The
LINCOLN LIBRARY
of
Essential Information

Named in honor of Abraham Lincoln,
whose inspiring example demonstrated
the possibilities of self-education

Revised With Each New Printing

THE FRONTIER PRESS COMPANY
COLUMBUS, OHIO

PREFACE

THE Lincoln Library of Essential Information has been prepared with two controlling ideas in view. One has been to embody the greatest amount of useful information for the average reader that could reasonably be placed in one work. The other aim has been to select, condense, arrange, and verify the material with a thoroughness and accuracy greater than that attained in any comparable work. The accomplishment of these aims ensures the production of a work in a class by itself.

NAME. The title of the work, The Lincoln Library of Essential Information, expresses the fact that it contains the essentials of a library of informational material. It signifies also that this information has been adapted to the needs of those who, following in the steps of Abraham Lincoln, will welcome every means of self-education.

SCOPE. This work is more than a source of information. It presents a range of knowledge greater than even experienced users of books would imagine possible. It offers a vast array of practical information on subjects that are fundamental. These include Geography, Economics, History, Government, Education, English, Literature, Fine Arts, Mathematics, Science, and Biography. The essentials of each are set forth clearly and completely. The field of human achievement is covered in Biography, the largest Department, which contains profiles of more than 4,000 of the world's noted men and women. Much information not directly referrable to the foregoing divisions has been grouped in the Miscellany. Review questions and bibliographies are given at the end of each section. Some idea of the scope of the encyclopedia lies in the fact that it covers more than 26,000 entries in the comprehensive Index.

METHOD AND PLAN. The plan of The Lincoln Library is in no sense an experiment, but is a development based on many decades of experience. The needs and desires of many million buyers and users of books containing useful information have been systematically studied. This study has shown that, for practically all readers, the most satisfactory source of general information is a comprehensive single reference work.

The careful planning by means of which this entire library has been published in two volumes obviates several obstacles to the average reader's use of the best reference works. Practically all such works are in many volumes, and the price is prohibitive to the great majority. There is also the matter of convenience.

Our study has shown also that the alphabetical arrangement followed in most encyclopedias is not suitable for a single work designed to contain the fullest possible information. When unrelated subjects are ranked next to each other in an A-to-Z arrangement, a large amount of information is unavoidably repeated.

It appeared desirable, also, to avoid the methods of the formal treatise, which often includes relatively unimportant matter. Elaborate refinements, which are seen in specialized textbooks, have been excluded. Without being a mere fact book, this work contains a larger number of carefully selected facts than similar works. It is not a dictionary, though it makes use of dictionary features wherever such treatment is of advantage. In short, adaptations of many widely used and tested methods have been worked out—in some instances, entirely new arrangements have been devised.

ACCURACY. In conformity with the policy of striving for the highest standards, care has been taken that the material should be based on primary sources and be as consistently accurate as possible. Many scholars and specialists have been enlisted, and all material has been subjected to intensive verification.

UP-TO-DATENESS. In no other age have advances in knowledge and in inventions so quickly rendered obsolete much that was accurate at the time it was published.

Whole new fields have been added to knowledge within the recent past. In this work, it has been a matter of care that such subjects should be adequately treated, and that the most recent positive contributions to knowledge should be duly recorded.

Social and political changes have made the 20th century a period of flux. National boundaries and governmental forms ebb and flow, making many older books of reference obsolete. The Lincoln Library meets this problem through its policy of thorough revision with each new printing.

For each new edition, the contents are systematically tested and revised. Not only facts, but also the perspective of the work, are kept abreast of a world constantly changing in aspect, interests, and viewpoint. On the whole, this work generally will be found to surpass larger encyclopedias in up-to-dateness, just as it goes beyond other compact works in completeness.

In the case of statistics regarding populations and other factors that vary continually, the most recent authentic figures are given rather than later estimates. It seems more desirable to present authoritative information rather than that which is recent but which lacks the essential of all statements of alleged facts—reliability.

MASS OF CONTENTS. By using every available centimeter of space, the mass of contents in The Lincoln Library had been made to exceed that of many more expensive encyclopedias of six to thirty volumes. This disparity in mass of contents, however, is only part of the difference between The Lincoln Library and the average multi-volume encyclopedia. Not only does the Lincoln excel in the amount of material presented, but the material itself is in a much more concise form. Consequently, this work contains from twice to many times as much information as the average work of many volumes.

By reason of these facts, The Lincoln Library holds a unique place in the world of books. The elaborate work of many volumes has had a recognized place since the 18th century, when Diderot and his colleagues in France produced, by twenty-one years of labor, their monumental *Encyclopédie*. The compact reference work of 800 to 1000 pages also has a well-established place. The Lincoln Library occupies a position intermediate between these types. It combines the advantages of lower cost and greater convenience in consultation with a completeness in essential information that closely approaches that of larger works.

INTRODUCTIONS. Preceding the treatment of each major subject, there is a useful preface giving the scope of the subject, its importance, and its function. In addition, many subdivisions, for example, Mythological Allusions, have instructive introductory sections and tables. These introductions give the user a clear idea of the value of the subject itself and lead to accurate knowledge of branches with which he has not previously been acquainted.

DICTIONARIES. In practically every department there is at least one dictionary, or group of selected topics in alphabetical order. These dictionaries effectively supplement the other material in the department. Following the discussions on government, there is a Dictionary of Political Terms and Institutions. The Department of Science is well provided with dictionaries, including alphabetically arranged sections on plants, animals, minerals, chemical terms, and added groups of subjects of importance.

TABULATIONS. As a base of condensed information, there is no superior to a well-constructed tabulation. This work has used carefully planned tables to an extent not found in other works, and has thus been able to display condensed information in readily accessible form. There are about 200 of these tables. Many, if expanded into descriptive text, would each provide material for a substantial volume.

ILLUSTRATIONS. Each department is introduced by appropriate full-page illustrations in color. The longer departments contain many pages of pictures, in color and black and white, covering thousands of subjects. Following the concept of presenting essential information, it has not been the aim to provide a heavily illustrated reference work. Rather, the intent is to provide a limited but useful array of photographs, maps, selected works of art, line drawings, graphs, and diagrams in locations where they will provide effective help and guidance. An example of such special selection and interest is the color sequence illustrating DNA, RNA, and the Cell in the section on Physiology.

MAPS. Recently prepared maps of the world, of the continents, and particularly of the United States and Canada precede the extensive descriptive material in the Department of Geography.

BIBLIOGRAPHIES. The user who may desire to extend his knowledge of some special subject will find, at the end of each department, a classified list of authoritative works. From these lists, he will be able to select books in which he may pursue a topic at greater length.

REVIEW QUESTIONS. At the end of each department will be found selected questions covering essentials of the topics treated. In all, there are more than 10,000 such questions, the answers to which, in themselves, constitute the foundations of a liberal education.

INDEX. The Master Index enables the reader to obtain information with speed and precision. While necessarily of extensive size because of the broad contents of the work, this index is simple and compact so that real ease will be found in its use.

CONTENTS

ATLAS

The World—North America—Canada—United States—Mexico—Central America—West Indies—South America—Western and Central Europe—British Isles—France—Germany—Scandinavia and Finland—Italy—Spain and Portugal—Balkan States—USSR—Asia—Southwest Asia—Southern Asia—East Asia—Southeast Asia—Indochinese and Malay Peninsulas—Australia and New Zealand—Pacific Ocean—Africa—Antarctica 1–48

I. GEOGRAPHY

Value of Geography—Geographical Discovery—General Facts about the Earth—North America—The United States—Growth of the United States—Largest Cities of the United States—Dictionary of American Geography—Canada—Mexico—Central America—West Indies—South America—Europe—Asia—Africa—Australia—Antarctica—World Statistics—Mountains and Volcanoes—Principal Islands—Important Rivers—Noted Waterfalls—World Travel Distances—Meanings of Place Names 49–250

II. ECONOMICS

Commerce—Commercial Raw Materials—Communication—Transportation—Labor Relations—Marketing—Advertising—Salesmanship—Insurance—Business Cycles—Investments—Money and Banking—Dictionary of Business, Banking, and Legal Terms—Agriculture—Horticulture—Forestry—Irrigation—Animal Industry—Fisheries—Mining and Mineral Production—Inventions—Engineering and Building—Manufacturing—Lumbering—Technology 251–438

III. HISTORY

American History: Exploration, Colonization, Revolutionary War, Territorial Growth of the United States, Civil War, Industrial Era, World Power, Historical Statistics, American Flags, Political Parties, Presidents, Dictionary of American History—Commonwealth of Nations History: England, Scotland, Wales, Canada, India, Australia, New Zealand—Latin American History—World History, Countries Ancient and Modern: Abyssinia (Ethiopia), Alsace-Lorraine, Austria, Babylonia, China, Czechoslovakia, Egypt, Finland, France, Germany, Greece, Holy Roman Empire, Italy, Japan, Norway, Persia (Iran), Poland, Rome, Russia, Spain, Sweden, Switzerland, Turkey, Yugoslavia—Ancient Cities—Peoples of the World—World War I—World War II—Dictionary of World History—Table of Periods, Events, and Movements of World History 439–726

IV. GOVERNMENT AND POLITICS

United States of America—Articles of Confederation—Constitution—Federal Government: The Congress, The President, The Supreme Court, Federal Agencies and Commissions—American State Government—Local Government—Commission Form of Government—Suffrage Requirements in All States—World Governments: Asian and African countries—Belgium—British Commonwealth—Central American States—China—France—Germany—Greece—Italy—Japan—Mexico—Netherlands—Norway—Poland—South American Countries—Soviet Russia—Spain—Switzerland—Dictionary of Political Terms and Institutions . . 727–840

V. EDUCATION

History of Education—Educational Institutions—Ancient Education—Medieval and Modern Education—Educational Reformers—Science of Education—Experimental Psychology—Intelligence Tests—School Surveys—Curriculum Studies—Job Analysis—School Systems of Various Countries—Education in the United States—Early Childhood Education—Elementary School—Junior High School—High School—Junior College—Universities—University Extension—Professional Schools—Vocational Education—Religious Education—Parent-Teacher Associations—Textbooks—Radio and Television in Education—Early Childhood Education 841–924

VI. ENGLISH LANGUAGE

The English Language—Good Usage—Word Building—Derivation of English Words from the Latin—Correct Spelling—Correct Pronunciation—Sentence Building—Prepositions—Conjunctions—Capital Letters—Punctuation—Language and Linguistics—Linguistic Theory—Writing and Speaking—Radio and Television Speaking—Forms of Literary Composition—Letter Writing—The Family Library—Synonyms and Antonyms—Foreign Words and Phrases—Abbreviations 925–1100

VII. LITERATURE

Modern Literature in the Western Nations—American Literature—English Literature: English, Canadian, and Australian Writers—Irish Literature—Romance Literatures: French, Italian, Spanish, Latin American—Germanic Literatures: German, Dutch, Scandinavian—Slavonic Literatures: Russian, Polish, Czech—Ancient and Oriental Literatures: Chinese, Japanese, Assyro-Babylonian, Hebrew, Arabic, Persian, Indian, Greek, Latin—Literary Plots, Characters, and Allusions—Mythological Persons, Places, and Stories 1101–1252

VIII. FINE ARTS

Environmental Design—Architecture—Interior Design—Crafts—Drawings—Painting—Print-making—Sculpture—Art Terms and Subjects—Photography—Music—Dictionary of Musical Terms—Leading Operas—Dance 1253–1476

IX. MATHEMATICS

History of Mathematics—Arithmetic—Mensuration—Plane Figures and Solids—Formulas—Graphs—Practical Problems—Weights and Measures—Metric System—Tables—Algebra—Logarithms—Geometry—Trigonometry—Calculus 1477–1540

X. SCIENCE

Value of Science—Methods of Science—Physical Geography: Land Forms, Continents, Islands, Mountains, Oceans, Lakes, Glaciers, Rivers, Volcanoes, Earthquakes, Climate, Wind—Meteorology, Oceanography—Geology: Kinds of Rock; Geological History of North America; Paleontology—Mineralogy: Minerals, Gems, and Precious Stones—Astronomy: History, Value; Earth, Sun, Moon, Planets, Stars, Comets, Nebulae, Telescope—Physics: Mechanics, Newton's Laws, Sound, Heat, Light, Electricity, Radioactivity, Atomic Energy, Magnetism—Chemistry: Principles; Chemical Substances, Metallic Alloys—Biology: History; Organic Evolution, Mendel's Law; Microbiology, the Cell—Anatomy, Physiology: Structure of the Human Body, Muscles, Circulatory System, Respiratory Organs, Nervous System, the Brain—Zoology: Classification of Animals, Dictionary of Animals—Botany: Classification of Plants, Dictionary of Plants—Ecology—Psychology 1541–1830

XI. BIOGRAPHY

Noted Men and Women of the Past and the Present: Statesmen—Rulers—Religious Leaders—Soldiers—Philosophers—Scientists—Authors—Orators—Jurists—Lawyers—Physicians—Educators—Discoverers—Explorers—Inventors—Financiers—Merchants—Manufacturers—Engineers—Architects—Painters—Sculptors—Composers—Musicians—Nobel Prize Winners, and Others 1831–2164

XII. MISCELLANY

Parliamentary Law—Orders, Societies, and Organizations—California Missions—Heroic Deeds—Sobriquets and Nicknames—Festivals and Holidays—Statistics of Religious Bodies—Psychiatry—Drawing and Design—Furniture—Games and Sports—Civilization: Problems and Progress—Space Exploration—General Miscellany 2165–2258

INDEX

How to Use—Illustrations—Master Index 2259

THE BUILDERS

This unique and comprehensive reference series owes its origin to the constructive foresight and untiring energy of Mr. M. J. Kinsella, founder and first president of The Frontier Press Company. Initially developed under his vigorous and able management, with the aid of a corps of workers who shared his vision, this organization has grown until it now stands in the foremost rank of American educational publishing houses. Beginning in 1908, with the publication of *The Standard Dictionary of Facts*, a compact digest of general information, this firm has concentrated during the following years on the presentation of organized knowledge brought together in a single reference work. The founder's aim of making a maximum quantity of useful knowledge readily available "under one roof," as a reviewer expressed it, led to the publication and later the continued improvement of the compact encyclopedia known everywhere as *The Lincoln Library*.

A Work for Desk Reference. Mr. Kinsella had completed a classical course at the Buffalo State Normal School and, in 1900, had received an A.B. degree from Cornell University. His experience as student, teacher, and businessman had impressed him with the need for having reference works on a desk at one's finger tips, not somewhere in a closet or on a shelf behind glass doors. While recognizing the importance of numerous volumes for leisurely reading and of specialized textbooks for formal study, he noted that busy people frequently have occasion to look for specific facts concerning an unlimited variety of subjects. To make it possible for them to obtain this information quickly, he conceived of a reference work in a few volumes that should be developed according to certain ideas derived from his personal experience and also from consultation with others. Briefly summarized, these ideas were as follows: first, the typical "handy" reference work, usually containing 800 to 1000 pages, should be greatly expanded if it was to fulfill its mission; second, in its enlarged form, such a work could be made readable and interesting as well as informative and could be particularly helpful to the large percentage of the general public who could not afford to purchase the multi-volume A-to-Z encyclopedias; third, because of its convenience for quick reference, it could usefully supplement the larger reference works and other books found in well-stocked private libraries; and fourth, if presented in an organized way, the content of such a work could provide the means for a thorough review of anyone's knowledge or for an effective program of self-education.

According to Ward Lamon, one of his early biographers, Lincoln's formal education did not amount to more than one year of schooling. Not only his professional studies in law and surveying but also literature, geometry and other elementary subjects were mastered by a process of self-instruction. While profiting from the historical facts concerning Lincoln's study, the Builders recognized the present and future needs throughout America that are created by an ever-expanding program of adult education. Conse-

quently, *The Lincoln Library* series, because of the organization of knowledge, became not only enlarged "fact books" but also an educational medium noted for effectiveness as a means of self-education.

CONTRIBUTORS AND EDITORS

The preliminary pages contain a list of men and women, occupying various positions of importance in the United States, Canada, and Australia, who have collaborated extensively in building The Lincoln Library series. After each name in this list is given the person's scholastic degree. Next is indicated the present or former position occupied by each collaborator, with a statement of the specific task performed.

In case a department, section, or article was prepared *in toto* by one of these collaborators, it is stated that he *contributed* it.

In case a section, prepared by the office editorial staff or by an outside contributor, was edited, revised, expanded, or approved by one of these collaborators, the exact service performed is specifically defined.

REVISIONS

One of the most serious problems facing the publishers of modern reference books is that of keeping abreast of the times. The policy adopted in that regard for The Lincoln Library series is in keeping with the high standards established when it was founded. At each new printing, those portions which are affected by the passage of events are thoroughly revised.

In some cases, the original contributor of a section or Department has made the necessary revisions. In other cases, the services of different outside editors have been secured, the list of editors being revised accordingly. A large part of this revision work, however, has necessarily been carried out by the editorial staff, which is engaged continually in surveying the progress of the world in order to select and report the most significant developments. In all such revisions, the original character of the articles has been left unaltered except insofar as necessary in order to present each topic in the perspective of the present time.

The policy of thorough revision at each new printing, inaugurated by M. J. Kinsella, has been carried on through a chain of leadership extending from his death in 1928 to the present. He was succeeded as president of The Frontier Press Company by his brother, Burt S. Kinsella, who served for nearly twenty years. Following his retirement the presidency was held from 1948 to 1958 by H. C. Goff, who was succeeded by Verne E. Seibert. On the latter's retirement in 1966, the reins were taken by his son William H. Seibert. Each of these men had worked closely with his predecessor, so that unbroken continuity of policy was assured. Even more important was the cumulative development of certain features of the encyclopedia. Care in the selection of contributors, vigilance on the part of the editorial staff, and the maintenance of high standards of accuracy have given The Lincoln Library a position of leadership in its field that has continued without serious challenge.

EDITORS AND CONTRIBUTORS

EDITOR-IN-CHIEF

WILLIAM J. REDDING, A.B., M.A., M.S. in L.S.

ASSISTANT EDITORS

NANCY V. SANDER

DOROTHY G. SUDDUTH

JOAN LONERGAN

DONALD SICO

DANIEL DUFFEE

ART EDITORS

MARY ANN LONERGAN

RICHARD SUMMERS

SUBJECT EDITORS

ROBERT BARTELS, B. S., M. B. A., PH. D.

BURVIL H. GLENN, B. S., M. A., PH. D.

JOHN W. TAYLOR, M. A., PH. D.

RESEARCH EDITORS

JOHN HABERMAN

ELAINE NIENHOUSE, A. B., M. L. S.

PARTIAL LIST OF CONTRIBUTORS

ABBOTT, FRANK FROST, Ph. D.
Late Kennedy Professor of Latin Language and Literature, Princeton University. Author: *A Short History of Rome.*
Contributed Roman History and Literature.

ALEXANDER, WILLIAM P., Ph. D.
Late Director of Extension Work, Buffalo Society of Natural Sciences; formerly, Department of Entomology, Cornell University.
Contributed articles on Ant and Honeybee.

ATWOOD, WALLACE WALTER, Ph. D.
Late President, and Professor of Physical and Regional Geography, Clark University, Worcester, Mass.
Revised and expanded Physical Geography.

BARRETT, JAMES M., B. S., M. S., Ph. D.
Assistant Professor of Zoology, Marquette University.
Contributed the material on The Cell, DNA, and RNA for the 28th edition.

BARROWS, DAVID PRESCOTT, Ph. D., LL. D.
Former President, and Professor of Political Science, University of California.
Contributed Government and Politics.

BARTELS, ROBERT, B. S., M. B. A., Ph. D.
Professor of Business Organization, The Ohio State University. Author: *Development of Marketing Thought.*
Contributed Marketing, 25th edition; and Salesmanship and Advertising, 26th edition; reviewed Economics, 34th edition.

BELL, ROGER A., B. Sc., Ph. D.
Assistant Professor of Astronomy, University of Maryland, College Park, Md.
Revised Astronomy, 28th and 30th editions.

BICKELHAUPT, DAVID L., B. S., M. S., Ph. D.
Professor of Insurance, The Ohio State University.
Revised Insurance for the 34th edition.

BICKLEY, JOHN S., B. A., M. B. A., Ph. D.
Professor of Business Organization, University of Texas.
Revised Insurance for the 24th edition.

BOTHNE, GISLE C., M. A.
Head of the Department of Scandinavian Languages, University of Minnesota.
Contributed articles on Norwegian, Danish, Swedish, and Icelandic Literatures; also Norwegian, Danish, and Swedish History.

BOURNE, HENRY ELDRIDGE, A. B., B. D., L. H. D.
Late Professor of History, Graduate School of Western Reserve University. Author: *Mediæval and Modern History.*
Revised the article on French History.

BROCK, REGINALD WALTER, M. A., LL. D., F. G. S., F. R. S. C.
Dean of the Faculty of Applied Science and Head of the Department of Geology and Geography, University of British Columbia.
Revised the section on Canadian Geography.

BRUMFIEL, CHARLES F., B. S., M. A., Ph. D.
Professor of Mathematics, University of Michigan.
Revised Arithmetic for the 28th edition.

BURNS, ROBERT E., A. B., C. P. A.
Member Association for Computing Machinery.
Contributed article on Computers for 30th edition.

CAMERON, HELEN ARNOLD, B. A., M. B. A., Ph. D.
Associate Professor of Economics, The Ohio State University.
Revised Business Cycles for the 34th edition.

CASE, ERMINE COWLES, PH. D.
Curator of the Paleontological Collection, University of Michigan.
Contributed Geology and Paleontology.

CHURCHILL, GEORGE MORTON, PH. D.
Late Professor of English History, The George Washington University.
Contributed the article on World War II and revised departments of History and Government for 11th and several later editions.

COHEN, PAUL P., B. A., LL. B.
Formerly Lecturer in Government, State University of New York at Buffalo.
Contributed Business, Banking, and Legal Terms.

COLE, DAVID W., M. B. A., D. B. A.
Associate Professor of Finance, The Ohio State University.
Revised Investments for the 34th edition.

CONANT, HOWARD S., B. S., M. S., Ed. D.
Chairman, Department of Art Education; Head, Division of Creative Arts, New York University.
Contributed articles on Crafts, Drawing, Painting, and Sculpture.

CRAIG, PAUL G., B. A., M. A., Ph. D.
Assistant Professor of Economics, The Ohio State University.
Revised Business Cycles for the 24th edition.

CURRAN, TERENCE, B. A., M. L. S.
Reference Librarian, Victoria Public Library, Victoria, B.C.; Member: *The American Name Society.*
Reviewed and revised Meanings of Place Names for the 28th edition.

DEWING, HENRY BRONSON, Ph. D.
President of Athens College, Athens, Greece.
Contributed Greek History and Literature.

DORFMAN, WILLIAM, B. S., M. A., Ph. D.
Counseling Psychologist, United States Army Medical Service Corps.
Revised and expanded the article on Psychology for the 34th edition.

FARMA, WILLIAM J., Ph. D.
New York University, Department of Education.
Reviewed and revised the Department of English for the 17th edition.

FINEGAN, THOMAS EDWARD, M. A., Ph. D., LL. D., Litt. D.
Superintendent of Education for State of Pennsylvania.
Reviewed, revised, and approved sections on Introduction to the English Language, Word Building, and Forms of Literary Composition.

FRANKLIN, EDWARD CURTIS, B. S., M. S., Ph. D.
Late Professor of Organic Chemistry, Stanford University.
Reviewed Chemistry for the first edition.

FREER, JAMES J., Ed. D.
Associate Professor, Department of Psychology, University of Detroit, Michigan.
Revised Psychology for the 28th edition.

FRUTKIN, ARNOLD W., B. A.
Assistant Administrator for International Affairs, National Aeronautics and Space Administration; author: *International Cooperation in Space.*
Contributed Section on Aeronautics and Space Exploration for the 30th edition.

FRYER, CHARLES EDMUND, M. A., Ph. D.
Professor of History, McGill University, Montreal, Canada.
Contributed the articles on the History of Canada and the British Commonwealth of Nations.

GAUSS, CHRISTIAN, A. M., Litt. D.
Late Dean of the College and Dean of the Alumni, Princeton University.
Contributed the Introduction to Literature and the table showing the Development of Modern Literature.

GIBBONS, OLIPHANT, A. B.
Supervisor of English, Secondary Schools, Buffalo, N.Y.
Reviewed, revised, and expanded the section on Synonyms and Antonyms.

GLENN, BURVIL HOLMES, B. S., M. A., Ph. D.
Professor of Education, State University of New York at Buffalo.
Revised the Department of Education for the 24th and subsequent editions.

GORDON, ELIZABETH M., B. S. in Ed.
Deputy Supervisor, Boston Public Library.
Revised Suggestions for the Family Library and The Children's Library for the 25th edition.

GRIFFITH, FRED R., Jr., A. B., M. A., Ph. D.
Formerly Head of the Department of Physiology, School of Medicine, State University of New York at Buffalo.
Revised Physiology for the 22d edition.

HALL, CALVIN SPRINGER, A. B., Ph. D.
Formerly Chairman, Division of Psychology, Western Reserve University.
Contributed the section on Psychology for the 17th edition.

HARPER, EDWARD O., A. B., M. D.
Assistant Dean and Associate Professor of Psychiatry, School of Medicine, Western Reserve University; Associate Physician, University Hospitals, Cleveland, Ohio.
Contributed the section on Psychiatry and revised it for the 25th and 32nd editions.

HAWORTH, PAUL LELAND, Ph. D.
Professor of History, Butler College; formerly Lecturer in History, Columbia University and Bryn Mawr College.
Contributed the section on World War I.

HILLS, E. JUSTIN, A. B., M. A., Ph. D.
Chairman, Mathematics and Science Dept., Cape Cod Community College.
Revised the Algebra, Geometry, and Trigonometry sections for the 28th edition.

HOEING, CHARLES, Ph. D.
Trevor Professor of Latin, and Dean of Graduate Studies, University of Rochester.
Reviewed and revised the section on English Words Derived from the Latin.

HOWARD, JOHN TASKER, A. M.
Late Musician, Composer, Author.
Revised Music for the 17th edition.

HUEBNER, SOLOMON S., B. S., M. S., Ph. D.
Professor of Insurance and Commerce, Wharton School of Finance and Commerce, University of Pennsylvania.
Contributed the section on Insurance.

HUNKER, HENRY L., B. A., M. A., Ph. D.
Professor of Geography, The Ohio State University.
Revised Commerce, Transportation, and Power for the 24th, 26th, and 34th editions.

JEWELL, WILLIAM McINTYRE, A. B.
Professor of Fine Arts, Boston University.
Revised Architecture for the 25th edition.

JOHNSON, EMORY RICHARD, B. L., M. L., Ph. D. (Sc. D.)
Late Professor of Transportation and Commerce and Dean of the Wharton School of Finance and Commerce, University of Pennsylvania.
Contributed the section on Transportation.

JOHNSON, ROSSITER, A. M., (Hon. Ph. D., LL. D.)
Author: *A History of the French War Ending in the Conquest of Canada.* Editor: *The Universal Cyclopædia.*
Contributed the original section on Meanings of Place Names.

JORDAN, DAVID FRANCIS, B. C. S.
Late of the Department of Finance, New York University.
Contributed the original sections on Investments and Money and Banking.

JUDD, CHARLES HUBBARD, Ph. D., LL. D.
Late Professor and Director of the School of Education; also Chairman of the Department of Psychology, University of Chicago.
Contributed the entire Department of Education for the first edition.

KARL, LINDA
Adjunct Professor of Art, Division of Creative Arts, New York University.
Contributed the article on Print-Making.

KIMBALL, STOCKTON, B. S., M. D.
Late Dean of the School of Medicine, State University of New York at Buffalo.
Reviewed the sections on Physiology and Anatomy for the 22d edition.

KLAIBER, G. STANLEY, B. A., M. A., Ph. D.
Associate Professor of Physics, State University of New York at Buffalo.

Revised section on Physics for the 25th through 28th editions.

KLUCKHOHN, LUCY WALES, A. B.
Writer on Anthropology. Editor: 1966 edition of Clark Wissler's *Indians of the United States*.

Contributed article on Indians of North America for the 30th edition.

KLUCKHOHN, RICHARD, A. B., M. A., Ph. D.
Associate Professor of Anthropology, San Fernando State College.

Contributed section on Peoples of the World.

LANCASTER, JOHN HERROLD, B. S., M. A., B. S. (L. S.), Ph. D.
Head Librarian, Baldwin-Wallace College, Berea, Ohio.

Revised the Bibliographies for the 25th and subsequent editions.

LEARY, DANIEL BELL, M. A., Ph. D.
Late Professor of Psychology and instructor in Russian, State University of New York at Buffalo.

Reviewed and revised Russian Literature and Russian History.

LEIGHTON, FREDERICK, B. S.
Late Superintendent of Schools, Oswego, New York. Author: *Students' Hand Book of Parliamentary Law.*

Contributed the section on Parliamentary Law for the first edition.

LEVIN, GILBERT V., A. B., Ph. D.
Director, Life Systems Division of Hazelton Laboratories.

Contributed article on Water Supply and Pollution Control for the 30th edition.

LEWIS, CALVIN LESLIE, A. B., A. M.
Professor of Rhetoric and Oratory, Hamilton College.

Reviewed and revised the section on Speaking and Writing in the first edition.

LINK, JOSEPH F., Jr., Ph. B., B. S., A. M., D. Ed.
Associate Professor of Economics and Head, Dept. of Commerce, Xavier University, Cincinnati, Ohio.

Contributed to revision of Department of Economics for the 18th and 30th editions.

LOPEZ, MANUEL LEON, A. B., A. M.
Department of Romance Languages, University of Oregon.

Reviewed and revised Spanish Literature and Spanish History; also Latin American Literature.

McCABE, LOUIS C., B. S., M. S., Ph. D.
President, Resources Research, Inc.; consultant to industry and government on air pollution.

Contributed article on air pollution for the 30th edition.

MacCRACKEN, HENRY NOBLE, Ph. D., LL. D., L. H. D.
Former President of Vassar College.

Reviewed, with constructive suggestions, the original manuscript on Sentence Building, Prepositions, and Conjunctions.

McCREA, ROSWELL CHENEY, Ph. D.
Late Dean of the School of Business, and executive officer of the Department of Economics, Columbia University.

Revised the sections on Inventions.

McGRATH, RUTH E., B. S., Ed. M., Ed. D.
Associate Professor of Education, Director of Laboratory School, State University of New York at Buffalo.

Contributed Early Childhood Education for the 25th and 28th editions.

MacIVER, ROBERT MORRISON, B. A., M. A., D. Phil., F. R. S. C.
Professor of Political Philosophy, Columbia University.

Contributed the Introduction to Economics and Useful Arts.

McLEOD, ALAN L., B. A., M. A., Dip. Ed., B. Ed., Ph. D.
Associate Professor of Speech and English, State University of New York at Fredonia.

Contributed article on Australian Literature and revised other articles on Australia for the 25th edition.

MADDEN, DOROTHY G., A. B., M. A., Ph. D.
Chairman, Department of Dance, University of Maryland.

Contributed the article on Dance.

MALLORY, V. STANDISH
Professor, Dept. of Geology, University of Washington.

Revised Geology for the 28th edition.

MATTERN, J. ARTHUR, B. S., M. S., Ph. D.
Associate Professor of Chemistry, State University of New York at Buffalo.

Reviewed and revised the section on Chemistry for 25th and subsequent editions.

MILJUS, ROBERT C., B. A., M. A., Ph. D.
Associate Professor of Management Science, The Ohio State University.

Revised Labor Relations for the 34th edition.

MILLER, GLENN W., B. Ed., A. M., Ph. D.
Professor of Economics, The Ohio State University.

Revised the section on Labor Relations for the 24th and 25th editions.

MOODIE, ROY LEE, Ph. D.
Professor of Paleodontology, College of Dentistry, University of Southern California. Author: *Paleopathology.*

Reviewed, revised, and materially extended the section devoted to Mineralogy.

MORGAN, BAYARD QUINCY, Ph. D.
Chairman of German Department, Stanford University.

Revised German Literature and History.

MORGENSTERN, JULIAN, Ph. D.
President Emeritus of The Hebrew Union College, Cincinnati, Ohio.

Contributed the article on Jewish History; also the articles on Hebrew, Syriac, Ethiopic, Arabic and Assyro-Babylonian Literatures.

MOULTON, FOREST RAY, Ph. D., Sc. D.
Formerly Professor of Astronomy, University of Chicago.

Contributed the original section on Astronomy.

NEEDHAM, JAMES GEORGE, Litt. D., Ph. D.
Former Professor of Entomology and Limnology, Cornell University. Author: *Outdoor Studies; General Biology.*

Revised and expanded the section on Zoology.

O'NEIL, WAYNE A., B.A., M.A., Ph.D.
Professor of Education and Linguistics, Harvard University.

Contributed Linguistics, 32d edition.

PARK, CLYDE W., A. M.
Formerly Professor and head of Department of English, College of Engineering, University of Cincinnati.

Supervision over 24th through 28th edition.

PARK, JULIAN, Ph. D.
Professor and Head of Department of History, State University of New York at Buffalo; also Dean of the College of Arts and Sciences.
Reviewed and revised World History; also the World History Tables for the first edition.

PFAHL, JOHN K., B. A., M. B. A., Ph. D.
Assistant Professor of Business Organization, The Ohio State University.
Revised Investments, 24th edition.

PHELPS, JEWELL, B. S., M. A., Ph. D.
George Peabody College for Teachers, Nashville, Tenn.
Revised Physical Geography, 26th edition.

PHILLIPS, LYLE W., B. S., M. A., Ph. D.
National Science Foundation, Washington, D.C. Former Professor and Head of Department of Physics, State University of New York at Buffalo.
Contributed the Department of Physics.

PINSON, WILLIAM H., Jr., Ph. D.
Research Associate, Department of Geology and Geophysics, Massachusetts Institute of Technology.
Contributed Astronomy for the 22d edition.

QUANTIUS, FRANCES WELLS, B. A., M. A., Ph. D.
Professor of Economics, The Ohio State University.
Revised Business, Banking, Legal Terms, 26th and 34th editions.

REEDER, WARD GLEN, A. B., A. M., Ph. D.
Professor of Education, Ohio State University.
Revised Education, 17th edition.

RHODENIZER, VERNON BLAIR, Ph. D.
Professor of English Literature, Acadia University, N. S.
Contributed article on Canadian Literature.

ROSS, WILBERT DAVIDSON, A. B., A. M.
Professor and Head of Department of History and Government, Kansas State Normal School, Emporia, Kansas.
Revised Central and South America.

RUDWICK, ELLIOTT M., B. S., M. A., Ph. D.
Professor of Sociology and Senior Research Fellow, Center for Urban Regionalism, Kent State University, Kent, Ohio.
Reviewed Negro studies for the 33rd edition.

SCHWENDEMAN, JOSEPH R., M. A., Ph. D.
Head of Department of Geography, University of Kentucky. Contributor to *World Political Geography.*
Revised Asia, Africa, and Australia, 18th edition.

SCOTT, ERNEST
Professor in the Department of History in the University of Melbourne, Australia.
Contributed the article on Australian History.

SEABORG, GLENN THEODORE, A. B., Ph. D.
Professor of Chemistry, University of California.
Revised Chemistry for the 17th edition.

SEIBERT, RICHARD HUNTER, A. B., M. D.
Senior Clinical Instructor in Medicine, School of Medicine, Western Reserve University.
Contributed article on War Against Disease for 30th edition.

SHEARER, RONALD A., B. A., M. A.
Instructor of Economics, The Ohio State University.
Revised Money and Banking, 24th edition.

SIMONDS, LOIS A., B. S., M. S., Ph. D.
Assistant Professor of Agricultural Economics, The Ohio State University.
Revised the Drainage, Fisheries, Horticulture, and Irrigation sections of Agriculture for the 34th edition.

SMITH, EDWARD S., M. E., M. S., Ph. D.
Professor of Mathematics, University of Cincinnati.
Revised Mathematics and contributed Calculus, 25th edition.

SNOW, ROYALL H., S. B., B. A., B. Litt.
Professor of English, Ohio State University.
Reviewed and revised American and English Literature and Literary Plots for the 17th edition.

JACK A. SOULES, B. S., M. S., Ph. D.
Dean of the College of Arts and Sciences, Cleveland State University.
Revised Chemistry and Physics, 34th edition.

STEELE, HOWARD L., B. S., M. S., Ph. D.
Associate Professor of Agricultural Economics, The Ohio State University.
Revised Agriculture for the 34th edition.

SULLIVAN, PEGGY, A.B., M.S. in L.S.
Director, Knapp School Libraries Project.
Revised the Family Library article and Literature in Early Childhood Education.

TAYLOR, G. GENE, B. S. M., A. M., Ph. D.
Professor of Music and Music Education, Capital University, Columbus, Ohio.
Revised the section on Music, 28th edition.

TAYLOR, JOHN W., M. A., Ph. D.
Contributed section on Mythology and numerous other articles, having been editor or contributor from the first edition.

VIZETELLY, FRANK HORACE, Litt. D., LL. D.
Late Managing Editor of New Standard Dictionary of the English Language.
Revised and expanded Good Usage.

WARFEL, JOHN HIATT, B. Sc., M. Sc., Ph. D.
Assistant Professor of Anatomy, School of Medicine, State University of New York at Buffalo.
Contributed the section on Anatomy for the 22d edition and reviewed for the 26th edition.

WESTON, GEORGE BENSON, A. M.
Associate Professor of Romance Languages, Harvard University.
Contributed article on Italian Literature.

WILLIAMS, EDWARD THOMAS, M. A., LL. D.
Late Agassiz Professor of Oriental Languages and Literature, University of California, 1918–27.
Contributed the articles on Chinese Literature and History, Japanese Literature and History.

WILSON, G. LLOYD, M. A., Ph. D., M. B. A.
Professor of Commerce and Transportation, Wharton School of Finance and Commerce, University of Pennsylvania.
Revised Transportation, 2d edition.

ZAPOLSKY, HAROLD S., A. B., Ph. D.
Assistant Professor of Physics, University of Maryland.
Revised Physics for the 30th edition.

ZENKERT, CHARLES ANTHONY, B. A., M. A.
Research Associate in Botany, Buffalo Museum of Science.
Revised Botany, Mineralogy, 16th, 26th editions.

DICTIONARIES

Abbreviations 1091
Africa, Political Divisions 212
American Geography 85
American History 479
Animals 1696
Art Terms and Subjects 1380
Asia, Political Divisions 201
Astronautical Terms 2237
Astronomy 1597
Australia, States 221
Biography 1833
Bus., Banking, and Legal Terms 329
Canada, Provinces of 145
Central American Countries 157
Chemical Substances 1629, 1659
Cities, Ancient 599
Cities, Popular Names 2251
Cities, Travel Interest Points:
  Africa 217
  Asia 207
  Australia 222
  Canada 151
  Central America 158

Cities, Travel Interest, Europe 182
  Mexico 157
  South America 166
  United States 85
Europe, Political Divisions 170
Festivals and Holidays 2197
Games and Sports 2213
Good Usage 927
Government, World 765
Heroic Deeds and Exploits 2189
Heteronyms 967
Homonyms 965
How Things Are Made 407
Hymns and Anthems, National 2248
Inventions 373
Latin American Countries 541
Latin Words and Phrases 1078
Literary Plots, Characters 1169
Metallic Alloys 1666
Miscellany, General 2165
Musical Terms 1441
Mythology 1224

Operas, Stories of Leading 1448
Orders, Societies,
  Organizations 2179
Peoples of the World 601
Physical Geography 1543
Place Names, Meanings of 233
Plants 1762
Political Terms and Institutions 805
Pronunciation, Correct 1008
Rocks, Minerals, Gems 1583
Sobriquets and Nicknames 2193
South America. Political Divisions 162
Synonyms and Antonyms 1038
U.S. Dependencies 757
  Government 739
Weights and Measures 1509
West Indies 159
Word Formations 948
Words and Phrases from Modern
  Languages 1802
Words Derived from the Latin 953
World History 641

TABULATIONS

Abdications 641
Agricultural Co-operatives 354
Agricultural Industry, U.S. 368–369
Agric. Prod'n, Chief Countries 365
Agricultural Products, Canada 355
  U.S. 351–352
Air Pollution, Cities 2226
Air Travel Distances 76
Animal Industry, Canada 363
  United States 366, 367
Atomic Numbers and Weights 1642
Australia, Statistics of 220–222
Band Instruments 1439
Banking, United States 323–325
Biological Sciences, Division of 1674
Birth and Death Rates 2219
Bridges and Viaducts 388
British Commonwealth 528
Business Crises, Important 313–314
Cabinet Members 743–748
Canada, Commerce 256
  Development of Provinces 536
  Governors-General 534–535
  Growth 142, 145, 148, 150
  Imports and Exports 257
  Prime Ministers 534–535
  Principal Productions 141
Canals, Important 269
Cattle, Dairy and Beef 366, 367
C.G.S. System of Units 1613
Cemeteries, Memorials 2239
Chemical Elements 1642–1643
Chemical Formulas 1646
Cities, Canada 148, 150
  U.S., Chief M'f'g 403–404
  U.S. Twenty-five Largest 71
  World, Principal 225
Coal Production, United States 1587
Coast Line, U.S. 59
College Education, by States 899
  Degrees Conferred 867, 853
Commerce, Leading Countries 259
Congress, Party Strength in 473
Consumer Price Index 320
Countries, Statistics of 231–232
Crop Production, Canada 355
  Leading Countries 365
  U.S. 351–352
Dams, Important 391
Death Rates, Important Causes 2219
Decimal Equivalents 1514
Deposits, U.S. Banks 323
Diseases, Bacterial 1686
Earth, General Facts about the 54
Education, Degrees Conferred 867
  Federal Funds 905
  Trends in School Districts 891
Electric Energy, U.S. 300
Electromagnetic Spectrum 1611
Farms
  Drainage of 356
  Income 353
  Population 350
Federal Government bet. 740–741
Federal Reserve System 326

Flowers, American Wild 1809–1810
  Symbolism 2255
Food, Civilian Consumption 351
Food Nutrients 1693–1694
Foreign Trade of Leading Countries 259
Forests, U.S. 360, 359
Geographical Discoveries 52–53
Geologic Time 1575
High Buildings 393
History,
  Chronological 502–515, 672–719
Illiteracy, Principal Countries 889
Immunity, Kinds of 1675
Indians, U.S., Canada 604
Industrial Production, Centers of 402
Industry, Divisions of 300
Instrumental Combinations 1436
Inventions 385–386
Irrigation in the U.S. 358
Islands, Principal 228
Junior Colleges 902
Lakes, Fresh and Salt Water 230, 58
Library, The Children's 1035–1036
  The Family 1033
Life Insurance, U.S., Canada 306, 305
Literature, American 1113–1115
  Canadian 1126
  Danish 1148
  English 1122–1124
  French 1132–1133
  German 1145–1146
  Greek 1166
  Italian 1138
  Latin 1168
  Modern 1105–1108
  Norwegian 1149
  Russian 1153–1154
  Spanish 1141
  Swedish 1150–1151
Locomotives, Standard Types 392
Logarithms, Common 1530
Lumber Production, U.S. 406
Manufacturing, U.S. 398–405
Meat Prod. Leading Countries 365
Memorial Coins, American 2246
Merchant Marine, World 267
Mineral Production, U.S. 1596
M.K.S. System of Units 1613
Money in U.S. 322
Mortality, Life Insurance 303–304
Motor Vehicle Laws, U.S. 2247
Motor Vehicle Registration, U.S. 276
Mountains, Passes, Volcanoes 227
Mythological Associations 1223
National Monuments 63–64
National Parks, U.S., Can. 62, 146
Negro Population, U.S. 467
Nobel Prize Winners 2145–2152
Observatories 1610
Orchestras 1437–1439
Parliamentary Rules 2177–2178
Party Strength, Comparative 473
Periodic Table of the Elements 1644
Petroleum Production, U.S. 372, 1593
Planets 1607

Popes 645–646
Populations, U.S. 137–140, 65, 70
Ports, World 218
Postal Service, U.S., Growth of 264
Poultry, Egg Production, U.S. 364
Powers, Roots, and Reciprocals 1514
Presidential Elections 478, 761–764
Presidents, United States 474–477
Prime Ministers, Britain 516
Public Debt, U.S. 321
Railroad Mileage, U.S. 272
Religions of the World 2204
Religious Bodies, United States 2204
Reserve Assets, by Country 328
Rivers, Important 229
Roads in the U.S., Rural 275
Roman Emperors 590
Rulers of England 530
  of France 563–565
  of Germany 568–569
  of Russia 593
Savings, Growth of in U.S. 325
School Course, Development of 894
School Enrollment 861–868, 871, 899
Schools, by States 864, 892
  Cost per Pupil 903, 905, 863
  Historical Statistics 868
  Trends in Districts 891
Seas, Bays, and Gulfs 2253
Speakers of the House 741
State Governments 759–760
State Parks 64
States, Historical Statistics 466
  Rank in Pop. 70
Statistics of the Nations 231–232
Supreme Court Justices 751
Temperature and Rainfall, Canada 1566
  Cities of the World 1564
  United States 1565
Traffic, Intercity Freight 274
  Passenger 273
Treaties 499–500, 668–670
Trigonometric Functions 1536
Tunnels, Important 394
United Nations 2222
U.S., Economic Dependence 260
  Exports and Imports 258
  Growth 72–75
  Historical Statistics 466
  Territorial Growth 456
Vice Presidents, United States 476
Wars, American:
  Civil 460–461
  Colonial 447
  Mexican 457
  Of 1812 455
  Revolutionary 450–451
  With Spain 464
Wars of History, Important 720–721
Waterfalls 226
Weights and Measures 1511–1514
World Expositions 2257
World Ports 218
World's Progress in Commerce 255
World Statistics 231–232

LIST OF ILLUSTRATIONS

A

Acropolis, Athens
  bet. 438–439
Adams, Ansel 1398
Adams, John 762
Adams, John Q. bet. 741–742
Admiralty Islands, Pacific 778
Admirals, American 908
Air Force Academy, U.S. 909
  Chapel 841, 1284
Airplane, Supersonic 1638
Alamo bet. 486–487
Alaska Map 79
Alba, Madonna · 1335
Albers, Josef 1342, 1360
Aldrin, Edwin E., Jr. 1541
Aleutian Islands, Caroli
  Volcano 199
Ali Baba 1016
Alice in Wonderland 1090
Altamira Plaza, Caracas 163
America, Historic 727,
  bet. 1100–01
  Scenic fol. xx
American Admirals 908
  Colleges 1615, 1632
  Educators 859
  Flags 486
  Generals 908
  Monuments 727
  Wild Flowers bet. 1766–67
Amer. Indian Heritage
  bet. 486–487
Andrea, John de 1378
Andromeda Galaxy
  bet. 1600–01
Annapolis, Md., U.S. Naval
  Acad. 909
Antares, Apollo 14 LM
  bet. 1540–41
Apollo 8 Earth View
  bet. 438–439
  (Spacecraft) bet. 1540–41
Apollo 11 Blastoff
  bet. 1540–41
  Earth View bet. 1540–41
  Landing Site bet. 1540–41
  Moonwalk bet. 1540–41
Apollo 14, Moon Landing
  bet. 1540–41
Aquilano, Paolo 1367
Arc de Triomphe 779
Archeology, N. Am. 487
Architecture 841
  Amer. Residences 1274,
  1276, 1278, 1280, 1298
Ardmore, Pa., Welsh Valley
  Jr. H.S. 891
Argentina 162
Arizona, Phoenix Public Lib.
  890
Armed Forces, U.S.
  Decorations, World
  War II bet. 486–487
Arp, Jean 1368
*Arthur and the Strange
  Mantle* 1172
Artifacts, Canadian Eskimo
  487
Asia, Views in 195
Aster, New England
  bet. 1766–67
Atget, Eugene 1394
Athens, Greece, Parthenon
  bet. 438–439, 1270
Atmosphere bet. 1600–01
Azalea bet. 1766–67

B

Babson House, Riverside,
  Ill. 1276
Baertling, Olle 1342
Baldessari, John 1328
Baler, Agricultural
  bet. 250–251
Balla, Giacomo 1320
Ballet 1464, 1466, 1468
Balthus 1322
Bangkok, Thailand 779
Banks, Nathaniel
  bet. 741–742
Barnard, Frederick 1091

Barnet, Will 1342
Bartholdi, Frederic
  Statue of Liberty
  bet. 2132–33
Baschet, Bernard and
  Francois 1372
Baskin, Leonard 1326, 1378
Baton Rouge, La., State
  lib. 890
Bayard Building 1276
Beardsley, Aubrey,
  ill. of Ali Baba 1016
  ill. Le Morte D'Arthur
  1172, 1173
  ill. of Volpone 1017
Becher, Bernd & Hilla 1374
Becky Sharp 1091
Beersheba, Israel 195
Bell, Liberty bet. 486–487
Bellingrath Gardens 1767
Bellini, Giovanni 1332
Benton, Thomas Hart 988
Bermuda, Hamilton,
  Parliament Bldg. 779
Bertoia, Harry 1372
Bethune, Mary 859
Betsy Ross Flag 486
Bewick, Thomas 1014, 1015
Big Ben, London 925
Birds, North American
  bet. 1720–21
Bismarck, N. Dak. 752
Black-eyed Susan
  bet. 1766–67
Black, Hugo L. 2031
Blackmun, Harry A. 2031
Blake, William 1354
Bluebonnet bet. 1766–67
Bochner, Mel 1374
Body (Skeleton) bet. 1684–85
Bolivia 163
Bookmobile 890
Boorstin, Daniel J. 1033
Borglum, Gutzon
  Mt. Rushmore Sculpture
  bet. 2132–33
Bosphorus Strait 194
Boston City Hall 1284
Boston, Mass., Brattle St.
  1264
Botero, Fernando 1345
Brady, Matthew 1392
Brancusi, Constantin 1368
Brattle St., Boston, Mass
  1264
Bravo, Claudio 1326
Brazil 163
Brazil, Brasilia 1286
Breckenridge, John C. 763
Brennan, Wm. J., Jr. 2031
Breuer, Marcel 1278
Bridalveil Falls, Cal. fol. xx
Bridge, Covered bet. 144–145
Bridge, Verrazano-Narrows,
  N.Y. 1284
Bristol House 1274
Brookhaven National
  Laboratory 1612
Brown, James 2216
Brueghel, Peter (the Elder)
  1332
Bryce Canyon Nat. Park,
  Utah fol. xx
Buckwheat, Golden
  bet. 1766–67
Buddha of Wat Doi Suteb
  778
Buddhist Temple 779
Buenos Aires 162
Buoy, Ocean bet. 1600–01
Burger, Warren E. 2031
Burr, Aaron 763
Butterflies bet. 1721–22

C

Cactus, Prickly Pear
  bet. 1766–67
Cairo, Egypt 779
Cajori, Charles 1324
Caldecott, R. 1090
Calder, Alexander 1368
  Sculpture bet. 1252–1253
Calhoun, John C. 763

California, Los Angeles,
  Dodger Stadium 2217
Callery, Mary 1378
Callot, Jacques 1352
Calzolari, Pier Paolo 1374
Camera Obscura 1390
Cameron, Julia Margaret
  1392
Canada:
  Maligne Lake bet. 144–145
  Montmorency Falls 198
  O'Keefe Centre 778
  Ottawa fol. xx
  Perce Rock bet. 144–145
  Quebec Parliament bet.
  144–145
  Ste. Rose du Nord bet.
  144–145
  Scenic bet. 144–145
  Toronto, Maple Leaf
  Gardens 2217
Canadian Artifacts 487
Canadian Parliament bet.
  144–145
Cape Town, S. Africa 778
Capital Cities, World 779
Capitols, State 752
Capitol, Washington
  bet. 731–732
Caracas, Venezuela 163
Cargo Vessel 268
Carjat, Etienne 1348
Caroli Volcano 199
Carpenter Shop, Egyptian
  1288
Carter, Jimmy bet. 741–742
Cartier-Bresson, Henri 1402
Cassatt, Mary 1358
Castagno, Andrea del 1332
Castle Geyser, Yellowstone
  Nat. Park, Wyo. fol. xx
Cave Painting 1330
Central America Mayan
  Temple 1260
Central Park, N.Y.C. 1266
Ceremonial Objects 1316
Cezanne, Paul 1336
Chagall, Marc 1360
Chamberlain, Wilt 2216
Charlemagne bet. 1830–31
Charlotte-Mecklenburg Co.,
  N.C., Public Library 890
Chartres Cathedral, France
  1273
Chase Manhattan Bank
  1256, 1274, 1282, 1294
Chaucer, Geoffrey 986
Chenonceaux, France
  bet. 438–439, 1273
Chicago, Ill., Byrd Elem.
  School 891
Chillida, Eduardo 1324
Chinese Scroll 1260
Chirico, Giorgio de 1320
Christo 1374
Christ of the Andes 163
Circulatory System
  bet. 1684–85
Circus Maximus, Rome 1260
Cities, World 779
Clinton, George 763
Cloisters, Ft. Tryon Park
  1273
Cloisters, Garden 1288
Close, Chuck 1345
Clouds 1546–47
Coal Mine, COSI 911
Coast Guard Academy, U.S.
  909
Colleges & Universities
  841, 858, 890, 891, 909,
  bet. 1252–53
Colorado Springs, Col. Air
  Force Academy 841, 909
Columbine bet. 1766–67
Columbus, Ohio Center of
  Science & Industry
  848–849, 910–911
Combines, Agricultural
  bet. 250–251
Conant, James B. 859
Congress bet. 740–741,
  741–742
Constantinople, Hagia Sophia
  1268

Continental Flag 486
Corinth, Lovis 1320
Cornell, Joseph 1338, 1377
Couelle, Jacques 1276
Coventry Cathedral 194
Covered Bridge bet. 144–145
Crafts Textile and Fiber
  1306
Crockett, Davy bet. 741–742
Cruikshank, George 1090
Cultivator, Farm Machinery
  bet. 250–251
Currier & Ives 1266, 1356
Cypress Gardens, Fla. 1767

D

Dallas, George M. 763
Daly, Norman 1372
D'Arcangelo, Allan 1340
Daumier, Honore 1320,
  1356, 1390
Davis, Stuart 1340
Degas, Edgar 1320, 1368
De Kooning, Elaine 1326
De Kooning, Willem 1378
Delaware State Capitol 752
Demuth, Charles 1322, 1340
Denver, Col., Convention
  Hall preceding 1477
Devil's Tower Nat. Mon.,
  Wyo. 1557
Dewey, John 859
DEW Line bet. 1600–01
Dickinson, E., Home
  bet. 1100–01
Dictionary, Facsimile Page
  of Samuel Johnson's 1078
Digestive System
  bet. 1684–85
Diller, Burgoyne 1342, 1370
Dine, Jim 1328, 1346
Dr. Seuss 1036
Dodger Stadium 2217
Dogwood, Flowering
  bet. 1766–67
Dolls, American 848
Dome of the Rock,
  Jerusalem bet. 144–145
Don Quixote 1090
Dore, Gustave 1090, 1170–71
Douglas, William O. 2031
Dover, Delaware 752
Dubuffet, Jean 1282
Duchamp, Marcel 1338, 1377
Duke University 858
Duncan, Isadora 1464
Durer, Albrecht 1350

E

Eagle, Bald bet. 1720–21
Earth Dynamics bet. 1568–69
  Erosion
  Glaciation
  Mountain Building
  Water Erosion
Earth Science, Photography:
  Ariz., Cal., Nev. fol. xx
Earth View, Apollo 8
  bet. 1540–41
Eclipses bet. 1600–01
Education 919
Educators, American 859
Egypt, Cairo 779
Einstein, Albert 1477
Eisenhower, Dwight D. 908
Eisenstaedt, Alfred 1400
El Camino (Cal.) College 891
Elementary School Students
  at work 919
Ellwood, Craig 1298
Emory Univ. Library,
  Atlanta, Ga. 841
England:
  Big Ben 925
  Coventry Cathedral 194
  London 779, 801
  Shakespeare Country
  bet. 924–925
  Stonehenge 925, 1258, 1392
  Views in 925
  Windsor Castle 925

English Manuscript, Early 985
English Spelling Book 1014
Epstein, Jacob 1368
Equador 162
Equator Monument 162
Equinox bet. 1600–01
Erechtheum, Fragment of 1270
Ernst, Jimmy 1338
Erosion, Earth Dynamics bet. 1568–69
Estes, Richard 1346
Europe, Scenes in bet. 144–145, 194

F

Famous Gardens 1767
Farm Machinery bet. 250–251
Farrell, Suzanne 1468
Feininger, Andreas 1402
Fenn, Henry 1266
Fiction Characters 1090
Fillmore, Millard 763
Fishing Boat, South American 163
Flags, American 486
  Bennington 486
  Betsy Ross 486
  Bon Homme Richard 486
  Bunker Hill 486
  Continental 486
  Fort McHenry 486
  "Old Glory" 486
  Stars and Stripes 486
Fleming, Peggy 2216
Flowers, Wild bet. 1766–67
Fontana, Domenico 1262
Foreign Scenes 778
Forests:
  Coniferous 1766
  Temperate 1766
France:
  Arc de Triomphe 779
  Chartres Cathedral 1273
  Chenonceaux Chateau bet. 438–439, 1273
  Luxembourg Gardens 194
  Versailles Palace bet. 144–145, 1274
Frankfort, Ky. 752
Frank, Mary 1326, 1378
Franklin, Benjamin bet. 1830–31
French Radio Center 194
Friedman, Milton 1033
Freud, Lucien 1326
Frost, A. B. 1090
Fuller, Buckminster 1284
Furniture, Hand-crafted 1308

G

Gabo, Naum 1368
Gainsborough, Thomas 1335
Galleria Vittorio Emanuele 1264
Gallo, Frank 1374
Gammage Auditorium bet. 1252–53
Gardens, Famous 1767
  Bellingrath, Mobile, Ala. 1767
  Cypress, Winter Haven, Fla. 1767
  Hodges, Many, La. 1767
  Versailles, France fol. xx, 1274
Gardner, John W. 859
Gaudi, Antoni 1276
Gauguin, Paul 1336
Geisel, Theodor Seuss 1036
Generals, American 908
George VI Falls 198
Germany:
  Moselle Wine Country 194
  Rhine River bet. 144–145
  Zugspitze, Mt. bet. 144–145

Gerry, Elbridge bet. 741–742, 763
Giacometti, Alberto 1322
Gilbert and George 1374
Gilray, James 1354
Glaciation, Earth Dynamics bet. 1568–69
Glen Head, L.I., N.Y., North Shore H.S. 891
Goddard, Robert H. 1601
Goltzius, Hendrik 1230
Goodman, Sidney 1326
Goodwin, Philip 1282
Gorky, Arshile 1322
Gottlieb, Adolf 1340
Governors-General of Canada, Residence bet. 144–145
Goya, Francesco 1335, 1354
Graham, John 1322, 1338
Graham, Martha 1466
Grand Canyon fol. xx
Grand Rapids, Mich., Children's Retreat & Training Sch. 891
Grant, Ulysses S. 908
Graves, Nancy 1372
Great Falls of Potomac 198
Greco, El 1335
Gris, Juan 1320
Gropius, Walter 1282
Grosvenor, Robert 1370
Grosz, George 1322
Guardi, Francesco 1318
Guggenheim Museum 1286
Guston, Philip 1324
Guyana 198

H

Hagia Sophia 1268
Hale Telescope, Mt. Palomar, Cal. bet. 1600–01
Hamilton, Bermuda 779
Hanson, Duane 1378
Harlan, John M. 2031
Harnett, William 1101, 1256, 1336
Harris County Sports Stadium 2217
Harrow, Farm Machinery bet. 250–251
Harvard University 858, 890
Hathaway Cottage bet. 924–925
Hawaii, Map 81
  Mauna Loa Volcano 199
Heavenly Bodies 1608, 1609
Held, Al 1342
Helsinki, Finland 2217
Hepworth, Barbara 1370
Hercules 1230
Hesburgh, Theodore M. 859
Hill, David O. 1392
Hine, Lewis W. 1396
Historic America bet. 1100–01
Historic England bet. 924–925
Hodes, Linda 1468
Hodges Gardens, Many, La. 1767
Hogarth, William 1352
Hokanson, Hans 1255, 1324, 1372
Hokusai, Katushika 1358
Holbein, Hans 1332
Holm, Hanya 1466
Homer 1231
Homes, Noted:
  Anne Hathaway bet. 924–925
  Babson 1276
  Bristol 1274
  Couelle 1276
  Conant 1278, 1298
  Dickinson bet. 1100–01
  Farnsworth 1278
  Geller 1278
  Hewlett 1274
  Irving bet. 1100–01
  Kaufman 1280
  Lowell bet. 1100–01, 1274
  Lyndhurst 1274

Mark Twain bet. 1100–01
  Paine 1276
  Robie 1280
  Shakespeare bet. 924–925
Hoover, Herbert bet. 740–741
Hopkins, Mark 859
Hopper, Edward 1345, 1360
Houses:
  Acorn 1280, 1298
  Egyptian 1258
  Glass 1278, 1298
  Maori Store House 778
Houston, Sam 741–742
Houston, Tex., Sports Arena 2217
Howard, Ebenezer 1264
Huckleberry Finn 988, 1090
Hudson River Museum 1294
Hufuf Airport 195
Hull, Bobby 2216
Hultberg, John 1338
Humphrey, Doris 1466

I

Iguassu Falls 198
Illinois Institute of Technology, Chicago 841
Implements, Handcrafted 1310
Indian bet. 486–487
Independence Hall bet. 486–487
Indiana, Robert 1328
Indianapolis Motor Speedway 2217
India, New Delhi 779
Indian Paintbrush bet. 1766–67
Indians, American, Map bet. 486–487
Indonesia, Mt. Kloet 1556
Irving, Washington, Home bet. 1100–01
Israel:
  American Embassy, Tel-Aviv 779
  Dome of the Rock bet. 144–145
  Keren Theater, Beersheba 195
  Memorial Shrine, Jerusalem 778
  Shrine of the Book, Jerusalem 1286
  Views in bet. 144–145
Istanbul 194
Italian Museum, Lima, Peru 162
Italy:
  St. Mark's Cathedral 1273
  St. Peters' Basilica 1273
  Vesuvius Volcano 199
Ivanowski, Sigismond de 1091

J

Jagger, Gillian 1377
Jane Eyre 1091
Japan: 195
  Komazawa Olympic Park 2217
Japanese Garden 1767
Japanese Supertanker 265
Jasper Nat. Park, Canada bet. 144–145
Java, Mt. Kloet 1556
Jefferson Memorial 727
Jefferson, Thomas 762
Jenkins, Paul 1340
Jerusalem, Israel:
  Dome of the Rock bet. 144–145
  Memorial Shrine 778
  Shrine of the Book 1286
Jewelry 1312, 1314
Jodrell Bank Experimental Station England bet. 1600–01
John Gilpin's Ride 1090

Johnson, Philip 1278, 1282, 1286, 1294, 1298
Johnson, Richard M. 763
Johnson, Samuel 1079
  Dictionary 1078
Jordan, David Starr 859
Jost, Amman 1262
Juarez Ave., Mexico City 162

K

Kahn, Louis 1286
Karnak, Temple of 1268
Kemble, E. W. 1090
Kentucky State Capital 752
Keren Theater 195
Kiesler, Frederick 1286
Kindergarten Students at Work 918
King, Martin Luther, Jr. bet. 2132–33
King, William R. 763
Kinigstein, Jonah 1338
Kircher, Athanasius 1390
Kitaj, R. B. 1328
Klee, Paul 1320
Klimt, Gustav 1320
Knossos, Crete, Palace 1268
Kohn, Gabriel 1370
Kokoschka, Oskar 1322
Kollwitz, Kathe 1360
Komazawa Olympic Park 2217
Kresge Auditorium, M.I.T. 858
Krushenick, Nicholas 1255
Kusama, Yayoi 1374

L

Lange, Dorothea 1396
Languages, Map bet. 2164–65
Languages of the World 2165
La Paz, Bolivia 163
Latin America bet. 162–163
Laurel, Mountain bet. 1766–67
Le Corbusier 1276
Lee, Robert E. 908
Leger, Fernand 1368
Lenin State Library 194
Lewitt, Sol 1374
Liberty Bell bet. 486–487
Libraries in the U.S.:
  Buffalo & Erie County, Bookmobile 890
  Charlotte-Mecklenburg County, N.C. 890
  Emory, Atlanta, Ga. bet. 840–841
  Lamont, Harvard 890
  Louisiana State 890
  Madison, N.J. bet. 840–841
  Phoenix, Ariz. 890
  Pius XII Memorial 890
  San Lorenzo, Alameda Co. Cal. bet. 840–841
  Scottsdale, Ariz. bet. 840–841
Library of Congress 890
Lichtenstein, Roy 1377
Lighthouse of the Mediterranean 199
Lily, Leopard bet. 1766–67
Lima, Peru 162
Limon, Jose 1468
Lincoln, Abraham 1037
  Lincoln and Tad 2030
Lincoln Library of Sports Champions 1032
Lipari Island 199
Lippi, Fra Filippo 1332
Literature:
  Characters from 1090
  Famous Names in 1091
London, England 779
Long's Peak, Colorado fol. xx
Los Angeles, Calif., Dodger Stadium 2217
Lost City of the Incas 162
Louisiana State Lib., Baton Rouge 890

Lowell, James Russell,
Home bet. 1100–01, 1274
Lucerne, Switzerland 194
Luxembourg Gardens 194
Lyndhurst 1274

M

MacArthur, Douglas 908
Machine, Experimental
bet. 250–251
McKinnell, Noel 1284
Machu Picchu, Peru 162
Madison, James bet. 741–742
Madison, N.J., Public
Lib. bet. 840–841
Madison, Wis., Hoyt
School 891
Madonna, Alba 1335
Maillol, Aristide 1368
Maligne Lake, Canada bet.
144–145
Manila Airport 195
Mann, Horace 895
Mantegna, Andrea 1350
Manupelli, George 1377
Manuscript, English 985
Manzoni, Piero 1374
Maple Leaf Gardens 2217
Maps:
Alaska 79
Hawaii 81
Indians, Amer.
bet. 486–487
Languages bet. 2164–65
Puerto Rico 84
United States
Presidential Election 761
Territorial Growth
bet. 486–487
Marc, Franz 1320
Marshall, George C. 908
Marshall, Thurgood 2031
Marsicano, Nicholas 1324
Martin, Agnes 1324
Masks 1316
Masks, New Guinea
Tribal 1253
Massachusetts Institute
of Technology 858
Mathematics preceding 1477
Matisse, Henri 1348
Matta 1338
Mauna Loa 199
Mayan Temple 1260
Mayon Volcano,
Luzon, P.I. 199
Mazur, Michael 1326
Meadmore, Clement
1255, 1370
Medals of Honor
bet. 486–487
Medicis Fountains, Paris 194
Meket-Re Tomb, Thebes
1288
Meryon, Charles 1262
Metalware, Handcrafted 1304
Mexico City, Mexico 162
Mexico, Paricutin
Volcano 199
Meyster Alman 1350
Michelangelo 1318
Midgette, Willard 1345
Mies van der Rohe,
Ludwig 841, 1278, 1282
Miki, Suizan 1326
Military Academy, U.S. 909
Ming Dynasty Art 1260
Miori, Luciano 1326
Miralda, Antoni 1374
Mitchell, Arthur 1468
Modigliani, Amadeo 1320
Moholy-Nagy Laszlo 1402
Mondrian, Piet 1297, 1320,
1342
Montevideo, Uruguay 162
Montmorency Falls 198
Montpelier, Vt. 752
Monument Valley,
Ariz. fol. xx
Moon bet. 1540–41, 1608
Moore, Henry 1322
Morgan, Edward P. 1033
Morning-Glory bet. 1766–67

Morris, Robert 1374
Morris, William 1033
Morte d'Arthur 1172–73
Mosaic, Roman 1270
Moscow 194
Motherwell, Robert 1340
Moths bet. 1720–21
Mountain Building,
Earth Dynamics
bet. 1568–69
Mount Kloet, Java 1556
Mount Rushmore fol. xx,
bet. 2132–33
*Mr. Darcy and Sir William
Lucas* 1091
Mummy Case 1330
Munch, Edvard 1356
Munson-Williams-Proctor
Institute 1294
Murch, Walter 1255, 1345
Muscular System
bet. 1684–85
Museum of Jade 195
Museum of Modern Art 1282
Musial, Stan 2216
Music and Literature 1101,
1256
Muybridge, Eadweard 1394

N

Nadar 1392
National War College 909
Naval Academy, U.S. 909
Neill John 1034–35
Nemeny, Geroge 1278, 1298
Nervous System bet. 1684–85
Nevelson, Louise 1255, 1370
New Delhi, India 779
New Guinea Tribal
Mask 1253
New London, Conn., U.S.
Coast Guard Acad. 909
New Mexico State Capitol
752
New York City:
Bayard Bldg. 1276
Central Park 1266
Chase Manhattan Bank
1256, 1274, 1282, 1294
Guggenheim Museum 1286
Museum of Modern
Art 1282
United Nations Bldg.
preceding 727
Verrazano-Narrows
Bridge 1284
World Trade Center
preceding 727
New Zealand: Maori
Store House 778
Niagara Falls 198
Nicklaus, Jack 2216
Niemeyer, Oscar 1286
Nimbus Satellite bet. 1600–01
Nimitz, Chester W. 908
Nolde, Emil 1320
North Carolina, Charlotte-
Mecklenburg County
Library 890
North Dakota State
Capitol 752
Nowicki, Matthew 1284
Nureyev, Rudolf 1468

O

Obelisk, Buenos Aires 162
Ocean Data Station
Buoy bet. 1600–01
O'Keefe Centre 778
Oldenberg, Claes 1377
Olympia 1258
Olympics Statue 2217
Oliver Twist 1090
Oppenheim, Dennis 1328,
1375
Oppenheim, Meret 1377
Orbiting Astronomical
Observatory bet. 1600–01
Orbiting of
Satellite bet. 1540–41

Oregon State Capitol 752
Oster, Gerald 1346
Oswego Tea bet. 1766–67
Ottawa, Ontario,
Canada bet. 144–145
Oud, J.J.P. 1276
Owens, Warren 1370
Oz, Scarecrow of 1034
Oz, Wizard of 1035
Ozenfant, Amedee 1340

P

Pacific Islands 778
Paine House 1276
Paintbrush,
Indian bet. 1766–67
Palmer, Arnold 2216
Pantheon 1270
Paricutin Volcano 199
Paris, France 194, 779
Parliament, Canadian
Buildings bet. 144–145
Parliament, London 925
Parthenon, Athens
352–353, 1270
Pearlstein, Philip 1255, 1345
Pearson, Henry 1377
Penn, Irving 1400
Perce Rock, Canada bet.
144–145
Pershing, John J. 908
Peru 162
Petrus a Merica 1262
Philadelphia, Pa.:
Independence Hall
bet. 486–487
Liberty Bell bet. 486–487
Philippines
Manila International
Airport 195
Mayon Volcano 199
Phlox, Meadow bet. 1766–67
Phoenix, Ariz., Pub. Lib. 890
Photography, Earth
Science: Ariz., Cal.,
Nev. fol. xx
Picabia, Francis 1338
Picasso, Pablo 1322, 1336,
1360, 1368, *por.* 1400
Piero di Cosimo 1332
Piranesi, Giambattista 1352
Planetarium, COSI 911
Planets 1608
Player, Gary 2216
Polar Regions 1766
Poppy, California
bet. 1766–67
Population Growth,
World bet. 2164–65
Portugal:
Quelez Gardens 778
Potomac River 198
Pottery 1300, 1302, 1330
Prairie 1766
Prairie Village, Kan.,
Shawnee-Mission East
High School 891
Presidential Election,
Map 761
Presidents, U.S.
bet. 740–742, 762, 848
Pride and Prejudice 1091
Puerto Rico, Map 84
Pyramid Model 1268
Pyramid of King Sahure at
Abusir 1268

Q

Quebec, Can., Citadel bet.
144–145
Queluz, Portugal, Palace
and Gardens 778

R

Radar Station, Alaska bet.
1600–01
Randolph, John bet. 741–742

Raphael's *Madonna* 1335,
bet. 1830–31
Ray, Man 1377
Rembrandt 1318, 1335, 1352
Renoir 1336
Rhine River bet. 144–145
Richardson, Henry
Hobson 1276
Rime of the Ancient Mariner
1170–71
Robbia, Luca della 1367
Robie House 1280
Rocket 1601
Rocky Mt. National
Park fol. xx
Roman Street Scene 1264
Rome:
Circus Maximus 1260
St. Peter's Basilica 1273
Rooms:
Art 1294
Connecticut 1292
Dormitory 1294
Franco-Flemish 1290
French 1292
Hart House 1290
Morse House 1292
Pennsylvania Dutch 1292
Roman 1288
Romanesque 1288
Spanish 1288
Venetian 1290
Victorian 1292
Wentworth House 1290
Roosevelt, F. D. bet. 740–741
Rosati, James 1370
Rotorua, N.Z. 778
Rouault, Georges 1255,
1336, 1348
Rowlandson, Thomas 1354
Rushmore, Mt. fol. xx, bet.
2132–33
Russia 194

S

St. Denis, Ruth 1464
St. Lawrence Seaway,
Map 270
St. Louis, Mo.,
Univ. Mem. Library 890
St. Mark's Cathedral,
Venice 1273
St. Peter's Basilica,
Rome 1273
Salem, Ore. 752
San Lorenzo Pub. Lib.,
Alameda Co.,
Cal. bet. 840–841
Santa Fe, N.Mex. 752
Sao Paulo, Brazil 163
Satellite, Nimbus 1600–01
Syncom 1638
Satellites, Orbiting of
bet. 1540–41
Saudi Arabia 195
Scarecrow of Oz 1034
Scenes in Europe 194
Scenic Canada bet. 144–145
Schoffer, Nicholas 1372
Schongauer, Martin 1350
School Bldgs, Modern 891
Schools, Armed Services 909
Science Experiment,
COSI 910
Scottsdale, Ariz., Public
Library bet. 840–841
Sculpture:
American 1362, 1368, 1370,
1372, 1374, 1377, 1378
Ancient Eastern 1362
Egyptian 1362
Medieval 1367
Prehistoric 1362
Primitive 1362
Renaissance 1367
Scuris, Stephanie 1255, 1370
Seasons bet. 1600–01
Segal, George 1378
Seley, Jason 1324, 1370
Selz, Dorothy 1374
Seurat, Georges 1336
Sense Organs bet. 1684–85
Shahn, Ben 1255, 1322

Shakespeare bet. 924–925
    Birthplace bet. 924–925
    Church bet. 924–925
    Theatre bet. 924–925
Sharaku, Tochusai 1358
Shaw, George Bernard 1121
Shaw, Kendall 1340
Shawn, Ted 1460
Shea Stadium 2217
Sherwood, Mills, & Smith
    1294
Shoemaker, Willie 2216
Shrine of the Book 1286
Singapore,
    Museum of Jade 195
Skeleton bet. 1684–85
Skidmore, Owings & Merrill
    841, 1282, 1284, 1294
Smith, David 1370
South Africa:
    Cape Town 778
    Victoria Falls 198
South America bet. 162–163
    Iguassu Falls 198
Space bet. 1600–01
    Man's Activities in
    bet. 1540–41, 1600–01
Space-Age Technology
    bet. 1540–41, 1600–01
Spacecraft bet. 1540–41,
    1600–01
Space Shuttle bet. 1600–01
Space Walk bet. 1540–41
Spalatin, Marko 1345
Speedway, Ind., Indianapolis
    Motor Speedway 2217
Spider Rock, Monument
    Valley, Ariz. fol. xx
Spiderwort bet. 1766–67
Spinning Wheels 849
Sports Centers 2217
Sports Champions 1032
Sports Stars 2216
Stadiums 2217
Stanford University 858
Stars 1609
Stars and Stripes 486
State Capitols 752
Statue of Liberty
    bet. 2132–33
Steichen, Edward 1398
Steinberg, Saul 1328
Stella, Frank 1324
Steppe 1766
Stewart, Potter 2031
Stockholm, Sweden
    bet. 438–439
Stone, Edward D. 1282
Stonehenge 925, 1258, 1362
Strand, Paul 1396
Stratford-on-Avon
    bet. 924–925

Stratosphere bet. 1600–01
Stromboli Volcano 199
Stuart, Gilbert 1335
Stubbins, Hugh 1256
Sugarman, George 1370
Suizenji Garden, Japan 1767
Sullivan, Louis 1276
Supersonic Research
    Plane 1638
Supertanker, Japanese 265
Supreme Court, U.S., 2031
Switzerland 194
Syncom Satellite 1638

T

Talbot, William Henry
    Fox 1390
Tania 1342
Tanker 265
    Universe Ireland 264
Taylor, Maxwell D. 908
Taylor, Paul 1468
Tel-Aviv, Israel 779
Telegraph 382, 383
Telephone Circuit 384
Temple of Artemis 1270
Temple of Karnak 1268
Tenniel, John 1090
Territorial Growth of U.S.,
    Map bet. 486–487
Thailand: Bangkok 779
    Buddha 778
Thomson, Hugh 1091
Tides bet. 1600–01
Tiepolo, Giovanni Battista
    1318
Tintoretto 1332
Tokyo, Japan 195
    Sports Arena 2217
Tomb of Per-Neb 1268
Tompkins, Daniel 763
Toulouse-Lautrec 1358
Tornado bet. 1600–01
Toronto, Canada:
    Maple Leaf Gardens 2217
    O'Keefe Centre 778
Tracking Station,
    Australia 1638
Trees, Birch 1760
    Pine 1761
Trova, Ernest 1372
Truman bet. 740–741
Tundra 1766
Tunnel 271
Twain, Mark, Clemens,
    S. L. 988, 989, 1090
    Home bet. 1100–01
Tyler, John 763

U

Uitshi River 198
Uncle Remus Stories 1090
United Nations
    Buildings preceding 727
Universe bet. 1600–01
Universe Ireland, tanker 264
Universities and Colleges
    see Colleges and Universities
U.S. Presidential Election
    Map 761
U.S. Territorial Growth,
    Map bet. 486–487
Urinary System bet. 1684–85
Uruguay 162
Utah, Bryce Canyon fol. xx
Utamaro, Kitagawa 1358

V

Van Buren, Martin 763
Van Gogh, Vincent 1336
Van Hoeydonck, Paul 1372
Vassar College 858
Vasarely, Victor 1346, 1360
Vegetation 1766
Velasquez 1335
Velde, Jan van de 1262
Venezuela 163
Venice, St. Mark's
    Cathedral 1273
Vermeer, Jan 1335
Vermont State Capitol 752
Verrazano-Narrows
    Bridge 1284
Verrocchio, Andrea del 1367
Versailles Palace 1274, bet.
    144–145
Vesuvius 199
Vice Presidents bet. 762–763
Victoria Falls 198
Villon, Jacques 1348
Vinci, Leonardo da 1318, bet.
    1830–31
Volcanoes, Famous 199
Vollmer, Ruth 1372
Volpone 1017
Von Weigand,
    Charmion 1342

W

Wagoner, Dan 1468
Wall Paintings:
    Egyptian 1288, 1330
    New Guinea 1330
    Roman 1330

Wall Street 1266
Ward, Lynn 1037
Warhol, Andy 1360
Washington, D.C.:
    Buildings 727, bet. 731–732
    Library of Congress 890
    White House 727
Washington Monument 727
Water Erosion, Earth
    Dynamics bet. 1568–69
Waterfalls 198
Waterspout bet. 1600–01
Watts, Robert 1377
Wayfarer's Chapel 1284
Weidman, Charles 1466
Wesselmann, Tom 1328,
    1346, 1377
Westmoreland, Wm. C. 908
West Point, N.Y.,
    U.S. Military Acad. 909
Weyden, Rogier van der 1332
Whistler, James 1356
White, Byron 2031
White House 727
White, Minor 1398
Wild Flowers bet. 1766–67
Wilson, Woodrow 740
Window, Early American
    1274
Windsor Castle 925
Wizard of Oz 1035
Wood, Grant 1345
World Population
    Growth bet. 2164–65
World Trade Center,
    N.Y. preceding 727
World War II:
    Decorations bet. 486–487
Wright, Frank Lloyd
    bet. 1252–53, 1280, 1284,
    1286
Wyoming:
    Devil's Tower 1557
    Yellowstone Falls 198
    Yellowstone Nat. Park
    fol. xx

Y

Yale University 858
Yeats, William B. 1120
Yellowstone Falls 198
Yellowstone Nat. Park,
    Wyo. fol. xx
Yosemite Nat. Park,
    Cal. fol. xx

Z

Zambesi River 198
Zugspitze, Mt. Germany
    bet. 144–145

KEY TO PRONUNCIATION

DIACRITICAL MARKS

ä, as in farm, father; à, as in ask, fast; ă, as in at fat; ā, as in day, fate; â, as in care, fare. ĕ, as in met, set; ē, as in me, see; ē̇, as in her, perform. ĭ, as in pin, ill; ī, as in pine, ice. ŏ, as in hot, got; ō, as in note, old; ô, as in for, fought; o͞o, as in cook, look; o͞o, as in moon, spoon. ŭ, as in cup, duck; ū, as in use, amuse; û, as in fur, urge. ou, as in out, about. oi, as in oil, boil.

å, ĕ, ȯ, u̇ represent the sounds ā, ē, ō, ū; they are of shorter quantity but do not lose the quality of the "long" vowel, as in senåte, ĕvent, ȯbey, lectu̇re.

TH indicates the sound of th in thee, though. In foreign words this symbol indicates a more distinct d sound than in English words, as in the Irish word

Dail. zh stands for the sound of z in azure.

ü cannot be exactly represented in English. The English sound of u as in *luke* and *duke* resembles the original sound of ü. ö cannot be exactly represented in English. The English sound of u in *burn* and *burnt* is perhaps the nearest equivalent to ö, or œ. K represents ch in German *ich*, *ach*. N represents the nasal tone (as in French) of the preceding vowel, as in *encore* (än′kōr′). H represents the guttural g or j in Spanish words, as in *jefe*.

The principal accent is indicated by a heavy mark,′, and the secondary accent by a lighter mark,′, placed at the end of the syllable

SPECIAL MARKS AND THEIR USES

PUNCTUATION:

, Comma		" " Quotation Marks	
; Semicolon		! Exclamation point	
: Colon		( ) Parentheses	
. Period		[ ] Brackets	
— Dash		' Apostrophe	
? Interrogation point, question mark		- Hyphen	

FOOTNOTE INDICATORS: Used when number of footnotes is small, otherwise numbers or letters are employed, or special indicator marks may be used double.

* Asterisk	§ Also used to mean section or clause
† Dagger	‖ Also used to mean "is parallel to"
‡ Double Dagger	¶ or ℙ Also used to indicate paragraph

PRONUNCIATION INDICATORS: More common signs used, in English and some foreign languages, usually to show the value or quality of a vowel. Letters are supplied below to show how sign is applied.

ĕ Breve. Pronounce vowel short	ê or â Circumflex accent (French)
ā Macron. Pronounce vowel long	ä Umlaut (German). Alters quality of vowels a, o,
aĕ Diaeresis. Pronounce vowels as separate sounds	or u
é Acute accent (French)	ç Cedilla (French). Converts hard c to soft c
è Grave accent (French)	ñ Tilde (Spanish). Gives effect of a following y

WORD SUBSTITUTES: Many signs are used as a species of shorthand. Some of the more commonly used follow. Where the sign has a name, the name precedes the meaning.

∧ Caret. Insert	+ Plus. Add
{ or } Brace. Lines belong together	− Minus. Subtract
═ Is equal to	× Multiply
☞ Index. See	÷ Divide
@ At or to	> Is greater than
% Per cent	< Is less than
° Degree	∴ Therefore
′ Minute (subdivision of degree) or foot (feet)	∵ Since
*** or . . . Ellipsis. Words are omitted.	: Is to (term used in expressing proportion)
″ Second or inch (inches)	:: As (term used in expressing proportion)
π Pi. The number 3.14159	√‾ Radical. Square root of
	℞ Take (used at beginning of prescriptions for drugs)

PROOFREADER'S MARKS: These are the more common signs used by publication and printing proofreaders.

ℬ Delete letters or words. Take it out.	✗ Broken letter or poor type.
# Insert space where indicated.	stet Let it stand. Disregard marks made.
ꝗ Turn inverted letter marked	cap replace letter marked with a capital.
tr Transpose letters or words indicated.	lc Replace With a lower case (small) letter.
⌒ Close up letters or words	bf Reset words in bold face type.
═ Straighten alignment of type.	ital Reset words in italic type.
[or] Move right or left to point indicated.	rom Reset words in roman (regular) type.
⊓ or ⊔ Raise or lower to point indicated.	⊙ Insert period where marked.
eq # Equalize spacing of words.	∧ Insert comma where marked
wf Wrong font. Incorrect size, weight or style of letter	⌄ Insert apostrophe per proofreaders mark.

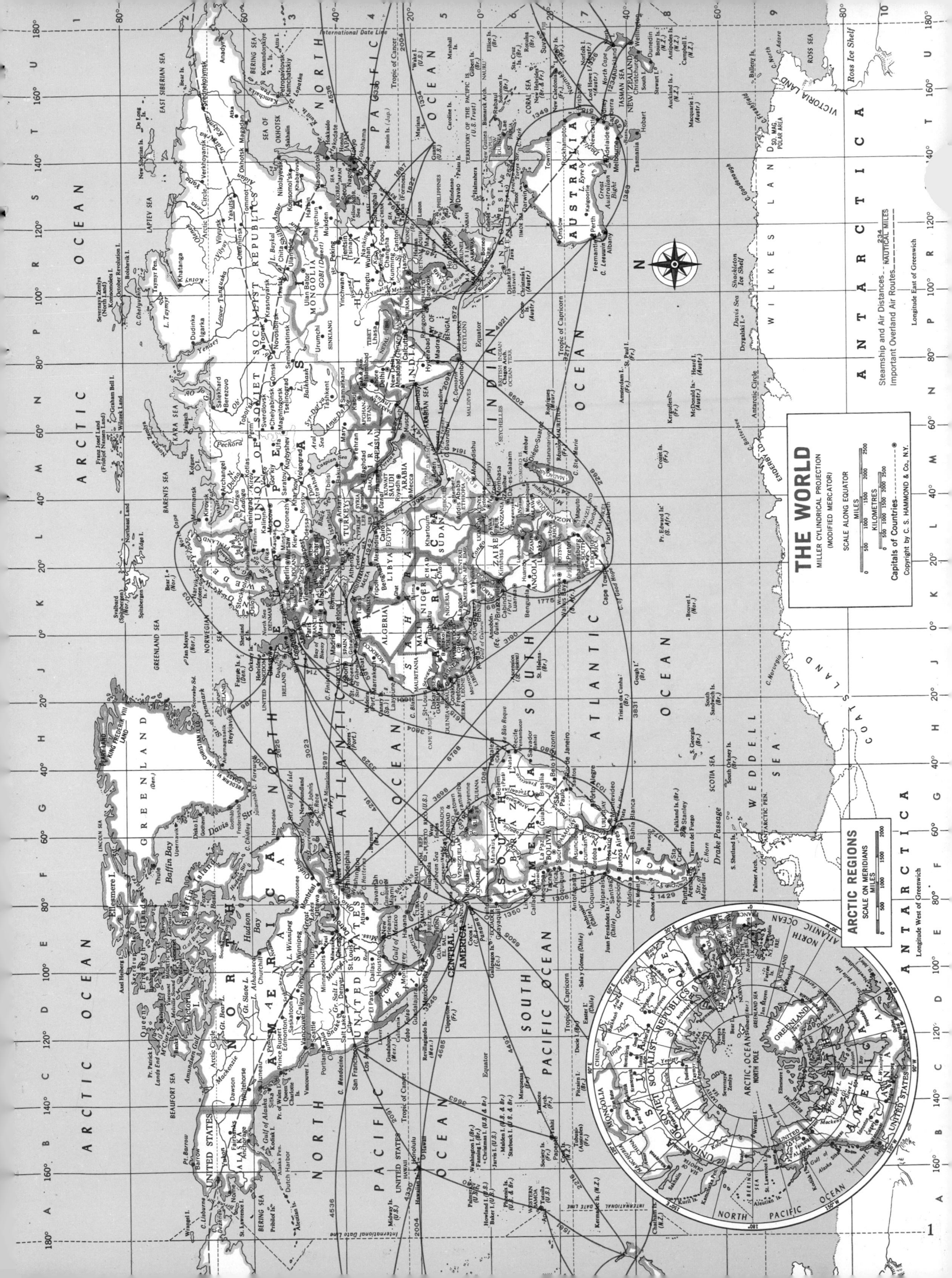

THE WORLD

MILLER CYLINDRICAL PROJECTION
(MODIFIED MERCATOR)

SCALE ALONG EQUATOR

MILES
0   500   1000   1500   2000   2500

KILOMETRES
0   500   1000   1500   2000   2500   3000

● Capitals of Countries

Copyright by C. S. HAMMOND & Co., N.Y.

Steamship and Air Distances... NAUTICAL MILES
Important Overland Air Routes...

ARCTIC REGIONS

SCALE ON MERIDIANS

MILES
0   500   1000   1500   2000

Longitude West of Greenwich

NORTH AMERICA

LAMBERT AZIMUTHAL EQUAL-AREA PROJECTION

SCALE OF MILES

0   100   200   400   600   800

SCALE OF KILOMETRES

0   200   400   600   800

Capitals of Countries..............☆
International Boundaries....._____
Other Boundaries................._____
Canals............................--------

© Copyright HAMMOND INCORPORATED, Maplewood, N.J.

Longitude   West of   Greenwich

CANADA

CONIC PROJECTION

SCALE OF MILES

0   50   100   200   300

SCALE OF KILOMETRES

0 50 100 200   300   400   500

Capitals of Countries . . . . ⭑

Provincial & Territorial Capitals . . . △

International Boundaries . . . .

Provincial Boundaries . . . .

Copyright by C.S. HAMMOND & Co., N.Y.

QUEEN ELIZABETH ISLANDS

Scale of Miles

0   50 100   200

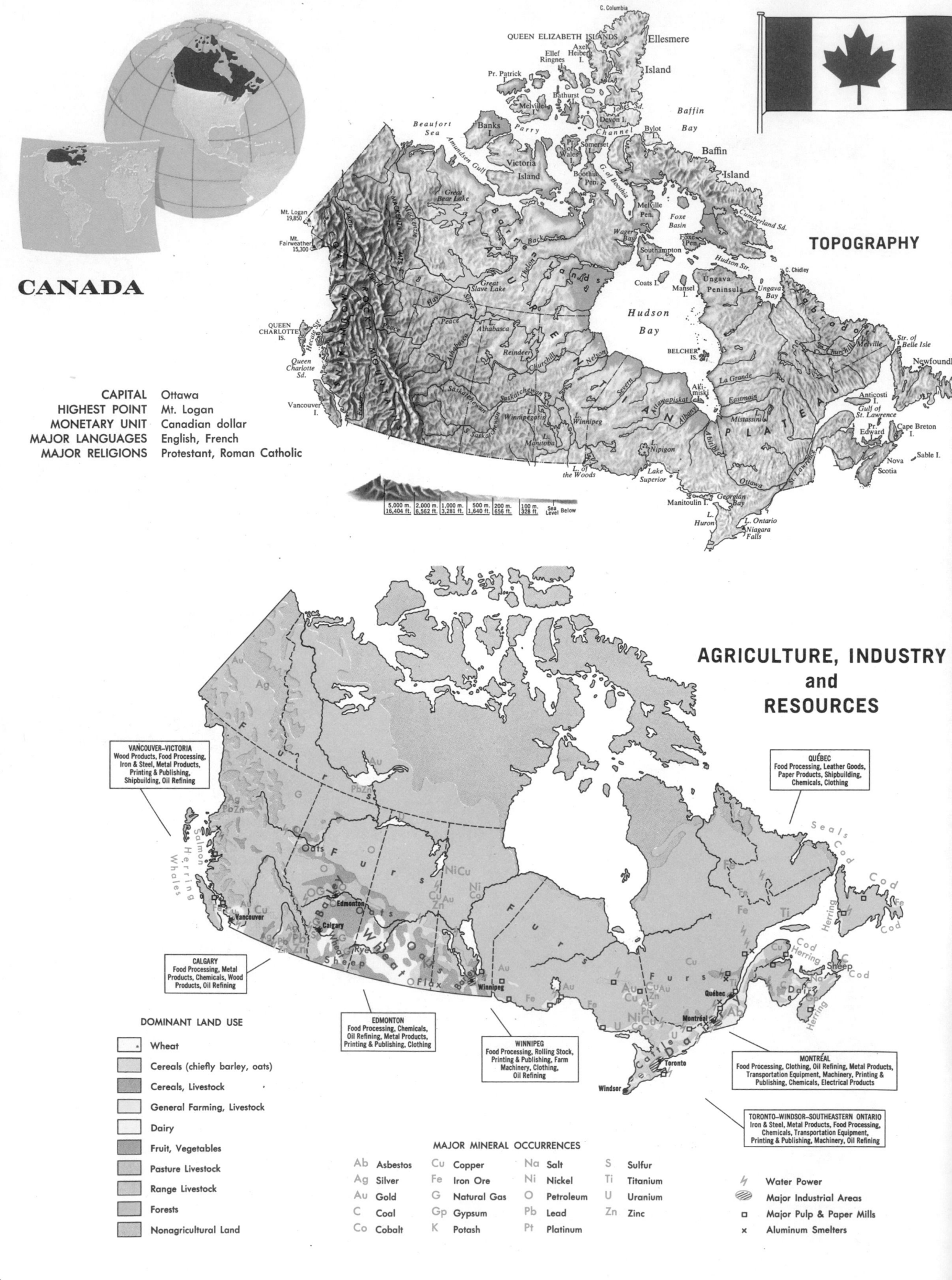

CANADA

TOPOGRAPHY

CAPITAL — Ottawa
HIGHEST POINT — Mt. Logan
MONETARY UNIT — Canadian dollar
MAJOR LANGUAGES — English, French
MAJOR RELIGIONS — Protestant, Roman Catholic

AGRICULTURE, INDUSTRY and RESOURCES

VANCOUVER–VICTORIA
Wood Products, Food Processing, Iron & Steel, Metal Products, Printing & Publishing, Shipbuilding, Oil Refining

CALGARY
Food Processing, Metal Products, Chemicals, Wood Products, Oil Refining

EDMONTON
Food Processing, Chemicals, Oil Refining, Metal Products, Printing & Publishing, Clothing

WINNIPEG
Food Processing, Rolling Stock, Printing & Publishing, Farm Machinery, Clothing, Oil Refining

QUÉBEC
Food Processing, Leather Goods, Paper Products, Shipbuilding, Chemicals, Clothing

MONTRÉAL
Food Processing, Clothing, Oil Refining, Metal Products, Transportation Equipment, Machinery, Printing & Publishing, Chemicals, Electrical Products

TORONTO–WINDSOR–SOUTHEASTERN ONTARIO
Iron & Steel, Metal Products, Food Processing, Chemicals, Transportation Equipment, Printing & Publishing, Machinery, Oil Refining

DOMINANT LAND USE

- Wheat
- Cereals (chiefly barley, oats)
- Cereals, Livestock
- General Farming, Livestock
- Dairy
- Fruit, Vegetables
- Pasture Livestock
- Range Livestock
- Forests
- Nonagricultural Land

MAJOR MINERAL OCCURRENCES

Ab	Asbestos	Cu	Copper
Ag	Silver	Fe	Iron Ore
Au	Gold	G	Natural Gas
C	Coal	Gp	Gypsum
Co	Cobalt	K	Potash

Na	Salt	S	Sulfur
Ni	Nickel	Ti	Titanium
O	Petroleum	U	Uranium
Pb	Lead	Zn	Zinc
Pt	Platinum		

- ⚡ Water Power
- Major Industrial Areas
- ▫ Major Pulp & Paper Mills
- ✕ Aluminum Smelters

4

TOPOGRAPHY

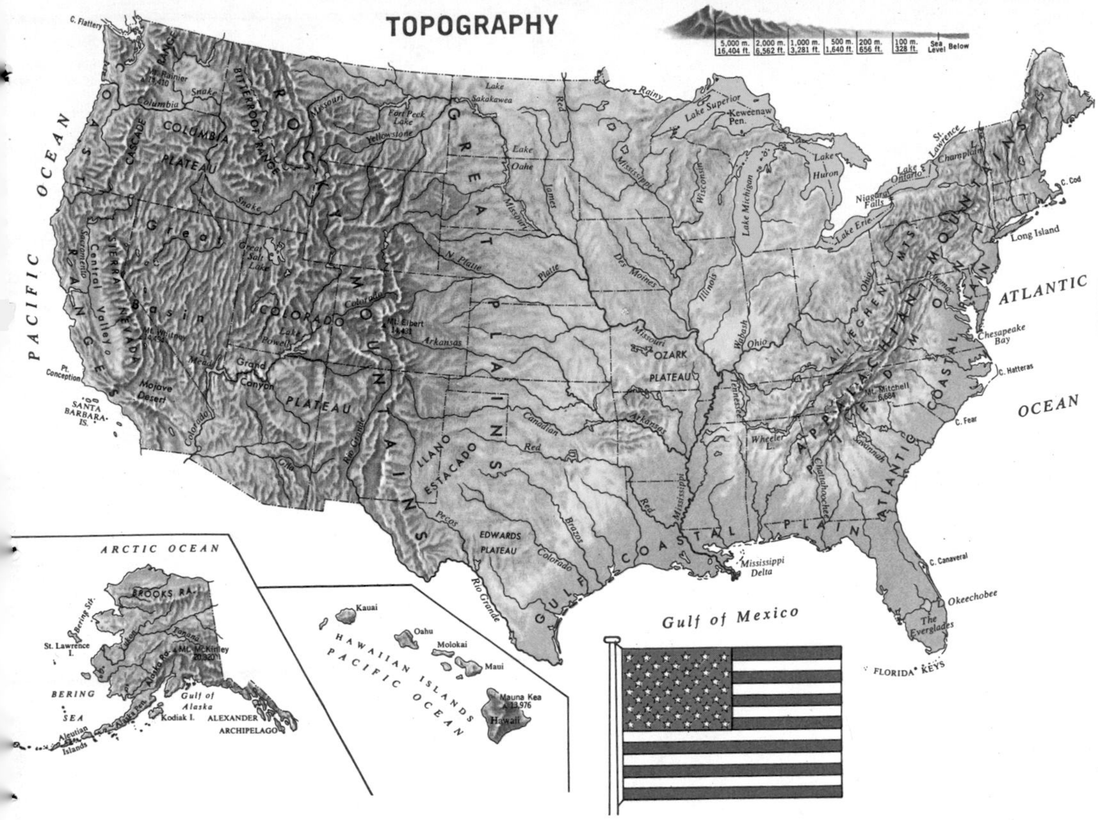

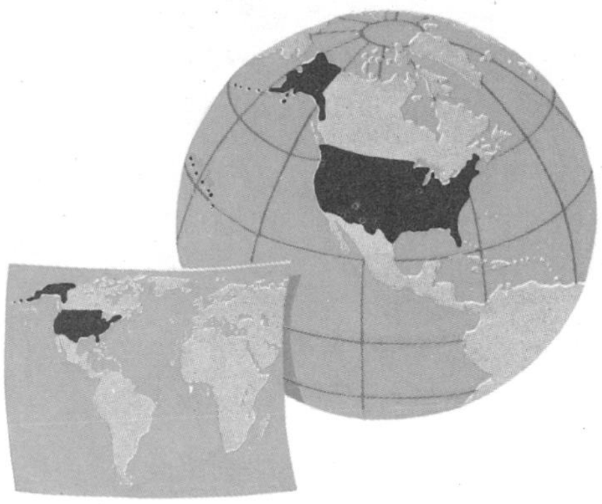

5,000 m. 2,000 m. 1,000 m. 500 m. 200 m. 100 m. Sea Level Below
16,404 ft. 6,562 ft. 3,281 ft. 1,640 ft. 656 ft. 328 ft.

PACIFIC OCEAN

C. Flattery

COLUMBIA PLATEAU

GREAT PLAINS

Lake Sakakawea
Fort Peck Lake
Yellowstone
Missouri

Lake Oahe

Rainy L.
Lake Superior
Keweenaw Pen.
Lake Michigan
Lake Huron
Lake Ontario
Lake Erie

St. Lawrence

Niagara Falls

C. Cod
Long Island

ATLANTIC OCEAN

Chesapeake Bay
C. Hatteras
C. Fear

GREAT BASIN
Humboldt
Pyramid L.
Salt L.

COLORADO PLATEAU

Grand Canyon

Mojave Desert

SANTA BARBARA IS.
Pt. Conception

Central Valley

PACIFIC RANGES

SIERRA NEVADA

Platte
N. Platte
Arkansas

LLANO ESTACADO

EDWARDS PLATEAU

Red

Canadian

Rio Grande

Pecos

Brazos

Colorado

OZARK PLATEAU

Missouri
Tennessee
Ohio
Wabash
Illinois

APPALACHIAN MOUNTAINS

Mt. Mitchell 6,684

ALLEGHENY MOUNTAINS

ATLANTIC COASTAL PLAIN

GULF COASTAL PLAIN

Mississippi Delta

C. Canaveral

Okeechobee
The Everglades

FLORIDA KEYS

Gulf of Mexico

ARCTIC OCEAN

BROOKS RANGE

BERING SEA

St. Lawrence I.
Mt. McKinley
Kodiak I.
Gulf of Alaska
ALEXANDER ARCHIPELAGO
Aleutian Islands

HAWAIIAN ISLANDS

Kauai
Oahu
Molokai
Maui
Mauna Kea 13,976
Hawaii

PACIFIC OCEAN

UNITED STATES

CAPITAL	Washington
HIGHEST POINT	Mt. McKinley
MONETARY UNIT	dollar
MAJOR LANGUAGE	English
MAJOR RELIGIONS	Protestant, Roman Catholic

AGRICULTURE, INDUSTRY and RESOURCES

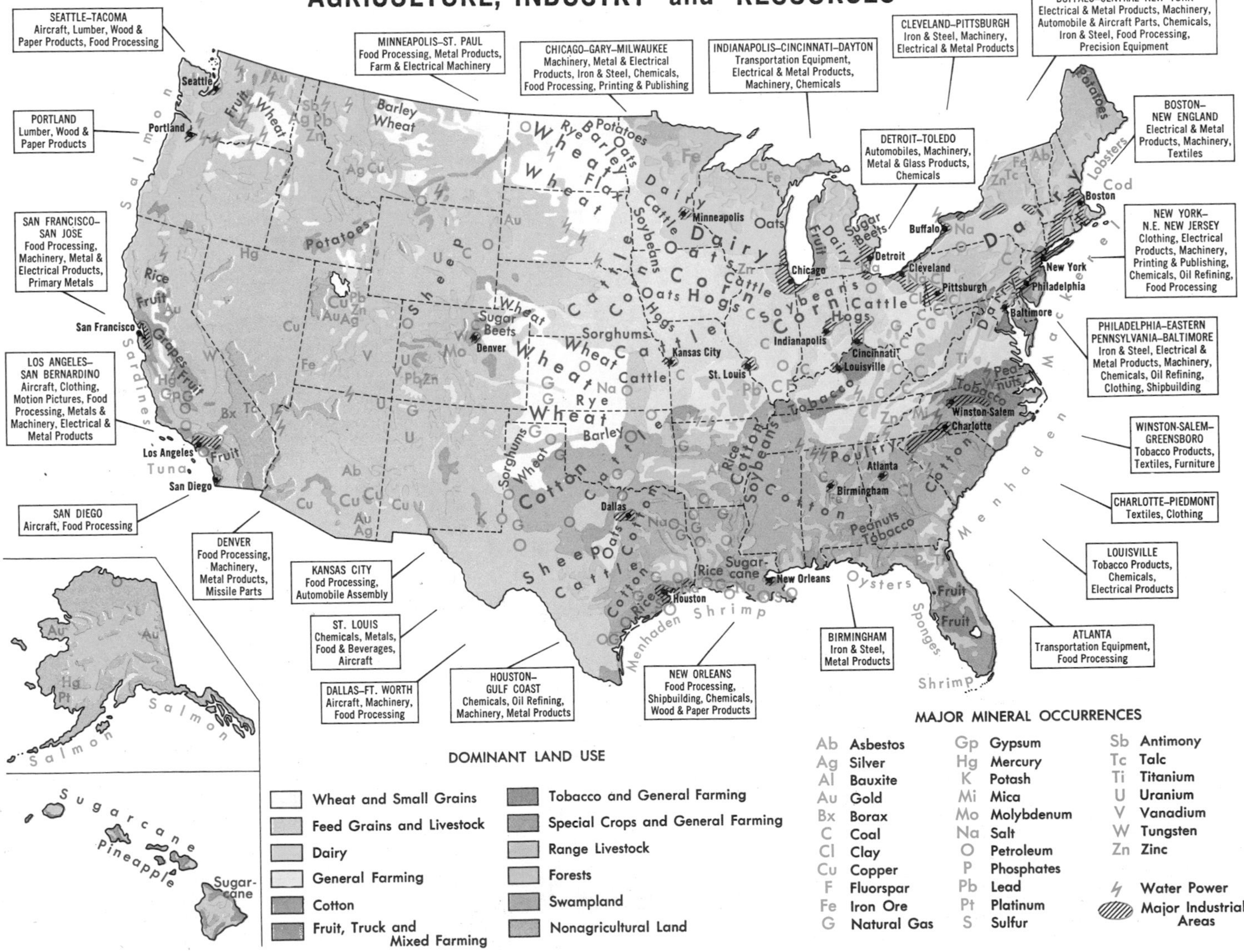

SEATTLE–TACOMA
Aircraft, Lumber, Wood & Paper Products, Food Processing

PORTLAND
Lumber, Wood & Paper Products

SAN FRANCISCO–SAN JOSE
Food Processing, Machinery, Metal & Electrical Products, Primary Metals

LOS ANGELES–SAN BERNARDINO
Aircraft, Clothing, Motion Pictures, Food Processing, Metals & Machinery, Electrical & Metal Products

SAN DIEGO
Aircraft, Food Processing

DENVER
Food Processing, Machinery, Metal Products, Missile Parts

KANSAS CITY
Food Processing, Automobile Assembly

ST. LOUIS
Chemicals, Metals, Food & Beverages, Aircraft

DALLAS–FT. WORTH
Aircraft, Machinery, Food Processing

HOUSTON–GULF COAST
Chemicals, Oil Refining, Machinery, Metal Products

NEW ORLEANS
Food Processing, Shipbuilding, Chemicals, Wood & Paper Products

MINNEAPOLIS–ST. PAUL
Food Processing, Metal Products, Farm & Electrical Machinery

CHICAGO–GARY–MILWAUKEE
Machinery, Metal & Electrical Products, Iron & Steel, Chemicals, Food Processing, Printing & Publishing

INDIANAPOLIS–CINCINNATI–DAYTON
Transportation Equipment, Electrical & Metal Products, Machinery, Chemicals

DETROIT–TOLEDO
Automobiles, Machinery, Metal & Glass Products, Chemicals

CLEVELAND–PITTSBURGH
Iron & Steel, Machinery, Electrical & Metal Products

BUFFALO–CENTRAL NEW YORK
Electrical & Metal Products, Machinery, Automobile & Aircraft Parts, Chemicals, Iron & Steel, Food Processing, Precision Equipment

BOSTON–NEW ENGLAND
Electrical & Metal Products, Machinery, Textiles

NEW YORK–N.E. NEW JERSEY
Clothing, Electrical Products, Machinery, Printing & Publishing, Chemicals, Oil Refining, Food Processing

PHILADELPHIA–EASTERN PENNSYLVANIA–BALTIMORE
Iron & Steel, Electrical & Metal Products, Machinery, Chemicals, Oil Refining, Clothing, Shipbuilding

WINSTON-SALEM–GREENSBORO
Tobacco Products, Textiles, Furniture

CHARLOTTE–PIEDMONT
Textiles, Clothing

LOUISVILLE
Tobacco Products, Chemicals, Electrical Products

ATLANTA
Transportation Equipment, Food Processing

BIRMINGHAM
Iron & Steel, Metal Products

DOMINANT LAND USE

- Wheat and Small Grains
- Feed Grains and Livestock
- Dairy
- General Farming
- Cotton
- Fruit, Truck and Mixed Farming
- Tobacco and General Farming
- Special Crops and General Farming
- Range Livestock
- Forests
- Swampland
- Nonagricultural Land

MAJOR MINERAL OCCURRENCES

Ab	Asbestos	Gp	Gypsum	Sb	Antimony
Ag	Silver	Hg	Mercury	Tc	Talc
Al	Bauxite	K	Potash	Ti	Titanium
Au	Gold	Mi	Mica	U	Uranium
Bx	Borax	Mo	Molybdenum	V	Vanadium
C	Coal	Na	Salt	W	Tungsten
Cl	Clay	O	Petroleum	Zn	Zinc
Cu	Copper	P	Phosphates		
F	Fluorspar	Pb	Lead	⚡	Water Power
Fe	Iron Ore	Pt	Platinum	▨	Major Industrial Areas
G	Natural Gas	S	Sulfur		

5

UNITED STATES

POLYCONIC PROJECTION

SCALE OF MILES

0   50   100   200   300

SCALE OF KILOMETRES

0   50   100   200   300

Capitals of Countries_____☆

State and Provincial Capitals_____△

International Boundaries_____

State and Provincial Boundaries_____

Copyright by C. S. HAMMOND & CO., N. Y

7

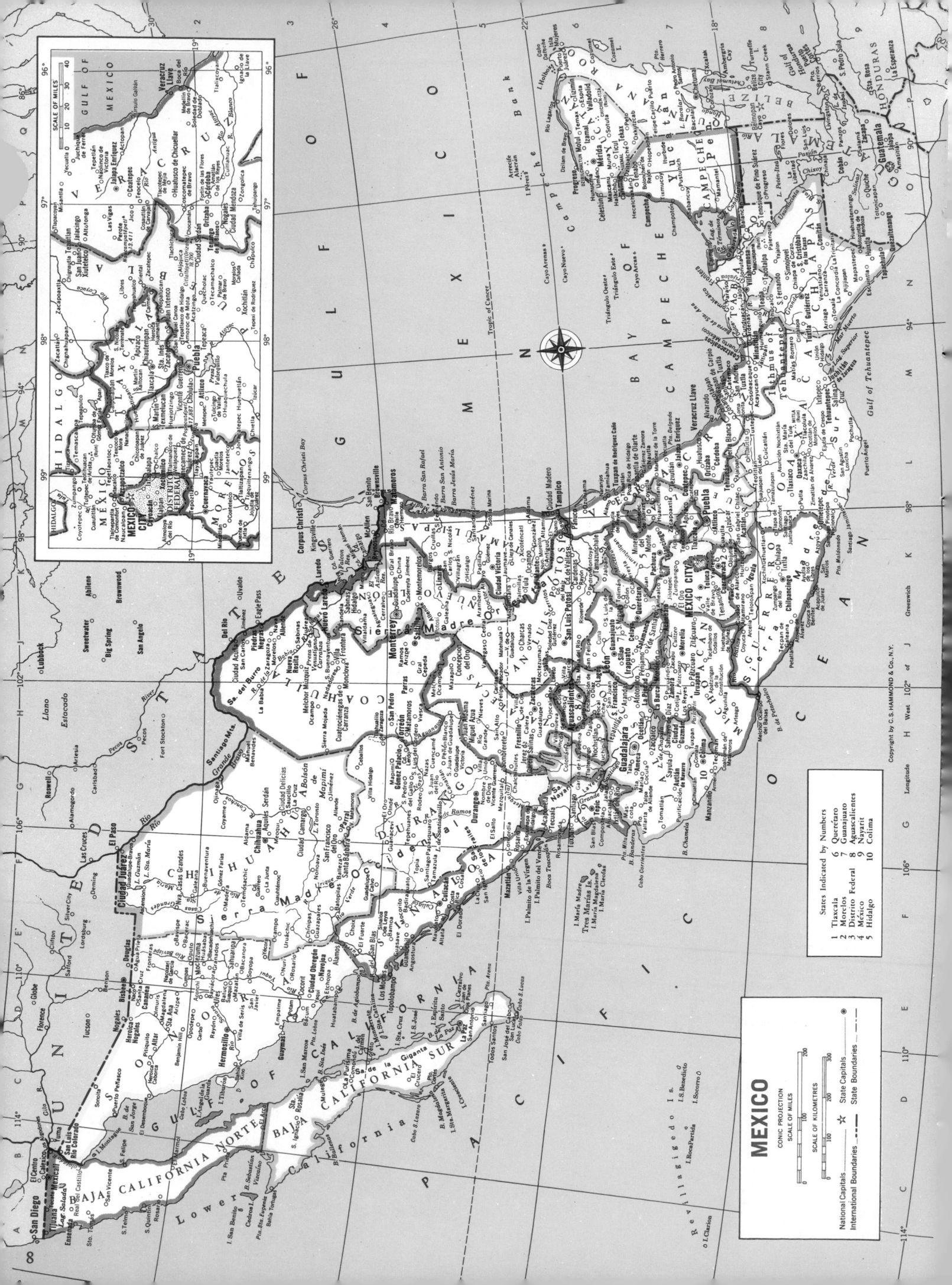

MEXICO

CONIC PROJECTION

SCALE OF MILES

SCALE OF KILOMETRES

National Capitals	⭐ State Capitals
International Boundaries	State Boundaries

States Indicated by Numbers

1 Tlaxcala
2 Morelos
3 Distrito Federal
4 México
5 Hidalgo
6 Querétaro
7 Guanajuato
8 Aguascalientes
9 Nayarit
10 Colima

Copyright by C.S. HAMMOND & CO., N.Y.

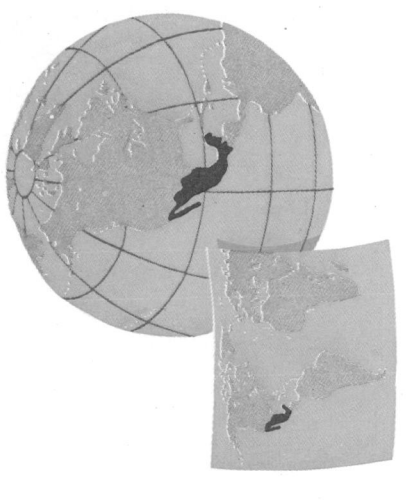

MEXICO

CAPITAL	Mexico City
HIGHEST POINT	Citlaltépetl
MONETARY UNIT	Mexican peso
MAJOR LANGUAGE	Spanish
MAJOR RELIGION	Roman Catholic

TOPOGRAPHY

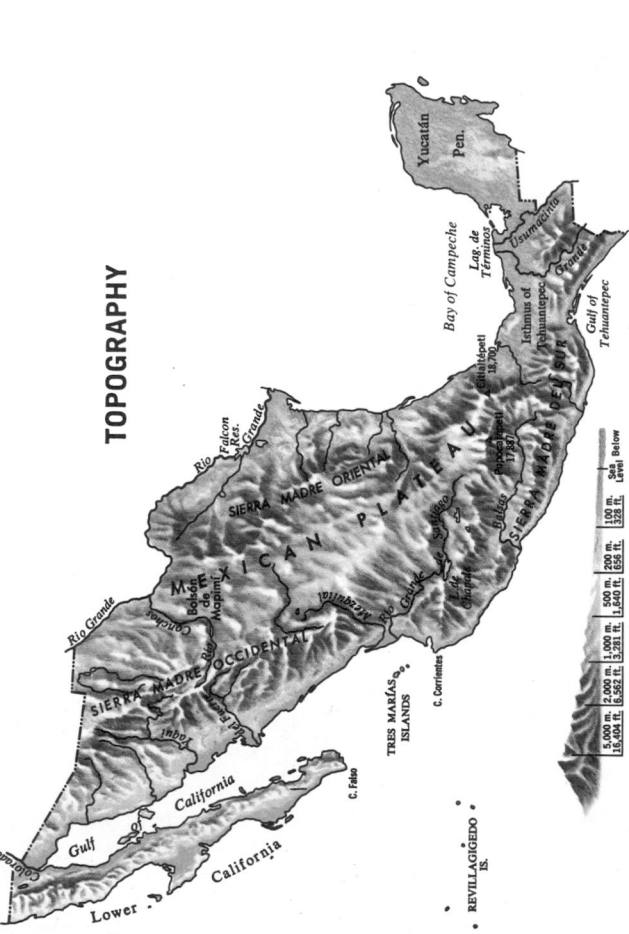

Yucatán Pen.

Bay of Campeche
Lag. de Términos
Usumacinta
Grijalva
Isthmus of Tehuantepec
Gulf of Tehuantepec
Citlaltépetl 18,700
Orizaba 17,340
SIERRA MADRE DEL SUR
MEXICAN PLATEAU
SIERRA MADRE ORIENTAL
SIERRA MADRE OCCIDENTAL
Rio Grande
Falcon Res.
Rio Grande
Bolsón de Mapimí
Gulf of California
Lower California
C. Falso
TRES MARÍAS ISLANDS
C. Corrientes
REVILLAGIGEDO IS.

5,000 m. 16,404 ft.	
2,000 m. 6,562 ft.	
1,000 m. 3,281 ft.	
500 m. 1,640 ft.	
200 m. 656 ft.	
100 m. 328 ft.	
Sea Level	Below

AGRICULTURE, INDUSTRY and RESOURCES

DOMINANT LAND USE

- Wheat, Livestock
- Cereals (chiefly corn), Livestock
- Diversified Tropical Cash Crops
- Cotton, Mixed Cereals
- Livestock, Limited Agriculture
- Range Livestock
- Forests
- Nonagricultural Land

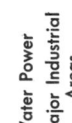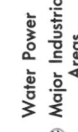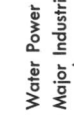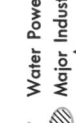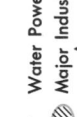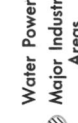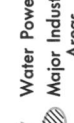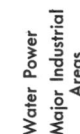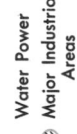

Water Power
Major Industrial Areas

MAJOR MINERAL OCCURRENCES

Ag Silver	O Petroleum		
Au Gold	G Natural Gas	Pb Lead	S Sulfur
C Coal	Gr Graphite		Sb Antimony
Cu Copper	Hg Mercury	Mn Manganese	Sn Tin
F Fluorspar	Mo Molybdenum		W Tungsten
Fe Iron Ore	Na Salt		Zn Zinc

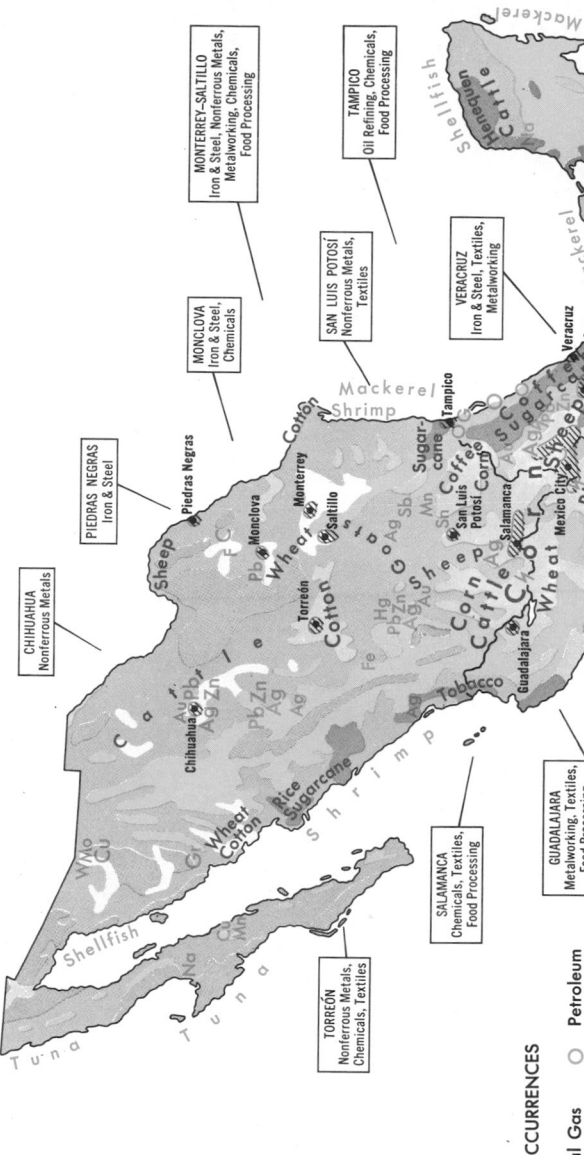

MONTERREY-SALTILLO
Iron & Steel, Nonferrous Metals, Metalworking, Chemicals, Food Processing

TAMPICO
Oil Refining, Chemicals, Food Processing

ORIZABA
Textiles, Cement

MONCLOVA
Iron & Steel, Chemicals

SAN LUIS POTOSÍ
Nonferrous Metals, Textiles

VERACRUZ
Iron & Steel, Textiles, Metalworking

PIEDRAS NEGRAS
Iron & Steel

CHIHUAHUA
Nonferrous Metals

MEXICO CITY-PUEBLA
Metalworking, Textiles, Leather Products, Food Processing, Chemicals, Automobile Assembly

GUADALAJARA
Metalworking, Textiles, Food Processing, Leather Products

SALAMANCA
Chemicals, Textiles, Food Processing

TORREÓN
Nonferrous Metals, Chemicals, Textiles

9

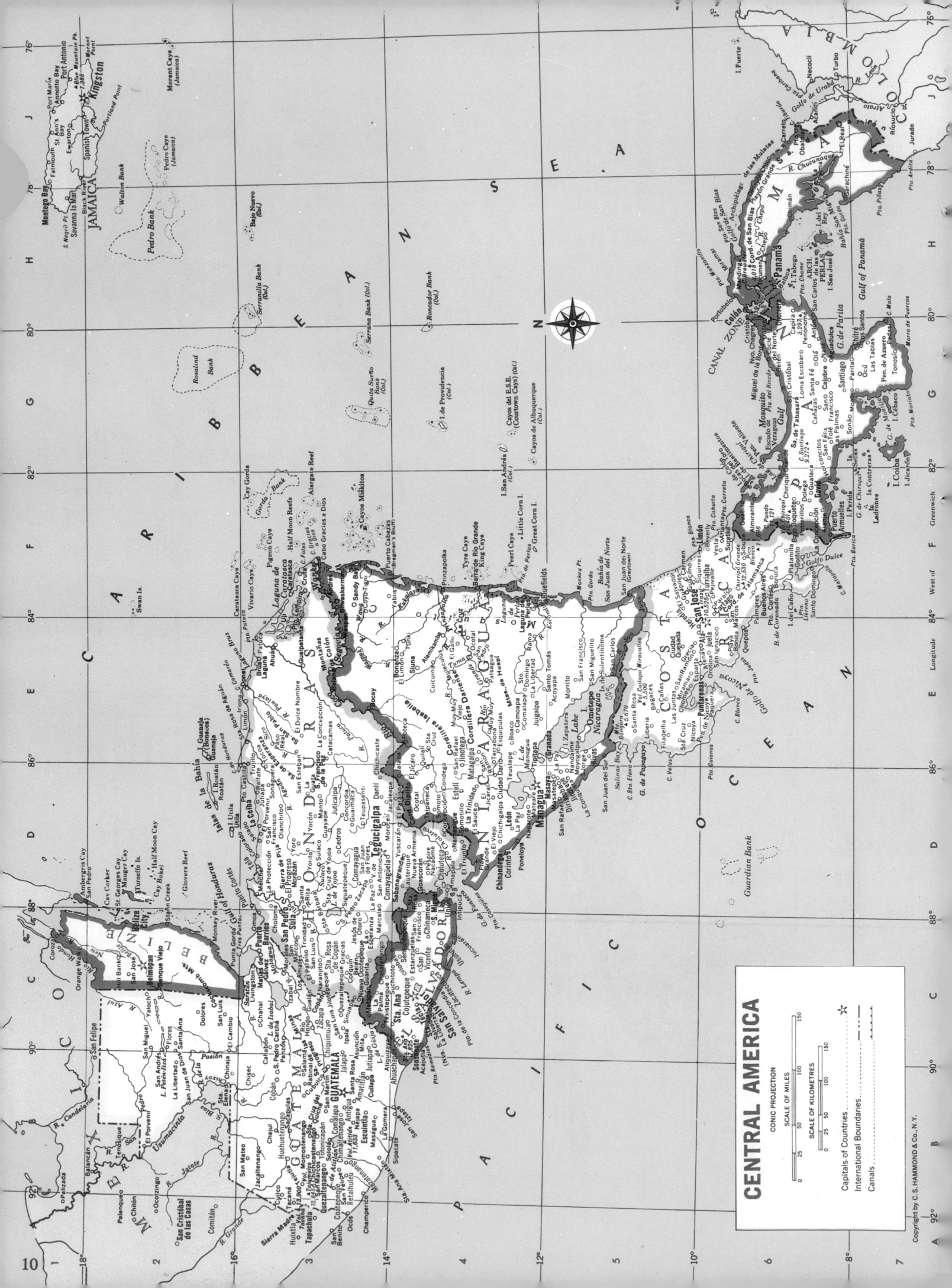

CENTRAL AMERICA

CONIC PROJECTION

SCALE OF MILES
0   25   50   100   150

SCALE OF KILOMETRES
0   25   50   100   150

Capitals of Countries........★
International Boundaries........
Canals........

Copyright by C.S. HAMMOND & Co., N.Y.

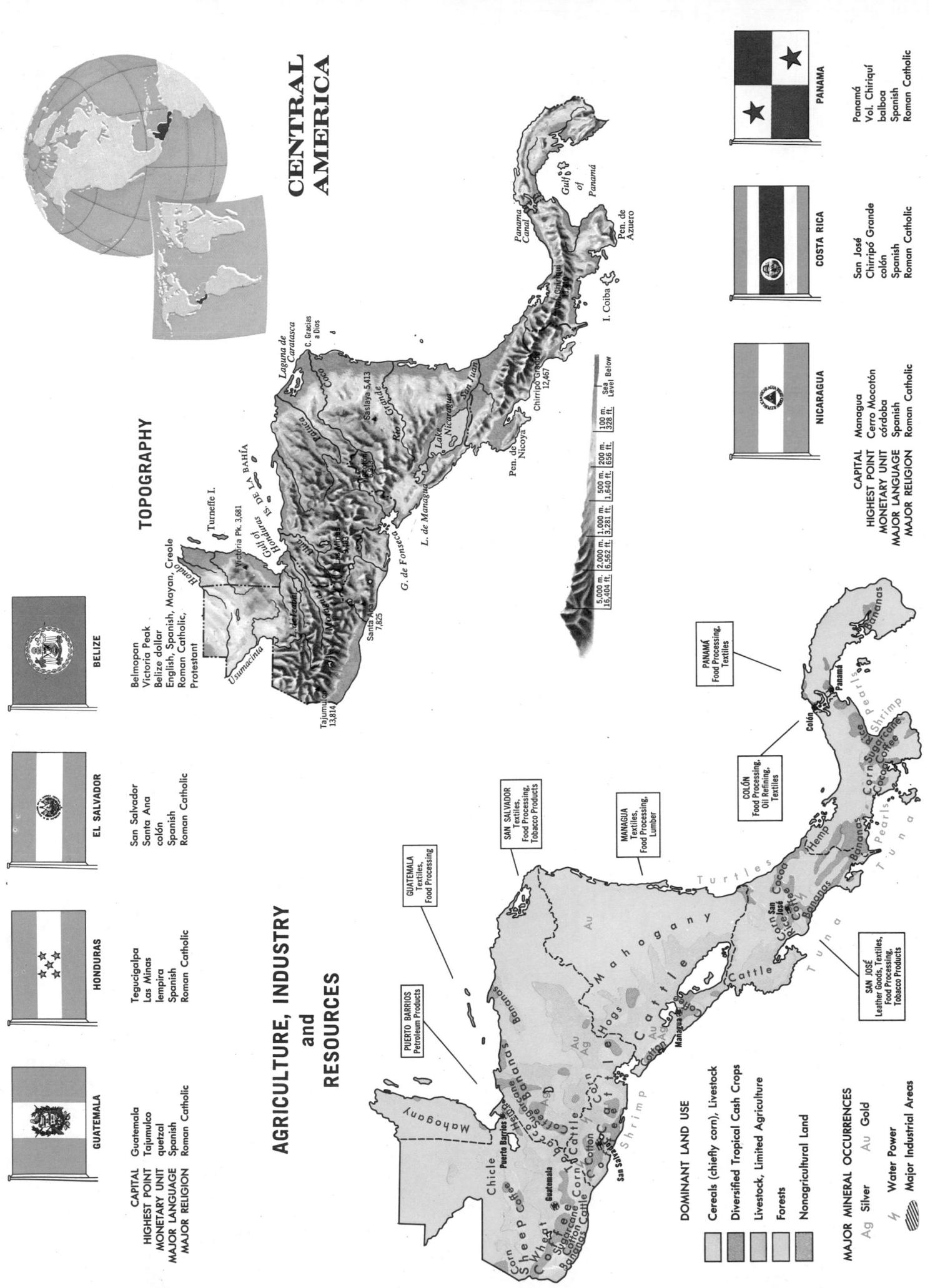

CENTRAL AMERICA

TOPOGRAPHY

5,000 m. 16,404 ft.	2,000 m. 6,562 ft.	1,000 m. 3,281 ft.	500 m. 1,640 ft.	200 m. 656 ft.	100 m. 328 ft.	Sea Below Level

BELIZE

Belmopan
Victoria Peak
Belize dollar
English, Spanish, Mayan, Creole
Roman Catholic, Protestant

PANAMA

Panamá
Vol. Chiriquí
balboa
Spanish
Roman Catholic

COSTA RICA

San José
Chirripó Grande
colón
Spanish
Roman Catholic

NICARAGUA

CAPITAL	Managua
HIGHEST POINT	Cerro Mocotón
MONETARY UNIT	córdoba
MAJOR LANGUAGE	Spanish
MAJOR RELIGION	Roman Catholic

GUATEMALA

CAPITAL	Guatemala
HIGHEST POINT	Tajumulco
MONETARY UNIT	quetzal
MAJOR LANGUAGE	Spanish
MAJOR RELIGION	Roman Catholic

HONDURAS

Tegucigalpa
Las Minas
lempira
Spanish
Roman Catholic

EL SALVADOR

San Salvador
Santa Ana
colón
Spanish
Roman Catholic

AGRICULTURE, INDUSTRY and RESOURCES

PUERTO BARRIOS
Petroleum Products

GUATEMALA
Textiles,
Food Processing

SAN SALVADOR
Textiles,
Food Processing,
Tobacco Products

MANAGUA
Textiles,
Food Processing,
Lumber

SAN JOSÉ
Leather Goods, Textiles,
Food Processing,
Tobacco Products

COLÓN
Food Processing,
Oil Refining,
Textiles

PANAMÁ
Food Processing,
Textiles

DOMINANT LAND USE

- Cereals (chiefly corn), Livestock
- Diversified Tropical Cash Crops
- Livestock, Limited Agriculture
- Forests
- Nonagricultural Land

MAJOR MINERAL OCCURRENCES

Ag Silver   Au Gold

⋔ Water Power   ▨ Major Industrial Areas

11

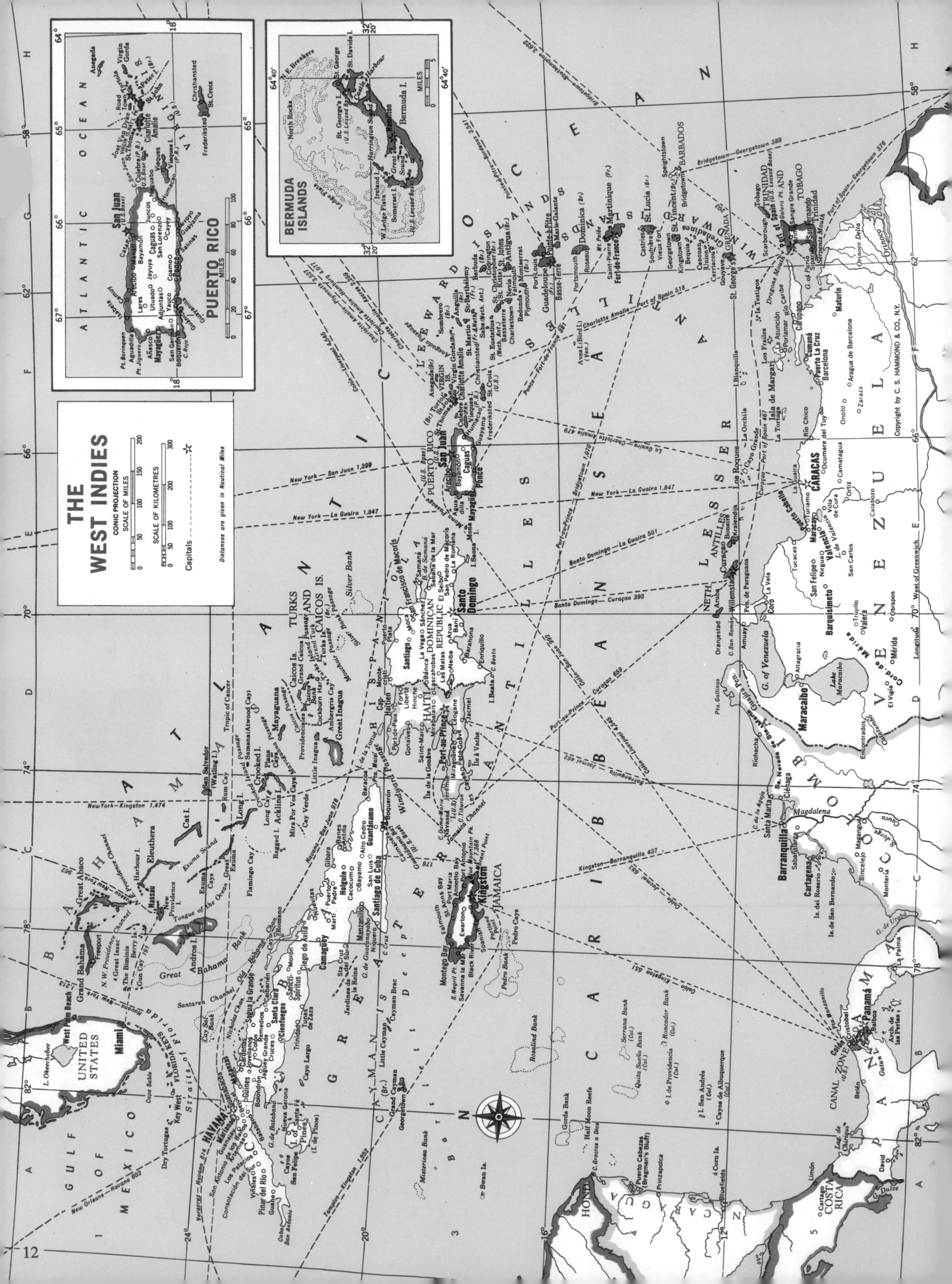

THE WEST INDIES

CONIC PROJECTION

SCALE OF MILES

SCALE OF KILOMETRES

Capitals .... ★

Distances are given in Nautical Miles

PUERTO RICO

ATLANTIC OCEAN

San Juan

BERMUDA ISLANDS

THE WEST INDIES

TOPOGRAPHY

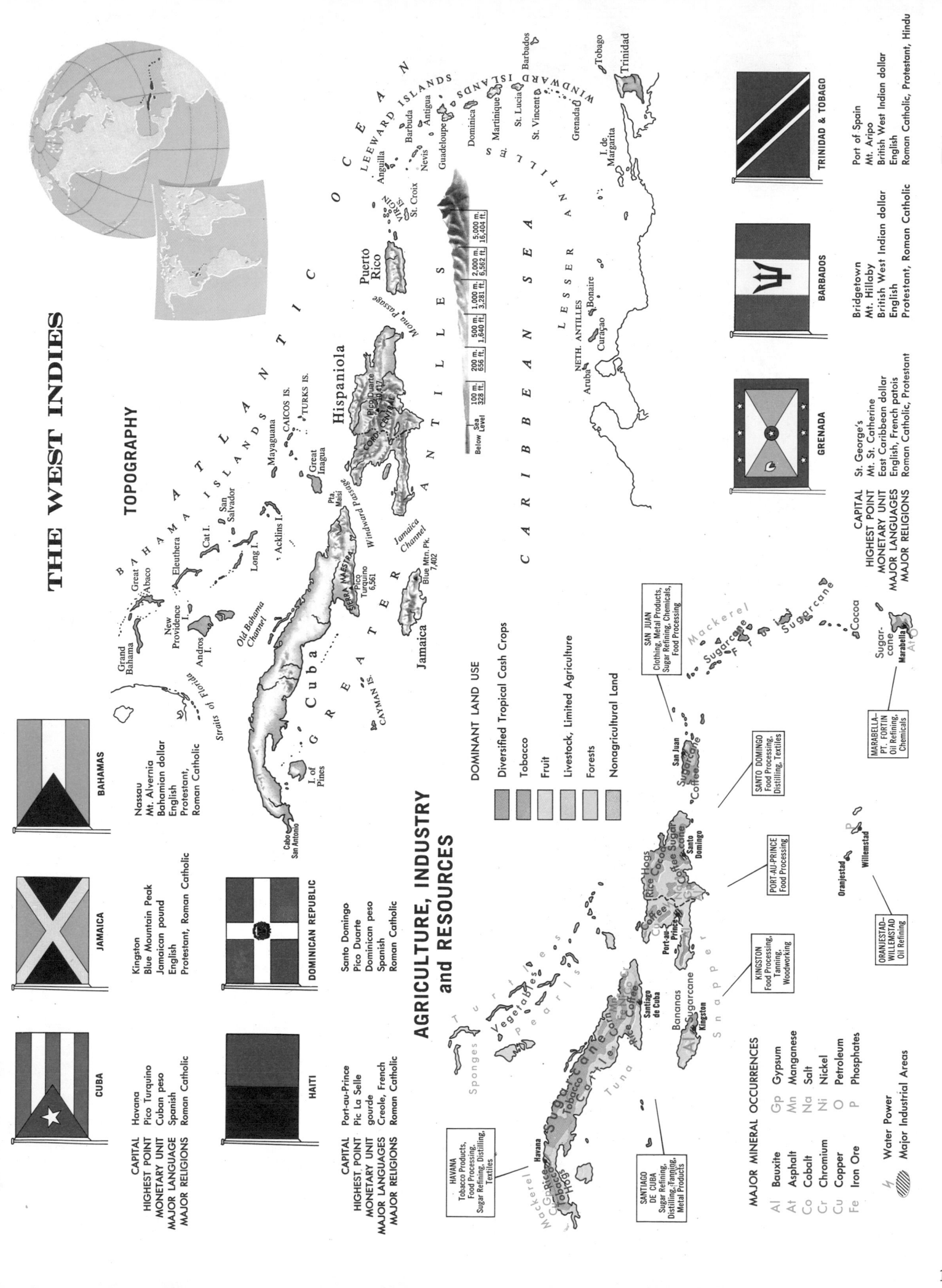

ATLANTIC OCEAN

LEEWARD ISLANDS
Anguilla
Nevis · St. Croix · Antigua · Barbuda
Guadeloupe
Dominica
Martinique
St. Lucia
St. Vincent · Barbados
Grenada
I. de Margarita
Tobago
Trinidad

WINDWARD ISLANDS

LESSER ANTILLES

VIRGIN IS.
Puerto Rico
Mona Passage

Hispaniola
Pico Duarte 10,417
CORDILLERA CENTRAL
CAICOS IS.
TURKS IS.
Mayaguana
Great Inagua

BAHAMA ISLANDS
San Salvador
Cat I.
Eleuthera
Long I.
Acklins I.
Pta. Maisi
Windward Passage

Great Abaco
Grand Bahama
New Providence
Andros I.
Old Bahama Channel

Cuba
SIERRA MAESTRA
Pico Turquino 6,561
GREATER ANTILLES

Jamaica Channel
Jamaica
Blue Mtn. Pk. 7,402

CAYMAN IS.

CARIBBEAN SEA

NETH. ANTILLES
Aruba · Curaçao · Bonaire

Cabo San Antonio
I. of Pines
Straits of Florida

5,000 m.	16,404 ft
2,000 m.	6,562 ft
1,000 m.	3,281 ft
500 m.	1,640 ft
200 m.	656 ft
100 m.	328 ft
Sea Level	
Below	

BAHAMAS
CAPITAL · Nassau
HIGHEST POINT · Mt. Alvernia
MONETARY UNIT · Bahamian dollar
MAJOR LANGUAGE · English
MAJOR RELIGIONS · Protestant, Roman Catholic

JAMAICA
Kingston
Blue Mountain Peak
Jamaican pound
English
Protestant, Roman Catholic

DOMINICAN REPUBLIC
Santo Domingo
Pico Duarte
Dominican peso
Spanish
Roman Catholic

CUBA
CAPITAL · Havana
HIGHEST POINT · Pico Turquino
MONETARY UNIT · Cuban peso
MAJOR LANGUAGE · Spanish
MAJOR RELIGIONS · Roman Catholic

HAITI
Port-au-Prince
Pic La Selle
gourde
Creole, French
Roman Catholic

TRINIDAD & TOBAGO
Port of Spain
Mt. Aripo
British West Indian dollar
English
Roman Catholic, Protestant, Hindu

BARBADOS
Bridgetown
Mt. Hillaby
British West Indian dollar
English
Protestant, Roman Catholic

GRENADA
CAPITAL · St. George's
HIGHEST POINT · Mt. St. Catherine
MONETARY UNIT · East Caribbean dollar
MAJOR LANGUAGES · English, French patois
MAJOR RELIGIONS · Roman Catholic, Protestant

AGRICULTURE, INDUSTRY and RESOURCES

DOMINANT LAND USE
- Diversified Tropical Cash Crops
- Tobacco
- Fruit
- Livestock, Limited Agriculture
- Forests
- Nonagricultural Land

SAN JUAN
Clothing, Metal Products, Sugar Refining, Chemicals, Food Processing

SANTO DOMINGO
Food Processing, Distilling, Textiles

MARABELLA–PT. FORTIN
Oil Refining, Chemicals

PORT-AU-PRINCE
Food Processing

KINGSTON
Food Processing, Tanning, Woodworking

ORANJESTAD–WILLEMSTAD
Oil Refining

HAVANA
Tobacco Products, Food Processing, Sugar Refining, Distilling, Textiles

SANTIAGO DE CUBA
Sugar Refining, Distilling, Tanning, Metal Products

San Juan
Sugarcane
Coffee
Santo Domingo
Coffee
Sugarcane
Cacao
Hogs
Rice
Coffee
Port-au-Prince
Kingston
Bananas
Sugarcane
Santiago de Cuba
Coffee
Sugarcane
Tobacco
Havana
Cattle
Hogs

Oranjestad
Willemstad
Marabella

Mackerel
Sugarcane
Fruit
Sugarcane
Cocoa

Turtles
Vegetables
Pearls
Sponges
Snapper
Tuna
Mackerel
Sugarcane, Coffee, Tobacco

MAJOR MINERAL OCCURRENCES
Al	Bauxite	Gp	Gypsum
At	Asphalt	Mn	Manganese
Co	Cobalt	Na	Salt
Cr	Chromium	Ni	Nickel
Cu	Copper	O	Petroleum
Fe	Iron Ore	P	Phosphates

Water Power
Major Industrial Areas

13

COLOMBIA

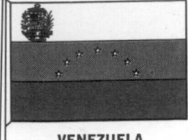
VENEZUELA

ECUADOR

PERU

BRAZIL

	COLOMBIA	VENEZUELA	ECUADOR	PERU	BRAZIL
CAPITAL	Bogotá	Caracas	Quito	Lima	Brasília
HIGHEST POINT	Pico Cristóbal Colón	Pico Bolívar	Chimborazo	Huascarán	Pico da Banderia
MONETARY UNIT	Colombian peso	bolívar	sucre	sol	cruzeiro
MAJOR LANGUAGES	Spanish	Spanish	Spanish, Indian	Spanish, Indian	Portuguese
MAJOR RELIGIONS	Roman Catholic	Roman Catholic	Roman Catholic	Roman Catholic	Roman Catholic

TOPOGRAPHY

| 5,000 m. 16,404 ft. | 2,000 m. 6,562 ft. | 1,000 m. 3,281 ft. | 500 m. 1,640 ft. | 200 m. 656 ft. | 100 m. 328 ft. | Sea Level | Below |

BOLIVIA

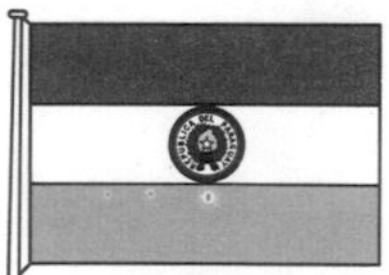

PARAGUAY

	BOLIVIA	PARAGUAY
CAPITAL	La Paz, Sucre	Asunción
HIGHEST POINT	Nevada Ancohuma	Amambay Range
MONETARY UNIT	Bolivian peso	guaraní
MAJOR LANGUAGES	Spanish, Indian	Spanish, Indian
MAJOR RELIGION	Roman Catholic	Roman Catholic

CHILE

	CHILE
CAPITAL	Santiago
HIGHEST POINT	Ojos del Salado
MONETARY UNIT	Chilean escudo
MAJOR LANGUAGE	Spanish
MAJOR RELIGION	Roman Catholic

ARGENTINA

URUGUAY

	ARGENTINA	URUGUAY
CAPITAL	Buenos Aires	Montevideo
HIGHEST POINT	Cerro Aconcagua	Mirador Nacional
MAJOR LANGUAGE	Argentine peso	Uruguayan peso
MAJOR LANGUAGE	Spanish	Spanish
MAJOR RELIGION	Roman Catholic	Roman Catholic

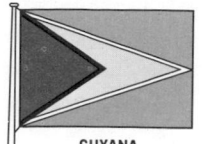

GUYANA

Georgetown
Mt. Roraima
Guyana dollar
English, East Indian
Christian, Hindu, Mohammedan

SURINAM

Paramaribo
Wilhelmina Mts.
Surinam guilder
Dutch
Christian, Mohammedan, Hindu

FRENCH GUIANA

Cayenne
Chaîne de Milthaide
French franc
French
Roman Catholic, Protestant

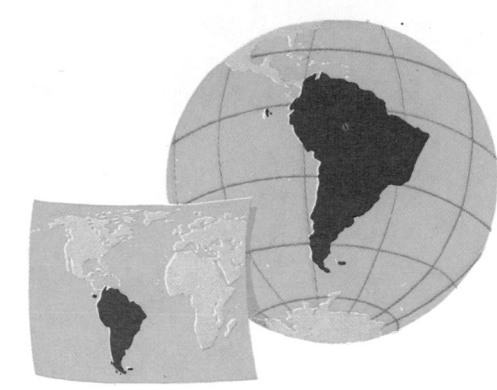

SOUTH AMERICA

AGRICULTURE, INDUSTRY and RESOURCES

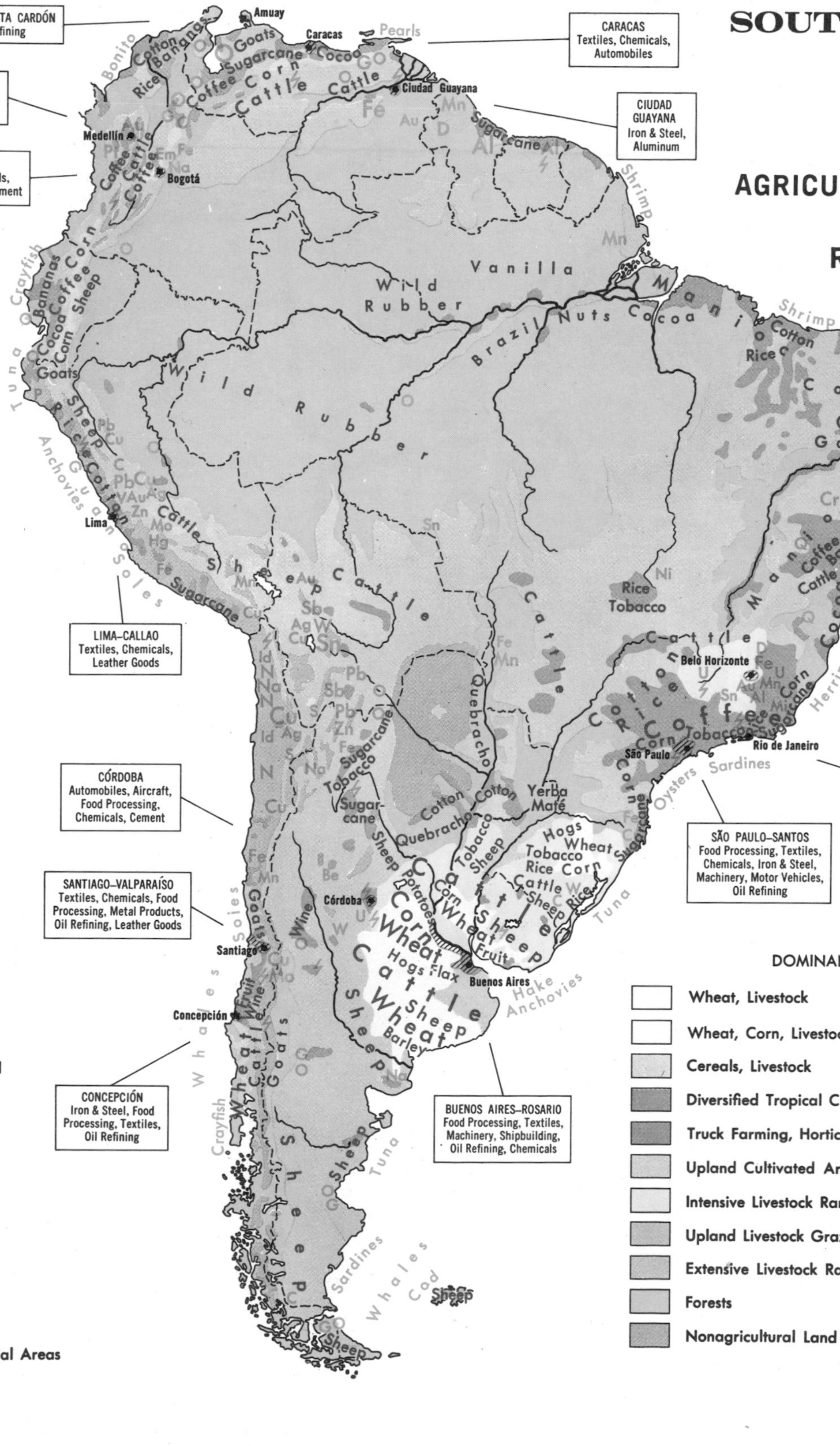

AMUAY–PUNTA CARDÓN
Oil Refining

MEDELLÍN
Textiles, Clothing, Leather Goods

BOGOTÁ
Textiles, Leather Goods, Cement, Electrical Equipment

CARACAS
Textiles, Chemicals, Automobiles

CIUDAD GUAYANA
Iron & Steel, Aluminum

BELO HORIZONTE
Iron & Steel, Textiles, Cement, Metal Products

RIO DE JANEIRO
Iron & Steel, Chemicals, Food Processing, Textiles, Glass Products, Cement, Oil Refining

SÃO PAULO–SANTOS
Food Processing, Textiles, Chemicals, Iron & Steel, Machinery, Motor Vehicles, Oil Refining

LIMA–CALLAO
Textiles, Chemicals, Leather Goods

CÓRDOBA
Automobiles, Aircraft, Food Processing, Chemicals, Cement

SANTIAGO–VALPARAÍSO
Textiles, Chemicals, Food Processing, Metal Products, Oil Refining, Leather Goods

CONCEPCIÓN
Iron & Steel, Food Processing, Textiles, Oil Refining

BUENOS AIRES–ROSARIO
Food Processing, Textiles, Machinery, Shipbuilding, Oil Refining, Chemicals

MAJOR MINERAL OCCURRENCES

Al **Bauxite**
Ag **Silver**
Au **Gold**
Be **Beryl**
C **Coal**
Cr **Chromium**
Cu **Copper**
D **Diamonds**
Em **Emeralds**
Fe **Iron Ore**
G **Natural Gas**
Hg **Mercury**
Id **Iodine**
Mi **Mica**
Mn **Manganese**
Mo **Molybdenum**
N **Nitrates**
Na **Salt**
Ni **Nickel**
O **Petroleum**
P **Phosphates**
Pb **Lead**
Pt **Platinum**
Q **Quartz Crystal**
S **Sulfur**
Sb **Antimony**
Sn **Tin**
U **Uranium**
V **Vanadium**
W **Tungsten**
Zn **Zinc**

⚡ **Water Power**

▨ **Major Industrial Areas**

DOMINANT LAND USE

☐ Wheat, Livestock
☐ Wheat, Corn, Livestock
☐ Cereals, Livestock
☐ Diversified Tropical Crops (chiefly plantation agriculture)
☐ Truck Farming, Horticulture, Special Crops
☐ Upland Cultivated Areas
☐ Intensive Livestock Ranching
☐ Upland Livestock Grazing, Limited Agriculture
☐ Extensive Livestock Ranching
☐ Forests
☐ Nonagricultural Land

SOUTH AMERICA

LAMBERT AZIMUTHAL EQUAL-AREA PROJECTION

Copyright by C. S. HAMMOND & Co., N.Y.

WESTERN and CENTRAL EUROPE

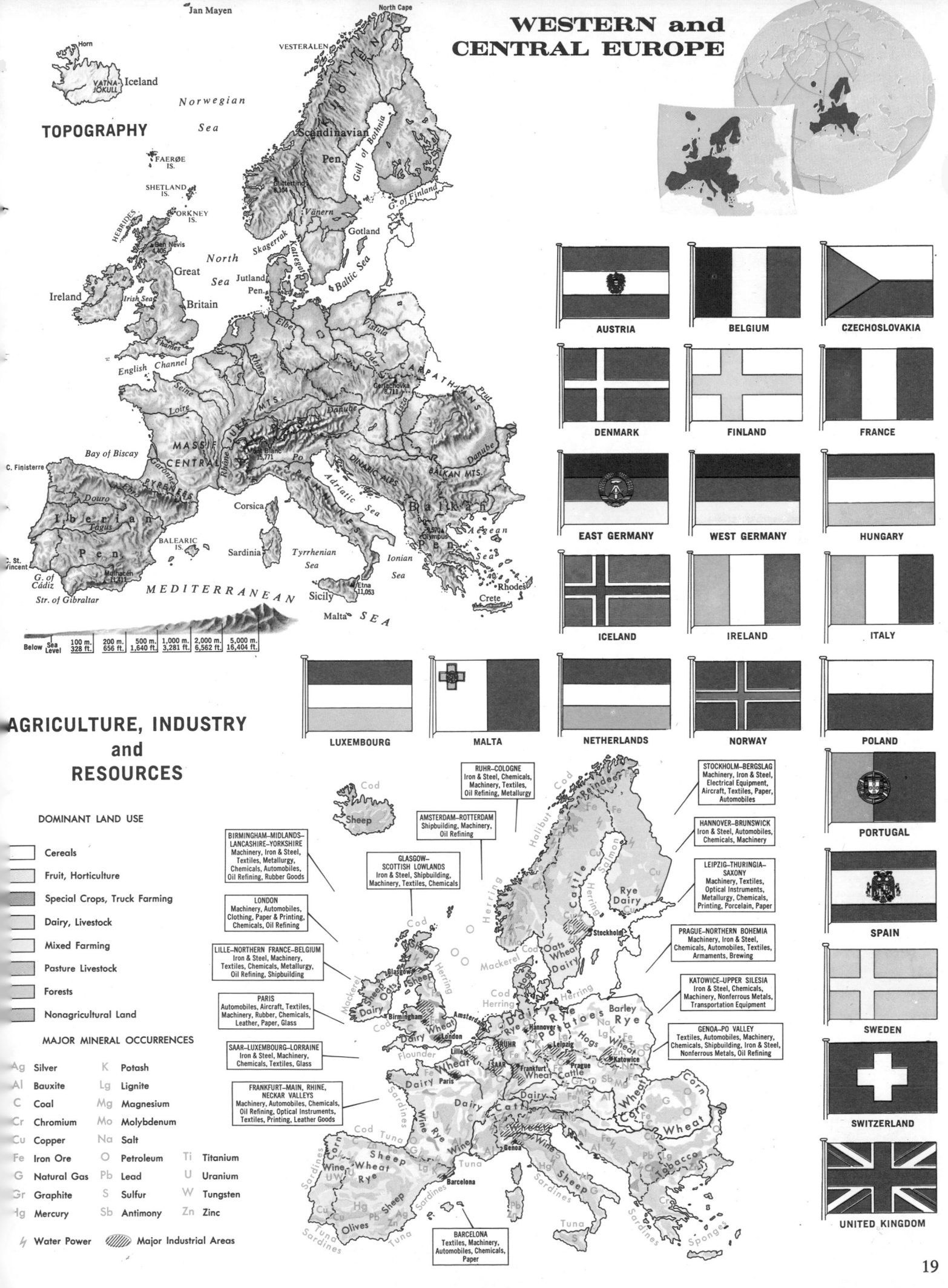

TOPOGRAPHY

Below Sea Level | 100 m. 328 ft. | 200 m. 656 ft. | 500 m. 1,640 ft. | 1,000 m. 3,281 ft. | 2,000 m. 6,562 ft. | 5,000 m. 16,404 ft.

AGRICULTURE, INDUSTRY and RESOURCES

DOMINANT LAND USE

- Cereals
- Fruit, Horticulture
- Special Crops, Truck Farming
- Dairy, Livestock
- Mixed Farming
- Pasture Livestock
- Forests
- Nonagricultural Land

MAJOR MINERAL OCCURRENCES

Ag	Silver	K	Potash
Al	Bauxite	Lg	Lignite
C	Coal	Mg	Magnesium
Cr	Chromium	Mo	Molybdenum
Cu	Copper	Na	Salt
Fe	Iron Ore	O	Petroleum	Ti Titanium
G	Natural Gas	Pb	Lead	U Uranium
Gr	Graphite	S	Sulfur	W Tungsten
Hg	Mercury	Sb	Antimony	Zn Zinc

Water Power   Major Industrial Areas

Flags

AUSTRIA — BELGIUM — CZECHOSLOVAKIA
DENMARK — FINLAND — FRANCE
EAST GERMANY — WEST GERMANY — HUNGARY
ICELAND — IRELAND — ITALY
LUXEMBOURG — MALTA — NETHERLANDS — NORWAY — POLAND
PORTUGAL
SPAIN
SWEDEN
SWITZERLAND
UNITED KINGDOM

Industrial Area Notes

RUHR–COLOGNE
Iron & Steel, Chemicals, Machinery, Textiles, Oil Refining, Metallurgy

STOCKHOLM–BERGSLAG
Machinery, Iron & Steel, Electrical Equipment, Aircraft, Textiles, Paper, Automobiles

AMSTERDAM–ROTTERDAM
Shipbuilding, Machinery, Oil Refining

HANNOVER–BRUNSWICK
Iron & Steel, Automobiles, Chemicals, Machinery

BIRMINGHAM–MIDLANDS–LANCASHIRE–YORKSHIRE
Machinery, Iron & Steel, Textiles, Metallurgy, Chemicals, Automobiles, Oil Refining, Rubber Goods

GLASGOW–SCOTTISH LOWLANDS
Iron & Steel, Shipbuilding, Machinery, Textiles, Chemicals

LEIPZIG–THURINGIA–SAXONY
Machinery, Textiles, Optical Instruments, Metallurgy, Chemicals, Printing, Porcelain, Paper

LONDON
Machinery, Automobiles, Clothing, Paper & Printing, Chemicals, Oil Refining

PRAGUE–NORTHERN BOHEMIA
Machinery, Iron & Steel, Chemicals, Automobiles, Textiles, Armaments, Brewing

LILLE–NORTHERN FRANCE–BELGIUM
Iron & Steel, Machinery, Textiles, Chemicals, Metallurgy, Oil Refining, Shipbuilding

KATOWICE–UPPER SILESIA
Iron & Steel, Chemicals, Machinery, Nonferrous Metals, Transportation Equipment

PARIS
Automobiles, Aircraft, Textiles, Machinery, Rubber, Chemicals, Leather, Paper, Glass

GENOA–PO VALLEY
Textiles, Automobiles, Machinery, Chemicals, Shipbuilding, Iron & Steel, Nonferrous Metals, Oil Refining

SAAR–LUXEMBOURG–LORRAINE
Iron & Steel, Machinery, Chemicals, Textiles, Glass

FRANKFURT–MAIN, RHINE, NECKAR VALLEYS
Machinery, Automobiles, Chemicals, Oil Refining, Optical Instruments, Textiles, Printing, Leather Goods

BARCELONA
Textiles, Machinery, Automobiles, Chemicals, Paper

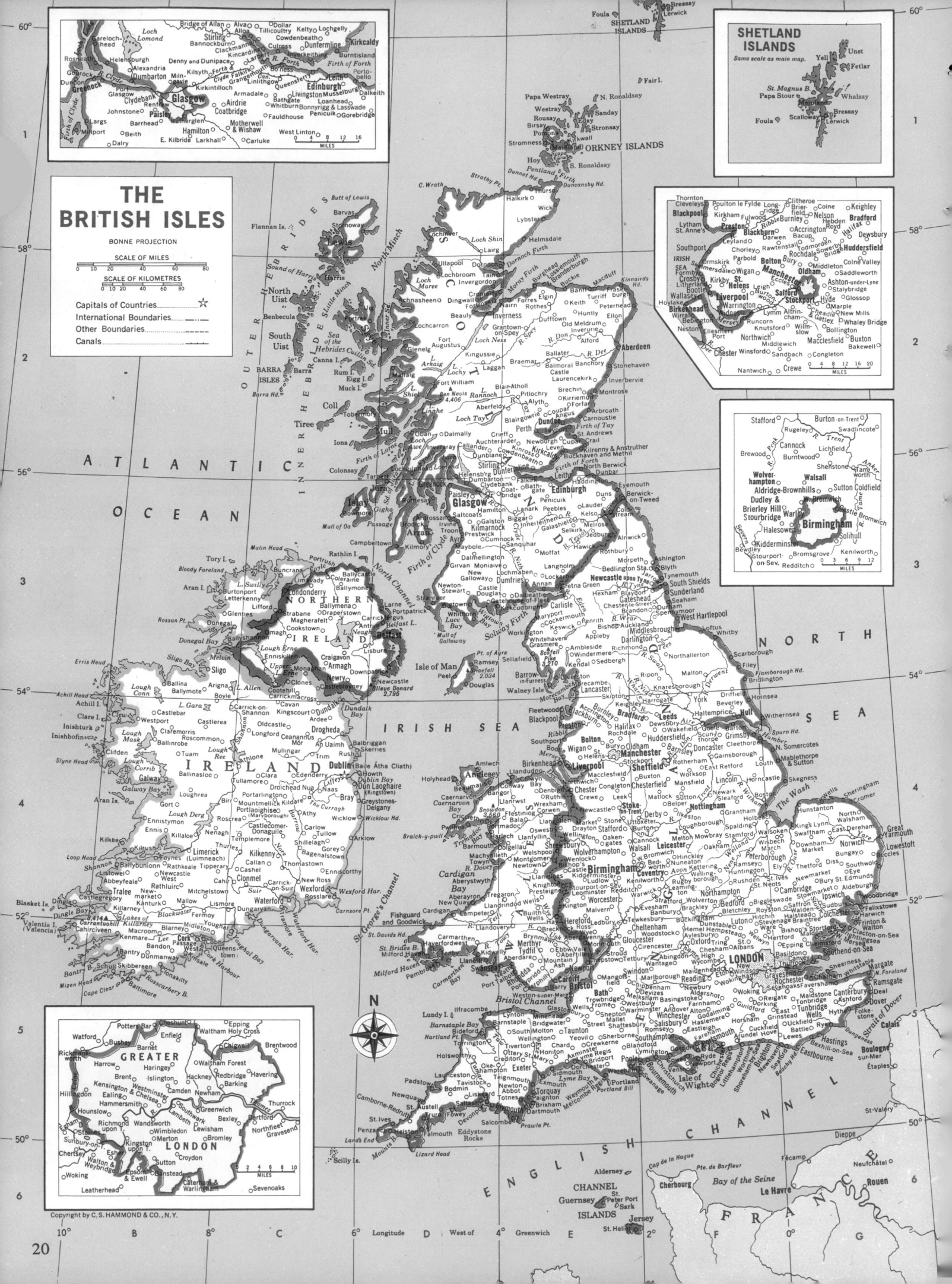

THE BRITISH ISLES

BONNE PROJECTION

SCALE OF MILES

SCALE OF KILOMETRES

Capitals of Countries .... ☆
International Boundaries ....
Other Boundaries ....
Canals ....

SHETLAND ISLANDS

Same scale as main map.

GREATER LONDON

20

GERMANY

CONIC PROJECTION

SCALE OF MILES

SCALE OF KILOMETERS

Capitals of Countries ....☆
State and District Capitals ....◉
International Boundaries ....
State and District Boundaries ......
Canals ....

East Germany is divided into districts bearing the
same name as their respective capitals.

© Copyright by C.S. HAMMOND & Co., Maplewood, N.J.

BERLIN

22

ITALY
CONIC PROJECTION

SCALE OF MILES

SCALE OF KILOMETERS

Capitals of Countries _____ ☆
Regional Capitals _____
Provincial Capitals _____ △
International Boundaries _____
Regional Boundaries _____

ITALY is divided for administrative purposes into 20 regions, shown on the map in separate colors. The regions are subdivided into provinces bearing the same names as their respective capitals, except:

PROVINCE	CAPITAL
MASSA-CARRARA	Massa
PESARO-URBINO	Pesaro

VATICAN CITY

ROME and ENVIRONS

Copyright by C.S. HAMMOND & Co., N.Y.

24

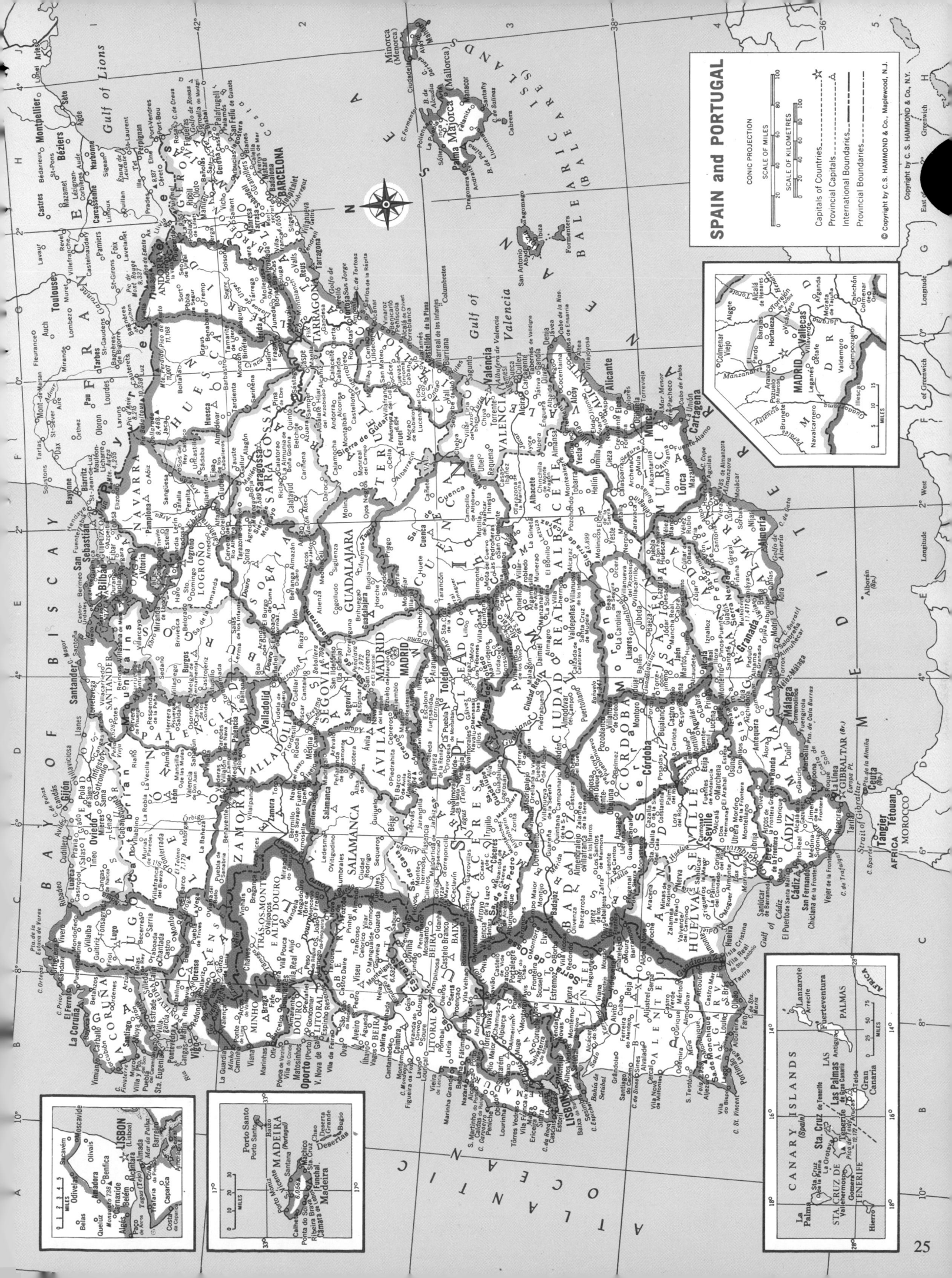

THE BALKAN STATES

CONIC PROJECTION

SCALE OF MILES

0   25   50   75   100   125   150   175

SCALE OF KILOMETRES

0   25   50   75   100   125   150   175

Capitals of Countries	☆
Administrative Centers	△
International Boundaries	
Major Internal Boundaries	
Minor Internal Boundaries	
Canals	

BULGARIA and GREECE are divided into counties and departments, respectively. Because of the scale no attempt has been made to delimit and name these sub-divisions; their administrative centers have, however, been designated.

The larger divisions named in Greece are well-known geographical regions, without administrative function.

RUMANIA consists of thirty-nine counties and three cities of regional status, Bucharest, Constanţa and Petroşeni. Scale does not permit delimiting these counties.

ALBANIA is divided into twenty-seven districts. Scale does not permit the delimitation of these divisions.

YUGOSLAVIA is a federation of six republics. The Serbian republic includes an autonomous province (Voyvodina), and an autonomous region (Kosovo-Mitohiyan).

26

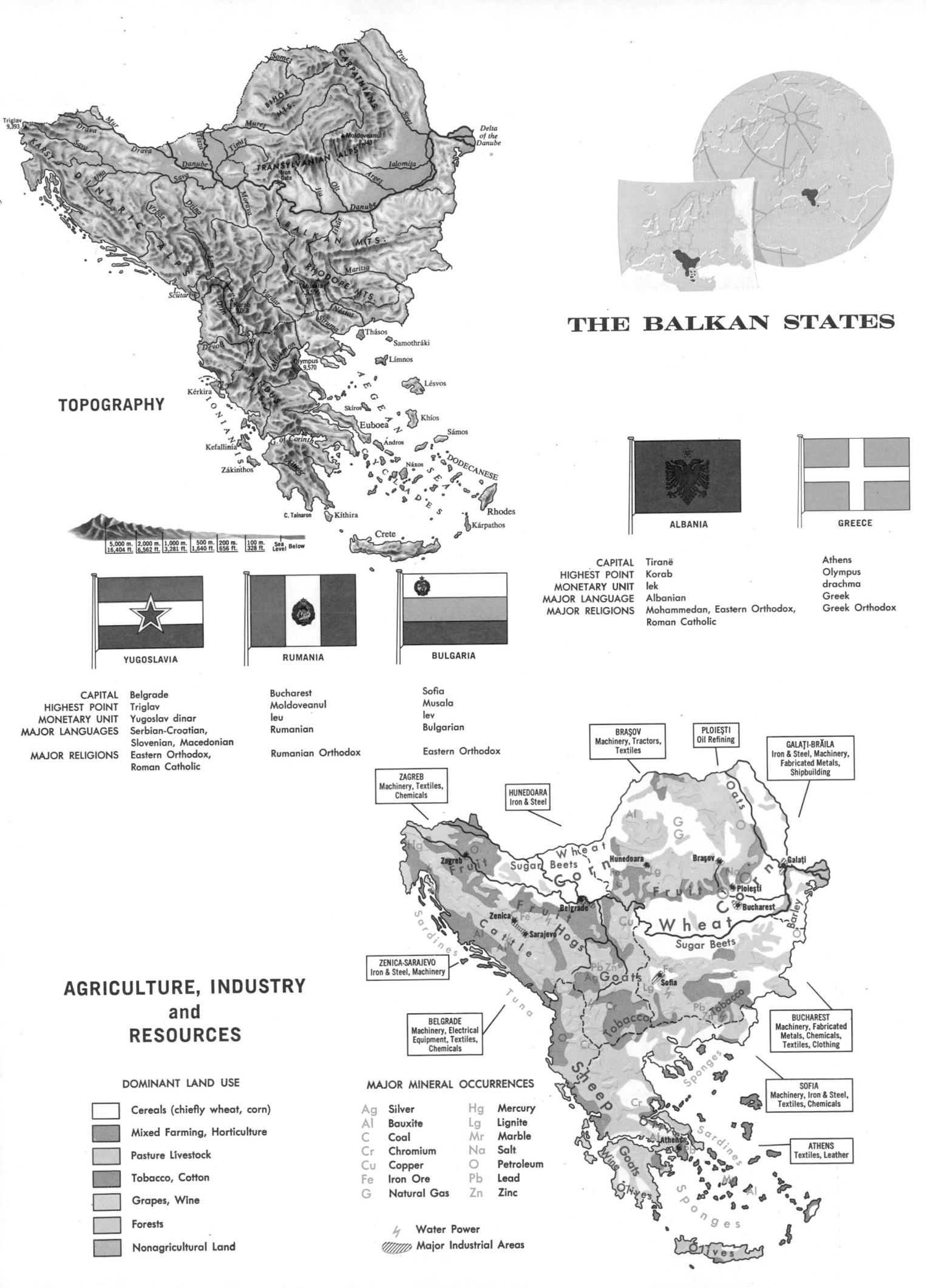

THE BALKAN STATES

TOPOGRAPHY

Triglav 9,393

Delta of the Danube

CARPATHIANS

BIHOR MTS.

Moldoveanul 8,343

TRANSYLVANIAN ALPS

Iron Gate

DINARIC ALPS

BALKAN MTS.

RHODOPE MTS.

Korab 9,068

Musala 9,595

Olympus 9,570

Thásos
Samothráki
Límnos
Lésvos
Khíos
Sámos
DODECANESE
Rhodes
Kárpathos

Kérkira
Skíros
Euboea
Ándros
Náxos
CYCLADES
AEGEAN SEA
IONIAN IS.
Kefallinía
Zákinthos
G. of Corinth
C. Taínaron
Kíthira
Crete

| 5,000 m. 16,404 ft. | 2,000 m. 6,562 ft. | 1,000 m. 3,281 ft. | 500 m. 1,640 ft. | 200 m. 656 ft. | 100 m. 328 ft. | Sea Level | Below |

Flags

ALBANIA   **GREECE**

	ALBANIA	GREECE
CAPITAL	Tiranë	Athens
HIGHEST POINT	Korab	Olympus
MONETARY UNIT	lek	drachma
MAJOR LANGUAGE	Albanian	Greek
MAJOR RELIGIONS	Mohammedan, Eastern Orthodox, Roman Catholic	Greek Orthodox

YUGOSLAVIA   **RUMANIA**   **BULGARIA**

	YUGOSLAVIA	RUMANIA	BULGARIA
CAPITAL	Belgrade	Bucharest	Sofia
HIGHEST POINT	Triglav	Moldoveanul	Musala
MONETARY UNIT	Yugoslav dinar	leu	lev
MAJOR LANGUAGES	Serbian-Croatian, Slovenian, Macedonian	Rumanian	Bulgarian
MAJOR RELIGIONS	Eastern Orthodox, Roman Catholic	Rumanian Orthodox	Eastern Orthodox

AGRICULTURE, INDUSTRY and RESOURCES

DOMINANT LAND USE

- Cereals (chiefly wheat, corn)
- Mixed Farming, Horticulture
- Pasture Livestock
- Tobacco, Cotton
- Grapes, Wine
- Forests
- Nonagricultural Land

MAJOR MINERAL OCCURRENCES

Ag	Silver	Hg	Mercury
Al	Bauxite	Lg	Lignite
C	Coal	Mr	Marble
Cr	Chromium	Na	Salt
Cu	Copper	O	Petroleum
Fe	Iron Ore	Pb	Lead
G	Natural Gas	Zn	Zinc

⚡ Water Power
▨ Major Industrial Areas

Industrial labels

- **ZAGREB** Machinery, Textiles, Chemicals
- **HUNEDOARA** Iron & Steel
- **BRAȘOV** Machinery, Tractors, Textiles
- **PLOIEȘTI** Oil Refining
- **GALAȚI-BRĂILA** Iron & Steel, Machinery, Fabricated Metals, Shipbuilding
- **ZENICA-SARAJEVO** Iron & Steel, Machinery
- **BELGRADE** Machinery, Electrical Equipment, Textiles, Chemicals
- **BUCHAREST** Machinery, Fabricated Metals, Chemicals, Textiles, Clothing
- **SOFIA** Machinery, Iron & Steel, Textiles, Chemicals
- **ATHENS** Textiles, Leather

27

UNION OF SOVIET SOCIALIST REPUBLICS

CONIC PROJECTION

SCALE OF MILES
0   100   200   300   400   500   600

SCALE OF KILOMETRES
0   100   200   300   400   500   600

Capitals
National .... ★
Union Republic .... ✪
A.S.S.R. .... ⊛
Autonomous Oblast .... ⊚
National Okrug .... ○

Boundaries
National ....
Union Republic ....
A.S.S.R. ....
Autonomous Oblast ....
National Okrug ....

ADMINISTRATIVE DIVISIONS NOT NAMED ON MAP

Division	Ref.	Division	Ref.
1. Abkhaz A.S.S.R.	E5	13. Khakass Aut. Oblast.	J4
2. Adygey Aut. Oblast	D5	14. Komi-Permyak Nat'l Okrug.	F4
3. Adzhar A.S.S.R.	E5	15. Mari A.S.S.R.	E4
4. Aginsk Nat'l Okrug	M4	16. Mordvinian A.S.S.R.	E4
5. Chechen-Ingush A.S.S.R.	E4	17. Nagorno-Karabakh Aut. Oblast.	E5
6. Chuvash A.S.S.R.	E4	18. Nakhichevan' A.S.S.R.	E5
7. Gorno-Altay Aut. Oblast.	H5	19. North Ossetian A.S.S.R.	E5
8. Gorno-Badakhshan Aut. Oblast.	H6	20. South Ossetian Aut. Oblast.	E5
9. Jewish Aut. Oblast.	O5	21. Tatar A.S.S.R.	F4
10. Kabardin-Balkar A.S.S.R.	E5	22. Tuvinian A.S.S.R.	K4
11. Karachay-Cherkess Aut. Oblast.	D5	23. Udmurt A.S.S.R.	F4
12. Kara-Kalpak A.S.S.R.	G5	24. Ust'-Ordynskiy Nat'l Okrug.	L4

© C. S. HAMMOND & Co., Maplewood, N.J.

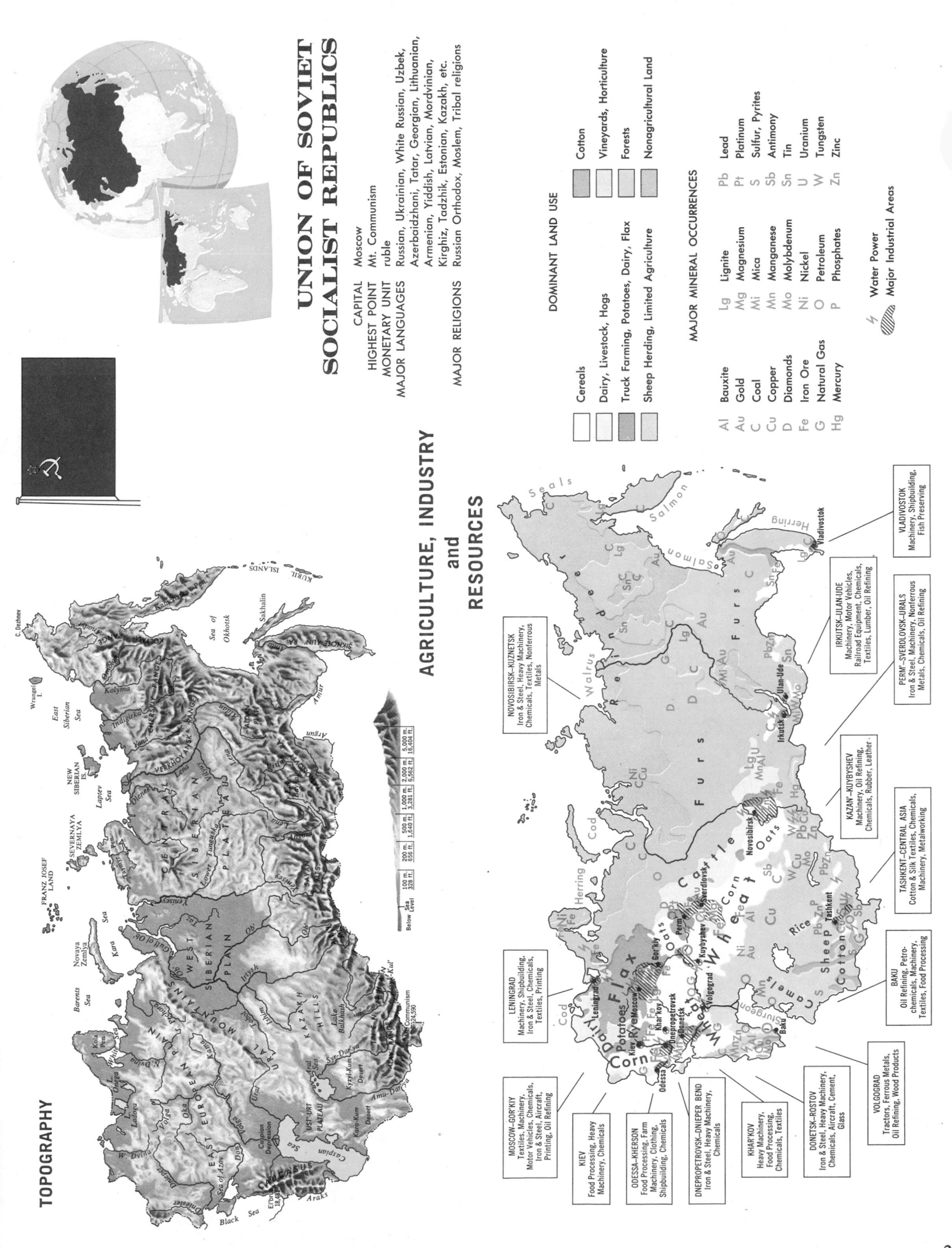

UNION OF SOVIET SOCIALIST REPUBLICS

CAPITAL Moscow
HIGHEST POINT Mt. Communism
MONETARY UNIT ruble
MAJOR LANGUAGES Russian, Ukrainian, White Russian, Uzbek, Azerbaidzhani, Tatar, Georgian, Lithuanian, Armenian, Yiddish, Latvian, Mordvinian, Kirghiz, Tadzhik, Estonian, Kazakh, etc.
MAJOR RELIGIONS Russian Orthodox, Moslem, Tribal religions

DOMINANT LAND USE

- Cereals
- Dairy, Livestock, Hogs
- Truck Farming, Potatoes, Dairy, Flax
- Sheep Herding, Limited Agriculture
- Cotton
- Vineyards, Horticulture
- Forests
- Nonagricultural Land

MAJOR MINERAL OCCURRENCES

Al Bauxite	Lg Lignite	Pb Lead
Au Gold	Mg Magnesium	Pt Platinum
C Coal	Mi Mica	S Sulfur, Pyrites
Cu Copper	Mn Manganese	Sb Antimony
D Diamonds	Mo Molybdenum	Sn Tin
Fe Iron Ore	Ni Nickel	U Uranium
G Natural Gas	O Petroleum	W Tungsten
Hg Mercury	P Phosphates	Zn Zinc

Water Power
Major Industrial Areas

TOPOGRAPHY

AGRICULTURE, INDUSTRY and RESOURCES

LENINGRAD
Machinery, Shipbuilding, Iron & Steel, Chemicals, Textiles, Printing

MOSCOW-GORKIY
Textiles, Machinery, Motor Vehicles, Chemicals, Iron & Steel, Aircraft, Printing, Oil Refining

KIEV
Food Processing, Heavy Machinery, Chemicals

ODESSA-KHERSON
Food Processing, Farm Machinery, Clothing, Shipbuilding, Chemicals

DNEPROPETROVSK-DNIEPER BEND
Iron & Steel, Heavy Machinery, Chemicals

KHAR'KOV
Heavy Machinery, Food Processing, Chemicals, Textiles

DONETSK-ROSTOV
Iron & Steel, Heavy Machinery, Chemicals, Aircraft, Cement, Glass

VOLGOGRAD
Tractors, Ferrous Metals, Oil Refining, Wood Products

BAKU
Oil Refining, Petrochemicals, Machinery, Textiles, Food Processing

TASHKENT-CENTRAL ASIA
Cotton & Silk Textiles, Chemicals, Machinery, Metalworking

KAZAN'-KUYBYSHEV
Machinery, Oil Refining, Chemicals, Rubber, Leather

PERM'-SVERDLOVSK-URALS
Iron & Steel, Machinery, Nonferrous Metals, Chemicals, Oil Refining

IRKUTSK-ULAN-UDE
Machinery, Motor Vehicles, Railroad Equipment, Chemicals, Textiles, Lumber, Oil Refining

NOVOSIBIRSK-KUZNETSK
Iron & Steel, Heavy Machinery, Chemicals, Textiles, Nonferrous Metals

VLADIVOSTOK
Machinery, Shipbuilding, Fish Preserving

UNION OF SOVIET SOCIALIST REPUBLICS
European Part
CONIC PROJECTION
SCALE OF MILES

SCALE OF KILOMETRES

National Capitals .... ★
Capitals of Union Republics .... ⊠
Administrative Centers .... △
International boundaries ....
Union Republic boundaries ....
A.S.S.R., Oblast, Kray boundaries ...
Autonomous Oblast boundaries .....
National Okrug boundaries ....
Canals ....

The government of the United States has not recognized the
incorporation of Estonia, Latvia and Lithuania into the Soviet
Union, nor does it recognize as final the de facto western limit
of Polish administration in Germany (the Oder-Neisse line).

**Administrative Divisions bear same
names as their respective Capitals
or Centers, except:**

Abkhaz A.S.S.R.	Sukhumi	F6
Adygey Aut. Oblast	Maykop	F6
Adzhar A.S.S.R.	Batumi	F6
Bashkir A.S.S.R.	Ufa	J4
Chechen-Ingush A.S.S.R.	Groznyy	G6
Chuvash A.S.S.R.	Cheboksary	G3
Crimean Oblast	Simferopol'	D6
Dagestan A.S.S.R.	Makhachkala	G6
Kabardin-Balkar A.S.S.R.	Nal'chik	F6
Kalmuck A.S.S.R.	Elista	F5
Karachay-Cherkess Aut. Obl.	Cherkessk	F6
Karelian A.S.S.R.	Petrozavodsk	D2
Komi A.S.S.R.	Syktyvkar	H2
Komi-Permyak Nat'l Okrug	Kudymkar	H3
Mari A.S.S.R.	Yoshkar-Ola	G3
Mordvinian A.S.S.R.	Saransk	G4
Nagorno-Karabakh Aut. Obl.	Stepanakert	G7
Nenets Nat'l Okrug	Nar'yan-Mar	H1
North Ossetian A.S.S.R.	Ordzhonikidze	F6
South Ossetian Aut. Obl.	Tskhinvali	F6
Tatar A.S.S.R.	Kazan'	G3
Trans-Carpathian Oblast	Uzhgorod	B5
Udmurt A.S.S.R.	Izhevsk	H3
Volyn Oblast	Lutsk	C4

Copyright by C. S. HAMMOND & CO., N.Y.

ASIA

LAMBERT AZIMUTHAL EQUAL-AREA PROJECTION

SCALE OF MILES

SCALE OF KILOMETRES

Capitals of Countries........ ✦   Canals.......
International Boundaries.......
Elevations in Feet

Copyright by C.S. HAMMOND & CO., N.Y.

31

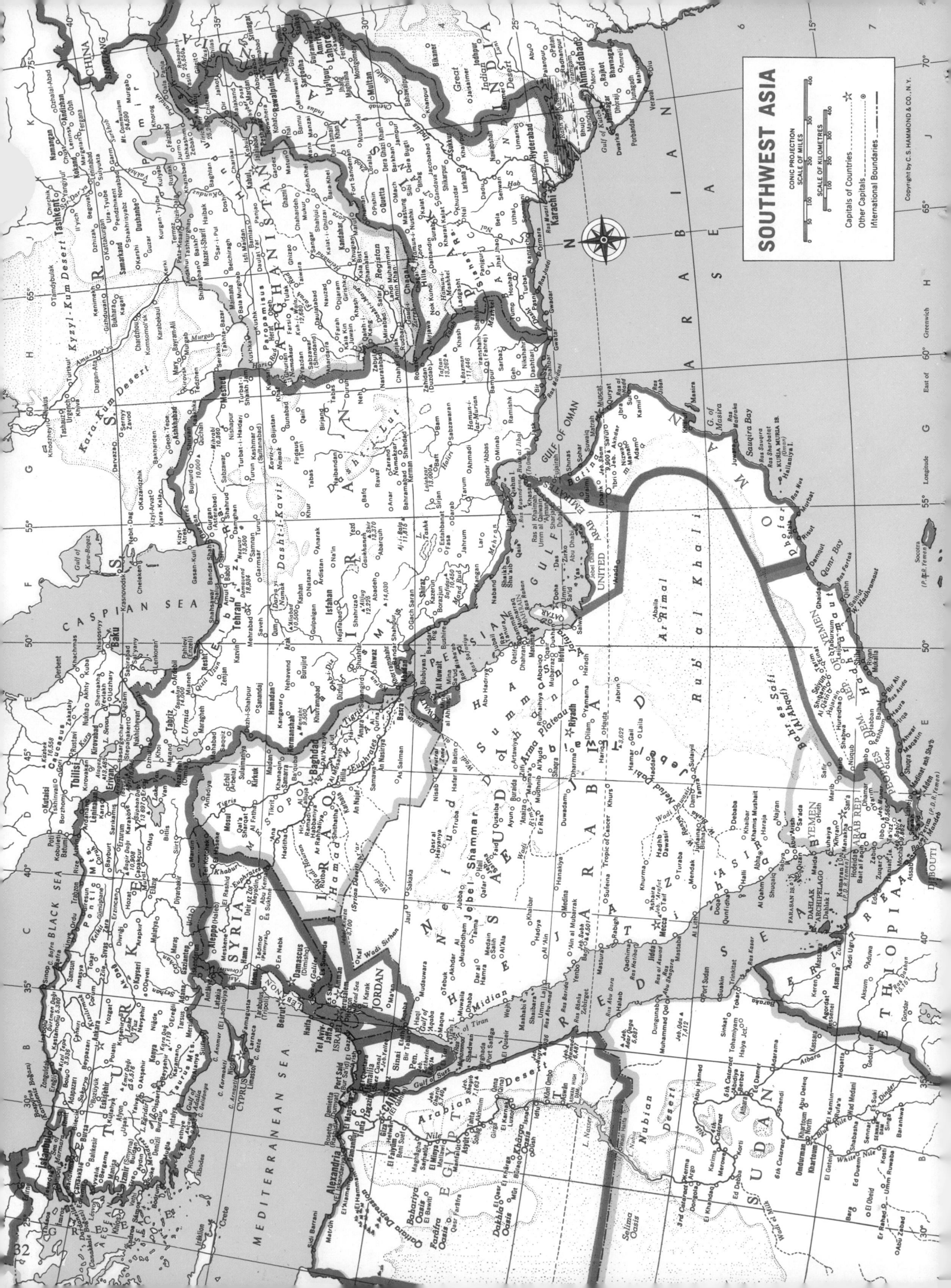

SOUTHWEST ASIA

CONIC PROJECTION
SCALE OF MILES
SCALE OF KILOMETRES

Capitals of Countries ★
Other Capitals ⊛
International Boundaries

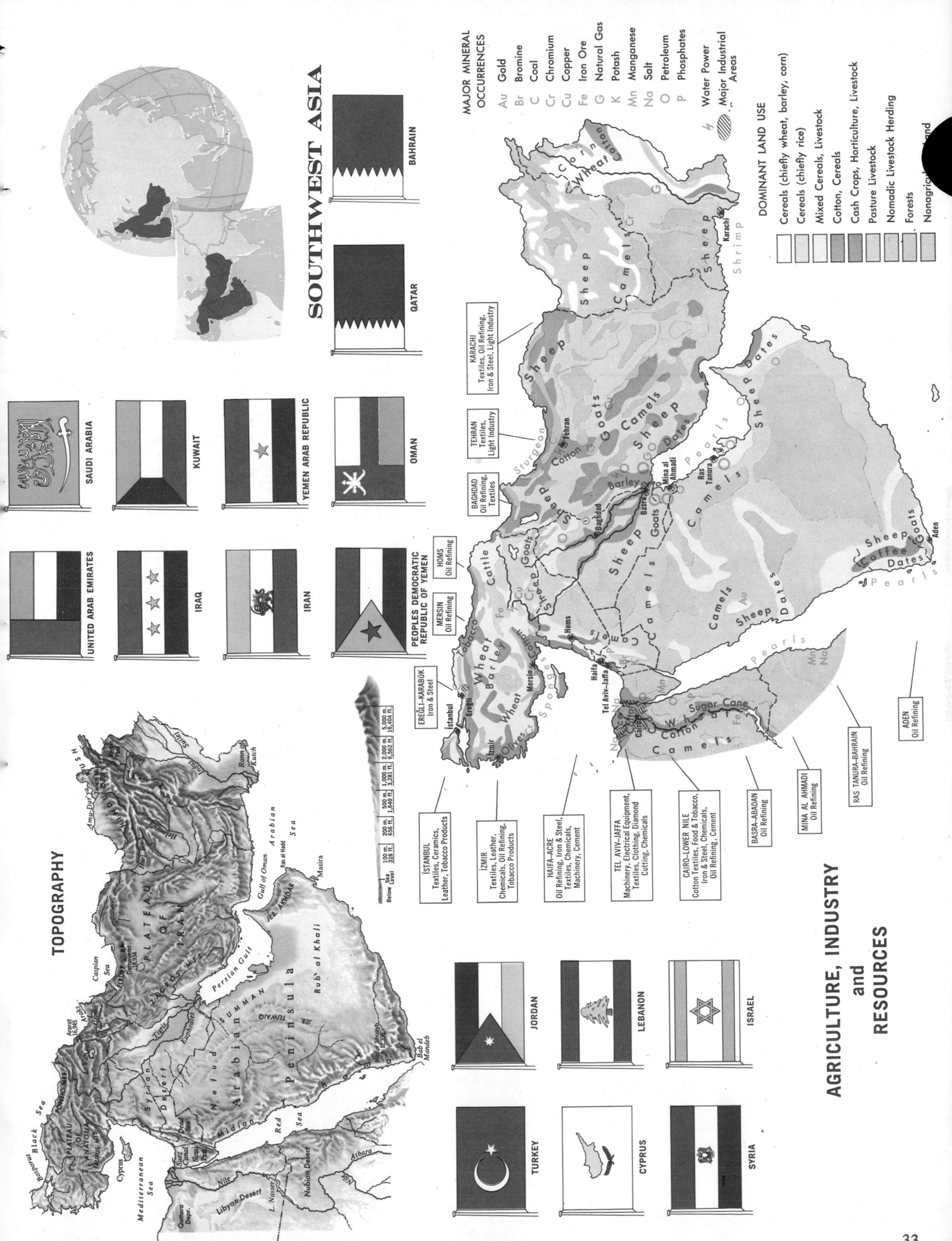

SOUTHWEST ASIA

BAHRAIN

QATAR

MAJOR MINERAL OCCURRENCES

Au Gold
Br Bromine
C Coal
Cr Chromium
Cu Copper
Fe Iron Ore
G Natural Gas
K Potash
Mn Manganese
Na Salt
O Petroleum
P Phosphates
⚡ Water Power
◫ Major Industrial Areas

DOMINANT LAND USE

Cereals (chiefly wheat, barley, corn)
Cereals (chiefly rice)
Mixed Cereals, Livestock
Cotton, Cereals
Cash Crops, Horticulture, Livestock
Pasture Livestock
Nomadic Livestock Herding
Forests
Nonagricultural Land

SAUDI ARABIA

KUWAIT

YEMEN ARAB REPUBLIC

OMAN

UNITED ARAB EMIRATES

IRAQ

IRAN

PEOPLES DEMOCRATIC REPUBLIC OF YEMEN

HOMS
Oil Refining

MERSIN
Oil Refining

EREĞLİ–KARABÜK
Iron & Steel

KARACHI
Textiles, Oil Refining, Iron & Steel, Light Industry

TEHRAN
Textiles, Light Industry

BAGHDAD
Oil Refining, Textiles

ISTANBUL
Textiles, Ceramics, Leather, Tobacco Products

İZMIR
Textiles, Leather, Chemicals, Oil Refining, Tobacco Products

HAIFA–ACRE
Oil Refining, Iron & Steel, Textiles, Chemicals, Machinery, Cement

TEL AVIV–JAFFA
Machinery, Electrical Equipment, Textiles, Clothing, Diamond Cutting, Chemicals

CAIRO–LOWER NILE
Cotton Textiles, Food & Tobacco, Iron & Steel, Chemicals, Oil Refining, Cement

BASRA–ABADAN
Oil Refining

MINA AL AHMADI
Oil Refining

RAS TANURA–BAHRAIN
Oil Refining

ADEN
Oil Refining

TOPOGRAPHY

100 m. / 328 ft.
200 m. / 656 ft.
500 m. / 1,640 ft.
1,000 m. / 3,281 ft.
2,000 m. / 6,562 ft.
5,000 m. / 16,404 ft.

Below Sea Level

JORDAN

LEBANON

ISRAEL

TURKEY

CYPRUS

SYRIA

AGRICULTURE, INDUSTRY and RESOURCES

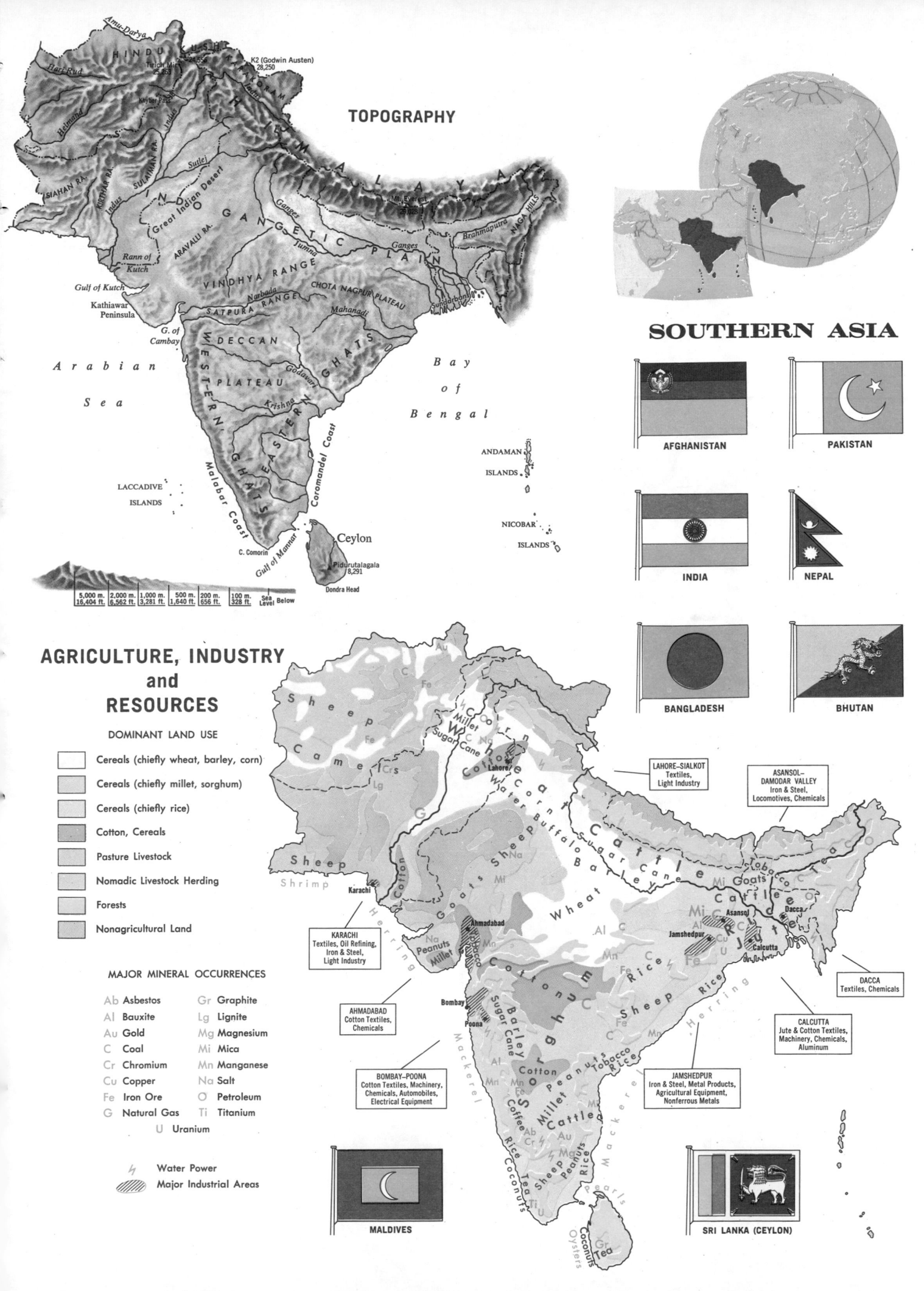

TOPOGRAPHY

SOUTHERN ASIA

AFGHANISTAN   PAKISTAN

INDIA   NEPAL

BANGLADESH   BHUTAN

MALDIVES   SRI LANKA (CEYLON)

AGRICULTURE, INDUSTRY and RESOURCES

DOMINANT LAND USE

- Cereals (chiefly wheat, barley, corn)
- Cereals (chiefly millet, sorghum)
- Cereals (chiefly rice)
- Cotton, Cereals
- Pasture Livestock
- Nomadic Livestock Herding
- Forests
- Nonagricultural Land

MAJOR MINERAL OCCURRENCES

Ab Asbestos   Gr Graphite
Al Bauxite   Lg Lignite
Au Gold   Mg Magnesium
C Coal   Mi Mica
Cr Chromium   Mn Manganese
Cu Copper   Na Salt
Fe Iron Ore   O Petroleum
G Natural Gas   Ti Titanium
U Uranium

⚡ Water Power
▨ Major Industrial Areas

LAHORE–SIALKOT
Textiles, Light Industry

ASANSOL–DAMODAR VALLEY
Iron & Steel, Locomotives, Chemicals

KARACHI
Textiles, Oil Refining, Iron & Steel, Light Industry

DACCA
Textiles, Chemicals

AHMADABAD
Cotton Textiles, Chemicals

CALCUTTA
Jute & Cotton Textiles, Machinery, Chemicals, Aluminum

BOMBAY–POONA
Cotton Textiles, Machinery, Chemicals, Automobiles, Electrical Equipment

JAMSHEDPUR
Iron & Steel, Metal Products, Agricultural Equipment, Nonferrous Metals

35

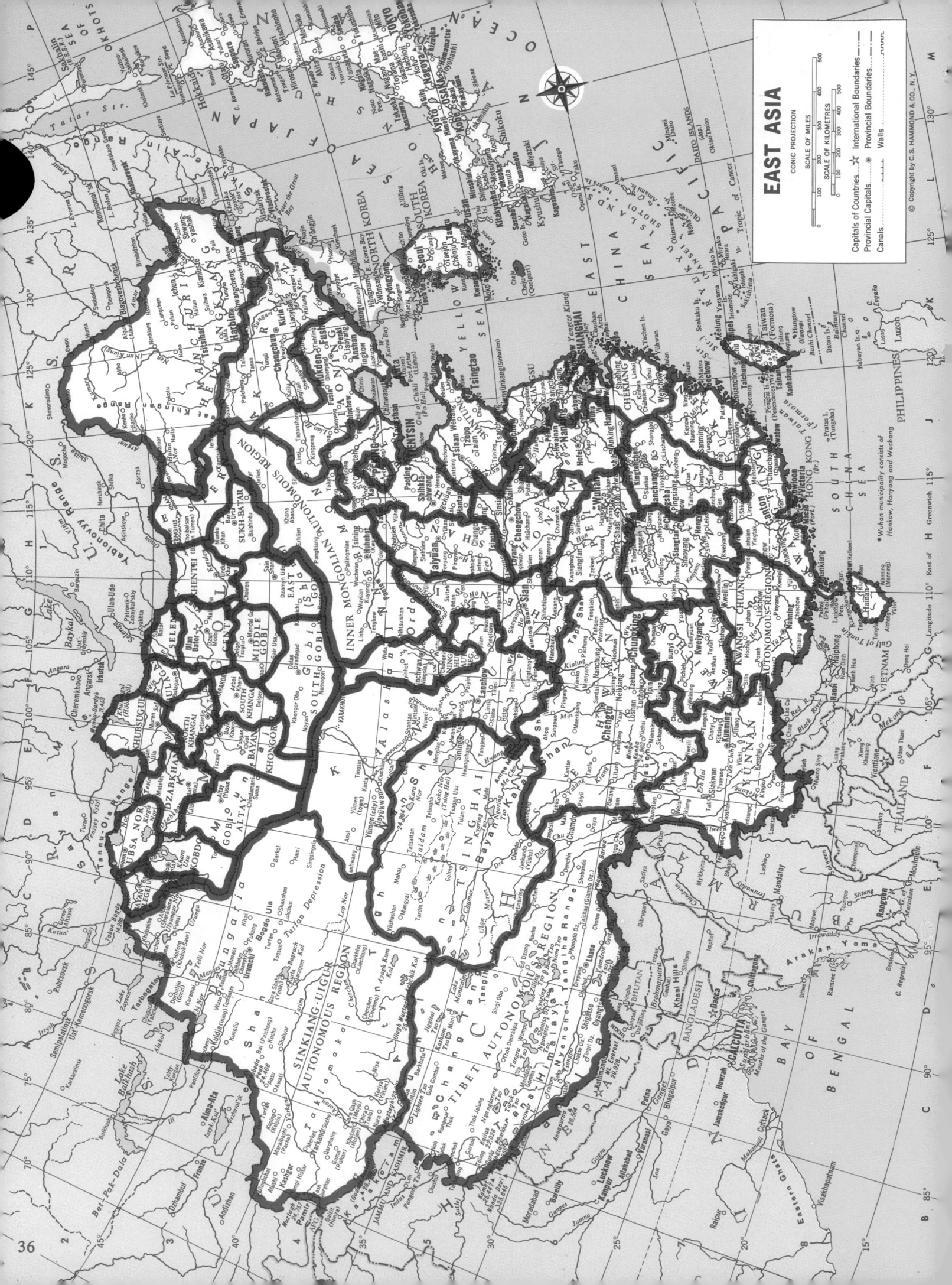

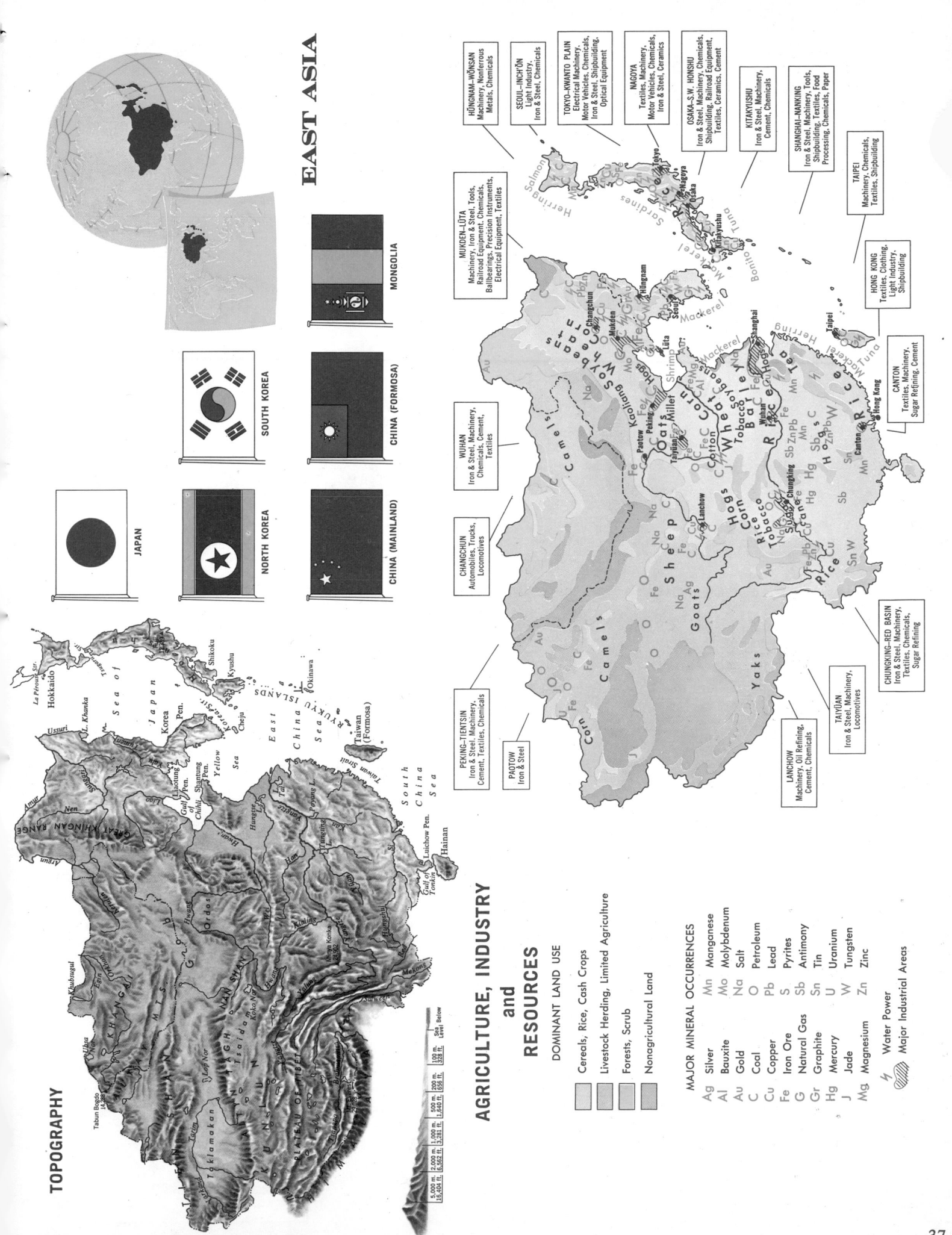

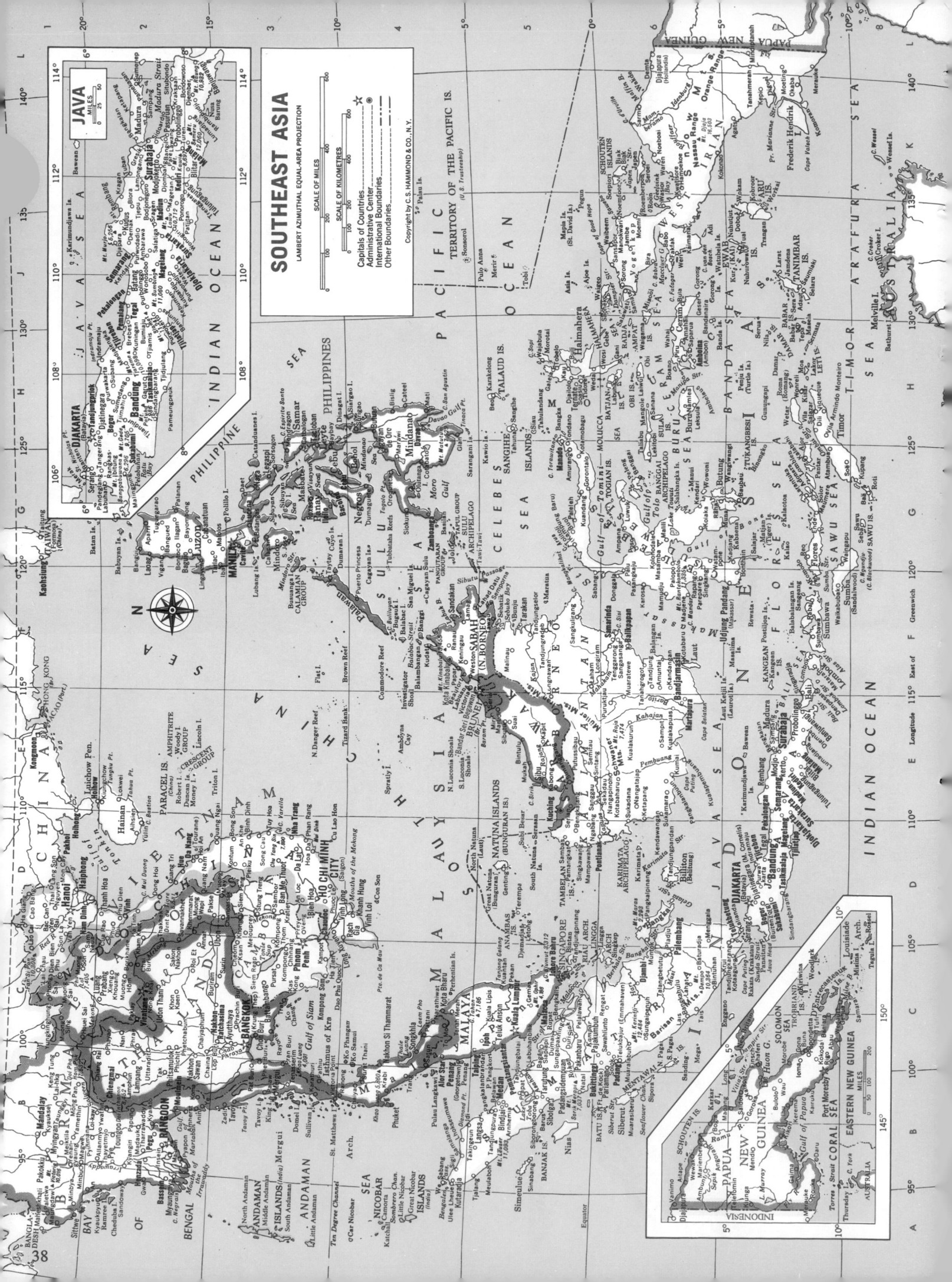

SOUTHEAST ASIA

LAMBERT AZIMUTHAL EQUAL-AREA PROJECTION

SCALE OF MILES

SCALE OF KILOMETRES

Capitals of Countries
Administrative Center
International Boundaries
Other Boundaries

TERRITORY OF THE PACIFIC IS.
(U.S. Trusteeship)

Copyright by C.S. HAMMOND & CO., N.Y.

JAVA

MILES
0 25 50

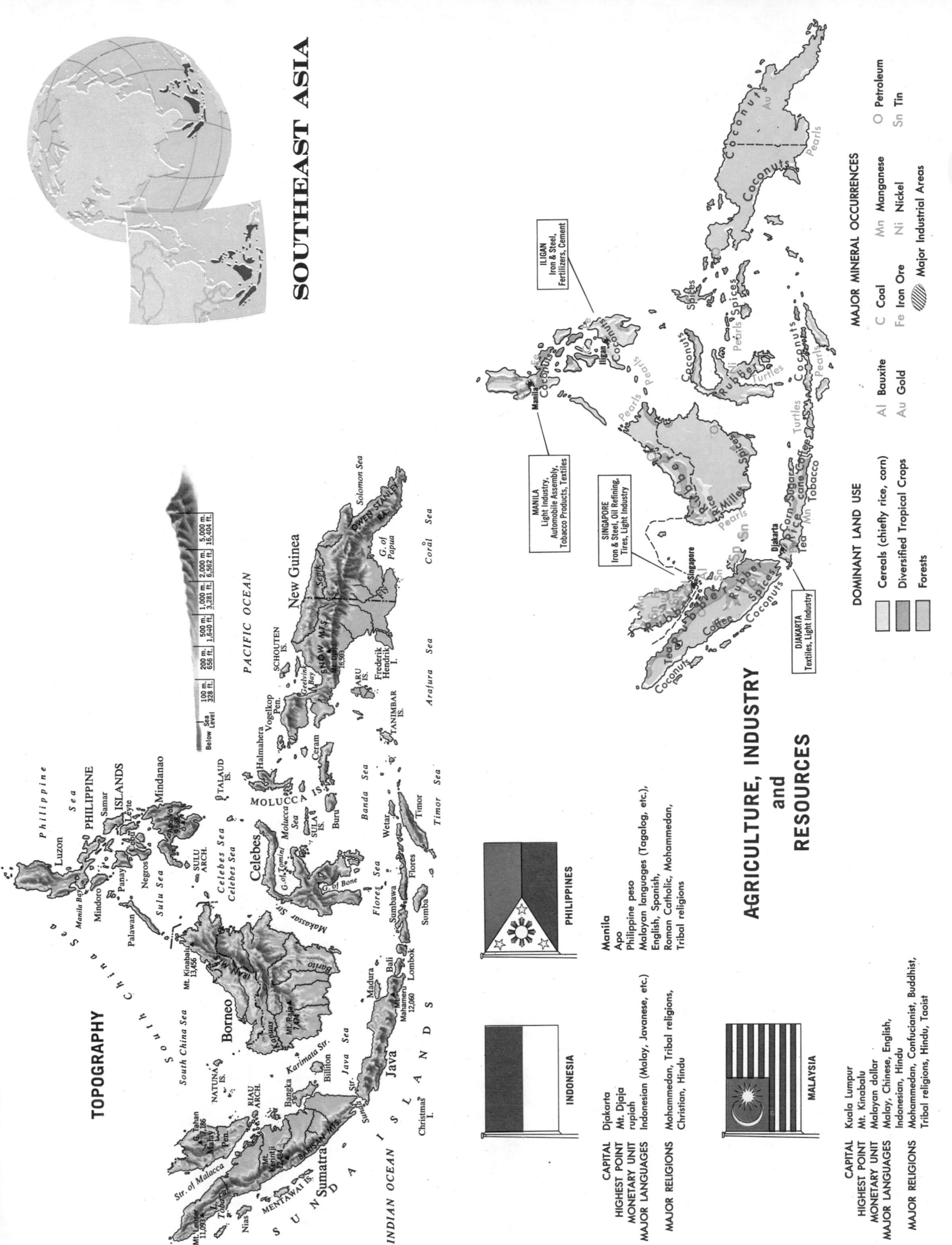

SOUTHEAST ASIA

TOPOGRAPHY

Below Sea Level | 100 m. 328 ft. | 200 m. 656 ft. | 500 m. 1,640 ft. | 1,000 m. 3,281 ft. | 2,000 m. 6,562 ft. | 5,000 m. 16,404 ft.

PACIFIC OCEAN

New Guinea

Philippine Sea

PHILIPPINE ISLANDS

Luzon
Samar
Mindoro
Mindanao
Panay
Negros
Leyte
Palawan
Mt. Apo 9,690

SULU ARCH.
Sulu Sea
Manila Bay

TALAUD IS.
MOLUCCA IS.
Halmahera
Ceram
Buru
Celebes
Celebes Sea
Molucca Sea
G. of Tomini
G. of Boni

Banda Sea
Flores Sea
Timor Sea
Arafura Sea

Borneo
Mt. Kinabalu 13,456

Java
Bali
Madura
Lombok
Sumbawa
Sumba
Flores
Wetar
Timor
Sumba

South China Sea

Sumatra
Bangka
Billiton
NATUNA IS.
RIAU ARCH.
Str. of Malacca
Nias
MENTAWAI IS.
Christmas I.
Mt. Leuser 11,093

INDIAN OCEAN

SUNDA ISLANDS

SCHOUTEN IS.
Vogelkop Pen.
Geelvink Bay
SNOW MTS.
Mt. Djaja 16,500
OWEN STANLEY RA.
Sepik
Fly
G. of Papua
Solomon Sea
Coral Sea

ARU IS.
Frederik Hendrik I.
TANIMBAR IS.

Makassar Str.

IRAN MTS.
Mt. Raja 7,474
Kapuas
Mt. Mahameru 12,060
Barito

BARISAN MTS.
Malay Pen.
G. of Tahan 7,186
Lake Toba
Mt. Kerintji 12,467

PHILIPPINES

CAPITAL	Manila
HIGHEST POINT	Apo
MONETARY UNIT	Philippine peso
MAJOR LANGUAGES	Malayan languages (Tagalog, etc.), English, Spanish
MAJOR RELIGIONS	Roman Catholic, Mohammedan, Tribal religions

INDONESIA

CAPITAL	Djakarta
HIGHEST POINT	Mt. Djaja
MONETARY UNIT	rupiah
MAJOR LANGUAGES	Indonesian (Malay, Javanese, etc.)
MAJOR RELIGIONS	Mohammedan, Tribal religions, Christian, Hindu

MALAYSIA

CAPITAL	Kuala Lumpur
HIGHEST POINT	Mt. Kinabalu
MONETARY UNIT	Malayan dollar
MAJOR LANGUAGES	Malay, Chinese, English, Indonesian, Hindu
MAJOR RELIGIONS	Mohammedan, Confucianist, Buddhist, Tribal religions, Hindu, Taoist

AGRICULTURE, INDUSTRY and RESOURCES

ILIGAN
Iron & Steel, Fertilizers, Cement

MANILA
Light Industry, Automobile Assembly, Tobacco Products, Textiles

SINGAPORE
Iron & Steel, Oil Refining, Tires, Light Industry

DJAKARTA
Textiles, Light Industry

Coconuts
Au
Pearls
Spices
Pearls Spices
Coconuts
Rubber
Turtles
Coconuts
Pearls
Coconuts
Turtles
Coconuts
Pearls
Rubber
Spices
Coffee
Tea
Coconuts
Sn
Rubber
Rice
Corn Sugarcane Corn
Mn Tobacco
Millet
Tea
Rice
Millet
Tobacco

DOMINANT LAND USE

Cereals (chiefly rice, corn)
Diversified Tropical Crops
Forests

MAJOR MINERAL OCCURRENCES

Al Bauxite
Au Gold
C Coal
Fe Iron Ore
Mn Manganese
Ni Nickel
O Petroleum
Sn Tin
Major Industrial Areas

39

INDOCHINESE and MALAY PENINSULAS

CONIC PROJECTION

SCALE OF MILES

SCALE OF KILOMETRES

International Boundaries ....
Division and State Boundaries ....
Capitals of Countries .... ☆
Division and State Capitals .... ⊛

40   Copyright by C.S. HAMMOND & Co., N.Y.   Longitude   East of   Greenwich

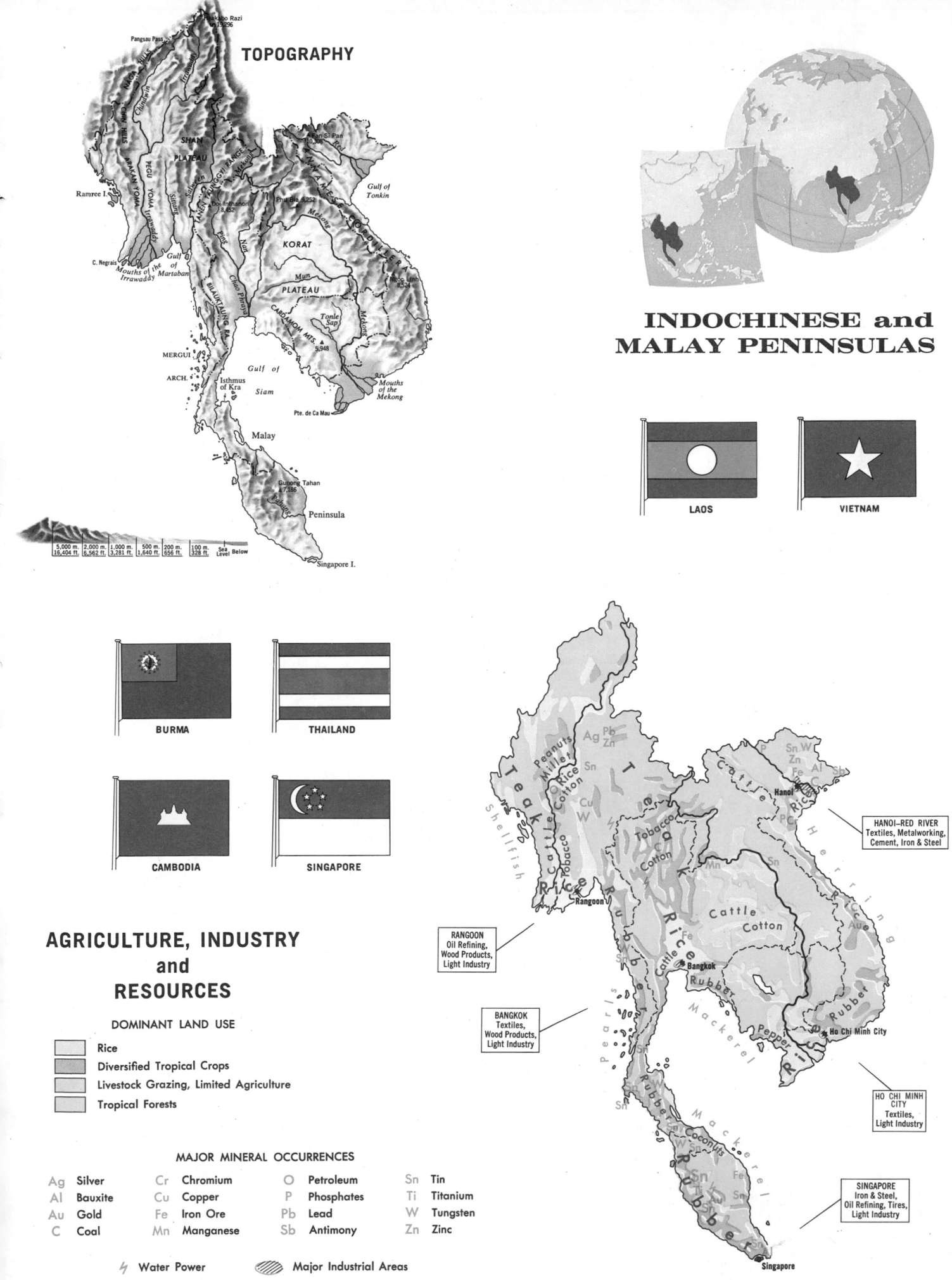

TOPOGRAPHY

Hkakabo Razi
15,296
Pangsau Pass

SHAN
PLATEAU

ARAKAN YOMA

PEGU YOMA

NAGA HILLS

CHIN HILLS

Chindwin

Irrawaddy

Sittang

Salween

Chao Praya

Ramree I.

Fan Si Pan
10,308

Doi Inthanon
8,452

TANEN TAUNGGYI RANGE

Nam

Mekong

Gulf of
Tonkin

Phu Bia 9,252

KORAT

Mun

PLATEAU

Ngoc Linh
8,524

CORDILLERA

BILAUKTAUNG RA.

C. Negrais

Mouths of the
Irrawaddy

Gulf
of
Martaban

CARDAMOM MTS.
5,948

Tonle
Sap

Mekong

MERGUI

ARCH.

Gulf of
Siam

Isthmus
of Kra

Pte. de Ca Mau

Mouths of the
Mekong

Malay

Gunong Tahan
7,186

Peninsula

Singapore I.

| 5,000 m. 16,404 ft. | 2,000 m. 6,562 ft. | 1,000 m. 3,281 ft. | 500 m. 1,640 ft. | 200 m. 656 ft. | 100 m. 328 ft. | Sea Level | Below |

INDOCHINESE and MALAY PENINSULAS

LAOS

VIETNAM

BURMA

THAILAND

CAMBODIA

SINGAPORE

AGRICULTURE, INDUSTRY and RESOURCES

DOMINANT LAND USE

- Rice
- Diversified Tropical Crops
- Livestock Grazing, Limited Agriculture
- Tropical Forests

MAJOR MINERAL OCCURRENCES

Ag	Silver	Cr	Chromium	O	Petroleum	Sn	Tin
Al	Bauxite	Cu	Copper	P	Phosphates	Ti	Titanium
Au	Gold	Fe	Iron Ore	Pb	Lead	W	Tungsten
C	Coal	Mn	Manganese	Sb	Antimony	Zn	Zinc

⚡ Water Power   ▨ Major Industrial Areas

RANGOON
Oil Refining,
Wood Products,
Light Industry

BANGKOK
Textiles,
Wood Products,
Light Industry

HANOI–RED RIVER
Textiles, Metalworking,
Cement, Iron & Steel

HO CHI MINH
CITY
Textiles,
Light Industry

SINGAPORE
Iron & Steel,
Oil Refining, Tires,
Light Industry

Teak

Peanuts

Millet

Cotton

Rice

Sn

Cu

W

Tobacco

Cattle

Shellfish

Rice

Rangoon

Rubber

Tobacco

Cotton

Rice

Fe

Sb

Cattle

Bangkok

Rubber

Pearls

Mn

Sn

Ag Pb Zn

Sn W Zn Al Sb Fe

Hanoi

Rice

Cattle

Herring

Cattle

Cotton

Sn

Rice

Ho Chi Minh City

Pepper

Rubber

Mackerel

Rubber

Coconuts

Rubber

Mackerel

Sn Fe

Singapore

41

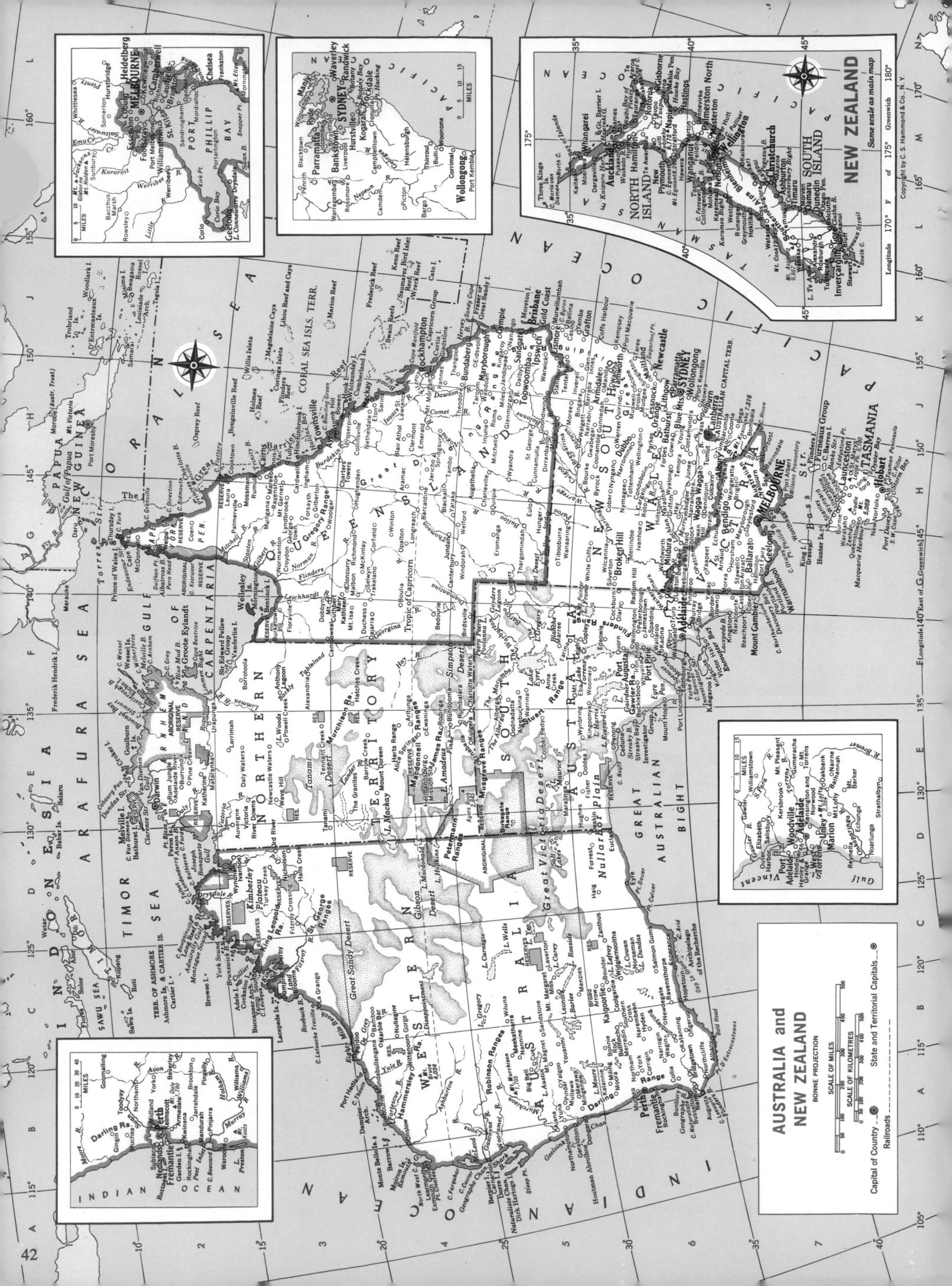

AUSTRALIA and
NEW ZEALAND

BONNE PROJECTION

SCALE OF MILES

SCALE OF KILOMETRES

Capital of Country........⊛
State and Territorial Capitals....⊛
Railroads.................

NEW ZEALAND

Same scale as main map

Copyright by C. S. Hammond & Co., N.Y.

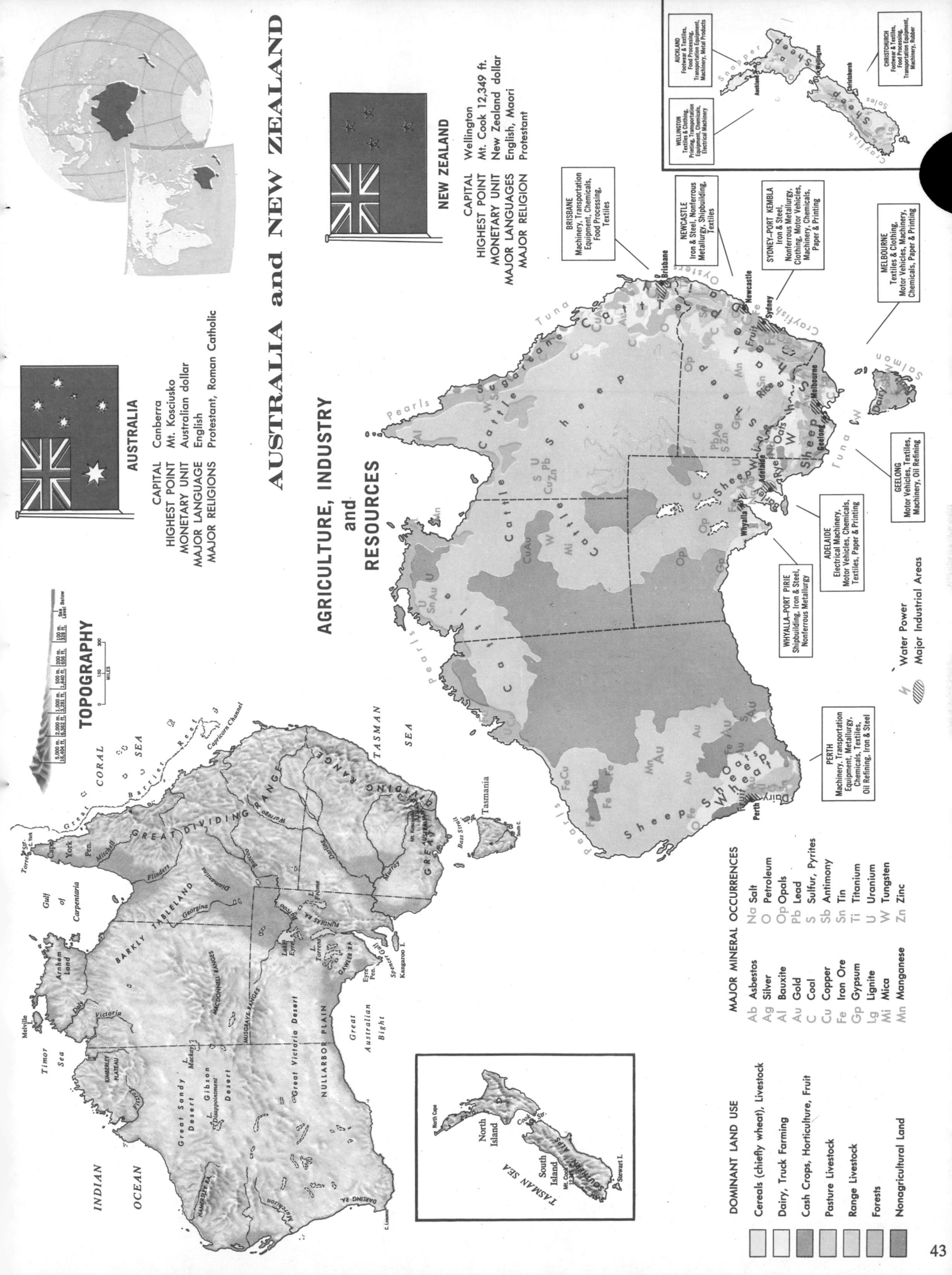

AUSTRALIA and NEW ZEALAND

AGRICULTURE, INDUSTRY and RESOURCES

AUSTRALIA

CAPITAL	Canberra
HIGHEST POINT	Mt. Kosciusko
MONETARY UNIT	Australian dollar
MAJOR LANGUAGE	English
MAJOR RELIGIONS	Protestant, Roman Catholic

NEW ZEALAND

CAPITAL	Wellington
HIGHEST POINT	Mt. Cook 12,349 ft.
MONETARY UNIT	New Zealand dollar
MAJOR LANGUAGES	English, Maori
MAJOR RELIGION	Protestant

TOPOGRAPHY

BRISBANE Machinery, Transportation Equipment, Chemicals, Food Processing, Textiles

NEWCASTLE Iron & Steel, Nonferrous Metallurgy, Shipbuilding, Textiles

SYDNEY–PORT KEMBLA Iron & Steel, Nonferrous Metallurgy, Clothing, Motor Vehicles, Machinery, Chemicals, Paper & Printing

MELBOURNE Textiles & Clothing, Motor Vehicles, Machinery, Chemicals, Paper & Printing

GEELONG Motor Vehicles, Textiles, Machinery, Oil Refining

ADELAIDE Electrical Machinery, Motor Vehicles, Chemicals, Textiles, Paper & Printing

WHYALLA–PORT PIRIE Shipbuilding, Iron & Steel, Nonferrous Metallurgy

PERTH Machinery, Transportation Equipment, Metallurgy, Chemicals, Textiles, Oil Refining, Iron & Steel

AUCKLAND Footwear & Textiles, Food Processing, Transportation Equipment, Machinery, Metal Products

WELLINGTON Textiles & Clothing, Printing, Transportation Equipment, Chemicals, Electrical Machinery

CHRISTCHURCH Footwear & Textiles, Food Processing, Transportation Equipment, Machinery, Rubber

⌇ Water Power   ▨ Major Industrial Areas

MAJOR MINERAL OCCURRENCES

Ab	Asbestos	Na	Salt
Ag	Silver	O	Petroleum
Al	Bauxite	Op	Opals
Au	Gold	Pb	Lead
C	Coal	S	Sulfur, Pyrites
Cu	Copper	Sb	Antimony
Fe	Iron Ore	Sn	Tin
Gp	Gypsum	Ti	Titanium
Lg	Lignite	U	Uranium
Mi	Mica	W	Tungsten
Mn	Manganese	Zn	Zinc

DOMINANT LAND USE

- Cereals (chiefly wheat), Livestock
- Dairy, Truck Farming
- Cash Crops, Horticulture, Fruit
- Pasture Livestock
- Range Livestock
- Forests
- Nonagricultural Land

43

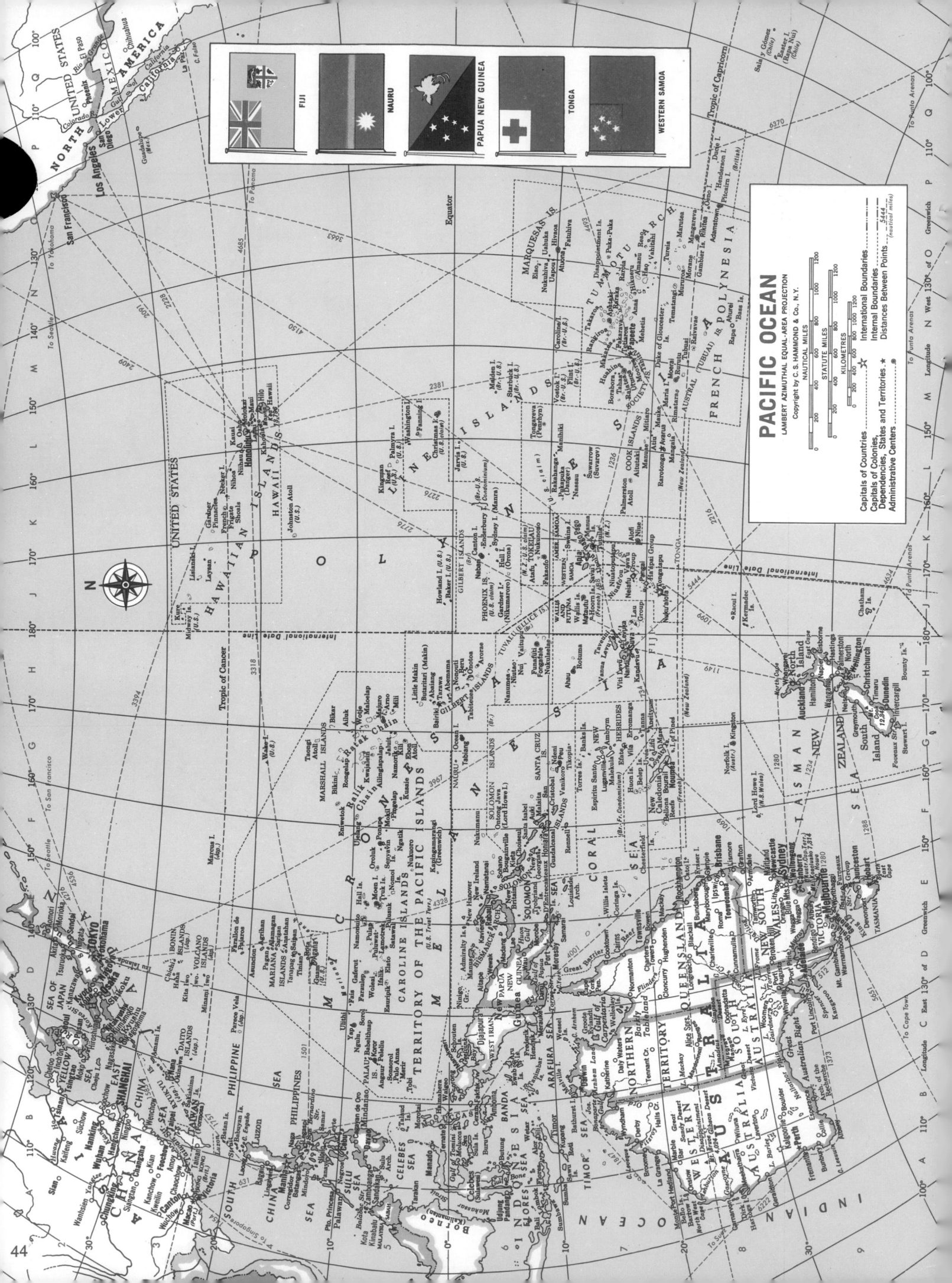

AFRICA

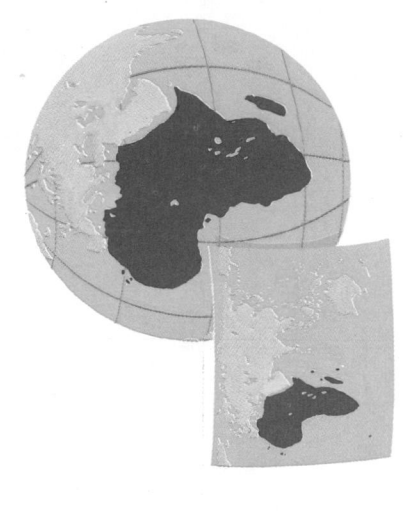

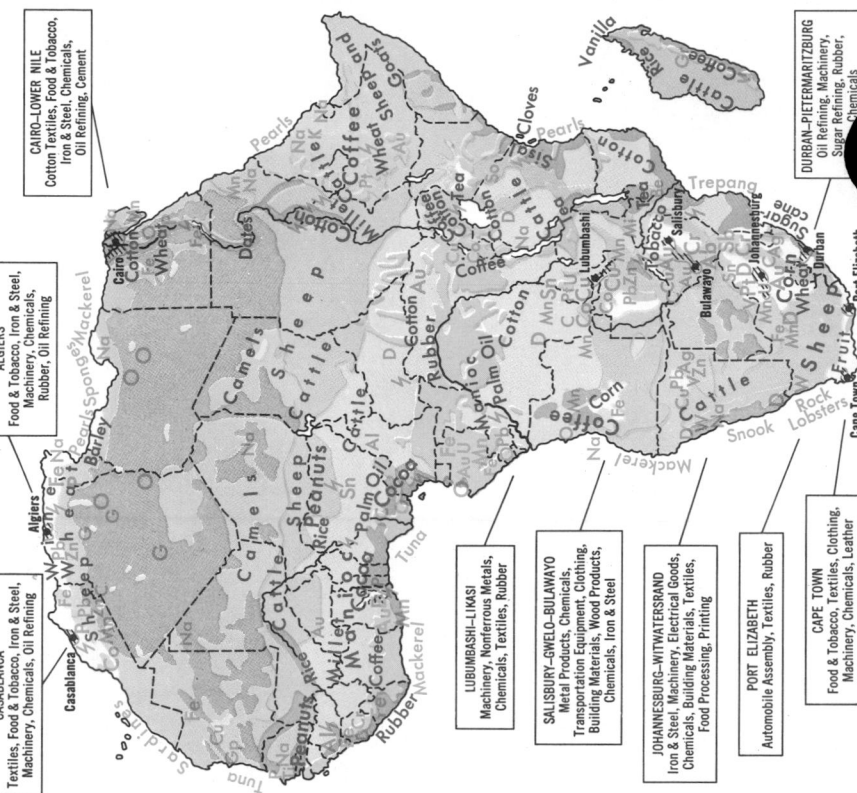

CAIRO–LOWER NILE
Cotton Textiles, Food & Tobacco,
Iron & Steel, Chemicals,
Oil Refining, Cement

ALGIERS
Food & Tobacco, Iron & Steel,
Machinery, Chemicals,
Rubber, Oil Refining

CASABLANCA
Textiles, Food & Tobacco, Iron & Steel,
Machinery, Chemicals, Oil Refining

DURBAN–PIETERMARITZBURG
Oil Refining, Machinery,
Sugar Refining, Rubber,
Chemicals

LUBUMBASHI–LIKASI
Machinery, Nonferrous Metals,
Chemicals, Textiles, Rubber

SALISBURY–GWELO–BULAWAYO
Metal Products, Chemicals,
Transportation Equipment, Clothing,
Building Materials, Wood Products,
Chemicals, Iron & Steel

JOHANNESBURG–WITWATERSRAND
Iron & Steel, Machinery, Electrical Goods,
Chemicals, Building Materials, Textiles,
Food Processing, Printing

PORT ELIZABETH
Automobile Assembly, Textiles, Rubber

CAPE TOWN
Food & Tobacco, Textiles, Clothing,
Machinery, Chemicals, Leather

TOPOGRAPHY

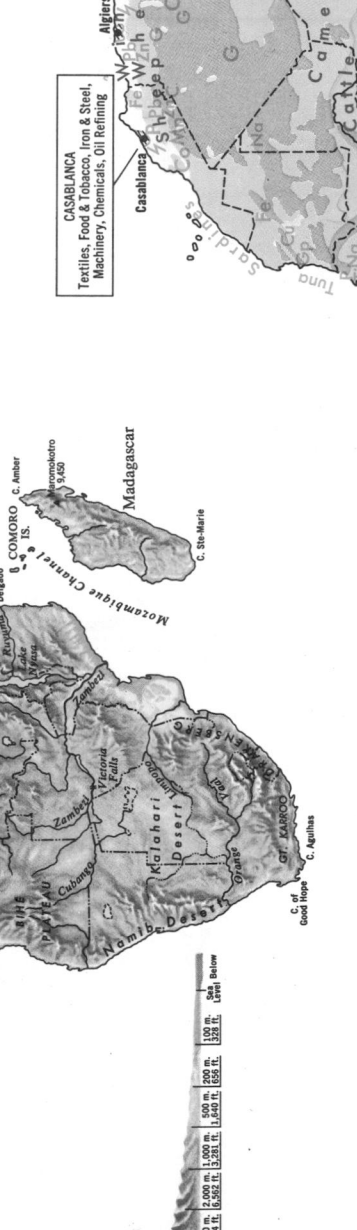

| 5,000 m. | 2,000 m. | 1,000 m. | 500 m. | 200 m. | 100 m. | Sea |
| 16,404 ft. | 6,562 ft. | 3,281 ft. | 1,640 ft. | 656 ft. | 328 ft. | Level | Below |

AGRICULTURE, INDUSTRY and RESOURCES

DOMINANT LAND USE

- Cereals, Horticulture, Livestock
- Cash Crops, Mixed Cereals
- Cotton, Cereals
- Diversified Tropical Crops
- Plantation Agriculture
- Oases
- Pasture Livestock
- Nomadic Livestock Herding
- Forests
- Nonagricultural Land

MAJOR MINERAL OCCURRENCES

Ab	Asbestos	G	Natural Gas	Sb	Antimony
Ag	Silver	Gp	Gypsum	Sn	Tin
Al	Bauxite	Gr	Graphite	So	Soda Ash
Au	Gold	K	Potash	Ti	Titanium
Be	Beryl	Mi	Mica	U	Uranium
C	Coal	Mn	Manganese	V	Vanadium
Co	Cobalt	Na	Salt	W	Tungsten
Cr	Chromium	O	Petroleum	Zn	Zinc
Cu	Copper	P	Phosphates	⩰	Water Power
D	Diamonds	Pb	Lead		Major Industrial Areas
Fe	Iron Ore	Pt	Platinum		

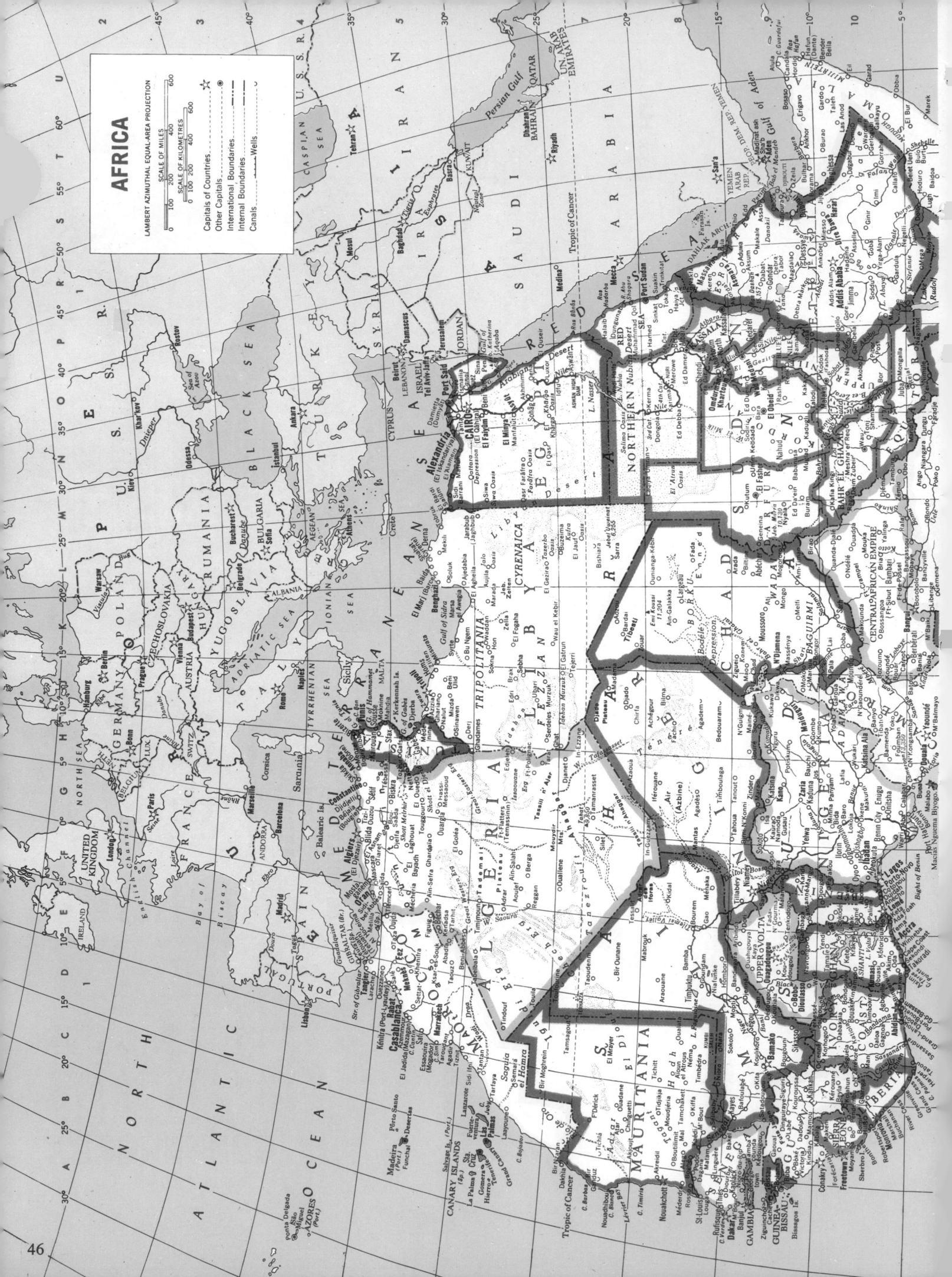

46

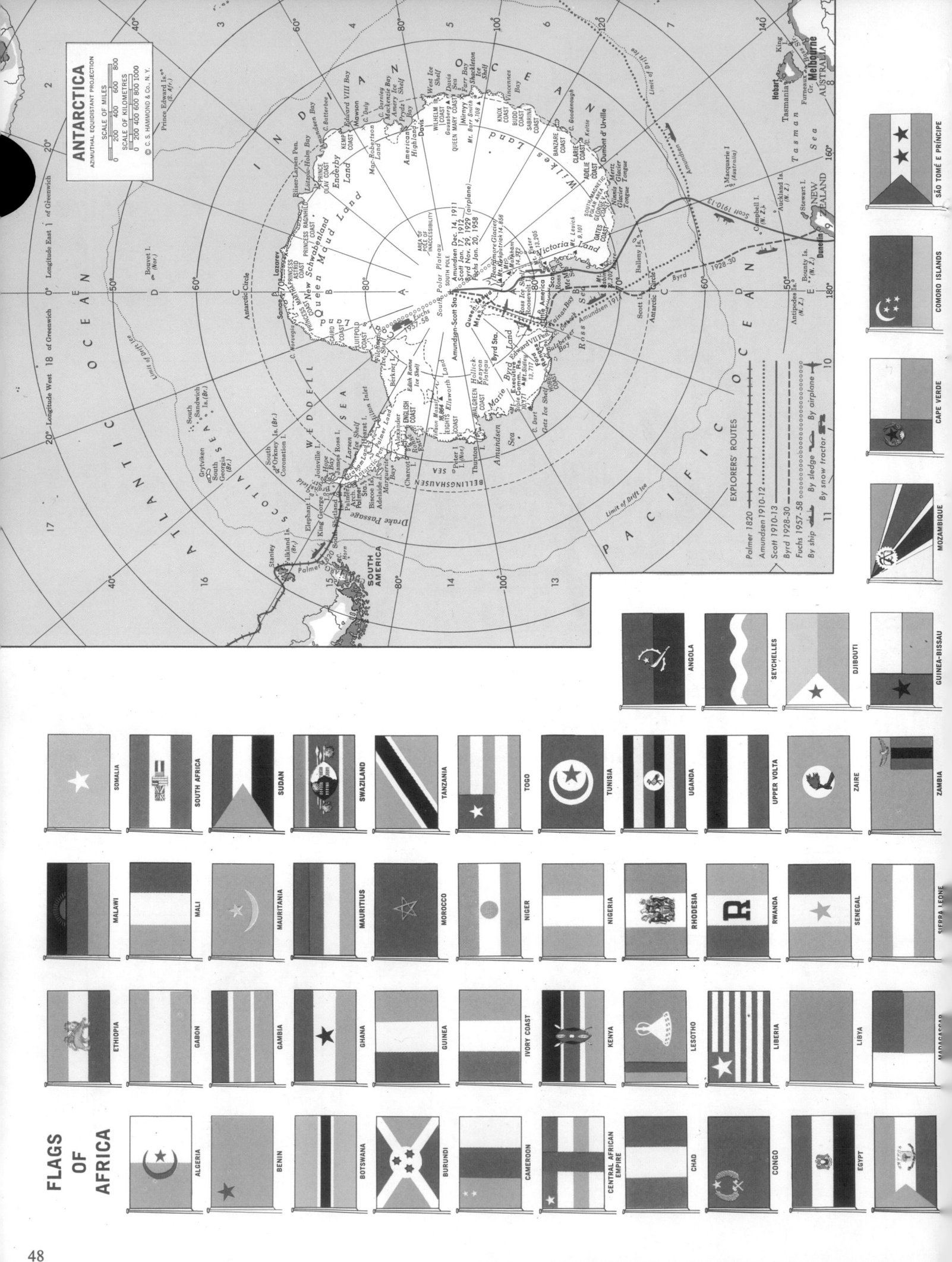

ANTARCTICA
AZIMUTHAL EQUIDISTANT PROJECTION

SCALE OF MILES
0 200 400 600 800

SCALE OF KILOMETRES
0 200 400 600 800 1000

© C. S. HAMMOND & CO., N. Y.

EXPLORERS' ROUTES

Palmer 1820
Amundsen 1910-12
Scott 1910-13
Byrd 1928-30
Fuchs 1957-58

By ship   By sledge   By snow tractor   By airplane

FLAGS OF AFRICA

SÃO TOMÉ E PRÍNCIPE

COMORO ISLANDS

CAPE VERDE

MOZAMBIQUE

ANGOLA

SEYCHELLES

DJIBOUTI

GUINEA-BISSAU

SOMALIA

SOUTH AFRICA

SUDAN

SWAZILAND

TANZANIA

TOGO

TUNISIA

UGANDA

UPPER VOLTA

ZAIRE

ZAMBIA

MALAWI

MALI

MAURITANIA

MAURITIUS

MOROCCO

NIGER

NIGERIA

RHODESIA

RWANDA

SENEGAL

SIERRA LEONE

ETHIOPIA

GABON

GAMBIA

GHANA

GUINEA

IVORY COAST

KENYA

LESOTHO

LIBERIA

LIBYA

MADAGASCAR

ALGERIA

BENIN

BOTSWANA

BURUNDI

CAMEROON

CENTRAL AFRICAN EMPIRE

CHAD

CONGO

EGYPT

48

Geography

C O N T E N T S   G U I D E

	Page		Page
Africa	211	Italy	24
African Geography Dictionary	217	Mexico	8
Air Travel Distances	76	New Zealand	42
American Geography Dictionary	85	North America	2
Antarctica	226	Scandinavia	23
Asia	199	South America	16–17
Asian Geography Dictionary	207	Spain and Portugal	25
Australia	219	Union of Soviet	
Bibliography	250	Socialist Republics	28
Canada:	141	United States	6–7
Cities	148, 150	West Indies	12
National Parks	146	World	1
Canadian Geography Dictionary	151	Mexico	156
Central America	157	National Parks and Monuments	62
Cities, U.S.: Over 30,000	137	New Zealand	223
25 Largest	71	North America	55
Dependencies, U.S.	82	Place Names, Meanings of	233
Elevation—Highest and Lowest		Population, Growth by States	65
Points by States	60	Population, Rank by States	70
Europe	169	Population, Urban Places	137
European Geography Dictionary	182	Questions, Review	242
Facts About the Earth	53	South America	161
Geographical Discovery	51	Geography Dictionary	166
Maps		State Parks, Number and Acres	64
Africa	46–47	United States:	59
Antarctica	48	Century of Growth	72–73
Asia	31	West Indies	159
Australia	42	World Statistics—Tables:	
Balkan States	26	Cities	225
British Isles	20	Countries	231
Canada	3	Islands	228
Central America	10	Lakes	230
Europe	18	Mountains	227
France	21	Ports	218
Germany	22	Rivers	229
Indochinese Peninsula	40	Waterfalls	226

Longs Peak, highest point in the snow-capped Front Range of the Rocky Mountains. Named for explorer Stephen Long, it rises 14,255 feet in Rocky Mountain National Park.

Mt. Rushmore National Memorial was established in 1929 and completed in 1941 in the Black Hills. Sculptor Gutzon Borglum and his son Lincoln carved the colossal busts of Washington, Jefferson, Theodore Roosevelt, and Lincoln.

Spider Rock, Canyon de Chelly, Monument Valley, Arizona. The giant sandstone pinnacle, in an area inhabited by Navajos, rises 800 feet from the canyon floor. The valley became a national monument in 1931.

Bryce Canyon (Utah), covering 56 square miles, was created a national park in 1928. Named for pioneer Ebenezer Bryce, it is noted for magnificent forests and the natural coloring of its eroded rock formations. (*Union Pacific Railroad*)

Above: **Castle Geyser,** Yellowstone National Park, Wyoming. The cone resembles the ruins of an old castle. Established in 1872, Yellowstone is the oldest national park. Left: **Bridalveil Falls** drops 620 feet to the floor of Yosemite Valley in California.

Below: **Grand Canyon,** Arizona, from Bright Angel Point, North rim. The Colorado gorge, 217 miles long and 4–18 miles wide, is a spectacular example of erosion. Discovered in 1540 by Garcia Lopez de Cardeñas, the canyon records vast geologic change.

PHOTOGRAPHY IN EARTH SCIENCE—This panorama of Nevada, Arizona, and California was taken from an aircraft at near-space altitude. Through infrared focusing, the camera defines earth characteristics not evident in normal color or black and white. The results aid in establishing earth resources criteria. The deep reds are reflected from chlorophyll in plant life. In the foreground above is Las Vegas, with scattered lawns and trees. The stream from Las Vegas to Lake Mead (center left) provides moisture for growth along its banks. Flowing from Lake Mead to Lake Mojave, the Colorado River moves through rocky areas without plant life. Right of Lake Mojave lies Needles, Cal., whose irrigated fields provide the large red pattern. At left are mountains tinged with red, indicating forests. For geologists, tonal differences provide a key to earth structure, stratification, and the location of river deltas. Such information is also useful to agronomists and foresters in preserving natural resources. Future applications include determining crop life-cycle states and yields. The data will also assist in locating hidden minerals and oil deposits. Other contributions will lie in expanding air and water pollution controls. (*Courtesy Hycon, Monrovia, Cal.*)

Geography

INTRODUCTION

THE word geography comes from *ge* and *grapho*, two Greek words which, in combination, mean a description of the earth. Geography differs from geology and other sciences of the earth in the fact that geography studies the earth as the abode of mankind. It is closely related, in certain of its aspects, to the sciences of economics, history, astronomy, botany, zoology, and meteorology.

Divisions. Geography is usually classified, on the basis of its subject matter, into mathematical geography, physical geography, or physiography, and biological geography. Mathematical geography concerns the size, shape, and movements of the earth; physical geography deals with the layers of the earth's surface—land, sea, and air; and biological geography studies the life conditions of plants and animals, on the one hand, and of man on the other.

The geography of man discusses the races of mankind and their distribution throughout the earth; it discusses also density of population and the various types of human occupation—fishing, hunting, pasturing, agriculture, mining, manufacture, and commerce. That part of human geography which is concerned with man's industries is classified as economic, or commercial, geography. The study of mankind by countries is known as political geography.

Development of Geography. Nearly all parts of the world have been inhabited by men from very early times and, consequently, have been known in a certain sense. Such knowledge, however, does not constitute geography. The science of geography begins only when people attempt to describe by word or chart the relations of one part of the earth's surface to other parts.

Advance in geographical knowledge has been due mainly to exploration and enterprise. The rate of advance, however, has been highly irregular. Three chief periods of progress may be roughly distinguished: first, that of ancient Greece, when the first serious attempts were made to describe and to explain scientifically the varied conditions of different localities; secondly, the age of discovery, from the 15th to the 19th century, when the main features of the earth were finally learned; and, lastly, the modern scientific period, more or less overlapping the second in time and continuing to the present, when the utmost resources of science have been systematically utilized to chart and to describe every part of the earth's surface.

As a descriptive and systematic science, geography is of comparatively recent origin. Its foundation is due in large part to Alexander von Humboldt, a German scholar who was born in 1769. He developed and supported with observed facts the concept of the earth in evolution, which had been previously set forth in outline by the philosopher Kant. Advancing from this fundamental conception, recent geographers have devoted much of their attention to studies of the effect of geographical environment on human settlement and ways of life.

The Earth and Mankind. The degree of man's dependence on the earth is apt to be obscured in a highly developed society. In point of fact, both in the state of savagery and of civilization, his activities and very life rest solely on the bounty of the earth. A sudden rise or fall of 100° in the mean temperature of the earth's surface would wipe out civilization and probably exterminate the human race.

Climate not only determines what plants and animals can thrive so as to enable any people to subsist, but it exerts decisive effects on their appearance, their stature, their vigor, and their health. The tropics, while bountiful, discourage activity. The polar regions restrict all manner of life. But the seasonal changes of the temperate zones not only predispose populations to activity but force them to make use of their resources to provide against the winters.

Mountains and coasts have served to restrict settlements; rivers and plains, to extend them. Each of these natural features has placed a characteristic imprint on the society which it dominated, largely fashioning its mode of life, its customs, morals, and temperament.

With the growth of inventions, however, the range of the earth's gifts to man has multiplied and has tended to free him from the effects of a restricted environment. Minerals and waterfalls, once useless, now provide shelter, heat, light, power, and transportation in extraordinary abundance. These developments, together with the world-wide exchange of commodities, processes, and ideas, multiply the bonds of man to the earth but also make these bonds much more elastic. To an ever greater degree the earth itself, rather than any particular locality, is becoming the environment of each person. One result is a tendency toward uniformity. Another is an extremely rapid increase of population, the growing pressure of which, in the opinion of many observers, is full of portent for human institutions and customs.

Geography in Schools. The first modern geography in English which was written explicitly for use in schools appeared in 1746. It was called *Introduction to Geography* and was published in England by J. Cowley, "geographer to his Majesty." The first professor of geography in an American university was Arnold Henry Guyot, appointed by Princeton University in 1854.

The study of geography has long held an important place in the public schools of America. The manner of teaching the subject, however, has changed considerably in the past 70 years. The major emphasis was first placed on the facts of political geography. More especially in the years following 1890, physical geography received greater attention. In the past few decades, the study of "home geography" has been favored, chiefly as a means of making pupils familiar with geographical causes operating in their own neighborhood; this familiarity in turn has enabled them to see how larger regions of the earth are affected by the same causes. Finally, with the development of human geography, regional studies are encouraged in order to determine the factors of all kinds which have affected human habitation in a particular region or may be expected to do so in the future.

Value of the Study. A knowledge of geography is necessary for the intelligent reading of newspapers and of books. Such knowledge enables one, as a citizen, to form sounder opinions of the foreign countries with which our government has relations or with which our merchants deal. The study may also impart a new interest to the materials which we handle, enabling us to picture, more or less accurately, the distant scenes from which have come our tin, cork, rubber, tea, chocolate, and other articles of common use.

Geography is, to a large extent, the study of causes. To learn many facts, more or less isolated, about countries, rivers, cities, and peoples has its value. It is more enlightening, however, to understand the *causes* behind the facts; to know, for example, *why* Arizona is dry, *why* northern Europe is warmer than Labrador, and *why* Chicago has grown up where it is. Familiarity with the reasons lying behind such facts gives us a new interest also in the conditions of our own locality.

Travel. Improved means of transportation within the past century have made it possible for hundreds now to travel for each one that did so in earlier times. Travel has become a new form of enjoyment and a new means of instruction. The novelty of unfamiliar scenes, the glamor of places famous in history, the fascination of nature in its most charming or its most desolate aspects, engage the mind and bring home to it the varied panorama of the great world in which we live.

Geography a Substitute for Travel. Many people, however, lack the financial means and the leisure necessary for extensive travel. For such people, geography provides the nearest equivalent of travel. By the printed word and by picture, one may visit the most interesting and the most remote parts of the world. He may see the head-hunters of Borneo, the crowded cities of China, the treeless steppes of central Asia, or the jungles of the Amazon. Under the guidance of what he reads, he may take a trip to the "land of the midnight sun," and he may enjoy the beauties of Yellowstone Park or of Paris.

Plan of Department of Geography. In the following pages, the geography of the world is treated by continents. This plan has at least two distinct advantages over an alphabetic arrangement of geographical topics. In the first place, it is possible in this way to bring into strong relief the contrast between the continents. Secondly, the reader is enabled to obtain a single view of each continent as a whole. There are certain aspects of geography which cannot be classified under continents. Such, for example, are the oceans, the zones, and the movements of the earth. A treatment of these general facts concerning the earth precedes the description of the continents.

Treatment of Countries. Following the general account of each continent, the countries and other political divisions within it are described in more detail. For the United States, the treatment has been made regional, each subdivision consisting of a group of states having a common geographic character. An exception is made of the off-shore states of Hawaii and Alaska, each of which is treated separately. Moreover, information regarding the individual states has been grouped in several tables, carefully prepared with a view to conciseness, easy visualization, and ready comparison.

Cities and Other Points of Interest. The description of countries or other divisions is followed by sections in which, under alphabetic arrangement, the cities, towns, and other places of interest are each accorded a special treatment. In the selection of such places, the guiding principle has been the importance of the place and its interest to the general reader. The lists contain the capitals of all countries as well as those of the American states and of the Canadian provinces. They contain also the important cities in all parts of the world. A very large number of other places are included. Some of these are notable for historic reasons, such as

Yorktown or Ypres. Others are chosen because their names have become associated with a particular industry, such as Waltham, Mass., or Limoges, France. Many places are described which are not incorporated settlements. These include such features as Pikes peak, Mammoth cave, and Lincoln highway in America or Belleau woods and the Riviera in Europe. An instructive section has been added also on the meanings of place names.

Scope. In mere extent of text, this department far exceeds the volume of the average school geography, being more thorough in treating each subject and more inclusive in the selection of topics, especially topics that have recently become important. The point of especial distinction, however, is the addition of material having a travel interest. The study of geography is thereby made more entertaining and far more helpful to the student.

Purposes. The department of geography is not intended to be used as a textbook for the schoolroom. It is too complete for that purpose. On the other hand, it does not purport to describe every place, without exception which appears on the map. In other words, it is not an atlas or a gazetteer. Consequently, it is neither dry nor mechanical. It is much more than a textbook or an atlas.

This treatment of geography has three principal purposes. In the first place, it contains a rich store of supplementary material both for the student and for the teacher of geography. Secondly, when used in connection with the review questions, it provides an extremely valuable aid for any person desiring systematically to study geography by himself. Lastly, it is an excellent source of general information for all ages and all classes of people.

Statistics. The figures published in this department have been prepared with unusual care. Those representing factors which constantly change, such as population and trade, are based, in all cases, on the latest official bulletins.

It is a fact that even in statistics representing such constant factors as the length of coast lines and areas of districts adjoining the sea, a considerable divergence often appears among geographical authorities. Such differences are frequently due to methods of measurement. A coast line, for example, may be surveyed from headland to headland, and the result obtained may be much less than the total arrived at by including all the insignificant inlets. Somewhat similar difficulties arise in statistics regarding lengths of rivers, heights of mountains, and many other such measurements.

These difficulties, however, detract nothing from the real value of statistics, which is to enable the reader to make comparisons. For ordinary purposes it is of no significance whether Mount Everest is 29,002 or 29,000 feet high or whether Mount McKinley is exactly 20,300 feet in altitude. The essential value of the figures is in showing that Mount Everest is about 9000 feet higher than Mount McKinley. In spite of such considerations, however, the statistics in this department represent the most painstaking efforts to reconcile authorities where they differ and to attain a degree of accuracy that is difficult to find in similar material.

Maps. Geographical position has been indicated throughout the text with a view to enabling the reader, by consulting the pertinent maps, to see at a glance the location of the principal places. The maps have been recently revised and take into account the numerous changes that have occurred during and since World War II.

Spelling of Names. The form of the names in the text has been made, in most instances, to conform with the spelling adopted by the United States Geographic Board. Those names which have not been made the subject of decisions by this board follow the spelling of the National Geographic Society, or, failing authority from either source, they conform to Webster's *Gazetteer*.

GEOGRAPHICAL DISCOVERY

ANCIENT ideas of the earth were vastly different from those of the present day. One of the earliest concepts of the earth is that revealed by the Homeric poems, written about 1000 B. C. In these poems, the earth is supposed to be a circular disk surrounded by a river, which was called Ocean.

Phœnicians. Such early views were probably based on the reports of the Phœnicians, who were the earliest navigators known to history. From these people, too, in all likelihood, came the information which the Hebrews had regarding such distant points as those called, in Hebrew literature, Gomer, Sinim, Cush, Sheba, Ophir, and Tarshish. Gomer is believed to mean the northern shores of the Black Sea; Sinim is conjectured to be southern Egypt; Cush is identified with Abyssinia; Sheba, with Yemen in southwestern Arabia; Ophir is placed in southeastern Africa; and Tarshish, in southeastern Spain.

Africa was circumnavigated as early as 600 B. C. by a Phœnician expedition. This expedition was dispatched by Necho, king of Egypt, with orders to sail through the Red Sea into the Indian Ocean and around Africa. After three years, the ships returned by way of the Strait of Gibraltar and the Mediterranean Sea.

Greeks. The earlier Greek geographers, Hecatæus and Herodotus, both of the 5th century B. C., did not advance beyond the idea of the earth conceived of as a disk. Hecatæus in his *Periodos*, "Trip around the World," and Herodotus in his *Histories*, added immensely to the available knowledge of different lands and peoples, each writer having traveled over most of the world as then known.

Aristotle, living in the 4th century B. C., has the honor of being the first to demonstrate that the world is a sphere. He based his proof on two facts which could be tested by observation: first, that the shadow of the earth thrown on the moon during an eclipse is always circular; and, secondly, that the horizon always retreats as the observer advances. To Aristotle also is due the division of the earth into a torrid zone bounded by two temperate zones with a frigid zone surrounding each pole.

It was in this period that maps of the world first showed the land surface of the earth surrounded by a wide expanse of sea instead of by a river. The name Ocean, which formerly designated the river, was applied to this sea. The sea was believed to extend around the globe, bathing on every side the great land mass in the eastern hemisphere. Our modern sense of ocean, as one of the major divisions of the water surface of the earth, arose since the 15th century, when it was learned that the universal sea was divided into parts by the continent of America and by other land areas previously unknown.

The inclination of the earth to the plane of its orbit was first measured by Eratosthenes, who lived in the 3d century B. C. His result was correct within 23 minutes of the angle as determined by the most accurate modern instruments. Eratosthenes also calculated the size of the earth and devised a system of indicating geographical position by drawing two lines of reference, one from east to west and the other from north to south. The location of any place could thus be indicated by giving its distance north or south of the one line and east or west of the other line.

The lines of reference drawn on the earth by Eratosthenes suggested to Hipparchus of Nicæa, in the 2d century B. C., the idea of drawing a series of circles of latitude and longitude. One circle was drawn for each degree on the earth's surface. In the 2d century A. D., Ptolemy, a Greek of Alexandria, compiled a work on geography which embraced all that was known of the earth until his day. This work formed the starting point of modern geography.

According to Ptolemy's geography, Africa extended southward and eastward, eventually joining Asia. The two continents thus enclosed the Indian Ocean. The farthest land to the north was called Thule, probably the Shetland islands. Something also was known of the Baltic Sea, western Russia, the great plains of Asia, and even the distant countries of China and Japan.

Romans. The Romans did little in the field of scientific geography. For the purpose of conquest and organization, however, surveys were made of practically all the territory surrounding the Mediterranean Sea, as well as of France, part of Britain, and Asia Minor. Nero dispatched an expedition in search of the source of the Nile river about 60 A. D. In the 6th century A. D., Justinian sent two monks to China, who returned with eggs of the silkworm concealed in a hollow cane. The culture of the silkworm was thus introduced into Europe.

Middle Ages. With the general decline of learning after the downfall of Rome, Ptolemy's work was forgotten in Europe, and people reverted to a primitive conception of the earth, believing it to be flat. Maps of this period frequently show Jerusalem as the center of the terrestrial disk.

The Arabs, however, translated Ptolemy's work into their own language, keeping alive a knowledge of geography as it had been developed. Arab astronomers measured a degree of latitude on the plains of Mesopotamia, deducing from it the approximate size of the earth. Prominent among Arabian books of travel was the *Meadows of Gold*, written by Masudi about 950 A. D. It contained geographical observations collected by its author, who, with this purpose in view, traversed all the countries lying between China and Spain. Ptolemy's geography became known to Europe by translation into Latin from the Arabic and later from the original Greek text.

Earliest Modern Discoveries. Before the period of the Renaissance, a number of notable voyages and discoveries were recorded. Greenland was sighted by Northmen in the 9th century, and, in the following century, men of the same race landed on the coast of North America. Little geographic interest, however, was aroused by these discoveries or by the trips of monks to remote parts of Asia and of Africa in search of a mythical Christian kingdom, ruled over by Prester John. The travels of Marco Polo, however, in the 14th century, did much to stimulate interest in distant lands. He visited the Far East, where he ruled a province of China for three years. A golden statue of him in a great temple at Soochow, China, still bears witness to his former influence in the Orient.

Age of Discovery. The 15th and the 16th century were distinguished by extraordinary activity in exploration. The previous invention of the mariner's compass did much to facilitate the sea voyages of the period.

Portuguese sailors discovered the Madeira islands and, by 1482, had sailed south as far as the Congo river. In 1486, a Portuguese ship sighted the Cape of Good Hope, and, 11 years later, Vasco da Gama doubled the cape and finally reached India.

In 1492, Columbus, sailing west, discovered the New World and thereby revolutionized the prevailing conception of the earth. Within 30 years from his historic landing on San Salvador island, the whole east coast of America from Greenland to Cape Horn had been explored, and the globe had been circumnavigated. Before the middle of the 16th century, America's west coast had been explored as far north as San Francisco bay, and Spanish colonists had settled in various parts of South America. On the other side of the world, progress had been made in knowledge of countries whose coasts were bathed by the Indian Ocean, including

Arabia, East Africa, India, and the great Malay archipelago. Apart from the Portuguese and the Spaniards, the nations most active in discovery at this period were the English, the Dutch, and the French.

The 17th and the 18th century witnessed the discovery of Australia, Tasmania, and New Zealand. Captain Cook, an English navigator, in the last quarter of the 18th century, explored widely in the Pacific Ocean, adding Hawaii and numerous other islands to the known world.

The task of geographical discovery was completed in the 19th and the 20th century. The chief accomplishments in this period were the exploration of Africa; the forcing of a passage by water northwest of America and of a passage through the ice-bound seas northeast of Asia; and, finally, the discovery of the north and south poles. The exploration of Africa is described in the section devoted to that continent.

Polar Exploration. Repeated efforts were made, from the 16th century on, to sail around North America's northern boundary. It was thought for many years that North America terminated in a northern cape, just as South America tapers to a cape at its southern extremity. As no such cape was found in the north, many later geographers believed that North America extended in an unbroken land mass to the north pole. The overland journeys of Hearne and Mackenzie, however, refuted that error and proved that an ocean washed the northern limits of the western continent.

Among the navigators who tried to effect this northwest passage from the Atlantic to the Pacific Ocean were Davis, Hudson, Baffin, Scoresby, Parry, Ross, and Franklin. Finally, in 1851-53, McClure, entering from Bering Strait, was forced to abandon his ship on Banks Land, but he and his crew were brought out to Baffins Bay by another expedition, thus demonstrating the northwest passage. In 1903-06, Roald Amundsen sailed by a more southern route from Baffins Bay to San Francisco. In 1878-79 Nordenskjöld sailed through the northwest passage from Sweden to Bering Strait.

The quest for the north pole engaged many explorers during the latter half of the 19th century. These include Greely, Nansen, and the duke of Abruzzi. The goal was actually reached, however, by Peary, who, on April 7, 1909, raised the American flag over the north pole.

Land was first found in the south polar region by Pierre Bouvet (French) in 1739. The first explorer known to have crossed the Antarctic Circle was Cook (British) in 1773. Further explorations were made by Bellingshausen, Biscoe, Weddell, Ross, Dumont d'Urville, and Borchgrevink. The pole was finally reached December 14, 1911, by the Norwegian explorer Amundsen. Just five weeks later, Captain Scott, an Englishman, arrived there. While returning, Scott perished a few miles from a relief station.

Recent Geographical Research. With the discovery of the two poles, the age of discovery came to an end. The next and more arduous step remained, to investigate and map regions already known only in outline. Mount Everest, the world's highest mountain, was first scaled in 1953 by Hillary (New Zealand) and Norkay (Nepal). Mapping of inaccessible regions was advanced rapidly by many countries through the use of aerial photography. Many geographical expeditions were sponsored by scientific societies, notably the National Geographic Society of Washington, D.C., which pioneered in reporting its findings in popular form. A spectacular example of Antarctic research was Richard E. Byrd's establishment of a "Little America" in 1929 not far from the south pole.

More systematic researches were undertaken in the so-called Geophysical Year (1957–58), when all the resources of science were brought to bear on the mysteries of the earth. Meanwhile, with an assist from atomic devices, geology and archeology were unlocking many of the secrets of historical geography, aiming to show what the earth was like in earlier ages. *See Antarctica, Geophysical Year.*

DATES OF GEOGRAPHICAL DISCOVERIES*

	B. C.
Phœnicians circumnavigate Africa	600
Himilco, Carthaginian merchant, at Ierne (Ireland)	500
Hanno, Carthaginian navigator, off Sierra Leone, Africa	470
Alexander the Great in the Punjab, India	327
Nearchus, Greek general, in the Indian Ocean	325
Pytheas of Marseilles at Ultima Thule (Shetland Islands)	320
Eudoxus, Greek sailor, crosses the Arabian Sea	118
Julius Cæsar in England	55
	A. D.
Cosmas Indicopleustes, Egyptian merchant, in India	550
Suleiman, Arab trader, voyages to China	850
Ottar, Norwegian explorer, rounds the North Cape, Europe	852
Sindbad the Sailor on the coast of India	9th c.
Al Masudi, Arab traveler, in China	920
Iceland colonized from Norway	930
Eric the Red colonizes Greenland	982
Benjamin of Tudela, Spanish traveler, visits India	1160–73
Friar John of Carpini, visits Karakorum, Asia	1246
Rubruquis, Flemish traveler, explores the Caspian Sea	1247
Marco Polo, the Venetian, at the Court of Kublai Khan, China	1270
Fr. Odoric, of Pordenone, Italian monk, enters Lhasa, Tibet	1320
Ibn Batuta, the Arab traveler, reaches Quiloa, E. Africa	1329
Ibn Batuta visits Timbuktu and the Niger River	1350
Clavijo, a Spanish knight, ambassador at Samarkand	1405
Zarco, Portuguese navigator, sights the Madeira Islands	1418
Conti, Italian traveler, explores southern China	1440
Cintra, Portuguese navigator, at Sierra Leone, Africa	1462
Cão, Portuguese navigator, discovers the Congo River, Africa	1484
Bartholomew Diaz, Portuguese navigator, doubles the Cape of Good Hope, South Africa	1488
Covilhão, Portuguese ambassador, penetrates into Abyssinia	1490
Columbus, Italian navigator, discovers San Salvador Islands, West Indies	1492
Vasco da Gama, Portuguese navigator, voyages to India by the Cape route	1497
John Cabot, Italian navigator in English service, lands on coast of North America	1497
Vespucci, Italian navigator, coasts along North American and South American shores†	1497–1503
Cabral, Portuguese explorer, discovers South America	1500
Pinzon, Spanish navigator, at the mouth of the Amazon, South America	1500
Columbus sights Central America	1502
Varthema, Italian traveler, visits the sacred city of Mecca	1503
Serrão, Portuguese sailor, reaches the Molucca Islands by way of India	1512
Balboa, Spanish explorer, discovers the Pacific Ocean	1513
Ponce de Leon, Spanish explorer, traverses Florida	1513
Solis, Spanish navigator, ascends the La Plata River, South America	1516
Grijalva, Spanish navigator, touches coast of Mexico	1518
Cortés, Spanish adventurer, in central Mexico	1518
Expedition of Magellan circumnavigates the globe	1521–22
Pizarro, Spanish adventurer, in Peru	1532
Cartier, French navigator, in the Gulf of St. Lawrence	1534
Coronado, Spanish explorer, marches from Mexico through Arizona and New Mexico to Kansas	1539–42
Alarcon, Spanish explorer, reaches the Colorado River, U. S.	1540
Cardenas, Spanish explorer, at the Grand Canyon, Arizona	1540

*Dates for ancient and medieval discoveries in various instances are only approximate.

†According to his narratives, the trustworthiness of which is disputed.

	A. D.
De Soto, Spanish explorer, discovers the Missis-sippi River	1541
Orellana, Spanish explorer, descends the Amazon	1541
Cabrillo, Portuguese navigator, on California coast	1542
St. Francis Xavier, Spanish Jesuit missionary, visits Japan	1549
Chancellor, English navigator, reaches the White Sea, Russia	1553
Willoughby, English navigator, sights Nova Zembla	1553
Gaetano, Spanish navigator, lands on the Hawaiian Islands	1555
Jenkinson, English traveler, reaches Persia	1561
Frobisher English navigator, in Frobisher Bay, Arctic North America	1576
Davis, English navigator, in Davis Strait, Arctic North America	1587
Barentz, Dutch navigator, at Spitzbergen, Arctic Europe	1594
Western Australia sighted by Portuguese sailors	1601
Gosnold, English navigator, at Cape Cod, United States	1602
Göes, a native of the Azores, traverses Central Asia	1603–05
Champlain, French explorer, on Maine coast, United States	1604
Torres, Spanish navigator, in New Guinea	1606
Smith, English colonist, in Chesapeake Bay	1608
Hudson, English navigator, ascends Hudson River to present site of Albany	1609
Champlain, French colonizer, discovers Lake Champlain	1609
Hudson, English navigator, discovers Hudson Bay, Canada	1610
Baffin, English navigator, in Baffin Bay	1616
Hartog, Dutch navigator, on the Australian coast	1616
Schouten, Dutch navigator, discovers Cape Horn, South America	1616
Nicolet, French voyager, reaches Lake Michigan	1634
Tasman, Dutch navigator, at Tasmania	1642
Deshnev, Russian navigator, sights Bering Strait	1648
Fr. Menard, French missionary, reaches Lake Superior	1660
Marquette and Joliet, French explorers, reach the Arkansas River	1673
Fr. Hennepin, Flemish missionary, at Niagara Falls, Canada	1678
Fr. Hennepin, at St. Anthony Falls, U. S.	1680
La Salle, French explorer, descends the Missis-sippi	1682
Fr. Kino, Spanish Jesuit, discovers the Casa Grande ruins, U. S	1694
Bering, Danish navigator. in Bering Strait	1728
Gwosdef, Russian sailor, lands on the Alaskan coast	1731
Verendrye, French explorer, reaches the Rocky Mountains	1740
Karstens Niebuhr, German traveler, explores Arabia	1761–67
Bruce, Scotch traveler, on the Blue Nile, Abys-sinia	1768–73
Hearne, English traveler, discovers Great Slave Lake	1772
Cook, English navigator, first to cross the Ant-arctic circle	1773
Cook, English navigator, explores the Hawaiian Islands	1774–79
Peter Pond, Canadian explorer, reaches Lake Athabaska	1778
La Perouse, French navigator, explores eastern coast of Asia	1787
Mackenzie, Scotch explorer, discovers the Mac-kenzie River, Canada	1789
Gray, American navigator, ascends the Colum-bia River, U. S.	1792
Mungo Park on the Gambia river, West Africa	1795
Humboldt, German scientist, explores South America	1799
Lewis and Clark explore the northwestern United States	1804–06
Colter, American trapper, discovers Yellow-stone Park, U. S.	1807
Hutchins, American pioneer hunter, discovers the Mammoth Cave, United States	1809
Bellingshausen, Russian navigator, on the Ant-arctic continent	1821
Clapperton and Denham, English travelers, cross the Sahara	1822
James Bridger, American explorer, discovers Great Salt Lake, United States	1824
Sturt, English explorer, traverses Australia	1828
Ross, English navigator, in Boothia Felix, Arctic North America	1831

	A. D.
Schoolcraft, American scientist, discovers Lake Itasca	1832
Wilkes, American navigator, on the Antarctic continent	1840
Abbé Huc travels in Tibet	1844
Krapf and Rebmann, German missionaries, at Mt. Kilimanjaro, East Africa	1848
McClure, Irish navigator, achieves the North-west Passage, Arctic Ocean	1851
Boling, American soldier, visits the Yosemite	1851
Livingstone, Scottish missionary, discovers Zam-besi River	1851–56
Kane, American explorer, on Grinnell Land, Arctic North America	1853
Livingstone, Scottish missionary, at Victoria Falls, Africa	1855
Barth, German traveler, explores the Sudan	1856
Burton and Speke, English explorers, discover Lake Tanganyika, Africa	1858
Speke, English explorer, discovers Victoria Nyanza, Africa	1858
Burke and Wills, Irish explorers, cross Australia from south to north	1860–61
Richthofen, German scientist, explores China	1868–72
Przhevalski, Russian traveler, crosses Mongolia	1871–73
Stanley, American explorer, traces the course of the Congo	1876–77
Nordenskjöld, Swedish explorer, accomplishes the Northeast Passage, Arctic Ocean	1878–79
Borchgrevink, Norwegian explorer, at the South Magnetic Pole, Antarctic continent	1899
Hedin, Swedish scientist, explores Central Asia.	1890–1908
Peary, American naval officer, proves the insular character of Greenland	1892
Roald Amundsen, Norwegian navigator, sails through Northwest Passage	1903–06
Peary discovers the North Pole	1909
Amundsen discovers the South Pole	1911

GENERAL FACTS ABOUT THE EARTH

The earth, or globe, is an oblate spheroid; that is, a sphere slightly flattened at two opposite points, called the poles. The two poles are the ends of the axis about which the globe rotates. The north pole is in the Arctic Ocean. The south pole is in the continent of Antarctica, which, directly at the pole, reaches an elevation of about 10,000 feet.

In order to make it possible to describe the exact location of any place on the earth, geographers have drawn around the globe certain circles, to which the position of any point may be referred. The equator is such a circle, encompassing the earth equidistant from the poles. Other circles are drawn parallel to the equator, dividing the distance between the equator and each pole into 90 equal parts. These circles are called parallels of latitude, and the distance between successive circles is called a degree. A degree (°) of latitude measures about 69 miles. Parallels of latitude are numbered from the equator north and south. Thus the north pole lies at 90° north latitude, and the south pole is at 90° south latitude. In passing from the north pole to the south pole, a traveler would traverse 180° of latitude and, in completing the circuit of the earth, he would pass through a total of 360° of latitude.

A second series of circles, 180 in number, is drawn about the earth, each circle passing through both poles. That half of each circle which extends from one pole to the other is called a meridian of longitude. Since each circle consists of 2 meridians, the 180 circles comprise a total of 360 meridians. Meridians are distant from each other about 69 miles at the equator. As one approaches the poles, however, the distance between two successive meridians decreases. Thus a degree of longitude is not constant, but varies from about 69 miles at the equator to zero at the poles. Meridians of longitude are numbered east and west from the meridian passing through Greenwich, England. The 180th meridian of east longitude coincides with the 180th meridian of west longitude, this meridian being the meridian in the western hemisphere corresponding to the Greenwich meridian in the eastern hemisphere.

The rotation of the earth takes place from west to east—the direction opposite to that in which the hands of a clock move. This movement of the earth causes the alternation of day and night.

A second movement of the globe is its revolution about the sun. The revolution takes place in an almost circular orbit. The earth's axis is not perpendicular to the plane of this orbit, but is inclined 23½° away from the perpendicular. To this inclination are due the varying lengths of day and night at different latitudes and in different seasons and also most of the seasonal variations in temperature. It provides the basis also for the division of the earth into zones, or "belts."

The boundaries of the zones are determined by the noonday inclination of the sun's rays to the surface of each zone. Thus the Torrid Zone comprises that part of the earth over which, at some time of the year, the sun is directly overhead. This zone extends for 23½° of latitude north and 23½° of latitude south of the equator, so that it has a total width of 47° of latitude. The North Frigid Zone and the South Frigid Zone, each of which extends 23½° of latitude from the poles toward the equator, comprise those parts of the earth in which, at some time in the year, the sun does not rise above the horizon at noon. Of the two remaining zones,—the North Temperate Zone and the South Temperate Zone,— each occupies 43° of latitude. In these zones, the sun never stands directly overhead and never remains for a whole day beneath the horizon. The variations of temperature between the different seasons are least in the Torrid Zone and are greatest in the two frigid zones.

The Torrid Zone is divided from the North Temperate Zone by the circle called the Tropic of Cancer and from the South Temperate Zone by the Tropic of Capricorn. The North Temperate Zone is separated from the North Frigid Zone by the Arctic circle. The corresponding line of division between the South Temperate Zone and the South Frigid Zone is called the Antarctic circle.

The following statistics regarding the earth are based on the latest research and are the nearest available approximations to the actual facts.

Equatorial diameter (miles) 7,926.6
Polar diameter (miles) 7,899.9
Circumference at the equator (miles) 24,901.7
Meridional circumference (miles) 24,859.4
Area of land surface approximately (square miles)
54,000,000
Area of water surface approximately (square miles)
143,000,000
Total area of the earth's surface approximately (square
miles) 197,000,000
Volume of the earth (cubic miles) 259,900,000,000
Mean density of the earth 5.53
Density of water 1.00
Density of surface rock 2.72
Density at the earth's center 10.87
Pressure at earth's center (tons per square inch) . 22,500
Weight of the earth (tons)   6,592,000,000,000,000,000,000
(Six sextillion five hundred ninety-two quintillion tons)

CONTINENTS, AREA AND POPULATION

The following table gives the area and the population of each of the continents, as estimated by the latest reliable authorities.

In the present state of geographical knowledge, it is impossible to obtain exact and strictly accurate statistics covering such large divisions of land as the continents. Even for North America, Europe, and Australia, all of which are inhabited by civilized peoples, no complete measurement of the area has been made. Only small parts of South America, Asia, and Africa have been surveyed. Consequently, it is impossible to obtain more than a careful estimate of the extent of land surface in each continent.

In arriving at the figures for population, somewhat similar difficulties have been encountered. It still remains impossible to obtain exact statistics for the number of inhabitants in large parts of Asia and of Africa. Official estimates have been utilized for these regions. In all places where regular censuses are taken, the figures here given are based on the latest returns except in a few instances, in which the most recent official estimates are used.

Name	Area Sq. Miles	Population
North America . . .	9,361,767	309,000,000
South America	6,885,321	180,000,000
Europe	1,903,000	455,000,000
U.S.S.R.	8,649,412	238,000,000
Asia	10,630,105	1,946,000,000
Africa	11,703,849	336,000,000
Oceania	3,286,097	18,500,000
Total	52,419,638	3,483,000,000

Source: United Nations, *Statistical Yearbook*, 1969. Land area includes land and inland waters but excludes uninhabited polar regions and some islands.

OCEANS, AREA AND DEPTH

Authorities differ widely in their estimates of the areas of oceans. This is owing in part to the absence of definite boundaries for separating the oceans. It is due also to the fact that, while some authorities include with the oceans various inland seas, such as the Mediterranean or Hudson bay, other exclude them. See *Ocean*.

Name	Estimated Area Sq. Miles	Greatest Depth Feet	Mean Depth Feet
Arctic	4,000,000	13,120	3,840
Atlantic	34,000,000	27,498	12,660
Indian	28,000,000	22,968	12,888
Pacific	71,000,000	36,056	13,440
Southern or Antarctic .	6,000,000	13,932	

HIGHEST, LOWEST, AND MEAN ALTITUDES OF THE CONTINENTS

The following table gives the highest and the lowest point in each of the continents. It will be observed from the figures given that the highest part of the land surface of the earth is the peak of Mount Everest, 29,002 feet above the sea, and the lowest point is the shore of the Dead Sea, which is 1290 feet below the level of the ocean. The land elevation of the world, therefore, varies within the limit of 30,431 feet, or about 5.7 miles. The figures for the mean elevations of the continents are approximations, being the latest estimates published by the United States Geological Survey.

Continent	Mean Elevation* (feet)	Highest Point — Name	Highest Point — Above Sea Level (feet)	Lowest Point — Name	Lowest Point — Below Sea Level (feet)
North America	2,000	Mount McKinley, Alaska	20,270	Death Valley, Cal. . . .	276
South America	1,800	Mt. Aconcagua, Chile-Arg.	22,835	Sea level	. . . .
Europe	980	Mt. Elbrus, Caucasus Mts.	18,481	Caspian Sea, Russia . .	86
Asia	3,000	Mt. Everest, India . . .	29,002	Dead Sea, Palestine . .	1,290
Africa	1,900	Kibo Peak, (Kilimanjaro) Tanganyika	19,565	Libyan Desert	440
Australia	1,000	Mt. Kosciusko, N. S. W.	7,305	Lake Eyre, South Aust. .	38

* Approximate

NORTH AMERICA

THE land mass of the western hemisphere with the adjacent islands is called America. The name was given in honor of Amerigo Vespucci, an Italian navigator who is said to have visited South America in 1499. It is often styled the New World because of its discovery and settlement in modern times by peoples from the eastern hemisphere, now commonly spoken of as the Old World.

Extent of America. The mainland extending from Alaska in the northwest and from Boothia Felix in the northeast to the south end of Patagonia is about 8700 miles long. This immense length is prolonged to about 9600 miles by the vast archipelago north of Hudson bay and by the island of Tierra del Fuego south of Patagonia. Cape Columbia in Grant Land and Cape Morris Jesup in Peary Land are within 450 miles of the north pole. Cape Horn, the southernmost point of Tierra del Fuego, is 2350 miles from the south pole. Greenland belongs to America, but Iceland, though partly in the western hemisphere, is associated with Europe. The area of America, including islands, is about 16 million square miles.

The Two Continents Compared. America comprises the two continents of North America and South America. These are connected by the narrow Isthmus of Panama. Each continent, like Africa, bears some resemblance to a triangle, the base, or shortest line, being along the northern border, and the apex, at the southern end. The climates, however, of the corresponding parts of the two continents are reversed. The northern part of North America is polar in character, while the northern part of South America is tropical. The physical features of America are displayed on a gigantic scale. There are great rivers, fresh-water lakes that are veritable inland seas, long, lofty ranges of mountains, and vast plains.

North America and South America alike have a chain of mountains extending from north to south along their western sides. Moreover, each continent has a broad central plain and a low eastern mountain range, and both continents have magnificent rivers affording access far into the interior. Vast, unbroken plains and immense forests are other characteristic features common to the two continents.

Extent of North America. The name, North America, is assumed by most geographers to mean all the continent, and all the outlying islands, north of the narrowest part of the Isthmus of Panama. Thus defined, North America includes Central America, Mexico, the West Indies, the United States, Canada, Alaska, and Greenland. For convenience of reference, Central America is often regarded as a separate section of the western hemisphere. The area of North America, including islands, is about 8.5 million square miles.

Oceans and Coasts. North America's shores are washed by the waters of three oceans—the Arctic on the north, the Atlantic on the east, and the Pacific on the west. On the south, the Gulf of Mexico and the Caribbean Sea are large bodies of water also associated with North America. Deep indentations mark the Atlantic coast and form many excellent harbors. The Pacific coast, for the most part, is without sheltered bays, and, in consequence, has fewer seaports.

Surface Features. Two mountain systems dominate the surface of the continent. On the east side is the Appalachian system. This is a series of worn-down mountains, very old geologically, which stretch from the coast plain of the Gulf of Mexico northeast to Labrador. On the west side of the continent rise the lofty ranges of the great Cordilleran system. These massive, rugged mountains are of relatively recent geological formation.

Cordilleran System. As a whole, this system extends in a northwest direction from Central America to the northern shores of Alaska. The most important ranges are the Sierra Madre of Mexico and the Rockies of the western United States, Canada, and Alaska. Between the Rocky mountains proper and the Pacific Ocean lie the Sierra Nevada of California, the Cascades of Oregon and Washington, the Selkirks of British Columbia, and the Coast ranges. Each of more than 30 peaks of the Rocky Mountain chain is over 14,000 feet high. Mt. Whitney, with an altitude of 14,495 feet, in California, is the highest peak in the continental United States. Mt. Logan, 19,850 feet high, in Yukon Territory, is the loftiest summit in Canada. Mt. McKinley, with a height of 20,270 feet, in Alaska, is the culminating point of North America.

Between the Appalachian system in the east and the Rocky Mountain system in the west lie the great medial plains. These occupy a central depression extending from the Arctic Ocean to the Gulf of Mexico. In this vast valley are situated Hudson bay, the Great Lakes, and the drainage basins of many large rivers.

Appalachian System. The Appalachian Mountain system, which trends generally northeast and southwest, consists of numerous ranges. Among these are the Great Smoky, the Allegheny, the Blue Ridge, the Catskill, the Adirondack, the Green, and the White mountains in the United States and the Notre Dame mountains in Quebec. The loftiest summit is Mt. Mitchell, 6684 feet high, in North Carolina.

Great Basin. A vast plateau, called the Great Basin, with an elevation of from 5000 to 7000 feet, lies between the lofty Wasatch range of eastern Utah and the still higher Sierra Nevada of eastern California. In this arid region, rivers disappear in sandy wastes or flow into saline marshes and salt lakes. North of the Great Basin is the less elevated and more fertile Columbia River plateau, situated between the Rockies and the Cascades. Between the Rocky mountains and the Coast ranges of Canada, a somewhat lower plateau, called the Northern Interior plateau, extends northwest to Alaska where it joins the Yukon plateau named for the great river which drains it.

Colorado Plateau. South of the Great Basin is an immense elevated tract called the Colorado plateau. This forms a plain that extends far into Mexico but attains its widest development in the southwestern United States. Much of this vast highland is from 7000 to 9000 feet above sea level. In it the Colorado river and its tributaries have carved the most stupendous examples of erosion in the world.

Mexican Plateau. This is the southeastern continuation of the great Colorado plateau. In shape, the Mexican plateau, called also the plain of Anahuac, resembles a broad wedge, with its widest portion adjoining the southwestern United States and with its narrowest portion extending to southern Mexico.

This interior plain is bordered both on the east and on the west by high ranges of the Sierra Madre, those on the west having an average elevation of 10,000 feet. On either side, the mountain slopes which face toward the sea are usually very steep and precipitous, while those which face inland toward the plateau are, for the most part, much more gentle.

The Mexican plateau increases in elevation southward, rising from about 3500 feet above sea level, opposite western Texas, to 9000 feet around the southern border. In the high southern portion lies the famous "valley of Mexico," containing Lake Tezcuco, on the shores of which were built the ancient Aztec capital and the present city of Mexico.

Medial Plains. Because of their immense extent in the northern part of the continent, the medial plains are sometimes called the Arctic valley. The width of this region, measured from the highlands of Labrador to the Rockies of northern Alberta, is fully 2000 miles. Between the Allegheny mountains of Pennsylvania and the Rocky mountains of Colorado, the plains region is about 1400 miles wide. This central depression extends south from the Arctic Ocean to the Gulf of Mexico, a distance of about 3000 miles. In this vast interior portion of the continent lie the drainage basins of large river systems. The most important of these are the Mississippi-Missouri draining into the Gulf of Mexico, the Saint Lawrence flowing into the Atlantic Ocean, the Nelson-Saskatchewan emptying into Hudson bay, and the Mackenzie-Athabaska with outlet to the Arctic Ocean. The total area drained by the four systems is about three million square miles.

Rivers. Numerous navigable rivers afford entrance to the interior of the continent. The Mackenzie and the Yukon, flowing into northern waters, are icebound during the greater part of the year. The Saint Lawrence, which flows into the Gulf of Saint Lawrence, is likewise frozen during the winter months. But portions of the Hudson, the Delaware, the mighty Mississippi with many important tributaries, are open practically all the year, as are also the navigable parts of the Rio Grande, the Colorado, the Sacramento, the Columbia, and numerous lesser streams. These provide transportation for much inland commerce and some furnish water for irrigation purposes.

Lakes. Besides the five Great Lakes in the east central part of the continent, there are several other large lakes. Of these, the most important are Great Bear lake, Great Slave lake, and lakes Winnipeg and Athabaska, situated in central and northwestern Canada. In the western United States is Great Salt lake. This is a relic of a former sea which, in geological times, occupied a large part of the Great Basin.

Glaciers. The most extensive remnants of the ice age on the mainland of North America are found in the coastal mountains of Alaska. Some of the great glaciers in the region bordering on the Gulf of Alaska are hundreds of square miles in extent. These continental glaciers, however, are very small when compared with the immense ice sheet that covers the greater part of Greenland. The higher mountains from Colorado and California northwestward to Alaska contain many glaciers.

Volcanoes. In North America, as in South America, there are extensive volcanic areas in the great mountain system bordering on the Pacific coast. Central America contains many active volcanoes, among the most noted of which are Coseguina, Izalco, Cerro Quemado, Santa Maria, Fuego, and Agua. On the Mexican plateau are situated some of the world's most gigantic volcanic mountains, as, for example, Orizaba, altitude 18,250 feet, and Popocatepetl, with an elevation of 17,876 feet. A short distance west of the plateau is Colima, a very active volcano, which rises to a height of about 13,000 feet. Another noted Mexican volcano is Jorullo.

In the United States, Lassen peak, in California, is the only active volcano. The Cascade range has many volcanic peaks but only a few display signs of volcanic activity. Mt. Saint Helens and Mt. Baker, both in the state of Washington, are said to have been in eruption between 1840 and 1850. Mt. Hood, in Oregon, exhales volcanic vapors. Of volcanic origin also are Mt. Shasta and Mt. Rainier, which rank among the grandest peaks of the continent. In the Rocky mountains, there are but few volcanic peaks, but evidence of volcanic activity is very marked in the geysers and in other wonderful features of Yellowstone national park.

Alaska contains numerous volcanoes, some of which are very active. These are found along the coast ranges of southern Alaska and in the Aleutian islands. Among the more noted of the active or the recently active volcanoes on the mainland are Mt. Fairweather, Mt. Wrangell, and Mt. Katmai. The Aleutian volcanic belt is a narrow chain of islands extending westward from the Alaskan peninsula for a distance of more than 1500 miles. Some 25 of these islands contain one or more volcanoes, either active or only recently extinct. On Unimak island, near the southern mainland, is Mt. Shishaldin, with a symmetrical cone rivaling that of Fuji, Japan, in graceful contour.

Climate. In so vast a continent, extending through 75 degrees of latitude, great variations of climate naturally occur. In the far north, arctic severity rules, while in southern Mexico and Central America the climate is tropical. Most of the central portion of the continent has a temperate climate. However, a marked difference exists between the temperatures of parts of the Atlantic and of the Pacific coast having the same latitude. The climate of Washington or of Oregon, on the Pacific coast, is much milder than the climate of Maine or of Massachusetts, which are Atlantic coast states situated in nearly the same latitudes.

In July, a great inland area in North America becomes much warmer than the waters on the east and west coasts. Compared with the weather then prevailing on the oceans, the summer heat of eastern North America is excessive. Moreover, the winter cold is severer than in European countries of the same latitude. For example, in January, Labrador is 40° F. colder than northern Germany.

As the great interior plain has no mountain ranges crossing it, cold winds from the north sometimes sweep unimpeded far to the south, suddenly causing a fall of many degrees in temperature. Occasionally, these winds destroy early plantings or belated harvests as far south as Texas. In the plains region east of the Rocky mountains, a drop of 110° F. within 48 hours has been recorded. Such great changes of temperature are unknown on the Pacific coast. In the eastern part of the continent, quick changes of temperature occur, especially in winter, but are much less extreme than in the Great Plains region.

Rainfall. Along the Gulf coast from 50 inches to 55 inches of rain fall every year. At some points near the Gulf of Mexico, the annual rainfall exceeds 60 inches. A rainfall of 80 inches in a year is not uncommon in the Puget Sound region, and in some localities on the northern Pacific coast the annual precipitation is more than 100 inches. From Manitoba and central Kansas eastward the annual rainfall averages about 35 inches. On the high plains immediately east of the Rocky mountains, the rainfall seldom exceeds 20 inches annually. In Wyoming west of the Rockies and in Nevada, the rainfall is rarely more than 10 inches. Arizona and southern California contain limited areas which are practically rainless.

Minerals. In mineral wealth, North America leads all the other continents. Gold, silver, iron, copper, lead, zinc, nickel, coal, and other minerals are produced in immense quantities. The continent is the world's chief source of petroleum. Large quantities of natural gas occur in many widely separated regions.

Flora. The flora of the temperate regions of North America is remarkable for the great number of species of trees which it contains. Forests, whose acreage totals hundreds of millions, yield enormous quantities of hard and of soft wood timber. The lowland flora of the North American countries which lie south of the United States is characterized by a profusion of tropical flowers, vines, and trees. Mexican and Central American forests produce mahogany, rosewood, ebony, and other fine cabinet woods. The plant life of the Pacific coast region differs in a marked degree from that of the eastern part of the continent. The pines, spruces, firs, and redwoods of the Pacific slope have no equals in size elsewhere in America. In bulk, the gigantic sequoias or "big trees" of California surpass all other known trees.

Fauna. Many of the animals native to North America closely resemble those found in the temperate parts of Europe and Asia. The bird fauna, for example, is strikingly similar. But the mocking bird, catbird, Baltimore oriole, wild turkey, turkey buzzard, bobolink, sage grouse, and various humming birds represent species found only in America. North America has various other distinctive animals which do not occur in the Old World. Among these are the American bison, popularly called buffalo, the grizzly bear, musk ox, bighorn sheep, Rocky Mountain goat, pronghorn, rattlesnake, Gila monster, and prairie dog.

GREENLAND

The largest island in the world, with the exception of Australia. The island lies northeast of Canada, from which it is separated by Baffin bay and Davis strait. It is almost wholly within the North Frigid Zone and stretches to a point within 450 miles of the north pole. Its estimated area is 840,000 square miles, and it has a maximum length north and south of 1400 miles, with a maximum width of 690 miles.

Physical Features. Greenland is bordered by a rocky shore rising abruptly several hundred feet above the water and cut by numerous deep fiords. The surface is a plateau having an average elevation of about 4500 feet but reaching, at a few points, an altitude of more than 10,000 feet. Spreading over about 85 per cent of the island's area is a covering of perpetual ice. This inland ice buries far below it all but the highest mountains, thereby affording an excellent example of such conditions as prevailed in the ice age. The ice constitutes a huge glacier flowing slowly toward the coasts. Each year it discharges into the ocean icebergs estimated to weigh in the aggregate more than one billion tons. The interior of Greenland contains one of the coldest areas on the globe, in which a temperature of 92° below zero has been recorded.

Area of Habitation. The southwest part of Greenland has a coastal strip which, in the summer, is covered with green lichens, trailing plants, and berries. The musk ox, white bear, wolf, arctic fox, and many varieties of birds subsist there.

This coastal strip was settled by Danes and is an integral part of the Commonwealth of Denmark. A large proportion of the 47,000 inhabitants are Eskimos, who although professing Christianity, still adhere to many of their pagan customs. The main occupations are fishing and hunting; whale oil, seal oil, skins, and eiderdown are exported. Greenland is the only source in the world of the mineral cryolite, or Greenland spar, used in making aluminum; lead, zinc, and wolfram are also mined.

Greenland was so named by Eric the Red, a Norseman who voyaged along the coast about 982 A. D. It was colonized by Scandinavians in the same century. Between 1410 and 1721, however, the island was neglected, and the European settlers disappeared, probably by intermarriage with the Eskimos. The present colony was planted in the 18th century. The capital is Godthaab, with a 1969 population of 3179.

HUDSON BAY

A large inland sea, situated in northeastern North America, and connected with the Atlantic Ocean by Hudson strait. From Fox channel, at the north, to the southern end of James bay, at the south, Hudson bay is about 1300 miles in length. In its main body, it is about 600 miles wide. It lies wholly within the Dominion of Canada, in a region of rigorous climate.

Area and Depth. The area of Hudson bay, estimated at 475,000 square miles, is about three times that of the Baltic Sea, and approximately half that of the Mediterranean. In its main portion, the bay varies in depth from 400 to 600 feet. The southern extension, called James bay, is very shallow except in the center.

Tides and Currents. On the extreme north, Hudson bay communicates with the Arctic Ocean through Fury and Hecla strait and the Gulf of Boothia. From this passage Hudson bay receives much arctic ice. In Fox channel the tide rises 40 feet, producing a strong current by which thick ice floes are driven southward into Hudson strait, where they menace navigation.

Character of Shores. The eastern shore, called the East Main, and the western shore north of Churchill are, for the most part, rocky and fringed with numerous small islands. The western shore is called the West Main. From Churchill southward it is low and flat. A low divide separates the drainage basin of Hudson bay from the two other great drainage basins of Canada, namely, the Mackenzie and the Saint Lawrence.

Tributary Rivers. The most important river system tributary to Hudson bay is the Nelson-Saskatchewan. Within this great drainage system lie the chief wheat producing areas of Manitoba, Saskatchewan, and Alberta. The system includes also the Red River of the North, which drains parts of North Dakota, South Dakota, and Minnesota, in the United States. This river flows north into Lake Winnipeg, the outlet of which is the Nelson river. The Nelson river empties its waters into Hudson bay at Port Nelson on the southwest coast.

Second in importance among tributaries is the Churchill river, which enters the bay at Churchill, about 125 miles northwest of Port Nelson. Its deep, capacious mouth forms the best harbor on the entire coast of Hudson bay. Among other affluents are the Albany river, on the southwest, flowing into James bay, and the Big, the Moose, and the Rupert river entering from the east shore. The total area of the Hudson Bay drainage basin is estimated at 1,486,000 square miles, or about one-half of the entire mainland of Canada.

Fisheries and Fur Trade. Hudson bay contains extensive and valuable fisheries. American whaling vessels often winter at Marble island in the northwest part of the bay, and the cod fisheries extend into Hudson strait. The Hudson's Bay Company has several stations, called factories, at various points on the coast. Of these, York Factory, at the mouth of Hayes river, is the leading trading post. For more than 200 years a cargo of valuable furs has been shipped annually from York Factory to England.

East and west of the northern part of Hudson bay are the Barren Grounds. These are dreary wastes where only stunted forms of vegetable life exist. But this desolate region is the feeding ground of caribou and musk oxen, and of various smaller animals hunted for their fur.

Commercial Importance. From Montreal and from Port Nelson the sailing distance to Liverpool is practically the same. Much of the grain produced in the Canadian Northwest is shipped to Montreal by way of Winnipeg and the Great Lakes. The distance from Winnipeg to Liverpool, by way of Port Nelson or Churchill, is more than 500 miles shorter than by way of Montreal. From Edmonton to Liverpool, by way of Hudson Bay ports, the distance is more than 1000 miles less than by way of Winnipeg and Montreal.

Other conditions being equal, it would be cheaper to export grain to Europe by way of Hudson bay. Wheat exports were begun over this route after the completion in 1929 of a railroad to Churchill. While neither Hudson bay nor Hudson strait is ever entirely frozen over, there is great danger to navigation from floating ice during the greater part of the year. For sailing ships, the season for safe navigation is from about July 15 to October 1.

THE GREAT LAKES

A chain of large fresh-water lakes, situated in the east central part of North America. They include lakes Superior, Huron, Michigan, Erie, and Ontario, and form a part of the boundary between the United States and Canada. None lies entirely within the territory of either country except Lake Michigan, which is situated wholly within the United States.

Area and Drainage Basin. The combined area of these lakes is about 94,600 square miles and constitutes the largest body of fresh water in the world. The land area in their drainage basins exceeds 185,000 square miles. No large river arising in the land flows into any of the Great Lakes; but the Saint Lawrence, the stream through which the system finally drains into the Atlantic, is one of the great rivers of the continent. The depressions occupied by the Great Lakes system are separated by low ridges from two other large drainage systems. One of these, lying on the north, drains into Hudson bay; the other, lying on the south and the west, drains through the Mississippi River system into the Gulf of Mexico.

Outlets and Connections. Lake Superior, situated at the head of the great chain, is the largest and deepest of the series. It empties through the Saint Marys river, 55 miles long, into Lake Huron. At Saint Marys rapids, called also Sault Sainte Marie, and the Soo, the river falls about 20 feet. The Sault Sainte Marie canals and locks, built on both the Canadian and the American side, permit deep-water navigation around these rapids. They form one of the most important artificial waterways in the world.

The outlet of Lake Michigan is the Strait of Mackinac, which empties into Lake Huron at a point near the mouth of the Saint Marys river. Lake Huron drains into Lake Erie through the Saint Clair river, 42 miles long; Saint Clair lake, 29 miles long; and the Detroit river, 28 miles long. Lake Erie empties into Lake Ontario through the Niagara river, 26 miles long. In its course between the two lakes, the Niagara river makes a descent of 326 feet, half of which occurs in one sheer drop at Niagara falls, the most noted of the world's great cataracts.

In order to establish navigation between Lake Erie and Lake Ontario, the Welland canal, 26 miles long, with an elaborate system of locks, was completed in 1833. This connected Port Colborne, on Lake Erie, with Port Dalhousie on Lake Ontario. Enlargements have transformed this early Canadian waterway into an important modern ship canal.

Lake Ontario drains through the Saint Lawrence river, about 750 miles long, into the Atlantic Ocean. In various rapids between the outlet of Lake Ontario and Montreal, the Saint Lawrence river descends nearly to sea level. As Lake Superior, with an altitude of 602 feet, is only 30 feet higher than Lake Erie, it will be seen that most of the descent to sea level is made in the Niagara and Saint Lawrence rivers between Buffalo and Montreal. Despite the rapids, the Saint Lawrence is navigable for downstream boats, including passenger steamers, but a series of canals has been constructed on the Canadian side to permit of upstream navigation.

The total length of the Great Lakes-Saint Lawrence water system is about 2200 miles. From Duluth to Buffalo the sailing distance is 997 miles; from Chicago to Buffalo, 929 miles; from Duluth to Ogdensburg, 1235 miles; and from Duluth to Montreal, 1350 miles.

Commercial Importance. In the industrial and commercial development of the eastern United States and Canada, the Great Lakes have been a factor of immense importance. For the early explorers, these lakes, with their river connections, furnished easy routes to the unknown interior. They also afforded avenues through which settlers reached the productive lands adjoining their waters. Later, these inland waterways provided efficient transportation of farm, forest, and mineral products throughout a vast region rich in natural resources. Thus the Great Lakes have contributed in a marked degree to the industrial supremacy of the United States. For example, the rapid development of the immense iron ore resources of the Lake Superior region was made possible by cheap water transportation.

From the times of the French-Canadian fur traders, with their flotillas of birch-bark canoes, the Great Lakes have been a water highway between eastern and western Canada. Down this waterway float much of Canada's huge surplus of wheat for export and also flour, iron, and lumber in vast quantities. In the opposite direction go coal and those manufactured articles for which the West exchanges its products with the East.

At Buffalo, on Lake Erie, is the western terminus of the New York State Barge canal. This gives the Great Lakes a very important connection with the seaboard by way of the Mohawk and the Hudson river to New York harbor. With no increase in capacity, the barge canal is capable of transporting every year millions of tons of grain and other staple products from the lake region to tidewater.

Magnitude of Lake Traffic. The total population of the eight American states and of the Canadian province bordering on the Great Lakes runs to scores of millions. The three largest inland cities of the New World are situated on their shores. In volume, the lake traffic is enormous. The tonnage passing annually through the Detroit river exceeds that which enters and clears in the foreign trade of both the Atlantic and the Pacific ports of the United States. The yearly traffic through the Sault Sainte Marie canal around Saint Marys falls is greater in point of tonnage than that of any other artificial waterway.

THE GREAT LAKES

ITEM	Superior	Michigan	Huron	Erie	Ontario
Latitude, north	46° 30' 49° 00'	41° 37' 46° 06'	46° 00' 43° 00'	41° 23' 42° 53'	43° 10' 44° 10'
Longitude, west	84° 30' 92° 06'	84° 45' 88° 00'	80° 00' 84° 45'	78° 50' 83° 30'	76° 10' 79° 53'
Elevation above sea level in feet	602.3	581.2	581.2	572.5	246.2
Greatest length in miles	360	307	206	241	193
Greatest breadth in miles	160	118	101	57	53
Maximum depth in feet	1,012	870	750	210	738
Area in square miles	32,060	22,336	22,978	9,968	7,243
Length of coast line in miles	1,500	745	1,165	657	540
Drainage basin in square miles	44,074	43,463	49,300	24,605	25,737
United States shore line in miles (approx.)	735	1,200	470	350	230
Boundary line in miles	280	None	220	250.	160
Outlet	St. Marys River	Str. of Mackinac	St. Clair River	Niagara River	St. Lawrence River
Discoverers or early explorers	Brulé	Nicolet	Brulé and Le Caron	Chaumonot and Brébeuf	Champlain
Date of exploration or discovery	1622	1634	1615	1640	1615
Largest port	Duluth	Chicago	Bay City	Cleveland	Toronto

THE UNITED STATES

The United States, a Federal republic, occupies the central part of North America, and extends from the Atlantic Ocean to the Pacific and from Canada to Mexico. The area of the continental United States, including Alaska, almost equals the area of Europe. Besides Alaska, the republic possesses various island dependencies. See *Territorial Growth of the United States.*

Character of Coasts. In the northeast, the Atlantic shore is rugged and has numerous inlets, but south of New York bay the coast belt is flat, sandy, and in only a few places rises more than 100 feet above the sea. Numerous lagoons, reefs, keys, and sandbars render the Gulf coast dangerous to navigation. Most of the Pacific shore is bold and rocky, San Francisco bay and Puget sound being the only important indentations. On the northern border are the Great Lakes—Superior, Huron, Michigan, Erie, and Ontario.

U.S. COASTLINE BY CHIEF DIVISIONS

(In Statute Miles)

Division	General Coastline	Tidal Coastline
United States . . .	12,383	88,633
Atlantic Coast	2,069	28,673
Connecticut	0	618
Delaware	28	381
Florida	580	3,331
Georgia	100	2,344
Maine	228	3,478
Maryland	31	3,190
Massachusetts	192	1,519
New Hampshire	13	131
New Jersey	130	1,792
New York	127	1,850
North Carolina	301	3,375
Pennsylvania	0	89
Rhode Island	40	384
South Carolina	187	2,870
Virginia	112	3,315
Gulf Coast	1,631	17,141
Alabama	53	607
Florida	770	5,095
Louisiana	397	7,721
Mississippi	44	349
Texas	367	3,359
Pacific Coast	7,623	40,298
Alaska	5,580	31,383
California	840	3,427
Hawaii	750	1,052
Oregon	296	1,410
Washington	157	3,026
Arctic Coast, Alaska .	1,060	2,521

Source: Department of Commerce,
Coastline of the United States.

Surface Features. Dominant physical features of the republic are the Appalachian Mountain system along the Atlantic side with a lowland between the mountains and the ocean; the great Rocky Mountain system in the west, extending nearly north and south; and the vast valley between these highlands.

Other important physical features are the Sierra Nevada, the Cascade, and the Coast ranges, situated between the Rocky mountains and the Pacific Ocean; the vast desert area, called the Great Basin, lying between the Rockies and the Sierra Nevada; and the narrow fertile valleys, extending north and south, between the Sierra Nevada and the Coast ranges. Flanking the Great Basin on the east and the south are the lofty plateaus of Utah and Arizona. To the north of the Great Basin lies the less elevated Columbia River plateau.

Mountains and Plateaus. The high plateaus and mountain ranges of the western United States are a part of the great Cordilleran system which dominates the whole western side of North America. This system extends entirely across the United States from Mexico to Canada, through New Mexico, Colorado, Wyoming, and Montana, and throughout the region between these states and the Pacific Ocean. Measured from the eastern base of the Rockies, across Colorado, Utah, Nevada, and California, to the western base of the Coast ranges, the Cordilleran system is about 1000 miles in breadth.

The northern section of this western mountain region, particularly the Columbia River plateau, contains more extinct volcanoes than are found in any other equal area in the world. Here lavas, from ancient fissure eruptions, overspread an area of 200,000 square miles.

Scenery. The sublimity of the scenery of the western mountains is celebrated. The Yosemite falls of the Merced river in the Sierra Nevada are the highest in the world. In grandeur the Shoshone falls of the Snake river in southern Idaho rival Niagara. No Alpine lakes surpass Crater lake and Lake Tahoe in scenic beauty. The wonderlands of the globe, Yellowstone national park and Glacier park, are in the Rocky Mountain country. The Grand Canyon, nature's most marvelous example of erosion, traverses the high plateau of northwestern Arizona.

Mississippi Basin. The vast valley between the Rocky mountains and the Appalachians, called the Mississippi basin, is chiefly a grassy plain, mostly treeless, rising gently from the Gulf of Mexico toward Canada and also toward the highlands east and west. Through this basin the great Mississippi river, rising near the Canada border, flows southward into the Gulf of Mexico. In the south-central part of the valley is the only elevated section. This is the Ozark plateau, mostly from 800 feet to 1000 feet above the sea, but with summits in Arkansas which reach an elevation of 2800 feet.

About one-half the total area of the United States lies within the Mississippi basin. This basin, on account of the great fertility of its central and its eastern parts, is the most important agricultural region of the globe. Much of the western part, known as the Great Plains, with an elevation of 6000 feet in some places, has only a light rainfall. This region affords excellent natural pasturage, and, when irrigated, the soil is very productive.

Drainage Systems. The drainage waters of the United States find their way into the adjoining oceans chiefly through streams grouped in four general drainage systems, namely, the Atlantic, the Gulf, the Great Lakes, and the Pacific. Parts of North Dakota, South Dakota, and Minnesota, however, are drained by the Red River of the North, whose waters, joining those of the Nelson-Saskatchewan, flow into Hudson bay. Of the river systems, the Mississippi-Missouri, with numerous tributaries, is by far the largest. Other important large river systems are the Rio Grande, the Colorado and the Columbia.

Climate and Rainfall. Situated within the Temperate Zone, but covering a vast area having lowlands and highlands, the United States has many varieties of climate. In general, however, the climate is that which normally prevails in temperate regions, though subject to greater extremes than those which occur in Europe. Intense heat prevails in the southwest deserts in summer. In the northwest, in winter, the mercury falls below −40° F. But the dryness of the air in these regions renders endurable extremes of both heat and cold. Within the same degrees of latitude, the Pacific coast is much warmer than the Atlantic coast. Over the central and eastern portions of the country, the climate is continental.

STATE OR POSSESSION	HIGHEST POINT Name	County	Elevation (feet)	LOWEST POINT Name	County	Elevation (feet)	Mean Elevation (feet)
Alabama	Cheaha Mt.	Clay-Talladega	2,407	Gulf of Mexico		S. l.*	500
Alaska	Mt. McKinley		20,300	Pacific Ocean		S. l.	
Arizona	San Francisco Pk.	Coconino	12,611	Colorado River	Yuma	100	4,100
Arkansas	{ Blue Mountain { Magazine Mt.	Polk-Scott Logan	2,800 } 2,800 }	Ouachita River	Ashley-Union	55	650
California	Mount Whitney	Inyo-Tulare	14,496	Death Valley	Inyo	−276†	2,900
Canal Zone	Cerro Galera	S. W. part of Zone	1,207	Pacific Ocean		S. l.	100
Colorado	Mount Elbert	Lake	14,420	Arkansas River	Prowers	3,350	6,800
Connecticut	Bear Mountain	Litchfield	2,355	Long Is. Sound		S. l.	500
Delaware	Centerville	New Castle	440	Atlantic Ocean		S. l.	60
Dist. Columbia	Tenleytown	Northwest part	420	Potomac River		S. l.	150
Florida	Iron Mountain	Polk	325	Atlantic Ocean		S. l.	100
Georgia	Brasstown Bald	Towns-Union	4,768	Atlantic Ocean		S. l.	600
Guam	Mt. Lamlan		1,334	Pacific Ocean		S. l.	
Hawaii	Mauna Kea	Hawaii	13,784	Pacific Ocean		S. l.	
Idaho	Borah Peak	Custer	12,655	Snake River	Nez Percé	720	5,000
Illinois	Charles Mound	Jo Daviess	1,241	Mississippi R.	Alexander	279	600
Indiana	Greensfork Tp.	Randolph	1,240	Ohio River	Vanderburg	316	700
Iowa	West boundary	Osceola	1,675	Mississippi R.	Lee	477	1,100
Kansas	West boundary	Wallace	4,135	Verdigris R.	Montgomery	700	2,000
Kentucky	Big Black Mt.	Harlan	4,150	Mississippi R.	Fulton	257	750
Louisiana	N. W. part of Co.	Claiborne	400	Gulf of Mexico		S. l.	100
Maine	Mt. Katahdin	Piscataquis	5,267	Atlantic Ocean		S. l.	600
Maryland	Backbone Mt.	Garrett	3,340	Atlantic Ocean		S. l.	350
Massachusetts	Mount Greylock	Berkshire	3,505	Atlantic Ocean		S. l.	500
Michigan	Porcupine Mts.	Ontonagon	2,023	Lake Erie		572	900
Minnesota	Mesabi Range	St. Louis	1,920	Lake Superior		602	1,200
Mississippi	Near Iuka	Tishomingo	780	Gulf of Mexico		S. l.	300
Missouri	Taum Sauk Mt.	Iron	1,800	St. Francis R.	Dunklin	230	800
Montana	Granite Peak	Park	12,850	Kootenai River	Flathead	1,800	3,400
Nebraska	S. W. part of Co.	Banner	5,300	S. E. part of Co.	Richardson	825	2,600
Nevada	Boundary Peak	Esmeralda	13,145	Colorado River	Clark	470	5,500
New Hampshire	Mt. Washington	Coos	6,288	Atlantic Ocean		S. l.	1,000
New Jersey	High Point	Sussex	1,805	Atlantic Ocean		S. l.	250
New Mexico	N. Truchas Peak	Rio Arriba	13,306	Red Bluff	Eddy	2,876	5,700
New York	Mount Marcy	Essex	5,344	Atlantic Ocean		S. l.	1,000
North Carolina	Mount Mitchell	Yancey	6,684	Atlantic Ocean		S. l.	700
North Dakota	Black Butte	Slope	3,468	Pembina	Pembina	790	1,900
Ohio	Campbell Hill	Logan	1,550	Ohio River	Hamilton	425	850
Oklahoma	Black Mesa	Cimarron	4,978	Red River	McCurtain	300	1,300
Oregon	Mount Hood	Clackamas-Hood River	11,253	Pacific Ocean		S. l.	3,300
Pennsylvania	Negro Mountain	Somerset	3,213	Delaware River		S. l.	1,100
Puerto Rico	Luquillo Mts.	Humacao	3,532	Atlantic Ocean		S. l.	
Rhode Island	Durfee Hill	Providence	805	Atlantic Ocean		S. l.	200
Samoa	Lata	Tau Island	3,056	Pacific Ocean		S. l.	
South Carolina	Sassafras Mt.	Pickens	3,548	Atlantic Ocean		S. l.	350
South Dakota	Harney Peak	Pennington	7,242	Big Stone Lake	Roberts	962	2,200
Tennessee	Clingmans Dome	Sevier	6,642	Mississippi R.	Shelby	182	900
Texas	El Capitan	Culberson	8,700	Gulf of Mexico		S. l.	1,700
Utah	Kings Peaks	Duchesne	13,498	Beaverdam Crk.	Washington	2,000	6,100
Vermont	Mt. Mansfield	Lamoille	4,393	Lake Champlain	Franklin	95	1,000
Virginia	Mount Rogers	Grayson-Smyth	5,719	Atlantic Ocean		S. l.	950
Virgin Islands	Crown Hill	Is. of St. Thomas	1,550	Atlantic Ocean		S. l.	
Washington	Mt. Rainier	Pierce	14,408	Pacific Ocean		S. l.	1,700
West Virginia	Spruce Knob	Pendleton	4,860	Potomac River	Jefferson	240	1,500
Wisconsin	Rib Hill	Marathon	1,940	Lake Michigan		581	1,050
Wyoming	Gannett Peak	Fremont	13,785	Belle Fourche R.	Crook	3,100	6,700
United States	Mount McKinley		20,300	Death Valley	Inyo, Cal.	−276†	2,500

* Sea level. † Below sea level.

The rainfall varies greatly in different sections. The northwest Pacific coast and the Gulf coast have a heavy annual rainfall. In the central Mississippi valley the rainfall is ample for crop production. Around the Great Lakes the precipitation is moderate, but sufficient for agriculture. Tornadoes occur from the Great Plains eastward, but are most destructive in the lower Mississippi valley. Tropical hurricanes, sweeping northward from the Gulf of Mexico, sometimes cause serious damage along the coast from Texas to Florida.

Minerals. No other country in the world is so rich in minerals. Coal, iron ores, lead, zinc, silver, tungsten, gold, quicksilver, and copper are mined. Petroleum, natural gas, clays, cement, building stone, sulphur, lime, salt, slate, and other minerals are also produced in the United States. The mineral industry has developed with extraordinary rapidity. In 1870, the value of mineral products was about $200,000,000; in 1900, $1,109,000,000; in 1920, $6,981,000,000; in 1948, $27,830,000,000; in 1962, $18,834,000,000.

Vegetation. A wide range of climatic conditions, many different soils, and a surface diversified with mountains and valleys produce a varied vegetation. Plants characteristic of the North Temperate Zone are well represented, and there are also many species peculiar to the United States. Large forests are found in the extreme northwest and also in the southern, north central, and eastern states. It is estimated that there are at least 150 species of trees of industrial importance.

The central and eastern United States has many forests containing oaks, elms, maples, chestnuts, hickories, ashes, walnuts, and other well-known species. Characteristic trees of the South are palmettoes, magnolias, tulip trees, sour gums, and yellow pines. Cypresses are abundant in the southern swamps. In the Great Lakes region, firs, pines, spruces, and larches abound. Pines, spruces, and junipers are common in the Rocky Mountain region and yuccas and cactuses in the southwestern deserts.

Cone-bearing trees attain their greatest development in the Pacific Coast region. Gigantic sequoias, believed to be the largest and the oldest of living plants, form groves in the Sierra Nevada. These remarkable trees are unknown elsewhere on the globe. Douglas firs, true firs, and various pines, cedars, hemlocks, and spruces also attain immense size, the Douglas fir and the sugar pine ranking with the sequoias among the great trees of the continent. There are many species of native grasses suitable for fattening live stock. Numerous kinds of berries, various species of nut trees, and hundreds of varieties of wild flowers are also found.

The original forests of the United States covered about 820 million acres and contained, it is estimated, over five trillion board feet of lumber. There remain now about 470 million acres of forested land, containing more than two trillion board feet. The annual growth of forest timber is only about one-sixth of the amount removed. The United States Bureau of Forestry is endeavoring to conserve the country's valuable timber resources and to grow new forests in suitable regions.

Animal Life. With the exception of arctic and tropical species, practically all the larger animals native to North America are found in the United States. Among grazing mammals now occurring wild are the moose, the wapiti or American elk, the bighorn, the Rocky Mountain goat, the pronghorn or American antelope, and various species of deer. Among native flesh-eating mammals are the black and the grizzly bear, the timber wolf, coyote, fox, puma, lynx, wolverene, raccoon, and cacomistle. Other interesting mammals are the beaver, porcupine, opossum, muskrat, woodchuck, badger, prairie dog, peccary, armadillo, numerous rabbits, hares, and squirrels, and various small fur-bearers, such as the skunk, mink, and ermine. The manatee or sea cow is found in Florida waters, and sea lions occur on the Pacific coast.

The birds are represented by several hundred species. Among game birds, the more highly prized are the partridge, sage hen, prairie hen, and other species of grouse; the mallard, teal, canvasback, and other kinds of ducks; the wild turkey, bobwhite, plumed quail, woodcock, and various kinds of geese, rails, plover, and snipe. Typical song birds are the robin, mockingbird, brown thrasher, wood thrush, bluebird, cardinal, goldfinch, and catbird; also several species of orioles, grosbeaks, and wrens. The birds of prey include the bald eagle (the American national emblem), the golden eagle, and numerous hawks, buzzards, owls, and vultures. Among birds of prey, the huge California vulture ranks second in size only to the condor of the Andes.

Of the large reptiles, the alligator is the best-known, though a true crocodile occurs in Florida. Numerous sea turtles, fresh-water terrapins, and land tortoises are found. The so-called horned toad, the chuckwalla, and the Gila monster are peculiar kinds of lizards inhabiting southwestern deserts. There are numerous species of snakes, but only the rattlesnakes, the copperhead, the water moccasin, and a few other species are venomous.

Both the coastal and the inland waters abound in fish. Cod, halibut, mackerel, bluefish, tuna, and many other valuable food fishes are taken in large quantities by the fisheries. Many inland streams teem with salmon, trout, shad, catfish, and sturgeon. In the larger lakes, various food fishes, such as whitefish, lake trout, ciscoes, bass, pike, and perch, occur in immense numbers. Along the north Atlantic coast, oysters and lobsters abound, the annual catch being one of the most valuable of American fisheries.

Manufacturing. In manufacturing, the United States surpasses all other countries. Immense natural resources—minerals, timber, water power, hydroelectric power—and an ample supply of skilled labor enable the republic to produce, year after year, a vast, varied, and increasing output of manufactures. In 1860, the total value of manufactures was less than 2 billion dollars; in 1963, it exceeded 150 billion dollars.

Commerce. The rapid development of the three great industries, mining, agriculture, and manufacturing, produced an equally rapid increase in railroad construction and also gave rise to an enormous foreign trade. The commerce of the United States is sure to increase to still greater dimensions because, in addition to its immense trade with countries in the temperate zones, the imports from tropical or subtropical countries are increasing. Rubber, tea, coffee, cacao, sugar, raw cotton, raw silk, tin, hides, nitrates, and gums come from countries lying within the Torrid Zone or near it. In 1860, the total foreign commerce of the U.S. was valued at about 700 million; in 1920, at about 13 billion; in 1960, over 20 billion; in 1970, over 42 billion; in 1975, over 106 billion.

GEOGRAPHICAL FACTS ABOUT THE UNITED STATES

The land area of the United States is 3,548,974 square miles.

The water area, exclusive of the Great Lakes, is 66,237 square miles.

The most northern point of conterminous United States is in Minnesota, latitude 49° 23′ N. and longitude 95° 9′ W.

The most southern point of conterminus United States is Cape Sable, Florida, latitude 25° 7′ N. and longitude 81° 5′ W. Hence Cape Sable is 49 miles farther south than the extreme southern point of Texas.

The most eastern point of the United States is West Quoddy Head, a Maine cape which projects into the Atlantic Ocean. This headland is in longitude 66° 57′ W. and latitude 44° 49′ N.

The most western point in conterminus U.S. is Cape Alava in Washington. This cape, which projects into the Pacific Ocean, is in longitude 124° 44′ W. and latitude 48° 10′ N.

The longest distance in a straight line from north to south is measured from the boundary between Canada and the United States, the 49th parallel of latitude, to the southernmost point of Texas—1598 miles.

The shortest distance from the Atlantic to the Pacific is a straight line drawn from a point near Charleston, South Carolina, to a point near San Diego, California. This distance is 2152 miles.

The longest distance in a straight line from the Atlantic to the Pacific is measured from West Quoddy Head to a point near Yaquina Head, an Oregon cape projecting into the Pacific Ocean. These points are 2807 miles apart.

The length of the boundary of the United States, as given by the United States Coast and Geodetic Survey, is 10,748 miles, divided as follows: Atlantic Ocean, 1883; Gulf of Mexico, 1639; Pacific Ocean, 1316; Mexico, 2013; Canada, 3897.

In the conterminus United States the temperature has fallen as low as 60° below zero in northern Montana and has risen as high as 134° in the shade in Death valley, California.

The annual rainfall on the north shore of the Gulf of Mexico exceeds 60 inches. Around Puget sound it reaches 100 inches. In the vicinity of the Great Lakes it ranges between 30 and 35 inches. At the eastern base of the Rocky mountains it is about 15 inches. In the deserts of the Great Basin it is usually less than 10 inches. At Yuma, in southwestern Arizona, it is only 3 inches.

The average yearly rainfall over all the continental United States equals 1300 cubic miles. This quantity of rain water would weigh six trillion tons.

The geographic center of the United States is a point 17 miles due west of Castle Rock, Butte county, South Dakota, approx. latitude 44° 58′ N., longitude 103° 46′ W.

The center of population in the United States in 1960 was at a point 50 mi. east of St. Louis, Mo., 6½ mi. northwest of Meridian Twp., Clinton Co., Ill. lat. 38° 35′ 58″N., long. 89° 12′ 35″ W., a movement of 57.0 mi. west and 16.5 mi. south since 1950.

The highest peak in the United States, including all territories, is the Alaskan mountain, Mt. McKinley, 20,300 feet.

The state having the lowest average elevation is Delaware. Its surface, if leveled, would be only 60 feet above the sea. Colorado has the highest average elevation, 6800 feet.

Geography

NAME	Location	Area Sq. Mi.	Estab-lished	Distinctive Characteristics
Acadia	Maine Coast . .	65.05	1919	Mountains and coastal area on Mount Desert Island.
Big Bend	West Texas . .	1106.60	1944	Last great Texas wilderness, in bend of the Rio Grande.
Bryce Canyon . .	Southwestern Utah.	56.26	1928	Massive mountain uplift; magnificent forests; fantastically eroded pinnacles; extraordinary natural coloring.
Canyonlands . .	S. E. Utah . . .	402.56	1964	Pinnacles, monoliths, deep gorges, rock formations.
Carlsbad Caverns	New Mexico . .	73.05	1930	Largest and deepest known cavern system.
Crater Lake . . .	Southwestern Oregon . .	250.45	1902	Lake of extraordinary blue in crater of extinct volcano. No known inlet or outlet. Sidewalls 500 to 2000 feet high.
Everglades . . .	Southern Florida	2188.33	1947	Part of the only subtropical area in the United States; vast forests, prairies, and watercourses; abundant bird life.
Glacier	Northwestern Montana . . .	1582.86	1910	Mountain region, 250 glacier-fed lakes of romantic beauty, 60 glaciers. Precipices thousands of feet high. Trout fishing. With the adjoining Waterton Lakes national park of Canada.
Grand Canyon .	North central Arizona	1052.46	1919	Greatest example of erosion and most wonderful scenic spectacle in the world. The stupendous gorge has average depth of about 1 mile and is from 4 to 18 miles wide.
Grand Teton . .	Wyoming. . . .	484.92	1929	Picturesque mountains in a great "dude ranch" district.
Great Smoky Mountains . .	North Carolina and Tennessee	801.05	1930	Picturesque mountains, including about 40 peaks.
Guadalupe Mountains . .	Texas	30.68	1968	Diversified and beautiful scenery.
Haleakala	Maui Is., Hawaii	41.25	1961	Huge dormant volcano, 10,023 feet high, has one of the largest and most colorful craters known.
Hawaii Volcanoes	Hawaii Island . .	344.28	1916	Kilauea, Mauna Loa, largest active volcanoes in the world.
Hot Springs . . .	Arkansas	1.61	1921	Forty-seven hot springs possessing curative properties.
Isle Royale . . .	Lake Superior N. Michigan .	842.73	1940	Extensive wilderness; habitat of one of the largest moose herds in America.
Kings Canyon . .	Middle eastern California . .	719.26	1940	Two canyons of the Kings River; mountain peaks to 14,000 feet; General Grant tree 40.3 feet in diameter.
Lassen Volcanic .	Northern California . .	167.08	1916	Lassen Peak, 10,453 feet in altitude. Only recently active volcano in conterminous United States. Hot springs; mud geysers; ice caves; majestic canyons.
Mammoth Cave .	S. W. Kentucky	80.24	1936	Large cavern including spectacular cave onyx formations.
Mesa Verde . . .	S. W. Colorado .	81.36	1906	Best preserved prehistoric cliff dwellings in United States.
Mount McKinley	S. C. Alaska . .	3030.45	1917	Highest mountain in North America (altitude 20,300 feet).
Mount Rainier. .	West central Washington . .	378.09	1899	Forty-eight square miles of glacier, 50 to 500 feet thick. Immense fields of wild flowers.
Olympic	N. W. Washington	1400.94	1938	Finest remnant of the Pacific Northwest rain forest; numerous glaciers; feeding ground for rare Roosevelt elk.
Petrified Forest .	Arizona	147.17	1962	Fossil tree trunks; colored rocks of Painted Desert.
Platt	So. Oklahoma . .	1.42	1906	Numerous well-known medicinal springs.
Rocky Mountain	North middle Colorado . . .	409.88	1915	Heart of the Rockies; snow-topped range; peaks 11,000 to 14,255 feet high; sublime scenery.
Sequoia	California . . .	604.47	1890	The Big Tree National Park; 12,000 sequoia trees ranging from 10 to 36 feet in diameter; towering mountain ranges; startling precipices.
Shenandoah . . .	N. W. Virginia .	331.72	1935	Region of scenic grandeur in the Blue Ridge mountains.
Virgin Islands . .	St. John Island .	23.67	1956	White sand beaches and semi-tropical climate. Embraces scenery and plant life totally different from any other national park. Area covers two-thirds of St. John Island.
Wind Cave . . .	South Dakota .	43.84	1903	Cavern having miles of galleries and numerous chambers containing many peculiar geological formations.
Yellowstone . . .	Wyoming, Montana, and Idaho	3471.52	1872	More geysers than in all rest of world; boiling springs; mud volcanoes; petrified forests; Grand Canyon of the Yellowstone; waterfalls; vast wilderness inhabited by deer, elk, bison, bear, mountain sheep, and other wild animals.
Yosemite	California . . .	1188.99	1890	Valley of world famed beauty; lofty cliffs; romantic vistas; waterfalls of extraordinary height; many snow-crowned peaks; good trout fishing.
Zion	Southwestern Utah.	229.74	1919	Magnificent gorge(Zion canyon), depth from 1500 to 2500 feet, with precipitous walls of great beauty; picturesque scenery.

Parks and Monuments. Modern public parks and monuments have these principal purposes: To provide enjoyment to visitors; to safeguard the property so as to afford like enjoyment to future generations; and to make use of them as illustrations in spreading popular education in geography, science, and history.

In the United States, national parks differ from national monuments in that the parks require acts of Congress for their establishment, while monuments may also be established by executive order pursuant to the Antiquities Act of 1906. In general, the national parks are large areas of scenic magnificence, while the national monuments and related areas are, with a few exceptions, smaller and more often are primarily of historic or prehistoric interest. The states also, as well as many municipalities, have set aside millions of acres in all as parks or monuments.

Of other countries, Canada has the largest system of national and provincial parks. South Africa, Holland, Czechoslovakia, Italy, Kenya, and France also have at least one large area each for the preservation of natural scenery and of certain animals and plants. In fact, though not in name, Italy, France, and most other European countries have numerous public areas administered much like the American parks and monuments for the preservation of historic sites, such as Pompeii in Italy and Stonehenge in England.

The number of areas supervised by the U.S. National Park Service as reported on Jan. 1, 1966, was 214, with a total area of 26,548,693 acres. Of this number, 32 were national parks, 77 were national monuments, 23 were national historic sites or parks, 28 were national military or memorial parks, 12 were national battlefields, battlefield parks, or battlefield sites, and the rest were national seashores, recreation areas, cemeteries, parkways, and other areas.

The table above gives data about the national parks. On the two pages following appears a tabulation of national monuments and related areas, followed by a summary of state parks and related areas showing by states the number and acreage of such areas.

Name	Location	Area (Acres)	Established	Distinctive Characteristics
Abraham Lincoln Birthplace (h)	Kentucky	117	1916	Contains log cabin where Abraham Lincoln was born.
Andrew Johnson (h)	Tennessee	17	1942	Andrew Johnson's home, tailor shop, and grave.
Antietam (b)	Maryland	784	1890	Scene of one of the greatest battles of the Civil War.
Appomattox Court House (h)	Virginia	972	1940	Scene of the surrender of the Confederate Army, April 9, 1865.
Arches (m)	Utah	34,010	1929	Natural arches, windows, and other effects of wind erosion.
Arkansas Post (m)	Arkansas	221	1965	Earliest permanent white settlement in region.
Aztec Ruins (m)	N. Mex.	27	1923	Pueblo ruins, one containing 500 rooms.
Badlands (m)	S. Dakota	111,530	1939	Spectacular exhibit of erosion—fantastic ridges, cliffs.
Bandelier (m)	N. Mex.	29,661	1916	Vast ruins of prehistoric cliff dwellings.
Bent's Old Fort (h)	Colorado	178	1963	Fort built about 1833, trading post in fur trade.
Big Hole (b)	Montana	666	1910	Scene of victory, 1877, over force of Nez Perce Indians.
Black Canyon of the Gunnison (m)	Colorado	13,683	1933	10 miles of deepest and most scenic portion of Black Canyon.
Booker T. Washington (m)	Virginia	218	1957	Plantation on which Booker T. Washington was born.
Buck Island Reef (m)	Virgin Is.	850	1961	Marine garden with coral, grottoes, tropical fish.
Cabrillo (m)	California	81	1933	Memorial to discoverer of San Diego Bay in 1542.
Canyon de Chelly (m)	Arizona	83,840	1931	Deep canyon; Indian cliff dwellings; very ancient ruins.
Capitol Reef (m)	Utah	39,173	1937	Cliff dwellings, fossils, imprints of prehistoric animals.
Capulin Mountain (m)	N. Mex.	775	1916	Cinder cone of geologically recent formation.
Casa Grande Ruins (m)	Arizona	473	1889	Buildings of a prehistoric race. Ruins discovered in 1694.
Castillo de San Marcos (m)	Florida	22	1924	Oldest masonry fort in continental U.S.; built 1672.
Cedar Breaks (m)	Utah	6,155	1933	Spectacular canyons and cliffs of vivid coloring.
Chaco Canyon	N. Mex.	21,509	1907	Numerous ruins of cliff dwellings, including communal houses.
Chalmette (h)	Louisiana	136	1907	Scene of battle of New Orleans, Jaunary 8, 1815.
Channel Islands (m)	S. Calif.	18,167	1938	Parts of Anacapa and Santa Barbara Islands; fossil elephants.
Chesapeake & Ohio Canal (m)	Md.-W.Va.	4,475	1961	Old American canal with minimum alterations.
Chickamauga and Chattanooga (b)	Ga.-Tenn.	8,190	1890	Beautiful scenic park, embracing battlefields of Chickamauga, Missionary Ridge, and other conflicts of the Civil War, 1863.
Chiricahua (m)	Arizona	10,646	1924	Wilderness of unusual rock shapes.
Christiansted (h)	Virgin Is.	27	1952	Danish colonial government buildings.
City of Refuge (h)	Hawaii	182	1961	Until 1819, sanctuary for individuals fleeing death.
Colonial (h)	Virginia	9,430	1936	Jamestown, Williamsburg, Yorktown, connected by parkway.
Colorado (m)	Colo.	17,362	1911	Many lofty monoliths; unusual scenic beauty.
Coronado (p)	Arizona	2,834	1952	Commemorates Coronado's exploration in 1540–42.
Craters of the Moon (m)	Idaho	53,545	1924	Volcanic region with weird landscape effects.
Cumberland Gap (h)	Ky.-Tenn.-Va.	20,169	1955	Pass explored by Boone and used by western settlers.
Custer Battlefield (m)	Montana	765	1946	Site of Battle of the Little Bighorn River, June 25, 1876.
Death Valley (m)	Calif.-Nev.	†2,981	1933	Arid tract containing lowest point in the western hemisphere.
De Soto (p)	Florida	30	1949	Commemorates explorer's landing in 1539.
Devils Postpile (m)	Calif.	798	1911	Spectacular six-sided aggregation of basaltic columns.
Devils Tower (m)	Wyoming	1,347	1906	865-foot rock tower of volcanic origin. First national monument.
Dinosaur (m)	Utah-Col.	206,233	1915	Deposits of fossil animal remains of great scientific interest.
Edison (h)	N. Jersey	21	1955	Edison's home and laboratory.
Effigy Mounds (m)	Iowa	1,468	1949	Indian mounds in shape of animals.
El Morro (m)	N. Mex.	1,279	1906	Rock containing inscriptions cut by early Spanish explorers.
Fort Caroline (p)	Florida	120	1953	Overlooks site of French colony planted in 1564.
Fort Clatsop (m)	Oregon	125	1958	Winter campsite of Lewis and Clark.
Fort Davis (h)	Texas	460	1963	Fort to protect frontier and early settlers.
Fort Donelson (p)	Tennessee	600	1928	Site of Civil War fort.
Fort Frederica (m)	Georgia	250	1945	Built (1736–48) by Gen. James E. Oglethorpe.
Fort Jefferson (m)	Florida	47,125	1935	Largest all-masonry fort in Western world, built 1846.
Fort Laramie (h)	Wyoming	586	1938	Center for migrants and explorers 1834–90.
Fort Matanzas (m)	Florida	258	1924	Early Spanish stronghold.
Fort McHenry (m)	Maryland	43	1925	Defense of this fort on Sept. 13–14, 1814 inspired the composition of our national anthem.
Fort Necessity (b)	Pa.	500	1931	Scene of opening battle of French and Indian War.
Fort Pulaski (m)	Georgia	5,517	1924	Brick fort built 1829–47, bombarded in Civil War.
Fort Raleigh (h)	N. C.	160	1941	Site of "Lost Colony" settlement in 1585–87.
Fort Smith (h)	Arkansas	14	1964	Early military post in Louisiana Territory.
Fort Union (m)	N. Mex.	721	1956	Ruins of key fort in southwestern settlement.
Fort Vancouver (h)	Wash.	90	1961	Western Headquarters of Hudson's Bay Co. 1825–49.
Fredericksburg and Spotsylvania (p)	Virginia	3,672	1927	Portions of four great battlefields of Civil War.
George Washington Birthplace (m)	Virginia	394	1930	Memorial mansion and gardens.
Geo. Washington Carver	Missouri	210	1951	Site of cabin where he was born. Museum with relics and records.
Gettysburg (p)	Pa.	3,672	1895	Beautiful natural park. Scene of great Civil War combat, 1863.
Gila Cliff Dwellings (m)	N. Mex.	533	1907	Highly interesting remains of cliff dwellings.
Glacier Bay (m)	Alaska	†3,554	1925	Tidewater glaciers of first rank.
Grand Canyon (m)	Arizona	198,280	1932	Adjoins Grand Canyon Nat. Park.
Grand Portage (m)	Minnesota	770	1960	Exploration route, fur trading post of North West Co.
Gran Quivira (m)	N. Mex.	611	1909	Important relic of Spanish missions in the United States.
Great Sand Dunes (m)	Colorado	36,740	1932	Sand dune 1000 feet high in San Luis Valley.
Guilford Courthouse (p)	N. Car.	224	1917	Near Greensboro. Scene of great battle of the Revolution, 1781.
Hampton (h)	Maryland	45	1948	Historic 18th century mansion.
Harper's Ferry (h)	W.Va.-Md.	1500	1955	Site of John Brown's raid before Civil War.
Home of Franklin D. Roosevelt (h)	N. York	188	1945	Roosevelt residence and library at Hyde Park.
Homestead (m)	Nebraska	163	1939	Site of first homestead in the United States.
Hopewell Village (h)	Pa.	848	1938	17th-century center of iron making, ruins.
Horseshoe Bend (p)	Alabama	2,040	1959	Site of Jackson's victory over Indians.
Hovenweep (m)	Utah-Col.	505	1923	Groups of prehistoric towers and pueblo ruins.
Independence (h)	Penn.	22	1956	Philadelphia's Independence Hall and other structures.

NATIONAL MONUMENTS AND ALLIED AREAS*—Continued

Name	Location	Area (Acres)	Established	Distinctive Characteristics
Jefferson National Expansion Memorial (h)	Missouri	85	1935	Commemorating westward expansion of U.S.
Jewel Cave (m)	S. Dakota	1,275	1908	Vast limestone cavern of extraordinary beauty.
Joshua Tree (m)	Calif.	557,992	1936	The Joshua tree, a spectacular feature of western desert land.
Katmai (m)	Alaska	†4,215	1918	Volcanic phenomena; "Valley of Ten Thousand Smokes."
Kennesaw Mountain (b)	Georgia	3,683	1947	Scene of battle in Civil War, June 27, 1864.
King's Mountain (p)	S. Car.	3,950	1931	Site of American victory, Oct. 7, 1780, in Revolutionary War.
Lava Beds (m)	Calif.	46,239	1925	Volcanic formations; battleground Modoc Indian War, 1873.
Lehman Caves (m)	Nevada	640	1922	Limestone caverns of much beauty and scientific interest.
Lincoln Boyhood (m)	Indiana	200	1963	Farm where Lincoln lived from 8th to 21st year.
Lincoln Memorial (m)	D.C.	164	1911	Parthenon-like structure with colossal statue of seated Lincoln.
Manassas (b)	Virginia	3,109	1940	Scene of two Civil War battles in 1861 and 1862.
Minute Man (h)	Mass.	750	1959	Scene of opening skirmish of Revolutionary War.
Montezuma Castle (m)	Arizona	842	1906	Prehistoric cliff-dwelling in the face of a high cliff.
Moores Creek (b)	N. Car.	50	1926	Scene of a memorable battle of the Revolutionary War.
Morristown (h)	N. Jersey	958	1933	Washington's headquarters in 1779–80.
Mound City Group (m)	Ohio	68	1923	Prehistoric mounds in Camp Sheridan military reservation.
Mount Rushmore (p)	S. Dakota	1,278	1925	Colossal figures of four presidents carved on cliff.
Muir Woods (m)	Calif.	503	1908	Noted redwood grove; located 7 miles from San Francisco.
Natural Bridges (m)	Utah	7,600	1908	Three natural bridges, largest 222 feet high; span 261 feet.
Navajo (m)	Arizona	360	1909	Numerous ancient pueblos, or ruins of cliff dwellings.
Ocmulgee (m)	Georgia	683	1936	Indian mounds in and around Macon.
Oregon Caves (m)	Oregon	480	1909	Vast caves of dazzling whiteness called "Marble Halls."
Organ Pipe Cactus (m)	Arizona	330,874	1937	Unique forms of native plant and animal life.
Pea Ridge (b)	Arkansas	4,283	1960	Scene of Civil War battle in 1862.
Perry's Victory (m)	Ohio	21	1936	Commemoration of victory over British fleet in 1813.
Petersburg (b)	Virginia	2,731	1926	Scene of Civil War conflicts.
Pinnacles (m)	Calif.	14,498	1908	Many spirelike rock formations, 500 to 1200 feet high.
Pipe Spring (m)	Arizona	40	1923	Historic fort built by Mormon pioneers.
Pipestone (m)	Minnesota	283	1937	Source of material for Indian peace pipes.
Rainbow Bridge (m)	Utah	160	1910	Natural bridge 309 feet above water; span is 278 feet.
Richmond (b)	Virginia	747	1944	Scene of battles in defense of Richmond during Civil War.
Russell Cave (m)	Alabama	310	1961	Archeological record of human habitation from 6000 B.C.
Sagamore Hill (h)	New York	85	1963	Theodore Roosevelt's home from 1885 till his death.
Saguaro (m)	Arizona	78,644	1933	Giant cacti of unusual scientific interest.
Saint Gaudens (h)	N. H.	86	1965	"Aspet," home of sculptor Augustus St. Gaudens.
Salem Maritime (h)	Mass.	11	1938	Nathaniel Hawthorne's place in Salem.
San Juan (h)	P. Rico	38	1949	16th-century Spanish fortifications.
Saratoga (h)	New York	5,500	1948	Scene of American victory over British, 1777.
Scotts Bluff (m)	Nebraska	3,084	1919	Landmark on Oregon trail.
Shiloh (b)	Tenn.	3,515	1894	Embraces the battlefield of Shiloh, near Pittsburg Landing.
Sitka (m)	Alaska	54	1910	Park of great natural beauty, scene of massacre of Russians.
Statue of Liberty (m)	N.Y.-N.J.	58	1924	Famous statue on Liberty Island, gift of the French people.
Stones River (b)	Tennessee	331	1927	Scene of Civil War battle.
Sunset Crater (m)	Arizona	3,040	1930	Volcanic crater with lava flows and ice caves.
Theodore Roosevelt (p)	N. Dak.	70,436	1947	Part of Roosevelt's Elkhorn ranch.
Thomas Jefferson (m)	D. C.	18	1934	Colonnaded rotunda in style favored by Jefferson.
Timpanogos Cave (m)	Utah	250	1922	Limestone cavern almost 600 feet in length.
Tonto (m)	Arizona	1,120	1907	Cliff dwellings in an unusually good state of preservation.
Tumacacori (m)	Arizona	10	1908	Spanish Mission established in late 17th century.
Tuzigoot (m)	Arizona	43	1939	Ruins of ancient pueblo with valuable relics.
Vanderbilt Mansion (h)	New York	212	1940	Palatial residence at Hyde Park.
Vicksburg (p)	Miss.	1,741	1899	Scene of the siege and surrender of Vicksburg, 1863.
Walnut Canyon (m)	Arizona	1,879	1915	Cliff dwellings of much scientific and popular interest.
Washington Monument (m)	D.C.	106	1848	Obelisk, 555 feet high, commemorating George Washington.
White Sands (m)	N. Mex.	146,535	1933	Sands resembling snow; interesting plant and animal life.
Whitman Mission (h)	Wash.	98	1940	Site of first mission in Pacific Northwest.
Wilson's Creek (b)	Missouri	1730	1965	Civil War battlefield of 1861 for control of Missouri.
Wright Brothers (p)	N. Car.	425	1933	Scene of first sustained flight by airplane.
Wupatki (m)	Arizona	35,233	1924	Prehistoric dwellings of ancestors of Hopi Indians.
Yucca House (m)	Colo.	10	1919	Mounds left by prehistoric people.

* Exclusive of areas less than 5 acres. † Square miles. (b) National military parks or national battlefields, battlefield sites, or battlefield parks. (h) National historical parks or national historic sites. (m) National monuments. (p) National memorials or national memorial parks.

STATE PARKS AND RELATED AREAS—1968

State	No.	Acres (1000)	State	No.	Acres (1000)	State	No.	Acres (1000)
Alabama	139	410	Louisiana	47	1,807	Ohio	492	358
Alaska	117	336	Maine	625	241	Oklahoma	88	491
Arizona	691	121	Maryland	99	198	Oregon	267	951
Arkansas	49	178	Massachusetts	574	340	Pennsylvania	495	3,033
California	216	921	Michigan	2,953	4,199	Rhode Island	101	31
Colorado	72	113	Minnesota	735	3,701	South Carolina	56	158
Connecticut	230	160	Mississippi	144	1,262	South Dakota	406	215
Delaware	35	24	Missouri	294	318	Tennessee	1,374	743
Florida	809	2,891	Montana	268	634	Texas	954	388
Georgia	312	773	Nebraska	122	131	Utah	123	241
Hawaii	90	1,302	Nevada	22	319	Vermont	161	152
Idaho	144	593	New Hampshire	285	76	Virginia	126	156
Illinois	129	1,008	New Jersey	134	291	Washington	1,546	4,148
Indiana	246	230	New Mexico	90	346	West Virginia	63	262
Iowa	513	160	New York	304	3,638	Wisconsin	1,075	944
Kansas	226	102	North Carolina	156	282	Wyoming	62	88
Kentucky	135	152	North Dakota	216	84	Total	18,610	39,701

State	Population 1900	Population 1940	Population 1950	Population 1960	Population 1970	% of inc. 1960–70	Rank	Largest City
Alabama . . .	1,828,697	2,832,961	3,061,743	3,266,740	3,444,165	5.4	21	Birmingham
Alaska	63,592	72,524	128,643	226,167	302,173	33.6	51	Anchorage
Arizona . . .	122,931	499,261	749,587	1,302,161	1,772,482	36.1	33	Phoenix
Arkansas . .	1,311,564	1,949,387	1,909,511	1,786,272	1,923,295	7.7	32	Little Rock
California . .	1,485,053	6,907,387	10,586,223	15,717,204	19,953,134	27.0	1	Los Angeles
Colorado . .	539,700	1,123,296	1,325,089	1,753,947	2,207,259	25.8	30	Denver
Connecticut .	908,420	1,709,242	2,007,280	2,535,234	3,032,217	19.6	24	Hartford
Delaware . .	184,735	266,505	318,085	446,292	548,104	22.8	47	Wilmington
Dist. Columbia	278,718	663,091	802,178	763,956	756,510	−1.0	41	Washington
Florida . . .	528,542	1,897,414	2,771,305	4,951,560	6,789,443	37.1	9	Jacksonville
Georgia . . .	2,216,331	3,123,723	3,444,578	3,943,116	4,589,575	16.4	15	Atlanta
Hawaii . . .	154,001	. . . .	. . . .	632,772	768,561	21.5	40	Honolulu
Idaho	161,772	524,873	588,637	667,191	712,567	6.8	43	Boise
Illinois	4,821,550	7,897,241	8,712,176	10,081,156	11,113,976	10.2	5	Chicago
Indiana . . .	2,516,462	3,427,796	3,934,224	4,662,498	5,193,669	11.4	11	Indianapolis
Iowa	2,231,853	2,538,268	2,621,073	2,757,537	2,825,041	2.4	25	Des Moines
Kansas . . .	1,470,495	1,801,028	1,905,299	2,178,611	2,249,071	3.2	28	Wichita
Kentucky . .	2,147,174	2,845,627	2,944,806	3,038,156	3,219,311	6.0	23	Louisville
Louisiana . .	1,381,625	2,363,880	2,683,516	3,257,022	3,643,180	11.9	20	New Orleans
Maine	694,466	847,226	913,774	969,265	992,048	2.4	38	Portland
Maryland . .	1,188,044	1,821,244	2,343,001	3,100,689	3,922,399	26.5	18	Baltimore
Massachusetts .	2,805,346	4,316,721	4,690,514	5,148,578	5,689,170	10.5	10	Boston
Michigan . . .	2,420,982	5,256,106	6,371,766	7,823,194	8,875,083	13.4	7	Detroit
Minnesota . .	1,751,394	2,792,300	2,982,483	3,413,864	3,805,069	11.5	19	Minneapolis
Mississippi . .	1,551,270	2,183,796	2,178,914	2,178,141	2,216,912	1.8	29	Jackson
Missouri . . .	3,106,665	3,784,664	3,954,653	4,319,813	4,677,399	8.3	13	St. Louis
Montana . . .	243,329	559,456	591,024	674,767	694,409	2.9	44	Billings
Nebraska . .	1,066,300	1,315,834	1,325,510	1,411,330	1,483,791	5.1	35	Omaha
Nevada . . .	42,335	110,247	160,083	285,278	488,738	71.3	48	Las Vegas
New Hampshire .	411,588	491,524	533,242	606,921	737,681	21.5	42	Manchester
New Jersey . .	1,883,669	4,160,165	4,835,329	6,066,782	7,168,164	18.2	8	Newark
New Mexico . .	195,310	531,818	681,187	951,023	1,014,979	6.7	37	Albuquerque
New York . .	7,268,894	13,479,142	14,830,192	16,782,304	18,190,740	8.4	2	New York
North Carolina .	1,893,810	3,571,623	4,061,929	4,556,155	5,082,059	11.5	12	Charlotte
North Dakota .	319,146	641,935	619,636	632,446	617,761	−2.3	46	Fargo
Ohio	4,157,545	6,907,612	7,946,627	9,706,397	10,652,017	9.7	6	Cleveland
Oklahoma . .	790,391	2,336,434	2,233,351	2,328,284	2,559,253	9.9	27	Oklahoma City
Oregon . . .	413,536	1,089,684	1,521,341	1,768,687	2,091,385	18.2	31	Portland
Pennsylvania .	6,302,115	9,900,180	10,498,012	11,319,366	11,793,909	4.2	3	Philadelphia
Rhode Island .	428,556	713,346	791,896	859,488	949,723	10.5	39	Providence
South Carolina .	1,340,316	1,899,804	2,117,027	2,382,594	2,589,891	8.7	26	Columbia
South Dakota .	401,570	642,961	652,740	680,514	665,507	−2.2	45	Sioux Falls
Tennessee . . .	2,020,616	2,915,841	3,291,718	3,567,089	3,924,164	10.0	17	Memphis
Texas	3,048,710	6,414,824	7,711,194	9,579,677	11,196,730	16.9	4	Houston
Utah	276,749	550,310	688,862	890,627	1,059,273	18.9	36	Salt Lake City
Vermont . . .	343,641	359,231	377,747	389,881	444,330	14.0	49	Burlington
Virginia . . .	1,854,184	2,677,773	3,318,680	3,966,949	4,648,494	17.2	14	Norfolk
Washington . .	518,103	1,736,191	2,378,963	2,853,214	3,409,169	19.5	22	Seattle
West Virginia .	958,800	1,901,974	2,005,552	1,860,421	1,744,237	−6.2	34	Huntington
Wisconsin . . .	2,069,042	3,137,587	3,434,575	3,951,777	4,417,933	11.8	16	Milwaukee
Wyoming . . .	92,531	250,742	290,529	330,066	332,416	0.7	50	Cheyenne
Total, U.S.	75,212,166	131,669,275	150,697,361	179,323,175	204,765,770	13.4		New York

Source: U.S. Bureau of the Census.

NEW ENGLAND STATES

The New England states, comprising Maine, New Hampshire, Vermont, Massachusetts, Rhode Island, and Connecticut, are situated in the northeastern part of the United States. The total area of these six states, 66,608 square miles, is less than the area of Oklahoma, 69,919 square miles, while the total population, 11,699,726, is more than four times the population of that state, 2,498,378.

Surface. The principal upland regions of New England are the old, worn-down White mountains in New Hampshire, the Green mountains in Vermont, and the Berkshire Hills in Massachusetts. Numerous harbors, formed from submerged valleys, indent the coast. Northern New England has many small lakes noted for scenic beauty. The Rangeley lakes in Maine and lakes Sunapee and Winnepesaukee in New Hampshire are popular resorts.

Rivers. New England is well watered. Many of the rivers are broken by falls or rapids, and some of these furnish hydroelectric power. The Connecticut, Penobscot, Kennebec, Mystic, Charles, and Thames are navigable for steamers.

Climate. The climate is continental. Winter, a very cold season, is rendered more unpleasant by the humidity of the air. Northeast winds passing over the cold Labrador current flowing along the New England shore are chilled and, blowing inland, bring heavy snows in winter and cause fogs and cold rains in summer. The southeast winds are much milder, as they sweep over warm ocean currents from the Gulf of Mexico.

Minerals. New England has but little mineral wealth. Building stones, feldspars, and various clays are found. Granite, basalt, marble, and slate are the chief quarry products, and rank in importance in the order named. Among these states, Vermont stands first in total value of quarry products, with Massachusetts second, and New Hampshire third. Besides leading in the production of granite, Vermont quarries large quantities of slate and much beautiful marble. In each of the New England states, except Connecticut in which basalt leads, granite is the most valuable quarry product.

Fisheries. Fishing early became a prominent industry, the nearness of rich fishing grounds attracting a large class of workers. Cod, halibut, mackerel, swordfish, haddock, hake, herring, and pollock are the principal catches. Oysters, clams, crabs, lobsters, and shrimps form important items in the total annual value of the fisheries. Menhaden are taken in immense quantities for oil and fertilizing material. In amount and value of sea fish taken, Massachusetts leads all other states in the Union.

Forests. Forests still cover large tracts of land in this section, especially in Maine, New Hampshire, and Vermont. The pine is the most common tree

Spruce is cut in Maine for making paper and wood pulp, the principal manufactures of the state. Maine still ships considerable lumber.

Agriculture. Much of New England is stony and difficult to cultivate, and abandoned farms are not uncommon. The Connecticut valley, however, has very fertile soil, and there is also considerable good farm land in the valleys of several smaller rivers. Hay is the chief crop. Potatoes, rye, corn, and oats are also raised. Connecticut Valley tobacco ranks second only to Cuban tobacco. Dairying is an important occupation, especially in Vermont. Market gardening is a profitable industry in recent years. Apples, pears, and cherries are the chief orchard fruits. More than half the world's supply of cranberries is grown in Massachusetts.

Manufacturing. In all these states, manufacturing is the principal occupation. Hundreds of different articles are made. Among the chief products are metal wares, boots and shoes, leather, paper, brass goods, machinery, electrical apparatus, clothing, rubber goods, barbed wire, carpets, and refined sugar. Although many textile mills have moved to the South, textiles are still important to the economy of New England. Every city in this division is a manufacturing center.

Many western states have counties each larger than southern New England. This section lacks coal, iron, copper, lead, zinc, timber, wool, cotton, hides—in short, all the basic materials of industrial work in mill, factory, or machine shop. Yet the intelligence, skill, energy, and inventiveness of its people have made southern New England the greatest center of diversified manufacturing in the Union. Massachusetts is a striking example. Forty-three states exceed it in area. Yet in population it stands ninth among the states, and its enormous manufacturing output gives it still higher rank in commerce.

Commerce. The seaboard states have a large commerce, both domestic and foreign, and the harbors of their important ports are crowded with shipping at all times of the year. Manufactures constitute the bulk of the exports; the imports consist mainly of raw materials from various parts of the globe. Numerous railroads link this section with the rest of the Union. The principal ports are Boston, Mass., Portland, Me., Providence, R. I., Portsmouth, N. H., and New Haven, Conn.

MIDDLE ATLANTIC STATES

Because of their medial position with reference to the seaboard, and on account of a general similarity in surface features, the states of New York, New Jersey, Pennsylvania, Delaware, Maryland, Virginia, and West Virginia are generally grouped together. The first four have been called the "Middle" states and the last three have been placed with "South Atlantic" or "Southern" states. By some, the first three are styled "Middle Atlantic" while all the others are called "South Atlantic" states.

The total area of the states comprising this group is less than one-sixteenth of the entire area of the country. Yet these seven states have about one-fourth of the population, own more than one-third of the manufacturing capital, and contain nearly two-fifths of the wage earners of the United States.

Surface. The Appalachian Mountain system extends across this group of states from northeast to southwest, and the coastal plain gradually widens southward. On the west side of the mountains is the Allegheny plateau. It is a rugged area, sloping toward the Mississippi, and is but thinly populated. Numerous bays and inlets indent the Atlantic Coast and several of them form excellent harbors.

The coastal plain is low and sandy, and much of it is bordered by swamps. Some of the rivers are navigable and add greatly to the transportation facilities of the region. Among the more important tidal streams are the Hudson, the Delaware, the Patapsco, and the James. The Ohio River on the west is a great artery of interstate trade. The shores of Chesapeake Bay are dotted with ports actively engaged in coastwise traffic.

Climate. Between the northern and southern limits of this division the distance is nearly 600 miles. This distance, together with variations in surface features, causes marked differences in the climatic conditions of the northern and southern parts. In northern New York the mean winter temperature is 17° F.; in southern Virginia, 35° F. The summer temperature averages 60° F. along the northern boundary of this group of states and 75° F. along the southern. The fruit belt of western New York owes its favorable climate to the equalizing influence of Lake Erie and Lake Ontario. The Gulf Stream passes near the Virginia coast and moderates the winds blowing from the ocean. In all the states of this division the rainfall is amply sufficient for farming.

Mining. Iron is found in all the states except Delaware. Enormous quantities of coal are mined in Pennsylvania, West Virginia, Maryland, and Virginia. Petroleum, first discovered in Pennsylvania in 1859, is produced in that state, in New York, and in West Virginia. Natural gas, piped from the gas fields, is utilized for heating and lighting in many cities.

Their vast supplies of coal, iron, petroleum, and natural gas, the basic materials of industrial wealth, have enabled these states to lead the nation in various steel and iron manufactures.

Forests. Northern New York is well forested, and much forest land in the Adirondack region is under the protection of the state. In the Appalachians, the United States government has reserved extensive forested tracts. Hemlock is the principal timber cut in New York and Pennsylvania. Spruce for making wood pulp is obtained chiefly in New York and in West Virginia. Oak, maple, poplar, walnut, and other broad-leaved trees are common in all these states. Yellow pine is an important source of lumber in Virginia, and cypress and cedar are found in the coastal swamps. Hardwoods produced in this group come mostly from West Virginia.

Agriculture. In these states, agriculture has always been an important industry. There is much fertile soil, and large crops of grains, potatoes, apples, peaches, pears, grapes, and strawberries are grown. Virginia ranks as one of the leading tobacco states. Peanuts also form an important crop in that state. Buckwheat is grown extensively in Pennsylvania and in New York. Peas, corn, tomatoes, berries, and orchard fruits are canned in enormous quantities. Market gardening is a profitable occupation near the large centers of population. Much attention is paid to dairying, especially in New York. The annual output of butter and cheese is very large. Vast quantities of milk are supplied to the great cities in this section. Besides cattle, the other large farm animals most commonly reared are horses, sheep, and hogs. Poultry raising is an important industry.

Fisheries. Fishing is an occupation of great importance. Oysters form the most valuable single item. Shad, bluefish, and mackerel are taken in the bays and rivers. Lakes Erie and Ontario furnish large quantities of lake trout, pike, ciscoes, and other food fish.

Manufacturing. In this section manufacturing is the foremost industry. New York, called the Empire State, ranks first in the Union in manufacturing as well as in population, wealth, and commerce. Of its long list of diversified manufactures, the most valuable single industrial product is wearing apparel. Other important manufactures of this division of states are iron and steel wares, foundry and machine shop products, chemicals, woolen goods, silk, glass, and leather goods. Oil refining is the leading industry in New Jersey.

Commerce. The commercial supremacy of this group of states arises from favoring geographic conditions and from abundant transportation facilities. Two-thirds of the foreign commerce of the United States passes through New York, Philadelphia, Baltimore, and other ports of this division. Unsurpassed facilities for collecting raw materials and for distributing manufactured goods account for the growth of the larger industrial cities. Equal facilities for gathering and for distributing exports have made several cities great seaports.

The Great Lakes aid the growth of the Middle Atlantic states by furnishing a waterway for transporting raw materials needed in many industries. Of high value also are the Hudson and Mohawk valleys. These furnish easy routes of rail, river, and canal communication between the Atlantic seaboard and the West. The New York State Barge canal connects the Hudson river with the Great Lakes. The Allegheny and Monongahela rivers, uniting to form the Ohio, afford water transportation between this group of states and the central and southern parts of the United States.

CENTRAL STATES

The large division of the Union called the Central states consists of Kentucky, Ohio, Indiana, Illinois, Michigan, Wisconsin, Missouri, Iowa, Minnesota, North Dakota, South Dakota, Nebraska, and Kansas.

Surface. Prairies occupy a large part of this division. They are level or gently rolling and for the most part are covered with a rich dark soil. On such plains modern farm machinery can be used to great advantage; hence the central and eastern parts have become the chief agricultural regions of the United States.

Along the western border there is considerable highland, including the Black Hills, noted for their gold mines. In the southwest corner of South Dakota are the famous Bad Lands. These consist of a maze of ridges and pinnacles of sandstone; the soil is mostly bare clay of different colors, and the whole region is very difficult of travel.

Rivers. Most of this division is drained by the Mississippi and its affluents. Six of the states, however, border on the Great Lakes and are in part in the Saint Lawrence basin. Some streams in Minnesota, North Dakota, and South Dakota flow into the Red River of the North. Hence the waters of the Central states find their way into the Atlantic through the Gulf of Mexico, the Saint Lawrence gulf, and Hudson bay. Besides the hundreds of streams that water this vast valley, there are thousands of small lakes that dot the surface, especially in Minnesota and in North Dakota. The principal rivers navigable by steamboats are the Mississippi, Missouri, Ohio, Wabash, Illinois, and Red River of the North.

Climate. In the north, the winter is long and extremely cold weather prevails, while the summers are short and hot. Along the southern border, in Kentucky, Missouri, and Kansas, the climate is milder. Snow seldom falls there and never stays on the ground long. The rainfall is sufficient for farming over all this division, except in the extreme western plains.

Minerals. This group of states is very rich in mineral wealth. Coal is mined extensively in Kentucky, Iowa, Indiana, Ohio, Kansas, and Illinois, the last ranking third among the coal producing states of the Union. Petroleum wells are in operation in Kentucky, Indiana, Kansas, and Illinois. Natural gas is produced in several states, notably in Illinois and Indiana. Gold, silver, lead, zinc, potter's clays, building stone, gypsum, asbestos, and graphite are obtained. Michigan has long been noted for its yield of copper and salt. In Minnesota and Michigan there are vast deposits of iron ore. Because of this supply, made available by cheap transportation, great centers of the iron industry have been developed on lakes Michigan and Erie.

Forests. Michigan, Wisconsin, and Minnesota, once leaders in the cutting of timber, are still important producers of lumber and pulp wood. Pine for lumber and spruce and hemlock for pulp wood are the principal items in the annual timber cut. Despite the destruction of the chief forests, large woodlands still exist in several of the states, and forest industries furnish employment for many workers.

Agriculture. Every crop known to the temperate zones can be grown in this division. Hundreds of millions of bushels of corn, oats, barley, rye, and wheat are raised annually. Hay, potatoes, vegetables, and orchard fruits are important crops. Tobacco is cultivated in the eastern part of this division. Kentucky is one of the leading states in the Union in tobacco production. Sugar beets are grown in ten states in this group; Nebraska, Michigan, and Minnesota lead in sugar beet production. Flax is grown in the northwest. No other section of equal area on the globe rivals the central Mississippi valley in agricultural productiveness. Even on the higher western plains, abundant harvests are reaped wherever the land is irrigated.

Live Stock. Cattle, horses, mules, and hogs (fattened on corn) are raised in immense numbers. Sheep are reared in every state, and the annual wool clip totals about one-third of that of the entire United States. Dairy interests, already very large, are becoming increasingly valuable. Butter, cheese, and condensed milk from this division now go to all parts of the civilized world. Poultry farming is a profitable occupation.

Manufacturing. The range in manufacturing is exceedingly extensive. In several states the manufactures surpass in value the farm products. More automobiles are made in this division than in all the rest of the world. Meat packing is so vast an industry that it influences prices in every city in the United States. Much of the world's supply of flour is milled in these states.

The iron and steel interests, concentrated in centers of industry in northern Ohio, Indiana, and Illinois, employ many thousands of workers. The yearly output of refined petroleum represents many millions of dollars. Glass, furniture, wearing apparel, foundry and machine shop products, pottery, lumber, agricultural implements, tobacco goods, chemicals, metal wares, farm machinery, boots and shoes, beet sugar, paints and varnishes are other products whose aggregate output is enormous.

Fisheries. The Great Lakes supply annually over 100 million pounds of fish. Whitefish, ciscoes or lake herring, and lake trout constitute the principal catch. The frozen fish industry has become extensive.

Commerce. The states in this division have excellent railway facilities. Within their borders are operated more than 100,000 miles of railways, or about two-fifths of the entire railway mileage of the United States. The Ohio river and the Mississippi river are important arteries of commerce. Fleets of steamers, handling an enormous tonnage, ply on the Great Lakes. In connection with the lake traffic, the New York State Barge canal is used to transport various raw materials to the Hudson river, which serves as the final link in an all-water connection with the seaboard. But by far the larger part of the foreign shipments reach the great eastern seaports, New York, Boston, Philadelphia, and Baltimore, by railroad.

SOUTHERN STATES

Alabama, Arkansas, Florida, Georgia, Louisiana, Mississippi, North Carolina, Oklahoma, South Carolina, Tennessee, and Texas comprise the Southern states.

This division of the Union is bounded on the north by the Middle Atlantic states and by the Central states; on the east by the Atlantic Ocean; on the south by the Gulf of Mexico and Mexico; and on the west by New Mexico. The shortest distance between the extreme eastern and western limits is about 1700 miles. The width from north to south varies from about 425 to 850 miles. The total area of these eleven states is 781,657 square miles, or more than one-fourth of the area of the continental United States. For convenience of reference this division is treated in two sections—an eastern section and a western.

EASTERN SECTION

North Carolina, South Carolina, Tennessee, Georgia, Florida, Alabama, and Mississippi constitute the eastern section of the Southern states.

Surface. The Appalachian Mountain system, occupying much of this section and broadening out in the north, reaches its highest point in Mt. Mitchell, 6684 feet high, in North Carolina. Southward the mountains diminish in height until, in Alabama, they become low hills. All Florida and Mississippi, and parts of North Carolina, South Carolina, Georgia, and Alabama, are in the coastal plain. The principal rivers, including the Mississippi, Savannah, Saint John's, and Cape Fear, are navigable for steamers.

Climate and Rainfall. Along the Gulf coast, a region of heavy rains, the temperature averages about 85° F. in summer and 50° F. in winter. On the Atlantic shore, the climate is almost as warm, though not so humid. The climate of the upland districts is cool and bracing. Flowers bloom the year round in the more southern section, and the mildness of the climate draws numerous visitors to the winter resorts along both the Atlantic and the Gulf coast. From 40 inches to 60 inches of rain a year falls in the seaboard districts.

Minerals. Coal and iron ore are mined in Tennessee and Alabama, and mica in North Carolina Georgia and Tennessee produce excellent marble. Granite, limestone, and sandstone are abundant. Florida has large deposits of phosphate rock. In all these states there are numerous beds of potter's clay and other minor minerals.

Forests. Forests overspread thousands of square miles, the trees including yellow pine, cypress, hickory, ash, maple, and other hardwoods. In size and variety of species the forest trees of this section exceed those of all other parts of the Union, except the Pacific states. Lumbering is an important industry in many sections.

Agriculture. The chief occupation is farming. All the crops of the Temperate Zone can be grown in these states. Cotton is the most valuable single crop. Sea-island cotton is grown along the Atlantic coast. Millions of acres are devoted to corn and tobacco. Oats, white potatoes, peanuts, sweet potatoes, hay, wheat, and fruits are also widely cultivated. Rice is raised in the coast belt. Apples, plums, pears, watermelons, strawberries, peaches, and grapes grow in abundance. Southern Florida produces pineapples, figs, oranges, grapefruit, avocados, guavas, and other subtropical fruits. Garden vegetables are grown extensively for northern markets. Strawberries are shipped north every spring by fast-freight trains. Similarly, oranges, grapefruit, and various vegetables are sent in winter. Georgia leads in the production of pecans.

Fisheries. Oysters are obtained along the Atlantic shore. Bluefish, mullet, shad, mackerel, kingfish, tarpon, and other sea fish are caught. Valuable fisheries, including sponge fishing, are established on the Florida coast.

Stock Raising. Hogs, horses, mules, sheep, and cattle are raised in every state. Dairying has become an important industry. Milk, butter, and cheese are produced in large quantities.

Manufacturing. Manufacturing is developing rapidly in this section. Among the important industrial products are cotton textiles, cottonseed oil, cottonseed cake, lumber, iron and steel, tobacco goods, and naval stores. Cigars and cigarettes are made in great quantities in North Carolina and in Florida. Cotton goods form the leading industrial product. North Carolina leads all other states of the Union in cotton manufacturing. Flour milling and woodworking are valuable industrial interests. Iron and steel products are made in Tennessee and in Alabama. Aluminum is produced in Tennessee and North Carolina. The canning of fruits and vegetables is a growing industry in all these states. In this group, North Carolina, Georgia, and Tennessee lead in manufactures in the order named. Among important industrial centers are Atlanta, Ga., Birmingham, Ala., Winston-Salem, N. C., Memphis, Tenn., and Nashville, Tenn.

Commerce. Much merchandise for export is shipped down the Mississippi to New Orleans, where it is transferred to seagoing vessels. Portions of other rivers are utilized to some extent as inland waterways. Cotton is the largest export of this section. Pine lumber, phosphate rock, and naval stores are also sent abroad in large quantities. There are ample facilities for transportation by rail to all parts of the Union. The principal seaports serving these states are Wilmington, N. C., Charleston, S. C., Savannah, Ga., Jacksonville, Fla., Tampa, Fla., Pensacola, Fla., Mobile, Ala., and New Orleans, La.

WESTERN SECTION

Arkansas, Louisiana, Texas, and Oklahoma form the western section of the Southern states.

Surface. The northeastern part of this section is included in the Ozark plateau. This upland extends into the northern part of Arkansas and into the eastern part of Oklahoma. Louisiana and southeastern Texas lie in the coastal plain. The elevated western parts of Texas and Oklahoma form the southern extension of the Great Plains. The principal rivers are the Mississippi, Red, Brazos, Sabine, Trinity, and Colorado. All these drain into the Gulf of Mexico.

Climate and Rainfall. An abundant rainfall occurs over the eastern and southern parts of this section, while on the western side, which is mostly an elevated plain, the rainfall seldom exceeds 20 inches annually. The extreme southwest is dry. The summers are long and hot, but the Gulf winds lower the temperature, and winter is a pleasant season.

Agriculture. Agriculture is the chief source of wealth. Rich soil and favorable climate make it possible to grow in this section any crop of the Temperate Zone. Cotton is the principal crop. Other important products are rice, corn, potatoes, sweet potatoes, hay, wheat, tobacco, and numerous fruits. Vegetables are grown in enormous quantities for the northern markets. Louisiana is the leading state in sugar production. Texas is a large producer in several lines of agriculture. It is easily the first state in cotton. Texas also leads all the other states in value of crops produced. These frequently approximate a billion dollars in total value.

Lumbering. There are great forests of pine and cypress in the coastal plain and immense forests of hardwoods in high lands in the interior. This section is one of the chief timber regions of the country. Louisiana is the second state in the Union in lumber production.

Minerals. Sulphur mining is important in Louisiana and Texas. These states now furnish the world's chief supply of sulphur. Bauxite, the most valuable ore of aluminum, is obtained in Arkansas. In Oklahoma, Texas, and Louisiana, immense quantities of petroleum and natural gas are found. The Oklahoma oil field yields a very substantial proportion of the annual output of the petroleum of the United States. Beds of rock salt are worked in both Louisiana and Texas. Oklahoma is one of the leading states of the Union in zinc production and a considerable amount of lead also is obtained there. Manganese, potter's clay, quicksilver, coal, and copper are other valuable minerals obtained in this section. Building stone is abundant in all the states.

Stock Raising. The farm animals reared in this section bring enormous sums annually. Texas is the chief cattle raising state. Mules, horses, hogs, and sheep also are raised in great numbers. Texas ranks as one of the foremost wool producing states. The wool clip of Texas normally exceeds 25 million pounds annually.

Manufacturing. The principal manufactures of this section are petroleum products, lumber, refined sugar, packed meats, flour, cottonseed oil, and cottonseed cake. The manufacture of ice and of textiles are growing industries. Louisiana leads the group in the refining of cane sugar and in rice polishing, rice and sugar cane being distinctive crops of that state. Oklahoma ranks highest in the production of flour. Texas leads in manufactures, and is followed by Louisiana, Oklahoma, and Arkansas in the order named.

Commerce. The eastern part of the section has ample transportation facilities, and the thinly populated western section is crossed by numerous railways. Railroads connect all the commercial centers with the large cities east and north, and the rivers furnish hundreds of miles of waterways navigable for steamboats. The chief seaports are New Orleans, La., and Galveston, Houston, and Port Arthur, Texas. Important inland cities are Little Rock, Ark., Shreveport, La., Oklahoma City and Tulsa, Okla., Dallas, Fort Worth, San Antonio, and El Paso, Texas.

PLATEAU STATES

The Plateau states division of the Union is composed of Arizona, Colorado, Idaho, Montana, Nevada, New Mexico, Utah, and Wyoming. These states cover more than 850,000 square miles, or more than one-fourth of the total area of the United States. Idaho, the smallest state in the group, is larger than all the New England states combined.

Surface. This division embraces most of the region occupied by the Rocky Mountain system in the continental United States. The surface is mainly a series of plateaus surmounted by lofty ranges, which attain their greatest height in Colorado. The mean or average elevation of the Plateau states is approximately 5300 feet, or slightly more than one mile, above sea level. Colorado and Wyoming have the highest average elevation; Montana and Arizona, the lowest. In all of the states there are mountains which rise above 12,000 feet. Peaks more than 13,000 feet high are found in Nevada, New Mexico, Utah, and Wyoming. In Colorado, many summits rise above 14,000 feet.

In geological times this vast upland was a scene of tremendous volcanic action. There are many extinct volcanoes, and ancient lava beds cover many thousand square miles. The great geysers of Yellowstone park are situated in a volcanic region.

Rivers. The Plateau states are drained chiefly by streams belonging to two great drainage systems, the Gulf and the Pacific. Important rivers whose waters reach the Gulf of Mexico are the Rio Grande, the Arkansas, the Platte, the Yellowstone, and the Missouri. The principal rivers whose waters finally flow into the Pacific are the Colorado, Green, Grand, Snake, and Clark Fork. The Green and the Grand are affluents of the Colorado; the Snake and Clark Fork are tributaries of the Columbia.

The streams of the Great Basin, a very dry region comprising much of western Utah and nearly all of Nevada, usually flow only during the brief rainy season. They either disappear in sandy valleys or discharge their scanty waters into alkaline lakes having no outlet. The Humboldt, the largest river in Nevada, flows nearly across the state from east to west. It empties into the Humboldt and the Carson sinks where its waters evaporate, leaving alkaline deposits. Similarly, the Sevier river, the longest stream in western Utah, flows into the salty Sevier lake. The Weber, the Bear, and the Jordan are small rivers which empty into Great Salt lake.

Climate. Because of a wide range in latitude, great variations in altitude, and marked diversity of surface features, the Plateau states have many varieties of climate. On the highest mountains, arctic conditions prevail. In the elevated plains at the base of the mountains there are severe extremes of heat and cold. In the far southwest are some of the hottest desert areas known.

The widest extremes of temperature are observed on the high plains of Montana, flanking the eastern base of the Rockies. Here temperatures ranging from about 60° below zero in winter to 108° above zero in summer have been noted. In southwestern Arizona, near the Mexican border, summer temperatures of 120° have been recorded, but in winter the thermometer rarely falls below freezing. The climate of the various interior parts of the Plateau states is similar, but with less pronounced extremes.

A noteworthy feature of the climate of the plateau region is the great daily variation in temperature which takes place, especially in summer. No matter how warm the days, the nights are almost invariably cool, even in the hottest deserts.

Strong winds, which prevail in many sections, often exercise a marked influence on the climate. A well-known example is the so-called chinook, a warm wind which, sweeping down the eastern slope of the Rockies and far out on the adjacent plains, sometimes melts heavy snowfalls within a few hours.

Notwithstanding severe extremes, the climate of the Plateau states is dry and invigorating, and, on the whole, unusually salubrious.

Rainfall. On one-fifth of the United States the rainfall is so light that agriculture cannot be successfully carried on without irrigation. Most of the dry area is in this division. Because of scanty rainfall, all these states have tracts of true desert. Thousands of square miles also are covered with alkali deposits. These dreary wastes have often no vegetation whatever. In other sections, the traveler may ride for hours over dusty plains, with yuccas, cactuses, greasewoods, or sagebrushes the only conspicuous plants in sight. These require but very little moisture.

Forests. In all of the Plateau states, forests are found on the slopes of the mountains. The trees are generally pines, spruces, firs, and other conifers. About one-sixth of the total area is more or less wooded. In each state there are large forested districts under government protection. These reserves, some 90 in all, are known as national forests. Their total area, about 140,000 square miles, is greater than that of any state in the group except Montana. Among the Plateau states, Idaho, with over 30,000 square miles of protected woodlands, has the greatest area in national forests. Montana ranks second, with Colorado, Arizona, Wyoming, New Mexico, and Utah following in the order named. Nevada, with reserves of 7780 square miles, ranks last. See *Forests, U. S. National.*

Minerals. The Plateau states are exceedingly rich in mineral wealth. Among important mineral productions are gold, silver, copper, coal, petroleum, lead, tungsten, uranium, vanadium, gems, and

STATE	1820	1830	1840	1850	1860	1870	1880	1890	1900	1910	1920	1930	1940	1950	1960	1970
Alabama	19	15	12	12	13	16	17	17	18	18	18	15	17	17	19	21
Alaska	..	..	..	..	..	..	..	..	..	..	..	..	..	..	51	51
Arizona	..	..	..	..	..	46	44	47	47	46	46	44	44	38	35	33
Arkansas	26	28	25	26	25	26	25	24	25	25	25	25	24	30	31	32
California	..	..	..	29	26	24	24	22	21	12	8	6	5	2	2	1
Colorado	..	..	..	..	38	41	35	31	32	32	33	33	33	34	33	30
Connecticut	14	16	20	21	24	25	28	29	29	31	29	29	31	29	25	24
Delaware	22	24	26	30	32	35	38	43	45	47	47	47	47	47	47	47
Dist. of Col.	25	25	28	33	35	34	36	40	41	43	42	41	37	36	40	41
Florida	..	26	27	31	31	33	34	32	33	33	32	31	27	20	10	9
Georgia	11	10	9	9	11	12	13	12	11	10	12	14	14	13	16	15
Hawaii	..	..	..	..	..	..	..	..	..	..	..	..	..	..	44	40
Idaho	..	..	..	..	..	44	46	46	46	45	43	43	43	44	43	43
Illinois	24	20	14	11	4	4	4	3	3	3	3	3	3	4	4	5
Indiana	18	13	10	7	6	6	6	8	8	9	11	11	12	12	11	11
Iowa	..	..	29	27	20	11	10	10	10	15	16	19	20	22	24	25
Kansas	..	..	..	..	33	29	20	19	22	22	24	24	29	31	28	28
Kentucky	6	6	6	8	9	8	8	11	12	14	15	17	16	19	22	23
Louisiana	17	19	19	18	17	21	22	25	23	24	22	22	21	21	20	20
Maine	12	12	13	16	22	23	23	27	30	31	34	35	35	35	36	38
Maryland	10	11	15	17	19	20	23	27	26	27	28	28	28	24	21	18
Massachusetts	7	8	8	6	7	7	7	6	7	6	6	8	8	9	9	10
Michigan	27	27	23	20	16	13	9	9	9	8	7	7	7	7	7	7
Minnesota	..	..	..	36	30	28	26	20	19	19	17	18	18	18	18	19
Mississippi	21	22	17	15	14	18	18	21	20	21	23	23	23	26	29	29
Missouri	23	21	16	13	8	5	5	5	5	7	9	10	10	11	13	13
Montana	..	..	..	..	..	43	45	45	43	40	39	39	40	43	42	44
Nebraska	..	..	..	..	..	39	36	30	26	27	29	31	32	33	34	35
Nevada	..	..	..	..	..	41	40	43	49	49	49	49	49	49	50	48
New Hampshire	15	18	22	22	27	31	31	33	37	39	41	42	45	45	46	42
New Jersey	13	14	18	19	21	17	19	18	16	11	10	9	9	8	8	8
New Mexico	..	..	..	32	34	37	41	44	44	44	44	45	42	40	37	37
New York	1	1	1	1	1	1	1	1	1	1	1	1	1	1	1	2
North Carolina	4	5	7	10	12	14	15	16	15	16	14	12	11	10	12	12
North Dakota	..	..	..	..	..	42	45	42	40	37	36	38	39	42	45	46
Ohio	5	4	3	3	3	3	3	4	4	4	4	4	4	5	5	6
Oklahoma	..	..	..	..	..	..	..	39	30	23	21	21	22	25	27	27
Oregon	..	..	..	34	36	38	37	38	36	35	34	34	34	32	32	31
Pennsylvania	3	2	2	2	2	2	2	2	2	2	2	2	2	3	3	3
Rhode Island	20	23	24	28	29	32	33	36	35	38	38	37	36	37	39	39
South Carolina	8	9	11	14	18	22	21	23	24	26	26	26	26	27	26	26
South Dakota	..	..	..	..	..	..	..	35	38	36	37	36	38	41	41	45
Tennessee	9	7	5	5	10	9	12	13	14	17	19	16	15	15	17	17
Texas	..	..	..	25	23	19	11	7	6	5	5	5	6	6	6	4
Utah	..	..	..	35	37	39	39	41	42	41	40	40	41	39	38	36
Vermont	16	17	21	23	28	30	32	37	39	42	45	46	46	46	48	49
Virginia	2	3	4	4	5	10	14	15	17	20	20	20	19	16	14	14
Washington	..	..	..	..	40	42	42	34	34	30	30	30	30	23	23	22
West Virginia	..	..	..	..	..	27	29	28	28	28	27	27	25	28	30	34
Wisconsin	..	..	30	24	15	15	16	14	13	13	13	13	13	14	15	16
Wyoming	..	..	..	..	..	47	47	48	48	48	48	48	48	48	49	50

precious stones. In gold production, Colorado, Utah, and Arizona rank highest in the group. Utah, Montana, and Idaho are the chief producers of silver in the United States. In copper production, Arizona stands first, while Utah and Montana also rank among the most important copper producing states of the Union. Colorado, Wyoming, Utah, and New Mexico have valuable coal deposits. Wyoming contains rich petroleum fields. Colorado is the world's chief source of molybdenum, and Nevada and Colorado stand first in the production of tungsten.

Agriculture. Dry farming is successfully practiced in some districts, but dependence is placed chiefly upon irrigated land. This will grow most of the standard crops of the temperate zones. Wheat, barley, oats, potatoes, and sugar beets are raised. Alfalfa is a highly profitable crop, several harvests being reaped in a year. Truck farm products, as Colorado and Arizona melons, bring high prices in eastern markets. Apple culture has become a valuable pursuit in Montana and Idaho. Peaches are grown in Colorado and Utah. In the southwest, the hot climate fosters the growth of dates, olives, figs, oranges, and other subtropical fruits. Egyptian or long-staple cotton has become a leading crop in Arizona.

Government irrigation work has already reclaimed millions of acres of arid land. Farms of irrigated soil are small, and intensive agriculture is practiced. Improved land in farms comprises about one-twentieth of the total area. Montana has the largest acreage of crop land, Colorado stands second, and Idaho is third.

Stock Raising. For many years, stock raising has been an important industry in this division, and much capital is invested in the rearing of cattle, sheep, and horses. These rank in value in the order named. The annual wool clip of these states amounts to about two-fifths of that of the entire United States. Native grasses afford excellent pasturage, and, in the southern and central parts, farm animals feed in the open all the year round. Large numbers of cattle are sent to Omaha, Kansas City, Chicago, and other meat packing centers, where they are slaughtered, the meat being packed and distributed largely in refrigerator cars.

Manufacturing. Copper, lead, refined ores, flour, beet sugar, butter, condensed milk, dressed meat, canned vegetables, railroad cars, foundry materials, and lumber are the principal industrial products of the Plateau states. Manufacturing to supply local needs is increasing. Immense water power is available for future development. Colorado stands first among these states in value of manufactures; Montana is second, Utah third, and Arizona fourth.

Commerce. Railroads afford ready transportation to all parts of the Union. Several transcontinental lines cross this section, and there are numerous local lines. Mine products, lumber, cattle, cotton, and fruits form the chief items of outgoing shipment. These are sent both to the East and to the West chiefly in exchange for manufactures and other staples which the plateau region does not as yet produce.

PACIFIC STATES—CONTIGUOUS

The Pacific States consist of (1) the three continental States of California, Oregon, and Washington and (2) the off-shore states of Alaska and Hawaii. The geography of the three continental Pacific states will be treated here as a unit, as with the preceding regions of continental United States. But since Alaska and Hawaii are separate geographic areas, each of them will be treated separately.

Surface. No other equal area in the continental United States displays such diversity in surface features as does this division. In its mountain ranges are found the highest peaks, and in its deserts occur the lowest depressions. The rivers plunge down from alpine valleys over the highest known waterfalls. Here also is the only active volcano in the country.

The Sierra Nevada range extends nearly north and south through eastern California and, under the name of the Cascade range, continues northward through Oregon and Washington. Near the Pacific shore, the Coast ranges traverse these states from north to south. Between the Sierra Nevada and the Coast ranges lies the great central valley of California. This is about 50 miles wide and 400 miles long and is remarkably fertile. In the southern part, irrigation is needed for successful farming. Farther north are the Columbia, Willamette, and Puget Sound valleys, all having soil of great fertility.

The extensive region lying east of the Sierra Nevada and the Cascades is mostly a barren desert. An exception is the fertile district situated between the Columbia and Snake rivers. A highland, largely of volcanic origin, known as the Columbia River plateau, occupies much of eastern Oregon and Washington. Parts of California adjacent to Nevada form the western rim of the Great Basin. East of the southernmost extensions of the Sierra Nevada and bordering on Arizona are the Mojave desert and the Colorado desert. On the Pacific side of the Sierra Madre, San Bernardino, and other ranges that form the western borders of these deserts, lies the valley of southern California, a coastal plain of remarkable productiveness under irrigation.

Rivers. The Columbia, which rises in Canada, is the only large navigable river in the Pacific states. Together with its tributaries, the most important of which are the Snake and the Willamette, the Columbia drains the greater part of Oregon and Washington. Next in importance are the Sacramento and the San Joaquin. The lower portions of each of these streams are navigable. These two rivers, with their affluents, drain the great central valley of California. There are numerous smaller streams, many of which are broken by rapids or falls. Some of these furnish hydroelectric power. Numerous streams supply water for mining and for irrigation purposes.

Climate. The great length of this division and its intersection by several mountain ranges result in many varieties of climate. These range from the very wet to the very dry, and from the arctic cold of high mountain tops to the torrid heat of California's southeastern deserts. Owing to the moderating influence of winds from the ocean, a mild climate prevails along the entire Pacific shore. This coastal climate ranges from subtropical and dry in southern California to temperate and moist in the Puget Sound region.

Rainfall. In western Washington, the rainfall over the valleys averages 65 inches a year and, in the mountain districts, reaches 100 inches. Western Oregon also has a heavy rainfall. But in the eastern sections of both states less than 20 inches of rain falls annually. In parts of the Colorado desert near the Arizona boundary, the average yearly rainfall is less than three inches.

Summer is a dry season in this division, and the winters are wet. In summer, trays of fruits are left outdoors, day and night, to dry, the drying period often lasting several weeks. Abundant rain falls in northern California, but, in the southern part of the state, irrigation is essential for crop raising.

Minerals. Gold was discovered in California in 1848, and since then the state has yielded every year millions of dollars worth of this precious metal. Though gold is now mined in several other states, California still leads in gold production.

At least 50 other minerals of high commercial value are found in this division. Among them are silver, lead, copper, bismuth, manganese, quicksilver, tungsten, chromium, zinc, magnesite, lithium, and arsenic. The southeastern deserts of California contain immense deposits of borax. Coal of good quality is mined in Washington. Building stone is quarried in all the states. But the most important product is petroleum. California's output of petroleum exceeds in value the yield of all her mines.

TWENTY-FIVE LARGEST CITIES OF THE UNITED STATES

City and Rank	Population 1900	Population 1910	Population 1920	Population 1930	Population 1940	Population 1950	Population 1960	Population 1970
1. New York, N.Y.†	3,437,202	4,766,833	5,620,048	6,930,446	7,454,995	7,891,957	7,781,984	7,867,760
2. Chicago, Ill.	1,698,575	2,185,283	2,701,705	3,376,438	3,396,808	3,620,962	3,550,404	3,366,957
3. Los Angeles, Calif.	102,489	319,198	576,673	1,238,048	1,504,277	1,970,358	2,479,015	2,816,061
4. Philadelphia, Pa.	1,293,697	1,549,008	1,823,779	1,950,961	1,931,334	2,071,605	2,002,512	1,948,609
5. Detroit, Mich.	285,704	465,766	993,678	1,658,452	1,623,452	1,849,568	1,670,144	1,511,482
6. Houston, Texas	44,633	78,800	138,276	292,342	384,514	596,163	938,219	1,231,394
7. Baltimore, Md.	508,957	558,485	733,826	804,874	859,100	949,708	939,024	905,759
8. Dallas, Texas	42,638	92,104	158,976	260,475	294,734	434,462	679,684	844,401
9. Washington, D.C.	278,817	331,069	437,571	468,869	663,091	802,178	763,956	756,510
10. Cleveland, Ohio	381,768	560,663	796,841	900,429	878,336	914,808	876,050	750,903
11. Indianapolis, Ind.	163,502	233,650	314,194	364,161	386,972	427,173	476,258	743,155
12. Milwaukee, Wisc.	285,315	373,857	457,147	578,249	587,472	637,392	741,324	717,099
13. San Francisco, Calif.	342,782	416,912	506,676	634,394	634,536	775,357	742,855	715,674
14. San Diego, Calif.	17,700	39,578	74,683	147,995	203,341	334,387	573,224	693,931
15. San Antonio, Texas	53,321	96,614	161,379	231,542	253,854	408,442	587,718	654,153
16. Boston, Mass.	560,892	670,585	748,060	781,188	770,816	801,444	697,197	641,071
17. Memphis, Tenn.	102,390	131,105	162,351	253,143	292,942	354,102	497,524	623,497
18. St. Louis, Mo.	575,238	687,029	772,897	821,960	816,960	856,796	750,026	622,236
19. New Orleans, La.	287,104	339,075	387,219	458,762	494,537	570,445	627,525	591,502
20. Phoenix, Ariz.	5,544	11,134	29,053	48,118	65,414	106,818	439,170	581,562
21. Columbus, Ohio	125,560	181,511	237,031	290,564	306,087	375,901	471,316	539,677
22. Seattle, Wash.	80,671	237,194	315,312	365,593	368,302	467,591	557,087	530,831
23. Pittsburgh, Pa.	451,512	533,905	558,343	669,817	671,659	676,806	604,332	520,117
24. Jacksonville, Fla.	28,429	57,699	91,558	129,549	173,065	204,517	201,030	518,131
25. Denver, Colo.	133,859	213,381	256,491	287,861	322,412	415,786	493,887	514,678

† Population of the city as now constituted.　Source: U.S. Bureau of the Census.

ITEM	1870	1880	1890	1900	1910
AREA, POPULATION, WEALTH, AND DEBT:					
Area . . . . Sq. mi.	3,026,789	3,026,789	3,026,789	3,026,789	3,026,789
Population	38,558,371	50,155,783	62,947,714	75,994,575	91,972,266
Wealth . . . . $	30,068,518,000	43,642,000,000	65,037,091,000	88,517,307,000	187,739,071,090 (a)
Wealth per capita . . . . $	779.83	870.20	1,035.57	1,164.79	1,965.00 (a)
Debt, national . . . . $	2,331,169,956	1,919,326,747	890,784,370	1,107,711,257	1,046,449,185
Debt, per capita . . . . . . $	60.46	38.27	14.13	14.55	11.34
Interest on debt . . . . $	118,784,960	79,633,981	29,417,603	33,545,130	21,275,602
AGRICULTURE:					
Farms, number of	2,659,985	4,008,907	4,564,641	5,737,372	6,361,502
Persons engaged in agriculture . . No.	5,922,471	7,713,875	8,565,926	10,381,765	12,659,203
Value farms and farm property . . . $	8,944,857,749	12,180,501,538	16,082,267,689	20,439,901,164	40,991,449,000
Value farm products . . . . . . $	1,958,030,927	2,212,540,927	2,460,107,454	4,717,069,973	8,498,311,413
Wheat produced . . . . . . bu.	235,884,700	498,549,868	399,262,000	522,229,505	635,121,000
Corn produced . . . . bu.	1,094,255,000	1,717,434,543	1,489,970,000	2,105,102,516	2,886,260,000
Cotton produced . . . . 500 lb. bales	4,024,527	6,356,998	8,562,089	10,123,027	11,608,616
Sugar (cane) produced . . . . . lbs.	87,043,000	178,872,000	301,284,395	322,549,011	750,400,000
Sugar (beet) produced . . . . . lbs.	806,000	2,688,000	4,934,720	163,458,075	1,024,938,000
Farm animals, value . . . . . . $	1,518,465,000	1,576,917,556	2,418,766,028	2,228,123,134	5,138,486,000
Wool produced . . . . lbs.	162,000,000	232,500,000	276,000,000	288,636,621	321,362,750
MINERAL PRODUCTION:					
Gold, value of . . . . $	50,000,000	36,000,000	32,845,000	79,171,000	96,269,100
Silver, value of . . . . $	16,434,000	34,717,000	57,242,100	35,741,100	30,854,500
Coal . . . . tons	29,496,054	63,822,830	140,866,931	240,789,310	447,853,909
Petroleum . . . . gals.	220,951,290	1,104,017,166	1,924,590,024	2,672,062,218	8,801,404,416
Iron ore . . . . tons	3,031,891	7,120,362	16,036,043	27,553,161	56,889,734
Pig iron . . . . tons	1,665,179	3,835,191	9,202,703	13,789,242	27,303,567
Steel . . . . tons	68,750	1,247,335	4,277,071	10,188,329	26,094,919
Copper . . . . tons	12,600	27,000	115,966	270,588	482,214
Total minerals . . . . $	218,598,994	364,928,298	606,476,380	1,107,031,392	1,991,216,220
MANUFACTURES:					
Establishments . . . . No.		253,852	355,405	207,514	268,491
Officials, clerks . . . . . . No.	. . . . .	. . . . .	461,001	364,120	790,267
Salaries paid . . . . $	. . . . .	. . . . .	391,984,660	380,771,321	938,574,967
Wage earners . . . . No.	. . . . .	2,732,595	4,251,535	4,712,763	6,615,046
Wages paid . . . . $	. . . . .	947,953,795	1,891,209,696	2,008,361,119	3,427,037,884
Cost of materials . . . . $	. . . . .	3,396,823,549	5,162,013,878	6,575,851,491	12,142,790,878
Products, value of . . . . $	. . . . .	5,369,579,191	9,372,378,843	11,406,926,701	20,672,051,870
Iron and steel manufactures . . . . $		296,557,685	478,687,519	803,968,273	1,377,151,817
Cotton manufactures . . . . . . $		192,090,110	267,981,724	339,200,320	628,391,813
Wood manufactures . . . . . . $		238,085,686	270,527,511	296,990,484	507,166,710
Electricity generated 1000 kwh				4,768,000 (c)	17,572,000 (d)
Radios manufactured, value . . . . $					
Rayon manufactured, value . . . . $					
TRANSPORTATION:					
Vessels built . . . . tons	276,953	157,409	294,122	393,790	342,068
Vessels, foreign trade . . . . . . tons	1,516,800	1,352,810	946,695	826,694	791,825
Vessels, coastwise trade . . . . . tons	2,729,707	2,715,224	3,477,802	4,338,145	6,716,257
Vessels, Great Lakes trade . . . . tons	684,704	605,102	1,063,063	1,565,587	2,895,102
Railways . . . . miles	52,922	93,262	163,597	193,346	240,293

* The information herein given has been derived from the Statistical Abstract of the United States and other authoritative sources. For various items satisfactory statistics covering some dates are unavailable. In such cases the spaces are marked with leaders, thus . . . . . In other cases, such as petroleum, the telephone, or beet sugar, in which the subject in question had not yet been discovered, invented, or brought to substantial production or use, the space corresponding to the date is left blank. The statistics of manufactures from 1880 to 1940, inclusive, are those of the Federal census, but, in each case, the figures are those of the preceding year, 1879, 1889, 1899, 1909, 1919, 1929, and 1939. The same applies to agricultural production.

merce, Industry, and Important Productions*

1920	1930	1940	1950	1960	1969 (prel.)
3,026,789	3,026,789	3,022,387	3,022,387	3,615,210	3,615,210
105,710,620	122,775,046	131,669,275	150,689,361	179,323,175	203,184,772 (u)
290,000,000,000 (b)	320,840,000,000 (j)	365,000,000,000 (o)	1,054,700,000,000	1,682,100,000,000	2,828,000,000,000 (r)
2,689.34 (b)	2,919 (j)	2,862 (o)	6,932	9,391.48	13,854 (r)
24,330,889,731	16,185,310,000	42,967,513,037	257,357,352,251	286,330,760,848	353,720,000,000
228.64	131.83	325.19	1,696.61	1,585.60	1,741
1,016,592,219	659,347,613	1,040,935,697	5,749,913,000	9,180,000,000	16,588,000,000
6,448,343	6,288,648	6,096,799	5,382,162	(p)3,707,846	2,971,000
10,661,410	10,482,323	9,162,547	10,351,000	6,316,336	4,514,000
77,924,100,338	57,245,544,269	33,641,738,726	75,830,000,000	127,855,000,000	202,600,000,000
21,425,623,614	11,387,396,953	9,583,000,000		30,656,524,000	44,386,000,000 (s)
833,027,000	806,648,955	816,698,000	1,026,755,000	1,363,443,000	1,576,000,000
3,208,584,000	2,130,751,782	2,449,200,000	3, 131,009,000	4,353,000,000	4,444,000,000
13,439,603	14,574,405	12,686,000	10,012,000	14,309,000	10,080,000
241,998,400	399,218,000	1,008,000,000	1,128,000,000	3,540,000,000	4,498,000,000
1,452,902,000	2,036,000,000	3,516,000,000	4,018,000,000	4,800,000,000	6,842,000,000
8,165,194,000	6,064,051,430	5,181,951,000	7,481,000,000	16,200,000,000	20,100,000,000
277,905,000	336,007,000	449,800,000	247,000,000	300,163,000	182,900,000
51,186,900	47,247,600	210,108,700	80,100,000	56,133,000	72,000,000
60,801,955	19,538,029	49,483,000	38,291,545	28,233,000	73,000,000
587,331,190	536,911,136	504,729,640	560,377,703	432,677,000	556,706,000 (s)
18,622,884,000	37,643,130,000	56,777,574,000	82,890,104,000	108,132,780,000	141,288,000,000
69,558,000	58,408,664	75,198,084	97,151,000	59,164,000	89,242,000
36,925,987	31,752,169	41,927,645	64,586,907	68,566,000	95,017,000
42,132,934	40,699,483	66,983,000	96,836,075	99,282,000	141,262,000
539,759	697,195	909,084	911,352	824,846,000	1,558,000
6,707,000,000	4,764,800,000	5,582,500,000	11,855,000,000	17,241,000,000	26,878,000,000
290,105	210,710	184,230	247,307	286,814	311,754 (r)
1,447,227	1,377,760	1,048,607	2,603,691	15,964,000	5,382,000
2,892,371,494	3,579,624,574	2,540,357,370	12,033,313,000	77,983,000,000	50,889,000,000
9,096,372	8,807,536	7,886,567	11,766,056	11,644,000	13,999,000
10,533,600,340	11,649,536,855	9,089,940,916	34,565,698,000	49,504,000,000	81,611,000,000
37,376,380,283	38,293,533,500	32,160,106,681		9,076,451,000	N.A.
62,418,078,773	70,137,459,352	56,843,024,800	89,675,779,000	141,270,297,000	215,383,000,000
3,623,368,934	7,138,007,000	4,779,866,341	N.A.	9,481,200,000	19,568,800,000
2,195,565,881	1,524,177,000	1,168,171,469	3,294,023,000	N.A.	N.A.
1,234,657,092	827,006,000	711,580,350	1,355,209,000	N.A.	N.A.
43,555,900	95,936,000	114,984,565	329,141,343,000	797,354,000	1,334,000,000
	411,637,000	275,870,165	675,000,000	N.A.	217,000,000
	149,546,000 (l)	247,065,556		N.A.	N.A.
3,880,639	254,296	449,221	404,617	409,736	418,000
9,928,595	6,303,000	3,047,000	8,352,000	325,670,000	12,268,000
6,395,429	9,765,000	10,654,000	3,924,000	205,535,000	⎱ 13,839,000
3,138,690	2,758,000	1,641,000	1,131,000	131,220,000	⎰
252,845	249,052	233,670	226,101	383,912	208,111 (t)

(a) 1912. (b) Estimate of Prof. David Friday. (c) 1902. (d) 1912. (e) Exclusive of rural delivery routes. (f) Includes food animals. (g) Includes foodstuffs. (h) Includes manufactures ready for consumption and manufactures for further use in manufacturing. (i) Ordinary disbursements which include disbursements for war, navy, Indians, pensions, payment for interest, and "civil and miscellaneous," but do not include payments for Panama Canal, public debt, special purposes, or postal service. (j) 1926. (k) 1927. (l) Includes "allied products," such as cellophane. (n) 1937. (o) 1938; estimate by National Resources Planning Board. (p) 1959. (q) 1968; 59.3% military. (r) 1967p. (s) 1968. (t) First track; excludes Alaska. (u) 1970.

Item	1870	1880	1890	1900	1910
TRANSPORTATION—Con.					
Automobiles manufactured . . . . No.				3,700 (c)	127,731 (d)
Automobiles in use . . . . No.				5,000	501,000
Aircraft manufactured, value . . . . $					
COMMUNICATIONS:					
Post Offices . . . . No.	28,492	42,989	62,401	76,688	59,580
Post Routes (e) . . . . miles	231,232	343,888	427,990	500,990	447,998
Air Mail Routes . . . . miles					
Telegraphs . . . . . . miles of line	. . . . . .	85,645	183,917	192,705	214,360
Telephones . . . . . . No. stations		47,880	227,857	1,355,911	7,635,367
COMMERCE:					
Imports, merchandise, total . . . . $	435,958,408	667,954,746	789,310,409	849,941,184	1,556,947,430
Imports, free . . . . $	20,140,786	208,301,863	265,668,629	367,236,866	755,311,396
Imports, dutiable . . . . $	415,817,622	459,652,883	523,641,780	482,704,318	801,636,034
Imports, per cent free	4.62	31.19	33.66	43.21	48.51
Imports, per capita . . . . $	11.06	12.51	12.14	10.91	16.52
Imports, agricultural . . . . $	191,559,361	314,617,480	384,100,435	420,139,288	87,509,115
Imports, foodstuffs (rude) (f) . . . . $	54,081,091	100,297,040	128,480,142	97,916,293	144,776,636
Imports, foodstuffs (mfg.) (g) . . . . $	96,081,635	118,125,216	133,332,031	133,027,374	181,566,572
Imports, raw materials for mfg. . . . $	55,615,202	131,861,617	170,637,250	276,241,152	566,270,770
Imports, manufactures (h) . . . . . $	229,183,959	307,366,921	347,609,661	337,348,386	652,861,740
Imports, sugar . . . . lbs.	1,196,773,569	1,829,291,684	2,934,011,560	4,018,086,530	4,094,545,936
Imports, coffee . . . . lbs.	235,256,574	446,850,727	499,159,120	787,991,911	873,983,689
Imports, tea . . . . lbs.	47,408,481	72,162,936	83,886,829	84,845,107	85,626,370
Imports wool (raw) . . . . . . lbs.	49,230,199	128,131,747	105,431,285	155,928,455	263,928,232
Imports, cotton (raw) . . . . . . lbs.	1,698,133	3,547,792	8,606,049	67,398,521	86,037,691
Imports, raw silk . . . . lbs.	583,589	2,562,236	7,510,440	13,073,718	23,457,223
Imports, rubber (crude) . . . . . lbs.	9,624,098	16,826,099	33,842,374	49,377,138	101,044,681
Exports, domestic, total . . . . . $	376,616,473	823,946,353	845,293,828	1,370,763,571	1,710,083,998
Exports, agricultural . . . . . . $	296,962,357	694,315,497	634,855,869	844,616,530	871,158,425
Exports, foodstuffs (crude) (f) . . . $	41,852,630	266,108,950	132,073,183	225,906,246	109,828,320
Exports, foodstuffs (mfg.) (g) . . . . $	50,919,666	193,352,723	224,756,580	319,696,334	259,259,654
Exports, raw materials for mfg. . . . $	213,439,991	238,787,934	304,566,922	325,244,296	565,934,957
Exports, manufactures (h) . . . . . $	70,040,845	121,818,298	178,982,042	485,022,156	766,981,245
Exports, iron and steel mfg. . . . . $	13,483,163	14,716,524	25,542,208	121,913,548	179,133,186
Exports, automobiles . . . . . . $					
Exports, meat and meat products . . $	21,396,050	113,769,604	123,880,422	175,226,535	128,382,362
Exports, wheat . . . . $	47,171,229	190,546,305	45,275,906	73,237,080	47,806,598
Exports, wheat flour . . . . $	21,169,593	35,333,197	57,036,168	67,760,886	47,621,467
Exports, cotton, quantity . . . . lbs.	958,558,523	1,822,061,114	2,471,799,853	3,100,583,188	3,206,708,226
Exports, cotton, value . . . . . . $	227,027,624	211,535,905	250,968,792	241,832,737	450,447,243
FINANCE:					
Money in circulation . . . . . . $	676,284,427	973,382,228	1,429,251,270	2,055,150,997	3,102,355,605
Circulation per capita . . . . . . $	17.51	19.41	22.82	26.93	34.33
Government receipts . . . . . . $	395,959,834	333,526,501	403,080,983	567,240,852	675,511,715
Receipts per capita . . . . . . $	10.26	6.65	6.43	7.43	7.48
Customs . . . . $	194,538,374	186,522,065	229,668,585	233,164,871	333,683,445
Internal Revenue . . . . $	184,899,756	124,009,374	142,606,706	295,327,927	289,933,519
Government disbursements (i) . . . $	293,657,005	264,847,637	297,736,487	487,713,792	659,705,391
Disbursements per capita . . . . $	7.61	5.28	4.75	6.39	7.30
Disbursements, war . . . . . . $	57,655,675	38,116,916	44,582,838	134,774,768	155,911,706
Disbursements, navy . . . . . . $	21,780,230	13,536,985	22,006,206	55,953,078	123,173,717
Pensions paid . . . . $	28,340,202	56,777,174	106,936,855	140,877,316	160,696,416
Pensioners . . . . No.	198,686	250,802	537,944	993,529	921,083

* The information herein given has been derived from the Statistical Abstract of the United States and other authoritative sources. For various items satisfactory statistics covering some dates are unavailable. In such cases the spaces are marked with leaders, thus . . . . . In other cases, such as petroleum, the telephone, or beet sugar, in which the subject in question had not yet been discovered, invented, or brought to substantial production or use, the space corresponding to the date is left blank. The statistics of manufactures from 1880 to 1940, inclusive, are those of the Federal census, but, in each case, the figures are those of the preceding year, 1879, 1889, 1899, 1909, 1919, 1929. The same applies to agricultural production.

merce, Industry, and Important Productions*

1920	1930	1940	1950	1960	1969 (prel.)
1,974,016	4,587,400	3,692,328	8,003,245	6,703,108	8,224,329
9,231,941	23,121,589	32,025,365	49,161,691	71,497,399	78,445,000
	72,019,000	550,000,000	N.A.	6,924,000,000	25,592,000,000
52,638	49,063	44,095	41,464	34,955	32,064
435,342	503,918	541,514	668,265	N.A.	N.A.
3,094	14,907	37,943	158,977	231,604	388,804
246,214	256,809 (k)	250,880 (n)	1,435,000	1,102,000	N.A.
13,329,379	20,201,576	20,830,950	38,045,000	62,683,000	96,099,000
5,238,352,114	3,060,908,000	2,625,445,000	8,743,000,000	14,562,000,000	35,870,000,000
3,405,233,003	2,051,110,000	1,648,285,000	4,766,786,000	5,780,000,000	13,017,000,000
1,833,119,111	1,009,798,000	892,004,000	3,976,304,000	8,872,000,000	22,853,000,000
65.01	67.0	65	54.5	39.45	36
47.22	24.90	19.93	N.A.	80.06	174.15
3,011,368,157	1,899,521,000	1,285,300,000	5,146,232,000	4,795,000,000	4,958,000,000
577,626,948	400,125,000	285,112,000	1,749,556,000	1,722,000,000	2,141,000,000
1,238,138,941	293,448,000	277,444,000	898,423,000	1,566,000,000	3,043,000,000
1,751,893,014	1,002,161,000	1,010,394,000	2,465,489,000	3,092,000,000	4,121,000,000
1,679,228,466	1,365,175,000	967,339,000	1,503,704	5,258,000,000	26,747,000,000
8,073,759,849	6,989,319,000	5,829,080,000	413,506,000	9,104,000,000	9,528,000,000
1,417,063,513	1,599,317,000	2,055,065,000		3,093,523,000	2,676,000,000
97,826,106	84,926,000	98,963,000	48,869,000	108,233,000	139,961,000
259,617,641	163,734,000	360,637,000	170,787,000	235,000,000	93,523,000
299,994,378	128,373,000	131,780,000		N.A.	21,952,000
30,058,374	81,993,000	47,600,000	22,450,000	4,757,138,000	1,904,000
566,456,136	1,089,830,000	1,824,722,000	742,740,000	1,384,000,000	1,311,000,000
8,080,480,821	3,843,181,000	4,021,564,000	12,584,000,000	20,300,000,000	37,444,000,000
3,466,619,819	1,495,823,000	516,856,000	3,411,000,000	2,271,000,000	5,936,000,000
917,990,828	178,533,000	74,019,000	759,753,000	1,639,000,000	2,086,000,000
1,116,605,173	362,650,000	166,881,000		1,117,000,000	1,782,000,000
1,870,767,054	829,098,000	456,078,000	1,886,042,000	3,522,000,000	3,476,000,000
4,163,354,637	1,898,089,000	3,237,687,000	5,773,238,000	11,435,000,000	30,101,000,000
1,112,835,237	1,186,827,000	515,595,000		858,000,000	940,000,000
	314,536,000	254,322,000	703,000,000	1,216,000,000	1,010,000,000
463,256,758	186,563,000	35,900,000	107,000,000	730,000,000	209,779,000
596,975,396	88,093,000	11,209,000	646,411,000		726,020,000
224,472,448	69,401,000	20,400,000	102,319,000	969,000,000	104,217,000
3,179,313,336	3,492,234,000	2,046,310,000	2,213,500,000	7,532,000	1,192,320,000
1,136,408,916	496,798,000	213,400,000	1,024,000,000	988,000,000	280,408,000
5,467,600,000	4,521,987,962	7,847,500,588	27,156,290,042	32,869,000,000	53,591,000,000
51.32	36.71	59.39	179.03	180.36	267.60
6,704,414,438	4,177,941,702	5,924,836,402	37,044,733,557	77,763,460,220	187,792,000,000 (o)
63.00	34.47	44.09	245.82	433.65	937.80
323,536,559	587,000,903	348,590,635	422,650,328	1,083,000,000	2,319,000,000
5,399,149,245	3,039,295,013	5,340,452,346	38,957,131,315	91,774,803,000	143,329,000,000 (p)
6,141,745,240	3,994,152,487	9,666,085,539	40,166,835,915	76,539,412,798	184,556,000,000 (q)
57.72	32.96	73.16	266.53	426.82	921.75
1,094,834,202	453,524,973	667,100,000	4,147,389,907	9,392,000,000	76,970,000,000
629,893,116	374,165,639	891,600,000	4,125,134,514	11,642,000,000	. . . .
213,344,204	418,433,000	556,700,000	2,009,462,298	3,605,000,000	26,175,600,000 (s)
592,190	451,433	600,848	3,026,361	4,173,921	24,877,900 (s)

(a) 1912. (b) Est. of Prof. David Friday. (c) 1902. (d) 1912. (e) Exclusive of rural delivery routes. (f) Includes food animals. (g) Includes foodstuffs. (h) Includes manufactures ready for consumption and manufactures for further use in manufacturing. (i) Disbursements for war, navy, Indians, pensions, interest payments, and "civil and miscellaneous," but not payments for Panama Canal, public debt, special purposes, or postal service. (j) 1926. (k) 1927. (l) Includes "allied products," such as cellophane. (m) 1937. (n) Total receipts, year ending June 30, 1969. (o) Federal funds, year ending June 30, 1969. (p) Total outlays, year ending June 30, 1969. (q) Military defense. (r) Social Security (OASDHI) payments and beneficiaries, year ending June 30, 1969.

AIR TRAVEL DISTANCES BETWEEN IMPORTANT CENTERS IN THE UNITED STATES

	Washington, D.C.	Seattle, Wash.	San Francisco, Cal.	Salt Lake City, Utah	St. Louis, Mo.	Portland, Ore.	Pittsburgh, Pa.	Philadelphia, Pa.	Omaha, Nebr.	Oklahoma City, Okla.	New York, N.Y.	New Orleans, La.	Nashville, Tenn.	Minneapolis, Minn.	Miami, Fla.	Memphis, Tenn.	Louisville, Ky.	Los Angeles, Calif.	Kansas City, Kansas	Jacksonville, Fla.	Indianapolis, Ind.	Houston, Texas	Detroit, Mich.	Denver, Colo.	Dal.-Ft. Worth, Texas	Cleveland, O.	Cincinnati, O.	Chicago, Ill.	Boston, Mass.	Atlanta, Ga.
Atlanta, Ga.	547	2,354	2,308	1,850	516	2,369	536	667	1,016	919	762	427	213	942	614	346	324	1,981	745	277	433	730	619	1,421	738	587	377	592	946	
Boston, Mass.	399	2,831	2,733	2,135	1,118	2,720	483	279	1,301	1,574	184	1,370	961	1,204	1,289	1,161	868	2,739	1,280	1,023	821	1,673	632	1,786	1,565	570	814	879		946
Chicago, Ill.	600	1,748	1,856	1,258	251	1,804	461	671	424	711	724	860	426	350	1,199	508	270	1,860	405	929	162	994	247	909	857	307	255		879	592
Cincinnati, O.	398	2,003	2,237	1,513	307	2,059	285	518	679	818	613	804	247	605	1,044	447	91	1,910	550	714	107	933	242	1,102	870	210		255	814	377
Cleveland, O.	310	2,259	2,163	1,565	491	2,150	124	363	731	1,002	458	1,097	457	657	1,109	657	301	2,054	712	779	263	1,405	91	1,216	1,080		210	307	570	587
Dallas - Ft. Worth	1,183	2,199	1,570	1,063	547	1,670	1,318	1,303	617	181	1,381	437	623	860	1,405	423	779	1,243	452	779	806	241	1,045	683		1,080	870	857	1,565	738
Denver, Colo.	1,519	1,074	956	380	781	987	1,349	1,578	485	676	1,633	1,120	1,084	840	1,911	1,115	1,046	838	552	1,758	1,011	924	1,156		683	1,216	1,102	909	1,786	1,421
Detroit, Mich.	398	1,947	2,103	1,505	463	2,003	214	442	671	942	486	987	489	549	1,200	635	333	2,052	692	870	252	1,121		1,156	1,045	91	242	247	632	619
Houston, Tex.	1,274	1,910	1,737	1,304	743	1,911	1,311	1,394	858	422	1,489	303	686	1,101	996	486	842	1,484	692	819	869		1,121	924	241	1,405	933	994	1,673	730
Indianapolis	500	1,998	2,146	1,420	230	1,966	338	580	589	692	658	735	251	512	1,040	383	109	1,819	451	710		869	252	1,011	806	263	107	162	821	433
Jacksonville	640	2,617	2,523	2,127	793	2,673	826	760	1,348	1,256	839	516	490	1,219	330	623	601	2,196	1,022		710	819	870	1,758	779	779	714	929	1,023	277
Kansas City	959	1,626	1,687	931	229	1,539	797	1,048	165	306	1,117	680	532	408	1,352	486	494	1,360		1,022	451	692	692	552	452	712	550	405	1,280	745
Los Angeles	2,426	956	327	575	1,589	821	2,157	2,467	1,323	1,259	2,624	1,680	1,791	1,768	2,611	1,666	1,947		1,360	2,196	1,819	1,484	2,052	838	1,243	2,054	1,910	1,860	2,739	1,981
Louisville, Ky.	469	2,032	2,181	1,528	265	2,113	376	589	694	727	684	655	156	620	931	356		1,947	494	601	109	842	333	1,046	779	301	91	270	868	324
Memphis	762	2,256	1,993	1,448	257	2,055	721	876	651	476	971	352	200	858	887		356	1,666	486	623	383	486	635	1,115	423	657	447	508	1,161	346
Miami, Fla.	922	2,947	3,055	2,457	1,123	3,097	1,108	1,042	1,623	1,586	1,106	693	820	1,549		887	931	2,611	1,352	330	1,040	996	1,200	1,911	1,405	1,109	1,044	1,199	1,289	614
Minneapolis	950	1,398	1,671	987	492	1,454	770	1,021	283	714	1,020	1,176	763		1,549	858	620	1,768	408	1,219	512	1,101	549	840	860	657	605	350	1,204	942
Nashville	562	2,161	2,118	1,452	303	2,217	532	676	697	616	771	499		763	820	200	156	1,791	532	490	251	686	489	1,084	623	457	247	426	961	213
New Orleans	971	2,608	2,007	1,434	609	2,664	928	1,091	933	618	1,186		499	1,176	693	352	655	1,680	680	516	735	303	987	1,120	437	1,097	804	860	1,370	427
New York	215	2,418	2,580	1,982	888	2,528	320	95	1,148	1,419		1,186	771	1,020	1,106	971	684	2,624	1,117	839	658	1,489	486	1,633	1,381	458	613	724	184	762
Oklahoma C'y	1,178	1,666	1,434	972	462	1,663	1,030	1,292	471		1,419	618	616	714	1,586	476	727	1,259	306	1,256	692	422	942	676	181	1,002	818	711	1,574	919
Omaha, Nebr.	1,034	1,533	1,434	839	394	1,422	844	1,093		471	1,148	933	697	283	1,623	651	694	1,323	165	1,348	589	858	671	485	617	731	679	424	1,301	1,016
Philadelphia	120	2,384	2,525	1,927	841	2,512	251		1,093	1,292	95	1,091	676	1,021	1,042	876	589	2,467	1,048	760	580	1,394	442	1,578	1,303	363	518	671	279	667
Pittsburgh	186	2,418	2,418	1,811	568	2,217		251	844	1,030	320	928	532	770	1,108	721	376	2,157	797	826	338	1,311	214	1,349	1,318	124	285	461	483	536
Portland, Ore.	2,453	135	552	637	1,678		2,217	2,512	1,422	1,663	2,528	2,664	2,217	1,454	3,097	2,055	2,113	821	1,539	2,673	1,966	1,911	2,003	987	1,670	2,150	2,059	1,804	2,720	2,369
St. Louis, Mo.	719	1,890	1,916	1,161		1,678	568	841	394	462	888	609	303	492	1,123	257	265	1,589	229	793	230	743	463	781	547	491	307	251	1,118	516
Salt Lake City	1,868	687	615		1,161	637	1,811	1,927	839	972	1,982	1,434	1,452	987	2,457	1,448	1,528	575	931	2,127	1,420	1,304	1,505	380	1,063	1,565	1,513	1,258	2,135	1,850
San Francisco	2,466	687		615	1,916	552	2,418	2,525	1,434	1,434	2,580	2,007	2,118	1,671	3,055	1,993	2,181	327	1,687	2,523	2,146	1,737	2,103	956	1,570	2,163	2,237	1,856	2,733	2,308
Seattle, Wash.	2,562		687	687	1,890	135	2,418	2,384	1,533	1,666	2,418	2,608	2,161	1,398	2,947	2,256	2,032	956	1,626	2,617	1,998	1,910	1,947	1,074	2,199	2,259	2,003	1,748	2,831	2,354
Washington		2,562	2,466	1,868	719	2,453	186	120	1,034	1,178	215	971	562	950	922	762	469	2,426	959	640	500	1,274	398	1,519	1,183	310	398	600	399	547

Source: Civil Aeronautics Board and U. S. Army Aeronautical Charts.

Forests. The coniferous forests of these states are the noblest in the world. In variety of species, in yield of merchantable timber, and in size, age, and beauty of trees, they are unsurpassed. Oregon and western Washington constitute the most important lumber region in the United States.

The heavy rainfall of the coast districts promotes forest growth. West of the Cascades the Douglas fir attains immense size. In dense, nearly pure forests, this tree covers large areas, and furnishes more than half of the available timber. Large spruces, cedars, and hemlocks also abound. East of the Cascades, western yellow pine and sugar pine are valuable timber trees, the former ranking second in importance to the Douglas fir.

The redwood, a magnificent conifer of the northern California coast, supplies excellent building material. Along the western slopes of the Sierra Nevada there are groves of giant sequoias, the most ancient and massive trees known. Many species of broad-leaved or deciduous trees are found, but native hard woods are of minor importance. In the plains districts of California, various species of eucalyptus provide quick timber and shade.

Agriculture and Horticulture. Farming is the chief industry in these states. Because of wide diversity in soil and climate, a greater variety of agricultural products is grown than in any other equal area in the United States.

In most of the large valleys of Washington, western Oregon, and north central California, sufficient rain falls to insure good harvests. In southern California and in the more arid parts of Oregon and Washington, irrigation is necessary. Among the principal crops are wheat, barley, oats, hay, alfalfa, potatoes, sugar beets, cotton, rice, beans, corn, and numerous fruits and vegetables. In total value the fruits outrank all the other agricultural products of this division. Next to fruits, wheat is the most important single crop, ranking first in value of all crops in Washington, second in Oregon, and third in California. Among hay and fodder crops, alfalfa leads. Although unsuited to the climate, corn, the great staple of the Central states, is grown to a limited extent.

California's great wheat ranches are disappearing, but intensive agriculture, especially fruit growing in connection with irrigation, is making notable progress. All of the Pacific states are famous for their fruits. Apples grown in the Hood River valley in Oregon and in the Yakima district in Washington command high prices in eastern markets Along the Willamette River thousands of acres are planted with apple, peach, pear, and plum trees. In western Oregon, loganberry culture is an extensive industry.

California ranks as the foremost fruit producing state in the Union. Contrary to general opinion in the eastern states, most of this state's great fruit harvest consists of the orchard and vineyard fruits of temperate latitudes,—apples, apricots, cherries, grapes, peaches, pears, plums, and prunes. The best varieties of the European grape flourish, and large quantities of grape juice and raisins are produced. The growing of citrus fruits is a large industry in southern California. From its extensive groves thousands of carloads of oranges, lemons, and grapefruit are shipped to the eastern states every year. Almonds, figs, olives, English walnuts, and melons are grown in large quantities. Among less common fruits whose cultivation has been established in California are the avocado, cherimoya, date, and feijoa.

Irrigation. By irrigation many arid areas in these states have been turned into highly productive lands. A half century ago southern California was mostly a dreary waste. Much that was then desert is now covered with groves of oranges and other fruits, or with fields of grain, alfalfa, melons, or cotton. In no other part of the United States is irrigation so extensively established or devoted to the production of such an immense variety of crops. California leads all the states of the Union in acreage under irrigation and in value of crops produced on irrigated land.

Animal Industry. Large areas in the drier sections are devoted to the raising of cattle and sheep. About one-sixth of the entire wool clip of the United States is produced in the Pacific states. Dairying is a profitable industry. Poultry raising is important, and in some localities, as at Petaluma, California, it has become highly specialized. In the production of honey California usually leads all the other states.

Fisheries. Salmon is the most valuable fish. Puget Sound and the Columbia River are the principal salmon fishing grounds. Millions of pounds of salmon are canned every year and exported to all parts of the world. Fresh salmon are also shipped in refrigerator cars to all the large cities of the Union. Halibut, tuna, herring, and other valuable food fish are taken along the Pacific coast.

Manufacturing. In the contiguous Pacific states, manufacturing ranks second to agriculture in importance. Among the chief manufactures are lumber, canned fruits, refined petroleum, flour, packed meats, and dairy products. Other important products of manufacture are refined sugar, canned fish, and mining machinery.

Manufacturing has been greatly stimulated by the extensive development of hydroelectric power, especially in California and Washington. Particularly since 1910, this factor has been one of rapidly increasing importance in the industry of the Pacific Coast. In southern California many factories use crude petroleum for fuel. Lumber, flour, slaughtering and meat packing, and paper and wood pulp are the leading products of manufacture in Washington; lumber and flour lead in Oregon; and petroleum products, canned fruits, and meat products rank in the order named in California. In total value of manufactures, California stands ninth among the states of the Union.

Commerce. The Pacific contiguous states occupy a position of great commercial advantage. They have fine harbors on the Pacific Ocean and an immense hinterland whose products of farm, forest, and mine are increasing every year. A great trade is carried on through Puget Sound ports. The Panama Canal has brought Europe and the Atlantic states much nearer to this division and thereby stimulated its commerce with those older manufacturing parts of the world. Since 1910 the trade of these states with Japan, the Philippines, Hawaii, New Zealand, Australia, and South America has made a marked gain.

PACIFIC STATES—NONCONTIGUOUS

The noncontiguous, or off-shore, Pacific states of Alaska and Hawaii are treated below in two separate articles. Both admitted into the Union in 1959, they are the only states situated outside of the mainland.

ALASKA

Alaska, the largest state of the United States, situated in the extreme northwestern part of North America. All of it lies to the north and to the west of the United States. Its northernmost point is about 1450 miles farther north than its southernmost point. From its easternmost point to its westernmost point, Alaska extends through a distance greater than that from New York to San Francisco.

Area and Location. Alaska embraces three distinct regions—the main territory, the panhandle, or southeastern Alaska, and the Aleutian Islands.

The main territory comprises all of continental North America lying west of the 141st meridian of west longitude. It is bounded on the east by Canada, on the north by the Arctic Ocean, on the west by the Arctic Ocean, Bering Strait, and Bering Sea, and on the south by the Pacific Ocean and the Gulf of Alaska. The panhandle of southeastern Alaska consists of a narrow fringe of mainland and various islands along the coast, between British Columbia and the Pacific Ocean, extending from Cape Muzon and the Portland Canal, at the extreme south, northward to Mount Saint Elias, where the panhandle joins the main territory.

The Aleutian Islands extend westward from the southwestern part of the main territory, as far as, and including, Attu, off the coast of Asia. Various islands in Bering Sea near the American mainland, including the Pribilof and the Saint Lawrence islands, also belong to Alaska.

The area of Alaska, about 590,000 square miles, is nearly one-fifth that of the "lower 48" states, or more than twice the size of Texas. The coast line of mainland Alaska has a total length of 6542 miles, measured along the tidal shore in units of 3 statute miles. The coast lines of all Alaska's islands measure 8590 miles. These two figures together, 15,132 miles, exceed the general tidal coast line of all the rest of the United States, including Hawaii.

Surface. There are four distinct natural surface divisions in the mainland of Alaska. From south to north, these are the Pacific Mountain system, the Central Plateau region, the Rocky Mountain system, and the Arctic Slope region.

The Pacific Mountain system comprises the Coast, the Mount Saint Elias, the Aleutian, and the Alaska ranges. These form great barrier walls along and near the southern shores. This rugged highland contains the loftiest mountains of the continent, culminating in Mount McKinley, in the Alaska range, the highest peak in North America.

East and north of these majestic ranges is the great central plateau, drained chiefly by the Yukon River. This plateau extends entirely across Alaska from east to west. North of it, the Rocky Mountain system, locally called the Brooks Range, which crosses the international boundary about 100 miles north of the Arctic Circle, extends westerly across Alaska nearly to the Arctic Ocean. North of the Rockies is the Arctic Slope, a barren, featureless, coastal plain.

For about 1000 miles southwestward from the Alaska peninsula extends the Aleutian archipelago which consists of about 70 treeless islands and numerous islets, mostly uninhabited.

Volcanoes. The Aleutian range, in the Alaska peninsula, contains a group of active volcanoes, which, in some respects, are the most remarkable in the world. The eruption of Katmai in this group, in 1912, was one of the most violent volcanic outbursts recorded in modern times. Katmai and its vicinity, including the famous "Valley of Ten Thousand Smokes," have been made a national monument. Aniakchak and Veniamin, with craters 21 and 20 miles in circumference respectively, rank first among active volcanoes in size of their vents.

Glaciers. The mountains bordering on the Gulf of Alaska are covered with perpetual snow. From their slopes, immense glaciers, which increase in size from Glacier Bay northward, extend down to the sea. On the shores between Glacier Bay and Kenai peninsula are found nine-tenths of the permanent ice fields on the mainland of the continent. Here are some 25 active glaciers which discharge their slowly flowing ice into the sea. Among the most noted is the Muir glacier, which has a seaward face 3 miles wide and 300 feet high. The greatest example of all is the Malaspina glacier, 1200 square miles in extent, which rests on the southern slope of Mount Saint Elias and reaches the ocean at Icy cape.

The Muir glacier has recently attracted much scientific attention because of its rapid recession due to melting. This has aroused speculation as to whether the world's climate is gradually becoming warmer.

This great glacier was first visited by John Muir in 1880 and has been named in honor of him. Net recession since then has been almost two miles with parts of the ice mass which melted having been nearly one-half mile thick. The formerly great central ice stream is all melted leaving now 12 separate glacial streams. This is reputed to be the best area in the world for study of glacial phenomena.

Rivers. The chief river in Alaska is the Yukon, the largest American river emptying into the Pacific Ocean. This magnificent river, some 2300 miles long, is formed by the confluence of streams having their headwaters in British Columbia. It flows northward in Yukon territory, and, about midway on the international boundary, enters Alaska. At the northernmost point in its bow-shaped course of about 1500 miles from the Canada boundary to Bering Sea, the Yukon swings slightly north of the Arctic Circle. Its chief tributaries are the Tanana, the Porcupine, and the Koyukuk. Other important Alaskan rivers are the Kuskokwim, the Copper, Matanuska, Kenai, Nushagak, Kobuk, Noatak, Colville, Stikine, Taku, and the Susitna.

Scenery. Alaska, with its great mountains, volcanoes, glaciers, and rivers, is noted for the magnificence of its scenery. The Portland Canal, Chatham strait, and the Lynn Canal, in southeastern Alaska, surrounded by snow-capped mountains rising above immense forests, rank among the finest scenic waterways in the world. Around the Gulf of Alaska, the coast is indented with deep bays resembling the noted fiords of Norway and which likewise include magnificent glaciers. The Taku glacier is only a few miles from the steamer track of the famous inside passage and can be seen from the largest ocean steamers that ply Alaskan waters. Mount McKinley national park, which includes the great mountain, affords some of the grandest mountain views on the continent.

Climate. According to the U. S. Weather Bureau, Alaska is climatically divided into 4 areas— (1) a maritime zone that includes southeastern Alaska, the south coast, and southwestern islands, (2) a transition zone between marine and continental influences (mostly a very narrow band along the southern portion of the Copper River and the northern extreme of the south coast—specifically the Chugach Mountains, Cook Inlet, Bristol Bay, and the coastal regions of west-central Alaska), (3) a continental zone made up of the remainders of the Copper River and west-central Alaska and the interior region, and (4) an arctic zone.

In the maritime zone a coastal mountain range coupled with plentiful moisture produces annual precipitation amounts up to 200 inches in the southeastern panhandle, and up to 150 inches along the northern coast of the Gulf of Alaska. Amounts taper to near 60 inches on the southern side of the Alaska Range in the peninsula and Aleutian Island sections. Precipitation amounts decrease rapidly to the north, with an average of 12 inches in the continental zone and less than 6 inches in the Arctic region.

Snowfall makes up a large portion of the total annual precipitation. For example, Yakutat averages 216 inches of snow annually, and has a total annual precipitation (rain plus water equivalent of snow) of about 130 inches. Along the Arctic slope, Barrow receives an average of 29 inches of snow annually and a total annual precipitation of slightly more than 4 inches. Total snow depths on the ground are controlled by the temperature of an area. Fortunately, most of the areas of heavy snow have relatively mild temperatures which prevent total depths from becoming excessive. The greatest annual precipitation occurred at Little Port Walter (in southeastern Alaska) in 1943, with a total of 269.30 inches. Snowfall extremes are all credited to one station, located at Thompson Pass. Mean annual temperatures in Alaska range from the low 40's under the maritime influence in the south to a chilly 10 degrees along the Arctic Slope north of the Brooks Mountain Range. The greatest seasonal temperature contrast between seasons is found in the central and eastern portion of the continental interior. In this area summer heating produces average maximum temperatures in the upper 70's with extreme readings in the 90's. The highest recorded temperature for the state, 100 degrees, occurred at Fort Yukon in June of 1915. In winter the lack of sunshine permits radiation to lower temperatures to the minus 50's and occasionally colder for two or three weeks at a time. Average winter minimums in this area are 20 to 30 degrees below zero. The coldest temperature ever recorded in Alaska was minus 76 degrees at Tanana in January of 1886. In Barrow, Alaska's northernmost town in the frigid arctic region, January temperatures average −18°F. Its minimum, −56°F is higher than at Fairbanks and points inland, due to its open coastal location. The sun circles the sky in Barrow without setting for about 2 months in summer and the Arctic night is also about 2 months in length.

Winter temperatures play a principal role in the flow of most of Alaska's rivers. Several cease to flow completely during the coldest months, generally from late October to early May.

Vegetation. The southern coastal region is heavily forested and contains much valuable timber, chiefly Sitka spruce and hemlock. The Tongass national forest comprises southeastern Alaska, and the Chugatch national forest extends from Controller bay to Cook inlet. Extensive forests of spruce and tamarack, interspersed with poplar, aspen, white birch, and alder, occur along numerous watercourses in the Yukon valley. These forests total nearly 21 million acres with practically all under National Forest Service Administration. In the remaining portions of Alaska, there are but few trees. The Alaska peninsula and the Aleutian islands are grasslands. These grasslands are composed of highly nutritious grasses and are available as pasturage the year round. Cattle and horses released on these areas have grown fat and sleek without attention from man.

The coastal region of Bering Sea and the Arctic Ocean is covered with tundra. The tundra furnishes very desirable pasturage for caribou, reindeer, and musk ox.

Animal Life. Alaska is rich in animal life, especially in game animals, fur bearing animals, and in food fishes. Among the larger land animals are moose, caribou, deer, bighorn, and mountain goat. There are also several species of bear, including the polar bear, the rare glacial bear, and the great Kodiak bear. The reindeer, introduced from Siberia to provide food for the native Indians and Eskimos, now abounds in great herds. It is reared like cattle, and reindeer meat is an article of export to the United States. In the coastal waters are found the walrus, the hair seal, and various whales. The fur bearing animals include the fur seal, sea otter, beaver, ermine, mink, marten, and wolverine. Salmon, cod, halibut, and herring are immensely abundant in Alaskan waters.

Minerals. Alaska possesses vast mineral resources, many of which are undeveloped. The most important mineral products are gold, oil, copper, and coal. Many other valuable metals and minerals are found, among which are silver, lead, antimony, tin, oil, tungsten, platinum, quicksilver, and marble.

Gold has been found chiefly in the Juneau district, the Copper River district, the Yukon valley, and in the Seward peninsula, or Nome region. Gold was first discovered in Alaska in 1861. The gold rush started in 1883, reached its peak about 1887, and experienced a resurgence in 1896. Gold mined in Alaska from 1880 until 1930 is valued at approximately $380 million. Annual production is in the neighborhood of $5 million.

The decline in gold production was accompanied

by a rise in the production of other minerals. The mining of copper, found in the coast region from Mount Saint Elias to Cook inlet, began in 1902 and soon surpassed gold in value of output. Copper exceeded all other mineral production until 1962, when it was surpassed by the production of petroleum. Alaska ranks eighth among the states of the Union in the production of oil, with the potential to rank higher. Alaska has sold leases to bidders, giving various companies oil exploratory rights to specified territory, for some $862 million, plus 12½% royalty tax and 4% severance tax on every barrel of oil taken out. The development of the oil industry in Alaska has been slow, with two wells now in operation, one at Prudhoe Bay, and the other at Snag River. The most attractive areas for drilling for oil are adjacent to the Pacific Ocean on the south and the Arctic Ocean on the north. Some of the most desirable areas, however, are not available for drilling or exploratory drilling.

Extensive coal fields are found in widely separated districts from southern Alaska to the Arctic coast. It is estimated that more than 12,000 square miles

ALASKA

are underlaid with coal deposits ranging in quality from anthracite to lignite. Silver and lead are also produced in significant quantities. Practically all the tin mined in North America comes from Alaska. Other mineral products include platinum, mercury, and marble. Natural gas, discovered in 1949, is marketed extensively.

Transportation. The development of Alaska's immense resources depends upon the establishment of quick and cheap transportation. The coasts have many good harbors, and the Yukon and other rivers provide some 3000 miles of inland waterways. But the water routes are long, are open only in summer, and do not reach some of the most important districts. Short railways have been built in connection with mining enterprises, but they were not constructed as correlated parts of a railway system designed to serve the needs of the whole territory.

The United States government has, however, completed a railway, some 470 miles long, from Seward, on the Gulf of Alaska, to Fairbanks, at the head of deep water navigation on the Tanana river, chief tributary of the Yukon. This connects the southern coast with the interior valley.

The Alaska Highway, originally called the Alcan Highway, was built by American army engineers for the defense of Alaska in 1942. It extends from Dawson Creek, British Columbia, to Fairbanks, Alaska, a distance of 1523 miles. Open to the public since 1948, tourist services are available along its entire length. Lodging and meal service are good and moderate in cost. Gasoline is available but as yet relatively costly. Autos may now make the round trip overland to Fairbanks; but a tourist seeking variety may drive from Fairbanks to Anchorage or Seward and take a boat over the attractive ocean route to Seattle.

Numerous airports have facilitated rapid transit to otherwise inaccessible points. There are 15 certified carriers and 50 or more irregular carriers. There are also 153 territorial fields. Outposts such as Nome are finding the quick connection by planes much more dependable and desirable than dog teams, which are costly to maintain, requiring constant feed and care.

Alaskans have been referred to as "the flyingest" of all Americans. The description is justified, not only on a per capita mileage basis for citizens of the 49th state, but also for the daring exploits of "bush pilots," who are not daunted by unfavorable weather or difficult terrain. Increasingly, this local use of air transportation is being matched by communication with distant points. Several Federal airports are maintained, and four air lines provide regularly scheduled service between Alaska and the other states.

Commerce and Industry. The industries of Alaska are chiefly in connection with mining, fisheries, and the fur trade, with a limited amount of lumbering. The dominant tree of the commercial timber type is western hemlock, with Sitka spruce a close second. Western red cedar and Alaska yellow cedar are produced to some extent. Local uses of forests are fuel, log cabins, mines, docks, salmon packing cases, etc. During World War II Sitka spruce provided airplane construction material. A more solid basis for Alaska's forest industry is the manufacture of pulp, which is exported mainly to Japan for making of paper and rayon. In value of production, fisheries rank first followed by products of the forests and the mines and oil and gas wells. Apart from pulp, exports include petroleum, canned salmon, copper ore, gold, and furs. Among the most important imports are foodstuffs, clothing, and machinery. As transportation facilities, particularly by air, are continually improving, tourism is becoming an important source of income for Alaska, which has scenic attractions not accessible elsewhere in the United States.

Fisheries. The salmon fisheries were formerly the most valuable in the world, but in the 1940's the catch fell off seriously. Cannery production of salmon reached a high of 8,454,948 cases in the 1930's, fell to an average of 2,797,699 cases for the years 1953–57, and remained in that range thereafter. Next in importance to salmon are herring, halibut, clams, and shrimp.

Furs and Game. Next in value below fishery, forest, and mineral products are furs. The most important land furs include red fox, white fox, blue fox, ermine, lynx, marten, mink, muskrat, and land otter. Fur farming, especially with foxes, is carried on extensively. The fur seal herds, on the Pribilof islands, increased, under government supervision, from 215,000 animals in 1912 to about nine times that number in the 30 years following.

The 1940 seal population of these islands was 2,185,136. Sealskins taken in 1941 were 95,013. The handling of this fur seal herd has been one of the most successful in wildlife administration. The total value of furs shipped from Alaska annually frequently exceeds 4.5 million dollars.

Fine and useful game animals are caribou; reindeer; moose; Dall mountain sheep; mountain goats; brown, grizzly, polar, and black bears; elk; deer; and, at present, a herd of musk oxen are being developed on Nunivak island and a herd of bison near Fairbanks. Immense numbers of ducks, geese, and

swans of several species breed abundantly throughout practically the entire territory. Other aquatic fowl form almost continuous coastal rookeries—auklets, murres, guillemots, puffins, cormorants, sheerwaters gulls, and kittiwakes. Eagles, owls, hawks, gyrfalcons are included among the land birds.

Agriculture. Owing chiefly to the shortness of the growing season, agriculture is successful only in limited areas and to a moderate degree. Vegetables are the most important products. These are grown in favored ground in the valleys of the Susitna, the Matanuska, the Kenai, the Koyukuk, the Copper, and the Tanana rivers. Hay, barley, and hardy fruits are also produced. Grazing and dairying are carried on in Kodiak island and other grassland districts. Reindeer thrive in moss covered and lichen covered areas. The government maintains four agricultural experimental stations,—a nursery at Sitka, a grain farm at Rampart, a dairy at Kodiak, and a demonstration farm at Fairbanks.

It is estimated that 65,000 square miles is potential farm land and 35,000 square miles is potential grazing land, not including the reindeer range which is very extensive. The area in farms rose from almost zero in 1900 to a peak of 2774 square miles in 1939 and then declined sharply, standing at 1356 square miles in the 1959 crop year. There were 623 farms in 1939 and 382 in 1964. But, despite this sharp decline in number of farms and area of farm land, the area actually cropped almost doubled—increasing from 12 to 23 square miles—and crops more than quadrupled, while farm animals approximately doubled.

Livestock in 1960 included 750 horses, about 6010 cattle, including 2800 dairy cows, 1200 hogs, and 27,000 sheep and lambs. The number of reindeer reported in herds declined from 712,500 in 1929 to 312,854 in 1939. There are about 38,540 reindeer now in western Alaska, of which 13,200 are located on Nunivak Island and are controlled by the Bureau of Indian Affairs. Individual Eskimo herders own the rest of the reindeer.

Farm production in 1967 was valued at $5,524,-000, including $1,931,000 for milk, $1,340,000 for grain crops, $607,000 for potatoes, and $214,000 for vegetables. The chief grains grown are oats and barley; hay is also produced. Fruits and vegetables harvested and sold, like other crops, have increased spectacularly, rising in value from $99,000 in 1949 to $214,000 in 1967. The types grown in quantity include strawberries, raspberries, beans, broccoli, cabbages, lettuce, onions, radishes, rutabagas, and turnips. Despite the fact that Alaska is suitable for farming, it is primarily a food-importing area.

Population. In 1970, the population of the state was 300,382, of whom about half were whites, the remainder Indians, with a few Negroes and Japanese.

The Indians of Alaska belong mainly to four great stocks—the Eskimos, the Aleuts, the Athapascans, and the Tlingits. The Eskimos, 15,576 in number, live near the seashore and on islands, chiefly along Bering Sea and the Arctic Ocean. The Pacific Eskimos live on the south coast around Kodiak island, Controller Bay, and Prince William Sound The Aleutian Eskimos occupy areas about the Alaskan Peninsula and extending along the Aleutian Islands. Asiatic Eskimos live on St. Lawrence Island which is part of the Alaskan Territory. The Bering Sea Eskimos live on Nunivak Island and the opposite mainland including the lower Yukon. The Colville Eskimos occupy the Arctic coast near Wainright Inlet, Cape Smyth, and Point Barrow. The Eskimos have proven good workers and are employed at such summer tasks as longshoremen in loading and unloading supply ships. Able bodied Eskimos were drafted for war service in Alaska in World War II.

Juneau, the capital, has a population of 6050. Other important cities and towns are Anchorage, 48,029; Fairbanks, 14,771; Ketchikan, 6994; and Seward 1587. Alaska has in all 70 incorporated places, among which may be mentioned, in addition to the above, Nome, 2488; Sitka, 3370; and Kodiak, 3798. Population for all of Alaska, 1970, 300,382.

History. In 1741, Vitus Bering, a Danish navigator in the employ of Russia, explored the coast of Alaska. Kodiak island was discovered in 1761 by the Russians, who made a settlement there in 1783. Captain James Cook, in 1778, and Vancouver, in 1793-94, made extensive coastal surveys. Sitka, founded in 1804, became the capital of the Russian territory. The Russians, who were engaged chiefly in fur sealing, did not extensively explore the interior.

In 1867, the United States purchased Alaska from Russia for the sum of $7,200,000—about $12 per square mile, or less than 2 cents an acre.

Preceding the discovery of the gold fields, there was little development, except in connection with the fur trade. Important events in the recent history of Alaska were the fur seal arbitration of 1893, the great gold rush of 1898, the settlement of the Alaska-Canada boundary dispute in 1904, and the construction of the government railway from Seward to Fairbanks, 1916–23.

During World War I, the white population of Alaska declined, but, following the completion of important portions of the government railway and the return of stable conditions, development was again stimulated. Growth of air travel provided an impetus.

In World War II the building up of the defenses of Alaska caused a boom. Numerous military and naval bases were built, especially air bases. Two of Alaska's islands, Attu and Kiska, were occupied by Japanese troops in June 1942. In May 1943, American troops invaded and retook Attu. In the following August, Kiska was bombarded. The landing force found the island had already been evacuated.

The development of atomic weapons and of long range missiles made Alaska a highly strategic point for defense of the United States. Elaborate systems for automatic warning of the presence of airplanes or missiles were constructed as part of lines extending also across Northern Canada, in which the Canadian and American governments pooled their efforts.

The Alaskan flag has a blue field on which gold stars represent the Big Dipper and the North Star. The forget-me-not is the official flower; the willow ptarmigan the official bird. In 1959, Alaska was admitted to the Union as the 49th state.

HAWAII

The state of Hawaii consists of a chain of nine inhabited and several uninhabited islands in the mid-Pacific Ocean. The chief islands are about 2100 miles southwest of San Francisco and approximately 3400 miles southeast of Yokohama, Japan. Their central position in relation to Pacific ports has won for Hawaii the sobriquet "crossroads of the Pacific."

Palmyra Island, 1½ miles in area, lying about 700 miles south of the main group, is officially considered as part of Hawaii. The extreme northwestern islets of the group are called the Midway Islands, being about halfway between Asia and North America. They are inhabited only by the employees of a United States cable station there.

The population of the Hawaiian Islands in 1970 was 768,561. The largest islands of the group are Hawaii, 4030 square miles; Maui, 728; Oahu, 604; Kauai, 555; Molokai, 260; Lanai, 141; Nihau, 72; Kalholawe, 45. The capital, Honolulu, on the island of Oahu, has 324,871 inhabitants.

The islands of Hawaii are of volcanic origin. Their surface is mountainous, reaching, in Mauna Kea, "White Mountain," a maximum altitude of 13,823 feet. If measured from the deep ocean floor, on which it stands, this volcanic giant is several hundred feet higher than Mt. Everest, the world's highest inland mountain. This peak and Mauna Loa

(13,675 feet), both in the island of Hawaii, are higher than any other mountain in the islands of the Pacific Ocean. Mauna Loa, "Long Mountain," shares with the near-by mountain of Kilauea the distinction of having active craters which rank among the largest in the world, covering 4.14 square miles. That of Kilauea is about 8 miles in circumference and is the seat of unceasing volcanic activity.

Haleakala, on the island of Maui, has one of the largest of all extinct craters. This crater is 20 miles around and is 2720 feet deep. A 41-square mile area containing it was made a national park in 1961. The island of Molokai is notable for its famous leper settlement. Lanai is owned by a pineapple company which constructed a harbor and a model city. Pearl Harbor, on the island of Oahu, is a United States naval base. It is landlocked, with an area of 10 square miles. The Hawaii Volcanoes National Park includes Kilauea and Mauna Loa on Hawaii Island and Haleakala on Maui.

The climate of the Hawaiian Islands is delightfully equable and invigorating considering its tropical position. Sea level temperatures average between 68.7° F. and 75.8° F. for the Islands. At Honolulu, the maximum recorded temperature is 90° F. and the minimum, 52° F. However, it is a rare summer day in which temperatures rise over 85° F. and a rare winter night when the low is 60° F. Especially noteworthy is the fact that damaging storms, such as hail, tornadoes, hurricanes, and typhoons, are practically nonexistent. Northeast

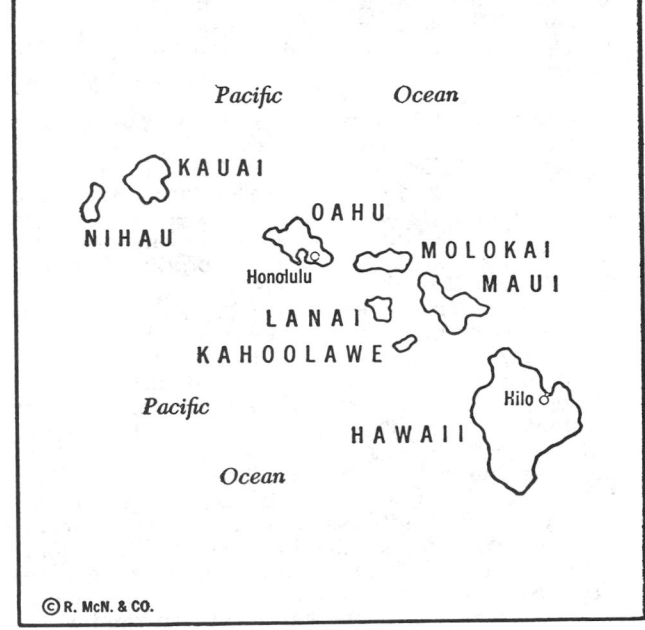

HAWAII

trade winds blow prevailingly for about 10 months in the year. On account of the mountainous character of the islands, much of the moisture in the winds is precipitated, falling mainly on the northeastern side of each island. As a result, the opposite side has insufficient rainfall and frequently suffers from drought. This rainfall variation is one of the largest in the world. Many rain-drenched windward towns officially report well over 200 inches a year. On the leeward side, averages of 20 to 30 inches are common (Honolulu, 25.8 in.) and are often inadequate for crops and water supply. Rain falls every month of the year, but the summer months are markedly drier. The prevailing sunniness of such lee locations as Honolulu is a notable attraction.

Another significant mountain influence is the change of temperature with altitude. In the land below 2500 feet (Tierra Caliente) frost never occurs and rarely forms even up to 4000 feet. Above 4000 feet (Tierra Templada) frost may occur, and at elevations of 6500 feet snow is occasionally reported.

Above 9000 feet (Tierra Fria) both frost and snow occur regularly and the higher peaks are frequently snow covered. Altogether the Hawaiian Islands are climatically among the most varied in the world.

Plant life is highly varied from tropical jungle to tropical steppe and desert. Only about 10 per cent is grazing land. Approximately four-fifths of the area is unused desert, semidesert, and volcanic waste with dense tropical jungle in favored spots. In the National Park area of the island Hawaii, locally called Big Island, is the world famous "Fern Forest" with some ferns attaining the height of 50 feet. Plant life in the inhabited areas is highly colorful and ornamental providing a major attraction. Among the most noted are royal palms, coconut palms, banyan trees, monkeypod trees, flame trees, bougainvillia, orchid, cacti, hibiscus, poinsettia, plumerias, and ilima. Many of these blooms are made into welcoming leis, a world famous Hawaiian custom with considerable commercial significance.

Although there are many kinds of fish and birds in Hawaii, there is only one mammal that is indigenous to the islands, and that is a species of bat. There are also lizards on the islands.

The soil along the coastal lowlands and in many valleys is very fertile and supports a flourishing agriculture of a tropical type. Since the soils are of volcanic origin they are deep rich clays high in mineral content and capable of sustained yields under cultivation. The staple crops are pineapples and sugar cane. Large quantities of cane sugar and of pineapples are shipped, principally to the United States. Other products exported include coffee, honey, hides, sisal hemp, bananas, rice, wool, tobacco, and cotton. Over half of the total area is in farms and ranches (2.5 million acres), yet only 10 per cent of the total area is cropped.

About 250,000 acres is kept in sugar cane, the major crop, using five times as much land as pineapples. Since the cane is allowed to grow 18 to 20 months before harvesting, the yield per acre is three times that of the annually harvested cane of the United States. Hawaiians annually cut just over half of the acreage in cane. Annual production varies from 700,000 to 1,000,000 tons.

Eighty to ninety per cent of the pineapple products of world trade originate in the Hawaiian Islands, making them world famous. This fame is justly merited, not only in quantity domination over all competitors, but also in leadership in methods of production and processing. Eight corporations dominate the field, led by the Hawaiian Pineapple Corporation founded by James D. Dole, 1922. Confronted by labor shortage, limited water supply, aridity, blowing soil erosion, soil and plant infestations and certain plant food deficiencies, these companies inaugurated far reaching conservation practices. Slopes are contoured; paper covers the soil, conserving moisture, preventing blowing and washing, checking weed growth, thus saving costly weeding. Water supply is obtained by wells, local galvanized roofs, and acres of galvanized sheds on the wetter upper slopes, from which the water can be channeled down as needed; machinery cultivates, plants, harvests, and transports the fruit to the processing factories where all of the pineapple is reduced to valuable products as canned fruit, juice, and citric acid. Cost of services in sanitation, health, and public utilities, formerly provided, must now be borne by the worker. Total sales of pine-

apples and sugar in 1967 exceeded $324 million, or about 63 per cent of total agricultural income.

Land tenure is a problem, with 60 per cent of the land owned either by the state or by large estates. The famous Bishop Estate owns 10 per cent and endows philanthropic enterprises such as the Kamehameha schools with the million dollar income. The Federal Government owns 429,076 acres, of which 373,384 is in National Parks and 55,559 is under the Navy.

The tourist industry ranks third after sugar and pineapples as an industry. Superior natural attractions are enhanced by luxurious accommodations to make this a world prominent resort. The Pan American Airways and United Air Lines contact the islands from San Francisco in a breakfast-to-dinner run. Several steamship lines connect the island with the United States, Canada, and the Orient. The Moana and Royal Hawaiian hotels on Waikiki beach are widely known.

Honolulu, on Oahu Island, is the capital and chief port of Hawaii. Its name means "quiet harbor." The harbor, which has excellent freight facilities, is almost entirely enclosed by a natural breakwater of coral reefs. The population of the state has a mixed character. More than half are Japanese and Chinese. White inhabitants number less than one-fourth of the total. The aborigines constitute a still smaller proportion. A similar complexity characterizes the language and the religion of the territory. The aborigines are mainly Protestant Christians, although some of their pagan beliefs and customs survive. The Hawaiian natives belong to the Polynesian race. When discovered, they had a well developed political system and a literature. Niihau is still maintained as a pure native asylum by the exclusive Robinson family

The Hawaiian Islands were first made known to the world by Captain James Cook, who discovered them in 1778. He called them Sandwich Islands after the earl of Sandwich. At that time, each island had its king, who exercised authority by a species of feudal organization. In 1790, Kamehameha, one of the kings, extended his sway over the entire group of islands. His successor, being opposed by those who upheld the native worship, abolished the old religion. Christianity was introduced as early as 1820. A system of universal, compulsory education is now established there.

In 1842, the kingdom of Hawaii was recognized by the United States. An internal struggle for constitutional rights arose and lasted, with interruptions, until 1893, when the reigning queen, Liliuokalani, was deposed. An appeal for annexation to the United States was made, but it was rejected by President Cleveland. A second appeal, made to President McKinley, resulted in the approval by Congress, July 7, 1898, of a treaty of annexation. In 1900, the islands were formally organized into the territory of Hawaii, and a territorial governor was appointed by the president. In 1959, Hawaii was admitted to the Union as the 50th state.

On Kealakekua Bay, Hawaii Island, stands an obelisk commemorating Captain Cook, who was slain near that point by natives in 1779. In 1928, a bronze tablet was dedicated in his honor and placed just below the surface of the water to mark the exact spot where he fell. The adjacent region, known as Kaawaloa, was made into a public park.

UNITED STATES DEPENDENCIES

Like the other powerful nations of the 19th century, the United States acquired a number of dependencies. Since America's independence had stemmed from revolt against colonialism, the name colony was never applied to these dependencies. Moreover, the question of their acquisition was the source of bitter political debate, particularly when the Philippines, Puerto Rico, and Guam were ceded to the United States in 1898, American Samoa was

acquired by treaty with Britain and Germany in 1899, and Hawaii was annexed in 1900. Alaska had already been purchased from Russia in 1867. The Panama Canal Zone was obtained by treaty with Panama in 1903; the Virgin Islands were purchased from Denmark in 1917.

It has been the official policy of the United States to provide stable government for the possessions and to encourage their economic and educational development with a view to their eventual self-government. Of the above dependencies, the Philippines was granted independence as the Philippine Republic in 1934, and Alaska and Hawaii became states in 1959.

This policy of development has entailed the building of railroads, highways, waterways, and harbor facilities, the introduction of improved methods of agriculture, and the founding of suitable manufacturing industries. Basic to such improvement was provision of free public schools and other educational facilities. The introduction of modern sanitation methods and of methods of preventing and treating diseases led, not only to improved well-being, but to rapid population increases that paced the economic advances.

In this section is treated the geography of American Samoa, Canal Zone, Guam, Puerto Rico, and the Virgin Islands. The small islands of Wake and Midway, and the South Pacific Islands which the United States received in trust under the United Nations for eventual return to Japan, are treated in the Department of Government and Politics.

AMERICAN SAMOA

A group of four inhabited and several uninhabited islands in the south Pacific Ocean, about 4200 miles southwest of San Francisco and about 2000 miles east of Australia. The inhabited islands are Tutuila, Tau, Swain's Island and those of the Manua group—Ofu and Olosega. The total area is 76 square miles.

The islands are largely mountainous in character, but much of the soil is extremely fertile. The moist tropical climate of the islands fosters a luxuriant vegetation. Agriculture is the principal occupation and is carried on mainly by family groups, each of which is directed and ruled by a patriarch, or *matai*. The chief products include copra, taro, breadfruit, yams, pineapples, oranges, and bananas. Copra and canned tuna are exported.

The only large port of American Samoa is Pago Pago. It is a United States naval station under a commandant. The population in 1970, 29,000 (est.). Schools were established in Samoan villages by Christian missionaries as early as 1830. Elementary education in English is available for all in schools supported by the government.

This group of islands came under American sovereignty in 1899 as the result of a treaty with Great Britain and Germany. Since the establishment of American control, the islands have made substantial gains in population and in social welfare.

CANAL ZONE

A strip of land ten miles in width, through the center of which runs the Panama canal. The Canal Zone divides the Republic of Panama into two parts.

The zone was obtained in 1903 from the Republic of Panama for the sum of $10 million with an annual payment of $250,000, changed in 1936 to 430,000 balboas after the American dollar had been devalued in terms of gold. Its affairs are administered by a governor appointed by the United States government. A railroad connects the two terminals of the canal—Balboa, the Pacific port, and Cristobal, on the Caribbean sea. Population 1970, 44,650. See *Panama Canal*.

GUAM

The largest and most southerly of the Mariana Islands, Guam is situated in the Pacific Ocean about 1700 miles east of Manila and some 6000 miles southwest of San Francisco.

The island of Guam is about 30 miles long, and varies in breadth from 4 to 8½ miles, its estimated area being 210 square miles. It is mountainous in the south but plateau-like in the north. Broken coral reefs fringe the shore.

There are only two seasons—a wet season and a dry one. Though the temperature averages 81° F. the year round, the climate is healthful. The soil is fertile, well watered, and yields abundant crops of copra, corn, sweet potatoes, taro, cassava, bananas, citrus fruits, and sugar cane. There are no import duties. Agana, the capital, is the chief city. Apra is the port of entry.

From 1898, when it was acquired from Spain, Guam was administered by the United States navy department, but in 1950 it came under the supervision of the department of the interior.

The natives are of a mixed race, called Chamorros, with the Malayan strain predominating. Chamorro, the native language, and also Spanish and English are spoken.

Guam was discovered in 1521 by Magellan. In 1565, the Spanish took possession of the island. It remained under Spanish rule until 1898, when, as a result of the Spanish American war, it was ceded to the United States. Its location has made it of great strategic importance both as a naval and an air base, and military establishments occupy about one-third of the usable land. During World War II, the Japanese held it from 1941 to 1944. Population, 1968 (est.), 101,000.

PUERTO RICO

A West India island lying about 70 miles east of Haiti and 1425 miles southeast of New York. The island is about 100 miles long and from 30 to 40 miles wide, and has about three times the area of the state of Rhode Island.

The climate of Puerto Rico is regarded as the most healthful in the tropics of the western hemisphere. Through the middle of the island, a broken range of mountains extends from east to west, their altitude varying from about 2000 feet to that of the culminating peak of El Yunque, 3532 feet high. These mountains are clothed to their summits with luxuriant vegetation. The coast belt is a broad, level alluvial plain. The soil is exceedingly fertile and, as the population is dense, most of the arable land is under cultivation.

On the eastern and on the northern slopes of the mountains there is abundant rainfall, the average yearly precipitation being 65 inches. But, in the southern part of the island, irrigation is required in some districts, as the mountains intercept much of the moisture in the trade winds. Puerto Rico is noted for its fine forest trees. Palms, Spanish cedar, ebony, mahogany, ausubo, laurel, sandalwood, and dyewoods abound.

The mineral resources of Puerto Rico, so far as developed, consist chiefly of limestone and volcanic boulders, used in building; various clays, used in making brick and pottery; and gypsum, used for stucco, plaster, and fertilizer. Deposits of marble and lignite occur; along the south coast there are extensive phosphate beds; and on the northern coast there are nearly pure silica sands, used in the manufacture of glass and china. Gold, copper ore, iron ore, and the ores of various other metals have been found in small quantities.

Agriculture is the chief industry, but in recent years manufacturing has rivaled it in value of output. Sugar is the most important crop, followed by tobacco, coffee, pineapples, grapefruit, oranges, and other tropical fruits. After World War II, the government put into effect a policy of purchasing farm land from large corporations and turning it over to individual farmers on a "proportional profit" basis. An aggressive policy of industrialization also was followed, and many United States corporations extended operations to Puerto Rico to take advantage of the tax incentives offered.

Nearly all the exports go to the United States. The chief one is sugar, which was valued at about $92 million in 1968–69. Textile fibers, rum, liquor, and molasses are also exported extensively.

Puerto Rico is densely populated, with about 800 inhabitants to the square mile. To encourage new industries and provide employment, the insular government in 1942 created the Industrial Development Company, which established a number of factories.

MAP OF PUERTO RICO SHOWING ✠ HOTELS. ★ RESTAURANTS.
● TOWNS AND OTHER POINTS OF INTEREST

Source: Office of Information, Economic Development Administration, San Juan, Puerto Rico

A bank with a liberal industrial loan policy was also set up, and in 1948 certain industries, old and new, were granted a twelve-year exemption from taxes. That same year the hydroelectric power of the island was increased by the completion of the Caonilas dam.

The principal cities and seaports are San Juan, the capital, on the north coast, with a population of 444,952; Ponce, on the south coast, population 125,926; and Mayaguez, on the west coast, population 69,485. The harbor at San Juan, which has been extensively improved by the United States government, is one of the best in the West Indies. A railroad, built near the coast, almost completely encircles the island, and there are branches into the interior. Surfaced highways, of which more than 3520 miles have been constructed, facilitate transportation in various parts of the island.

Under the school system, education is free and compulsory. In 1968–69, there were 720,313 pupils enrolled in Puerto Rican schools. There is also a well-distributed system of night schools and kindergartens. Colleges include the University of Puerto Rico, at Rio Piedras; the Catholic University of Puerto Rico, at Ponce; the Inter-American University, at San German; and the College of the Sacred Heart, at Santurce. The percentage of illiteracy has declined from 83 per cent in 1889, to 14 percent in 1966.

Puerto Rico was discovered in 1493 by Columbus. The first settlement was made at Pueblo Viejo in 1508 by Ponce de Leon, who, in 1509, was appointed governor by King Ferdinand of Spain. Although attacked at various times by the English and the Dutch, Puerto Rico remained in the possession of Spain until 1898, when, at the close of the Spanish American war, it was ceded to the United States. Since the establishment of American methods of agriculture, American public schools, improved highways and railways, and various civic improvements, Puerto Rico has made remarkable progress. Population. 2,739,000.

VIRGIN ISLANDS

A group of some 50 tropical islands and islets formerly called the Danish West Indies. They lie about 40 miles due east of Puerto Rico. The total area of the group is about 149 square miles, of which 132 is comprised in the three largest islands— Saint Thomas, Saint John, and Saint Croix (Santa Cruz). Almost all the inhabitants are Negroes or mulattoes. Population, 1967, 54,545 (est.).

Saint Thomas is the best known of the islands because its principal town, Charlotte Amalie, population 12,880, is located on one of the finest harbors in the West Indies. The surface of the island is rugged and elevated, and the soil is poor. The exports are principally rum and hides. Most of the imports are foodstuffs and wearing apparel. The College of the Virgin Islands is located on St. Thomas. The area of the island is about 28 square miles. Population, 1967, 28,705 (est.).

Saint Croix, the largest and wealthiest of the islands, lies about 40 miles southeast of Saint Thomas, and has two well-known towns, Frederiksted (Westend) and Christiansted (Bassin). The latter was the capital of the islands under Danish rule. Sugar cane is the chief crop. Longstaple cotton is grown, and cattle are raised. The area of the island is about 84 square miles; population, 1967, 24,295 (est.).

Saint John, the smallest of the three main islands, grows bay leaves for the distillation of bay oil and also has a considerable acreage devoted to cotton, sugar cane, and tobacco. The entire population is considered rural. The area of Saint John is about 20 square miles; population, less than a thousand.

The Virgin islands were discovered in 1493 by Columbus. Saint Thomas was first colonized in 1672 by the Danes. Saint Croix, first occupied in 1625 by Dutch and English settlers, came into the possession of Denmark in 1733. With the exception of two periods—1801-02 and 1807-15—during the Napoleonic wars, when they were seized and held by the English, most of the islands were under the Danish flag for a period of 245 years. In 1917, upon payment of $25 million, they came into the possession of the United States by purchase.

During the days of sailing ships, especially about 1820, Saint Thomas was a supply point of great importance in the West Indian trade. Before the abolition of slavery, in 1848, in the islands, sugar growing was a substantial industry. With the decline of the sugar industry, the population decreased, falling gradually from about 40,000 in 1850 to about 26,-000 when the United States took possession in 1917. Tourism has become the chief industry.

The value of the Virgin islands now lies chiefly in their geographic location and their exceptionally fine harbor facilities. Their situation with reference to the Panama canal makes Saint Thomas of great strategic importance as a naval base and as a coaling station.

DICTIONARY OF AMERICAN GEOGRAPHY

In the selection of topics for this section of American geography, the following considerations have governed:

Capital Cities. All capitals of states, territories, and dependencies of the United States are given an item because of their political importance.

Largest Cities. Size in itself would dictate the selection of a large proportion of the cities of United States for special articles. But with size normally go commercial and industrial importance and numerous cultural activities which make their inclusion doubly essential.

Smaller Cities and Places. Various cities and towns with a population of less than 50,000 have been included for specific reasons, such as historical associations like those of Gettysburg, Plymouth, and Ticonderoga, or proximity to features of travel interest, as in the case of Adamana and Grand Junction.

Other cities, such as Butte, Cohoes, Hibbing, Riverside, and Anaconda, are included because they are leading centers in some important economic enterprise. Still others have been selected primarily because they are seats of universities, colleges, or other important educational institutions. Examples of this kind are Ithaca, Oberlin, and Princeton.

The more important Indian towns of the Southwest are given brief treatment. Among these are Isleta, Laguna, and Zuni. Selections of resorts have also been made, including Lake Placid, Palm Beach, and Saratoga Springs. Of the less populous states, the largest and, usually, the second and third largest cities have been included.

Cities of the continental U.S. whose population exceeds a half-million have generally been given special topical treatment. Descriptive matter is divided into topics under separate subheadings. The treatment follows a uniform plan, beginning with a description of the locale, then describing streets, parks, buildings, educational institutions, industries, and other leading features, and ending with important points in the city's history.

Populations figures are based on final U.S. Bureau of the Census reports. At the end of the section appears a tabulation of cities having a population of 30,000 or more in 1970, with populations in that year and in 1960.

Scenic and Travel Interest. Among topics of scenic and travel interest will be found descriptions of some of the most noted features of the continent, including mountains, lakes, deserts, islands, waterfalls, gorges, cliffs, and caves. Examples of the mountains are Mount Rainier, Mount Shasta, Lassen Peak, and Mount Washington. The lakes include Lake Champlain, Lake George, Itasca Lake, and Lake Tahoe. Among the deserts described are Death Valley, the Mojave, the Colorado, and the Painted Desert. Representative of the other scenic features mentioned above are Niagara Falls, Luray Cavern, Mammoth Cave, and the Palisades.

Numerous features, combining both scenic and historic interest, include Harpers Ferry, Lookout Mountain, Stone Mountain, and Starved Rock. Various special regions, such as the Cotton Belt, the Corn Belt, the Wheat Belt, the Citrus Belt, the Blue-Grass Region, and the Inland Empire, are also described. Although the numerous national parks and national monuments are given tabular treatment elsewhere, some of the most noted are described in greater detail in this section; as, for example, Yellowstone Park and the Grand Canyon

Aberdeen. A city of South Dakota, situated in the northern part of the state at the junction of U.S. highways 12 and 281. Aberdeen is the commercial center of a rich agricultural district, producing large crops of wheat, corn, hay, and potatoes. Its industries include meat packing, flour milling, and the manufacture of machinery. The city is the seat of Northern State College, which has a large open-air theater. Population, 1970, 26,476.

Aberdeen. A city of western Washington, on Grays harbor, 50 miles west of Olympia. Aberdeen is a timber, dairy, and agricultural center, with lumber and plywood mills, fish-curing houses, canning establishments, and excellent port facilities. It adjoins Hoquiam on the west and Cosmopolis on the east. Its inhabitants have a large Scandinavian element. Population, 1970, 18,489.

Abilene. This city in Kansas, 100 miles west of Topeka, was established in 1860 as a shipping point at the end of a trail over which cattle were driven from the Southwest. It has become a flourishing trade center for livestock and grain, particularly wheat. The boyhood home and burial site of Dwight D. Eisenhower, Abilene is the seat of the Eisenhower Museum. A part of old Abilene is being restored as it was in pioneer days. Population, 1970, 6,661.

Abilene. A city located in west central Texas. Long known as an agricultural and livestock center, it has added manufacturing (including aerospace components and ladies' garments), and oil production. Nearby is the Dyess Air Force Base. Educational institutions are Hardin-Simmons University, McMurry College, and Abilene Christian College. Population, 1970, 18,563.

Adamana (ä'dä-mä'na). A small village on the Santa Fe railway in eastern Arizona. Near it are located the celebrated "petrified forests." Of the three forests which together constitute the Petrified Forest national park, two lie at distances of from 6 to 9 miles south of Adamana. Here some thousands of acres are covered with fragments of petrified wood and with wonderfully preserved fossil tree trunks, many of which are 4 feet in diameter. One of these large mineralized trunks, by spanning a ravine 45 feet wide, forms a natural bridge.

The third forest, usually called "Rainbow Forest," is more readily reached by automobile road from Holbrook, a railway town 20 miles west of Adamana. In this petrified forest there are several hundred whole trees, some of which are more than 200 feet long and 6 feet in diameter, all partially embedded in the ground. These are the remains of great cone-bearing trees that grew in geological times.

Agaña (ä-gän'ya). The capital and chief town of Guam, situated on the west coast of the island. Official buildings such as the Governor's Palace, Administration Building, and Post Office are situated here. The people are principally merchants or are in professional trades. Nationalities include Guamanians, Americans, Filipinos, and Japanese. In 1940 Agaña was annexed to Sinajana. Population, 1968, 2400.

Akron. A rubber manufacturing city of Ohio, located 35 miles southeast of Cleveland, with a grain producing region to the south and rich dairy country to the north.

Akron has long been noted for its clay products. With the rise of the automobile industry, the city became the center of the world's most extensive manufacture of automobile tires and of rubber goods in general. It produces also synthetic rubber, fishing tackle, zinc oxide, machine shop products, sulphur, salt, and children's books and is the principal center for the manufacture of sheet metal products, defense equipment, and airships. A huge dirigible air dock, The Goodyear Air Dock, adjoining the municipal airport and covering 9 acres, was opened in 1930. Truck transportation is a major activity.

Within the city there are 26 beautiful parks; these cover a total area of 2200 acres. The Portage Lakes, a 2250-acre state park, lies just south of the city. A steel bridge, 190 feet high, spans the Cuyahoga River within the city, and the North Hill viaduct, 135 feet high and 2810 feet in length, provides the main approach from the north and east. Symbolic of Akron's prominence as a rubber center is the Harvey S. Firestone Memorial, created by architect Eric Gugler and sculptor James Earle Fraser, and dedicated in 1950 to commemorate half a century of progress since the founding of the Firestone Company. The chief educational institution is the state University of Akron. "Derby Downs" is the scene each August of the International Soap Box Derby. Population, 1970, 275,425.

Alameda (ăl'à-mä'dà; -mē'dà). A city of California, occupying a narrow island on the east side of San Francisco Bay, opposite San Francisco and directly south of Oakland. An underwater tube and five bridges link the city to the mainland and major highway systems. Alameda is a beautiful residential city, with numerous fine streets and homes. It also maintains substantial industries, among which are potteries, shipbuilding, and the manufacture of motors, pumps, engines, airplanes and lumber. A large naval air station is located there. Alameda's seven miles of municipal beaches, two yacht harbors, and seven parks provide recreational facilities. Population, 1970, 70,968.

Albany. The capital of New York State, situated on the west bank of the Hudson River, near the head of the Tidewater, 145 miles north of New York City.

Albany is the connecting link between the state's barge canal system and ocean navigation via the Hudson River. A feature of its terminal facilities is a grain elevator covering eight acres. Because of its extensive railway connections, the city is one of the leading transfer points in the United States for passenger, express, and mail traffic. Albany is said to have been the first American city to have a municipal airport, having provided one in 1917. The city's manufactures are extensive and varied. Among the chief products are car heaters and other metal wares, clothing, knit goods, paper products, flour, printing, meat-packing products, and felts.

The city occupies a commanding site, affording superb views of the Hudson River valley. Washington Park, the largest of the 27 units in the city's park system, is noted for its natural beauty.

The most imposing building is the State Capitol, which cost over $29 million. The structure, 400 feet long and 300 feet wide, is built of Maine granite in the Renaissance style. The State Office Building, 34 stories high, is the city's tallest structure. Among other noteworthy buildings are the Albany Institute of History and Art; the old Schuyler Mansion, dedicated in 1917 as a historical monument; and Saint Peter's Church.

Albany's educational institutions include the State University of New York at Albany, Albany Law School (Union University), Albany Medical College, and the College of St. Rose.

Established by the Dutch as a trading post in 1614, Albany is said to be the second oldest permanent settlement within the limits of the thirteen Colonies. Its charter, granted in 1686, is said to be the oldest in the United States. The city was Burgoyne's objective before the battle of Saratoga. Population, 1970, 114,873.

Albuquerque (ăl'bū-kûr'kê). A city of New Mexico, on the Rio Grande River, slightly northwest of the center of the state. It lies at an elevation of 5000 feet, in a bracing, sunshiny climate, and is a noted health resort. The old town, founded in 1705 by the Spanish, remains as a division of the modern city, which dates from 1879.

Albuquerque is the trade center of a rich timber, livestock, and irrigation farming district. A leading occupation is the entertainment of tourists. The University of New Mexico is located here. The more notable structures include a Federal Building and the Harvey Indian Museum. Features of interest in the vicinity are the ancient church of San Felipe de Neri, built in 1735, and the Isleta Indian pueblo. Population, 1970, 243,751.

Alcatraz. An island in San Francisco Bay, about a mile from the mainland. Its shores rise precipitously from the sea. It had been fortified by the Spaniards. From 1858, it was used by the United States government to intern military prisoners. Beginning in 1933, it was used to incarcerate prisoners convicted of kidnaping, murder, and other serious charges, mostly involving life sentences. It was chosen for the purpose as being practically escape-proof and was designed for punishment rather than reformation. Its use as a prison was discontinued in 1963.

Alexandria. A historic city of northern Virginia on the west bank of the Potomac River, six miles below Washington, D. C. Among its many quaint old buildings are Old Christ Church, which George Washington and Robert E. Lee attended; Carlyle House, where Braddock, in 1775, organized his expedition against Fort Duquesne; and the home of Robert E. Lee. The George Washington National Masonic Memorial, erected at a cost of $5 million, is the most imposing modern building. Alexandria's freight classification yard is one of the largest in the country. Refrigerator cars are made in the city. Population, 1970, 110,938.

Allentown. A manufacturing city of Pennsylvania, 50 miles north of Philadelphia. The products of Allentown's industries include electronic components, trucks, fire engines, communication equipment, textiles, shoes, food and beverages, paints, furniture, and numerous items of metal and paper. Founded in 1762 by William Allen, Chief Justice of Pennsylvania, the city has interesting historical traditions. During the Revolutionary War, the Liberty Bell was concealed here to prevent its capture by the British. The city is the seat of Muhlenberg, Cedar Crest, and Pennsylvania Wesleyan colleges. Population, 1970, 109,527.

Altoona. A railroad city of central Pennsylvania picturesquely situated in a mountainous district about 100 miles east of Pittsburgh. The major industry is railway shop construction and repairs, enormous car shops of the Pennsylvania railroad being located in the city. Other products are textiles and clothing. Population, 1970, 62,900.

Amarillo. This leading commercial and industrial center in the northwestern or "panhandle" section of Texas, is a focal point by rail, air, and highway for one of the richest gas and oil regions in the United States. Helium-bearing sands are found nearby, and the city is the chief producer of this gas for airships. Other industries include oil refining, zinc smelting, meat packing, and flour and cottonseed oil milling. Educational institutions include Amarillo College. Population, 1970, 127,010.

Anaconda. A mining city of southwestern Montana, 26 miles northwest of Butte. Anaconda was founded in 1884 by the Anaconda Copper Mining Company, which has there one of the world's largest non-ferrous reduction plants. It is often called the smelting city and is said to have the tallest smokestack in the world. Population, 1970, 9,771.

Anaheim. A city 28 miles southeast of Los Angeles in the Santa Ana Valley of California. Chief among its diversified industries is the packing and canning of citrus fruits, especially oranges. Population, 1970, 166,701.

Anchorage. A city of Alaska which was founded in 1914 and became construction headquarters for the railroad between Seward and Fairbanks. Reflecting the interests of a growing community, it has expanded to include a land office, an international airport, shipping agencies, oil-producing companies, and varied manufacturing and commercial enterprises. Population, 1970, 48,029.

Anderson. A city in Indiana on the White River, 35 miles northeast of Indianapolis. It is in an agricultural region for which it is a business and industrial center, manufacturing steel products and appliances, among other things. It is the seat of Anderson College. Population, 1970, 70,787.

Annapolis. The capital of Maryland, situated on the right bank of the Severn River, near the center of the western coast of Chesapeake Bay. The city was first settled in 1649, and was called Providence. In 1694, it was named after Queen Anne and was made the capital of the colony of Maryland. The first Federal Constitutional Convention met in Annapolis in 1786. The city is the seat of the United States Naval Academy, on a beautiful site of 200 acres, organized in 1845, and of Saint John's College, founded in 1696. The industries include an oyster packing plant. Population, 1970, 29,592.

Ann Arbor. A city on the Huron River, 36 miles southwest of Detroit. It is an industrial and trading center in the midst of an agricultural region. It is the seat of the University of Michigan. Population, 1970, 99,797.

Appalachian Trail. A wilderness foot trail extending 2050 miles from Mount Katahdin, Maine, to Mount Oglethorpe, Georgia. The longest marked foot path in the world, it follows in general the ridge of the Appalachian Mountains. The project was begun in 1921, largely through the initiative of Benton MacKaye, forester and specialist in regional planning; it was completed in 1938.

Asbury Park. A city of New Jersey, on the Atlantic Ocean, about 40 miles south of New York City. Asbury Park is noted chiefly as a seaside resort and residential city. It has, however, various small industries, including the manufacture of silk, women's apparel, electronic equipment, and leather clothing. Population, 1970, 16,533.

Asheville. A mountain resort and city of North Carolina, picturesquely situated in "The Land of the Sky," a plateau of the southern Appalachian Mountains, 2300 feet above sea level, at the western extremity of the state. It is near Great Smoky Mountains National Park, Mount Mitchell, and numerous other points of scenic interest. Near Biltmore Forest, a suburb, is situated the magnificent estate of George W. Vanderbilt, which is open to the public. Other features of the city include Pack Memorial Library, Grove Arcade, covering an entire block, and the civic center on Pack Square. Craggy Rhododendron gardens, 600 acres of royal purple rhododendrons 15 miles from the city, is one of the finest natural gardens in the world.

Asheville provides a market for nearby producers of fruit and is an important distribution center. Manufactured products include furniture, plastics, mica, rayon, cotton textiles, and blankets. The city was incorporated in 1797. Population, 1970, 57,681.

Astoria. A port of northwestern Oregon, located on the Columbia River, about 10 miles from its mouth. It is noted chiefly for the catching and canning of salmon on an immense scale. Tuna also is caught and packed there. Other industries include lumber mills, and creameries. Astoria has river, rail, and bus transportation to Portland, 105 miles distant, and also considerable ocean commerce, with exports of lumber, grain, fish, and flour. It has also a large tourist traffic. Astoria was named for John Jacob Astor, who founded it in 1811. The first post office and the first customhouse west of the Rockies were located here. Population, 1970, 10,244.

Athens. A city of northern Georgia, on the Oconee River, some 70 miles east of Atlanta. Its industries produce electronic components, non-woven fabrics, textiles, clocks, transformers, baseball bats, and precision parts for the aerospace industry. Athens is a noted educational center and is sometimes styled the "classic city of the South." Its leading institutions include the University of Georgia (the oldest state-chartered university) and the Georgia Center for Continuing Education. The city is known for its ante-bellum homes and memorial gardens. Population, 1970, 44,342.

Atlanta. The capital of Georgia, situated in the north central part of the state, about 300 miles northwest of Savannah.

The ridge on which the city is built is a part of a watershed dividing streams that flow into the Atlantic from those that flow into the Gulf of Mexico. The city lies about 1050 feet above sea level. The Chattahoochee River, flowing within 8 miles of the city, is the source of its water supply.

Atlanta is admirably, though somewhat irregularly, laid out, and contains many beautiful avenues and streets. The city covers about 34 square miles, and includes a park system embracing a total area of more than 1200 acres and containing 75 parks, squares, and open spaces. In Grant Park there is a great cycloramic painting of the battle of Atlanta. About 15 miles to the east of Atlanta is situated Stone Mountain, on the face of which is a huge sculptured memorial to the valor of the Confederate soldiers. The commercial district contains many notable buildings, giving the city a metropolitan aspect. Among these are the State Capitol, the Atlanta Public Library, the Federal Building, the Terminal Station, the Federal Reserve Bank, and numerous imposing office buildings.

Atlanta is a prominent educational center and contains many widely known institutions of learning. Among the leading institutions of higher learning are the Georgia Institute of Technology, Emory University, Oglethorpe University, and Columbia Theological Seminary. The institutions for women include Agnes Scott College, located in the adjoining suburb of Decatur. Among the institutions for Negroes are Atlanta, Clark, and Morris Brown universities, Morehouse College, and Gammon Theological Seminary. There are excellent libraries, and the city is one of the chief centers of printing and publishing in the South.

Because of its advantageous situation and excellent railway facilities, Atlanta has become the chief inland commercial city of the southeastern states. It is the distributing center for a large region and has developed extensive industries, ranking first in the state in manufactures. The leading products include cotton mill products, automobiles, aircraft, confectionery and ice cream, Coca-Cola, furniture, mattresses and bed springs, lumber, clothing, and fertilizers. The city conducts a large merchandising trade.

The growth of Atlanta dates from the building of the first railroads in northern Georgia. The site was settled about 1839. In 1843 it was incorporated as Marthasville. This name was changed to Atlanta in 1845, and in 1847 a city charter was granted. Because of its location, it was one of the most important cities of the Confederacy, and in 1864 was the objective of General Sherman's campaign from Chattanooga. The battle of Atlanta and other severe engagements were fought near the city, which was finally taken by the Union forces and largely destroyed. It was quickly rebuilt after the war and grew rapidly. In 1878, it was made the capital of the state. Population, 1970, 496,973.

Atlantic City. An all-year seaside resort on Absecon Beach, a sandy island five miles off the southeastern mainland of New Jersey, about 55 miles southeast of Philadelphia. There are about 1200 hotels and motels for the accommodation of visitors, the number of which often exceeds 15 million annually. The attractions include many miles of beaches, six large recreation piers, a $28 million convention hall covering 12 acres and seating 41,000 people in its auditorium, and the "Boardwalk," a magnificent promenade, 60 feet wide, extending along the ocean front for a distance of five miles. Permanent population, 1970, 47,859.

Augusta. A commercial and manufacturing city of eastern Georgia, located at the head of navigation on the Savannah river, about 132 miles northwest of Savannah. Augusta is the trade center of a rich agricultural district and one of the leading cotton markets in the United States. Water power and hydroelectric power are extensively used in the city's substantial industries, the chief of which are the manufacture of cotton goods and cottonseed products. Other manufactures include brick, lumber, and fertilizers. A United States arsenal is located there. Augusta was established in 1735, and for a time during and after the Revolutionary War was the capital of Georgia. Educational institutions include Paine College, for Negroes, and the University of Georgia Medical College. Population, 1970, 59,864

Augusta. The capital of Maine, situated on both banks of the Kennebec River, about 40 miles from its mouth. The State Capitol is a handsome structure, built of granite quarried locally. Excellent water and rail transportation facilities have made the city the trade center of a large district. It is also a leading air travel center. Local industries include cotton, paper, and lumber mills. Population, 1970, 21,945.

Aurora. A city of northeastern Illinois, occupying a beautiful site on the Fox River, 38 miles west of Chicago. It is an important manufacturing and railroad center, producing road-building machinery, pumps, drills, and other metal products. Its educational institutions include Aurora College. Aurora was settled in 1834 and chartered as a city in 1857. Population, 1970, 74,182.

Ausable (ô-sä′b′l) **Chasm.** A narrow gorge of great scenic attractiveness, situated in northeastern New York, about midway between the Adirondacks and Lake Champlain. The rocks forming the walls are of hard Potsdam sandstone, traversed by numerous fault lines or displacements. Through these the Ausable River has worn a zigzag course about 2 miles long and, in places, 175 feet deep.

Austin. The capital of Texas, located on both sides of the Colorado River, in the south central part of the state. The State Capitol, situated in the ten-acre Capitol Square, is one of the largest in the U.S. Austin is the seat of the University of Texas.

A chain of seven lakes begins within the city limits and winds 150 miles through wooded hills. Called the Highland Lakes, they were created by Colorado River dams as a system for flood control, irrigation, power development, and provision for recreation. The city is the center of a considerable wholesale and shipping business, and carries on an extensive trade in agricultural products, wool, and livestock. Its industries include the manufacture of furniture, electronic instruments, office equipment, food products, finished stone, and fiberglass boats and motor homes. The "association center" of the Southwest, Austin is the headquarters for more than 225 state and national organizations. Austin was incorporated in 1839 and named for S. F. Austin, the "Father of Texas." The site had been selected in 1837 by a state commission instructed to find the most attractive spot for the capitol. Population, 1970, 251,808.

BALTIMORE. The principal city of Maryland, and the largest on the Atlantic seaboard south of Philadelphia. It is situated on the estuary of the Patapsco River, 12.5 miles from Chesapeake Bay and about 170 miles by water from the Virginia capes on the Atlantic. Washington, D. C., lies about 40 miles southwest, and Philadelphia, 97 miles to the northeast. The area of Baltimore is about 79 square miles.

BUILDINGS. Many of the public buildings are noted for size and architectural beauty. Among these are the Peabody Institute, the Roman Catholic Cathedral, said to be the oldest in the United States, the First Presbyterian Church, the Enoch Pratt Free Library, the Walters Art Gallery, the Baltimore Museum of Art, the City Hall, the Federal Building, and the Masonic Temple. The Baltimore Trust Company Building, 509 feet high, affords a landmark of conspicuous beauty.

PARKS AND MONUMENTS. Many fine parks are scattered throughout the city. Of these, Druid Hill Park is the largest and finest. Other noteworthy parks are Clifton, Patterson, Carroll, Herring Run, and Gwynns Falls. A statue of Columbus, unveiled in 1792, the first in any American city to be dedicated to the great discoverer, stands on the grounds of the old Ready school. Mount Vernon Place, the nominal center of the city, is the site of the Washington Monument, a stately column of marble 210 feet high. This monument, the cornerstone of which was laid July 4, 1815, was the first erected by any city in memory of George Washington. Edgar Allen Poe is buried in Westminster Cemetery, one of the oldest and smallest in Baltimore.

EDUCATIONAL INSTITUTIONS. Baltimore is the seat of Johns Hopkins University, a leading institution of higher learning. Connected with it is the widely known Johns Hopkins Hospital. Among other important educational establishments are the University of Maryland, Goucher College for Women, Loyola College, Morgan College, St. Mary's Seminary, and Notre Dame Academy. The Peabody Institute contains a valuable historical library.

TRANSPORTATION AND COMMERCE. In its magnificent system of railroads, its excellent harbor, and its extensive docks, Baltimore has every facility for railway and overseas transportation. Baltimore harbor, one of the largest on the continent with a minimum depth of 35 feet, is capable of accommodating large ocean steamers. Ocean steamers load and unload directly from and into railroad cars at the piers. Baltimore is the chief mercantile and jobbing city of the south Atlantic states and ranks as one of the leading export and import centers of the country. There is an extensive coastwise and intercoastal trade.

MANUFACTURES. Baltimore ranks among the leading cities of the United States in total value of manufactures produced. The principal industries are the making of iron and steel products (the largest single group), shipbuilding, copper, petroleum and sugar refining, and the manufacture of clothing, aircraft, malt and distilled beverages, tin plate, fertilizers, chemicals, and copper products. There are also large establishments for canning fruits and for packing meats and oysters.

Baltimore owes its commanding position as regards manufactures to its easy access to domestic and foreign raw materials and to principal American and world markets.

HISTORY. The first settlement within the present limits of the city was made in 1662. The city was founded in 1729 and was incorporated in 1796. At the time of the American Revolution and especially during the Napoleonic wars, Baltimore attained prominence as a seaport. Its fame was spread throughout the world by its fast-sailing ships called "Baltimore clippers." During an unsuccessful attack by the British on Ft. McHenry, which guarded the city, Francis Scott Key, in 1814, wrote the "Star-spangled Banner."

Baltimore was the first American city to be lighted by gas (1821). The first gas company in America was established there in 1816. The construction of the first important line of railway in the United States, the Baltimore and Ohio railroad, was begun in Baltimore in 1828. Here, also, the first iron steamship was built. In 1844, the first electric telegraph line ever operated was strung between Baltimore and Washington. The first complete, practical electric street railway in the world was installed in Baltimore in 1888. Population, 1970, 905,759.

Bar Harbor. A summer resort in Maine, on the east shore of Mount Desert Island, which lies near the center of the state's coast line. Bar Harbor is partially within Acadia National Park. The scenery in the vicinity is enriched by mountains, by numerous small inlets on the coast, and by many picturesque lakes. Population, 1970, 3,716.

Baton Rouge (băt'ŭn rōōzh'). The capital of Louisiana, located on the east bank of the Mississippi River, about 85 miles northwest of New Orleans. The river is spanned at this point by a $10 million bridge. The city occupies a picturesque site on the river bluff, and receives additional charm from its sub-tropical foliage trees and old houses in the Spanish style. The imposing Capitol, dedicated in 1932, has a 33-story tower. South of the city on a 3100-acre campus is the State University. Baton Rouge also is the home of Southern University, said to be the largest and oldest primarily Negro university. By reason of its fine deep-water harbor, Baton Rouge carries on an extensive shipping trade. Its manufacturing interests include sugar and rice mills, wood-working factories, and extensive chemical and petroleum plants. Population, 1970, 165,963.

Battle Creek. A city of south central Michigan, situated about midway between Detroit and Chicago. The city lies in the center of a rich agricultural region and has become noted for its manufacture of cereals. Other manufactures include industrial trucks, valves, cartons, and therapeutic appliances. The Battle Creek Sanitarium is visited by thousands of persons yearly. Population, 1970, 38,931.

Bay City. A city of eastern Michigan, on the Saginaw River, some 4 miles from Saginaw Bay, an arm of Lake Huron, and about 100 miles northwest of Detroit. Bay City has excellent transportation facilities, both by rail and by water, the river being navigable for the largest lake vessels. The surrounding farming district produces large crops of sugar beets. Among the principal industries are automobile parts, electrical and other machinery, fabricated houses, cement, and beet sugar. Recreation fa-

cilities include the large Bay County Veterans Memorial Park. First settled in 1837, Bay City received its charter in 1865. Population, 1970, 49,449.

Bayonne (bā'yōn'). An industrial city of New Jersey, situated on New York harbor 7 miles southwest of New York City. Bayonne is one of the world's most important centers for the refining of petroleum. It is the terminal of oil pipe lines leading to New York and other eastern cities. The Bayonne Port terminal offers docking facilities among the finest in the New York area. Population, 1970, 72,743.

Beaumont (bō'mŏnt). A deep-water port of southeastern Texas, on the Neches River, about 84 miles northeast of Houston. Beaumont is the center of an important rice growing district, and there are great oil fields and large pine and cypress forests in the vicinity. The chief industries are oil refining, lumbering, shipbuilding, and the cleaning and the marketing of rice. Beaumont is the seat of Lamar State College of Technology. Population, 1970, 115,919.

Bellingham. A port of northwestern Washington, located on a natural harbor on Bellingham Bay. It is the commercial center of an extensive agricultural, poultry and lumbering region. Salmon fishing is an important industry. The leading manufacturing establishments include lumber, pulp, and paper mills, salmon and fruit canneries, and cement and sugar beet factories. The city is the seat of the Western Washington State College. Population, 1970, 39,375.

Berkeley (bûrk'lĭ). A city of California, situated on San Francisco Bay opposite the Golden Gate and adjoining Oakland, which lies to the south. Berkeley's site overlooking the bay and the equable climate unite to make the city highly attractive from a residential point of view.

Berkeley is the seat of the University of California, the largest university in the world. Excellent transportation facilities and low-priced electrical power have favored the development of various industries. The manufactures include soap, toilet articles, drugs, inks and printing material, pastry products, and chemicals. Berkeley was first settled in 1868, and was incorporated as a town in 1878. Population, 1970, 116,716.

Bethlehem (běth'lê-hěm; -lê-ěm). A manufacturing city of eastern Pennsylvania, 52 miles northwest of Philadelphia. It is built on two hills separated by the Lehigh River. The leading industries are steel, foundry and machine products, and silk. Other products include flour, knit goods, radios, electrical equipment, and furniture. Founded in 1741 by Moravians, Bethlehem is the center of the Moravian sect in America. The city celebrates an annual musical festival which is sometimes styled the American Bayreuth. Bethlehem is also the seat of Lehigh University and Moravian College. Population, 1970, 72,686.

Billings. A city in southern Montana on the Yellowstone River, in the heart of an irrigated region noted especially for the raising of sugar beets. Tourist attractions include Beartooth National Forest, the Black Otter Trail, and the Yellowstone Historical Museum. Principal industries are oil refining and diversified manufacturing. Rocky Mountain and Eastern Montana colleges are located in Billings. Population, 1970, 61,581.

Biloxi. A city of Mississippi, about 12 miles east of Gulfport, on a peninsula extending into the Gulf. It is known as a seafood center, with extensive seafood canneries, as well as being a resort area. Biloxi is the site of Keesler Air Force Base and of Beauvoir, the last home of Jefferson Davis. At three times, Biloxi was the capitol of the French province of Louisiana. It was founded by the French in 1699. Population, 1970, 48,486.

Binghamton. A city located in a heavily industrialized area of New York, about 125 miles southwest of Albany. Binghamton is situated at the confluence of the Chenango and Susquehanna rivers. It is the seat of New York State University of Binghamton and Roberson Center for the Arts and Sciences. The birthplace of International Business Machines (IBM), Binghamton is also noted for its manufacture of shoes and photographic equipment and supplies. Binghamton was founded in 1800 by Joshua Whitney, land agent for William Bingham, a wealthy Philadelphia merchant and U.S. Senator from Pennsylvania. It was incorporated as a village in 1834 and became a city in 1867. Population, 1970, 64,123.

Birmingham. A city of Alabama, slightly north of the center of the state. Being situated in the midst of immense coal and iron deposits, Birmingham has risen to high rank among the iron and steel producing centers of the country. Steel and steel products and coke account for a high percentage of the city's extensive output of manufactures, although in recent years the industries of Birmingham have become considerably diversified. The tonnage of its freight is said to be greater than that of all the rest of the South combined. Birmingham is also the trade center of a large and highly productive agricultural district.

The city is substantially and handsomely built, and has many fine streets. beautiful residences, and imposing public buildings, and also numerous commercial structures of the skyscraper type. The municipal park system contains upwards of 39 public parks. Among the most prominent of these are Wilson, North Birmingham, East Lake, Lake View, and Highland parks.

Birmingham is a notable product of the industrial transformation that has taken place in the South since the Civil War. In 1870, the site of the city was a cotton field. In 1871, following the discovery of valuable coal and iron ore deposits in the vicinity, a land company founded Birmingham. Growth at first was slow, but the population rose from about 3000 in 1880 to more than 26,000 in 1890. Population, 1970, 300,910.

Bismark (*bĭz'märk*). The capital of North Dakota, situated on the east bank of the Missouri River, slightly southwest of the center of the state. The most notable buildings include the State Capitol and the Bismarck Civic Arena. The Missouri River is spanned at Bismarck by a bridge. The city's industries include printing, trucking, and the manufacture of farm machinery and concrete products. Population, 1970, 34,703.

Black Hills. A picturesque, mountainous region in South Dakota and northeastern Wyoming. Its 6000 square miles are rich in minerals, particularly gold, and embrace the Black Hills National Forest (970 square miles) and Custer State Park (168 square miles). The highest point is Harney Peak (7216 feet). On Mount Rushmore was begun in 1927 a huge memorial depicting in colossal sculpture the figures of Washington, Jefferson, Lincoln, and Theodore Roosevelt

Black Rock Desert. A dreary waste fully 70 miles long and in some places 20 miles wide, extending northeast from Pyramid Lake in northwestern Nevada. This area, which embraces nearly 1000 square miles, is an alkaline flat or sink, practically devoid of vegetation. During winter, portions are covered with shallow water, whence the name "mud lake," sometimes applied to the region.

Bloomfield. Located 4 miles northwest of Newark, New Jersey, and 11 miles west of New York City, Bloomfield was a part of Newark until 1812. The city is heavily industrialized, with such manufactures as paper and paper products, plastics, rubber goods, textiles, and tile. There is a Revolutionary War soldiers' training ground, now a park, in Bloomfield. Population, 1970, 52,029.

Bloomington. A city about 50 miles southwest of Indianapolis in Indiana. Bloomington is the center of a rich dairy farming region and of the limestone industry, with many quarries in the area. The city has various manufactures. Incorporated in 1876, Bloomington is the seat of Indiana University. Population, 1970, 42,890.

Blue-Grass Region. A district in central Kentucky, lying between the low plains of the west and the mountains on the east. This region is devoted largely to stock raising and is famous for its thoroughbred horses. It is so named because of the prevalence and fine quality of its blue-grass pastures, a common feature of the landscape.

Boise (*boi'sĭ*). The capital of Idaho, located on the Boise River in the southwestern quarter of the state. The surrounding country is rich in minerals and in agricultural products, and the city is an important inland wool market. The varied industries utilize hydroelectric power from the celebrated Arrowrock Dam, constructed 22 miles east of the city and having a height of 349 feet. Boise is unique among cities in possessing a natural supply of hot water from a flowing well. This is used for heating houses and in part for supplying one of the city's outdoor swimming pools. Population, 1970, 74,990.

BOSTON. The capital of Massachusetts, the chief city of New England, is situated on Boston Bay, at the mouth of the Charles and the Mystic rivers, about 230 miles northeast of New York City.

SITE. The original site of Boston was a peninsula marked by three historic hills, Beacon hill. Copp's hill, and Fort hill, and contained about 780 acres. By leveling portions of the hills and by filling in various inlets and tidal marshes, this original area was gradually expanded to 1800 acres. The city now contains an area of more than 30,000 acres, or about 50 square miles.

METROPOLITAN DISTRICT. Modern Boston consists of the city proper and of the populous metropolitan district of which it is the center. The cities of Somerville and Cambridge extend almost to the heart of Boston, and the fine suburb of Brookline lies almost wholly within the city. These are closely surrounded by other large suburban communities. The center of population in the state of Massachusetts lies within the metropolitan district.

STREETS. The narrow, irregular streets, characteristic of the old town, now form but a small section of the North End, mainly an Italian center. The modern city contains about 700 miles of paved streets, which, in the newer districts, are handsomely laid out. Beacon Street, rich in historic associations, and Commonwealth Avenue, one of the finest boulevards in America, are representative of Boston's finest residential avenues.

PARKS. Boston ranks high among American cities in the development of parks and playgrounds. This has two distinct phases, municipal and metropolitan. The municipal park system covers 3500 acres, or more than one-tenth of the city's total area. It embraces the historic Common, 48 acres in extent, set aside in 1634, now in the heart of the city, and includes a chain of parks in various other sections, connected by beautiful parkways. These almost encircle the city.

The Metropolitan parks district includes, with Boston, about 40 municipalities. These are administered by a state commission. The Metropolitan parks plan includes such reservations as the Middlesex Fells, 1900 acres; the Blue Hills, 4900 acres; Stony Brook Woods, 460 acres; and Lynn Woods, 2000 acres. The scheme embraces reservations with connecting parkways covering upwards of 10,000 acres.

MONUMENTS. Boston is noted for its monuments and statues, embracing some of the finest sculptural work in America. The most striking is Bunker Hill Monument, a granite obelisk, about 220 feet high, in Charlestown. In the Common is the great Army and Navy Memorial, by Milmore, and the monument commemorating the Boston Massacre, by Kraus. In the Public Gardens is an equestrian statue of Washington, by Ball; and the Ether Monument, commemorating Dr. W. T. G. Morton's experiments, by J. Q. A. Ward. Facing the Capitol is the impressive Shaw Memorial by Saint Gaudens. There are many others.

BUILDINGS. The newer portions of Boston contain some of the finest examples of modern architecture in the United States. Among many notable buildings may be mentioned the Capitol, the Public Library, Federal Building, Prudential Center, Trinity Church, Holy Cross Cathedral, the First Church of Christ Scientist, and the Museum of Fine Arts. The Customhouse, with a tower 505 feet high, is one of the landmarks of the city.

EDUCATIONAL INSTITUTIONS. Boston is unsurpassed as an educational center. Among its leading institutions are Boston University, Boston College, Simmons College, the New England Conservatory of Music, the Harvard Medical and Dental schools, Northeastern University, and the art school in connection with the Museum of Fine Arts. Harvard University, Radcliffe College, and the Massachusetts Institute of Technology are located across the Charles River in Cambridge. Tufts College, Wellesley College, and other noted institutions are in nearby suburbs. Boston is the home of many important historic, scientific, literary, and musical societies. The Boston Symphony Orchestra is one of the leading organizations of its kind.

TRANSPORTATION. In large measure, Boston owes its commercial prominence to excellent transportation facilities. It is the chief railway center of New England, and its harbor is one of the finest and best equipped on the continent. It has 8 miles of wharfage, giving 40 miles of berthing space.

COMMERCE. Boston is the chief seaport of New England and one of the foremost in the United States. The exports are chiefly provisions and manufactures of cotton, wool, leather, iron and steel, and rubber. Among the principal imports are wool, cotton, fibers, sugar, hides, tea, tin, wood products, and chinaware. There is an extensive coastwise trade, and the city has become the leading fish market in the United States. Among the world's wool markets, Boston ranks second only to London. As a chief distributing point for New England, Boston conducts an enormous wholesale trade. The city is also the center of immense mining, railway, and insurance interests.

MANUFACTURES. As a manufacturing center, the Boston area ranks about tenth among the industrial regions of the United States. While no single industry predominates, the city is a leading center for the manufacture of boots and shoes, clothing, confectionery, cocoa products, books, textile and electrical machinery, edge tools, shipbuilding, and numerous specialties.

POINTS OF INTEREST. Boston, with its environs, offers the traveler an immense number of points of historic and literary interest. Many of the more famous of the earlier buildings have been carefully preserved. Among these are Christ Church (Old North), dating from 1723, Faneuil Hall, the old statehouse, King's Chapel, and the Old South Meetinghouse. Bunker Hill Monument and the navy yard are within the city. In the environs to the northwest are Concord and Lexington, and farther away to the southeast are Plymouth and Plymouth Rock.

Many great writers and scientists lived in or near Boston, including Longfellow, Lowell, Emerson, Holmes, Hawthorne, Thoreau. Dana, Aldrich, Parkman, Prescott, Motley, and Agassiz. Numerous homes and other places of interest connected with the lives of these men are readily accessible.

HISTORY. In a large sense, the history of Boston is the history of New England. Founded in 1630 by Puritans under the leadership of Governor John Winthrop, it was made the capital of the Massachusetts Bay Colony, and has since remained the dominant center of New England. In 1704 the *Boston News Letter*, the first regular newspaper printed in America, began publication. In 1765 began the resistance to the Stamp Act, which culminated in the Revolution. In 1770 occurred the "Boston Massacre," and, in 1773, the famous "Boston Tea Party." At the beginning of the Revolution, Boston was occupied by British troops who defeated the colonists at the battle of Bunker Hill, 1775, but early in 1776 Washington forced the British to evacuate the town Boston received its charter as a city in 1822. During the greater part of the 19th century, Boston was regarded as the literary center of America. Population, 1970, 641,071.

Boulder. A city of northern Colorado, 30 miles northwest of Denver, at the foot of the Rocky Mountains. It is a research and development center, most notably in the area of atmospheric sciences. Manufactures include computer components, technical equipment for satellites, cutlery, and chemicals. The city owns 6000 acres of mountain park land, including Arapahoe Glacier, from which the municipal water supply is obtained. Boulder Canyon nearby possesses great scenic interest. The city is a noted summer and health resort, and is the seat of the University of Colorado. Population, 1970, 66,870.

Bridgeport. The chief manufacturing city of Connecticut, situated in the southwestern part of the state on a natural harbor of Long Island Sound. The city is noted for the diversity of its manufactures, which include electrical machinery, sewing machines, and airplanes. It first attained importance as the seat of the manufacture of sewing machines and as the headquarters of P. T. Barnum's circus. The park system includes Seaside Park, with its two-mile boulevard along the sea wall. The University of Bridgeport has cooperated with the American Shakespeare Festival Theatre to form the Shakespeare Institute, bringing cultural interest to the area. Bridgeport is also the seat of Sacred Heart University. Population, 1970, 156,542.

Brockton. A manufacturing city of eastern Massachusetts, about 20 miles south of Boston. Brockton was one of the largest shoe manufacturing centers in the United States. Other industries include the manufacture of elastic goods, shoe machinery, shoe blacking, nails, and tools. Brockton was settled in 1700, became a town in 1821, and a city in 1881. Population, 1970, 89,040.

Brookline. A town of eastern Massachusetts, on the Charles River, about 3 miles west of Boston. Brookline is chiefly a residential place and ranks among the most beautiful and wealthy suburban towns in America. It produces some manufactures, among which may be mentioned furniture, scientific instruments, and textile products. Brookline is the seat of Cardinal Cushing College and Hebrew Teachers College. Population, 1970, 58,886.

Brooklyn. See *New York*.

Brownsville. A city of southern Texas, located on the Rio Grande River. It is an important port of entry, tourist resort, industrial center, shipping point, and agricultural area. It has excellent transportation facilities, manufactures bricks, and cans fruits and vegetables grown in the surrounding area. Founded in 1848 on an old Mexican settlement, Brownsville was an important port during the Civil War. Population, 1970, 52,522.

BUFFALO. A city of New York state, situated at the eastern end of Lake Erie, 22 miles south of Niagara Falls. It occupies a commanding site facing westward on Lake Erie and the Niagara River, and southward to the valley of Buffalo Creek.

STREETS AND BUILDINGS. The city is regularly laid out, with mostly broad streets crossing each other usually at right angles. There are, however, several great diagonal thoroughfares radiating from the commercial center.

Among the many fine edifices are the Federal Building, an impressive granite structure in the French Romanesque style; the County Courthouse; Buffalo and Erie County Public Library; the 32-story City Hall costing $7 million; New York State Building; the William J. Donovan State Office Building; Roswell Park Memorial Institute; the Liberty National Bank, Rand, Marine Midland Trust, Federal Reserve, and Tishman buildings; the 174th Infantry and the 106th Field Artillery armories; the Museum of Natural History and Science, the Buffalo Historical Society Building; the Albright-Knox Art Gallery, an excellent example of refined classical architecture; the modern Kleinhans Music Hall, a $8.7 million Memorial Auditorium; and Saint Joseph's Cathedral. In the adjoining suburb of Lackawanna is the beautiful Basilica of Our Lady of Victory, a national shrine of the Roman Catholic Church.

PARKS AND MONUMENTS. The municipal park system consists of a chain of parks and parkways which nearly encircle the city, covering in all an area of more than 1250 acres. In these are golf links, lakes and ponds, and numerous other facilities for recreation. Delaware Park, 365 acres, with an artistic blending of lake, field, and natural forest, ranks scenically among the leading American parks. The Front and Centennial park, two beautifully landscaped tracts, overlook the outlet of Lake Erie into the Niagara River.

The principal public memorials are the McKinley Monument in Niagara Square and the Soldiers' and Sailors' Monument in Lafayette Square. In Forest Lawn Cemetery, there are monuments in memory of the Indian-chief Red Jacket and of President Fillmore.

EDUCATIONAL INSTITUTIONS. The chief educational institutions are the State University of New York at Buffalo, Canisius College, D'Youville College, the Buffalo Seminary, State University College at Buffalo, Roswell Park Memorial Institute, and the Buffalo Fine Arts Academy which runs the Albright-Knox Art Gallery. In nearby suburbs are Rosary Hill College in Snyder and Erie County Community College in Williamsville.

TRANSPORTATION. Buffalo's unique situation on the Great Lakes, combined with highly developed transportation facilities, gives the city its rank as a world port. The harbor, protected by an immense breakwater, is one of the best on the Great Lakes. The New York State Barge Canal forms a continuous water route to the Hudson River. The Welland Canal, 20 miles northwest of Buffalo, gives water connection with Lake Ontario and the Saint Lawrence Seaway. A railroad bridge and the Peace Bridge for general traffic connect the city with Canada. Moreover, Buffalo is one of the most important railway centers of the nation, being served by 7 major railroads. Thus, by rail as well as by water, Buffalo is on the direct line of communication between the lake ports and the Atlantic seaboard. A segment of the New York State Thruway passes directly through Buffalo.

COMMERCE. In tonnage and in extent of traffic, Buffalo ranks with the leading American and European ports. The water-borne traffic from the West consists principally of grain, iron ore, flour, and general merchandise. Wheat is the chief commodity received, with iron ore second, the two constituting more than half of the total. The water-borne traffic to the West is comprised mostly of manufactured goods, sugar, and anthracite. The total value of goods entering and leaving the port exceeds a billion dollars annually. Besides this large lake and barge canal traffic, immense quantities of merchandise are received and distributed by rail. The city is an important center for the transshipment of grain, its grain elevators having a capacity of about 30 million bushels. Buffalo is also the general trade and wholesale distributing center of a large and highly populous region.

MANUFACTURES. In manufactures, Buffalo usually ranks eighth among the cities of the United States. The city's industries are extensive and varied and their growth has been substantial and enduring. The production of iron and steel and various iron and steel products constitutes one of the chief industries. Storage and milling of grain have always been major activities along Buffalo's busy water front. Among other noteworthy manufactures are automobile parts, rubber tires, chemicals, food preparations, books, linseed oil, and furniture. Buffalo owes its eminence in manufactures to an abundance of electric power, to large supplies of natural gas, and other readily available fuel; and to unexcelled transportation advantages for the distribution of its products.

POINTS OF INTEREST. The pre-eminent feature of scenic interest in the vicinity of Buffalo is Niagara Falls. There are also many points of historical interest in connection with the early settlement of the Niagara frontier and of the conflict with the British and Indians in the War of 1812–14.

HISTORY. La Salle visited the site of Buffalo as early as 1679. The first white settlement was made about 1788 by Indian traders. In 1801–02, a village called New Amsterdam was laid out at the mouth of Buffalo Creek. This village was incorporated and renamed Buffalo in 1810. Three years later it was captured and practically destroyed by the British. It was rebuilt but grew slowly until the completion of the Erie Canal in 1825. Since that date.

Buffalo's progress has been continuous and substantial. In 1832, Buffalo received its charter as a city. The first grain elevator in the world was built in Buffalo in 1843. The city has given to the United States two presidents, Millard Fillmore and Grover Cleveland. In 1901, the Pan-American Exposition was held at Buffalo. Population, 1970, 462,768.

Burbank. A city of southern California, 12 miles north of Los Angeles, noted for its motion-picture and aviation industries. Population, 1970, 88,871.

Burlington. A city of Vermont, located at the approximate center of the east shore of Lake Champlain. Among its manufactures are textiles, armament systems and components, dyes, and apparel. In the vicinity are large quarries of limestone. The city is the seat of the University of Vermont, chartered in 1791, Trinity College for Women, and St. Michael's College. It is headquarters of the Champlain Transportation Company, reputedly the oldest steamship corporation in the world. Greenmount Cemetery contains the grave of Colonel Ethan Allen. Population, 1970, 38,633.

Butte (*būt*). A city of Montana, situated in a mountainous region at an elevation of 5500 feet above sea level. Incorporated in 1879, Butte is the center of an extremely rich copper mining region. Recognition of the city's indebtedness to Marcus Daly, discoverer of the rich copper veins, is expressed in the form of a statue by St. Gaudens. The famous Anaconda mine, said to be the largest copper mine in the world, and many other valuable mining properties are located within a radius of a few miles. Besides copper, the principal product, manganese, gold, silver, lead, and zinc are obtained. The total value of the mineral output to date is approximately $2 billion. The city has an extensive local trade, entertains numerous tourists, and is the seat of the Montana College of Minerals and Technology. Population, 1970, 23,368.

Cambridge. A city of Massachusetts, situated on the Charles River opposite Boston. Cambridge is exceedingly rich in historical, literary, and educational associations.

The Washington elm, under which Washington took command of the American army, stood in Cambridge until 1923, when it was blown down. Elmwood Park commemorates the home of James Russell Lowell Craigie House, once the headquarters of General Washington, became the home of Henry Wadsworth Longfellow. Among the illustrious figures once resident in Cambridge were Oliver Wendell Holmes, Louis Agassiz, and John Fiske. The city is the seat of Harvard University, the oldest university in the United States, of Radcliffe College, of the Massachusetts Institute of Technology, and of the Andover Theological Seminary. A beautiful system of parks includes nearly the entire river front.

The city has numerous important industries, among which are printing and publishing, and the manufacture of electrical machinery, rubber goods, structural ironwork, chemicals, soap, candy, and bakery products.

Cambridge was settled in 1630 by Governor Winthrop and others as Newe Towne. In 1638, Newe Towne was renamed Cambridge; in the same year, Harvard College (founded in 1636) was opened. In 1639, the first printing press in English-speaking North America was set up in Cambridge. The first book printed here was "The Bay Psalm Book," which appeared in 1640. Population, 1970, 100,361.

Camden. A city of southwestern New Jersey, located on the east bank of the Delaware River, opposite Philadelphia. The city occupies a level site, covering an area of about 10 square miles. The park system contains Farnham Park and about 40 other parks or playgrounds. Among the leading industries are shipbuilding and the manufacture of radios, phonographs, canned soups, and worsted goods. Other important manufactures include iron and steel forgings, foundry products, linoleum, chemicals, and pens. In the suburbs are immense market gardens. The city is connected with Philadelphia by steam ferries and by two great bridges: one, the Benjamin Franklin bridge, on its completion in 1926, was the greatest suspension bridge in the world; the other, the Walt Whitman bridge costing $86 million, was opened in 1957.

First settled by Quakers, Camden was organized and named in 1773, and became a city in 1828. Population, 1970, 102,551.

Canaveral, Cape. See *Kennedy, Cape.*

Canton. An industrial city of northeastern Ohio, famed for its manufacture of roller bearings and other iron and steel products, particularly those made from stainless steel. Second only in importance to its metal-working plants are its brick and tile factories. Canton was the home and is the burial place of President McKinley, in whose honor a national memorial has been erected in West Lawn Cemetery. The first home of the National Football League, Canton is now the seat of the Professional Football Hall of Fame. Population, 1970, 110,053.

Carlsbad Caverns National Park. A cavern in southeastern New Mexico, believed to be the largest and deepest in the world. It is entered at the foot of a cliff in the Guadalupe Mountains about 20 miles south of Carlsbad, New Mexico, and 130 miles east of El Paso, Texas.

The cave was formed by water filtering through overlaid rocks and slowly dissolving out beds of rock salt, limestone, and gypsum. The dripping water carrying dissolved minerals has formed stalagmites and stalactites of unrivaled beauty. One of the most impressive portions is the "Big Room," about 4000 feet long with a maximum width of 625 feet. At one point the ceiling is 300 feet high. The "Giant Dome" resembles the leaning tower of Pisa. It is estimated to be 60 million years old. The lowest known point in the cave is some 1350 feet below the earth's surface.

The cave is known to extend at least 25 miles, approximately a third being accessible to the public over carefully marked trails. Artistically concealed electric flood lights emphasize the natural beauty of the cavern. The temperature is constant throughout the year at 56°F.

The most interesting feature of animal life within the cave is a huge colony of bats, estimated to number 3 million, which issues forth from the entrance each evening of summer like a thick cloud. It was this cloud of bats which led to the discovery of the cave in 1901 by Jim White, a cowboy. Milk-white crickets have been found in the cave.

In 1923, an area of about 719 acres surrounding the mouth of the cavern was set aside as a national monument. This was made into a national park in 1930, and its area was subsequently enlarged to about 73 square miles.

Carson City. The capital of Nevada, picturesquely located near the foot of the Sierra Nevada, 14 miles from Lake Tahoe. It contains the Capitol, a Federal building, and a museum containing a series of mastodon skeletons which were discovered nearby. In the vicinity are the State Penitentiary and a government Indian school. Population, 1970, 15,468.

Casa Grande (*kä'sä grän'dä*). The remains of a prehistoric building, situated near the south bank of the Gila River, about 12 miles west of Florence, Arizona. The first white man to visit this impressive structure was Father Kino, a Jesuit missionary. In 1694, he said Mass there. It became a national monument in 1918.

The principal edifice is about 45 by 60 feet in extent. The height of the walls indicates that there were at least three stories, each having various rooms. Above the third story was a smaller room, apparently a watch tower. This structure is only one of many blocks of buildings whose former existence nearby is marked by mounds of debris. The exterior walls of the Casa Grande building are rough and very much eroded. The interior walls, however, are smoothly plastered. The structure is built of a natural cement, called *caliche* by the Mexicans, composed of lime, earth, and pebbles. This was made into blocks laid in courses.

Casa Grande was probably built about 1350 by the Salado Indians and was occupied by them and the Hohokams for nearly a century before being abandoned.

Casper. A city of Wyoming, in the east central part of the state, on the North Platte River, 150 miles northwest of Cheyenne. It is the site of Fort Caspar, and has extensive commercial interest in the cattle, sheep, wool, and petroleum produced in the surrounding districts. The refinement of petroleum is the chief industry. Casper owns a 440-acre mountain park 5 miles south of the city. Population, 1970, 39,361.

Castle Gate. The entrance to Price River Canyon in central Utah, 115 miles southeast of Salt Lake City. This gatelike passage is formed by two immense pinnacles of sandstone, 450 to 500 feet in height. These pinnacles, strikingly colored, rise like two castles sheer from the narrow canyon bed, barely leaving room for the railway and the river to pass.

Catskill Mountains. A group of mountains in the southeastern portion of New York State about 100 miles north of New York City. The system is about 50 miles long, north and south, and has a breadth of some 30 miles. The highest peak is Slide Mountain, 4204 feet in elevation. In order to supply New York City with water, two creeks on the southern slopes of the Catskills have been impounded: the Esopus by the Ashokan Dam and the Schoharie by the Gilboa Dam. From the resulting reservoirs, which connect by the 18-mile Shandaken tunnel, water is conveyed to New York City by the Catskill aqueduct, which includes a 17-mile tunnel.

Cedar Rapids. A manufacturing city and railway center of east central Iowa, situated on the Cedar River, 220 miles west of Chicago. Its 200 industries include meat packing and the manufacture of cereals, corn products, machinery, and electronic equipment. In total value of manufactures, Cedar Rapids ranks first among the cities of the state. The city is the mercantile center for a rich agricultural region, and enjoys an extensive wholesale trade. The first settlement was made in 1838 at the rapids of the Cedar River. These furnish the water power which has been an important factor in the city's growth. Cedar Rapids is the seat of Coe College. Population, 1970, 110,642.

Champaign. A city in a rich agricultural region of Illinois, about 127 miles southwest of Chicago. It adjoins Urbana, Illinois, Urbana being primarily a residential area, and Champaign, an industrial and commercial area. The University of Illinois is located in Urbana. Champaign manufactures drop forgings, soybean oil, road machinery, deep freezers, air conditioners, and many other items. Population, 1970, 56,532. Population of Urbana and Champaign, 89,332.

Champlain, Lake. An important lake, lying between New York and Vermont, draining through the Richelieu River into the Saint Lawrence. Lake Champlain is about 110 miles long and, at its broadest northern portion, about 13 miles wide. It has a total area of about 600 square miles, two-thirds of which is in Vermont. Its greatest depth is about 300 feet, and it is navigable for the largest vessels.

Lake Champlain is connected with the Hudson River by a canal from Whitehall and serves as a link in New York's extensive system of inland waterways. Among the towns along its shores are Rouses Point, Plattsburg, Port Henry. Crown Point, and Whitehall in New York, and Burlington in Vermont.

Discovered by Champlain in 1609, the lake and its environs became the scene of many stirring events in the French and Indian War and in the Revolutionary War. The decisive naval battle of Lake Champlain was fought off Plattsburg in 1814.

Charleston. The only seaport city of South Carolina, situated 7 miles from the ocean on a peninsula between the Ashley and Cooper rivers. The estuary of these rivers forms a fine landlocked harbor—one of the deepest and most spacious on the Atlantic coast.

The attractive appearance of the city is enhanced by such features as Washington Park, with its pre-Revolutionary statue of William Pitt; Hampton Park; the Customhouse, built of white marble at a cost of $3.4 million; White Point Gardens; and the Esplanade, comprised of the broad, beautiful promenade of the Battery seawall drive.

Manufacturing in Charleston County is widely diversified, including products of wood, metal, tobacco, concrete, paper, asbestos, rubber, chemicals, plastics, and fabrics. An average of more than one hundred ships per month enter and leave the Port of Charleston, and the value of imports and exports is in excess of $200 million annually. Wool is a very important item, with two large wool scouring plants nearby. The port facilities, being fully modernized, handle everything from heavy machinery to tropical fruits. Charleston is one of the country's leading banana ports.

The vicinity of Charleston was the scene of the earliest attempts at colonization in South Carolina. A temporary settlement was made by the French in 1562. The first settlement on the present site of the city was made by English colonists in 1670, who were joined in 1686 by groups of Huguenot refugees. In 1755, a colony of 2000 deported Acadians settled in Charleston.

During the American Revolution, Charleston was captured by the British. The city suffered immense damage in the final campaign of the Civil War in 1865. On August 31, 1886, a heavy earthquake caused great destruction of life and property. After each period of devastation, the city was rebuilt more substantially than before. Charleston has preserved, to a remarkable degree, her interesting historic places and features.

Possessing a well-equipped navy yard, Charleston is an important center of military activity. Located in the immediate vicinity are the Minecraft Base, the Charleston Air Force Base, the U.S. Naval Ammunition Depot, and the U.S. Army Transportation Corps Depot. The system of harbor defenses includes Fort Sumter, whose bombardment in 1861 marked the beginning of the Civil War.

Among the city's leading educational institutions are the College of Charleston, the Medical College of South Carolina, and the Citadel, or State Military College. Population, 1970, 66,945.

Charleston. The capital of West Virginia, situated at the junction of the Kanawha and Elk rivers in a region rich in coal deposits and in petroleum and natural gas. In addition to steel manufactures the city has become noted as a source of nylon, synthetic rubber, resin, and various other chemical products, particularly those having to do with defense. The ready accessibility of silicon,

salt brine, and coal-tar products has made this a natural location for such industries. The city's increased activity has been reflected in the completion of the Kanawha County Airport, located on Coonskin Hill. A local educational institution is Morris Harvey College. Charleston was incorporated in 1794, and became the capital of the state in 1870. Population, 1970, 71,505.

Charlotte (shär'lŏt). A cotton manufacturing city of North Carolina, located in the rich cotton growing district of the southwestern part of the state. It is at the heart of the hydroelectrical development in the state, and, besides cotton textile mills, has dye and engineering works and automobile assembly plants. The city has a monument erected to the memory of those who, at Charlotte in 1775, signed the Mecklenburg Declaration of Independence. The leading educational institution is Queen's College. Charlotte is the birthplace of President Polk. Population, 1970, 241,178.

Charlotte Amalie. The capital of the Virgin Islands, on the southern side of the island of Saint Thomas, about 40 miles east of Puerto Rico and 1440 miles southeast of New York. Situated on Saint Thomas harbor, one of the finest in the Antilles, it commands strategically the important Virgin Passage.

Charlottesville. A city of central Virginia, built on the Rivanna River, about 70 miles northwest of Richmond. Charlottesville is the seat of the University of Virginia. This was founded by Thomas Jefferson, whose home at Monticello is only 3 miles distant. The city is beautifully located in a rich agricultural and fruit growing region. It was settled in 1744, and the vicinity abounds in historical associations connected with the Revolutionary War. Population, 1970, 38,880. See *Monticello*.

Chattanooga (chăt'à-nōō'gà). A railroad center and manufacturing city of southeastern Tennessee, situated on the south bank of the Tennessee River. Nearby deposits of coal and iron together with abundant hydroelectric power, marketed at low cost by the Tennessee Valley Authority, facilitate the operation of many industries. Of these, the most important are the manufacture of steel, steel products, and textiles. Near the city stands Lookout Mountain, from whose summit seven states can be seen. Several important battles of the Civil War were fought in the vicinity of Chattanooga. The educational institutions include the University of Tennessee at Chattanooga and the Chattanooga State Technical Institute. Population, 1970, 119,082.

Chautauqua (shà-tô'kwà) **Lake.** A small lake in the extreme southwestern part of New York. It is about 18 miles long and 2 miles wide, and drains through Conewango Creek into the Allegheny River. It lies about 1300 feet above sea level, and 730 feet above Lake Erie, which is only a few miles distant but separated by a range of hills. Chautauqua Lake is noted for its beautiful surroundings and for the widely known Chautauqua summer school located on its banks.

Chelsea (chĕl'sè). A city of eastern Massachusetts, situated on the Mystic River, about 3 miles northeast of Boston. Chelsea has substantial industries. These include the manufacture of lithographs, shoes, paper, car wheels, and rubber products. First settled in 1642, as Winnisimmet, Chelsea was incorporated under its present name in 1739. In 1908, a great fire destroyed a large portion of the city. The devastated area, however, was rapidly rebuilt. Population, 1970, 30,625.

Chester. A manufacturing city of southeastern Pennsylvania, located on the Delaware River, about 13 miles southwest of Philadelphia. The chief industrial interests include steel products, munitions, locomotives, automobiles, chemicals, paper, petroleum, machinery, and textiles. It has also one of the largest shipbuilding yards in the country. The city has three parks, also the Deshong Memorial grounds. It is the seat of Pennsylvania Military College. Chester was first settled about 1640 by Swedes. Of historic interest are the City Hall, built in 1724, and the house of William Penn. Population, 1970, 56,331.

Cheyenne (shi-ĕn'). The capital of Wyoming, site of America's first ICBM base, is situated in the southeast part of the state, 106 miles north of Denver. The city was founded in 1867 by engineers of the Union Pacific railroad. Because of its central location in an extensive stock-growing section, the city is an important shipping point for beef cattle and for sheep. Among the chief buildings are the State Capitol, the Federal Building, and the governor's mansion. A three-mile boulevard extends from the city to Fort Francis E. Warren, an important government military post. Population, 1970, 40,914.

CHICAGO. The chief city of Illinois, the metropolis of the Middle Western states, and the second most populous city in the United States. It is situated on the southwestern shore of Lake Michigan and on the Indiana boundary, about 185 miles northeast of Springfield, the capital of the state.

SITE. Chicago occupies a remarkably level site, extending along the lake shore for 24½ miles. The city extends inland, at its widest point, for a distance of about 10 miles and embraces a total area of some 212 square miles.

By the Chicago River, a small stream, and by its two branches, the city is divided into three principal districts. The branches of the river unite about a mile west of the lake and approximately midway between the north and the south boundaries of the city. The district lying north of the river and the north branch is called the North Side; that lying south of the river and the south branch is called the South Side; and the much larger district lying west of the two branches is known as the West Side.

STREETS. With few exceptions, Chicago's streets cross at right angles and in east-and-west and in north-and-south directions. Chicago is noted for its exceedingly long and straight streets. Many continue in a direct line for from 5 to 10 or more miles. Some, as, for example, Western Avenue and Halsted Street, extend without deviation for practically the entire length of the city, a distance of 25 miles.

The chief commercial and mercantile center lies south of the river between its south branch and the lake. Here, in an area approximately a mile square, are found most of Chicago's great public edifices, office buildings, and department stores. Many of these are grouped within the so-called "loop," a section surrounded by elevated railroads. On the north it is bounded by the two-level Wacker Drive. State Street contains the great department stores, and, with Wabash and Michigan avenues, constitutes the chief shopping district. LaSalle Street, the center of the financial district, is sometimes styled the "Wall Street" of Chicago. Franklin and Market streets are the principal center of the wholesale trade. The most notable street of the commercial district is Michigan Avenue. For more than a mile this overlooks Grant Park, and its massive buildings, when viewed from Lake Michigan, dominate the city's sky line. Extending northward over the Link Bridge, which spans the Chicago River, it becomes the beautiful Lake Shore drive.

BUILDINGS. Near the center of the business district is the magnificent Civic Center. This is a twin structure of limestone and granite, built in the French Renaissance style. The United States Courthouse, one of the largest structures erected by the United States government outside of Washington, covers an entire city square, about 320 by 400 feet. It is built of granite, 16 stories high, and is surmounted by a massive dome nearly 300 feet high. The Field Museum, on the lake front, erected at a cost of $8 million, ranks among the finest museum buildings of the world. Nearby, on an artificial island, is the Adler Planetarium, the first to be erected in America (1930). Among other notable structures are the Public Library, the great stadium, on West Madison street, the Municipal Pier, the Wrigley Building, the Tribune Tower, the Pure Oil Building, the Board of Trade Building, the Field Building, the Hilton Hotel, the Merchandise Mart, and a $21 million Post Office.

PARKS AND MONUMENTS. Chicago has a magnificent park system embracing about 486 large and small parks, with a total area of more than 7300 acres. The major parks are connected by a system of boulevards and parkways, aggregating 162 miles in length. The circuit through the park system affords one of the finest drives in America. The larger units of the system are Lincoln, Humboldt, Garfield, Douglas, Marquette, Washington, Jackson, Burnham and Grant parks. Among the parkways and drives which link these units into one organic whole are Lake Shore Drive, Sheridan Road, the Outer Drive, and Diversey Avenue on the North Side; Humboldt, Jackson, and Washington boulevards on the West Side; and Eriksen Drive, Michigan Avenue, Grand, Drexel, South Shore Drive, and Garfield Boulevard on the South Side.

Grant Park, on the lake, in front of the business district, contains the Art Institute and the beautiful Buckingham Fountain. Lincoln Park contains a large conservatory and zoological garden and notable statues of Grant and Lincoln, the latter an impressive work by Saint Gaudens.

Jackson Park, the largest of all, overlooks the lake on the South Side. Along the Midway plaisance, connecting Jackson and Washington parks, are the buildings of the University of Chicago. In this plaisance is the impressive sculptural group "Fountain of Time," by Lorado Taft.

Besides the extensive recreation grounds within the city, a metropolitan park district has been created outside of the city. For the purpose of establishing an outer ring of parks, several large forested areas, aggregating more than 37,800 acres, have been purchased.

EDUCATIONAL INSTITUTIONS. Chicago is one of the important educational centers of the country. It is the seat of the University of Chicago, noted for its large postgraduate school. Northwestern University, in the adjoining suburb of Evanston, has most of its professional departments in the city. Other important institutions are Loyola University, De Paul University, the Illinois Institute of Technology, the Lewis Institute, and the art school in connection with the Art Institute.

TRANSPORTATION. Chicago is the chief railway center of America, being the terminus of railway systems embracing about half the total railway mileage of the country. No railroad runs through Chicago, for all of the 22 trunk lines, radiating to all parts of the United States, have terminals in the city. The business district is surrounded by a ring of great passenger stations. A series of belt lines around the city connects the different railroads, forming a complete transfer system. Chicago's 640-acre O'Hare airport is the terminus of numerous converging airplane routes. Meigs and Midway airports are also located in Chicago.

Chicago has also the advantage of inland water transportation, and ranks as one of the chief ports on the Great Lakes. There is a well protected harbor, with docking facilities furnished by the Municipal pier, which extends 3000 feet into the lake. The river and its branches have been deepened so that an immense tonnage, greater than that passing through the Panama Canal, is handled at wharves within the city. By the construction of the Chicago drainage canal, whereby the waters of the river are made to flow outward from the lake into the Des Plaines river, an all-water route to the Mississippi and to the Gulf of Mexico has been made possible.

Local transportation is served by an extensive system of elevated electric railway. The elevated railways radiate from the central loop in the commercial district to all sides of the city. In addition, there is an extensive system of motor bus transportation. Chicago is served also by a large number of suburban electric lines.

COMMERCE. Chicago owes its supreme position in American inland commerce to superior advantages of location and to marvelously developed facilities for transportation. It is situated at the crossroads between the populous industrial sections of the northeastern states and the rich agricultural districts of the Mississippi valley and the great Northwest. The city is the center of shipment of western produce to the East and of eastern manufactures to the West. It is the greatest distributing point in the United States for dry goods, foodstuffs, clothing, household articles, and general merchandise. In Chicago was developed the now extensive business of mail order merchandising.

MANUFACTURERS. Chicago is the industrial as well as the commercial metropolis of the Mississippi Valley region. Among American cities, it stands second only to New York in value of manufactures. Chicago's manufactures normally exceed $3.5 billion in value, or more than two-thirds that of New York's manufactures. Chicago is the world's greatest meat packing center, and leads the country in the manufacture of farm implements, farm machinery, and railroad cars. Its other industries are extensive and exceedingly varied.

HISTORY. In 1803, John Kinzie, the first American settler, built a house on the north bank of the river. In 1804, Fort Dearborn was erected. During the War of 1812, this fort was captured and the settlers massacred by the Indians. Fort Dearborn was reconstructed in 1816, but the village around it grew very slowly until the building of the Illinois and Michigan canal in 1830.

Made a town in 1833, Chicago was incorporated as a city in 1837 with a population of 4170. In 1852, the first railway from the East reached Chicago. Following this event the city's growth was rapid, rising from 28,000 in 1850 to 109,000 in 1860, and to 298,000 in 1870. Since 1870, Chicago has increased in population at the rate of more than a half million in each decade.

In 1871 occurred the "great fire," the most appalling disaster that as yet had befallen an American city. Within a few years the devasted areas were rebuilt and made more substantial than before. In 1893 was held the World's Columbian Exposition, erected at a cost of about $43 million. The centennial of Chicago's incorporation as a town was celebrated by the Century of Progress Exposition in 1933. Population, 1970, 3,366,957.

Chicopee. A manufacturing city of southwestern Massachusetts, located on the Connecticut River, at the mouth of the Chicopee, about 4 miles north of Springfield. Abundant water power is furnished by the Chicopee River for the city's varied and extensive industries. These include the manufacture of firearms, cotton and knit goods, bronze statuary, knitting machines, rubber goods, athletic goods, regalia, swords, and many other articles. Westover Air Base is located nearby. Population, 1970, 66,676.

Chillicothe (*chĭl'ĭ-kŏth'ē*). Capital of the former Northwest Territory and once capital of Ohio, Chillicothe is situated on the Scioto River 45 miles south of Columbus, in the middle of a rich agricultural region. It is also in the center of the Mound City group of prehistoric earthworks which have yielded many artifacts revealing some early American civilization. Chillicothe's manufactures include aluminumware, paper and paper products, shoes, and floor tiling. Camp Sherman was built here during World War I. The city is the site of the Chillicothe Correctional Institute and a U.S. Veterans' hospital. Population, 1970, 24,842.

Cicero. A town of Illinois, partially surrounded by Chicago, of which it is an industrial suburb, being about 7 miles west of Chicago's "loop." Manufactures comprise chiefly electrical equipment, pumps, engines, iron castings, and enamel ware. Population, 1970, 67,058.

CINCINNATI (*sĭn'sĭ-năt'ĭ*). A city in Ohio, situated on the north bank of the Ohio River, 120 miles southwest of Columbus.

SITE. Cincinnati is environed by a semicircular range of high hills. From the river bank, it rises in two great terraces or steps, finally reaching a height of 450 feet above the river. Several fine bridges connect the city with Covington, Newport, Ludlow, and other towns on the Kentucky side. Through the center of the city passes Central parkway, a 4½-mile boulevard on the site of the old Miami and Erie canal. The picturesque residential sections of Mount Auburn, Mount Adams, Fairview, Avondale, Hyde Park, College Hill, and Clifton are reached by motor bus lines and by splendid highways.

BUILDINGS AND INSTITUTIONS. Among the more notable buildings are the Post Office, the Public Library, the Music Hall, the County Courthouse, Carew Tower (48 stories, 574 feet high), the Union Central Life building (34 stories, 495 feet high), Saint Peter's Cathedral, and a magnificent terminal station costing about $42 million. Of public monuments, the most artistic are the Tyler-Davidson Fountain, in Fountain Square, and the Barnard Lincoln statue, in Lytle Park. The extensive park system, embracing over 2800 acres, includes Mount Airy Forest, Eden Park, Burnet Woods, Ault, Mount Echo, and various smaller parks.

The city has been long known as an educational, art, and musical center. Among the principal institutions are the University of Cincinnati, a state university; the Ohio Mechanics' Institute; the Art Academy and Art Museum, in Eden Park; Saint Xavier University; Hebrew Union College, Our Lady of Cincinnati College; and the Cincinnati College Conservatory of Music. For many years the May Musical Festivals, held annually, and the annual season of summer opera at the municipally owned Zoological Gardens, have been an indispensable feature of the city's cultural life. The widely known Cincinnati Symphony Orchestra is a well-endowed, permanent organization.

MANUFACTURES. Cincinnati ranks high as a manufacturing city, and owes much of its success as such to its advantageous location midway on the great Ohio River. In addition, the city has the service of eight trunk lines of railway, one of which, the Cincinnati Southern, 338 miles long, is owned by the municipality itself. It is an important airroute center and is an outlet for the bituminous coal fields of Kentucky and West Virginia and for fruits and vegetables grown in the South. Cincinnati's most important manufactures include machine tools, playing cards, soap, building materials, cans, chemicals, clothing, coffins and burial cases, conveyors, cosmetics, electric motors, food products, jet engines, malt and distilled liquors, mattresses, motor vehicles and parts, paper, pianos and organs, plastics, inks, meat products, printing, metal products, shoes, and ceramic products, including the famous Rockwood pottery.

HISTORY. In 1788, a village called Losantiville was laid out on the present site of the city. The name of this village was changed in 1790 to Cincinnati, which, in 1802, became incorporated as a town. Its steady growth dates from 1816, when steam navigation was inaugurated on the Ohio River. Cincinnati was incorporated as a city in 1819. Few large cities in the United States have a larger proportion of native-born inhabitants. Population, 1970, 452,524.

Citrus (*sĭt'rŭs*) **Belt.** The name applied to those parts of the states of California and Florida in which the leading citrus fruits—oranges, lemons, and grapefruit—are chiefly produced. Many counties in various parts of California grow oranges on a small scale, but by far the largest part of the state's commercial crop of all citrus fruits is grown in seven counties in the southern part of the state. These are Los Angeles, San Bernardino, Orange, Tulare, Riverside, Ventura, and San Diego counties. Santa Barbara County is an important producer of lemons, and, farther north, Fresno, Sacramento, Butte, Tehama, and Glenn counties produce and market substantial quantities of oranges.

The citrus belt of Florida comprises about 15 counties in the central part of the peninsular portion. It extends across the state from the Gulf of Mexico to the Atlantic Ocean, its center lying a short distance north of Tampa. In this belt the chief citrus fruits produced are oranges and grapefruit. The leading counties in the production of oranges are Polk, Orange, DeSoto, Brevard, Lake, Hillsborough, Volusia, and Pinellas. These counties produce about two-thirds of the total orange crop of the state. The counties leading in grapefruit are Polk, Manatee, Pinellas, Lee, DeSoto, and Saint Lucie. These counties produce about two-thirds of Florida's total yield of grapefruit.

California produces practically all of the lemons, about 70 per cent of the oranges, and some 13 per cent of the grapefruit grown in the United States. Florida grows about 60 per cent of the grapefruit and about 28 per cent of the oranges produced in the country. Texas and Arizona also rank high in grapefruit production, each growing between 10 and 20 per cent of the nation's crop.

Clarksburg. A trade center in the north central part of West Virginia. Among various manufactured products it is noted for articles made of glass, particularly glass tumblers. Clarksburg was founded in 1782. It is the birthplace of "Stonewall" Jackson, after whom one of its leading hotels is named. A Veterans' hospital was opened in 1951. Population, 1970, 24,864.

CLEVELAND. The chief city of Ohio, situated on Lake Erie at the mouth of the Cuyahoga River. It is located in the northeastern part of the state, about 625 miles by rail northwest of New York, and some 360 miles east of Chicago.

SITE. Cleveland occupies a beautiful site on elevated ground sloping gently toward the lake, along which it has a frontage of 14 miles. The city is divided unequally by the windings of the Cuyahoga River into a larger portion on the east side and a smaller portion on the west side. The highest point reaches an elevation of about 300 feet above the level of the lake; the lowest points are in the valley of the river and along the lake shore. Immense viaducts, spanning the deep valley of the river, connect the eastern and the western sections. Among the most notable of these are the High Level and Main Avenue bridges and the Abbey Street, Clark Avenue, Lorain-Central, and Harvard-Denison viaducts.

STREETS AND BUILDINGS. Cleveland is well laid out with many broad, well shaded streets and handsome boulevards. At the intersection of Superior Avenue and Ontario Street, in the heart of the city, is the Public Square. There are also streets connecting with the great viaducts leading to the west side of the city. The chief business section extends from the lower part of the river eastward. The manufacturing districts are mostly along the lake front, in the low flat valley of the river, and along various lines of railway.

A notable architectural feature in the heart of the city is the array of buildings forming the "Municipal Group," or civic center. The project, designed by leading American architects, includes the erection of structures of beautiful and harmonious architecture on a T-shaped tract of land, known as the Mall. The buildings include the County Courthouse, the City Hall, the Federal Building, the Auditorium, the Board of Education Building, and the Public Library. The city is noted for its superb office buildings. Among noteworthy structures are the Museum of Art, the Auditorium, the Keith Building, Federal Reserve Bank, the Union Station with its associated buildings, including the 708-foot Terminal Tower building, the Medical Arts Building, and the Builders Exchange.

PARKS. Cleveland's public park system covers a total area of about 3000 acres and includes upwards of 40 miles of connecting boulevards. Important units in the park system are Gordon, Edgewater, Brookside, Garfield, Monumental, Washington, Rockefeller, Wade, and Woodland Hills parks. Among attractive drives are Euclid Avenue, Fairmont and Shaker boulevards on the east side and, on the west side, Lake Avenue and Clifton Boulevard. About the three landward sides of the city extends a belt of boulevards and natural park lands, known as Metropolitan Park.

EDUCATIONAL INSTITUTIONS. Prominent among Cleveland's cultural institutions are Case-Western Reserve University, John Carroll University, Cleveland State University, Fenn College, the Museum of Art, and the Museum of Natural History. Unique as a means of public education is Cleveland's "Health Museum." In 1949, two new theaters were constructed in the city by nonprofit groups. The Cleveland Orchestra is nationally known.

TRANSPORTATION. The harbor, which is protected by an immense breakwater nearly 6 miles long, is one of the most spacious on the Great Lakes. There is a total lake dock frontage of more than 13 miles, and the Cuyahoga River is also lined with docks. These are equipped with facilities for handling iron ore, coal, and lumber, and there is ample dockage at special piers for the extensive passenger service. Cleveland is also one of the great railway centers of the country, with direct lines to most of the leading cities of the United States. It is also an important point of transcontinental air routes. To its already commodious airport facilities for large commercial craft, the city has added a lake-front landing field for light planes.

COMMERCE. Cleveland owes its commanding position in commerce and industry to superior advantages of location. It is situated at the economic focus for the assembly of the raw materials of iron and steel. It is said to be the largest ore market in the world. Within a short distance to the southeast lie iron mines, limestone quarries, and immense coal fields. From the northwest, by cheap all-water transportation, are received enormous supplies of Lake Superior iron ore. In consequence, the city's railways and lake steamer lines handle an immense tonnage of raw materials and distribute manufactured products valued at hundreds of millions of dollars. It is estimated that the total shipments handled at Cleveland aggregate in value more than a billion dollars annually.

MANUFACTURES. Cleveland is one of the great manufacturing centers of America. It ranks fifth among the cities of the United States, being surpassed only by New York, Chicago, Philadelphia, and Detroit. While there is an immense diversity of manufactures, the chief industries are concerned with the manufacture of iron and steel and their products. Other important manufactures are automobile parts, machine tools, household appliances, packed meats, clothing, electrical machinery, and refined petroleum. The Standard Oil Company, which began its operations in Cleveland, has immense refineries in the city. Cleveland is one of the greatest wire and bolt manufacturing centers in the world.

HISTORY. Cleveland was laid out in 1796 and was incorporated in 1814. In 1818, the first newspaper began publication. The Ohio Canal was opened to Akron in 1827, and in 1832 was completed to the Ohio River. This stimulated the growth of Cleveland, which received its city charter in 1836. Since the discovery of iron ore in the Lake Superior region and the construction of the first railroads, 1850-60, Cleveland's growth has been rapid and continuous. The centennial of its status as a city was celebrated by the Great Lakes Exposition in 1936. Population, 1970, 750,903.

Cleveland Heights. A city of northeastern Ohio, being a residential suburb of Cleveland, which it adjoins at Cleveland's eastern boundary. Between 1920 and 1930 it increased in population from 15,236 to 50,945. Population, 1970, 60,767.

Cohoes (*kô-hōz'*). A manufacturing city of eastern New York, located on the Hudson River and the State barge canal, at the mouth of the Mohawk River, about 9 miles north of Albany. Abundant water power and hydroelectric power have led to the development of extensive industries. Cohoes leads all other cities of the United States in the manufacture of knit underwear. Other industries include the manufacture of paper products, shirts and collars, machinery, and building materials. Population, 1970, 18,613.

Colorado Desert. An arid region in southeastern California. It is separated from the Mojave Desert, which lies to the north, by the San Bernardino and the Chocolate ranges, and is bounded on the south by the San Jacinto, the Santa Rosa, and the Superstition mountains.

From the eastern entrance of San Gorgonio pass, the desert extends to the Colorado River, from which it takes its name. It is more than 100 miles long, in some places more than 20 miles wide, and covers an area of about 2000 square miles. Much of this region lies below the sea level. The lowest portion is known as the Salton Sink. In this lies the salt lake, called the Salton Sea, the surface of which is about 280 feet lower than that of the Gulf of California. Parts of the desert show traces of volcanic activity, and there are mud volcanoes and numerous thermal springs.

As in the case of the Mojave Desert and Death Valley, lofty mountain ranges on the west cut off the vapor-laden breezes from the Pacific. Consequently, the Colorado desert is a region of extreme aridity,—in fact, one of the driest and hottest in the world. The normal rainfall ranges from 3 to 4 inches, and summer temperatures as high as 130° have been recorded.

The scanty vegetation is typical of southwestern deserts, it includes the creosote bush, mesquite, cat's-claw, smoke tree, paloverde, and numerous kinds of cactus. In a few canyons at the western end of this desert are the only known groves of the native American fan palm, or Washington palm. Among characteristic desert animals are the chuckwalla lizard and the sidewinder, or horned rattlesnake.

Wherever irrigation is practicable, much of this seemingly worthless desert will produce immense crops of fruits, alfalfa, cotton, and grains. In consequence, prosperous towns and agricultural communities grew up in various parts, notably the rich and populous Imperial Valley. In many points this California desert resembles Arabia or Egypt. Here, as in those ancient countries, the date palm, long-fiber cotton, and alfalfa flourish. The desert is traversed from end to end by the Southern Pacific railway, and by the Los Angeles-Yuma and other highways. See *Mojave Desert, Palm Canyon, Salton Sea.*

Colorado Springs. A city of central Colorado, situated near the eastern base of Pikes Peak at an elevation of 6000 feet above the sea. The city is a noted health and pleasure resort and has a beautiful system of parks, covering some 3000 acres. Among places of historic and scenic interest in the vicinity are Pikes Peak, Ute Pass highway, the Garden of the Gods, Cave of the Winds, Manitou Springs, Phantom Cliff Canyon, and Will Rogers shrine, halfway up Cheyenne Mountain. The city is the seat of Colorado College, the Colorado Springs Art Center, and the United States Air Force Academy. Population, 1970, 135,060.

Columbia. A city of Missouri, located about 125 miles northwest of St. Louis. Columbia is primarily an educational center, the seat of the University of Missouri and Stephens College for women. The city is in an agricultural area and has light manufacturing. Columbia was incorporated in 1826. Population, 1970, 58,804.

Columbia. The capital of South Carolina, situated near the center of the state on the high eastern bank of the Congaree River. The State capitol, built of granite at a cost of $6 million, is modeled after the national Capitol. Radiating from the capitol are four wide, well-shaded avenues. The most important industry is the manufacture of cotton. Electricity is provided by large hydroelectric developments in the vicinity, including the huge Saluda Dam. The city is the seat of the University of South Carolina and five colleges. The site of Columbia was settled about 1700; it was chosen for the capital, and the town was laid out in 1786. The legislature first met there in 1790. Population, 1970, 113,542.

Columbia River Highway. An important scenic highway constructed along the south side of the Columbia River in Oregon. It extends west from Portland through Astoria to Seaside on the Pacific Ocean, and east from Portland to Hood River, northeast of Mount Hood, a total distance of about 150 miles. This skirts the Columbia River by running around mountains, over hills, through tunnels, across viaducts, and along embankments.

At some points the highway reaches a height of 700 feet above the river, affording magnificent views. The highway passes near many beautiful cataracts, running immediately beside the celebrated Multnomah Falls, 607 feet high, and so close to Horse Tail Falls that the spray keeps the roadway moist.

Columbus. A city of southern Georgia, about 95 miles southwest of Atlanta, situated at the head of navigation of the Chattahoochee. The falls of this river provide power for the city's industries, and a channel connects the river with the Gulf of Mexico. Columbus played an important role in manufacturing army supplies for the Confederate Army during the Civil War, and is still an important industrial city, producing chiefly cotton textiles among its many manufactures. Fort Benning, the largest infantry post in the United States is located nearby. Population, 1970, 154,168.

Columbus. The capital of Ohio, located in the central part of the state, about 135 miles southwest of Cleveland and 120 miles northeast of Cincinnati. Surrounded by a productive agricultural region and by rich coal, iron, and natural gas fields, the city has developed into an important industrial and commercial center. The leading manufactures include agricultural, electrical, mill, and mining machinery, steel and steel products, boots and shoes, drugs, caskets, meat and other food products.

Columbus is laid out in a form somewhat resembling a Maltese cross. Parks and public grounds cover more than 9300 acres. Columbus is the seat of Ohio State University, which has a stadium capable of seating nearly 100,000 persons. Other educational institutions are the Capital University, Ohio Dominican College, the Josephinum College, and the Columbus College of Art and Design. On spacious grounds in the center of the city is the massive Doric capitol. Bordering the beautiful civic center is the Le Veque Lincoln Tower. Civic center buildings also include the City Hall and state and federal government buildings. An important junction point of the nation's airways, Columbus is the site of Port Columbus and the Rickenbacker Base Hospital for the U.S. Air Force.

Comparable to the growth of its educational institutions is the development of related activities which have made Columbus a center of scientific research. The internationally known journal *Chemical Abstracts* is published at the Ohio State University. The Battelle Memorial Institute, a foundation with affiliated laboratories in Frankfurt and Geneva, conducts basic research in chemistry, metallurgy, physics, fuels and combustion, and ceramic technology.

The first permanent settlement on the present site of the city was made in 1797. Columbus was laid out and was made the capital of the state in 1812. In 1816, the legislature first met in Columbus. Population, 1970, 539,677.

Concord. A town of Massachusetts, rich in historical and literary interest, situated some 20 miles northwest of Boston. Concord was founded in 1635. It was the British objective in the fighting at Lexington and Concord, which was the first armed conflict of the Revolution. The battle of Concord began at the Old North bridge. Here, April 19, 1775, the "embattled farmers fired the shot heard round the world." The town contains various memorials of the struggle, the most notable of which is the statue of "The Minute Man." Concord is celebrated also as the home of a number of distinguished figures in American literature, including Emerson, Hawthorne, Thoreau, and Louisa M. Alcott. Antiquarian House contains many mementos of the city's rich history. Population, 1970, 16,148.

Concord. The capital of New Hampshire, located in the Merrimack River Valley on a rolling and varied terrain. Industries include printing, electronics, research and development, and the manufacture of paper carton machinery. The famous Concord stagecoaches were made here during the days of Westward expansion in the United States. The impressive State Capitol is built of fine white native granite. Settled in 1725, the village, first called Pennacook and then Rumford, later changed its name to Concord. It became a city in 1853. It was the home of Mary Baker Eddy, founder of Christian Science. Population, 1970, 30,022.

Coney Island. A narrow island five miles in length, situated at the southwestern point of Long Island, near the entrance to New York harbor. The island is the most popular seashore resort in the United States. Coney Island is divided into four well-defined districts: West Brighton, which is provided with numerous popular means of amusement; Brighton Beach, containing a race track; Manhattan Beach, which is partly residential; and Sea Gate, the home station of the Atlantic Yacht Club.

Continental Divide. The crest or height of land in the United States which separates the waters draining into the Atlantic Ocean from those draining into the Pacific. This extends from the Mexican boundary northward across western New Mexico and then somewhat eastward to Rocky Mountain National Park in north central Colorado, its easternmost point. Thence the "great divide" trends northwest through northern Colorado and western Wyoming to Yellowstone National Park. Continuing westward and northward across Montana, it passes through Glacier National Park to the Canadian boundary. In some parts of its course, the Continental Divide is at the crest of the loftiest ranges; in others, it is on gently rolling uplands at the summit of high plateaus, usually 7000 feet or more above sea level.

Corn Belt. The fertile region in the east central United States which is largely devoted to the growing of corn. The most productive area embraces western Ohio, Indiana, Illinois, Iowa, Missouri, eastern Nebraska, eastern Kansas, and southeastern South Dakota. Adjoining parts of Kentucky, northern Oklahoma, and southern Minnesota, which produce large yields of corn, are usually considered as belonging to the Corn Belt. More than half of the corn crop of the United States is grown in this central zone.

Corpus Christi. A city and seaport of southern Texas, situated at the mouth of the Neuces River on Corpus Christi Bay. A deep-water channel to the Gulf of Mexico gives access for ocean ships to the city's well-equipped port facilities, opened in 1926. Corpus Christi Harbor Bridge spans the channel and is the highest bridge in Texas. Corpus Christi's industries and its exports, which include cotton, aluminum, petroleum, and seafoods, are based largely on the resources of the surrounding territory. Corpus Christi was chartered as a city in 1876. After the opening of the port, it grew rapidly, almost doubling its inhabitants in the decade of 1930–40. The University of Corpus Christi is located here. Population, 1970, 204,525.

Cotton Belt. The extensive region in the southern United States in which the immense cotton crop is produced. The zone of greatest productivity embraces eastern North Carolina, most of South Carolina, Georgia, Alabama, and Mississippi, parts of Arkansas, western Tennessee, northern Louisiana, and southern Oklahoma, and much of the northeastern half of Texas. Texas, Missis-

sippi, and Arkansas are the leading states. The Cotton Belt produces about three-fifths of the world's supply of cotton.

Council Bluffs. A railroad, manufacturing, and commercial city of southwestern Iowa, located on the Missouri River opposite Omaha, Nebraska. For the most part, the city, which is well laid out, lies upon a plain largely surrounded by lofty bluffs. There are several parks, of which the chief one is Fairmount. Railroads, and vehicle bridges over the Missouri River, and also electric lines, connect the city with Omaha. Served by 8 major railroads, the city is a leading grain marketing center and has varied industrial interests, including the manufacture of truck bodies, farm implements, freight car wheels, bee supplies and cereals. The name Council Bluffs is said to have been given because of the council held at this point in 1804 between the Indians and the explorers Lewis and Clark. Population, 1970, 60,348.

Covington. A city of Kentucky, situated on the Ohio River, opposite Cincinnati. Covington occupies a beautiful site, partly surrounded by lofty hills, and contains many fine streets and homes. It has excellent transportation facilities by rail and by river, and is connected with Cincinnati by three bridges. While largely residential, Covington has substantial industries, including meat packing and the manufacture of machine tools, canvas goods, hardware, and structural iron. Devon Park, 550 acres, on the outskirts, has a large natural amphitheater. St. Mary's Cathedral, patterned after Notre Dame in Paris, has one of the largest stained-glass windows in the world. Covington, the seat of Thomas More College, was settled in 1812, and became a city in 1834. Population, 1970, 52,535.

Crater Mound (now **Meteor Crater**). A remarkable geological formation in central Arizona, about 40 miles southeast of Flagstaff. First known as Coon Butte and later as Meteorite Mountain, Crater Mound ranks as one of the most remarkable geological features of the West.

Viewed from the Santa Fe railway, which passes some miles to the north, it appears as a low ridge. Upon close approach, this ridge is found to be circular in form and to enclose an immense crater-like hole or depression 4000 feet in diameter and 600 feet deep. The encircling ridge, 100 to 150 feet in height, is composed of fragments of rock and sand blown up from the hole. The beds of rocks in the walls of the hole are limestone above and sandstone below, both more or less upturned near the hole and in part considerably shattered.

The cause of this great hole was long a mystery. The occurrence of many small masses of meteoric iron in the vicinity suggested that it was made by the impact of a meteorite. All efforts to locate the main body of such a meteorite failed until 1932, when with the aid of electrical instruments, geophysicists located the metallic mass at a depth of 680 feet.

Crawford Notch. A picturesque gorge between Mount Webster and Mount Willey, in the White Mountains of New Hampshire. In a narrow passage, at an elevation of about 1900 feet, the Saco River traverses the Notch, which is notable for its fine rock scenery.

Cumberland. A city of western Maryland, situated on the Potomac River, about 155 miles northwest of Baltimore. Cumberland is located in a mountainous region near important coal fields. It ships immense quantities of semibituminous coal, highly valued for steaming purposes, and has other extensive industries. The principal manufacturing establishments are railway repair shops, rubber tire, cellulose and glass factories, and silk, flour, and lumber mills. Population, 1970, 29,724.

Cumberland Road, or the National Road or Great National Pike. Originally envisioned by George Washington, the project to connect the East and the central West was initiated by Thomas Jefferson in 1806. Beginning as a federal government project, it was completed as such only from Cumberland, Md., to Wheeling, W. Va. It was then connected with older pikes in the East and with newer ones in the West, with individual states assuming responsibility for maintenance of the road. The Cumberland Road is still a means of travel from Chesapeake Bay, its easternmost point, to St. Louis, Mo., its western limit.

Currecanti Needle. One of the striking scenic features of the Black Canyon of the Gunnison River, in southwestern Colorado. It is a massive pinnacle of highly colored rock, hundreds of feet in height, and tapering at the top to a somewhat pointed spire, whence the name "needle."

Dallas. The second largest city of Texas, located on Trinity River, in the northeastern part of the state, about 185 miles northeast of Austin. Dallas is located in an exceedingly fertile agricultural region, the chief cotton growing district of the state. The city is in the center of the world's largest oil field. It is the largest inland cotton market in the United States, and the leading wholesale and jobbing center southwest of Saint Louis. Dallas is the chief distributing point in the Southwest for farm implements and automobiles. In manufactures, Dallas ranks first among the cities of the state. The principal industries include oil refining, meat packing, printing and publishing, the manufacture of oil well and cotton ginning machinery, airplanes, automobiles, cottonseed oil, saddlery, harnesses, and cotton goods. Its fine commercial structures include the 42-story Southland Tower and the 36-story Republic National Bank Building.

The city's parks embrace an area of more than 15,500 acres, and there are extensive boulevards and drives. The state fair, held annually in the city, attracts more than three million visitors. The city is the seat of the Southern Methodist University, University of Dallas, Baylor Dental School, Dallas Art Institute, and museums of fine arts and natural history. Dallas was settled in 1841 and chartered as a city in 1856. Population, 1970, 844,401.

Danbury. A city of Connecticut, about 13 miles northwest of Bridgeport. Danbury is noted for manufacturing hats, especially felt ones. It was the site of several significant incidents during the Revolutionary War. Danbury was chartered as a city in 1889. Population, 1970, 50,781.

Davenport. A commercial and manufacturing city of eastern Iowa, situated on the slope of a steep bluff of the Mississippi River, opposite Rock Island, Illinois. The chief manufactures include aluminum products, meat products, and farm implements. An extensive business is carried on in flour and grain by river as well as by rail transportation. The city has a municipal art gallery, a public museum, and an excellent park system. Educational institutions include St. Ambrose College, Marycrest College, and Palmer College of Chiropractic. Founded in 1835, Davenport was incorporated as a town in 1838 and received its charter as a city in 1851. Population, 1970, 98,469.

Dayton. A manufacturing city of southwestern Ohio, situated on both banks of the Miami River, about 50 miles northeast of Cincinnati. Among the leading manufactured products are cash registers, envelopes, electric motors, electrical refrigeration machinery, and automobile accessories. A great contribution to the city's prestige has been made by the airplane industry, founded by the Wright brothers, to whose memory a beautiful monument has been erected in the city. Other structures of note include the Art Institute and Museum and the Deeds' Carillon Tower with 32 bells. Wright field accommodates the experimental laboratories of the U. S. Air Corps. Patterson Field and the Fairfield Air Depot are also located here.

First settled in 1796, Dayton became a city in 1841. In 1913 a disastrous flood caused great destruction of property and loss of life. The devasted sections were rebuilt, and a system of five reservoirs, costing $32,000,000, was constructed to prevent a repetition of the disaster. Population, 1970, 243,601.

Daytona Beach. A year-round resort city of Florida, situated on the Halifax River, 53 miles south of St. Augustine. Well-known automobile speed trials are held on the city's 23-mile, hard-packed, white sand beach. Tourism is the chief industry. Population, 1970, 45,327.

Dearborn. A city of southeastern Michigan, ten miles west of Detroit, of which it is a residential suburb. Henry Ford had his home there, his birthplace being on a farm in the vicinity. This farm he restored to its early appearance and he built there a village museum, "Greenfield village," consisting of old buildings collected from all parts of the United States and from England. An outstanding example of modern architecture is the Ford Rotunda exhibit hall. Population, 1970, 104,199.

Death Valley. An extremely arid desert in eastern California, near the Nevada boundary, containing the lowest point of dry land in the Western Hemisphere. The name was given by a survivor of a party of 30 "forty-niners," most of whom perished of thirst in its sands. It lies in a north-and-south direction, is about 150 miles long, and varies in width from 4 miles to 16 miles. On the west it is bordered by the high Panamint Range; on the east it is flanked by the Funeral, the Black, and the Grapevine mountains. The lowest point in Death Valley is 282 feet below sea level. In a direct line, this lowest point is about 86 miles east of Mt. Whitney, 14,496 feet high, the loftiest peak in the United States outside Alaska.

The valley is in the sink of the Amargosa River, a stream that is dry for the greater part of the year throughout much of its course. The eastern side of the valley was formerly the bed of a salt lake. In the entire area, drinkable water can be obtained in only a few places. The salty bottom of the valley is destitute of vegetation, but the bordering slopes have a sparse growth of desert shrubs. The annual rainfall averages 1.66 inches; the average humidity is very low—no dew ever forming, and the summer temperatures, reaching 134°, being the hottest authentically recorded in America. See *Colorado Desert, Mojave Desert.*

Decatur (dē-kā′tŭr). Located on the Sangamon River, almost in the center of Illinois, Decatur lies in the corn and soy bean belt. The city's chief industrial establishments include railway shops, metal and wood-working plants, soy bean processing plants, and factories for the making of tractors, graders, air conditioners, window glass, and gas and water systems. Decatur is the seat of Millikin University. Recreation is afforded by a 160-acre park system and by a lake 12 miles long formed by a dam across the Sangamon River. The city was named for Stephen Decatur, naval hero. Population, 1970, 90,397.

Delaware Water Gap. A picturesque gap and narrow gorge in the Kittatinny Range, near Stroudsburg, Pa., on the borders of Pennsylvania and New Jersey. The steep sides of the mountain here rise to an elevation of 1400 feet above the Delaware River, which flows through the gap.

Denver. The capital of Colorado. It is situated at the junction of Cherry Creek and South Platte River. The site, which has an altitude of one mile above the level of the sea, slopes back from both banks of the river and commands a magnificent view of the Rocky Mountains. Denver is the largest city between the Missouri River and the Pacific coast. It is also one of the most important railway centers of the West, to which fact, in great measure, it owes its growth and prosperity.

The city is handsomely planned and contains many fine public buildings and substantial private residences. Among the former may be noted the State Capitol, the Auditorium, the United States Mint, and the Civic Center, whose 5 million-dollar City and County building is said to have the largest bronze doors in the world. The Fitzsimons General Hospital for army tubercular patients is one of the largest buildings in Colorado. Some of the principal educational institutions are the University of Denver, Regis College, Westminister College, and Colorado Woman's College. The City Park, which covers 408 acres, has a zoological garden, a lake, a museum, aviary, and speedway. The park system, including about 40 parks in all, is one of the finest in the United States and is supplemented by a system of 38 municipal mountain parks in the vicinity.

Denver is the principal center of mercantile supply for the agricultural, stock raising, and mining districts of Colorado and New Mexico. The chief industries include meat packing, flour milling, railway car construction, printing and publishing, and the manufacture of iron and steel products, structural iron, clothing, paints, automobile accessories, and chemicals. Population, 1970, 514,678.

Des Moines (dĕ moin′). The capital of Iowa, built on both banks of the Des Moines River, in the central part of the state. Des Moines is the commercial center of an exceedingly fertile farming region, with which it carries on an extensive marketing and wholesale trade. Surrounded by rich farm lands, the city has developed numerous and varied industries, prominent among which is the production of machinery, food products, and clothing. Many important farm journals and other publications are printed in Des Moines, which is also the center of large insurance interests.

Chief among many imposing public buildings is the Capitol, built on a slight eminence, and approached by Capitol Extension park. Adjoining this park is the fine State Historical Building. The city's park system includes 58 parks and covers 1500 acres. To this total may be added the 600 acres comprising the State fairgrounds. Des Moines is the seat of Drake University and of the Des Moines College of Osteopathy and Surgery.

By reason of its central location, together with ample hotel and auditorium facilities, Des Moines is a favorite meeting place for conventions. The city's unique civic center consists of a landscaped area taking in the opposite banks of the river. In the group of buildings are the Post Office and Library, the City Hall, the Federal Court Building, the Y.M.C.A., and the municipal armory.

Around Fort Des Moines, which was established in 1843, settlers, in 1846, built a village. This village was incorporated in 1851 as the town of Fort Des Moines. In 1856, the town was made the capital of the state. In the following year, it was chartered as the city of Des Moines. Population, 1970, 200,587.

DETROIT. The chief city of Michigan and the fifth most populous in the United States, situated on the Detroit River, 18 miles from Lake Erie. It lies some 90 miles southeast of Lansing, the capital of the state, and is about 250 miles west of Buffalo and 285 miles east of Chicago. The city occupies a nearly level but gently rising site, extending some 12 miles along the river front, and containing an area of about 138 square miles.

STREETS AND BUILDINGS. The city is regularly laid out, with wide streets, most of which cross at right angles on the checkerboard plan. There are, however, several broad avenues, 100 to 200 feet wide, which radiate from the Campus Martius and the Grand Circus in the heart of the city.

The commercial district is located mainly around and near the Grand Circus and the Campus Martius. The former is a small, semicircular park, and the latter is a large plaza. These are situated near each other and give an air of openness and spaciousness to the business center of the city. Griswold Street, lined with great office buildings and banking houses is the "Wall Street" of Detroit.

The chief public buildings are located on or near the Campus Martius. Within it is the Michigan Soldiers' and Sailors' monument, facing the City Hall. Nearby is the skyscraper City-County Building. Numerous great office buildings, of the finest modern type, are built around portions of the Grand Circus. Among many notable buildings may be mentioned the General Motors Building, the Veterans Memorial Building, the Ford Auditorium, the Fisher Building, the Federal Building, the Board of Commerce, the Michigan Central Station, the Masonic Temple, the Ford, Penobscot, Stroh, First National Bank, and Majestic buildings, the Public Library, Bank of the Commonwealth, and the Detroit Institute of Art.

PARKS AND BOULEVARDS. The municipal system contains upwards of 242 parks, embracing an area of about 3600 acres. The most notable of these is the island park, Belle Isle, with an area of 1000 acres, where is situated one of the country's best zoological gardens. This lies opposite the eastern part of the city, with which it is connected by a bridge. River Rouge Park is the largest, 1204 acres in area. In addition to the numerous small parks, many triangles at diagonal street intersections have been improved and ornamented, and there are numerous boulevards.

EDUCATIONAL INSTITUTIONS. Detroit is the seat of Detroit University, Wayne State University, the Detroit College of Law, the Michigan College of Medicine, the Michigan State Auto School, and various other educational institutions.

TRANSPORTATION. The city owes its greatness, in a large part, to unique advantages in transportation both by lake and by rail. It is situated midway on the inland waterway system of the Great Lakes. The deep Detroit River, sometimes called the "Dardanelles of America," affords a spacious harbor, accommodating the largest lake vessels. There is a numerous passenger fleet, and the city is a port of call for all steamers from Buffalo to the upper lakes. The tonnage passing through the Detroit River is more than double that passing through the Suez Canal, and is immensely greater than the tonnage arriving at and leaving any other inland seaport in the world.

Local transportation is effected by a comprehensive system of municipally owned street railways and bus lines. The city is connected with Windsor, Canada, by a tunnel and the great Ambassador suspension bridge.

COMMERCE. Enormous quantities of iron ore, copper products, grain, and coal are handled by the lake traffic. There is a large export trade to Canada and Europe, chiefly foodstuffs, automobiles, and steel products. The city is the commercial center of a great interior district with which it carries on an immense distributing trade. In addition, it ships the products of its vast industries to all parts of the country.

MANUFACTURES. Detroit is the greatest automobile manufacturing center in the world. Its phenomenal growth in the early 20th century corresponded with the vast development of the automobile industry. In value of manufactures, Detroit stands fourth among the cities of the United States. The greater part of this production is automobiles and automobile accessories and parts. There are numerous other substantial industries. Detroit is a leading center for the manufacture of aircraft, brass and bronze products, adding machines, stoves and furnaces, malleable iron, and aluminum castings. Other important manufactures include railway cars, machine tools, electrical apparatus, drugs, chemicals, engines, paint, tobacco, and rubber goods.

HISTORY. The first settlement at Detroit was made in 1701 by Cadillac, the French governor of Michillimackinac, who built Fort Pontchartrain. During the French and Indian War, this was captured, 1760, by the British. The first act of Pontiac's conspiracy, 1763, was an unsuccessful attempt to seize this important fort. Detroit was incorporated in 1802 and became the capital of Michigan territory in 1805. In 1812, William Hull surrendered the town to the British, who evacuated it the following year.

Detroit was chartered as a city in 1824, continued as the capital of the territory until 1835, and was the capital of the state, 1835-47. Its growth until 1910 was continuous and substantial. In the decade 1910-20, the city more than doubled in population and more than quadrupled in value of manufactures. Population, 1970, 1,511,482.

Diablo (dê-ä′blō; dǐ-ăb′lō), **Mount.** A mountain of west central California, situated on the edge of the great interior valley, about 30 miles air-line distance nearly due east of San Francisco. Its general domelike outline and isolated position have given the erroneous impression that Mount Diablo is an old volcano. It is, in fact, the higher portion of a great overturned arch of sedimentary rocks.

Because of its visibility for long distances in many directions, Mount Diablo has been a noted landmark since the days of the "forty-niners." Through it run the meridian and the base line from which the land surveys of a large part of California are reckoned. While of moderate height, the elevation being 3849 feet, its unique situation makes it one of the finest scenic viewpoints in the state.

Dismal Swamp, Great. A tract of marshy land in southeastern Virginia and northeastern North Carolina. It begins a short distance south of Norfolk, Virginia, extends southward for about 30 miles, and embraces a total area of some 750 square miles. Near its center is Lake Drummond, about 2 miles in diameter and very shallow. The remainder of the swamp is covered, for the most part, with heavy timber and a thick tangled undergrowth. The swamp originally contained an area of about 2200 square miles, but much of it has been reclaimed and placed under cultivation.

Dobbs Ferry. A village of New York State, on the Hudson River 20 miles north of New York City. Here are located two schools for girls—the Masters School and the Sacred Heart Academy. In the Livingston Manor here Washington and Rochambeau planned the Yorktown campaign. Opposite this village the American flag was saluted for the first time by a British sloop of war. Population, 1970, 10,353.

Dover. The capital of Delaware, located slightly north of the center of the state. Dover is surrounded by a rich fruit growing country, the chief crops being apples, grapes, melons, and peaches. The principal industry is the canning of plum pudding, poultry, and other foods. There is an impressive State Capitol and a handsome monument erected to the memory of Cæsar Rodney, one of the signers of the Declaration of Independence. The Archives Building houses Delaware's earliest records. Silver Lake Park and Dover Green are other features of interest. Dover was laid out in 1717 and became the capital of Delaware in 1777. It became a town in 1829; a city in 1925. It is the seat of Delaware State College. Population, 1970, 17,488.

Dubuque (dŏŏ-būk′). A city of northeastern Iowa, built on the west bank of the Mississippi River, about 200 miles northeast of Des Moines. Dubuque lies in a fertile farming district and the surrounding region is rich in lead and zinc deposits. Dubuque has substantial manufacturing industries, and is the center of a large marketing and distributing trade by river and by rail. The city is situated partly on a terrace 20 feet above the river and partly on a hill, which rises to a height of 200 feet.

Among the notable features are Eagle Point park which has a very large ledge garden. There is also a monument to Julien Dubuque, who settled on the site of the city in 1788. The first permanent settlement dates from 1833. The village was incorporated as a town in 1837, and, in 1840, was chartered as a city. The educational institutions include Loras and Clarke colleges and the University of Dubuque. Population, 1970, 62,309.

Duluth. An important lake port and the third largest city of Minnesota. It is built on steep and picturesque slopes overlooking a fine natural harbor at the western end of Lake Superior. Enjoying the advantages of exceptional railroad and port facilities, Duluth handles an annual tonnage of grain and iron ore of stupendous proportions. Impetus to its further expansion has come from the newly-developed Taconite industry and the completion of the St. Lawrence Seaway. Hydroelectric power, available in abundance, contributes to a large industrial activity, which includes the manufacture of steel, wood products, clothing, cement, and food products.

The city's natural beauty is enhanced by 106 miles of scenic drives, by 3216 acres of parks, 74 in all, including Minnesota Point, which extends 7 miles into the lake, and by facilities for summer and winter sports. The chief public buildings cluster about the attractively designed civic center. Population, 1970, 100,578.

Durham. A city of central North Carolina, 25 miles northwest of Raleigh. It is one of the leading tobacco centers of the country, both for marketing and manufacturing. Cotton and hosiery mills constitute a second industry of large proportions. Durham is the seat of Duke University, developed from Trinity College and richly endowed by James B. Duke, a large tobacco manufacturer and developer of hydroelectric power. The city contains also North Carolina College at Durham and is the headquarters of the country's leading life insurance company for Negroes. General Johnston surrendered to Sherman at Durham in 1865. Population, 1970, 95,438.

East Chicago. A city of northwestern Indiana on Lake Michigan. It adjoins Hammond, Gary, and Whiting and is 20 miles southeast of the center of Chicago, of which it is an industrial suburb. The part of the city along the lake is known as Indiana Harbor, and handles a large traffic of incoming coal, iron ore, and limestone with shipments of gasoline and steel products. The chief industries are steel manufacture and oil refining. Population, 1970, 46,982.

East Orange. A city of northeastern New Jersey, adjoining Newark, and about 11 miles west of New York City. East Orange is mainly residential, being populated largely by persons doing business in New York and Newark. The city has wide, well shaded streets, and contains many attractive homes and public buildings. There are substantial industries and the chief manufactures include electrical machinery, valves, tools, sewer pipe, and knit goods. East Orange was separated from Orange in 1863 and became a city in 1899. It is the seat of Upsala College. Population, 1970, 75,471.

East St. Louis (*lōō′ĭs; lōō′ĭ*). A city of southwestern Illinois, built on the east bank of the Mississippi River, opposite Saint Louis. The city is an important railway and manufacturing center. It is also a leading market and distributing point for live stock, especially horses, mules, and hogs. The leading industries include meat packing, flour milling, and the manufacture of iron and steel products, aluminum, baking powder, glass, paints, chemicals, and refined petroleum. Population, 1970, 69,996.

Edison. A rapidly growing residential and industrial suburb in Middlesex County, New Jersey, 27 miles southwest of New York City. Here are located the Menlo Park Museum and the Edison Tower, erected on the site of Thomas A. Edison's laboratories, where the incandescent lamp, the phonograph, and other inventions were developed. Industries include an automobile assembly plant and factories for the fabrication of electronic equipment and plastic and ceramic products. Population, 68,000 (est.).

Elizabeth. A manufacturing and suburban residential city of New Jersey, lying 12 miles southwest of New York City. It is connected with Staten Island by Goethals Bridge, opened in 1928. Among important industries are oil refining and the manufacture of sewing machines, chemicals, and electrical machinery. Elizabeth was settled in 1664 and still preserves many examples of colonial architecture. From 1755 to 1757 the city was the capital of New Jersey. Population, 1970, 112,654.

Elmira (N.Y.). From the village originally called Newtown, which was established in 1790, Elmira grew into a flourishing center of commerce, with water shipping connections by way of the Chemung and Susquehanna rivers and the Chemung Canal. The Erie Railroad was built here in 1849. Elmira's most famous citizen, by marriage and adoption, was Mark Twain, whose wife, Olivia Langdon, lived here. During many summers which they spent at Quarry Farm, the home of Mrs. Theodore Crane, Olivia's sister, Mark used a study that was built for him in the shape of a pilot house on a Mississippi River steamboat. The study is now on the campus of Elmira College. In Woodlawn Cemetery is a monument to Mark Twain, erected at his burial site.

Elmira has extensive manufacturing industries. The more important products include steel bridges, prefabricated houses, television tubes, milk containers, coaster brakes, and aviation equipment. A glider contest is held annually on Harris Hill nearby. Population, 1970, 39,945.

El Monte. A city in California, located 13 miles east of Los Angeles Civic Center, settled by pioneers who found water here at the end of the Sante Fé Trail. There are many hop fields and walnut groves in the area. Although El Monte is primarily residential, nearby South El Monte is heavily industrialized. Population, 1970, 69,837.

El Paso (*ĕl păs′ō*). An important railway center and manufacturing and commercial city of western Texas, about 1200 miles by rail from New Orleans and 800 miles from Los Angeles. El Paso is situated on the Rio Grande River opposite Ciudad Juarez, and is the largest city on the Mexican border.

The chief industries include smelting, flour milling, railway car repairing, box making, meat packing, cotton milling, and the manufacture of cement and garments. The city has extensive wholesale and jobbing establishments, and carries on a substantial trade in copper, silver, lead, wool, hides, and live stock. Trade with Mexico amounts to many millions of dollars annually.

Located at an elevation of about 3800 feet in a region of almost perennial sunshine, El Paso has become a noted health resort. Buildings show a pronounced Mexican influence. Much of the surrounding district is irrigated by the great Elephant Butte Dam, and produces large crops of grains, fruits, vegetables, and cotton, which are marketed chiefly through El Paso. El Paso is the seat of The University of Texas at El Paso.

The first settlement was made in 1829, the town was incorporated in 1869. Population, 1970, 322,261.

Enchanted Mesa (*mā′să*). A remarkable castle-like rock or, more accurately speaking, a butte, situated near the Indian pueblo of Acoma, in west central New Mexico. It is an immense mass of buff sandstone, with perpendicular sides, rising boldly from an arid plain. In shape it is elongated, the length measuring about 2000 feet and the width from 100 to 350 feet. At the base there is a sloping heap of rock debris, 100 to 200 feet high, above which towers the vertical wall to an elevation of 430 feet above the plain.

Evidence of former human occupation is slight, but Acoma Indians believe that their remote ancestors inhabited a pueblo built on the flat-topped summit.

Endless Caverns. A large cave two miles south of New Market, Virginia. Its name indicates that its farthest reaches are unknown.

The cave was discovered by two boys on October 1, 1879. Among the marvelous formations within the cave are "Skyland," recalling by its coloring the play of sun and cloud in the sky, "Alpine Pass," the "Arctic Circle," "Diamond Lake," and "Oriental Palace."

Erie. A manufacturing city of northwestern Pennsylvania, situated on a large natural harbor on Lake Erie. The harbor is protected by Presque Isle, a peninsula about 11 miles long and a mile wide, on which there is a 3100-acre forested state park. There is considerable lake commerce; the leading articles of shipment include pulpwood, sand and gravel, petroleum, and manufactured goods. Among the city's varied manufactures are foundry and machine shop products, engines, excavating machinery, and paper. Erie has 19 parks, one of which, Presque Isle State Park, near the harbor entrance, is the site of an old French fort, erected in 1753. The original site is now occupied by a blockhouse, built by the state in order to commemorate Anthony Wayne, who died at the old fort in 1796. In the War of 1812, Erie was Commodore Perry's headquarters. Population, 1970, 129,231.

Eugene (*û-jēn′*). A city of western Oregon, located at the head of navigation on the Willamette River, 110 miles south of Portland. It is the commercial center of an extensive farming and stock raising region, and its industrial products include lumber products and canned fruit and vegetables. Eugene was first settled in 1864 and is the seat of the University of Oregon. It is at the head of the Willamette flood control basin. Population, 1970, 76,346.

Evanston. A city of northeastern Illinois, situated on Lake Michigan at the northern boundary of Chicago, of which it is a residential suburb. Evanston is the seat of Northwestern University, including a large technological institute. It is also the national headquarters of the Women's Christian Temperance Union. Manufactures include steel tubing, toys, chemicals, and paper. Population, 1970, 79,808.

Evansville. A manufacturing and commercial city of southwestern Indiana on the Ohio River, about 180 miles southwest of Indianapolis. The city is situated on a high bank of the river and has many fine parks, streets, and drives. It is surrounded by a rich agricultural district, and within the vicinity of the city are numerous coal mines. The chief industries include the manufacture of agricultural equipment, refrigerators, steam shovels, and grain products. Founded in 1816, Evansville became a city in 1847. Population, 1970, 138,746.

Everett. A city of eastern Massachusetts, located on the Mystic River, about 3 miles north of Boston. While mainly a residential suburb, containing many fine streets and homes, Everett is also the seat of important industries. Among these are the manufacture of coke and petroleum products. Everett was settled in 1643, but until 1873 was known as South Malden. In 1892, it was chartered as a city. Population, 1970, 42,485.

Everett. A city of northwestern Washington, with a good harbor on Puget Sound, about 28 miles north of Seattle. The surrounding region is heavily timbered, and there are extensive agricultural, mining, sporting and fishing interests. With these, the various enterprises of the city are chiefly connected. Among leading industrial products are the manufacture of lumber, pulpwood, paper, aircraft, stoves, and machinery. Population, 1970, 53,622.

Everglades. An immense marshy tract in southern Florida, covering an area about 140 miles by 50 miles. Drainage canals have been cut through various parts of the swamp, and some of the higher portions have been rendered suitable for agriculture. It is estimated that some 5000 square miles may eventually be reclaimed. Over 2000 square miles of it was made a national park in 1947.

Fairbanks. A city of Alaska lying in the Tanana River valley, on the banks of the Chena River. It is the terminus of the government railway from the coast, has a large airport, and was once the center of an extensive gold-mining district. It is also the seat of the University of Alaska. Population, 1970, 14,771.

Fall River. A manufacturing city and seaport of southeastern Massachusetts. It is built on the shore of Mount Hope Bay, at the mouth of Taunton River, about 50 miles south of Boston. Fall River is a leading center for dyeing and finishing textiles and for the manufacture of garments, curtains, lighting fixtures, and latex and aluminum products. The city is well laid out and substantially built. Many of the buildings are constructed of fine granite quarried in the vicinity. There are several parks with beautiful drives. The population in 1970 was 96,898.

Fargo. A city of North Dakota, situated on the Red River, somewhat south of the center of the state near the Minnesota boundary. Fargo is the commercial center of a large wheat growing and mixed farming region, and is a leading distributing point for farm implements. Industries include meat packing and manufacture of steel products. It is the seat of North Dakota State University and other educational institutions. There are a number of fine parks totaling 480 acres in area and several beautiful drives. Population, 1970, 53,365.

Finger Lakes. The name given to a group of beautiful lakes in west central New York. These lakes, which are long, narrow, and somewhat finger-like in shape, were formed by the blocking up of deep river valleys with glacial materials. They lie somewhat parallel to each other, extend in a general north and south direction, and give a distinctive character to a fine scenic region.

The largest are lakes Seneca and Cayuga, each of which is about 40 miles long and from 2 to 3 miles wide. Others of the group are lakes Canandaigua, Owasco, Skaneateles, and Otisco. Oneida lake, northeast of Syracuse, and Lake George, in eastern New York, are of similar formation.

Fitchburg. A manufacturing city of northeastern Massachusetts, built on a branch of the Nashua River, about 48 miles northwest of Boston. Fitchburg is attractively located and has many fine homes, public buildings, and parks. The city's extensive manufactures include cotton and woolen goods, turbines, plastics, furniture, paper, saws, bicycles, hardware, and shoes. The city is the seat of Fitchburg State College. Fitchburg was settled in 1719, was incorporated in 1764, and became a city in 1872. Population, 1970, 43,343.

Flagstaff. A city of north central Arizona, located at an altitude of 6907 feet, near the southern base of the San Francisco Mountains. It is the commercial center of a lumbering, mining, and stock-raising district, has large lumber mills, and carries on a trade in Indian curios and blankets. Lowell Observatory is situated on a high mesa near the city.

By reason of its fine climate and varied scenic attractions, Flagstaff is also a tourist resort. Ten miles north are the San Francisco Peaks, of which Humphrey's Peak is the highest, 12,670 feet. The mountains are remnants of an extinct volcano. The region contains ancient lavas and is interspersed with numerous cinder cones. One of the most conspicuous is Sunset Crater, a large cone tipped with bright red cinders, giving it the appearance of being illumined by the setting sun.

About 8 miles east of Flagstaff are the remarkable sink holes in the Kaibab limestone, known as the "Bottomless Pits." In the near vicinity also is the Walnut Canyon national monument containing prehistoric cliff dwellings. Population, 1970, 26,117.

Flint. A manufacturing city of southeastern Michigan, situated on the river of the same name, about 70 miles northwest of Detroit. Flint is, after Detroit, the world's largest center of automobile manufacture. Its industries center around various subsidiaries of the General Motors Corporation, including the Chevrolet, Buick, and Fisher Body divisions. The 42 public parks of the city have a total area of 1275 acres. Population, 1970, 193,317.

Fort Knox. A United States fort in eastern Kentucky directly south of Louisville and 600 miles west of New York City. It is noted as the repository of the greater part of the monetary gold stock of the United States, its location west of the Allegheny Mountains making it comparatively secure from a hypothetical invader from the East. The gold storage building is constructed with walls of solid granite two feet thick, behind which are fabricated coils of steel set in concrete. The building, having a floor area of 10,000 square feet, is two stories high, the second set back so as to leave a parapet at each corner of which machine guns are mounted. The gold vault is 90 feet long, 50 feet wide, and two stories high. All parts of the vault's exterior are visible to guards from all angles by means of mirrors. Microphones and automatic alarms communicate with the guard room, from which messages may be sent to a motorized unit of the army in the adjacent fort. The first shipment of gold was taken to Fort Knox in 1937. Population, 1970, 37,608.

Fort Lauderdale. A flourishing commercial, industrial, tourist, and residential center in the lower east coast area of the Florida peninsula. Its business district is between two and three miles of the Atlantic Ocean. The city's transportation needs are served by two railroads and by major bus and truck lines. Adjacent are the Ft. Lauderdale-Hollywood International Airport and the steamship terminal, Port of Everglades. Because of its favorable climate and excellent visitor accommodations and the transportation facilities, Ft. Lauderdale has become a favorite convention center. Population, 1970, 139,590.

Fort Wayne. A railroad center and manufacturing city of northeastern Indiana. It is built at the confluence of the St. Joseph and the St. Mary's rivers which here join to form the Maumee River. Car shops, car wheel works, foundries, hosiery mills, clothing, motor truck, copper and enamelled wire factories, electrical machinery works, and oil tank shops are among the chief industrial interests. Among the largest buildings is the office of the Lincoln National Life Insurance Company, occupying an entire block. The city encloses the site of a fort built in 1794 by Anthony Wayne, to whom a monument has been erected. Population, 1970, 177,671.

Fort Worth. An important commercial city and railway center of northeastern Texas, situated in the midst of a rich agricultural and oil producing territory. The city is one of the great cattle and grain markets of the United States and one of the world's greatest petroleum pipe-line centers. Seventeen railways enter the city. Industries include oil refining, meat packing and the manufacture of flour, textiles, cement, and cottonseed products.

Of unique distinction is the Casa Manana Theatre, a structure of geodesic design built of aluminum and supported by steel struts. Educational institutions include the Texas Christian University and the Texas Wesleyan College. The city has 101 parks, covering 10,116 acres. Population, 1970, 393,476.

Franconia Notch. A narrow picturesque passage in the Franconia range of the White Mountains in New Hampshire, through which the Pemigewasset River flows. Entering the notch from the east is a narrow passage excavated in the rock, called the "flume." Nearby is the "great stone face" celebrated by Hawthorne. The territory is embraced in a 6000-acre state park.

Frankfort. The capital of Kentucky, situated on the Kentucky River, in the rich "Blue-Grass" and limestone region, somewhat northwest of the center of the state. Its manufactures include lumber, shoes, brooms, twine, tobacco, and concrete pipe. Many thoroughbred trotting horses are raised in the vicinity. In a setting of rare beauty is the State Capitol, behind which is the large Capitol Annex Building.

Frankfort was founded in 1786, and, in 1792, when it had a population of less than 500, was made the capital of the state. The city contains the grave of Daniel Boone and is rich in historical associations. Population, 1970, 21,356.

Fresno (frĕz'nō). Commercial center of a noted fruit growing district, Fresno is located in the irrigated portion of the fertile San Joaquin Valley, about 200 miles southeast of San Francisco. In addition to peach growing, in which it excels, the country surrounding Fresno has a high yield of grapes and raisins. Other important crops are alfalfa, flax, cotton, sugar beets, grain, vegetables, and some tropical fruits.

The industrial and commercial activities of the city are centered chiefly upon handling and marketing the county's staple productions. Places of interest in the vicinity are King's River Canyon, Roeding Park, and Kearney Park, the last an irrigated experimental farm belonging to the University of California. Population, 1970, 165,972.

Gadsden. A city of northern Alabama, on the Coose River, 58 miles northeast of Birmingham, to which Gadsden is second in importance in Alabama in industry, manufacturing iron and steel products, rubber products, and many other items. The city has good transportation facilities and is in the midst of an agricultural and mining region. Population, 1970, 53,928.

Gainesville. A city of Florida, located about midway between the Atlantic Ocean and the Gulf of Mexico. It is noted for manufacture of tung oil, used in paints, and as a shipping center for many of the products (such as tobacco, citrus fruits, and pecans) grown in the area. Located in Gainesville are the Florida State Museum and the University of Florida. Population, 1970, 64,510.

Galveston. The world's largest cotton and sulphur port, situated in southeastern Texas. It is built on the east end of Galveston Island between Galveston Bay on the north and the Gulf of Mexico on the south.

The excellent natural harbor facilities have been further improved at vast expense, and the port has been fortified by modern coast defensive works. Manufactures include flour, ships, and steel wire. Since a disastrous flood, caused by a hurricane in 1900, the level of the city has been raised, a sea wall has been built along the shore facing the Gulf, and two 2-mile causeways have been constructed joining the city with the mainland. The Medical School of the University of Texas is situated in the city. In 1901, Galveston adopted the commission form of government, which has since been widely adopted by other American cities. Population, 1970, 61,809.

Garden of the Gods. A small region of about 500 acres, near Colorado Springs, Colorado, noted for its curiously shaped rock formations and for its magnificent views of Pikes Peak. By the action of wind and water, the red and the white sandstone strata have here been worn into many grotesque shapes. To these, various fanciful names have been given, such as "Cathedral Spires," "Balanced Rock," "Siamese Twins," and the "Seal and the Bear." The gateway to these interesting examples of erosion consists of two massive pinnacles of red rock, 300 feet high, which, at their bases, leave barely room for a vehicle to pass between them.

Gary. A steel manufacturing city of northwestern Indiana, at the southern end of Lake Michigan, about 30 miles southeast of Chicago. The city was founded in 1906 and is virtually the creation of the United States Steel Corporation. It contains immense steel works, tin and rail mills, and a cement plant, each of which is among the largest of its kind. The city is well planned with broad boulevards, giving an air of spaciousness. Its 18 parks cover 700 acres, Marquette Park being particularly attractive. A civic gateway, flanked by twin-designed Courthouse and City Hall, leads to the great steel mills over an area traversed by trunk-line railroads. Nearby is the Indiana Dunes State Park. The so-called Gary plan of elementary education originated in the public schools of the city. Population, 1970, 175,415.

Gettysburg. A town of southern Pennsylvania, located about 35 miles southwest of Harrisburg. Gettysburg occupies a picturesque site in a hilly but fertile farming country. President Eisenhower, bought a farm here shortly after his election.

In the vicinity was fought, July 1-3, 1863, one of the most decisive battles of the Civil War. Here the Union army under General Meade defeated the Confederate forces under General Lee. The entire battlefield, comprising 3409 acres, has been converted into a national military park, in which are marked the sites where particular actions took place; a cyclorama painting within a circular building depicts the battle. On Cemetery Hill is the National Cemetery, dedicated by Lincoln in his famous Gettysburg Address. An eternal light peace memorial was dedicated on the battlefield by President Roosevelt in 1938. Population, 1970, 7275.

Glendale. A city of southern California, adjoining Los Angeles on the north. Its elevation varies from 400 feet to 2400 feet. It is a popular residential suburb, but has rapidly expanding industrial interests which include pottery, electronic equipment, and drugs. A feature of particular interest in Forest Lawn Memorial Park, the court of which has a stained glass window design copied from Da Vinci's "Last Supper." Glendale was incorporated in 1906. Population, 1970, 132,752.

Gloucester (glŏs'tĕr). A seaport of northeastern Massachusetts, built on the south side of the Cape Ann peninsula, about 30 miles northeast of Boston. The city is an important fishing port, with a large fleet engaged in taking cod, haddock, halibut, redfish, and mackerel. There are various other industries, largely connected with the fisheries. By reason of its picturesque location, quaint, old-fashioned streets, and interesting historic associations, the city is a favorite travel and summer resort, especially for artists. A well-known piece of sculpture there is the famous Fisherman's Memorial. Gloucester was founded in 1623, incorporated in 1642, and became a city in 1874. Population, 1970, 27,941.

Gloversville. A city of east central New York, noted as the chief glove manufacturing center in the United States. Its factories, together with those of the neighboring town of Johnstown, produce a substantial percentage of the gloves made in the country. The leather glove industry is said to have been first introduced into the United States by Sir William Johnson, who, in 1760, settled several families of Scotch glove makers on his lands near the site of Gloversville. Other manufactured products include silk and knitted goods, phonograph records, leather, and lumber. Population, 1970 19,677.

Grand Canyon of the Colorado. The most magnificent scenic spectacle of its kind in the world. This immense

gorge, the greatest example of stream erosion known, has been cut by the Colorado River in the high plateau of northern Arizona. The deeper portion is 217 miles long; its vast chasms range from 4000 to 6000 feet in depth from the uppermost rim to the river; and its width from rim to rim varies from 4 to 18 miles.

The canyon consists of two distinct parts: the broad, outer, upper portion, which has been eroded through stratified rocks; and the narrow, inner, lower portion, which has been worn down through unstratified rocks. The outer or upper walls are carved in alternating layers of limestones, sandstones, and shales. These descend in successive benches or escarpments, displaying a multitude of beautifully castellated, temple-like forms, banded in splendid colors, and finally reach the top of the gloomy inner gorge. This is irregularly cut in tough dark granite, and, at its bottom, extending usually from wall to wall flows the foaming, torrential river.

The descent throughout the entire length of the canyon is so great that the river is broken into many rapids and semirapids. These, rushing between almost vertical walls of rock, make navigation, even for the staunchest boats, exceedingly dangerous. The current rolls great boulders along the bottom of the narrow channel, and, at some points, the noise of their grinding in the rocky river bed can be heard above the roaring of the waters.

The most impressive portion of the canyon is included in Grand Canyon National Park. Its area, 1052 square miles, embraces 105 miles of the Grand Canyon, stretching from east to west from its beginning at the mouth of the Little Colorado River. From rim to rim this part of the canyon is from 8 to 15 miles wide; it is more than a mile deep measured from the north rim, which averages nearly 1000 feet higher than the south rim. The eastern boundary includes the lofty, richly colored walls east of which lies the Painted Desert. The western boundary of the park includes the broad Cataract canyon, entering from the south. In this tributary canyon is the Havasupai Indian reservation and a group of five waterfalls.

The first white man to see the Grand Canyon was Cardenas, a member of Coronado's party, who, in 1540, visited the south rim. The first successful passage of the Grand Canyon by boat was made in 1869 by Major John Wesley Powell. An isolated plateau known as Shiva's Temple, believed to have been cut off in the glacial age 12,000 to 35,000 years ago, was explored for the first time in 1937 by Dr. Harold E. Anthony who conducted an investigation into the effects produced on animal life there by its long separation from outside influences.

Grand Coulee Dam. One of the largest dams in the world, backing up the Columbia River in Washington into a lake that extends 151 miles to the Canadian border. The height of the dam is 553 feet and its length is 4200 feet. Into its construction went 11.5 million cubic yards of concrete, an amount of construction unmatched by any other engineering work. The dam is designed to produce 1,974,000 kilowatts of electricity and to irrigate 1,250,000 acres of land. The cost of the dam and power plant, opened in 1941, was 181 million dollars. An additional 209 million dollars was allocated to irrigation canals.

A peculiarity of the dam is that, to be useful for irrigation, a reservoir of water must be created 280 feet above the level to which the dam raises the river. Power developed at the dam is used to pump water into such a reservoir, which, when full, is 23 miles long and covers 2300 acres.

Grand Junction. A city of southwestern Colorado, 255 miles southwest of Denver, at the junction of the Colorado and the Gunnison rivers. Located in the midst of uranium-producing industries, it is also the commercial center of a fertile farming and fruit growing district, watered by a large irrigation canal. The city lies 4600 feet above sea level, and is surrounded by some of the most noted scenic points in Colorado, notably Colorado National Monument and Grand Mesa. Population, 1970, 20,170.

Grand Rapids. A city of Michigan, built on both banks of the Grand River, about 150 miles west of Detroit. The city takes its name from the rapids of the river, which here descends 18 feet in about a mile. While maintaining numerous important industries, Grand Rapids is noted chiefly as a center for the manufacture of furniture. Although exceeded in volume by New York and Chicago, Grand Rapids is distinguished for the design, quality, and finish of its product. In the heart of the city there are large exposition buildings for displaying furniture samples for wholesale buyers.

Among other leading manufactures are automobile parts, carpet sweepers, house furnishings, chemicals, textiles, and gypsum plasters. Public parks cover 1245 acres.

Grand Rapids was settled in 1833, became a village in 1838, and a city in 1850. Educational institutions include Aquinas and Calvin colleges. Population, 1970, 197,649.

Great Falls. The leading manufacturing city of Montana, picturesquely situated at the Great Falls of the Missouri River, about 100 miles north of Helena. The development of immense hydroelectric power in the center of a rich mining and agricultural region has been the chief factor in the growth of the city's manufactures.

Among the leading industrial establishments are copper reduction works, smelting and refining works, and flour and cereal mills. The city is also an important market for wool, shipping several million pounds annually. The municipal park system embraces 48 parks with a total area of 952 acres. Great Falls is a "jumping off" point for motorists driving north to connect with the Alaska Highway. Population, 1970, 60,091.

Great Salt Lake. A salt-water lake in northwestern Utah. Situated at an altitude of 4218 feet above sea level, it has an area of about 1750 square miles with a maximum length of 75 miles and a width of from 30 to 50 miles. Its mean depth is about 20 feet with a maximum of 40 feet. The lake has no outlet, but is fed by the Jordan, Weber, and Bear rivers. Variations in rainfall have a very pronounced effect on its size and on its salinity, the latter fluctuating from 12 to 27 per cent accordingly as the water is high or low. Since the salinity of the ocean is about 3.44 per cent, Great Salt Lake is from four to six times as salty as the ocean. Common salt is the chief mineral constituent of the water, and its recovery is the basis of an active industry. Sodium sulphate and gypsum are also obtained. It is impossible for a bather to sink in the water of the lake.

Great Salt Lake was first accurately described by John C. Frémont in 1845. Geological observations indicate that the lake is the shrunken remnant of an inland sea, Lake Bonneville, which, centuries ago, covered some 20,000 square miles. Great Salt Lake contains nine islands, the longest being 16 miles in length. It is crossed by the Southern Pacific railroad over the Lucin cutoff, a trestle and gravel fill about 27 miles long.

Greeley. A city of northern Colorado, 50 miles north of Denver, on the Cache la Poudre River. It is situated in a fertile agricultural district, and its industries are chiefly based on agriculture. They include sugar refining, flour milling, cold storage warehousing, and canning. Named for Horace Greeley, the place was settled in 1870 by the "Union Colony," composed mainly of New England people. By establishing irrigation, these pioneers transformed an almost barren wilderness into a highly productive region. Greeley is the seat of the University of Northern Colorado. Population, 1970, 38,902.

Green Bay. A city of eastern Wisconsin on high level ground on both sides of the Fox River where it empties into Green Bay, an arm of Lake Michigan. Dating from 1745, it is the oldest settlement in Wisconsin, and Tank Cottage, in Washington Park, is said to be the oldest house in the state. Paper manufacture is prominent among the varied industries. The city is a busy port, shipping chiefly cheese, grain, and fish, and receiving coal, sulphur, steel, and motor cars. Green Bay became a city in 1854. Population, 1970, 87,809.

Greensboro. A manufacturing city in the north central part of North Carolina. The chief products are textiles, cigarettes, machinery, furniture, and hosiery. The city is spacious and open, with 425 acres of parks. It is the seat of Guilford College and two colleges for women—Greensboro and North Carolina. Greensboro was founded in 1809 and named for General Nathanael Greene, hero of the battle of Guilford Court House, which is memorialized by a national military park six miles to the northwest. Population, 1970, 144,076.

Greenville. A city of northwestern South Carolina, built on the banks of the Reedy River, about 110 miles northwest of Columbia. Greenville is an important textile manufacturing center and contains many large cotton mills. Other industrial establishments include foundries, dye works, and garment, textile machinery, and furniture factories. Greenville is the seat of Furman University. Population, 1970, 61,208.

Greylock, Mount. The highest summit in Massachusetts, situated in the Berkshire Hills, on the western border of the state, about 5 miles southwest of North Adams. The broad, flat top, which rises to an elevation of 3500 feet, is accessible by highway and by many beautiful trails. A tract of about 8600 acres on the upper part of the mountain has been purchased by the state for a permanent park.

Gulfport. A port, city, and resort of southeastern Mississippi, on Mississippi sound, an arm of the Gulf of Mexico. It is about midway between New Orleans and Mobile. The shore is protected by a 26-mile concrete sea wall surmounted by a four-lane scenic highway. Gulfport is the second largest banana terminal in the world and also receives sugar, hemp, and other products. It ships locally produced chemicals and fertilizer. Population, 1970, 40,791.

Hagerstown. A city of western Maryland, built on Antietam Creek, 72 miles northwest of Baltimore. It is the trade center for a large agricultural district and has extensive and varied industries. The city's industrial products include silk and knit goods, shoes, pipe organs, aircraft, cement, fertilizers, and sheet metal. In the vicinity are Fort Frederick and the battlefields of Antietam and Gettysburg. Population, 1970, 35,862.

Hamilton. A manufacturing city of southwestern Ohio, on the Miami River, 25 miles north of Cincinnati. Its principal manufactures are machinery, machine tools, paper, stoves, office fixtures, safes and bank vaults, engines, and woolen goods. The city is said to have been the first in the country to own its waterworks, gas plant, and electric light plant. Hamilton was the boyhood home of novelist William Dean Howells. Population, 1970, 67,865.

Hammond. A city of northwestern Indiana, on Lake Michigan, 18 miles southeast of the center of Chicago, of which it is an industrial suburb. Hammond arose as a packing center, George Hammond having established a plant there in 1868. After 1900, steel and railroad car manufacture became of chief importance, and immense oil refineries were built. Other industries include printing, bookbinding, and the making of railroad equipment and chemicals. Population, 1970, 107,790.

Hamtramck (hăm-trăm'ĭk). A city of southeastern Michigan, existing as an island municipality within the city of Detroit. Hamtramck owes its rapid growth to the immense development of automobile industries. The city has extensive manufactures of automobile accessories, iron and aluminum castings, wheels, radiators, brass goods, and paints. Population, 1970, 27,245.

Hannibal. A city of northeastern Missouri, situated on the Mississippi River, about 120 miles above Saint Louis. It is the trade center of an agricultural district, and there are coal mines in the vicinity. The chief manufactures include Portland cement, lime, structural steel, lawn mowers, and food products. Hannibal was settled in 1819 and became incorporated in 1839. During boyhood, Mark Twain lived in Hannibal, and his early home is the property of the city. A statue of him stands in the 200-acre Riverview park. The Mark Twain memorial bridge spans the Mississippi at Hannibal. Population, 1970, 18,609.

Harpers Ferry. A historic town 60 miles northwest of Washington in the extreme eastern part of West Virginia, where the state line borders Virginia and Maryland. It occupies a site of remarkable scenic beauty at the junction of the Shenandoah and Potomac rivers, at the point where the latter stream flows through a gap in the Blue Ridge Mountains. Here, in 1859, John Brown attempted his famous raid. During the Civil War, the town was alternately in the possession of the Union and of the Confederate forces. In 1944, it was authorized as a National Monument, and in 1963, made a National Park. Population, 1970, 423.

Harrisburg. The capital of Pennsylvania, situated on the Susquehanna River, in the southeastern part of the state. The city is noted for its diversified manufactures, chiefly of steel and of steel products, and for the extensive railway roundhouses, repair shops, and freight yards, which have made Harrisburg a great distribution center.

The most beautiful of the city's fine buildings is the State Capitol. This impressive edifice, constructed of steel and faced with granite and marble, and decorated with elaborate sculptures, was erected at a cost of $13,000,000. East of it lies Memorial Park, where there are four monumental-type office buildings and a half-mile viaduct in memory of Pennsylvanians who served in the World Wars. Since 1900, extensive civic improvements have won for Harrisburg the sobriquet of the "Model City." The park system covers 1100 acres, of which 666 acres are included in the picturesque Wildwood Park. A beautiful riverside park and boulevard borders on the Susquehanna.

Harrisburg was named for John Harris, an English trader, who settled on its site in 1719. It was incorporated in 1791, and in 1812 became the capital of the state. Population, 1970, 68,061.

Hartford. The capital of Connecticut, built on the west bank of the Connecticut River, in the north central part of the state. The city occupies a commanding site on rolling ground, affording fine views of the Connecticut valley.

Hartford is laid out with wide, well shaded streets and beautiful boulevards. The city is noted for its artistic homes and for its excellent public buildings. In the old State House, designed by Bulfinch, the Hartford Convention of 1814 met. The State Capitol adjoins Bushnell Park, and nearby are the State Library and Supreme Court Building, the State Office Building, the State Armory, Bushnell Memorial Hall, and the Soldiers' and Sailors' memorial arch. Five highway bridges span the Connecticut River.

Its important industries include the manufacture of firearms, typewriters, brushes, precision tools, oil burners, and counting devices. For a long period, Hartford has been one of the leading insurance centers of the country, containing the home offices of nearly 50 companies. The Travelers Insurance Company tower is 527 feet in height. Hartford is the seat of Trinity College and the Wadsworth Atheneum, said to be the oldest free public art museum in America. It has a famous municipal rose garden and celebrates a rose festival annually.

Prior to the settlement of the town in 1635–36 by English colonists from Massachusetts Bay under the leadership of Reverend Thomas Hooker, the Dutch had a trading post and fort at Hartford. Here, in 1639, were drawn up and adopted the "Fundamental Orders of Connecticut," said to be the first written constitution of modern times. In 1687 occurred the attempt of Governor Andros to seize the charter of the colony, and its alleged concealment in the famous "Charter Oak." Hartford was the capital of Connecticut colony until 1701, when it was made joint capital with New Haven. In 1873, Hartford became the sole capital of the state. Population, 1970, 155,868.

Haverhill (*hā'vēr-ĭl*). A manufacturing city of northeastern Massachusetts, built on both banks of the Merrimack River, about 30 miles north of Boston. Haverhill is one of the chief centers in the United States for the manufacture of boots and shoes. The city was settled in 1640–41 and almost since its founding has been noted for the manufacture of shoes. It now makes about one-sixth of all the women's shoes produced in the United States. The city contains many fine parks, lakes, and drives; also many handsome residences and public buildings. It is the birthplace of John Greenleaf Whittier. Population, 1970, 46,120.

Helena (*hĕl'ê-nȧ*). The capital of Montana, situated in the west central part of the state. The city overlooks an arable valley, the scene of extensive cattle raising, and is surrounded by a mountainous region, rich in gold and other valuable metals. Helena was founded by mining prospectors in 1864 on Last Chance gulch and was incorporated in 1881. From this gulch gold was extracted to the value of $40 million. The industries include lead and zinc smelting.

The per capita wealth of the inhabitants is very high and is reflected in the many fine residences of the city. Among the chief buildings are the State Capitol, the Federal Building, Consistory Temple, Civic Center and Saint Helena Cathedral. Especially noteworthy are the Veterans' and Pioneers' Memorial Building and the Russell Art Gallery. Many points of scenic interest exist in the neighborhood, notably the "Gates of the Mountains," named by Lewis and Clark in 1805. The educational institutions include Carroll College. Population, 1970, 22,730.

Hibbing. A mining village of northeastern Minnesota, in the center of the state's Mesabi Iron Range, 75 miles north of Duluth. It is the site of the world's largest open-pit iron-ore mine and the nation's only "triple divide" watershed. The Greyhound Bus Company originated here in 1914. Population, 1970, 16,104.

Highland Park. A city of southeastern Michigan completely within Detroit, of which it is an industrial suburb. Highland Park was at one time the headquarters of the Ford Motor Company and owes its growth largely to the automobile industry. In 1900, it was a village of 427 inhabitants. Population, 1970, 35,444.

High Point. A manufacturing city of central North Carolina, 99 miles northwest of Raleigh. It is the chief southern center for the manufacture of furniture. The Southern furniture exposition, held there four times annually, is visited by buyers from all parts of the United States. Other important industrial products include textiles, tile, and tobacco. Population, 1970, 63,204.

Hoboken (*hō'bō-kĕn*). A manufacturing city of northeastern New Jersey. It is situated on the Hudson River opposite New York, with which it is connected by ferries, and the Holland and Lincoln vehicular tunnels. Hoboken is a large seaport, and is the terminus of several important transatlantic steamship lines. Its industrial output includes coffee, marine equipment, furniture, and pencils. The city is the seat of the Stevens Institute of Technology. The first steam-propelled ferry-boat was invented and put in operation at Hoboken. Population, 1970, 45,380.

Hodgenville. A town of central Kentucky, situated about 50 miles almost due south of Louisville in a fertile region devoted to growing grain, tobacco, and live stock. Three miles distant from the town is the national historic site, Abraham Lincoln Birthplace. Here a beautiful memorial building preserves the log cabin in which President Lincoln was born. Population, 1970, 2562.

Hollywood. A residential and winter resort community in southeastern Florida, 18 miles north of Miami, and 7 miles south of Fort Lauderdale. It has two yacht basins and Port Everglades, a port of entry for southern Florida. Industry is growing in the city, and there are numerous citrus groves in the area. Hollywood was founded in 1921 and incorporated as a city in 1925. Population, 1970, 106,873.

Holy Cross, Mountain of the. A high peak of the Rockies, 30 miles northwest of Leadville, Colorado. The emblem from which this mountain takes its name appears about midsummer. At that time the snow has melted from the higher slopes and ridges and is retained only in two deep canyons, which, by their intersection, form an immense cross high up on the side of the mountain. This white cross remains in view until late autumn, when the entire crest is again covered with snow.

Holyoke (*hol'yok*). A planned industrial city of southwestern Massachusetts, built on the west bank of the Connecticut River, 97 miles southwest of Boston. Immense water power, derived from falls in the river, promoted the rise of extensive industries. These are concerned chiefly with the manufacture of paper, paper products, and textiles. Holyoke is one of the largest producers of fine writing papers and envelopes in the United States. Because of the number and size of its mills, it has long been styled the "Paper City."

The total value of the city's paper products is, however, exceeded by that of its textile products. These include cotton and woolen goods, thread, knit goods, alpaca, and silk. Among other important manufactures are machinery, blank books, and school supplies. Mount Tom and Mount Holyoke are among the many points of interest in the vicinity. Population, 1970, 50,112.

Homestead. A manufacturing city of western Pennsylvania, located on the Monongahela River, about 7 miles southeast of Pittsburgh. Its chief manufacture is steel, and its vast steel plants rank among the largest in the country. Among the "Homestead steel mills," in and around Homestead, is the Carnegie-Illinois strip steel mill, costing 60 million dollars, one of the largest of its kind in the world. Homestead was settled in 1871 and in 1880 was incorporated. Population, 1970, 6309.

Honolulu (*hō'nō-lōō'lōō*). The capital and chief commercial center of Hawaii, situated on a good harbor on the south coast of Oahu. Honolulu is noted for its delightful climate and for its luxuriant tropical gardens. It possesses fine clean streets, spacious open squares, and many handsome public buildings. The University of Hawaii, a state institution, is located in Honolulu.

Representative of the city's industries are pineapple canneries, sugar factories, iron foundries, and artificial ice plants. The native population is industrious and self-supporting. Honolulu occupies a vantage ground of immense importance on the trade routes of the Pacific, and, from a strategic point of view, is of great value as a naval station of the United States. Honolulu harbor was discovered in 1794. The modern town was founded in 1816, and in 1820 it was made the capital of the islands. The population is composed of a mixture of various races, among which predominate Hawaiians, Japanese, Chinese, and Portuguese. Population, 1970, 324,871.

Hood, Mount. A peak of the Cascade range in northern Oregon, about 50 miles east of Portland. It is of volcanic origin and rises symmetrically to a height of 11,225 feet, the loftiest elevation in the state. The lower slopes are forested but the peak is snow capped and there are glaciers on the upper slopes. The summit, which may be ascended without serious difficulty, commands magnificent views of the Columbia River valley and also of many great peaks of the Cascades, including mounts Rainier, Adams, and Jefferson.

Hood River. A town of northern Oregon on the Columbia River, 67 miles east of Portland. It is the trade center and shipping point of the Hood River valley, which extends southward 25 miles to Mt. Hood. This valley, protected by Cascade ranges and provided with a constant flow of gravity-irrigation water, is excellently adapted to fruit growing. Hood River apples and pears are famed throughout the continent and command maximum prices. The Bonneville Dam, 24 miles down the Columbia River, backs the water up to Hood River, thus forming a pool for water sports and recreation. Population, 1970, 3991.

Hoquiam (*hō'kwĭ-ăm*). A city of western Washington, situated on Gray's Harbor, about 90 miles by rail southwest of Tacoma. It adjoins Aberdeen, with which it shares the distinction of being one of the greatest seaports of the world for shipment of forest products. The industries include lumber mills. wood product factories, and fisheries. Population, 1970, 10,466.

Hot Springs. A health and travel resort, located in central Arkansas 53 miles southwest of Little Rock. The city is picturesquely situated in a narrow valley sheltered by two ridges of the Ouachita Mountains. It surrounds Hot Springs National Park, celebrated for its numerous hot springs having valuable medicinal properties. There are numerous large hotels, sanitariums, and sumptuous bathhouses. Hot Springs Medical Center is one of the tallest buildings in Arkansas. The resort is nearly surrounded by Lakes Catherine and Hamilton, created by power dams in the Ouachita River. Population, 1970, 35,631.

Houston (*hūs'tŭn*). A city of Texas, situated in the southeastern part of the state. It is about 50 miles northwest of Galveston, on a sluggish stream formerly known as Buffalo bayou. This has been widened and deepened into a canal called the Houston ship channel, which permits large ocean steamers to reach the city's wharves.

Houston is the commercial center of a rich agricultural and lumbering region and is one of the world's richest oil producing territories. The city is one of the greatest cotton markets and ports in the United States. In manufactures Houston ranks first among the cities of the state. Its varied industries include petroleum refining, sugar, rice and flour milling, and the manufacture of fertilizers, cement, and chemicals.

The city is laid out with wide, shaded streets, beautiful parks, handsome residences, and imposing public and commercial buildings. The Humble Oil and Gulf buildings are among the tallest in the south. Houston is the seat of Rice University, the University of Houston, and the University of St. Thomas, and has a magnificent Museum of Fine Arts. Houston's Astrodome, built at a cost of $31.6 million, was the world's first air-conditioned all-weather stadium. Its plastic dome is 208 feet high. Houston was settled after the battle of San Jacinto, which was fought near its site in 1836. Incorporated in 1837, it became the capital of the former republic of Texas in 1840. Population, 1970, 1,231,394.

Huntington. A city in West Virginia, located on the Ohio River in the western part of the state. It lies in a rich coal and oil producing region and is an important trade and manufacturing center. It has extensive railroad shops and manufactures nickel, clay products, textiles, optical goods, and mining cars. Huntington is the seat of Marshall College. Population, 1970, 74,315.

Huntsville. An historically interesting city in northern Alabama. In 1811, its earlier name of Twickenham was changed to honor John Hunt, early settler and Revolutionary soldier. At present Huntsville's typical industrial activities are overshadowed by its contribution to America's space program through the Redstone Arsenal. Population, 1970, 137,802.

Imperial Valley. A former desert area in southeastern California, which has been made remarkably productive by irrigation. It lies east and south of the Salton Sea and extends southward to the Mexican border. The improved district is about 40 miles long, with a maximum breadth of 30 miles, and embraces a total area of approximately 500,000 acres.

Water for irrigation is taken from the Colorado River near Yuma, and conducted to the south end of the valley. Thence it is distributed in a network of waterways covering the district. The soil is largely composed of the silts of an ancient delta of the Colorado river. It is of unmatched and seemingly of inexhaustible fertility. Owing to the warm climate and almost continuous sunshine, the growing season is not only very long but also very rapid. By rotation, two or more crops a year are often produced from the same field.

The Imperial Valley has become widely noted for the production of long-staple cotton of unexcelled quality. The district produces also immense quantities of melons, lettuce, asparagus, onions, grapes, oranges, and various other vegetables and fruits. Date culture on a commercial scale is becoming established.

Independence. A city in the western part of Missouri, located in an agricultural district adjacent to Kansas City. Recently, it has become well known as the home of President Harry S. Truman and the site of the Harry S. Truman Library. In an earlier period it was important as a supply point for caravans of pioneers who were going west over the Oregon Trail or the Santa Fe Trail. Population, 1970, 111,662.

Indianapolis. The capital of Indiana, situated on the White River, near the center of the state, about 185 miles southeast of Chicago. In population, transportation facilities, and volume of business transacted, Indianapolis is a major wholesale and retail trade center.

The city occupies a nearly level site, is regularly laid out, for the most part with broad streets, and is substantially and handsomely built. Indianapolis, preeminently a city of homes, is widely noted for its advantages as a residential city.

The park system, which embraces a total area of more than 4564 acres, contains 90 parks. Of these, Eagle Creek, is the largest, covering some 2600 acres. The soldiers' and Sailors' Monument, in Monument Place, a lofty shaft of stone and bronze, 285 feet high and richly decorated with sculptures, is one of the notable military memorials in America. Among numerous fine buildings are the Capitol,

the Federal Building, the Riley Public Library, Christ Church, the Indianapolis Art Museum, the Scottish Rite Cathedral, and Indiana State Library. A 15-million dollar World War Memorial Plaza occupies five blocks in the downtown district of the city. The principal structure is the magnificent Shrine Building. A cenotaph stands in the north square at the head of a mall two blocks long. In the northeast corner is a four-story building of Greek architecture which houses the national headquarters of the American Legion. The city's educational institutions include Butler University, Indiana Central College, several professional schools of Indiana University, and several schools of Purdue University.

Indianapolis owes its prominence largely to three important advantages. First, it is the center of a large and highly productive agricultural region; second, it lies near immense supplies of coal, insuring cheap fuel, and third, it possesses unusually excellent transportation facilities. The city is served by numerous railway and air lines radiating in all directions and by very extensive truck and bus systems. A feature for which the city is widely noted is the Indianapolis Motor Speedway. Among the chief industries are meat packing and the manufacture of drugs, motor vehicle engines and parts, aircraft engines, refrigerators, electrical and telephone equipment, television and radio sets, apparel, furniture, and inner tubes for tires.

The site on which the city is located was selected for the state capital and named Indianapolis in 1821. The legislature first met there in 1825. Population, 1970, 743,155.

Inland Empire. A name popularly given to a rich agricultural, stock raising, and mining region of the northwestern United States, lying between the Rocky and the Cascade mountains. It embraces a considerable part of the Columbia River plateau, including eastern Washington, northeastern Oregon, the northern part or "panhandle" of Idaho, and the extreme western part of Montana. The chief railway and commercial center in this large region is Spokane.

Iowa City. A city of eastern Iowa, on the Iowa River, about 120 miles east of Des Moines. The city is primarily a college community (the seat of the State University of Iowa) in the midst of a rich farming and cattle-raising region. The university has excellent medical-research departments cooperating with local hospitals to provide medical service for the state. This city was once the capital of the Territory of Iowa, and from 1846 to 1857 was capital of the state of Iowa. Population, 1970, 46,850.

Irvington. A town of northeastern New Jersey. It is a residential suburb of New York and Newark, which it adjoins on the southwest. It has various industries, including foundries and facilities for the manufacture of chemicals, tools, plastics, and electronic equipment. Settled in 1692, it was called Camptown until 1852, and was then renamed in honor of Washington Irving. Its incorporation as a village dates from 1835, and, as a town, from 1898. Population, 1970, 59,743.

Isleta (*ês-lā'tä*). An Indian town situated on the west bank of the Rio Grande River, about 10 miles south of Albuquerque, New Mexico. The present town was founded early in the 18th century. The inhabitants, who are of Tanoan Indian stock, retain much of their aboriginal social organization. By primitive means of irrigation, they produce from an arid soil excellent crops of corn, fruits, and vegetables. Population, 1970, 1080.

Itasca (*i-tăs'kä*), **Lake.** A small lake in north central Minnesota. It consists of three long narrow arms, from the northern one of which emerges the Mississippi River. The region immediately surrounding the lake, embracing an area of about 35,000 acres, has been made a state park. Its waters abound in many kinds of fish, beavers are abundant, and a band of elks has been established in the park.

Ithaca. A city of west central New York, located at the south end of Cayuga Lake, about 40 miles south of Syracuse. While the city conducts a substantial trade and maintains various local industries, it is noted chiefly as the seat of Cornell University, with which is connected the New York State Agricultural College. This important educational institution occupies a magnificent campus on East Hill, an eminence rising about 400 feet above the lake and lower city, and commanding unexcelled views of a highly picturesque region. Ithaca was founded in 1789, and was chartered as a city in 1888. Population, 1970, 26,226.

Jackson. A city of southern Michigan, built on both banks of the Grand River, about 70 miles west of Detroit. Jackson is an important railway center, and is situated in the midst of a rich agricultural region. It carries on an extensive trade in grain, fruit, and vegetables, and has substantial industries. The city's manufactures include automobile parts, tires, machine tools, machinery, airplane wheels, and food products. Nearby is a cascade 500 feet long and 64 feet high which is illuminated each night in summer. Jackson was settled in 1829, became a village in 1843, and a city in 1857. The Republican party was organized and named at Jackson in 1854. Population, 1970, 45,484.

Jackson. The capital of Mississippi, located on the Pearl River, about 40 miles east of Vicksburg. Possessing both railway and water transportation, Jackson has become a commercial center for agricultural and manufactured products, with an extensive trade in cotton. The chief local industries include cottonseed oil mills, foundries, lumber mills, and woodworking shops. Among the prominent public buildings are the Capitol and the Carnegie Library. Jackson is the seat of Millsaps College, Bellhaven College, and the James Observatory.

The site of Jackson was chosen for the state capital in 1821. During the Civil War, Jackson was the scene of many conflicts, and in 1864 was largely destroyed by General Sherman. Population, 1970, 153,968.

Jackson. A city of western Tennessee, about 80 miles northeast of Memphis. Jackson is the trade center of a rich farming and fruit growing district, is an important cotton and fruit market, and has substantial local industries. Among the city's manufactures are cotton goods, cottonseed oil, lumber, aluminum products, and furniture. Jackson is the seat of Union University and of Lambuth and Lane colleges. Population, 1970, 39,996.

Jacksonville. A city and commercial center of Florida, situated on Saint Johns River, about 27 miles from its mouth. It has an excellent harbor, with a 30-foot channel to the ocean, and carries on an extensive coastwise and foreign trade in lumber, cotton, phosphates, fruits, and vegetables. The leading industries include shipbuilding and the manufacture of fertilizers, lumber, cigars, chemicals, and naval stores; also fruit packing, crab meat packing, and spice milling.

The city's streets, parks, and private residences are rendered attractive by the luxuriance of semi-tropical vegetation. By reason of its mild climate and nearby ocean beaches, Jacksonville is a favorite winter resort. Population, 1970, 518,131.

Jamestown. A manufacturing city of western New York, about 75 miles southwest of Buffalo. Jamestown occupies a hilly site on the outlet of Chautauqua Lake, with abundant water power. It is a leading center for the manufacture of furniture. Other important industries make bearings, automatic voting machines, metal office furniture, and automobile parts. The city is also an important dairy center. Population, 1970, 39,795.

Jamestown. The first permanent English settlement in the United States. It was founded in 1607 on the banks of the James River, in Virginia, about 32 miles above its mouth, and nearly opposite the present town of Williamsburg. The first legislative assembly held in America met at Jamestown in 1619, and here, in the same year, slaves were first introduced into the colonial territory.

During Bacon's Rebellion, 1676, Jamestown was burned to the ground. It was rebuilt and remained the capital of Virginia until 1698, when it was again destroyed by fire and was never reconstructed. The site of the settlement, originally a peninsula, later became an island. Of the former town, there remain only the ruins of the tower of the church of 1639, but the old church has been reconstructed, the foundations of many early structures have been exposed and marked, lot lines and streets have been re-defined, and a modern Visitor Center containing exhibits and an orientation film has been added.

Jefferson City. The capital of Missouri, situated on the south bank of the Missouri River, about 110 miles west of Saint Louis. The city is a trade and commercial center of a rich farming district and contains large railway shops. The chief manufacturing interests include shoe factories, flour mills, machine shops, and foundries. A fine steel bridge spans the Missouri at Jefferson City. Among prominent buildings are the State Capitol, erected at a cost of $4,215,000, the State Supreme Courthouse, and the State Office Building. The site was chosen for the state capital in 1821, the town was laid out in 1822, and the legislature first met here in 1826. Population, 1970, 32,407.

Jersey City. A city of New Jersey, built on the west bank of the Hudson River. It occupies 20.2 square miles directly opposite lower New York City, with which it is connected by four tubes under the Hudson and by the Holland vehicular tunnel.

Jersey City is the terminus of a large number of railroads, which link it with the South and West. As a shipping and receiving port, it is probably second in importance to New York. Among its numerous manufactures are electrical and scientific apparatus, jewelry, musical instruments, soap, radios, and drugs.

The city has many notable public buildings and several parks. John F. Kennedy Boulevard, 19 miles long and 100 feet wide, follows the crest of Bergen Hill, extends past

West Side Park, and gives a splendid view of the river and upper New York. Population, 1970, 260,545.

Johnstown. A manufacturing city in southwestern Pennsylvania, about 75 miles east of Pittsburgh. Johnstown is located in a picturesque valley at the foot of the Allegheny Mountains, in a rich coal mining and iron producing region.

The city is one of the leading centers in the state for the manufacture of steel and steel products. Other manufactures include silk, radios, radiators, and paint. Johnstown has 230 acres in 14 public parks. On May 31, 1889, as a result of a flood caused by the bursting of a dam on the south fork of the Conemaugh River, Johnstown was largely destroyed and 2000 lives were lost. A reminder of this tragic occurrence is the Unknown Plot in Grandview Cemetery, where 777 unidentified victims of the flood are buried. Prompt outside aid was extended, and the city was soon rebuilt and its industries re-established. Population, 1970, 42,476.

Joliet (jŏ'lĭ-ĕt). A manufacturing city of northeastern Illinois, situated on the Des Plaines River, about 40 miles southwest of Chicago. The manufacture of steel products, chiefly rods and wire, and of wall paper are major industries. Other products include refined oil, chemicals, and stoves. The American Institute of Laundering is located there. Joliet is also noted for its quarries of fine building stone, known as Joliet limestone. Population, 1970, 80,378.

Juneau (jōō'nō). The capital of Alaska, and the supply center of mining, fishing, and lumbering camps. It is situated on a good harbor on the Gastineau Channel, in the "panhandle" portion of southeastern Alaska. Huge quantities of salmon, halibut, and other fish are shipped, mainly within the United States. A decline in gold mining has been accompanied by a growth of the pulp and lumber industry and fur farming. Population, 1970, 6050.

Kalamazoo. A manufacturing center of southwestern Michigan, in a rich agricultural district. Principal industries include metal working and the manufacture of pharmaceuticals, paper, printing machinery, and paper boxes. The city is the seat of Western Michigan University and Kalamazoo and Nazareth colleges. Population, 1970, 85,555.

Kansas City. A city of Kansas, built on both banks of the Kansas River at its junction with the Missouri. It lies adjacent to Kansas City, Missouri, with which communication is facilitated by a two-mile intercity viaduct connecting the higher levels of the cities. It is the second greatest live stock market and meat packing center in the United States. Flour milling is second in importance among the city's extensive industries, which include petroleum refining, soap making, car repairing, and the manufacture of structural ironwork, boxes, chemicals, cooperage, and fertilizers. Parks cover 330 acres, and nearby is Wyandotte County Park of 1400 acres with a 333-acre lake created by an earthen dam. First settled as a trapping post in the 1820's, it became a gateway to the West and was incorporated as a city in 1889. Population, 1970, 168,213.

Kansas City. A city of Missouri on the western border of the state, some 230 miles west of Saint Louis. It occupies a commanding site on the south bank of the Missouri River, at its junction with the Kansas River. The city is built on three levels, in a landscape of high bluffs. Kansas, City, Mo., and Kansas City, Kans., though separate in government, form a continuous settlement at the center of a six-county metropolitan area. Because of its location near the geographical center of the United States and its excellent transportation facilities, including an international airport, Kansas City is one of the most important warehousing and distribution centers in the United States.

Known for its leadership in agricultural enterprise, the city also has a strong and diversified industrial base and ranks high as a center for consulting engineering firms. Also important are its wheat market, cold storage facilities, production of vending equipment, distribution of vending machinery, and automotive assembly plants. Chief industrial products are refined oil, iron and steel products, paints, and chemicals.

Among prominent buildings are the municipal auditorium, city hall, the federal building, and the Nelson Gallery of Art. Here also are the Kansas City Philharmonic Orchestra, the Museum of History and Science, the Midwest Research Institute (operating in 20 fields of science), the Hall Library of Science and Technology, and the University of Kansas City. Population, 1970, 501,859.

Katahdin (kȧ-tä'dĭn), **Mount.** The highest mountain in Maine, located in Piscataquis county, slightly northeast of the center of the state. It rises to an elevation of 5267 feet, with precipitous slopes and massive cliffs of richly colored granite. The bare summit furnishes a grand view of forests, rivers, lakes, and mountains.

Kennedy, Cape. A cape on Florida's east coast midway between Jacksonville and Miami where the U.S. government maintains a launching site for space explorations. Its name was changed from Cape Canaveral in honor of President Kennedy after his assassination in 1963. In 1973 the cape was renamed Cape Canaveral. The space launching facility will still be known as the John F. Kennedy Space Center.

Kenosha (*ke-no'sha*). A city of fine homes and choice industrial sites in southeastern Wisconsin, overlooking a fine harbor on Lake Michigan, 34 miles south of Milwaukee. The city's extensive industries include the manufacture of automobiles, brass and copper products, tools, stainless steel fittings, wire rope, hosiery, and knit goods. Population, 1970, 78,805.

Key West. The southernmost city of continental United States, situated on Key West Island, one of the Florida Keys. This small coral island lies in the Gulf of Mexico, about 50 miles southwest of Cape Sable, Florida. It is connected with the mainland by an overseas highway built, in part, upon the chain of low islands, of which Key West is the terminal, and, in part, upon huge concrete causeways connecting the islands. There are large shipping interests and important fisheries. Population, 1970, 27,563.

Kings Mountain. A ridge 100 feet high and a mile long in South Carolina, about 30 miles southwest of Charlotte, N. C. Here on October 7, 1780, a British force of 1100 troops was defeated and captured by less than 1000 mountaineers, who thereby spoiled the strategy of Cornwallis and prepared the way for victory at Yorktown.

Knoxville. An industrial and educational center in eastern Tennessee, built on the north bank of the Tennessee River, about 160 miles east of Nashville. It lies between the Cumberland and Great Smoky mountain ranges in a rich coal mining, iron producing, and marble quarrying region, with which it conducts an extensive trade. Knoxville's industrial products include textiles and clothing, iron and steel products, furniture, plastics, and marble. The city is the seat of the University of Tennessee and Knoxville College. It is headquarters of the Tennessee Valley Authority. Population, 1970, 174,587.

La Crosse. A city of western Wisconsin, on the Mississippi River at the mouth of the La Crosse and Black rivers. Its site is on level ground extending about 2½ miles back from the Mississippi to bluffs which command fine views. Lumber manufacture, formerly the leading industry, has been replaced by a great variety of new industries including the manufacture of motor car instruments and farm machinery. It is the trade center for a rich dairying district. The numerous lakes, picturesque crags, and winding valleys nearby make La Crosse a popular center for tourist travel. Population, 1970, 51,153.

Laguna (*lä-goo'nä*). The second largest Indian pueblo in New Mexico, located near the San Jose River, in an arid desert, 67 miles west of Albuquerque. The inhabitants, who are of Keresan stock, are industrious and self-supporting. By primitive methods of irrigation, they produce crops sufficient for their needs. Wool also is grown.

Lake Charles. A city of southwestern Louisiana, situated on the lake of the same name, about midway between New Orleans and Houston. It is an important seaport, connected with the Gulf of Mexico by a 33-mile deepwater channel. Principal industries are oil refining and chemical manufacturing. McNeese State College is located here, and just north of the city is the 1220-acre Sam Houston Park. Population, 1970, 77,998.

Lake Geneva. A summer resort town of southern Wisconsin, situated on a lake of the same name, about 40 miles southwest of Milwaukee. The lake is a fine body of water, 9 miles long and from 1 to 3 miles wide. Many residents of Chicago have villas on its shores. The town is the seat of a large sanitarium and a military school. Nearby is Yerkes Observatory, containing the great Yerkes 40-inch refracting telescope. Population, 1970, 4890.

Lake George. A small lake in eastern New York, one of the most picturesquely beautiful in America. It is fed chiefly by cold springs, and its waters flow into Lake Champlain through a series of cascades, with one abrupt fall of 30 feet at Ticonderoga.

Lake Mohonk (*mô-hŏngk'*). A popular summer resort, charmingly situated on a small lake of the same name in the Catskill Mountains, of Ulster County, about 75 miles north of New York City. Lake Mohonk is noted also as the seat of a long series of annual conferences on international arbitration, the first of which was held in 1895

Lake Placid. A beautiful small lake in the Adirondacks of northeastern New York. It is situated at the foot of Whiteface Mountain, some 10 miles northeast of Mount Marcy. The lake lies at an altitude of about 2000 feet.

Lakewood. A city of northern Ohio on Lake Erie and adjoining the western limits of Cleveland, of which it is a residential suburb. Lakewood was incorporated in 1911. Population, 1970, 70,173.

Lancaster. A city of southeastern Pennsylvania, about 65 miles west of Philadelphia. Lancaster is the trade center of one of the most productive tobacco and grain growing counties in the United States, and has varied and extensive industries. It is noted for its output of watches, umbrellas, locks, linoleum, cork, silk goods, cotton goods, and leather. Franklin and Marshall College and the Theological Seminary of the Reformed Church are located here. First settled in 1718, Lancaster became the center of a progressive community whose important historic contributions include the Pennsylvania rifle and the Conestoga wagon. It was the home of James Buchanan, 15th president of the United States. Population, 1970, 57,690.

Lansing. The capital of Michigan, built at the junction of the Grand and Cedar rivers, about 85 miles northwest of Detroit. Power developed from these streams is utilized in the city's extensive industries. In value of manufactures, Lansing stands fourth among the cities of the state. Of its industries, the manufacture of automobiles is the most important. Other manufactures are machine shop products and chemicals. Among important public buildings are the new capitol and the Lansing Public Library. Parks cover 1802 acres. East Lansing is the seat of Michigan State University. Lansing was settled in 1837, was laid out for the capital in 1847, and became a city in 1859. Population, 1970, 131,546.

Laredo (*le,ra'do*). A city of southern Texas, on the Rio Grande River, opposite Nuevo Laredo, Mexico, and connected with it by two international bridges. It is the largest port of entry on the U.S.-Mexico border, the distribution center for an area rich in petroleum production, cattle raising, and truck crops. Laredo is a tourist attraction with historical interest. It was founded in 1755 by the Spanish. Population, 1970, 69,024.

Lassen Peak. A volcanic mountain in northern California, situated at the north end of the Sierra Nevada range, about 135 miles north of Sacramento It stands at the extreme southwestern border of the great ancient lava beds which cover more than 200,000 square miles in the Columbia River plateau.

Long inactive and regarded as extinct, Lassen Peak in 1914 began to emit immense clouds of steam and smoke. An area of 167 square miles surrounding and including Lassen Peak has been created a national park. In this are smaller volcanoes, lava fields, cinder cones, fumaroles, hot springs, solfataras, boiling lakes, and other features characteristic of a volcanic region.

Las Vegas. A city in Nevada, located in the southeastern tip of the state. Having advantages of climate and nearness to points of scenic interest, such as Hoover Dam, it has become known as a residential, tourist, and convention city, specializing in entertainment for visitors. Its industries serve the AEC Nevada Test Site and other U.S. bases. Population, 1970, 125,787.

Lawrence. A city in eastern Kansas, on both banks of the Kansas River, about 40 miles west of Kansas City. Lawrence is the trade center of a rich agricultural region and has various local industries, including flour mills, pipe organ and box factories, nurseries, and canning works. It is the seat of the University of Kansas, and the Haskell Institute for Indians is also located here. Founded in 1854 by settlers from New England, Lawrence was the first of the Kansas Free State towns, and became an antislavery stronghold. It was sacked by a band of bush rangers from Missouri in 1856. In 1863, Quantrell, the Confederate raider, attacked the town, killing more than 100 of its citizens. Population, 1970, 45,698.

Lawrence. A manufacturing city of northeastern Massachusetts, built on both sides of the Merrimack River, about 26 miles north of Boston. The Merrimack Falls of the river at this point originally played an important part in building up the city's industries. In the production of worsted cloth, Lawrence leads all other cities of the United States. Here are located the huge mills of the American Woolen Company as well as the Pacific and Arlington mills Other manufactures include foundry and machine shop products, shoes, and paper. Population, 1970, 66,915.

Leadville. A mining city of central Colorado, located near the Continental Divide, at an elevation of 10,200 feet. First settled by gold prospectors in 1860, it was a prosperous gold mining center for a few years until the deposits at that time known were exhausted. Thereupon the place was practically abandoned. In 1877, exceedingly rich lead and silver ore bodies were discovered. As a result, the population, which had declined to about 300, increased to more than 6000 in 1878, and to about 35,000 in 1879. For a time thereafter, Leadville held first place in the United States in lead and silver production. During the period

1879–1940, the total value of its mineral output exceeded $550 million. Mineral production has declined to a small fraction of its former value. Nearby is a mine producing most of the world's molybdenum. Population, 1970, 4314.

Lewiston. A leading manufacturing city of Maine, built on the east bank of the Androscoggin River opposite the city of Auburn, about 35 miles north of Portland. The river here falls 60 feet; at the five million dollar Gulf Island dam it furnishes immense hydroelectric power which is utilized in the city's extensive industries. The chief manufacturing establishments are cotton and woolen mills, shoe factories, dye works, and bleacheries. The city is the seat of Bates College. Population, 1970, 41,779.

Lexington. The chief city of the "Blue-Grass region," situated about 80 miles southeast of Louisville. It is located in a highly productive agricultural and stock-raising district and is an important market for grain, tobacco, and livestock, especially thoroughbred horses. Lexington, named for the first battle of the Revolutionary War, is surrounded by beautiful countryside. It is the seat of Kentucky University, Transylvania University, and other educational institutions. It is also the site of a U.S. Veterans' Hospital and a U.S. hospital and farm for the treatment of drug addicts. Lexington was the home of Henry Clay, Mary Todd Lincoln, and General John Hunt Morgan. Population, 1970, 108,137.

Lexington. A town of northeastern Massachusetts, situated about 12 miles northwest of Boston. Lexington village, now chiefly residential, is noted as the scene of the first conflict between the colonists and the British in the Revolutionary War. In the village and its vicinity are many points of great historic interest. Among these are the first battleground of the Revolution; numerous houses, taverns, and other buildings associated with the conflict; and various monuments in commemoration of the men and of the events that made Lexington famous. Lexington was settled about 1642 and for some 50 years was known as Cambridge Farms. In 1839, the first normal school in the United States was opened in Lexington. Population, 1970, 31,886.

Lima. A city of western Ohio and center of oil pipe lines, located on the Ottawa River, 79 miles south of Toledo. Among its chief industrial products are cigars, locomotives, power shovels, electric motors, diesel engines, bus bodies, and steel castings. Population, 1970, 53,734.

Lincoln. The capital and second largest city of Nebraska, situated on a gently sloping site, about 55 miles southwest of Omaha. It is the center of a productive agricultural and stock-raising section, with which it carries on an extensive trade. The industrial products include food products, chemicals, brick, cement, and machinery. The city is regularly laid out, with wide streets. The Capitol is among the great architectural achievements of America. Parks, numbering 42, cover 4028 acres.

Lincoln is the seat of the University of Nebraska, Wesleyan University, and Union College. Fairview, the estate of William Jennings Bryan, is used as a hospital. The first permanent settlement on the site of the city was made in 1856, and in 1864 a village was laid out, called Lancaster. This, in 1867, was selected for the state capital and renamed Lincoln. Population, 1970, 149,518.

Lincoln Highway. A road extending entirely across the northern United States and named in honor of Abraham Lincoln. It was laid out in 1913 with the purpose of establishing a modern vehicular highway, national in character and free to the public at all points, connecting New York and San Francisco. For most of its length, the road is now known as U.S. 30 (Philadelphia to Salt Lake City). From Utah across Nevada into California, it is replaced by U.S. 50.

Little Rock. The capital and largest city of Arkansas, on the Arkansas River, near the center of the state. The name has reference to a bold cliff rising 50 feet above the river at this point. The city is the commercial center of a rich lumbering and cotton-growing district. It became an inland port in 1968 as part of the $1.2 billion Arkansas River Navigation Project. Two new navigation locks and dams are located only a short distance from the city. There are many fine public buildings, among which is the Capitol, built of native Arkansas marble. The park system covers 400 acres. Because of its profusion of roses, Little Rock is often called the "City of Roses." The city is the seat of Little Rock University and the University of Arkansas schools of medicine, nursing, pharmacy, and law. Population, 1970, 132,483.

Lockport. A city of western New York, situated on the State Barge canal, 26 miles northeast of Buffalo and in the center of the highly productive Niagara fruit belt. It occupies a commanding though somewhat uneven site, part of the city being built on a sloping terrace known as "Mountain Ridge." At this point the canal drops some 66 feet, from the level of Lake Erie to that of the Genesee River, by massive locks of masonry, and is crossed by one of the widest bridges in the world. The varied industries include numerous manufactures, notably automobile parts and pulpwood products, chemicals, and high-grade steel. There is a large trade in fruit and grain. The Niagara County Historical Center is located here. Population, 1970, 25,399.

Logan. A city of northern Utah, on Logan River, about 70 miles north of Salt Lake City. Logan is the commercial center of the Cache valley, a rich agricultural district, with some mineral deposits. Its industrial establishments include flour mills, cheese plants, and beet sugar and knitting factories. Utah State University is located there, and a Mormon temple with grounds of great beauty overlooks the city from a hilltop. Population, 1970, 22,333.

Long Beach. An industrial and tourist center on the coast of California, 22 miles south of Los Angeles. It is beautifully located, looking out on the harbor of San Pedro, while the beach from which it takes its name is one of the finest along the Pacific coast. Its harbor, elaborately improved, is the base of the Pacific battle fleet. It accommodates a large trade in fruit, canned fish, petroleum, and lumber, the last two being the chief products of the city's industry. Petroleum is extensively produced within the city limits and is used as fuel for an electric generating plant, one of the largest on the continent. Population, 1970, 358,633.

Lookout Mountain. A steep ridge which rises to an elevation of 2100 feet, overlooking the city of Chattanooga, Tennessee. This rocky height was the scene of the famous battle of the Civil War, sometimes called the "Battle above the Clouds." The summit commands a superb view of the Tennessee River and its valley, the city of Chattanooga, and the surrounding mountainous region.

LOS ANGELES (lōs ăng' gĕl-ĕs; lŏs ăn'jĕl-ĕs). The chief commercial center of southern California and the third most populous city in the United States, Los Angeles is situated on the Pacific coast, about 475 miles southeast of San Francisco and about 10 miles south of the Sierra Madre mountains. Through it passes the Los Angeles River, a dry bed in summer but a considerable stream in winter.

SITE. The city lies, for the most part, in a gently sloping plain, with an average elevation of about 270 feet. The site is fairly level, though there are a few steep eminences, and the northern suburbs extend into the foothills. Including extensions to the ocean and taking in San Pedro harbor, the total area of the city exceeds 457 square miles.

STREETS AND BUILDINGS. The city is regularly laid out, with wide, straight streets, and an extensive system of boulevards and drives. About the old Plaza is the civic center, which includes the $10 million City Hall with a 464-foot tower surmounted by the Lindbergh beacon. Near the plaza is the union station, an $11 million structure. The railway terminals and manufacturing districts lie chiefly to the east and south of the business center, while the large and handsomely built residence sections flank it on the west and north. Los Angeles is preeminently a city of beautiful homes, with the Mission style of architecture, adopted from the Spanish, and the bungalow as characteristic types. The broad avenues and spacious grounds are luxuriant with evergreen foliage and a profusion of flowers which bloom throughout the year.

PARKS AND BOULEVARDS. There are 112 public parks embracing a total area of more than 9600 acres. Among the more noteworthy of these are Griffith, Elysian, Westlake, Lincoln, Echo, Hollenbeck, Exposition, Central, and Plaza parks. Griffith park, a hilly, wooded tract of 4109 acres, is one of the largest municipally-owned parks in the United States. Many handsome boulevards and driveways connect the parks with various parts of the city and with fine scenic roads to the ocean, fruitful valleys, and mountain wildernesses.

EDUCATIONAL INSTITUTIONS. Los Angeles is the seat of the University of Southern California, the University of

California at Los Angeles, Occidental College, Loyola University, and Los Angeles City College, The Museum of History and Science in Exposition Park, has a large display of skeletons of extinct animals. The County Museum of Art and the Music Center of the Performing Arts are recent additions to Los Angeles' cultural attractions.

TRANSPORTATION. Los Angeles owes its great growth in part to unusually complete transportation facilities. The city contains terminals of three transcontinental railways which enter the magnificent Union Station, completed in 1939 at a cost of $11 million. There is also a capacious harbor for coastwise and foreign shipping in its municipally-owned wharves at San Pedro. It is connected with the surrounding country by a system of bus lines, some of which reach towns 60 miles distant. Well paved public freeways form a huge network over country districts in all directions. One of the finest is the Arroyo Seco Parkway. These serve as thoroughfares for extensive regularly operated systems of autobuses and autotrucks.

COMMERCE. Los Angeles is the commercial center of the far Southwest and has extensive fruit growing, petroleum producing, manufacturing, and shipping interests. Its foreign and intercoastal shipping vies with that of New York City. The chief imports are lumber and raw materials such as rubber, silk, coffee, and cacao. Exports are largely petroleum and other minerals, food products, and factory goods. The city is a general market for one of the most productive horticultural and agricultural sections of the country. Among leading products handled are oranges, lemons, walnuts, olives, vegetables, beet sugar, beans, cereals, and cotton. Citrus fruits and petroleum are the chief products of the immediate district.

MANUFACTURES. By reason of cheap fuel, in the form of crude petroleum, and abundant hydroelectric power derived from the Hoover Dam, Los Angeles has grown at a prodigious rate as a manufacturing city. The motion picture industry is the best known. Hollywood, the chief center of this industry, is famous throughout the world. The Los Angeles area leads the country in aircraft manufacture. Other important manufactures include petroleum and metal products, lumber, packed meats and other food products, and furniture. The outdoor life and the importance of the motion picture industry have made Los Angeles a style center for sports and other clothes, and the manufacture of women's clothing has become a large industry.

FEATURES OF INTEREST. With its picturesque setting between the mountains and the sea, its numerous historic associations, and its many attractive suburbs, Los Angeles presents an immense number of points of interest. Among those within the city are the Old Plaza Church, China City and Chinatown, Griffith Observatory and Planetarium, Memorial Coliseum, with a seating capacity of 105,000, and the Hollywood Bowl, seating 18,000, Dodger Stadium, the Pilgrimage play, Radio Center, and La Brea pits in Hancock Park. In the near vicinity are San Gabriel Mission with its Mission Play theater, Mount Lowe, and Mount Wilson Observatory, Huntington Library and Art Gallery, and Palos Verdes hills. Attractive beach resorts include Santa Monica, Venice, Redondo Beach, Long Beach, and Santa Catalina Island. Interesting suburban cities include Pasadena, Riverside, Alhambra, Universal City, Glendale, Orange, Pomona, and San Bernardino.

HISTORY. In 1781, Los Angeles was settled by Spanish colonists from Mexico who named it *El Pueblo de Nuestra Senora la Reina de Los Angeles* (the City of Our Lady the Queen of the Angels). Until its final capture in 1847 by United States troops under General Stephan W. Kearny, it served alternately with Monterey as capital of the Mexican province of California.

Los Angeles was chartered as a city in 1850, and attained its first railway connection with San Francisco in 1876. Following the completion, in 1885, of the Santa Fe railway, giving direct access to the East, the growth of Los Angeles was rapid.

The genial climate, the great fertility of the surrounding region under irrigation, and large local supplies of natural gas and petroleum have been influential factors in this development. Two important municipal achievements have also contributed substantially to its rise as a great city. The first was the extension, in 1909, of the city to the ocean at San Pedro, making possible the establishment of a commodious, municipally controlled harbor. The second was the completion, in 1913, at a cost of $25 million, of a great aqueduct from the slopes of Mount Whitney in the Sierra Nevada, across the Mojave desert, and through the Sierra Madre range, by tunnel, to the city. In the 1930's, water from the Colorado River was made available through a 250-mile aqueduct, 108 miles of which was tunneled through the rock, the total cost being $220 million. A third source of supply was secured with the completion of the Mono Basin project in 1940 at a cost of $20 million. Population, 1970, 2,816,061.

Louisville (*loo'ĭ-vĭl*). The chief city of Kentucky, located on the south bank of the Ohio River, 110 miles south of Cincinnati. Louisville occupies a commanding site opposite the rapids or "falls" of the river, at which point is an enormous fossil reef containing what is said to be the world's only exposed relic of the Devonian era, dating from 300 million years ago. A system of locks and dams has recently been added in the falls area.

The city's park system covers some 2177 acres. Cherokee Park, 409 acres, is cut into ravines by Beargrass Creek. Iroquois Park, the largest, 676 acres, rises to eminences of nearly 300 feet, affording views of the city and of the river.

Louisville has excellent transportation facilities by air, expressway, rail, and the Ohio River. It is the commercial center of a large agricultural region. Its leading manufactures include tobacco products, electrical appliances, farm implements, packed meats, whiskey, railroad cars, sanitary plumbing supplies, and gasoline. It leads the U.S. in the production of bathtubs, baseball bats, hickory handles, and wagons. The city is the seat of the University of Louisville and other educational institutions. It is widely known as the site of the Kentucky Derby and the Kentucky State Fair.

The town of Louisville was laid out and named in 1779 and became a city in 1828. Its growth, favored by river traffic, was greatly stimulated by the completion, in 1830, of the Louisville and Portland canal around the rapids. Near the city is the home and the grave of Zachary Taylor. Population, 1970, 361,472.

Lowe, Mount. A peak of the Sierra Madre in southern California. It is situated some 15 miles in direct line northeast of Los Angeles and rises to an elevation of 5650 feet above sea level. An electric scenic railway ascends almost to the summit, which affords superb views of the surrounding region.

Lowell. A manufacturing city of northeastern Massachusetts, situated at the junction of the Merrimack and Concord rivers, about 30 miles northwest of Boston. While electronics has replaced textiles as the main industrial base (many of the textile mills having moved south), manufactures are diversified, including food products, shoes, medicine, clothing, plastics, and paper products. Various civic improvements have recently been made within the city. Lowell is the seat of Lowell Technological Institute and Lowell State College. It is the birthplace of the artist James McNeill Whistler, whose home is now a museum. Population, 1970, 94,239.

Lubbock. A city in the Great Plains area of Texas, 295 miles northwest of Fort Worth. Located in a rich oil region, it is also in the center of an agricultural section whose major products are cotton, cottonseed, and sorghum. Principal educational institution, Texas Technological University. Population, 1970, 149,101.

Luray Cavern. A remarkable cave, situated near the town of Luray, Virginia, in the foothills of the Blue Ridge mountains. There are numerous galleries, rising above one another in tiers to a height of nearly 300 feet. Some contain stalactites and stalagmites of great size and unusual beauty of coloration. The cavern was discovered in 1878.

Lynchburg. A city of central Virginia, on the James River, 112 miles west of Richmond. The city is picturesquely located, sloping in steep terraces upward from the river, with the Blue Ridge and the Peaks of Otter as background. It is situated in a tobacco producing district, of which it is the trade center. Power developed from the river is utilized in various local industries, chiefly in the manufacture of shoes and clothing. Educational institutions include Randolph-Macon Woman's College and Lynchburg College. Population, 1970, 54,083.

Lynn. A manufacturing city of eastern Massachusetts, located about 10 miles northeast of Boston. The city is beautifully situated and admirably laid out. The commercial and industrial districts extend for about 3 miles along Massachusetts Bay, on which the city has a well-developed harbor, while the residential sections occupy the higher portions overlooking the harbor.

Lynn is one of the chief centers in the United States for the manufacture of women's and children's shoes. The city has other important industries, chiefly the manufacture of electrical machinery, jet engines, measurement devices, adhesives, boxes, and proprietary medicines. Lynn was settled in 1629 but was known as Saugus until 1637, when it was given its present name. Its great shoe industry had its beginnings about 1750. Population, 1970, 90,294.

McKeesport. A manufacturing city of Pennsylvania, on the Monongahela River, 14 miles southeast of Pittsburgh. Advantageously situated in a region rich in bituminous coal, iron, and natural gas, the city has become a leading center for the manufacture of iron and steel. It possesses one of the greatest steel tube and iron pipe works in the world, which has earned for it the name of the "Tube City." Among other industrial products are chromium sheet, tools, and other steel products. Population, 1970, 37,977.

Macon (*mā'kŏn*). A city of central Georgia, built at the head of navigation on the Ocmulgee River, about 80 miles southeast of Atlanta. Macon is the commercial center of a highly productive farming and fruit district, and is a leading market for peanuts, pecans, and peaches. Hydroelectric power, derived from the river, is utilized in the city's extensive industries, which include the manufacture of cotton and knit goods, cottonseed oil and cottonseed cake, brick, tile, lumber, flour, fertilizers, foundry and machine shop products, and packed meats. Macon has a municipal auditorium with a huge copper dome.

The city is the seat of Mercer University and Wesleyan College. Macon was first settled in 1822 and was incorporated as a city in 1832. It was the home of the poet Sidney Lanier. Population, 1970, 122,423.

Madison. The capital of Wisconsin, situated in the south central part of the state. The city occupies a picturesque site between lakes Mendota and Monona, in the so-called "Four-Lakes region." It is surrounded by a rich agricultural district, of which it is the trade and industrial center. Madison is noted for its beautiful parks, wide, heavily shaded streets, and scenic lake shore drives. Its industrial output includes meat and dairy products, dry cell batteries, and machine tools. There are many fine public buildings, the most imposing of which is the capitol, built of granite in the Renaissance style.

The city is the seat of the University of Wisconsin, which occupies a magnificent campus, more than a mile in length, bordering on Lake Mendota. Madison has a United States forest products laboratory, opened in 1910, the first in the world. The site of Madison was chosen for the state capital in 1836. Population, 1970, 173,258.

Malden. A city of eastern Massachusetts, built on the Malden River, 5 miles north of Boston. Malden is noted for its extensive manufactures of rubber boots and shoes, and contains some of the largest rubber shoe factories in the United States. Among numerous other manufactures may be mentioned knitted goods, soap, paints, chinaware, and precision instruments. Malden was first settled in 1641, was incorporated in 1649, and was chartered as a city in 1881. Population, 1970, 56,127.

Mammoth Cave. The second largest known cavern in the world, being exceeded in size only by Carlsbad Cave in New Mexico. Situated near the Green River, about 100 miles south of Louisville, Kentucky, it is located in a region which abounds in large caverns and whose surface is marked by thousands of sink holes. Through these depressions, drainage waters find their way to underground streams whose solvent and erosive action has largely produced the caves.

To the geologist, the cave is a laboratory and museum inexhaustibly rich in materials for the study of rock formations and the effects of erosion. For the tourist, the processes of geologic change have created a picturesque setting unlimited in interest and variety. In the St. Louis limestone, a layer of soluble rock capped by sandstone and sometimes reaching a thickness of 300 feet, underground waters have carved a series of pools and streams that are bordered by cathedral-like rooms and ornamental passageways. The walls are lined, not only with the usual rows of stalactites and stalagmites, but also with a panorama of symmetrical statues and grotesque gargoyles.

In more matter-of-fact terms, Mammoth Cave may be described as a complex series of caverns, including more than 200 so-called rooms, chambers, domes, pits, abysses, grottoes, avenues, and galleries, which extend for 9 miles underground. In the lower portions, there are rivers, waterfalls, and small lakes. Among the most interesting features are the vast pits or domes, which are caverns of unusual height. The largest of these, called the Chief City, is 450 feet long and 130 feet wide.

Cleveland Avenue, which extends for fully 2 miles, presents wonderful displays of crystals and incrustations. Stalactites and stalagmites in a great variety of grotesque shapes, many of which resemble architectural forms. When the incrustations are covered with crystals, as in Star Chamber, their sparkling effect when the cavern is lighted is impressive. Among the larger bodies of water within the cavern are the so-called Dead Sea, the Styx, Lethe Lake, Roaring River, and Echo River.

In the waters of the cave are 2 species of blind fish. These, together with crayfish and a few insects, make up the animal life. The temperature remains almost constant at about 54°. The cavern was discovered in 1809 by a hunter named Hutchins. In 1936, a tract including the site of the cave was created Mammoth Cave National Park, covering over 80 square miles.

Manchester. A city of New Hampshire, built on the Merrimack River, 18 miles south of Concord. A fall of some 50 feet in the river, formerly used as direct water power, now provides one of the units in a superpower system. The city's extensive industrial output includes cotton textiles, worsted dress goods, rayon mixtures, shoes, brushes, and cigars. The city has many fine parks, municipal buildings, and educational institutions, including the Manchester Institute of Arts and Sciences and the Currier Art Gallery. Recreation is provided by 35 parks. Population, 1970, 87,754.

Manitou (*măn'ĭ-tōō*) **Springs.** A health and pleasure resort, located at the foot of Pikes Peak, 6 miles northwest of Colorado Springs, Colorado. The town lies at an elevation of about 6300 feet in a region noted for picturesque scenery. The numerous features of interest in the locality include Pikes Peak, the Cave of the Winds, Soda Springs Park, the Garden of the Gods, and various canyons, Cliff Dwellers' ruins, waterfalls, and scenic drives. The famous radioactive mineral springs flow at the rate of a quarter million gallons daily. The summer population is estimated at 25,000. Resident population, 1970, 4278.

Mansfield. A city of north central Ohio, situated in an agricultural region, about 65 miles northeast of Columbus. Its manufactures include appliances, brass products, tires, and plumbing products. Of interest in and around Mansfield are two winter ski resorts; a monument to Johnny (Chapman) Appleseed, who is said to have used his influence to save the settlement from Indians; the Richland County Museum; Malabar Farm, a successful experiment of novelist Louis Bromfield's from the 1930's in farming on ecological principles; and Kingswood Center, a beautiful exhibit of flora and fauna. Population, 1970, 55,047.

Marcy, Mount. The loftiest summit of the Adirondack mountains and the highest peak in the state of New York. It is situated about 10 miles south of Lake Placid, and 30 miles southwest of Lake Champlain. It is a dome-shaped mountain rising to an elevation of 5344 feet. The slopes, except near the summit, are generally wooded. The summit and a portion of the upper northern slope are above timber line. The vegetation above the zone of trees consists of dwarfed and stunted heaths and willows and other plants peculiar to an arctic-alpine vegetation.

Marietta. The oldest town in Ohio, was founded, 1788, by General Rufus Putnam, acting for the Ohio Company. Located at the junction of the Ohio and Muskingum rivers, the city has enjoyed a flourishing river trade and a substantial industrial development. Its chief manufactures are furniture and metal products. It is the site of Marietta College. Population, 1970, 16,861.

Marion. A city of central Ohio, situated 44 miles north of Columbus, in a rich agricultural and limestone quarrying region. The city's extensive industries include the manufacture of power shovels, steel products, road rollers, farm implements, conveying machinery, cereal products, and electric refrigerators. Marion has many fine streets and buildings. The city was the home of President Harding. His tomb stands near the city within a circular colonnade surrounded by a beautifully landscaped tract of 100 acres. Population, 1970, 38,646.

Medford. A city of eastern Massachusetts, 5 miles northwest of Boston, of which it is a residential and manufacturing suburb. Medford was founded in 1630. It has some of the oldest examples of colonial architecture, including Wellington House, dating from 1657, and the Cradock House, built 1677–80. Medford is the seat of Tufts University, which has a campus of 80 acres. Population, 1970, 64,397.

Memphis. The chief city of Tennessee, built on the east bank of the Mississippi River, about 210 miles southwest of Nashville. The city occupies an undulating site, on Chickasaw bluff, about 450 miles by river south of Saint Louis and 740 miles by river north of New Orleans.

At Memphis, the river is spanned by three immense cantilever bridges, and railways radiate from the city in all directions. Because of its advantageous situation on the Mississippi River, in a rich agricultural and lumbering region, Memphis has become an important marketing, manufacturing, and distributing center. It is the chief center of hardwood lumber production in the United States, and is the principal inland cotton market of the South. The city's varied and extensive industries include the manufacture of cottonseed oil and cake, food preparations, lumber, cooperage, window screens, flavoring extracts, television sets, drugs, and automobile tires. The city owns its electric generating and distribution system.

Memphis is regularly laid out, with wide, well shaded streets and handsome residences, and contains many excellent public and commercial buildings. The city's park system, connected by a boulevard 11 miles long, is one of the finest in the South. This system covers a total area of 2500 acres. Important units are Riverside Park, 349 acres, and Overton Park, 357 acres, the latter containing an art gallery and a large zoological garden.

The city is the seat of Memphis State University and of the medical and law schools of the University of Tennessee. Memphis was laid out in 1818 by General Andrew Jackson and associates. It was incorporated in 1826, and, in 1849, received its charter as a city. Population, 1970, 623,497.

Meriden. A heavily industrialized city of Connecticut, 18 miles from Hartford, surrounded by a truck-farming region. It is the home of the International Silver Company, largest manufacturer of sterling and plated silverware in the world. Other manufactures include aircraft products, electronics, plastics, and printing presses. Population, 1970, 55,959.

Meridian. The second largest city of Mississippi, in the east central part of the state. It is the market center of a rich cotton, vegetable, and cattle district. The principal industries include the manufacture of cottonseed oil, cotton gins, lumber, bricks, knitted goods, and airplane tail assemblies. Population, 1970, 45,083.

Miami (*mī-ăm'ĭ*). A commercial and year-round resort city on the lower east coast of Florida on the shores of Biscayne Bay, an inlet of the Atlantic Ocean.

The second largest city in Florida, Miami is in a subtropical region of luxuriant vegetation, producing grapefruit, oranges, limes, guava, pineapples, avocados, mangoes, and coconuts. It is an important center for shipping fruit and winter vegetables to northern markets. Light industry has become increasingly important to Miami's development in recent years, with products ranging from novelties to garments, metal products, and furniture.

Miami, a terminus for two rail lines, has steamer connections with Nassau and other Caribbean ports. The Miami International Airport is said to handle more foreign cargo than any other airport in the United States. Its $26 million terminal was dedicated in 1958, and the $30 million Port of Miami, in 1967.

In adjacent Coral Gables is the University of Miami. Politically, Miami is the hub of a rapidly growing metropolitan center comprised of 27 municipalities, whose activities are co-ordinated by a central county government housed in the 27-story Dade County Court House. Population, 1970, 334,859.

MILWAUKEE. The chief city of Wisconsin. It is situated on Lake Michigan 93 miles north of Chicago. Its area is 96 square miles.

SITE. Milwaukee occupies a commanding site overlooking Lake Michigan. Within the city three small rivers join before emptying into the lake—the Milwaukee from the north, the Kinnickinnic from the south, and the Menomonee from the west.

STREETS AND BUILDINGS. Noteworthy streets include Lincoln Memorial Drive on the shore of Lake Michigan and Wisconsin Avenue, the leading business thoroughfare. MacArthur Square is the civic center plaza around which various public buildings are grouped.

Prominent among the city's imposing edifices is the Municipal Auditorium and Arena, comprising eight halls and covering an entire city block. Other impressive buildings include the City Hall, the Courthouse, the Federal Building, the Public Library, the Art Gallery, the Public Museum, and Northwestern Mutual Life Insurance Building.

PARKS. The park system of Milwaukee covers about 1300 acres. Among its 100 units are Mitchell Park, noted for its floral displays; Washington Park, containing a fine zoological garden; and Gordon Park, with recreational facilities.

COMMERCE. The city's harbor is protected by a long breakwater. Its facilities are well suited to the handling of increased commerce resulting from the opening of the St. Lawrence Seaway. Shipping trade is very extensive and embraces an immense tonnage of coal, grain, and manufactured products. The transportation facilities include several railroad, steamship, bus, and airplane lines, and also a daily car ferry service which transports railroad trains to the east shore of Lake Michigan.

INDUSTRY. Milwaukee is one of the leading industrial centers of the country, ranking among the first ten cities of the United States in value of manufactures. These include hosiery, electrical control apparatus, power shovels, electric generators, automobile frames, packed meats, railway cars, engines, beer, shoes, and knit goods.

EDUCATIONAL INSTITUTIONS. Milwaukee has many educational institutions, including Marquette University; University of Wisconsin, Milwaukee; Mount Mary College; and Cardinal Stritch College.

HISTORY. The site of Milwaukee was visited in 1673 by Fathers Marquette and Joliet. The first permanent settlement dates from 1818. The village was organized in 1837, and, in 1845, it became a city. Population 1970, 717,099.

MINNEAPOLIS. The chief city of Minnesota, built on both banks of the Mississippi River, at the Falls of Saint Anthony. Immediately below lies Saint Paul, which adjoins Minneapolis.

SITE. Minneapolis attained industrial and commercial importance primarily by reason of the immense water power derived from the falls. This was first utilized principally in sawmills and flour mills. Until about 1870, lumber was the leading product, but since that date the milling of grain has become a pre-eminent industry. One of the great mills situated around the Falls of Saint Anthony is the largest single flour mill in the world. Other important manufactures are linseed oil, cereal foods, agricultural implements, machinery, knit goods, and dairy products. Over recent years, Minneapolis is being recognized as one of the leading centers of electronics equipment manufacturing.

The city is served by 29 railroads, 10 of which are trunk lines, and stands at the head of navigation on the Mississippi River. By reason of its extensive transportation facilities, Minneapolis has become the wholesale distributing center for the Northwest. It is also one of the chief wheat markets of the country.

Minneapolis is predominantly a city of homes, with wide, well shaded streets, handsome residences, charming parks, and beautiful drives. The park system, containing 153 parks, covers 5897 acres. It includes Lake Calhoun, Lake Harriet, Lake of the Isles, Lake Nokomis, Cedar Lake, and 17 smaller lakes and lagoons. By means of canals connecting several lakes, a scenic waterway 9 miles long has been made available for canoes and launches. Minnehaha Park contains the beautiful Minnehaha ("falling water") Falls, immortalized by Longfellow. Here Minnehaha Creek, the outlet of Lake Minnetonka, plunges over a 50-foot cliff just before joining the Mississippi.

BUILDINGS. There are many notable buildings, among them the Public Library, the City Hall, the Art Institute, the Pro-cathedral, Saint Mark's Church, Hennepin Avenue Methodist Church, the Federal Reserve Bank, the 32-story Foshay Tower, the $4 million Post Office, and the Minneapolis Auditorium. Another feature of the city is the large number of handsome bridges across the Mississippi River. The city is the seat of the University of Minnesota, De La Salle Institute, Dunwoody Institute, Augsburg Seminary, the MacPhail and Minneapolis schools of music, and the Minnesota Symphony Orchestra.

HISTORY. Father Hennepin, a French missionary, discovered and named the Falls of Saint Anthony in 1680. In 1766, the site of the city was visited by Jonathan Carver, an American traveler, and, in 1805, by Lieutenant Z. M. Pike, who purchased the site of Fort Pike from the Indians. Fort Saint Anthony, later called Fort Snelling, was established in 1819. The first sawmill at the falls was erected in 1822 to provide lumber for the fort. The village of Saint Anthony, on the east side of the river, was incorporated in 1855, and Minneapolis, on the west side, in 1856. In 1872, the two places were united. Population, 1970, 434,400.

Missoula (*mĭ-zōō'là*). A city of western Montana, on the Clark Fork River, about 125 miles by rail northwest of Helena. It is the distributing center for a large farming and fruit growing, lumbering, and mining region, and is the seat of the University of Montana. The National Bison range and the extensive Flathead Indian reservation lie to the north of the city. Population, 1970, 29,497.

Mitchell, Mount. The highest point in the state of North Carolina, and the loftiest summit of the eastern United States. It is a massive, dome-shaped mountain, sometimes called Black Dome, rising to an elevation of 6684 feet, with many high cliffs and precipitous slopes. It is named for Elisha Mitchell, a distinguished scientist who lost his life while attempting, in 1857, to scale the mountain. A large tract of land, including the summit and surrounding spruce forests, has been created a state park, which provides accommodations for travelers.

Mobile. The second largest city and only seaport in Alabama, located on Mobile Bay, 26 miles north of the Gulf of Mexico. It is a leading cotton market and has varied industries, among them shipbuilding, cotton, lumber, and paper mills, chemical and steel factories, oil refineries, and seafood canneries. The harbor has been elaborately improved, and the bay is spanned by the Cochrane bridge. The Bankhead tunnel beneath the Mobile River accommodates vehicular traffic. The chief exports include logs, hewn timber, pine lumber, rosin, cotton, paper, metals, machinery, and coal; the leading imports are bananas, ores, sugar, and chemicals. There is also an extensive local trade in vegetables, fish, and oysters.

The city has broad, regular streets, shaded with live oaks and magnolias and lined with beautiful residences. Important structures are the Mobile County Court House and the Ladd Memorial Stadium. Mobile was founded in 1702 by the French. Later, it was in the possession of the English, the Spanish, and again of the French. It became a part of the United States by the Louisiana Purchase in 1803. Population, 1970, 190,026.

Modesto. A processing, shipping, and marketing center for a rich agricultural region, located 93 miles southeast of San Francisco. Nearby Don Pedro Dam provides the irrigation power that waters the area, which abundantly produces peaches, melons, and other fruits and vegetables. Modesto is a gateway to Yosemite National Park. Population, 1970, 61,712.

Mojave (*mô-hä'vā*) **Desert.** A desert of southeastern California, situated chiefly within the boundaries of San Bernardino county and embracing an area of about 15,000 square miles. It lies south and east of the Tehachapi mountains and north of the Sierra Madre and the San Bernardino mountains. These high ranges intercept the moisture-laden winds from the Pacific, and, in consequence, the Mojave is an exceedingly arid region. The average annual rainfall is only 5 or 6 inches, and the temperature in summer sometimes reaches 120°.

The surface is that of a more or less elevated plateau, broken by numerous small mountains, with intervening valleys and plains. From an elevation of about 4000 feet on the west, this plateau slopes down to 1500 feet elevation or less toward its eastern border. Much of the southwestern portion drains into the Mojave River, which, after flowing in a definite channel for some 50 miles, entirely disappears in valley sands to the eastward.

For the most part, the Mojave Desert presents an aspect of extreme barrenness and desolation. The smaller mountains are mostly jagged masses of naked rock. Many plains are interspersed with saline sinks and dried-up lakes. Some of the valleys are covered with dark-colored sheets of anciently erupted lavas. These volcanic areas also contain numerous cinder cones and small craters.

There are valuable mineral deposits, and, where water for irrigation is available, a few small areas yield good crops. The Santa Fe and the Salt Lake railway cross this desert, as do several well constructed automobile highways. See *Colorado Desert*.

Moline. A city of western Illinois, situated at the junction of the Rock and Mississippi rivers, about 180 miles southwest of Chicago. The city of Rock Island adjoins Moline on the west, and across the Mississippi River from Rock Island is Davenport, Iowa. Moline has one of the largest steel plow plants in the country. Manufacture of agricultural implements is Moline's chief industry. A feature of interest in the vicinity is the United States arsenal on Rock Island. Between this island and Moline is a large roller dam for flood control. Nearby are the Quad-City Airport and the Black Hawk State Park. Population, 1970, 46,237.

Monadnock, Mount. A noted mountain of southwestern New Hampshire, situated about 10 miles southeast of Keene. It is a bold granitic peak with precipitous walls and extremely rugged contour, rising to an elevation of 3186 feet. Because of its isolated position and unusual form, it is one of the most impressive mountains in New England.

Monroe. Originally called Fort Miro, and later renamed for President Monroe, Monroe is situated in northeastern Louisiana, midway between Memphis and New Orleans. It is styled the "Crossroads of Pipelines," being the point where more major pipelines converge than at any other spot in the U.S. Monroe produces chemicals, paper, furniture, and strawberries. It is the seat of Northeastern Louisiana State University. Population, 1970, 56,374.

Monterey (*mŏn'tĕ-rā'*). Second-oldest city in the state, Monterey is a famous tourist attraction situated on the bay side of a peninsula on the California coast, 125 miles south of San Francisco. Fringing the Bay of Monterey is a landscape of great scenic beauty. Among many notable buildings visited by tourists are the old Custom House, built in the Mexican period, the Royal Presidio Chapel, and the home of Robert Louis Stevenson. Nearby are the artist colony of Carmel-by-the-Sea and a grove of ancient cypress trees not known to occur native anywhere else in the world and confined to a small area on Cypress Point. The chief industries are fishing and sardine packing.

Six miles from the city, in 1770, Father Junipero Serra, Spanish missionary to the Indians, established the mission of San Carlos Borromeo. After more than 75 years of Spanish and Mexican occupation, the American flag was run up at Monterey in 1846 and, in 1847, it became the capital of the military government of California. Population, 1970, 26,302.

Montgomery. The capital of Alabama, located on the Alabama River slightly southeast of the center of the state, is the hub of a highly productive grain, fruit, vegetable, cotton, and livestock region, for which it is the central market. A balanced industrial growth has resulted from the combination of favorable climate, excellent water supply, abundant electric power, and an ample labor force. Industries include cotton mills, car shops, foundries, fertilizer plants, machine works, and plywood fabricators.

Montgomery was founded in 1817 and became the state capital in 1846. The Confederate government was organized here in 1861, and this city was the seat of government until the capital was moved to Richmond, Virginia. Historic landmarks are numerous, including spacious antebellum homes and churches and the Confederate White House, occupied by Jefferson Davis, which is now a museum. Montgomery's educational institutions include Huntingdon College and Alabama State University. Population, 1970, 133,386.

Monticello. The residence and estate of Thomas Jefferson, situated in Albemarle County, Virginia, about 3 miles east of Charlottesville. Standing on the summit of a hill (whence the name Monticello, "little mountain"), it commands an extensive view of the surrounding country and has long been regarded as one of the most elegant and picturesque residences in the South. It was constructed from designs made by Jefferson himself, was first occupied in 1770, and remained his home for 56 years. In 1926, it was purchased by patriotic admirers of Jefferson for $500,000 and presented to the nation.

Montpelier (*mŏnt-pēl'yẽr*). The capital of Vermont, located in the north central part of the state. It is the center of an agricultural district and there are many valuable granite quarries in the vicinity. The finest building is the capitol, a granite structure surmounted by a handsome dome. Among its notable institutions are the State Library and the Wood Art Gallery. The town was first settled in 1787, and, in 1805, was selected as the capital of the state. It was made a city in 1895. Population, 1970, 8609.

Moundsville. A city of West Virginia, on the Ohio River 12 miles south of Wheeling. It is in the center of an important agricultural, coal mining, and oil producing district and has varied local industries, including the manufacture of glass. Moundsville is noted for a huge, prehistoric mound, a famous relic of the Mound Builders, after which the city is named. Population, 1970, 13,560.

Mount Clemens. A city and health resort on the Clinton River, about 20 miles northeast of Detroit, Michigan. It has numerous medicinal springs, which attract thousands of persons suffering from chronic ailments, especially rheumatism. Its commercial interests include the growing of roses and the manufacture of tools and dies, metal products, paint, and pottery. Population, 1970, 20,476.

Mount Rubidoux. A bold rocky summit rising abruptly from the Santa Ana valley at Riverside, California. At its crest is a cross dedicated to the memory of Father Junipero Serra, the heroic Franciscan missionary to the Indians. An impressive sunrise service is held on its summit each Easter Sunday.

Mount Tom. A small mountain in Massachusetts which rises precipitously in the Connecticut Valley, opposite Mount Holyoke and about 4 miles south of Northampton. The summit, 1200 feet high, is reached by highway and an incline railroad and affords exceptionally fine views of the surrounding region. A tract of 1700 acres on the mountain has been created a state park.

Mount Vernon. A residential city bordering on the Bronx River and adjoining the northeast section of New York City. Mount Vernon occupies an attractive site, and has wide, well shaded streets and handsome lawns and gardens. While a large portion of the city is restricted to residential purposes, there are several important industrial establishments and a considerable local trade. St. Paul's, the oldest Episcopal Church in America, established in 1665, is located here. Population, 1970, 72,778.

Mount Vernon. The home and burial place of George Washington, situated on the right bank of the Potomac River, in Fairfax county, Virginia, 15 miles south of the National capital. Located on an eminence 200 feet high, the mansion house commands a beautiful view of the river. It is constructed of wood, 2 stories high, 96 feet long, and 30 feet deep, with a high piazza along the front, and is painted white to resemble stone. The main part was built in 1743 by Lawrence Washington, Washington's elder brother, who named it in honor of Admiral Vernon of the British navy. In 1754, soon after the death of his brother Lawrence, the estate came into the hands of George Washington, who added the wings to the house.

In 1858, a tract of 200 acres of the original estate, including the mansion and the brick tomb containing the remains of George and Martha Washington, came into the possession of an association of Southern women which holds it in trust as a shrine of national interest. The six rooms on the ground floor contain many objects of historic value, including the key to the French Bastille, and various pieces of furniture used by the family.

Muncie. A city of eastern Indiana, trading center of an agricultural region, with meat packing and dairying plants. Its manufactures include foundry and machine-shop products, glass, auto parts, and electrical equipment. It is the seat of Ball State University. Population 1970, 69,080.

Muscle Shoals. A series of shallow rapids in the Tennessee River where the stream has a fall of about 134 feet within 37 miles, forming the one interruption to navigation of the river within Alabama.

A canal around the rapids was opened in 1890. In 1918, further development was undertaken by the Federal government for the purpose of improving navigation, generating electric power, and manufacturing a part of the nitrates needed for explosives during World War I. In 1925, Wilson Dam, one of the largest in volume in the world, was completed. Except for sale of current from this dam, the costly property remained idle until 1933. By that time the process for which the nitrate factories had been equipped had become obsolete.

The Tennessee Valley Authority was established in 1933 to take over the properties and to use them in a demonstration of regional planning for the Tennessee River watershed. Other dams were built, making possible a regulated flow the year round, and the nitrate factories were adapted to development of phosphate fertilizers of a superior type. The former home of Helen Keller is in nearby Tuscumbia.

Muskogee (*mŭs-kō'gê*). A city of eastern Oklahoma, situated in the valley of the Arkansas River, about 130 miles east of Oklahoma City. Muskogee is the trade center of a rich agricultural region devoted to the production of cotton, wheat, fruits, and vegetables, and to cattle raising. It has, in addition, large supplies of petroleum and natural gas. Its manufactured products include cottonseed oil, oil well supplies, and refined petroleum. There are several educational institutions. Population, 1970, 37,331.

Nashville. The capital of Tennessee, built on both banks of the Cumberland River, in the north central part of the state. Nashville is situated in a productive agricultural region, near extensive coal fields. These advantages have contributed to make it an important commercial and manufacturing city. It carries on an extensive wholesaling trade. Its leading industries include printing and publishing, meat packing, and the manufacture of glass, aero structures, shoes and boots, food products, clothing, stoves, and furniture. The city is well known for its recording studios (ranking second in the U.S. as a recording center).

Nashville occupies a hilly site, with eminences commanding fine views. On the most lofty hill, stands, like the Acropolis at Athens, the imposing State Capitol. The city has 42 parks and playgrounds covering 5500 acres. They include Centennial Park, where there is an exact replica of the Parthenon in Athens, Greece.

The city is one of the most important educational centers in the South. It is the seat of Vanderbilt University, Belmont College, Peabody College for Teachers, Fisk University, Meharry Medical School, and other public and private institutions.

The first settlement on the site of Nashville was made in 1780, and, in 1806, the city received its municipal charter. From 1812 to 1815 it was the seat of the state legislature. In 1843, it was made the permanent capital of the state. In the park surrounding the State Capitol is the tomb of James K. Polk. The Hermitage, the former home of Andrew Jackson, is about 10 miles east of the city. In 1864, one of the great battles of the Civil War was fought in the environs of Nashville. Population, 1970, 436,044.

Natural Bridge. A bridge of natural rock spanning Cedar Creek 13 miles southeast of Lexington, Va. It is 90 feet long, 50 to 150 feet wide, and about 215 feet above the creek bed. It consists of horizontal limestone strata, which are the remains of the roof of an underground tunnel or a cave through which the creek once flowed. The bridge is crossed by a public road.

Newark (*nū'ẽrk*). A city of New Jersey, situated on the Passaic River and Newark Bay, about 8 miles west of New York City, with which it is connected by several railways, an electric high speed line, and the Holland and Lincoln vehicular tunnels.

The city extends some 3 miles along the west shore of Newark Bay and about 7 miles up the west bank of the Passaic River, from its mouth in Newark Bay to the suburb of Belleville. The site of the city occupies an area of about 24 square miles. For a mile inland from the water front, the surface is fairly level and it then rises gently in a series of plateaus.

Immediately adjoining the city on the north, west, and southwest is a group of smaller municipalities, including Belleville, Bloomfield, East Orange, Orange, West Orange, South Orange, and Irvington. Opposite Newark, on the east bank of the Passaic, are East Newark, Harrison, and Kearny. These and other suburbs are intimately connected with the city and, with it, form a greater Newark whose total population exceeds 1,000,000.

The port of Newark is a deep water harbor 700 feet wide, extending 7000 feet inland. Because of favorable location and fine transportation facilities, including a subway, Newark has become a great manufacturing center, sometimes styled the "Birmingham of America." Its industries are numerous and varied. Among important products are jewelry, electrical machinery, chemicals, paints, varnishes, malt liquors, ships, and meat products. The city is the headquarters of some of the largest life insurance and fire insurance companies.

Newark is a city of fine buildings, wide streets, and spacious parks. Military Park contains Borglum's colossal sculptural group in bronze known as "The Wars of America." Among Newark's most noted buildings are the Public Library, the County Courthouse, City Hall, Federal Building, Newark College of Rutgers University, and the Roman Catholic Sacred Heart Cathedral. Newark was settled in 1666 by Puritans from Connecticut. It was first called Milford but was soon after given its present name. In 1836, it was chartered as a city. Population, 1970, 382,417.

New Bedford. A seaport and manufacturing city of Massachusetts, situated on the Acushnet River, at its mouth in Buzzards Bay, about 55 miles south of Boston. New Bedford was formerly the principal whaling port in the world. This stage of its history is memorialized by the Bourne Whaling Museum and by a rich collection of whaling material in the public library, one of the first free libraries established in the country. After the decline of the whaling industry, it became the leading city in the United States in the manufacture of cotton yarn and cotton cloth. Less important industries include the manufacture of silk goods, fine tools, sperm and whale oil, rayon, shoes, rope cordage, toys, and rubber and paper goods. Educational institutions include Southeastern Massachusetts University and the Swain School of Design. New Bedford was settled in 1652, on land purchased from Massasoit by a company from Plymouth. Population, 1970, 101,777.

New Britain. A manufacturing city of Connecticut, situated in the central part of the state, about 10 miles southwest of Hartford. Because of its extensive production of cutlery, edged tools, and other kinds of hardware, New Britain is sometimes styled the "Hardware City." Other important manufactures include electrical appliances, knit goods, and machine shop products. The city is the seat of Central Connecticut State College and has a unique World War Memorial. New Britain was settled in 1687 but remained a part of Berlin until 1850, when it was incorporated as a town. In 1871, New Britain received its charter as a city. Population, 1970, 83,441.

New Castle. A manufacturing city of western Pennsylvania, built at the junction of the Shenango and the Neshannock rivers, about 50 miles northeast of Pittsburgh. The city's industrial products include chinaware, bronze bearings, strip steel, tin plate, and clothing. New Castle is situated in a fertile agricultural district, rich in coal, limestone, and other mineral deposits. Population, 1970, 38,559.

New Haven. A city of Connecticut, on an inlet of Long Island Sound, some 70 miles northeast of New York City. It occupies a level site partly enclosed by a range of precipitous hills, from 300 to 400 feet high. While a commercial city with extensive shipping interests, the leading industry is manufacturing. In its exceedingly varied industries, there are more than 600 separate manufacturing establishments. Among important manufactures are firearms, clocks, rubber goods, electrical machinery, and an immense variety of iron and steel goods.

The city is well laid out with many imposing public buildings, beautiful parks, and broad, shaded streets. Because of the great number of elms formerly planted in the older sections, New Haven has been called the "City of Elms." It is the seat of Yale University, founded at Saybrook in 1701 and removed to New Haven in 1716. The Harkness Memorial Tower at Yale is one of the finest Gothic towers erected in modern times. The Yale Bowl seats 70,896 people. The first settlement, made by a company of Puritans in 1638, was known as Quinnipiac, but in 1640 it was renamed New Haven. The city is the burial place of S. F. B. Morse, Eli Whitney, Noah Webster, and other noted men. Population, 1970, 137,707.

NEW ORLEANS (ôr'lê-ănz). The chief city of Louisiana, the commercial metropolis of the Gulf states, and, after New York City, one of the greatest centers of domestic and foreign trade in the United States. It is situated on the Mississippi River 107 miles above its mouth in the Gulf of Mexico.

The city originally was built along the bend of the river in a semicircular curve and became known as the "Crescent City"; later, its growth up the river followed a backward curve toward Lake Borgne and Lake Pontchartrain, which is spanned by two concrete highway bridges, each about 5 miles in length. Lake Pontchartrain is also spanned by a 24-mile causeway, the world's longest overwater highway bridge.

New Orleans is connected with nearly all the important ports of the world by direct steamship lines, the markets of Asia and western South America being accessible through the Panama Canal. The city forms the gateway to the Mississippi Valley, the greatest agricultural region in the world. It has one of the safest harbors in existence, with a deep water canal from the river through the city to Lake Pontchartrain. More than 100 steamers from 400 to 500 feet in length can be berthed along seven miles of steel docks. Besides public wharves, grain elevators, and coal tipples, the port facilities include also a municipally owned and operated belt line railway.

New Orleans is a leading market for cotton, sugar, molasses, coffee, rice, burlaps, cigars, nitrate, sulphur, timber, and cereals, these products being among its principal exports. It is, moreover, one of the principal manufacturing cities in the South. It makes over three-fourths of the men's wash clothing worn in the United States.

The park system of New Orleans includes the 280-acre Audubon Park, City Park, covering 1500 acres, and a 1400-acre "made" area of boulevards, parks, and bathing beaches on the southeast shore of Lake Pontchartrain. The parks are ornamented with palms, live oaks, magnolias, and a profusion of subtropical shrubs and flowers. The newer residential districts have broad streets, spacious grounds, handsome gardens, and pretentious houses. The old French quarter is a city by itself, with narrow streets lined with rows of quaint old dwellings, built over a hundred years ago in the style of the houses of southern Europe. The Mardi Gras carnival, held yearly, is another heritage of the Latin Old World. New Orleans is often styled the "birthplace of jazz."

Among the buildings of historic interest are the Cabildo, the old archbishop's palace, and the Saint Louis Cathedral, one of the best-known churches in the United States. The principal educational institutions are Tulane and Loyola universities and Newcomb Memorial College for Women.

HISTORY. New Orleans was founded by the French in 1718, and came into the possession of the United States with the Louisiana Purchase of 1803, of which territory it was the capital. It remained the capital of the state of Louisiana until 1849. Population, 1970, 591,502.

Newport. A city and seaside resort of Rhode Island. It has a fine harbor which serves as a naval base for the United States Atlantic fleet. Its palatial private residences, public buildings, parks, fountains, and old-time historic structures render it one of the most attractive cities in the country. In Touro Park is the old Stone Mill, or "Round Tower," mentioned by Longfellow in his "Skeleton in Armor." Other features of interest include a Jewish Synagogue dating from 1763. There are various local industries, including manufactures of furniture and brass goods, and extensive fisheries. Population, 1970, 34,562.

Newport News. A city in Virginia, situated on the north side of Hampton Roads near the mouth of the James River, about 12 miles northwest of Norfolk. Newport News is one of the leading ports of the Southern states and an important coaling station. It has enormous shipbuilding yards, drydocks, and ironworks, and is the center of much agricultural and fishing trade. Points of interest include Fort Monroe, Langley Air Field, one of the greatest in the United States, and the Huntington Mariners Museum. Hampton Roads off Newport News was the scene of the battle between the *Monitor* and the *Merrimac* in 1862. Population, 1970, 138,177.

New Rochelle. A city of southern New York on Long Island Sound 16 miles northeast of Grand Central Station in New York City, of which it is a residential suburb. The city consists characteristically of modern residential districts of beautiful parklike contour. Besides several parks and bathing beaches, the city contains 153 "parklets," or open spaces. New Rochelle is named for the French city of La Rochelle, the home of Huguenots who settled on the site in 1688. Iona College is in New Rochelle. Population, 1970, 75,385.

Newton (nū'tŭn). A city of eastern Massachusetts, built on the Charles River, 8 miles west of Boston. Newton is chiefly a residential city but maintains substantial industries. The city is admirably laid out, with fine streets, parks, and drives, and contains many beautiful homes. Among the city's manufacturing establishments are silk mills, printing works, worsted mills, curtain factories, and rubber works. The city is the seat of Boston College, Newton Theological Seminary, and other educational institutions. Newton was settled in 1630 as a part of Cambridge. In 1688, it was made a separate town, called New Cambridge, but, in 1692, it received its present name. In 1873, Newton became a city. Population, 1970, 91,066.

NEW YORK. The chief city of the state of New York, the commercial metropolis of the United States, and the most populous city in the western hemisphere. It is situated on New York Bay at the mouth of the Hudson River, about 205 miles in direct line northeast of the National capital at Washington.

SITE. No metropolis in the world is more strikingly or more beautifully situated than is the city of New York. It is built on three islands, Manhattan, Staten, and Long Island, with a portion on the adjacent mainland, the Bronx.

The Hudson River, here nearly a mile wide, sweeps majestically down the western side of Manhattan and pours its vast waters into the landlocked harbor of New York Bay at the south end of the island. The bay is connected with the ocean by a mile-wide channel running between Long Island on the east and Staten on the west. Between the Bronx and Manhattan is the Harlem River which is connected with the Hudson by Spuyten Duyvil Creek. Separating Manhattan and the Bronx from Long Island is East River, properly an arm of Long Island Sound.

On the west bank of the Hudson, opposite the upper part of the city, the picturesque Palisades tower to a height of from 300 to 400 feet. The surface of the various divisions of the city is fairly level but rises in some parts, as in upper Manhattan, to commanding elevations affording magnificent views of the city and the harbor.

MAIN DIVISIONS. Originally, the city was confined to Manhattan Island. This is 13½ miles long, with a maximum width of 2¼ miles and an area of about 22 square miles. In addition to Manhattan, Greater New York, by consolidation, has since come to embrace Staten Island, called Richmond, with an area of about 60 square miles; the western end of Long Island, known as Brooklyn, 80 square miles; an adjoining part of Long Island, known as Queens, 120 square miles; and the portion of the mainland known as the Bronx, 40 square miles. Each of these divisions includes several small adjacent islands. Officially, New York consists of five boroughs, Manhattan, Brooklyn, Queens, Richmond, and the Bronx, and contains a total area of some 325 square miles.

Manhattan is the heart of New York and contains its great commercial, financial, and mercantile institutions, and also its famous museums, libraries, cathedrals, railway stations, and imposing residences. Brooklyn is a residential district with a large number of industrial establishments. Staten Island is mainly residential, with an increasing number of industries; the Bronx is also chiefly residential, while Queens, containing more than a third of the total area of Greater New York, is the "home" borough. Long Island City, in Queens borough, is its industrial center, while the remainder of the borough is principally a district of suburban homes.

STREETS AND AVENUES. In the older portions of various divisions of the city there are narrow, short, irregular streets. The newer sections, however, have been admirably planned, and contain many magnificent thoroughfares.

At the south end of Manhattan, the streets are cramped and irregular but, north of Washington Square, they cross at right angles. The great, long north-and-south streets, usually 100 feet wide, running lengthwise of the island, are called avenues. The shorter east-and-west thoroughfares, mostly 60 feet wide, are called streets. Differing from the plan of most American cities, the blocks are solid, having practically no alleys.

An exception to this regular street plan is Broadway, the "greatest street in the world." This noted thoroughfare runs diagonally through the city, in a northwesterly direction, from the Battery, at the sea front, to the extreme northern boundary, a distance of about 16 miles. It traverses the entire length of Manhattan Island and continues through the Bronx into Yonkers, completely changing its character in the different portions of the city through which it passes.

Equally famous with Broadway is Fifth Avenue, the most beautiful thoroughfare in the city, and one of the finest streets in the world. It begins at Washington Arch, about a quarter of a mile west of Broadway, and extends northward for 6 miles, crossing to the east of Broadway at 23d street. It is lined with fashionable shops, beautiful churches, elegant clubs, immense hotels, and palatial residences. Above 59th street, it is restricted to residences by a zoning ordinance.

Other beautiful streets are Morningside Drive, which passes Saint John's Cathedral; and Riverside Drive along the Hudson, passing Grant's Tomb and commanding excellent views of the Palisades. A considerable portion of this drive accommodates two levels of traffic.

Beginning at Trinity Church on Broadway and extending eastward to East River is Wall Street, long the money center of America and, since World War I, the chief financial center of the world. In Brooklyn, Ocean Parkway and Flatbush Avenue are magnificent drives; Northern Boulevard, Queens Boulevard, and Hillside Avenue, in Queens, are noteworthy thoroughfares.

PARKS. Lying in the center of Manhattan Island is Central Park, one of the most beautiful pleasure grounds in the world. On its eastern border is the magnificent Metropolitan Museum of Art, and on the west side is the great American Museum of Natural History. This park embraces 840 acres, is largely forested, and contains a reservoir, small lakes, and scores of miles of charming drives, roadways, and footpaths. In it are located the Obelisk, or Cleopatra's Needle, and many fine works of sculpture.

Other important parks are Prospect Park, Brooklyn, with an area of 526 acres, noted for the natural beauty of its wooded hills and broad meadows; Bronx Park, 719 acres, containing superb zoological and botanical gardens; Van Cortlandt Park, embracing 1132 acres and containing immense recreation grounds; Pelham Bay Park, containing ›1788 acres, with a shoreline of 9 miles; and Marine Park, covering 1522 acres.

MONUMENTS. In New York are many of the most noted monuments, memorials, and other fine sculptural works of America. The famous Statue of Liberty, designed by Bartholdi and presented to the American people by the French nation, stands on Bedloe's or Liberty Island in New York Bay. Grant's Tomb, a mausoleum of great dignity, overlooks the Hudson from Riverside Park, as does the beautiful Soldiers' and Sailors' Monument from Riverside drive. At the entrance to Prospect Park, Brooklyn, there is an imposing memorial arch, surmounted by a large quadriga by Macmonnies, erected in honor of the soldiers and sailors of the Civil War.

On the Plaza, at the southeast corner of Central Park, stands an impressive equestrian statue of General Sherman by Saint-Gaudens. By the same noted sculptor is the fine statue of Peter Cooper, at Cooper Union, and the noble monument to David Farragut, in Madison Square.

BUILDINGS. New York excels all other cities in the size, height, elegance, and costliness of its buildings. These include immense commercial structures, towering temples of finance, imposing public edifices, monumental railway stations, beautiful cathedrals and churches, magnificent apartment houses, and palatial residences. There is a greater number of large and costly buildings on Manhattan Island than upon any other equal area on the globe. For miles, the buildings contain from 12 to 30 or more stories, rising from 200 to 500 feet in height, with some towering higher than the pyramids or the loftiest cathedrals.

Among the large number of great commercial structures may be mentioned the Metropolitan Building, 50 stories and 700 feet high; the Woolworth Building, 55 stories, more than 792 feet high; R. C. A. Building at Rockefeller Center, the largest office building in the world, 69 stories, 853 feet high; Bank of the Manhattan Building, 70 stories, 927 feet high; Sixty Wall Tower (Cities Service Building), 67 stories, 950 feet high; the Chrysler Building, 77 stories, 1046 feet high; and the Empire State Building, 102 stories, 1248 feet high.

Prominent among public edifices is the Municipal Building 41 stories high, covering two city blocks and surmounted by a tower and statue which rise to a height of 580 feet. Among structures noted for their architecture are the marble Stock Exchange, the New York Clearing House, the Chamber of Commerce, the Hall of Records, the Tiffany building, the United Nations Secretariat Building, and the New York Public Library.

The Grand Central Station and the Pennsylvania Station were each great achievements of architectural and engineering skill. Other notable buildings include the Metropolitan Museum of Art, the American Museum of Natural History, the Columbia University Library, and the Eighth Regiment Armory. A unique architectural unit is Rockefeller Center, or "Radio City," covering three city blocks. Its ten building units, ornamented with hanging gardens and artificial waterfalls, house elaborate broadcasting and theatrical facilities and magnificent stores and offices.

Among hundreds of beautiful churches may be mentioned Saint Patrick's Cathedral built of white marble with spires rising 332 feet. This ranks among the finest Gothic structures in America. Other noteworthy churches are the cathedral of Saint John the Divine, Saint Thomas's Church, Saint Bartholomew's Church, the Temple Emanu-El, the great church of Saint Paul the Apostle, and the Riverside Church, containing one of the finest carillons of bells in the western hemisphere.

INTERCOMMUNICATION. East River is spanned by 6 bridges, ranking among the largest in the world. Four of these—Brooklyn Bridge, Manhattan Bridge, Williamsburgh Bridge (connecting New York and Brooklyn), and the Triborough Bridge, joining Queens with the Bronx— are suspension bridges. The Queensboro Bridge, connecting New York and Queens, is a cantilever structure. Hell Gate Bridge, an immense steel arch, connects the Bronx with Queens. Staten Island is connected with New Jersey by three bridges, Kill van Kull at Bayonne, Goethals at Elizabeth, and Outerbridge Crossing at Perth Amboy. Washington Memorial Bridge crosses the Hudson and connects 178th Street with the New Jersey shore. The Verrazano-Narrows Bridge stretches across the entrance to New York's harbor from Staten Island to Brooklyn. The world's longest single-span bridge, it was opened in 1964.

An extensive ferry service and two pairs of subway tunnels for electric cars connect Manhattan with Brooklyn. as does also the Brooklyn-Battery vehicular tunnel, and two pairs also connect Manhattan with Queens. The Holland and Lincoln vehicular tunnels. under the Hudson River, connect New York City with Jersey City, and a 3½-mile viaduct connects it with Elizabeth, New Jersey.

Most of New York's local transportation system is municipally owned. The city operates 250 route miles of rapid transit subway lines and 80 miles of bus routes. Running north and south in the narrow island of Manhattan, there are two 4-track subway lines, both of which continue under the East River to Brooklyn where they connect with steam and electric rapid transit to all parts of Long Island. The Long Island railroad transports more commuting passengers than any other railroad in the world.

EDUCATIONAL INSTITUTIONS. New York is the seat of two great universities, Columbia University, on Cathedral Heights, and New York University in the Bronx, overlooking the Harlem River. With the former is affiliated Barnard College, the Teachers' College, and the Horace Mann School. Connected with New York University is the Hall of Fame for noted Americans.

Among many other prominent educational institutions are the College of the City of New York, Hunter College, Manhattan College, Brooklyn College, Fordham University, the College of Saint Francis Xavier, Cooper Union, the College of Physicians and Surgeons, and the Rockefeller Institute for Medical Research. Of great influence in the educational life of the city are the Public Library, with more than 40 branches, the Metropolitan Museum of Art, the Guggenheim Museum, the American Museum of Natural History, the Planetarium and the Brooklyn Institute of Arts and Sciences. The Medical Center on Washington Heights, overlooking the Hudson River, takes the first place among institutions of the kind throughout the world.

TRANSPORTATION. New York Bay, nearly enclosed by islands, forms one of the finest harbors in the world. The city of New York, built around it, has a total water front of some 771 miles, of which more than 345 miles are developed with port facilities. About 100 ocean steamship lines, affording service to all parts of the world, have headquarters in New York. Some 40 lines of river and coastwise steamers likewise operate from the port. New York has water connections to the Great Lakes through the Hudson River and the State Barge Canal. The great railway systems of the New England and the Middle Atlantic states, and also various western railroads, have terminals, either within the city or across the Hudson on the New Jersey shore. The Pennsylvania Railway is connected with New York City by tunnels under the Hudson River.

COMMERCE. New York's commercial supremacy is owing to its magnificent harbor facilities and to its geographical location. The largest ships are accommodated at its wharves, and railway and inland water routes afford quick collection and distribution of goods throughout the richest and most populous region in America. The commerce of New York is several times greater than that of any other port in the New World, and, in value, usually embraces about one-half the total imports and exports of the United States. The volume of the coastwise trade usually greatly exceeds that of the foreign trade. The wholesale and jobbing trade is enormous, as is also the distribution of the city's immense manufactures. In 1936, a zone in Staten Island was made a free port.

FINANCE. During the present century, New York has become the dominant money center of the world, with annual banking transactions aggregating more than $300 billion. Here are located the greatest financial institutions of the country, including powerful banks, trust companies, and insurance companies, the New York clearing house, the stock exchange, the cotton exchange, and casualty, credit, fidelity, and surety companies.

MANUFACTURES. In value, the manufactures of the metropolis exceed those of any other manufacturing center in America. Usually about one-tenth of the total manufactures of the United States is produced in New York City. This supremacy is owing to an immense volume of light manufacturing, for the most part carried on in small factories. The industries are exceedingly diversified, including some 30,000 establishments and representing about 90 per cent of all the industries listed in the country. The largest single product is clothing; more than half of the clothing worn in the United States is made in the city. The second largest industry is the printing and publishing of newspapers, magazines, periodicals, and books. Other important industries are meat packing, sugar refining, petroleum refining, and the manufacture of millinery, lace, fur goods, jewelry, tobacco, drugs, shoes, and machinery.

HISTORY. In 1609, Henry Hudson, employed by the Dutch, sailed up the river which bears his name. Dutch fur traders began operations along the Hudson in 1613 and soon after built a fort, near which the first white settlement developed. The first permanent colonists, mostly Walloons, arrived in 1624. Peter Minuit, in 1626, bought Manhattan Island from its Indian owners for $24, and named the settlement New Amsterdam. There were difficulties with the Indians, but, under the rule of Peter Stuyvesant, 1647-64, the settlement grew to a village of 1000 inhabitants.

In 1664, New Amsterdam was captured by the English, who renamed it New York. Despite political conflicts, the town in 1700 had increased to 5000 inhabitants, about half Dutch and half English. During the Revolutionary War, British armies occupied the town for 7 years, 1776–83. In this unfortunate period, New York lost about half its inhabitants and was largely destroyed by fire. Within 8 years, however, the population trebled, commerce revived, and for a year and a half, 1789–90, New York was the capital of the Federal government. Washington, the first president of the United States, was inaugurated, April 30, 1789, in Federal Hall on Wall Street.

The completion of the Erie Canal in 1825, furnishing a waterway from the Hudson to the Great Lakes, made New York the gateway for the commerce of the rapidly developing nation. This so accelerated the city's growth that, in 1835, New York numbered 200,000 inhabitants. The first railway to the Great Lakes was completed in 1851, and thenceforward the history of New York is a record of continuous and monumental growth.

More recent achievements were the consolidation of the five boroughs into Greater New York, the construction of the subway system with tunnels under East River and the Hudson, and the completion of the gigantic Catskill aqueduct, insuring an adequate water supply to the expanding metropolis. Population, 1970, 7,867,760.

Niagara Falls. The grandest cataract in America and the second largest in the world, being exceeded in combined height and volume only by Victoria Falls in South Africa. It is situated about 22 miles north of Buffalo, New York. The Niagara River in its northerly course of over 26 miles descends 326 feet from the level of Lake Erie to that of Lake Ontario. By far the greater part of this descent occurs at the falls and at the rapids immediately above and below them. For the first 2 miles after leaving Lake Erie the river is troubled and rapid. It then expands into a broad, placid stream, from 1 to 2 miles wide, and encircles several islands.

After flowing nearly 20 miles and descending only about 20 feet, the river suddenly narrows and enters a series of beautiful rapids. In about a half mile the river descends 52 feet, in seething, boiling torrents and eddies in which the whole surface is torn and tossed into white spray. The waters then reach the edge of an abrupt declivity, the Niagara escarpment, and make a sudden plunge to the bottom of an immense gorge. A short distance above the brink of the falls, Goat Island separates the river into two unequal streams. The narrow, shallower one, on the American side, discharges over the American Fall, 167 feet in height and 1060 feet wide. The main part of the river swings to the west of Goat Island and discharges over the Canadian or Horseshoe Fall, 158 feet high, with a deep retreating curve in the center and measuring about 2500 feet along the crest. A feature of interest is the illumination of the cataract each evening by shifting lights of rich and varied color.

The water flowing over the American Fall is from 1 to 4 feet deep, but that plunging over the Horseshoe Fall is estimated at about 20 feet in depth. The main cataract carries over fully 90 per cent of the water, while the American Fall discharges less than 10 per cent. The volume of flow is normally about 500,000 tons of water a minute.

The edge of the American Fall is receding at a rate estimated at from 2 to 7 inches a year. In 1954 hundreds of tons of rock, loosened by the seepage of river water, fell into the gorge from the point of land adjoining the falls. Measurements by the U.S. Geological Survey indicate that the Horseshoe Falls have been receding at the rate of about 5 feet a year for nearly a century. In 1969 the water flowing over the American Fall was temporarily diverted with a cofferdam so that the recession could be studied

with the intention of "repairing" the fall to prevent its rapid erosion.

For about 7 miles below the foot of the falls, the river descends between nearly perpendicular cliffs, 200 to 300 feet high, through a series of magnificent rapids, the famous Niagara Gorge. In width, the gorge varies from 1700 feet, opposite the American Falls, to 700 feet, opposite the Whirlpool. The river at the bottom of the gorge is considerably narrower, with depths believed to range from 100 to 500 feet, and with a speed in some places estimated at 30 miles an hour.

About 3 miles below the falls the river rushes into the Whirlpool. This is a huge circular indentation worn into the Canadian side of the river and surrounded by walls 300 feet high. The river plunges into this great excavation in a northwesterly direction and is forced to leave it in a northeasterly direction, forming one of the most impressive maelstroms in the world. At the end of the gorge, near Lewiston, the river again widens and flows tranquilly for about 7 miles to its mouth in Lake Ontario.

Niagara Falls is the most accessible to the traveler of any of the great cataracts. Fine parks, with many conveniences for the public, have been established on both sides of the river. There is a bridge to Goat Island. An aerial cable tramway spans the chasm over the Whirlpool, giving a unique view of this natural wonder.

While several early French missionaries, visiting the Niagara region, wrote accounts of the falls received from the Indians, the first white man to describe and depict the great cataract was Father Hennepin, who accompanied La Salle to the Niagara frontier in 1678. French domination of the region continued until 1759, when Fort Niagara was surrendered to the British. The region was controlled by the British until 1796 and was the scene of many conflicts during the War of 1812.

Niagara Falls. A manufacturing city of western New York, situated on the Niagara River at the falls from which it takes its name. By utilizing immense power generated at the cataract, the city has developed extensive manufactories and has become an important center of electrochemical industry. Among the leading manufactures are chemicals, electrical machinery, aluminum ware, carborundum, paper and wood pulp, flour, shredded wheat biscuit, roofing materials, and metallurgical products.

The hydroelectric power is developed by the Power Authority of the State of New York as an agent under the St. Lawrence Waterway Treaty of 1950 with Canada. In order to take maximum advantage of the fall, two intakes were constructed 2½ miles above the falls to convey the water about four miles to one of the world's largest power plants, where nearly 2 million kilowatts of power is developed. Only half of the diversionary flow is taken during the day in the tourist season so as to interfere as little as possible with the scenic attraction of the falls. When demand for current is low, the surplus current is used to pump water into an 1800-acre reservoir above the power plant, and this water in turn, in falling back, develops additional current at times of peak demand.

Because of the falls, which rank among the world's greatest scenic wonders, the city is visited yearly by tens of thousands of travelers. Niagara Falls and Suspension Bridge, formerly two villages, were, in 1892, united as the city of Niagara Falls. Population, 1970, 85,615.

Nogales (nö-gä'lĕs). A city on the southern boundary of Arizona, 65 miles south of Tucson. A fence, with gates always open, separates it from the Mexican city of the same name. Nogales is the trade center of a mining and grazing district and is an inland gateway to the western coast of Mexico. A feature of historical interest in the vicinity is the ruin of the Tumacacori Mission. This was founded in 1691 by Father Kino, a Jesuit missionary, was taken charge of by Franciscan fathers in 1769, and is now a national monument. Population, 1970, 8946.

Norfolk. A city and the principal seaport of Virginia, with about 50 miles of waterfront on the Elizabeth River, Hampton Roads, and Chesapeake Bay.

Norfolk, together with Portsmouth, forms the largest naval station in the Union. It is the base for the Atlantic fleet. The harbor is capable of giving anchorage to the largest class of vessels.

A little to the east of the city is a terminus of the Chesapeake Bay bridge-tunnel, completed in 1964 at a cost of $200 million. It provides a 17.6 mile roadway crossing to Cape Charles, the roadway descending from the bridge into tunnels at two points so as to permit passage of ships at these points.

The port carries an extensive shipping trade in cotton, tobacco, lumber, corn, cattle, horses, fish, oysters, fruits, vegetables, and peanuts. The principal manufactures include ships, airplane parts, fertilizers, agricultural implements, lumber, cotton goods, flour, and roasted peanuts.

Among the public buildings may be noted the Custom house, the City Hall, and the Cotton Exchange. The educational establishments include old Dominion University and

Virginia Wesleyan College. Popular seaside resorts nearby include Virginia and Ocean View beaches. Norfolk was first settled in 1682, incorporated as a borough in 1736, and chartered as a city in 1835. Population, 1970, 307,951.

Norwalk. A city of Connecticut, 14 miles southwest of Bridgeport, on Long Island Sound. An industrial center since before the Revolutionary War, Norwalk now manufactures hats, pumps, leather goods, electronic equipment and other items. Norwalk is also a research center and a summer resort. The area is rich in colonial history. Population, 1970, 79,113.

Oakland. The fifth largest city of California, situated on the mainland shore of San Francisco Bay and connected with San Francisco by the 8¼-mile San Francisco-Oakland Bay Bridge. Oakland's metropolitan area extends for 23 miles along the San Francisco Bay eastward to the San Joaquin Valley, consisting of an almost unbroken chain of factories, waterfront industries, commercial trading centers, and residences. Mild year-round temperatures are an outstanding feature of the area.

Oakland is the terminus for three major railroads. Inland waterways and ocean-freight service is provided by the Port of Oakland. The freeway system has also helped to make Oakland a distribution center. Manufactures include processed foods, passenger cars and trucks, office equipment, tin and glass containers, metal products, floor coverings, chemicals, and paints.

Oakland has 65 parks covering 1600 acres. Lake Merritt, a 155-acre body of salt water, is located in the center of the city, surrounded by Lakeside Park. A recent addition to the city is the new $9 million Oakland Museum, featuring a design developed by a competition of the world's leading architects. Among Oakland's educational institutions are Mills College for women, the College of the Holy Names, and the California College of Arts and Crafts. Oakland was founded on a Spanish grant in 1850, was incorporated as a town in 1852, and as a city in 1854. Population, 1970, 361,561.

Oak Park. A village of northeastern Illinois, about nine miles west of the center of Chicago, of which it is a residential suburb. Oak Park was incorporated in 1901. Population, 1970, 62,511.

Oak Ridge. A community in eastern Tennessee, one of the three so-called "atomic cities," which mushroomed during World War II, when it became a center for the development of materials for the atomic bomb. At that time it had an estimated population of 75,000. Oak Ridge sprang from practically nothing, as did also the other two places, Richland, Washington, and Los Alamos, New Mexico. Population, 1970, 28,319.

Oberlin. A town of northeastern Ohio, situated about 35 miles southwest of Cleveland. While it conducts a substantial trade with the surrounding agricultural districts and has local industries, it is chiefly noted as the seat of Oberlin College, the first American college to adopt coeducation. The town is well laid out, with broad, shady streets and fine residences. Population, 1970, 8761.

Ogden. The second largest city of Utah, situated at the junction of the Ogden and Weber rivers, at the foot of the Wasatch Mountains, about 35 miles north of Salt Lake City. It is noted for its picturesque scenery. A boulevard passes through the scenic Ogden Canyon a distance of 8 miles to Ogden Valley and Pine View Dam, which afford various recreational opportunities. Ogden is the distributing center of a productive agricultural, fruit growing, and stock raising district. Electricity for light, heat, and industrial purposes is supplied to the city by the waterfalls from surrounding canyons. Meat packing, fruit and vegetable canning, oil refining, and the manufacture of beet sugar and flour are among the chief industries. Ogden was founded in 1848 and in 1850, under the direction of Brigham Young, was laid out as a city. Population, 1970 69,478.

Oklahoma City. The capital of Oklahoma, situated on the north branch of the Canadian River in the central part of the state. Lying in the midst of a rich oil producing, agricultural, and stock raising country, the city has grown into a community of diverse industry, aviation, manufacturing, distribution, petroleum, utilities, transportation, science and medicine, wholesale and retail trade, finance and various commercial enterprises, and business services. The city's 83 parks and playgrounds cover 9924 acres. An architecturally outstanding addition to the capitol, in Ionic style, and to many large business buildings, is the National Cowboy Hall of Fame and Museum. Oklahoma City was granted its charter in 1891 and was made capital of the state in 1910. Population, 1970, 356,661.

Old Point Comfort. A favorite watering place in Virginia, situated on a neck of land where Hampton Roads at the mouth of the James River joins Chesapeake Bay. Fort Monroe is situated here.

Olympia. The capital of the state of Washington, situated on the southernmost inlet of Puget Sound. The city is the port for a district rich in lumber and in agricultural products. Industries include boat building, the manufacture of plywood, the brewing of beer, and the oyster industry. Manufacturing interests are promoted by the abundant hydroelectric power available, the chief industry being the production of lumber. The noteworthy buildings include the Capitol, the Federal Building, and four other governmental buildings costing in all $15 million. The first settlement was made at Olympia in 1845. The town was laid out in 1851, and became the territorial capital in 1853. Population, 1970, 23,111.

Omaha. The chief city of Nebraska, situated on a commanding site on the west bank of the Missouri River, opposite Council Bluffs, Iowa.

Omaha owes its position as the commercial and manufacturing metropolis of the state to the fact that it is one of the greatest gateways of the West, having the facilities afforded by several great railroad systems and the deepened channel of the Missouri River. The industries of the city, especially those based on agricultural products, are enormous. Its live stock market is the second in the world, while its creameries and macaroni factories are among the largest in the country. It is one of the greatest meat packing centers in the United States. Other industries and manufactures include ore smelting and refining, railway car repairing, flour, steam engines, machinery, and dairy equipment. It is also an insurance center.

Omaha has 3646 acres of parks and many fine public buildings. Among the city's numerous educational institutions may be mentioned the University of Nebraska at Omaha, Creighton University, and the Joslyn Memorial Art Museum. From 1854, the date of the first permanent settlement, to 1867, Omaha was the capital of Nebraska. Population, 1970, 347,328.

Oraibi (*ō-ri′bĭ*). A village of the Hopi Indians in northeastern Arizona, believed to be the oldest continuously inhabited community in the United States. It lies about 100 miles north of Winslow. The community existed as early as 1370, this fact being inferred from a study of the annual growth rings of timbers in the ruins. Population about 100.

Orlando. A city and winter resort of Florida, situated amidst numerous small lakes, some 2000 in all, about 40 miles inland from the approximate center of the state's Atlantic coastline. There are 33 lakes within the corporate limits. Palms, magnolias, and laurels impart a subtropical beauty which joins with the mild climate in attracting winter visitors.

Orlando lies in the center of a rich citrus fruit country, which also produces truck crops and raises cattle. Its primary industries are processing citrus fruits and the manufacture of electronic and defense equipment. Educational institutions include Rollins College and Florida Technological University. Population, 1970, 99,006.

Oshkosh. A city of eastern Wisconsin, situated on the western shore of Lake Winnebago at Fox River, about 75 miles north of Milwaukee. It is located in a once densely wooded region, and the woodworking industry is still a leading commercial interest of the city. Other industries include the manufacture of furniture, travel goods, overalls, and trucks, Oshkosh is a well-known pleasure resort. Lake Winnebago is noted for its game fishing; yachting in the summer and ice boating in the winter are favorite sports. Population, 1970, 53,221.

Pago Pago (*pang′ō-pang′ō*). A fine natural harbor on the south coast of Tutuila, principal island of the American Samoa group. On the shores of this bay are the village of Pago Pago, government offices in the villages of Fagatogo (the constitutional seat of government), business districts, and key industries. Chief exports are copra and canned tuna. Population 1970, 3800 in the bay area—more than 29,000 for all of American Samoa.

Painted Desert. An area of plateaus and low mesas in north central Arizona. It extends from the top of the Marble Canyon of the Colorado River southeastward along the east side of the valley of the Little Colorado for about 100 miles, varying in width from 15 to 40 miles. At the south, it ends near the Santa Fe railway, which crosses it between Holbrook and Winslow. This desert lies at an altitude of about 5000 feet and has an exceedingly arid climate. In consequence, vegetation is so scant that vast areas of rocks are bare or very nearly so. These rocks, mostly Triassic shales and sandstones, exhibit a great variety of colors, whence the name "painted."

Situated on the margin of this desert, about 60 miles north of Winslow, are the seven villages of the Hopi Indians, the best known of which are Walpi and Oraibi. See *Walpi*.

Palisades, The. The name given to a series of massive cliffs on the west bank of the Hudson River. From near Haverstraw, New York, these extend south to Weehawken, New Jersey, a distance of about 30 miles. For the most part, these precipitous cliffs rise almost directly from the water's edge, varying in height from 200 to 550 feet. They consist of basaltic trap rock or diabase, which exhibits marked columnar effects, forming a striking feature in the beautiful scenery of the lower Hudson. The Palisades Interstate Park in New York and New Jersey embraces some of the finest portions of the Palisades.

Palm Beach. A noted winter resort on the southeast coast of Florida, about 64 miles north of Miami. It is situated on Lake Worth, opposite West Palm Beach, the nearest railway town. Its delightful climate, together with its bathing, boating, and fishing facilities, makes Palm Beach one of the most desirable of pleasure haunts. Palatial hotels, spacious parks, and golf links attract thousands of visitors. Population, 1970, 9086.

Palm Canyon. A narrow, rocky gorge opening upon the extreme western end of the Colorado Desert, at the southeastern base of San Jacinto Mountain, about 7 miles south of Palm Springs, California. Near the mouth of this canyon, growing along the small watercourse at its bottom, is one of the largest existing groves of the stately Washington palm, many trees being from 40 to 60 feet high. Their brilliant green foliage makes a striking contrast with the arid, barren rocks forming the canyon walls.

Palo Alto (păl′ō ăl′tō). A city 32 miles south of San Francisco, California. Favored by location and climate as a residential site, it is noted as a center of education and research. Large areas of the city are occupied by Stanford University, with its Hoover library of history, its medical center, its art gallery, and its research laboratories, particularly in electronics and biophysics. Some local industries are related to the research in high-energy physics. Population, 1970, 55,768.

Parkersburg. A city of West Virginia, located on the Ohio River, at the mouth of the Little Kanawha, in a region rich in oil, coal, natural gas, and fire-clay. Its manufactures include glass, petroleum products, chemicals, viscose, rayon, lumber, steel products, earthenware, and electrical porcelain. Besides having river and rail transportation, it is an important highway center, being situated at the junction of U.S. routes 50 and 21. Parkersburg was founded in 1789. Population, 1970, 44,208.

Pasadena. A residential city and widely known winter resort of southern California, northeast of Los Angeles and touching its boundaries at several points. It occupies a beautiful site in the foothills of the Sierra Madre, in a region luxuriant with palms, orange groves, eucalyptus, and other subtropical vegetation. The city is noted for its spacious avenues, fine public buildings, and handsome residences, and is the seat of many educational institutions, including the California Institute of Technology.

Among the many features of interest within or near the city are the Huntington Library and Art Gallery, the Rose Bowl, Mount Wilson Observatory, a beautiful public library with outdoor reading rooms, Mount Lowe, San Gabriel Mission, and a mile-long avenue of deodars known as "Christmas Tree Lane." Its 13 parks cover 500 acres, the largest, Brookside, being within a great natural gorge, the Arroyo Seco, which is spanned at Colorado Street by one of the country's most beautiful bridges. The city is widely known for its annual festival, called the "Tournament of Roses," celebrated on New Year's Day. In 1874, a colony from Indianapolis, Ind. settled on the site of Pasadena and began raising fruit; in 1886, Pasadena received its charter as a city. Population, 1970, 113,327.

Pasadena. A large residential suburb of Houston, Texas, Pasadena was the site of the capture of the Mexican General Santa Anna after the Battle of San Jacinto. Population, 1970, 89,277.

Passaic (pă-sā′ĭk). A manufacturing city of New Jersey, situated on the Passaic River, about 12 miles northwest of New York City. The chief industry is the manufacture of woolen and worsted goods. Passaic is said to make one-third of the handkerchiefs produced in the United States. Other important industrial establishments include cigar factories, rubber, metal, and dye works. Population, 1970, 55,124.

Paterson. A city of New Jersey, located on the Passaic River, about 16 miles northwest of New York City. Immense power, developed from Passaic Falls, 50 feet in height, is utilized in the city's numerous industries. Paterson is the leading producer of silk fabrics in the United States. It has also cotton and woolen mills, dyeing and finishing establishments, airplane engine factories, and machine shops.

Paterson owes the beginnings of its great industrial growth to the "Society for Establishing Useful Manufactures," promoted largely through the efforts of Alexander Hamilton, in 1791, when he was secretary of the treasury. In 1792, the site, "by the Great Falls of the Passaic," was chosen for the location of the mills which were to be used in bringing about the commercial independence of the United States from Europe. Population, 1970, 144,824.

Pawtucket. A city of Rhode Island, built on both banks of the Pawtucket River, about 4 miles northeast of

Providence. The city was the birthplace of the cotton goods industry of the United States. The original mill, founded by Samuel Slater in 1790, is now a museum. Pawtucket produces wire and cable, textiles, toys, and electronic components. Its fine parks, public squares, and imposing bridges across the river serve to make Pawtucket an attractive city. Population, 1970, 76,984.

Pendleton. A city of northeastern Oregon, on the Umatilla River, 225 miles east of Portland. Pendleton is the supply center for the Umatilla irrigation district and has an extensive trade in grain, fruit, and live stock. Pendleton has become widely known through its annual exhibition festival "The Round-Up." Population, 1970, 13,197.

Pensacola. A seaport of Florida, situated on Pensacola Bay, 10 miles north of the Gulf of Mexico. It has a fine landlocked harbor and conducts an extensive domestic trade. Industrial products include paper, fertilizers, wood products, cottonseed oil, and naval stores. A huge navy aviation school is located there. The city was settled by Spaniards in 1559. Points of interest include forts Barrancas, San Carlos, and Pickens, and numerous recreational facilities. Population, 1970, 59,507.

Peoria (pê-ō′rĭ-à). A manufacturing city of Illinois, built on the west bank of the Illinois River, 160 miles southwest of Chicago. Peoria is the commercial center of a rich agricultural district, in close proximity to large coal fields. The manufactures include agricultural implements, packed meats, paper goods, stoves, barrels, woven wire fence, cordage, stock foods, and chemicals. Peoria has one of the largest truck-in stockyards in the country. Parks cover about 6810 acres. Lake Peoria and other natural features of the city's environment provide beautiful scenery within and around it. The city is the seat of Bradley University. Population, 1970, 126,963.

Pepin (pē′pĭn), **Lake.** An expansion of the upper Mississippi River, situated in a fine scenic region, about 30 miles south of Saint Paul, Minnesota. The lake is about 30 miles long and from 1 to 2 miles wide. It is surrounded by imposing bluffs of limestone, rising about 400 feet above the water and carved by erosion into many remarkable shapes. The town of Red Wing with a population, 1970, of 10,441 is situated at its northern end.

Perth Amboy. A city of eastern New Jersey, located on Raritan Bay, about 20 miles southwest of New York City. Perth Amboy, by reason of its good harbor, has extensive shipping interests, and is an important commercial and industrial center. Among the chief industries are chemical works, copper and silver refineries, and the manufacture of clothing and hats. The city is connected with South Amboy by the Victory Bridge, and with Staten Island by a bridge completed in 1928 at a cost of $16 million. Perth Amboy was settled in 1683, and, for a long period, was the capital of New Jersey province. It became a city in 1718. Population, 1970, 38,793.

Petersburg. A city of southeastern Virginia, situated on the south bank of the Appomattox River, 23 miles south of Richmond. Its chief industries consist of the manufacture of tobacco products, trunks, optical lenses, and cotton clothing. The city is located in an extensive tobacco growing region at the northern end of the peanut belt, and carries on a substantial trade in these products. Historic reminders of the Civil War are found in the Battlefield National Park and the Lee Memorial Park. Population, 1970, 36,103.

Petrified Forests. See *Adamana*.

PHILADELPHIA. The chief city of Pennsylvania, and the fourth most populous in the United States. It is situated at the junction of the Schuylkill and the Delaware River, some 50 miles from the mouth of the Delaware in Delaware Bay and 85 miles by water from the Atlantic Ocean.

SITE. From the confluence of the rivers, Philadelphia extends northerly along the Schuylkill for more than 20 miles and northeasterly along the Delaware for nearly the same distance, and has an irregular northern boundary. The site embraces a total area of about 130 square miles. At the south, between the two rivers, the surface is level. The old city was laid out on this peninsula. This section is now the principal business center.

To the north, the surface rises, culminating in Chestnut hill, 430 feet high, and other similar eminences. The manufacturing districts were developed in this northern area, with Germantown, now within the city limits, occupying the heights above them. That section west of the Schuylkill river is called West Philadelphia and is largely residential.

STREETS. Philadelphia was the first modern city to be

laid out, with broad, long, straight streets, intersecting at right angles, and with small parks and squares located at suitable intervals.

Broad Street, one of the greatest streets of America, bisects the city from north to south. The Benjamin Franklin Parkway extends northwest from the City Hall at Broad and Market streets. Fountains, shade trees, and flower beds make this drive one of the most beautiful in the world.

PARKS AND MONUMENTS. The city park system, including 140 parks, squares, and parkways, embraces an area of about 8000 acres. The finest unit is Fairmount Park, the largest municipal park in the nation, containing some 3600 acres along the Schuylkill River, and connected with the City Hall by the magnificent Benjamin Franklin Parkway. Wissahickon Drive, 6 miles in length, along Wissahickon Creek in Fairmount Park is regarded as one of the finest scenic drives within the limits of an American city. Among other important parks are League Island, 300 acres; Pennypack, 726 acres; Tacony, 250 acres; Cobb's Creek, 288 acres; Hunting, 86 acres; Burkolme, 69 acres; Whitehall Commons, 35 acres; Bartram's Garden, 27 acres; and the Cope Arboretum, 22 acres. Roosevelt Boulevard, 300 feet wide, is a part of the Lincoln Highway.

Important monuments are the Soldiers' and Sailors' Memorial in Fairmount Park, the imposing Washington Monument at the main entrance to the park, and the World War Memorial on the Parkway. Noted statues within the commercial district are: of Washington, in front of Independence Hall; of Franklin, at the Post Office; and of Girard, Muhlenberg, Leidy, and McClellan, on the city hall plaza. On the plaza stands also Saint-Gaudens's statue of "The Pilgrim." Other noteworthy sculptural works in various parts of the city are Wolff's "Wounded Lioness," Remington's "Cowboy," and statues of Lincoln, Grant, Meade, Garfield, Columbus, Goethe, Schiller, Humboldt, and Joan of Arc.

BUILDINGS. The monumental City Hall, an immense marble structure, is about 470 feet square, and covers 4½ acres. The tower, some 548 feet high, is surmounted by a colossal statue of William Penn.

Among the older buildings, Christ Church and Independence Hall exemplify the Colonial style of architecture, the buildings of Girard College illustrate the Neo-Greek style, and Saint Mark's Church is an example of the Gothic.

United States government buildings include the Federal Building; the United States Mint, one of the greatest in the world; the Post Office; and the Customhouse. Other noteworthy structures include the Reading depot, the immense Pennsylvania railroad station, costing over $100 million, the $16 million Museum of Art on an eminence at the end of the Parkway, and Convention Hall. Among numerous fine commercial buildings may be mentioned the Philadelphia Savings Fund, new Penn Center Plaza buildings, the Girard Trust, the Curtis, the Bell Telephone, the Arcade, the Atlantic, the Morris, and the 35-story Lewis tower, and the Wanamaker, the Gimbel Brothers, the Strawbridge and Clothier, and the Lit Brothers stores. A stadium seating 100,000 people, is a legacy of the Sesquicentennial Exposition, held in 1926 in south Philadelphia.

HISTORIC STRUCTURES. No city in the United States, except Boston, has preserved a larger number of important buildings associated with the early history of the nation. Chief among these is Independence Hall, built 1729–34, America's most famous landmark. In this notable building, the second and the third Continental Congress met; here Washington was chosen commander in chief; in it the Declaration of Independence was signed; and from its tower the Liberty bell, still preserved in the building, pealed forth its message of freedom.

To the west of Independence Hall is Congress Hall, where the United States Congress met from 1790 to 1800, and where George Washington, in 1793, and John Adams, in 1797, were inaugurated. East of Independence Hall is the old City Hall, first occupied in 1791, now used as a historical museum. The three buildings—Independence Hall, Congress Hall, and the old City Hall—form what is known as the State House group in Independence Square. A mall around the group is a national monument.

In the same vicinity is Carpenters Hall, where, in 1774, the first Continental Congress met, and where, in 1787, the Constitutional convention framed the Constitution of the United States. On Arch Street stands the home of Betsy Ross, who is said to have made the first American flag.

Among historic churches are Old Swedes' Church, built 1698–1700; Christ Church, begun in 1727; Old Saint Joseph's Church, dating from 1729; and Saint Mary's Church, built in 1762.

The Penn Mansion, built in 1682, was the first brick house erected in Philadelphia. It originally stood between Market and Chestnut streets, in the heart of the city. With the encroachment of great business structures, it was taken down and carefully re-erected in Fairmount Park.

EDUCATIONAL INSTITUTIONS. Philadelphia is the seat of Temple University, the University of Pennsylvania, and Drexel Institute. It is also a noted center of medical and dental education. Among its prominent medical schools are the Jefferson, the Hahnemann, the Woman's Medical College, and the medical departments of Temple and Pennsylvania universities, which also have important dental schools. Other noteworthy institutions are the planetarium, the schools of the Pennsylvania Academy of Fine Arts, the Franklin Institute, the Curtis Institute of Music, the Spring Garden Institute, the Public Library, Rodin Musuem, the Franklin Memorial Museum of Graphic Arts, Girard College, La Salle College, Saint Joseph's College, and the William Penn Charter School, founded in 1701. In the suburbs are Bryn Mawr, Haverford, Villanova and Swarthmore colleges, Ogontz School, and Overbrook Seminary.

TRANSPORTATION. Although ships from its wharves sail nearly 85 miles before entering the ocean, Philadelphia is an important seaport. It is the largest fresh water port in the world and America's second busiest. It has more than 35 miles of water front on the Delaware River, which admits the passage of ocean-going ships. The Schuylkill is also navigable.

Philadelphia is also a great railroad center, with a huge network of lines extending, not only into the nearby coal and iron districts, but also into the Ohio and the Mississippi valley and into the South. The city is served chiefly by the Pennsylvania, the Reading, and the Baltimore and Ohio systems, and has the most direct connections with the Middle West of any great Atlantic port. Two municipal airports, including International Airport, rank Philadelphia as a leading aviation center for foreign and domestic flights. Eleven major airlines, including a number of jet lines, provide the city with nearly 400 flights daily.

Local transportation consists of an immense system of surface electric railways, supplemented by both subway and elevated high-speed lines, together with an extensive electric suburban service. Subways beneath Broad Street, Ridge Avenue, Eighth and Locust streets were constructed at a cost in excess of $140 million.

Of numerous fine bridges, the most noteworthy are the Fairmount Avenue bridge, a double-deck truss structure completed in 1895, the great Benjamin Franklin Bridge across the Delaware River, which was completed in 1926 at a cost of nearly $25 million, and the Walt Whitman Bridge over the same river, completed in 1957 and costing $86 million.

COMMERCE. Philadelphia's high rank as a commercial city is primarily owing to its importance as a port; and its favorable location near vast supplies of raw materials has led to the development of immense industries. The city ranks first among the leading ports of the United States in the value of its foreign import commerce, and conducts a large coastwise trade, especially in oil and coal. Hog Island was purchased from the Federal government by the city in 1930 to be made into a huge sea, rail, and air terminal.

MANUFACTURES. Three factors have made Philadelphia a great manufacturing center—nearness to the sources of raw materials, its advantageous situation as the natural outlet of great coal and iron fields, and excellent transportation facilities.

The city has the largest shipbuilding plant in the United States. The city leads in the quantity of rolling mill, foundry, and machine shop products, and in the manufacture of hats, carpets, and hosiery. In production of woolen and worsted goods, leather goods, and chemicals, in printing and publishing of books, newspapers, and periodicals, and in sugar refining, Philadelphia ranks among the chief manufacturing centers of the country. The League Island navy yard plant includes one of the country's largest aircraft factories.

HISTORY. The earliest settlement within the limits of Philadelphia was made in 1636 by a company of Swedes. Late in 1681, William Markham, deputy governor for William Penn, organized an English settlement, and, in 1682, under Penn's supervision, the city was laid out and named. In 1683, a colony of Germans, invited by Penn, settled at Germantown, now a part of the city. In 1723, Benjamin Franklin came to Philadelphia, and in 1729 began the publication of the *Pennsylvania Gazette*. Philadelphia took a leading part in resisting British aggression, and the most important official events of the Revolutionary War occurred in the city. The battle of Germantown was fought in 1777. Philadelphia was occupied by British armies, 1777–78, while Washington's army was at Valley Forge.

Philadelphia was the capital of Pennsylvania from 1683 to 1799, was the seat of the Federal government, 1790–1800, and was the financial center of the country until 1836. The first daily newspaper in the United States, the *Pennsylvania Packet*, appeared in Philadelphia in 1784. The Centennial Exposition, celebrating the centenary of American independence, was held in Fairmount Park in 1876. Philadelphia is called the "Quaker City" and also the "City of Brotherly Love," the latter being the meaning of its name, which is Greek. A popular New Year festivity in Philadelphia is the Mummers parade, a survival from an Old-World custom with modifications coming from American pioneer life. Population, 1970, 1,948,609.

Phoenix. The capital of Arizona, in the south central part of the state, about 400 miles east of Los Angeles. Phoenix is the commercial center of the Salt River Valley, the most productive agricultural region in the state. After the immense extension of irrigation following the construction of the Roosevelt Dam in 1911, the city grew rapidly. Among the crops are Egyptian cotton, alfalfa, cereals, oranges, grapefruit, figs, olives, cantaloupes, strawberries, and winter vegetables. The total value of the crops produced in Maricopa County, of which Phoenix is the county seat, far exceeds that of all the remainder of the state.

The city lies in a wide, irrigated plain surrounded by mountains. It has a mountain park of 14,000 acres 6 miles to the south. Its broad streets are ornamented with palms and other subtropical plants. Prominent public buildings are the Capitol and the City Library. By reason of its dry, salubrious climate, Phoenix is an important winter resort. In the vicinity are numerous points of interest, including Cactus Park, petroglyphics, and the ruins of Aztec community houses. Phoenix was settled in 1870 and became the capital of the territory in 1889. Population, 1970, 581,562.

Piedmont. The name used in the United States to designate that part of the Atlantic plain which lies between the low, flat coastal plain and the true Appalachian highland. It consists chiefly of rolling, rugged lands with deeply eroded valleys. The rocks are a harder formation than those underlying the coastal plain. In consequence, there is a definite line of escarpments, over which most of the rivers descend in rapids or cataracts. This is known as the "fall line." The piedmont plain reaches its greatest extent in Virginia, South Carolina, and North Carolina, being about 300 miles wide in the latter state.

Pierre (*pēr*). The capital of South Dakota, situated on the Missouri River in the central part of the state. It is located in an agricultural and stock raising district and is an important cattle shipping center. Besides the Capitol, Pierre has the State Library, a Federal school for Indians, and a fine Federal Building. The city's parks include the 1500-acre Farm Island in the Missouri River. Four miles upstream is Oahe Dam, the world's largest earth-rolled dam. Fort Pierre, established in 1832, was for many years the chief fur trading post of the Upper Missouri River country. Pierre was laid out in 1880 and was incorporated in 1883. Population, 1970, 9699.

Pikes Peak. A mountain in Colorado, 14,108 feet high, situated in the easternmost range of the Rockies immediately west of Colorado Springs. It was discovered in 1806 by General Zebulon M. Pike of the United States army, and was first successfully ascended in 1819 by Major S. H. Long. In 1891, a cogwheel railway was completed to the summit, which is now reached also by a well constructed automobile road.

While not the highest mountain in Colorado, Pikes Peak is one of the most majestic and imposing. Pine and spruce forests cover the slopes to an elevation of about 11,700 feet, above which there is a fringe of beautiful alpine flowering plants bordering the snow. The summit consists of bare granite rocks. The view from the top is one of unusual magnificence, including rugged mountains, vast plains, and numerous lakes and rivers in a landscape which extends 100 miles in all directions.

Pine Bluff. A distribution center for an agricultural region that produces cotton, livestock, and lumber, situated about 45 miles southeast of Little Rock, Arkansas. Most of the industry within the city is related to the products grown in the area. Pine Bluff is the seat of Arkansas Agricultural, Mechanical, and Normal College. Local residents claim the Civil War actually began in Pine Bluff. Population, 1970, 57,389.

Pinehurst. A noted winter resort of southern North Carolina, about 60 miles southwest of Raleigh. It is 125 miles from the seacoast and 13½ hours ride by rail from New York City, and possesses a mild and equable climate. It was founded as a winter resort in 1895 by James W. Tufts, of Boston, and is famous for the beauty and excellence of its parks, bridle paths, polo grounds, golf links, tennis courts, and other facilities for recreation. The

permanent residential population is about 1500, but the winter visitors number 10,000 or more annually.

Piqua (*pĭk'wā*). A city in Miami County, Ohio, about 70 miles west of Columbus, in the center of a rich agricultural district. Its manufactures include knit underwear, walnut veneer, industrial fans and heating equipment, and other wood products. The first settlement was made in 1797. The outpost known as Fort Piqua, at this point, was an important supply base during the War of 1812. Population, 1970, 20,714.

PITTSBURGH. A city of Pennsylvania, situated at the junction of the Monongahela and Allegheny rivers, which here unite to form the Ohio. Pittsburgh lies in southwestern Pennsylvania, about 340 miles west of Philadelphia.

SITE. Pittsburgh occupies the most irregular and uneven site of any on which a great American city is built. The three rivers flow through deep narrow valleys and the highlands bordering upon them are broken into a large number of hills. These rise to heights of from 500 to 740 feet above the rivers and are separated by great ravines.

The Monongahela River, from the southeast, is joined by the Allegheny, from the northeast; and the Ohio River, formed by their union, flows northwesterly to the city limits. The chief business district and the greater part of the city lies between the Monongahela and the Allegheny.

By annexation, there have been absorbed into the city more than 40 boroughs and townships. The names of many of these are still in common use locally, as, for example, Esplen, Beltzhoover, Sheraden, and Spring Garden.

STREETS AND BUILDINGS. After World War II, Pittsburgh began a rebuilding program which converted the older downtown section into a "golden triangle." A 35-acre Point Park was created, and a civic arena was built with a retractable stainless-steel dome 415 feet in diameter and 136 feet high. The Boulevard of the Allies, a magnificent roadway overlooking the Monongahela, sweeps along the precipitous face of a cliff eastward from the business district to Forbes Avenue, which leads to Schenley Park.

By reason of its extremely hilly site, Pittsburgh has perhaps more bridges and viaducts than any other city in the world. The city owns and maintains over 125, including the Liberty bridge, which connects the business section with the South Hills district via the Liberty tubes. These are twin tubes 5714 feet long and cost nearly $6 million to construct. The Bloomfield bridge, spanning a deep valley between Herron Hill and the Bloomfield district, is nearly a mile long. The Larimer Avenue viaduct and the George Westinghouse bridge in East Pittsburgh have concrete arches ranking among the longest in America.

The commercial district, largely concentrated in "The Point," where the Monongahela and Allegheny rivers converge, is noted for its many fine office buildings of the skyscraper type, including the Grant, Koppers, Gulf, and Gateway Center buildings. Other imposing structures are the Courthouse, the Federal Building, Saint Paul's Cathedral, and Trinity Church.

PARKS. The municipal park system includes 24 parks, covering a total area of more than 6000 acres. Of these, the finest is Schenley Park containing, within its 422 acres, the Carnegie Institute and Library, and the Phipps Conservatory. Highland Park, covering 366 acres, commands a superb panoramic view of the Allegheny valley. In this park, which contains a large zoological garden, there is a memorial building to Stephen C. Foster, author of "Old Folks at Home," who was born and lived in Pittsburgh. At the entrance of Riverview Park is the Allegheny Observatory. Other noteworthy parks are McKinley, Grandview, and Allegheny.

PUBLIC INSTITUTIONS. Foremost among the public institutions of Pittsburgh are the magnificent buildings of the Carnegie Institute, which includes library, museum, art gallery, and music hall. This beautiful structure, which covers nearly 6 acres, is built in the Italian Renaissance style. Memorial Hall, containing a war museum and a large auditorium, is a notable structure. The Cathedral of Learning, a 40-story building 523 feet high and costing $6 million, houses the University of Pittsburgh. The Phipps Conservatory is one of the largest in America. All the above and many other buildings constitute a civic educational and social center at the entrance to Schenley Park.

EDUCATION. The chief educational institutions of the city are the University of Pittsburgh. Carnegie-Mellon University, Duquesne University, Chatham College, the Allegheny Observatory, and the Buhl Planetarium and Institute of Popular Science.

TRANSPORTATION. Transportation, provided by the rivers and by railroads, and abundant fuel, in the form of coal, petroleum, and natural gas from nearby fields, are some of the factors which have made the city of Pittsburgh one of the great "workshops of the world." The rivers afford connections with an immense system of inland waterways, including not only those of the state, but also those of the Midwest and the South. There is extensive river traffic between Pittsburgh and Cincinnati, Saint Louis, and New Orleans. The city is served by three passenger and five freight railway carriers. Because of the character of the commodities handled, largely coal, ores, and iron and steel products, the tonnage handled at Pittsburgh greatly exceeds that of any other inland river port.

MANUFACTURES. Pittsburgh, long known as "Steel City," is one of the leading centers of the world for the manufacture of iron and steel. About one-fifth of the steel made in the Western hemisphere is made in the Pittsburgh district. Pittsburgh leads all other cities in the manufacture of steel rails, aluminum, pressed steel cars, iron pipe and tubing, and pressed steel plates for shipbuilding. The city is also the chief center in the U.S. for the manufacture of coke, plate glass, window glass, and bottles, and produces a high quality of optical glass. Other important manufactures include aluminum wares, bronze and copper wares, refined petroleum, and aerospace materials. Adjacent to Pittsburgh is the world's first full-scale nuclear plant.

HISTORY. In colonial times, the vicinity of Pittsburgh was the scene of many struggles with the French and Indians. In 1753, the site of Pittsburgh was visited by George Washington who regarded it "extremely well situated for a fort." The French and Indians, however, drove off the Virginians, and built Fort Duquesne. Endeavoring, in 1755, to capture it, Braddock, with a strong British force, met disastrous defeat. In 1758, General Forbes, marching from Philadelphia, took the fort, and, at Washington's suggestion, renamed it in honor of William Pitt. The Block House, built in 1759, the oldest building in the city, is preserved as a relic of colonial days. Pittsburgh was laid out in 1784, was incorporated in 1794, and became a city in 1816. Population, 1970, 520,117.

Pittsfield. A city of western Massachusetts, situated in the Berkshire valley, near Pontoosuc Lake, with a background of fine mountain scenery. It is the largest city in the Berkshire Hills region, and is particularly noted for its wide, shaded streets, fine public buildings, and historic tradition. Its Museum of Natural History and Fine Arts contains the "one hoss shay," made famous by Oliver Wendell Holmes's poem. Holmes, Melville, and Longfellow resided for a time at Pittsfield, and H. W. Shaw ("Josh Billings") lived nearby. The city's industries produce plastics, transformers, bank note paper, textiles, machine tools, and silk. Population, 1970, 57,020.

Plymouth. A town on Plymouth harbor, Massachusetts, about 37 miles southeast of Boston. Founded by the Pilgrim Fathers in 1620, it is the oldest town in New England. Plymouth Rock, on which the Pilgrims are said to have landed, is preserved under a beautiful portico. Pilgrim Hall contains many interesting relics and historical paintings. A full-sized replica of the *Mayflower* has been moored at State Pier. The city is a port of entry, has varied local manufactures, and ships large quantities of cranberries grown in the vicinity. Population, 1970, 18,606.

Pocatello (pŏ′kȧ-tĕl′ō). A city of southeastern Idaho, about 170 miles north of Salt Lake City, Utah. Pocatello is situated in a region largely arid and volcanic, but highly productive by reason of irrigation. The city's industries consist largely of processing farm and dairy products. Pocatello is the seat of Idaho State University. Population, 1970, 40,036.

Pomona. A city in California, about 30 miles east of Los Angeles. Pomona ships the citrus fruits, walnuts, and various agricultural products grown in the area. Oil refineries are among its industrial establishments. Population, 1970, 87,384.

Ponce. The second largest city in Puerto Rico, located on the dry, southern coast of the island, about 8 miles southwest of San Juan. Its manufactures include clothing, textiles, paper, shoes, and canned tuna, fruits, and vegetables. It is a seaport and the seat of the Catholic University of Puerto Rico. Population, 1970, 125,926.

Pontiac. A city of southeastern Michigan, on the Clinton River, about 25 miles northwest of Detroit. Pontiac is the trade center of a rich farming and dairying region, and has developed extensive industries. The chief manufactures include automobiles, automobile accessories and parts, trucks, buses, paints and varnishes, tools, and machine shop products. Pontiac was settled in 1818, was incorporated in 1837, and, in 1861, was chartered as a city. It was named after the Indian chief. Population, 1970, 85,279.

Port Arthur. A seaport of southeastern Texas, situated on Sabine Lake, 12 miles from the Gulf of Mexico. Port Arthur is one of the largest oil refining centers in the United States. Since the completion of the Port Arthur ship canal, affording passage for large ocean vessels to its

fine landlocked harbor, Port Arthur has become a leading port. The Neches River is spanned there by Rainbow Bridge (said to be the tallest bridge in the South over a navigable waterway), connecting Port Arthur and Orange. The city is the seat of Port Arthur College. Population, 1970, 57,371.

Portland. The commercial metropolis of Maine, located on Casco Bay, 108 miles northeast of Boston. It is built on two peninsulas, some encircling territory on the mainland, and islands totaling 2585 acres. Portland is an important seaport and possesses one of the finest harbors on the Atlantic coast. It occupies a picturesque site, with handsome buildings and streets closely bordered with trees. Its industries are extensive and varied, including iron forging, shoe manufacturing, cod and mackerel fishing, the canning of fish and vegetables. and lumber milling. Longfellow was born here. Population, 1970, 65,116.

Portland. The chief city of Oregon, situated on the Willamette River, about 12 miles from its junction with the Columbia, and approximately 100 miles by water from the Pacific Ocean. It occupies a commanding site on the sloping banks of the river, with the snow-capped peaks of Mount Hood, Saint Helens, and Mount Adams in the eastward background.

Portland owes its growth and importance to great natural advantages of situation. It is surrounded by highly fertile valleys and heavily timbered mountains, and has an excellent fresh-water harbor with 27 miles of deep water frontage. The exports consist mainly of grain, flour, lumber, and salmon.

In manufactures, Portland ranks among the leading cities of the Pacific states, its favorable situation enabling it to utilize vast resources of hydroelectric power, as well as natural gas. Among important manufactures are lumber, pulp, paper, clothing, automobile tires, and flour. The city's industries include also fruit canning and meat packing.

The city contains many imposing public buildings and is noted for its fine residences. It is the seat of Reed College and several schools of the University of Oregon besides various other educational institutions. Among features of interest are Council Crest, affording a panoramic view of the city and its surroundings; Terwilliger Boulevard on the west side of the city; Willamette Boulevard on the east side; and Washington Park, containing famous rose gardens and a fine statue of Sacagawea, a Shoshone Indian woman who guided the Lewis and Clark expedition. The environs of the city are reached by numerous scenic roads, including the famous Columbia River Highway, which extends 120 miles east, and 110 miles west to the sea. Portland is called the "Rose City." Its Rose Festival is a beautiful annual pageant.

Settlers from New England founded the city in 1844, naming it after Portland, Maine. Population, 1970, 382,619.

Portsmouth (pŏrts′mŭth). The only seaport of New Hampshire, built near the mouth of the Piscataqua River, opposite the Maine boundary, about 60 miles north of Boston. The city carries on a substantial coastwise trade especially in coal, and has various local manufactures. Portsmouth was settled in 1623, and incorporated in 1849. It is a quiet city with a quaint, old-fashioned appearance, and contains many fine colonial houses rich in historic and literary interest. The Portsmouth navy yard, on an island in the river, is situated within the boundaries of Maine. In 1905, the Treaty of Portsmouth, ending the Russo-Japanese War, was signed in the "Peace Building" on Seavy's Island. Population, 1970, 25,717.

Portsmouth. A city of southern Ohio, built on the north bank of the Ohio River, at the mouth of the Scioto River, about 90 miles south of Columbus. It is protected from floods by a concrete wall 77 feet above normal water stage. The city is located in an agricultural and industrial region, of which it is the commercial center. Other important manufactures are steel and lumber products, shoes, paper boxes, and furniture. Portsmouth is near the Shawnee state forest, the Goodyear atomic plant, and the Roosevelt game preserve. In the Scioto valley, north of the city, are interesting remains of the ancient Mound Builders. Population, 1970, 27,633.

Portsmouth. A seaport of southeastern Virginia, occupying the mainland side of the important harbor of Norfolk-Portsmouth. Here the larger railway systems of the South have deep-water terminals and are connected with Norfolk, just across the harbor, by passenger and railroad car ferries. An immense tonnage, both foreign and domestic, passes through the port of Norfolk-Portsmouth. This consists chiefly of cotton, coal, lumber, fruits, vegetables, oysters, fertilizers, grain, coffee, and peanuts. This port is the greatest peanut market in the world. There are extensive industries, including railroad shops, fertilizer works, barrel factories, cottonseed oil mills, and lumber mills.

A few blocks south of the center of Portsmouth is the navy yard, officially known as the Norfolk navy yard. This occupies 350 acres, contains immense dry docks, and is the most important naval establishment in the United States. Population, 1970, 109,827.

Poughkeepsie (*pô-kĭp'sĭ*). A city in New York State on the east bank of the Hudson River, about 75 miles north of New York City. It is picturesquely situated on high ground commanding a fine view of the Hudson River, which is here crossed by two magnificent bridges. The city conducts an extensive local trade. The chief manufactures include farm machinery, ball bearings, cough drops, cigars, and electronic data-processing machines. Poughkeepsie is the seat of Vassar College. Population, 1970, 32,029.

Princeton. A university town of central New Jersey, about 50 miles southwest of New York City. Founded in 1696, Princeton remained a straggling village until the College of New Jersey, now Princeton University, was removed, in 1756, from Newark to Princeton. It soon became a center of higher education and has remained distinctly a university town. Early in 1777, the battle of Princeton was fought in the vicinity. From June to November, 1783, Congress sat in Princeton. The town is built on an elevated site, commanding fine views of the surrounding country. It has broad, well shaded streets, and the architecture of its colonial period has been largely preserved. Besides the university, Princeton is also the seat of Princeton Theological Seminary, the Institute for Advanced Study, and the Westminster Choir College. Population, 1970, 12,311.

Providence. The capital of Rhode Island, and the second largest city of New England. It is situated on Narragansett Bay, about 45 miles southwest of Boston. The city has excellent railway facilities and a fine harbor.

While maintaining a substantial coastwise shipping trade, Providence is pre-eminently an industrial city, with extensive and varied manufactures. It is a leading center for the manufacture of jewelry, and for similar articles requiring a high degree of artistic skill. Among other important industrial products are abrasives, chemicals, precision tools, plastics, knit goods, pens, pencils, and rubber products.

The city is substantially built, and contains many fine parks and public buildings, including an imposing State Capitol and the beautiful Roger Williams Park. Brown University, chartered in 1764, and other important institutions are located in the city. Providence was founded and named in 1636 by Roger Williams, and here, in 1639, he organized the first Baptist Church in America. Population, 1970, 179,213.

Provincetown. A small town in Massachusetts, at the extreme outer edge of Cape Cod Bay, known to history as the first landing point to which the Pilgrims came in November of 1620, and the place where the Mayflower Compact was signed before the settlers sailed on to Plymouth. Once a thriving center of the whaling trade, the town is still engaged mainly in fishing industries, particularly in the marketing of cod and mackerel. In recent years, Provincetown has become well known as a gathering place for various artist groups, who make up a considerable part of its summer population. Some years ago, through the Provincetown Players, it gained fame as a proving ground for budding playwrights, of whom probably the best known were Susan Glaspell and Eugene O'Neill. Population, 1970, 2911.

Provo. A city of north central Utah, picturesquely situated in a fertile valley at the foot of the Wasatch Mountains, 44 miles south of Salt Lake City. Provo is the trade center of a rich irrigated district devoted to agriculture, fruit growing, and stock raising, and is the seat of Brigham Young University. Population, 1970, 53,131.

Pueblo (*pwĕb'lō*). The second largest commercial and industrial city in Colorado, located on the Arkansas River, about 120 miles south of Denver. Pueblo has immense iron and steel works, and is near a region rich in coal and oil. The city has also various other manufactories and extensive stockyards. There are many fine public buildings, including the State Historical Museum. Population, 1970, 97,453.

Quincy (*kwĭn'sĭ*). A manufacturing city of western Illinois, on the Mississippi River, about 110 miles northwest of Saint Louis. Built on the top of a limestone bluff, Quincy overlooks an enchanting panorama of river, valley, and surrounding hills. The city is the commercial center of a rich agricultural region. Its manufactures include electronic equipment, air compressors, pumps, ranges, truck and trailer bodies, poultry equipment, pulp-board, shoes, containers, and various dairy products. There are numerous fine parks, boulevards, and public buildings. The Mississippi is spanned here by a great bridge. Population, 1970, 45,288.

Quincy (*kwĭn'zĭ*). A city of eastern Massachusetts, situated on Quincy Bay, about 8 miles south of Boston. While essentially a residential suburb of Boston, Quincy has a large granite quarrying industry, and also huge shipyards, engine works, brass and iron works, rivet mills, and soap and aluminum factories. The city contains many fine streets and homes, and the park system covers 2614 acres.

Settled in 1625 as Mount Wollaston, Quincy ranks among the oldest permanent settlements in New England. Until 1792, when the community was incorporated under its present name, it was a part of Braintree. The first commercial railway in America was constructed here 1826–27 to transport granite used in building Bunker Hill Monument. Quincy enjoys the distinction of being the birthplace of two presidents, John Adams and John Quincy Adams, and also of John Hancock. Population, 1970, 87,966.

Racine. A manufacturing city of southeastern Wisconsin, located on a fine harbor on Lake Michigan, 65 miles north of Chicago. In value of its manufactures, Racine ranks second only to Milwaukee among the cities of the state, and is noted especially for the manufacture of threshing machines and farm implements. Other important manufactures include automobiles, machine shop products, furniture, hardware, and electrical equipment. Noted for its beautiful residential sections, Racine also has a park system covering 635 acres. More than one-third of the inhabitants are of Danish descent. Population, 1970, 95,162.

Rainier (*rā-nēr'*), **Mount.** The loftiest peak in the Cascade range, situated in southwestern Washington about 50 miles southeast of Tacoma. It rises to an elevation of 14,408 feet, overtopping all other summits in the Pacific states except Mount Whitney in California.

Like Fuji in Japan, Mount Rainier rises majestically in graceful lines that proclaim its volcanic origin. Its summit lies in perpetual snow and on its upper slopes there are numerous glaciers. These are from 50 to 500 feet thick and cover a total area of about 50 square miles. Some of these glaciers are from 4 to 6 miles long, and in size and beauty rival those of the Alps.

The lower slopes of the mountain are clothed with luxuriant forests, containing trees of unusual size. Above the forests, which extend to an elevation of about 7000 feet, are many picturesque mountain meadows. In summer, these bear a profusion of beautiful alpine flowers that follow the retreating snow banks almost up to the line of perpetual frost. The summit rises about 8000 feet above the general level of the Cascades and affords excellent views of the Puget Sound region. Mount Rainier, in 1899, was created a national park.

Raleigh (*rô'lĭ*). The capital of North Carolina, situated in the central part of the state. Raleigh is a large cotton and tobacco market and has varied industries, the manufacture of textiles, fertilizers, and cottonseed oil being among the more important. The city contains some 13 park areas, including Pullen Park, a 74-acre semiforest tract of exceptional beauty. Nearby is the house in which Andrew Johnson was born. The city's streets are wide and, for the most part, lined with beautiful shade trees. Among the more notable buildings are the State Capitol on grounds covering four acres, the Federal Post Office and Court Building, the State Agricultural Building, Sir Walter Hotel, Christ Church, and the Municipal Auditorium. Raleigh is the seat of North Carolina State University. The site of the city was selected for the state capital in 1792, and the city was founded in that year. Population, 1970, 121,577.

Reading (*red'ĭng*). A city of southeastern Pennsylvania, on the Schuylkill River, 58 miles northwest of Philadelphia. Situated in a rich agricultural region and near large fields of anthracite coal and iron ore, Reading possesses unusual commercial advantages. The chief industries are the manufacture of machine products, auto frames, and electric components. Other industries include railway maintenance and the manufacture of iron and steel, hosiery, castings, copper products, caskets, sweaters, paints, optical products, and building and fire brick.

Reading occupies a site between the base of Mount Penn and the Schuylkill River. The summits of Mount Penn, to the east, and Neversink Mountain, to the south, both rise to elevations of about 800 feet and command magnificent views. The city was laid out in 1748 in accordance with the plans of Thomas and Richard Penn, sons of William Penn. Daniel Boone was born near here. The early inhabitants were mostly German. Population, 1970, 87,643.

Redlands. A city of southern California, picturesquely situated in the foothills of the San Bernardino Mountains, about 60 miles east of Los Angeles. Redlands is a noted residential city, health resort, and educational center, in the heart of an immensely productive orange growing district. Smiley Heights, one of the city's numerous parks, affords a magnificent view of the surrounding region, embracing orange and lemon groves, grain fields, forests, and snow-capped mountains. The city is the seat of the University of Redlands. Population, 1970, 36,355.

Reno. The chief commercial and industrial city of Nevada, located near the western boundary of the state, about 30 miles northwest of Carson City. Reno lies in a sheltered valley near the eastern base of the Sierra Nevada mountains at an elevation of 4500 feet. It is on the Truckee River, which feeds the Truckee-Carson Canal, a government irrigation project that waters more than 100,000 acres. The city is the distributing center of an extensive region devoted to mining, farming, and stock raising. Reno's biggest single industry is tourism, with its related gaming and entertainment operations. The University of Nevada at Reno is located here. Population, 1970, 72,863.

Richmond. An important deep-water Pacific coast port across the bay from San Francisco. Settled on the coming of the railroad in 1899, its industries have shown remarkable development. These include oil-refining, food-processing, and metal fabrication. The Santa Fe railroad's western terminal shops are located here. Many persons are employed in research agencies and distributive industries. Large shipyards were constructed at Richmond during World War II. Population, 1970, 79,043.

Richmond. The capital of Virginia, located at the head of navigation on the James River, about 100 miles almost directly south of Washington. Richmond is an important railway center and has excellent air transportation facilities and a new deep-water river terminal. It is a leading tobacco market and one of the chief manufacturing centers of the South. Industries include packaging of many kinds, and the manufacture of tobacco in various forms, synthetic fibers, chemicals, drugs, paints, food, metals, and men's clothing.

The city occupies a commanding site, covering seven hills, and is sometimes styled the "Modern Rome." It is regularly laid out, rising in terraces from the river. There are many beautiful parks and imposing public buildings. Among the most noteworthy of the latter is the Capitol, designed after the Maison Carrée at Nimes, France, and built 1785–92. The city possesses many fine monumental and sculptural works, including the equestrian statue of Washington at Capitol Square.

Richmond is exceedingly rich in historic associations, and in colonial days, like Boston in New England, it played a prominent part in shaping the destinies of the country. In Saint John's Episcopal Church, in March 1775, Patrick Henry made his noted speech containing the famous exclamation, "Give me liberty or give me death!" From May 8, 1861, to April 2, 1865, it was the capital of the Confederate states. The executive mansion, occupied by Jefferson Davis, 1862–65, has been transformed into a Confederate Museum. The former residence of John Marshall, built in 1795, still stands; also the Lee mansion, occupied by General R. E. Lee's family during the Civil War. Richmond was established as a town in 1733, and chartered as a city in 1782. Population, 1970, 249,621.

Riverside. An important orange-growing center of southern California, situated on the Santa Ana River, 53 miles east of Los Angeles. Much of Riverside's beauty lies in thousands of acres of orange groves and in its 130,000 street trees. The city is noted for its distinctive "Indian rain cross" street lights, patterned after an ancient heathen symbol, prayed to for rain by the Navajo and Central American Indians. The "Parent" Naval Orange tree, from which all navel oranges in California's multimillion dollar citrus industry descended, still flourishes in a park in the center of the city.

Riverside conducts a substantial local trade, has large Portland cement works, and ships annually from its warehouses thousands of carloads of oranges. Riverside is widely known for the Mission Inn, containing numerous exhibits connected with the early Mission days of California. Riverside is the seat of the University of California at Riverside, California Baptist College, and Sherman Indian High School, among other educational institutions. Population, 1970, 140,089.

Roanoke. The chief industrial and mercantile city of southwestern Virginia is situated on the Roanoke River, 150 miles west of Richmond, in a picturesque valley between the Blue Ridge and the Allegheny mountains. As an electric power and transportation center, it affords ample facilities for the development of extensive industries which are diversified in character and number more than 250. Roanoke is a tourist mecca and is the headquarters of the Blue Ridge Parkway. Both Roanoke College and Hollins College are located here. Population, 1970, 92,115.

Rochester. A city of southeastern Minnesota, on the Zumbro River, about 80 miles southeast of Saint Paul. It is the trade center of a rich agricultural district and has substantial industries. The city is the seat of Saint Mary's Hospital and of the Mayo Clinic, founded by the surgeons Charles and William Mayo. The 19-story Plummer Building, which houses part of this clinic, has, in its tower, a 23-bell carillon as a soldiers' memorial. Population, 1970, 53,766.

Rochester. A city of west central New York, built on both banks of the Genesee River, at the Genesee Falls, and extending to Lake Ontario. Rochester ranks second in population and third in manufactures among the cities of the state. Factors which have contributed to its eminence as an industrial center are abundant power, derived from the falls of the river, and excellent transportation facilities afforded by Lake Ontario, the State Barge Canal, numerous rail and bus lines. It has a port on Lake Ontario.

The city's extensive manufactures embrace more than 350 different commodities. These are produced in upwards of 1700 factories and consist largely of articles requiring the employment of a high degree of mechanical skill. Rochester leads the world in the manufacture of photographic, optical, dental, check-protecting, industrial fluid-mixing, and gear-cutting equipment; process-control and recording instruments; enameled steel tanks; mail chutes; and thermometers.

Rochester occupies a nearly level site and is divided into two almost equal parts by the Genesee River, which is spanned by 12 bridges, some of which are 200 feet high. In the center of the city is the Upper Falls, 96 feet in height; below them the river flows in a deep gorge to the Lower Falls, 80 feet high. The park system, covering nearly 2000 acres in 12 units, is one of the most beautiful in America. Highland Park is world-famous for its displays of over 1500 lilac bushes of more than 500 varieties.

The city is the seat of the University of Rochester, Saint Bernard's Seminary, Rochester Institute of Technology, Colgate Rochester Divinity School, St. John Fisher College, Nazareth College, and other important educational institutions, and affords exceptional advantages for the study and enjoyment of art and music, particularly at the Eastman School of Music.

First permanently settled in 1812, Rochester was incorporated as a village in 1817 and chartered as a city in 1834. The completion, in 1825, of the Erie Canal greatly stimulated the city's growth. During the early period, when the Genesee valley was the chief wheat belt of the country, Rochester was known as the "Flour City." With the decline of milling and the rise of the nursery industry this sobriquet was changed to the "Flower City." Since the development of its great camera and photographic supply business, it has been styled the "Kodak City." Population, 1970, 296,233.

Rockford. A manufacturing city of Illinois, on the Rock River, about 90 miles northwest of Chicago. Abundant power, furnished by a great dam in the river, is utilized in its large and varied industries. Among these are the manufacture of machine tools, farm implements, furniture, and hardware. The city is the seat of Rockford College. A park in the center of the city contains the Turtle Indian mound. First settled in 1834, Rockford was chartered as a city in 1852. Population, 1970, 147,370.

Rock Island. A city of western Illinois, on the Mississippi River, adjoining Moline, and opposite Davenport, Iowa, with which it is connected by bridges including the four-lane Centennial bridge. These three cities with East Moline are called the Quad-City area. The city takes its name from an island in the river opposite the upper section of the town. Abundant hydroelectric power, provided by a government dam, has aided in the development of the city's substantial industries, which include the manufacture of agricultural implements, rubber footwear, food products, wood products, clothing, and concrete products. An immense government arsenal is located on the island. Rock Island was chartered as a city in 1841. Population, 1970, 50,166.

ROCKY MOUNTAIN NATIONAL PARK. An area of about 410 square miles in the heart of the Rocky Mountains, reserved as a national park in 1915. It is in north central Colorado about 50 miles northwest of Denver. It is traversed by the Continental Divide, which here rises to a height of over 14,000 feet and provides scenery of unsurpassed grandeur.

SIZE AND SURFACE. The park extends about 25 miles north and south, and from 12 to 20 miles from east to west. Altitudes within it range from 8000 to 14,256 feet above sea level, the highest point being Longs Peak, in the southeastern portion of the park, a mountain of the Snowy range. This range follows a general north and south direction. On its west side this mountain chain slopes gently down in a lovely region diversified by streams and charming lakes, the largest and deepest being Grand Lake. The eastern slope, however, is precipitous and awe-inspiring, bold summits standing out in daring relief separated by gorges with walls often 1000 to 2000 feet high. In the northern portion of the park are several peaks over 13,000 feet in height, including Hagues Peak and Mummy and Ypsilon mountains. Mount Copeland at the extreme south also exceeds 13,000 feet.

GLACIERS. There are few places on the earth where the effects of glacial erosion can be seen and understood so easily as in Rocky Mountain Park. Andrews glacier is the largest of those which still exist, but numerous huge moraines attest the stupendous force of these mountain-carving agents in past ages, when they were vastly more extensive. At Moraine Park is a ridge 800 feet high marking the lower edge of an ice-age glacier which crept down from Forest Canyon. The Mills moraine, at the foot of Longs Peak precipice, is 1000 feet high and four miles long. Glaciers still active seldom extend below an altitude of 12,000 feet. The timber line is reached at about 11,000 feet.

TRAVEL FACILITIES. There are four principal approaches to Rocky Mountain Park, three from the east converging at the hotel village of Estes Park, and one western approach known as the Grand Lake route. Motor highways also give access to the park from Denver, Boulder, and Grand Junction over these same approaches.

The park has over 300 miles of trails, but the principal scenic road is the Trail Ridge Road, which connects the western approach via Grand Lake with Estes Park. Following the crest of the Continental Divide for about three miles at an altitude of 11,800 feet, it is one of the highest roads in North America. It commands superb views of mountain peaks, chasms, waterfalls, glaciers, and mountain lakes.

ANIMALS. Rocky Mountain Park contains many bighorns, which particularly frequent Bighorn mountain, descending daily to drink from Sheep Lake in Horseshoe Park. Beavers are numerous, and much land on valley floors is marshy by reason of dams built by these animals. Deer abound and there are elk herds and some bears. The streams and lakes are stocked with fish from a hatchery in Estes Park.

Rome. A manufacturing city on the Mohawk River in New York, about 90 miles northwest of Albany. Its industrial output includes many items, but Rome is particularly noted for its copper and brass products, and has the largest fish hatchery in New York. Located in or near the city are the Rome State School for Mental Defectives; Griffiss Air Force Base; Fort Stanwix, claimed to be the place where, during the Revolutionary War, the Stars and Stripes were first flown in battle; and the grave of Francis Bellamy, author of the "Pledge of Allegiance to the Flag." Population, 1970, 47,655.

Roswell. This city in the Pecos valley in southeastern New Mexico owes its origin chiefly to its abundant water supply, having been known as an oasis even before the discovery of artesian wells there. A city of homes, with tributary cattle raising and oil industries, it is also prominent as a tourist center, one of its attractions being Bottomless Lake State Park. Educational institutions include Eastern New Mexico University at Roswell and New Mexico Military Institute. Population, 1970, 33,908.

Royal Gorge. The deepest part of the Grand Canyon of the Arkansas River. It is situated in central Colorado, 45 miles west of Pueblo. The entire canyon, about 8 miles long, has precipitous walls of eroded granite which rise to an immense height. In the portion a mile and a half long called the Royal Gorge, these titanic walls tower almost perpendicularly 2600 feet above the foaming torrent of the river. At the narrowest part, the stream fills the canyon nearly from wall to wall, and the railway passes through it over a bridge hung from transverse girders mortised into the rocks of both sides of the canyon.

Sacramento. The capital of California, located on the Sacramento River 90 miles northeast of San Francisco. Sacramento lies in the midst of a very rich farming and fruit growing region, and the most important of the city's varied industries is the canning of fruit. Among the other establishments are large railroad shops; factories making missile engines; flour, rice, and lumber mills; meat packing houses; and a huge air corps supply depot of the army. The city is built on the site of Sutter's Fort, the first settlement in California reached by the gold seekers of 1849 and 1850. The fort, rebuilt, houses relics of the pioneer days.

The handsome Capitol and a number of other state buildings form a multi-million dollar group in a beautiful 38-acre park in the center of the city. The park system covers about 1200 acres, the largest unit being Del Paso Park of 828 acres. Sacramento was incorporated in 1849 and became the state capital in 1854. A state college is located here. Population, 1970, 254,413.

Sagamore Hill. The country estate and residence of Theodore Roosevelt, situated near the town of Oyster Bay, on the northern shore of Long Island, about 30 miles northeast of New York City. In 1963, it was established as a national historic site. Young's Memorial Cemetery, which contains the grave of the former president, is also situated at Oyster Bay.

Saginaw. A city of southeastern Michigan, built at the head of navigation on the Saginaw River, 85 miles northwest of Detroit. The city lies in rich coal and oil fields and has immense supplies of hydroelectric power. There are many salt wells in the vicinity. Its industries produce, among other commodities, automobiles and parts, foundry and machine shop products, furniture, coal, beet sugar, and oil. Saginaw has extensive car shops. There are fine parks and public buildings, including hospitals and educational institutions. Population, 1970, 91,849.

Saint Augustine (ô′gŭs-tēn′). The oldest city in the United States, situated on the east coast of Florida, about 30 miles southeast of Jacksonville. Saint Augustine was founded in 1565 by the Spanish under Pedro Menendez de Aviles, sent by Philip II of Spain. With the exception of 20 years, 1763–83, when it was in the hands of the British, Saint Augustine remained a Spanish city until 1821, when the United States acquired Florida. In the old part of the town, the quaint, narrow streets are lined with ancient houses built of the shell material known as coquina. Many of these houses have overhanging balconies and are set amid gardens luxuriant with semitropical vegetation.

Among the many historic buildings are Fort Marion, the oldest fort in the United States, begun in 1656; the remodeled governor's palace; the Old Spanish Treasury; and the famous city gates. Saint Augustine is a noted winter resort and contains many fine hotels. Among these are the Alcazar and the palatial Ponce de Leon hotel, built in the Spanish Renaissance style. Population, 1970, 12,352.

Saint Joseph. A city of Missouri, built on the east bank of the Missouri River, about 60 miles north of Kansas City. The city lies picturesquely along the bluffs of the river. It is the center of a rich agricultural region with which it carries on a large merchandising and marketing trade. Saint Joseph is one of the leading live stock markets of the country, and contains several meat packing establishments. Its chief manufactures are packing-house products and flour products, including pancake flour. Other important manufactures include chemicals, malt beverages, paper products, and cans. Parks occupy about 1350 acres. A park about the Civic Center has a pony express monument, commemorating this service which began in 1860 between St. Joseph and Sacramento, Cal. Saint Joseph was first settled in 1826 by Joseph Robidoux, a French fur trader; it was incorporated in 1845 and became a city in 1851. Population, 1970, 72,691.

SAINT LOUIS (loō′ĭs). The chief city of Missouri, situated on the Mississippi River, about 20 miles below the mouth of the Missouri.

SITE. Saint Louis occupies a commanding site, rising in a succession of gently sloping hills and depressions, each ridge toward the west ascending higher and finally reaching, at the western limits, an elevation of some 300 feet above the river. The boundaries are two curved lines, the crescent-like bend of the Mississippi on the east and an arbitrary boundary on the west. The total frontage on the river is more than 19 miles, the length of the western boundary is about 21 miles, and the maximum width is nearly 7 miles. The total area slightly exceeds 61 square miles.

STREETS AND BUILDINGS. In the small, older portion of the city, the streets are narrow and more or less irregular. The modern parts of the city have been laid out, wherever possible, with wide streets, crossing at right angles, and in north-and-south and east-and-west directions.

The Old Cathedral on Walnut Street is the most noteworthy example of the French period in the history of Saint Louis. Among the many notable modern buildings are the City Hall, which resembles an old French hotel de ville; the Union Station, in Renaissance style; the buildings of Washington University, in Tudor Gothic style; the Public Library, built of Maine granite in the early Italian Renaissance style, and the Art Museum and the Jefferson Memorial, in the classic style. Other noteworthy structures are the immense Saint Louis Cathedral, distinctly Romanesque; the Protestant Episcopal Cathedral, in modified Gothic; and the impressive Shaare Emeth Synagogue. A group of imposing buildings on Lindell Boulevard includes the Masonic Temple, the Shriners' Moolah Temple, and the Scottish Rite Cathedral. The tallest buildings include the Civil Courts Building and the 31-story Southwestern Bell Telephone Building.

No city in America excels Saint Louis in the beauty of its exclusive residential districts, called "places." In these are magnificent homes with spacious grounds reflecting the highest skill of the architect and the landscape gardener. Washington Terrace, Westmoreland, Kingsbury, and Portland rank among the most noted of the places. Other fine residential sections are found in Compton Heights, Hortense Place, Parkview, and in Hillcrest, and also along Forsyth and Lindell boulevards.

Saint Louis is distinctively a city of brick, and, with few exceptions, even the most elaborate mansions are built of this material. Owing to comparative cheapness of local building materials, especially brick and limestone, a large percentage of the inhabitants live in separate homes.

CIVIC IMPROVEMENTS. A unique recreation facility is the Open Air Municipal theater located in Forest Park. A civic center on a memorial plaza, occupying 9 downtown blocks, accommodates an auditorium and other city buildings. A 37-block river-front area constitutes the Jefferson National Expansion Memorial, which commemorates the Louisiana Purchase and Westward expansion in the U.S., with a Gateway Arch, 630 feet high and from base to base, and a rich underground historical museum. Completed in 1966, the steel and concrete arch weighs 16,678 tons. Visitors may ride to the top of the arch in transit gondolas and from there view the city.

PARKS. The city has 68 parks, covering an area of more than 3000 acres. Forest Park, the largest, containing 1381 acres, lies almost directly west of the business center. Other important recreation grounds are the Missouri Botanical Garden, Tower Grove, O'Fallon, Carondelet, and Lafayette parks. Forest Park has one of America's finest zoos and a $1.5 million planetarium. Several of the parks are ornamented with noteworthy works of sculpture, including statues of Shakespeare, Columbus, Jefferson, and St. Louis, the crusader king of France, for whom the city was named.

EDUCATIONAL INSTITUTIONS. Among the leading educational institutions are the University of Missouri at St. Louis, Washington University, Saint Louis University, and Concordia and Eden seminaries. The Missouri Botanical Garden, founded by Henry Shaw and usually called Shaw's Garden, is now maintained for the public. It contains a fine arboretum and a collection of native and foreign plants, especially orchids, rivaling those of Kew Gardens in London.

TRANSPORTATION. Two great advantages make Saint Louis pre-eminent as a commercial and industrial center. The first is its location in the heart of the great Mississippi valley, the most fertile agricultural region in the world. The second lies in its unsurpassed facilities for transportation. Barge lines handle an immense tonnage between Saint Paul and Minneapolis on the north and New Orleans on the south. Additional facilities include 16 trunk-line railroads, 9 scheduled airlines, and 5 major highways having access to 7 steel bridges across the Mississippi River.

COMMERCE. Saint Louis is the most important distributing center of the Mississippi valley, handling products representing the entire country. It is a great grain, live stock, horse, tobacco, and wool market and conducts an immense wholesaling trade.

MANUFACTURES. In value of manufactures, Saint Louis ranks among the nine leading cities of the United States. Its extensive industries embrace the manufacture of an exceedingly wide range of products. It is one of the greatest shoe and tobacco manufacturing centers of the United States and has one of the world's largest breweries. Other important manufactures include packed meats, coke, blast furnace, foundry, machine shop, and rolling mill products, refined petroleum, clothing, chemicals, medicinal compounds, locomotive parts, aircraft, railway and rapid transit cars, jute goods, hot-air furnaces, stoves, clay products, automobiles, furs, and furniture.

HISTORY. Saint Louis was established in 1764 as a fur trading station by Pierre Laclède Liguest, assisted by Auguste Chouteau. Though under the control of Spain from 1770 to 1804, the place remained essentially French. In 1804, Saint Louis came into the possession of the United States by the Louisiana Purchase. The first newspaper was published in 1808, and, with the arrival of the first steamboat in 1815, a new era in the history of Saint Louis was opened. From 1840 to 1880, it passed 38 other American cities in population, and was passed by only one—Chicago. In 1904, the Louisiana Purchase exposition was held in the city. A feature of interest is the annual festival of the Veiled Prophet, somewhat similar to the Mardi Gras of New Orleans. Population, 1970, 622,236.

Saint Paul. The capital of Minnesota, built on both banks of the Mississippi River, immediately below Minneapolis. A part of the western boundary of Saint Paul is contiguous with the eastern limits of Minneapolis, but the commercial centers of these "Twin Cities" are about 10 miles apart.

The city is built chiefly on the left or east bank of the Mississippi, and occupies three terraces, rising in all from 100 to 200 feet above the river. The lowest section contains railway yards, stock yards, wholesale houses, and factories. Lying above this, on the middle terrace, is the commercial district and a part of the residential section. On the uppermost terrace, crowning the highest bluffs, is the fine residence section.

Saint Paul is admirably laid out, with many handsome streets, among the most scenic of which are Kellogg Boulevard and Summit Drive. The various parks, playgrounds, and connecting boulevards cover a total area of more than 2240 acres. In Como and Phalen parks there are picturesque lakes. Indian Mound Park affords unsurpassed views of the Mississippi River.

Foremost among the city's notable buildings is the beautiful State Capitol, constructed of marble and granite and containing many fine sculptural and mural decorations. Other fine structures are the Roman Catholic Cathedral, the Hill Memorial Library, the Minnesota Historical Building, and the Union railway station, completed in 1926 at a cost of $15 million. The beautiful buildings and grounds of the Minnesota Horticultural Society are at the northern end of the city. The annual state fair held here is one of the largest in the United States. Within the city are several important educational institutions, including Hamline University, Macalester College, Concordia College, Saint Thomas College, and the Saint Paul College of Law.

Saint Paul enjoys exceptional transportation facilities, both by rail and by river. On the completion of extensive canalization work in the Mississippi River, a barge service was opened in 1928. For a long period prior to this the river had scarcely been used for freight transfer although it had earlier been the main artery of commerce.

The St. Paul area is one of the great wholesale and jobbing centers of the country, with a total annual trade exceeding $500 million. The city is also an important market for live stock and, in manufactures, ranks second among the cities of the state. Prominent among the city's manufactures are railway cars, boots and shoes, fur goods, refrigerators, cordage and twine, law books, automobiles, glass, butter, and packed meats.

Settled in 1839, Saint Paul was made the territorial capital in 1849, and, upon the admission of Minnesota into the Union in 1858, was made the capital of the state. From about 1870, following the extensive building of railways and the settlement of the Northwest, the city grew rapidly. Population, 1970, 309,980.

Saint Petersburg. A summer and winter resort of western Florida, about 20 miles southwest of Tampa. The city is charmingly situated on Pinellas Peninsula with the Gulf of Mexico on the west and, on the south and east, Tampa Bay, which is here spanned by the 6-mile Gandy highway bridge. Extending 2400 feet into the bay is a million-dollar recreation pier. The city has 65 parks and 33 miles of water front. The post office is an open-air building, appropriate for the equable, sunny, subtropical climate which attracts an immense number of winter residents. Thousands of green benches on Central Avenue are a feature of the city. Population, 1970, 216,232.

Salem. A city of eastern Massachusetts, built on a peninsula between two inlets of the Atlantic Ocean, 16 miles northeast of Boston. Though irregularly laid out, Salem occupies an attractive site, with a fine drive along the north shore, and contains several beautiful parks. There are several very early colonial houses, numerous old mansions, dating from the period of the city's commercial supremacy, and many fine modern homes.

From early colonial years until about 1860, Salem was an important trading port. With the advent of steam navigation, its foreign commerce was largely transferred to Boston. The city still maintains an extensive coastwise trade, especially in coal. The substantial manufactures include cotton goods, games, radio tubes, leather, and shoes.

Salem is the seat of the Essex Institute, Peabody Museum, and Salem State College. Founded in 1626, Salem is one of the oldest cities of New England, and is rich in historical associations. In 1692, it was the scene of the Salem witchcraft delusion. Many early dwellings are well preserved, as, for example, Hawthorne's birthplace, the House of Seven Gables, and the witch jail, built in 1684. Population, 1970, 40,556.

Salem. The capital of Oregon, situated on the Willamette River in the northwestern portion of the state. Salem is the trade center of a fertile agricultural region; the industrial interests center about hop products, peppermint oil, linen, fruit and meat packing, mobile homes, and wood products. Wide streets and two public parks enhance the appearance of the city. Among the principal buildings are the Capitol, the Federal Building, and the Supreme Court Building. The city is the seat of Willamette University and of various state institutions. Salem was settled in 1840, was incorporated in 1853, and became the state capital in 1860. Population, 1970, 68,296.

Salt Lake City. The capital of Utah, the chief commercial city between Denver and San Francisco. The city is magnificently situated at the western base of the Wasatch Mountains, at an elevation of about 4300 feet above the sea, some 12 miles southeast of Great Salt Lake. It occupies a gently sloping site at the edge of a wide plain made highly fertile by irrigation. A noteworthy feature of the city is its unusually wide streets, at the sides of many of which run conduits bringing water from the mountains for freshening the vegetation of parks, lawns, and gardens. It has 7000 acres set aside as public parks.

Salt Lake City is the distributing center for a vast and rich region devoted to mining, stock raising, and agriculture. There are important mining interests, with large smelters and mineral mills in the city and vicinity. The city's industrial output includes petroleum and steel products, woolens, beet sugar, candy, salt.

In the heart of the city is Temple Square, containing the famous Mormon Tabernacle, a huge oval building capable of seating 8000 people; the impressive granite temple which took 40 years to erect (1853–93); and the large assembly hall built to accommodate 3000 persons. Among other fine buildings are the State Capitol and City and County building. Memory Park, east of the Capitol, commemorates local veterans of World War I. The city is the seat of the University of Utah, a State Normal school, and several other educational institutions.

Approximately 28 miles southwest of Salt Lake City at Bingham Canyon is the Bingham Copper Mine, the largest surface copper mine in North America.

Salt Lake City was founded by Brigham Young, the leader of a party of Mormons who arrived in the valley in 1847, and it has since been the headquarters of the Church of Jesus Christ of Latter-Day Saints. About 40 per cent of the people are Latter-Day Saints, who have more than 54 places of worship in the city. Population, 1970, 175,885.

Salton Sea. A brackish lake in the central depression of the Colorado Desert in southeastern California. Prior to 1905, this was a salt marsh interspersed with shallow saline ponds and lakes, covering an area about 30 miles long and 12 miles wide, with the surface lying about 280 feet below sea level. During the spring rains, however, the lake usually expanded into a body of water occupying an area of some 60 or 70 square miles, which, with the coming of the dry season, rapidly receded.

In 1905 and 1906, by an accidental inflow of water from the Colorado River, through defective irrigation canals, this watery marsh expanded into a lake 40 miles long, from 10 to 16 miles wide, and 90 feet deep, covering in all some 515 square miles. At its greatest height, the surface of the lake was only 194 feet below sea level.

After the inflow of water from the Colorado River was stopped in 1907, the lake receded as a result of evaporation until, by 1920, it covered only 265 square miles. Its surface was then approximately 250 feet below sea level. Since that time it has remained fairly stable, due to the inflow of natural drainage and a large volume of seepage and waste water from the irrigated lands in the Imperial Valley.

San Angelo. A city built near old Fort Concho on the river of that name in western Texas. It is a wool and mohair market and a distributing and shipping center for cattle, agricultural products, and oil. Manufactures include cottonseed oil, petroleum, surgical sutures, ceramic tile, skins and hides, and dairy products. Angelo State University is located here. An outstanding educational institution is the campus-type Central High School. Population, 1970, 63,884.

San Antonio. Next to San Augustine, the oldest city of Texas, situated on a river of the same name, 80 miles southwest of Austin. San Antonio is noted for its delightful and healthful climate and is the pleasure resort of thousands of visitors. On all sides are spacious grounds, luxuriant gardens, and an abundance of subtropical foliage and flowers. The 56 public parks and plazas cover 2200 acres. San Pedro Park, with its picturesque live oaks and its famous springs, is the original site of the Indian settlement of San Antonio. Many of the old buildings, especially the Alamo and San Fernando Cathedral, are full of historical interest. Fort Sam Houston is now the headquarters of the U.S. Fourth Army. Nearby are four important Air Force centers including Randolph Field and Kelly Air Force Base.

San Antonio is the commercial center of a large oil producing, agricultural and stock raising region, and is an important cattle, horse, and mule market. Its industrial establishments include oil refineries, flour mills, foundries, packing houses, cement works, and garment manufacturing.

The first permanent settlement was established in 1718 with the founding of the mission of San Antonio de Valero and the presidio of San Antonio de Bexar. In 1809 this settlement became a city. San Antonio was the scene of stirring events in the early history of Texas. Population, 1970, 654,153.

San Bernardino (săn bûr'när-dē'nō). A commercial and industrial city of southern California, about 60 miles east of Los Angeles. San Bernardino is situated in a beautiful valley surrounded by snow-capped mountains, near the entrance of the Cajon pass into the Mojave Desert. It is the trade center of a rich, irrigated district devoted chiefly to growing citrus fruits, grapes, and orchard crops. Its industrial establishments include large railroad shops, foundries, machine shops, and planing mills. First settled by Mormons in 1852, San Bernardino was incorporated as a town in 1868 and, in 1886, was chartered as a city. Population, 1970, 104,251.

San Diego (dē-ā'gō). Third largest city of California, with an excellent harbor on San Diego Bay, about 125 miles southeast of Los Angeles. The climate is mild and equable. Subtropical fruits flourish in the area. Among the leading industries are fish canning, the handling of fruits and fruit products, shipbuilding, and the growing of flowers, tomatoes, avocados, and citrus fruits. The manufactures include aircraft. The chief exports are fruits, honey, and citrus products.

San Diego is a United States naval base and one of the greatest naval aviation bases in America. It is also an important commercial aeronautical center, the airport, Lindbergh Field, being within five minutes' drive of the central business district. San Diego possesses many fine parks, Balboa Park alone having an area of 1400 acres. San Diego State College is located here. By reason of its climate and location, San Diego is a prominent health and travel resort. Among local points of interest are Coronado Beach, Fort Rosecrans, Point Loma, and Palomar Observatory. Population, 1970, 693,931.

SAN FRANCISCO. The principal seaport and manufacturing city of the Pacific coast of America, and second only to Los Angeles in population among the cities of the Pacific states. San Francisco is situated about 600 miles northwest of San Diego and about 900 miles south of Seattle.

SITE. San Francisco occupies a magnificent site overlooking one of the finest natural harbors in the world. The city is built on the northern end of a semimountainous peninsula lying between the ocean on the west and San Francisco Bay on the east. The site, though generally sloping toward the east, is irregular, and embraces many bold hills, of which the highest, Twin Peaks, 925 feet high, separate the business district from the newer residential sections. The entrance from the ocean to the bay is through the Golden Gate, a narrow, rock-bound waterway whose attractive setting recalls Istanbul and Gibraltar. The city is connected with the north and east shores of the bay by two of the greatest suspension bridges in the world— Golden Gate and San Francisco-Oakland Bay.

STREETS AND BUILDINGS. In general, the streets of the city are broad and straight, in some cases leading directly up steep hills. The district bounded approximately by Kearney and Stockton streets and by California and Pacific avenues, in the heart of the commercial section, is Chinatown, long a picturesque feature of the city. The level section south of Market Street contains the manufacturing district.

Of many imposing public buildings, the most important are those of the group forming the Civic Center, including the City Hall, the Public Library, and the Auditorium. Other notable buildings are the Post Office, the United States Mint, and the Union Ferry Building. Among the larger office buildings are the Southern Pacific Building, the Federal Reserve Bank, the Russ Building, 30 stories high, the Standard Oil Building, 22 stories high, the Hobart Building, 21 stories high, and the Claus Spreckles Building, 19 stories high, which withstood the ravages of the great fire of 1906.

PARKS AND BOULEVARDS. The municipal park system includes 127 public recreation and park units covering 4043 acres. The chief of these, Golden Gate Park, covering 1013 acres, extends from near the center of the city west to the ocean. The principal points of scenic and historic interest are reached by an extensive system of boulevards and driveways. Those passing through the Presidio and Lincoln Park give fine views of the Golden Gate. These lead also past Sutro Baths and the Cliff House to the Great highway which runs close to the ocean for 3 miles. The historic Mission Road, the city's oldest thoroughfare, has been modernized. A boulevard extends to the top of Twin Peaks, whose lofty crest affords a splendid view.

EDUCATIONAL INSTITUTIONS. Among the important educational and scientific institutions are the Memorial Museum, the California School of Fine Arts, the Mechanics Institute, the School of Mechanical Arts, the Cogswell Polytechnic Institute, and the San Francisco State College. The University of California is at Berkeley, across the bay; in San Francisco are located the affiliated colleges, which include the departments of medicine, dentistry, and pharmacy. Leland Stanford University is at Palo Alto, 33 miles distant.

TRANSPORTATION. The harbor of San Francisco, completely sheltered from the sea by coastal hills, is one of the largest and safest on the globe. It has extensive docks, and is equipped with dry docks and other facilities for the care of vessels. The city is connected, by regular lines of steamships, with all ports on the Pacific coast of North and South America, with Atlantic seaports by way of the Panama Canal, and with Hawaii, the Philippines, Australia, China, and Japan.

San Francisco is the terminus of the Southern Pacific railway from New Orleans. Oakland, on the eastern side of the bay, is the terminus of three transcontinental systems, and connection with San Francisco across the bay is afforded by ferry and bridge services. Two systems of street railways and buses, one municipally owned and operated, provide local transportation.

COMMERCE. In foreign commerce, San Francisco ranks among the chief seaports of the country. The leading articles of export usually include canned fruits, canned salmon, raw cotton, iron and steel manufactures, grain, and oils. Among the principal imports are sugar, coffee, copra, burlap, tea, rubber, silk, and tin. The city also conducts an extensive coastwise commerce with other ports of the United States, and much Western produce is collected at San Francisco for distribution by rail.

FINANCE. San Francisco is the financial center of the Pacific coast. It is noted for the size and strength of its banking institutions, and is the headquarters of two of the largest banking organizations in America.

MANUFACTURES. San Francisco is, after Los Angeles, the leading city of the western United States in the total value of manufactured products. Crude petroleum, piped from vast oil fields, is extensively used for fuel. Among important industries are printing and publishing, meat packing, ship-building, coffee roasting, fruit canning, and the manufacture of paper products, furniture, confectionery, and paint.

FEATURES OF INTEREST. Among many noteworthy places of interest within the city and its environs are the Presidio, a large military reservation; the Cow Palace, Telegraph hill, Russian hill, and Twin Peaks, affording excellent views; Chinatown, with its Oriental character and aspect; the ocean shore at Cliff House; the celebrated Seal rocks, Mission Dolores, Mount Tamalpais and Muir Woods north of the Golden Gate; and Angel and Alcatraz islands the latter formerly a Federal prison island.

HISTORY. The site of San Francisco was visited in 1769 by Spaniards who called the place Yerba Buena. The first settlement began in 1776 with the establishment of Mission Dolores. In 1846, the United States took possession of California, and, in 1847, the name of the town was changed to San Francisco. Following the discovery of gold in California in 1848, the development of the town was spectacular, and, in 1850, it became a city. In 1862, telegraphic communication with the East was established, and, in 1869, the first transcontinental railway was completed. The most momentous event in the history of San Francisco was the earthquake of April 18, 1906, followed by a tremendous conflagration which almost totally destroyed the buildings on an area of more than 4 square miles, including the chief commercial and residential districts. Notwithstanding this enormous loss, the devastated area was rapidly rebuilt, and the city reconstructed on a grander and more substantial scale. Population, 1970, 715,674.

San Jose (*săn hŏ-sā'*). A city of west central California, situated in the beautiful and fertile Santa Clara valley, 50 miles southeast of San Francisco. It is in the midst of an important fruit growing region, and its principal commercial and industrial interests are connected with the cultivation of deciduous fruits. San Jose is noted for its salubrious climate and delightful gardens. Alum Rock Park, 776 acres in area, has 22 mineral springs, each with a grotto. San Jose possesses many fine buildings, including the San Jose State College. Lick Observatory, situated on Mount Hamilton, about 25 miles east of the city, attracts many visitors. The Ames Aeronautical and Space Research Laboratory is 9 miles north of the city. Population, 1970, 443,950.

San Juan (*săn hwăn'*). The capital city and chief seaport of Puerto Rico. It is built on two small islands, San Juan and Santurce, connected by five modern bridges. It possesses an excellent harbor and several fine plazas and gardens. The Capitol is a beautiful building of white marble in the classic style. The chief industry is the manufacture of tobacco and the handling of sugar, grapefruit, pineapples, and other fruits. Various industries have sprung up and flourished under favorable leigslation known as The Industrial Incentives Act.

San Juan was founded about 1519 by Ponce de Leon. The main part of the city is surrounded by medieval ramparts. Morro Castle, built in 1584, stands on a promontory to the west. San Juan came into the possession of the United States by cession at the close of the Spanish American War. Population, 1970, 444,952.

Santa Ana. A city of California located about 80 miles northwest of San Diego. Once a citrus center, Santa Ana now has diversified industry, including electronics and beet sugar refining. Population, 1970, 156,601.

Santa Barbara (*săn'tă băr'bă-ră*). A city of southern California, situated on Santa Barbara channel, about 90 miles northwest of Los Angeles. Santa Barbara lies in a beautiful valley opening southward to the sea, but encircled on the north and east by the Santa Ynez Mountains. Closely paralleling the shore, the high coast range extends for many miles in an east-and-west direction, resulting in a remarkably mild and salubrious climate. The city is in the midst of an important farming, lemon growing, walnut growing, and stock raising region. A large proportion of the lima beans grown for market in the United States are produced in this district. The city is zoned to prohibit industries that are not "smokeless."

The Santa Barbara Mission, founded in 1786, stands in the northern part of the city, and is still occupied by Franciscan monks. Santa Barbara is widely known for its attractive buildings in Spanish architecture. An "Old Spanish Days" fiesta is held each August at the full of the moon. Santa Barbara is a noted all-year resort. Population, 1970, 70,215.

Santa Catalina (*kăt'ă-lē'nă*). An island of southern California, separated from the mainland of Los Angeles county by San Pedro channel, some 20 miles wide. Santa Catalina is about 25 miles long and the average width is about 4 miles. The surface is semimountainous. Many interesting trees, shrubs, and other plants grow on the island, some of which do not occur elsewhere. The clear waters, remarkable for the beauty and variety of their marine life, are famous game-fishing grounds. Sea lions inhabit the south coast; flying fish are numerous in the channel, and whales are sometimes seen. The only town, Avalon, is a noted resort.

Santa Clara. A town in California, 47 miles southeast of San Francisco. Santa Clara was known for its fruits in the early mission days of California, and is still an important fruit-growing and packing center. It is the seat of the University of Santa Clara. Population, 1970, 87,717.

Santa Fe (*săn'tă fā'*). The capital of New Mexico, situated in the north central part of the state. First established in 1610, Santa Fe has ever since been the capital of New Mexico. The city was taken from Mexico by the United States in 1846. Stock raising is the main industry of the surrounding district. Indian pottery in large quantities is made by the Pueblo Indians.

The older part of the city has narrow, crooked streets with houses made of adobe or sun-dried brick. There are many buildings of historic interest: the Palace, beside a central plaza, where the Mexican governors resided; San Miguel Church; Cristo Rey Church; Scottish Rite Temple; and the State Art Museum, built in a mission style of architecture. The new capitol is round and styled as an Indian kiva. Population, 1970, 41,167.

Santa Monica. A city of southern California, on the Pacific Ocean, 16 miles west of downtown Los Angeles. By reason of its climate, bathing beaches, and boating facilities, Santa Monica is a popular year-round resort. Distinctive features include the Palisades Park and many fishing piers. Leading industries are electronics, aerospace research and development, missile production, plastics, ceramics, furniture making, and cosmetics manufacture. Population, 1970, 88,289.

Saratoga Springs. A city and famous watering place of eastern New York, about 30 miles almost directly north of Albany. It is noted for its numerous medicinal springs, which have made it one of the most attractive health resorts in America. The waters are bottled and shipped to various parts of the world. There are many recreational facilities.

Saratoga Springs was founded in 1789 and is the seat of Skidmore College for women. In a 30-acre park is the curious geological display known as the Petrified Sea Garden. The Saratoga battlefield, scene of Burgoyne's surrender and now a national historical park, is located 12 miles east of the city. Population, 1970, 18,845.

Sault Sainte Marie (*sōō' sănt mă-rē'*). A city of northern Michigan, on the Saint Mary's River, and opposite a town of the same name in Ontario. At this point are the famous rapids (the *Sault* or "rapids" of Saint Mary), which make navigation impossible for lake vessels. However, between Lake Superior and Lake Huron, navigation has been made possible for ships of the heaviest tonnage by an extensive system of canals and locks. Some 25,000 ships, carrying about 100 million tons of freight, pass through this waterway every year. Immense hydroelectric power, generated at the rapids, is utilized in the city's growing industries, the chief of which is the manufacture of calcium carbide. Other manufactories include planing, paper, and machine shops. Sault Sainte Marie is the oldest settlement in Michigan. Population, 1970, 15,136.

Savannah. The second largest city of Georgia, situated on the Savannah River, about 18 miles from the sea. It occupies a fine level site and has an excellent harbor. Savannah is the leading port on the southern Atlantic coast of the United States, and has also large exports of lumber, fertilizers, tobacco, and naval stores. It has extensive industries, which include the manufacture of cottonseed oils, fertilizers, resin, turpentine, refined sugar, foundry and machine shop products, paper, cloth and paper bags, and aircraft.

Savannah is noted for its well shaded streets and for its beautiful parks and gardens luxuriant with subtropical vegetation. The city was founded in 1733 and received its municipal charter in 1789. During the Revolutionary War it was captured by the British, and in the Civil War it was the objective of Sherman's march to the sea. Population, 1970, 114,155.

Schenectady. A city of eastern New York, located on the Mohawk River and the State Barge Canal, 16 miles northwest of Albany. The older parts of the city are built along the river, but the more modern sections occupy the surrounding hills. Schenectady is unique among American cities of its size in that about 90 per cent of its industry grew up through the building of locomotives and the manufacture of electrical machinery, apparatus, and supplies. It contains the laboratories and headquarters of the General Electric Company.

Schenectady was settled in 1661 and chartered as a town in 1798. In 1690, an attacking force of French and Indians massacred most of the inhabitants. The city is the seat of Union College, the second college incorporated in the state. Population, 1970, 77,859.

Scottsdale. A prosperous, residential suburb of Phoenix, Arizona. It is primarily a resort city, part of which has been reconstructed as an old Western town. Population, 1970, 66,852.

Scranton. A city of Pennsylvania, situated on the Lackawanna River, about 100 miles northwest of Philadelphia. Scranton occupies an undulating site surrounded by low mountains. It is the richest coal mining city in the world, being the center of the chief anthracite producing region of the United States.

Scranton is also a leading silk manufacturing center, and its other noteworthy industries include the manufacture of locomotives, iron and steel goods, knit goods, cotton lace, women's clothing, and tobacco products. The fine parks and the lake resorts in the nearby mountains make the city and its environs attractive. Scranton was founded in 1840, incorporated as a borough in 1854, and was chartered as a city in 1866. Population, 1970, 103,564.

Seattle. The chief city of Washington, and the second largest seaport of the Pacific states. It is built on the hilly eastern shore of Puget Sound, 933 miles by water north of San Francisco. The city occupies a commanding site between the Cascade and the Olympic range, with Puget Sound forming its western front, and Lake Washington lying on its eastern border. Evergreen Point floating bridge, 7518 feet long, connects Seattle with Bellevue.

Surrounded by a tributary region rich in timber, fisheries, minerals, and agricultural resources, and possessing exceptional facilities for transportation, Seattle has become one of the foremost commercial centers of the Pacific coast. It is the terminal point of several transcontinental railroads and has regular steamship connections with all parts of the world by way of the Panama Canal and the transpacific routes. In addition to other fine harbor facilities, a ship canal, 8½ miles long, situated wholly within the city, connects Puget Sound with Lake Union and Lake Washington. The leading exports of the port are wheat, flour, lumber, refined copper, automobiles, machinery, and fish; the imports are chiefly silk, rice, tea, coffee, sugar, copper ore, furs, and various Oriental products.

Seattle has one of the largest municipally owned hydroelectric power systems in the world. Industries include flour milling, food processing, shipbuilding, meat packing, lumber and wood products, airplanes, iron and steel products, and machinery. The fishery interests of Alaska and Puget Sound are largely centralized in Seattle which handles enormous quantities of canned salmon and other preserved fish.

Seattle contains many noteworthy buildings, among which are the Cathedral of Saint James, the Public Library, Art Museum, Northern Life Tower, and the Smith Tower, 42 stories high. The park and boulevard system embraces more than 1800 acres and includes upwards of 25 miles of scenic boulevards. The latter afford magnificent views of Mount Rainier and other snow-capped peaks of the Cascades. The campus of the University of Washington, covering 582 acres and situated between lakes Union and Washington, lies entirely within the city. Other educational institutions are Seattle University and Seattle Pacific College.

Seattle, named for a local Indian chief, was first settled in 1851. It was incorporated in 1865, and, in 1869, was chartered as a city. It was the site of the World's Fair in 1962. Population, 1970, 530,831.

Shasta, Mount. A majestic peak in the Sierra Nevada of northern California, situated about 40 miles south of the Oregon boundary. This great mountain, one of the most imposing on the continent, is an extinct volcanic cone which rises to an elevation of 14,380 feet. The summit is continuously covered with snow, and on the north slope there are several glaciers. About 1400 feet below the summit there is a crater nearly 4000 feet in diameter and 2500 feet deep.

Although regarded as extinct, Mount Shasta still shows vestiges of volcanic activity. At the summit there is a sulphurous fumarole which emits hot gases, and on the north slope there is another similar opening. During one of the prehistoric eruptions of Mount Shasta, a stream of lava flowed down its southern slope, entered the channel of the Sacramento River, and followed the bed of that stream for a distance of 50 miles.

The influence of temperature and moisture upon the distribution of plant life is well illustrated in the strong contrast between the vegetation of Mount Shasta and that of Shasta valley. The summit of the mountain is devoid of vegetation because of cold; the Shasta valley, 10 miles distant, is treeless because of a lack of moisture. Between these extremes lies the great forest belt of Mount Shasta. In this heavily forested area the different species of trees are arranged in zones, according to the requirements of each species as regards temperature and moisture. For example, yellow pine and sugar pine predominate in the Transition zone at the foot of the mountain; Shasta fir in the Canadian zone midway on the slope; and whitebark pine in the Hudsonian zone, immediately below the upper limit of trees, at about 9500 feet altitude. Small alpine plants are found as high as 13,000 feet.

Mount Shasta may be ascended with little difficulty. From the city of Mount Shasta, a good trail, about 6 miles in length, leads to Timberline camp. From this camp, the summit may be reached and the return journey made to Mount Shasta city in a single day. The view from the summit of Mount Shasta is unsurpassed by that from any peak in the Cascade range.

Sheboygan (*shê-boi′găn*). A city of eastern Wisconsin, situated on Lake Michigan, 52 miles north of Milwaukee. The city is the trade center of a dairy and farming region and has diversified industries which include stainless steel and enameled kitchen ware, leather, knitted clothing, furniture, toys, molded plastics, shoes, electric sprayers, and hydraulic machinery. Fishing interests process large quantities for national distribution. Population, 1970, 48,484.

Sheridan. A mining and trade center of northern Wyoming. It is an important shipping point for farm products and livestock, and also for coal, which is mined extensively in the neighborhood. Industries include flour mills, sugar refineries, brick and tile works, and concrete plants. The Indian battles of Wolf Creek, Massacre Hill, and Great Wagon Box were fought in the vicinity, 1865–67. population, 1970, 10,856.

Shoshone (*shô-shō′nê*) **Falls.** A great cataract of the Snake River, in southern Idaho, about 120 miles southeast of Boise. This magnificent waterfall is exceeded in grandeur, in the United States, only by Niagara and by the falls in the Yosemite Valley. After coursing through a rocky canyon, some 1200 feet in depth, the deep river, here nearly 800 feet wide, first descends about 30 feet through several rocky channels. The waters then unite and the full volume of the river, in a single sheet, plunges over a precipice about 200 feet high, into the bottom of a narrow gorge. The cataract is easily reached from Twin Falls, about 5 miles distant.

Shreveport. The second largest city of Louisiana, on the Red River, in the northwestern part of the state, about 300 miles from New Orleans. The city has excellent railway facilities and is the commercial center of a large region, rich in oil, gas, lumber, and agricultural products. There is an extensive trade in cotton, corn, peanuts, pecans, fruit, truck crops, and live stock. The local industries include oil refineries, lumber, cotton, and cottonseed oil mills, glassworks, foundries, and machine shops. Industrial output includes also sulphur, salt, and glass. The Caddo Parish Court House is an 8-story building of unusual beauty, having a jail on the two top stories. Population, 1970, 182,064.

Sioux (*soo*) **City.** A city of Iowa, located on the Missouri River, 200 miles northwest of Des Moines. Sioux City occupies a commanding site embracing parts of the river valley and the encircling bluffs. It is the commercial center of a highly productive agricultural region and has extensive wholesaling and shipping interests. It stands at the head of navigation in the Missouri River. The city is one of the important livestock markets of the country and has large meat packing establishments, creameries, and numerous other substantial industries. In total value of manufactured products, Sioux City ranks first among the cities of the state. There are many fine streets and public buildings, and the municipal park system covers an area of 1519 acres. The largest unit is Stone Park, a 915-acre natural wooded tract on the northwestern edge of the city. Grand View Park contains a music pavilion in a natural amphitheater.

Sioux City was founded in 1849 as an outfitting station for expeditions to the Black Hills, and received its municipal charter in 1857. It is the seat of Morningside College and of Briar Cliff College. Population, 1970, 85,925.

Sioux Falls. A city of South Dakota, on the Big Sioux River, about 320 miles southwest of Minneapolis. The river here falls nearly 100 feet. In the vicinity are extensive beds of quartzite, usually called jasper or red granite. Many buildings, both public and private, are built of this native pink stone. Meat packing, stone quarrying, and the manufacture of plastics and farm equipment are among the chief industries. Augustana College and Sioux Falls College are located here. Population, 1970, 72,488.

Sitka. A city on the west coast of Baranof Island, of southeastern Alaska. The chief industry is the processing and packing of salmon. Though located in a high northern latitude, the winters are not severe, and the general climate is healthful. Across the channel is a large naval air base. Nearby is the Sitka National Monument, a 54-acre park of great natural beauty and the scene of a massacre of Russians by Indians in 1802. Sitka was founded by the Russians in 1799 and later became the capital of the Russian territory of Alaska. From 1867 until 1906, Sitka was the capital of the United States territory of Alaska. Population, 1970, 3370.

Somerville. A residential city of eastern Massachusetts, on the Mystic River, two miles northwest of Boston. It is built on a series of hills and has many historic associations connected with the War of Independence. Paul Revere on his memorable ride passed through Somerville along a road now known as Broadway. Prospect Hill is said to be the scene of the first unfurling of the American flag. Meat packing, food processing, and the manufacture of paper bags are among the city's leading industries. Population, 1970, 88,779.

South Bend. A city of northern Indiana, built at the south bend of the Saint Joseph River, about 85 miles east of Chicago. South Bend has excellent railway facilities, is the commercial center of a rich agricultural and peppermint growing district, and has developed extensive manufacturing industries. The city contains large factories making airplanes and agricultural implements. Other important manufactures include lathes, knit goods, roofing, men's clothing, sewing machine parts, stoves, watches, and washing machines. There are 34 parks covering 623 acres. South Bend was founded in 1823 and was incorporated in 1865. The University of Notre Dame is situated in the environs of the city. Population, 1970, 125,580.

Southern Pines. A noted winter resort of North Carolina, situated some 70 miles south of Raleigh. It is located in a fruit growing region, producing berries, peaches, and grapes. By reason of its mild and equable climate, it is a favorite place of winter residence for people from the Northern states. Population, 1970, 5937.

Spartanburg. An industrial city of South Carolina, about 100 miles northwest of Columbia. It is located in a rich cotton-growing section, and has large cotton and textile mills. Other manufactures include machinery, office furniture, food products, ceramics, and apparel. Peaches and other fruit are grown nearby in large quantities and account for much of the income of the area. Spartanburg is the seat of Wofford College for men and Converse College for women. Population, 1970, 44,546.

Spokane (spō′kăn′. A city of Washington, located near the eastern border of the state. It occupies a site at the falls of the Spokane River, which, with other falls in the district, provide immense hydroelectric power for manufacturing. Served by three transcontinental railroads, Spokane has become the chief industrial city of the rich mining, lumbering, stock-raising, and agricultural region known as the "Inland Empire." Among important manufactures are aluminum, lumber products, dairy and meat products, apparel, metal products, flour, and cereals. The city has a system of parks embracing an area of more than 3000 acres, and is the seat of several educational institutions, including Whitworth College and Gonzaga University. The first settlement at Spokane was made in 1872 and, in 1881, the city was incorporated as Spokane Falls, becoming simply Spokane in 1890. Population, 1970, 170,516.

Springfield. The capital of Illinois, situated in the south central part of the state, 185 miles south of Chicago. The city is the center of a highly productive agricultural and coal mining district and has extensive manufacturing interests. Its industries include flour milling and textiles and the manufacture of electrical apparatus, agricultural implements, shoes, tractors, garage equipment, and road grading machinery. The Capitol, erected at a cost of $4.5 million, is built in the neoclassic style of architecture and surmounted by a lofty dome.

Among the points of historic interest are the former residence of President Lincoln and the Lincoln National Monument. The mausoleum in the latter contains the remains of the president. Springfield was first settled in 1818 and was made the capital of Illinois in 1837. Population, 1970, 91,753.

Springfield. A city of southwestern Massachusetts, built on the Connecticut River, about 100 miles southwest of Boston. Springfield occupies a site of great natural beauty on the east bank of the river, and possesses many fine public buildings. Among the most impressive of these is the municipal group, including the Administration Building, the Auditorium, and the Campanile. The top of the Campanile, 300 feet high, affords a magnificent view of the Connecticut valley. Other noteworthy structures are the Public Library, the Art Museum, the Science Museum, the United States Armory, and Trinity Church with a carillon of 61 bells.

Of the city's park system, embracing 1268 acres, the largest unit is the 757-acre Forest Park with a zoological garden. In Merrick Park stands the famous statue of "The Puritan" by Saint Gaudens. Springfield is the seat of the American International College, the Springfield Y. M. C. A. Training College, Springfield College, and Western New England College. Springfield's Naismith Basketball Hall of Fame enshrines many memorabilia of basketball.

The industries of the city are extensive and varied. Among the principal manufactures are firearms, chemicals, envelopes, electrical machinery, toys, and automobile tires.

Springfield was first settled in 1636 and was called Agawam. It assumed its present name in 1640 and, in 1852, was chartered as a city. The city was the center of hostilities in King Philip's War, 1675, and was the scene of various conflicts which took place during Shays's Rebellion, 1786–87. Population, 1970, 163,905.

Springfield. A city of southwestern Missouri, located on a plateau in the Ozark Mountains, about 230 miles southwest of Saint Louis. The city is the commercial center of a large farming, fruit-growing, dairy, and poultry region.

The city is the seat of Drury College, Southwest Missouri State College, Evangel College, and Central Bible College. Springfield was laid out in 1843 and, in 1847, was chartered as a city. In 1956, Springfield was designated as an "All America" city by the National Municipal League. Population, 1970, 120,096.

Springfield. A city of southwestern Ohio, 45 miles west of Columbus. It carries the trade of a rich agricultural region but is primarily an industrial center. Among its chief manufactures are farm implements, metallic caskets, motor trucks, gas engines, automobile parts, and electrical machinery. Here are located the state home of the Masons, the Knights of Pythias, and the Odd Fellows. Springfield is the seat of Wittenberg University. The first settlement was made here in 1799, when a fort was built on the site by Simon Kenton. Population, 1970, 81,926.

Stamford. A manufacturing and residential city of southwestern Connecticut, situated on Long Island Sound, 33 miles from New York City. Stamford is noted especially for the manufacture of mailing machines. Other important products are automobile parts, electric motors, furniture, oil burners, engines, and chemicals. The city was first settled in 1641 by a colony from New Haven, became a borough in 1830, and, in 1894, was chartered as a city. Population, 1970, 108,798.

Starved Rock. A perpendicular cliff of white sandstone, on the south bank of the Illinois River, near the town of Utica, about 90 miles southwest of Chicago. This cliff overhangs the water's edge and rises sheer to a height of about 160 feet. The walls of the fortress-like rock slope precipitously in all directions, and the top is reached by a single narrow rocky stairway. The flat summit, about half an acre, commands an excellent view of the fertile river valley, bordered by wooded hills and grassy slopes.

This almost inaccessible rock was the scene of many interesting events in the early history of Illinois. In 1673, Father Marquette and Joliet spent many weeks at Kaskaskia, the great village of the Illini Indians, in the valley near the rock. In 1681, La Salle and Tonti built a palisaded stronghold on the top of the rock, which they named Fort Saint Louis.

About 1770 occurred the tragic events which gave the cliff its present name. Here perished by starvation the last remnant of the once powerful Illini tribe. At a council at Cahokia, Pontiac, the famous chief of the Ottawas, was stabbed to death by an Illini warrior. Pontiac's followers swore a war of extinction against the Illini, finally entrapping the last survivors of the tribe in this natural fortress. An area of more than 800 acres, including Starved Rock and other historic points, is a state park.

Stockton. An industrial and commercial city of central California, situated 78 miles east of San Francisco on the San Joaquin River, which is deepened so as to be accessible to ocean-going ships. Stockton has important fruit, grain, and livestock interests. Leading manufactures include canned and frozen foods, agricultural implements, and paper products. Stockton is the seat of the University of the Pacific. The settlement which became Stockton was founded in 1847 and was an outfitting point for miners during the gold rush. Population, 1970, 107,644.

Stone Mountain. A huge, cone-shaped hill of granite, located near the town of the same name, about 15 miles east of Atlanta, Georgia. It rises about 1000 feet above the surrounding country and covers an area of some 2 square miles. The surface is almost wholly naked rock. At the base of the northern slope there is an almost vertical cliff, about 800 feet high and 5000 feet long. In 1916, work was begun on a project for transformation of this cliff into a Confederate memorial by chiseling in bold relief figures of Confederate soldiers, centered on colossal figures of Lee, Davis, and Jackson. After many delays, the three central figures were completed and dedicated in 1970, although work remained to be done. The composition as it stands is 190 feet high and 305 feet long.

Superior. A city of northwestern Wisconsin, situated on Lake Superior and lying adjacent to Duluth, Minnesota. Possessing a fine harbor and excellent railway facilities, Superior shares with Duluth the advantages of location at the head of navigation on the Great Lakes. The city ships large quantities of iron ore and grain by water and receives coal to be distributed by rail to inland districts. Among the chief industries are planing and flour mills, iron and steel works, and shipyards. Superior is the seat of Wisconsin State University, Superior.

The early explorers, Radisson and Groseilliers, are supposed to have made their headquarters on the site of Superior in 1661. The explorer Du L'Hut, after whom Duluth was named, established a trading post here about 1680. Superior was laid out as a town in 1853, and, in 1889, was chartered as a city. Population, 1970, 32,237.

Syracuse. A city of New York State, located in the central part of the state, almost exactly midway between Albany and Buffalo, being about 150 miles from each of these cities. It occupies a fine, gently undulating site on Onondaga Lake, 35 miles south of Lake Ontario.

Syracuse owes its prominence as a commercial and industrial city to its central location in a highly productive region and to its superior transportation facilities. It is served by numerous railways which radiate in all directions and by the State Barge Canal system, which affords water transportation north to Lake Ontario, west to Lake Erie, and east to the Hudson River. The city has extensive shipping interests and conducts a large wholesale trade.

Syracuse has upwards of 750 industrial establishments, producing a great variety of articles. Among important manufactures are typewriters, air conditioning equipment, soda ash, tool steel, candles, agricultural implements, chemicals, ceramics, and washing machines.

The commercial district is substantially built, largely of brick and of the native Onondaga limestone, and contains many imposing buildings. The residential sections are noted for their broad, well-shaded streets, and handsome residences and grounds. There are about 60 public parks, ranging in size from small plots at street intersections to spacious tracts such as Burnet Park, on the west, covering 120 acres. Lincoln Park on the east, affords a beautiful view of the city and its environs.

The city is the seat of Syracuse University, with which is connected the State College of Forestry. Le Moyne College also is located here. Another institution, located permanently at Syracuse, is the State Fair.

The site of Syracuse originally belonged to the Onondaga Indians, whose survivors occupy a small reservation south of the city. The salt springs, long known to the Indians, became known to white settlers in 1789. The first settlement on the present site of the city was made about 1805. This was named Syracuse in 1819 and was chartered as a city in 1847. Population, 1970, 197,208.

Tacoma (tȧ-kō'mȧ). A city and port of western Washington, built on a fine harbor on Puget Sound, about 30 miles south of Seattle. It occupies a commanding site, rising to an elevation of several hundred feet overlooking the sound, in a beautiful scenic region between the Olympic and the Cascade mountains. Mount Rainier lies about 56 miles southeast.

The city has a substantial wholesale trade, large manufacturing industries, and an extensive coastwise and foreign commerce. The leading manufactures include lumber, furniture, pulp and paper, and machine shop products. Tacoma contains many fine public buildings, has several picturesque parks, in all covering 1200 acres. It is the seat of University of Puget Sound and Pacific Lutheran University. Old Tacoma, founded in 1868, and New Tacoma, founded in 1873, united in 1883 to form Tacoma. Population, 1970, 154,581.

Tahoe (tä'hō; tȧ'hō), **Lake.** A beautiful lake, situated at the eastern base of the Sierra Nevada mountains, at an elevation of 6275 feet above sea level. The boundary line between California and Nevada passes through the lake, which lies about 85 miles (direct) northeast of Sacramento and 12 miles west of Carson City. It is about 20 miles long and from 8 to 12 miles wide, with an extreme depth exceeding 1650 feet. Its remarkably clear waters are discharged through the Truckee River, eastward into Pyramid Lake, Nevada. Lake Tahoe is a favorite summer resort.

Tallahassee. The capital of Florida and seat of Florida State University and Florida Agricultural and Mechanical University. It is the trade center of a rich dairying and poultry region, which also grows corn, tobacco, cotton, vegetables, pecans, figs, grapes, and blueberries. Tallahassee is located 20 miles from the Gulf of Mexico, on rolling hills. Among the principal buildings are the State Capitol, the Governor's Mansion, and the Federal Building. Tallahassee became the state capital in 1824. It was the only capital not captured by Union troops during the Civil War. Population, 1970, 71,897.

Tamalpais (tăm'ȧl-pīs'), **Mount.** A mountain in the Coast range of California, situated on the Marin Peninsula, about 15 miles in direct line northwest of San Francisco. The triple summit, about 2600 feet high, affords unsurpassed views of the surrounding region.

To the south are the Golden Gate, the city of San Francisco, and, far beyond them, Mount Hamilton, 4444 feet high, on which the Lick Observatory is situated. To the east is San Francisco Bay, with Oakland, Berkeley, and other cities on its eastern shore. Beyond these are the Contra Costa Hills and Mount Diablo, the latter rising nearly 4000 feet high. Close by to the north is the reservoir called Lake Lagunitos, and in the distance are ridge after ridge of the Coast range. On the west is the ocean and the rocky Farallon Islands, lying far out at sea. Within walking distance from West Peak is Muir Woods, with its superb forest of sequoias, many of which are 300 feet high. Muir Woods is a national monument.

Tampa. A manufacturing city and winter resort of west central Florida, located at the head of Tampa Bay, an inlet of the Gulf of Mexico. The city has a good harbor and is served by various steamer lines. A large part of the world's supply of Havana cigars is manufactured at Tampa. Other products include cement, phosphate fertilizer, canned citrus fruit, and beer. Among the city's features are the semitropical Plant Park, where Tampa University is situated; and the Tampa Greyhound Track. Davis Island, a fine residential district, is a result of an extensive reclamation project. Two universities are located in Tampa. Population, 1970, 277,767.

Taos (tä'ôs). An Indian pueblo and village of northern New Mexico, built near the Rio Grande River, about 50 miles north of Santa Fe. The inhabitants are of Taonan Indian stock. Like all pueblo dwellers, the people of Taos are industrious and self-supporting. Population, 1970, 1030.

Tarrytown. A village of New York State on the Hudson River 25 miles north of New York City. It is noted as the scene of numerous skirmishes in the Revolutionary War. Major John André was captured in the vicinity. The village contains "Sunnyside," the home of Washington Irving, who made famous the neighboring valley, Sleepy Hollow. Its factories include an automobile assembly plant. Nearby is the Tappan Zee Bridge, connecting with the New York Thruway. Population, 1970, 11,115.

Terre Haute (tĕr'ē hōt'). A railroad center and manufacturing city of west central Indiana, situated on a high bank of the Wabash River, 73 miles southwest of Indianapolis. The city is the commercial center of a rich agricultural and manufacturing district. Among the chief industries are paper mills, foundries, and the manufacture of plastics, chemicals, and phonograph records. Parks, 20 in number, cover 717 acres. The city is the seat of the Rose Polytechnic Institute, Indiana State University, and, just west of the city, St. Mary-of-the-Woods College. Population, 1970, 70,286.

Thousand Islands. A numerous group of islands in the Saint Lawrence River, located immediately northeast of Lake Ontario. They are situated in an expansion of the river, 40 miles long and from 3 to 7 miles wide. Some of the islands are many acres in extent, but many are mere rocky islets. A large number belong to Canada, 14 of them forming part of the Saint Lawrence Islands National Park, and others are a part of the State of New York. Their attractive scenic setting, together with their cool climate, make the Thousand Islands an ideal place for summer recreation.

Ticonderoga. A village of northeastern New York situated on the creek connecting Lake George with Lake

Champlain, about 95 miles north of Albany. Paper and lumber are its chief industrial products. Because of its many associations with the French and Indian War and the Revolutionary War, Ticonderoga and its environs possess great historic interest. At this point, the French erected, in 1755, a fort which they called Fort Carillon. In 1757, this was heavily garrisoned by Montcalm, but, in 1759, it was taken by the English under General Amherst.

In the Revolutionary War, this stronghold, renamed Fort Ticonderoga, was captured from the English by Ethan Allen and his "Green Mountain Boys." Later, it was retaken by Burgoyne and held until his surrender. The fort fell into disuse but has since been restored and contains a valuable museum. Population, 1970, 3268.

Toledo. A city of Ohio, located about 95 miles directly west of Cleveland and abutting Michigan. It occupies both banks of the Maumee River at its mouth in an inlet of Lake Erie, which provides a seven-mile commercial channel.

Toledo owes its commercial and industrial prominence to its advantageous location at the head of direct water transportation to the East and to its good railway facilities. It is surrounded by a rich agricultural region, with which it maintains an extensive trade, particularly of wheat and soybeans. Toledo is one of the largest distributing points of the Great Lakes for soft coal and is an important oil-refining center.

Toledo has more than 1000 industrial establishments, whose chief products include refined petroleum, auto parts, glass, tools, electrical machinery, ships, and scales.

There are many notable public buildings, among which are the Museum of Art and Our Lady of the Holy Rosary Cathedral, an outstanding example of Spanish architectural design. The park system, covering more than 1500 acres, includes several large parks and some 45 smaller ones. Among noteworthy educational institutions is the University of Toledo, maintained by the state. Toledo was founded in 1837 by the consolidation of two earlier settlements. Population, 1970, 383,818.

Topeka. The capital of Kansas, situated on Kansas River about 70 miles west of Kansas City. It is an important railroad center, being served by four railroad systems and having the extensive car shops of the Santa Fe railroad. An outstanding industry is the publication of farm journals which circulate widely throughout the Middle West. Meat packing, flour milling, and the manufacture of butter are other important industrial interests. The Capitol stands in the center of a beautiful park area. Among other features of the city are a 9-acre rose and rock garden and the 572-acre Lake Shawnee Park. Educational institutions include Washburn University and the Mulvane Art Museum.

Topeka was laid out in 1854 as one of the "free state" towns. In 1856 an antislavery convention there adopted the Topeka constitution, establishing a Topeka government, which was broken up by Federal troops. It became a city in 1857 and capital of the state in 1861. Population, 1970, 125,011.

Trenton. The capital of New Jersey, built on the eastern bank of the Delaware River, at the head of tidewater navigation, about 30 miles northeast of Philadelphia. Proximity to the coal fields of Pennsylvania and to the markets of New York and Philadelphia has contributed to its growth as an industrial center. Among its extensive and varied manufactures, the most noted is that of pottery, which ranks among the finest produced in the United States. Other important industries include the manufacture of wire cables, bridge sections, engines, electric lamps, rubber products, and linoleum.

The city is regularly laid out with many fine public buildings and residences. Among the more notable public buildings are the State Capitol, the Federal Building, the Courthouse, the new State Cultural Center, and Trenton State College. A landmark of historic interest is Battle Monument surmounted by a colossal statue of Washington, which commemorates his command on the battlefield of Trenton. Trenton became a city in 1792. Population, 1970, 104,638.

Troy. A manufacturing city of east central New York. It is situated six miles north of Albany at the head of tidewater navigation on the Hudson River. Once famous as a center for the manufacture of collars and shirts, Troy's manufactures now include ordnance, abrasives, shirts, springs, radiators, brake linings, silicone products, and steel. The chief educational institutions are Rensselaer Polytechnic Institute and Russell Sage College for women. The beautiful Hart-Cluett mansion is maintained as a museum.

The vicinity of Troy was the scene of internecine struggles between the Mohawk and the Mohican Indians, and during the Revolutionary War was the theater of stirring American activities in resisting Burgoyne's invasion. Henry Burden founded his famous ironworks here in the early nineteenth century. Population, 1970, 62,918.

Tucson (*too-sŏn'*). A city of Arizona, situated in the southern part of the state, about 65 miles north of the Mexican border. It is the commercial center of a large district devoted to stock raising, mining, and farming. Many new companies engaged in research and engineering science have located in Tucson recently. Tucson is the seat of the University of Arizona and other educational institutions. The warm, dry climate makes it a tourist and health center. A replica of the walled city of Tucson as it looked in 1859 stands 13 miles away, having been erected in making the motion picture *Arizona*, and still being used for similar purposes. Population, 1970, 262,933.

Tulsa. A city of Oklahoma, on the Arkansas River, about 100 miles northeast of Oklahoma City. Tulsa is situated in one of the richest oil and natural gas fields in America. To the immense development of these resources, the city owes its remarkably rapid growth. More than 500 operating and refining oil companies are located in the city. The surrounding district also contains valuable deposits of coal.

The city is the trade center of a large outlying region devoted to farming, stock raising, and dairying, and, by reason of cheap and abundant fuel, has developed substantial industries. Among the chief of these are oil refining, flour and lumber milling, and the manufacture of aircraft, boilers, tools, stoves, and glass.

Tulsa occupies a fine, gently rolling site, and is well laid out, with many beautiful parks, boulevards, and handsome homes built by fortunes made in the oil fields. Mohawk Park covers 2400 acres. The business district is noted for its impressive array of modern office buildings, including the 21-story Philtower Building and the 27-story tower of the Exchange National Bank Building. The city is the seat of Tulsa University and the Philbrook Art Center and Indian Museum. Tulsa was founded in 1887 and was first chartered as a city in 1902. Population, 1970, 330,409.

Tuscaloosa. Located on the Black Warrior River in Alabama, 58 miles southwest of Birmingham, Tuscaloosa is the seat of the University of Alabama and Stillman College. Manufactures, such as paper, lumber, iron, chemicals, building materials, and food products, have become more important to the area than the cotton crop that once made it prosper. Population, 1970, 65,773.

Union City. A city of eastern New Jersey, adjoining Hoboken and Jersey City. It was formed in 1925 by a consolidation of the old towns of West Hoboken and Union. Weehawken, adjoining Union City on the east and fronting on the Hudson River, is the railroad terminal and port. Union City is a residential place for persons employed in New York City and Jersey City. It has also many local industries, their output including embroidery, silk, cement products, and rubber goods. Population, 1970, 58,537.

Utica. A city of central New York, situated on the Mohawk River and the State Barge Canal, about 95 miles west of Albany. Utica is the commercial center of a rich dairy-farming district. Important manufactures include fabricated metal products, men's clothing, textiles, heating and ventilating apparatus, and iron and steel forgings. Utica is an important railway center and transfer point, and is often called the "Gateway to the Adirondacks." Its $4 million Munson-Williams-Proctor Institute has brought new cultural opportunities to Utica. Population, 1970, 91,611.

Vallejo (*văl-yā'hō; vă-lā'ō*). A city of western California, located on an arm of San Pablo Bay, opposite Mare Island, about 25 miles northeast of San Francisco. Mare Island Navy Yard contributes substantially to the commerce of the city. The city's industrial products include flour, lumber, and dairy products. Vallejo was founded in 1851 and was planned as the capital of the state. The legislature held sessions in Vallejo, 1851–53. Population, 1970, 66,733.

Valley Forge. A village on the Schuylkill River, in eastern Pennsylvania, about 20 miles west of Philadelphia. Valley Forge is famous as the place where Washington and the Colonial army of about 11,000 men endured terrible privations during the severe winter of 1777–78. The area with the trenches thrown up by the "ragged Continentals" remains substantially unchanged, and the old stone house where Washington made his headquarters still stands. An area of 2048 acres, including the old camp site, comprises Valley Forge State Park. The site is occupied by replicas of soldiers' huts and by monuments to generals Washington, Wayne, and von Steuben.

Vancouver. A city of southwestern Washington, on the Columbia River, about 8 miles north of Portland, Oregon. The chief manufactures include lumber, aluminum, pulp and paper, canned fruit, metal castings, and machine shop products. A long interstate bridge over the Columbia River connects Vancouver with Oregon. Vancouver was established in 1825 by the Hudson's Bay Company and was incorporated in 1858. Population, 1970, 42,588.

Vicksburg. Located on high bluffs overlooking the Mississippi River, Vicksburg is an important tourist, industrial, and river port city 45 miles west of Jackson, Miss. The U.S. Army Corps, with three major agencies, is the city's largest employer. The chief industries, most of which depend on the river for cheap transportation or processing water, produce lighting fixtures, earth-moving equipment, chemicals, hardwood lumber and flooring, feeds, house trailers, and boats.

Incorporated in 1825, Vicksburg gained special prominence during the Civil War. Its capture by the Union forces after a prolonged campaign was one of the decisive events of the great struggle between the North and the South. The Vicksburg National Military Park, of 1648 acres, with 30 miles of driveways and many monuments, restores the battleground as it was in 1863. Population, 1970, 25,478.

Vincennes (vĭn-sĕnz'). A city of southwestern Indiana, on the Wabash River. It is the oldest settlement in the state, dating from 1727, when Sieur de Vincennes built a fortification there. A French trading post had been erected on the site as early as 1702. The city is in a rich agricultural region and has varied industrial interests, including structural steel, storage batteries, paper products, glass, shoes, and flour.

Vincennes was under the French flag until 1777, was held by the British until 1779, and was taken by American troops in 1779 under George Rogers Clark, to whom is erected a $2 million memorial on the river front. The house still stands where the first territorial legislature met in 1805, Vincennes having been capital of Indian Territory from 1800 to 1813. Crossing of the Wabash River at this point by the Lincoln family in 1830 while migrating to Illinois is memorialized by a bridge, a marble shrine, and life-size bronze statue of Abraham Lincoln. Population, 1970, 19,867.

Waco. A city of east central Texas, on the Brazos River, 100 miles south of Dallas. Waco is the trade and shipping center of a rich agricultural region. The city is a leading cotton market for the interior of the state and has substantial industries. The principal manufactures are textiles, twine, woodwork, tents, awnings, camp furniture, clothing, and cement. Waco is the seat of Baylor University. The city was laid out in 1849 and was named for the Huaco Indians. Population, 1970, 95,326.

Walla Walla. A city of southeastern Washington, situated near the Oregon boundary. Walla Walla is the trade center of a fertile agricultural district. The manufactures include farm machinery, flour, and lumber. The city is the seat of Whitman College and Walla Walla College. At Waiilatpu, seven miles west, is a national monument park commemorating the first white family settling in the Pacific Northwest, that of Dr. Marcus Whitman, who founded a mission there in 1836. The original Fort Walla Walla is now a veterans' hospital. Population, 1970, 23,619.

Walpi. A Hopi Indian village built on a lofty mesa, several hundred feet high, overlooking an arid desert in north central Arizona. The inhabitants are among the most interesting of the Pueblo tribes. These peaceful village dwellers steadfastly adhere to their aboriginal culture and ancient customs. Their houses are constructed of adobe or of stone set in clay mortar, with square rooms and flat roofs, through which trap doors provide entrances.

The elaborate ceremonials of the Hopi people include the celebrated snake dance, in which the performers carry living rattlesnakes. The Hopi are industrious farmers, and maintain abundant stores of corn, beans, and vegetables. They also weave excellent blankets and baskets and display great skill as potters and wood carvers. The village contains about 150 inhabitants.

Waltham (wŏl'thăm). A city of eastern Massachusetts, situated on the Charles River, about 10 miles west of Boston. Here in 1854 was made the first successful attempt to manufacture watch movements, on an extensive scale, by machinery. Industries in Waltham are engaged in the manufacture of watches, clocks, knit goods, precision machinery, radar equipment, batteries, and jewel bearings. Other manufactures include emery wheels and furniture.

A point of interest is Norumbega Tower, named in allusion to a fabulous city said by early explorers to be located in New England. Waltham was incorporated in 1738 and was chartered as a city in 1884. A mill established there in 1814 is said to have been the first complete power mill for the making of cotton cloth in America. Population, 1970, 61,582.

Warren. An industrial city in northern Ohio, situated on the Mahoning River, 14 miles northwest of Youngstown. It has good transportation facilities and manufactures steel, automobile parts, tires, electrical products, fire protection equipment, drinking fountains, and many other items. Population, 1970, 63,494.

Warwick. This city is a residential suburb of Providence, Rhode Island, and is situated on the Pawtuxet and Providence rivers in a region of quiet towns and villages. It has some industry, including the manufacture of textiles and the shipping of clams, oysters, and scallops. It was the birthplace of General Nathanael Greene, a hero of the American Revolutionary War. Population, 1970, 83,694.

WASHINGTON. The capital of the United States, situated on the left bank of the Potomac River, about 100 miles from its mouth. Washington is coextensive with the District of Columbia. It is the administrative, legislative, and judicial center of the nation.

SITE AND PLAN. The site was chosen by a commission headed by George Washington, and the city was planned by L'Enfant, a noted French engineer. Congress transferred its sittings from Philadelphia to the new capital in 1800. The city was captured and burned in 1814 by the British. At the time of the Civil War, it was fortified and made the headquarters of the Northern army. Following 1871, important improvements were made in the city, mainly in accordance with the original plan drawn up by L'Enfant. In the 1930's still greater improvements were made particularly the construction of monumental government offices occupying a triangle south of Pennsylvania Avenue. In 1962, President Kennedy appointed a commission to draw up plans for a much more radical improvement. One aspect of the plans called for a second triangle of buildings north of Pennsylvania Avenue, some governmental and others privately owned but architecturally suitable. In addition, an immense National Square would be created at the White House end. The plans envisaged several levels of construction, including underground parking areas, arcades for shopping facilities, and large areas accessible only to pedestrians. To President Kennedy is due also initiation of the Kennedy Cultural Center to the west on the Potomac River.

From 1802 until 1871, Washington's affairs were managed, under a charter, by its own citizens. In 1871 the charter was revoked, and the city was placed directly under the management of the Federal government. In 1961, the XXIII amendment gave residents of the District of Columbia the right to vote in presidential elections.

AREA AND SURFACE. The District of Columbia is about 70 square miles in area, including 8 square miles of water surface. The surface, on the whole, is gently undulating and the elevation of the land in the District varies within a range of approximately 400 feet.

STREETS. The streets are laid out on a rectangular plan modified by a system of 26 avenues, which intersect the streets at different angles. A number of avenues converge on the two focal points of the city, namely, the Capitol and the executive mansion, or White House, the line of Pennsylvania Avenue passing through both points of intersection. The streets and avenues are from 80 to 160 feet in width, many of them adorned on each side with a double row of trees.

PARKS AND MALLS. In a central square stands a lofty monument erected to the memory of George Washington. Extending north, east, and west from this square are long, parklike areas, or malls. The north mall leads to the White House; the area to the east is the approach to the Capitol; and to the west of the monument along a reflecting pool stretches a vista terminating in the Lincoln Memorial. Small parks and open squares or circles are found in various parts of the city. Potomac Park consists of about 723 acres of land which has been largely reclaimed from the Potomac River. The "tidal basin" is partially surrounded by Japanese cherry trees. Rock Creek Park, covering approximately 1600 acres, is a hilly tract of great natural beauty extending along both sides of the creek, which flows south, and widening at one point to form the picturesque National Zoological Park, covering 170 acres.

MONUMENTS. The monuments and buildings of Washington befit the dignity of the national capital. The Washington Monument, already mentioned, is a majestic obelisk 555 feet in height. The stately Lincoln Memorial takes the form of a Greek temple of the Doric order. It is surrounded by a peristyle of 36 columns, one for each of the states of the Union at the time of Lincoln's presidency. In the interior is a statue, heroic in size, of the martyred president. On the shore of the tidal basin rises the circular, dome-crowned memorial to Thomas Jefferson. A striking monument in the Washington area is the U. S. Marine Corps War Memorial showing the flag-raising on Iwo Jima. Most of the numerous circles throughout the city where avenues cross are adorned with colossal statues of national heroes.

BUILDINGS. The buildings of Washington, which are among the most beautiful in America, are characterized in general by the neoclassical type of architecture. The Capitol, a magnificent structure of the Corinthian order, having two immense wings and surmounted by a beautiful dome, occupies a commanding position on an eminence east of the Mall. The White House exhibits a pleasing and noble simplicity. The Library of Congress, containing one of the world's largest collections of books, is an imposing structure in the Renaissance style, near which stands the annex, modernistic in design. The Treasury, like the Supreme Court building, is an example of pure Greek architecture. One of the city's most exquisite structures is the Folger Shakespearean library.

The diverging lines of Constitution and Pennsylvania avenues form a triangular wedge of monumental buildings extending from the Apex Building, nearest the Capitol, to the Department of Commerce Building and the Treasury Building, near the White House. This group includes the Archives and Internal Revenue buildings and structures housing the justice, post-office, labor and interior departments. South of this group are the Department of Agriculture building, the Smithsonian Institution, and the Natural History and History and Technology museums. Nearer to the Capitol is the National Gallery of Art. West of the triangle are the Federal Reserve and Interior Department buildings.

Other notable structures include the Pentagon, the Corcoran Art Gallery, Constitution Hall, the State, War and Navy Building, the State Department Building, National Academy of Sciences, Pan-American, Red Cross, and Bureau of Engraving and Printing Buildings. The Health, Education and Welfare building and the National Aeronautic and Space Administration building are on Independence Avenue facing the Mall. Notable too are the National Geographic building with its fine exhibits and numerous high-rise office and apartment buildings in newer architectural styles. Ford's Theater, where President Lincoln was assassinated has been completely restored.

The Naval Observatory is the source from which the official time is telegraphed to all parts of the country. Among Washington's many fine churches are the National Cathedral of Saint Peter and Saint Paul, Gothic in architecture, where President Wilson is buried, and the Franciscan Monastery, which contains a replica of part of the catacombs at Rome. In the northeastern part of the city is the Catholic Shrine of the Immaculate Conception, crowned with a colored tile dome, which is offset by a bell tower 329 feet high with a carillon of 56 bells.

COMMERCE. The industries of Washington are devoted largely to the service of the government and to the supplying of local needs. The city's mercantile business, however, is very extensive. Scientific research plays a large role. Local travel is facilitated by a high-speed belt highway. As a national and international center of travel, it is served by three airports, of which Dulles airport is one of the world's finest.

EDUCATIONAL INSTITUTIONS The institutions of learning and research are numerous. They include George Washington University, Catholic University of America, American University, the Smithsonian Institution, the Carnegie Institution of Washington, Georgetown University, and Howard University. The Washington Academy of Sciences serves as "federal head" for many learned societies.

POINTS OF INTEREST. The city and its environs are rich in historical associations. Mount Vernon, the home of Washington, lies on the right bank of the river, about 15 miles below the city. Across the Potomac from the Lincoln Memorial, in Virginia, is Arlington National Cemetery, containing a beautiful memorial amphitheater and the grave of three of the nation's Unknown Soldiers. This cemetery is connected with Washington by the beautiful Arlington Memorial Bridge. To the north of the city lie the Naval Hospital with its conspicuous tower, the widespreading National Health Institutes, the impressive Bureau of Standards building, and the headquarters of the Atomic Energy Commission.

During the Civil War, Washington was surrounded by a ring of 68 forts. Of these, only Fort Myer on Arlington Heights opposite the city is occupied, being used as a training center. Population, 1970, 756,189.

Washington, Mount. The highest peak in the White Mountains of New Hampshire, and the loftiest summit in the northeastern United States. It rises from the massive Presidential range, in the central part of the White Mountain group, and reaches an elevation of 6288 feet. It lies east of Crawford Notch and is about 140 miles almost directly north of Boston.

The mountain is composed chiefly of granite. The east and north sides are gashed with deep gorges and the west slope is precipitous. The rocky summit, which rises many hundred feet above timber line, has a scant covering of alpine vegetation; the lower slopes are extensively forested. Trails, highways, and a rack-and-pinion railroad make it easy for travelers to reach the summit, on which are a government meteorological station and a commodious hotel.

Waterbury. A city of southwestern Connecticut, on the Naugatuck River, 32 miles southwest of Hartford. Abundant water power has contributed largely to the city's industrial prominence. Waterbury is the leading center for the manufacture of brass ware in the United States, and is often styled the "Brass City." It is noted also for the production of clocks and watches. In value of manufactures, Waterbury ranks among the first two or three cities of the state. The city occupies a hilly site and contains parks of great natural beauty. Population, 1970, 108,033.

Waterloo. A city in Iowa on the Cedar River about 110 miles northeast of Des Moines. The surrounding country produces grain, hogs, cattle, and dairy products in great abundance. It is one of the largest manufacturing centers in the state, being noted especially for the manufacture of tractors and other agricultural implements. Waterloo is served by four railroads, one air line, and 32 trucking lines, and is on three federal highways. It is the home of the National Dairy Cattle Congress. Population, 1970, 75,533.

Watkins Glen. A narrow gorge of unusual scenic beauty, situated near the village of Watkins Glen, New York, not far from the head of Seneca Lake, and about 20 miles north of Elmira. Through this chasm, which, in places, is 300 feet deep, a narrow stream flows over a series of charming cascades and rapids. The rocks, which are Devonian shales, were worn into deep gorges by glacial ice.

Waukegan. A lake port and industrial city in the northeast corner of Illinois. Although it has distinct individuality and local pride in educational and other civic enterprises, Waukegan is closely associated with North Chicago in matters of commerce, industry, and transportation. Population, 1970, 65,269.

West Point. A strong military post and noted military educational center in New York State. It occupies a picturesque site on the west bank of the Hudson River, about 50 miles north of New York City. The government reservation, including Constitution Island, covers 3574 acres and is the seat of the United States Military Academy. It has a great repository for the storing of monetary silver. Among many fine buildings and monuments are Memorial Hall, containing trophies of war, and a handsome equestrian statue of George Washington. West Point was a position of great strategic importance in the Revolutionary War. Benedict Arnold plotted, while in command here, to betray it to the British, but this result was prevented by the timely discovery of the plot.

Wheat Belt. The name applied to the section of the United States in which more than three-fourths of the nation's wheat crop is grown. In reality, there are two wheat belts, the winter wheat belt and the spring wheat belt.

The winter wheat belt has two parts. One stretches from Ohio to eastern Colorado, and the other consists of north central Montana and the Pacific Northwest. The chief producing area for winter wheat includes southern Nebraska, Kansas, western Oklahoma, northern Texas, eastern Colorado, north central Montana, Idaho, eastern Washington, Missouri, Illinois, Indiana, and Ohio. The spring wheat belt consists chiefly of North Dakota, South Dakota, Minnesota, and eastern Montana.

Wheeling. A city of West Virginia, on the Ohio River, in the northern "panhandle," about 65 miles southwest of Pittsburgh, Pennsylvania. Wheeling owes its industrial and commercial importance to large supplies of natural gas, to extensive nearby coal fields, and to abundant raw materials, made available by excellent facilities for transportation, both by rail and by water. There are more than 200 manufacturing establishments in Wheeling, and the total value of its products is greater than that of any other city in the state. The leading manufactures include iron and steel products, plastics, glass, tobacco, tin plate, and aluminum ware. There are also print works, packing houses, and large proprietary remedy works.

The city occupies an excellent site, rising gradually from the river, and contains many fine streets and public buildings. Oglebay Park, of 1200 acres, is a country recreational center. Wheeling Island is connected with the main part of the city by a historic suspension bridge.

The first settlement on the site of Wheeling was made in 1769 by Ebenezer Zane. Fort Henry, named for Patrick Henry, was built in 1774 and, during the Revolutionary War, was repeatedly, but unsuccessfully, attacked by the Indians and the British. Wheeling was incorporated in 1795 and was chartered as a city in 1836. From 1863 to 1870, and again from 1875 to 1885, Wheeling was the capital of the state. Population, 1970, 48,188.

White Plains. A city of southern New York about 25 miles north of midtown New York. Here in 1776, Washington's army was attacked by a superior force of British and succeeded in withdrawing across the Hudson River. Population, 1970, 50,220

White Sands National Monument. Located in south central New Mexico, in the vicinity of White Sands Proving Ground (a rocket test site) and about 15 miles from Alamogordo (the site of the explosion of the first atomic bomb in 1945). This national monument is 140,247 acres of dazzling white dunes, which extend far beyond the boundaries appropriated for the monument itself. The dunes range from 5 to 50 feet high and consist of 95% pure gypsum, grading into quartz sand in the north. The dunes are not continuous, but occur in waves, with bare ground showing between them. They move constantly, always in a northeasterly direction and very slowly, shifting a few feet a year. There is a strange, boggy lake bed, Lake Lucero, in the southwest corner of the monument area. It is said that no life can exist in it. Mice, insects, and beetles, which are numerous in the White Sands area, are white or nearly white, apparently a protective coloration. Plant life is confined to the outer stretches of the sands and differs from similar species elsewhere.

White Sulphur Springs. A health and pleasure resort of southeastern West Virginia, located in picturesque Greenbrier County. Famed for its numerous mineral springs, this historic spa and fashion center, dating back to Revolutionary War times, is visited annually by thousands of tourists. Japanese diplomats in Washington at the time of the attack on Pearl Harbor were interned here during World War II. Population, 1970, 2396.

Whitney, Mount. The highest peak in the United States, excluding Alaska. It is situated in the main range of the Sierra Nevada, in eastern California, and is surrounded by a region of unusual scenic magnificence. Its eastern slope rises precipitously nearly 11,000 feet above Owens Valley, and the peak itself towers to an elevation of 14,495 feet above sea level. The lowest land in North America, Death Valley, much of which is below sea level, lies only 86 miles east of this gigantic mountain.

Whittier. A city of California, situated about 12 miles southeast of Los Angeles. It was founded by Quakers and named for the poet John Greenleaf Whittier. It is a residential city, once a citrus empire, now a hub of industry and a packing and shipping point for agricultural products grown in the area. It is the seat of Whittier College and the world's largest Quaker church. Population, 1970, 72,863.

Wichita. A city of Kansas where 64% of the world's private aircraft are manufactured. Beech Aircraft Corporation, the Boeing Company—Wichita Division, Cessna Aircraft Company, and Gates Learjet Corporation are major aircraft plants located in the city. Wichita is also a milling and meat-packing center. Wichita's industry is varied, with manufactures of farm machinery, heating equipment, amusement park equipment, hotel and motel equipment, and camping equipment. The city occupies an excellent site on the banks of the Arkansas River in central Kansas. Three institutions of higher learning are located here—Friends University, Sacred Heart College, and Wichita State University. The city's name was derived from the Wichita tribe of Indians. Settled in 1870, Wichita was incorporated in 1871. A living historical monument recalls the city's origin in a section called "Cowtown," which contains many of the original structures of early Wichita. Population, 1970, 276,554.

Wichita Falls. A city of northern Texas, on the Wichita River, about 100 miles northwest of Fort Worth. Wichita Falls is the distributing point for a large agricultural and stock raising region, and is the center of a rich petroleum oil and gas field. Its principal manufactures are window glass, auto trucks, flour, and oil well machinery. The refining of petroleum is one of the most important industries. Wichita Falls was settled in 1882 and was chartered as a city in 1884. It is the seat of Midwestern University. Population, 1970, 97,564.

Wilkes-Barre (*wĭlks′ băr′ĭ*). A city of northeastern Pennsylvania, on the Susquehanna River, about 100 miles northwest of Philadelphia. It is situated in the picturesque Wyoming Valley and is the center of one of the richest anthracite coal fields in the world. Its manufactures include electronic components, furniture, cigars, pencils and writing supplies, aircraft and missle parts, perfumes, malt beverages, clothing, fiber glass, shoes, wire rope, and boilers.

Wilkes-Barre is the seat of Wilkes and King's colleges. Two major annual events include the Fine Arts Fiesta and the Cherry Blossom Time festival, both held in May.

Wilkes-Barre was settled in 1769 by New Englanders, and named in honor of John Wilkes and Isaac Barre, members of the British Parliament. It was the scene of desperate struggles with the British and Indians during the Revolutionary War; the Wyoming massacre took place four miles from its site. The city is noted as the birthplace of the anthracite coal industry. Here "stone coal," as it was called, was first used for domestic purposes. Population, 1970, 58,856.

Williamsburg. A historic city of eastern Virginia, 48 miles east by south of Richmond, in a peninsula between the James and York rivers. It was settled in 1632 and was known as Middle Plantation until 1699. From 1699 to 1780 it was the capital of Virginia. It is the seat of William and Mary College, opened in 1693, which, after Harvard, is the oldest college in the United States.

In 1927, under the active interest of John D. Rockefeller, Jr., the restoration of the colonial area of Williamsburg was undertaken. Among the many restored structures are the original college building, designed by Sir Christopher Wren, and the Raleigh Tavern, where the Virginia assembly met when dissolved by royal governors. Recently erected business structures are made to conform with the earlier architectural style. Here in 1776 the Phi Beta Kappa society was organized. Population, 1970, 9069.

Willimantic. A city of Connecticut, located 28 miles east of Hartford, at the junction of the Willimantic and Natchaug rivers. It has been styled the "Thread City," having produced thread extensively since 1822. The city has other industry and is in the midst of a fertile farm area. It is the seat of Eastern Connecticut State College. Population, 1970, 14,402.

Wilmington. The chief city of Delaware, located on the Delaware River, at its junction with Christina River, about 27 miles southwest of Philadelphia.

The favorable location, excellent transportation facilities, nearness to the great coal fields and the sources of raw material, together with water power furnished by the Christina, have combined to make the city an important manufacturing center. The Du Pont chemical industries center in Wilmington, the city of their origin. They began as a powder mill, established in 1802, the first in America. Other important manufactures are braided rubber hose, leather belting, castings, cork products, iron and steel articles, hosiery, machinery, paper, and petroleum products. Immense powder and dye mills, across the river in New Jersey, contribute substantially to the city's trade.

The town was founded in 1638 by Swedes and was known by various names. Nearby Winterthur Museum, formerly the residence of Henry Francis du Pont, contains a collection of American decorative arts from the seventeenth century through the early nineteenth century. Population 1970, 80,386.

Wilmington. The chief port of North Carolina, situated on the Cape Fear River, 20 miles from the Atlantic Ocean. Wilmington has an excellent harbor, accommodating large seagoing vessels, and is an important commercial city with an extensive shipping trade. The city is located in a highly productive agricultural district, of which it is the mercantile center. Wilmington has a number of textile mills for the manufacture of cotton goods, pile fabrics, hosiery, and wearing apparel. The city is the home of the U.S.S. North Carolina Battleship Memorial and the annual North Carolina Azalea Festival.

Wilmington was first settled in 1730 and incorporated in 1739. Here, in 1765, was the first armed resistance to the British Stamp Act. During the Civil War, the port was the chief gateway between the South and foreign nations. It was the principal resort of the blockade runners. It is the seat of Wilmington College. Population, 1970, 46,169.

Wilson, Mount. A peak in the Sierra Madre range of southern California, about 10 miles northeast of Pasadena. On its summit, which rises to an elevation of 5750 feet, is the Mount Wilson Observatory, containing the famous Hooker 100-inch reflecting telescope and other powerful instruments for astronomical research. An automobile road leads from Pasadena to the summit, which affords excellent views of the surrounding region.

Wind Cave National Park. Tom Bingham discovered Wind Cave in 1881 when he thought he felt wind blowing up from the ground and stopped to determine the source. The narrow entrance to the cave lets wind in when the outside pressure rises, and expels air when the pressure drops, creating a strong current of air and the illusion that the wind is blowing out of the ground. The cave was made a national park in 1903, and is located 12 miles northwest of Hot Springs in South Dakota. Its extensive galleries with many beautiful crystal formations are unusual because there are relatively few stalactites and stalagmites. There is a 44-square-mile game preserve surrounding the cave, with herds of bison, antelope, elk, and deer.

Winona. A city of southeastern Minnesota, situated on the Mississippi River, about 110 miles southeast of Minneapolis. A shipping point for agricultural products grown in the area, Winona is also important for limestone quarrying. Manufactures include sheet metal, glue, automotive equipment, and medicines. It is the seat of Winona State College, College of St. Teresa, and St. Mary's College. Population, 1970, 26,438.

Winston-Salem. A city of North Carolina, situated 108 miles west of Raleigh. It is located in a region noted for tobacco growing, and has become the most important center for the manufacture of tobacco in the United States. Its immense factories are said to turn out more manufactured tobacco products than those of any other city in the world. In value of manufactures, Winston-Salem outranks practically all other cities of the South. Other products include hosiery, underwear, air conditioning machinery, and furniture.

The business and industrial establishments are, for the most part, centered in Winston, while Salem is chiefly residential. The city is the seat of Wake Forest University, Salem College for young women and Winston-Salem State College. Salem was founded in 1766 by Moravians and long remained under the direct control of the Moravian Church. Winston was founded in 1849 and received its municipal charter in 1899. The two communities were consolidated in 1913. Population, 1970, 132,913.

Woodbridge. A large town of New Jersey, located 14 miles south of Newark, on the Arthur Kill, a channel separating New Jersey from Staten Island, New York. Rich clay deposits in the area supply the pottery, tile, and brick industry. Other industries include oil refining and the manufacture of chemicals, tools, and radio tubes. In the vicinity are the Bible Gardens, an outdoor museum of small replicas of the Holy Land's gardens and orchards as they were in Biblical times. Puritans from Massachusetts and New Hampshire settled the town in 1665. Woodbridge was incorporated in 1669. Population, 1970, 98,000 (est.).

Woods Hole. A village in Massachusetts within the town of Falmouth on Cape Cod. Formerly a whaling and shipbuilding center, the village is now widely known as the location of the Woods Hole Oceanographic Institution and Marine Biological Laboratories, which study tides, currents, and marine life.

Woonsocket. A city of Rhode Island, on the Blackstone River, about 16 miles northwest of Providence. The great waterfalls that gave Woonsocket its Indian name have been replaced by a huge dam with hydraulically operated gates as part of a $15 million flood-control system along the entire course of the Blackstone River. Textiles are the city's dominant industry, but other manufactures include plastics, rubber gear, canvas footwear, machine tools, and garments. Woonsocket is a consolidation of several factory villages, was chartered as a village in 1837, and incorporated as a city in 1888. Population, 1970, 46,820

Wooster. A city of northern Ohio, about 30 miles southwest of Akron. It is the trade center for a productive farm country, and is also important industrially, with manufactures ranging from paint brushes to truck bodies. It is the seat of the College of Wooster and the Ohio Agricultural Research and Development Center, which has 1900 acres used in experiments to improve and increase the world's plant and animal production. The city claims to have had the nation's first Christmas tree. Population, 1970, 18,703.

Worcester (woos'ter). A city of Massachusetts, built on both banks of the Blackstone River, about 40 miles west of Boston. The city occupies a picturesque site covering the river valley and a number of the surrounding hills.

Worcester is preeminently a manufacturing city and is one of the greatest machine tool centers in the world. Among noteworthy manufacturing establishments are immense rolling mills, wire factories, envelope factories, and loom works. Other manufactures include aviation pressure suits, firearms, abrasives, paper products, athletic shoes, pharmaceuticals, and steam turbines.

The city ranks high among the cities of the state in general civic improvements. There are 17 public parks and many other recreation sites. Lake Quinsigamond forms part of the eastern boundary of the city.

Worcester is the seat of Clark University, College of the Holy Cross, Assumption College, Worcester Polytechnic Institute, and Massachusetts State College, Worcester. There is an excellent art museum; the library of the American Antiquarian Society, founded in 1812, is rich in historical material.

First settled in 1673, Worcester was twice abandoned because of the hostility of the Indians, especially during King Philip's War. It was incorporated in 1722 and was chartered as a city in 1848. Within the vicinity of Worcester were born Eli Whitney, inventor of the cotton gin; Erastus Bigelow, inventor of the carpet-weaving machine; Elias Howe, inventor of the sewing machine; Lucius Knowles, who perfected the modern power loom; and George Bancroft, the historian. Population, 1970, 176,572.

Wyandotte. A city of Michigan, 12 miles southwest of Detroit, of which it is a residential suburb. It is noted for its important chemical industry, which is largely based on the extensive salt beds that underlie the city. It was also important in the development of the steel industry in the U.S., having established the first steel analysis laboratory in 1862, and producing the first commercial Bessemer steel in the U.S. as early as 1864. Population, 1970, 41,061.

Wyandotte Cave. A natural formation in Crawford County, southern Indiana, five miles northeast of Leavenworth. Wyandotte Cave is the third largest cave in the U.S. after Carlsbad Cavern and Mammoth Cave and has a greater number and variety of stalactites and stalagmites than any other known cave in the U.S. Besides the numerous chambers and galleries, the 23 miles of the cave that have been explored contain Monument "mountain," rising 175 feet from the floor, and the Pillar of the Constitution, a large stalagmite 30 feet high and 75 feet in circumference.

Yakima (yăk'ĭ-mả). A city of central Washington, situated 142 miles southeast of Seattle. Yakima, formerly called North Yakima, is the commercial center of the Yakima Valley. This valley contains one of the largest areas of irrigated land in the western United States and is widely noted for the excellent apples and other fine fruits which it produces. The city's chief industrial establishments include fruit canneries, fruit packing houses, sugar, and lumber mills. Fort Simcoe is a nearby historical attraction. Population, 1970, 45,588.

Yellow Springs. A village of Ohio about 18 miles east of Dayton. It is noted as the seat of Antioch College, which operates on a cooperative plan of work and study. The Fels Research Institute and the Kettering Research Laboratory in Yellow Springs study human development. The village is also the seat of the national headquarters for the American Humanist Association. Population, 1970, 4624.

YELLOWSTONE NATIONAL PARK. The largest national park in the United States, situated mainly in northwestern Wyoming but encroaching slightly upon adjoining portions of Montana and Idaho. It is approximately 62 miles long and 54 miles wide, and covers an area of 3472 square miles. Of this area, 3200 square miles are in Wyoming, 236 square miles are in Montana, and 36 square miles are in Idaho.

RIVERS AND LAKES. Within the limits of the park are the headwaters of several large rivers, including the Yellowstone, the Snake, the Lewis, the Madison, and the Shoshone. The Continental Divide, passing through the park from southeast to northwest, marks the line of separation of the waters draining into the Atlantic from those flowing into the Pacific. There are also numerous lakes, the largest of which is Yellowstone Lake, some 20 miles long and from about 5 to 15 miles wide. Below timber line, the less precipitous mountains, as well as the more level portions of the park, are beautifully forested with pine, spruce, and other evergreen trees.

SURFACE AND ORIGIN. The central part of the park is essentially a high plateau, lying at an average elevation of about 8000 feet above sea level. Except on its southwestern border, this plateau is surrounded by massive, snow-capped mountains, whose culminating peaks and ridges rise from 2000 to 4000 feet above the enclosed tableland.

In its origin, the whole region is volcanic. Not only the encircling mountains but also the interior plains are made up of volcanic ash and lava, ejected in some former geologic age from far below the surface. Striking evidences of this are seen in the black glass of Obsidian cliff, in the contorted lavas along the road near the summit of Mount Washburn, and in the fused, highly colored sands composing the walls of Yellowstone Canyon.

SCENIC FEATURES. The entire park is a scenic wonderland. Its chief features are the geysers, which are the greatest in the world; the Grand Canyon of the Yellowstone, which, in beauty though not in size, rivals the Grand Canyon of the Colorado; Yellowstone Falls, ranking among the finest of American cataracts; and the remarkable fossil forests along the Lamar River.

GEYSERS. There are five active geyser basins—the Norris, the Upper, the Lower, the Heart Lake, and the Shoshone—all lying in the west and south central parts of the park. The numerous geysers in these various fields differ greatly in size, character, and action. Some, as, for example, Old Faithful, spout at nearly regular intervals, longer or shorter, while others are exceedingly irregular. Some burst upward to a great height, displaying immense power; others shoot tiny streams or bubble and foam while in eruption.

HOT SPRINGS. Besides the geysers, there are marvelously colored hot springs, mud volcanoes, and other strange formations. At Mammoth Hot Springs, and also at Norris and at Thumb, the hot water has brought to the surface immense quantities of white mineral deposits. These have built up high terraces containing beautifully incrusted basins, over the edges of which the hot water pours. Microscopic plants, growing on the edges and on the sides of these basins, color them with brilliant hues of pink, red, and bluish gray. The surface of many hot springs appears brilliantly colored, and the deeper pools in the terraces are often intensely green.

GRAND CANYON AND FALLS. Because of the vivid coloration of its walls, in some places 2000 feet high, the Grand Canyon of the Yellowstone is a scenic feature of the first order. The colors vary from pearly white and pale lemon to orange, pink, and crimson. With the deep green of the forest above, these give a beautiful setting to the Yellowstone Falls, which are twice as high as Niagara. The view of the canyon and of the cataract is one of the most impressive in America.

FOSSIL FORESTS. The fossil forests along the Lamar River contain many petrified tree trunks which stand upright in the faces of nearly vertical cliffs that rise to a height of nearly 2000 feet above the valley floor. These petrified trunks are found at different depths, indicating a succession of forests, which, from time to time, have been overwhelmed, like Pompeii, with volcanic materials.

ANIMAL LIFE. The park is a great wild-animal refuge or natural zoological garden. It contains protected herds of elk, moose, deer, antelope, and American bison. There are also numerous groups of brown, cinnamon, and grizzly bears, some of which have become remarkably tame and friendly. Yellowstone Lake and the other waters of the park abound in trout.

HISTORY. In 1806 John Colter, a member of the Lewis and Clark expedition, struck out on his own and in 1807 entered what is now Yellowstone National Park, thus becoming in all probability the first white man to see the region. The area was occasionally visited by hunters and trappers, and their reports of the fantastic sights, along with Colter's accounts, were regarded as pure imagination. Myth and legend grew around the bona fide reports, and the area was often derisively labeled "Colter's Hell." In 1870 the State of Montana organized an expedition, headed by Surveyor-General H. D. Washburn, to explore the area. His associate, N. P. Langford, wrote glowing descriptions of what they saw, confirming what had been regarded as fiction. In 1872 the American geologist Ferdinand Vandeveer Hayden surveyed the area and was influential in its establishment as a national park to guard against private exploitation of the area. In 1872 it became the world's first national park. Even after it became a national park, however, Yellowstone was unsafe for tourists. Indians raided and murdered visitors, hunters, trappers, and explorers. From 1886 to 1916 it was administered by the Army, with headquarters at Fort Yellowstone.

ACCESSIBILITY. Yellowstone Park is reached by bus at Gardiner, Montana, on the north, and also at West Yellowstone, Montana, on the west. The eastern entrance to the park is reached by auto stage from Cody, Wyoming, 55 miles distant. The southern or Snake River entrance is reached by an auto road from the main north-and-south highway in Idaho. The southern entrance may be reached also by various auto routes.

TRAVEL FACILITIES. Automobile roads and trails reach all the important features of the park. There are hotels, camps, stores, auto-transportation lines, and various other facilities and accommodations for travelers. The various park utilities are operated during the tourist season, which extends usually from June 20 to September 20.

Yonkers. A residential and manufacturing city of southeastern New York, on the Hudson River, 14 miles north of the center of New York City. It is situated along the east bank of the Hudson River, its site rising in a gradual slope to an elevation of 400 feet, from which may be obtained splendid views of the river and of the towering Palisades. Of the many industries of Yonkers, the principal are the manufacture of machine shop products, elevators, drugs, clothing, wire and cable, and chemicals.

Yonkers was chartered as a city in 1872. Points of interest include the Philipse Manor House and Andrus Planetarium. Population, 1970, 204,370.

York. A town on the Atlantic coast of Maine, at the mouth of the York River, 40 miles southwest of Portland, in an area of cliffs, beaches, and pine groves. It is composed of several villages, including the well-known summer resorts of York Beach and York Harbor. One of the oldest communities in Maine, it was settled in 1624 under a grant from the Plymouth Company. It became the first English municipal corporation in America when it was chartered as a city in 1642 and named Gorgeana, after a member of the Plymouth Company, Sir Ferdinando Gorges. The city's name was changed to York in 1652. Frequently attacked by Indians, the community was almost annihilated in 1692. There are several buildings of historical note in the town, including the Old Gaol, one of the oldest in the U.S., and now a museum. Population, 1970, 5690.

York. A manufacturing and commercial center of southeastern Pennsylvania, 25 miles southeast of Harrisburg. York is situated in the midst of a highly productive agricultural district with which it conducts an extensive trade. Its chief industries are the manufacture of foundry and machine products and of bakers' machinery. Other manufactures include agricultural implements, safes and vaults, refrigeration machinery, silk goods, and hosiery.

York was first permanently settled in 1735 by a German colony. It was laid out in 1741 by the sons of William Penn, was incorporated in 1787, and received its city charter in 1887. In 1777–78, the Continental Congress held sessions in York while the British were occupying Philadelphia. Population, 1970, 50,335.

Yorktown. A village of southeastern Virginia, situated on an arm of Chesapeake Bay, about 70 miles southeast of Richmond. Yorktown is famous as the scene of the surrender, October 19, 1781, of the British army, by Lord Cornwallis. This virtually ended the Revolutionary War, and there is an impressive monument commemorating the event. The Yorktown battlefield area, reconstructed with fortifications and marked with explanatory signs, forms part of the Colonial national historical park. In 1862, General G. B. McClellan, with a large Union army, besieged the place and compelled its evacuation by the Confederate forces under General J. E. Johnston. On the principal street of the village stands the oldest customhouse in the United States. Population, 1960, 311.

YOSEMITE (yô-sĕm'ĭ-tê) **NATIONAL PARK.** A national park, containing some of the most magnificent scenery in America. It lies immediately west of the summit of the Sierra Nevada, in central California, about 160 miles east of San Francisco.

AREA AND SURFACE. The park occupies a mountainous tract, some 50 miles long, north and south, with an extreme width, east and west, of about 35 miles, the whole embracing an area of 1189 square miles. This region, in general, slopes to the west, and is traversed by two main rivers, the Merced and the Tuolumne, and by their numerous tributaries.

The surface varies from deep valley floors on the west, which lie at an elevation of less than 4000 feet above the sea, to snow-capped peaks which tower to heights of 13,000 feet, along the eastern boundary. Extensive areas are covered with noble forests of immense evergreen trees. These are interspersed with charming mountain meadows and many beautiful lakes. There are innumerable canyons, gorges, and narrow valleys, with rushing streams, cascades, and cataracts, fed, in large part, from the glaciers and snow fields on the higher mountains.

The surface features that give to the park its most striking character were mainly formed by glacial action and by river erosion. These natural agencies, working through long periods of geological time, have produced the deepest valleys and the highest waterfalls on the continent.

SCENIC FEATURES. Like Yellowstone Park, the Yosemite region presents a long succession of scenic wonders. The chief of these are included in the celebrated Yosemite Valley, in the Tuolumne Canyon with the Hetch Hetchy, and in the famous Mariposa grove of "big trees."

YOSEMITE VALLEY. This incomparable valley is about 7 miles long, with an average width of about a mile. Through the bottom of this valley, the Merced River flows. On either side, the valley is bordered with a succession of vast cliffs and lofty granite domes which rise almost vertically to immense heights. Among the most noted of these massive rock formations, with the heights of their summits above the valley floor, are: Cathedral Rocks, 2591 feet; El Capitan, 3604 feet; Sentinel Dome, 4157 feet; Half Dome, 4892 feet; and Clouds Rest, 5964 feet.

WATERFALLS. Over the edges of towering precipices in the rock walls that enclose the Yosemite Valley plunge some of the most remarkable cataracts known. The Upper Yosemite Falls drop 1430 feet in one sheer descent. Immediately below, the stream cascades through a drop of 620 feet, known as the Middle Yosemite Falls, and then takes a drop of 320 feet over the Lower Yosemite Falls. These three falls, which are parts of one great cataract, make a drop of 2370 feet, equal to 14 Niagaras, before their waters reach the Merced River. Bridal Veil Falls has a drop of 620 feet; Vernal Falls, 320 feet; Illouette Falls, 370 feet; and Nevada Falls, 594 feet. The Ribbon Falls, the highest of all, drops 1612 feet sheer, a straight fall about ten times as great as that of Niagara. Nowhere else in the world is there such an array of stupendous waterfalls.

TUOLUMNE VALLEY. With the opening of roads and trails, making this region of the park accessible, the fine scenic features of the Tuolumne basin are also becoming celebrated. These include the beautiful Hetch Hetchy Valley, the Grand Canyon of the Tuolumne, and the remarkable Waterwheel Falls, in which enormous arcs of water are flung from 50 to 80 feet into the air.

BIG TREES. The greatest grove of giant sequoias outside of Sequoia National Park is the Mariposa grove in the southern area of Yosemite Park. The monster tree of this grove is the Grizzly Giant, whose girth is 93 feet, whose diameter is 29½ feet, and whose height is 204 feet. In massiveness, this immense tree is exceeded only by the General Sherman tree, 36½ feet in diameter and 280 feet high, in Sequoia National Park, and by the General Grant tree, 35 feet in diameter and 264 feet high, in General Grant National Park. Other noted trees in the Mariposa grove are the Washington tree, slightly smaller than the Grizzly Giant; the Columbia tree, 294 feet high; and the Wawona tree, through whose trunk ran an automobile road 26 feet wide until the tree fell in 1968. There are two minor sequoia groves in the park—the Merced and the Tuolumne.

HISTORY. The Yosemite National Park region was once the stronghold of the Awani, or Yosemite (Grizzly Bear), Indians. The first white men to see it were probably Captain Joseph R. Walker's party, who came to the area in 1833. In 1851 a band of militia, the Mariposa Battalion, led by James D. Savage, entered Yosemite seeking retribution for Indian raids, and tried to drive out Chief Tenaya. James Hutchings led the first tourist party through Yosemite and later used his publication, the *California Magazine*, to encourage others to come to see the beautiful Yosemite valley. In 1864 an act of Congress set aside the valley and Mariposa Grove of Big Trees to be administered by California. John Muir, noted American naturalist, lived here in 1868–74 and helped to establish it as a national park. In 1890 a national park was created around the Yosemite Grant, as the section ceded to California in 1864 was called, and in 1906, California returned this grant to the Federal Government as a part of Yosemite National Park.

ACCESSIBILITY. Yosemite Park is reached by bus and car through El Portal, near the western boundary of the park, and thence into Yosemite Valley. The park is reached also from Merced by auto stage to Mariposa and Wawona, thence to the Mariposa grove of "big trees," and into Yosemite Valley. It may be reached by auto roads from various other points.

TRAVEL FACILITIES. Automobile roads and trails have been built to the chief places of interest. There are hotels, camps, stores, auto-transportation lines, saddle horses, camping and hiking equipment, and various other facilities and accommodations for travelers. Yosemite Valley is always open. The higher mountain roads usually are not open until early June.

Youngstown. A city of northeastern Ohio, on the Mahoning River, about 65 miles southeast of Cleveland. Youngstown owes its importance as a steel manufacturing center to its advantageous situation near necessary raw materials and to excellent transportation facilities. In the vicinity are coal mines and limestone quarries. Iron ore from Minnesota is available with a short haul from lake ports.

The city's chief industrial establishments are its immense blast furnaces, steel works, and rolling mills. Other manufactures include many subsidiary steel products, such as sheets, pipes, and engine boilers; also tin plate, coke, fireproofing, rubber goods, and electrical machinery. The Youngstown district produces about one-sixth of the pig iron and about one-eighth of all the steel made in the United States. The city has 2633 acres in public parks, including the beautiful Mill Creek Park, covering 2383 acres. Among the public buildings of especial note are the Stambaugh Memorial Auditorium and the Butler Art Institute.

Youngstown was settled in 1796, was incorporated in 1848, and received its city charter in 1867. A blast furnace was built in 1805 and a rolling mill was erected in 1845. Population, 1970, 139,788.

Ypsilanti. A city of Michigan, situated on the Huron River, 28 miles west of Detroit. It is the commercial center of a fertile agricultural region. Primary among its manufactures are automobiles and automobile parts. The site was established as a French fur-trading post in 1809, and as a permanent settlement in 1823. It was named for Alexander and Demetrios Ypsilanti, leaders of the Greek war for independence, which was raging at the time. Ypsilanti is the seat of Eastern Michigan University and Cleary College. Population, 1970, 29,538.

Yuma. A city of southwestern Arizona, built on the east bank of the Colorado River, at the mouth of the Gila, about 7 miles from the Mexican boundary. The surrounding region is remarkable for its almost continuous sunshine and for the extreme dryness of its climate. The annual rainfall of 3.13 inches at Yuma is the lowest recorded at any station of the United States weather bureau. Summer temperatures of 110° to 120° in the shade are recorded. Yet, owing to the low humidity, sunstroke is practically unknown. Yuma was established in 1700 by Spanish missionaries. It is the trade center of a district in which large quantities of alfalfa seed and other irrigated field crops and fruits are produced the year round because of the uniformly warm climate. Yuma is a popular winter resort and the site of the Yuma Indian Reservation and Vincent Air Force Base. Population, 1970, 29,007.

Zanesville. A city in Ohio, located on the Muskingum River at the mouth of the Licking, 58 miles east of Columbus. The Muskingum River is here spanned by a "Y" bridge, branches going to both sides of the Licking River. Zanesville occupies an attractive site, surrounded by lofty hills. Its varied industries include the manufacture of pottery, glass, tiles, electrical transformers, steel, cement, and barrels.

Zanesville was founded in 1797 by Ebenezer Zane and others, and, during 1810–12, it was the capital of the state. It was incorporated in 1814 and was chartered as a city in 1850. Population, 1970, 33,045.

ZION NATIONAL PARK. A national park, 230 square miles in area, containing picturesque mountains, bizarre rock formations, and a long, narrow canyon three-fourths of a mile deep.

HISTORY. It is evident from the remains of cliff dwellings in and near Zion National Park that it was inhabited long before the white man arrived. Nephi Johnson, a young Mormon missionary and interpreter for the Paiute Indians, the native inhabitants of the area, was probably the first white man to view the area extensively. The reports of Captain John C. Fremont, who explored the Southwest in 1843–44, influenced some Mormon pioneers to come to the area in 1847. They settled around the Virgin River and named the region Zion, "the heavenly city of God."

The park area, located in southwestern Utah, was set aside in 1909 as Mukuntuweap National Monument. It was enlarged and renamed Zion in 1918, and became a national park in 1919. It was enlarged in 1956 by the addition of the adjoining Kolob Canyon area. The name Zion was first given to the canyon by Mormon settlers in 1850, and many natural features of the area bear names reminiscent of the Mormon faith.

FEATURES. The North Fork of the Virgin River, flowing from north to south, has cut through mountains a narrow gorge eight miles long whose sides rise 2500 to 3500 feet above the bed. The rocky walls are vermilion at the bottom and white at the top, exhibiting a geological history of the rise and fall of the land over a period of 15 million years. A road runs along the bed to a northern observation point 6508 feet high, from which one may see mountains called the Temple of Sinawava, Cathedral, and Majestic, among others. Other high mountains in the park are the Sentinel (7157 feet) and East Temple (7110 feet). The highest point is West Temple (7795 feet). Utah Route 15 passes east and west through the park beside Clear Creek, passing through a mile-long tunnel. To the north of this road is the Great Arch, carved out by millennia of erosion by water and wind.

The park is open throughout the year, and the highways are kept free of snow. There are some 155 miles of trails.

Zuñi (*zōō′nyê*; *sōō′-*). The largest of the Pueblo Indian villages, situated near the western boundary of New Mexico, about 40 miles south of Gallup. The inhabitants, who possess a distinct language, call themselves Ashiwi. They are descendants of the people of "Cibola," mentioned by the earliest Spanish explorers.

Like Pueblo Indians generally, the Zuni people are peace-loving, devoted chiefly to agriculture, and adhere with great tenacity to their ancient culture and customs. In the construction of their adobe and stone houses, in their methods of irrigation and agriculture, in weaving, in jewelry, in pottery making, and in other arts, as well as in their elaborate ceremonials, they closely resemble the other village-dwelling Indians of the Southwest.

The Zuñi people were first visited by the Spaniards under Coronado in 1540. Later, Spanish missionaries gained considerable influence with them. Population, 1970, 3958.

City	Pop. 1970	Pop. 1960
Alabama		
Anniston	31,533	33,657
Bessemer	33,428	33,054
Birmingham	300,910	340,887
Decatur	38,044	29,217
Dothan	36,733	31,440
Florence	34,031	31,649
Gadsden	53,928	58,088
Huntsville	137,802	72,365
Mobile	190,026	194,856
Montgomery	133,386	134,393
Prichard	41,578	47,371
Tuscaloosa	65,773	63,370
Alaska		
Anchorage	48,029	44,237
Arizona		
Glendale	36,228	15,893
Mesa	62,853	33,772
Phoenix	581,562	439,170
Scottsdale	67,621	10,026
Tempe	62,907	24,897
Tucson	262,933	212,892
Arkansas		
Fayetteville	30,729	20,274
Fort Smith	62,802	52,991
Hot Springs	35,631	28,337
Little Rock	132,483	107,813
North Little Rock	60,040	58,032
Pine Bluff	57,389	44,037
California		
Alameda	70,968	63,855
Alhambra	62,125	54,807
Altadena†	42,380	40,568
Anaheim	166,701	104,184
Arcadia	42,868	41,005
Arden-Arcade†	82,492	73,352
Bakersfield	69,515	56,848
Baldwin Park	47,285	33,951
Bellflower	51,454	45,909
Berkeley	116,716	111,268
Beverly Hills	33,416	30,817
Buena Park	63,646	46,401
Burbank	88,871	90,155
Carmichael†	37,625	28,075
Carson	71,150	38,059
Castro Valley†	44,760	37,120
Chula Vista	67,901	42,034
Compton	78,611	71,812
Concord	85,164	36,208
Costa Mesa	72,660	37,550
Covina	30,380	20,124
Culver City	31,035	32,163
Cypress	31,026	1,753
Daly City	66,922	44,791
Downey	88,445	82,505
East Los Angeles†	105,033	104,270
El Cajon	52,273	37,618
El Monte	69,837	13,163
Escondido	36,792	16,377
Fairfield	44,146	14,968
Florence-Graham†	42,895	38,164
Fountain Valley	31,826	2,068
Fremont	99,665	43,790
Fresno	165,972	133,929
Fullerton	85,826	56,180
Gardena	41,021	35,943
Garden Grove	122,524	84,238
Glendale	132,752	119,442
Glendora	31,349	20,752
Hacienda Heights†	35,969	15,600
Hawthorne	53,304	33,035
Hayward	93,004	72,700
Huntington Beach	115,960	11,492
Huntington Park	33,744	29,920
Inglewood	89,985	63,390
La Habra	41,350	25,136
Lakewood	82,973	67,126
La Mesa	39,178	30,441
La Mirada	30,808	22,444
Lancaster†	30,948	26,012
La Puente	31,092	24,723
Livermore	37,703	16,058
Long Beach	358,633	344,168
Los Angeles	2,816,061	2,479,015
Lynwood	43,353	31,614
Manhattan Beach	35,352	33,934
Modesto	61,712	36,585
Monrovia	30,015	27,079
Montebello	42,807	32,097
Monterey Park	49,166	37,821
Mountain View	51,092	30,889
Napa	35,978	22,170
National City	43,184	32,771
Newport Beach	49,422	26,564
North Highlands†	31,854	21,271
Norwalk	91,827	88,739
Novato	31,006	17,881
Oakland	361,561	367,548
Oceanside	40,494	24,971
Ontario	64,118	46,617
Orange	77,374	26,444
Oxnard	71,225	40,265
Pacifica	36,020	20,995
Palo Alto	55,768	52,287
Palos Verdes Peninsula†	39,616	......
Paramount	34,734	27,249
Pasadena	113,327	116,407
Pico Rivera	54,170	49,150
Pomona	87,384	67,157
Rancho Cordova†	30,451	7,429
Redlands	36,355	26,829
Redondo Beach	56,075	46,986
Redwood City	55,686	46,290
Richmond	79,043	71,854
Riverside	140,089	84,332
Rosemead	40,972	15,476
Sacramento	254,413	191,667
Salinas	58,896	28,957
San Bernardino	104,251	91,922
San Bruno	36,254	29,063
San Diego	693,931	573,224
San Francisco	715,674	740,316
San Jose	443,950	204,196
San Leandro	68,698	65,962
San Mateo	78,991	69,870
San Rafael	38,977	20,460
Santa Ana	156,601	100,350
Santa Barbara	70,215	58,768
Santa Clara	87,717	58,880
Santa Cruz	32,076	25,596
Santa Maria	32,749	20,027
Santa Monica	88,289	83,249
Santa Rosa	50,006	31,027
Seaside	35,935	19,353
Simi Valley	56,464	......
South Gate	56,909	53,831
S. San Francisco	46,646	39,418
South Whittier†	46,641	......
Stockton	107,644	86,321
Sunnyvale	95,408	52,898
Thousand Oaks	36,334	22,000
Torrance	134,584	100,991
Upland	32,551	15,918
Vallejo	66,773	60,877
Ventura (San Buenaventura)	55,797	29,114
Walnut Creek	39,844	9,903
West Covina	68,034	50,645
Westminster	59,865	25,750
Whittier	72,863	33,663
Colorado		
Arvada	46,814	19,242
Aurora	74,974	48,548
Boulder	66,870	37,718
Colorado Springs	135,060	70,194
Denver	514,678	493,887
Englewood	33,695	33,398
Fort Collins	43,337	25,027
Greeley	38,902	26,314
Lakewood	92,787	19,338
Pueblo	97,453	91,181
Connecticut		
Bridgeport	156,542	159,748
Bristol	55,487	45,499
Danbury	50,781	22,928
East Hartford	57,583	43,977
Enfield	46,189	31,464
Fairfield	56,487	46,183
Greenwich	59,755	53,793
Groton	38,523	29,937
Hamden	49,357	41,056
Hartford	158,017	162,178
Manchester	47,994	42,102
Meriden	55,959	51,850
Middletown	36,924	33,250
Milford	50,858	41,662
New Britain	83,441	82,201
New Haven	137,707	152,048
New London	31,630	34,182
Norwalk	79,113	67,775
Norwich	41,433	38,506
Southington	30,946	22,797
Stamford	108,798	92,713
Stratford	49,775	45,012
Torrington	31,952	30,045
Trumbull	31,394	20,379
Wallingford	35,714	29,920
Waterbury	108,033	107,130
West Hartford	68,031	62,382
West Haven	52,851	43,002
Delaware		
Wilmington	80,386	95,827
District of Columbia		
Washington	756,189	763,956
Florida		
Clearwater	52,074	34,653
Coral Gables	42,494	34,793
Daytona Beach	45,327	37,395
Fort Lauderdale	139,590	83,648
Gainesville	64,510	29,701
Hialeah	102,297	66,972
Hollywood	106,873	35,237
Jacksonville	518,131	201,030
Kendall†	35,497	......
Lakeland	41,550	41,350
Melbourne	40,236	11,982
Miami	334,859	291,688
Miami Beach	87,072	63,145
North Miami	34,767	28,708
North Miami Beach	30,723	21,405
Orlando	99,006	88,135
Panama City	32,096	33,275
Pensacola	59,507	56,752
Pompano Beach	37,724	15,992
St. Petersburg	216,232	181,298
Sarasota	40,237	34,083
Tallahassee	71,897	48,174
Tampa	277,767	274,970
Titusville	30,515	......
West Palm Beach	57,290	56,208

† Unincorporated places.   Source: U.S. Bureau of the Census.

City	Pop. 1970	Pop. 1960
Georgia		
Albany	72,623	55,890
Athens	44,342	31,355
Atlanta	496,973	487,455
Augusta	59,864	70,626
Columbus	154,168	116,779
East Point	39,315	35,633
Macon	122,423	69,764
Rome	30,759	32,226
Savannah	118,349	149,245
Valdosta	32,303	30,652
Warner Robins	33,491	18,633
Hawaii		
Honolulu	324,871	294,194
Kailua	33,783	25,622
Idaho		
Boise City	74,990	34,481
Idaho Falls	35,776	33,161
Pocatello	40,036	28,534
Illinois		
Alton	39,700	43,047
Arlington Heights	64,884	27,878
Aurora	74,182	63,715
Belleville	41,699	37,264
Berwyn	52,502	54,224
Bloomington	39,992	36,271
Calumet City	32,956	25,000
Champaign	56,532	49,583
Chicago	3,366,957	3,550,404
Chicago Heights	40,900	34,331
Cicero	67,058	69,130
Danville	42,570	41,856
Decatur	90,397	78,004
De Kalb	32,949	18,486
Des Plaines	57,239	34,886
Downers Grove	32,751	21,154
East St. Louis	69,996	81,712
Elgin	55,691	49,447
Elmhurst	50,547	36,991
Evanston	79,808	79,283
Galesburg	36,290	37,243
Granite City	40,440	40,073
Harvey	34,636	29,071
Highland Park	32,263	25,532
Joliet	80,378	66,780
Kankakee	30,944	27,666
Lombard	35,977	22,561
Maywood	30,036	27,330
Moline	46,237	42,705
Mount Prospect	34,995	18,906
Niles	31,432	20,393
North Chicago	47,275	22,938
Oak Lawn	60,305	27,471
Oak Park	62,511	61,093
Park Forest	30,638	29,993
Park Ridge	42,466	32,659
Pekin	31,375	28,146
Peoria	126,963	103,162
Quincy	45,288	43,793
Rockford	147,370	126,706
Rock Island	50,166	51,863
Skokie	68,627	59,364
Springfield	91,753	83,271
Urbana	32,800	27,294
Waukegan	65,269	55,719
Wheaton	31,138	24,312
Wilmette	32,134	28,268
Indiana		
Anderson	70,787	49,061
Bloomington	42,890	31,357
East Chicago	46,982	57,669
Elkhart	43,152	40,274
Evansville	138,764	141,543
Fort Wayne	177,671	161,776
Gary	175,415	178,320
Hammond	107,790	111,698
Indianapolis	743,155	476,258
Kokomo	44,042	47,197
Lafayette	44,955	42,330
Marion	39,607	37,854
Michigan City	39,369	36,653
Mishawaka	35,517	33,361
Muncie	69,080	68,603
New Albany	38,402	37,812
Richmond	43,999	44,149
South Bend	125,580	132,445
Terre Haute	70,286	72,500
Iowa		
Ames	39,505	27,003
Burlington	32,366	32,430
Cedar Rapids	110,642	92,035
Clinton	34,719	33,589
Council Bluffs	60,348	55,641
Davenport	98,469	88,981
Des Moines	200,587	208,982
Dubuque	62,309	56,606
Fort Dodge	31,263	28,399
Iowa City	46,850	33,443
Mason City	30,491	30,642
Sioux City	85,925	89,159
Waterloo	75,533	71,755
Kansas		
Hutchinson	36,885	37,574
Kansas City	168,213	121,901
Lawrence	45,698	32,858
Overland Park	76,623	21,110
Salina	37,714	43,202
Topeka	125,011	119,484
Wichita	276,554	254,698
Kentucky		
Bowling Green	36,253	28,338
Covington	52,535	60,376
Fort Knox†	37,608	
Lexington	108,137	62,810
Louisville	361,472	390,639
Owensboro	50,329	42,471
Paducah	31,627	34,479
Louisiana		
Alexandria	41,557	40,279
Baton Rouge	165,963	152,419
Bossier City	41,595	32,776
Houma	30,922	22,561
Lafayette	68,908	40,400
Lake Charles	77,998	63,392
Metairie†	135,816	
Monroe	56,374	52,219
New Iberia	30,147	29,062
New Orleans	591,502	627,525
Shreveport	182,064	164,372
Maine		
Bangor	33,168	38,912
Lewiston	41,779	40,804
Portland	65,116	72,566
Maryland		
Baltimore	905,759	939,024
Bethesda†	71,621	56,527
Bowie	35,028	1,072
Catonsville†	54,812	37,372
Chillum†	35,656	
Dundalk†	85,377	82,428
Essex†	38,193	35,205
Glen Burnie†	38,608	
Hagerstown	35,862	36,660
Parkville†	33,897	44,800
Randallstown†	33,683	
Rockville	41,564	26,090
Silver Spring†	77,496	66,348
Suitland-Silver Hill†	30,355	10,300
Towson†	77,809	46,000
Wheaton†	66,247	54,635
Massachusetts		
Arlington	53,524	49,953
Attleboro	32,907	27,118
Beverly	38,348	36,108
Billerica	31,648	17,867
Boston	641,071	697,197
Braintree	35,050	31,069
Brockton	89,040	72,813
Brookline	58,886	54,044
Cambridge	100,361	107,716
Chelmsford	31,432	15,130
Chelsea	30,625	33,749
Chicopee	66,676	61,553
Everett	42,485	43,544
Fall River	96,898	99,942
Fitchburg	43,343	43,021
Framingham	64,048	44,526
Haverhill	46,120	46,346
Holyoke	50,112	52,689
Lawrence	66,915	70,933
Leominster	32,939	27,929
Lexington	31,886	27,691
Lowell	94,239	92,107
Lynn	90,294	94,478
Malden	56,127	57,676
Medford	64,397	64,971
Melrose	33,180	29,619
Methuen	35,456	28,114
Natick	31,057	28,831
New Bedford	101,777	102,477
Newton	91,066	92,384
Norwood	30,815	24,898
Peabody	48,080	32,202
Pittsfield	57,020	57,879
Quincy	87,966	87,409
Revere	43,159	40,080
Salem	40,556	39,211
Somerville	88,779	94,697
Springfield	163,905	174,463
Taunton	43,756	41,132
Waltham	61,582	55,413
Watertown	39,307	39,092
Westfield	31,433	26,302
Weymouth	54,610	48,177
Woburn	37,406	31,214
Worcester	176,572	186,587
Michigan		
Allen Park	40,747	37,494
Ann Arbor	99,797	67,340
Battle Creek	38,931	44,169
Bay City	49,449	53,604
Dearborn	104,199	112,007
Dearborn Heights	80,069	71,551
Detroit	1,511,482	1,670,144
East Detroit	45,920	45,756
East Lansing	47,540	30,198
Ferndale	30,850	31,347
Flint	193,317	196,940
Garden City	41,864	38,017
Grand Rapids	197,649	177,313
Highland Park	35,444	38,063
Inkster	38,595	39,097
Jackson	45,484	50,720
Kalamazoo	85,555	82,089
Lansing	131,546	107,807
Lincoln Park	52,984	53,933
Livonia	110,109	66,702
Madison Heights	38,599	33,343

† Unincorporated places.

City	Pop. 1970	Pop. 1960
Midland	35,176	27,779
Muskegon	44,631	46,485
Oak Park	36,762	36,632
Pontiac	85,279	82,233
Portage	33,590	27,642
Port Huron	35,794	36,084
Roseville	60,529	50,195
Royal Oak	85,499	80,612
Saginaw	91,849	98,265
St. Clair Shores	88,093	76,657
Southfield	69,285	31,501
Southgate	33,909	29,404
Sterling Heights	61,365	
Taylor	70,020	49,658
Troy	39,419	19,402
Warren	179,260	89,246
Westland	86,749	
Wyandotte	41,061	43,519
Wyoming	56,560	45,829
Minnesota		
Bloomington	81,970	50,498
Brooklyn Center	35,173	24,356
Coon Rapids	30,505	14,931
Crystal	30,925	24,283
Duluth	100,578	106,884
Edina	44,046	28,501
Mankato	30,895	23,797
Minneapolis	434,400	482,872
Minnetonka	35,776	25,037
Richfield	47,231	42,523
Rochester	53,766	40,663
Roseville	34,518	23,997
St. Cloud	39,691	33,815
St. Louis Park	48,883	43,310
St. Paul	309,980	313,411
Mississippi		
Biloxi	48,486	44,053
Greenville	39,648	41,502
Gulfport	40,791	30,204
Hattiesburg	38,277	34,989
Jackson	153,968	144,422
Meridian	45,083	49,374
Missouri		
Cape Girardeau	31,282	24,947
Columbia	58,804	36,650
Florissant	65,908	38,166
Fort Leonard Wood†	33,799	
Independence	111,662	62,328
Jefferson City	32,407	28,228
Joplin	39,256	38,958
Kansas City	501,859	475,539
Kirkwood	31,890	29,421
Lemay†	40,115	
Raytown	33,632	17,083
St. Charles	31,834	21,189
St. Joseph	72,691	79,673
St. Louis	622,236	750,026
Springfield	120,096	95,865
University City	46,309	51,249
Montana		
Billings	61,581	52,851
Great Falls	60,091	55,244
Nebraska		
Grand Island	31,269	25,742
Lincoln	149,518	128,521
Omaha	347,328	301,598

City	Pop. 1970	Pop. 1960
Nevada		
Las Vegas	125,787	64,405
North Las Vegas	36,216	18,422
Reno	72,863	51,470
New Hampshire		
Concord	30,022	28,991
Manchester	87,754	88,282
Nashua	55,820	39,096
New Jersey		
Atlantic City	47,859	59,544
Bayonne	72,743	74,215
Belleville	34,643	35,005
Bergenfield	33,131	27,203
Bloomfield	52,029	51,867
Camden	102,551	117,159
Clifton	82,437	82,084
East Orange	75,471	77,259
Elizabeth	112,654	107,698
Fair Lawn	37,975	36,421
Fort Lee	30,631	21,815
Garfield	30,722	29,253
Hackensack	35,911	30,521
Hoboken	45,380	48,441
Irvington	59,743	59,379
Jersey City	260,545	276,101
Kearny	37,585	37,472
Linden	41,409	39,931
Long Branch	31,774	26,228
Montclair	44,043	43,129
Newark	382,417	405,220
New Brunswick	41,885	40,139
Nutley	32,099	29,513
Orange	32,566	35,789
Passaic	55,124	53,963
Paterson	144,824	143,663
Perth Amboy	38,793	38,007
Plainfield	46,862	45,330
Sayreville	32,508	22,553
Trenton	104,638	114,167
Union City	58,537	52,180
Vineland	47,399	37,685
Westfield	33,720	31,447
West New York	40,627	35,547
West Orange	43,715	39,895
New Mexico		
Albuquerque	243,751	201,189
Las Cruces	37,857	29,367
Roswell	33,908	39,593
Santa Fe	41,167	33,394
New York		
Albany	114,873	129,726
Auburn	34,599	35,249
Baldwin†	34,525	30,204
Binghamton	64,123	75,941
Buffalo	462,768	532,759
Central Islip†	36,369	
Deer Park†	31,120	16,726
East Meadow†	46,252	46,036
Elmira	39,945	46,517
Franklin Square†	32,156	32,483

City	Pop. 1970	Pop. 1960
Freeport	40,374	34,419
Hempstead	39,411	34,641
Hicksville†	48,075	50,405
Jamestown	39,795	41,818
Levittown†	65,440	65,276
Long Beach	33,127	26,473
Mount Vernon	72,778	76,010
New Rochelle	75,385	76,812
New York City	7,867,760	7,781,984
Niagara Falls	85,615	102,394
North Babylon†	39,556	
North Tonawanda	36,012	34,757
Oceanside†	35,028	30,448
Plainview†	32,195	27,914
Poughkeepsie	32,029	38,330
Rochester	296,233	318,661
Rome	47,655	51,646
Schenectady	77,859	81,682
Syracuse	197,208	216,038
Troy	62,918	67,492
Utica	91,611	100,410
Valley Stream	40,413	38,629
Watertown	30,787	33,306
White Plains	50,220	50,485
Yonkers	204,370	190,634
North Carolina		
Asheville	57,681	60,192
Burlington	35,930	33,199
Camp Lejune Central†	34,549	
Charlotte	241,178	201,564
Durham	95,438	78,302
Fayetteville	53,510	47,106
Fort Bragg†	46,995	
Gastonia	47,142	37,276
Greensboro	144,076	119,574
High Point	63,204	62,063
Kannapolis†	36,293	28,448
Raleigh	121,577	93,931
Rocky Mount	34,284	32,147
Wilmington	46,169	44,013
Winston-Salem	132,913	111,135
North Dakota		
Bismarck	34,703	27,670
Fargo	53,365	46,662
Grand Forks	39,008	34,451
Minot	32,290	30,604
Ohio		
Akron	275,425	290,351
Barberton	33,052	33,805
Boardman†	30,852	
Brook Park	30,774	12,856
Canton	110,053	113,631
Cincinnati	452,524	502,550
Cleveland	750,903	876,050
Cleveland Heights	60,767	61,813
Columbus	539,677	471,316
Cuyahoga Falls	49,678	47,922
Dayton	243,601	262,332
East Cleveland	39,600	37,991
Elyria	53,427	43,782
Euclid	71,552	62,998
Fairborn	32,267	19,453
Findlay	35,800	30,344
Garfield Heights	41,417	38,455
Hamilton	67,865	72,354
Kettering	69,599	54,462
Lakewood	70,173	66,154
Lancaster	32,911	29,916

† Unincorporated places.

City	Pop. 1970	Pop. 1960	City	Pop. 1970	Pop. 1960	City	Pop. 1970	Pop. 1960
Lima	53,734	51,037	Warwick	83,694	68,504	**Vermont**		
Lorain	78,185	68,932	Woonsocket	46,820	47,080			
Mansfield	55,047	47,325				Burlington	38,633	35,531
Maple Heights	34,093	31,667						
Marion	38,646	37,079	**South Carolina**					
Massillon	32,539	31,236						
Mentor	36,912	4,354	Charleston	66,945	65,925	**Virginia**		
Middletown	48,767	42,115	Columbia	113,542	97,433			
Newark	41,836	41,790	Greenville	61,208	66,188	Alexandria	110,938	91,023
North Olmsted	34,861	16,290	Rock Hill	33,846	29,404	Arlington†	174,284	
Norwood	30,420	34,580	Spartanburg	44,546	44,352	Charlottesville	38,880	29,427
Parma	100,216	82,845				Chesapeake	82,616	73,577
Sandusky	32,674	31,989				Danville	46,391	46,577
Shaker Heights	36,306	36,460				Hampton	120,779	89,258
Springfield	81,926	82,723	**South Dakota**			Lynchburg	54,083	54,790
Steubenville	30,771	32,495				Newport News	138,177	113,662
Toledo	383,818	318,003	Rapid City	43,836	42,399	Norfolk	307,951	304,869
Upper Arlington	38,630	28,486	Sioux Falls	72,488	65,466	Petersburg	36,103	36,750
Warren	63,494	59,648				Portsmouth	110,963	114,773
Youngstown	139,788	166,689				Richmond	249,621	219,958
Zanesville	33,045	39,077	**Tennessee**			Roanoke	92,115	97,110
						Virginia Beach	166,729	8,091
			Chattanooga	119,082	130,009			
			Clarksville	31,719	22,021			
Oklahoma			Jackson	39,996	34,376			
			Johnson City	33,770	31,187	**Washington**		
Enid	44,008	38,859	Kingsport	31,938	26,314			
Lawton	74,470	61,697	Knoxville	174,587	111,827	Bellevue	61,102	12,809
Midwest City	48,114	36,058	Memphis	623,497	497,524	Bellingham	39,375	34,688
Muskogee	37,331	38,059	Nashville	436,044	170,874	Bremerton	35,307	28,922
Norman	52,117	33,412				Everett	53,622	40,304
Oklahoma City	356,661	324,253				Fort Lewis†	38,054	
Stillwater	31,126	23,965	**Texas**			Lakes District†	48,195	
Tulsa	330,409	261,685				Seattle	530,831	557,087
			Abilene	89,653	90,368	Spokane	170,516	181,608
			Amarillo	127,010	137,969	Tacoma	154,518	147,979
Oregon			Arlington	90,643	44,775	Vancouver	42,493	32,464
			Austin	251,808	186,545	Yakima	45,588	3,284
Corvallis	35,153	20,669	Baytown	43,980	28,159			
Eugene	76,346	50,977	Beaumont	115,919	119,175			
Portland	382,619	372,676	Brownsville	52,522	48,040			
Salem	68,296	49,142	Bryan	33,719	27,542	**West Virginia**		
			Corpus Christi	204,525	167,690			
			Dallas	844,401	679,684	Charleston	71,505	85,796
			Denton	39,874	26,844	Huntington	74,315	83,627
			El Paso	322,261	276,687	Parkersburg	44,208	44,797
Pennsylvania			Fort Hood†	32,597		Wheeling	48,188	53,400
			Fort Worth	393,476	356,268			
Allentown	109,527	108,347	Galveston	61,809	67,175			
Altoona	62,900	69,407	Garland	81,437	38,504			
Bethel Park	34,791	23,605	Grand Prairie	50,904	30,386			
Bethlehem	72,686	75,408	Harlingen	33,503	41,207	**Wisconsin**		
Chester	56,331	63,658	Houston	1,231,394	938,219			
Easton	30,256	31,955	Irving	97,260	45,985	Appleton	57,143	48,411
Erie	129,231	138,440	Killeen	35,507	23,377	Beloit	35,729	32,846
Harrisburg	68,061	79,697	Laredo	69,024	60,678	Brookfield	32,140	19,812
Hazleton	30,426	32,056	Longview	45,547	40,050	Eau Claire	44,619	37,987
Johnstown	42,476	53,949	Lubbock	149,101	128,691	Fond du Lac	35,515	32,719
Lancaster	57,690	61,055	McAllen	37,636	32,728	Green Bay	87,809	62,888
McKeesport	37,977	45,489	Mesquite	55,131	27,526	Janesville	46,426	35,164
New Castle	38,559	44,790	Midland	59,463	62,625	Kenosha	78,805	67,899
Norristown	38,169	38,925	Odessa	78,380	80,338	La Crosse	51,153	47,575
Philadelphia	1,948,609	2,002,512	Pasadena	89,277	58,737	Madison	173,258	126,706
Pittsburgh	520,117	604,332	Port Arthur	57,371	66,676	Manitowoc	33,430	32,275
Reading	87,643	98,177	Richardson	48,582	16,810	Menomonee Falls	31,697	18,276
Scranton	103,564	111,443	San Angelo	63,884	58,815	Milwaukee	717,099	741,324
State College	33,778	22,409	San Antonio	654,153	587,718	Oshkosh	53,221	45,110
Wilkes-Barre	58,856	63,551	Temple	33,431	30,419	Racine	95,162	89,144
Williamsport	37,918	41,967	Texarkana	30,497	30,218	Sheboygan	48,484	45,747
York	50,335	54,504	Texas City	38,500	32,065	Superior	32,237	33,563
			Tyler	57,770	51,230	Waukesha	40,258	30,004
			Victoria	41,349	33,047	Wausau	32,806	31,943
			Waco	95,326	97,808	Wauwatosa	58,676	56,923
			Wichita Falls	97,564	101,724	West Allis	71,723	68,157
Rhode Island								
Cranston	73,037	66,766	**Utah**			**Wyoming**		
East Providence	48,151	41,955						
Newport	34,562	47,049	Ogden	69,478	70,197			
Pawtucket	76,984	81,001	Provo	53,131	36,047	Casper	39,361	38,930
Providence	179,213	207,498	Salt Lake City	175,885	189,454	Cheyenne	40,914	43,505

† Unincorporated places.

CANADA

Canada is a completely sovereign or independent state and member nation of the Commonwealth of Nations.

Size. Canada, having an area of 3,852,000 square miles, covers a surface nearly as large as Europe and larger than the United States, excluding Alaska. The country measures from east to west at its widest extent more than 3000 miles and from north to south about 1600 miles. A number of islands, which are territory of the state, lie off the northeastern coast. The most northerly island extends to a latitude of 85° N. A large inland sea, connected with the north Atlantic Ocean by Hudson strait, extends into the country from the northeast a distance of about 600 miles. Canada's southern boundary follows the 49th parallel of latitude from the western coast eastward to the Lake of the Woods. Inclining slightly southward to Lake Superior, it passes through the Great Lakes and part of the Saint Lawrence river, which it leaves at the 45th parallel. It then runs with an irregular course eastward to the Atlantic Ocean.

Topography. Canada may be divided into five natural divisions, based on the character of the land surface. These divisions are commonly called (1) the Acadian or Appalachian region, (2) the Canadian shield or Laurentian plateau, (3) the Saint Lawrence lowlands, (4) the great plains, and (5) the Cordilleran region.

1. The Acadian or Appalachian region embraces southeastern Quebec and the maritime provinces. This region is the extension into Canada of the Appalachian mountains of the United States.

2. The Canadian shield or Laurentian plateau is a huge V-shaped area of 2½ million square miles, which encloses Hudson bay at its center. It forms practically all of northern Canada, and covers the area lying northeast of a line drawn from the Mackenzie River delta to the Lake of the Woods and northwest of a line which passes thence north of the Saint Lawrence River basin. Its southern and Atlantic borders are elevated and outwardly steep, forming the Laurentian mountains. From this outer rim its surface slopes gradually to its low center, Hudson bay. The western portion inclines similarly from an elevated rim toward Hudson bay and the

Arctic Ocean. In detail, the surface of the plateau is often broken and rocky with innumerable lakes.

3. The Saint Lawrence lowlands, which run from Lake Huron down the Saint Lawrence valley between the Laurentian plateau and the Acadian highlands, are a northeasterly extension of the central plain of North America drained by the Mississippi valley.

4. The great plains form a northern extension of the topographical division which occupies all North America within the limits of the Appalachian mountains, the Canadian shield, and the Rocky mountains. At the international boundary line, this division has a width of 800 miles, but becomes narrower farther north. For 300 miles north of the boundary the region is prairie, but beyond this latitude it is forested. In the southern portion, traversed by the railway lines, three prairie steppes are clearly marked: an eastern steppe, the basin of the Red river, lying between the Canadian shield and the Manitoba escarpment and having an elevation of 800 feet above the sea; a central steppe, between this escarpment and the Missouri coteau, with an elevation of from 1600 feet in the east to about 2500 feet in the west; and a western steppe, rising to a height of 3000 or 4000 feet, which extends from the Missouri coteau to the Rockies.

5. The Cordilleran region, about 500 miles broad, is made up of a succession of mountain ranges running parallel to the Pacific coast and of the well marked longitudinal valleys which separate the ranges. In the south, where the mountains have been adequately explored, the district falls into three subdivisions: (1) an eastern group of mountain systems, consisting of the Rocky mountains, the Selkirk system, and the Columbian mountains, or Gold ranges; (2) the interior plateaus; (3) the coastal mountains, consisting of the Coast range and the Vancouver range, the latter being in places submerged. In the south the Rocky mountains are the highest, but in the north the coastal mountains far exceed them. Mount Logan, in the St. Elias range, Yukon, 19,850 feet elevation, is the highest point in Canada.

Climate. Canada covers so many degrees of latitude and possesses such vast areas of highland and lowland that it has many varieties of climate.

PRINCIPAL PRODUCTIONS OF CANADA*

PROVINCES	Field Crops 1966	Livestock & Poultry 1966	Dairy Products 1966	Fisheries 1966	Mineral Products 1967	Lumber** 1966	Manufactures 1966
Alberta	726,488,000	565,115,700	50,065,000	1,383,000	973,327,000	18,188,000	1,429,020,000
Rank	2	2	3	10	2	5	4
British Columbia	45,372,000	97,688,400	42,850,000	123,715,000	379,986,000	521,196,000	3,063,675,000
Rank	6	6	4	1	4	1	3
Manitoba	310,905,000	198,839,100	27,570,000	7,082,000	184,679,000	2,042,000	1,019,000,000
Rank	4	5	5	7	7	8	5
New Brunswick	26,860,000	22,325,500	12,961,000	45,268,000	90,419,000	25,850,000	547,197,000
Rank	7	8	8	4	9	4	7
Newfoundland	....	2,868,400	....	58,473,000	266,365,000	1,181,000	194,102,000
Rank		10		3	6	9	9
Nova Scotia	12,017,000	26,492,000	14,705,000	97,807,000	77,226,000	14,912,000	612,466,000
Rank	9	7	7	2	10	6	6
Ontario	477,924,000	674,586,200	245,046,000	6,744,000	1,194,545,000	72,289,000	19,452,570,000
Rank	3	1	1	8	1	3	1
Prince Edward Is.	24,830,000	20,282,700	6,677,000	9,164,000	2,606,000	139,000	46,781,000
Rank	8	9	9	6	11	11	10
Quebec	198,237,000	350,868,900	220,408,000	13,345,000	734,142,000	105,589,000	10,464,530,000
Rank	5	4	2	5	3	2	2
Saskatchewan	1,216,586,000	389,851,900	27,536,000	4,858,000	362,194,000	6,064,000	470,381,000
Rank	1	3	6	9	5	7	8
Yukon and Northwest Territories	....	26,200	....	1,225,000†	133,182,000	325,000	3,734,000
Rank		11		11	8	10	11
	3,037,219,000	2,348,945,000	647,818,000	355,590,000‡	4,398,671,000	767,773,000	37,303,455,000

* Showing value in dollars for provinces, with rank.
** Includes other sawmill products, but not manufactured products.
† Yukon Territory included with British Columbia rather than with Northwest Territories here.
‡ Lower than sum of provincial totals because duplications resulting from intershipments between provinces are removed..
Source: Dominion Bureau of Statistics

ITEM	1911	1931	1941	1951	1961	1966
POPULATION . . .	7,206,643	10,353,778	11,506,655	14,009,429	18,238,247	20,014,880
IMMIGRATION . . .	311,084	88,223	11,496	194,391	71,689	194,743
AGRICULTURE:						
Wheat . . . . bu.	215,841,300	298,000,000	540,190,000	562,395,000	283,394,000	827,338,000
Oats . . . . . bu.	348,187,600	331,243,000	346,154,000	492,683,000	283,965,000	374,678,000
Barley . . . . bu.	40,641,000	67,972,000	116,659,000	252,795,000	112,640,000	301,235,000
Corn . . . . . bu.	18,772,700	5,643,000(5)	12,036,000(5)	15,662,000	33,262,000	72,971,000
Potatoes . . . bu.	66,023,000	91,815,000	65,206,000	66,647,000	55,436,700	91,131,000
Tame Hay . . tons	12,694,000	113,961,000	12,245,000	17,316,000	20,812,000	26,049,000
Horses . . . no.	2,266,400	3,129,058	2,881,400	1,306,634	512,021	380,000
Cattle . . . . no.	7,086,600	7,990,947	8,797,800	8,370,991	10,900,000	9,747,000
Sheep . . . . no.	2,389,300	3,608,340	3,550,500	1,478,737	1,563,534	1,094,000
Swine . . . . no.	2,792,200	4,716,761	5,994,000	4,915,987	5,332,736	5,443,000
Cheese . . . . lbs.	199,904,205	113,956,639	148,913,300	90,615,000	131,408,000	193,863,000
Butter . . . . lbs.	64,489,398	225,955,246	286,109,500	246,400,000	364,286,000	342,423,000
FISHERIES:						
Total value. . . $	29,965,433	30,517,306	62,258,997	204,912,000	222,800,000	355,953,000
MINERALS:						
Total production $	103,220,994	230,434,726	560,241,290	1,245,483,595	2,582,300,000	3,972,480,919
Gold . . . . . oz.	473,159	2,693,892	5,345,179	4,392,751	4,474,000	3,319,474
Silver . . . . oz.	32,559,044	20,562,247	21,757,408	161,872,873	31,382,000	33,417,874
Copper . . . . lbs.	55,648,011	292,304,390	608,825,570(6)	539,941,589	878,175,000	1,012,152,458
Lead . . . . . lbs.	23,784,969	267,342,482	388,569,550(6)	316,462,751	460,860,000	599,244,120
Nickel . . . . . lbs.	34,098,744	65,666,320	226,105,865(6)	275,806,272	465,983,000	447,219,823
Pig Iron . . . tons	917,535	420,038	1,364,336	2,552,696	4,946,000	7,212,000
Coal . . . . tons	11,323,388	12,243,211	18,225,961	18,586,823	10,398,000	11,391,569
Cement . . . bbl.	5,692,915	10,161,658	8,368,711	17,007,812	32,800,000	47,740,000
MANUFACTURES:						
Capital . . . $	1,247,583,609	3,705,701,893	4,095,716,836(7)	4,921,500,000(4)	8,172,000,000†	15,090,000,000†
Employees . . . no.	515,203	528,640	762,244(7)	1,258,375	1,352,605(1)	1,646,024(1)
Salaries and Wages $	241,008,416	587,566,990	920,872,865(7)	3,276,281,000	5,701,651,000	8,695,890,000
Products . . . $	1,165,975,639	2,555,126,448	4,529,173,316(7)	16,392,187,000	25,895,611,000	37,303,455,000
Electric power . kwh.	793,162,316	16,330,867,000	33,445,000,000	54,851,844,000	113,713,318,000(3)	158,135,232,000(3)
COMMERCE:						
Exports . . . . $	297,196,365	599,560,460	1,640,454,541	3,914,460,376	5,895,215,000(4)	10,325,320,000(4)
Imports . . . . $	472,247,540	628,098,386	1,448,791,650	4,084,856,478	5,768,578,000	9,866,439,000
Exports, Domestic—						
Wheat . . . bu.	45,802,115	217,243,037	177,967,532	237,060,505	358,000,000(8)	515,300,000(8)
Wheat flour . . bbl.	3,049,046	7,218,188	10,288,327	12,078,671		
Oats . . . . . bu.	5,431,662	3,258,501	14,396,287(7)	59,272,650	3,500,000	4,800,000
Hay . . . . . tons	326,132	156,722	74,598(7)	100,429	78,771	54,106
Bacon . . . . lbs.	56,068,607	12,177,000	345,604,200(7)	61,325	3,896,000	4,142,600
Butter . . . . lbs.	3,142,682	1,162,900	1,337,600(7)	543,700	27,252,000(12)	35,949,000
Cheese . . . . lbs.	181,895,724	79,590,400	106,631,100(7)	30,653,200	19,508,000	35,947,000
Fisheries . . . $	15,675,544	28,894,983	31,650,889(7)	117,464,445	144,215,000(9)	221,719,000
Forest products . $	45,439,057	97,369,461	348,006,396(7)	1,399,076,131	1,639,300,000	*
Manufactures. . $	35,283,118	494,562,000	580,963,000(7)	1,497,235,000	3,622,900,000	6,672,100,000
Mineral products $	42,787,561	155,697,504	374,120,171(7)	684,535,336(2)	2,235,200,000(10)	3,100,000,000(10)
Newsprint . . tons	. . . . .	2,098,241	3,242,789(6)	5,112,061	6,216,000	7,821,481
Imports(4)—						
Agricultural . . $	35,304,683	177,628,778	157,249,495(7)	411,260,000	754,749,000(12)	*
Animal products $	23,258,364	45,995,705	35,365,835(7)	278,983,000	136,898,000(12)	*
Fisheries . . . . $	1,995,091	2,885,203	3,503,450(7)	6,425,108	19,156,000(12)	*
Forest products . $	12,873,875	46,042,029	40,688,785(7)	140,007,000	291,475,000(12)	*
Manufactures. . $	310,514,144	690,106,000	723,690,140(7)	2,774,766,000	4,344,645,000(12)	*
Mineral products $	44,020,074	408,090,364	560,156,309(7)	2,383,173,000	710,851,000(12)	*
TRANSPORTATION:						
Steam Railways. mi.	25,400	42,075	42,441	42,956	43,689	43,003
Electric Railways mi.	1,224	1,386	1,040(7)	595	. . . . . .	. . . . . .
Urban Transit System, Passengers no.	. . . . .	. . . . .	. . . . .	. . . . .	987,319,165	1,036,423,243
Shipping, sea going, cleared tons	22,297,186	26,535,387	34,865,229(7)	52,750,461	77,140,524	99,852,760
COMMUNICATION:						
Telephones . . no.	302,759	1,402,861	1,397,272	3,108,437	6,014,015	7,882,628
Telegraphs . . . mi.	42,351	53,228	52,246	53,580	48,675	50,538
Postal revenue . $	9,146,952	30,416,106	40,383,366	90,454,678	173,645,658	237,538,585
Postal expenditure $	7,954,223	36,292,603	38,699,674	91,781,466	178,371,716	240,206,458
Postal money orders issued . . $	70,614,862	167,749,651	173,565,550	511,915,621	886,976,976	965,095,390
FINANCE:						
Revenue . . . . $	117,780,410	349,587,299	872,169,654	3,112,535,948	6,249,358,000	9,425,407,000(11)
Expenditures . . $	87,774,198	440,057,336	1,249,641,446	2,901,241,698	7,022,623,000	9,732,839,000(11)
Gross debt . . . $	474,941,487	2,610,265,698	5,011,399,120	16,923,307,028	22,907,814,464	30,340,137,314(11)
Net debt . . . $	340,042,052	2,261,611,936	3,648,691,449	11,433,314,949	13,228,127,045	15,964,950,478(11)
Bank deposits . $	1,073,298,505	2,568,683,245	3,464,781,844	8,464,510,837	15,163,000,000	21,497,000,000

(1) Based on the revised standard industrial classification and new establishment of total activity concepts. Using earlier classification, figures would be 6–7% lower. (2) Nonmetallic minerals. (3) Based on new series; includes power produced by industrial establishments for their own use. (4) Includes re-exports of 140 million for 1961 and 255 million for 1966. (5) Exclusive of fodder corn. (6) 1939; military restrictions prevented publication of detailed figures for copper, lead, and nickel after 1939.(7)1940. (8) Includes bushel equivalent of wheat flour. (9) 1959. (10) Minerals and metals. (11) Year ended March 31, 1967, DDB statistics. (12) 1962. *Not available; new classifications were instituted in January 1961 for exports and in Jan. 1964 for imports. †Expenditure for new stock. Source (main): *Canada Year Book* (annual editions).

Over the larger part of the country, especially over the great interior plain, a continental climate prevails, the temperature in Fort Simpson, for example, varying from a recorded minimum of 73° below zero to 101° above. In other sections, however, the extremes of heat and cold are modified by the presence of vast bodies of water, as the Atlantic Ocean, the Pacific Ocean, the Great Lakes, and Hudson Bay.

In the maritime provinces, spring is retarded by the presence of the cold arctic current on the Atlantic Coast. The summer climate, however, is equable and the autumn is long and open. British Columbia has one of the finest climates in North America. At New Westminster the mean temperature of the coldest month is 36° F. and that of the hottest is 58° F. The lowest recorded temperature of Vancouver is only 2° lower than that of San Antonio, Texas. The recorded rainfall reaches a higher figure on the Pacific Coast than in any other part of Canada. The region of the Great Lakes has a temperate climate with a fairly high precipitation. The interior plains have a comparatively dry climate, but fortunately the precipitation occurs mainly in the summer, when it can be of value for agriculture.

Waterways. The rivers of Canada are of exceptional magnitude and number. They belong to four large drainage basins: (1) the Atlantic, including the Saint John, the Saint Lawrence and its tributaries, and the Hamilton; (2) the Hudson Bay, including the Moose, the Albany, the Nelson and its tributary,—the Saskatchewan,—the Churchill, and many others; (3) the Arctic, including the Banks, the Coppermine, and the Mackenzie with its tributaries—the Liard, the Peace, and the Athabaska; (4) the Pacific, including the Columbia, the Fraser, the Skeena, the Stikine, and the Yukon, the last emptying into Bering Sea.

Rimming the outer border of the Laurentian plateau are the greatest lakes of the world, the lakes of the Saint Lawrence system—Lake Ontario, Lake Erie, Lake Huron, and Lake Superior. Other large lakes of Canada are Lake Winnipeg, Lake Athabaska, Great Slave Lake, and Great Bear Lake.

The Great Lakes system is the waterway of the most importance for transportation, although the Nelson-Saskatchewan river, flowing into Hudson Bay, and the Mackenzie-Athabaska river, flowing into the Arctic Ocean, were well traveled water highways known to fur traders long before settlements had advanced as far west as Lake Ontario.

By means of enlarging the channel of the Saint Lawrence River, the Canadian government has made it possible for ocean steamers to reach Montreal, which is situated at a distance of 700 miles from the Atlantic Ocean. By the further construction of 117.2 miles of canals, an uninterrupted communication by water has been established from the head of Lake Superior to the Atlantic Ocean, an aggregate distance of 1594 miles.

Minerals. Canada is the world's chief source of nickel, platinum and the platinum metals, and asbestos; it ranks second in gold, aluminum, and zinc, and fourth in copper and lead.

The chief minerals of the maritime provinces are coal and iron, mined mostly in Nova Scotia. These provinces also produce gypsum in large amounts.

Canada's nickel, gold, and cobalt come mainly from northern Ontario, where platinum, copper, and silver also represent a large proportion of Ontario's annual output of minerals. Oil, natural gas, and salt are produced in southern Ontario. Quebec is one of the world's chief sources of asbestos. Other minerals produced in Quebec are mica, copper, gold, building stone, and clay for bricks.

The prairie provinces, particularly Alberta, have large coal deposits. Alberta also produces oil and natural gas in important quantities. From Manitoba come gold and copper.

The mineral output of British Columbia comprises chiefly copper, coal, gold, silver, lead, and zinc.

Yukon territory has long been famous for its gold and silver mines. Important discoveries of silver, cobalt, and radium ore deposits were made in 1931 in the Northwest Territories, northeast of Great Bear Lake, and the first shipments of radium ore were made in 1932 for reduction in Port Hope, Ont.

Flora. In Ontario and Quebec, south of a line running from Georgian Bay to Montreal, the flora is of a southern forest type. North of this line to latitude 50°, from the Gulf of Saint Lawrence to Manitoba, a Temperate Zone forest type prevails. In Manitoba the forest disappears, giving place to the prairie grasses and herbage. Prairie vegetation spreads west as far as the foothills of the Rockies. Farther north, along a line drawn from latitude 55° on the Athabaska river to the south end of Lake Winnipeg, the prairie gradually gives place to the northern forest.

This northern forest belt extends from the Atlantic Ocean and the Gulf of Saint Lawrence to the Rockies. It covers all the country, extending from the temperate forest and the prairies northward as far as the Barren Grounds. In its southern half, this area is densely forested, but in the northern half the forest gradually becomes more open and the trees become smaller. The line between the forest and the Barren Grounds runs from Richards Island in the Arctic Ocean to the general region of Churchill on Hudson Bay, and from Richmond Gulf on the east side of the bay to Ungava Bay. In the Barren Grounds, the subsoil is permanently frozen.

In the Cordilleran belt, the flora varies according to climatic conditions. It is characterized by a tropical luxuriance on the coast and on the western slopes of the high ranges but, in the dry areas east of the ranges, it takes on forms typical of the American desert.

Forests and Lumbering. Canada's forests cover 1,151,454 square miles, nearly one-third of the country's total surface. They are included more or less roughly in three areas: (1) the giant fir forest of the Rocky Mountains and the Pacific Coast; (2) the northern coniferous forest, lying between the prairies and the Barren Grounds; and (3) the deciduous, hardwood forest, extending from Lake Huron through southern Ontario and southern Quebec to New Brunswick and the Atlantic Coast.

The chief timber trees of the Pacific Coast area are Douglas fir, red cedar, Alaska pine, Sitka spruce, and Engelmann spruce. The dominant types of the northern forest include white spruce, balsam fir, tamarack, and black spruce. The more valuable trees of the southeastern forest area are yellow birch, white pine, red pine, eastern cedar, maple, elm, ash, oak, and hickory.

The forests of Canada are owned mainly by the provincial governments. Leases are extended to lumber or pulp companies to cut the timber, usually with the condition that the logs be sawed or manufactured into pulp in Canada.

The products of the forest which represent the largest value are pulp wood, lumber, and firewood. A large part of the lumber and pulp wood or paper manufactured from pulp wood is exported to the United States.

Fauna. The fauna of Canada resembles that of northern Europe. The carnivora are represented by several species of the weasel family, such as the ermine, the marten, and the mink. The lynx, bear, fox, wolf, and skunk are common at a distance from the settled districts. In the prairie provinces, small rodents, called gophers, are so numerous as to constitute a pest. The beaver is a characteristic Canadian animal and has been adopted, along with the maple leaf, as a national emblem. Otters and muskrats are numerous. Caribou range over the northern plains, which are also the habitat of the unique musk ox, an animal almost as large as the domesticated ox but having a close resemblance to the sheep. Moose and deer are found in the forested areas, and goats, sheep, and grizzly bears make the mountains their habitat. White bears, seals, and walruses are common along the northern coasts. Snakes are rare except in the extreme south.

Fur-bearing Animals. The animals which provide the largest aggregate value in pelts are the fox, muskrat, beaver, mink, ermine, and marten. Approximately one-fifth of all Canadian furs come from fur farms. The silver fox is the animal most successfully raised in captivity, but many fur farms are stocked with minks, raccoons, skunks, martens, coyotes, and badgers.

The fur trade constituted Canada's earliest commercial interest. It was formerly a monopoly of the Hudson's Bay Company, which controlled most of the northwest region until 1859. The company still has the largest share of Canada's fur trade, maintaining posts throughout the vast territory of the north.

Fisheries. Canada's sea fishing waters, including bays and inlets, total over 200,000 square miles. Conservation methods to protect the country's immensely valuable fishing industry have been adopted both by the Federal government and by provincial governments. It is officially estimated that the government hatcheries plant annually in suitable waters about two billion fish fry.

Salmon are taken on the Pacific coast; lobsters are obtained from the shore waters of the maritime provinces and of Quebec. Herrings are caught both on the Atlantic coast and on the Pacific coast. Hake, pollock, mackerel, and paddock are products of Atlantic deep-sea fishing. Halibut were formerly plentiful in Atlantic waters, but they now come mostly from the Pacific coast. British Columbia and New Brunswick have developed sardine canning industries. In the Pacific Coast waters, are found the eulachon, or candlefish. Smelts are also abundant there as well as along the shores of the maritime provinces. Alaska black cod is highly prized but is not plentiful.

Prince Edward Island Malpeque oysters were formerly famous for size and quality, but the beds have been greatly depleted as a result of overfishing and of disease. Clams are found on the coasts of both oceans. Large quantities of fresh-water fishes are taken, such as perch, bass, pickerel, pike, tullibee, and whitefish, the last constituting the most valuable food fish obtained from the Great Lakes.

Agriculture. Agricultural land in Canada lies directly north of the American border in a strip extending east and west across the country with a width of several hundred miles. The fertile portion of this strip is interrupted by a large rocky territory in northern Ontario and by the mountains of British Columbia, where cultivation is confined mainly to the valleys. The total area of land under field crops is about 62,000,000 acres, although approximately six times this area is said to be of value for agriculture.

In the maritime provinces, fruit and potatoes are the most important cash crops, although hay, clover, and oats command the largest acreage. Farming in Quebec is mixed and largely self-contained; potatoes and buckwheat are the leading cash crops. Ontario supports dairy farming chiefly in the east; wheat, apples, tobacco, and sugar beets are the principal cash crops in the south; and the Niagara region specializes in the cultivation of peaches, grapes, cherries, and other fruits. The prairie provinces raise the bulk of Canada's wheat crop, which reached a high point of 567 million bushels in 1928. Canada leads the world in wheat exports, and its wheat production is exceeded only by those of Russia and the United States. British Columbia cultivates fruits intensively and raises poultry and cattle.

Livestock. Stock raising is still an exclusive occupation in some parts of Alberta, Saskatchewan, and British Columbia, but elsewhere it is made a part of mixed farming. Specialization in stock raising, just as in grain growing, is being superseded by mixed farming. This change, however, has resulted in an increase rather than in a decrease of the number of live stock raised.

Dairying is an important industry, Canada being one of the largest exporters of cheese in the world. The factory system has been adopted in all the provinces. Experimental farms distributed across the continent are maintained by the government.

Manufacturing. Industrial development has proceeded rapidly in Canada during recent years, partly as a result of the increased availability of cheap hydroelectric power. This expansion has been largely confined to the older provinces. Ontario ranks highest in manufacturing, Quebec comes next, and British Columbia takes the third place. Montreal heads the list of industrial cities with Toronto a close second, Hamilton, Windsor, and Vancouver following in the order named. The industrial output exhibits a wide variety of products, the most important of which is newsprint paper, in the production of which Canada leads the world. Flour manufacture, meat packing, sawmill operations, and automobile and textile manufacture follow. Canada is one of the largest manufacturers of rubber products in the world.

Water Power. The water power available in Canada is enormously extensive, the total available for electric generation being estimated at 33,113,200 horse power at ordinary 6 months flow. Over 80 per cent of all power used in Canada is in the form of electricity, and of this over 98 per cent is generated by water power. This situation is due chiefly to the fact that water power is available close to the centers of population. In the use of electricity Canada is exceeded only by the United States; in its use per capita, Canada leads the world.

Transportation. There are in Canada over 40,000 miles of railroad in operation, of which the government owns more than 20,000 miles. Two transcontinental systems span the country from east to west.

Roads and highways in Canada open to traffic in 1953 had a total mileage of 512,795, of which 181,306 miles were classified as improved highways. They include the Trans-Canada highway, 4860 miles in length, said to be the longest highway in the world. Opened in 1962, it connects all ten provinces of Canada. From its eastern terminus at St. John's, it traverses 500 miles in Newfoundland, utilizes a ferry to Cape Breton Is., N.S., crosses the world's deepest causeway at the Canso Strait into Nova Scotia, and is joined by a ferry-served feeder section from Prince Edward Island. It proceeds through Ottawa, Winnipeg, Calgary, Rogers pass in the Rocky Mountains, and, via ferry to Vancouver island, finds its western terminus at Victoria, B.C.

Shipping. The principal seaports of Canada include Montreal, Vancouver, Victoria, Halifax, Saint John, Sydney, and Quebec. The countries with which Canada has the heaviest sea-borne commerce are the United States, Australia, and Great Britain. The shipping on the Great Lakes is heavy, traffic being mainly of grain, lumber, and ores passing east and of coal and manufactures going west. See *St. Lawrence Seaway*.

Population and Language. More than one-half of the population of Canada is of British descent; about one-third is composed of the descendants of French colonists. In the prairie provinces large numbers of Americans have settled as well as a certain proportion of people from continental Europe. The majority of the latter, however, live in the industrial centers. There are more than 100,000 American Indians, mostly on reserves. The population in 1971 was estimated at 21,681,000.

French shares with English the status of an official language in Canada. Its use is confined mainly to

SCENIC CANADA

Percé Rock, an offshore bird sanctuary in Quebec's fishing region, is 1500 ft. long, 288 ft. high, and pierced by a 60-ft. central arch.

View of the city of Quebec, capital of the Province of Quebec
(*Quebec Province Tourist Branch & Film Bureau*)

A primitive wooden bridge in rural Canada. About 600 of these structures, covered for protection from the weather, still survive.

Sainte Rose du Nord, a village on the shore of the Saguenay River. Supported by fishing and forestry, it was settled about 1860.

Canadian Government Scenes: Quebec. The Citadel rises 350 feet above Quebec—the only fortified city in North America. Controlling the St. Lawrence waterway, it was built between 1823 and 1832, and was the site of wartime conferences in 1943 and 1944 between Churchill and Roosevelt. Below: In a colorful ceremony the Guard is changed. Garrisoned by the Royal 22nd Regiment, the fortress is the official Quebec residence of Canada's Governor General. (*Quebec Department of Tourism*)

Canadian Parliament, Ottawa—Winter view of the Parliament through the iron tracery of the central gate. The three Gothic-style buildings stand on a promontory over the Ottawa River. The original center building was designed mainly by Thomas Fuller. Begun in 1860, the group was completed in 1865. In 1916 the center was swept by fire, but rebuilt by 1920. The central Peace Tower, with a carillon of 53 bells, is 291 feet high, patterned after the famous Big Ben clock-tower of Britain's Parliament. The center section contains the Senate Chamber, House of Commons, and government offices. (*Canadian Dominion Bureau of Statistics*)

GEOGRAPHY AND TRAVEL

The Rhine, one of Europe's most famed rivers in history and legend, rises among the Swiss Alps and falls some 7000 feet. (*German National Tourist Office*)

Versailles Palace, a national museum near Paris, built by Louis XIV. The city is the capital of the Seine-et-Oise Department. (*French Govt. Tourist Office*)

Maligne Lake, in Jasper National Park (largest in North America—4200 square miles), a region of majestic peaks, canyons, lakes, icefields, and hot springs. Located in the Canadian Rockies, the park was established in 1907 as a wildlife sanctuary. (*Canadian Government Travel Bureau*)

The Dome of the Rock, site of Solomon's Temple in Jerusalem, dates from A.D. 687. It is believed that it was built by Omar, second Moslem Caliph. By tradition, it is the place where the Hebrew patriarch Abraham prepared to sacrifice his son Isaac. (*Courtesy Robert Bartels*)

Province	1901	1911	1921	1931	1941	1951	1961	1966	1971
Alberta	73,022	374,295	588,454	731,605	796,169	939,501	1,331,944	1,463,203	1,628,000
British Columbia	178,657	392,480	524,582	694,263	817,861	1,165,210	1,629,082	1,873,674	2,190,000
Manitoba	255,211	461,394	610,118	700,139	729,744	776,541	921,686	963,066	985,000
New Brunswick	331,120	351,889	387,876	408,219	457,401	515,697	597,936	616,788	629,000
Newfoundland	......	......	......	289,588	321,819	361,416	457,853	493,396	523,000
Northwest Terr.	20,129	6,507	7,988	7,133	12,028	16,004	22,998	28,738	36,000
Nova Scotia	459,574	492,338	523,837	512,846	577,962	642,584	737,007	756,039	770,000
Ontario	2,182,947	2,527,292	2,933,662	3,431,683	3,787,655	4,597,542	6,236,092	6,960,870	7,795,000
Prince Edward Island	103,259	93,728	88,615	88,038	95,047	98,429	104,629	108,535	111,000
Quebec	1,648,898	2,005,776	2,361,199	2,874,255	3,331,882	4,055,681	5,259,211	5,780,845	6,030,000
Saskatchewan	91,279	492,432	757,510	921,785	895,992	831,728	925,181	955,344	927,000
Yukon Territory	27,219	8,512	4,157	4,230	4,914	9,096	14,628	14,382	17,000
Total	5,371,315	7,206,643	8,788,483	10,374,196	11,506,655	14,009,429	18,238,247	20,014,880	21,641,000

Quebec and to a few French settlements in other provinces.

Education. The education of Indian and Eskimo children of school age is a responsibility of the Federal government; the provincial governments are responsible for exercising all other education. Elementary and secondary education is free and compulsory to age 14. As the need for qualified tradesmen, technicians, and professionals has increased, numerous vocational schools and community colleges have come into existence, making nearly 400 institutions of higher education in Canada in 1968. In the same year, more than 3,000,000 adults were enrolled in the large adult education program.

PROVINCES

Canada is divided into ten organized provinces, Yukon Territory, and the Northwest Territories comprising the districts of Franklin, Keewatin, and Mackenzie. The provinces, enumerated from east to west, are Newfoundland, Nova Scotia, Prince Edward Island, New Brunswick, Quebec, Ontario, Manitoba, Saskatchewan, Alberta, and British Columbia.

Alberta. A province of Canada, situated between British Columbia on the west and Saskatchewan on the east and stretching from the American border about 750 miles north to the 60th parallel of north latitude. The southwestern border follows the summit of the Rocky mountains, thereby leaving in Alberta the western mountain slope and the foothills. From the foothills in the southern portion of the province, a plain slopes eastward, forming a part of the Saskatchewan River basin. The northern part of the province consists of a plain of northern drainage, belonging to the Mackenzie-Athabaska basin. A fringe on the extreme south drains into the Missouri river. The elevation varies from 12,294 feet on the top of Mount Columbia in the Rocky mountains to 568 feet at Slave river in the north. Except in the south, Alberta is well watered by numerous rivers, large and small. Lakes abound in the central and northern parts. The area of the province is 255,285 square miles.

The climate of Alberta is continental, involving great extremes of temperature. The air is dry and healthful. In southern Alberta the chinook winds, descending from the ridge of the Rocky mountains, often clear the ground rapidly of snow in the early spring, thus reviving the grasses which serve as sustenance for large herds of cattle.

A dark mold, mostly humus, overlying a clay subsoil, covers the surface of Alberta from six inches to several feet in depth. Such a soil, being exceedingly fertile and at the same time capable of retaining a large amount of moisture, supports a highly developed agricultural industry. Wheat and oats are the principal crops. Mixed farming has tended in recent years to replace specialized grain growing, with the result that potatoes, dairy products, flax, sheep, hogs, and poultry contribute a considerable amount to the total of the agricultural production.

In the southwest of the province, there is an area which requires irrigation in order to insure crops. Over 5400 miles of irrigation canals and ditches have been constructed.

The mineral resources of Alberta are of considerable importance. Immense areas of lignite and of a high grade bituminous coal have been discovered. Anthracite coal is also mined. The output of all kinds of coal amounts normally to over six million tons, a total exceeded by none of the other provinces. Petroleum and natural gas have been found both in the northern and in the southern part.

The capital and largest city of Alberta is Edmonton, in which is located the University of Alberta, supported by the province. The chief industries are those related to agriculture, such as meat packing. Population, 1971, 1,628,000.

British Columbia. The most western province of Canada, extending from the international boundary line to latitude 60°. The province is bounded on the east by Alberta; the western boundary is the Pacific Ocean, for a distance of 500 miles, and, for an additional 600 miles, the province borders on the coast strip of Alaska. British Columbia includes Vancouver island, the Queen Charlotte islands, and numerous other islands off the Pacific coast. The area is 366,255 square miles.

With the exception of a portion of the Peace River country in the northeast, the whole of British Columbia lies within the Cordilleran mountainous belt. The highest point is Mount Fairweather, 15,300 feet. Between the ranges, and occasionally cutting through them, are deep fertile valleys. Between the coastal mountains and the next important range to the east is an interior plateau having much agricultural or grazing land.

A submergence of the coast has resulted in an archipelago of innumerable islands, deep sounds, and fiords, many of them excellent harbors. As a result, the province has a coast line of 7000 miles. Of the rivers, the Fraser, 800 miles long, is the largest. The Columbia river rises in British Columbia and has a course of 500 miles before crossing the boundary line. Beautiful fiordlike lakes are a feature of many of the valleys. The islands and the coast region have a mild climate, rainy in winter but dry in summer. The interior plateaus are dry and subject to greater extremes of temperature.

British Columbia has one of the greatest forests of merchantable timber in North America, besides

Name	Location	Area Sq. Miles	Established	Distinctive Characteristics
Scenic and Recreational Parks:				
Banff	Alberta	2,564	1885	Ideal mountain playground containing the two famous resorts, Banff and Lake Louise.
Cape Breton Highlands	Nova Scotia	390	1936	Northern part of Cape Breton island; rugged coast line with mountain background.
Fundy	New Brunswick . .	80	1948	Recreational area. Forested region, wildlife sanctuary, rugged terrain.
Georgian Bay Islands	Ontario	5.37	1929	Thirty islands in Georgian bay, scene of bloody inter-tribal Indian war in 1649; includes Flowerpot Island reserve.
Glacier	British Columbia . .	521	1886	Summit of the Selkirks; Illecillewaet and Asulkan glaciers; Nakimu caves; Marion lake; Rogers and Baloo passes.
Jasper	Northern Alberta . .	4,200	1907	Immense mountain wilderness; unclimbed peaks, glaciers, snow fields, canyons, lakes; Mt. Edith Cavell, Miette Hot Springs, Mt. Robson.
Kootenay	British Columbia . .	543	1920	Mountain scenery, Briscoe range, Ice lake, Sinclair canyon, and Radium Hot Springs.
Mount Revelstoke .	British Columbia . .	100	1914	Panoramic views of Columbia and Illecillewaet valleys, Clach-na-Coodin ice field.
Point Pelee	Lake Erie, Ontario .	6	1918	Most southerly point in Canada; resting place of many migratory birds; recreational area; unique flora.
Prince Albert	Saskatchewan . . .	1,496	1927	Recreational reserve and wild life sanctuary.
Prince Edward Island Shore	North Shore, P.E.I. .	7	1937	Twenty-five mile strip of bathing beaches.
Riding Mountain . .	Western Manitoba .	1,148	1929	Rolling wooded hills. Abundance of large game.
Saint Lawrence Islands	Ontario	189.4*	1914	Thirteen islands and one mainland reservation among the Thousand Islands.
Tar Sands Reservation	N. Alberta	3.2	1926	Four areas reserved for National Parks Branch to supply materials for road building.
Waterton Lakes . .	Southern Alberta . .	204	1895	With adjoining U. S. Glacier park forms international park. Mountains noted for beauty of coloring; lovely lakes, waterfalls, and snow peaks; excellent trout fishing; favorite camping resort.
Yoho	British Columbia . .	507	1886	Rugged scenery of west slope of Rockies; Yoho valley with falls over 1200 feet in height; natural bridge; Emerald lake.
Animal Parks and Reserves: Buffalo	Near Wainwright, Alberta	197.5	1908	Government's buffalo herd—over 3000 buffalo also moose, elk, deer, yak, and catalo.
Elk Island	Near Lamont, Alberta	75	1913	Smaller fenced enclosure, containing about 2000 buffalo; also moose, elk, and deer.
Nemiskam antelope Reserve	Southern Alberta . .	8.5	1922	Fenced reserve containing about 300 pronghorned antelope.
Wood Buffalo . . .	Alberta and N. W. T.	17,300	1922	Home of the wood buffalo.
Historic Parks: Fort Anne	Nova Scotia	31*	1917	Fort Annapolis Royal was the center of the struggle between France and England for the possession of the continent.
Fort Beauséjour . .	New Brunswick . .	81*	1926	Site of a fort built by the French in 1750-51.

* Acres.

millions of acres of pulp wood yet untouched. Douglas fir, cedar, spruce, western hemlock, larch, and pine attain an unusual diameter and height. Logs 30 feet in girth are not uncommon. In value of output lumbering ranks highest among the industries of the province, providing support for two-fifths of the population and entitling British Columbia to the first place among the lumber producing provinces.

In the fishing industry, British Columbia likewise ranks first among the provinces, supplying 47 per cent of the Canadian production. The salmon fisheries are the most important, and have given rise to a large salmon canning industry. Halibut, herring, and black cod form a considerable part of the annual catch.

The discovery of gold in 1858 in the Fraser River district was the occasion for the earliest settlements in British Columbia. The mineral production since that time has continued to be important, copper, gold, coal, and silver being among the more valuable products of the industry. Nearly all the lead produced in Canada comes from British Columbia, which has one of the greatest lead-zinc deposits in the world. The province mines about one-fourth of the country's mineral output by value.

In recent years agriculture, fruit growing, stock raising, dairying, and poultry raising have made rapid advances. The chief fruits include apples, grapes, peaches, apricots, plums, strawberries, and cherries.

British Columbia has a native supply of coal and of iron, and the province is favorably situated for shipping goods to the markets of Australia, of South America, and of Asia. Mainly as a result of these facts, manufacturing has become important, entitling British Columbia to the third place in regard to industrial output among the provinces.

The public school system is nonsectarian. Instruction must be given in English. The provincial university, called the University of British Columbia, is situated at Vancouver, which is the largest city of the province. The capital is Victoria, on Vancouver Island. Population, 1971, 2,190,000.

Keewatin (kĕ-wä'tĭn), **Mackenzie, Franklin.** Three divisions, each known as a provisional district, formed on January 1, 1920, out of the vast Northwest Territories. The total area of these districts is 1,309,682 square miles, of which 1,258,217 square miles are land and 51,465 square miles are water. In 1966, the population numbered 28,738.

The land is a rolling plain. The principal lakes are Great Bear lake and Great Slave lake, both in Mackenzie; the largest river, the Mackenzie, flows for most of its course through that district, emptying into Mackenzie bay, an arm of the Arctic Ocean. Furs are obtained in all the districts, and minerals—radium, gold, copper, lead, zinc, petroleum, and coal—have been found.

Manitoba (măn'ĭ-tō'bà). A province of Canada, situated in the south central part of the country between Ontario and Saskatchewan, stretching about 750 miles northward from the American border to 60° north latitude. The eastern boundary follows the 95th meridian about 275 miles northward, then cuts across at an angle of about 45° to Hudson Bay, so that the northeastern part of the province has a coast line on the bay. In the southern part, the drainage is from the southeast and the west to Lake Manitoba and Lake Winnipeg and thence northeast by the Nelson River to Hudson Bay. In the north, the Churchill River basin drains eastward into Hudson Bay. Duck mountain, 2727 feet in altitude, is the highest point. The area of the province is 251,832 square miles.

A large part of the soil is alluvial, a vast lake having occupied the southern part of the province in geological times. This alluvium, a black loam of great fertility, has a very high content of potash, nitrogen, and phosphoric acid, and is, therefore, peculiarly well adapted to the growth of cereals. The southeastern part of the province is rocky and slopes rapidly from the highlands of northern Ontario. This fact has made possible the development, on the Winnipeg River, of extensive hydroelectric power.

The chief primary industry of Manitoba is agriculture. The growing season has a duration of from 85 to 105 days. This period, however, by reason of the long, bright summer days, is sufficient to ripen a hard type of spring wheat which holds a position in the world's markets second to none. Oats, barley, and potatoes are grown also in considerable quantities. The dairy products of Manitoba are important and a great deal of butter and cheese are shipped. Cattle and swine are raised.

Manufacturing in Manitoba has been promoted by the availability of cheap hydroelectric power. In the value of industrial output, the province normally ranks fourth.

The capital and largest city of Manitoba is Winnipeg, which is also the seat of the University of Manitoba. The first permanent settlement was made in 1812 in the Red River district by a company of Scotch colonists. A unique feature of Manitoba's winter life is the annual dog derby, a race in which various dog teams compete on a course some 200 miles in length. Population, 1971, 985,000.

New Brunswick. A maritime province in the southeastern part of Canada, having an eastern coast line on the Gulf of Saint Lawrence and a southeastern coast line on the Bay of Fundy. Maine lies to the southwest of the province, and Quebec, to the northwest. The total coast line is 500 miles long and is indented with many fine harbors. Most of the surface is a rolling plain, lying between the low hills which, in the south, skirt the Bay of Fundy and the subdued mountains of the northwest. The highest point is Carleton mountain, which reaches an altitude of 2716 feet. The area is 27,985 square miles.

A number of navigable rivers traverse the province: the Saint John flows southward into the Bay of Fundy; the Mirimichi and Restigouche follow an eastward course into the Gulf of Saint Lawrence. At Grand Falls on the Saint John River is the spectacular 225-foot cataract which, now harnessed, supplies power for a large hydroelectric plant. At the river's mouth in Saint John Harbor is the famous 'reversing falls" which, lighted at night, is an impressive sight.

New Brunswick's climate is subject to extremes. The thermometer has ranged from 95° F. in summer to –30° F. in winter.

Agriculture is the leading industry. The principal crops are hay, potatoes, oats, and turnips. Orcharding is important, apples forming the most valuable item. There are numerous cheese factories and creameries. Most of their products are exported to England. The province has much fertile land which has not yet been occupied.

Forests cover a large part of New Brunswick. Lumbering is an important industry, entitling the province to the fourth place in the nation in regard to lumber production. Spruce, pine, fir, maple, hemlock, birch, beech, ash, and elm are among the principal timber trees. At present, spruce is the principal commercial wood and is exported in large quantities.

New Brunswick ranks third among the provinces in the fishing industry. Oysters, lobsters, herring, codfish, haddock, and smelts are caught. The canning of lobsters and oysters and the curing of codfish add greatly to its economy.

The principal manufactured products include lumber, woodenware, wood pulp, boots and shoes, paper, cottons and woolens, nails, mill machinery, and leather. Fredericton is the capital. Saint John, the largest city, is an ice-free harbor at which two transcontinental railways reach tidewater. Population, 1971, 629,000.

Newfoundland. A former British dominion, consisting of the island of Newfoundland, lying across the mouth of the Gulf of Saint Lawrence, and a portion of the Labrador peninsula. Being situated 1640 miles west of Ireland, Newfoundland commands the shortest route from North America to Europe.

The island has an area of 42,734 square miles. In form it resembles a triangle with approximately equal sides of about 325 miles in length. The coasts are, in general, high and rocky, indented by innumerable fiords. Newfoundland's Labrador territory covers about 232,400 square miles, covering the land draining into the Atlantic. Of this, 112,400 square miles came to Newfoundland in 1927 through the favorable outcome of a boundary dispute. Its value lies in the coast fisheries, in pulpwood, and in potential hydroelectric development.

The interior of Newfoundland is a rolling plain, interrupted by a few isolated peaks and rising on the northwest to a ridge of hills, called Long range. From this ridge eastward flows Exploits River, the country's longest stream. The Humber River has cut its way westward through Long range and flows into the Gulf of Saint Lawrence. The rivers are not navigable.

The climate is subject to less extreme variations of temperature than those occurring in any part of the interior of Canada. The mean temperature is lowered by the proximity of the arctic current, which brings melting icebergs from the north and occasions dense fogs along the coasts.

Large portions of the island consist of marshes and of rocky soil supporting lichens and low shrubs of pine and of larch. The river valleys, however, contain large tracts of arable land and extensive areas heavily forested with conifers, birch, and red maple. The wild animals include the black bear, the wolf, the beaver, the deer, and the fox. The Newfoundland dog was developed by a cross between European species and a woolly-coated dog used by the Indians of Labrador.

City or Town	1951	1971	City or Town	1951	1971	City or Town	1951	1971
Alma, Que.	22,195[1]	22,353	Lindsay, Ont.	9,603	12,090	St. Hubert, Que.	17,215[1]	21,753
Anjou, Que.	22,477[1]	33,842	London, Ont.	95,343	221,430	St. Hyacinthe, Que.	20,236	24,192
Barrie, Ont.	12,514	26,985	Longueuil, Que.	25,593[1]	97,483	St. James, Man.		70,768
Belleville, Ont.	19,519	34,498	Magog, Que.	12,423	13,280	St. Jean, Que.	19,305	32,484
Boucherville, Que.	15,338[1]	20,000	Medicine Hat, Alta.	16,364	26,058	St. Jérôme, Que.	17,685	26,131
Brampton, Ont.	36,264[1]	41,238	Mississauga, Ont.		155,667	St. John, N. B.	50,779	87,910
Brandon, Man.	20,598	30,832	Moncton, N. B.	27,334	47,781	St. John's, Nfld.	52,873	86,290
Brantford, Ont.	36,727	62,853	Montreal, Que.	1,021,520	1,197,753	St. Laurent, Que.	59,479[1]	63,067
Brockville, Ont.	12,301	19,707	Mont-Royal, Que.	21,845[1]	21,470	St. Léonard, Que.	25,328[1]	52,013
Burlington, Ont.	65,941[1]	86,125	Moose Jaw, Sask.	24,355	31,284	St. Thérèse, Que.	15,628[1]	17,161
Calgary, Alta.	129,060	400,154	Nanaimo, B. C.	15,188[1]	14,762	St. Thomas, Ont.	18,173	25,062
Cap de la Madeleine, Que.	18,667	31,120	New Glasgow, N. S.	9,933	10,792	St. Vital, Man.	29,528[1]	32,613
Charlottetown, P. E. I.	15,887	18.631	New Waterford, N. S.	10,423	9,549	Sarnia, Ont.	34,697	56,727
Chatham, Ont.	21,218	34,601	New Westminster, B. C.	28,639	42,083	Saskatoon, Sask.	53,268	125,079
Chicoutimi, Que.	23,111	32,900	Niagara Falls, Ont.	22,874	65,271	Sault Ste. Marie, Ont.	32,452	78,175
Cornwall, Ont.	16,899	46,429	North Bay, Ont.	17,944	49,063	Sept Iles, Que.	18,950[1]	24,289
Dartmouth, N. S.	15,037	64,002	Oakville, Ont.	52,793[1]	61,365	Shawinigan, Que.	26,903	27,502
Dollard-des-Ormeaux, Que.	12,297[1]	25,284	Orillia, Ont.	12,110	24,016	Sherbrooke, Que.	50,543	80,457
Drummondville, Que.	14,341	31,537	Oshawa, Ont.	41,545	91,113	Sorel, Que.	14,961	19,317
East Kildonan	28,796[1]	29,722	Ottawa, Ont.	202,045	298,087	Stratford, Ont.	18,785	23,863
Edmonton, Alta.	159,631	434,116	Outremont, Que.	30,057	28,402	Sudbury, Ont.	42,410	153,959
Fredericton, N. B.	16,018	23,612	Owen Sound, Ont.	16,423	18,281	Sydney, N. S.	31,317	32,459
Galt, Ont.	19,207	38,134	Pembroke, Ont.	12,704	16,130	Sydney Mines, N. S.	8,410	8,957
Gatineau, Que.	17,727[1]	22,356	Peterborough, Ont.	38,272	57,498	Thetford Mines, Que.	15,095	21,662
Glace Bay, N.S.	25,586	22,276	Pierrefonds, Que.	27,924[1]	33,046	Three Rivers, Que.	46,074	55,240
Granby, Que.	21,989	33,958	Pointe aux Trembles, Que.	29,888[1]	35,521	Thunder Bay, Ont.		107,805
Grand' Mere, Que.	11,089	17,144	Pointe Claire, Que.	26,784[1]	27,310	Timmins, Ont.	27,743	28,252
Greenfield Park, Que.	12,288[1]	15,277	Port Arthur, Ont.	31,161		Toronto, Ont.	675,754	698,634
Guelph, Ont.	27,386	58,364	Prince Albert, Sask.	17,149	27,613	Transcona, Man.	19,761[1]	22,085
Halifax, N. S.	85,589	121,086	Quebec, Que.	164,016	182,418	Trenton, Ont.	10,085	14,405
Hamilton, Ont.	208,321	307,473	Red Deer, Alta.	26,171[1]	27,428	Truro, N. S.	10,750	12,968
Hull, Que.	43,483	62,842	Regina, Sask.	71,319	137,759	Valleyfield, Que.	22,414	29,776
Joliette, Que.	16,064	19,497	Richmond Hill, Ont.	19,773[1]	32,399	Vancouver, B. C.	360,520	419,433
Jonquière, Que.	21,618	28,080	Rimouski, Que.	20,330[1]	26,546	Verdun, Que.	77,391	74,520
Kingston, Ont.	33,459	61,870	Rivière du Loup, Que.	9,425	12,423	Victoria, B. C.	51,331	60,897
Kitchener, Ont.	44,867	109,954	Rouyn, Que.	14,633	17,804	Victoriaville, Que.	13,124	22,088
Lachine, Que.	27,773	44,345	St. Boniface, Man.	26,342	46,661	Waterloo, Ont.	11,991	37,245
LaSalle, Que.	48,322[1]	72,916	St. Catherines, Ont.	37,984	109,636	Welland, Ont.	15,382	44,222
Laval, Que.	196,088[1]	228,101	Ste. Foy, Que.	48,298[1]	67,834	West Kildonan, Man.	22,240[1]	23,728
Lethbridge, Alta.	22,947	40,706				Westmount, Que.	25,222	23,570
Lévis, Que.	13,162	16,566				Whitby, Ont.	17,231[1]	25,291
						Windsor, Ont.	120,049	199,784
						Winnipeg, Man.	235,710	243,208
						Woodstock, Ont.	15,544	25,559

Source: Statistics Canada, preliminary 1971.   [1] 1966.

Approximately one-fifth of Newfoundland's population is engaged in fishing and curing codfish. Nearly half the exports are codfish products.

The most important manufactures are pulp and paper. A very small fraction of the arable land is cultivated, in spite of the steps taken by the government to encourage agriculture. The chief crops are potatoes and turnips. Iron, zinc, and copper are mined.

The population of Newfoundland in the 1971 census was 523,000, concentrated mainly in the coast region of the southeast. This figure excludes 5,000 inhabitants of Labrador, mostly Indians. Nearly all the inhabitants are of British descent and Protestants. The schools are denominational.

The government has been undergoing changes since 1934, when the British government suspended the constitution and took over on account of internal financial difficulties. Union with Canada as a tenth province was carried by a small majority in a referendum conducted in Newfoundland July 1948, and was mutually agreed to in December of that year. Canadian and British parliaments and the Newfoundland government ratified this agreement, which came into force March 31, 1949. The population of St. John's, the capital, fishing, industrial, and educational center, in 1971 was 86,290.

Nova Scotia. A maritime province in the extreme southeast of Canada, consisting of a narrow peninsula and of the Island of Cape Breton, which was connected with the mainland by a large rail-highway causeway completed in 1955. The greatest length is 350 miles and the greatest breadth, 100 miles. The maximum elevation of 1500 feet is reached at North Cape plateau, Victoria County. The area of the province is 21,428 square miles.

The main peninsula is a long highland cut by transverse valleys. An important longitudinal valley, the Annapolis valley, runs parallel to the Bay of Fundy, being separated from it by a narrow ridge known as North mountain. The seacoast line is 1500 miles in length, and is indented by several inlets which form excellent harbors.

Bras d'Or lake in Cape Breton is a magnificent landlocked body of salt water. It has become a popular resort for wealthy summer residents. Minas basin, the east arm of the Bay of Fundy, penetrates 60 miles inland. Here the tides, rising some 50 feet, rush in with great force, forming "bores."

Nova Scotia has a healthful climate, with a mean summer temperature of 65° F. and a mean winter temperature of 25° F. Winter weather is variable, and spring is late.

Agriculture is the chief occupation, hay, potatoes, turnips, and oats constituting the principal crops. Fruit growing, dairying, and stock raising are important.

Coal is mined extensively in Cape Breton island and in the northern part of the mainland. Copper tungsten, lead, gold, and manganese are found, and there are enormous beds of iron ore. Gypsum occurs in immense masses. Nova Scotia normally ranks fourth among the provinces in mineral output.

The fisheries of Nova Scotia are among the most productive in the world. The annual value is second only to that of British Columbia, among the Canadian provinces. Mackerel, cod, herring, haddock, and lobsters abound in the coast waters. Lobster canning has become a large industry.

Products manufactured in the province include iron and steel products, cotton and woolen goods, boots and shoes, machinery, farm implements, furniture, paper, sugar, condensed milk, and vehicles. Wood pulp is exported. Lumbering, formerly the chief industry, is still important.

The province is well supplied with railroads, chiefly lines of the Canadian National Railway. Shipping is important, especially in winter, when navigation on the Saint Lawrence is closed. There are three universities. The capital and largest city is Halifax. Population, 1971, 770,000.

Ontario. The most populous and most wealthy province of Canada. It is situated in the southeast of Canada, between Quebec and Manitoba and between the international boundary and Hudson Bay. The province consists of a large northern area joined to a smaller but populous southern area by a narrow neck between Georgian Bay and the Quebec border. The southern portion is part of the Saint Lawrence lowlands, belonging to the Saint Lawrence River basin. This basin is separated by a flat and ill-marked watershed, called the height of land, from the Laurentian plateau, which is an area of southern drainage sloping toward Hudson Bay. The bulk of the population is to be found in the lowlands, where the soil is adapted to agriculture. The northern country is rocky. Tiptop Hill, 2120 feet high, in Thunder Bay district, is the highest point in Ontario. The province is well watered by lakes and rivers. The area is 412,582 square miles.

Since Ontario extends from Hudson Bay to Lake Erie, a distance of about 1000 miles, there is considerable climatic variation. Extreme cold in winter is experienced about the watershed. The southern part, however, has a much milder climate, while the climatic severity of the northern section is tempered by the lowness of its altitude.

In value of mineral production, Ontario leads all the other provinces. The chief products mined are gold, silver, nickel, copper, cobalt, platinum, lead, iron, and arsenic. Nickel and cobalt are distinctive of Ontario's mineral output. Nickel is produced in no other part of the world in similar quantities.

Farming is the most important primary industry. In value of field crops, Ontario usually ranks second among the provinces. The land under cultivation is almost entirely in the lowlands, although agriculture is practicable in parts of the Laurentian plateau, including the clay belt in northern Ontario, through which the Canadian National railway has been constructed. Oats, wheat, barley, and corn are the chief grains. Minor crops are peas, rye, sugar beets, tobacco, potatoes, and turnips. About half the fruit raised in Canada is produced by Ontario. Approximately one million barrels of apples of the high grade are annually shipped to Europe. Similarly, in the output of dairy products and in the number of live stock owned, the province holds the leading position.

In lumbering, Ontario yields the first place to British Columbia, and, in the production of pulp wood, the province ranks third to Quebec. Immense forests cover almost one-fourth of the area of the province. Spruce, pine, and poplar are the principal woods cut, although maple, birch, and elm are also found over considerable areas. Oak and hickory occur in the more southern parts.

The Great Lakes fisheries employ hundreds of vessels. Trout, whitefish, pickerel, and fresh-water herring form most of the catch, a part of which is canned for market.

Ontario is Canada's most highly developed industrial section, manufacturing industries supporting nearly one-half the population. Hydroelectric power is available in large quantities due mainly to the development of the water power of Niagara Falls. The manufactures of the province include machinery, electrical equipment, automobiles, rubber products, farm implements, ironware, railroad rolling stock, metals and alloys, leather, furniture, paper, soap, boots and shoes, sewing machines, woodenware, and textiles. Milling, fruit canning, and meat packing employ many thousands of hands.

Ontario has seven universities, besides a number of church and technical colleges and agricultural schools. The province was formerly called Upper Canada. Its population was considerably augmented by the United Empire Loyalists. The capital and largest city is Toronto. The province also contains Ottawa, the capital of the country. Population, 1971, 7,795,000.

Prince Edward Island. An island province of Canada, situated in the southern part of the Gulf of Saint Lawrence. Prince Edward Island is the smallest and most densely populated province of the nation. The island is about 145 miles long and varies in width from 5 miles to 34 miles. The coast line is a succession of bays and headlands. The surface is gently rolling, the greatest height being 306 feet, at Fredericton Station, Queens County. The area is 2184 square miles.

Due to the influence of the surrounding sea, the province is singularly free from extremes of heat and cold. Fogs are less frequent than on the mainland. The soil is fertile and produces, besides other crops, hay, potatoes, oats, and turnips.

The fisheries provide employment for a large part of the population. Lobsters and oysters of superior quality are canned for market. Cod, herring, hake, and mackerel are also taken.

Dairying receives much attention, and the island's creameries and cheese factories export large quantities of their products. Rivaling it in importance is the production of poultry and eggs. In recent years, silver fox farming has developed into a highly important industry.

Prince Edward Island attracts many summer residents by its pleasant summer climate and its facilities for surf bathing. Higher education is furnished by two colleges. Charlottetown, the capital, is the largest city. Population, 1971, 111,000.

Quebec. A province in eastern Canada, lying between the Gulf of Saint Lawrence on the east and Hudson Bay and Ontario on the west and extending north about 1200 miles from the international boundary to Hudson strait and the Atlantic coastal strip known as Labrador. Quebec is the oldest as well as the largest province in the country and was formerly known as Lower Canada. Its area is 594,434 square miles.

Except for a narrow strip along the Saint Lawrence River, the whole northern part of the province belongs to the Canadian shield with a drainage toward Hudson Bay. To the south of the river rise the Notre Dame Mountains, a continuation of the Appalachian system. Mount Jacques Cartier, on the Gaspe Peninsula, is the highest point in Quebec, with an altitude of 4230 feet.

The climate of Quebec is continental in severity, partly on account of the influence of cold arctic currents and of winds blowing above them and passing over the land. The air is dry, clear, and bracing.

The mining industry of Quebec is confined mainly to the eastern townships and to the district along the Ottawa River. Asbestos is a distinctive product, Quebec supplying over half of the world's market. Other products are copper, gold, chromic iron, cement, magnesite, mica, graphite, apatite, marble, serpentine, roofing slates, and building stone.

The lumber industry has always been of great importance in Quebec, which contains millions of acres covered with commercial timber. The lumber and the pulp industry yield approximately the same returns as in Ontario.

Agriculture and dairying form the chief occupations. The principal crops are hay, oats, and potatoes. Quebec is a close second to Ontario in the production of creamery butter and of factory cheese. Cattle are exported to Europe. The making of maple sirup and of maple sugar centers in this province.

The seacoast fisheries yield cod, mackerel, and lobsters as the principal items of the catch. Large amounts of salt fish are exported.

Quebec ranks second to Ontario as a manufacturing province. Wood pulp, timber products, machinery, cottons and woolens, aluminum, refined sugar, leather, and boots and shoes are included among the principal manufactures. Hydroelectric power installations exceed in horsepower those of any other province. Among the largest plants and ranking among the greatest in the world are those at Arvida near Lake St. John, at Gouin Dam on the St. Maurice River, near Quebec, and at the Beauharnois Dam, near Montreal.

Elementary instruction is free. Catholics and Protestants have separate schools. There are four universities in the province and several agricultural, technical, and trade schools. The capital is Quebec. The largest city is Montreal, which is also one of the largest wheat shipping ports of the world, in spite of the fact that it is icebound during the winter.

Most of the people are descendants of early French settlers, and in most of the rural districts French is the language in common use. Roman Catholicism is the predominant religion. Population, 1971, 6,030,000.

Saskatchewan (*săs-kăch'ĕ-wŏn*). A province of Canada, situated in the south central part of the country between Manitoba and Alberta and extending from the international boundary about 750 miles north to latitude 60° N. The southern half belongs to the great central plains region; the northern portion is part of the Laurentian plateau. South of the North Saskatchewan and of the Saskatchewan River, the surface is prairie, but north of these rivers the province is heavily forested with spruce, pine, tamarack, poplar, and birch. The eastern portion of the prairie belongs to the second prairie steppe; the western section forms a part of the third steppe, which angles across the province and stretches in rolling plains through Alberta to the Rocky Mountains. On the plains, the soil is a rich loam. Excepting for the southwestern section, the province is well watered with rivers and lakes, which are especially numerous in the Laurentian area, in the northern and central parts. The surface covers 251,700 square miles.

On account of Saskatchewan's great length, there is a considerable diversity of climate and of temperature. The southern third has a moderate and changeable climate. The western portion of this section is dry, being subject to the warm chinook winds, and requires irrigation; the eastern part has more moisture and a steadier winter. The central third has a steady winter and a greater precipitation. The climate of the northern region is of a continental severity.

Agriculture is the great, almost the exclusive, industry of Saskatchewan. In point of wheat production in Canada, the province holds the first place. Its fields are free from rust and from insect pests which attack wheat. In the production of oats, Saskatchewan normally ranks first or near the first among the provinces. Mixed farming is increasing in the south. In the north, too, cattle raising is gradually giving place to mixed farming. Dairying is encouraged by the government, especially through the improvement of breeds of stock. Agricultural products are marketed by means of more than 6000 miles of railway, which have been constructed in the province. A government experimental farm, with headquarters at Indian Head, has performed valuable services in the agricultural development of Saskatchewan.

The capital and largest city is Regina. Other important cities are Moosejaw, Prince Albert, and Saskatoon, the last-mentioned city being the seat of the University of Saskatchewan. Population, 1971, 927,000.

Yukon. A territory in the northwest of Canada between British Columbia and the Arctic Ocean. Ranges of the Rocky Mountain system traverse the northeastern portion of the territory, and are separated by the Yukon River basin from the Coast range and the Saint Elias range in the southwest. The Yukon River basin is a plateau country with a general slope toward the northwest. In the extreme southwest, Mt. Logan, the highest peak in Canada, reaches an elevation of 19,850 feet. The area of the territory is 207,076 square miles.

Mining is the principal occupation, gold and silver being the chief products. From 1895 to 1931 the value of the gold output was $211 million. The annual yield has greatly diminished, causing a decline in population from 27,219 in 1901 to 4157 in 1921. The development of a rich silver district later caused a fresh influx of settlers, but the inhabitants numbered only 17,000 in 1971.

A railroad connects Whitehorse, the capital of the territory, on the upper Yukon with Skagway in Alaska. Some of the hardier crops, as barley, oats, rye, potatoes, and turnips, are grown, and, in sheltered valleys, peas, cabbages, lettuce, and other garden vegetables thrive. Dawson, in the west central section, is the center of the Klondike gold region.

TWENTY LARGE CITIES OF CANADA

Showing Growth 1891-1971

CITY	POPULATION									
	1891	1901	1911	1921	1931	1941	1951	1961	1966	1971
Montreal, Que.	254,278	325,653	490,504	618,506	818,577	903,007	1,021,520	1,191,062	1,222,255	1,197,753
Toronto, Ont.	181,215	218,504	381,833	521,893	631,207	667,457	675,754	672,407	664,584	698,634
Edmonton, Alta.		4,176	31,064	58,821	79,197	93,817	159,631	281,027	376,925	434,116
Vancouver, B.C.	13,709	29,432	120,847	163,220	246,593	275,353	344,833	384,522	410,375	419,433
Calgary, Alta.	3,876	4,392	43,704	63,305	83,761	88,761	129,060	249,641	330,575	400,154
Hamilton, Ont.	48,959	52,634	81,969	114,151	155,547	166,337	208,321	273,991	298,121	307,473
Ottawa, Ont.	44,154	64,226	87,062	107,843	126,872	154,951	202,045	268,206	290,741	298,087
Winnipeg, Man.	25,639	42,340	136,035	179,087	218,785	221,960	235,710	265,429	257,005	243,208
London, Ont.	31,977	37,976	46,300	60,959	71,148	78,264	95,343	169,569	194,416	221,430
Windsor, Ont.	12,607	15,198	23,433	55,935	98,179	105,311	120,049	114,367	192,544	199,784
Quebec, Que.	63,090	78,118	78,710	95,193	103,594	150,757	164,016	171,979	166,984	182,418
Regina, Sask.		2,249	30,213	34,432	53,209	58,245	71,319	112,141	131,127	137,759
Saskatoon, Sask.		113	12,004	25,739	43,291	43,027	53,268	95,526	115,892	125,079
Halifax, N.S.	38,437	40,832	46,619	58,372	59,275	70,488	85,589	92,511	86,792	121,086
St. John, N.B.	39,179	40,711	42,511	47,166	47,514	51,741	50,779	55,153	51,567	87,910
St. John's, Newf'd.						44,603	52,873	63,633	79,884	86,290
Sherbrooke, Que.	10,097	11,765	16,405	23,515	28,933	35,965	50,543	66,554	75,690	80,457
Verdun, Que.	296	1,898	11,629	25,001	60,745	67,349	77,391	78,317	76,832	74,520
Victoria, B.C.	16,841	20,919	31,660	38,727	39,082	44,068	51,331	54,941	57,453	60,897
Three Rivers, Que.	8,334	9,981	13,691	22,367	35,450	42,007	46,074	53,477	57,540	55,240

Source: Statistics Canada, preliminary 1971.

CITIES, TOWNS, AND OTHER POINTS OF INTEREST

The following section contains articles on some cities of Canada having a population in excess of 25,000. It includes also descriptions of the capital cities of the country and of all the provinces. Since Canada is scenically one of the most attractive countries of the world and draws annually many hundreds of thousands of travelers, many of the places especially worth visiting are described. These include Banff in the Rocky Mountains and Muskoka in Ontario. A number of other places are included for special interest attaching to them, such as the famous shrine center at Sainte Anne de Beaupré and Churchill, the sub-arctic port.

Banff. A health and pleasure resort of southwestern Alberta, picturesquely situated in Banff National Park on the eastern mountain slope. It has a boiling sulphur spring and is the point of departure for numerous scenic features in the vicinity, including Bow Falls, many rocks of unusual formation, and glacier fed lakes. The most beautiful of the lakes is Lake Louise, enclosed by gigantic pine-clad mountains. Lying about a thousand feet above Lake Louise are Lake Agnes and Mirror Lake. Banff itself was the first national park in America, an area of five square miles dedicated in 1885 but since enlarged to over 250 square miles. The town's permanent population is engaged almost exclusively in the tourist trade, the summer visitors numbering over 15,000 a day. Local attractions include the Canadian wax gallery and an annual four-day celebration of "Banff Indian days." The town is governed by a federal park superintendent, but a locally elected council serves in an advisory capacity. Population, 1971, 3,608.

Brandon. A commercial and railway city of southwestern Manitoba, the second largest city in the province. Industries are based primarily on agriculture, including meat and vegetable packing and manufacture of dairy products and fertilizers. Situated 130 miles west of Winnipeg, it is the trade center for Western Manitoba and part of Saskatchewan. Other industries include oil refining and the manufacture of electrical equipment. Brandon College is affiliated with McMaster University in Hamilton, Ont. A Dominion experimental farm and an Indian residential school are located in the vicinity. Population, 1971, 30,832.

Brantford. A manufacturing city on the Grand River in southern Ontario. Its leading manufactures are agricultural implements, binder twine, refrigeration units, and truck bodies. The city is named for the Mohawk chief, Joseph Brant, for whom a beautiful monument has been erected. His body is buried beside Queen Anne's Chapel of the Mohawks, built in 1785. Alexander Graham Bell resided at Brantford when he first demonstrated his telephone in 1874. A handsome monument to his memory stands in Victoria Park, and his homestead is preserved as a public museum. Population, 1971, 62,853.

Calgary. A commercial and manufacturing city of southern Alberta at the junction of the Bow and Elbow rivers. It is the gateway to Banff and the Canadian Rockies, 77 miles distant.

Calgary, incorporated as a town in 1884 and as a city in 1893, owed its early growth to cattle marketing and meat packing. Irrigation of the farm lands to the east brought other industries based on agriculture. The discovery of oil in 1914 and of rich gas fields in 1948 made it a magnet for a wide variety of industries and accelerated its growth. Situated along the east side of the city, these include oil refining and the manufacture of petrochemicals, fertilizers, farm machinery, rubber products, and oil-well equipment. Shops of the Canadian Pacific Railway are located in the city.

Calgary's leading educational institution is the University of Alberta, Calgary. Its 110-acre exhibition ground features an annual stampede and provides sporting and art facilities. There is a 400-acre recreation area known as Happy Valley. Among the more imposing buildings is the Provincial Jubilee Auditorium, a center for concerts and art exhibitions. Population, 1971, 400,154.

Charlottetown. The capital of Prince Edward Island, occupying a high site at the head of Hillsborough Bay at the junction of three tidal rivers. The city has an excellent harbor. The fisheries are extensive. Manufacturing interests include frozen-food processing, meat and poultry packing, iron and brass founding, metal fabricating, and manufacture of industrial and special machinery, concrete and stone products, and chemical fertilizers. Charlottetown has two colleges and several fine public buildings, including the Fathers of Confederation Memorial Centre.

The city was founded in 1756 by French settlers but passed to Great Britain with the cession of Canada in 1763. Two American privateers raided the town in 1775; but the property seized was returned, and the prisoners were restored to their homes by order of General Washington. Charlottetown was incorporated in 1855. Population, 1971, 18,631.

Churchill. A port of northern Manitoba on Hudson Bay. The first commercial shipments of wheat were made through this port in 1932. A railroad connects this point with Winnipeg, and large grain elevators and port facilities have been constructed. By using the route through Hudson Bay during its open season of three or four months, shippers between Western Canadian points and Liverpool same 600 miles over the route via Montreal. Population, 1971, 1,612.

Cobalt. A mining town of Ontario, situated near Lake Timiskaming on the upper Ottawa River. Cobalt was the center of one of the richest silver producing regions in the world. The deposit was discovered in 1903, and production reached its peak in 1911, with shipment of 31,507,791 ounces of silver. In the 1930's the town went into a sharp decline although the district continued to produce a large proportion of the world's cobalt, with nickel and arsenic as by-products. Population, 1971, 2,191.

Dawson. Former capital of Yukon Territory, located in the west central part of the territory on the Yukon River just below the Klondike. At the height of the Klondike's gold-mining prosperity, Dawson had a population of over 20,000; but, when the rich claims in the district were worked out, the number of inhabitants decreased greatly. The name commemorates Dr. G. M. Dawson, the geologist, who first reported on the gold prospects of the district. Population, 1971, 745.

Edmonton. The capital of Alberta, a trading, manufacturing, and oil production center. It occupies a picturesque site on the North Saskatchewan River, which is here spanned by six bridges, one of them 200 feet above the river.

A fur trading station and fort was founded on the site in 1795. In 1891, when a railroad line reached it from Calgary, the population was 400, which was temporarily swollen to 3000 as the starting point of the Klondike gold rush. It became Alberta's capital in 1906, and settlers poured in as the surrounding rich agricultural lands were occupied. Coal mines attracted industries, chiefly those related to agriculture and lumbering.

The discovery of oil nearby in 1947 brought a period of spectacular growth. Edmonton found itself the center of the richest oil and gas field in Canada, and gas was piped to points as far away as Ontario. A mushrooming chemical industry grew up, followed by satellite secondary industries.

The city is regularly laid out with wide streets crossing at right angles. In the early 1960's work was begun on a civic center, its focal point being the strikingly modern city hall. Other structures include the ultra modern Centennial public library, an art gallery, and the Chateau Lacombe hotel. In one of the city's 86 parks is a planetarium, the first to be constructed in Canada. Other imposing buildings are the Parliament Buildings and the buildings on the 300-acre campus of the University of Alberta. Population, 1971, 434,116.

Fort William. A transshipping point and flour milling city of northwestern Ontario, situated on Thunder Bay in Lake Superior at the head of Canadian navigation in the Great Lakes. It is the Great Lakes terminal of Canada's Lake Superior, Canada's western terminus of the St. Lawrence Seaway. It is contiguous with its sister city, Port Arthur, the two being popularly known as the Canadian Lakehead Cities. The economy of both is based on their location, the point where the grain from the prairie provinces is loaded on ships. Although ice-bound for six months a year, the port's tonnage ranks with the largest in Canada. It has a grain storage capacity of 110 million bushels. Its industries include pulp and paper milling and shipbuilding.

The cities' water supply comes from Loch Lomond, a nearby lake 320 feet above the city situated behind Mt. McKay. Eighteen miles to the west is the magnificent Kakabeka Falls, where the water of the Kaministikwia River falls 128 feet into a rocky gorge. In 1966, the population of Fort William was 48,208; that of Port Arthur was 48,340.

Fredericton. The capital of New Brunswick, situated in the southwest part of the province at the head of navigation for large ships in the Saint John River, about 84 miles from its mouth. The leading industries include the manufacture of lumber, machine shop products, and shoes.

Fredericton is the seat of the University of New Brunswick, in whose organization the first step was taken in 1785 on petition of the first settlers, United Empire Loyalists driven from the United States. Several of its buildings were erected through the benefaction of Lord Beaverbrook, whose earliest years were spent in New Brunswick and who became a publisher and peer in England. He donated also the Beaverbrook Art Gallery and the Playhouse, the latter opened in 1964.

Fredericton was incorporated in 1845. Its Parliament buildings, old and impressive, are supplemented by the Centennial Building of ultra-modern construction in the downtown area, which houses most government departments. Population, 1971, 23,612.

Halifax. The capital of Nova Scotia, located on a natural harbor at the center of the southeast coast of the province. Halifax is an important naval base, an ice-free port, and the winter terminus of several steamship lines. The Canadian National railways also use the city as their eastern terminus. The steamship and railway terminal facilities are among the finest on the continent.

The chief interests of Halifax include transportation and shipping, fisheries, and manufacturing. The foreign trade of the port normally approximates $140 million in value. Fish cured in the city are extensively exported to the West Indies and to South America. The leading industries are car shop production, sugar refining, and the manufacture of textiles, furniture, cordage, and foundry products.

The northwest arm of the harbor is used as a pleasure resort by citizens of Halifax. The educational institutions include Dalhousie University, King's College, Technical College, Mt. St. Vincent University, and St. Mary's University. The city was founded by Lord Cornwallis in 1749 under orders to create a bastion to offset France's Port Royal. In 1917, a collision of two ships in the harbor, one loaded with ammunition, caused an explosion that destroyed the north part of the city, killing 1158 persons and injuring 4000 others. Population, 1971, 121,086.

Hamilton. A manufacturing and railroad city and lake port of southern Ontario, the fifth largest city of Canada. It is situated on Burlington Bay, a land locked harbor at the extreme western end of Lake Ontario. The Niagara escarpment, a height of land passing through the south of the city, imparts a picturesque effect which is further enhanced by the presence of numerous shade trees. The greater part of the city lies in the plain between the waterfront and the escarpment, known locally as the mountain.

Numerous railroads and highways enable the city to profit by its central location in the most populous region of Canada with electric power abundant and cheap. The St. Lawrence Seaway makes it an ocean port, whose tonnage places it among Canada's largest shipping centers. It is the center of Canada's steel industry. Other important industrial products include electrical equipment, farm implements, glass, and textiles. Canning is also an important industry.

The city has numerous parks, the finest being Dundurn, which contains a historic castle and is equipped for "sound and light" productions. Other parks include Victoria, with its famed Royal Botanical Garden; Confederation park with beach areas on Lake Ontario; and Cherokee Winter Sports park. The educational institutions include McMaster University, Ontario Teachers College, and Institute of Technology. There is also a fine art gallery. Hamilton was incorporated as a city in 1846. Population, 1971, 307,473.

Hull. A lumber and manufacturing city of southwestern Quebec, on the Ottawa River opposite the city of Ottawa, with which Hull is connected by three bridges. Pulp wood, matches, paper, lumber, cement, and knitted goods are the chief items of manufacture. The city was incorporated in 1875. Population, 1971, 62,842.

Kingston. A city of Ontario, situated at the northeastern extremity of Lake Ontario, where the waters of the lake enter the Saint Lawrence river. The city's manufactures include locomotives, textiles, and leather goods. A natural harbor and excellent railway facilities make Kingston an important point for the transshipping of grain. The Rideau canal connects the city with Ottawa.

Kingston is the seat of Queen's University and of the Royal Military College. The university buildings on a beautiful campus, the Roman Catholic and the Anglican cathedral, the streets adorned with numerous shade trees, and several parks make Kingston an attractive city. Numerous limestone buildings give a distinctive character to the architecture. The historic associations of the city are emphasized by the elaborate fortifications, including the fort and martello towers, which command the harbor.

Kingston was founded in 1673 by Frontenac and La Salle and formed one of the chief French centers of authority and trade with the West. It became the center of loyalist settlements in the West after the Revolutionary War.

It was a British naval and military base, until the treaty by which the United States and Great Britain abolished naval establishments on the lakes. From 1841 to 1844 Kingston was the capital of the United Provinces of Upper and Lower Canada. Population, 1971, 61,870.

Kitchener. A prosperous manufacturing city in Waterloo County, southern Ontario. The chief manufactures include automobile tires, shoes, and meat products. Kitchener was incorporated as the village of Berlin in 1854. Its earliest inhabitants were Mennonites who left Pennsylvania shortly after the Revolutionary War. Their German origin and frugal, industrious habits left a lasting impression on the population. Made a city in 1912, it changed its name to Kitchener in 1916.

Among the city's features are the Memorial Auditorium, used for exhibitions, sports, and theatrical productions; Doon, a pioneer village; and the Homer Watson Memorial Park. Adjacent to Kitchener on the north is the city of Waterloo, an insurance center and the seat of Waterloo University. The population of Kitchener in 1971 was 109,954; that of Waterloo was 37,245.

Klondike. A gold mining district in the Yukon Territory near the center of the Alaskan boundary. It covers an area of about 800 square miles. The principal settlement became notable for the discovery of gold there in 1896, since which time it has yielded about $211 million worth of the metal.

London. A commercial, manufacturing, educational, and ecclesiastical center of southwestern Ontario. London is situated midway between Toronto and Detroit in a rich agricultural district. The chief industrial interests include printing, electrical apparatus, hosiery, sheet metal products, machinery, chemicals, and cereals. London is also a financial center. It is the seat of the University of Western Ontario and has two cathedrals, Anglican and Catholic. London was founded in 1826 and was incorporated as a city in 1855. Population, 1971, 221,430.

Moncton. A manufacturing, railroad, and lumbering city of southeastern New Brunswick, standing at the head of navigation on the Petitcodiac River. Moncton is the headquarters for the Atlantic division of the Canadian National railways. It has a large lumber trade and manufactures stoves, engines, and boilers. Moncton has three parks, from one of which, Bore View Park, may be obtained an excellent view of the famous tidal bore from the Bay of Fundy. The University of Moncton is located here. Population, 1971, 47,781.

Montreal. The largest city of Canada, situated in south central Quebec on Montreal Island at the confluence of the Saint Lawrence and Ottawa rivers. The city lies mainly on the east and southern parts of the island and extends north and west to encircle Mount Royal, a magnificent park which commands a panoramic view of the area.

Montreal's harbor is the eastern terminus of the St. Lawrence Seaway, providing access for ocean ships to the head of the Great Lakes. The port, with 131 berths along its 12-mile waterfront is the world's second largest inland port, after Rotterdam. The island city is also a train and truck transportation center and is served by 17 airlines. The Metro, a 16-mile subway system, was first opened in 1966.

Montreal has progressed faster in redevelopment than any other city. While a few narrow streets still exist in the old part, restoration of them is under way to retain the atmosphere dating back to its early days. Other parts of the city are modern in all respects. Chief industries are oil and sugar refining, meat packing, brewing, and the manufacture of aircraft, iron and steel products, tobacco and leather goods, textiles, cement, and flour. The financial center of the nation's economy depends on the Montreal and Canadian Stock Exchanges at Place Victoria in the heart of the city. Place Ville Marie comprises a 42-story office complex and underground city of 40 acres filled with shops, restaurants, and theaters, where some 80,000 people shop and browse daily in a climate-controlled atmosphere. Place d'Armes has an imposing monument to Maisonneuve, founder of Montreal. It is surrounded by several noted buildings, one being Notre Dame Church, the most famous of the city's 300 churches and one of the largest in America. Rising in midtown Montreal is Mary Queen of the World Cathedral, a half-size replica of St. Peter's in Rome.

Place des Arts, with two theaters and a 3000-seat concert hall, is the home of the Montreal Symphony Orchestra. Other cultural centers are the Montreal Museum of Fine Arts, Redpath Museum of McGill University, Contemporary Arts Museum, the Institute of Applied Arts, and the Mount Royal Art Center.

Two man-made islands in the St. Lawrence were the scene of the world's fair Expo '67. At the close of the fair, a large permanent exhibit, Man and His World, and a 135-acre amusement park, La Ronde, became enormously popular as tourist attractions.

Montreal is the seat of McGill University, Montreal University, and a number of colleges. A majority of the population is bilingual. About one-half the inhabitants are of French descent. The prevailing religion is Catholicism.

Montreal was founded in 1642 by Maisonneuve as a religious colony; but, as the outpost of civilization at the door of the Iroquois country, it became a military post, fur trading center, and base for explorations. It was taken by the British in 1760 and was held by the American Continental army in 1775–76. Population, 1971, 1,197,753.

Moose Jaw. A commercial and manufacturing city of south central Saskatchewan, the center of a rich mixed farming district. The city has large stockyards. The industrial products include flour and cereals, oil refining, brick, clothing, millwork, steel products, roofing materials, and insecticides. A potash mine operates nearby. Population, 1971, 31,284.

Muskoka. A lake region of Ontario. It embraces about 4000 square miles lying east of Georgian bay and about 100 miles north of Toronto. Of its 800 to 1000 lakes, the chief are Muskoka, 19 miles long, Rosseau, 12 miles long, and Joseph, 14 miles long. These three lakes are connected and have regular steamship service in summer. The region has extensive forests. Its numerous rivers, lakes, and islands make it an extremely popular playground for summer residents and visitors. The eastern part of the territory is sometimes called the Lake of Bays region, after the largest lake in it. Farther to the northeast lies the Algonquin provincial park, an untamed region of over 2000 square miles.

New Westminster. A port and lumbering center of southwestern British Columbia, situated on the Fraser River 17 miles from its mouth. With an excellent harbor and retail facilities, it is a thriving port, particularly for lumber, which is the city's leading manufacture. Others include paper, fish products, and canned goods. Population, 1971, 42,083.

Niagara Falls. A city of Ontario on the Niagara River beside the cataract. Hydroelectric power developed at and near the city on the Canadian side totals about 3,000,000 horsepower. As in similar developments on the American side, water is pumped electrically by night to a huge reservoir, from which the water is used during the day to develop additional power. The reservoirs are used also in drawing off additional water from the river above the falls at night and in the winter for power purposes. Thus the drain on the cataract's volume of water is kept at a minimum for sightseeing purposes, while at the same time the erosion at the brink of the falls is reduced.

In June 1969 the waters of the Niagara were diverted to the Horseshoe Falls to allow geologists to study how best to curb rock falls on the American side before the waters resumed their normal flow in December 1969.

The city commands a magnificent view of the entire falls from Victoria Park, color illumination being provided for 2½ hours nightly. A panoramic view may be had from three observation towers; a close-up view of the Horseshoe (Canadian) Falls from Table Rock House. At Rainbow Bridge, leading to Niagara Falls, N.Y., is Carillon Tower, containing a 55-bell carillon. The Oakes Garden Theatre has gardens and an open-air amphitheater.

The city's chief manufactures include abrasives, cereals, insulators, and metal products. Incorporated as the village of Elgin in 1853 and the town of Clifton in 1856, Niagara Falls was given this name in 1881 and became a city in 1904. Population, 1971, 65,271.

Oshawa. A manufacturing city of Ontario, situated on Lake Ontario about 30 miles east of Toronto. It is the chief center in Canada for the manufacture of automobiles, particularly of those made by Canadian subsidiaries of the General Motors Corporation. Other industrial products include leather, foundry products, canned goods, glass, and bathing suits. In a large block near the center of the city is the Canadian Automotive Museum, which visually reconstructs the history and prospects of this type of transportation. Oshawa has a huge shopping center laid out in the form of a landscaped mall, with an undergound trucking concourse. Population, 1971, 91,113.

Ottawa. The capital and one of the largest cities of Canada, lying in southeastern Ontario and picturesquely situated on the high southern bank of the Ottawa River about 120 miles above its mouth at Montreal. The river, following a winding course between wooded banks and dropping 40 feet at the magnificent Chaudière Falls, presents a beautiful view from Parliament Hill, upon which stands the Parliament Building. Rideau Canal separates Ottawa into west and east parts, known as Upper Town and Lower Town, and inhabited by French and English people respectively.

The Parliament Buildings, Gothic in style, front and flank Confederation Square. The central tower, 291 feet high and known as the "Peace Tower," houses a carillon of 53 bells, one of the finest on the continent. The old, impressive Governor-General's house, Rideau Hall, contrasts with the modern city hall. Among the numerous churches are the Catholic Basilica of Notre Dame and the Anglican Christ Church Cathedral. The famous hotel Chateau Laurier evokes the lines of a castle in old France. Notable also are the National Gallery of Canada, the Dominion Observatory, the Supreme Court of Canada, and the University of Ottawa. The National Arts Center, a 2300-seat concert hall and a theater, was opened in 1969. Winter and summer sports are held at the $9 million Civic Center arena-stadium.

A National Capital Commission was created in 1958 to develop the city and its environs. Among its most impressive achievements was the development of the 100-square-mile Gatineau Park immediately across the Ottawa River from the city. This includes the estate of the former prime minister Mackenzie King, who had re-erected there a number of historic buildings. The commission supervises the tulip festival with its million plants from Holland and provides the many parks and connecting driveways with flowers blooming from spring to late fall. The manufacture of paper products is the city's only sizable industry.

Ottawa was formerly called Bytown in honor of its founder, the engineer in charge of the construction of Rideau Canal, which provides direct communication by water between the Ottawa River and Lake Ontario. The settlement was chartered as a city under the name of Ottawa in 1854 and was selected as the capital of Canada in 1858. Population, 1971, 298,087.

Outremont ($\overline{oo}'tr'$-môN'). A city of Quebec on Montreal Island, surrounded by the city of Montreal. It is almost entirely residential in character, having very few industries. Population, 1971, 28,402.

Prince Rupert. A seaport of west central British Columbia, situated on an island connected with the mainland by a steel bridge. It has a natural harbor formed by an inlet of the Pacific Ocean. Prince Rupert forms a western terminus of the Canadian National railways. It is the southern terminus of the Alaska Marine Ferry System and the northern terminus of the ferry system from Vancouver Island. It ships large quantities of grain as well as the output of its halibut processing and its lumber and pulp mills. Its Centennial Museum has a famous collection of carved totem poles. Population, 1971, 15,355.

Quebec. Capital of the province of Quebec and one of the largest cities of Canada. It is picturesquely situated on a bold promontory at the head of the Saint Lawrence estuary. The city was founded by Champlain in 1608 and was long the center of exploration and of government by the French in the northern part of the continent. In 1759, as a result of the battle of the Plains of Abraham, the city, along with the rest of French Canada, fell into the hands of the British. It was unsuccessfully attacked in 1775 by an American force under Montgomery.

The city's importance was due partly to its strong natural defenses and partly to its strategical position, which commanded the entrance to the river leading to the interior of the continent. Quebec is still the point of entry for immigrants from Europe and is the terminus of larger ocean liners. It has one of the largest dry docks in the world. The chief industrial interests include iron castings, pulp and paper, machinery, cutlery, steel, woolens, lumber, tobacco, and rope. Hydroelectric power is available from the Montmorency and Shawinigan falls. The Saint Lawrence River is crossed at Quebec by a bridge which has one of the longest cantilever spans in the world.

The appearance of Quebec reflects the history of the city. The highest point, Cape Diamond, is 333 feet above the river and is crowned by a citadel within a walled enclosure covering 40 acres. On these defensive works over $30 million were spent in the early decades of the 19th century. The upper town, containing the citadel, is used as a residential district and has many of the finer churches and public buildings. Dufferin Terrace, a magnificent promenade, a half mile long, overlooks the Saint Lawrence, which lies 200 feet below. The upper town is reached from the other division of the city, called the lower town, by roads cut in the rock, by flights of steps, and by an elevator. The streets of the lower town are narrow and winding, and they recall the appearance of certain provincial towns of France.

The city's most noteworthy edifices include the Parliament buildings; Château Frontenac; the church of Notre Dame des Victoires, built in 1688; the handsome Franciscan convent; the Ursuline convent, which contains the remains of Montcalm; the Anglican Cathedral; and the Notre Dame de Quebec built in 1647, which contained many valuable pictures and relics. The last-named building was burned in 1922 but has since been rebuilt on the original model. There are numerous statues and monuments of historic interest. In the governor's garden, stands a plain granite column erected to the memory of Wolfe and of Montcalm, both generals having fallen in action at the battle which decided the city's fate.

Quebec is the seat of Laval University, which was chartered by Queen Victoria and Pope Pius IX and is an outgrowth of the Grand Seminary founded in 1663. In the immediate vicinity are Battlefields Park, Wolfe's Cove, the Shrine of Sainte Anne de Beaupré, and many other points of interest. The city is reputed for a famous winter carnival. It has a literary and historical society founded in 1824. The great majority of the population are of French descent, and the prevailing religion is Catholicism. Population, 1971, 182,418.

Regina. The capital and largest city of Saskatchewan, lying in the south central part of the province. Regina was formerly the capital of the Northwest Territories, and is still the western headquarters and training center for the Royal Canadian Mounted Police.

The Regina Campus of the University of Saskatchewan is the city's leading educational institution. Other impressive buildings are the Legislative Building, the curvilinear Saskatchewan Power Corp. Building, the Museum of Natural History, and the Mackenzie Art Gallery.

Founded in 1883, Regina is a service and distribution center for a rich wheat-farming, potash-mining, and oil-producing district. Its chief industries include steel, steel pipes, cement, meat packing, farm machinery, and petroleum products. Population 1971, 137,759.

Sainte Anne de Beaupré (sȧnt än dĕ bô′prȧ′). A village and famous Catholic pilgrim resort 20 miles east of Quebec. A chapel was built there in 1658, on which occasion a devout inhabitant of Beaupré who suffered from rheumatism, after laying three stones on the foundation, found himself free from his affliction. This occurrence was the first of many instances of miraculous healing credited to the saint at the shrine. In 1676 the chapel was superseded by a church, which was replaced by a much larger one in 1876. In 1922 the building was destroyed by fire, but was replaced by a new church, which is one of the finest in Canada. The shrine is annually visited by pilgrims numbering upward of one million. Population, 1971, 1474.

Saint Catharines. A trading and manufacturing city of south central Ontario in the Niagara peninsula on the south shore of Lake Ontario and 12 miles west of Niagara River. It is set in a rich fruit-growing district and celebrates each September as Grape and Wine Festival Time. St. Catharines owes its early growth to the Welland Canal, which was opened in 1829 and was subsequently reconstructed and enlarged to become a key canal in the St. Lawrence Seaway. The Garden City Skyway carries traffic above the canal to avoid delays due to the lift bridge spanning the busy waterways. Manufactures include paper, automobile parts, and a wide variety of other products. It is the seat of Brock University. The Lakeside Amusement Park fronts on Lake Ontario. Population, 971, 109,636.

Saint John. The largest city of New Brunswick, situated at the mouth of the Saint John River on the Bay of Fundy. In the vicinity is the noted "reversing falls," spanned by a steel arch bridge.

St. John is the geographical hub of three Canadian provinces. It is the rail and highway link between east and west besides being an ocean port with a year-round ice-free harbor which handles large shipments of grain and miscellaneous commerce. It has one of the world's largest dry docks and shipbuilding yards. Manufactures include sugar, brushes and brush making machinery, pulp and newsprint, brass goods, petroleum products, lumber, wire and cable, and large thermal electric installations. Parks and public gardens cover more than 500 acres.

St. John was a village of a few hundred people in 1783, when some 9000 refugees from the United States arrived after the Revolutionary War. The coming of these United Empire Loyalists is commemorated in the Loyalist House, built in 1810 and restored a century and a half later. The city was incorporated in 1785 under royal charter—the first city in Canada. Population, 1971, 87,910.

Saint John's. Provincial capital of the island province of Newfoundland. Situated on the coast near the easternmost point of land in North America, Saint John's has a superb harbor capable of accommodating the largest ships. It is the trading center of the province, but its main business is the fishing industry. The Roman Catholic and Anglican cathedrals are both named for St. John the Baptist, on whose feast day, June 24, John Cabot is traditionally believed to have discovered the harbor in 1497, and honored it with the saint's name. Sir Humphrey Gilbert established an English settlement here in 1583. Captured and destroyed twice by the French, Saint John's was finally taken by the English in 1702. Here Marconi received the first wireless message sent across the ocean, 1901. Also the English aviators Alcock and Brown took off from here in 1919 for the first nonstop trans-Atlantic flight. It is the eastern terminus of the Trans-Canada Highway. Population, 1971, 86,290.

Sarnia. An oil refining and petrochemical manufacturing city in southern Ontario situated at the southern tip of Lake Huron. It is connected with Port Huron, Mich., by a tunnel under the St. Claire River, opened in 1891, and by the high-level Blue Water Bridge. Extensive salt deposits and oil wells in the vicinity gave Sarnia its start, but its importance as an industrial center began with the establishment of a synthetic rubber plant and large oil refineries after World War I. Other manufactures include a wide variety of chemicals, foundry products, fiber glass, and plastics. The opening of the St. Lawrence Seaway made it an ocean port.

Among the city's features are Canatara Park on the lake shore and its city hall of strikingly modern construction. Population, 1971, 56,727.

Saskatoon (săs′kȧ-tōōn′). The second largest city of Saskatchewan, situated on both sides of the South Saskatchewan River, which is here spanned by six bridges. It lies about 150 miles northwest of Regina. The city is the center of rich farming lands, for irrigation of which a 210-foot-high earth dam on the South Saskatchewan River was constructed in the 1960's. The largest known potash mines anywhere contribute to the city's industrial interests, which include oil refining and the manufacture of machinery, cement, chemicals, and flour. The University of Saskatchewan, Saskatoon, occupies a 3200-acre campus. Other features include the 18-story CN Towers, the Jubilee Auditorium, and the Western Development Museum. Saskatoon was incorporated as a city in 1906. Population, 1971, 125,079.

Sault Sainte Marie (sōō′ sȧnt mä-rē′). A manufacturing city of Ontario, situated on the Saint Mary's River, which is here crossed by a bridge one mile in length. Navigation in the river, which connects lakes Superior, Michigan, and Huron, depends on a ship canal. The first one was first opened in 1895; after frequent enlargements it finally became a key link in the St. Lawrence Seaway. The city's largest industry is steel manufacturing. Other industrial products include paper, chemicals, lumber, and beer. The city owns the 75-acre Point des Chenes Park, 12 miles to the west. Population, 1971, 78,175.

Sherbrooke. A manufacturing city of southeastern Quebec about 85 miles east of Montreal. Among its varied manufactures are textiles, machinery, pulp and paper, and machinery. It has two universities—the University of Sherbrooke (French) and Bishop's University (English). Population, 1971, 80,457.

Stratford. A city of southern Ontario, about 90 miles west of Toronto. Stratford arose as a trade center for the surrounding agricultural region. The principal industrial products are furniture and automotive supplies. The city is best known for its Festival Theater, where Shakespearean and other dramas are given during four months each summer, attracting visitors from many countries. The beautiful circular theater is located in Queen's Park, part of a 750-acre system of parks on both sides of the river Avon throughout its course traversing the city. Population, 1971, 23,863.

Sudbury. A mining city of Ontario about 60 miles north of the northern shore of Georgian Bay. Here is mined the greater part of the world's output of nickel; also most of the copper produced in Ontario. The city is the seat of Laurentian University and has an art gallery and a government school of mines. Population, 1971, 153,959.

Sydney. A city in northeastern Nova Scotia, situated on a natural harbor on the east coast of Cape Breton Island. Sydney is noted as a center for coal mining and for the manufacture of steel. It is also a well-known summer resort. Population, 1971, 32,459.

Thetford Mines. A mining town about 75 miles south of Quebec City, noted, along with Black Lake in the vicinity, as a center of the district which produces a large proportion of the world's supply of commercial asbestos. Population, 1971, 21,662.

Three Rivers (Trois Rivières). A manufacturing city of Quebec, situated on the north bank of the Saint Lawrence River where the two mouths of the Saint Maurice River enter it. It is 78 miles southwest of the city of Quebec. Long the center of a large lumber, cattle, and grain trade, it began to grow rapidly with the development of hydro-electric power from nearby waterfalls. Paper and pulp manufacture became the leading industry. With its three large paper mills, it is said to be the world's largest center of newsprint production. Other manufactures include electric lamps, chemicals, cement, and structural steel. Three Rivers was founded in 1634 by Samuel de Champlain. Population, 1971, 55,240.

Toronto. The capital and largest city of Ontario and the second largest city in Canada, situated on the northwest shore of Lake Ontario. Its natural harbor in recent years has been greatly enlarged and improved. About 2000 acres at the waterfront, largely reclaimed land, is municipally owned and used for industrial establishments, railroad sidings, waterways, and parks. The offshore Toronto Island accommodates the city's airport.

As an industrial, railroad, financial, and commercial center, Toronto ranks second only to Montreal. *Turbo*, the new turbine-train runs between these two cities. Toronto's leading manufactures are lumber, farm implements, automobiles, car shop products, packed meats, rubber goods, food products, clothing, hosiery and knit goods, soap, iron castings, and musical instruments. The Toronto hydroelectric system is one of the largest municipal supply undertakings on the continent.

The city rises from the shore to an elevation of about 300 feet. This variation in level lends itself to the construction of many beautiful driveways and boulevards, connecting a large number of parks, the largest being High Park, near which is an elaborate pleasure resort.

The Parliament buildings, in Queen's Park, are the government headquarters of Ontario's more than seven million people. This massive complex is constructed of red stone in the Romanesque style of architecture. Opposite these buildings is the Sigmund Samuel Canadiana building of the Royal Ontario Museum, which houses a fine collection of Canada's historic treasures. Nearby are the many colleges and professional schools of the University of Toronto. Other buildings are the O'Keefe Centre for the performing arts; the main branch of the Public Library, where the Robertson Historical Collection is displayed; and the Art Gallery of Toronto, containing masterpieces by Rembrandt, Gainsborough, Picasso, and several French Impressionists. Riverdale Zoo is notable for its exotic animals and jungle birds. Maple Leaf Gardens is one of Canada's largest auditoriums.

The modern city hall was the first project in Toronto's comprehensive redevelopment program. Dominating the 11½-acre civic center, Nathan Phillips Square, it is in the form of two tall, marble-veneer buildings facing each other in a concave outline embracing a low-lying cupola—the council chamber and auditorium set between them. The square has reflecting pools embellished with fountains, ornamental trees, and an imposing sculpture by Henry Moore. One of Canada's tallest buildings, a 56-story structure, is the headquarters of the Toronto-Dominion bank. By mid-1969, a still higher office building, to be the nation's tallest, was well under way for the Canadian Imperial Bank of Commerce. Many international business firms have headquarters in the city.

The Canadian National Exhibition, an annual fair, is normally visited by more than three million people. On the Exhibition grounds, the Hockey Hall of Fame honors outstanding figures of the country's national sport.

While Toronto owns its own surface transportation system and subway, it does so subject to a larger metropolitan municipality which takes in also 12 suburban areas, the whole covering 240 square miles. The latter has legislative power over finances, roads, education, parks, police, housing, welfare, and pollution control.

Toronto was founded in 1749 as York, and became the capital of Upper Canada in 1793. York was captured by the Americans in 1813. In 1834 it was incorporated under the name of Toronto. Population, 1971, 698,634.

Vancouver. The largest city of British Columbia and one of the largest in Canada, situated at the southwest extremity of the mainland on Burrard inlet, a deep arm of the Strait of Georgia. The harbor is one of the finest on the globe and has helped to place Vancouver among the leading ports of the continent. The area of the harbor is 48 square miles, of which 28 are landlocked. Here Canada's two transcontinental railroads meet the transoceanic shipping lines. Wheat is the chief export. Shipbuilding, lumbering, and salmon-canning are major industries. Vancouver is the commercial metropolis of British Columbia. It has launched an extensive redevelopment program.

The city has several parks and recreation areas. Stanley Park is a partly cleared forest area of 1000 acres, situated on a cape and surrounded by a 9-mile drive along the shore. The city's highest point is the 410-foot Little Mountain in Queen Elizabeth Park, which affords a panoramic view of the city, harbor, and North Shore Mountains. The B.C. Hydroelectric Building (all glass and perpetually lighted), the courthouse, the general hospital, and numerous high-rise office and apartment buildings give the city a striking skyline.

The University of British Columbia and the Simon Fraser University are located here. There are also two community colleges and several art galleries and museums. The Queen Elizabeth Theatre complex affords a variety of year-round entertainment. The Pacific National Exhibition, similar to Toronto's is an annual event for western Canada. Ferry service links Vancouver Island, across the Strait of Georgia, with the mainland.

Incorporated in 1886 with 600 inhabitants, the city, named for Capt. George Vancouver, a British naval officer, grew rapidly when it was connected by railroad with eastern Canada in 1887. Population, 1971, 419,433.

Verdun. A city of Quebec on Montreal Island. It is a residential suburb of Montreal, the southern border of which it adjoins. Population, 1971, 74,520.

Victoria. The capital of British Columbia, occupying the extreme southeastern point of Vancouver Island on the Strait of Juan de Fuca. Possessing a commodious harbor, and being advantageously located from a commercial standpoint, Victoria ranks as one of the four largest ports of Canada. It is the western terminus of the Trans-Canada Highway. Victoria's economy is supported mainly by service industries, including government, trade, and entertainment of tourists. The other industries include manufacture of wood products, fishing, and market and flower gardening. There are three large shipbuilding yards. An extensive trade is carried on in coal, timber, and canned salmon.

The city has fine streets with many beautiful residences, and its delightful climate and beautiful environment attract numerous summer visitors. Beacon Hill Park is the city's chief recreation ground. The provincial Parliament buildings of gray stone are of high architectural merit. The Dominion Astrophysical Laboratory in the city has one of the world's largest telescopes. Adjoining Victoria is Esquimalt, the naval base and dockyard.

Fort Victoria was erected on the present site of the city in 1843 as a trading post of the Hudson's Bay Company. The place was incorporated as Victoria in 1862 and became the capital of British Columbia in 1868. The inhabitants are predominantly of British birth or descent. Population, 1971, 60,897.

Whitehorse, capital and chief city of the Yukon, is in the southern part of the territory. It has an airport and is connected by rail with Skagway, Alaska, and by the Alaska Highway with Dawson Creek, B. C. Population, 1971, 11,084.

Windsor. The most southerly city of Canada, lying in southern Ontario on the Detroit River, opposite Detroit, Mich., with which it is connected by a vehicular tunnel and by the Ambassador suspension bridge, which has a central span of 1850 feet. Windsor is the chief center of automobile production in Canada. Other industrial products are iron and steel, paints and varnishes, salt, drugs, and prepared foods. It is the seat of the University of Windsor and has also the Willistead Art Gallery and Hiram Walker Historical Museum. Windsor became a town in 1858 and was incorporated as a city in 1892. Population, 1971, 199,784.

Winnipeg. The capital of Manitoba and one of the largest cities of Canada. It is located in the southern part of the province at the junction of the Red and Assiniboine rivers. In commerce, Winnipeg occupies a strategic position, comparable to that of Chicago. All traffic between eastern and western Canada is routed through Winnipeg. The city is served by the two Canadian transcontinental railways, with western headquarters here; by several American lines; and by many railroads radiating throughout the rich agricultural district in which it is situated. It is the largest cash grain market in the world, the Winnipeg Grain Exchange having one of the busiest "trading pits" anywhere. Besides being a valuable livestock market, it is the base of the Canadian Wheat Board, which handles the sale of the country's vast wheat crop.

Winnipeg ranks among the leading manufacturing cities of Canada, partly by reason of the availability of cheap hydroelectric power, which is developed from the Winnipeg River rapids. Among the chief industrial products are flour, farm machinery, processed foods, lumber, pulp, and paper. Printing and publishing are also important.

Winnipeg has grown rapidly, its economy being based on its rich agricultural and mineral resources. The modern city hall complex is indicative of its long-range renewal schedule. In 1968 a new concert hall was opened, and completion of a new 6-story museum was scheduled before 1971. The city has one of the most modern air terminals on the continent.

Of the several parks, Fort Garry Park has the greatest historical interest, while the 362-acre Assiniboine Park, containing a zoo and a horticultural conservatory, is the largest. Outstanding in another park is the provincial Legislative Building, built in classic Greek style with a 255-foot dome.

The suburb of Saint Boniface is the Roman Catholic headquarters of the West. It has a magnificent cathedral, the archbishop's palace, and the Catholic College of Saint Boniface. It is the birthplace and burial place of Louis Riel, leader of the Red River rebellion in 1869-70.

The University of Manitoba (1877) and the University of Winnipeg (1871) are the oldest institutions of higher education in western Canada.

In 1733, on the site now occupied by Winnipeg, the French explorer, La Verendrye, built Fort Rouge, a name now used to designate a favorite residential section of the city. In 1821, the Hudson's Bay Company built Fort Garry. The population in 1870 was 250. In 1873 the place was incorporated and the name was changed from Fort Garry to Winnipeg. Population, exclusive of suburbs, 1971, 243,208.

MEXICO

A federal republic of North America, lying south of the United States and extending southeast to Guatemala. The outline of the country resembles a cornucopia modified by two irregularities,—the peninsula of Yucatan in the southeast and the peninsula of Baha California in the northwest. Its area is 760,375 square miles, about half of which is in the Torrid Zone. Its maximum length is over 1900 miles, and its width varies from 1833 miles, along the northern boundary, to 134 miles, at the Isthmus of Tehuantepec. The coast line on the Gulf of Mexico and the Caribbean Sea measures 1727 miles, while the coast line on the Pacific Ocean and on the Gulf of California has a total length of 4574 miles.

Surface and Drainage. The greater part of Mexico consists of a central plateau, called the *tierras templadas*, having an elevation of from 3000 to 8000 feet. It is flanked on the east by a high range of mountains called the Sierra Madre Oriental. At the Isthmus of Tehuantepec, this range converges with the Sierra Madre Occidental, which flanks the central plateau on the west. The mountains of the Isthmus of Tehuantepec belong to the Central American system. The lofty areas above an altitude of 8000 feet are known as the *tierras frias*. On each side of the country, lowlands, or *tierras calientes*, form a fringe between the coast and the mountain range. The peninsula of Yucatan is, for the most part, a low, sandy plain. Baja California is mountainous and consists of a southern extension of the Sierra Nevada range.

The central plateau is of volcanic origin and the sierras contain a large number of volcanoes. The highest, Citaltepetl (Orizaba), has not been active since the 16th century. Its elevation is 18,700 feet. Popocatepetl, "Smoky Mountain," and Iztaccihuatl, "White Woman," are extinct. Violent earthquakes are frequent. In 1920, in the Orizaba Volcano district, about 3000 people were killed by seismic disturbances and ten towns were partially or wholly destroyed.

The drainage system of Mexico is simple. The central plateau has a number of lakes but no large rivers. Several short streams flow from the mountain ranges into the sea. The Rio Grande, on the northern border, receives little water from the Mexican side. No river of Mexico is navigable throughout the year.

Climate and Flora. The *tierras calientes*, on the east, are subject to great heat and a heavy rainfall. They support a luxuriant vegetation and valuable food plants. The banana, coconut, pineapple, pomegranate, vanilla, cacao, and ginger are produced in abundance. Sisal hemp is grown in Yucatan and is exported in large quantities to the United States to be used in the manufacture of rope. Mexico's forest areas, which are estimated to cover 95 million acres, are mainly in the lowlands. Mahogany, ebony, rosewood, and rubber are among the more valuable products of the tropical forests. The Pacific lowlands are arid in the north but have a more copious rainfall in the south.

The plateau has a temperate climate and is well adapted for the cultivation of cotton, tobacco, coffee, rice, sugar cane, corn, wheat, and potatoes. The rainfall in general is light but varies considerably in different parts. The north portion is dry; the cactus appears as a characteristic plant, and irrigation is necessary for successful agriculture. In some parts. however, two or three crops a year may be raised. The forest areas of the plateau contain oak, myrtle, fir, spruce, and pine. The higher mountain regions support an alpine flora.

Animal Life. The lowlands are the habitat of monkeys, pumas, jaguars, ocelots, sloths, armadillos, parrots, parakeets, humming birds, alligators, venomous snakes, and many other animals char_ acteristic of a tropical fauna. The wolf, coyote, otter, and deer are found in the central plateau.

Minerals and Mining. The mineral resources of Mexico make her potentially one of the richest countries in the world. Mining is the chief industry, and petroleum is the chief product. It is estimated that Mexican mines have yielded over $3 billion worth of silver. Mexico is also one of the world's greatest copper and lead producing countries. Gold, zinc, antimony, tungsten, molybdenum, mercury, and opals are also exported. Near the city of Durango is a large hill, the Cerro de Mercado, composed almost entirely of pure iron ore. Improved transportation facilities and development of the vast mineral deposits have been possible with capital from increased tourism.

Other Industries. The production of coffee exceeds a value of $100 million each year. Other large crops are corn, rice, sugar cane, wheat, beans, tomatoes, oranges, and bananas. Irrigation is essential for much of the production and a number of large dams have been constructed for this purpose and to develop electric power. The area employed for grazing purposes is about four times that devoted to agriculture. The chief manufactures are cotton and wool textiles, tobacco and rubber products, iron and steel, cement, shoes, glass, silver and leather handicraft, and pottery.

Inhabitants. The population of Mexico in 1970 was 48,313,438. The language is Spanish, and the prevailing religion is Roman Catholicism. Elementary education is free and compulsory. The largest and oldest university, the University of Mexico, was founded in 1552. The chief cities, in addition to those described below include Monterrey (1,177,361), Ciudad Juarez (436,054), Leon (453,976), Torreon, (257,045), Tijuana (335,125), and Mexicali (390,411).

Ruins in Yucatan. In Yucatan, the extreme eastern state of Mexico, are to be found the most impressive of the monuments left by the civilizations which flourished in America prior to its discovery by Europeans. Here was centered the New Mayan Empire, which was established by the Mayas after the fall of the Old Empire, the territory now known as Guatemala. The Old Empire flourished from the beginning of the Christian era until the 6th century A. D.

The causes of its fall form one of the fascinating enigmas of early American history. Mayan settlers entered Yucatan as early as the 4th century A. D., but the New Mayan Empire was not definitely established until about 1100 A. D. It continued until the coming of the Spaniards in the early 16th century. The chief centers were the capital, Uxmal, and the cities of Mayapan and Chichen-Itza.

The buildings are of one story in height, but in nearly all cases are situated on terraces or pyramids constructed of earth. They are faced with stone and have masonry steps for ascent and descent. The Temple of the Magician at Uxmal crowns a majestic pyramid 80 feet high and 240 by 180 feet at the base. The exterior is richly ornamented with carvings and relief work. Such carving was executed by stone tools, the only metals known to the builders being gold, silver, and copper. Since the true arch was unknown, roofs of Mayan buildings were either flat or, more often, vaulted. The buildings are very narrow, and the walls are usually from three to nine feet thick.

In central Mexico also are numerous pyramids surmounted by stone temples or palaces built by the Toltecs and Aztecs.

It was in what is now Mexico that corn was first cultivated and improved some 4000 to 2000 years before our era. It is believed that this provided a first basis for the civilizations that arose there.

Guadalajara (*gwä'THä-lä-hä'rä*). The second largest city of Mexico, situated about 150 miles inland from the center of the country's Pacific Coast. The climate is agreeable, the range of the temperature being limited to a few degrees. Guadalajara is an important mining center. The large waterfall of Juanacatlan near by furnishes electric power for street railroads, city lighting, and manufacturing. Among the manufactures are cotton goods, art pottery, tiles, leather articles, and cordage.

The city is well built and has spacious streets and several large parks embellished with fountains and statues. The principal building, the cathedral, noted for its ornamentation and magnificent interior, contains one of Murillo's masterpieces. Aqueducts, eight miles long, bring water to the city. Population, 1970, 1,196,218.

Mexico City. The capital and largest city of Mexico, situated somewhat southeast of the geographic center of the country at an elevation of 7415 feet. Majestic, snow-crowned mountains encircle the city, presenting a scene of surpassing grandeur. The climate is delightful; the air is dry, and the range of temperature seldom exceeds 15°.

Mexico City is the social, literary, financial, and industrial center of the country. Manufactures include textiles, chemicals, paper, boots and shoes, and foundry and tobacco products.

The city, founded by Cortez in 1521 on the site of the Aztec town Tenochtitlan, is regularly laid out with wide, well-paved streets, shaded boulevards, numerous parks and driveways embellished with statues and monuments, and several ornate squares. Mexico City abounds in churches. Fronting Plaza Mayor Square is the great cathedral, a magnificent structure in Spanish Renaissance style, the foundations of which were laid in 1573 on the site of an Aztec temple.

Tourism has greatly increased as a result of much improved roads and highways and the convenience of air travel. The visitor will find in Mexico City numerous buildings (with elaborate façades) and places noted for their beauty and historical associations. A few of these are the National Palace, which has several murals by Diego Rivera; the Palace of Fine Arts; the National Museum of Anthropology; Chapultepec castle, the executive mansion; Xochimilco and its "floating gardens"; the National University, founded in 1551; and the famous 22-ton Aztec calendar stone, noted for its remarkable accuracy.

The modern city has many tall buildings, some with entire walls of glass, others with colorful mosaics, which present an interesting contrast to the older buildings most of which are only one story high. The city, once the hub of Aztec civilization, has become a mecca for thousands of visitors each year. In less than forty years, it has grown from less than one million inhabitants to an estimated population of 3,025,564 in 1970.

Puebla (*pwä'blä*). An important city of Mexico, situated in the vicinity of several of the highest mountains in the country about 60 miles southeast of Mexico City. The manufactures include textiles, soap, glass, straw hats, pottery, and leather goods. Onyx articles, made from the stone quarried nearby, form an important article of export.

The city is well built and has all modern improvements. Besides several professional schools, there are three libraries, an imposing cathedral of Spanish architecture, an art gallery, a museum, an observatory, and many other institutions of note. A short distance from the city are the famous mineral springs of Tehuacan and the prehistoric pyramid of Cholula, 177 feet high and covering nearly 45 acres. The city was founded by the Franciscans in 1532. It was captured by the Americans in 1847 and was taken by the French in 1863. Population, est. 360,576.

Tampico (*täm-pē'kō*). The best equipped port of Mexico, on the Panuco River near its mouth in the Gulf of Mexico. Petroleum is produced in large quantities in the vicinity and forms the chief article of export. Ores, hides, wood, wool, and hemp are also exported; manufactured goods, mainly from the United States, are imported. Modern warehouses, offices, and municipal improvements give Tampico a thoroughly up-to-date appearance. Population, 1970, 196,147.

Vera Cruz. An important seaport of Mexico, situated on the Bay of Campeche, an arm of the Gulf of Mexico. An enervating climate and the prevalence of yellow fever once gave Vera Cruz the name of the City of the Dead. Modern sanitation measures, however, have completely transformed living conditions.

Twenty-five million dollars have been spent on the improvement of the harbor. On a reef near its entrance stands the fortress of San Juan de Ulua. The exports consist chiefly of ore, chicle, dyewoods, and hides, and the imports include textiles, hardware, and other manufactured goods. Fishing is carried on extensively, and there is a considerable manufacturing industry. Population, 1970, 242,351.

A geographical term used to designate the neck of land which connects North America and South America. It stretches in a southeast and northwest direction, lies entirely within the Torrid Zone, and comprises the area between the Isthmus of Tehuantepec, in southern Mexico, on the north, and the Isthmus of Panama, immediately north of Colombia, on the south. Its area is approximately 200,000 square miles. Its width varies from about 30 miles at the Isthmus of Panama to 450 miles in southern Mexico.

Surface. The southwestern coast of Central America is skirted by a broken chain of mountains, which reach a maximum elevation of 13,000 feet. Their formation is distinct from that of the Rocky Mountains and of the Andes range. Volcanic eruptions and violent earthquakes are very frequent. The largest interruption of the mountainous highlands is the basin of Lake Nicaragua, which has a water area in excess of 3500 square miles. The northeastern side of the isthmus slopes gradually toward the sea and has a fertile and well watered soil.

Climate and Flora. The climate varies, according to elevation, from a tropical heat to an arctic rigor. The lava areas are extremely fertile and, where the climate is favorable, produce coffee, sugar, corn, pineapple, bananas, and other products of tropical agriculture. The forests of the lowland are rich in dyewoods and valuable cabinet woods. The higher districts have a characteristic temperate-zone and alpine flora.

Inhabitants. The total population is estimated at more than 15,000,000, mostly of Indian and Spanish blood. The majority live on the southwestern coastal area. Agriculture is the chief occupation, although vast mineral and forest resources await development. Textiles and other manufactured goods are imported. More than 80 per cent of the trade is with the United States.

Politically, Central America comprises the countries lying between Mexico on the north and Colombia on the south. Apart from the Panama Canal Zone and Belize, a member of the British Commonwealth, they consist of six independent republics—Guatemala, Honduras, El Salvador, Nicaragua, Costa Rica, and Panama. Roman Catholicism is the prevailing religion and Spanish is the common language.

Belize (British Honduras). Bordering on the Caribbean Sea, Mexico, and Guatemala, the area of Belize is 8598 square miles. Most of the surface is covered with tropical forests yielding mahogany, chicle, and logwood. Bananas and coconuts are also exported in considerable quantities. The coastal area is low, marshy, but not unhealthful. The estimated population in 1970 was 130,000, of whom about 98 per cent were of Negro and Indian origin. The capital is Belmopan. Control of the region was long disputed by the Spanish and it was not secured by Britain until 1836. The settlement was proclaimed a British colony in 1862. In 1884 it became an independent colony of Britain and was made self-governing in 1964.

Canal Zone. A strip of land ten miles wide, from the Atlantic Ocean to the Pacific. Through the zone runs the Panama Canal, finished by the U.S. in 1914. The Canal Zone divides the Republic of Panama into two parts. See *United States Dependencies* and *Panama Canal*.

Costa Rica (*kŏs'tà rē'kà*). A country occupying the section of Central America between Nicaragua and Panama. The area is about 20,000 square miles, a large part of which is an irregular tableland in which some mountain peaks attain an altitude of more than 10,000 feet. Many mountains are volcanic and have caused a considerable loss of life.

Coffee is the staple product of the subtropical plateau, but cacao, tobacco, and sugar are also grown and exported. Costa Rica is one of the chief banana producing countries of the world. The fruit is grown extensively in the hot, tropical lowlands. Other important industries include lumbering, gold and silver mining, and cattle raising. The manufacture of fiber glass products, textiles, and fertilizers are among the newer industries.

The estimated population in 1970 was 1,800,000, a large number being of Spanish origin. San José is the capital. *Costa Rica* means "rich coast" and was given the name by Christopher Columbus in 1502.

El Salvador. The smallest, but next to Guatemala, the most populous republic of Central America, and the only one without an Atlantic coastline. It is southwest of Honduras, with a coastline of about 160 miles on the Pacific Ocean. Its area is about 8000 square miles. San Salvador is the capital.

There is a level coastal strip that rises, farther inland, to a mountainous plateau containing a number of active volcanoes. One of these, called the Izalco, or "lighthouse," began to rise from the plateau about a century ago and, by means of its own lava, has reached the height of a mile.

The volcanic area is extremely fertile and produces large crops of coffee, sugar, cotton, tobacco, and cacao. Coffee is the chief export, with cotton making great gains. Balsam and hardwoods are the principal forest products sent abroad. Cattle raising and gold and silver mining are carried on extensively. U.S. aid has helped the economic growth of the country considerably. The 1970 population estimate was 3,534,000.

Guatemala (*gwä′tä-mä′lä*). The second largest and the most populous country of Central America, lying between Mexico and the republic of Honduras. Its area is 45,452 square miles. A mountain ridge, which includes a number of volcanoes, divides the long eastern slope from the narrower but more thickly populated Pacific drainage area. Lake Peten, in the northern part of the country, is noted for being the habitat of 30 species of fish not found elsewhere.

The hot lowlands in the north and east are unhealthful but produce large crops of cacao, sugar cane, and bananas. The dense forests of the valleys yield valuable hardwoods, chicle, and rubber. The staple export of the country, however, is coffee, grown principally on the rich, volcanic soil of the plateau and the western slope. Two annual crops of wheat and three of corn are raised in this district. Cotton is a crop of more recent importance, and by 1961 had become the second largest export, after coffee. At the higher altitudes, apples and potatoes are grown and many cattle are raised. Beginning in 1952, a program of agrarian reform was put into operation, under which land not under cultivation might be expropriated, with eventual compensation, and divided into small holdings.

The population of Guatemala, 1970 est., was 5,188,981, more than half of whom are pure Indians. Guatemala is the capital and lies on the interoceanic railway which connects Puerto Barrios, the port on the Gulf of Honduras, with San José and other ports on the Pacific coast.

Honduras. A country of Central America, lying between Guatemala and Nicaragua, with a coast line of 400 miles on the Caribbean Sea. The southwestern boundary is El Salvador and the Gulf of Fonseca, an inlet of the Pacific Ocean. The surface covers 44,275 square miles, the greater part of which is a plateau ranging in elevation from 5000 to 10,000 feet.

The hot, malarial coastal region produces the bulk of the country's staple export—bananas. Coconuts are grown there also, and, farther inland, large crops of sugar, tobacco, and coffee are produced. Corn is cultivated as the chief article of domestic consumption. Stock raising is one of the principal industries. The dense forests of the coast area and of the valleys yield rubber, dyewoods, and medicinal plants. Cigars and Panama hats are manufactured for export.

The mineral resources of the country are extensive but production is confined to silver, lead, and zinc. Foreign concessionaires must employ Hondurans up to at least half of their labor force. Railroads, totaling about 850 miles, are used mainly to transport bananas. The normal means of transport for both passengers and freight is by airplanes, which are treated as casually as buses. There is one large international airport, at Tegucigalpa, which is the capital and largest city.

The population of the country in 1970 (est.) was 2,582,000. While Spanish is the official language, a number of aboriginal tribes speak languages of their own.

Nicaragua (*nĭk′à-rä′gwà*). The largest country of Central America, situated at the center of the intercontinental neck. Its surface is mountainous in the northern and western part, where there are several volcanoes. The eastern section is low, and, in the south, there is a depression forming the basin of Lake Nicaragua, Central America's largest inland body of water. The area of the country is 57,143 square miles.

Most of the population is found in the fertile, volcanic valleys of the uplands on the western side of the country, of which the chief agricultural products are coffee, cacao, sugar cane, and corn. Cattle are raised and the export of hides is important. Bananas are grown in large quantities in the eastern lowlands. Forest industries rank second in importance, timber, dyewoods, gums, oils, fibers, and rubber being obtained on both coasts of the country. Gold and silver are mined. The chief manufactures are Panama hats and cigars.

The estimated population of Nicaragua in 1970 was 1,984,000. The two principal cities are Managua and Leon, the former being the seat of the national government. The Pacific Coast ports of Corinto and San Juan del Sur handle most of the foreign trade. In 1916 the U. S. purchased from Nicaragua the right to build an interoceanic canal through the country. The treaty ended in 1970.

Panama (*păn′à-mä′*). The most eastern country of Central America, stretching from Costa Rica about 480 miles east to Colombia. It occupies the narrowest part of the intercontinental neck and is divided into two parts by the Canal Zone, ten miles in width, controlled by the United States. The area of the country is 28,576 square miles.

Panama is traversed by two broken mountain chains, which are overgrown with dense forests containing rubber trees and valuable hardwoods. Bananas and coconuts are produced in the hot lowlands, and sugar cane, coffee, cacao, and tobacco are grown at higher altitudes. A considerable number of cattle are raised, and hides form a valuable article of export.

The population of Panama, exclusive of the Canal Zone, was estimated to be 1,463,500 in 1970. The city of Panama is the seat of government.

Belize City (*bĕ-lē′z*). The chief seaport of Belize is situated at the mouth of the Belize river near the center of the country's seacoast. The climate is hot but not unhealthful. The exports go mainly to the United States and consist chiefly of mahogany, logwood, coconuts, and bananas. Population, 1965, 45,055.

Guatemala City. The capital of the country of the same name. Guatemala is an inland commercial city, situated in the southern part of the country about 85 miles from the Pacific coast on a plateau 5000 feet above the sea. A large part of its trade is in coffee. The city has various professional schools, a university, and a cathedral, which is the seat of the archbishop. Guatemala has been destroyed four times by earthquakes, most recently in 1976. Pop. 1970, 730,991.

Leon (*lā-ōn'*). A metropolis of Nicaragua and formerly its capital, situated about 15 miles from the coast in the western portion of the country. It has a cathedral built in the Renaissance style, and is the seat of a university. Population, about 47,000.

Managua (*mä-nä'gwä*). The capital of Nicaragua, situated about 25 miles inland from the center of the state Pacific coast line. It is a commercial center for the marketing of coffee grown in the region. The city is the seat of the Central University of Nicaragua. Managua was almost entirely destroyed by earthquake in 1972, but rebuilding was begun at once. Population 262,047.

Panama City. The capital of the Republic of Panama, situated at the head of Panama Bay near the southern terminus of the Panama Canal.

Panama, founded by Pedro Arias in 1519, was one of the first European settlements in the western hemisphere. It was long the capital and Pacific metropolis of Spain's vast possessions in America. Population, 1970, 418,013.

San José (*sän hô-sā'*). The capital of Costa Rica situated in a rich coffee growing region. The city is regularly built and has broad streets, fronted for the most part by one-story brick houses. The principal buildings include the national palace, the university, and the national theater. Population, 1970, 203,148.

San Salvador. The capital and largest city of El Salvador, situated in a fertile valley about 25 miles from the coast. It is about three miles from the volcano of San Salvador, which destroyed most of the city three times. The houses are surrounded by open ground and built low in order to minimize the danger during possible earthquakes. The city carries on an active trade in tobacco, and other products of the region. It has a university, a national library, and a fine botanical garden. Salvador is one of the oldest settlements of the western hemisphere, being founded in 1528 by Alvarado. Pop. 1970, 349,333.

Tegucigalpa (*tä-gōō'sê-gäl'pä*). The capital of Honduras, situated in the southern part of the country about 50 miles from San Lorenzo, its port on the Gulf of Fonseca. The agricultural and mining interests of the surrounding region center in the city, which is also the seat of a national university and of several colleges. Tegucigalpa was formerly an Aztec city. It was made the capital of Honduras in 1880. Population, 1970, 232,276.

THE WEST INDIES

A large group of islands lying between North America and South America and forming the barrier between the Atlantic Ocean and the Caribbean Sea. They stretch in a great curve from Florida east and south to the mouth of the Orinoco river in Venezuela. Their total area is about 92,000 square miles; their population, more than 25,000,000. Most of the islands are rocky. They receive copious rain, brought principally in the summer by the northeast trade winds, which at times develop into destructive hurricanes.

The largest island is Cuba, which, like the two republics on the island of Hispaniola, is an independent country. Puerto Rico belongs to the United States.

Cuba, Hispaniola, Jamaica, and Puerto Rico are sometimes referred to as the Greater Antilles, and the other West India islands, except the Bahamas, as the Lesser Antilles. Antilles is an Anglicized plural of Antilia, a name given on early maps to a mythical island in the Atlantic Ocean.

British West Indies. Islands of the West Indies which are dependencies in, or members of, the British Commonwealth of Nations. They may be divided into the following five groups: The Bahamas, Barbados, Jamaica and its dependencies, the Leeward Islands, and the Windward Islands. Trinidad and Tobago are sometimes added as a sixth group, but their proximity to South America makes it more natural to count them as insular parts of that continent. The total area of the islands is estimated at 12,000 square miles.

The chief occupation of the inhabitants is agriculture, although valuable hardwoods are to be found in the forested areas. English is the common language. The population, 1970, est., was 4,221,000.

Bahama Islands. A group of low islands in the British West Indies, extending from a point near the east coast of Florida, in a general direction parallel with the Cuban coast, to within 100 miles of the island of Hispaniola. While the group includes several hundred islands, only twenty have permanent settlements. These twenty cover an area of 4404 square miles. The population, in 1970, was estimated at 161,000. The islands are an independent nation within the commonwealth, with a capital at Nassau in New Providence island. The staple products are sponges and sisal hemp. Pineapples, both fresh and canned, oranges, and tomatoes are also exported.

Barbados. (*bär-bā'dōz*). The most easterly of the West India islands. The climate is healthful, fever being almost unknown. About two-thirds of its area of 166 square miles is under cultivation. The crop of paramount importance is sugar, exported chiefly to Canada and the United States.

The population in 1970 was 256,000. Washington's visit to Barbados in 1751 was the only foreign journey he ever made. It became an independent member of the British Commonwealth in 1966.

The capital and seaport is Bridgetown. Its houses are built of coral rock and of wood. Pop., 1970 est., 238,000.

Jamaica. The largest island of the British West Indies, lying about 100 miles south of the eastern end of Cuba. Its area is 4411 square miles. Jamaica, including some smaller islands with a total area of 224 square miles, is an independent country within the British Commonwealth.

Jamaica is traversed by low hills, which, at the eastern end, culminate in the Blue Mountains with a maximum altitude of 7362 feet. The island is one of the world's largest sources of bauxite, some of which is processed locally into aluminum. Other exports include sugar, bananas, fruit juice, and rum.

The tourist trade is large. The population estimate in 1968 was 1,913,000.

The capital and chief port is Kingston, situated on a landlocked harbor on the southeast coast of the island. The city is well built. It has modern improvements and attractive suburbs. In one of its old parish churches stands the tomb of Admiral Benbow, an English seaman who distinguished himself in a battle with a French fleet in 1702. In 1907, Kingston was almost entirely destroyed by an earthquake. Pop., 1969 est., 1,972,130.

Leeward Islands. A group of West India islands forming a chain which begins to the east of Puerto Rico and curves southeast to the island of Saint Lucia. The majority of the islands are British. France, however, controls Guadeloupe, Martinique, Saint Bartholomew, and part of Saint Martin. The remainder of Saint Martin and the islands of Saint Eustatius and Saba belong to the Netherlands. The British dependencies are Antigua, Dominica, British Virgin islands, Saint Kitts, Montserrat, Barduda, Redonda, Sombrero, Nevis, and Anguilla. The British islands form one colony, having its seat of government at Saint John in the island of Antigua. The islands of the colony cover an approximate area of 428 square miles and support a population, principally Negroes, of more than 145,000. The chief articles of export are cotton, sugar, molasses, cocoa, limes, and coconuts. The name was given in allusion to the fact that the islands are not swept by the northeast trade winds as much as are the Windward Islands to the south.

Windward Islands. A group of British West India islands forming the eastern barrier of the Caribbean Sea, with a total area of 811 square miles. Population, 1970 est., 389,759. The four chief islands are Grenada, Saint Vincent, Saint Lucia, and Dominica. These islands have separate administrative bodies. The products include excellent grades of cotton and of arrowroot; also sugar, cocoa, lime juice, and spices. Most of the trade is with Great Britain.

Bermuda Islands. A group of low coral islands belonging to Great Britain, about 880 miles due east of Charleston, South Carolina, and 699 miles from New York. Twenty of the 150 islands are inhabited. They supported in 1970, on an area of 21 square miles, a population of 54,000. The chief exports are lilies and onions, sent almost entirely to the

United States. Hamilton, situated on Bermuda island, is the capital. During World War II the United States built a naval and air base at Bermuda under a 99-year lease. The climate is genial and attracts numerous visitors from the United States and from Great Britain. The islands are named after the Spaniard, Bermudez, who discovered them in 1515. They were first settled in the 17th century by Somers, an Englishman.

Cuba. The largest island of the West Indies, which, with the Isle of Pines and smaller adjacent islands, constitutes the independent republic of Cuba. Cuba is in the Torrid Zone and lies 92 miles south of Key West in Florida, the most southern town of the United States. The island has an average width of 50 miles and stretches about 730 miles in a general east and west direction. Its area is 44,206 square miles.

The surface of Cuba is in general low and undulating. Hills border the northern coast and in the southeast a short range of mountains, the Sierra Maestra, skirts the sea and reaches at one point an elevation of 8320 feet. The rivers are short. Many of them, however, are noted for disappearing throughout part of their courses. The Moa cascade in eastern Cuba is formed by a river which drops 300 feet into a cave. A number of springs of fresh water are found in the sea rising through the salt water. These are believed to be emerging rivers which disappeared inland.

The climate of Cuba is hot and moist. Improvements in sanitation have virtually banished yellow fever, which formerly afflicted the inhabitants as a yearly epidemic. The soil is rich and supports a luxuriant vegetation. Palms and valuable hardwood trees flourish in forests covering nearly half the island. Bananas and other tropical fruits provide food for the inhabitants and are exported in great quantities. The fauna includes the tarantula, chameleon, scorpion, vulture, scavenger buzzard, and, among the numerous species of snakes, a boa, which often attains a length of 18 feet. The rare insectivore, the almiqui, is indigenous to the island. Alligators infest the waters. Coral insects have produced coral reefs about the coasts in such number as to endanger navigation in many parts.

The chief industry of Cuba is the cultivation of sugar cane and of tobacco. Cuba leads the world in the production of sugar cane. After a Communist-type government was set up in 1959, all land and industries were nationalized. Sugar and other exports, which had gone chiefly to the United States, were taken under barter arrangements by Russia, China, and other Communist countries. Since that time, crops of rice, corn, and beans have increased markedly. Coffee also is an important crop. Rayon and cement are among recent manufactures.· Sugar refining remains the leading industry; cigars and cigarettes rank second.

The population of Cuba, 1970 est., was 8,553,395. Spanish is the prevailing language, and the Roman Catholic religion predominates. In 1961, when education was nationalized, many Catholic schools were seized. Elementary education is free and obligatory from ages 6 to 14. There are many vocational schools and a national university. The capital is Havana.

Havana. The capital of Cuba, situated on an excellent natural harbor on the northern coast. The city lies directly south of Florida. Havana is the chief commercial city of the West Indies. It is the focus of Cuba's enormous trade in sugar and in tobacco, and has tobacco factories which are among the largest in the world.

The older section of the city, lying between the harbor and the sea, has narrow, irregular streets. The newer parts have wide, asphalt-paved streets and contain picturesque parks and promenades adorned with shade trees. The most attractive street is the Prado, which has in the center a parkway shaded by laurels and palms. Most of the public buildings are of limestone. They include the costly presidential palace, on the Prado; the Tacon theater, which is one of the largest playhouses in the western hemisphere; and the cathedral, said to have contained the remains of Columbus from 1796 to 1898. The city is a popular winter resort. The chief educational institutions include the University of Havana and the Jesuit College of Belen.

The harbor is equipped with three forts of obsolete construction. In 1898 the American battleship, the *Maine*, was blown up in the harbor. After the expulsion of the Spaniards in 1899, a program of improvements in sanitation was carried out which freed the city from the pestilential scourges to which it was formerly subject. Havana was founded in 1519. Population, 1970, 1,565,700.

Camagüey (*kä′mä-gwä′*). The largest inland city of Cuba, situated in the midst of rich savannas somewhat east of the center of the island. Its port, Nuevitas, located about 50 miles northeast on the Atlantic coast, is the outlet for the products of the live stock industry centering in the city. The sugar interests of Camagüey are also considerable.

Founded in 1516, the city retains an antiquated appearance with narrow, winding streets and poor houses. During the American occupation of Cuba, good water was provided by means of artesian wells and a drainage system was introduced. The city is sometimes known as Puerto Principe. Population, 1970, 170,500.

Cienfuegos (*syĕn-fwä′gōs*). A seaport of Cuba, situated on a landlocked harbor near the center of the island's southern coast. The commerce consists largely of sugar exports. Population, 99,530.

Matanzas (*mä-tän′zäs*). A city on the northern coast of Cuba, 55 miles east of Havana. It has tobacco factories, distilleries, and iron foundries, and ranks next to Havana in the export of sugar and tobacco. Population, 82,619.

Santiago de Cuba (*sän′tê-ä′gō dä kōō′bä*). A city of southeastern Cuba, situated on a deep, landlocked harbor on the Caribbean Sea. The port is the outlet for the tobacco raised in the district, for forest products, and for iron, manganese, and copper ores. The city was founded in 1514 by Diego Velasquez. In the Spanish-American War, Spain's fleet under Cervera took refuge in Santiago harbor and was destroyed while attempting to escape. San Juan hill nearby is a national park memorializing Theodore Roosevelt's assault in 1898. Population, 1970, 249,600.

Hispaniola. The second largest island of the West Indies, a short distance southeast of Cuba. It is divided between two republics, Haiti and the Dominican Republic, which have a total population of more than 9,000,000. It was discovered on December 6, 1492, by Christopher Columbus, who named it La Española. It was later known as Haiti.

The island, about 405 miles long and 165 miles wide, has an area of about 29,400 square miles. The surface is rugged and has three mountain ranges running east and west. In the Dominican Republic is Hispaniola's highest peak, Pico Duarte, altitude 10,417 feet; a large salt lake, called Enriquillo; and a number of hot mineral springs. The mountains are rich in undeveloped mineral deposits. Abundant rainfall fosters luxuriant vegetation—valuable hardwood trees in the tropical forests, and, in the cultivated areas, large crops of coffee, cacao, cotton, tobacco, and sugar. Coffee is the chief export.

Haiti. A republic occupying the western third of the island of Hispaniola. Its area is 10,700 square miles. Most of the inhabitants live in the hot, unhealthful lowlands, and the death rate is high. The chief industry is the cultivation of coffee and other products of tropical agriculture. The mineral and forest wealth is little developed.

The population, 1970 estimate, was 4,867,000, of whom about 90 per cent have no admixture of white blood. The spoken language is a corrupt dialect of French known as Creole French. The official religion is Roman Catholicism.

The capital and largest city is Port au Prince, situated at the head of the Bay of Haiti. It has a population of about 250,000. It has a university, created in 1921. Port au Prince is sometimes called Port Républicain.

Dominican Republic. A republic of the West Indies, occupying the eastern two-thirds of the island of Hispaniola. Its 18,700 square miles have a subtropical climate.

The chief industry is agriculture. Sugar, cocoa, coffee, livestock products, and tobacco are exported, mainly to the U.S. Forest and mineral resources are extensive, but undeveloped. In 1968 several U.S., Japanese, and European companies formed a trust with the Dominican government to aid in technical training and industrial development.

The common language is Spanish, and Roman Catholicism is the prevailing religion. Customs collections from 1907 and the general administration of the country from 1916 were in the hands of the United States until 1934. The American receivership was abolished in 1941. Population, 1970, 4,325,000.

The capital is Santo Domingo (formerly Ciudad Trujillo) and is situated near the center of the republic's southern coast. The city had a cathedral, in which the bones of Christopher Columbus were entombed from 1542 to 1796, and a statue of him stands in the public square. The settlement was founded in 1496 by the brother of the great discoverer, and, after Isabela on the northern coast, it is the oldest European settlement in the western hemisphere. Population, 822,862.

Curaçao (*kōō′rä-sä′ō*). A political name applied to a Dutch colony which comprises two groups of islands in the West Indies. Curaçao, the largest island, and two others lie about 40 miles off the northwestern coast of Venezuela, while the remaining three form part of the Leeward Islands southeast of Puerto Rico. The total area of the colony is 403 square miles. Population, 1970 est., exceeded 220,000. The chief industry is oil refining. These islands, along with Surinam (formerly Dutch Guiana) were sometimes referred to as the Dutch West Indies.

SOUTH AMERICA

THE southern continent of the western hemisphere, situated, for the most part, south of the equator. It lies east of a line drawn directly south from Florida and extends east to a point about 1000 miles west of Africa's most western meridian. South America is joined to North America by a narrow isthmus, called Central America. The continent extends north and south a distance of about 4550 miles and has a maximum width of approximately 3200 miles. The area is slightly less than that of North America, being commonly estimated at 7,500,000 square miles.

Contour. In outline, the continent has a general resemblance to a triangle. It is widest in the north and tapers in the south to a point several hundred miles farther south than any other large body of habitable land in the world. The coast line is simple, having no major indentations, such as Hudson Bay in North America. There are, however, many small inlets, especially on the southwest coast of Chile, two large estuaries, that of the Amazon river and of the Plata river, and a number of bays and gulfs, of which the principal ones are: the Gulf of Guayaquil, Golfo Corcovado, and Golfo de Penas on the west; Bahia Grande, Gulf of Saint George, Golfo de San Matias, and Bahia Blanca, on the southeast; and on the north the Gulf of Paria and the Gulf of Venezuela, the latter being connected with the inland sea, Lake Maracaibo.

Surface and Drainage. Along the western side of the continent extends a continuous mountain system, known as the Cordillera of the Andes. This system differs from the Rocky Mountain system of North America in being higher and in containing a large number of volcanoes. Numerous short rivers flow down the narrow west incline of the Andes into the Pacific Ocean. On the east, the mountains slope rapidly down to three great plains drained by three of the greatest rivers of the world. The most northerly plain is the basin of the Orinoco River, a level, grass-covered stretch called the llanos. Separated from it by the plateau of Guiana are the silvas, the vast forested plain of the Amazon Valley. The llanos and the silvas drain to the east. The third great plain drains to the south. It is the basin of the Plata-Parana, consisting of undulating tracts, called pampas, adapted to pasturage.

The pampas are separated from the Amazon Valley by a low plateau, which, extending westward branches into a subdued mountain range skirting the Atlantic coast northeast almost to the Amazon and southwest to the mouth of the Plata. This range is cut in the north by a valley through which flows the Francisco river. South of the Plata-Parana River several streams drain into the Atlantic from the eastern slope of the Andes mountains. The largest of these are the Colorado River, the Rio Negro, and the Chubut River.

Islands. A number of islands are reckoned with the continent. In the southwest, numerous small islands are formed by the partially submerged Andes range. The group of islands at the extreme south is called the Archipelago of Tierra del Fuego and is separated from the continent by Magellan strait. Cape Horn is the most southerly of these islands and forms the most southerly point of the continent. The Galapagos islands lie about 600 miles off the Ecuador coast. The island of Trinidad is close to the delta of the Orinoco river. The Falkland Islands are situated about 350 miles east of the continent at its southern extremity.

Climate. The greater part of South America lies within the tropics. Over this region the moist trade winds blow westward from the Atlantic, providing the country with a copious rainfall as far west as the Andes range. Impinging on the mountains, the winds rise and become cooled, thereby losing their moisture, which is precipitated as rain. They descend as hot, dry winds on the Pacific Coast region, in which, consequently, desert conditions prevail. The Atacama desert in northern Chile is said to be the driest area in the world. Farther south, moist winds blow from the Pacific, giving the western slope of the Andes Mountains a heavy rainfall and rendering the pampas to the east a semi-desert country.

South America does not experience such extremes of temperature as does North America, except on the mountains. The temperature in the moist Amazon valley is consistently high, varying little from about 80° F. The southwestern coast similarly has a fairly constant temperature, but the dry region of the western coast and that of the pampas show greater variation. The mean winter temperature in parts of the south falls to 35° F. The hottest mean midsummer temperature is 85° F. and is found in northern Argentina. The higher mountain peaks, however, are snow-capped even under an equatorial sun.

Flora. The hot, moist region at the extreme north of the continent has a characteristic tropical vegetation. Palms, bamboos, and tree ferns are predominant, giving place to conifers on the mountains and to tall grass in the Orinoco River basin. The silvas of the Amazon valley form the largest heavily forested area in the world. The pampas are luxuriantly grassed in their northern portions, but in the south the aridity occasions a stunted vegetable growth. The potato is indigenous to the continent, which is also the world's chief source of coffee. Rubber and quinine come from the tropical forests, and the Temperate Zone region is one of the world's principal wheat growing and stock raising areas.

Fauna. The animal life of South America includes a number of characteristic species. Among them are alpacas, vicuñas, llamas, condors, tapirs, and a number of toothless quadrupeds—sloths, anteaters, armadillos, and bloodsucking bats. Llamas are used as beasts of burden in the mountains, and alpacas provide a superior quality of wool. Birds of brilliant plumage abound in the tropical regions; many monkeys and reptiles and innumerable species of insects and of fish are found, especially in the Amazon basin. The electric eel and the caribe, a savage fish, are among the more noteworthy.

Minerals. The mineral resources of the continent, although great, have been very imperfectly developed, largely on account of difficulties of transportation and of climate. The Cordillera of the Andes contains the bulk of such minerals, although many are found in the Brazilian plateau. Silver and gold were produced extensively before Europeans came to South America. Brazil was long the chief source of diamonds, and Chile exports nitrates to all parts of the world. South America is also the chief source of monazite and of vanadium. Immense quantities of oil come from Venezuela, copper from Chile, and tin from Bolivia. Aluminum ore comes from the Guianas, and platinum and emeralds from Colombia.

Inhabitants. The population of South America in 1969 exceeded 180 million. The largest city is Sao Paulo, with a population of 5,900,000. The majority of the continent's inhabitants are a mixture of white races with native Indians. Possibly one-fifth are pure Indians. Those of unmixed European origin are comparatively few, although they predominate in Argentina and comprise almost the whole of the population in Uruguay. Pure Indians predominate in Paraguay and Bolivia.

Most of the inhabitants speak Spanish, being descended from Spaniards, except in Brazil, where the European strain in the population is Portuguese and the Portuguese language is spoken. The Catholic religion prevails throughout the continent.

The Andes Mountains. The system of mountains running north and south on South America's western border. This system, wide and high in the northern and central part, where it divides into three chains, becomes narrower toward the south and gradually sinks to the level of the sea at the continent's southern extremity. The highest peak is Aconcagua, in west central Argentina, which reaches a height of 22,835 feet. Mt. Huascaran in Peru has an elevation of 22,205 feet. Several of the world's gigantic volcanoes belong to the Andes mountains, such as Chimborazo, Cotopaxi, Antisana, and Misti. Glaciers are found on the tall peaks, even those within the equatorial regions.

The continent's largest lake and one of the highest in the world, Lake Titicaca, lies among the Andes mountains at a level of about 12,500 feet above the sea. The lake, which has no outlet, has an area of 3200 square miles and a maximum depth of about 900 feet. Near its shores, there are many ruins of temples and other relics of a former civilization.

The Amazon River. The largest and one of the longest rivers of the world, draining a tropical basin in South America eastward from the Andes Mountains and emptying into the Atlantic Ocean through an estuary which expands to a width of 150 miles.

The river has several tributaries which are themselves among the major rivers of the world. The Rio Negro is the largest affluent on the north; on the south the chief tributaries are the Purus, the Tapajoz, the Xingu, the Araguaia, and the Madeira, the last of which has an affluent explored by Theodore Roosevelt and named, after him, the Roosevelt River.

The Amazon River is navigable for ocean steamers over a distance of 2300 miles, and 486 miles farther for smaller vessels. The river system affords navigable waterways of 27,000 miles.

Rising tides produce large tidal waves, or bores, which rush up the river with a loud roar and often endanger shipping. The effect of the river's current can be detected 200 miles out at sea. In the flood season the river rises 30 to 40 feet in some parts, inundating the banks for several months of the year.

Plata-Parana. The second largest river system of South America, consisting of the Parana River and the Uruguay River, which unite their streams in the Rio de la Plata, "Silver river," an estuary conducting the water of the system to the Atlantic Ocean, about 20° of latitude north of Cape Horn.

The basin has a southern drainage, sloping from the Brazil plateau in the north. The estuary is 135 miles wide at its outlet. The Plata-Parana stream measures altogether about 2500 miles, of which about 1200 miles are navigable. The chief tributary is the Paraguay river, which flows into the Parana.

Orinoco River. One of the three large rivers of South America, draining a tropical territory in the northern part of the continent. The river rises in the Parima Mountains between Venezuela and Brazil. After traversing immense flat, treeless plains in a course running first west, then north, and finally east, the river winds through a dense tropical forest area and empties into the Atlantic Ocean through several mouths forming a delta south of the island of Trinidad. About 150 miles from its source the river discharges part of its water into the Rio Negro, an affluent of the Amazon River. The Orinoco River is navigable to a cataract 870 miles from its mouth. Its tributaries are very numerous, the chief navigable ones being the Guaviare, the Meta, and the Apure. The system has 4300 miles of navigable streams. See *Venezuela*.

POLITICAL DIVISIONS

Located on the mainland of South America are the nations of Argentina, Bolivia, Brazil, Chile, Columbia, Ecuador, Guyana (formerly the colony of British Guiana and now an independent member of the Commonwealth), Paraguay, Peru, Surinam (formerly the colony of Dutch Guiana), Uruguay, and Venezuela—and the colony of French Guiana. Brazil has the largest land area and Surinam the smallest. Among the islands, Trinidad and Tobago are an independent member of the British Commonwealth, while the Falkland Islands are dependencies of Britain. The Galapagos Islands belong to Ecuador.

Argentina. The most highly developed country of South America and second largest in area, occupying the greater part of the southern portion of the continent. The country has an Atlantic seaboard of 1565 miles and a western land boundary of about 3000 miles, following the continental watershed formed by the Andes. Argentina measures about 2285 miles from north to south and has a maximum width of 930 miles, with an area of 1,084,-120 square miles.

The country is drained in the north by the Plata-Parana River. In the south the surface slopes from the ridge of the Andes toward the Atlantic Ocean. The climate varies from the tropical warmth in the low plains of the north, where 120° F. has been recorded, to the more moderate conditions existing in the south, where 3° F. is the lowest temperature officially noted. The rainfall decreases from the eastern coast to the base of the Andes Mountains.

The flora of Argentina shows variations following the differences in climate. In the partly unexplored tropical forests of the north, algaroba trees are especially numerous, and many medicinal shrubs and other plants abound, including the *yerba maté*, or Paraguay tea plant. The mountains are wooded, those around the Strait of Magellan and Tierra del Fuego being covered with immense forests of beech. The most valuable product of the forest is quebracho extract, a dye. The pampas are treeless but are covered with grass. Such tropical and subtropical fruits as oranges, lemons, grapes, and peaches are grown. The animals characteristic of Argentina include the viscacha and the hare of Patagonia.

The chief industries of Argentina are grazing and agriculture, for which the extensive pampas are admirably suited. Wheat and corn are the most valuable crops. Grain and meat form more than 75 per cent of the exports. Argentina is the world's largest exporter of beef, corn, and flaxseed. Lumbering and mining are carried on to some extent. Oil fields yielded 123,076,000 barrels of petroleum in 1968. There are 27,301 miles of railway, all of which are now state property, a greater mileage than that of any other South American country.

Argentina is divided into 22 provinces and 1 federal district. The capital is Buenos Aires. The country has received a great many European immigrants, principally from Italy, Spain, and Germany. The Indian strain in the population is comparatively slight. The population, according to the 1970 estimate, was 24,352,000.

Bolivia. An inland country in the west central part of South America. The southwestern border follows the ridge of the western range of the Andean Cordillera, which in this section spreads out into the Bolivian plateau and occupies nearly half the surface of Bolivia. The average elevation of the plateau is 12,000 feet, but it contains some of the highest peaks of the continent, such as Ancohuma, Sajama, Illampu, and Illimani. In this plateau lies the lofty Lake Titicaca, with which is connected Lake Aullagas. East of the plateau, the surface slopes down in vast undulating plains toward the Amazon River valley in the north and, in the south, toward the llanos of the Parana River basin. The area of the country is estimated at 424,162 square miles.

Buenos Aires, capital of Argentina, is the largest city in South America. This obelisk is a copy of that on the Rue de la Concorde, Paris.

This view of Juarez Avenue in Mexico City illustrates the typical broad avenues in the city's regular layout. Shaded boulevards, ornate squares, and numerous parks embellished with sculpture characterize this great city built more than a mile above sea level.

Right Machu Picchu, the "Lost City of the Incas," near Cuzco, Peru, where it is believed that survivors of the Spanish conquest took refuge and eluded the victors in this inaccessible fastness.
Braniff Airways

This is the Equator Monument at zero latitude in Ecuador. The northern hemisphere on the left, southern hemisphere is on the right.

Many of the newer buildings in South America are daringly modern in design. This striking apartment house is in Montevideo, Uruguay.

Italian Museum, Lima, Peru, a gift of Lima's Italian citizens on the occasion of the centenary of Peru's independence in 1921.

Pan American Union

LATIN AMERICA II

Christ of the Andes, a colossal statue on the Chile-Argentina border, celebrating settlement of an old dispute.

Pan American Airways

South American Indians still use primitive methods. This fishing boat on a high Andean lake is made of balsa wood, including the sail.

Altamira Plaza, in Caracas, reflects the spirit of progress in Venezuela and the increase in national wealth that has made possible many modern improvements.

Courtesy—Ministry of Development,
Tourist Dept., Caracas, Venezuela

Modern and progressive, Sao Paulo, largest city in Brazil, is a leading manufacturing and business center.

Brazilian Gov't. Trade Bureau

This shadowy, ancient street in La Paz, Bolivia, is typical of many old South American cities, where buildings hundreds of years old rub shoulders with modern architecture.

Bolivia is entirely in the Torrid Zone, but the climate of the upland is of an almost arctic severity. Parts of this plateau support grazing flocks of sheep, llamas, and alpacas, but it is for the most part arid and of value only for its minerals. The fertile eastern slope of the Cordillera, being warmer and well watered, produces wheat, corn, barley, peaches, grapes, and figs. The lowlands support a tropical vegetation. Coffee, cacao, rice, sugar cane, and medicinal plants are cultivated, and vast forests yield rosewood, mahogany, ebony, cedar, and rubber, the last being produced in quantities which entitle Bolivia to rank next to Brazil as a rubber exporting country.

Bolivia's principal industry is mining, and the principal mineral product is tin, in the export of which Bolivia ranks second among the countries of the world. Silver, gold, and copper are also mined in large quantities, and wolfram, vanadium, bismuth, lead, zinc, salt, and antimony are obtained in smaller amounts. Potosi, where the tin and silver mining interests center, is the highest city in the world, having an elevation of 14,350 feet. At such an altitude, operations can be carried on only by the natives. Population, 1970 est. at more than 98,000.

Railroad transportation is limited by the natural obstacles in the way of construction. Some 2200 miles of track, however, are in operation. There is communication by airplane between the principal cities. Llamas are used for carrying light loads over mountainous districts.

The majority of the inhabitants live on the eastern slopes of the mountains. About one-half are pure Indians, and the white race forms about 12 per cent of the population of 5,600,000 (1975 est.). La Paz is the largest city and the seat of Congress, and Sucre is the statutory capital and seat of the supreme court. The country possesses many impressive remains of a vanished civilization. Bolivia was deprived of access to the sea by a disastrous war with Chile which ended in 1883.

Brazil. The largest country of South America, occupying the entire east central part of the continent and having a westward extension which reaches almost to the Andes Mountains. The country's maximum extent north and south is 2660 miles and east and west it measures about 2700 miles, with a total area of 3,289,000 square miles, exceeding that of continental United States.

In the north the climate is moist and tropical in character, while toward the south it becomes more temperate and the rainfall is lighter. The northern region is drained by the Amazon River, south of which lies one of the world's largest unexplored forest areas. The eastern part of the country is a highland through which the river Francisco flows, and the southern district is drained by the Uruguay River and by the upper reaches of the Parana River system.

The mineral resources of Brazil are very great but are largely undeveloped. The production of gold and of diamonds was formerly of great importance. The Morro Velho gold mine, having a depth of 7000 feet, is one of the deepest mines in the world. The deposits of iron are very extensive. Brazil provides the greater part of the world's supply of monazite.

The tropical flora of Brazil includes trees producing an extraordinary variety of useful and of ornamental woods, 200 different kinds of timber having been shown at the national exhibition in Rio de Janeiro in 1922. These woods include mahogany, rosewood, brazilwood, and logwood. The rubber tree and the pine are among those of the greatest commercial value. The rank forests of the Amazon basin abound in brilliantly colored flowers and in countless monkeys, lizards, fish, gaudy butterflies, and other tropical animals. The portions of the country farther south are suitable for agriculture, and produce a large amount of coffee, sugar, cocoa, tobacco, and cotton. About three-fourths of the world's supply of coffee comes from Brazil. The country continues to supply substantial quantities of rubber to world trade. Large areas provide fertile pasture land for raising livestock, notably Brahman cattle.

Brazil exports mainly the products of the forest and farm, and imports some manufactured goods. The textile industry includes the manufacture of silk, woolen, cotton, and jute goods. Other industries rapidly developing are ceramics, glass, electrical appliances, plastics, and cement. There are many tobacco factories and sugar refineries. Carnauba wax, produced only in Brazil, insures a high hard polish and long-wearing protection on furniture and floors.

The population of Brazil, according to the 1970 estimate, was 95,305,000, making the country the most populous in the western hemisphere after the United States. Many Negroes and about 100,000 Indians live in the Amazon valley. In the south there are a number of settlements of Germans, Spaniards, and Italians. The majority of the inhabitants, however, are of Portuguese origin, and the language of the country is Portuguese.

Politically, the country consists of 21 federated states, one federal district, and four territories. The most populous and most prosperous states are Bahia, Minas Gerais, and Sao Paulo, all bordering on the central part of the southeastern coast. These states produce the bulk of the minerals, coffee, sugar, cotton, and live stock. The most extensive state is Amazonas, occupying the upper Amazon valley. From it come most of the valuable woods. The largest city of the country is Sao Paulo and the capital is Brasilia. The port Pernambuco, on the eastern coast, is nearer to Lisbon than to New York.

Chile (*chĭl'ê*). A country of South America, lying on the western coast and extending, with an average width of about 87 miles, from the southern extremity of the continent northward about 2700 miles to Peru. The area is estimated at 286,397 square miles. The eastern boundary follows in general the ridge of the Andes mountains.

A high plateau rises abruptly from the sea along the greater part of the coast, leaving a lofty plain between the sea and the foot of the Andes. There is a gentle slope from the north to the south. The rivers are short and drain into the Pacific Ocean. A number of natural harbors are found among the fiordlike indentations and the numerous islands of the southern coast. The country is subject to severe earthquakes followed usually by destructive tidal waves. One of the most disastrous occurred in 1922. In 1751, the former city of Concepcion was sunk in the Pacific Ocean.

The climate of Chile is hot and extremely arid in the north, where a whole year often passes without rain. The central region, having a more moderate temperature and a greater precipitation, supports a flourishing agricultural industry and contains most of the population. In the south the increased rainfall permits the growth of forests of beech, cypress, and oak, the last of which has been introduced from abroad. In the extreme south the growth of the trees is stunted by the prevailing low temperatures.

The northern third of Chile is the world's chief source of natural nitrate of soda, which is used as a mineral fertilizer and in the production of explosives and of most of the world's supply of iodine. Chile is also one of the leading producers of copper. Other minerals mined in important quantities include iron ore, gold, silver, sulphur, borate, and salt. A large portion of the government's revenue is derived from the export of nitrate.

Agriculture provides employment for about half the population. The principal crops are grapes and wheat. Stock raising also is important. Most of the textiles and other manufactured goods consumed are imported. The United States and Great Britain receive most of the foreign trade.

Chile has a longitudinal railway system of some 6000 miles in length. The Trans-Andean railroad connects Valparaiso, on Chile's Pacific coast, with the Atlantic seaboard at Buenos Aires. Parts of it climb grades of a steepness nowhere else attempted by railroad engineers. The total length is nearly 6000 miles. Air transportation is well developed.

The population of Chile in 1972 was 10,044,940, of whom about one fourth were of Spanish descent. The influence of the Church is greater than in most other countries of the continent. Chile has a powerful fleet and is politically one of the three strongest countries of South America. The capital and largest city is Santiago. Valparaiso is the chief port.

Colombia. A country of South America, occupying the extreme northwestern part of the continent. Colombia borders on the Pacific Ocean for a distance of about 500 miles and on the Caribbean Sea for 700 miles. Its area is 439,520 square miles.

The country is traversed from northeast to southwest by the Cordillera of the Andes, which here consists of a western, a central, and an eastern range separated by fertile plateaus. The eastern slope of the Cordillera drains in the north into the basin of the Orinoco river and, farther south, into the basin of the Amazon river. The central plateaus drain northward by the Magdalena River system into the Caribbean Sea. The western slope of the Cordillera has a number of short rivers emptying into the Pacific Ocean. The Magdalena river is navigable for steamers to La Dorada, a point about 560 miles above its mouth.

The climate of Colombia varies from the intense tropical heat of the coast regions, the valleys, and the llanos, to the temperate conditions of the plateaus and the mountains. There are two wet seasons and two dry seasons over most of the country. The llanos, however, have two seasons only. The rainfall there is deficient and does not permit the growth of trees. The west coast, however, has a large rainfall. The mountain sides are covered with forests of a tropical character, containing, among many other varieties of plants, the wax palm, the rubber tree, and several species of cinchonas.

The mineral wealth of Colombia is great. Gold, platinum, copper, petroleum, and emeralds are exported, the last being produced in Colombia in greater quantities than in the rest of the world. The salt mines are a government monopoly and provide a considerable part of the national revenue.

The chief industries are agriculture and stock raising. Temperate zone cereals are grown on the plateaus, and coffee, sugar, bananas, and cocoa are produced in the valleys and the lower regions. Colombia provides most of the world's supply of mild coffee. Panama hats are produced extensively, although the industry is not centralized in factories. In addition to coffee, the chief exports are petroleum, bananas, gold, and platinum. The bulk of the foreign trade is with the United States. The mountainous surface of the country and the prevalence of tropical forests make transportation difficult except on the rivers and by air. Overhead ropeways are also a feature of Colombia's transportation facilities.

Colombia is divided into 23 departments, 3 intendancies, and 5 commissaries. The capital and largest city is Bogota. The population of the country, 1972 estimate, was 23,210,000.

Ecuador. A country in the northwest portion of South America, bordering on the Pacific Ocean and stretching south from Colombia to Peru. Its area is estimated at 104,516 square miles. Ecuador's coast line is broken by the Gulf of Guayaquil, the only large inlet on the south side of the continent.

The country is traversed from north to south by two ranges of the Andean Cordillera. Between the ranges lies a plateau, which has an average elevation of 9000 feet but in the south falls to a level of about 2000 feet. This plateau contains most of the cultivated land and has a delightful climate. The mountain ranges have many peaks of exceptional height, including Cotopaxi, the world's loftiest active volcano.

The coastal strip in Ecuador is not an arid waste, as in Peru and northern Chile, but is a stretch of tropical jungle with an excessive rainfall. Dense forests are found on the mountain slopes both on the west and on the east of the Cordillera. The east slope gives rise to several navigable rivers of the Amazon basin. One of the largest is the Napo, down which the explorer Orellana sailed in 1541 to the mouth of the Amazon River.

The immense virgin forests of Ecuador yield rubber, ivory nuts, dyewoods, cinchona bark, and many valuable kinds of cabinet wood. The distinctive products of the country, however, are cocoa and toquilla. The latter is the fabric from which Panama hats are made. It is shipped extensively to Colombia where the actual weaving is an important industry. Other products of the tropical agriculture pursued on the coastal strip are coffee, tobacco, and sugar. In the plateau, hay, cereal crops, and fruits and vegetables of a temperate zone character are cultivated, and cattle are raised in large numbers. Alligator skins are exported. Gold and petroleum are produced and silver, copper, iron, lead, coal, and sulphur are found. The production of salt is a government monopoly.

The population, 1974 census, was 6,500,845, the great majority of whom are of Indian origin. The coinage of the country is minted in England and the United States. The country owns the Galapagos, or "turtle", islands, lying 600 miles to the west. The capital of Ecuador is Quito and the principal seaport and largest city is Guayaquil. The name of the country is the Spanish word for equator.

French Guiana. An overseas department in the French Community with an area of about 34,740 square miles in northeastern South America. It is bounded by the Atlantic Ocean, Brazil, and Surinam, and consists of two districts—Cayenne and Inini. Cayenne (the coastal strip 25 miles deep), along with Devil's Island and other islands, was used by France as a penal settlement from 1931 until 1944, when it was closed. Inini, the hinterland district, is rich in valuable hardwoods and has much mineral wealth, including gold, silver, iron, and phosphates. Corn, rice, bananas, and sugar cane are among the principal crops. The population of French Guiana was estimated to be about 44,200 in 1971, most of the people living in the coastal strip, Cayenne. The capital and chief port is also called Cayenne.

Guyana. A former British colony of continental South America, lying between Venezuela and Surinam near the center of the continent's northeastern coast line. Its area is 83,000 square miles. The interior is covered with dense forests as far as the highlands in the southwest. The rivers are not navigable, except for short distances, because of rapids and falls. In the Potaro River are the famous Kaieteur Falls, having a drop of about 800 feet. The coast district, about 40 miles wide, is low, and part of it is protected by dikes. It is very fertile and produces large crops of sugar cane, rice, and coconuts. Gold and diamonds are mined in the highlands. Bauxite, the ore of aluminum, is exported.

The climate of the country is generally hot and moist. It was estimated that the population in 1975 was more than 794,348, about one-half of whom are East Indians, who were brought in to work on the plantations. The capital is Georgetown. England's sovereignty over the colony was disputed by the Dutch and the French until 1815, when the territory finally passed into her possession. The Venezuelan boundary was fixed after a dispute arbitrated in 1899 by jurists of Great Britain and of the United States. Guyana became independent in May, 1966.

Paraguay. An inland country of central South America, bounded by Brazil, Argentina, and Bolivia.

Paraguay is a low-lying country situated between the Parana River and the Paraguay River, with the exception of a district to the northwest, the Gran Chaco. By arbitration with Bolivia in 1930, Paraguay received 91,800 square miles of the Gran Chaco, making her total area about 157,000 square miles.

Apart from the disputed territory, which is subject to alternate floods and droughts, the climate is delightful for the greater part of the year. During the three hottest months, however, the temperature not infrequently rises above 100° F. The rainfall is moderate, but sufficient to foster the growth of dense forests, and rich groves of tropical fruit, particularly oranges, bananas, and lemons. Fine cabinet timbers, dyewoods, drugs, gums, and oils are obtainable from the forests on the hills and in the valleys of the northeast part of the country. Occasional stretches of savannas afford rich pasturage, and flat marshes in the south are adapted to rice culture.

The chief cultivated plants are orange and other tropical fruit trees, corn, sugar cane, rice, tobacco, and cotton. Agricultural methods, however, are still primitive. *Yerba maté*, or Paraguay tea, found wild in great abundance and also cultivated to some extent, is exported. Stock raising is the second industry of the country. Iron, copper, manganese, and marble are to be found in the northeast of the country, but they are not mined extensively.

Transportation facilities for this land-locked country improved noticeably in 1968–69. A new highway to Brazil was completed, new roads were built, and a large hydroelectric project was begun. Access to the sea is by river navigation through Argentina and by a railroad service to Buenos Aires. Chief exports are oranges, tobacco, beef hides, quebracho logs and extract, and vegetable oil. Increased tourism has helped raise the country economically.

The population of Paraguay was estimated in 1972 to be 2,354,071, a very small proportion of whom are white, these being mainly Italian and German immigrants. The settlements are largely confined to the vicinity of the Paraguay River. About one-seventh of the inhabitants are pure Indians, and the native Guarani language is more widely used than Spanish. The percentage of illiteracy is high. The capital, chief port, and the largest city is Asuncion.

Peru. A country of west central South America, bordering on the Pacific Ocean and stretching northward from Chile to Ecuador. Its area is 496,223 square miles.

Peru is traversed from north to south by the Cordillera of the Andes, which, under the name of the Sierra or uplands, constitutes one of the three physiographical divisions of the country. The uplands consist of three ranges, ill defined in parts, and of the intervening plateaus. There are several large volcanoes in this region and violent earthquakes are not uncommon. The rainfall is unevenly distributed.

Between the foothills of the Andes and the Pacific Ocean is a dry coastal strip averaging about 30 miles in width. This strip is cut by several rivers, which foster vegetation along their banks and afford means of irrigation. The civilization of the country centers about these rivers. Sloping eastward from the uplands is the Montana, a forest area with a heavy rainfall, in which the Amazon River system takes its rise.

Peru lies wholly within the Torrid Zone. The climate is not oppressively hot, however, except in the eastern valleys and lowlands. The greater part of the Sierra enjoys an equable temperature, and the heat of the coastal strip is moderated by the antarctic currents. Dense fogs frequently hang over the coast.

The eastern part of the Montana, being hot and well watered, supports a tropical vegetation. The cinchona tree is native to Peru and rubber trees grow in abundance but are comparatively inaccessible. Peru is the chief source of the coca shrub, from which cocaine is obtained.

The watered sections of the Sierra and of the coastal area produce sugar and cotton. Other agricultural products include coffee, grapes, palms, cocoa, corn, and wheat. A large number of sheep are raised in the Sierra, and wool, taken in part from sheep but to a great extent from llamas and alpacas, is exported in large quantities. The llama is the principal beast of burden. Mules are used extensively for traveling, the railway mileage being small on account of the mountainous character of the country. The various lines embrace about 2800 miles of track.

Mining ranks second to agriculture among the industries. The chief minerals are petroleum, copper, and silver, but over four-fifths of the world's supply of vanadium comes from Peru. The chief manufactures are sugar and cocaine, other necessary industrial products, such as textiles, lumber, wheat, and coal being imported. Peru has an important fishing industry, the main catch being anchovies, most of which are made into fish meal for cattle and poultry feed. This makes fish meal the leading export, with copper second.

Peru is the seat of the vanished civilization of the Incas, by whom Cuzco is said to have been founded in the 10th century. The population, according to the latest estimate, was 15,400,000, about 53 per cent being white and mestizos, and 46 per cent Indian.

The capital and largest city is Lima. The chief port is Callao on the Pacific Ocean. The steamship service between Peruvian and Bolivian ports on Lake Titicaca is unique in operating at an altitude unequalled on any other navigable body of water. Iquitos, on the upper reaches of the Amazon river, has steamer connections with the Atlantic Ocean, 2500 miles distant.

Surinam. This former Dutch colony became fully independent in 1975. It is situated at the center of the continent's northeast coast between Guyana and French Guiana. Its area—54,291 square miles—makes it the smallest South American nation.

The cultivated area is confined to a coastal strip about 20 miles in width, the interior region being covered with a dense tropical forest as far as the highlands of the southeast. The chief agricultural products are bananas, sugar, cacao, coffee, and rice. Gold is exported also, much of it obtained from alluvium.

The estimated population in 1971 was 384,900, and consists largely of Negroes and people of East Indian origin, who were brought in to work on the plantations. The capital is Paramaribo. The name Surinam is a corruption of Surreyham, which was the original designation given in honor of the Earl of Surrey.

Uruguay. A country south of Brazil between the Atlantic Ocean and the Uruguay River. Its southern coastline is on the Rio de la Plata. The total area is 72,172 square miles.

The surface is rolling and has several chains of hills reaching a maximum elevation of 2000 feet. The climate is equable in the south, but in the north it becomes continental, admitting of greater heat in the summer and of occasional frosts in the winter. The northern hills and valleys are covered with a subtropical forest, while the south and east form extensive fertile plains suited for agriculture and for stock raising. Deer, otters, wild hogs, and wildcats are indigenous. Rheas, or American ostriches, are found; and fur seals, protected by the government, inhabit Lobas island and Castillos island near the coast. There are also storks, swans, cranes, and wild turkeys.

Stock raising is the principal industry of Uruguay, animal products forming nearly nine-tenths of the exports. Wheat, oats, flaxseed, and grapes are also grown and exported. Less than 10 per cent of the country's area, however, is devoted to agriculture, in spite of the fact that the government encourages the industry by supporting agricultural schools. Hailstorms, destructive hurricanes, and occasional droughts occur as factors unfavorable to the raising of crops.

Gold mines are worked, and there are deposits of copper, iron, manganese, and lignite. Manufactures are very slightly developed, the population relying on importation for such industrial products as textiles and hardware. Transportation in Uruguay is facilitated by several hundred miles of navigable river streams and by more than 1700 miles of railway.

The population of Uruguay, according to the latest official estimate, was 2,763,964, of whom about nine-tenths are of European descent, mainly Spaniards and Italians. The earliest settlements were made by Spaniards in 1624 on the Rio Negro, a tributary of the Uruguay River. The capital, foreign port, and largest city is Montevideo.

Venezuela. The most northern country of South America, having a northern coast line of about 1700 miles on the Caribbean Sea and a land boundary separating the country from Guyana, Brazil, and Colombia. Its area, including the islands off the north coast, is 352,143 square miles.

Apart from the small basin of Lake Maracaibo in the northwest, Venezuela is drained by the Orinoco River system. This system flows eastward from the Andes mountains between the Guiana highlands to the south and a northeastern extension of the Andes mountains on the north, and enters the sea through a large estuary overgrown with a mangrove swamp. The upper portion of the river system traverses the llanos. A major irrigation project became a reality with the completion in 1968 of the Guri Dam, 512 feet high, located near the confluence of the Caroni and Orinoco rivers. The tributaries of the Orinoco are numerous and, with the main stream, provide the country with about 4000 miles of navigable waterways.

The climate in the lower levels of Venezuela is tropical but becomes temperate in the highlands and frigid on the higher mountain peaks. The rainfall is copious in the east and in the northwestern parts near the mountains. On the llanos the comparative dryness during one season of the year prevents the growth of trees.

The flora of the eastern lowlands and of the better watered territory in the northwest consists of tropical forests similar to those of the Amazon valley. The forests include many plants from which are available such products as rubber, vanilla, brazil nuts, dyewoods, and drugs. Grasses form the characteristic vegetation of the llanos. The fauna of Venezuela is tropical and rich, and includes such species as the howling monkey, the spectacled bear, the vampire bat, the flamingo and other brilliantly colored but usually songless birds, the anaconda and other snakes, a frog with a voice resembling a human shout, the electric eel, and the caribe.

Venezuela is rich in minerals. It ranks among the world's largest producers of petroleum. Also produced in quantity are gold, salt, and asphalt, the last being found in lakes containing extensive remains of prehistoric animals. Pearl fishing is an industry on a number of islands off the north coast.

In the northern and western parts of Venezuela, where most of the population is concentrated, agriculture is carried on, the chief products being coffee, sugar, and cocoa. Grazing is the chief industry on the llanos. Most of the foreign trade is with the United States.

The name Venezuela is Italian, meaning Little Venice. It was given by early Italian explorers who found, on Lake Maracaibo, an Indian tribe inhabiting huts which were supported by piles driven into the bed of the lake. Reminded of Venice, they gave the region its name.

Venezuela is divided into 20 states, 2 territories, and a federal district. The capital and largest city is Caracas. The 1971 estimated population was 10,721,522, excluding 31,800 Indians.

CHIEF CITIES AND OTHER PLACES OF INTEREST IN SOUTH AMERICA

The preceding articles on South America deal with the larger features of the continent. Other points of interest, including the principal cities, the national capitals, the trade centers, certain islands, and regions of especial note are covered below.

Asuncion (ä-sōōn'syōn'). The capital and metropolis of Paraguay, situated on the east bank of the Paraguay River in the west central part of the country. The city is the port and trading center of Paraguay, and is connected by railroad with Buenos Aires. It has foundries, shipyards, and distilleries. The exports include Paraguay tea and lace, the latter a beautiful product of the industry of Indian women. Population, 392,753.

Bahia (bä-ē'ä). A city of east central Brazil, picturesquely situated on a high peninsula which partly encloses an excellent natural harbor. Bahia, also called Salvador, is a notable port, shipping coffee, sugar, rubber, cotton, and other products raised in the state. The manufactures are varied, the principal one being cotton cloth. Bahia was formerly the center of the world's largest diamond trade.

The lower part of the city, devoted to commerce, has narrow streets. The upper, or residential, part is accessible by elevators and is attractively built. The churches are very numerous. The cathedral of the archbishop of Brazil is situated in Bahia and is one of the finest basilicas in Brazil. The city has a university, a medical college, and a museum. The culture of seedless oranges was introduced into the United States from Bahia. Founded in 1510 by Correa, a Portuguese navigator, the city was the capital of Brazil until 1763. Population, 863,000.

Barranquilla (bär'rän-kēl'yä). The chief port of Colombia, situated on the Magdalena River about 7½ miles from its mouth. The mouth of the river is not navigable. Traffic borne down the river to Barranquilla for export, therefore, is sent by rail to Puerto Colombia, a seaport on the Caribbean Sea. Population, 721,000.

Belem. A seaport of northeastern Brazil, situated on the Rio Para about 85 miles from the Atlantic Ocean. On the land side, it is flanked by dense forests. Belem is the headquarters for the navigation on the Amazon. Exports include cocoa, rice, cotton, rubber, and various forest products of the Amazon valley. Population, 633,000.

Bogota (bō'gô-tä'). The capital and largest city of Colombia, situated near the geographical center of the country on a fertile table-land at an elevation of about 8700 feet above the sea. There are many mountains in the vicinity and the mining interests of the city are considerable, the government's salt mines being a short distance north of the city. Coal, iron, and manganese mines lie to the north and east.

The more important edifices of Bogota include the government buildings and the cathedral, the latter being a structure in the Corinthian style of architecture. The city is the seat of the national university, of three endowed colleges, and of a museum containing many relics of the civilization of the Incas. The streets are narrow but well paved. Population, 2,978,000.

Brasilia (brä-sīl'i-ä). Brazil's new capital, located in the Central Plateau in the state of Goias, is designed to integrate 6 million square kilometers of the interior into the general progress of the country. The city's daringly modern buildings are the work of sixty Brazilian architects. Population, 537,000.

Buenos Aires (bwä'nōs ī'rās; bō'nŭs ā'rĭz). The capital of Argentina and one of the largest cities in South America, situated on the south shore of the estuary of the Rio de la Plata about 170 miles from the Atlantic Ocean.

Buenos Aires handles the bulk of Argentina's foreign commerce and is one of the largest ports of the world, the harbor having been improved at a cost of about 50 million dollars. Near the wharves is the central fruit market, one of the largest warehouses in the world. The manufacturing industries produce mainly for home consumption.

The oldest part of Buenos Aires has narrow streets. The city is divided from east to west by the magnificent Avenida de Mayo, which is 100 feet wide and connects two beautiful squares. At the eastern end lies the Plaza de Mayo, having an area of more than four acres and fronted by several imposing buildings, including the executive palace and the cathedral. At the western end, the view terminates in the House of Congress, erected at a cost of $6 million. The office of the newspaper *La Prensa* is one of the most handsome buildings of the city.

Buenos Aires has a system of more than 100 parks which cover a total area of over 3000 acres. Numerous monuments have been erected in the city, including a statue of George Washington set up in Palmero park by American residents of the city. The chief educational institution is the University of Buenos Aires.

Buenos Aires was founded by Pedro de Mendoza in 1535. It was destroyed by the Indians and was re-established in 1580 by Juan de Garay, the governor of Paraguay. The city has grown very rapidly in the past half century. Population, 2,966,816.

Callao (*kăl-yä'ô*). The principal seaport of Peru, situated on an island-sheltered bay near the center of the country's Pacific coast line. The city is connected by steam and electric railroads with Lima, distant seven miles inland. The chief exports are sugar, cotton, cocaine, minerals, and wool. In 1746 the former city of Callao was submerged with all its inhabitants, and on calm days the ruins are still distinguishable under water. Population, 335,000.

Cape Horn. The most southerly point of South America. The name is applied to a small, rocky island and to the most southerly point of the island, a headland having a height of 600 feet. The cape was discovered by the Dutch navigator, Schouten, who named it after Hoorn, his native town in the Netherlands.

Caracas (*kä-rä'käs*). The capital and largest city of Venezuela, occupying a mountainous site 7 miles from La Guaira, a port near the center of the country's northern coast. The city is an important exporting center for cocoa, coffee, tobacco, and other products of the country. Its principal square contains a large statue of Bolivar. The capitol building covers an area of two acres. The city has all modern improvements. An earthquake in 1812 killed more than 12,000 inhabitants. Population, 1,764,274.

Cayenne (*kā-ĕn'*; *kĭ-ĕn'*). A fortified seaport, the capital of the colony of French Guiana. The town is built on a low island between the Cayenne River and the Mahury River. The harbor is insecure and shallow. Sugar, gold, hides, woods, spices, and cacao are the principal exports. Thirty miles northwest is the Isle du Diable, "Devil's island," where Captain Dreyfus was imprisoned from 1894 to 1899. Population, 24,000.

Christ of the Andes. A bronze statue of Christ, by Mateo Alonzo, on the border of Chile and Argentina erected to commemorate the peaceful settlement in 1902 of a boundary dispute between the two countries. The statue, more than twice life-size, stands on a pedestal roughhewn from the natural rock near the summit of Uspallata Pass in the Andes at an altitude of 12,796 feet. It was cast from bronze obtained by melting cannon.

Cordoba (*kôr'dô-bä*). A commercial city of central Argentina, situated on the Rio Primero, about 400 miles northwest of Buenos Aires. Live stock, wool, and hides are shipped from this city. Cordoba has a cathedral, a massive Jesuit Church, a National Observatory, two national colleges, and a university, the last founded in 1613. The city dates back to the year 1573. It was formerly the head of the Jesuit missions in South America. Population, 589,153.

Easter Island. An island possession of Chile, lying about 2000 miles to the west in the Pacific Ocean. It contains many colossal stone images, which, according to archaeological evidence, were carved during several centuries after 1100 A.D. Masonry remains go back to about 300 A.D. When Easter Island was discovered by the Dutch captain Roggeveen on Easter Sunday, 1722, it had a population of about 4000, probably of Polynesian origin. Present inhabitants number about 1135. Its area is 45 square miles.

Falkland Islands. A group of about 100 small islands, forming a British crown colony situated in the south Atlantic Ocean, about 300 miles east of the Strait of Magellan. Only two of the islands are inhabited—East Falkland, with an area of 2610 square miles, and West Falkland, having 2090 square miles of surface.

The surface of the larger islands is treeless. Sheep farming was formerly the chief industry, but in recent years whaling has become more important. The climate is equable but cool and damp. South Georgia, the South Orkneys, the South Shetlands, the Sandwich group, and Graham's Land, all lying some hundreds of miles to the southeast, are regarded as dependencies of the Falkland Islands. In 1967 the population of the islands was about 2122. The capital is Stanley, East Falkland. During World War I, a British fleet defeated a German fleet near these islands.

Galapagos (*gä-lä'pä-gôs*) **Islands.** A group of small volcanic islands, sometimes called the Colon Archipelago, lying about 600 miles west of the coast of Ecuador. They have an estimated area of 2868 square miles and a population of about 2412. Politically, they are a dependency of Ecuador. The United States has a naval base there.

The name means turtle islands, and was given because of the prevalence of large turtles described in 1858 by Darwin as capable of carrying several men on their backs. The flora and fauna are distinctive, about one-half of the species of plants being found nowhere else.

Georgetown. The capital and seaport of Guyana, situated near the center of the nation's coast line. The city lies at the mouth of the Demarara river, which can be entered, however, by boats of light draft only. The chief exports are sugar, rice, coconuts, bauxite, gold, and diamonds. The streets cross each other at right angles. Some are 100 feet wide and have, in the center canals leading to the roadways. Most of the better residences are surrounded by private groves of palms and other forest trees. Population, 167,000.

Guayaquil (*gwî'ä-kēl'*). The largest city and chief port of Ecuador, situated on the Guayas River about 30 miles from its mouth in the Gulf of Guayaquil. The principal export is cocoa. The climate is hot and unhealthful. Manufactures, including lumber, machine shop products, and artificial ice, are mainly for local consumption. Population, 814,000.

Juan Fernandez Islands. A group of islands belonging to Chile in the Pacific Ocean, lying 400 miles west of Valparaiso. Alexander Selkirk lived here in solitude for four years. This fact is said to have suggested to Defoe the theme of *Robinson Crusoe*.

La Paz (*lä päs'*). The largest city of Bolivia and the seat of Congress, situated in the west central part of the country about 40 miles southeast of Lake Titicaca. The city has an elevation of 12,470 feet and is flanked by ranges of the Andes mountains. It is connected with the sea by two railroads, terminating at ports in Chile. The streets are narrow and irregular. There are, however, fine public promenades, a university, and a museum containing a valuable collection of Inca antiquities. Population, 697,000.

Lima (*lē'mä*). The capital of Peru. It is situated in the west central part of the country on the Rimac River seven miles from Callao, its port, with which it is connected by two railroads, one on each side of the river. Lima is the western terminus of a transcontinental railroad which, at one point, is 15,000 feet above the sea. Earthquakes have destroyed large parts of the city a number of times.

There are several beautiful squares and promenades lined with trees and flowering plants and ornamented with statues and fountains. The University of San Marcos, founded here in 1551, is the oldest university in the western hemisphere. Of the numerous churches, the largest and finest one is the cathedral. It contains the tomb of Pizarro, the founder of the city. The manufactures include textiles, leather, furniture, cement, chemicals, and rubber, aluminum, tobacco, and petroleum products.

During the war between Chile and Peru, the Chileans held Lima from 1881 to 1883 and in that time destroyed the national library and many monuments, statues, and other works of art. This city was the home of Saint Rose of Lima, the first native inhabitant of the Americas to be canonized. Population, 3,318,000.

Manaus (*mä-nä'ŭs*). A city of Brazil on the Rio Negro, 12 miles above its junction with the Amazon and about 1000 miles from the Atlantic. Manaus is the trading metropolis of the upper Amazon valley, upon which it draws for such articles of export as rubber, brazil nuts, and dyewoods. Manaus became the capital of the city of Amazonas in 1852. Population, 312,000.

Montevideo (*mŏn'tê-vĭd'ê-ō*). The capital and chief city of Uruguay, situated on a chain of hills overlooking a harbor on the north side of the Rio de la Plata.

The principal streets are wide and straight, and the city bears, in general, a European appearance, having all the modern municipal improvements and many fine residences. The Cagancha Plaza and the Solis Theater are among its more notable features. An equable climate makes possible an extensive cultivation of roses.

The city is cosmopolitan and handles all the foreign trade of the country. The chief industries are those connected with stock raising—the drying and packing of meats, and creamery and tannery operations. Montevideo is the seat of a military college and of the University of Uruguay. The name is a corruption of *montem video*, "I see the mountain," said in allusion to the Cerro, a picturesque mountain on the opposite side of the city's harbor. Population, 1,230,000.

Paramaribo (*păr'ä-măr'ĭ-bō*). The capital of Surinam, situated at the head of navigation on the Surinam River 16 miles from its mouth in the Atlantic Ocean. The climate is very hot, the mean yearly temperature being over 80° F. The town has regularly laid out streets, shaded by tamarind and orange trees and bordered by well built houses. A commodious harbor lined with wharves enables the handling of international commerce, most of which is with the Netherlands, Great Britain, and the United States. The chief exports are rice, sugar, rum, coffee, bananas, and gold. Population, about 102,000.

Patagonia. A name formerly applied to the portion of South America stretching from the Strait of Magellan about 1200 miles north to the latitude of the Rio Negro. It was claimed both by Argentina and by Chile, and was divided between them in 1881 by a line of demarcation following the ridge of the Andes mountains. From that time the name has been restricted to southern Argentina, the part of the disputed territory sloping in terraces eastward from the mountains to the Atlantic Ocean.

Port of Spain. The capital of Trinidad and Tobago, situated in the northwest extremity of Trinidad. It has a fine harbor, and a large part of the products of the Orinoco basin are shipped from the port. The streets are wide and there are a number of fine residences and public buildings; also a university and a botanical garden. Population, 62,680.

Punta Arenas (*poon'tä ä-rä'näs*). The most southerly city in the world, a port in southern Chile on the Strait of Magellan. Surrounded by plains affording excellent grazing, it was the point where sheep-raising was first introduced into South America from the Falkland Islands and it is still an important center of sheep raising. It serves also as a fueling harbor for ships. Population, 67,600.

Quito (*kē'tō*). The capital of Ecuador, situated in a mountainous plateau somewhat north of the country's geographical center and about 114 miles from the Pacific Ocean. The city is less than ten miles south of the equator, but its climate is rendered equable by its elevation of 9000 feet. It is built at the foot of a volcano and is traversed by two deep ravines.

Quito was very difficult of access until the completion in 1903 of a railroad connecting the city with tidewater near Guayaquil. There are a university, an astronomical observatory, and a botanical garden which has the distinction of being the highest in the world. Quito was the central town of an ancient Indian nation until it was taken by the Incas in 1470. It was captured from the Incas by the Spaniards in 1534. Population, 557,000.

Recife (*rä-sē'fĕ*) (**Pernambuco**). A commercial city and port of Brazil situated on the Atlantic Coast at the extreme eastern point of the continent. The harbor is protected from the sea by a long reef and by a breakwater constructed at a cost of about 28 million dollars. Its distance from Lisbon is less than that between New York and Lisbon. The chief exports are sugar and cotton. The imports are mainly foodstuffs, textiles, and iron products.

The city consists of three parts, one built on a peninsula, one on an island, and a third, a pleasant residential section on the continent. Recife is therefore often called the Venice of South America. The climate is tropical.

The city has many fine churches and a celebrated law school. The name Recife means "reef." The first settlement on the site was made in 1535 by Pereira, a Portuguese adventurer. Population, 1,056,000.

Rio de Janeiro (*rē'ō dā zhä-nā'rō*). The second largest city of Brazil, situated on a natural harbor near the center of the country's southeastern coast. Spurs from nearby mountains penetrate into the heart of the city, which spreads into the valleys and up the hillsides. Sugarloaf peak rises abruptly above the city.

The interests of Rio de Janeiro are chiefly commercial. The leading export is coffee and the principal imports include cereals, coal, textiles, and machinery. Manufactures are confined mainly to textiles and flour.

Many of the streets in the older section of Rio de Janeiro are too narrow for wheeled vehicles. The newer portions, however, have wide, well paved avenues adorned with tall palm trees. Avenida Beira-Mar, a beautiful 20-mile boulevard, skirts the edge of the harbor. On the Avenida Presidente Wilson stands a colossal bronze figure representing Amicitia, "friendship," which was presented by the government of the United States. At the base of the pedestal are four statues representing Washington, Lincoln, Bonifacio, and Branco. On Corcovado Mountain, above the city, stands a statue of Christ, 130 feet in height.

There are several fine parks and squares. The Praça 15 de Novembro is surrounded by imposing buildings, among which are the Senate house and the city hall. In the neighborhood is the former Imperial Palace, occupied from 1808 to 1821 by the court of Portugal and now used as a national museum. Other institutions of education and research include the national library, the botanical garden, the historical and geographic institute, the observatory, and the University of Rio de Janeiro. The city was founded by Portuguese colonists in 1567 and from 1762 to 1960 it was the capital of Brazil. Population, 4,252,000.

Rosario (*rô-sä'rê-ō*). A commercial city of Argentina, situated on the left bank of the Parana River, about 230 miles above Buenos Aires. Rosario is the trade center for northern Argentina, being served by six railroads which connect at the city with ocean steamers. The chief exports are wheat and animal products, and the imports consist mainly of manufactured goods, mostly textiles. The city has modern improvements and attractive residential districts. Population, 807,000.

Santiago (*sän'tê-ä'gō*). The capital and largest city of Chile, situated near the center of the country about 50 miles from the Pacific Coast. The city lies at the northern edge of a rich agricultural district for which it is a distributing point and market.

Santiago's location is highly picturesque by reason of the surrounding mountains. A rock within the city, over 200 feet in height, once used as a citadel and a refuge from attacking Indians, is now a park, irrigated and supporting a luxuriant growth of vegetation. The city is traversed by a wide, ornate boulevard, the Avenida de las Delicias, which has a width of more than 300 feet.

Among the city's more impressive buildings are the exposition palace, the hall of Congress, the municipal theater, the cathedral, and the university building. At the head of the institutions of education and research stand the University of Chile and the agricultural school farm, an institution which embraces a zoological garden, a museum of natural history, and various schools for teaching different branches of rural industry. The city was founded in 1541 by Pedro de Valdivia. Population, 3,700,000.

Santos (*sän'tōōsh*). A large seaport of Brazil, situated on Santos Bay on the Atlantic Coast about 200 miles southwest of Rio de Janeiro. Santos is the world's largest coffee shipping port, being the outlet for the coffee collected at Sao Paulo. Population, 300,000.

Sao Paulo (*sounm pou'lōō*). The capital of the state of Sao Paulo and largest city in Brazil, situated in the southeastern part of the state 25 miles inland from Santos, its port on the Atlantic Ocean. The city is the headquarters of the country's vast coffee industry. The coffee is transported from the plantations by a network of railroads leading to Sao Paulo, whence it is sent on by rail to Santos.

Among the more imposing buildings are the cathedral, the government building, and the Ypiranga palace, erected to commemorate Brazil's declaration of independence. The city has a modern appearance, having grown very rapidly in the decades following 1900, when numerous immigrants were attracted to it. Population, 5,900,000.

Sucre (*sōō'krä*). The statutory capital of Bolivia and the seat of the supreme court, picturesquely situated on a wide plateau about 150 miles south of the country's geographical center. The city is a trade center for a rich agricultural and mining region and has rail connection with La Paz, and with Mollendo and Antofagasta on the Pacific Coast. Sucre is the seat of an archbishop and has a normal school and an ancient university. Since 1898 Congress has met at La Paz. The city is 9328 feet above the level of the sea. Population, 88,000.

Trinidad and Tobago. Two islands constituting a member state of the British Commonwealth of Nations. Trinidad is about ten miles off the northeast coast of Venezuela near the delta of the Orinoco River, and the small island of Tobago is 22 miles northwest of Trinidad.

Trinidad has an area of 1864 square miles; that of Tobago is 116 square miles. The interior of Trinidad is a series of rolling, fertile, well watered plains, partly covered by forests of palms, breadfruits, tamarinds, and bamboo trees. Low mountain ranges parallel the north and the south coast. Tobago is a single mountain mass rising to a height of 1800 feet and covered with dense forest.

The most valuable products include petroleum, asphalt, sugar, cocoa, coconuts, and lumber. The asphalt comes mainly from a 114-acre reservoir known as Pitch Lake. The trade is principally with Great Britain and the United States.

Negroes and people of East Indian origin make up the majority of the population, which in 1973 was 1,061,000. Columbus discovered Trinidad in 1496 and Tobago in 1498. They passed from Spanish into British possession early in the 19th century, were colonies, later consolidated, and, in 1962, became an independent member of the British Commonwealth.

Valparaiso (*väl'pä-rī'sō*). The chief seaport of Chile, situated on a bay at the approximate center of Chile's coast line. The port is strongly fortified. The chief imports are textiles and other manufactured goods. The leading articles of export include agricultural products and Chile saltpeter. Its trade increased considerably as a result of the opening of the Panama Canal.

The city was one of the first in South America to introduce the use of street cars, of gas, and of aqueducts for the water supply. There are a number of wide streets and a fine square adorned with many statues. Population, 296,000.

EUROPE

THE continent consisting of the northwestern portion of the vast land surface in the eastern hemisphere. Europe may be regarded as a western peninsula of Asia, from which it is divided, more or less arbitrarily, by the Ural mountains, the Caspian Sea, the Caucasus mountains, the Black Sea, the Bosporus strait, the Sea of Marmora, the Dardanelles strait, and the Ægean Sea. To the south of Europe lies the Mediterranean Sea, which separates the continent from Africa. This inland sea communicates with the Atlantic Ocean by the Strait of Gibraltar, where Europe's most southern point, Cape Tarifa, is no more than nine miles from Africa's northern extremity. The continent is bounded by the Atlantic Ocean on the west and by the Arctic Ocean on the north. The continental part of Europe, as distinct from the islands, is often referred to as "the continent" by people in the British Isles and in America.

Size. With the exception of Australia, Europe is the smallest of the continents, covering about 3,900,000 square miles, or very little more than the area of the United States and Alaska. It includes, with all its outlying islands, little more than 7 per cent of the total land surface of the globe. Its greatest length from east to west is 3300 miles, and its maximum extent north and south is about 2400 miles.

Outline and Islands. Europe has a contour diversified by so many irregularities, great and small, that the coast line, winding about all the indentations of the mainland and of the chief islands, has a length of nearly 48,000 miles. The islands and peninsulas, occupying about one-third of the total area of the continent, partially enclose a number of large gulfs and inland seas. Thus, while the small inlets provide numerous harbors, the inland seas make all parts of the continent comparatively easy of access from the sea.

In the extreme northeast, the islands of Nova Zembla separate the Kara Sea from Barents Sea, the latter being shut off from the Arctic Ocean by the islands of Spitsbergen. From the southwest corner of Barents Sea, a strait, called the Gorlo, leads into the White Sea, a three-pronged gulf sheltered behind the Kola peninsula. The Kola peninsula is, itself, part of the huge Scandinavian peninsula, which encloses the Baltic Sea and its three major inlets, the Gulf of Bothnia, the Gulf of Finland, and the Gulf of Riga. The Scandinavian peninsula trends in a general southwestern direction and terminates in two diverging extensions, which open like jaws above the peninsula of Jutland and are separated from it by two straits, the Kattegat and the Skagerrack. The Jutland peninsula and part of the Scandinavian peninsula form the eastern shore of the North Sea, which, stretching westward to the British Isles, has a southwestern outlet through the English channel to the Atlantic Ocean. The British Isles consist of two principal islands, Great Britain and Ireland, separated by the Irish Sea. Dunmore Head on the southwestern coast of Ireland is the most westerly point of Europe. The Bay of Biscay is the only large western inlet.

The southern coast has three major peninsulas—the Iberian peninsula, Italy, and the Balkan peninsula. Between the Iberian peninsula and Italy, in the Mediterranean Sea, lie the Balearic islands, and the three islands—Corsica, Sardinia, and Sicily—which, with Italy, enclose the Tyrrhenian Sea. The Gulf of Taranto stretches inland between the toe and the heel of the bootlike peninsula of Italy, and the whole peninsula is separated by the Adriatic Sea from the Balkan peninsula, which, on its eastern side, is washed by the Ægean Sea, the Black Sea, and the smaller bodies of water connecting the two. The Ægean Sea is dotted with small islands, most of which cluster in archipelagoes known as the Cyclades and the Sporades.

At a distance from the continent, about 700 miles northwest of the Scandinavian peninsula, lies the large mountainous island of Iceland.

Surface. The average elevation of Europe is less than that of any other continent. The highest point is Mount Elbrus, in the Caucasus range, the peak of which reaches a height of 18,481 feet. Marked changes in land level at the coast have been observed within historical times. The land about the Gulf of Bothnia has risen, and the southern shore of the North Sea has subsided. On the eastern side of the Adriatic Sea near modern Rovigno, the island town of Cissa, which was flourishing in the 7th century, is now 85 feet below the sea.

Apart from the Ural and the Caucasus range, there are two chief systems of mountains in Europe—the Kiolen range, forming a longitudinal ridge in the Scandinavian peninsula, and an irregular group of ranges trending in a general east and west direction across southern Europe. This latter group consists of the Pyrenees range, which cuts across the neck of the peninsula of Spain; the Alps, forming a central highland north of Italy; the Apennines, extending to the southern extremity of Italy and finding a continuation in the mountainous regions of Sicily; the Carpathian mountains, extending northeast of the Alps for some distance and then turning southeast toward the Black Sea; the Pindus range, which forms the backbone of Greece; and the Balkan mountains passing eastward north of the Ægean Sea. Other mountainous regions are Iceland, Scotland, and Spain.

Volcanic activity is confined to Iceland and to the Mediterranean region and is most marked in southern Italy, Sicily, and the adjacent islands. Here are situated Mount Stromboli, Mount Etna, and Mount Vesuvius, the last being notable for the eruption which, in 79 A. D., buried the cities of Herculaneum and Pompeii. No part of the continent, however, is free of earthquakes except the great plains of Russia.

A large part of Europe's area consists of fertile plains. Western and northern France, northern Germany, and almost the whole of European Russia constitute what is sometimes called the Great Lowland Plain. Other plains are the Central Plain, occupying Ireland and England; the Plain of Lombardy, south of the Alps; the Hungarian Plain, hemmed in by the Carpathian mountains and by the highland extending from the Alps southeastward into Greece; and the Wallachian Plain, between the southern Carpathians and the Black Sea.

Drainage. Of the many rivers of Europe, only one, the Volga, is more than 2000 miles in length, and, of the others, only the Danube, the Dnieper, and the Don exceed a length of 1000 miles. With few exceptions, however, the rivers admit of navigation and contribute toward making the interior of the continent readily accessible from the coasts.

The chief rivers draining northward, named in order from east to west, are the Pechora, the Dvina, the Duna, the Vistula, the Oder, the Elbe, the Rhine, and the Seine. The Loire and the Gironde River system flow westward into the Bay of Biscay. The plateau of Spain is drained toward the Atlantic Ocean by the Douro, the Tagus, the Guadiana, and the Guadalquivir and, toward the Mediterranean Sea, by the Jucar and the Ebro river. Of the rivers of southern drainage, the Rhone flows into the Golfe du Lion, an inlet of the Mediterranean Sea; the Po, into the Adriatic Sea; the Danube, the Dniester, and the Dnieper, into the Black Sea; the Don, into the Sea of Azof, a northern inlet of the Black Sea; and the Volga, into the Caspian Sea.

Fresh-water lakes are particularly numerous in three regions—the highlands of the Alps, the British Isles, and the territory east and northwest of the Baltic Sea. The last-mentioned region contains by far the most lakes, including the two largest of the continent—Ladoga and Onega.

169

Climate. Europe lies almost entirely in the temperate zone, a small portion only projecting into the arctic region. The northern part, however, has a warmer climate than other regions of the same latitude on account of warm ocean currents which wash its shores. The southern limit of drift ice from the polar regions nowhere approaches within 50 miles of the Scandinavian peninsula. The northern interior plains, however, suffer much greater extremes of temperature than those occurring near the coast. The southern part of Europe has a subtropical climate.

Europe is the only continent which has no desert region. Warm, moisture-laden winds blow prevailingly from the southwest. In the absence of a mountain wall running north and south, these winds carry their moisture far inland, instead of being intercepted and losing it by precipitation near the coast.

Plant and Animal Life. There are three chief plant regions in Europe—the arctic, possessing scanty vegetation; the intermediate, comprising forest areas,—largely coniferous,—and level steppes which resemble the North American plains; and, lastly, the Mediterranean region in the south. The last is noted for the great variety and economic importance of its flora.

Next to Asia, Europe has contributed to the human race more cultivated plants than any other continent. The more important include, among the grains, oats and rye; among the vegetables, asparagus, beet, cabbage, carrot, endive, horseradish, lettuce, pea, and turnip; the forage plants, clover and timothy; and such fruits as the currant, gooseberry, and fig.

The fauna likewise is rich. It has a general similarity to that of North America. The characteristic mammals include the bear, lynx, badger, wolf, fox, otter, marten, ermine, polecat, squirrel, hedgehog, and rabbit. The desman and chamois are peculiar to the continent. In the south, the fallow deer, ibex, alpine marmot, and civet are found. Of the domesticated animals, Europe is the original home of the goose, pigeon, rabbit, reindeer, and swan.

Minerals. The geology of Europe reveals an immense wealth of mineral resources. Coal and iron are produced in the greatest aggregate value. The chief coal fields are those in Great Britain, in Upper Silesia, in the Ruhr district in Germany, in northeastern France, and in Russia. The Lorraine district in France, the Saar valley in Germany, and northern and central England are the most important iron producing regions. Spain and Upper Silesia produce the world's chief supply of zinc, as Russia does of platinum. Spain and Italy supply a large part of the world's market for quicksilver. Gold and asbestos are obtained from the Ural Mountain region in large quantities. Other mineral products of the continent include salt, sulphur, silver, lead, aluminum, tin, copper, and marble.

Industry. The industrial output of Europe exceeds that of any other continent. Industrial development, however, is concentrated largely in a few regions, chiefly those where coal and iron are found in close proximity. Among the principal industries are those making steel, fertilizers and other chemicals, glass, pottery, perfumes, and scientific instruments. There are also many highly specialized products exported, such as art objects, specially designed clothing, and time pieces.

Inhabitants. Human habitation in Europe is very ancient. In various districts, remains of prehistoric men have been found, the earliest going back probably 250,000 years to the second interglacial period. The population of Europe, now numbers over 500 million. With few exceptions, the languages of Europe belong to one family, called by philologists Indo-European. Peoples of Asia speaking related languages are believed to have migrated from Europe to Asia. Counter migrations from Asia brought some Oriental types into Europe, such as the Magyars and Huns.

POLITICAL DIVISIONS

Europe has more old established countries than any other continent. The countries are: Albania, Andorra, Austria, Belgium, Bulgaria, Denmark, Finland, France, Germany, Great Britain and Northern Ireland, Greece, Hungary, Iceland, Eire, Italy, Liechtenstein, Luxembourg, Monaco, the Netherlands, Norway, Poland, Portugal, Rumania, Russia, San Marino, Spain, Sweden, Switzerland, Vatican City, and Yugoslavia.

Of these divisions, Eire is a part of the island of Ireland, and its geography, along with that of Northern Ireland, is treated under the head of Ireland. Vatican City is 109 acres of papal territory within the city of Rome. Andorra is a mountainous, pastoral country between France and Spain; Luxembourg is surrounded by France, Germany, and Belgium; and Liechtenstein is a small principality hemmed in by Austria and Switzerland. These countries, as well as San Marino, an ancient state surrounded by Italian territory in the northeastern part of the peninsula, will be found described from a geographical point of view in the departments of history and government.

In addition to the independent states, there is a territory north of the Sea of Marmora forming part of Turkey. Gibraltar, a bold promontory at the south of the Iberian peninsula is a dependency of Great Britain.

Albania. A mountainous republic on the west of the Balkan peninsula with a coast line on the Adriatic Sea. It has an area of 10,629 square miles and a population, 1974 estimate, of 2,400,000. The people support themselves mainly through agriculture devoted chiefly to livestock. There are vast tracts of undeveloped forests and considerable unexploited mineral wealth, consisting largely of copper, salt, coal, and oil.

Tirana is the capital and largest city. Durrës, the chief port is equipped with modern facilities.

Austria. An inland republic of central Europe, bounded on the north by Germany and Czechoslovakia and on the remaining sides by Hungary, Yugoslavia, Italy, and Switzerland. The western part, known as the Tyrol, is a mountainous region, widely celebrated for its bold, picturesque scenery. In the north, Austria is traversed by the Danube River, which provides a navigable waterway several hundred miles in length.

On an area of 32,366 square miles, Austria supports a population numbering, in 1971, 7,456,403. Agricultural products comprise chiefly wheat, rye, barley, oats, potatoes, and sugar beets. Dairying is a thriving industry. Austria is one of the world's chief sources of graphite. Petroleum also is produced. Manufactures include lumber, textiles, glass, sugar, paper, furniture, pianos, and chemicals. Most of the industry is nationalized. Tourism is a leading source of income. German is the language of Austria.

Most of the inhabitants are Roman Catholic. There is a system of compulsory elementary education. The largest of the three state universities is situated in the capital, Vienna, a city which has for centuries been a center of learning and of art.

Belgium. A small kingdom of Europe with a coast line on the North Sea. The country is bounded by France, Luxembourg, Germany, and the Netherlands. Its area is 11,750 square miles, its latest population figure 9,651,000.

Nearly all of the surface of Belgium is arable and is intensively cultivated. The country is also industrially one of the most highly developed in the world, being favored in this respect by the occurrence of coal and of iron deposits in close proximity to each other. The recovery of Belgium since its liberation in 1944 is extraordinary. Increases in the output of grains, potatoes, beet sugar, milk, meat, coal, chemicals, machinery, glass, paper, beer, textiles, and zinc are outstanding. Diamond cutting is an important industry.

Two languages are spoken in Belgium—French in the south by the Walloons, a people of Celtic origin, and Flemish in the north by the Flemings, who are of the Teutonic race. The majority of the inhabitants professing a religion are Roman Catholics. Of the country's four universities, Louvain is the most celebrated. The capital and largest city is Brussels. Other cities of note are Antwerp, Ghent, Liège, and Ostend.

Bulgaria. A mountainous republic of southeastern Europe, with an eastern coast line on the Black Sea. Bulgaria lies between Rumania on the north and Greece on the south and stretches westward to the borders of Yugoslavia. Its area is 43,000 square miles.

The Balkan mountains divide southern Bulgaria from the northern zone, in which a cool climate and a fertile soil foster agriculture of a temperate zone type. The perfume attar of roses is a distinctively Bulgarian product. Apart from it the chief products are grains, tobacco, livestock, cotton, hemp, flax, silk, beans, sugar beets, fruits, rice, and various flowers. The manufacturing of textiles is the chief industry. The Danube River, which constitutes the northern border of Bulgaria, provides, with its affluents, important water highways for trade.

Agriculture of various kinds engages the activities of about one-fifth of Bulgaria's population, which the latest census listed as 8,706,000. The prevailing religion is Greek Catholicism. Elementary instruction is free and obligatory. Sofia is the capital and largest city of the country.

Czechoslovakia (*chĕk′ô-slô-vä′kĭ-à*). An inland republic of central Europe, closely allied with the Soviet Union. The country is narrow and elongated, lying in a general east and west direction. It is bordered by Poland, Germany, Austria, Hungary, and Russia. The area, 49,359 square miles, is about the size of the state of New York. The population, in 1974, was estimated to be 14,738,377. Approximately three-fourths of the people are Czechs and Slovaks.

About one-third of its area is covered with valuable forests and by 1946 the pulp and paper industry had reached 80 per cent of prewar output. The soil is fertile and supports extensive and intensive agriculture; the chief crops are potatoes, sugar beets, wheat, barley, rye, oats, hops, tobacco, and various fruits and vegetables. The coal deposits are extensive and provide a surplus for export. Gold, silver, copper, lead, and rock salt are also found. The textile, porcelain, glass, furniture, sugar, chemical, and metal factories place Czechoslovakia among the more important manufacturing countries of Europe. By decrees of October 1945 all national resources, public utilities, and other important branches of industry and trade were nationalized. Transportation is provided by the Elbe and Danube rivers, and by more than 13,241 km. of railway and about 73,538 km. of highway.

Approximately seventy-five per cent of the inhabitants are Roman Catholics in spite of the fact that the provinces of Bohemia and Moravia constituted one of the earliest centers of Protestantism. The Moravian Church in America was founded by emigrants from this region. In 1975, universities had a total attendance of 144,325. The capital and largest city is Prague, with a population in 1975 of 1,161,000.

Denmark. A small kingdom of northern Europe, consisting of the greater part of the Jutland peninsula and of several adjacent islands, the largest of which are Zealand and Funen. The Faroe Islands, lying nearly midway between Scotland and Iceland, are administratively a part of Denmark. The total area of the country is 16,619 square miles. Greenland is an integral part of Denmark.

The surface of continental Denmark is a low rolling plain nowhere exceeding 570 feet in altitude. Sand dunes fringe much of the coast line, often extending five or six miles inland. Considerable areas of peat bog provide fuel for the inhabitants. Forests, mainly of beech trees, cover about 750 square miles. Apart from lumbering, the principal industries are agriculture, dairying, and fishing. The value of the annual catch of fish is considerable. The farm produce is marketed largely by co-operative societies. Copenhagen porcelain is a distinctive product of the country's manufacturing industry.

The population of Denmark is 5,054,410, most of whom are Lutheran Protestants in religion. Illiteracy is virtually nonexistent, elementary education having been obligatory since 1814. The University of Copenhagen stands at the head of the educational system, which is of the most enlightened type and is well adapted to the interests of the people. The capital, Copenhagen, is situated on the island of Zealand. With a population of 1,380,204, it contains nearly one-fifth of the inhabitants of the country.

A territory known as Northern Schleswig was added to Denmark in 1920 as a result of the Treaty of Versailles. This territory had been wrested from the Danes by Germany in 1864.

Finland. One of the most northern countries of Europe, lying between the Gulf of Finland and the Gulf of Bothnia and extending northward almost entirely across the neck of the Scandinavian peninsula. The Aland islands off the southern coast are governed as part of Finland. About one-fourth of the country's 130,127 square miles of surface is within the Arctic circle. In the north, mountains rise to a height of 4000 feet, but the remainder of the country is, for the most part, a plateau having an average elevation of about 500 feet. The numerous lakes of glacial formation, which occupy 11 per cent of the area of the country, have won for Finland the name of "the land of the thousand lakes."

Although agriculture employs more workers, forest products, chiefly timber, pulp, and paper, account for a large part of the country's export trade. Nearly two-thirds of the country is covered with pine forests.

The population of Finland in 1974 was 4,691,556. Lutheran Protestantism is the prevailing religion. The country has a well developed system of elementary, secondary, technical, and higher education. The capital and largest city is Helsingfors (Helsinki), a city of 502,383 inhabitants, situated in the southern extremity of the country. Other important towns are Turku (Abo) and Tampere (Tammerfors).

The inhabitants of Finland are mostly of the Finnic race, which is believed to have occupied formerly the whole of northern Asia and northeastern Europe.

France. A republic of western Europe, bounded on the north by the English channel and on the west by the Bay of Biscay. On the south, France is separated from Spain by the Pyrenees mountains and has a southern coast line on the Mediterranean Sea. On the east and northeast, France adjoins Italy, Switzerland, Germany, Luxembourg, and

Belgium. The island of Corsica in the Mediterranean Sea is politically a part of France. The coast line of the country is nearly 2000 miles in length, but, being either sandy or high and rocky, it affords few good harbors. The total area of the republic is 212,919 square miles.

Since World War II France has been successful in securing certain boundary changes. On the Italian border they acquired the pass and enclave of Tenda and Briga in 1947. France also secured minor border rectifications in the areas of Little St. Bernard Pass, Mt. Cenis Pass, and Mt. Thabor and Chaberton. Other eastern continental boundaries reflect the great zone of transition between western and central Europe. After both wars of this century the French were eager to have the Saar with its coal mines under their political, or at least economic, control. In the Rhineland the French have wanted to see an independent unit separate from Germany, and in the industrial Ruhr they have favored international control.

The most elevated part of France is in the southeast, where the Jura mountains and the Alps divide the country from Switzerland and Italy. Mont Blanc, an Alpine mountain within the French border, is the second highest peak in Europe, having an altitude of 15,781 feet. The lower, forest-clad Vosges ridge farther north separates Alsace from the rest of France. These mountain groups form the eastern side of the Rhone-Saone River valley, which is flanked on the west by the Cevennes mountains. The Rhone, rising in Switzerland and being augmented by the Saone river, flows southward into the Mediterranean Sea. The Saone River is connected by a canal with the upper reaches of the Seine river, which, with its tributaries,—the Marne and the Oise,—drains northward into the English channel. The other chief rivers of France flow westward and empty into the Bay of Biscay. They are the Loire, to the north, and, farther south, the Garonne and the Dordogne, which mingle their waters in the broad estuary called the Gironde River.

The principal rivers are all more or less navigable and afford shelter for such seaports as Havre and Rouen on the Seine, Saint Nazaire and Nantes on the Loire, and Bordeaux on the Garonne. The rivers as highways of inland commerce are supplemented by numerous canals.

France has considerable deposits of coal centering around Valenciennes near the northeastern border. The mines of this region were wrecked by the Germans during World War I, and from 1920 to 1935 the French operated the German coal mines in the Saar basin. France controls more iron than does any other European country, the mines being located in Lorraine, from which about one-tenth of the world's supply of iron ore is obtained. Other minerals produced in important quantities include gold, antimony, salt, potash, manganese, and bauxite, the ore of aluminum.

Of the surface of France, about one-fifth is forested, and approximately three-quarters is devoted to agriculture and grazing. Wheat, oats, potatoes, rye, barley, corn, and sugar beets are the leading crops. In the south, the climate is subtropical and fosters the cultivation of olives, peaches, apricots, oranges, mandarins, lemons, walnuts, and almonds. Apples, pears, cherries, plums, and berries are also produced in important quantities. The abundance of grapes grown in France enables her to rank as the leading wine producing country of the world. The cultivation of silkworms is an important industry in the south.

The fisheries of France are among the more important in the world. Large fleets are sent each year to catch cod about Newfoundland and about Saint Pierre and Miquelon, which lie off the south shore of Newfoundland. These two small islands constitute the sole remaining part of France's former empire in North America. Sardines are caught on France's northwestern coast and anchovies and tunny fish are obtained from the Mediterranean Sea.

The textile industries of France are famous the world over. The city of Lyon is the greatest silk center in Europe. Rayon also is manufactured there in large quantities. Rouen, on the Seine River, is noted for its cotton cloth made mainly from cotton grown in the United States. A large wool industry flourishes in the northeast. Paris is the seat of manufacture for the most costly products, including tapestries, shawls, jewelry, watches, and scientific instruments. Other manufactured products include chemicals, iron and steel, automobiles, electrical equipment, fine leather goods, the exquisite porcelains of Sèvres and of Limoges, cut glass, pottery, perfumes, and similar articles requiring skill and taste for their production.

After World War II, the French government stimulated agricultural and industrial production by means of agricultural price supports and tax incentives for industry. Chemical, fertilizer, tractor, shipbuilding, electricity, and automobile industries were greatly expanded. New industries included oil refining and atomic energy. Social welfare measures included old-age pensions, unemployment and medical benefits, and family allowances.

The population of France in 1968 was 49,795,000. The great majority of those professing a religion are Roman Catholics. Illiteracy is almost unknown. At the head of the educational system stand 23 universities, of which the University of Paris is the most notable. Apart from Paris, the capital, the great emporiums of trade include Lyon, Lille, Saint Etienne, Toulouse, Strasbourg, and Reims. The more attractive maritime ports are Marseille, Bordeaux, Le Havre, and Cette.

City	Population	City	Population
Paris	2,590,771	Le Havre	199,509
Marseille	889,029	Lille	190,546
Lyon	527,800	Rennes	180,943
Toulouse	370,796	Toulon	174,746
Nice	322,442	Montpellier	161,910
Bordeaux	266,662	Grenoble	161,616
Nantes	259 208	Brest	154,023
Strasbourg	249,396	Reims	152,967
St. Etienne	213,468	Clermont-Ferrand	148,896

Source: UN *Demographic Yearbook*, 1968.

French Community. Until the beginning of World War II France controlled a colonial empire second only to that of Great Britain. The combined area of French dependencies was more than twenty-one times that of European France. In geographical range, the colonies, mandates, or protectorates administered by France extended from neighboring North Africa to America, to Southeast Asia, to Oceania, and to huge sections south of the Sahara desert, some of them in West Africa along the Atlantic coast, and some in the interior, particularly in Equatorial Africa. Added to these was the large island of Madagascar in the Indian Ocean.

From the war France emerged weakened but determined to retain her empire. However, the tide of the future was against her until she learned from two costly wars how to ride it. The wave of the future was the spirit of racial equality which inspired the peoples of Africa and Asia to throw off colonial status and to seek by their own efforts to obtain the higher standards of living which modern science had made possible.

France initially surrendered control of Morocco and Tunisia, but held tenaciously to Algeria, where a century of colonization and settlement had resulted in a French population of over ten per cent of the total. Algeria was regarded as administratively a part of France. Independence was refused, and for many years the resistance of the rebels tied down a large portion of the French army. When it became apparent to the French government that it could not win the war, negotiations began looking to Algerian independence. Immediately the French settlers and many of the leaders of the Army opposed the French policy, and civil war was averted only by turning control of the government over to Charles de Gaulle and granting him almost dictatorial power for a limited period.

Meanwhile a similar struggle had gone on in French Indo-China, where the forces seeking independence were assisted by the Chinese Communists. The French were defeated and withdrew before the crisis in Algeria had come to a head.

De Gaulle, having subdued the army insurrection, proposed to France and to all French dependencies a new political formula modeled after the British Commonwealth of Nations. As part of the new constitution adopted by popular vote in 1958 by France and most French territories overseas, each of the latter might choose either to retain its status, to become a department of France, or to be an independent member of the French Community.

Most of the territories elected membership in the Community. Guinea alone rejected the constitution and was cut off from France. Algeria was given complete independence in 1962. Much of the French population in Algeria returned to France to live.

The French Community is organized as follows:

Member States—France (including Corsica), Central African Empire, Congo, Gabon, Malagasy, Senegal, Chad.

Overseas Departments—Martinique, Guadeloupe, Reunion, French Guiana.

Overseas French Territories—French Polynesia, New Caledonia, Southern and Antarctic Territories, Wallis and Futuna Islands, Saint-Pierre and Miquelon.

Condominium—New Hebrides.

Independent Countries with Special Agreements—Algeria, Benin, Cameroon, Ivory Coast, Mali, Mauritania, Niger, Togo, Upper Volta.

Germany. A historic and heavily populated commercial and agricultural area in north central Europe. Following the surrender of Nazi Germany in 1945, the country was divided into four zones. The United States occupied the southwest, Great Britain the northwest, France the west, and Russia the east. When the four Allied Powers of World War II were unable to reach a postwar agreement as to the future administration of Germany, the country became permanently split. The three zones occupied by the United States, Britain, and France became the Federal Republic of Germany (West Germany) on May 23, 1949. The Soviet-occupied zone became the German Democratic Republic (East Germany) on October 4, 1949. Former German territories east of the Oder and Reisser rivers—Silesia, East Prussia, and most of Pomerania—were given to Poland by the U.S.S.R. at the close of World War II.

East Germany. The German Democratic Republic covers 41,648 square miles and had a 1975 estimated population of 16,820,249. The country is bordered by the Baltic Sea on the north, on the east by Poland, on the southeast by Czechoslovakia,

and on the southwest and west by the Federal Republic of Germany. The northern part of the land is characterized by lakes and low hills. Most of the country's farming is done on the fertile plain of the central region. The heavily forested middle range mountains in the southern area are one of the most scenic parts of Germany. There are five major rivers in East Germany. They are the Elbe, Oder, Saale, Havel, and Spree.

East Germany is largely dependent on industry although there are few natural resources and a great deal of raw material must be imported. The chief industries are iron and steel products, chemicals, fertilizers, synthetic rubber, drugs, and plastics. The East Germans are large food producers and rank in the top ten nations of the world in the production of rye, barley, and oats. Other major crops include potatoes, sugar beets, and wheat. The major trading partners of East Germany are the U.S.S.R. and Czechoslovakia.

The capital city of the German Democratic Republic is East Berlin, with a 1973 population of 1,088,828. Other major cities with their 1973 populations are: Leipzig (574,432), Dresden (506,067), Karl-Marx-Stadt (302,409), and Magdeburg (274,146).

West Germany. The Federal Republic of Germany is bordered by the North Sea and Denmark on the north, East Germany and Czechoslovakia on the east, Austria and Switzerland on the south, and by France, Luxembourg, Belgium, and the Netherlands on the west.

The country covers an area of 95,959 square miles; its estimated 1975 population was 61,644,600. The land is generally flat in the north and hilly in the central and western regions. The Bavarian Alps and the Black Forest make the southern part of the country a major tourist attraction. The principal rivers of West Germany are the Rhine, Danube, Ems, Weser, and the Elbe.

West Germany is one of the most highly industrialized countries in the world. It is rich in natural resources—including coal, iron ore, lead, and zinc. The chief industries are the manufacture of iron and steel products, chemicals, electricity, machinery, and aluminum products. Advanced farming techniques have made West Germany a leader in food production and its farms produce a high yield of rye, wheat, oats, barley, and potatoes. West Germany also has major forestry and fishing industries. Its main trading partners are France, Belgium, the Netherlands, and the United States.

The historic capital and largest city of Germany is Berlin. Bonn is the seat of the West German government. The leading cities in West Germany, with their estimated 1975 populations are as follows:

City	Population	City	Population
Berlin (West) .	1,984,837	Stuttgart . . .	600,421
Hamburg . . .	1,717,383	Duisburg . . .	591,635
Munich . . .	1,314,865	Bremen	572,969
Cologne . . .	1,013,771	Hanover . . .	552,955
Essen	677,568	Nuremberg . .	499,060
Dusseldorf . .	664,336	Bochum . . .	414,842
Frankfort . . .	636,157	Wuppertal . .	405,369
Dortmund . .	630,609	Gelsenkirchen .	322,584

Gibraltar (*jĭ-brŏl'tẽr*). A rocky promontory near the southern point of the Iberian peninsula and commanding the western entrance to the Mediterranean Sea. It is a possession of Great Britain. It covers about two square miles and consists mainly of a fortified rock, 1439 feet high, at the foot of which is the town of Gibraltar with a population in 1967 of 25,281. The fortress was obtained by Great Britain from Spain in 1713. From 1779 to 1783, it withstood a siege of 3 years, 7 months, and 12 days at the hands of a Spanish fleet.

Great Britain. An island kingdom lying north and slightly west of France and separated from it by the English channel, which narrows from a maximum width of 150 miles near the west end to a neck in the east, 21 miles wide, called the Strait of Dover. Geographically, the term Great Britain has reference to the one large island divided, for historical reasons, into England and Wales in the south and Scotland in the north. As a political division, however, Great Britain, officially known as the Kingdom of Great Britain and Northern Ireland, includes also Northern Ireland, the Orkney islands, the Shetland islands, and the Hebrides,—three groups lying north of Scotland,—the Scilly islands and the Isle of Wight in the south, and nearly 800 smaller islands. The Isle of Man in the Irish Sea and the Channel islands,—Guernsey, Jersey, and their dependency, Sark island,—are not subject to British legislation unless specifically designated in particular enactments. The area and the population of Great Britain and of its principal divisions are given in the table of *The British Commonwealth*.

The island of Great Britain is about 700 miles long from north to south, and its width varies from 280 miles in the extreme south to 30 miles in northern Scotland, where Dornoch Firth and Loch Broom penetrate deeply into the land from opposite sides of the island. The coast line is well in excess of 4000 miles, being deeply indented by the estuaries of tidal rivers and, especially in northern and western Scotland, by deep, rocky fiords. The chief of these inlets on the eastern side, named from south to north, are the estuary of the Thames, the Wash, the Humber River estuary, the Firth of Forth, the Firth of Tay, Moray firth, and Dornoch firth. On the western side, the principal inlets are Bristol channel, Cardigan bay, the Dee River and the Mersey River estuary, Morecambe bay, Solway firth, the Firth of Clyde, and the Firth of Lorne with its continuation known as Loch Linnhe.

The seas surrounding Great Britain are shallow, rarely exceeding 300 feet in depth. This circumstance has the effect of protecting the island from the cold arctic currents, so that the country enjoys a climate much milder than that in corresponding latitudes of America. The shallow waters provide a feeding ground for fish, thereby supporting fisheries of great value.

Great Britain has been the most active colonizing nation in Europe. As islanders, the British turned readily to seafaring and were among the first to explore the Americas, Australia, the Orient, Africa, and other regions. The settlers succeeded in carrying their institutions to many distant parts of the world and thus laid the foundation for the present British Commonwealth of Nations and the system of dependencies which are found in every continent. The English language and English basic institutions were transplanted to North America, Australia, and New Zealand. Through the rapid growth of these settlements, in population and power, and particularly of the United States, the influence of the English heritage is widely spread throughout the world.

The worldwide demand of underdeveloped countries throughout the world for political independence had a sharper impact on Great Britain than on any other country for the reason that her commitments among them were the greatest. Drawing on prior experience and modifying old formulas of association, she succeeded in transforming her empire into a commonwealth with a minimum of conflict and political unsettlement. Nearly all such territories after attaining independence requested Great Britain to sponsor their admittance to the British Commonwealth of Nations, and the body consisting of the heads of member states acted favorably on their application.

ENGLAND. A division of Great Britain comprising most of the southern part of the island and divided from Scotland on the north by a low ridge, called the Cheviot hills. The maximum length of England is 425 miles, and the width varies from 280 miles to 62 miles. The surface is, in general, a rolling plain, rising in the north to the low mountains in Derbyshire, Yorkshire, Westmoreland, and Cumberland. In the northwest is the "lake district," where occur the largest lake and the highest mountain in England—Lake Windermere, 10½ miles long, and Sca Fell, 3210 feet high. The chief rivers flowing into the North Sea on the east are the Thames, the Humber, the Tees, and the Tyne. Those flowing west include the Severn, Dee, and Mersey.

England is one of the leading exporting countries in the world. The richest coal fields are located in the region of Newcastle in northeastern England and in an area 100 to 150 miles farther south, where the proximity of large iron deposits has resulted in the growth of such huge manufacturing cities as Sheffield and Birmingham. In production of iron, England ranks among the world's leading producers. Her manufactures, however, require the importation of additional ore, which comes mainly from Spain and Sweden. The southwestern extremity of England has been the chief European source of tin since the days of the Phœnicians. Lead, silver, and zinc are mined in the northeast.

About 5 per cent of England is covered with forests, of which certain tracts, such as Epping forest near London, were formerly set aside as royal deer forests. Epping forest is now open to the public as a park. The greater part of the country's surface is fertile, and, being tilled according to the most advanced methods, it is highly productive. The live stock of England and of Great Britain generally is of a superior quality. No country has produced more standard breeds of domestic animals.

England was the first country in the world to become industrialized and still remains one of the greatest manufacturing nations. In the making of cutlery and other steel products and of cotton, woolen, and linen textiles, England is excelled by no other country. The shipbuilding industry of Great Britain, favored by the numerous harbors of the island, is likewise unsurpassed. British ships do a large part of the carrying trade of the world. The foreign trade of the country exceeds that of any other country of the world. The total length of canals is about 2,500 miles, and of railways, nearly 20,000 miles.

World War II and the political and economic developments which followed had the effect of weakening England's relative position in the world. But the people accepted years of austerity to safeguard the country's position in commerce and trade, many of the most attractive manufactured products being kept from the home market and reserved for export.

At the same time, welfare measures such as old-age pensions, unemployment compensation, and family allowances were enlarged by a system of health insurance. The educational system was modified to make advanced training more available to persons of all classes of society.

The population of England is about 95 per cent Protestant, the majority belonging to the Anglican, or Protestant Episcopal, Church, which is the "established church" of the country. No civil disabilities, however, attach to any British subject on account of religion. The outstanding universities of England are Oxford, Cambridge, and the University of London. Illiteracy is almost unknown. By an act passed in 1918, part time attendance at free continuation schools is required of all people up to 16 years of age, and, when the necessary facilities are provided, the age limit is extended to 18 years.

London, the capital of Great Britain, is one of the largest cities in the world. The chief cities with estimated populations are as follows:

City	Population	City	Population
London	7,880,760	Wolverhampton	266,890
Birmingham	1,101,990	Enfield	266,640
Liverpool	705,310	Westminster	258,930
Manchester	616,520	Newham	257,350
Sheffield	534,100	Islington	254,580
Bristol	518,640	Haringey	254,120
Leeds	507,780	Newcastle upon	
Lambeth	338,130	Trent	251,650
Coventry	333,830	Havering	251,160
Wandsworth	330,470	Hackney	249,140
Croydon	328,290	Plymouth	247,400
Barnet	315,210	Redbridge	245,300
Nottingham	309,740	Camden	238,020
Bromley	302,660	Waltham Forest	237,910
Ealing	302,570	Hillingdon	234,470
Southwark	300,720	Greenwich	231,150
Bradford	296,860	Sunderland	219,270
Kingston upon		Portsmouth	219,110
Hull	295,900	Bexley	215,330
Brent	293,370	Kensington &	
Lewisham	289,700	Chelsea	213,310
Cardiff	289,320	Hammersmith	211,720
Leicester	282,800	Southampton	209,790
Stoke on Trent	275,703	Harrow	208,200
		Hounslow	206,870

WALES. The roughly rectangular land projection west of England, which lies between the Irish Sea on the north and Bristol channel on the south. Its surface is more mountainous than that of England, the highest peak being Mount Snowdon, 3560 feet in altitude. Wales contains some of the most valuable coal beds in Great Britain, and its largest city, Cardiff, exports more coal than any other city of the world. The inhabitants are of Celtic origin rather than Germanic, and about 40 per cent of them can still speak the native Welsh language. In religion, most of the Welsh are nonconformists, principally Methodists and Presbyterians.

SCOTLAND. The portion of Great Britain north of the Cheviot hills. It is, in general, a more mountainous country than England. The chief rivers flowing to the east are the Tweed, the Forth, and the Tay. The Clyde is the only important river draining westward. Scotland has many beautiful lakes, of which Loch Lomond, 24 miles long, is the largest. The country is divisible, by the nature of its surface, into the highlands of the north, the central lowlands, and the southern uplands.

The highlands of Scotland occupy nearly half the country. They are remarkable for their mountainous masses, which are especially rugged along the western coast. The region is cut into two parts by the Great Glen of Scotland, a depression in which lie the elongated lakes, Loch Ness and Loch Lochy. These have been connected and made part of the Caledonian canal, which provides a waterway from Moray firth in the east to the Firth of Lorne in the west. Southwest of the Great Glen are the Grampian hills, which culminate in Ben Nevis near the center of the western coast. This mountain, having an altitude of 4406 feet, is the highest peak in Great Britain.

The southern uplands constitute a region of low mountains, none exceeding 3000 feet in height. Between them and the highlands of the north lies a fertile plain, which supports a dense population and flourishing industries.

The minerals of Scotland include coal, iron, and oil shale. Of the last named, Scotland has about 80 per cent of the amount in the world known to be available. Agriculture in Scotland is often handicapped by an excessive rainfall. Of the chief crops,—oats, barley, turnips, and potatoes,—oats are grown in the most important quantities. The southern uplands are excellently adapted to grazing, and sheep are raised in large numbers. Cheviot sheep and the Ayrshire, Galloway, Polled Angus, and Jersey cattle were first bred in Scotland, while the Shetland breed of ponies originated in the Shetland islands lying to the northeast.

The industries of Scotland are similar to those of England, consisting chiefly of textiles steel products, and shipbuilding. At Glasgow on the Clyde are located the world's largest shipbuilding yards. Most of the Cunard liners have been built in these yards. The country is noted also for its production of whisky and of preserved fruits.

Scotland is the original home of Presbyterianism, the form of Protestantism professed by the established church of Scotland. The Roman Catholic Church is relatively stronger than in England. There are four universities in the country—Edinburgh, Glasgow, Aberdeen, and Saint Andrews. Scotland enjoys the same system of continuation schools as that described under *England*. The county authorities are empowered to provide educational books for the use of the adult population. The Gaelic language is still spoken in parts of Scotland.

Three-quarters of Scotland's 5,188,000 inhabitants live in towns or cities. The largest urban center is Glasgow, population 960,527. Edinburgh, population 467,986, is the seat of the supreme court, Scotland having courts and a system of law differing from those of England and based on French models

Greece. A maritime country occupying the southern part of the Balkan peninsula and including about 500 near-by islands, of which Crete is the largest. The shores of the mainland are bold, rocky, and deeply indented. The Gulf of Ægina, stretching inland from the east, is connected by a canal with the Gulf of Corinth, which is an inland continuation of the Gulf of Patras on the west coast. The resulting peninsula, called the Peloponnese in ancient times, is now known as Peloponnisos. The total area of the country is about 51,180 square miles.

About four-fifths of the surface of the mainland is crumpled by a complex system of mountains, which divide the surface into a number of small plains. The chief range, running north and south, is called the Pindus. The highest peak is Mount Olympus, in northern Greece, which has an altitude of 9570 feet. Mount Parnassus, celebrated in literature as the home of the Muses, is 8062 feet high. It is situated just north of the Gulf of Corinth and is sometimes known as Mt. Liakura. The progressive deforestation which has taken place in Greece is believed to have made the country drier than it formerly was. The climate is otherwise marked by intensity of heat in the summers and occasionally by severe cold in the winters.

The small plains of Greece provide the major part of the arable land. Agriculture, though practicable on only one-third of the country's surface, is the leading industry of the country. By the draining of Lake Copais in central Greece, about 53,000 acres were reclaimed in 1894. The chief crops are olives, wheat, grapes, corn, currants, figs, tobacco, oranges, lemons, barley, and oats. Currants constitute a distinctive product. The English word currant is a corruption of Corinth, the name of a Greek city from which the fruit is exported. Other industries are the raising of sheep and of goats. Lignite, magnesite, iron, salt, lead, emery, and zinc are mined. Slag from the silver mines at Laurium is being worked over for lead that the ancient Athenians failed to extract.

The Greeks are a commercial people. Along with the manufacture of textiles, leather, and soap, shipbuilding ranks high among the industries. The Greek trader has for more than 2500 years been found everywhere throughout the Levant, as the countries washed by the eastern Mediterranean Sea are sometimes called. Seventy-five per cent of the Greek ocean-going ships were lost during World War II, the coastal fleet was ruined, and Greek ports were severely damaged. Railways and highways suffered similar losses.

Most of Greece's 8,803,000 (1968 est.) inhabitants profess the Greek Catholic faith. The spoken language, known as Romaic, is related to ancient Greek much as Italian is related to Latin; the literary language, however, is much closer to classical Greek. Athens is the capital and largest city of Greece, with a population of 1,852,709. Other notable cities are Salonika, Piræus, which is the port of Athens, and Patrai. Elementary education is nominally obligatory, but the percentage of illiteracy is high. There are government commercial schools and two universities at Athens, where also schools of archeology are maintained by American, British, French, Italian, and German learned societies. The Greek ministry of education is charged with the duty of conserving, repairing, and excavating ancient monuments.

The most notable architectural monuments of Greece date back more than 2000 years. Many of the finest buildings have been seriously mutilated, but some remain almost complete and still retain the dignity of their former state. Apart from Athens, the places containing the more interesting ruins are Olympia, Delphi, and Mycenæ.

Hungary. An inland agricultural republic in the eastern part of central Europe, bounded by Austria, Czechoslovakia, Russia, Rumania, and Yugoslavia. Hungary was defeated in both world wars and as a result, her territory has been reduced from over 60,000 square miles to 35,912, and her population has declined from more than 13,000,000 to 10,510,000.

The chief crops raised in Hungary are corn, wheat, sugar beets, barley, rye, oats, grapes, and tobacco. Most of the industries are those based on agriculture, such as flour milling and sugar refining. There are also iron and steel works. Hard and soft coal and bauxite are mined. Forests cover about 6 per cent of the surface. Important quantities of fish are obtained from Lake Balaton, the largest lake in central Europe, and from the rivers.

The majority of the people are Roman Catholics. There is a well developed educational system with compulsory attendance between the ages of 6 and 14. There are many fine universities and colleges. Budapest is the capital and largest city.

Iceland. An island state situated in the north Atlantic Ocean about 500 miles northwest of Scotland and 150 miles southeast of Greenland. The Arctic circle touches the most northern point of the island. The cold is not extreme, however, being moderated by the proximity of the ocean.

Almost the whole of Iceland's 39,758 square miles of surface is of volcanic origin, magnificent as scenery but unproductive. The ice-strewn plateaus, of which the island consists, average more than 2000 feet in altitude. The most celebrated of the island's 100 volcanoes is the Hekla, 4707 feet in height. The Great Geyser is 60 feet in diameter and, at intervals of several hours, projects immense quantities of hot water about 150 feet into the air. Boiling water from geysers is piped to the capital to heat buildings. About one-eighth of the island is covered by glaciers.

Nearly all the inhabitants of Iceland are dependent for their living on agriculture, stock raising, or fishing. Less than 1 per cent of the island is cultivated. The chief crops are hay, potatoes, and turnips. The exports consist almost entirely of live stock, mainly sheep and horses, and of fish and fish products. Trade is mainly with Great Britain, Russia, and the United States.

The population of Iceland in 1974 was 216,628. The national church is Lutheran. There is a complete system of education culminating in a university situated at Reykjavik, the capital of the republic.

Ireland. The large island lying immediately west of Great Britain and separated from it by the Irish Sea, which is connected with the Atlantic Ocean by Saint George's channel and by North channel. In the narrowest part of North channel, Ireland is separated from Great Britain by 14 miles. The area of the island is about 32,000 square miles. It has a maximum length of 300 miles and a maximum width of 180 miles. Politically, the island is divided into two parts. Eire occupies the whole island except a comparatively small district in the north. This district, under the name of Northern Ireland, constitutes a division of the Kingdom of Great Britain and Northern Ireland. For the area and the population of Northern Ireland, see the table of *The British Commonwealth*. Since 1850 nearly 4,500,000 Irish have emigrated to other countries, by far the greatest number having settled in the United States. The Irish are Celtic in origin. The Irish language was spoken by about 13 per cent of the population in 1920, and since then its use has been actively fostered by the government. Along with English, it is the official language of that state.

About two-fifths of Ireland's surface consists of bog. Most of the remainder is fertile. The humidity of the climate and the equability of the temperature foster a verdant clothing of vegetation, which has earned for Ireland the name of the "emerald isle." The island is drained by the Shannon river, which, having a course of 250 miles, is the longest river in the British Isles. The enchanting and romantic scenery of the lakes of Killarney in the south attracts visitors from all parts of the world.

EIRE. This portion of Ireland is predominantly agricultural in its interests, being Great Britain's most important single source of foodstuffs. Marketing is accomplished largely through co-operative societies. The chief crops are potatoes, oats, turnips, barley, and wheat. Dairying and stock raising form an important part of the farm operations. There are also valuable sea and fresh-water fisheries, the catches including salmon, mackerel, cod, and herring. The chief manufactures are food products, beer, ale, and tractors.

The population of Eire, estimated in 1971 at 2,978,000, is predominantly Roman Catholic. At the head of the educational system stand two universities, both situated in Dublin, the capital and largest city of the country. Other cities of note include Cork and Limerick.

NORTHERN IRELAND. In addition to agriculture and fishing, the northern division of Ireland has a large manufacturing industry. This industry, which has been developed in spite of the lack of coal and of iron in the island, consists chiefly of shipbuilding, distilling, and the manufacture of linen and of other textiles.

The prevailing religion of Northern Ireland is Protestantism. The educational system is distinct from that of the other divisions of the United Kingdom. Belfast, the largest city, is the seat of a university and of the legislature and the judiciary of Northern Ireland. Londonderry is another important center of manufacture and of trade.

Italy. A republic occupying the large bootshaped peninsula of southern Europe. Italy includes also the islands of Sicily, Sardinia, Elba, and about 70 smaller islands in the surrounding seas. The land boundary at the north follows, in a roughly semicircular course, a mountain wall, which separates Italy from France, Switzerland, Austria, and Yugoslavia. To the east of the mainland lies the Adriatic Sea, at the head of which is the Gulf of Venice. The sea narrows toward the south to the Strait of Otranto, 45 miles wide at its narrowest point. Italy's western coast is washed by the Tyrrhenian Sea and by the Ligurian Sea, the latter having a broad northern inlet called the Gulf of Genoa. On the south, Italy is bounded by the Ionian Sea with its inlet, the Gulf of Taranto. The "toe" of Italy is separated from Sicily by the Strait of Messina, which has a minimum width of two miles. The mainland of Italy has an average width of about 100 miles and a maximum length of 780 miles. The total area of the country is 116,304 square miles.

Italy is mountainous and includes the only part of the European mainland which contains active volcanoes. Spurs of the Alps mountains, extending into Italy from the northern mountain wall, form the beautiful scenery of the celebrated Italian Tyrol. The range of the Apennines passes from the Gulf of Genoa to the southern extremity of the mainland. Vesuvius, a mountain of the latter range, Etna on Sicily, and Stromboli on one of the Lipari islands, north of Sicily, are volcanoes which are seldom quiescent. An earthquake at Calabria, southern Italy, in 1783, destroyed 100,000 lives, and another, about the Strait of Messina in 1908, resulted in the death of some 96,000 people.

The most important river of Italy is the Po, which drains the fertile, well watered plain of Lombardy in the north and discharges near the head of the Adriatic Sea. The Tiber, which empties into the sea near the center of the western coast, is richer in historical associations.

The mineral resources of Italy are comparatively small and insufficient for domestic use except for mercury and sulphur, which are exported. Petroleum, however, is found in quantity in Sicily, where there is one of Europe's largest oil fields. The output, however, is not sufficient to meet Italian demand, and imports are extensive, usually processed in Italian refineries. Other mineral products include marble, copper, zinc, iron, and manganese. The fisheries employ more than 150,000 workers.

The leading industry of Italy is agriculture. The climate, ranging from subarctic in the Alps to subtropical in the south, permits the cultivation of such varied crops as wheat, corn, potatoes, sugar beets, oats, grapes, olives, rice, beans, barley, and rye. Northern Italy is the most productive region, being cultivated by the most improved methods. Over 400,000 acres were reclaimed for agriculture in central Italy in the decade 1920–30. Silk culture is also a considerable industry. Wine, olive oil, and cheese are important exports of Italy.

Italian agriculture consists typically of small farms intensively cultivated but with a minimum of farm machinery, the farmers living in villages or even cities and traveling each day to their outlying farms. Under land reform laws of 1950, the government acquired and made available to farmers about one and a half million acres in lots of less than 12 acres each. A large number of Italian farm laborers have migrated in recent years to France and other members of the Common Market.

The chief manufacturing centers are in the north, where abundant hydroelectric power is available. The principal products include cotton and silk textiles, lace, straw hats, metal products, chemicals, sugar, rayon, leather goods, glass, pottery, perfumes, and paper. Shipbuilding is also an important industry. Among the distinctive products of Italian craftsmanship are cameos and marble statuettes. From Murano, near Venice, comes glass whose unrivalled beauty gives it a secure market throughout the world. The secret processes of manufacture go back at least to the 1200's. To protect them the Venetian rulers made it a capital offense for an artisan to emigrate.

The population of Italy in 1971 was 53,744,737 (est.). The prevailing religion is Roman Catholicism. Elementary instruction is compulsory. Italy has over 40 universities, many of them among the oldest in Europe. In addition, there are many technical colleges, art schools and learned societies. Everywhere throughout Italy are to be found monuments, more or less ruined, which bear witness to the fact that Italy was the chief center of European civilization from the 2d century B. C. to the 16th century A.D. The Italian government has capitalized on this fact by protecting the historical sites and prescribing for guides licenses granted only after rigorous training, thereby attracting tourists who normally exceed 18 million each year. Apart from the government's care for the more obvious historical attractions such as Pompeii, the ancient Roman structures in Rome, and still earlier Greek structures in Sicily, it assists in the archeological study and preservation of hundreds of underground Tuscan tombs which only in recent years have been known to exist.

Rome is the capital and largest city of Italy. The chief cities with their populations are given in the following table:

City	Population	City	Population
Rome	2,856,309	Cagliari	235,892
Milan	1,732,451	Brescia	215,317
Naples	1,224,274	Leghorn	177,526
Turin	1,202,846	Modena	176,796
Genoa	807,138	Parma	176,617
Palermo	661,235	Reggio di	
Bologna	492,700	Calabria	174,462
Florence	464,897	Salerno	159,302
Catania	399,635	Ferrara	155,478
Bari	374,521	Foggia	150,725
Venice	365,431	Prato	150,580
Trieste	271,536	Ravenna	137,020
Verona	270,815	Perugia	134,288
Messina	259,858	Reggio	
Padua	239,250	nell 'Emilia	129,787
Tarento	238,749	La Spezia	122,754

By the peace treaty signed at Paris February 10, 1947, Italy ceded four of her frontier districts to France, and most of the province of Venezia Giulia to Yugoslavia. She also gave up her former colonies, all in Africa, where her possessions were second in extent only to those of Great Britain and France. The United Nations supervised the reorganization of this colonial empire. Ethiopia, which Italy had conquered in 1936, was restored to independence, and the former Italian colony of Eritrea was joined to it. The former Italian colony of Libya was erected into an independent kingdom in 1951. Italian Somaliland was joined with British Somaliland to form the Somali Republic.

Monaco (mŏn'à-kō). One of the smallest states in Europe. Monaco is a constitutional monarchy, lying in southeastern France and bordering on the Mediterranean Sea. The surface, about 2 miles long and half a mile wide, is mountainous and highly picturesque. The chief occupation of the 23,000 (1968 est.) inhabitants is to provide accommodation and entertainment for the visitors who, in numbers exceeding 1,500,000 each year, are attracted by this famous winter resort and gambling center. Despite popular misconception, the famous Monte Carlo gambling casino now furnishes less than 10 per cent of revenues. While tourist trade remains of chief importance, local industries include making electrical appliances, radios, pharmaceuticals, and cosmetics.

Netherlands, The. A kingdom of northwestern Europe, roughly triangular in shape, with a northwestern coast line on the North Sea. The country, sometimes called Holland after the name of two of its provinces, borders on Belgium to the south and Germany on the east. No point in it is more than 120 miles from the sea, which forms more than one-half the total of its boundary. Its seacoast is 465 miles in length.

The surface of the Netherlands, 12,529 square miles in area, is, in large part, too low for natural drainage, portions of it being from 16 to 20 feet below the level of the sea. The population of 13,733,578 averages about 1,059 persons to the square mile, which makes the Netherlands the most densely populated country on the earth.

The former Zuider Zee, a large shallow gulf, formed by an inundation from the sea in the 13th century, was cut off from the sea by dikes in 1932, in order to be drained to one-third its former size, leaving a lake, Ijsselmeer. This reclamation project is the largest ever undertaken anywhere in the world. It adds 523,000 acres of arable land to the Netherlands, an increase of nearly one-tenth.

Part of the coast is bordered by sand dunes, which keep out the sea from the lowlands. In other parts, artificial embankments, or dikes, are erected for that purpose. In the interior of the country, also, such dikes are used to enclose swampy land, from which the water is pumped by windmills, leaving the soil of these so-called "polders" available for cultivation.

The Netherlands has a network of river mouths through which the Rhine, the Meuse, and the Scheldt rivers discharge their waters. These rivers are supplemented as trade highways by some 2000 miles of canals, which, both in mileage and in utility, vie in importance with the railroads. More than 50,000 people live on barges which ply along the waterways.

The distinctive products of the Netherlands are cheese, butter, margarine, and flower bulbs. More than one-half of the land is arable. It produces among other crops, rye, oats, potatoes, sugar beets, flax, and barley. Dairying is one of the leading occupations of the country. The Holstein breed of cattle, developed first in Holland, is one of the best milk producing varieties in the world. Herring and oysters are the chief products of the deep-sea fisheries, which formerly constituted the foundation of the country's wealth. The industries include shipbuilding, tobacco products, and pottery, and the refining of sugar, cocoa, and chocolate.

Until after World War II, the Netherlands had colonial possessions more than 50 times the area of the country itself, but practically all of them became independent. The Dutch merchant marine is among the world's largest.

The majority of the inhabitants are Protestants, but there is a strong Catholic minority. Both churches, as well as the Jewish religious bodies, receive grants from the government. Illiteracy is virtually unknown. The educational system provides widely different kinds of training. There are four state universities. Amsterdam was formerly the capital and is still the scene of the royal coronation. The seat of government, however, is The Hague. The following table gives the chief cities with their population in 1976:

City	Population	City	Population
Amsterdam	987,205	Utrecht	464,357
Rotterdam	1,031,403	Eindhoven	358,234
The Hague	682,452	Haarlem	232,048

Norway. A kingdom of northern Europe, occupying that portion of the Scandinavian peninsula which lies west and north of the ridge of the Kiolen Mountains. The country extends 300 miles within the Arctic circle to a latitude farther north than that of any other part of the European mainland. Norway possesses as a dependency the Spitsbergen Islands, a coal producing archipelago which is situated some 600 miles north of the country's northern extremity and stretches to a point about 650 miles from the north pole. The area of the archipelago is estimated at 25,000 square miles.

The surface of Norway, 125,065 square miles in area, is mountainous and, for the most part, barren. About one-fifth is covered with forests, mainly of pine and fir. The arable portion comprises a scant 4 per cent of the total area. The coast line is cut by deep, picturesque fiords, and is fringed by some 150,000 islands, the larger ones being in the north.

The climate is moderated by the warm ocean currents which flow past the coast. The Arctic coast settlement, Hammerfest, which is the most northern town in the world, has a mean winter temperature higher than that of New York. Numerous summer tourists visit the country, attracted by Norway's scenic beauty and by the spectacle of the "midnight sun." In the north, the sun never sets between the middle of May and the last of July.

The chief occupations of Norway's inhabitants are lumbering and fishing. Herring, cod, mackerel, salmon, whale, walrus, seal, and lobsters form the most valuable part of the catch. Ships from Norway carry on most of the whaling in the Antarctic. The merchant marine of Norway ranks, in tonnage, among the great commercial fleets of the world. The manufacturing industries of the country are largely dependent on water power, which is available in great abundance. The most important industrial products are pulp, paper, and chemicals.

The population of Norway, (4,017,101, 1976 est.) is almost entirely Protestant in religion. The Lutheran Church is endowed by the state. Education is obligatory and illiteracy is almost unknown. The one university is situated in Oslo (463,022), the capital and largest city. Other cities include Bergen (213,594), Trondheim, and Stavanger.

Poland. A nation of eastern Europe, the Polish People's republic was established after World War II. Poland covers an area of 120,665 square miles between Russia on the east and East Germany on the west. Poland borders on Czechoslovakia on the south and the Baltic Sea on the north. Apart from the Carpathian foothills in the south, with a maximum elevation of 2000 feet, the surface is a gently rolling plain, most of it drained northward by the Vistula River and its tributaries.

Since World War II Poland has become highly industrialized, using its abundance of coal, lignite, sulphur, copper ore, and zinc to produce manufactured goods. The major Polish industries are mining, machine manufacture, chemicals, power production, and food production. Poland is also the world's ninth largest producer of ships.

The people of Poland have exerted great effort to restore agricultural production since the war. Collective farming is being phased out by the government and a majority of the land is being turned over to private owners. The major crops of Poland are wheat, rye, potatoes, oats, barley, and sugar beets. The country's main trade partners are the U.S.S.R., Czechoslovakia, East and West Germany, and Britain.

Poland's 1976 estimated population was 34,300,000, 95 per cent of whom are Roman Catholic.

Education is free and compulsory between the ages of 7 and 15, and there are 89 institutions of higher education. Warsaw is the capital and largest city, with a 1973 estimated population of 1,388,000. Other major cities include Lodz (781,000), Krakow (657,000), Wroclaw (560,000), and Poznan (499,000).

Portugal. A republic occupying the most western part of the Iberian peninsula and washed on the south and on the west by the Atlantic Ocean. On the land side, to the north and the east, Portugal adjoins Spain. The area of Portugal is given as 34,500 square miles, little more than half of which is productive.

The country is traversed from east to west near its center by the Tagus River, the estuary of which forms one of the best harbors in the world. North of the river, the surface is a mountainous plateau, which is crossed by the deep, gorgelike bed of the Douro River. On the left of the Tagus River, a plain stretches southward to an irregular group of mountains in the southwestern extremity of the country. Between this group and a mountain ridge on the eastern border, the Guadiana River, rising in Spain, flows south to the Atlantic Ocean.

About 26 per cent of Portugal's surface is forested, mainly with pines, chestnuts, oaks, and cork trees. Cork is one of the chief sources of the national wealth. The acorns of the oak forests serve to fatten large herds of swine. The central part of the country produces enormous amounts of grapes, from which is made port wine, so called from Oporto, its point of export. In the south, olives, figs, oranges, lemons, and other tropical fruits are grown. Products of the fisheries—sardines and tuna fish—form, next to wines, the principal article of export. The mineral wealth is considerable. Wolfram, iron, copper, manganese, antimony, lead, tin, and gold are found. A characteristic industry is the manufacture of porcelain tiles. The chief manufactures are textile products.

The population of Portugal is 9,505,000. There is freedom of worship, but Roman Catholicism prevails almost to the exclusion of any other religion. Elementary education is compulsory and, since Portugal became a republic in 1910, has been rigorously enforced. There are three universities and several schools of technology and of art. The two principal cities are Lisbon—the capital—and Oporto.

Rumania. A republic of southeastern Europe with an eastern coast line on the Black Sea. Russia is its immediate neighbor to the north; Hungary and Yugoslavia, to the west; and Bulgaria, to the south. The area of the country is 91,671 square miles.

Rumania is divided into an eastern and a western part by the Carpathian mountains, which, in Rumania, trend south and southwest. This ridge is often known as the Transylvanian Alps, and the western part of the country is known as Transylvania. The remainder of the country is a plain drained by the Danube. This river has 595 miles of its course in Rumania and along the southern border.

After being joined by the Pruth, its great tributary from the north, the Danube empties through several mouths into the Black Sea. Navigation on the Danube according to the peace treaty of 1947 is free and open to all countries on an equal footing.

About four-fifths of the inhabitants of Rumania support themselves by stock raising and by agriculture of the usual temperate zone type, corn and wheat being the leading crops. Rumania is, next to Russia, the most important oil producing country of Europe. Other minerals obtained are lignite, coal, iron, copper, and salt, the mining of the last being a government monopoly. Flour milling, brewing, and distilling are the chief industrial interests. Apart from oil, the leading exports are grain, salt, coal, timber, and hides. In 1947 Rumania's transport services, oil, industry, and entire export-import trade were taken over by Soviet-controlled agencies.

The predominant religion of Rumania's 19,721,-000 people is Greek Catholic. There are six universities in the country. Bucuresti (Bucharest) (1,372,937) is the capital and largest city of Rumania. Other cities of importance include Iasi (Jassy), Galati (Galatz), and Cluj.

Russia. The largest country in the world, occupying nearly half the total area of Europe and the whole northern portion of Asia. Including its Asiatic territory, Russia covers an area of 8,599,776 square miles, of which about 2,500,000 are in Europe. Officially known as the Union of Soviet Socialist Republics (U.S.S.R.), it is divided into the Russian Socialist Federated Soviet Republic (R.S.F.S.R.), which occupies about 78 per cent of the entire country, and fifteen other republics, of which seven are in Europe and eight in Asia.

The areas and population of the constituent republics, as estimated in 1969, were as follows:

Republic	Area in sq. miles	Population
RSFSR*	6,593,391	128,526,000
Ukrainian	232,046	46,752,000
Byelorussia (White Russia)	80,154	8,897,000
Moldavia	13,012	3,531,000
Estonia	17,413	1,316,000
Latvia	24,695	2,323,000
Lithuania	26,173	3,103,000
Azerbaijan	33,436	5,042,000
Georgia	26,911	4,710,000
Armenia	11,306	2,363,000
Turkomen	188,417	2,085,000
Uzbek	158,069	11,669,000
Tadzhik	54,019	2,823,000
Kazakh	1,064,092	12,877,000
Kirghiz	76,642	2,926,000
Total	8,599,776	238,943,000

*The first republic listed, the RSFSR, includes territory in Europe and Asia. The next 6 listed are in Europe. The last 8 are in Asia.

The surface of European Russia is a vast rolling plain, which rises, in the Ural mountains on the east, to an altitude of about 8000 feet and, at Mount Elbruz in the Caucasus range, to a maximum height of 18,465 feet. Almost the whole surface, however, is less than 600 feet above the sea.

Extreme cold in winter and extreme heat in summer constitute a general characteristic of Russia's climate. The Valdai hills in the west central part of the country form the chief watershed and give rise to the Don, the Dnieper, and the Volga, all flowing southward. The Dvina, the Neva, and the Volkhof are the most important rivers of northern drainage. The Volga river is navigable for 1800 miles. Canals join the principal rivers, making a system of navigable waterways having a total length of about 90,000 miles. The northern region abounds in lakes of glacial formation. Lake Ladoga near the border of Finland, with an area of 7000 square miles, is the largest lake in Europe.

Prior to the revolution of 1917, Russia was predominantly an agricultural country. In the next 40 years, it became also one of the world's leading industrial nations with over 80 per cent of the output nonagricultural, although the farm and nonfarm population were about evenly divided. But this industrial emphasis led to trouble, and Russia was compelled to import grain on a large scale in 1964. Farm land is partly owned and operated by the state, but most is operated by co-operatives with state-appointed managers. Individual workers are allowed small tracts to raise their own produce.

The official explanation for disappointing returns was that manufacture of fertilizers had been neglected; others attributed them also to inadequate investment and lack of incentive to produce.

Russia is one of the world's largest producers of wheat, barley, rye, flax, and oats. Other important crops are hemp, sugar beets, rice, cotton, tea, and tobacco. The richest soil lies in the so-called black earth belt, which extends from the Carpathian Mountains through the Ukraine in southern Russia to the borders of China. This is by far the greatest single wheat growing land on the face of the globe. In production of farm animals, Russia vies with the United States for the first place.

Industrialization in Russia was carried out by means of governmental planning and control, which extends to every aspect of its economic life. Frequently entirely new cities were created in the process, such as Magnitogorsk for the manufacture of steel. Dneprostroy, where Europe's largest hydroelectric station was erected, became a center for aluminum, ferroalloy, coke, and cement plants. Production of tractors was centralized in Volgograd (formerly Stalingrad) and Chelyabinsk. Russia is one of the world's largest producers of petroleum. Among the older centers of industry are Leningrad, which produces chemicals, matches, and rubber products, and Moscow, where the textiles and publishing industries are centered. Kharkov is a leading center of heavy industry. Centers of the atomic energy industry are scattered and unpublicized.

From the forests of the north come lumber, pulp, tar, turpentine, resin, and fur. Russia is the world's largest exporter of lumber. There are important fisheries in the Arctic Ocean and in the seas. The fisheries of the Volga River and of the Caspian Sea supply most of the sturgeon, whose eggs are salted and made into Russian caviar. From the Ural Mountains come asbestos and platinum. Here, too, is produced gold, making Russia a rival of South Africa as the world's chief source of the yellow metal. One of the chief sources of manganese is southern Russia, where there are also very rich deposits of coal and of iron. Copper is mined in the north.

The population of Russia, 1969 est., was 239,000,-000. All forms of religion are permitted in Russia, but atheism is officially encouraged. Following the revolution in 1917, an ambitious and comprehensive system of education was inaugurated. Education is compulsory and even advanced education is free. Medical care and many other social services are provided by the government. The role of women in all phases of Russian life is greater than in any other large country.

The capital and largest city in Russia is Moscow. Other large cities of European Russia are Leningrad, Kiev, Odessa, Kharkov, Dnepropetrovsk, Saratov, and Gorkiy.

See also *Russia in Asia.*

Spain. A country in southwestern Europe, occupying about four-fifths of the Iberian peninsula. It is separated from France on the northeast by the Pyrenees Mountains and, in the southwestern part of the peninsula, surrounds Portugal on the land side. Spain is otherwise bounded by the Atlantic Ocean and the Mediterranean Sea, which are connected, at the southern extremity of the country, by the Strait of Gibraltar. Spain has an area of 194,945 square miles. It extends north and south 540 miles and, east and west, about 620 miles.

Next to Switzerland, Spain has the most elevated surface in continental Europe. Most of the interior is a table-land varying from 2000 to 3000 feet above the sea level. It is divided irregularly by low mountain ranges, of which the Cantabrian Mountains parallel the northern seacoast, the Sierra Nevada range skirts the Mediterranean coast, and the Sierra Morena trend east and west in the interior. Of Spain's rivers, the Douro, the Tagus, and the Guadiana have their mouths in Portugal. The Guadalquivir flows east and south into the Atlantic Ocean, while the Jucar and the Ebro empty into the Mediterranean Sea. The Guadalquivir and the Ebro are the only navigable rivers.

In the interior, the rainfall is light, and the climate is harsh, with cold winters and hot summers. The northern coast has the heaviest rainfall in Europe, and the southern coast has the warmest winter climate of any part of the continent. About one-sixth of the acreage is under forest, the more characteristic trees being the Spanish chestnut and the cork oak.

The leading occupations of the people are agriculture, grazing, fruit culture, mining, fishing, and manufacturing. Cereal crops are raised especially in the north and include, in order of importance, wheat, barley, rye, corn, and oats. Huge flocks of sheep and of goats graze on the dry, treeless plateau, where esparto grass is a characteristic type of vegetation. From this plant, rope and paper are made. In the southern part, which is known as Andalusia, grapes, oranges, olives, figs, peaches, dates, almonds, and other fruits and nuts are grown in abundance.

Spain is one of the chief wine producing countries of Europe. Mulberries are cultivated as a food for silkworms. Valencia in the south is the chief center of the Spanish silk industry. Raisins form a considerable item of export. Saffron and licorice are distinctive products of the region.

The mineral resources of Spain are among the richest in Europe. Iron ore is extensively exported. Spain is the chief European source of lead. Coal, copper, mercury, salt, zinc, tin, and potash are produced in important quantities. With the exception of steel and textiles, there are no important manufacturing industries. The country is deficient in petroleum. One of the chief products is cork, made from the bark of the cork oaks. The fisheries employ over 100,000, the chief catches being sardines, tunny fish, and cod. Oranges, olive oil, wines and cognacs, preserved fruits and fish, and almonds are among the chief exports.

The population of Spain is 33,823,918, practically all of whom are adherents of the Roman Catholic Church. The Basques, living near the head of the Bay of Biscay and numbering about 400,000, are believed to be descendants of a pre-Aryan people known to the Romans under the name of Iberians. Spain has also some 50,000 gypsies. Elementary education is compulsory. There are 13 universities. The capital and largest city is Madrid. Other important urban centers are Barcelona, Valencia, Seville, Malaga, Saragossa, Murcia, Bilbao, and Granada.

Spain was formerly one of the chief centers of Roman civilization. Bullfighting, the most popular national sport, is a survival of the ancient Roman wild beast shows.

Sweden. A republic of northern Europe, occupying the eastern and larger part of the Scandinavian peninsula. The country is 950 miles long and tapers to a blunt point at the north and at the south. It is bounded on the west by Norway and the Kattegat, and, on the east, by the Baltic Sea, the Gulf of Bothnia, and Finland. Its average width is about 190 miles, and its surface covers 173,436 square miles. The country includes many adjacent islands, the largest being Gottland and Oland.

Sweden is mountainous in the west, but the remainder of the country is flat. Most of the rivers are fed by lakes at the base of the Kiolen Mountains, which form the greater part of the Norwegian boundary. Toward the south, four large lakes occur, — Väner, Vätter, Mälar, and Hjälmar, — of which Lake Väner is the third largest in Europe. The first two are part of the Göta Canal system, which, giving access between the Baltic Sea and the Kattegat forms one of the chief arteries of Swedish commerce. The climate of Sweden is cold in winter and hot in summer; other seasons are short.

The most southern part of the country, known as Götaland, is the richest agricultural and industrial region and is the center of the shipping interests. North of Götaland lies Svealand, the center of the political and intellectual life of the country. Norrbotten, stretching to the northern extremity of Sweden, furnishes minerals and timber.

About one-half of the population of Sweden is supported by agriculture. Hay, oats, and rye are the leading crops. Timber is one of the chief sources of Sweden's wealth, and the lumber and pulp wood manufactures hold the leading place among the industries. The iron of Sweden is of a particularly high grade. Rich gold mines in northern Sweden, began production about 1930. Manganese, lead, silver, copper, and zinc are also mined. The industries suffer from lack of coal, being compelled to utilize charcoal or hydroelectric power. The largest hydroelectric plant in Western Europe on the Ume river has helped to increase the output of numerous manufactured goods.

The population of Sweden (1970 cen.) was 8,076,-903. Lutheran Protestantism is the established form of religion. There is an excellent system of education, at the head of which are six state universities. Illiteracy is almost unknown. The capital and largest city is Stockholm. Other cities of note are Göteborg and Malmö.

Switzerland. A mountainous inland republic of south central Europe, bounded on the north and east by Germany and Austria, on the west by France, and on the south by Italy. The surface of Switzerland, 15,941 square miles in area, has a greater average elevation than any other European country and contains the headwaters of four great European river systems,—the Rhine, the Rhone, the Po, and the Danube.

The northwestern half of the country is a rolling plateau hedged, near the northwestern border, by the Jura mountains. It drains northward toward the Rhine river and contains the lakes of Neuchatel, Bienne, Zurich, Lucerne, Thun, and Constance. The southeastern half is a region of picturesque mountains that has long been famous for its scenic beauty. The Southern Alps form much of the southern border of the country. Here are found the highest mountains, including Monte Rosa, 12,-203 feet in height; Matterhorn, a towering pyramid of solid rock 14,701 feet high; Simplon, with an elevation of 11,117; Saint Bernard, 8110 feet high, near which the Saint Bernard breed of dogs was developed, the animals being used to help in the rescue of travelers lost in the snow. This range descends on the north to the valley in which the Rhone river rises and, flowing westward, broadens into Switzerland's largest body of water, the Lake of Geneva. At the southeastern border lies Lake Maggiore, which has a southern drainage into the Po river.

South of the Rhone valley rise the irregular Burnese Alps, the highest peak of which is the Jungfrau, "The Maiden," so called from the blush which suffuses its snowy peak at sundown. Its height is 13,653 feet.

The mountains of Switzerland are cut by some 40 passes, and over 1000 glaciers furrow the rocky slopes. The mountains are burrowed by several railroad tunnels, that at Mount Simplon, 12½ miles in length, being one of the longest in the world. A warm wind, known as the foehn, often, by rapidly melting the snow and ice, causes avalanches.

Partly as a protection against avalanches, the forests of the country, covering about one-sixth of the republic's area, are carefully guarded by the government. Maples, oaks, and chestnuts flourish at the lower levels. Higher up occur birches, and still higher, firs, pines, and larches. In this region, the characteristic alpine animals, the chamois and the ibex, may be seen. The edelweiss and certain other flowering plants grow almost as far up the mountain side as the summer snow line.

Switzerland is one of the most highly industrialized countries in Europe. Agriculture and dairying rank next as occupations of the inhabitants. Grapes, rye, barley, potatoes, oats, flax, hemp, and tobacco are grown in the valleys and on the plains, while the mountain sides provide abundant pasturage for cattle, goats, horses, and sheep. Swiss cheese, Swiss clocks, watches, and Swiss chocolate form some of the more distinctive products of the country. Machinery, textiles, clothing, chemicals, metals, and watches are the industries that employ the greatest number of people. The entertainment of tourists is one of the major industries.

The inhabitants of Switzerland, 6,269,783 in 1970, are a unit neither in race, language, nor religion. German, French, and Italian are spoken. Illiteracy, however, is virtually nonexistent. The Protestants are slightly more numerous than the Catholics. Higher education is cared for by seven universities, that at Zurich dating from 1460. A distinctive type of dwelling is used in Switzerland, known as the chalet. It has a projecting roof under which are placed balconies and staircases.

Berne is the capital and Zurich is the largest city. Geneva is headquarters of many international organizations.

Turkey. The European territory of Turkey consists of the territory north of the Sea of Marmora extending to the borders of Bulgaria and of Greece. It includes Adrianople and Istanbul, formerly Constantinople. Istanbul is treated among the cities of Europe, but the geography of Turkey is dealt with under *Asia*.

Yugoslavia (*yōō′gō-släv′ĭ-à*). A republic of southern Europe with a southwestern coast line on the Adriatic Sea. On the land side, the country adjoins Italy, Austria, Hungary, Rumania, Bulgaria, Greece, and Albania. Its area is 98,725 square miles. In the peace treaty of 1947, Yugoslavia gained the state of Venezia Giulia plus the enclave of Zara and the islands of Cherso (Cres), Lussino (Losinj), Pelagosa (Pelagruz), and Pag at the expense of Italy.

Much of the coast is rocky and precipitous, rising inland to a mountainous plateau covering the western and southern part of the country. The eastern portion of the country contains a southern spur from the Carpathian mountains. The greater part of the surface is drained toward the east and the north by the Drava, Sava, and Morava rivers, which empty into the Danube. The Danube River, traversing the northern part of Yugoslavia and forming part of the country's Rumanian boundary, cuts through the eastern mountain barrier at the Iron Gate. The Iron Gate is a mountain pass through which the river formerly rushed over a plateau of rock 1400 feet wide. This point has been made navigable by extensive blasting at a cost of more than $10 million. The river valleys provide most of the country's arable land. Nearly one-half of the surface of Yugoslavia is covered with forest. Lumber leads the exports. The chief minerals are coal, lignite, iron, copper, lead, zinc, gold, salt, chromium, and antimony.

The most important industry is agriculture. The chief crops are wheat, corn, potatoes, barley, oats, sugar beets, tobacco, and temperate zone fruits. Silk culture employs many people. Large numbers of swine are fattened on the beechnuts and the acorns of the wooded land, while cattle and sheep graze on the higher mountain slopes. Flour milling, sugar refining, carpet weaving, tanning, and pottery are important industries. State ownership and control characterize the nation's postwar economic and agricultural systems. Tourism contributes immeasurably to the economy.

The inhabitants of Yugoslavia, estimated at 20,523,000 in 1971, are divided among three chief forms of religion, Greek Catholic, Roman Catholic, and Moslem. There are three universities. Belgrade is the capital and largest city.

CITIES AND OTHER POINTS OF TRAVEL INTEREST

The cities of Europe are distinguished by the richness of their historic associations, and, in many cases, by the wealth of their artistic adornment. Some of them, such as Athens and Rome, still preserve the visible evidences of the brilliant civilization which flourished in the southern part of the continent as early as 600 B. C. In others, the remains of outstanding interest are medieval structures—sublime cathedrals, or castles and dungeons of more sinister memories. Cities of southern Spain tell of Mohammedan enterprise; those of Italy remind us of the flowering of art known as the Renaissance; while the industrial cities of northern Europe often afford a curious blending of old interests and of new.

In World War II many European cities were largely destroyed or suffered extensive damage. In some places the historic buildings and monuments have been rebuilt or repaired, though many which were familiar to generations of American tourists have vanished forever.

The scenic beauties of Europe are not only grand in themselves but have the prestige that comes from centuries of description by travelers. The Alps have given us the term alpine, applicable to mountainous scenery of impressive beauty. The natural charm of the pleasure resorts is supplemented by all the attractions that can be suggested by ingenuity aiming to please vast numbers of tourists. The more noteworthy of these resorts are described in the following section, along with the cities and other places of especial interest on the continent.

In many instances, a city is known in English by a name different from that used by the inhabitants of the country in which it is located. In all such cases, the native name is given in bold-face type in parenthesis after the name commonly used by English-speaking people.

Alps. An irregular mountain system of south central Europe, occupying most of Switzerland and parts of France, Italy, Austria, and Germany. The system is 600 miles in length and has a width varying from 75 to 150 miles. It covers an area of about 85,000 square miles. The highest point is reached by Mont Blanc, 15,781 feet high. Other notable peaks with their heights are Monte Rosa, 15,203; Mischabel, 14,935; Lyskamm, 14,889; Weisshorn, 14,804; Matterhorn, 14,701; Dent Blanche, 14,318; Grand Combin, 14,164; Finsteraarhorn, 14,026; Aletschhorn, 13,803; and Jungfrau, 13,653.

The glaciers of the Alps number about 1200 and cover an area of 1600 square miles. The largest, called the Aletsch, has an area of 50 square miles. Other well-known Alpine glaciers are the Unteraar, the Gorner, the Viesch, the Mer de Glace, and the Miage, the last two being on Mont Blanc. The glaciers give rise to a number of mountain lakes, several of which have become proverbial for their beauty. The chief ones are Lucerne, Geneva, Como, Garda, and Maggiore. Water is often drawn from the bottoms of Alpine lakes to secure an all-year flow to develop electric power.

The Alps are cut by many passes, of which the principal ones have been pierced by tunnels for railroads or vehicular traffic. Under Saint Bernard pass, a two-lane tunnel 3.6 miles through the rock provides a roadway supported for an additional ten miles by concrete pylons. Railroad tunnels pierce the Brenner and Simplon passes and the Saint Gotthard and Mont Cenis mountains. A vehicular tunnel through 7.25 miles of rock under Mont Blanc was completed in 1964 to connect Italy and France. In 1976 a 10-mile, 120-yard vehicular tunnel, the world's longest, was completed in Switzerland. It runs from Goschenen on the northern side of the Alps beneath the St. Gottard range to Airolo in the Ticino area.

There are also numerous scenic railroads in the Alps and automobile roads which are marvels of engineering skill. These supplemented by cable cars giving access to mountain peaks make the Alps the most accessible region of superb mountain scenery in the world. The Swiss Alps and the Tyrol, in Italy and Austria, are among the most popular regions.

Amiens (F. *á'myăɴ'*; E. *ăm'ĭ-ĕnz*). A cathedral city of northern France, lying about 80 miles north of Paris. The Cathedral of Amiens, for magnificence and for richness of decoration, is not surpassed by any other Gothic building of the world. The city has important textile manufacturing interests and is widely known by tourists for its macaroons. During World War I, Amiens was made the headquarters of the British armies in France. Population, 101,677.

Amsterdam. The largest city and the statutory capital of the Netherlands, although the actual seat of government is The Hague. Amsterdam occupies a low site at the southwestern extremity of the Ijsselmeer and is connected with tidewater by the North Sea canal. The numerous canals, which divide the city into some 90 islands connected by almost 300 bridges, have given rise to the city's characterization as "the Venice of the North." Amsterdam's defenses consist of dikes, by the opening of which the whole district may be flooded.

The city is named after a dam built in 1240 across the river Amstel. Part of the site originally occupied by this dam is now the central square of the city and is called the Dam. From it the principal streets radiate in a semicircle. Nearby stand the New Church and the Royal Palace. In the former, a Gothic structure dating from 1408, the sovereigns of the Netherlands are crowned. The Royal Palace, belonging to the city, is the residence of the country's sovereigns when they are guests of Amsterdam. The Ryks, or State Museum, contains a number of paintings by Rembrandt, who, with the philosopher Spinoza, was among Amsterdam's most famous citizens. The city maintains a municipal abattoir, theater, pawnshop, and museum.

Amsterdam is the chief center of Dutch industry, commerce, and finance. Its diamond-cutting factories are the largest in the world. There are also shipbuilding yards, sugar, and oil refineries, and factories for making dyes, chemicals, glass, liquor, tobacco and steel products. The Bank of the Netherlands, situated in Amsterdam, is one of the leading financial institutions of Europe. The city is the seat of the University of Amsterdam and is the headquarters of the National Academy of Arts, the Royal Academy of Sciences, and the Royal Dutch Geographic Society. Amsterdam's botanical gardens are among the foremost in Europe. Population, 861,034. Greater Amsterdam, 911,248.

Antwerp (Antwerpen). A large city of Belgium, situated on the Scheldt River about 50 miles from its mouth in the North Sea. The river, 2200 feet wide at this point, provides Antwerp with one of the best harbors in the world. By means of 28 miles of quays, 3½ miles being granite and equipped with all modern appliances, the port handles merchandise often exceeding an annual total of one billion dollars. Besides its commerce, Antwerp is important for diamond cutting, sugar refining, and the manufacture of liquors, textiles, and cigars. Urban traffic is facilitated by two tunnels under the Scheldt River.

The most conspicuous building in the city is the Cathedral of Notre Dame, the construction of which was begun in the 14th century. It has a tower 400 feet high and contains three celebrated paintings by Rubens, whose tomb is contained in the splendid Church of Saint James. The richly decorated town hall was built in the 16th century. The art gallery contains a priceless collection of masterpieces by Rubens and Van Dyck, the latter having been born in the city. The Steen, part of an old castle dating from the 10th century, was formerly the seat of the Inquisition, but is now used as an archeological museum. Fine boulevards follow the line of the old city walls.

The city has had a stormy history. Founded in the 8th century, it had become, by the 16th century, the financial center of Europe and one of the chief commercial cities of the world. It was destroyed by the Spaniards in 1576. Napoleon revived the city. By improving its harbor, he hoped eventually to make Antwerp a rival of London. Population, 661,697.

Appian (*ăp'ĭ-ăn*) **Way.** A Roman road running from Rome to Brindisi in southern Italy, 446 miles. Begun in 312 B. C. by Appius Claudius as a public work, it is still in use over a considerable portion of its course. For several miles from Rome it is bordered by ancient tombs and the ruins of monumental buildings.

Arcadia. An inland district of the peninsula of Morea in Greece. Its ancient inhabitants long retained their primitive customs, unaffected by the Dorians who invaded the peninsula in the 12th century B. C. A pastoral poetry arose there in the last centuries of the pre-Christian era and gave support to a literary tradition, which represented Arcadia as a land of primitive simplicity and idyllic happiness.

Argonne Forest. A rocky wooded area northwest of Verdun in northeastern France. It was the scene, in September and October 1918, of one of the bloodiest battles ever waged by American troops. The capture of this forest by the Americans threatened the line of retreat of the German army.

ATHENS (Athēnai). The capital and largest city of Greece, situated in the southeastern portion of the country about five miles from the port of Piræus on the eastern shore of the Gulf of Ægina. The city stands in a plain surrounded on three sides by mountains. Athens is a financial, railroad, and commercial city of importance, but its industrial interests center chiefly in Piræus, where there are establishments for manufacturing cotton, flour, leather, chemicals, and rugs. Near Piræus lies Phalerum, the sea resort of Athens. Athens is named after Athena, the ancient Greek goddess of wisdom.

THE MODERN CITY. For several centuries following 500 B. C., Athens was the intellectual and artistic center of the civilized world and, architecturally, was one of the most beautiful cities on the earth. After many centuries of misfortunes, it was finally reduced to a Turkish village. When, in 1832, Greece became independent, Athens was chosen its capital and was rebuilt as a modern city.

The Square of Harmony forms a center from which radiate wide boulevards, two of them ending in Constitution square—the site of the royal palace and gardens. Between the two squares stand the government offices, the buildings of the Academy of Sciences, the National university, the National library, and the archeological colleges. Other notable modern structures include the Parliament buildings, the Palace of Justice, and the National Archeological Museum, the last housing a priceless collection of Greek antiquities. The city contains also the University of Athens, a beautiful library known as the Gennadeion, and the impressive Temple of Youth, headquarters of the Greek Y.M.C.A. There is a large stadium, in which the Olympic games were held in 1896.

The white marble, which is used in most of the public edifices, imparts to the city's architecture a distinctive and impressive brilliancy. The marble used in the ancient buildings has, through age, become tinged with a russet hue.

ANCIENT BUILDINGS. The ancient city centered about a flat-topped hill, called the Acropolis. This hill is surrounded by a wall and contains four beautiful structures: the Propylæa, a building of mixed Doric and Ionic style, which serves as a stately entrance to the enclosure; the Temple of Victory, a small Ionic edifice beside the Propylæa; the Parthenon, which is the classic example of a pure Doric temple and is justly famed as one of the world's most beautiful buildings; and, finally, the Erechtheum, known best for its Porch of the Maidens, in which the columns take the form of Greek maidens, often called Caryatids. These four buildings were all erected in the 5th century B. C., but they still preserve much of their original impressiveness. The Parthenon was partially restored in 1930.

The chief of the ancient buildings outside the Acropolis are the arch of Hadrian, the Theseum, the open-air theater of Dionysus, the Temple of Zeus, the Tower of the Winds, and the monument of Lysicrates, the last being the earliest extant example of the Corinthian style. The Theseum is the best preserved of the ancient Greek structures. Of the 104 Corinthian columns of the Temple of Zeus, each of them 56 feet in height, only 15 remain erect today.

These ruined structures are the original models for the Greek style of architecture as it has been revived in recent times and employed in the erection of many modern buildings. Excavations are going forward continuously, the most stupendous project being that for unearthing the ancient Agora. Population, 1,852,709.

Athos (ăth'ŏs). A mountain of northern Greece, 6670 feet high, occupying the extremity of a peninsula in the northern part of the Ægean Sea. In ancient times it was noted as the scene of the shipwreck of Xerxes' fleet, which sailed to attack Greece in 492 B. C. Since the 9th century A. D., the mountain has been occupied by a group of fortified monasteries, now 20 in number. The control of the mountain was handed over by the Byzantine emperors to the monasteries, which have continued to exercise their rights of self-government to the present day. Under a constitution dated in 1045 A. D., women and female animals are excluded from the holy mountain. The monks, numbering 4800, support themselves by agriculture, fishing, and various handicrafts.

Avignon (à'vē'nyôN'). A town of southeastern France, situated on the Rhone River about 30 miles from the Mediterranean Sea. Avignon is notable as the former residence of the popes, who made it their seat from 1309 to 1376. The city is built on a wall-girdled height, from the summit of which rise the cathedral and the impressive mass of the old papal palace. Population, 64,581.

Barcelona. The chief manufacturing center and, with the exception of Madrid, the largest city of Spain, located near the northeastern extremity of the country on the Mediterranean Sea. The city has a fine harbor and ranks as the second seaport in Spain. It is the commercial center of a rich fruit growing district. The chief manufactures are cotton, silk, and woolen goods, lace, leather, machinery, furniture, dyes, soaps, and drugs. Fruit, wine, olive oil, as well as manufactured goods, are among its exports.

The city dates from the 3d century B. C., when it was founded by the Carthaginian Hamilcar Barca, after whom it was called Barcino. From the 2d century A. D., the city has, in spite of varying fortunes, remained one of the chief commercial cities of southern Europe.

The older part of the city was formerly surrounded by walls, which have since been replaced by promenades. This section has, in general, narrow, irregular streets. Its chief thoroughfare, however, the Ramblas, which connects it with the "new town," has a handsome promenade on which are situated many of the principal buildings of the city, including one of the finest theaters in Spain. At the highest point of the Ramblas stands a famous 13th century cathedral in Spanish Gothic style. The "new town" is regularly laid out and has all modern improvements. Among the more recent buildings is the terminal station, one of the finest in Europe. The chief educational institution is the University of Barcelona. Population, 1,696,750.

Belfast. The capital and metropolis of Northern Ireland, situated on a small inlet in the northeastern part of the island. The city has an excellent harbor and contains immense shipyards, in which most of the White Star liners have been built. In addition to the linen textile industry, manufactures include the making of rope, liquors, tobacco goods, machine shop products, flour, and chemicals.

Belfast was incorporated as a city in 1888. It is the seat of Queen's university and Campbell college and has several fine churches, an art gallery, and a museum. Population, 399,270.

Belgrade (bĕl'grād') (Beograd). The capital and largest city of Yugoslavia, situated near the center of the country's northeastern boundary at the confluence of the Save and the Danube rivers. Belgrade is an important railway junction and is the chief trade center of the country. The city is modern in appearance and has several institutions for higher education, including a university, a national library, a museum, and an academy of sciences. There are several fine Greek Catholic churches. Prior to its capture by the Austrians on Oct. 9, 1915, Belgrade was the capital of Serbia. Population, 585,234.

Belleau (bĕl'ō') Woods. A forest of northeastern France, 5 miles northwest of Chateau Thierry and about 42 miles east of Paris. It is celebrated for a bitterly contested battle waged there in June 1918, when American marines and regulars dislodged a strongly entrenched German force and captured the village of Bouresches, 2 miles south of the woods. The battle ground was dedicated in 1923 as a permanent memorial to the Americans who fell there. It was named Bois de la Brigade de Marine.

Bergen (bûr'gĕn). A seaport and codfish market on the southwestern coast of Norway. Bergen's fish exports are nearly half those of all Norway. The chief manufactures are ships, paper, and ropes. The buildings include a naval academy, an observatory, and a fishery museum. The city maintains a noted marine biological station and is annually the scene of an international fishermen's fair. Edvard Grieg, the composer, was born there. Population, 117,353.

BERLIN. The capital of prewar Germany. After World War II, it became a divided city, 188 of its 342 square miles being an enclave of West Germany and the remaining 154 square miles being the capital of East Germany. It lies about 50 miles from the Polish border to the east and nearly 100 miles from West Germany, which has access to it by railroad, by a principal highway from Helmstedt, by waterway from Hamburg, and by an air corridor. In 1961 the East Germany government built a concrete wall separating the sectors and mounted armed guards on it to prevent escape to the West.

COMMERCE AND INDUSTRY. The old Berlin was the distributing point for a vast inland trade, being served by 12 trunk railroads and several waterways. Since the war, manufacturing has been concentrated chiefly in West Berlin, whose industries produce mainly clothing, electrical apparatus, locomotives, machinery and other steel products, pharmaceuticals, dyestuffs, porcelain, railroad cars, toys, and liquors.

Three-quarters of the old Berlin was destroyed by bombing and artillery fire in World War II. In 1948-49 the western sector was blockaded by the Russian military government, but the blockade was broken by a massive airlift from the west. Thereafter, restoration went forward rapidly, and manufacturing, commerce, and other civic activities grew apace.

STREETS, BUILDINGS, AND MONUMENTS. Streets are regularly laid out and flanked by handsome residences combined with numerous squares, parks, playgrounds, monuments, fashionable promenades, and splendid public buildings.

Berlin's most famous boulevard is Unter den Linden, so called from the double rows of lime, or linden, trees with which it is planted. The street is 196 feet wide and leads from the former imperial palace, with its 600 rooms, to the Brandenburg Gate, which is the official point of passage between the East and West sectors. This gate is a triumphal arch, modeled on the Propylea in Athens and surmounted by a colossal bronze car of victory. On the boulevard is situated, among other impressive buildings, the palace of William I.

The Brandenburg Gate leads west into the Tiergarten, a magnificent park of 600 acres, which contains one of the largest zoological gardens in the world. The continuation of Unter den Linden into East Berlin is Liebknecht-strasse, formerly Wilhelmstrasse. It passes the Chancellery, once administrative center of Germany and scene of Hitler's suicide. The Reichstag building, erected in the Italian Renaissance style, remains as when gutted by fire in 1933.

EDUCATIONAL INSTITUTIONS. Berlin is the chief intellectual center of Germany. The University of Berlin, founded in 1810, has numbered among its teachers Hegel, Fichte, Grimm, Niebuhr, Lipsius, Mommsen, and Einstein. Besides numerous technical institutions, there are free astronomical observatories, academies of art and of music, public libraries, botanical gardens, and many learned societies. Population of West Berlin, 2,190,577.

Berne. The capital and fourth largest city of Switzerland. The city is in the northwestern part of the republic and is picturesquely situated on a rocky bluff surrounded on three sides by the river Aar, a tributary of the Rhine. The name Berne is a corruption of the German word for bears, a number of the animals having been slain on the site when Berne was founded in 1191. A den of tame bears is maintained by the city, which has adopted the bear as its emblem.

Berne is noted for its manufacture of toys, engines, scientific instruments, and chocolate. It is the center of the international postal, telegraphic, railroad and copyright associations. The chief edifices are the magnificent Parliament building and a Gothic cathedral begun in 1421 but not completed until 1894. Population, 166,000.

Bingen (bĭng'ĕn). A town on the west bank of the Rhine River in Germany, 17 miles west of Mainz. Like many other towns on the Rhine, it has several picturesque ruins of feudal castles, the most notable of which is the Mouse Tower. In this tower, Archbishop Hatto is said to have been devoured by mice in 969 A. D. The Bingenloch, a famous whirlpool, is found a short distance down the river. Population, 20,210.

Birmingham. The second largest city of England, situated near the geographic center of the country. Being in close proximity to rich coal fields and large iron deposits, it was known for its iron products as early as the 16th century, and it has since become famous for its steel manufactures. Other industrial products include glass, jewelry, chemicals, automobiles, railroad cars, plated articles, pins, and hydraulic presses.

Birmingham has led the cities of England in municipal improvements. There are 17 parks and recreation grounds. An excellent school system provides elementary education, while museums, libraries, art galleries, botanical gardens, technical colleges, and an amply endowed university afford means for higher study. James Watt, John Bright, and Joseph Chamberlain are some of the distinguished names connected with the city. Population, 1,102,570.

Bologna (bô-lōn'yä). A city of northern Italy, located in a fertile plain at the foot of the Apennine mountains, almost midway between the Gulf of Genoa and the Gulf of Venice. It is an important railroad junction and has a large trade and extensive manufactures. The products for which the city is especially noted are macaroni, Bologna sausages, liquors, and canned fruit. Other industrial establishments include sugar refineries, rice mills, and railroad shops.

Bologna is believed to have been founded in the 8th century B. C. It figures in the career of Hannibal, Alaric, Charlemagne, and Napoleon. The city uses an aqueduct built by Augustus Cæsar. By a popular vote in 1860, Bologna became a part of the kingdom of Italy.

There are some 130 churches, several dating from the 11th century. One of the most noted is the San Domenico, where lies the body of Saint Dominic, the founder of the Dominican order. Bologna's art treasures include Raphael's portrait of Saint Cecilia. Two leaning towers survive from among 180 which Bologna possessed in the Middle Ages. One of the two is 163 feet high and inclines 10 feet from the perpendicular. The University of Bologna is the oldest existing university in Europe. Founded in the 11th century, it became famous as a law school and in 1262 had about 10,000 students, among whom were Dante and Petrarch. Galvani, one of the earliest investigators of electricity, was born in Bologna and lectured in the university. Population, 481,527.

Bonn (bŏn). A university city of central Germany, beautifully situated on the Rhine River, now the seat of government of the Federal Republic of West Germany. Establishment of the capital here has led to great expansion of departmental buildings. The University of Bonn, second only to that of Berlin among German universities, occupies the former palace of the electors of Cologne. The city also has a venerable cathedral and a Beethoven museum, the latter containing relics of the famous musician, who was born in the city. The principal manufactures are porcelain, office furniture, and stoneware. Population, 140,482.

Bordeaux (bôr'dō'). A commercial city of southwestern France, situated on the Garonne River at the point where it widens to form the Gironde River. It is connected by canal with the Mediterranean Sea. The chief article of export is wine, besides which hides, sugar, rice, cotton and woolen cloth, salt fish, and fruit are shipped abroad, mainly to South America. The city's industries include shipbuilding, canning, sugar refining, and the manufacture of casks, liquors, chemicals, leather, machinery, and pottery. Bordeaux is an important center for fishing fleets which annually visit the shores of Newfoundland and of Iceland.

The University of Bordeaux was founded in 1441. Among the more notable buildings of the city are the Grand Theater, the Church of Saint Croix, Saint Michael's Church, and the Cathedral of Saint André, the last dating from the 11th century. Montesquieu, Montaigne, and Rosa Bonheur were residents of Bordeaux.

Bordeaux was used as a port of disembarkation by the American forces during World War I. For a short period in 1914, it became the seat of the French government when Paris was menaced. Population, 249,688.

Boulogne (F. bōō'lôn'y'; E. bōō-lōn'). A fortified seaport of northern France, situated at the eastern extremity of the English channel. The city is the chief French station of the North Sea fisheries. It consists of a lower town,—the business part close to the harbor,—and an upper town built on a hill, from which, on clear days, the English coast may be seen. As a center for passenger traffic with England, Boulogne rivals Calais. During World War I, many American troopships landed their passengers in Boulogne. Population, 49,036.

Bradford. A manufacturing city in the north central part of England, the chief center in England for the manufacture of woolen textiles, and the leading wool market of the world. Silks, velvets, and foundry products are also manufactured. Bradford is substantially built, mainly of stone. Among the public buildings are Saint Peter's Church, the Mechanics Institute, the large, covered markets, and the Cartwright Memorial Hall, erected in memory of the inventor of the power loom. Population, 298,220.

Bremen (E. brĕm'ĕn; G. brā'mĕn). The second largest seaport of Germany. It lies in West Germany about 38 miles from the North Sea on both banks of the Weser River. The "old town" on the right bank is the business district, while the "new town" on the left is a well built residential section. The chief industrial products include ships, iron castings, machinery, refined sugar, tobacco, and cordage. It is the leading German fishing port.

Bremen is the capital of a small state of the same name, which retained its rights of self-government when it entered the German Empire. Population, 598,957.

Breslau (brĕs'lou) (**Wroclaw**). An important commercial and manufacturing city of Poland, situated on both banks of the Oder River. It has a large trade in raw materials and holds three annual fairs. The chief manufactures are textiles, steel products, railway cars, paper, and furniture. Breslau consists of an old town surrounded by five modern suburbs. One of the most notable buildings is the Protestant church, with a 300-foot steeple, founded in 1250 and dedicated to Saint Elizabeth. Population 477,300.

Brest. A strongly fortified seaport and one of the chief naval stations of France, located on a wide rock-bound harbor at the northwestern extremity of France. Most of the working population are engaged in industries related to naval maintenance. Between the town and the harbor mouth, the Cours d'Ajot, one of the finest promenades in Europe, skirts the shore. Brest was one of the principal ports used by the American Expeditionary Forces in World War I. A telegraph cable connects the city with Duxbury, Mass. Population, 130,867.

Brighton. The most celebrated seaside resort in England, situated on the English channel, 51 miles due south of London. A magnificent 4-mile promenade and driveway with two fine piers borders the coast. The most noteworthy building is the Royal Pavilion, in Oriental style, occupied by George IV and succeeding British sovereigns. Population, 162,650.

Bristol. A maritime city of southwestern England, situated seven miles south of the estuary of the Severn, with which it is connected by the navigable river Avon. The city has long been noted for its extensive commerce and for its glassworks, potteries, sugar refineries, soap works, tanneries, tobacco, chocolate, shoe, and chemical factories, and shipyards. In the shipyards of Bristol was built, in 1838, the early steamship *Great Western*.

The city is the seat of Bristol university and two colleges. Besides libraries, museums, and art galleries, there are several churches of which the finest architecturally is that of Saint Mary Redcliffe, dating from the 14th century. From Bristol came the first settlers of Newfoundland as well as the island's discoverer, John Cabot. The city was at one time the residence of Southey and of Coleridge. Population, 429,370.

Bruges (E. *broo'jĕz*; F. *brüzh*). A decadent commercial city of western Belgium. Prior to the 16th century, Bruges was a flourishing center of woolen manufacturing. Among the many medieval structures which the city has preserved from its more prosperous days are the Church of Notre Dame and les Halles, the Market Hall, whose tower, 352 feet in height, contains a chime of 48 bells. This tower was celebrated by Longfellow in his poem "The Belfry of Bruges." The port of Bruges is Zeebrugge, 8 miles distant, which was a German submarine base during World War I. The name of the city means bridges and was applied in allusion to the 54 bridges constructed across the numerous canals which intersect the city. Population, 52,220.

Brünn (*brün*) (**Brno**). An important commercial city of south central Czechoslovakia. Its manufactures include woolen goods, hardware, flour, refined sugar, and machinery. Brünn has several churches of attractive medieval architecture and a beautiful synagogue built in the Saracenic style. The city is a trading center for a thickly populated district. Population, 328,316.

Brussels (**Bruxelles**, or **Brussel**). The capital and largest city of Belgium, situated in the central part of the kingdom. It consists of an upper town,—the new and fashionable quarter,—and the lower, or old, town, devoted to commerce and industry.

Its magnificent boulevards, beautiful squares and parks, and imposing buildings make Brussels one of the most beautiful cities of Europe. The more notable buildings include the Hôtel de Ville, with its open-stonework spire, 374 feet high, and the sumptuous Greco-Roman Palais de Justice. The Church of Sainte Gudule, begun in 1220, is celebrated for its marvelous stained-glass windows. The royal library, the museums, and the art galleries contain many masterpieces of Flemish painters. The University of Brussels is one of the very few European universities which have been founded without the co-operation of church or state. The city has numerous schools and scientific societies.

Brussels suffered severely from the German occupation during World War I. Since that time, however, its industries have resumed their production of Brussels lace, carpets, furniture, steam engines, and other articles manufactured before the war. The city is also the railroad center of the country. Population, 1,074,586.

Bucharest (*boo'kȧ-rĕst'*; *bū'-*) (**Bucaresti**). The capital and largest city of Rumania, located in the central southern part of the country. Since 1948 it has been the seat of the Cominform (Communist Information Bureau). Bucharest has an extensive commerce in petroleum, cereals, and timber. The industries include oil refining and the manufacture of flour, liquors, chemicals, and brick.

The city's chief attractions are the splendid public gardens and the bright cupolas of the numerous Greek Catholic churches. Among the more imposing structures are the Royal Palace, the National university, the Palace of Justice, and several fine monuments. The customs of the inhabitants exhibit a blending of Oriental and Western influences. The name Bucharest is a corruption of a Rumanian word meaning city of joy. Population, 1,372,937.

Budapest (*boo'dȧ-pĕst'*). The capital and largest city of Hungary, situated in the central northern part of the country on the banks of the Danube river. Budapest comprises the former city of Buda on the right bank and of Pest on the left bank. The two are connected by six bridges, including two suspension bridges which are among the longest in Europe. These bridges were bombed by the U.S. Air Force in 1944–45.

Buda, the older section, which was founded by the Romans in the 2d century A.D., is built on two hills and contains the royal castle, the government offices, and the former residences of the aristocracy. The newer town, Pest, founded by the Huns under Attila in the 5th century A.D., is built on a low plain. Pest is the commercial, industrial, and intellectual center of the city. The city was largely in ruins in 1945 when the Russians expelled the occupying Germans.

The city's commercial interests are of great importance. Budapest is the railroad center of Hungary and is further served by the Danube, the chief waterway of the country. Population, 1,960,000; with suburbs, 1,970,000.

Cadiz (*kȧ'dĭz*). An Atlantic port on the south coast of Spain. Cadiz is one of the most ancient cities in Europe. Founded by the Phœnicians, 1100 B.C., Cadiz was captured in turn by the Carthaginians, Romans, Goths, Moors, and Spaniards. The town is still protected by walls and fortresses. When Spain was mistress of most of the New World, Cadiz was the emporium of American commerce and was a city of vast wealth and importance. Today its trade is small, the exports being principally salt, wines, olive oil, and fruits. Population, 117,871.

Calais (*kăl'ā*; *kăl'ĭs*). A fortified port of northeastern France, situated on the Strait of Dover near its narrowest part. Calais is the chief point of disembarkation for travelers from England, being only 21 miles from the English coast. It has considerable commercial, manufacturing, and shipbuilding interests and is the chief center in France for the making of lace.

Calais was held by England from 1347 to 1558. During World War I, it was used by England as the principal point of disembarking troops for France. Population, 70,707.

Cambrai (*käN'brĕ'*). An industrial town of northern France, noted for its manufacture of linen and of cotton textiles. The city has given its name to the fabric known as cambric.

In the vicinity of Cambrai, on Nov. 20, 1917, was fought the battle in which tanks were first used on a large scale. Population, 32,601.

Canterbury. A cathedral city in the southeast of England, lying south of the Thames and about 56 miles east of London. Christchurch Cathedral is the crowning architectural feature of the city. Although the cathedral was a target for German bombers during World War II, it was not directly hit. Nearby buildings, however, were destroyed. The Archbishop of Canterbury is, next to the king, the highest official of the Anglican Church. Among the distinguished Catholic archbishops who, prior to the Reformation, presided over the see, were Saint Augustine, Lanfranc, Anselm, and Thomas à Becket, the one last mentioned having been murdered in the cathedral. The building contains, among other tombs, that of Henry IV and of the Black Prince. The city has many interesting ruins, including those of Canterbury castle, a fortress of Norman construction. A public drinking fountain commemorates Marlowe, who was a native of Canterbury. Population, 32,020.

Cantigny (*kän'tēN'y'*). A village of northern France, 18 miles south of Amiens. On May 28, 1918, it was the scene of the first American offensive in World War I.

Capri (*kä'prē*). A beautiful, rocky island at the entrance of the gulf of Naples, Italy, visited annually by more than 60,000 tourists. Its area is nearly 6 square miles, and its highest point is about 2000 feet above the sea. One of its most remarkable features is the Blue grotto, the roof and sides of which are composed mostly of stalactites. The grotto is on the coast and is called blue because the light, refracted in passing through the water at the cave's mouth, causes the interior of the grotto to appear blue. Capri is the scene of Norman Douglas's famous modern novel, *South Wind* (1917).

Capri was anciently famous for the palace there to which the Roman emperor Tiberius retired in order to spend his last years in pleasures. It had also a large Roman lighthouse, the remains of which are still visible. A more recent ruin is that of Barbarossa, a castle named after a pirate who partially destroyed it in 1544. Population, about 7000.

Cardiff. The principal seaport and largest city of Wales, situated at the southeastern extremity of the principality near the northern coast of Bristol channel. The city is the largest coal exporting port in Europe and ranks among the largest ports of England in its total shipping tonnage. Besides coal, its chief exports are iron and steel products, machinery, railroad cars, and vehicles. Its docks cover more than 200 acres, and there are 7 miles of wharves. In Cathays park, at the center of the city, is one of the finest groups of public buildings in Great Britain. Near by is Cardiff castle, which embraces structures dating from Roman and medieval times. Cardiff is also the seat of University College of South Wales. Population, 259,700.

Carrara (*kär-rä'rä*). A city of northern Italy celebrated for its marble quarries. It is situated 3 miles inland from the eastern extremity of the Gulf of Genoa in a valley surrounded by marble hills. Most of the city's buildings are of marble, and there is a museum containing numerous statues and Roman antiquities discovered in the vicinity. Population, 37,386.

Cartagena. A Mediterranean port and strong naval station in the southeastern part of Spain. The chief industries are tunny fishing, shipbuilding, lead smelting, glass blowing, ironworking, and the manufacture of cordage and of other esparto grass products. The city is well built and is still surrounded by walls.

Cartagena was named after the city of Carthage. The city was founded about 243 B. C. by Hasdrubal, a Carthaginian general, who called the city *Carthago Nova*, "New Carthage." It was captured by the Romans in 210 B. C. and afterward was occupied successively by the Vandals, Moors, Spaniards, English, and French. Population, 42,424.

Catania (*kä-tä′nyä*). An Italian city on the eastern coast of Sicily, situated at the southeastern base of Mount Etna. The city has broad, well kept streets and many fine public buildings. A large trade in agricultural products is carried on in Catania, and there are important manufactures of linen, cotton, silk goods, and art objects of lava, wood, and marble. The chief attraction is Mount Etna. The city contains the remains of an ancient theater.

Catania was founded by Greeks in 729 B. C. and was held successively by the Carthaginians, Romans, Goths, Saracens, Normans, and the rulers of Aragon, from whom it passed to Italy. Population, 391,709.

Channel Islands. A cluster of islands lying in the English Channel near the northwestern coast of France, of which the principal ones are Jersey, Guernsey, Alderney, and Sark. Originally a part of the Duchy of Normandy, they have belonged to Great Britain since the Norman Conquest. Although rocky, about half of their 75 square miles is arable.

The Channel Islands are much frequented by tourists. Jersey contains a gorge more than 1000 feet deep in the cliffs at Crabbe. Other features of the islands include a picturesque natural archway of rock on Dixcart bay; a feudal manor house at Samares, dating from the 11th or 12th century; and Mousterian caves which, when explored recently, exhibited the remains of Neanderthal men, of the woolly rhinoceros, the cave hyena, and other animals now extinct. The state of New Jersey was named after the island of Jersey. Population, 113,416.

Chateau Thierry (*shä′tō′ tyĕ′rē′*). A town in the northern part of France, on the Marne River 47 miles east and slightly north of Paris. At this point, in June 1918, American troops engaged German forces advancing toward Paris and effectively checked their progress. Several weeks later, a general counter attack swept the Germans back a distance of many miles. The town is named after a castle in the neighborhood, which was built by Charles Martel for the Frankish king Thierry IV. On July 15, 1923, a monument commemorating the American victory was erected in a square of the town, renamed United States place. Population, 9356.

Chemnitz (*kĕm′nĭts*) (**Karl-Marx-Stadt**). An industrial city of East Germany situated at the base of the Erzgebirge Mountains. The principal manufactures include locomotives and engines, textiles, hosiery, carpets, chemicals, and dyestuffs. Founded as a market town in 1143, Chemnitz has a varied but unbroken history as an industrial city extending from the 13th century until the present. Population, 294,973.

Cherbourg (*shĕr′bŏŏr′*). A strongly fortified French naval station near the center of the country's northern coast on the English channel. Its ocean railroad station, opened in 1933, is one of the largest buildings in France. It was from this port that the Confederate cruiser, the *Alabama*, was forced by the French authorities to put out to sea before it was sunk by the United States vessel, the *Kearsarge*. Population 37,096.

Coblenz (**Koblenz**). A commercial and manufacturing city of West Germany, beautifully situated at the confluence of the Moselle and the Rhine River. It was rich in old churches and art monuments until World War II, when most of the city was destroyed.

Coblenz has an active trade in grain. Its manufactures consist mainly of Moselle wine, ships, hats, machinery, pianos, and lacquered wares. The finest edifice is the government building, in which are centered the administrative activities of the province of Rhenish Prussia. Saint Castor's church, founded in 836, ranks among the oldest in Germany. Population, 99,240.

Cologne (*kŏ-lōn′*) (**Köln**). A large commercial and manufacturing city of central West Germany, beautifully located on the left bank of the Rhine river. *Eau de Cologne* is a distinctive product. The chief manufactures are leather goods, chemicals, starch, textiles, rubber goods, machinery, metal wares, beet sugar, tobacco products, and chocolate.

The outstanding feature of Cologne's architecture is the Gothic cathedral, begun in 1248 and completed in 1880. Two of its towers rise to a height of 512 feet. The cathedral, though damaged, survived World War II, in which most of the other Romanesque and Gothic buildings perished.

The Church of Saint Ursula is reported to contain the bones of 11,000 British virgins who were massacred near Cologne on their way to Rome. The Virgin islands in the West Indies owes its name to this tradition.

Cologne was founded in the 1st century A. D. under the name of Colonia Agrippina, of which its modern name is a corruption. Rubens, the painter, lived in the city, and one of the local churches contains the tomb of John Duns Scotus. Population, 861,027.

Copenhagen (*kō′pĕn-hā′gĕn*) (**Köbenhavn**). The capital and largest city of Denmark, situated on a deep, safe, and capacious harbor on the northeast shore of the island of Zealand. Across the harbor, on the island of Amager, is the modern suburb of Christianshavn. Copenhagen commands the sea highway from the Baltic to the North Sea and was at one time the chief distributing mart of the Baltic trade. To offset the advantages given by the Kiel canal to Germany's seaports, Copenhagen, in 1894, made part of its harbor a free port. Shipbuilding is the chief industry. Among the manufactures are agricultural machines, porcelains, textiles, sugar, watches, and chemicals.

A characteristic feature of Copenhagen is the large number of spires, which occur on many public buildings as well as on the churches. The Church of Our Redeemer has a winding staircase built outside the spire 295 feet to its top. Copenhagen is the seat of the University of Copenhagen and is the headquarters of many learned societies. The Thorvaldsen Museum contains over 300 works executed by Thorvaldsen, Denmark's greatest sculptor. Hans Christian Andersen was one of the city's most distinguished residents. Population, 1,377,605.

Cordoba (*kôr′dō-vä*). An inland city of southern Spain, located on the Guadalquivir River. The city was founded by the Phœnicians and attained to considerable importance under the Romans. It later became the metropolis of the Moors in Spain and, from the 9th to the 12th century, was one of the greatest centers of commerce in the world. The Mosque of Cordoba, now used as a Catholic cathedral, is the most magnificent example of Mohammedan architecture in Europe. The city is now in decline, its manufactures being confined largely to textiles, gold and silver filigree work, and cordovan leather. The last named article obtained its name from Cordoba. Cordoba was the birthplace of the Roman poet Lucan, of the two Senecas, and of the Arab philosopher Averroës. Population, 214,296.

Cork. A port of central southern Eire, situated on a capacious natural harbor formed by the estuary of the River Lee. It has a lower harbor, Cobh, formerly Queenstown, located at the river's mouth, an important Irish port of call for trans-Atlantic liners. A heavy trade in foodstuffs is carried on with England. The city's chief manufactures are leather, liquors, gloves, fertilizers, and textiles.

Among the finest buildings are the Anglican and the Catholic cathedral, both dedicated to Saint Finn Barr, who founded the city in 622 A. D. The Church of Saint Anne Shandon has a notable peal of bells. Other features of the city are University college, a school of science and of agriculture, and a public park, 240 acres in extent. Population, 122,146.

Coventry. An industrial city of central England, noted for its manufacture of automobiles, ribbons, artificial silk, telephone equipment, and electric motors. Coventry is a very old town and was for centuries the scene of an annual pageant commemorating the ride of Lady Godiva. According to tradition, she agreed to ride naked through the streets in order to save the citizens from certain exactions, her husband, Earl Leofric, having demanded this action as a condition of relieving the townspeople. The pageant was last celebrated in 1887. Saint Mary's Hall, built in 1450, is one of the finest examples of ornamental architecture in England. Much of the city, including a 14th century cathedral, was destroyed by bombing in World War II. The latter was replaced by a magnificent cathedral in modern architectural style. Population, 331,950.

Dardanelles. A narrow channel, 42 miles long and 1 to 5 miles wide, joining the Sea of Marmora and the Ægean Sea. The territory about the strait, affording an excellent defense of Istanbul from the West, was the scene of a costly offensive against Turkey during World War I. After the war, it was placed under the control of an Allied commission, but Turkey resumed control in 1936.

The ancient name of the Dardanelles was Hellespont, across which, in spite of its strong current, the mythical Leander is said to have swum each evening to visit Hero. Lord Byron swam the Hellespont at the point where Xerxes crossed it in 480 B. C.

Dnepropetrovsk. A large and rapidly developing industrial city of the Russian Ukraine located at the junction of the Dnieper and Donets rivers. Its major industries are iron and steel, machine construction, chemicals, and food products. The city shared in the hydroelectric development of the vast Dnepr dam, destroyed in 1941, but since restored. Its population is 738,000, more than double that of 1926.

Dortmund (dôrt'mōont). A railway center and manufacturing city of central West Germany in the northern part of the Ruhr district. Located in the midst of rich coal mines, the city has become an important point for the manufacture of steel products, including machinery, wire ropes, rails, mining equipment, and safes. Among other products are flour, lumber, and liquors. Since 1900, its population has more than tripled, standing, according to the latest reports, at 657,087. Largely devastated in World War II, it was promptly rebuilt.

Dover. A heavily fortified port and favorite summer resort of England, situated at the southeastern extremity of the country. White chalk cliffs tower nearly 400 feet above the harbor, and, on clear days, afford a view of the opposite coast of France, 21 miles distant. The chief industrial products are ships, sails, rope, and flour. Towering 375 feet above the sea is Dover Castle, covering 35 acres, which includes within its ancient walls a Roman lighthouse. Population, 36,080.

Dragoman. Picturesque Bulgarian town at the easterly end of the Dragoman Pass, near the Yugoslavian frontier. Bernard Shaw made it the scene of his play, *Arms and the Man*, which was later turned into the opera, *The Chocolate Soldier*. The famous international train, the Orient Express, stops at Dragoman for customs inspection.

Dresden. An industrial city of East Germany. It is situated on the Elbe River and is an important railway center. The chief manufactures include pianos, confectionery, silverware, jewelry, chemicals, glassware, and metal goods. Dresden china is made at Meissen, a suburb.

In World War II about 60 per cent of the city, with most of the art and architectural monuments, was destroyed. Since then many art treasures, including Raphael's "Sistine Madonna," which were safely stored outside the city during the war, have been transferred to Russia. Population, 507,470.

Dublin. The capital and largest city of Eire, situated on an inlet near the center of Ireland's eastern coast. A large part of the country's exported foodstuffs are handled through the port of Dublin. Liquors are made in considerable quantity.

Dublin as a whole, with its fine bay, wide streets, spacious squares, magnificent 2000-acre park, massive public buildings, and beautiful suburbs, is one of the handsomest capitals in Europe. Christ Church, in Early English Gothic style, was begun in 1038 by a Danish king of Dublin. Saint Patrick's Cathedral is about 700 years old. The city has statues of O'Connell, Burke, Goldsmith, and many other famous Irishmen. The University of Dublin is the chief educational institution. Population, 568,772.

Duisburg (düs'bōorк). A manufacturing city of central West Germany, in the Ruhr district. Its quays, built along canals and on the Rhine and the Ruhr rivers, are said to constitute the largest river harbor in the world. The chief commodities handled are coal and the products of the city's industries—iron and steel products, chemicals, liquors, asphalt, varnish, furniture, and tobacco. The former cities of Duisburg and Hamborn were combined in 1929. Population, 483,993.

Düsseldorf (düs'ĕl-dôrf). A manufacturing city of West Germany, situated on the right bank of the Rhine at the influx of the Düssel River. The harbor is spacious and well equipped, and there is a large export trade. The city has great iron and steel industries and textile manufactures. Chemicals, tobacco goods, chocolate, beer, paper, glass, and musical instruments are also made.

Destruction of Düsseldorf in World War II was widespread and drastic. In a situation between the Ruhr coal and steel area and the Federal capital at Bonn, Düsseldorf is becoming more and more the industrial and banking center of West Germany. It is also tending to lead in German commercial development of women's fashions. Population, 698,421.

Edinburgh (ĕd"n-bŭr-ô). The second largest city of Scotland. It is built near the south shore of the Firth of Forth, which is here spanned by a bridge 1½ miles in length. Edinburgh is the seat of the supreme court of Scotland and was the seat of government before the country united politically with England. The chief industries include printing and publishing, and the manufacture of liquors, leather, flour, and rubber goods.

Edinburgh consists of an old and a new section. Through the latter runs the magnificent Princes street, one of the finest thoroughfares in Europe. Near it stands the beautiful Scottish American war memorial. Among the city's points of interest are Holyrood Palace; Saint Giles Church, which has a memorial tablet to R. L. Stevenson designed by Saint-Gaudens; a magnificent monument to Sir Walter Scott; a small Greek temple erected to the memory of Robert Burns; and Calton cemetery, which contains a statue of Abraham Lincoln with a freed slave kneeling at his feet. Edinburgh has a handsome library donated by Andrew Carnegie. There are numerous educational institu-

tions, the most famous of which is the University of Edinburgh. The predominance of literary elements in the city's population, combined with its picturesque location, has won for it the name of "modern Athens."

The city was named after Edwin, king of Northumbria, who seized it in the 7th century A. D. and built a fortress on Castle rock, a precipitous height which dominates the city. The Royal Castle now stands on the site of Edwin's fortress. Population, 467,986.

Essen. A steel manufacturing city of West Germany, situated in the Ruhr district and surrounded by rich coal and iron deposits. The recent industrial growth of the city is due mainly to the activities of the Krupp corporation. The town, however, traces its origin to 873 A. D., when construction began on the cathedral, which is one of the oldest churches in Germany. Population, 721,182.

Etna. The largest active volcano in Europe. It is an isolated mountain, 10,705 feet high, in northeastern Sicily near Catania and has a base 90 miles in circumference. On its eastern side is a former crater, now a vast amphitheater with nearly precipitous sides 3000 feet in height.

The first recorded eruption of Etna was in the 8th century B. C. Another, occurring in 477 B. C., is graphically described in Æschylus' *Prometheus Bound*. Later eruptions of a violent character took place in 1169, 1527, 1669, 1693, 1852, 1864, 1879, 1911, 1923, and 1928. In that of 1669 more than 20,000 people were killed. An observatory and a house for the convenience of travelers have been erected near the chief crater. A large part of the world's supply of sulphur came formerly from Mount Etna.

Fingal's Cave. A remarkable cave of basalt formation, on Staffa, a small island off the central western coast of Scotland. The cave extends from the shore a distance of 227 feet within a rocky height and has an arch 66 feet high. Its maximum width is 42 feet. The color effects of the columnar basalt formation are no less striking than the weird sounds produced by the action of wind and wave as they play upon the opening of the huge cave.

Florence (Firenze). A city of north central Italy, lying in a fertile valley near the Apennine mountains. Florence is, next to Rome, the most celebrated Italian city, being noted for its illustrious history and its art treasures.

The Cathedral of Florence is the city's outstanding structure. Founded in 1296, it occupied about 200 years in construction. Its dome was planned by Brunelleschi. The bell tower of the cathedral was built by Giotto. This tower and the bronze doors of the baptistery, designed by Ghiberti, have enjoyed renown for centuries. The Franciscan church Santa Croce contains the tombs of Galileo, Michelangelo, Machiavelli, and many other distinguished men. The picture galleries contain some of the best works of Titian, Andrea del Sarto, Botticelli, Rubens, Raphael, and other great painters. Among the notable statues are the "Venus de' Medici," "Dancing Faun," and "Knife Grinder."

The city has famous academies of art, a museum of natural history, a university, a botanical garden, a large astronomical observatory, and a number of libraries, chief of which is the Laurentian library founded by Lorenzo de Medici. Florence was the birthplace of Dante and of Florence Nightingale.

The industries of the city include the manufacture of silks, glassware, porcelain, and objects of art, especially mosaics, wood carvings, majolica chinaware, stained glass, and jewelry. Florence was founded in the 2d century B. C., but the period of its greatest prosperity was in the 13th century A. D., when it was an independent city-state. Population, 454,858.

Flushing. A strongly fortified Dutch seaport, built on an island at the western extremity of the Netherlands. There is a large passenger traffic between Flushing and English ports. The city was the birthplace of Admiral de Ruyter, one of Holland's greatest naval heroes. Population, 29,141.

Folkestone. An ancient town and seaport of southeastern England, situated on the Strait of Dover. Folkestone has daily steamer communication with Boulogne in France and is also popular as a summer resort. Harvey, the discoverer of the circulation of the blood, was born in this city. Population, 43,470.

Frankfurt (Frankfort). Important commercial, industrial, and transportation center in central West Germany, on both sides of the lower Main River, an eastern tributary of the Rhine. It is the headquarters of the American armed forces in Europe, and of the U. S. zone high commissioner. The city has important literary and historical associations.

About 55 per cent of Frankfort was destroyed in World War II, but some of the most famous buildings, including Goethe's birthplace, have been rebuilt. It has a university, and other colleges and institutes. There is a monument to Gutenberg, the inventor of movable type. Frankfort was formerly the electoral city of the Holy Roman Empire, and, after 1816, the German Parliament held its sessions there. Population, 684,798.

Freiburg (*frī'bŏŏrк*). A city in the southwestern extremity of Germany, noted for its magnificent Gothic cathedral. This edifice, built of red sandstone, was begun in 1122 and was completed in 1513. It is admired for the delicate symmetry shown in its design as well as for its splendid tower, which is 386 feet high. Population, 150,437.

Geneva (**Genève**). A beautiful city of western Switzerland, situated at the lower end of Lake Geneva where its waters flow into the Rhone River. The city covers two islands in the river, one of which, called Rousseau's island, is a public pleasure ground commemorating the revolutionary writer, who was a native of the city. The left bank of the river is occupied by the old city and the business section, while, on the right bank, is the quarter called Saint Gervais, mainly residential in character. The latter district contains numerous hotels for the accommodation of the many tourists who enter Switzerland by way of Geneva.

The University of Geneva was originally founded as an academy in 1559 by Calvin, who made Geneva the chief center of Protestantism in the 16th century. Swiss heroes of the Reformation are further commemorated in Geneva by a recently erected monument entitled the "Wall of the Reformers." The manufactures of the city consist principally of clocks, watches, jewelry, enameled ware, and scientific instruments. Geneva, formerly the headquarters of the League of Nations, is now the European headquarters of the United Nations, and of many other international organizations, including the Red Cross. The city is predominantly French in language and culture. Population, 169,700.

Genoa (*jĕn'ô-ȧ*) (**Genova**). A commercial city of northeastern Italy, picturesquely situated at the head of the Gulf of Genoa. The city is strongly fortified against attacks by sea or land. Rail connections render it the sea outlet for much of the foreign trade of northern Italy, Switzerland, and southern Germany. The manufactures include foundry and other metal products, leather, cotton, cement, motor cars, crystallized fruits, and hats, and the city is also noted for its production of works of art in gold, silver, ivory, alabaster, and coral. It has large shipbuilding facilities and the largest dry dock in the Mediterranean Sea.

Among the notable examples of Genoa's many fine edifices are the ducal palaces, the residences of the doges in the days of the city's independence; the Cathedral of San Lorenzo, containing what is said to be the Holy Grail; the Church of Santissima Annunziata; and the Teatro Carlo Felice. The last named edifice was built in 1828 and ranks among the largest theaters in Italy. Genoa has an imposing sculptural group in honor of Columbus. Population, 845,427.

Ghent (**Gent** or **Gand**). A city of western Belgium, located on the Scheldt River and connected with the North Sea by a ship canal. The city is divided into islands by smaller canals, which are spanned by numerous bridges. The older part of Ghent has narrow, gloomy streets, but the newer part is laid out with wide avenues, flanked by fine houses.

Ghent contains the Cathedral of Saint Bavon, in which is the celebrated "Adoration of the Magi" by Van Eyck. There is also a great walled and moated nunnery, which, since its foundation in the 13th century, has been known for the production of exquisite lace. Ghent's principal manufactures are cotton and linen textiles, leather, and refined sugar, and the city has an active export trade in flowers. The emperor Charles V was born in Ghent, where, also, was signed the treaty which closed the War of 1812. Population, 232,736.

Giant's Causeway. A line of three perpendicular cliffs on the northeastern coast of Ireland. According to a legend, they were the beginning of a causeway to be built by giants across the channel to Scotland. They are formed of vertical basalt columns, mainly hexagonal in form and fitting closely together. The three cliffs are called the Little Causeway, the Middle Causeway, and the Grand Causeway. The last has a width of 60 to 120 feet and extends about 500 feet into the sea. On the Middle Causeway is the famous "wishing chair." The vicinity abounds in special points of interest, such as an amphitheater of natural formation and ruined castles perched on the top of isolated crags.

Glasgow. The third largest city in Great Britain situated on the Clyde River somewhat southwest of the geographical center of Scotland. Its harbor has been elaborately improved at the cost of 40 million dollars and has some 8 miles of quays. Glasgow's shipyards are the largest in the world. The industrial development is due partly to the city's location in the midst of extensive deposits of coal and of iron. The chief manufactures, apart from ships, comprise iron and steel products, textiles, coal, paper, chemicals, and whisky.

Glasgow is conspicuous for its successful management of civic operations and improvements, which include the erection of large numbers of modern apartment houses. There are many institutions for technical and higher education, of which the most important is the University of Glasgow. The municipal art gallery contains the finest collection of paintings in Great Britain outside of London, including Whistler's portrait of Carlyle. Saint Mungo's Cathedral, built between 1197 and 1446, is a beautiful example of Early English architecture. It stands on the site of a church erected in the 6th century by Saint Mungo, the patron saint of Glasgow. Population, 960,527.

Gorkiy, formerly **Nizhni Novgorod.** A city of Russia, on the Volga River about 270 miles east of Moscow. From remote antiquity, the city has been famous for its annual fair, one of the greatest of the entire world. Prices of many important commodities throughout Russia depended on those prevailing on this market. Merchandise totaling in some years over 20 million tons changed hands between August 1 and September 15.

The Soviet government chose this city as its chief center for the manufacture of automobiles. About fourteen miles from the old town, an enormous automobile factory, the largest in Europe, was placed in operation in 1931. About it was built a model soviet city designed for 60,000 inhabitants. One-third its area was devoted to parks. Residential units were built to accommodate 200 people per unit, each being equipped for communal meals and provided with facilities for amusement and instruction. The name Nizhni Novgorod was changed in 1932 to Gorki in honor of the famous writer, who was born there in 1868. Population, 1,120,000.

Göteborg (*yû'tĕ-bôr'y'*). The second largest city of Sweden, situated in the southwestern part of the country at the mouth of the Göta River, which discharges into the Kattegat. The town was founded in 1618 by Gustavus Adolphus, but, in consequence of numerous fires, it has been largely rebuilt in recent times. It has numerous fine buildings and broad, well shaded streets, those near the river having canals running through their centers. Favored by an excellent harbor open all the year round, Göteborg conducts much of the country's foreign commerce. The industries comprise shipbuilding, textile weaving, dyeing, iron-working, brewing, and the manufacture of tobacco, furniture, paper, and leather. Population, 443,292.

Granada. An inland city of southeastern Spain, lying at the base of the Sierra Nevada about 40 miles from the Mediterranean coast. The city, having been formerly one of the chief centers of Moorish civilization in Spain, has a partially Oriental appearance. The residential section of the Moorish nobility is now in ruins and is occupied largely by gypsies. Granada's outstanding edifice is the Alhambra, a magnificent Moorish palace celebrated in America by Washington Irving's book *The Alhambra*. The cathedral, begun in 1529, commemorates the reconquest of Spain by the Christian powers. Granada has a university founded in 1531 by the emperor Charles V.

The city is in a fertile district containing groves of orange, lemon, and fig trees. Its manufactures include textiles, paper, leather, flour, macaroni, chocolate, and soap. Population, 150,186.

Graz (*grät's*). A commercial and industrial city of Austria, situated in a beautiful valley at the eastern extremity of the Alps Mountains. The principal architectural attractions include a Gothic cathedral dedicated to Saint Ogidius and noted for its exquisite stained-glass windows, a mausoleum containing the remains of Emperor Ferdinand II, and the parish church, which, built in 1520, is adorned with an altarpiece by Tintoretto. Graz has a university, founded in 1573.

A rich coal district is near the city. The manufactures comprise iron and steel goods, optical instruments, chemicals, paper, and lithographs. Graz is an important railroad and trade center. Population, 237,080.

Hague, The (**'s Gravenhage**). The capital of the Netherlands, situated in the southwestern part of the kingdom about two miles from the North Sea. The city is chiefly occupied with the business of governing, although there are manufactures of gold and silver lace, jewelry, and articles of iron, brass, and copper.

The Hague has broad, shaded streets, intersected by picturesque canals and lined by many fine edifices. One of the most noted buildings is the Mauritshuis, which contains masterpieces by Rembrandt, Rubens, Van Dyck, and others. The city is the headquarters of the Permanent Court of International Justice and of the International Court of Arbitration. These courts sit in the Carnegie Peace Palace, which was erected in 1913, partly through the generosity of Andrew Carnegie. Other features of the city are the royal library, the various government buildings, Willem's park, and the royal villa Huis-ten-Bosch, "House in the Woods," which stands in the suburbs amid the magnificent forests separating the city from its seaside resort, Scheveningen. Population, 589,862.

Hamburg. The largest city of West Germany, excluding Berlin, and one of the largest seaports in the world. In northwestern Germany south of the Baltic peninsula, it is connected with Cuxhaven on the North Sea, 75 miles distant, by the Elbe River. Hamburg's two harbors are on two small lakes made by damming the Alster, a stream flowing through the city. The docks are 20 miles in length and are among the best equipped in the world. Hamburg is one of the chief coffee markets of the world and handles immense quantities of wool, grain, cotton, ironware, tobacco, coal, and paper. It is also the headquarters of the Hamburg-American steamship line. The manufactures include ships, tobacco products, liquors, flour, chocolate, rubber, chemicals, electrical goods, motor cars, and steel products. Workingmens' sections were devastated in World War II.

Hamburg was one of the principal cities of the Hanseatic League in the 13th century. In 1842, a large part of the city was destroyed by fire and was since rebuilt in a modern fashion. As a memorial of the fire, the Church of Saint Nicholas was erected, with a spire rising 482 feet above the ground. Hagenbeck's private zoological gardens contain one of the largest collections of wild animals in captivity. The city is the capital of the state of Hamburg, some 160 square miles in area, which has self-governing rights within the German republic. It is also the seat of the University of Hamburg. Population of city, 1,851,327.

Hammerfest. The most northerly incorporated town in the world, situated on an island off the northern coast of Norway 300 miles north of the Arctic circle. The inhabitants support themselves by fishing, raising reindeer, and entertaining tourists, large numbers of whom annually visit the town in order to view the spectacle of the midnight sun. The sun does not set on Hammerfest from May 13 to July 29. Population, 3470.

Hanover (Hannover). An industrial city of northern West Germany, about 150 miles west of Berlin. The leading manufactures are iron and steel products, musical instruments, machinery, rubber, cotton, cork, chocolate, tobacco, furniture, chemicals, and leather. Among the features of Hanover are the city forest, lying in the suburbs and containing a zoological garden; the Grosse Garten, a pleasure ground richly adorned with statuary; Herrenhausen Castle; the Marktkirche, a 14th century church with a tower 300 feet high; and a veterinary school founded by George III of England. It is now capital of the state of Lower Saxony. Hanover was formerly the capital of the Kingdom of Hanover, a state which, from 1714 until 1837, had the same rulers as England. Population, 547,767.

Havre, Le (E. *hȧ'vēr*; F. *lĕ ȧv'r'*). One of the largest seaports of France, situated at the mouth of the Seine river near the center of the country's northern coast. Its exports are mainly silk and cotton goods. The manufactures include chemicals, rope, machinery, flour, dyes, textiles, toys, and refined oil.

The importance of Havre dates from 1517, when the improvement of its harbor was begun. During World War I, the city was temporarily made the seat of the Belgian government. Population, 183,776.

Heidelberg. A university town of Baden in southern West Germany. The university was founded in 1385 and numbers among its graduates Melanchthon, Gervinus, Kuno Fischer, and Bunsen. The town has an ancient castle, which contains in its cellar a cask with a capacity of 46,732 gallons. Near Heidelberg, in 1907, the lower jawbone of a prehistoric man was found, and the city has given its name to the racial type which, on the basis of this bone, is believed to have existed many hundreds of thousands of years ago. Population, 124,401.

Helsingfors (*hĕl'sĭng-fôrs'*) (**Helsinki**). The capital and largest city of Finland, located in the south part of the country on a peninsula projecting into the Gulf of Finland. The city is strongly fortified. It is regularly laid out and has many fine buildings and handsome parks adorned with monuments. The University of Helsingfors was originally founded at Abo in 1640 and was moved to Helsingfors in 1827. Helsingfors is the chief industrial city of Finland, manufacturing tobacco, liquors, and carpets. It has a considerable commerce in timber, paper, and dairy products. In 1952, the Olympic Games were held here. Population, 501,474.

Hull. A large seaport of central eastern England, situated at the mouth of the Hull River in the estuary of the Humber. It is the chief outlet for most of England's exports to Denmark, Norway, and Sweden. Its docks cover 200 acres. The city has extensive fishing interests, and its manufactures comprise iron goods, engines, ships, chemicals, soap, cement, paper, cotton goods, and leather. William Wilberforce was a native of Hull. Population, 300,320.

Istanbul, formerly **Constantinople.** The largest city of Turkey. It is built on a peninsula on the northern side of the Bosporus Strait at its outlet into the Sea of Marmara. Istanbul occupies a key position, commanding a vast commerce between the East and the West. It has an excellent natural harbor in the Golden Horn, a northwestern inlet of Bosporus Strait.

Stamboul, or the Turkish section, has a typically Asiatic character, being surrounded by walls, now partly ruined, and having unimproved, crooked streets, picturesque mosques, and extensive, colorful bazaars. There are two suburbs—Galata, the foreign business quarter, built mainly

of stone; and Pera, a modern residential section of the foreign inhabitants, which is separated from Stamboul by the Golden Horn. The finest street in the city is the Grande Rue, in Pera, which is lined with fashionable shops and large hotels. Educational institutions include Stamboul university and Roberts college.

The most notable buildings of Istanbul are the mosques. Saint Sophia, originally built by Justinian as a church, and later converted by the Turks into a mosque, is being restored to its original beauty and is to be used as a museum. The Suleymanieh Mosque is the city's outstanding example of genuine Turkish architecture.

Secular buildings of historic interest include the Castle of the Seven Towers, once used as a state prison; the hippodrome completed by Constantine; and the old seraglio, now transformed into a museum, in which is stored an extremely valuable collection of Greek antiquities. Water for the city's use is conveyed long distances by aqueducts, some of which date from the 3d century A. D., and is held in reservoirs until required. One of these reservoirs is covered with a roof supported by 420 marble columns and is said to be the largest work of its kind in the world.

Large manufacturing establishments in Istanbul are few in number, producing mainly ironwares, leather articles, and tobacco goods. The handmade products, however, are important both in variety and in quantity. The chief exports of the city are carpets and rugs, lambskins and wool, attar of roses, embroidery, and filigree work.

Istanbul was often referred to formerly as the Sublime Porte. This is a French term meaning the lofty gate and referred to an elaborate entrance into the enclosure containing the government buildings. This name was used to designate the city as a political capital.

The city was founded in the 6th century B. C. by Greek colonists, who gave it the name Byzantium. In 330 A. D., Constantine the Great made it the capital of the Roman Empire, changing its name to Constantinople. Taken by the Turks in 1453, the city became the capital of the Ottoman empire and the residence of the head of the Moslem religion. In 1920, however, the Turkish Nationalists revolted, choosing as their capital Ankara, in Asia Minor. The name Constantinople was then changed officially to Istanbul. It is now Turkey's chief link with the Western world. Population, 1,750,642.

Jena (*yā'nä*). A university town within East Germany. The university, founded in 1558, has numbered among its professors Humboldt, Hegel, Fichte, Schiller, Haeckel, and Eucken. Goethe resided here at one time. The city is also noted for its production of lenses. Jena was the scene of a disastrous German defeat in the Napoleonic wars. Population, 82,113.

Karlovy Vary. Formerly known as Karlsbad, this is one of the most celebrated fashionable watering places of Europe, situated in Czechoslovakia. It is famous for its hot mineral springs, the daily flow of which is estimated at 2 million gallons. The name means Charle's Bath, Charles IV of France having bathed there.

The principal buildings of Karlovy Vary are an iron and glass structure, called the Sprudel colonnade, and an edifice in the Greek style, called the Muhlbrunnen colonnade. The city is noted also for porcelain manufacture. The resort is visited annually by upwards of 65,000 guests. The permanent population of the town is about 43,091.

Kharkov. An industrial city of southern Russia and the administrative center of the Ukraine soviet republic. Being near to the Donetz coal field and to important iron ore deposits, it has become one of the chief Russian centers of heavy industry. The manufactures include iron and steel, machinery, agricultural implements, tractors, elevators, dynamos and electric motors, rope, coal tar products, and airplanes. Kharkov has an Institute of People's Education, an agricultural and economic institute, and museums for the demonstration of improved agricultural methods. Population, 1,125,000.

Kiev (*kē'yĕf*). One of the oldest cities in Russia, attractively situated amid wooded hills on the Dnieper River in the southwestern part of the country. The Dnieper is here spanned by a suspension bridge, 3510 feet long. In the upper town is the famous Petchersk monastery. The city has numerous churches, whose gilded cupolas, seen at a distance, impart to it an almost Oriental effect. It suffered severely from civil war and famine in 1917-20, during which period it changed hands six times.

Christianity was first preached in Russia at Kiev, which has long been the chief eastern center of the Greek Catholic religion. There is a large trade in flax, wool, wine, cattle, timber, grain, and fruits. The manufactures include sugar, hardware, tobacco goods, machinery, glass, leather, and yeast. Population, 1,413,000.

Königsberg (*kü'nĭ͡ĸs-bĕrĸ*), **Kaliningrad.** A city located in western Russia near the border of Poland, lying on the river Pregel, about 4 miles from its mouth in the Frisches bay, a southern inlet of the Baltic Sea. It was almost entirely destroyed in 1945. Its manufactures include locomotives, chemicals, cork, tobacco, sugar, malt liquors, and pianos. Amber articles constitute a distinctive product. The University of Königsberg was founded in 1544. Kant, who was born in Königsberg in 1724, was a member of the university's professional staff. Population, 238,000.

Krakow (*krä′kō*). A city of southwestern Poland, situated at the head of navigation on the Vistula River. It was annexed by Germany in 1939. Krakow was the capital of Poland from 1320 to 1609. Favored by its position as a river port and railroad terminal, Krakow has become the trade center of a large territory. The city was founded in 700 A. D. by the Polish Duke of Krak. Population, 525,000.

Lapland. An area of indefinite extent at the northern extremity of Europe. The region has no separate political existence, but includes parts of Norway, Sweden, Finland, and Russia. Reindeer provide sustenance, clothing, and transportation. The people are called Lapps. They belong to an Asiatic race and average about 5 feet in height.

Lausanne (*lō′zän′*). A city of western Switzerland, built on five hills rising from the north shore of Lake Geneva. The city is a railroad and educational center and has a large tourist trade. The manufactures include chocolate, machinery, tobacco goods, and sugar.

The Protestant Cathedral of Notre Dame is the city's most notable church. It dates from the 13th century and was intimately associated with the rise of Protestantism. The University of Lausanne, founded as an academy in 1537, was one of the first schools established for the training of Protestant ministers. The city has been the scene of many important international conferences of statesmen. The language of the citizens is French. Gibbon wrote most of his *Decline and Fall of the Roman Empire* while a resident of Lausanne. Population, 132,500.

Leeds. A woolen and steel manufacturing city of north central England. The woolen industries especially have been famous for centuries. The chief products of the city, apart from textiles and steel, include machinery, agricultural implements, leather, furniture, artificial silk, and ready-made clothing.

In the midst of the factory district stand the celebrated ruins of Kirkstall Abbey, founded in the 12th century. The city also has a fine university and is noted for a great music festival held every three years. Population, 508,000.

Leghorn (**Livorno**). A seaport and commercial city of northwestern Italy, situated on a spacious, improved harbor on the northeastern coast of the Tyrrhenian Sea. The industries include shipbuilding and the manufacture of copper and brass products, coral ornaments, glass, porcelain, chemicals, electrical apparatus, and flour. The city is noted also as a summer resort. The architectural monuments are comparatively few, the most notable being the cathedral, dating from the 17th century. There is a handsome synagogue founded in 1581. Population, 152,517.

Leicester (*lĕs′tẽr*). A manufacturing city of central England, about 100 miles northwest of London. The chief industrial products are woolen hosiery, boots and shoes, bricks, and dyes. The city lies in a rich coal mining and sheep raising district.

Leicester is a progressive municipality, providing adequately for the health, education, and recreation of its inhabitants. Saint Nicholas church was constructed partly of bricks taken from a Roman wall in the vicinity. The assize court of Leicester is held in a building which was formerly the banquet hall of a Norman castle. Population, 283,540.

Leiden. A city of the Netherlands about 10 miles east of The Hague and 6 miles inland from the North Sea. It has a famous university founded in 1575 by William of Orange. Leiden is also known as the birthplace of Rembrandt and as the city which received the persecuted English emigrants, some of whom sailed later in the *Mayflower* to Plymouth, Massachusetts. Population, 95,964.

Leipzig (E. *lῑp′sῐk*; G. *lῑp′tsῐκ*). A city of East Germany, noted as the chief center of the country's publishing industry. There are about 1000 establishments engaged in the business. The city is also a world market for furs, which, along with glass, cloth, and leather, are sold in great quantities at fairs, three of which are held each year.

It was the birthplace of Richard Wagner, and Bach is buried in the church of St. John. Many old buildings were damaged or destroyed by bombs in World War II, but one interesting survival is Auerbach's cellar, represented by Goethe as the scene of part of his *Faust*. The city was captured by American forces in April 1945, but is now in the Russian zone. Near Leipzig, in 1813, was fought the battle in which Napoleon was defeated prior to his banishment to Elba. Population, 595,712.

Lemberg (**Lvov**). A city of the Ukraine, almost surrounded by strongly fortified hills. Formerly known as Lemberg, it is the seat of three archbishops and has three cathedrals—a Roman Catholic, an Armenian, and a Greek Catholic. There are many educational institutions, chief of which is a university founded in 1784, when the city was a part of Austria. Lvov was annexed by Russia in 1939.

Lvov has numerous manufactures, including iron-wares, musical instruments, bricks, flour, and spirits, and conducts a large trade in linen, flax, hemp, and wool. The Fair of the Three Kings is held here each January. Population, 469,000.

Leningrad (E. *lĕn′ῐn-grȧd*) (R. *lyĕ′nῐn-grȧt*). One of the largest cities of Russia, situated at the head of the Gulf of Finland on the delta of the Svir River. The port and fortress of the city is Kronstadt, on a near-by island. Canals connect the city with the White and Black seas.

Leningrad, formerly called Saint Petersburg, and, after 1914, Petrograd, was the creation of Peter the Great of Russia, who built it at enormous cost of labor and of life, in order to obtain communication with Western Europe. He populated it, in part, by compelling his wealthier subjects to spend a portion of each year in the city. Its name was changed to Leningrad in 1924.

From the Admiralty, in the center of Leningrad, radiate three great avenues, one of which—Prospekt of the 25th of October—ranks among the finest streets in Europe. Near the Admiralty stands the Winter Palace. It is connected by a gallery with the Hermitage, which houses an art collection of rare value. Across the Neva river from the palace is situated the prison of Saint Peter and Saint Paul, infamous for the many political prisoners formerly confined within its walls. The city has one of the finest subways in the world.

Leningrad was formerly the capital and the greatest commercial and industrial city of Russia, being the outlet for enormous exports of wheat. The Revolution of 1917 broke out there. In 1918, the national government was removed to Moscow. After a period of industrial paralysis, during which the city's population fell from over 2,300,000 to 722,000 it recovered rapidly as an industrial center. Its chief products are metal and machinery, chemicals, textiles, rubber, leather, tobacco, paper, furniture, matches, and foodstuffs. Population, 3,296,000.

Liége (*lê-ĕzh′*) or **Luik.** The chief manufacturing city of Belgium, situated amid rich coal mines in the eastern part of the country and built on both banks of the Meuse river. The chief industrial products are guns, steam engines, machinery, motor cars, and textiles. The city has numerous educational institutions, including Liége university, the museum of which contains the skeletons of many prehistoric animals found in the vicinity.

Liége is the center of the Walloon culture, akin to the French. A chapel built in the 6th century furnished the nucleus about which the city began to grow. The German attack on the surrounding fortresses was one of the first battles in World War I. Population, 450,387.

Lille (*lēl*). An industrial city in northern France, connected by a canal with the North Sea. 30 miles distant. The chief manufactures are linen and cotton textiles. locomotives, structural steel, sugar, chemicals, tobacco, and soap. Lisle thread derives its name from the city.

The city is modern in appearance and well built. Its features include the Church of Saint Maurice, the Palais des Beaux Arts with its extremely valuable collection of paintings, and Lille university, at which Pasteur was a professor. Lille suffered severely during World War I, part of the laboring population having been deported to work in German factories. Population, 193,096.

Limerick. A port of Eire in southwestern Ireland, at the head of the Shannon estuary. Butter and condensed milk are the most important exports. The industries include flour milling, the curing of bacon, and the manufacture of lace, fishhooks, leather, and clothing. Limerick is an ancient city, known to Greek geographers as Regia. It has given its name to the type of nonsense verse known as a limerick. Population, 50,786.

Limoges (*lē′mōzh′*). An old city of France, situated somewhat southwest of the geographical center of the country. It is famous for its porcelain industry, Limoges china being known in all parts of the world. Other important industries are printing and the manufacture of liquors, leather goods, hats, and gloves. The city has a museum of ancient pottery. Every seventh year, the Fête d'Ostension is celebrated to commemorate a plague, which, in the 10th century, destroyed 40,000 people. Limoges was the ancient capital of Limousin, a former French province, which gave its name to the limousine. Population, 113,378.

Lisbon. The capital and largest city of Portugal, beautifully situated at the head of the Tagus estuary about seven miles from its mouth in the Atlantic Ocean. Its harbor has few superiors and facilitates a large commerce. The city has manufactures of cork, textiles, pottery, paper, chemicals, sugar, iron castings, and machine-shop products.

Although founded by the Phœnicians, Lisbon has a modern appearance, having been almost entirely rebuilt after the earthquake and tidal wave which, in 1755, destroyed most of the city and took nearly 40,000 lives. Between the terraced levels of the city, elevators carry people up and down. The Avenue of Liberty, 300 feet wide with a double row of shade trees down the middle, commemorates the freeing of Portugal from Spain in 1640. Other features of the city include the Botanical Garden, the Estrella Garden, the Estrella Church, a university, and numerous other educational and scientific institutions. Camoëns and Vasco da Gama were born in Lisbon. Population, 825,800.

Liverpool. The third largest city of England, situated near the center of the country's western coast on the northeastern side of the Mersey River estuary. Among British cities, its total commerce is second only to that of London, while its foreign trade exceeds London's by a considerable margin, giving it the distinction of having the largest foreign commerce of any city in the world. The harbor has been elaborately improved. By a system of locks, the water level of the inner harbor is rendered independent of the tides. Docks cover an area of 660 acres, and there are about 40 miles of quays. The storage facilities include a 13-story tobacco warehouse with 36 acres of floor space. There are also installations for storing over 100,000 tons of oil and spirits in bulk.

Liverpool is connected with Birkenhead on the opposite side of the Mersey River by a railway tunnel nearly a mile long and a vehicular tunnel which ranks with the greatest in the world. Beneath the city, also, there are five tunnels used by railroads. Liverpool university is widely known for its school of tropical medicine. One of the most noteworthy of the city's buildings is Saint George's Hall, a structure of the Corinthian order, erected with the proceeds of dock profits. The Anglican cathedral, begun in 1904, is designed to be the largest in England. Also under construction is a Catholic cathedral of Christ the King, to be surmounted by a dome 168 feet in diameter, the largest in the world. Liverpool was the first city in England to provide municipal baths, having maintained such establishments since 1794. Population, 712,040.

Lodz. The second largest city of Poland, located in the west central part of the country on a site which, in 1800, was covered with impenetrable forest. It has grown with remarkable rapidity, having become, since 1870, largely through the activity of Germans, the chief center of the textile industry in Poland. Other manufactures include chemicals, beer, machinery, and silk. Population, 745,400.

LONDON. The capital of Great Britain and Northern Ireland, the commercial, financial, artistic, and intellectual center of the kingdom, and the second largest city in the world. It is situated in southeastern England on both banks of the Thames River about 60 miles from its mouth. London consists of three parts: "the City," a space one square mile in area; the County of London; and the "Outer Ring," or metropolitan district. The whole constitutes Greater London, which covers an area of 693 square miles lying within a radius of 15 miles from Charing Cross, a central point in the heart of London.

COMMERCE. London handles one-third of Great Britain's commerce. The docks cover about 650 acres, and the quays have a total length of 28 miles. Each dock is an interior basin accessible by means of a lock. The port officials and their staffs are accommodated in a domed edifice completed in 1922 at a cost of ten million dollars. London's foreign commerce amounts to nearly four billion dollars annually. Products handled by the port come from all parts of the world and exhibit an extraordinary variety. Wool represents the greatest bulk.

INDUSTRY. London easily leads all other cities of Great Britain in the aggregate value of manufactures. The clothing industries engage the greatest number of workers. Other important manufactures are furniture, machinery, silks, and leather products. Printing and bookbinding employ nearly 50,000 persons. The industrial establishments are mainly confined to the eastern and southern parts of the city.

TRANSPORTATION. All the trunk railway lines of England converge in London, which is, also, connected with European points by airplane service. Electric railways operate subways, or "tubes," and cross beneath the river by means of tunnels. The river is spanned by numerous bridges, of which London bridge, Tower bridge, Blackfriars, Waterloo, and Westminster are among the more noteworthy.

STREETS. The thoroughfares of London are not laid out on straight lines but parallel the winding of the Thames river. The more famous streets include a popular promenade along the Thames embankment; Lombard street, the financial center of the city; Fleet street and Paternoster row, both devoted to printing and bookselling; Whitehall street and Downing street, where the government offices are located; Haymarket, a street of theaters and cafes; the Strand, an avenue of retail stores, hotels, and places of amusement; Regent street, with handsome shops; Piccadilly, lined with shops and hotels; and Bond street, also noted for its shops. Large sections of London were devastated during World War II.

SQUARES, PARKS, AND MONUMENTS. Charing Cross, standing in the center of Greater London, is named after a memorial cross erected in 1290 by Edward I in the former village of Charing. The cross has disappeared, and its place has, since 1675, been occupied by a statue of Charles I. Popularly, the name is associated with a near-by railroad station, in the courtyard of which stands a modern reproduction of the cross.

Trafalgar square contains a lofty column in memory of Nelson and a statue of Washington, the latter a gift from the state of Virginia in 1922. Hyde park with the adjoining Kensington gardens covers 630 acres and contains a large statue of the duke of Wellington and the national monument to Queen Victoria. Whitehall has a magnificent cenotaph erected "To the Glorious Dead," a memorial to the English soldiers who fell in World War I. In Regent park is located one of the greatest zoological gardens in the world. Other pleasure grounds include Saint James park and Epping forest, the latter being a tract of 5600 acres northeast of London purchased by the city and thrown open to the citizens.

BUILDINGS. The Tower of London, erected by William the Conqueror, stands guard over the eastern entrance of "the City." Formerly used as a prison, it serves now chiefly as a museum and contains the crown jewels of the British sovereigns. The Houses of Parliament, known as Westminster Palace, cover 8 acres on the bank of the Thames river. The building has 1100 rooms and two towers, one with an altitude of 340 feet. The other is 318 feet high and contains a clock which rings "Big Ben," a famous bell weighing 13 tons. Saint Paul's Cathedral, planned by Sir Christopher Wren, is surmounted by a dome which reaches a point 364 feet above the street. Buckingham palace is the residence of the royal family when in London.

Westminster Abbey, dating from 1220, is the coronation church of the British sovereigns. It has a length of 531 feet, a width of 203 feet, and a tower rising 225 feet above the ground. The building is the burial place of many of the country's rulers, and has monuments to famous British warriors and statesmen. The "Poets' Corner," in the south transept, contains the tombs of most of England's great writers from Chaucer to John Ruskin.

Among the other notable buildings and institutions of the city are the British Museum, which contains three million volumes and priceless treasures of ancient art and antiquities; London university, adjoining the British Museum; the Bank of England building, covering four acres of ground; the South Kensington Museum, where classes are conducted in art and in industrial sciences; the Temple, a group of buildings long known as the residences of law students; and the People's Palace, used for recreation and for education of the poorer classes. London university comprises upwards of 30 different colleges located in various parts of the city.

London has many reminders of America. A statue of Lincoln faces Westminster Abbey, and within the famous edifice is a bust of Longfellow and a window and tablet to Lowell. John Harvard, the founder of Harvard university, was baptized in Southwark's cathedral. John Quincy Adams was married in All Hallows church, where, too, William Penn was baptized. Theodore Roosevelt's second marriage was solemnized in Saint George's church, Hanover square. In Saint Margaret's church, Americans have installed a beautiful window to the memory of Phillips Brooks, Episcopal bishop of Massachusetts. Pocahontas is commemorated by a window in a small Gravesend church, where she was buried in 1617. Christ church has a Lincoln tower with the Stars and Stripes cut in the stone. In Westminster Abbey, a tablet was erected in 1923 commemorating Walter Hines Page, American ambassador to Great Britain during World War I. In 1950, a statue of Franklin D. Roosevelt was erected in St. James's Square.

GOVERNMENT. Greater London has no mayor, but, in most matters, is directly under the control of Parliament. "The City," however, is nominally independent even of the sovereign, who may not enter until he receives the key of admission from the lord mayor. London county consists of a large number of boroughs, each having its mayor and alderman.

HISTORY. London is first mentioned in history by the Romans, who built walls about the city. It was later burned by the British queen Boadicea, sacked by the Danes, and later was taken by William the Conqueror, who granted the city its charter. In 1666, the Great Fire destroyed four-fifths of the buildings. In 1851, the first international industrial exhibition took place in London. Population, 7,880,760.

Lourdes (lo͞ord). A town of southwestern France, situated at the foot of the Pyrenees mountains and about 80 miles from the head of the Bay of Biscay. It is one of the chief places of Catholic pilgrimage in Europe, being visited annually by upward of 600,000 people.

The fame of Lourdes dates from 1858, when the Virgin appeared to a young girl, Bernadette Soubirous. The grotto near which the apparition took place is now surmounted by the magnificent Church of the Rosary, containing a shrine dedicated to the Virgin, "Our Lady of Lourdes." The church contains numerous crutches, tablets, and gifts, which memorialize cures credited to the Virgin. A near-by spring, which appeared at the time of the apparition, is diverted into several basins, in which the pilgrims bathe. On August 20 each year, a national pilgrimage is conducted to Lourdes.

The inhabitants of Lourdes are economically dependent on the pilgrims. The chief products are souvenirs. Population, 15,691.

Louvain. A city of central Belgium, formerly the center of a thriving textile industry. In recent times, the city has been chiefly noted for the University of Louvain, founded in 1425-26, and for several fine buildings, a number of which were burned while the city was under German occupation during World War I. A new library building, erected mainly by American generosity, was dedicated in 1928. Population, 32,524.

Lucerne (Luzern). A city of north central Switzerland, having a location of rare beauty at the northwestern extremity of the Lake of Lucerne. The inhabitants are occupied chiefly in providing accommodation and services for tourists, who throng the city's 70 hotels in numbers exceeding an annual total of 140,000. The most noted memorial of the town is the famous "Lion of Lucerne." It is in a nearby grotto and consists of a colossal figure of a lion transfixed by a spear but still defending the lilies of France. The figure is carved from the solid rock and was executed in memory of the 781 Swiss guards of Louis XVI, who were slain in 1792 during the attack on the Tuileries in Paris. Population, 72,400.

Lyon. A commercial and manufacturing city of France, situated southeast of the country's geographical center at the junction of the Rhône and the Saône rivers. The rivers are crossed by 24 bridges, one of which, opened in 1918, is called President Wilson bridge.

Industrially, Lyon is second only to Paris among the cities of France and is the foremost silk manufacturing city of the world. Other important products include rayon and cellophane, chemicals, machinery, macaroni, hats, chocolate, leather, jewelry, and tobacco goods.

Lyon's importance dates from the period of the Roman republic. The ruins of a Roman bath and of a Roman theater still remain. The city's oldest edifice, the Church of Saint Martin d'Ainay, utilizes several columns of a Roman temple which formerly occupied the site. The Cathedral of Saint Jean, begun in 1110, is one of the finest examples of early Gothic in France. Other notable structures are the Hôtel de Ville, the Bourse, and the Palais des Arts. The University of Lyon ranks next to that of Paris among French universities in number of students. The Roman emperors Claudius and Caracalla were born in Lugdunum, as Lyon was called by the Romans. Population, 528,535.

Lvov. See *Lemberg*.

Madrid. The capital and largest city of Spain, situated 2100 feet above sea level on a plateau near the center of the country. In this city are centered most of Spain's governmental, educational, and artistic activities. Since 1890, manufactures have increased greatly and now include leather, chemicals, pottery and porcelain, matches, cork, paper, glass, foundry products, furniture, and carpet.

Madrid centers about a plaza lined with impressive buildings. The ten most important streets radiate from this plaza. The magnificent Liberty Avenue, traversing the city in a north and south direction and ornamented with four to six rows of trees and with numerous monuments, is one of the finest promenades in the world. The Royal Palace, built of granite and white marble, stands on a hill which overlooks the city from the west. The adjoining armories contain the armor of Columbus and that of Cortés. Other features of the city are the National library, the University of Madrid, the Press Palace of skyscraper-like construction, a magnificent bull ring seating over 13,000 persons, and the National art gallery, the last containing, next to the Louvre, the world's most valuable collection of paintings. Population, 2,599,330.

Maelstrom (māl'strŏm). The literary and former name of Moskenstrom, a celebrated tidal eddy, occurring between two small islands at the western end of the Lofoten group off Norway's northwestern coast. The eddy is caused by the tidewaters passing through a narrow channel between the ocean and Vestfiord. The Maelstrom was memorialized by Schiller in his poem "The Diver." When the current flows fastest and the wind blows directly against it, the sea for miles around becomes so agitated that small vessels cannot survive in it. Ordinarily it may be traversed without danger The name is often used as a synonym for whirlpool.

Magdeburg (G. mäg'dĕ-bo͝ork; E. mäg'dĕ-bûrg). A commercial city of East Germany, situated on the Elbe River 88 miles southwest of Berlin. The chief manufactures include steel products, sugar, chemicals, tobacco goods, gloves, fertilizers, cement, glass, and rubber. The old royal palace is now used as a museum. Magdeburg was the birthplace of Otto von Guericke, the inventor of the air pump. The city sided with the Protestant powers during the Thirty Years' war and, in 1631, was sacked and burned, 30,000 of the inhabitants being put to the sword. Population, 268,048.

Malaga (S. mä'lä-gä; E. măl'à-gà). An ancient city of southern Spain, picturesquely located on a fine harbor opening into the Mediterranean Sea. A mountain range surrounds the town on three sides. The principal architectural feature is the vast cathedral dominating the whole view of the city from the sea. Malaga is known for Malaga wine, grapes, and raisins. The site was first settled by Phœnicians. Population, 312,018.

Malmö (mälm'ŭ'). A seaport of southern Sweden, situated on The Sound opposite Copenhagen. Malmö is an important railroad terminal and manufacturing center and has grown rapidly in recent years. Among its industrial products are iron castings, railroad cars, and textiles. The city has a large artificial harbor and exports much farm produce. Population, 253,502.

Manchester. A manufacturing city and third largest port of England, lying about 200 miles northwest of London and 35 miles inland from the western seaboard. It is connected with the sea by the Manchester ship canal, which was the first ship canal to be built in England.

Manchester is the largest cotton manufacturing city in the world and the center of one of the world's greatest industrial areas. Besides cotton, the manufactures include structural steel, electrical machinery, chemicals, glass, paper, rubber, and silk. The city has 1600 acres devoted to parks. Victoria University of Manchester is the city's leading educational institution.

The more important buildings include the town hall, a Gothic structure costing over $5 million; the Royal Exchange; The Royal Institution, an art gallery in the Doric style; Free Trade Hall; and Ship Canal House, the tallest commercial building, constructed on American design. Population, 625,250.

Mannheim (män'hĭm). A manufacturing city of West Germany, situated at the confluence of the Rhine and the Neckar River, 43 miles south of Frankfort. Mannheim is said to be the most regularly built city on the continent of Europe. It consists of 136 square sections, the whole surrounded by a semicircular boulevard, known as the Ring Strasse. Outside the semicircle are numerous suburbs. Nearly all historic buildings were destroyed in World War II.

Mannheim's commerce consists chiefly of grain, coal, petroleum, tobacco, sugar, and ironware. The manufactures include machinery, celluloid, carpets, chemicals, furniture, glass, and leather goods. Population, 329,911.

Marseille (mär'sâ'y'). The second largest city of France and the republic's principal seaport, located in the southeastern part of the country on an inlet of the Mediterranean Sea. Southwest of the harbor lies the islet Chateau d'If, celebrated in Dumas's *Count of Monte Cristo*.

Marseille's trade is largely with eastern countries and with the French Community in northern Africa. It consists mainly of woolen goods, ribbons, sugar, and wines. The city has large shipyards and factories for making soap, vegetable oils, and numerous other products.

The national anthem of France, "The Marseillaise," received its name in Paris when a battalion of Marseillais, or citizens of Marseille, sang the song at the storming of the Tuileries. Massilia was the name given to the city by the Romans when the settlement was already many centuries old, having been founded by Phœnicians prior to 600 B. C. It was the home of Pytheas, a Greek explorer who visited Britain in the 4th century B. C. The city's importance in modern times dates from 1848, when the surrounding region was irrigated by a canal from the Durance River about 100 miles distant. Marseille has the finest modern cathedral in France. Population, 778,071.

Milan (mĭl'ăn; mĭ-lăn') (Milano). The second largest city of Italy. It lies in the northwestern part of the country about 40 miles from the border of Switzerland. Milan is the chief financial center of Italy and ranks high as an industrial community and as a seat of art and learning. The more important manufactures include locomotives, automobiles, electrical supplies, and rubber articles. The silk, printing, and furniture making trades of Italy are centered in the city,

The Cathedral of Milan, dating from 1386, is the third largest in Europe. Built of white marble, it is 486 feet long and 356 feet high. It contains 3000 statues, and its stained-glass windows are said to be the largest in the world. The edifice has a capacity for 40,000 people. Other features of the city are the Church of Sant' Ambrogio, dating from the 4th century A. D.; the former convent of Santa Maria delle Grazie, which contains Leonardo da Vinci's "Last Supper"; the Brera Palace, one of the finest picture galleries in Italy; the Teatro della Scala, the second largest opera house in Europe; and a celebrated archeological museum.

Milan was captured from the Gauls by the Romans in 222 B. C. It has frequently been sacked and burned, but its position at the northern entrance to Italy has insured its continued importance as a commercial city. Population, 1,228,092.

Monte Carlo. A city in the principality of Monaco, beautifully situated on a sheltered bay in the Mediterranean coast. Monte Carlo is best known for its Casino, a palatial building on a promontory in the east of the city. It is the chief fashionable gambling resort of Europe. The principal games played are roulette and *trente et quarante*, "thirty and forty." In the latter game, the minimum stake is 20 francs and the maximum is 12,000, while, for roulette, the stakes may range from 5 francs to 6000. Tickets are obtained free, and playing takes place between 11:30 A. M. and 11:30 P. M. The inhabitants of Monaco are not allowed to participate.

Adjoining the Casino is the *tir aux pigeons*, "pigeon shooting range," where expert marksmen compete in shooting pigeons released for the purpose. A prize of 20,000 francs is offered for a competition held each January. Population, 9516.

MOSCOW (*mŏs'kō*) (**Moskva**). The capital and largest city of Russia, situated somewhat north of the geographical center of the country's European territory. Built at the intersection of six important highways, the city has long been an important market for grain, hemp, oil, tea, sugar, hides, wool, timber, metal, drugs, and silk. Its leading manufactures are textiles, chemicals, metal and food products, glass, and leather.

Moscow is a city of striking contrasts, with its old wooden houses of the suburbs, the many-storied apartment buildings for workmen recently erected, the low dwellings of the former aristocracy with their pillared porticoes, huge factories, gilded domes of Oriental-like cathedrals, and magnificent palaces of old Russian or ultra-modern design.

THE KREMLIN. This is the old citadel of Moscow, and is the city's outstanding feature. It is a triangular enclosure surrounded by walls 1½ miles in length. Its walls are surmounted by 18 towers and pierced by 5 gates. The main entrance opens on the Red square, and is fronted by the massive mausoleum of Lenin, within which lies his embalmed body in a glass case. Within the Kremlin stand the government offices and a number of palaces and cathedrals. In the Great Kremlin Palace, built of white stone with a gilded cupola, are held the congresses of the Communist, or Third, International.

Other points of interest in the Kremlin are the Tower of Ivan the Great, which is 322 feet high and contains 34 bells with a total weight of 290 tons; several monasteries of considerable antiquity; and the Czar Bell, cast in 1733, which is the largest bell in the world. It weighs 220 tons and measures 22 feet in diameter and 19 feet 3 inches in height. The bell was never hung, having been cracked by a fire before it left the foundry.

RECONSTRUCTION. Beginning in 1935, a reconstruction of Moscow was begun, with plans calling for its expansion from 68 to 234 square miles and accommodation for five million inhabitants. Eleven miles of a new subway had already been completed in that year.

Under this plan, the Kremlin, preserved and restored, will remain the central feature of the city. Along one side the magnificent Lenin boulevard will be constructed, flanked by many of the finest new buildings in Russia. At one end is the site of the Palace of the International Soviets, planned to be the world's tallest building. Residential and industrial sections form a circular band about the central portion and the entire city will be ringed with parks and forests. One feature of the city as it is being rebuilt is the manner in which large factories dominate districts, each factory, workers' residences, and facilities for living being planned as a unit. Cultural institutions include the Moscow Art theater, the University of Moscow, and the Lenin institute and library.

HISTORY. The earliest reference to Moscow dates from 1147. It was made the capital of Russia, and, in spite of many sieges, conflagrations, and pestilences, it remained the seat of government until 1712, when Saint Petersburg, now called Leningrad, became the capital. In 1812, the Russians burned the city in order to deprive Napoleon of a winter base. In 1918, Moscow was again made the capital of Russia. Population, 6,422,000.

Munich (*mū'nĭk*) (**München**). One of the largest cities of West Germany and the capital of the state of Bavaria, situated near the southern extremity of the country on the Isar river, a tributary of the Danube.

Largely through the effort of King Ludwig I of Bavaria, Munich became, in the 19th century, one of the best built cities of Europe and, architecturally, one of the most beautiful. It is lavishly adorned by numerous squares and pleasure gardens and by buildings constructed in the leading styles. The English Garden, a park of 500 acres adorned with small temples and towers, was designed by Count Rumford, a native of Massachusetts. Other features of the city are the former Royal Palace, the National Theater, the Art Union, numerous museums, and the Old Castle, the last dating from 1253. The art collections in Munich are among the richest on the continent. The University of Munich is one of the leading educational institutions of Germany. Many buildings were destroyed in World War II.

Apart from art and education, the great industry of Munich is the brewing of beer. Other products of the city's workmanship are bronze founding, glass staining, silversmiths' work, wood carving, and lithographing. Railway machinery, wallpaper, gloves, and artificial flowers are also made. Population, 1,231,458.

Nantes (E. *nănts*; F. *nänt*). A seaport of northwestern France, located at the head of the Loire River estuary and about 50 miles from the sea. The industries include the canning of sardines, sugar refining, shipbuilding, and the manufacture of iron products and of tobacco goods. In history, the city is known for the Edict of Nantes, by which, in 1598, Henry IV granted toleration to the Huguenots. Population, 240,028.

Naples (**Napoli**). The third largest city of Italy, situated near the central part of the kingdom on the Bay of Naples, which opens into the Tyrrhenian Sea. On one side of the bay rises Mt. Vesuvius, and on the other side is the picturesque height of Posilipo. The city has a safe and deep harbor. It is an important naval station and commercial emporium and possesses numerous industrial establishments. The manufactures include steel products, textiles, glass, macaroni, and chemicals. The port is a noted embarkation point for emigrants.

Naples is visited yearly by upwards of 30,000 tourists. Its features include the cathedral, built in 1272; the National museum, containing a priceless collection of antiquities, most notably those obtained from the excavated site of Pompeii and of Herculaneum; the San Carlo opera house, one of the largest in Europe; the most complete marine aquarium in the world; and the University of Naples, founded in 1224. Naples was originally a Greek colony, established about 450 B. C. under the name of Neapolis, "New City." Population, 1,228,092.

Newcastle. One of the largest coal exporting cities of Great Britain, situated in northeastern England on the Tyne river 8 miles from its mouth in the North Sea. Quays and factories line both banks of the river for a distance of 10 miles. There are also large shipbuilding yards and locomotive, engineering, and ordnance works. Other industrial products include Portland cement, chemicals, grindstones, and refined lead. The city's pre-eminence as a coal exporting center is reflected in the popular expression, "carrying coals to Newcastle," indicating superfluous activity.

Newcastle was the site of a Roman fort built to defend the eastern end of the wall that Hadrian constructed across Britain. The city was named from a castle built here in the 11th century by Robert, the son of William the Conqueror. Population, 253,780.

Nice. A city and tourist resort of southeastern France on the Mediterranean coast and at the foot of the Alps Mountains. Its industries produce perfume, liquors, soap, silk, straw hats, and rubber, metal, and tobacco goods. An 8-acre harbor accommodates an active coastal shipping trade. An equable climate, varying from a winter mean of 49°F. to a summer mean of 72°F., lends Nice an attractiveness which is further enhanced by the meeting of sea and mountain scenery in a subtropical setting. The city is famous for its carnivals, especially the battle of flowers.

Nice is about 2000 years old, having been founded by Greek colonists. The name is Greek for Victory. It was subject at various times to Saracen, German, Italian, and Spanish power, but was confirmed in French possession in 1860. Population, 292,958.

Nottingham. A manufacturing city of central England, 125 miles northwest of London. It is built on the slope and at the foot of a rocky eminence, which is crowned by an ancient castle, now used as a museum. Nottingham college is on a fine 220-acre campus, called Highfields. The chief manufactures include lace, hosiery, clothing, machinery, tobacco, and bicycles. Population, 310,280.

Nuremberg (Nürnberg). A city of southwestern Germany, noted especially for its manufacture of toys, electrical machinery, and lead pencils.

Because it was an important center for the manufacture of tank, airplane, and marine engines, a majority of this picturesque medieval city was destroyed in World War II, including most of the architectural monuments. Hans Sachs and the artist Dürer were born in the city. Watches were first made here, being known as "Nuremberg eggs." Air guns and geographical globes are also claimed as Nuremberg inventions. Population, 470,778.

Oberammergau (ō'bĕr-ăm'ĕr-gou'). A village in the extreme south of Germany, celebrated for the Passion play, which takes place there once in each ten years, the most recent performance having been given in 1970. The play represents the crucifixion and the ascension of Jesus. It takes place each Sunday during the summer on a large wooden stage open to the sky, and it usually lasts eight hours. The performance was originally undertaken in fulfillment of a vow made in 1633 by the villagers, who thereby expressed their gratitude for the cessation of an epidemic of the plague. Oberammergau is also famous for wood-carving crafts.

Odessa. A city of southwestern Russia, situated on the north shore of the Black Sea. Its commodious harbor is divided by moles into six ports. Odessa became great as the point of export for vast quantities of grain, wool, sugar, and lumber. Its industrial products include salt, glass, motion picture apparatus, and canned goods.

Odessa was founded in 1794 by Catherine the Great as a stepping-stone to Constantinople. The city is well built and is adorned by many pleasure grounds and fine buildings. The Victims of the Revolution square contains tombs of the fallen, the city having changed hands eight times in 1917-20. Population, 892,000.

Olympia. A plain in the western part of the Morea peninsula, Greece. It contains many ruins, including those of a temple of Zeus and of a stadium in which the Olympic games were originally held. In ancient times, the temple of Zeus contained a colossal statue of this god, the work of Phidias. Carved in ivory and embellished with gold, this statue was one of the seven wonders of the world.

Oporto (Porto). A city of northwestern Portugal, beautifully situated on both banks of the Douro River about 3 miles from its mouth in the Atlantic Ocean. The river is spanned by several bridges, one of which, having an arch of 560 feet, is counted among the great bridges of the world. Manufacturing is the most prominent industry. The city's products include leather, woolens, pottery, corks, hats, and tobacco. Prominent among the exports is port wine, which received its name from Oporto. Population, 324,400.

Oslo. The capital and largest city of Norway, situated at the head of Oslo fiord in the southeastern extremity of the country. The city is the trade center for southern Norway and has large shipyards and important manufactures of woolens, matches, pulp, and nails. Hydroelectric power is abundant and cheap.

Oslo is surrounded on the land side by picturesque hills. The chief edifices are the Parliament buildings, the National Theater, the University of Oslo, the Museum of Art, and a historical museum. Oslo was founded in 1048. Having been destroyed by fire, it was rebuilt in 1624 and named Christiania. The original name was restored in 1925. Population, 487,600.

Ostend (ŏst-ĕnd') (**Ostende**). A fashionable summer resort of northern Belgium, on the North Sea. The city is also a well-known gateway to continental Europe for travelers from England. During World War I, Germany used Ostend as a naval base. Population, 57,230.

Oxford. A university city of England, with a population, in 1969, of 109,720. It is situated about 50 miles northwest of London. The city is the seat of Oxford university, which was founded as early as the 12th century. This university is of especial interest to the English-speaking world on account of the Rhodes scholarships tenable at Oxford and open to students from the British dominions and the United States. The Bodleian library, connected with the university, is one of the world's richest collections of early printed books and of ancient manuscripts.

The university consists of a federation of 31 colleges, each with its own government and teaching staff. Degrees are granted by the university, not by the colleges. Shown below are the names of the colleges and the dates of their founding:

University	1249	All Souls	1438
Balliol	1263	Magdalen	1458
Merton	1264	Brasenose	1509
St. Edmund Hall	1278	Corpus Christi	1517
Exeter	1314	Christ Church	1546
Oriel	1326	Trinity	1554
Queen's	1340	St. John's	1555
New	1379	Jesus	1571
Lincoln	1427	Wadham	1612
Pembroke	1624	St. Catherine's	1962
Worcester	1714	WOMEN'S COLLEGES	
Keble	1868	Lady Margaret Hall	1878
Hertford	1874	Somerville	1879
St. Peter's	1929	St. Hugh's	1886
Nuffield (coed)	1937	St. Anne's	1893
St. Antony's	1950	St. Hilda's	1893

Palermo. An Italian seaport, located on the northwest coast of Sicily. The exports are mainly oranges, lemons, dried fruits, oils, sulphur, and wines. Tuna fishing and shipbuilding are the chief industries. The city ranks third among the seaports of Italy. Palermo has many architectural monuments dating from the periods when Sicily was held successively by the Saracens, the Normans, and the Spaniards. The city was founded by the Phoenicians and was captured in 254 B.C. by the Romans, who called it Panormus. Population, 653,533.

PARIS. The capital of France and the third largest city in Europe, situated on both banks of the Seine River about 110 miles from its mouth in the English channel. Paris is the commercial, artistic, and intellectual center of France and is generally acknowledged to be the most beautiful city in the world.

STREETS AND BOULEVARDS. The streets of Paris do not follow any unified plan. There are, however, several systems of magnificent boulevards. Boulevard is a French word originally meaning bulwark. As the old walls encircling Paris were from time to time torn down to be replaced by others embracing a larger circle, the site of the demolished walls was converted into beautiful driveways, to which the term boulevard was still applied. The boulevards of Paris consist of several concentric systems of roughly circular courses, having their common center in the Ile de la Cité, an island in the Seine river. The longest and most recent of these boulevards owes its origin to the leveling of the 22-mile wall which, until 1919, encircled the city.

Paris is traversed from north to south by an irregular thoroughfare, which, like all the longer streets and boulevards of Paris, is known by different names in different sections of its course. The more important portions of the thoroughfare are called the Boulevard de Sebastopol and the Rue Saint Michel. The latter section passes through the so-called Latin quarter, a district south of the Seine inhabited mainly by students and given its name when university lectures were delivered in Latin.

A straighter thoroughfare crosses the city from east to west on the north side of the Seine river. This thoroughfare, which passes many of the most famous squares, gardens, and buildings of Paris, is known, in different sections, under six different names. The more noteworthy sections are the Rue de Rivoli, the Avenue des Champs Elysées, and the Avenue de la Grande Armée. Other famous streets of Paris are Saint Germain, Rue Royal, and Rue du Faubourg Saint Honoré.

SQUARES, PARKS, AND MONUMENTS. On the north bank of the Seine, near the center of the city, lie the famous gardens of the Tuileries, a 75-acre park with numerous statues. It adjoins the Place de la Concorde, adorned by sculptured fountains and by a huge obelisk brought by Napoleon from Luxor, Egypt. The adjacent Champs Elysées, "Elysian Fields," contain the Grand Palais, built in 1718. Farther west lies the Place de Charles de Gaulle, formerly the Place de l'Etoile, which contains the world's largest triumphal arch. From this square radiate 12 avenues, including the Rue Foch, which leads to the beautiful 2100-acre park in the suburbs called the Bois de Boulogne. A southeastern suburb contains the Bois de Vincennes, an ornamental park with an area of 2300 acres.

Other notable squares and parks of Paris are the Luxembourg gardens, laid out in the 17th century; the Jardin des Plantes, 58 acres in area, where the principal scientific museums of the city are located; the Place de Rivoli, with an equestrian statue of Joan of Arc; the Place de la République; the Place d'Iena, containing a large statue of George Washington; the Place de la Bastille, near the site of the historic prison of the same name; the Place Vendôme, which has a brazen column made by melting 1200 cannon captured by Napoleon; the Square des Innocents, where stands the famous sculptured Fontaine des Innocents; the Place des Etats-Unis, in which stands a bronze monument erected in 1923 to the memory of American volunteers who fought in French armies during World War I; and the Champ de Mars, in which the Eiffel Tower rises to a height of 984 feet. It is named for Alexandre Eiffel, the engineer who constructed it as a feature of the Paris International exposition in 1889. One of France's most beautiful war memorials is a white marble temple in the Parc de Villeneuve-l'Etang, commemorating 67 American aviators who died in French service during World War I.

BUILDINGS. The Ile de la Cité in the Seine contains three remarkable buildings: the Hôtel Dieu, which, founded in A.D. 600, is said to be one of the oldest hospitals in Europe; the Palais de Justice, architecturally one of the finest structures in Paris; and the Cathedral of Notre Dame, the

SCENES IN EUROPE

A peaceful valley near Lucerne, Switzerland
European Travel Commission

The Medicis Fountains in the Luxembourg Gardens in Paris, noted for its art, architecture, and works of sculpture.

French Radio Center, Paris, France
French Gov't. Tourist Office

Istanbul, in Europe at Bosphorus Strait
—as viewed from Asia
European Travel Commission

Lenin State Library, Moscow, USSR

SOVFOTO

This modern cathedral at Coventry, Eng. incorporates ruins of its predecessor bombed in World War II.

Moselle Wine Country, Burg Kochem, Germany
European Travel Commission

VIEWS IN ASIA

A street scene in Tokyo, now the largest city in the world (pop. 8,302,565; Greater Tokyo 9,311,774).

The modern administration building at the Hufuf Airport in Saudi Arabia.

Museum of Jade in Singapore, former home of late millionaire ointment king Aw Boon Haw.
Keystone Press

The luxurious Keren Theater, Beersheba, Israel
Israel Gov't. Tourist Office

International Airport at Manila, Philippines

construction of which was begun in 1163. A few of the other great edifices of Paris are the Louvre, which houses the richest collection of art in the world; the palace of the Luxembourg, which contains the world's greatest collection of contemporary art, the American exhibits ranking second in number after the French; the Grand Opéra, one of the most beautiful theaters in the world; the government buildings, fronting the Seine embankment and known as the Quai d'Orsay; the Palais de l'Elysée, where the president of France resides; the Bibliothèque Nationale, one of the world's greatest libraries; the Pantheon, where many of France's most notable citizens have been buried; the Church of the Madeleine, built by Napoleon in the Greek style as a "temple of glory;" and the Hôtel des Invalides, which contains Napoleon's tomb. The railway car in which the armistice was signed on November 11, 1918, was housed in the Hôtel des Invalides until 1927, when it was transferred to a special shelter in Compiégne woods.

OTHER FEATURES. Paris was spared the fate of many European cities during World War II, suffering scarcely any damage. No other city of the world makes a feature of its sewers. Those of Paris, 9 to 20 feet in diameter and nearly 700 miles in length, are kept so clean and are so well ventilated that there is a regular tourist route through the system by boat and electric car. The University of Paris, which includes the Sorbonne, is one of the oldest and most famous educational institutions in Europe.

COMMERCE AND INDUSTRY. Paris is the largest industrial and commercial center in France, and has a worldwide reputation for the manufacture of articles of taste and elegance, such as gold and silver ornaments, furniture, scientific instruments, toys, and perfumes. These industries, as well as the clothing industry of Paris, which largely sets the standard for the Western world in women's apparel, are carried on mainly in small establishments. The manufacture of machinery, railroad supplies, chemicals, beer, porcelain, and leather is centralized in larger factories.

Paris was one of the first cities of the world to establish large departmental stores, the better known ones being Galeries Lafayette and the Bon Marché. The banks of the Seine are lined with docks over which passes a volume of trade exceeding annually one billion dollars in value. There are more than 65 public markets in the city, the largest of which is the Halles Centrales, soon to be replaced by a modern complex and subway. The stock exchange of Paris is called the Bourse.

HISTORY. Paris was known to Julius Cæsar, about 50 B. C., as Lutetia. It was then the chief city of the tribe of the Parisii, from whom the city, in the 4th century A. D., adopted the name Paris. In the 10th century, it became the capital of the French monarchy. Paris suffered from an English conquest during the Hundred Years' war and endured several disastrous sieges, the last at the hands of the Germans in 1871. Henry of Navarre, Louis XIV, Napoleon Bonaparte, and Napoleon III contributed most toward the improvement and adornment of the city, thereby making Paris not only a symbol for light-hearted enjoyment, but entitling it also to the claim of being the chief focus of European civilization. Population, 2,790,091.

Pisa (*pē'sä; pē'zä*). A town of northern Italy, 11 miles northeast of Leghorn. Pisa is noted for a leaning tower, 179 feet in height, which inclines 16½ feet from the perpendicular. The tower is built entirely of white marble with walls 13 feet thick at the base. Its construction was begun in 1174, and it was originally intended as a bell tower for the white marble cathedral near by. Within the past century, the inclination of the tower has increased one foot.

Pisa was formerly notable for the victory which its citizens won over the invading Saracens in the 11th century. In the 13th century, it controlled an extensive territory and had a population of 150,000. In recent centuries it has declined in importance, but its walls and its citadel still stand. The only large industry is the manufacture of cotton textiles. Pisa was the birthplace of Galileo, who used the tower in experiments to determine the velocity of falling bodies. Population, 76,846.

Plymouth. A naval station and seaport of southwestern England. Situated on a commodious harbor, Plymouth has a large commerce. Apart from naval equipment, the chief manufactures are chemicals. Sir Francis Drake set out from Plymouth for his voyage around the world. The town has a *Mayflower* commemoration stone, which records the fact that Plymouth was the last point touched by the Pilgrim Fathers on their way to America. Facing the waterfront is the Hoe, one of the finest pleasure grounds in Europe. Population, 213,800.

Portsmouth (*pörts'mŭth*). A seaport and the chief naval arsenal of Great Britain, situated on Portsea, a small island separated by a creek from the south coast of England. Portsmouth has the most complete fortifications in Britain. Its harbor lies close to Spithead, a capacious naval anchorage in the shelter of the Isle of Wight. The government dockyard covers about 500 acres.

The principal industries of the city are connected with the naval establishment. There is considerable traffic in timber, coal, cattle, and agricultural produce. Portchester castle, a ruined Norman fortress to the north of the harbor, occupies the site of the Roman Portus Magnus, "Great Port." Charles Dickens and George Meredith were natives of the city. Population, 221,470.

Prague (*präg*) (**Praha**). The capital and largest city of Czechoslovakia, situated on both banks of the Moldau River, a tributary of the Elbe. It belonged to Germany from 1938 to 1945. Its manufacturing establishments, located mostly in the suburbs, produce railway cars, machinery, flour, chemicals, leather goods, sugar, and furniture. Prague is the focus for the rail and river trade of southern Germany.

The most impressive edifice of Prague is the ancient palace of Hradcany, adjoining which is the Cathedral of Saint Vitus, where the Bohemian kings used to be crowned. The University of Prague, founded in 1348, had, as one of its earliest graduates, John Huss, famous as a martyr to Protestantism. Prominent features of the city are the Charles bridge, 546 yards long, spanning the Moldau and ornamented with two medieval towers and with many statues of saints; the 14th century Tyn church; and a famous clock, one of the oldest in Europe, having, for figures, representations of Jesus and his apostles. Population, 1,022,621.

Ravenna. An ancient city of northern Italy, lying 45 miles east of Bologna and 6 miles inland from the northwestern extremity of the Adriatic Sea. In the 1st century B. C., Ravenna was a naval base and seaport. Subsequent changes in the coast line, which left Ravenna an inland city, diminished its importance. A canal gives it access to the sea. Wine, silk, sugar, and lace are its chief products.

Reminiscences of Ravenna's former greatness are the Church of Sant' Orso, which, although largely rebuilt since, dates back to Roman times; twelve basilicas used as churches and erected between the 5th and the 8th century; a two-storied mausoleum of Theodoric, the Ostrogothic king who subjected Ravenna to a 3-year siege; and the tomb of Dante. Population, 56,815.

Reims (E. *rēmz*; F. *răns*). A cathedral city of northeastern France, lying about 80 miles east of Paris. The Cathedral of Reims, in which the French kings used to be crowned, was built between 1212 and 1430 and is considered to be the finest example of Gothic architecture in the world. During World War I, the structure suffered much damage, which has been largely repaired. Reims is also noted for its wines. Population, 133,142.

Reykjavik (*rā'kyȧ-vēk'*). The capital and largest city of Iceland, located on the island's southwest coast. The city has a university and a cathedral; also a museum containing a collection of Icelandic antiquities. Population, 90,792.

Riga. A city of Russia situated on the Duna River about 10 miles above its mouth at the head of the Gulf of Riga in the Baltic Sea. It was capital of Latvia when the latter was an independent country from 1919 to 1940. By means of canals connecting the Duna with the Volga and Dnieper rivers, Riga has access to Russia's vast regions producing timber, grain, and flax.

The principal manufactures are paper and wood pulp, matches, paints, textiles, shoes, rubber goods, cement, and tobacco. Saint Peter's church is notable for its lofty spire, which rises 440 feet above the street. Riga was founded in 1201 and became important as a member of the Hanseatic League. Nearly half the inhabitants are German. Population, 680,000.

Riviera (*rê-vyȧ'rä*). A popular name for the narrow but beautiful coast line of Italy and France, mainly about the Gulf of Genoa. Its mild climate, charming subtropical vegetation, and vistas of rare attractiveness make it one of the most popular parts of Europe for winter tourists. The chief resorts along the Riviera are Cannes, Nice, Mentone, Monte Carlo, and San Remo.

ROME (Roma). The capital and largest city of Italy, and, historically, the most famous city in the world. Rome is situated on both banks of the Tiber River about 15 miles above its mouth in the Tyrrhenian Sea near the center of Italy's western coast. The traditional date of the founding of Rome is April 21, 753 B. C. April 21 is still celebrated annually in Rome as the anniversary of the city's origin. Rome was successively the head of the Roman Republic, the Roman Empire, and the western branch of the Catholic Church. In 1871, it became the capital of the Kingdom of Italy. This long career of uninterrupted greatness has earned for Rome the title of "the eternal city." In 1929, a tract of 109 acres within the city was granted the status of an independent state under papal rule. It is known as Vatican City. This area is in the northwestern section of Rome and includes the former site of Nero's gardens.

THE MODERN CITY. The Tiber, meandering through the city, divides the more populous eastern part from the western section. The eastern part comprises the Campus Martius, "Field of Mars," and the seven hills of ancient Rome—the Capitoline, Palatine, Aventine, Quirinal, Viminal, Esquiline, and Cælian. The western section consists of the hill anciently known as the Janiculum and of the eminence on which the Vatican is situated. The river is spanned by ten bridges, three being of ancient construction. Rome is 15 miles in circumference and is surrounded by a brick wall 55 feet high, constructed mainly by Aurelian about 275 A. D. The wall is pierced by 12 gates. The Porta del Popolo in the north opens upon a road anciently called the Flaminian way, while the famous Appian way leaves the city through a southern gate.

STREETS AND MONUMENTS. The streets are irregular in plan. From the Plaza del Popolo in the north of the city three important thoroughfares diverge—the Corso, the Ripetta, and the Babuino. The Corso terminates at the Piazza di Venezia at the Capitoline hill, which has a colossal monument to Victor Emmanuel II. The Piazza del Campidoglio is adorned by a large statue of Marcus Aurelius, the Roman emperor who erected the so-called Antonine column, which stands in the Piazza Colonna on the Corso. An obelisk, 104 feet high, brought from Heliopolis, Egypt, has been placed in the Piazza di San Giovanni. Garibaldi, the liberator of modern Italy, is memorialized by a huge equestrian statue on the Janiculum hill. An equestrian statue of Victor Emmanuel II in a magnificent setting towers above the Piazza Venetia. Most conspicuous of all is a 180-foot bronze statue of Mussolini. The Fontana Trevi is among the grandest of the city's many sculptured fountains.

MODERN BUILDINGS. The most famous structures associated with modern Rome are those within Vatican City, notably the Vatican and Saint Peter's Church. The Vatican, or papal residence, consists of a group of palaces, covering 13½ acres and containing about 1100 rooms. It houses a library, museum, and picture gallery, each of inestimable value. The decorations of the Vatican were executed by the best artists of the Renaissance, including Raphael and Michelangelo. Saint Peter's Church is generally admitted to be the world's largest and grandest church. Its construction occupied 126 years. The building is 727 feet in length and is surmounted by a huge dome, which rises to a height of 405 feet above the level of the beautiful colonnaded court before the church's entrance.

Other notable buildings of modern Rome include the Quirinal palace, where the Italian sovereigns reside; the Villa Medici, housing the French Academy of Art; the Santa Pudenziana, the oldest church in Rome; and the palaces called Doria, Ruspoli, Corsini, Orsini, Giustiniani, Altieri, Cicciaporci, Farnese, Berberini, and Colonna. On the Capitoline hill are three palaces appropriated for the assemblies of the magistrates, for the observatory, and for the fine arts collection. There are several palaces, which, being surrounded by extensive gardens, are called villas. The most notable of these is the Villa Borghese, the gardens of which form the most fashionable promenade in the city.

EDUCATIONAL INSTITUTIONS. Rome is the seat of the University of Rome, founded in 1244. In addition to the Vatican library and the 10 public libraries, there are the libraries called Nazionale Centrale, Casanatense, and Angelica, and the libraries of the Barberini and of the Corsini palace. No city of the world has richer collections of Roman antiquities and of Renaissance art. The United States and several European countries maintain archeological schools in the city.

ANCIENT BUILDINGS The level of the ancient city of Rome is, except where excavated, from 20 to 60 feet below the level of the present city. Within the past century, a considerable portion of the ruins have been uncovered. These ruins include temples, palaces, public halls, theaters, baths, porticoes, and monuments and indicate that, in the first centuries of the Christian era, Rome was a still more impressive city than it is today.

The best preserved ancient building is the Pantheon, now used as a church, which has a dome larger than that of Saint Peter's Church. The Colosseum had a seating capacity of 45,000. The outer wall alone is said to have cost the equivalent of 50 million dollars to construct. The Forum has been despoiled of most of the palatial buildings, the 1200 marble columns, and the 1000 colossal statues which once adorned its 25 acres of surface. Other impressive ruins are the Mausoleum of Hadrian, used for 15 centuries as the fortress of medieval Rome; the triumphal arches of Titus, Severus, and Constantine; and the baths of Caracalla and of Diocletian, those of the latter having originally covered nearly 9 acres. The outlines of the Circus Maximus are still traceable—a building capable of seating 260,000 spectators.

One of the stateliest buildings of ancient Rome was the residence of the emperors on the Palatine hill. It was called the Palatium, a name from which the word palace is derived. The great drains of ancient Rome are still in use today. Dating from early Christian times are the catacombs, underground passages used as places of burial and

of refuge by the persecuted Christians. About 75 groups have been found, having a total length of about 750 miles.

INDUSTRIES. Rome, noted for its fine silks and knit goods, has become a leading center for both men's and women's fashions, with many outstanding designers. Other manufactures are gloves, jewelry, mosaics, cameos, and artificial flowers. The city is also the chief railroad center of Italy and, since World War II, has experienced a vigorous economic growth. Population, 2,484,737.

Rotterdam. The chief commercial port of the Netherlands, situated in the western part of the country, about 10 miles southeast of The Hague. It is on the Meuse River 15 miles above its mouth in the North Sea. The leading articles of commerce are coffee, tea, tobacco, flour, sugar, spices, coal, oil, and foodstuffs. The most important manufactures are ships, refined sugar, margarine, paint, ropes, and leather.

A labyrinth of tree-bordered canals runs through the city, and most houses are built on piles on account of the city's low site. Rotterdam was the birthplace of Erasmus. The central part of the city was completely destroyed by German bombs in 1940. The city was reconstructed according to the most advanced principles of city planning. The port also was reconstructed and soon became one of the world's busiest, being a gateway to the "common market" of Europe, as symbolized by its landmark "Euromast"—a high tower in the form of a mast and forecastle, which houses a restaurant. Population, 727,207.

Rouen (rwän). A commercial and manufacturing city of northern France on the Seine River, about 70 miles northwest of Paris. Ocean-going ships ascend the river to Rouen. The industrial products include textiles, machinery, and refined oil. The Cathedral of Rouen has a spire 487 feet in altitude, said to be the highest in France. The Place du Vieux Marché is adorned by a statue of Joan of Arc, who, in 1431, was burned there at the stake. Population, 118,775.

Ruhr (rōōr), **The.** An irregularly oval strip of land in the northern part of West Germany, extending eastward from the Rhine for about 40 miles along both sides of the Ruhr River. The district includes the great industrial centers of Essen, Dortmund, Bochum, Gelsenkirchen, Mülheim, Oberhausen and Duisburg. It is the largest single industrial area in Europe and the most thickly populated. The reason for this great concentration of industry in the Ruhr is to be found in the rich coal mines, and the excellent transportation facilities by rail and water. The center of Germany's mining, steel, power, and chemical industries, it suffered serious damage during World War II, and afterwards many of the heavy industrial plants were dismantled. Light industries, however, sprang up, such as coal-tar derivatives, pharmaceuticals, textiles, ceramics. In 1949 France, England, the United States, and the Benelux countries established an international authority over the Ruhr, in which later the West German republic participated. German trustees supervised production, which soon approached the pre-war output.

Saint Gallen (sânt gäl'ěn). A city of northeastern Switzerland, situated 12 miles from the south shore of the Lake of Constance. The city is the highest in Europe, having an elevation of 2196 feet above the sea. Its ancient Benedictine monastery, an architectural masterpiece which is now used for government offices, was founded by the Irish missionary Saint Gall, who settled here in 614. Population, 78,300.

Saint-Mihiel (săn' mē'yěl'). A town of northeastern France, situated on the Meuse River 23 miles southeast of Verdun. The capture of Saint-Mihiel and the annihilation of the German salient about the town in September 1918 constituted the first military operation carried out independently by the American army in France during World War I. Population, 5,203.

Salzburg. A resort city in western Austria, beautifully situated on the Salzach River. It is one of the most attractive cities of central Europe and the scene of the famous music and theatrical festival held in honor of Mozart, who was born here. There are a Renaissance cathedral, two archiepiscopal palaces, and a castle, which overlooks the city. Salzburg is a manufacturing center for musical instruments. Population, 117,400.

Salonika (E. să'lô-nē'kä); (**Thessalonikē**). A city of northern Greece, the second largest in the country, situated at the head of Salonika Bay, a northern inlet of the Ægean Sea. Salonika, having a capacious, improved harbor, is the sea outlet for Bulgarian and Yugoslavian products. Among the squalid houses which fill most of the city arise lofty spires and minarets, and numerous ruins dating from Greek, Roman, and Byzantine times.

Salonika was founded in 315 B. C. and has been held successively by Macedonia, Rome, the Byzantine Empire, Turkey, and Greece. It was the seat of an early church, to which Saint Paul addressed two epistles. Population, 378,444.

Sarajevo (*sär'ȧ-yä-võ*). A city of Yugoslavia, 122 miles southwest of Belgrade. It is partially Oriental in appearance, having an extensive bazaar, but, in recent decades, many modern improvements have been introduced. The chief industries are the manufacture of metal ware, silk weaving, and the making of pottery. At Sarajevo in 1914 occurred the incident which precipitated World War I, and thereby brought independence to Yugoslavia. This was the assassination of Franz Ferdinand, heir to the throne of Austria-Hungary, by F. Princip. A statue of Princip was erected in 1930. Population, 143,117.

Seville (*sĕv'ĭl; sê-vĭl'*) (**Sevilla**). A city and port of south western Spain, situated on the Guadalquivir River, about 50 miles above its mouth in the Atlantic Ocean. Seville was an important center of the Moorish civilization in Spain. The Alcazar, now partly in ruins, was a Moorish royal palace. The Cathedral of Seville, one of the largest Gothic churches in the world, retained, as a belfry, the Giralda tower, erected by the Moors. Other notable structures include the Moorish Renaissance palace of the duke of Medinaceli; the Museum of Painting, which houses the largest collection of the masterpieces of Murillo, a native of Seville; the buildings of the University of Seville, founded in 1502; a tobacco factory covering 6 acres; and a bull ring with a seating capacity of 12,000.

Seville was a prosperous seaport in Roman times. It had a monopoly of trade with America for a considerable period. The chief articles of trade at the present time are metals, fruits, cork, grain, and glazed tiles, the last being manufactured in a suburb, Triana. Population, 474,082.

Sheffield. An industrial city of north central England about 30 miles east of Manchester. It is noted for its manufacture of cutlery, armor plate, artillery, scientific instruments, and other steel products. The famous silver Sheffield plate is no longer made, the process being a lost art, but a high quality of silverware is made by a new process. Other industrial products include leather, bicycles, paper, brass goods, brushes, chemicals, and paints. Sheffield university was founded in 1905. The city was a target for German bombs in 1940. Population, 486,490.

Sofia (*sô'fê-yȧ; sô-fē'ä*) (**Sofiya**). The capital and largest city of Bulgaria, situated at an altitude of 1800 feet in the western part of the country. Sofia is the commercial and industrial center of Bulgaria and is connected by rail with Vienna, Salonika, and Istanbul. It has an important export trade in agricultural products and attar of roses. The city has been largely rebuilt since 1878. Its principal features include famous baths with hot springs; the ruined Sofia Mosque; and the University of Sofia, founded in 1888. Population, 810,300.

Southampton. A city and port of southern England, 79 miles southwest of London. It was a royal borough before 1086, its fine natural harbor making it at one time a rival of London. After a decline of trade in the 16th century, it was improved in the 1800's and, in 1914, was the chief port of embarkation for British armies. In 1940 it suffered severe damage from repeated German air raids. From this port, in 1620, the *Mayflower* began its voyage for America. Population, 208,710.

Spa (*spä; spô*). A famous watering place and town in central eastern Belgium. Its mineral springs are said to be the oldest in Europe, having been discovered in 1326. The town has been a fashionable resort for centuries. The principal buildings are the Casino and the Pouhon. Population, 9,055.

Stettin (*shtĕ-tēn'*) (**Szczecin**). A seaport and manufacturing city of northwestern Poland, built on both banks of the Oder river, 17 miles from its mouth in an inlet of the Baltic Sea. The largest industries are shipbuilding and the manufacture of clothing. Other products are cement, locomotives, sewing machines, and glass. The chief exports are grain, spirits, lumber, sugar, and cement. Population, 299,200.

Stockholm. The capital and largest city of Sweden, situated on a group of hilly islands and peninsulas at Lake Mälar's outlet into the Baltic Sea. Surrounding forests advance almost to the city's confines. On account of the varied levels prevailing in different parts of the city, tunnels and elevators are utilized by the citizens in passing from one part to another. Stockholm's capacious harbor facilitates a large commerce. The chief manufactures are ships, iron and steel products, leather, textiles, and pottery. The features of the city include the Royal Palace; Saint Nicholas Church, where the Swedish sovereigns are crowned; the city hall, one of the finest modern structures in Europe; Skansen, a 70-acre park illustrating the fauna, flora, and peasant customs of various parts of Sweden; an equestrian statue of Gustavus Adolphus; and a colossal bronze figure of Linnæus. Population, 777,115.

Stoke. A manufacturing city of central England, about 30 miles south of Manchester, noted chiefly for its porcelain and pottery industry. Other industrial products are iron, machinery, electrical and rubber goods, and bricks. The chief public buildings are the town hall, New Market hall and Minton Memorial building. Population, 263,910.

Stonehenge. The most famous prehistoric monument in Great Britain. It is in Wiltshire county, England, about 32 miles inland from the center of the southern coast. It consisted originally of upright stones in two concentric circles surrounding two elliptical groups. The height above ground of the largest stone is 22 feet. The outer, or Sarsen, circle is 97 feet in diameter and consisted of 30 stones, 16 of which are standing, some weighing as much as 40 tons. They were joined by superimposed lintel stones attached by mortise and tenon, of which 6 are in their original position. The inner circle, 76 feet in diameter, had 60 stones, of which 20 remain and 8 are standing. The origin of most of the stones has been identified at two sites, 23 and 240 miles distant. From the center of the circles at a distance of 256 feet is set a stone whose tip is aligned with the rising sun at the summer solstice.

Stonehenge was built over a period from 1800 to 1400 B. C., probably in part by the so-called Beaker people, who distributed the first bronze beakers from Spain and are believed to have erected the thousands of stone menhirs in Brittany, similarly aligned with the sunrise at the summer solstice. It is surmised that an architect of Stonehenge came from Mycenae, Greece, since traces have been observed on a stone of an incised dagger ornament found elsewhere only in Mycenae around 1400 B. C.

Stratford. A town of south central England on the river Avon, chiefly noted as the birthplace and burial place of William Shakespeare. Located here is the Royal Shakespeare Theatre, endowed by popular subscription from people in many countries. In the vicinity are the cottages where Mary Arden, Shakespeare's mother, and Anne Hathaway, his wife, were born. Population, 17,400.

Stuttgart. A well built and beautiful city of southwestern Germany. Stuttgart is the capital of the German state of Württemberg. The city's finest structures center about a large square, called the Schlossplatz. There are exceptionally valuable collections of paintings and of antiquities in the city.

Stuttgart is the chief printing and book publishing city of South Germany. The industrial products include automobiles, furniture, machinery, paper, leather, chemicals, tobacco goods, and textiles. Population, 630,494.

Turin (*tū'rĭn; tū-rĭn'*) (**Torino**). A commercial and manufacturing city of northwestern Italy, situated on the Po River within view of the Alps. It is about 70 miles inland from the Gulf of Genoa and 40 miles from the French border. Turin is the center of the automobile industry in Italy. Other manufactures are machinery, cotton, silk, rayon, leather, and chemicals. Hydroelectric power for the industries is generated from near-by mountain torrents.

Turin is the only large Italian city having streets laid out on a rectangular plan. Among the features of the city are the Piazza Castello, the chief square of Turin; the palace and park once occupied by the rulers of Piedmont; the Palazzo Carignano, in which the Italian Parliament met from 1860 to 1864; and an imposing monument of Cavour, one of the liberators of Italy. The University of Turin was founded in 1405. Population, 1,111,659.

Valencia (*vȧ-lĕn'shĭ-ȧ; -shä*). A Mediterranean seaport of Spain near the center of the country's eastern coast. The older part of the city has narrow, winding streets, while the new portion is laid out with wide thoroughfares and well shaded squares. Its features include the cathedral La Seo, with a splendid octagonal tower; the University of Valencia, founded in 1411; the Silk Exchange, a beautiful Gothic structure; the Plaza de Toros, a richly ornamented bull ring, said to be the best in Spain.

The commerce of Valencia consists principally of rice, fruits, silk, wine, and olive oil. The manufactures include tobacco, metal and leather products, glazed tiles, and textiles of silk and of linen. Population, 501,795.

Venice (**Venezia**). A seaport of northeastern Italy, situated on 120 small islands at the head of the Adriatic Sea. Some 177 canals serve as streets, spanned by 400 bridges. Houses are built on piles. The Grand canal divides the city into two equal parts. A bridge, about 2½ miles long, connects Venice with the mainland and, passing as a viaduct over the city, slopes downward to a large open square.

Venice's greatest building, the Cathedral of Saint Mark, dating from 1047 A. D., resembles the Church, now the Mosque, of Saint Sophia in Istanbul. It is surmounted by five Oriental domes and contains four gilded, bronze horses, taken originally from Nero's triumphal arch in Rome. The bell tower of the church, standing separate from the main structure, is 322 feet high. Its construction was begun in 874 A. D. The tower collapsed in 1902 but has since been restored. The Doge's Palace, the building of which occupied the two centuries following 1301, is one of the most picturesque buildings in the world.

Among the many other features of this unique and beautiful city are the Royal Palace; a curious clock tower, built in 1496, upon which two colossal bronze figures strike the hours on a large bell; the Bridge of Sighs, connecting the Doge's Palace with a prison; the Rialto, a marble bridge, on which are situated many busy shops; numerous churches and art galleries containing rich collections of paintings by Italian masters, including many by Titian, a native of Venice; and the museum of the city's arsenal, which exhibits a model of the *Bucentaur*. This was the ship from which, each year, the doge of Venice cast a ring into the Adriatic, thereby representing symbolically the marriage of Venice with the sea.

Venice manufactures heavy machinery, clocks, cotton and woolen goods, glassware, lace, brocades, tapestry, wood carvings, and jewelry. The city is a first-class naval station and has an excellent harbor.

Venice is said to have been founded in 452 A. D. by refugees in flight before Attila the Hun. It became prosperous by trading with the East and with the crusaders. The city's importance declined with the fall of Istanbul, but was revived when the Suez canal opened up a Mediterranean route to Asia. Population, 361,980.

Verdun (*věr'dŭn'*). A strongly fortified town of northeastern France, about 140 miles east of Paris. It was the objective of desperate German attacks in 1916 and 1917, which, for bitterness and carnage, were unequaled by any other conflict of World War I. The French army retained its hold on the town. Population, 21,406.

Verona (*vē-rō'nà*). A fortified city of northern Italy, lying 71 miles west of Venice. It has an important trade with Switzerland, Austria, and Germany in wines, fruits, rice, and marble. The chief manufactures are cotton, paper, flour, and nails.

Verona was a Gallic town before it passed into the hands of the Romans in 89 B. C. From the Roman period dates the amphitheater, still in use, which the emperor Diocletian built. It is about 500 feet long and 160 feet high with accommodation for 20,000 people. Numerous weather-stained palaces of white marble, mostly built in the period of the Renaissance, give to certain parts of the city an air of sumptuous decay. Population, 175,581.

Versailles (F. *věr'sä'y'*; E. *věr-sălz'*). A city of north central France, situated about 12 miles southwest of Paris. Versailles is chiefly noted for its palace and park of unparalleled magnificence.

The palace dates mainly from 1661, being mostly the work of Louis XIV. It consists of a central block, surrounding three sides of a large court, and of two immense wings, each enclosing two or more courts. The total length of the building with its dependencies is nearly one-half mile. It houses a picture gallery upon which alone Louis XIV spent 5 million dollars. The play of colored lights in the evening upon the waters of the sculptured fountains within the gardens constitutes a spectacle of rare beauty. An apartment of the palace, called the Hall of Mirrors, was the scene, in 1871, of the coronation of William I as emperor of Germany. In the same hall, in 1919, the representatives of Germany subscribed to the Treaty of Versailles. Population of city, 84,860.

Vesuvius (**Vesuvio**). An active volcano of Italy, 3891 feet high, near the Bay of Naples and about 10 miles from the city of that name. Prior to 79 A. D., it was not known that the mountain was volcanic. In that year, however, the top of the mountain blew off and ashes, stones, and mud were ejected, burying the Roman cities of Pompeii and Herculaneum in 20 feet of débris. The elder Pliny perished in this eruption, of which the younger Pliny left a detailed description. Other notable eruptions occurred in the years 203, 472, 512, 685, 983, 1631, 1822, 1855, 1865, 1872, 1878, 1880, 1895, 1906, 1929, 1944.

Vichy (*vē'shē*). Health resort and formerly temporary capital of France. Situated 72 miles northwest of Lyon and about 180 miles south of Paris. It owes its location to a group of about 40 springs of warm water having medicinal properties. Heavily charged with sodium bicarbonate and minerals, the water from some of the springs has a temperature as high as 120°F. About 2½ million gallons are bottled and exported annually. The 11 largest springs are state owned and supply public hospitals for treatment of soldiers and of civilians unable to pay for private treatments. The Romans built baths at Vichy, but the modern development, dating from the 17th century, owes much to Napoleon Bonaparte and Napoleon III. When the Germans in 1940 overran France and occupied Paris, the new chief of state, Marshal Pétain, then 84 years old, chose Vichy as the seat of his government. Population, 30,610.

VIENNA (**Wien**). The capital and largest city of Austria, built on the south bank of the Danube River. Vienna was the capital of the former empire of Austria-Hungary and, from 1938 to 1945, was a part of Germany. Since the 13th century, Vienna has been the chief artistic and cultural center of east central Europe.

BOULEVARDS AND PARKS. The most notable driveway of Vienna is the Ringstrasse, which follows the line of old fortifications, demolished in 1858. It separates the old, inner city from the more modern portions. The Prater, a 2000-acre park, is the largest of the many ornamented open spaces which, in the aggregate, cover more than 50 per cent of Vienna's surface.

BUILDINGS. The Cathedral of Saint Stephen is the most famous structure in Austria. It was founded in 1144 and has great catacombs beneath it. The cross on its steeple attains a height of 441 feet. Other great buildings are the Imperial opera house, one of the most superb art temples of Europe; the stately Grecian Houses of Parliament; the lavishly decorated Gothic city hall; the Imperial Palace; and the Votivkirche. Most of the inhabitants live in apartment houses, some of which are built on a magnificent scale, adorned with painting and sculpture.

INSTITUTIONS OF ART AND EDUCATION. The University of Vienna, founded in 1365, enjoys a world-wide reputation. The most notable of the many public and private museums of Vienna is the Imperial Art-History museum, which contains an extraordinarily rich collection of ancient and medieval antiquities and numerous masterpieces of art, embracing nearly every school in the world.

INDUSTRIES. The manufactures of Vienna include jewelry, ornaments of gold and silver, musical and optical instruments, leather goods, furniture, machinery, textiles, and chemicals. A large commerce in corn, flour, cattle, wine, and sugar is facilitated by a network of railways centering in the city and by the navigable Danube river.

HISTORY. Under the name of Vindobona, Vienna was a city of strategical importance to the Romans. It was taken successively by the Huns, the Avars, and the Franks; attained to prosperity in supplying the needs of the crusaders; and, in 1296, became the residence of the Habsburg emperors. Vienna was besieged by the Turks in 1529 and, again, in 1683, but on neither occasion was the city taken. The treaty of peace following the Napoleonic wars was drawn up in Vienna. Population, 1,638,100.

Vimy Ridge. An elevated region of northeastern France, 100 miles north of Paris and about 4 miles northeast of Arras. In May 1917, it was the scene of one of the most bitterly contested struggles in which Canadian troops were engaged during World War I. The ridge had been fortified by the Germans but was relinquished as a result of the battle, which is commemorated by an impressive monument erected by the Canadian government in 1936.

Warsaw (**Warszawa**). The largest city of Poland, situated on the left bank of the Vistula River. It was the capital of Poland prior to its seizure by Germany in 1939. The old part of Warsaw has many dark, narrow, and squalid lanes, but the new section is quite modern, with wide streets flanked by rows of fine buildings. There are numerous squares, parks, and public gardens. The city has over 30 Catholic and 7 Russian churches, the Catholic Cathedral of Saint John being the largest. Iron bridges connect the city with the prosperous suburb of Praga on the opposite bank of the Vistula.

Among the manufactures are textiles, metal wares, tobacco articles, malt liquors, chemicals, and furniture. Small factories and home industries give employment to many thousands. Population, 1,261,300.

Windsor. A town of southeastern England, on the Thames River about 21 miles west of London. Its interest lies chiefly in its parks and its castle, which, since before the time of William the Conqueror, have been a favorite retreat of the English monarchs.

Windsor Castle covers 12 acres of ground in the Home park, which is about 4 miles in circumference. A tree-lined avenue connects this park with the Great park, which has a circuit of 18 miles. The castle, consisting of numerous chapels, cloisters, and apartments, is dominated by the Round Tower, built by Edward III. Population, 29,030.

Ypres (*ē'pr'*). A town of western Belgium about 20 miles from the North Sea. It was the scene of a large number of battles in World War I, being held by the British armies in the face of the most desperate German attacks, made over a period of four years. One of the chief squares contains a monument erected by the Canadian government as a memorial to Canadian soldiers who perished in the sanguinary conflicts near Ypres. The town, almost obliterated as a result of military operations, has a population of 18,121.

Zurich (*zōō'rĭk*) (**Zürich**). The largest city of Switzerland, beautifully situated in the northern part of the country on both banks of the Limmat River as it issues from Lake Zurich. In the older quarter, the streets are narrow, but the newer section is very attractively laid out, its main thoroughfare being a broad boulevard lined with shops comparing well with those of Paris. Zurich is the seat of the Swiss National museum, of the University of Zurich, and of several splendid medieval churches and monasteries. The cathedral known as the Grosse Münster, founded in the 11th century, had Zwingli as one of its pastors.

Zurich is the financial center of Switzerland. Its manufactures include silks, cottons, machinery, paper, and musical instruments. Population, 433,200.

NOTED WATERFALLS

The Great Falls of the Potomac River, in Maryland, is an interesting and picturesque example of the cascade type of waterfall.

At George VI Falls, in tropical Guyana, the Uitshi River drops 1600 feet.

Niagara Falls undoubtedly is the world's best known waterfall. This view shows the American side of the falls, which drops 167 feet.

Montmorency Falls, 265 feet, is one of Canada's most beautiful waterfalls. It is eight miles from Quebec.

Iguassu Falls is on the river which is the boundary between Argentina and Brazil. The water drops 215 feet.

Victoria Falls, on the Zambesi River in South Africa, is 343 feet high and is one of the world's most spectacular.

There are two great falls on the Yellowstone River in Wyoming. This is the Lower Falls. It is 310 feet high.

FAMOUS VOLCANOES

The beautifully shaped Mayon volcano rises 8000 feet on Luzon, P. I. It has a perfect cone and is the most active of the Philippine volcanoes. Mayon erupted 26 times during the 19th Century and in 1914 destroyed several villages and killed several persons. The volcanoes in this area are a part of the volcanic mountain chain known as the Circum-Pacific system, often called the "Circle of Fire."

Vesuvius is the world's best-known volcano. It is in Italy, southeast of Naples, and is the only active volcano on the mainland of Europe. Its earliest recorded eruption was in A.D. 79, when it buried Pompeii. Its latest eruption was in 1944.

Caroli is a beautiful but dangerous Aleutian volcano. A wisp of smoke at its top shows that it is active. The most recent Aleutian eruption was Shisaldin volcano, which burst into action in 1947.

On the Lipari Islands, north of Sicily, is Stromboli volcano. It is about 3000 feet high and is called the *Lighthouse of the Mediterranean* because of its activity. In ancient times, these islands were identified with Vulcan, fire god of Roman myths.

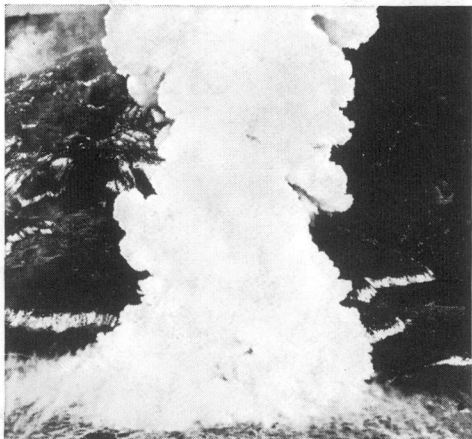

Of immense size, the active volcano Mauna Loa on the island of Hawaii is interesting both to tourists and to scientists. It has averaged one eruption every 3½ years since 1832.
Hawaiian Visitors Bureau

Beginning in 1943 with smoke, then lava, issuing from the surface of a cornfield near San Juan, Mexico, Paricutin rose within a year to a height of over 2000 feet.

ASIA

THE largest and the most populous of the continents. It lies entirely in the northern hemisphere and, beginning near the equator, stretches 5270 miles northward to a point within 800 miles of the north pole. Its maximum extent east and west is 6820 miles. Having an area of 17,200,000 square miles, it occupies nearly one-third of the land surface of the globe and is larger than North America and South America combined.

With the exception of Europe on the northwest and of the narrow Isthmus of Suez, Asia is entirely surrounded by water. It has the Arctic Ocean on the north, the Pacific Ocean on the east, and the Indian Ocean on the south. In the southwest, the continent is divided from Africa by a line passing through the Isthmus of Suez, the Red Sea, and the Gulf of Aden. At the northeast extremity, Asia is separated from North America by Bering strait, a neck of water less than 40 miles in width at its narrowest point. The coast line of the continent aggregates about 33,000 miles.

Outline and Islands. The line of demarcation on land between Asia and Europe follows roughly the Ural Mountains and the Caucasus Mountains. The remainder of the western boundary passes through the Caspian Sea and through the three seas which wash the shores of Asia Minor, the continent's farthest westward extension. These three seas are the Black Sea, the Ægean Sea, and the Mediterranean Sea. The Black Sea and the Ægean Sea are connected by the small Sea of Marmora, which communicates with the Black Sea by the Bosporus strait and with the Ægean Sea by the Dardanelles strait.

The coast line has many irregularities. Those on the north are mainly the enlarged mouths of rivers, the only major inlet being Nordenskjöld Sea. On the south, however, there are three large peninsulas separated by two deep indentations. Between Arabia, the most western peninsula, and India, in the center, lies the Arabian Sea, which has two important inlets, each connected by a strait with an inland sea. The Gulf of Aden in the west is joined to the Red Sea by the strait of Bab-el-Mandeb, and the Gulf of Oman at the north of the Arabian Sea communicates by the strait of Ormuz with the Persian gulf. The third great peninsula is Indo-China with its southern extension known as the Malay peninsula. It is separated from India by the Bay of Bengal.

The eastern coast is notable for a series of deep inlets and for an irregular chain of islands stretching from the north to the south. This configuration results in a number of island-bound seas. Bering Sea at the north is confined by the Aleutian islands, which are geographically a part of Alaska. South of Kamchatka peninsula lies the Sea of Okhotsk. The Sea of Japan is enclosed by Sakhalin island and by the islands of Japan, which stretch southwestward toward the southern end of the peninsula of Chosen. The Yellow Sea and the China Sea extend southward to the Taiwan strait, as the channel is called which lies between the island of Formosa and the mainland. The South China Sea, bounded on the east and south by the Philippine Islands and by Borneo, has two large inlets, the Gulf of Tonkin and the Gulf of Siam.

South and east of the continent lies, in an elongated cluster, the largest group of islands in the world. This group, known as the Malay archipelago, extends as far as Australia. This archipelago, together with the numerous smaller islands which continue to dot the Pacific for more than 2000 miles still farther east, is sometimes embraced under the term Oceania. The only other large island off the southern coast is Ceylon, near the southern tip of India. The New Siberian islands and Wrangell island lie well within the Arctic circle to the north.

Surface. Asia has the greatest mean elevation of any of the continents except Antarctica, its surface being, on the average, more than 3000 feet above the sea. Moreover, the continent contains the highest mountain, the highest plateau, the most extensive lowland, the lowest lake, and the deepest lake, in the world.

About 2000 miles north of the southern tip of India lies the plateau of Pamir, often called the roof of the world. This plateau, 11,000 feet in height, forms a central point from which mountain chains radiate, most of them trending in a general east and west direction.

The highest range is that of the Himalaya Mountains, curving from the Pamir plateau to the south and east, where it forms a northern wall of India. Mount Everest, in this range, is the highest peak in the world, having a height of 29,002 feet.

North of the Himalaya Mountains lies the world's highest plateau, Tibet, which has an elevation ranging from 9000 to 17,000 feet. The region is volcanic. To the north of the plateau of Tibet lies, at a lower level, the plateau of Mongolia, largely occupied by the Gobi desert. This plateau is separated from Tibet by the Kunlun mountains. The plateau of Mongolia is confined on the northwest side by an irregular group of mountain ranges stretching northeast from the Pamir plateau. Among these mountains lies the deepest body of fresh water in the world, Lake Baikal, in which soundings of 5306 feet have been taken. Both the plateau of Tibet and the plateau of Mongolia widen toward the east and eventually slope downward to the plains of China in the south and, farther north, to the plains of Manchuria.

Westward from the Pamir plateau, a broad mountainous highland stretches to the extreme western part of the continent in Asia Minor. This region contains the lofty Hindu Kush range and, farther west, Mount Ararat, on which Noah's ark is said to have landed. The highland slopes, on the south, down to the plains of Iraq, which drain toward the Persian gulf. South and west of this drainage basin rises the plateau which occupies the greater part of the Arabian peninsula. The northwestern extremity of the plateau falls rapidly to a basin of inland drainage, which constitutes the most remarkable depression on the face of the earth. The lowest point is occupied by the Dead Sea, the surface of which is almost 1300 feet below the level of the sea.

To the north of Asia's great central highland lies the world's vastest plain. Occupying the whole northern part of the continent, it is sometimes called the Great Northern Lowland. Most of it inclines in steppes very gently toward the north, but in the southwest there is an area of inland drainage, part of which slopes toward the Caspian Sea and part toward the Aral Sea.

To the south of the Himalaya Mountains lie the plains of India. These plains rise on the southern side to a table-land of moderate height, sometimes called the Deccan. On the east, the plains are confined by a number of mountain ridges, which constitute a southern spur from the plateau of Tibet. These mountains lose themselves in the plains of Indo-China and in the Malay peninsula.

The plateau of Mongolia sends a similar spur to the northeast, known as the Stanovoi Mountains, which stretch as far as Bering strait. From this extreme northern point, a partly submerged mountain chain passes south through the ocean, emerging in various places to form the numerous islands off the east coast. Many of these mountains, particularly those in Japan, are actively volcanic.

Drainage. The great central highlands of Asia feed six rivers which exceed 2000 miles in length. Two of them, the Yangtze and the Yenisei, rank among the six longest rivers of the world.

199

The Ob River, the Yenisei River, and the Lena River are the largest of the streams which take their rise in these highlands and wind slowly through the immense steppes down to broad estuaries at the Arctic Ocean. Their lower courses are icebound eight months in the year. For 100 miles above the mouth of the Lena lies a stretch of frozen silt in which are embedded the remains of numerous mammoths and of other animals which were engulfed in quagmire thousands of years ago.

The three greatest rivers flowing to the east are the Amur, the Hwang, and the Yangtze. Each follows a long, meandering course in the central plateau before descending to the plains and emptying into the waters of the Pacific Ocean. Destructive annual floods frequently follow the melting of the upland snows, particularly in the Hwang river in China, which for that reason is often called "China's sorrow."

The southeastern spur of the plateau of Tibet gives rise to three rivers of southern drainage. Named in order from east to west, they are the Mekong River, the Salwin River, and the Irrawaddy River. The Ganges River and the Brahmaputra River both rise in the Himalaya Mountains and mingle their waters in a common delta at the head of the Bay of Bengal. The Brahmaputra River flows eastward along the northern edge of the Himalayas in the plateau of Tibet and, bending southward and westward, passes through a plain which has a heavier rainfall than any other region of the world. The Ganges throughout most of its course flows eastward. The Indus River rises to the north of the Himalaya Mountains and, passing around the western end of the range, empties into the Arabian Sea.

The plains of Iraq are drained toward the Persian Gulf by the Tigris River, which is joined about 100 miles above its mouth by the celebrated Euphrates River. The Ural River flows into the northern end of the Caspian Sea. The Caspian Sea has no outlet but is itself 86 feet below the level of the ocean. The Aral Sea is the center of another basin of interior drainage. Such basins cover, in Asia, a larger area than in any other continent.

Climate. On account of its range of latitude and of altitude, Asia is subject to a great variety of climate. In the interior of Siberia, temperatures of 92° below zero have been recorded, although in summer on the Arctic coast the thermometer sometimes registers 100°. The hottest part of the continent is in Arabia, where the temperature has reached 120° F. and the average for the year is 93°.

While parts of Assam, in the basin of the Brahmaputra River, have a rainfall of about 500 inches, the rainfall of Asia as a whole is scanty. An arid desert, in which the annual precipitation is less than 10 inches, extends in a broad sweep through the center of the continent from east to west. Beginning with the desert of Gobi in the plateau of Mongolia, it passes through central Asia, Iran, and Arabia. Siberia also has a light rainfall. Japan, the plains of China and of the Indo-China peninsula, the Malay peninsula, and eastern and southern India have a copious and, in parts, an excessive precipitation.

Vegetation. Asia is the original source of more of our important economic plants than all other parts of the world combined. From it come wheat, barley, sugar cane, alfalfa, cotton, flax, jute, hemp, tea; such fruits as the apple, cherry, peach, prune, apricot, banana, olive, orange, lemon, grapefruit, date, and pomegranate; and, in the list of vegetables, the radish, cucumber, muskmelon, onion, parsnip, rhubarb, spinach, and eggplant.

Northern Siberia from east to west contains a strip of tundra, or frozen desert, stretching 150 to 500 miles southward from the Arctic Ocean. In this tundra, a permanently frozen subsoil permits the growth of few plants other than mosses and lichens. Coniferous forests and, farther south, forests of deciduous trees cover the steppes. South of the forests lies an immense belt of treeless plains covered with grass. The grass is replaced by a desert flora toward the arid zone of central Asia.

In the regions of copious rainfall, the plant life is extraordinarily rich, India having more species than any other region of equal area in the world. The sacred peepul and the banyan tree, plants producing ginger, members of the pea family, medicinal plants, orchids, gourds, figs, timber trees, gum producing trees, sago palms, bamboos, and teak are representative of the rich flora south of the Himalaya Mountains. On these mountains grow magnolias and large rhododendrons; higher up, pines are found, and also the deodar, a species of cedar similar to that growing on Mount Lebanon in southwestern Asia. The better watered parts of Arabia still produce, in limited amounts, the spices and fragrant plants which, in earlier days, won for the peninsula the poetic characterization of "Araby the blest."

Animal Life. Asia is the original home of most of the world's domesticated animals, including the horse, ox, sheep, pig, goat, camel, chicken, and goose. The humped ox, the water buffalo, and the yak are used as draft animals by the inhabitants of the continent. The elephant of Asia, unlike the African elephant, is easily domesticated.

The Himalaya Mountains form a barrier north of which the climate is unfavorable to animal life. In the north, however, bears, foxes, and wolves are found, as well as other wild animals which inhabit the corresponding latitudes of Europe. South of the barrier, the fauna is extremely rich. Nearly all the families of tropical birds are represented. India is the home of the tiger. There are several species of the rhinoceros. The deadly cobra takes a yearly toll of many thousands of human lives.

Minerals. The natural resources of Asia have been very inadequately explored. There is reason to believe, however, that the continent is extremely rich in minerals. Coal and iron exist in large quantities in China, and the world's richest source of petroleum is in southwest Asia. Most of the world's supply of tin comes from the Malay peninsula and the islands lying near it.

Inhabitants. It is generally acknowledged that it was in Asia that man first turned to agriculture and built cities. From Asia have come all the most wide-spread religions of the world. It justifiably claims the earliest use of writing. Today it supports a larger population than any other continent, its estimated 1900 million inhabitants being about 60 per cent of the human race.

Asiatic peoples comprise about seven-tenths of the total population of the continent. About one-tenth of the population, however, consists of Caucasians, living in Siberia, India, and southwest Asia. From these regions, the Caucasians emigrated at an early period, spreading over northern Africa and Europe, whence they came later to America. The aborigines of America are believed to have reached the western hemisphere by way of northeastern Asia.

Religion. The most widely embraced religions of Asia today are Buddhism, Confucianism, Mohammedanism, Hinduism, Taoism, and Shintoism. Buddhism, Confucianism, and Taoism center principally in China. Shintoism is the chief religion of Japan. In India, Hinduism competes with Mohammedanism, which is the dominant religion of southwestern Asia. Christianity is strongest in northwestern Asia, chiefly Siberia, and in the islands of the Malay archipelago, in many of which it dominates to the virtual exclusion of others. It has also been introduced by missionaries into China, Japan, and India.

POLITICAL DIVISIONS

Asia is a continent most of whose nations have only recently come into existence. This was due to the conquest of most of Asia by European nations in early modern times and the liquidation of those conquests after World War II.

The following are the chief national states of the continent: Afghanistan, Burma, Cambodia, China, Cyprus, India, Indonesia, Iran, Iraq, Israel, Japan, Jordan, Korea, Kuwait, Laos, Lebanon, Malaysia, Maldive Islands, Pakistan, Philippines, Saudi Arabia, Singapore, Sri Lanka (Ceylon), Syria, Thailand (Siam), Turkey, Vietnam, and Yemen.

In addition, a large section of Asia is part of Russia, whose Asiatic territory is about three times the area of European Russia.

Afghanistan. A republic of south Asia, hemmed in by India, Iran, and Turkestan. Its area is about 250,000 square miles. The surface is, for the most part, a dry, mountainous plateau. It is traversed by the Hindu Kush and by other ranges, which in some places attain a height in excess of 17,000 feet.

The mountainsides have forests of cedar, pine, walnut, and other trees; the valleys support crops of cereals and a variety of fruits. Wheat, rice, and mutton are staple foods. Sheep raising is one of the chief occupations.

The population of Afghanistan is about 16,113,000. The capital is Kabul, a city of about 300,000, which is a center of caravan trade with India and central Asia. There are no railroads in Afghanistan. Herat, in the northwest, contains ruins of many buildings erected by Timur, the Mogul warrior who overran Asia in the 14th century.

Bangladesh. Formerly the East Bengal province of Pakistan, the People's Republic of Bangladesh became independent in December 1971. Bangladesh covers 55,126 square miles and has a population of 71,300,000. The country is bordered by India on the north, east, and west, and by the Bay of Bengal on the south.

Bangladesh is largely a subtropical alluvial plain with many river valleys, deltas, and swamps. The chief rivers are the Ganges and Brahmaputra. In November 1970 the southern Ganges Delta region was destroyed by a cyclonic tidal wave. More than 220,000 people were reported dead and an estimated 350,000 dwellings were either damaged or destroyed.

The country is agricultural, with some 80 to 90 per cent of the population engaged in agriculture. The major crops are rice, jute, sugar cane, tea, tobacco, and oilseeds. Large reserves of natural gas and some coal deposits are being developed by the government through loans from India.

The capital and largest city of Bangladesh is Dacca (1,310,972). Other major cities are Chittagong (416,733) and Chalna (436,000).

Burma. A republic of southeast Asia on the Bay of Bengal adjoining India and Pakistan on the west and China, Laos, and Thailand on the north and east. Its area is 261,789 square miles.

Burma consists of a central basin with the Arakan Yoma mountains to the west on the India border and the Shan plateau in the east. The central basin is watered by the Irrawaddy River running south through a fertile delta and emptying by nine mouths into the Bay of Bengal. Minerals include lead, silver, zinc, nickel, copper, tin, gold, rubies, sapphires, and jade. The forests produce teak and other valuable hardwoods.

Agriculture is the leading occupation, and Burma normally is a heavy exporter of rice. Sugar cane and peanuts are also produced in quantity. Industries include silk weaving, rice husking, oil refining, and wood carving. The Baluchaung hydroelectric plant, completed in 1960, is one of the largest in southeast Asia. Buddhism is the established religion. The leading cities are Rangoon, the capital and chief port, and Mandalay, a river port of Upper Burma.

Burma was given independence in 1948 by Great Britain and dissociated itself from the Commonwealth. Population, 26,389,000.

Cambodia. A republic of southeast Asia bounded north by Thailand and Laos, east by Vietnam, and southwest by the Gulf of Siam. Its 69,884 square miles consist chiefly of an alluvial plain watered by the Mekong River.

Agriculture of a subsistence type is the chief occupation, and rice is the principal crop. Other products include rubber, cotton, tobacco, kapok, and corn. Cattle breeding is an important activity.

From the 9th to the 13th century A.D., Cambodia was ruled by the Khmers, whose monarchs constructed at Angkor magnificent shrines and temples. Their ruins, among the most impressive in southeast Asia, were threatened in 1970 during the Vietnam conflict. Angkor Wat is the best known.

Cambodia was part of French Indochina until 1953 and was a constitutional monarchy for several years thereafter. In 1970 it became a republic. The capital and largest city (pop. 393,995) is Phnom Penh. Population, 6,557,000.

Ceylon. See *Sri Lanka.*

China. The immense, roughly triangular country in eastern Asia lying between Asiatic Russia on the northwest and India, Pakistan, Burma, Laos, and Vietnam on the southwest. It is about 3,000 miles from east to west, and its maximum extent from north to south is 2400 miles. The area of continental China is 3,754,210 square miles. Known as the People's Republic of China (Communist China), it claims but does not control Taiwan (Formosa), which is ruled by the National Republic of China.

People's Republic. Communist China consists of six regions, which include 23 provinces, 4 autonomous regions (including Tibet, conquered in 1950, and Inner Mongolia), and the 2 administrative areas of Peking, the capital, and Shanghai, the largest city.

Three-fifths of the territory of China is inhabited by about 1 per cent of the population. This sparsely settled part, occupied mainly by nomadic tribes, consists of the lofty, mountainous plateau of Tibet, the desert plateau of Mongolia, and the arid depression of inland drainage known as Sinkiang. The remainder of the country embraces the extremely fertile eastern plains, watered by three great rivers, the Hwang, the Yangtze, and the West river. In China proper as well as in the outlying territories, the surface is mainly mountainous. While practically all of the level lands are fertile flood plains, they are subject to disastrous floods.

The climate of China proper, where practically all of the Chinese live, is divided into two main regions, northern and southern. The northern region extends from the crest of the Tsingling and Haiyang mountains to the northern border. It is a temperate region supporting wheat as a major cereal as compared to rice in the southern region. The southern region includes the great Yangtze basin and southward area, with rice as the major climatic adjustment. Northern China is temperate with hot summers, cold winters, and moderate rainfall, while southern China differs by having mild winters and heavy rainfall. China's rainfall is sharply seasonal, falling mainly in summer.

All of China suffers greatly from droughts and floods which are caused by variations in the Monsoon winds which control China's weather. A 1911 flood of the Yangtze affected 50,000,000 people, directly causing the death of upwards of 100,000 and destroying vast properties. Typhoons, earthquakes, and locusts also plague China.

The deposits of coal, of iron, and of copper in China are among the richest in the world. More than one-half of the world's supply of antimony and tungsten comes from China. The proximity of the coal and the iron deposits in the northeastern district of Shan-si has resulted in a large steel industry. The manufacture of porcelain, centering since 220 A. D. in Kingtehchen, a city of about 266,000 inhabitants, is still a distinctive industry of the country. Lacquered ware and textiles of silk and of cotton are other native manufactures for which China has long been noted. In the north are vast deposits of oil shale which are being processed. This region also has a large share of China's coal and iron reserves plus considerable industrial development.

The chief occupation of the Chinese, however, is agriculture, which is carried on more intensively than anywhere else in the world. The soil is very fertile, and irrigation by canals and by irrigation wheels or even by hand is employed where necessary. Rotation of crops has been practiced for centuries. The chief crops include rice, corn, tobacco, soy beans, tea, cotton, and sugar cane, the last three being grown in the southern part of the country. The mulberry tree is cultivated largely for the silkworms which feed on it and from which silk is obtained. Soy beans and silk are the most valuable articles of export. Other important exports are textiles, tea, coal, and cotton. Chickens and pigs are raised everywhere in China, and pig's bristles have become an important article of export. China's farm problems are complex also because 80 per cent of the people live on farms and must depend on farming for their existence. Farm land per capita is only a fraction of an acre (0.45) or 1485 people for each square mile of agricultural land. While her total production of such important crops as wheat and rice are among the largest in the world, probably totaling upwards of 3 billion bushels, it scarcely suffices to feed her huge population who depend upon cereals for 90 per cent of their diet. The Communist government attacked the problem by nationalizing land and trying, in the 1960's, to industrialize farm work by so-called communes.

By 1960, about 20,000 miles of railroad had been constructed in China. The so-called Grand Canal, running from the city of Hangchow a distance of 600 miles north to the Gulf of Chihli, was built 2500 years ago. Parts of it are choked with silt. In 1960, there were more than 250,000 miles of highways. A large part of the country's transportation is provided by the rivers, along which ply numerous "junks" and other boats. Thousands of people live on the rivers in house boats, which are often equipped with gardens made in soil laid on the floors of the boats.

Chinese civilization is ancient and distinctive. For thousands of years, the veneration of parents remained a cardinal principle of Chinese religion, law, and social customs. These cardinal principles of Chinese religion and philosophy were tremendously impressed upon the Chinese people by the zealous teaching of the great philosopher Confucius and his disciple Mencius. This principle encouraged a high birth rate, which, despite recurrent famines, has kept the population of China well above the limits which the country could readily support. The chief

religions are Buddhism, Confucianism, and Taoism. About 4 per cent are Mohammedans, and less than 1 per cent are Christians.

As a people, the Chinese have adapted themselves to both cold and hot countries, having settled in large numbers both in the northern remote border regions and in the countries of southeast Asia. In several of the latter countries, they form the principal class of traders. A 30-letter alphabet of the Latin type is gradually replacing the 30,000 characters of the Chinese script.

The impact of western civilization plunged China into social and political chaos. Industrialization, beginning with the manufacture of textiles, flour, and steel, tended to break up the authority of the family. Western ideas of freedom were followed by Communism as a means of catching up with the western economy. But none of the desperate expedients was as effective as, for example, the parallel modernization of Japan's economy.

Apart from the capital, Peking, and Shanghai, the largest city, Communist China's leading cities are Tientsen, Shenyang (formerly Mukden), Wuhan (including former Hankow), Chungking, Canton, and Nanking, which was the capital before the Communist regime. Population, 1968 UN est., 730,000,000.

National Republic. The government of the Chinese National Republic, taking refuge from the Communists, retreated in 1950 to Taiwan (Formosa), an island 13,890 square miles in area, 110 miles off the east coast of the mainland. Lying in a generally north-and-south position, it is 225 miles long and 80 miles across at its widest point. It is traversed axially by a mountain range, steep on the eastern side but sloping gradually on the west to a fertile plain, which is intensively cultivated and produces exportable surpluses of rice and sugar cane. Its extensive forests are the world's chief source of camphor. Mineral output includes gold, silver, copper, and coal. Taiwan's rapidly growing industry produces steel, aluminum, lumber, flour, cement, paper, fertilizers, and refined oil.

Taiwan was held by Japan from 1895 until 1945. After the Nationalist Chinese government took refuge there, the economy of the island was rapidly expanded, partly with aid from the United States, which guaranteed the island's independence and strengthened its armed forces. The capital is Taipei, with a population of 1,155,191. Population of Taiwan, 13,466,000.

Cyprus. An island republic in the northeastern part of the Mediterranean Sea, 3572 square miles in area, with a length of 140 miles east and west and a maximum width of 60 miles. Agriculture is the predominant industry, which provides exports of tropical fruits, wine, potatoes, and tobacco. The most valuable export is copper concentrate, as it was in ancient times, the name of the island being the Greek word for *copper*. The inhabitants are partly Greek and partly Turks. The capital is Nicosia. Population, 622,000.

India. A republic occupying the large southern Asiatic peninsula separating the Indian Ocean on the east and the Arabian Sea on the west. Its northern boundary lies against China and Nepal; the land boundary to the west is Pakistan and to the east are Bangladesh and Burma. India has an area of 1,262,275 square miles.

India has a northern mountain wall, south of which the surface falls to a great plain arid in the extreme west but well watered in the central and eastern regions. Through this plain, which is shared by Pakistan, pass the Indus River and the Ganges River, the latter being joined at its delta by the Brahmaputra River. From the head of the Bay of Bengal, a mountain barrier runs north to the Himalaya Mountains and divides India from Pakistan.

On India's side of the Himalayas are two nominally independent mountain kingdoms, Nepal to the west and Bhutan to the east, with a feudal form of organization. Nepal, with an area of about 56,400 square miles, supports a population estimated at 11,700,000. Livestock is the basis of its economy, which includes manufacture of cement and chemicals. Bhutan has an area of 18,000 square miles and about one million inhabitants. It barters rice, cloth, elephants, and swords.

The central plains of India are the hottest part of the country. The year is divided into three seasons, the hot season, the monsoon rains, and the cold season. The hot season is from late March to early June. In central India temperatures rise daily to over 100° F. in the shade and at times 120° F. Day and night the temperature stands between 95° F. and 115° F. and little outside work can be accomplished during midday.

With the coming of the rainy season, June to mid-September, the temperatures fall appreciably and daily rains prevail. A secondary heat period follows the rainy season, from mid-September to November, when the cold season sets in. This "cold" season is about like summer in northern United States except that no rain falls in India.

Over most of India frost and snow are unknown. Only in the far northwest and in high altitudes do temperatures descend below freezing.

India is a land of great climatic extremes. The droughts caused by failure of the monsoon rains cause famines when literally millions have starved to death. Typhoons bring havoc to both coasts of the Deccan. During the rainy season the heaviest rainfall known in the world falls on the windward side of the Khasi Hills. Over 38 feet (457.8 in.) of rain falls here annually between late March and early October. During a particularly wet year 905 inches (75 feet) of rain fell at the station of Cherrapunji and on one day 41 inches, the equal of a year of rainfall in central United States. A great climatic variation is provided by the towering Himalayas which provide important summer resorts, as at Simla. The eastern regions and a strip along the western coast have a heavy rainfall, confined mainly to the rainy season— June to November. The northwestern section is dry, but the land is productive under irrigation. Irrigation works in India dwarf those of any other country except China. Over 50 million acres of crop land is thus served, mainly by means of canals.

The vegetable and animal life of India is extremely rich, comprising nearly all the tropical species of the continent. Venomous snakes are numerous, and every year their human victims are numbered by the thousand. Man-eating tigers have been known to cause whole villages to be deserted. Crocodiles infest the malarial swamps at the mouths of the large rivers. A species of loud-voiced lizard abounds in all the moister regions.

More than two-thirds of the population of India supports itself by agriculture and stock raising. India is the world's chief producer of jute and one of the largest producers of cotton and tea, the latter being the leading export. The other chief crops are wheat, rice, sugar cane, lac, wool, and nuts. The livestock consists mainly of humped oxen, buffaloes, sheep, and goats. Buffaloes are far more numerous as beasts of burden than are horses, donkeys, or camels. India possesses more cattle than any other country in the world, but, by reason of low quality, their value is not comparable.

Mineral production includes gold, petroleum, manganese, salt, chromium, copper, titanium, china clay, gypsum, and iron. Steel, cement, and fertilizers are among the significant manufactures but textiles form the leading industrial product. Traditionally, India has absorbed enormous amounts of gold and silver for ornaments and treasure.

The estimated population of India is 605 million, of whom about 80 per cent are Hindu, 10 per cent Mohammedan, and 2 per cent Christian. Some 220 different languages are spoken, but the prevailing one is Hindi, and English is known to several million people, a legacy of 200 years of British rule. About 70 per cent of the population is illiterate. Religion plays a large role in Indian life, a feature of which is the prevalence of pilgrimages to the holy city of Benares and bathing in the sacred waters of the Ganges to remove physical and spiritual ills. Agra has a world-famed mausoleum, the Taj Mahal, built in 1629–50 by Emperor Shah Jehan as the burial place for his favorite wife, Mumtaz Mahal.

India became a sovereign republic in 1950 after a long period of struggle, in the course of which the former British India was divided into India, which was predominantly Hindu, and Pakistan, which was predominantly Mohammedan. Extensive population changes took place after the boundaries were agreed upon. India was the first republic to adhere to the British Commonwealth of Nations.

The capital of India is New Delhi, and Bombay is the largest city. Other important cities include Calcutta, Madras, Bangalore, and Kanpur.

Indonesia. A republic of southeastern Asia consisting of seven principal islands and 3000 islets of the Malay Archipelago. It stretches 3000 miles from the Malay Peninsula eastward toward Australia and lies across the equator between the Indian and Pacific oceans. The republic's area is 575,450 square miles. The island of New Guinea is divided between Indonesia and Malaysia.

The western islands of the archipelago, Sumatra, Java, Bali, and Borneo, lie in a shallow sea. This fact and their common flora and fauna indicate that the islands were once a part of the continent of Asia. The eastern islands of the Indonesian Republic offer a striking contrast to the western group. The eastern islands comprise Celebes, the Moluccas, and the lesser Sunda chain from Lombok to the Tanimbar group. These rise abruptly from deep sea basins. They have steep, rugged mountains, short rivers, and narrow coastal plains.

The islands are fertile, warm, and well watered. They show an extraordinary degree of productivity, the exports in some years exceeding $500 million in value. Rice, corn, cassava, tea, sugar, quinine, coffee, rubber, tobacco, indigo, copra, petroleum, and tin are the chief products. Coal is mined also, the annual production exceeding one million tons. Among the more noteworthy forest trees are the teak and the upas.

The island of Java, with 60 million inhabitants, is one of the three most populous islands of the world. Its beauty and tropical luxuriance have won for it the characterization of the "pearl of the East Indies." At Boro Budor in Java stands one of the architectural marvels of the world, the largest and one of the most elaborate Buddhist temples in existence. The island of Bali, east of Java, is a mecca for tourists because of its beauty and picturesque inhabitants.

The capital of Indonesia is Jakarta. Until after World War II, Indonesia was a dependency of the Netherlands. Population, 132 million, est.

Iran (ē-rän'). A constitutional monarchy of southwest Asia, formerly known as Persia, with a southern coast line on the Persian Gulf and Arabian Sea. Its northern border, interrupted by the Caspian Sea, adjoins Russia. It is bounded west by Turkey and Iraq and east by Afghanistan and Pakistan. Its surface, covering 627,000 square miles, is a plateau rimmed by mountains on every side except the east. Mount Demavend is 18,500 feet high.

A narrow plain on the southern coast of the Caspian Sea has a heavy rainfall and supports a luxuriant vegetation. Nearly all the remainder of the country is dry and barren. The former name, Persia, gave its name to the peach, the English word being a corruption of the Latin word for Persian. The chief products of the country include petroleum, cotton, tobacco, rice, silk, wool, gums, fruits, opium, cereals, and the famous Persian rugs, the last being made entirely on looms operated by hand. Petroleum accounts for about half the total value of the exports.

The population of Iran is 26,985,000. Of this number, about one-third lead a nomadic life. Most of the inhabitants are Mohammedans, although there is a group of about 10,000 Parsis, or Ghebers, adherents of the ancient Persian religion that flourished as early as the 6th century B.C. Tehran is the capital and largest city of Iran.

Iraq. Formerly known as Mesopotamia, this country of 172,000 square miles stretches northwest from the Persian Gulf to Turkey and Syria. It lies between Iran and Arabia, and occupies the Tigris-Euphrates valley, where 19th-century excavations uncovered very complete records of an ancient civilization. The rich soil yields crops of dates, cotton, and wheat. Petroleum, the chief mineral product, provides most of the national income. The population, mainly Arabs and Kurds, is about 8,634,000. The capital is Baghdad.

Israel. A republic situated on the southeastern coast of the Mediterranean Sea and occupying most of the territory historically designated as Palestine. It is bounded north by Syria and Jordan and south by Saudi Arabia and Egypt. Israel, with a 7993-square-mile area, was established by its founders in 1948 as a national home for the Jews. In the 6-day Israeli-Arab war, June 1967, Israel successfully occupied the Sinai Peninsula, the Gaza Strip, the western bank of the Jordan, and a small area in Syria. Israel still held these areas in 1970, pending direct Arab negotiations and assurance from Egypt of the same shipping rights to the Suez Canal as other nations.

Agriculture in Israel consists of mixed farming under irrigation, dry farming, and grazing of farm animals, most of its area giving returns if properly irrigated. The industry is carried on in several ways—by communal settlements, cooperative settlements, and villages where each settler owns his own land. Products include grain, cotton, grapes, bananas, and especially citrus fruits, which form the chief item of export.

Manufactures include chemicals, building materials, textiles, glass and ceramics, tobacco products, leather goods, precision instruments, and electrical goods. Electric power is distributed from Tiberias, Haifa, and Tel Aviv.

The capital is Jerusalem. A Hebrew university there was founded in 1925. Military service is required of both men and women. Nearly 90 per cent of the inhabitants are Jews, and about half of the remainder are Arabs. Population, 2,745,000.

Japan. An ancient empire, consisting of a chain of mountainous islands off the eastern coast of Asia. The largest island is called Honshu. To the north lies Hokkaido, or Yezo; to the south, Shikoku and Kyushu. Its area is 142,726 square miles.

The islands of Japan, being the projecting portions of an immense submarine mountain range, have a mountainous surface, traversed from end to end by a high ridge. Numerous spurs from the mountains, descending to the coasts, result in a highly irregular coast line. There is, consequently, an abundance of good harbors, most of which are on the Pacific side.

The highest mountain in Honshu is Fuji, 12,388 feet in altitude. There is probably no region of its size in the world which has so many active volcanoes and is subject to such violent earthquakes as Japan. The largest active volcanic peak is Asama in central Honshu, which has a crater 600 to 800 feet deep with absolutely perpendicular sides.

The climate of Japan varies from subarctic to subtropical conditions. The cold northwestern winds from Siberia bring heavy snows in winter on the western side of the northern islands. Farther south, and more especially on the eastern side, the ocean exerts a moderating influence on the temperature and provides a copious rainfall. Violent and destructive windstorms, known as typhoons, usually mark the end of the hot, moist summers.

Japan has a very rich flora. The forests contain such trees as bamboos, camphor trees, oaks, maples, walnuts, laurels, and willows. The cultivation of flowering plants is very extensive, the Japanese being noted for their appreciation of floral beauty. Their national emblem is the chrysanthemum.

The animals include bears, monkeys, hares, wild boars, deer, foxes, wildcats, and pheasants. The buffalo is used for food and for plowing. The crane is considered sacred, being regarded as a symbol of longevity. The silkworm and numerous kinds of fish are of great economic importance.

Japan's mineral resources are gold, silver, copper, and petroleum. The chief occupations are agriculture—rice, fish, wheat, barley, rye, and poultry being the staple foods; fishing, which supports almost a million workers; and manufacturing. Export products are textiles, machinery, motor vehicles, electronic equipment, optical and other precision instruments, sewing machines, pianos, and organs. Japan leads the world in shipbuilding, and ranks second in auto production. Despite the lack of iron ore, it is also a leading producer of steel.

There is complete freedom of religion. The chief forms are Shintoism and Buddhism. Nine years of education are compulsory. There are 37 universities in the empire.

The capital and largest city is Tokyo. Osaka, the principal port, was the site of Expo '70. Other important cities are Kobe, Kyoto, Nagoya, Yokohama, and Nagasaki. The government is a constitutional monarchy under an emperor. Population, 101,090,000.

Jordan. A semi-desert Arab kingdom in Palestine east of Israel. It is bounded north by Syria and south and east by Saudi Arabia and Iraq. More than half the country's 37,301 square miles is desert. Crops of citrus fruits, vegetables, olives, barley, and wheat are grown in the fertile western part of Jordan. Industrial products are tobacco, olive oil, flour, textiles, plastics, and cement. Its only minerals are potash from the Dead Sea, and phosphate, a valuable export. Aqaba is the only port. The capital is Amman.

Education is progressing slowly. Arabic, the official language, and English are taught in the schools. Population, 2,039,000.

Korea. The peninsula of Korea in eastern Asia extending southeast about 600 miles from China and separating the Sea of Japan from the Yellow Sea is occupied by a nation divided as an aftermath of World War II. The dividing line is the 38th parallel of latitude, which separates South Korea from North Korea. The peninsula, 85,266 square miles in area with a maximum width of 350 miles, is a beautiful land of sparkling streams and high mountains. The northern part has cold winters and short summers, but the southern part has a warm, moist, rich climate. The Korean people have a history going back before Christ. China seized Korea in 1667; Japan annexed it in 1910.

South Korea. The Republic of Korea, 38,452 square miles in area, is predominantly agricultural in character, with rice the leading product, but other cereal grains are raised as well as cotton and tobacco. The country is one of the world's chief suppliers of tungsten and graphite. Manufacturing is concentrated in light consumer goods. Fishing is a leading industry.

The capital of South Korea is Seoul, with a population of 3,800,000. Pusan is the leading port. The population of South Korea is 30,470,000.

North Korea. The Democratic People's Republic of Korea, covering 46,814 square miles, is a Communist regime. It is richer in minerals than South Korea, the leading products being iron, coal, tungsten, gold, silver, and petroleum. Agriculture, largely mechanized since the war, produces temperate zone crops. Manufacturing, powered partly by several large hydroelectric projects, turns out steel, chemicals, cement, textiles, and fertilizers. As with South Korea, fishing is a leading occupation. The capital is Pyongyang, with 653,100 inhabitants. Population, 13,000,000.

Kuwait. A small, oil-rich sheikdom on the northeast corner of the Persian Gulf and adjoining Saudi Arabia and Iraq. Its 9375 square miles are waterless and barren except for their petroleum. Constitutional government on the British model was established in 1963. Population, 540,000.

Laos. A kingdom of southeastern Asia bounded north and east by China and Vietnam, south by Cambodia, and west by Thailand and Burma. Its area of 88,780 square miles is covered in the north by tropical forests and, in the south, by agricultural land producing rice, corn, tobacco, citrus fruits, and opium. About 90 per cent of the inhabitants are engaged in agriculture. There are rich iron ore deposits, but they are not mined. The forests produce teak and other valuable hardwoods.

Laos was part of French Indochina until after World War II, when it declared its independence and was a cockpit of strife between Communists and their foes. French is still one of the official languages. The capital is Vientiane. Population, 2,825,000.

Lebanon. A country on the eastern end of the Mediterranean Sea immediately north of Israel. It is bounded north and east by Syria. North to south it measures about 135 miles with a width of 20 to 35 miles. Most of its area of 3400 square miles is mountainous. About one-fourth is cultivated, the principal crops being oranges, apples, grapes, olives, wheat, and potatoes. Tripoli and Sidon are the terminals of oil pipe lines from Iraq and Saudi Arabia, respectively.

The capital is Beirut. Lebanon has a population of 2,580,000, and was a French dependency until after World War II.

Malaysia. A constitutional monarchy of southeastern Asia comprising most of the southern portion of the Malay Peninsula. It included also Singapore at the southern tip of the peninsula prior to 1965, when Singapore separated. Malaysia's area is estimated at 128,338 square miles.

The wealth of Malaysia is based in considerable part on rubber and tin. Agricultural products comprise chiefly rice, coconuts, and tea. Exports pass mainly through the port of Singapore.

The population is predominantly Malay, whereas in Singapore the Chinese were in the majority and controlled trade there and in Sarawak and North Borneo. This divergence underlay the separation. The capital is Kuala Lumpur in the State of Malaya. Malaysia's population is estimated at 10,384,000.

Maldive Islands. A republic occupying a coral island in the Indian Ocean 300 miles southwest of India. It was a British dependency until 1965. The area is 115 square miles. Population, 106,000.

Pakistan. A civil war in 1971 caused the separation of East and West Pakistan. West Pakistan became the Islamic Republic of Pakistan; East Pakistan became Bangladesh. Pakistan covers 310,403 square miles and is bounded on the south by the Arabian Sea, on the east by India, on the north by China and Afghanistan, and on the west by Iran. The country's landscape varies greatly. The northern part of the country is dominated by the Karakoram and Himalaya mountain ranges; from the foothills of these mountains stretches a barren plain. The fertile Indus plain of the southern and central region is watered by the country's only major river—the Indus.

Pakistan is largely agricultural, much of its exports are grains. The major crops are wheat, cotton, maize, sugar cane, rice, fruits, and dates.

The development of reserves of crude oil and large reserves of natural gas supplies the expanding industries of Pakistan. Principal industries include woolen and cotton products, cement, and refined sugar. Fishing is also a major source of income. Pakistan's chief trade partners are the U.S., Japan, West Germany, and Britain.

Pakistan's 1972 population was 64,890,000, with 235,000 living in the capital city of Islamabad. Other major cities include Karachi (3,469,000), Lahore (2,148,000), Lyallpur (820,000), and Rawalpindi (615,000).

Philippines. An island republic forming the most northern division of the great Malay archipelago. The Philippines lie southeast of China, about 500 miles from its coast, and are bounded on the north and the east by the Pacific Ocean, on the south by the Celebes Sea, and on the west by the South China Sea. The island group is situated north of the equator but entirely within the tropics. It extends north and south for a distance of 1150 miles and east and west for a distance of 650 miles.

There are upwards of 7000 islands and islets, of which only 466 have areas of one square mile or over. Luzon, 40,420 square miles, and Mindanao, 36,537 square miles, rank among the large islands of the world.

Besides the two largest islands, there are 9 others of importance. Their names and approximate areas in square miles are as follows: Samar, 5100; Negros, 4900; Palawan, 4500; Panay, 4450; Mindoro, 3800; Leyte, 2800; Cebu, 1700; Bohol, 1550; and Masbate, 1250. The total area of the entire Philippine group is approximately 115,507 square miles. The population of the islands, 35,993,000.

The islands of the Philippine Archipelago are largely volcanic. There are 12 volcanoes which have been more or less active in modern times, and slight earthquakes are of frequent occurrence. The islands are traversed by irregular mountain ranges, the main ridges of which extend usually in a north-and-south direction. In Luzon, the mountains rise to heights of from 3500 to 4500 feet. Mount Apo, in southern Mindanao, with an elevation of 9690 feet, is the highest peak in the Philippines.

In the larger islands, there are extensive drainage systems. The Cagayan River, in Luzon, 220 miles in length, with a drainage basin of some 10,000 square miles, is the largest river in the Philippines.

The principal minerals are gold, silver, lead, zinc, copper manganese, chromite, iron, mercury, coal, and salt, though none is extensively exploited.

The plant life is distinctly tropical in character and is especially rich in trees. Primeval forests cover about half the area, abounding in dyewoods, cedars, ebonies, wild rubber, and many other valuable trees. The most valuable native plant is the abaca, which yields the fiber called manila hemp. Other products of the Philippine flora include coconuts, cinnamon, pepper, cloves, rattan, and gums.

The islands, while poor in native mammals, are rich in birds, about half of their 700 species being found only in the Philippines. Bright hued tropical birds include parakeets, cockatoos, firebirds, fairy bluebirds, and sunbirds. Among the larger mammals are the timariu (related to the water buffalo), monkeys, deer, wild hogs, civet cats, and fruit bats.

The commonest domestic animal is the water buffalo. Agriculture employs about 60 per cent of the inhabitants. The chief products are rice, manila hemp, copra, sugar cane, corn, tobacco, sweet potatoes, and bananas.

Manufacture is chiefly in homes, though there is factory production of coconut-oil, rice, cigarettes, shoes, sugar, and cement. Home industries turn out embroidery, hats, cloth, baskets, and pottery.

About 90 per cent of the 35,993,000 inhabitants are of the Malay race and profess Christianity, the Filipinos being the only Asiatic people who, in modern times, have in large part embraced Christianity. The other inhabitants are largely Mohammedans and pagan tribes living in the mountains. The original inhabitants were Negritos, a low-statured race of whom about 25,000 remain. Mohammedan Malays are called Moros. The official language is based on Tagalog, although English is the main language of instruction.

The Philippine Islands were discovered in 1521 by Magellan. A Spanish expedition in 1542 named them in honor of Philip II of Spain. Spain began their conquest in 1565 and founded Manila in 1571. They were ceded to the U.S. in 1899 as a result of the Spanish-American War. In 1934, the U.S. granted semi-independent status, effective in 1935, intended to lead ten years later to independence. On July 4, 1946, the islands became independent as the Republic of the Philippines.

In 1970, several powerful typhoons roared across the islands with an estimated 300 deaths and property loss in the millions. Manila, hardest hit, is the largest city, population about 3,100,000. The capital is Quezon City, population 501,800.

Russia in Asia. Russian territory in Asia covers 5,816,000 square miles, which is nearly three times the area of European Russia. The larger part is comprised in the Russian Socialist Federal Soviet Republic (R.S.F.S.R.), subdivided into the Far Eastern area, the Yakutsk autonomous republic, the Siberian area, and many smaller units. In addition, Asiatic Russia comprises eight states which are federated with the R.S.F.S.R. in the Soviet Union. These are the three Transcaucasian republics of Armenia, Georgia, and Azerbaidzhan, between the Caspian and Black seas; and the Turkmen, Uzbek, Tadzhik, Kazakh, and Kirghiz republics, situated north of India, Afghanistan, and Iran (Persia).

Geographically, this huge territory may be divided into three parts—the Great Northern Lowland, over four million square miles in area, which has mainly a northern drainage into the Arctic Ocean; the semi-arid region of Central Asia, some 1,700,000 square miles in area, with an interior drainage into the Caspian and Aral seas; and Transcaucasia, a dry, mountainous, subtropical region of about 75,000 square miles.

The Great Northern Lowland, formerly comprised largely under the name of Siberia, has on the whole a severe winter climate. The northern belt is barren tundra. An intermediate belt of forested land, stretching east and west, is suitable for dairying and flax culture and has enormous lumber resources. The southernmost belt is an immense grassland plain, potentially one of the great wheat areas of the world. The two latter belts, until recently very sparsely inhabited, are in the process of rapid settlement. They are served by the Trans-Siberian railroad. The Ural area, in the west, contains one of the richest iron deposits of the world. One of the world's largest steel plants was erected in 1932 at Magnitogorsk.

Transcaucasia has a subtropical climate. Its principal industry is the production and refining of petroleum, which centers about Baku.

The principal cities of Transcaucasia include Baku, Tiflis, and Batumi; those of Central Asia, Tashkent, Bukhara, and Samarkand; and those of the Great Northern Lowland, Omsk, Sverdlovsk, Novosibirsk, Vladivostok, and Irkutsk.

Saudi Arabia. A desert kingdom occupying four-fifths of the Arabian peninsula in southwestern Asia. Having an area of about 870,000 square miles, it is bounded west by the Red Sea and Egypt, north by Jordan and Iraq, east by Kuwait and the Persian Gulf, and south by Yemen, Southern Ye-

men, and Oman, which border on the Arabian Sea.

The highlands of the west, 9000 feet high, slope down to 2000 feet at the Persian Gulf. This plateau is an arid, barren desert, inhabited by wandering tribes of Bedouins. Camels are the chief form of wealth among the tribesmen, who maintain themselves at oases. Mainly from the oases also come agricultural products, including dates, honey, hides, wool, barley, and clarified butter known as ghi.

Saudi Arabia is one of the richest oil-producing regions of the world, and oil royalties provide most of the income of the country, paying expenses of government and providing free medical service to the inhabitants.

The capital is Riyadh. Mecca and Medina are the two sacred cities of the Mohammedan world, and pilgrims and tourists visit them in great numbers. The country is an earlier amalgamation of two kingdoms, Hejaz and Nejd. Several other shiekdoms are associated with Saudi Arabia, including Oman at the southeastern extremity of the peninsula. Population of Saudi Arabia, about 7,100,000.

Singapore. See *Malaysia* and article on the city of Singapore.

Sri Lanka (Ceylon). An island member of the Commonwealth of Nations in the Indian Ocean near the southern tip of India. The surface (25,332 square miles) is mainly a rolling plain, about one-fifth being mountainous and covered with forests. The island is famous for gems, although the export of tea, rubber, and coconuts exceed in value any other export. Other products are cocoa, cinnamon, and coffee. Graphite is mined and salt and cement are produced. The capital and largest city is Colombo. Some 70 per cent of the people are Buddhists and of Singhalese origin; 20 per cent are Hindus of Tamil extraction and originally from India. The population is 12,711,000.

Syria. A republic of western Asia bounded west by the Mediterranean Sea and Lebanon, north by Turkey, east by Iraq, and south by Jordan and Israel. It has an area of 71,210 square miles and a population of 5,738,000. Although most of the people are Sunni Moslems, some 500,000 are nomadic Bedouins. It is traversed by the Orontes and Euphrates rivers. Damascus, the capital, with a population of 618,457, is the oldest inhabited city in the world. Syria was under French rule before World War II. In 1958, it joined Egypt to form the United Arab Republic, but a revolt in 1961 broke the tie.

Only about half of the area is suitable for farming. Sandy deserts are common. Tobacco, wheat, fruits, cotton, barley, corn, sorghums, hemp, and silk are produced. Besides foodstuffs, manufactures include matches, alcohol, soap, cotton cloth, and cement. There are agricultural, engineering and teacher-training colleges as well as universities in Damascus and Aleppo.

Thailand (*tī'lănd*) **(Siam).** An independent kingdom of southeastern Asia, bounded west by Burma, north and east by Laos, and south by Cambodia. It has a southern coast line on the Gulf of Siam. The area of the country is 200,148 square miles.

The richest part of Thailand is the wet, tropical valley of the Menam River. This river valley lies between a western mountain wall and a central plateau that divides the Menam River basin from the western reaches of the Mekong River system. The valley produces valuable timber and dyewoods. Agriculture is carried on intensively. Rice is the national food and is the staple article of export. The live stock of the country consists mainly of oxen and buffaloes but includes several thousand elephants. The white elephant, really a light ashy gray in color, is considered sacred by the inhabitants. Tin is the chief mineral produced on a commercial scale.

The population of Thailand is 33,693,000 (1968 est.). Buddhism is the prevailing religion. Thailand has, in recent years, introduced many of the methods of Western civilization, having employed the services of European and American advisers in finance, education, drainage, and many other departments. The capital is Bangkok.

Turkey. A republic of west Asia occupying the whole of Asia Minor and extending eastward to Transcaucasia and Iran. It includes also a number of islands off the coast and a small district of Europe, in which the city of Istanbul is situated. Asiatic Turkey is sometimes called Anatolia.

The area of Turkey is 296,108 square miles, including 9257 square miles in Europe. It consists mainly of a plateau which, except in the mountainous eastern region, sinks on all sides to wooded foothills cut by valleys leading to the sea. The northern coast district is most heavily wooded; the chief region of cultivation is on the west. The interior, particularly the eastern part, is hot and dry.

The principal occupation of the Turks is agriculture. Tobacco, cereals, cotton, figs, grapes, olives, and sugar beets are the chief products of the soil. Mineral wealth is considerable but is undeveloped. Meerschaum is a distinctive product. Manufactures are confined mostly to handmade articles, including rugs and copper utensils, although lumber mills, cement works, and an automobile assembly plant have been opened in recent years.

The population of Turkey is 40,197,669 (1975 est.). The seat of government is Ankara.

Vietnam. A country of southeast Asia fronting eastward and southward on the South China Sea and extending from China on the north along the borders of Laos and Cambodia on the west. Formerly a part of French Indochina, it was occupied by the Japanese in World War II, and French efforts to reassume their control ended in defeat, after eight years, by local Communist forces aided by the Chinese. A role of neutrality was agreed on in 1954 by interested powers, including the United States, and a commission was set up to establish a government. The northern part refused to cooperate and set up a Communist government on the Chinese model. The southern part set up a republic in 1954, and hostilities continued between the two parts.

After more than two decades of warfare, U.S. troops were withdrawn from the North-South conflict in 1973. In 1975 South Vietnam was defeated and the country was united under the Socialist Republic of the North.

South Vietnam. The former republic of Vietnam has an area of 66,263 square miles. Predominantly agricultural, it exports rice, rubber, tea, coffee, quinine, tobacco, cinnamon, and silk. There is no heavy industry, but light industry includes weaving and the manufacture of textiles, pens, bicycles, radios, sewing machines, and many other articles. The capital was Saigon (now Ho Chi Minh City). The inhabitants are concentrated in the fertile delta of the Mekong River. Population, over 20 million in 1976.

North Vietnam. The Democratic Republic of Vietnam, 63,344 square miles in area, contained the richer part of the former French dependency. Its mineral output includes coal and phosphates. Rice is the chief agricultural product and practically all is grown by peasants grouped in agricultural cooperatives. All business is state-owned. Manufactured products include cement, cotton, and silk textiles, chemicals, and plywood. Hanoi is the capital and Haiphong is the chief port. Population, 23,787,375 (1974).

Yemen. A mountainous republic at the tip of the Arabian peninsula, bounded north by Saudi Arabia, east by Southern Yemen, and west by the Red Sea. Grown in the most fertile part of its 75,000-square-mile area are coffee and grain. Hides, dates, herbs, and fruit are exported. Hodeida, on the Red Sea, is the chief port. Sana, its capital, is an archeological site. Population, 6,500,000.

The following articles describe the principal cities of Asia. Most of these cities present an appearance in which the marks of ancient civilizations contrast strikingly with the changes introduced by a rapidly penetrating industrialization. A number of other notable features are described, such as the Dead Sea, the world's lowest and saltiest body of water; Tai Shan, the sacred mountain of Confucianists; and the Malay archipelago, the largest group of islands in the world.

Agra (ä'grä). A walled city of northern central India. The Mogul emperors left in Agra several monuments of striking magnificence, including the Taj Mahal, "Gem of Buildings," a white marble mausoleum, the construction of which is said to have engaged 20,000 workmen for 22 years. The city has a large trade. Its industries include gem setting and inlaid mosaic work. Population, 637,785.

Amernath. A cave in the Himalaya mountains near the extreme northern border of India. In the cave stands the sacred symbol of the god Siva, which is the object of pilgrimages from all parts of India.

Ankara. The capital of Turkey, officially chosen as such in 1923, replacing Istanbul. It was rapidly transformed from an oriental hamlet in a malarial plain to a modern city with sanitary improvements and well laid-out streets. Railroads connecting with other parts of the country were constructed, electric power was provided, and manufacturing industries arose, notably for producing tiles and cotton and linen textiles. A park was laid out, and attractive government buildings were erected. Population, 1,236,152.

Baghdad. The capital of Iraq, situated on the Tigris River near the geographic center of the country. Like many other Oriental cities, Baghdad has a striking appearance at a distance. There are many ruined mosques, monuments of the city's former splendor. It was, in the 8th century, the capital of the caliphate of Haroun-al-Raschid, a hero of the *Arabian Nights*. Population, 2,969,000.

Bangkok. The capital and chief seaport of Thailand, on the Menam River 25 miles from the Gulf of Siam. It is noted for many elaborate temples and palaces. The streets, intersected by small canals, are made attractive with gardens and tall palm trees. The city's location on a far-reaching waterway system enables it to carry on an extensive foreign trade in rice, sugar, silk, peanuts, and cotton. Its modern airport, Don Muang, one of the largest in Southeast Asia, is served by 24 international airlines. Population, 3,967,081.

Beirut. Capital and principal seaport of Lebanon, also the seat of the American University and the Lebanese National Museum. Beirut has rail connections with Damascus and with Haifa and Tripoli. Population, about 700,000.

Benares. See *Varanasi.*

Bethlehem. A town of Jordan about five miles southwest of Jerusalem. Its chief center of interest is the basilica of Constantine, built in the 4th century at the spot where Jesus was believed to have been born. A chapel nearby commemorates Jerome, the maker of the Vulgate edition of the Bible, who resided and died in Bethlehem. Population, 22,453.

Bombay. The second largest city of India, situated on a small island near the center of the country's southwest coast. By reason of its industrial development and of its modern improvements, Bombay is the most European in appearance of the cities of India. It has one of the six federal universities of the country. The characteristic Oriental features remain, however, in much of the city, where decorated houses, tea shops, bazaars, and temples bear witness to the more ancient civilization of the Hindus. Bombay was the birthplace of Rudyard Kipling. Population 5,970,575.

Calcutta. The largest city and, until 1911, the capital of India, about 85 miles from the sea at the west of the enormous delta of the Ganges River. Calcutta is the terminus of many railroads and canals and handles about one-third of the entire foreign trade of India. The European section has numerous splendid buildings. Cotton mills, sugar refineries, sawmills, silk mills, flour mills, and shipbuilding yards are among the more important industrial establishments.

The city is the seat of the University of Calcutta, founded in 1857. Victoria Memorial, one of the finest buildings in Calcutta, contains documents and pictures illustrating Indian history. Thackeray, the novelist, was born in Calcutta. Population, 7,031,382.

Canton (Kwangchow). A commercial city of southeastern China, situated about 70 miles northwest of the island of Hong Kong. The city is one of the chief centers of the Chinese silk trade. The industries include the manufacture of paper, lacquered wares, textiles, and glass, and the painting of porcelain.

The city is surrounded by a brick wall and partitioned by a cross wall into the old town and the new town. The latter has many wide, paved streets, Canton being one of the most progressive cities of China. Among the pagodas is one covering an area of seven acres. There is a Mohammedan mosque dating from the 9th century. Population, 1,840,000.

Chinese Wall. The most gigantic defensive work in existence, consisting of a wall more than 1500 miles in length, which was begun by the rulers of China in the 3d century B. C. and received its last addition in the 16th century A. D. A part, now destroyed, began near the Gulf of Liaotung in northeast China. The wall follows a general western direction along the southern border of Mongolia. The average height is about 22 feet. The base is from 15 to 25 feet wide, narrowing to 12 feet at the top. Its course passes through valleys and over mountains irrespective of the difficulties of construction.

Colombo. The capital of Sri Lanka (Ceylon), situated on the eastern coast of the island. The city was founded by the Portuguese in 1517 and was named in honor of Columbus. The European section is well built and modern in appearance. Population, 510,947.

Damascus. The capital of the republic of Syria. It is one of the few very ancient cities of the Mediterranean region which have survived until the present day. It is situated in a fertile region 53 miles southeast of its port, Beirut, on the Mediterranean coast. At the time of the Crusades, Damascus produced a famous type of ornamented steel, which has given the name damascening to modern steel etching.

The city has been often destroyed and rebuilt. The Ommiad, the largest of the city's 200 mosques, was formerly a church, which had earlier replaced a temple said to have contained the head of John the Baptist. Damascus, on account of its beautiful surroundings, is believed to have been the model for the paradise described in the *Koran.* The city contains the burial place of Fatima, the only child of Mohammed. Population, 618,457

Dead Sea. A salt-water lake in Palestine. It is 47 miles long and 10 miles wide. Its area is 340 square miles and it has a maximum depth of 1280 feet. Lying 1290 feet below sea level, it is the lowest body of water on the surface of the earth. Its principal affluent is the Jordan river. It has no outlet, its excess water being taken off by evaporation, estimated at about 6,000,000 tons daily. The salinity of the Dead Sea is 23 to 27%, which is about 5 times that of the ocean. The economic value of the various salts in solution is very great.

Delhi (*děl'ē*). The capital of India, situated in the north central part of the country. Delhi was formerly the largest city of India. The Mogul emperors made it their capital, and erected many fine buildings, the ruins of which still attest their original grandeur. The Great Mosque, built in 1650, still stands, and is regarded by Mohammedans as one of the wonders of the world. In the vicinity of the city is the Kutb Minar, a tower 238 feet high built of stone, ranging in color from red at the bottom to orange at the top.

The transfer of the seat of government from Calcutta to Delhi in 1911 was the occasion for building a new division of the city, known as New Delhi. This centers about Raisina, a hill six miles south of the walls of old Delhi, with which it is connected by broad, tree-lined avenues. Over $150 million was spent on this city building project, which is the most magnificent the Orient has witnessed in modern times. Population, 3,647,023.

Hangchow (*häng'chō'*). A city of mainland China near the center of the country's eastern coast and standing at the head of Hangchow bay, an inlet of the China Sea. The city is near the southern terminus of the Grand canal, which serves as an artery of the commerce centering in the city. The chief manufactures are silk and fans.

Hangchow is one of the best-built cities of China. The city is surrounded by a massive wall, 12 miles in circuit. The western part of this wall is washed by West lake, a beautiful sheet of water 8 miles in circumference dotted with islands on which are built monasteries, memorial halls, and shrines. To the west of the lake are numerous Buddhist temples. Population, about 784,000.

Hankow (*hän'kō'*). See *Wuhan.*

Hiroshima. A large city near the southern end of the island of Honshu, Japan. It was an important political and commercial center having rail, air, and ocean connections. As a victim of the first atomic bomb, it was almost completely demolished but has been rebuilt. Population, 515,000.

Irkutsk (*ĭr-kōōtsk'*). A commercial city of south central Siberia, situated near the south end of Lake Baikal. It has a large caravan trade from Mongolia and is one of the three important points on the Asiatic section of the Trans-Siberian railroad. Articles of commerce include tea, silk, porcelain, dried fruit, fur, and fossil ivory. Population, 420,000.

Islamabad. The capital of Pakistan, situated in the north of West Pakistan 15 miles north of Rawalpindi. The latter was provisional capital until 1966 while the new governmental city of Islamabad was being built. Population, 235,000.

Izmir. See *Smyrna.*

Jakarta (Raya). The capital of the Republic of Indonesia, situated on the north coast of Java Island. It forms the chief outlet for the numerous products of the former Netherlands East Indies. The European section, in the higher, more healthful part, contains the Museum of the Batavian Society of Arts and Sciences, a beautiful structure in the Greek style which houses the largest collection of Javanese art in existence. The University of Indonesia is located here. Population, 4,600,000.

Jerusalem. The capital of Israel, as it had been of the ancient Israelites from about 1000 B.C. It is on an elevation of 2500 feet between the Mediterranean and Dead seas. About it has centered the devotion of Jews, Christians, and Mohammedans. It is the seat of Hebrew University.

The city is surrounded by ravines on three sides. The water and drainage facilities were greatly improved after the city was occupied by the British in 1918. The most prominent building of the city is the Mosque of Omar, standing on the site of Solomon's temple. The Church of the Holy Sepulchre and the Via Dolorosa are of interest for their connection with the crucifixion of Jesus. The "wailing wall," said to be a vestige of Solomon's temple, is sacred to Jews as a place for prayer and lamentation. Population, 344,200.

Kabul. The capital and largest city of Afghanistan It is near the center of the eastern frontier. Surrounded on three sides by mountains, it commands passes leading to India and Russia. Well built roads connect the city with these countries. The city itself is unattractive but it has a fine palace in a magnificent setting overlooking fruitful plains. It has also a small arms factory. Population, 289,703.

Karachi. A seaport in Pakistan, formerly the capital of the country. It is the chief outlet for wheat and raw cotton. Population, 2,721,200.

Keijo (Seoul). The capital and chief port of South Korea, situated near the center of the west coast of Chosen, of which it is the chief port and the capital. It is connected with the Trans-Siberian railroad. Silk, tobacco, mats, paper, and fans are made in the city. During the Korean war, it was the scene of bitter fighting and was partly ruined. Population, 3,800,000.

Kobe (*kō'bě*). A seaport of Japan, situated on the southern coast of Honshu Island. It is the chief center of Japan's silk export trade. Prominent among the industrial establishments is an imperial ship-building yard. Population, 1,228,000.

Kyoto (*kyō'tō*). An inland commercial and industrial city of Japan, situated near the southern coast of Honshu Island. Kyoto was formerly the capital of Japan and bears evidence of the fact in the regularity of its plan and in its magnificent monuments and temples. Its industries include the manufacture of porcelain, brocade, toys, metal products, and silk fabrics. The city is the seat of an imperial university. Population, 1,379,000.

Lhasa (*läs'ă*). The sacred city of the Lamaists, members of a widespread, ascetic sect of Buddhism. The city is situated in south central Tibet on a plateau having an altitude of 11,830 feet. Being forbidden to the uninitiated, Lhasa was seen by no more than three Europeans before 1904, when the British forced an entrance. Just outside the city stands the imposing former residence of the head of the religious sect, the Dalai Lama. The Chinese took over the city in 1958, destroying the monastic institutions, and the Dalai Lama escaped to India the next year.

Madras. One of the largest cities of India, situated on the southeastern coast of the country. The industrial output includes textiles, cigars, iron, cement, and dyes. The city contains an ornamental park, many fine buildings and monuments, an observatory, museums, a university, and a number of colleges. Population, 3,169,930.

Malay Archipelago. The largest group of islands in the world, lying at the extreme southeastern corner of Asia. The principal islands are Sumatra, Java, Borneo, Celebes, and the Philippine group. Of these, Sumatra, Java, and Borneo are on a continental shelf less than 600 feet deep, which connects with the Philippines by two submarine banks; the others are surrounded by water of great depth. Nearly all the islands present bold profiles and have mountains which are actively volcanic.

The equator passes through the center of the group. A rich soil and the warm, moist climate combine to make these islands extraordinarily fertile. They abound in tropical fruits of many kinds. Among the cultivated crops are rubber, rice, tea, sugar, coffee, kapok, cinchona bark, and coconuts. The mineral wealth of the islands is important, including tin in Banka and other islands near Sumatra, petroleum in Sumatra, coal in Borneo and Sumatra, and lead in all the larger islands. The inhabitants are largely Malaysians. Chinese tradesmen are numerous. The total area of the archipelago is estimated at 1,094,857 square miles, supporting a population of over 60 million.

Mandalay. A city of central Burma, standing on the Irrawaddy River. There are a number of Buddhistic shrines, the most remarkable of which is the Kuthodaw, a square surrounded by 450 pagodas. Within each pagoda is inscribed a part of the Buddhist scriptures, the aggregate of the inscriptions constituting the whole of the sacred writings. A walled section of the city encloses Fort Dufferin, formerly a royal palace. Population, 1968 est., 195,348.

Manila. The former capital and chief city of the Philippines, on the west coast of the island of Luzon. It is built on both banks of the Pasig River at its entrance to Manila Bay. On the south side of the river is the ancient Spanish town, surrounded by a wall, with the cathedral, monastic buildings, and numerous quaint Spanish houses; also the principal residential section, hospitals, and government buildings. On the north side is Binondo, containing the principal shopping and financial district. Manila is important for its foreign and coastwise commerce. It is the world's greatest shipping market for hemp. The Spanish city of Manila was founded in 1571. In 1898, Admiral Dewey destroyed a Spanish fleet in Manila Bay. Population, 1,402,000; Greater Manila, 3,100,000.

Mecca. The most sacred city of the Mohammedans, situated in a barren valley in the southern part of the Saudi Arabia, of which kingdom it is one of the two capitals. It is about 50 miles inland from Jidda, its port on the Red Sea. Most of the inhabitants find support from lodging the pilgrims who, in numbers exceeding 100,000 annually, flock here from all parts of the Mohammedan world to visit the Sacred Mosque, which marks the birthplace of Mohammed. Population, about 185,000.

Medina. An inland city of central Hejaz, sacred to the adherents of Mohammedanism. Mohammed's flight there from Mecca in 622 A. D. marks the year in which the Mohammedan calendar begins. The prophet died in Medina, and a large mausoleum, said to contain his undecayed body, attracts numerous pilgrims. Population, about 72,000.

Mukden. See *Shenyang.*

Nagasaki. An old and large Japanese port of just over 420,000 people. It is important in both trade and industry with steel work and shipbuilding predominant. It is located on the extreme west of the southernmost Japanese island of Kyushi and was the second target of the atomic bomb.

Nagoya. The fourth largest city of Japan, 235 miles southwest of Tokyo. It is one of the greatest centers of Japanese pottery manufacture. Other industries include cotton and silk mills. Many people are engaged in the embroidering of handkerchiefs. Nagoya has a very fine Buddhist temple and a castle dating back to 1610. Population, 1,954,000.

Nanking. The former capital of China. It is about midway between Peking in the north and Canton in the south and lies on the south bank of the Yangtze River 235 miles from the sea. The first sovereign of the Ming dynasty chose it as his capital in 1368. From 1403 until 1928, the Chinese government had its seat at Peking, but returned in the latter year to Nanking. Most of the magnificent buildings of earlier days were destroyed in the Taiping rebellion in 1853. The Republican government in 1928 proceeded to modernize the city. A boulevard has replaced the ancient city wall. On Purple mountain near by, a magnificent monument was erected to Sun Yat Sen, founder of the Chinese republic. Population 1,419,000.

Nazareth. A town of northwestern Israel, about 20

miles from the Mediterranean seacoast. It is memorable among Christians as the early residence of Jesus. A richly decorated basilica, the Church of the Annunciation, stands on what is said to be the site of the residence of Mary, the mother of Jesus, her house allegedly having been miraculously transported to Loreto, Italy. The town was captured from the Turks by Australians in 1918. Population, 26,400.

New Delhi. See *Delhi.*

Omsk. A city of southwestern Siberia on the Trans-Siberian railroad. It is a noted trading center for wheat and for dairy products. Manufactures include agricultural machinery, cloth, and sausages. Population, 774,000.

Osaka (ō'zä'kä). The second largest city of Japan, situated on Osaka Bay in the southern part of the island of Honshu. Being intersected by the Yodo River and by numerous canals spanned by hundreds of bridges, the city has been styled the Venice of the East. Ironworks, cotton and sugar mills, shipyards, and a large government mint are among the more important industries. The city is regularly laid out and contains many notable temples. Population, 3,133,000.

Pacific Islands or **Oceania.** Under these terms are included the numerous islands of the Pacific Ocean east of the Malay archipelago and north and east of Australia. On racial grounds they are frequently divided into three groups—Polynesia, Melanesia, and Micronesia. Melanesia lies directly north and east of Australia and west of the international date line. It includes the Solomon, Santa Cruz, New Hebrides, New Caledonia, and Fiji islands. North of this group lies Micronesia, comprising the Caroline, Marshall, Gilbert, Guam, Nauru, and neighboring islands. Polynesia includes most other islands of the Pacific Ocean east of the groups described above. Among the more important are the Hawaiian, New Zealand, Friendly (Tonga), Society, Cook, Samoan, Marquesas, Manahiki, and Union islands.

Peking. The capital of Communist China. It is located about 80 miles west of the Gulf of Chihli, an inlet of the Yellow Sea. Peking consists of an old city and a new city, usually called the outer city and the inner city. Each is surrounded by a wall, which, in one section, separates the two cities. The new city is larger and more populous. The old city contains a walled imperial city, within which lies the "purple forbidden city," the former palace and court of the emperor. These divisions are now traversed by a broad thoroughfare which passes through Peking from north to south. The finest building in the old city is the famous Temple of Heaven. To the west of the city, on the so-called Mountain of Ten Thousand Ancients, stands the emperor's summer palace, near which, upon a lagoon, floats a marble boat, built as a pleasure house. The grounds contain the celebrated camel back bridge, and near by is a pagoda built of porcelain.

Peking is a great educational center. It is the seat of Yenching University, established by American philanthropy, a number of technical and professional schools, and the oldest observatory in the world. Population, 4,010,000.

Pichola. A small lake near Udaipur in central west India. Each of two small islands in the lake is enclosed by marble walls, within which is erected a marble palace. These marble palaces were built by rulers of Rajputana and exhibit a grace and elegance which are equaled in very few of the great buildings of the world.

Rangoon. The capital and leading port of Burma, located on the southern coast near the Gulf of Martaban. The chief industrial establishments include lumber, rice, and oil mills, the products of which are exported in large quantities. Rangoon has a Buddhist pagoda, 370 feet high and covered with gold leaf, the foundation of which is said to have been laid in 588 B. C. This pagoda, called the Shoay Dagon, contains objects sacred to Buddhists and is annually visited by thousands of pilgrims. A university is situated in the city. Population, 3,662,312.

Rawalpindi. See *Islamabad.*

Samarkand. A historic city in the former Uzbek Republic, USSR. Its ancient name was Maracanda. It was destroyed by Alexander the Great in 329 B.C. After its capture by the Moslems in 911-12 A.D., it became a brilliant seat of Arabic civilization. Jenghis Khan destroyed it in 1221. Timur made it his capital in 1369. The palace and tomb of Timur are among the finest of the city's buildings. The Rigistan square is surrounded by four ancient structures, formerly Moslem colleges. The modern part of the city has broad, shaded streets. Its industries include cotton ginning and the manufacture of leather, flour, brick, pencils, and liquor. Population, 233,000.

Seoul. See *Keijo.*

Shanghai. The largest city, principal port, and chief industrial center of Communist China. It lies at the junction of the Huang River and Soochow creek 12 miles from their mouth in the estuary of the Yangtze River. It is the sea gate for the trade of the richest portion of China and is the spearpoint of its advancing industrialization. Flour and rice milling, shipbuilding, publishing, and the manufacture of engines, machinery, cotton and silk textiles, paper, cigarettes, leather, and food products are the leading industries.

A portion of the city is modern and well built, having grown up entirely since 1854. In 1932 Japan captured a part of the city and held it for a short time. Population, 10,820,000 (est.).

Shenyang (Mukden). A city of Communist China, located about 150 miles north of the Yellow Sea. It is a railroad junction and a point of convergence of several caravan routes. Near the city are the tombs of the Manchu emperors, who, in the 17th century, made Mukden their capital. Huge stone elephants stand on guard over the tombs. Near Shenyang was fought the decisive battle of the Russo-Japanese war. Population (Western est., 1965) 4 million.

Singapore. City and member country of the British Commonwealth, situated on an island at the southern tip of the Malay Peninsula. It is the smelting point for the immense amount of tin mined in adjoining Malaysia and ships a major part of the world's block tin. A strong British naval station is maintained there by agreement with the Singapore government. About two-thirds of the estimated 2,278,200 inhabitants are Chinese. See *Malaysia*.

Smyrna (Izmir). A seaport and commercial city of west central Turkey, standing at the head of the Gulf of Izmir, an inlet of the Ægean Sea. The rugs for which Smyrna is famous are made, for the most part, in the surrounding towns. Other articles of trade are silks, cottons, olive oil, gums, and figs. Smyrna is one of the oldest continuously inhabited cities in the world. It was assigned to the Greeks as a mandate in 1920. In 1922 the Greeks were driven out, and the city was put to flames. Population, 1,660,529.

Srinagar (srē'nà-gŭr'). The capital of the native kingdoms of Jammu and Kashmir in the northern extremity of India. In the picturesque scenery of the surrounding country was located the "Vale of Cashmere," celebrated in Moore's poem entitled *Lalla Rookh*. Population, 403,612.

Tai Shan. A sacred mountain about 120 miles southwest of the Gulf of Chihli, an inlet of the Yellow Sea. On its summit are several temples, beneath one of which Confucius is said to have been buried. Each year during February and March as many as 10,000 pilgrims in a single day ascend to the summit, 4700 feet in height. The ascent is facilitated by a six-mile mountain road, paved and provided with steps in the more precipitous stages.

Tashkent. A city of southern Russia, capital of the Uzbek Republic. It is situated in a vast surrounding plain of arid land on which cotton is grown with the aid of irrigation. Its industrial interests include cotton ginning and lumber mills and tobacco, leather, machinery, and rayon factories. The city has up-to-date water, electric, and street railway systems. Population, 1,643,000.

Tbilisi (Tiflis). The capital and largest city of the Georgian Republic, in the Soviet Union, situated midway between the Black Sea and the Caspian Sea. It is the distributing center for the country and has manufactures of bricks, tobacco, leather, soap, flour, cotton, and furniture. In picturesque contrast to its many wide streets and modern water, electric, and transport services are the Oriental bazaars and markets, where merchants from the East display their silverware, swords, rugs, dried fruits, and silk goods. It was founded as Tiflis in A.D. 379. Russia obtained it in 1799. Population, 1,030,000.

Tehran (tĕ-h'rän'). The capital of Iran, lying on an elevated plain in the north central part of the country about 66 miles south of the Caspian Sea. Manufactures include rugs, silks, cotton goods, and ironware. It has a citadel, called the Ark, within which is the handsome palace of the shah. The principal street is the Boulevard des Ambassadeurs, running through the foreign section. Tehran was founded in the 12th century and became capital of Persia (now Iran) in 1788. Population, 3,150,000.

Tel Aviv. Mediterranean port of Israel, forming, with Jaffa, a joint municipality having a combined population of 389,700. It grew rapidly after World War II with the influx of displaced European Jews.

Tientsin. A commercial city and port of Communist China on the Pei River about 70 miles from its mouth in the Gulf of Chihli. It is 70 miles southeast of Peiping. The waterfront has buildings resembling the commercial structures of Western cities. The remainder of the city, which lies on a low plain, has small buildings and narrow, ill-kept streets, although municipal services have been much improved since 1900, when the city walls were destroyed in the Boxer uprising. Tientsin has an immense trade in salt, rice, and tea. Population, 4,280,000, estimated.

Tokyo. The capital of Japan and largest city in Asia. It stands at the head of Tokyo Bay near the center of the eastern coast of Honshu Island.

The city was largely destroyed in 1923 by earthquake and fire, which laid waste 25 square miles. This catastrophe provided the opportunity for rebuilding according to modern plans. The streets were widened, at the cost of moving some 200,000 houses; sewers were installed; public school playgrounds were enlarged; and a subway for rapid transit was constructed. Buildings in general are low or made of reinforced concrete to minimize danger of damage from earthquakes. The Hall of the Nameless Dead commemorates 33,000 victims of the great fire of 1923.

The chief of the city's many parks is called Tukiage, which contains the palace of the emperor built in a mixed Japanese and European style of architecture. The University of Tokyo is an institution of higher learning of the most advanced type. The eastern portion of the city contains regions known to visitors for their display of flowers.

The site of the city was a fishing village in the 13th century. It first became important in 1457 as the residence of the feudal lord. The name was changed in 1868 from Yedo to Tokyo, meaning Eastern Capital. Population, 8,643,000.

Trans-Siberian Railroad. A railroad which traverses Russia in an east-west direction, connecting Leningrad in Europe with Vladivostok on the extreme edge of Asiatic Russia. Over 5,500 miles in length, it occupied 11 years for initial construction, which cost $172 million. It was practically completed by 1902.

At a point east of Lake Baykal the road was divided, finally meeting at a point near Vladivostok. One line passed east of Lake Baykal entirely in Russian territory. The other line, passing through Manchuria, was known as the Chinese Eastern Railway and was owned jointly with China. In 1931 it was seized by Manchuria, and a small indemnity was paid to Russia.

The railroad is now double tracked. With feeders and connections running to southern Russia, it has been the central factor in one of the greatest migrations of people in history—settlement of the Siberian plains. Strategically, it makes eastern and western Russia a unit.

Varanasi (Benares). A city of north central India on the Ganges River. It is sacred to the Hindus, who come from all parts of India to wash away their sins in the Ganges. There are more than 1500 temples in the city, which abounds in beggars. The river banks are lined with stone and have many landing places, often highly ornamented. The city is a center of trade. Gold brocades, gold and silver thread, brassware, and lacquered toys are manufactured. The Benares Hindu university is situated there. Population, 582,915.

Victoria. The capital of the British island of Hong Kong by which name it is usually called. Victoria is a free port and the center of British commerce with China and Japan. The British fleet used the island as a naval base in the first Opium war, 1839-42. Then practically uninhabited, it was ceded to Great Britain in 1841.

Its numerous industries include the manufacture of ships, cement, paper, rope, glass, soap, cigars, and knitted goods. Population of Victoria, 633,138; of Hong Kong island and adjacent leased territory, 3,927,000.

Vladivostok (vlä'dyĭ-vŏs-tôk'). The chief Pacific Ocean port of Russia and the eastern terminus of the Trans-Siberian railroad. The city is situated in the extreme southeastern part of Asiatic Russia, in the vicinity of valuable iron deposits. The chief products handled are the numerous derivatives of the soy bean. Vladivostok was settled in 1860, two years after its site was acquired by Russia. Population, 526,000.

Wuhan. A city of China, standing at the head of ocean navigation on the Yangtze River about 680 miles from its mouth in the East China Sea. Under the Communist government, this city was formed by the amalgamation of the former Hankow with the neighboring cities of Wuchang and Hanyang. The city contains large iron and steel works, which utilize the extensive iron and coal deposits in the vicinity. Cotton goods, flour, and leather are also manufactured. The chief exports of the city are normally black tea, wood oil, and sesame seed. Population, 2,411,000.

Yokohama. A leading seaport of Japan, situated on Tokyo Bay near the center of the western coast of Honshu Island. The chief exports are silk and tea. Yokohama was the first Japanese port open to foreigners and it is still the headquarters for most tourists who visit Japan. The city was almost totally destroyed in 1923 by earthquake and fire. It was reconstructed with wide streets, concrete buildings, and bridges. Population, 2,622,000.

AFRICA

THE second largest continent of the world, situated in the eastern hemisphere south of Europe and southwest of Asia, with which it is connected by the Isthmus of Suez. It is separated from Europe by the Mediterranean Sea, an inland body of water which narrows to a width of nine miles at the Strait of Gibraltar. Between Africa and Asia, lie the Red Sea and the Gulf of Aden. The Atlantic Ocean on the west and the Indian Ocean on the east meet at the southern point of the continent.

Africa lies farther to the north than South America. In length, the continent is almost equally divided between the northern and the southern hemisphere. On account of its shape, however, about two-thirds of Africa's surface lies north of the equator. Its most northern point is in the latitude of Washington, D. C., and it extends nearly 5000 miles south to the approximate latitude of Buenos Aires. It has an area of about 11,500,000 square miles, being about 1⅓ times as large as North America and second only to Asia in extent.

Outline. As in the case of South America, the maximum width of the continent is in the north. By reason of a huge western extension, Africa attains a width of 4600 miles, just 400 miles less than its length. Between the western extension and the southern portion of the continent, lies the Gulf of Guinea. The only other major indentation is the Gulf of Sidra near the center of the northern coast. On the eastern coast, the Somali Republic projects as a cape, separating the Gulf of Aden from the Indian Ocean. The coast line is remarkably regular and, consequently, affords very few good harbors.

Surface. Africa is, for the most part, a plateau surrounded by a very narrow strip of coastal lowlands. The southern and the eastern parts of the plateau are higher than the western and the northern parts. The latter contain certain sections, in the interior of the Sahara desert, where the elevation is that of the sea level or even less.

In the extreme southern part of the continent, a ridge rims the plateau, rising, on the eastern side, to a height of nearly 9000 feet. The east central part of the continent consists of a wide, irregular highland cut longitudinally by the so-called Great Rift valley, which contains lakes rivaling in size the Great Lakes of North America. Lake Victoria is the largest, being second only to Lake Superior in area. Lake Tanganyika, farther south, is the longest lake in the world, having a length of 400 miles. Lake Nyasa, the most southern of the group, has the extraordinary depth of 2580 feet. In this region are to be found also the highest mountains of the continent, usually rising abruptly from the surface of the plateau. Mount Kilimanjaro, situated about 200 miles south of the equator and 200 miles from the east coast, reaches an altitude of 19,710 feet. Mount Kenya and Margherita mountain are other notable peaks of the district. Continuing northward, the highland narrows to form the lofty, mountainous region of Ethiopia. An elevated ridge skirts the Red Sea as far as the Isthmus of Suez.

The mean level of the northern and the western parts of Africa is below 2000 feet. Isolated mountain ridges, however, occur in various parts. The highest is the Atlas range at the extreme northwest, running parallel with the coast and attaining to an altitude of 14,000 feet.

Drainage. The absence in Africa of a pronounced continental divide has had the effect of producing two kinds of rivers. Those on the outer slopes of the continental plateau are short and rapid, while those rising in the interior follow a long, winding, inland course. Then, penetrating the mountain rim, they make their way over cataracts and through narrow channels to the sea, where a sand bar is often formed by sediment carried down the stream.

The four largest rivers of Africa are the Nile, the Congo, the Niger, and the Zambezi. The basins of inland drainage, which occupy more than three million square miles in northern Africa, are usually too arid to give rise to large bodies of water. There is a notable exception, however, in the case of Lake Chad.

The Nile is, next to the Mississippi-Missouri, the longest river of the world. Rising in a stream that flows into Lake Victoria, it wends its way northward, and, after passing over six cataracts and traversing a distance of 4000 miles, it empties through a large delta by seven mouths into the Mediterranean Sea. Its lower course lies through the desert region of Egypt, a strip of which it renders productive by means of its annual flood. The river is navigable about 590 miles above its delta to the foot of the first cataract at Aswan and, with interruptions, for a distance of 1550 miles farther toward the source.

The Congo River is the second river of the world in volume of water discharged and in the area of its basin. By means of numerous tributaries, of which the Ubangi is the largest, the Congo drains a tropical basin of central Africa in a general westward direction and discharges its waters into the Atlantic Ocean through a mouth ten miles in width. The river admits of navigation, with some interruptions, for a distance of 2000 miles above its mouth.

The Niger River offers greater facilities for navigation than any other river of Africa. It drains a comparatively low plain in Africa's westward extension. Rising within a few hundred miles of the Atlantic coast, it flows inland toward the northeast, then, bending southeast, it follows a meandering course to an immense delta on the Gulf of Guinea.

The Zambezi River rises on a ridge near the west coast of southern Africa, and flows eastward across the continent to Mozambique channel. Near the middle of its course, it plunges over Victoria Falls, the greatest cataract in the world. Here, over a width of a mile, the river drops 343 feet.

Lake Chad, situated about 850 miles northeast of the head of the Gulf of Guinea, has no outlet. During the rainy season, it occupies an area of about 40,000 square miles, but it diminishes during the dry season to one-sixth of this area.

Climate. Africa extends almost equal distances north and south of the equator. It is, therefore, subject to a smaller variation in temperature than any other large division of land. At the extreme north and at the extreme south, there are belts of temperate or subtropical climate. Between these limits the heat is greater.

The rainfall is greatest in the basin of the Congo. On each side of this equatorial belt of abundant and well distributed rainfall, stretches a zone in which the rainfall is seasonal, a short, wet season being followed by a long, dry one. These two zones pass gradually into the two great desert areas of the continent, Kalahari desert in southern Africa and the Sahara desert in the north. Beyond these arid regions, in the extreme north and in the extreme south of Africa, there are narrow coastal lowlands having a moderate, or even a copious, rainfall.

The Sahara Desert is the largest continuous arid region of the world. Its area, about 3,500,000 square miles, is larger than that of the United States. It occupies all that part of northern Africa from the Atlas mountains on the northwest to the mid-course of the Nile river on the southeast. The small amount of rain which does fall occurs in one season only and, as a rule, sinks immediately into the sand to issue here and there as springs. These springs foster islets of vegetation, known as oases, which are estimated to cover one-fortieth of the desert's surface.

Vegetation. The plant life of Africa varies in a manner determined mainly by the rainfall. The extreme northern section has a flora resembling that of Europe. The forests in this part consist largely of oaks, while the olive, vine, fig, and the cereals of Europe thrive. The extreme southern region, being comparatively isolated, has a characteristic vegetation marked by the prevalence of heaths and of other plants producing brilliant flowers. Forests are scarce, but there is abundant pasturage for sheep.

The equatorial belt, except in the eastern highlands, is covered with dense tropical forests. These forests contain an immense variety of trees, including the wine palm, the oil palm, the silk-cotton tree, and the camwood, besides ebony, mahogany, and many other valuable cabinet wood trees.

Animals. Africa is the home of many distinctive types of animals, including a number of large mammals. The giraffe, okapi, hippopotamus, gorilla, and chimpanzee are among the more notable of African mammals which occur nowhere else. Lions, leopards, two-horned rhinoceroses, zebras, antelopes, and African buffaloes are representative of the large animals which attract hunters. The conservation of such animals was, in 1900, made the subject of an international conference, as a result of which game preserve areas were established in British Africa, Somaliland, and other countries. The African elephant is hunted for its ivory tusks, which for centuries have been brought from the interior of Africa by caravans.

The ostrich is found in the drier regions. Other birds are the maribou stork, the secretary bird, and the parrot. Crocodiles are found in the large rivers and tropical lakes. Insects include the formidable white ant and the deadly tsetse fly.

A European type of fauna characterizes the extreme north, where the bear, the jackal, and the fox are found. The wild ass of east central Africa is said to be the ancestor of the domesticated ass. Camels were introduced very early into the northern desert regions from Asia. In Egypt, the inhabitants anciently regarded as sacred the ibis, the crocodile, and the cat.

Minerals. Africa produces nearly all of the world's supply of diamonds and more than one-third of the world's yearly output of gold. South Africa is the region most productive of both minerals, although gold is also obtained from the Gulf of Guinea region and elsewhere. Some of the richest copper deposits in the world exist west of the great interior lakes, and iron has from the earliest times been worked by the natives. Salt is abundant. Oil is found in the Sahara and elsewhere.

Inhabitants. Although the city civilization of northeastern Africa is probably the world's earliest, the rest of the continent continued as a pastoral and agricultural society organized on a tribal basis until the 20th century. The aborigines of most of the continent are negroid and are believed to have remained relatively immune from foreign conquest because Africa's rivers did not afford ready navigation into the interior. Arabs established themselves on the northern and northeastern regions in the 7th century; the Dutch settled in the south in the 17th century; and the French infiltrated the Mediterranean coast in the 19th century, followed by colonization of most of the continent by Britain, Belgium, Italy, and other European nations. By the middle of the 20th century the colonial empires were almost entirely liquidated.

The Pygmies of the equatorial forests and the Bushmen of the southern arid districts are believed to represent the earliest African races extant. They live by hunting; their dwellings are of the most primitive type. The Hottentots stand, in culture, as in location, between the Bushmen and the Bantus. The Bantus constitute the southern half of a negroid race which inhabits most of Africa from the region of the great lakes northward to the Sahara Desert.

The native Africans speak a language belonging to a family known as Bantu. One branch, spoken chiefly in the east, is Swahili. It has obtained a wide currency as a trade language.

The total population of the continent is estimated at 336 million. It is estimated that less than half the population has been affected by religions of foreign origin. Of this proportion by far the most are Mohammedans.

Discovery. The valley of the Nile river was the seat of what is perhaps the world's earliest civilization. The interior of the continent, however, remained unknown until the 19th century.

As early as the 7th or 6th century B. C. a Phœnician ship sailed around Africa. The possibility of circumnavigation, however, was forgotten until 1486, when the Cape of Good Hope was rounded by Diaz.

Numerous early attempts were made to penetrate the interior of Africa. The first European to cross Africa from ocean to ocean was David Livingstone, who completed the journey in 1856.

POLITICAL DIVISIONS

The last quarter of the 19th century witnessed the partition of Africa into protectorates and colonies of various nations of Europe. By 1976, practically all these colonies had become independent nations, leaving a small residue as dependencies.

Algeria. A republic of northern Africa stretching 640 miles east and west along the Mediterranean Sea between Libya and Tunisia on the east and Morocco on the west and extending south about 340 miles. Its area is 113,883 square miles.

Algeria is divided longitudinally by the Atlas mountains, north of which lies a fertile well-watered plain 50 to 100 miles wide. The rest of the arable land is dry and is productive only with the aid of irrigation. Crops raised include wheat, barley, oats, corn, tobacco, dates, oranges, figs, and grapes, from which wine is made in large quantities. Wool is a leading product of Algeria's agriculture, which is particularly rich in farm animals, including camels.

The population in 1968 was 12,934,000. The capital is Algiers. Other leading cities are Oran, Constantine, and Bone.

Angola. Formerly Portuguese West Africa, Angola has a 1000-mile coastline along the Atlantic and is bounded by Zaire on the north and east, by Zambia on the east, and South West Africa (Namibia) on the south. Its area is 481,351 square miles. Most of Angola's land is desert and plains, although in the northeast there are heavily forested valleys that provide the main exports—diamonds and hardwoods. Along the coast palm trees are grown for their oil and kernels. Angola's population is 5,673,046 (1970)—of whom 475,328 live in Luanda, the capital and largest city.

Benin (Dahomey). A republic of central western Africa, Benin consists of a narrow strip 77 miles wide and 415 miles long. With its southern boundary on the Gulf of Guinea, it is bounded on the west by Togo, on the north by Niger and Upper Volta, and on the east by Nigeria. Benin's 44,290 square miles are devoted mainly to animal industry and agriculture; the chief products are corn, manioc, and yams. Benin's capital is Porto Novo (population: 2,571,000). The nation is a member of the French Community.

Botswana. A land-locked republic of southern Africa. Botswana is bounded by South West Africa (Namibia) on the north and west, Zambia and Rhodesia on the east, and South Africa on the south and southeast. Its area is 222,000 square miles. Most of the country is a tableland with the Kalahari desert in the southwest. In the northwest the Okavango river forms a great inland delta and the swamplands of the river cover 6500 square miles. The Orapa diamond mine in the south contains one of the largest gem deposits ever found. Agriculture and animal raising account for almost half of the national income, but there are also rich deposits of manganese, copper, nickel, coal, and salt. The population was 656,737 in 1973. Gaborone is the nation's capital. Botswana is a member of the British Commonwealth.

Burundi. A republic of east central Africa, 10,744 square miles in area, bounded north by Rwanda, east and south by Tanzania, and west by Congo. Coffee is the principal crop. The capital is Bujumbura. Population, about 3,406,000.

Cameroon. A republic of West Africa, whose west coast lies on the Gulf of Guinea. It is bounded north by Nigeria and Chad, east by the Central African Empire, and south by Congo (Brazzaville), Gabon, and Equatorial Guinea. The republic, 181,476 square miles in area, is a federation of a former French dependency, which was given independence in 1960, and the southern part of a former British dependency, which voted in 1961 to join the Cameroon republic.

The population is made up of about 200 tribes, which support themselves by agriculture and husbandry. There is normally an exportable surplus of cocoa, coffee, rubber, bananas, cotton, palm oil, and timber. Most of the trade is with France and Britain. The capital is Yaounde. Population, about 5,562,000.

Central African Empire. A land-locked country at approximately the geographical center of Africa, bounded north by Chad, east by Sudan, south by Congo and Zaire, and west by Cameroon. Its 238,000 square miles form a rolling plain about 2000 feet in altitude draining southward toward the Congo basin and thence into the Atlantic Ocean. It lies about 300 miles inland from the Gulf of Guinea.

The population of about 1,488,000 is organized on a tribal basis. Cotton, coffee, and peanuts are raised in exportable quantities, and meat is imported. The capital is Bangui. It was formerly part of a French dependency.

Chad. A land-locked republic of north central Africa, 495,000 square miles in area, bounded north by Libya, east by Sudan, south by Central African Empire, and west by Cameroon and Niger. The northern part of the country is a sandy desert, but agriculture, featured by cotton raising and animal husbandry, is carried on in the central steppe land and a southern grassland with scattered trees. The population of about 4,000,000 has a large element professing the Moslem faith. The capital is N'djamena. It is a member of the French Community.

Comoro Islands. A former French dependency, the islands lie off the eastern coast of Africa about 300 miles northwest of Malagasy. The nation is an archipelago of four islands—Mayotte, Anjouan, Grande Comore, and Moheli. The total area is 838 square miles. The islands are of volcanic origin and are extremely mountainous. The highest peak is Mt. Karatab at 7900 feet. Grande Comore island is heavily forested and the timber is used for building. Although there is fishing and animal raising, the country is largely agricultural. The main crops are vanilla, copra, cacao, sisal, coffee, and cloves. The capital is Moroni, on Grande Comore island, and the population of the Comoro Islands is about 300,000.

Congo. The country has about 60 miles of coast on the Atlantic Ocean and stretches some 800 miles northeast with a maximum width of about 400 miles. It is bounded west by Gabon and Cameroon, north by Central African Empire, and east by Zaire, from which it is separated in part by the Congo River.

More than half its 139,000 square miles is covered by forest, from which considerable timber is exported. Other products are palm oil and peanuts. Gold and lead are mined. The chief port, Pointe Noire, as well as the capital, Brazzaville, have modern airports. Population, about 870,000.

Egypt. An Arab republic, situated in the extreme northeast of Africa. Its area is about 386,198 square miles, most of which is arid and unproductive. The population, numbering some 32 million, is almost entirely concentrated in the fertile valley of the Nile River, and is devoted principally to agriculture. The area of the cultivated region is about 13,600 square miles, which includes not only the Nile valley but the delta and oases in the desert. Much of this area has been reclaimed by irrigation.

The chief crop is cotton. The papyrus plant of Egypt was used in the making of paper more than 4000 years ago. Today, however, Egypt imports practically all her paper.

The productivity of the Nile River valley is due to the annual flooding of the river banks in September and October. The area of cultivation has been greatly extended by the construction of irrigation works, consisting of canals, of several barrages, and of the great Aswan and Sennar dams, each over a mile in length, which now regulate the flow of water.

The Nile proper which flows through Egypt is formed by the junction of the Blue Nile and the White Nile at Khartoum in the Sudan. The Blue Nile rises in the mountains of Ethiopia, the White Nile in Uganda. It descends by a series of six cataracts or rapids, and, after flowing through the Nile delta, empties into the Mediterranean by two main channels, one near Alexandria, the other near Port Said. The Nile is one of the world's longest rivers.

Southern Egypt has a dry, healthful climate, which makes it desirable as a resort for tourists. A further attraction is found in the pyramids, the sphinx, various tombs, and other remains of the ancient civilization of the Nile. The northeastern extremity of the country has one of the world's two most celebrated ship canals, the Suez, which connects the Mediterranean Sea with the Red Sea.

Equatorial Guinea. This former Spanish dependency of western Africa consists of Rio Muni on the mainland. It is bounded by Cameroon on the north, Gabon on the east and south, and the Atlantic Ocean on the west. The offshore islands of Marcias Nguema and Pigalu in the Gulf of Guinea are added territories of Equatorial Guinea. The total area is 9,828 square miles. Rio Muni is characterized by a coastal plain and further inland the foothills of the Crystal Mountains. There are 2 volcanos on Marcias Nguema. The country depends greatly on agriculture as there are few industries. The main crops are cocoa, coffee, and wood. Uranium deposits have been found but they have not yet been developed. The capital is Malabo and the population is about 307,500.

Ethiopia. A country of northeast Africa with a northeast coast line on the Red Sea. It is bounded east by French Somaliland and Somali Republic, south by Somali Republic and Kenya, and west by Sudan.

Its area is about 350,000 square miles and is the most mountainous country of Africa. Most of the surface is covered by the Highlands of Ethiopia which reached their greatest height in Ras Dashan, 15,160 feet. The country is naturally rich with fertile soil and abundant rainfall. The climate is cool and bracing because of the high elevation. The chief rivers of Ethiopia, the Blue Nile and Atbara are tributary to the Nile and mainly responsible for its floods. The population is estimated at nearly 24 million.

The commercial products include hides, cattle, and coffee. Musk from the civet is used in perfumes. Gold is washed in the beds of the Atbara and its tributaries. Addis Ababa is the capital.

Gabon. A republic of equatorial Africa with 500 miles of western coast line on the Gulf of Guinea. It is bounded north by Cameroon, and east and south by Congo (Brazzaville). Most of its 102,290 square miles are covered with forest. Its products include timber, plywood, and veneer. Exploitation of its rich mineral resources has raised the economy of Gabon. Gabon, with a population of about 480,000, is a member of the French Community. The capital is Libreville.

Gambia. A republic of west Africa on the Atlantic Ocean and otherwise surrounded by Senegal. Its area is 4005 square miles; its population 494,279. Peanuts, rice, and palm kernels are the chief products. Banjul is the capital.

Ghana. A republic of western Africa with a southern coast line on the Gulf of Guinea. It is bounded west by Ivory Coast and Upper Volta, north by Upper Volta, and east by Togo.

About one-third of Ghana's 92,100 square miles is forested, from which comes such valuable timber as mahogany and other tropical woods. The rest of the country is devoted to agriculture. Ghana is the world's largest exporter of cocoa, the production of which is Ghana's major industry. Diamonds, bauxite, and manganese are Ghana's most important mineral exports. The Volta Dam, 370 feet high, was completed in 1966. It backs up the Volta River 300 miles to form Lake Volta, 3500 square miles in area. The hydroelectric plant generates nearly a million kilowatts of electricity.

The capital, Accra, is the seat of a research institute supported by Ghana and some of its neighboring republics, whose purpose is to discover the best methods of land use and disease control. Ghana is a member of the British Commonwealth. Population, 8,545,561.

Guinea. A republic of Africa with a western coast line on the Atlantic Ocean. It is bounded north by Guinea-Bissau, Senegal, and Mali, east by Ivory Coast, and south by Liberia and Sierra Leone.

Most of Guinea's area of 96,865 square miles is devoted to agriculture and animal husbandry. Agricultural products include rice, cassava, bananas, palm nuts, coffee, pineapples, and oranges. Guinea has one of the world's richest deposits of bauxite, and this, together with alumina, iron ore, and aluminum are the leading exports.

Guinea was one of the few former French dependencies which elected to separate itself from the French Community, although French remains the official language and French technical assistance is provided under an agreement made in 1963. The capital is Conakry. Population, about 4,010,000.

Ivory Coast. A republic of western Africa with a southern coast line of 34 miles on the Gulf of Guinea. It is bounded west by Liberia and Guinea, north by Mali and Upper Volta, and east by Ghana. Its area is 127,520 square miles.

About 90 per cent of the population is engaged in agriculture, animal husbandry, fishing, and forestry. The leading products are yams, cassava, bananas, corn, and rice. Mahogany is obtained from the forests. Diamonds and manganese are exported. The population numbers about 4,100,000. The capital is Abidjan. The Ivory Coast is a member of the French Community.

Kenya. A constitutional democracy of East Africa with an eastern coast line on the Indian Ocean. It is bounded south by Tanzania, north by Sudan and Ethiopia, west by Uganda, and east by Somali Republic and the Indian Ocean. Its area is 224,960 square miles.

The northern three-fifths of the country is arid. Production comes chiefly from the south, which consists of a low coastal plain and a plateau varying from 3,000 to 10,000 feet in altitude. The forests of the uplands are preserved to conserve the water supply. Kenya is the largest source of tea in Africa. Other products are coffee, cereals, cotton, sisal, dairy products. Copper, gold, and salt are among the products of the mines.

The capital is Nairobi. Kenya is a member of the British Commonwealth of Nations. Population, 10,209,000.

Lesotho. An enclave within South Africa, known as Basutoland before emerging in 1966 from colonial status to Great Britain. Agriculture and stock raising are the chief occupations. Its area is 11,716 square miles and the capital is Maseru. Population, 1,081,000.

Liberia. A republic of western Africa with 350 miles of southern coast line on the Atlantic Ocean and stretching inland from 75 to 190 miles. It is bounded west by Sierra Leone, north by Guinea, and east by Ivory Coast. Its area is about 43,000 square miles.

Most of the country is covered with tropical forest. Rubber is the chief export, Liberia providing the United States with about one-tenth of its imports of natural rubber. Iron ore also is exported.

Liberia was founded by settlement of American slaves at the site of the present capital, Monrovia, by philanthropic societies, beginning in 1822. English is the official language, although the many indigenous tribes speak their own languages. Population estimated at 1,500,000.

Libya. A republic of north Africa on the Mediterranean Sea between Egypt and Algeria. Its southern, desert region borders Chad and Niger. The northern region is fertile and produces dates, olives, almonds, figs, and grapes. Petroleum is the most important mineral and accounts for nearly all of Libya's exports. Its area is 679,358 square miles; the population, 2,260,000. Tripoli is the largest city and shares with Benghazi the governmental administration.

Malagasy. An island republic in the Indian Ocean off southeast Africa, from which it is separated by the Mozambique channel, 240 miles wide at its narrowest point. The island, formerly known as Madagascar, is 980 miles long in a generally north-and-south direction with a maximum width of 360 miles and an area of 229,975 square miles. The interior is a plateau 3000 to 5000 feet in height, rising in the northwest to mountains with a maximum height of 9490 feet. Around the plateau are extensive plains, up to 50 miles wide on the eastern side and up to 100 miles on the western side.

Cattle breeding and agriculture are the chief occupations. The principal farm animal is the humped zebu. Agricultural products of the greatest importance are rice, cassava, sugar cane, coconuts, and bananas. Others include corn, vanilla, and potatoes. Among mineral products are graphite, mica, and phosphates. Cotton and silk weaving are carried on as well as food-processing industries.

The capital is Tananarive. The republic is a member of the French Community. Population, 7,185,000.

Malawi. A land-locked republic of southeastern Africa. It is bounded north by Tanzania, west by Zambia, and south by Mozambique. Its area is 46,686 square miles. Until 1964 it was the British dependency of Nyasaland. Principally an agricultural country, tea, tobacco, cotton, and peanuts are its leading products. Lilongwe is the capital. Population, 5,175,000.

Mali. A land-locked republic of western Africa, bounded north by Algeria, east by Niger, south by Upper Volta, Ivory Coast, and Guinea, and west by Senegal and Mauritania. Its area is about 450,000 square miles. It is traversed west to east by the upper reaches of the Niger River. On this river small steamboats connect Gao and Timbuktu with a railway leading through the capital Bamako and continuing in Senegal to Dakar, which port Mali has the right by treaty to use. Agriculture is being organized on collective principles. Cattle number about 4,000,000. The chief exports are peanuts, gum, dried fish, and hides. Mali is a member of the French Community. Population, about 5,600,000.

Mauritania. An Islamic republic of west Africa with a western coast line on the Atlantic Ocean. It is bounded east by Mali and south by Mali and Senegal. The area is 418,810 square miles, much of which is desert. Agriculture and animal husbandry are the main occupations, products including millet, rice, and corn. There are about 700,000 camels. Iron and copper have been discovered. The capital is Nouakchott. Population, about 1,500,000.

Morocco. A constitutional monarchy on the northwest coast of Africa and separated from Spain by the Strait of Gibraltar. With a northwestern coast line on the Atlantic Ocean and a northern coast line on the Mediterranean Sea, it is bounded east and south by Algeria. At the north facing Gibraltar are the Riff mountains and behind them run the Atlas mountains. The rest of the area consists of fertile alluvial plains and plateaus, but in the south and west the land is arid—the beginning of the Sahara desert. The area is estimated at 171,305 square miles.

Agriculture is the leading industry, supporting 70 per cent of the population, but phosphates make up the bulk of the exports. Farm products include wheat and barley, vegetables, canary seed, olives, almonds, and citrus fruits. Morocco is the world's leading producer of cork. Wine is produced in quantity, and sardines are exported. Mineral products, in addition to potash, include coal, iron, manganese, silver, and zinc. Islam is the established state religion. The capital is Rabat, and the largest city is Casablanca. Population, 16,309,000.

Mozambique. Formerly a Portuguese colony, Mozambique is bordered on the north by Tanzania, Zambia, and Malawi; on the west by Rhodesia and South Africa; and on the east by the Mozambique channel. The land area is 303,070 square miles. The eastern region is mostly coastal lowlands, while the interior is highland plains. Aluminum, asbestos, tin, tungsten, and coal are mined in the northwest, but the chief exports are cashew nuts, sugar, and cotton. Many Mozambicans travel to South Africa to work in the mines. The population is estimated at about 9,300,000; the capital city is Maputo.

Niger. A land-locked republic of north central Africa, bounded north by Algeria and Libya, east by Chad, south by Nigeria, and west by Benin, Upper Volta, and Mali. Its area of 490,000 square miles lacks water except in the west, which is watered by the Niger River and its tributaries, and in the south, where water is obtained from wells. The country is a plateau, and access is chiefly by air.

Agricultural products include peanuts, millet, cassava, cotton, and rice. The capital is Niamey. Niger is a member of the French Community. Population, about 4,239,000.

Nigeria. A republic of west central Africa with a southern coast line on the Gulf of Guinea, into which flows the country's principal river, the Niger. It is bounded west by Benin, north by Niger, east by Chad and Cameroon. Its area is 356,669 square miles. The coast is a belt of mangrove swamps, behind which is a belt of tropical forest 50 to 100 miles wide. Farther north the level rises, and open woodland and treed plains afford facilities for agriculture. The extreme north is desert.

Agriculture and stockraising are the principal industries, the northern regions producing peanuts, cotton, and hides, while cocoa, timber, and rubber come from the south. Minerals produced include tin, gold, coal, and petroleum. Among leading manufactures are soap, cigarettes, beer, margarine, textiles, cement, and canned foods. Of the estimated 62,650,000 inhabitants, nearly 14 million are Moslems and about 7 million are Christians. Nigeria is a member of the British Commonwealth. The capital is Lagos.

Rhodesia. A land-locked, south-central African republic, Rhodesia covers 150,820 square miles. It is bounded on the north by Zambia, on the east by Mozambique, on the south by South Africa, and on the west by Botswana. Most of the country is a high, rolling plateau; the chief rivers are the Zambezi and Limpopo. The land abounds in minerals—asbestos, coal, chrome ore, copper, gold, iron, lithium, nickel, phosphate, and tin. The Wankie colliery is the largest coal mine in the world. Tobacco is the main export yield; corn is the staple food and most important crop. Major industries include textiles, chemicals, and metal products. The population is 6,530,000; of these, 569,000 live in Salisbury, the capital, largest city, and industrial center of Rhodesia.

Rwanda. A republic of east central Africa, 10,169 square miles in area, bounded north by Uganda, east by Tanzania, and south and west by Zaire. Its agricultural industry produces coffee and cotton. The capital is Kigali. Formerly a Belgian trusteeship, it asserted its independence in 1962. Population, about 5,500,000.

Senegal. A republic of west Africa, on the Atlantic Ocean. Its capital, Dakar, is the extreme western point of Africa. Senegal is bounded north by Mauritania, east by Mali, and south by Guinea and Guinea-Bissau. Its area is 76,000 square miles. The surface is mainly sandy and supports an agriculture of which peanuts are the leading product. Dakar is the country's port and has a considerable concentration of industry, including cement and titanium concentrates. Peanuts and phosphates are exported in quantity. Senegal is a member of the French Community. Population, about 4,500,000.

Sierra Leone. A republic of western Africa with a southwestern coastline 212 miles long on the Atlantic Ocean. Having an area of 27,925 square miles, it is bounded north and east by Guinea and southeast by Liberia. The principal occupation is agriculture. Exports include palm kernels, coffee, cocoa, iron ore, and diamonds. The capital, Freetown, is one of the finest ports in Africa. It was founded in 1787 by the British government as a home for destitute free slaves. Sierra Leone is a member of the British Commonwealth. Population, about 3,002,400.

Somali Republic. A republic of east central Africa with a northern coastline on the Gulf of Aden and a southeastern coastline on the Indian Ocean. Its eastern tip is the most easterly point of the continent. Having an area of 262,000 square miles, it is bounded west by Kenya and Ethiopia. About 80 per cent of the inhabitants depend on the livestock industry, most of the country being adapted to grazing rather than agriculture. Large uranium deposits were found in 1968. The capital is Mogadisho. It was previously an Italian colony. Population, about 3,221,050.

South Africa. A republic at the southern extremity of Africa, 472,494 square miles in area, with the Atlantic Ocean westward and Indian Ocean eastward meeting off its southern coast. South Africa is bounded north by its own dependency of South West Africa, Botswana, Rhodesia, and Mozambique. Lesotho and the former British dependency of Swaziland are enclaves within South Africa.

The surface is, for the most part, a high plateau, interrupted by isolated flat-topped hills called kopjes. The plateau slopes rapidly down near the coasts. A ridge, low in the west, passes around the southern and eastern parts of the plateau, reaching its highest point in the east central region of the country. This eastern ridge is the divide separating a large number of short rivers, draining toward the east and the south, from the Orange river, which flows westward across the country and empties into the Atlantic Ocean. Farther north, the Limpopo river rises on the interior plateau and makes its way north of the eastern ridge; then, turning southeast, it flows into the Indian Ocean.

The climate of South Africa is warm, and the soil is fertile. The precipitation varies greatly, being nearly 50 inches on the southeastern coast and falling to less than 3 inches farther north on the western coast. In the western part of the country, semiarid conditions prevail, and grazing rather than agriculture is the principal industry. Wool is one of the chief exports, and about half the world's supply of mohair comes from the Republic. Corn, wheat, oats, barley, and tobacco are also grown, and such products of subtropical agriculture as cotton, tea, and sugar cane are raised in the lower and moister coastal regions. The operation of ostrich farms constitutes a distinctive industry.

The exports of the greatest value are the products of the mining industry. South Africa is the world's chief source of diamonds and is by far the greatest gold-producing region of the world. The output of gold is several times that of Canada, the country which ranks second to South Africa. Other minerals obtained in important quantities include coal, tin, and copper.

The white population in 1961 was 3,067,638, while the native population stood at 10,807,809. The 1970 estimate of the total population was 21,402,470. About one-half those of the white race are of Dutch descent. The religion is predominantly Protestant. There are 16 universities, 11 for whites, 5 for non-whites. Most of the country's 13,284 miles of railway is owned by the government.

South Africa is divided into four provinces. Cape of Good Hope is in the extreme south, and Transvaal, on the eastern side of the country, lies farthest north. Between the two lie the inland province, called Orange Free State, and Natal, which borders on the Indian Ocean. In eastern Transvaal is the Kruger national park, a 5-million acre sanctuary for big game, which attracts thousands of visitors each year. The center of governmental administration is Pretoria, but the legislature sits at Cape Town, which is the terminus of the partially constructed "Cape to Cairo" railway. The largest city is Johannesburg, situated in the Witwatersrand, which is among the richest gold-mining districts of the world. Kimberley is the chief diamond-mining center.

Spanish Africa. The possessions of Spain in Africa were diminished when, in 1968, it granted independence to *Equatorial Guinea*, which includes Rio Muni, Marcias Nguema, and a number of small islands in the Gulf of Guinea. The capital of the new Republic of Equatorial Guinea is Malabo. Ifni, an enclave on the Atlantic coast of Morocco, was turned over to that country by Spain in 1969.

The following is the only remaining province in Africa belonging to Spain:

Canary Islands, 2807 square miles in area, in the Atlantic off the coast of Morocco, with an estimated population of 1,138,800.

Sudan. A republic of northeast Africa lying directly south of Egypt and with a northeastern coast line on the Red Sea. With an area of 967,000 square miles, it is the largest country in Africa. It is bounded east by Ethiopia, south by Uganda, Zaire, and the Central African Empire, and west by Chad and Libya.

Nearly half the country is desert or semidesert, and grazing of cattle, sheep, goats, and camels is a principal occupation. Cotton is by far the most important crop and provides most of the exports, although the Sudan is the world's chief source of gum arabic. The Nile River flows north through Sudan, and its waters are used for extensive irrigation works, an agreement having been made with Egypt for diversion of the available water.

About four-fifths of the 14,770,000 inhabitants are Moslem Arabs. The capital is Khartoum.

Tanzania (*Tăn-zȧ-nē'ȧ*). A united republic of eastern Africa, formed in 1964 of the former Tanganyika, fronting on the Indian Ocean and the large island of Zanzibar off its eastern coast. The republic has a combined area of 362,820 square miles, and has a population of 12,590,000. The capital is Dar es Salaam.

The mainland is bounded by Kenya and Uganda on the north; Malawi, Mozambique, and Zambia on the south; Lake Tanganyika, Burundi, and Rwanda on the west. Its area is 361,800 square miles. The surface slopes upward from the coastal plain on the east to a high plateau and the western mountain slopes. The forests produce camphor and mahogany. About half the world's supply of sisal, Tanzania's chief agricultural product, is grown here. As Tanganyika, the country was colonized by Arabs as early as the 8th century A.D. and was a possession of Germany before World War I.

The island of Zanzibar lies about 22 miles off the coast east of the mainland. Politically it includes also the island of Pemba, 25 miles to its northeast. The total area of the two islands is 1020 square miles. Often referred to as the "Isle of Cloves," the islands supply about 80 per cent of the world's cloves. Coconuts are also produced in quantity. Chief port is the city of Zanzibar. Population about 354,360.

Togo. A western African republic fronting southward on the Gulf of Guinea and stretching northward to Upper Volta with Ghana on the west and Benin on the east. Its area is about 22,000 square miles. The surface is hilly, rising to a maximum altitude of 3600 feet. It is partly forested. The rest of the surface consists of plains, some dry and others cultivated. Coffee is the main export, but Togo produces also cocoa, copra, cotton, kapok, peanuts, and cassava. The capital is Lome. It was a German colony before World War I and is now a member of the French Community. Population, about 2,197,000.

Tunisia. A republic of north Africa with the Mediterranean Sea on the north and east. It is bounded southeast by Libya and west by Algeria. Its area is 63,362 square miles. The principal occupation of its estimated 5,270,000 inhabitants is agriculture, with large estates predominating. Chief products of the soil are cereal grains, olives and olive oil, citrus fruits, dates, grapes, and wine. Phosphates, iron ore, and silver ore are mined. Local and cottage industries produce wool, textiles, carpets, leatherwork, pottery, and copper ware. The population is predominantly Arab and Berber, but there is a large French minority. The capital is Tunis.

Uganda. An inland republic of central east Africa with an area of 91,343 square miles. It is bounded north by Sudan, east by Kenya, south by Tanzania and Lake Victoria, the world's second largest fresh-water lake, and west by Zaire. Its territory is traversed by the Nile River. Uganda is the largest coffee producer in the British Commonwealth, of which it became a member in 1962. Other products are tea, cotton, peanuts, sisal, and sugar. Copper and tin are the leading mineral products. Fresh-water fish are caught in large quantities commercially. The capital is Kampala. Population, about 11,171,900.

Upper Volta. An inland republic of western Africa, about 500 miles north of the Gulf of Guinea. It is bounded north and west by Mali, east by Niger, and south by Benin, Togo, Ghana, and Ivory Coast. Its area is 105,900 square miles. The surface is mainly a plateau of 600 to 1000 feet in altitude, on which are raised cattle, cotton, rice, and peanuts. The capital is Ouagadougou. Upper Volta is a member of the French Community. Population, about 5,870,000.

Zaire. With 904,757 square miles, it is the second largest country in Africa. It is bounded north by Central African Republic and Sudan, east by Uganda, Rwanda, Burundi, and Tanzania, south by Zambia and Angola, and west by the Atlantic Ocean and Congo.

The country is one of the richest sources of copper in the world, and its mineral wealth places it at the forefront of the African countries. Besides copper, it exports gold, radium, uranium, diamonds, cobalt, tin, zinc, tungsten, manganese, and silver.

The Congo River flows through the country. It and its tributaries provide transportation and extensive hydroelectric power. Tropical forests cover a considerable part of the country, and from them are exported mahogany, ebony, teak, and other valuable woods. Wild life includes elephants, lions, leopards, chimpanzees, apes, gorillas, giraffes, rhinoceroses, hippopotami, buffalo, hyenas, crocodiles, pythons, cobras, parrots, flamingoes, heron, and vultures. Ivory is exported.

Animal husbandry and agriculture form the occupation of most of the approximately 21,638,000 inhabitants, the chief exportable products being animal and vegetable oils, cotton, coffee, rubber, bananas, and manioc.

Zambia. An inland republic of south central Africa bounded north by Zaire and Tanzania, east by Malawi and Mozambique, south by Rhodesia and South West Africa, and west by Angola. The area is 290,586 square miles. Part of the southern boundary is the Zambesi river, from which hydroelectric power is developed in large quantities, particularly near Victoria falls, the world's largest cataract. The area is mostly a plateau with an equitable climate. The leading agricultural products are corn and tobacco. The country is one of the largest copper producing regions of the world.

Zambia, formerly a British protectorate, became in 1964 an independent republic within the British Commonwealth. The capital is Lusaka. Population, 4,751,000.

The following section contains descriptions of the principal cities and of other places in the continent which merit especial attention.

Addis Ababa. The capital of Ethiopia, situated in the center of the country at an elevation of about 8000 feet. It is connected by a 486-mile railway with Djibouti on the Gulf of Aden. It has a vast central market place where native and imported goods are sold. Population is estimated at 560,000.

Alexandria. The chief seaport of Egypt situated at the west of the Nile delta. The city has an industrial district with asphalt works and oil, rice, and paper mills. The chief exports are cotton, grain, rice, and sugar.

Alexandria was founded in 332 B. C. by Alexander the Great and was, for several centuries, the chief commercial city of the world. In ancient times, its harbor was famous for the Pharos, or lighthouse, a huge structure completed in 282 B. C. and regarded as one of the seven wonders of the ancient world.

In the 7th century, Alexandria was captured and sacked by the Arabs. Its importance in modern times dates from the construction of the Suez canal. Population, 1,801,056.

Algiers. The capital and chief seaport of Algeria. It lies near the center of the country's Mediterranean coast. The lower part, built by the French, has modern hotels, spacious squares, and ornamented parks, which present a marked contrast to the narrow streets and characteristic mosques of the Moorish section.

Algiers is one of the most important coaling stations on the Mediterranean Sea. It has an important trade, mainly with France. The chief exports are wine, fruits, olive oil, and cork. Population, 943,142.

Aswan Dam. A dam on the Nile River in Egypt at Philae about 700 miles up-stream from its mouth in the Mediterranean Sea. A dam was first completed there in 1902 and was heightened several times before construction was begun in 1960 on the "high dam." The "high dam" which required 10½ years to build at a cost of more than a billion dollars, partly supplied by Russia, was designed to increase 25-fold the water impounded for irrigation, to raise the water level 600 feet above sea level, and to back up the Nile for 300 miles, including 100 miles in Sudan. Development of over 9 million KW of power was envisaged, and Egypt's arable land would be enlarged by 30 per cent. Since the flood waters were scheduled to cover some 58 historic monuments, archeologists and governments hastened to devise and execute plans for their preservation. With an American contribution of a third toward the $31-million project, work was begun in 1964 on the dismantling at Abu Simbel of a temple hewn in rock containing four 65-foot statues of Rameses II. This monument, dating from 1300 B. C., was reconstructed from its parts on the heights above. At Philae, dikes were built to preserve a temple of Isis about 2000 years old.

Cairo (*ki'ro*). The capital of Egypt, and the largest city of Africa, situated on the Nile River about 100 miles from its outlet in the Mediterranean Sea. The city is an important center of trade.

Chief of the numerous sacred edifices of Cairo is the Sultan Hassan Mosque, which is regarded as the finest example of the Byzantine-Arabian architecture in existence. The El Azhar university, situated in the city, holds the leading place among the world's institutions for Mohammedan education. Cairo's site covers the remains of many cities that had fallen into ruins before the founding of the present city in 968 A. D. Population, 4,219,853.

Cape Town. The legislative capital of South Africa, occupying a picturesque site on the southwestern coast of the Republic. It stands at the head of Table bay, an inlet of the Atlantic Ocean. The city and several beautiful suburbs extend along a narrow coastal strip between the water and a group of precipitous mountains.

Cape Town is the chief seaport of South Africa, the exports ranking highest in value being diamonds and bar gold. Among the notable features of the city are the Parliament buildings, the public library; a 14-acre botanical garden; the Cape observatory; and the Castle. The last-named edifice was built as a defensive work in 1666, 14 years after the founding of a Dutch colony on the present site of the city. Cape Town passed into the hands of the English in 1806. Population, 807,211.

Casablanca. The chief city and seaport in Morocco. It has a large airport as well as a fine harbor. Following its capture by American forces in 1942, Casablanca became headquarters for the movement of Allied troops on their way to North Africa and the Mediterranean region. Population, 1,120,000.

Dakar. The capital and chief port of Senegal. It is the westernmost point on the coast of Africa and terminus of transatlantic flights between Africa and South America. Prior to Senegal's independence, Dakar was the administrative center of French West Africa. It has numerous industrial establishments. Population, 374,700.

Dar es Salaam. The capital and chief port of Tanzania. It is carefully laid out with wide streets and substantial buildings—features which it owes to the Germans, who made it the administrative center of German East Africa. The British took it in 1916. Population, 250,000.

Giza (gē′zĕ). A village of Egypt about three miles from Cairo. It is notable for the pyramids which stand in the vicinity. The largest was erected by Cheops, an Egyptian king who lived about 3000 B. C. According to Herodotus, 100,000 men were employed for 20 years in building it, while 10 years were occupied in transporting the stones. It is about 480 feet in height with a base 764 feet square. The pyramid is believed to have been originally encased with marble. Since 1000 A. D., however, the exterior stones have been removed, leaving visible a structure of rough limestone blocks forming steps with a platform of considerable area at the top. This pyramid was one of the seven wonders of the ancient world and is the only one of the seven still in existence. Two other major pyramids and nearly 40 minor ones are included among the pyramids of Giza. They were intended to serve as tombs for their builders. The great sphinx is located in the approach to Giza, where it might serve to frighten evil spirits away from the pyramid tombs near by. The sphinx is an image of the head of the god Harmachis attached to the body of a lion. The whole figure is 66 feet high and about 172 feet long and is carved out of the solid rock.

Johannesburg (yô-hän′ĕs-bŭrg). The largest city and commercial metropolis of South Africa, lying in the south central part of the Transvaal province. The city was founded in 1886 and owes its importance to its location on the Witwatersrand, in the midst of the richest gold field in the world. Johannesburg is regularly laid out and well built, presenting a more completely modern appearance than any other city on the continent of Africa. It contains the University of the Witwatersrand.

Johannesburg was the center of the agitation which resulted in the Boer war. The days of the Boer régime are recalled by a dismantled fortress overlooking the city and by a monument, which stands in a nearby field, commemorating the Boer declaration of independence in 1880. The city was occupied by the British in 1900. Population, 1,152,525.

Karnak, El (kär′nȧk). A village of Egypt on the right bank of the Nile River about 400 miles southeast of Cairo, famed for its ruins of ancient Egyptian temples. The chief one is the temple of the god Amen-Ra. It was erected about 4000 years ago and is the largest temple in the world. There is comfortable standing room for as many as 90 people on the top of many of the columns still erect.

Luxor. A village of Egypt near the Nile River a short distance southwest of El Karnak and about 400 miles above Cairo. Luxor is known for the numerous tombs nearby, which contain the mummies and treasures of ancient Egyptian monarchs. These treasures, which were intended to serve the spirits of their deceased owners, amount to millions of dollars in value. The tombs are hewn in the rock and usually have, on their walls, elaborate carvings, which have done much toward the unfolding of early Egyptian history. One of the more remarkable of such tombs was that of Tutankhamen, discovered by Lord Carnarvan in 1922.

In Luxor stand two colossal statues, one of which is said to represent the god Memnon. It is a Roman restoration of a former statue, which, before its destruction by an earthquake, is said to have given forth a sound each morning when struck by the rays of the rising sun.

Nairobi. The capital of Kenya, situated about 300 miles inland from Kenya's port Mombasa, with which it is connected by rail. Its altitude is 5000 feet, and its climate is favorable. Population 314,760.

Port Said (pōrt sä-ēd′). A seaport of Egypt at the Mediterranean end of the Suez canal. It has an export trade in cotton and is an important coaling station. Its features include a large lighthouse, whose light is visible 24 miles out at sea, and a colossal statue of De Lesseps, the French engineer under whose direction the Suez canal was constructed. Population, 282,977.

Pretoria. The administrative capital of the Republic of South Africa. It is an inland city, situated in the northeastern part of the Republic in the Transvaal province. Its streets are broad and regularly laid out. The outstanding architectural feature of the city is the large group of government offices. They are in the Renaissance style of architecture and have a central tower surmounted by a statue of Liberty. Pretoria is the seat of Transvaal University college. Population, 1960, 422,590.

Timbuktu. An inland city of Mali near the southern border of the Sahara desert and on the edge of the marshes of the Niger River. The city was formerly one of the chief centers of Mohammedan influence in Africa, the center of an immense caravan trade in gold, ivory, wax, salt, hardware, beads, and cloth. The principal buildings—a large Mohammedan library and several mosques of striking appearance—date back beyond the 18th century. Population, about 8735.

PRINCIPAL WORLD PORTS*

Port traffic statistics for ocean-borne cargoes are difficult to make comparable owing to the different methods used in measuring cargoes. The following table showing ship entrances with net registered tonnage gives a fair idea of the traffic and importance of the ports listed. Figures are from the Bureau of Foreign and Domestic Commerce.

Rank	Port and Country	Number of Vessels	Net Register Tons	Rank	Port and Country	Number of Vessels	Net Register Tons
9.	Antwerp, Belgium	11,125	18,730,000	15.	Marseille, France . . .	9,135	16,612,000
6.	Baltimore, U.S.A.	56,067	21,008,000	38.	Melbourne, Australia . . .	3,396	7,613,000
41.	Bombay, India	33,731	6,547,000	36.	Montevideo, Uruguay . .	1,631	8,087,000
17.	Boston, U.S.A.	7,340	14,978,000	33.	Montreal, Canada	5,725	8,516,000
20.	Buenos Aires, Argentina .	14,826	13,435,000	29.	Naples, Italy	9,008	10,809,000
48.	Calcutta, India	1,296	4,059,000	32.	Newcastle, England . . .	8,532	8,596,000
43.	Capetown, South Africa .	1,629	5,454,000	21.	New Orleans, U.S.A. . . .	16,287	13,319,000
50.	Charleston, S.C., U.S.A. .	10,668	3,226,000	1.	New York, U.S.A.†	92,032	68,598,000
42.	Cherbourg, France	952	6,478,000	24.	Norfolk, U.S.A.	7,089	12,222,000
7.	Colombo, Ceylon	2,708	20,425,000	8.	Osaka, Japan	18,999	19,600,000
39.	Copenhagen, Denmark . .	25,432	7,452,000	11.	Philadelphia, U.S.A.‡ . . .	8,302	17,907,000
49.	Curacao, Dutch West Indies	5,047	3,700,000	37.	Piraeus, Greece	13,396	7,758,000
22.	Duluth, U.S.A.	2,807	12,882,000	40.	Portland, Oregon, U.S.A. .	9,548	7,051,000
44.	Galveston, U.S.A.	1,762	5,383,000	27.	Rio de Janeiro, Brazil . .	3,924	11,226,000
28.	Genoa, Italy	5,421	10,860,000	5.	Rotterdam, Netherlands. .	110,406	22,415,000
10.	Hamburg, Germany . . .	16,141	18,418,000	18.	San Francisco, U.S.A. . .	17,353	14,974,000
25.	Havre, France	9,018	11,572,000	47.	Savannah, U.S.A.	1,395	4,075,000
16.	Hong Kong, China§ . . .	5,947	15,340,000	35.	Seattle, U.S.A.	3,416	8,210,000
30.	Houston, U.S.A.	7,275	10,091,000	12.	Shanghai, China	8,488	17,418,000
46.	Jacksonville, U.S.A. . . .	1,810	4,523,000	19.	Singapore, Straits Settlements	5,934	14,800,000
45.	Jakarta, Indonesia	2,183	5,338,000	23.	Southampton, England . .	15,628	12,509,000
3.	Kobe, Japan	26,776	28,334,000	31.	Sydney, Australia	6,855	10,057,000
14.	Liverpool, England	14,614	16,640,000	26.	Vancouver, Canada . . .	16,970	11,488,000
2.	London, England	29,137	29,673,000	4.	Yokohama, Japan	5,757	26,785,000
13.	Los Angeles, U.S.A.	5,369	17,211,000				

*Statistics for United States ports include barges but exclude tugs and ferries. †Upper bay shipping only. ‡On Delaware River, Philadelphia to the sea. §Excluding 9,304 junks.

AUSTRALIA

A N island continent lying southeast of Asia between the Indian and the Pacific Ocean. The western portion of Australia forms one of the oldest land surfaces of the globe. The continent is about one-fourth less in area than Europe, but is nearly as large as the continental United States and, with the exception of Antarctica, is the only continent lying wholly in the southern hemisphere. Australia is 1800 miles from Asia, 4500 miles from Africa, 6300 miles from South America, 6700 miles from the United States, and 11,000 miles from England. The island lies between 10° 39' and 39° 11' south latitude and between 113° 5' and 153° 16' east longitude, and from east to west is 2400 miles long and from north to south, 1971 miles. The total area is 2,971,081 square miles, of which 1,149,320 square miles, or about five-thirteenths, are within the Torrid Zone. The population is 12,099,100.

Surface. Strong contrast in elevation above sea level is strikingly absent in Australia. The highest point is Mount Kosciusko, which has an elevation of 7328 feet. The greater part of Western Australia consists of a low plateau averaging about 1000 feet in height. This plateau extends eastward into South Australia and Northern Territory. To the eastward of this plateau lie the lowlands of the Lake Eyre and Murray River basins. Along the eastern coast of the continent the land rises to an average elevation of from two to three thousand feet, forming the Great Dividing range. This range extends practically the full length of the eastern coast. At the southern end of the coast, the range turns westward and disappears in western Victoria. The most elevated area, the Australian Alps, is in the southeastern part of the continent, near the border of New South Wales and of Victoria. The low-lying coastal strip is very narrow along eastern Australia, but it widens about the Gulf of Carpentaria in the north and around Western Australia. The main watershed of the continent is formed by the Great Dividing range, from which practically all the rivers of importance rise. The country around Lake Eyre is a basin of internal drainage. The West Australian plateau is an arid region with only a few short streams flowing down the western scarp.

Climate. The climate of northern Australia is tropical, and the mean annual temperature rises in places to 85° F. The range of temperature in the interior is very great. In central Australia, heavy frosts occur at night during the winter, while in summer the temperature in the shade may rise above 130° F. The southern part of Australia lies within the South Temperate Zone and near the south coast the mean annual temperature is about 60° F. In summer, the southern coastal areas are tempered by sea breezes, but are subject to extremely sudden changes of temperature. Hot north winds from the interior may be replaced by cold south winds, the thermometer showing a fall of 20° or more in about 20 minutes. These southerly changes rarely occur in the inland districts, and within 100 miles of the coast the temperature at midday may rise to 100° F. or over for days or even for weeks.

Snow may lie for months on the higher portion of the Australian Alps, but over the greater part of the continent snow is rarely, if ever, seen.

Rainfall. A line running generally from Sharks' bay on the west coast to Sydney on the southeast coast divides the northern area of summer rains from the southern area of winter rains. In the winter months, June to September, areas of low pressure move northward from the antarctic region to a latitude sufficiently low to bring rain to Tasmania and the southern projections of the continent. In the summer, however, these areas do not move so far to the north. As a result, summer rains seldom occur, except on the west coast of Tasmania. In summer, the thermal equator is over northern Australia, and the northwest monsoons bring rain to the northern coast line, January and February being the wettest months. Monsoonal tongues sometimes extend southward as far as northern Victoria and produce extremely useful rains.

The rainfall in the remaining portion of Australia is governed mainly by the southeast trade winds. These winds bring summer and autumn rains to the eastern coast. The greater part of the moisture is deposited on the eastern highlands. The trade winds pass on as dry winds and, becoming heated, absorb moisture rapidly, thereby causing the aridity which characterizes large parts of central and western Australia. Cairns, on the northeast coast, receives over 100 inches per annum, while a large portion of the interior receives less than 10 inches. Wheat may be grown in some areas in the south, which have about 10 inches of rain, because the rain that does fall comes at the right time.

The rains of northern and of southern Australia are fairly reliable, but the central area shows great variation, and disastrous droughts sometimes occur over a large portion of the continent. During such drought periods, there is an immense loss of cattle and sheep, as it is impossible, under present conditions of transportation, to move the vast numbers of stock to the better-watered areas. Artesian wells have improved conditions somewhat by affording a supply of drinking water for the stock; but unfortunately the water is not suitable for irrigation.

Irrigation. Owing to the small rainfall over large portions of Australia, irrigation is impracticable except in limited areas, such as the Murray River basin. In recent years considerable areas in New South Wales and Victoria have been irrigated as a result of progress on the Snowy Mountains Project which diverts waters from the Australian Alps into the Murray-Murrumbidgee Irrigation Area. The Goulburn valley is served from the Waranga basin. Water for the Mildura and Red Cliff fruit growing settlements is pumped from the Murray River.

Rivers. The interior of the continent being dry, there are comparatively few rivers. Australia has only the one small snowfield, which feeds the Murray River. Of the streams flowing into the Pacific, the Burdekin and the Fitzroy, both in Queensland, are the largest. Each drains an area of about 55,000 square miles. The chief river of the north, the Roper, flowing into the Gulf of Carpentaria, is navigable for 75 miles from its mouth. The largest river system is the Murray with its tributaries—the Darling, the Murrumbidgee, and the Lachlan. These rivers drain south Queensland, western New South Wales, and northern Victoria. There are other streams, such as Cooper's Creek, which, in time of abnormal rains, carry enormous volumes of water inland to lakes which have no outlet, such as Lake Eyre, Lake Gairdner, and Lake Frome. Generally, however, these streams contain water in their upper courses only, because, by evaporation and soakage, the water is lost, and the remainder of their channels is marked by occasional water holes, which also dry up in time of drought.

On the east, north, and west coasts, short rivers flow from the mountain slopes to the sea. But there are no long navigable waterways penetrating far into the interior, like the Mississippi in North America and the Nile in Africa. Hence the development of the continent has been much retarded.

Minerals. Australia is fairly rich in mineral resources. Gold, discovered here in 1851, has yielded the most valuable returns. In the early days most of the gold was obtained from alluvial deposits or gold placers. Deep leads or deeply buried alluvial deposits also gave splendid returns. When the alluvial areas were worked out, the miners turned their attention to the quartz reefs from which the alluvial gold had been derived, and more costly methods of winning the gold were introduced. Copper, tin, lead, silver, zinc, manganese, antimony, wolfram, and bismuth have been mined, and important deposits of such minerals as gypsum and phosphates are being worked.

Precious stones, including diamond, sapphire, topaz, and opal, are found. Agates are fairly abundant.

Black coal occurs in large areas in eastern Australia and in Tasmania. Western Australia draws its supply largely from the Collie coal field, situated in the state. Thick seams of brown coal occur in southeastern Australia, especially near Morwell in Victoria. Building stones have been quarried in all the states.

MINERAL PRODUCTION OF AUSTRALIA, 1967

ITEM	Quantity	$A1,000*
Black coal	34,799,000 t.	160,099
Brown coal	23,386,000 t.	20,686
Copper	90,252 t.	72,515†
Gold	801,000 f.oz.	24,371†
Iron ore	18,536,000 t.	82,994
Lead	375,031 t.	73,654†
Silver	19,783,000 f.oz.	N.A.
Zinc	399,582 t.	29,354†

Value of all mining & quarrying 696,701

* Value at mine; includes value of materials used in production process. † Value of all minerals containing the metal.

Vegetation. The continent has over 7000 species of plants found nowhere else in the world. Many of them have fossil representatives in America and in Europe. Characteristically Australian are the gum trees, or eucalyptus, and the acacias. Eucalypts number over 230 species and are found in all places capable of supporting vegetation. Some are only a few feet in height, as the mallee and snow gum; some rival California's giant sequoias. Oil is secreted in the leaves of numerous species, and a gumlike resin exudes from the trees when the bark is injured. Some of the most durable timber known is furnished by various eucalypts, as the jarrah, red gum, and ironbark.

Much sunshine and too little rain compel many Australian trees to hang their leaves vertically, only the edges being turned to the sun. By this means the amount of evaporation from the leaves is diminished. The eucalypts are evergreens, but in many cases they shed their bark. The acacias, or wattles, constitute another important group, the members of which vary, according to their environment, from small shrubs to trees 100 to 150 feet in height. The bark of some varieties is used for tanning. The golden wattle is regarded as Australia's national flower.

Other forms of natural vegetation include the grass tree, resembling a tall stump from which grass sprouts at the top; tree ferns as large as palm trees; the banksia or Australian honeysuckle; and the native cherry, noted for having the stone outside the fruit.

Fodder Plants. Many acacias provide fodder for sheep and cattle. Other shrublike fodder plants, growing in the dry interior, are saltbushes, cotton bushes, and bluebushes. Australia's saltbushes have proved so valuable as sheep foodplants that they have been introduced into the arid regions of the southwestern United States.

Timber. Forest areas occupy 24,500,000 acres, which is about one-twentieth of the surface of Australia. Of this total, 15,895,781 acres are held as timber reserves. Soft woods, such as kauri pine, red cedar, silky oak, and Queensland maple, are found in the tropical forests of Queensland. Murray pine and Huon pine, the latter growing in Tasmania, are other important soft woods. The hard woods include many species of eucalypts, such as ironbark, red gum, gray box, yellow box, blue gum, and stringybark. These grow mainly on the highlands of eastern and southeastern Australia. Jarrah and kauri flourish in southwestern Australia. Blackwood, a species of acacia, is used extensively for furniture.

Grassland. The eastern half of the interior is a vast sheep pasturing country, though the rainfall is light. The soil is rich alluvium, and in good seasons grass is abundant. In time of drought the grass dries and is scattered by the wind, leaving the land perfectly bare. When the drought breaks, the grass springs up and grows with great rapidity. European fodder grasses have been planted over considerable areas. Farther west, plants needing but little water, wattles and saltbushes, mallee and mulga scrub, and the wiry spinifex, or porcupine grass, cover a large part of Australia's semidesert.

Jungles. In the northern part of Australia, a region of tropical heat and of heavy rains, there are found, in all the lowland districts, dense forests containing eucalypts, bamboos, palm trees, beautiful orchids with singular flowers, and gigantic lilies six to eight feet high, bearing dark red blossoms. Such jungle growth is variously known as bush, brush, or scrub. The term "bush" is frequently applied to any area in which the natural trees have not been cleared off to any extent.

Fauna. The fauna of Australia is quite distinct from that of the northern hemisphere. It is most closely related to that of South America. The characteristic mammalian forms are the marsupials, which, with few exceptions, are found elsewhere only in the fossil state. The higher mammals are represented only by the dingo, or native dog, probably introduced by the aborigines, and by a few rodents. The marsupials, or pouched animals, include the kangaroo and the wallaby, which are typically Australian. Other forms are the wombats, bandicoots, opossums, or possums, and the native bear, or koala. The Tasmanian wolf and Tasmanian devil are marsupials now confined to Tasmania. Outside the Australian area the only living pouched animals are the Patagonian opossum-rat and the North American opossum. The Monotremes, which are the lowest order of the mammals, have no living representatives outside Australia. The Australian forms include the duck-billed platypus and the echidna, or anteater. Both are egg laying forms and constitute a link between the mammals of today and the great reptile family from which the birds and mammals have developed.

Among the more remarkable birds are the emu, cassowary, kookaburra (laughing jackass or giant kingfisher), native turkey, black swan, lyre bird, and bower bird. Brilliant plumaged parrots and the yellow-crested cockatoo are abundant.

Two species of crocodiles are found in north Queensland. The largest lizard is called the "iguana" or "goanna" and may reach a length of 5 feet. Snakes, both venomous and nonvenomous, are fairly abundant.

Fish. Excellent food fish of many kinds abound in Australian coastal waters and in most of the rivers. The remarkable ceratodus or lungfish occurs in the Burnett and the Mary River in Queensland. Several species of European fish have been acclimatized. Trout may now be caught in a number of the mountain streams.

Pearling. Pearl fishing is a lucrative occupation off the northern and northwestern coasts of the continent. Some of the nearer pearl-oyster banks, however, have been practically exhausted, owing to persistent gathering of the shellfish and failure to allow the beds time enough to restock.

Sheep Raising. Gold brought Australia into the circle of the nations, but her greatest source of wealth is her merino sheep. Sheep raising is the continent's main industry. Pasturage for sheep is less dependent on rainfall than is pasture for cattle; sheep thrive where cattle would starve. Australian wool is the thickest and finest in the world. Hence wool growing is a profitable industry in the east central part of Australia. Wire fencing is used to enclose the "stations" or "runs" on which sheep are grazed. Merino sheep, improved wonderfully from the old Spanish stock, form the largest flocks. The stations vary greatly in size and in the number of sheep carried. Many of the very large stations have been subdivided, but recently, in the Riverina, there was one station which carried 150,000 sheep. Australia has over 120,000,000 sheep and exceeds in number any other sheep raising area in the world.

Large cattle stations are situated in the northern parts of Australia, especially Queensland. Dairy farms are abundant in the well watered districts of eastern and southern Australia. Horses and pigs are also raised.

ANIMAL INDUSTRY OF AUSTRALIA

ITEM	Season 1967–68	Season 1960
Cattle, No.	19,218,000	16,503,000
Pigs, No.	2,056,000	1,424,000
Sheep, No.	166,912,000	155,171,000
Butter produced, lbs.	432,284,000	436,633,000
Wool produced, lbs.	1,769,688,000	1,680,000,000

Agriculture. The area under cultivation in Australia is gradually extending. In the southern coastal regions the rainfall is generally good; and oats, barley, maize, and lucerne are the principal crops. Apples, pears, peaches, and other such fruits are largely grown. Inland, wheat is extensively cultivated, the area under cultivation increasing as means of communication are improved. Apples, oranges, lemons, peaches, apricots, grapes, and currants are readily grown in the irrigation areas. In the coast regions of Queensland, sugar cane, bananas, pineapples, and other tropical fruits are cultivated. Rice, cotton, and tobacco have been grown in various portions of the Commonwealth.

Manufacturing. Manufacturing is rapidly developing. Flour, woolen goods, leather, boots and shoes, furniture, iron and steel goods are among the products made for home consumption; and an export trade in manufactured articles is gradually developing.

VALUE OF CHIEF CLASSES OF PRODUCTS

ITEM	Value 1965–66 $A1,000	Value 1967–68 $A1,000
Agricultural	861,115	925,941
Pastoral	1,188,536	1,059,600
Dairying, Poultry and Bee-Farming	416,003	453,381
Forests and Fisheries	170,152	165,717
Mining	441,558	564,386
Manufacturing	6,275,355	7,430,738
Total	9,354,369	10,599,763

Commerce. Imports are principally European manufactures. Most of the trade is with Great Britain. Australia exports more wool than any other country. Among the other exports are wheat, butter, hides, tallow, and dressed meats, comprising chiefly beef, mutton, and rabbit. Summer dairy products, shipped on fast steamers with cold-storage chambers, reach Great Britain in a few weeks when the cows in that country are housed for the winter.

Canada and New Zealand are linked by cable with Australia. Most of the foreign capital invested in Australia is British. The country has about 28,000 miles of railway, of mixed gauges. A railway gauge unification scheme is being considered. The state governments own the railways while the Federal government owns the telegraph and telephone services, an interstate and the overseas airline.

The Federal District. In 1911, the Commonwealth acquired from New South Wales an area of approximately 912 square miles to be used as a Federal district. An additional area of 28 square miles on Jervis bay was obtained in 1917 to be used as a naval station. This Federal district was named Canberra. Building operations began in 1923, and the Australian parliament convened there for the first time in May 1927.

Inhabitants. The population of Australia in 1968 was estimated at 12,099,100. Protestants constitute the larger proportion of the inhabitants, but there is an influential Catholic minority. The Federal constitution forbids the establishment of any state-supported religion. In all parts of the Commonwealth, education is free, secular, and obligatory. Illiteracy is virtually unknown. The population is almost entirely of British origin, less than 5 per cent being of any other extraction. These figures do not include about 50,000 aborigines.

Name. The continent was formerly called New Holland. *Australia*, from the Latin word for southern, was suggested by Captain Matthew Flinders (1774–1814), an English navigator, who had explored the southern part of the island. The name came into use in 1817.

STATES OF THE COMMONWEALTH

The Commonwealth of Australia, a self-governing British Commonwealth member, was formed Jan. 1, 1901. It consists of six states—New South Wales, Queensland, South Australia, Tasmania, Victoria, and Western Australia—the Northern Territory, and the Australian Capital Territory. The following section contains a brief description of the states and of the Northern Territory.

New South Wales, a state of southeastern Australia. The Great Dividing range extends along the east side at a distance of 20 to 100 miles inland. On the west is a magnificent pastoral country which gradually changes to arid plains farther inland. The pastoral area is the basis for Australia's great sheep industry. There are 48,000,000 sheep in this area alone. Also this state includes Australia's most important mining, farming, and industrial developments. Coal, gold, silver, lead, tin, antimony, manganese, bismuth, and copper are locally mined and iron ore is nearby and available. Farm crops are wheat, maize. barley, oats, potatoes, lucerne, tobacco, sugar cane, and grapes. Sydney, Newcastle, Broken Hill, Tamworth, Bathurst, Goulburn, Wagga Wagga, and Albury are important urban centers.

Forests cover the western slopes of the mountains and include such trees as the red cedar, eucalyptus, red gum, and murray pine. Acacias and mulga are shrubs of the arid regions. Unusual animal life is found, as kangaroos, platypuses, and echidnas. Rabbits introduced from Europe have multiplied and become a serious menace to sheep grazing since they also are herbivorous.

Queensland lies in the northeast part of the continent. The climate is subtropical to tropical. Along the coast and on the windward eastern side of the Great Dividing range the rainfall is heavy. Across the mountains and inland to the "Never, Never Country" the land is arid, again supporting immense herds of cattle and sheep. Tropical crops, as sugar cane, bananas, and rice, are grown along the coastal plains. Wheat is prominent about Brisbane. Natural forests still abound including such valuable trees as cedar, kauri, pine, silky oak, and maple. Leading cities are Brisbane, Rockhampton. Towns-ville, Maryborough, Gympie, Ipswich, Toowoomba, and Charters Towers.

South Australia lies in south central Australia. The Flinders range, Spencer's Gulf, and a series of shallow saline lakes divide it into eastern and western sections. The east is well watered and fertile; the west is desert. The Murray River flows through the southeastern corner. Temperatures are extremely high in desert sections in summer but frosts occur in the higher lands in winter. Ranching prevails, with sheep the most prominent. Adelaide is the state capital and most important city. Other cities are Whyalla, Port Pirie, Port Augusta, and Gawler.

Tasmania, originally called Van Diemen's Land, is an island state lying to the south of Victoria, from which it is separated by Bass strait. It consists of one large and numerous small islands. The climate is temperate and moist. Mines produce silver, lead, copper, gold, zinc, tin, and coal. Besides metals, Tasmania exports fruits, dairy products, potatoes, wool, hides, and timber. Hobart is the capital and principal port.

Victoria is a comparatively small state on the southeast corner of Australia. The section of the Great Dividing range known as the Australian Alps is in the eastern part. The coastline is 680 miles long on the south and the Murray River forms the north boundary. As in Tasmania, just across the straits, the climate is temperate with moderate temperatures and sufficient rainfall for cropping except in the northwest. Grazing is important with sheep raising first. Farming and manufacturing are rapidly developing. Melbourne is the capital. Other important cities are Ballarat, Bendigo, and Geelong.

Western Australia comprises all of western Australia to the 129° Meridian east. It is a huge area with greatest dimensions being 1480 miles north-south and 1000 miles east-west. It is largely an arid tableland with a narrow strip of coastal lowland. The southwest corner of the state has moderate temperatures and sufficient rainfall, crops and livestock. The extreme north is tropical with abundant rainfall. Gold is the most valuable in mineral output. About Perth, the capital city, a wide variety of temperate and subtropical crops are grown, such as wheat, oranges, grapes, lemons, and olives. Other important cities are Fremantle, Midland, Albany, Coolgardie, Kalgoorlie, Geraldton, Northam, Collie, Bunbury, and the port of Broome.

Northern Territory is the northern central section of the continent and includes the Arnhem Land peninsula. Its dimensions are 900 miles north-south by 560 miles east-west. The coastline is 1040 miles in length. The area is largely tableland with a low narrow tropical coastal plain in the north. This state is not especially well developed because of heat and aridity. The northern part has tropical rainfall mainly in summer. Darwin is a port, has an important international airport and is the center of the Territory Administration. Alice Springs is the other important town in the Territory.

STATISTICS OF AUSTRALIA

States and Territories	Area in sq. mi.	Pop. 1968 est.	Capital
New South Wales	309,433	4,430,200	Sydney
Victoria	87,884	3,356,900	Melbourne
South Australia	380,070	1,136,400	Adelaide
Queensland	667,000	1,751,800	Brisbane
Tasmania	26,215	386,000	Hobart
Western Australia	975,920	930,800	Perth
Northern Territory	520,280	64,000	Darwin
Federal District (A.C.T.)	939	117,200	Canberra

PRINCIPAL CITIES

The following section contains a brief description of the chief cities of Australia, including each of the state or territorial capitals. The population of Australia shows a marked tendency to concentrate in the cities, the five largest of which contain almost 50 per cent of the country's inhabitants.

Adelaide. The capital of South Australia, situated in the southern part of the state on the Torrens River, about six miles from its mouth in the Gulf of St. Vincent. A dam here forms the river into a lake a mile and a quarter long. The city stands on a wide plain near the base of the Mt. Lofty range and is divided by the Torrens into South Adelaide and North Adelaide.

The manufactures comprise iron wares, leather, woolens, pottery, starch, soap, flour, and malt liquors. Adelaide is the trade emporium of South Australia and has a large commerce. Port Adelaide, the seaport of the city, is about 7 miles distant by rail. It is the seat of considerable manufacturing; is a port of call for vessels from Europe; and is connected by railway with the principal cities of the Commonwealth. Near by is the summer resort of Glenelg.

Adelaide was founded in 1836 and was named in honor of Queen Adelaide, consort of King William IV of England. Population, 794,300.

Ballarat. A prosperous inland city of Victoria, Australia, the center of a rich gold yielding district. It was the finding of gold nuggets near the present site of Ballarat in 1851 that started the rush of gold seekers into Australia. At Bakery Hill, there was found, in 1858, a nugget that was sold for about $50,000. Population, 41,037.

Brisbane. The capital of Queensland, Australia, situated in the southeastern part of the state on the Brisbane River, about 25 miles from Moreton bay. Brisbane is the center of commerce and of manufacturing for southern Queensland.

Steamers ascend the river and berth at the wharves. There is a regular steamer communication with other ports in Australia and with the chief ports of Europe, and of the United States. Among the manufacturing establishments are flour mills, tobacco factories, breweries, tanneries, and shoe factories. Coal is mined in the vicinity.

The climate is healthful though the mean yearly temperature is 68.9° F. in the shade. Higher education is afforded by a Teachers College, a Technical College, and the University of Queensland. Population, 813,300.

Canberra (kăn'bĕr-à). The capital of Australia. It is a Federal territory, 912 square miles in area, situated about 150 miles southwest of Sydney and 60 miles inland from the east coast of Australia. The city is built on the Molonglo River and is picturesquely surrounded by mountains. It was laid out by W. Burley Griffin, of Chicago, whose plans were adjudged the best in a world-wide competition. These plans call for streets in concentric circles with radiating avenues. The National War Memorial Museum, Institute of Anatomy, overseas embassies, Australian National University (1949), National Observatory and Canberra University College (1932), and government buildings are tourist attractions. Population, 110,000.

Darwin. A port city, named after Charles Darwin, and the government seat of the Northern Territory, Australia. Almost 2000 miles from the nearest metropolis, Darwin is the terminus of the overland telegraph and of the cable to Java and Singapore. In 1974, a cyclone struck Darwin, leaving 50 dead and destroying 90 per cent of the city. Reconstruction started immediately and it was estimated that it would take 5 years to complete. Population, 45,000.

Hobart. The capital of the Australian island state of Tasmania. The city is situated on the Derwent estuary.

The manufactures include woolens, hats, flour, pottery, leather, and jam.

Most of the exports consist of fruits, hops, grain, wool, and timber. Many Australian visitors are attracted to Hobart by the cool and invigorating climate. The city is the seat of the University of Tasmania.

Hobart was founded in 1804 and was named Hobart Town in honor of Lord Hobart, then secretary of state for the colonies. In 1881 the name was changed to Hobart. Population (with suburbs), 144,000.

Melbourne. The capital of Victoria, on the Yarra River about two miles from its mouth in Hobsons bay, an arm of Port Phillip bay. The river is navigable by vessels drawing less than 22 feet of water, but large steamers usually anchor in the bay at Port Melbourne.

The University of Melbourne stands in the foremost rank of institutions of higher learning.

Melbourne has large docks. Served by regular steamer communication with ports in Asia, Europe, and America, the city is a great emporium of foreign commerce. Railroads connect it with all the chief cities in Australia.

From 1901 to 1927 it served as the temporary capital of the Commonwealth. Population, 2,319,700.

Perth. The capital of Western Australia, occupying a picturesque site in the southwestern part of the state on

Melville water, an expansion of the Swan river. The city is 12 miles by rail from its port, Fremantle, a town at the mouth of the river on the Indian Ocean.

The University of Perth was founded in 1912. Population, (with suburbs) 499,494.

Sydney. The largest and oldest city in Australia and the capital of New South Wales. Sydney is picturesquely situated on Port Jackson, a magnificent expanse of water, which forms a landlocked harbor extending 20 miles inland. The harbor is spanned by a steel arch bridge having a main span of 1650 feet, one of the longest in the world. The water in the harbor is deep enough to permit ocean-going ships to dock at the wharves and quays. Favored by this advantage, the city has become a naval station of the first rank.

Sydney has an enormous commerce. The harbor is crowded with shipping from foreign ports, and the staple Australian products are exported in immense quantities. Favored by the proximity of vast coal deposits, Sydney is also a manufacturing city. Cars, locomotives, hardware, foundry and machine shop products, clothing, boots and shoes, textiles, machinery, and malt and distilled liquors are some of the manufactures. An annual sheep show is an event of great commercial importance.

Sydney has 647 acres of parks within the city boundary and 680,000 acres of reserves and commons in the metropolitan area.

Adjoining Victoria park stands the sumptuous main edifice of the University of Sydney with the Macleay museum of natural history.

The city's mean annual temperature is about 63.1° F., which is nearly the same as the average yearly temperature of Lisbon. Sydney was founded in 1788 by Captain Arthur Phillip, who had been sent by the British government to select a site for a colony. Population, 2,444,735.

NEW ZEALAND

A self-governing country consisting of two large islands to which are attached politically a number of small islands lying at some distance from the main group. New Zealand is situated in the south Pacific Ocean about 1200 miles east of Australia. It lies 7000 miles almost due south from Alaska and is 4000 miles west of the coast of Chile. It is 5400 miles by direct route from San Francisco. The two large islands are called North island and South island and are separated by Cook strait, which has a width varying from 16 to 90 miles. The two islands lie entirely in the South Temperate Zone and form a group stretching about 1000 miles in a general northeast and southwest direction and having a maximum width of 180 miles. The total area of New Zealand including Stewart Island and the Chatham Islands is 103,736 square miles.

North Island. The northern portion of New Zealand has an area of 44,281 square miles. It is 515 miles long, and its greatest breadth is 180 miles. The island may be likened to an inverted shoe the toe of which is a long irregular peninsula extending to the northwest. This peninsula is attached to the rest of the island by a narrow isthmus, consisting of a neck six miles in width separating Hauraki gulf on the east from Manukau harbor on the west. The arch of the shoe is represented by the Bay of Plenty in the north. The only remaining inlet of any considerable size is Hawke bay on the east. North island has the two best ports of New Zealand, Port Nicholson in the south and Waitemata at the isthmus in the northwest.

Most of the surface is gently undulating with low, heavily forested hills. A volcanic area, beginning in the south, passes through the center of the island as far as the Bay of Plenty. Much of this region will not support grasses, but trees cover parts of it. It occupies the southern extension of the island from coast to coast, but, where the width of the island increases, a fertile area spreads out on each side and runs along each coast in a belt averaging about 40 miles in width. These tracts are well adapted for grazing. The northwestern peninsula is in large part covered with a heavy clay, which yields returns only in response to intensive cultivation. The peninsula has areas of rich alluvium, however, in which the mangrove, the orange tree, various palms, and the giant kauri pine flourish. The partially fossilized resin of this pine is excavated and exported in quantity to be used in the manufacture of varnish and of linoleum.

The volcanic area of North Island contains many notable features. The highest volcano is Mount Ruapehu, which has an altitude of 9175 feet. It is situated in Tongariro national park, about 20 miles southwest of Lake Taupo, New Zealand's largest inland body of water. Stretching north from the mountain is a region of about 5000 square miles abounding in hot springs, geysers, pools of boiling mud, and colored lakelets. This region formerly contained a famous series of pink and white terraces of volcanic formation. In 1886, however, they were blown up in an eruption which tore a chasm in the earth nine miles in length. Farther south, on Cook strait, stands one of the most beautiful mountains of the island, Mount Egmont, an extinct volcano 8340 feet in height. No country has so large a proportion of its area incorporated in national parks as New Zealand. Covering over 2,500,000 acres, these reserves embrace a variety of scenery unmatched in any other park system of the world.

The rivers of the island are short. The longest is the Waikato River, which drains the waters of Lake Taupo northward to an outlet on the west coast. It is navigable for 70 miles of its course, but it shares with nearly all the other rivers of New Zealand the disadvantage of having at its mouth a bar which obstructs navigation.

South Island. The southern portion of New Zealand is slightly larger than the northern, having an area of 58,092 square miles. Off its southern coast, and separated by Foveaux strait, lies Stewart Island, which has an area of 670 square miles. About 350 miles to the east lie the Chatham Islands, 372 square miles in area. The length of South Island is 530 miles. It has a fairly uniform breadth of about 100 miles.

The outstanding feature of the surface is a mountain range called the Southern Alps, which runs from end to end near the western coast of the island. The mountains reach a maximum elevation at Mount Cook, which has an altitude of 12,349 feet. The scenic grandeur of the region is comparable to that of the European Alps. On the western slope, many glaciers flow down to the edge of the coniferous forests which cover a large part of the mountain sides. East of the divide are several long glacial lakes. The largest, Lake Wakatipu, has a depth of more than 1500 feet, and its wild, mountainous surroundings impart to it a beauty rivaling that of Lake Lucerne in Switzerland. The eastern slope descends to a plateau flanked on the east by a ridge of mountains passing through the center of the island. East of this ridge the land inclines toward the sea in grassy terraces, which provide the largest stretch of arable land in New Zealand.

Other Islands. New Zealand controls a number of islands in the south Pacific Ocean. They have a total area of about 500 square miles and a population of approximately 15,000. The more important of these islands are Cook Islands, about 1500 miles northeast of North Island, and Auckland Islands, uninhabited, 200 miles south of New Zealand. The Cook Islands support about 21,000 inhabitants, mainly of Polynesian race, who export tropical fruit and coffee. New Zealand formerly held a mandate over Western Samoa, which became independent in 1962. This group of fertile islands of 1130 square miles is about 1000 miles to the north and had an estimated population of 137,000 in 1968.

Climate. The prevailing winds of New Zealand blow from the west. They carry sufficient moisture to foster everywhere on the islands a vegetation of a uniform greenness that recalls the verdure of Ireland. In South island, where the mountains reach a greater height, much of the moisture is precipitated as rain on the plateau, and the warm, dry winds, descending from the elevated regions into the eastern plains, occasionally cause droughts of sufficient duration to injure the crops. Except in the mountains, New Zealand is free from severe frosts, while in North island, where two-thirds of the population is concentrated, the climate is subtropical. Tempering breezes, however, blow incessantly from the ocean; yellow fever is unknown, and there are few mosquitoes or other pests usually found in subtropical regions. As a result, the mortality rate of New Zealand is one of the lowest in the world.

Flora and Fauna. The most characteristic plant of New Zealand is the fern, which flourishes in great variety everywhere. The so-called tree fern often reaches a height of 40 feet. About two-thirds of the indigenous species of vegetation are found nowhere else, and most of the others resemble those of Australia. The eucalyptus and acacia, however, which predominate in Australia, are not found in New Zealand. The nikau palm occurs even on South island, which is the southern limit for true palms. The kauri pine, the beech, and many other hardwood trees formerly covered much of the region's surface. Phormium, or New Zealand flax, is the country's outstanding contribution to the economic plants of the world. The fiber is used for binder twine and ropes. The cultivation of phormium has been introduced into Ireland, America, and several other regions of the earth. A noticeable feature of New Zealand's flora is the comparative absence of brilliant flowers.

New Zealand has not a single indigenous mammal. The dog and the rat, however, were brought by Polynesian settlers, and wild pigs, rabbits, and many other forms of animal life have been introduced by Europeans. There are no snakes, but there are a few lizards peculiar to the country. The area is the sole habitat of many species of birds, including the kiwi, or apteryx, a wingless and tailless bird the size of a hen. The kiwi is related to the moa, a bird which was formerly very numerous in New Zealand but which has been exterminated within the past few centuries.

Stock Raising. The bulk of New Zealand's wealth is derived from sheep and cattle. The wool clip normally amounts to more than 200 million pounds, approximately 20 to 25 per cent of that of Australia. Sheep skins to the value of 10 to 15 million dollars are exported annually. Frozen meat exports are valued at more than 50 million dollars, and 60 to 80 million dollars worth of butter and cheese is shipped. The stock is carried and fattened mainly on cultivated grasses, although in North island most of the pasturage is unplowed.

Agriculture. The greater part of the land sown to field crops is in South island. The produce, absorbed almost entirely by the domestic market, consists principally of wheat, oats, barley, and potatoes. Grain growing is not a specialized occupation, but is carried on along with stock raising. About two-thirds of New Zealand's surface is said to be capable of successful cultivation.

Mining. The four minerals produced in quantity by New Zealand are coal, gold, kauri gum, and silver. Most of the coal is mined in South island, but very little is sent out of the country. Gold is found in both islands, and heads the list of mineral exports. Gold mining was an attraction which drew large numbers of settlers in the decade 1861-71.

Manufacturing and Trade. The chief manufactures of New Zealand are connected with stock raising and dairying. After meat packing and the making of dairy products, the most important industries are lumber mill operations, printing, and the manufacture of flour, textiles, leather, and metal products. Industrial disputes are settled by compulsory arbitration.

Most of the trade is with Great Britain. The United States, Canada, and Australia rank next in order. The exports normally amount to over 300 million dollars in value, most of which is represented by the products of New Zealand's characteristic industry, the raising of sheep and other livestock. The imports usually approximate the same value as the exports, the chief articles being iron and steel products, textiles, motor cars, oils, clothing, paper, and tobacco products.

Internal Communications. New Zealand has about 3450 miles of railroads, practically the entire mileage being owned and operated by the government. The greater part of the mileage is on South island. The telephone and the telegraph system are also under government ownership.

Inhabitants. The aborigines of New Zealand are called Maoris, a Polynesian people which is believed to have displaced an earlier race some six centuries ago. They were polygamous, and occasionally indulged in cannibal feasts. Among them, it was supposed that the seat of the soul was the left eye. In warlike arts, wood carving, dyeing, and tattooing, they had developed a considerable skill. After a desperate resistance to the British settlers, they accepted the religion and the manner of life of the newcomers. In 1968, the Maoris in New Zealand numbered 219,042.

The population of New Zealand, 1968 estimate, was 2,776,266, nearly all of whom were of British descent. A little less than two-thirds of the population resides in North Island, the rest living in South Island and the dependencies. The capital is Wellington and the largest city is Auckland, both of which are in North Island.

There is an excellent educational system, at the head of which stands the University of New Zealand with four affiliated colleges. The university is not a teaching body. It has the power of granting degrees and is charged with conducting the examination of students prepared by the colleges. Over one-third the population are members or adherents of the English Church. The Catholics number about 11 per cent of the total.

New Zealand is divided into nine provincial districts, of which four are in North island, five are entirely in South island, and one is partly in South island and partly in other islands. Those in North island are Auckland, Wellington, Hawke's Bay, and Taranaki. Within South island are the provincial districts of Canterbury, Nelson, Westland, Marlborough, and the greater part of Otago. Otago includes also Stewart and other outlying islands.

PRINCIPAL CITIES

Auckland. The largest city of New Zealand, beautifully situated on a cluster of extinct volcanoes at the neck of the northwestern peninsula of North Island. The isthmus is six miles in width, thus providing the city with two natural harbors, one on each side of the isthmus. The eastern harbor is protected by a volcanic cone rising to a height of 1000 feet. This harbor has been elaborately improved and is the point of export for kauri gum and a large part of the lumber shipped abroad. The chief industries include shipbuilding, sugar refining, and the manufacture of rope and of machine shop products.

Auckland is the seat of Auckland University College and has an art gallery, a library with a valuable collection of rare manuscripts, and a museum containing many Maori relics. The mountain sides in the vicinity are terraced by former Maori fortifications. The Domain, one of the four parks of the city, contains a fine botanical garden. Auckland was until 1865 the capital of New Zealand. Population, 548,293.

Christchurch. The capital of the provincial district of Canterbury and the second largest city of New Zealand, situated near the center of the eastern coast of South island on the Avon River seven miles from its mouth. The city lies on a fertile plain and is the center of the surrounding agricultural and grazing interests. Frozen meats, wool, and lumber are exported. The chief manufactures include agricultural machinery, leather goods, furniture, and clothing.

Christchurch was founded by the "Canterbury pilgrims," a group of churchmen who left England about 1849. Many of the streets are named after English dioceses. Canterbury college is the leading educational institution. The Anglican cathedral with its dominating spire is the finest piece of church architecture in New Zealand. A museum contains numerous remains of the moa, an extinct wingless bird which is peculiar to New Zealand. Population, est., 250,000.

Dunedin. The capital of the provincial district of Otago, situated on Otago harbor, an inlet on the southeastern coast of South Island. The chief exports are wool, frozen meat, and gold. Dunedin is the seat of Otago College, the largest institution for higher education in New Zealand.

Dunedin is connected by rail with Christchurch to the north and with Invercargill to the south. The population is about 80,000.

Invercargill (ĭn′vẽr-kär′gĭl). A port and city at the southern extremity of South Island. Invercargill is the regular starting point for journeys to Lake Wakatipu and other glacial lakes of the Southern Alps. It has several woolen and lumber mills. Population, 43,800.

Wanganui (wŏ′ngȧ-nōō-ê). The principal port on the west coast of North island, lying about 120 miles north of Wellington. It is regularly laid out at the foot of low hills, from the summit of which may be seen the snow-clad volcano of Mount Ruapehu. Wanganui is the export center for a pastoral and agricultural region. Population 36,000.

Wellington. The capital and third largest city of New Zealand, situated at the geographical center of the country, on a mountainous site at the southern end of North Island. It fronts on Lambton harbor, the most commodious in New Zealand. The port is equipped with modern facilities for handling the city's extensive commerce, which includes a large export trade in wool, meat, hides, skins, butter, cheese, and hemp. Wellington's manufactures embrace chiefly packed meats, woolen goods, soap, matches, rope, and brick. Printing and the assembling of motor vehicles are other important industries.

The government and principal office buildings are substantial, modern structures. The city has a university, two museums, an art gallery, and a modern research laboratory. Besides 1613 acres of parks and reserves in the city, Wellington owns a 970-acre belt of grazing land, accessible to the public, and Williams park, a seaside resort on Days bay. The 30-mile drive around the Wellington waterfront is one of the finest scenic routes in Oceania. Population, 167,859.

GREAT CITIES OF THE WORLD

City and Country	Population		City and Country	Population	
	City Proper	Urban Agglom.		City Proper	Urban Agglom.
Ahmedabad, India	1,585,544	1,950,000	Los Angeles, USA	2,750,000	8,960,000
Alexandria, Egypt	2,032,000	2,250,000	Madras, India	2,469,449	3,200,000
Algiers, Algeria	1,503,720	1,800,000	Madrid, Spain	3,247,108	3,785,000
Amsterdam, Netherlands	770,805	1,780,000	Manchester, England	516,100	2,865,000
Athens, Greece	867,023	2,540,541	Manila, Philippines	1,435,500	5,000,000
Bagdad, Iraq	1,300,000	2,183,800	Marseille, France	889,029	1,015,000
Baku, USSR	927,000	1,555,000	Melbourne, Australia	74,400	2,620,400
Baltimore, USA	847,000	1,920,000	Mexico City, Mexico	7,768,000	10,700,000
Bangkok, Thailand	1,867,297	3,125,000	Milan, Italy	1,743,427	3,725,000
Barcelona, Spain	1,800,274	3,365,000	Milwaukee, USA	685,000	1,388,000
Belgrade, Yugoslavia	770,140	1,150,000	Montevideo, Uruguay	1,202,757	1,300,000
Berlin (W.), Germany	2,047,948	3,860,000	Montreal, Canada	1,214,352	2,743,408
Beirut, Lebanon	470,870	1,010,000	Moscow, USSR	7,469,000	10,650,000
Birmingham, England	1,086,500	2,660,000	Munich, Germany	1,336,576	1,895,000
Bogota, Colombia	2,855,065	2,925,000	Nagoya, Japan	2,082,235	3,500,000
Bombay, India	5,970,575	6,750,000	Nanking, China	1,455,000	
Boston, USA	601,000	3,855,000	Naples, Italy	1,221,859	1,975,000
Brussels, Belgium	153,405	2,020,000	New Orleans, USA	569,000	1,131,000
Bucharest, Rumania	1,528,562	1,642,651	New York, USA	7,605,000	17,150,000
Budapest, Hungary	2,049,100	2,475,000	Odessa, USSR	1,002,000	1,050,000
Buenos Aires, Argentina	2,972,453	8,625,000	Osaka, Japan	2,802,065	14,350,000
Cairo, Egypt	4,961,000	6,600,000	Paris, France	2,290,900	9,150,000
Calcutta, India	3,148,746	9,100,000	Peking, China	4,800,000	7,570,000
Canton, China	1,867,000		Philadelphia, USA	1,820,000	5,280,000
Caracas, Venezuela	1,658,500	2,475,000	Pittsburgh, USA	472,000	2,240,000
Casablanca, Morocco	1,506,373	1,575,000	Prague, Czechoslovakia	1,091,449	1,230,000
Chicago, USA	3,115,000	7,655,000	Pusan, Korea	1,880,710	
Chungking, China	2,165,000		Rangoon, Burma	1,854,000	
Cleveland, USA	750,903	2,361,100	Rio de Janeiro, Brazil	4,252,009	7,000,000
Cologne, Germany	832,396	1,700,000	Rome, Italy	2,833,103	3,075,000
Copenhagen, Denmark	562,405	1,515,000	Rotterdam, Netherlands	635,910	1,100,000
Dallas, USA	859,000	2,470,000	Saigon, Vietnam	1,804,880	2,750,000
Denver, USA	506,000	1,285,000	St. Louis, USA	538,000	2,270,000
Delhi, India	3,706,558	4,500,000	San Diego, USA	765,000	1,355,000
Detroit, USA	1,355,000	4,530,000	San Francisco, USA	675,000	4,450,000
Genoa, Italy	813,256	880,000	Santiago, Chile	517,473	2,925,000
Glasgow, Scotland	905,032	1,925,000	São Paulo, Brazil	5,921,796	8,050,000
Gorki, USSR	1,283,000	1,775,000	Seattle, USA	490,000	1,788,000
Guadalajara, Mexico	1,411,900	1,800,000	Seoul, Korea	5,536,377	5,900,000
Hamburg, Germany	1,751,621	2,300,000	Shanghai, China	7,900,000	10,820,000
Harbin, China	1,814,000		Shenyang, China	2,423,000	
Havana, Cuba	1,755,400	1,800,000	Singapore, Singapore	2,074,507	2,225,000
Houston, USA	1,369,000	2,140,000	Sofia, Bulgaria	919,000	1,035,480
Hyderabad, India	1,607,396	2,000,000	Stockholm, Sweden	1,353,359	671,226
Istanbul, Turkey	2,376,300	3,250,000	Sydney, Australia	55,770	2,898,330
Jakarta, Indonesia	4,576,009	4,650,000	Taipei, Taiwan	2,003,604	3,050,000
Johannesburg, S. Africa	654,682	2,550,000	Tehran, Iran	3,858,000	4,400,000
Kanpur, India	1,154,388	1,320,000	Tel Aviv, Israel	367,600	1,215,000
Karachi, Pakistan	2,850,000	3,498,634	Tientsin, China	3,800,000	4,280,000
Kharkov, USSR	1,357,000	1,625,000	Tokyo, Japan	8,678,642	23,800,000
Kiev, USSR	1,947,000	2,140,000	Toronto, Canada	712,786	2,628,043
Kobe, Japan	1,351,651		Tsingtao, China	1,144,000	
Kyoto, Japan	1,438,714		Turin, Italy	1,199,006	1,670,000
Lahore, Pakistan	2,050,000	2,200,000	Victoria, Hong Kong	521,612	3,575,000
Leningrad, USSR	3,850,000	5,000,000	Vienna, Austria	1,614,841	1,940,000
Lima, Peru	340,339	3,350,000	Warsaw, Poland	1,410,000	1,875,000
Lisbon, Portugal	774,500	1,800,000	Washington, D.C., USA	715,000	3,190,000
Liverpool, England	561,100	1,595,000	Wuhan, China	2,226,000	
London, England	7,167,600	10,475,000	Yokohama, Japan	2,562,291	

The source of the above data was the *Rand McNally Commercial Atlas & Marketing Guide*, 1976. The figures for the cities in the U.S. are 1975 Rand McNally estimates. The populations for the foreign cities were derived from censuses, official estimates and unofficial estimates.

ANTARCTICA

Isolated, inaccessible, and for a long time undiscovered, the continent of Antarctica received special attention from several nations during the International Geophysical Year of 1957–58. Improved equipment and techniques made possible the accumulation of much new data concerning the area, topography, sea bottom, weather, depth of ice, mineral resources, animal and vegetable life, fossils, and other aspects of the great Ice Age land mass which surrounds the South Pole.

To analyze and evaluate all the information thus obtained is a major undertaking which may require several years during which important additional findings are certain to be made in the continuation of some investigations beyond the time originally fixed for the IGY studies.

Conditions are such as to make international cooperation in Antarctic exploration cordial and promising. It is true that some overlapping territorial claims here have been made by different countries from time to time, dating back to Kerguelen's identification of "South France" at longitude 50 in 1771 and English explorer Cook's discovery of new land in 1773, when he made the first recorded crossing of the Antarctic Circle. As additional land masses were discovered, other claims were entered, particularly by Britain, Australia, and New Zealand and, by implication, the United States through the establishment of outposts in "Little America" by Admiral Richard Byrd. However, since the continent is not suitable for colonizing, and since the utilization of its mineral resources is not feasible at this time, there has been comparatively slight political rivalry between the nations that have sent exploring parties.

Because of Antarctica's remote location, immense area, and forbidding climate, its exploration is a major challenge to world scientists. Being an irregular land mass of 6,000,000 miles, extending roughly in a circle from the South Pole to meet the Atlantic, Pacific, and Indian oceans, it contrasts sharply with the Arctic region, whose center is an ice-covered sea and whose land boundaries within the Arctic Circle are marked by Canada, Alaska, and Siberia. People, timber, vegetation, and rich animal and mineral resources are found within the Arctic Circle, but not within the Antarctic, where winds reaching 100 miles an hour blow across snow-covered plateaus and temperatures of -80 are not uncommon. In earlier periods of exploration, sailing through "pack ice" or traversing frozen surfaces by dog sledges called for unexampled heroism and hardihood. More recently, the problem of transportation has been made easier by the use of airplanes and motor-driven vehicles such as the modern "snocats" and "weasels," but the storms and crevasses remain, and also the "white-out" peril to flyers.

For the United States, "Operation Deepfreeze," organized by the late Admiral Byrd and commanded by Admiral George Dufek brought to the task of IGY exploration the experience gained by Admiral Byrd's epoch-making 1928 expedition and such later ones as "Operation Highjump" of 1947 and its sequel "Operation Windmill." For the British, a Commonwealth Transantarctic expedition featured cooperation and friendly rivalry between Dr. Vivian Fuchs and Sir Edmund Hillary of New Zealand, best known as the conqueror of Mount Everest. In their race by separate overland routes to the South Pole, Hillary arrived first, on January 4, 1958, and Fuchs on January 19. Explorers had flown over the Pole not long before, but Hillary and Fuchs were the first in 46 years to reach it by the land route. In fact, there was a striking resemblance between this latest venture and the one that led to the reaching of the South Pole five weeks apart by Amundsen and Scott in the Antarctic "summer" of December-January, 1911–12. The tragic fate of Captain Scott soon after his triumph and his personal record of the last days have made his story one that is both inspiring and poignant.

To review the less dramatic and more prosaic aspects of the latest Antarctica explorations, we may note a few of the observations and estimates that have so far been reported. It is too soon to use the word "conclusions," for scientists are notably careful about expressing final judgments. However, some typical researches and their tentative results may be cited at this early stage of the investigation. For example, studies of the sea bottom were made to determine approximately when the Ice Age took over. It was believed that the seas were free of ice until about 3000 B. C. The Geomagnetic South Pole was relocated about 600 miles west of its earlier assumed location. Ore specimens of high-grade manganese silicate were found on Clark Peninsula. Seismic soundings proved some ice-covered land to be 7,000 feet above sea level. In addition to previously-known mountain peaks 15,000 feet high, new ones ranging up to 11,000 feet were sighted. Bedrock at the South Pole was estimated to be 903 feet above sea level but covered by 8,297 feet of snow and ice. Along a bank of the Upper Mawson Glacier, a New Zealand party found a coal field of six seams, each 6 to 12 feet thick. A Japanese party reported finding uranium. Valleys almost free of ice and snow were found extending north from the Hill Glacier in the Great Antarctic Horst Mountains. One party discovered a glacier-made gorge 9,000 feet deep and 30 miles long. When these countless other facts have been brought together and studied, the hitherto mysterious continent of Antarctica will be much better understood.

NOTED WATERFALLS

Name	Location	Height (feet)
Angel	Venezuela	3,300
Bridal Veil	Yosemite, Cal.	620
Cuquenan	Venezuela	2,000
Gastein	Austria	480
Gavarnie	Pyrenees	1,385
George VI	Guyana	1,600
Grand Falls	Labrador	316
Great Falls	Montana	526
Great Falls	Potomac River	35
Great Umgeni	Natal	364
Harsprang	Sweden	110
Iguassu	Argentina	215
Ililouette	Yosemite, Cal.	370
Juanacatlan	Mexico	70
Kar Kloof	Natal	350
Krimmler	Austria	1,300
Minnehaha	Minnesota	60
Montmorency	Quebec	265
Multnomah	Oregon	607
Nevada Falls	California	594
Niagara Falls	New York	167
Portage Falls	Portageville, N. Y.	110
Rhine Falls	Schaffhausen	710
Ribbon Falls	Yosemite, Cal.	1,612
Roraima	Guiana	2,000
Ruikanfos	Norway	805
St. Anthony	Minnesota	50
Seculéjo	Pyrenees Mts.	820
Sellesche	Switzerland	128
Seneca Falls	New York	50
Shoshone	Idaho	210
Skykjefos	Norway	660
Snoqualmie	Washington	267
Staubbach	Switzerland	870
Sutherland	New Zealand	1,904
Takakkow	British Columbia	1,400
Taughannock	New York	215
Tequendama	Colombia, S. Am.	475
Terni	Italy	650
Trollhattan	Sweden	108
Twin Falls	British Columbia	400
Vernal Fall	California	320
Victoria	Africa	343
Voringsfos	Norway	520
Widow's Tears	Yosemite, Cal.	1,170
Yellowstone (2 falls)	Wyoming	420
Upper	Wyoming	110
Lower	Wyoming	310
Yosemite (3 falls)	California	2,370
Upper	California	1,430
Middle	California	620
Lower	California	320

NOTED MOUNTAINS AND VOLCANOES

The following list is a selection representative of important mountains. It contains one or more of the higher peaks in various regions of the world, includes some of the greatest volcanic mountains, and embraces also a number of the most active volcanoes. All volcanic mountains, including extinct, quiescent, and active volcanoes, are in italics; some of the more active volcanoes are indicated by an asterisk thus, Stromboli*.

NAME OF MOUNTAIN OR PEAK	Location	Height Feet
Aconcagua	Chile-Argentina	22,835
Adams	Washington	12,307
Altar	Ecuador	17,300
Ancohuma	Bolivia	21,489
Antisana	Ecuador	18,714
Apo	Philippine Is.	9,690
Ararat	Turkey	16,945
Arequipa (Misti)	Peru	20,013
Asama*	Japan	8,200
Aso-San*	Japan	5,225
Baker	Washington	10,750
Baldy Peak	New Mexico	12,491
Bandai-San*	Japan	5,968
Ben Nevis	Scotland	4,406
Blackburn	Alaska	16,140
Borah Peak	Idaho	12,655
Bruce	Australia	4,024
Cayambe	Ecuador	19,014
Cenis, Mt.	France	11,755
Chimborazo	Ecuador	20,577
Chinati Peak	Texas	7,730
Clingmans Dome	Tennessee	6,642
Colima*	Mexico	14,240
Cook	New Zealand	12,349
Cosiguina	Nicaragua	2,776
Cotopaxi*	Ecuador	19,344
Cradle	Australia	5,069
Crillon	Alaska	12,725
Demavend	Iran	18,600
Dhaulagiri	Nepal	26,810
Elbert	Colorado	14,431
Elbrus	Russia	18,481
Elgon	Uganda-Kenya	14,178
Erebus*	Antarctica	13,202
Etna*	Sicily	10,705
Everest	Nepal	29,002
Fairweather	British Columbia	15,300
Fuego*	Guatemala	12,582
Fuji	Japan	12,388
Galdhoppigen	Norway	8,097
Gannett Peak	Wyoming	13,785
Godwin-Austen (K 2)	Kashmir	28,250
Haleakala	Hawaii	10,032
Hekla*	Iceland	4,707
Hermon	Syria-Lebanon	9,232
Holy Cross	Colorado	13,986
Hood	Oregon	11,245
Huascaran	Peru	22,205
Humphreys Peak	Chile-Argentina	19,130
Illampu (Sorata)	Bolivia	21,275
Illimani	Bolivia	21,185
Izalco*	El Salvador	6,184
Iztaccihuatl	Mexico	17,342
Jorullo	Mexico	4,330
Jungfrau	Switzerland	13,653
Kanchenjunga	India-Nepal	28,156
Katahdin	Maine	5,268
Katmai*	Alaska	7,000
Kenya	Kenya	17,040
Kilauea*	Hawaii	4,000
Kilimanjaro (Kibo Peak)	Tanzania	19,565
Kings Peak	Utah	13,498
Kosciusko	Australia	7,305
Lassen*	California	10,453
Lebanon	Lebanon	10,131
Llullaillaco	Chile	22,015
Logan, Mt.	Yukon	19,850
Loma Tina	Dominican Rep.	9,239
Longs Peak	Colorado	14,255
McKinley	Alaska	20,270
Maipu	Chile-Argentina	17,355
Marcy	New York	5,344
Margherita	Uganda-Congo	16,795
Matterhorn	Switzerland	14,701
Mauna Kea	Hawaii	13,825
Mauna Loa*	Hawaii	13,675
Mercedario	Argentina	21,885
Mitchell	North Carolina	6,684
Mont Blanc	France	15,781
Monte Rosa	Italy	15,203
Morrison	Formosa	14,000

NAME OF MOUNTAIN OR PEAK	Location	Height Feet
Mount of Olives	Jordan	2,680
Olympus	Greece	9,570
Orizaba	Mexico	18,700
Orohena	Tahiti	7,618
Parnassus	Greece	8,062
Peaks of Otter	Virginia	4,001
Pelée*	Martinique, W.I.	4,429
Perdu, Mont	France	10,997
Perote, Cofre de	Mexico	14,048
Pico, Peak of	Azores	7,611
Pikes Peak	Colorado	14,110
Popocatepetl	Mexico	17,877
Rainier	Washington	14,408
Robson	British Columbia	12,972
Rogers	Virginia	5,720
Roraima	Venezuela	9,219
Ruapehu	New Zealand	9,175
Sajama	Bolivia	21,047
Saint Elias	Alaska	18,008
Saint Helens	Washington	9,671
San Francisco	Arizona	12,655
San Miguel*	El Salvador	7,064
Shasta	California	14,162
Simplon	Switzerland	11,117
Sinai, Mt. (Jebal Musa)	Egypt	7,359
Sir Sanford	British Columbia	11,590
Snehaetta	Norway	7,550
Snowdon	Wales	3,560
Soufrière, La*	St. Vincent, W.I.	4,048
Spruce Knob	West Virginia	4,860
Stromboli*	Lipari Is., N. of Sicily	3,038
Teide	Canary Is.	12,000
Terror	Antarctica	10,750
Tolima	Colombia	18,438
Toluca	Mexico	15,020
Truchas	New Mexico	13,110
Tungurahua*	Ecuador	16,512
Tupungato	Chile-Argentina	21,490
Vancouver	Alaska-Yukon	15,700
Vesuvius*	Italy	3,891
Washington	New Hampshire	6,288
Wheeler Peak	Nevada	13,058
Whitney	California	14,495
Wrangell	Alaska	14,005

IMPORTANT MOUNTAIN PASSES

PASS	Location	Altitude (feet)
Athabaska	Alberta	5,736
Berthoud	Colorado	11,314
Bolan	Baluchistan	5,880
Brenner	Austrian Alps	4,495
Cajon	California	3,800
Chilkat	Yukon	4,950
Chilkoot	Alaska	3,500
Crownest	Alberta	4,450
Donner	California	7,135
Fremont	Colorado	11,318
Kearsarge	California	11,823
Khyber	Afghanistan	3,500
Kicking Horse	Alberta-Br.Col.	5,339
Kootenay (North)	Alberta	6,774
Kootenay (South)	Alberta	7,100
La Veta	Colorado	9,382
Logan	Montana	6,664
Loveland	Colorado	11,992
Mont Cenis	France	6,831
Rabbit Ears	Colorado	9,680
Raton	Colorado	7,834
Rogers	British Columbia	4,340
St. Bernard, Great	Swiss Alps	8,100
St. Gotthard	Swiss Alps	6,936
San Gorgonio	California	2,804
Shipka	Bulgaria	4,166
Simplon	Swiss Alps	6,589
Simpson	Alberta	6,650
Tehachapi	California	3,790
Tennessee	Colorado	10,424
Truckee	California	5,800
Uspallata (Cumbre)	Chile	12,650
Vermilion	Alberta	5,264
White Pass	Alaska-Br.Col.	2,888
Wolf Creek	Colorado	10,850
Yellowhead (Tete Jaune)	Alberta-Br.Col.	3,711

Name	Location	Dependency, Territory, or part of	Discovery, Conquest, or Settlement By Whom †	Date	Area Sq. Mi.	Population	Chief City or Town
Aleutian	Bering S.-Pac. O.	Alaska	Russians	1741	6,821	8,500	Unalaska
Azores	Atl. O. W. of Port.	Portugal	Cabral, *P.*	1432	893	603,000	Ponta Delgada
Baffin	Arctic O.	Canada	Baffin, *E.*	1616	183,870	2,052	Cape Dorset
Bahama	Atl. O. E. of Fla.	Bahama*	Columbus, *S.*	1492	5,353	168,812	Nassau
Balearic	Mediterranean S.	Spain	Romans	123‡	1,936	542,000	Palma
Barbados	West Indies	Barbados*	British	1625	166	254,000	Bridgetown
Bermuda	Atl. O. N. of W. Ind.	Great Britain	Bermudez, *S.*	1515	21	53,000	Hamilton
Borneo	East Indies	Indonesia, Malaysia	De Gomez, *P.*	1518	288,150	5,200,000	Banjermasin
Bornholms	Baltic Sea	Denmark	Norse	B.C.?	217	47,017	Rönne
Canary Is.	Atl. O. W. of Afr.	Spain	French	1334	2,807	1,160,000	Las Palmas
Cape Verde	Atl. O. W. of Afr.	Portugal	Cadamosta, *P.*	1456	1,557	272,071	São Vicente
Ceylon	Ind. O. S. of India	Sri Lanka*	Portuguese	1505	25,332	12,711,143	Colombo
Corsica	Mediterranean S.	France	Phocaeans	560‡	3,367	219,300	Bastia
Crete	Mediterranean S.	Greece	Prehistoric	3400‡	3,218	456,642	Heraklion
Cuba	West Indies	Cuba*	Columbus, *S.*	1492	44,206	9,170,000	Havana
Cyprus	Mediterranean S.	Cyprus*	Egyptians	1500‡	3,572	631,778	Nicosia
Elba	Mediterranean S.	Italy	Romans	B.C.	86	28,500	Portoferraio
Falkland Is.	Atlantic O.	Great Britain	Davis, *E.*	1592	4,700	1,759	Stanley
Faroe	N. Atlantic O.	Denmark	Norwegians	9th c.	540	40,441	Thorshavn
Fiji	S. Pacific Ocean	Fiji*	Tasman, *D.*	1643	7,055	535,357	Suva
Gotland	Baltic Sea	Sweden	Swedes	9th c.	1,225	54,174	Visby
Great Britain	Atl. O.-North Sea.	Great Britain	Romans	55‡	88,752	53,978,538	London
Greenland	Arctic O.	Denmark	Norwegians	982	840,000	49,502	Julianehaab
Guadeloupe	West Indies	France	Columbus, *S.*	1493	657	334,000	Pointe-à-Pitre
Guam	East Indies	United States	Magellan, *P.*	1521	209	86,926	Agana
Hawaiian Is.**	Pacific Ocean	United States	Jas. Cook, *E.*	1778	6,425	769,913	Honolulu
Hispaniola	West Indies	Haiti Dom. Rep.*	Columbus, *S.*	1492	29,400	8,456,005	Port au Prince
Iceland	No. Atlantic O.	Iceland*	Norwegians	870	39,758	216,628	Reykjavik
Ireland	Irish S.-Atl. O.	British Isles	Ancient Celts	B.C.	32,598	4,514,313	Dublin
Isle of Man	Irish Sea	Great Britain	Ancient Celts	B.C.	211	56,289	Douglas
Isle of Wight	English Channel	Great Britain	Romans	43	147	109,284	Newport
Jamaica	West Indies	Jamaica*	Columbus, *S.*	1494	4,411	1,861,300	Kingston
Japan ††	S. of Japan-Pac. O.	Japan*	Portuguese	1542	142,726	108,430,000	Tokyo
Java	East Indies	Indonesia	Portuguese	1511	51,032	76,000,000	Jakarta
Long Island	Long Is. So.-Atl. O.	New York	Hudson, *E.*	1609	1,723	6,403,852	Brooklyn
Macias Nguema	G. of Guinea, Afr.	Equatorial Guinea	Portuguese	1486	782	62,612	Malabo
Madagascar (Malagasy)	Ind. O. E. of Afr.	Malagasy*	Portuguese	1506	229,233	7,185,000	Tananarive
Madeira	Atl. O. W. of Afr.	Portugal	Portuguese	1419	308	269,000	Funchal
Malta	Mediterranean S.	Malta*	Phœnicians	1000‡	122	317,980	Valletta
Manhattan	Hudson R.-East R.	United States	Verrazano, *I.*	1524	22	1,509,327	New York§
Marshall Is.	N. Pacific	U. S. Trustee	British	1788	160	25,044	Jabor
Martinique	West Indies	France	Spanish	1493	420	342,000	Fort de France
Mauritius	Ind. O. E. of Afr.	Mauritius*	Portuguese	1505	720	826,199	Port Louis
Nantucket	Atlantic O.	Massachusetts	Gosnold, *E.*	1602	57	3,824	Nantucket
New Caledonia	Oceania	France	Jas. Cook, *E.*	1774	7,374	131,665	Noumea
Newfoundland	Atlantic O.	Canada	Cabot, *E.*	1497	143,045	522,104	St. John's
New Guinea	East Indies	Australia	Portuguese	1526	316,615	2,489,935	Port Moresby
New Zealand‡‡	Tasman S.-S. Pac.O.	New Zealand*	Tasman, *D.*	1642	103,736	3,105,400	Auckland
Novaya Zemlya	Barents S.-Kava S.	Russia	English	1556	31,900	100	
Orkney	Atlantic Ocean	Scotland	Ancient Picts	B.C.?	376	17,462	Kirkwall
Philippines§§	East Indies	Philippines*	Magellan, *P.*	1521	115,830	42,517,330	Manila
Prince Edward	G. of St. Lawrence	Canada	Cabot, *E.*	1497	2,184	111,641	Charlottetown
Puerto Rico	West Indies	United States	Columbus, *S.*	1493	3,435	2,712,033	San Juan
Réunion	Ind. O. E. of Afr.	France	Portuguese	1513	969	476,700	St. Denis
Saint Helena	S. Atl. O. W. of Afr.	Great Britain	Portuguese	1502	47	4,952	Jamestown
Sakhalin	Okhotsk S.	Russia	Dutch	1650	24,560	631,000	Alexandrovsk
Samoa, Amer.	S. Pacific Ocean	United States	Roggoveen, *D.*	1722	76	27,159	Pago Pago
Santa Catalina	G. of St. Catalina.	California	Cabrillo, *P.*	1542	85	1,457	Avalon
Sardinia	Mediterranean S.	Italy	Carthaginians	500‡	9,301	1,473,800	Cagliara
Shetland	Atl. O.-North Sea.	Scotland	Ancient Picts	B.C.?	550	18,445	Lerwick
Sicily	Mediterranean S.	Italy	Phœnicians	1000‡	9,925	4,680,715	Palermo
Spitsbergen (Svalbard)	Arctic Ocean	Norway	Barents, *D.*	1596	24,294	3,472	Longyearbyen
Staten	New York Bay	United States	Verrazano, *I.*	1524	60	221,981	New York§
Sulawesi (Celebes)	East Indies	Indonesia	Portuguese	1512	72,986	8,500,000	Makassar
Sumatra	East Indies	Indonesia	Portuguese	1508	167,480	20,800,000	Medan
Tahiti	S. Pacific Ocean	France	Spain	1606	402	84,552	Papeete
Taiwan (Formosa)	China Sea	Nationalist China	Portuguese	1590	13,892	16,500,000	Taipei
Tasmania	Bass St.-Ant. O.	Australia	Tasman, *D.*	1642	26,215	400,431	Hobart
Tierra del Fuego	St. of Magellan-Antarctic O.	Chile-Argentina	Magellan, *P.*	1520	8,074	8,000	Ushuaia
Trinidad	West Indies	Trinidad and Tobago	Columbus, *S.*	1498	1,864	892,317	Port of Spain
Vancouver	St.of Georgia-Pac.O.	Brit. Columbia	Vancouver, *E.*	1792	12,408	333,950	Victoria
Victoria	Arctic O.	Canada			81,930	41,878	
Virgin Is.	West Indies	United States	Columbus, *S.*	1493	133	63,200	Charlotte Amalie
Zanzibar	Ind. O. E. of Afr.	Tanzania	Egyptians	B.C.	640	190,117	Zanzibar

* Independent state. † Capital letters in italics, following names, indicate nationality of the discovery, thus *D.* signifies Dutch; *E.*, English; *I.*, Italian; *P.*, Portuguese; *S.*, Spanish. ‡ Before Christ. § Island forms part of New York City. ** Seven inhabited is., largest being Hawaii (4,021 sq.m.), Maui (728 sq.m.), Oahu (589 sq.m.). †† Four main islands, largest being Honshu (88,925 sq.m.). ‡‡ Two largest islands in group: South I. (58,093 sq.m.) and North I. (44,281 sq.m.). §§ Two largest islands in group: Luzon (40,420 sq.m.) and Mindanao (36,537 sq.m.).

NAME	Location	Length Miles	Drainage Basin Sq. Miles	Outlet	Largest City or Town on Banks
Amazon	South America	3,400	2,500,000	Atlantic Ocean	Pará
Amur	Northeastern Asia	2,700	780,000	Sakhalin Gulf	Blagovieschtchensk
Arkansas	United States	2,000	189,000	Mississippi R.	Tulsa
Assiniboine	Manitoba-Saskatchewan	450	52,600	Red R. of North	Winnipeg
Athabasca	Alberta	765	58,910	Lake Athabasca	Athabaska
Brahmaputra	India-Pakistan	1,800	425,000	Bay of Bengal	Dibrughur
Clyde	Scotland	100	1,480	Irish Sea	Glasgow
Colorado	United States-Mexico	2,000	250,000	G. of Cal.	Yuma
Columbia	Canada-United States	1,400	298,000	Pacific Ocean	Vancouver, Wash.
Congo	W. Equat. Africa	3,000	1,500,000	Atlantic Ocean	Kinshasa
Connecticut	New England	350	11,000	Long Is. Sound	Hartford
Cumberland	S. E. United States	688	18,000	Ohio River	Nashville
Danube	Southeastern Europe	1,750	300,000	Black Sea	Vienna
Darling	Australia	1,160	200,000	Murray River	Bourke
Delaware	E. United States	360	12,012	Delaware Bay	Philadelphia
Dnieper	S. European Russia	1,400	202,000	Black Sea	Kiev
Don	S. E. European Russia	1,300	166,000	Sea of Azov	Rostov
Douro	Spain-Portugal	500	37,500	Atlantic Ocean	Porto
Dvina	Russia	1,000	140,000	White Sea	Archangel
Ebro	Spain	470	30,000	Mediterranean Sea	Saragossa
Elbe	Germany	700	55,000	North Sea	Hamburg
Euphrates	Syria, Iraq	1,700	260,000	Persian Gulf	Basra
Fraser	British Columbia	750	91,700	Strait of Georgia	New Westminster
Ganges	India	1,500	400,000	Bay of Bengal	Cawnpore
Hudson	New York	300	13,000	New York Bay	New York
Hwang	China	2,600	400,000	Gulf of Pechili	Lanchow
Indus	Pakistan	1,800	372,000	Arabian Sea	Hyderabad
Irrawaddy	Burma	1,250	158,000	Bay of Bengal	Mandalay
Jordan	Jordan	200	1,500	Dead Sea	
Kuskokwim	Alaska	700	50,000	Bering Sea	Bethel
Lena	Siberia	2,800	900,000	Arctic Ocean	Yakutsk
Loire	France	650	45,000	Bay of Biscay	Nantes
Mackenzie	N. W. Terr., Canada	2,525	680,000	Arctic Ocean	Ft. Providence
Marne	France	325	4,894	Seine	Chalôns-sur-Marne
Mekong	Indo-China	2,600	280,000	South China Sea	Phnom Penh
Meuse	Belgium-France	575	12,740	North Sea	Liège
Mississippi	United States	2,500	725,000	Gulf of Mexico	Saint Louis
Missouri	United States	3,000	525,000	Mississippi R.	Kansas City
Missouri-Mississippi*	United States-Canada	4,200	1,250,000	Gulf of Mexico	Saint Louis
Murray	Australia	1,450	270,000	Indian Ocean	Albury
Nelson*	Canada	1,660	370,000	Hudson Bay	Port Nelson
Niger	Western Africa	2,600	600,000	Gulf of Guinea	Bamako
Nile	Cent. and N. E. Africa	4,145	1,100,000	Mediterranean Sea	Cairo
Ob	N. W. Siberia	2,500	1,125,200	Gulf of Ob	Barnaul
Oder	Germany-Poland	560	43,000	Baltic Sea	Breslau
Ohio	Eastern United States	975	214,000	Mississippi R.	Pittsburgh
Orange	Southwestern Africa	1,300	400,000	Atlantic Ocean	Hopetown
Orinoco	South America	1,500	368,000	Atlantic Ocean	Ciudad Bolivar
Ottawa	Ontario-Quebec	685	86,000	St. Lawrence R.	Ottawa
Peace	British Columbia-Alberta	1,065	117,000	Slave River	Peace River
Plata-Parana*	South America	2,500	1,200,000	Atlantic Ocean	Rosario
Po	Italy	420	27,000	Adriatic Sea	Turin
Potomac	Eastern United States	450	15,000	Chesapeake Bay	Washington
Red	Texas-Arkansas	1,200	90,000	Mississippi R.	Shreveport
Red River of the North	United States-Canada	545	63,400	Lake Winnipeg	Winnipeg
Rhine	N. W. Europe	800	75,000	North Sea	Cologne
Rhone	France	500	38,000	Mediterranean Sea	Lyon
Rio Grande	S. W. United States	2,000	240,000	Gulf of Mexico	El Paso
Sacramento	California	400	27,100	Suisun Bay	Sacramento
Saguenay	Quebec, Canada	405	35,900	St. Lawrence	Chicoutimi
St. Lawrence	United States-Canada	750	500,000	Gulf of St. Law.	Montreal
San Francisco	Eastern Brazil	1,800	200,000	Atlantic Ocean	Penedo
San Joaquin	California	350	30,000	Sacramento R.	Stockton
Seine	France	480	30,000	English Channel	Paris
Shannon	Ireland	250	4,500	Atlantic Ocean	Limerick
Susquehanna	N. E. United States	500		Chesapeake Bay	Harrisburg
Tagus	Portugal	565	31,850	Atlantic Ocean	Lisbon
Tennessee	S. E. United States	1,200	44,000	Ohio River	Knoxville
Thames	England	215	6,000	North Sea	London
Tiber	Italy	240	6,840	Mediterranean	Rome
Ural	Russia	1,400	85,000	Caspian Sea	Orenburg
Vistula	Poland-Danzig	650	76,000	Baltic Sea	Warsaw
Volga	Russia	2,300	563,300	Caspian Sea	Saratov
Weser	Germany	300	18,530	North Sea	Bremen
Yangtze	China	3,300	650,000	East China Sea	Nanking
Yenisei	Mongolia-Siberia	3,000	1,000,000	Arctic Ocean	Krasnoyarsk
Yukon	Alaska-Canada	2,300	330,000	Bering Sea	Dawson
Zambezi	South Africa	2,200	600,000	Indian Ocean	Livingstone

* River system.

PRINCIPAL FRESH-WATER LAKES OF THE WORLD

NAME	Location	Area Sq. Miles	Elevation Above Sea Level	Depth	DISCOVERY OR EARLY EXPLORATION	
					By Whom	Date
			Feet	Feet		
Albert	Central Africa	1,800	2,100	20	Speke and Grant	1862
Athabasca. . . .	Alberta	2,762	697	Shallow	Hearne	1771
Baykal	Eastern Siberia, Asia . .	13,200	1,500	5,306		
Bangweulu . . .	Central Africa	1,670	3,700	15	Livingstone	1868
Cayuga . . .	New York	75	381	400		
Chad	French Sahara-Nigeria .	10,000	850	20	Denham and Clapperton	1823
Champlain . .	New York	600	93	300	Champlain	1609
Chapala . . .	Mexico	1,400	6,000			
Chautauqua . .	New York	35	1,300	. . . .	La Salle	1669
Como.	Italy	55½	650	1,365	Mentioned by Virgil . .	30 B. C.
Constance . . .	Switz.-Ger.-Aust. . . .	208	1,309	827	Lake Dwellers	Stone Age
Crater	Oregon	20	6,177	2,001	Hillman	1853
Edward	Central Africa	1,500	3,000	. . . .	Stanley	1876
Erie	United States-Canada .	9,968	573	210	Chaumont and Brebeuf .	1640
Garda	Italy	189	216	1,916	Described by Virgil . .	35 B. C.
Gatun	Panama, Cent. Amer. .	164	85			
Geneva	Switzerland-France . . .	225	1,230	1,095	Lake Dwellers	Stone Age
George	New York	50	323	400	Friar Jogues	1642
Great Bear . . .	N. W. Terr., Canada . .	12,200	450	270		
Great Slave . . .	N. W. Terr., Canada . .	11,170	391	650	Hearne	1771
Huron	United States-Canada .	22,978	581	750	Brulé and Le Caron . .	1615
Itasca	Minnesota	2	1,457	50	Schoolcraft	1832
Ladoga	European Russia	7,000	55	730		
Lake of the Woods	Ontario-Manitoba . . .	1,485	1,058	. . . .	De Noyon	1688
Lucerne	Switzerland	49	1,435	700	Scene of Tell legends . .	
Maggiore	Italy	82	636	1,220	*L. Verbanus* of Romans .	B. C.
Managua	Nicaragua, Cent. Amer. .	560	154	Unknown	Cordoba	1522
Michigan	United States	22,336	581	870	Nicolet	1634
Mweru	Congo (Kinshasa)-Zambia	1,700	3,189	. . . .	Livingstone	1867
Neuchatel . .	Switzerland	90	1,420	472	Lake Dwellers	Stone Age
Nicaragua . . .	Nicaragua, Cent. Amer. .	3,000	106	260	Cordoba	1522
Nipigon	Ontario	1,590	850			
Nipissing	Ontario	330	640	. . . .	Brulé and Le Caron . .	1615
Nyasa	Equatorial Africa . . .	14,200	1,645	2,580	Livingstone	1859
Okeechobee . . .	Florida	730	16	15	Spaniards—Fontaneda? .	1552?
Onega	European Russia	3,764	125	400		
Ontario	United States-Canada .	7,243	246	738	Champlain	1615
Rangeley	Maine	80	1,350			
Reindeer	Manitoba-Saskatchewan .	1,765	1,150			
Rudolf	Equatorial Africa . . .	3,500	1,250	. . . .	Count Teleki	1888
Seneca	New York	75	445	630		
Simcoe	Ontario	271	130	. . . .	Champlain	1615
Superior	United States-Canada .	32,060	602	1,012	Brulé	1622
Tahoe	California	200	6,275	1,650	John C. Fremont	1844
Tanganyika . . .	Equatorial Africa . . .	12,700	2,600	2,000	Speke and Burton . . .	1858
Tezcuco	Mexico	85	7,300	2	Cortes	1519
Titicaca	Bolivia-Peru	3,200	12,500	900	Ancient Incas	
Victoria	Equatorial Africa . . .	27,000	3,775	270	Speke	1858
Winnepesaukee .	New Hampshire	178	475	300	Johnson and Willard . .	1652
Winnipeg	Manitoba	9,398	710	70	Verendrye	1733
Winnipegosis . .	Manitoba	2,086	828	40	Verendrye	1736
Yellowstone . . .	Wyoming	140	7,740	300	Colter	1807

PRINCIPAL SALT-WATER LAKES OF THE WORLD

NAME	Area Square Miles	Location	Elevation Above Sea Level*	Depth
			Feet	Feet
Aral, Sea of	26,200	Kirghis-Khiva, W. Asiatic Russia	155	220
Balkash	8,600	Russian Central Asia	780	135
Caspian Sea	170,000	S. E. Europe-Western Asia	−86	3,000
Dead Sea	340	Palestine, S. W. Asia	−1,290	1,280
Eyre	3,600	South Australia	−35	Shallow
Great Salt Lake	1,750	Utah, W. United States	4,218	40
Issyk-Kul	2,230	Asiatic Russia	5,400	Unknown
Kuku-nor	2,300	Central China	10,000	Unknown
Maracaibo†	8,000	Venezuela, South America	Sea level	500
Salton Sea	266	S. E. California, North America	−280‡†	Shallow
Urumia	1,795	Azerbaijan, S. W. Asia	4,100	40
Van	1,400	Armenia, S. W. Asia	5,214	Unknown

* A minus sign indicates below sea level. † Partially fresh. ‡ Approximate level before the inflow from the Colorado river in 1905-06.

Country	Area (sq. miles)	Population		Capital	Largest City	Form of Gov't[1]
		Thousands	No. Per Sq. Mile			
Afghanistan	252,000	18,796	74.6	Kabul	Kabul	P.D.
Albania	11,100	2,578	214.2	Tirana	Tirana	P.R.
Algeria	896,593	16,275	18.2	Algiers	Algiers	Isl. Rep.
Argentina	1,072,168	25,050	23.4	Buenos Aires . .	Buenos Aires . .	M.O.
Australia	2,967,900	13,339	4.5	Canberra	Sydney	P.D.
Austria	32,375	7,528	282.5	Vienna	Vienna	Rep.
Bahamas	5,382	197	36.6	Nassau	Nassau	B.C.R.
Bahrain	256	239	933.6	Manama	Manama	
Bangladesh	55,126	74,991	1,360.4	Dacca	Dacca	B.C.R.
Barbados	166	244	1,469.9	Bridgetown . . .	Bridgetown . .	B.C.R.
Belgium	11,782	9,772	829.4	Brussels	Brussels	C.M.
Benin (Dahomey) . . .	43,475	3,029	69.7	Porto-Novo . . .	Cotonou	M.O.
Bhutan	18,000	1,146	63.7	Thimphu	Thimphu . . .	A.M.
Bolivia	424,165	5,470	12.9	Sucre[2]	La Paz	Rep.*
Botswana	222,000	661	3.0	Gaberones	Kanye	B.C.R.
Brazil	3,286,488	104,243	31.7	Brasilia	Sao Paulo . . .	M.O.
Bulgaria	42,823	8,706	202.7	Sofia	Sofia	P.R.
Burma	261,789	30,310	115.8	Rangoon	Rangoon	M.O.
Burundi	10,747	3,678	342.2	Bujumbura . . .	Bujumbura . . .	Rep.
Cambodia (Khmer Rep.)	69,898	7,888	112.9	Phnom Penh . . .	Phnom Penh . .	Rep.
Cameroon	179,558	6,282	35.0	Yaounde	Douala	Rep.
Canada	3,851,809	22,479	5.8	Ottawa	Montreal . . .	P.D.
Cape Verde Is.	1,557	291	186.9	Praia	Mindelo	Rep.
Central African Empire	241,305	1,752	7.3	Bangui	Bangui	M.O.
Chad	495,750	3,949	8.0	Fort-Lamy . . .	Fort-Lamy . . .	Rep.
Chile	292,258	10,405	35.6	Santiago	Santiago . . .	Rep.
China (Communist) . .	3,691,500	824,961	223.5	Peking	Shanghai . . .	P.R.
China (Nationalist) . .	13,893	15,701	1,130.1	Taipei	Taipei	Rep.
Colombia	439,737	23,952	54.5	Bogota	Bogota	Rep.
Comoro Islands . . .	863	298	345.3	Moroni	Moroni	Rep.
Congo (Brazzaville) . .	132,047	1,313	9.9	Brazzaville . . .	Brazzaville . .	Rep.*
Costa Rica	19,652	1,921	97.7	San Jose	San Jose . . .	Rep.
Cuba	42,827	9,090	212.2	Havana	Havana	Rep.*
Cyprus	3,572	641	179.5	Nicosia	Nicosia	B.C.R.
Czechoslovakia	49,374	14,686	297.4	Prague	Prague	S.R.
Democratic Yemen . .	61,890	1,590	25.7	Aden	Aden	Rep.
Denmark	16,630	5,045	303.4	Copenhagen . . .	Copenhagen . .	C.M.
Dominican Republic .	18,658	4,562	244.5	Santo Domingo	Santo Domingo .	Rep.
Ecuador	109,484	6,552	59.8	Quito	Guayaquil . . .	Rep.*
Egypt	386,900	36,417	94.1	Cairo	Cairo	Rep.
El Salvador	8,124	3,980	489.9	San Salvador . .	San Salvador .	Rep.
Equatorial Guinea . .	10,830	303	28.0	Santa Isabel . . .	Santa Isabel . .	Rep.
Ethiopia	471,800	27,239	57.7	Addis Ababa . . .	Addis Ababa . .	C.M.
Fiji	7,055	560	79.4	Suva	Suva	B.C.R.
Finland	130,129	4,682	36.0	Helsinki	Helsinki	Rep.
France	210,039	52,507	250.0	Paris	Paris	Rep.
Gabon	103,347	1,106	10.7	Libreville	Libreville . . .	Rep.
Gambia	4,467	510	114.2	Bathurst	Bathurst	B.C.R.
Germany, East	41,768	17,166	411.0	East Berlin . . .	East Berlin . .	D.R.
Germany, West (F.R.)	95,985	62,041	646.4	Bonn	Hamburg . . .	F.R.
West Berlin	186	2,173				
Ghana	92,100	9,607	104.3	Accra	Accra	Rep.
Greece	50,960	8,962	175.9	Athens	Athens	C.M.*
Grenada	133	107	804.5	St. George's . . .	St. George's . .	B.C.R.
Guatemala	42,042	5,175	123.1	Guatemala City .	Guatemala City	Rep.
Guinea	94,926	4,309	45.4	Conakry	Conakry . . .	Rep.
Guinea-Bissau	13,948	517	37.1	Bissau	Bissau	Rep.
Guyana	83,000	774	9.3	Georgetown . . .	Georgetown . .	B.C.R.
Haiti	10,714	4,514	421.3	Port-au-Prince . .	Port-au-Prince .	Rep.*
Honduras	43,277	2,654	61.3	Tegucigalpa . . .	Tegucigalpa . .	Rep.
Hungary	35,920	10,458	291.1	Budapest	Budapest . . .	P.R.
Iceland	39,769	215	5.4	Reykjavik	Reykjavik . . .	Rep.
India	1,266,602	586,266	462.9	New Delhi	Bombay	B.C.R.
Indonesia	782,663	127,586	163.0	Jakarta	Jakarta	Rep.
Iran	636,000	31,955	50.2	Teheran	Teheran	C.M.
Iraq	168,928	10,765	63.7	Baghdad	Baghdad	Rep.*
Ireland (Eire)	27,136	3,086	113.7	Dublin	Dublin	Rep.
Israel	7,992	3,299	412.8	Jerusalem	Tel Aviv-Jaffa .	Rep.
Italy	116,313	55,361	476.0	Rome	Rome	Rep.
Ivory Coast	123,484	6,673	54.0	Abidjan	Abidjan	Rep.
Jamaica	4,244	1,998	470.8	Kingston	Kingston . . .	P.D.
Japan	145,747	109,671	752.5	Tokyo	Tokyo	C.M.
Jordan	36,832	2,618	71.1	Amman	Amman	C.M.
Kenya	224,961	12,912	57.4	Nairobi	Nairobi	B.C.R.
Korea, North	46,800	15,439	329.9	Pyongyang . . .	Pyongyang . . .	P.R.
Korea, South	38,130	33,459	877.5	Seoul	Seoul	Rep.
Kuwait	6,880	929	135.0	Kuwait	Kuwait	R.M.
Laos	91,400	3,257	35.6	Vientiane	Vientiane . . .	C.M.
Lebanon	3,950	2,782	704.3	Beirut	Beirut	Rep.
Lesotho	11,720	1,016	86.7	Maseru	Maseru	R.M.*

Country	Area (sq. miles)	Population Thousands	Population No. Per Sq. Mile	Capital	Largest City	Form of Gov't[1]
Liberia	43,000	1,667	38.8	Monrovia	Monrovia	Rep.
Libya	675,000	2,352	3.5	Tripoli & Benghazi	Tripoli	M.O.
Luxembourg	999	342	342.3	Luxembourg	Luxembourg	C.M.
Malagasy, Rep. of	226,444	7,785	34.4	Tananarive	Tananarive	Rep.
Malawi	45,747	4,900	107.1	Zomba	Blantyre-Limbe	B.C.R.
Malaysia	127,316	11,700	91.9	Kuala Lumpur	Kuala Lumpur	C.M.
Maldive Islands	115	129	1,121.7	Male	Male	Rep.
Mali	478,822	5,557	11.6	Bamako	Bamako	Rep.*
Malta	122	298	2,442.6	Valletta	Valletta	B.C.R.
Mauritania	398,000	1,290	3.2	Nouakchott	Nouakchott	Isl. Rep.
Mauritius	787	872	1,108.0	Port-Louis	Port-Louis	B.C.R.
Mexico	761,604	58,118	76.3	Mexico City	Mexico City	Rep.
Mongolia	604,000	1,403	2.3	Ulan Bator	Ulan Bator	P.R.
Morocco	177,117	16,880	95.3	Rabat-Sale	Casablanca	C.M.
Mozambique	308,642	9,029	29.3	Maputo	Maputo	Rep.
Nepal	54,362	12,321	226.6	Katmandu	Katmandu	C.M.
Netherlands	15,892	13,541	852.1	Amsterdam[3]	Amsterdam	C.M.
New Zealand	103,736	3,027	29.2	Wellington	Christchurch	P.D.
Nicaragua	50,000	2,084	61.7	Managua	Managua	Rep.
Niger	489,000	4,476	9.2	Niamey	Niamey	Rep.
Nigeria	356,669	61,219	171.6	Lagos	Lagos	Rep.*
Norway	125,053	3,987	31.9	Oslo	Oslo	C.M.
Oman	82,000	743	9.1	Muscat	Salalah	Rep.
Pakistan	307,374	68,214	221.9	Islamabad	Karachi	Isl. Rep.
Panama	29,209	1,631	55.8	Panama City	Panama City	Rep.*
Papua New Guinea	178,260	2,652	14.9	Port Moresby	Port Moresby	B.C.R.
Paraguay	157,048	2,572	16.4	Asuncion	Asuncion	Rep.
Peru	496,224	14,531	29.3	Lima	Lima	M.O.
Philippines	115,800	41,457	358.0	Quezon City	Manila	Rep.
Poland	120,725	33,691	279.1	Warsaw	Warsaw	P.R.
Portugal	35,383	8,735	246.9	Lisbon	Lisbon	Rep.
Qatar	4,400	170	38.6	Doha	Doha	Rep.
Rhodesia	150,873	6,100	40.4	Salisbury	Bulawayo	B.C.R.
Rumania	91,700	21,029	229.3	Bucharest	Bucharest	S.R.
Rwanda	10,169	4,123	405.4	Kigali	Kigali	Rep.
Sao Tome & Principe	373	79	212.4	Sao Tome	Sao Tome	
Saudi Arabia	872,000	8,702	10.0	Riyadh	Riyadh	Mon.
Senegal	78,685	4,231	53.8	Dakar	Dakar	Rep.
Seychelles	107	58	542.1	Victoria	Victoria	B.C.R.
Sierra Leone	27,925	2,707	96.9	Freetown	Freetown	B.C.R.
Singapore	227	2,219	9,775.3	Singapore	Singapore	B.C.R.
Somalia	246,300	3,086	12.5	Mogadisho	Mogadisho	M.O.
South Africa	471,445	24,920	52.9	Pretoria[4]	Johannesburg	Rep.
Spain	194,885	35,225	180.7	Madrid	Madrid	C.S.
Sri Lanka (Ceylon)	25,332	13,679	540.0	Colombo	Colombo	B.C.R.
Sudan	967,500	17,324	17.9	Khartoum	Omdurman	M.O.
Surinam	70,060	385	5.5	Paramaribo	Paramaribo	Rep.
Swaziland	6,704	478	71.3	Mbabane	Mbabane	R.M.
Sweden	173,732	8,161	47.0	Stockholm	Stockholm	C.M.
Switzerland	15,943	6,481	406.5	Bern	Zurich	Rep.
Syria	71,772	6,303	99.6	Damascus	Damascus	Rep.*
Tanzania	364,943	14,763	40.5	Dar es Salaam	Dar es Salaam	B.C.R.
Thailand	198,250	39,950	206.7	Bangkok	Bangkok	C.M.
Togo	21,925	2,171	99.0	Lome	Lome	M.O.
Trinidad & Tobago	1,980	1,062	536.4	Port-of-Spain	Port-of-Spain	B.C.R.
Tunisia	63,379	5,641	89.0	Tunis	Tunis	Rep.
Turkey	300,948	38,270	127.2	Ankara	Istanbul	Rep.
Uganda	91,452	11,172	122.2	Kampala	Kampala	B.C.R.
U.S.S.R.	8,649,500	252,064	29.1	Moscow	Moscow	S.R.
United Arab Emirates	37,000	430	11.6	Abu Dhabi	Dubayy	Rep.
United Kingdom	94,217	56,056	595.0	London	London	C.M.
United States	3,615,122	211,909	58.6	Washington, D.C.	New York	Dem.
Upper Volta	105,869	5,895	55.7	Ouagadougou	Ouagadougou	Rep.
Uruguay	68,536	2,764	40.3	Montevideo	Montevideo	Rep.
Venezuela	352,144	11,557	32.8	Caracas	Caracas	Rep.
Vietnam	130,653	43,349	331.8	Hanoi	Hanoi	D.R.
Yemen Arab Rep.	77,200	5,238	67.8	Sana	Sana	Rep.
Yugoslavia	98,766	21,153	214.2	Belgrade	Belgrade	F.R.
Zaire	905,365	24,222	26.8	Kinshasa	Kinshasa	Rep.*
Zambia	290,586	4,751	16.3	Lusaka	Lusaka	B.C.R.

Present (1970) form of government, which may differ from the form that is supposed to exist. An asterisk (*) indicates that the basic form of government is being influenced by the military; the actual difference between Rep.* and M.O., thus, may be very little in many cases. Abbreviations used: B.C.R.—British Commonwealth member with republican government; C.M.—Constitutional Monarchy; C.S.—Corporate State; D.R.—Democratic Republic (Communist); F.R.—Federal Republic; I.P.—Indian Protectorate; Isl. Rep.—Islamic Republic; M.O.—Military Oligarchy; P.D.—Parliamentary Democracy; P.R.—People's Republic (Communist); Rep.—Republic; R.M.—Representative Monarchy; S.R.—Socialist Republic (Communist). [2] Actual seat of government is La Paz. [3] Actual seat of government is The Hague. [4] Administrative capital. Legislative capital is Capetown; judicial is Bloemfontein.

Source: 1969 population estimates by UN; local estimates used when no UN figures were available.

MEANINGS OF PLACE NAMES

IT is part of man's inquiring nature to be interested in the origin of things, but it was not until the 19th century that scholars began to investigate the origin of place-names by using scientific method. Before this, legend was usually employed to give meaning to a name whose origin was no longer self-evident. Historical documents are now carefully searched to find the earliest written form of a name and this is then interpreted by the language or dialect spoken in the area at that time. Even this is not valid if the meaning does not correspond with geographical or historical fact. Thus it is that many of the ancient names are still unintelligible.

This science of place-name study is called *toponymy* and it is a branch of *onomastics*, or the study of names in general. Apart from its intrinsic value in satisfying man's natural curiosity, toponymy also serves the student of language and history. Place-names often contain the only record of an extinct language and they can supply much valuable information on the origins and social customs of early peoples.

There are three main types of place-names and most names may be so classified, whether they originated in 10th century Asia, 15th century Europe, or 20th century America. *Habitation* names have evolved from the name of a tribe who once inhabited the area, or from the name of an individual who once owned the land. The countries of Iran, Bulgaria, Finland, France, and Belgium are but a few which have received their names from tribes who lived there. Nearly all the major tribes of the American Indians have left their trace on the map. Usually the names of individuals are commemorated in the names of villages or small towns.

Nature names describe the place itself, its surroundings, or its position relative to an outstanding landmark or other town. Often these names are composed of only one element, such as Bonn, Vigo, Chester, and Mons, which mean simply "the city," "the village," "the castle," "the mountain." More often they have a qualifying element as is found in the names of Tallahassee, Casablanca, and Reykjavik, which mean "old town," "white house," and "smoky bay."

Commemorative or *historical* names form the final group. These may recall either an historical event, a famous person, or another place. Nice and Tirana, Washington and Constantinople, New York and New Orleans, are all names of this type.

The map of North America contains a rich variety of names because they have been contributed by men of many nationalities. The French in Quebec and Louisiana, the Spanish in California and the Southwest, the Dutch in New York, as well as the native Indians have all left their mark. In addition, the names of many towns were given by settlers to recall their homes in Europe.

Acapulco (*ä'kä-pōōl'kô*). Mexican town. From the Aztec *acatl,pul,co*, "place covered with thick reeds."

Accra (*ăk'rà*). Capital of Ghana. The original tribe of fishermen who lived here were known to the natives of the interior as *Accras* derived from *nkran*, "ant."

Addis Ababa (*ăd'ĭs ăb'à-bä*). Ethiopian city. Founded in 1887 as the new capital and named by the Empress Taitu. The name is Amharic for "new flower" and refers to its ideal situation.

Adirondacks. The Algonquin Indians who lived in these mountains were nicknamed *Ratirontakeke*, "they eat, i.e., live from, the forest." Adirondack is a Mohawk variation.

Alcantara (*ăl-kăn'tà-rà*). Town in Spain. Arabic *Al-Kantara*, "the bridge." The Romans built a famous bridge here which was constructed without the use of mortar.

Alcatraz. Island in San Francisco Bay. Site of former U.S. penitentiary. Spanish *Isla de Alcatraces*, "island of pelicans." The Spaniards found the place covered with these birds when they discovered it in 1769.

Al-Mausil. City in Iraq. Arabic for "place of connection." It is the meeting place of the ancient trade routes. The cloth called *muslin* was formerly made here.

Amalfi (*ä-mäl'fê*). Italian resort. Arabic *Al-Marfa*, "the port, landing-place."

Amarillo. Texas city. Suggested by the yellow banks of the nearby creek or the yellow flowers that cover the prairie in the spring. Buildings were painted bright yellow after the town was named. *Amarillo* is Spanish for "yellow."

Amritsar (*ŭm-rĭt'sĕr*). Sacred city of India. Built around a pool named "nectar of immortality." The name is Sanskrit.

Amsterdam. Dutch city. Low German name meaning "dam of the people living on the Amstel River." Amstel itself means "water-bank."

Anaconda. City in Montana. The mine here was named from a newspaper account during the Civil War when "Grant circled Lee like a giant anaconda."

Anacortes (*ăn'à-kôr'tĕs*). City in Washington State. Originally named after the wife of the founder, Anna Curtis. Later altered to agree with the Spanish sound of other local names.

Anatolia. Ancient name of Asia Minor. From the Greek *anatole*, "rising of the sun."

Andes. South American mountain range. This Quichu Indian name means "metal" but refers especially to the copper which is mined here.

Androscoggin (*ăn'drŭs-kŏg'ĭn*). Maine river. Abnaki Indian for "place where fish are cured" by drying or smoking.

Angostura. Now Ciudad Bolivar, Venezuela. Located on the narrowest point on the Orinoco, it receives its name from the Spanish word for "narrow." Angostura bitters are from here.

Anticosti. Large island in the Gulf of St. Lawrence. Most authorities see in the name a transposition of the Montagnais Indian name *Natiscotec* which means "place where bears are hunted."

Antigua (*ăn-tē'gà*). West Indian island. Columbus named the island in honor of the church of Santa Maria la Antigua ("the old") in Seville.

Antofagasta. City in Chile. "Place where copper is hidden" in the Quechuan Indian language.

Antwerp. Belgian port. Old Low German *aend-werp*, "against the dike or dam" referring to the original site of the city.

Aorangi (*ä'ô-räng'ê*). Maori name for Mt. Cook, highest peak in New Zealand. Maori *ao*, "cloud" and *rangi*, "sky." The peak is often covered with clouds.

Aral Sea. U.S.S.R. Its many willow-covered islands give this large inland sea its name. From the Kirghiz *aral*, "willow-plot."

Arctic (*ärk'tĭk*). The northern constellation known as the Great Bear is seen in this region. From the Greek *arktos*, "bear."

Argentina. The poet Barco Centenera first used the word Argentina in his poem of the same name in 1602. He was referring to the country's situation on the banks of the Plata River. The name is Spanish for "silvery."

Aroostook. River in Maine. Micmac Indian for "shining river."

Ascot. Village in England, the home of the Royal Ascot races. "Eastern cottage or sheep shelter." From Old English *east-cot*.

Asuncion. Capital of Paraguay. Named in honor of Our Lady of the Assumption. The name is Spanish.

Atacama. Desert in Chile. The Spanish form of Quechua Indian *tacama*, a type of black duck. These birds inhabit the area near the coast.

Atchafalaya (*à-chăf'à-lī'à*). River and bay in Louisiana. "Long river" in the Choctaw language.

Atlantic. The ocean is named after the mythical island of Atlantis which was supposed to lie in the waters west of Mt. Atlas from which the name originated.

Australia. As early as the 16th century, various terms derived from the Latin *australis*, "southern," were applied by mapmakers to lands south of Asia.

Austria. Latinized form of German *Oster-reich*, the "eastern kingdom" of the Franks.

Azores. Islands in the Atlantic. Portuguese *Ilhas do Acores*, "Islands of hawks."

Bahrein (*bä-rīn'*). Islands in the Persian Gulf. Arabic "two seas," applied to land having water on both sides.

Baikal (bī-käl'). The largest lake of Siberia. The lake has an abundance of fresh-water salmon. The term *bai-kol* is Turko-Tatar for "rich take."

Balkan. Mountain range and peninsula in southeastern Europe. This Turkish term meaning "mountain" was first used in 1808.

Ballarat. City of Australia. Officially *Ballaarat*, an aboriginal name meaning "camping-place." A swamp which was here was a favorite with the natives.

Baltimore. Maryland city. Cecil Calvert, Lord Baltimore, opened up the colony of Maryland. The barons of Baltimore came from *Bailena-tigh-mhor*, "town of the large house" in Ireland.

Bangkok. Capital of Thailand. In the Thai language this means "the place where the wild olives grow."

Basel (bä'zĕl). Swiss city. This name is derived from Celtic word which means "boar." The Gauls were devoted to a God in the form of a pig whose image has been found on many coins.

Beirut (bā-root'). Capital of Lebanon. From the Phoenician *b'eroth*, "wells."

Belem. City in Brazil. Named in honor of Our Lady of Bethlehem, Portuguese *Belém*. The mental hospital in London, England called St. Mary of Bethlehem is the origin of our word *bedlam*.

Belfast. City in Northern Ireland, hence the town in Maine. Gaelic *Beal-feirste*, "ford at the sandbar" was the place where the Lagan River was crossed.

Belgrade. Capital of Yugoslavia. Serbian *Beograd*, "White City." In olden times the city shone white in the sun.

Belleek. Town in Ireland famous for its pottery. Gaelic *Beal-leice*, "ford-mouth of the flagstones."

Berezina. Russian river. Scene of battle during Napoleon's retreat from Moscow. Old Slavic *beréza*, "birch tree." The river banks were formerly covered with birch.

Berlin. German city. A wooden scaffolding was formerly erected over the river and was used to collect floating timbers and for fishing. Old Slavic *bruleni*, "water-rake."

Bethlehem. A village in Palestine. The name is from the Syrian *beit el lehm*, "house of bread." The city in Pennsylvania was named while some German settlers were singing carols in a stable here on Christmas Eve in 1741.

Biarritz (byà'rĕts'). French city. "Place of the twin oaks," from the basque *haritz*, "oak-tree."

Bihar (bē-här'). Town and state in India. The Sanskrit word *vihara* means "monastery." There was formerly a large Buddhist monastery here.

Bismarck. Capital of North Dakota. Originally Edwinton, but the name was changed by an overseas shipping agent in 1873 in honor of the German Chancellor. It was hoped that German settlers would thus be attracted.

Biwa. Largest lake in Japan. The lake is similar in shape to the Japanese *biwa*, a mandolin-type musical instrument.

Bizerte (bē'zĕrt'). Tunisian city. A gross Arabic corruption of *Hippo Diarrhytus*, a hybrid name from Phoenician *hippo*, "city" and a Greek term meaning "traversed by running waters."

Blarney. Castle in Ireland containing the Blarney stone. Irish *Blárna*, diminutive of Middle Irish *blár*, "field."

Blenheim. German *Blindheim*. Village in Bavaria; site of famous battle in 1704. "Settlement in a blind valley."

Bombay. City in India. Portuguese corruption of the vernacular name *Mumbai*. There was a temple here dedicated to the goddess of the Koli fishermen, *Mumba*, or the "Great Mother."

Bonin Islands. South of Japan. Corrupted from Japanese *Munin*, "uninhabited." There were no natives on the islands when discovered by the Japanese about the year 1600.

Bonn. Capital of West Germany. Originally a Gaulish settlement whose name is simply a Celtic word for "city."

Bothnia. Gulf between Sweden and Finland. Lies on the eastern shores of *Botten*, a Swedish district. Old Norse *botn* means "valley bottom."

Bowery. Street in New York City. English spelling of Dutch *boererij*, "farm." Originally this was a lane which led to the farm of Peter Stuyvesant.

Brazos. River of Texas. Originally Spanish *Brazos de Dios*, "Arm of God." A mission on the river was destroyed by the Indians but the Spaniards believed it to be the work of God.

Bremen. German port. Middle High German *brëme*, "bank, shore."

Britain. From the Old French Bretaigne. Great Britain refers to the British Isles as opposed to Little Britain or *Brittany* in France. Both names refer to the home of the *Britons*, who were a Celtic people. The name is related to the Welsh word *pryd*, "picture," and refers to the custom of the Britons of tattooing themselves.

Brooklyn. Named by Dutch settlers after the town of Breukelen in the Netherlands. This name, originally *Broklede*, means "water-course through a swamp."

Bruges (broozh). City in Belgium. Although this name is usually associated with Low German *brügge*, "bridge," it is actually the Old Norse *bryggja*, "quay or landing-place." Named by the Vikings.

Brussels. Capital of Belgium. Records of the year 1107 show *Brucsella*, "house in the swamp."

Bryn Mawr. Suburb of Philadelphia. The railway station here was named after a local country estate which was so called after an ancestral seat in Wales. It is Welsh for "great hill."

Buffalo. This city in New York State was built on Buffalo Creek. The creek name is probably derived from the name of a local Seneca chief rather than from the animal itself.

Bulawayo. City in Southern Rhodesia. Zulu for "place of killing." Rebellious members of the Indunas tribe were formerly executed here.

Bulgaria. "Country of the Bulgars." From the Old Turkish *bulgar*, "mongrol, cross-breed," alluding to the mixture of races in this people.

Cadiz. City in Spain. Arabic *Gades*, from a Phoenician word related to the Hebrew *gader*, "protecting wall."

Cairo. Capital of Egypt. A Venetian corruption of the Arabic *Qahir al-Falak*, "The Triumphant of Heaven." The planet Mars was in the ascendant when the city was laid out.

Calcutta. City in India. Sanskrit *Kali-ghat*, "ghat of the Goddess Kali." A ghat is a flight of stairs leading to a river for the convenience of ritual bathers.

Calicut. City in India. Officially *Kozhikode*, meaning "cockfort." On his retirement, the last king of Malabar gave the Zamorin of Calicut as much land as was within earshot of a cock's crow.

Callao. Peruvian seaport. A Spanish word meaning "gravel" referring to the stony nature of the beach.

Calumet. River in Illinois which has given its name to the industrial district at the southern end of Lake Michigan. The name is French for "reed." The reeds which grew along the banks of the river were made into "pipes," *calumets*, by the Indians.

Cambodia. Republic in southeast Asia. A European form of *Kambuja*. Kambu was the mythical founder of the Khmer race which settled here.

Cambridge. University town in England and city in Massachusetts. Old English *Grantebrycg*, "Bridge on the Granta River." *Granta*, which is from a Celtic root meaning "muddy," was altered to *Cam* through Norman French influence.

Cameroon. African republic. Named for the Cameroon River. Early navigators found many prawns here and called the river, *Rio dos Camaroes*, "River of shrimps, or prawns."

Canada. Apparently derived from the Huron-Iroquois *kanata*, "village, collection of tents." The name is first mentioned in Jacques Cartier's narrative of 1534 and referred to a village called Stadacona where Quebec City now stands. Gradually extended to southern Ontario and Quebec and thence to the whole dominion.

Cannes (kăn). Resort on the French Riviera. This was originally a Phoenician settlement and contains the same Semitic root found in the name of the Biblical town of Cana. The name means "place of reeds." The English word *cane* is related.

Canton. City in China. This is a variation of *Kwangtung*, the Chinese province of which Canton is the capital. The area in southern China formerly known as *Kwang* was divided into the two provinces of *Kwangtung*, "Eastern Kwang," and *Kwangsi*, "Western Kwang."

Canton. City in Ohio. Named in the mistaken belief that it was directly opposite the city of Canton in China.

Cardiff. Chief city of Wales. The Welsh name is *Caer ar Daf*, "Fort on the Taff River." A Roman station was established here during the conquest of Britain.

Carlow. County in Ireland. Irish *Cetherloch*, literally "Quadruple Lake." The Barrow River anciently formed four lakes here.

Carmel. Mountain in Israel and many places in America. In historical times Mount Carmel was famous for the luxurious growth of plants on its slopes. Hebrew for "garden, orchard."

Carnegie. Old Scottish barony which was the seat of the Carnegie family. Gaelic *Cathair-an-eige*, "Fort at the Gap." This would refer to a mountain pass.

Carrara (*kà-rär'à*). Italian town famous for its marble. From the Ligurian *caris, cararis*, "rock, stone."

Cartagena. City in Spain whose name has been transferred to cities in South America. Named after the ancient city of Carthage in North Africa. Phoenician for "new city."

Castile. Medieval kingdom of Spain. Spanish *Castilla* means "place of many castles."

Catamarca. City and province in Argentina. From the Kechua Indian *q'atamarca*, "village of the mountain slope." This city lies at the foot of the Sierra de Ambato.

Catskill. Creek and mountains in New York. *Kill* is a Dutch word for "creek" and the name means "creek of the cats or panthers."

Caucasus. Mountain range in southeastern Europe. The modern name comes from the Greek *Kaukasia*. The basic Indo-European root is seen in the Lithuanian word *kaukas*, "hill," and the English word *high*.

Chattanooga. City in Tennessee. A simplification of the Cree Indian *Chat-to-to-noog-gee*, "rock rising to a point." This was the native name for Lookout Mountain.

Cheddar. Gorge in England famous for its cheese. Earlier recorded as *Ceodre*, from the Old English *ceod*, "pouch." This would refer to the shape of the gorge.

Chemnitz. City in East Germany. A Slavic name meaning "stony river."

Chesterfield. Town in England. Old English *Cestrefeld*, "field by the Roman fortification." The word *cestre* is derived from Latin *castrum*, "fort" which is the origin of the French *chateau* and place-names such as *Castile, Lancaster, Winchester*.

Cheyenne. Capital of Wyoming. Named after the Cheyenne Indians. This is a French version of the name given to them by the Dakota Indians meaning "the red-talkers," that is, "those who speak in a strange tongue."

Chicago. French rendition of a native name. It is Algonquin Indian for "wild-onion place." The wild-onion or garlic formerly covered the low, marshy plain.

Chimborazo. Volcano in Ecuador. From the Kechua Indian *cimpu*, "multi-colored woolen threads" and *rasu*, "snowy peak." The debris on the slopes resembles the woolen threads in the *llautu* or headband worn by the Incas.

China. Named after the Ts'in Dynasty which ruled in China in the Third Century B. C.

Cimarron. River in New Mexico. Originally the Spanish word *cimarron* meant "wooded; mountainous," but later it was applied to anything that was wild or unruly.

Cincinnati. This city in Ohio was named in honor of the Society of the Cincinnati. This society was formed in 1783 by a group of officers in the Continental Army before its disbanding and was named after the Roman hero Cincinnatus.

Clare. Town and county of Ireland. A board was once used to cross over the River Fergus at this point. *Clar* is the Irish word for "plank."

Clyde. Scottish river famous for its shipbuilding. From a Celtic root meaning the "cleanser." Possibly in honor of a river goddess.

Coburg. City in West Germany. Formerly *Choburg* from a Slavic *chov*, "shelter." It means "the fort of refuge."

Cochabamba. City and department in Bolivia. Literally, Kechua Indian for "lake-plain." The natives used the term *bamba* (from which the word *pampas* is derived) for any barren expanse,

Cochise. Town and county in Arizona. Named in honor of Chief Cochise, the leader of the Chiricahua Apaches.

Coeur D'Alene. City in Idaho. This is the French name of the Skitswash Indians and means "awl-heart." It is said to have been applied by an Indian chief to indicate the size of a trader's heart.

Coleraine. Town in Northern Ireland. Gaelic *Cuil Raithin*, "ferny nook or corner."

Cologne. West German city where *eau-de-cologne*, or "water of Cologne" was originally made. Established by the Emperor Augustus as *Colonia Agrippina*, "colony or settlement of Agrippina." It was the birthplace of Agrippina, the wife of Augustus.

Colon. City in the Canal Zone. This place-name, like Columbus, Colombia, British Columbia, etc., was named in honor of Christopher Columbus. It is the Spanish form of the name.

Concepcion. City in Chile. Like many places in South America, this name commemorates a Feast of the Blessed Virgin. Concepcion alludes to her Immaculate Conception.

Connemara. District in the west of Ireland. Gaelic *Conmacne-Mara*, "place by the sea where the descendants of Chief Conmac reside."

Constantinople. Old name of Istanbul, Turkey. A Greek name meaning "City of Constantine." The Emperor Constantine made the old city of Byzanz the capital of Eastern Roman Empire in the year 330. The Greek word *polis*, "city" enters into the names *Naples, Tripoli*, and others.

Copenhagen. Capital of Denmark. Old Danish *København*, "Port of merchants." Copenhagen was the center of commerce for the western Baltic.

Corcovado. Mountain at Rio de Janeiro whose summit supports a famous statue of Christ. Portuguese *corcovado*, "hunchbacked," describes the shape of the peak.

Cork. City and county of Ireland. Originally *Corcachmor* which is Gaelic for "great swamp." A district in the city is still known as "The Marsh."

Corregidor. Island at the entrance to Manila Bay, Philippines. Ships formerly stopped here to have their paper checked and corrected. Spanish *corregidor* means "corrector."

Correggio. Town in northern Italy; home of Correggio, the artist. In the dialect of northern Italy the word *coréza*, from which this place-name is derived, means "a strip of land in the middle of a marsh."

Corvallis. Town in Oregon. From the Latin words *cor*, "heart" and *vallis*, "of the valley." Corvallis lies in the middle of the Willamette Valley.

Cotopaxi. Volcano in Ecuador. Kechua Indian *q'utu p'asi*, "smoky mound."

Couchiching. Ontario lake. The lake discharges the waters of Lake Simcoe into the Severn River. From Algonquin *kotchichi*, "discharge, emptying."

Coventry. English cathedral city. Old English *Cofentreo*. The town grew up around a tree belonging to a man called Cofa.

Crimea. Russian peninsula in the Black Sea. At the time of the Bosphoran Empire a protective moat and embankment were built across the isthmus here. From the Turkish word for "trench," *kyrym*.

Croatia. Ancient kingdom, now a federated republic of Yugoslavia. "Land of the Croats." The Croats are a Slavic people whose name originally derives from Old Persian *haurvata*, "shepherd." The French form of the name, *Cravate*, is the origin of our word *cravat*. This was originally a neckpiece worn by Croatian soldiers.

Cuba. Arawak Indian for "land." The apparent reference is to the island as the Mainland as opposed to the Lesser Antilles.

Cumberland. County in England, thence Cumberland Gap in Tennessee and many American place-names. "Land of the Cumbrians." The Cumbrians were Britons who inhabited the ancient kingdom of Strathclyde, which embraced Cumberland. Their name derives from Welsh *Cymry*, "compatriots."

Curitiba (*kōō'rê-tê'và*). City in Brazil. Guarani Indian *curi*, a type of pine tree, probably the Araucaria. Literally, a "place of pine trees."

Cusco. City in Peru; former capital of the Incas. From the Kechua Indian word *qusqu*, "navel." The city lies in the middle of a valley.

Dachau (*däk'ou*). City in West Germany. From Old High German *daha*, "clay," and *aue*, "watery place." The site of the original settlement was in a clay-rich swamp.

Dahomey. Republic of Africa. In the native language this is literally "the belly of Dan." In the 17th century a native king murdered a petty chief and built a house over his corpse. The chief's name was Dan, hence the original name, *Danhomé*.

Dalmatia. Coastal region of Yugoslavia. Home of the Illyrian tribe called *Delmatae* or "shepherds." Dalmatian dogs originated here.

Danube. European river. Its Celtic name was *Danuvius*, from an Indo-European root with the basic meaning of "that which flows or gushes."

Dar es Salaam. African seaport. Arabic *Bandar es Salaam*, "Harbor of Peace." So called by the Sultan of Zanzibar when he established a base here in the mid-19th century.

Darjeeling. Indian town in the Himalayas. From the Tibetan *Rdo-rje-gling*, "place of the dorje." A *dorje* is a mystical thunderbolt in Lamanist religion.

Darmstadt. City in West Germany. "Town on the Darm River." The Darm is named from Old High German *darm*, "intestine." There are many twists and turns in the river.

Denmark. Old Norse *Danmork*, "Country of the Danes." The Danes were originally a Germanic people who inhabited the marshy hollows of southern Jutland. Their name is related to the Old English word *dene*, "hollow, small valley."

Denver. English village. Ancestral home of the Denver family. From Old English *Dena faer*, "passage or road of the Danes." Denver, Colorado was named in honor of J. W. Denver, a Governor of Kansas Territory.

Derbent. City of the U.S.S.R. on the Caspian Sea. A defile here, called the Caspian Gates, locked the route through the Caucasus Mountains. From Persian *derbend*, "bolt, lock."

Derby. County town of Derbyshire, England. The 12th Earl of Derby established the Derby stakes at Epsom Downs; hence any similar annual race is called a *derby*. From Old Norse *djur-byr*, "homestead frequented by deer."

Detroit. City in Michigan. Founded in 1701 as Fort Pontchartrain du Detroit. The French word *detroit*, "straight, narrows," refers to the Detroit River.

Dnepr, Dnestr. Two great rivers of the U.S.S.R. Formerly *Danapris* and *Danastius*, which are Scythian names with the probable meaning of "nearer river" and "further river."

Dominica. Island in the West Indies. Spanish for "Sunday." It was discovered on a Sunday by Columbus.

Donegal. Irish county. English version of *Dun-na-nGall*, "fort of the foreigners." The "foreigners" were the Danes, who had an earthen fortification here before the 12th century.

Dordrecht. City in the Netherlands. Middle Dutch *Thur-drecht*, "through-channel." The city was built on a short stretch of water between the Dubbel and Mewerde Rivers.

Drammen. Norwegian river and city. Old Norse *Drofn*, related to the German word *trübe*, "gloomy." Indo-European rivers often have names signifying "dark, dismal, gloomy."

Dresden. City in East Germany. A Slavic name from Wendish *Drazhdzhanj*, "home of the forest-people."

Dublin. Capital of the Republic of Ireland. Irish *Dubhlinn*, "black pool." This was the name of that part of the Liffey River on which the city is built. Irish-speaking people refer to the city as *Baile-atha-cliath*, "town of the ford made of hurdles."

Dubuque. City in Iowa. Julien Dubuque, a French-Canadian trader settled here in 1788 in order to mine.

Dundee. Scottish city. Gaelic for "Fortress on the Dee River." The Dee, originally *Devona*, honors a river goddess.

Dunkirk. Town on the Belgian coast. Flemish *Dunkerque*, "church on the sand-dunes."

Durham. English city and county. Norman corruption of Old English *Dun-holm*, "hill-island." The city is built on a rocky hill nearly surrounded by the Wear River.

Durham. City in North Carolina. Originally Plattsburg, the name was changed in 1851 to honor Dr. Bartlett Durham whose forebears were from Durham, England.

Dusseldorf. City in West Germany. German *dorf* means "village." The name of the Dussel River derives from Old High German *doson*, "to rage, roar." Hence, "village on the banks of the roaring river."

Eboli. Town in Italy. Modern form of Celtic *Eburum*, "place of the yew tree."

Edmonton. Town in England and city in Alberta. Old English *Eadhelmstun*, "the homestead of Adhelm."

Egypt. Probably from an epithet of the city of Memphis, "Hi-ku-Ptah," which means "house of the spirit of Ptah." Ptah was one of the chief gods of ancient Egypt.

El Paso. City in Texas. In the year 1598, the Spaniards crossed the Rio Grande here and called the ford *El Paso del Norte*, "The Pass of the North."

El Salvador. Republic of Central America. So named in 1524 by Pedro de Alvarado in honor of Our Blessed Saviour (Span. *Salvador*).

Engadine. Swiss alpine valley. *En co de Ino* is the Raeto-Romansch form of Latin *in capite Eni*, land lying at "the head or source of the Inn River."

Erfurt. East German city. "Ford on the Erf River." *Erf* is a Germanic river-name meaning "brown-colored."

Erie. One of the Great Lakes and a city in Pennsylvania. Named after the Erie Indians. It is a French form of their original name of *Yenrish*, "Long-tailed." This tribe held the panther sacred.

Eritrea. Self-governing state in the Ethiopian federation. This territory lies on the shore of the Red Sea and its name is derived from the Greek *Ereuthre thalassa*, "Red Sea."

Essen. Industrial city in West Germany. In 898 written *Astnide* from Middle Low German *ast*, "forge." Therefore, "place of the forge."

Essex. County in England and many towns in North America. Old English *East Seaxe*, "East Saxons" as distinguished from the West and South Saxons.

Estonia. One of the Baltic states. "Land of the *Aestii*." This was a Germanic tribe who once lived on the shores of the Gulf of Riga and whose name possibly derives from the Latin *aestuarium*, "tidal waters, estuary."

Ethiopia. Republic in northeast Africa. From the Greek *aithein*, "to burn," and *ops*, "sight, face." This is the land of the people who have dark skin, literally, "burnt faces."

Faroe. Danish islands in the North Atlantic. Old Norse *faer*, "sheep." The islands still support large herds of sheep.

Foggia. Italian city. This name is derived ultimately from the Latin word *fossa*, "ditch, trench." In the dialect of North Italy, however, it refers to a place for threshing grain.

Formosa. The name the Portuguese navigators gave to the island of Taiwan in 1590. It is Portuguese for "beautiful."

Forth, Firth of. The long estuary of the Firth River, Scotland. Gaelic *Foirthe* from a Celtic *Vo-ritia*, "running under," hence, "the river with strong undercurrents."

France. "The land of the Franks." The name of the Franks is probably derived from a Germanic word related to Old English *franca*, "spear, javelin."

Frankfurt. The name of two German cities. German for "Ford of the Franks." The *frankfurter* originated here.

Fresno. City and county in California. From Spanish *fresno*, "ash-tree."

Funchal. City in the Madeira Islands. "Place where fennel grew," from the Spanish word for fennel, *funcho*.

Fundy. Bay between New Brunswick and Nova Scotia. It is an Anglicized form of the name *Fond de la Baie*, "far end of the bay," which appeared on French maps.

Galapagos (gȧ-lä′pȧ-gŭs). Pacific islands belonging to Ecuador. This is the Spanish name for a species of turtles found here.

Galilee. Sea in Israel and district of Palestine in Biblical times. From the Aramaic *galil*, "ring or circle," with reference to the fact that it was surrounded by Gentiles or foreigners.

Galle. Seaport of Ceylon. The place is built on a rocky promontory and named Haycock Hill. In the Sinhalese language, *gala* means "rock, hill." The Portuguese confused this with the Latin word for "rooster," *gallus*.

Garda. Lake in northern Italy. Named after the Veronese castle which *guarded* the military road near here.

Gaspe (gȧs′pā). Peninsula in the province of Quebec. Micmac Indian for "end of the earth."

Gaza. Town and strip of land between Egypt and Israel. A stronghold of the Phoenicians in ancient times, the place derives its name from their word *'azzah*, "firmness, strength." Gauze is said to have been first made here.

Gdansk. Polish city on the Baltic Sea. Germanic *Gutiskandje* means "end or coast of the Goths." Danzig is the German name.

Gdynia. Polish city. German *Gdingen*, from *G(u)dingen*, "place of the Goths."

Geneva. Swiss city. Originally *Genava*, a Ligurian name which means "knee or bend." The city is situated in a deep corner at the east end of Lake Geneva.

Gethsemane. Garden outside Jerusalem. This is the Aramaic name for a vat in which oil was stored after being pressed from olives. There was probably such a vat here as it is close to the Mount of Olives.

Gibralter. Named after Tariq Ben Zaid, the Moorish conqueror of the Visigoths. Arabic *Gabal Tariq*, "Mount of Tariq."

Gilead. Mountainous region of Palestine. Aramaic for "rugged country" as opposed to the fertile plain of Bashan.

Ginza. Main street of Tokyo. Literally "silver place." It derives the name from the silver mint which was located here.

Gonzaga. Town in northern Italy; home of St. Aloysius Gonzaga. Originally *Verecundiaca* or "property of Verecundius." Verecundius is a Latin personal-name meaning "modesty."

Gouda. Dutch town famous for its cheese. The town lies near the Gouwe River which was called *Golda* in the 12th century. It is Low German for "gold river" and refers to the yellowish-colored, muddy water.

Gramercy Park. New York City. Known to the Dutch settlers as *Krum Marisje*, "crooked little swamp."

Greenland. An English literal translation of Old Norse name. It actually means "new land" and not "green-colored land."

Guiana. Region in northern South America shared by the English, French, and Dutch. English spelling of Spanish *Gauyana*. The parrot which is native to the area is called by the Carib Indians *wayana*, and this is the origin of the place-name.

Guinea. Republic in northwestern Africa. The name is a European form of a Berber phrase meaning "land of the black men."

Hague, The. Capital of the Netherlands. Officially 's Gravenhage, "The Count's Hedge." First mentioned in the year 1242 as the residence of Count William II of Holland, *Die Haghe*.

Hainan. Chinese island. From the Chinese *hai*, "sea," and *nan*, "south." It lies in the sea south of the southern mainland.

Hainault. Province of Belgium. "Meadow on the Hagna River." The name Hagna comes from a Low German word meaning "hedge."

Haiti. Republic in the West Indies. The Arawak natives called the country *Aiti*, which in their language meant "mountainous."

Halifax. Cities in England and Nova Scotia. In the 12th century, *Haliflax*, Old English for "sacred flax field."

Hamburg. City in West Germany. From Old Saxon *hamme*, "enclosed place." The fort built here in the 9th century was once surrounded by trees.

Hanover. Cities in Germany and the United States. The German spelling is *Hannover*. From the German phrase *zum hohen Ufer*, "at the high bank." The city is built on the bank of the Leine River.

Hardwar (hŭr'dwär). Sacred town in India. Sanskrit *Hari dwara*, "capital of Hara." Hara is a title of the Hindu god Siva.

Harlech. Welsh castle and town. The Romans built a castle on a rock here. Welsh *hardd*, "beautiful," and *llech*, "rock." The same Celtic root may be seen in the name *Belleek*.

Hartford. City in Connecticut. Founded by settlers from Massachusetts led by Samuel Stone who was born in Hertford (originally *Hartford*), England. It means "Ford of the stag."

Heidelberg. City in West Germany. "Mountain of the heathberry." This is the same as the English bilberry.

Hereford. Town and county in England; many American towns. Old English *here-ford*, "army ford." This would be where a marching column could cross the river in closed order.

Hialeah. Suburb of Miami with famous racetrack. Named by Willie Willie, an Indian chief, whose town occupied the site until the end of the 1920's. Seminole-Creek Indian *haiyakpo-hili*, "pretty prairie."

Himalayas. Asian mountain range. The peaks are perpetually covered with snow. The name is Sanskrit for "abode of the snows."

Hiroshima. Japanese city. In 1594 a feudal lord built his castle here and named it *Hiro-shima-jo*, "Castle of the Broad Island."

Hoboken. City in New Jersey. Dutch settlers named the place after the town of Hobuechen, Holland. It means "place of the tall beech tree."

Holland. Former name of the Netherlands and still the name of a region. Originally *Holtland*, "wood-land." This part of the country was densely wooded in ancient times.

Holstein (hōl'stīn). Former duchy of Denmark and now part of the province of Schleswig-Holstein, West Germany. The Old Low German name was *Holt-seten*, "home of the forest-dwellers."

Honduras. Republic in Central America. Spanish for "depths." It is not known if the reference is to the coastal waters or to the inland valleys.

Hong Kong. British colony off the Chinese coast. Chinese *H'eng K'eng*, "Water-channel or harbour of the fragrant flowers."

Honolulu. Capital of Hawaii. The first element *hono* is common to many Hawaiian place-names and means "bay, gulch, or valley." Honolulu is "the sheltered bay."

Honshu. Largest island of Japan. Japanese for "main-land."

Hunan. Chinese province. Region "south of the lakes."

Hungary. The area was settled by the Ten Tribes of Oguz, Turkish *on ogur*, whose name was Latinized to *Ungari*. The initial *H* is by attraction to the name of the Huns.

Innsbruck. City in Austria. German for "bridge on the Inn River." The river-name is Celtic but the meaning is doubtful.

Iran. Old Persian *Airyana*, "Land of the Aryans." The Aryans were an Indo-European people who occupied the major portion of the country in historical times.

Iraq. That part of the Tigris-Euphrates Valley known as Babylonia was once called *'Iraq*, which is Arabic for "cliff."

Irrawaddy. River of Burma. Sanskrit *Iravati*, "giver of refreshment."

Israel. The origin of the name given in Genesis 32:22 is merely folk-etymology. More probably from the Semitic root *ishr*, "reliable, happy," referring to an ancient Canaanite god of fertility.

Istanbul. Capital of Turkey. The Byzantines referred to Constantinople, which was the former name, simply as *The City*. Hence the Greek phrase, *eis ten polin*, "to or in the city," from which the modern name is derived.

Italy. "Land of the Itali." The tribal name is derived from the Oscan dialect *Viteliu*, "young cattle," honoring Mars who was the god of bulls.

Iwo Jima. Japanese island. Japanese *iwo-shima*, "sulphur island." At one time there were important sulphur mines here.

Jaffa. City in Israel. A city established by the Phoenicians and mentioned in the Bible as *Joppa*. The name is Semitic and means "beautiful place."

Jakarta. Capital of Indonesia. It was named *Jayakarta*, "prosperous on account of victory," in 1527 after a successful battle there.

Jamaica. The abundance of springs on this West Indian island prompted the Arawak Indians to call it *Jaymaca* or "Island of Springs."

Japan. This is a 15th century Dutch corruption of the Chinese name *Jih-pen*, "Place of the Sun's Origin."

Jena. City in East Germany. Middle High German *jan*, "row of mowed hay or compost."

Jerusalem. Shalem was the local god of pre-Israelite Jerusalem. The name may be interpreted as "the foundation or city of Shalem."

Jodhpur. City in India. It was established by Rao Jodha in the year 1459 and called "City of Jodha." Riding breeches known as *jodhpurs* originated here.

Jordan. River of the Bible; thence the country through which it now flows. The river drops 1300 feet in its course and was known to the Hebrews as "the descender."

Kalgoorlie. Town and famous gold field in Australia. A shrub known to the aborigines as *galgurli* was a prominent feature of the local landscape.

Kanchenjunga (kŭn'chĕn-jŭng'gä). Mountain in the Himalayas and the 3rd highest in the world. Its five peaks are perpetually covered with snow, hence the Tibetan name, "the five repositories of the great snow."

Kandahar. City in Afghanistan. Founded in 330 B. C. by Alexander the Great. The name is a corruption of the original *Alexandria Arachosiarum*, "Alexandria of the Arachosian people."

Kanpur. City in northern India known as Cawnpore during the British rule. Sanskrit for "City of Kahn." Kahn is one of the names of the Hindu god Krishna and means "husband."

Katmandu. Capital of Nepal. A wooden temple was built here in 1596 for religious mendicants. Sanskrit *kath*, "wood," and *mandu*, "palace, temple."

Kennebec. River in Maine. The Abnaki Indian name meaning "long water" originally referred to the stretch between Skowhegan and Merrymeeting Bay.

Kent. County in England, and the name of many American towns. Known to Julius Caesar as *Cantium*, the area's name probably derives from Celtic *canto-*, "rim, border" as applied to a coastal district.

Khartoum. Capital of the Sudan. The Arabic name is *Rasel-Khartum*, "Cape of the Elephant's Trunk." At high water on the Nile, a spit of land having the shape of an elephant's trunk appears near here.

Kiel. City and canal in Germany. From the Low German phrase *tom Kyle*, "on the creek or inlet," referring to its position on Kiel Bay. The same word is the second element of the *Catskills*.

Kilimanjaro. Mountain in Tanganyika; highest in Africa. A native name which may be roughly translated as "mountain of the cold devils."

Killarney. Town and lakes in Ireland. Irish *Cill-airne*, "church of the sloes or blackthorn bushes."

Kirghiz. Soviet Republic in Asia. Home of the Kirghiz people. Their name comes from Kirghiz *kyr*, "wilderness" and *gizmak*, "to wander." It refers to their nomadic life.

Klondike. River and gold field in the Yukon Territory. This is a mispronunciation of the Indian *Thron-diuk*, "hammer-water." The natives hammered stakes across the shallow mouth of the river on which they hung their nets.

Koevorden. Town in the Netherlands. From Dutch *koe-voord*, "ford of the cows or oxen." This is the ancestral home of Capt. George Vancouver whose family name was originally Van Koevorden.

Kostroma. River, city and oblast of the U.S.S.R. Russian *koster'* is a type of sturgeon which abounded in the river.

Kuala Lumpur. Capital of Malaysia. In the Malayan tongue, *kuala* refers to any place where a river empties. *Lumpur* means "muddy." The waters here were muddied by the work of Chinese miners.

Kuwait. A shiekdom on the Persian Gulf. The name, which is a diminutive of Arabic *kut*, and meaning "small fort," was given by early settlers to the stronghold built in the center of the original tented village.

Labrador. That part of the Province of Newfoundland which is on the Canadian mainland. First noted on a map of 1534 as "land of the Labrador." The pilot on the English ship which sighted land here was a labrador (Spanish for "laborer") from the Azores.

Ladoga. Large lake in northwestern U.S.S.R. From the Finnish *aaldokas*, "tossed, disturbed." The waters of this lake are extremely rough in bad weather.

Lagos. Capital of Nigeria. Named by Portuguese explorers for the many lagoons and coastal lakes in the neighborhood. Portuguese *lago* means "lake."

La Jolla. Suburb of San Diego, California. This is a variant spelling of Spanish *hoya*, "pit, cavity," hence the pronunciation. It was the name of a rancheria in a hollow.

Lancaster. County town of Lancashire, England and a city in Pennsylvania. Old English *Loncestre*, "Roman fort on the River Lune." Lune is a Celtic river-name meaning "health-giving."

La Paz. Capital of Bolivia. Originally, in Spanish, *Pueblo Nuevo de Nuestra Senora de la Paz*, "New Town of Our Lady of the Peace." The name commemorates the treaty signed between two rival groups of Spanish *conquistadores* in 1548.

Laredo. Village in Spain and city in Texas. Nuevo Laredo is a Mexican city across the Rio Grande from Laredo. The name is related to Spanish *gleria*, "gravel" and refers to the stony river banks.

Las Vegas. City in Nevada and town in New Mexico. The Spanish word *vega*, "open plain," aptly describes the surrounding desert.

Latakia (*lăt'ȧ-kē'ȧ*). City and territory of Syria, famous for its tobacco. The Greek name was *Laodicea*, given by Seleucus Nicator in honor of his mother Laodice.

Latvia. Former Baltic state now part of the U.S.S.R. The country is named for the Late River near the Lithuanian border. The river-name is Lettish for "marshy, swampy."

Lausanne. City in Switzerland. Like many names in this area, this one is Celtic and proves that the Celts were here in ancient times. It means "river of the flat stones."

Lebanon. A country in Western Asia on the Mediterranean. From a Semitic word meaning "the white." It probably refers to the snowy peaks of the Lebanon Mountains.

Leipzig. City in East Germany. This is the German form of Slavic *Lipsk*, from *lipa*, "linden tree."

Lepanto. Strait in Greece where a famous naval battle was fought between the European powers and Turkey in 1571. An Italian corruption of Modern Greek *Epaktos*, originally *Naupaktos*, "place where ships were built."

Levant. Name applied to the eastern regions of the Mediterranean. A French term from the Latin *levans*, "rising," referring to the rising of the sun.

Lhasa. Capital of Tibet. Long known as "The Forbidden City" because of its inaccessibility. Tibetan *lha-sa*, "land of God." It is a holy city and the residence of the Dalai Lama.

Liberia. Republic of western Africa. The American Colonization Society settled emancipated American slaves here in 1822. The Latin name, meaning "land of the free," commemorates their new-found freedom.

Lido. Island reef off Venice, Italy, famous as a resort. Latin *litus*, "beach."

Lille. French city where lisle fabric was first made. In the 11th century Flemish counts built a chateau here in the midst of a marsh. French *l'isle* is an old spelling for "island."

Lima. Capital of Peru. Spanish corruption of *Rimac*, the name of the river on which it lies. It is Kechua Indian *rimaq*, "talking," hence "noisy."

Limburg. Provinces of Belgium and the Netherlands famous for Limburger cheese. The castle of *Lintburch*, "fortress of the linden tree," gives the modern name.

Limehouse. District of London. There were many limekilns here from medieval times until quite recently. From Old English *lim-ast*, "lime oast or kiln."

Limerick. City and county of Ireland. Irish *Luimneach*, a diminutive form of *lomm*, and meaning "little bare spot of land."

Limoges. French city famous for its porcelain. In ancient Gaul this was the home of the tribe of *Lemovici*, or "warriors of Lemos." The modern name is derived from the tribal name.

Lincoln. Cities in England and Nebraska. The Latin name was *Lindon colonia*, "colony or settlement of Lindon." Lindon is a Celtic name meaning "lake" and refers to the widening of the Witham River here.

Lithuania. Former Baltic state now part of the U.S.S.R. This is a Latinization of Lithuania *Lietuva*, "coastland."

Liverpool. English seaport and towns in New York and Pennsylvania. The name refers to a pool of thick, clotted water.

Lorelei. Rock in the Rhine River on which a siren is supposed to have sat and lured sailors to their destruction. From Middle High German *lure-lei*, "ambush-rock."

Los Angeles. Originally *Reina de los Angeles*, "Queen of the Angels," a name given by the Spanish in honor of Our Lady of the Angels of Portiuncula. The stream on which the city was built was discovered on this feast-day.

Lourdes. French town and shrine. From the Basque *lorr-d-e*, "rocky height extending into space."

Loyola. Castle in Spain where St. Ignatius Loyola was born. From the Basque *lloi-ola*, "muddy place."

Luxembourg. Duchy in Europe and province of Belgium. Formerly *Lutzelburg*, from Old High German *luzzil-burh*, "little fortress."

Madeira. Portuguese islands off the coast of Morocco. They are famous for their wines. Early navigators were impressed by the forests of large, unusual trees which they brought back to the King of Portugal. It is the Portuguese word *madeira*, "wood."

Madrid. Capital of Spain. First mentioned as *Magrit*, a name from a north African dialect meaning "aqueduct." There were many aqueducts built here by the Arabs to bring water from the mountains to the dry plains.

Majorca. The largest of the Balearic Islands in the Mediterranean. From the Latin *major*, "older, larger," as opposed to Minorca from the Latin *minor*, "younger, smaller."

Malaga. City in Spain. Founded as a commercial center by the Phoenicians and called by them *Malaka*, "workshop, factory."

Mali. Republic of northwest Africa. The Mandingo tribe called any capital city *Mali*, or "place where the king lives." The name was later extended to their entire empire.

Managua. Capital of Nicaragua. Named after the Barbados cherry tree which grew there. It is a name given by the Arawaks.

Mangalore. City in India. Sanskrit *Mangalapura*, "City of Good Fortune."

Manila. Former capital of the Philippines. Tagalog *ma-nilad*, "place of nilads." The nilad is the plant *Ixora Manila*, a white, blossoming shrub which once grew here in profusion.

Mauna Loa. Semi-active volcano of Hawaii. A native name which means "long mountain."

Mayo. Irish town and county. St. Colman established a monastery here in the 12th century which he called *Magh-eo*, "plain of the yew trees."

Mazatlan. City on the west coast of Mexico. "Place of deer," from the Aztec word *mazatl*, "deer."

Mecca. One of the capital cities of Saudi Arabia. Arabian *Makkah*, "Sanctuary." This holy city of the Moslems is surrounded by an inviolable territory.

Mecklenburg. Former German state and the name of two American counties. *Mikilinburg* was the chief fortress of the Obortites, a Slavonic tribe who succeeded the Teutons in the 6th century. Its name is Germanic, however, and means "large fortress."

Melanesia. One of the three great divisions of the Pacific islands. The name is a Greek formation and means "island of the blacks." The Papuans, who are the prevailing tribe, have very dark skin.

Memphis. Capital of ancient Egypt and largest city in Tennessee. The old name, *Menfi*, is from the Egyptian name of the pyramid of Pepi I, *Men-nefer*. It probably means "his goodness endures."

Menlo Park. Village in New Jersey where Thos. Edison lived, and city in California. From Menlo Castle, Ireland, whose Irish name is *Mion Loch*, "small lake" as contrasted with Lough Corrib.

Menominee. River in Wisconsin. From the name of an Indian tribe which means "wild rice men." They lived mainly on the wild rice found in the lakes and rivers of their country.

Merrimack. River in Massachusetts and New Hampshire. This is a Pennacook Indian name meaning "deep place." The river is navigable as far as Haverhill.

Mesopotamia. Historical region now occupied by modern Iraq. The area between the Tigris and the Euphrates, hence its Greek name meaning "in the middle of the rivers."

Miami. City in Florida. Fontaneda spelled the name *Mayaimi* in 1575 and stated that it meant "very large." It is probably a compound of Choctaw *maiha*, "wide," and *mih*, "it is very." The Laguna de Mayaimi, which gave its name to the city, is now Lake Okeechobee.

Milan. City in northern Italy. Those who imported silks and ribbons from Milan for making hats, etc., were called Milaners; hence our word *millinery*. The Gaulish name was *Mediolanum*, "cleared portion of a wood."

Milwaukee. A Wisconsin river and city at its mouth. From Algonquin Indian *milo-aki*, "good land," referring to the country through which the river flows.

Minneapolis. Largest city in Minnesota. A name formed by adding the Greek word *polis*, "city," to the root of *Minnehaha*, "curling water," the name of the falls which are in the city still.

Mobile. City in Alabama. Name of an Indian tribe. It is probably connected with the Choctaw word *moeli*, "to row, paddle;" hence "the rowers."

Mojave. River and desert in California. Named after the Mojave Indians who lived here. Their name *Hamak-hava* referred to the center of tribal activities in the vicinity of the mountains known as the Needles and means "three mountains."

Moluccas. Indonesian islands. The Arabians gave them the name *Jazirat-al-Malik*, "Islands of the Kings." Each island used to have its own king.

Monaco (mon'à-kō). Independent principality in southern France. Originally a Phoenician settlement dedicated to *Melkarth*, "The Solitary One," a god corresponding to the Greek god Herakles. The Greeks later translated this as *Monoikos*, hence the present name.

Mongolia. Region in central Asia. "Land of the Mongols." The name of these people is generally believed to come from the Tartar word *mong*, "brave." The word *mogul* derives from the Persian form of their name.

Monrovia. Capital of Liberia. Named in honor of President James Monroe "as an acknowledgment of important benefits conferred on the Settlement by the present illustrious chief magistrate of the United States," in the words of the founders.

Monterey. City and bay in California. **Monterrey.** City in Mexico. Both named after the Count of Monterrey who was Viceroy of Mexico 1595–1603.

Moose Jaw. City in Saskatchewan. The Moose Jaw River makes a 90-degree turn here resembling the outline of a moose's jawbone.

Mostar. City in Yugoslavia. Serbo-Croatian *most*, "bridge," and *stary*, "old." The Turks built a bridge over the Neretva here in 1556.

Mourne. Mountains in Northern Ireland. Irish *Mughd-horna*, the tribal name of the MacMahons who lived here. They are descendents of the Celtic *Mugdornai*, "wearers of ankle-bands."

Multnomah. County in Oregon. This is the former name of the Willamette River and referred to that part of the river below the falls. It is a corruption of the Chinook *nematlnomag*, "down-river."

Munich. City in West Germany. The German name, *München*, is from the phrase *bei den Mönchen*, "near the monks." The reference is to its proximity to a monastery on the Tegernsee.

Murmansk. Port in the northern U.S.S.R. The name is a Russian corruption of Old Norse *Northmadhr*, "Northmen." It is literally "place of the Northmen," referring to the foundations of the early Vikings.

Muskegon. River and city in Michigan. Chippewa Indian *muskig*, "grassy bog." The course of the river through swamp land. The same Indian word has given us the word *muskeg*.

Mysore. City and state in India. From *Mahisur*, "buffalo town."

Nagasaki. Japanese city. In the latter part of the 12th century the district was given as a fief to Nagasaki Kotaro by the founder of the Kamakura Shogunate Government.

Nanking. Chinese city. "Southern Capital." This was the capital of China from 1928–1949.

Naples. City in Italy. From the Greek *Neapolis*, "New City." This type of name was often given to a place in a new colony.

Natchez. City in Mississippi. This is the name of an extinct Indian tribe who lived in the area. From Caddo Indian *Na'htcha*, "forest, timber-land."

Netherlands. European kingdom. Often called Holland from the name of two of its provinces. The name means "low-lying lands" and much of the country is below sea-level. Belgium and the Netherlands were once called the Low Countries.

Nevis. River and mountain in Scotland and island in the West Indies. A Celtic name meaning "misty, watery river."

Newark. Towns in England and city in New Jersey. Old English *niwe*, "new" and *(ge)weorc*, "fortification."

New Guinea. Island in the southwest Pacific. Named by the Spaniard Ynigo Ortiz de Retes in 1545 because he thought the natives resembled the Negroes of Guinea in Africa. Also called **Papua**.

New Orleans. Originally named by its French founders *La Nouvelle Orleans* after a city in France. See *Orleans*.

New Zealand. English form of the Dutch *Nieuw Zeeland*. Tasman gave this name to the islands to commemorate the Dutch province of *Zeeland*, "land reclaimed from the sea."

Niagara. River and falls between Canada and the United States; also two cities named after the falls. From Iroquois *Ongniaahra*, "point of land cut in two." Once a place near Lake Ontario where the wide river cut through the land.

Nice (nēs). City on the French Riviera. Founded by the Greeks and called by them *Nikae*, "victory." They won a battle against the coast-dwellers here and erected a defensive bastion in 300 A. D.

Nimes (nēm). French city. Originally *Nemausus*, from a Celtic root meaning "holy place, sanctuary." The fabric *denim* was once called *serge de Nimes*, or "serge from Nimes."

Niobrara. River in Nebraska. Corruption of Omaha Indian *ni*, "water" and *bthatha*, "spreading."

Nome. Town in Alaska. When the chart of this area was being drafted, attention was drawn to the fact that the cape here had no name. The notation *? name* was made and this was misread as Nome.

Norway. Old Norse *Norvegr*, "the north-way." This refers to the coastal route used to travel to the northern regions.

Novgorod. City of the U.S.S.R. Russian for "New City."

Nubia. Former kingdom in northeastern Africa. From Egyptian *noub*, "gold." Gold was found here in historical times.

Nunassiaq. Territory of northern Canada. In 1963 the Northwest Territories Council named the eastern part of the Territories *Nunassiaq*, an Eskimo name for "beautiful land."

Nuremberg. The English spelling of Nurnberg, West Germany. From Middle High German *knur*, "rock, cliff or any barren spot of ground."

Nyasaland. Former British protectorate in Africa. Named after Lake Nyasa on which it borders. This is a corruption of the Bantu name Nyanza from the root word *anza*, "body of water."

Oahu. One of the Hawaiian Islands. From a Polynesian word *ahu*, "heap." In this case it refers to a storehouse or place where things gathered were kept in a heap.

Oaxaca. Mexican city and state. Spanish transcription of Nahuatl *Huaxinyacatl*, "place where the guaje trees start to grow."

Oberammergau. Town in Bavaria famous for its Passion Play. "Upper district of the Ammer River."

Odense. City in Denmark. Old Norse *Odin's ve*, "place sacred to the god Odin."

Odessa. City in the Ukrainian S.S.R. Founded as a Russian trading center in 1795 on the site of the Turkish fortress of Hadzhibej. Named in memory of the ancient city of Odessa which was near the present site of Varna, Bulgaria. This name was from the Thracian word *bedu*, "water."

Okefenokee. Swampy region in Georgia. From Hitchiti Indian *oki-finoki*, "shaking water."

Okhotsk. Sea east of Siberia, really an arm of the Pacific. The name of the sea derives from that of the Okhot River which empties into it. The Tungus word *okat* means simply "sea."

Okinawa. Island between Japan and Formosa. The literal meaning of this Japanese name is "rope offshore." It refers to the shape of the long, low island which suggests a knotted rope.

Omaha. City in Nebraska. Commemorates the Omaha Indians whose name is Siouxan for "those going against the current or wind." They once lived on the banks of the Ohio and Wabash rivers, but later migrated up the rivers to the west.

Orense (*ô-rän′sâ*). City of Spain. From the Latin name *Auriensis*, a derivative of *aurum*, "gold." Gold was formerly found there.

Orinoco. River of Venezuela. The Carib Indians made pottery along the banks. This would verify the meaning of "clay river."

Orkney. Islands north of Scotland. A translation of Old Irish *Insi Orc*, "islands of the Uirc tribe." The tribal name means "pigs" and has pagan connotations.

Orleans. City in France. *Aurelianum* was the name given to the ancient Gaulish city of Genabum in honor of Aurelianus, Emperor of Rome, 270–75 A. D.

Osaka. Japanese city. In 1583 the great Japanese warrior, Hideyoshi, built a magnificent castle on a hill here. He called it *O-saka* or "great hill." The name of the castle was later given to the entire city.

Ottawa. Capital of Canada situated on the Ottawa River. The river-name is Iroquois and means "boiling" with reference to its many rapids and falls.

Oxford. City and county in England and town in Mississippi. "Place where the oxen forded the river."

Ozarks. Range of mountains in the Southern States. The French had a custom of shortening long Indian names, thus Arkansas became Ark. The phrase "aux Arks," referred to the range of mountains which lay in the direction of the Arkansas River.

Pakistan. Moslem students in England during the 1930's took the first letters of Punjab, Afghania, Kashmir and Sind, which are all regions of Pakistan, and added the suffix *-stan*, "land."

Palestine. From the name of the Peleshtim or Philistines, one of the tribes of sea peoples who invaded the coastal plain in the 12th century B. C.

Palomar. California mountain which supports a famous observatory. A Spanish name meaning "place of doves."

Panama. Central American Indian word meaning "butterflies." During the migration of butterflies in the summer months the multitudes were so vast that the sky was darkened for days.

Papua. British territory on the island of New Guinea. Portuguese explorers named the aborigines *Papuas* from the Malayan word for "frizzled or curly hair." During World War II, the Australian soldiers in New Guinea called them "fuzzy-wuzzies."

Paris. Name of the French capital and of many American towns. Commemorates the Gaulish tribe of the *Parisii*, "the bold ones."

Passamaquoddy. Bay in Maine. Malecite Indian for "place where pollack abound." The pollack is a fish related to the cod.

Pawtucket. City in Rhode Island. Narragansett Indian for "at the falls on the tidal stream." The Pawtucket Falls on the Blackstone River are here.

Pecs. City in Hungary. Known in ancient times as *Quinque Ecclesiae*, "Five Churches." From Old Slavic *piec*, "five."

Peking. Capital of the People's Republic of China. "Northern Capital," as opposed to Nanking. From 1928 to 1949 the city was known as *Peiping* or "Northern Peace."

Pembroke. Welsh town and county and many towns in America. Old Welsh *pen-brog*, "head of land." It is at the western extremity of Wales.

Pensacola. City in Florida. It is the name of a Muskhogean Indian tribe, who were called by the Choctaws *panshi-okla*, "hair people." Both men and women of the tribe wore their hair long.

Pernambuco. Former name of Recife, city of Brazil. From the Guarani Indian *paranambuku*, "long river."

Persia. Historical name of Iran. Named for the Parsa, an Indo-European people who lived here. Their name probably derives from Sanskrit *parashu*, "battle-axe," and refers to their use of these weapons in battle.

Perth. City in Scotland, Australia, and America. From a Pictish word related to the Welsh word *perth*, "bush, hedge."

Peru. The Spanish heard of a place called Viru by which entrance to the Incan Empire was presumably gained. The name was ultimately given to the entire country in a corrupted form. It is from Kechua Indian *wiru*, a species of South American bamboo.

Phoenicia. Ancient kingdom in vicinity of modern Syria and Israel. Famous for its purple dye industry, the name is from the Greek *phoenix*, "purple."

Platte. River in Nebraska. This is a misspelling of the French word *plate*, "flat." The river is extremely shallow and wide.

Polynesia. Pacific islands. Greek for "many islands."

Pomerania. Former German province on the Baltic; home of the pomeranian dog. Old Slavic *po-morije*, "seacoast."

Pondicherry. City in India, formerly a French dependency. Earlier *Podutscheri*, from Dravidian *podu*, "new," and *tscheri*, "city."

Popocatepetl (*pō-pô-kăt′ĕ-pĕt′l*). Mexican volcano. An Aztec name meaning "smoky mountain," referring to its volcanic activity.

Portugal. From *Portucale*, the name given to the region behind the "port of Cale." The name Cale is Celtic and means "shelter."

Potomac. American river. Name of an Algonquin town erroneously applied to the river. It means "where things are brought," probably tributes to a neighboring tribe.

Prague. Capital of Czechoslovakia. An Old Slavic word meaning "clearing burnt by the sun."

Recife (*rĕ-sē′fĕ*). City in Brazil. An enormous reef (Portuguese *recife*) encloses the harbor.

Regina. Capital of Saskatchewan. Honors Queen Victoria, called Victoria Regina in Latin.

Reykjavik (*rā′kyä-vēk′*). Capital of Iceland. Old Norse *reykr-vik*, "smoky bay." The first settlers mistook the clouds of steam from local hotsprings for smoke.

Riga. Capital of Latvia. From Lithuanian *ringa*, "something crooked," with reference to the stream on which the city was built.

Rostock. City in East Germany. Old Slavic *rastok′*, "fork in a river."

Rotorua. Thermal spa in New Zealand. It was the second big lake discovered by the Maori explorer Ihenga, hence its Maori name, "Second Lake."

Rotterdam. City in the Netherlands. Low German for "dam on the Rotte River." Rotte is the river "of duckweed."

Ruhr. German river and valley. Old High German *ruora*, "following with a strong, swift course."

Russia. Swedish tribes living around Kiev were called *Rus*. The name was gradually extended to the whole country.

Santos. City in Brazil. From the Portuguese *Hospital dos Santos*, "Hospital of the Saints." This was a hospital for sailors built in the 16th century.

Saskatoon. City in Saskatchewan. A kind of Juneberry called by the Cree Indians *missaskatoomina* grew here in abundance.

Saxony. Former German kingdom. "Land of the Saxons." The tribal name derives from Old High German *sahso*, "one-edged sword." This was their battle-weapon.

Sedalia. City in Missouri. Named by George R. Smith after his daughter Sarah, whom he called "Sed."

Shanghai. Chinese for "upper sea." Two arms of the sea extended inland at one time and Shanghai was on the upper arm.

Shantung. Chinese province famous for its silk. Chinese *shan*, "mountains" and *tung*, "east." It is the province "east of the mountains" while Shansi is "west of the mountains."

Sheffield. City in England. "Field by the River Sheaf." The *Sheaf* is Old English for "boundary river" and it separates Derbyshire and Yorkshire.

Sorrento. City in Italy. Modern form of Latin *Surrentum* from Greek *Seiren*, "siren or sea-nymph." The city faced the Sea of the Sirens.

Staten Island. Between New Jersey and Long Island. Named *Staaten Eylandt* during the Dutch period in honor of the States (Staaten) General, the governing body of the Netherlands at that time.

Stockholm. Capital of Sweden. Old Norse *stokkr* is the first element of Stocksund, "Sound of stakes or stumps." Stockholm is the *holm*, or island, in Stocksund.

Strasbourg. French city. Formerly *Stratesburg*, "fortress on the Roman street or road."

Sudan. African republic. Arabic *Blad-es-Soudane*, "Country of the Blacks." Originally referred to people not of Semitic stock but later extended to the entire area.

Susquehanna. River in Pennsylvania. Delaware Indian *Assisku-hanne*, "muddy stream."

Sussex. County in England and counties in the U.S. Old English *Suth-Seaxa*, "South Saxons."

Syracuse. Cities in Sicily and New York State. From the Greek *Syrako*, the name of a swamp in Sicily where the Greeks established a colony. It means "sour or brackish water."

Tahoe. Lake between California and Nevada. Corrupted form of the Washoe Indian word for lake, *da'au*.

Tallahassee. City in Florida. Creek Indian *talwa-hasi*, ' old town."

Tasco. Mexican town and art colony. The name is related to the native word *tlachtli*, "ball." The place was once consecrated to the ritual games of the Aztecs.

Thames. River in England and rivers in North America. A British river-name, formerly *Tamesis*, "dark river."

Ticonderoga. Fort and town in New York State. Lake George empties into Lake Champlain here, hence the Mohawk name "where two currents join."

Timor. Indonesian island. Malayan word for "east." Timor is the most easterly of the Sunda Islands.

Tirana. Capital of Albania. Founded in the early 17th century by the Turks and named after Teheran, Persia, after a Turkish victory there.

Titicaca. Lake in Bolivia. Kechua Indian *titi*, "lead," and *gaga*, "rock." The name was originally applied to the rocks which surround the lake.

Tobruk. Town in Libya. Arabic pronunciation of the Greek *Antipyrgos*, "opposite the rock." A firm rock in the harbor protected ships from the east wind.

Tokyo. City in Japan. "New Capital." Kyoto was the the "Old Capital."

Toronto. City in Ontario. An Iroquois name meaning "tree or stump projecting out of the water."

Transvaal. Province of the Republic of South Africa. Named by the Boers when they settled "across the Vaal River." *Vaal* is Dutch for "yellow."

Tripoli. Capital of Libya. A union of three ancient cities called Oea, Leptis Magna, and Sabata. Greek for "three cities."

Tucson. City in Arizona. Derived from the Papago Indian name of *Tuqui-son*, "black-based." The base of the Sentinel Mountains here is darker in color than the summit.

Tunis. Capital of Tunisia, Africa. The Berber root *ENS*, "to sleep" suggests that this was once a place for passing the night; an encampment.

Turkey. "The country of the Turks." These people were originally inhabitants of Mongolia and received their name from living near a hill called *Turku*, "helmet." The hill was helmet-shaped.

Tuskegee. City in Alabama. From the name of a Muskhogean tribe. They were "warriors" and Creek Indian word for warriors, *taskialgi*, is related.

Ukraine. Part of the U.S.S.R. From the Slavic *ukrai*, "on the edge," hence "boundary." This territory separated the Poles from the Mongolian Tartars.

Vaduz. Capital of Liechenstein. Formerly *Valdulz*, from *Vallis Dulcis*, which is Latin for "Sweet Valley."

Valparaiso. Seaport in Chile. Spanish for "valley of paradise," referring to the beautiful situation and lush plant growth.

Vancouver. Cities in Washington State and British Columbia and island off British Columbia. Named after Capt. George Vancouver, an English navigator who explored this coast 1792–94.

Venezuela. South American republic. When Spanish explorers saw the native huts built on pilings off Maracaibo, they were reminded of the city of Venice, Italy, and gave the name *Venezuela*, which is Spanish for "Little Venice."

Waco. City in Texas. Named after the Waco Indians. Their name was originally *Wehiku*, a corruption of Mexico, and they were so-called because they were always fighting the Mexicans.

Waikiki. Beach at Honolulu. Hawaiian for "spouting water."

Wichita. City in Kansas. From an Indian tribe of that name which means simply "the men."

Winchester. City in England and many places in America. Earlier *Ventacestre*, Old English for "fort on the Venta River." *Venta* is a Celtic river-name meaning "smiling, pleasant."

Windsor. Town in England and city in Ontario. Old English *Windlesora*, "windlass-shore." This was a landing-place with a windlass for pulling the boats up the river-bank.

Winnebago. Wisconsin lake. The name signifies "dirty, stinking water," in the Fox and Sauk Indian languages. The English called the Winnebago Indians "The Stinkards.'

Winnipeg. Capital of Manitoba. The name is Cree Indian *win*, "dirty" and *nipi*, "water." The reference is to the waters of Lake Winnipeg which lies to the north.

Yemen. Independent kingdom in Arabia. From the Arabic *yaman*, "to the right-hand." Yemen is on the right side of the region of Hejaz, while Syria is on the left or north side.

Yokohama. City and seaport of Japan. Japanese for "sheltered beach."

York. City and county of England; hence New York. In the year 730 the name was *Eburacum* which is Celtic for "place of the yew tree." Later the Old English word *wic*, "village" was added and finally the Scandinavians contracted the name to its present form.

Yosemite. National park in California. This is a name which was given to a band of renegades from various tribes who once lived here. In the local Indian dialect it means "killers."

Yugoslavia. The name of this European republic is Serbo-Croatian for "South Slavs," as distinguished from East and West Slavs to the north.

Yuma. Town in Arizona. The Yuma tribe received their name from their habit of making huge fires to induce rain. It derives from the Spanish *umo*, "smoke."

Zaragoza. City in Spain; often spelled *Saragossa*. An Iberian city which received the name *Caesaraugusta* in 27 B.C. in honor of that emperor. Zaragoza is an Arabic corruption.

REVIEW QUESTIONS

Give the derivation of the word geography. State the name and the subject matter of each of the principal divisions into which the science of geography is classified 49

Characterize the three chief periods of geographical progress 49

Name one of the founders of the science of geography 49

Give two reasons based on climate for the superior state of civilization in the temperate zones . 49

State four benefits that may be derived from the study of geography 49-50

Who were the earliest navigators known to history? Name a notable discovery made by each of them 51

Mention six Greek geographers and state the chief contributions made by each to the science of geography 51

What conception of the world's shape prevailed in Europe during the middle ages? How was the geographical knowledge possessed by the Greeks transmitted to Western Europe? . . 51

What chief discovery was made·by each of the following men: Marco Polo, Vasco da Gama, Captain Cook, McClure, Nordenskjöld, Peary, and Amundsen? 51-52

What is meant by the poles of the earth? Contrast the character of the earth's surface at the north pole with that at the south pole . 53

Of what use are circles of latitude and of longitude? How does a degree of latitude differ in length from a degree of longitude? 53

What is the cause of the alternation of day and night? of the difference in length of day at different seasons? 53-54

Explain how an observer may tell in what zone he is by observing the noonday position of the sun throughout the year 54

NORTH AMERICA

To what part of the earth is the name America applied? In whose honor was it so named? Explain the use of the term New World . . 55

Give the north-and-south length of America. How near does America approach to the north pole? to the south pole? 55

Compare North America and South America as regards shape and climate. Name prominent features common to both continents 55

What oceans and other bodies of salt water border the shores of North America? Describe the character of the North American coasts. On which coast are the harbors most numerous? 55

What great mountain systems form the chief surface features of the North American continent? Locate these systems and indicate the extent of each. Name the highest mountain peak in North America 55

Describe the Great Basin, the Colorado plateau, the Mexican plateau. What noted valley lies in the Mexican plateau? 55

Give the location and extent of the Medial plains. By what important river systems are these plains drained? 56

In what part of the continent are volcanoes found? Name one or more active volcanoes in Central America, in Mexico, in the United States, in Alaska 56

Describe in general the climate of North America. Characterize the climate of Central America; of Mexico; of the Great Plains. Where, in North America, is the region of greatest rainfall? of least rainfall? 56

State the rank of North America among the continents in respect to mineral wealth. Name 10 important mineral products of this continent. 56

Indicate the extent and the general character of North American forests. In what respect are the trees of the Pacific slope remarkable? . 56-57

Compare the bird and animal life of North America with that of Europe and Asia. Name several birds and larger animals characteristic of North America 57

State the chief facts about Hudson bay, mentioning its location, its size, the character of its waters, shores, and tributary rivers. Describe its fisheries and fur trade, and point out its commercial importance 57

Name and describe the Great Lakes, in the order of size, giving outlets and connections. State the commercial importance of the Great Lakes, naming the largest port on each . . 58

THE UNITED STATES

State the location of the United States, naming the countries and the oceans between which it lies. Describe briefly the character of the Atlantic coast; of the coast of the Gulf of Mexico; of the Pacific coast 59

What mountain system extends along the Atlantic side of the United States? along the western side? Where is the Great Basin located? the Columbia River plateau? . . . 59

Name the chief drainage basins of the United States. Into what oceans, seas, or gulfs do their drainage waters flow? How large a part of the United States lies in the Mississippi basin? Estimate the agricultural importance of this region 59

Describe in general the climate of the United States. Where do the greatest extremes of heat and cold occur? Where are the regions of greatest rainfall? 59-60

Discuss the mineral wealth of the United States, naming several important minerals produced. In what parts of the United States are extensive forests found? Name several important forest trees 60-61

Mention some of the larger native animals of the United States. Name six well-known song birds; six highly prized game birds; eight valuable food and game fishes 61

State the rank of the United States in manufactures among the countries of the world. Give reasons for its position 61

Locate the northernmost point in the United States; the easternmost; the southernmost; the westernmost. Where is the geographic center of the country? Indicate the location of the center of population 61

Locate the following national parks and mention a prominent feature of each: Glacier, Lassen Volcanic, Rocky Mountain, Mount Rainier, and Sequoia 62

New England States

Locate the group of New England states and give their names. To what single western state are they nearly equal in total area? Compare them with that state in respect to population 65

Describe the surface, the rivers, and the climate of the New England states 65

What are the chief mineral productions of these states? Which of these states leads in the value of quarry products? 65

Describe briefly the fisheries of New England. Which state stands first in value of sea fish taken? 65

What is the leading occupation of the people of New England? Mention ten important products of New England factories. Give four reasons for the success of New England as a manufacturing region. Compare Massachusetts with other states of the Union with respect to manufactures and commerce . . . 66

Describe the commerce of the New England states. Name five leading New England seaports 66

Middle Atlantic States

Name the states usually called the Middle Atlantic states. Which of these are sometimes called the Middle states? 66

What fraction of the total area of the United States do the Middle Atlantic states embrace? what proportion of the total population? of the total manufacturing capital? of the total number of wage-earners? 66

Describe in general the surface of the Middle Atlantic states. Through what part of this group does the Appalachian Mountain system extend? Describe the coastal plain. Name four important tidal rivers found in this group. What large river on the west serves as an interior waterway? 66

State in general the climate of the Middle Atlantic states. To what influence does the fruit belt of western New York owe its favorable climate? 66

In what does the mineral wealth of the Middle Atlantic states consist? Where and when was petroleum first discovered? In what manufactures do these states, by reason of their mineral resources, lead all other states? . . 66

Describe the development of agriculture in the Middle Atlantic states. Name the leading agricultural products. What state pays special attention to dairying? In what state do peanuts and tobacco form an important crop? 66

Name the most valuable single product of the salt-water fisheries of the Middle Atlantic states 66

Give two reasons for the commercial supremacy of the Middle Atlantic states. In what respects does the state of New York rank first among the states of the Union? What important waterway connects the Hudson river with the Great Lakes? 66

Central States

Name the states included in the division called the Central states. Describe the character of their surface and the nature of their soil . 67

By what river systems are the Central states chiefly drained? Name some important navigable rivers. Describe the climate and rainfall of the Central states 67

Compare this group of states, as regards mineral wealth, with other parts of the United States. In which of these states is coal mined? iron ore? In which are petroleum and salt obtained? 67

State the importance of the Central states as an agricultural region. Name the principal crops produced. What state leads in the production of tobacco? What state leads in production of sugar beets? 67

Name the principal farm animals raised in the Central states. What proportion of the country's wool clip is produced in these states? . 67

In what article of manufacture do the Central states lead the world? Name other important manufactures. In which of the Central states is the manufacture of iron and steel chiefly centered? 67

What proportion of the railway mileage of the country is located in the Central states? Name the rivers and lakes that form important inland waterways 67

Southern States

Give the boundaries, extent, and area of the Southern states. What proportion of the total area of the United States do these states form? 68

Name the states comprised in the eastern section of this group; in the western section. Describe the surface of each section 68

Summarize the chief features of the climate of the Southern states. Which parts receive the heaviest rainfall? the lightest rainfall? . . . 68

Describe the forests of each section of the Southern states. Compare these forests with those of other parts of the United States. 68

Name the principal mineral deposits found in the eastern section; in the western section. What important minerals are found in Alabama and in Tennessee? in Florida? Indicate the leading state or states in the production of petroleum and natural gas; of sulphur; of rock salt 68

State the chief occupation of the people of the Southern states. What is the most valuable crop produced in the Southern states? What fruits does southern Florida produce? Which of the Southern states leads in cotton growing? in sugar production? in cattle raising? in wool production? 68

Estimate the importance of stock raising in the eastern section; in the western. Name the chief animal products of each section . . . 68

State the principal manufactures of the eastern section. Name the three states which lead in manufactures. Which states in this group lead in the manufacture of iron and steel? of cotton goods? of tobacco? . . . 68

What are the chief manufactures of the western section? Which of these states leads in manufactures? 68

What are the chief articles of export of the Southern states? Name the principal seaports of each section 68–69

Plateau States

Name the Plateau states. Describe their surface. Which state has the highest elevation above sea level? the lowest? Which contains the highest mountains? 69

By what drainage systems are the states in this division drained? Name four important rivers in each system 69

Describe the climate of the different parts of this region, stating reasons for the great diversity. Which parts are hottest? which are coldest? Why does each of these states contain tracts of desert? Describe these desert areas 69

In what locations are the forests in these states found? Of what trees do they chiefly consist? How many national forests are located in these states? State their total area 69

State the chief mineral productions of this region. Name the states which lead in the production of gold; of silver; of copper; of tungsten 69–70

By what methods is agriculture carried on in the Plateau states? What are the chief crops produced? In what states or sections are apples grown? melons? long staple cotton? . 70

State the importance of stock raising in these states. Name the most important animals reared. What proportion of the total wool clip of the United States do these states produce? 70

Contiguous Pacific States

Name the states which form the contiguous portion of this group. Describe in general their surface. Name and locate three important mountain ranges. Mention five important valleys noted for their fertility 71

Name the chief navigable rivers of the contiguous Pacific states. Name three important uses of the rivers of these states 71

Describe the climate of the contiguous Pacific states, giving its chief characteristics. What sections receive the greatest rainfall? . . . 71

Name important mineral products of these states. Indicate the present rank of California among the states in gold production . 71

For what characteristics are the forests of these states noted? In which of the states is the most important lumber region located? . 77

State the importance of agriculture in these states. Mention leading crops. What class of crops outranks all others in value? . . . 77

Which of these states leads in fruit production? Of what classes of fruits does this state's production chiefly consist? In what district are citrus fruits extensively grown? Of what three kinds of fruits does this production principally consist? 77

Discuss the value and extent of irrigation in the contiguous Pacific states. What is the position of California as regards irrigation? . . . 77

Where are the principal fishing grounds? Name the most important food fish taken. . 77

Point out factors that have stimulated manufacturing in the contiguous Pacific states. Name the chief classes of manufactured products. Describe the commerce of these states. Indicate the value of the Panama canal to this region 77

Alaska, Hawaii, U.S. Dependencies

Locate and give the extent of Alaska. Describe the chief surface divisions of the mainland. Describe also the principal river 77–78

List Alaska's principa volcanoes, glaciers, straits, canals and other points of scenic interest, including her largest mountain. What special characteristic distinguishes the Muir glacier? What is the "Valley of Ten Thousand Smokes?" 78

According to climate, into what principal districts is Alaska divided? What varieties of vegetation and animal life are found in these different regions? 79

Name the chief mineral products of Alaska. State the value of its fisheries. What parts of Alaska does the government railway connect? Sketch briefly the history of Alaska 79

Briefly describe Hawaii, mentioning location, extent, surface, soil, and climate. Name the capital. What are the chief productions of Hawaii? Outline its history 81

Describe American Samoa. Name its chief seaport. Locate and give important points about Guam 83

Name the dependencies of the United States. 82

Locate Puerto Rico. Briefly describe its surface, climate, vegetation, and soil. Name the principal industry and products of the island. What city is the capital? Name three other important cities. Outline the history of Puerto Rico 83

Briefly describe the Virgin islands. Sketch their history. In what does the chief value of the Virgin islands now consist? 84

DICTIONARY OF AMERICAN GEOGRAPHY

What noted features of travel interest are situated near Adamana? Describe them briefly. State the chief industry of Akron, O.; give reasons for the city's growth 85

Describe briefly the city of Albany, mentioning noteworthy features. What widely known educational institution is located at Annapolis? at Ann Arbor? at Athens, Georgia? . 85–86

Of what state is Augusta the capital? Austin? Compare these cities with respect to manufactures and commerce. Briefly describe Baltimore. State its rank in population and give reasons for its industrial and commercial prominence 87–88

Locate and describe Black Rock desert, Blue-Grass Region. For whom was Berkeley named? For what is the city noted? State the chief industries of Bayonne; of Beaumont; of Bethlehem; of Binghamton; of

Birmingham 88–89

Briefly describe Boston, giving important points regarding its site, parks, monuments, buildings, and educational institutions. State its rank in population, in manufactures, and as a seaport. Mention features of historic and literary interest. Outline the history of the city. 89–90

In what manufacture does Brockton rank high among American cities? What are the chief manufactures of Bridgeport? 90

Give a brief description of Buffalo, covering important features. State its rank in population; in manufactures. What great commercial advantages does the city possess? Near what celebrated point of interest is it located? 90

Locate and give points of travel or other interest regarding Carlsbad Cave, Casa Grande, Castle Gate, and Lake Champlain. Of what importance is Cambridge? Locate and describe Charleston, South Carolina . . . 91–92

Describe in brief the city of Chicago, giving chief points regarding its site, area, streets, parks, and buildings. State the rank of the city in population, in manufactures, in commerce, and as a railway center. To what advantages does Chicago largely owe its commanding position? Give six important events in the history of Chicago 93

Where is Cincinnati located? Describe its site. Mention fine residence districts, parks, buildings. Name its leading manufactures. . . . 94

Locate and describe the city of Cleveland. State its rank in population and in manufactures. Of what does its civic center consist? With what are the city's chief industries concerned? Point out factors which have greatly aided the city's growth 94–95

Name points of interest in the vicinity of Colorado Springs. Describe the Columbia River highway. For what is Concord, Mass., noted? What and where is the Continental Divide? 95–96

Describe the Corn Belt; the Cotton Belt. . . . 96

Briefly describe Detroit. State its rank in population and manufactures. Of what great industry is it the world center? Of what importance is the lake traffic of Duluth? What are the chief manufactures of Elizabeth? of El Paso? 97–99

For what special industry is Fresno noted? Gary? Gloucester? Gloversville? Of what political importance is Frankfort? Harrisburg? Hartford? Where is the Grand Canyon? Describe some of its principal features. For what historic associations is Gettysburg widely known? Harpers Ferry? Hodgenville? 100–103

Describe Honolulu. Of what races and nationalities is its population composed? Where and of what importance is Houston? Locate and describe the Imperial valley. What is the Inland Empire? Briefly describe Indianapolis, giving important points regarding its commerce and industries. Mention factors aiding its development 103–104

Describe and give the commercial importance of Kansas City, Mo., and Kansas City, Kans. Of what great industries do these cities form a leading center? For what is Key West remarkable? 105–106

Trace the route of the Lincoln highway. For what is Lookout mountain noted? Of what political importance is Lincoln, Nebr.? Little Rock? 107

Briefly describe Los Angeles. State its rank in population, in manufactures, in commerce. Mention factors which have contributed to its growth. Name notable features and places of interest in its vicinity. State the commercial importance of Louisville. For what product is the city a leading market? 107–108

Locate and briefly describe Madison. For what is the city mainly important? Of what production is Memphis the chief center in the United States? State the rank of Milwaukee in manufactures. Briefly describe its site, harbor, parks, buildings, manufactures, commerce 109–110

Give a short description of Minneapolis. In the manufacture of what product is it a leader among American cities? Locate and describe the Mojave desert. For what historic associations is Monterey noted? 110–111

Why are Monticello and Mount Vernon, Virginia, places of national interest? Mention important points concerning Moundsville, Mount Clemens, Mount Rubidoux, Mount Tom, Muscle Shoals 111–112

In what manufacture does New Bedford lead? Of what commercial importance is New Orleans? 112–113

In what characteristics of its buildings does New York excel other cities? What are the chief means of transportation within the city? Describe the harbor and its connections by water and by rail. Discuss the rank of New York in commerce, in finance, in manufactures. Give reasons for the city's supremacy . 113–115

Locate and describe briefly Niagara falls. What important industries are located at the city of Niagara Falls? By what means is the power of the cataract transformed into electric power? Name cities to which this electric power is distributed 115

Locate Philadelphia. Describe its site and street plan. Mention important public edifices and commercial buildings. Name and locate the city's most famous historic landmark 117–118

On what rivers is Pittsburgh located? State its chief industries. In what manufactures does it lead? Give reasons for the city's industrial prominence 119–120

For what is Pittsfield noted? Plymouth? Port Arthur? Portland, Maine? Portland, Oregon? 120

Locate and compare three cities named Portsmouth. Name an important educational institution at Poughkeepsie; at Princeton; at Providence 120–122

For what historic associations is Portsmouth, N. H., noted? Quincy, Mass.? Richmond, Va.? 120–122

Briefly describe Saint Louis. Discuss its commercial importance. State its rank as a manufacturing center. Name leading industries. Sketch the city's history 123–124

What is the standing of Saint Paul as a wholesale center? Mention historic associations of Salem, Mass. Describe Salt Lake City. 124–125

Describe the site and harbor of San Francisco. What is the Golden Gate? State the importance of San Francisco in commerce, in finance, in manufactures. Mention features of scenic or historic interest 125–126

State the rank of Seattle in commerce and manufactures. Give reasons for the city's importance. In what lines does Shreveport lead? Sioux City? South Bend? 127–128

Locate and compare briefly four cities named Springfield. For what is Starved Rock noted? Stone mountain? 128–129

Describe Syracuse as a manufacturing center. Mention factors which have aided the city's growth. Locate and name features of interest regarding Lake Tahoe; Mount Tamalpais; Thousand Islands; Ticonderoga . . . 129–130

For what special product is Trenton noted? Troy? Tulsa? Utica? Waltham? Give points of historic interest regarding Trenton, Valley Forge, Vicksburg 130–131

By whom was the city of Washington planned? How were these plans finally carried out? with what result? Name four of the most noted public buildings. Describe the Washington monument; the Lincoln memorial . . 131

Locate and briefly describe Mount Washington; Watkins Glen; Mount Whitney, Mount Wilson 132–133

Of what industry was Wilkes-Barre the birthplace? Locate the Wheat Belt. Of what manufacture is Winston-Salem the leading center? 132–134

Locate Yellowstone park. Name and briefly describe its chief scenic features. Where is Yosemite park? What remarkable scenic attractions does it contain? Describe its waterfalls; its big trees 134–136

Where and what is Zuñi? Compare it with Laguna, Walpi 136, 106, 131

CANADA

Is the area of Canada greater or less than that of the United States? How far does Canada extend east and west? how far north and south? 141

Into what five natural divisions may the surface of Canada be divided? Characterize each briefly 141

How does the climate of the interior plains of Canada differ in temperature and in rainfall from the climate of British Columbia? Describe the climate of the arctic region in Canada 143

What are the four chief drainage basins of Canada? Name the chief rivers belonging to each basin 143

Indicate the approximate extent and location of the different vegetation areas in Canada . . 143

What are the three chief forest areas of Canada? What kind of timber is obtained from each? What steps have been taken by the government to preserve the forests? Where is the principal market for Canadian forest products? 143

Name 20 animals commonly found in Canada; one animal distinctive of the Canadian fauna; the animal which is a national emblem of Canada 143

Indicate the location and extent of land in Canada suitable for agriculture. How much of it is under field crops? 144

Name in order the four cities of Canada which rank highest as industrial centers 144

Mention distinctive features of Canada's railroad system; language conditions 144

Provinces

Mention a distinctive feature of the climate of Alberta. What recent trend is noticeable in the province's agricultural industry? What minerals are found in Alberta? 145

What are the two chief industries of British Columbia? 146

Describe the conditions of soil and of climate which make Manitoba an important wheat growing region 147

What are the three principal industries of New Brunswick? 147

State the area of Nova Scotia, its population, and the length of its coast line. Name a large island and a productive fruit district of the province. Where are its richest coal mines? province. Where are its richest coal mines? . 148

How does Ontario rank with other Canadian provinces in each of the following respects: population, wealth, mineral production, value of field crops, output of dairy products, lumbering, and manufactures? 149

What is the maximum elevation of Prince Edward Island? What distinctive industry has recently become important there? 149

Give the boundaries of Quebec. Mention an important factor influencing its climate. Name a distinctive mineral obtained in the province. Discuss Quebec's rank among the Canadian provinces in forest products and manufactures. What is the predominant religion and the language of Quebec? . 149–150

Describe the climate of Saskatchewan. What is the most important product? 150

Name the highest mountain in the Yukon. State the approximate value of gold which has been obtained from the territory 150

Cities and Points of Travel Interest

Name three lakes of great scenic beauty in the vicinity of Banff. 151

What are the leading industries of Brantford? of Calgary? of Charlottetown? 151

Where is Churchill? For what reason is it notable? 151

Locate Edmonton, Fort William, and Halifax. For what is Cobalt noted? Dawson? . .151–152

State reasons for Hamilton's growth as a manufacturing city. 152

Discuss Kingston from the point of view of transportation, education, and historical associations 152

Name two respects in which Montreal exceeds in importance any other city of Canada. Specify two notable examples of engineering skill, three squares, and two great buildings of Montreal 152

For what are the following places chiefly noted: Hull, New Westminster, Niagara Falls, Oshawa? 152–153

How large is Muskoka? What provincial park lies near it? 153

When was Ottawa made the capital of Canada? Mention an outstanding scenic feature near the city. Name six buildings of note. What is the chief industry? 153

Describe Quebec under the heads of location, history, industries, great buildings, and educational institutions 153–154

For what is Sainte Anne de Beaupré noted? . 154

What is the distinctive industry of each of the following places: Sherbrooke, Sudbury, Sydney, Thetford Mines, and Three Rivers? . . 154

For what institution is Stratford best known? On what river is the city situated? 154

How does Toronto rank among the cities of Canada in each of the following: industry, commerce, and finance? What distinctive annual institution has Toronto? 154–155

What are the leading industries of Vancouver? Name the principal park of Vancouver; the chief recreation ground of Victoria. 155

What is the most southerly city of Canada? . 155

Show how Winnipeg's location is favorable to its growth. Mention the city's outstanding edifice, the largest park, and a distinctive feature of the municipal supply service 155

MEXICO, CENTRAL AMERICA, AND WEST INDIES

How much of Mexico is in the Torrid Zone? What is the length of the country? its greatest and its least width? 156

What name is applied to the portion of Mexico between 3000 and 8000 feet elevation? to that above 8000 feet? Name the chief mountain ranges and volcanoes. Give 10 products of Mexico's agriculture or forestry 156

State the reasons for saying that Mexico is potentially one of the richest mineral producing countries in the world. What are the chief manufactured products? 156

Give the names of the two largest cities of Mexico. Describe the situation of Mexico City. For what is its museum famous? What three notable features are there in the vicinity of the city? 157

Describe Central America under the heads of mountains, climate, and inhabitants 157

Who named Costa Rica? What are the staple products of Costa Rica? of Guatemala? 157–158

Name the chief article of domestic consumption in Honduras; a distinctive fact regarding its capital; the largest lake in Central America; and the volcano of Salvador that has risen one mile in height in the past century 158

What are the chief exports of Belize? of Managua? Why is the cathedral of Guatemala noteworthy? Give interesting historical facts about San Salvador and Tegucigalpa . .157–159

Explain the meaning of the terms British West Indies, Greater Antilles, Lesser Antilles. What is the origin of the name Antilles? . . 159

What is the prevailing racial strain in the population of each of the following islands or island groups: Bahama, Leeward, Cuba, and Haiti? 159–160

Mention distinctive features of the rivers and of the fauna of Cuba. What is Cuba's outstanding economic interest? What language is spoken in Cuba? in the republic of Haiti? Name five cities of Cuba 160

SOUTH AMERICA

Compare South America with North America in regard to location, area, coast line, and western mountain system 161

Name the three great plains of South America; the three greatest rivers. What is the most southerly point of the continent? 161

Where are the most arid parts of the continent? What part has the greatest rainfall? 161

Give the names of four important economic plants which flourish in South America; ten characteristic species of animals native there. 161

Name three distinctive mineral products of South America. What countries have a population predominately of the white race? of pure-blooded Indians? What is the prevailing religion? the most widespread language? 161

What are the two highest peaks of the Andes mountains? four volcanoes in this range? For what is Lake Titicaca remarkable? . . . 162

Name the chief tributaries of the Amazon river; of the Plata-Parana River system; of the Orinoco river 162

What is the maximum range of temperature recorded in Argentina? For what economic products is the country noted? Mention two respects in which Argentina leads all other South American countries 162

Specify four of the highest mountains of Bolivia. Discuss the mining and transportation difficulties of Bolivia. What are the chief minerals produced? 162–163

State the area, chief products, and population of Brazil. Describe its climate. Name a notable gold mine of Brazil 162

Give a distinctive mineral product of Chile; of Colombia; two distinctive products of Ecuador. Name and locate the highest active volcano in the world 163–164

What are the chief exports of Paraguay? three distinctive products of Peru? State the principal industry of Uruguay; the origin of the name Venezuela 165–166

Name the largest city of South America. Describe the city's principal avenue. Mention interesting features of Easter island, Galapagos islands, Juan Fernandez island, and Santos. What city of South America was recently built as a national capital? 167–168

EUROPE

State the boundaries of Europe. Compare the continent's area with that of the United States. What is the most noticeable characteristic of Europe's coast line? How has this feature proved advantageous for settlement? Name the principal islands of Europe . . . 169

Describe two changes of elevation that have occurred in parts of Europe within historical times. Name six mountain ranges of southern Europe; four plains of the continent. What are the chief volcanic regions? 169

Specify the four longest rivers of Europe. Into what body of water does each empty? What are the two largest lakes of Europe? 169

Account for the warm climate on Europe's northern coast; for the absence of deserts in Europe 169

Name 16 cultivated plants and 5 animals the original habitats of which were in Europe . 169

Indicate the chief areas of Europe which produce each of the following minerals: coal, iron, zinc, platinum, and quicksilver 169

What are the principal mammals found on the continent of Europe? Which domesticated animals originated there? 169

How does Europe's industrial output compare with that of other continents? Account for the concentration of her industries in a few areas 169

Mention five products which European countries export in substantial amounts to countries in other continents 169

What basis is there for the saying that Europe is a collection of small, stubbornly independent states? Give some examples of these autonomous countries 169

Bound Austria. What is her latest estimated area and population? On what industries do the inhabitants depend chiefly for support? 169

Countries

What is the density of Belgium's population? Name the chief manufactures; the most celebrated university. Indicate a peculiarity of the racial and linguistic conditions of Belgium 170–171

Give the boundaries of Bulgaria. Name a distinctive product of Bulgaria; the chief waterway; the prevailing religion; the three largest cities 171

Describe the political relation of Denmark to the Faroe islands; to Greenland. Characterize the agricultural industry of Denmark. Specify a change in Denmark's territory occasioned by World War I 171

State the boundaries of France. How does the character of the coast and of the rivers affect the location of French ports? Name the highest mountain of France; the leading minerals produced; the principal manufactures. What is the prevailing religion of France? the most notable university? .171–172

Give the names of a high mountain in Germany; five rivers; five minerals obtained; the two leading field crops; two products for which German industry has shown special aptitude 173

How high is Gibraltar? Describe a memorable siege which it endured 174

Distinguish between Great Britain as a geographical entity and as a political division. Name the principal coastal indentations of Great Britain. What benefits accrue to Great Britain from the shallowness of the surrounding seas? 174

Name the chief rivers of England; the largest lake; the highest mountain. Discuss the rank of England among European countries in coal exporting, iron production, shipbuilding, and the manufacture of cutlery and of textiles. Name the four largest cities . . 174–175

What is the chief economic interest of Wales? . 175

Into what three parts may Scotland be divided by the nature of its surface? Where is the densest population? What are the chief industries? the leading crop? the established religion? the four largest cities? 175

Specify the largest island of Greece; the ancient and the modern name of the chief peninsula; the largest mountain range; a notable drainage project; and a distinctive product. Describe the climate of Greece 175–176

Give the boundaries of Hungary. Why are the people sometimes called Magyars? 176

Describe and locate Hecla and the Great Geyser 176

How many people emigrated from Ireland since 1850? Approximately what percentage of the inhabitants can speak the Irish language? What is the island's longest river? a district which attracts numerous tourists? Give a reason for Ireland's designation as the "emerald isle" 176

Contrast Eire with Northern Ireland in regard to economic interests and religion 176

State the boundaries of Italy; two notable rivers of the country; the leading industry; two distinctive artistic products 177

Mention a method by which many Italian city dwellers combine city and country life. What two disastrous earthquakes have visited Italy in modern times? 177

Why is the Netherlands sometimes called Holland? Characterize the surface of the country. Describe the formation and the reclamation of the former Zuider Zee. Indicate the country's canal mileage, three distinctive products, a breed of cattle developed there, a chief source of raw material for the industries, and the seat of government . . . 178

Mention a distinctive attraction for tourists in Norway. What are the chief occupations of the inhabitants? 178

Specify three characteristic products of Portugal. Mention a noteworthy political fact concerning the country 178

State the boundaries of Rumania; the chief exports; the predominant religion 178

How much of the Danube river lies in Rumania? Give the name of one of its large tributaries . 178

Name and locate the highest mountain in Russia. Name the constituent republics of the Soviet Union. What is the principal watershed in Russia, and what rivers of southern drainage rise from it? Describe some of the measures taken by the Soviet government to bring about the industrialization of the country. From what is Russian caviar made? Specify the chief minerals produced . . 179–180

Characterize the surface of Spain. Name six rivers of the country. Which ones are navigable? What are the principal economic values of the plateaus in Spain? Where is Andalusia? What does it produce? Name two distinctive products of Spain. Describe the mineral wealth of the country 180

Name four great lakes of Sweden. Characterize the three principal divisions of the country. Specify three important industries; the three principal cities 180–181

Describe the surface and drainage of Switzerland. Name five notable mountains. Discuss avalanches in Switzerland, stating their cause and some precautions taken against loss due to them. Mention a famous tunnel of Switzerland; the chief industries; three distinctive products. What characteristics distinguish a Swiss chalet? 181

Describe the surface of Yugoslavia. What is the Iron Gate? How much of the country's area is forested? What are the three chief religions of the inhabitants? 181

Cities and other Points of Travel Interest

Name five glacial lakes in the Alps mountains. State an important item of interest concerning each of the following places: Amiens, Arcadia, Argonne forest. In what industry does Amsterdam lead the world? How long is the Appian way? 182

Give the names of two important squares in the city of Athens; the four ancient edifices on the Acropolis. Specify an important fact regarding Mount Athos; Avignon; Belleau woods 183

What is the most famous boulevard of Berlin? Mention a great park, six important buildings, and 10 industries of Berlin . . . 183–184

State the origin of the name Berne. Mention an interesting fact concerning Bingen. What is the chief industry of Birmingham? of Bradford? of Brest? 184

Name a famous ship which was built at Bristol. Specify two important industries of Budapest. When was Cadiz founded? State an important point of interest regarding each of the following: Calais, Cambrai, Canterbury, Cantigny, Capri, Cardiff, Carrara 185

What American state was named after one of the Channel islands? Indicate at least one interesting fact regarding Chateau Thierry; Chemnitz; Cherbourg. Describe briefly Cologne cathedral 186

Name the chief museum of Copenhagen; the founder of Cork; the principal art gallery of Dresden; the finest public garden of Düsseldorf; a thoroughfare of Edinburgh . . . 186–187

Describe Fingal's cave. Discuss Florence as an art center. Mention some of the literary and historical associations of Frankfort and important religious and political associations of Geneva; a sculptural group in Genoa. . 187–188

State at least one outstanding fact regarding Hammerfest. Indicate the chief commercial interest of Hanover; of Le Havre 189

Explain the terms Stamboul, Sublime Porte, Golden Horn, Byzantium, Galata, and Pera. Name the two greatest mosques of Istanbul 189

What great philosopher lived at Königsberg. Name the two chief industries of Leeds; the principal manufacture of Limoges . . . 189–190

Who founded Leningrad? 190

Name the three divisions of Greater London; eight important streets of London; three parks or pleasure grounds; ten famous buildings of the city. For what is Lourdes noted? 191–192

Describe the "Lion of Lucerne" and the Maelstrom. What is the largest industry of Lyon? of Manchester? What are the chief attractions of Monte Carlo? 192–193

Give a description of the Kremlin in Moscow. Mention a famous opera house of Naples; important facts regarding Nuremberg, Oberammergau, and Olympia 193–194

What is the chief interest in Ostend? in Oxford? Explain the plan followed in the construction of the boulevards of Paris. What is the Latin quarter? the Louvre? the Quai d'Orsay? the Sorbonne? the Bon Marché? the Bourse? 194–195

What is Pisa's most celebrated building? Mention famous persons connected with Portsmouth; Prague; Ravenna 195

Justify Rome's designation as "the eternal city." Name the seven hills of Rome; three important thoroughfares; a fashionable promenade of the city. Describe the Vatican briefly 195–196

Discuss the industrial importance of the Ruhr district to Germany. Name its chief cities. . 196

State interesting facts about the Cathedral of Seville and the Cathedral of Saint Mark in Venice. What is the most famous prehistoric monument in Great Britain? 197

Name the most notable driveway and the largest park of Vienna. For what is Verdun noted? Versailles? Windsor? 198

ASIA

Compare the area of Asia with that of North and South America. Name the three great peninsulas on the south of Asia. What is meant by the term Oceania? 199

Name and locate the world's highest plateau; highest mountain; deepest lake; vastest plain 199

Describe briefly the course of the following rivers: Lena, Hwang, Brahmaputra, Indus. 200

Specify the coldest part of Asia; the hottest part; the area of the greatest rainfall; the desert portion 200

Name 25 cultivated plants and 8 domesticated animals that are believed to have originated in Asia. Indicate the chief minerals known to exist in Asia 200

Name the independent countries of Asia . . . 201

Name five minerals found in Burma; three industries followed there 201

Who constructed the Angkor temples of Cambodia? 201

Describe the mineral wealth of China; Chinese agriculture; transportation; religion; government 201–202

Cyprus is named for its chief export. Explain what is meant by this 202

Name two semi-independent kingdoms on India's northern border. In the possession of what domestic animal does India lead the world? . 203

What was the first republic to adhere to the British Commonwealth of Nations? 203

Name the capital of Indonesia 203

Specify five products of Iran 204

Tell three kinds of farm communities in Israel. 204

Compare North Korea and South Korea in respect to manufacturing; materials . . . 204

Indicate the two highest mountains of the Japanese empire; the highest active volcano; the chief market for Japanese silk . . . 204

What is the established religion of Pakistan? . 205

Name the two largest islands of the Philippines; five distinctive trees; five distinctive birds; the principal crops; three leading manufactures 205

Characterize the agricultural resources of Russia's Great Northern Lowland; the agricultural industry of Turkey 206–207

Indicate the nature of the religious interest centering in Amernath; in Bethlehem. Mention a striking historical fact regarding Agra; Ankara; Baghdad; Calcutta 207

What is the chief commercial interest of Canton? Kobe? Madras? To what religion is each of the following places sacred: Lhasa, Mecca, Jerusalem, Medina? 208–209

AFRICA

What is the distinguishing characteristic of Africa's coast line? How does this continent compare in size with North America? What is the Great Rift Valley? Name three lakes in this valley. Locate Africa's highest mountain 211

Name four great rivers of Africa; the greatest cataract in the world. Mention a remarkable fact concerning Lake Chad 211

Indicate the two desert areas of Africa and the region of the greatest rainfall. Describe the surface of the Sahara desert. Name five native cultivated plants of Africa; five distinctive species of mammals; a deadly insect; two important mineral products 212

Contrast the Bantus and the true Negroes in Africa. What religion of outside origin has the greatest following in the continent? . . 212

What is Egypt's principal crop? What part of the country is most productive? What is the chief cause of its productivity? 213

Name the world's largest source of tea in Africa 214

What country is the world's leading producer of cork? 215

Of what country is Dakar the capital? 215

For what purpose was Freetown in Sierra Leone founded? 216

Specify the leading industry and a distinctive industry of South Africa; three products of which the country provides a large part of the world's supply 216

Who founded Alexandria? Name a famous building which distinguished the city in ancient times. What is the largest city of Africa? Indicate two notable edifices of Cairo. 217

What are the chief attractions of Giza? of Karnak? of Luxor? 218

Of what importance is Casablanca? Dakar? Dar es Salaam? Johannesburg? Nairobi? . . 218

AUSTRALIA

Compare the area of Australia with that of the United States; that of Europe. What is the highest mountain in Australia? What regions are arid? 219

Account for the fewness of Australian rivers. Name the largest river system; three lakes of inland drainage systems. What two minerals are obtained in the greatest value? Name six other minerals produced in the continent 219–220

Mention two distinctive families of plants found in Australia. Note an adaptation by many Australian plants to their arid environment. What is Australia's national flower? Give the names of four valuable fodder plants of Australia 220

Indicate four soft woods and six hard woods obtained from Australian forests; two characteristic mammals and five remarkable birds found in the continent 220

What is the main industry of Australia? an export in which Australia leads the world? What is the meaning of the name Australia? What was the continent called before 1817?. 221

Locate New South Wales; describe its surface, rainfall, forests, and chief industry. What is its capital? Describe Queensland 221

Mention a noteworthy fact about the lakes of South Australia. What is the chief industry? 222

Where are the "Australian Alps?" Which state of the Australian Commonwealth has the largest area? The greatest population? . . . 222

What parts of Western Australia have sufficient moisture for agricultural purposes? What are the principal crops? The chief mineral product? 222

Name five manufactures of Adelaide; a prominent summer resort near the city; the chief industrial interest of Ballarat 222

What is the mean annual temperature of Brisbane? State facts of the city's early history. Name a notable square of Hobart 222

What is the population of Melbourne? Name four colleges affiliated with the University of Melbourne 222

Point out an important advantage of location enjoyed by Sydney. Name three outstanding manufactures 223

NEW ZEALAND AND ANTARCTICA

Describe an interesting volcanic region in North island. What is the chief mountain range of South island? the largest lake? the highest peak? 223

Name the most characteristic plant of New Zealand; an outstanding contribution to the world's economic plants; a distinctive wingless bird; the chief industry. Mention a noticeable feature of the country's industrial life; of the transportation system 224

What are the aborigines of New Zealand called? Specify the chief exports of Auckland; of Dunedin. Who founded Christchurch? . 224–225

Compare the area of Antarctica with that of Australia. Why have south polar expeditions landed on the side of Antarctica nearest New Zealand? Describe the climate of the continent. Name six recent expeditions which set out to explore Antarctica 226

PLACE NAMES

In what century did scholars begin the scientific investigation of place-names? 233

What is the study of place-names called and of what science is it a branch? 233

What useful purpose does this study serve? . 233

How is the scientific method applied, and what are the three main types of place-names? 233

What natural surroundings led to the naming of the following: Andes, Biwa, Cameroon, Carlow? 233–234

From what languages do these places derive: Alcatraz, Amalfi, Anatolia, Angostura, Aorangi, Aral Sea, Arctic, Beirut, Bethlehem, Bihar, Cadiz, Carrara, Chimborazo, Cimarron, Corvallis, Dachau? 233–235

What tribes or peoples are commemorated in the following names: Britain, Dalmatia, Denmark, Estonia, France, Hungary, Iran, Italy, Kirghiz, Limoges? 234–238

What events suggested the following names: Dar es Salaam, El Paso, Kuwait, Labrador, Liberia, Monrovia, Nice? 236–239

Explain the origin of each of the following names: Managua, Mauna Loa, Menlo Park, Moluccas, Mongolia 239

What English words derive from the following places: Al Mausil, Derby, Gaza, Jodhpur, Lille, Milan, Nimes, Phoenicia? 233–240

What have the following names in common: Omaha, Orinoco, Ottawa, Passamaquoddy, Pensacola? 240

After what individuals are these places named: Monterey, Regina, Sedalia, Vancouver, Zaragoza? 239–241

What do the following place-names mean: Staten Island, Tucson, Waikiki, Yosemite? . 241

State the reason for the application of each of the following place-names: Russia, Santos, Saskatoon, Shantung, Sudan, Syracuse, Ticonderoga, Tunis, Ukraine, Windsor, Winnipeg 241

BIBLIOGRAPHY

The following titles of books have been selected chiefly from lists of standard works recommended by librarians for the guidance of general readers.

GENERAL GEOGRAPHY

Chase, Ilka—Second Spring and Two Potatoes.
Doubleday '65 (around the world)
Davies, Clarice S.—Exploring the World . *Roy '66*
Hall, Ernie—Flotsam, Jetsam, and Lagan from the Seven Seas, the Five Great Lakes, and Our Inland Rivers . . . . . *Cornell Maritime '65*
James, Preston E.—A Geography of Man. 2nd ed.
Blaisdell '66
Jones, Emrys—Human Geography; an Introduction to Man and His World . . . . . . *Praeger '66*
Perpillou, Aime V.—Human Geography .*Wiley '66*
Rand McNally New Cosmopolitan World Atlas.
Rand McNally '65
Scott, Jack D.—Passport to Adventure *Random '66*

REGIONAL GEOGRAPHY AND TRAVEL

United States
Brooks, Maurice G.—The Appalachians.
Houghton '65
Carpenter, John A.—Alaska, From Its Glorious Past to the Present . . . Chicago, *Children's Pr.* '65
Davenport, William W.—Hawaii, 1966 *McKay '66*
Ford, Norman D.—What to See in All America.
Crown '64
Hollon, William E.—The Great American Desert, Then and Now. . . . . *Oxford '66*
Mandell, Muriel—The 51 Capitals of the U.S.A. (grades 5–8) . . . . *Sterling '65*
Paterson, John H.—North America, 3rd ed.
Oxford '66
Perry, George S.—Cities of America . . *McGraw*
Platt, Rutherford Hayes—The Great American Forest . . . . *Prentice '65*
Road Atlas and Travel Guide . *Rand McNally '66*
Steinbeck, John—Travels with Charley; in Search of America . . . . . *Viking '62; Banton '63*

Canada
Canadian Almanac and Directory for 1966 (119th yr.). . . . . *Pittman '66*
McDougall, Robert L., ed.—Canada's Past and Present . . . . . *U. of Toronto Pr.* '65
Myers, B. R.—North of the Border . *Vantage '64*
Nicholson, N. L.—Canada in the American Community . . . . *Van Nostrand '63*
Scarfe, N. V. & others—A New Geography of Canada . . . . *Gage '63*
Wilson, George W.—Canada; an Appraisal of Its Needs and Resources . . . *Twentieth Century '65*

Mexico, Central America, West Indies
Fodor's Guide to the Caribbean, Bahamas, and Bermuda, 1966. . . . . *McKay '65*
MacPherson, John—Caribbean Lands; a Geography of the West Indies . . . . . . *Longmans '65*
Nicholson, Irene—The X in Mexico; Growth Within Tradition . . . . *Doubleday '66*
Rodman, Seldon—The Road to Panama.
Hawthorne '66
Woodman, Jim—Discovering Yucatan.
Doubleday '66
The World and Its Peoples: the Caribbean Region and Central America . . . .*Greystone '65*

South America
Clark, Sydney A.—All the Best in South America, East Coast . . . . *Dodd '66*
Clark, Sydney A.—All the Best in South America, West Coast . . . . *Dodd '66*
Clissold, Stephen—Latin America; a Cultural Outline . . . . *Harper '65*
Fodor's Guide to South America, 1966. *McKay '66*
Johnson, William W.—The Andean Republics: Bolivia, Chile, Ecuador, Peru . . . *Time, Inc.* '65
MacEoin, Gary—Colombia and Venezuela and the Guianas . . . . *Time, Inc.* '65

Schneider, Ronald M.—An Atlas of Latin American Affairs . . . . *Praeger '65*

Europe
Clark, Sydney A.—All the Best in France. *Dodd '66*
Fielding's Travel Guide to Europe, 1966.
Morrow '66
Fodor, Eugene, ed.—Britain and Ireland.
McKay '66
Fodor's Guide to Europe, 1966; a Comprehensive Handbook of 34 countries . . . . . *McKay '66*
Houston, James M.—A Social Geography of Europe. Rev. . . . . *Hillary House '66*
Latham, Peter—The German Federal Republic.
Blackie '65
Latham, Peter—Italy . . . . *Blackie '65*
Salisbury, Harrison E.—Russia . . *Macmillan '65*
Shakleton, Margaret Reid—Europe; a Regional Geography. 7th ed . . . . *Praeger '65*
Waldo, Myra—Travel Guide to Europe, '66–'67.
Macmillan '66
The World and Its Peoples: Austria, Hungary, Czechoslovakia, Poland . . . . *Hawthorne '65*

Asia
Gary, Dorothy H.—Splendors of Asia. .*Viking '65*
Gellhorn, Eleanor C.—McKay's Guide to the Far East and Hawaii . . . . *McKay '65*
Gellhorn, Eleanor C.—McKay's Guide to the Middle East . . . . *McKay '65*
Hammer, Ellen Joy—Vietnam, Yesterday and Today. . . . . *Holt '66*
Lamb, Beatrice (Pitney)—India; a World in Transition. Rev. ed. . . . . *Praeger '65*
Langer, Paul F.— Japan, Yesterday and Today.
Holt '66
Lindqvist, Sven—China in Crisis . . *Crowell '65*
McCune, Shannon B.—Korea, Land of Broken Calm . . . . *Van Nostrand '66*
Tayyeb, Ali—Pakistan; a Political Geography.
Oxford '66
Tregear, Thomas R.—A Geography of China.
Aldine '66
Walz, Jay—The Middle East . . . *Atheneum '65*

Africa
Ady, Peter H.—Africa . . . . . *Clarendon Pr.* '65
Nelson, Nina—Your Guide to Egypt.
Intl. Pubns. Serv. '66
Sillery, Anthony—Africa; a Social Geography.
Humanities '65
Steffen, Don Carl—The Splendor of Africa.
Walker '65
Wattenberg, Ben and Smith, Ralph—The New Nations of Africa . . . . *Hart '63*

The Pacific
Berney, Maurice, ed.—Australia.
Rand McNally '65
Briggs, Donald S.—Orient-Hawaii Guide; Introducing Hawaii, Japan, Hong Kong, and the Philippines . . . . *Crown '62*
Corpuz, Onofre D.—The Philippines. *Prentice '66*
Horne, Donald—The Lucky Country: Australia in the Sixties. 2nd ed. London, *Angus & Robertson '66*
Waldo, Myra—Travel Guide to the Orient and the Pacific . . . . *Macmillan '65*

Polar Regions
Debenham, Frank—In the Antarctic; Stories of Scott's Last Expedition . . . . *Verry '65*
Dukert, Joseph M.—This is Antarctica. *Coward '65*
Eklund, Carl R. and Beckman, Joan—Antarctica.
Holt '63
Silverberg, Robert, ed.—Antarctic Conquest; the Great Explorers in Their Own Words . *Bobbs '65*
Simmons, George—Target: Arctic; Men in the Skies at the Top of the World . . . *Chilton '65*

Space Exploration
Alexander, Thomas W.—Project Apollo: Man to the Moon . . . . *Harper '64*
Emme, Eugene M.—A History of Space Flight.
Holt '66
Faget, Maxime A.—Manned Space Flight. *Holt '65*
Hilton, William F.—Manned Satellites, Their Achievements and Potentialities . . *Harper '66*

Economics

CONTENTS GUIDE

	Page
Aeronautics	277
Agricultural Statistics	350
Agriculture	347
Air Transportation	277
Animal Industry	361
Bibliography	438
Bridges and Viaducts	388
Buildings and Towers Table	393
Business Cycles	311
Business, Banking, and Legal Terms	329
Canals, Important	269
Collective Bargaining	284
Commerce	253
Communication	262
Dairying	362
Dams	391
Drainage and Reclamation	356
Economic Dependence, U.S.	260
Employer Associations	286
Engineering and Building	387
Federal Reserve System	325
Fisheries	363
Foreign Trade	259
Forestry	357
Highways, Public	276
Horticulture	354
How Things Are Made Dictionary	407
Insurance:	
Fire	309
Life	303
Transportation	311

	Page
Inventions Dictionary	373
Investments	315
Irrigation	357
Labor Acts	284
Labor-Management Act	284
Labor Relations	279
Labor Unions	285
Lumbering	406
Manufacturing	395
Marketing	289
Merchant Marine, the World's	267
Mining	370
Modern Inventions Table	385
Monetary Units	328
Money and Banking	319
Motor Vehicle Registration	276
Power	299
Questions, Review	431
Railroads	271
Raw Materials:	
Animal Products	262
Mineral Products	262
Vegetable Products	261
Saint Lawrence Seaway	270
Soil Erosion Prevention	359
Transportation	265
Tunnels	393
Unemployment	288
Wage and Hour Regulation	287

Picture Guide: Farm Machinery in the Field—Modern Farm Machinery—Modern Mechanical Research Machine.

Machines in the Field. Top: **Tractor-Pulled Harrow**—Used to break up clods of earth and destroy weeds in preparing land for seeding. Lower left: **Cultivator**—In operation to loosen and aerate the earth during the early stage of growth of field crops. Lower right: **Field Baler**—The sweep moving through the fields of cut straw feeds the crop into a pressure chamber to make firm, square bales for easy handling and storage. (*Courtesy Sperry Rand and Caterpillar Tractor Company*)

Modern Farm Machinery. Top. **Combine:** A self-propelling machine for harvesting that cuts, threshes, and cleans the grain while moving through the fields. Bottom. **Automatic Baler:** Pickup balers such as this lift the hay to a conveyor that carries it to a baling chamber, where it is compressed into bales weighing as much as 125 pounds and automatically bound with heavy twine or wire. Balers handle such crops as alfalfa, maize straw, or prairie hay. (*Sperry Rand/New Holland*)

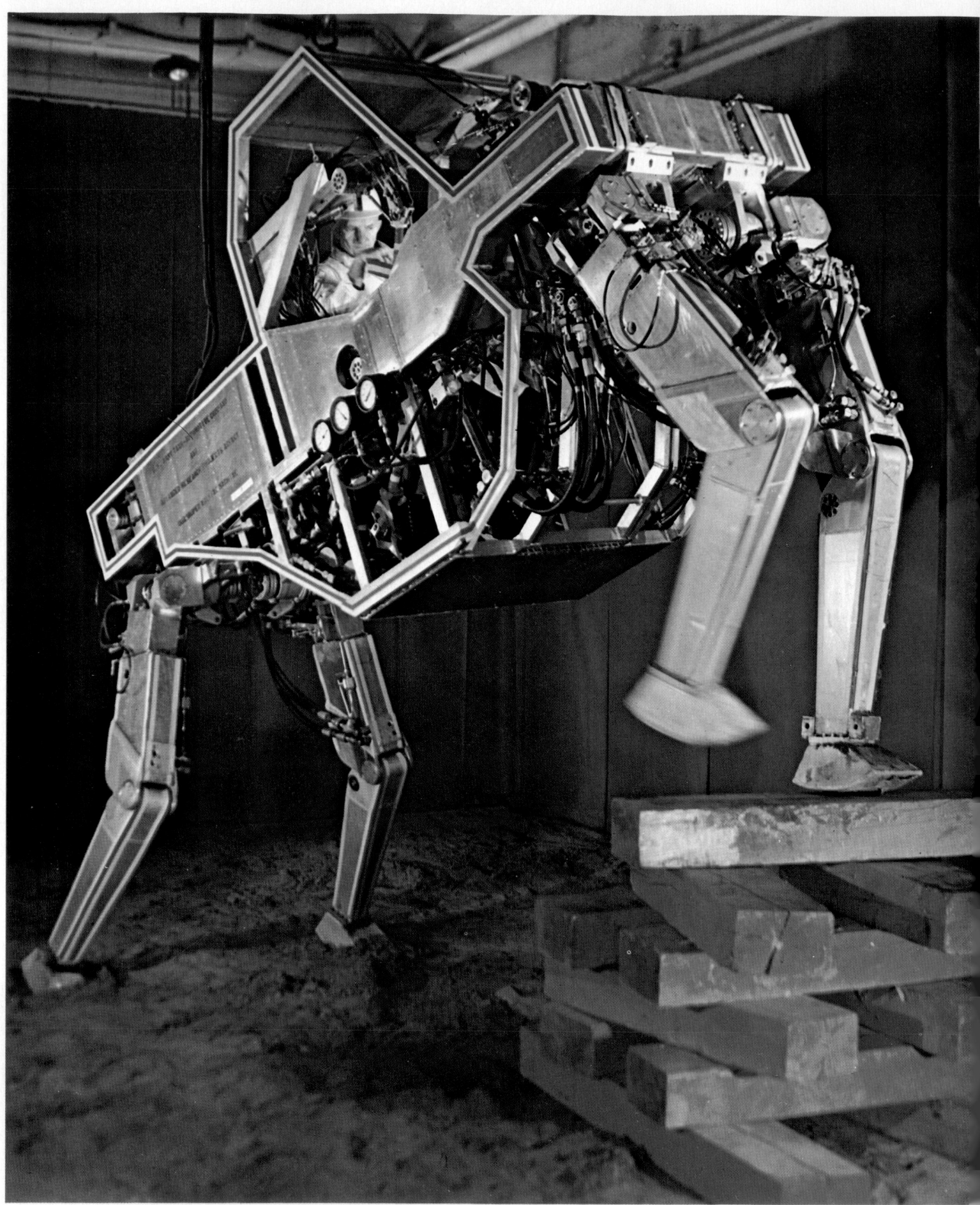

Modern Mechanical Research. This prototype of a 4-legged quadruped machine was developed by General Electric engineers. It was designed to spur development of equipment to improve the mobility and materials-handling capabilities of workers under the most severe conditions. By an advanced control system, the machine mimics and amplifies the linear movements of the operator. The front legs of the unit are controlled by the operator's arms and the rear legs by his legs. The research prototype—11 feet high and 3000 pounds in weight—was built by GE under a joint U.S. government agency contract.

Economics and Useful Arts

INTRODUCTION

ECONOMICS is the study of the means by which people obtain their livelihood and satisfy their wants. Many thinkers maintain that the economic system under which a people lives largely determines the form of all its institutions, including its morality, family life, religion, and art. Whether or not this view is entirely correct, there can be no doubt that, along with political government, economic conditions constitute a factor of supreme importance in the life of man.

The economic system touches the life of every man, woman, and child, primarily through their jobs or other sources of income or support and through the prices which must be paid in securing what they want. When jobs fail or prices fluctuate unduly, the average person senses that something is wrong. On giving it proper attention, he begins to perceive that he is part of a vast system of world-wide sweep. If he is to be an intelligent citizen and understand the forces which have such a large part in determining his well-being, it is essential that he study the economic system under which he lives.

The Economic System. In the normal course of events, every one of us, unless he is altogether dependent on others, contributes something to the common store of goods and services. In return, he receives, through the agency of money, the right to a certain share of that common store.

The present economic system of production, distribution, and consumption has been built and rebuilt by many generations, the results differing according to each generation's degree of intelligence, skill, and invention, its command over nature, and its social relationships. The system rests on such institutions as property and contract, the division of labor, competition, and combination. Behind all the factors of an economic system are the laws of human nature. These laws, working through the instincts to acquire, to possess, and to provide for family and dependents, operate to convert the vast resources and powers of the earth into human service.

Under the impact of two world wars, the economic system has been subjected to tremendous strains and shocks of abnormal periods. We have seen inflation and deflation at their greatest extremes, high prices, scarcity of raw materials, rationing and governmental price fixing, excess profits tax, and other programs and policies necessitated by world conflict. The divergent interests of workers and employers, labor and capital, have frequently set class against class, while the intensive research in products and methods has given us great improvements in machines and time-saving devices, all of which have displaced great numbers of workers from one form of employment into other forms, causing a change in the personal life of the individual affecting his housing, type of employment, wage, and social position.

The economic system of a democratic country must assume that the right of private property is an inalienable right. With this right of ownership and possession for use, man becomes a dignified human being and possesses initiative and an incentive to achieve a better education, and a better position so that he may provide more adequately for himself and his family

Today, millions of people live under one or the other of two world economic systems designated as Capitalism and Communism. In the "free world," where people are self-governed, Capitalism prevails. The economic life of the country is carried on by private enterprise instead of government directives. The individual citizen can choose his own occupation, invest his savings as he wishes, and otherwise manage his personal and business affairs. Competition is essentially free, and the hope of profit provides an incentive for industry and thrift. In Russia, which operates under a system of modified Marxist Communism, production has been placed on a basis of use rather than profit, and the strong central government allocates production, regulates prices, and assigns positions. Under this "controlled economy" the individual surrenders his independence and initiative and has his entire future education, work, and leisure time planned for him. While Russia has recently made some concessions to the individual citizen by increasing the supply and availability of consumer goods, an extreme form of Communism exists in mainland China.

In the United States of America, which has the world's highest standard of living, it is recognized that the government, as a servant of all the people, must provide for laws and regulations so that all persons, regardless of race, creed, or color, may have the opportunity of training and work so that they in return may provide for themselves and their families. The purpose of a government in our economic system is simply to outline the rights and responsibilities of each group, so that no one transgresses upon the rights of others.

The Division of Labor. This is the key to the understanding of the whole economic order. If every man or every family produced only for himself or itself, there would be no exchange, no markets, no money, no means of transportation; in fact, no economic system. Some such situation actually existed in the more primitive ages of the world where each household was almost self-sufficient. With the advance of civilization, however, came the division of labor. Men have discovered that it is far more profitable to co-operate with one another, each finding and keeping to his own special task.

Ours is an age of specialization. To provide the breakfast of even the humblest family in a modern country, all parts of the earth are drawn upon. To serve our needs we have thus built up the vast network of modern trade and commerce.

Linking the World. The greatest benefits of the division of labor are reaped when cities and districts and countries exchange with one another those products which they can produce most advantageously. Such advantages in the production of certain commodities may arise in a particular place by reason of its climate, soil, natural resources, and the capacities of its inhabitants. The United States, with its wide range of soil and climate, is more self-sufficient than most countries. But it needs the rubber and tin of the East Indies, the silk of Japan, the nickel of Canada, and a thousand other products which commerce brings to our shores.

In a similar way, different parts of the same country specialize and create domestic trade. Indiana specializes in corn; South Dakota, in wheat; California, in oranges. Each produces the crops which it can raise to the greater advantage. Likewise, the city depends on the country, but so also does the country depend on the city.

By aid of the means of communication, we have today markets that are nation-wide and even world-wide for the main articles of commerce—wheat, cotton, wool, rubber, and so forth. By aid of the system of transportation, the resources of the world are exploited and brought wherever there is a demand for them. Nowhere have these agencies been more highly developed than in the United States, and nowhere have they been such important factors in the building up of a national life.

Capital and Labor. We often speak of capital as a form of wealth. It also has another aspect, which appears when we contrast capital with labor. The relationships among these two contributors to economic production constitute one of the most interesting and dynamic aspects of society. Before the Industrial Revolution, workers generally owned the tools of their craft. The mechanization of industry, however, separated workers from the tools of production, which became too costly and impersonal to be owned by each man. Ownership passed to the company or corporation employing the workers. Consequently, interest in the products of the economic unit became divided, with portions going to both owners and workers. During the 20th century, ownership claims became further separated from management, as a third specialized contributor to economic activity. The expectations of all three have now to be balanced and reconciled.

The diverse interests of all contributors and claimants against the economic product or output are in conflict among themselves, but coordination of them is essential in the harmonious functioning of the economic system. They *must* work together. The dominance of any one of the interests shifts the balance of power. Owners originally held dominion —with the rise of labor unions, however, control over economic processes passed more to workers collectively. More recently, managers have enjoyed a type of supremacy. Inability to resolve conflicts among these parties has led to the government's increasingly mediating and regulating their respective activities. These issues are treated in the *Labor Relations* section.

From Producer to Consumer. When production takes place on a large scale, the consumer is no longer in direct and personal relation to the producer. Hence arises the need for agencies to bring the two together. Modern business makes necessary a system of commission houses, jobbers, wholesalers, and retailers. They all have their parts to perform in the division of labor, and, as such, they serve useful economic functions. The practical aspect of this subject is taken up in the discussion of *Marketing*, and *Selling and Advertising*.

Money as the Medium of Exchange. All this interchange requires a scale of value and an exchange system. This is achieved through the modern use of money. Direct barter, various commodities, and silver and gold have served as means of exchange, but today money serves this function and, depending upon a convention or custom, it includes anything *generally* acceptable as a means of making payments. Thus, in the U.S. today, money includes coins, paper bills, and demand (or checking) accounts.

For the creation and control of money, a vast system of institutions has arisen, consisting in the U.S. of individual banks and other financial institutions, as well as the Federal Reserve System— and, on the international level, there are such institutions (with the U.S. and other nations as members) as the International Monetary Fund and the International Bank for Reconstruction and Development, generally known as the World Bank.

Pervading the monetary system is the very important element of credit. In effect, credit is a special form of money which expands and contracts as loans are made and then repaid. It permits purchase in advance of immediate ability to pay, thereby generating a chain of economic activity from borrower, to retailer, to manufacturer or builder, and thence to employees and purchasers.

The control of credit is the key to the expansion of the means of production, the level of employment, and the scale of living. Governments ultimately hold this key. In the modern world they recognize this responsibility and devote much of their attention to it in order to keep as even a keel as possible between inflation with rising prices and deflation with attendant unemployment and loss of purchasing power. These subjects are treated under *Insurance, Investments, Money and Banking.*

The Stages of Production. In a study of Useful Arts, we begin with the land, for on it or out of it (including, as economists do, the oceans and inland waters as part of the "land") are produced all the raw materials which the labor and organization of men turn into the means of satisfying their numerous wants. Thus we have first in order the extractive industries, which are described under the titles *Agriculture, Animal Industry, Fisheries,* and *Mining and Mineral Production.*

Most raw materials—wheat, cotton, wool, silk, iron, copper, lumber, and a host of others—go through many and elaborate processes before they are ready for their final use. They must be conveyed by land and water, they must pass through many hands, they must be treated by complicated machinery. Production calls for the work of the inventor and of the engineer no less than that of the farmer and of the miner. Hence the division on *Inventions* and on *Engineering and Building.*

Then comes the last stage, that of manufacturing. In the plant of the manufacturer, the work of the farmer, the miner, the inventor, and the engineer is brought together. Out of the factory the results of their labor pass at last as finished goods, and the whole roundabout process of production is complete. The more important aspects of this last step are treated under *Manufacturing.*

The Age of Industry. One man today can do the work which hundreds or even thousands were needed to perform in the pre-industrial age. Power has been harnessed and applied in countless ways. Steam and electricity and oil and gasoline serve the desires of man. The blast furnace, the power loom, the self-binding reaper, the linotype machine—to mention at random a few of our innumerable inventions—make possible an efficiency of production which surpasses the wildest dreams of the past. The standard of living of ever-greater populations has risen vastly. The ordinary man has at his command commodities that in earlier times were the rare luxuries of kings. Thus has industry, aided by invention, revolutionized the world. The Industrial Revolution is well named because, of all the great changes society has known, none has been at once so rapid and so extensive as this development. A period of much less than a hundred years saw the transformation of the everyday life of our Western civilization, saw a remarkable change in the habits and thoughts and modes of work of many millions, saw a new power over nature created, and saw the very face of the country completely altered.

To understand these things is to understand our own age and civilization. Through a study of economics and the arts of production, we may attain this understanding and learn in a new way the meaning of the world and the society in which we live.

Mass Production. A logical modern extension of the Industrial Revolution has been the introduction of large-scale manufacturing operations. These cut unit costs, thus permitting lower prices, wider markets, and greater profits. The next step is investment of part of the profits and new money in developing new products through research and utilization of the advances of science.

As a final stage comes the application of the computer for making automatic numerous steps in manufacture, control of operations, and even many decisions of management.

COMMERCE

COMMERCE consists of all those processes of trade involved in the general distribution of commodities from the producer to the consumer. However, the term generally implies an exchange of large volumes of merchandise between different places or communities rather than the trade carried on between individuals. Traffic passing from one nation to another is *foreign*, or *international*, commerce; that moving between localities included within national boundaries is *internal*, or *domestic*, commerce. In the United States, commercial shipments of merchandise from one state to another are said to enter nto *interstate* commerce.

Origins. The desire of man to satisfy his wants as easily as possible supplies the primary reason for commercial transactions. However, there can be comparatively little exchange between countries or districts inhabited by people who produce the same type of commodities; for then, neither locality has anything required by the other. Commerce, therefore, depends upon existing differences in temperature and climate, in natural resources, in industrial development, or in racial and cultural characteristics.

Transportation and Commerce. Wherever such differences exist, the inhabitants of one district will generally have a surplus of certain commodities which they are anxious to exchange for the surplus from other places. But, before the exchange can be accomplished, the goods must be transported to the locality where they are needed. For this reason commerce and transportation are mutually dependent to such an extent that the condition of one is almost invariably indicated by a corresponding degree of development in the other.

Because of this intimate relationship, the history of commerce may be divided into three fairly distinct periods: First, that in which transportation was accomplished by man or by beasts of burden on land, and by coasting vessels on the water. Second, that in which mariners, by the aid of the compass, were able to guide their sailing vessels upon the open seas. Third, that in which transportation depended chiefly on the power of steam, internal combustion, and other forms of engines. The first period, of possibly 5000 years' duration, extended from the beginning of commerce well into the 15th century, in spite of the fact that the compass was known in parts of Europe as early as 1200; the second period, of about 400 years' duration, may be said to have terminated in 1838, when the first line of commercial steamships began. The third period is that of the past century.

ANCIENT COMMERCE

Early exchange centered on Mesopotamia, the "Great Road" between Central Asia, the Mediterranean Sea, and Egypt. Commerce was related to geographic location and raw material shortages. Metals, semiprecious stones, building stone, timber, and aromatic woods and spices were important commodities. Manufacturing of woolen cloth and bronze work occurred. Until 3000 B.C., trade was by barter and controlled by the temple. Early legal codes, and even the beginning of civil law, evolved from the commercial experience and early guilds were formed. In this period, Damascus in Syria emerged as a major trade center for the caravan routes crossing the region from the Mediterranean and Red Seas to the interior.

The Phœnicians. The first people devoted chiefly to commerce were the Phœnicians, who inhabited a strip of land about 100 miles long and 10 miles wide on the eastern coast of the Mediterranean. Forced upon the sea as fishermen, these people gradually developed commercial fleets which in time extended their voyages to the Strait of Gibraltar and even north to England. The ships brought back ivory, tin, copper, and precious metals, while caravans sent inland brought spices and frankincense from India. Manufacturing produced glassware, linen and woolen cloth, and metal work. Profits from commerce and manufacturing supported the merchant and leisure class. Great cities such as Sidon and Tyre emerged and extensive colonization, such as the founding of the great city of Carthage, took place on Mediterranean shores and parts of the Atlantic coast. For perhaps 1000 years, the Phœnicians dominated commerce and served not only to exchange commodities but ideas and cultures, as well.

The Greeks. Eventually, the commercial supremacy of the Phœnicians passed to the Greeks, who excelled both as sailors and as business men. Their homeland, which in area was smaller than the state of Maine, nevertheless offered great incentives to commerce. It was sufficiently fertile to afford a surplus of some products, such as wine, figs, and olive oil, but it did not produce enough grain to feed the population. Mountains on the north protected it fairly well from attack by land; it was centrally located in relation to other countries of the Mediterranean; and its extensive coast line afforded many good harbors.

The conditions of living in a small, well populated country having an insufficient supply of grain were conducive to emigration; ships furnished an easy means of travel. Consequently, for a period of about 500 years, the Greeks followed a consistent policy of founding and of developing settlements in fertile sections of foreign lands, notably on the Black Sea, in Asia Minor, and in southern Italy and Sicily. Malaga, in Spain, and what is now Marseille, in France, were sites of thriving Greek colonies. From these colonies, grain and raw materials were supplied to the mother country, which developed many manufacturing industries, especially the production of bronze, clay, marble, and woolen products.

The Greeks were quick to adopt new devices for facilitating commerce. From contact with the Phœnician traders, they acquired an alphabet, which they greatly improved. From the Lydians of Asia Minor, they learned to mark pieces of silver with an official seal and to use these coins as money.

In spite of the success of the Persians, who broke the Greek power in the East, the Western colonies developed more rapidly than before, while Greece itself, under the leadership of Athens, reached the pinnacle of its power.

Empire of Alexander. The enormous eastern empire held by the Macedonian, Alexander the Great, took away from Athens the control of commerce and led to the development of great commercial cities farther east. Of these, the largest was Alexandria, located near the western corner of the Nile delta. As the greatest of Hellenistic cities, it surpassed all previous commercial centers in volume of trade and was a cosmopolitan economic and intellectual center. The Pharos, the 370-foot-high harbor lighthouse, was considered one of the seven wonders of the ancient world.

The Romans. The expansion of Roman power outside of Italy is said to have begun in 241 B. C., when Sicily was taken from the Carthaginians. Ninety-five years later, the great commercial cities of Carthage and Corinth were destroyed by Roman soldiers, and Greece and Macedonia were reduced to the position of Roman provinces.

Although Rome ruled the Western world, she never became a commercial city. Captives of war were extensively sold as slaves, and great quantities of foodstuffs, manufactured products, and luxuries were sent to the capital by sea, and over the fine roads that were constructed by Roman engineers, even in the farthest provinces. These products, however, to a large extent, did not represent commercial transactions but were the tributes and taxes imposed upon conquered peoples. What Rome gave in return was almost five centuries of comparative peace and security, during which time commerce developed wherever conditions permitted.

MEDIEVAL COMMERCE

During the "dark ages" that followed the fall of Rome, commerce was almost entirely in the hands of the Mohammedans, with centers at Baghdad, Damascus, Cairo, Alexandria, and the Moorish cities in Spain.

Western and northern Europe became divided under the feudal system into thousands of tiny units, each attempting to be complete within itself, and entirely independent of all external sources of supply. Roads were totally neglected; strangers were regarded with suspicion; robbery was a common practice; and commerce, under such conditions, was quite naturally almost nonexistent.

Growth of Towns. Soon after 1000 A. D. the need for places where an interchange of commodities might be carried on was filled by the widespread development of towns. In these growing communities, manufacturing and trading not only became possible, but were necessary in order to provide something to exchange for the food and raw materials brought in at first from the surrounding country, and, later, from other parts of the world.

Under these conditions some men were enabled to devote all of their time to trading and dealing in commodities. The fear of the townspeople that these traders would take undue advantage of their opportunities, coupled with the prevalent suspicions of all strangers, next led to the establishment of *public markets*, where commercial transactions might be carried on under official supervision. As the markets increased in size and prosperity, traders customarily united for mutual benefit, forming *merchants' guilds*. Somewhat later, the craftsmen also combined, according to their special trades, to form *craftsmen's guilds*. The guilds provided the merchants and artisans with a position in the social order, a monopoly of the town's trade, and considerable power in local government.

Fairs. European trade expanded in the 11th century to meet the demand for goods from beyond local regions. This led to the establishment of fairs, usually held annually and under the protection of powerful lords. Participants were guaranteed protection and safe conduct, and efforts were made to ensure honest dealings. The fairs of Champagne, in northern France—in a fertile region crossed by major trade routes—were the most famous. Each country and region, however, had its own fair. As the most important form of commercial activity in their time, medieval fairs had a profound influence: they served to promote Western civilization by destroying the provincialism and bigotry of the "Dark Ages," and by establishing the basis for expanded trade, monetary economies, and commercial law.

Risks of Medieval Commerce. The extensive commerce of the latter part of the medieval period was carried on at very great risk, because of constant rivalry and open warfare between great commercial cities. There was no central government sufficiently powerful to enforce its laws and to guarantee security. Shipments on land and by inland waterways were subject both to innumerable and excessive tolls and to constant danger from highway robbers. Similarly, coasting vessels always had to be ready for battle with pirates or with ships from rival cities.

Venice and the Hanse. In the north of Europe, during the 13th and the 14th century, the great commercial cities of Lubeck, Hamburg, Cologne, Danzig, and many others united, for mutual protection, into an organization known as the Hanse, or Hanseatic league. This league became extremely powerful and had complete control of commerce with the countries on the Baltic and, to a large extent, with those on the North Sea.

On the Mediterranean the struggle for supremacy was largely between Venice and her chief rivals, Genoa and Pisa. Leadership was secured to Venice by the crafty manner in which the doge, Enrico Dondolo, directed the energies of the Fourth Crusade, first to the capture of Zara, a rival Christian city, and next, in 1203, to the subjugation of Constantinople. Venice then completely dominated the trade with the East, and developed commerce to a degree never before attained. Venetian methods of banking and bookkeeping represented standards that were copied throughout the commercial world.

Between Venice and northern Europe, commerce was carried on in two ways: Traders from central and southern Germany were permitted to bring their metals, furs, coarse textiles, twine, and leather over the Alps by way of the Brenner or the Saint Gotthard pass, to Venice. By sea, the Venetian galleys, with their precious cargoes of spices, dyes, alum, fine textiles, weapons, and paper, traveled to Flanders. Bruges, which was succeeded in the 15th century by Antwerp, was the common center at which the wares of Venice were traded for the fish, furs, coarse textiles, wax, grain, and salt meat brought by the ships of the Hanseatic league, and for the wool, tallow, leather, tin, and lead of England. English exports at this time were almost entirely under the control of the "Merchants of the Staple," a society composed chiefly of foreigners.

MODERN COMMERCE

During the 14th and the 15th century, England, France, and Spain were becoming nations in which many loosely connected feudal divisions were gradually merged under comparatively strong central governments. Then, for the first time, the individual cities of Italy and the weak organization of the Hanse came into conflict with commercial rivals who had less experience but were more powerful and determined than themselves.

Portugal, under the direction of wise rulers, had already attained the leadership in navigation; not because the Portuguese were better sailors than the Venetians, the Genoese, or the mariners of the Hanseatic league, but because they received encouragement and assistance from their government.

New Trade Routes. In the East, the ancient land routes by which the commerce of India and of China had reached Venice were gradually cut off by the spread of Turkish power. As a result, each of the important European nations was actively searching for the "Eastern passage" by which their ships could reach the fabulously rich countries of the Orient.

In 1492, Columbus, a Genoese in command of Spanish vessels, sailed west until he reached the New World, which blocked the direct route to Asia. Cabot, an Italian master of an English ship, reached North America in 1497. Finally, by sailing around Africa, Vasco da Gama, a Portuguese, established trade by sea with India in 1498, and returned home the next year with goods that sold for sixty times the cost of the voyage. In 1522 the expedition which had set out from Spain three years before under command of Magellan completed the first voyage around the world.

The Portuguese obtained the rewards due the winner of the race to the East, for to them Pope Alexander VI assigned all of Africa and of Asia, with the exception of the Philippines. The Americas, except Brazil, were allotted to Spain.

The Struggle for Supremacy. The open seas now became the highway on which the ships of Portugal, Spain, France, and England speeded in order to obtain as much as possible from the newly found sources of wealth. Portuguese ships brought back great quantities of Eastern products which, because of the increased supply, eventually sold at prices low enough to change such important commodities as tea, coffee, and sugar from luxuries to necessities. Lisbon for a time succeeded Antwerp as the most important city of commerce.

Spain. During the century which followed the discovery of America, Spain became the richest and most important country on the earth. From her colonies she received enormous quantities of gold

Year	Population	Total Commerce $	Commerce per Capita $	Ships, Sail Tons	Ships, Steam Tons	Railways Miles
1850	1,075,000,000	4,049,000,000	3.76	11,470,000	864,000	24,000
1860	1,205,000,000	7,246,000,000	6.01	14,890,000	1,710,000	67,400
1870	1,310,000,000	10,663,000,000	8.14	12,900,000	3,040,000	139,900
1880	1,439,000,000	14,761,000,000	10.26	14,400,000	5,880,000	224,900
1890	1,488,000,000	17,519,000,000	11.80	9,166,000	8,295,000	390,000
1900	1,543,000,000	20,105,000,000	13.02	6,674,000	13,857,000	500,000
1910	1,616,000,000	33,634,000,000	20.81	4,624,000	22,046,000	637,000
1920	1,730,000,000	61,277,000,000	35.42	4,066,000	32,092,000[3]	710,600
1930	2,000,000,000	69,526,000,000[1]	34.28[1]	....	69,734,310[4]	706,090
1940	2,170,000,000	27,706,000,000[2]	12.92[2]	....	69,439,659[5]	756,781[6]
1950	2,400,000,000	58,400,000,000	24.31		75,718,000	783,679
1960	3,005,000,000	264,000,000,000[10]	113.80	61,655,000[11]	74,261,000	N.A.
1968	3,483,000,000	491,000,000,000[10]	141.00	119,889,000[12]	74,263,000	N.A.
1974	3,690,000,000	1,584,500,000,000[13]	407.32	215,979,000[12]	126,184,000	N.A.

Year	Telegraphs Miles	Cables[8] Miles	Cotton Pounds	Coal Short tons	Pig Iron Long tons	Gold Production $
1850	5,000	25	1,435,000,000	81,400,000	4,700,000	363,900,000
1860	100,000	1,500	2,551,000,000	142,300,000	7,200,000	1,334,000,000
1870	281,000	15,000	2,775,000,000	213,400,000	11,900,000	1,263,000,000
1880	440,000	49,000	3,601,000,000	340,000,000	18,000,000	1,150,800,000
1890	768,000	132,000	5,600,000,000	466,000,000	27,200,000	1,060,100,000
1900	1,180,000	200,000	6,247,000,000	800,000,000	40,400,000	2,100,000,000
1910	1,307,000	291,000	9,013,000,000	1,141,600,000	65,800,000	3,780,700,000
1920	1,592,000	....	9,405,000,000	1,305,000,000	68,300,000	4,253,800,000
1930	7,119,665	360,613	12,900,000,000	1,196,003,000	80,289,000	3,846,848,000
1940	6,730,500[7]	344,079[2]	14,770,820,000	1,615,972,000[2]	104,000,000	8,562,100,000
1950	5,089,000	344,079[2]	13,750,000,000	1,441,257,000	112,800,000	8,610,000,000
1960	N.A.	N.A.	22,000,000,000	2,170,000,000	286,000,000	1,175,000,000
1968	N.A.	N.A.	25,000,000,000	2,217,000,000	425,000,000	1,420,000,000
1974	N.A.	N.A.	27,000,000,000	1,870,000,000	485,000,000[13]	1,371,000,000

[1] 1929. [2] 1938. [3] Includes motor ships. [4] Gross Tons, includes motor and sail ships. [5] Includes barges, motor and sail ships, 1939. [6] 1937. [7] 1939. [8] Nautical miles. [9] For decade ending year named. [10] Imports and exports. [11] Motor, 1961. [12] Motor. [13] 1975.

and silver, and also many valuable cargoes of hides, drugs, dyes, cocoa, vanilla, and sugar. Manufacturing industries at home were developed on a large scale for the production of silk and woolen textiles, wines, soap, salt, and many other commodities. In addition to manufactured articles, Spain exported figs, raisins, olives, olive oil, iron ore, and large amounts of mercury for use in obtaining gold and silver at the mines of Mexico and Peru.

All of these great advantages were nullified and finally destroyed by a prolonged period of bad government, marked especially by exorbitant taxes of every kind, and by a policy of exploitation rather than assistance in connection with the colonies. So serious were the results that the population declined rapidly, and some great commercial cities retained only one-fourth of their former inhabitants.

Portugal. The commercial greatness of Portugal was open to attack by her rivals, because it lacked the firm foundation of domestic production. The Portuguese were excellent traders, but their country was small and was not developed industrially. Manufactured articles for export were not made at home but had to be purchased from other European countries. Consequently, England and the Netherlands were eventually able to cut off Portugal's supply of export goods, and to fill the Eastern demand themselves. In addition to this fundamental lack of commercial stability, Portugal fell under the harmful rule of Spain during the 60 years between 1581 and 1640. By the time the Spanish yoke was cast off, England had broken Portuguese control in India, and the Netherlands had taken the islands of Ceylon, Sumatra, Java, and the valuable Moluccas, or Spice islands.

The Netherlands. Dutch traders were quick to take advantage of the opportunities offered by the decline of Spain and Portugal. Their ships traveled to India and to the Eastern islands, and were equally active in European trade. Most of the wool exported by Spain was carried to northern countries by Dutch vessels, which also entered the Baltic and returned with cargoes from Russia.

At home, large business companies grew up, the manufacture of silk and of leather was developed,

the fishing industry increased until more than 2000 fishing boats were regularly employed, and business of all forms was greatly stimulated. The Netherlands became the financial center, and Amsterdam the most important commercial city, of Europe.

Unfortunately for the country, a strong central government was lacking, corruption became common among high officials, and taxes were greatly increased. The volume of commerce ceased to grow after 1730. In 1798 the Dutch East India Company, which had ruled all of the Eastern possessions and for 180 years had paid average annual dividends of over 18 per cent, came to an end. Its debts of more than 50 million dollars were assumed by the government.

France. Among the five European nations that achieved commercial power during the modern period of 1500 to 1800, France was one of the two which a historian in the 16th century would probably have selected as most likely to reach and to keep first place. Portugal and the Netherlands were obviously handicapped by their lack of area and domestic resources. But France and Spain were the largest and richest countries of western Europe, and both had extensive coast lines. In exploration, France surpassed both the English and the Dutch, while in area of foreign colonies, she was second only to Spain.

France did develop a prosperous trade with the Levant and with Italy and Spain, but this could not become of first importance because faulty political organization raised almost insuperable obstacles to the free flow of commerce.

The greatest checks to commerce within the country were due to the existence of feudal divisions which prevented national unity, to the continuance of the guilds long after these organizations had been displaced in more progressive nations, and to the establishment of an absolute monarchy wherein the correction of existing evils was impossible unless the ruler was unusually strong and wise. High customs duties were collected whenever goods entered the country and also when they crossed from one internal division to another. The quarrels and the strict regulations of the numerous guilds

CANADIAN SHIPPING, 1972
Cargo Loaded and Unloaded, 15 Major Ports
(in 1,000-ton units)

PORTS	International		Coastwise		Total
	Loaded	Unloaded	Loaded	Unloaded	
Vancouver, B.C.	24,358	2,918	3,546	4,074	34,987
Sept.-Iles, Que.	17,779	391	3,418	734	22,324
Montreal, Que.	4,738	5,779	5,171	10,024	25,513
Port Arthur, Ont.	4,533	148	17,599	812	23,094
Hamilton, Ont.	350	7,619	219	4,991	12,680
Port Cartier, Que.	11,594	650	38	2,804	15,088
Halifax, N.S.	3,685	5,434	1,885	710	11,715
Quebec, Que.	4,323	5,772	1,512	3,226	14,385
Toronto, Ont.	267	2,298	122	1,579	4,267
St. John, N.B.	2,346	6,019	1,818	133	10,317
New Westminster, B.C.	728	352	994	946	3,020
Sault Ste. Marie, Ont.	212	2,755	185	1,764	4,917
Baie Comeau, Que.	3,768	1,240	181	2,724	7,826
Port Alfred, Que.	445	3,589	4.4	472	4,512
Sorel, Que.	2,624	4,607	2,531	604	8,085

Source: *Canada Year Book, 1974.*

largely prevented any improvements in methods of manufacture, and, finally, selfish monarchs entered upon a series of wars which gained nothing at home and lost most of the colonies abroad.

England. In spite of serious wars and intense commercial competition with larger countries, England, by 1750, had become the dominating factor in world commerce. Of the various reasons for her success, two may be considered as fundamental: First, she was a part of Europe and yet was separated from the continent by a wide channel which effectively prevented invasion by land; this condition made the possession of a powerful navy a primary necessity for national safety. Second, England acquired a coherent central government much sooner than did her rivals, and this government was far more flexible and democratic than theirs.

As a basis for exchange with other countries, England had from very early times the products of her sheep industry and of her mines. Manufacturing industries were gradually developed, which changed these raw materials into cloth and metal products. Ships were required to carry the excess production to other countries, and ships were needed also for protection and to supply trained sailors to the navy in time of war. The government, therefore, adopted the policy of encouraging shipping and

commerce. Whenever possible, special privileges were secured by the state for English merchants, and success in battle usually meant the addition of foreign colonies in which an extension of trade could be expected.

English Trading Companies. During the 17th century, English commerce was to a large extent controlled by trading companies such as the East India Company, the Guinea Company, the Virginia Company, and the Hudson's Bay Company. A trader who was not a member of one of the companies could deal only with France, Spain, or Portugal. The strict control and regulations of the companies provoked so much antagonism that they finally lost their power and disbanded. The Hudson's Bay Company, however, still exists as an ordinary business corporation.

Having extensive colonies which supplied raw materials and required manufactured articles in return, together with a powerful merchant marine for the distribution of her products, England experienced at home a high degree of industrial development. Textiles and products of iron and steel were the chief commodities manufactured and exported. Homeward bound ships brought wool, cotton, naval stores, grain, sugar, tea, coffee, spices, tobacco, and rum; also silk, linen, and other foreign

CANADIAN COMMERCE
Imports and Exports to Selected Countries, 1930–1973
(add 000's)

YEAR	IMPORTS (in dollars)					EXPORTS (in dollars)				
	From U.K.	From Commonwealth	From U.S.	From Others	Total	To U.K.	To Commonwealth	To U.S.	To Others	Total
1930	227,816	*	653,676	126,987	1,008,479	316,342	*	373,424	173,917	863,683
1935	173,889	*	312,417	64,009	550,315	377,644	*	261,685	85,648	724,977
1940	267,383	*	744,231	70,336	1,081,950	655,957	*	442,984	80,013	1,178,954
1945	271,668	*	1,202,418	111,689	1,585,775	1,486,848	*	1,196,977	534,506	3,218,331
1950	400,811	240,988	2,089,531	393,901	3,125,231	467,896	184,362	2,020,703	431,055	3,104,016
1951	415,194	305,522	2,752,087	532,136	4,004,939	630,124	239,982	2,296,235	730,741	3,897,082
1952	351,541	183,911	2,887,628	493,338	3,916,418	744,461	260,788	2,302,673	974,339	4,282,261
1953	445,441	169,666	3,115,301	517,400	4,247,808	663,785	231,412	2,413,318	788,596	4,097,111
1954	382,229	180,759	2,871,279	533,134	3,967,401	651,033	193,768	2,308,670	706,746	3,860,217
1955	393,117	208,940	3,331,143	634,554	4,567,754	767,642	235,867	2,547,636	707,183	4,258,328
1956	476,371	220,437	4,031,394	818,749	5,546,951	811,113	242,011	2,803,085	904,233	4,760,442
1957	507,319	237,937	3,887,391	840,704	5,473,351	720,898	231,637	2,846,646	989,699	4,788,880
1958	518,505	208,702	3,460,147	863,138	5,050,492	771,576	281,435	2,808,067	930,358	4,791,436
1959	588,573	239,240	3,709,065	972,043	5,508,921	785,802	273,305	3,083,151	879,414	5,021,672
1960	588,930	279,069	3,693,189	931,160	5,492,348	915,290	326,958	2,932,171	1,089,633	5,264,052
1967	673,050	435,291†	8,016,341	1,950,517	11,075,199	1,169,053	638,201†	7,079,396	2,224,930	11,111,580
1973	1,005,397	1,991,296†	16,483,587	3,822,294	23,302,574	1,581,845	2,477,608†	16,611,868	4,629,694	25,301,005

† Commonwealth and preferential countries.   Source: *Canada Year Book, 1974.*

textiles. It must not be thought that all of this commerce depended on the colonies, for, at the end of the 18th century, more than half of England's trade was carried on with Europe. The trade with America ranked second in value. That with Africa was very much smaller, but was considered important because it furnished a supply of slaves for sale in America and the West Indies.

Canadian Commerce. The early commerce of Canada was controlled largely by monopolistic companies chartered by France. After the English conquest, control passed to British traders who confined their commerce almost entirely to the homeland. Early trade with the United States was by smuggling until Great Britain removed restrictions on normal traffic.

In 1975, Canada's foreign trade amounted to over $66 billion, with about two-thirds of its exports going to the United States, compared to about 6% to Great Britain. The United States supplies Canada with about 60% of its imports, while Great Britain supplies about 4½%. Major exports to Great Britain include foodstuffs and tobacco (about 20% of the total in value), aluminum, copper, nickel, newsprint, and lumber. Exports to the United States include raw materials, petroleum, lumber, and wood pulp. Canadian imports are largely manufactured goods, such as auto parts, machinery, and vehicles. The accompanying tables indicate the character of Canadian trade.

In 1975, Canada ranked 11th in world trade. It has enjoyed the trade advantages associated with membership in the British Commonwealth. In 1974 Canada entered into a comprehensive trade agreement with the European Common Market. This was an attempt to reduce its commercial dependence on the United States.

Class of Merchandise	Imports of Canada, 1973 (Thousand dollars)			Exports of Canada, 1973 (Thousand dollars)		
	From United Kingdom	From United States	From All Countries	To United Kingdom	To United States	To All Countries
Live Animals	1,527	131,007	137,105	1,433	117,821	144,688
Food, Feed, Beverages and Tobacco	68,164	861,073	1,844,380	332,575	861,562	3,007,857
Crude Materials, Inedible	33,115	780,215	2,016,253	311,685	2,733,613	5,019,059
Fabricated Materials, Inedible	252,470	2,823,959	4,281,513	774,718	5,697,755	8,194,083
End Products, Inedible	638,765	11,695,214	14,776,578	160,591	7,161,256	8,308,116
Special Transactions— Trade	11,356	192,119	246,747	843	39,855	45,355
Total	1,005,397	16,483,587	23,302,576	1,581,845	16,611,869	24,719,157

Source: *Canada Year Book, 1974.*

UNITED STATES

The preceding sections relate the story of commercial progress on the earth, from the days of ancient Babylon to the beginning of the 19th century. At the conclusion of this 4800-year period of development, world commerce had reached a yearly value of about one and one-half billion dollars. Of the total, the United States of America was credited with about one-tenth.

World commerce, due to advanced methods of transportation and communication, increased tremendously from 1800 to the present time, while from 1800 to the beginning of World War I the rise of American foreign commerce was almost proportional to that of the rest of the world. Assembly line methods in production of ships and planes enabled America to lead the world in World War II in its merchant marine tonnage, rail transportation, and air transport.

In the following paragraphs, the development of foreign commerce in the United States is given especial attention. The corresponding growth in other nations is indicated by the commercial relations of these countries with America, and by the comparative importance of each in world trade.

The commerce of the English colonies in North America was such as would be expected between fertile, newly discovered lands, and the older, more advanced countries. Food and raw materials, consisting chiefly of flour, grain, tobacco, lumber, fish, potash, and indigo, were exported in exchange for textiles and other manufactured articles, and for colonial products such as sugar, molasses, coffee, and tea.

It is surprising to note that after the Revolution the United States continued to trade chiefly with England, although that country closed the ports of the West Indies to American ships. The European wars between England on one side, and France, Spain, and the Netherlands on the other, afforded the new nation its first great commercial opportunity. Having ships and sailors equal to any in the world, the American merchant marine developed rapidly, and carried a large share of the world's commerce while Europe was busily engaged in warfare.

This commercial growth received serious checks when France and England both placed arbitrary restrictions on neutral shipping. A general embargo, ordered by the American government in 1807 as a means of retaliation, proved even more disastrous. Commerce declined until the conclusion of the War of 1812, and then, after a few years of sharp fluctuations, experienced a long period of slow growth.

Expansion and Development. This period was, for the United States, one of active territorial expansion and economic development. The West grew rapidly, and in various parts of the country improved highways, new canals, or steamboats on the large rivers supplied better means of transportation. At the same time, more and better manufactured commodities were produced by industries which had originated or developed during the seven years between the passing of the Embargo act and the end of the War of 1812. Domestic manufacturers fought hard to retain the home market which had been created by the temporary shortage of foreign goods. They succeeded to a notable extent because their increased *production* was accompanied by an even greater increase in *demand*, together with great improvements in the natural means of *distribution*. Although the *per capita* consumption of foreign goods decreased, the total amount of foreign trade continued to increase, and was carried chiefly by American ships. During this period the American merchant marine approached very closely in size that of Great Britain, and was second to none in skill and efficiency.

The change in the economic condition of the country is well shown by the changes in the list of exports. In 1800, grain amounted to one-third, and cotton to less than one-fourteenth, of all exported merchandise; in 1860, cotton accounted for four-sevenths of the total, and grain for only one-thirteenth. Manufactured goods, which stood low on the earlier list, were second only to cotton in 1860.

Triangular Exchange. The South gave all of its energies to the production of cotton. The North developed extensive manufacturing industries, but it also produced sufficient grain and meat to supply the entire nation and still had a surplus for export. From New Orleans, enormous quantities of cotton were shipped to Europe. Europe returned to New York textiles, articles manufactured from iron and steel, and luxuries. Finally, the cycle was completed and the South received compensation for its cotton in the form of food and manufactured products sent from the North.

Effects of Civil War. Intersectional warfare checked for a time the development of American commerce. With the war's end, slavery had been abolished and the nation was again a political unit. The war also had the effect of influencing the economic futures of the two opposing sections. The world demand for cotton, and the consequent high prices paid for this staple, forced the South to resume the production of white fiber as rapidly as possible. In the North, a shortage of labor accentuated the advantages that were to be obtained by the extensive use of machinery in the factories and on the farms.

1850 to 1900. During the second quarter of the 19th century the annual production of coal increased from one-half million to six million tons, and the economic value of railroads was clearly demonstrated. Between 1850 and 1860, thousands of miles of track were laid, especially in the Middle West. Our domestic exports, which amounted to 316 million dollars in 1860, averaged less than 225 million dollars a year until 1870; but by 1880 they became 824 million, and in 1892 they exceeded one billion dollars for the first time.

The last half of the 19th century was marked throughout the civilized world by the expansion of industrial and commercial activities. That the United States was able to hold a position of decided commercial importance is shown by the tables, *A Century of Growth of the United States* and *World's Progress in Commerce and Production*.

Merchant Marine. This position was retained in spite of a great decline in American shipping. Many conditions contributed to this marked decrease in tonnage. The country was expanding and developing so rapidly that there were unusual opportunities for profits in domestic rather than in foreign trade. Higher tariff rates gave protection to home industries but did not help the merchant marine. Lower priced, foreign-built ships were not purchased because, according to the law, they could not obtain American registry. And, finally, we were not prepared to build iron ships at a cost that could compete with those built in England.

In 1860, 70 per cent of our exports and 63 per cent of the imports were carried by American vessels. These ratios fell to about 10 per cent in 1910 but rose to more than 35.8 per cent by 1935. The foreign commerce of the United States amounted to $21.26 *per capita* in 1860. Fifty years later, although population was three times as great, the figures had increased to $34.78. In 1920, following World War I, the amount became $120.81, but fell to $77.59 by 1929. It was $48.92 in 1940; $137.63 in 1964.

U.S. Exports and Imports. Historically, U.S. exports were characterized by large quantities of relatively few products, largely agricultural in nature. In 1860, 80% of the exports were in this category, reflecting the impact of colonialism upon the country. In 1975 exports from the U.S. amounted to over $106 billion, consisting largely of manufactured products. Principal exports included various machinery (almost one-third of the total), grain, industrial chemicals, iron and steel mill products, automobiles and aircraft.

While major imports emphasize raw materials and food requirements, the U.S. also purchases manufactured goods abroad. While manufactured items accounted for more than half the imports in 1860, by 1975 they accounted for only slightly more than one-third. Major imports include machinery and vehicles, petroleum, electrical apparatus, iron and steel products, wood pulp and paper products, metals, chemicals, sugar and coffee. Many of these items come from the uuderdeveloped countries of the world.

UNITED STATES EXPORTS AND IMPORTS,
1974 (Million Dollars)

EXPORTS		IMPORTS	
RANK	$ VALUE	RANK	$ VALUE
1. Total Machinery	38,189	1. Petroleum & products	24,210
2. Grains and preparations*	11,898	2. Total machinery	11,862
3. Chemicals	8,822	3. Automobiles (and parts)	10,640
4. Automobiles (and parts)	7,878	4. Iron & steel mill products	5,013
5. Aircraft (and parts)	5,766	5. Chemicals	3,991
6. Iron & steel mill products	2,500	6. Nonferrous base metals	3,925
7. Coal	2,487	7. Pulp, paper, and products	2,572
8. Textiles and apparel	2,196	8. Sugar	2,256
9. Cotton	1,335	9. Metal manufactures	2,053
10. Nonferrous base metals and alloys	1,300	10. Coffee	1,504
Total	82,371	Total	68,026

* Including soybeans.

U. S. Foreign Trade. The foreign trade of the United States amounted to $4.2 billion in 1913. Principal participants included Great Britain, an 18% share, Canada 13%, Germany 12.5%, France 7%, and several other nations significant largely in terms of a single commodity—Cuba and sugar, Brazil and coffee.

By 1975, not only had total U.S. foreign trade increased to nearly $200 billion, but the importance of the various countries had changed. Canada continues to develop as a major source of trade, with more than 20% of the total. Other large participants include Japan, with about 10%; West Germany, about 6%; the United Kingdom, about 5%; and Mexico, about 4%.

Internal Commerce of the U. S. Although the United States ranks high in world commerce, the internal or domestic trade is of far greater importance. Within American boundaries, sections of widely diversified economic and geographical character specialize in the production of commodities to which the locality is best adapted. Excess production may be transported to any part of the country, or may be shipped out without any hindrance of toll or tariff except the cost of transportation. The great size of this free market has been a vital factor in American economic development.

Europe's Common Market. The existence of this huge free market in the United States provided the basic argument for the economists and statesmen who created the European Common Market. Western Europe possessed a pool of skilled labor, capital, and population greater than that of the United States, but their potential was not realized because of trade and political barriers. The Treaty of Rome in 1957 provided for gradual reduction of tariffs and aimed at unified labor and social-welfare conditions and freedom to travel, trade, employ, and invest without border hindrances. Political integration was set as the ultimate goal.

Governments as Traders. Meanwhile world commerce contended with a refractory element— the Communist regimes which barred private trading and channeled all exchange of goods through their governments. The element of political policy

was thus injected into the global market place. Lacking also was the element of stability since the Communist market might disappear overnight. Commerce between the free world and the Communist powers tended to be dictated by the needs of the latter and by their ability to pay in gold, since the goods they had available for export were severely restricted.

To a limited extent, the proliferation of new and underdeveloped nations had a like effect, since many of them had no individuals or business organizations capable of foreign trade. The rulers perforce set limits on what could or could not be bought or sold.

This situation forced on governments of the United States and other freely trading nations the task of handling a considerable part of the distribution of goods where such nations were involved.

FOREIGN TRADE (COMMERCE) OF LEADING COUNTRIES, 1975
Showing their trade with the United States

Country	Exports Total ($000,000)	Exports Per Cap. ($)	Exports to U.S. ($000,000)	Exports to U.S. %	Imports Total ($000,000)	Imports Per Cap. ($)	Imports from U.S. ($000,000)	Imports from U.S. %
Algeria	4,377	254.50	1,359	29.5	4,035	234.60	632	15.6
Argentina	3,191	131.60	215	6.3	3,656	141.90	628	17.1
Australia	11,575	857.40	1,147	9.9	9,811	726.25	1,816	18.5
Austria	7,518	1002.40	238	3.1	9,319	1252.10	181	1.9
Belgium/Luxembourg	28,807	2880.45	1,190	4.1	30,691	3069.10	2,247	7.3
Bolivia*	548	96.10	89	16.2	196	34.35	138	70.4
Brazil	8,656	82.45	1,464	16.9	13,558	129.10	3,056	22.5
Canada	31,881	1518.10	21,747	67.7	34,306	1559.40	21,756	61.7
Chile	2,408	204.80	138	5.7	1,911	191.10	533	27.8
China (Taiwan)	5,232	337.50	1,938	37.0	6,906	445.50	1,660	24.0
Colombia	1,358	56.55	590	43.4	1,558	64.90	643	41.2
Costa Rica	454	227.05	195	42.9	637	318.50	212	33.2
Czechoslovakia	8,358	597.00	NA	NA	9,081	648.60	NA	NA
Denmark	8,716	1743.25	461	4.5	10,366	2073.20	445	3.8
Ecuador	844	125.95	461	54.6	943	140.70	414	43.9
Egypt	1,402	36.80	28	1.9	3,951	103.95	683	13.0
El Salvador	463	115.80	180	38.8	562	140.50	194	34.5
Finland	5,487	1192.80	148	2.6	7,602	1652.65	261	3.4
France	52,214	1004.10	2,137	4.0	54,247	1043.20	3,031	5.5
Germany, West	91,620	1527.00	5,382	5.7	64,925	1082.00	5,194	8.0
Germany, East	10,088	600.50	NA	NA	11,290	672.00	NA	NA
Ghana	720	72.05	150	20.8	805	80.55	100	12.5
Greece	2,288	254.20	111	4.8	5,457	606.30	450	8.2
Guatemala*	586	97.60	173	29.5	700	116.60	255	36.4
Honduras	283	94.30	145	57.2	400	133.30	151	37.7
Hungary	6,091	609.10	NA	NA	7,176	717.65	NA	NA
India	4,365	7.30	548	12.5	6,094	10.10	1,290	21.1
Indonesia	7,103	54.60	2,221	30.9	4,708	36.20	810	17.2
Iran	20,249	613.60	1,400	14.4	10,343	313.40	3,242	31.0
Iraq	8,756	796.00	19	0.02	2,365	215.00	310	13.1
Ireland	3,177	1024.80	176	5.5	3,768	1215.45	190	5.0
Israel	1,835	539.70	313	17.0	4,140	940.90	1,551	37.4
Italy	34,821	633.15	2,397	6.6	38,366	697.60	2,867	8.0
Japan	48,452	440.40	11,260	23.0	47,825	434.70	9,565	20.0
Korea, Rep. of	4,948	145.50	1,416	28.5	7,275	213.90	1,761	23.6
Libya	6,454	2581.60	1,046	15.6	2,762	1104.80	232	8.3
Mexico	5,821	92.30	3,059	53.0	6,331	105.30	5,144	77.0
Morocco	1,542	88.10	10	0.06	2,560	146.30	200	7.8
Netherlands	35,075	2598.15	1,083	2.8	34,573	2560.00	4,183	11.8
New Zealand	2,152	694.20	246	11.4	3,152	1016.80	414	13.1
Nicaragua	376	167.10	131	34.8	517	229.80	156	30.1
Nigeria	8,078	126.20	3,282	40.6	6,103	98.45	536	8.7
Norway	7,207	1801.75	403	5.5	9,718	2429.50	510	5.2
Pakistan	1,005	13.95	49	4.8	2,125	29.50	372	17.5
Peru	1,514	94.60	NA	NA	1,531	95.70	904	59.0
Philippines	2,241	52.10	754	33.6	3,375	78.50	832	24.6
Poland	10,283	302.45	NA	NA	12,536	380.70	NA	NA
Portugal	1,939	228.10	194	10.0	3,840	451.75	349	9.0
Rumania*	4,874	232.10	NA	NA	5,144	244.95	NA	NA
Singapore	5,376	2443.60	532	9.9	8,133	3696.80	994	12.1
South Africa, Rep. of	12,026	462.50	841	7.0	8,137	312.95	1,302	16.0
Spain	7,691	219.75	831	10.8	16,097	459.90	2,161	13.4
Sweden	17,439	2179.90	877	5.0	17,874	2234.25	925	5.1
Switzerland	3,317	518.30	867	26.1	13,305	2078.90	1,153	8.6
Thailand	2,485	60.60	217	8.7	3,143	76.65	357	11.3
Turkey	1,401	35.00	145	10.3	4,640	116.00	608	13.1
United Kingdom	43,760	781.40	3,784	8.6	53,232	951.10	4,525	8.4
Uruguay*	382	127.30	24	6.2	487	162.30	51	10.4
U.S.S.R.	33,310	130.10	NA	NA	53,262	951.10	NA	NA
Venezuela	10,214	851.15	3,624	35.4	5,359	446.60	2,243	41.8
Yugoslavia	4,061	193.40	260	6.4	7,697	366.50	328	4.2

* 1974
Sources: Data for calculating information from Department of Commerce, Domestic and International Business Administration, and from *Statistical Yearbook (UN), 1976.*

Hence the rise of so-called foreign aid, under which credit or outright grants of money were extended to foreign governments to purchase goods. An example is the sale of American agricultural surpluses to India. Since such countries lacked exportable goods with which to make payment, the United States accepted payment in local currency and left it there on deposit.

Balance of International Payments. This term refers to the net result of a nation's transactions with the outside world in a given period. It is derived from statistics showing to what extent domestically produced goods and services have been exchanged with foreign countries, and how the differences in credits have been financed. The chief factors producing the balance are 1) exchanges of merchandise, services, and income on investments, 2) unilateral transactions like individual gifts and government grants, 3) transfers of long-term capital, and 4) movements of gold and short-term capital.

ECONOMIC DEPENDENCE OF THE UNITED STATES

The United States is more favorably situated in regard to raw materials than any other country. Nevertheless, her high scale of living and enormous consuming power create many needs that cannot be satisfied by materials obtainable within her own territories. The following table presents some of the commodities for which she is dependent chiefly on foreign sources of supply. Those in *italics* are of especial importance for national defense in the event of war. An asterisk (*) appears after those of which there is practically no supply native to the United States.

Material	Chief Uses	Quantity Imported 000 omitted	Chief Sources	Material	Chief Uses	Quantity Imported 000 omitted	Chief Sources
Abaca	paper products	36 tons	Philippines	Nutgalls*	dyeing, inks, color printing	N.A.	China
Aluminum	construction of airplanes, automobiles	457 tons	Japan, Canada	Nux Vomica*	medicinal agent	N.A.	Korea, Cambodia, India, Laos
*Antimony**	printing glass	2,174 tons	Mexico, Bolivia	Palm Oil	soap, tin plate	900,000 lbs.	Singapore
Arsenic	pesticides, medicines	13 tons	France, Sweden	*Petroleum*, (crude)	fuel oils, gasoline, lubricants	1,498,181 bar.	Saudi Arabia, Nigeria, Canada
Barley	food, livestock feed	2,000 bushels	Canada				
Bismuth	glass, clothing, paint, medicines	1,331 lbs.	Japan, Peru, Bolivia	*Petroleum*, (refined)	gasoline, fuel oils, lubricants	666,858 bar.	Saudi Arabia, Iran, Canada
Black Pepper	food seasoning	51,049 lbs.	Indonesia, India, Malaysia				
Cadmium	plating for mechanical equipment	5,928 lbs.	Canada, Australia	*Platinum*	electrical equipment, jewelry, chemical industries	1,900 oz.	Canada, United Kingdom
Chinawood Oil (Tung)	paints, varnishes, insulation	21,000 lbs.	Paraguay, Argentina	Rattan*	furniture	N.A.	Indonesia, Philippines, China, Malaysia
Chromite	hard steel, paint	1,350 tons	USSR, S. Africa, Philippines				
*Cobalt**	steel alloys, colored enamels	5,200 tons	Belgium, Zaire	Rubber (crude)	footwear tires, electrical equipment	657 tons	Thailand, Ceylon, Indonesia, Liberia, Malaysia
Cocoa	candy, beverages	233 tons	Ghana, Brazil				
Coconut Oil	food, cooking materials	890 lbs.	Philippines	*Sisal Hemp*	binder twine	N.A.	Mexico, Brazil, Haiti
Coffee*	beverage	2,683 lbs.	Colombia, Brazil, Portugal	Tea*	beverage	159,467 lbs.	India, Ceylon, China, Japan
Hides and skins	shoes, leather, travel goods	69,000 lbs.	Canada, Brazil, India, New Zealand				
Jute	twine, burlap, linoleum, carpet bags	250,000 lbs.	Pakistan, Thailand, India	*Tin*	canning, dyeing, textile manufacturing, solder	43,663 tons	Malaysia, Thailand
Kapok	lifeboats, buoys, mattresses	9.8 tons	Thailand, Philippines	Wool (carpet)	rugs	119,600 lbs.[1]	Argentina, Pakistan, India, New Zealand, Australia, Syria, Lebanon, Iraq
Lumber	construction	6,114,000 bd. ft.	Canada				
Manganese	structural steel	766 tons	Brazil, West Germany, France, S. Africa				
				Wool (unmanufactured)	clothing	33,600 lbs.	Argentina, Uraguay, Brazil, New Zealand, Australia
Mercury	electrical apparatus, medicinal agent	3,380 lbs.	Canada, Spain				
*Nickel**	steel, electroplating	162,000 tons	Canada, Norway				

Data concerning imports are mostly 1975 figures taken from *Commodity Year Book, 1976*, or 1974 figures taken from *Statistical Abstracts, 1975*. [1] 1968.

COMMERCIAL RAW MATERIALS

By far the most important commercial raw materials are those commodities which are utilized for food, for clothing, for the production of machinery and of power, and for structural purposes. These are obtained from all parts of the earth as contributions from the three kingdoms of nature—the vegetable, the animal, and the mineral.

The following classification is based primarily on this natural division, and secondarily on the purpose for which each commodity is generally employed. In the various groupings are included the most important commercial raw materials, together with representative examples of a vast number which are of minor importance.

VEGETABLE PRODUCTS

Cereals: Wheat—including emmer and spelt—rice, corn, oats, rye, barley, the sorghums, millet, and buckwheat (not a true cereal but used as such).

Other Starchy Foods: Potatoes, yams, sweet potatoes, arrowroot, cassava (tapioca). See *Starch*.

Pulses: Peas, beans, lentils, soy beans.

Sugars: Cane sugar, beet sugar, maple sugar, palm sugar (jaggery), and glucose.

Vegetables: Artichoke, asparagus, beans (string), beet, cabbage, carrot, cauliflower, celery, cucumber, eggplant, endive, garlic, kohl-rabi, leek, lettuce, mushrooms, okra, onion, parsnip, peas (green), pumpkin, radish, rhubarb, spinach, rutabaga, squash, tomato, turnip, and various others.

Fruits: Orchard fruits—apple, apricot, cherry, peach, pear, plum, prune, and quince; various grapes—table, raisin, wine, and currant; berry fruits—blackberry, blueberry, cranberry, currant, gooseberry, huckleberry, loganberry, mulberry, raspberry, and strawberry; melon fruits—cassaba melon, muskmelon, watermelon; citrus fruits—citron, grapefruit, kumquat, lemon, lime, and orange; subtropical fruits—carob (Saint-John's-bread), date, fig, olive, persimmon, and pomegranate; tropical fruits—avocado, banana, guava, mango, papaw, soursop, and prickly pear.

Nuts: Almond (sweet and bitter)—Jordan almonds are a choice hard-shelled variety of sweet almond from Malaga, Spain; chestnut, native to the eastern United States, also imported from southern Europe; cashew nut, from India and Brazil—poisonous until roasted; coconut, commonly grown in tropical countries; filbert, grown in southern Europe; hickory nut, native to the eastern United States; litchi nut, a dried fruit from China; peanut, not a true nut but the fruit of a legume; pecan, both wild and cultivated in the southern United States; pine nuts, oily seeds of pines native to southern Europe and southwestern Asia; pinons, nuts from pines native to the southwestern United States and Mexico; pistachio, grown in Mediterranean countries; and the English walnut, extensively cultivated.

Beverages. The plant materials chiefly used for making beverages are coffee, the cleaned seeds of the coffee tree; cocoa, prepared from the seeds of cacao; maté, the dried leaves of a South American holly; and tea, the variously cured leaves of the Asiatic tea shrub. With these are sometimes grouped fermented beverages, such as beer, wine, sake (Japan), and pulque (Mexico), and also distilled liquors, such as whisky, brandy, rum, gin, mescaline (Mexico), arrack (Orient), and vodka (Russia), which, strictly speaking, are manufactured products.

Timber. Of imported woods, the most valuable include mahogany, teak, lignum-vitæ, Spanish cedar, Circassian walnut, rosewood, or Jacaranda (from Brazil), satinwood (from the East Indies and West Indies), ebony, greenhart (from South America), lancewood (from Jamaica), and rule boxwood (from West Indies and South America).

Fibers. Textile and cordage fibers include cotton, flax, hemp, jute, ramie, manila hemp, sisal hemp, bowstring hemp, sunn hemp, coir, pineapple fiber, and raffia. Among brush fibers are broom corn, piassaba (from the West Indies and from Brazil), saw palmetto (from Florida), and palmyra (from Ceylon). Other fibers or fiber-like products are kapok, or silk cotton; luffa, a vegetable sponge; Spanish moss, from the southern United States, used for upholstery; rattan, from the East Indies, used in making furniture, baskets, and whips. Fibers used for paper making are exceedingly numerous (See *Paper*.). Panama hat straw, or toquilla, is prepared from the young leaves of a South American screw pine.

Alkaloidal Stimulants and Narcotics. These include tobacco, the most extensively used narcotic, cola leaves, chewed by the Indians of South America; pituri leaves, used by the natives of Australia; the kola nut, containing caffeine, chewed by the natives of Africa; betel leaf and betel nut, widely used by Malayan peoples; hashish, from Indian hemp, used by the peoples of southern Asia; and opium, the dried juice of the poppy, used widely in the Orient.

Medicinal Plants. Many plants contain medicinal principles which experience has proved to be of such value that they are employed more or less widely by all civilized nations. Among plants used for their leaves are belladonna, one source of atropin; coca, the source of cocaine; digitalis, or purple foxglove, grown in Europe and in America; and senna, from Egypt and India. Some of the best-known medicinal roots are aconite, hydrastis (golden seal), gentian, ginseng, licorice, may apple, rhubarb, and sarsaparilla.

Among the most highly prized medicinal barks are cascara sagrada, native to California and Oregon, and cinchona, or Peruvian bark, the source of quinine, now obtained chiefly from cultivated trees in Java. Nux vomica (the source of strychnine), chaulmoogra, and the castor oil plant are valued for the medicinal properties of their seeds. Plants yielding medicinal juices include aloes and also the poppy, the source of opium. Among medicinal resins are asafetida, balsam of Peru, and guaiac.

Gums and Resins: Rubber, gutta-percha, balata, chicle, gum arabic, gum Senegal, gum tragacanth, turpentine, rosin, and copal.

Tanning Materials. These include various barks, woods, roots, fruits, and nuts which contain tannin. Among these are oak bark, hemlock bark, chestnut bark and wood, sumac leaves, canaigre root, myrobalans (unripe fruit), divi-divi (seed pods), quebracho wood, gambier (twigs and leaves), mangrove bark, and oak galls.

Dyestuffs: Logwood, fustic, Brazilwood, Lima wood, Osage orange, indigo, archil, and cudbear.

Vegetable Oils. *Drying oils*, used extensively in paints and varnish, include linseed oil, perilla oil, Chinese wood oil (tung oil), candlenut oil, hempseed oil, walnut oil, soy bean oil, poppy-seed oil, and sunflower oil. *Semidrying oils*, used for various purposes, include corn oil, cottonseed oil, sesame oil (benne oil), rape oil (colza oil), olive oil, apricot kernel oil, peach kernel oil, almond oil, castor oil, and peanut oil.

Vegetable Fats. These substances, which are solid at ordinary temperatures, include cocoa butter (See *Chocolate*.), coconut oil, palm oil, palm kernel oil, and Japan wax.

Essential Oils. Many of these form the basis of natural perfumes; as, for example, attar of roses, geranium oil, lemon-grass oil, lavender oil, neroli, ylang-ylang oil, and patchouli oil. Peppermint oil and spearmint oil are widely used for many purposes.

Spices and Condiments: Allspice (or pimento), cinnamon, cloves, mace, mustard, pepper, tonka bean, and vanilla.

ANIMAL PRODUCTS

Food. Beef, pork, mutton, poultry, and game form the chief items in the meat supply of most countries. In some parts of the world, meat from the whale, horse, camel, and reindeer is also used. Eggs, almost universally an important article of food, are a commercial source of albumin and are used also in tanning. Milk is the source of butter, cheese, casein, milk sugar, and various fermented beverages, such as koumiss and leben. Butter, cheese, condensed milk, preserved meats, canned meats, and meat extracts, though often classified as manufactured products, may also be listed here.

Fish, oysters, clams, lobsters, crabs, and shrimps, marketed fresh, dried, canned, or otherwise preserved, are used in great quantities for food. See *Fisheries*.

Animal Oils. Oils used for food include butter, lard, tallow, and oleo oil (See *Oleomargarine*.). Medicinal cod-liver oil is expressed from the livers of freshly caught cod. Large amounts of other fish oils are obtained, especially menhaden oil. (See *Fisheries*.) Sperm oil, valued as a lubricant, is obtained from the sperm whale. Wool wax, widely used in making salves and ointments, is the natural grease from sheep's wool.

Animal Fibers. Wool, produced chiefly by the sheep, is obtained also from the alpaca in Peru and from the Kashmir goat of central Asia. Silk, produced by the silkworm, ranks next in value to wool among animal fibers. Long hair from the tails of cows and from the manes and tails of horses is used in making bows for musical instruments, for weaving into haircloth, and for stuffing mattresses. Short hair from various animals is used as stuffing material and in making plaster. Swine bristles from Russia and China are largely used in making brushes. The hair of the Australian rabbit is one of the most important materials entering into the manufacture of felt hats.

Hides and Skins. See *Leather*.

Furs. The most expensive furs are probably those of the sea otter, the Russian sable, and the silver fox. Among other valuable furs are those of the seal, ermine, marten, weasel, mink, skunk, mole, chinchilla, beaver, muskrat, karakul sheep (yielding the Persian lambskin), various species of fox, wolf, and bear, and the larger cats, such as the lion, the tiger, and the leopard.

Horns, Hoofs, Bones, and Tusks. Ivory is obtained chiefly from the tusks of the elephant but also from the tusks of the hippopotamus, the horn of the narwhal, the tusks of the walrus, and the tusks of the extinct mammoth whose remains are still found in Siberia. Horns and hoofs are utilized for the production of buttons, combs, ornaments, and of cyanide compounds. Bones are used for making buttons and ornaments, for the production of fertilizer, and for the preparation of bone black and bone charcoal.

Bird Products. Besides eggs, the most important bird products include feathers, plumes, edible birds' nests, eider down, and guano (See *Fertilizer*.).

Insect Products. In addition to silk, the most valuable of all, insect products include honey, beeswax, lac, and cochineal.

MINERAL PRODUCTS

The immense number of commercial products obtained from the mineral kingdom may be classified as metals or nonmetals. The first group supplies the materials from which tools and machines are constructed. The second group is divided into mineral fuels (liquid, gaseous, solid) and other non-metallic minerals, which includes building and chemical materials; abrasives; refractory materials; and precious and semiprecious stones.

COMMUNICATION

By communication is meant the transference of thoughts and of information from person to person. Underlying, as it does, all human co-operation, it has an importance which can scarcely be exaggerated. The initial step, and unquestionably the most important in making possible an unimpeded exchange of ideas, was the invention of spoken and, later, of written language.

A great length of time elapsed during which communication between distant points could be effected only by means of messages, oral or written, which were carried by messengers. The great development of electrical signaling devices and the vast improvements which have taken place during the past century in the means of transportation have reduced to comparative insignificance the time element in communication. With the help of the printing press, radio, television, and satellite, they can bring to all nations a knowledge of the events of importance in the whole world within a few hours of the time of their occurrence.

Early Postal Systems. The complicated postal organization of today had its origin in the system of private messengers employed by ancient rulers. Each messenger was given a fixed station where he should always hold himself in readiness to receive a message and to carry it to the next post. The emperor Diocletian was apparently the first to establish such a post open to the use of private persons. In the 12th century a commercial post was organized by the Hanse Towns of northern Germany, and in the 13th century a postal system was developed by the University of Paris for the benefit of its students. The national postal system in France was established by Louis XI in 1464.

Postal System in England. In England, private postal systems were used in the 14th century, but it was not until 1533 that Sir Brian Tuke was appointed the first "Master of the Post" by Henry VIII. Improvements in the service were gradually made, but, in 1812, the cost of sending a single sheet varied from 8 cents to 35 cents according to the distance. A money order system was begun in 1792 for the convenience of soldiers and sailors.

Due to reforms initiated by Sir Rowland Hill, a rate of one penny was established throughout the United Kingdom in 1840. The first adhesive postage stamp was issued in May of that year. This one-penny stamp was black and carried the profile of Queen Victoria. It had to be cut from the printed sheet. Perforated stamps were not officially issued until 1854. If the postage was not prepaid by means of a stamp, a double rate was charged upon delivery of the letter. The use of postage stamps made possible the mailbox, which was first introduced in 1855.

Universal Postal Union. In 1874 an International Postal Union was organized at Berne, Switzerland. This was followed in 1878 by a larger organization known as the Universal Postal Union. It became a specialized agency of the UN in 1947 and includes practically all countries of the world. All member nations are declared to be "a single postal territory for the reciprocal exchange of correspondence." The UPU regulates mailing procedures and aids governments in improving their mailing systems. UPU headquarters are in Berne, Switzerland.

Postal System in America. The general court of Massachusetts in 1639 ordered that the house of Richard Fairbank was to be the official distributing point for overseas mail. In 1691, Thomas Neale was by royal patent granted authority for the establishment and control of an American post, and, in 1693, Andrew Hamilton was appointed the first colonial postmaster general. In 1707, control of the post was purchased from Neale by the English government, which held it until the Revolution.

Under the new order, Benjamin Franklin was appointed the first postmaster by the Continental Congress in 1775. The first Federal postage stamps were issued in 1847, although in 1845 the postmasters of various large cities were permitted to issue five- and ten-cent stamps at their own expense. Stamped envelopes were first used in 1853.

It was not, however, until 1856 that prepayment was required and stamps came into general use. In 1851 the rate was reduced to three cents up to a distance of 3000 miles, and in 1863 under Lincoln, this rate was established for all distances and free delivery was begun in some of the larger cities. A money order system was established in 1864; postal cards came into use in 1873; a two-cent rate went into effect for the first time in October 1883; a special delivery service, for which an extra charge was made, began in October 1885; and rural free delivery was inaugurated in 1896. In 1971 the Post Office Department was replaced by an independent U.S. Postal Service in the executive branch.

Parcel Post. By the provisions of the general parcel post act which took effect January 1, 1913, and by its subsequent revision, the transportation of parcels within certain limits of size and weighing up to 70 pounds is undertaken by the post office department. By facilitating the cheap transit of merchandise, this service has opened up throughout the entire country a market for goods sent by mail. For rate making purposes, the United States and certain other territories are divided into units of area which are the basis of eight postal zones. The zones represent an area having a mean radial distance of 50, 150, 300, 600, 1000, 1400, 1800, all beyond 1800, miles from the center of any given unit of area which is the mailing point.

The value of the parcel post service is enhanced by the privilege of insuring the contents of the parcel against loss by the payment of a small additional fee. Parcels may also be sent C. O. D., special delivery, or as first class mail.

Air Mail Service. In 1918 the regular use of airplanes was initiated by the United States government for the carrying of air mail. By 1969, each of the 50 states had air mail service and many foreign countries were included in regular air mail service with the United States.

Since the first air mail service, accomplished by the U.S. Army for the government in 1918 with one round trip a day between Washington, D.C. and New York, delivery and receipt of mail by air has grown immensely. From time to time, Congress has authorized increased air mail rates to help the Post Office department reduce operating losses. In 1977 the air mail rate for a letter was 13¢ an ounce and for an air postal or post card, 9¢ each, when mailed from any point in the U.S. to any other point in the U.S. or its possessions. The same air rates apply also to 1) first class letters and cards addressed in care of an APO and/or a Fleet Post Office for delivery outside the U.S., and 2) Canada and Mexico. The air mail rate to all countries besides Canada and Mexico is 31¢ for each half ounce. Aerogrammes may be sent by air to all countries and purchased at the post office for 22¢ each.

Dead Letter Office. Every year about 23,000,000 pieces of mail matter are received by the Post Office so carelessly or incorrectly addressed that they cannot be delivered. These are sent to the Dead Letter Office at Washington, D. C. where, by means of maps and directories, skilled clerks are able to guess correctly the destinations of about one-half the items. The others are opened and those with addresses inside are returned to the sender.

Currency, checks, and money orders amounting to more than $1 million are received annually. Merchandise which cannot be delivered or returned to the sender is sold at auction, letters are burned, and thousands of magazines, picture cards, and holiday cards are sent to hospitals. Insured parcels are held for six months; ordinary parcels for 60 days. Parcel sales are held periodically at each Dead Letter branch post office from two to six times a year. The fees from return postage from unclaimed packages along with the money which was inclosed in some of the letters amounts to about $250,000, which is only $20,000 less than the entire operating expense. The Dead Letter office originated in 1825.

Postal Service in Canada. The postal system of Canada is similar to that of the United States in its main features, and includes the services comprised under the headings of registration, insurance, money orders, postal savings, parcel post, and C. O. D. delivery systems. Rural free delivery was inaugurated in 1908, and an air mail service in 1927. The latter is of especial value in Canada in establishing communication between isolated settlements and the more populous portions of the country. Thus in 1929 an air mail route was established southward from Aklavik, which lies 300 miles within the Arctic Circle.

Telegraphic Communication. Postal communication depends for its speed on the available means of transportation. Although modern air mail service has effected great improvements in speed, it was preceded by Morse's telegraph, which began commercial operations in 1844.

The advantages of a land telegraph system quickly became apparent and in 1861 the first transcontinental system opened between San Francisco and New York. Telegraphic communication between water-separated places was first attempted in 1842 in New York harbor; by 1851, a line crossed the English Channel. After unsuccessful efforts, the first transatlantic cable was completed in 1866. Since then, 21 cables (about 1½″ thick) have been laid in the North Atlantic. A lesser number cross parts of the Pacific Ocean.

Telephony. Vocal communication over long distances became possible when Bell invented the telephone in 1876. Improvements on the original device were made by many of the greatest inventors of the world. The advantages of the telephone have been so obvious that in the United States there is an average of one telephone for every 1.5 persons. Sweden has one telephone for every 1.6 persons. In the per capita use of telephones the following nations rank in order after the United States and Sweden: Switzerland, Canada, New Zealand, Denmark, United Kingdom, Finland, Norway, Australia, the Netherlands, and Japan.

COMMUNICATIONS OF PRINCIPAL COUNTRIES
(add 000's)

Country	Telephones*	Radio Sets*	Television†
United States	143,972	368,000	121,100
Japan	39,405	70,794	25,500
United Kingdom	20,536	39,000	17,725
Germany, Fed. Rep.	18,767	20,586	17,600
U.S.S.R.	15,782	110,300	50,000
Canada	12,454	19,133	9,800
France	12,405	17,034	13,712
Italy	13,695	12,448	12,805
Sweden	5,178	262	4,115
Spain	7,043	8,000	6,125
Australia	5,000	2,815	4,250
Netherlands	4,679	3,811	3,545
Switzerland	3,790	2,003	1,800

* For 1974. Source: *Statistical Yearbook, 1975 (UN)*.
† For 1975. Source: *Encyclopedia Year Book, 1976*.

Teletypewriter. A service was inaugurated in 1931 by which two-way communication by typewriter became possible over telephone or telegraph wires. By this system, two people, equipped with teletypewriters, on being connected through a central exchange, can converse in type, the words of both parties being recorded for future reference. This instrument, operating at about 60 words per

264

Economics

ITEM	1900	1920	1940	1960	1975
Post offices, no.	76,688	52,638	44,095	35,238	30,754
City carriers, no.	15,322	36,142	58,551	109,749	166,946
Money orders.	$255,670,027	$1,365,659,884	$2,094,543,479	$5,030,614,549	$5,194,000,000
Gross revenue	$102,354,579	$437,150,212	$766,948,627	$3,276,818,000	$11,585,400,000
Gross expenditures	$107,740,267	$454,322,609	$807,629,180	$3,873,953,000	$12,574,205,000
Total Number Pieces of Mail Handled	7,129,990,000	. . . .	27,749,467,000	63,674,609,000	89,270,000,000

Source: *Annual Report of the Postmaster General.*

minute, is employed extensively also for one-way communication, where it is desirable to send the same message to numerous places throughout the country. Market quotations, financial news, and weather reports for airports are broadcast by wire in this manner.

Radio Communication. With the beginning of the 20th century, radiotelegraphy became a practical means of transmitting messages, so that ships at sea were enabled to keep in continuous communication with each other and with many stations ashore. Navigation became at once more safe and more accurate, because a captain could obtain the exact time and, during a fog, could usually obtain his bearings from a land station equipped with direction-finding apparatus known as the radio compass. All seagoing passenger ships must now be equipped with radio apparatus.

Long distance conversation by means of the radiotelephone became possible in 1915. Owing to developments made in the research laboratory of the American Telephone and Telegraph Company, the wire systems may be used in connection with the radiotelephone. By this method it is now possible to establish communication with a properly equipped ocean liner at sea from any commercial telephone in North America. On January 7, 1927, a regular transatlantic radiotelephone service was inaugurated between New York and London. This was followed by extensions which made possible direct vocal communication between any telephone in North America with any telephone in Europe. See *Cable, Submarine; Radio; Telegraph; Telephone; Phototelegraphy.*

Newspapers. The preceding articles have outlined the development of two-way communication. But of no less significance for the world's history is the growth of one-way communication from its primitive forms to the high-speed printing presses and radio broadcasts of the present day.

The prototype of the modern newspaper is to be seen in the *Acta Diurna* ("Daily Events") issued during the Roman Empire and posted in a public place. Copies were made by hand and dispatched to subscribers at a distance.

The invention of printing made possible the first genuine newspaper to be regularly published. It was the *Avisa Relation oder Zeitung*, printed first in 1609 in Germany. In 1622 appeared the first newspaper in England, *The Weekly Newes from Italy, Germany, etc.*, published in London. The earliest news sheet to appear in the Western Hemisphere was the *Relación*, issued in 1594 at Lima, Peru, but it was not until 1620 that a regular newspaper was published there. The first regular newspaper in British America was *The Boston News-Letter*, begun in 1704.

Before the days of the telegraph, enterprising newsmen employed carrier pigeons, fast ships, pony expresses, and even semaphore signaling systems for gathering news. With the rise of telegraph and telephone systems, this task was greatly simplified and was put on an organized basis. See *Newspaper Press Associations.* With the development of phototelegraphy, it has become possible to transmit news in picture form with practically the same speed as verbal messages. Improvements in printing presses make it possible now to issue editions containing latest news within a few minutes.

Broadcasting. Within the decade 1920–30, a second means of rapid dissemination of information grew into effective rivalry with newspapers. This was the system of radio broadcasting.

Experimental dissemination of speech and music from a central sending station to owners of receiving sets began some years prior to 1920. Lee De Forest was one of the leaders in this development. Station KDKA, operated by the Westinghouse Electric and Manufacturing Company at East Pittsburgh, Pa., broadcast the presidential election returns in 1920. The popularity of this broadcast led the way for a phenomenal increase in the number of receiving sets owned and for a corresponding increase in broadcasting stations. By 1940, there was an average of one radio receiving set for each 2.4 persons in the United States, and programs for every taste and purpose had become routine.

By utilizing telephone wires, chains of stations may be connected so as to send out identical programs. In this manner, nation-wide and world-wide "hook-ups" afford opportunities for statesmen, entertainers, or advertisers to reach the ears of millions of listeners. By 1940, there were 675 broadcasting stations in the United States. Canada and Russia ranked next in number, the total for the world being a little fewer than 2000.

Radio broadcasting has remained an important means of communication even with the introduction of television in 1939, when the first station (WRGB) began operating in Schenectady, New York. By 1976 there were 7,307 radio stations operating in the United States, a 110% increase since 1960. Television stations increased from 50 in 1950 to 961 in 1975. Nearly every city in the U.S. is served by one of the three major networks: the American Broadcasting Company, the Columbia Broadcasting System and the National Broadcasting Company. In addition, there were 152 non-commercial stations in operation at the end of 1975. By 1973, more than 368 million radios and 120 million televisions were in use in the U.S.

Communication Satellites. These are satellites of the earth which (1) have an approximately circular orbit and travel at such a speed that they remain a constant distance above a given point on the earth's surface and (2) are able to receive, amplify, and reflect electrical impulses produced on the earth by radio and television transmitters. By means of a number of such satellites properly spaced, impulses may be transmitted from any point on earth and reflected to any point without having to contend with difficulties created by the curvature of the earth's surface. The first such satellite designed as a part of this system was Early Bird, launched April 6, 1965. Since that time the growth of the communications satellite system has been spectacular. In 1975, 15 satellites were launched by governments, private industries and international organizations.

The Universe Ireland, a 327,000 deadweight tonnage mammoth tanker, built in Japan. *(Courtesy Japanese Embassy)*

Supertanker under construction—The bulbous bow of a mammoth ship near completion. (*Courtesy Japanese Embassy*)

TRANSPORTATION

TRANSPORTATION is conducted chiefly by the use of vehicles operated upon the water, upon the land, and, more recently, through the air. Water transportation was early conducted by means of sailing vessels. Land transportation, except upon pack animals, required the construction of roads and railways, as well as the invention and improvement of appropriate vehicles.

Sailing Vessels. Long before the Christian era, the Egyptians, the Phœnicians, and the Greeks made use of sails to propel the small vessels of their time. To a large extent the Greeks, and especially the Romans, propelled by oars the ocean craft with which they navigated the Mediterranean. In the larger boats, called galleys, the oars were arranged in two or three rows or banks. The largest type of vessel widely used in ancient times for commercial or war purposes was the trireme, equipped with three banks of oars. The life of the oarsmen in these galleys was a hard one, and slaves were commonly employed. This practice gave rise to the term "galley slave."

The sailing vessels employed by the Venetians, Italians, Spanish, Portuguese, Danes, Norsemen, and the early English navigators were small craft, which seldom ventured far from sight of land. But beginning with the 14th century, the increasing use of the mariner's compass made it possible for sailing vessels to make voyages of great length.

According to present standards, the ships then employed seem small. Few people now living would willingly undertake a transatlantic voyage in a ship of the size of the *Mayflower*, in which the Pilgrims, early in the 17th century, came to their new home in America. But, in small sailing vessels of these or similar types, men in those days were making voyages halfway round the world, and, in a few instances, daring sailors circumnavigated the globe.

Steamships. The great revolution in transportation came when mechanical power was substituted for wind power on the ocean and for muscle power on the land. In performing the service of transportation, mechanical power was first applied to vessels. As early as 1787, John Fitch, a Pennsylvania farmer, propelled a boat on the Delaware by steam power. The *Charlotte Daudas* in 1802 towed two vessels of 140 tons 3½ miles an hour against a strong wind in the Forth and Clyde canal. Robert Fulton five years later ran the *Clermont* from New York to Albany by steam power and demonstrated the practical success of steam navigation.

A few years more were to pass before a vessel crossed the ocean entirely by steam power. The first transatlantic voyage of a steamer was the one made by the *Royal William*, which sailed from Quebec to the Isle of Wight in 1833. This was a wooden vessel, but in 1845 an iron steamer, the *Great Britain*, built by I. K. Brunel, a celebrated British engineer, was put in operation upon the transatlantic service.

The latter vessel is notable also because it was the first large merchant ship driven with a screw propeller. While its basic principle had long been known, the modern practical screw propeller was invented almost simultaneously in 1836 by Francis B. Smith, an English farmer, and by John Ericsson, a Swedish engineer.

Highways. The extensive use of vehicles upon the land could not precede the building of roads. The earliest road building on a large scale was carried on by the Romans. By maintaining order and by building permanent highways in the lands about the Mediterranean and in far-away Britain, the Romans made possible the development of Western civilization.

The first of the modern nations to undertake road building on an extensive scale was France. Beginning in 1597 under Sully, this progressive country proceeded to construct 15,000 miles of surfaced road. Colbert, who became prime minister in 1661, introduced the corvée system of forced labor upon the roads. The method was bad, but it gave France good roads in advance of other nations.

Two Scottish engineers, Thomas Telford and John L. McAdam, who did their work between 1800 and 1830, have fixed their names permanently to types of roads now largely built. Both men emphasized the necessity of providing adequate drainage for roads. Telford roads have a foundation of large broken stones surfaced by more finely broken or crushed rock; macadam roads are built without the foundation of larger stones. Hard surfaced roads are now constructed of the following materials: Sand clay, gravel, water bound macadam, surface treated macadam, bituminous macadam, cement concrete, brick and other block paving materials. The development of the motor car has given great impetus to road construction.

Canals. Canals are nearly as old as human history. The Assyrians built them. The Egyptians connected the Nile with the Red Sea by a canal. The Chinese are said to have constructed canals more than 2000 years ago. They built their Grand Canal, a system about 1000 miles long, in the 13th century. In the 15th century the famous artist, Leonardo da Vinci, invented the canal lock which was introduced into the canals of Milan. France began her existing system of canals early in the 17th century. England built her canals in the 18th century. In the first half of the 19th century numerous canals were built in North America.

Along with the construction of canals went the canalization of rivers until various countries, such as France and England, were equipped with a co-ordinated system of canalized rivers connected by canals. During the early development of the United States and Canada, however, it was impossible, because of physical obstacles, to create a fully co-ordinated system of inland waterways.

Railways, Steam and Electric. Before the system of inland navigation was completely worked out in the United States and Canada, the superiority of the railroad had been demonstrated. In 1829, the steam locomotive was perfected by the English engineer, George Stephenson, whose famous "Rocket" was successfully developed. By 1830, the Baltimore and Ohio, the Mohawk and Hudson, predecessor of the present New York Central, and a few other railroad systems began to operate in a small way. The completion of the Union Pacific in 1869 opened the first transcontinental span of railroad in America.

By 1890 the electric railway became commercially important for its passenger travel and cargo transport. Today, because of its cleanliness in operation and speed, it is utilized in mountainous areas throughout the world where hydroelectric power is available and on such heavily travelled passenger lines as in Washington and New York.

OCEAN TRANSPORTATION

Ocean Vessels in Colonial Times. The *Mayflower*, in which the Pilgrims came to America, was a typical sailing vessel of its time. It was a three-masted, square-rigged ship, only 100 feet long, and between 20 and 25 feet wide. It was registered as of 180 tons burden or, as it would be measured today, of about 160 tons gross register. Aboard this ship were 102 Pilgrims and the crew. The *Speedwell*, which started across the ocean with the *Mayflower* but which had to turn back, was only one-third the capacity of the *Mayflower*.

At the beginning of the 19th century, many ships were owned and operated by the merchant princes of America; as, for example, Elias Haskett Derby of Salem, Mass., and Stephen Girard of Philadelphia. The ships were square-rigged sailing vessels— ships and barks with three masts and brigs with two masts—of 100 or 200 tons register, a few being as large as 300 tons. The American merchants, lumbermen, planters, and fishermen of that period usually operated their own vessels instead of employing the services of common carriers. Derby, with his fleet of small sailing vessels, built up an extensive trade with the East Indies. Stephen Girard used forty sailing ships to carry on his trade with the West Indies and other parts of the world. The small vessels which these men used were well adapted to the service requirements of their time and brought fame and wealth to their owners.

Common Carriers on the Ocean. In American commerce, the common carrier on the ocean dates from 1816, when the Black-Ball Line was established from New York to England. Even in Great Britain the common carrier was hardly known until the beginning of the 19th century. For hundreds of years men had owned ships for hire or for charter to those who desired to use them, but transportation services on the ocean were not organized and conducted by common carriers until the early 1800s. The early common-carrier lines employed sailing vessels, but, from about 1840 in England and from about 1870 in America, steamship lines began to replace sailing vessels.

American Clipper Ships. In the 1840's the Cunard and other British companies began to use steamships and iron vessels. Thereupon the shipbuilders and seamen of America sought to increase the size and speed of the wooden sailing vessel so as to enable it to compete successfully with its new rival. Out of this competition grew the famous American clipper ships of the late 1840's and early 1850's. These were square-rigged sailing vessels, some of them between 2000 and 3000 tons gross register—fifteen times the size of the *Mayflower*. They derived their name from their long, overhanging prow and their sharp lines forward.

For a time the swift-sailing clippers held their own in competition with the steamship. But, as the marine engine became more efficient and iron and steel vessels of increasing dimensions were constructed, sailing tonnage rapidly declined. The last serious effort to enable the sailing vessel to maintain its place on the high seas was made at the close of the 19th century. About that time huge six- and seven-masted, steel-hulled sailing vessels of over 5000 tons register were built. Some of these vessels could carry 7000 tons of cargo.

Ocean Steamships. The steamship has had an interesting history. The marine engine, first successfully employed in the 1830's to propel vessels entirely across the Atlantic, was installed in wooden vessels with paddle wheels. English builders began to use the screw propeller for transoceanic service in the 1840's. It was more than a decade later before American builders substituted the screw for the less efficient paddle wheels. Indeed, even some of the British lines, such as the Cunard, kept to the use of paddle wheels until after 1860. The celebrated *Great Eastern*, completed in 1859, was equipped both with screw and with paddle wheels. This ship marked the transition from the older to the newer type of steam vessel. The *Great Eastern* was too large to be successfully driven by the engines of its day.

The Marine Engine. Most steamships are equipped with the inverted direct-acting marine engine. This type was used first in 1854, and most of the early engines were single expansion, although from the beginning some double expansion engines

FOREIGN COMMERCE AT SELECTED U.S. PORTS: 1974

(Figures in thousands of short tons of cargo)

PORT	IMPORTS	EXPORTS
Baltimore Harb. & Channels, Md.	25,231	12,876
Baton Rouge, La.	12,427	7,660
Beaumont, Tex.	6,205	4,232
Charleston Harbor, S.C.	3,113	1,302
Coos Bay, Oreg.	1	5,467
Corpus Christi, Tex.	11,143	4,598
Galveston, Tex.	1,093	4,110
Houston, Tex.	18,763	15,908
Jacksonville Harbor, Fla.	5,329	1,707
Long Beach Harbor, Calif.	11,943	6,125
Los Angeles Harbor, Calif.	10,463	3,348
Marcus Hook & vicinity, Pa.	9,515	146
Mobile Harbor, Ala.	9,416	3,963
New Castle & vicinity, Del.	4,652	—
New Orleans, La.	13,537	37,188
Norfolk Harbor, Va.	8,913	33,345
Paulsboro & vicinity, N.J.	13,191	63
Philadelphia Harbor, Pa.	33,112	6,025
Port Arthur, Tex.	7,789	3,021
Port Everglades Harbor, Fla.	3,778	319
Portland Harbor, Maine	22,791	17
Port of Boston, Mass.	8,397	881
Port of Longview, Wash.	331	3,986
Port of Newport News, Va.	1,063	10,482
Port of New York, N.Y. & N.J.	58,666	7,862
Port of Portland, Oreg.	2,245	6,821
Richmond Harbor, Calif.	3,432	634
San Juan Harbor, P.R.	4,208	451
Savannah Harbor, Ga.	4,252	1,981
Seattle Harbor, Wash.	3,670	2,020
Tacoma Harbor, Wash.	2,178	3,169
Tampa Harbor, Fla.	5,803	12,883

Source: U.S. Corps of Engineers.

were constructed. The triple expansion marine engine made its appearance in 1881. However, it was not until 1894, when the *St. Louis* and the *St. Paul* of the American Line were built by the Cramps of Philadelphia, that the quadruple expansion marine engine was constructed.

During this same year, 1894, an entirely new type of engine, the turbine, was also applied to the propulsion of vessels. The first large ocean vessel to be equipped with turbines was the *Carmania* of the Cunard Line, built in 1905.

The Diesel Engine. Earlier types of marine engines are, however, being displaced by an entirely different kind of engine, which is far more efficient and requires much less fuel. This is the internal combustion engine, named after its inventor, Rudolf Diesel. This engine has no boilers or furnaces but burns oil as fuel in the cylinders. The principal limitation upon the immediate use of the Diesel engine is its relatively large cost, but, in 1927, the tonnage of new ships being equipped with this type of engine exceeded for the first time that of steamship construction. See *Internal Combustion Engine.*

The Diesel driven engines were extensively constructed and used in World War II and proved so efficient that in 1948 practically every major railroad line in America had Diesel engines on order.

Ocean Leviathans. The large vessels of today have little resemblance to the ocean vessels of a century ago. The remarkable increase in the size of vessels is indicated by the developments of the first thirty years of the 20th century. The *Mauretania* (I), which began operation in 1908, was considered a marvel because she registered nearly 30,700 tons gross. She held the transatlantic speed record until 1929. In 1910 the *Olympic* was launched. This ship's length was slightly over 850 feet; its gross registered tonnage was 46,439.

Then, in 1912 and shortly thereafter, came the *Imperator* (renamed the *Berengaria*), the *Vaterland* (renamed the *Leviathan*), and the *Bismarck* (renamed the *Majestic*), all approximately 900 feet long.

The *Bremen* (1st), also about 900 feet long, was launched in 1929. It crossed the Atlantic in nearly 9 hours less time than the *Mauretania*. The first liner to exceed this length substantially was the *Normandie*, (renamed *Lafayette*), which was launched in 1932, and later burned in New York harbor. The greatest speed attained by any Atlantic (screw) steamship was 35.59 knots per hour in 1952 by the American-built liner *United States* on her passage from New York to Bishop's Rock in 3 days, 10 hours, and 40 minutes, a total of 3144 sea miles.

Oil Tankers. An outstanding development of marine traffic is the oil tanker. The evolution of super-tankers reflects increased world demand for petroleum products and a drastic reduction in transport costs. When the 38,000-ton *W. Alton Jones* joined the Cities Service fleet in June 1954, it was the largest tanker afloat. By 1960, the *Universe Apollo*, a 106,416-ton super-tanker built in Japanese shipyards by a U.S. company, exceeded in tonnage any other vessel. The largest super-tankers are now 1135 feet long, with a tonnage of 327,000 deadweight tons. Tankers of nearly a million tons are now on order. The world's tanker fleet has grown to more than 3,825 vessels and total capacity has risen to about 150 million tons. The super-tanker has been developed to transport more economically the oil products of the Middle East to the industrial powers. Japan is the world leader in construction of the tankers.

The majority of the world's tanker fleets are controlled by individuals such as the Onassis family and Stavros Niarchos, the Greek shipowners, and Daniel Ludwig, owner of National Bulk Carriers, Inc., an American firm. Major oil companies operate about 30 per cent of the fleet and national governments 10 per cent.

Although some countries may appear to have large merchant fleets most of the ships using their flags are owned by foreigners. The Liberian government, for example, requires only a small registration fee and an almost nominal annual charge. They maintain no control over the operation of ships flying the Liberian flag. Ships registered in Panama have the advantages of low fees and lenient labor laws.

The American Marine. The British colonists in America were a maritime people. They had to build ships in order to market their products in the West Indies and in Europe. With low-priced material for shipbuilding from the abundant forests, American shipping prospered until the Civil War.

During the Civil War there was a shrinkage of nearly a million tons in American shipping on the high seas. Four-fifths of this shrinkage was due to war losses and to the transfer of American vessels to foreign flags to escape the hazards of war. Moreover, this blow to the American marine came at the time when the steamship was taking the place of the sailing vessel, and when iron was supplanting wood in the shipyards of the world.

The American merchant marine of 1860 was composed largely of wooden sailing vessels; by 1870, the marine engine provided the steamship with a basis for superiority over the sailing vessel. The American marine began a decline that was to continue to the present due to the relatively high cost of shipbuilding and operation in the U.S. Generally, this reflects high labor costs and expensive material costs. Federal subsidization of construction and operating expenses amounting to 40 to 50 per cent of the total cost is required.

In 1975, the U.S. operated 3.9% of the world's 22,600 merchant vessels. In 1968, the U.S. operated 21.5% of the combination passenger-cargo vessels, 14% of the freighters, 8.7% of the tankers, and 2.8% of the bulk carriers. Of the 622,900,000 tons of cargo shipped and received by the U.S. in

1973, only 6.4% was carried on U.S. vessels. In 1950, U.S. vessels carried 39.3% of the much smaller total tonnage.

WORLD'S MERCHANT MARINE

Flag	Merchant Fleet as of June 30, 1975 (In 1000 tons)		
	Number	Gross Tons	Dwt. Tons
United States	891	12,359	17,608
Albania	10	50	68
Algeria	27	212	288
Argentina	158	1,310	1,805
Australia	88	1,032	1,492
Austria	19	77	115
Bangladesh	15	82	119
Belgium	76	1,265	2,000
Brazil	256	2,583	4,098
Bulgaria	114	851	1,230
Burma	10	58	73
Canada	69	365	503
Chile	44	390	588
China (Rep.)	370	2,763	3,994
China (Nat'l)	153	1,382	2,117
Colombia	38	212	281
Costa Rica	1*	5*	8*
Cuba	61	404	544
Cyprus	575	3,302	4,839
Czechoslovakia	12	123	180
Denmark	314	4,179	6,997
Ecuador	16	122	170
Egypt	57	287	402
Ethiopia	5†	35†	52†
Finland	186	1,740	2,740
France	436	10,382	17,740
Germany (West)	620	8,110	12,948
Germany (East)	147	1,180	1,706
Ghana	19	127	166
Greece	1,802	22,118	36,563
Honduras	11	52	53
Hungary	14	46	64
Iceland	26	50	73
India	301	4,065	6,395
Indonesia	164	595	750
Iran	39	458	696
Iraq	17	278	455
Ireland	17	164	247
Israel	49	453	587
Italy	630	9,772	15,427
Ivory Coast	17	124	170
Japan	2,033	36,090	60,720
Korea (South)	154	1,294	2,154
Kuwait	39	936	1,617
Lebanon	46	139	194
Liberia	2,491	66,709	125,308
Malaysia	24	322	459
Mexico	49	465	689
Monaco	4†	35†	51†
Morocco	19	62	93
Netherlands	442	5,107	7,793
New Zealand	35	121	160
Nicaragua	5†	14†	21†
Nigeria	18	118	170
Norway	985	26,054	45,180
Pakistan	55	479	633
Panama	1,499	12,972	20,809
Peru	41	358	536
Philippines	153	781	1,123
Poland	285	2,542	3,726
Portugal	106	1,090	1,625
Rumania	92	747	1,118
Saudi Arabia	20	66	85
Singapore	376	3,926	6,295
Somalia	243	1,810	2,625
South Africa	56	451	579
Spain	437	4,599	7,642
Sweden	325	7,125	11,968
Switzerland	26	233	342
Thailand	28	149	244
Tunisia	12	37	52
Turkey	106	847	1,229
United Kingdom	1,592	32,240	53,121
Uruguay	17	155	240
U.S.S.R.	2,375	13,920	17,758
Venezuela	42	417	597
Yugoslavia	218	1,784	2,586
Zaire	10	96	137
Total	22,591	320,275	530,669

* 1968 † 1969

Source: Maritime Administration, U.S. Dept. of Commerce.

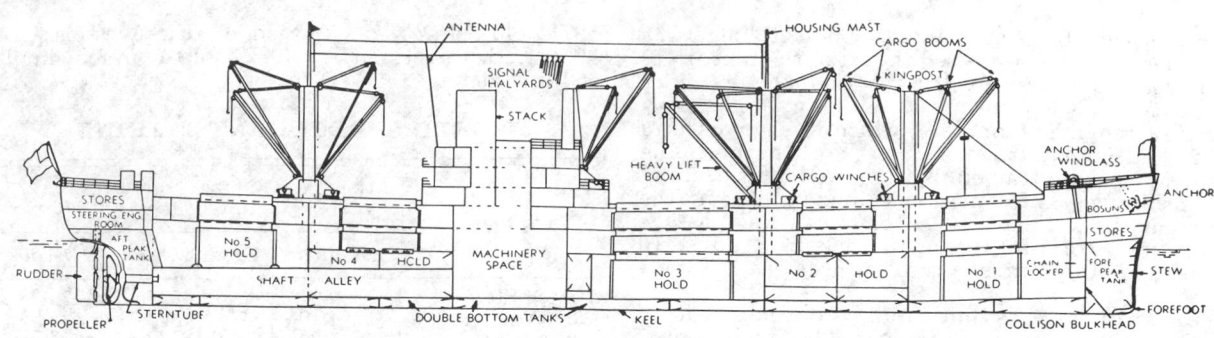

TYPICAL CARGO VESSEL, UNITED STATES MERCHANT MARINE

During the year 1935 the water-borne foreign commerce of the United States was valued at $3,786,000,000, of which 35.8 per cent was carried in American vessels and 64.2 per cent in foreign. If the commerce is measured by tonnage, however, the proportion of the total commerce carried in ships of American registry rises to approximately 40 per cent, indicating that a larger amount of goods bulky in relation to their value, such as grain and petroleum, are carried in American ships. These figures show clearly that, in the overseas commerce of the United States, American vessels in 1935 were playing a minor rôle. This rôle, which had diminished steadily since 1830, expanded remarkably during and immediately after World War I, then fell, but climbed precipitately during World War II.

TRANSPORTATION ON LAKES, RIVERS, AND CANALS

River Navigation. Long before men had the capital or the knowledge required for the construction of highways, and centuries before railroads were thought of, rivers and lakes were used wherever possible for inland transportation. Not only in ancient Egypt, Babylonia, and China, but in modern European countries, such as Austria, Germany, France, Holland, England, and others having navigable streams, the rivers were the only avenues over which traffic could move from interior points to seaboard markets.

For a long time rivers were used without improvement. Later their channels were improved by the removal of obstacles and, to some extent, by the construction of dams, locks, and canals past the rapids in the streams. The importance of rivers as avenues of inland transportation in Europe during the middle ages is indicated by the practices established by the feudal barons. These medieval rulers often maintained their power by constructing castles and barriers along the rivers. Possessing these strategic strongholds, they secured their revenues by exacting tolls from all those who used the streams for commercial purposes.

Canal History. As a result of improving their rivers and of constructing canals during the 17th and the 18th century, Holland, France, and England in turn acquired the economic leadership of other European countries. By building canals to connect their natural waterways, each of these countries was able to develop industrially, to accumulate capital, and successively to play an important rôle in international affairs.

Canal construction in the Netherlands required no special engineering skill, and it was to be expected that the people of that country would extend their numerous natural waterways by artificial channels. In countries like France and England,

however, superior engineering skill was required. To France first credit must be given, for in that country as early as 1605, during the reign of Henry IV, construction was begun on the Briare canal to connect the Seine and the Loire rivers. It took until 1642 to finish the work. In 1675 the Orleans canal connected the same rivers by another route, and in 1681 the celebrated Languedoc canal was completed, connecting the Bay of Biscay with the Mediterranean. The summit level of this canal was 600 feet above the sea.

The greatest names in English canal history are Francis, duke of Bridgewater, and his engineer, James Brindley. The Bridgewater canal, connecting Manchester and Liverpool, was begun in 1759. During the succeeding 75 years one inland canal after another was constructed in England and Scotland until the principal streams of the island were connected by a network of waterways. Until after the middle of the 19th century, the waterways of Great Britain, France, and of several other European countries were far more important as freight carriers than were the railways.

Canals in the United States. River and canal transportation in the United States dates from colonial days. The first great leader in the development of inland waterways was George Washington. Washington was a surveyor, and the knowledge he gained in the French and Indian war, which took him as far west as the Ohio river, gave him a lifelong interest in waterways. In 1774, before the Revolution, he brought about the establishment of a company, chartered by Virginia and Maryland, for the improvement of the Potomac river. The ultimate purpose of this company was to connect the Chesapeake bay and the Ohio river by a canal, if possible, or at least by a portage road westward from Cumberland on the Potomac river.

The Revolutionary War interrupted the plans of the colonies for joining the Potomac and Ohio. However, upon the termination of the Revolution, Washington again returned to the prosecution of the project, only to be interrupted once more by being called to the presidency of the new republic. Much later, and in a different manner than Washington had planned, the Chesapeake bay and the Ohio river were connected by the construction of the Baltimore and Ohio railroad which reached Wheeling on the Ohio river in 1851. Forty years earlier, a highway, called the National Pike, had joined the two waterways.

The first man to plan a comprehensive system of inland navigation and of inland waterways and highways in the United States was Albert Gallatin, who for twelve years served as secretary of the treasury under Jefferson and Madison. In the year 1808 Gallatin made a report to Congress outlining

Name	Location	Length (miles)	Width (feet)*	Minimum Depth (feet)†	Number of Locks	Opened	Approximate Cost
Albert	Antwerp–Liège, Belgium	76	52.5	11.5	6	1939	$ 80,000,000
Amsterdam Ship	Ijsselmeer—North Sea, Netherlands	16.7	164	32.1	5	1876	12,700,000
Cape Cod	Buzzards Bay—Barnstable Bay	7.68	250	27	none	1914	13,500,000
Chesapeake-Delaware	Delaware and Maryland	13.63	24	19	none	1829	‡9,000,000
Chicago Drainage and Ship	Chicago—Lockport, Ill.	38.6	174	22	1	1900	55,250,000
Corinth	Gulf of Corinth—Ægina Gulf	4	69	26	none	1893	13,750,000
Cronstadt	Leningrad—Bay of Cronstadt	18.75	275	22	none	1884	10,000,000
Hohenzollern	Berlin—Stettin, Germany	136	32	9.8	19	1914	12,500,000
Houston Ship	Galveston Bay—Houston, Texas	50	150	30	none	1925	20,000,000
Kaiser Wilhelm (Kiel)	Baltic—North Sea, Germany	61	147.6	36	2	1895	95,000,000
Lake Washington	Seattle—Puget Sound	8	80	34	1	1916	3,500,000
Languedoc	Garonne R.—Mediterranean, France	148	19.7	6.5	119	1681	3,500,000
Manchester	Manchester—Mersey River, England	35.5	80	28	4	1894	90,000,000
Moscow-Volga	U.S.S.R. Moscow to Volga River	80	279	18	11	1937	
New Orleans	Mississippi River—Lake Pontchartrain	5.5	300	30	1	1923	20,000,000
New York Barge	Lake Erie—Hudson River	540.8	44.44	12	57	1918	168,000,000
Panama	Through Isthmus of Panama	50.5	110**	41	6	1914	400,000,000
Port Arthur	Taylor's Bayou—Sabine Pass, Texas	7	150	26	none	1899	1,500,000
Sabine Neches	Sabine River—Port Arthur Canal	23	150	30	1	1926	18,100,000
Sault Ste. Marie, U.S.	Lake Superior—Lake Huron	1.6	100	25	1	1896	17,500,000
Sault Ste. Marie, Can.	Lake Superior—Lake Huron	1.41	60	19.5	1	1895	5,000,000
Suez	Mediterranean to Red Sea	104.5	196	46	none	1869	136,000,000
Great Lakes Canals, including St. Lawrence Seaway							
Lachine	Lachine—Montreal, St. Lawrence R.	8.7	45	14	5	1826	14,043,000
Soulanges	St. Lawrence River	14.6	45	15	5	1899	7,897,000
South Cornwall	St. Lawrence River at Cornwall Is.	2	500	29.5	none	1958	17,000,000
Trent	Georgian Bay—Lake Ontario	275.4	33	6	42	1826	19,951,000
Welland Ship	Lake Ontario—Lake Erie	27.6	80	30	8	1930	131,860,000
Wiley-Dondero	St. Lawrence R., south of Long Sault Island	9	442	27.5	2	1958	11,000,000
Williamsburg	St. Lawrence River	12.5	45	14	6	1847	13,550,000

*Width of locks or bottom of channel.   †A depth greater than 20 feet indicates a ship canal.   ‡Converted, 1926, from lock to sea-level canal.   **300 feet minimum through the Divide.

in detail a plan for a system of inland waterways and of highways extending throughout the then settled portion of the United States. But again an armed conflict, the War of 1812, interrupted transportation development.

History of "Internal Improvements." During the War of 1812–15 the United States had great difficulties in conducting land campaigns. The practical failures of most of the land campaigns of that war made it clear to everyone that both military and economic considerations demanded the development of transportation facilities. The railroad had not been invented, and the public naturally turned to improving the rivers, constructing canals, and building highways. The movement for "internal improvements" was led by the ardent young statesman Henry Clay, and was supported by John Quincy Adams. For a time, leaders of the South, such as John C. Calhoun, advocated Federal support for canals and roads.

But, from 1820 on, the conflict over slavery and state rights caused the leaders of the South to oppose internal improvements by direct action of the Federal government. During the administration of John Quincy Adams, 1825–29, the Federal government gave active support to canal and road building. But after Andrew Jackson became president he supported the strict constructionists, and took the position that the Federal government could not constitutionally carry on works of internal improvement within the states. His popularity and powerful personality put an end to the policy of Federal aid for canals and roads.

During the year that Andrew Jackson was inaugurated president, the construction of railroads was begun in the United States. Within a decade it became evident that the railroads were to be efficient carriers of freight as well as of passengers,

and that the inland waterways must at least share their traffic with the railroads. Indeed, as time went on, the waterways lost most of this traffic to the rival railroads. Nevertheless, the states which had begun works of internal improvements during the two decades following the War of 1812 continued to carry on such works until the Civil War and in some cases beyond that period. See table *Some Important Canals*.

River and Harbor Works. The Civil War settled the controversy as to the power of the Federal government. After 1865 no question was raised as to the power of the United States to expend funds upon the improvement of harbors, upon the channels of the Hudson, the Mississippi, the Ohio, and other rivers, and upon the connecting channels and the ports of the Great Lakes. From 1870 on, the Federal government regularly appropriated funds for rivers and harbors.

River Traffic. Railroads are now so generally used for freight traffic and passenger travel that it is hard to realize the great role played by the Mississippi, Missouri, Ohio, Kentucky, Tennessee, and other rivers, in the development of the country from 1840 to 1870. The steamboat, which began to run on the Hudson in 1807, made its appearance on the Ohio in 1811, and its use increased with the settlement of the Mississippi Valley states. St. Louis, on the Mississippi, near the mouth of the Missouri, became the principal trading city of the Mississippi valley, and New Orleans became the chief export city of the United States. The traffic of the great Middle West and of much of the South moved with the river currents to the Gulf, borne by the busy steamboats.

The Erie Canal. The canal which most influenced economic development in the United States was DeWitt Clinton's "Big Ditch"—the Erie

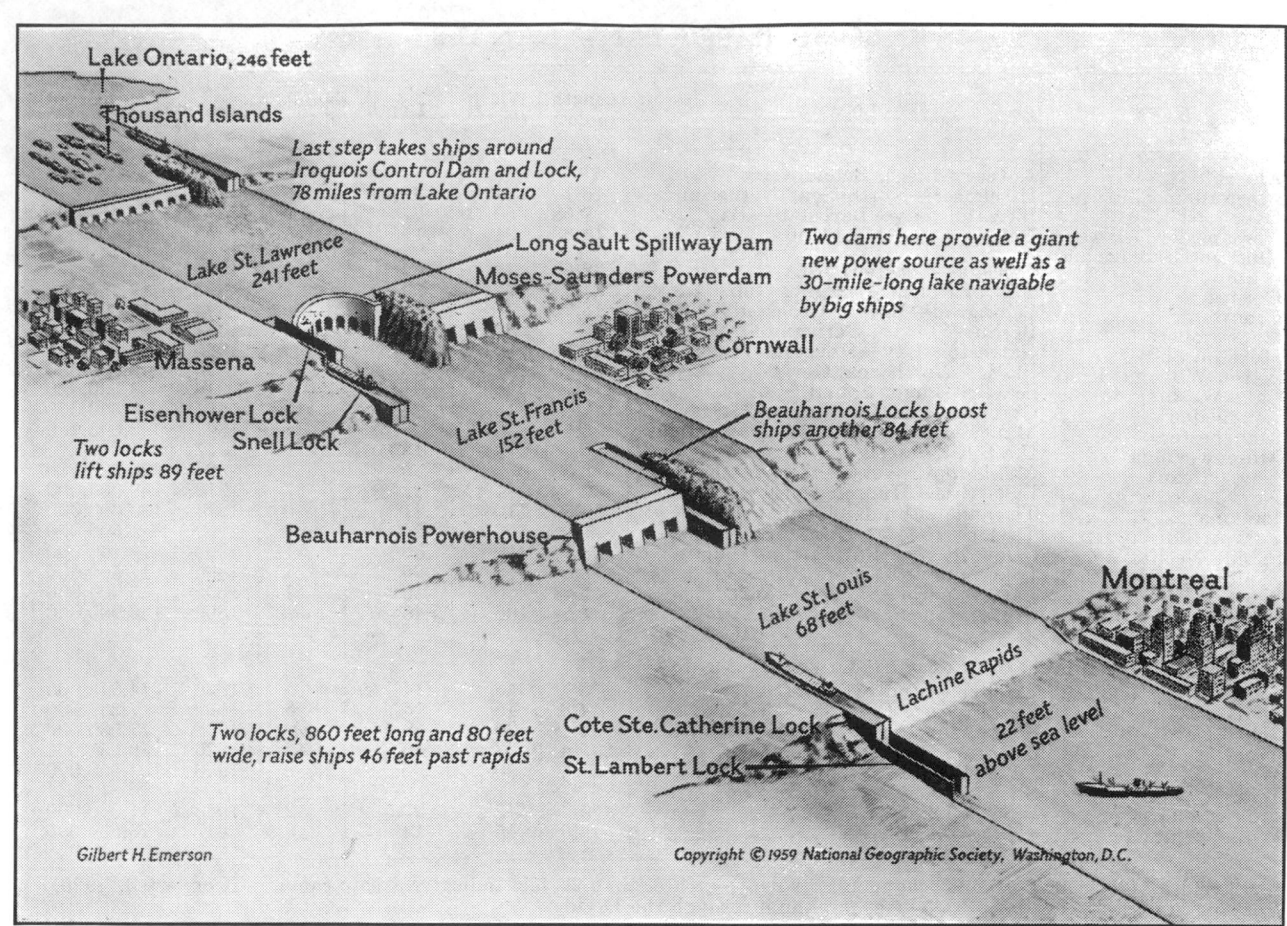

Lake Ontario, 246 feet

Thousand Islands

Last step takes ships around
Iroquois Control Dam and Lock,
78 miles from Lake Ontario

Lake St. Lawrence
241 feet

Long Sault Spillway Dam

Moses-Saunders Powerdam

Two dams here provide a giant
new power source as well as a
30-mile-long lake navigable
by big ships

Cornwall

Massena

Eisenhower Lock

Snell Lock

Two locks
lift ships 89 feet

Lake St. Francis
152 feet

Beauharnois Locks boost
ships another 84 feet

Beauharnois Powerhouse

Montreal

Lake St. Louis
68 feet

Lachine Rapids

Two locks, 860 feet long and 80 feet
wide, raise ships 46 feet past rapids

Cote Ste. Catherine Lock

St. Lambert Lock

22 feet
above sea level

Gilbert H. Emerson

Copyright © 1959 National Geographic Society, Washington, D.C.

"Drawn by Gilbert H. Emerson. Reprinted by special permission from the March, 1959, National Geographic Magazine."

DIAGRAMMED STEP-DOWN OF SEAWAY IN ST. LAWRENCE RIVER

Canal—constructed by the State of New York from 1817 to 1825. By connecting the Hudson River and New York City with the Great Lakes via the Mohawk Corridor, it permitted the expansion of trade between the mid-west and eastern coast. New York City emerged as the great metropolis of the nation and its leading port. In the Midwest, the success of the Erie Canal stimulated the construction of numerous canals, notably in Ohio and Indiana. By the 1870's, competition from the railroads and rate wars caused canal traffic to decline.

New York State Barge Canal System. Presently, the Erie Canal is part of this System. The entire System, including the Champlain, Oswego, and Cayuga-Seneca canals in addition to the Erie, extends over 801.3 miles. The canals are at least 12 feet deep with a minimum bottom width of 75 feet when dredged through earth and of 94 feet where cut through rock. The 56 concrete locks built by the state are 300 feet long and 45 feet wide. The Federal lock at Troy is 44.4 feet wide. The largest barge that can be accommodated would be 300 feet long and 43 feet wide with a 4000-ton capacity.

The lock at Little Falls has a 40½-foot lift, one of the highest in the world. The five locks at Waterford raise a vessel 169 feet, twice as great as that to the summit of the Panama Canal.

Canals in Canada. Canada had an exceptional opportunity for the development of river and lake transportation by canalizing the St. Lawrence River and by connecting Lake Erie with Lake Ontario. The possibility of connecting Georgian Bay with the Ottawa River, and thus with the St. Lawrence River at Montreal, was also early apparent.

The St. Lawrence River has four rapids, which render upstream navigation impossible except by the construction of canals and locks along the river past the rapids. The Lachine Rapids are just above

Montreal, and a canal past those rapids was begun in 1824. At later dates, canals past the other rapids of the river were constructed. These were equipped with locks 270 feet by 45 feet, and 14 feet deep.

The first Welland Canal, enabling boats to pass from Lake Erie to Lake Ontario, was opened in 1829. This waterway has been enlarged from time to time, and work completed in 1930 gave the waterway the dimensions of an ocean ship canal. In addition to one guard lock, there are seven lift locks, each of which is 800 feet in length by 80 feet in width, with a depth of 30 feet of water above the sills, each lock having a lift of 46½ feet. The canal connects Port Colborne, on Lake Erie, with Port Weller, on Lake Ontario. The total cost exceeded $122 million.

The St. Lawrence Seaway. The feasibility of a Seaway was studied in 1895 but not until May 13, 1954 was legislation signed authorizing the U.S. to join Canada in its construction. Congress acted after Canada announced plans to construct the Seaway within its boundaries. Passage of the bill was urged for reasons of national security.

The dredging of the St. Lawrence River and construction of locks and canals permits 27-foot draft ocean-going vessels (80 per cent of the world's shipping) to proceed beyond Montreal to Detroit and on to Duluth, Minnesota.

In 182 miles from Lake Ontario to Montreal, the river drops 224 feet. Canada undertook construction of facilities in the 68-mile section from Montreal to the International Rapids. The U.S. built the Wiley-Dondero Canal and three locks in the 46-mile International Rapids section between Cornwall, Ontario, and Ogdensburg, New York.

Another project, the joint development between

New York and Ontario in the International Rapids section of hydro-power facilities capable of producing 13 billion k.w.h. annually, began operations on July 1, 1958. The cost of the power project exceeded $600 million.

Chesapeake and Delaware Canal. In 1824, the Chesapeake and Delaware Canal Company constructed a canal connecting the Chesapeake and Delaware bays. This canal was acquired by the United States government in 1919. The Engineer Corps of the Army took in hand the work of improving the canal by the elimination of curves and the removal of locks, converting it into a sea-level canal. These improvements, completed in 1926, were calculated to reduce a ship's transit time from ten hours to four hours or less.

The Panama Canal. Encouraged by their success at Suez, the French sought to build a canal across the Isthmus of Panama. Under a concession from the Colombian government, work was begun in 1881. Unexpected physical obstacles and the prevalence of malaria and yellow fever caused the enterprise to be abandoned in the late 1880's. About this time an American company was considering the construction of a canal across Nicaragua, but this project, too, was abandoned and it became evident that if a canal was to be built it would have to be done by the United States government. As between the two locations, the United States in 1902 decided in favor of the Panama route after the French agreed to sell their interest for $10 million. In this same year Congress authorized the President to negotiate with the Colombian government for a concession to build the Canal. However, the two governments were far apart in their valuations of this permission. Colombia wanted $50 million and the United States considered the concession to be worth $10 million.

During the delay thus caused, the Republic of Panama declared its independence from Colombia. The United States promptly recognized the new government and made a treaty with it whereby permission was granted for building the Canal and for permanent occupancy of a strip ten miles wide along the canal route. The U.S. Secretary of War, assisted by a commission, began the construction in 1904.

This time, under the leadership of Col. Wm. C. Gorgas, measures were taken to prevent the diseases that had plagued workers on the French project. Sanitary precautions that eliminated disease-carrying mosquitoes made the Canal Zone completely safe from a health standpoint. U.S. Army engineer Col. George W. Goethals was equally successful in overcoming the many physical obstacles that had baffled the French. Both men were raised to the rank of Major General in recognition of their services.

The length of the Panama Canal is about 44 nautical miles or 50 statute miles. The minimum depth is 41 feet, and the minimum bottom width through the Divide is 300 feet. Navigation for most of the distance is in lake channels. A vessel passing from the Caribbean Sea to the Bay of Panama proceeds through a sea-level channel across the swamp district to Gatun, where by means of three locks the vessel rises to the level of the lake. Thence, the channel is through the lake to the Continental Divide, where, through a cut nine miles in length, the vessel passes to within a few miles of the ocean. At Pedro Miguel the vessel is lowered 30 feet to Miraflores Lake. Two locks at Miraflores lower the vessel to mean sea level.

Transit from sea to sea occupies 7 to 8 hours, with passage through the locks 3 to 3½ hours. In 1974 there were 15,269 transits carrying a record of 147,907,000 tons of cargo. Tolls on commercial ships totaled $119,419,878. The canal is operated and regulated financially by the Panama Canal Company, a governmental agency.

The total cost of the Panama Canal has been over $400 million. Under a new treaty signed with Panama in 1955, the United States raised the annuity paid Panama for the use of the Canal Zone from $430,000 to $1,930,000 annually and, among other concessions, agreed to return land no longer needed for canal operation. In 1974, a U.S.-Panamanian agreement set guidelines for the negotiation of a new treaty under which the Canal Zone would eventually revert to Panama.

The Suez Canal. The Suez Canal, connecting the Mediterranean with the Red Sea, was the first inter-ocean canal constructed. Begun in 1859 and opened in 1869, it was constructed by the Suez Canal Company under the leadership of Ferdinand de Lesseps.

This sea-level canal, 105 miles in length, is the world's busiest international waterway. Originally 26 feet in depth and with a bottom width of 72 feet, successive enlargements have given it a depth of 46 feet (capable of handling 35-foot draft vessels) with a minimum bottom width of 196 feet. The original cost was $80 million; total capital investment, approximately $136 million.

Canal use developed slowly since sailing vessels, the only ones employed in the Europe and Orient traffic in the mid-1800's, could not use the route. Traffic increased considerably with the introduction of steam vessels and stockholders realized dividends of 25 to 30 per cent. Approximately 176,000 shares of Canal stock, including that held by Egypt, were purchased by Disraeli for the British government in November 1875. The British government became the largest stockholder, although never controlling the majority of the 400,000-share stock.

Tonnage on the Canal increased from 20 million tons annually prior to World War I, to over 270 million tons in 1966. Nearly three-fourths of the northbound traffic is petroleum. The distance from the Persian Gulf to London via the Canal is 7000 miles; via South Africa, 12,900 miles. A 30,000-ton tanker saves over $100,000 by using the Canal.

The Canal company's 99-year concession was to revert to Egypt in 1968, but in July 1956 the Egyptian government seized and nationalized the Canal. Warfare followed in which Egypt was attacked by Israel, Britain, and France. From October 1956 until mid-April 1957, the Canal was closed while war-damage was being repaired. Since then Egypt has operated the Canal. From 1967 to 1975 the canal was closed due to the Arab-Israeli wars.

RAILROAD TRANSPORTATION

When in 1829 Stephenson succeeded in running "The Rocket" at the rate of 44 miles an hour in the contest at Rain Hill near Liverpool, England, he inaugurated a new epoch in the world's history. The effect of Stephenson's achievement was greater even than that of Watt, for the influence of the locomotive upon the industrial and social life of the world has been more fundamental than that of the stationary engine. The locomotive has made possible the rapid settlement and development of the continents of North and South America and of Australia, and is rapidly opening up Africa.

History of American Railroads. The railroad has had its most rapid and its largest development in the United States. The chartering of railroad companies in the United States began in 1826, and construction, on a small scale at first, soon followed.

The first locomotives were run in 1830. Several roads, the antecedents of the present Baltimore and Ohio, New York Central, and Pennsylvania systems, started at about the same time. The Baltimore and Ohio was chartered in 1827, and the first rail of this historic road was laid July 4, 1828, by Charles Carroll who was then the only surviving signer of the Declaration of Independence.

The Mohawk and Hudson, from which the great New York Central system has developed, was chartered in 1826. Construction was begun in 1830, and the first 17 miles of the line were opened in 1831. These early roads developed slowly, but Buffalo was reached in 1842. The Baltimore and Ohio reached Wheeling in 1851. The most active center of railroad construction in the 1830's was Philadelphia, which was connected with the Susquehanna River by rail in 1834 and thus with Pittsburgh by rail and canal lines. The Camden and Amboy connected the Delaware River with New York bay in 1837, and Baltimore was reached by rail in the same year.

Between 1830 and 1835 three lines were built out from Boston, one north to Lowell, one south to Providence, and the other west to Worcester. By 1841 this third line had been extended to Albany, and before the close of the following year one could travel from Boston to Buffalo by an all-rail route.

Periods of Railroad Construction. The historic growth of American railroads and the decline in mileage since World War I may be observed in the table *Railroad Mileage in the United States, 1845–1974.* Slow initial growth was followed by a 240 per cent increase in mileage in the decade 1850–1860. In no subsequent period did the railroads experience such a rapid rate of increase. In this decade prior to the Civil War, growth occurred principally in two regions, the South and the trans-Appalachian west. Vigorous railroad construction by the southern states provided them with the economic strength to wage four years of Civil War. The extension of northern railroads west beyond the Appalachian Mountains to the Mississippi River and to some extent beyond enabled the North to defeat the South.

From the close of the Civil War to 1880, rapid construction of railroads and the westward extension of the lines were plagued by intermittent panics. The severe panic of 1873, whose effects lasted for five years, resulted in large measure from the over-extension of railroads into the west in advance of traffic requirements. This distinctive railroad panic and its effects were ended by 1880.

From 1880 to 1890, more than 70,000 miles were added to the railroad network of the United States, the largest total in any 10-year period. Expansion occurred in all parts of the country but notably in the new states of the central west.

RAILROAD MILEAGE OF THE UNITED STATES BY STATES

STATE	Miles of Line 1940	Miles of Line 1960	Miles of Line 1974
Alabama	4,996	4,647	4,541
Alaska	536	572	538
Arizona	2,228	2,166	2,034
Arkansas	4,482	3,950	3,559
California	7,947	7,758	7,335
Colorado	4,552	3,786	3,499
Connecticut	887	825	656
Delaware	295	293	291
District of Columbia	35	30	....
Florida	5,218	4,670	4,143
Georgia	6,334	5,864	5,414
Hawaii*	192	25	....
Idaho	2,746	2,685	2,659
Illinois	11,949	11,211	10,607
Indiana	6,889	6,601	6,419
Iowa	8,950	8,569	7,644
Kansas	8,564	8,239	7,621
Kentucky	3,691	3,543	3,518
Louisiana	4,357	3,938	3,752
Maine	1,882	1,786	1,667
Maryland	1,367	1,146	1,099
Massachusetts	1,793	1,654	1,405
Michigan	7,303	6,665	6,032
Minnesota	8,421	8,205	7,382
Mississippi	3,919	3,659	3,645
Missouri	7,042	6,595	6,082
Montana	5,149	4,969	4,900
Nebraska	6,044	5,721	5,334
Nevada	1,941	1,647	1,573
New Hampshire	1,002	869	751
New Jersey	2,108	1,915	1,708
New Mexico	2,812	2,473	2,087
New York	7,739	6,541	5,325
North Carolina	4,668	4,310	4,115
North Dakota	5,266	5,255	5,079
Ohio	8,501	8,334	7,746
Oklahoma	6,302	5,802	4,946
Oregon	3,385	3,149	3,041
Pennsylvania	10,328	9,126	8,064
Rhode Island	194	184	139
South Carolina	3,466	3,282	3,016
South Dakota	4,006	3,920	3,363
Tennessee	3,573	3,402	3,207
Texas	16,356	14,769	13,320
Utah	2,082	1,734	1,734
Vermont	919	811	765
Virginia	4,261	4,133	3,873
Washington	5,243	4,979	4,807
West Virginia	3,831	3,680	3,508
Wisconsin	6,639	6,191	5,832
Wyoming	2,008	1,881	1,780

Source: Interstate Commerce Commission; annual reports, *Statistics of Railways in the U.S.,* and *Transport Statistics in the U.S.*

* Figures do not include approximately 670 miles of plantation railway lines.

By 1890, the principal railway systems required to meet the commercial needs of the nation had

RAILROAD MILEAGE IN THE UNITED STATES, 1845-1974

YEAR	Miles of Line in Operation	Change in Mileage	YEAR	Miles of Line in Operation	Change in Mileage	YEAR	Miles of Line in Operation	Change in Mileage
1845	4,633	......	1890	163,597	35,277	1935	241,822	−7,230
1850	9,021	4,388	1895	180,657	17,060	1940	233,670	−8,152
1855	18,374	9,353	1900	193,346	12,689	1945	226,696	−6,974
1860	30,626	12,252	1905	218,101	24,755	1950	223,779	−2,917
1865	35,085	4,459	1910	240,293	22,192	1955	220,670	−3,109
1870	52,922	17,837	1915	253,789	13,496	1960	217,100	−3,570
1875	74,096	21,174	1920	252,845	− 944	1965	211,384	−4,284
1880	93,262	19,166	1925	249,398	−3,477	1970	205,782	−5,602
1885	128,320	35,058	1930	249,052	− 346	1974	201,555	−4,227

Statistical Abstract of the United States, 1975.

PASSENGER TRAFFIC, 1930–1974
Millions of Passenger Miles and Percentage of Total*

YEAR	Rail-roads	%	Busses	%	Air Carriers	%
1930	26,876	68.5	7,100	18.1	73	0.2
1940	23,816	64.5	9,800	26.5	1,052	2.8
1950	31,790	45.3	26,436	37.7	10,072	14.3
1960	21,284	27.2	19,896	25.5	33,958	43.5
1961	20,308	26.3	19,703	25.6	34,642	44.9
1963	18,600	21.6	21,700	25.3	42,900	49.9
1968	13,265	9.4	26,211	18.6	101,189	72.0
1974	10,500	5.9	26,700	15.1	135,474	76.7

* Excludes miles traveled in private automobiles. Sources: *Railroad Information Yearbook* and *Statistical Abstracts*.

been built. From that time on, most additions were built to supplement or extend existing systems. Peak mileage was reached in 1916 when the net extended to 254,037 miles. Since then, nearly 53,000 miles of line have been abandoned, primarily because of the growth of other forms of transportation. The change also reflects the decline in passenger traffic and efforts to economize by reducing redundant services.

Distribution of Railroad Mileage. Approximately 29 per cent of the railroad mileage of the world is in the United States. The combined countries of Europe have approximately 30 per cent and the remainder of the world 40 per cent of the total.

The mileage by state is given in an accompanying table. Texas, with 13,951 miles of railway, surpasses the mileage of France or Germany. New Jersey ranks first among the states in the number of miles of railroad per hundred square miles of area whereas Nevada has the lowest ratio.

Standard Gauge. The standard gauge of railroads is 56.5 inches from the inside of one rail to the inside of the opposite rail, measurement being made about ⅝ of an inch from the top of the rail head.

History of Canadian Railroads. In many respects the development of Canadian railways corresponds with that of the United States. As was the case in the States, the Canadian colonies devoted their attention first to canal building and the establishment of inland waterways. During the first half of the 19th century, these were the chief improvements made in transportation.

The first railway in Canada was placed in operation in 1836. This was a line 16 miles in length, connecting Montreal and St. John's on the Champlain route to New York. Up to 1850 only 50 additional miles of railway had been constructed. But the great activity in American railroad building during the 1840's convinced the Canadians that they too must have railroads to supplement their canals.

In 1849 the Canadian government adopted a vigorous policy regarding railway construction by undertaking to guarantee 6 per cent interest on a sum not to exceed one-half the cost of railways 70 miles in length or longer. As a result, the St. Lawrence and Atlantic railway, connecting Montreal and Portland, Maine, was completed in 1853, and, during the same year, the Northern railway from Toronto to Collingwood was placed in operation. In 1854 the Great Western railway, connecting Niagara and Detroit, was opened. The Grand Trunk railroad, chartered in 1852, operated the St. Lawrence and Atlantic under a lease, and, in 1856, completed the main line from Toronto to Montreal, thereby connecting the chief commercial districts of Canada with the Atlantic seaboard.

By 1860 more than 2000 miles of Canadian railways were in operation. These were constructed largely by heavy outlays of British capital. But the financial crisis of 1857, together with the pecuniary embarrassments of most of the lines, prevented

extensive railway construction for the ensuing 10 years. Except for the completion of local lines, there was but little additional railway building until after the confederation of the various provinces of the Dominion was effected in 1867.

Fulfilling a condition of Confederation in the East, the Dominion government undertook the completion of the Intercolonial railway between the province of Quebec and the ice-free Atlantic ports of Nova Scotia and New Brunswick. In 1876, at a cost exceeding $20,000,000, this line was completed. A corresponding condition of western federation, demanded by British Columbia, was fulfilled by the construction of the Canadian Pacific railway. At a cost to the country of $62,000,000 in cash and 25,000,000 acres of land, this notable enterprise in railway transportation was begun in 1881 and completed in 1885. It is worthy of note that in the United States at this time only three transcontinental railway connections with the Pacific coast had been established. These were the Central Pacific, from Ogden to San Francisco, finished in 1869; the Southern Pacific, from the Texas seaboard to San Francisco, completed in 1877, and the Atchison, Topeka, and Santa Fé, from the Missouri river to Los Angeles, opened in 1885.

The railways of Canada have been built largely under various forms of government aid, consisting of land grants, cash subsidies, loans, and guarantee of bonds or interest. The total so granted, up to 1940, exceeded 47,000,000 acres.

Government Railways in Canada. A feature wherein railway development in Canada sharply differs from that in the United States is found in the large mileage owned or controlled by the national government. The Prince Edward Island railway, completed in 1875, and the Intercolonial railway, completed in 1876, were the earliest government owned lines. In 1903 the national government began the construction of the eastern division of the National Continental railway from Moncton, N. B., to Winnipeg. This line was to be leased to the Grand Trunk railway. Upon the failure of the latter to operate the new road after it had been completed at a cost of $165,000,000 up to 1919, the national government undertook its operation.

At the beginning of 1918 the Canadian government railways had a total mileage of 5150, comprising the Intercolonial, 2305 miles; St. John and Quebec railway, 128 miles; Prince Edward Island railway, 314 miles, and National Continental railway, 2403 miles. During 1918 branch lines in New Brunswick aggregating 143 miles were taken over for operation. In the same year the national government acquired the capital stock and control of the Canadian Northern Railway Company. The Canadian Northern system at this time had a total mileage of 9566 miles. With the later acquisition of various subsidiaries, including the Hudson Bay railway, the Canadian Northern system, as controlled by the government, comprised fully 10,000 miles of line. In 1920, the Grand Trunk Pacific railway, having a mileage of about 2700 miles, was taken over and operated by the government. The Grand Trunk railway, also, with about 3600 miles, was placed under government management in 1921.

In this manner the government acquired about 21,500 miles of railway; the total was increased to over 24,000 in 1935. This is over one-half the total mileage in Canada, which in 1973 amounted to 44,230, of which 90% is controlled by the government-owned Canadian National and the privately owned Canadian Pacific.

Technical Triumphs of American Railroads. The triumph of American railroads has been as significant in the development of equipment as in track construction. The success of U.S. railroading depended upon the ability to move heavy loads over long distances and over such grades as were required to surmount the Appalachian and Rocky mountains.

In a country of three million square miles, resources are scattered and occasionally remote. The great distances and the diversity of economies and resources suggest the complex nature of the transport problem which the railroads solved. With major markets in the northeastern quarter of the country and on the west coast fringe, extensive transportation systems became a necessity. The wheat and corn of the mid-west and Great Plains must travel 1000 to 1500 miles to the markets and ports of the east. Vast quantities of coal move from the Appalachian fields by rail to the industrial centers of the interior; non-ferrous metals cross the nation from the mines of the west to eastern markets; and the forests of the west, south, and north-central states transport their products by rail to the rest of the nation.

Steam Locomotives. To provide transportation for the products of forests, mines, and fields, the steam locomotive was enormously increased in size and tractive power. From the tiny locomotives of the 1830's and 1840's, weighing from 5 to 20 tons, was developed the huge triplex articulated locomotive of recent years, which had 24 driving wheels and a total weight of 853,000 pounds. This extraordinarily large locomotive was intended for work on heavy mountain grades. But the standard freight locomotives, with eight driving wheels, had a total weight of about 500,000 pounds. The average tractive power of locomotives in the United States more than doubled in the first 40 years of the 20th century, being over 50,000 pounds in 1940. The number in use was 44,333. The maximum of 65,358 was attained in 1924.

Since World War II, however, there has been a sudden and dramatic change from steam locomotives to Diesel engines. By 1957 the railroads owned only 2,404 steam locomotives as against 27,211 Diesel units. Diesels now perform almost all freight, passenger, and switching service. The average traction power of over-the-road locomotives increased from 45,225 pounds in 1930 to 60,311 pounds in 1964.

The Car. Such heavy trainloads would not be possible except for the size and the strength of the freight cars now in use. At the close of the Civil War, the standard freight car had a capacity of about 20 tons. By the end of the 19th century the standard had been raised to 40 tons. The average capacity climbed from 42.5 in 1921 to 58.2 tons in 1964. The only limit to the size of the car is the strength of the tracks and bridges.

The Electric Locomotive. The earliest electric locomotive was used to haul cars in mines in 1882, but the most important early use of this form of traction was in subways and tunnels, where it has obvious advantages in the fact that electric locomotives do not emit smoke and noxious gases. The first tunnel in which electric locomotives were used was that of the City and South London Railway under the Thames River, opened for traffic in 1890.

Other situations in which electric locomotives have proved of value sufficient to justify the high initial cost are: in terminals and suburban divisions; on steep mountain grades; and on routes carrying heavy traffic and requiring fast service.

Diesel-Electric Locomotive. Although electrically driven, this type of locomotive does not require that tracks be electrified so as to transmit current from a central station. On the contrary, it generates its own current by means of a dynamo driven by a Diesel engine. The current drives motors geared to the wheels. The Diesel uses much less fuel than the steam locomotive. It also requires less maintenance and inflicts less wear and tear on tracks. It allows easier starting for heavy loads, and can maintain higher speeds for longer periods. The first Diesel-Electric locomotive for commercial use was built in 1925, the Jersey Central Railroad's No. 1000.

Streamlined Passenger Trains. The streamlining of passenger trains has the primary purpose of economy through reduction of air resistance at high speeds. A second advantage of molding the outline of locomotive and cars is to increase the beauty of the train as an attraction to customers. The first completely streamlined train in America was the "Zephyr," put into service by the Chicago, Burlington & Quincy Railroad on November 11, 1934, to run between Lincoln, Nebraska, and Kansas City, Missouri. Lightweight low-slung coaches able to take curves faster and cars with observation domes and with rubber used to make a smoother ride were other improvements designed to offset the attraction of transport by air, bus, and private automobile. In the years of explosive growth in travel, the number of passengers carried by railroads declined between 1950 and 1975 from 488 million to 269 million.

Competition with Trucks. In the years after World War II, the tonnage of goods hauled by trucks gained rapidly on the static or declining volume of goods hauled by railroads. The answer of the railroads was directed toward the twofold goal of cutting expenses and making its service more efficient and attractive. These developments included (1) discontinuance of uneconomic runs, with government consent, (2) conversion to Diesel locomotives, and (3) construction of larger and more specialized freight cars. These latter included cars adapted for transporting automobiles and particularly those which could carry truck trailers deliv-

INTERCITY FREIGHT TRAFFIC, 1930–1974*
(Millions of Freight in Ton-Miles)

Year	Railroads	%	Motor Vehicles	%	Inland Waterways**	%	Oil Pipeline	%
1930	389,648	74.3	20,345	3.9	86,453	16.5	27,900	5.3
1940	379,201	61.3	62,043	10.0	118,057	19.1	59,277	9.6
1950	596,940	56.2	172,860	16.3	163,344	15.4	129,175	12.1
1955	631,385	49.4	222,254	17.5	116,508	17.0	203,244	15.9
1960	579,130	43.7	297,662	22.4	220,253	16.6	228,626	17.2
1961	569,997	42.9	313,141	23.6	209,706	15.8	233,172	17.6
1962	599,977	43.1	331,319	23.8	223,089	16.0	237,723	17.0
1963	629,457	43.1	347,865	23.8	240,000	16.4	243,286	16.6
1964	666,207	43.5	347,470	22.7	250,165	16.3	265,826	17.4
1965	721,055	43.67	359,218	21.76	262,421	15.89	306,393	18.56
1966	761,044	43.71	380,917	21.85	265,000	15.20	332,916	19.10
1968	768,538	41.63	396,300	21.46	287,000	15.55	391,300	21.20
1974	855,700	38.6	495,000	22.3	354,882	16.1	506,000	22.8

* Airlines percentage of total was less than 1/10 of 1% before 1964; slightly above thereafter.
** Inland waterways consist of Great Lakes and Rivers & Canals. In the 35-year period, the share of traffic carried on the Great Lakes dropped from 14.8% to 6.7% whereas the share of traffic carried by Rivers & Canals increased from 1.7% to 9.3%.
Source: *Statistical Abstract.*

ered to the railroad by trucks and delivered again to trucks to take them to their ultimate destination. This was known as "piggy-back" service; it represented a measure of co-operation instead of competition. Similar in effect was the increasing use of standardized freight containers that could be reloaded directly for truck, ship, or air transportation.

Other improvements by the railroads were (1) the use of machines in laying rails, which could be fused into lengths of 2000 feet or more, and (2) the use of computers to make up freight trains in switchyards and to keep hour-by-hour record of where each shipment was.

TRANSPORTATION UPON ELECTRIC RAILWAYS

Tramways. The first electric railways were built to take the place of horse-car lines or tramways in the cities. The tramways had been preceded by bus lines, which began to run in New York City in 1830 and in Philadelphia the following year. It was not until 1832 that the first horse car was built in the United States. The first street railway in Boston dates from 1853, and, in Philadelphia, from 1858. Chicago's first line was started in 1859. These horse-car lines provided a service of four or five miles an hour, and were fairly adequate for the transportation needs of the times.

Cable and Elevated Roads. By 1870, more rapid transit than could be provided by horse-car lines had become necessary, and in one important city, San Francisco, steep hills made horse cars impracticable. The cable lines were the first to provide rapid transit. San Francisco opened a cable line in 1873, Chicago in 1878, Philadelphia in 1884.

In New York City, rapid transit was provided by the construction of elevated railways. The franchise for the first of these elevated railways was granted in 1867. Construction followed in due course, and by 1879 New York City had a fairly complete system of elevated roads. It was intended at first to use cable traction upon these elevated lines, but, before operation began, it was decided to use dummy locomotives. Twenty-five years later these steam locomotives were displaced by electric locomotives. Chicago began the construction of elevated roads in 1888; Boston, in 1903; and Philadelphia, in 1907.

Subways. The earliest underground railway for passengers was opened in London in 1863. It was operated with steam locomotives at first, but electric traction began to be used in 1890. The term "tube" is ordinarily applied in England to these railways. Budapest and Glasgow followed with the inauguration of electric train subways in 1896. A subway was opened in Boston in 1898. A subway service in Paris was initiated in 1900. The first line of the New York subway system was opened in 1904. Construction in this city presented peculiar difficulties. The subways had usually to be blasted through rock and, in certain sections, buildings of enormous weight had to be safeguarded while tunnels were driven beneath them. In later years, Philadelphia, Rochester, Toronto, Berlin, Tokyo, Moscow, Stockholm, and Montreal constructed transit facilities of this type. Chicago has a freight subway with a network of tunnels beneath the street level.

Technical Development. The electric railway was made possible by the dynamo, which was developed for practical use shortly after the middle of the nineteenth century. However, it was not until 1888 that an electric trolley line was actually demonstrated to be commercially practicable. After its introduction during that year, the electric railway made rapid progress in all cities. By the end of the century it had almost completely displaced horse-car lines.

Early in the 20th century, long-distance electric railway and electric interurban traffic developed rapidly and served as a decentralizing force. The

increasing use of the automobile and motor bus, and the economic impact of the depression of the 1930's upon the over-extended lines resulted in their decline.

Transportation in Cities. The popularity of the private automobile caused a rapid and long decline in rapid-transit systems using electric power to carry people from one part of a metropolitan area to another. Transit companies in practically all cities converted to the use of buses, although electrically driven trains continued to operate in subways.

But the rapid growth of cities and the increase in car ownership produced transit difficulties of crisis proportions. Streets were widened; elevated roads were constructed; beltways were built around

RURAL ROADS IN THE UNITED STATES—1973

State	State Control	Local Control	Federal Control	Total Mileage
Alabama	19,831	47,741	275	67,847
Alaska	4,351	1,559	1,701	7,611
Arizona	5,590	21,156	18,100	44,846
Arkansas	13,779	52,758	1,802	68,339
California	14,263	71,477	37,137	122,877
Colorado	8,493	67,119	95	75,707
Connecticut	1,518	3,908	......	5,426
Delaware	4,348	......	......	4,348
Florida	13,349	57,035	1,390	71,774
Georgia	15,857	68,356	1,003	85,216
Hawaii	895	1,680	77	2,652
Idaho	4,741	25,462	22,504	52,707
Illinois	13,389	88,856	242	102,487
Indiana	10,224	65,078	56	75,358
Iowa	9,089	89,922	69	99,080
Kansas	10,081	113,098	94	123,273
Kentucky	23,846	39,314	609	63,769
Louisiana	14,231	28,160	323	42,714
Maine	10,960	7,841	162	18,963
Maryland	4,964	17,541	144	22,649
Massachusetts	1,193	4,908	49	6,150
Michigan	8,014	88,035	2,660	98,709
Minnesota	11,107	98,054	1,539	110,700
Mississippi	9,742	49,863	239	59,844
Missouri	29,908	68,451	740	99,099
Montana	12,158	53,823	9,471	75,452
Nebraska	9,793	80,719	563	91,075
Nevada	6,161	41,577	......	47,738
New Hampshire	3,056	7,006	111	10,173
New Jersey	1,579	12,005	13	13,597
New Mexico	11,666	46,575	6,819	65,060
New York	12,518	44,130	35	56,683
North Carolina	71,537	......	1,829	73,366
North Dakota	6,692	95,035	1,298	103,025
Ohio	17,036	68,971	29	86,036
Oklahoma	11,513	81,948	34	93,495
Oregon	9,279	35,213	50,179	94,671
Pennsylvania	42,491	46,784	858	90,133
Rhode Island	500	519	......	1,019
South Carolina	32,123	20,637	490	53,250
South Dakota	8,823	69,260	1,623	79,706
Tennessee	8,162	59,202	1,211	68;575
Texas	61,578	136,172	1,021	198,771
Utah	4,826	22,151	16,110	43,087
Vermont	2,593	10,129	185	12,907
Virginia	49,687	870	2,337	52,894
Washington	14,335	39,598	17,177	71,110
West Virginia	31,902	......	776	32,678
Wisconsin	10,772	78,871	68	89,711
Wyoming	5,918	20,879	12,500	39,297
Total	710,461	2,249,446	215,747	3,175,654

Source: Dept. of Transportation, Federal Highway Adm., *Highway Statistics, 1973.*

many cities; even hours of work were staggered in some places to avoid traffic tie-ups at the rush hours. Space had to be found for parking the automobiles. One result was a trend for businesses to move into the suburbs.

The problem was attacked in some cases by a revival of public mass transportation systems. San Francisco began construction of a suburban electric rail system with maximum train speed of 80 miles an hour, the tracks going overhead in some places and underground in others. Montreal and Stockholm constructed subways. Los Angeles also began work on a rapid transit system. Many other cities proceeded to enlarge their existing surface systems or subways, including Chicago, Cleveland, Boston, Detroit, and Toronto. Tokyo put up a monorail system as a partial answer, and Seattle continued to operate the monorail trains used for its world's fair.

TRANSPORTATION ON THE PUBLIC ROADS

Highway History. In colonial days and until within a few decades, road building in the United States was carried on mainly by local governments. The work of construction was done by townships and towns in the middle and eastern states, and by counties and subdivisions of counties in the southern states. These local highways were mostly dirt roads and were not suitable for the handling of freight and passenger traffic between distant points. The first long distance or through-transportation highways were the turnpike roads, built by corporations chartered by the several states. The first important turnpike was the one from Philadelphia to Lancaster, Pa., begun in 1792 and completed two years later. Early in the 19th century, turnpike roads in large numbers were built in Pennsylvania, New York, and other states.

For a time the government of the United States gave aid to highway construction. Works of internal improvement then included highways as well as canals. But the policy of national aid to public highways came to an end in the 1830's, when it was held that Federal works of internal improvement were unconstitutional. By 1850 most of the states had come upon financial difficulties in attempting to build or aid canals, railroads, and highways.

Good Roads Movement. About 1890 a "good roads" movement started in Massachusetts, New Jersey, New York, and other states. Following 1910, this movement was powerfully re-enforced through the need for roads more suitable for motor vehicles, which by that time were coming

into general use. The way had been prepared abroad, where the first asphalt highway was constructed in Paris in 1870 and the first cement highway was built in Grenoble in 1876.

Motor Trucks and Buses. The decade of 1920-30 saw public conveyances on the highways developed to the point of near approximation with the railroads in the transportation picture. This was due to improvements both in trucks and buses and in the highways on which they traveled. The highways were, of course, built at public expense. The federal government alone was soon spending a billion dollars a year to construct a system of national (United States) highways and assisting states and municipalities to improve their roads. Truck and bus lines were made subject to regulation by the Interstate Commerce Commission in 1935.

In 1940, the first motor toll road was opened, the Pennsylvania Turnpike, a divided highway with restricted entry and no traffic lights. It was followed by many others, constructed by state governments which expected to liquidate the cost by toll revenues. The private automobile was the beneficiary even more than the public conveyance.

The Motor Age. Before the mid-20th century, the private automobile had become a necessity rather than a luxury. Its appeal was irresistible, giving its occupants a sense of being at home wherever the car traveled. The result was more and more intolerable traffic congestion. Again the federal government stepped in.

In 1956, Congress passed the Federal Aid Highway Act authorizing expenditure of $33 billion over 13 years, primarily for a 41,000-mile system of *interstate* highways, multi-lane divided roads with limited access and engineered for maximum speed and safety. Ninety per cent of the cost was borne by the federal government, as was the case also for improvement of 190,000 miles of state roads and 510,000 miles of secondary roads. Gasoline and other taxes were imposed to produce the needed revenue. Traffic on the interstate system was enabled to pass between, into, and around the larger cities; railroad and highway crossings were eliminated by overpasses. The original cost authorizations were later substantially increased. Apart from the direct transportation benefits of lower operating cost of vehicles, increased safety, and saving of time for travelers and shippers, the system had an important impact on the pattern of economic life. The new highways attracted industrial, commercial, and residential development with consequent enlargement of economic opportunities.

MOTOR VEHICLE REGISTRATION IN UNITED STATES
Privately Owned Vehicles*

Year	Passenger Cars	Trucks Number	% of total	Buses	Total
1900	8,000	......	...	......	8,000
1910	458,377	10,123	2.2	......	468,500
1915	2,332,426	158,506	6.4	......	2,490,932
1920	8,131,522	1,107,639	12.0	......	9,239,161
1925	17,439,701	2,483,215	12.5	17,808	19,930,724
1930	22,972,745	3,518,747	13.3	40,507	26,531,999
1935	22,494,884	3,675,865	14.0	58,994	26,229,743
1940	27,372,397	4,590,386	14.3	72,641	32,035,424
1945	25,691,434	4,834,742	15.8	112,253	30,638,429
1950	40,333,591	8,604,448	17.5	223,652	49,161,691
1955	52,135,583	10,302,987	16.4	255,249	62,693,819
1960†	61,558,847	11,937,589	16.2	272,129	73,768,565
1961	63,260,416	12,286,430	16.4	279,668	75,826,514
1962	65,928,547	12,809,150	16.2	285,219	79,022,916
1963	69,026,690	13,423,327	16.2	297,864	82,747,881
1964	71,984,540	14,019,143	16.2	305,415	86,309,098
1966	78,331,488	15,522,114	16.4	323,197	94,176,799
1969	86,710,000	17,155,000	16.3	‡	105,404,000
1974	104,898,256	24,598,284	18.0	446,547	134,904,676

* Figures from 1950 through 1974 are for privately and publicly owned vehicles, excluding military vehicles. † Increase over 1955 due in part to addition of Alaska and Hawaii. ‡ Buses included with figure for trucks.
Source: Dept. of Transportation, Federal Highway Adm.; annual reports, *Highway Statistics*, *Drivers Licenses*, and unpublished data.

TRANSPORTATION BY AIR

Early History of Aircraft. The earliest *attempts* at flight were made with craft heavier than air. This fact was probably due to the every-day example of the flight of birds.

The Greek inventor Archytas is said to have constructed, about 400 B. C., a wooden pigeon which maintained itself for a short time in the air. About 1500 A. D., Leonardo da Vinci constructed models of helicopters, with propellers rotating in a horizontal plane, which hovered in the air. He is, therefore, properly credited with the invention of the helicopter and also of the propeller with rotating blades. He first conceived also of the parachute and he drew plans for ornithopters, that is, for aircraft to be propelled by flapping wings. These were to be operated by the arms and legs of the aeronaut. Many later inventors continued to experiment on these lines despite the fact that Giovanni Borelli (1606-79) pointed out that man's pectoral muscles have less than one-tenth the power possessed by the wing-operating muscles of birds when the weight of the body is taken into consideration.

Attempts at gliding are said to have been made in Rome in the time of Nero. About 1660, a French acrobat named Allard undertook a gliding flight in Paris before Louis XIV. These and many subsequent attempts ended in injury or death to the would-be aeronauts.

Aeronautics. Mechanical flight is pre-eminently a development of the 20th century. Its success demanded the improved gasoline engine, a light, strong metal, such as duralumin, and a knowledge of air dynamics. These discoveries led to the evolution of the airship from the balloon and to the building of successful heavier-than-air machines, or airplanes. See *Airplane* and *Airship*.

The flight of an airplane is analogous to that of a kite. The string by which the kite is drawn forward corresponds to the forward drive of the propeller, and the upward pressure of the air on the kite corresponds to the lift exerted on the wings of the airplane. This lift is due partly to the pressure exerted on the under side of the wings, and partly to the suction caused by a partial vacuum on the upper side of the wings. Neither surface of the wing is flat. The cross section of the wing follows certain streamline designs which are a balance between three requirements—maximum lifting power, strength, and minimum resistance in passing through the air. The last mentioned requirement demands also that the body of the airplane should conform to streamline design.

To exert effective lifting power the wings must be driven forward at a certain minimum speed and must be inclined upward at an angle of from 2° to 20°. Below this limit, or above it, the air resistance, or "drag," causes the plane to "stall;" that is, to fall below the minimum speed necessary for horizontal flight or control. The minimum speed required to keep the average plane in the air is about 35 miles an hour. Airplanes driven by piston engines travel from 200 to 350 miles per hour at top speed. But those propelled by jet, which were introduced into commercial flying in the 1960's, attain speeds of from 500 to 600 miles per hour. This velocity approaches the speed of sound, which is approximately 770 miles per hour. Plans soon were laid for introducing supersonic turbojet planes which would operate at nearly 2000 miles an hour.

The jet planes are pushed forward, not by revolving propellors pressing against air, similar in principle to the screw of a ship, but by thrusting backwards an explosive mixture of compressed air and fuel. Their propulsion is independent of air. Hence at high altitudes, up to 42,000 feet, where air is rarified and presents much less resistance to the plane's forward movement, far greater speeds can be obtained with the same expenditure of fuel. This is the chief factor in making their flight more economical.

The mechanisms for stabilizing the airplane's course include a vertical tail fin and a horizontal tail plane. Control of its course is effected through an "elevator," jointed to the tail plane, a rudder, jointed to the fin, and ailerons, or adjustable wing flaps. Landing on rough ground is facilitated by the use of pneumatic tired wheels on axles fitted and designed for maximum shock absorbing capacity.

While the control of an automobile involves only two main factors—speed and steering in a horizontal plane—the control of an airplane involves at least two additional factors. One is steering in a vertical plane; that is, going upward, downward, or on the level. The other is maintaining an even keel; that is, avoiding undue tipping, or "banking." Most planes have a so-called stick control. Moving the "stick" forward or backward causes a fall or rise in height; moving it sideways causes tipping to the right or left. Steering right or left is accomplished by a foot bar.

Important Dates in Aircraft History.

Aug. 27,1783—Hydrogen first used in a balloon by Prof. J. A. C. Charles, of Paris.

Jan. 7, 1785—The first crossing of the English channel in a balloon, by J. J. Blanchard, a Frenchman.

Jan. 9, 1793—The first ascent of a balloon in America, at Philadelphia, by J. J. Blanchard, in the presence of George Washington.

1848—The first power-driven airplane which actually flew, a 9-pound model, steam-driven, constructed by John Stringfellow, an Englishman. It flew 120 feet.

Dec. 17, 1903—First successful piloted flight in a power-driven airplane, at Kitty Hawk, N.C., by Wilbur Wright, 120 feet in 12 seconds. Nine days previously Samuel P. Langley's 'aerodrome" had crashed in a take-off, but was later proved capable of flight by Glenn Curtiss and flown successfully at Hammondsport, N.Y. Sept. 17, 1914.

1904—The first airship built in the United States, the *California Arrow*, by Captain T. S. Baldwin.

Aug. 22, 1906—First successful flight in Europe and first in the world without launching aids, by Alberto Santos-Dumont at Bagatelle, France.

July 25, 1909—First airplane flight across the English Channel, by Louis Bleriot, 20 miles in 37 minutes.

June 22, 1910—The first flight of an airship on a regularly operated transportation service, by Count Zeppelin at Friedrichshaven, Germany.

May 15, 1918—First regular air mail route in America inaugurated, between New York and Washington.

June 14, 1919—First non-stop transatlantic airplane flight, by Alcock and Brown, Newfoundland to Ireland, 1936 miles in 15 hours, 57 minutes.

1924—First aerial circumnavigation of the globe, by United States Army planes in 175 days.

1930—Development of "blind flying."

1931—Aerial circumnavigation of the earth in 8 days, 15 hours, 51 minutes, by Post and Gatty, as compared with the first circumnavigation in 1519 by Magellan, which required 37 months.

1934—First west to east crossing of the Pacific, by Sir Charles Kingsford-Smith and Capt. P. G. Taylor, 7365 miles in 51 hours flying time.

Nov. 1935—First transpacific air mail service—San Francisco to Manila.

June 17, 1939—Transatlantic passenger service inaugurated between U.S. and Europe.

1940-45—World War II mass production of aircraft; emergence of the helicopter as a useful craft; development of jet aircraft and V-2 rockets by German scientists.

1950-53—Korean War saw the military use of advanced jet aircraft.

1953-57—Development of turbo-prop, turbo-jet, and pure-jet commercial aircraft; experimental VTOL (vertical take-off and landing craft) introduced; advanced development of military rockets and missiles.

1958—First U.S. commercial jet aircraft capable of speeds up to 615 mph and reducing flying times by nearly one half.

1965-67—Pilot studies by the United States and jointly by France and Britain for development of commercial supersonic planes.

1968—The U.S.S.R.'s supersonic transport (SST), TU-144, designed to travel at 1,550 mph and carry 135 passengers 4,000 miles, made its first test flight.

1969—The Concorde, a British-French supersonic airliner designed to carry 140 passengers at 1,450 mph, made its first test flight. The Boeing 747 "jumbo" jet, with a 490-passenger capacity, made its first public flight—from Seattle to New York.

1973—The British-French Concorde landed in the U.S. (Dallas-Ft. Worth Airport) for the first time.

1974—The Concorde set two records: from Paris to Boston in 3 hours, 9 minutes; from Boston to Miami in 80 minutes.

Air Travel. Air transportation is mainly passenger transportation, although carrying of mail has played a large role in development of the line. Volume of air freight is insignificant in comparison with passenger traffic.

The development of air travel was slow at first since it represented such a sharp break with past habits. Fear had to be overcome by confidence based on proven safety. European airlines, with government subsidies, progressed rapidly in the 1920's. In 1930, Congress authorized air-mail subsidies, and the routes selected by the postmaster general helped develop the pattern of routes which formed the basis for today's system. The government established beacons and radio stations for the guidance of fliers. Terminals were constructed by municipalities, usually with government assistance.

Established in 1938, the Civil Aeronautics Board was given broad powers to regulate nonmilitary flying and to lend assistance to commercial airlines. This law and the sale of surplus military aircraft after World War II provided the impetus for a crescendo in air travel which, by the 1960's, placed it at the head of all forms of travel except the private automobile. Transoceanic air passengers far exceeded in number those using ships. The use of private planes also grew apace. Traffic congestion at the larger airports became a serious problem.

Airplane safety depends on numerous sophisticated instruments. The pilot uses a radio range instrument to keep to a course marked by a radio beam, any deviation from which is registered on the panel instruments. An "omnibearing instrument" gives him his exact location. When he is near an airport landing, his instrument landing system enables him to follow a radio beam sent from his landing point. At the airport, a control officer, by means of radar, is made aware of every aircraft within range and issues instructions for orderly landing.

Planes that fly above 10,000 feet are equipped with pressurized cabins. Those going more than 25,000 feet are equipped with separate facilities to distribute oxygen to all occupants should the pressure system fail.

Commercial Air Transportation. At the end of the second decade of commercial air transport in the U.S. in 1940, the airlines were transporting about 3,185,278 passengers per year. This number rose to 126,700,000 by the early 1970's. Also at that time, approximately 750 airlines were in operation in the world. Their air routes covered over 9,670,000 miles, with an estimated 236,750,000 passengers per year.

Federal Control. Federal promotion and regulation of civil aviation are carried out by two bodies—the Civil Aeronautics Board and the Civil Aeronautics Administration. The Civil Aeronautics Board is an independent agency concerned primarily with the issuance of certificates of public necessity, economic regulation, the formulation of safety regulations, and the investigation of accidents in civil aircraft. The Civil Aeronautics Administration is an operating agency of the Department of Commerce. Its principal activities are the building and operation of air navigation aids and the enforcement of safety regulations.

TRANSPORTATION VISTAS

The demand for fast transportation in a world rapidly filling with people pointed by the middle of the 20th century to intolerable traffic congestion on highways and in the air. Radical new methods came under study and testing. Some of these are described below.

Air Cushion Vehicles (ACV). These operate on the principle of the jet. Air is forced downward so as to exert a lift on the car or boat sufficient to free it of contact with the surface of the ground or water. Propulsion also is by jet action.

This type of craft was invented by the British engineer Christopher S. Cockerell. His air-cushion boat, the hovercraft, was demonstrated successfully with the financial aid of the National Research Development Corporation of Great Britain. A land vehicle was developed also to follow a rail in the form of a V.

In France, a so-called aerotrain (or tracked ACV) was built which uses a rail embedded in the center of a smooth reinforced concrete roadway. This rail also fits into a deep groove in the car but, when the car attains operating speed, does not touch the surfaces of the groove. Jets of air prevent the contact. Thus there is no friction either with the roadbed or the rail. In 1967 an aerotrain reached a speed of 215 mph; a speed of 300 mph is considered a feasible maximum.

In the United States a similar vehicle known as the levacar was constructed by the Ford Motor Company in 1961. It, however, utilizes two rails instead of one but is raised so as to have no direct contact with them, as in the aerotrain. A possible speed of 500 mph was claimed for it.

Train in a Tube. A more radical device worked out by the Lockheed Corporation replaces the roadbed and guide rails with a giant tube within which the vehicle is propelled. The car would be fitted with precision to the walls of the tube. No attention is paid to getting rid of friction since at high speeds this would be at a minimum. The work of the engine is to take the air ahead and force it at great pressure to the rear. This jet effect would propel the car at a speed which theoretically could be supersonic.

Another device, using both a tube and air cushion, is one developed by the Rensselaer Polytechnic Institute. The air cushion centers the car in the tube so as to avoid contact with the walls of the tube, and the car is propelled by sucking in the air ahead and ejecting it in the rear.

The RRollway. This word is formed from "railroad" and "tollway." It is applied to a proposed electric train of cars about 24 feet wide operated on four tracks. Its purpose is to provide a rapid mode of transporting passengers and also, if they wish, their automobiles, which can be driven in and parked transversally across the car. The width of the track assures stability. Speeds up to 300 mph are envisaged. Operation would be automatic by computer so that a service as frequent as one each 90 seconds could be maintained. According to the developer, General American Transportation Corporation, the terminals would be outside cities in view of the wide tracks required and the requisite large areas of the terminals.

LABOR RELATIONS

SINCE the days of feudalism, much of the world's work has been done under what is known as the system of free contract which means that the employee delivers his work to his employer for a stipulated price. Forced labor, as under slavery, and labor exacted as a duty because of social status, which prevailed under feudalism, theoretically at least have no part in labor relations today among democratic nations.

Before the rise of large-scale industry, as on many farms today, the relation between employer and employee was close and personal. But as the small property owner yielded to the large corporation as the typical employer, the relation of employee to employer became rather that of production worker to manager with personal acquaintance replaced by rules and policies. In a corporation, the management itself consists of employees of the corporation. Its interests, however, lie chiefly with the owners of the corporation rather than with the production workers. This fact provides the setting for the problems of labor relations in industry.

Management and Workers. The interests of management and workers conflict in so far as each group seeks to obtain a larger share of the revenue of the enterprise. Their interests overlap, however, in that neither could operate the enterprise without the aid of the other and both stand to prosper by enlarged revenue. Under normal conditions, ownership and management have the initial advantage in that they do not need workers as much as the workers need them. That is to say, the workers are usually much more dependent upon the weekly or monthly pay check than the owners of capital are upon profit or dividends from business. The owners are likewise able, as a group, to employ their superior money resources as a purveyor of power through political activity, use of the courts, and publicity. To offset this advantage, workers eventually built up strong organizations—labor unions—to mobilize countervailing economic and political power.

Role of the Government. For these reasons the labor problem in an industrialized nation enters vitally into government itself. Two groups, one wealthier and the other more numerous, compete for control. But the government, which represents all other interests as well as these, has a primary concern in seeing that industrial peace is preserved, that production and distribution of goods and services are promoted and that causes of strife are kept to a minimum. The government also has an interest in seeing that the health and the physical and mental well-being of its citizens are not impaired by substandard conditions of work, prolonged unemployment, and discriminatory employment practices.

INDUSTRIAL CONFLICT

In the early 19th century, the legal relation of employer and employee was still that of master and servant, a relic of the feudal system. Concerted action by employees to obtain better wages or working conditions was punishable by the courts as conspiracy, for which prison sentences might be imposed. In 1842, however, the Supreme Judicial Court of Massachusetts, then perhaps the most influential court in the country, ruled that employees might lawfully organize for mutual aid.

This right was slow in obtaining recognition. Its practical exercise, however, and the use of it to better the conditions of labor provide the key to most of the economic conflict between capital and labor both before and since.

The ultimate weapons of industrial conflict are the strike on the part of employees and the lockout on the part of employers. These simple forms of economic pressure, however, are usually supplemented by other actions intended to break the resistance of the opposing parties. Strikes, cessation of work by a group of employees until certain issues are settled, are usually accompanied by picketing and may be supplemented by boycotts. In the past, especially in the late 1930's, the stay-in or sit-down strike technique was used. Lockouts are much rarer than strikes. Most employer action in industrial disputes, therefore, takes the form of combating strikes.

Early History of Unions. The first recorded strike in America took place in the colonial period, when in 1741 New York bakers quit work as a protest against a municipal ordinance regulating the price of bread. The earliest known strike for higher wages took place in 1786, when the Philadelphia printers ceased work as a means of enforcing their demand for a minimum weekly wage of six dollars. A sympathetic strike took place in 1799, when the shoemakers, belonging to the organization known as the Federal Society of Journeymen Cordwainers, were compelled to lay down their tools in order to aid the bootmakers, who were seeking an increase in wages. This action may be regarded also as the first *organized* strike in America. Sympathetic strikes, however, did not play an important part in industrial disputes until the last two decades of the 19th century.

A successful attempt to establish a 10-hour working day was made by the unions of Philadelphia in 1835. Fifty-one years later, in 1886, occurred the first nation-wide strike for an eight-hour day.

Many trade unions were formed in the period between 1792 and 1810, especially in the cities of New York, Baltimore, Philadelphia, and Pittsburgh. The first central organization of trades in one city was formed at Philadelphia in 1827. It was called the Mechanics Union of Trade Associations.

In 1833, there were 29 organized trades in New York City. Many of these affiliated to form the New York Trades Union. Similar organizations followed quickly in other cities, so that when a convention was called in New York in August 1834, delegates were present representing the trades unions of Boston, Brooklyn, Philadelphia, Poughkeepsie, New York, and Newark. At this convention was inaugurated the National Trades Union. A trades union, comprising as members *unions* in various trades, must be distinguished from a trade union, which comprises as members *individual workers* in *one* trade only.

The printers were apparently the first craft to unite their local units into a national association, so that the Typographical Union, organized in 1850, is the oldest *national* trade union in America. The Stonecutters effected a national organization in 1853; the Hat Finishers, in 1854; the Molders, and the Machinists and Blacksmiths, in 1857.

In addition to unions of the workers in a particular trade, two organizations on a national scale arose prior to 1870, each of which admitted workers of any trade. The first was known as the National Labor Union, founded in 1866. The second, established in 1869, was called the Noble Order of the Knights of Labor. It began as a secret society, but the policy of secrecy was abandoned in 1878. Dissensions within these organizations led, in 1881, to the formation at Pittsburgh of the Federation of Organized Trades and Labor Unions of the United States and Canada. This federation merged with a separate trade union conference on December 8, 1886, forming the present American Federation of Labor. In 1889, the new federation recognized the continuity of its existence by dating its records from 1881.

Strikes. A strike is a concerted cessation of work on the part of the employees to compel an employer to meet their wishes as to wages or other conditions. It is a two-edged weapon, however; sometimes it cuts three ways. While its purpose is to cause loss to the employer, it also cuts off earnings of employees and may entail serious consequences for the public.

To enable employees to stand the loss of wages, labor organizations usually accumulate strike funds from which payments may be made to needy strikers in the form of strike benefits.

When the effect of strikes on the public goes beyond mere inconvenience and threatens disorganization of customary ways of living, as when electric power is cut off, the government is likely to intervene. Some states make strikes against public utility companies unlawful. The Federal government has the power by law to delay strikes which the president finds to imperil the public health or safety.

Sit-down Strike. This is a term applied when strikers, instead of leaving their jobs, remain at their places and refuse to work. Such action amounts practically to taking over the shop. When first used, in 1937, the sit-down strike brought workers some conspicuous successes, but in 1938 it was held by the U.S. Supreme Court to be illegal, and participants were deprived of the protection of Federal labor laws which they would otherwise have enjoyed.

Sympathetic Strike. This is a strike called by a union against an employer with whom the union has no quarrel, the purpose being to aid a sister union involved in a dispute with another employer.

Picketing. The picket line is the commonest means of adding to the effectiveness of a strike. It usually takes the form of a file of strikers carrying signs near a plant entrance, the signs conveying in simplified form the strikers' version of the dispute. The signs, for example, may read, "Unfair to organized labor." Sometimes sound trucks are pressed into service to give the public a more detailed account of the strikers' case.

The effectiveness of a picket line may be much greater than the number involved would lead one to expect. This is because crossing a picket line is regarded by large numbers of people as a species of treason to the employee class or the labor movement. The picket line helps to make a strike complete.

When feelings run high, picketing may become much more than an advertisement of the strikers' case. The pickets may attempt forcibly to prevent nonstrikers or customers from entering the employer's premises. This is sometimes known as obstructive or violent picketing as opposed to peaceful picketing.

Peaceful picketing has been declared by the United States supreme court to be a right protected by the Constitution as a form of free speech. On the other hand, courts ordinarily take the view that violent picketing is unlawful and may be forbidden by injunction. Even peaceful picketing when engaged in for unlawful purposes falls under the ban of many laws which define such purposes.

Boycotts. In addition to picketing, unions frequently seek to exert pressure on employers with whom they are in controversy through destroying their markets by means of boycotts. That is to say, members and others are asked not to patronize the employer concerned.

Secondary Boycott. A boycott is secondary when it is aimed only indirectly at the employer with whom the union has a quarrel. It seeks to reach him by forcing his customers, suppliers, or employees to cease doing business with him until he consents to what the union wants. An example would be picketing a radio store to prevent it from handling radios made by a company against which the union was striking. Such tactics are forbidden by Federal law and by some state laws.

Union Label. The use of a special label for goods made in factories where labor is unionized is another form of aiding a consumer's boycott. In another sense it is a form of advertising so as to permit preferential buying, comparable to the plea to "buy home goods."

Strikebreaking. The usual strategy of the employer in combating a strike, the picket line, and boycott is to attempt to operate his business with nonstrikers or new employees and weaken the morale of the strikers. Injunctions against illegal picketing and boycotts may be sought.

If the strike is "economic," that is, not motivated by the employer's unfair labor practices, the employer may lawfully seek to replace the strikers by new employees. Otherwise, the strikers may be entitled to job reinstatement with regular pay for the time they were on strike. For this reason, employers have largely abandoned the cruder forms of strikebreaking formerly used. In most large strikes, there is no attempt to operate until the dispute is settled. But sometimes picketing continues even years after the business has been operating normally.

LABOR INJUNCTIONS

It is impossible to understand industrial conflict without appreciating that, while the objective of employees is better pay and working conditions, these can be achieved as a rule only when the employees are able to act together effectively. Only by concerted action can strikes, picketing, or boycotts be made into effective instruments.

For this reason, in the earlier stages of the industrial age, employers' efforts to combat employee demands were aimed at preventing employees from organizing. One method used was to insist that new employees sign what came to be called "yellow-dog contracts." These were undertakings not to join a labor organization on pain of discharge. Even without such contracts, many employers considered membership in such organizations ground for discharge.

When conflicts came into the open through strikes and picketing, the weapon of court injunctions was relied on. An injunction is a court order usually issued to prevent the violation of someone's right. If it is disobeyed, the violators may be punished at the court's discretion through fines or imprisonment.

The first labor injunction by a Federal court was issued in 1885 (*U. S. v. Kane*) to prevent an act threatening a bankrupt property which was directly under the guardianship of the court. This precedent was extended to protect private property rights in the case of Casey v. Cincinnati Typographical Union, decided in 1891. Thereafter injunctions were used freely to prevent picketing and other strike action, frequently without the union being notified or given a chance to reply.

Antitrust Laws. In 1890 Congress passed the Sherman Antitrust act designed to break up combinations of capital. Combinations in restraint of interstate commerce were made subject to injunctions and to suit for triple damages by persons injured by such combinations. This law was utilized to prevent picketing and boycotts where interstate commerce was affected.

The supreme court of the United States, in 1906 and 1908 respectively, decided that a boycott conducted by a labor union against goods of a manufacturer with which the union has a dispute and a boycott against retailers buying from such a manufacturer fall under the prohibitions contained in the Sherman act. (See *Buck Stove and Range Case* and *Danbury Hatters' Case*.) The Clayton act, amending the Sherman act in 1914, provided that the antitrust laws should not apply to labor unions acting lawfully in pursuit of their legitimate purposes. The courts held, however, that action which interfered with interstate commerce was not part of the legitimate activity of unions, thus leaving the earlier decisions of the supreme court in effect.

Norris-LaGuardia Anti-Injunction Act. This act, passed in 1932, attempted, among other things, to do what the Clayton act failed to do. It forbids Federal courts to issue injunctions in labor disputes except under narrowly defined circumstances. The result was that labor organizations were to a large extent freed of injunctions issued by Federal courts. A seeming exception was the 1947 injunction to prevent a coal strike, but this applied to a government-operated industry.

Injunctions Under Taft-Hartley Act. The Labor-Management Relations act, 1947, popularly known as the Taft-Hartley act, punched at least two holes in the Norris-LaGuardia act. First, it allows injunctions in labor disputes at the instance of the National Labor Relations Board (NLRB), an agency established for regulating labor relations. This federal agency is *required* to seek orders to stop secondary boycotts and certain other kinds of "unlawful" acts by unions, and is *permitted* to seek such orders to stop "unfair labor practices." (See *Taft-Hartley Act* below.)

The other major modification in the Anti-Injunction act is a provision of the Taft-Hartley act under which the attorney general of the United States may obtain injunctions to delay up to 80 days any strikes found by the president of the United States to affect the public health or safety.

RIGHT TO ORGANIZE

As stated above, a key objective of employees in industrial conflict is the right to organize for mutual aid and protection. The chief obstacles to the exercise of this right have been these: (1) the discharge of employees known to be members of unions or active in forming unions; (2) refusal by employers to recognize and deal with unions organized by employees to act as their agents; and (3) undermining the unions of employees by organizing so-called company unions which the employer could control.

After decades of costly controversies in which these tactics were combated by unions through the use of their economic weapons of strikes, picketing, and boycotts, Congress adopted legislation to curb those employer practices which undercut the right of employees to organize. The six principal steps in this legislation are as follows:

In 1926, the Railway Labor act asserted the duty of railroads to deal with freely chosen representatives of their employees for the establishment of wages, hours, and other conditions of employment. In 1929, the United States supreme court held that railroad employers violate this law by forming company unions and dealing with them as if they were the freely chosen representatives of employees (*Railway Clerks v. Texas & New Orleans Ry.*). The Railway Labor act was amended in 1934 to provide for the designation, following a vote, of employees' bargaining agents by a government agency, the National Mediation Board. In 1936, this act was extended to cover airlines and their employees.

In 1932, the Norris-LaGuardia act, already referred to, forbade "yellow-dog contracts." It thereby put an end to the practice of requiring employees to consent in advance to their discharge if they joined a union.

In 1933, the National Industrial Recovery act authorized industry codes in which it was obligatory to incorporate terms which (1) prohibited employers from discriminating against employees for union activity and (2) required employers to recognize as bargaining agent of employees any union selected by the majority of the employees. The act was declared unconstitutional in 1935.

Wagner Act. In 1935, Congress adopted the National Labor Relations act, popularly known as the Wagner act. This law served as a basic guarantee of the right to organize and bargain collectively. There were two principal reasons for its effectiveness.

First, it brought under Federal regulation nearly all forms of business except small local enterprises.

Second, the act provided an enforcing agency, the national labor relations board, which prosecuted violations at government expense and without cost to the complainant.

In 1947, this basic labor law was made still more sweeping by a new act. At the same time its emphasis was changed. While the purpose of the Wagner act was to remove certain causes of labor strife by restraining conduct of employers, the Labor Management Relations act, 1947, was designed to guard rights of the public, of employers, and of individual employees. In doing so, it abridges in some respects the collective rights of employees which had been guaranteed by the Wagner act.

TAFT-HARTLEY ACT

The Taft-Hartley act, officially known as the Labor Management Relations act, 1947, contains as Title I the National Labor Relations act (the Wagner act of 1935) as amended in 1947. The other titles, or divisions, of the act relate to restrictions on payment of benefits to employees or unions, outlawry of certain kinds of union conduct, suability in the Federal courts for breach of agreements, and handling of disputes imperiling the national health or safety. The act also establishes the United States mediation and conciliation service and defines its rôle in the settlement of labor disputes.

The most publicized part of the law is Title I. This is the part which forbids as "unfair labor practices" certain types of conduct on the part of employers and of unions. It describes the methods by which the conduct may be stopped through action by the national labor relations board and the courts. It also prescribes means by which the union chosen by the majority of employees may be given official status through "certification." Finally, it imposes certain conditions with which unions must comply before they are permitted to use the services of the board.

Unfair Labor Practices. According to Title I of the act, there are five principal unfair labor practices of employers and six unfair labor practices of unions or their agents. Those of employers were forbidden by the Wagner act and are carried forward with a few changes into the later law. Those of unions were added by the Taft-Hartley act.

Practices Forbidden Employers. Employers are forbidden to engage in the following practices:

(a) *Discrimination for Union Activity.*—This prohibition acts as a limitation on the right of employers to hire and fire at will. It means in practice that employers may not discharge or otherwise discriminate against workers for the reason that they are or are not union members or that they have engaged in concerted activity (or refused to do so) to advance their interests.

(b) *Domination of a Labor Organization.*—This means organizing, or encouraging employees to organize, an inside labor union or it may mean merely giving financial or other support to a union which the employees have organized on their own initiative. The reason which frequently actuates employers in supporting inside unions is the desire to forestall organizers from outside. When organized from outside, employees typically affiliate their local organization with a national union and draw strength and support from it in dealing with their employer. An inside group dominated by the employer is frequently referred to as a "company union."

(c) *Refusal to Bargain.*—This is an unfair labor practice which has an exact counterpart among those forbidden to unions. The meaning of it will be described below.

(d) *Interference with Employee Rights.*—This also has its counterpart among unfair practices of unions. The rights with which interference is forbidden are the rights to join, and refrain from joining, unions formed for the purpose of dealing with employers. As applied to employers, the term has a very broad meaning. It may include the conduct described in (a), (b), and (c) above and many other acts. Some acts which have been forbidden under this head include: Insisting on employees' signing of individual contracts in place of bargaining collectively through a union; espionage and questioning employees about their union membership; and maneuvers to weaken unions, such as transferring production from a plant where the union is strong to a plant where it has not obtained a foothold.

Discrimination for Giving Testimony.—The employer may not discriminate against an employee for filing charges or giving testimony under the Act.

Practices Forbidden Unions.—Unions and their representatives are forbidden to engage in these unfair labor practices:

(a) Coercion of employees in their right to join or refrain from joining labor organizations formed for the purpose of collective bargaining or coercion of employers in the selection of their agents in dealing with employees either when bargaining or handling grievances.

(b) Causing or attempting to cause an employer to discriminate against a worker who has been denied membership in a union for reasons other than certain ones specified in the Act.

(c) Refusal to bargain with employers, provided the union represents the majority of employees.

(d) Participation in secondary boycotts or striking and picketing for three other specified improper purposes. The purposes which are declared improper or unlawful are: (1) Organization from the top down through picketing, as when a union, without any members among employees, goes to their employer and compels him, by picketing, to give it a contract covering his employees; (2) supplanting an officially certified bargaining agent by compelling the employer to recognize the picketing union instead; and (3) forcing the solution of a dispute over work jurisdiction, as when a carpenters' union pickets an employer to compel him to let its members do work which he is having members of a machinists' union do.

(e) Charging excessive or discriminatory fees to members where the employee is permitted to hold his job only if he joins the union. There are special rules under the law which govern such compulsory membership. They are explained below.

(f) Compelling an employer to pay money, in the nature of an exaction, for work which is not intended to be performed.

Some of these unfair labor practices—those of employers—have been defined more concretely by judicial interpretation over a period of years. The one known as refusal to bargain, which is forbidden both to employers and unions, is defined at some length in the law itself. Important points in the elaboration of "discrimination," "domination," and "refusal to bargain" follow.

Discrimination Interpreted. In determining whether the discharge of an employee was for union activity or for some reason not forbidden by the law, such considerations as the following are taken into account.

1. Did the employer know of the employee's union membership? If he did not, the discharge could not have been for this reason.

2. If the alleged ground of discharge is inefficiency, were non-union employees of less efficiency for the same kind of job retained? If so, the employer's defense is weak.

3. If the discharge is said to be because the employee broke a rule against engaging in union activity on company time, are other rules against outside activity similarly enforced? If not, there is a presumption that the discharge is unlawful.

When persons unlawfully discharged are ordered reinstated, persons hired to replace them must be dismissed by the employer if necessary to make room for them. The same applies when employees are ordered reinstated after participating in a strike caused by an employer's unfair labor practice. If the strike, however, is economic, that is, for the purpose of obtaining better wages or working conditions, the strikers are entitled to their jobs back only if the jobs are still available.

Strikers or unlawfully discharged employees are not entitled to reinstatement if they have been guilty of crimes in connection with the labor dispute, have participated in sit-down strikes, or have, through their union, breached a contract with an employer.

Unlawful Aid to Unions. Support or aid which the law forbids employers to give to organizations of employees has been held to include the following procedures:

1. Suggesting the formation of a union, either personally or through supervisors, or facilitating its formation by advice or by provision of space or supplies free of charge.

2. Pressure placed on employees to join, particularly if the pressure includes threats of reprisals or promises of benefits.

3. Paying officers of the organization for time spent on the activities connected with it.

4. Eagerness in recognizing and executing a contract with the organization or giving it credit for wage increases granted, particularly if an outside union claims at the same time to represent a majority of the employees.

Duty to Bargain. The courts have held that, by making unlawful a refusal to bargain, Congress has created a positive duty to bargain in good faith. The Taft-Hartley act imposes this duty on both employers and unions, whereas the Wagner act imposed it on employers only.

The Taft-Hartley act defines the duty to bargain to include meeting at reasonable times, conferring in good faith on conditions of employment, negotiating an agreement or a dispute arising out of an agreement, and executing a written contract on request embodying the points agreed upon. The law, however, does not compel either party to agree to a particular proposal or to make a concession.

Freedom of Speech. The unfair labor practice of interference with employees' organizational rights was interpreted in the early years of the Wagner act to prevent employers or supervisors from expressing their views to employees about unions. The courts held that the words of employers were "loaded" in view of the employers' economic power over their employees. The Taft-Hartley act, however, provides that an employer may lawfully express his opposition to unionism in general, provided that he does not promise special benefits or suggest that employees will be penalized for failing to adopt his views.

Union Security. This term is applied to agreements between employers and unions under which employees must belong to the union if they are to continue in their jobs. It has a very special relation to the unfair labor practice of discrimination.

It should be explained first that carrying out such an agreement by discharging an employee who is not a union member amounts on its face to discrimination in respect of union membership. The Taft-Hartley act, however, permits this exception to its ban on discrimination but hedges it about with a number of conditions.

In the first place, the law forbids the closed shop.

The *closed shop* is an arrangement under which the employer is restricted to hiring persons who are members of the union.

The law does permit the union shop or a membership-maintenance agreement—but with some "ifs."

The *union shop* is an arrangement whereby employers may hire regardless of union membership, but employees, to keep their jobs, must join the union within a stated period (30 days under the Taft-Hartley act) and must thereafter remain members in good standing. Otherwise, the employer is required to discharge them.

Membership maintenance is an arrangement whereby those employees who are members of the union on a given date or who later become members must remain members if they are to keep their jobs. An "escape period" of limited time is usually provided to allow members to renounce membership. Hence, all employees need not be members of the union.

Preferential hiring requires the employer to hire union members to the extent that the contracting union is able to supply a sufficient number of qualified employees. This provision is lawful today, under certain conditions.

The agency shop does not require union membership, but does require as a condition of employment the payment of the same lawful union dues required of members.

While the Taft-Hartley act allows the negotiation of the union shop, the agency shop, and membership-maintenance provisions, it permits individual states to outlaw such clauses.

This recognition of states rights is a one-way affair. A state may not enact a law that allows greater union security, say a closed shop, and have this law take precedence over the Taft-Hartley prohibition of such clauses. The federal law specifies that it is to be superseded by state law only if the state law is more restrictive of union security than the federal enactment. In 1970 nineteen states had enacted so-called "right-to-work" laws which outlawed any kind of union security clause.

Under the Taft-Hartley law, failure of the employees to continue their membership for any reason other than nonpayment of dues will not justify discharge. For example, if a member is expelled from the union for violating its rules of conduct but offers to pay his dues, he may not be discharged from his job by the employer.

If these conditions are ignored, it becomes an unfair labor practice for the employer to discharge the employee for nonmembership in a union and it becomes an unfair labor practice for the union to try to force the employer to make the discharge. Either the employer or the union or both may be required to make good the wages lost by an employee discharged under these circumstances.

Bargaining Agents. It is a basic principle of labor law that, if a majority of the employees concerned select a union to represent them in bargaining, the employer has the duty of dealing with that union. But the determination of whether a particular union is the majority's choice is beset with difficulties.

The first problem is, who are the "employees concerned"? Are they the employees in one department, in the entire plant, or in some other grouping? To solve this problem, the national labor relations board is given the duty of deciding which employees are in a bargaining unit.

The second problem is, do the employees really wish the union to represent them? The difficulty is solved by having a secret election conducted by the national labor relations board to determine the free choice of the employees.

Unit for Bargaining. Establishing the unit appropriate for collective bargaining corresponds, in its field, to determining in political life what classes of persons are eligible to vote in an election. The process, however, is frequently much more complicated. Bargaining units fall principally into one of the following types:

1. *Craft unit*, which consists of those employees of a firm who follow one craft or occupation, such as carpenters, molders, or machinists.

2. *Plant unit*, which consists of all employees working in one plant. Supervisory personnel are excluded by law, while guards or watchmen and professional employees have separate provisions.

3. *Employer unit*, which consists usually of all those working for one employer, who has a number of plants. The term is sometimes extended to include all persons working for members of an associa-

tion of employers, which is authorized by its members to bargain for them.

The term *industrial unit* is sometimes applied to cover plant and employer units. It is used to point a contrast with craft unit, since the industrial unit takes in all workers without distinction of special skills.

Craft unions ordinarily seek to have craft units established, while industrial unions prefer plant or employer units. In practice, however, a number of craft unions may act together through a joint council in a form very similar to an industrial union. Industrial unions, on the other hand, may make special contracts for special classifications of their members, with a result similar to that secured by cooperating craft unions.

Determination of Units. In establishing units for bargaining, the National Labor Relations Board first excludes all persons whose interests are held to lie with the employer rather than with the other employees. These ordinarily include executives, supervisors, secretaries, and personnel directors. The rule is that those who have power to hire and fire or whose recommendations on employment are given weight are considered to be on the side of management. Supervisory employees are excluded from bargaining units because the law excludes them from the definition of "employee."

The law also provides that plant guards may not be in the same unit with other employees, nor may they be represented by a union which is affiliated in any way with a union representing the other employees in the plant. Professional employees and office workers must be given the option of inclusion with other employees or constituting a unit of their own. Craft employees also are usually given a choice of bargaining in a separate unit.

Within these limits, the labor board usually decides the question of unit by the test of effectiveness in bargaining. This test has been interpreted to mean:

1. Where bargaining has been effectively carried on in the past, the unit used should not be disturbed. This is sometimes known as the history-of-bargaining rule.

2. When a union and an employer differ as to the proper unit, the union's preference is usually given the greater weight, provided it does not do violence to the way the employer's business is organized.

Employee Elections. An election to choose a bargaining agent will usually be held if a union can show that it has a following of 30 per cent of the employees concerned. An employer may ask for an election if one or more unions claim to represent the majority of employees. Individual employees also, with support of 30 per cent of their unit, may secure elections. If there is no legal obstacle, the NLRB sets up a polling booth and the election is on.

Where only one *bona fide* union is seeking to be certified as agent for employees, the ballots present a choice for the union or against it. If two or more unions compete, the employee is permitted to vote for either or for no union. If no one choice receives more than 50 per cent of the votes, the choice obtaining the lowest number is eliminated and a run-off election is held.

If a union wins an election which the board directs, it is "certified" as bargaining agent. If no union is selected, collective bargaining need not take place.

A union once certified remains the bargaining agent until displaced by another in a subsequent election or until it is "decertified." Decertification by the board takes place only after a decertification election, which may be asked for by 30 per cent of the employees or by another union. If the challenge fails, the union is recertified.

NLRB. This federal agency, the National Labor Relations Board, is responsible for the application of the Taft-Hartley act and related labor legislation. Its main responsibilities are: (1) the determination of employee representation (described earlier), and

(2) handling unfair labor practice charges—which may be initiated by an employee, a union, or an employer. The board is composed of 5 members appointed by the President of the U.S., with Senate approval, for 5-year terms.

The regional directors of the NLRB investigate charges brought for unfair labor practices. If the charges appear valid, the directors seek informal settlement or issue a "complaint" and hearing notice. Trial attorneys of the NLRB's general council prosecute the charge before a trial examiner appointed by the board. Following such a hearing, the trial examiner prepares an "intermediate report," with a recommended order, which normally becomes final after 20 days, unless appealed to the board within that time. If the order is contested, the NLRB itself reviews the charge and issues a "Decision and Order." Compliance with the order may be voluntary or it may be forced by a circuit court of appeals or a district court. The court's decree is final, subject to petition to the U.S. supreme court.

Injunctions to Stop Unfair Labor Practices. As stated above, the labor board gets its orders enforced by securing a decree from a United States circuit court of appeals. Disobedience to such orders may be penalized by fine or imprisonment. But the board has recourse also to United States district courts to secure speedier action.

The general counsel of board is authorized to seek injunctions to stop any unfair labor practice after he has issued a "complaint," that is, after he has begun formal action in prosecuting a violation.

In respect of one group of unfair practices, however, the board is directed to seek an injunction as soon as it is determined that a complaint should be issued. This group comprises the practices listed under **Practices Forbidden Unions,** paragraph (d). They may be roughly identified as secondary boycotts, organizational picketing, striking to displace a lawful bargaining agent, and striking over a work-jurisdiction dispute.

National-Emergency Disputes. The Taft-Hartley act lays down special procedures for postponing or halting national-emergency strikes, that is, strikes affecting all or a large part of an industry and imperiling the national health or safety. If the president so identifies a dispute, he may appoint a board of inquiry to report on the issues. The government may then go into court for an injunction to stop or postpone the strike until these three steps are taken: (1) The parties negotiate with governmental assistance through mediation; (2) if no agreement is reached in 60 days, the board of inquiry reports the position of the parties, which is made public by the president; and (3) the national labor relations board in the next 15 days polls employees on acceptance of the employer's last offer. If the offer is rejected, the injunction is dissolved, and the parties are left to the arbitrament of economic weapons, unless Congress intervenes. Settlement of the dispute, of course, at any time in this period would also lead to dissolution of the injunction.

LABOR-MANAGEMENT REPORTING AND DISCLOSURE ACT OF 1959

Presumably this law, popularly referred to as the Landrum-Griffin act, was to correct abuses in union and management behavior publicized by the McClellan Committee hearings. However, it went further than simply correcting abuses—it made a number of changes in prior labor legislation and significantly modified Federal labor policy.

The Act sought to protect the rights of union members and insure democratic union administration. Local unions must elect officers at least every three years, and nationals at least every five, by secret ballot. Locals may not raise dues without majority approval by secret ballot and certain restrictions are put on dues increases by organizations other than locals. Members are insured freedom of speech in union meetings, the right to nominate candidates, to vote in union elections, and to examine union books records, and accounts.

Unions must adopt constitutions and by-laws and file with the Secretary of Labor copies of these and a variety of reports on finances and administrative practices. Union officers are required to file reports which would show financial connections that could influence their dealings with management; employers must make reports showing dealings with union officials. Labor relations consultants must also report compensation, disbursements, and the nature of their activities.

Some modifications in the Taft-Hartley law are technical. Employment, by unions, of Communists is prohibited for five years after membership. Revisions insure that, if the National Labor Relations Board does not take jurisdiction in an issue, a State agency may do so, thus eliminating a "No Man's Land" that evolved under Taft-Hartley. Secondary boycotts, attempts by a union to persuade persons not involved directly not to patronize the boycotted concern, were restricted further, but in construction and garment manufacture the provisions were softened. The act declared "hot cargo agreements" between employers and unions an unfair labor practice. In such agreements, the employer agrees not to handle, use, sell, transport, or otherwise deal in any of the products of another employer.

In general, violations of the Act are punishable by fines and imprisonment. Administration of the Act throws a major responsibility on the Secretary of Labor. The Secretary is empowered to conduct investigations when it is believed that violations (other than those arising from the "Bill of Rights of Members") have occurred or are threatened. The numerous reports and other data required under the Act go to the office of the Secretary; he must supervise the internal affairs of unions much more closely than ever before. The results of the law depend primarily on the actions of the staff of the Secretary.

PUBLIC EMPLOYEE UNIONISM

The Lloyd-LaFollette act, of 1912, allowed postal employees to join unions. In 1962, Executive Order 10988 specifically recognized the right of employees in the administrative branch to organize and to present their views on employment terms to agency management.

Organizational rights and certain bargaining privileges were further spelled out in Executive Order 11491, in 1969. A Federal Labor Relations Council and a Federal Service Impasse Panel were established to implement the labor-management program.

The various states have also adopted legislation regulating unionism within such public agencies and institutions as elementary and secondary schools, hospitals, correctional institutions, police and fire departments, mental institutions, public health services, and others. In general, the laws are aimed at controlling strikes that would hamper the effective provisions of such institutions and services.

COLLECTIVE BARGAINING CONTRACTS

The purpose of collective bargaining is to arrive at a contract between employer and union which will govern relations between the parties for a definite period of time—usually a year. Among the subjects which collective bargaining contracts typically cover are these:

1. Union recognition, with a description of the unit of employees represented by the union.
2. Wage rates, possibly with provision for renegotiation after a certain time.
3. Hours of work, with provision for premium rates of pay for hours in excess of the standard day or week.
4. Holidays, with the rate of pay when work is performed on holidays.
5. Vacations, showing eligibility and length, with the amount of vacation pay to be given.

6. Seniority and other ground for promotions and for the selection of those to be laid off and rehired in business fluctuations.

7. Employee benefits, such as sick leave or pension plans.

8. Guarantees of various kinds, such as (1) an employer's undertaking not to discriminate among employees on specified grounds or (2) a union's promise not to strike.

9. Grievances, with procedures for settlement. The procedures usually culminate in arbitration of unsettled grievances arising out of disputed points in the contract or even of all disputes.

10. Union security, which might include the union shop or checkoff.

11. Management prerogatives, outlining management's authority relative to such functions as plant layout and location, product design, production processes, work scheduling, new product development, pricing policies, and other areas of decision.

12. Termination, often with a provision for automatic renewal if neither party gives notice before a certain date that it desires a change in terms.

Limitations on Contracts. The Taft-Hartley act, as noted above, forbids closed-shop clauses. Other contract terms limited by the law are those providing for the checkoff and employee welfare funds.

Checkoff.—This is an arrangement whereby the employer holds back from the employees' pay envelopes the amount of union dues and pays the proceeds over to the union's treasurer. The law permits the checkoff only if the employee authorizes the employer in writing to make such deductions from his pay. The authorization may not be made irrevocable for longer than one year.

Welfare Funds.—The law permits the setting up of trust funds under contracts, but, if the employer contributes to such a fund, the money must be used only for genuine welfare purposes of employees and their families. Management must be given an equal voice in control of the fund, disputes to be resolved by having a third, neutral member on the governing committee.

AVOIDANCE OF DISPUTES

In advance of the acceptance of collective bargaining, a large number of employers put into practice arrangements designed to give employees a sense of unity with the enterprise, thus mitigating or obscuring any division of interest which might lead to disputes. Under collective bargaining, the approach toward elimination of controversy takes typically the form of methods for disposing of grievances. In some instances, a more positive step has been taken through mutual arrangements to increase efficiency or expand markets on the understanding that wages are to be increased, or not decreased, if the efforts are successful.

Methods adopted on employer initiative are usually considered as part of personnel management. Undertaken as a long-range means of increasing efficiency, this form of management aims to keep employees satisfied, loyal to the company, and disposed to give their best services. Methods include wage incentive systems, and granting of special benefits, such as insurance and profit sharing. Labor leaders frequently oppose their use on the ground that they detract from loyalty to the labor movement on which employees in general, it is stated, must depend for safeguarding of their interests.

Settlement of Grievances. Nearly all collective bargaining contracts prescribe steps to be taken for settlement of disputes arising under their terms and provide that no strike or lockout is to take place during the life of the contract when such steps are available. Some contracts go still further and prohibit all work stoppages. Under most contracts the final step in settlement of disputes is arbitration, both sides binding themselves in the contract to abide by whatever award is made.

The following generalized description illustrates the manner in which a dispute arising under a contract may be settled.

Workman Smith complains that, having been told to report for work, he did so, found no work available, and yet was not paid for four hours as required under terms of the contract applying to this situation. The foreman giving no satisfaction, Smith carries the complaint to the shop steward. The shop steward is a union member elected by the "local" for the purpose of taking up grievances of employees with supervisors. The status of shop steward is recognized by the company under the contract.

The steward is told by the foreman that he had not notified Smith to report. The dispute thus hinges on a question of fact, which must be decided on the basis of evidence, if any.

At the next meeting of the union's grievance committee, the status of which also is recognized under the contract, the steward reports the complaint, the statements of Smith and the foreman, and the evidence which each is able to adduce. If the committee, possibly after discussion with both parties, thinks Smith was mistaken, the complaint is dismissed. If it disbelieves the foreman, the chairman of the grievance committee takes up the matter with the supervisor or other superior official. Failing settlement here, an officer of the national union may be called in to speak with the highest executive officer of the company. This completes the grievance procedure where there is no absolute prohibition of strikes or arbitration clause.

Arbitration. This term applies to the settlement of a dispute by the decision of an umpire or impartial committee, both sides agreeing in advance, or being required by law, to accept the award. If acceptance is required by law, the arbitration is said to be compulsory; if by agreement, the arbitration is called voluntary.

There are two different kinds of situations to which arbitration of labor disputes is applied. One is a dispute over rights arising under a contract, such as the dispute outlined above. Arbitration in such a situation is sometimes known as arbitration of rights. This is the most usual type of arbitration.

The other type of dispute—interest—arises during the negotiation of contract terms. Here the services of the Federal Mediation and Conciliation Service may be utilized in the search for a compromise solution.

Railway Labor Disputes. The Railway Labor act of 1926 set up a special procedure for avoiding strikes which was the precedent for the Taft-Hartley act's provision respecting national-emergency disputes described above. If a strike is threatened, the president may appoint an "emergency board" to investigate the dispute and make recommendations within 30 days. For that period and an additional 30 days the parties are forbidden to make any change in conditions, but no penalties are prescribed for violating the prohibition.

LABOR UNIONS—A SUMMARY

As indicated in the foregoing account, labor unions have evolved into major types through a long period of strife, adjustment, and progress. As their membership has increased in numbers and in variety of occupation, the interests which they represent have ceased to be limited to labor and management and have involved a third party, the general public, whose disapproval or sense of unfairness could place either of the bargaining groups at a serious disadvantage. Although in most cases the leaders have been responsive to the challenge and have moved to correct injustices by or within their own organizations, there have been instances in which pressure from the public has been exerted to insure reasonableness and equity in the conduct of one group or the other. Practices on either side that the public considered arbitrary, monopolistic, or unduly selfish have sometimes led to stringent regulation by Federal authorities or to proposals for local remedies such as the "right to work" laws that have recently been enacted in several states. Both the efforts of unions to achieve economic betterment and those of management to obtain productivity with economy have become increasingly subject to public scrutiny.

Types of Unions. Organizationally, unions may be divided into craft unions and industrial unions.

A *craft union* embraces workers in a single craft, irrespective of industry, plant, or employer. Thus all carpenters are eligible in one union whether hired by a building firm, a mining company, or a ship builder. Craft unions frequently provide insurance and unemployment benefits for members.

An *industrial union* embraces workers in a single plant or industry regardless of the type of work done by members. In mass-production industries, this type of union has advantages over craft unions, since modern factory production breaks down the older classifications of skill and craft and opens the way for enrollment of all workers.

The existence of these two types of labor organization has given rise to numerous disputes since a given craft employee may be claimed by both types.

Jurisdictional Disputes. These are controversies between two unions as to which one is entitled to enroll a certain type of worker. The term is sometimes applied to conflicts between craft and industrial unions, but it more typically describes a conflict between craft unions. Some long-standing jurisdictional disputes include one over drivers of beer trucks as to whether they belong to the brewery workers (industrial union) or to the truck drivers (craft or class union). Another involves two crafts—carpenters and machinists—and concerns work on a considerable number of jobs which had not been envisioned when the unions were chartered, such as installation of metal-frame windows.

Strikes over work-jurisdiction disputes are forbidden as unfair practices by the Taft-Hartley act, which authorizes the National Labor Relations Board to settle the question at issue unless the parties work out some other acceptable method of settlement.

National Labor Unions. The earlier unions in the United States adopted the craft form of organization. The Knights of Labor championed the industrial type, but the ascendency of the American Federation of Labor, representing the craft type predominantly, gave this type the advantage until the formation of a rival group in 1935, which later became the Congress of Industrial Organization. The latter body and the Federation embrace the great majority of organized workers.

The American Federation of Labor (A. F. of L.). This organization was an association of trade unions in the United States and its dependencies. Some unions, however, known as international unions, had local units in Canada also.

The basic unit in the Federation was the local union. Most local unions belonged to national or international unions, which were associated in the A. F. of L. as more or less autonomous bodies. They were chartered by the A. F. of L., and the charters could be revoked for non-payment of dues or assessments.

Other local unions were directly affiliated with the A. F. of L. and were known as federal unions. They belonged to crafts or industries for which no national union had been chartered.

Congress of Industrial Organizations (C.I.O.). Formally organized on November 16, 1938, this rival labor group stems from the Committee for Industrial Organization, a committee of the A. F. of L. formed for the purpose of promoting the industrial type of union. Its members were A. F. of L. unions of the industrial type. In 1936, these unions were suspended and later expelled. Meanwhile, many new unions were chartered by the C. I. O. before it had adopted a constitution.

The formation of the C. I. O. was in protest against the failure of the A. F. of L to organize mass production industries, this failure being attributed to a desire to protect the jurisdictions of craft unions over skilled workers within these industries. The first fruits of the C. I. O.'s efforts were the organization of most of the steel and automobile industries.

In many other industries the C. I. O. and A. F. of L. directly competed for members, the A. F. of L. frequently opening membership to all employees irrespective of craft and thus competing on an industrial union basis.

AFL—CIO Merger. On December 5, 1955, these two great unions were merged in a single federation, The American Federation of Labor and Congress of Industrial Organizations.

Following the merger at the national level, began the slow process of merging state federations of labor (of the former A. F. of L.) and state industrial union councils (of the former CIO) and city organizations of like nature. Most, but not all, local unions are affiliated with the appropriate state and city "central labor body." The mergers of state and city bodies progressed slowly.

There remained also the problem of many international unions affiliated with the AFL-CIO with seriously overlapping jurisdiction. For example both AFL and CIO had affiliates that assumed jurisdiction over workers in aircraft manufacturing. The same situation prevailed in many other industries. Also certain craft unions of the old AFL felt they should have jurisdiction over some workers organized by industrial unions of the former CIO. Thus jurisdictional problems abound within the merged labor body.

Railway Brotherhoods. Traditionally workers on the railways were in unions unaffiliated with either the AFL or CIO. The major unions of this group are the Brotherhood of Locomotive Engineers, Brotherhood of Locomotive Firemen and Enginemen, Brotherhood of Railroad Trainmen, Order of Railway Conductors and Brakemen, and the Yardmasters of North America. The Switchmen's Union of North America is affiliated with the A. F. of L.

These are sometimes referred to as operating brotherhoods to distinguish them from unions of other railroad employees who do not actually operate trains. After the merger of AFL and CIO the Brotherhood of Locomotive Firemen and Enginemen and the Brotherhood of Railroad Trainmen affiliated with the merged federation. In addition, most of the unions of non-operating railroad employees are affiliated with the A. F. of L. Nevertheless for purposes of negotiations these unions and the operating brotherhoods frequently act through a joint body known as the Railway Labor Executives' Association.

In addition to the above there are a number of independent unions, most of them being plant or local organizations. A considerable proportion of them are successors of company-supported unions, reorganized after withdrawal of employer support.

In addition some major unions of national importance are non-affiliates of AFL-CIO. These include the United Mine Workers and the Teamsters (Chauffeurs) Union, the latter expelled from the AFL-CIO in 1957 because of its failure to remove corrupt officials from positions in the union. In 1968, the powerful United Automobile workers (UAW) joined the ranks of the non-affiliates by splitting away from the AFL-CIO.

EMPLOYER ASSOCIATIONS

When unions become strong, employers frequently form their own organizations to bargain on behalf of their members with the unions and to take concerted action if necessary in resisting union demands or pressing their own. Such associations may be formed on an industry basis, as among coal mine owners, or on a regional basis, taking in employers in a given area, as is done in San Francisco.

When collective bargaining has reached this stage, individual employers no longer negotiate with unions but accept the terms reached in conversations between the association and the union. Disputes become fewer. The magnitude of a possible strike or lockout tends to impress a sense of caution on both sides. Well defined procedures are usually established for handling disagreements under the contracts negotiated. Not infrequently a permanent arbitrator is appointed whose duty is to settle such disagreements, building up a body of precedents into an accepted code of labor practices. Unions and associations in some instances work out programs of joint action to aid the industry.

WAGE AND HOUR REGULATION

While, in general, employment conditions are a matter of free arrangement between employers and employees, there are several segments of economic life in the United States in which such freedom of contract is rigidly limited by law.

Industrial employment of children is limited by all states and is prohibited for interstate enterprises by the Federal government.

Hours which women may be permitted to work are restricted in a majority of the states.

A lower limit is placed on the wages for which women may be permitted to sell their labor in approximately half the states.

Both hours and wages of industrial workers in interstate commerce, men and women, are regulated by the Federal government under the Fair Labor Standards Act of 1938.

Child Labor. The first child labor law in the United States was adopted by Massachusetts in 1836. It required that children under 15 years of age employed in manufacturing establishments should be required to attend school at least three months in the year.

In 1842, the hours of children under 12 were limited to ten a day in Massachusetts; in Connecticut this provision was applied to children under 14. Rhode Island in 1853 restricted hours of labor for children under 12 to eleven a day.

In the decade of 1850-60, a number of states prohibited altogether the employment of children under certain ages in manufacturing industries. Other states limited their employment with varying requirements as to age and hours.

In 1907 the Federal government took cognizance of the problem in a comprehensive investigation into the condition of women and child wage earners. The findings of this report, added to years of effort to secure a Federal child-labor law, culminated in the passage of the Keating-Owen bill by Congress in September 1916. This act was declared unconstitutional in a 5-to-4 decision by the supreme court on June 3, 1918 (247 U. S. 251). An attempt was next made to achieve the same purpose by levying a tax of 10 per cent on the annual net profits of any establishment employing child labor in violation of the standards it set. But on May 15, 1922, this act was declared unconstitutional by an 8-to-1 decision of the supreme court (259 U. S. 20).

In 1924, Congress approved a resolution for submitting to the states a proposed amendment to the Federal constitution giving Congress the power to "limit, regulate, and prohibit the labor of persons under 18 years of age." By 1938, only 28 out of the requisite 36 states had ratified the proposed amendment. In that year the United States supreme court upheld a wage regulation law of the State of Washington in terms which led to the belief that the earlier child labor decisions would be reversed. The same year Congress passed the Fair Labor Standards act, which forbids interstate shipment of goods made at a plant where, within the previous 60 days, minors below 16 years of age (18 in hazardous occupations) were employed.

Regulation of Hours by States. The earliest law in America regulating hours of work for women was passed by New Hampshire in 1847. This measure became a dead letter through the practice of employers in requiring employees to contract away their rights under the act as a condition of employment. The next such law was passed by Massachusetts in 1874. It limited hours worked by women in manufacturing to 10 daily and 60 weekly.

All such state laws until recent years applied to women and children only. Then men in certain occupational groups began to be given similar protection. Pennsylvania in 1937 passed a law applying to both men and women in all occupations. It was declared unconstitutional on technical grounds.

Regulation of Wages by States. The pioneer in legislation setting minimum wages was Massachusetts, which passed the first law of this type in 1912. It covered only women and children with provision for gradual application from industry to industry. The first such law to be applied also to men was passed by Oklahoma in 1938. It was held unconstitutional on technical grounds but upheld in other respects. Connecticut in 1939 became the first state to extend the coverage of its minimum-wage law to men. As of 1968, 39 states, Puerto Rico, and the District of Columbia had enacted minimum wage laws, almost all of which covered both men and women.

The prevailing pattern of state wage laws of general application calls for appointment of committees to study the need for wage minima in different occupations. The recommendations of such committees, if accepted by a designated administrative agency, become effective as wage orders. In some cases the wage order is "directory" for a period, during which violation incurs the penalty of publicity only. It later became "mandatory," and violations then are punishable by criminal penalties.

Fair Labor Standards Act. Effective October 24, 1938, this law established in general a 44-hour week, hours worked in excess of the standard calling for pay at the rate of time and one-half. After one year, the standard week was reduced to 42 hours and a year later reached the permanent form of 40 hours. A 1965 amendment also required the time-and-one-half rate for hours over 8 a day, a practice that was already almost universal in most industries.

A "floor" was placed beneath wages, it being unlawful to pay an employee engaged on work for interstate commerce a wage less than 25 cents an hour. This figure was raised to 30 cents after the first year and to 40 cents by the end of the seventh year. Provision was made for increasing the minimum wage in individual industries to the 40-cent level in less than the seven years.

The federal minimum wage rate was raised to the hourly rate of 75 cents in 1949, $1.00 in 1956, $1.25 in 1961, $1.40 in 1967, and $1.60 in 1968.

In 1974 legislation was passed covering new minimum wage rates for nonfarm workers, farm workers, federal, state, and local government workers, domestic service, and retail and service employees of chain-store operations. The minimum wage is to be increased in stages until 1978, when all are to receive $2.30.

Enforcement. For violation of the law, fines may be levied and second offenders may be imprisoned. Injunctions also may be issued against such practices in violation of the law as failure to pay the minimum wages or pay for overtime work, failure to keep records or falsification of records, employment of minors without permits, and shipment in interstate commerce of goods produced in violation of the law. Also, employees who believe they have been underpaid on the basis of the law may sue to recover wages allegedly due. If successful, they are entitled to collect double the amount due as wages and reasonable legal expenses in addition.

Public Contracts. Another way in which the government influences wages and hours is through the power of its purse. By requiring that all enterprises doing business with it should stipulate that, in carrying out the contract, they will observe specified standards, the government is able to extend these standards at least as widely as work done under such contracts. In practice, the influence extends much further, since a firm filling contracts both for the government and other customers frequently finds it impossible to separate the work and maintain one standard for government work and a lower standard for other work.

This form of leverage is applied by the Davis-Bacon act, of 1931. It requires contractors in construction work valued at $2000 or more, and paid for by federal funds, to pay at least the prevailing minimum wage to all construction employees. This type of regulation was extended in 1965, by the O'Hara-McNamara Services act, to government contract on-site services other than construction.

Portal-to-Portal Act. This act, amending the Fair Labor Standards act and Public Contracts act, was passed in 1947 to limit liability of employers for wages of employees. Primarily it was to mitigate the effect of a decision by the United States supreme court in *Anderson v. Mt. Clemens Pottery Co.* The court held that time spent by employees in subsidiary activities outside their principal jobs, such as traveling from entrance to job and back, must be paid for as time worked. The law forbids courts to treat such time as working time unless it has been so treated by contract, custom, or practice.

Wage Stabilization. During World War II, a somewhat flexible ceiling was placed over wages as a means of controlling inflation. Employers were forbidden by the Economic Stabilization Act of 1942 to increase or decrease compensation except by permission of designated government agencies, especially the National War Labor Board. While wage rates were stabilized, employees increased their earnings by overtime, promotion increases, shift differentials, and other benefits, such as paid holidays and health and welfare plans. During the Korean conflict, wages and prices were temporarily frozen in 1951, and a Wage Stabilization Board promulgated regulations outlining conditions under which such increases as those based on merit, seniority, promotion, inequity, and other factors could be granted.

UNEMPLOYMENT

Defenses against Unemployment. In seasonal employments. the laborer has tried to prolong his job by curtailing daily production until the piece-work system has been substituted for the day wage. Similarly, low employment periods have been met by union men through restriction of days of work so as to make available work go around among the existing number of trained workers in the craft. Monopoly of labor supply through restricted apprenticeship and membership is another means used to prevent unemployment.

Labor-saving Machinery. There is an increasing realization among labor leaders that machinery, by increasing possible production per hour, increases possible earnings per hour. On the other hand, not only may the impact of rapid mechanization on a society geared to private profit be disastrous to those whose skill is rendered useless, but it is believed by many to be a cause in recurrent depressions.

Technological Unemployment. This is a term used to describe unemployment which results from the introduction of labor-saving machinery. In some favorably situated industries, those displaced through machinery may be equalled in number by those absorbed again into employment by the industries as mechanization brings enlarged demand.

Featherbedding. This term is used to mean employment and payment of a worker, pursuant to a union contract, for work not intended to be performed. Typically, it means payment of a worker whose task has disappeared because of technological changes, such as firemen no longer needed when Diesel locomotives replaced steam locomotives. It is an extreme form of union efforts to limit output of work so as to limit unemployment.

Seasonal Unemployment. To a certain extent, unemployment of this type is inevitable, as for instance in farming, where the chief demand for labor is at seeding or harvest time. In other cases, buying habits of the public are responsible.

Cyclical Unemployment. The use of this term is based on the expression "business cycle," referring to the cycle, or recurrent sequence, of booms and depressions. Loss of work opportunities is the most serious feature of depressions. Not only does it fall with cruel force on those who are denied the opportunity of earning a living, but, by drastically cutting the productivity of all industry, it decreases the wealth available for distribution.

Measurement of Unemployment. The United States Labor Department publishes monthly figures on the percentage of the labor force actively seeking jobs. It is based on the survey of a sample of about 35,000 households. It is possible, however, that total personal income may rise even when reported unemployment is increasing. Reasons include the facts that unemployment compensation is paid and that the figures take no account of many persons having second or part-time jobs.

Employment Act of 1946. Consideration of the losses occasioned by cyclical unemployment was behind the declaration of congressional policy contained in the Employment act of 1946. The declaration states that it is the responsibility of the Federal government to use all practicable means, consistent with other aspects of national policy, to coordinate its efforts with those of industry, agriculture. labor, and state governments to promote maximum employment, production, and purchasing power.

In the early 1960's, Congress passed a sequence of acts—the Area Redevelopment act in 1961, the Manpower Development and Training act in 1962, and the Economic Opportunity act in 1964—aimed at the expansion of employment opportunities, providing for the training of workers and attacking the roots of poverty. In 1968, the "Job Opportunities in the Business Sector" (JOBS) program was launched in a widespread attempt to combat hard-core unemployment.

The first national fair employment or equal employment opportunity legislation was incorporated as Title VII of the 1964 Civil Rights act. In general, Title VII makes it unlawful for an employer to refuse to hire or to discharge or otherwise to discriminate against an individual on the basis of race, color, religion, sex, or national origin.

Unemployment Compensation. The most common measure designed to aid in meeting the problem of involuntary idleness is unemployment compensation. Each state, prompted by the offset provision of the Social Security act of 1935, has enacted unemployment compensation legislation. Extensive variation exists among these laws with respect to their coverage, eligibility requirements, and benefit amounts. Generally, these laws exempt farm workers, casual workers, and frequently workers in very small establishments. Benefit funds are raised by employers' payment of taxes on wages earned during periods of employment. Benefits allowed tend to be roughly half of lost wages, and generally may not be paid for more than 26 weeks in a year, but some states responded to encouragement by the federal government to extend the benefits to 39 weeks.

In response to severe recessions and resultant lengthy periods of unemployment, Congress in 1958 and again in 1961 enacted temporary legislation urging states to lengthen the duration of benefit payments. The first such legislation provided federal loan assistance, while benefits provided by the second legislation were financed by a temporary increase in payroll taxes.

Some of the more powerful industrial unions, notably those in automobile, rubber, and steel manufacturing, have negotiated agreements with employers to pay supplemental unemployment benefits in addition to the unemployment compensation payment. These supplemental benefits are financed by the employer based on employee hours worked. The benefits are retained in a trust fund, added to state benefits to constitute from about 80% to 95% of take-home pay, and are usually payable up to 52 weeks.

MARKETING

Marketing is a specialized type of economic activity that has been developed during the 20th century, largely in the United States. The broad activity of which "marketing" is the specialized name, however, is common to all people and all times. This basic activity of distributing products that people consume arises from the separation of producing and consuming as specialized economic activities.

Thus, the term "marketing" has several meanings: it covers a highly specialized consumer-related service, a type of business undertaking, a far-reaching economic process, or a form of social activity.

A Social Institution. When a pattern of activity and personal relationships spreads throughout and characterizes a society, it is regarded as an institution. As marketing forms a meaningful element in present-day society, it may be said to be institutionalized. However, while marketing has been an important influence on society, it is society which has created and approved the manner in which distribution is performed. Marketing is an expression of society's values and goals, as well as forming the best judgment of how to attain those goals and to relate the activity with other social patterns. Every society has its own structure, relationships, goals, values, and resources, and marketing is the product of all of them. Therefore, the distributive processes and systems of one society may not be appropriate for another. Nevertheless, every society will work out some form of distribution, and one of the more highly specialized and technical forms of distribution is termed "marketing."

Viewed in this sense, marketing is not merely the means by which *businessmen* meet the needs of society for consumer goods and services, it is also a means by which *society*, acting as a whole, meets its own needs.

An Economic Process. As an economic process, marketing is the manner in which economic resources are organized by society for reaching its consumption goals. Marketing is the manner in which factors of economic production—land, labor, capital, and management skill—are combined in the processes of distribution. Marketing is the process of creating additional values in products by making them available to the market at the time, in the place, and in the manner desired. Marketing is the carrying into effect by suppliers of the conception, creation, and communication of a standard of living for society. It is the means by which a uniform pattern of consumption is provided through mass distribution to a large community. It is the process of effecting through the market mechanism the assignment and use of scarce resources.

Viewed thus, marketing is concerned mainly with economic factors such as values, prices, costs, utility, scarcity, economies, profits, production, and efficiency. It is not thereby concerned with some of the broader social implications.

A Business Undertaking. Business is a managed aspect of the market economy, and marketing is a phase of business management: that which relates to the analysis of markets, the conception of marketable products, their physical distribution, and transfer of title.

As a business undertaking, marketing is a broad technical activity; the general function of assembling, sorting, and dispersing goods; the control of the flow of values through successive stages of ownership; the utilization of the mechanism of the market for private and public economic and social ends. Marketing is typically a seller-initiated management process.

From the conception of "marketing" early in the 20th century, it has always been a *compound* activity and not merely the *single* process of selling, distributing, etc.

A Consumer-Oriented Service. Finally, marketing is management of business enterprise based upon primary motivation to render a customer service. Marketing is characteristically a matter of viewpoint, and nothing less than consumer orientation is marketing in the highest sense.

Adoption of this viewpoint in marketing management is a contemporary development. It has long been held that business is primarily for producing profit, that it performs best when "let alone" (*laissez faire*), and that buyers should look after their own defense (*caveat emptor*). Marketing practice in the United States has shown the fallacy of this philosophy and the profitability of conforming business undertakings to the needs and wishes of the market. This viewpoint has evolved with development of scientific marketing practice.

Thus marketing is the conduct of the distributive function in business, approached from the interest of the market served. This concept of marketing is consistent with the idea of marketing as a social institution, for society approves only institutions which meet its needs. The marketing mechanism which is consumer-oriented fulfils both a business and a social purpose.

HOW SOCIETIES SUPPLY THEIR NEEDS

The role which marketing plays in modern society is outlined more boldly by contrasting the marketing process with its counterparts in other societies. In ancient societies, as in some underdeveloped ones even today, needs were met through exchange carried on *without markets* and *without marketing*. The market economy has evolved only during the past 400 years, since the Industrial Revolution. The practice of modern marketing began about 1900.

In general, older societies have accomplished the distribution of products by three principles of human behavior which are not primarily economic in nature: reciprocity, redistribution, and householding. A fourth principle, which is primarily economic, is that of the market organization; marketing relates only to this.

Reciprocity is that conduct of society whereby one gives from the harvests of his production, not for immediate material benefit in exchange, but for the approbation which society places on good husbandry and fine citizenship. Credit due to good behavior and civic virtue is the well-spring of motivation in such dissemination of one's goods. The recipients, according to the society and the scale of the operation, may be one's sister and her family, or a paired counterpart in another tribe or village. Supply for one's own needs is assured in the measure that he has earned social esteem through his own generosity. Social values are paramount; the economic effect is secondary. This system has been effective where society is organized on a family or kinship basis.

Redistribution is the principle employed in societies of a territorial character, under a common chief, whereby a substantial part of production is delivered to village headmen who keep it in storage. Redistribution of the provision is made according to a plan of differentiated rations to both producing and non-producing parts of the population and to members of other distant communities on ceremonial and festival occasions. Redistribution was practiced in the kingdom of Hammurabi in Babylonia and in the New Kingdom of Egypt as well as in medieval feudal systems, which were also based on this principle.

Householding is that principle of economic organization whereby production is carried on by a closed group, such as a family, a village settlement, or a political unit, for supplying the needs of the group. *Personal* self-sufficiency has never existed, and such *group* self-sufficiency is achieved only in a fairly advanced stage of agriculture; it is not more primitive than systems of reciprocity and redistribution. Production in a householding economy is for use, not for exchange; storage may or may not be performed. In certain circumstances, surpluses may be sold, but inasmuch as gain through sale is not the motive for producing, the essential character of the economy is not disturbed thereby.

In these three forms of the economy, there is no instance of trade or markets, where equivalencies are determined and expressed as a price. Where there is no market, there obviously is no marketing.

However, before markets developed, trade existed and was widely carried on. The development of markets antedated the rise of the market economy. And the existence of the market economy was prerequisite to the modern conception of marketing.

Trade developed in three distinct and separate realms: foreign trade, local trade, and national trade. Foreign or long-distance trade arose originally out of exploration, adventure, hunting, piracy, and war. Later, it was characterized by barter, and ultimately markets for trade developed at seaports, fords, riverheads, caravan junctures, and sites of fairs. Such trade was external to the economy of a society. Its transactions were consummated by rulers and headmen; its functionaries were not middlemen, but hired servants; and its markets were segregated from local distribution by regulations prohibiting retail sale of goods by long-distance traders.

Local markets were within the towns and did not extend into the countryside. In them were dispersed products which could not stand long travel and which supplied the common needs of the community. While foreign trade was conducted *outside* the economy, local trade was made to conform to the prevailing principles of economic and social behavior. Trade was restricted in the community to prevent its encroaching upon the prevailing economic organization of society. The values of society superseded those of the local market place.

National or interior markets were not the outgrowth of either local or long-distance trade. Regulations specifically prevented such spread of trade. Rising territorial states, however, adopting a policy of mercantilism, removed barriers to trade and opened the countryside and provinces to the competitive commerce. The impetus to this move was political, for the national state was forced to draw its resources from a wider territory and to foster more extensive interchange among its regions. Freeing trade from restrictions which confined it to the town or to long-distance dealing, however, did not remove all restrictions from it. On the contrary, the national market was still kept subordinate to social objectives; practices in the new market did not interfere with the prevailing manorial economy.

Between the development of national markets and the later rise of the market economy, prevailing concepts of the relationship between the economy and society were changed. Production was carried on primarily for sale on the market; incomes were derived from sales on the market; personal gain became the principal motivation of exchange; and social values became subordinated to economic value. Such was the conceptual transition from the non-market to the market economy accompanying the Industrial Revolut on.

In their early stages, the market economy and market society were fraught with commercial tyranny and social depredations. Such was the character of trade in the United States, even until the late 19th century. Then social resistance to predatory business practices began to express itself in legislation and in other ways intended to improve trade and market practices. At the same time, scientific methods were introduced into business management. These several circumstances led to the development of the body of thought and practice known as Marketing.

SOCIAL ORIENTATION OF MARKETING IN THE UNITED STATES

The nature of marketing in any country is determined largely by two factors: 1) the character of society which determines the behavior of people in the market as consumers and as businessmen, and 2) the types and quantities of products which must be distributed.

Marketing in the United States is affected by certain basic facts, one of which is that ours is a theistic society, predicated upon the principle of man's divine rights. Precocious and preoccupied with success, however, it presents paradoxes as a market economy. Ours is a new culture. It has not been weighted with historical precedents that have hampered many countries of Western Civilization and the Oriental societies. Not only have we been receptive to new ideas, we have been quick to translate ideas into institutions, products, and practices. Willingness to experiment and to find better ways of doing things has characterized our life. This attitude has accustomed us to continual change, to anticipation that, although present achievements are good, better ones are on the threshold. While this youthful attitude has encouraged progress, it has left some traditional values undeveloped. Short-lived values have been preferred to more permanent ones; appearance has been more important than quality; and mere change has been accepted in place of improvement.

Notwithstanding the youthful character of our society, many of our attitudes are deeply rooted in ancient Judeo-Christian concepts, one of which relates to the importance and the dignity of individual man. From this stems our ideal of equality—that all men are created equal and that men should enjoy equal opportunity. This concept relates to the absence of formal class or caste structure in our society, to the provision of education for the masses, to freedom of initiative in business undertakings, to equality of the sexes, to uniformity of living level among different groups. It is interpreted in our concept of the "average man," in glorification of the "middle income" group, in protection of the "little" fellow.

Our society emphasizes also the importance of mental enlightenment. Respect for the ability to think things through has produced theories of rationalism and pragmatism and placed great hope upon science for meeting human needs. It is related to the fact that in the United States more than 38 million pupils are enrolled in elementary and secondary public and private schools, and more than 3 million in institutions of higher education. It is related also to the vast and numerous programs of adult education and executive development. Logic and reason are replacing ignorance, mysticism, and emotionalism. It has been assumed, therefore, that individuals are rational in the market place as well as in their other behavior. Standards of fairness, justice, and ethics also stem from rationality.

In an environment offering opportunity and equipped with rationalism, man in our society is under social pressure to produce—to achieve, to get ahead. Fortunately, we have been exceedingly inventive in our scientific pursuits, and rich rewards have befallen individuals. Rewards, however, rather than contributions have become the social criterion for bestowing homage and respect. Ability to show affluence and material possessions has become an important end and motivation; when satiety with things is reached the quest for power and prestige continues. The urgency to evidence success has encouraged aggression and risk taking, countenanced brashness and egoism, and deplored weakness and failure.

Toward the end of achieving its objectives, our society has widely adopted the concept of specialization. We are a society of interrelated parts and individuals, but specialization rather than integration is stressed. Occupations in both the professions and trades have taken on assembly-line characteristics. Even education has become compartmented and not dedicated to development of the whole man. Society exploits specialized talents and personal idiosyncracies. The effect has been an increased dependence of the individual upon the whole, loss of pride in craftsmanship, and resort to hobbies, adult education, and vicarious enjoyment as compensation for the imbalances of over-specialization.

As the basic needs of our people have become satisfied, we have indulged in leisure, diversion, mobility, and pleasure. Approximately 20 per cent of the American families change their dwelling place every year. We travel widely. We seek comfort, ease, and entertainment, on the assumption that *now* is the time for *enjoyment*. Abstinence, sacrifice, and self-discipline are unpopular. Pleasure is pursued vigorously, usually with gadgets and extra equipment. While there has been an increase in reading and educational undertakings, we often reach for fragments of knowledge which are not integrated. Personal interests have often precluded interest in broader social issues, and satisfaction with our own institutions has prevented us from becoming sufficiently informed about those of other people.

The family, long a significant social unit, has some unique characteristics in our society. It is typically a small group expressing considerable independence, both economically and socially. It consists typically of parents and their unmarried children, although the latter often establish independent households. Since 1900, private households have increased 205 per cent, while population has increased 120 per cent. Although about one-third of our families have liquid savings and no debt, personal debt in general is commonplace. Consequently, training in personal finance and encouragement in economic independence is begun early in one's life. The family is often a unit of decision, action, and consumption.

THE AMERICAN MARKET

In this social setting lies the American market, which is the object of the marketing task. It consists of approximately 213,000,000 individuals, about two-thirds of whom reside in urban areas. In 1975, the per-capita income was $5,834. The per-capita personal income in 1975 was as follows:

Alabama	$4,557	Montana	$5,434
Alaska	8,815	Nebraska	6,175
Arizona	5,329	Nevada	6,524
Arkansas	4,383	New Hampshire	5,210
California	6,555	New Jersey	6,629
Colorado	5,839	New Mexico	4,482
Connecticut	6,854	New York	6,603
Delaware	6,800	North Carolina	4,801
Dist. of Columbia	7,750	North Dakota	5,855
Florida	5,517	Ohio	5,883
Georgia	4,969	Oklahoma	4,996
Hawaii	6,426	Oregon	5,611
Idaho	4,980	Pennsylvania	5,874
Illinois	6,750	Rhode Island	5,917
Indiana	5,587	South Carolina	4,521
Iowa	5,899	South Dakota	4,980
Kansas	5,968	Tennessee	4,766
Kentucky	4,668	Texas	5,387
Louisiana	4,729	Utah	4,819
Maine	4,785	Vermont	4,926
Maryland	6,437	Virginia	5,671
Massachusetts	6,159	Washington	6,226
Michigan	6,240	West Virginia	4,815
Minnesota	5,754	Wisconsin	5,627
Mississippi	4,041	Wyoming	5,941
Missouri	5,387		

Source: Bureau of Economic Analysis, 1976.

Although personal consumption is regarded as household consumption, not all of it occurs in the home. In addition, people consume in restaurants, hotels, private clubs, schools, trains and airplanes, churches, student organizations, boarding houses, and in welfare, charity, and emergency institutions. The durable and nondurable goods and services consumed through *personal* expenditures are about 62 per cent of the Gross National Product.

Business institutions constitute another large market, buying products which they either convert into other products or which they consume in their business activities. Such industrial consumers are the market for 45 per cent of all manufactured goods, 80 per cent of all farm products, about 50 per cent of all imports, the bulk of products mined and quarried, and practically all products of wells, fisheries, and hunting and forest industries.

Personal and business domestic investment accounts for another 15 per cent of the Gross National Product. This includes new construction—residential, non-farm, and other; producers' durable equipment; and changes in business inventories.

Governmental agencies—federal, state, and local—are the market for about 19 per cent of the Gross National Product. They consume vast quantities of commodities in performance of administrative work, in military activity, in carrying out public projects, in fulfilling price support programs, and in granting foreign aid assistance.

Finally, the market for some 4.5 per cent of the Gross National Product is abroad, where American products are marketed to personal consumers, business establishments, and government organizations.

PRODUCTS TO BE MARKETED

Another factor affecting the marketing task in the United States is the variety and quantity of products which are produced. In 1975, the Gross National Product amounted to approximately $1,500 billions. The magnitude of the marketing task, however, is a multiple of the value either of goods produced or consumed, for in the channels of distribution one product may be resold several times. For example, agricultural products may be sold at the farm, through a broker, to wholesalers, then to jobbers, then to retailers, and ultimately to consumers.

THE MARKETING TASK

Whatever the form of society and the nature of its products and disposition of its consumers, the responsibility for distributing its products constitutes a collective undertaking. In our society, this responsibility for effecting distribution and exchange is known as *the marketing task*. When transaction occurs and goods are acquired, the marketing task is fulfilled.

The performance of the marketing task in our society is a vast and complex undertaking. It employs uncounted millions of people in the marketing activity of manufacturers and other producers, in advertising agencies, research organizations, credit information bureaus, market news agencies, and transportation companies, as well as in almost 2,100,000 marketing establishments. The number employed in retail and wholesale establishments alone comprise more than 20 per cent of our gainfully employed citizens.

The task to which these people are dedicated is the creation of those services required to make desired products available to consumers at the place, at the time, and in the manner preferred. The task of marketing is twofold: first, to distribute physical products; second, to provide with those products such service or services as the market may wish. Such services may include personal salesmanship, credit, delivery, adjustments, guarantees, assortment, continuous availability, convenience, pleasant surroundings, and the like. The *primary* task of marketing is the distribution of *commodities*. The performance of related services is secondary and incidental but in our society highly important.

THE MARKETING FUNCTIONS

Circumstances of the market define the need for marketing, and this need prescribes the types of marketing service supplied. Thus because they are *functions* or variants of the marketing task to be performed, these services or processes are known as "marketing functions." The following functions are implicit in a concept of marketing:

> Market Research
> Conception and Identification of Products
> Selling
> Buying
> Transporting
> Storing
> Market and Marketing Finance
> Merchandising
> Market Risk Bearing

Not all of these functions must be performed in every instance of marketing. In the simplest market situations, a minimum of marketing activity occurs. It must be remembered that, insofar as the marketing of products is concerned, it is the *product* that is wanted. The services which constitute marketing are desired and bought only in order that the *product* may be obtained at the time, in the place, and in the manner desired. The *transaction* conveying the product is the object of primary interest. Marketing services are performed only in order that the transaction may occur. Marketing, therefore, is the means by which a transaction is brought about; it is not primarily the transaction itself.

Market Conditions. A market may be defined as demand and supply existing in a relationship which results in transaction and in transfer of goods. Markets, however, have a variety of demand-supply relationships, and the state of the market determines the functions to be performed. When buyers and sellers have mutual knowledge of each other's need, transaction or fulfillment of the market may depend upon only negotiation and establishment of a price. It is impossible that such markets exist to any large extent in a vast economy, for several reasons. First, mutuality of knowledge does not exist; consequently, both buyers and sellers are obliged to share an information function. Sellers seek to know what needs exist, what capacities are unsatisfied, where markets are located. Buyers at the same time study their needs and the offerings of which they know, and they seek additional information about the market. Sellers interpret their market information into products, whose qualities they make known through means of identification and communication.

When knowledge of the market is shared by traders, transaction may still not occur because of other maladjustments of demand and supply. Space and time factors may prevent the fulfillment of a transaction, until additional services have been performed. When buyers and sellers are separated by space, transaction is dependent upon transportation. When time interferes, transaction depends upon products being stored if supply antecedes demand, or upon the transaction being financed if demand antecedes effectual demand. Acts counteracting time and space facilitate transaction and bring markets to fulfillment.

In addition to the relationship existing be ween any pair of demanders and suppliers who may make an individual transaction, there are other significant factors affecting the need for marketing in the *aggregate market*. A single transaction occurs at but one place and at a particular time. Satisfaction of the demand which constitutes the aggregate market requires making products available *within the bounds of the market* in the assortment, at the place, and at the time preferred by a *variety* of buyers. Transaction thus depends upon merchandising, or the pro-

viding of products for the *collective* market. To the physical product is thus added *availability*.

The service of availability is provided by the function of merchandising and also by the bearing of market risk. Unless market risks are borne, the responsibility for making goods available to the market is not undertaken.

Utility Created. In the mass market economy, marketing in some form or combination of functions is practically indispensable, for there is almost always need for one or more of the functions of transportation, storage, finance, or availability. Because value is placed upon these services, marketing, through the functions which produce these services, creates five types of economic utilities:

> *Information Utility*, by market research, product identification, selling, and buying
> *Place Utility*, by transporting
> *Time Utility*, by storing
> *Possession Utility*, by market and marketing finance
> *Availability Utility*, by merchandising and bearing of market risk

Creation of form utility is the province of production, in contrast to marketing. The greater the demand for marketing service, the greater is the justification for incurrence of functional costs, and the greater the value which is added to products through the performance of marketing functions.

The nature of the marketing functions needs to be understood in detail, for upon them depends the system of marketing institutions and policies governing the practice of marketing.

Market Research. Research in connection with marketing includes both market research or investigation of characteristics of the market, and marketing research or inquiry into the means and practices of marketing. Both represent the quest for information to guide the economic processes of production and distribution to maximum satisfaction of society's wants and needs.

The nature of research has varied throughout the years, depending largely upon the nature of marketing problems and the prevailing concept of marketing. Its fields of study include the consumer, internal functions of business management, economics of the market, marketing channels, and trade practices. It employs both quantitative and qualitative data drawn from private and public, internal and external sources. Its methods are those of scientific inquiry developed in the physical and social sciences, including survey, observation, and experimentation. Techniques are borrowed from fields of statistics, accounting, engineering, mathematics, economics, psychology, and sociology. Among the methods of analysis employed are questionnaire survey, ratio analysis, depth interviewing, simulation, business games, correlation analysis, cost and budget analysis, copy testing, opinion research, and others.

Conception and Identification of Products. Information gathered through research is a guide to the invention and production of products for which there is a market. Products produced, however, must be recognizable as possessing qualities desired by buyers. For some products this assurance can be gained only by first-hand inspection. For others with less perceptible qualities, assurance depends upon adequate identification of the products. This is achieved through establishment of standard grades for products, through informative labeling and sales promotion, and through branding.

Standards developed in the interest of the public pertain to various aspects of identification and are usually the product of the collective efforts of agencies and businessmen. Standards convey information concerning size, quality, number of units, composition, strength, purity, etc. Among the agencies co-operating in the development of standards are the Agricultural Marketing Service of the U.S. Department of Agriculture, the Commodity Standards Division of the U.S. Department of Commerce, the Food and Drug Administration, the Federal Trade Commission, and the American Standards Association.

The identity of products is also established by the use of brand labeling. Using private marks of identification, producers distinguish their products both through word descriptions and through association and imagery. Symbols as well as words convey to buyers information which sellers wish them to have about their products.

Selling. Selling is the communication to a prospective buyer of information intended to show the likelihood of a product's meeting a buyer's need. It ranges in type from the mere listing of sales facts to aggressive presentation of sales claims or to efforts designed to create wants rather than merely to satisfy known needs. It includes personal selling, advertising, and other forms of sales promotion such as contests, displays, premiums, sale events, sampling, dealer aids, demonstrations, trading stamp plans, and the like.

The need for selling arises from 1) the separation of buyers and sellers, 2) buyers' unfamiliarity with new products, 3) sellers' opportunities for lowering costs through increased scale of operation, and 4) the stimulus given improvement of products and services through open announcement of offerings.

Although vast sums of money and effort are expended in selling—more for personal selling than for advertising—the beneficial contributions of this function are greater in value than the cost of performing it. Advertising expenditures are estimated to amount to between 3 and 4 per cent of personal consumption expenditures; the advertising expenses of most retail stores amount to between 1 and 2 per cent of their sales.

Buying. Buying is, in part, performance of the information function on the part of the buyer and, in part, the buyer's effort to consummate a transaction. It is a function known as procurement, purchasing, shopping, or simply "buying." It may be carried on for purposes of one's own use or as an intermediary activity on behalf of another.

Personal buying stems from the level of living which one maintains or from that to which he aspires. It is likely to conform to the pattern of consumption of the economic or social level with which one associates himself. The order in which one buys various products is determined by the priority of his need, by the channels in which his living flows, and by the appearance of especially favorable buying opportunities. Buying usually requires, first, choice between two or more potentially satisfying prospects. This may be followed by selection of a particular brand or style of produce, and by selection of the vendor from whom the purchase is to be made. Rational and emotional motivations enter into the buying calculation.

Business buying is somewhat predetermined for a distributor by what he can sell, and for an institutional consumer by the operation he conducts. The rate and timing of purchases is affected by the necessity of maintaining an inventory of supply or stock, by seasonal factors, by costs of acquisition, special buying opportunities, discounts, condition of one's liquid working capital, and the like.

Transporting. Movement of products from one place to another is feasible simply because 1) a market for them exists at a distance, in addition to or in place of a market for them at their origin, and 2) the value of the product in the distant market is sufficiently higher than in the other to warrant the incurrence of the necessary transportation costs. Such markets in different positions may be called "space markets." They are linked by transportation, the performance of which in accommodating distant markets creates place utility.

The extent to which transportation is performed in marketing depends upon several factors. If production costs are identical in different markets, products will tend to be produced in each market

and not to move between them. If there is a differential in production costs, producers in the two markets compete in the intervening space to the extent that production costs plus transportation costs become equal. The differential may be so great as to permit one producer to compete even in the local market of the other. The sum of production plus transportation costs, however, may not exceed any fixed sense of value in a distant market, else it may be found that for products delivered at prices above that value no market exists. Value in the buyers' minds justifies incurrence of costs; transportation may create place utility, but it cannot create a market for that utility.

Market patterns change with changes in the variables of which transportation is a function. Thus changes in production costs, in freight rates, in methods of shipment, in insurance rates, etc. affect the markets for products and for transportation service.

Storing. The need for storage arises from the separation of markets by time. Producers frequently have a choice in disposing of their goods in the present local market, in the present distant market, or in a future market, be it local or elsewhere. Value of the product at a future time, however, must exceed present value by at least the cost of storage. Through storage, therefore, is created time utility or the service which is warranted by anticipated values in a future market.

The performance of the storage function is affected by the cost of storing, by production cost differentials at different times, and by the relative competition between time and space markets.

An important factor in storing is the financing of the investment in products during the storage period. The development of means in recent years whereby this is facilitated has made storing more feasible and has thus prolonged markets. These facilities have included bonding of public warehousemen, field warehousing, and the rise of companies financing particularly goods in storage.

Financing. Many transactions would never materialize if immediate payment of cash were always necessary. The ability to obtain goods before paying for them is often important to both businessmen and consumers. Only by so obtaining goods may businessmen have them to sell or fabricate, and so conduct their business. Likewise is this the means by which consumers may have enjoyment of products sooner than they would if cash were required. Possession, therefore, has a value to both business and household buyers, and the financing of possession creates possession utility.

Financing the market involves assuming three responsibilities: 1) providing capital for receivables, 2) assuming credit risk, and 3) performing investigation, authorization, collecting, etc. inherent in the operation. Thus is produced credit service, a utility for which there is a wide market, a variety of prices, and definite production costs. Both vendors, in connection with sale of goods, and lenders, in connection with loans, provide such credit service. All or part of these responsibilities may be shifted from vendors and lenders to an array of credit specialists which have arisen in the banking and commercial fields.

The basis of a system providing credit service is confidence in the promise to pay extended by the one who offers his credit. One's credit is good in proportion to his ability to redeem his credit through ultimate payment. Thus it is directly related to potential income, although moral considerations and other resources are also important.

Merchandising. Merchandising is that service provided in distribution which makes products available in the market at the time, at the place, and in the manner desired. In contrast to transporting and storing, which carry products into *other markets*, merchandising provides for the availablity of goods with a *given market*. It is a function which is performed in storekeeping, stock keeping, etc. It caters to the desire of consumers that goods be available when they are in the market for them.

Aggregate markets, unlike single transactions, embrace a period of time and a span of space, in which all buyers desiring to make a transaction may do so. For example, the "Christmas market" covers a period of two or three months, during which some people prefer to buy early, others late. Markets for automobiles, clothing, and garden equipment are also periodic; those for grocery staples, birthday cards, and gasoline are continuous. Providing availability satisfies a value and creates a utility in addition to the mere value of the product itself. This is the contribution of the merchandising function. Merchandising differs from mere storing for value increases with storage time, whereas no such increase occurs during the time goods are in inventory for availability. To the contrary, if value does not remain constant, it may even decline toward the end of a market period.

Similarly, markets have spatial dimensions embracing a city, a metropolitan area, or a neighborhood, in which products are transported for the simple reason of making them available *in the market* rather than moving them to *other markets* where they have greater value.

Merchandising provides products not only at the time and place, but also in the manner desired. By this function are assembled goods in assortment making choice possible, goods so related as to make shopping convenient, and goods surrounded with an environment pleasant and appropriate for buying. All of these functions of merchandising provide in some way the service of availability.

Market Risk Bearing. In a broad sense, products are brought to the market only because someone assumes entrepreneurial responsibilities, including the risks which are inherent in the market situation. In a market economy, it is normal and to be expected that transactions will be consummated. It is normal also, however, that failure in the fulfillment of other marketing functions sometimes prevents the occurrence of transactions. Lack of information, faulty communication, improper estimation of the market, failure to provide goods at the place and time and in the manner desired—these occasion risk which must be borne in an economy such as we have. The dynamic nature of the market imposes also risks which result from price changes.

Marketing Processes: Wholesaling and Retailing. Although the concept of marketing may be refracted into the spectrum of marketing functions, the distributive operation itself occurs neither as a composite activity of marketing nor as the separate activities of the marketing functions. It consists rather of the complementary processes of retailing and wholesaling, retailing being selling to ultimate, household, or personal users, and wholesaling being selling to all others—to distributors and to business and institutional buyers. All of the marketing functions are performed on both levels of distribution, but the two levels represent the performance of dissimilar processes.

The wholesaling process, in general, is one of assembling products, of moving them toward their markets in bulk, to points where bulk is broken by making them available in smaller quantities to industrial buyers or to subsequent distributors. It is that stage of distribution wherein time utility is generally created and wherein major responsibility for financing distribution *within the channels* is assumed. It is the stage wherein purchases are large, consisting of great quantities of given products, but sales are large consisting of a great number of smaller quantities of a variety of products. The assembly process of wholesaling may also combine small quantities at the point of origin, as in distribution of agricultural products, before moving them on in bulk.

The retailing process, on the other hand, is essentially one of dispersion. It is a further step in the breaking down of homogeneous or heterogeneous bulk which has moved through wholesaling processes. It provides for satisfaction of the individual want or need at the termination of mass production and mass distribution. It offers availability, both through variety and assortment of products and through presentation in keeping with the time and space dimensions of the market. It furnishes information not only as to what supplies are available, but also as to where they may be obtained. It provides for, although it does not generally assume, responsibility for financing the consumer market.

MARKETING FUNCTIONARIES—THE MARKETING SYSTEM

When functions must be performed, there emerge individuals and institutions to perform them. Marketing functions are performed by a variety of functionaries. While the needs for functionaries differ with the combinations of functions inherent in different market situations, needs differ also depending upon the manner in which the functions are performed in any given situation. A range of choices lies between extremely specialized functionaries, on the one hand, and highly integrated functionaries, on the other.

One classification of functionaries is made on the basis of the extent to which they combine or segregate production and marketing. Some producers perform no marketing functions, even in connection with their own products; they are obviously specialists solely in production. Other producers undertake a full range of functions in connection with their products, some marketing them to the first specialist in the channel of distribution, others marketing them to their final market destination; thus they combine production and marketing. Still others market not only their own products, but also some purchased for resale. If their sales of purchased goods exceed the sales of goods produced, they cease to be classifiable as a producer and are in fact distributors, or specialized marketing functionaries.

Apart from producers (manufacturers, farmers, extractive industries, and others) who perform some marketing functions, the bulk of the marketing work is done by functional specialists. Some perform single marketing functions, such as transportation by carriers, storage by warehouses, financial assistance by banks, sales information by advertising agencies. Others perform not only such functions, but also through selling contribute directly to the transfer of title of goods. Those are known as *marketing establishments*.

Marketing establishments are of two types: middlemen and others. Middlemen are independent, autonomous organizations—*merchant middlemen*, who take title to the goods they handle, and *functional middlemen*, who do not take title to goods in whose distribution they assist. Other than the middlemen, there are marketing establishments which are not independent entrepreneurs, inasmuch as they are owned by producers (manufacturers' branches), by consumers (consumer co-operatives), by independent distributors (chain store warehouses), or by governmental agencies (military post exchanges). To be classifiable as marketing establishments, even those owned by producers must be physically separate from the parent producers, a separate place of business specializing in marketing.

Marketing establishments are also distinguished as *retailing establishments* and *wholesaling establishments*. Retailing establishments are those the bulk of whose sales are made to ultimate consumers. Wholesaling establishments are those whose business is primarily with industrial buyers and distributors.

Determination of the type and identity of marketing functionaries is of practical significance. Whether one is engaged in retailing or wholesaling determines prices at which he buys and sells, wages which he is required by law to pay, taxes levied upon him, the market which he can reach, and the nature of his business operation. Whether he is independently or producer-owned determines the character of his competition, whether he must earn a full measure of operating profit on his distributive activity, the risks he bears, or the price at which he obtains his merchandise.

A Marketing Establishment. Collectively, the various types of marketing establishments comprise what is known as the marketing structure or marketing system. An understanding of their varying roles, their differences, and their competitive advantages requires understanding of the essential character of a marketing establishment.

Basically, it is an entrepreneurial business venture. In the process of meeting a market need, it represents an effort to maximize profit through the utilization of invested and borrowed funds in the usual fixed assets (building and equipment) and current assets (inventory, accounts receivable, and cash). Gross profits tend to be maximized by increasing the volume of sales of the enterprise. Maximization of net profit depends upon the most favorable relation between sales volume and operating costs. It may be achieved by increasing sales without a proportionate increase in costs, or by a decrease in sales with a greater than proportionate decrease in operating costs.

This expansion and contraction of income and costs results from the efforts of management to manipulate several of the fundamental characteristics of the business: the variety and assortment of items handled, the number of store units operated, the number and types of services provided, the types of clientele or markets served, the radius of the market, and the types and intensity of promotional effort employed. An infinite number of combinations of these factors is possible, but certain combinations of them have become common, and enterprises so characterized are familiar to us as our well-known types of retail and wholesale establishments: department stores, chain stores, single-line stores, merchant and functional wholesalers, manufacturers' sales branches, etc.

THE RETAILING STRUCTURE

While there is no such thing as a standard variety or assortment of goods offered in a given establishment, a large part of our marketing effort and structure has been based upon the concept of a "line" of goods. This signifies a group of products which are related through common physical properties, in use, in purchase, or in origin. The traditional "lines" have been the grocery, drug, hardware, and dry goods line. During the 19th century, those products were the principal ones marketed, and they were typically segregated in distribution and made available through what have been called "single-line stores": grocery, drug, hardware, and dry goods stores.

Multiple-Line Stores. The efforts of management to increase volume through expansion and combination of lines, thus providing a broader base for the allocation of overhead, has resulted in the fusions represented by the general store, the department store, the modern drug store, mail order house, and others, wherein products of different lines are combined, as in supermarkets, automotive supply stores, and variety stores. There has been a strong tendency in recent years for many retail stores to offer items from different lines in the name of providing shopping convenience known as "one-stop shopping."

Simultaneously, there has been a contrary trend toward line specialization through reduction of items handled. Thus have arisen such specialized retailing establishments as those handling only neckties, paint, millinery of a particular price, die-

tetic foods, toys, and the like. Through such restriction of the line, it is expected either that costs will be disproportionately cut or that volume will be increased through more effective promotional emphasis.

Multiple-Unit Stores. Historically, retail establishments have been operated as single units, even though several may have fallen under common ownership. Contemporary marketing, however, exploits the merchandising potentialities of multi-unit establishments linked in horizontal integration. Chain organizations and branch establishments are typical. Not only is increased volume made possible by the addition of outlets, but multiple-unit operations also provide for economies through large-scale buying, apportionment of overhead, experimentation, research, and risk. Thus have developed on the basis of multiplicity of horizontally integrated units four types of retail enterprises: 1) the corporate chain store organization, which is typically found among single line and specialty stores, although also among the smaller department stores; 2) voluntary chain organizations representing independent ownership but integrated merchandising; 3) ownership groups, as among large department stores, representing centralized ownership but decentralized merchandising; 4) branches, also typical of department stores, representing the integration not of comparable and equal units, but of dominant and subordinate ones, with centralization of both ownership and merchandising.

In addition to their horizontal linkage, retail stores have also been affiliated in vertical channels by several means: in corporate systems initiated by producers, wholesalers, and retailers alike; in contractual systems, such as wholesale-sponsored voluntary chains, retailer-cooperative organizations, and franchising organizations; and in administered systems wherein vendor-developed comprehensive programs for distribution integrate the entire channel.

Multiple-Service Stores. Throughout a century, the principal service provided by retail establishments has been that of availability. Additions and subtractions of other services have from time to time been made to accommodate the market and to maximize profit. Chain stores originally represented not only a multiplicity of units, but also a reduction of the services of credit and delivery which were customarily provided by retail groceries. The department store, on the other hand, epitomizes the combination of a full range of services with merchandise: credit, delivery, returns, adjustments, guarantees, nursery facilities, club rooms, restrooms, shopper service, etc. Discount houses are typically a withdrawal of services customary in connection with durable goods, including personal salesmanship and even convenient availability, insofar as the discount house is located more or less remotely. Mail order establishments, by the very nature of their operation, curtail the service of availability, while attempting to compensate for non-store inconvenience by substitution of the service of catalogue selling, telephone ordering, and liberal adjustments.

Multiple Customers. Markets are stratified on several bases, and the effort to serve either more or fewer market classifications is a management decision which also has helped to form the retailing structure. Some establishments sell at both wholesale and retail. Some cater to high, medium, and low income classes. Some solicit the patronage of minors as well as adults. Some make direct solicitation of the consumer while concurrently selling also to other distributors. Conversely, managements contrariwise minded follow the opposite policy of serving selective types of customers in their effort to achieve their operating objectives.

Multiple Territories. As with customer types, merchants differ with respect to the distance they will go in seeking customers. Some operate wholly on a local basis, customarily providing over-the-counter sales service. Supermarkets have greatly extended the circumference of the market formerly served by the neighborhood grocer. Department stores draw patronage from large metropolitan markets and, even more extensively, through the use of mail order selling. Some enjoy even a national patronage as a result of advertising placed in such media as the *New York Times* Sunday edition.

Thus it is apparent that, while physically retail establishments may be characterized by size, location, and commodities handled, conceptually from the management standpoint they represent so many integrations and specializations of line, unit, service, market, and territory. The manner of merchandising which these combinations provide determines the market appeal of the establishments and their competitive stature among the trade.

Environmental Influences. The managerial concept of the best way in which to perform the necessary marketing functions is not the sole determinant of the nature of the establishments which are created. Environmental influences also determine the manner in which the various factors may profitably be combined as a market offering. This is the influence which social change holds over the entire marketing process.

One need go back no more than one hundred years to observe some of the principal environmental influences which have helped to shape the retailing establishments of our marketing system.

1. DEPARTMENT STORES. Following the Civil War, four circumstances contributed to the growth of department stores: a) the increase of urban population, b) increased manufacture of textiles, c) increasing disposition of consumers to buy ready-made clothing, and d) a growing higher income class which constituted a market for the more luxurious commodities and services which department stores were offering.

Late 19th century improvements in urban transportation augmented department store growth by making downtown shopping areas more readily accessible to people in all sections of the widening metropolitan areas. These factors continued almost uninterrupted until the 1930's with post-war migration from rural to urban areas and with growing markets for department store type merchandise. However, growth of large metropolitan family-owned department stores was paralleled by growth of chains of smaller department stores locating particularly in the rising number of small towns. At the same time, the financial merger movement of the 1920's stimulated integration of large department stores in ownership groups for both financial and merchandising advantages. Enlargement of cities gave rise in the 1930's to department store branches in secondary shopping areas, and in the 1950's to branches in shopping centers. Complex downtown traffic problems have posed a counteracting influence upon central department store popularity and accessibility, but this has been compensated somewhat by the department store's development of parking facilities.

2. CHAIN STORES. The growth of retail chains, particularly in groceries, was the result of population growth prior to 1920, and of widening realization of advantages to be gained through horizontal and vertical integration and through elimination of some services. During the early 19th century, the number of chain organizations increased rapidly. They too were influenced by the mergers of the 1920's with resulting reduction in the number of chains but increase in the number of stores comprising chains. Depression conditions of the 1930's, coupled with punitive graduated license taxes imposed upon chains and the rising competition of supermarkets in the grocery field, wrought enlargement of the chain stores and reduction of their number. Later, chain groceries adapted themselves to expanding use of the supermarket techniques.

3. MAIL ORDER ESTABLISHMENTS. The custom of American farmers to live on their farms, in contrast to the European practice of settling in villages adjacent to agricultural areas, contributed to the crossroads location of numerous general stores combining the lines of consumer goods common in the 19th century. Their unwillingness or inability to handle the increasing number of products, or to satisfy farmers' desire for urban contacts which would break their isolation, prepared the way for the catalogue-promoted mail order selling. Such business was made feasible by improvements in rail transportation, by provision of rural free delivery and parcel post service, and by achievement of a high rate of literacy through general educational programs. The popularity of mail selling, however, met head-on the counteracting influence of automobiles and improved rural highways in the 1920's, which shifted much buying from home ordering to small town shopping. The adaptive response of mail order establishments to that development was their opening in towns of catalogue order offices, display rooms, and ultimately retail stores, which are in fact chain department stores.

4. CONSUMER CO-OPERATIVES. Co-operative establishments differ from those privately owned mainly in ownership and not in merchandising conception. In a given field, both have responded to the same external influences. However, co-operatives have felt the added stimulus of depression-born emphasis upon low price and savings and of socialistic philosophies antagonistic to capitalistic enterprise. Consequently, those influences, particularly during the 1930's, stimulated growth of co-operatives, but their competitive status and service to consumers are to be judged primarily from a managerial rather than from a legal standpoint.

THE WHOLESALING STRUCTURE

Social circumstances affect first that level of marketing practice which directly serves society, namely, retailing. Changes in retailing and in the retailing system in turn affect wholesaling practice and wholesaling establishments.

Whereas in retailing the character of marketing establishments is determined almost wholly by decisions made locally within those establishments, in wholesaling their character is the effect of the joint and/or separate decisions of producers and wholesale middlemen. Between them occurs such a play of integration and specialization of activities, whereby the functions inherent in a given market situation are divided, that a producer's assumption of wholesaling functions is usually attended by a corresponding reduction in wholesaling functions performed by independent wholesale middlemen. This process whereby functions of wholesaling sometimes performed by wholesale middlemen are shifted backwards or forwards in the distributive channel is termed *circumvention*, indicating a tendency to "go around" but signifying management decisions making a new allocation of the functions involved.

The performance of wholesaling occurs in three stages representing degrees of specialization and integration: 1), producers performing the entire function of wholesaling involved in the distribution of their goods; 2), producer-owned marketing establishments physically separate from the production facilities; 3), independent wholesale undertakings representing complete separation of production and marketing functions.

Channels. In a market as large and diversified as that of the United States, competitive initiative has produced a variety of combinations of marketing establishments involved in the performance of the functions. These combinations are called "channels" for the flows of various elements. Some handle the flow of products, others the flows of title, information, payments, service, and the like.

The circumstances of the market—of the buyer, of the seller, and of the product—prescribe the functions which must be performed. Differences in market situations result in a variety of channels functioning side by side, even in the same line or trade. Dissimilar channels are also found serving in *identical* market situations, as a result of differences in competitive strategy and efficiency.

Wholesaling components of vertical channels include both *wholesale middlemen* and *other wholesale establishments*. They range from those establishments performing a minimum of functions (such as brokers and drop shippers) through those middlemen performing a wide range of functions (such as the selling agent and the regular wholesaler) to producers' own distributive outlets, with or without stocks.

The regular wholesaler represents a full combination of marketing functions; other establishments represent a lesser combination, and therefore a relegation of residual functions to other buyers and sellers in the channel.

In the channels for manufactured products, the following are the principal establishments and their functions:

I. Limited Function Middlemen
a) Not taking title.

1) *Brokers.* One of the most highly specialized independent middlemen is the broker, whose almost sole function is representation of buyers and sellers in negotiations. He does not take title, handle goods, render financial assistance, or determine the sale price. He is engaged either by buyers or sellers on a temporary basis and is paid a commission for his service. He is most useful in the sale of highly standardized goods, particularly of a seasonal nature, and in negotiating between widely scattered buyers and sellers.

2) *Commission Merchants.* Commission merchants also do not take title, but, in addition to the negotiatory functions of the broker, they may handle, or temporarily store commodities, and on occasion render financial assistance to buyers. They serve mainly in distribution of grocery specialities, and in the wholesale marketing of dry goods.

b) Taking title.

1) *Drop Shippers.* Buying, selling, and financing of marketing are the principal functions of drop shippers, who do not handle physically the commodities they sell. They deal primarily in the distribution of bulky products bought in large quantities.

2) *Cash and Carry Wholesalers.* Buying, selling, and storing are the main functions of cash and carry wholesalers, who omit delivery and marketing financing.

3) *Wagon Distributors.* Simultaneous sale and delivery are the chief functions of the wagon distributor, who omits storage and financing in the limited line of specialty items which he carries.

II. Full Function Establishments
a) Not taking title.

1) *Manufacturers' Representatives.* Manufacturers' representatives are, with selling agents, one of the two types of functional middlemen who maintain continuous contractual relations with producers whom they represent. They sell, handle products, and provide market information, but they do not buy, render financial assistance, select the market in which they sell, or determine the selling price. They serve the principal in the manner and place of his determination. This middleman is employed by producers needing economical sales assistance in selling a narrow line of products in sparce, scattered, distant, or new markets.

2) *Selling Agents.* Selling agents are independent, multiple-line establishments substituting for a manufacturer's own sales organization. They may perform all functions except buying. Handling the producer's entire output, they sell, store, finance, gather market information, determine price and territory. Combining the product with non-competing lines of other producers, particularly in the field of textiles but also in other lines, they serve manufacturers who are least able or willing to perform any of the marketing functions themselves.

b) Taking title.

1) *Regular Wholesalers.* Independent merchant wholesalers perform in some channels the dual processes of assembly and disposition. They are most useful in distributing products which, for efficiency and economy, must be gathered from many sources and distributed to many outlets and buyers. They take title, buy, sell, store, break bulk, deliver, and both gather and disseminate market information. When handling manufactured goods intended for the household consumer market, this middleman is called a wholesaler; when handling products for the industrial or institutional market, he is known as an industrial distributor. Regular wholesalers provide economical distribution for a great number of related products.

Producer-Owned Establishments. Producers desiring to perform and control their own marketing activity find certain circumstances favoring the establishment of a distributive branch, in contrast to direct distribution from the place of production. Such branches may be either with or without stocks, being in the latter case sales offices. When branch distribution is undertaken, existing circumstances must warrant it. Branches without stocks are made feasible by the production of a diversified line of products, by concentrated markets, and by technical products requiring expert salesmanship. Branches with stocks are inspired by the market's need for accessible inventories for repair and replacement, for installation and repair service, and for small-scale delivery of products moved major distances in bulk for reasons of economy.

Distribution of Agricultural Products. The markets, horizontal outlets, and vertical channels for agricultural products differ from those of manufactured goods. Markets for agricultural products impose a marketing task in some respects unique. Primary production, in contrast to manufacturing, is generally on small scale, requiring assembly of products into marketable quantities before they can be economically moved long distances to urban markets where they are disseminated in vertical channels to retail outlets. On the other hand, many industrial users of agricultural raw materials, such as canners, meat packers, tanners, cotton mills, etc., are located in the vicinity of farms and purchase directly from the producers of those materials.

For agricultural commodities which must be assembled in the local areas, the establishments which have arisen there to perform this function include independent cash buyers, traveling buyers, cooperative assemblers, representatives of distant merchants and industrial consumers. Depending upon the product, these local agencies in the channel may buy, sell, store, transport, grade, finance, bear market risk, and provide market information. In the central market, where the process of dispersion begins, an important role is played by functional middlemen: brokers, commission merchants, and auction houses. Negotiating and dealing in large quantities, they facilitate the distribution of farm products to wholesalers, jobbers, and large retail chain organizations.

MARKETING MANAGEMENT

While marketing is a social phenomenon and its institutional structure is an example of economic specialization, the management of marketing is a role in business which has become highly professionalized. Within a business organization, the function of marketing is an area of decision making, corresponding in importance to production, finance, and personnel, with which it must be integrated for effective and profitable operation. Responsibility for the marketing function, itself a complex and co-ordinated activity, is being placed in modern organizational structures with a position known as "Vice President in Charge of Marketing," "Director of Marketing," or "Marketing Manager." In top management deliberations, the marketing manager has a leading responsibility, inasmuch as the total undertaking of the individual firm must begin with the market—with understanding of its needs and wants, its character, size, location, etc. Marketing management is responsible for preserving this viewpoint in the various undertakings of the firm.

The Marketing Mix. Within the scope of its own technical responsibility, marketing management is charged with planning, organizing, and controlling a variety of activities which, combined in different proportions, constitute the "marketing mix." It is the administration of the means of accomplishing the marketing objective. Those means include personal selling, advertising, credit selling, product styling, packaging, branding, choice of both horizontal and vertical channels, price structure, guarantees, service policies, etc. Specialization in the performance of marketing gives rise to subordinate organizational specialization in the positions of sales manager and salesmen, director of marketing research, advertising manager, merchandising manager, manager of credit sales, service manager, adjustments manager, etc. It is the duty of the co-ordinative manager of marketing to proportion and combine these various activities of the "mix" in the manner most appropriate to the prevailing circumstances.

The actual management of marketing is regarded as a process of decision making, primarily in determination of policies and secondarily in the application of them. Decisions must be based upon a knowledge of theory and facts. Theory, embracing concepts and principles, is drawn from economic theory, sociology, psychology, law, accounting, finance, management, statistics, and mathematics, not to speak of marketing theory. The facts upon which marketing decisions are based are ascertained both within and without the business organization.

The actual processes of marketing decision making are too complex for a brief treatment of them; however, the following are some of the areas of decision and a few of the factors which management takes into consideration.

1) Market and Product Decisions. Every marketing venture begins with an assumption that a market exists. The entrepreneur must determine, however, whether it is a household or industrial market, whether demand is elastic or inelastic, whether it is an effectual or potential market, whether its wants have been articulated or must be cultivated with information, whether it is of such dimensions that it can be reached economically. It must be considered whether a product of desired character can be made to sell at an acceptable price, whether a single item or a line of products should be made, whether they should be of staple or changing characteristics, sold in bulk, packaged, or branded.

2) Channel Decisions. As the necessary channel is a function of the market, the producer, and the product, marketing management must ascertain the functions required for the distribution of a product, the costs involved, and the likelihood of selling at a price which justifies the costs. If multiple channels are required, the manufacturer's price structure must provide for both the functions performed and the functionaries that are essential in different channels.

3) Price Decisions. Price is a focal point of a variety of administrative decisions. It is in one sense an expression of the vendor's concept of his costs; it is also an indication of the buyers' valuation of the goods. Administratively, price determination is not a simple task. It is the effect of policies embodied in accounting practices, implicit in the marketing structure of the firm, or expressed in its promotional strategy. Price may be stated simply and directly as a net amount, or as a gross sum subject to trade, functional, quantity, cash, and other discounts. It may be a mill-based or a delivered price. In many other ways, price decisions are a means of management for achieving its marketing objectives.

MARKETING LEGISLATION

While sanctioning the general institution of marketing in our market economy, society has not completely surrendered control over it to the competitive business mechanism. Evidence to the contrary implied by attitudes of *laissez faire* and *caveat emptor* in trade during recent centuries, is refuted by reconstruction of social sanctions through legislation in the United States beginning about 1890. At that time, in the name of the Sherman Antitrust Act, appeared the beginnings of social policy which have since then been amplified and clarified by legislative, judicial, administrative, and "semi-judicial-administrative" agencies, in both federal and state governments. While aimed at "business," the regulation has pertained specifically to marketing—both wholesaling and retailing.

Underlying the philosophy of marketing regulation are the principles of the superiority of the interests of consumers over those of business, of the freedom to undertake and carry out business enterprise, and of conformity to fair play, insofar as that can be defined in business practice. Several lines of social policy are apparent in marketing legislation:

First, a concept of fairness in competitive price determination underlies portions of the following related statutes: The Sherman Antitrust Act (1890), the Clayton Act (1914), the Robinson-Patman Act (1936). They deal in part with the question of trade-restraining price discrimination, sanctioning price differences based upon, and to the extent of, differential distribution costs incurred in selling different quantities or under different conditions. Restraint is exercised over competition-impeding dealership contracts of vendors and horizontal agreements among competitors relating to price and trade practices.

Second, vertical agreements relating to price maintenance have been sanctioned, with exceptions in some states, by the Miller-Tydings Act (1937) and the McGuire Act (1952), as well as by similar state legislation. Such laws undertake to prevent socially undesirable predatory price-cutting practices through the interest which sellers claim to have in protection of their brand name and distributive organizations.

Third, protection of the public against false, deceptive, and misleading statements in advertising is provided in the Federal Trade Commission Act (1914) and the Wheeler-Lea Act (1938) whereby jurisdiction over this area of business practice is established with the Commission. Similar guard over statements made in product labels is effected through the Pure Food and Drug Act (1906) and the Food, Drug and Cosmetic Act (1938).

Fourth, encouragement as well as discouragement of certain marketing practices is given in the Webb-Pomerene Act (1918) and the Capper-Volstead Act (1922), which sanction agreements among competitors otherwise prohibited by the Sherman Act, in certain matters relating to export trade practice and the establishment of agricultural marketing co-operatives, respectively.

Fifth, a variety of regulation is provided in a number of lesser acts such as the Wool Products Labeling Act (1939), the Fur Products Labeling Act (1951), the Lanham Trademark Act (1946), unfair trade practice acts, municipal vending ordinances, and the like.

POWER

THE satisfaction of human needs rests fundamentally on labor. Consequently, the more labor procurable at the least cost in human energy, the greater is the human energy set free for other purposes—for the enjoyment of leisure, for progress, for civilization. Past civilizations were built up and supported largely on the labor of slaves maintained at a subsistence level. Modern civilization rests on the utilization of mechanical power, which, in an ever increasing degree, is made to do work formerly done by human beings. Revolutionary changes in the development and use of power have done more than any other factor to raise the standard of well-being in the 20th century.

The application of mechanical power to human productivity multiplies the amount and the value of goods which each individual worker can produce. The following table, showing the estimated daily output of various kinds of workmen in the year 1800 and in 1925, brings home vividly the advantages created largely by the use of power-driven appliances.

ESTIMATED DAILY PRODUCTIVITY PER WORKMAN IN 1800 AND 1925

Product	1800	1925
Iron	500 lbs.	5000 lbs.
Lumber	100 bd. ft.	750 bd. ft.
Nails	5 lbs.	500 lbs.
Shoes	¼ prs.	10 prs.
Coal	½ ton	10 tons
Paper	20 sq. ft.	200 sq. ft.
Bricks laid	500	3600*

*By electric brick layer.

No degree of finality is to be expected of such figures as the above. They depend first on the degree to which various labor saving devices, available to an industry, are actually adopted by the industry. They depend also on the continued discovery of still newer devices, a process which, while going on constantly, is nevertheless very unequal and largely unpredictable. An example is the mechanical blowing of glass bottles, which almost overnight multiplied many-fold the output per man. The flour milling and automobile industries represent continuous and progressive advances over decades. The figures given are regarded as conservative. Their value is chiefly in illustrating the most fundamental fact in the evolution of our economic system—the multiplication of productive capacity by the development of mechanical power.

Early Sources of Power. The adoption of draft animals as a substitute for human labor was an extraordinary advance in the economy of primitive man. This change dates from prehistoric times. Draft animals performed heavy work on the farms, as well as providing power for transportation throughout the world during the entire period of recorded history. They were also employed by the Romans and later peoples in turning mills for grinding grain. Comparatively little additional progress in the utilization of non-human power was made until the invention of steam-driven appliances for pumping water in the late 17th century. The Romans, however, are credited with the first use of the water wheel to turn grinding mills. The wheel was connected with the mill stone by a horizontal spindle through the intervention of bevel gearing.

The water wheel of the Romans was introduced into various parts of Europe and into Britain. At the time of the Norman Conquest of England, 1066 A. D., two counties alone, Norfolk and Suffolk, had 500 mills driven by water power. Windmills were introduced from the East by the Crusaders.

Steam Engines and the Industrial Revolution. The 18th century is notable for the invention of the steam engine and for the beginnings of its application to industries, notably mining, textile and steel manufacture, and flour milling. This development occurred first in England, where, in the 19th century, an industrial society first began to take shape. Urban population increased rapidly. Despite recurrent crises of overproduction, unemployment, booms, and panics, British wealth grew rapidly, due to the fact that machines driven by steam multiplied the productive power of each laborer. Steam power at the same time was vastly increasing the facilities for transportation on land and sea. By the close of the century, Germany and Belgium had been largely industrialized, but the most striking transformation of all was under way in the United States.

The Early Twentieth Century. In 1900, the United States contained two-fifths of the steam railway mileage of the world—about 198,000 miles of track. The country's installed power, not used for transportation, was about 15,278,000 horse power, of which nearly two-thirds was used for manufacturing, the balance being divided almost equally between public utility plants and mineral production. For about 88 per cent of the power the prime mover was steam, that for the balance being practically all water power.

The beginning of the 20th century was notable for two developments in the utilization of power which were of fundamental importance.

The first was the adaptation to wide practical use of the internal combustion engine. The world is most largely indebted for this device to Nicholas Otto, who in 1877 developed the first successful engine of this type, and to Gottlieb Daimler, who in 1884 adapted this engine for use in road vehicles. In 1900, Rudolf Diesel exhibited at Paris the Diesel engine, a much more economical type, particularly for heavy uses. In the following quarter-century the internal combustion engine made possible the universal employment of the automobile for transportation and travel; it also led to the solution of the problem of air travel. In marine transportation, the Diesel engine made rapid inroads on the use of steam. By 1927, the tonnage of ships constructed with oil-burning motors exceeded the year's construction of ships equipped for steam propulsion. Petroleum, the chief source of the motive power for these engines, took its place with coal as one of the most indispensable of raw materials.

The second epochal development of the 20th century in the use of power was the wide utilization of electricity as a means of distributing energy and of making it flexible in application.

Dynamos and electric motors respectively are the instruments by which power is made to take the form of electricity and by which electricity is reconverted to mechanical energy. The principle governing these machines was discovered by Michael Faraday in 1831. Important improvements were made by Werner Siemens in 1854 and by H. Wilde in 1863. In the period from 1880 to 1900, electric railways were constructed in most of the principal cities. It was not until the 20th century, however, that the importance of electricity as a form of power was adequately realized.

Technical improvements in the steam engine, the internal combustion engine, and electrical machinery were largely responsible for the phenomenal growth of power used in the 20th century. The total installed horsepower in the U.S. increased rapidly after 1900, but changes since World War II have been even more phenomenal. The total horsepower of all prime movers was 2.8 billion in 1940, with just over 90% produced by automotive engines. The total increased by more than 500% by 1968 to 17.9 billion; more than 94% was produced by automotive engines. All other sources of horsepower production, including factories, power plants, railroads and other forms, contribute only about 6% of the total horsepower, an indication of the tremendous importance of the automotive engine to society.

PRODUCTION OF ELECTRIC ENERGY IN THE U. S., 1930–1970

Source: *The Federal Power Commission.*

Year	Electric Energy Produced				Fuel Consumed in the Year		
	Total	Hydro	Steam	Internal Comb't'n	Coal	Oil	Gas
	1,000 Kw. hrs.	1,000 Kw. hrs.	1,000 Kw. hrs.	1,000 Kw. hrs.	Short tons	42 Gal. Barrels	1,000 Cu.ft.
1930	91,111,548	31,189,554	59,293,363	628,631	40,277,989	8,804,530	119,552,711
1935	95,287,390	38,372,154	56,144,412	770,824	32,714,761	11,256,565	124,117,769
1940	141,837,010	47,321,278	93,001,735	1,531,997	51,473,881	16,325,122	180,096,185
1945	222,486,283	79,970,312	140,435,268	2,080,703	74,724,956	20,228,215	326,211,969
1950	329,141,343	95,938,317	229,543,366	3,659,660	91,870,770	75,420,490	628,918,834
1951	370,672,814	99,750,579	267,251,680	3,670,555	105,768,006	63,944,724	763,898,241
1952	399,223,620	105,102,458	290,384,847	3,736,315	107,071,241	67,218,426	910,116,741
1953	442,664,515	105,233,348	333,541,535	3,889,632	115,897,204	82,237,712	1,034,272,333
1954	471,686,354	107,068,508	360,834,386	3,783,460	118,384,671	66,744,754	1,165,498,360
1955	547,037,985	112,975,069	430,119,086	3,943,830	143,759,195	75,273,862	1,153,279,586
1956	600,667,750	122,028,608	474,552,045	4,087,097	158,278,996	72,710,841	1,239,310,686
1957	631,507,224	130,232,457	497,212,384	4,082,383	160,769,232	79,692,910	1,336,140,626
1958	645,098,000	140,262,000	500,764,000	4,072,000	155,724,000	77,668,000	1,372,853,000
1959	710,006,000	137,782,000	567,839,000	4,385,000	164,431,000	88,263,000	1,628,509,000
1960	753,350,000	145,516,000	603,342,000	4,492,000	176,634,000	85,340,000	1,724,762,000
1966	1,144,350,138	194,755,781	944,430,145	5,164,212	266,476,823	140,948,854	2,609,948,660
1967	1,211,749,276	220,043,018	986,782,770	4,923,488	273,972,576	161,274,680	2,743,251,360
1970	1,529,581,307	247,327,890	1,260,580,532	6,038,373	322,357,138	332,104,404	3,894,017,643

Electrification. Electricity is not a primary source of power, like steam, waterfalls, and gas engines. It is a means of making prime movers more useful. Through the generation of electricity by prime movers and the subsequent reconversion of this electricity into power through electric motors, primary energy can be used with greater flexibility in time and space. Power through electricity can be used *when* and *where* it is wanted far more readily than power delivered directly from steam engine or water wheel.

Not only may factories using electricity for power be located at points more advantageous for utilizing raw materials, markets, and labor, but electricity enables power to be used in private homes and on farms. This results in two chief developments of great social significance. First, labor in homes and on farms for the first time in the world's history may be largely freed from drudgery, thereby releasing an incalculable amount of human time and energy for other purposes. Secondly, factories need no longer be located in centers of congested population. New centers of industry may be semi-rural in character, with marked improvement in living conditions. Individual factories need not, as a rule, have their own power plants. Expensive and dangerous beltings and shaftings may be dispensed with. The control of machine processes is more exact and is effected with less labor.

Electricity has the further merit of being instrumental in turning power into other useful forms of service. The most obvious of these is light. The first electric lighting plant was established by Thomas Edison in Brooklyn, beginning operation on September 4, 1882. By November 1883, only 508 premises were wired for 12,732 lamps, none being in private homes. By 1937, about 21,500,000 homes in the United States were served with electricity, in addition to more than 4,000,000 commercial or industrial establishments. Since then, of course, millions of other homes and business establishments have been provided with electrical energy. Lighting now takes a variety of forms developed from the incandescent carbon lamp and the tungsten. Fluorescent lighting and neon lights have become quite common, the latter used especially for advertising purposes.

In addition to light, electric power is essential for the operation of telephones, telegraphs, and radio, where it results in the production of sound. As heat, it performs essential work in electric ranges, furnaces, irons, toasters, grills, and numerous other devices. As an agent of chemical change through electrolysis, it plays a necessary part in the chemical industry. Another important use is for the precipitation of dust from the air in factories. It is essential to the production of talking motion pictures. By facilitating automatic control of numerous processes, it releases an enormous amount

DIVISIONS OF INDUSTRY

Industry	April 1970			Total 1965
	Male	Female	Total	
Employed Persons	48,686,000	29,722,000	78,408,000	72,179,000
Professional and technical workers	6,890,000	4,431,000	11,322,000	8,883,000
Managers, officials, and proprietors	6,896,000	1,301,000	8,198,000	7,340,000
Clerical workers	3,497,000	10,337,000	13,834,000	11,166,000
Sales workers	2,724,000	1,990,000	4,714,000	4,715,000
Craftsmen, and foremen	9,737,000	290,000	10,027,000	9,221,000
Operatives	9,539,000	4,272,000	13,811,000	13,390,000
Private household workers	26,000	1,559,000	1,585,000	2,251,000
Other service workers	3,185,000	4,954,000	8,139,000	7,091,000
Farmworkers	2,692,000	472,000	3,164,000	4,265,000

Source: *Statistical Abstract of the U.S., 1970.*

of human labor. Finally, electricity has given the world automatic refrigeration and the control of atmospheric humidity through air conditioning.

Growth of Electric Power in American Industry. The first quarter of the 20th century witnessed the electrification of over three-fourths of American industry. The following summary presents the factual basis for this statement:

In 1899, the total horsepower in electric motors was 492,936 out of a total of 10,097,893 primary horsepower—4% of the total.

In 1927, the total horsepower in electric motors was 30,361,106 out of a total of 39,040,563 of primary horsepower—78% of the total.

In other words, electrification in American industry rose from 4% in 1899 to 78% in 1927.

In the same period the amount of power developed in factories and used directly without being transformed into electricity showed only a moderate increase, reaching a high point in 1909 (13,734,597) and steadily declining thereafter. On the other hand, electricity developed in individual factories increased from 310,374 horsepower in 1899 to 11,216,111 in 1927—36-fold. Electricity used in the factory but developed in central stations increased from 182,562 horsepower in 1899 to 19,144,995 in 1927—105-fold.

Electric Power in the World. According to 1974 UN statistics, the United States ranked as the world's number-one producer of electric energy. The U.S.S.R. was second, followed by Japan, West Germany, and Canada. In terms of per-capita electric energy consumption, the United States was tenth among the nations of the world. Norway, Panama, New Caledonia, Luxembourg, and Guam were the top five consumers.

Chief Sources of Electricity. In presenting the available information on this subject, it must be remembered that for a substantial part of the electricity generated there are no authentic records. Every gasoline automobile, for instance, generates electricity for setting off the cylinder explosions and for other purposes. Motor ships generate electricity which in turn drives the propelling machinery. Most electricity, however, is generated in central plants or by individual industrial concerns which report their production.

Fossil fuels are used in steam-power plants to produce electric energy. The fuel is burned, steam is created, and this force drives the electric generator. Fossil-fuel plants use coal, natural gas, and oil. Of the electric energy produced by this method in the United States, in 1970, 46% was from burning coal, 24% from natural gas, 12% from oil. In 1969 56% of the coal consumed in the United States was for electric energy generation, 17% of the natural gas, and 6% of the oil. The fourth chief source of electricity is water. In 1970 hydroelectric power plants produced 16% of the electric needs of the United States. In Canada electric power is almost synonymous with hydroelectric power.

Conservation, economics, and environmental factors are some of the determinants in the production of electric energy. Conservation of fuel is a long-range motive for preferring water power to coal or oil as a source of electricity, yet immediate economic factors are necessarily the ones which determine the development of the electric industry. Chief among these factors are the location of mineral fuels and of water-power sites in relation to the centers of population. The cost of transmission of current rises rapidly with increase of distance, not only on account of the cost of transmission lines but through losses of energy in transmission.

Since three of the four major sources of electric energy are depletable energy sources, new sources must be developed. Among these are nuclear fission and fusion, geothermal power, solar power, tidal power, wind power, and waste heat. In 1970

nuclear fission accounted for about 2% of the electricity generated in the United States, geothermal about 0.05%. (See *World Energy Crisis*.)

Electricity Generated by Fuel. Electric generating plants operated by steam are normally located in or near industrial centers, in order to be close to their customers and in order to have available a water supply for use in condensing steam as required by the turbine type of steam engine.

Unlike hydroelectric power, the output of steam-driven generators can be counted on at all times irrespective of season. Installations may be added, unit by unit, as the market requirements demand. Operating costs of fossil-fuel plants are higher than hydroelectric plants, however, because of high fuel prices and the high costs of handling waste products.

Fossil-fuel plants have certain environmental disadvantages. About 60% of the available heat produced by these plants is lost as waste heat. They also release to the environment undesirable combustion by-products. Coal-burning plants give off large amounts of smoke or particulate matter. Properly operating electrostatic precipitators can remove 99% to 99.5% of the particulate matter. Coal-burning plants emit gaseous pollutants—carbon dioxide, sulfur dioxide, nitrogen dioxide. Oil-burning plants also release sulfur dioxide. Low-sulfur coal and oil, and tall stacks, effecting a dispersal of undesirable gases, are among the proposed solutions to this problem. Natural gas-burning plants emit nitrogen dioxide—a highly visible element of smog.

Hydroelectric Power. By this term is meant electricity developed by water power, usually through the medium of water turbine generators.

The first hydroelectric plant began operation at Appleton, Wisconsin, in 1882, a few weeks after the opening of Edison's electric lighting plant in Brooklyn. The Appleton plant had a capacity of 250 sixteen-candlepower lights.

The economic advantages of hydroelectric power include the low cost of operation, since no fuel is required and a very small labor force is needed to operate the plant. On the other hand, hydroelectric plants require a large initial investment, since complete installation for all requirements must be made at the outset, even though much of it may be usable only for a brief flood season or may not be required for years. It is often necessary also to construct dams and artificial water channels, and the power houses themselves must be more substantially built in order to withstand the surge of the water. Eventually the growth rate of hydroelectric plants will lessen. This slowdown will be the result of environmental pressures against the building of new dams and the decreasing number of acceptable sites for hydroelectric power plants.

Nuclear Fission and Fusion. Nuclear energy is released during nuclear fission—disintegration of nuclei during an atomic reaction—and during nuclear fusion—joining of nuclei.

Nuclear fission power plants are thermal plants. The energy produced heats water to steam; the steam passes through a steam turbine; the turbine drives an electric generator. In addition to using a thermal cycle to generate electricity, projected nuclear fusion plants will convert reactor energy directly to electric energy.

In 1954 the Atomic Energy Commission launched an experimental program to test different types of reactors to produce electric power. Although strongly criticized, five plants, to cost about $120 million, were developed. The first nuclear power reactor was started up at Shippingport, Pa., in 1957. The first atomic-powered submarine, the USS *Nautilus*, was launched early in 1955.

Nuclear energy presents several environmental problems, among these are the release of radiation, possible theft of nuclear fuel, and the handling of nuclear wastes. The economic factors involved in the construction, operation, and maintenance of nuclear power plants are difficult to determine precisely because nuclear energy is a relatively new development.

Other Sources of Electricity. Electricity can be generated by *geothermal power* through the same steam cycle as that used in fossil-fuel power plants. The source of heat used to produce the steam is found in the earth's interior. The Geysers area in northern California is one example of geothermal power.

Energy from the sun far exceeds the expected future needs of the world. Methods for controlling *solar power* to generate electricity are in the developmental and experimental stages. Systems currently being studied include: (1) a satellite system that involves a satellite rotating at a speed equal to the earth's rotation; collecting the sun's energy and converting it into electricity by way of a large solar panel; and transmitting the electric energy to earth by a microwave beam; (2) a ground-based plant that stores heat from the sun and transfers the heat to a steam generator.

Tidal power makes use of the changes in water level. Proposed tidal power projects include water wheels and large floating objects, which would rise and fall, and in turn drive an electric generator. *Wind power* can be used to drive wind machines that generate electricity. Energy lost as *waste heat* can be used for, among other things, heating homes and offices and for sewage treatment plants.

Tennessee Valley Authority. The Tennessee Valley Authority act was approved May 18, 1933. Under this act, a government corporation, the Tennessee Valley Authority, was created not only for the purpose of improving navigation and controlling floods, but to generate and sell power with a view to determining the relative cost of public and private power operations. For this reason, the corporation (TVA) was designated by President Roosevelt as a "yardstick of power costs." The private utility industry bitterly contested the validity of the "yardstick," maintaining that the two costs were not on a comparable basis.

Another part of the TVA's purpose was declared to be the maximum utilization of electricity within its territory, this to be brought about partly by low promotional rates and partly by education of residents in the advantages of greater use.

The TVA operates in 40,600 square miles of territory drained by the Tennessee River. It comprises parts of seven states—Alabama, Georgia, Kentucky, Mississippi, Tennessee, and the Carolinas—embracing an area inhabited by two million people, with four million more in territory within transmission range of its electric power. TVA took over Wilson Dam and proceeded to build more than 20 major dams providing, in part, a 750-mile waterway, nine feet deep, between Knoxville, Tennessee, and Paducah, Kentucky, where the Tennessee River joins the Ohio.

Electrical energy is produced by water power and by steam, with coal-generated steam plants producing most of the energy today. By the early 1970s over 2 million electricity consumers were being served by distributors that buy power from TVA. In 1971 the average annual household use of electricity by consumers served by TVA was twice the national average for that year.

The TVA has provided cheap electric power, flood control, improved river navigation, and extensive recreational facilities. The TVA power system has grown to be the largest in capacity in the United States.

Municipal Power Systems. Prior to 1933, about 1,750 municipalities operated their own electric systems as compared with 13,665 communities which were served by privately operated systems. Most of these municipal plants were small, however, and they generated little more than 4.8% of total power produced. The largest included those in Los Angeles, Seattle, Cleveland, and Springfield, Ill.

With the establishment of the TVA and the building of large governmental dams in the Columbia basin and elsewhere, a powerful impulse was given to municipal power distribution. Numerous federal loans and grants were made to local bodies for building or buying the necessary facilities, this being a means of finding a market for power developed at the dams.

Transmission of Electricity. One of the chief advantages of electricity as a form of power is its ability to be transmitted long distances. In 1889, seven years after the construction of the first electric plant, it was a notable achievement to transmit electricity 13 miles at a pressure of 4,000 volts.

High voltage transmission systems usually employ overhead conductors. These ordinarily consist of twisted strands of copper or of aluminum wire with steel cores, supported either by poles or steel towers with arms, to which the wires are attached through the medium of insulating porcelain plates.

High voltages used for long distance transmission are transformed to lower voltages at distributing stations and substations until the current is of the proper character for the ultimate user.

Interconnection of Electric Systems. This is frequently referred to as superpower, which may be defined as a system of hydroelectric and steam generating plants within a given territory interconnected into a power pool, which draws on the various generating stations according to their capacities, subject to the dictates of economy, and dispenses electricity to various communities according to their needs. The policy of interconnecting power systems took shape in the period from 1917 to 1919.

Electric Power Industry. Approximately 25% of the world's energy resources goes into the production of electricity. The production of electric energy in the United States amounted to an estimated 1.1 trillion kilowatt-hours in 1960; 1.5 trillion kilowatt-hours in 1970; and 1.9 trillion kilowatt-hours in 1975. Approximately 78% of the electricity produced in 1975 came from privately owned utilities. Of the electric power produced by publicly owned utilities, 51% came from federal sources, 30% from cooperatives, power districts, or state projects, and 19% from municipal power plants.

Operating companies in the United States which produce electric power are required by law to be local monopolies under the control of a state regulating commission. The standard method is to place each local monopoly under the regulation of a state commission charged with the duty of seeing that the service is adequate and that the prices are just and reasonable. Other state and federal agencies oversee the activities of electric power companies to control radioactive materials and the use of water and to protect the environment.

In the 1930s, the federal government became a factor in the production and distribution of electric power. Although faced with opposition from private power groups contending that they could not compete with the nonprofit operations and low-interest financing of the government, public power has expanded. Major developments include the Tennessee Valley Authority and various Columbia River projects.

INSURANCE

THE gigantic nature of the private insurance business in the U.S., in the early 1970's, is summarized in the following figures: about 5,000 insurance companies had more than $250 billion in assets, received $70 billion a year in premium volume (sales), and employed 1,400,000 persons.

In addition, various forms of social (government) insurance required the expenditure, largely in taxes paid by employers and employees, of more than $40 billion a year. About three-fourths of social insurance costs were accounted for by the federal Old Age, Survivors', Disability and Health Insurance (OASDHI) program, which provides basic retirement, death, and disability protection for hospital and medical costs of the elderly, was also a rapidly expanding part of OASDHI. Other important social insurance programs were administered through the states: unemployment compensation, workmen's compensation (for work injuries and diseases), and temporary nonoccupational disability income insurance.

A more detailed review of the private sector of the field is best approached by a division into (1) *life* insurance, (2) *health* insurance, and (3) *property-liability* insurance. The basic purpose of all these types is the reduction of risk or uncertainty in regard to economic losses. The principle of loss sharing among large groups of exposures is used to apportion equitably the dollar value of losses for such events as death, disability, medical treatment, automobile collision, fire, windstorm, theft, riot, and a variety of other causes of loss. Many of these occasions (difficult to predict for individuals or businesses) become reasonably predictable through the institution of insurance.

LIFE INSURANCE

Life insurance has for its basis the *potential income-earning* ability of an individual. This is one of the greatest assets that individuals and families have. Few other assets begin to compare with the importance of this "human life value." Life insurance protects the insured, his family, creditors, and others against the financial loss occasioned by death. Almost $1.5 trillion dollars of life insurance in force—with more than 1800 companies holding $200 billion of assets to guarantee future payment to 130 million individual policyholders—is clear evidence of the popularity and significance of the field of life insurance.

Purpose and Extent. In the vast majority of instances, life insurance is taken to protect the family against the loss of the earning capacity of the breadwinner through untimely death. But, in recent years, business uses of life insurance have also shown marvelous growth. Life insurance can help offset financial loss when a key man in the firm dies. Partners can insure each other so that funds will be available to buy out the interest of the one dying first. Stockholders in closely held corporations often hold life insurance to provide funds for the firm's purchase of the shares of a deceased shareholder.

Increasingly, also, businesses are using group forms of life insurance, whereby large groups of employees are protected under a single policy for a stated amount for each employee, usually the equivalent of one or two years' wages. The "Life Insurance in the U.S." table will make clear the extent of this extraordinary growth. Annual income of U.S. life insurance companies grew nearly eight-fold between 1940 and 1970, doubling during the last decade. Benefits increased from $2.7 billion in 1940 to $15.5 billion in 1970. Assets grew from $30 billion to $200 billion, while total life insurance in force rose from $.1 billion to $1.4 billion during the same period.

Group life insurance accounted for almost 40% of the total insurance in force in 1970 with legal reserve life insurance companies. From 23,000 policies involving 8.8 million certificates and $15 billion of life insurance in 1940, the field expanded to include 289,000 policies involving 75 million certificates and $483 billion of life insurance at the beginning of the 1970's. Group life insurance has been among the fastest-growing types of insurance. More than $500 billion of such insurance is in force, providing at least some basic protection for many families. The principle of group insurance is also used in the sizable Servicemen's Group Life Insurance and Federal Employees Group Life programs. Another type with rapid growth from 1950 to 1970 is group credit life insurance, used to repay a loan when an individual borrower dies.

In Canada, life insurance ownership equals 197% of national income, the highest such ratio for any country. The total life insurance in force as of 1970 was $110 million, of which 54% was individual life insurance and 46% was group life insurance. Eleven million Canadians owned life insurance in 1970, with some 70% held in Canadian companies. Benefits paid during the year totaled $1.3 billion; death payments were $425 million, while "living benefits," such as annuities, surrender values, dividends, and matured endowments made up the remainder.

Additional forms of life insurance in the U.S. at the end of 1969 included veterans life insurance, with $38 billion in force; fraternal life insurance, with $23 billion (including Canada); and savings bank life insurance, with $3.6 billion in force.

Basic Principles. Life insurance differs from other forms of insurance in one vital respect. In other forms, the contingency insured against may never happen, and, as regards the great majority of policies written, does not happen. Life insurance, however, protects against the event of death, which, under a whole-life policy, is a "hazard converging into certainty." It is, therefore, necessary to provide not only against the risk of death each year, but also "to accumulate a fund sufficient not only to meet a claim whenever occurring, but also to provide at the ultimate limit of human life an absolutely certain claim.

To accomplish this, it is necessary to have life insurance companies base their premium charges upon a mortality table, which includes the death rate per 1000 persons and the expectation of life for each age. The U.S. death rate as a whole has remained approximately the same from 1955 to 1970. However, considerable improvement in the rate came early in the century with advances in medicine. Life expectancy at birth is now close to 70 years.

MORTALITY TABLE

Age	Number Living at Beginning of Designated Year	Number Dying During Designated Year	Deaths per 1,000	Expectancy Years	Per Cent Living to 65
0	1,000,000	7,080	7.08	68.30	68.01
1	992,920	1,747	1.76	67.78	68.49
2	991,173	1,507	1.52	66.90	68.61
3	989,666	1,445	1.46	66.00	68.72
4	988,221	1,384	1.40	65.10	68.82
5	986,837	1,332	1.35	64.19	68.91
6	985,505	1,281	1.30	63.27	69.01
7	984,224	1,240	1.26	62.35	69.10
8	982,984	1,209	1.23	61.43	69.18
9	981,775	1,188	1.21	60.51	69.27
10	980,587	1,186	1.21	59.58	69.35
11	979,401	1,205	1.23	58.65	69.44
12	978,196	1,233	1.26	57.72	69.52
13	976,963	1,289	1.32	56.80	69.61
14	975,674	1,356	1.39	55.87	69.70
15	974,318	1,423	1.46	54.95	69.80
16	972,895	1,498	1.54	54.03	69.90
17	971,397	1,574	1.62	53.11	70.01
18	969,823	1,639	1.69	52.19	70.12
19	968,184	1,685	1.74	51.28	70.24
20	966,499	1,730	1.79	50.37	70.36

MORTALITY TABLE—Con.

Age	Number Living at Beginning of Designated Year	Number Dying During Designated Year	Deaths per 1,000	Expectancy Years	Per Cent Living to 65
21	964,769	1,765	1.83	49.46	70.49
22	963,004	1,791	1.86	48.55	70.62
23	961,213	1,817	1.89	47.64	70.75
24	959,396	1,832	1.91	46.73	70.88
25	957,564	1,848	1.93	45.82	71.02
26	955,716	1,874	1.96	44.90	71.16
27	953,842	1,898	1.99	43.99	71.30
28	951,944	1,932	2.03	43.08	71.44
29	950,012	1,976	2.08	42.16	71.58
30	948,036	2,019	2.13	41.25	71.73
31	946,017	2,072	2.19	40.34	71.89
32	943,945	2,124	2.25	39.43	72.04
33	941,821	2,185	2.32	38.51	72.21
34	939,636	2,255	2.40	37.60	72.37
35	937,381	2,353	2.51	36.69	72.55
36	935,028	2,469	2.64	35.78	72.73
37	932,559	2,611	2.80	34.88	72.92
38	929,948	2,799	3.01	33.97	73.13
39	927,149	3,013	3.25	33.07	73.35
40	924,136	3,262	3.53	32.18	73.59
41	920,874	3,536	3.84	31.29	73.85
42	917,338	3,826	4.17	30.41	74.13
43	913,512	4,138	4.53	29.54	74.44
44	909,374	4,474	4.92	28.67	74.78
45	904,900	4,841	5.35	27.81	75.15
46	900,059	5,248	5.83	26.95	75.56
47	894,811	5,691	6.36	26.11	76.00
48	889,120	6,179	6.95	25.27	76.49
49	882,941	6,710	7.60	24.45	77.02
50	876,231	7,291	8.32	23.63	77.61
51	868,940	7,916	9.11	22.82	78.26
52	861,024	8,576	9.96	22.03	78.98
53	852,448	9,283	10.89	21.25	79.78
54	843,165	10,033	11.90	20.47	80.65
55	833,132	10,831	13.00	19.71	81.63
56	822,301	11,685	14.21	18.97	82.70
57	810,616	12,597	15.54	18.23	83.89
58	798,019	13,566	17.00	17.51	85.22
59	784,453	14,583	18.59	16.81	86.69
60	769,870	15,659	20.34	16.12	88.33
61	754,211	16,774	22.24	15.44	90.17
62	737,437	17,927	24.31	14.78	92.22
63	719,510	19,117	26.57	14.14	94.52
64	700,393	20,340	29.04	13.51	97.10
65	680,053	21,592	31.75	12.90	100.00
66	658,461	22,874	34.74	12.31	
67	635,587	24,178	38.04	11.73	
68	611,409	25,484	41.68	11.17	
69	585,925	26,724	45.61	10.64	
70	559,201	27,842	49.79	10.12	
71	531,359	28,773	54.15	9.63	
72	502,586	29,477	58.65	9.15	
73	473,109	29,929	63.26	8.69	
74	443,180	30,189	68.12	8.24	
75	412,991	30,301	73.37	7.81	
76	382,690	30,302	79.18	7.39	
77	352,388	30,200	85.70	6.98	
78	322,188	29,983	93.06	6.59	
79	292,205	29,568	101.19	6.21	
80	262,637	28,885	109.98	5.85	
81	233,752	27,898	119.35	5.51	
82	205,854	26,590	129.17	5.19	
83	179,264	24,986	139.38	4.89	
84	154,278	23,143	150.01	4.60	
85	131,135	21,131	161.14	4.32	
86	110,004	19,011	172.82	4.06	
87	90,993	16,846	185.13	3.80	
88	74,147	14,700	198.25	3.55	
89	59,447	12,630	212.46	3.31	
90	46,817	10,681	228.14	3.06	
91	36,136	8,881	245.77	2.82	
92	27,255	7,248	265.93	2.58	
93	20,007	5,788	289.30	2.33	
94	14,219	4,502	316.66	2.07	
95	9,717	3,413	351.24	1.80	
96	6,304	2,525	400.56	1.51	
97	3,779	1,846	488.42	1.18	
98	1,933	1,291	668.15	.83	
99	642	642	1,000.00	.50	

The assumption is that the death rate of the future will be approximately that demonstrated by the past. Given the age of the insured, the kind and amount of the policy desired, and the maximum rate of interest which the company will guarantee on its funds, it is possible to compute a premium based on the particular mortality table in use. That premium is known as the "net premium," and is intended to cover only the actual mortality cost of the company. To this "net premium" the company must add a percentage to cover expenses of operation and contingencies, thus giving the so-called "gross premium," actually charged the policyholder.

Should the premium be found to be too large, owing to a more favorable death rate than was indicated by the mortality table, or because expenses are smaller and interest earnings larger than anticipated, the company may have agreed to return to the policyholder all or a portion of such gains in the form of a "dividend." When this is done, the insurance is known as "participating." When the insurance is "nonparticipating," the premium charged the policyholder is usually considerably smaller. This is due to the fact that the company, as distinguished from the policyholder, remains entitled to all the gains which may accrue.

While the premium may be increased from year to year as the age of the insured increases, this is seldom done. Experience has shown that life insurance, in order to be practicable, must be based on a uniform annual premium during the premium-paying period. Such a plan requires the company, during the early years of the policy, to charge a premium more than sufficient to pay the current cost of insurance. The excess portions of the annual premiums are thus accumulated in a fund, known as the "reserve." This will be drawn upon in later years when, owing to the increasing hazard connected with increasing age, the uniform annual premium becomes insufficient to meet the current cost.

When a large number of policies are considered, the reserve (the overcharge or unearned premium) may be defined as representing that "sum which, together with future premiums paid by policyholders, will just enable the company to meet its claims according to the mortality table in use." Accumulation of such a reserve fund is fundamental to any sound plan of life insurance. Its absence in the past has been the cause of failure of many insurance institutions. Even today, it is the one great distinguishing feature between the sound and the unsound. It is for this reason that all regular life insurance companies are required by law to operate on the so-called "legal reserve basis."

Who Can Be Insured. Unlike the various kinds of property insurance, life insurance has not been construed by the courts as furnishing contracts of indemnity for loss suffered. It is well settled in the law that an individual possesses an insurable interest in his own life to an unlimited extent. Likewise, the insured may make his life insurance payable to his own estate, or to any beneficiary he may choose.

In view of the above ruling, it is necessary for insurance companies to protect themselves against the acceptance of risks which are either substandard in quality or which involve amounts of insurance greatly out of line with the earning capacity of the applicants. The protection needed is secured in several ways. A medical examination of the prospect is often required in the case of individual applicants. This precaution may be dispensed with in the case of policies of limited size or for group insurance. The prospect is required also to give true answers to numerous questions, relating to his health, family history, habits, and other points, contained in the application for his insurance. Where the insurance applied for is apparently too large, inquiry will also be made into the financial status of the applicant.

The problem of providing insurance for substandard applicants is receiving careful study in insurance circles. It is recognized that applicants for insurance are by no means equal in the quality of the risk involved. Numerous features, involving occupation, state of health, nationality, stature, weight, family history, and various other points, need to be considered if due allowance is to be made for the actual merits of the case. It is now felt that substandard lives should be given the benefits of life insurance, although at premiums sufficiently increased to meet the additional hazard associated with the substandard character of the applicant.

Almost all applicants for life insurance today are able to obtain policies. About 97% of applications for individual contracts are accepted. Only 3% are rejected because of serious health impairments or extremely hazardous occupations. Only 5% of policyholders pay higher than standard rates for "extra risks," such as heart disease, weight problems, or work hazards.

Who May Be a Beneficiary. As already noted the insured has an insurable interest in his own life to any extent. Further, in the absence of policy conditions to the contrary, he may name his own estate, or any individual he chooses, as beneficiary. But what is the situation when the insurance is taken out by a person other than the one insured?

Here we unfortunately meet with a great variety of judicial decisions. With respect to ties of affection, blood, or marriage, the courts have generally held that certain of such ties create an insurable interest even though the element of financial dependence is not present. The weight of authority holds that a parent has an insurable interest in the life of a child. Husband and wife are conclusively presumed to have an insurable interest in each other's life.

As regards all other relations, however, the courts have generally taken the position that the interest of the beneficiary, when taking out the insurance, must be based upon a reasonable expectation of deriving pecuniary benefit from the continuance of the insured's life. The weight of legal opinion is to the effect that the insurable interest of a beneficiary taking out insurance "must exist at the time the contract is made and that a policy valid at its inception will not, therefore, be voided if it should happen that the interest ceases before the maturity of the contract, unless the provisions of the policy are such as to bring about that result."

A creditor has an insurable interest in the life of a debtor. This interest has been held even to survive a discharge of a debtor in bankruptcy. The only question about which there is variance relates to the amount of insurance that the creditor may obtain on the life of the debtor. Usually, the creditor may only take out insurance up to the amount of the debt. Some states allow an additional amount to repay the creditor for the insurance premiums and/or the loss of interest.

What Type of Policy to Select. When considering the fundamental whole type of policies—term, life, and endowment—the average applicant unfortunately gives too little thought to the importance of making the proper selection. No one type of contract serves all persons equally well. In every case the applicant's special circumstances should be considered by the salesman, and the insurance recommended should be such as will meet the needs of the prospect.

The size of the premium varies greatly with the kind of policy, depending mainly on the extent to which a savings fund is provided for in addition to the current cost of protection. When a term policy grants protection only, and contains no savings fund accumulation, the premium outlay is small. The company's promise is limited to $1000 in the event of death during the term, nothing being paid in case of survival. The whole life policy, on the contrary, promises, not only $1000 upon death at any time, but also the same amount upon survival at age 100. As compared with short term policies, it represents a gradually increasing savings fund,

thus requiring a higher premium to be paid throughout life.

The whole life policy offers permanent rather than temporary protection. There are two basic types: the "ordinary" (or "straight") life insurance contract, and the "limited-payment" contract. The ordinary life contract is based on the assumption that premium payments will be continued as long as the insured is living.

The limited-payment whole life policy resembles the ordinary whole-life contract in every respect, except that premium payments are limited to a term of years, like 20 years, instead of being continued throughout life. Since the liability is the same under the two contracts, the insurance company must collect the same amount, considering an assumed rate of interest. If all payments are, therefore, completed within 20 years, as under a 20-payment life policy, the premium rate must necessarily be higher than when the payments continue indefinitely for life. As distinguished from the above, endowment insurance—using a 20-year endowment for illustrative purposes—promises $1000 upon death during the 20-year term as well as an equal amount upon survival at the end of the term. Since this policy involves, in addition to the term insurance, a rapidly increasing savings fund (amounting to $1000 in 20 years), the premium must be correspondingly large. The difference in cost between the aforementioned types of policies may be illustrated at age 25 with the following rates charged by a certain company per $1000 of insurance: 10-year level term (renewable to age 70), $6.20; ordinary life, $15.20; 20-payment life, $25.20; and 20-year endowment, $45.50.

Owing to the low premium, term insurance gives the largest protection for the smallest possible outlay. It, therefore, meets the insurance needs of the young man with a small income and with a family on his hands. Here no surplus earnings exist to pay for the accumulating savings fund under other types of policies. Even where there is some small surplus, it may probably be used to better advantage in the profession or business, which are in the formative stage. Moreover, in the average man's family there is a peculiarly hazardous period, the child-raising period, when the death of the income producer proves a calamity. Accordingly, many who carry a substantial line of higher premium insurance supplement the same with additional 10- or 20-year term insurance to cover the period mentioned. The total insurance is thus substantially increased without undue strain.

The essential purpose of term insurance is to protect a *known temporary hazard*, under conditions when no other form of policy can be purchased in adequate amount. Its great disadvantage lies in the

LIFE INSURANCE IN CANADA

(Millions of Canadian Dollars)			
	1960	1974	1975
Insurance in Force:			
Ordinary	$31,016	$ 37,673	$ 98,478
Group	14,739	100,998	121,865
Industrial	1,112	...	...
Total	$46,867	$188,671	$220,343
Benefit Payments:			
Death Benefits	$ 197	$ 614	$ 700
Matured Endowments	46	80	82
Disability Payments	6	23	26
Annuity Payments	71	393	486
Surrender Values	128	269	271
Policy Dividends	113	303	336
Total	$ 561	$ 1,760	$ 1,984
Income:			
Premium Income	$ 953	$ 3,099	$ 3,549

Source: *1976 Life Insurance Fact Book* (New York: Institute of Life Insurance).

LIFE INSURANCE IN THE UNITED STATES

INCOME, PAYMENTS, ASSETS AND RESERVES OF LIFE INSURANCE COMPANIES 1900–1975 (000,000 Omitted)

Date	Premium Income	Investment Income	Total Income	Benefit Payments	Assets	Reserves
1900	N.A.	N.A.	$ 401	$ 169	$ 1,742	$ 1,443
1910	N.A.	N.A.	781	387	3,876	3,226
1920	$ 1,381	$ 383	1,764	745	7,320	6,338
1930	3,517	1,077	4,594	2,247	18,880	16,231
1935	3,673	1,399	5,072	2,535	23,216	20,404
1940	3,887	1,771	5,658	2,664	30,802	27,238
1945	5,159	2,515	7,674	2,667	44,797	38,667
1950	8,189	2,075	11,337	3,730	64,020	54,946
1951	9,040	1,948	12,012	3,984	68,278	58,547
1952	9,883	2,160	13,076	4,146	73,375	62,579
1954	11,563	2,590	15,280	4,947	84,486	70,903
1955	12,546	2,801	16,544	5,382	90,432	75,359
1956	13,584	3,063	17,865	5,878	96,011	79,738
1960	17,365	4,304	23,007	8,119	119,576	98,473
1961	18,258	4,668	24,397	8,811	126,816	103,285
1967	28,277	7,917	38,248	13,300	177,361	142,217
1969	33,996	9,354	45,628	15,525	197,208	158,550
1975	58,575	16,488	78,022	22,536	289,304	235,057

Before 1947 the business of accident and health department of life companies was not included.　　N.A.—Not available.
Source: *1976 Life Insurance Fact Book.*

fact that the temporary nature of the hazard may be misjudged. At the expiration of the term policy, insurance protection may still be needed, and yet be unobtainable because of inability to meet the medical standard. For this reason term policies usually contain a renewable provision allowing extensions of the original term period. Term policies may also be convertible, which means they may be exchanged for higher premium form by paying the extra cost. Both of these provisions are recommended if the insured's needs so dictate.

The shortcomings just noted with respect to term insurance are obviated by the ordinary policy. This represents *permanent* protection at a very moderate cost. It also combines protection with reasonable saving. Whenever possible, this type of insurance should be preferred to the term plan. Many who take term insurance could, through a little additional effort, pay the extra premium on an equal amount of ordinary insurance. Many argue that they prefer to place the difference in premium in bonds, stocks, real estate, or some other investment. Yet this seems inadvisable, even assuming the resolution is carried out, owing to the absolute security of the life insurance investment and the approximate return of 4–5½%. Careful evaluation of the net effects (after taxes) over a long period of investment, such as 20–40 years, is necessary to justify a decision to purchase term insurance only. The normal family situation suggests a combination of both term and whole-life protection for the husband.

A substantial variety of special forms have become important in life insurance. The so-called "preferred risk" or "special" policies are sold at a reduced rate per $1,000 of insurance because the insured agrees to buy a certain minimum amount, such as $5,000, $10,000, or $25,000. The reduced rate represents a discount for a quantity purchase and recognition of the more careful selection process followed in reviewing applications for insurance. These contracts contain essentially the same provisions as ordinary life forms.

Another development which has appealed to many buyers of life insurance is the "family plan" under which standard packages of coverage apply to all members of the family. The insurance is generally an amount of ordinary life, such as $5,000, on the father, with perhaps $1,000 of term on the life of the wife and each child (to age 18). The premium remains constant even if the wife dies or additional children are born.

Methods of Paying the Proceeds at Maturity of the Policy. The proceeds of life policies may be paid either in a lump sum or in installments. In the latter case, commonly known as the annuity option, monthly installments are usually paid for ten or

twenty years, irrespective of the life of the beneficiary and, therefore, as much longer as the beneficiary may survive the 10- or 20-year period.

The lump sum payment plan has little to commend it where the purpose of the insurance is to give an income to dependents. The fairness of giving 20 or 50 thousand dollars in one lump sum to a widow may well be questioned. The underlying purpose of life insurance is to *assure an income* to dependents *as long as needed.* This the lump sum payment method does not guarantee. The life annuity plan, on the contrary, "insures the insurance," and is just as necessary a form of protection to the beneficiary as the original insurance itself.

Under the life annuity plan the policy proceeds constitute an "insurance estate" administered by the insurance company. It relieves the beneficiary of all expenses of reinvestment, and of all exercise of judgment in the placing of investments and of their supervision thereafter. Administration of the insurance estate by the insurance company also compares very favorably with the administration of an estate through other channels. There are no legal contests between heirs, no legal expenses of administration, no income taxation, and no fluctuation in either the value of or the income obtained from the estate. Moreover, there is no danger of loss of the principal. The only significant danger is that the value of the proceeds will diminish due to inflation. The dollars paid the beneficiary continue at a constant amount while the purchasing power of these dollars diminishes. Thus, in many situations it may be advisable to use a portion of the total estate values for other investments—such as stocks, bonds, or mutual funds—to hedge against the inflationary trend of the economy.

Disposal of Policy before Maturity. In many instances, however, life insurance policies terminate

INSURANCE IN FORCE, 1900–1969 (000,000 Omitted)

Year	Ordinary	Group	Industrial	Credit	Total
1900	$ 6,124	. .	$ 1,449	. .	$ 7,573
1910	11,783	. .	3,125	. .	14,908
1920	32,018	$ 1,570	6,948	$ 4	40,540
1930	78,576	9,801	17,963	73	106,413
1935	70,684	10,208	17,471	101	98,464
1940	79,346	14,938	20,866	380	115,530
1945	101,550	22,172	27,675	365	151,762
1950	149,071	47,793	33,415	3,889	234,168
1951	159,054	54,398	34,870	4,818	253,140
1952	170,795	62,913	36,448	6,435	276,591
1954	198,419	86,395	38,664	10,241	333,719
1955	216,600	101,300	39,682	14,750	372,332
1960	340,268	175,434	39,563	31,183	586,448
1961	364,347	192,202	39,451	33,493	629,493
1966	538,992	343,362	39,663	62,672	984,689
1969	678,887	483,240	38,614	83,788	1,284,529
1975	1,083,421	904,695	39,423	112,032	2,139,571

Source: *1976 Life Insurance Fact Book.*

by lapse or surrender instead of by death. Various circumstances may be responsible for this, such as inability to pay premiums, death of the named beneficiary without leaving other dependents to be protected, or impairment of the insured's health to such an extent as to make further payments of premiums inadvisable in view of the "extended insurance option" granted by the policy.

Cash or Loan Value.—When a policy terminates by surrender, the insured has the option of selecting any one of a number of "guaranteed values," set forth in the contract. One of these values is called the "cash" or "loan value." This value represents the amount of the reserve value of the policy which may be borrowed, if it is intended to keep the policy alive, or which may be taken in cash, if the policy is to be terminated. Usually, such a value is granted after the second annual premium has been paid. Competition is now leading many companies to offer cash values after the first year of the policy. The amount, however, will not represent the full reserve value, in most cases, until a considerable number of years have elapsed. Usually, the full reserve value is given or loaned after the payment of ten annual premiums. With the rise of interest rates after 1969, the policy loan feature of permanent contracts became more valuable to policyowners. A loan rate of 5% is guaranteed in most such contracts, while alternative sources of credit may cost much more.

Paid-up and Extended Insurance.—Instead of the cash value of the policy, the insured may, upon terminating his policy, take either "paid-up insurance" or "extended insurance." The "paid-up insurance" represents that amount of insurance which may be purchased with a net single premium equal to the amount of the cash value of the policy. "Extended insurance," on the contrary, means insurance of the same kind on a term basis and for the original amount for as long a period as may be purchased with a net single premium equal to the cash value at the attained age.

In a typical case, the cash value of a $10,000 20-payment life policy at age 35 amounts to $682 at the end of the third year. Instead of taking the $682 in cash, the policyholder may obtain $1540 of paid-up whole-life insurance, or $10,000 of extended term insurance for a period of 7 years and 334 days. In other words, all three of these options are mathematically equivalent, assuming a given mortality table and a stipulated interest rate. Aside from these options, many companies give the insured, upon termination of his policy, the privilege of utilizing the cash value to purchase an annuity, or some other type of life insurance contract.

Industrial Insurance. As its name implies, industrial insurance is a form of life insurance especially adapted for wage-earners. Its purpose is to enable the large industrial portion of our population to have the funds necessary to meet the expenses connected with medical attendance during their last illness and to assure a decent burial. But, while these are its special purposes, industrial insurance has proved a great educator to the masses in that it has conveyed a proper appreciation of the value of ordinary life insurance.

Although originally sold on the basis of units of premiums of 5 cents a week or multiples thereof, with collection by the agent each week, improved machine accounting techniques and rising income levels for policyholders have resulted in policies being stated in terms of their face amount (usually $250–$1,000) and in monthly premium collections. Such insurance is more expensive than ordinary life, but it has served a real need in the insurance market. The average size policy in the U.S. in 1969 was just under $500. Although this type of life insurance decreased during 1950–70 from 15% of all life insurance in force to less than 3%, 79 million persons held such contracts for a total of $39 billion in protection by 1970.

Industrial life insurance contracts contain a few provisions that differ from other individual policies, but they are based on the same general principles that serve as the foundation for ordinary life insurance. The legal reserve basis is used and the contracts contain practically all of the leading provisions found in regular policies. Premiums are calculated upon an actuarial basis, although a different mortality table is necessary to indicate the higher death rate that prevails among this type of policyholders.

Group Insurance. This form of insurance was introduced in 1911. It is designed to enable an employer to insure employees under one policy. The employer holds a master policy, which covers the employees insured, and each of the employees so insured holds an individual policy. The premium may be paid entirely by the employer or its cost may be shared between employer and employee. At least 10 to 25 employees (depends on state law) must be covered, although so-called wholesale policies are written covering from 5 to 9 employees. Most group insurance policies are for term insurance. No medical examination is necessary. Consequently this is the only form of insurance which some people can obtain. For employees advanced in years, the cost is much less than for equivalent insurance in any other form. In case of the termination of employment, the holder of an individual policy ordinarily has the privilege of converting his insurance into some other type, on which, of course, he pays the premiums.

The employer ordinarily receives whatever dividends are paid on group policies. These may in some cases equal the amount the employer has contributed toward meeting the premium. If the dividends are less than the amount paid by the employer, the difference may be regarded as an increased wage payment or an investment in employee good will.

An important recent development is group creditor insurance under which a lending institution purchases a group contract on all borrowers to cover the loan in the event of the borrower's death. The average credit life insurance policy is written for about $1000, compared with the average contract for other group life insurance, which is $6500.

Fraternal Insurance. Fraternal societies usually observe some ritual, and their government is purely democratic. With respect to insurance, their chief purpose has been to enable the members to secure protection at the smallest possible cost.

Owing to this desire, many of the societies ignored the "reserve basis" of life insurance and charged premiums wholly inadequate to prevent numerous failures. This situation led to the adoption in many states of laws making it compulsory for the orders to employ the legal reserve basis. In 1970 fraternal insurance in force in the U.S. and Canada was only about $23 billion, and assets of these companies were $4.7 billion.

Whereas an ordinary life policy is a definite promise to pay a stated sum in return for a fixed annual premium, the benefit certificate of a fraternal society has, in the past, merely recognized the holder's rights as a member in the society to share in its benefits if the same can be paid out of the assessments levied on the membership. With the adoption of actuarial methods, however, a fraternal benefit certificate can be made as definite a promise as an ordinary life policy.

Usually, the holder of a certificate can name as beneficiary only some member of his family, or other dependent recognized by the society, and for an amount not to exceed a limited sum, such as two or three thousand dollars. Many societies also extend to their members sickness and accident benefits.

HEALTH INSURANCE

Just as life insurance serves to protect dependents against financial need through the death of the insured, so health and accident insurance are intended to protect dependents against a similar need arising out of the incapacitation of the insured through sickness or accident. For the average family this form of protection is indispensable. Industrial accidents are covered today in most states by workmen's compensation insurance. But the largest number of accidents do not occur in industry and must be covered by private insurance. Moreover, loss due to sickness is equal to many times the loss resulting from accidents. It is estimated that about 250,000,000 working days are lost annually in the United States through sickness.

Various methods of granting protection against sickness and accident have been adopted by private insurance companies. Most life insurance companies grant protection, in the form of a monthly income for life, in the event of the total and permanent disability of the insured. But fully 97 per cent of all sickness and accident claims are for temporary disability. Many accident and health companies also issue "limited policies" at comparatively small premiums since the coverage is confined to a limited number of diseases or accidents and the compensation to a comparatively short period.

Much more adequate are the health and accident policies which are "general" in their coverage. These cover against disability from every variety of sickness or accident. They may be issued either separately or in combination, that is, as either health or accident policies or both.

Under accident policies a certain principal sum, such as $5,000, is paid in the event of death, the loss of sight, both hands, both feet, or one hand and one foot. Smaller sums are paid for the loss of one eye, or one hand, or one foot. Weekly or monthly compensation is also provided either for a definite period or for life, in the event of permanent disability, and a smaller compensation when the disability is only partial. Almost invariably indemnities are doubled if the accident occurs on a public conveyance.

In health insurance no principal sum is paid in case of death, and the payments are limited to a weekly compensation for a stipulated period. Often, both health and accident policies provide for extra payments covering hospital and surgical expenses. Until recently all health and accident policies were subject to cancellation by the company. But recently various companies have undertaken to issue so-called "non-cancellable policies," which may be renewed from year to year at the option of the insured until a stipulated age is reached.

More than 85% of all Americans have one or more forms of private health insurance. By 1969 the coverage was: hospital expense, 170 million; surgical expense, 156 million; regular medical expense, 129 million; major medical expense, 67 million; disability income loss, 63 million. One of the fastest-growing was major medical insurance, offering maximum benefits of $5000 to $20,000 or more. In 1955 fewer than 5 million persons had this coverage—by 1969 the number had grown by more than 13 times.

For those 65 and over, federal Medicare, since 1966, has provided considerable protection against rising costs. Compulsory coverage of most hospital expenses is provided by employer and employee taxes. A second part of the program (physician's expenses and other medical costs) is financed by the government and by voluntary contributions by participants (95% of all eligible have chosen this coverage). More than 20 million persons are covered by Medicare, in which selected companies and Blue Cross-Blue Shield organizations participate as intermediaries to pay benefits of more than $5 billion a year.

PROPERTY-LIABILITY INSURANCE

Property-liability insurance in the U.S. includes more than 2500 companies. Some firms write many or all kinds of "multiple-line" insurance; others cover only a few specialized lines (or types) of insurance, such as automobile or fire insurance. Most of the $29 billion of annual premiums in this sector are written by approximately 1000 companies, operating in all or many states.

Automobile Insurance. The "automobile economy" of today is reflected in the more than $12 billion a year of the direct insurance cost of the mobile society of the U.S. Nearly 60,000 automobile accident deaths and 5 million annual injuries emphasize the need for improved motor vehicle safety as one of the most vital current issues.

Numerous industry proposals and government regulations are aiming at solutions to the "automobile problem," which is really a complex of related problems of increasing costs, difficult apportionment of individual and societal responsibility, dissatisfaction with present conditions, and evolving changes in the legal and economic systems. Some current criticism is directed at auto manufacturers, while other comment takes to task the liability system on which auto insurance is based, the rating structure used by insurers, enforcement of traffic safety by government, and the irresponsibility of some drivers.

Kinds of Automobile Insurance. Under this area of coverage there are six headings:

Bodily injury liability insurance protects against legal claims arising from personal injuries or death caused by the use of a motor vehicle. The policy covers the person or corporation responsible for the operation of the car. It usually also covers any licensed driver the policyholder or adult members of his family permit to drive the car. Usual protection covers defense of all claims and suits for injury and payment of any costs assessed against the insured, up to the policy limit, which may range from $5000 for one person and $10,000 for all claims from one accident to as much as $300,000 and $1 million limits, respectively.

Property damage liability insurance protects against losses incurred through damage done in use of the car to the property of other people. In case the damaged property cannot be used and its withdrawal from use imposes additional losses to its owner, these losses, assessed against the insured, are also covered by the policy. But the policy does not cover damage done to the car of the policyholder.

Collision insurance covers damage to the policyholder's car caused by collision with any other object, moving or stationary. If the driver strikes a tree, the policy protects him no less than if he collides with another car. The amount he can collect, however, is limited to the actual cost of repairs or the actual value of the car at the time of the accident. Moreover, the accident must have taken place within certain geographical areas. Under many policies, no indemnity can be collected unless the damages are over a certain minimum amount, such as $50 or $100, called the deductible.

Comprehensive insurance pays for all physical damage to the vehicle, with certain exceptions specified in the contract. Such losses to the insured car as fire, hail damage, lightning, theft, riot damage, or glass breakage are covered to the extent of the actual cash value of the item damaged.

Medical payments coverage provides for reimbursement to the insured for any medical expenses incurred by him or by persons in the car, to the limits stated. Some automobile policies also include a lump sum payment for death and a weekly benefit for total disability.

Uninsured motorists' coverage is a recent and important part of most present contracts. On either a mandatory or optional basis, the insured is protected against bodily injury losses (medical expenses, loss of income) caused by negligent but uninsured motorists. The coverage applies to "hit-and-run" and stolen-car accidents, including protection up to specified limits for the insured, his family, and other riders in the car of the insured.

Workmen's Compensation Insurance. Accidents and diseases affect thousands of employees each year. Without insurance, many would suffer severely as a result of medical expenses and income loss.

Workmen's compensation insurance provides benefits through a combination of social and private insurance. State laws require most employers to purchase workmen's insurance. Some states provide funds for writing this protection, but in 44 states most of the policies are written by private insurers.

Standard contracts include: (1) a promise by the insurer to pay the employees those benefits provided in the law, and (2) employers' liability coverage for basic limits of about $25,000. Most benefits are paid under the workmen's compensation portion of the contract—in which the employer pays the employee regardless of fault, or of who is to blame for the loss. The concept of employer liability, based on negligence and proven fault by the employer, is important in understanding the derivation of the present workmen's compensation system.

Laws Formerly Adverse to Employees.
Employers' liability insurance indemnifies "against loss from liability imposed by law upon the insured." Thus, it is important to note the nature of the law of the particular jurisdiction under consideration as it governs the liability of employers.

In the 1800's, a mass of special law between employer and employee—so-called judge-made law—developed both in England and in America.

The adverse character of this law from the employee's standpoint is indicated by the following doctrines or practices: (1) the *contributory negligence doctrine*, which held that an employee must show his freedom from negligence, and cannot collect if he has failed to use reasonable care and if that neglect contributed to his injury; (2) the *fellow-servant rule*, which provided that an injured employee could not recover from the employer if the injury was caused by the negligence of a fellow servant; and (3) the *assumption of risk rule*, which was to the effect that "an employee entering employment is held to assume and consent to the ordinary and obvious risks incident to the employment."

With the increasingly harsh application of these rules, various statutes were enacted with a view to increasing the employee's protection. But this tendency was soon counteracted by the development of the "*contracting-out privilege*," according to which the employer could request his employees to contract away their rights under the law, thus relieving the employer of all liability in case of injury.

Under such a system of law it naturally followed that little financial redress was obtainable for injured employees. Criticism of the system was well merited, but should have been directed against the law itself, and not against the form of insurance which merely sought to protect against the law as it existed. The fault was with the system of law. This forced upon the employee the burden of proof and yielded substantial compensation to only a small proportion of injured employees. This system led also to excessive delay owing to the slow operation of court trials.

Workmen's Compensation Laws.
In view of such shortcomings it was only natural that the public should demand a more definite and rational system of law with respect to employers' liability for industrial accidents. This was accomplished through the passage of so-called workmen's compensation laws. Within the decade 1910–20 practically every state enacted such legislation.

While lacking uniformity in details, the various laws have a common purpose. All of the objectionable doctrines mentioned in the preceding paragraphs are abrogated. Employers who refuse to come under the act are compelled to take their chances in a court of law without the support of any of the aforementioned legal rules.

At first, only hazardous occupations were covered by workmen's compensation laws, but gradually coverage has been extended to more than two-thirds of all U.S. workers. Some smaller employers and agricultural, domestic, and casual help are usually excluded. Basic benefits are for medical expenses, loss of income due to death or disability, and rehabilitation expenses resulting from all work accidents and from many diseases caused by work conditions. Although medical expenses are usually paid without limit, income payments normally aim at replacing about two-thirds of income within a stated maximum duration.

All features of administration are clearly defined and are designed to overcome the delay occasioned under the previous system. Specific payments are provided for each of the following: death, total disability, partial disability, or specific injuries. The compensation is based upon the wage of the injured person; and, in addition, in the event of death, upon the number and the degree of consanguinity of the dependents.

All employers, if choosing to come under the act, are compelled to protect their legal obligation under the law through insurance. In most states, the insurance may be taken either with a state fund or with an insurance company. In most instances self-insurance is permitted only when authorized by the administrative authorities, and may subsequently be revoked at any time. A few states make it compulsory to take the insurance in the state fund. Whatever insurance institution is selected, the policy must be based on the compensation law under consideration, and any provisions to the contrary are declared null and void.

FIRE AND MULTIPLE-PERIL INSURANCE
Fire insurance is an important form of indemnity in the field of property insurance. This line of insurance also embraces such perils as windstorm, riot, explosion, water overflow, vandalism, and collapse. Also, contracts protecting the insured against consequences of such perils which cause his business or residence to be closed are part of the fire insurance field.

A significant development since the early 1950's has been the expansion of many contracts to include multiple-peril insurance of fire, theft, and liability perils. Package policies insuring these basic perils have become popular, and the average home now has the broad protection of a homeowner's policy. A variety of commercial multiple-peril policies are also available to most firms and institutions, in which broad coverage, convenience, and lower cost are obtained in a single contract.

Purpose of Fire Insurance.
Like other forms of insurance, fire insurance has for its fundamental purpose the "substitution of certain for uncertain loss." As regards a great and everpresent hazard, it serves to stabilize business, to reduce all costs to consumers, and to enhance production by eliminating fear of loss and by increasing initiative.

Fire insurance also serves as the support of commerce and of industry, in so far as it and its companion, marine insurance, are the basis of our whole credit system. The significance of this function becomes apparent when we reflect that fully 90 per cent of the world's business is conducted on credit, and that nearly all transactions involving goods, buildings, and ships, are confronted with the danger of ruinous loss through fire or marine disaster.

As has been elsewhere stated: "It can be shown in a hundred ways that fire and marine insurance have become absolute necessities of trade, without the assuring protection of which the large undertakings of today would be a gigantic gamble and would never be attempted if liable to miscarry through a single fire or marine disaster. As it is, enormous sums are borrowed on stocks and bonds and warehouse receipts; merchants sell their wares on credit; investors furnish millions for the upbuilding of vast industries supporting whole towns;

capitalists make loans on buildings worth many times the value of the ground upon which they are built—all being willing to do this because they know that the insurance policy stands between them and loss."

Personal Character of the Contract. Fire insurance policies are personal contracts, that is, strictly speaking, they do not insure the property but the persons who own the same or have an interest therein. Two buildings may be just alike in all respects, except that one is owned by an honest person whereas, with respect to the other, the owner may be grossly careless or even inclined to profit from a dishonest fire. The importance of this factor cannot be overemphasized. Probably no other type of contract places one party (the insurer) so much at the mercy of the other (the insured). With reference to over-insurance, therefore, as well as the determination of rates, it is highly important that the insurance company know the character of the property-owner.

Nature of the Indemnity. The fire insurance contract is also one of indemnity for actual loss. Irrespective of any value stated in the policy, insurance companies are not liable for more than the "actual value of the property at the time of the fire." Any other rule might work the greatest injustice to companies, and might even result in fraud, owing to the constant and frequently great fluctuations in values as regards both buildings and goods. Should companies be obliged to pay the full face of the policy in the event of total loss, irrespective of an actually lower value, the policyholder would be enabled to profit from a fire. Such a result is contrary to the very idea of "indemnity," which "implies that the insured should be compensated for loss actually incurred, but should never find the insurance contract a source of profit."

Two other concepts, relating to the nature of the indemnity, should be mentioned. Only the loss of material values is indemnified, i. e., the fair cash market value of the property at the time of the fire. Sentimental values, such as those associated with gifts, documents, and objects of art, are not covered unless there is an express agreement to the contrary. In case of inability to reach a fair settlement with the insured as to the fair value of the property damaged or destroyed, the insurer is given the option, under the terms of the policy, of replacing or reconditioning the property. Moreover, in the event of agreement as to the value of all the property, damaged and undamaged, the insurer is given the option of settling at that figure and taking title to the undamaged portion.

Restriction of Liability. The company's liability is also limited to "loss or damage directly traceable to fire." Small fires, working through a chain of circumstances, such as charged wires and explosives, may result in enormous loss for which the insurer becomes liable. In all such cases the question is: "Is fire the real cause, and if so, is the sequence of events between the origin of the fire and the destruction of the property an unbroken one or has some outside force, such as an act of God, intervened to bring about or increase the loss?"

Who May Insure. Since fire insurance policies are contracts for indemnity and not for profit, it follows that only those who have a pecuniary interest—an insurable interest—in the property under consideration have a right to insure. Insurable interest, however, has been given a very broad meaning by our courts. Eliott defines it as "every interest in property or in relation thereto, or liability in respect thereof, of such a nature that a contemplated peril may directly damnify the insured."

Such an interest does not necessarily imply ownership or even possession of the property. Thus insurable interest has been held to extend to the following: (1) custodians of property intrusted to their care, to the extent of their interest or liability, such as administrators of estates, agents in property held for the principal, assignees in insolvency, trustees, common-carriers, warehouse men, and commission merchants; (2) creditors or debtors, such as mortgagees, debtors with respect to property seized for debt, pledgees to the value of the property pledged, and those who have by agreement expended money on the property of others; and (3) those possessing contract rights depending upon the preservation of the property, such as consignees and consignors, contractors whose payment is deferred until completion of the contract, patentees possessing a right to royalties, and even insurers in the property they have insured.

The last illustration serves as the basis for the important practice of reinsurance, whereby an insurance company may reduce its risk by reinsuring all or a part with other insurers.

Use of a Standard Policy. In probably no form of insurance is it so essential to have a uniform or standard policy as in fire insurance. Prior to 1870 there was an utter lack of uniformity. The first state to attempt a remedy was Massachusetts, which adopted a standard form in 1873. New York followed in 1887, and the so-called New York Standard Fire Policy, although improved from time to time, has been adopted as the standard in all but a few states on a mandatory basis. Even where not enacted into law, this policy is generally used by all the companies.

Standard policies are necessarily drawn to meet a general situation, and cannot be designed to cover the numerous special needs surrounding the many different types of property or the various insurable interests therein. All such exceptional circumstances must be arranged for through so-called "endorsements" attached to the policy.

Coinsurance. With comparatively few exceptions, fire insurance on commercial and industrial properties is written subject to coinsurance. This means that the insured will have any claim paid in the proportion that the insurance taken bears to the insurance required. The advantage offered the insured for accepting a coinsurance clause is a reduced rate per $100 of insurance.

For example, with a building valued at $10,000, let us assume that the insurance required is $8000 (80 per cent), that only $4000 of insurance was taken, and that a loss of $2000 occurred. Under the circumstances the $2000 loss is paid only in the proportion that $4000 (the insurance taken) bears to $8000 (the insurance required), or to the extent of only one-half, or $1000.

Usually the amount of insurance required is 80% of the value, representing the proportion of the property value subject to destruction by fire. Where, however, the property is subject to total destruction, a 100% coinsurance clause may be used. In other cases much lower percentages, as, for instance, 70 or even 50% are applied.

Where property appreciates materially during the term of the policy, it is highly important that the owner should correspondingly increase his insurance in order to comply with the coinsurance requirement. The purpose of coinsurance is to secure justice between property owners and to enable the companies to derive an adequate premium income. The overwhelming majority of fires result merely in partial losses.

Without a coinsurance requirement, many of those insured would be encouraged to purchase only small amounts of insurance in relation to their exposed property values. With coinsurance, all of the insured are encouraged to purchase amounts that will provide protection against serious losses. Equity among policyholders is achieved in applying the fire insurance rate, as if the rate were proportionally decreased when larger amounts were purchased.

TRANSPORTATION INSURANCE

Often referred to as "marine" insurance, transportation insurance has two basic divisions: (1) ocean marine insurance, and (2) inland marine insurance. The first primarily covers sea perils of ships and cargoes; the second generally covers a wide variety of movable property in transit, as well as fixed property used in connection with transportation, such as bridges, docks, and tunnels. Ocean marine insurance is used here to illustrate the unusual aspects of transportation insurance.

Ocean marine insurance has for its purpose the indemnification of interested parties "against loss, damage, or expense, occasioned accidentally in connection with vessels, cargoes, and freight charges, through any of the numerous perils incident to transportation by water." In fact, the so-called "warehouse-to-warehouse clause," used in insuring cargo, covers goods from the time they leave the shipper's warehouse in the interior—through all the various stages of the journey, rail, truck, dock, ship, and port of destination—until they reach the warehouse of the consignee in the foreign country.

Types of Losses Covered. Policies of marine insurance may vary according to the type of losses they cover. Marine losses are either "total" or "partial." Total losses, in turn, may be either "actual" or "constructive," the latter comprising those cases where the property has not actually been destroyed but where the cost of repairing or reconditioning is so great, as compared with the restored value, as to make the attempt financially inadvisable.

Partial losses may be classified as "general average," "particular average," and "salvage." General average has been defined as comprising "losses and expenditures which result from the sacrifice of any interest voluntarily made by the master of the vessel, in time of real distress, for the common safety of vessel, cargo, and freight, and which must be repaid proportionately by all the parties benefited." Any partial loss which does not meet this definition is regarded as a "particular average loss." "Salvage" represents the remuneration recoverable under maritime law by a salvor for saving property at sea.

SURETY, FIDELITY, TITLE AND CREDIT INSURANCE

In the field of property insurance, there should be mention of surety and fidelity bonds, and title insurance, and credit insurance. A surety bond is a guarantee, and has been defined as a "written obligation to pay a sum of money under one or more expressed conditions, among which may be found negligence, breach of trust, disobedience of a law, failure to pay a judgment, failure to pay a debt voluntarily assumed, and other conditions under which losses may be sustained by personal acts." Hundreds of kinds of policies are issued to meet every possible variety of obligation. Some bonds are much like insurance, protecting against crime perils such as fidelity losses due to employee dishonesty. Broadly speaking, bonds may be classified as falling under fidelity, judicial (court bonds), license and permit, contract, and depository bonds.

Title insurance, as defined elsewhere, "promises to protect the owner of real estate, or the lender of money thereon, against loss or damage, not exceeding the amount stated in the policy, sustained by reason of any defect of title assumed under the policy, or because of the unmarketability of the title or by reason of unknown liens or encumbrances against the property at the time the policy is issued."

Credit insurance has for its purpose "the indemnification of losses, coming within the coverage of the policy and exceeding the normal loss of the business under consideration, suffered by manufacturers and jobbers through the insolvency of their customers."

BUSINESS CYCLES

It is a matter of historical observation that aggregate business activity pursues a distinct course of expansion and contraction, prosperity and depression. This more or less rhythmic succession of business conditions is known as the *business cycle*. The layman refers to its alternative phases as good times and bad times.

Prosperity is characterized by full employment. Consumers and businesses spend freely, frequently with borrowed money, and prices are firm or rising. Profit margins are generally favorable. New enterprises are undertaken and old businesses expand. The total output of the economy increases and a spirit of optimism prevails. Depression is associated with opposite conditions. There is widespread unemployment and jobs are scarce. There is a reluctance to spend, accompanied by a contraction of credit. Prices usually decline and profit margins narrow or disappear. Business firms contract, some failing altogether. Total output of goods and services declines and optimism gives way to fear and pessimism.

Business Crises. The change in business from prosperity to depression used to be abrupt and decisive. Now, with government assistance in moderating crises, it is usually more gradual.

Frequently in the 18th and 19th centuries, the prosperity phase of business cycles was associated with the doubtful and unscrupulous promotion of some particular enterprise accompanied by excessive and unsound credit expansion. Normal business was displaced by frenzied speculation. Ultimately, some prominent firm or individual became overextended in the speculation and was forced to liquidate its holdings. Thus, the speculative mania was broken.

The abrupt reversal of outlook resulted in the calling of loans, a desperate scramble for money, frantic sale of securities, and sharp declines in prices. Instead of the pessimism of a normal business crisis, the community was gripped by overpowering fright. When crises became thus violent, they were called panics. There have been 11 such panics in the U.S., the last one in 1929.

Since then, instead of panics, there are periods of reduced activity such as in 1957–58, 1960–61, and 1969–70, when stock markets decline, unemployment increases, and business activity in general slows down. These are called recessions.

True, the business cycle has become milder as a result of a favorable conjuncture of structural changes and because of better and wider understanding of the requirements of business cycle policy. However, the forces that tend to generate cyclical movements have not vanished.

Causes. The annals of business record crises from the beginnings of commercial capitalism. There is little doubt that crises are as old as trade itself. However, up to the Napoleonic era of the early 19th century, and to a limited extent thereafter, each crisis had a special cause usually of a non-business nature. The business reversals were attributable to what we would now call random events such as a bad harvest, riots, wars, or acts of God. The periods of depression were viewed as abnormal deviations from the normal course of prosperous economic growth.

As capitalism matured and modern industrial economies developed, crises became more regular in occurrence and more similar in nature, especially in their financial aspects. Instead of being viewed as random abnormal events, they became recognized as a recurrent and inherent feature of a business economy. Statisticians detected a rhythm and regularity which seemed periodic and the concept of a business cycle evolved. Although modern data do not support the thesis of periodic recurrence, the name "business cycle" has remained, and more or less regular fluctuations are considered a normal attribute of modern business societies.

A problem of such long standing and such social

importance has attracted many great minds to its study. Consequently there are many theories or explanations of business cycles.

Since many of the theories differ more in their emphases than in fundamentals, most of them may be classified under one of three headings: business economy theories, monetary theories, and savings and investment theories.

Business Theories. These explanations rest on the general hypothesis that prosperity, through its effects on business expectations, breeds maladjustments which ultimately undermine prosperity. They run somewhat as follows. Business is speculative by nature and therefore prosperity breeds overoptimism and overexpansion. Productive capacity and goods are created in anticipation of future markets and inventories are accumulated. This process strains the capacity of the whole economy. Labor efficiency declines as marginal workers are employed, wage rates rise, raw materials rise in price, credit becomes scarce, and interest rates rise. Eventually costs rise faster than selling prices, profits are reduced, and some of the weaker businesses fail. These conditions convert overoptimism into overpessimism and contraction begins. Inventories are reduced, loans cancelled or paid off, and prices decline. These developments set the stage for recovery, optimism returns, and the process is repeated. These theories are realistic and conform with observed behavior, but they are somewhat superficial. They are more descriptive than explanatory.

Monetary Theories. These explanations emphasize the key role of the money supply and bank policies. They may be summarized in the following manner. Economic activity expands and contracts with changes in total spending, and this spending is done with money. Spending is influenced largely by changes in the supply of money. In a modern credit economy, bank deposits constitute the main form of money. Consequently the behavior of banks in expanding and contracting the money supply is responsible for business fluctuations.

In the early phases of prosperity, banks extend credit at low interest rates. This leads to business expansion, inventory accumulation, and the spread of optimism. This process gains momentum until the banks are unable or unwilling to continue the credit expansion and interest rates rise. Businesses are forced to curtail activities and reduce inventories. The decline begins. When contraction has gone far enough, bank reserves are adequate for a new round of expansion. Theories of this type make the monetary system and its interest-rate movements the sole originating force in cycle turns. However, once the turn has been taken and a new direction of movement charted, the economic system will respond with a complex interplay of other forces which further influence interest rates and are influenced by them in a cumulating movement away from equilibrium.

Savings and Investment Theories. These theories are more general and analytical than the others. They do, however, usually incorporate elements of the other two in them. Most currently accepted explanations are of this type. A general outline of such theories is as follows.

In a modern business economy, any given level of production generates a flow of money income equal to it. That is, the total market value of the goods produced is distributed among the populace in the various forms of income payments such as wages, rents, profits, etc. If the total of income payments is spent, the spending will exactly absorb the output, and that level of production will be perpetuated. This exact balancing of the flow of production and the flow of spending would constitute an equilibrium from which the economy would not fluctuate. The existence of business cycles stems from imbalances

between these two flows. The imbalances occur through the savings and investment processes.

Since, historically, business cycles have not been government caused but are distinctly an attribute of a private enterprise economy, we may, for purposes of analysis, assume government to be non-existent. Or, more realistically, we may assume government to be neutral in its effects on business fluctuations, which it would tend to be, if its budget were in balance.

Total spending in the private sector of the economy is the sum of consumer spending plus business investment spending. Total private spending must equal private incomes after taxes, if the economy is to remain in equilibrium. Income receivers as a group typically save part of their incomes; thus consumer spending is less than total income and production. This leaves some income, the savings, available for investment spending. If businesses decide to invest an amount exactly equal to these savings, the total flow of consumer and business spending will equal the flow of incomes. The economy would not fluctuate under such conditions.

Saving out of income is carried on by the populace at large, including business firms, for various reasons, many of them habitual in nature. The decisions to save are changeable and largely independent of business investment plans. Investment is carried on by business firms mainly to exploit the profit opportunities of new resource discoveries, new technology, new products, and population growth. These decisions are largely independent of the savings plans of the public.

Thus savings decisions and investment decisions are carried out by different groups with different motivations and independent of each other. Furthermore, the nature of each is such that both are quite variable. There is no assurance that plans to save will match plans to invest. For this reason the flow of total spending can have a tendency to either exceed or fall short of the total income flow. Since equilibrium requires a balance of the two flows, this imbalance leads to fluctuations.

If technological developments, discoveries, population growth and related stimuli are such as to cause investment plans to exceed planned savings, banks can create money through credit expansion—thus lending non-saved money. This permits the total spending flow to exceed the income flow. Equilibrium is destroyed and the economy expands until the flow of production and income rises to a level equal to the new spending level. At first such expansion is usually real in that physical output expands along with the monetary expansion. Once all labor and other resources are employed, any further expansion must be strictly monetary, and inflation sets in. Whether the expansion is real, monetary, or both, it continues until the income and spending flows are again in balance. At this point, savings out of the enlarged income flow would equal the investment spending and equilibrium would be reestablished. The expansion or the new equilibrium may continue for an indefinite period of time— business cycles vary in duration.

If for some reason investment plans should become less than planned savings, due either to an increase in savings or to a decline in investment, savings will begin to pile up in banks and other financial institutions. The spending flow becomes less than the income flow. Inventories accumulate and production is reduced. The income flow declines until it is in balance with the spending flow. At this lower level of income, savings would be reduced to equal investment and the contraction would cease. Equilibrium would exist at this depressed level until either savings or investment decisions changed so as to set off a new expansion.

This analysis stresses the divergence between the plans to save and the plans to invest. Actually it is possible that savings and investment may be planned equal, and still turn out unequal, causing fluctuations in the economy. In some instances new products and new technology may stimulate investment plans which equal savings. But the actual investment may require such radical shifts in the structure of output that it is impossible to move the men and resources quickly enough. In such instances actual investment would be forced to fall short of plans and thus be less than savings.

Possibility of Control. In view of past experience and the nature of business activity, it is not considered entirely possible to eliminate business cycles while still maintaining a private enterprise economy. However, some control is possible and fluctuations may be modified.

To the extent that cycles are accentuated by overoptimism and speculation during prosperity, government, through the control of banking, can curtail credit whenever signs point to excessive borrowing. In this way purely monetary and inflationary expansion can be curbed. This should make less severe the declines following an expansion. Likewise, centrally-controlled banks can be liberal in their credit policies during a decline, thereby relieving some of the stress on business and reducing the number of failures. It was to facilitate such policies that the Federal Reserve system was revamped in 1935. See *Federal Reserve System.*

A balanced budget means that taxes are equal to government spending, which means that the government extracts from the income flow by taxation an amount equal to what it extracts from the production flow by its spending. Under such conditions any imbalance between total spending (including government spending) and total income (including taxes) would stem from the private sector.

Economic contraction and expansion are situations of imbalance between income and spending. If the economy is declining, income is greater than spending because savings are greater than investment. The government can counteract the decline by unbalancing its budget so as to spend more than it taxes, financing the difference by borrowing. In this manner government increases public spending more than it reduces private spending, thereby causing total spending to rise. This brings spending and income into equality, halting the decline.

If the economy is in an expansion running into inflation, spending is greater than income because savings are less than investment. The government can curb the inflationary expansion by unbalancing its budget so as to tax more than it spends. The excess revenue can be used to pay off past borrowing or to add to the government's cash balance. This action would decrease private spending more than it increased public spending, causing total spending to decline. Income and spending are made equal and the expansion ceases.

Since periods of depression and prosperity are approximately balanced in duration, the government could alternately increase and reduce its debt, thus acting as a stabilizer without going progressively farther into debt. The policy then becomes essentially one of timing public expenditures. However, for this policy to control the business cycle completely, the government would need the ability to forecast business conditions perfectly and the administrative and political flexibility constantly to adjust its taxing and spending activities.

Built in "Stabilizers." There are, however, certain means of control that act more or less automatically. When times are good, progressive income taxes, both personal and corporate, and taxes for unemployment compensation usually take more from spendable income than is paid out in benefits and subsidies, thus acting as a brake. When times are bad, less is collected from both personal and corporate income taxes and more is paid out in unemployment insurance and other forms of social security. The result increases purchasing power, thus stimulating demand and employment.

Explanatory Table. In the examination of the table which follows, the above discussion should be borne in mind. Under the heading "Special Causes," attention is drawn only to particular events which precipitated the crisis, it being unnecessary to mention in each case the general causes of overspeculation and its concomitants. Similarly, in the column headed "Special Consequences," no mention is made of the normal features accompanying and succeeding the crisis—the fall in prices, slack trade, unemployment, and so forth—unless these features showed some special character.

IMPORTANT BUSINESS CRISES

Date	Countries Chiefly Affected	Special Causes	Special Consequences	Period of Depression
1809	England, United States	Speculation connected with Napoleonic war which led to credit and note inflation.	Bullion committee's recommendation for resumption of cash payments not accepted; depreciation of notes continued.	2 years
1815	England . .	Close of Napoleonic wars; vast production of English manufactured goods which European countries were too much impoverished to buy.	Much unemployment, machine-breaking, fall of prices.	About 2 years
1836–1839	England, U. S. A., France, Belgium . .	Railway speculation in England and U. S. A. Land speculation and paper money inflation in U. S. A. Collapse occurred simultaneously in England, Ireland, and U. S. A., in 1836. Bad harvest of 1838 caused another crisis in which Bank of England was threatened with ruin.	Failure of many banks and speculators; much unemployment. Drain of bullion from England was finally checked by raising discount rate and by aid of Bank of France. Bank Act of 1844.	7 years
1857	United States, nearly all other countries . . .	American crisis due to great discoveries of gold, railroad extension, development of banking and speculation.	Suspension of Bank Act in England. Very great unemployment in all countries.	3 years
1866	England . .	Wild speculation in limited liability companies, excessive borrowings by means of "finance bills," unsound banking practices.	Universal distrust of English investments. The failure of the weaker banks left the well-established banks stronger.	About 1 year
1869	United States	Operations of Jay Gould, made possible by unsound paper money system.	Many failures. (Black Friday, Sept. 24, 1869).	
1873	Nearly all countries .	Payment of French indemnity to Germany loosed a speculative mania in Germany and Austria; railway boom in U. S. A.; excessive construction of permanent works and "overproduction" at high prices.	Failures of banks and commercial houses; unemployment (3,000,000 "tramps" in U. S. A. during winters of 1873 and 1874). Shrinkage of prices, stagnation, glut.	6 years

Date	Countries Chiefly Affected	Special Causes	Special Consequences	Period of Depression
1882	France, England . . .	Wild speculation inspired by Union Generale, a company promoted among French and Austrian Catholics to destroy financial supremacy of Jews.	Collapse of this company and of the boom in general. Long period of depression.	5 years
1884	United States	Railroad speculation; large foreign wheat crops caused low prices for US grain and lessened US railroad earnings.	Very low prices.	2 years
1890–1894	England, Germany, France	Speculation in South America. Revolution in Argentina.	Support of Bank of England, aided by Bank of France, averted panic.	4 years
1893	United States	Good harvest of 1891 stimulated business; smaller harvest of 1892, low agricultural prices, heavy gold exports, fear that gold standard might be abandoned, and doubtful bank loans occasioned crisis.	Widespread failures, unemployment, and industrial unrest; march of Coxey's Army. Political and tariff uncertainties prevented thorough recovery until latter part of 1897.	4 years
1900	England, Germany, France	Great prosperity in England in 1898; business further stimulated by war in 1899 till it reached highest point in 1900 and then receded; high taxation and dear coal (both due to South African war) held responsible.	In England, unemployment but no spectacular failures. In Germany alarming failures occurred.	4 years
1903–4	United States	Decline of security prices after speculation of 1900 and 1901, precipitated by withdrawal of European funds—("Rich man's panic").	A few corporations failed, idle money accumulated in banks, but abundant harvests of 1904 hastened recovery.	About 1 year
1907	United States, Europe . .	Failure of Knickerbocker Trust Co. inaugurated panic in New York which spread over the whole country. American panic caused rise of bank rates in London, Paris, Berlin, and intensified depression there.	Failures, but not extensive scale. US government aided banks; Clearing House certificates issued; gold shipped to US from Europe. This crisis strengthened movement to Federal Reserve System.	1½ years
1914	United States, Europe . .	Crisis due to overspeculation transformed into special financial crisis by outbreak of World War I.	Many normal features of depression disappeared in the increased business activity due to the war.	About 2 years
1920–1922	United States, England, Europe . .	Increase of productive capacity in victorious countries accompanied with loss of purchasing power in defeated countries partly due to collapse of national currencies.	Widespread unemployment and business losses; famines and pestilence in some countries.	Less than 2 years in the US. Continued depression in Europe
1929–1933	World wide except in Russia . . .	Cumulative result of over expansion in agricultural and industrial productiveness. Reparations and war debt payments combined with trade restrictions.	Unprecedented unemployment. Practically all countries off gold standard. Banking crisis in United States. Free play of economic forces curbed by governments.	About 8 years
1937–1938	United States	Sharp change of federal fiscal policies from deficit to balanced budget. Excessive credit restraint by Federal Reserve Banks.	Renewed large government deficits	About 1 year
1945	United States	Reconversion from a war to a peacetime economy. Sharp reduction in defense spending.	None. Surprisingly rapid recovery.	Less than 1 year
1948–1949	United States	Rapid inflation following end of wartime price controls.		About 1 year
1953–1954	United States	Close of Korean War and sharp reduction of military spending.	Exceedingly liberal credit policies.	1 year
1957–1958	United States	Excess industrial capacity developed in preceding boom. Cutbacks in defense spending.	Large Federal deficit.	About 1 year
1960–1961	United States	Unemployment caused by restrictive monetary policy, automation, and monopoly in the bear markets.	Chronic unemployment.	About 1 year
1970	United States	Efforts to counteract inflation characterized by restrictive monetary policy.	Very high interest rates.	
1971		Vietnam war limitations reduced military spending. Aerospace cut also brought lower federal outlays.	The US balance-of-trade deficit was triple that of 1970. Import taxes rose, and wage-price freezes were imposed. The US Gross National Product continued upward, despite inflation. World inflation continued.	
1972		The US move toward a peacetime economy spurred growth. Wage-price controls were continued.	US inflation increased 3.5%; consumer prices rose, and employment increased. Interest rates rose and the foreign-trade deficit moved higher. The Gross National Product again moved upward.	
1973–1976	United States	Arab oil embargoes and shortage of domestic fuel caused "energy crisis" and programs for development of other sources of energy. The change from war to peacetime economy slowed. Urban centers faced financial difficulties.	Inflationary trends continued and unemployment rose to highest rates since the great depression of the 1930s. The housing industry suffered as homeowners faced increasing mortgage rates. The federal government was forced to aid urban areas. Despite the struggling economy, the Gross National Product continued upward.	

INVESTMENTS

Investment is the exchange of capital for property rights from which a return is expected. The investor releases his capital for use by the issuer or seller of a security. In exchange, the investor receives either a creditor's claim, as in a note or bond, or an owner's interest, as in a share of stock. The investor's primary purpose in releasing his capital is to produce a return on the investment. The return is normally in the form of periodic interest or dividend payments. However, in certain cases, the return may be a combination of periodic payments and realized increase in value in the market price of the security. A true investment is productive in that it produces income to the security holder.

In making any investment, the individual investor should be primarily concerned with the safety of the principal amount invested and with the certainty and regularity of income. In addition, the investor will be interested in marketability and yield. An absolutely safe investment does not exist. Since safety is a relative term, all securities have a certain element of risk. This risk, which is typically referred to as financial risk, is the possibility that the issuer of a security will be unable to repay the amount invested at the time of maturity of the security. The yield that the safest security offers may be considered as the true rate of investment income. The higher yield obtainable from all other securities may be considered as a profit received for the additional risk assumed in the purchase of securities less desirable than the best. The yield on long-term U.S. government bonds may be accepted as the "true" rate at any given time.

Since no securities, except possibly U.S. government issues, are safe from financial risk, a basic principle of investment is "diversification," or variety of investments. Diversification involves selecting investments in several different securities or areas so that gain in one may be used to offset losses in another. Diversification is obtained by investing in different types of securities (bonds, stocks, etc.), securities in different industries (railroads, utilities, steel, etc.), securities with different maturity dates (short-term, long-term, no maturity, etc.), or securities in companies operating in different geographic areas.

Determination of Yield. The annual return or yield of an investment is the percentage relationship between the amount of the annual income obtained therefrom and the current market value of the investment. In the case of stocks, the method of determining current yield is fairly simple. The rule is to divide the number of dollars received in annual dividends per share by the current market price per share. To illustrate: a certain stock pays dividends at the rate of $9 per share and is quoted at $180; 9 divided by 180 gives 5 per cent, which is the current yield.

The determination of bond yields is somewhat more involved as the good bond will be paid at par at maturity date regardless of the purchase price. If the bond is purchased below par, it is assumed that the holder will receive, in addition to the annual interest, an increase in the value of the bond as the bond approaches the due date. On the other hand, if the bond is purchased above par, the holder is obliged to charge against his current income a certain amount to cover the decrease in the value of the bond as it nears maturity.

To illustrate: a 6 per cent bond due in ten years is quoted at 105; from the annual income of $60 on a thousand dollar bond, a deduction of $5 must be made for premium write-off, leaving $55 net return. This is divided by the average investment of $1025 (average of $1050 cost price at time of purchase and $1000 maturity value) for a yield of 5.37 per cent net to maturity. The amount of the premium write-off was determined by dividing the number of dollars paid as premium ($50) by the number of years (10) in the period during which the bond will run.

Classes of Securities. Investment securities may be divided into two classes, owner obligations (preferred and common stocks) and creditor obligations (bonds, notes, debentures, etc.). A fundamental difference exists between owners and creditors. The owners (stockholders in a corporation) are a part proprietor in the enterprise and must be prepared to share both in profits and in losses according as the business prospers. The stockholder in a corporation is normally limited in loss absorption to the amount of his investment in the corporation. The creditor (bondholder, etc.) has legally loaned money or capital to the business and, therefore, expects the payment of interest regularly and of principal at maturity, regardless of the incidental prosperity of the company. If the company cannot pay the creditor his interest when due or his principal at maturity, the creditor has the right to sue and demand foreclosure on the assets of the business.

The income of a bondholder is said to be fixed, regular, and certain within limits. This is because the bond bears a fixed rate of interest, such as 5 per cent; because the interest must be paid regularly irrespective of earnings; and because default in payment to the bondholder usually brings foreclosure upon the corporate property or a reorganization of the enterprise.

The income of the stockholder is not so satisfactorily assured. The amount will depend upon the prosperity of the company and the discretion of the directors of the corporation. During poor years, his income may cease entirely. His right to receive income is subordinate to that of all others who have a claim against the corporation.

Preferred stockholders are owners who normally have a preference to earnings over other stockholders (common stockholders). Preferred holders will receive their stated dividend before common stockholders receive anything. However, their dividend income is normally limited to a stated maximum amount, while common stockholders have no limit on the amount they may receive. While preferred stockholders have a right to receive their dividend before common stockholders, they do not have the right of foreclosure on property for nonpayment as creditors do. If the company pays no dividends to its common stockholders, it is under no obligation to pay anything to preferred stockholders. Preferred stockholders normally have a preference over common stockholders as to assets in the event of dissolution. However, in dissolution, creditors would have to be paid in full before preferred stockholders could receive anything.

Creditors are divided into two major classes: secured and unsecured. Secured bondholders are protected by a mortgage or certain corporate property in addition to the legal promise to pay. Holders of unsecured bonds (debentures) do not have a lien on specific property but do have all the rights of general creditors including the right of suit and foreclosure.

Tests of Investments. What comprises a good investment? Of many attributes, the most important are: (1) safety of the principal; (2) satisfactory income; (3) marketability; (4) a favorable tax position; (5) a satisfactory denomination and maturity date; and (6) a good collateral value.

Safety of principal depends chiefly upon the true value of the assets of the company which is, in turn, dependent upon the earning power of those assets. Satisfactory income comprehends both stability and amount of income. This depends upon the nature of the business and the efficiency of the management. The amount of income received on any investment should be adequate to compensate the investor for the risk he undertakes. Marketability of a security means that it can be disposed of at a fair price in a reasonable time. Marketability depends in part upon the volume of the security outstanding in the hands of the public, but much more largely upon the reputation of the company. These are the three major tests, and unless the prospective security meets each of these satisfactorily, the other tests may be eliminated.

Public Bonds. Public bonds may be divided into two classes: federal and municipal. Federal bonds are the bonds of the United States government. They are regarded as the premier investment security of the country because they are secured by the credit of the United States. Bonds guaranteed as to principal and interest by the United States government are in the same class. No question exists as to the ability of the government to arrange payment at maturity. The market price of the bonds will change from month to month with changes in the market rate of interest, but this is in no way attributable to fear concerning their repayment.

Municipal bonds comprise state, county, city, and all local government obligations. These bonds are often desirable investment securities. They are secured by the taxing power of the communities. While it is true that the respective states are sovereign powers and, as such, cannot be sued in the event of default of payment of their bonds, it is also true that constitutional restrictions upon the creation of debt have kept the bond issues within conservative limits. There has been no default in the payment of state bonds since the early 1890's. The value of a state bond depends upon (1) the good faith of the people, (2) the financial standing of the state, and (3) the constitutional restrictions on the amount and purpose of issue.

County and city bonds are also highly regarded as investment securities. Unlike a state, a municipality may be sued. The first test, therefore, is ability to pay. Experience has shown that a net debt of ten per cent of the value of the taxable property marks the ordinary limit of safety in municipal borrowing. For small communities, seven per cent is a safer limit. The second test is validity of issue. Unless the bonds have been issued in accordance with existing laws, there is constant danger that the issue may be declared invalid. The average investor is not in a position to pass upon questions of validity. His chief protection is to buy municipal bonds only through reliable bond houses which have had the advice of counsel in this respect. The third test is the good faith of the citizens of the municipality with regard to the payment of their debts. State, county, city, and local government bonds are regarded as tax-exempt securities, as the income received is exempt from Federal income taxes.

Corporate Securities in General. Corporate securities include the stocks and bonds of all privately-owned profit corporations. They are generally divided into railroads, public utilities, financial, and industrial. From the standpoint of investment desirability, corporate securities range from very good to very bad. In general, the nature of the business has material effect upon the prosperity of the companies. The income of public utility companies has a greater inherent stability than that of industrial companies. Consequently, the utilities are more highly regarded in the investment field.

The stability of income depends upon the product the corporation makes or the service it sells and upon the character of the management. The bonds of Pacific Gas and Electric Company are better than those of Bethlehem Steel Company because there is a more constant demand for electricity than for steel products. Also, the bonds of a company that is efficiently managed is generally of better quality than those of another company that is less fortunate in this respect.

The strength of a corporate security may best be judged from the financial statements of the company and from past payment records. The balance sheet shows the assets and liabilities; the income statement shows the income and expense items and the profit or loss for the period covered. Past payment records give an indication of future payments and trends. From the balance sheet may be determined the book value of assets that represent the capital behind the stocks and bonds. From the income statement may be judged the earning power of the company. Of the two, the earning power is by far the more significant.

Before purchasing any security an individual investor should make a careful study of all available information pertaining to the particular industry, company, and security. In the case of many large companies, there is a considerable volume of material available through banks, brokerage houses, and libraries. Certain financial services are available through the above sources which summarize information on securities and/or corporations of interest to the general public. These services offer up-to-date data through daily, weekly, or monthly supplements to annual publications. The leading services are Fitch Investors Service, Moody's Investors Service, and Standard & Poor's Corporation. A considerable amount of investment information can also be obtained from current business magazines and newspapers.

Railroad Securities. From the time railroads were first constructed in the U.S. until the time of World War I, railroad stocks and bonds enjoyed a high rating in investment circles. With the introduction of other forms of motive transportation (especially automobile, truck, and plane) railroad earnings have trended downward. The tremendous increase in traffic during World War II greatly improved the position of railroads and enabled many of them to pay off millions of dollars of indebtedness. This improvement in financial position carried into the early postwar period, but competition from other forms of transportation continued to increase and the railroads again experienced a long-run downward trend.

The roads sought to combat this trend by such moves as abandoning unprofitable passenger runs, use of specialized types of cars for freight, and application of computers to speed freight shipments. In the 1960's, a number of railways worked out mergers into fewer but larger systems to reduce overlapping services and strengthen the financial position of the corporations. Such moves were subject to approval of the Interstate Commerce Commission, which has the duty of regulating rates and services from the public's point of view. This includes consideration of the interests of displaced employees.

Railroad companies issue more different classes of securities than any other enterprise. The senior bonds are those which are protected by a first lien or mortgage on the property. Junior bonds follow senior issues in their claim and are given names such as consolidated, general, refunding, and debenture. The rolling stock is usually bought on the installment plan and is financed through the sale of equipment trust certificates which are generally safe investments. Most railroads issue both preferred and common stock.

Public Utility Securities. Public utility securities comprise those issued by electric light and power companies, by natural and artificial gas companies, by water companies, by electric railways, and by telephone and telegraph companies. The types of securities issued are much simpler than in the case of the railroads. They comprise mortgage bonds, collateral trust notes, debenture bonds, preferred stocks, and common stocks.

The utility companies (particularly the electric and gas companies) enjoy many advantages over other corporations. They operate under public service commissions in the different states which set rates sufficiently high to insure a fair return. They have a virtual monopoly in supplying their product under the franchises granted by the communities in which they operate. The demand for their products is growing steadily. Rate increases seem to have little effect on demand for their products. High grade public utility bonds have taken the place formerly held by railroad bonds as the safest corporate bonds.

Before World War II, the best-known public utility securities were those issued by the large holding companies in the field. These holding companies did not conduct any direct operations but simply bought and sold the securities of operating companies, frequently managing them and financing them through other subsidiaries. Since the enactment of the Public Utility Holding Company Act of 1935, holding companies have become much less important in the field and the leading companies today are primarily operating companies or holding companies with only one layer of operating companies beneath them.

The chief tests of the quality of public utility securities are the earnings record and rate of return. Operating companies should have earned the total interest charges an average of 4 times a year during the preceding 7 years. The rate of return tends to be lower than for comparable rail and industrial securities due to the reduced risk of public utility investment. A third test of importance is the location of the communities served. In this connection the effect of competition with publicly-owned utilities along with the rate of growth of the community should be considered.

Industrial Securities. Industrial securities comprise the stocks and bonds issued by all privately-owned corporations outside the railroad, public utility, and finance fields. Industrials include agriculture, manufacturing, wholesaling, retailing, service, mining and petroleum industries. Thus, it is difficult to generalize about the field as a whole due to its diverse nature. Generally, industrial corporations issue primarily common stock. Only a small percentage of the companies have preferred stock or bonds outstanding. When bonds are outstanding, they are generally less important percentage-wise to the company than they are for utilities and railroads.

The profits of industrial companies vary to a marked degree with changing business conditions. When business is booming, most industrial companies realize large profits; when business is dull, many suffer losses or barely avoid them. Retailing, service, food processing, and tobacco companies tend to fluctuate less with business conditions than do other types of industrials.

Industrial securities, notably the common stocks of companies which are leaders in essential and growing industries, are popular investments for both individuals and institutional investors. Common stocks of these companies are particularly popular as a hedge against inflation, as it is anticipated that their earnings and market price will increase as prices increase. Considerable caution is necessary in choosing good industrial securities.

In testing industrial securities, consideration should be given to the nature of the industry and the type of product or service handled. The growth rate of the industry as well as of the specific company should be considered along with past dividend record. Stability and trend of earnings becomes particularly important in choosing a good industrial investment.

Investment Companies. Investment companies or trusts are financial organizations which make a business of investing the funds supplied by their shareholders in selected stocks and bonds, the investors sharing in the income and profits from the securities held by their company, according to the number of shares they own. These companies have proved attractive to small investors, with perhaps little knowledge of financial markets, because the companies are managed by specialists in the investment field, and because the "mutual fund" permits the buying of a diversity of investments, thus minimizing the risk of loss of principal.

There are two main types of investment companies, the "closed-end" company which has a set capitalization, and the "open-end" company which keeps offering new shares for sale. The companies are regulated by the Federal Investment Company act of 1940, and have, since 1950, been obliged to conform to the rulings of the Securities and Exchange Commission in their dealings with the public and with their stockholders.

Real Estate Mortgages. Real estate mortgages have long been one of the most popular forms of investment in this country. The chief concern of the investor should be to secure ample margin of safety. In no case should the mortgage exceed four-fifths of the conservative value of the property pledged. The average investor should avoid all but first mortgages and then only on property which is more likely to appreciate in value than to decline. Moreover, he should invest with particular care during times when rents are abnormally high as this condition makes for inflated real estate values. The mortgage should contain a condition that the entire principal becomes immediately due and payable in the event of default. The average investor in mortgages should confine his holdings to residential property. "Special utilizations," such as office buildings, hotels, and stores, are likely to have wide fluctuations in value. Mortgages on vacant land are likewise inadvisable as true investments.

Foreign Securities. Two primary reasons exist for foreign investing: At times, the return available from foreign securities exceeds by a considerable margin the yield available on domestic investments. For some investors, the increased yield available on foreign securities is adequate to compensate for the greater chance of loss of money invested. The second reason is the desire to facilitate the financing of foreign trade. Long-term credits make a strong appeal in international trade and are made possible through the willingness of the nationals of the exporting countries to advance the necessary funds by purchasing foreign securities offered directly or indirectly in payment.

Foreign investment (other than in Canadian securities) is not recommended for the average investor due to the high degree of risk involved and the possible problems of fluctuating exchange.

Effect of Taxation. Present tax laws materially affect investment income. The Federal normal and surtax applies on all bond interest with the exception of municipal and certain government bonds. In addition to the federal taxes, many states and cities impose added taxes upon income.

Current income taxes are established on a graduated scale under which those having the largest income are generally required to pay the highest rate of tax. The maximum is 70 per cent for the federal tax. This means that an investor in the highest tax bracket may pay as much as 70 per cent of his marginal income to the federal government. Because of the high marginal tax rates, wealthy investors have purchased large amounts of tax-exempt securities. Consequently, tax-exempt securities normally sell at too high a price (and, on the other hand, too low a yield) to make them attractive to the average investor in the lower tax brackets.

The fact that capital gains are taxed at a maximum of twenty-five per cent has made them more desirable to wealthy investors than dividend or interest income. Thus, certain investors will give up stability of income for gains made through buying and selling securities.

Economic Conditions. Business conditions are constantly changing. Periods of prosperity and depression or recession have followed alternately during the entire commercial experience of the U.S. Interest rates are high when business is active, and low when business is dull. Stock prices are high when business is booming, and low when business is poor. Bond prices, peculiarly, are low during periods of activity and high during periods of inactivity. See *Business Cycles.*

The most favorable time to buy stocks is when prospective earning power is good but has not yet been reflected in the market, and the most favorable time to sell is when the price already discounts a long period of increasing profits. Generally, the most advantageous time to buy bonds is when market interest rates are high, and the best time to sell bonds is when interest rates are low.

Needless to say, there is no unfailing method of telling when the conditions are ripe for buying and selling, since only later events can provide the answer to the question of whether given conditions are the end of a "movement" or midway within it.

Security Regulation. The Federal securities acts consist of a series of measures passed in the period 1933–40 inclusive with amendments since that time. These statutes are all concerned with the subject of investment and are designed to protect the investor against dishonest and misleading practices as well as against irrational actions on his own part. The first of these measures is the Securities Act of 1933 which calls for registration of most large new issues of securities. The Act does not attempt to control the quality of the issues, but rather it is an attempt to give the investor complete and accurate information regarding possible investments. The Securities Exchange Act of 1934 was designed to control certain types of manipulations on security exchanges and to make information available on issues traded on organized exchanges. Other Acts in this group deal with public utility holding companies, over-the-counter securities, corporate reorganizations, bond indentures, investment companies, and investment advisers.

The administration of these Acts is in the hands of the Securities and Exchange Commission. This is a Commission of five members appointed by the President with the consent of the Senate. The SEC accepts all registrations of new issues and polices the organized security exchanges and security dealers. The basic philosophy of the commission and the legislation which it has fostered is to place the potential security purchaser on a more equal plane with the seller so that the purchaser may make rational and intelligent investment decisions.

Security Middlemen. Corporate securities are purchased generally through investment bankers, security dealers, and brokerage houses. Publicly-traded securities are normally not purchased direct from the issuing company. Investment bankers act as dealers rather than brokers and normally handle new issues of securities or very large offerings in the secondary market. Brokerage houses act as agents for buyers and sellers and accept a commission for their services. They deal primarily in the secondary markets. Secondary markets are those in which securities are bought and sold after the original sale by the issuing corporations. Organized security exchanges (such as the New York Stock Exchange) are the major secondary markets. However, large numbers of securities are bought and sold in the secondary market outside the organized exchanges by brokers and security dealers. This is called the over-the-counter market.

UNITED STATES SAVINGS BONDS

The tremendous amount of governmental borrowing in World War II and since has been met to some extent by United States Savings Bonds. As a medium of investment for people of moderate means, these securities have proved highly popular.

Among the reasons for their attractiveness to the mass of the people are:

1. They are made available in small denominations.

2. They can be liquidated without loss at any time after a minimum period.

3. Their purchase is supported by patriotic motives.

4 During most periods of time, they have offered the best return available for minimum risk fixed-value investment.

Purpose of Savings Bonds. Savings bonds grew out of the old postal savings system bonds. Before 1935, persons with postal savings accounts could exchange their savings for postal savings bonds. When issuance of postal savings bonds was discontinued in 1935, the government brought out savings bonds to take their place. Series E savings bonds were first issued in 1941. The guaranteed redemption value forestalled losses to the investor while the graduation of yield, rising in later years, discouraged liquidation before maturity.

An additional merit in this type of financing for government is that, unlike borrowing through the banking system, it does not create inflationary tendencies. Savings bonds may not be purchased by commercial banks and, therefore, cannot be used as a base for further credit expansion.

During World War II, the savings bond, renamed defense savings bond and later war savings bond, assumed an additional function of great importance. The war economy brought a huge increase in purchasing power accompanied by a diminution of goods and services available for purchase. To avoid the bidding up of prices, a draining off of purchasing power became essential. The leading instrument available for this purpose was the war savings bond.

Following World War II, the bonds were renamed savings bonds and have continued to be important in government finance although the total amount outstanding has not risen to any great extent in recent years.

Features of Savings Bonds. There are two major series of savings bonds of interest to the average investor. These are Series E and Series H bonds.

Series E bonds are discount bonds. They are sold at 75 per cent of their face value. Interest is not paid semi-annually as in the case of most bonds; instead, bonds are redeemed at face value at maturity with the gain on cost representing the interest on the bonds. Since the introduction of E bonds, Congress has several times shortened their maturity to increase the yield and make it competitive with that available to investors on other types of fixed-income securities. Series E bonds purchased on or after December 1, 1973, return 6 per cent interest, compounded semiannually, when held to maturity of 5 years. Outstanding E bonds that as of December 1, 1973 had not reached their first maturity receive a ½-percent increase in yield for semiannual interest periods beginning on or after December 1, 1973, payable as a bonus at maturity. Series E bonds may be redeemed at any time after 2 months after purchase and be purchased in amounts up to $5,000 per investor per year. They are non-negotiable, but a fixed market for them is maintained at all times since they are redeemable at set prices.

Series H bonds are current income bonds. They are issued in larger amounts (the smallest is $500) and mature in 10 years. The interest checks vary in amount from small to large as the period of time the bond is held increases. Series H bonds purchased on or after December 1, 1973, yield 6 per cent from date of issue to date of maturity.

All existing Series E and H savings bonds have provision for extension beyond the stated maturity if the investor so desires. They may be held for additional periods with the same yield to maturity. A substantial number of matured bonds have been held by investors for continued investment.

MONEY AND BANKING

Money plays a substantial and significant role in the determination not only of the welfare of individuals, but also of the growth and stability of the entire economy. Available and quite reliable statistics for the last century indicate that major economic fluctuations in the United States have been characterized by significant monetary and banking disorders.

Without an understanding of the monetary powers and operations of the Federal Reserve system and certain government departments, particularly the Treasury, it is impossible to comprehend the nature of domestic monetary policy problems and their international ramifications, as well as the underlying theories of the ways in which money affects the economy. While monetary policy actions are directed primarily at commercial banks, they also have an impact in varying degrees on other financial institutions.

The world is becoming increasingly characterized as one global market in which multinational industrial corporations and banks participate. The types of monetary and fiscal policies pursued by the various countries are associated with and largely determine flows of funds in financial markets within and among nations, the relative amounts of individual commodities and services produced and marketed, the total volume of employment and output, and the distribution of income and wealth. In the international realm, also, the policies and operations of two institutions with common membership, the International Monetary Fund and the International Bank for Reconstruction and Development, popularly known as the World Bank, have an important bearing upon the world economy.

What Is Money? Because of the difficulties of direct barter of goods for other goods or services and the obvious advantages of the division of labor and specialization, even primitive societies developed money relatively early in their existence. In bygone days commodities such as wheat, tobacco, or salt have served as media of exchange. The American Indians used wampum, or shells, for money. Gourds were formerly used as money in Haiti, and the monetary unit of Haiti still carries that name. The Latin word for money, *pecunia*, is derived from *pecus*, "cattle," and survives in the English word pecuniary, thus reflecting an early use of cattle as money. For thousands of years silver was a rival of gold in the coinage systems of most advanced countries of the world and was not decisively replaced by gold until the 19th century.

Gold was first coined by Croesus, King of Lydia in the 5th century B. C., and was long the most popular form of actual money. It had many attributes that made it especially valuable, both as money and as a monetary standard. These included beauty, indestructibility, high value in small bulk, homogeneity, malleability, and scarcity. The annual production, even under the most favorable conditions, never exceeded five per cent of the existing stocks. This tended to give to gold a stability in value greater than that of any other commodity. Other commodities had certain of these attributes of gold, but in the case of no other metal did the combination exist so favorably.

Today, money is no longer defined in terms of its physical substance. Instead, economists favor a broad, functional definition. Within a single society, money may take more than one form at any one time; within the same society at some other time, money may take other forms. Thus, in a given society at a given time, what is money depends upon a convention or custom and includes anything *generally* acceptable as a means of making payments. Following this definition, in the United States today, the Federal Reserve and most economists define money to include coins, paper bills, and demand (or checking) deposits. The last form is the most popular form of money, mainly because of its convenience. Some economists would even broaden the definition of money to include, for example, savings accounts and time deposits, which usually have been classified as "near monies" because they are not immediately spendable in their present form, but may ordinarily be converted to money in a short time and at little or no financial loss.

Functions of Money. Money serves several important functions quite well. It is used as a medium of exchange, as a standard of value, as a store of value, and as a standard of deferred payment. While money does not perform these functions perfectly and, indeed, at times may not perform some of them as well as something else might, the important thing to note is that money has performed this combination of functions better than any substitute.

Money is most popularly known as a medium of exchange. Without money, men with commodities and services to dispose of would be compelled to exchange them directly for other commodities or for other services. The farmer who produces wheat and desires shoes would be obliged to find someone who had shoes to exchange and who wanted wheat. Under a monetary system, producers simply exchange their production for money, and exchange the money for the commodities and services desired. The barter system of exchange is both slow and inconvenient; the money system has made possible a method of exchange infinitely more efficient.

Complementary with its use as a medium of exchange, money serves as a standard of value. Value is expressed in terms of price. Other things being equal, when the quantity of money is increased, the general price level tends to rise, and when the quantity of money is decreased, the general price level tends to fall. The general price level may change, since the values of all of its components are expressed in terms of money, whose quantity varies in accordance with central banking policy. The function of money in acting as a common denominator of values for individual commodities is decidedly useful also in enabling one to remain acquainted with the relative values of different goods without necessarily desiring immediately either to buy or to sell.

Money also serves as a store of value. People often have goods or services to dispose of without a concurrent desire for other commodities or services. By exchanging the goods immediately for money, one may hold the money indefinitely, awaiting the desired time for exchanging it. In the meantime, the money represents so much stored value. The modern form of hoarding money consists of more than holding of coins and paper notes and includes the holding of idle demand (checking) deposits.

Finally, money serves as a standard of deferred payment. All credit transactions represent the postponed payment of money. If the transaction is not immediately completed, there must be some agreement between the buyer and the seller, or between the borrower and the lender, as to the method of settlement at the due date. The purchasing power of the money may substantially change in the meantime: nevertheless, the number of dollars agreed upon remains the basis of the settlement.

The Purchasing Power of Money. The purchasing power of money is its worth in exchange for goods and services. It is highly desirable that this power be stable, but experience has shown that such is far from the case. When prices advance, the purchasing power of money falls; when prices decline, the purchasing power rises. For example, prices were much lower in 1958 than in 1970. It required $1.36 in 1970 to buy what $1 bought in 1958.

Changes in price levels represent concurrent changes in the value of money. It is important to appreciate the large influence these changes exert on business conditions. They profoundly affect credit transactions because they create risk for all parties.

They affect production, as changes in the value of materials during processing interfere with expected profits. Since interest on debt and some other charges are fixed, the effect on profits is much greater proportionately than the alterations in price level would suggest.

But most important is the fact that prices do not change uniformly. There is a wide variance, both in degree and in time. The position of the farmer in 1932, for example, was especially unfavorable because the prices of farm products had fallen much lower than other prices. This uneven variance is the main reason that many people favor a program for price stability.

CONSUMER PRICE INDEX— SELECTED ITEMS

All index figures are based on an arbitrary figure of 100 for 1967.

Item	1960	1965	1970	1975 May
Food	88.0	94.4	114.9	171.8
Meats	87.2	93.9	117.6	167.9
Dairy Products	88.4	90.0	111.8	153.6
Housing	90.2	94.9	118.9	165.3
Gas & Electricity	98.6	99.4	107.3	167.3
Health & Recreation	85.1	93.4	116.2	152.3
Medical Care	79.1	89.5	120.6	166.8
Movie Admissions	65.0	86.5	130.0	170.0
Transportation	89.6	95.9	112.7	147.4
Cars, new	104.5	100.9	107.6	126.8
Bus Fares	NA	93.7	118.4	175.5
All Items	88.7	94.5	116.3	159.3

Source: *Statistical Abstracts 1975.*

The Measurement of Prices. The general level of prices is measured through the use of index numbers. Current prices on a great many commodities are taken and a general average is secured after giving weight in accordance with the importance of each commodity. This permits one to judge the general trend of prices, not only from week to week, but also over a period of years. The Bureau of Labor Statistics issues monthly indices of wholesale prices for some commodities, consumer prices for some commodities and services, and a weekly index for a few commodities. The wholesale price index, begun in 1890, is the oldest continuous statistical series issued by the government. Since January 1971, it has been relative to the arbitrary figure of 100 for the average price of commodities in 1967. Whenever possible, the prices used are collected directly from sellers and apply to the first large-volume commercial sale of each item. The consumer index is also relative to 100 for 1967 and the prices used are for the weights of commodities that the average consumer might buy. It is with this index that the variation in the cost of living is calculated.

What Establishes the Value of Money? Money's value is determined by the relationship between demand and supply. The demand for money constantly varies. Of course, in the popular sense, there is no limit to the demand for money. The ordinary person really does not demand money, but rather the goods or the services which money commands. The demand for money depends upon the volume of transactions, upon the population, and upon the extent of the use of credit. In the period before World War II the famous British economist J. M. Keynes developed an analysis of the motives for holding money. The transactions demand for money depends largely upon the quantities of goods and services produced in the community, and thus upon the level of national income. Also, there is a precautionary motive for holding money. It arises from the desire to be able to meet possible emergencies. While the size of one's precautionary balance is related to income, it is also related to the level of interest rates, that is, to the income that would be forgone if money were held idle. Lastly,

there is a demand for money for speculative purposes. This will be small when interest rates are already high. When rises in interest rates are expected, there is a preference for holding cash in order to speculate, in effect, on bond prices.

In the post World War II period, building upon the Keynesian analysis, economists have viewed money as an asset. In this light, they regard monetary demand as the choice of money from among other assets by those holding wealth in various forms. Thus, one's demand for money is related to his total wealth and to the rate of return he expects on money in comparison with other kinds of assets. Therefore, monetary theory is part of the theory of wealth.

For the most part, the supply of money is determined by the Federal Reserve through its control over the monetary base, especially the reserve component of this base.

Formulations of the Quantity Theory of Money. The quantity theory in its various versions is perhaps the oldest of monetary theories. Dating from before the Middle Ages, it survives today and has recently had an upsurge in popularity.

Earlier forms of the theory were directed toward explaining movements of the price level by relating them to changes in the quantity of money. Modern quantity theorists are less interested in price levels and more interested in the relation between fluctuations in monetary growth and changes in the volume of economic activity and, thus, income. These, of course, have a bearing on price levels.

In their statements of causation, quantity theorists make use of the equation of exchange, an identity or truism, expressed in algebraic terms. This equation, though not a theory itself, sets forth the factors involved in the traditional theory. The equation is the most convenient approach to the study of the interdependent and interacting forces that effect changes in the level of prices in general. The most familiar form of the equation of exchange, expressed in algebraic terms, is that developed by Irving Fisher as follows: $MV + M'V' = PT$. In this equation, M equals the average quantity of money, including metallic and paper money, in circulation during a year's period, V represents the velocity or speed of circulation of money, which means the number of times the total supply of money turns over during the course of a year in facilitating trade. If the velocity of circulation of money happens to be twenty-five, only one twenty-fifth as much money is required as if its velocity were one.

The rapid turnover of money increases the efficiency of its use. M' stands for demand deposits. Actually, the "dollar on deposit" as represented by M', directly facilitates much more trade than the dollar represented by M. V' represents the velocity of circulation of bank deposits, the number of times on the average that the "dollar on deposit" does duty in an exchange transaction annually. P represents the average price paid for all units of goods acquired in an exchange transaction, and T represents the total number of units so exchanged, or the volume of trade.

If the algebraic symbols are translated into their meanings, the equation of exchange may be expressed as follows: the average quantity of money in circulation, multiplied by its velocity of circulation, plus the average quantity of bank deposits for checking, multiplied by their rate of turnover, equal the average price per unit paid for goods multiplied by the volume of trade. The total of money payments must equal the total value of all the goods acquired in exchange. Quantity theorists, by transposition, often wrote the equation: $P = \dfrac{MV + M'V'}{T}$. This equation indicates that prices vary directly with the quantity of money and of substitutes for money, together with their velocities of circulation, and inversely with the volume of trade. In general, it was then concluded, after examining the factors in the equation, that M + M were the causal factors, and the ultimate effect of changes in the quantity of money was to change the price level in the same direction and even, according to the earliest theorists, in the exact proportion.

In this transactions form, the quantity theory proved relatively useless to policy makers because they had incomplete data to analyze T, P, and V. Also, many transactions involved merely a transfer of existing goods.

Since modern quantity theorists are vitally interested in the rate of economic growth, which is measured by changes in GNP (gross national product), for which the government has reliable data reflecting the output of currently produced goods and services, it became customary to use an income version of the quantity theory. Thus, more recently, the equation of exchange has been condensed and refined. Usually it is now written as either $MV_y = P_yT_y$ or $V_y = \dfrac{GNP}{M}$. M is the money supply as defined today; P_yT_y or GNP represents currently produced output (or income); and V_y refers to the income velocity of money, the number of times on the average and for the period (usually one year) that a dollar is spent for final goods or services produced during this period. In recent years, V_y has been quite constant and has averaged about 3, as calculated by dividing GNP by the money supply. In other words, on the average, $1 has accounted for $3 of income for the annual period. Because of the relative constancy of V, the modern quantity theorist argues that changes in M are the usual factor in the determination of the level of GNP.

Two leading present-day quantity theorists, Milton Friedman and Anna Schwartz, have analyzed a century of statistics comparing fluctuations in business activity with the rate of growth of the money stock and have found close correspondence between the two, as evidenced by variable lags in which monetary changes consistently have led changes in economic activity by periods of at least months and sometimes a year or more.

The Use of Credit. The extent of the use of credit has been given as one of the factors affecting the demand for money. Credit is also an economic contrivance enabling society to allocate resources. It is a device that not only makes it possible for individuals to spread their consumption over time, but also provides business with large-scale capital formation, and the economy with technological progress and economic growth.

It is important to note that credit and debt are two aspects of the same thing. For every creditor (lender) there is a debtor (borrower). A potential debtor's ability to obtain credit is based upon his present and expected future income, the amount and nature of his assets and collateral, and, of course,

PUBLIC DEBT OF THE UNITED STATES
Source: *U.S. Treasury Department*

June 30	Amount in Millions of Dollars	Per Capita Dollars
1800	83	15.87
1900	1,263	16.56
1920	24,299	228.33
1930	16,185	131.49
1940	40,440	308.29
1950	257,357	1,696.11
1955	274,374	1,660.56
1956	272,825	1,621.82
1959	284,706	1,607.57
1960	286,331	1,586.07
1961	288,971	1,574.80
1962	298,201	1,600.53
1963	305,860	1,619.32
1964	312,526	*1,627.00
1965	317,864	*1,634.00
1967	326,221	*1,637.00
1969	353,720	*1,741.00
1970	382,603	*1,875.00
1975	544,131	*2,542.00

*Based upon Bureau of Census est. of pop.

upon his character, particularly his willingness to meet obligations promptly.

Credit or debt is usually evidenced by either open-book accounts or by written instruments such as promissory notes, drafts, acceptances, or bonds. Oral agreements are much less satisfactory, partly because there is difficulty in proving their existence. Bank loans, as well as loans extended by other financial institutions, are, of course, examples of credit transactions.

The Gold Coin Standard and the Limited Gold Bullion Standards. In 1900 the United States legally established the gold coin standard and remained on it until 1933. Many other countries also have made use of this standard. Each nation had its own distinctive unit of account. In order that commerce could be carried on readily among nations, it was essential that there be some common standard for determining the relative values of these national currencies. That standard was provided by gold. Nations defined their units of account as a definite weight of pure gold. Thus, par value could be expressed for the various currencies by comparing their gold equivalents.

The gold content of the dollar was originally 24.75 grains, being so defined in 1792. In 1834, it was altered to 23.22 grains.

The gold dollar retained its 1834 value for a century. In 1933 Congress voted to end the gold coin standard and authorized the president to reduce the dollar's gold equivalent by as much as 50%. On January 31, 1934, President Franklin D. Roosevelt established a $35 price per ounce (480 grains) of gold and defined the American dollar, therefore, as equivalent to 13.71 grains of gold. At this time, the country changed to the limited gold bullion standard, under which gold coins and gold certificates were exchanged for other money, and gold was henceforth kept in bar form in several depositories, of which Fort Knox, Kentucky, is the best known. Gold certificates became the legal reserves of the twelve Federal Reserve banks.

Modifications of a Full Gold Standard. A nation may be legally on a gold standard, and yet the circulation of gold may be modified in various degrees. The chief restrictions include:

1. Circulation of coinage is forbidden, but paper money is convertible into gold bars or bullion. Countries having this system are said to be on the *gold bullion standard*. The purpose is to discourage the circulation of gold, which can be used more economically as a basis for credit money.

2. All domestic circulation of gold is forbidden, both that of coin and of bullion.

3. Export of gold is forbidden except under governmental license.

Devaluation. When the United States suspended the operation of the gold coin standard in 1933, restrictions numbered 2 and 3 were used. At the same time all gold was nationalized. By this move the Federal government obtained all "profit" from the procedure by which the same amount of gold was made to represent 69 per cent more dollars.

Of this profit, amounting to about 2,800 million dollars, approximately two billion dollars was used as a *stabilization fund*, the purpose of which was to keep on an even keel the foreign exchange rate between the dollar and other currencies.

Other things being equal, devaluation of the currency has a tendency to raise domestic prices. It acts most quickly on those of goods which are bought abroad, the effect then spreading slowly to other prices. Until this process is completed, there is a stimulus to export trade.

Stabilization of Currencies. The chief purpose of a freely operating gold standard was to make possible the conversion of one national currency into others at an approximately constant level. Foreign currencies or short-term credit instruments payable in them are known as pieces of foreign exchange when held by residents of other countries.

In practice, conversion was a market transaction, the price of each currency being determined by supply and demand. Price changes in foreign exchange, however, usually received an automatic check when they rose above, or fell below, a certain point. When gold flowed freely, this point was known as the *gold export point*. Under managed currencies, it is known as the point of support or the *stabilization point*.

The gold export point under a full gold standard may be defined as the point of price increase in a foreign currency at which it becomes more profitable to ship gold instead of buying the foreign currency.

In theory, inequalities in the distribution of gold among nations should be self-correcting. When one country receives an unduly large supply, prices would normally rise. This rise would make it easier for foreign countries to sell in that market and harder for producers there to sell abroad. Hence the imports would tend to be larger than the exports, and would have to be paid for by the export of gold. This in turn would tend to lower domestic prices and encourage export trade.

Difficulties in Maintaining a Full Gold Standard. Many obstacles to this self-corrective process arose. In the first place, the increase of gold may or may not be followed by a proportional increase of currency and credit, which are actual determinants of price level. Central bank policies and national habits may prevent such increases in money and credit. The normal effect of the gold influx is thereby "sterilized." This result occurred in France and, to a certain extent, in the United States in the years 1928-30, when these two countries together acquired about two-thirds of the world's monetary gold.

Even though the price level does rise, tariff barriers and other restrictions may be imposed to prevent the inflow of goods. Other countries, therefore, have no opportunity to acquire claims to the excessive gold so as to bring about its redistribution.

Balance of Payments. The United States "balance of payments" is an expression used to designate an estimated (by the Commerce Department) and itemized account of all the transactions that lead to flows of funds between U.S. residents and those of other countries.

Balance of payments accountants use a double-entry format showing the goods, services, and securities that are exported or imported, as well as how these transactions are financed. Since the means of finance is not always known for particular transactions, some estimates are incomplete. Others are inconsistent because they are based upon a number of statistical sources. For these reasons an errors-and-omissions entry is used to make the balance of payments actually balance.

Even though receipts and expenditures relative to other countries are equal, the balance of payments may be said to be in disequilibrium if the U.S. either loses or gains monetary reserves, or if its short-term monetary liabilities to foreigners are increased or decreased. The prevalence of these situations means that payments and receipts are equal only because of "induced" or "accommodating" capital flows in the form of movements of official reserves, that is, gold and convertible currencies. Autonomous outflows do not equal autonomous inflows when induced capital flows are necessary. The country is said to be in a state of surplus when it acquires monetary reserves, and in deficit when it loses monetary reserves.

Managed Currencies. The great depression beginning in 1929 led to partial or complete suspension of full gold standards by every nation in the world. Stability of exchange rates was made to depend on action by governments or central banks. Such action is known as currency management, and nations were said to be on managed, inconvertible paper standards domestically, whereas gold was used chiefly as an international monetary reserve.

The plan adopted by the United States, as by Great Britain and France, was the use of a stabilization fund. Thus when the dollar price of the pound or franc deviated by a certain amount from a point chosen as normal, the Treasury of the U.S. would buy or sell pounds or francs until the normal price was restored. This action was called "pegging" or "supporting" the foreign exchange rate.

Many other countries met the situation by limiting transactions in foreign currencies so as to make purchases balance sales. German nationals, for instance, could not obtain dollars until Americans had purchased an equivalent value of marks.

International transactions after 1950 multiplied many times in volume while gold stocks increased very moderately. A world-wide credit shortage developed into crisis proportions in 1966. Remedies proposed included devaluation of gold in terms of the leading currencies to creation of an international medium of exchange. Ultimately, through the auspices of the International Monetary Fund, the SDR (special drawing rights) plan was adopted, under which bookkeeping entries known as SDR's were created for use by governments and central banks to serve as an addition to the existing pool of international reserves.

The Rate of Interest. Interest is the cost of borrowing money. The rate changes with conditions of business, and is determined by the demand for and the supply of loanable funds. The businessman seldom withdraws actual money at his bank when arranging a loan. He secures a credit to his deposit account which he draws against in payment of his obligations.

The average business man is a constant borrower at his bank. He needs additional capital for the operation and expansion of his business, and secures it through his banks and other institutional lenders or through the selling of negotiable short-term, intermediate, or long-term credit instruments in the open market. The extent to which he borrows depends upon the relationship between the cost of borrowing—the rate of interest—and the return he can obtain in his business from the added investment. There must be or appear to be a profit margin, or he will not borrow. Low rates of interest therefore tend to encourage borrowing by businessmen and make

MONEY IN CIRCULATION, BY DENOMINATION: 1960 TO 1974
(In millions of dollars. As of December 31.)

Denomination	1960	1965	1970	1972	1974
Total*	32,869	42,056	57,093	66,516	79,743
Coin and small denomination currency	23,521	29,842	39,639	45,105	51,606
Coin†	2,427	4,027	6,281	7,287	8,332
$1	1,533	1,908	2,310	2,523	2,720
$2	88	127	136	135	135
$5	2,246	2,618	3,161	3,449	3,718
$10	6,691	7,794	9,170	9,827	10,503
$20	10,536	13,369	18,581	21,883	26,197
Large denomination currency	9,348	12,214	17,454	21,411	28,137
$50	2,815	3,540	4,896	5,868	7,444
$100	5,954	8,135	12,084	15,118	20,298
$500	249	245	215	193	179
$1,000	316	288	252	225	209
$5,000	3	3	3	2	4
$10,000	10	4	4	4	4

* Outside Treasury and Federal Reserve Banks.   † Paper currency only; $1 silver coins reported under coin.
Source: *Statistical Abstracts, 1975.*

for increased business activity. High rates of interest may, depending upon profit prospects, discourage borrowing and make for decreased business activity.

Money in the United States. The present monetary standard of the United States may be described from the domestic standpoint as an inconvertible managed paper standard, and from the international standpoint as a restricted or limited gold bullion standard.

Credit Money in the United States. Credit money is also called representative money. All money which circulates freely in the United States is credit money. This applies to metallic coins as well as to paper money.

By far the greatest part of representative money in the United States consists of Federal Reserve notes, described below. These and subsidiary coins are the backbone of the money system, although there are a number of other types, most of which are gradually being withdrawn from circulation.

National bank notes in the later 19th century constituted a principal form of currency, supplemented by gold certificates and silver certificates. Gold certificates were withdrawn from circulation in 1934, when the dollar was devalued in terms of gold. Silver certificates, however, in that year were given a larger role in credit money. The treasury was directed by the Silver Purchase Act to buy silver and add it to the total money stock until its value, computed at $1.29 an ounce, was equal to one-fourth of the money stock or until its market price reached $1.29 an ounce.

In 1963, however, when the market price did reach about $1.29 an ounce, the act was repealed, and the treasury was directed to gradually withdraw silver certificates from circulation and replace them by Federal Reserve notes. Other metals were substituted also for silver in subsidiary coins to prevent them from being melted down for the silver in them. Redemption of silver certificates ended on June 30, 1968.

Advantages of Credit Money. The wide use of credit money as a substitute for standard money is due to two important advantages:

It is more economical. The use of credit money, which is easily and quite inexpensively manufactured, relieves the demand for gold, which is much more difficult and costly to produce.

It makes possible an elastic currency supply. In view of the fact that the demand for money is constantly changing, it is highly desirable that the supply be regulated accordingly; otherwise, price levels will constantly fluctuate. Elasticity of currency means the power to expand and to contract according to the needs of business. The supply of gold currency in circulation may be increased or decreased only with extreme difficulty; the supply of paper currency and other credit money may be easily regulated, as in the case of Federal Reserve notes. Yet paper currency has value because its supply is controlled.

Federal Reserve Notes. The most important currency used in the United States today is the Federal Reserve note. These are issued by the Federal Reserve banks and are essentially promissory notes of these banks. For each of these notes outstanding the Federal Reserve Bank must maintain certain assets. The reserve for these notes is no longer partly gold certificates as in the past.

An example of a traditional rediscount (or discount, the term preferred by the Federal Reserve) follows. This particular example results in the creation of Federal Reserve notes. Jones, a rancher in Montana, borrows $500 from the National Bank of Butte for sixty days to enable him to market his wool crop. The banks may rediscount the promissory note given by Jones with the Federal Reserve Bank of Minneapolis, receiving Federal Reserve notes. When Jones repays his loan, the rediscount can be paid off, and the Federal Reserve notes retired.

DEPOSITS IN U.S. COMMERCIAL BANKS
December 31, 1974
(In millions of dollars)

STATE	Total	Demand	Time
Alabama	8,367	3,669	4,698
Alaska	1,004	494	510
Arizona	5,710	2,147	3,563
Arkansas	5,428	2,477	2,951
California	79,184	27,916	51,268
Colorado	6,989	3,360	3,629
Connecticut	6,983	3,584	3,399
Delaware	1,840	816	1,024
Dist. of Columbia	3,586	2,069	1,517
Florida	24,094	10,694	13,400
Georgia	12,157	5,905	6,252
Hawaii	2,444	964	1,480
Idaho	2,433	999	1,434
Illinois	58,610	21,729	36,881
Indiana	16,513	6,271	10,242
Iowa	10,589	4,127	6,462
Kansas	7,964	3,662	4,302
Kentucky	9,090	4,412	4,678
Louisiana	11,017	4,897	6,120
Maine	1,825	730	1,095
Maryland	8,012	3,557	4,455
Massachusetts	14,788	7,407	7,381
Michigan	28,101	9,263	18,838
Minnesota	13,887	5,263	8,624
Mississippi	5,144	2,335	2,809
Missouri	16,159	7,781	8,378
Montana	2,617	977	1,640
Nebraska	5,767	2,681	3,086
Nevada	1,752	710	1,042
New Hampshire	1,485	546	939
New Jersey	20,882	8,215	12,631
New Mexico	2,651	1,115	1,536
New York	132,712	65,943	66,769
North Carolina	11,895	5,177	6,718
North Dakota	2,235	907	1,328
Ohio	29,636	11,194	18,442
Oklahoma	9,210	4,111	5,099
Oregon	5,577	2,281	3,296
Pennsylvania	42,661	15,480	27,181
Rhode Island	3,099	905	2,194
South Carolina	3,867	2,193	1,674
South Dakota	2,614	911	1,703
Tennessee	12,287	4,849	7,438
Texas	42,516	20,692	21,824
Utah	2,959	1,269	1,690
Vermont	1,237	349	888
Virginia	13,084	4,914	8,170
Washington	8,699	3,549	5,150
West Virginia	4,980	1,855	3,125
Wisconsin	13,951	4,899	9,052
Wyoming	1,422	572	850
United States	741,713	312,858	428,855

Source: *Statistical Abstract of the United States, 1975.*

Thus the commercial bank rediscounted its customers' promissory notes with the Federal Reserve Bank. The provision of this facility was one of the most important innovations of the Federal Reserve Act. However, today banks do not have to rediscount their customers' promissory notes in order to obtain funds from the Federal Reserve Banks. They can obtain advances secured by government securities. Under the Banking Act of 1935 the Federal Reserve Banks can also make longer-term advances secured by any assets which the Federal Reserve banks approve.

Rediscounts and advances normally do not result in the creation of Federal Reserve notes. The funds may merely be added to the reserve balances, which the member banks are required to hold with the Federal Reserve banks. (Part of a member bank's deposit balance constitutes required legal reserve. The rest is called an excess legal reserve. The sum of the two constitutes the bank's total portion of legal reserve on deposit. The remainder of its legal reserve consists of vault cash.) Similar results can be obtained through purchases of government bonds by the Federal Reserve system. See *Open Market Operations.* Today most money is created by the latter method.

Legal Tender. Any form of currency which the law states must be accepted in payment of obligations is known as legal tender. Since 1933 all forms of United States currency have been fully legal tender. Before that date, a large proportion of it was not, notably Federal Reserve notes and silver certificates. Some of the coins had only limited legal tender qualities. But since all forms of currency bore the promise of the government to redeem in lawful money on demand, the distinction between what was and what was not legal tender was of little practical importance.

Money and the Banks. In the popular sense, banks are institutions where money is stored for safe-keeping. This is far from being the case, however. A bank may be holding many thousands of dollars on deposit for its patrons. But, under ordinary circumstances, only a very small fraction of this amount is carried as money in the vaults of the bank. One may wonder why banks are willing to safeguard the funds of their depositors without making a charge for the service. The answer is that the bank lends money to depositors and others and receives interest payments upon the loans. In some cases, the bank shares this revenue with its patrons by paying interest on the deposits. American banks are forbidden to pay interest on demand deposits.

Kinds of Banks. Just as there are different kinds of stores at which we may purchase various kinds of commodities, so there are various kinds of banks with which to do business. The percentage of the country's banking strength represented in the Federal Reserve system is evidenced by the following statistics:

NUMBER OF COMMERCIAL BANKS IN U.S.

June 30, 1975

Member banks		5,794
National banks	4,730	
State banks	1,064	
Non-member banks		8,779
Insured	8,526	
Non-insured	253	
Total number of banks		14,573

Numerically, over one-third of the banks of the country are members of the Federal Reserve system, but these banks hold approximately 80% of all commercial assets.

Commercial Banks. Commercial banks are unique in that their demand or checking deposits circulate as money and are the largest component of our money supply. The name "commercial" was first widely applied to these banks over a century ago when the view was held in both England and the United States that institutions accepting and creating demand deposits should restrict their lending for the most part to short-term, self-liquidating business loans extended for working capital purposes such as meeting the payroll or acquiring raw materials. However, these banks today are allowed to lend for a wide variety of purposes and to extend loans in all maturity ranges.

Since depositors may at any time without notice draw against their demand deposits by writing checks, the banks must exercise extreme caution in lending because they often cannot tell in advance just when the depositor is going to withdraw or transfer his funds. Banks know from experience, however, that it is extremely unlikely that all the depositors will ask repayment on the same day. They know also that the new deposits each day tend to equal the amount of the withdrawals. Consequently they feel safe in lending an amount equal to the larger share of their deposits.

Sometimes a rumor of unsatisfactory conditions at a bank will cause depositors to become apprehensive of the safety of their deposits and will result in large withdrawals in short intervals. This is known as a "run" on the bank. Unless the bank can meet the sudden demand, it will be obliged to suspend operations. The Federal Reserve banks enable a solvent but hard-pressed bank to turn some of its loans and other assets into cash to pay in-sistent depositors. Also, existence of the Federal Deposit Insurance Corporation makes runs less likely.

This machinery, particularly as recently liberalized to permit rediscounting of "approved" assets instead of "commercial paper" only, is designed to make longer-term loans no less safe for commercial banks than the 60- and 90-day loans to which they largely confined themselves in the past.

Bank Deposits. Banks accept funds on deposit from their patrons and make a corresponding credit in the deposit book of the patron and on their own books of account. It should be appreciated that the funds deposited immediately become the property of the bank and that the depositor becomes a creditor of the bank to that amount. Items which are payable at other banks are credited conditionally, subject to collection. If payment is refused at the other bank, the credit at the first bank is canceled.

Deposits are of two kinds, demand and time or savings. A demand deposit is subject to withdrawal at any time at the option of the depositor. A time deposit may not be withdrawn before the expiration of the definite period for which the deposit was made. Time deposits are more satisfactory to the bank, because the institution knows in advance when withdrawal may be expected. Savings accounts may be withdrawn after advance notice is given unless this requirement is waived by the bank.

Deposit Insurance. Through an agency known as the Federal Deposit Insurance Corporation, the United States government insures all deposit accounts in all member banks of the Federal Reserve system and in other banks which are willing and able to pay for the service. On the failure of one of these banks, depositors are paid up to the amount insured.

Each deposit is insured up to $20,000. Cost of the insurance is defrayed by assessing a modest premium, usually 1/12 of 1% of total deposits. All national banks having deposits insured are required to join the Federal Reserve system, but state banks may insure without joining.

Bank Checks. A check is an order drawn upon a bank by one who has funds in that bank to pay a certain sum to another party upon demand. The party to whom the check is payable may possibly present the check to that bank and secure cash from the bank. More probably, he will deposit the check in his own bank for credit to his account. Each day the banks exchange these checks, usually through a clearing house. In this way, the payee receives his funds without being obliged personally to present the check for payment, and the banks are relieved of the obligation of carrying large cash reserves to meet checks presented by individuals for payment. The depositors in a certain bank may during one day draw checks aggregating $10,000; yet that same day the bank may receive in deposits $15,000 in checks on other banks. The net result is an increase of $5000 in the funds of the bank, despite the fact that checks for $10,000 were drawn against it.

Payment by check is the most popular method in this country. At least three-quarters of the daily business transactions are settled on this basis.

Bank Loans. From the banker's viewpoint, he is in business to make loans and investments. Deposits and withdrawals are simply a service which he offers as an inducement for customers, but which, of themselves, bring no profit to the bank unless service charges are set high enough to do so. The bank profits, as has been stated before, from the interest it receives upon its loans and securities.

Loans differ in thousands of ways. One man desires to borrow $1000 for ten days to meet his payroll at a time when his cash balance is low; a second man desires to borrow $10,000 to finance the purchase of one hundred shares of United States Steel Common Stock as a speculation for an indefinite period; a third man wishes to borrow $5000 for five years to buy a home; and so on.

Commercial loans should never exceed one year initially, but they may be renewed. A depositor is usually permitted to borrow in proportion to his bank balance. If he is well and favorably known, he will secure the credit upon his simple promissory note; otherwise, he may be obliged to pledge collateral as security. The more marketable the collateral, the more satisfactory it is to the banker. The interest charge is often collected in advance when the loan is made. The bank is usually less interested in what the borrower is going to do with the funds than it is in the chance for repayment; yet the two are closely interrelated. Often the depositor is expected to allow a part of his loan—about one-fifth —to remain on deposit. This portion is called a compensating balance. For the ordinary bank, the loans average about three-quarters of the deposits in prosperous periods.

The total loans outstanding in the commercial banks of the United States run into enormous figures. At the present time, the total is over $750,000,000,000.

Rediscounting Loans. Banks which are members of the Federal Reserve system are permitted to rediscount customers' promissory notes. All loans are not eligible for this purpose, especially those which are made for stock speculation. The Cleveland Trust Company may lend $5000 to a manufacturer in Cleveland, and then have the Federal Reserve bank of Cleveland rediscount it, in the same manner as was previously mentioned in connection with the Montana bank. The rediscount privilege greatly increases the lending power of the member banks. But, more important, it allows the bank quickly to convert loans into cash in times of emergency. This rediscount privilege used to be much more important than it is today. The Federal Reserve now has more effective ways to increase the lending power of banks.

Other Forms of Loans. Other forms of loans handled by commercial banks include drafts and acceptances. Brown in Albany buys merchandise from White in Buffalo on terms of thirty days. White may immediately draw an order upon Brown, payable in thirty days, and have this order, or draft as it is called, discounted at his Buffalo bank in the same manner in which he would discount his personal promissory note. An acceptance is a draft which bears the written acceptance of the party upon whom it is drawn that payment will be made when due. Many firms now have their customers sign acceptances upon receipt of goods. In this manner the firm is able to receive immediate payment through discounting the acceptance at its local bank. Otherwise the firm would have to wait until the invoice was due before receiving the money.

Types of Commercial Banks. Commercial banks are divided into two classes, depending upon the method of incorporation. National banks receive a Federal charter. State banks receive charters from the states in which they are located.

National banks are required to operate under the provisions of the National Banking Act, as amended. Minimum capital requirements are established for country and city banks. With certain exceptions, loans cannot be made to any individual in an amount in excess of 10% of the capital of the bank. In addition, there are other loan limitation provisions. These banks were formerly permitted to issue circulation notes backed by government bonds, but this privilege was discontinued on August 1, 1935.

National banks are permitted to have branches under the same terms as state banks within states which grant this privilege to state banks. National banks must be members of the Federal Reserve system and of the Federal Deposit Insurance Corporation.

State banks operate under the banking laws of the respective states. These laws vary widely but, in the main, follow closely the Federal law. State banks are permitted, though not required, to join the Federal Reserve system if they can qualify.

Item	1950	1974
Number of Banks	14,164	14,448
Assets	170.5	927.5
Loans & Securities	128.0	750.3
Cash, balances with banks, etc.	40.4	128.8
Liabilities & Capital Accounts	170.5	927.5
Deposits	156.1	753.6
Demand	118.8	317.5
Time	37.3	436.1
Business & Personal	129.4	608.9
Government	12.6	74.6
Capital Accounts	11.7	64.0
Capital Notes and Debentures	0.0	4.4
Equity Capital	11.6	59.6
Stock	3.6	15.0
Surplus	5.3	25.3
Undivided profits & reserves	2.7	19.1

Source: *Federal Reserve Bulletin.*

Federal Reserve System. The Federal Reserve system is the machinery by which a central control may be exercised over the expansion and contraction of the money supply and credit. The Reserve system may be said to be the most potent instrument for good or ill in American economic life.

Before this machinery for credit control is described, it should be noted that it cannot actually produce credit if there is no demand for credit, that is, if people do not wish to borrow. What it can do is to make credit easier or more difficult to obtain.

The Reserve system comprises 12 Federal Reserve banks and about 6400 member banks. The Federal Reserve banks are located in the following cities: Boston, New York, Philadelphia, Cleveland, Richmond, Atlanta, Chicago, Saint Louis, Minneapolis, Kansas City, Dallas, and San Francisco. Each Reserve bank may have branches under certain conditions.

The Federal Reserve banks are bankers' banks. Except under emergency conditions, they deal only with banks and governments. Their capital is subscribed to by the member banks to an amount equal to 6 per cent of the capital and surplus of each subscribing bank. Each Reserve bank is permitted to pay to stockholders from its earnings a cumulative dividend of 6 per cent of its paid up capital. The balance is transferred to reserve.

Purposes of the System. The two most important dates in the history of the Federal Reserve system are 1914 and 1936.

On the first of these dates, the system was established and most of the control mechanisms were established.

On the second date, 1936, additional controls were provided, and all of them were placed in the guiding hands of one authoritative commission, known as the Board of Governors of the Federal Reserve System. The enabling law was passed in 1935. Since that time there have been many more amendments to the Act.

The Reserve banks were created in the first place to prevent recurrence of the "money squeeze" known as the currency panic of 1907. They provided elasticity or flexibility of the currency supply.

The system was strengthened in 1936 to avoid, as far as possible, a recurrence of an unstable boom, such as that which preceded 1929, and the collapse of credit which followed.

The following paragraphs outline the chief features of the system. Under the headings *Legal Reserves*, *Rediscount Rate* and *Open Market Operations* are described the credit control methods originally provided. The additional controls established in 1936 are explained under the heading *Margin Requirements*, while, under *Board of Governors*, is described the way in which central control may be excercised.

Legal Reserves. Each member bank is required to keep on deposit with the Federal Reserve Bank of its district a sum which, in addition to its vault cash, constitutes the member bank's legal reserve. This reserve must be maintained at a certain minimum percentage of deposit liabilities, the percentage depending on the type of deposit and the location of the bank, and being subject to change by the Board of Governors of the Federal Reserve System. See *Raising of Reserves.*

Lower reserves are required against time deposits than against deposits payable on demand. The pooling of a part of reserves in central institutions has one distinct advantage. It reduces to a minimum the transfer of actual cash from one part of the country to another. When a check on a member bank in Bangor, Maine, is paid by a member bank in Fresno, California, money is not sent from Bangor to Fresno in settlement, but the transfer is effected by a debit and credit entry in the Federal Reserve books. This entry signifies the transfer of a definite amount of ownership in the so-called gold settlement fund, which is held in Washington. It is due to this procedure that there is usually no collection charge for checks drawn on member banks. All member banks have been classified according to their location as either Reserve City or Country banks.

FEDERAL RESERVE SYSTEM
ASSETS AND LIABILITIES OF ALL MEMBER BANKS

(All money in $ millions)	1947	1960	1970	1974
Loans	$32,628	$99,933	$253,936	$429,537
U.S. Treasury Securities . .	57,914	49,106	45,399	38,921
Other Security Investments .	7,304	16,579	66,604	100,073
Total Deposits .	122,528	193,029	384,596	575,563
Cash Assets .	32,845	45,756	81,500	106,995
Borrowings . .	54	130	18,578	52,850
Capital Accounts	8,464	17,398	34,100	48,240
Number of Banks	6,923	6,174	5,767	5,780

Source: *Federal Reserve Board.*

Rediscount Rate. The Federal Reserve banks may exert a considerable effect on the expansion or contraction of business by two devices intended as general or quantitative controls. One is raising or lowering of the rediscount rate. The other is known as open-market operations.

A member bank may command the liquid resources of its reserve bank by rediscounting "eligible paper" that it holds. Or it may borrow on its own promissory note secured by eligible paper or United States government obligations, such as bonds and Treasury certificates.

By raising the rate of interest charged member banks when they wish to borrow on eligible paper, a reserve bank tries to discourage borrowing and serves notice to the business community that it regards current expansion as excessive. On the other hand, by lowering the rediscount rate, it tries to encourage borrowing and the consequent expansion of credit.

Open-Market Operations. By this term is meant the purchase or sale of government securities, bankers' acceptances, foreign exchange, and a few other things by the Federal Reserve banks. These operations automatically expand or contract the nation's monetary base and money supply. When Jones sells a $1000 bond to Smith, there is merely a transfer of funds or credit from one individual to another. But when a Federal Reserve bank buys a $1000 bond, it issues new funds in payment. When it sells a bond, it withdraws the funds it receives. Since the funds so created or destroyed may be the basis of many times their face value in bank credit, one can see how large an influence the reserve banks can exert on economic activity.

Variation of Reserve Requirements. All member banks have been classified as either reserve city or country banks. Congress has fixed a range of

from 10 to 22% for reserve requirements against net demand deposits (gross demand deposits less balances due from other domestic banks and cash items in process of collection) for reserve city member banks and 7 to 14% for country member banks. For all member banks, Congress has set a range of 3 to 10% against time and savings deposits. The Board of Governors of the Federal Reserve System may vary reserve requirements within these limits to offset or to prevent undesirable changes in the money supply. If it wishes, the Board may apply differential reserve requirements; that is, it may break each type of deposit into two or more brackets and apply a lower percentage to, for example, the first $5 million of deposits than to amounts above that. Reserves are now computed on a weekly basis. Weekly average required reserves are not based on average net customers' deposits and average vault cash held two weeks earlier but on the bank's own average deposits at the Federal Reserve as of the current week. There is a 2% carry-over of excesses or deficiencies.

While originally reserve requirements were meant to compel banks to maintain adequate liquidity, today they are used for purposes of control. In general, this tool is used relatively infrequently because of its uneven impact on banks and the serious side effects associated with it.

Margin Requirements. To check speculation on the stock exchanges, the Board of Governors of the Federal Reserve is empowered to set rules to govern the amount of money which may be lent to finance the purchase of a given value of securities. This applies both to member banks and to brokers doing business on stock exchanges. See *Margin.*

Board of Governors. The most important change in the banking system effected in 1936 was to place more authority in the hands of the reserve board. The old board had the right to recommend use of controls and to see that policies pursued by the twelve Reserve banks were within the law. Actually, control over each of the twelve banks was exercised by officers of those banks, who were private bankers and not public officials. Concerted action by the entire system was difficult if not impossible to effect.

The new board, consisting of seven members appointed for 14-year staggered terms by the president, with the advice and consent of the Senate, is armed with actual control. Its decisions are mandatory in setting the rediscount rate, reserve requirements, and margins for security speculators. Policies for open-market operations are set by a committee consisting of these seven board members and five senior officers of the reserve banks, chosen regionally on an alternating basis.

Furthermore, the presidents of the twelve Reserve banks must be acceptable to the board of governors. Additional assurances that the system shall be operated in the public interest rather than for the profit of bankers include a provision that members of the board of governors may not return to the private banking business for two years after the expiration of their terms of office.

The policy of the board is insulated from influence of the executive branch of the government through a requirement that the terms of members expire in rotation at two-year intervals. It would take six to eight years for a president to have his appointees form a majority of the board.

The reason for this precaution is to prevent the government from using the banking system as a source of indefinitely large Federal loans if the Federal Reserve board does not agree with government policy. It should be noted that, while the Federal Reserve banks are privately owned, the central banks of other major nations are owned by their governments. The Federal Reserve system is legally and structurally independent of the national government, yet it was created by Congress and can be abolished by Congress.

Government as Banker. The Federal government began providing credit for its citizens with the establishing of the Farm Loan Banks in 1916. See *Farm Loan Banks*. These banks were provided for farmers who demanded mortgage money for farm property at rates comparable to those prevailing in cities.

World War I, the Depression of the Thirties, and World War II brought a vast expansion in government lending. Through the War Finance Corporation, Federal funds were advanced to private corporations for the purpose of enabling them to forestall serious failures in financial institutions during the deflation period of the early 1930's. Banks, insurance companies, and later, railroads, states, school districts, and even private individuals were beneficiaries. The Federal Deposit Insurance Corporation was created by the Act of 1933 and made permanent in the Banking Act of 1935. Through this act the insurance of deposits was made mandatory for members of the Federal Reserve system and optional for sound non-member banks. Deposits in insured banks are fully protected up to $20,000 for each depositor. This provides 100 per cent insurance coverage to the vast majority of all the depositors in the insured banks of the country.

Two forms of credit constitute the credit structure of American business, namely: investment credit and commercial credit. The Federal government adopted the National Banking Act of 1863, by which it chartered national banks; about 5000 such banks were in existence at the beginning of 1951. Twelve Federal Reserve banks were chartered by the U. S. Government in 1914 and since then have established 24 branches. In 1916, the Federal Farm Loan act authorized the creation of special types of mortgage banks, designed to help finance agriculture. In 1932 a system of Federal Home Loan banks was established to provide a nationwide credit facility to mortgage lending institutions to help meet extraordinary needs of savers and borrowers. In the same year the Reconstruction Finance Corporation was created by Congress to help meet an emergency situation. With a capital of 500 million dollars, the RFC loaned to banks themselves funds to liquidate frozen credits and to strengthen their capital structures. The Home Owners Loan Corporation provided capital for individual home purchasers and, in the financial operations of World War II, the Reconstruction Finance Corporation, through such affiliates as the Defense Plant Corporation and the Defense Supplies Corporation, provided investment of billions of dollars.

In 1933 there were organized the Federal Farm Mortgage corporation, to refinance farm mortgages in distress, and the Home Owners Loan Corporation, to provide emergency relief to home owners under threat of foreclosure of their homes, and to refinance their homes on easier terms that they might retain ownership. During their statutory lending period, 1,017,821 loans were made in the aggregate amount of $3,093,451,321. Financial institutions and individual lenders received $2,750,-000,000 from the HOLC for frozen mortgages and paid $490 million to local cities and towns for delinquent taxes of its borrowers, and taxes on its own acquired properties. 800,000 homeowners were saved from loss of their property through foreclosure. Liquidation of the Corporation was completed in October 1950, and in the following year $14,023,649.82 was paid to the Treasury of the United States.

Additional banking aid for farmers includes: 12 intermediate credit banks, which discount agricultural paper as the Federal Reserve banks do commercial paper; 12 production credit corporations, which lend money for general farm transactions much as the Federal Land banks do for purchase of farms; and one central bank and 12 regional banks for financing farm co-operatives. In all these agencies, the government owns the stock but most of the capital comes from private investors.

Thousands of co-operative savings and loan associations have been organized pursuant to the Federal Credit Union act of 1934 and subsequent amendments, and pursuant to similar legislation enacted in all but a few of the 50 states.

Truth-in-Lending. A bill passed by Congress in 1968 requires lenders to list credit costs of all transactions in terms of approximate "effective annual" rates. Credit information must be complete, true, and comparable—that is, calculated at annual rates under the same specifications by all lenders. "Extortionate extension of credit" was barred by the bill and made punishable by imprisonment and fine. A significant provision also required disclosure of "true" annual interest rates on first mortgages on housing.

Credit Cards. These cards permit holders to obtain goods or services without immediate payment. Of plastic or cardboard, the cards are numbered and often carry photographs for identification. In the 1960's millions used them for travel, telephone calls, and to buy all types of goods. Cards are issued to those with good credit, and businessmen are heavy users since the cards provide full expense records. Bank, hotel, restaurant, auto rental, airline, and oil company cards are among the most common. Charges are usually billed for the preceding month and prompt payment is normally expected.

Savings Banks. As the name indicates, savings banks aim to provide a place to safeguard the savings of the people. The funds are invested in securities of the highest class, and the income is distributed to the depositors in the form of interest. In New York State, all savings banks are mutual, which means they are owned by and operated for the depositors. The entire investment income becomes the property of the depositors after the payment of expenses. The entire amount is seldom distributed, however, as a certain part is placed in a surplus account for the protection of the accounts. It is the custom to limit the maximum balance to a few thousand dollars.

Savings and Loan Associations. This type of financial institution is chartered by both state and Federal governments. All federally chartered associations use "Federal" as a part of their corporate name. In certain areas state-chartered associations use building and loan association, building association, homestead association, and co-operative bank, as a part of their corporate name. The major function of savings and loan associations is to accept savings from the public in large and small amounts, regularly or irregularly, at the convenience of the savings customers. Investments are generally limited by Federal or State law to loans for building or buying homes, and U. S. Government obligations. To a limited degree funds can be invested in loans on other types of real estate. As a result of specialization in home financing, savings and loan associations provide more home loans than any other type of financial institution.

The channeling of these funds into home financing not only encourages and makes home ownership possible, but performs a basic economic function by providing jobs for construction workers, income for suppliers of materials and orders to factories.

All Federally chartered associations are required by law to be members of the F.S.L.I.C. State-chartered associations are insured upon application and meeting the F.S.L.I.C. requirements. Of the 6300 associations in existence, 4500 are members of the F.S.L.I.C. The Federal Home Loan Bank System (see below), of which all insured associations are members, makes available credit to meet unusual demands and for seasonal mortgage lending.

Federal Savings and Loan Insurance Corporation. This Corporation was created in 1934 by an Act of Congress to insure savings accounts in savings and loan associations, up to the legal authorization of $20,000. The original capital of $100 million was provided by the Federal government. This has been retired in full by the Corporation. The premium for insurance protection is paid by the insured associations at a rate fixed by law, currently $\frac{1}{12}$ of 1% of aggregate liabilities.

In the event of default by an insured institution, the Corporation, as soon as possible, pays the saver up to 100% of insurable limit in cash or makes available an insured account in another insured association. In order to prevent default, the Corporation is authorized to take steps to restore an insured association, to normal operating conditions.

Federal Home Loan Bank System. Federal Home Loan Banks were established in 1932 by an Act of Congress to provide a system of reserve credit banks for thrift institutions of the savings and loan type engaged in long-term home mortgage financing. Eleven regional Federal Home Loan Banks, and the districts they serve, are designated by the Federal Home Loan Bank Board. Membership in a Federal Home Loan Bank is by approval by the Federal Home Loan Bank Board, upon meeting eligibility requirements.

Principal functions of these banks are to provide additional liquidity for members by making advances when needed to meet unusual or heavy withdrawal demands and to meet seasonal mortgage lending demands. The Federal government supplied the initial capital of $125 million; this has been fully retired. Each member association is required to hold stock equal to 1 per cent of its total mortgage loans and is entitled to obtain advances on an unsecured basis for a term up to one year or on a ten-year term basis where the loans are secured by mortgage loans. The system raises its funds through consolidated obligations of the eleven banks in the system. Members of the bank system may deposit funds with the Bank of which it is a member.

Federal Housing Administration. This corporation was established in 1934 to insure mortgage loans made to finance the construction, improvement or purchase of all types of residential property. Loans made on the FHA plan are originated by any type of financial institution that is making mortgage loans. The loans to be insured are submitted to the FHA and upon acceptance a premium of $\frac{1}{2}$ of 1 per cent per annum is paid by the borrower. The protection of insurance is given to the lender in return for his willingness to make high-percentage, long-term loans tailored according to standards set by the Federal Housing Administration. Whereas most lending institutions are confined, on their loans on residential property, to 60 to 80 per cent of value, FHA loans can be made for as high as 95 per cent.

The Veterans Loan Guarantee. As a part of the Veterans Rehabilitation Act of 1945, provision was made for loans to be made by private lending institutions to honorably discharged veterans for as much as 100 per cent of the purchase price or the construction cost of homes for terms up to 25 years at a rate of 4 per cent. Also, certain business and farm loans to honorably discharged veterans could be insured. The lenders making these loans were originally protected with a guaranty up to $2000 or 50 per cent of the loan. These guaranties were increased in 1950. In the first five years of the operation of this program, $2\frac{1}{2}$ million veterans acquired homes on this plan.

TOTAL RESERVE ASSETS: 1970 TO 1974

Figures are in millions of U.S. dollars. Assets include gold stock, holdings of convertible foreign currencies, special drawing rights and reserve position in International Monetary Fund.

Country	1970	1972	1974	Country	1970	1972	1974
All countries[1]	92,449	158,067	217,912	Libyan Arab Rep.	1,590	2,925	3,616
				Malaysia	664	981	1,618
United States	14,487	13,150	16,058	Malta	158	275	402
				Mexico	744	1,164	1,395
Algeria	339	493	1,689	Morocco	140	237	417
Argentina	673	465	1,315				
Australia	1,693	6,141	4,269	Netherlands	3,241	4,785	6,958
Austria	1,751	2,719	3,430	New Zealand	258	833	566
Belgium	2,847	3,870	5,345	Nigeria	224	385	5,629
				Norway	813	1,325	1,929
Brazil	1,187	4,183	5,252	Oman	129	164	225
Canada	4,679	6,050	5,825				
Central Africa	102	84	(NA)	Pakistan	190	281	460
China (Taiwan)	480	1,039	1,191	Panama	17	44	(NA)
Colombia	206	325	449	Peru	329	460	(NA)
				Philippines	251	551	1,504
Cyprus	209	320	269	Portugal	1,504	2,312	2,354
Denmark	484	855	935				
Ecuador	83	143	350	Saudi Arabia	662	2,500	14,285
Egypt	167	149	104	Singapore	294	873	(NA)
Finland	480	758	708	South Africa	1,012	1,290	1,159
				Spain	1,817	5,014	6,485
France	4,960	10,015	8,851	Sweden	761	1,575	1,735
Germany, F. R. of	13,610	23,785	32,399				
Ghana	58	107	94	Switzerland	5,132	7,488	9,011
Greece	310	1,032	936	Syria	55	135	835
India	1,006	1,180	1,325	Thailand	906	1,052	1,855
				Tunisia	60	223	418
Indonesia	160	574	1,492	Turkey	431	1,401	1,861
Iran	208	960	8,383				
Iraq	462	782	3,273	United Kingdom	2,827	5,647	6,939
Ireland	697	1,126	1,266	Uruguay	175	198	217
Israel	449	1,222	1,202	Venezuela	1,021	1,732	6,529
				West Africa	259	323	338
Italy	5,352	6,079	6,941	Yugoslavia	140	733	1,139
Japan	4,840	18,365	13,519				
Jordan	256	270	350				
Korea, Rep. of	610	740	1,056	Zaire	186	178	140
Kuwait	203	363	1,397	Zambia	514	165	172
Lebanon	386	675	1,674				

NA—Not available. [1] Includes countries not shown separately.
Source: *Statistical Abstracts 1975.*

BUSINESS, BANKING, AND LEGAL TERMS

THE everyday life of the average man or woman brings frequent occasions which demand the ability to understand and use many terms peculiar to business, banking, or the law. To know the nature and the meaning of commercial forms and legal instruments is to be acquainted with the necessary working tools of the business world. Every person needs to know what these tools are and how they are used.

The treatment of the topics in the following dictionary of business, banking, and legal terms is adapted to meet such everyday needs. This alphabetic list will supply definite information upon specific subjects, and it will supplement with greater detail the chapters that precede it in the department of Economics.

Acceptance. A term designating any bill of exchange which has been accepted by the drawee—the party upon whom it is drawn.

The term is used with reference to the act of the drawee in accepting the bill of exchange, by writing upon the face of the bill the word "accepted" and signing his name as acceptor. The date of acceptance and the place of payment are generally added. These, however, are not essential to the validity of the acceptance. After the bill has been accepted, it becomes the direct obligation of the acceptor, and the drawer of the bill then becomes liable to pay the amount of the bill only in the event that the acceptor does not pay it.

A bank or banker's acceptance is a bill of exchange of which the acceptor is a bank or trust company or some other financial person, firm, or corporation which makes a business of lending its credit by accepting bills of exchange.

A trade acceptance is a bill of exchange drawn by a seller upon a purchaser to cover a current sale of goods. Ordinarily, the trade acceptance is drawn by the seller payable to himself, and the acceptance of the bill by the purchaser converts the bill into what is substantially the same as a promissory note. The trade acceptance, however, bears upon its face the statement: "The obligation of the acceptor hereof arises out of the purchase of goods from the drawer"; and it is made a crime under the Federal laws to use a trade acceptance in interstate commerce for any other purpose than in payment for an original purchase of goods. See *Bill of Exchange, Payee.*

Acceptor. One upon whom a draft or bill of exchange is drawn, and who, by writing his acceptance upon the face of the bill, has undertaken to pay the amount of the bill.

Acceptor for Honor. One who accepts a bill drawn upon another, in order to prevent the bill from being protested for nonacceptance or nonpayment. Thus the acceptance is deemed to be for the "honor" of the person upon whom the bill is drawn.

Accommodation Paper. An instrument by which one person lends his credit to another. Usually, but not necessarily, the transaction involves no financial profit to the person lending his credit. The accommodation may take the form of signing a note as maker or endorser, or of drawing, accepting, or endorsing a draft or bill of exchange, or otherwise affixing one's name to a commercial instrument in such manner as to become liable in the event that the instrument is not paid when due by the person receiving the accommodation.

Accounts Payable. Sums owed by a person, partnership, or corporation to others upon open account, the obligations not being represented by notes, bills, or other instruments of indebtedness. See *Bills Payable.*

Accounts Receivable. Sums due to a person, partnership, or corporation from others upon open book account, the obligations not being represented by notes, bills, or other instruments of indebtedness. See *Bills Receivable.*

Accrued Dividends. A term improperly applied to dividends which have not been paid or declared, but which are loosely regarded as having "accrued" because the stock upon which the dividends are payable entitles the holder to cumulative dividends at a specified rate. In fact, a stockholder can have no right to dividends until they have been declared by the board of directors of the company. See *Preferred Stock.*

Accrued Interest. While interest upon an obligation usually becomes due and payable at the termination of some definite period or periods of time, the interest upon the obligation, in fact, accrues from day to day. In the purchase and sale of securities between interest payment dates, the amount of interest accrued must be added to the face value of the obligation in order to determine the actual present value. Similarly, an exact statement of the financial condition of a business at any particular moment must include among the liabilities of the company the item of accrued interest upon interest-bearing obligations of the company held by others. A similar item will also be included among its assets, representing interest accrued upon interest-bearing obligations of others held by the company. Interest already due and unpaid is not properly included in the item of accrued interest.

Active Stocks. Stocks that are frequently bought and sold in considerable quantities upon the general market.

Actuary. One whose business is the calculation of insurance risks and premiums.

Ad Valorem Duties. Tariffs imposed upon articles according to their value.

Affidavit. A written statement sworn to or affirmed before some person who has authority by law to administer an oath. Affidavits are prescribed by law for proper execution of many documents. They are frequently used in place of oral evidence at court trials. Their proper substance is confined to statements of fact regarding which the witness has certain knowledge. Making a false statement in an affidavit is the crime of perjury.

Agent. One hired to carry on certain activities for an employer. The person employing the agent is known as the principal, and is bound by any acts performed by the agent within the scope of the agent's employment. The principal is liable also for any damages sustained by third persons from wrongful acts committed by the agent in the course of his employment.

Frequently it is difficult to distinguish an agent from an independent contractor. Under a mere agency, the employer may direct and supervise the work of his agent, both in large matters and in details. In the case of the independent contractor, this power of supervision does not exist.

Amortization. The periodic setting aside of revenue or earnings in a definite proportion to the initial cost of machinery, plant, or other capital investment, for the purpose of providing a fund with which to replace the machinery or equipment when it has become worn out.

The term is applied also to the building up of a fund for the retirement of a loan when it becomes due.

Ancillary Receiver. A receiver appointed in a state or a district other than the one in which the principal or original proceedings have been begun. The duties of an ancillary receiver are to gather in and administer property in the state or the district of his appointment. See *Receiver.*

Annuity. An annuity has been defined as a series of equal payments made or due at equal intervals of time. Although the term is most commonly associated with payments made at stated intervals to insurance policy holders or beneficiaries, it applies also to bond coupons, preferred stock dividends, and other periodic payments.

Arbitrage. The almost simultaneous purchase and sale of foreign exchange, securities, or commodities in two or more different markets with the motive of making a profit.

Assessed Valuation. The value placed upon property by government officials as a basis for the imposition of taxes. Frequently the assessed valuation of property is considerably below its real or market value.

Assessment. (1) A charge imposed upon properties to defray a part of the cost of a local improvement by which most, if not all, of the properties are directly benefited. Assessments for paving and cleaning streets, for installing sewers, and for widening streets are of this character.

(2) A levy made by a company upon its shareholders for the purpose of securing additional capital. The stock of most business corporations is today nonassessable if the par value of the stock has once been fully paid in cash or its equivalent.

Assets. Anything of value belonging to a person, firm, or corporation. The term includes, not merely real property and tangible personal property, but also good will, copyrights, patent rights, and all other rights, privileges, franchises, and property interests having value.

Assignee. One to whom any contract, right, security or interest has been assigned.

Assignment. The transfer to another of one's interest in a contract, security, or any other thing of value. Except in the case of negotiable instruments, an assignee receives no better title to the thing assigned than his assignor had.

A "general assignment for the benefit of creditors" is sometimes made by a debtor who is insolvent or financially embarrassed. The assignment takes the form of a transfer, by the debtor, of all his assets to a trustee. The purpose of such an assignment is to show the good faith of the debtor and his willingness to distribute his assets among his creditors. If satisfied that the debtor has not withheld assets from the trustee, the creditors will join in a composition agreement whereby each creditor agrees to accept, in satisfaction of the debt, a certain percentage of the amount due him. If all the creditors join in the composition agreement, the property of the debtor can be equitably distributed among the creditors, without the stigma and the wastage of assets which bankruptcy proceedings would entail. Any group of creditors, however—sometimes one creditor is sufficient—may refuse to enter into this plan for an informal distribution of the debtor's assets, and may insist upon formal bankruptcy proceedings; and the general assignment is itself a sufficient ground for the institution of bankruptcy proceedings against the debtor.

Assumed Bonds. Bonds issued by one corporation and assumed by another, as a result of a merger or consolidation of the two companies, or as a result of the acquisition of the control of the former company by the latter. The bonds so assumed become the liabilities of the second corporation as though originally issued by it.

Attachment. A writ issued by a court of competent jurisdiction, authorizing the seizure of a person or of designated property.

Audit. An official examination of the accounts and records of a person, firm, or corporation, to determine whether there are any arithmetical errors or fraudulent entries in the accounts, or whether any improper methods of accounting have been employed.

Available Assets. Unencumbered real or personal property that can be sold, pledged, or mortgaged as security for a proposed indebtedness.

Balance of Trade. A part of the balance of payments, the relation between the merchandise exports and imports of a country. When the exports exceed the imports during any period, the balance of trade is said to be "favorable." When imports exceed exports, the balance of trade is "unfavorable." It is so regarded largely because an excess of exports is likely to be accompanied by an influx of gold or other international reserves in payment of the excess of products sent abroad. And, vice versa, an excess of imports may result in an outward flow of international reserves.

In actuality, however, an excess of imports frequently indicates merely that the citizens of a country have lent or invested heavily abroad and are receiving the income upon their investments, or repayment of the principal, in merchandise. When this is the case, there can be no harm in an "unfavorable" balance of trade.

Balance Sheet. A statement of the assets, liabilities, and net worth of an individual, firm, or corporation as of a certain date.

Bank Acceptance. See *Acceptance.*

Bank Balance. The amount credited to a customer by a bank at any particular time. This sum does not represent actual currency in the custody of the bank to the amount of the balance; rather, it represents the amount of an obligation due from the bank to the customer. In the ordinary deposit in a commercial bank, the amount of this balance is subject to withdrawals upon written orders called checks, drawn by the depositor upon the bank.

Bank Discount. Simple interest deducted in advance from the face value of a loan, the principal of which is payable at a definite future date. By thus taking the interest before it is earned, a slightly higher rate of interest than the rate nominally charged is actually received by the bank, since the full amount of the principal is never turned over to the borrower, who does repay the full amount.

Bank Draft. An order in writing, drawn by one bank upon another, directing the latter to pay a designated sum of money to a third person. The draft may be payable at sight, that is, on demand, or at a definite or determinable future time.

Banker's Acceptance. See *Acceptance.*

Bank Examiner. Both state and national banks, as depositories of the funds of the general public, are subjected to stringent control and supervision by state and/or federal authorities. This control is exercised by examinations of the banks, made periodically by bank examiners acting under the authority of the Comptroller of the Currency, the Federal Reserve, the Federal Deposit Insurance Corporation, or the banking department of a state. Such examinations supplement and check the statements which banks are required to furnish, setting forth in detail their financial condition. Any fraudulent or false entries or unsafe practices discovered by the bank examiners are reported to the proper officials, and the bank guilty of the improper practice or false entry is promptly required to rectify the situation or sometimes to drop its membership in the FDIC, Federal Reserve System, or both. In extreme cases banks may be placed in receivership or reorganized.

Bank Holding Company. Any company which holds a controlling interest in one or more banks and often provides certain services for the members of the group. This type of organization is also referred to as group banking.

Bankruptcy. Proceedings under which the property of an insolvent debtor may be distributed ratably among his creditors under the supervision of a court, and the bankrupt be thereupon discharged of his debts. Bankruptcy proceedings thus serve two purposes: (1) the equitable distribution of the property of the debtor among his creditors; (2) the release of the debtor from his obligations, giving him a fresh start in the business world.

Bankruptcy proceedings in the United States are governed by the Federal Bankruptcy act of 1898 and the amendments thereto. Under this act, proceedings may be either "voluntary" or "involuntary." In the former, the debtor himself institutes the proceedings by filing a voluntary petition showing that he owes debts to the amount of at least $1000, which he is unable to pay. In involuntary proceedings the creditors file the petition. Three or more creditors with unsecured claims amounting to at least $500, or, if there are fewer than twelve creditors, one creditor with a claim amounting to $500 may institute the proceedings.

A debtor may be adjudicated an involuntary bankrupt only if, within four months prior to the filing of the petition, he has done one or more of the following acts: (1) concealed, removed, or otherwise fraudulently disposed of property with intent to hinder, delay, or defraud his creditors; (2) transferred property, while insolvent, to any creditor, with intent to prefer that creditor over others; (3) permitted a creditor to obtain a preference by legal proceedings, as by attachment or levy upon goods of the debtor, and failed to vacate the preference at least five days before a sale under the levy or attachment; (4) made a general assignment for the benefit of creditors; (5) being insolvent, applied for a receiver, or if a receiver has been appointed at the request of creditors.

Bank Statement. A statement issued by a bank or trust company, setting forth in detail its assets and liabilities, together with its capital accounts.

Basing-Point Price. This term means primarily the price for a commodity plus transportation charges. Thus more distant customers pay more than nearer ones. However, a company with widely separated plants may average total shipping charges and, by adding this average to the factory price, sell at a uniform price everywhere. The Supreme Court has held that this practice may violate the antitrust laws.

Bear. A stock or commodity speculator who gambles on the prospect of prices going down. The "bear" sells, for future delivery, stock or wheat which he does not then have, expecting to cover, that is, buy in, at a lower price than that for which he has agreed to sell, at some time before delivery must be made.

Bear Market. A condition of declining prices in securities or commodities, generally accompanied by little activity in the market and by a general depression in trading.

Bear Panic. When those who have sold "short" in any security or commodity find that the market is rising, they attempt to cover in order to keep their losses as low as possible. When the rise in prices is very sudden or very pronounced, the haste of the "bears," to cover their sales by buying in on the market, reaches the point of a veritable panic. See *Cover, Selling Short.*

Bear Raid. A concerted movement by those traders who make a business of selling "short" on stock or commodity exchanges, the purpose of which is to cause the market price of a certain stock or commodity to fall. This result is effected by sales of the stock, against which the raid is directed, at prices below the true market value of the stock. In the case of a successful "bear raid," these sales, which usually provide for delivery at some future time, result in a very pronounced temporary fall in the price of the stock, the public being afraid to hold a stock, the price of which is apparently on the down grade. When the market price has thus been hammered down to an artificially low price, the bears "buy in" and so cover at a profit their earlier sales for future delivery.

Bids and Offers. The rules of the New York stock exchange provide definite terms upon which bids and offers must be made and construed in dealings upon the exchange. These are: "cash," that is, for delivery upon the day of contract; "regular way,"—for delivery upon the business day following the contract; "at three days,"—for delivery upon the third day following the contract; "buyers' or sellers' options,"—for not less than four days nor more than sixty days. Unless otherwise specified, bids and offers are deemed to be "regular way."

Bill of Exchange. An unconditional order in writing, addressed by one person (called the drawer) to another (called the drawee), ordering the person to whom it is addressed to pay on demand, or at a fixed or determinable future time, a definite sum of money to the bearer or to the order of a third party (called the payee). Often the term "draft" is used in the United States particularly with respect to domestic bills of exchange.

A check is in effect a bill of exchange drawn upon a bank, payable upon presentation or at sight. See *Acceptance, Check, Draft*.

Bill of Lading. A receipt and contract and, in some forms, a document of title given by a railroad or other carrier, stating that the goods described have been received by the carrier for transportation to a designated point, and setting forth the terms of the contract between the carrier and the shipper under which the goods are transported. There are two kinds of bills of lading in use in the United States. One is the so-called "order (or negotiable) bill of lading," and the other the so-called "straight (or non-negotiable) bill of lading."

In the "order bill of lading," the carrier undertakes to deliver to the *order of* a designated person, and only upon the surrender of the document. In the "straight bill of lading," the carrier merely undertakes to transport and to deliver to the person named as consignee in the bill of lading; the surrender of the bill of lading is not made a condition precedent to the surrender of the goods by the carrier.

The distinction between the order bill and the straight bill has become very important by reason of the effect which the law has given to order bills of lading. Since the order bill may be negotiated from one holder to another by mere endorsement and delivery, and since the carrier undertakes to deliver the goods represented by it only upon a surrender of the document, the order bill has come to be dealt with commercially as the symbol of the goods. Thus loans are frequently made upon the security of properly endorsed bills of lading, the lender being protected by the assurance that the carrier will not deliver the goods represented by the bill of lading except upon the surrender of that instrument properly endorsed.

In order to further the use of the order bill of lading as an instrument in commerce and as the basis for the advance of credit to owners of goods in transit, all states have passed the Uniform Bill of Lading act, which makes the order bill of lading in effect a negotiable instrument and protects from loss all bona fide purchasers of such bills, as well as persons who lend upon the instruments, even though the bill of lading itself may have been lost by, or even stolen from, the true owner. The Uniform Bill of Lading act also forbids any attachment of, or interference with, goods in transit represented by an order bill of lading, unless the negotiation of the bill has first been enjoined and thus its transfer to a bona fide purchaser or lender has been rendered impossible. The Uniform Bill of Lading act has been passed by Congress, and has thus been made applicable to all shipments in interstate and foreign commerce.

The straight bill of lading possesses none of these peculiar attributes that the law has given to the order bill. The straight bill of lading, therefore, does not in any sense represent the property in the possession of the carrier, and cannot form the basis for a loan upon the goods. The duty of the carrier, where a straight bill of lading has been issued, is merely to deliver to the person named as consignee, and this duty remains unchanged and unaffected by any attempted dealing with the bill of lading.

Bill of Sale. A written instrument transferring or assigning, from one person to another, personal property or an interest therein.

Bills Payable. Obligations owing to others, represented by bonds, notes, or other instruments of indebtedness.

Bills Receivable. Obligations due from others, represented by notes, bills, or other instruments of indebtedness.

Bimetallism. A monetary standard in which the monetary unit is defined in terms of two metals. All provisions with regard to such metals—coinage, redeemability, legal tender characteristics, etc.—apply equally to both metals.

Black Friday. September 24, 1869. A day when the "bears" of the New York stock exchange were practically ruined by a "bull" movement engineered by Jay Gould and Jim Fisk, which caused an unprecedented rise in the prices of speculative stocks upon the exchange. The movement was precipitated by the redemption by the United States of $4,000,000 of its bonds in gold.

Blanket Mortgage. A mortgage which covers several different properties, or one mortgage which is issued in place of several existing mortgages. Such a mortgage is not necessarily a first mortgage.

Block of Stock. A number of shares of stock held by an individual or by a group in a particular corporation.

Bond. A long term instrument by which a person, corporation, or government agrees to pay a certain sum of money on a determinable date. Bonds are usually given under seal and, in many states, are enforceable for a period of twenty years after their maturity; while the ordinary promissory note, or contractual obligation, is not enforceable after the lapse of six years from the date when the obligation matured.

Bonded Debt. The amount of the indebtedness of a government, a corporation, or an individual, represented by bonds issued and outstanding. The bonded debt is taken to represent the fixed or permanent indebtedness, as opposed to current or short time indebtedness, which must be paid or renewed currently.

Books Closed. The books of a corporation are usually closed as of a certain date, for the purpose of determining what persons are entitled as stockholders to share in a dividend to be declared, or in other distributions to be made by the company, or to determine who are entitled to vote as stockholders in any stockholders' meeting of the company. During the period when the books are closed, no transfers of stock are made on the books of the company. For all corporate purposes, the holders of record, as of the date upon which the books are closed, are deemed the stockholders of the company until the books are again opened to transfers of stock.

The term "books closed" is sometimes used also with reference to subscriptions to a new issue of securities, when the issue has been fully subscribed. In the event of oversubscription, the issue is frequently prorated among all who have sent in subscriptions. But, unless the right to prorate the issue among the subscribers has been specifically reserved in the offer of sale of the securities to the public, a subscriber is not obligated to accept less than the full amount called for by his subscription.

Book Value. The value of the assets of a company as set forth upon the books of the company.

The book value of a share of stock issued by a company, as distinguished both from its par value and from its market value, or selling price on the market, may be obtained by dividing the net assets of the company by the number of outstanding shares. If the books of the company are accurately kept, the book value of any share of stock is thus a closer approximation to the amount of capital investment represented by each share than either the par or the market value of the stock.

Boom. Unusual activity and enthusiasm in any line of business, or prosperity in business generally, resulting in a marked rise in prices, employment, output, and profit.

Bottomry. Lending money upon the security of vessels or their cargo.

Bourse. The stock exchange of Paris; by extension, any exchange in continental Europe.

Break-even Point. Point in a firm's operations where revenue from sales just equals overhead and current costs, thus showing neither profit nor loss. It is usually expressed as a percentage of maximum productive capacity.

Break in the Market. A sharp and rapid decline in the prices of stocks or bonds, generally coming at the end of a period of violent speculation and rising prices.

Broker. One who, for a commission or other fee, buys or sells personal or real property for others.

Brokerage. Fee charged by a broker for his services.

Bull. A speculator in the stock market who gambles upon the expectation of a rise in prices; one who manipulates the market in such a manner as to bring about a rise in prices.

Bullion. Uncoined gold or silver, generally in the form of bars or ingots, ready to be turned into coins. Bullion is frequently used in payment of obligations due from persons of one country to those in another. See *Dollar Exchange*.

Bull Market. A bull market is one of activity and rising prices. The term is particularly applied to such a condition in the stock market.

Buyer's Option. A special term applied to a contract permitted by the rules of the New York stock exchange, whereby the buyer of stock is not compelled to accept and pay for the securities purchased until the expiration of a specified time. The buyer has the privilege, however, of demanding delivery of the stock upon one day's notice. The rules of the New York stock exchange provide that such a contract must be for a term of not less than four days and not more than sixty days. A buyer's option, the term of which is four days, is called "buyer's four"; if the term is ten days, it is called "buyer's ten"; and so forth.

Buying Outright. A purchase of stock or other security by a payment of the full purchase price at once or within a definite period after the purchase. This is distinguished from buying "on margin," where only a portion or percentage of the purchase price is paid by the purchaser, the remainder of the price being loaned to the purchaser by the broker. See *Margin*.

Callable Bonds. Bonds issued with a right reserved by the issuing corporation to redeem or "call" the issue, in whole or in part, after a specified date, at a designated price. The "call" price is generally five to ten points above par. A redemption provision is now commonly inserted also in issues of preferred stock.

Call Loan. The lending of money repayable on demand. Loans of this character used to be very common in New York City, where brokers and speculators upon the various exchanges borrowed large sums of money from the banks upon securities as collateral. In this type of loan, both the borrower and the lender have the right to terminate the loan at any time. The advantage to the bank of such a loan is that it enables the bank to make some profitable use of its available funds during any period of temporary abundance; while leaving the bank free to terminate the loan at any time, should any extraordinary demand for cash arise. Its advantage to the borrower is that, as soon as the temporary need of cash or credit has passed, the loan may be repaid and the incurring of interest may at once be terminated.

Calls. Transactions upon stock and commodity exchanges in which one person is given an option to require another to deliver a specified amount of stock or of a commodity at a particular price at any time within a specified period. A "call" is frequently referred to as a "buyer's option."

The term "call" is used also with reference to a notice issued to stockholders or subscribers to the stock of a corporation, requiring payment to the corporation of sums upon stock purchased or held by them. In this sense a "call" may be issued either before or after the stock has been paid in full. If issued prior to full payment, it is nothing more than a notice that an installment is due upon the purchase price of the stock. Where a call is issued after the stock has once been fully paid for, it amounts to an assessment of stockholders to enable the corporation to carry on its business. Most stock is now issued as nonassessable after it has once been paid for in full. In that event, a "call" of the latter character cannot be made.

Capitalism. The economic system of private enterprise in industry and trade in which capital and capitalists play the chief rôle, subject to regulation by the state. Capitalism emphasizes freedom of individual initiative in business. Its greatest development has been since the Industrial Revolution in the 19th century, but it has been known to most civilizations.

Carrier. Any person or company that purports to engage in the business of transporting passengers or freight for hire. The more appropriate term is "common carrier," the term "carrier" being used as a colloquial abbreviation of the longer term. Included within the general class of common carriers are railroads, steamships, ferries, street railways, airplanes, trucks, and other vehicles which make a business of carrying persons or property from one place to another. An elevator has been held not to be a common carrier.

From the early days of feudal England down to the present time, common carriers have been subjected to special rules of law, at least with respect to the transportation of property.

From early times, too, the law limited the charge which a common carrier may make, for transporting persons or property, to such sum as was deemed a reasonable compensation for the service rendered. In modern times, common carriers have come to be strictly regulated by statutes administered by governmental commissions; and the more important carriers, such as the huge railroad systems and steamship lines, as well as street railway systems, are looked upon as quasi public corporations. The Interstate Commerce act, originally enacted by Congress in 1887, and amended from time to time since then, created a commission with power to regulate the service rendered and the rates charged by any carrier engaged in interstate traffic. The commission may also prescribe rules to insure safety of operation. In most states, there are similar regulatory statutes.

Carrying Charges. Interest on moneys advanced by banks or brokers, insurance, storage charges, and similar costs incurred by one who has purchased goods or securities on credit or on margin.

The term is sometimes used also as the equivalent of "fixed charges," that is, costs incurred regardless of the volume of operations or the amount of business done.

Cartel. This is a formal or informal agreement between rival firms controlling production and distribution of certain products to divide the market regionally so as to maintain prices. This is a form of monopoly barred by antitrust laws in the United States, but it is not uncommon in Europe. Its economic effect is to retard consumption and to place little premium on efficiency of operations.

Cashier's Check. A check, sometimes called an officer's check, issued by a bank, usually signed by the cashier (whence the name is derived), and drawn against the bank itself or against a metropolitan bank with which the drawing bank keeps an account. New York funds are generally provided in the form of cashier's checks. The cashier's check differs radically from an uncertified check drawn by a depositor of the bank. The cashier's check gives the holder an obligation against the bank itself, while the ordinary check gives the holder no claim against the bank, but only a claim against the depositor in the event that the check is not honored.

Center Spread. A preferred position for advertisements, since the two facing pages offer a continuous surface and the double-page text and illustrations can be printed on a large sheet with no interference from center margins or "gutters."

Certificate of Deposit. A certificate or receipt, in which a commercial bank or savings and loan association acknowledges that it has received a certain sum of money from the person to whom the certificate is issued, and agrees to pay the sum to the person named in the certificate, or to his endorsee, upon demand or at a definite future date. Such a certificate bears interest and is often negotiable, and the amount represented by a certificate of deposit is generally not subject to withdrawal by check. In the case of a negotiable time certificate of deposit, that is, one payable at a definite future date, the holder of the certificate may not be a depositor of the bank, but may have purchased his instrument through the open market.

Certified Check. A check having the word "certified" stamped or written upon it, and bearing the signature of an official of the bank upon which the check is drawn. The effect of the certification is merely to furnish a guarantee from the bank that the amount to the credit of the drawer of the check is adequate to meet the check, and that the amount of the check will be set aside for the purpose of paying the check when presented for payment. It is not true, as is sometimes thought, that a certified check constitutes a direct obligation of the bank to pay the amount of the check. Thus, if the check is a forgery, the bank may subsequently refuse to pay the check, even though it be certified, without liability to any holder or endorsee. Or, if the amount of the check has been fraudulently raised before certification, a subsequent holder of the check can recover only the amount for which the check was originally drawn.

Chain Banking. The control of two or more banks by an unincorporated individual or group of individuals through stock ownership in the various banks and/or interlocking directorates.

Chattel Mortgage. A lien given upon personal property, generally as security for a loan or other obligation. Nominally, a chattel mortgage takes the form of a transfer of title of the personal property to the person to whom the mortgage is given (called the mortgagee). In almost all states, however, a chattel mortgage is now regarded, not as a transfer of the title to the property, but as merely giving a lien upon the property.

Generally, a chattel mortgage, to be valid against creditors of the mortgagor or against subsequent transferees of the property, must be recorded in the city or town where the mortgagor resides. Chattel mortgages usually provide for a sale of the property in the event of nonpayment of the debts they are given to secure. The method of sale, however, is usually expressly prescribed by statute.

Check. A check is a written order directed to a bank, ordering the bank to pay a specified sum of money to the order of the person named in the check or to the bearer of the check.

A check payable to "cash" is equivalent to a check payable to bearer, and may be negotiated from one person to another without endorsement. It is the practice of banks, however, to require one who presents a check payable to bearer or payable to cash to endorse the check. Such an endorsement, however, merely operates as a receipt to the bank.

Checks should be presented promptly for collection or payment. Where a check is not presented promptly for payment and the bank upon which it is drawn becomes insolvent during the interval, the holder may in some cases be compelled to shoulder the loss. Moreover, death or bankruptcy of the drawer of the check renders the instrument void, and relegates the holder to the status of a mere general claimant against the drawer's estate.

C. I. F. An expression used in quoting prices, particularly in the export trade, to indicate that the price includes the cost of the goods plus insurance and freight.

Clearing House. The place at which the banks of a particular city or region customarily present checks drawn upon each other. A definite debit or credit balance against or in favor of each of the member banks is made on the basis of these balances.

The method by which the local clearing house operates is as follows: Each bank sends a messenger to the clearing house with the checks which it has received that are drawn against the other members of the clearing house. Each bank assorts the checks it receives, placing all of the checks drawn against one bank in an individual folder, to which is attached an itemized statement of all of the checks contained and their total amount. Each bank has a designated desk as the clearing house, and, at an appointed time the messenger of each bank distributes to the desks of the other banks the checks drawn upon the latter, retaining a duplicate memorandum of each amount. When the distribution is complete, each bank is in possession of all the checks which have been drawn upon it and deposited in other banks. The amount of such checks is then totaled, and, in the event that this total exceeds the amount of the checks presented by it against the other banks, a debit balance is entered against the bank. In the event that the amount of checks presented by any bank against the other banks exceeds the amount of checks presented by the other banks against it, a credit balance is entered for the particular bank.

If there is a debit balance, the amount thereof is paid by the particular bank to the clearing house; if there is a credit balance, the amount of the credit is received by the bank having the credit balance from the clearing house. Under the Federal Reserve system, member banks may use the reserve banks as clearing houses. Under special arrangements non-member banks also may clear checks through the regional reserve banks.

In the larger cities, clearing house organizations have functions wider than those of the ordinary clearing house.

Clearing House Balance. Applied both to an amount due from a clearing house to a creditor bank and to an amount due from a debtor bank to the clearing house. In the former case the balance is called a favorable balance, and in the latter it is called an adverse balance, at the clearing house.

Co-insurance Clauses. Under a co-insurance clause, the insured party agrees to maintain other insurance in an amount equal to a specified percentage of the property's total value. If the insured should carry less than this designated percentage, the payment for any loss he incurs would be reduced in proportion to the percentage by which he has fallen below the co-insurance requirement stipulated by the insuring company.

Collateral Loan. A loan secured by a pledge of securities or other personal property.

Collateral Note. A form of note commonly used by banks and other financial institutions making secured loans. This type of note not merely recites the promise of the borrower to pay but also sets forth the terms upon which the security is deposited with the lender. The terms of the collateral note are designed to relieve the bank or other lender from the obligations imposed by law upon pledgees who undertake to sell the pledged property.

Collision Deductible Insurance. If an insuring company should assume entire coverage for loss resulting from automobile collisions, the premium it would have to charge would be very high, and to many owners would seem almost prohibitive. However, if the insured agrees to assume liability for a certain amount of the damage, for example, the first $100, the premium can be greatly reduced. In that case, a great many small claims would not need to be brought to the attention of the insuring company. Its only liability would be for damage in excess of the deductible amount.

Commercial Agencies. Organizations which make a business of compiling and furnishing to their subscribers information with respect to the assets and liabilities, promptness of payment of obligations, and general solvency and credit of individuals, firms, and corporations engaged in business. This information is given out in the form of general ratings, furnished to all subscribers, and in special reports with respect to any particular concern, furnished upon the special request of a subscriber.

Dun and Bradstreet, Inc. is the leading commercial agency in the United States. The credit ratings and reports given by this agency constitute an important basis for extending or withholding of credit to prospective borrowers or to purchasers on credit.

Commercial Paper. Short-term notes of business concerns and sales finance companies of national reputation, which either may be purchased by dealers and then distributed by them among various banks and other investors throughout the country, or may be placed directly with interested buyers, usually by telephone. Dealers usually make a profit or commission of one-quarter of one per cent upon the principal of these notes. By using this type of commercial paper, these large borrowers may supplement their bank loans and at times borrow at a lower rate than they would be compelled to pay for current loans obtained from local banks.

This type of security, by reason of its general marketability, has come to be highly regarded throughout the banking community as an excellent mode of investment for secondary reserve purposes. The notes, commonly in amounts of $2500 and $5000, run for periods varying from one month to one and one-half years, and can be made to bear such a maturity as will fit in with the needs of the banks purchasing the securities. While these notes are not guaranteed by the houses which buy and sell them, the larger note brokerage houses have made a practice of virtually protecting their purchasers against loss, both by thorough examination of the businesses of those whose notes are purchased and by taking control of such businesses, if necessary, in order to save purchasers from loss.

Commission House. A firm which buys and sells commodities or securities, as a broker or agent for others, receiving a commission on the purchases or sales, or upon both, in compensation for the service rendered.

Common Stock. That class of stock which is entitled to receive dividends or otherwise share in the earnings of a company only after all preferential rights to payments out of the earnings of the company have been satisfied. The term common stock is also used with reference to all of the stock issued by a corporation where only one class of stock has been created. Usually the control of the company is vested in the holders of the common stock. This, however, is not necessarily so, and sometimes the holders of preferred stock are given an equal or greater share in the control of the corporate affairs.

While the common stock usually receives no dividends until the preferential dividends to which any class or classes of preferred stock may be entitled have been paid, the common stock is normally entitled to receive all of the surplus after the preferential payments to the preferred stockholders have been made. The relative rights of holders of any particular issue of preferred or common stock depend, however, upon the special provisions of the certificate of incorporation of the company which issues the stock, and, to determine what these rights are, resort must always be had to the certificate.

Usually, the holder of preferred stock is assured the more continuous and steady return upon his investment. On the other hand, the common stock carries with it the possibility of great profits, in the event that the enterprise proves especially profitable. See *Preferred Stock.*

Congeneric. In the banking field, the term is applied to only bank holding companies whose non-bank subsidiaries engage in financial activities other than commercial banking.

Conglomerate. A merging of a company in one industry with one or more companies in other unrelated industries. In the field of banking, a one-bank holding company having subsidiaries which engage in business activities unrelated to the financial field. It is now illegal for holding companies controlling two or more banks to have affiliates in either nonfinancial fields or even in most financial fields, though in the latter case there are certain exceptions.

Consignee. A person named in a bill of lading as the one to whom goods are to be delivered by a railway or other carrier.

Consignment. Goods are said to be shipped upon "consignment" when they are forwarded by a seller, called the principal in the transaction, to a broker or sales representative, pursuant to an arrangement whereby the broker is to sell the goods and remit to his principal the proceeds less his commission, the broker undertaking no responsibility for the purchase price of the goods until they are actually sold. However, when a sale has in fact been made, if the goods were shipped upon consignment, the broker becomes personally responsible for the sale price, less the commission to which he is entitled. In this respect, such a broker is similar to a "*del credere factor*" who insures the financial responsibility of his purchasers.

Consignor. One who delivers goods to a railway or other carrier for transportation to a designated point.

Consols. The name applied to the 3 per cent "consolidated annuities," sometimes referred to as "consolidated threes," issued by the government of Great Britain, entitling the holder to a certain sum from the government annually. These annuities are obligations of the British government, but differ from other bonds in that they have no definite date of maturity. The government, however, reserves the right to pay the principal represented by the securities at any time. They are, therefore, callable. See *Callable Bonds.*

The full name, "3 per cent consolidated annuities," had its origin in the fact that this form of obligation was issued to replace the entire or consolidated debt of Great Britain, and a purchaser received 3 per cent annually upon the amount paid to the government for the consol.

Controlling Interest. A phrase used to indicate a person, or a body of persons united in mutual interest, who have secured the right, by purchase or by proxy, to vote a majority of the shares of capital stock in a corporation at any stockholders' meeting.

Convertible Bonds. Bonds which are issued subject to a provision for their surrender and cancellation at some future time and the issuance of stock in their place. The provision for conversion may make the conversion optional in the bondholder or in the company, or may be made absolute upon the fulfillment of some condition, depending in each case upon the particular provision contained in the bond.

Corner. The acquisition by an individual, or by a group of speculators, of the larger part or of all of the available supply of a particular stock, or of a commodity such as cotton, wheat, copper, or sugar. When a corner has been successfully effected, one who has sold the stock or commodity short, or who must have the commodity to carry on his business, is compelled to pay any price demanded.

The most notable corners in American financial history were the successful corner of Harlem Railroad stock by Commodore Vanderbilt in 1863 and the attempted corner of gold by Jay Gould in 1869.

Corporation. A corporation is a legal creation whose rights and liabilities as a single person are stated in its charter. The most common form is the joint stock corporation, which is organized for the profit of its members, known as stockholders. Stockholders are not liable for the corporation's debts. Consequently, capital may be invested in a corporation without jeopardizing the estate of the investor. Stockholders have no claim on the corporation's assets. Hence the corporation may carry on indefinitely, irrespective of the death or withdrawal of any of the investors. Through these two advantages, the corporate form of organization has made possible the concentrations of capital on which modern industrial society rests.

A corporation is formed by applying to the state or Federal government for a certificate of incorporation. When granted, this document entitles the corporation to carry on the type of business described therein. The business is managed by officers chosen by a board of directors, who have previously been elected by the stockholders. A typical set-up would be a board of directors consisting of three or more people and executive officers known as president, vice president, secretary, and treasurer.

The owners of a corporation are the stockholders. Their degree of ownership depends on the number of shares of stock they hold and on the special rights which these shares may confer. Profits are distributed to the shareholders at the discretion of the directors. See *Common Stock, Preferred Stock.*

Cost, Insurance, Freight. See *C. I. F.*

Country Banks. A term used to designate Federal Reserve member banks in small communities. They are required to hold lower legal reserves than are city member banks.

Coupon. A certificate attached to a bond, representing the interest for a given period, to be detached and forwarded to the corporation or government which has issued the bond when such interest becomes due. The coupon generally bears the name of the debtor or obligor upon the bond, the number of the bond, the rate of interest, and the amount due or payable upon the coupon.

Coupon Bonds. Bonds issued with coupons attached, representing the interest falling due from time to time. The interest upon coupon bonds is obtained by detaching or clipping the coupons as they fall due and forwarding them to the debtor corporation for payment.

Cover. Where a person has sold for future delivery stocks or commodities which he does not actually own at the time he makes the sale, he is said to "cover" when he buys in such stocks or commodities.

Curb. The name given originally to the group of brokers who formerly made a practice of meeting daily in Broad street, New York, one block from the New York stock exchange. There they bought and sold securities of both the better and the cheaper grades. This practice of congregating at a point near the financial center of New York City, for the purpose of engaging in stock transactions, began as early as 1869, and continued until 1920, when an ordinance was passed by the city of New York prohibiting the carrying on of brokerage transactions upon the public streets. As a result of the enforcement of this ordinance, the so-called curb brokers organized and erected their own exchange, which is called the American Stock Exchange. Here is now carried on the business which formerly was transacted upon the street and sidewalks of Broad Street.

Currency Denominations. Identification of denominations of U.S. currency is made in terms of the portraits they carry as well as the amount printed on their face. Historical celebrities associated with the different denominations are as follows: $1, Washington; $2, Jefferson; $5, Lincoln; $10, Hamilton; $20, Jackson; $50, Grant; $100, Franklin; $500, McKinley; $1,000, Cleveland; $5,000, Madison; $10,000, Chase; $100,000, Wilson. There are now plans to drop the large denominations.

Current Assets. Assets which are readily convertible into cash and which change in amount from day to day. Cash on hand, bank deposits, merchandise, and accounts and bills receivable are all regarded as current assets.

Current Liabilities. Obligations which fall due from day to day or which will mature in the near future. Included within this designation are accounts payable, notes payable, wages unpaid, interest due or accrued, and similar obligations which are immediately payable or of short term duration.

Dating. An agreement between a buyer and a seller of goods, providing that the date of purchase shall be deemed to be of a later date than the actual date of purchase. The purpose of "dating" is to extend the period or term of credit beyond that normally allowed.

Debenture Bonds. In the United States, an evidence of indebtedness issued by a corporation and not secured by a mortgage or other lien upon property of the corporation. Such a bond is similar to an ordinary promissory note, except that it normally runs for a longer period.

Deed. An instrument signed and sealed, purporting to convey an interest in real property from one person to another.

A *quitclaim deed* is one in which the grantor purports merely to convey such right, title, or interest as he may have in the property described in the deed. Such a conveyance does not carry with it any representation of ownership vested in the grantor, and, in the event that it is later discovered that the title to the property is encumbered or was vested in some other person than the grantor, no recourse can be had against the grantor.

A *warranty deed* is one in which the grantor covenants that he is the owner of the property and that there are no encumbrances upon the property (except such as are expressly excluded from the covenants), and that the grantee will enjoy quiet and peaceful possession of the property. A grantor who executes a warranty deed may be called upon to defend the title to the property, should the grantee's title or possession be attacked. He may also be compelled to respond in damages, should the title prove to be defective.

Deferred Dividend. When dividends are not regularly paid upon preferred stock, carrying cumulative dividends, such unpaid dividends are regarded as "deferred," and ordinarily must be paid before any dividends can be paid upon the common stock.

Demurrage. A charge imposed upon a shipper for detaining a railroad car, or other vehicle of transportation, for a longer time than that allowed by the agreement with the carrier for loading or unloading the cargo.

Deposit. Funds deposited with a bank, entailing an obligation upon the bank to repay an amount equal to the sum deposited. The ordinary deposit with a commercial bank involves an undertaking by the bank to honor withdrawals, in the form of checks drawn upon the account, until the amount of the deposit is exhausted. A deposit of this character is a "demand deposit," being payable at any time upon presentation of a check drawn upon the bank. Interest is not paid on demand deposits; a service charge may be imposed if the balance is too small in relation to the checks drawn. Time deposits, on which interest is paid, are those which must be left with the bank for a definite period.

Depreciation. Diminution in the value of any property, real or personal, whether due to ordinary wear and tear or to any other cause resulting in the lessened value of the property, during any period of time

Diminishing Returns. The law of diminishing returns was formulated by Malthus (1766–1834). Land, he said, becomes more productive with the application of more fertilizers and more labor but only up to a point. Beyond this point their application is not justified by the increase in production. The law has been generalized and applied to production generally.

Direct Mail Selling. This term usually applies to letters, booklets, brochures, or a combination thereof, addressed to individual prospects and designed to secure an order without the necessity of visits by a salesman. Successful selling by direct mail depends upon several factors, including an article, product or service that is not too expensive, yet costing enough to absorb its share of the selling campaign; a list of prospects carefully selected and with verified up-to-date mailing addresses; and a sales presentation that is interesting in content and attractive in form, besides being complete enough to answer a prospect's questions. The usual sequence of 1) getting attention, 2) arousing interest, and 3) creating desire is essentially the same in direct mail campaigns as in personal selling.

Discount. This term has several meanings. It is applied to a loan made by a bank to a customer upon his note, where the interest which is to accrue upon the loan during the term of the note is deducted in advance. Thus, if a customer wishes to borrow $1000 for six months at 6 per cent, the bank "discounts" his note and credits him with the sum of $970. The $30, which is deducted from the principal of the loan, is termed discount or unearned interest, and the entire transaction is called a "discount."

The term discount is applied also to the purchase by a bank, from the payee or holder, of a note having a definite maturity. In such a purchase, as in a direct loan upon the paper of the borrower himself, the interest to become due upon the note during the term it has to run is deducted in advance, and the net proceeds only are credited to the seller of the note.

Another use of the term discount is with reference to the amount or percentage by which the market price of a particular kind of domestic or foreign currency, or of a bond or other obligation, falls below its nominal or par value. Thus, when bonds of the United States government, having a face value of $100, sell for $98, they are said to sell at a discount of $2 or of 2 per cent.

Dishonor. The refusal of one upon whom a draft or bill of exchange is drawn to pay or to accept the bill in accordance with the terms of the instrument.

Disintermediation. Direct investment by individuals in assets, such as Treasury bills, other government securities, acceptances, and commercial paper, as opposed to indirect investment through deposits in banks and other savings institutions. In the last decade, interest rate ceilings on the savings deposits of commercial banks have been set by the Board of Governors of the Federal Reserve system under its Regulation Q. At times when interest yields on open market instruments have risen above these ceilings, disintermediation has occurred. Savings and loan associations faced a similar problem during much of this period because, for one thing, the depressed state of the construction industry made them unable to compete with either commercial banks or open market instruments.

Disposable Income. This refers to income after taxes, which is available for purchase of goods or services and for savings. It is not necessarily the same as "take-home pay," since this may be smaller by reason of "check-off" items that are part of voluntary expenses or savings. Disposable income on a national scale is a key factor in planning for stabilization of prices. An increase of taxes will curtail disposable income and therefore reduce private demand; and this in turn will tend to lower certain prices. Lowering taxes operates in the opposite direction.

Dividend. A proportionate distribution of past and/or present earnings by a corporation among its stockholders. Where the stock of the company has a nominal or par value, the dividend will be payable in terms of a certain per cent of this nominal or par value. Where, however, the stock has no nominal or par value, the dividend merely represents a distribution of cash among the stockholders, out of the earnings or surplus profits of the company, in proportion to their respective holdings in the company. The laws of practically all the states prohibit the payment of dividends to stockholders except out of earnings or surplus profits, in order that the capital of the corporation may be kept intact for the benefit of creditors. Any violation of this prohibition usually renders the directors participating in the declaration or payment of the dividend guilty of a crime.

A stock dividend is entirely different from a cash dividend, and represents merely a distribution of additional evidences of ownership in the corporation, no property of the company being turned over to the stockholders.

Dollar Exchange. Bills of exchange, drawn in foreign countries upon banks or business concerns of the United States, and payable in United States money.

Domestic Exchange. Drafts or bills of exchange, drawn upon banks or commercial houses located in New York or other important commercial centers, used in making remittances from one part of the country to another. Bank drafts upon New York City formerly constituted the greater part of domestic exchange. In recent years, however, bank drafts upon Federal Reserve banks have in large measure replaced drafts upon New York.

Double Taxation. Frequently the same person or the same property is taxed by more than one governmental authority. The most common instance of double taxation of this sort is taxation by both the Federal and the state government. But sometimes the same person or interest in property may also be taxed by more than one state. Thus, where a person residing in the state of New York owns property which is physically present in the state of Ohio, a tax may be imposed by both states, one by reason of jurisdiction over the person owning the property, and the other by reason of jurisdiction over the property or "*res*" itself.

Likewise, where two different states or countries impose income taxes, a tax may be imposed by one state or country, by reason of the income being derived within the limits of its territorial sovereignty; and an income tax may be imposed upon the same income by another state or country, by reason of its jurisdiction over the person earning the income. Frequently, too, succession or inheritance taxes seem to operate to impose double or multiple taxation, where the decedent was a resident of one state and had property subject to the jurisdiction of other states. Double or multiple taxation of this sort may sometimes appear to operate unjustly, but the courts have uniformly held that such taxation is entirely lawful and constitutional.

Draft. A written order drawn by one party (drawer) directing a second party (drawee) to pay a definite sum of money to a third party (payee). The drawer and the payee may be the same person. Also, the drawee and the payee may be the same person. Thus three parties, but not necessarily three persons, are involved. A draft may be drawn payable at sight or on demand, that is, upon presentation; or it may direct payment at a definite or determinable future time. A draft is a bill of exchange. In the United States, however, the term draft has come to be applied to ordinary domestic bills of exchange, as distinguished from bills of exchange used in foreign commerce.

Duebill. A written nonnegotiable acknowledgment of a credit to the account of the person to whom the bill is addressed. This type of instrument is usually given by merchants to persons who have purchased goods and have subsequently returned them.

E. & O. E. Abbreviation for "errors and omissions excepted." This term appearing upon any financial statement negates any representation of the one furnishing the statement that it is absolutely accurate. Its use absolves the one furnishing the account from personal liability for errors in the statement, other than those due to fraud or willful misrepresentation.

Employee Benefit Plans. In the policy and practice of an increasingly large number of companies, there is a tendency to supplement the direct payment of wages or salaries to employees by "fringe benefits" of various kinds. Examples are group insurance, pension plans, and profit-sharing, either current or deferred. Such items are incorporated in "package agreements" between the firm and its employees.

Endorse. To write one's name upon the back of a note, check, or other instrument, for the purpose of transferring the instrument to another, or for the purpose of lending one's credit as a guarantor of the payment of the obligation. An endorsement by one whose name already appears upon the instrument as a payee or endorsee should be made without variation from the form in which it first appears upon the instrument. An endorsement, however, is legally sufficient if, in fact, the person who endorses the instrument is the same person as the one to whom the instrument was payable as payee or endorsee.

Endorsee. One to whom a note or other negotiable instrument has been transferred by endorsement by the holder of the instrument.

Endorsement, Anomalous. Where one who is not a party upon the face of a note or other instrument writes his name upon the back of the instrument, as a guarantor of its payment at maturity, such endorsement is termed anomalous.

Endorsement, Restrictive. An endorsement which indicates that the holder or endorsee of the instrument is not the owner of the instrument, but has merely been intrusted with it for certain definite purposes specified in the restrictive endorsement. Thus, a note or check may be restrictively endorsed, "Pay to the First National Bank for collection only," or "Pay to John Jones as agent," signed by the holder of the instrument.

Endorsement, Special. Where a payee or endorsee of a note or other instrument, upon transferring it, designates upon the back of the instrument the particular person to whom or to whose order the instrument shall be paid, such endorsement is termed a special endorsement. When an instrument has been thus endorsed, it may be further negotiated or transferred only by an endorsement of the person named in the special endorsement.

Endorser. One who has signed his name upon the back of a note, check, or other commercial instrument, to lend his credit to the maker or to the holder of the instrument, in which case he may be an anomalous endorser; or one who, being the holder of the instrument, endorses the instrument in order to negotiate it or sell it to another. Unless an endorser has signed his name "without recourse," he may be held liable for the payment of the instrument, in the event that the maker fails to pay it at maturity. The endorser may, however, be released from liability if the instrument is not duly presented to the maker and protested, and notice of the protest given to the endorser within 24 hours.

Engel's Law. This is a rule formulated by the German statistician Ernst Engel (1821–96) to the effect that, as a family's income increases, the proportion of it spent for food decreases, the proportion spent for advancement (education, luxuries, and savings) increases, and the other items remain about the same.

Escrow. An instrument deposited with a third party, to be delivered to the grantee named in the instrument upon the performance of some condition or upon the happening of a certain event.

Eurodollars. Bank demand and/or time deposits denominated in United States dollars and located in banks outside the United States (but not necessarily in Europe).

Excess Profits Tax. A federal levy imposed several times throughout the twentieth century during war periods. The tax base is that portion of profit that is above normal for the industry, each firm being given a choice of alternative methods of defining abnormal profit.

Exchange. Claims upon foreign merchants or banking institutions, usually in the form of bills of exchange or drafts accepted or drawn upon them, arising out of the export of goods to foreign countries or out of other international transactions. These instruments are bought by persons who are obliged to make remittances to such countries. The result of this buying and selling of "exchange" is that claims by individuals in one country against individuals or banks in another country are offset by claims which individuals in the latter country have against individuals and banks in the former country.

Excise. Any tax imposed by a government upon commodities manufactured, sold, or used, or upon activities carried on, within its territorial jurisdiction. The tax upon cigars and cigarettes, and the tax upon liquors, formerly constituted the most important excise taxes in the United States. In recent years the scope of excise taxes in the United States has been very much widened.

Ex Dividend. Literally, without dividend. When stock is sold during a period when the stock books of the particular company are closed in anticipation of the payment of a dividend, no transfers of ownership being recorded by the company during this period, the stock is said to sell on the market "ex dividend." This is because the purchaser of the stock during such a period will not be entitled to receive the dividend about to be paid by the company.

External Loan. A loan which a country obtains by selling its bonds or other obligations to investors in other countries; it is to be distinguished from an internal loan, which is obtained by the sale of securities to the country's own citizens. Frequently, in the case of an external loan, securities are made payable in the currency of the country in which they are intended to be sold.

Face Value. The value noted upon the face of a check, note, bond, certificate of stock, bank note, or unit of currency. The term "face value" is used in contradistinction to the actual value of the instrument, which may be either greater or less than its face value. See *Par*.

Factor. One who sells goods for another upon commission. See *Agent, Consignment*.

Fair Trade Laws. These are laws designed to limit price cutting. The Robinson-Patman Act bars discrimination between purchasers unless based on specified economic reasons. The Miller-Tydings Act permits states to enact laws for maintenance of resale prices by manufacturers. Courts decisions have severely curtailed the scope of such laws.

Farm Loan Bank. Banks organized pursuant to the Federal Farm Loan act of July 17, 1916. This act provided for the creation of a Federal land bank in each of eleven designated farm loan districts. Most of the original capital was provided by the Federal government, but now all the capital of the banks is owned by national farm loan associations. The act provides for the lending of funds to farmers, but only upon the security of first mortgages on farm land; and the loans are to be made, not directly to the farmer, but through advances to local farm loan associations. In order to obtain a loan under the provisions of this act, an intended borrower has to become a member of one of these associations and subscribe to stock in the association to an amount equal to at least 5 per cent of the amount to be borrowed.

F. A. S. Free alongside ship. This term is used to indicate the extent of the obligation of the seller with respect to delivery of goods sold. Where the goods are sold "F. A. S.," the seller's obligation is fulfilled when the goods are delivered to a wharf from which the goods can be loaded into a vessel for transportation to the port of destination. Where it is necessary to carry the goods from the wharf to the vessel by means of small tugs or lighters, the seller would be obligated to bear the expense of this part of the transportation in addition to carrying the goods to the wharf.

Federal Funds. Funds on deposit and immediately available at the twelve Federal Reserve banks. These are largely the excess reserves of member banks. Federal funds are the customary means of settling certain transactions in the short-term money market. Important among these is the demand for Federal funds by certain commercial banks, which pay interest to borrow the funds, and then make use of them to avoid deficiencies in legally required reserves.

Federal Reserve Bank Notes. Currency formerly issued by Federal Reserve banks in denominations of one, two, five, and ten dollars, secured by deposit, with the Secretary of the Treasury, of certain issues of United States bonds to an amount equal to the bank notes issued. In 1945 the Federal Reserve banks lost the right to issue these notes.

Federal Reserve Notes. Currency issued by Federal Reserve banks, for which these banks pledge collateral consisting of certain assets. The Federal Reserve note has introduced an elastic element into the currency of the

United States. Its volume can be increased or decreased in accordance with seasonal and extraordinary demands. At present these notes account for 90 per cent of the total amount of currency in circulation.

Fee Simple. The absolute, unconditional ownership of real property. The fee simple is the highest estate known to the law. The ownership of the fee simple in any particular parcel of property is not inconsistent with the existence of restrictions or encumbrances upon the property.

Fiduciary. One who occupies a position of trust, or who receives and dispenses funds for another. Executors, administrators, trustees under wills and deeds of trust, directors of corporations, agents, committees of the estates of lunatics, and guardians of infants are all within the general class designated as fiduciaries.

First Mortgage Bond. A bond secured by a first or prior lien upon a part or all of the assets of the company issuing the bond. The extent of this lien depends upon the particular terms of the mortgage in each case. Some so-called "first mortgage bonds" cover only a very limited part of the tangible assets of the issuing company. Others purport to cover not merely specific physical property described in the mortgage, but also property both tangible and intangible which may subsequently be acquired. In the event of a default in the payment of interest or principal upon first mortgage bonds, a foreclosure of the mortgage securing the bonds would bar all secondary or subsequent liens or mortgages upon the property.

Fiscal Year. Any twelve consecutive months used as a period of financial accounting by an individual or a corporation. The fiscal year of any business concern may or may not coincide with the calendar year.

Fixed Charges. The fixed expenses of a business, which can be determined in advance, and which do not vary in proportion to the amount of business carried on. Fixed charges include interest upon bonds or other fixed or long-time indebtedness, taxes upon property, rent, insurance, and depreciation.

F. O. B. Free on board. This term is used in price quotations to indicate the extent of the undertaking of the seller with respect to defraying the cost of transportation, at the price quoted. Thus, if flour is quoted at ten dollars a barrel, f. o. b. cars Buffalo, the seller undertakes merely to deliver the flour to the railroad company at Buffalo, and the cost of transportation from that point on must be borne by the purchaser.

Foreclosure. A remedy provided by the law for realizing upon the security given for a loan or other obligation, in the event of a failure of the obligor or debtor to comply with the terms of his agreement. The usual mortgage upon real property, for example, provides that in the event of a failure to pay any installment of principal when due, or to make any payment of interest within thirty days after the payment is due, the mortgagee may sell the property at a foreclosure sale and receive payment out of the proceeds of the sale. If, upon a mortgage foreclosure, the amount received from a purchaser is more than sufficient to satisfy the claim of the mortgagee and the expenses of sale, the surplus is turned over to subsequent lienors or, if there are none, to the mortgagor.

The term foreclosure applies, not merely to the sale of real property to realize upon sums advanced upon real property as security, but also to sales of personal property under like circumstances. A foreclosure sale may take place also to satisfy a judgment obtained against the owner of the property or to obtain payment of taxes which have been imposed upon the property.

Fractional Currency. Coins of less than one dollar.

Fully Paid. Stock is "full paid" or "fully paid" when it has been completely paid for by the stockholder and no further payment or assessment can legally be demanded from or imposed upon the stockholder by reason of his ownership of the stock. In order that stock be fully paid, it must have been issued in exchange for cash, property, or services having some reasonable relation in value to the par value or amount of the stock issued.

The practice of issuing so-called fully paid stock, bearing a par value of a particular amount, for worthless patents, fictitious good will, and highly overvalued services of promoters, together with the associated practice of issuing shares of stock as bonuses to subscribers or purchasers of stock, has rendered this term in practice almost meaningless. The misleading character of issues of this sort has led to the introduction of non-par-value stock. This becomes fully paid when any sum, however small, is paid to the cor-poration for the stock, if the agreement between the stockholder and the corporation does not require any further or other payment.

Funding. The floating of a new issue of securities to pay off obligations which have matured or are about to mature. The term is used also with reference to the replacing of a number of outstanding issues of securities by a single new issue, generally for a longer term than the outstanding issues. Such a funding plan frequently provides economies in administration, in addition to extending the period during which the obligations will remain outstanding.

Futures. Contracts for the delivery of stocks or commodities at a future date. Dealing in futures is a very legitimate and even a necessary element in the conduct of some businesses. Thus, a flour manufacturer, in order to make his plans of production for the ensuing quarter or half year, must make his purchases in advance of his actual needs. Only by so doing can he, with any safety, make quotations to his customers for future delivery to them. But speculators upon the commodity and stock exchanges deal in futures in a manner which amounts to plain gambling. These speculators, however, by selling for delivery in the future, relieve the business man of the risks incident to possible fluctuations in prices, and enable him to do business upon a safe, carefully calculated basis.

Garnishee Proceedings. Legal proceedings by which a creditor reaches an obligation owed to his debtor by a third person. Thus, if A owes B $50 and C owes A $50, B may garnishee the sum which C owes to A and thus obtain payment of B's claim against A. In these proceedings, C, the debtor's debtor, is known as the garnishee

Gold Bond. Long-term debt instruments payable in gold coin and issued by governmental units and by private corporations in the days of the gold coin standard. The term "gold" in this connection was intended to promote the sale of such bonds by promising their redemption in the legal tender of that day. After the gold coin standard was abandoned and the dollar was devalued (1934), the Supreme Court refused to enforce payment of the bonds in an amount of dollars having the same total gold equivalent as the dollars originally lent. The Court held that the value of the dollar is determined by its purchasing power rather than its gold equivalent.

Gold Certificates. Paper money issued by the Treasury and which was formerly circulated as legal tender and later, under the limited gold bullion standard, served as legal reserves of the Federal Reserve banks. Recently this requirement has been removed so that the gold certificate is merely a warehouse receipt for gold owned by the Treasury, most of which is part of our international monetary reserve.

Gold Reserve. The term applied to the stocks of gold in the various government depositories, the largest being Fort Knox in Kentucky.

Good Will. Reputation enjoyed by a company or its product, which gives to the product a ready and wide marketability and attracts repeat customers. Frequently, good will constitutes the most valuable single asset a business possesses. Where the good will has been acquired through the expenditure of large sums in advertising, it is deemed proper accounting to set forth as an asset the good will achieved by the advertising at a valuation approximately equal to the sum spent in advertising.

Greenbacks. See *United States Notes.*

Gresham's Law. The principle that, if there is money of different kinds in a country, the better appearing money, or that which intrinsically is more valuable, will either go out of circulation into hoarding or into industry or will be exported, and that that kind of money which is less attractive or of less intrinsic value will tend to become the sole currency of the country.

Gross National Product. This is the market value of all goods and services produced by a nation in a given year. It is the obverse of gross national income, which is the total money value received by the nation for the gross product. The two are equal. The gross national income is measured by (a) compensation to employees, (b) income of proprietors, (c) rental income, (d) corporate profit, including adjustment of inventory values, and (e) net interest received. Gross national product consists of (a) personal consumption expenditures, (b) gross private domestic investment, (c) net export of goods and services, and (d) government purchases of goods and services. In order to show year-to-year trends, the total values are adjusted by price indexes so as to be expressed in dollars of constant value. The totals, as computed by the Commerce Department, have excluded all goods and services that do not enter the market, such as do-it-yourself projects and unpaid housework.

Guarantee. The undertaking by one who is not a direct party to a transaction to perform the promise or obligation made or assumed by another, in the event that the latter does not himself perform the promise or obligation. Bonds of subsidiary corporations are frequently guaranteed by the principal or holding corporation. It is not legally possible, however, for a company to guarantee the payment of the principal or interest upon its own bonds or the payment of dividends upon its own stock. For, in order to have a true guaranty, there must be three parties in the transaction,—the creditor, the debtor, and the guarantor.

Hedging. Either buying or selling in such a manner as to curtail threatened losses through speculative sales or purchases in stocks or commodities. Thus, for example, a speculator agrees to deliver a certain number of units of stock or of a commodity at a certain price at a future time. He intends to cover the sale by purchasing at some time before delivery is due, at a price lower than that named in his contract of sale. Prices then begin to advance in such a manner as to indicate that there probably will be a continuous advance rather than any decline in prices. The speculator will then at once "cover" by buying in the amount of stock or commodity that he has sold, and thus limit his loss to the difference between the price at which he has sold and the price at which he has covered.

Holder in Due Course. One who has acquired a promissory note or other negotiable instrument for value, without notice of any defect in the instrument or in the title of the transferor. A holder in due course may ordinarily recover upon the instrument, regardless of defenses claimed by the maker or by other parties to the instrument. The defense of forgery, however, is available even against a holder in due course.

Holding Company. A corporation whose chief function is the holding of stock in other corporations, the latter being sometimes referred to as its "subsidiaries."

Hypothecation. Depositing stocks or bonds with a creditor as security for the payment of a debt.

Income. Gains received in any form capable of valuation, including compensation for services rendered, interest, dividends, gains from sales and exchanges of personal or real property, profits derived from the conduct of a business, and any other thing of value received during any period.

Income Tax. Federal, state, or city levies imposed upon a person and measured by the income he receives. A state may impose an income tax by reason of the fact that gain has been derived from sources within that state's jurisdiction, even though the person upon whom the tax is imposed has never been, by citizenship or residence, or otherwise, personally subject to the jurisdiction of the state imposing the tax. Income taxes are direct and usually are characterized by progressive rates.

A second type of income tax is one imposed on corporations. As levied in the United States, it presents two differences from the income tax on individuals.

First, the rate is not increased to so high a figure for large incomes. Prior to 1934, a flat rate on earnings was applied irrespective of the amount of earnings. In that year for the first time a slightly higher rate was imposed on larger profits. The change was designed to encourage small enterprises.

Second, higher rates have at times been imposed on companies which retain larger proportions of their earnings to add to surplus. First used under the Revenue act of 1936, this principle is for the purpose of encouraging larger distributions in dividends during the depression period. The money thus distributed is taxable under the individual income tax schedules.

Indenture. An agreement or deed under seal, executed by two or more persons. The origin of the term was in the practice, now obsolete, of executing an agreement in duplicate, or in as many counterparts as there were parties, the copies being separated unevenly in such manner as to create indentures, those in one copy fitting into those in another.

Inheritance and Estate Taxes. Federal and state levies upon the succession to property of a deceased person. Thus, the term "transfer" tax or "succession" tax is sometimes applied to this tax.

Usually, an estate tax is imposed upon the entire estate of the decedent by the state in which he resided at the time of his death, regardless of the situs or physical location of the property left by him. Most states, however, also impose a so-called inheritance tax upon the transfer of property from a deceased person to his heirs at law, or other beneficiaries, if any of the property of the deceased lies within the territorial limits of those states. A so-called inheritance tax is sometimes imposed upon a beneficiary also, by reason of his succession to property, whether under a will or by operation of law, even though the property had no situs or physical presence within the taxing state and the decedent had no residence or domicile there.

Insolvent. Formerly one was deemed insolvent if he was unable to meet his obligations as they matured. The repeated failure of anyone engaged in business to pay definitely maturing obligations upon their due dates was regarded as conclusive evidence of his insolvency.

The term has acquired a new meaning. This meaning has been legislated into legal and commercial usage by the Federal Bankruptcy act of 1898. This act defines an insolvent as one whose liabilities exceed his assets at a fair market valuation. Obviously, under this latter definition, one who fails to meet his obligations as they mature may nevertheless be solvent.

Interest. A periodical return paid for the use of money or other capital. Fundamentally, interest is regarded as a compensation paid to those who deprive themselves of the present use of their funds or capital, in order that these funds may be put to productive and profitable employment. The average rate of interest has been viewed by economists to be determined by two factors—the amount necessary to induce individuals to sacrifice the present for the future, and the amount of additional value that can be created by using the capital thus set aside in producing goods to be consumed in the future. With reference to business loans made by banks, the most important variable in determining the rate is probably the size of the loan, interest rates being scaled upward from the prime rate, that rate which is extended to the top business firms.

Interim Certificates. Frequently, in the reorganization of corporations, considerable time is consumed in carrying into effect the plans of reorganization. It is then customary for stockholders who join in the plan of reorganization to deposit their certificates of stock with designated trustees or with a stockholders' committee, who act for the participating stockholders. These trustees—commonly a single trust company is designated to perform this function—issue to the stockholders interim certificates in exchange for the stock certificates deposited with the trustees. The interim certificate is issued only as a temporary evidence of the interest of the holder.

Interlocking Directorate. The holding by the same persons, of directorships in two or more corporations. When the corporations have dealings with each other, the results may be prejudicial to the interests of one corporation or the other, or outsiders. This circumstance has given rise to criticism of the practice and to restriction of it by Federal law in several fields.

International Bank for Reconstruction and Development (World Bank). A sister institution to the International Monetary Fund (see below), with which it has common membership. This bank makes long-term productive loans to member countries, chiefly for developmental purposes; however, it supplements rather than replaces private investment.

International Monetary Fund. An international financial institution created near the end of World War II and now having 116 members. This bank has the resources to substantially aid members facing temporary balance of payments problems, with the result that these countries have less need to resort to any of the various forms of foreign exchange controls that distort international trade and investment. The Fund extends short and intermediate term loans to members who meet the qualifications.

Internal Loan. A government loan, the securities for which are intended by the government for flotation and sale primarily among its own citizens; as distinguished from an external loan, which is intended primarily for foreign investors. See *External Loan.*

Inventory. An itemized statement or schedule of the assets of an individual, a firm, or a corporation, usually accompanied by a statement of the value of each of the separate items set forth in the schedule.

Investment Banker. One who buys securities wholesale and sells them retail. It is the practice of the well established investment bankers to underwrite or purchase blocks of new securities of corporations and then to market them to their customers. The investment banker is thus the connecting link between persons who have funds in large amounts to invest and persons actively engaged in existing industries or in the promotion of new enterprises.

Invoice. Statement furnished by a seller to a buyer, setting forth in detail the character, quantity, and price of goods sold, and any other terms of the sale.

Jetsam. Goods thrown overboard to lighten a vessel in distress; also called jettison.

Judgment. A determination of a judicial tribunal, reached at the conclusion of legal proceedings. The judgment may impose upon the defendant an obligation to pay a certain sum of money; it may order him to do or to refrain from doing certain acts; or it may merely state a conclusion of law as to what are the rights of the parties.

Judgment Debtor. A debtor against whom a creditor has obtained from a court a judgment which has been placed on record.

Judgment Note. A promissory note containing a power of attorney, authorizing the holder of the note to confess judgment on behalf of the maker or obligor in the event the note is not paid at maturity. The purpose of such a provision is to avoid the necessity of bringing formal legal action against the maker for the recovery of the amount due upon the note. In many states such a power of attorney, if incorporated in the note itself, is given no legal effect.

Killing. The making of exceptionally large profits in a speculative transaction. The word "coup" is sometimes used in a similar sense.

Kiting. A method of obtaining from banks the use of funds for a short period, without paying interest therefor, by the exchange of checks between two or more individuals having accounts in different banks. Thus, if A desires the use of $1000 and is unable or unwilling to borrow the sum from a bank, he may, by prearrangement with a friend, B, who has an account in another bank, request the friend to forward to A a check for $1000. A deposits B's check in the bank with which A keeps his account, and receives credit therefor immediately. A then draws upon the amount thus placed to his credit in his bank, either by obtaining cash from the bank or by issuing checks, to pay his current obligations.

Before B's check reaches the bank with which B keeps his account—and several days may elapse between the deposit of the check in A's bank and its presentation to B's bank—A forwards to B a check drawn upon A's bank for a similar sum, and B deposits the check of A in B's bank, thus obtaining a credit upon the books of the bank sufficient to meet the check drawn by B in A's favor. B then draws a second check in favor of A in the sum of $1000, or in some other sum, which A again deposits in the bank with which A deals. Again A forwards a check to B in a similar amount, which B deposits in time to meet the second check drawn by B in favor of A. By continuing this exchange of checks, it is possible for A to carry indefinitely a fictitious credit in his favor, upon which he can draw in the form of cash or otherwise, depending upon the practice and rules of the particular bank.

Kiting is, therefore, merely a method of taking advantage of the delay incident to the collection of checks. Ordinarily, depositors are not expected to draw checks unless they have on deposit, at the time the check is drawn, sufficient funds to meet the checks. Improved check clearance methods make this practice less prevalent, as will the checkless society of the future. It is now predicted that by about 1980 the transfer of funds may be entirely automated at reasonable cost to the public. One making a payment will merely dial his bank's computer.

Lamb. An amateur speculator upon the stock market who is shorn of his money as the lamb is shorn of its fleece. Thus, buyers of worthless securities, or others deprived of their savings in near-fraudulent transactions, are said to have been "fleeced."

Latin Union. Agreement in 1865 of France, Belgium, Italy, Greece, and Switzerland to adopt a common gold monetary unit as the basis of their systems of currency. In Italy this monetary unit was called the lira; in Greece, the drachma; and in France, Belgium, and Switzerland, the franc. The unit was equivalent to 19.3 cents in United States currency. World War I disrupted the agreement.

Lawful Money. A term covering broadly any form of currency in common use and accepted by government for payment of taxes and fees, whether or not it be legal tender in a technical sense. Prior to 1933, Federal Reserve notes, silver certificates, and national bank notes were lawful money but were not legal tender. In that year the distinc-

tion was wiped out as affecting currency in the United States. See *Legal Tender*.

Legal Investment. By law, savings banks, commercial banks, and insurance companies are required to invest their funds in limited classes of high grade securities. These securities consist of Federal, state, county, and municipal bonds; first mortgages on real estate in an amount not exceeding, under the laws of most states, 60 per cent of the value of the real property; and bonds of certain designated companies. A further limitation with respect to investment in railroad and municipal bonds is frequently imposed, to the effect that the bond of a particular municipality or of a particular railroad may not be the subject of investment if there has been, at any time during the preceding five years, or sometimes a longer period, a failure to pay interest upon its bonds; and, in the case of some railroad bonds, if there has been, for a certain period preceding the investment, a failure to pay dividends.

Either by statute or by repeated rulings of the courts, fiduciaries (in which class are included trustees under wills and under deeds of trust, executors and administrators, and guardians of the estates of minors and incompetents) are required to invest the funds of the trust estate in securities which are legal investments for savings banks. This rule, where not prescribed by statute, is not an absolutely hard and fast limitation upon the investments of fiduciaries. But, if investments are made in any other securities or property than the so-called "legal investments," the fiduciary runs a very serious risk of being held liable personally for any diminution or depreciation in the value of the principal of the estate.

Legal Rate of Interest. The maximum rate of interest fixed by the laws of a state or country as a lawful charge for the use of money. Each state in the Union may fix its own lawful rate of interest. Where individuals of different states, having different legal rates of interest, are involved in a transaction, that rate governs, which is fixed by the laws of the state in which the transaction takes place, or in which it is to be performed.

Where interest in excess of the rate allowed by law is charged, the rate is usurious, and the lender is guilty of usury. Under the laws of most states, if the facts are proved, the lender can then recover neither the interest nor the principal. In some states usury is also made a misdemeanor, punishable under the penal law.

Legal Tender. Currency which a creditor is compelled to accept in payment of a debt, in the absence of an express agreement prescribing the specific kind of money to be paid by the debtor, or no further interest on the debt may be collected.

Before 1933, when all lawful money in the United States was made fully legal tender, gold certificates, gold coin, United States notes, originally issued during the Civil War and known as greenbacks or legal tenders, United States treasury notes of 1890, and silver dollars were full legal tender in unlimited amounts. Silver coins of less than one dollar had limited legal tender qualities.

Letter of Advice. A formal notification sent by the drawer of a bill of exchange to the one upon whom the bill is drawn, generally a banking house with which the drawer has made arrangements for the acceptance of bills drawn by him, advising the latter of the drawing of the bill and of the amount and terms of the instrument.

Letter of Credit. A formal letter, issued by a bank or banking firm on behalf of a customer, requesting correspondents of the bank to honor drafts drawn by the person named in the letter of credit, and to charge the amounts thereof to the issuing bank.

Letters of credit are of two general classes—travelers' letters of credit and commercial letters of credit. The traveler's letter of credit is merely a letter addressed generally to the correspondents of the issuing bank, introducing the person for whose benefit the letter has been issued, and requesting that his drafts be honored up to a named amount by any correspondent bank. The signature of the one in whose favor the letter is issued is written at the bottom of the letter at the time it is issued. With this letter in his possession, a traveler may, at the office of any correspondent bank, obtain currency in any sum up to the amount named in the letter of credit, by writing a draft for the amount desired. The signature upon the draft is compared with the signature upon the letter of credit, and, if it appears to be in proper form, the desired funds will be paid to the holder of the letter of credit in any form of currency he may desire. Whenever any payment is made pursuant to the letter of credit, an entry is made on the reverse side of the letter, showing the date of payment, the bank making the payment, and the amount paid.

Commercial letters of credit are drawn by a bank at the request of a customer, usually in order to facilitate purchases abroad. Thus, if an importer desires to purchase goods in a foreign country on credit, he obtains a letter of credit from his bank or from another bank with which his bank has made arrangements for the issuance of letters of credit. This document may be addressed to a foreign correspondent of the issuing bank, or it may be addressed by the issuing bank directly to the foreign exporter.

The letter in effect is an undertaking or a guaranty that the issuing bank will accept and/or pay all drafts drawn in accordance with the terms specified in the letter of credit. Where the letter specifies that drafts will be honored only when accompanied by negotiable bills of lading, consular invoices, and, sometimes, also by policies of insurance, the instrument is called a "documentary" letter of credit. Where there is no requirement that drafts shall be accompanied by bills of lading or other instruments of title, the letter is called a "clean" letter of credit.

The letter may be a "revocable" letter of credit or an "irrevocable" letter, depending upon the particular terms of the instrument. In the former, the bank reserves the privilege of withdrawing the credit at any time before drafts have been drawn against it. Where the letter is "irrevocable," it remains in effect until it is exhausted or expires by its terms.

Where the letter of credit is forwarded first to a correspondent of the issuing bank, and the correspondent notifies the exporter and undertakes on behalf of the issuing bank to accept drafts drawn by the exporter, pursuant to the letter of credit, the letter is said to be "confirmed." Where, however, the correspondent or notifying bank merely advises the exporter of the receipt of the letter of credit, without itself undertaking to accept or guarantee drafts drawn against it, the letter is "unconfirmed."

Lien (lē'ĕn; lēn). A legal right of a person to detain or control property belonging to another until certain charges upon it have been paid, or until some pecuniary claim against the owner has been satisfied.

Lighterage. Transferring goods from a dock or wharf to a lighter or barge, and then from the lighter or barge to a ship, or vice versa. The term is applied also to the expense involved in thus loading or unloading a vessel, This expense will be incurred whenever the shallowness of the water or the lack of proper dock facilities makes it impossible to load or unload directly from wharf to ship.

Limited. See *Ltd.*

Limited Partnership. A partnership in which the liability of one or more of the members is limited to the amount invested in the business. Such a partner, in the event of the insolvency of the partnership, cannot be held liable for any of its obligations beyond the amount which, under the partnership agreement, he has undertaken to place at the disposal of the business.

Usually, limited partnerships are strictly regulated by statute, the purpose of such regulation being to provide adequate notice to the public of the limited liability of one or more of the partners. These laws generally provide that the active management of the partnership shall be vested solely in the general partners—those members of the firm who are liable, without limitation, for any and all debts contracted by the partnership.

Liquidation. The conversion of the assets of a corporation, firm, or partnership into cash, and the distribution of its assets among the creditors and stockholders or other persons having an interest in the company or business.

A liquidation is known as a "voluntary" liquidation where it results from the mere desire of the owners of the business, or the stockholders of a corporation, to terminate the business and distribute its assets. The liquidation is a "forced" liquidation where the pressure of creditors has thrown the business, or has threatened to throw it, into receivership, and liquidation is the only method by which creditors can receive payment of the sums due them.

Listed. Before a stock or bond may be bought and sold on any of the larger stock exchanges, the security must be submitted to the governors of the exchange or to a special committee appointed to pass upon the character of the security and the qualifications of the corporation issuing the stock or bond. Certain definite requirements usually must be met to qualify the security for listing. When the stock or bond has been approved as fulfilling these requirements, it becomes "listed" on the particular exchange.

Sometimes the term listed is used with reference solely to listing on the New York stock exchange.

Lombard Street. The name applied to the financial section of London, of which Lombard street forms a part. The use of this term corresponds to the use of the term "Wall Street" in this country, as expressive of the entire metropolitan financial district.

Ltd. Abbreviation for the word limited, required to be included in the names of companies organized under limited liability statutes in Louisiana, Great Britain, Canada, and in some other countries. The term "Ltd." is used with the same purpose and effect as the abbreviation "Inc."—which is more commonly used in the United States—to indicate that the company is one in which the liability of the stockholders is limited to the amount invested in the corporation.

Manifest. A complete list of the passengers or freight carried upon each voyage made by a vessel. This list must be signed by the captain or other person in charge of the ship. If a passenger ship, it must contain, in addition to the name of every passenger, a complete record of the voyage, including particularly the name of the port of embarkation and that of the port of landing. Where the manifest covers a shipment of freight, it must contain the name of each shipper or consignor, the character of the freight, the number of packages, and the ports of loading and destination.

Margin. A sum deposited with a broker for the purchase of stocks or commodities on speculation. The "margin" so deposited constitutes a protection against loss to the broker, in the event of a fall in the value of the securities purchased. The amount of the margin required by the broker varies with the speculative quality of the security or commodity to be purchased for the customer. In the case of stocks traded on national exchanges and certain other securities, margin rules are set by the Federal Reserve Board of Governors.

Whenever the price or quotation of a security purchased for a customer on margin falls to such a point that the margin is reduced below the stipulated percentage, the broker calls upon the customer for additional margin. If this is not forthcoming, the broker "sells out" the customer before the fall in price has completely wiped out the margin deposited.

Matched Order. An order to buy, given simultaneously with an order to sell a similar number of shares of the same stock or an equal quantity of a commodity. Such an order really amounts to a fictitious sale and gives an appearance of activity in the particular stock or commodity which has no basis in actual demand. The purpose of "matched orders" is usually to cause an artificial or temporary rise in prices. Penalties are prescribed against traders on national exchanges who use this device. Detection is a duty of the Securities and Exchange Commission.

Mechanic's Lien. Under the laws of many states, one who performs labor or provides materials used in the construction of a building may obtain a lien upon the building for the value of the labor or materials rendered, by filing a notice in the office of the county clerk or registrar of deeds. Such a lien is called a mechanic's lien. The purpose of these statutes is to provide security and some assurance of ultimate payment to those who render services or provide materials by which the owner of the building benefits.

In order to obtain a mechanic's lien, it is not necessary that the work or materials be rendered directly to the owner at his request. A notice of lien may be filed by one who performs work for a contractor or subcontractor. But, in that event, under the laws of most states, the lien is valid only to the extent to which money is or may become due from the owner to the contractor or subcontractor, by reason of work performed upon the structure. The filing of a notice of a mechanic's lien, therefore, operates as a notice to the owner that, if any sums are or may become due to his contractor, he must set aside out of these sums, an amount sufficient to pay the mechanic's lien asserted against the building. To avoid double payment, it is customary for the owner to require a contractor to file a bond, protecting the owner against the possibility of having his property subjected to liens of persons hired by the contractor to perform services upon the building.

Middleman. One who stands between the producer or manufacturer and the consumer. Distributors of all kinds, such as jobbers, wholesalers, retailers, brokers, factors, and commission merchants, are included within this class.

Money. Any generally recognized medium of exchange. In a more limited sense, and as the term money is now commonly used, it applies to the currency or coin either issued or recognized by governmental authority, whether or not it is legal tender, and to demand deposits. See *Legal Tender*.

Money Order. An order payable at sight to a person designated in the instrument, the amount to be charged to the account of the drawer. Money orders are issued by express companies and by the post-office department of the United States government, and, more recently, also by bankers' associations. They are quite similar to cashiers' checks in their essential character and in the purpose which they serve. By reason of their almost universal acceptability and further by reason of the fact that they are made payable to a designated party—so that one not entitled to the money order cannot avail himself of it—they provide a safe and convenient means for transmission of payment through the mails.

Moratorium. An act of the government providing that, during a certain period, creditors shall have no right to bring proceedings against debtors for the collection of debts.

Mortgage. Technically, a transfer of title to real or personal property as security for a loan or other obligation.

Formerly a mortgage was deemed to convey to the mortgagee the ownership in the property subject to defeasance; that is, subject to termination upon payment of the debt for which the mortgage was given as security. Today, however, mortgages, upon either real or personal property, are commonly regarded as giving to the mortgagee merely a lien upon the property mortgaged, and not as conveying any actual rights of ownership.

In most states, statutes provide specifically how mortgages may be foreclosed in the event of nonpayment of the debt for which the mortgage was given, the purpose of these statutes being to protect the mortgagor—the one who gives the mortgage—from a forfeiture of his interest in the property.

In order that the mortgagee shall have a valid lien upon the property mortgaged, as against a person to whom the property may be sold by the mortgagor, or, in most states, even as against judgment creditors of the mortgagor, the mortgage must be recorded. If the mortgage is upon real property, it will be recorded in the office of the clerk or the registrar of deeds of the county where the property is located. Chattel mortgages must generally be recorded in the office of the clerk of the town or municipality in which the mortgagor resides.

Mortgage, Insured. Congress set up in 1934 a Federal Housing Administration, one of whose functions is to insure approved mortgages on homes. The mortgage is insured in favor of the lender of the money, and the insurance is paid for by the borrower. If the borrower defaults, the housing administration makes good the loan. One purpose of the law is to create a class of negotiable mortgages. Insurance eligibility requirements vary from time to time, depending upon economic conditions.

Mortgage Bond. A bond secured by a mortgage upon real or personal property.

Municipal Bonds. Obligations of a city, school district, incorporated village, or other municipality, issued to provide funds for municipal purposes. The term is often used more broadly to include the obligations of the state as well.

National Bank. A bank organized under the National Banking Act of the United States, and subject to regulation by the Comptroller of the Currency and Administration of National Banks, United States Treasury Department. The present national banks have been organized pursuant to acts passed on February 25, 1863 and June 3, 1864, as a part of the general financing plan of the Northern states during the Civil War. These banks were specifically given the power to issue bank notes upon depositing with the Treasury certain types of bonds of the United States. When the eligible types of bonds were called for redemption in 1935, the note-issuing privilege of the national banks lapsed. All national banks are required to be members of the Federal Reserve system and of the Federal Deposit Insurance Corporation.

National Income. See *Gross National Product.*

Negotiable Paper. A check, draft, bill of exchange, or other commercial instrument payable to bearer or to order, the title to which may be transferred by delivery or by endorsement. An instrument is not negotiable unless it is payable to "bearer" (or a recognized equivalent of the term bearer, such as "cash") or to "the order of" a designated person. In order to be negotiable, the instrument must have also a definite or ascertainable date of maturity, and must contain an unconditional obligation to pay a definite sum of money. One who acquires a negotiable instrument for value, prior to maturity and without notice of any defect in the title of previous holders of the instrument, usually may recover against those who appear to be liable upon the instrument, irrespective of any defenses which they may claim against previous holders of the instrument.

Negotiable Securities. Bonds payable to bearer and therefore transferable by delivery, as distinguished from registered bonds, which can be effectively transferred only by changing the registration of the bond at the office of the issuing corporation.

Net. A term applied to a price or to an amount after all discounts and other deductions have been made.

The net weight of a commodity sold in a container is the weight of the contents alone, free from the container.

No Account. When a check, drawn upon a bank in which the drawer is not a depositor, is presented at that bank, it is stamped with the words "no account."

Nonassessable. A term applied to stock in a "limited liability" corporation, which has been paid for in full, and the owner of which, under the terms of the issuance of the stock, cannot be required to make further contributions to the capital or business of the corporation. When such stock has once been fully paid for, the ownership of it entails no further liability on the part of the owner, either to the corporation or to its creditors.

No Protest. An instrument that is not subject to protest is marked with these words. See *Protest.*

Note. An unconditional written promise to pay a specific sum of money at a definite or determinable future date, signed by the person making the promise.

Oath. In law, an oath is a solemn affirmation, usually accompanied by a set formula, such as the words "I do hereby solemnly swear that", etc. One who swears falsely is liable to criminal penalties in nearly all jurisdictions.

Option. A right or privilege to buy (or sometimes to sell) property upon designated terms. An option differs from a contract in that the person to whom the option is given is under no obligation to buy or to sell, whichever the case may be. He may or may not exercise his privilege, as he chooses. In order that an option may be valid and binding, usually something of value must be given to the person granting the option. Otherwise, it is a mere offer, which may be withdrawn at any time.

Outlawed. A colloquial term applied to the barring of rights by the failure to enforce them within a certain period.

The practical administration of justice requires that a definite limitation be placed upon the time within which those who claim rights against others shall enforce these rights in courts of justice. The principle upon which statutes of limitation rest is that the facts about a matter are likely to be obscured by the lapse of time, and also that it is socially desirable that a long existing situation should not be disturbed by reason of long past events.

The period within which an action must be commenced upon a note or other contractual obligation is, under the laws of most states, six years. An instrument under seal, however, does not become outlawed in some states until twenty years have elapsed from the date when the obligation matured. Tort actions—actions for injuries to person or property—are usually "outlawed" in two, three, or four years, the term varying in different states.

Overdrawn. When a depositor draws checks to an amount in excess of the credit to his account, his account is said to be overdrawn. Where such an overdraft is permitted by a bank, it constitutes, in effect, a loan by the bank to the depositor. Such a loan, however, often is not represented by any written instrument from the depositor to the bank.

Paper Money. Any paper currency, whether or not it is legal tender.

Par. The face value of a note, security, or other instrument. A stock or bond is said to sell at par, above par, or below par, accordingly as its sale price is equal to, greater than, or less than, the nominal value stated upon the instrument itself.

Parity Price. This term, used in connection with American farm legislation, means the price of a farm commodity which has the same purchasing power as the price which that commodity had, as an average, in a selected base period. Thus, if a bushel of wheat sold at $1.00 in the base period and the consumer price index later doubled, the parity price would be $2.00 a bushel.

Pass Book. A term sometimes applied to a bank book. See *Bank Book.*

Payable to Bearer. An instrument payable to "bearer" is payable to the holder of the instrument, and may be transferred from one holder to another by mere delivery, without endorsement. Where an instrument is made payable to "cash," it is regarded as payable to bearer.

Payee. The one to whom a note, draft, or other instrument is made payable.

Payor (Payer). The maker or drawer of a promissory note, or of a similar instrument.

Personal Property. Any property, whether tangible or intangible, that is not affixed to land. Stocks, bonds, jewelry, furniture, live stock, automobiles, trade-marks, good will, patents, and leases for definite periods of years are all included within the general class of personal property.

Pit. The trading room of the Chicago board of trade, in which grain, rye, oats, barley, and other commodities are bought and sold.

Point. The unit used in designating the extent of a rise or fall in the market price of a security or a commodity. A point may indicate different amounts for different securities or commodities. Thus, a rise or fall of a point in the quotation of a stock ordinarily indicates a rise or fall of one dollar. In quotations of cotton, a point is $1/_{100}$ of a cent, and a rise of 25 points in the price of cotton would indicate merely an increase of one-quarter of a cent per pound.

Pool. A combination of individuals or interests for the purpose of creating an artificial rise or fall in the price of securities or commodities dealt in upon the stock or commodity markets. The members of the pool combine their resources and, under the management of a designated individual or group of men, buy and sell in a particular stock or commodity with the purpose, either of hammering down the price of the stock or commodity, or of artificially raising the price to a point that will enable them to unload the security or commodity upon the public at a profit.

Operations of these types on national security exchanges were forbidden by law in 1933; those on the commodity exchanges, in 1936. Security traders are now required to obtain licenses from the Securities and Exchange Commission; commodity traders, from the Commodities Exchange Commission. The penalty for engaging in pool operations may be revocation of the trader's license.

Postdated Check. A check bearing a later date than the date upon which it was actually drawn. A postdated check will not be honored by a bank until the date indicated upon the check arrives.

Power of Attorney. A writing or instrument signed by one person and giving to another person authority to perform certain acts on behalf of the signer of the instrument. A power of attorney, in most states, must either be witnessed, or be acknowledged before a notary public or other official authorized to take acknowledgments. The power of attorney may be very general in its scope, or it may be limited to a single specific act.

A power of attorney may be terminated at any time by the grantor of the power, unless the holder of the power of attorney has some pecuniary interest of his own which would be violated or infringed by the termination.

For some purposes, a power of attorney may be conferred by one person upon another by mere oral or parol authorization, without any instrument in writing. An authority conferred in this manner is more properly termed a mere agency rather than a power of attorney.

Preferred Creditor. A creditor entitled to payment of his claims before the claims of mere general creditors are paid. Whether a creditor has a preferred claim becomes important where a debtor has become insolvent or has been adjudicated a bankrupt. Claims arising out of personal services rendered within two years of the filing of a petition in bankruptcy are entitled to a preference, and such claims must be paid in full before other debts may be paid.

Preferred Stock. Stock in a corporation, which confers upon the holder a prior right to dividends or to payment out of the assets of the corporation, in the event that the corporation is dissolved.

The usual preference given to holders of preferred stock is one entitling the holders to dividends of a certain per cent upon the par value of their stock in each year, before any dividends shall be paid to holders of the common stock. This preference as to dividends may be either cumulative or noncumulative. If the dividend preference is cumulative, then, if no dividends, or dividends less than the amount of the dividend preference, are paid in any year upon the preferred stock, the amount unpaid must be paid to the holders of the preferred stock before any dividends can be paid upon the common stock in any subsequent year. If the preference as to dividends is noncumulative, then, if no dividends are paid upon the preferred stock in any year, such omission of dividends does not affect the relative rights of the holders of preferred and common stock in any subsequent year, the prior omission of payment of dividends to the preferred stockholders being disregarded.

Generally, the dividends which holders of preferred stock may receive from the corporation are limited to a definite rate or amount. Thus, if the preferred stock entitles the holder to dividends of 7 per cent upon the par value of the stock, all of the profit in any year, in excess of the dividends to which the preferred stock is entitled, goes to the holders of the common stock. This, however, is not necessarily the case. For, in the absence of a provision limiting the holders of preferred stock to dividends of a certain per cent, preferred stockholders are entitled to share equally with the common stockholders in any excess profits distributed by the corporation, after the common stockholders have received dividends at a rate equal to that paid to the holders of the preferred stock. See *Common Stock.*

Premium. When any security having a par value sells at a price above par, it is said to be quoted at a premium. The term is used also in transactions in international or foreign exchange, with reference to the amount above the normal exchange rate at which any particular currency is quoted.

Price Index. This term applies to a measure of prices. To prices in a base period is assigned the number 100 on the scale, and a change of one point represents a change of one per cent of the prices in the base period.

The prices are weighted by the amount of each commodity or service usually purchased. From time to time the items priced are reviewed and altered or changed in weight to reflect current spending habits.

Both consumer and wholesale price indices are calculated and used by the federal government to compute the present purchasing power of the dollar as compared with its purchasing power in other years.

Principal. The capital sum due upon a bond or other obligation as distinguished from the interest which accrues or becomes due upon the principal from time to time.

Profit. This is the excess of a firm's revenue in a given period over all operating and overhead costs, including depreciation and pro-rated cost of capital invested. If revenue is insufficient to cover the costs, there is a loss.

It is from profits that dividends normally are paid. On the average, about two-thirds of profits are paid in dividends and one-third is retained for reinvestment in the business. This fact helps account for the long-term upward bias in stock prices, since capital is continually accumulated in this way for further earnings.

Corporations are taxed by the federal government on the basis of their profits. Profits after taxes form the chief determinant of the market value of the firm's stock. Since rising stock values facilitate the raising of new capital, as well as benefiting the stockholders, management has a strong incentive to increase profits by improving and diversifying the products offered for sale and by reducing the costs of doing business. It is this characteristic of the profit system that is responsible for the dynamic nature of capitilistic economies in comparison with communistic regimes, in which the profit motive is discouraged.

Profiteering. Selling goods or services at a price yielding an unusually large profit. In 1918, Congress passed a law designed to prevent and punish profiteering in certain businesses. This law, however, was held unconstitutional.

Promissory Note. An instrument containing an unconditional promise to pay a definite sum of money to a particular person or to his order, or to bearer, either on demand or at a definite future time. A promissory note may be either negotiable or nonnegotiable. It is nonnegotiable when it is payable to a definite person only, and not to his order or to bearer, or when it does not meet any of the other requirements of the negotiable instruments law.

Promoter. One who makes a business of floating or financing new enterprises or of obtaining additional capital for already existing enterprises.

Pro Rata. In proportion to their respective rights or liabilities. Thus, it is the policy of the law that creditors of an insolvent debtor shall share pro rata in his assets; that is, in proportion to their respective claims. Conversely, where several persons are engaged in a joint enterprise, it is the policy of the law that they shall, as among themselves, be liable pro rata for any obligations incurred; that is, they share the burden in proportion to their interests in, or contributions to, the entreprise.

Protest. The formal step necessary to fix the liability of the endorsers of a check, note, or other instrument which has been presented to the maker or acceptor for payment and has been refused. In the case of a note or of a draft or bill of exchange payable at a definite future date, the instrument must be presented formally to the maker or acceptor during business hours upon the date of maturity. If the instrument is not paid before the close of business on that day, the notary who made the formal presentation of the instrument for payment certifies over his seal and signature that the instrument was presented and payment was refused. This certification is the "protest" of the instrument.

It is usually not necessary, particularly in domestic, as opposed to foreign, business, that the note or draft be presented and protested for nonpayment in order that the maker shall remain liable upon the instrument.

Proxy. An authorization from one person to another to act in his place and on his behalf. It is customary for stockholders of a corporation to vote their stock by proxy; that is, by executing a written authority authorizing another to act on their behalf at a meeting of the stockholders.

Put. An agreement to accept and pay for a certain amount of a stock, or of a commodity, at a fixed price at any time before the expiration of a designated period.

Pyramiding. Buying additional blocks of a particular stock or commodity upon margin, with the book profits yielded by a rise in prices. Thus, a customer requests a broker to buy 100 shares of a particular stock at 25 dollars a share, on a five-point margin, that is, a margin of 20 per cent, and gives directions to the broker to buy additional stock upon the same margin upon each advance in the market price of the stock. If the stock advances five points, the broker, under his instructions, will buy another hundred shares upon a similar margin upon the basis of the five-point paper profits yielded by the first purchase. As the stock continues to rise in price, the paper profits furnish additional margin for further purchases, until a large quantity of the stock has been purchased; and, if the stock so purchased is unloaded before a fall in the price of the stock, a very handsome profit upon the original investment will result.

Quotation. A price bid or asked for a stock, bond, or commodity. Sometimes a quotation may represent an actual market price based upon actual sales.

Rate of Exchange. The actual price at which a unit of currency of one country exchanges for a unit of currency of another country. Under normal conditions, the monetary unit of one country has a definite par in terms of the currency of any other country, generally based upon the amount of pure gold represented by the respective monetary units. When exchange is at par—one of the possible rates—, then the currency of one country has a value, in transactions with persons of the other country, equal to the relative amount of gold represented by the monetary units when operating under gold standard conditions.

Where paper currency which is not redeemable in gold, circulates within a country, a new element is introduced. The currency of such a country will be exchangeable for the currency of other countries at a rate established by other factors. Under "managed currencies," such as Great Britain's became in 1931 and that of the United States became in 1933, the par may be set by tacit agreement and with an eye to its effect on internal prices. Sometimes each government, in such cases, uses a large "stabilization fund" to support at a definite level the value of its own currency through buying or selling those of other countries. In other cases an international financial institution may carry on these support or pegging operations.

Rating. The credit worth of an individual, firm, or company, as estimated by Dun and Bradstreet, Inc., or any other recognized mercantile agency.

Real Property. Land and all things permanently attached to the land. Thus, real property includes structures erected upon the land and intended to remain affixed for an indefinite time, minerals, water flowing through the land, trees and other issues of the soil (excepting crops which are planted and reaped yearly or more frequently), rights of way and other easements, and rights of every nature in land and in waters, not including, however, leases for years or mere licenses.

Rebate. A return of part of a sum received for goods, for services rendered, or for taxes overpaid. Some uses of the rebate device are now illegal. For example, at one time it was customary for railroads to make rebates to large or favored shippers. The result of this practice was that certain large corporations were able to save sufficiently upon their transportation costs to undersell their smaller or less favored competitors. The result of this was to crush the smaller concerns out of existence. The Interstate Commerce Act of 1887 and the amendments which have since been made to that act have had, as one of their chief objects, the prevention of this practice. Under this act, the giving of a rebate by any railroad or other common carrier in interstate commerce was made a crime.

Receiver. Person appointed by a court to manage the property of a person or a company, pending the termination of legal proceedings affecting the property or its owner. Thus, a receiver may be appointed to receive the rents and profits of a property with respect to which mortgage foreclosure proceedings have been instituted. Similarly, a receiver may be appointed to receive the rents and profits of property the ownership of which is disputed.

The type of receiver that is most common, however, is the receiver who is appointed ostensibly to take over the assets and continue the business of a corporation, pending its dissolution. Frequently this means of preserving the property of a corporation until its affairs can be liquidated is abused by those in charge of the affairs of the corporation. Thus, the receiver may be appointed at the behest of friendly creditors, with the sole purpose of preventing unfriendly creditors from pressing their claims and levying execution upon the property of the company. No bona fide purpose to dissolve the corporation or to liquidate its affairs then exists; but the protection which receivership proceedings provide against the collection of claims by creditors is obtained. In these cases, therefore, a receivership merely grants the corporation a moratorium —a suspension of payment of its debts—and serves no other purpose than to carry the corporation through temporary financial straits.

Refunding. Floating a new issue of securities to replace outstanding issues which are about to mature.

Registered Bonds. Bonds payable to a definite person designated in the face of the bond, and transferable only by endorsement properly witnessed and by an entry of the transfer upon the books of the issuing corporation. Where the bond is registered not merely as to principal but also as to interest, the interest is paid by check to the record holder of the bond, without the necessity of the transmission of any coupons to the corporation. When the bond is registered as to principal only, and not as to interest, it usually bears coupons representing the interest due or to accrue upon the bond, the coupons being payable to bearer and cashed upon presentation as they mature.

Registrar. One who records original issues and transfers of stock or bonds of a corporation. The functions of the registrar generally include the duty of safeguarding against a fraudulent or erroneous overissue of stock or bonds by the officers of the corporation. The registrar must then make certain that no certificates of stock or bonds are issued unless they are part of a duly authorized original issue or are issued in place of surrendered and canceled certificates of like amount.

Reserve. Funds set aside to meet a contingent or definite future expenditure.

Most corporations have a reserve for obsolescence and depreciation, the purpose of which is to provide a fund with which to replace capital assets when they have become worn out or useless. Where a company carries its own insurance—that is, does not take out insurance with regular insurance companies, but carries its own risks as to fire loss or other damage—a reserve will be accumulated from year to year so that, in the event of a loss by fire or otherwise, there will be sufficient funds set aside to cover the loss. It is also customary for companies that have issued bonds or other long-term notes to set aside annually a certain amount as a so-called reserve, with which to fund or pay the bonds or notes when they become due. Banks are required by law to maintain a reserve consisting of cash or its equivalent, amounting to a certain proportion or percentage of their deposits. See *Bank Reserves*.

Rights. The term applied to the privilege given to existing stockholders of a corporation to purchase a proportionate number of shares of any new issue of the company's stock.

Under the law which has grown up with respect to the rights of stockholders in corporations, a stockholder is entitled to subscribe to any new issue of stock that the corporation may make, in proportion to his holdings in the corporation, before the stock may be offered to the general public. Where the outstanding stock of the corporation has a market value higher than par, this privilege of purchasing stock of the new issue, at par or at any price lower than the market quotation for the outstanding stock, is a valuable one. Thus, assuming that there are 10,000 shares of the stock of a corporation outstanding, the shares having a par value of $100, but selling on the market at $150, if a new issue of 5000 shares is to be offered at $100 per share, each stockholder would be entitled to purchase one share of the new issue for each two shares which he already owns in the corporation. The holder of 100 shares would then be the owner of 50 so-called "rights," a right being the privilege of purchasing one share of stock of the new issue. If the new stock is issued at $100 and the stock outstanding is quoted at $150, then the value of a right would be something less than $50. These rights may be bought and sold and, in the case of stocks having a wide market, are sometimes the subject of considerable speculation.

Savings Banks. Banks organized for the purpose of receiving deposits from small savers, and utilizing these savings in the form of investments in high-grade bonds and in loans upon real estate. Savings banks are very strictly regulated by statute in nearly all states, with the purpose of insuring the utmost safety to depositors. Thus, savings banks are generally prohibited by law from investing their funds in other than Federal, state, or municipal bonds and bonds of certain designated railroads, and in loans secured by first mortgages upon real estate, where the loan is not in excess of 60 per cent of the value of the property. Generally, deposits in savings banks are not subject to check or to withdrawal upon demand, although banks frequently waive the requirement that they receive a certain period of notice of an intended withdrawal.

Scrip. A form of promissory note or certificate of indebtedness, issued by a corporation to its stockholders in lieu of cash dividend payments. A corporation will resort to the use of scrip dividends when, although the profits of the company are such as to warrant some return being made to the stockholders upon their holdings in the company, the amount of actual cash on hand is not enough to permit immediate payment of cash to the stockholders.

Second Mortgage. A mortgage upon property which is already subject to a prior or first mortgage. Mortgages are called first, second, third, or fourth mortgages, according to the order in which they have been placed upon the property, and they are entitled to payment out of the property in order of their priority. Thus, if a second mortgage is foreclosed on default in the payment of interest or principal, the property can be sold only subject to the first mortgage. In other words, only the equity of the owner above the first mortgage can be relied upon to pay the amount of the second mortgage. In the event that the interest or principal due upon the first mortgage is not paid when due, the first mortgage may be foreclosed, and, in that event, the amount of the first mortgage must be paid out of the proceeds before any sum will be paid to the holders of the second or subsequent mortgages. If, after payment of the amount of the first mortgage and the expenses of the foreclosure sale, there is any residue, this will be paid to the second and subsequent mortgagees or lienors, in order of their priority.

Secured Creditor. A creditor who has security or collateral, in the form of personal or real property, for a sum due him from a debtor.

Securities. Stocks, bonds, and other evidences of long-term indebtedness or of ownership in a corporation.

Seigniorage. A profit-yielding charge made by a government for coining bullion into money.

Sellers' Option. A contract entered into in a stock or commodity exchange, whereby the seller is given the option of delivering at any time during a specified period upon one day's notice to the buyer. Under New York Stock Exchange rules, the period of a sellers' option cannot be less than four days nor longer than sixty days. "Sellers' option four" or "sellers' option ten" designates the period during which delivery may be made. See *Bids and Offers, Buyer's Option.*

Selling Short. Selling for "future delivery." One who sells short makes an agreement whereby he agrees to deliver at a future time, a stock or commodity which he does not possess at the time he enters into the contract to deliver, with the expectation that he will be able to purchase the stock or commodity, before delivery is due, at a lower price than he sold for. One who habitually sells short is called a "bear." See *Bear.*

Sight Draft. An order due and payable upon presentation to the person upon whom it is drawn. The ordinary bank check is, in effect, a sight draft. See *Draft.*

Silent Partner. One who has money invested in the business of a partnership and shares in its profits and losses, but whose interest in the business is not known to the general public. A silent partner is usually liable without limit for all of the debts of the partnership but only for those incurred while he maintained his interest in the business. He may, however, retire from the partnership at any time without giving notice to the public. See *Limited Partnership.*

Silver Certificate. Prior to the summer of 1968, this was paper currency issued by the government of the United States as a substitute for, and representative of, silver dollars deposited with the United States treasury.

Simple Interest. Interest computed on the principal only. Simple interest is to be distinguished from compound interest. In the latter, at regular intervals, interest due or accrued is added to the principal, and interest is computed thereafter upon the principal plus the interest so credited.

Single Standard. A phrase used to describe a monometallic monetary system in which one metal is used as the sole standard of value. Formerly, nearly all countries had a bimetallic system, or double standard, in which both silver and gold were freely coined at a certain ratio. Values were then determined in terms of either silver or gold. England was the first country formally to adopt the single gold standard, the act accomplishing this reform having been passed in 1816. The single gold standard was formally adopted by the United States in 1900.

Sinking Fund. A fund created by setting aside periodically, out of earnings or revenue, sums with which to pay bonds or other long-term obligations when they mature. A sinking fund may be created also for the purpose of replacing worn-out machinery or other capital assets. See *Amortization.*

SDR (Special Drawing Rights). Reserve assets created in the form of book entries by the International Monetary Fund and divided among member countries in proportion to their present IMF quotas. Within limits, each member country is required to accept SDR balances in exchange for convertible currency, from other countries offering them in the settlement of balance of payments obligations. In general, the SDR's may be used by national governments in the same ways as gold and other international reserve items are used.

Specie. Coined money.

Spot. A term used in quotations on commodity exchanges to indicate that the price is for immediate delivery and cash payment.

Standard Weight and Fineness. A phrase referring to the weight and purity of the metal in a monetary unit established by law. Thus, the gold dollar, existing since 1934 only in the form of bullion, has a standard weight of $15^5/_7$ grains, $^9/_{10}$ fine, that is, $^9/_{10}$ pure gold and $^1/_{10}$ copper alloy, or $13^5/_7$ grains of pure gold.

State Banks. Banks organized under the laws of a particular state and subject to state regulation.

Sterling. Abbreviation for the pound sterling, the unit of account of the English monetary system. For nearly a century the pound sterling at par was equivalent to $4.86. Its par is now $2.40.

Sterling Exchange. British money or bills of exchange payable in British money.

Stock. The capital stock of a corporation represents the amount invested by stockholders in the business of a corporation. From the point of view of the law, the capital so invested represents a fund to which creditors may look for payment of debts incurred by the corporation.

The capital stock of a corporation is usually divided into a number of shares which are held by the various stockholders of the company. These shares, evidenced by certificates of stock, represent the proportionate interest which each stockholder has in the corporation.

Stock Certificate. A printed or engraved certificate issued as an evidence of ownership of stock in a corporation. This certificate must be signed by authorized officials of the company; sometimes also by a "registrar of transfers."

Stock certificates may be transferred by endorsement upon the reverse side of the certificate, or by a separate instrument of transfer. The transfer, however, vests no rights in the one to whom the transfer is made, as against the corporation, until a record of the transfer has been made on the books of the corporation.

Under these statutes, if a certificate is endorsed in blank by the holder of record, it becomes similar to a negotiable instrument, the ownership of which can be transferred by mere delivery from one person to another. Under the Uniform Stock Transfer act, which has been adopted in a majority of states, one who, in good faith, purchases a certificate which bears a valid endorsement may obtain a good title even though the certificates have been stolen from, or lost by, the true owner.

Stock Dividend. Nominally, a distribution of surplus or earnings to stockholders, in the form of additional stock, rather than in the form of cash. The use of the term distribution, in connection with stock dividends, is, however, misleading. For, in a stock dividend no property is turned over by the corporation to its stockholders. The stockholders merely receive additional evidences of their ownership or interest in the company. Thus, if a stock dividend of 100 per cent has been declared and made by a corporation, each stockholder merely holds two shares of stock where he formerly held one. The net assets of the company remain unchanged, and the proportionate interest of each stockholder in the net assets of the company remains the same. His interest in the company, however, is evidenced by a greater number of shares of stock.

Where the stock has a par value, a stock dividend operates to convert surplus on the books of the company into capital stock.

Stop-loss Order. An order left by a customer with his broker directing the broker to sell stock owned by the customer in the event of a fall in the price of the stock below a certain point. The object of such an order is to check further loss where there appears a definite tendency to a decline in the price of the stock.

Where a stock or commodity has been sold short by the customer, an order would be placed with the broker to buy as soon as the price had risen to a definite point, in order to avoid greater losses, which would be incurred if the customer were compelled to cover at a still higher price.

Stop Payment. An order by a customer to a bank, directing it to refuse payment of a check or other instrument drawn by the customer upon the bank, or made payable at the bank.

A bank owes no obligation to the holder of a check drawn upon the bank by a customer, in the absence of a certification of the check by the bank. The bank may, therefore, with entire impunity, refuse payment of a check upon which the drawer has stopped payment. If the check, however, has been transferred by the payee or any other holder to a bona fide purchaser, either by endorsement or, if payable to bearer, by delivery, then the drawer of the check may be held liable to such a transferee for the amount of the check. No claim, however, can be made against the bank by any holder or transferee of the instrument.

Subpœna. A writ issued by a court of law commanding a person to appear on a certain day and at a place designated under a penalty for nonappearance or default.

Subpœna Duces Tecum (*sŭb-pē′na dū′sēz tē′kŭm*). A court order in an action, directing a witness to bring with him any books, documents, or other papers in his possession or control which may or can be used as evidence. Such an order must describe with reasonable clearness what is wanted.

Supplementary Proceedings. A statutory remedy brought against a judgment debtor in aid of execution, for the purpose of locating and setting apart property of his to be applied in satisfaction of the judgment.

Surplus. The net worth of a firm or corporation, above its capital or capital stock. The term nominally includes both earnings from business operations and increases in the value of capital assets.

Tare. The difference between the gross and the net weight of an article in a container or vehicle. The gross weight of a barrel of flour is the total weight, including the container. The net weight is the weight of the flour itself. The difference between the gross and the net weight is the "tare."

Teller. A paying teller is an officer of a bank who pays out cash over the counter upon checks and other instruments made payable at the bank.

A receiving teller is a bank officer who receives and counts sums deposited with the bank, giving receipts for the funds deposited.

Ticker. An instrument, operated by telegraph, which automatically types messages transmitted from a central station. The instrument is used in brokers' offices, primarily for receiving prompt information with regard to stock transactions.

Time Deposit. A deposit of funds with a bank, under an agreement that the bank shall be entitled to the use of the funds for a definite period, or until a certain number of days have elapsed after notice has been given of an intention to withdraw the deposit.

Trade Acceptance. See *Acceptance*.

Trade Discount. A deduction, usually on a percentage basis, from the retail or "list" price of goods, allowed to a merchant by the manufacturer or jobber.

Trade-Mark. A special mark or symbol used for the purpose of identifying a certain product, or the products of a certain merchant or manufacturer. A trade-mark is protected under the law against use or appropriation by others than the one first to use the particular mark. The purpose of this protection given by the law is chiefly to prevent fraud upon the public.

Trade-marks may be registered at the United States patent office. Such registration does not add to the rights already possessed, without registry, by the owner of a trade-mark. Registration, however, provides conclusive evidence of a time since which the trade-mark has been used, and may prove of considerable value in the event of any litigation respecting the particular trade-mark.

Transfer Agent. Custodian of the stock book of a corporation, whose duty is to record transfers of stock and to issue new stock certificates in place of the surrendered certificates.

Transfer in Blank. Normally, stock is transferred by delivery, accompanied by an endorsement upon the reverse side of the stock certificate, made by the one in whose name the certificate has been issued. Where the name of the person to whom the stock is transferred is left blank, the stock certificate is said to be endorsed "in blank," and may then be transferred from one person to another by mere delivery, without further endorsement.

The stock is not effectually transferred, as against the corporation, however, until an entry of the change of ownership has been made upon the books of the corporation. And all rights of participation in benefits accruing to stockholders, including the right to dividends and the right to vote at stockholders' meetings, are determined by the record of stock ownership kept by the corporation.

Treasury Certificates. Short-term obligations bearing interest, issued by the United States government.

Treasury Notes. Certain paper currency issued by the United States government at intervals beginning in 1862 and now mostly retired. Today the term is used mainly to denote an intermediate credit instrument issued and sold by the United States Treasury.

Trust Companies. Corporations organized under state and federal laws, usually with powers to carry on a general commercial banking business and to act in various fiduciary capacities. These fiduciary capacities include acting as an executor under a will; administrator of the estate of a deceased person; trustee under a will, a deed of trust, or a mortgage indenture; guardian of the estate of an infant; committee of the estate of an incompetent; registrar and transfer agent of a corporation; and fiscal agent for a person, a corporation, or a municipality.

Trustee. One to whom property or rights are transferred, to be administered for the benefit of a certain person or group of persons known as the beneficiaries of the trust, or the *cestuis que trustent*.

A trustee under a will or a deed of trust is usually given the custody of property or securities, for the purpose of collecting and distributing the income for a designated period—during the minority of an infant or during the life of the beneficiary—the principal to be preserved intact by the trustee and distributed to certain persons at the termination of the trust.

A trustee under a corporate mortgage is appointed to safeguard the interests of numerous bondholders scattered throughout the country. It is the duty of such a trustee to see that the corporation which has given the mortgage does nothing to lessen the value of the property which forms the security for the bonds issued.

Underwriting. An agreement to share in the risk of a proposed venture or undertaking. Before the rise of the large insurance corporation, it was customary for a group of capitalists to underwrite a policy of fire, marine, or other insurance, each underwriter, or person who subscribed his name to the agreement, undertaking to pay a definite proportion of the loss.

The term is now frequently applied to an agreement by private banking houses, or by other dealers in securities, to provide a market for a proposed issue of bonds or other securities. Such an underwriting agreement normally contains a promise by the underwriters that they will dispose of a certain proportion of the securities to the general public on or before a certain date, and, if all of the securities are not taken up by the general public, that the underwriter will himself purchase the remainder. Where the proposed issue is large, a number of private banking houses form a "syndicate" and together underwrite the issue. They then proceed to use their joint efforts to dispose of the stock to the public. A generous commission is usually paid to the underwriters for the service rendered.

Unearned Increment. The increase in the value of land, resulting from an increase in population or from any other cause not traceable to the expenditures or efforts of the individual owner.

United States Notes. Paper money of the United States, originally issued under the act of February 25, 1862. This currency was merely a promise by the government to pay the bearer, on demand, the face amount of the note in gold. In fact, however, the notes were not redeemable until 1879, when specie payments were resumed by the government. These notes, when issued, were expressly made legal tender for all debts, and were received in payment for all public dues except customs and excise taxes. By reason of their legal-tender quality, they were popularly called "legal tenders." They were also called "greenbacks," from the color of the reverse side of the notes. Some of these notes still circulate, having been replaced when worn out as required by special and long-standing legislation.

Unlisted Securities. Stocks and bonds not listed upon the recognized stock exchanges. Frequently the term is applied to any security not listed upon the New York stock exchange. See *Listed*.

Upset Price. The price below which a security or a commodity will not be offered; as, for example, by an auctioneer at a public sale.

Voucher. A receipt, evidencing a payment of money, together with a statement of the items for which the payment was made.

Wall Street. Name popularly given to the financial district of New York City, of which Wall street itself forms the center.

Warehouse Receipt. A receipt issued by a warehouseman, evidencing a deposit of certain goods with him. The warehouse receipt may be negotiable; that is, it may run to the bearer or to the order of the depositor of the goods, in which case it may be transferred by delivery or by endorsement from one holder to another. When a negotiable receipt has been issued, the goods will be surrendered by the warehouseman only upon a surrender of the receipt. For many purposes, such a receipt may then be dealt with in commerce as though it were the goods themselves, since the possession of the receipt gives control over the goods. Thus, banks frequently make loans upon these negotiable receipts as collateral, and the goods themselves are bought and sold in the market by mere negotiation or delivery of the receipt.

The Uniform Warehouse Receipt act, which has been passed in most states, is designed to further the commercial dealing in negotiable warehouse receipts as the representatives of the goods. This act, however, differs from that governing negotiation of "order bills of lading," in that a pledgee or purchaser of a warehouse receipt from or through a thief or a finder gets no title to the receipt or to the goods represented by it.

Warrant. In law, a warrant is a precept, or writ, issued by a court, authorizing a public official to do some special act; as, for example, to make an arrest. In business, a warrant is a written authorization proceeding from a competent source to a proper individual, conveying power to receive either money, its equivalent, or other personal property, or to pay money to one who is entitled to receive it. In England, the term is in general use to designate a receipt for goods which have been deposited in a warehouse, showing the date of entry, the person or persons to whom the goods are deliverable, the date upon which rent commences, and all other details necessary to identify the particular parcels for which the warrant is issued. The warrant is transferable by endorsement.

Warrant, Bench. A warrant issued by a court "in bench," authorizing an officer to arrest and bring before the court persons who are in contempt, or who have disobeyed a court order, or who have been indicted. The name distinguishes this writ from warrants issued by inferior judicial officials.

Warrant, Search. A written authority of state, issued by a court, directing some judicial officer to examine a named place for articles alleged to be unlawfully concealed there. The articles most commonly searched for are stolen and embezzled goods, counterfeit money, gambling implements, and other unlawful possessions.

Wash Sales. Fictitious sales made for the purpose of creating an artificial market price for a stock or commodity. Wash sales on national exchanges are now forbidden under penalty of law. See *Pool, Bear*.

Watered Stock. Where stock has been issued, having a total nominal or par value in excess of the capital actually invested in a corporation, the stock is said to be "water." And the amount of stock issued in excess of the actual assets held by the corporation is called "water." The result of watering stock is to mislead creditors of the corporation and the general public who form a market for the sale of the stock of the corporation.

When, As, and If Issued. Frequently, when a corporation plans to issue stock or bonds to the public, a campaign for the sale of the securities will be undertaken before the necessary legal steps involved in creating the new issue of securities have been completed. The corporation, or the banking house through which it has arranged to dispose of the securities, in order to safeguard itself against the possibility of some legal obstacle preventing the proposed issue, will then offer the securities to the public "when, as, and if issued." In the event that, for any reason, the securities are not issued, the corporation or the banking house through which it operates will then not be liable to those who have given orders for the proposed stock or bonds.

Will. A formal, written instrument executed pursuant to provisions prescribed by law, providing for the distribution of the property of the testator—the person making the will—at his death. Normally, a will may be revoked or amended by the testator at any time before his death.

Under the laws of most states, a will is invalid unless it is subscribed by the testator and declared by him to be his last will and testament, in the presence of two witnesses who, at his request, also subscribe their names to the will in the presence of the testator and in the presence of each other. In some states, three witnesses are necessary. Under exceptional circumstances, as in the case of a soldier dying on the field of battle, the ordinary formalities necessary to render a will valid may be omitted.

Without Recourse. One who endorses a note, check, or other commercial instrument is usually liable to subsequent holders of the instrument, in the event of the non-payment of the instrument at maturity, if proper presentation and protest of the instrument is made. If one desires to relieve himself from this liability, he must prefix or append to his endorsement the words "without recourse." His endorsement then merely operates to transfer such title as he has to the instrument, and carries with it no implied promise to pay the instrument in the event that the maker does not pay it at maturity.

AGRICULTURE

The story of modern agriculture is one of man's inventive mind, his observation, experimentation, innovation, and adaptation. The annual abundance created by modern agriculture is often taken for granted in Western society. It should not be, as it is a triumph only recently achieved by man in managing nature's elements. Furthermore, world population pressures are constantly challenging man's ingenuity in the food production-consumption cycle.

Today the skilled commercial farm operator in the United States has the resources and ability to produce enough food for himself and at least 50 others. Only five percent of the nation's people live on farms and ranches, yet they produce ample food and fiber for themselves and the other 95 per cent of the population. In addition, there is enough left to export to other areas of the world. American consumers are the primary beneficiaries of this agricultural production-marketing miracle, since they need spend only about 17 per cent of their disposable income for food, the lowest in man's experience.

The background of modern agriculture, like that of the human race itself, begins in prehistoric times. Nevertheless, to a certain limited extent, it can be told. Through the discovery of various tools used by the ancient races, scientists have been able to trace the development of man, from the stone ages, through the periods when bronze implements were substituted for stone and when iron displaced bronze. By a somewhat similar method, the story of prehistoric agriculture has been pieced together.

Emerson has written that "the first farmer was the first man," but, according to archeological records, the earlier man knew nothing of agriculture. He was a hunter who was probably forced by hunger to eat wild fruits, grasses, and roots, when he could capture no game. Such was the condition of the men of the Paleolithic or Old Stone Age. They were hunters and fishers who had fire and probably the bow and arrow, but no domestic animals, with the possible exception of the dog.

Prehistoric Agriculture. Sometime during the Paleolithic period, possibly some 25,000 to 50,000 years ago, man acquired his first ideas of planting the edible seeds from wild plants, thus producing crops of grain. The men of the next period, the Neolithic or New Stone age, not only polished their stone tools and kept dogs, sheep, goats, and oxen, but also learned to raise wheat, barley, and millet. Where wheat was first found is an unsolved question that has provoked much discussion. Many scientists now believe that it originated as a wild grass, somewhere in the region of the eastern Mediterranean. The grain was gradually improved and ultimately carried to all parts of the earth. It did not reach the American continent until after Columbus' voyage, nor was it known in Australia until 1788.

Although Neolithic man had learned some of the benefits of keeping domestic animals and of planting grain, he nevertheless depended on hunting and fishing for a large part of his food and clothing. But the hunters slowly changed their modes of living to those of shepherds or farmers. Some tribes increased their herds of cattle and sheep, and adopted the nomadic life necessary to guarding their animals and leading them to new pastures. Others found that in certain rich valleys food was most easily obtained by erecting permanent dwellings and devoting their energies to tilling the soil. From farming settlements of this kind, made in Mesopotamia and Egypt, came the first civilized communities of which any record can be found.

Ancient Agriculture. Five thousand years before Christ, both in the valley of the Nile and in the rich country between the Tigris and Euphrates rivers, crops of bearded wheat, six-rowed barley, millet, flax, and durra, which is a variety of sorghum, were raised by tillage and irrigation. The earliest Egyptians seem to have known onions, garlic, radishes, beans, chick-peas, lentils, and the castor bean. Cattle grazed on the grass-covered range; poultry and swine were well known; sheep were raised for their wool, goats for their milk, and camels and donkeys for burden-bearers. Horses were not introduced until 1900 B. C., when the nomadic shepherd kings from Asia conquered the country. For fruit the Egyptians had watermelons, grapes, olives, figs, pomegranates, and dates.

On coming further down the scale of time, we find that the Greeks raised wheat and barley as their chief cereals, and that they had hemp as well as flax. They had mules and commonly kept swarms of bees. To the vegetables known to the Egyptians, the Greeks added beets, cabbage, lettuce, turnips, kidney beans, and garden peas. Naturally they did not have the date palm, but they had the almond tree, and also apples, quinces, cherries, pears, and plums. The Greeks are said to have been the first to apply manure to the fields, and to plow under a growth of green lupine in order to enrich the land.

The Romans gave much attention to agriculture, and fortunately left many accurate records telling of their crops and the methods used to produce them. They carefully plowed and harrowed their fields and were acquainted with methods of drainage. Oxen were used as work animals on the Roman farms, and mules as beasts of burden. Much attention was given to breeding fine horses, sheep, swine, cattle, many kinds of poultry, and even hares, fish, snails, and dormice. Oats and rye, celery, peaches, apricots, and melons were added to the list of products known to the older nations, and alfalfa was raised for fodder. Milk was obtained chiefly from sheep and goats, and was made into cheese by curdling with lamb's or kid's rennet. As the Romans came into possession of great tracts of land taken from vanquished nations, they developed an extensive system of working large foreign estates by means of slaves. The popular demand for the division among the common people of these great holdings of state-owned land was resisted by the aristocratic possessors, and this dispute led to one of the greatest internal struggles in the history of Rome.

Medieval Period. During the dark ages that followed the conquest of Rome, agriculture made very little progress, for the conquerors were a warlike people who had reached a stage of development not far above the pastoral. There were, however, two agencies that carried on agricultural work with great activity. In Spain, the Moors, or Arabs, who were also great engineers, brought in rice, cotton, and sugar, and when necessary used irrigation to bring the land to a high degree of cultivation. At the same time, in western Europe, the members of many religious brotherhoods studied the manuscripts left by the Romans, and worked with great energy to improve on the crops and the methods of producing them. Much later, toward the end of the Middle Ages, the people of the Low Countries— the Netherlands and Belgium—gained a great reputation as farmers and dairymen, and northern Italy was so intensively cultivated during the 13th and 14th centuries that it not only supported a large population, but it also exported much grain.

Contemporary with the development in Europe, the Chinese, and the Incas of Peru had reached a very high state of agricultural production. Both nations understood the use of fertilizers and of methods of irrigation. The important crops of the Chinese have for centuries been wheat, rice, tea, cotton, and silk for which large amounts of mulberry leaves are required. The ancient Peruvians terraced the hillsides in order to make use of all available ground. Their principal crops were corn, potatoes, and cotton; much coca also was grown for the alkaloid contained in its leaves. The chief beast of burden was the llama, and the alpaca was raised for its hair. Neither of these nations has made any permanent impression on modern methods of agriculture. The civilization of the Incas is extinct, and the typical Chinese farmer of today still prefers the methods of cultivation used by his ancestors of one or two thousand years ago.

Modern Improvements. The two greatest innovations in modern agriculture may be said to be the proper rotation of crops and a chemical knowledge of fertilizers. The value of the first was demonstrated when Lord Townsend established in England the Norfolk system, consisting of the annual rotation of wheat, turnips, barley, and clover. This permitted half of the land to be used for grain, while the other half produced fodder with which to fatten cattle. Under this system, the land was neither exhausted by the continuous growth of one crop nor unproductive from lying fallow, cattle-raising was promoted, and much of the product of the land was returned to it as manure.

A knowledge of the chemical composition of plants and of soils came at first from the work of Liebig in the beginning of the 19th century. This led to the scientific use of artificial fertilizers containing potash, phosphorus, and nitrogen. Breeding experiments have led to better types of all farm animals, and, by means of modern methods of transportation, the most satisfactory breeds of plants or animals can be quickly sent to any part of the world.

Investigations in agricultural science are promoted by the governments of practically every civilized nation, with the result that modern agricultural practice is based on knowledge rather than on the Chinese system of adherence to the ways of their ancestors.

AGRICULTURE IN THE UNITED STATES

The first farmers of North America were the Indians, who, long before the coming of the white race, were accustomed to raising beans, pumpkins, squashes, peppers, onions, sunflowers, tobacco, and, most important of all, maize or Indian corn. This was most fortunate for those pioneers who arrived in 1607 and 1620, for, without the corn which they obtained from the Indians, the settlers both of Jamestown and of Plymouth would have starved during their first winters in America.

First Experiments. The early history of agriculture after the arrival of the settlers is one of adaptation and adjustment. The summers at Jamestown were so warm that it seemed that semitropical vegetation should be successful. Consequently, pineapples, French grapes, olives, figs, ginger, and sugar cane were planted, and attempts were made to raise silkworms. Naturally these undertakings, begun in ignorance of the colder winters, were failures. Furthermore, because of the high summer temperature and very rich earth, the wheat plant grew luxuriantly but failed to produce much grain. Tobacco was an early success and proved so profitable that all other crops were neglected until laws were made requiring each planter to raise a certain amount of corn and other food products.

In New England, a friendly Indian named Squanto taught the newcomers to plant corn. The earth was exposed to the sun by girdling the trees and burning the branches and underbrush. Four grains of corn and two beans were then dropped at four-foot intervals into openings made with an ax or hoe. If possible, a fish was placed in each hill for fertilizer. Later, when the plants were high enough, the ground was piled up around the base of the stalks. White potatoes, which are native to South America, were brought from England by the settlers and were not previously cultivated by the Indians, although the natives in the South were well acquainted with the sweet potato. Cattle and hogs, both in the North and in the South, were allowed to run wild in the woods, where they developed rapidly and often formed large herds.

Experiments gradually taught what crops were most satisfactory and profitable in each section. Buckwheat was introduced into New York by the Dutch in 1625. Apples were planted on Governors Island in Boston Harbor, and the first fruit was picked October 10, 1639. Cherries were brought first to Virginia, in 1641. Rice, which in 1647 had been a failure in Virginia, was tried at Charleston in 1693, and, together with indigo, soon became the principal crop of South Carolina and Georgia. Long fiber or sea-island cotton was introduced into these states in 1786, and, by this time, the best crops were so well established that, except for sorghum and alfalfa, nothing new was introduced during the next century.

Regional Differences. Agriculture as practiced in the southern colonies soon became differentiated from that in the North.

In New England the growing season was shorter. Land was harder to prepare for use because of its stony character and the extensive forests. Help was hard to obtain and the climate did not lend itself to any one highly profitable crop. Consequently each family raised most of the products necessary for its subsistence—grain, vegetables, fruit, cattle, swine, and other farm animals. Lumbering, fishing, and shipbuilding sometimes provided auxiliary sources of income.

In the South, however, the land was richer and the growing season was long and warm. Rice, indigo, sugar cane, and cotton proved highly profitable, especially when cultivated on a large scale with the help of cheap labor. This was supplied by indentured servants, convicts, and, later, by Negro slaves. The typical farm, or plantation, was about 5000 acres, about 50 times the size of the Northern farm. It was operated as a source of profit for the owner rather than as a means of family subsistence.

Cotton. The use of the newly invented spinning jenny and power loom between 1767 and 1790 produced a large demand in England for American cotton. In 1793 the difficult problem of separating the cotton fiber from the seeds was solved by Eli Whitney's invention of the cotton gin. The result was a vast increase in cotton production, exports rising 200-fold between 1791 and 1803. Its cultivation, formerly confined to Georgia and North Carolina, had, by 1815, spread north to Virginia and west and south to Alabama and Mississippi. As the soil became exhausted under this one-crop agriculture, new land was brought under cultivation in Louisiana, Texas, and Oklahoma. The United States instantly assumed and maintained a position of dominance in the world's cotton production. The cotton crop was admirably adapted to Negro labor, a fact which made Negro slavery the outstanding feature of Southern economic life until the Civil War.

Wheat and Corn. While the South was devoting all its energies to the production of cotton, settlers were moving west across the northern and central states. By its policy in granting small homesteads, the government encouraged family-sized holdings. Labor was difficult to obtain, since few men cared to work for others when they could take up new government land at a very small cost and work for themselves. The farmers produced principally corn, wheat, and other grains, besides potatoes, fruit, and live stock. Much of the grain was fed to live stock, which commanded a ready and profitable market. Excess production was sold in the South.

In the meantime the cultivation of corn in the region lying roughly between the winter wheat area and the spring wheat area increased rapidly. This region became known as the corn belt. It included chiefly western Ohio, Indiana, Illinois, Iowa, Missouri, eastern Nebraska, and southeastern South Dakota. Some corn was exported, but principally it was used to fatten hogs. The United States thus became the largest producer of corn and of hogs.

Farm Animals. Cattle and hogs were first brought to Florida from the West Indies in 1638; to Newfoundland by the Portuguese in 1553; and to Canada and Virginia in 1608. Although horses were taken to Florida in 1527, all of these were killed, and it was not until much later that others were imported. In the early days the sheep were small, with a light coat of coarse wool, the hogs were long-legged and thin, the cattle were light and wiry, and the cows produced only enough milk for their calves. Gradually, however, fine animals were imported from Europe, and, from these, careful breeding produced the splendid present-day herds of dairy and beef cattle, the large meat-type hogs, sheep that yield from 15 to 30 pounds of wool at a clip, and flocks of hens that average approximately 240 eggs per year instead of one or two dozen.

In the second half of the 19th century the western plains supported huge herds of cattle on unfenced ranges. As the area of cultivation was extended, the ranges were fenced off, but the amount and the quality of beef production increased as a result of better breeding. The fattening of cattle for market, like the raising of hogs, became especially important in the corn-growing regions because, by feeding the grain to animals, a higher-priced product was obtained. For the same reason the combination of grain raising and milk production was profitable near the large cities.

Farm Machinery. In the first half of the 19th century, farming was carried on almost entirely by hand labor with the help of a few simple tools, much as it had been since the dawn of history. From 1830 to 1860, horse-drawn implements were made available in considerable variety, but only after the Civil War was there a sweeping adoption of them. Seeders and cultivators replaced the hoe; mowing machines, the scythe; reapers, the cradle; threshing machines, the flail. Among scores of other important farm machines are cream separators and milkers, corn cutters, hay loaders, and manure spreaders. Illustrative of the economic and human value of such devices is a statement issued by the United States Department of Agriculture, that the human labor required to produce a bushel of grain had decreased on the average from 3 hours and 30 minutes in 1830 to 10 minutes in 1896, the cost of this labor declining from 17¾ cents to 3⅓ cents. By the 1960's the application of new technology to mechanization had reduced the average time to produce a bushel of corn to 4.8 minutes and wheat to 6.6 minutes.

Power Farming. In 1870, practically the entire non-human power on farms was in the form of farm animals. Even in 1900 they represented about 80 per cent of the available power, the remainder being steam engines, gas engines, and windmills. By 1919, however, the number of horses and mules on farms reached its maximum, 26,436,000, and thereafter declined with increasing rapidity. By 1923, mechanical power exceeded animal power, the principal forms being stationary gas engines, gasoline tractors and trucks, steam engines, electricity, and windmills. In the years from 1920 to 1940, the number of tractors on farms increased over 14-fold, and had increased to 4,263,000 by 1975. The total power available on the farm is approximately equal to that at the service of the combined factories, public utility plants, and mines of the country—over 60 million horse power.

The use of the tractor has made it possible for individuals to work much larger areas than formerly. Plowing and cultivating can be done much more quickly and at the most suitable time. Harvesting grain with the combine, which cuts and threshes or husks in a single operation, greatly reduces the cost of this process when a sufficiently large area of suitable land is worked. There were approximately 678,000 such combines on United States farms in 1975. Even in the raising of cotton,

mechanical methods have made rapid headway, particularly in western Texas and Oklahoma. The tractor-drawn plow, the "sled", which strips the cotton bolls, opened and unopened, at a single operation, and the cotton cleaner, used in connection with the gin, radically reduce the unit cost of production.

Automobiles and trucks effect great saving of time in marketing and in moving about the farm, making possible the cultivation of more land at a greater distance from shipping points. Electricity has been made increasingly available to farms, so that many minor operations can be performed through electric motors, particularly dairying and household operations, by which much of the former domestic drudgery is eliminated.

Economic Change. The pressure of demand, the scarcity of labor, and the attractive prices for farm products occasioned by World Wars I and II hastened the adoption of labor-saving devices and the use of power machinery on the farm. The result after World War I was a world-wide surplus, despite Russia's withdrawal from the export market, and prices fell rapidly. War-impoverished importing nations lacked purchasing power and the increasing replacement of the horse by the automobile cut down the market for hay and oats. The productive capacity of Canada, Argentina, Australia, and certain other countries had increased at even faster rate than that of the United States. The result was a market in which only the most efficient producers could make a profit. Road and other improvements increased taxes while farm income decreased. Small-scale farmers were forced, in large numbers, to abandon their farms. The earlier scale of land values was completely upset, with the resulting failure of many banks.

Between 1920 and 1930 there was a net decrease of farm population in the United States of about 3 millions, which was only slightly increased later. Cultivated land also decreased by more than 13,-000,000 acres. Yet, in the same period the total crop production increased about 20 per cent and the productivity of each worker increased by about 30 per cent. This situation indicated, after World War I, heightened efficiency of agriculture, but the distress caused by the process made the relief of agriculture a political question of importance.

Today American farms are outstanding in producing food to feed, not only Americans, but people more or less dependent upon the United States for subsistence since World War II.

International Trade. The typical farm in the U.S. has increased average production rapidly in the past several decades, and has an absolute production advantage in total resources used. Specialization and trade, in the absence of political or other barriers, are based on the principle of comparative advantage. That is, each nation produces those products for which it has the greatest comparative advantage, and trades its surplus to other nations that can only produce at a comparative disadvantage.

Thus, the U.S. was a net exporter of agricultural products in 1975, exporting some $21.6 billion worth, while importing $9.6 billion. The primary U.S. agricultural exports are oilseeds and products, wheat and flour, feed grains, animal and animal products, and tobacco, in that order. Principal imports are coffee, meats and poultry, sugar, rubber, and vegetables. Major receivers of American agricultural products in 1975 were Japan, Canada, the Netherlands, and West Germany. The principal sources of American agricultural imports in that year were Brazil, Mexico, Australia, and the Philippines.

An estimated 17 per cent of all U.S. farm products are sold to other countries. For some commodities, such as wheat and soybeans, the percentage may be as high as 50 or 60 per cent. International trade in agricultural commodities produced in the U.S. is important to the American economy and to world consumers.

Year	Total Population 000 omitted	Farm Population		Year	Total Population 000 omitted	Farm Population	
		Number 000 omitted	% of total			Number 000 omitted	% of Total
1917	103,052	32,326	31.4	1940	131,820	29,047	22.0
1918	104,266	31,741	30.4	1941	133,076	28,786	21.6
1919	104,935	30,886	29.4	1942	134,483	27,895	20.7
1920	106,089	31,556	29.7	1943	136,278	25,757	18.9
1921	108,023	31,638	29.3	1944	138,016	24,647	17.9
1922	109,676	31,558	28.8	1945	139,584	24,342	17.4
1923	111,476	30,873	27.7	1946	141,032	25,543	18.1
1924	113,573	30,493	26.8	1947	143,478	26,147	18.2
1925	115,402	30,440	26.4	1948	146,044	25,093	17.2
1926	117,007	30,162	25.8	1949	148,562	25,134	16.9
1927	118,628	29,647	25.0	1950	151,132	24,335	16.1
1928	120,135	29,599	24.6	1951	153,699	23,276	15.1
1929	121,453	29,564	24.3	1952	155,761	24,283	15.6
1930	122,775	29,447	24.0	1953	158,313	22,679	14.3
1931	123,841	29,723	24.0	1954	161,191	21,890	13.5
1932	124,658	30,229	24.2	1955	164,303	22,158	13.4
1933	125,401	31,198	24.9	1956	167,261	22,257	13.3
1934	126,192	31,071	24.6	1957	170,293	20,396	11.9
1935	127,057	30,887	24.3	1958	173,260	20,827	12.0
1936	127,886	30,420	23.8	1959	177,131	21,172	12.0
1937	128,649	29,903	23.2	1960	179,323	13,475	11.4
1938	129,589	29,573	22.8	1969	201,921	10,307	5.1
1939	130,642	29,388	22.5	1974	211,523	9,264	4.4
				1975	213,135	8,864	4.2

RURAL POPULATION BY STATES, 1970*

State	Population	State	Population	State	Population
Alabama	1,432,224	Louisiana	1,235,156	Ohio	2,626,320
Alaska	154,870	Maine	487,891	Oklahoma	819,092
Arizona	362,036	Maryland	917,436	Oregon	688,681
Arkansas	962,430	Massachusetts	922,477	Pennsylvania	3,363,499
California	1,817,089	Michigan	2,321,310	Rhode Island	122,422
Colorado	473,948	Minnesota	1,277,663	South Carolina	1,366,018
Connecticut	686,657	Mississippi	1,230,270	South Dakota	368,879
Delaware	152,535	Missouri	1,398,818	Tennessee	1,618,380
Florida	1,321,306	Montana	323,733	Texas	2,275,784
Georgia	1,821,501	Nebraska	570,733	Utah	207,801
Hawaii	129,878	Nevada	93,402	Vermont	301,441
Idaho	327,133	New Hampshire	321,641	Virginia	1,713,653
Illinois	1,884,155	New Jersey	794,759	Washington	932,701
Indiana	1,821,609	New Mexico	315,420	West Virginia	1,064,746
Iowa	1,207,971	New York	2,633,254	Wisconsin	1,506,854
Kansas	779,625	North Carolina	2,796,891	Wyoming	131,305
Kentucky	1,534,653	North Dakota	344,319	Total	53,884,804

* Figures include persons living on farms or in places of less than 2500 population.
Source: Bureau of the Census

CIVILIAN CONSUMPTION OF PRINCIPAL FOODS
(in pounds per capita)
Source: *Agricultural Statistics 1975*, ERS, USDA

Foods	1959	1966	1974 (prel.)
Meat	146.6	151.4	165.0
Poultry	35.6	44.3	50.7
Fish	13.7	13.9	15.0
Eggs	44.7	39.7	36.4
Dairy Products including butter	393.0	371.0	343.0
Fats and oils excluding butter	41.7	47.2	51.3
Fruits, fresh	92.1	79.6	78.1
Fruits, processed	48.4	41.4	54.4
Vegetables, fresh	146.7	138.4	142.6
Vegetables, processed	50.4	56.1	64.3
Flour and other cereal products	148.0	143.0	138.0
Sugars and other sweeteners	107.7	113.0	121.5
Coffee, tea, cocoa	15.2	15.1	13.2
All foods, total	1,450.0	1,427.0	1,428.0

Agricultural Adjustment. The first governmental attack on the problem was an attempt to support prices of farm products. Tried out in 1929-33, it failed because of uncontrolled production.

The second attack was through the Agricultural Adjustment act of 1933. This law empowered the secretary of agriculture to pay producers for withholding a proportion of their normal acreage from production of certain basic crops. The law was declared unconstitutional by the Supreme Court in January 1936. This act was supplemented by the Agricultural Adjustment Act of 1938, which had the following principal features designed to provide an "ever normal granary":

Acreage allotments are made annually for growing these major crops—corn, wheat, cotton, rice, and tobacco. Farmers who consent to abide by the allotments and who observe specified soil-conserving practices obtain benefit payments based on various factors and preference in access to federal crop loan facilities. If any major crop is estimated to be above normal by a certain amount, marketing quotas are set which, if made effective, may not be exceeded by farmers without payment of a fine. Such quotas become effective only if approved in a referendum by at least two-thirds of the farmers affected. Wheat crops may be insured with the Federal Crop Insurance Corporation on payment of a premium either in cash or wheat. The secretary of agriculture is authorized to make so-called parity payments to producers of the major crops if funds are appropriated for the purpose.

Parity payments are payments designed to raise farm per capita income to the point at which it bears the same relation to non-farm per capita income as farm income bore to non-farm income in the period from August 1909 to July 1914.

The Agricultural Act of 1948 introduced the concept of a "flexible price support" feature in farm legislation. This allowed the price of peanuts, corn, wheat, cotton, rice, and tobacco to vary, depending on the amount of the commodity that was produced. The range of flexibility was set at 60 to 90 per cent. If the supply of the crop were 70 per cent (or below normal), the support level would be the maximum 90 per cent of parity. The 1948 act also introduced the new parity formula, designed to eliminate distortions due to changes in the cost of production.

Legislation in the 1960's was by no means limited to the basic commodities. Efforts were begun early in 1961 to expand the existing program authorizing food distribution to needy persons. A pilot food stamp program was begun. Expansion of the School Lunch and Special Milk programs was undertaken. The Feed Grain Act (March 22, 1969) and the Agricultural Act of 1961 (August 8, 1961) provided the basic framework for legislation in the next decade. Also undertaken were specific programs for wheat and feed grains, with provisions for crop acreage diversion to soil-conserving crops and methods (practiced extensively in the Soil Bank Program of the late 1950's), authorization of marketing orders for specific crops, and extensions of the National Wool Act of 1954 and Public Law 480 to help supply needy nations with surplus American food stocks.

The Food and Agriculture Act of 1965 broke the tradition of annual Congressional battles and outlined legislation covering a four-year period. Essentially, the 1965 Act carried forward many of the provisions of previous legislation.

Co-operatives. The procedure of pooling farm produce in America for the purpose of selling it to better advantage is carried on voluntarily by farmers through associations known as Co-operatives.

The Capper-Volstead act of 1922 protected these associations at first, when properly conducted, from

CHIEF CROPS FOR UNITED STATES 1930-1974
Source: *Economic Research Service; Dept. of Agriculture*

Year	All Corn	Oats	Barley	Sorghums for grain	Wheat	Rye	Buckwheat	Rice
	1,000 bushels	1,000 bushels	1,000 bushels	1,000 bushels	1,000 bushels	1,000 bushels	1,000 bushels	1,000 bags
1930	2,080,130	1,274,592	301,619	37,561	886,522	45,383	6,967	20,218
1935	2,299,363	1,210,229	288,667	57,610	628,227	56,938	8,488	17,753
1940	2,457,146	1,246,450	311,278	85,824	814,646	39,725	6,476	24,495
1944	3,087,982	1,149,240	276,275	184,978	1,060,111	22,525	8,956	30,974
1945	2,868,795	1,523,851	266,994	96,063	1,107,623	23,708	6,467	30,668
1946	3,217,076	1,477,573	265,059	106,025	1,152,118	18,487	6,812	32,497
1947	2,354,739	1,176,142	281,868	93,217	1,358,911	25,497	7,177	35,217
1948	3,605,078	1,450,186	315,537	131,384	1,294,911	25,886	6,085	38,275
1949	3,238,618	1,254,855	237,071	148,299	1,098,415	18,102	4,956	40,737
1950	3,057,803	1,410,464	303,533	233,278	1,019,389	21,257	4,439	38,689
1951	2,941,423	1,316,396	254,668	159,265	987,474	21,410	3,340	43,805
1952	3,279,403	1,260,127	226,014	83,024	1,298,957	16,046	3,205	48,107
1953	3,192,491	1,209,458	242,544	109,353	1,169,484	18,163	3,193	52,607
1954	2,964,639	1,499,579	370,126	204,087	969,781	23,688	2,719	58,853
1955	3,229,743	1,503,074	401,225	242,526	934,731	29,055	1,934	55,902
1956	3,455,283	1,163,160	376,873	206,205	1,004,272	21,155	2,032	49,459
1957	3,422,231	1,300,954	437,170	564,324	950,662	27,243	1,871	42,935
1958	3,799,844	1,422,164	470,449	614,845	1,462,218	32,485	1,783	47,015
1960	3,908,070	1,555,312	431,309	619,867	1,357,272	33,052	810	54,591
1961	3,625,530	1,011,398	395,669	479,751	1,234,743	27,476	864	54,198
1969	4,578,000*	950,000	417,000	743,000	1,458,900	31,000	N. A.	91,300
1974†	4,651,167*	620,539	308,077	628,081	1,793,322	19,293	N. A.	114,096

* Corn raised for grain. † Preliminary data.

Year	Flaxseed	Cotton Lint	Cotton Seed	Tobacco	Hay	Sorghums for forage	Sorghums for silage	Beans dry edible
	1,000 bushels	1,000 bales	1,000 tons	1,000 pounds	1,000 tons	1,000 tons	1,000 tons	1,000 bags
1930	21,673	13,932	6,028	1,648,037	74,527	6,326	572	14,341
1935	14,914	10,638	4,634	1,302,041	90,364	12,052	3,133	14,335
1940	30,924	12,566	5,286	1,460,441	96,050	16,110	6,217	16,945
1944	21,665	12,230	4,902	1,950,940	102,889	11,552	5,644	16,147
1945	34,557	9,015	3,664	1,991,108	107,438	9,543	3,570	13,091
1946	22,588	8,640	3,513	2,314,807	99,518	8,181	3,587	15,840
1947	40,618	11,857	4,681	2,107,160	100,576	5,666	3,338	17,268
1948	54,803	14,877	5,945	1,979,581	96,172	3,633	4,318	20,816
1949	42,976	16,128	6,559	1,969,100	95,055	5,729	3,626	21,379
1950	40,236	10,012	4,105	2,030,645	102,340	6,592	4,926	16,886
1951	33,802	15,290	6,186	2,282,386	108,351	6,410	5,622	17,446
1952	30,174	15,139	6,109	2,254,271	104,345	4,358	3,821	16,235
1954	41,534	13,569	5,568	2,200,134	104,380	6,431	6,890	18,899
1955	41,243	14,721	6,043	2,192,852	112,736	6,877	9,402	16,649
1956	48,009	13,310	5,407	2,175,556	108,680	4,613	8,843	17,218
1957	25,919	10,964	4,609	1,667,544	120,977	7,508	15,157	15,626
1958	39,543	11,512	4,798	1,736,204	121,924	4,936	12,268	18,981
1960	30,402	14,272	5,886	1,944,175	118,236	3,859	12,547	17,917
1961	22,178	14,318	5,978	2,061,392	116,819	3,413	12,996	20,287
1969	27,264	10,015	4,186	1,807,000	127,000	9,567†	10,948†	19,000
1975	14,557	8,326	3,030	2,184,237	132,917	. . .	7,259	17,196

Year	Peas dry field	Peanuts picked and threshed	Soybeans	Potatoes	Sugar cane Sugar and seed	Sugar cane Sirup	Sugar beets	Oranges and Tangerines
	1,000 bags	1,000 pounds	1,000 bushels	1,000 bushels	1,000 tons	1,000 gallons	1,000 tons	1,000 boxes
1930	2,114	697,350	13,929	343,817	3,153	16,602	9,199	55,060
1935	3,385	1,152,795	48,901	378,895	4,954	24,509	7,908	52,073
1940	2,192	1,766,590	78,045	376,920	4,218	13,360	12,194	85,510
1944	8,894	2,080,825	192,121	383,926	6,144	19,897	6,718	113,210
1945	5,915	2,042,235	193,167	419,399	6,707	28,251	8,616	104,350
1946	6,679	2,038,005	203,395	487,315	5,962	23,335	10,560	118,540
1947	6,322	2,181,695	186,451	388,985	5,289	18,545	12,503	114,510
1948	3,640	2,335,840	227,217	449,895	6,768	11,245	9,424	104,120
1949	3,212	1,864,780	234,194	402,353	6,541	9,745	10,196	108,465
1950	3,206	2,021,730	299,279	429,896	6,944	9,230	13,535	121,610
1951	3,763	1,595,025	280,512	325,708	5,601	5,140	10,584	122,900
1952	2,610	1,366,225	298,052	349,098	7,605	6,005	10,169	125,080
1954	3,484	1,043,560	342,795	355,099	6,940	4,795	14,027	141,475
1955	2,525	1,548,010	373,522	227,046	7,248	4,910	12,228	137,015
1956	4,639	1,607,810	449,446	243,716	6,483	3,895	12,993	136,705
1957	3,326	1,435,945	483,715	239,539	6,750	3,225	15,530	111,155
1958	2,475	1,864,725	574,413	265,729	6,681	3,770	15,183	130,620
1960	3,241	1,786,266	555,307	257,435	16,456	3,558	16,421	121,535
1961	3,543	1,742,960	679,566	293,594	19,737	3,425	17,704	138,095
1969	3,738†	2,553,000	1,117,000	511,666	22,615	2,482†	28,518	188,090
1975	2,731	3,857,122	1,521,370	315,647	28,499	. . .	29,270	237,910

Year	Grape-fruit	Lemons	Apples	Peaches	Pears	Grapes	Cran-berries	Straw-berries
	1,000 boxes	1,000 boxes	1,000 bushels	1,000 bushels	1,000 bushels	1,000 tons	1,000 barrels	1,000 crates
1930	18,690	7,950	. . . . . .	56,392	27,167	2,458	584	9,143
1935	18,347	7,787	140,398	55,440	25,943	2,477	516	10,811
1940	42,883	17,236	111,436	57,832	29,590	2,466	570	12,319
1944	52,180	12,550	121,266	78,191	31,337	2,712	376	4,366
1945	63,450	14,450	66,796	81,548	33,042	2,781	656	5,201
1946	59,520	13,800	119,410	86,643	34,447	3,160	856	7,004
1947	61,630	12,870	113,041	82,270	35,312	3,036	790	8,895
1948	45,530	10,010	88,407	65,352	26,334	3,078	968	10,224
1949	36,500	11,360	133,742	74,818	36,404	2,650	840	8,795
1950	46,580	13,400	123,126	53,485	31,140	2,707	984	11,295
1951	40,400	12,900	112,935	70,265	32,687	3,281	932	11,846
1952	38,360	12,590	92,489	62,560	30,947	3,164	804	11,794
1954	46,120	14,600	103,773	60,794	30,077	2,607	1,012	11,874
1955	45,380	13,250	107,157	51,852	29,622	3,241	1,026	223*
1956	44,790	16,200	100,852	70,079	32,322	2,912	970	275*
1957	39,780	16,900	118,548	61,518	31,676	2,599	1,050	277*
1958	43,500	17,000	126,610	71,069	28,890	3,026	1,166	267*
1960	43,300	14,340	108,515	74,315	25,621	2,997	1,341	233*
1961	42,910	16,740	126,565	77,895	27,080	3,092	1,236	255*
1969	54,170	15,810	140,873	77,000	29,625	3,874	1,468†	243*
1975	61,370	29,400	7,087,100a	2,818,000a	739*	4,300	2,075	5,420b

* Thousand tons.   † 1968 preliminary.   a lbs.   b cwt.

FARM INCOME AND GOVERNMENT PAYMENT BY STATES—1974

Source: *Economic Research Service; Department of Agriculture*

State	Cash Receipts from farming (000 omitted)				Farm Income (000,000 omitted)		
	Livestock and Products	Crops	Government Payments	Total	Gross Income	Expenses	Total Income *
Alabama	$679,000	$511,000	$9,220	$1,199,220	$1,352.5	$1,165.7	$264.4
Alaska	4,000	2,000	59	6,059	7.3	6.6	0.6
Arizona	583,000	613,000	5,252	1,201,252	1,255.5	903.2	337.8
Arkansas	827,000	1,260,000	7,417	2,094,417	2,240.5	1,741.9	650.4
California	2,788,000	5,863,000	18,285	8,669,285	8,963.0	6,399.4	2,733.0
Colorado	1,409,000	744,000	12,533	2,165,533	2,264.7	1,705.9	494.3
Connecticut	125,000	88,000	505	213,505	234.1	195.3	52.9
Delaware	164,000	108,000	254	272,254	282.8	199.1	83.5
Florida	549,000	1,695,000	12,548	2,256,548	2,362.2	1,604.5	858.5
Georgia	1,027,000	1,072,000	10,364	2,109,364	2,280.8	1,767.9	598.3
Hawaii	58,000	579,000	8,310	645,310	661.9	245.1	419.1
Idaho	411,000	1,043,000	11,151	1,465,151	1,556.5	1,008.9	604.4
Illinois	1,789,000	3,937,000	9,755	5,735,755	6,173.6	4,489.8	1,250.2
Indiana	1,162,000	1,888,000	6,591	3,056,591	3,395.7	2,494.8	547.1
Iowa	3,786,000	3,495,000	16,596	7,297,596	7,658.0	5,650.4	1,204.4
Kansas	1,835,000	2,140,000	22,457	3,997,457	4,186.0	2,973.1	944.6
Kentucky	585,000	903,000	5,813	1,493,813	1,729.5	1,249.3	639.0
Louisiana	335,000	1,046,000	13,591	1,394,594	1,478.0	957.5	567.1
Maine	226,000	213,000	1,656	440,656	473.3	316.4	212.6
Maryland	369,000	253,000	1,023	623,023	693.1	549.0	136.1
Massachusetts	105,000	96,000	487	201,487	223.8	185.1	45.7
Michigan	707,000	1,050,000	10,438	1,767,438	1,952.2	1,352.0	656.0
Minnesota	1,950,000	2,591,000	18,420	4,559,420	4,849.6	2,851.5	1,752.4
Mississippi	602,000	873,000	7,944	1,482,944	1,630.9	1,284.7	385.0
Missouri	1,441,000	1,289,000	22,549	2,752,549	3,024.7	2,407.4	513.5
Montana	430,000	760,000	14,998	1,204,998	1,294.1	872.2	694.2
Nebraska	2,265,000	1,964,000	20,970	4,249,970	4,396.2	3,188.1	681.1
Nevada	101,000	35,000	305	136,305	151.1	118.8	30.1
New Hampshire	51,000	20,000	654	71,654	82.6	65.9	17.6
New Jersey	114,000	236,000	660	350,660	393.2	299.3	98.6
New Mexico	410,000	156,000	13,341	579,341	627.7	552.1	93.8
New York	1,026,000	506,000	6,003	1,538,003	1,737.0	1,458.7	367.6
North Carolina	920,000	1,712,000	8,125	2,640,125	2,925.9	1,858.5	1,087.8
North Dakota	490,000	2,080,000	30,968	2,600,968	2,706.8	1,314.6	1,126.0
Ohio	998,000	1,508,000	7,419	2,513,419	2,833.3	2,242.4	646.3
Oklahoma	1,117,000	830,000	14,355	1,961,355	2,124.4	1,835.1	397.8
Oregon	328,000	775,000	4,137	1,107,137	1,212.9	815.1	408.0
Pennsylvania	1,097,000	504,000	4,916	1,605,916	1,801.5	1,469.6	407.1
Rhode Island	12,000	14,000	63	26,063	28.4	22.0	6.6
South Carolina	255,000	572,000	5,591	832,591	924.6	685.5	243.0
South Dakota	1,279,000	816,000	33,443	2,128,443	2,218.3	1,403.6	572.3
Tennessee	459,000	546,000	8,979	1,013,979	1,213.0	1,091.3	234.5
Texas	2,972,000	2,848,000	80,552	5,900,552	6,335.8	5,275.4	813.4
Utah	220,000	101,000	2,946	323,946	351.9	286.2	82.8
Vermont	197,000	17,000	1,573	215,573	240.7	198.7	42.6
Virginia	453,000	519,000	7,825	979,825	1,157.3	869.3	316.1
Washington	458,000	1,525,000	9,829	1,992,829	2,108.4	1,236.4	908.8
West Virginia	100,000	43,000	1,496	144,496	191.5	174.7	27.2
Wisconsin	1,919,000	526,000	13,298	2,458,298	2,718.0	2,007.7	750.3
Wyoming	237,000	132,000	4,784	373,784	410.2	359.9	67.6
Total	$41,424,000	$52,097,000	$530,448	$94,051,448	$101,112.0	$73,405.0	$26,072.0

* Of farm operators (net income).

prosecution under the antitrust laws. They are fostered by the Farmer Co-operative Service of the U.S. Department of Agriculture which disseminates information concerning supply, demand, prices, and those practices found advantageous by co-operative organizations.

Another form of co-operative enterprise which, in America, has developed chiefly in farm communities is the so-called "consumer" co-operative. Its aim is to secure for members the price benefits of large-scale buying. In many cases, these associations own their own stores, warehouses, and factories. Business done through them by farmers reached a pre-war high of $250,000,000 in 1938. They have been chiefly active in the purchase of gasoline, seed, and fertilizer and in the building and operation of rural electric distribution systems under the encouragement of the rural electrification administration.

The increase in business done by farmers' marketing and purchasing co-operatives since 1915 is shown by the following table:

AGRICULTURAL CO-OPERATIVES

Source: *Farmer Cooperative Service*

Marketing Season*	Number	Estimated Membership (thousands)	Estimated Business (Millions of $)
1915	5,424	651	636
1925	10,803	2700	2400
1930	11,950	3000	2400
1935	10,500	3660	1840
1940	10,600	3400	2280
1941	10,550	3600	2840
1942	10,450	3850	3780
1943	10,300	4390	5160
1944	10,150	4505	5645
1945	10,150	5010	6070
1946	10,125	5436	7116
1949	10,035	6584	8,726
1954	9,903	7604	9,642
1959	9,345	7273	12,036
1964	8,583	7082	14,742
1967	7,940	6445	17,034
1970	7,790	6355	19,080

*Ends June 30 of the following year.

OPERATIONS OF COOPERATIVES, 1972-73

Leading States	Associations Number	Membership Number	Business ($1000)
California . .	308	91,850	2,655,901
Iowa	499	373,385	1,827,430
Minnesota . .	1,117	591,990	1,766,161
Wisconsin . .	538	422,040	1,763,497
Illinois . . .	329	318,285	1,427,847
New York . .	296	135,900	1,238,710
Texas	484	142,630	964,329
Kansas . . .	288	202,980	959,004
Ohio	218	217,630	929,699
Nebraska . .	374	263,870	841,790
All others . .	3,403	3,366,190	12,123,374
Total . . .	7,854	6,126,750	26,497,742

Source: *Agricultural Statistics 1976.*

HORTICULTURE

Originally the term horticulture meant the cultivation of a garden. It now includes the art and science of vegetable growing or *olericulture*, fruit growing or *pomology*, flower growing or *floriculture*, and landscape gardening. Horticulture, therefore, might justly be called applied botany, and it bears much the same relationship to botany as do any of the branches of engineering to mathematics and physics.

In a new and undeveloped country, horticulture, as a branch of agriculture, usually receives comparatively little attention. But it increases rapidly in importance as the primary problems of producing a sufficient supply of grain, potatoes, and live stock are gradually solved. The phenomenal development of horticulture in America is shown by the great and increasing number of horticultural publications, by the extent to which the subject is taught in the schools, by the obvious importance of the canning and preserving industries, greenhouses, nurseries, and seed raising, and by the accompanying tables. Factories devoted to the manufacture of boxes, baskets, barrels, glass jars, and tin cans depend for their existence largely on the success of horticultural enterprises.

Robert Squibb's *Garden Kalendar*, published at Charleston, South Carolina in 1787, was probably the first separate book on horticulture printed in America. Since that time, more than 10,000 books have been published (a conservative estimate), in addition to numerous journals, many of which are still in circulation. There are also a number of national or regional horticultural societies and many local organizations.

Elementary instruction in horticulture is often given in both primary and secondary schools of cities, as well as in rural districts. This training is given not only to teach horticulture, but also to help develop growing minds. Advanced courses in horticulture are given by some 70 colleges and universities located in every state and territory of the United States.

Vegetables. The chief sources of fresh vegetables are large commercial farms, often distant from market areas, and greenhouses, usually located near large cities. With intense cultivation, $1,500 to $2,500 worth of crops for fresh market may be taken from a single acre. Other farms are devoted to raising vegetables for commercial processing. Numerous families have home gardens.

Modern transportation facilities and refrigeration have made possible large-scale truck farming at a distance from cities. For some time the South and West have specialized in supplying the North with out-of-season vegetables. A great deal of the marketing is done co-operatively, shipments in carload lots being made up with the produce of a number of growers, who might separately have difficulties in filling a freight car as their crops are harvested.

Fruits and Nuts. The orange is the most important fruit produced in the United States, both in quantity and in value. Apples rank second in value, while grapes are second in quantity produced. Citrus production has become the most highly organized of the fruit industries. Much of the fruit produced in the U.S. is processed, as consumers use more fruit canned, frozen, dried, and in juice form, than in the fresh form. Nut production has declined in recent years. English walnuts, pecans, and almonds are the most important ones, in that order.

Flowers. In the commercial production of flowers, the chrysanthemum is the most valuable crop, followed by the carnation, and then the rose. An important branch of this industry is the forcing of bulbs and plants in order to produce potted flowers for sale, not only for holidays, but during the entire year. Although it has been demonstrated that bulbs can be produced in America, they are nearly all imported from Holland.

Landscape gardening consists in the arrangement of growing trees, shrubs, and other ornamental plants in connection with walks, drives, and other features of the landscape, so that together they form an artistic and pleasing view.

Crop	Acreage (1,000) 1974*	Acreage (1,000) States Leading	Production (tons) 1974*	Production (tons) States Leading	Value ($1,000) 1973	Value ($1,000) 1974*
Artichokes	10.8	Calif.	35.1	Calif.	8,699	12,152
Asparagus	112.5	Calif., Wash.	130.2	Calif., Wash.	66,411	74,277
Beans, lima	72.2	Calif., Del.	86.0	Calif., Del.	20,714	26,786
Beans, snap	372.1	Wisc., N.Y.	887.4	Oreg., N.Y.	130,430	167,765
Beets	18.5	Wisc., N.Y.	240.7	N.Y., Wisc.	5,520	9,636
Broccoli	48.7	Calif., Oreg.	188.2	Calif., Oreg.	42,476	52,859
Brussels sprouts	6.3	Calif.	33.1	Calif.	8,894	11,524
Cabbage	106.2	Tex., Fla.	953.4	Tex., Fla.	121,416	92,519
Cantaloupes	69.9	Calif., Tex.	473.0	Calif., Ariz.	91,322	94,686
Carrots	79.0	Calif., Tex.	1,154.3	Calif., Tex.	105,450	124,017
Cauliflower	34.6	Calif., N.Y.	147.6	Calif., N.Y.	33,902	38,771
Celery	32.4	Calif., Fla.	805.6	Calif., Fla.	101,352	91,806
Corn, sweet	628.1	Wisc., Minn.	2,705.4	Minn., Wisc.	157,334	211,748
Cucumbers	177.3	N.C., Mich.	820.9	Mich., Calif.	98,879	124,626
Eggplant	3.3	Fla., N.J.	30.0	Fla., N.J.	5,164	6,969
Escarole	8.3	Fla., N.J.	55.7	Fla., N.J.	13,943	12,191
Garlic	9.0	Calif.	58.5	Calif.	10,522	14,284
Honeydew melons	11.4	Calif., Tex.	91.5	Calif., Tex.	18,324	15,610
Lettuce	226.2	Calif., Ariz.	2,486.1	Calif., Ariz.	374,923	352,731
Mint for oil	87.1	Oreg., Wash.	2.4	Oreg., Wash.	36,112	61,274
Onions	109.9	Calif., Tex.	1,670.8	Calif., Tex.	207,046	158,494
Peas, green	425.6	Wisc., Wash.	572.7	Wisc., Wash.	59,694	112,071
Peppers, green	47.8	Fla., Calif.,	238.3	Calif., Fla.	65,739	70,110
Spinach	34.5	Calif., Tex.	204.5	Calif., Tex.	17,579	19,108
Strawberries	39.6	Calif., Oreg.	266.6	Calif., Oreg.	131,592	152,759
Tomatoes	464.5	Calif., Fla.	8,013.8	Calif., Fla.	561,233	797,625
Watermelons	215.2	Tex., Fla.	1,159.8	Fla., Tex.	77,465	88,468

* Preliminary.   Source: *Statistical Abstract of the U.S. 1975.*

PRINCIPAL CANADIAN AGRICULTURAL CROPS

Crop	Area in Acres 1974	Area in Acres 1975	Yield per Acre (Bushels) 1974	Yield per Acre (Bushels) 1975	Total Production (Bushels) 1974	Total Production (Bushels) 1975
Winter wheat	420,000	455,000	45.4	50.0	19,070,000	22,750,000
Spring wheat	18,807,300	19,337,800	21.9	25.5	412,043,000	492,450,000
Durum wheat	2,850,000	3,650,000	20.1	25.1	57,400,000	91,500,000
All wheat	22,077,300	23,442,800	22.1	25.9	488,513,000	606,700,000
Oats for grain	6,106,000	6,058,000	41.7	47.5	254,745,000	287,898,000
Barley for grain	11,799,500	10,991,200	34.3	38.6	404,286,000	423,797,000
Fall rye	801,000	746,000	22.7	26.4	18,164,000	19,698,000
Spring rye	42,000	42,000	17.9	20.6	750,000	865,000
All rye	843,000	788,000	22.4	26.1	18,914,000	20,563,000
Mixed grains	1,810,900	1,835,400	44.6	48.5	80,754,000	88,991,000
Flaxseed	1,450,000	1,400,000	9.5	12.2	13,800,000	17,100,000
Rapeseed	3,160,000	4,020,000	16.2	17.8	51,300,000	71,600,000
Corn for grain	1,460,000	1,539,000	69.8	83.6	101,910,900	128,624,000
Buckwheat	63,600	47,200	19.1	20.3	1,216,000	959,000
Peas, dry	78,500	74,500	21.4	24.6	1,680,000	1,834,000
Beans, dry	171,500	147,000	20.7	18.3	3,548,000	2,695,000
Soybeans	445,000	390,000	24.8	31.0	11,040,000	12,090,000
Potatoes*	282,600	257,300	193.9	169.0	54,783,000	43,482,000
Tame hay†	13,033,000	13,014,000	1.95	1.95	25,402,000	25,342,000
Fodder corn†	1,048,000	1,021,000	10.56	12.35	11,070,000	12,606,000

Source: Statistics Canada.   * In cwt.   † In tons.

LEADING AGRICULTURAL PRODUCTS OF CANADA, 1974*
By Provinces on Basis of Bushels Produced
(000 omitted)

PROVINCE	Wheat	Oats	Barley	Grain Corn	Tame Hay	Potatoes	Fodder Corn	Mixed Grain
Alberta	110,000	80,000	188,000	....	6,700	4,000	....	14,600
British Columbia	1,900	3,500	6,400	....	1,600	3,200	330	300
Manitoba	63,000	43,000	53,000	190	2,400	4,900	210	6,000
New Brunswick	144	2,295	447	....	277	13,398	....	252
Nova Scotia	120	920	271	....	317	638	....	369
Ontario	19,370	23,415	15,470	90,200	6,320	8,120	8,485	43,800
Prince Edward Island	444	2,805	1,048	....	225	10,304	....	4,358
Quebec	1,535	23,810	1,650	11,250	4,980	8,425	2,045	4,675
Saskatchewan	326,000	75,000	128,000	....	3,200	378	....	6,400
Canada	522,513	254,745	394,286	101,910	26,019	53,363	11,070	80,754

* Estimated.

DRAINAGE AND RECLAMATION

In agricultural practice the term drainage generally refers to the removal of excess water from the soil by means of open ditches, or to drainage below the surface using drain tile or tubing (plastic is sometimes used for this purpose today) in which the water collects and is carried away under the force of gravity. Where the ground is so low that the water collected by the system must be removed with pumps, the process is termed pump drainage.

Drainage was used to a certain extent by the Romans, and during the 17th century attention was occasionally called to its advantages; but the methods practiced by James Smith, of Perthshire, England, about 1823, are generally considered to have introduced the modern systems of farm drainage. In America, John Johnson imported tiles from Scotland in 1835 and placed them in the wet ground of his farm near Geneva, New York. The improvement in his crops was so noticeable that the advantages of draining were quickly appreciated.

The simplest way of draining wet soil is to dig ditches from 3 to 5 feet deep and connect these with a main ditch that is somewhat deeper. Because this method cuts up the ground, tubing or 4- to 7-inch tiles are generally placed at the bottom of the ditches, which are then refilled. The ground water filters through openings into the tile or tubing, then flows through drains of larger diameter, and thence to the outlet.

Among the more important advantages of drainage are:

1. Excess water is removed from the ground, providing aeration of the root zone.
2. Nutrients are made more readily available to plants.
3. Farmers are enabled to prepare soil for planting earlier in the spring and to perform field operations at the appropriate time.
4. Better environment is provided for plants, resulting in higher yields of better-quality crops.
5. Drained regions provide a more healthful environment.
6. Excess soluble salts are more efficiently removed from alkaline land.

Drainage in the United States. In the United States about 9 percent (nearly 100 million acres) of all farmland had drainage in 1960. The number of drained acres in cropland amounted to around one-fourth of the total cropland in the country. However, since a large part of the drainage in the country operates in land not now used as farms for the raising of crops, the above figures give a very inadequate picture of drainage enterprises.

In order to drain a farm, an entire district often must be embraced in a drainage operation, known officially as an enterprise. Such enterprises are organized under state laws and may be undertaken by state governments, counties, or townships. If supported and operated by organizations having their own executive officers, enterprises are known as drainage districts. There were 8,461 drainage enterprises in the United States in 1960. Other enterprises are individually owned, being constructed for various uses by the land owner.

Nearly two-thirds of the lands in drainage enterprises are located north of the Ohio and Missouri rivers. These are usually small enterprises and, with the exception of those draining swampy areas in Wisconsin and northern Michigan, they were undertaken to improve farm land already under cultivation.

The enterprises along the lower Mississippi and in the plains along the southern Atlantic and Gulf of Mexico coast lines are, in the main, large scale undertakings. They have been instrumental in draining huge swamps and making them fit for cultivation.

Drainage enterprises in the arid southwestern states are practically all located on irrigated land. Their purpose is to prevent damage from seepage of water and to carry off excess salts from the soil. Frequently, the water drained off is collected in drainage wells and is pumped from them to be used again for irrigation.

Old World Projects. The Fens on the east coast of England, the valley of the Po, in Italy, the south of France, and Egypt have all benefited from extensive reclamation projects. These are not as famous as those in the Netherlands, where, by an elaborate system of dikes and canals, many marshes have been changed to fertile regions known as "polders." In the Haarlem Meer, 44,724 acres which had been covered with 13 feet of water were surrounded by a dike, and, after 39 months of pumping, the water was removed. Even this project is dwarfed by the reclamation of the Zuider Zee, a branch of the North Sea which was formed in 1170 when a terrific storm broke down the sand dunes on the coast. An 18-mile dike was completed in 1932, which cut off the inland water. The pumping out of this water provides 523,000 acres of reclaimed land, leaving a lake named Ijsselmeer.

DRAINAGE OF FARMS IN THE UNITED STATES*

STATE	Area Drained and Used for Agriculture (acres)	Cost of Draining: Works and Services incl. maintenance, repairs & administration, 1950–59 (dollars)
Alabama	65,901	31,061
Arkansas	4,680,966	20,488,266
California	1,911,251	29,065,257
Colorado	55,496	178,196
Delaware	340,922	476,944
Florida	4,855,327	91,627,636
Georgia	93,228	118,012
Idaho	110,982	2,011,573
Illinois	5,563,426	28,691,965
Indiana	11,053,446	13,598,832
Iowa	6,871,339	21,032,299
Kansas	373,110	1,665,416
Kentucky	888,799	897,753
Louisiana	7,110,624	45,796,344
Maryland	350,447	409,398
Michigan	9,877,049	37,186,074
Minnesota	10,560,808	41,809,993
Mississippi	3,040,607	9,557,061
Missouri	3,097,316	12,138,381
Montana	60,112	721,491
Nebraska	739,220	1,388,581
Nevada	41,521	219,902
New Jersey	10,956	40,617
New Mexico	31,593	127,433
New York	49,616	202,013
North Carolina	1,320,503	2,959,290
North Dakota	1,641,183	1,672,790
Ohio	8,809,415	8,268,377
Oklahoma	133,796	249,053
Oregon	270,454	5,002,268
South Carolina	338,066	824,238
South Dakota	658,580	298,591
Tennessee	590,879	2,136,236
Texas	5,691,130	28,895,392
Utah	66,910	558,392
Virginia	92,778	401,765
Washington	241,182	4,404,324
Wisconsin	584,093	1,579,398
Wyoming	23,833	145,293
United States	92,296,864	416,875,865

* Last reported in the *1959 Census of Agriculture*, Vol. III.

IRRIGATION

The practice of supplying water to the fields by artificial means has been known for thousands of years. The ancient Egyptians, the Babylonians, the Chinese, and the natives of India—all made use of irrigation. In the western hemisphere, the Incas of Peru, the Aztecs of Mexico, and the Pueblo Indians of New Mexico employed artificial methods of watering very similar to those of the Old World.

In many parts of the earth, the soil is extremely fertile, but vegetation is scanty because the annual rainfall either is less than 20 inches or is concentrated in a relatively short season and followed by a long period of drought. In such regions, the ability to obtain water and distribute it to the fields when needed means the difference between a comparative desert and a rich region capable of supporting a large population.

Water is usually obtained from a river having its source in a more humid region. Lakes, wells, and springs also serve as sources of water. During the rainy season in India, many small reservoirs, called tanks, become filled by the floods.

Irrigation is practiced more extensively in India than in any other country. However, in the Middle East, United States, and other countries with large areas having arid and semi-arid climates, irrigation systems are being expanded with governmental assistance.

Methods of Irrigation. A large proportion of all irrigated lands receive water from rivers and streams. During the season of flood, these streams usually carry far more water than can be used, while later in the year their volume is much less than is needed by the surrounding country. By means of a dam equipped with control gates, a reservoir can be created which may be filled when the river is high and gradually emptied when the river would otherwise be too low.

Most of the great dams of the world, that at Aswan, Egypt, being a notable example, have been constructed as the most important feature of some irrigation project. The force of falling water is frequently sufficient to generate electric power, which is especially valuable in irrigated regions where fuel is generally scarce. The water is usually distributed from the river by main canals, with ditches branching from it to carry the water to the fields. Irrigation is accomplished by running the water in shallow channels until it is absorbed by the earth, or by flooding the entire field. Another method of irrigation is effected with sprinklers. Water is lifted from its source—well, stream, or reservoir—and pumped through pipes to sprinklers.

Irrigation in America. In the United States, irrigation was at first carried on by private enterprise, but the capital required was so great and the payments were necessarily spread over such a long period that the work on many projects was finally undertaken by the government. By the terms of the National Reclamation act, which was passed in 1902, a large part of the money received from the sale of public lands in sixteen Western states was to be used for the construction of reclamation projects under the direction of the department of the interior. But, when the equipment has been paid for, the control passes to the owners of the irrigated land.

More irrigated acres are devoted to raising alfalfa than to any other crop. Much of the irrigated land, however, is concentrated in specific areas: in the cotton-, fruit-, and vegetable-producing areas of California; in the high plains and the lower Rio Grande valley of Texas; in southern Idaho; in a few valleys in Oregon, Washington, and Colorado; and on livestock ranches scattered throughout the West, where irrigated land produces hay for use between grazing seasons. More than half of the 11.2 million-acre increase in irrigated land from 1950 to 1964 occurred in the Great Plains states. As a result, cereals account for about one-third of the total crops irrigated.

The Arrowrock dam on the Boise project, built in Idaho in 1915, was long the highest in the world (350 feet), but the Hoover (Boulder) dam, finished in 1936, is more than twice as high (726), and a dozen or more other dams also outrank Arrowrock. Many of these, in addition to irrigation, are used for flood control, power production, and river regulation. The total area of irrigated land in the United States approaches 35 million acres. Nearly 10 per cent of all U.S. farms have some irrigation. For details, see tables on *United States Government Irrigated Land Enterprises*. Large-scale irrigation projects are also being carried out in western Canadian provinces.

Old World Irrigation. As already stated, India is the most extensively irrigated country in the world, with a total area of projects in excess of 80 million acres, or more than 20 per cent of the total area occupied. The Sukkur barrage in the Sind province is designed to irrigate 5,500,000 acres. It is part of a larger plan for impounding the waters of the Indus river by works estimated to cost 250 million dollars. The annual value of crops on irrigated land in India approximates an average of 1½ times the total cost of the works.

Virtually 100 per cent of the cultivated land in Egypt is irrigated because of the arid climatic conditions. In 1955 this amounted to more than 7 million acres, with another 2 million acres in the planning stages for irrigation. The Aswan Dam, constructed in 1902 and more than doubled in storing capacity in 1912, is credited with having saved Egypt from famine and economic disaster in the low-flood year of 1913. Russia and Japan rank ahead of Egypt, however, in the total area of their irrigated soil. France, Italy, and Spain follow in the order named. China has a large area of irrigated land, but no authentic statistics are available by which its extent may be determined.

FORESTRY

Forestry is the art and the science of the economical management of existing communities of trees, and the development of new forests upon land unsuited to agriculture.

Value of Forests. Forests supply fuel and timber; they break the force of strong winds; they are warmer in winter and cooler in summer than open country; they afford parks for amusement; and they protect game for the hunter. Finally, forests exert a very noticeable influence upon the flow and character of neighboring streams. This effect has three principal causes: First, the trees break the direct force of the rainfall so that the earth on wooded hillsides is not cut up and washed into the valley. Second, water accumulates in the porous bed of a forest, and escapes to the stream gradually, thus tending to produce a continuous flow rather than a series of sudden, disastrous floods. Third, trees draw from swampy ground a large amount of water, which is evaporated through their leaves, thereby substantially decreasing the volume to be drained off by streams.

The purpose of forestry is to secure the greatest possible utilization of forests and forest products for the present, and, at the same time, to provide new growth for the future. To attain these results, existing forests must be protected from their chief enemies, fire and insects; lumbering operations must be performed with a minimum of waste; and cut-over areas must be replanted. Replanting may be done by allowing seed trees to remain standing, by artificial distribution of seed, or by setting out young trees which have been raised in nurseries.

Forestry has been practiced in Europe for several centuries, especially by the Germans and the French. England depended largely upon her commercial organizations to provide a supply of timber from foreign lands, but for a time during the World War she could obtain only that wood which France was able to spare. Because of this experience, England, shortly after the war, planned

UNITED STATES GOVERNMENT IRRIGATED LAND ENTERPRISES*

| STATE | Area Irrigated (in acres) | | | | Capital Invested 1959 ($1,000) |
	1949	1959	1964	Percent Increase 1959–64	
Alaska	N.A.	N.A.	158	. . .	N.A.
Arizona	979,014	1,152,450	1,125,376	−2.3	168,000
Arkansas	418,644	974,297	711,812	36.9	N.A.
California	6,618,595	7,395,570	7,598,698	2.7	898,000
Colorado	2,940,502	2,684,757	2,690,018	0.2	204,000
Florida	362,909	413,526	1,217,192	194.3	N.A.
Hawaii	. . .	141,179	143,940	2.0	N.A.
Idaho	2,168,323	2,576,580	2,801,500	8.7	148,000
Kansas	140,992	762,101	1,004,210	31.8	43,000
Louisiana	598,056	484,850	580,687	19.8	11,000
Mississippi	. . .	99,686	123,398	23.8	N.A.
Montana	1,809,908	1,874,520	1,893,360	1.0	96,000
Nebraska	887,505	2,077,926	2,169,317	4.4	56,000
Nevada	722,896	542,976	824,511	51.9	17,000
New Mexico	691,429	731,835	812,723	11.1	59,000
North Dakota	35,759	40,000	. . .	. . .	N.A.
Oklahoma	44,189	197,632	302,081	52.9	N.A.
Oregon	1,338,226	1,384,284	1,607,659	16.1	71,000
South Dakota	84,356	115,629	130,050	12.5	10,000
Texas	3,148,115	5,655,638	6,384,963	12.9	88,000
Utah	1,166,659	1,061,683	1,092,270	2.9	92,000
Washington	617,362	1,006,969	1,149,842	14.2	369,000
Wyoming	1,475,069	1,469,911	1,571,192	6.9	79,000
All Others	. . .	2,217,800	1,121,126	. . .	. . .
Total	26,248,508	33,021,799	37,056,083	12.2	2,411,000

* Statistics from Census Bureau, 1950, and *U.S. Census of Agriculture, 1964.*

| | Diversion Dams number | Reservoirs number | Reservoirs with capacity reported | | Canals miles | Pipe Lines miles | Wells number | |
			Reservoirs number	Total Capacity acre-feet			Flowing	Pumped
Arizona	562	269	237	3,625,629	4,898	316	245	4,361
Arkansas	108	86	74	40,431	684	19	27	3,662
California	4,706	1,687	1,507	8,711,658	20,188	10,091	572	72,163
Colorado	7,713	1,182	1,105	2,021,343	18,833	251	1,451	4,988
Florida	355	180	168	3,343	692	485	4,181	3,381
Idaho	5,108	366	313	5,124,969	15,321	437	490	887
Kansas	127	52	42	25,505	546	14	12	1,340
Louisiana	319	61	56	31,249	3,675	61	844	7,590
Montana	8,134	629	577	1,598,898	15,498	109	100	142
Nebraska	488	117	96	133,934	4,628	90	100	7,176
Nevada	4,046	202	176	687,179	3,390	124	293	254
New Mexico	1,286	476	448	3,186,401	5,769	167	106	3,832
North Dakota	15	11	6	1,101	92	7	—	4
Oklahoma	20	29	27	148,945	355	20	—	160
Oregon	6,218	528	470	2,369,138	8,395	573	148	2,770
South Dakota	281	100	94	204,693	968	7	14	27
Texas	439	570	508	1,402,689	9,892	758	163	15,065
Utah	3,080	511	474	2,424,093	9,622	299	1,920	565
Washington	1,859	224	205	6,436,541	3,977	1,515	87	2,098
Wyoming	5,237	458	415	4,370,844	9,724	59	225	248
Total	50,101	7,738	6,998	45,548,583	137,147	15,402	10,978	130,713

to plant one million acres of forest within forty years, and appropriated 17 million dollars to be used for this purpose within a period of ten years.

Forestry in the United States. During the early days of American history, the entire country, with the exception of the treeless plains of the mid-continent, was heavily wooded. Forestry, therefore, received little attention. In 1962 there were approximately 508 million acres of commercial forest land in the United States. Of this, 72 per cent was owned privately and 28 per cent by local, state, and federal governments.

In recognition of the pressing need for conservation of a dwindling national asset, Congress, in 1891, empowered the president to create forest reserves. Yellowstone Park Timberland reserve, the first to be established under the new law, was created by President Harrison. There are now national forests in 44 states and Puerto Rico, with a total area of approximately 226.5 million acres. These are under the control of the forest service of the Department of Agriculture and are chiefly located in the Western states.

Within the national forests, cutting of mature trees and replanting of new crops is continually going on. Fuel and fencing may be obtained free by local settlers, but most of the timber is sold. Grazing of live stock within the areas of the national forests is a practice of great importance. About 5 per cent of the cattle and 17 per cent of the sheep and lambs slaughtered annually are fed on national land during some part of the year.

Possibly the most important function of the national forests is to safeguard the streams which supply water for the famous Western irrigation projects. Without water there can be no irrigation, and without the forests the supply of water would be irregular and uncertain.

TOTAL AREA OF NATIONAL FORESTS EXTENDING INTO TWO OR MORE STATES

Forest	States	Net Area Acres
Apache	Arizona and New Mexico	1,569,090
Ashley	Utah and Wyoming	1,076,367
Bitterroot	Idaho and Montana	1,900,814
Black Hills	South Dakota and Wyoming	660,085
Cache	Idaho and Utah	712,890
Caribou	Idaho and Wyoming	845,497
Cherokee	North Carolina and Tennessee	547,489
Coronado	Arizona and New Mexico	1,442,277
Custer	Montana and South Dakota	1,201,317
Eldorado	California and Nevada	600,526
George Washington	Virginia and West Virginia	920,647
Harney	South Dakota and Wyoming	539,147
Inyo	California and Nevada	1,582,046
Kaniksu	Idaho, Montana, and Washington	1,487,698
Klamath	California and Oregon	1,511,832
Kootenai	Idaho and Montana	1,800,782
La Sal	Colorado and Utah	534,299
Lolo	Idaho and Montana	1,692,392
Minidoka	Idaho and Utah	592,968
Mono	California and Nevada	1,262,773
Ouachita	Arkansas and Oklahoma	1,491,818
Rogue River	California and Oregon	906,195
Siskiyou	California and Oregon	1,379,479
Tahoe	California and Nevada	606,154
Targhee	Idaho and Wyoming	1,365,574
Umatilla	Oregon and Washington	1,303,208
Wasatch	Utah and Wyoming	845,296
White Mountain	Maine and New Hampshire	704,196

In addition to national forests, there are forested tracts totaling about 8 million acres which have been created as reserves by a number of the states. New York State leads with forest reserves in excess of 2 million acres, chiefly in the Adirondack and Catskill parks. Pennsylvania and Washington have about 1.3 million acres of state forest land each. Other states with forest reserves over 500,000 acres are Montana and Michigan.

According to estimates made by the U. S. Department of Agriculture, about one-third of the total land area of the U.S. is forested, or 758 million acres out of 2.2 billion acres in the 50 states. Of this total, 508.8 million acres are classified as commercial forest land, either incapable of producing in excess of 25 cords of timber growth per acre per year, or protected by statute from commercial use. Of the 508.8 million commercial acres, 151 million acres are on farms, 216 million are owned by forest industry firms, and the balance are owned by state, local, and federal governments.

Progress of Forestry. By the enactment, in 1924, of the Clarke-McNary forestry law, the United States government became committed to a definite national forestry policy, embracing alike the publicly and the privately owned forest lands of the nation. The provisions of this act insure increased protection to immature forests and a larger measure of Federal assistance in fire prevention. Provision is made for the systematic study of the problems of forest taxation with the specific purpose of developing equable laws to encourage timber growing. Appropriations also are authorized for supplying nursery stocks of young forest trees to the farmer and for aiding him in caring for his tree plantations, the latter work to be carried out in co-operation with the agricultural extension service and forestry department of his own state.

The aim of forestry is to make the forest lands a perpetual source of needed supplies of wood. This will be accomplished when the annual growth equals or exceeds the amount of timber cut, and lost through fire, insects, and disease.

Civilian Conservation Corps. A major step in forestry conservation was taken in 1933, when provision was made for a "forest army," or Civilian Conservation Corps (CCC), employed by the Federal government to plant trees, combat fire and tree diseases, and otherwise to add to the value of the forest domain. A project was begun in 1935 for planting a tree shelter belt 100 miles wide from the Texas Panhandle to Canada to check erosion by the wind, the trees being designed to retard the evaporation of moisture from the soil. Trees are planted in strips 70 feet wide, spaced at one-mile intervals. The CCC was disbanded during World War II.

Forestry in Canada. Approximately 94.4 per cent of Canada's forested land is publicly owned. The Canadian government administers about 12,000 square miles of forest within national parks. Apart from these areas, there are no national forests in Canada. The other publicly owned forests belong to the provinces, whose governments administer a total of 97,600 square miles of provincial forest reserves and, in addition, about 13,000 square miles of forested lands within the provincial parks.

Forest reserves are intended to supply timber for local use and to protect the watersheds. The export of unmanufactured timber or pulpwood cut from public lands is prohibited in every province except Nova Scotia.

All the provinces provide means of protection against forest fires, including the patrolling of the forest areas, building of roads and telephone lines, and the maintenance of airplane and motor service for reporting or combating fires. Many millions of trees are distributed annually free of charge from governmental nurseries.

PREVENTION OF SOIL EROSION

Agricultural scientists estimate that 64 per cent of the cropland in the United States is in need of better conservation practices. Approximately 16 million acres need to be converted from cropland to permanent cover of trees or grass.

Removal of forest and grass cover to permit intensive cropping of the land has had a triple effect. First, a large proportion of the rain, instead of being held back and absorbed to form a sub-surface reservoir, runs off, forming gullies and carrying

State or Dependency and Forest	Net Area Acres**	State or Dependency and Forest	Net Area Acres**	State or Dependency and Forest	Net Area Acres**
ALABAMA:		**ILLINOIS:**		**OREGON:**	
Wm. B. Bankhead	178,736	Shawnee	210,953	Deschutes	1,659,380
Conecuh	83,790	Total for State	229,248†	Fremont	1,254,608
Talladega	357,726	**INDIANA:**		Klamath*	29,795
Tuskegee	10,777	Hoosier	125,000	Malheur	1,204,834
Total for State	631,317†	Total for State	146,169†	Mount Hood	1,115,327
ALASKA:		**KENTUCKY:**		Ochoco	845,880
Chugach	4,726,082	Cumberland	459,661	Rogue River*	837,235
Tongass	16,015,912	Total for State	538,893†	Siskiyou*	1,047,101
Total for State	20,734,673†	**LOUISIANA:**		Siuslaw	622,180
ARIZONA:		Kisatchie	591,566	Umatilla*	1,075,959
Apache*	1,190,068	Total for State	593,416†	Umpqua	983,982
Coconino	1,800,786	**MAINE:**		Wallowa	979,279
Coronado*	1,724,147	White Mountain	41,004	Whitman	1,511,613
Kaibab	1,718,043	Total for State	50,016†	Willamette	1,665,835
Prescott	1,247,622	**MICHIGAN:**		Winema	908,963
Sitgreaves	768,994	Hiawatha	476,653	Total for State	15,471,213†
Tonto	2,894,314	Huron	414,918	**PENNSYLVANIA:**	
Total for State	11,429,833†	Manistee	446,403	Allegheny	471,077
ARKANSAS:		Marquette	354,270	Total for State	479,762†
Ouachita*	1,321,689	Ottawa	861,459	**PUERTO RICO:**	
Ozark	1,046,649	Total for State	2,633,127†	Caribbean	21,499
St. Francis	20,611	**MINNESOTA:**		Total for Territory	27,916†
Total for State	2,442,924†	Chippewa	594,292	**SOUTH CAROLINA:**	
CALIFORNIA:		Superior	1,929,533	Francis Marion	245,650
Angeles	648,739	Total for State	2,784,143†	Sumter	341,610
Cleveland	391,312	**MISSISSIPPI:**		Total for State	588,928†
Eldorado*	640,872	Bienville	175,657	**SOUTH DAKOTA:**	
Inyo*	1,774,236	Delta	58,956	Black Hills	1,047,106
Klamath*	1,667,669	De Soto	500,405	Custer	73,707
Lassen	1,667,669	Holly Springs	145,432	(Norbeck Wildlife	
Los Padres	1,749,082	Homochitto	189,070	Preserve)	(46,000)
Mendocino	867,433	Tombigbee	65,232	Total for State	1,982,433†
Modoc	1,688,789	Total for State	1,134,495†	**TENNESSEE:**	
Northern Redwoods		**MISSOURI:**		Cherokee	594,770
(Purchase Unit)	14,491	Clark	824,118	Total for State	603,601†
Plumas	1,147,415	Mark Twain	391,702	**TEXAS:**	
Rogue River*	49,261	Total for State	1,400,811†	Angelina	154,392
San Bernardino	613,886	**MONTANA:**		Davy Crockett	161,563
Shasta	986,585	Beaverhead	2,130,936	Sabine	183,844
Sequoia	1,118,508	Bitterroot*	1,113,814	Sam Houston	158,205
Sierra	1,295,745	Custer*	1,097,784	Total for State	775,375†
Siskiyou*	31,740	Deerlodge	1,134,572	**UTAH:**	
Six Rivers	935,266	Flathead	2,336,388	Ashley*	1,282,829
Stanislaus	895,820	Gallatin	1,700,139	Cache*	391,720
Tahoe*	694,123	Helena	966,613	Dixie	1,851,341
Toiyabe	629,745	Kaniksu*	447,142	Fishlake	1,415,665
Trinity	1,051,173	Kootenai*	1,769,404	Manti-La Sal*	1,237,128
Total for State	19,994,773†	Lewis and Clark	1,862,018	Sawtooth*	71,117
COLORADO:		Lolo*	2,076,641	Uinta	774,901
Arapaho	984,489	Total for State	16,699,099†	Wasatch*	822,197
Grand Mesa	360,963	**NEBRASKA:**		Total for State	8,000,169†
Gunnison	1,660,147	Toadstool Park		**VERMONT:**	
Manti-La Sal*	26,631	(National		Green Mountain	231,825
Pike	1,084,873	Grassland)	100	Total for State	235,558†
Rio Grande	1,800,322	Nebraska	339,716	**VIRGINIA:**	
Roosevelt	776,882	Total for State	349,543†	George Washington*	903,748
Routt	1,144,792	**NEVADA:**		Jefferson	543,501
San Isabel	1,103,859	Eldorado*	400	Total for State	1,495,080†
San Juan	1,849,635	Humboldt	2,507,870	**WASHINGTON:**	
Uncompahgre	957,004	Inyo*	60,576	Colville	928,312
White River	1,960,714	Toiyabe	2,489,181	Gifford Pinchot	1,263,300
Total for State	14,319,757†	Total for State	5,073,657†	Kaniksu*	287,684
FLORIDA:		**NEW HAMPSHIRE:**		Mount Baker	1,818,294
Apalachicola	556,496	White Mountain	677,660	Okanogan	2,042,213
Ocala	361,243	Total for State	678,807†	Olympic	621,756
Osceola	157,233	**NEW MEXICO:**		Snoqualmie	1,207,815
Total for State	1,075,712†	Apache*	542,443	Umatilla*	313,780
GEORGIA:		Carson	1,225,408	Wenatchee	1,205,437
Chattahoochee	679,660	Cibola	1,690,738	Total for State	9,710,815†
Oconee	96,056	Coronado*	69,567	**WEST VIRGINIA:**	
Total for State	806,063†	Gila	2,715,706	George Washington	98,259
IDAHO:		Lincoln	1,087,909	Monongahela	805,721
Bitterroot*	460,812	Santa Fe	1,233,419	Total for State	920,212†
Boise	2,633,534	Total for State	9,153,364†	**WISCONSIN:**	
Cache*	262,897	**NORTH CAROLINA:**		Chequamegon	827,067
Caribou*	963,939	Croatan	152,351	Nicolet	640,448
Challis	2,447,363	Nantahala	448,334	Total for State	1,478,984†
Clearwater	1,250,772	Pisgah	479,722	**WYOMING:**	
Coeur d'Alene	723,408	Uwharrie	43,391	Big Horn	1,113,768
Kaniksu*	891,348	Total for State	1,127,418†	Black Hills*	199,466
Kootenai*	48,851	**NORTH DAKOTA:**		Bridger	1,699,878
Lolo*	426,062	Total for State	1,104,958†	Caribou*	7,829
Nezperce	2,196,029	**OHIO:**		Medicine Bow	1,069,283
Payette	2,307,328	Wayne	113,000	Shoshone	2,430,028
St. Joe	868,650	Total for State	127,381†	Targhee*	344,573
Salmon	1,768,728	**OKLAHOMA:**		Teton	1,700,766
Sawtooth	1,731,563	Ouachita	180,977	Wasatch	36,880
Targhee*	1,319,293	Total for State	287,119†	Total for State	9,165,186
Total for State	20,347,244†			Aggregate for the	
				National Forests	186,921,196

* Forest extending into more than one state.

** Acreage includes land area and water.

† Totals include National Grasslands land utilization projects and other special areas administered by the Forest Service.

top soil into streams and rivers. Secondly, the soil, containing a smaller amount of permanent moisture, is more susceptible to drought. Thirdly, during dry spells, high winds strip off enormous amounts of top soil, carrying it away as dust.

As compared with plowed land, it is estimated that grass-covered soil retains two to three times as much water from a given rainfall and that forests in turn retain twice as much as do pastures. Prescriptions to retard damage include:
1. Contour farming across the slopes, rather than up and down the slopes.
2. Building brush and log dams across gullies and small streams.
3. Retention and/or development of woodlots on farms and planting of trees to serve as windbreaks to prevent wind erosion.
4. Rotation of crops, including in the cycle the raising of grasses and soil-enriching plants, such as clover and other legumes.

Partly to encourage this form of conservation, Congress passed a Soil Conservation Act in 1936. The Soil Conservation Service was established as a result of this act, making technical service available to farmers for the development of soil and water conservation practices. In addition to this technical assistance from the U.S. Soil Conservation Service and local Soil and Water Conservation Districts, farmers also receive payments from the Federal government to help share the cost of establishing soil and water conservation practices.

ANIMAL INDUSTRY

During the early period of man's development, wild animals were a valuable source of food and of clothing. Later, certain of the larger animals were tamed and used as beasts of burden. Fine furs are still taken chiefly from wild animals; but, as the population of the earth increased in numbers and advanced in the arts of civilization, man learned that better meat, more comfortable clothing, and superior types of motive power could be obtained from domestic animals. By careful selection and breeding, he gradually developed these animals to suit his needs.

Nevertheless, the number of species used by man is very small. Swine, cattle, sheep and goats, horses, mules, and asses comprise more than 99 per cent of all live stock exclusive of poultry. These animals are extensively distributed throughout the temperate zones, the type or species most suitable to any locality depending almost entirely on the climate and on the condition of the soil.

Swine. The total number of swine in the U.S. in 1969 was 57 million. This was more than double the number of sheep and lambs, estimated at 21 million, but only about one-half of the 110 million cattle and calves on farms that year. Nevertheless, because of its rapid growth and great rate of reproduction, the hog is the chief meat-producing animal of the world. Hogs cannot live upon grass, but require a more concentrated food. They are found, therefore, wherever grain is raised, because the feeding of grain to hogs usually results in a more valuable food product. A large part of the American corn crop goes to market as pork. In fact, the corn belt is the center of the hog-raising industry.

Modern breeds of swine are meat-type hogs. The Hampshire, Duroc, Yorkshire, Chester White, and Poland China breeds are popular domestic types and produce excellent hams, bacon, and other cuts. Breeding stock, such as the Landrace breed, developed in Denmark, have also been introduced into the U.S. from Europe since World War II as the newer meat-type animals have gained in popularity over older lard-type strains. In number of swine produced, China, Brazil, the United States, and Russia are the four leading countries.

Sheep. Just as pork is the principal meat of grain-producing countries, so mutton and wool are the chief animal products of all dry, rough, and thinly settled, grass-growing regions. Tunis, Algeria, and Morocco are known as the "sheep countries," and for centuries the shepherd has been representative of one of the most important industries of Syria, Palestine, and the great dry steppes of southern Russia and the Crimea. The semiarid regions of western United States and the high plateaus of Mexico are largely devoted to sheep raising. Australia leads all countries in number of sheep, Russia is second, United States third, and Argentina fourth. The number of sheep in the United States reached its maximum in 1903.

Draft Animals. The horse is the most important and the most valuable of all draft animals; nevertheless, for this purpose, it is exceeded in numbers, even at the present time, by the ox. In the production of horses, Russia is first, followed by the United States, Argentina, Brazil, China, Germany, and Canada. In Canada, horse raising is of unusual importance. The number of horses sometimes exceeds that of sheep and is almost equal to that of swine.

The United States produces more than half of the world's supply of mules. The greatest horse and mule market in the world is at East Saint Louis, Illinois.

The Percheron, which is considered by many to be the finest type of draft horse, was developed by French breeders in the south of Normandy. The English Shires are the largest of all horses. The breeding of thoroughbreds is most extensive in Great Britain.

As a beast of burden, the camel is especially well adapted to traveling in the desert, the reindeer to the plains of the arctic regions, and the yak to cold places of high altitude, such as Tibet. The llama performs in the Andes the same services as does the yak in the Himalayas. The elephant is extensively used in India as a draft animal, and his great power is utilized by almost every traveling circus. The dog is very useful for drawing sleds in the snow regions of North America, and is commonly used for hauling wagons in the densely populated sections of northwestern Europe.

Cattle. India, the United States, Russia, Argentina, Brazil, Germany, and China are the chief cattle producing countries of the world; but the chief beef exporting nations are Argentina and Australia. The cattle of India consist largely of the humped Brahman variety, and of the water buffalo. They are not used to any great extent for food. Cattle raising is quite generally divided into the production of beef cattle of the Hereford, Angus, Shorthorn, and newer cross-breed types such as the Santa Gertrudis, and of milk-producing breeds, such as the Holstein, Guernsey, and Jersey. In a new, level, thinly settled country, well covered with rich grass, beef cattle are raised on a large scale for the export of meat, hides, and tallow. Fresh beef can be shipped to any part of the world because of modern methods of artificial refrigeration. But, as the population increases, cattle ranges give place to farms, and the type of cattle gradually changes from beef producers to dairy animals. In order to produce more beef from fewer animals, the tendency of modern breeding is towards early maturing cattle. In Europe, where extensive pastures are no longer available, practically all cattle are stall-fed.

Poultry. Poultry raising is the most universal form of animal industry. All countries raise poultry, chiefly chickens. China leads in the production of eggs, with Russia second. The average commercial egg farm in the U.S. has 10,000 hens in its flock; some have as many as 2 million hens under single management with automated facilities. The U.S. produces in excess of 69 billion eggs per year. The U.S. is also a world leader in the production of turkeys, some 106 million in 1969, valued at nearly $415 million. Today in the United States, egg-producing hens, called layers, are either hybrids or

Leghorns. Meat-type birds come from highly specialized breeders; some breed only for the male line and others for only the female line.

Silk Culture. Annual production of silk amounts to about 75 million pounds, of which Japan produces more than half. Other important silk-producing countries include China, Russia, India, and Korea. The silk industry has become relatively less important as synthetic fibers have been developed and accepted. Annual importation of silk into the United States exceeds $300 million in value.

Bees. The production of honey is an industry that depends upon the food-storing instinct of the honeybee, and upon a supply of growing flowers to provide the nectar. Total production of honey in the U.S. is over 200 million pounds annually. This amount has declined steadily in recent years. Of even greater value is the service performed by bees in pollinating flowers of fruit trees and other useful plants.

Farm Animals in U. S. In 1940, each of the 6.1 million farms of the United States had on the average seven swine, ten cattle, seven sheep, two horses or mules, and 55 chickens, valued in all at $740.49. These animals produced, besides what was consumed on the farms, 399 dozen eggs, 49 pounds of wool, and 1916 gallons of milk, including that sold for making butter and cheese. The farm value of these products amounted to an average of $275.77 for each farm. The inhabitants of the Oceanic countries are the greatest meat-eaters in the world, with an average annual consumption exceeding 200 pounds per person. Per-capita consumption of meat in the United States in 1969 was 182 pounds. Beef consumption, in particular, has increased in recent years in the U.S.—from 82.1 pounds in 1957–59 to 110.5 pounds per person in 1969.

The most important breeding grounds of beef cattle in the United States are the western portion of the Corn Belt, the Great Plains, the valleys and high plateaus of the Far West, and the Gulf coast from Georgia to Texas.

Milk. The insuring of an adequate daily supply of fresh milk of standard quality in the large centers of population necessitates elaborate organization, specialized transportation, and rigid inspection. Most milk offered for sale is pasteurized, that is, heated to 161 degrees Fahrenheit for 15 seconds, or to as high as 190 degrees for one-half second in the flash pasteurization process, to kill all pathogenic bacteria. Many municipalities have insisted on a unified system of grading milk as A, B, and C. Grade A, either raw or pasteurized, must have not more than 10,000 bacteria per cubic centimeter; grades B and C, not more than 50,000. Grade B must be pasteurized under official supervision; grade C is pasteurized, but not under official supervision. By the Babcock test, devised in 1890 by S. M. Babcock, the proportion of fat in milk is readily determined. This normally varies from 3 to 6%. Large amounts of milk are concentrated and shipped in air-tight tins for use in the home or food factories. Wisconsin and New York are the leading states in milk production.

Serums and Vaccines. Employment of animals for the preparation of serums and of vaccine used in the treatment and prevention of diseases is a small but exceedingly important branch of animal industry. For example, diphtheria antitoxic serum is developed within the blood of healthy horses, while the vaccine used for preventing smallpox is generally obtained from calves.

There is a marked difference between antitoxin and vaccine. Diphtheria antitoxin, as its name implies, contains substances which, when injected into the blood of a person suffering from diphtheria, neutralize the poisons already produced in the blood by the active germs of that disease. A vaccine is the exact opposite of an antitoxin. Smallpox vaccine, for example, contains, in a greatly diluted or weakened form, the virus which tends to produce smallpox, or, rather, cowpox. When, by the process of vaccination, a minute quantity of vaccine is allowed to enter the system, the blood soon proceeds to develop within itself quantities of antitoxin which neutralize the virus.

In the preparation of diphtheria antitoxin, a very small amount of the poison produced by growing diphtheria germs is injected into a healthy horse. The horse develops a very mild fever, which soon disappears. Successively larger doses are administered at intervals until the horse receives without injury an amount of the toxin many hundreds of times that which would kill an ordinary animal.

Smallpox vaccine is obtained by vaccinating healthy young calves with smallpox or cowpox virus. The virus is applied in long narrow scratches, which, in about a week, develop the characteristic swelling that contains vaccine lymph. The virus produced in these lesions is collected, purified, diluted with glycerin, and quickly distributed.

Insulin. This extract, secured chiefly from the pancreas of cattle and hogs, is used extensively in the treatment of diabetic patients. It occurs in certain interior portions of the pancreas, known as the "islands of Langerhans." Diabetes is caused by a failure of the liver to act normally in transforming sugar into glycogen, and as a result the blood becomes surcharged with unassimilated sugar. Insulin, when injected into the blood, temporarily enables the liver to take this sugar from the blood.

DAIRYING

This term embraces the production of milk and the manufacture of milk products. While goats, sheep, camels, reindeer, mares, and the Asiatic buffalo are sometimes used as a source of milk, the cow alone is bred for the purpose and supports a huge dairy industry. The dairy industry was revolutionized in the late 19th century by the introduction of the centrifugal cream separator and of the Babcock test for determining the fat content of milk. The latter, invented in 1890, made possible the purchase of milk, for manufacture and distribution, on the basis of quality and greatly stimulated the improvement of herds.

The same period saw the rise of education in dairy management. A school of agriculture was opened in 1873 at Copenhagen, Denmark, which country has shown the most marked improvement in the quality of its milch cows. In 1890, at Madison, Wis., the first American school for dairying was opened, under the direction of W. A. Henry. Since that time numerous schools for dairying, experimental stations, and co-operative cow-testing associations have come into existence in the United States, Canada, and other countries. Australia, New Zealand, Argentina, Russia, and Switzerland are also large producers of milk and milk products.

Dairying in North America. In 1969 there were about 13 million dairy cows on U.S. farms, and the average milk produced per cow was 9,000 pounds. A United States gallon of milk weighs about 8.6 pounds; the Canadian gallon, about 10.3 pounds. Each person in the United States annually consumes about 5.4 pounds of butter, 10.8 pounds of margarine, 10.9 pounds of cheese, and 18.1 pounds of ice cream, in addition to 271 pounds, or about 31.5 gallons, of fluid milk and cream.

The chief dairying states are Wisconsin, New York, Iowa, Minnesota, California, and Pennsylvania. Wisconsin produces the greatest amount of butter, cheese, and condensed milk; New York, the most milk for market. The dairy production of the United States is valued at about $6.2 billion, or $31 per capita. Among the Canadian provinces, Ontario leads in the production of cheese and butter; Quebec ranks second.

Cheese and Other Milk Products. Cheese was a common article of diet at least as early as 1400 B. C. It is made from milk by separating the curd, or casein, portions of the fat, and other constituents from the whey, shaping the mass into different forms, and usually curing it. The separation is ordinarily effected by rennet, prepared from the stomachs of young calves or pigs. Upward of 150 kinds of cheese are made in Europe and America, the differences being dependent on the kind and condition of milk used, the manufacture, the seasoning, and especially the curing.

Milk is preserved either in the form of powder; as a sweet, slow-flowing liquid; or as an unsweetened, creamlike liquid. In these forms, which were first made about 1855, milk is now susceptible of much wider use than was formerly the case. It has become an important article of international commerce, and its use by bakers has resulted in a marked improvement in the quality of factory-made bread.

When used for ice cream, milk is generally *homogenized*, the fat globules being thereby rendered so small that they do not rise in the form of cream.

Casein obtained from milk is used in the manufacture of glue and also, in a plastic form, as a strong, elastic, noninflammable product resembling celluloid. Its uses include electric insulation and ornamental objects.

FISHERIES

The three greatest commercial fishing grounds of the world are located near the coasts of northwestern Europe, northeastern North America, and northeastern Asia. In these places, where the ocean is comparatively shallow, enormous "schools" of valuable food fishes congregate in order to obtain the food that they find near the bottom. A second important type of fisheries takes advantage of the spawning habits of certain fish, which, at the spawning season, travel up rivers or to the shores, where they are easily caught. The cod and haddock are chief examples of bottom feeders, while salmon and shad are the most valuable of the second group.

The rank of various nations in order of the size of their fish catch is approximately: Peru, Japan, Russia, Norway, United States, India, Spain, Canada, Denmark, and South Africa. In terms of value of catch, Japan ranks first, followed by the United States, the Philippines, Spain, and France. Data regarding value of the catch in mainland China and Russia are not available. Although the United States is among the top-ranked nations, the fishing industry is of less relative importance than in many other countries. The total catch of fish in the United States in 1974 was 4.9 billion pounds, valued at $898 million. In addition, 2.2 billion pounds of fish were imported from other countries, at a value of nearly $1.5 billion.

The development of the freezing process has increased the consumption of fish to an annual total of 15.01 pounds per person in the United States.

Fisheries in the U.S. Because of its great extent, the United States affords almost all kinds of fishing, from seal-fishing in Alaska to sponge-gathering in Florida. Shrimp are the most valuable product of the country's fisheries, with salmon second, tuna third, crabs fourth, and oysters fifth. The menhaden, though inedible, is important for its use in manufacturing fertilizer and for the industrial use of its oil.

Canadian Fisheries. Salmon caught in the Pacific regions of Canada are the most valuable product of the country's fisheries. Lobster and cod are second and third in value, with flounder and haddock together in fourth place. The total Canadian catch amounts to some 2.3 million tons annually, valued at nearly $545 million.

Secondary Products. In addition to food, there are many other uses for fishery products. From the whale are obtained the ordinary whale oil and whalebone, and also sperm oil, spermaceti wax, and ambergris, which is highly valued for use in fine perfumes. True caviar is prepared from the roe of the sturgeon, and the swimming bladder of the same fish is the source of the finest isinglass. Liquid glue is prepared from fishskins and offal, while crushed oyster, clam, and other shells are used for poultry grit, for surfacing roads, and for making lime. Sealskin, pearls, and corals are among the luxury products of the fisheries. Fish scales enter into *essence d'orient*, used in making artificial pearls.

ANIMAL INDUSTRY IN CANADA, 1974

PROVINCE	Milk Cows	Other Cattle	Sheep and lambs	Swine	Poultry
Alberta	190,000	3,920,000	181,000	1,195,000	3,132,000
British Columbia	109,000	490,000	34,000	56,000	4,215,000
Manitoba	118,000	1,076,000	21,000	635,000	3,735,000
New Brunswick	39,000	65,000	8,000	45,000	715,000
Nova Scotia	50,000	82,000	19,000	72,000	1,330,000
Ontario	847,000	2,464,000	138,000	1,900,000	13,375,000
PEI	28,000	73,000	5,000	87,000	159,000
Quebec	1,125,000	687,000	42,000	1,215,000	5,295,000
Saskatchewan	93,000	2,562,000	91,000	660,000	1,530,000
Canada	2,080,000	12,898,000	784,000	6,564,000	34,996,000

LEADING UNITED STATES CATTLE STATES, 1975

Rank	State	Number	Rank	State	Number	Rank	State	Number
1	Texas	15,600,000	6	Oklahoma	6,400,000	11	Kentucky	3,450,000
2	Iowa	7,500,000	7	California	5,000,000	12	Illinois	3,400,000
3	Missouri	6,600,000	8	Wisconsin	4,550,000	13	Colorado	3,250,000
4	Nebraska	6,550,000	9	South Dakota	4,500,000	14	Montana	3,150,000
5	Kansas	6,450,000	10	Minnesota	4,430,000	15	Tennessee	3,100,000

Source: U.S. Department of Agriculture.

POULTRY AND EGG PRODUCTION IN THE UNITED STATES, 1975

Source: Department of Agriculture, Statistical Reporting Service; annual report, *Agricultural Statistics.*

STATE	Eggs Produced on Farms (millions)	Chickens Raised on Farms (1,000)	Commercial Broilers Produced (1,000)	Turkeys Raised (1,000)	Chicks Hatched by Commercial Hatcheries (1,000)
Alabama	2,951	14,330	398,303	17	432,399
Alaska	5	36	.....	.....	.....
Arizona	159	518	.....	.....	.....
Arkansas	3,594	20,092	482,399	7,100	561,820
California	8,467	22,122	90,377	15,771	148,157
Colorado	473	2,188	.....	3,620	.....
Connecticut	798	3,100	1,836	36	4,733
Delaware	115	650	146,945	.....	145,462
Florida	2,779	11,300	59,727	.....	116,557
Georgia	5,284	20,800	426,857	1,216	487,191
Hawaii	209	565	1,900	.....	.....
Idaho	184	760	.....	.....	.....
Illinois	1,483	5,500	.....	445	10,750
Indiana	2,609	12,500	11,679	5,135	51,087
Iowa	2,006	10,600	3,615	6,260	20,645
Kansas	599	2,900	780	154	5,830
Kentucky	518	3,000	6,885	.....	.....
Louisiana	658	3,100	54,443	2	.....
Maine	1,650	8,300	77,426	6	98,510
Maryland	331	1,500	189,709	39	210,603
Massachusetts	541	1,800	.....	125	.....
Michigan	1,303	6,000	577	700	10,675
Minnesota	2,209	9,572	10,815	22,752	34,095
Mississippi	1,707	10,300	227,220	.....	248,419
Missouri	1,241	7,078	19,796	8,125	17,683
Montana	197	1,050	.....	.....	.....
Nebraska	782	2,400	2,312	487	4,173
Nevada	4.3	17	.....	.....	.....
New Hampshire	283	1,300	.....	21	.....
New Jersey	620	2,200	.....	74	.....
New Mexico	234	1,300	.....	.....	.....
New York	1,984	8,500	1,580	145	9,560
North Carolina	2,802	14,000	286,558	14,400	316,756
North Dakota	132	800	.....	911	.....
Ohio	1,999	8,900	11,900	2,835	.....
Oklahoma	430	2,100	29,560	1,370	1,698
Oregon	519	1,640	14,253	1,025	28,522
Pennsylvania	3,299	12,440	63,649	2,838	107,227
Rhode Island	69.5	220	.....	9	.....
South Carolina	1,385	6,180	31,552	2,585	32,645
South Dakota	702	3,550	.....	860	.....
Tennessee	949	2,300	42,586	4	.....
Texas	2,360	11,000	173,588	8,845	201,949
Utah	321	922	.....	3,446	883
Vermont	105	350	.....	7	.....
Virginia	765	4,400	77,220	5,972	95,921
Washington	1,068	4,460	16,730	225	18,825
West Virginia	256	1,050	18,293	1,530	.....
Wisconsin	1,194	4,300	11,274	4,894	.....
Wyoming	29.7	95	.....	.....	.....
Total	64,362	274,085	2,992,344	124,255	3,622,875

Source: *Statistical Abstract of the United States, 1970.*

In Thousands of Short Tons

Country	Wheat	Rice	Cotton	Corn	Potatoes	Sugar	Meat
Argentina	6,327	312	79	7,231	2,168	1,028	3,248
Australia	16,189	244	21‡	222	737	3,086	1,932
Austria	1,152	—	—	440	3,828	330	511
Belgium	942	—	—	3	1,726	634	668
Brazil	944	7,332	657	14,125	1,770	4,824	2,446
Canada	19,495	—	6	2,261	2,655	130	1,615
Chile	1,345	103	—	354	799	187	280
China (mainland)	28,329*	101,412†	1,602	N.A.	N.A.	2,756	N.A.
Colombia	143	860	132	970	937	731	530
Cuba	—	210	—	132†	116†	5,859	270
Denmark	511	—	—	—	955	376	1,020
Ecuador	84	—	—	220	389	—	—
Egypt (UAR)	1,652	2,851	482	2,532	520	456	482
Finland	569	—	—	—	1,001	54	193
France	16,144	91	—	5,897	11,016	2,536	3,289
Germany, Fed. Rep.	6,832	—	—	316	21,154	2,176	3,677
Greece	1,670	119	82	413	714	132	226
Hungary	3,704	45	82	4,204	1,799	465	517
India	18,232	65,743	1,195	6,284	4,665	2,618	642
Indonesia	—	17,093	—	3,368	46‡	661	227
Iran	5,486	1,055	176	......	......	......	......
Iraq	1,500	384	......	......	......	......	......
Ireland	448	—	—	—	1,791	168	430
Italy	10,571	704	2	4,396	4,365	1,422	1,372
Japan	1,116	20,685	—	56	4,471	669	847
Korea, Rep. of	94‡	2,756‡	4	69	680	—	108
Mexico	2,088	502	592	10,318	441	2,575	653
Netherlands	748	—	—	1†	5,561	787	1,006
New Zealand	487	—	—	227	331	—	1,048
Norway	......	......	—	—	1,005	—	146
Pakistan	7,341	22,118	585	693	993	473	408
Paraguay	......	......	11	198	11	41	159
Peru	165	441	111	650	1,874	829	163
Philippines	—	5,326	—	1,603	13†	1,819	358
Poland	5,148	—	—	14	56,016	2,041	2,008
Portugal	879	169	—	583	1,147	15	192
Rumania	5,344	66	—	7,832	4,085	457	449
South Africa	1,350	2†	17	5,700	548†	1,895	685
Spain	6,041	399	78	1,624	4,118	789	902
Sweden	1,167	—	—	—	1,570	326	438
Switzerland	411	—	—	—	1,210	75	353
Syria	661	9	......	......	......	......	......
Turkey	10,584	226	480	1,102	1,990	772	205
U.S.S.R.	102,947	1,172	2,255	9,731	112,637	10,784	11,739
United Kingdom	3,824	—	—	—	7,546	1,033	2,230
United States	47,289	5,265	2,737	122,493	14,700	5,626	17,618
Uruguay	534	115	—	76	103†	77	459
Venezuela	—	299	14	661	175	373	250
Yugoslavia	4,809	20	3	7,507	3,186	477	713
World Total	366,100	314,300	12,500	275,800	346,500	73,700	85,600

* 1966.   † 1967.   ‡ 1965.   — None or negligible.

	Horses and Mules 1959	All Cattle		Milk Cows		Sheep and Lambs 1975	Hogs and Pigs 1975
		1964	1975	1964	1974		
Alabama	93,000	1,848,000	2,700,000	160,800	95,000	4,400	820,000
Alaska	N.A.	8,000	9,300	2,000	1,700	12,400	700
Arizona	51,000	1,104,000	1,170,000	46,000	62,000	510,000	97,000
Arkansas	77,000	1,574,000	2,680,000	132,000	92,000	5,500	302,000
California	77,000	4,303,000	5,200,000	732,000	797,000	1,100,000	138,000
Colorado	65,000	2,499,000	3,375,000	93,000	76,000	990,000	290,000
Connecticut . . .	4,000	123,000	110,000	72,000	55,000	5,500	6,800
Delaware	3,000	37,000	33,000	18,000	12,200	1,900	55,000
Florida	27,000	1,822,000	2,950,000	176,000	201,000	4,200	240,000
Georgia	71,000	1,747,000	2,420,000	153,000	130,000	3,500	1,300,000
Hawaii	7,000	218,000	250,000	14,000	12,800	. . . .	58,000
Idaho	50,000	1,603,000	2,150,000	165,000	149,000	595,000	90,000
Illinois	74,000	3,751,000	3,200,000	422,000	262,000	229,000	5,600,000
Indiana	53,000	2,053,000	2,125,000	328,000	220,000	196,000	3,900,000
Iowa	81,000	7,285,000	7,350,000	736,000	407,000	460,000	12,600,000
Kansas	68,000	5,150,000	6,400,000	241,000	147,000	200,000	1,650,000
Kentucky	145,000	2,341,000	3,750,000	407,000	297,000	40,000	1,000,000
Louisiana	87,000	1,867,000	1,832,000	187,000	37,000	15,000	170,000
Maine	8,000	158,000	138,000	76,000	60,000	13,000	7,300
Maryland	15,000	415,000	444,000	175,000	136,000	17,000	235,000
Massachusetts . .	5,000	127,000	107,000	79,000	54,000	7,900	55,000
Michigan	36,000	1,725,000	1,640,000	574,000	420,000	167,000	700,000
Minnesota . . .	58,000	4,281,000	4,430,000	1,237,000	890,000	390,000	3,000,000
Mississippi	141,000	2,351,000	3,000,000	248,000	129,000	7,000	351,000
Missouri	102,000	4,522,000	6,800,000	461,000	314,000	194,000	3,200,000
Montana	86,000	2,873,000	3,340,000	55,000	28,000	710,000	145,000
Nebraska	68,000	5,987,000	6,900,000	250,000	158,000	280,000	2,700,000
Nevada	19,000	609,000	657,000	13,000	14,000	151,000	9,000
New Hampshire .	4,000	82,000	71,000	44,000	32,000	5,600	8,700
New Jersey . . .	7,000	153,000	117,000	97,000	50,000	10,100	98,000
New Mexico . .	43,000	1,203,000	1,720,000	35,000	31,000	578,000	53,000
New York . . .	47,000	1,959,000	1,875,000	1,134,000	905,000	79,000	90,000
North Carolina .	145,000	906,000	1,120,000	198,000	152,000	11,000	1,900,000
North Dakota . .	57,000	2,465,000	2,635,000	229,000	125,000	315,000	350,000
Ohio	74,000	2,164,000	2,350,000	544,000	407,000	517,000	1,675,000
Oklahoma	90,000	4,200,000	6,500,000	168,000	124,000	89,000	300,000
Oregon	44,000	1,620,000	1,470,000	126,000	91,000	415,000	90,000
Pennsylvania . .	58,000	1,789,000	1,960,000	791,000	687,000	125,000	660,000
Rhode Island . .	1,000	16,000	12,000	10,000	5,900	2,500	9,000
South Carolina .	68,000	555,000	710,000	77,000	57,000	1,400	540,000
South Dakota . .	61,000	4,144,000	4,950,000	223,000	164,000	792,000	1,400,000
Tennessee	139,000	2,136,000	3,300,000	370,000	218,000	19,000	920,000
Texas	237,000	9,766,000	16,600,000	392,000	349,000	2,688,000	780,000
Utah	30,000	748,000	900,000	75,000	78,000	697,000	43,000
Vermont	9,000	368,000	336,000	230,000	193,000	6,300	4,500
Virginia	84,000	1,312,000	1,750,000	246,000	159,000	177,000	660,000
Washington . . .	38,000	1,376,000	1,420,000	192,000	181,000	93,000	71,000
West Virginia . .	38,000	482,000	540,000	84,000	42,000	128,000	50,000
Wisconsin	59,000	4,384,000	4,640,000	2,083,000	1,801,000	105,000	1,150,000
Wyoming	49,000	1,348,000	1,690,000	23,000	13,200	1,350,000	30,000
Total	2,953,000	105,558,000	131,826,000	14,623,000	11,219,000	14,512,000	49,602,000

Source: *1959 data, 1959 Census of Agriculture; 1964 data, Dept. of Agriculture, Statistical Reporting Service; 1975 data, Agricultural Statistics, 1976.*

PUREBRED BEEF AND DUAL-PURPOSE CATTLE
Source: *Breeder's Gazette, March 1964*

Number of new registrations each year, as reported by breed associations, United States

Year	Aberdeen Angus	Devon	Hereford	Polled Hereford	Red Poll	Shorthorn	Brahman
1936	15,023	208	124,278	8,000	1,382	36,521	....
1937	17,278	236	134,679	6,732	1,418	34,424	....
1938	19,248	214	135,454	7,946	1,624	33,575	....
1939	25,308	259	159,408	8,717	2,350	41,025	....
1940	40,778	285	191,405	10,848	2,876	41,431	4,409
1941	38,737	336	207,517	15,244	2,724	50,120	4,132
1942	46,820	338	250,527	17,372	2,522	54,471	[1]
1943	52,432	398	288,675	17,034	3,155	52,845	8,536
1944	57,717	443	298,421	18,881	4,267	60,504	7,054
1945	66,020	401	316,081	31,863	3,958	63,988	10,954
1946	71,968	397	336,193	24,200	4,088	69,418	10,623
1947	81,992	403	356,530	33,000	4,366	80,853	14,928
1948	84,548	365	352,888	37,121	4,296	58,538	15,145
1949	87,722	...	370,015	37,179	4,689	73,986	17,220
1950	110,442	601	426,971	44,263	4,782	76,965	19,177
1951	138,896	511	506,061	61,513	5,093	108,565	20,610
1952	164,329	500	548,418	71,580	5,011	47,938	24,013
1953	160,754	710	560,794	78,152	4,225	47,674	17,873
1954	213,410	534	552,554	80,020	3,834	48,487	17,010
1955	186,316	560	522,639	101,084	3,443	48,963	16,564
1963	345,576	5,308	513,076	174,575	2,135	38,294	13,791

[1]No report of registration received.

PUREBRED DAIRY CATTLE
Number of new registrations, by breeds, United States

Breed	1948	1949	1950	1951	1952	1953	1954	1955	1963
Ayrshire:									
Bulls	4,175	3,904	3,412	3,458	2,604	2,357	2,178	2,018	*
Cows	21,938	22,413	20,824	22,005	20,604	22,013	20,815	21,017	*
Total	26,113	26,317	24,236	25,463	23,208	24,370	22,993	23,035	14,605
Brown Swiss:									
Bulls	6,295	5,637	5,759	5,827	*				
Cows	16,330	15,678	16,962	19,936	*				
Total	22,625	21,315	22,721	25,763	23,385	21,854	22,854	21,667	16,854
Guernsey:									
Bulls	18,939	17,227	16,013	14,181	13,669	9,622	7,882	7,589	*
Cows	77,956	72,679	78,888	79,448	100,240	79,986	73,663	73,977	*
Total	96,895	89,906	94,901	93,629'	113,909	89,608	81,545	81,566	55,670
Holstein-Friesian:									
Bulls	35,576	36,329	36,662	36,629	32,424	25,752	23,539	23,469	*
Cows	132,762	141,596	147,584	155,009	157,266	163,810	172,424	174,139	*
Total	168,338	177,925	184,246	191,638	189,690	189,572	195,963	197,608	258,568
Jersey:									
Bulls	12,152	11,273	10,654	9,145	7,934	7,841	6,041	5,777	*
Cows	56,974	54,701	58,325	59,506	62,924	79,741	54,555	54,483	*
Total	69,126	65,974	68,979	68,651	70,858	87,582	60,596	60,260	43,363

*Individual figures not available.

State	Electricity*	Electric water pump*	Telephones*	Distance to trading Center most frequently used		
				1 to 4 miles	5 to 9 miles	10 miles and over
Alabama	144,589	31,857	17,442	80,801	56,360	50,501
Arizona	8,062	4,630	4,408	3,421	2,308	3,176
Arkansas	121,916	30,808	19,201	77,044	50,517	34,350
California	124,613	85,194	78,720	64,636	32,625	20,450
Colorado	36,541	18,623	27,048	13,828	11,349	16,298
Connecticut	14,425	11,175	13,081	6,940	4,795	1,835
Delaware	6,112	4,665	4,990	3,263	2,662	491
Florida	40,535	24,235	10,253	19,220	16,776	13,711
Georgia	149,271	52,916	18,624	73,390	66,754	40,656
Idaho	37,232	25,874	22,264	14,457	12,433	9,832
Illinois	169,645	105,237	127,618	81,116	65,093	31,351
Indiana	152,864	99,299	102,904	68,422	57,180	26,767
Iowa	184,787	116,983	166,380	78,935	73,690	32,858
Kansas	97,668	41,245	89,760	41,610	44,185	32,347
Kentucky	145,246	28,940	45,808	90,410	52,607	41,129
Louisiana	83,191	30,485	14,364	53,779	29,948	20,187
Maine	26,200	14,798	19,467	12,821	8,568	5,370
Maryland	30,302	20,765	19,457	15,749	10,121	6,348
Massachusetts	20,365	10,294	17,319	10,930	5,526	2,306
Michigan	146,902	114,255	83,136	66,687	55,320	22,426
Minnesota	150,755	101,391	107,359	65,896	69,101	33,833
Mississippi	140,695	36,188	16,425	97,035	75,862	55,320
Missouri	159,165	53,461	106,673	91,862	72,121	41,903
Montana	26,335	15,134	9,995	7,353	7,956	17,636
Nebraska	83,309	38,115	69,541	34,285	38,741	24,949
Nevada	2,184	1,457	1,550	949	700	1,056
New Hampshire	12,696	7,904	10,055	5,690	4,150	2,118
New Jersey	23,281	19,427	17,829	10,922	7,567	3,113
New Mexico	14,037	5,595	3,500	6,381	4,500	9,657
New York	117,262	79,735	87,767	55,746	38,471	16,417
North Carolina	219,417	71,021	23,347	111,337	85,498	62,154
North Dakota	44,200	19,812	27,214	15,894	22,791	22,711
Ohio	185,681	118,286	119,721	85,869	65,452	31,115
Oklahoma	93,315	30,512	47,161	45,054	47,291	38,594
Oregon	56,618	37,762	30,104	22,740	16,072	14,970
Pennsylvania	133,919	85,391	77,211	58,291	46,106	28,561
Rhode Island	2,411	1,862	1,998	1,011	746	489
South Carolina	95,025	32,961	11,901	51,902	47,985	29,191
South Dakota	45,898	16,631	37,221	16,690	22,242	23,650
Tennessee	165,541	41,694	43,541	94,713	57,025	45,843
Texas	260,373	89,647	79,080	106,288	100,888	93,197
Utah	21,602	5,448	12,515	8,397	4,574	4,460
Vermont	17,533	7,595	13,267	8,899	5,133	2,591
Virginia	114,273	40,701	35,853	56,202	37,830	38,524
Washington	64,599	42,293	40,166	29,037	19,397	14,287
West Virginia	59,141	13,915	21,724	32,736	19,683	19,003
Wisconsin	156,382	121,229	99,821	71,273	61,036	24,004
Wyoming	9,432	4,716	4,735	2,958	2,284	6,428
Total	4,213,563	2,011,162	2,059,625	2,072.940	1,640,239	1.117.473

* Latest available statistics. Based on reports for sample of farms.

Motor Trucks*		Tractors*		Automobiles*		Farms Operated by Full Owners	State
Farms Reporting	Number	Farms Reporting	Number	Farms Reporting	Number		
56,000	70,000	53,000	79,000	64,000	82,000	92,530	Alabama
5,000	17,000	4,000	14,000	5,000	11,000	6,477	Arizona
60,000	81,000	54,000	105,000	53,000	65,000	79,898	Arkansas
64,000	126,000	62,000	158,000	36,000	49,000	80,852	California
27,000	56,000	26,000	68,000	27,000	39,000	29,798	Colorado
5,000	10,000	5,000	13,000	6,000	9,000	6,068	Connecticut
3,000	5,000	4,000	10,000	4,000	6,000	4,401	Delaware
24,000	41,000	24,000	46,000	31,000	43,000	40,542	Florida
57,000	77,000	59,000	97,000	67,000	90,000	83,366	Georgia
26,000	48,000	27,000	66,000	27,000	37,000	29,661	Idaho
99,000	121,000	125,000	335,000	125,000	166,000	132,822	Illinois
78,000	99,000	98,000	231,000	99,000	137,000	108,082	Indiana
97,000	107,000	144,000	352,000	149,000	201,000	154,162	Iowa
80,000	134,000	85,000	194,000	86,000	115,000	92,440	Kansas
74,000	90,000	88,000	144,000	102,000	131,000	133,038	Kentucky
40,000	51,000	36,000	65,000	46,000	56,000	62,466	Louisiana
9,000	15,000	10,000	20,000	11,000	15,000	12,875	Maine
14,000	21,000	18,000	45,000	18,000	28,000	20,760	Maryland
6,000	11,000	6,000	14,000	7,000	10,000	8,019	Massachusetts
63,000	80,000	88,000	204,000	88,000	122,000	93,504	Michigan
91,000	113,000	125,000	308,000	126,000	175,000	131,163	Minnesota
61,000	75,000	53,000	95,000	71,000	88,000	109,141	Mississippi
100,000	123,000	126,000	256,000	124,000	150,000	141,315	Missouri
25,000	58,000	25,000	69,000	25,000	35,000	27,020	Montana
64,000	93,000	75,000	190,000	77,000	106,000	80,163	Nebraska
2,000	4,000	2,000	6,000	2,000	3,000	2,156	Nevada
3,000	6,000	4,000	8,000	4,000	6,000	4,648	New Hampshire
9,000	17,000	9,000	26,000	10,000	15,000	10,641	New Jersey
12,000	23,000	9,000	19,000	11,000	15,000	14,206	New Mexico
43,000	63,000	62,000	157,000	61,000	84,000	66,510	New York
84,000	101,000	102,000	164,000	116,000	151,000	148,202	North Carolina
45,000	82,000	47,000	130,000	46,000	65,000	48,836	North Dakota
74,000	91,000	109,000	249,000	111,000	160,000	120,381	Ohio
73,000	105,000	66,000	116,000	71,000	87,000	88,726	Oklahoma
32,000	54,000	34,000	76,000	36,000	49,000	39,757	Oregon
54,000	70,000	75,000	173,000	75,000	110,000	83,086	Pennsylvania
1,000	2,000	1,000	2,000	1,000	2,000	1,100	Rhode Island
30,000	39,000	33,000	54,000	44,000	58,000	56,248	South Carolina
39,000	57,000	47,000	125,000	47,000	66,000	49,703	South Dakota
74,000	86,000	86,000	138,000	97,000	122,000	133,446	Tennessee
152,000	211,000	152,000	285,000	163,000	205,000	205,110	Texas
13,000	20,000	13,000	25,000	14,000	19,000	15,759	Utah
6,000	8,000	8,000	19,000	8,000	12,000	9,247	Vermont
46,000	59,000	56,000	103,000	59,000	78,000	80,354	Virginia
36,000	64,000	39,000	83,000	42,000	60,000	45,574	Washington
20,000	24,000	23,000	39,000	24,000	29,000	34,504	West Virginia
82,000	97,000	113,000	285,000	113,000	154,000	116,816	Wisconsin
8,000	18,000	8,000	23,000	8,000	11,000	9,038	Wyoming
2,167,000	3,030,000	2,520,000	5,486,000	2,675,000	3,593,000	3,157,857	Total

* Based on reports for sample of farms.   ** Source: U.S. Census of Agriculture 1964 Vol. II.

MINING AND MINERALS

Mining includes all methods and processes involved in obtaining valuable mineral materials—organic and inorganic—from the earth's crust. Technically defined, minerals are earth substances with definite chemical compositions; however, in common usage the term mineral includes all elements and compounds occurring naturally. Consequently, coal and petroleum, which do not have definite chemical compositions, are classified as minerals. Most minerals must be treated, refined, or purified before they can be used. The processing of mined products is included in the science of metallurgy.

Mining is purely an extractive process. For this reason it is the most destructive of the primary industries by which man satisfies his wants. A ruined forest may be replaced, if necessary, within a few generations; even the number of fish in the sea may be greatly increased by artificial propagation. But, when a ton of coal or of iron ore has once been mined, the store available to future generations has been decreased by just so much. There can be no replacement. Mineral reserves may, however, be enlarged by new discoveries, mining improvements, and new economic developments.

The distinctive character of modern commerce, industry, and civilization is due largely to the extensive employment of mined products. In addition to the important role mineral resources have in establishing living standards, they also have been and continue to be an extremely important element of international politics.

Historical. In human development, the acquirement of a knowledge of mining and metallurgy marks the change from savagery to barbarism. This change has not been made by all peoples at the same time. Copper was obtained from the mines of Sinai by the Egyptians 5000 or more years ago, while this stage was not reached in Europe until about 2000 B.C. Gold and meteoric iron, which are found as free metals, were used even earlier. Similarly, the natives of North America employed copper which they found near Lake Superior.

Copper was the first metal to be reduced from its ore. The Phoenicians, about 1000 B.C., obtained copper from Cyprus and Spain. They also got silver from Spain, and, for the tin needed to alloy with copper in making bronze, they sailed to the British Isles. The Romans mined iron on the island of Elba. In the 16th century the search for gold drew the Spanish to South America. There they found gold in vast quantities, although the Aztecs still used weapons and tools of bronze.

Mining Products. These important substances may be classified as metals or nonmetals. The first group supplies the materials from which tools and machines are constructed. Examples of metals are: iron ore, manganese ore, copper, aluminum, gold, and uranium.

Nonmetals are divided into mineral fuels and other nonmetallic minerals. The mineral fuels include liquid (petroleum), gaseous (natural gas), and solid (hard and soft coal) minerals. The nonmetallic minerals include building, chemical, fertilizer, ceramic, and insulating materials; refractory (or heat-resistant) materials used in making asbestos fabrics, insulation, and furnace linings; abrasives; pigments and fillers; and precious and semiprecious stones.

Types of Mines. Heavy minerals, of which gold is the most important, are frequently found disseminated throughout an alluvial or a glacial deposit. A mineral-bearing bed of this type is known as a placer, from the Spanish word *placel*, meaning sand bank. The simplest form of placer mining consists in shaking the gold-bearing earth in a pan of water with such a motion that the heavier particles sink to the bottom while much of the lighter material can be thrown over the side.

In *sluicing*, an operation which depends on the same principle, a stream of water flows through a wooden trough or other form of channel provided with corrugations, or riffles, on the bottom. Mercury is placed in the riffles. When placer dirt is shoveled into the sluice, the current carries away the lighter substance while the gold settles into the riffles, where it amalgamates with the mercury and is retained. The amalgam is collected and heated in a retort, from which the mercury distills, leaving the gold.

Hydraulicking is placer mining on a large scale. In this process the gravel bank is washed down into sluices by means of a stream of water under a pressure of 250 to 400 pounds per square inch. Huge dredges are also used on placer deposits, the buckets dropping the sand on screens, from which the fine particles pass to sluices, where the gold is recovered.

Where bodies of ore are to be found comparatively near the surface, *open-pit* mining is frequently most satisfactory. By this process the overburden of useless earth is removed so that the ore may be taken up by steam shovels and dropped directly into railroad cars. *Quarrying* is removing nonmetallic rock from shallow open-pit mines.

Drilled wells are used chiefly to obtain petroleum, natural gas, salt, and sulphur.

Underground mines are reached by tunnels entering the side of a hill or mountain, by shafts sloping gradually, or by vertical shafts. When the veins of mineral are reached, various systems of cutting away the ore are used so as to obtain as much of the valuable material as possible, consistent with economy, safety, and ease of working. Some of these methods are known as *stoping, room-and-pillar* mining, the *longwall* method, *milling*, and *caving*. Removal of the coal or ore may be accomplished by pick-and-shovel methods or by machines.

Development. The search for valuable bodies of minerals in the earth is known as prospecting. An oily spot on the surface of the ground an outcropping vein, rusty places, or a strip of unusually rich or poor vegetation may call attention to a useful deposit. Modern methods of prospecting are generally carried out by large companies in the light of geological knowledge supplied by scientific experts. Any region that gives indication of mineral wealth may be tested by means of core drills which bring up a section of the material through which they pass. Careful geological and chemical examination of the core forms a basis for a fairly accurate estimate of the amount and the quality of ore that may be expected.

Having established a promising location, shafts must be sunk, the ore blocked out by further drilling, and provision made for drainage and ventilation of the tunnels. If early indications are confirmed, machinery is installed, a mill or a cleaning house is constructed, and the mine is placed in operation.

Technical Processes. Magnetic ores are frequently separated from nonmagnetic substances by passing the powdered material through a magnetic field. A similar separation of conducting and nonconducting minerals may be produced by means of an electrostatic field. Gold-bearing ore taken from the lodes of underground mines usually consists chiefly of quartz. This hard material is reduced to powder by stamp mills or by other types of machinery and is then passed over copper plates coated with mercury. Much of the gold is retained by these plates. The remainder of the metal may be obtained by treating the powder with chlorine gas.

Production in the U.S. Although the U.S. has never been self-sufficient in minerals its total mineral production, since at least 1900, has been greater than total mineral imports. The Depression of the 1930s drastically slowed mineral production but before that, from 1900 to 1929, the U.S.

produced 89 per cent of all the minerals it consumed. After 1939 U.S. mineral production began to increase and has continued to increase; however, production has not increased at the same high rate as consumption.

In 1971 the U.S. was self-sufficient in molybdenum, phosphate, diatomite, talc, vermiculite, magnesium, bromine, clay, feldspar, boron minerals, coal, lime, and cement. Metal production is low in the U.S.; in 1972, the U.S. was self-sufficient in only two metals, molybdenum and magnesium.

For some time the U.S. was the world's principal market for raw minerals; but, since 1945 world mineral production has increased more rapidly than U.S. production. In the early 1970s the value of U.S. mineral imports was more than three times the value of U.S. mineral exports. The U.S. is still an important supplier of coal, molybdenum, phosphate, boron minerals, and sodium minerals. Of 35 major mineral commodities, the U.S. ranked first in production of 12, including natural gas, in 1974; the U.S. ranked second in production of 4, including coal and crude petroleum, in 1974.

In the early 1970s the U.S. consumed about one-quarter of the world's annual mineral production. Every year the U.S. is demanding more raw mineral materials than it can produce.

Bureau of Mines. This branch of the Department of the Interior was established by an act of Congress that became effective July 1, 1910.

It is the duty of the bureau to conduct scientific investigations with the objectives of improving technical processes and conditions of labor involved in the production and use of mineral wealth, and assisting industries in the reduction of pollution due to the mining and processing of minerals. As a result of the bureau's efforts, legislation has been passed to improve safety conditions and reduce pollution.

Economic Significance. Among the scores of minerals which the world produces, certain ones stand out as pre-eminently important by reason of their utility in our civilization. Among them are coal, gas, petroleum, iron, and gold.

Coal, gas, and petroleum are the basic fuels for the production of power, on which industrial civilization rests. Coal and gas are of primary importance for industrial power, and petroleum for motive power in transportation by sea, highway, and air.

Iron is by far the most essential metal in the machine age. When iron deposits are found close to coal deposits, the material elements are present for building up an economic empire. These conditions account to a large extent for the industrial growth of the U.S., Britain, Western Europe, and Russia.

Gold is placed among the premier minerals because of its unique value as a promoter of trade and commerce.

World Energy Crisis. By 1973 a grave and persisting crisis in energy faced the Western world. The problem was rooted in widespread wastage of power and was marked by factors of limited choice. The U.S., representing 6 per cent of the world's population, was consuming 30 per cent of the available world energy supplies. At the same time, three-quarters of current U.S. energy needs were met by gas and oil. American production of both of these sources of energy was declining, and only sharply limited resources remained for future production. Other sources of energy for the U.S. were more abundant in the form of adequate coal deposits, oil-rich rock shale, and the virtually unlimited resources of nuclear and solar energy. Yet the inherent restrictions in the complex of use, demand, price, choice, and availability of energy resources—and the long-standing reliance on imported sources of energy—endangered the economic security, as well as the foreign and domestic policy independence of the U.S., Japan, and other nations of the Americas, Europe, and Africa.

The situation worsened in 1973. That year war broke out once more between Egypt and Syria and

Israel. Arab countries had been taking over more and more control of their own oil production and had formed the Organization of Petroleum Exporting Countries to control the price and distribution of oil. In the years that followed, world oil prices were quadrupled and embargoes were established against Western nations in an attempt to force Israel to withdraw from Arab lands. The rise in oil prices and the cutback in production increased world inflation, and intensified the already existent crises in energy and food supplies.

At the peak of the crisis the need was clear for a shift to new and primary forms of energy production. Such major changes had occurred twice before—from the use of wood as fuel in the mid-1800's to coal in the early 1900's, and a later shift from coal to oil and gas fuels. The two change-overs had each required some 60 years to accomplish. But in the troubled world of the mid-1970's it was clear that the West could not afford any such span of time to complete the needed shift in fuel use and sources.

Another factor emerged in the harsh winter of 1976-77. When record-breaking sub-zero weather hit the Eastern part of the country, natural gas companies found they did not have adequate supplies to meet the heavy demand. Some factories and schools had to close so that private homes could remain heated. Although many were surprised by these drastic measures, others had been predicting a crisis in natural gas. In preceding years, industry had begun to rely heavily on gas for their energy needs. In 1962, 45% of all energy consumed by manufacturers was natural gas; in 1974, the amount had risen to 54%. During the same period, the use of coal resources dropped from 24% to 10%. Natural gas use increased not only because it is efficient and non-polluting, but also because the price of gas passing through interstate pipelines was regulated by the federal government and did not increase at the same rate as other energy resources, such as coal. Under controlled prices, gas suppliers claimed they lacked "incentive" to develop more of the known reserves. From 1969 to 1976, total production remained about the same while demand greatly increased. The shortages of supplies became apparent to the public in late 1976. A short-term answer proposed was the deregulation of gas prices. Others thought the crisis had been artificially created to achieve a price increase. But almost everyone agreed that the country could no longer count on abundant supplies of natural gas.

Faced with these problems, three sets of priorities emerged. For the present near-term (until 1985) and beyond, the priorities were: (1) To preserve and expand major existing energy systems—coal, nuclear reactors (industrial furnaces for converting energy in atomic nuclei into heat energy), and gas and oil from new sources, together with improved methods of recovery. (2) To increase conservation and to improve the efficiency of energy use in all sectors of national economies.

For the mid-term (1985 to 2000) and beyond, the priorities were: (1) To accelerate the development of new processes to produce synthetic fuels from coal, to extract oil from rock shale, and to find alternate sources, such as the production of fuel alcohols from plant life. (2) To increase the use of underdeveloped energy forms such as natural springs of hot water and steam from underground, to make solar-energy devices available, and to extract more usable energy from waste heat.

For the far-term (past the year 2000), the following priorities appeared: (1) To pursue vigorously other possible technologies that would make available the unlimited resources of nuclear power reactors. (2) The fuller exploitation of solar energy through collection and transmission by space satellites. (3) The development of major devices to use wind power. (4) The perfection of other devices to harness the energy potentials of ocean forces.

CRUDE PETROLEUM PRODUCTION

(Crude oil and natural gas liquids; in 1,000 metric tons)

	1950	1960	1970	1975*		1950	1960	1970	1975*
NORTH AMERICA					**EUROPE**				
Canada†	3,800	27,480	69,954	80,000	Austria	1,600	2,440	2,798	2,000
U.S.A.†	285,200	384,080	533,677	485,500	Germany (West)	1,120	5,560	7,536	5,750
Mexico	10,296	14,125	21,877	37,500	Netherlands	700	1,920	1,919	1,400
					U.K.	40	90	84	1,130
CARIBBEAN					France	120	2,260	2,308	1,050
Trinidad	2,980	6,075	7,225	10,000	Italy	8	1,990	1,408	1,030
Colombia	4,850	8,100	11,071	8,000	Spain	—	—	156	1,888
Venezuela‡	78,140	148,690	193,209	124,000	Norway	—	—	—	9,350
					Denmark	—	—	—	160
SOUTH AMERICA									
Brazil	40	4,050	8,009	8,400	**AFRICA (EXCLUDING EGYPT)**				
Ecuador‡	360	390	191	8,050	Algeria‡	80	8,630	47,253	42,600
Peru	2,050	2,680	3,450	3,500	Tunisia	—	—	4,151	4,500
Bolivia	80	450	1,128	2,000	Libya‡	—	—	159,201	71,000
Chile	80	990	1,620	1,200	Gabon‡ and Congo	—	850	5,460	13,800
Argentina	3,460	9,160	19,969	19,550	Angola	—	70	5,066	7,000
					Nigeria‡	—	880	53,420	87,800
MIDDLE EAST									
Turkey	30	350	3,461	3,150	**OCEANIA**				
Iraq‡	6,650	47,480	76,600	111,300	Australia	—	—	8,292	19,250
Iran‡	32,260	52,065	191,663	268,200					
Saudi Arabia‡	26,620	61,090	176,851	337,300	**COMMUNIST COUNTRIES**				
Kuwait‡	17,290	81,860	137,397	93,300	U.S.S.R.	37,500	148,000	352,667	490,000
Kuwait neutral zone‡	—	7,270	26,724	25,400	Rumania	4,100	11,500	13,377	14,600
Bahrain	1,560	2,250	3,834	3,100	Yugoslavia	110	1,040	2,854	3,700
Qatar‡	1,640	8,210	17,257	20,000	Hungary	500	1,215	1,937	2,000
Abu Dhabi‡	—	—	33,288	64,600	Poland	175	195	424	550
Dubai‡	—	—	4,306	12,600	Albania	395	600	1,199	2,300
Oman	—	—	17,169	16,500	Bulgaria	—	200	334	120
Syria	—	—	4,350	9,000	Czechoslovakia	50	140	203	150
Egypt§	2,370	3,600	16,404	15,750	Germany (East)	—	—	60	200
Sharjah	—	—	—	2,000	China||	—	5,000	20,000	78,000
FAR EAST									
India	315	440	6,809	8,300					
Pakistan	250	360	486	400					
Burma	125	530	750	900					
Indonesia‡	6,450	20,560	42,102	63,000	**ESTIMATED TOTAL WORLD**				
Brunei	4,340	4,690	6,916	9,550	**PRODUCTION#**	538,470	1,090,680	2,336,153	2,702,140
Japan	350	510	750	600					

* Provisional estimates. † 1970–1975 figures refer to all hydrocarbon liquids; 1950–1960 figures refer only to crude oil proper. ‡ OPEC member. § Including the Sinai fields. ||From 1963 the figures include shale and coal-based oil. # Estimates differ widely because of conversion difficulties of barrels to metric tons.

U.S. PETROLEUM IMPORTS: 1974–1976

(Quantity in barrels; value in dollars)*

GENERAL IMPORTS†

COUNTRY OF ORIGIN	December 1974		December 1975		March 1976	
	NET QUANTITY	VALUE	NET QUANTITY	VALUE	NET QUANTITY	VALUE
Canada	26,969,377	$326,091,774	22,721,799	$279,553,321	13,132,845	$164,411,764
Mexico	377,899	3,764,951	3,156,195	38,168,038	3,210,824	38,907,792
Trinidad	3,282,182	41,341,215	3,670,862	48,061,359	4,810,299	64,046,723
Venezuela	15,616,059	169,825,698	13,639,749	156,345,865	8,310,679	93,830,057
Ecuador	940,139	10,211,009	2,793,733	31,184,728	895,590	10,361,323
Iran	13,415,077	146,539,707	10,454,630	125,840,817	9,335,058	112,796,424
Kuwait	—	—	1,743,276	18,866,564	—	—
Saudi Arabia	22,462,804	242,298,573	30,528,842	351,257,167	35,046,306	411,718,075
Qatar	864,238	10,114,219	—	—	668,383	8,062,856
Arab Emirates	2,709,830	30,792,378	4,744,160	54,422,302	6,270,627	74,853,370
Indonesia	10,802,857	137,479,884	11,201,073	142,445,953	17,070,905	218,116,923
Algeria	8,309,887	103,486,750	6,162,862	78,325,606	12,390,951	159,719,111
Tunisia	49,119	610,057	443,458	5,654,089	414,282	5,364,952
Libya	—	—	10,616,623	131,485,522	11,649,986	143,854,909
Nigeria	24,685,879	294,709,315	24,469,311	309,065,517	28,312,098	363,826,669
Angola	295,278	3,428,178	1,587,453	18,557,326	41,734	521,675
Norway	—	—	839,397	9,713,148	624,474	7,930,819
Oman	443,181	4,879,425	491,367	5,827,613	51,668	617,949
Egypt	153,733	1,583,307	686,886	6,900,294	1,148,527	13,017,306
Gabon	702,419	7,716,930	968,631	11,206,006	1,081,177	12,508,990
Bolivia	—	—	273,031	3,677,728	—	—
Malaysia	—	—	220,620	2,786,431	225,994	2,854,304
TOTAL	132,079,958	$1,534,873,370	151,413,958	$1,829,345,394	154,692,407	$1,907,316,991

Source: Social and Economic Statistics Administration, U.S. Dept. of Commerce. * Data for U.S. Trade Statistics commodity numbers 475.0510 and 475.1010 combined. † General imports are a combination of entries for immediate consumption and entries into bonded warehouses. Imports for consumption are a combination of entries for immediate consumption and withdrawals from warehouses for consumption.

INVENTIONS

PRIMITIVE man became safely established in his supremacy over the lower animals when he invented the bow and arrow. Since that prehistoric time, millions of inventions have been made, each adding a part to the total sum of knowledge by which mankind is gradually achieving mastery of space and control of the forces of nature. Some inventions are of trifling importance; others are so fundamental that their development affects the lives of all civilized people. The history of human progress has been marked by a series of epoch-making inventions.

At Ghent, in Flanders, on December 14, 1814, a treaty was signed which formally declared at an end the War of 1812 between England and the United States. Nevertheless, fighting was still going on in Louisiana 59 *days* later, because news of the treaty had not yet arrived. Few examples could more strikingly illustrate the progress of invention during the last century. Today, an event of similar importance could be known throughout the country in less than 59 *minutes*.

An invention is considered to be any new and useful machine, art, manufacture, or composition of matter, or any new and useful improvement thereon. All civilized nations recognize the right of an inventor to his product, and, when all requirements have been fulfilled, will issue a written contract or *patent*, guaranteeing to him the exclusive right to the use of his invention for a definite period of time. The life of a United States patent is 17 years. Approximately 3.5 million patents have been issued by the United States patent office. Comparatively few have shown themselves to be valuable.

SOME NOTED INVENTIONS OF MODERN TIMES

Certain inventions have proved to be of special importance because of their marked influence upon the welfare and the progress of mankind. Talking machines, telephones, and motion pictures, for example, are so much a part of our daily life that the wonderful principles governing their operation usually receive but little attention. Some of the more noteworthy of these inventions are given special treatment in the articles that follow.

Air Brake. A device, invented by George Westinghouse, Jr. in 1869, for applying the brakes to the cars of a railroad train by means of compressed air. Although the original system has been greatly improved in many ways by Westinghouse and others, the following description applies to the mechanism common both to passenger and to freight trains.

Each car is equipped with a *brake cylinder*, in which there is a piston connected to the brake shoes by a rod; an *auxiliary reservoir* to hold compressed air; a *triple valve*; and a train pipe with flexible couplings at each end. On the locomotive, in addition to its own brakes, are a steam driven *air compressor* which supplies air to the whole system, a *main air reservoir*, and the *control valve* operated by the engineer.

Under normal conditions, equal pressures of about 70 pounds are maintained in the train pipe and in the auxiliary reservoirs, and this condition of equal pressure holds the triple valve in a position closing the brake cylinder. To *set* the brakes, the engineer allows air to *escape* from the train pipe, thus reducing the pressure below that of the auxiliary reservoir. The triple valve then changes so that air enters the brake cylinder and forces the brake shoes against the wheels.

To *release* the brakes, the engineer allows air from the main reservoir, which has about 110 pounds pressure, to enter the train pipe until it again has a pressure equal to that in the auxiliary reservoir. The triple valve then resumes its normal position and the pressure is removed from the brakes.

It is obvious that, if the coupling of a car becomes detached or broken, the train pipe pressure is lowered and the brakes are immediately applied.

This system has been of great importance in the development of the railroads because it allows the engineer to have complete control of his train, and permits of quick stops at high speed, either in an emergency or under ordinary running conditions.

Airplane, or **Aeroplane.** A heavier-than-air flying machine that flies because of the lifting effect of *moving* air upon a surface inclined to the wind at a small angle. The necessary movement of the air is relative to that of the airplane. For example; a speed of about 35 miles per hour *with respect to the air* is generally required before a flying machine can leave the ground. If the air is still, the machine will have to travel along the ground at 35 miles per hour, but, if a 20-mile wind is blowing, the machine can rise when moving into the wind at only 15 miles per hour.

Airplanes are usually classified, according to the number of their supporting surfaces, as *monoplanes* or *biplanes;* the latter type is becoming less common. The planes are not flat, but are curved upward, with the greatest curve near the front edge. A two or three bladed propeller at the front is driven by a gasoline motor. The larger military and cargo planes have two or four engines.

Among notable attempts to solve the problem of artificial flight was the work of Lilienthal and Chanute, with gliders; and of Ader, Maxim, and Langley, who, with the aid of their respective governments, built power driven machines which were usually destroyed by accidents at the first trial.

Orville and Wilbur Wright, bicycle manufacturers of Dayton, Ohio, were interested in aviation, and they found after many tests that the current theories were partly correct and partly guesswork. The Wrights devoted their attention chiefly toward a means of securing stability of a machine when in the air. They succeeded in developing a system of maintaining balance and control by bending or warping the ends of the planes, and using an elevating rudder in front. On December 17, 1903, they achieved flights of from 12 to 59 seconds, Wilbur being the first to fly successfully in a heavier-than-air machine. Reports of this work traveled to Europe and encouraged the French school of enthusiasts to continue their efforts. Alberto Santos-Dumont was the first of these to succeed, when in 1906 he made flights of several hundred feet. The French airplanes differed from the Wright type in having a tail, which was not adopted by the Wrights until about seven years later. Glenn H. Curtiss, in America, developed a type of biplane, and in 1911 and 1912 he developed the hydro-airplane and flying boat, capable of rising from and landing on the water.

From 1908 the development of the airplane was very rapid, especially in France and Germany. Improved engines also supplied greater power although they weighed much less. Of these, the rotary engines are most peculiar because the cylinders are placed like the spokes of a wheel, and revolve around a fixed crank shaft. The motors commonly used average two pounds in weight per horse power; some racing motors are as light as .8 pounds per horse power.

In World War I airplanes carried machine guns and even small cannon. These guns were often geared to fire between the revolving blades of the propeller. In World War II the armament was greatly increased. Bombing planes can carry bombs weighing up to 4000 pounds. Photographic equipment is used for reconnaissance and for checking the damage done by bombing. Radio keeps the aviator in communication with other planes. By the use of gliders, engineless planes towed by another plane, an entire army may be transported by air and set down behind the enemy's lines. Since World War II the development of jet-propelled planes, particularly the propellerless jet and the turbo-propeller jet, has given military planes supersonic speed. In September 1948 the U. S. Air Force F-86 made 670 m.p.h., and the F-110 is capable of going 1500 m.p.h. Experimental craft have gone 4100 m.p.h.

Noteworthy aerial achievements include the first non-stop flight across the Atlantic Ocean, 1930 miles from Newfoundland to Ireland, in 16 hours, 12 minutes, made in 1919 by English aviators, Alcock and Brown; a discontinuous flight of 26,103 miles around the world in 365 hours, 11 minutes, of flying time, made in 1924 by U. S. Army Air Service planes; and an altitude record of 310,000 feet by Major Robert M. White, an American, in 1962. The first American passenger air line service was begun on November 1, 1920, between Key West and Havana.

Various types of airplanes have been built for vertical ascent. The most successful is the autogiro, invented in 1923 by De la Cierva, a Spaniard. It differs from all other heavier-than-air craft in the source of its lifting power. This lift is given, not by wings, but by four rotating blades hinged to a nearly vertical spindle and moving in a horizontal plane. They rotate by wind pressure, and are not driven by the engine, the sole function of which is to propel the machine. The autogiro can climb steeply and descend almost vertically at a speed less than a man with a parachute, thereby eliminating the hazards of landing which attend the usual type of airplane. Moreover, it is proof against falling into a spin, and can maintain itself in the air at a forward speed as slow as 25 miles an hour. See *Aeronautics, Transportation by Air*.

Airship. A dirigible balloon as distinguished from an airplane. Ordinary balloons were invented by the Montgolfier brothers in 1783, and in the same year Pilâtre de Rozier made the first ascension. Attempts were made, almost from the beginning, to control the direction of flight. However, the first successful dirigible was not built until 1852 when Henri Giffard propelled a balloon at six miles per hour by means of a three horse power steam engine. Alberto Santos-Dumont constructed 14 dirigibles. As all of the earlier airships were handicapped by lack of light, powerful motors, it remained for the Lebaudy brothers, Major Parseval, and Count Ferdinand von Zeppelin to develop dirigibles capable of fulfilling the requirements for military use.

Dirigible balloons may be classified as rigid, semirigid, and nonrigid. The rigid type has a strong skeleton or framework inside the envelope; the semirigid is held by a network of wires and rods; the nonrigid is merely a large bag of gas. Successful development of the rigid type is due largely to Zeppelin, whose airships were all rigid.

The zeppelin was developed commercially for mail and passengers before World War I and in that war was used for bombing expeditions. The United States tried dirigibles, but gave them less attention after several accidents. They proved of great value, however, in World War II in combating submarines. Captive balloons were used for observation during World War I, and, in World War II, to support cables and nets for air raid protection. Blimps are non-rigid airships. A U. S. Navy blimp set a world record in 1954 by staying aloft more than 8 days.

The lifting power of airships has customarily been provided by the use of hydrogen, although in recent years helium has been increasingly employed. The buoyancy of helium is somewhat less and the cost is higher, but it has the merit of not being inflammable. This advantage of helium received a tragic confirmation in 1937, when the German zeppelin *Hindenburg* was destroyed by flames, with most of its passengers, its hydrogen having ignited from an unknown cause as the craft was mooring at Lakehurst, N. J.

Amplifier. This is a general term applied to devices for magnifying variations in electric currents. The commonest form is the three-electrode vacuum tube. It has made possible such recent achievements as transatlantic radiotelephony, phototelegraphy, television, speaking motion pictures, a radically improved type of phonograph, and the "loud speaker."

The idea is already familiar that the sound variations constituting speech or music can be rendered as equivalent grooves on the record of a phonograph and then reconverted into sound. It is equally true that a modulated electric current can be produced which will represent such sound variations. The current may also represent light variations, through the agency of the photoelectric cell, the action of which is explained under *Phototelegraphy*. The amplifier is used to magnify the modulated electrical current to such a degree that, when this is converted to equivalent sound or light variations, the results will be easily heard or seen.

In speaking motion pictures, sound is converted to an equivalent band of light and shade, which is placed so accurately beside the pictures on the film that, on reconversion to sound, it produces an effect remarkably close to real life. The amplifier is essential to the process. Phonographs also owe much to the amplifier, both in improving the quality, and in enlarging the volume, of the sound reproduced.

Automobile. A self-propelled, four-wheeled vehicle designed to travel on highways. As steam and electric automobiles comprise less than 2 per cent of the total number, the term refers, when used without qualification, to a motor vehicle propelled by a gasoline engine. In Great Britain, gasoline is commonly called *petrol*; in Germany, *benzin*; and, in France, *essence de pétrole*, or simply *essence*.

Most standard automobiles of today consist essentially of a steel frame, attached through springs and axles to four pneumatic tired wheels. A four-cycle gasoline engine is mounted at the front, just behind a radiator through which water for cooling the engine is pumped. By means of a *clutch* operated by a left-foot pedal, the flywheel may be connected with the *transmission gears* which transmit the power through a driving shaft to bevel and differential gears attached to the middle of the rear axle.

Speed of the car is varied by shifting from one to another of the transmission gears, and by changing the amount of fuel supplied to the engine. The *differential gear* permits the rear wheels to revolve at different rates when the car rounds a curve and the outside wheel must move faster than that on the inside. The engine is started by means of an electric motor which receives power from a storage battery and is geared to the flywheel. When the engine is running, the battery is charged by a generator driven by the fan belt.

The front axle does not turn, but the wheels are attached to it by movable joints which are connected by a bar called a tie rod. The bottom of the post on which the steering wheel is mounted is fitted with a screw thread which causes a vertical *steering arm* to move forward or backward. This movement is transmitted to the *steering knuckle* by a rod.

The engine usually has from 4 to 12 cylinders, runs at from 800 to 4000 revolutions per minute, and weighs from 5 to 15 pounds per horse power. Some of the speed records which have been made are: 1 mile in 17.7 sec.; 10 miles in 4 min. 9.31 sec.; 50 miles in 26 min. 23.4 sec.; 100 miles in 54 min. 17.8 sec.; and 500 miles in 5 hr. 7 min. 26 sec.

It is probable that Siegfried Markus, a German, should be called the inventor of the gasoline automobile, for in 1875 he built a crude machine which carried him about the streets. Gottlieb Daimler is often called the "father of the automobile" because of the great improvement which he made in the gasoline engine, about 1884. In 1885 both Daimler and Karl Benz used gasoline engines to propel bicycles and tricycles. The first commercially manufactured car, made by Panhard and Levassor in 1891, used the Daimler engine. But the first automobile imported into the United States was a Benz, taken to the Chicago World's Fair in 1893.

The first successful American automobile was built by Charles E. and J. Frank Duryea in 1892. Henry Ford built a car in 1893, and Elwood Haynes in 1894. In 1896 these three cars and the imported Benz were the only ones in the United States; in 1948 there were 33¼ million passenger cars alone. The first public auto race was run in 1894 from Paris to Rouen; the first in the United States took place in 1895 from Chicago to Waukegan. The commercial history of gasoline automobiles in the United States may be said to date from 1898, when a Winton was the first car sold. The first commercially successful Ford was sold in 1903.

In 1879, George B. Selden, of Rochester, N. Y., applied for a fundamental patent on a road vehicle driven by a gasoline motor. The application was kept active, by perfectly legitimate methods, for 16 years, when a patent was taken out in 1895. Because of this patent, many of the leading manufacturers were forced to pay royalties of from .8 to 1.25 per cent of the retail price. Others refused to pay and, led by Henry Ford, carried the question to the United States circuit court of appeals which in 1911 decided in their favor and freed the industry of this burden. See *Internal Combustion Engine.*

Colorscope. This is an electrical device for matching colors. Each of two colors to be matched is placed before a photoelectric cell, which generates an electric current proportional in intensity to the light waves received by the cell. When the colors are exactly matched, the two currents are equal and register zero on a galvanometer. The instrument was invented by Dr. H. H. Sheldon and exhibited first in 1930.

Compass. A device designed to hold a certain definite direction, from which a ship or airplane may establish and maintain a true course. Prior to the 20th century, the only compass known was the magnetic, or *mariner's*, compass. This acted imperfectly in the presence of magnetized iron on ships, and the gyrocompass was devised to overcome this difficulty. The development of aeronautics demanded a different type. Several have been invented, of which the earth inductor compass is best known.

Magnetic Compass.—The action of this kind of compass depends on the magnetic force of the earth. The earth is a huge magnet, one pole being approximately at 70° N. lat. and 97° W. long. and the other at 72° S. lat. and 153° E. long.

One or more magnets, or needles, are mounted to move in a horizontal plane within a circular framework, the flat upper side of which is called the compass card. The magnet sets itself in line with the earth's "lines of force," thereby pointing in the general direction of the earth's magnetic poles. In order that motion may be as free as possible, the needle with its framework may be floated on a nonfreezing liquid within the compass bowl. This is the so-called liquid compass. In the dry compass, the entire weight of the needle and framework rests on a pivot within the bowl.

Since the compass needle points to the magnetic poles of the earth, not the geographic poles, it shows, for most places, a variation, or declination, from the true north and south. This angle of variation is known as the compass error. To enable navigators to make necessary corrections for declination, magnetic charts are prepared. They are revised periodically, since the location of the magnetic poles varies slightly from time to time.

Gyrocompass.—In the construction of this non-magnetic compass, use is made of the fact that the axis of a freely suspended gyroscope wheel will tend to turn parallel to the earth's axis of rotation.

The most successful type of gyrocompass is that known as the *Sperry compass*, perfected about 1910 by Elmer A. Sperry.

The instrument consists essentially of a gyro wheel mounted so as to be free to spin, free to tilt about a horizontal axis, and free to turn about a vertical axis. The gyro wheel is about 9 inches in diameter and weighs 50 pounds. It revolves in a vacuum inside a metallic casing at a speed of about 8500 revolutions per minute.

Upon starting the gyro wheel in motion, it gradually assumes a position parallel to the earth's axis. In the course of a few hours it establishes a north and south direction, which is maintained with marked accuracy so long as the wheel is kept rotating at the right speed. As usually mounted, the instrument carries a compass card similar to that of the magnetic compass. See *Gyroscope.*

Earth Inductor Compass.—This instrument was invented by scientists in the United States bureau of standards. It consists of a generator, a direction controller, and a steering indicator. The generator is pivoted on a vertical axis. It contains two pairs of brushes, which are revolved in the magnetic field of the earth at the rate of 1400 revolutions per minute. Each pair of brushes collects a direct current.

When the generator is oriented properly, the currents are equal and register zero on a galvanometer, known as the steering indicator. If the generator is oriented at an angle to this position, one current is stronger than the other and deflects the steering indicator to the right or left. The direction controller is a crank for orienting the generator by reference to a compass card.

If the aviator wishes to change his direction, he moves the direction controller to the compass point indicating the desired direction. This changes the current strengths and deflects the steering indicator to the left or right until the plane is headed in the direction for which the control crank is set. To continue in this direction the aviator must steer so that the steering indicator remains at zero.

Boxing the Compass.—Around the outer edge of the circular compass card the degrees are marked from 0 to 360, beginning at north and numbering in the same direction as the hands of a clock move. Besides being marked in degrees, the compass card is marked also in points (11¼°), half points, and quarter points. The four primary directions—north, south, east, and west—are called the *cardinal* points. The points intermediate between these—northeast, southeast, southwest, and northwest—are called *intercardinal*. The point halfway between north and northeast is north-northeast, that between northeast and east is east-northeast, and so on for like subdivisions. Other points are named north by east, northeast by north, and similarly, according to the following table.

COMPASS CARD

N.	E.	S.	W.
N. by E.	E. by S.	S. by W.	W. by N.
N. N. E.	E. S. E.	S. S. W.	W. N. W.
N. E. by N.	S. E. by E.	S. W. by S.	N. W. by W.
N. E.	S. E.	S. W.	N. W.
N. E. by E.	S. E. by S.	S. W. by W.	N. W. by N.
E. N. E.	S. S. E.	W. S. W.	N. N. W.
E. by N.	S. by E.	W. by S.	N. by W.

Composing Machine. A machine which sets either type or type molds and arranges them in lines of the proper order and length for printing. The true typesetting machine has been almost entirely supplanted by those which set type molds from which castings are automatically produced. Of this second class, the linotype and monotype are best known, and, because of their extensive use in printing, are of greatest economic importance.

The linotype was invented in 1885 by Ottmar Mergenthaler, a German living in Baltimore. It is operated similarly to a typewriter, from a keyboard having 90 or more keys. When a key is pressed, the corresponding brass matrix is released from its compartment in a magazine and falls on a moving belt which carries it to a collector. At the end of each word a wedge-shaped spacer is inserted. When the molds for one line of type are assembled they are carried to a casting wheel and placed in front of a slot.

At this time the wedge-shaped spacers are pushed up between the matrices so that the words are spread until they exactly fill one line. A pump then forces molten type metal into the slot and against the matrices. The metal cools rapidly, so that the molds may be almost instantly removed and redistributed into the proper section of the magazine. The slug of metal is trimmed to exact size between knives and placed with others to form a column of type. Should any error be discovered, a whole line must be reset. Linotype machines may be operated electrically by the so-called teletypesetter, first used in 1928. This device makes use of ticker tape perforations transmitted by telegraph. These, corresponding to words, are fed into the teletypesetter, which depresses the proper keys of the linotype keyboard so as to reproduce the words of the message.

The monotype, as indicated by its name, casts each letter separately. It also differs from the linotype in that the composing and the type casting are done on different machines. The composing mechanism has a keyboard of 225 keys which cause holes corresponding to the proper letter to be punched in a moving strip of paper. When words have been set almost to fill a line, an automatic indicator shows the operator what size space is required to *justify*, or exactly fill the line. When this ribbon is passed through the casting machine, each type is cast separately and delivered in proper order of lines.

Photocomposition utilizes a filmsetting machine. A tape controls the movements of a matrix case through which a beam of light photographs each required letter. When the line is completed, the strip of film advances on a revolving drum. See *Books*.

Dynamo and Electric Motor. The dynamo, sometimes called a generator, is a machine for producing electric current. It is driven by mechanical power, usually steam or water power. The same machine, when reversed in action, is an electric motor. Driven by an electric current, it is capable of performing work, such as driving machinery or providing traction for cars. The dynamo and motor are sometimes referred to under the single term dynamo-electric machine.

Michael Faraday in England discovered, in 1831, the principle on which the dynamo is based, namely, that, if the lines of force between the poles of a magnet are cut by an electric conductor moving across them, an electric current is induced in the conductor. The dynamo consists essentially of one or more coils of insulated copper wire about a ring of soft iron, which revolves rapidly on its diameter between the poles of a magnet. The revolving part is called the *armature*. The ends of the wire lead to metal *collecting rings*, from which two metal brushes, connected through an external circuit, pick up the current. In this simple form, at each complete revolution of the armature, the current flows first in one direction and then in the opposite direction. The change from one point of maximum intensity in one direction to the next in the same direction is called a cycle. By adding two or more rings to the armature, a so-called two or many-phase current is produced, in which, for every revolution of the armature, there are two or more points of maximum current intensity in each direction.

If the collecting rings are replaced by a *commutator*, that is, by insulated ring segments placed opposite each other, a one-direction, or direct, current may be produced. It will fall to zero once during each revolution of the armature, but this pulsation may be virtually eliminated by increasing the number of armature rings and coils.

The magnets used for the early dynamos were permanent magnets, but later the electromagnet was substituted. For alternating currents, this is actuated by a separate circuit, but, with direct current machines, the current produced by the dynamo may be used in whole or part to actuate, and regulate the strength of, the magnet.

Designs of modern dynamos differ widely. One or many magnets may be used and either the magnets or the armature may revolve, the other remaining stationary. Motors have been adapted to innumerable uses, including electric railways, elevators, machine shops, and household appliances.

For long distance transmission, the alternating current is almost exclusively used in America, since this current may be readily transformed to a high potential and so transmitted over a much smaller copper or aluminum conductor than would otherwise be necessary. At the point of use, the current is "stepped down" by transformers and distributed to the users. It is common to transmit in this way currents of 220,000 volts over hundreds of miles.

When the peak requirements for electricity at different using centers occur at different times, economies can be effected by connecting many generating stations and consuming centers, thereby making available the surplus from any station for the center needing it.

Electric power is generated most economically where coal, natural gas, oil, or water power are readily available. The chief generating centers or regions in the United States include Niagara Falls; New York City; Chicago; Los Angeles; San Francisco; Pittsburgh; Muscle Shoals, Ala.; Butte, Mont.; and the North Pacific states. The electric power produced in the United States was over 1500 billion kilowatt hours in 1970, and the number of residential customers exceeded 63 million.

Electron Tube. A vacuum tube very similar in appearance to an incandescent electric lamp, but generally containing, in addition to the filament, a flat metallic plate and an irregularly shaped grid. When the filament is heated to glowing by means of an electric current, it emits *electrons* or negative charges of electricity, which ordinarily would return to the wire. If, however, a battery is connected to the filament and to the plate so that the plate is *positively* charged, the electrons will be attracted to the plate and a current of electricity will flow through the vacuum and around the circuit. If the plate is negatively charged, no current will flow; consequently, when connected with an alternating current, the tube acts as a valve which allows the electricity to pass through in one direction only, thus producing a direct current.

The grid is placed between the filament and the plate, so that, if a charge of varying strength is applied to the grid, corresponding changes will also be imposed on the current flowing through the tube. A weak current is thus enabled to control one that is much stronger. Because of these properties, electron tubes are used as relays, which make long-distance telephony possible; as converters, by which direct current may be obtained from an alternating source; as detectors, which amplify weak radio telegraph or telephone signals and make them audible; and as transmitters, which can be used to send out a continuous train of ether waves of almost any desired frequency.

Fathometer. An instrument for measuring the depth of water in the process of echo sounding. An electric oscillator on a ship makes a characteristic sound which is transmitted to the water. The instrument clocks the time of its production and the time when the echo, reflected from the floor of the ocean, returns to the instrument. Since sound travels about 4700 feet a second in water, the depth is calculated from the lapse of time, an indicator showing the result. By thus making possible the almost instantaneous recording of the contour of the sea floor, the instrument multiplies the speed and the economy with which the ocean bed can be mapped.

Gyroscope. A mechanical device invented early in the 19th century, and at first used chiefly to illustrate certain laws of rotating bodies. It consists essentially of a wheel with a heavy rim, mounted on an axis which is pivoted at both ends within a light circular framework. Instruments of this type are frequently sold as toys under the name *gyro-top*. The more scientific form of gyroscope is so mounted that it is free to revolve about three mutually perpendicular axes, whose common center is the center of gravity of the spinning wheel.

When the wheel of a gyro-top is made to rotate rapidly,—usually by pulling away a string coiled about the axis,—two characteristics are noticeable. First, any attempt to change the direction of the axis meets with a surprising amount of resistance. Second, this resistance is so great that, if the gyroscope is turned on its side and supported at only one end, it will not fall, but will move in a horizontal circle about its point of support, apparently in contradiction of the laws of gravity. This circling movement, known as *precession*, takes place in the direction opposite to that in which the wheel is rotating.

A gyroscope resists any force which tends to change the direction of its axis for the same reason that the passengers on a moving train are jerked forward when the brakes are suddenly applied; that is, because of inertia The amount of inertia depends upon the speed of the wheel, its mass, and the average distance of the mass from the axis.

The act of precession is explained by the fact that a body moving under the influence of two forces must respond to both. The wheel which is rotating on one axis is also pulled downward because of gravitational attraction. The gyroscope then tends to place its axis parallel to a third, intermediate axis, and, as a result, moves backward. As the third axis also changes its position at the same time, precession continues as long as the inertia of the wheel is sufficient to prevent falling.

The earth acts as a huge gyroscope, spinning on an axis which points toward the polestar, and also rotating around the sun. As these two axes of rotation do not coincide, the earth, like the top, is forced to precess, thus causing the pole to move west in a small circle which is completed once in 25,900 years. For this reason, the star which indicated true north when the Egyptians built the pyramids is not the polestar of today.

The tendency of a gyroscope to rotate in one plane has been utilized for many purposes. By means of a gyroscope, Léon Foucault, about 1852, was able to demonstrate the rotation of the earth.

Gyroscopes are no longer scientific toys. The *Brennan monorail car* is capable of retaining perfect equilibrium upon a single rail, because of two heavy, motor-driven gyroscopes, which spin in opposite directions. Somewhat similar devices are used upon ships to prevent rolling, while, for ice-breaking vessels, the gyroscope is fastened so as to cause the vessel to roll. Torpedoes are held to their course by means of a controlling gyroscope which begins to spin when the torpedo is released. Gyroscopic apparatus for stabilizing airplanes is also in use. This stabilizing influence becomes more comprehensible in the light of Newton's third law of motion—to every action there is an equal and opposite reaction. Probably the most important application of the gyroscope is the gyrocompass which indicates true north regardless of any change in the magnetic field. See *Gyrocompass*.

Internal Combustion Engine. A heat engine which performs work because of the expansive energy of hot gases formed within a closed chamber. The fuel used may be a natural or an artificial gas, a volatile liquid such as gasoline or alcohol, a poorly volatile liquid such as kerosene, or heavy oils and tars. An engine is usually named for the fuel to which it is best adapted.

In order that such engines may operate continuously it is necessary that the fuel, together with the proper amount of air, be placed in the cylinder, compressed, burned, and allowed to expand, after which the spent gases must be removed

and the series of operations repeated. When these processes are performed during four strokes of the piston the machine is called a *four-cycle* engine.

The action of a four-cycle gas or gasoline engine is as follows: At the first, or *intake stroke*, with the exhaust valve closed and the intake valve open, the piston moves away from the closed end of the cylinder, and fuel is sucked into the chamber. With both valves closed, the piston then returns on the *compression stroke* which forces the confined gas into a small space. The compressed gas is then ignited by means of an electric spark, and the chemical action of burning raises the temperature so that the gases expand and force the piston outward. After this *power stroke*, the exhaust valve opens and the piston returns on the *exhaust stroke*, forcing out the burned gas.

In a *four-cycle* engine there is one power stroke during two revolutions of the flywheel. In a *two-cycle* engine the same operations are performed during two strokes of the piston, so that there is an explosion at each revolution of the crank shaft. This is usually effected by making the crank case gas-tight and filling this space with the proper mixture of gas and air. At the end of the power stroke, two valves or ports are uncovered. One opens to the exhaust and the other to the crank case, which is under slight pressure, so that the burned gas flows out and fresh fuel is forced into the cylinder. As the piston returns, it covers the valve openings and compresses the gas, which is then ignited and the series repeated.

It is obvious that power thus imparted by a blow on the piston at every second or fourth stroke will be jerky. In order to prevent excessive vibrations a single-cylinder engine usually has a heavy flywheel, while larger engines have several cylinder, connected to one crank shaft and firing in rotation so that the pressure is more continuous. For automobile and aircraft engines, four and six vertical cylinders in a straight line, or eight and twelve cylinders in two equal rows inclined so as to form a V, have been most generally satisfactory. In some aircraft engines vibration is almost eliminated by having the cylinders rotate like a flywheel about a fixed crank shaft.

In gas engines the proper amounts of gas and air are easily adjusted in a mixing chamber; in the gasoline engine a jet of the volatile liquid is sprayed into a current of air as it is drawn through a *carburetor* into the cylinder. With kerosene or other less volatile fuels, a hot bulb or other form of heating device is often necessary. Ignition is almost universally caused by means of an electric spark produced by an induction coil or a high tension magneto.

The *Diesel* type of engine, which operates with heavy hydrocarbons such as tar oil, usually requires no ignition system when once in operation. Instead, air is drawn into the cylinder and highly compressed. The great pressure raises the temperature of the air to such a degree that, when the fuel is forced into the cylinder by means of a pump, spontaneous combustion occurs. The great advantage of the Diesel engine due to the low cost of fuel is partly offset by the heavier construction necessary to provide for the great pressure.

A theoretical plan for the four-cycle engine was originated by Beau de Rochas in 1862. The same plan was independently invented by Nicholas A. Otto, of Cologne, and was developed into a practical machine in 1877.

The power which a four-cycle engine will deliver is generally calculated by means of the formula,

$$DHP = \frac{D^2 \times S \times RPM}{18,000}$$

For example: the *delivered horse power* (DHP) of an engine having a 3-inch bore (D), a 4-inch stroke (S), and running at 1000 *revolutions per minute* (RPM) equals $3 \times 3 \times 4 \times 1000 = 36,000 \div 18,000$ or 2 horse power. The power of a two-cycle engine is obtained by dividing by 13,500 instead of 18,000.

For multicylinder engines the result is multiplied by the number of cylinders.

Microscope. An optical instrument consisting of a lens or combination of lenses, used to obtain a magnified image of minute objects. A *simple microscope* consists of a single convex lens composed of one or more parts, and is often called a magnifying glass. Instruments of this class have been known and used for centuries.

A *compound microscope* is composed of two lenses,—the objective and the eyepiece, or ocular,—mounted in opposite ends of a metal tube. The objective, being of short focus, is placed close to the object, of which it produces a magnified image within the tube. The eyepiece, which is generally of low power, magnifies this image a second time.

The first instrument of this type seems to have been made, about 1590, by Zacharias Janssen, a native of Holland. The magnifying power of a compound microscope depends on the power of the objective, the power of the eyepiece, and the distance between the two. It would thus seem possible to produce images of any magnification, but greatly enlarged images lack detail and sharpness, so that a power of 2000 diameters is seldom exceeded for visual work. It should be remembered that, as area increases with the square of the diameter, 2000 diameters means 4,000,000 times the area of the object.

The usual form of compound microscope consists of the lenses in an adjustable tube fastened above a platform having an opening in the center, across which the object is to be placed. Beneath the platform is a mirror which reflects rays of light from some source of illumination upward through a condenser. This, as its name indicates, concentrates the light from the mirror into a small bundle of rays which pass up through the stage, object, and lenses. For opaque objects the lighting must be from above.

Eyepieces which magnify from 4 to 20 diameters are generally used with objectives having a focal length of $\frac{2}{3}$, $\frac{1}{6}$, or $\frac{1}{12}$ inch and a corresponding power of about 10, 44, and 90 diameters. A $\frac{1}{12}$ inch objective with a 10-power ocular would therefore produce a magnification of 900 diameters. To prevent loss of light when using objectives of very short focus, a drop of cedar oil or similar fluid is placed so that it touches both the object and the lens. Objectives constructed to operate under such conditions are called *oil-immersion* lenses.

No microscope can show directly the true form of any object smaller than one-half the wave length of light by which it is seen. Much smaller objects, however, may be observed indirectly by means of two devices—the *ultramicroscope* and the *electron microscope.*

The ultramicroscope consists of an arrangement by which minute objects may be made visible as spots of light against a dark field. Light is sent across the field instead of up through it, so that any ultramicroscopic particles reflect light and are seen like dust in the air of a dark room through which a ray of sunshine is passing. In this way particles about six-millionths of an inch have been detected.

The electron microscope, invented in 1938, is a revolutionary contribution to microscopy. It employs the principle that electrons are, like light, reflected from what they strike. The electrons are focused, by a magnetic field within a cylindrical coil of electric wires, upon a glass plate treated chemically so as to become fluorescent where the electrons converge. The fluorescence reproduces the pattern of the minute object scanned.

The instrument is steel, about five feet high, with glass windows. Its interior is a vacuum. Within the vacuum a cathode-ray tube sends out a stream of electrons which strike the object to be scanned. Those reflected by the object are picked up by the magnetic field created by the coil of electric wire and are converged upon the chemically treated glass. The image may be projected in enlarged form on a phosphorescent screen.

Motion Pictures. A series of separate pictures projected upon a screen, and changed so rapidly that the eye receives the effect of continuous motion. This effect is due to a physiological property of the eye called *persistence of vision*, which causes an image to remain apparent for about $\frac{1}{5}$ second after it has really disappeared. Standard pictures are projected at the rate of 16 per second. Each picture is shown perfectly still for $\frac{5}{96}$ second, and the screen is dark for $\frac{1}{96}$ second three times in the period during which one picture passes before the source of illumination.

After the invention and the development of photography, many investigators worked over the problem of picturing motion. Edward Muybridge, using methods devised by John D. Isaacs about 1872-73, studied the movements of a trotting horse by means of a row of 24 cameras, exposed in order as the horse passed before them. The photographs were projected in such a way as to simulate movement, but his apparatus was necessarily clumsy as he had only glass plates. A light, flexible, continuous film was needed as a substitute for the glass, and this was invented by Goodwin and produced by Eastman.

In 1894, Edison placed on the market his kinetoscope, which successfully depicts motion by means of photographs printed on an endless strip of celluloid film. But the pictures in this machine can be viewed by only one person at a time. In 1895, Thomas Armat of Washington was the first to produce motion pictures by modern methods. The essential point in the improvement made by Armat, with whom C. F. Jenkins was for a while associated as experimenter, was a device by which the film moved intermittently, having periods of rest and illumination largely in excess of the period of movement from image to image. Other projectors were made and exhibited in 1896. From 1897 to 1907 a violent war of litigation over patents disturbed the industry.

Motion picture film is so standardized that pictures made by one company may be exhibited on any machine in the world. It is usually prepared in strips 200 feet long by $1\frac{3}{8}$ inches wide. On each side there is a margin of $\frac{3}{16}$ inch in which perforations are cut. There are 16 photographs and 64 perforations to the foot. Each picture is thus 1 x $\frac{3}{4}$ inches. One thousand feet is the standard length to fill one reel.

The motion picture camera is equipped with a very fast, high grade lens of 2 to 3 inch focus. The shutter is a revolving, perforated disk driven by a crank which the operator usually turns at the rate of two revolutions per second. Eight exposures are made at each turn of the handle. Within the box the film passes from the original coil over several rolls. It is carried behind the lens, over other rolls which preserve an even tension and prevent tearing, and finally is rewound on a second reel. A delicate mechanism, catching in the perforated edges, holds the film firmly while the shutter is open and jerks it forward just $\frac{3}{4}$ inch when the shutter closes.

The exposed film is wound spirally on racks and is developed in huge tanks in a dark room. From the negative, any number of positives may be printed at the rate of from 5 to 8 pictures per second. These are made on similar strips of film coated with an emulsion which is not so sensitive but which gives greater contrast.

In the projecting machine, an electric arc is the usual source of illumination. The light passes first through heat filters and condensing lenses, and then through the film and the projecting lenses to the screen, where the picture is enlarged about 10,000 times. Most films are made of celluloid and are consequently highly inflammable. Noninflammable films may be produced from cellulose acetate, but even these are melted by the heat from the arc if they are held too long between the lenses. The used and the unused reels of film are therefore held in asbestos lined boxes, and a safety shutter is provided, which automatically protects the picture from the light if the machine accidentally stops. The mechanism for moving the film is similar to that used in the camera, but the shutter disk which revolves once for each picture has two large openings instead of a single small one.

Animated cartoons are made by photographing a great number of single drawings each showing a different stage of the action. Colored "movies" are made by exposing through a series of color screens and projecting through similar screens in reverse order—the technicolor process. These pictures must usually be shown at about twice the normal speed. "Talking movies" depend for their success on the exact timing of picture and voice. This problem was solved by the use of the photoelectric cell and the amplifier. See *Amplifier, Photoelectric Cell*.

The motion picture industry as organized today has three principal divisions: production, distribution, and exhibition. Forty-five years after its birth, in about 1895, the industry in the United States had grown to such proportions that it employed nearly 300,000 people. Nearly one-fifth of the total of the world's motion picture theaters, approximating 100,000, are in the United States. Russia is credited with the largest number, about 30,000. It is estimated that one-eighth of the world's population attend motion picture theaters each week.

The first studio for making motion pictures was a little, black, paper covered shanty built by Edison near his factory in New Jersey. Today a whole community in California is given over to the staging and filming of picture stories. This community, Hollywood, in Los Angeles, produces over two-thirds of the world's output.

Phonograph. An instrument which records and reproduces sound by means of a moving diaphragm that is caused to vibrate by sound waves in the air. A stylus or chisel-like needle connected with the diaphragm is allowed to trace or engrave a spiral line upon a revolving cylinder or disk. The slightest movement of the diaphragm is thus recorded on the path of the needle. To reproduce the sound, the record is again revolved at the same speed and a smooth needle attached to a second diaphragm is allowed to travel over the engraved line. The irregular motion of the needle then forces the diaphragm to vibrate and produce sound waves similar to those first recorded.

The first phonograph, or "talking machine," was invented by Thomas A. Edison in 1877. It consisted of a cylinder having a spiral groove cut on its surface, and mounted on a screw passing through its center. A smooth layer of tin foil was placed on the cylinder, which was then revolved so that the groove was always under the point attached to the diaphragm. The movements of the diaphragm thus produced irregular indentations in the tin foil, which would impart similar vibrations when the stylus was again allowed to travel over the cylinder.

The *graphophone*, invented in 1885 by Chichester Bell and Charles Tainter, improved on the phonograph by substituting a wax tube for the tin foil. The *gramophone*, invented by Emile Berliner in 1887, differed fundamentally from the first two, in producing a tracing of the sound waves as a zigzag line of even depth, rather than an up-and-down engraving. This system was found more satisfactory on disks than on cylinders. Modern practice tends toward the use of wax cylinders for temporary records, such as those used for commercial dictation, and of hard disks for all permanent records. Some machines employ reproducing needles which are used but once, while others have a permanent diamond or sapphire point.

In preparing commercial records the original is recorded directly upon a wax tablet. This is carefully covered with graphite in order that it may conduct electricity, and is then electroplated with copper. The copper shell is stripped from the wax and then nickel-plated in order to harden it.

From this *master record*, a second, mother record is prepared in the same way, and from the mother record several matrices are made which are used for molding the familiar commercial disks. These are generally composed of shellac, together with charcoal, barium sulphate, and other substances.

In the *auxetophone*, an ordinary record is used to control the action of a delicate valve which impresses the proper vibrations on a stream of air generated by an air compressor. The recorded sound is thus *reproduced* without the aid of a vibrating diaphragm.

Great progress has been made within the past few years in the recording and transmission of sound. A new accuracy and realism has been achieved by the introduction of high-fidelity (hi-fi) equipment, which reproduces sound with an amazing degree of faithfulness to the original. This has been accomplished largely by eliminating sound distortion caused by electronic deficiencies in the making of a record and in the transmitting equipment. Its popularity, especially among lovers of music, has proved a stimulus to the industry.

Photoelectric Cell. This device, often called the electric eye, is used for translating variations in the intensity of light into variations in intensity of an electric current. Since the electric current, properly amplified by electron tubes, can be made to perform innumerable operations, the photoelectric cell makes it possible to produce these results by changes in the light which falls on the cell. Possible applications are almost innumerable.

The effect of light on an electric current was first noted by Heinrich Hertz in 1887. Julius Elster and Hans Geitel constructed in 1890 the first photoelectric cell. In modern practice, this cell consists essentially of a glass bulb or tube, either evacuated of air or filled with an inert gas, such as argon or neon, having an anode of platinum or some other suitable metal. The cathode is usually a very thin coating of an alkali metal, such as potassium or cæsium, which has been found to emit particles of negative electricity, or electrons, when exposed to light. When an electric current is passed from the anode to the cathode, this current is decreased by the action of light on the cathode. This effect varies with the amount and the wave length (color) of the light, which is admitted through a small window. The current used is necessarily of extremely low voltage and must be magnified enormously by an amplifier before being put to effective use in the production of sound or the operation of mechanical devices. Another type of cell utilizes a property of selenium, which is a very poor conductor of electricity when in the dark but, when exposed to light, conducts an electric current much more readily.

Photoelectric cells differ in their sensitivity to light of different colors or wave lengths. Some are adapted to respond to infra-red light rays, which are invisible to the human eye. Such cells can "see" in the dark, and the resulting current fluctuations can be made to produce visible photographs of invisible objects.

The first important application of the photoelectric cell was in the production of audible motion pictures. It is the basic element in phototelegraphy and television. It may be used also for mechanically counting objects passing before its "eye," for sorting objects by their color, for analyzing and matching colors, for measuring illumination and ultra-violet radiation, for transforming the printed page into intelligible sound, and for picking up obscure or invisible light signals and performing operations in accordance with the signals. All these operations it can perform better than the human eye. With the development of television, it promises to enable man to see in the dark or through fogs.

Photography. The process of forming and fixing images of objects upon a sensitized surface by means of the physical and chemical properties of light. The question "Who invented photography?" is often asked, but cannot be definitely answered because modern photographic methods have been developed by contributions from many.

J. H. Schultz, in 1727, made the first photographic copy of writing. In 1802, Thomas Wedgwood copied pictures by the action of light. Joseph Nicéphore Niepce produced the first permanent pictures in 1814. Louis Jacques Daguerre, in 1839, made public the details of his *daguerreotype* process of sensitizing a silver plate with iodine, and developing, with vapors of mercury, the image produced on exposure. The next year Professor John W. Draper of New York university made by this method the first photograph of a human face. William H. F. Talbot, in 1841, presented his calotype process, which permitted many copies to be made from one paper negative.

In 1851, Scott Archer introduced the process in which sensitive silver salts are produced in a film of *collodion* supported on a glass plate. The American photographer Mathew Brady began using the new wet-plate process, called *ambrotypes*, in his New York studio around 1853. Later utilizing that method and a variant called *tintypes*, Brady documented the Civil War in over 7000 pictures. Because exposures required several seconds, he was unable to take action photography, but his portraits captured the destruction and desolation of the war.

The gelatin-silver bromide emulsion, the basis of modern dry plates, was discovered in 1871 by Dr. R. L. Maddox. In 1884, George Eastman patented a successful roll film of paper, and, in 1887, Rev. Hannibal Goodwin applied for a patent on a transparent, sensitive, celluloid-like pellicle which was the basis of the modern roll and cut film. Both films and glass plates are coated with gelatin containing bromide and iodide of silver.

Modern photographic apparatus usually consists of a light-tight box or camera, equipped with a lens which focuses an image upon the sensitive surface of a plate or film when the shutter is opened. No change can be seen on the exposed plate until it is *developed* by immersion in an alkaline, oxygen-absorbing solution of pyrogallol, metol, or similar reducing agent. In this solution the plate gradually darkens and the image appears. But, as the parts of any object which reflect the most light cause the greatest change in the silver salts, a reversed image, called a *negative*, is produced, in which the high lights of the object appear dark, and the shadows, light. Developing is done in the dark or in a red light, which does not affect ordinary plates. The negative is next *fixed* with a solution of sodium thiosulphate, commonly called *hypo*, which dissolves all *unchanged* silver salts. After further washing in fresh water, the negative is dried. Satisfactory negatives are produced almost mechanically by the system of *tank development*, in which the exposed plates are treated with a developer of known strength, for a definite time at a fixed temperature.

The final step consists in making a positive *print* by placing sensitized paper behind the negative and exposing these to the light. The dark parts of the negative hold back more light than the lighter shadows, so that the resulting image has the same light values as the original object. The principal kinds of photographic paper are: those which are printed by artificial light, developed, and fixed in the same way as the negative; and ordinary *printing out paper*, which is exposed to the sun until the image appears, and is then fixed, washed, and often given further treatment to improve the color.

Photographs in natural colors are generally produced by means of screens or filters which separate light into its red, green, and violet components. The finished photograph must usually be viewed through similar screens. The processes of Ives, Joly, Wood, and the Lumière brothers are best known. On the Lumière autochrome plate a permanent screen is formed by a layer of starch particles colored red, green, and violet.

By use of highly sensitized film, photography will produce results which far outdistance the capacity of the human eye. Rays, for instance, invisible to the eye may nevertheless produce pictures from objects which appear to be completely in the dark. In astronomical work, by long exposure, stars are photographed which are completely invisible to the human eye. In warfare, photographs made from airplanes will reveal changes in enemy forces which camouflage conceals from the eye. X-ray photography is one of the most valuable aids to surgery. Another important use is the photographing of documents or pages of books. The pictures are produced on a very small scale in a non-inflammable film, from which they may be projected by a lantern on a screen. The so-called candid camera depends on the use of very sensitive films and high speed exposure.

In 1947, American Edwin H. Land invented the Polaroid Land camera. This camera develops and prints the picture within seconds after it was taken.

Phototelegraphy. A process for sending photographs by telegraph or telephone, perfected in the Bell Telephone laboratories, New York City, about 1925. The apparatus consists of a transmitter and a receiver, which may be used at the ends of any telephone line. A positive film of the photograph to be transmitted is rolled into cylindrical form and inserted in the transmitter. This film is revolved, at the same time moving forward very gradually with a screwlike motion. A small intense ray of light is focused on the film and shines through it with intensities varying according to the lightness or shade of the portion traversed. The varying currents thus set up control a similar cell and a beam of light directed upon an unexposed photographic film at the receiving end which is geared to rotate synchronously with the film at the transmitting end.

Radar. This term means "radio direction and ranging," operating on the principle of high tension radio impulses sent out in a straight line and reflected directly back to the sending instrument. The time of travel gives the distance. A joint Army-Navy release proclaimed the existence of Radar April 25, 1943. The system operates with ultra-high-frequency radio waves and was discovered in September, 1922, by Dr. A. H. Taylor and Leo C. Young of the U. S. Naval Aircraft Radio laboratory. The battleship *New York*, in 1938, was the first ship to be equipped for its use.

Radio. This term is used to describe the transmission and reception of signals by means of radiated electromagnetic rays (radio waves).

The utilization of radio waves for sending messages by code is known as radiotelegraphy or wireless telegraphy. It may be accomplished by a series of interrupted waves to indicate dots and dashes, as in wire telegraphy. To transmit the tones of the voice or music, a continuous wave is required. To produce such radiations, an alternating current of very high frequency is necessary. This is supplied by electron tubes or transistors. Communication of this type is known as radiotelephony, or simply as radio.

The basis of modern systems of wireless or radiotelegraphy was laid down in 1864 when Clerk-Maxwell, by mathematical reasoning, predicted the existence of electromagnetic waves in the ether. In 1887 Professor H. Hertz proved by experiments that such waves existed, and later Edouard Branly and Sir Oliver Lodge each developed an instrument called a coherer, by which these waves could be detected. Hertz found that they could be produced in the ether by the discharge of an electric spark. The shortest of these waves is many times longer than the longest light wave, but they travel at the same speed, 186,284 miles per second.

Guglielmo Marconi, in 1895, was the first to combine the discoveries of earlier scientists into a practical method of signaling. In 1901 he signalled the letter S across the Atlantic. This achievement was surprising, since it meant that the waves must have changed their direction with the curvature of the earth. Professor Kennelly in the United States and Dr. Heaviside in England later proved that the Hertzian waves were reflected by a layer of ionized atoms produced about 50 to 100 miles above the earth's surface by ultra-violet rays from the sun. The existence of this celestial mirror, the so-called ionosphere, makes possible long distance communication by radio.

Marconi produced his signals by means of sparks formed by an induction coil and condenser. One side of the electric discharge was connected with the earth; the other, with a series of aerial wires or antennæ supported from tall poles. The current producing the spark was controlled by a telegraph key, so that long and short trains of waves, corresponding to the dashes and dots of the telegraph code, were radiated from the antennæ. At the receiving station, similar aerial wires conducted the incoming waves to a coherer which under their influence operated a local telegraphic circuit.

The coherer was soon replaced by electrolytic detectors and by crystals of carborundum, silicon, galena, and other minerals which, when used with telephone receivers, were much more sensitive. These in turn have been largely superseded by electron tubes and transistors which are used both for receiving and for transmitting.

A message sent out is radiated in every direction. To insure that the receiving station obtain only that message intended for it, the so-called wave antenna is employed, having a length approximately that of the wave used and pointed in the direction of expected messages. The antenna is not sensitive to waves coming crosswise. The large transatlantic stations are able to transmit two and receive six messages simultaneously. This result is possible partly through the use of different wave lengths and partly through the so-called barrage receiver, by which interfering waves from near-by stations are neutralized and the desired waves are amplified. In the short-wave "beam" system, reflectors are used at the sending and receiving ends, thereby greatly increasing the energy of the waves received.

The development of wireless telegraphy has been rapid. Three large systems are those of the Marconi and Telefunken companies, and of the Radio Corporation of America. In 1902 the first transatlantic message was sent, and later the value of the wireless telegraph on shipboard was proved by incidents such as the rescue of the survivors of the *Titanic* in 1912. Commercial service is regularly carried on throughout all parts of the world. All ships except the smallest are required to carry the necessary sending and receiving equipment.

Radio Broadcasting. Although all transmission by radio is broadcast in all directions, as distinguished from wire telegraphy and telephony, the term radio broadcasting is not applied to radiotelegraphy but only to wireless transmission by high frequency electromagnetic waves, or radiotelephony. These waves with their modulations corresponding to different sounds are produced through the medium of electron tubes or transistors in the sending instruments. Receiving instruments, also by means of electron tubes or transistors reconvert the modulations into air vibrations recognized by the ear as sounds.

The waves used in transmission differ in length according to the instruments producing them. If messages are sent out over waves having the same or not greatly different lengths the messages will "interfere." Consequently, to avoid "interference" no two or more stations within range of each other may be allowed to transmit over approximately the same length at the same time. For this reason, sending stations are licensed to broadcast with waves of a definite length and to broadcast at certain hours. Licensing is done by governments according to rules agreed on at international conventions. A high-power receiving station near Grand Island, Nebr., checks on American broadcasting stations to see that they observe the terms of their license.

Ordinary radio waves have lengths varying from 30,000 to 10 meters. "Short" radio waves have lengths from 10 meters down to lengths of microscopic proportions. The term *frequency*, measured in *kilocycles*, as applied to radio waves is the inverse of wave length. If a wave length is doubled, the frequency is halved.

Short-wave broadcasts have the advantage of being more readily reflected along the ionosphere. A system known as the national "hook up" is accomplished by the transmission of programs by wire to distant points where they are broadcast on long waves. Static refers to static electricity causing imperfect reception.

On September 29, 1915, the same year in which the first transcontinental telephone line was completed, a conversation over the wireless telephone occurred between New York and San Francisco and was heard in Panama and Honolulu. A regular transatlantic radiotelephone service was inaugurated in 1927. See *Electron Tube, Radio*.

Frequency Modulation. (F.M.) A circuit designed by Major E. H. Armstrong. The practical effect is to do away with static and man-made noises and interferences, also to permit a large number of stations to use a wave length.

Television. The method of broadcasting both sound and pictorial effects simultaneously. Transmission by wire or wireless of scenes or moving-pictures by conversion of light rays to electrical waves, which are reconverted to reproduce the original image.

Refrigeration. While ice has been used at least as early as the Christian era to chill foods, and the addition of salt has been known for centuries to add to its effectiveness, the invention of a device to lower temperatures by mechanical means opened an entirely new chapter in refrigeration.

The first patent for a refrigerating machine was granted to Dr. John Gorie, Apalachicola, Fla., in 1851, and the first refrigeration plant to be operated commercially was opened in New Orleans in 1866.

Refrigerating machines are based on the principles (1) that a liquid absorbs heat ("produces cold") when it turns into a gas and (2) that a gas tends to turn into a liquid when the pressure upon it is increased and to return to a gaseous state when the pressure is lowered. These principles are applied as follows:

A gas is chosen as a "refrigerant" which will liquefy at a pressure not far above that of the atmosphere. Pressure is increased upon the gas, thus liquefying it. The liquid is led into pipes not subject to the higher pressure. The liquid becomes a gas, absorbing heat from the walls of the pipes and their surroundings, thereby cooling the surroundings. The gas is returned to the compression chamber, where it is again liquefied and the cycle repeats itself.

Gases commonly used as refrigerants include sulphur dioxide, ammonia, and carbon dioxide. They are usually compressed by a pump driven by an electric motor, although an alternative method is to heat a solution of ammonia gas in a closed boiler, the gas driven off increasing the pressure. Refrigerating machines are ordinarily automatic. This requirement involves (1) use of a thermostat to start the application of power when the temperature of the commodities to be chilled rises above a certain point and to stop the power when the temperature falls below another point and (2) valves which permit the flow of the refrigerant from the compression chamber to the cooling tubes and on to the compression chamber again when certain temperature conditions prevail.

Refrigeration machinery was first used in breweries and later was applied to the manufacture of ice. Its employment for the direct cooling of food storage chambers has had an influence on the diet of the world's population which is difficult to exaggerate. It has made possible, for instance, the storage and long-distance shipping of meat, fruits, and vegetables. The process of very rapid freezing of fresh fruits and fish has been found to preserve the original flavor without change.

One of the most important applications of refrigeration is so-called air conditioning, which usually involves the cooling of air and regulation of its humidity. The process involves sending air through a water spray chamber, the water ordinarily being cooled by refrigeration equipment.

For certain purposes, refrigeration is applied through the medium of solidified carbon dioxide, or "dry ice." The dry ice is produced under high pressure by refrigeration machinery, its temperature being about 110° F. below zero. In view of its low temperature, a much smaller bulk is required for a given amount of cooling than would be required if ordinary ice were used. As heat is absorbed, the dry ice turns into gas, leaving no liquid residue. The resulting carbon dioxide gas, being heavier than air, forms a protecting blanket around the solid, thus decreasing loss of heat to the surrounding air.

Sewing Machines. Modern sewing machines may be divided into two classes, chain stitch and lock stitch. The great majority of domestic machines make the lock stitch because the chain stitch is liable to ravel. Both types use a needle having the eye near the point, and usually a groove along the side so that the thread will not bind.

In making the chain stitch the needle plunges through the cloth and returns to its first position, leaving a loop of thread on the underside of the cloth. The material is advanced automatically, and the needle descends through the first loop, which is tightened while another loop is left. Through this the needle passes on the next stitch. The upper side of chain stitching appears as a straight line; the lower side forms a series of chainlike links. A second type of chain stitch machine employs a rotating hook to make a twisted loop.

Two threads are necessary to form the lock stitch. One passes from the spool, over various guides, and through the eye of the needle. The other is wound upon a bobbin that is attached beneath the sewing table to a vibrating shuttle or at the center of a rotating hook. When the needle descends, it throws out a loop, through which the shuttle or the hook passes with the second thread, thus locking the stitch. With a properly adjusted tension on the thread, the end of the loop is drawn to the middle of the cloth, so that both sides of the stitching present the same appearance.

An important device used on all domestic machines is the four-motion feed plate which lies under the material and moves it forward between stitches. The surface of this plate is covered with forward-pointing teeth which engage the cloth and with the first motion pull it toward the needle. The plate next drops down from the cloth, moves backward, then upward, and again travels forward for the length of the stitch.

Several hundred different types of sewing machines are used for commercial purposes. There are machines which sew on buttons, others which make the buttonholes, and delicate machines, having from four to a dozen needles, for sewing gloves. Carpet-sewing machines travel along the seam, because the material is too large and heavy to be moved to the needle. Sewing machines have had a predominating influence upon the garment making industry. The McKay stitching machine, invented by Lyman Blake, and the Goodyear welt-sewing machine have revolutionized shoemaking. By the Goodyear method, the insole of a shoe is fastened to the upper, and a narrow strip, called the welt, is sewed around the edge of the insole. The sole is then sewed to the welt.

The first sewing machine was invented in 1790 by Thomas Saint, an Englishman. Saint probably never built a machine, but a model constructed from his plans has been shown to be entirely practicable. In 1830, Barthelemy Thimonnier, a French tailor, produced a machine which was used for sewing uniforms for the French army. It was Thimonnier's factory that was destroyed by a mob. Later improvements of the sewing machine were made almost entirely by Americans.

About 1832–34, Walter Hunt, a machinist, first combined an eye-pointed needle with a lock stitch machine. He sold his interest in his invention to a blacksmith, who refused to apply for a patent. In 1853, Hunt himself applied, but the courts held that in waiting so long he had abandoned his rights to protection.

Elias Howe, in September 1846, received a patent for a sewing machine on which he had been working for three years. Howe's machines were the first to become a real competitor of hand labor. As the courts sustained the fundamental principles of Howe's patent, he is generally considered to be the inventor of the modern sewing machine. Howe was also the first to patent a lock stitch machine. He used in it an eye-pointed, grooved needle that moved horizontally.

In 1849, John Bachelder produced the first machine having a horizontal sewing table and a continuous feed. This feed consisted of an endless leather belt studded with pins.

Isaac Merritt Singer, in 1851, received patents for the first machine with a rigid, overhanging arm and a vertical needle. His machine made the lock stitch and was operated by a foot treadle.

The four-motion feed was invented in 1850 by Allen B. Wilson, a cabinetmaker. In 1857, A. E. Gibbs, a Virginia farmer, invented a rotary hook for making a chain stitch. As the fundamental patents have gradually expired, the most satisfactory features of the older machines have been adopted by all modern sewing machine manufacturers.

Steam Engine. A machine by which the expansive power of steam is transferred into mechanical energy and useful work.

The use of steam as a driving force is not new, for, in the first century A. D., Hero of Alexandria described a toy which revolved because of escaping steam. During the 17th century, steam appliances were used for pumping water, and, in 1705, Newcomen built for the same purpose the first practicable engine in which pressure was applied to a piston. In 1765, James Watt invented the separate condenser, and later made many other improvements of the greatest importance.

Modern steam engines may be divided into two types: the *reciprocating engine* and the *steam turbine*. In the first and more common type, steam acts alternately on either side of a *piston* which is forced back and forth within a hollow cylinder.

The piston is attached by a *piston rod* to a *crosshead*, which is in turn connected with the *flywheel* by a *connecting rod*. Through the action of valves, the steam is admitted behind the piston, while that part of the cylinder in front is connected with the exhaust. The piston moves toward the opposite end, and at the proper moment the steam is cut off, the piston finishes its stroke, and the valves automatically change so that the action is reversed. In a noncondensing engine the exhaust steam is forced out into the air against the atmospheric pressure of 14.7 pounds per square inch. In a *condensing engine* the exhaust steam is drawn off into a vacuum and condensed. By thus avoiding back pressure, more power is developed. In *expansion* engines the exhaust steam is forced into a second, larger cylinder, where it expands further and does more work. Marine engines are frequently of the *triple expansion* and even *quadruple expansion* type in which the steam, before it is exhausted, is allowed to expand into a third and a fourth cylinder, each larger than that preceding.

In spite of the great commercial importance of the reciprocating engine, it is very far from being efficient. In the best engines only about 12½% of the energy in the fuel is delivered as mechanical

Assembly of telegraph sounders, largely a hand operation, for special uses by Western Electric. *(Photo courtesy Western Electric Photographic Services, N.Y.)*

Telegraph keys and sounders manufactured by Western Electric for special test and service functions. The design has hardly changed since 1915. *(Photo courtesy Western Electric)*

Telegraph Office—1861. At this office on Main Street in Salt Lake City, Utah, telegraph lines from the East and West coasts were joined on October 24, 1861, to complete the first transatlantic telegraph line. *(Photographs courtesy Western Electric Photographic Services, N.Y., N.Y.)*

Modern Telegraphic Equipment. On similar equipment though more primitive, the inventor of the telegraph, Samuel B. Morse, sent the first public telegram on May 24, 1844. His message, tapped out in Washington, D.C. and received in Baltimore, was the Scriptural message "What hath God wrought."

energy. The largest single units of this type are of about 10,000 horse power.

In the steam turbine, steam flows from an opening against vanes attached to a *rotor*, which revolves under the pressure of the moving steam. As the steam leaves the moving vanes, it strikes stationary blades, which again deflect it against another row of the vanes. The turbine is the most nearly perfect of all steam engines. It operates at very high speed and is especially effective in driving dynamos and in propelling ships. Turbine generators may attain a capacity of 160,000 kilowatts, or 251,000 horse power. The first vessel driven by turbines developed a speed of 34 ½ knots, so that large vessels were soon equipped with the new engines which give greater power and require much less space.

A further development in ship propulsion which provided greatly increased power with much greater economy in space was the introduction of atomic reactors, as in the pioneer U.S. ship *Nautilus* (See *Submarine Warfare*). The record of this vessel for long cruises submerged was enhanced when she made history, in 1958, by passing the North Pole under Arctic ice. Power plants similar to the one successfully demonstrated by the *Nautilus* are now standard for the U.S. submarine fleet.

The steam necessary for turbines is produced by heating water in a boiler. *Saturated steam* is in such a condition that any lowering of its temperature or increase of pressure will cause part of it to condense to water. One pound of such steam normally occupies 26.36 cubic feet. Saturated steam holding in suspension less than 3 per cent of water is called *dry steam*. Steam at a temperature higher than its normal condensing point is known as *superheated steam*. By its use and through improvements in design and fueling, boilers have been constructed to operate at a pressure of 3375 pounds to the square inch. Variant types of boilers include those which employ electricity for heating or which use mercury vapor instead of steam.

Telegraph. In its simplest form the telegraph is composed of a *line* of wire, usually galvanized iron; a key for sending; a sounder to make the signals audible; and some source of current such as a battery or dynamo. All are connected so that the current must pass through each one. Only one wire is generally used because the earth serves as a return wire to complete the circuit.

The *key* is merely a lever held in place by a spring. It has an insulated knob on one end, and carries a contact point underneath. The *sounder* consists of two electromagnets with a piece of iron mounted close to their ends. The iron armature is attached to a pivoted arm which strikes a brass anvil when it moves either up or down. When the key is *open*, no current can flow, but, when the knob is depressed, a contact is made which closes the circuit. The current then flows through the magnets, which pull the iron toward them, causing a click when the arm strikes the anvil. When the key is raised, the arm springs away from the magnets with another click.

The signals depend upon the time between the sounds of an up and a down click. A short period corresponds to a dot, a longer period to a dash, with a definite arrangement of dots and dashes for each letter. The Morse code, which is used in the United States and Canada, also makes use of a space in order to simplify the combinations. To avoid errors, the Continental Morse code using only dots and dashes is generally employed in Europe, and also in radiotelegraphy.

A commercial Morse telegraph key is equipped with a switch which is closed when the instrument is not in use. A current thus flows continually through all the instruments on a line until some operator wishes to send a message. He then opens his switch and sends the signals which are repeated in every office connected with the line. As the current flowing over a long line is usually too weak

to operate a sounder, the main line is connected with a *relay*, which operates in the same way but is much more sensitive. The moving arm of the relay acts as a key to close a local circuit and operate a sounder. Very long lines, such as those from New York to Chicago, are generally divided into sections by *repeaters* which act as a reversible relay to repeat the signals with a stronger current.

By using currents differing in strength or direction, or both, it is possible by the *duplex* system to send a message in both directions at the same time. In 1873, Edison invented the *quadruplex* system whereby two messages may be sent in both directions at the same time. The *synchronous multiplex* system permits six operators to send over the same wire. Machines, such as the Wheatstone automatic telegraph, which use a perforated tape, are capable of transmitting 300 to 400 words per minute as compared with 25 to 40 by a good operator. With the multiplex *printing telegraph* system, messages are sent by pressing keys on a machine resembling a typewriter, and are automatically printed on telegraph blanks at the receiving end. Most telegrams are now sent in this way. Facsimile telegrams may be sent by phototelegraphic instruments. (See *Phototelegraphy*.)

The supreme court of the United States has decided that Samuel F. B. Morse was the inventor of the electromagnetic telegraph. Other famous scientists who worked on the same problem were the Englishmen, Wheatstone and Cook, whose five-wire system was the first to be tried commercially, and Professor Joseph Henry, an American, who in 1831 operated the first sounding electric telegraph. Steinheil of Munich also developed a similar system about 1837. Morse began his work in 1832. His first commercial line was constructed with government aid. It extended between Washington and Baltimore and was opened to the public April 1, 1844.

Morse Code. A · — B — · · · C · · · D — · · E ·
F · · — · G — — · H · · · · I · · J · — — · K — · —
L · — · · M — — N — · O · · P · · · · · Q · · — · R · · ·
S · · · T — U · · — V · · · — W · — — X · — · ·
Y · · · · Z · · · ·

Continental Code. A · — B — · · · C — · — · D — · ·
E · F · · — · G — — · H · · · · I · · J · — — — K — · —
L · — · · M — — N — · O — — — P · — — · Q — — · —
R · — · S · · · T — U · · — V · · · — W · — —
X — · · — Y — · — — Z — — · ·

Telephone. An instrument used for the purpose indicated by its name, which means a "voice from afar." Many inventors worked on the problem of an electric telephone. On February 14, 1876, Alexander Graham Bell applied for a patent, granted on the following March 7, which is fundamental for this method of transmitting speech by means of electricity.

Although it follows the basic principles of Bell's telephone, today's set possesses far better sending and receiving qualities. The telephone consists of two basic parts: 1) the handset which contains a receiver and transmitter, and 2) the base housing a ringer, an electrical network, a switch, and often a dial.

When the handset is lifted off the base, an electrical circuit is established through the telephone instrument. In the transmitter, this circuit passes through carbon granules in a chamber located immediately behind the diaphragm. Sound waves cause the diaphragm to vibrate, which in turn exerts pressure upon the granules, compressing them in varying densities. The varying resistance of the granules regulates the current flow. An electrical pattern of the voice is sent through a switching center to the other telephone.

In the receiver of the other telephone, a permanent magnet, surrounded by an electromagnet, exerts force on an iron-rimmed fabric diaphragm. As current passes through the electromagnet (coil), the magnet's attraction on the iron rim and attached diaphragm varies and the diaphragm moves accordingly. The surges of current dispatched from the transmitter set the pattern of vibration. This vibration sets sound waves in motion which the listener hears.

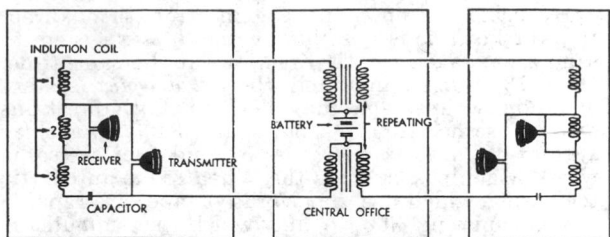

DIAGRAM OF A TELEPHONE CIRCUIT

One telephone is connected to another automatically (dial) or by hand in the switching center, called a central office. Today almost 90 per cent of all Bell telephones are dial operated. Three main types of dial apparatus are in use. Step-by-step, a switching system which connects a call in stages as each figure is dialed, is used mostly in smaller communities. In larger cities, or where switching requirements are complicated, "panel" and "crossbar" systems are most often found. Panel equipment has largely been replaced by "crossbar" for new installations. Unlike step equipment, crossbar switching of a call does not begin until the number is completely dialed. Then the entire operation is completed almost instantaneously. In conjunction with automatic accounting equipment, crossbar systems have opened the way for such modern, time-saving arrangements as operator long distance dialing and customer dialing to distant points. In 144 cities, in mid-1956, approximately 1,500,000 customers could dial long distance calls on a nationwide basis. Telephone connections now span the Atlantic and Pacific oceans.

Telephone conversations are carried over various types of voice highways. *Wire* transmission, the best known, basically depends on a pair of wires, providing metallic circuit. Two pairs form a quad and, when suitably arranged, can carry three conversations simultaneously. Telephone cables are made up of quads and pairs of various sizes. *"Carrier"* systems are today the principal method of long distance transmission. "Carrier" is the term given to a method by which a pair of wires, or other transmission medium, can be adapted to carry many simultaneous conversations. Conversations are put on different frequency bands. Filters at the receiving end sort out and "demodulate" (restore) the frequencies to those of the original voice band

"Coaxial" cable is one of the transmission media used for long distance carrier systems. Such cables usually have eight tubes. Tubes and a copper wire within have a common axis, or are coaxial. Voice signals are sent through the tubes on different frequency bands at speeds approaching light. With today's equipment, 1860 separate conversations or 660 conversations plus TV signals in each direction can be carried on a pair of tubes. Since two tubes are kept for emergencies, a coaxial cable thus can carry a maximum of 5580 separate simultaneous conversations. *Radio Relay*, a narrow beam radio system of super high frequencies (microwave), is another carrier communications system. The principal Bell Company radio relay systems can handle as many as six broad band communications paths in each direction. Two such highways in opposite directions can carry up to 600 conversations or two television programs. *V.H.F.(Very High Frequency) Radio* is used for communicating to and from moving vehicles, while *high frequency radio* is used for many overseas calls. In 1956, the first two major trans-

oceanic telephone cable systems were laid—one between North America and Great Britain and the other between Alaska and the United States. The Trans-Pacific cable between U.S. and Japan was completed in 1964.

Television. This term is applied to the reproduction, transmission, and reception, through the medium of electromagnetic rays, of a series of rapidly succeeding photographic pictures which give the impression of a scene from life. The word means "seeing from a distance."

The central element in the process is a specialized form of electron tube known in different forms as an iconoscope or an image dissector. It contains a screen consisting of numerous minute light-sensitive cells. A photographic image is focused on the light-sensitive cells. The screen is scanned by an electronic beam, which has the effect of setting up in the cells currents proportional to the amount of light received. The currents on transmission to a receiving instrument are used to reconstruct the light pattern in the original image. A standard picture calls for the electronic beam passing across the image 440 times and making 30 complete pictures in a second.

Transmission requires the simultaneous use of numerous telephonic channels, a requirement which is met by the coaxial cable for wire transmission and short wave bands for wireless transmission.

Color television cameras contain three orthicon (image-dissecting) tubes. A system of mirrors and color filters enables the first tube to form a red image; the second, a green image; and the third, a blue image. Through use of an electronic transmission system, the three primary color signals are fed to three color picture tubes where they are simultaneously converted back into color images. A system of mirrors superimposes the three pictures so that the viewer sees one color-blended picture.

Thermostat. An instrument for automatically regulating the temperature produced by heating apparatus. When the temperature to be regulated rises to a certain point it causes an element of the thermostat, either a fluid or a metal bar, to expand and touch off a control which closes a draft or the fuel feed supplying the heat. Then when the temperature falls to a certain point, the sensitive element of the thermostat contracts and the control is actuated in such a way as to cause more heat to be supplied.

Thermostats in household use are ordinarily placed in a living room. The control actuated by the expanding or contracting element is connected electrically with a device for regulating the furnace. In a hot air furnace, if coal is burned, the device closes or opens the drafts; if oil or gas is used, the device partially cuts off the feed. In hot water furnaces, the action of the thermostat is to cut off or turn on an electric current operating a pump which, when in action, causes the hot water to circulate. A second thermostat regulates the temperature of the water.

Typewriter. An instrument for writing in characters similar to those used for printing. Christopher Latham Sholes is generally considered to be the inventor of the modern typewriter. On his first machine, completed in September 1867, many letters were written and sent to friends. One of these letters induced James Densmore, of Meadville, Pa., to take a large financial interest in the new invention, which was patented in 1868.

A famous firm of gunmakers, E. Remington and Sons, was then persuaded to manufacture the machine, which, in 1874, appeared on the market as the Remington typewriter.

Most of the standard modern typewriters are operated by 42 keys arranged in what has been found to be the most convenient order. This arrangement is known as the *universal keyboard*. Scores of other arrangements are used for writing in foreign languages, or for the use of special characters. Each key controls a steel type bar which carries two characters near the free end.

Selection of the desired character is obtained by means of a shift key.

The type bars are hinged in a basket-like group, so that each one may strike on a common center when the proper key is depressed. The paper is placed upon a rubber cylinder, which is mounted on a carriage moving from right to left. Under the control of a pawl and ratchet, the carriage moves one space to the left after each letter is printed or when the space bar is used. At the end of a line the carriage is pushed to the right by the operator. This pressure also serves to advance the paper for a new line.

Just before the type bar reaches the cylinder, an inked ribbon is raised into place so that the key strikes the ribbon and leaves a sharp impression upon the paper. Key and ribbon then drop back so that the writing is always visible. The ribbon, which is usually about 25 feet long, is stretched between two spools and moves at the same speed as the carriage. When most of the ribbon has been wound upon one spool, the direction of winding is automatically reversed.

The average operator writes about sixty words per minute, which is about three times as fast as the ordinary penman. Special typewriters are in use for bookkeeping and similar operations.

Outstanding among typewriter improvements was the early introduction of the warning bell which tells the typist the end of the line is approaching, the coming of the noiseless machine in 1909, and the advent of the electric typewriter about 1935.

The teletype or teletypewriter records messages by electrical transmission, as does also the machine known as the stock market ticker.

MODERN INVENTIONS

Invention, Inventor, and Country	Date	Invention, Inventor, and Country	Date
Adding machine; Blaise Pascal; France	1642	Improved carbon filament; Thomas A. Edison; United States	1879
Recording; Burroughs; United States	1888	Ductile tungsten filament; W. D. Coolidge; United States	1910
Air brake; George Westinghouse, Jr.; United States	1869	Electric motor, split phase; Tesla; United States	1887
Airplane; Orville and Wilbur Wright; United States	1903	Alternate current; Tesla; United States	1892
Airplane compass; Mendenhall and Williamson; United States	1917	Electric welding, resistance process; Elihu Thompson; United States	1886
Air pump; Otto von Guericke; Germany	1654	Electrocast blocks; G. S. Fulcher; United States	1927
Airship; Henri Giffard; France	1852	Electromagnet; Wm. Sturgeon; England	1824
Aluminum, Hall process of making; Charles M. Hall; United States	1886	Electron tube, practical; J. A. Fleming; England	1904
Aniline dyes; W. H. Perkin; England	1856	Three-electrode; Lee De Forest; United States	1906
Autogiro; J. de la Cierva	1920	Electroplating; Luigi Brugnatelli; Italy	1805
Automobile, gas engine; Siegfried Markus; Germany	1875	Electrotyping; Moritz H. von Jacobi (Germany) and Thomas Spencer (England)	1838
First commercial; Levassor; France	1891	Elevator, power; Elisha G. Otis; United States	1852
Babbitt metal; Isaac Babbitt; United States	1839	Flotation process, ore refining; Elmore; United States	1899
Bakelite; L. H. Baekeland; Belgium-United States	1907	Food preservation, canning process; Appert; France	1810
Balloon; J. E. and J. M. Montgolfier; France	1783	Fourdrinier paper-making machine; Louis Robert; France	1798
Barbed wire machine; Glidden and Vaughan; United States	1874	Galvanometer; Sweigger; Germany	1820
Barometer; Torricelli; Italy	1643	Gas engine, electric ignition; Barsonti and Matteucci; Italy	1857
Bicycle; Macmillan; Scotland	1840	Four-cycle; Nicholas August Otto; Germany	1877
Modern type; James Starley; England	1884	Successful; Gottlieb Daimler; Germany	1884
Bifocal lens; Benjamin Franklin; United States	1780	Gaslighting system; Wm. Murdock; England	1792
Calcium carbide, commercial production of; Thomas L. Willson; United States	1892	Gas mantle, incandescent; von Welsbach; Austria	1885
Carborundum; E. G. Acheson; United States	1891	Gas meter, wet; S. Clegg; England	1815
Car coupler, automatic; E. H. Janney; United States	1873	Dry, modern; Wm. Richards; United States	1843
Carding machine; Whittemore; United States	1797	Gatling gun; R. J. Gatling; United States	1861
Cartridge, metallic; Houiller; France	1847	Gauge, steam pressure; Bourdon; France	1849
Cash register; J. Ritty; United States	1879	Gramophone; Emile Berliner; United States	1887
Caterpillar tractor; Benjamin Holt; United States	1900	Graphophone; Bell and Tainter; United States	1885
Caustic soda, Castner process; Hamilton Y. Castner; United States	1890	Guncotton; Schönbein; Germany	1846
Cellophane; J. E. Brandenberger; France	1912	Gyrocompass; H. Anschutz-Kampfe; Germany	1906
Celluloid; J. W. and Isaac Hyatt; United States	1869	Improved; Elmer A. Sperry; United States	1910
Chrome tanning; Schultz; United States	1884	Gyroscope; Foucants; France	1852
Clock, pendulum; Huygens; Netherlands	1657	Harvester and thresher, combined; S. C. Matteson; United States	1888
Coach, steam; Richard Trevithick; England	1801	Holography; Dennis Gabor; England	1947
Coal, liquefaction of, for producing gasoline; Friedrich Bergius; Germany	1914	Hydraulic press; Joseph Bramah; England	1795
Coherer, for detecting "wireless" waves; E. Branly; France	1892	Hydrogenation, catalytic; Sabatier and Senderens; France	1902
Color photography; F. E. Ives; United States	1892	Hydroplane; Glenn H. Curtiss; United States	1911
Ruled screen process; John Joly; Ireland	1894	Ice machine, compressor system; Jacob Perkins; United States	1834
Autochrome process; A. and L. Lumiére; France	1906	Absorption system; F. P. E. Carré; France	1860
Cotton gin; Eli Whitney; United States	1793	Induction coil, modern; Ruhmkorff; Germany	1851
Cream separator, centrifugal; De Laval; Sweden	1880	Injector, steam, for boilers; Henri Giffard; France	1858
Cultivator, rotary disc; Mallon; United States	1878	Iron, galvanizing process; Henry Craufurd; England	1837
Cyanide process for gold and silver ore; Forrest and MacArthur; Scotland	1890	Knitting machine; William Lee; England	1589
Dental plate, rubber; Charles Goodyear, Jr.; United States	1855	Circular; M. I. Brunel; England	1816
Depth bomb; Unge; Sweden	1903	Latch needle; Townsend and Moulding; England	1858
Improved; Godfrey Tait; United States	1916	Kodak, roll-film hand camera; Eastman and Walker; United States	1888
Diesel engine; Rudolf Diesel; Germany	1893	Lacquer, synthetic—nitrocellulose; W. P. Field; United States	1890
Dynamite; A. Nobel; Sweden	1866	Cellulose acetate; C. F. Cross, E. J. Bevan; England	1892
Dynamo-electric machine, first; Michael Faraday; England	1831	Laser; Charles Townes, Arthur Schawlos; U. S.	1958
Drum wound armature; Werner Siemens; Germany	1854	Lathe, turret; Stephen Fitch; United States	1845
Separately excited field; H. Wilde; England	1863	Lawn mower; A. M. Hills; United States	1868
Electric arc lighting, practicable system; C. F. Brush; United States	1878	Lewis gun; I. N. Lewis; United States	1912
Electric battery, primary; Alessandro Volta; Italy	1799	Leyden jar, modern; John Bevis; England	1746
Electric battery, storage; Gaston Plante; France	1859	Lightning conductor; Benjamin Franklin; United States	1752
Nickel-iron type; Thomas A. Edison; United States	1903	Linotype; Ottmar Mergenthaler; United States	1885
Electric furnace, arc type; Pichou and Johnson; France and England	1853	Lithography; Alois Senefelder; Bohemia	1798
Resistance type; W. Borchers; Germany	1880		
Electric lamp, carbon filament; Joseph W. Swan; England	1860		

Invention, Inventor, and Country	Date	Invention, Inventor, and Country	Date
Locomotive, steam, on rails; Richard Trevithick; England	1804	Self-binding reaper, twine; J. F. Appleby; United States	1875
First successful; George Stephenson; England	1829	Sewing machine; Elias Howe; United States	1846
Loom, pattern; M. J. Jacquard; France	1801	Four-motion feed; Allen B. Wilson; United States	1854
Power; Edmund Cartwright; England	1785	Shoe-sewing machine, McKay; Lyman Blake; United States	1858
Locomotive, electric; Vail; United States	1851	Welt-sewing; Charles Goodyear, Jr.; United States	1871
Machine rifle; John M. Browning; United States	1916	Shotgun, practical breech-loading; Casimir Lefaucheux; France	1836
Maser, Charles Townes; United States	1954	Hammerless, ejecting; J. Needham; England	1874
Matches, friction; John Walker; England	1827	Silencer for firearms; Hiram P. Maxim; United States	1909
Safety; Lundstrom; Sweden	1855	Smokeless powder; J. F. E. Schultze; Germany	1867
Mercerized cotton; John Mercer; England	1844	Spectroscope; Kirchhoff and Bunsen; Germany	1859
Mercury vapor lamp; Peter Cooper Hewitt; U. S.	1900	Spinning machine, jenny; James Hargreaves; England	1767
Microphone; Emile Berliner; United States	1877	Roll-drawing; Richard Arkwright; England	1769
Microscope, compound; Zacharias Janssen; Netherlands	1590	Mule-jenny; Samuel Crompton; England	1779
Electron; E. Ruska, B. von Boris; Germany	1938	Ring spinner; John Thorp; United States	1828
Monotype; Talbert Lanston; United States	1887	Stainless steel; Brearley; England	1914
Motion picture machine; Thomas Armat; United States	1895	Steamboat, successful; Robert Fulton; United States	1807
Mowing machine; Manning; United States	1831	Steam engine, atmospheric; Thomas Newcomen; England	1705
With differential gear; Eickemeyer; United States	1876	With separate condenser; James Watt; Scotland	1765
Multiplying machine; G. W. Leibnitz; Germany	1671	Double action, use of expanding steam; James Watt; Scotland	1782
Nails, machine cut; Ezekiel Reed; United States	1786	Compound; Jonathan C. Hornblower; England	1781
Naval telescope gun sight; Bradley A. Fiske; United States	1891	High-pressure; Oliver Evans; United States	1799
Nernst lamp; Walter Nernst; Germany	1897	Steam hammer; James Nasmyth; Scotland	1839
Nitrogen fixation electric arc; C. Birkeland; Norway	1903	Steam turbine; Charles A. Parsons; England	1884
Catalytic process; Haber and Bosch; Germany	1911	Steel, Bessemer process; William Kelly; United States	1847
Cyanamid process; Caro and Franke; Germany	1908	Independently by Henry Bessemer; England	1855
Nylon; E. I. du Pont de Nemours & Co., U. S.	1937	Crucible process; Robert Huntsman; England	1740
Oleomargarine; H. Mege-Mouries; France	1869	Open-hearth process; Siemens and Martin; England	1866
Opthalmoscope; Helmholtz; Germany	1851	High speed; F. W. Taylor and M. White; United States	1900
Optophone, by which blind can read type; E. E. Fournier d'Albe; England	1914	Manganese; Hadfield; England	1884
Pen, steel; Samuel Harrison; England	1780	Stereoscope, lenticular; Sir David Brewster; England	1849
First successful fountain; L. E. Waterman; U. S.	1884	Stereotyping; William Ged; Scotland	1725
Percussion cap; Shaw; United States	1816	Stethoscope; Laënnec; France	1819
Phonograph; Thomas A. Edison; United States	1877	Submarine boat, first successful; John P. Holland; United States	1900
Photoelectric cell; J. Elster and H. Geitel; Germany	1895	Submarine detector; Max Mason; United States	1917
Photography, daguerreotype process; L. Daguerre; France	1839	Tack machine; Blanchard; United States	1806
Bichromate process; Mungo Ponton; Scotland	1839	Tank, military; Gen. E. D. Swinton; England	1914
Use of hypo; John Herschel; England	1839	Telegraph; S. F. B. Morse; United States	1837
Collodion process; Scott Archer; England	1851	Duplex system; J. B. Stearns; United States	1872
Gelatin-silver bromide emulsion; R. L. Maddox; England	1871	Quadruplex system; Thomas A. Edison; United States	1873
Roll-film, modern; Hannibal Goodwin; United States	1887	Submarine, siphon recorder; Wm. Thompson; England	1874
Phototelegraphy; Bell Telephone Laboratories; United States	1925	Telephone; A. G. Bell; United States	1876
Piano; Bartollomeo Cristofori; Italy	1709	Automatic; A. B. Strowger; United States	1889
Piano player, first pneumatic; M. Fourneaux; France	1863	Long-distance, by loading coils; Michael I. Pupin; United States	1900
Pin-making machine; L. W. Wright; United States	1824	Telephone transmitter, microphone; Emile Berliner and Thomas A. Edison, United States	1877
Plow, cast-iron, modern shape; Jethro Wood; United States	1819	Telescope; Jan Lippershey; Netherlands	1608
Disk; Hardy; United States	1896	Teletypesetter; Morkrum-Kleinschmidt Corporation; United States	1928
Pneumatic tire; R. W. Thompson; England	1845	Television; J. L. Baird; England	1925
Independently by John B. Dunlop; Ireland	1888	Independently by C. F. Jenkins; United States	1925
Pneumatic tool; George Law; England	1865	Thermit mixtures; H. Goldschmidt; Germany	1897
Portland cement; Joseph Aspdin; England	1824	Thermometer; Galileo; Italy	1593
Printing from movable type; J. Gutenberg; Germany	1450	Threshing machine; Andrew Meikle; Scotland	1786
Printing press, cylinder; F. Konig; Germany	1811	Torpedo, self-propelled; Whitehead; England	1868
Double cylinder; R. Hoe & Co., United States	1845	Radio controlled; Bradley A. Fiske; United States	1897
Rotary; Thomas Nelson; England	1850	Transistor; John Bardeen, Wm. B. Shockley, Walter H. Brattain, United States	1948
Gordon; George P. Gordon; United States	1850	Trolley car, practical system; F. J. Sprague; U.S.	1888
Pulmotor; Alexander B. Dräger; Germany	1911	Tunnel shield; M. I. Brunel; England	1818
Radar; Dr. A. Hoyt Taylor and Leo C. Young of the Naval Aircraft Radio laboratory; United States	1922	Turbine, hydraulic; J. B. Francis; United States	1849
Radiotelegraph; G. Marconi; Italy	1895	Turret, revolving, for floating battery; Theodore Timby; United States	1862
Radiotelephone; Lee DeForest; United States	1906	Typewriter, first practicable; C. L. Sholes; U.S.	1868
Long-distance; American Tel. & Tel. Co.; United States	1915	Vacuum bottle; James Dewar; England	1892
Rail, flanged; T. R. L. Stevens; United States	1831	Valve gear, Stephenson link; William Howe; England	1843
Rayon; H. de Chardonnet; France	1889	Walshaert gear; Egide Walshaert; Sweden	1844
Reaper, McCormick; Cyrus H. McCormick; United States	1831	Vulcanized rubber; Charles Goodyear; United States	1844
Refrigerating machine; John Gorie; United States	1851	Watches, machine-made; Dennison and Howard; United States	1850
Revolver; Samuel Colt; United States	1835	Water gas, modern process; T. S. C. Lowe; United States	1873
Rifle, spiral grooves; Koster; England	1620	Wood pulp, for paper, mechanical process; Keller and Voelter; Germany	1844
Breech-loading, successful; John M. Hall; United States	1810	Sulphite process; B. C. Tilghmann; United States	1867
Bolt action, military; Dreyse; Germany	1839	Sulphate process; Dahl; Sweden	1883
Repeating; Henry; United States	1860		
Rock drill, percussion; J. J. Couch; United States	1849		
Diamond bit; Herman; United States	1854		
Safety lamp, miner's; Sir Humphry Davy; England	1815		
Saw, band, wood; William Newbery; England	1808		
Circular, wood; Samuel Miller; England	1777		
Screw propeller, successful application; John Ericsson; Sweden	1841		

ENGINEERING AND BUILDING

AN engineer directs the natural forces of nature to the uses of mankind. He must therefore be a scientist; for mathematics, physics, and chemistry are the foundation of most engineering training. Nevertheless, the pioneer of science who devotes his energies to solving the problems of physics or chemistry is not an engineer. To qualify as such, he must apply the knowledge obtained by research and testing, to the design, construction, and operation of works, machines, or processes.

The mathematician studies the mutual relations between the sides and the angles of a triangle; the engineer uses the knowledge thus obtained to measure the distance across a river or to the top of a distant peak. The physicist studies the laws of centrifugal force; the engineer applies these laws when he raises the outer rail at a curve, to prevent a train from leaving the track. The chemist discovers that starch can easily be changed into glucose; the engineer then designs and operates a factory where table sirups are made from corn or potatoes. Because of this practical side of his work, an engineer has been described as one who can accomplish with one dollar what an untrained worker can do, indifferently, with two.

The practice of engineering is not new, for the pyramids of Egypt with their perfectly placed masses of stone compare well with the greatest of modern structures; and some of the bridges and aqueducts constructed by the Romans are still in use. The earliest engineers were chiefly surveyors. Later, engineering became largely a military profession, because the chief demand of the time was for men who could plan strong fortifications and construct tunnels and the engines of war necessary to reduce opposing forts.

With the advance of civilization and the development of commerce, engineering projects, such as bridges and harbors, dams, roads, and canals, were required even more for civil than for military purposes. As a result, men capable of filling this need gradually developed the profession of *civil engineering*, which is now generally recognized as the first and largest division of engineering practice. Next, the rapid increase in the application of power to mechanical operations caused men to specialize in the design and the use of machines. Thus developed the second great branch of the engineering field—that of *mechanical engineering*.

Branches of Engineering. Civil and mechanical engineering represent the fundamental divisions of engineering practice. Mining, electrical, chemical, and sanitary engineering are specialized branches, each applying general engineering principles in connection with a particular division of science. The electrical engineer is probably the most highly specialized, but that each branch is closely related to every other is shown by the training given to students of engineering in the great technical schools. For the first two or three years of their work, students of electrical, mechanical, or chemical engineering study almost the same subjects; later they are permitted to specialize.

More than a hundred well recognized subdivisions might also be named, such as heat, hydraulic or water power, railway, locomotive, automotive, ventilation, highway, telephone, and aeronautical engineering.

Civil Engineering. The civil engineer may be compared to a general at war with the elements, for he strives to bring the land and the sea under his control. He is a builder, in order that commerce and industry may be more easily carried on. He designs, locates, and builds highways and railroads, and, if these are interrupted by a deep gorge or by wide rivers, bridges and tunnels are constructed under his direction. He deepens harbors, protects them from the open waters by means of breakwaters, places lighthouses to guide ships to safety, and builds docks at which cargoes can easily be handled.

Construction of canals and the development of inland waterways, the building of dams for purposes of irrigation and water power, the erection of a single skyscraper or the building of an entire city and of aqueducts to supply the city with water—all come directly within the province of the civil engineer.

Mechanical Engineering. The division of engineering which is concerned with the design, construction, and operation of machines. A civil engineer may plan and lay out a railroad, and a naval architect may design a fast and beautiful steamship, but it is the mechanical engineer who designs the locomotive that hauls the trains and the boilers and engines that drive the vessel. While an architect designs, and a civil engineer constructs, a mighty office building, the mechanical engineer provides for a suitable power plant, pumps, elevators, hot water, ventilation, heat, and often a system of refrigeration. A steel mill, with its enormous power plant and giant engines for handling and shaping iron and steel products, is one of the most impressive examples of mechanical engineering.

When a new type of machine is required for some special purpose, it must be designed by a mechanical engineer. However, standardized machines for many purposes are already on the market, so that in factory operation the mechanical engineer must frequently select and arrange the proper machines to produce a certain result in the most economical manner. The design and the improvement of automobiles have become so important that specialists in this branch of mechanical work are called *automotive engineers*.

Another important duty of the mechanical engineer is the testing of structural materials. The builder of a bridge knows that it will carry its load because a mechanical engineer has designed machines capable of testing steel beams by the application of enormous forces. In this age of machinery, no engineering problem of any considerable importance can be carried through without the aid of the mechanical expert.

Mining Engineering. A branch of engineering devoted to the surveying, testing, and evaluation of mineral deposits, and the planning and execution of the methods by which the mineral is obtained and treated. The mining engineer must decide on the methods to be used in removing the ore, in strengthening tunnel walls to prevent accidents, in providing drainage and ventilation for the mine, and in quickly and efficiently hoisting the mineral to the surface. He must, therefore, be especially trained in civil and mechanical engineering, and in chemistry, geology, and mineralogy.

Electrical Engineering. Engineering principles applied to the designing, building, and operating of dynamos and batteries, electric light and power systems, electric railways, motors, heating apparatus varying in type from a toaster to a giant furnace, telegraph and telephone systems including radio transmission, and various other types of electrical apparatus.

In co-operation with the mechanical engineer, the electrical engineer has done important work in providing mechanical equipment with electrical control. And, in co-operation with the chemical engineer, he has developed the important division of *electrochemical* engineering, which deals with the use of electricity in chemical processes. The products of the electrochemical industries include some of the most indispensable materials employed in manufacture, such as ferro-alloys, aluminum, electrolytic copper, caustic soda, chlorine, hydrogen, oxygen, carborundum, cyanamid, and calcium carbide.

SOME NOTED BRIDGES AND VIADUCTS OF THE WORLD*

Kind and Name	Location	Com-pleted	Length Feet	Main Span Feet	Height Feet	Approximate Cost
Bascule [(1) one leaf; (2) two leaf]:						
Canadian Pacific Ry. (2)	Sault Ste. Marie canal (U. S.)	1914	426	336		$ 250,000
Michigan Ave. (2)	Chicago R., Chicago, Ill.	1920	300	256	16.5	
Wells S. (1)	Chicago R., Chicago, Ill.	1921		268		
Outer-Drive (2)	Chicago R., Chicago, Ill.	1937		264	24	1,800,000
St. Charles Air Lane (1)	Chicago R., Chicago, Ill.	1931	277	219.3	20	705,000
Arlington Memorial (2)	Potomac R., Washington, D. C.	1932	2,163	216	35	7,360,000
Tower (2)	Thames R., London, Eng.	1894	2,980	200	30	5,000,000
Cantilever:						
Quebec	St. Lawrence R., Quebec	1917	3,240	1,800	150	9,000,000
Forth	Firth of Forth, Scotland	1890	8,095	1,700	150	16,000,000
Rip Van Winkle	Hudson R., Catskill, N. Y.	1935	5,040	1,600	142	2,165,000
Victoria	St. Lawrence R., Montreal	1898	8,440	1,250	150	6,000,000
Longview	Columbia R., Wash.	1930	3,740	1,200	196	5,800,000
Queensboro	East R , New York City	1909	7,449	1,182	135	13,000,000
Carquinez	Carquinez Str., Cal.	1927	4,482	1,100	158	7,800,000
South Shore	St. Lawrence R., Montreal	1929	9,137	1,097	162	18,639,000
Cooper River	Charleston, S. C.	1929	14,313	1,050	160	6,000,000
Bluewater	St. Clair R., Port Huron	1938	6,539	871	210	3,250,000
Concrete Arch:						
Plougastel-Brest	Elorn R., France	1930	2,625	612	118	440,000
Westinghouse Memorial	Turtle Creek Valley, East Pittsburgh	1931	1,560	460	200	1,480,000
Pont de la Caille	Cruseilles, France			458.5		
Cappelen Memorial	Mississippi R., Minneapolis	1923	1,032	435	88	900,000
Pierre du Vauvray	Seine R., Ande, France	1924		432		
Royal Tweed	Tweed R., Edinburgh, Scot.	1928	1,400	361.5	45	800,000
Resorgimento	Tiber R., Rome, Italy	1911	492	328	47	238,000
Masonry Arch:						
Plauen	White Elster R., Germany	1903	492	295.2	58	125,000
Sidi Rached	Constantine, Algeria	1915	1,468	227	300	366,000
Cabin John	Cabin John Creek, Washington, D. C.	1864	420	220	101	237,000
London	Thames R., England	1831	928	152	56	7,241,500
Steel Arch:						
Kill van Kull	Staten Is.—Bayonne, N. J.	1931	5,780	1,652	150	18,000,000
Sydney Harbor	Sydney, Australia	1932	3,770	1,650	170	35,000,000
Birchenough	Sabi R., Southern Rhodesia	1935	1,080	1,080		500,000
Glen Canyon	No. Central Arizona	1964	1,271	1,028	700	
Hell Gate	East R., New York City	1917	17,868	977.5	135	15,000,000
Rainbow	Niagara R., Niagara Falls	1941	1,240	950	189	3,760,000
Henry Hudson	Harlem R., New York City	1936	2,000	800	142.5	1,137,876
McKees Rocks	Ohio R., near Pittsburgh	1930	3,600	750	100	6,000,000
West End	Ohio R., Pittsburgh	1931	1,889	780	73	
Suspension:						
Verrazano-Narrows	Brooklyn-Staten Island	1965	13,700	4,260	228	125,000,000
Golden Gate	San Francisco Bay, Cal.	1937	8,500	4,200	220	32,815,000
Mackinac	Straits of Mackinac, Michigan	1957	26,444	3,800	148	96,400,000
Washington Memorial	Hudson R., New York City	1931	8,243	3,500	213	60,000,000
Tagus River	Lisbon Harbor, Portugal	1966	3,323		230	75,000,000
Firth of Forth	Edinburgh, Scotland	1966	3,300			30,350,000
Severn River	Aust, England	1966	3,240		120	22,400,000
Bolivar	Orinoco R., Venezuela	1965	2,336		177	18,500,000
Transbay	San Francisco Bay, Cal.	1936	22,720	2,310†	200	77,600,000
Delaware Memorial	Delaware R. near Wilmington	1951	10,750	2,150	442	44,000,000
Ambassador	Detroit R., Detroit, Mich.	1929	8,000	1,850	152	22,500,000
Delaware River	Camden-Philadelphia	1926	9,570	1,750	135	24,600,000
Bear Mountain	Hudson R.	1924	2,257	1,632	155	5,000,000
Williamsburg	East R., New York City	1903	7,308	1,600	135	15,000,000
Brooklyn	East R., New York City	1883	7,580	1,595.5	135	18,000,000
Lions Gate	Vancouver Harbor, Vancouver, B. C.	1938	5,820	1,550	200	6,000,000
Mid-Hudson	Hudson R., Poughkeepsie, N. Y.	1930	4,200	1,500	135	5,622,700
Manhattan	East R., New York City	1909	6,855	1,470	135	17,000,000
Triborough‡	East and Harlem Rs., N.Y.C.	1936	4,318	1,380	135	42,000,000
Truss [(s) simple; (c) continuous]:						
Metropolis (s)	Ohio R., Ill.	1917	5,700	720	53	3,000,000
Paducah (s)	Ohio R., Ohio	1929	9,000	716	100	
St. Louis (c)	Mississippi R., Mo.	1930	5,350	700	55	
Tanana River (s)	Alaska	1923	700	700		1,370,000
Cincinnati (c)	Ohio R., Ohio	1929	1,575	675	104	1,750,000
Cape Girardeau (c)	Mississippi R., Mo.	1930	2,339	671	99	
Vertical Lift:						
Buzzards Bay	Cape Cod Canal, Mass.	1936	806	544	139	2,000,000
Marine Park	Jamaica Bay Channel, N. Y.	1937	4,802	540	55	3,800,000
Burlington-Bristol	Delaware R., N. J.—Pa.	1931	3,027	534	61	1,300,000
Kansas City	Missouri R., Kans.—Mo.	1912	5,340	428	65	2,200,000
Boonville, Mo., M.K.T.R.R	Missouri R.	1932	1,638	408	27	1,000,000
Hackensack River	P.R.R. near Jersey City	1930	2,950	331.5	40	
Suisun Bay	California	1930	5,603.5	328	70	12,000,000

*The bridges in this table are divided according to the type of their main span. In each division, the bridges are arranged in the order of the length of the main span.

†Two joined spans of 2310 feet each; also a main cantilever span of 1400 feet.

‡Suspension span over East River; vertical lift span, 310 feet long, over Harlem River.

Many bridges which are not remarkable for their main spans are nevertheless noteworthy on account of their lengths or their heights. Among the longest bridges in the world are the following:

Chesapeake Bay Bridge-Tunnel, length 17.6 miles, from Cape Charles to Chesapeake Beach, Va.

Transbay, 8 miles long.

Great Salt Lake cutoff, a railroad trestle 20 miles long.

San Mateo bridge across San Francisco bay, 7.1 miles.

Lake Pontchartrain railroad bridge, Louisiana, 7 miles.

James River Highway bridge, near Newport News, Va., with approaches, 6 miles; without approaches, 4½ miles.

Lake Pontchartrain highway bridge, Louisiana, 5 miles.

Huey Long cantilever bridge over Mississippi at New Orleans, completed 1935, totaling 4½ miles.

Rainbow Bridge, Niagara River, is the longest hingeless arch span in the world.

Among the highest bridges are the following:

Royal Gorge, a suspension bridge over the Arkansas River at Canon City, Colo., 1050 feet high; steel arch bridge over the Colorado River at Glen Canyon Dam, Arizona, 700 feet high; Snake River cantilever bridge near Twin Falls, Idaho, 502 feet high; Marble Canyon, a steel arch bridge over the Colorado River at Lee's Ferry, Arizona, 467 feet high.

Chemical Engineering. A chemical engineer designs and operates the process and special equipment necessary for commercial preparation of chemical substances. His field includes the production of acids and alkalies, dyes, fertilizers, gases, explosives, synthetic drugs and perfumes, and also of many products, such as leather, paper, soap, starch, glucose, and sugar, which frequently do not suggest the chemical methods by which they are prepared.

Sanitary Engineering. A branch of civil engineering which deals with problems such as providing a community with pure water, and disposing of sewage, garbage, and other refuse, in such a manner as to avoid danger to the public health. In addition to the fundamental civil engineering, a sanitary engineer must, therefore, have special training in biology, bacteriology, and chemistry.

Military Engineering. This consists in the application of engineering principles to military problems. The military engineer is essentially a civil engineer who has specialized in the design and construction of permanent forts, military bridges, roads, railroads, barracks, and camps. The plans for dugouts, trenches, tunnels, barbed wire entanglements, and the placing of mines and big guns are all under the direction of the military branch called, in the United States army, the Corps of Engineers. On graduation at West Point, the cadets ranking at the head of their class are usually assigned to this corps, which, in addition to purely military duties, has charge of navigable rivers and harbors, and also of the bridges and roads in Crater Lake and Yellowstone national parks.

The mechanical engineering involved in the production of guns and ammunition for the United States army is done under the direction of the department of ordnance. The magnitude of the work may be best appreciated after considering the size of one of the 16-inch guns guarding the Panama canal. It weighs 130 tons and is 49¼ feet long, tapering from a diameter of 28 inches at the muzzle to 5 feet at the breech. The projectile weighs 2400 pounds, and, when driven by a full charge of 667 pounds of powder, leaves the bore at the rate of about half a mile per second. When the gun is fired, the gas pressure on the base of the shell equals 19 tons to the square inch, or about 180 times the pressure on the foundations of a great skyscraper. If the tallest known building were placed on top of the earth's highest mountain, ten miles away from this gun, the engineers in charge could fire a shell over the obstacle with a fair chance of striking a target 21 miles distant.

Graduates of the United States Naval Academy are all trained as mechanical engineers. Those wishing to specialize in the designing of warships are given advanced courses in *naval architecture*; those who are to have control of a ship's engines, are given special courses in *naval engineering*. It is these specialists who decide upon the number and size of the guns, the type and size of the power plant, and the thickness of armor plate on a battleship; the size and equipment of submarines; the design of torpedoes, mines, depth bombs; and similar engineering problems relating to the navy.

Aqueduct (Latin, *aqua*, "water"; *ducere*, "to lead"). An artificial channel or system of conduits through which a large volume of water may flow for a long distance under the action of gravity. Aqueducts are generally used when a city is unable to obtain a near-by supply of water. And, because water is absolutely necessary, aqueducts were used by some of the most ancient cities of which there is any record.

The earliest aqueducts were tunnels, but the Romans developed the use of masonry conduits carried across the country on tall, arched piers. It is this type of structure which is generally associated with the name aqueduct. Modern engineers are returning more and more to the use of tunnels, preferring siphons—which are U-shaped tunnels—instead of bridges, for carrying the water across a river or a low level.

Rome was supplied with water by eleven aqueducts, constructed between 312 B. C. and 226 A. D. The longest of these, the *Anio Novus*, had a length of 62 miles. The *Aqua Virgo*, or *Aqua Vergine* as it is called in the modern Italian language, was restored by the popes Nicholas V and Pius IV and now supplies water for several fountains in Rome. Among the many aqueducts built throughout the Roman Empire, that at Segovia, Spain, and the Pont du Gard at Nimes, France, are probably most famous.

There are many modern aqueducts of great length. In England, Liverpool has a 68-mile aqueduct and Manchester one of 96 miles. Vienna, Austria, obtains water through a conduit 114 miles in length. Longest of all is the Pugliese aqueduct, which supplies 536 Italian towns with water, and has a total length of 1175 miles. The city of Winnipeg, Canada, has a 100-mile aqueduct, and Denver, Colorado, brings a part of its water a distance of 20 miles through large wooden pipes.

The Catskill aqueduct, built to supply New York City with an additional 600 million gallons of water per day, was completed in 1917 at a total cost of 177 million dollars. The water, obtained from the Esopus and Schoharie watersheds, is first stored in the Ashokan reservoir, which has sufficient capacity to cover all of Manhattan island to a depth of 30 feet. The aqueduct proper, 92 miles long, is composed of 55 miles of cut-and-cover conduit, 31 miles of tunnel, and 6 miles of steel pressure tubing. The cut-and-cover sections are made by excavating a channel, in which a 17-foot concrete conduit is built and then covered with earth. The water is carried under the Hudson river at Storm King, about 4 miles above West Point, by means of a siphon consisting of a tunnel 3022 feet long, bored through solid rock at a depth of 1100 feet below sea level. The aqueduct ends at Hill View reservoir, and the water is distributed to the city from a pressure tunnel 18 miles long, which passes the length of Manhattan island and into Brooklyn at a depth of 200 to 700 feet below the streets.

The Los Angeles aqueduct, built between 1908 and 1913, begins at the Owens river, which, with about 35 contributing streams, drains an area of 2800 square miles in the Sierra Nevada. The total length of the aqueduct is about 233 miles. For 60 miles the water is carried in open canal to the Haiwee reservoir. From the end of the reservoir, which is 3760 feet above sea level, the water flows to its destination through 98 miles of covered conduit, 43 miles of tunnel, and 12 miles of steel siphon. As Los Angeles has an elevation of only 275 feet, the water, in coming from the reservoir, has a total drop of almost 3500 feet and thus serves as a source of electrical energy capable of producing 120,000 horse power. The aqueduct is designed to carry 260 million gallons of water per day, and, as there is not yet need for so great an amount, the excess is used for irrigation purposes. The total cost of the aqueduct was about 24 million dollars.

The great Hetch Hetchy project for supplying water for the city of San Francisco involves the construction of an aqueduct 170 miles long.

Bridge. The first artificial bridges were probably tree trunks or strong vines used by primitive man to cross some narrow gorge or stream. Simple bridges, consisting of logs of wood or slabs of stone supported at each end, were used by the earliest known groups of mankind.

The arch bridge was probably first used by the Chinese. Simple brick arches have been discovered among Egyptian ruins, but whether or not the Egyptians used arch bridges is unknown. Bridges are not mentioned in the Bible, but according to other records a brick arch was erected across the Euphrates river within the city of Babylon. *Pontoon* bridges, which are carried on boats or other floating supports, were used for military purposes by Cyrus and other Persian kings as early as the 6th century B. C.

The stone arch was developed by the Romans, who used it especially for strong monumental bridges, some of which are still standing. Smaller Roman bridges usually consisted of wooden beams resting either on stone or on timber foundations. In the 16th century Leonardo da Vinci and Palladio invented the wooden truss and used it in constructing bridges. The first metal arch bridge was made of cast iron and erected at Coalbrookdale, over the Severn river, in 1776. Cast iron was displaced by wrought iron after the investigation carried out for Robert Stevenson when planning the famous tubular bridge across Menai Strait. Later, steel displaced wrought iron, and now ordinary steel is gradually giving way to special alloy steels. At the present time the principal structural materials for bridges are steel, concrete, and masonry.

Bridges may be classified, according to the methods used for supporting the weight, as girder or truss, suspension, arch, and cantilever.

A modern *girder bridge* rests upon strong beams or girders of steel or re-enforced concrete, supported by firm foundations at either end. The girders may be single steel I-beams for small crossings, or *plate girders* built up from steel plates carefully riveted together. Plate girder bridges are the standard type for distances of 20 to 100 feet. The longest plate girder is 130½ feet; another, of 122½ feet, is heavier, weighing 170 tons.

A *truss bridge* may be considered as one composed of enormous girders from which all excess material has been cut away, leaving only a network of braces and connecting members. The ribs of a truss are always arranged to form triangles, because triangular bracing gives the most rigid structure obtainable. Simple truss bridges have been built with spans up to 720 feet in length.

A *suspension bridge* is carried by ropes, chains, or cables, fastened at both ends. This type of bridge has frequently been used by primitive people; it is occasionally used for military purposes; and it has been employed for some of the most famous bridges in the world, notably those of New York City, San Francisco, Philadelphia, and Detroit. Of these, the Oakland Bay bridge at San Francisco, completed in 1936, has the longest span, 4620 feet. The weight of the cables supporting the Delaware River bridge connecting Philadelphia and Camden is 7000 tons. They contain a total of 25,100 miles of wire, a length exceeding the circumference of the earth. The oldest suspension bridge in the United States is the 1057 foot suspension bridge connecting Cincinnati, Ohio, with Covington, Kentucky, completed in 1867.

Arch bridges are so constructed that the load imparts an outward thrust which must be carried at each end by heavy structures, called abutments. In building a bridge of this type, false work or centering of some sort is necessary to carry the load until the arch is completed. It is interesting to note that the first masonry arch across the river Tiber—the Pons Æmilius—was begun about 179 B. C., and in 1911 the longest re-enforced concrete arch then built—the Risorgimento arch, with a span of 328 feet, 1 inch—was completed over the same river. One of the largest arch bridges in America is that over Hell Gate, New York City. It is made of steel, with a hinge at each end to relieve excessive strains. When the foundations for one of the abutments were being sunk, it was discovered that there was a wide crack in the rock, which had been thought to be solid. In order to prevent any settling, a concrete arch was built across the gap, so that the Hell Gate bridge is partially supported by another bridge that is buried 90 feet underground. The Kill van Kull bridge, New York, has the longest steel arch in the world, 1652 feet.

Cantilever bridges consist of trusses arranged like a bracket on a wall, that is, they are supported at one end, while the free arm reaches out over the space to be bridged. In practice, the heavy columns which are to carry the weight are usually erected on strong foundations, with an arm extending in opposite directions so as to give a balanced structure. The shore arm is then fastened to heavy anchor foundations. By placing a cantilever on opposite sides of a river, panel after panel can be added to the free arms until they meet at the center. The greatest bridge in the world of this type crosses the St. Lawrence river at Quebec, with a distance of more than one-third of a mile between the central piers. Construction was begun in 1903. In 1907, when the south cantilever was almost finished, one of the main supporting members gave way and the structure fell into the river. In the new bridge, begun in 1911, an opening of 640 feet was left between the arms. The truss to fill this span was constructed on the shore, floated out under the bridge, and lifted by means of hydraulic jacks. When about 15 feet above the water, the connections at one corner slipped, and the truss, weighing 5000 tons, collapsed and fell into the water. The following year, a second span was successfully raised into place. Seventy-four men were killed at the first accident, and eleven at the second.

The ordinary *bascule* or *jackknife bridge* is a girder or truss, hinged at one end and counterbalanced by weights so that it may be swung up like the blade of a pocketknife.

A *rolling lift bridge* is a bascule which turns up on the rounded ends of its own base instead of on a hinge.

A *vertical lift bridge* usually consists of a truss placed between two towers. Cables or levers connect the truss to counterbalancing weights, so that the power of a comparatively small motor is sufficient to raise the bridge straight up.

A *swing bridge*, erected on a turntable at its center, is sometimes preferred because it gives two channels, one on either side of the open bridge. When closed, a swing bridge is usually a simple truss, but the open bridge is a cantilever.

Viaducts, in the ordinary use of the term, are bridges carried across a valley or other low level, on towers. The towers may be high or low, and the spans are usually comparatively short.

A girder or truss bridge pushes down on its foundation piers, a suspension bridge pulls inward, and an arch pushes outward. A cantilever pushes down on its main pier, but may pull up on the anchorage. In addition to the *dead load* or weight of the bridge itself, the engineer must include in his calculations the *live load* which it is to carry, together with the added strain due to starting and stopping of trains, and a possible wind pressure of 30 or more pounds on each square foot of surface.

Canal Locks. Among the most important structures connected with a canal are the locks. These act as a step or as an elevator to raise or to lower a vessel from one water level to another. They are used where there is a change in the elevation of a canal.

An ordinary lock consists of a rectangular basin provided with heavy, water-tight gates at both ends. The sides of the lock and the top of the gates extend above the highest part of the canal. When the gates at one end are open, those at the other end must be closed in order to hold back the water.

When a vessel, traveling upstream, enters a lock, the gates are tightly closed behind it. Water is then admitted to the lock chamber, and the boat gradually rises until it reaches the upper level of the canal. The gates in front are then swung open, and the way is clear. To lower a vessel, the process is reversed, and the water flows from the lock until the lower level is reached.

Locks are occasionally constructed so that the entire chamber is raised or lowered. Sometimes two such chambers are connected and balanced so that one is raised when the other is lowered. In such cases only sufficient water is transferred to make the upper chamber slightly heavier than the other, so that the change in position is caused by gravity.

Dam. Any barrier used to stop the flow of a liquid is called a dam. In engineering, however, the term refers to a structure built across a watercourse, and provided with a spillway over which the water confined behind the wall can flow when it rises to the proper level.

By means of a dam, the depth of a shallow stream may be increased until it is sufficient for the passage of boats and barges; water can be stored for the use of municipalities, for manufacturing, or for irrigation; and power can be generated.

The design and construction of large dams requires a high degree of engineering skill because of the enormous pressure exerted by the water. This pressure depends not on the volume, but on the height, of the water held behind the dam. Each vertical foot of water imparts a pressure of .433 pounds on every square inch of surface, so that at the bottom of a dam where the water is 100 feet deep there is a pressure of 3.1 tons per square foot.

Few dams are more famous than that across the Nile river at Aswan. Since the dawn of civilization, the years of rich harvests and the periods of famine in the Nile valley have depended on the height to which the river would rise during the annual flood. The average rise has been about 25 feet; 30 feet meant destruction and ruin, while 18 feet meant poor crops and starvation. But now the reservoir behind the dam not only affords control of the river's flow, but supplies enough water to irrigate 6 million acres that formerly were desert.

Dams are built of timber, earth, concrete, masonry, and occasionally of steel. Earth dams frequently have a thin core of concrete, which prevents the water from trickling through the earth and ruining the dam. The center of the Gatun dam was pumped into place by hydraulic dredges which took up the mud from the river bottom and deposited it between walls of stone. The water drained away, leaving a very firm structure.

Automatic dams are frequently used on canals where it is desired to keep the water level as high as possible. Movable dams of the "bear-trap" type

SOME IMPORTANT DAMS OF THE WORLD

NAME	LOCATION	Completed	Type	Height Feet	Length on Top Feet	Width in Feet	
						Top	Base
Arrowhead	California	1909	Earth *	222	850	20	950
Arrowrock	Boise R., Idaho	1916	Concrete (a)	349	1,100	15½	238
Ashti	Ashti R., India	1878	Earth	58	12,709	6	182
Aswan	Nile R., Egypt	1934	Masonry	174	6,970	36	92
Barossa	South Australia	1903	Concrete (a)	112	472	4½	42
Bartlett	Verde R., Ariz.	1939	Multiple arch	287	750	20	1,700
Belle Fourche	South Dakota	1909	Earth	122	6,493	19	650
Bonneville	Columbia R., Wash., Ore.	1937	Concrete	170	1,282	40	180
Camarasa	Spanish Pyrenees	1920	Concrete	333	460	21	250
Cataract	Sydney N. S. W.	1908	Concrete (a)	192	811	16½	158
Cheoah	Little Tennessee R.	1918	Concrete	225	725	12	175
Cobble Mountain	Little R.,Springfield, Mass.	1930	Earth	245	700	50	1,505
Columbia	Susquehanna R., Pa.	1875	Timber	11	6,847	16	30
Conowingo	Susquehanna R.	1928	Concrete	105	4,700	22	105
Coolidge	Gila R., Arizona	1928	Multiple dome	251	550	4	20
Dalles, The	Columbia R., Oreg.-Wash.	1961	Concrete-Earth	260	8,875	..	...
Daniel-Johnson	Canada	1970	Multi-arch	703	4000		
Diablo	Skagit R., Rockport, Wash.	1930	Concrete arch	446	1,180	16	140
Dix River	Kentucky	1925	Rock-fill	278	1,020	20	650
Dnieprostroy‡	Dnieper R., Ukraine, Russia.	1932	Arch gravity	200	5,000	73	140
Don Pedro	Tuolumne R., Cal.	1923	Concrete	280	1,040	16	177
El Azucar	San Juan R., Mexico	1945	Earth	138	19,360	26	1,661
Elephant Butte	Rio Grande R., New Mex.	1916	Concrete (a)	305	1,310	18	215
Fort Peck	Missouri R., Mont.	1939	Earth *	242	20,000	13	2,875
Gatun	Panama	1913	Earth	105	7,800	400	2,600
Gilboa	Schoharie Creek, N. Y.	1926	Concrete, earth	160	2,300	15	158
Glen Canyon	Colorado R., Ariz.	1964	Concrete	710	1,550	25	340
Grand Coulee	Columbia R., Wash.	1942	Concrete	553	4,200	30	490
Grimsel	Central Switzerland	1930	Concrete gravity	373	656	15	224
Hetch Hetchy	Tuolumne R., Cal.	1922	Concrete	427	600	15	298
Hoover	Colorado R., Ariz. Nev.	1935	Concrete gravity	727	1,244	45	660
Kensico	White Plains, N. Y.	1917	Masonry	307	1,843	28	235
Keokuk	Miss. R., Keokuk, Ia.	1913	Concrete	53	4,649	29	42
Lake Cheesman	S. Platte R., Colo.	1904	Masonry	236	700	18	176
Morena	San Diego, Cal.	1909	Rock-fill	278	520	16	357
Norris	Clinch R., Tenn.	1936	Concrete	265	1,872	30	405
Necaxa No. 2	Necaxa R., Mex.	1911	Earth	190	1,220	54	975
New Croton	Croton R., N. Y.	1906	Masonry	297	1,168	18	206
Oahe	South Dakota	1958	Earth	242	9,360	..	...
Olive Bridge(Ashokan)	Esopus Creek, N. Y.	1913	Masonry	252	1,000	26	200
Owyhee	Owyhee R., Oregon	1932	Concrete	417	1,010	30	265
Pacoima	San Fernando, Cal.	1928	Concrete	372	640	10.4	100
Pardee	Mokelumne R., Cal.	1929	Concrete arch	358	1,337	..	241
Poona	India	1872	Masonry	108	5,136	14	61
Roosevelt	Salt R., Ariz.	1911	Masonry	280	1,125	16	158
Salt Spring	Mokelumne R.,Cal.	1932	Rock-fill	332	1,300	15	900
Saluda R.	S. Carolina	1930	Earth	208	7,838	25	1,150
Sautet	France	1934	Concrete arch	414	263	..	...
Seminoe	North Platte R.,Wyo.	1939	Concrete arch	261	560	15	85
Sennar	Nile R., Upper Egypt	1926	Masonry	130	9,915	15	50
Shasta	Sacramento R., Cal.	1945	Concrete gravity	602	3,500	..	...
Shoshone	Shoshone R., Wyo.	1910	Masonry	328	200	10	108
Sukkur	Indus R., India	1932	Masonry	185	4,725	..	...
Tansa	India	1891	Masonry	118	8,800	12	100
Tieton	Yakima project, Wash.	1925	Earth *	232	900	25	1,200
Wachusett	Nashua R., Mass.	1906	Masonry	228	1,476	25	187
Wilson Dam	Muscle Shoals, Ala.	1925	Concrete	137	4,860	..	105
Yellowtail	Big Horn River, Mont.	1965	Concrete	525	1,450	..	...

*With concrete core. ‡Destroyed by Russian army in 1941 to prevent use by invading Germans and later rebuilt.
(a) Called also cyclopean masonry, because, where possible, enormous boulders are set in the concrete.

are equipped at the top with hinged, floating leaves, which rise and fall with the water level so that the depth of flow over the dam is always about the same. On small structures the water usually flows directly over the top, but, in large dams, the excess water passes through control gates and over a spillway. The highest dam in the world is the Hoover dam at Black canyon in the Colorado river, which rises 727 feet above the river bed.

The multiple arch, hollow, concrete dam is a form of structure which is coming into extensive use. The ability of this type to withstand great water pressure depends on the strength of comparatively thin, concrete arches, rather than on the weight of massive walls. The same principle is involved in the multiple dome dam, consisting of concrete forms facing upstream, each one shaped like one quarter of an egg shell cut axially.

Cofferdams are water-tight enclosures open at the top and used where it is necessary to work in places that would ordinarily be covered with water. In order to examine the sunken battleship *Maine*, which lay in Habana harbor at a depth of about 37 feet, an oval cofferdam was built around the vessel so that the water could be pumped away.

Embankments placed parallel to the course of a stream so as to prevent the flooding of the surrounding country are known as *levees*.

The term *dike* originally referred to an artificial ditch or canal. Later, it was also applied to the mound of earth thrown up beside the excavation, and eventually to any embankment or wall, especially one used to prevent floods.

Jetties are dikes built, usually at the mouth of a river or harbor, to direct the flow of the tide or the river current in such a way as to scour out a deeper channel. One of the most important uses of jetties has been to make navigable the mouth of the Mississippi river. The longest jetty in the world, 42¾ miles in length, was built to preserve a channel at the mouth of the Columbia river.

Locomotive. The first locomotive used commercially in the United States was called the *Stourbridge Lion*. It was built in England and was put into service in 1829. The first to be built in America for commercial purposes was the *Best Friend*, which was manufactured for the Baltimore and Ohio railroad in 1830. It was destroyed by an explosion after about seven months of service. In 1831, the *De Witt Clinton* was put into operation. On its first run from Albany to Schenectady, a stretch of 17 miles, it covered the distance in 1 hour and 45 minutes, but the return trip was accomplished in 38 minutes. Its weight was 12,098 pounds, or less than that of a single pair of driving wheels on a standard Pacific type engine of today.

The chief improvements in the locomotive have been devices to secure greater pulling power and more efficiency. These purposes have been effected partly by the use of stronger boilers and *greater steam pressure*. Some locomotives now operate at a boiler pressure of 250 pounds per square inch. Certain ones in Germany have been constructed to use a pressure of 750 pounds. A second improvement has resulted from *superheating the steam*. Superheated steam acts as a gas under pressure and can do a certain amount of work without condensing. A third improvement has been the introduction of *compound cylinders*, by which the engine is changed from the simple to the expansion type. See *Steam Engine*.

Among the largest and most powerful steam locomotives in the world is one built for the Northern Pacific railroad in 1928. It is 175 feet long, weighs 500 tons, generates 6000 horse power and is capable of hauling on the level a train over two miles long. It is driven by two pairs of cylinders, each connected with eight drive wheels. Electric locomotives weighing 600 tons and having a length of 150 feet are not unusual. The greatest speed attained by a locomotive, is 112 miles per hour, which was made in 1893 by the New York Central engine number 999 while hauling the Empire State Express.

In 1937, there were about 47,000 locomotives operating in the United States. This represents a decrease from the maximum of 65,358 in 1924 and indicates a trend toward fewer and more powerful locomotives, but since 1944 there has been a great upsurge in the use of Diesel-electric motive power. In 1952 it handled 65.5 per cent of freight traffic, compared with 32.6 per cent for steam locomotives and 1.9 per cent for other locomotives. The same advance has been made in passenger traffic, with Diesels hauling 71.5 per cent of the traffic in 1952.

In recent years, there has been a conspicuous trend toward the electrification of railroads. In a test made at Erie, Pa., an electric locomotive was pitted against two large steam locomotives of the New York Central railway in a pushing contest. It was found that the electric locomotive was able, not only to stop the two steam locomotives, which had been allowed first to develop a high speed, but forced them backward against the full force of their driving power.

The ordinary electric locomotive takes its power from an electrified line. Some locomotives, however, develop their own electric power either from Diesel engines or from a steam turbine engine.

Locomotives designed for high speed are usually streamlined to reduce air resistance. The necessity of providing for locomotives and cars a level track over or through natural obstacles has set for civil engineers many of the most difficult problems they have had to solve. Most of the great bridges and tunnels of the world have been built for railways and have been among the greatest triumphs of civil engineering.

The following table shows the standard types of American steam locomotives:

Symbol*	Type	Special Use
0–6–0	6-wheel switcher	Switching
2–8–0	Consolidated . .	General freight
2–8–2	Mikado	General freight—sharp curves
2–10–0	Decapod . . .	Heavy freight
2–10–2	Santa Fe	Heavy freight—sharp curves
2–10–10–2	Mallet articulated†	Heavy freight
2–8–8–8–2	Mallet articulated triplex† . . .	Heavy freight
4–4–0	American . .	Passenger and freight
4–6–0	Ten-wheeler .	Passenger, fast freight
2–6–2	Prairie	Heavy passenger, fast freight
4–4–2	Atlantic . . .	High speed passenger
4–6–2	Pacific	Fast heavy passenger, fast freight
4–8–2	Mountain . . .	Heavy passenger

* The first figure in each entry indicates the number of smaller wheels under the front; the last figure denotes the number of trailing wheels under the rear; the intermediate figures indicate the number and the grouping of the driving wheels.

† In this type, the frame is jointed, or articulated, to facilitate the passing of curves.

Skyscraper. The first requirement of a modern skyscraper, and one of the most important, is a firm foundation. If possible, the foundation should rest on bed rock, but, where a heavy structure must be located over sand, soft clay, or peat, the difficulties of obtaining a solid foundation are often very great.

One of the most satisfactory methods is to drive piles through the soft earth until they reach solid rock. Or, if the ground is comparatively firm, a great number of piles may be driven until the total resistance of the earth to further settling of the piles is sufficient to carry the weight of the building. The Illinois Central Railway passenger station in Chicago is thus supported on about 1700 wooden piles, driven to a depth of from 40 to 60 feet by means of one-ton to two-ton drop hammers. In 1920, when an American firm received a contract to build modern steel office buildings in Japan, 13,000 piles of Oregon pine were shipped across the Pacific to form foundations in the city of Tokyo.

HIGHEST BUILDINGS AND TOWERS

Name and Location	Height in feet
Canadian National Tower, Toronto	1,815
Sears Tower, Chicago	1,454
World Trade Center, New York City	1,353
Empire State Building, New York City	1,250
Television Center, Moscow	1,179
Standard Oil Co. of Indiana Bldg., Chicago	1,136
John Hancock Center, Chicago	1,107
Chrysler Building, New York City	1,046
Eiffel Tower, Paris	984
60 Wall Tower, New York City	950
First Canadian Place, Toronto	935
40 Wall Tower, New York City	927
Bank of Manhattan, New York City	900
United California Bank, Los Angeles	858
Transamerica Pyramid, San Francisco	853
RCA Building, New York City	850
Water Tower Plaza, Chicago	850
U.S. Steel Building, Pittsburgh	841
One Chase Manhattan Plaza, New York City	813
John Hancock, Boston	812
Pan Am Building, New York City	808
First National Bank, Chicago	800
Woolworth Building, New York City	792
Gaspar Libero, São Paulo, Brazil	787
M. V. Lomonosov State University, Moscow	787
MLC Building, Sydney, Aus.	786
Commerce Court, Toronto	784
Bank of America, San Francisco	778
Canadian Imperial Bank of Toronto, Toronto	766
IDS Center, Minneapolis	752
Prudential Tower, Boston	750
Detroit Plaza Hotel, Detroit	748
U.S. Steel, New York City	743
City Bank Farmers Trust, New York City	741
Palace of Culture and Science, Warsaw	741
Toronto Dominion Bank, Toronto	740
Security Pacific, Los Angeles	738
Marine Midland Building, New York City	724
Peachtree Center Plaza Hotel, Atlanta	723
Exxon Building, New York City	720
First International, Dallas	710
Terminal Tower, Cleveland	708
Union Carbide Building, New York City	707
General Motors Building, New York City	705
One Penn Plaza, New York City	700
Metropolitan Life Building, New York City	700
One Shell Plaza, Houston	700
American Tobacco Building, New York City	700
500 Fifth Avenue, New York City	697
One Shell Square, New Orleans	697
IBM Building, Chicago	695
9 W. 57th Street, New York City	688
Chemical Bank New York Trust, New York City	687
McGraw-Hill Building, New York City	685
Chanin Building, New York City	680
Gulf and Western Building, New York City	679
55 Water Street, New York City	678
Lincoln Building, New York City	673
1633 Broadway, New York City	670
Atlantic Richfield Plaza (twin bldgs.), Los Angeles	667
National Bank of Tulsa, Tulsa	667
Civic Center (City Hall), Chicago	662
National Cathedral Tower, Washington, D.C.	660
Irving Trust Building, New York City	654
1100 Milam Building, Houston	651
One Astor Plaza, New York City	651
Ukraine Hotel (including tower), Moscow	650
American Brands, New York City	648
Lake Point Towers, Chicago	645
Burlington House, New York City	645
345 Park Avenue, New York City	634
Gateway Arch, St. Louis	630
1114 Avenue of the Americas, New York City	630
Home Insurance, New York City	630
Monsanto, New York City	630
One New York Plaza, New York City	630

Piles may be of wood, concrete, or steel. One of the most effective types consists of a hollow steel tube, driven with a pile driver. Earth and stones are blown out of the cylinder by compressed air, and the interior is filled with concrete.

When the piles are all in place, the tops are cut off at exactly the same height, and care must be taken that wooden piles are entirely below water level, because, when covered with water, wood is preserved almost indefinitely. The platform type of foundation usually consists of steel beams piled in layers to form a pyramid. Each layer is placed at right angles to that below, and all are covered with concrete.

To support the enormous weight of the skyscrapers of New York City, the foundations are sunk to bed rock by means of open cofferdams or closed pneumatic caissons. The caisson may be a huge timber box or steel cylinder, open at the bottom, but closed at a height of 8 or 10 feet so as to form a working chamber. Above the working chamber the caisson is filled with concrete, which is pierced by vertical shafts for the passage of men and materials. The top of each shaft is closed by an air lock, for, as the earth is removed at the bottom and the structure gradually sinks, the pressure of the air must be ra sed to prevent the surrounding water from flowing into the working chamber. When the edges of the caisson reach rock, the working chamber and shafts are filled with concrete, thus forming a solid pillar.

After the foundations have been completed, the steel skeleton is rapidly placed in position. First the massive columns are erected and bolted temporarily to the crossbeams that form the floor. At each floor the girders extend beyond the wall columns in order to form a short shelf, on which the wall for that floor is carried. Because of this arrangement, each floor supports its own wall. Floors are formed by brick or hollow tile arches, or by concrete slabs, placed between or over the beams.

Tunnel. The term tunnel, as generally used, refers to an artificial passageway, horizontal or nearly so, open at both ends, and constructed without removing the surface soil. Tunnels cut through solid rock with simple hand tools were built by many ancient nations, including the Egyptians, Assyrians, Greeks, Aztecs, Peruvians, and the natives of India. The oldest known tunnels were used as the entrance to a royal tomb or for religious purposes, but by 500 B. C. the Greeks were using tunnels for mining.

The Romans, who surpassed all previous nations as engineers, built tunnels for use as roads, aqueducts, sewers, and mine galleries, not only at Rome, but in what is now France, Switzerland, Spain, Portugal, Algeria, and Turkey. In order to drain Lake Fucinus, the emperor Claudius, about 52 A.D., completed a three-mile tunnel, 9 feet wide and 19 feet high. The Romans understood *fire setting*, which consists in first heating a rock surface by means of fires and then cooling it suddenly with water in order to produce cracks.

In the construction of large rock tunnels, small sections are first drilled and blasted out. These openings are then gradually enlarged to full diameter. In building the Connaught tunnel, a small pioneer tunnel, parallel to the main boring, was constructed first, so that, by cutting cross passages, work could be carried on in several sections at the same time. Of an entirely different type was the railroad tunnel under the river between Detroit, Michigan, and Windsor, Ontario. This tunnel was built on land in twenty sections having the form of enormous, hollow, steel cylinders. Each section was closed at both ends, floated into position, and then sunk to foundations which had been dredged on the river bed. The sections were joined, covered with concrete, and also given a concrete lining.

The first of the great transalpine tunnels, the Mont Cenis, was driven from both ends. The work was so accurate that, when the borings met after 13 years of labor, there was a difference in alignment of only one inch. During the construction of the St. Gotthard tunnel, conditions were so severe that 800 of the workers died. The Simplon tunnel, which now consists of two parallel tunnels 16½ feet in diameter, was most difficult of all. This tunnel passes through the mountains at a depth of 5000 to 7000 feet below the peaks. The pressure was so great that in places great steel beams were necessary to hold the rock walls in place. Cold springs at times poured as much as 17,000 gallons of water a minute into the first tunnel, and, near the center, hot springs were encountered which raised the temperature of the air to such a degree that it was necessary to spray the walls with cold water. The second tube was completed in 1921.

The many miles of tunnel under New York City represent one of the greatest achievements of engineering skill. The New York City extension of the Pennsylvania railroad, which crosses from New Jersey, under the Hudson river to the Pennsylvania terminal, and then under East river to Long Island, has a total length of only 13.68 miles. Yet the average cost of this short extension was almost 6 million dollars a mile. One of the chief engineering problems in the construction of the Holland vehicular tunnel was to provide proper ventilation. Powerful fans change the air completely 42 times each hour.

Construction of tunnels, such as the Pennsylvania and the Hudson and Manhattan tubes, through clay and silt, under a river bed, is much more difficult and dangerous than blasting through solid rock. The use of compressed air is often necessary in the head of the tunnel to balance the pressure of the surrounding water.

One of the greatest aids in soft ground tunneling is the *shield*, which is a short, hollow cylinder slightly larger in diameter than the tunnel. The forward end is closed and is provided with several strong doors through which the workman may pass to excavate, if the nature of the ground permits. The shield is pushed forward by hydraulic rams, and the cast-iron or concrete lining of the tunnel which is thus formed is constructed under the protection of the rear walls of the cylinder. Various unusual expedients are sometimes necessary. In tunneling through soft clay, huge torches have been used to bake the ground hard. In order to drive an opening through wet quicksand, the earth has been frozen by artificial refrigeration.

The largest tunnel in the world is the Rove, which forms a part of the canal between the Rhone river and Marseille, France. It is 4½ miles long and, with a height of 40 feet and a width of 72 feet, it is almost six times as large in cross section as an ordinary railroad tunnel.

The first transportation tunnel in the United States was a part of the Schuylkill Navigation canal, opened in 1821. The first railway tunnel in the United States was 901 feet long. It was constructed in Pennsylvania, between 1831 and 1833, for the Allegheny Portage railroad. Neither tunnel is now in existence.

SOME IMPORTANT TUNNELS OF THE WORLD

Name	Location and Use	Length Miles	Years in Construction	Approximate Cost
Appenine	Italy; Florence Bologna R. R.	11.5	1923–1928	$24,735,000
Arlberg	Austrian Alps; R. R.	6.23	1880–1884	7,500,000
Arthur's Pass	South Island, N. Z.; R. R.	5.38	1908–1912	3,000,000
Brooklyn-Battery	Brooklyn-Manhattan; under East R.; vehicular	1.72	1940–1950	80,000,000
Caldera	Peru, S. A.; R. R.	1.75	–1893	
Cascade	Cascade Mts., Wash.; Gt. N. R. R.	2.6	1897–1900	1,250,000
Cascade, New	Berne-Scenic, Wash.; R. R.	7.78	1925–1928	10,000,000
Choacella	Part of 240-mile Colorado River—Los Angeles aqueduct, costing $230,000,000	18.3	1933–1936	
City No. 1	New York City; Aqueduct	18.11	1911–1914	26,400,000
City No. 2	New York City; Aqueduct	20.0	1928–1932	42,700,000
Connaught	Selkirk Mts., B. C.; Can. Pac. R. R.	5.0	1913–1916	6,500,000
Detroit River	Detroit, Mich.—Windsor, Ont.; R. R.	1.6	1906–1910	10,000,000
Detroit International	Detroit, Mich.—Windsor, Ont.; vehicular	.95	1928–1930	10,000,000
Elizabeth Lake	Los Angeles Aqueduct, Cal.	5.1	1907–1911	1,088,000
Florence Lake	Southern Cal.; Aqueduct	12.8	1920–1925	17,000,000
Gravehals	Oslo—Bergen, Norw.; R. R.	3.3	1904–1909	
Great St. Bernard	Italy-Switzerland	3.6	–1964	35,000,000
Grenchenberg	Jura Mts., Switz.; R. R.	5.3	1912–1915	3,500,000
Gunnison	Montrose, Colo.; Aqueduct	5.8	1905–1909	2,170,000
Hetch Hetchy	San Francisco Aqueduct, Calif.	18.0	1920–1923	
Holland	New York—New Jersey; under Hudson R.; vehicular	1.75	1920–1927	48,400,000
Hoosac	Hoosac Mts., Mass.; R. R.	4.31	1856–1873	11,000,000
Hudson & Manhattan	New York City—New Jersey	8.50	1875–1911	75,000,000
Jungfrau	Swiss Alps; R. R.	4.47	1897–1912	1,375,000
Khojak Pass	Quetta-Chaman, India; R. R.	2.44	1889–1891	
Loetschberg	Bern-Brig, Swiss Alps; R. R.	9.05	1906–1913	10,000,000
Mersey	Liverpool-Birkenhead; vehicular	2.16	1925–1934	40,000,000
Moffat	James Peak., near Denver, Colo.; R.R.; water system	6.1	1922–1927	14,500,000
Mont Blanc	France-Italy	7.25	1959–1965	
Mont Cenis	France—Italy; R. R.	7.97	1857–1872	15,000,000
Mont d' Or	Jura Mts., France—Switz.; R. R.	3.8	1910–1915	4,060,000
Mt. Royal	Montreal, Can.; Can. North. R. R.	3.22	1910–1916	
Newhouse	Idaho Springs, Colo.; drainage and transportation	4.17	1893–1910	
N. Y. City Extension	New Jersey—Long Island; Penn. R. R.	11.7	1905–1910	100,000,000
Pirahy River	Rio de Janeiro, Brazil; Aqueduct	5.25	1911–1913	
Posey (Oakland-Alameda)	San Francisco bay; vehicular, trolley	.67	1926–1928	4,500,000
Ricken	Swiss Alps	5.35	1904–1910	2,500,000
Rothschönberg	Freiberg, Sax.; mine drainage	18.0	1844–1887	
Rove	On Rhone canal, France	4.5	1901–1927	27,000,000
Saint Gotthard	Switzerland—Italy; R. R.	9.33	1872–1882	11,500,000
Severn	England—Wales	4.36	1873–1886	
Shandaken	Gilboa—Allaben, N. Y.; Aqueduct	18.0	1919–1923	12,138,000
Simplon	Switzerland—Italy (Second tunnel built 1912–1921)	12.45	1898–1906	21,000,000
Sutro	Virginia City, Nev.; drain mines	3.79	1869–1878	
Tanna	Japan; under mountains for Tokkaido R. R.	4.85	1918–1932	
Tauern	Austrian Alps; R. R.	5.31	1901–1909	6,062,500
Tequixquiac	Drains City of Mexico	6.25	1880–1898	6,760,000
Transandine	Chile—Argentina	5.0	–1911	

MANUFACTURING

THE word manufacture is derived from the Latin *manus*, "hand," and *facere*, "to make." Literally, it means "made by hand." However, in modern usage, the term no longer imparts its intrinsic meaning, but almost invariably refers to the making of articles by power driven machinery rather than by hand-operated tools. This change in language is representative of far greater and more important changes in social and economic conditions, which were consequent to the Industrial Revolution that originated in England during the latter part of the 18th century.

For proper appreciation of the extraordinary effects of the Industrial Revolution, it is first necessary to consider the systems of manufacturing and the social conditions which this revolution displaced.

The Domestic System. Primitive manufacturing consists of the elemental processes involved in the preparation, for individual or family use, of food, shelter, clothing, ornaments, weapons, and tools. Manufacturing in the home, of products intended solely for domestic consumption, was customary in the earliest times of which there is any record. It was equally characteristic of the pioneers who settled the American West, and is always to be found where individual families must depend upon their own resources. The first advance in manufacturing practice came when some member of a household was able to produce a surplus of meal, cloth, leather, or other commodity, which could be sold outside of the home.

Origin of Handicrafts. Later, with the rise and development of large communities, specialization became possible. Men who were unusually skillful in building, weaving, metal working, or other handicraft were enabled to devote all their energies to their chosen occupations. Thus originated the numerous trades, such as those of carpenter, wheelwright, coppersmith, weaver, fuller, tanner, butcher, and baker. Eventually, the expert workers learned to combine for mutual benefit according to their distinctive handicrafts. Such combinations, which in Europe were known as craft guilds, gradually became very powerful and were able to exercise strict control over the individual members and their products.

As a rule, a master craftsman labored at home or in a shop connected with his dwelling place, carrying on his trade with the aid of apprentices and the help of journeymen who formed the intermediate grade of workers. His products were made to suit the demands of his customers, or were offered for sale to the public under regulations prescribed by the guild to which he belonged. The master generally owned his shop and tools, purchased his raw materials, changed them into the finished product, and disposed of the goods himself.

The Outwork System. The next step in the organization of manufacturing came with the growth of the outwork system. By this arrangement, raw materials owned by a merchant were distributed or "put out" among home workers, who made and returned the finished product and received payment for their labor. Under these conditions, the buying of raw materials and the selling of completed goods were controlled by the merchant. The workman, however, owned the tools required for production and was, to a certain extent, master of his time. He usually owned his home and a piece of ground, so that a shortage of work at his craft allowed him to give more time to his farm.

Hand Power and Machines. All of the foregoing systems of domestic production are still in existence. Bread is baked and clothing is made in many homes. And, frequently, a woman who has acquired unusual skill as a cook or as a seamstress devotes her spare time to preparing food or clothes for her neighbors.

In almost every town, carpenters, cabinetmakers, tinsmiths, blacksmiths, tailors, and many other skilled craftsmen are to be found working with their own tools and in their own workshops in order to fill custom orders. Panama hats, Turkish rugs, Navajo blankets, and the fine laces of Switzerland, Italy, and Ireland are still prepared by the painstaking action of skilled fingers. Nor has the outwork system been entirely discarded. In a modified form it is still the basis of modern, successful, merchandising concerns which sell knitting machines and yarn to home workers, and buy, for resale, all of the hosiery which they are able to produce. Nevertheless, all of the foregoing examples are exceptions to the general rule that, today, manufacturing is done in factories equipped with complicated, power driven machinery. This change from handwork to the factory system of production was the outstanding feature of the Industrial Revolution.

Manufacturing before 1780. In the chapter on the history of commerce, it has been shown that manufacturing, transportation, and commerce are interdependent and have developed together from the earliest historical times. When, by 1750, England had become the chief commercial nation of the world, the most important products of her industries were woolen textiles, fabricated to a large extent from the fleece of domestic sheep.

Cloth making was a domestic industry in which the wool was washed, carded, and spun into yarn by women. The processes in use differed from those employed in the days of ancient Greece only because the spinning wheel had been substituted for the distaff and spindle sometime during the 15th century. Almost every cottage contained a loom, on which the yarn was woven into cloth by the master of the house. The methods of weaving, like those of spinning, had changed very little for centuries, although in 1733 John Kay invented the "fly shuttle," which made the process much more easy and rapid.

As several spinners were required to keep a weaver supplied with yarn, the weavers were usually glad to make cloth from yarn "put out" by a merchant. In this way the workers were able to keep continuously occupied, while the merchant insured a steady supply of cloth with which to meet the increasing demands of commerce. Fulling and finishing of woolen fabrics were generally done in a fulling mill located on the banks of a stream.

Practically all other operations were performed in the homes, although occasionally a merchant would erect and equip a weaving shed wherein a considerable number of hired weavers could work together under his supervision. Production of cotton cloth was small, the finest cotton goods being imported from India.

In the iron industry, charcoal furnaces were still extensively used, although the practice of smelting with coke, as introduced by Abraham Darby about 1735, was gradually spreading. This new demand for coke stimulated production of coal. In operating the coal mines, Newcomen's engine was found to be valuable for pumping out water which accumulated in the tunnels and galleries. Power for the operation of slitting mills and for producing the air blast for furnaces was obtained by water wheels. For this reason, ironworks were usually located beside streams.

Economic Conditions. A review of the general economic conditions existing in England about 1763 shows that commerce was actively increasing, transportation was being facilitated by the construction of turnpikes and canals, capital was accumulating, and industrial production, while very important in the aggregate, represented the contributions from farm homes and from many small shops or works, quite widely dispersed throughout the land. The country as a whole was fundamentally agricultural.

Living conditions were comparatively stable, because, if unable to obtain employment at his trade, a skilled worker could generally depend upon his small farm for the necessities of life.

At home, England possessed what seemed to be an adequate supply of coal, iron ore, and wool; her colonies were capable of producing large quantities of cotton, sugar, and natural dyes. All of these raw materials are adapted to large scale operations, and, as the demands for commercial products continued to increase, the need for machinery and improved methods of production was commonly recognized.

Epoch-making Inventions. In 1767, James Hargreaves invented his spinning jenny, capable of spinning eight threads of cotton instead of one. Arkwright, a barber by trade, followed, in 1769, with the roll-drawing spinner, which operated by water power, and therefore became known as the water frame. This machine produced thread strong enough to be used for the warp of cotton cloth, but insufficiently fine for the higher grades of muslin.

Ten years later, Samuel Crompton combined the best features of the jenny and the roll-spinner in a new power machine which, because of its hybrid origin, he called a "mule." The mule established the muslin industry in England. It also made it possible to spin cotton thread faster than the weavers could change it into cloth on the hand looms.

Improvements in the speed of weaving began in 1785 when Edmund Cartwright, a clergyman, obtained a patent for a power loom. This machine at first was far from successful; in fact, a practicable power loom did not come into use until about 1803. The great demand for cotton, caused by the application of the power loom, could not have been supplied at a reasonable cost had not Eli Whitney, in 1793, invented his cotton gin, whereby cotton fiber could be quickly separated from the seeds. It is interesting to note that these great inventions were all concerned with the manufacture of cotton, rather than of woolen fabrics. The use of power for spinning and weaving wool did not become general for several years after the beginning of the 19th century.

Water Power and Steam. In order to use the new textile machinery, many cotton mills were erected in the northern parts of England, where water power was most available. But the necessity of locating beside a waterfall was removed by Watt's condensing engine, invented in 1765 and greatly improved in succeeding years. Steam boilers heated by coal fires became a source of unlimited power. As the cost of transporting coal was greater than that of moving textiles or other finished commodities, the coal fields gradually became the center of manufacturing industries.

The iron trade also was greatly stimulated by the use of coal and of steam power. For example, the annual production of iron was doubled within eight years after the substitution of the steam engine for water power as a source of the air blast required in smelting. In 1783, Henry Cort invented the grooved rolling mill, and, in the following year, introduced the puddling process for making wrought iron from pig iron.

Thus, in response to the demands of commerce for large quantities of cheap textiles, we find that, in the last half of the 18th century, machines were invented which permitted of an increased volume of production. Steam engines were developed to drive the machinery. Cort's inventions made possible a more extensive application of iron, and from the improved iron many new types of machines and more efficient engines were constructed.

Effects of the New Inventions. Manufacturing by machinery, in buildings especially designed for that purpose, required a far greater outlay of capital than was necessary to provide the simple tools used by manual laborers. Nevertheless, costs of production were so greatly reduced by this method that a development of the factory system was inevitable. The widespread domestic system practically disappeared, because necessity forced the workers to leave their rural homes and to concentrate near the factories. The laboring population was gradually transplanted from the land to the cities. Master craftsmen, skilled in all branches of their trade, were no longer needed. For the factory system of production depends upon the use of labor-saving machinery wherever possible, and upon a systematic division of any complete manufacturing process into the proper number of parts. Each succeeding step is then performed by a worker who is able to acquire a high degree of skill in the accomplishment of a single operation. Under this system, production increased enormously, old industries expanded, and new ones came into existence.

Automation. Industrial development since World War II has been marked by the rapid progress made by automation, a new word meaning the use of machinery or mechanical devices instead of men in a production system. By the use of electronic equipment, the flow and quality of production can be regulated and co-ordinated. Production principles found effective in speeding the output of war materials are now used in civilian industries. Machines can operate continuously at higher speeds and more efficiently than men, and they do not tire as men do.

New models of specialized automatic labor-saving machines are constantly being introduced into industrial plants engaged in the mass production of standardized products. Development of mechanical ways of moving and handling materials has likewise contributed to the reduction of labor engaged in these operations. By the wider use of automatic controls, or the control of machines by other machines, many industries are becoming self-regulated. Not only does automation save labor, but it makes possible a better quality product. High-speed electronic computers and data-processing machines have helped to cut down the large clerical forces formerly required for the important work of handling information.

Whether automation presents an opportunity for labor or is a threat to it remains to be seen. If our economy continues to expand, the new machines may, through increased production, create more jobs than they eliminate. It seems inevitable that some readjustments will be necessary, but, as Norbert Wiener remarked, automation wisely applied holds promise of "more human use of human beings."

Industrial Advantages. Europe became the workshop of the world, and, until 1894, England surpassed all other nations in manufacturing. The advantages which caused her superiority are worthy of note because they are those which, today, will insure the success of any properly directed manufacturing concern. England controlled a plentiful supply of cheap *raw materials*. Her *workers* were skillful and adaptable. Her methods of *production*, because of the many great inventions and the early adoption of the factory system, were the most efficient known. She had, in her colonies and also in continental Europe, a ready *market* for her finished goods. And, as a means of *distribution*, her highly skilled commercial organization was second to none.

British Industrial Centers. Textiles are, as they always have been, the chief product of British manufacture. Before the advent of machinery, wool was the principal fiber used, but, early in the 19th century, cotton took the lead. Cotton was first imported into England in 1298 for use in making candlewicks. By 1801, England produced more cotton goods than did all of continental Europe. Manchester became the cotton manufacturing center of the world. Leeds is now the center of the

British woolen industry, of the manufacture of ready-made clothing, and of leather. Leicester is renowned for the production of woolen hosiery, as Nottingham is for cotton hosiery and for machine-made net. Silk weaving and dyeing is located chiefly in Derbyshire.

The iron and steel industry in England is second in importance only to that of textiles. Blast furnaces and rolling mills are concentrated at Middlesbrough, Newport, and Barrow, while Birmingham and Sheffield have become world famous for their manufactures of fine steel and of steel products. An example of extreme specialization is Redditch, whence a large part of the world is supplied with needles and fishhooks. The greatest shipbuilding district in the world is located along the banks of the Clyde river. The heart of the British ceramic industry is at Burslem in north Staffordshire.

INDUSTRIAL GERMANY

Germany's industrial revolution did not begin until the formation of the empire in 1871. But, when once begun, the transformation from an agricultural to an industrial basis was the most rapid and complete ever known. In 1845 Germany mined less coal than either France or Belgium. In 1880, Spain had more steam tonnage than Germany. Even as late as 1882, more than one-fourth of the German textile workers operated under the domestic system. But, by 1895, over 90 per cent were employed in factories. In 1871, about 64 per cent of the population of Germany was rural, while 36 per cent lived in cities. During the succeeding 40 years the intensive development of manufacturing caused towns to grow rapidly while the rural population remained stationary. In 1910, 60 per cent of the people lived in cities.

Fuel and Iron. Germany possessed or controlled abundant supplies of iron and coal. Nevertheless, her iron ore, derived chiefly from Lorraine and Luxemburg, contained a high proportion of phosphorus and was thereby rendered unsuitable for the production of Bessemer steel. This difficulty was removed in 1878 when Thomas and Gilchrist invented their basic method of making steel, by which phosphorus is removed from the molten metal and retained in the slag. When finely ground, "Thomas slag" becomes valuable as a fertilizer, so that the invention stimulated both manufacturing and agriculture, and was of fundamental importance to Germany.

Chemical and Other Industries. The German dye and fine-chemical industry, although depending primarily on the by-products from the coke ovens, is quite widely distributed, with the chief factories located on waterways at Ludwigshafen, Leverkusen (near Cologne), Frankfort, Hochst, and Berlin. The heavy-chemical industry is centered about the potash beds of Stassfurt. The largest salt works in the country is at Schonebeck.

Most of Germany's electrical machinery is made at Berlin and Nuremberg. Porcelain is produced chiefly at Meissen, Zwickau, and Berlin. Crefeld rivals Lyon as a center of the silk industry. Shipbuilding is important at Stettin, Hamburg, Kiel, and Lubeck. Textile factories tend to concentrate near the coal fields, but the industry as a whole is scattered over the entire country. Chemnitz is called the Saxon Manchester. As a nation devoted to manufacturing, Germany's policy has been to produce highly finished goods in which the greatest proportion of the cost is due to the application of skilled labor.

OTHER EUROPEAN NATIONS

France. In France the innovations which had so quickly transformed industrial conditions in England were adopted with much less haste. In 1848, factory methods of production were not yet customary, and typical French manufacturing was done in private workshops or in small establishments. One of the chief reasons why steam power was not more quickly applied in France was an insufficient supply of coal.

The famous French steelworks at Le Creusot were founded by royal charter in 1782, but this enterprise was not financially successful until the management was taken over by the Schneider family in 1836.

Production of textiles and of clothing is the most important branch of French manufacturing. Roubaix, Tourcoing, Fourmies, Reims, and Amiens are the chief centers of the wool industry. Mulhausen, in Alsace, and Rouen lead in the production of cotton fabrics. Paris has become the center of the production of jewelry, perfumes, gloves, shoes, and porcelain. Lyon is at the heart of the great French silk trade. Saint Etienne is known for the production of silk ribbons; Troyes, for hosiery; and Grenoble, for kid gloves. Lille is the largest manufacturing city of the North.

Switzerland. Switzerland, with very little coal or iron, is distinctly a manufacturing country which is forced, by a shortage of raw materials, to produce highly finished articles, such as silks, fine shoes, watches, and intricate machinery. The famous Geneva watches are so named because Geneva is the commercial center of the watch trade. They are made chiefly in the towns of Le Locle, La Chaux de Fonds, Bienne, Saint Imier, and Porrentruy. A shoe factory at Schonenwerd, near Olten, is said to be the largest in Europe. Saint Gallen is noted for the production of embroidered linen. Zurich and Basel are centers of the silk industry. Electricity generated by water power is extensively employed, notably in the production of aluminum at Rheinfelden.

Belgium. This country, where both coal and iron are available, was the only section of Europe which was able to follow the industrial pace set by England during the first half of the 19th century. Liege is one of the most successful metallurgical and manufacturing cities in Europe. It is famous for the production of all types of steel products, especially firearms. The production of textiles is even more important than that of steel and machinery. Cotton manufacturing is centered at Ghent, the making of linen at Ghent and Tournay, and the spinning and weaving of wool at Verviers.

Scandinavia. Sweden and Norway are noted for the production of wood pulp, matches, and paper, and for their electrochemical industries. In Norway electricity is used to manufacture large amounts of nitrogenous fertilizer at Odde, Notodden, and Sarpsborg. Stockholm, Goteborg, and Norrkoping are the chief industrial towns of Sweden. Perhaps the most famous manufactured product is the pure Swedish iron, reduced from domestic ore with charcoal from the extensive forests.

Czechoslovakia. This nation possesses a better supply of coal than of iron. Bohemia, however, is noted for its iron industry and especially for the manufacture of fine glassware, of which Eger is the center of production. Small articles of glass, such as buttons, beads, and imitation jewels are produced in enormous quantities at Gablonz.

Western Europe was the most important manufacturing district in the world. In 1880 the United Kingdom led all the other nations in this branch of industry, but by 1894 the United States assumed first place.

The highly developed production in Czechoslovakia far exceeds its domestic needs, and agricultural products, led by sugar, provide raw materials of great importance to its industry. The beer industry is world famous as are the spirits, malt and foodstuff industries. Metallurgical industry thrives here because of the abundant supply of iron ore and coal. Output of steel in 1970 was approximately 11 million metric tons (1 metric ton = 1.02 short tons). The Skoda steel works at Pilsen are among the largest in Europe. Other industries are glass, porcelain, pottery making, timber, paper and cellulose industries.

MANUFACTURING STATISTICS BY STATES, 1972

States	All employees		Production workers			Value added by manu- facture million dollars
	Number (average for the year) 000 omitted	Salaries and wages, total million dollars	Number 000 omitted	Man- hours, total millions	Wages total million dollars	
Alabama.	323	2,397	262	519	1,731	5,065
Alaska	8	75	6	12	57	170
Arizona	94	855	62	121	482	1,880
Arkansas	181	1,152	150	298	853	2,800
California	1,546	15,483	1,020	1,975	8,430	31,195
Colorado	133	1,298	89	177	770	2,504
Connecticut	399	3,860	258	521	2,069	6,828
Delaware	69	755	38	74	304	1,292
Dist. of Columbia. . .	19	215	9	16	92	376
Florida	343	2,750	242	482	1,581	5,787
Georgia	468	3,336	369	738	2,243	7,386
Hawaii	25	191	18	33	114	410
Idaho	43	340	34	66	245	821
Illinois	1,306	12,801	901	1,780	7,675	25,849
Indiana	704	6,882	526	1,042	4,641	14,112
Iowa	216	2,039	157	311	1,355	4,758
Kansas	137	1,181	101	203	783	2,915
Kentucky	259	2,160	200	393	1,480	5,682
Louisiana	179	1,601	134	275	1,072	4,273
Maine	100	699	83	162	513	1,383
Maryland	256	2,386	176	346	1,428	4,707
Massachusetts	619	5,486	416	812	3,027	10,678
Michigan	1,076	12,745	768	1,583	8,095	23,376
Minnesota	302	2,889	196	383	1,555	5,524
Mississippi	200	1,302	167	332	959	2,825
Missouri	434	3,897	300	584	2,305	8,169
Montana	21	185	17	34	138	463
Nebraska	85	704	63	128	469	1,733
Nevada	10	92	7	14	57	208
New Hampshire . . .	90	663	68	131	414	1,279
New Jersey	836	8,107	547	1,071	4,354	16,409
New Mexico	24	157	17	33	96	358
New York	1,679	16,222	1,076	2,068	8,174	30,404
North Carolina . . .	744	4,929	604	1,211	3,427	11,015
North Dakota . . .	10	79	7	14	48	201
Ohio	1,346	13,810	940	1,888	8,717	27,171
Oklahoma	143	1,188	96	186	659	2,270
Oregon	179	1,627	142	271	1,170	3,490
Pennsylvania	1,418	12,794	1,015	1,954	7,886	23,519
Rhode Island.	118	888	91	174	566	1,764
South Carolina	345	2,345	283	582	1,679	4,966
South Dakota . . .	17	135	13	25	89	285
Tennessee	467	3,352	367	725	2,295	7,662
Texas	736	6,345	517	1,031	3,763	15,259
Utah	57	486	39	74	287	1,069
Vermont	37	311	26	52	176	576
Virginia	375	2,826	293	583	1,902	6,178
Washington	226	2,308	160	303	1,411	4,721
West Virginia	121	1,098	93	182	765	2,647
Wisconsin	501	4,722	361	721	3,063	9,443
Wyoming	7	57	5	10	39	144
Total	19,029	174,206	13,528	26,699	105,502	353,994

Source: *Statistical Abstract of the United States, 1975.*

Industry	All Employees		Production Workers		Value added by manufacture (millions)
	Number (000 omitted)	Payroll (millions)	Number (000 omitted)	Wages (millions)	
Food and kindred products	1,553	$14,788	1,075	$9,196	$44,948
Tobacco manufactures	67	604	58	477	3,179
Textile mill products	933	6,684	813	5,195	13,199
Apparel and related products	1,317	7,642	1,147	5,793	14,926
Lumber & products, exc. furniture	675	5,490	583	4,294	11,561
Furniture and fixtures	459	3,570	381	2,577	6,983
Paper and allied products	646	6,995	507	4,995	18,957
Printing and publishing	1,076	11,139	639	6,131	23,610
Chemical and allied products	866	10,547	542	5,697	44,488
Petroleum and coal products	146	1,920	101	1,241	9,951
Rubber products	661	6,203	523	4,303	14,826
Leather and leather products	256	1,604	223	1,229	3,120
Stone, clay and glass products	637	6,414	508	4,720	14,566
Primary metal industries	1,248	15,900	1,001	12,102	37,297
Fabricated metal products	1,575	16,570	1,208	11,469	35,221
Machinery, except electrical	2,126	24,713	1,497	15,431	52,495
Electrical machinery	1,776	18,093	1,242	10,509	36,902
Transportation equipment	1,738	22,609	1,250	14,554	44,973
Instruments and related products	524	5,560	338	2,851	13,627
Miscellaneous manufactures	435	3,477	337	2,254	7,667
All industries, total	19,844	$208,312	13,927	$124,977	$452,497

Source: Bureau of the Census, *Annual Survey of Manufactures, 1974*, "General Statistics for Industry Groups and Industries."

MANUFACTURING CORPORATIONS—RELATION OF PROFITS TO SALES: 1960—74
(Averages of quarterly figures at annual rates, after taxes.)

Industry Group	Profits per dollar of sales (in U.S. cents)			
	1960	1965	1970	1974
Total	**4.4**	**5.6**	**4.0**	**5.5**
Durable goods[1]	**4.0**	**5.7**	**3.5**	**4.7**
Motor vehicles and equipment	5.9	7.2	2.6	2.6
Aircraft and parts	1.4	3.3	2.0	3.0
Electrical machinery, equip., & supplies	3.5	4.8	3.3	3.9
Machinery, except electrical	3.9	6.2	4.6	6.0
Fabricated metal products	2.4	4.5	3.0	4.6
Primary iron and steel	5.1	5.7	2.5	6.3
Primary nonferrous metal	5.4	7.3	6.2	7.0
Stone, clay, and glass products	6.6	5.9	3.6	4.4
Furniture and fixtures	2.1	3.7	2.5	(NA)
Other lumber and wood products	1.7	4.0	2.5	(NA)
Instruments and related products	5.9	8.6	7.3	9.2
Misc. manufacturing, inc. ordnance	3.5	3.8	3.4	(NA)
Nondurable goods[1]	**4.8**	**5.5**	**4.5**	**6.4**
Food and kindred products	2.3	2.7	2.5	2.8
Tobacco manufactures	5.5	5.9	5.8	9.1
Textile mill products	2.5	3.8	1.9	2.5
Apparel and related products	1.4	2.3	1.9	(NA)
Paper and allied products	5.0	4.9	3.4	7.1
Printing and publishing	3.6	4.8	4.2	4.7
Chemicals and allied products	7.5	7.9	5.9	8.4
Petroleum refining	9.9	11.1	9.3	12.6
Rubber and misc. plastic products	3.6	4.3	2.7	5.0
Leather and leather products	1.6	2.8	2.5	(NA)

NA—Not available. [1] Includes industries not shown separately. Source: *Statistical Abstracts 1975*.

MANUFACTURING IN THE UNITED STATES

The development of successful manufacturing requires, among other things, an adequate supply of capital and of labor, a steady market for the finished products, and regular means of transportation. None of these was available in the American colonies during the early period of their existence. Furthermore, almost all of the colonies were founded as commercial enterprises which were expected to serve their promoters and the homeland by becoming a source of raw materials and a market for manufactured goods.

First Colonial Manufactures. In the early colonial days of America, each home was of necessity self-sufficient. Grain was ground, wool was spun and woven, and hides were tanned only in order to supply the needs of the family. However, as the population increased and towns developed, these industries were divided among the members of each community. Each settlement was soon furnished with mills for grinding grain, for sawing lumber, and for the fulling and finishing of woolen cloth. Tanneries, also, were erected in many communities. The first sawmill was built at Dorchester (Mass.) in 1628. The first New England tannery was located at Lynn in 1629, and the manufacture of shoes was begun there in 1635.

Expansion of New England Industry. The American colonies as a group were essentially agricultural. But, in New England, where the land was not well adapted to farming, a large proportion of the settlers were forced to gain a livelihood by other means. Fishing, which, from the first, was an industry of primary importance, gave rise to a demand for ships. The finest materials with which to construct ships were available in the forests, and shipbuilding soon became one of the chief industries.

From fishing and shipbuilding, the New Englanders quite naturally advanced to maritime trade, which was carried on at first chiefly with the West Indies. These islands were glad to exchange their surplus sugar and molasses for salt fish and lumber. Thus, in addition to purely local manufacturing industries which sprang up in all of the settlements, New England developed others which were based on the necessity of equipping the ships, supplying food for the sailors, providing cargoes for export, and utilizing the commodities that were imported.

A ropewalk to supply vessels with cordage was erected in Boston in 1641, and, at many places along the coast, salt for the preservation of meat and fish was prepared by evaporating sea water over wood fires. Bakers found employment in shops devoted to the production of sea biscuit, or hard-tack. Rum was so extensively used on shipboard that the expense for liquor issued regularly to sailors was generally as great as the cost of their bread, and the production of rum by fermenting and distilling the West Indian molasses became a thriving New England industry. Since practically all commercial commodities, whether liquid or solid, were packed and shipped in barrels, the manufacture of barrels and barrel staves, buckets, and similar forms of cooperage from the white oak of New England became exceedingly profitable.

Ironworks. Iron was sorely needed in the colonies, not only to provide ships with anchors, bells, cannon, and shot, but also to supply the population with nails, hardware, cooking utensils, iron barrel hoops, and similar products. The earliest successful attempt to meet the demand was made at Lynn, Massachusetts, where a company organized by the son of Governor Winthrop erected a blast furnace in 1644. The first product from the furnace was a cast-iron kettle of about one quart capacity, made in 1645. In 1648 a refining forge was added to the equipment, so that refined iron products then became available. The making of nails, hammered from rods of iron obtained from slitting mills, was a domestic industry almost as widespread as the production of textiles

Growth of Manufacturing. The colonial population, which in 1640 numbered 25,000, increased to one million during the succeeding century, and amounted to 2¼ million in 1775. Manufacturing developed at a corresponding rate. Iron furnaces and refining forges became almost as common as sawmills, gristmills, and fulling mills. The abiilty of the colonial foundrymen is shown by the fact that in 1753 they melted and recast the bell for the Pennsylvania statehouse, which afterward became famous as the Liberty Bell. Four of the signers of the Declaration of Independence were financially interested in the iron industry. The Washington family owned a one-twelfth interest in the Principio ironworks of Maryland.

England encouraged the manufacture of pig iron, but passed laws against the production of steel and steel products, as well as that of other articles which competed with British industry. Although these prohibitory laws checked the growth of manufacturing industries, enforcement of them was found to be almost impossible except in the vicinity of the larger cities where the crown officers were stationed.

The Revolutionary War greatly stimulated American manufacturing, because raw materials accumulated and the supply of English products, on which the country had largely depended, was cut off. Necessity caused the growth of various industries. But, when peace was concluded, English manufacturers flooded the country with their products at prices so low that many American concerns were ruined.

Textiles. Competition of American made cloth with that of British manufacture was especially difficult, because the colonies were at first unable to utilize the newly invented textile machinery. England not only prohibited the exportation of designs or models of the machines, but even endeavored to prevent the emigration of mechanics skilled in the industry. However, in 1789, Samuel Slater, who had been employed in Arkwright's factory, came to America. He went first to Philadelphia, where a comparatively large amount of cotton spinning was carried on. Failing to interest the manufacturers in that city, he went to New York and then to Rhode Island, where, in 1790, on the falls of the Pawtucket river, he built for Moses Brown the first power driven cotton spinning mill in the United States. Andrew Jackson called Slater the "father of American manufacturers."

In 1805, there were only four cotton mills in America. But the passing of the Embargo act of 1807, followed by the Nonintercourse act and the War of 1812, prevented foreign commerce and again stimulated manufacturing. Twelve new spinning mills were opened in 1808; in 1811, spindles to the number of 80,000 were in use, and 10,000 bales of cotton were spun; in 1815, the spindles numbered 500,000. In 1814, Francis Cabot Lowell devised a power loom similar to those which he had seen while visiting England, and erected at Waltham, Massachusetts, the first complete cotton factory in the world. Practically all power mills were located on waterfalls, although steam engines came into use as a source of power after 1810. Most of the early mills obtained their cotton from the West Indies, because the Southern states marketed their product in Liverpool.

Tariffs and Railroads. At the close of the War of 1812, British manufactures were for a second time thrown on the American market at prices which brought disaster to many growing industries. After 1816, these industries received protection through a series of tariff acts, and manufacturing again expanded.

Even more important than the tariff, however, in its influence upon manufactures, was the development of railroads. The iron industry was directly affected, because the railroads proved to be the greatest consumers of iron products. Iron T rails were first rolled in 1844, in Maryland. Bessemer steel was first made on a commercial scale in 1864; in the following year, the Chicago Rolling Mills produced the first American Bessemer steel rails. Besides thus stimulating iron and steel manufactures, through enlarging the market for their products, the railroads promoted many types of industry by furnishing the necessary means for the interchange of goods between manufacturing centers and distant agricultural regions. The cotton growing South and the rapidly expanding agricultural regions of the West afforded rich markets where the demand for manufactured products seemed unlimited. By 1860 the annual production of agricultural implements alone amounted to $17.8 million.

Inventions and Industrial Progress. While the development of such agricultural machinery as the McCormick reaper added greatly to the farmers' ability to raise grain on a large scale, many other great inventions opened the way for new forms of manufacturing. (See table of *Modern Inventions*.) To choose a single example, the invention of the sewing machine laid the foundation for the great modern clothes making industries, and, when the machine was developed, it revolutionized the process of making shoes.

Manufacturing after the Civil War. During the Civil War, the lack of the customary supply of raw material from the Southern states checked the production of cotton goods, although other branches of manufacturing were unusually active. The coming of peace introduced an era of industrial progress in which large scale production was developed to a degree never before attained, and the United States advanced steadily to first rank among manufacturing nations. In 1820, America produced only 2 per cent of the world's pig iron; a century later the proportion had increased to 54 per cent.

GREAT MANUFACTURING INDUSTRIES

Group and Important Divisions	Value Added[1]
Machinery (except electrical)	$52,494,900,000
Construction, Related Machinery	8,886,900,000
Metalworking Machinery	7,395,900,000
General Industrial Machinery	7,147,100,000
Office and Computing Machines	7,141,100,000
Special Industry Machinery	5,071,600,000
Refrigeration and Service Machinery	4,715,300,000
Farm and Garden Machinery	4,214,000,000
Transportation Equipment	44,973,300,000
Motor Vehicles and Equipment	22,300,700,000
Aircraft and Parts	12,459,900,000
Guided Missiles, Space Vehicles[2]	4,314,600,000
Ship, Boat Building and Repairing	3,061,300,000
Food and Kindred Products	44,947,500,000
Beverages	7,583,600,000
Meat Products	5,986,900,000
Preserved Fruits and Vegetables	5,416,700,000
Bakery Products	5,385,500,000
Grain Mill Products	4,942,400,000
Dairy Products	4,823,600,000
Chemicals, Allied Products	44,488,100,000
Industrial Organic Chemicals	9,384,200,000
Drugs	7,269,100,000
Plastic Materials, Synthetics	7,086,400,000
Soaps, Cleaners, Toilet Goods	7,072,700,000
Primary Metal Industries	37,297,300,000
Blast Furnace, Basic Steel Products	20,060,800,000
Nonferrous Rolling and Drawing	6,291,500,000
Iron and Steel Foundries	4,724,200,000
Electric, Electronic Equipment	36,901,500,000
Communication Equipment	9,978,900,000
Electronic Components, Access	6,963,000,000
Electrical Industrial Apparatus	4,532,400,000
Electric Lighting, Wiring Equipment	3,946,600,000
Fabricated Metal Products	35,221,000,000
Fabricated Structural Metal Products	9,153,300,000
Metal Forgings and Stampings	6,356,400,000
Misc. Metal Products	6,006,300,000
Cutlery, Handtools and Hardware	3,616,600,000
Metal Cans, Shipping Containers	2,986,000,000
Printing and Publishing	23,610,300,000
Newspapers	7,044,900,000
Commercial Printing	6,627,600,000
Books	3,009,400,000
Periodicals	2,435,800,000
Paper and Allied Products	18,957,200,000
Misc. Converted Paper Products	5,781,200,000
Paperboard Containers & Boxes	4,800,200,000
Apparel, Other Textile Products	14,925,800,000
Women's Outerwear	4,700,000,000
Men's Furnishings	3,703,300,000
Rubber, Misc. Plastics Products	14,826,200,000
Misc. Plastics Products	8,106,600,000
Tires and Inner Tubes	3,065,000,000
Stone, Clay, Glass Products	14,566,000,000
Concrete, Gypsum, Plaster Products	4,353,300,000
Misc. Nonmetal Mineral Products	3,065,000,000
Instruments, Related Products	13,627,400,000
Photographic Equipment, Supplies	5,075,000,000
Measuring, Controlling Devices	3,656,200,000
Textile Mill Products	13,199,000,000
Knitting Mills	3,268,900,000
Weaving Mills, Handmade Fiber	2,192,300,000
Lumber and Wood Products	11,561,200,000
Sawmills and Planing Mills	3,736,600,000
Millwork, Plywood, Struc. Mills	2,764,000,000
Petroleum and Coal Products	9,951,100,000
Petroleum Refining	8,363,500,000
Misc. Manufacturing Industries	7,666,500,000
Toys and Sporting Goods	2,285,900,000
Furniture and Fixtures	6,983,400,000
Household Furniture	4,249,000,000
Tobacco Products	3,179,100,000
Cigarettes	2,689,100,000
Leather, Leather Products	3,120,200,000
Footwear	1,859,600,000

[1] 1974 figures. [2] Not including government owned.
Source: *Annual Survey of Manufactures 1974.*

Distribution of Manufacturing. As the preceding table shows what manufactures in the United States have the greatest annual value, the next point of interest is, "Where are these industries chiefly located?" Inspection of the table, *Manufacturing Statistics by States*, shows that 40 states each had in 1972 an annual production exceeding $1 billion in value. To these states is to be credited over 95 per cent of all national manufactures.

According to the Bureau of the Census, the first census of manufactures covered the year 1809, and was then taken at ten-year intervals up to 1899. From 1904 to 1919 it was taken every five years, and from 1921 to 1939 every other year. The 1947 census of manufactures was the first since 1939. Present legislation provides for a complete census covering 1953 and every fifth year thereafter. An annual survey is part of this program.

Localization of Manufacturing. Economic factors such as raw materials, supply of power and labor, markets, and distribution facilities usually determine the location of manufacturing industries. Cotton and woolen mills require a moist atmosphere, while other industries depend on skilled labor or raw material supply. Water power and access to cheap coal were formerly major factors in attracting industry. Due to electric power today and its easy transmission, power requirements no longer force industries into certain areas. The West Coast today, with only 4 per cent of American industry, promises a future because of climate, availability of hydroelectric power, and future market demands.

Westward Movement of Industry. As the center of American population has moved westward, it has been followed, although with less speed, by the center of manufacturing. The early settler in the "West" obtained his ax, spade, and kettles from New England. Today the Western farmer obtains his plow or thresher from Illinois. The center of production of flour and gristmill products has moved from New York to Minnesota. Here the mills are close to the great wheat producing areas, power is available, and markets are easily accessible. Slaughtering and meat packing, which, as a separate industry, originated in Cincinnati about 1818, is now centered in Chicago. Kansas City, Kansas, ranks second in this industry, with Omaha, Nebraska, third. In these locations, the industry is close to the Western cattle raising area, its source of raw material.

Manufacturing in the South. One of the most notable developments connected with American manufacturing progress has been that of the production of cotton goods in the Southern states. North Carolina and South Carolina both rank in value of cotton manufactures above Massachusetts, which in 1920 was easily the leader. In 1880, North Carolina, South Carolina, and Georgia, together produced only 6.2 per cent of American cotton products. In 1910, their combined output equaled 29.7 per cent, and, in 1939, 58.8 per cent, of the total. In the production of iron and steel also the South is advancing steadily. A process by which paper may be made from slash pine grown in the South is the basis of an expanding industry. Large increases in chemical and other industries requiring cheap power took place as the result of the development of the Tennessee Valley, begun in 1933 under government initiative.

Easy access to raw materials and the shortage of energy supplies have been leading causes of the migration of certain industries to the South. The hope of obtaining labor at low wages was an important motive until government studies revealed that wage differences between the North and South had leveled out.

GROWTH AND SPECIALIZATION OF INDUSTRY

The 20th century witnessed a remarkable increase in specialization and an extraordinary rise in industrial efficiency. These were largely the result of the application of inventive genius and scientific research to the problems of production. Of chief importance was the exploitation of the possibilities in electricity as a means of transmitting power.

The Electrical Age. Power in the form of electricity can be used *when* and *where* it is wanted far more readily than power delivered directly from steam engine or water wheel. It facilitates the ready and precise control of machine processes, thereby making possible an increasing use of automatic machinery. In the first quarter of the 20th century electrification in American industry rose from 4 per cent to 70 per cent. It later became almost universal. Electricity used in factories but developed in central stations increased from 182,562 horse power in 1899 to 15,868,828 horse power in 1925—87 fold. The result has been a pronounced growth in production accomplished by a decreasing number of workmen. Wages have risen, yet many manufactured articles have become cheaper. At the same time, by making power available at long distances from its generating source, electricity has obviated the need for locating industries in centers of congested population. New industrial communities may be semirural in character, with marked improvement in living conditions.

The marked advance in the field of electric energy production in the United States is shown by the fact that the total production in 1950 was 389 billion kilowatt hours, while in 1970 it had risen to 1,640 billion. Production by the type of prime mover used in 1970 was hydro 247 billion KWh, steam 1,262 KWh, gas turbine 16 billion KWh, and internal combustion 6 billion KWh. Fuel consumed in the production was coal 321 million tons, oil 336 million barrels, and gas 3,932 billion cubic feet. By far the greater proportion of this energy was supplied by privately owned public utilities. The total number of power-generating plants in 1970 was 3,519, of which 1,183 were hydro, 1,009 were steam, 321 were gas, and 1,006 were internal combustion.

Specialization and Mass Production. The automobile industry and possibly the assembly line methods of shipbuilding and plane construction in World War II are the best examples of specialization and mass production. Operations are analyzed into their simplest constituent parts and each of these is performed by a worker, with or without a special machine. His work is confined, mechanical, and highly specialized.

MANUFACTURING, EMPLOYMENT AND VALUE ADDED—PER CENT DISTRIBUTION, BY GEOGRAPHIC DIVISIONS: 1947 TO 1972

Item	1947	1950	1954	1958	1963	1967	1970	1972
Employment								
New England	10.3	9.8	9.0	8.7	8.4	8.1	7.6	7.2
Middle Atlantic	27.7	26.9	26.6	25.7	24.0	22.6	21.8	20.7
East North Central	30.2	30.0	28.6	26.6	26.4	26.7	26.0	25.9
West North Central	5.5	5.6	6.0	6.0	6.0	6.2	6.2	6.3
South Atlantic	10.7	11.1	11.0	11.8	12.5	12.9	13.6	14.4
East South Central	4.4	4.4	4.5	4.9	5.2	5.7	6.1	6.6
West South Central	3.9	4.0	4.5	5.0	5.1	5.6	6.1	6.5
Mountain	1.0	1.1	1.1	1.4	1.7	1.6	1.8	2.0
Pacific	6.4	7.0	8.8	10.0	10.6	10.6	10.3	10.4
Value Added								
New England	9.2	8.3	7.8	7.4	7.1	7.2	6.8	6.4
Middle Atlantic	28.0	26.2	26.0	24.6	22.6	21.9	21.4	19.9
East North Central	31.6	33.2	31.2	28.9	29.3	28.6	27.5	28.2
West North Central	5.5	5.7	6.1	6.3	6.1	6.4	6.9	6.7
South Atlantic	9.3	9.4	9.1	10.1	11.0	11.2	11.8	12.5
East South Central	3.9	3.8	4.0	4.5	4.8	5.2	5.7	6.0
West South Central	4.1	4.3	4.9	5.5	5.7	6.3	6.7	7.0
Mountain	1.1	1.2	1.2	1.6	1.8	1.7	1.9	2.1
Pacific	7.5	7.9	9.7	11.1	11.5	11.3	11.1	11.3

Source: *Statistical Abstracts 1975.*

New Industries and Research. Through the expenditure of many millions of dollars on organized scientific research, industrial firms have evolved or perfected many important new materials and new products which have become the basis of new industries. Examples are the camera, synthetic lacquer, the radio, and a cheap method of producing aluminum. The electrical, rubber, and automobile industries have risen in the 20th century from very small beginnings to gigantic proportions, automobiles reaching the first place among American industries in 1925. Synthetic nitrates, rayon, and airplanes have likewise forged ahead under the powerful stimulus of well-directed research.

Manufacturing and Agriculture. In 1899, one out of every 16 persons in the United States, or 6.2 per cent of the population, was employed in manufacturing. The proportion increased moderately thereafter whereas the proportion of persons engaged in agriculture steadily declined. Not only, therefore, is manufacturing becoming more important because of the largely enhanced value of its product, but it produces a growing proportion of the total output of the country's industries, and it employs an increasing percentage of the working population. This condition became almost inevitable when the last of the rich American agricultural lands were settled. Fear is frequently expressed that manufacturing is making progress at the expense of agriculture. For any given locality this may at times be true, but, considered more broadly, manufacturing and agriculture must develop together. The great industrial cities could not exist for more than a day, or at most a week, if their incoming supply of food should be cut off, while the agriculturist, who finds his chief market in the industrial centers, would be unable to produce and distribute his crops if he did not have the advantages afforded by countless factory products.

The situation has been further affected by the recent enormous increase in the population of the United States, which between the 1950 and 1960 censuses increased nearly 28 millions, the greatest rise in the nation's history.

MANUFACTURES—STATISTICS FOR STANDARD METROPOLITAN AREAS WITH 40,000 OR MORE MANUFACTURING EMPLOYEES, 1973

Source: *Bureau of Census; 1973 Census of Manufactures*

STANDARD METROPOLITAN STATISTICAL AREA*	Rank	Establishments[4]	All employees[1] Number	All employees[1] Payroll $million	Value added by Manufacture[2] $million	Capital Expenditure new[3] $million
Akron, Ohio	54	991	96,200	1,094.4	1,926.9	148.7
Albany-Schenectady-Troy, N.Y.	43	732	68,000	713.6	1,459.0	73.7
Allentown-Bethlehem-Easton, Pa.-N.J.	59	1,118	113,500	1,083.5	2,185.3	176.1
Anaheim-Santa Ana-Garden Grove, Calif.	19	2,820	144,300	1,536.9	3,085.7	149.6
Atlanta, Ga.	18	2,259	134,700	1,257.1	2,906.0	144.4
Baltimore, Md.	14	2,026	184,900	1,907.9	3,873.9	233.1
Binghamton, N.Y.-Pa.	112	361	42,200	463.9	617.5	56.7
Birmingham, Ala.	44	947	69,600	651.1	1,341.2	84.8
Boston, Mass.	8	5,229	280,800	2,917.6	5,283.2	284.7
Bridgeport, Conn.	86	926	63,800	643.4	1,286.0	45.2
Buffalo, N.Y.	26	1,632	160,300	1,838.6	3,720.4	242.9
Canton, Ohio	84	580	62,800	681.0	1,390.9	146.5
Charlotte-Gastonia, N.C.	62	1,197	91,100	679.3	1,331.8	104.3
Chattanooga, Tenn.-Ga.	90	635	57,300	481.4	989.2	69.7
Chicago, Ill.	2	14,004	953,100	10,119.7	19,938.8	1,015.6
Cincinnati, Ohio-Ky.-Ind.	23	2,046	164,600	1,805.6	3,960.1	198.0
Cleveland, Ohio	16	4,359	284,100	3,213.9	5,937.2	326.8
Columbus, Ohio	35	1,199	104,500	1,063.7	2,226.3	155.4
Dallas-Ft. Worth, Tex.	10	4,234	250,000	2,307.9	4,569.6	261.7
Davenport-Rock Island-Moline, Iowa-Ill.	96	417	46,000	549.0	980.4	51.9
Dayton, Ohio	42	1,149	118,100	1,382.5	2,427.9	184.2
Denver-Boulder, Colo.	24	1,808	95,700	1,001.5	1,967.9	178.3
Detroit, Mich.	5	7,510	589,500	8,234.8	13,563.7	872.1
Erie, Pa.	126	480	45,500	462.9	857.7	52.6
Gary-Hammond-E. Chicago, Ind.	57	456	106,500	1,311.8	2,792.7	276.4
Grand Rapids, Mich.	66	1,212	80,600	829.2	1,759.3	104.1
Greensboro-Winston-Salem-High Point, N.C.	46	1,559	144,000	1,129.3	2,847.5	165.2
Greenville-Spartanburg, S.C.	72	837	105,100	767.8	1,792.7	145.1
Hartford, Conn.	51	1,192	89,100	1,015.7	1,774.6	58.9
Houston, Tex.	13	3,169	170,600	1,834.9	4,797.2	530.3
Indianapolis, Ind.	31	1,506	129,500	1,487.3	2,830.7	179.0

For footnotes, see following page.

MANUFACTURES—STATISTICS FOR STANDARD METROPOLITAN AREAS WITH 40,000 OR MORE MANUFACTURING EMPLOYEES, 1973—Con.

Source: *Bureau of Census; 1973 Census of Manufactures*

STANDARD METROPOLITAN STATISTICAL AREA*	Rank	Estab-lish-ments[4]	All employees[1]		Value added by Manu-facture[2] $million	Capital Expendi-ture new[3] $million
			Number	Payroll $million		
Jersey City, N.J.	60	1,909	91,500	858.8	1,885.7	88.5
Kansas City, Mo.-Kans.	27	1,883	125,000	1,260.9	3,223.1	158.8
Lancaster, Pa.	107	719	56,100	513.3	1,084.7	73.5
Los Angeles-Long Beach, Calif.	3	18,025	816,700	8,376.5	18,136.0	750.0
Louisville, Ky.-Ind.	39	1,005	117,800	1,222.0	3,273.2	175.4
Memphis, Tenn.-Ark.	41	1,046	68,200	587.3	1,548.1	119.8
Miami, Fla.	25	2,890	89,100	661.7	1,286.8	86.8
Milwaukee, Wis.	21	2,623	211,600	2,324.2	4,186.6	296.8
Minneapolis-St. Paul, Minn.	17	3,217	215,400	2,283.3	4,530.3	179.6
Nashville, Tenn.	52	1,124	77,400	618.4	1,295.8	105.3
Nassau-Suffolk, N.Y.	9	4,193	157,000	1,590.9	2,936.2	102.7
New Haven, Conn.	82	818	47,600	444.7	933.3	44.5
New Orleans, La.	33	934	53,600	498.1	1,083.9	63.1
New York, N.Y.	1	28,419	938,700	9,146.0	15,666.2	524.5
Newark, N.J.	15	4,600	276,700	3,001.9	6,086.3	282.5
Oklahoma City, Okla.	49	856	42,300	377.5	813.0	54.6
Paterson-Clifton-Passaic, N.J.	74	1,591	77,600	697.4	1,304.9	55.9
Peoria, Ill.	98	364	48,300	634.1	1,336.9	136.8
Philadelphia, Pa.-N.J.	4	7,890	503,500	5,112.9	10,055.7	620.1
Phoenix, Ariz.	32	1,367	80,700	794.6	1,757.1	100.2
Pittsburgh, Pa.	12	2,531	269,900	3,171.4	5,070.9	246.3
Portland, Oreg.-Wash.	34	2,006	94,900	957.7	1,862.5	95.8
Providence-Pawtucket-Warwick, R.I.-Mass.	38	2,991	138,200	1,097.1	2,204.6	98.9
Reading, Pa.	111	631	53,300	471.6	978.1	52.5
Richmond, Va.	65	684	52,100	489.2	1,229.0	175.9
Rochester, N.Y.	36	1,292	151,300	1,836.4	5,196.8	282.8
St. Louis, Mo.-Ill.	11	3,215	264,100	2,870.4	5,644.2	262.4
San Bernardino-Riverside-Ontario, Calif.	29	1,311	62,100	581.9	1,190.1	63.1
San Diego, Calif.	20	1,400	70,000	737.7	1,332.1	83.5
San Francisco-Oakland, Calif.	6	4,933	188,900	2,109.2	4,429.5	308.1
San Jose, Calif.	30	1,743	145,400	1,804.2	3,317.3	236.6
Seattle-Everett, Wash.	22	2,159	121,400	1,390.3	2,729.5	127.8
Springfield-Chicopee-Holyoke, Mass.-Conn.	68	1,002	63,200	571.7	1,248.5	68.8
Syracuse, N.Y.	56	732	63,300	666.2	1,361.3	98.7
Tampa-St. Petersburg, Fla.	28	1,455	65,800	539.4	1,150.9	91.9
Toledo, Ohio-Mich.	45	1,197	95,600	1,113.3	2,156.2	129.8
Tulsa, Okla.	64	957	52,300	508.7	842.7	107.4
Washington, D.C.-Md.-Va.	7	1,727	58,900	668.8	1,107.2	79.9
Wichita, Kans.	94	564	45,900	435.1	982.0	54.5
Wilmington, Del.-N.J.-Md.	71	492	66,600	844.6	1,271.9	119.1
Worcester, Mass.	91	817	47,400	447.1	865.0	38.5
York, Pa.	104	699	58,800	510.0	1,062.4	53.2
Youngstown-Warren, Ohio	69	603	92,300	1,112.3	2,146.2	86.7

* A standard metropolitan statistical area is a county or group of counties (except in New England) which contains at least one city of 40,000 inhabitants or more, or "twin cities" with a combined population of at least 40,000. In New England, towns and cities are the units used in defining standard metropolitan statistical areas.

[1] Includes central administrative offices or units which serve the manufacturing establishments of a company.

[2] Value of shipments less cost of materials, supplies, fuel, electricity, and contract work.

[3] Includes expenditures for plants in operation and plants under construction.

[4] Figures for 1972.

By Selected Representative Industry Groups

INDUSTRY GROUP	Value Added by Manufacture (in millions, dollars)	Value of Products Shipped (in millions, dollars)	INDUSTRY GROUP	Value Added by Manufacture (in millions, dollars)	Value of Products Shipped (in millions, dollars)
Agricultural chemicals	2,097	4,649	Metal forgings, stampings . . .	5,971	11,542
Aircraft and parts	11,460	18,533	Metalworking machinery . . .	6,281	9,099
			Millwork, plywood, and		
Bakery products	4,632	8,578	structural members . .	3,279	7,683
Beverages	6,690	14,663	Motorcycles, bicycles, and parts	309	722
Blast furnace and basic steel			Motor vehicles and equipment .	25,518	74,799
products	14,935	36,240	Musical instruments	379	715
Books	2,762	4,207			
Building paper and board mills	238	489	Newspapers	6,677	8,868
Cement, hydraulic	1,224	1,988	Office and computing machines	5,959	10,320
Children's outerwear	732	1,452	Office furniture	781	1,288
Cigarettes	2,454	4,181	Optical instruments and lenses .	386	595
Cigars	187	334*			
Commercial printing	6,183	10,195	Paints and allied products . . .	1,960	-4,268
Communication equipment . .	9,363	14,751	Paperboard containers and		
Concrete, gypsum, plaster			boxes	4,197	9,315
products	4,160	8,435	Paperboard mills	2,291	4,862
Construction and related			Paper mills, except building		
machinery	6,997	13,144	paper	3,416	7,514
Cutlery, handtools, hardware	3,468	5,649	Paving and roofing materials		
Cut stone and stone products .	196	317	(petroleum and coal		
			products)	876	2,114
Dairy products	4,414	18,016	Pens, pencils, office and art		
Drugs	6,628	8,750	supplies	617	1,049
			Periodicals.	2,344	3,856
Electric lighting and wiring			Petroleum refining	6,519	31,846
equipment	3,600	6,315	Photographic equipment and		
Electronic components, accessories	6,596	10,783	supplies	4,736	6,435
Engineering, scientific			Plastic materials, synthetics . .	6,068	11,720
instruments	818	1,244	Plumbing and heating, except		
Engines and turbines	3,267	6,312	electric (fabricated		
			metal products) . . .	1,209	2,315
Fabricated rubber products . .	1,825	3,265	Pottery and related products. .	676	961
Fabricated structural metal			Printing trades services	861	1,047
products	7,461	15,738	Pulpmills	383	849
Farm and garden machinery . .	3,246	6,868			
Fats and oils	2,013	10,378	Radio and television receiving		
Footwear (leather products),			equipment	2,569	5,712
except rubber	1,855	3,384	Railroad equipment	1,246	2,771
Fur goods	63	209	Refrigeration, service machinery	4,846	9,819
			Rubber, plastics footwear . . .	338	556
Glass, glassware, pressed or			Rubber, plastic hose, belting . .	618	1,052
blown	2,539	3,717			
Grain mill products	4,175	16,096	Sawmills and planing mills . . .	4,189	8,759
Greeting card publishing . . .	531	817	Screw machine products, bolts,		
Guided missiles, space vehicles .	4,283	6,413	etc.	2,337	3,919
			Ship and boat building and		
Handbags and personal leather			repairing	2,780	5,140
goods	351	621	Soap, cleaners, toilet goods . .	6,484	10,578
Household appliances	3,886	7,749	Sugar and confectionery		
Household furniture	4,219	8,217	products	2,563	7,245
Industrial chemicals	3,730	6,773	Textile finishing, except wool .	1,166	2,927
Industrial organic chemicals . .	6,904	13,448	Tires and inner tubes	3,518	6,542
Iron and steel foundries	4,066	6,858	Tobacco stemming and redrying	148	1,631*
			Toys and sporting goods . . .	1,987	3,744
Jewelry, silverware, and plated					
ware	963	2,158	Watches, clocks, and		
			watchcases	546	1,053
Leather gloves and mittens . .	52	120	Weaving, finishing mills, wool .	249	485
Leather tanning and finishing .	336	1,082	Weaving mills, cotton	1,322	2,742
Logging camps and contractors .	1,608	3,333	Weaving mills, synthetics . . .	2,030	4,369
			Women's, children's		
Measuring and control devices .	3,246	4,678	undergarments	1,087	2,102
Meat products	6,341	37,942	Women's and misses' outerwear	4,602	9,354
Medical instruments and			Wood buildings and mobile		
supplies	2,033	3,162	homes.	1,544	4,593
Men's and boys' suits and coats	1,442	2,492			
Metal cans, shipping containers	2,312	5,491	Yarn and thread mills	2,001	4,999

Source: U.S. Department of Commerce, Bureau of the Census.   * Represents value of production.

**Manufac-
turing**

LUMBERING

The lumber industry of the United States began in pioneering days in Maine, which held the lead for more than 200 years. With the increase in population and the westward trend of the people, the industry grew rapidly and the center of production shifted, first to New York about 1850, and then to Pennsylvania in 1860. From there it moved to Michigan, Minnesota, and Wisconsin, which from 1870 to 1895 were the principal lumber-producing states. Then the South sprang into the lead, notably Mississippi and Louisiana, but it was overtaken in 1920 by the West, particularly Oregon and Washington, an area which still dominates the industry. Oregon has been the leading lumber state since 1938.

The production of lumber is divided between the coniferous, or softwood, trees and the broadleaf, or hardwood, trees. In a general way, softwoods may be considered as the structural material used by carpenters, while hardwoods are more extensively utilized by cabinetmakers. The distinction, however, is not sharp, because some of the so-called "hardwoods" are, in fact, softer than certain of the so-called "softwoods."

Total lumber production in 1973 was 38,595,000,-000 feet board measure, of which 31,586,000,000 feet was softwood and 7,009,000,000 was hardwood.

Industries depending on forest products are widely distributed throughout the United States. California manufacturing plants use the largest amount, followed by New York, Washington, Illinois, and Michigan.

On the basis of the quantity cut, yellow pine has been for many years the most important timber, although the amount of Douglas fir standing in forests in the United States is greater than that of any other single kind of wood. For the first time, in 1949, more Douglas fir was cut than yellow pine.

In recent years, the lumber industry has come to realize that trees are a crop and it engages in extensive tree planting, even maintaining nurseries to supply the seedlings.

LUMBER PRODUCTION AND CONSUMPTION

(In millions of board feet, except per capita.)

Item	1965	1973[1]
Total Production	36,762	38,595
Softwoods:		
Production[2]	29,295	31,586
Cedar	633	785
Douglas fir	8,783	8,686
Hemlock	2,576	2,494
Ponderosa pine	3,776	4,030
Redwood	1,087	1,227
Southern yellow pine	6,628	7,895
White fir	2,422	2,438
White pine	693	1,069
Hardwoods:		
Production[2]	7,467	7,009
Ash	141	140
Beech	182	176
Cottonwood	198	326
Elm	206	145
Maple	786	623
Oak	3,356	3,227
Sweet gum	387	342
Tupelo and black gum	385	309
Yellow poplar	681	701
Domestic consumption	40,782	45,919
Softwoods	32,701	38,452
Per capita (bd. ft.)	172	183
Mill stocks, yearend	4,539	3,998
Exports	777	1,773
Imports	4,895	9,002
Hardwoods	8,081	7,467
Per capita (bd. ft.)	39	35
Mill stocks, yearend	1,066	460
Exports	145	222
Imports	338	558

[1] Preliminary data.
[2] Includes kinds of wood not shown separately.
Source: *Statistical Abstracts 1975.*

SELECTED TIMBER PRODUCTS—WHOLESALE PRICE INDEXES: 1950–1974

(Based on an arbitrary designation of 100 for 1967. Prior to 1965, production in Alaska and Hawaii is not included.)

Product	1950	1955	1960	1965	1970	1974
All Lumber	**87**	**95**	**92**	**94**	**114**	**207**
Softwood lumber	88	98	93	93	113	211
Douglas fir	88	98	89	92	109	214
Southern pine	88	94	94	91	115	185
Ponderosa pine, #3 boards	100	110	104	94	116	246
Hardwood lumber	82	86	91	97	115	190
Oak, red, flooring, select	93	100	99	108	113	203
Gum #1, common	74	62	68	82	93	159
Poplar #1, common	77	83	80	86	105	173
Birch #1, common	71	80	89	96	91	140
Plywood	122	120	110	104	108	161
Softwood	148	143	113	106	114	187
Hardwood	99	100	105	101	103	130
Insulation board	83	101	114	98	111	134
Woodpulp	81	96	102	100	110	218
Paper	68	83	93	95	111	149
Paperboard	81	98	105	102	101	152

Source: *Statistical Abstracts 1975.*

TECHNOLOGY: HOW THINGS ARE MADE

THE history of civilization is frequently divided into periods distinguished by the materials used among the people then living. Thus a period when only skins of animals were worn for clothing is regarded as more primitive than a period when cloth was woven of wool, cotton, or some other substance.

Judged by such a standard, the present age far excels all previous ones. Materials that were used earlier are now prepared in more efficient ways and are applied to more various purposes. The ancient art of pottery, for example, has been enriched in modern times by many new processes and products. Moreover, many materials have in recent times been discovered, and many others have been created by aid of the science of chemistry. The latter include such substances as aniline dyes, linoleum, and Portland cement.

The almost infinite number of different objects manufactured and the additions to that number that are being made practically from day to day render it quite impossible to give an exhaustive record of these products. Those, however, that are among the best known and most widely employed have been selected and treated in the following section, where each will be found described in such a way as to show clearly and concisely its source, history, manufacture, and uses.

Arc Lamp. A device producing intense, bluish-white light that is much used for illuminating streets, factories, and large, open spaces. Light is produced by the flow of an electric current between the slightly separated ends of two carbon rods. The tips of the rods become white hot and give off carbon vapor, which serves to conduct the current across the gap. This flaming path, in which the temperature is above 6,500° F., is curved in the form of an arc, hence the name *arc light*.

The carbons are usually made from petroleum or gas coke. They are gradually burned away and must be renewed after from 100 to 150 hours of service. Should the arc become broken, the upper rod automatically drops against the lower and is again pulled up to the proper distance by means of a magnet. When the carbon rods contain some salt, such as calcium fluoride, the vapor becomes intensely colored and is known as a *flaming arc*.

Because the arc light requires rather frequent cleaning, and renewal of the carbons, it is being replaced in many cases by gas-filled tungsten lamps, which give more light from the same amount of electricity.

Bakelite. An artificial material used in the preparation of varnishes and as a substitute for amber and hard rubber. It is formed by chemical reactions between carbolic acid and formaldehyde, and was discovered by L. H. Baekeland. It is made in two initial forms, distinguished in name by the letters *A* and *B*. *Bakelite A* is soluble and fusible; *Bakelite B* is insoluble, but plastic, so that it can easily be molded. Both of these initial forms are changed under the action of heat and pressure to *Bakelite C*, which is hard, insoluble, infusible, and possessed of high insulating properties.

Baking Powder. A mixture of chemicals substituted for yeast in order quickly to make light and porous cakes, biscuits, and similar foods. Nearly all such powders are combinations of *baking soda*, or *sodium bicarbonate*, with some acid substance. Starch constituting about 25 per cent of the whole serves to keep the mixture dry. The acid material is usually cream of tartar, a salt of phosphoric acid, or alum. When the powder becomes wet, a chemical reaction takes place which results in the production of carbon dioxide. This gas is also produced when bread is raised by yeast. As the gas cannot escape when generated within a thick dough or batter, it produces a porous, open structure in the cooked product, making it lighter and more easily digestible.

Bell. A hollow, cup-shaped vessel suspended from the closed end and giving forth sound when struck. The materials used in small bells range from glass to steel, but large bells are usually cast by pouring melted *bell metal* into molds of clay. Bell metal is an alloy of copper with various proportions of tin, to which small amounts of other metals may be added. Sometimes several weeks must elapse before the metal is cool enough to allow the removal of the mold without danger to the casting. The characteristic tone by which one bell is distinguished from another depends, not only on its size, shape, and thickness, but also on the proportion in which the constituent metals are alloyed.

The heaviest bell ever made, the 216-ton Tsar Kolokal of Moscow, was never rung because, before it was finished, an 11-ton piece fell from its side. The first large bell, 6½ tons in weight, was cast in 1400. The heaviest bell in the Western Hemisphere is the Bourdon, weighing 18¼ tons, in the Rockefeller carillon, Riverside Church, New York City. One of the most famous is Big Ben, weighing 13 tons, in Westminster Palace, London. The Liberty Bell is the most famous of all bells in the United States.

Bells, as known today, were used first during the 4th century as a summons to religious exercises. At present, most of the large and famous bells belong to churches, but the uses of bells, especially for sounding signals, are very numerous. Sound is usually caused by rocking the bell until it strikes a metal clapper. Very large bells remain at rest and are struck by a moving hammer. Many famous clocks have tuned bells that strike the hours, while, on ships, each half hour is indicated by a fixed number of strokes on a bell. Sailors are often warned of dangerous waters by a wave-rocked *bell buoy*. A *curfew* bell was sounded originally in England as a signal that it was time to "cover the fire" with ashes and to retire for the night.

Books. The earliest known records in the form of writing are the inscriptions on tablets of baked clay that were excavated from the ruins of the ancient Chaldean city of Nippur. Such tablets were probably in use about 6000 B.C. Inscriptions cut in stone, wood, or other more or less durable substances continued to be employed for special purposes long after more convenient materials were in general use. One of the earliest of these materials was papyrus, made from a plant that grew chiefly in Egypt. An extant Egyptian papyrus manuscript, called the *Papyrus Prisse*, dates from about 2000 B.C. From 400 B.C. to A.D. 600, the greater part of all writing was done on papyrus. Another material often used in this period was parchment, which was made principally from the skins of sheep, goats, or calves. Scrolls made of papyrus or parchments were prepared in the form of strips, sometimes 120 feet long. For convenience, these long strips were rolled on two sticks. The change from rolls to piles of leaves came with the more general use of parchment. The books of the Christian monasteries were usually written on this material.

Printing on paper by means of engraved blocks was practiced by the Chinese as early as 50 B.C. The name of the first European to print from movable type has been the subject of controversy for several hundred years. According to the Dutch, the honor belongs to Lourens Janszoon Coster, of Haarlem, Holland; but works printed by Coster have never been identified. In 1450, at Mainz, Germany, Johannes Gutenberg operated a printing shop, where he first experimented with letters carved from wood and later used types carved or cast from metal. Some books may have been printed from movable type at an earlier date, but the first book known to have been so printed is the Gutenberg Bible in Latin, completed about 1455.

The first book printed in English was a history of Troy, probably made at Bruges, Flanders, in 1474, by William Caxton. Early in 1476, Caxton established a press in the almonry of Westminster, London, and the next year brought out *Dictes and Sayings of the Philosophers*, the first book printed in England. The first press in the New World was established at the city of Mexico in 1544; the first one in the territory now embraced by the United States was built at Harvard college in 1639.

MODERN BOOK MANUFACTURE

The author's manuscript is examined by the copy editor, who looks for errors in spelling, punctuation, grammar, and clarity of meaning.

Edited and typemarked copy is sent to the typesetter (the *compositor*), who uses a *linotype* machine to set it into lines of solid type or a *monotype* machine to set it into lines of individual letters. In either case, hot metal is used for casting the type, and the type is delivered in columns on long trays called *galleys*. For making customer proofs, the face of the type is inked while it is still in the tray, and a *galley proof* is printed by pressing a sheet of paper over the inked type. A newer, faster, but generally more expensive, method is a computerized system called *photocomposition*. This method uses a camera, a computer, and a case containing transparent matrices ("cold" type) to "set" type photographically; in this case, a copy of the film is the customer's proof. This method is invaluable for certain jobs.

Customer proofs are examined by the author and editor and necessary alterations made. Then the editor marks the long proofs for separation into pages and adds chapter headings, running heads, and folios. If any illustrations appear in the text he now allows room for them. While typesetting was being done, his illustrations were prepared.

If the original copy for the illustration is all black or white a *line engraving* is made, usually smaller than the copy. If there are many gradations of black, as in a photograph, a *halftone* is made. For this an ordinary negative is shot to the desired size, but with a transparent screen of very fine lines at right angles to each other placed in front of the film. The lines on this screen are very close together, usually 100, 110, 120, or 133 lines to the inch. When a photograph is exposed through this screen the negative resulting is composed of many small dots, large where the illustration is light and small where the illustration is dark.

When the printing plate is made, by exposing it to light through the negative, the condition is reversed. The dark dots of the negative become light on the plate and the light ones become dark, so the printed result duplicates the original copy but is composed of many little dots and is called a halftone.

There are two important kinds of printing—letterpress and offset. Letterpress printing is done by inking a relief surface, such as the face of a page of type matter or the dots on a halftone engraving, and pressing the paper against the inked surface. Offset printing is done from a flat surface on which the image of the type or illustration is in the form of a greasy ink. The surface of the printing plate, a sheet of aluminum or zinc clamped around a cylinder, is somewhat porous. A dampener roller coats the plate with water, then another roller inks the wet form. Because the water sticks only to the plate surface where there is no ink and the ink sticks only to the greasy image, only the image area will print. In practice, the plate prints onto a rubber blanket on a cylinder which runs in contact with the plate, and the inked image on the blanket is transferred, or offset, onto the paper. Hence the term offset printing.

If the book is to print letterpress, 2, 4, or 8 pages of type are locked up together and a mold of wax or plastic is pressed against the type face. This mold is dusted with graphite or sprayed with silver to make a conductive surface and is immersed in an electrolytic bath to plate it with cooper. When the copper deposit is thick enough, the wax is melted off, or the plastic mold removed, the back of the copper cleaned, filled with melted lead, cooled, shaved to about 1/7th inch thick and cut to page size. These plates are then locked on the bed of the press, 32 to 64 or more at a time, in position so that when printed and folded the folios will be in sequence.

The offset plate is a large sheet of zinc or aluminum which is coated to make it light sensitive and over which the negatives for the whole form (or parts of it at a time) are laid. When exposed to light an image is formed on the plate which can be developed and inked to make a printing surface.

The book now comes out of the printing presses in large sheets ready for the bindery to take over. About twenty different machines are ordinarily used to bind a single book.

BINDING

THE FIRST FOUR BASIC BINDING STEPS are folding, sheetwork, gathering, and sewing. Sheetwork is subdivided into tipping, inserting, stripping, and guarding.

FOLDING. If 32 pages are printed on each side of a sheet, the form contains 64 pages. The folding machine will make several folds in this sheet, slit it apart and deliver four *signatures* of 16 pages each or two of 32 pages. A signature is a folded section of a book with pages in correct order.

TIPPING is done by running a narrow line of paste along the binding edge of a leaf to attach it to a signature. Smyth endsheets, maps, and colored inserts are processed in this manner. *Endsheets* are folded sheets of heavy paper at front and back of the book, pasted to the cover and tipped to the body to make the book hold together.

INSERTING is placing one part of a signature inside another, as putting a 16-page text section within an 8-page illustration section to make a 24-page signature.

STRIPPING is the attachment of a narrow piece of paper or cloth along the binding edge of a signature as a reinforcement.

GUARDING is the attachment of a narrow extension of paper or cloth so it projects along the binding edge. This is done for double spread maps in side-sewed books so all of the map is visible when the book is opened.

The *Gathering* machine has a long row of "pockets" or bins. Each bin holds a different pile of identical signatures. Signature 1 is in the first bin, signature 2 in the second, and so on. A conveyor belt or chain travels in a long trough under the bins. Grippers take a signature from the bottom of the pile in each bin and drop it onto the conveyor. By the time the grippers have returned and pulled out another group of signatures the conveyor has moved forward one step and the second signature is deposited on the first, and the third on the second, and so on. When the conveyor reaches the last bin a complete book has been assembled and, with each operating cycle, another book is delivered.

SEWING. There are two methods of thread sewing—*Smyth* and *Side*. Smyth-sewed books usually have a rounded back and the book opens relatively flat. Side-sewed books are stronger and this method is used for textbooks and titles subject to hard use. The Smyth sewing machine punches a number of holes along the backbone of each signature and through them sews each signature to the next in several places at once. Each signature is fed in the sequence it is gathered and is thus attached to the rest of the book.

Side-sewing of books up to about ¾ inch thickness is done by a heavy type of household sewing machine, using a lock stitch and sewing through the entire book from front to back, about ¼ inch from the backbone. For thicker volumes the drill-and-stitch method is used. These stitches are about an inch long. The book is pushed along, one stitch at a time. First a small drill bores a hole halfway up from the bottom. As the book moves forward, a hole is next bored down from the top to meet this. Another inch and the needle, more like a crochet hook, comes up through the hole, hooks the thread and pulls it down through, holding the loop until the next hole comes along. Then the needle goes up through this hole, catches the thread again and pulls it down through the preceding loop. Thus a single thread is used to make a chain stitch. The loops are pasted down so the stitches do not pull loose. Most drill-and-stitch books are also stapled with wire as they are gathered.

FORMING THE BOOK is done in five basic steps: smashing, glueing, trimming, rounding and backing, and lining.

SMASHING. Sewing makes many books bulge along the backbone. The heavy smasher squeezes and flattens them to a uniform thickness.

GLUEING OFF. This machine supplies a thin coating of glue to the backbone of Smyth-sewed books. This keeps the thread from unravelling and forces a layer of glue between signatures. This helps the book to keep its shape.

The *Trimmer* cuts off the uneven folded edges on three sides of the book to trim it to final size. After trimming, the edges of some books are decorated by staining, gilding, or sprinkling.

The *Rounding and Backing* machine curves the back of the book and bends over the edges of the outer signatures. Turning over these edges is called backing, and is important if the book is to open easily and for the cover to fit well.

LINING. The liner glues to the backbone a strip of stiff muslin, called "super," almost the length of the book and about an inch beyond each backbone edge. A liner of heavy kraft, the width of the backbone, is then glued over the super on the backbone. If the book has headbands, these are glued to the kraft liner. The super, liner, and headbands all feed from rolls and are cut to proper width automatically.

CASEMAKING. While these operations were going forward the cover, or *case*, has been made. Sheets of strong, heavy cardboard are cut to the proper size for front and back. Cloth is slit into rolls or cut into rectangles, depending upon the machine used. In the roll-fed machine the cloth is coated with glue on its inner side. As the cloth moves along, boards are pulled from hoppers and positioned on the glued surface. A strip of heavy paper liner for the backbone goes between each pair of boards. Rollers turn in the edges, and corners of the cloth are cut off to make a neater fold. Other forms of casemakers use pre-cut cloth, but perform essentially the same operations.

STAMPING. Cases may be decorated by being printed with ink, may be embossed or may be stamped with pigmented foil, using heated dies. They may also be silk screen printed. If the casemaking machine uses pre-cut material, this may be printed by offset and lacquered; or the covering material may be paper, printed in several colors and laminated with transparent plastic.

The *Casing-in* machine now applies paste to the joints and over the endsheets, and the cases are placed on the books. The extensions of the case beyond the body are called squares and the operator checks books as they come from the machine to make sure the squares are even all around.

BUILDING IN. The paste and glue in the books must now be dried by a building-in machine, a sort of hot presser and dryer. The books are pressed between heated plates and the joints or hinges are shaped. These machines have, in most binderies, taken the place of the practice of pressing between boards without heat, which took many hours to do.

The binding operations are now complete and the books are inspected. If the books are to be sold through bookstores, a jacket is normally added. They are then wrapped, packed and shipped.

Bread. A staple form of baked food, made from the flour or meal of some grain, in such manner that the product has a more or less porous structure. This is the modern *leavened*, or raised, bread. In general, the term bread includes any product made by baking a mixture of flour or crushed cereal and water. Wheat flour, because of its gluten, makes the best bread, although there are many special kinds made from other cereals. The common and standard form in the United States consists of a light-colored loaf made from wheat flour and raised with yeast. It is essentially a starch food as it normally contains a little more than one-half its weight of starchy compounds, about one-tenth of protein, 1.1 per cent of salts, 1 per cent of sugar, and only 1.3 per cent of fat, the remainder being water. Because of its low fat content, bread is usually eaten with butter. Corn bread and hot bread are familiar forms in those Southern states where, because of climatic conditions, the ordinary loaf will keep but a short time.

To understand the well-known process of bread making, it is necessary to know of what flour is composed and why yeast causes the dough to rise. Good wheat flour contains about 75 per cent starch and between 11 and 12 per cent of a nitrogenous material called *gluten*. Starch mixed with water must be heated to form even a weak paste; but wet gluten is very tough and elastic, acting somewhat like soft rubber in binding the flour and water into a dough. A cake of *yeast* contains thousands of microscopic yeast cells. These will grow rapidly in a dilute solution of sugar if certain salts and substances containing nitrogen are also present. See *Yeast; Microbiology.*

When yeast is stirred into dough and warmed, it finds conditions exactly suitable for growth and proceeds to develop rapidly. During growth, the yeast produces certain substances which cause the sugar to break down into *alcohol* and *carbon dioxide*, which is the same gas that causes the bubbles in soda water. As the carbon dioxide cannot escape through the heavy elastic mass, the dough *rises*, that is, swells up, because of the internal pressure of the gas. It is then *kneaded* in order to break up the large irregular bubbles and to distribute them evenly through the mass. Raising and kneading are repeated, usually two or three times, until the dough seems sufficiently light. It is then cut, and worked into pieces which about half fill the pans. When set in a warm place, the dough rises to the top of the pan and is ready for the oven. During the foregoing process of fermentation, the gluten becomes much less tough and rubbery. A temperature between 78° and 82° F. is best for the growth of yeast. Greater heat often leads to the development of bacteria which produce acetic and lactic acids, thus causing the bread to become *sour*.

The first effect of the heat of baking is to expand the small bubbles of gas so that the loaf becomes larger, lighter, and more porous. The yeast is killed, and much of the alcohol and water are driven off as vapor. The starch grains expand and break, thereby becoming much more digestible. The starch on the surface, which is exposed to the high temperature of the oven, is largely changed to dextrin and some is still further changed to caramel. To these chemical changes are due the distinctive color and taste of the crust. Within the loaf, the temperature does not rise much above 212° F. because of the presence of water, which cannot exceed that temperature, the excess heat being exhausted in converting the water into steam.

As bread is a starchy food, it should be well chewed in order that the starch may be changed by saliva to simpler and more digestible compounds. Bread ranks among the most nutritious of staple foods; a pound loaf contains more energy-producing units (calories) than a pound of fish, a pound of potatoes, and a quart of milk, combined.

Brick. A building material made by shaping, drying, and baking a prepared mixture of clay and sand. Brick was made and used in Babylon, where there were neither forests nor quarries, over six thousand years ago, and was probably the first material used for permanent construction. The earlier forms, like the present adobe brick used by the Indians of the Southwestern states, were merely sun dried and could be used only in regions where rain seldom fell. Straw was customarily mixed with the clay in order to bind it together. This was the case among the ancient Egyptians, who, according to the Biblical account, forced their Israelite captives, not only to make the customary number of bricks, but also to find the necessary straw.

At present, bricks are made chiefly by machinery. The clay is mixed with the proper amounts of sand and water, pressed into form, dried in the air or in drying tunnels, and finally heated to a cherry red in kilns which are usually about 30 feet in diameter by 12 feet high. The firing requires from 6 to 10 days. Some kinds of brick are formed from dry clay by enormous pressure, but most kinds are made by the wet process. In one type of machine, capable of an average daily production of 10,000 to 150,000 brick, the clay is compressed by a screw and is forced out in a long bar that is cut to the proper length by wires. The size varies somewhat but approximates $2\frac{1}{4} \times 4 \times 8\frac{1}{4}$ inches.

The red color of common brick is due to iron oxide. Brick that is almost white may be obtained by adding lime to specially selected clay. Other shades are obtained by the addition of various minerals. *Facing brick* is carefully finished by re-pressing and is used on the exterior of buildings where a fine appearance is desired. *Fire brick* is made from special clay which will undergo a very high temperature without softening or fusing.

Butter. A food product consisting chiefly of fat which is separated from milk by churning and is worked into a compact mass. Fat in the form of tiny globules is found in the milk of healthy cows in amounts which vary from 2 to 6 per cent, the average being somewhat under 4 per cent. The process by which it is changed into butter is much the same whether carried on in the farmhouse or at the butter factories, or *creameries*. It consists of separation, ripening, churning, and working.

Butter can be churned from milk, but it is much more satisfactorily made by separating the cream from the milk and churning the cream. This is frequently done by allowing the milk to stand until the lighter particles of fat rise to the top, where they may be collected. A much quicker and more efficient method involves the use of a *centrifugal separator*, in which the milk flows into a bowl or hollow spindle rotating from 6000 to 17,000 times per minute. The heavier skim milk is thrown towards the edge and passes out by one pipe, while the cream runs from another pipe near the center. Cream containing 30 to 33 per cent of fat is considered the best for churning.

Because sweet cream yields a butter of very mild flavor, it is usually allowed to sour or ripen, before churning. Ripening is due to bacterial growth which, to a large extent, develops the typical butter flavor and also causes better churning. Cream that has become sour in the natural way often contains harmful bacteria which produce unpleasant flavors. This danger is avoided by using, as a *starter*, a culture containing only such bacteria as have been found to give good results.

When sufficiently ripened, the cream may be churned by hand or in the large revolving, power-driven cylinders used in creameries. Churning causes the tiny particles of fat to combine and become larger, finally attaining such size that they can no longer remain suspended in the liquid. The butter then *breaks*, or separates from the buttermilk in grains about the size of wheat.

The natural yellow color of the fat is due to coloring matter absorbed from the green food of the cows. If their food is changed to dried grass and grain, as often happens in winter, the color of the butter becomes much lighter. In order that the appearance may be uniform, artificial color is often added. The most important butter color is made by boiling the seed of the *annatto* plant with an oil such as cottonseed. A small amount of this colored

oil is usually added to the cream before churning. Standards for color vary greatly. Butter exported to South America is often almost red.

When churning is complete, the buttermilk is drawn off and the butter is washed with clean, cool water. Salt is then added, chiefly for flavor, in amounts which are usually between $\frac{3}{4}$ and $1\frac{1}{2}$ ounces per pound of fat. Salted butter does not become moldy so quickly as the unsalted product.

The grainy mass of butter is then worked by hand or under rollers. The purposes of this process are to eliminate any remaining buttermilk, to mix the salt evenly, and to incorporate the proper amount of water so thoroughly that it will not separate. Too much working spoils the grain and leaves a soft, oily butter. The finished product is usually packed in tubs or one-pound cartons.

Renovated, or *process* butter, is prepared by melting strong butter which is no longer acceptable for food, refining the clarified fat, and rechurning it with milk or skimmed milk.

Button. A piece of metal, bone, ivory, or other substance, usually employed for fastening clothing by being pushed through an opening called a button-hole. The term is used also to designate any small knoblike projection or similar object.

Buttons were first used as ornaments in Europe during the 13th or the 14th century. Later, they served to hold loops of cord, a practice which led to the modern buttonhole. The two principal types are perforated buttons, meant to be attached by sewing, and buttons having on the reverse side a projection or shank, by which the attachment is made. Buttons are usually disk-shaped, but they may have many other forms.

Bone buttons have long been known, but many modern substitutes have also come into use. Several factories, located chiefly at Rochester, N. Y., and at Newark, N. J., are devoted to the production of *vegetable ivory* buttons, made from the kernels of *tagua* or *corozo* nuts, the seed of a South American palm tree. These become hard when heated. Pearl buttons are cut from the lustrous shells of certain species of oysters and mussels. Many of these come from Japan and from the Mississippi river. Disks are drilled from the shell, which is first softened by soaking. Holes are then bored in the disks, the rough back is ground or split away from the mother-of-pearl, and the back and edges are polished. The finished buttons are fastened to cards. Metal buttons and cloth covered buttons are made by machinery.

Buttons of special pattern or design are often worn to indicate membership in some organization or adherence to some political party. The rank of a mandarin is shown by the color and the material of a button worn on his hat.

Cable, Submarine. A telegraph line laid under water. The earliest experimental cables of this type were laid across rivers and ponds, but the first commercially successful cable was laid across the Strait of Dover in 1851. Scotland and Ireland were connected in 1853, and the next year saw Sweden joined with Denmark and Italy with Corsica. The success of these comparatively short lines encouraged attempts to lay a transatlantic cable. Such a line was completed in 1858, but, after a few weeks of use, it ceased to give satisfactory service.

Through the perseverance of Cyrus W. Field, a successful cable was finally completed in 1866 between Heart's Content, Newfoundland, and Valentia, Ireland. These places were selected because they permitted the smallest mileage of cable and because the intervening ocean bed was soft and level. There are now several cables between North America and Europe.

A cable consists of a central strand of twisted copper wires, called the core, which is covered with gutta percha or rubber. Next comes a layer of jute wrapping surrounded by galvanized steel wires. These add strength and afford protection against anchors, sharp stones, and the attack of fishes. The outer layer is of jute filled with material to make it waterproof. In deep water, such a cable may be less than an inch thick, but, in shallow places, where there is more danger from waves and from ships' anchors, it is usually much better protected.

In 1902, an English cable was completed in the Pacific Ocean between British Columbia and Australia. In 1903, an American cable was laid between San Francisco and the Philippines.

A small strand of wire, over 2000 miles long, can carry only currents which are far too weak to operate ordinary telegraph instruments. The effectiveness of the current is multiplied by surrounding the copper core with a thin layer of permalloy. Two sending keys are used in cabling. One sends a signal corresponding to the dots of the telegraph code; the other sends the dashes. The receiver, called a *syphon recorder*, consists of a slender, carefully adjusted, hollow needle, one end of which dips in ink while the other marks on a moving band of paper. Dot signals move the needle to one side, and dashes pull it to the other. The result is a wavy line, from which the message can be deciphered.

With the first cables, it was possible to telegraph in one direction at the rate of about 7 words per minute. At present, messages can be automatically sent in both directions at the same time at the rate of 2500 letters each minute.

Calico. Cheap cotton cloth printed with a colored pattern. The name comes from Calicut, a city of India, whence the process of decorating cloth by means of a hand stamp moistened with dyes was introduced into Europe. Calico printing is now done almost entirely by machinery.

Cambric. A thin, finely woven, linen cloth, which receives its name from the town of Cambrai, France, where it was originally made. It is used chiefly for handkerchiefs and fine underclothing and as an embroidery linen. Cotton cambric is a similar fabric of plain weave, one surface of which is smooth and easily sheds dust.

Canvas. A strong, coarse cloth, originally made from hemp but now woven also from linen and cotton. Canvas is used to a large extent for awnings, sails, and tents. For oil painting, artists require a canvas of heavy linen. Fine, light grades, called *duck*, are made into summer clothing.

Castor Oil. A clear, thick, almost colorless oil, chiefly known as a reliable cathartic. It is obtained by crushing and pressing the seeds of the castor oil plant. Castor oil is an important ingredient in many transparent soaps. When properly treated with sulphuric acid and ammonia, it is used, under the name of *Turkey red oil*, to prepare cotton for dyeing and printing.

Cellophane. A transparent, paper-like substance widely used for wrapping articles placed on sale. While protecting the articles, it does not interfere with their display to customers and often enhances their attractiveness. The invention of cellophane is due to J. E. Brandenberger, a Frenchman, whose experiments extended from 1900 to 1912. A moisture-proof product was developed in the Du Pont laboratories in 1927.

Cellophane, like rayon, is made from cellulose obtained from wood pulp or cotton linters. By treatment with acids or other chemicals, the raw material is made soluble in alcohol or ether. The solution, after purification, is pressed through a thin slit and emerges as a sheet, which becomes solid on the evaporation of the volatile solvent.

Celluloid. An artificial material which was invented in 1869 by the Hyatt brothers of Newark, N. J. It is used as a substitute for more expensive substances, such as bone, ivory, and hard rubber, which it can be made to resemble very closely. It is produced from some pure form of cellulose, such as tissue paper or cotton fiber, which is treated with a mixture of nitric and sulphuric acids. The resulting *nitrocellulose* is carefully dried and is then kneaded in a mixing machine with alcohols and camphor until it becomes plastic. It is then worked between rollers and afterward pressed and dried. The final product may be transparent or opaque and can be given any desired color. Celluloid can be applied to paper, cloth, or leather to produce a very smooth, waterproof surface. It has a high degree of inflammability, but this may be markedly decreased by mixing with the celluloid a proportion of plastic casein.

Cement, Portland. A fine gray or white powder made by heating and grinding definite proportions of lime and clay. After mixture with water, it gradually sets to form a rocklike mass. The white variety is made from specially selected clay. The name portland is due to Joseph Aspdin, a bricklayer of Leeds, England, who, in 1824, patented the method of making cement and thought that the hardened product bore a slight resemblance to a famous building stone found on the Isle of Portland.

Sometimes the raw materials are found already combined in the proper proportions in certain kinds of rock. But usually clay and some substance rich in lime, such as limestone, chalk, or marl, after being dried and weighed, are carefully mixed and finely ground. Then the powdered product goes to the kilns, which are revolving steel cylinders sometimes 200 feet long. These are lined with fire brick and heated within by a burning blast of pulverized coal, crude oil, or natural gas to a temperature between 2500° and 3000° F. This intense heat causes the powder to fuse slightly, and, as the kilns have a slight slope, the mass works its way downward through the flame and is discharged as clinkers. After cooling, the clinker is ground sufficiently fine to meet the standard requirement—that at least 78 per cent of it shall pass through a sieve having 40,000 holes to the square inch. Before the grinding is complete, a small amount of plaster of Paris or gypsum is added in order to control the time required for the cement to harden.

This exceedingly fine powder is portland cement. When mixed with water, the cement sets rather slowly. Within a few hours, it becomes stiff enough to resist the pressure of a finger and thereafter gains rapidly in strength for the first 30 days, continuing to gain, though much more slowly, for at least two years. Cement sets because of a chemical action that takes place when water and the dry powder are mixed. The exact nature of this change, however, is not known.

Portland cement is used in enormous quantities in making concrete for the construction of buildings, bridges, dams, tunnels, and conduits, as well as for sidewalks and permanent roads. Because of its more extended use, cement is now marketed increasingly in bulk shipments and ready-mixed form. See *Concrete*.

Chocolate. A valuable food product obtained from the seeds of the cacao tree, which is indigenous to the tropical parts of the western hemisphere. Chocolate was used by the natives of Central America long before Columbus crossed the ocean, and it is said that, when Cortez conquered Mexico, he found the emperor of that country drinking chocolate from a golden cup. When cultivated, the cacao attains a height of about 20 feet, although the wild trees are sometimes twice this size. The fruit is a red or yellow melon-shaped pod, between 6 and 8 inches long, which grows directly from the trunk or older branches. It has a rough, thick rind that covers a mass of seeds embedded in a sweet, sticky pulp. The seeds, from which chocolate, cocoa, and cocoa butter are made, are about the size and shape of an almond kernel and are covered with a thin brown shell.

When the fruit is ripe, the rind is cut open, and the seeds and pulp are removed and thrown into piles or into sweating-boxes, where they are allowed to ferment for several days. After the fermentation, which improves the flavor and makes the pulp easily removable, the seeds are cleaned, dried, packed in bags, and shipped to the markets of the world.

When the cocoa beans arrive at the factory, they are first roasted like coffee in long revolving cylinders. This develops a pleasant aroma and also makes the shell dry and brittle. After roasting, the beans pass first to crushing machines, where they are broken, and then to cleaners, where the germ of each bean and the shells are removed. The clean, broken kernels of the roasted beans, called *cocoa nibs*, are then ground to a smooth paste under heavy stone rollers. If this pasty mass is run into flat molds, it hardens to the well-known dark cakes of *bitter chocolate*. When the chocolate mass is ground with a large proportion of sugar, the resulting product, which is sometimes flavored with vanilla or spices, is *sweet chocolate*. When milk or milk powder is included in the mixture, the result is *milk chocolate*.

Cocoa nibs and bitter chocolate contain about 50 per cent of a hard, yellowish white fat called *cocoa butter*. Because of the large amount of fat, many people find that the drink made from chocolate is too rich. In making *cocoa*, about one-half or two-thirds of the cocoa butter is squeezed out from the warm chocolate by means of a hydraulic press. The resulting cake is broken and ground very fine, giving *cocoa powder*, which usually contains only 20 or 25 per cent of fat.

Candy is covered with a coating of chocolate by being dipped into the soft, warm material. Ordinary sweet chocolate cannot be used for this purpose because it will not melt easily. For candy making, a special product called *dipping* or *coating* chocolate is prepared by adding extra cocoa butter to sweet chocolate. This mixture can be melted in hot water.

Chocolate contains a stimulating alkaloid called theobromine, which is closely related to the caffeine of coffee and tea. For this reason, some people find it difficult to sleep after drinking cocoa. But the various drinks and other products prepared from chocolate have a high food value and are usually considered wholesome and nutritious.

Coke. The substance which remains when the volatile matter has been expelled from soft coal by heating it under controlled conditions. Coke is usually hard, gray, and porous, and it burns with intense heat and a smokeless flame. It was first made to supply the need of a smokeless fuel, but today a large proportion of all coke is used for the production of iron from its ore. It is more satisfactory than anthracite for this purpose because it burns freely in the blast furnace and contains only a small amount of sulphur, which is harmful to iron.

The original method of making coke was to pile soft coal in heaps, which were lighted and allowed to burn until most of the volatile matter was given off. Next came the practice of heating the coal in dome-like furnaces, which were known as *beehive ovens* because of their shape. These ovens make good coke, but, because they allow the volatile matter to escape, they are being supplanted by modern *by-product* coke ovens, which recover gas, ammonia, and coal tar. The gas is burned for heating purposes; the ammonia is used for refrigeration or is made into a valuable fertilizer; and, from the coal tar comes a long list of dyes, medicines, explosives, and roofing and paving materials. A ton of coal gives 5 to 6 pounds of ammonia and from 8 to 10 gallons of tar.

There are many areas in the United States which supply good coking coal, the most important being Pennsylvania, West Virginia, and Kentucky. Much non-coking coal can be processed and blended to produce good-quality metallurgical coal.

Concrete. Artificial stone produced by the setting, or hardening, of a mixture of portland cement, sand, pebbles or broken stone, and water. When steel rods or other forms of steel are placed within this mass in order to add to its strength, we have *re-inforced concrete*. The sand used should be clean and free from dust. The stone, preferably sharp, should range in diameter from $\frac{1}{4}$ to not more than $1\frac{1}{4}$ inches. The cement, sand, and water form a mortar which fills up the air spaces and binds the stone to a rocklike mass. The materials are mixed in various proportions, depending on the strength required and the amount of wear the surface will receive.

A 1-2-4 mixture, so called because it contains one part of cement, two of sand, and four of stone, all by volume, is generally used for re-inforced concrete walls and engine foundations. For basement walls and foundations, grain and coal bins, and the lower layer of sidewalks and of floors, a ratio of 1-2$\frac{1}{2}$-4 is satisfactory. A 1-2 mixture, without stone, is used for the wearing surface of walks and floors. Walks and floors of but one layer, fence posts, and watering tanks are best made of the proportions 1-2-3. The ingredients are carefully mixed and wet with the least amount of water that will allow the mixture to run together, if the maximum strength is desired. It is then spaded into molds, or *forms*, and requires three to ten days to set. An especially hard, quick-setting concrete, which will take a polish like granite, is made by putting the mixture into forms and adding a minimum of water, which is distributed throughout the mass by a process of high-frequency vibration. Concrete continues to gain in strength for about two years.

Concrete is a structural material of great value because it can be made into almost any desired shape and because when set, it has the strength and permanency of stone. It is comparatively cheap and can be prepared when and wherever needed from materials that are usually available. Roads, dams, bridges, and foundations for buildings provide its largest uses. See *Cement*.

Corduroy. A thick, strong, cotton cloth characterized by a corded or ribbed surface of velvet-like texture. Its excellent wearing qualities make it especially suitable for clothing subject to hard usage. The name, meaning king's cord, was first applied to the material in the 17th century, when it composed the uniform of the French king's huntsmen. Because of the ridged appearance, the name corduroy is sometimes applied also to a road or bridge made of logs laid transversely.

Cork. The outer layer of the bark of an evergreen species of oak. The larger proportion of good cork comes from Spain and Portugal, although the cork oak grows throughout northern Africa and southern Europe. It attains an average height of about 30 feet with a thickness of 2 feet through the trunk.

As the tree grows, layers of dead cells accumulate on the surface of the bark. This growth is cork. It is gathered by making cuts around the trunk just below the branches and just above the ground. These are joined by several vertical cuts, so that each layer of cork can be pried loose. The first stripping, known as virgin cork, is taken when the tree is about 20 years old. It is of poor quality. Succeeding growths are cut at periods of 8 to 10 years, with an average yield of about 45 pounds. The best cork is produced after the tree is 40 years old, and, when carefully done, the process is not injurious to the tree, which lives for 150 years or more.

The slabs of cork are dried for a few days and then steamed or placed in boiling water. This treatment softens the rough outer coating so that it may be scraped off. It also extracts tannin and other soluble matter, increases the bulk and elasticity, and flattens the curved pieces so that, after drying, they may be packed in bales.

Cork is a soft, light, elastic material that is highly resistant to the passage of electricity, heat, water, or air. It is so generally used as stoppers for bottles and jugs that stoppers made of other substances are usually called corks. Because it weighs only one-fourth as much as water, it is used for floats on fishing nets, in life preservers, and for artificial limbs. Insoles for shoes are often made of cork. Ground cork affords an excellent insulating material and, mixed with thickened linseed oil, is used in the manufacture of *linoleum*. A valuable black pigment is made from burnt cork.

Cotton. A product of the cotton plant, which is probably more generally useful than any other textile fiber. Wool is required chiefly for warm clothing, and silk is demanded because of its beauty, but, while cotton can be made into products almost as warm as wool or as attractive as silk, it also serves for countless purposes where the cost of other fabrics would be prohibitive. Under the microscope, each cotton fiber is seen to resemble a flattened, twisted tube, and it is this characteristic twisted structure which makes cotton so satisfactory for spinning into threads. Columbus found it used by the natives of South America for making cloth, and it had already been employed in India for at least 3000 years. It is a tropical plant, but grows best in a reasonably moist, temperate climate which is free from frost for at least 6 months of the year. North and South America, Egypt, China, India, and Russia all produce important parts of the world's cotton crop, most of which grows between the 36th parallels north and south of the equator.

The plant is a perennial and, in tropical countries, often produces crops for many years; but, in the southern part of the United States, where a large proportion of all cotton is grown, it is treated as an annual. Seeds are planted early in the spring, and the plant, which belongs to the same family as the hollyhock, attains a height of from 2 to 10 feet but is usually about 4 feet tall. When the flowers open, they are cream or yellow, but the color changes to pink on the second day. Before the end of the third day, they usually fall to the ground, leaving a tiny green boll, or seed pod, which grows to about the size of a hen's egg. When ripe, the bolls burst open, and the cotton is ready for gathering. If the bolls were all to ripen at the same time, a great saving could be made by mechanical picking. Although about one-fourth of the picking is now done by machine, none of the machines has so far been a complete success, and the expense of harvesting the crop by hand is one of the largest items in the cost of production. An expert can pick 200 pounds or more in a day, but the average is only about 100 to 125 pounds. Cotton picking time in the Southern states extends from about August 25 to December 10.

The cotton worm, the boll weevil, and the pink cotton-boll worm are the worst enemies of the cotton plant and have caused enormous losses. The most generally used remedies have been insecticides such as paris green and kerosene emulsions. More recently, calcium arsenate, applied as a dust or powder, has proved of great value.

The collected cotton is taken to a ginning mill where the fiber is separated from the seeds and compressed into bales. There are two kinds of gins,— the *saw gin*, which is most generally used, and the *roller gin*, used for treating long-fibered cotton. The saw gin, invented by Eli Whitney in 1793, consists of a set of circular saws with fine teeth which catch the fiber and pull it through an opening too small for the seed to follow. The standard domestic, 500-pound bale, of about 28 × 42 × 56 inches, is covered with coarse jute cloth and bound with steel straps. For export these bales are compressed to about 30 pounds per cubic foot. The average production of cotton in the United States is about 185 pounds per acre.

There are many varieties of cotton, all of which are graded according to the length and the fineness of the fiber. A rough commercial classification may be made into four general types. *Upland* cotton is the standard product and fills about ⅔ of the world's cotton requirements. Its fiber is between ¾ and 1¼ inches long, white, and easy to work.

Peruvian cotton is long, rough, hairy, and well adapted for mixing with wool. *Egyptian* cotton has strong, silky fibers between 1⅛ and 1⅝ inches in length. Much of it has the tawny color characteristic of balbriggan underwear and natural ecru curtains, but one of the most widely cultivated varieties is white, so that these products are now usually dyed. Egyptian cotton of the finest quality is grown by irrigation in the Imperial valley of California and the Salt River valley of Arizona.

The finest and longest fibers are those of sea-island cotton, which grows chiefly on the sea islands and coast regions of South Carolina, Georgia, and Florida. It averages 1¾ inches in length and is suitable for the finest thread and lace. The seeds of this variety are smaller than those of the upland cotton and are black instead of green.

When the bales reach a cotton mill, they are opened as needed and are mixed so that the quality will be uniform. The packed fiber is then loosened and passed through many mechanical processes, technically known as carding, drawing, slubbing, roving, spinning, and doubling. In the various machines the cotton is formed into a lap much like that of cotton batting. The fibers are carded until they all run in the same direction, and the broad lap is divided into narrow slivers, which are reduced, combined, and redrawn until uniform in size, when they are twisted into yarn or thread. The spinning machines are of two types, called ring spinners and mules. They often have thousands of threads, or bobbins.

The finished threads are then fitted to the great looms and woven into cloth. Preparation of spool, or sewing, thread is also an important branch of the industry. *Mercerized* cotton, invented by John Mercer of Lancashire, England, is produced by treating the thread or cloth, while under tension, with caustic alkali. The fibers shrink and become stronger, more transparent, and almost like silk in appearance. *Absorbent* cotton is made by dissolving from the fibers the natural waxlike material which they contain, so that they become soft and very porous. Cotton is almost pure *cellulose* and is used in great quantities for making artificial silk, celluloid, and many explosives.

Cottonseed Oil. The most valuable product obtained from the seed of the cotton plant. It is occasionally extracted by means of gasoline or some other volatile liquid that will dissolve fat, but usually it is squeezed out of the carefully prepared seed under the enormous power of the hydraulic press. The *crude* oil so obtained is *refined* by treatment with a dilute solution of caustic soda, which removes most of the coloring matter and all of the sharp-tasting fatty acids. These impurities settle to the bottom of the refining tank in a thick, soapy mass, called *foots*, from which the oil is drawn off and washed with water to remove all traces of alkali.

The dark, foggy liquid that runs from the press becomes, by this process, a clear, golden yellow oil with a pleasant taste and odor. If it has been carefully prepared from good seed, it will probably be classed as *prime summer yellow* cottonseed oil, which is the standard grade in the markets of the world. When the color or odor is below standard, it is called *off* oil. Refined oils are classed commercially as summer yellow, summer white, winter yellow, and winter white. The white oils are made from the yellow by bleaching with fuller's earth. At a temperature of 38° to 32° F., summer oils become thick because of the formation of palmitin crystals. For this reason, they are not considered satisfactory salad oils. *Winter* oils have been chilled and pressed to remove these crystals and, consequently, will remain bright and clear at 32° F. Any of the refined products may be *deodorized* by blowing the liquid with steam at high temperatures.

Enormous quantities of prime cottonseed oil are used in the manufacture of oleomargarine and lard compounds. The winter oils are prepared chiefly for table use. Grades below edible standard in color or flavor are usually made into toilet soap. The foots are used in the preparation of laundry soaps and soap powders. If treated with acid and distilled, the foots yield light-colored fatty acids for the soap industry and a residue of pitch used in roofing tars.

Cottonseed oil was first produced by Dr. Otto, of Bethlehem, Pennsylvania, in 1768, but its value as a food product was not generally appreciated until about 1855. Since that time, the industry has had a remarkable growth due to the continuous discovery of new uses for the various crude products.

Cottonseed Products. For every pound of cotton that is grown, about two pounds of cottonseed are produced. This seed was for many years considered a nuisance and was wasted or burned. It is now a very important part of the cotton crop because it yields food for man, food for cattle, and food, or fertilizer, for growing plants. The dark greenish seeds, about the size of a pea, are covered with short fiber, or *linters*, which is removed by machinery after the seeds have been carefully sifted and cleaned. After delinting, they pass to the *huller*, where they are cut into pieces, beaten, and sifted until the *hulls* are separated from the meats which they contain. The meats are then crushed between heavy rolls, cooked with steam, formed into cakes, and placed in a hydraulic press, where the oil is squeezed out under a pressure of almost 4000 pounds per square inch. The hard, dry cakes which remain are ground into *cottonseed meal*.

One ton of seed yields about 315 pounds of oil, 920 pounds of meal, 600 pounds of hulls, 80 pounds of linters, and 85 pounds of dirt and waste which have no value. The linters are used as a filler for pads and cushions, for making paper, for mixing with wool in shoddy and cheap felt, and in the manufacture of celluloid, guncotton, and smokeless powder. The hulls often serve, like sawdust, for a packing material and are added to concentrated cattle foods to give bulk. The meal is valuable both as a fertilizer and as a rich food for all farm animals, while the oil, which is most important of all, has many uses in the production of edible and technical products. See *Cotton, Cottonseed Oil.*

Dyes and Dyeing. The art of dyeing, or applying color in a more or less permanent form to cloth and other substances, is very ancient. In 1000 B. C., the city of Tyre was already famous for its purple dye, which later became the badge of royalty.

The dyes formerly used were natural products obtained from many sources. *Indigo* was prepared from a plant; *logwood*, from the heart of a tropical tree; *madder*, which gave the famous *Turkey red*, from a root; *cochineal*, from the dried bodies of female insects which live on certain cactus plants; and *Tyrian purple*, from a species of shellfish.

Artificial dyes originated in England in 1856, when Perkin first prepared from aniline the lilac color *mauve*. Similar products which followed were accordingly known as aniline dyes. The term *coal-tar dyes* is now more customary because the basis for most of these colors is benzol, carbolic acid, naphthalene, and other compounds obtained from the tar which results when coal is distilled for the production of gas and coke. Thousands of artificial dyes have been made by chemists, so that the production of madder, indigo, and other natural products is now of minor importance.

Silk and wool combine directly with dyes much more readily than does cotton. In order to produce fast colors, certain substances, called *mordants*, are often used, which can combine both with the fiber and with the dye. Alum, iron salts, and tannin are among the many materials used for this purpose. The fabric is first dipped into a solution of the mordant and is then passed to the dye vat, where it takes up the desired color.

Eau de Cologne. A famous perfume, called in English Cologne water, which was originally made in Cologne by an Italian named Farina. It consists of pure alcohol to which are added several aromatic oils that impart a pleasant and refreshing odor.

Enamel. A glasslike substance fused upon the surface of metal, glass, or other material as a means of protection or of decoration. The familiar enameled kitchen ware is made by baking a smooth coating of enamel upon an iron base. Transparent enamels are usually called glaze. The art of enameling was practiced even in the time of the Egyptians and the Babylonians. It has led to the production of exceedingly beautiful articles, many of which have the appearance of gold covered with a pattern of bright-colored jewels. Enamel is used for glazing some varieties of pottery and of brick. Clock and watch dials are usually enameled. The type of paint known as enamel gives, when dry, a hard, glossy surface resembling that obtained by fusion.

Fire Extinguisher. Any device intended for use in stopping combustion and in extinguishing flame. Under ordinary conditions, fire is due to a violent chemical reaction between combustible material and oxygen of the air. Therefore, any means which will cut off the supply of oxygen from the flame will usually put out the fire.

One of the most common and easily available fire extinguishers is a bucket of water. The water should be spread over the burning material with a sweeping motion, rather than hurled in a mass at the flame. A well-known type of extinguisher consists of a strong metal tank partly filled with a solution of baking soda in water. A hose and nozzle is connected with the top of the tank, and a small, loosely stoppered bottle of sulphuric acid is placed above the solution. When the container is inverted, the acid reacts with the soda to form carbonic acid gas under considerable pressure. This forces out the water in a steady stream.

Many of the most dangerous fires result from the careless handling of gasoline and kerosene. For fighting such fires, water is of little value, but *carbon tetrachloride* is very effective when sprayed from a hand pump or even when sprinkled from a bottle. This chemical, however, should not be used in closely confined or unventilated places, because it may generate dangerous gases. Sand is often successfully used to smother an oil fire which has spread out over a large surface. *Quick action* is most important in fighting a small fire. Consequently, the prompt application of several handfuls of flour, cement, or similar powder may often prevent serious damage.

A bucket of slightly moistened sawdust mixed with two or three pounds of washing soda will often serve to extinguish an oil fire in a deep container where sand would sink and be of no value. When clothing is afire, a blanket, a rug, or an overcoat wrapped closely about the person will usually extinguish the flame.

Fireless Cooker. A cooking device which usually consists of an oven surrounded on all sides by thick layers of insulating material. It is designed to keep the heat where it is needed and thus maintain the proper cooking temperature without wasting fuel.

Heat may be produced within the oven by means of electrical resistance coils, but it is usually supplied by placing stones, heated to the proper temperature, at the top and the bottom of the oven with the container of food between them. As the heat from the stones cannot quickly escape through the nonconducting walls, the temperature of the oven falls very slowly, and the food is thus cooked with a minimum amount of fuel.

Flour. The finely ground meal of wheat or other grains. When used alone, the word refers to wheat flour. *Graham flour* is made from the entire wheat kernel, but, if the outer layer of bran is removed before grinding, *whole wheat* flour is produced.

The white flour most used for bread making is no longer prepared, as it was for centuries, by crushing the grain between moving stones. In a modern flour mill, wheat which has been carefully cleaned and then moistened or dried to the proper condition is passed through a series of four or five steel rolls, each of which is adjusted to break the pieces a little smaller than the one before. Between each *break*, the fine particles of flour are sifted out, and the coarser pieces, or middlings, are also cleaned and sifted. The purpose of this complicated process is to get as much high grade flour as possible and to eliminate the bran.

After being sifted through fine silk bolting cloth, as many as forty different streams of flour are finally reunited into standard grades called first patent, second patent, first clear or bakers, second clear or low grade, and red dog, the lowest grade of flour made. Standard patent flour, which is the bread flour usually found on the market, includes the first three grades. About 25 per cent of the wheat, consisting of shorts and bran, is classed as offals. Shorts are the fine particles of bran mixed with some flour. The germ is also separated because it contains much fat and, if ground into flour, is likely to develop an unpleasant flavor.

Because of the gluten which it contains, wheat flour makes better bread than that made of other cereals. But the quality of the gluten is just as important as the quantity. Red dog contains about 50 per cent more gluten than the high grade patent flours, but it will not make good bread. The quality of the bread which it yields is the final test of a flour. Crackers and macaroni are important food products made almost entirely from flour. Macaroni flour, or *semolina*, is rather coarsely ground from *durum* or other hard wheat.

During World War I, the United States Food Administration ordered that 100 pounds of wheat should be milled so as to yield at least 74¼ pounds of a product which was officially called 100 per cent flour and popularly known as *war flour*. This should not be confused with 100 per cent extraction flour, which, as previously explained, is Graham flour. Rye flour is an important food product, especially in Europe. Corn flour and potato flour find limited uses, and banana flour is well known in the countries where the fruit grows. See *Bread*.

Gas, Artificial. A combustible gas used for light or heat. It may be classified according to its methods of production as coal gas, water gas, oil gas, air gas, and acetylene.

When soft coal is heated in a closed container, it gives off inflammable gas. *Coal gas* produced in this manner was known as early as 1691, but it was first used in 1792 by William Murdock to light his home in Cornwall, England. Pall Mall, London, was, in 1807, the first street to be lighted with gas, while Baltimore, in 1821, was the first American city to use the new system.

Much coal gas is obtained as a by-product in the manufacture of coke. Large amounts are also produced in retorts built specially for that purpose. Before it can be used, the gas passes through cleaning devices which remove such impurities as tar, ammonia, sulphur, and carbon dioxide. It is then stored in huge tanks, from which it passes to the distributing pipes.

Water gas, which is used in many cities, is made by blowing steam through a furnace full of white hot anthracite or coke. The steam is decomposed and combines with the carbon of the fuel to produce hydrogen and carbon monoxide, gases which burn with great heat. Coal gas and water gas are of chief importance in public gas systems.

Oil gas is produced by heating suitable oils until they break down into permanent gases. These may be purified and compressed into cylinders. *Pintsch* and *blau* gases are of this type. *Air gas* is formed by blowing air through a volatile, inflammable liquid such as gasoline, until the air contains enough vapor to burn. This type is often used in detached houses.

When it was the custom to obtain light directly from burning gas, it was often necessary to add to the gas quantities of hydrocarbons such as ethylene and benzene in order that the flame should produce a certain fixed degree of brightness or candle power. The use of the more efficient incandescent mantles, which require only that the burning gas supply heat sufficient to make them glow, made desirable a standard for gas which should be based on *heating value* rather than on candle power. The change to such a standard was hastened by the World War, when all available benzene was needed for the production of explosives.

Gelatin. A hard, transparent, yellowish white, nitrogenous substance, without taste or smell, which swells when in contact with cold water. It dissolves in hot water and, when the solution is cooled, sets to a stiff, jelly-like mass. Gelatin is formed by the action of boiling water on connective tissue, cartilage, ligaments and tendons, skin, hoofs, and bones. By one commercial process, the selected tissues are washed, soaked in warm diluted soda lye for about ten days, and then heated in an airtight compartment. They are next washed in revolving drums, bleached by fumes of burning sulphur, and rewashed to remove all sulphur, after which the gelatin is dissolved out with boiling water. Color is removed by means of bleaching charcoal, and the clear hot solution is poured out in thin layers, which, after setting, are cut into small sheets and dried on nets.

Isinglass is a very pure form of gelatin, obtained from the swimming bladders of sturgeon and other fish. It should not be confused with the thin, transparent sheets of mica, which are sometimes incorrectly called isinglass. Ordinary *glue* is impure gelatin, of great value as an adhesive. Many photographic processes require gelatin, which is used to hold the sensitive silver salts on plates and films.

The value of gelatin as a food was for a long time greatly overestimated, for it has been shown that animals, when fed on it exclusively, die of starvation.

Glass. A hard, noncrystalline, artificial substance, usually transparent or translucent, made by melting together a mixture of various materials. The principal ingredients used in glassmaking are: *sand* or other forms of pure silica; *lime* or lead oxide; and some form of *alkali*. Many other materials enter into the production of special kinds of glass. Bottle glass usually contains aluminum. The addition of manganese gives a brown color; cobalt yields a blue; and even gold has been used to produce a particularly beautiful ruby glass. One of the most important characteristics of glass is that it does not melt at any fixed temperature, but softens gradually as the heat increases, and loses plasticity as it cools.

Great care is taken that the materials used shall be as free as possible from iron, which imparts a green color to the finished product. The selected ingredients are melted in a furnace together with a small amount of broken glass or *cullet*, which lowers the melting point of the mixture. The furnaces were formerly huge pots of clay, but now are usually large rectangular tanks.

Plate glass is made by casting molten glass upon large iron tables, where it is flattened by rollers, and then placed in annealing ovens to cool. For mirrors and windows, the sides of the rough plate are ground and carefully polished, but the unfinished plate is quite satisfactory for use as a cheap roofing glass.

In the process of making *window glass*, a large lump of the molten substance is gathered from the furnace on the end of an iron pipe and is then blown by compressed air to a bubble which gradually stretches out in the form of a great bottle. The bottom is then softened by heating and is blown open by air pressure. The blowpipe is broken from the neck, and the shoulder of the bottle is cracked off, thus leaving a cylinder. The cylinder is opened by being cut on the inside with a diamond, cracked along the cut by means of a piece of hot metal, and placed in a kiln where the heat is sufficient to soften the sides so that they may be flattened. The process is now performed almost entirely by machinery.

Flint glass, in spite of its name, is the softest of the ordinary types. It is usually made from silica, potash, and lead oxide and, because of its brilliancy, is used for tableware and cut glass. A flint glass containing a large proportion of lead forms the *strass* used for making imitation jewels.

Optical glass must be cooled very slowly to prevent distortions due to internal stresses which are caused by unequal contraction.

Safety glass is made by inserting between two sheets of plate glass a sheet of transparent celluloid, which is securely attached to the two glass plates by adhesive material. Glass of this type has become standard for motor car windows.

Float glass comes close to plate glass quality without the polishing and grinding steps. It is a continuous process lending itself to automation. The molten glass mixture runs from the furnace onto the surface of a pool of molten tin. As it floats, it cools with a fine polished surface.

Fiber glass is produced by drawing out molten glass into filaments a few ten-thousandths of an inch in diameter and generally 10 to 12 inches long. The result is extremely flexible fibers that can be woven or felted into a wide variety of durable fabrics that are resistant to fire and water. Popular uses are in draperies and upholstery, electrical and heat insulation, and acoustical materials. When layers of glass fabric are interspersed with plastics, they can be molded into durable and lightweight objects such as armor plate, boat hulls, and automobile bodies.

Other new types of glass include a "shrunk" glass with an extremely low rate of expansion when heated and an "invisible" glass, which transmits light with more than 99 per cent completeness and will not reflect light from any angle. The last named glass consists of plates fastened together by an invisible varnish in a layer having a thickness of one-fourth of the wave length of light. Waves of reflected light are cancelled, as it were, when meeting waves of oncoming light in the layer of varnish.

Glass which transmits ultra-violet rays is made by including as ingredients boric oxide, excluding lead, and diminishing the proportion of ferric oxide.

Expert glassblowers can work the material into almost any form. Frosted effects are obtained by using a sand blast or hydrofluoric acid. *Cut glass* has its designs sunk into it by sharp edged wheels, or the pattern may be molded and the slightly rounded edges sharpened on a grinding wheel.

Glucose. Commercial glucose is a clear, thick, sirupy liquid, which is about two-thirds as sweet as sugar. In Europe it is made chiefly from potato starch, but in the United States it is produced almost entirely from corn, whence the name corn sirup. The corn is ground under water to obtain the starch, which, after being cleaned, is treated with hydrochloric acid. Under the influence of the acid, the starch molecules combine with water and break down into glucose together with some dextrins and other products. The acid is then neutralized, and the thin liquid is bleached, filtered, and finally concentrated under vacuum to the required consistency.

Experiments by government experts have shown that glucose is in no way inferior to cane sugar in healthfulness. For table use, it is usually flavored with about 15 per cent of sirup obtained from sugar refineries. Large amounts of glucose are required by canning, preserving, and candy industries.

Glycerin. A sweet sirupy liquid without color or odor. It is the principal by-product of the soap- and candle-making industries, resulting from the decomposition, under heat, of fats with alkali or acid. Glycerin can be obtained from any fat, such as cottonseed oil, lard, or butter. It is purified by distillation with superheated steam, the pure substance boiling at a temperature (554° F.) higher than the melting point of tin. It does not evaporate easily, but takes moisture from the air. For this reason, it is added to tobacco, shredded coconut, candy, and inking pads, to prevent drying.

Glycerin is a good solvent for many organic materials and may be used instead of alcohol in the preparation of flavoring extracts. Tea and coffee stains can often be removed by first moistening the spot with glycerin and then applying soap and water. Mixed with litharge, or lead oxide, glycerin makes a valuable cement. Glycerin is used in medicine to allay inflammation. It is valuable also as a cosmetic and is used extensively in the preparation of nitroglycerin for explosives.

Gold Leaf. Extremely thin sheets of gold, used chiefly for gilding. These sheets average $\frac{1}{200000}$ inch in thickness, so that, in this form, an ounce of gold will cover almost 100 square feet.

In making gold leaf, an ingot of gold about an inch wide is first flattened between steel rollers to a long ribbon having the thickness of very thin paper. This ribbon is cut into squares, which are stacked with a sheet of vellum or tough paper between adjacent pieces. The pile is enclosed in a parchment case, placed on a marble table, and beaten with a heavy hammer until each piece has spread to a square having a size of about 3½ inches. These squares are quartered.

Each small piece is next placed between layers of *goldbeater's skin*, a tough membrane prepared from the intestines of cattle. The skins are dusted with fine plaster of Paris to prevent sticking, and beating is continued with a lighter hammer until the gold is again about 3½ inches square. Another quartering and beating then yields foil of the proper thickness. The final pieces are trimmed to about 3¼ inches square and are packed between leaves of dusted paper in books, each containing 25 pieces.

Gold used for beating is about 23 carats fine. A small amount of alloy gives the desired color, but, as impure gold does not yield so much foil, adulteration with cheaper metals is seldom practiced.

Gunpowder. An explosive mixture of saltpeter, charcoal, and sulphur. The origin of this product is unknown. The Chinese apparently knew of the mixture at the beginning of the Christian era, but, in Europe, Friar Roger Bacon, of Oxford, seems to have been the first to write of its properties. About 1313, a German monk named Barthold Schwartz demonstrated that it might be used for propelling missiles. Cannons existed at least as early as 1326. However, gunpowder was not generally used in warfare until the 16th century.

Standard United States Army black powder contains 75 per cent saltpeter, 15 per cent charcoal, and 10 per cent sulphur. When such a mixture explodes in the breech of a gun, about 43 per cent of it is changed to hot gases, which, by their expansive force, exert an enormous pressure. The large amount of smoke is due to the remaining 57 per cent of solid particles which are thrown out.

In the manufacture of gunpowder, the materials are mixed dry. They are then moistened, and ground under heavy rollers. After grinding, the *meal* is placed between plates of hard rubber in a hydraulic press. High pressure yields a dense, quick-burning powder; lower pressure gives one that acts more slowly. The cakes from the press are broken up into grains, which are sifted and then polished in revolving barrels. After a second sifting, the grains are dried and packed in containers.

Brown, or *cocoa*, *powder* was developed for use in heavy guns. It is usually in the form of prisms about 1⅓ inches long and having a hole through the center to increase the burning surface. Partially charred rice straw, which gives a brown color to the powder, is used instead of charcoal. *Blasting*, or *mining*, *powders* are coarser products and usually contain a smaller proportion of saltpeter. Chile saltpeter, or sodium nitrate, is sometimes used instead of the more expensive potassium salt.

These explosives have been almost entirely supplanted by superior products of the smokeless powder type, which are made so that practically all the products of explosion are gases. Smokeless powders are more powerful and less bulky than the black gunpowder and do not leave a large residue of mineral matter. They are usually prepared from materials of the type of guncotton and nitroglycerin modified in such a manner as to retard the speed of explosion. The first smokeless powder for sporting purposes was made in 1867 by Schultze, a German. A Frenchman named Vieille produced the first successful military smokeless powder in 1886, and, in 1889, Richard von Freeden invented a hard-grained sporting powder.

Heating and Ventilating Systems. Heating is ordinarily accomplished by means of open fireplaces, stoves, hot-air furnaces, steam, hot-water, and the vacuum-vapor systems. The hot-air furnace is an *indirect* heater, because the air is warmed by it before entering the room. The other systems are *direct*, because they are placed within the rooms to be heated. A radiator or other heating unit located within a room at the opening of a fresh air intake would be classed as a *direct-indirect* system.

The open fire is a pleasant source of warmth, but it is exceedingly expensive because most of the heat goes up the chimney. It does, however, afford good ventilation. A base-burner stove furnishes one of the most efficient methods of heating, but it requires a large amount of space and is unpleasant on account of the dust that arises when coal is applied and ashes are removed.

With the hot-air furnace, air is generally admitted from outside the building through an intake pipe and passed over a heating surface connected with the fire box. The heated air expands, becomes lighter, and, rising up through the distributing pipes, passes through registers, or grated openings in the floor or wall, into the rooms to be warmed. This system has the advantage of providing fresh air, but it is not always reliable. When a strong wind is blowing, it is a common experience to find that rooms on the windward side cannot be heated. This is usually because the wind leaks into the room through small cracks around the windows and baseboards. The slight pressure then becomes sufficient to prevent warm air from rising in the pipes. The use of storm sash during cold weather has often seemed to double the value of a hot air furnace.

A pipeless furnace has but one large register, placed in the floor directly above the heating plant. From the center of the register, the warm air rises to the ceiling, spreading in all directions. The outer edge of the register is connected as an intake through which the cool air near the floor is drawn to the furnace. The pipeless furnace can heat thoroughly only those rooms into which the warm air finds an easy path. It is therefore most satisfactory where the rooms are few—though not necessarily small—and where the door openings extend to the ceiling.

Steam, hot water, and vacuum-vapor systems use hollow radiators to give off the heat, and a furnace to generate it. The two are connected by a series of pipes. These systems deliver heat where it is needed, without reference to the direction of the wind. Steam radiators do not operate until the water in the boiler has been heated to the boiling point and sufficient pressure generated to force the steam through the pipes. Hot-water systems begin to radiate soon after a fire is started, because, as the water in the furnace becomes warmer, it becomes lighter and is pushed upward through the radiator by the heavier, cooler water entering the furnace from below. Hot-water radiators must be larger than steam radiators to warm the same space because they usually operate at 140° F. to 180° F. compared with 212° F. for steam.

At the ordinary atmospheric pressure of 14.7 pounds per square inch, water boils at 212° F. If, by creating a partial vacuum, this pressure is reduced to 1 pound, the boiling point becomes 101.8° F. The vacuum-vapor system takes advantage of this fact and is practically equivalent to a steam system operating under a vacuum produced by automatic valves or other devices. Under these conditions the water gives off vapor at comparatively low temperatures, and the vapor, meeting but little resistance, quickly flows to the radiator.

COMPARATIVE COST OF HEATING

System	Initial Cost	Fuel Required
Hot air	1.0	1.0
Pipeless furnace	2/3	1.0
Steam	2.0	3/4
Hot water	2 2/3	2/3
Vacuum-vapor	3 2/3	3/5 – 2/3

It is impossible to say which system is the best because the answer depends on the conditions and surroundings. An approximation of the relative cost is given in the above table.

Distribution of heat from a central station as practiced in various communities is often very satisfactory, especially where exhaust steam is available from some large power plant. The use of gas for fuel is convenient, but in some regions gas is more expensive than coal. Electric heating is almost ideal in terms of efficiency, cleanliness, and maintenance. In many areas, however, electric heating is still considerably more expensive than other methods.

According to various calculations, the hourly supply of fresh air in a living room should be from 700 to 1000 cubic feet for each person. But the problem of ventilating the house ordinarily receives very little attention because doors and windows are so frequently opened that the air seldom becomes unwholesome. However, the air in most American homes generally contains about one-half as much moisture as it should contain, or, in technical terms, the *relative humidity* is too low. A living room temperature of 68°–70° with a relative humidity of 60–70 is considered best from the standpoint of health and efficiency.

The prevalence of colds, sore throat, and pneumonia in the United States can to a large extent be attributed to the custom of living in dry, overheated rooms. If the percentage of moisture in the air of these rooms were increased, a lower temperature would be used, for, when the air is very dry, the temperature must be from 7° to 10° higher than would otherwise be comfortable.

In hospitals, theaters, and schools, fresh air is usually provided by means of power driven fans. This air is sometimes cleaned and provided with the proper amount of moisture by means of washing devices. Many commercial establishments, such as candy factories, weaving mills, and offices where color printing is done, find it necessary to install air-conditioning apparatus so that, in winter and in summer, the atmosphere of the operating rooms shall always have the same degree of temperature and humidity. By this means the quality of their product is kept uniform.

Ink. A colored fluid used for writing or printing. Standard writing ink is usually prepared from an extract of nutgalls, a solution of copperas or iron sulphate, and a solution of some gum, such as gum arabic. The gum is added to the extract, which contains gallic acid, and the iron salt is then poured into the mixture. A fine, light-colored precipitate is formed, which is prevented by the gum from settling. A small amount of disinfectant is generally added to prevent the growth of molds.

Such an ink produces writing of a light blue color, which, from the action of oxygen in the air, changes in about a week to intense, permanent black. In order that the writing may immediately have a strong, dark color, a solution of some coal-tar color is often added. Fountain pen inks should contain no sediment. Therefore, in making this type of ink, certain aniline colors, especially nigrosine, are extensively used.

Red ink may be prepared by dissolving eosin and a small amount of gum in water. Gold, silver, and bronze inks may be made by grinding the metallic leaf to extreme fineness in a heavy sirup, such as honey or glucose. The powder is then washed, and suspended in a solution of gum arabic. India ink consists of a stick of finely divided carbon mixed with gum, which is rubbed with water.

Inks used for printing usually consist of the proper color or pigment mixed with linseed oil or resinous varnish. Lampblack and gas black are the best pigments for printing black, while the colored inks are generally made with coal-tar dyes.

Lacquer. This term is generally used today of the synthetic, quick-drying lacquers having a pyroxylin base, which came into wide use about 1923. In distinction from paints and varnishes, its base is an artificially prepared material, pyroxylin. This is made by stirring cotton linters or high grade tissue paper in sulphuric and nitric acid. The excess acid is separated out by centrifugal machines, leaving pyroxylin, a nitrate of cellulose. This is dissolved in wood alcohol, ethyl acetate, acetone, or some other solvent, and pigments are added. The first of these lacquers to be marketed was called duco.

The principal advantage in the use of lacquer is the speed with which it dries. It reduces the time necessary for finishing automobile bodies from several weeks to three days or less. It is also much more durable and less susceptible to scratching than varnish. Its employment on automobiles has made possible the use of colors at moderate prices, since baked enamel, formerly used on metal bodies, lent itself only to black, colors being affected by the baking heat. However, lacquers do not take as high a gloss as varnishes and baked enamel.

Lactic Acid. A clear, sirupy liquid formed when the lactose (white, crystalline sugar) in milk ferments, causing it to sour, or when sugar ferments. Commercially, lactic acid is prepared by the fermentation of carbohydrates, such as corn sugar and starch. It is important to a wide range of industries, including foods, beverages, candy, leather, and synthetic resins.

Lead Pencil. The ordinary lead pencil consists of a long, narrow stick of "lead" held in a small circular case, usually composed of wood, but which is frequently made of paper or of metal. The "lead" pencil contains no lead whatever, the marking element being in reality graphite. This was introduced about 1565, when a graphite mine was discovered at Barrowdale, in Cumberland, England. The black mark of a graphite pencil was much superior to that made by metallic lead, which had been used for this purpose from early times by the Romans, the Aztecs, and many other peoples. The new material, called black lead, gradually displaced the older type.

In the process of manufacture, the graphite is first reduced to an extremely fine powder by crushing. It is then suspended in water and mixed with the proper amount of fine clay. The water is removed by filtering the mixture, and the paste is then forced through perforated plates until it is sufficiently smooth. Finally, the pasty mass is forced, under hydraulic pressure, through a die, from which it emerges as a continuous string of the required size. This string is straightened and is cut into pieces which are packed in trays and baked in ovens.

Red cedar or other soft wood is prepared for the casings by being cut into slats 7 inches long, 2 inches wide, and $\frac{1}{4}$ inch thick. On the surface of the slats, grooves are cut parallel to the long side and just deep enough to receive half the thickness of the lead. Glue is then applied to the grooved surface; a strip of lead is placed in the groove; and a second grooved slat is placed over the first so as to form an oblong block. The dried blocks are then fed to a milling machine, from which they emerge as perfectly shaped lead pencils. These are varnished or painted, the ends are trimmed smooth and, frequently, tipped with a metallic cap holding a rubber eraser.

Leather. The skin from an animal, tanned or treated so that it is more or less soft and flexible when dry. It differs from raw skin in that it does not decompose quickly and does not yield glue when treated with boiling water. Leather may be prepared from any skin, but cattle, sheep, and goats are the chief sources of supply. The skins of the larger animals, such as cattle and horses, are called hides.

A raw skin consists of three layers. That on the outside is hard and scaly; that on the inside is composed of connecting and fatty tissues. Between these is the true skin, a layer of gelatinous fibers from which leather is made.

In preparation for tanning, skins are softened by soaking in water, the hair is loosened by treatment with milk of lime, and the layers of hair and fatty tissues are scraped off with knives. Further soakings are usually given to remove any excess lime. After these preliminary treatments, the inner skin is ready to be *tanned*, or changed to leather.

This change is usually accomplished in one of three ways: by soaking the skin in a solution of tannin extracted from oak or hemlock bark, sumac leaves, quebracho, or other vegetable material; by soaking in a solution of metallic salts, such as aluminum or chromium; by treatment with fish oils. The first method is called *tanning*; the second, *tawing*; and the third, *chamoising*. As the use of tannin is much older than other methods, the word tanning is used as a general term to include all processes.

The tannin process often requires from 4 to 8 months, while tawing with chromium salts can sometimes be completed in a few hours or days. As chrome tannage yields a very durable leather that is soft, light, and almost waterproof, it has become very popular in this country. Most glazed kid, such as that used for women's shoe tops and gloves, is chrome tanned. *Vici kid* is a proprietary name now generally used to describe any black, glazed, chrome-tanned kid. *Sole leather*, *harness leather*, and *belting leather* are produced from heavy cowhides by both methods of tanning.

Chamoising yields soft, pliable, light-colored wash leather of the chamois, doeskin, and suède type. These are made by working fish oil into the skins until all of the moisture is displaced. An oxidation process then occurs, during which the skins are changed to leather. The excess fat, known as *degras* when pressed from the skins, and as *sod oil* when washed out, is highly valued for dressing leather. *Chamois* was originally made from the skin of a small antelope of that name, which lives on the highest mountains of Europe and southwestern Asia. It is now made mostly from sheepskins. *Ooze* refers to leather having a suède finish.

Patent leather is made by applying many coats of oil and nitrocellulose varnish to well tanned skins tightly stretched on frames. The process is not controlled by a patent. *Cordovan leather* is soft, firm, fine-grained, and nearly waterproof. It was originally made in the Spanish city of Cordoba, but is now prepared in many countries from horsehide. Any required color is produced by dyeing. *Russian leather* is tanned with willow and birch bark. It has a peculiar odor due to the oil of birch bark tar with which it is finished.

Morocco was originally a fine red leather made in the vicinity of Morocco from goatskins. Today it is colored leather made from sumac-tanned goatskins which have been worked to bring out the grain. It is considered by bookbinders to be both the most durable and the most beautiful covering for books. *Levant morocco* is the finest and most expensive grade. When the grain of Levant morocco is crushed until the surface is smooth and polished, it is known as *crushed levant*. *French morocco* is made from sheepskin. *Buffing* is the grain, or outside split, from calfskin. It is much used for binding books.

Artificial leather, which has the appearance and many of the characteristics of the more expensive material. is usually made of cloth coated with some waterproof, flexible substance, such as a preparation of cellulose nitrate. The surface is grained by means of a die.

Lighting Devices, Electric. Illumination by electricity is accomplished by three principal types of lamps,—filament, gaseous, and phosphorescent. The oldest and commonest is the so-called incandescent or filament lamp, in which a current flows through a filament, usually of tungsten, inside a glass bulb either empty of gas or filled with an inert gas. The current heats the filament until the filament glows brilliantly. The filament is looped, each end being connected with a small wire sealed into the neck of the glass bulb.

The gaseous type depends on sending a current of electricity through a glass tube filled with an inert gas, the current causing the gas to glow throughout its entire volume. The terminals for the current are placed at opposite ends of the tube. Different gases produce different colors. They also vary greatly in illuminating efficiency per unit of current. Mercury vapor gives off white light with a bluish tinge, neon a reddish-orange light, argon lamps a green glow, sodium vapor a yellowish light. The glass tubes may be molded to spell words, thus making these lights especially adaptable for advertising signs.

The phosphorescent lamp consists of a glass tube whose inner surface is coated with a phosphorescent substance. Upon the inner surface of the tube are projected invisible ultraviolet rays, which, upon striking the phosphorescent coating, causes it to glow. The advantages of the phosphorescent electric light include greater approximation to daylight, a wider range of possible color, high lighting efficiency, and long life.

The earliest electric lamps used platinum-wire filaments. In 1860, J. W. Swan, an Englishman, exhibited lamps using carbonized threads of paper. Thomas A. Edison, working independently, produced in October 1879 a carbon filament lamp, which was the first to succeed commercially.

In carbon filament lamps it was necessary to exhaust the air from the glass bulb in which the filaments were placed. Otherwise the carbon would burn.

Edison's early lamps used a filament of carbonized bamboo fiber. Later, the filaments were made by forcing a solution of cotton through a fine hole. The threads thus formed were hardened and were changed to carbon by heating. Improvements followed steadily. In 1907, a lamp with a filament made from powdered metallic tungsten was placed on the market; in 1911, stronger filaments of drawn ductile tungsten appeared; and, in 1913, the efficiency was greatly increased by filling the bulb with an inert gas, formerly nitrogen but now chiefly argon. These gas-filled bulbs, unlike the vacuum lamps, become hot when in use because the gas conducts some of the heat from the center to the sides. Nevertheless, they last longer and give more light for less cost than any of the older types.

Lime. A caustic, infusible material which, when pure, consists chiefly of calcium oxide. It is made by roasting limestone, chalk, marble, shells, or other forms of *calcium carbonate*, to a bright red heat. *Carbon dioxide gas* is given off and the residue is lime, or, as it is often called, *quicklime*. The burning is done in lime kilns, some types of which operate continuously while others must be cooled and emptied before another batch can be made.

When lime is mixed with water, chemical combination takes place. Much heat is given off and the lime swells to a powder known as *slaked lime*, or, chemically, as calcium hydroxide. *Milk of lime* consists of slaked lime suspended in a large excess of water. Ordinary *whitewash* is milk of lime to which a size, such as glue or flour, is usually added. *Air slaked lime* has been exposed to the atmosphere, from which it absorbs carbon dioxide and moisture until it falls to a powder. Pure lime which combines easily with water and makes a smooth stiff paste is known as a *fat lime*.

Lime is used principally for making mortar. It is also extensively employed for softening hard water, for neutralizing acid soils, for making bleaching powder and glass, for purifying sugar, in metallurgical operations, and for many other purposes.

Linen. Thread or cloth made from fibers of the flax plant. It is noted for its smoothness, luster, strength, and durability. Well preserved linen cloths have been found in Egyptian mummy cases which were more than 4000 years old. Linen is not easily dyed, consequently it does not hold stains so permanently as cotton, wool, or silk.

In preparing the fiber, the seeds are removed from the plant and the flax is placed either in pools of stagnant water, in streams, or upon a moist meadow. The wet straw ferments, and, during this process, called *retting*, the woody core becomes soft, so that it may be easily removed. When retting is complete, the flax is passed through machines which break the hard parts without injuring the fiber, which is then *scutched*, or beaten until clean and free of foreign materials. The purified flax is combed, or *heckled*, so as to separate the long, straight fibers, called *line*, from the short tangled *tow*. The line is then ready for spinning and weaving, and the tow is used in making cordage or the cheaper fabrics.

Linen thread is used almost exclusively in the manufacture of handmade lace. Table linen, when woven so as to show a pattern, is known as *damask* because of a resemblance to the famous patterned silks of Damascus. The snow white color is obtained by bleaching. Other linen fabrics include fine cambric, shirting, and handkerchief cloth, as well as the coarser butcher linen, crash, and huckaback.

Linen is much used for towels because it absorbs water quickly. As the result of this property, a spot of moisture usually shows on the opposite side of a linen fabric more quickly than it does on cotton. A more reliable method of distinguishing between the two is to put a drop of salad oil on the cloth and press it between blotting paper. Linen becomes more transparent than cotton.

Linoleum. A floor covering made by fixing on a sheet of canvas a mixture of oxidized linseed oil, ground cork, and other materials. The oxidized oil alone is also known as linoleum.

When thin layers of linseed oil are exposed to air, or when air is blown through the oil under proper conditions, oxygen is absorbed and the fluid gradually changes to a tough, elastic solid somewhat similar to rubber. This oxidized product is ground by machinery, mixed with cork, resin, and coloring materials, and fixed upon burlap by means of hot rollers. A decorative pattern is usually printed on the smooth surface.

Better grades of linoleum are made up of a mosaic of colored pieces so that the pattern extends through to the back. These pieces are united into a single layer by the pressure of hot rolls. Good linoleum provides a smooth insulating floor covering which is comfortable to walk on, easy to clean, and much more durable than oilcloth, which it has largely displaced.

Linseed Oil. The most useful of all paint oils. It was probably known in ancient times and was undoubtedly used for paint in the 7th century, but its real value was not generally appreciated until about 1400, when oil painting came into general use.

Linseed oil is dissolved from the crushed seed with naphtha, which has a low boiling point and can easily be removed from the oil by heating. The product is known as *raw linseed oil*. It ranges in color from light amber to dark yellow-brown and has rather an unpleasant odor and taste. Enormous quantities are used in making paint; at least seven and one-half gallons are required for every 100 pounds of white lead. *Boiled linseed oil* is produced when the raw oil is boiled with the addition of certain chemicals, such as manganese dioxide, which hasten the rate of the drying. This form is used chiefly for interior paints. *Refined linseed oil* receives special treatment which removes any sediment-forming material and gives the lighter color which is demanded by the makers of fine varnish.

Besides its exceptional value in the paint industry linseed oil is required for the manufacture of patent leather, for waterproofing cloth, such as oiled silk, and for making many of the imitation leathers which are often used for automobile tops and book bindings. It is an important ingredient in linoleum and oilcloth, while thousands of gallons are used in printing and lithographic inks. The value of the oil for these purposes is due entirely to its ability to absorb oxygen from the air and thereby change from a liquid to a tough, elastic solid. Oils having this property to a high degree are called drying oils. In addition, linseed oil has minor uses in medicine.

After the oil has been removed from the seed, the residue is known as *linseed oil cake.* When ground, this is called *linseed meal,* a very rich and valuable cattle food, at least four times as nutritious as hay. Linseed meal is also used to some extent as a fertilizer.

Liquid Air. A pale blue liquid, similar to water in density, used for producing very low temperatures. As the name indicates, it is prepared by liquefying air through subjection to high pressure, about 120 times the atmospheric pressure being required for air at normal temperatures. As pressure increases, the temperature falls. The oxygen in the air liquefies at $-182.9°$ C., and the nitrogen at $-195.7°$ C. In evaporating, the liquid absorbs heat, thereby producing very low temperatures. If the oxygen from liquid air is allowed to boil and evaporate off, the nitrogen still remains. Nitrogen is thus obtained for the manufacture of ammonia, cyanamid, and other compounds.

Luminous Paint. A mixture usually consisting of barium sulphide and zinc sulphide together with an exceedingly minute amount of some salt of radium. It has the valuable property of being visible in the dark. The mixture is used as a paint, or as a powder in small glass containers, to mark the hands and dials of clocks and watches, and the position of keyholes, lighting fixtures, gun sights, and other objects the visibility of which in the dark is often desirable.

Before the discovery of radium, luminous paint was generally prepared from mixtures of calcium sulphide with bismuth, from calcium tungstate, or from other materials phosphorescent only after an exposure to daylight. During the World War, the radium paint was extensively used in the front line trenches as it is visible for only a very short distance.

Radiolite is a commercial preparation containing the hexagonal zinc sulphide, called Sidot's blende, and radium. On the hands and dial of a "radiolite" watch there is less than $\frac{1}{1000}$ milligram of radium. Reckoning radium at about $100,000 per gram, there is from five to ten cents' worth of the element on such a watch. This radium gives off each second some 30,000 alpha particles, which strike the zinc sulphide and cause it to become luminous.

Match. A short, slender piece of wood or other inflammable material tipped with some combustible substance which will ignite by friction. Modern matches come under two general classes: safety matches, which must be rubbed on a specially prepared surface; and "strike anywhere" matches.

One of the earliest types of match consisted of a long splinter of wood tipped with sulphur. These were lighted by pressing the tip into glowing tinder. Later the sulphur tip was covered with a mixture of potassium chlorate and sugar, which ignited when dipped into a bottle containing asbestos saturated with strong sulphuric acid. The first true friction match was invented in 1827 by John Walker, an Englishman. It had a sulphur tip covered by a mixture of potassium chlorate and antimony sulphide. Fire was produced by drawing the head of the match between folded sandpaper which was supplied with each package.

Walker's matches were known as *congreves,* while imitations of these, called *lucifers,* were made by several competitors. White phosphorus was first used on the tips of friction matches by Walker and other manufacturers, in 1833. In the United States, improved friction matches were first made at Springfield, Massachusetts, in 1836.

For many years the tips of ordinary matches consisted of sulphur and white phosphorus, often with some chlorate or nitrate. Because of the unpleasant fumes of burning sulphur, these were largely displaced by *parlor matches,* having a more inflammable tip with much less sulphur. A machine for automatically preparing the sticks was invented in 1842.

In 1855, safety matches were introduced by a Swede named Lundstrom. He omitted white phosphorus from the tip and instead placed a friction surface of red phosphorus and sand on the side of the box. Safety matches ignite only when rubbed on this surface.

White phosphorus is an intense poison which was the cause, among match workers, of many cases of necrosis, or rotting of the jawbones. The dangers attendant on its use can be avoided by substituting in its place red phosphorus or phosphorus sesquisulphide. For this reason, the use of white phosphorus in matches has been forbidden in many countries.

Patents covering the use of phosphorus sesquisulphide in the United States were owned by the Diamond Match Company, which in 1911 surrendered these patents so that the process might be employed by anyone. The Esch-Hughes Non Poisonous Match act, passed in 1912, placed a tax of two cents per hundred on matches containing white phosphorus, thus making the use of this material commercially impossible. The exact composition now used for the tips of matches is a carefully guarded trade secret. Safety matches often have potassium chlorate and dichromate on the head, with red phosphorus, manganese dioxide, and glass powder on the rubbing surface. "Strike anywhere" matches generally contain phosphorus sesquisulphide together with such oxidizing materials as red lead, lead peroxide, manganese dioxide, and potassium chlorate. The mixture is often colored, and is held by a binder of glue or dextrin.

In North America, matches are usually made from white pine or California sugar pine which has been seasoned and dried for almost two years. The wood may be cut into planks about two inches thick, which are then sawed into blocks the length of a match. The blocks are fed into a machine which rapidly splits them into match sticks. A second important method of preparation consists in cutting the pine log into a long roll of veneer having the thickness of a match. The veneer is then reduced to splints by machinery.

The splints are automatically fixed in rows on an endless belt, which carries them until the free ends, having been heated and dipped in paraffin, receive the composition that forms the head. This is dried by a blast of warm air. They are then mechanically packed into boxes. Ordinarily, they are from $1\frac{7}{8}$ to $2\frac{1}{4}$ inches long. Matches made of waxed taper, called *vestas,* as well as the small books of cardboard matches so much used for advertising are also made by machinery. Impregnated matches have been dipped in solutions of alum or magnesium sulphate to prevent smoldering of burnt stems. In France the manufacture of matches is a government monopoly. Prior to 1918 practically no safety matches were made in the United States, the entire supply being imported from Norway, Sweden, and Japan.

Mortar. A building material ordinarily made by mixing slaked lime, sand, and water. It becomes hard because of chemical action in which the lime absorbs carbon dioxide from the air and changes to calcium carbonate. Lime is prepared by roasting limestone, or calcium carbonate, until the carbon dioxide which it contains is driven off. Thus the hardening of mortar is due to a change in which the lime again becomes limestone. Unlike cement, mortar does not harden until fairly dry. Consequently, it should not be used in very damp places.

Nails. Slender pieces of metal usually pointed at one end and flattened or enlarged at the other to form a head. Nails are classified, according to the method of manufacture, as wrought, cut, and wire. All nails were formerly made by hand, but, with the exception of some horseshoe nails, hand wrought products have been displaced by machine made nails.

The first machine for making cut nails was patented in 1786 by Ezekiel Reed, an American. Machines of this type cut the nails from sheets or narrow strips of heated metal, form the head by pressure or by hammering, and drop the flattened nail into a receiving trough. Wire-nail machines seem to have been a French invention, but the process received little recognition until 1876, when, at the Centennial exposition, American made machines were awarded medals over those of foreign manufacturers. These machines are fed from coils of wire, which they grasp, straighten, cut, and form into nails of any size or type, with great rapidity. At present the wire-nail industry produces the greatest proportion of all nails used.

The size of a standard common nail ranges from 2 d. or *two penny*, to 60 d. This odd method of describing nails, which originated in England, finds two explanations. One is that four penny and ten penny nails sold respectively for four pence and ten pence per hundred. According to the second explanation, 4 d. and 10 d. applied to nails, 1000 of which weighed four pounds and ten pounds respectively. The abbreviation "d.," which now means penny, was in earlier times used for pound. The standard size of the common wire nails is shown in the accompanying table.

A *spike* is three inches or more in length and is thicker than a corresponding nail. For example, a 40 d. spike has the same length as a 40 d. nail but is as thick as a 60 d. nail. *Common brads* have the same length and thickness as nails but have a small, thickened head instead of one that is large and flat. *Finishing nails*, made from 2 d. to 20 d., have the same shape and length as brads but are much thinner.

Wire nails are made into hundreds of special forms, such as roofing nails, plaster board nails, basket nails, wagon nails, hinge nails, and boat nails. Sterilized lath nails are marketed because lathers customarily carry nails in their mouths while working. Special nails may be smooth or may have rough, corrugated surfaces. Cement coated nails are extensively used because they have much greater holding power. Nails are generally sold in 100-pound kegs and in boxes of smaller weight. Those of 20 d. size and larger sell for the same price per pound; the cost of smaller nails increases as the size decreases.

COMMON WIRE NAILS

SIZE	Length Inches	Steel Wire Gauge	Diameter Inches	Number Per Pound
2 d.	1	15	.072	876
3 d.	1¼	14	.080	568
4 d.	1½	12½	.099	316
5 d.	1¾	12½	.099	271
6 d.	2	11½	.112	181
7 d.	2¼	11½	.112	161
8 d.	2½	10¼	.131	106
9 d.	2¾	10¼	.131	96
10 d.	3	9	.148	69
12 d.	3¼	9	.148	63
16 d.	3½	8	.162	49
20 d.	4	6	.192	31
30 d.	4½	5	.207	24
40 d.	5	4	.225	18
50 d.	5½	3	.244	14
60 d.	6	2	.263	11

Needle. A slender, pointed instrument of metal or other material, used to carry the thread in sewing, knitting, and similar operations. Most needles are pierced with a hole called the *eye*, through which the thread is passed. The earliest needles were really pins, for they had no eye but were used simply to make an opening through which a thong of leather or vegetable tissue could be passed. Stone needles having an eye at one end have been found among the relics of the Stone age. Delicate needlework was produced by the Egyptians and ancient Greeks, and both common and surgeons' needles were found in the ruins of Pompeii.

It is believed that the Chinese were the first to use steel needles and that knowledge of this practice was eventually carried into Europe by the Moors. By 1370 a needle making industry had become established at Nuremberg. The manufacture of needles in England developed during the reign of Queen Elizabeth. Not until 1885 were needles made and finished by machine.

Most modern needles are made from high grade steel wire cut into pieces two needles long. The pieces are straightened, both ends pointed against a grindstone, the eyes stamped out, and the double needle broken at the center. The rough needles thus formed have the heads ground to the proper shape and are tempered and polished. The eyes may be smoothed with fine emery and waxed thread, and, in the finest needles, are often gilded. Sewing machine needles are often pressed from short blanks of thick wire.

Knitting needles have no means for holding the thread. Crochet needles have a hook on the end. Surgeons' needles are generally curved, and the needles on many welting machines are curved in the arc of a circle. Sewing machine needles have the eye near the point, with grooves on the sides to prevent binding the thread.

Nitroglycerin. A powerful explosive made by treating pure glycerin with a mixture of concentrated nitric and sulphuric acids. The oily product has a yellowish color, is about 1.6 times as heavy as water, and is slightly volatile. It was discovered by Sobrero in 1846. Both the liquid and its fumes are poisonous and usually cause violent headaches, but persons working in the nitroglycerin factories often become immune to its effects. In medicine it is used as a heart stimulant. Pure nitroglycerin is not very sensitive to friction or to a moderate blow. When frozen it is less sensitive than when liquid. A small quantity, when freely exposed to a flame, burns brilliantly without explosion. Somewhat larger amounts, under the same conditions, usually explode, so that all experiments of this sort are uncertain and dangerous.

Liquid nitroglycerin is used in torpedoes for *shooting* wells, to start or hasten the flow of oil. Because of the danger attending its transportation, the liquid is usually absorbed in some very porous material, such as kieselguhr or sawdust, and pressed into sticks, which are carefully wrapped in paraffin paper. This product, which is known as *dynamite*, was invented by Alfred Nobel in 1866. Nitroglycerin is also an ingredient in other explosive compounds such as *gelatin dynamite* and the *smokeless powders*, which include *ballistite* and *cordite*. Dynamite, as well as nitroglycerin, is most effective when exploded by a *detonating cap* fired either by the ordinary fuse or by electricity. Such a detonator acts as a very quick, powerful blow. The safest way to destroy nitroglycerin is to treat it with a solution of ammonium sulphide.

Nylon. A synthetic textile having many properties similar to those of silk. The word is a coinage of E. I. duPont de Nemours & Co., which obtained the patent in 1937. Nylon is defined as the generic name for "synthetic fiber-forming amides having a protein-like chemical structure; derivable from coal, air, and water or other substances; and characterized by extreme toughness and strength and the peculiar property to be formed into fibers and into various shapes, such as bristles and sheets." Like rayon, nylon filaments are made by pressing a liquid through small holes. The filaments then become solid but may be cold-drawn to an extreme fineness.

Nylon differs from rayon in that it is not made from cellulose. It has greater strength and elasticity, but is less absorbent than cotton, wool, linen, rayon, or silk. Fabrics knitted from nylon hold their shapes better than those made from any other fabric and excel them in wearing qualities. Nylon takes dyes as well as wool, cotton, or silk. The dye may be incorporated in the yarn or added after it is spun. Among its chief uses are as hosiery and other knitted wear, tooth brush bristles, fish lines. Being relatively non-absorbent, fabrics made from nylon dry quickly and feel cool to the skin.

Oleomargarine. A mixture of edible fats churned with milk, salted, and worked to a butter-like consistency. This product was invented in 1869 by a Frenchman, Hippolyte Mège-Mouries, in order to secure a prize offered by Napoleon III for a cheap and wholesome butter substitute.

Oleomargarine is made by churning carefully prepared fats with milk which has been pasteurized and then ripened or fermented until it has a strong butter flavor. Oleo oil and neutral lard, or simply *oleo* and *neutral*, are the most important ingredients used, although some vegetable oil, such as cotton-seed or coconut, is often added. The term oleo oil is somewhat misleading, as the fat is not an oil at ordinary temperatures. Oleo is prepared from selected beef tallow by slowly cooling the melted fat until it begins to thicken. The pasty mass is wrapped in porous cloths and placed under pressure. This forces out the softer portion into tanks of cold water, where it is chilled to a granular, slightly yellowish solid. Neutral is made from choice lard by a similar process, which has for its purpose the removal of the crystalline portion of the fats so that the final product will be smooth instead of grainy. *Nut margarines* are prepared entirely from vegetable fats by substituting coconut and palm kernel oils for oleo and neutral.

The fats are first melted at low temperatures, weighed out in the exact amounts required by the formula, mixed, and thoroughly churned with the ripened milk. The contents of the churn are then sprayed into ice water, becoming solid so quickly that crystals do not have time to form. This chilled mass is allowed to stand for some time in order that the butter flavor may develop further. Its color is white. It is then salted and worked by machinery until smooth and firm like butter.

A household test which will usually distinguish between butter and margarine consists in heating a spoonful of the material over a small flame. Butter foams quietly, while margarine sputters noisily and produces very little foam.

Paint. A suspension of finely ground pigment in a liquid or other medium, which is applied to objects for decoration or protection. Thus, calcimine and whitewash are paints in which the pigment is suspended in water. However, as generally used, paint refers to a suspension of pigment in a fatty oil. Paint was formerly used only as a means of decoration, but its value as a protection against corrosion and decay is now quite generally recognized. Since the invention of water-soluble thermoplastic resins, water-base paints, such as Lucite, may be used both indoors and outdoors.

A good house paint generally contains about 65 per cent by weight of pigment and about 35 per cent of a liquid vehicle, or pigment carrier. The vehicle consists of a mixture of an oil, a solvent or thinner, and a liquid drier. The oil is usually linseed oil, which has the property of absorbing oxygen from the air and of drying to a tough elastic film when spread out. China wood, perilla, soy bean, poppy, fish, and other oils are also used in paints. The solvent is added to make the product penetrate and spread more readily. Among the best solvents are turpentine and benzol. The principal driers are composed chiefly of lead and manganese soaps, which by their presence cause the oil to take up oxygen and to dry more rapidly.

The chief pigments are white lead, zinc oxide, and lithopone. Certain proportions of inert fillers such as barytes, asbestine, silica, and calcium carbonate are often added; but, as a rule, small amounts of these are found in good paint and large amounts in a cheap product. A single pigment in oil does not usually produce the best paint. White lead combined with zinc oxide, with or without a small amount of inert pigments, has been shown by many experiments to give the most satisfactory results. Any desired color may be produced by the addition of natural earth colors, such as sienna and iron oxide, or of artificial pigments, such as lead chromate, prussian blue, and carbon black.

In making prepared paints the pigments are thoroughly mixed by machinery with a small amount of oil. The mixture is then ground to a smooth paste between heavy revolving plates of stone or steel. One barrel of pigment, when ground with oil, yields only $\frac{1}{3}$ barrel of paste. Paint is produced by mixing this paste with linseed oil together with the proper amounts of turpentine, liquid drier, and coloring pigments, which have also been ground in oil. The finished product is then sealed in containers and is packed for shipment.

Enamel paints generally consist of zinc oxide and lithopone in blown linseed oil and high grade varnish. Flat wall paints, often called sanitary flat wall paints, usually contain lithopone and zinc oxide ground in treated china wood oil and thinned with turpentine substitute made from petroleum. Floor paint contains a larger proportion of the inert pigments barytes and silica, which are highly resistant to abrasion, while good mixing varnish is added to the vehicle in order to produce a hard, glossy surface. Paints intended for the protection of iron and steel must prevent corrosion. Red lead containing about 15 per cent litharge, zinc oxide, zinc chromate, basic lead chromate, and basic lead sulphate are especially valuable as rust preventives. Steel hulls of ships usually receive a coat of anti-corrosive paint followed by a coat of antifouling paint, which, in order to prevent the growth of animal and vegetable organisms, contains a poison such as cyanide of copper or mercuric oxide. See *Linseed Oil, Turpentine, Varnish.*

Paper. A substance composed chiefly of cellulose fibers matted or felted into thin sheets. As cellulose is of vegetable origin, the raw materials used for making paper are numerous and include cotton or linen rags, wood pulp, cotton linters, esparto grass, straw, hemp, jute, and old papers. The word "paper" is derived from *papyrus*, a Latin word applied to writing material made from an aquatic plant of that name which was used by the Egyptians as early as 2400 B. C.

The manufacture of paper was known to the ancient Chinese, who during the second century B. C. prepared it from the pulp of the mulberry tree. Chinese prisoners taken by the Moslems introduced paper to the Arabs, who at first utilized ramie extensively in its manufacture. Ramie is a plant having tough fibers similar to linen or flax fibers but stronger. After the 14th century, linen fiber predominated. The Arabs passed the invention on to the Western nations, among whom the making of it has been developed into a highly mechanized process. Fine handmade papers are still produced in China, Japan, and Italy. But the same principle is used whether paper is made by machinery or by hand. A film of fibers suspended in water is spread over a flat surface and the water drained off. In making paper by hand, the mixture of pulp and water is dipped from a vat with a shallow tray or mold with a screen bottom. The vat man dips with a shaking motion to interlock the fibers, and most of the water drains out through the bottom of the mold. He then hands it to the coucher who lays the wet sheet on the "couch" or piece of felt. The pile of alternate layers of felt and paper is pressed and re-pressed to remove more water, and, after sizing with animal glue, the sheets are hung up until thoroughly dry.

At least 250 kinds of paper have been made in the United States. Seventy-five per cent of the total volume is produced from wood pulp; about five per cent, consisting of the highest grades, from rags. The rags are carefully sorted and cut into small pieces, cleaned by boiling with lime, washed, ground in a machine called a *hollander*, bleached with some form of chlorine, and then beaten to a mass of fibers. These fibers are ready to be made into paper.

Wood pulp is classified, according to the method of preparation, as mechanical and chemical. *Mechanical pulp* is made by forcing logs of wood against a revolving grindstone, from which the torn fibers are carried away by a stream of water. *Chemical pulp* is prepared by cutting barked logs into chips, which are cooked with a liquid under pressure until most of the impurities have dissolved. The product is known as *soda*, *sulphite*, or *sulphate pulp*, according as the liquid contained caustic soda, lime and the gas from burning sulphur, or sodium sulphate. Soda pulp lacks strength, while sulphite pulp has good strength and color. Sulphate pulp gives a strong, brown product known as *kraft paper*. Spruce, poplar, pine, and hemlock are the chief pulp woods. Newspaper is usually made from mechanical pulp with which a certain amount of chemical pulp is mixed to impart strength.

The strained pulp, to which has been added any necessary coloring and filling materials, is made into paper on a complicated mechanism called a *Fourdrinier* machine. Wet pulp is first deposited on a long, endless, moving screen of fine wire, from which the water drains rapidly, leaving a soft sheet. A *water mark* is formed at this time by lightly pressing the moist layer with a roller having a raised design. From the moving wire the paper passes to felt rollers, where it is pressed; then to drying rollers; and from these to other rollers, which impart the desired finish to the surface. The edges of the sheet are trimmed and it is wound on a reel. Some Fourdrinier machines can make an endless sheet of paper 180 inches wide at 1000 feet per minute.

Papers to be used for printing and writing are filled with various materials and sized with glue so they will not absorb ink. *Tissue* and *blotting paper* are loosely made without sizing. *Manila paper* was originally made from hemp, jute, or old rope, but it is now produced from wood. The genuine product is called *rope manila*. *Paraffin paper* is made by passing the material through melted paraffin and then through rolls which remove the excess wax.

The skins of various animals when treated so as to afford a smooth surface for writing are known as *parchment*, and a soft, white variety made from calf- or kidskin is called vellum. *Vegetable parchment*, which resembles the animal product, is prepared by rinsing and drying an unsized paper that has been treated with dilute sulphuric acid.

Coated paper is a development of recent years to meet the exacting requirement of the printer so that half tones may be well printed. This paper is mechanically coated on both sides or on one side as may be desired, by either running it through a bath of coating liquid or flowing the liquid onto the paper. The materials used in the coating mixture are largely mineral in character. The mixture may have in it satin white (calcium sulphate and aluminum hydrate), English china clay, blanc fixe (barium sulphate), glue, casein, and starch.

Pins. The first pin was very probably a long thorn, pushed by some primitive man through the animal skins with which he covered himself. Pins made of bone and of bronze have been found among the remains of the ancient Lake Dwellers who inhabited central Europe in prehistoric times. Some of these relics are entirely similar to the present day safety pin. The Egyptians, the Greeks, and the Romans were all familiar with long pins of bronze, bone, and other hard materials.

Development of the process for making wire led to the production of modern pins, which were made first in France and Germany. The manufacture of brass wire pins was introduced into England in 1826. These early pins were cut and sharpened by hand, and the head was formed by wrapping fine wire around one end of the shank. Such handmade pins were expensive, but were considered so necessary an item of dress that the money received or set aside by a woman for her personal expenses came to be known as *pin money*.

The first machine for making solid-headed pins was the invention of an American, Lemuel W. Wright, in 1824. A more satisfactory machine was invented in 1831 by John Ireland Howe, a physician of New York City. A machine for sticking the pins into folded paper, invented by Samuel Slocum, was used in Howe's factory as early as 1841.

The great majority of common pins are made from brass wire; the best are made from fine steel. Coils of wire are placed in the machine, which cuts off and straightens a piece of proper length, holds it in viselike jaws until the head is formed by the blow of a die, and moves the lower end against grinding wheels, which sharpen the point. The pins are next cleaned, coated with tin, and polished. Other automatic machinery arranges them and sticks them into papers. Birmingham is the center of the industry in England; Connecticut, in the United States.

Plastics. A term applied to a group of synthetic chemical products. Their distinctive quality is their capacity to be molded into any shape by moderate heat and pressure and to retain it at ordinary temperatures. They may also be dissolved and used as lacquers, pressed into sheets and panels, or drawn out in threads. They are obtained by chemical treatment from such substances as cellulose (cotton), phenol, or carbolic acid (coal tar), and formaldehyde (wood alcohol). The caseins come from milk; the ureas from ammonia and carbon dioxide (coal, air, and water). The qualities which make these products desirable are their strength, hardness, and electric resistance, the variety of color and finish obtainable, and the possibility of reproducing with exact uniformity.

During World War II, when there were numerous shortages, the plastics industry came to the front by supplying many engineering materials. Considered then to be merely substitutes for older materials, plastics have since won recognition on their own merits, and production has soared from about a billion pounds a year to several times that figure. The development of plastics has had a marked effect on numerous industries. See *Bakelite*, *Cellophane*, *Celluloid*, *Lacquer*, *Nylon*, *Rayon*.

Porcelain. The most highly valued type of fine pottery, differing from inferior grades because of its glasslike, translucent body. It is usually very hard and white. Its common name of *china* indicates the place of its origin; the time is uncertain, perhaps because of the gradual development of the art. The Chinese may have made porcelain of a sort as early as the 7th century A.D. But it is generally acknowledged that not until the Ming dynasty (1368–1644) did their ceramic products develop the qualities for which they became famous.

Porcelain is generally classified, according to the materials of which it is composed, as hard paste, artificial soft paste, and natural soft paste. True hard paste porcelain is made from kaolin, or china clay, and feldspar, which imparts translucency; quartz and special sands are sometimes added. The feldspar is often called Cornish stone because Cornwall, England, has been an important source of this material. From the time that Chinese porcelain first appeared in Europe, great efforts were made to produce a similar product. Articles which resembled porcelain, but were chiefly glass, were made in Florence about 1580. In France, about 1670, artificial soft paste porcelain was first produced.

This contained no kaolin, but was a glasslike substance composed of sand, niter, gypsum, alum, soda, salt, and marl or chalk. It was usually covered with a rich, waxlike glaze. Very little porcelain of this type was produced after 1780. Natural soft paste porcelain, or *bone china*, was an English invention developed during the 18th century. The standard mixture, containing ball clay, kaolin, feldspar, and notable quantities of bone ash, was apparently fixed by Josiah Spode, about 1800. Since that time, it has been the principal product of the chief English potteries.

Hard paste porcelain was first produced in Europe, about 1709, by the alchemist Johann Friedrich Böttger. The factory which he established at Meissen became the source of the famous Dresden china. Manufacture of hard paste was begun at Plymouth, England, in 1768; at Sevres, France, in 1769; and at Philadelphia, U. S. A., in 1825.

Hard porcelain ware is usually baked at a rather low temperature. The resulting biscuit is decorated if desired, covered with glaze, dried, and then fired at temperatures so high that the body almost fuses. Kiln temperatures range from 2000° to 3200° F. The glaze is composed of the same ingredients as the body, although in different proportions. Care is necessary to prepare a glaze which will not crack and separate when the piece cools. When the cracking or crazing of the enamel is uniform and is produced intentionally, the product is known as *crackle ware.*

Parian is a fine grade of thin, unglazed porcelain which receives its name from a resemblance to an ivory tinted marble found on the island of Paros. *Belleek* is thin, light weight porcelain having a beautiful iridescent or pearly glaze. It takes its name from a town in Ireland where it has been made for many years.

The French factories at Sevres and Limoges, the German potteries at Meissen and Berlin, and the Royal Copenhagen factories are recognized as producers of much of the world's finest porcelain. Japan and Austria are also known for their porcelain. The production of high grade porcelain in the United States is constantly increasing, the output of certain potteries being considered by experts equal to the best made in the Continental factories. During World War I a very satisfactory porcelain for use in scientific laboratories was developed in America. See *Pottery.*

Pottery. Any article or product formed from soft, moist clay or claylike material and hardened by means of heat. The term thus includes products ranging in character from ordinary brick to finest porcelain. In common usage, however, *pottery* generally refers to the class of clay or ceramic products which comes between these extremes.

Production of pottery depends chiefly, first, on the fact that moist clay is so plastic that it may be worked or molded into almost any form; secondly, on the fact that, under the action of heat, the plasticity is destroyed, and soft clay becomes hard and durable.

After an article of pottery has been heated or *fired*, it has either a porous, open structure or a nonpermeable, vitrified, or glasslike, body. Porous ware includes terra cotta, fired refractories such as fire brick, and earthenware. *Terra cotta* includes all permeable, unglazed, clay products which fuse or lose shape if heated to 1650° C. The term is applied more narrowly to red-brown or yellowish red ceramic ware used for architectural or decorative purposes. Refractories are similar to terra cotta but must endure a temperature of 1650° C. without fusing or losing shape. Ceramic products having a permeable body covered with a glaze or enamel are classed generally as earthenware. Pottery having a *vitrified body* is divided into *stoneware* and *porcelain*. Stoneware is *opaque* and has usually more or less color; porcelain is *translucent* or partly transparent and is generally white.

The potter's art was known thousands of years before the Christian era. Wherever clay was to be found, man learned in prehistoric times to fashion it into useful articles and to harden these by heat. Thus, pottery was developed independently by the Egyptians, the Chinese, and the Aztecs or their ancestors.

Raw clay must be purified and tempered before satisfactory pottery can be made. For this purpose weathering or exposure to the elements for several months is often practiced. Stones and coarse material may be removed by screening and washing, and uniform plasticity obtained through grinding, kneading, and mixing, usually by machinery. Fine clays are often mixed with large amounts of water so that any coarse particles settle out. The thin mixture is then pumped through filter presses, which retain the clay and allow the water to escape. There are many kinds of clay; the finest—white burning china clay—is called *kaolin*. Iron is the most common impurity, imparting the red color characteristic of terra cotta and brick. Kaolin lacks plasticity; *ball clay* is highly plastic and, when burned, gives rise to white products; *slip clay* melts at low temperatures and is often used as a natural glaze.

When clay has been reduced to proper consistency, it is formed into pottery by *throwing* on a potter's wheel, or by means of molds. A potter's wheel is merely a horizontal, rotating table driven either by power or by the foot of the operator. A lump of clay is placed on the center of the table, and, as it turns under his hands, a skillful potter can produce almost any desired circular form, such as a flat plate or hollow vessel. The surface is smoothed with a wet sponge or a piece of leather and the piece is removed from the wheel. When dry, it may be made perfectly symmetrical by turning in a lathe. Rotating forms called *jiggers* are generally used when many pieces of the same size and shape are to be produced. Irregular shapes are molded, and large vessels may be made up from several molded pieces. Thin pieces are sometimes cast from a mixture of clay and water in a porous plaster of Paris mold, which absorbs much of the moisture. Small parts, such as spouts and handles, are cemented on by means of a thin suspension of clay in water.

When the pieces have dried, they are carefully packed in oven-like, clay containers called *saggers*, which are stacked up in the kiln. Firing requires from 24 to 60 hours, after which the pottery is allowed to cool very slowly. The ware is now in the stage known as *biscuit*. It may be decorated and is then glazed by being dipped into thin, watery mixtures of enamel, dried, and again fired for several hours. During the second firing, most enamels change to a transparent glass through which any decoration is plainly seen. Decoration may also be applied to the unfired enamel or to the fired glaze. Enamels containing tin are white and opaque, while lead enamels are softer and transparent. Very hard, transparent, lead glazes are produced by addition of feldspar, borax, and flint. Salt glaze is made by volatilizing salt in the furnace. The salt vapors combine with the surface of the biscuit ware, yielding a cheap, comparatively soft, but quite effective glaze.

Particular kinds of enamel and types of decoration often characterize the products of certain potteries. Thus Delft, a town in the Netherlands, has long been famous for its decorated, tin enameled pottery. *Majolica*, named from the island of Majorca, is another highly decorative, tin enameled ware. *Yellow ware* is earthenware made from clay which burns to a buff color, covered with transparent glaze. *Rockingham ware* is usually yellow ware covered with a dark brown glaze. It resembles pottery first made on the estate of the marquis of Rockingham. *White granite* or *ironstone* is a bluish white stoneware from which most of the ordinary American crockery is made.

Building bricks were made in Virginia as early as 1612, and white ware was first produced in America about 1684. White ware with underglaze decorations was first produced about 1770, and hard porcelain in 1825. Architectural terra cotta was made in the United States about 1870, and eggshell porcelain, in 1884. Possibly the most famous pottery in America is made at the Rookwood Pottery, of Cincinnati, Ohio. See *Porcelain*.

Pressure Cooker. One of the most popular devices for quick and convenient cooking in the modern American kitchen is the pressure cooker. It is usually made of aluminum or appropriate metal, which may be sealed for cooking or sterilizing under high-pressure superheated steam.

Raisin. A dried grape of special type. All grapes will not make raisins, one requirement being a high content of sugar which not only imparts the characteristic sweet taste but also acts as a preservative. Raisins are produced chiefly in the countries which border on the Mediterranean Sea and in California. The principal varieties of grapes used are the Muscat, Thompson seedless, and Sultana, which is also without seeds.

When the grapes are ripe, the bunches are usually cut from the vines and exposed to the sun on trays, with occasional turning so that drying will be uniform. About three weeks is the average time of curing, and, to hasten the process and avoid the danger of rain, some growers complete the process in artificial dryers.

Rayon. A manufactured textile fiber resembling silk in appearance and sometimes called artificial silk. The material from which it is made is either cotton linters or wood pulp. The raw material is treated with acids or other chemicals in order to make it soluble. It is then dissolved in alcohol and ether, or other suitable solvents, and, after purification, is forced through very small openings. It emerges as fine threads, which become solidified by evaporation of the volatile solvents or by passage through a setting bath.

There are four principal processes in use, of which the above is a generalized description. All are derived from the process devised by a French scientist, Chardonnet, about 1889.

The use of rayon has grown at an amazing rate. In 1922, the consumption of rayon in the United States was by weight about half that of silk. In 1926, the two were about equal. In 1931, 150 million pounds of rayon were used and 79 million pounds of silk. The United States leads the world in rayon production and is followed by Great Britain and Italy.

Rayon is smooth and lustrous, like silk, providing a beautiful fabric at a low cost. Most rayons, being pure cellulose, are very durable if not subject to wear in excess of their strength. Rayon yarn has comparatively low tensile strength, which is still further reduced when the fiber is wet. For this reason, it is frequently mixed with cotton or wool. The resulting fabric usually has better wearing qualities than rayon and is more decorative than cotton or wool.

Rifle A firearm having spiral grooves cut on the surface of its bore. When a shot is fired, the bullet follows the path of the grooves until it leaves the barrel. It consequently receives a spinning motion, which greatly increases the accuracy of its flight.

A rifle usually means a small gun which is fired from the shoulder. But, with a few exceptions, all modern firearms, from the smallest pistol to the great guns of a battleship, are rifled. *Automatic rifles* and *pistols* are automatic only in the sense that they are self-loading; the trigger must be pulled before each shot. A loaded *machine gun*, however, continues to operate automatically as long as the trigger is depressed.

Rubber or **Caoutchouc.** An elastic gum obtained from the milky juice, or latex, of many tropical trees, vines, and shrubs. This latex contains the rubber as small suspended globules. In 1770, when it was learned that a piece of the material was useful for rubbing out pencil marks, it received the name rubber. The principal source of rubber has been the rubber tree, which is native to the valley of the Amazon.

Early experimenters tried to make shoes and clothing waterproof by covering the fabric with raw rubber. In 1823 Charles Macintosh produced rainproof garments by sewing a thin sheet of rubber between two of cloth. Such articles could not be generally useful because the gum became soft in hot weather and brittle in cold.

This difficulty was solved by Charles Goodyear in 1844, when he patented his process of *vulcanization*, in which rubber is mixed with powdered sulphur and heated. A low temperature and a small amount of sulphur produce a soft, elastic rubber; greater heat and much sulphur produce a completely vulcanized, hard rubber. *Vulcanite*, from which combs and thousands of other articles are made, contains about 32 per cent of sulphur.

Persistent experiments under British initiative in the East Indies resulted, during 1890–1900, in the successful cultivation of the Brazilian rubber tree in that region. As a result of scientific research, the quantity of the latex from each tree was increased and the quality was improved. The latex is coagulated on the plantation by the use of acetic acid or by other methods, thereby improving the texture of the rubber and shortening the time required for treatment in the factories. The coagulated rubber, washed, rolled into sheets, sun dried, and usually smoked to kill enzymes, is then shipped to the factories. Often, however, the latex itself is sent to the factory, where it is sprayed into heated chambers. The moisture evaporates from the latex in the process, and the rubber falls in flakes at the bottom of the chamber.

At the factory, the rubber is heated to make it plastic, and sulphur, fillers, accelerators, and pigments are added. When mixed to a homogeneous mass, it is then shaped into the required forms and heated with steam, which causes it to react with the sulphur and become vulcanized. Rubber spread on cloth, for producing rubberized fabrics, is vulcanized by the "cold" process, being hung in the vapor of sulphur monochloride.

Rugs and Carpets. Patterned fabrics generally employed as floor coverings. A floor rug differs from a carpet by being woven usually in one piece of a definite shape and design. A rug, also, unlike a carpet, is not intended to cover the whole floor. Both fabrics are usually woven with a pile, or raised surface of tufts, either cut or looped.

The weaving of rugs is one of the most ancient of industries. Rare specimens of decorative textiles in the Cairo museum dating from the 15th century B. C. indicate that the more ancient rugs made in Egypt did not have a pile, or nap, but were woven like tapestries. The earliest extant examples of rugs having a piled surface date from the 3rd or 4th century A. D. They were made in Egypt and are now in the Victoria and Albert museum, England.

From time immemorial, China and southwestern Asia have been noted for their beautiful rugs, and this industry remains today in almost the precise form under which it was carried on thousands of years ago. The rugs are laboriously woven by hand in the most primitive manner. By reason of the skill of the weavers, however, rugs of the Orient hold a unique place in the world's markets, being unsurpassed for coloring, artistic patterns, and durability.

Oriental rugs are woven on a simple frame consisting of two poles supporting two rollers. The poles are usually fixed upright in the ground with one roller attached to the top of the poles and the other below it at a distance about equal to the desired length of the rug. To the rollers is fastened a warp of strong threads, the number of which determines the width and fineness of the rug. To each thread of the warp, short pieces of colored wool, silk, or hair of camels or goats are knotted in such a way that the two ends project toward the worker. The arrangement of these tufts by color produces the design in the finished product. A weft thread is then run in across the warp. A second row of knots are made on the warp threads, and a second weft thread is run in. The rows of tufts and the weft threads are pressed together by a comblike instrument, thus producing a compact textile with a pile. The projecting tufts are carefully clipped to make an even surface. The number of knots to the square inch varies ordinarily from about 50 to 400, although a few rugs are still more closely woven. The royal Ispahan prayer rug, made in the 18th century for the shah of Persia, has more than 1000 knots in each square inch of surface. The designation prayer rug has reference to the wide use of rugs among Mohammedans as a fabric upon which to kneel during prayer. Their designs generally have a religious significance.

Oriental rugs are usually classified according to the geographical divisions in which they are produced. Fabrics from each locality still have a distinctive character, although, in recent years, the sharpness of the distinctions have tended to be obscured because of the demand for rugs made to order. An account of the outstanding types is given in the following paragraphs.

Chinese rugs are readily distinguished by their looser texture and beautiful background of blue, gold, red, or tan. The designs are usually detached figures of dragons, kilins, lion-dogs, the animal signs of the Chinese zodiac, or emblems of Buddhism and are wrought predominantly in grayish blues, yellows, and creams, as well as in delicate pastel pinks and shades borrowed from Chinese silks and porcelains. The warp is always of cotton.

Bokhara rugs are woven by tribes, still largely nomadic, living in Bokhara, a district of Central Asia north of Afghanistan. They are made of fine durable wool with a liberal mixture of goats' hair. A Bokhara rug may be recognized by its wide selvages and long fringes at the ends and by its octagonal patterns on a field of rich maroon or dull crimson. *Afghan rugs* have a somewhat similar design on a deep red background. The choice of red as the dominant color is said to be determined by the religion of the weavers, who are worshippers of fire. *Beluchistan rugs* also are red and have simple floral or mosaic patterns. They come from western India.

Caucasian rugs are lighter in tone than those described in the preceding paragraph. They are made in the district lying between the Caspian Sea and the Black Sea. The finest of them are the *Daghestan rugs*, which are usually made of lambs' wool. The ground color is deep blue or ivory and is always well covered by geometrical designs, including octagons, hooks, crosses, and eight- or six-pointed stars. Daghestan rugs never exceed four by seven feet in size. Other Caucasian rugs are the *Shirvan rug*, very similar to the Daghestan; the *Kazak*, made by brigand Cossack tribes and distinguished by an unusually thick, heavy pile, which gives the fabric great durability; the *Cabistan*, which is long and narrow; the *Soumak*, or *Kashmir*, known by its straight lines and somewhat whitish effect; and the *Saruk* rug, which is richly ornamented with floral designs on a warm red or brown background.

Turkish rugs include the *Bergamo rug*, made near ancient Pergamum and distinguished by an open bold design with rosettes placed here and there and by a wide selvage at each end. The warp and woof are made of colored wool. *Smyrna rugs*, having a linen or hempen warp and filling and a pile on both sides, have been extensively imitated in America by machine processes, although the patterns in the American products are much simplified.

Persian rugs are the finest rugs made. Among the finest Persian rugs are those of *Kirmanshah*, a province on the Arabian Sea. These rugs are closely woven, often having more than 400 knots to the square inch. They usually have a central figure consisting of a floriated medallion on a rich background of old ivory, rose, or blue, and the borders are variegated with a maze of floral designs.

Other Persian rugs include *Mossoul rugs*, *Mahal rugs*, *Serebend rugs*, *Serape rugs*, *Meshed rugs*, *Saruk rugs*, and *Kurdistan rugs*. The last named are readily distinguished by their field color of deep blue or strong, rich red, on which is placed a large central figure. The design of this figure is matched by similar ornamentations at the corners of the rug. The Serebend rug also is easily recognized. On a field of rich blue or red is woven a small uniform loop pattern, which is said to have been intended originally to represent a bend in the sacred river Indus. Mahal rugs come from Sultanabad, in northwestern Persia. The name means "made to order," and, in America, many weaves properly designated by other names are sold as Mahal rugs because they are made at or near Sultanabad in fulfilment of orders. Persian rugs are noticeable in general for the profusion of their conventionalized floral figures.

The weaving of rugs and carpets was introduced into Europe by the Moors, but it was not practiced on a large scale before the 17th century. Ingrain carpet was manufactured at Kidderminster, England, as early as 1735. This carpet is woven with two or more colors of yarn, the design appearing in different colors on different sides of the fabric. It is known as *Kidderminster* or *Scotch carpet*.

Brussels carpet, made in imitation of floor tapestries then manufactured at Brussels, was first produced in England in the middle of the 18th century. It has a warp and a weft of cotton or jute, which serve as a body for extra warps of worsted. These warps are looped over wires and thus produce the characteristic ridges of Brussels carpet. The designs are made by the use of one layer of worsted thread in the warp for each color required in the design, all threads being concealed in each part of the fabric except the one having the desired color.

Wilton carpets and *rugs* are made like Brussels carpet, but the loops are cut so that a velvety appearance results. The materials used are generally better, and the weaving is finer. The designs are largely adaptations of Oriental models.

Tapestry and *Velvet rugs* have only one worsted warp instead of several. The designs may be printed on the warp before weaving, allowance being made for the distortions due to looping the worsted threads over the wires. A more recent process is to print the design on the rug after the weaving is completed.

Axminster rugs are distinguished by a loose, soft texture, and the colors in the patterns are not limited by the number of layers of threads in the warp. American Oriental rugs are modifications of Axminsters, the pattern being brought through to the back. They are distinguished from true Orientals by the fact that the tufts are looped about the warp threads instead of being knotted. *Smyrna rugs*, originally woven near Smyrna, Turkey, are made in America by weaving chenille, that is, tufted cords of wool, cotton, or worsted, as an extra weft into a body of cotton or jute warp and weft. They are made with Oriental patterns and are reversible. *Chenille Axminster rugs* are the richest and most costly of machine-made rugs. They are made like the Smyrna rugs, except that the chenille cord is steamed and flattened into a braid with fuzz on one side only. The pile of these rugs varies from three-eighths of an inch to one inch. Most of them have plain fields with two or three tone effects.

Other American rugs include those made by the *Navajo* Indians. These rugs are usually known as blankets, but, on account of their firm texture, they are often employed as floor coverings.

The first carpet factory to be established in America began operation in 1791 at Philadelphia, where now more carpets are produced than in any other city of the world. The best and most costly rugs, however, continue to come from Oriental countries.

Silk. A fine, strong fiber produced by certain insects, usually for the purpose of providing themselves with a protective covering, or cocoon. Most commercial silk is produced from the cocoon made by the larva of the mulberry-eating silk moth, which is cultivated chiefly in China, Japan, Syria, Persia, Italy, India, and France. According to Chinese history, the industry was begun by Si-ling-Chi, wife of the third emperor, about 2600 B. C. It developed to such a high state of perfection that Chinese silks were sold in Greece and Syria for their weight in gold. Death was the penalty for taking the eggs of the silkworm out of the country, and the secret was so well guarded that the true origin of the beautiful fabrics was unknown in Europe for many centuries. About 550 A. D., at the direction of the Roman emperor Justinian, two monks who had been missionaries in China brought to Constantinople a supply of the eggs concealed in their hollow bamboo staffs.

The silk moth is a small insect having broad, white wings marked with black lines parallel to the sides. In summer, the female, which cannot fly, lays about 500 sticky eggs and dies a few days later. The eggs hatch in the next spring, producing worms about ⅛ inch long, which feed almost continuously on fresh mulberry leaves, and grow so rapidly that they shed their skins 4 times within 6 weeks. At that time the green worms, which have reached a length of about 3 inches, begin to spin their cocoons. The thread is produced from a gluelike material secreted by two narrow glands which connect with an opening on the upper lip, called the spinneret. On exposure to air, the fluid hardens, forming a sticky thread which the worm winds about itself by a continuous, regular motion of the head.

Spinning is completed in about 3 days, and, if the cocoon is left for 2 or 3 weeks, a moth will force its way out through one end. The escape of the moth breaks so many threads that only enough cocoons are saved to provide another crop of eggs, and the remainder are heated so as to kill the pupa.

They are then assorted according to color and texture, the loose, irregular floss is removed from the outside, and the compact, creamy ovals placed in hot water in order to soften the gum which binds the threads together. Here they are stirred by means of a brush until the loose end of each coil is found. The threads from 4 or more cocoons are twisted together into one strand and then reeled into skeins of *raw silk*. A single thread is usually from 400 to 800 yards long. Only about 70 per cent of a cocoon can be reeled. The remainder, together with damaged cocoons, is combed and spun like wool into *spun silk*. There are about 35,000 silkworm eggs to the ounce. These will yield about 100 pounds of cocoons and 11 pounds of raw silk.

The skeins of raw silk are placed in linen bags and soaked in warm soapsuds to soften the gum; they are then dried and wound on spools. The next process, known as *throwing*, prepares the silk for weaving. That fiber called *organzine*, which will form the *warp* of cloth, is twisted, then doubled and twisted again so as to form a strong thread. *Tram*, or the material for filling the warp, is not twisted so tightly. The threads to be used for crêpes are very highly twisted. After throwing, the thread is stretched evenly on a special machine and then rewound into skeins to be dyed.

The dyer boils the skeins in soapy water until the gum is removed and the threads are soft and lustrous. They are then rinsed and passed to the dye vat. The boiling process causes a loss in weight of about 25 per cent. The desire to avoid this loss resulted in the process of *loading*, by which the fiber is made to unite with chemicals such as compounds of tin, which sometimes weigh several times as much as the silk. This process is generally injurious to the fabric and is not now practiced to such an extent as formerly.

Two of the chief requirements for commercial production of silk are a supply of cheap labor and of mulberry leaves. Lack of the former explains why silk growing has never been successful in the United States. However, silk weaving, performed by very complicated machinery, is a thriving industry. In modern factories two pieces of silk velvet or plush are woven face to face and then separated by a sharp knife, which cuts the pile threads. *Crêpe-de-chine* is produced by alternating right and left twisted threads in the warp and filling with a soft tram. *Georgette crêpe* has hard twisted threads in both warp and filling. Sewing silks are highly twisted threads, while floss and embroidery silks are loosely twisted.

A green tinted silk, used in China and Japan, is produced by the Japanese oak-feeding silk moth. The natives of India manufacture *tussah silk* from the hard grayish white cocoon of the undomesticated tussah moth. Several other varieties are also known.

Artificial silk is produced by several processes which usually depend on dissolving cotton or wood pulp to a thick liquid. This is forced through fine holes into some material that will cause the threads to harden. It is not usually so soft, nor has it the strength and elasticity of true silk, but improvement is taking place rapidly and the product is becoming more and more important. See *Rayon*.

Soap. A cleansing agent usually prepared by the action of caustic alkali on vegetable and animal fats. A fat is a chemical compound of glycerin with one or more fatty acids. In the presence of a caustic alkali, the fat breaks down; the acids combine with the alkali to form soap, while the glycerin remains in the solution. The alkalies used are caustic potash, which yields *soft soap*, and caustic soda, which gives the ordinary hard soap. The fats come from many sources and are usually of low grade, but some of the finest soaps are made from edible oils. Coconut, castor, corn, cottonseed, and soy bean oils are consumed in enormous quantities, together with various animal fats and tallows.

The lye and fat may be mixed in the proper proportions and allowed to react without being heated. This produces *cold process* soap. In the *Krebitz* process, the fats are saponified with milk of lime, and the resulting calcium soap is changed to soda soap by boiling with sodium carbonate. But 90 per cent of the soap used in the United States is made by boiling the fat with a solution of caustic soda. When the action is complete, salt is added until the soap is thrown out of solution and floats at the top of the kettle. The spent lye is drawn off and concentrated in vacuum pans in order to recover the glycerin. The soap is then given a second boiling with a small amount of fresh caustic, again salted out, and settled for some time before it is drawn off into *crutchers*, where it is very thoroughly mixed. *Filling*, such as water glass, washing soda, borax, or naphtha, is often added during this so-called *crutching* process. *Floating soaps* are produced by operating the crutcher in such a manner as to incorporate a large amount of air in the soap and thus make it slightly lighter than water. From the crutchers the pasty liquid is drawn into narrow iron boxes called *frames*, where it stands until cool and hard. The iron shell is then removed and the huge slab is cut into cakes by pressing against a series of tightly drawn wires.

Toilet soaps are usually produced by milling. This consists in passing the soap between heavy rollers which reduce it to narrow ribbons. The ribbons may be dried and perfumed and are then forced by a powerful screw press through an opening about the size of the cake into which the pieces are pressed. Transparent soaps are made in various ways; for example, by adding sugar to a soap made with much castor oil, or by dissolving ordinary soap in alcohol and then evaporating the solvent.

Marine soap and *hard water soaps* usually contain a large amount of coconut oil. Cold process soap contains all the glycerin of the original fat. Pure *castile soap*, named from the province of Castile in Spain, is made from olive oil. The best soaps usually result from a mixture of tallow with some coconut and other vegetable oils. Many soaps contain rosin, but with one or two exceptions rosin is seldom used in a product intended for toilet purposes. *Shaving soap* is prepared chiefly from coconut and palm kernel oils, which impart its lathering qualities. Great care is taken to avoid retaining any free alkali, which irritates the skin.

The term *detergent* usually refers to a material whose molecule (structure) is made up of a hydrophobic, or water-hating, group (a hydrocarbon chain of 10–18 carbon atoms) and a hydrophilic, or water-loving, group. Thus, detergents clean by emulsification—one group attaches itself to the dirt, while the other one clings to the water.

The term *soap* refers specifically to a detergent whose hydrophilic group is sodium or potassium carboxylate. All similar compounds whose hydrophilic groups are other than the carboxylates are *synthetic detergents*, commonly called simply *detergents*. The vast array of different hydrophilic groups attached to the hydrocarbon chains has made available detergents having a wide variety of properties. Their great popularity is threatened, however, by their contributing to the pollution of water and streams.

Soda Water. A slightly acid beverage having a peculiar pungent taste due to carbon dioxide gas which has been forced into the water under pressure. When the liquid is drawn into a glass and the pressure released, the gas forms characteristic bubbles as it escapes from solution.

Starch. A white, granular substance, insoluble in cold water, that is found in all green plants, where it serves as a reserve food supply. Large amounts are found in many seeds and in certain roots and tubers, especially corn, wheat, rice, beans, potatoes, sweet potatoes, and cassava, or manioc. Food starches also include *arrowroot*, obtained from a West Indian plant; *sago*, from the pith of various palm trees; and *tous-les-mois*, from certain varieties of canna. Pure starch alone will not sustain life, but, in its natural forms or as products made from them, it constitutes the greater proportion of human food.

The grains of starch from different sources generally have a characteristic shape and size by which they can be readily identified when seen under the microscope. Starch turns blue when treated with tincture of iodine, as may be shown by placing a drop of this solution upon a piece of potato or bread. Hot water causes the grains to swell until they burst, and, on cooling, the paste sets to a stiff gelatinous mass.

In Europe, much starch is produced from potatoes, but, in the United States, over 90 per cent is made from corn, usually by the sulphur dioxide process. The grain is soaked from two to four days in water containing one per cent of the gas from burning sulphur. When sufficiently soft, it is ground, and carried by a stream of pure water over sieves, which permit the starch to pass but retain the germs and husks. As the germs float, they are skimmed off and pressed to recover the valuable oil which they contain. The residue is sold for cattle food. The water with its suspended starch is passed over a series of gently sloping surfaces, on which the heavier particles are left. The remainder flows to settling tanks, from which the starchy sediment is collected to be further refined by washing and straining until sufficiently pure. The separated starch is dried by artificial heat until the mass breaks into lumps.

Besides its chief uses for food and laundry purposes, starch is employed in the preparation of glucose and dextrin, in printing and finishing calico and other cloths, and in making special kinds of paste. See *Bread, Flour, Glucose, Sugar.*

Sugar. A sweet crystallizable substance found in the juices of many plants. The term includes a group of chemically related compounds such as *grape sugar, fruit sugar, milk sugar,* and *malt sugar*; but, except in a technical sense, sugar means the very valuable food called *cane sugar* or *sucrose*. Any substance having a sweet taste was formerly called sugar, hence the name *sugar of lead* for poisonous lead acetate. A sugar of some sort appears to be the first carbohydrate formed in green plants, where it serves as a food for the growing parts or is changed into starch and stored as a reserve. The principal sources of sugar are the *sugar cane* and *sugar beet*.

The use of sugar and of sugar cane seems to have originated in India at a very early period. During the middle ages it was carried by Arabs to Egypt and southern Europe, whence it was introduced into Louisiana in 1751. The first refined sugar was made about 1791, and the first commercial crop was harvested in 1795.

Sugar cane is a giant grass, raised chiefly in Cuba, Puerto Rico, Louisiana, Hawaii, the Philippines, Java, and India. It is usually from 6 to 15 feet high, with narrow cornlike leaves at the top. The stalk is from 1 to 2 inches thick and is composed of short jointed sections which may be yellow, green, purple, or striped, depending on the variety. The plant may be raised from seed, but usually pieces of stalk are planted in shallow furrows running the length of the field. At each joint there is an eye, or bud, from which a new stalk springs up.

In Louisiana the harvesting occurs between October and January; in tropical countries, from January to June. The cane is cut close to the ground with a broad knife about 18 inches long which has a sharp hook on the back. The leaves are stripped off with the hook, the top cut away at the last mature joint, and the cane stacked until it can be taken to the factory. New crops will grow from the stubble for several seasons, but the general practice is to replant a part of the field each year.

At the factory the canes are shredded and then passed through a series of heavy rolls, which squeeze out the juice. Water is usually sprinkled upon the cane before the second pressing in order that the extraction may be as complete as possible. The crushed cane, called *bagasse*, is used for fuel. The juice is a gray or green liquid which contains, in addition to sugar, many impurities, such as glucose, gum, albumin, acids, and ash. These are removed by treatment with lime, other chemicals, and heat.

Sugar is obtained by evaporating the purified juice, usually under vacuum, to a heavy sirup. This is run to another vacuum kettle called the *strike pan*, where boiling is continued until crystals of sugar form and grow to the proper size. The mixture of sugar and sirup, called *massecuite*, is stirred and fed to centrifugal machines lined with fine screen, which retains the crystals and allows the molasses to escape. A second and a third yield of soft sugar are often obtained from the molasses, of which the uncrystallizable residue is ultimately sold to distilleries or for cattle food. A certain amount of the best grade is used in cooking. If the molasses is separated from the massecuite by draining rather than by centrifugal force, the sugar is not so pure and is called *muscovado*.

Brown, or *raw*, *sugar*, so prepared, is usually shipped in bags to a refinery, where it is dissolved, filtered, treated with chemicals, decolorized by means of bone black, and again boiled under vacuum until the small white crystals of granulated sugar are formed. These are dried and sifted into the standard sizes. *Loaf sugar* may be made by molding the sticky grains under centrifugal pressure, then drying and sawing the resulting blocks to the proper size. By a more recent process, however, the individual blocks are molded in presses, from a specially prepared soft, white grain. *Powdered* and *confectioners' sugars* are prepared by passing the crystalline variety through a disintegrator that reduces it to very fine particles, which are graded by sifting.

The sugar beet, which is extensively cultivated in Europe and the United States, grows best in a temperate climate where the soil is suitable and where the average summer temperature is about 70° F. It is white and usually contains 12 to 18 per cent sugar, compared with 10 to 16 per cent in Louisiana cane. The seeds are usually planted in April and May. At harvest time, which begins in August or September, the beets are pulled up, and the leaves cut off just below the top or neck. The beets are then carried to the factory to be carefully washed and weighed. The clean beets are cut into very thin slices, packed into a series of tanks, and treated with warm water, which dissolves the sugar together with many impurities. The exhausted chips are pressed, dried, and sold for stock food or fertilizer.

The solution is purified with lime, bleached with sulphur fumes, crystallized, and the sugar is refined in much the same way as that from cane. Special efforts are made to obtain as much sugar as possible from the molasses. Neither the raw beet sugar nor the molasses are fit to eat, but, when the raw product has been properly refined, it is impossible to tell whether it came from beet or cane.

Jaggery, the sugar obtained from several varieties of the palm, has been used in India since very ancient times. It is obtained by tapping a hole in the tree and collecting the sap which runs out. This is boiled with a little lime, until a sirup forms which will harden on cooling. A large tree will yield 30 to 40 pounds of sugar per year. The sirup has long been an article of commerce under the name *date honey*.

Maple sugar is made in North America wherever the sugar maple is found, but Quebec, Ontario, New York, Vermont, Ohio, and Pennsylvania are the most important producing centers. Sap begins to flow in the trees at the end of winter and is collected by drilling into the base of the trunk one or more small holes about 1½ inches deep. A spile or trough is driven into each hole to conduct the sap into a bucket. The juice, which is unusually free from impurities, contains an average of 3½ per cent of sugar. It is boiled down over an open fire or in a modern evaporator to a heavy sirup, or, if sugar is wanted, until the liquid will become solid on cooling. The average amount of sugar from each tree varies from 2 to 3 pounds. Maple sugar is highly valued because of its characteristic flavor, and is sold as raw sugar and as sirup. If it were refined, it would be exactly the same as the product of cane or beet.

Thermos Bottle. The trade name for a practical device invented by Sir James Dewar about 1892 for the purpose of containing intensely cold, liquefied gases. It is also called a *vacuum bottle*, as it consists essentially of a double walled bottle or flask in which there is a high vacuum between the walls. Radiation is prevented by silvering the walls, and there is of course nothing to conduct heat across the vacuum. The small opening to the flask is usually stoppered with a thick cork, this material being a very poor conductor of heat.

Hot substances stay hot for long periods in a vacuum bottle because the heat cannot get out, and cold substances remain cold because heat from the outside cannot get in. Such containers have generally been made of glass, which requires careful handling. An improved type is constructed of metal, thus avoiding the fragility of the glass product.

Time-pieces. Modern time-pieces are known chiefly as watches or clocks. Watches, being for personal use, are smaller and are driven by a spring. Clocks are driven either mechanically, by spring or gravity (by means of weights), or by electricity.

Mechanically driven time-pieces consist essentially of a system of wheels controlling indicators, or "hands", on a dial, the wheels being actuated by a force and their revolutions made uniform in speed by a governing device, known as an *escapement*.

The escapement is ordinarily a rod curved in the arc of a circle, each end being provided with a specially shaped cog, or detent. The rod is pivoted at the center. The escapement, being driven usually by the actuating force of the clock, oscillates on its pivot. The ends of the escapement alternately engage and release cogs of a wheel, which is also driven by the actuating force of the clock. The result is to cause the wheel to revolve in equally timed jumps. In gravity clocks, a pendulum governs the movement of the escapement.

With the revolutions of a master wheel thus made uniform in time, a system of cog gears is used to make the axis on which the hands are set revolve at the requisite speed to indicate hours and minutes marked on a dial.

The invention of the first mechanical clock is ascribed to Pope Silvester II in 996 A.D. Watches were first made about the time of the discovery of America in 1492. The chief contribution of America to the development of time-pieces has been the devising of mass production methods of manufacture.

The electric clock in common use in America is driven by a small motor so constructed that it revolves once for each "beat" of an alternating current or in some other fixed relation to the beat. Its uniformity of speed is thus dependent on the accuracy of the dynamo which produces the current. The desired speed of rotation of the hands is secured by gearing from the motor to the axis of the hands. The most accurate of all now is the atomic clock.

Turpentine. The resinous exudate of several species of pine trees. In America it is obtained during the spring by cutting and scarring the trunk of the long-leaf pine, which grows abundantly in the Southern states. The sap which runs from the cuts is collected, placed in copper stills, and heated until the volatile products are driven off as vapors. These are condensed by means of cold water to *spirits of turpentine*, which, when pure, is a colorless liquid having a penetrating, aromatic odor, and a bitter, burning taste. After distilling off the "turps," the residue, while still hot, is run into barrels, where it hardens to a brittle, transparent mass of *rosin*.

Turpentine is much used in varnishes to hasten drying and in paints for thinning and for producing a dull surface. It is also used in medicine, internally, as an antispasmodic, as a stimulant, and to stop hemorrhages; externally, as a remedy for ringworm and to relieve inflammation. Rosin is used in the manufacture of varnish, soap, sealing wax, cement, sizing, and for many other purposes.

Varnish. A solution of gums or resins which dries to a hard, smooth, transparent film. Varnishes give a pleasing appearance to most surfaces, protect them against the weather, and bring out the beauty of wood even better than polishing. The many kinds of varnish are classified according to the solvent used. Shellac dissolved in alcohol forms the best-known example of a *spirit varnish*. It dries rapidly to a hard, brittle surface. *Turpentine varnishes* also dry rapidly and, being more brilliant and less brittle, are sometimes used in oil paintings.

Oil varnishes, the most important for general use, are made by adding the proper amount of boiling oil to melted gums and boiling the mixture until it becomes clear. It is then thinned with turpentine, cooled, filtered, and pumped to storage tanks to age for at least six months.

Linseed oil and *copal*, a hard resin found as a fossil and on living trees chiefly in Zanzibar and New Zealand, are the principal ingredients of a good oil varnish. Poppy and tung oils are of increasing importance, while available gums include lac, mastic, sandarac, amber, asphalt, and various synthetic resins. Coloring matter, such as dragon's blood, cochineal, or artificial dye, is often added. *Japanese lacquer* is a natural varnish prepared from the sap of a plant. See *Lacquer.*

Veneer. A thin layer of valuable wood, or occasionally other material, glued to furniture or cabinetwork in order to produce a surface more attractive than that which it covers.

Veneers that are sawed from the solid wood are known as *saw cut*; those that are pared, as *knife cut*. Both are made by machinery. Saw cut veneer varies from 1/32 to 1/16 inch thick, while knife cut veneer is usually much thinner. The use of veneer does not imply cheapness or poor quality. It is the only method by which some rare and beautiful woods such as curly mahogany and burled walnut can be applied to surfaces.

Vinegar. A sour liquid varying in color from light yellow to brownish red, much used as a condiment and for pickling. It is made from weak alcoholic liquors such as hard cider, wine, beer, beetroot juice, or fermented molasses. When liquids of this sort stand exposed to the air at a temperature of about 76° F., a slimy scum usually forms on the surface. This scum, commonly known as *mother of vinegar*, is a bacterial growth, in the presence of which the dilute *alcohol* combines with *oxygen* of the air to form *acetic acid*. The sourness of vinegar is due to this organic acid, but the characteristic odor and taste are due to the materials out of which it is made.

In the *new* or *quick* process, now generally used, vinegar is produced by draining the alcoholic liquor over some substance such as beech-wood shavings, or clean charcoal which has been previously soaked in strong vinegar. Such a material provides a very large surface on which thin films of liquid are exposed to the action of the "mother" and to the air. By this method vinegar is produced in from 24 to 36 hours as compared with several weeks required by the old process. Vinegar and foods containing it should be kept in glass or other nonmetallic containers, because acetic acid slowly attacks such metals as tin, copper, and brass, forming soluble compounds highly injurious to health.

The strength of commercial vinegar is usually expressed in *grains*. Each grain represents $\frac{1}{10}$ per cent of acid, so that a bottle of vinegar marked 45 grain contains 4.5 per cent acetic acid.

Water Glass. A heavy, colorless solution of sodium or potassium silicate, which becomes hard and glossy when exposed to the air. It is usually prepared by heating fine sand together with washing soda and charcoal, and extracting the fused mass with boiling water. Uses for the alkaline liquid include painting on glass, protecting wall decorations, glazing, and fireproofing. It is an important ingredient in fireproof cement, and is valuable as a coating material for the inside of barrels because it fills any small holes and leaves a smooth, water-tight coating. Large quantities are used for filling cheap soaps. When mixed with sand, it hardens to a useful artificial stone. Eggs are often preserved by keeping them covered with a dilute solution of water glass.

Wool. A soft, wavy, modified form of hair, which grows on domestic sheep. No wild wool-bearing animals are known, and, when sheep are raised without care or protection from the elements, the wool rapidly becomes coarse and hairlike. Wool differs from other textile fibers and from hair chiefly in being covered with scales which can interlock and thus cause the fibers to mat together. Wool is elastic, it does not readily absorb water, and the scales hold air in the spaces of a woolen garment, making it very warm for its weight. These characteristics make wool so valuable that the quantity used each year is second only to cotton. Longer fibers very similar to wool are found on the llama and the alpaca of South America; on the Kashmir goats of India; and on the Angora goat, which yields the wool used in weaving *mohair*.

Sheep are not native to America, but were imported by the earliest settlers, who were accustomed to weave their own clothes from homespun yarn. Practically all standard breeds are now raised in this country, wool from the merino sheep being the finest but not the longest.

The wool is generally clipped from the sheep in the spring, and, when there are large flocks, the clippers are power driven, so that an experienced operator can trim 150 to 200 animals each day. All the clippings from one sheep are called a *fleece* and usually weigh from 5 to 8 pounds. Wool taken from the shoulders and back is the best in quality. Lambs' wool is softer and more wavy than sheep's wool. *Pulled wool* is that removed from pelts of dead animals. It is usually of inferior quality because of the treatment given the skins in order to loosen the fibers. Consequently it is necessary to sort the fleeces into various grades. A certain amount is sorted at the clipping sheds, but most of this work is done at the warehouses and factories.

There are many grades and qualities, and several systems of classification, but in general the fibers may be grouped as *combing wool* when over $2\frac{1}{2}$ inches long and rather straight; as *carding wool* when short, fine, and wavy; and as *carpet*, or *blanket*, *wool* when coarse and stiff. *Woolen* goods are made from carding wool, while *worsteds* are woven from combing wool. The chief difference is that woolen thread is soft and composed of crisscross fibers, while worsted thread is twisted hard after the fibers have been combed until they are parallel. Worsted is firm and shows a definite pattern, while woolens are soft, having the pattern almost concealed by the nap.

When the wool reaches the factory, the fleeces are pulled apart, graded, and beaten to remove dust and dirt. The reason wool does not form a mass of felt on a healthy sheep's back is that each fiber is coated with a mixture of greasy materials called *yolk* and *suint*, secreted by the animal. This is removed from the clipped wool by careful *scouring* with soap and soft water. From the wash water *potash* and *lanolin* are obtained. Lanolin serves as a basis for salves and ointments. Most wool is white, but some is black, gray, fawn, or brown. The fiber can be dyed in the form of wool, yarn, or cloth. After scouring is complete, the material may be "dyed in the wool," and dried.

The matted wool is loosened by revolving, toothed drums, and any seeds or burs are removed either mechanically or by a chemical process, which chars the impurities. Oil is added to restore the natural softness; then all the material is uniformly mixed and passed to a series of *carding machines*. These are cylinders covered with projecting teeth, which arrange the fiber in a continuous flat band. This is divided by a *condensing* machine into narrow strips, or *slivers*, somewhat larger than heavy yarn. The sliver is usually spun into twisted thread on a *mule-jenny* and is then ready for the loom.

After weaving, various processes are used to give a cloth the desired surface and finish. In the first step, *fulling*, the fabric is wet with soap and water and pressed or worked between rolls until the shrinkage and degree of felting are satisfactory. It is then rinsed and supported on hooks until dry. The nap of woolens is raised by means of a conelike spike head covered with sharp hooks, which grows on the teasel plant. Artificial *teasels* are frequently used for this purpose.

The fibers for making worsted, unless very long, are also carded and are then put through *combing* and *gilling* machines, which leave them parallel and free from the short, curly pieces called *noil*. They are then spun to a hard, wiry thread, and are woven. *Felt* is a warm, dense fabric made by pressing and beating together unwoven wool fibers. It is much used for making hats. *Shoddy* might be called secondhand wool, for it is obtained by tearing refuse woolen fabrics into fibers which can be rewoven. It is of great value, and is objectionable only when used to adulterate new wool.

Broadcloths and *beavers* have the nap raised and spread in one direction over the face of the cloth. On *overcoatings* the nap is often formed in little curls. In some goods it is left standing as in velvet, and, in the bare-face finish, it is entirely sheared off. *Tweed* is a soft, rough-finished material originally made in the villages along the Tweed river, Scotland. It is usually woven from two or more different colored yarns. The cloth is finally brushed, stretched on drums under hot water, and steamed while in a hydraulic press in order to develop the luster.

REVIEW QUESTIONS

Point out several reasons for the widespread interest in economics. Define the term economics. Discuss some industrial effects of *division of labor* 251

Illustrate commercial co-operation among states and countries 251–252

From what circumstances does the conflict between capital and labor arise? 252

Discuss the function of money as a medium of exchange 252

In what sense is credit money? 252

Point out some characteristics of the "age of industry" 252

COMMERCE

In what does commerce consist? What does the term commerce generally imply? Distinguish between *foreign* and *domestic* commerce. Explain the phrase "interstate commerce" 253

State some of the conditions upon which commerce depends. Explain the interrelation between transportation and commerce . . 253

Describe the commercial system of the ancient Phœnicians. What were the economic conditions that gave rise to the extensive commerce of the Greeks? 253

What service to commerce did Rome render for five centuries? 253

What people controlled commerce during the period immediately after the fall of Rome? Summarize the conditions that prevented commerce in Europe in this period 254

Explain the rise of markets and guilds in the towns of medieval Europe. Indicate the use and importance of the medieval fairs . . . 254

Indicate the purpose and the power of the Hanseatic league. Point out some events to which Venice owed her commercial supremacy in the Mediterranean 254

What states became strong commercial powers in the 14th and 15th centuries? 254

What new sea routes were opened about the end of the 15th century? To what city did commercial supremacy fall at this period? . 254

By what influences was the commercial power of Spain destroyed? How did Portugal lose her greatness in trade? 255

Outline the growth and decline of Dutch commerce in the 17th and 18th centuries . . . 255

Point out the commercial advantages possessed by France between 1500 and 1800. Explain her failure in world commerce 255–256

To what two chief factors is the commercial success of England in the 17th and 18th centuries ascribed? Name the most important English trading companies of this period. What were the staple articles of English commerce? 256–257

Summarize the chief features of the growth of Canadian commerce. What are the chief articles of Canadian export? 257

Outline the leading facts about American commerce down to 1812 257

Describe the important economic development of the United States in the period from 1812 to 1860. Compare the list of chief exports in 1800 with that of 1860 257–258

Explain the phrase "triangular exchange" . 258

What were the most notable effects of the Civil War upon the economic development of the United States? 258

Show by statistics the growth of United States export trade from 1870 to 1892. Account for the decline of the American merchant marine. Give figures which show the growth of the foreign commerce of the United States after 1860 258

How does the internal commerce of the United States compare in importance with the foreign trade of the United States and of the world? 259

State the changes in the ranking of leading nations in foreign commerce. How was the foreign trade of the United States affected? 259–260

COMMUNICATION

What emperor first opened the postal system to private use? 262

By whom were three early European postal systems established? Who was the first "Master of the Post" in England? By whom was he appointed? When and for what purpose was the English money order system established? 262

Give the date of the introduction of the following in England: penny rate of postage; perforated stamps; mail boxes 262

Outline the history and some of the regulations of the Universal Postal Union . . . 262

Outline the history of the colonial postal system in America before the Revolution. Summarize the important reforms and extensions of the United States postal system, giving the date of each 262–263

Mention some of the chief conveniences afforded by the parcel post service in the United States 263

Indicate the rapid development of the air mail service 263

State examples of the extensive practical development of radio communication 263

TRANSPORTATION

What methods of propelling their vessels were used by ancient peoples around the Mediterranean Sea? Account for the phrase "galley slave" 265

Review the early history of the building and use of steamships 265

Name two Frenchmen and two Scotchmen who are famous in the history of modern road building 265

Summarize important facts about the history of canal building 265

State approximately in tons the size of ocean-going ships of American colonial times. Name two famous American shipowners of the beginning of the 19th century . . . 265–266

Show the conditions that brought about the building of the American clipper ships . . 266

Outline the development of the chief types of engines used in ships 266

Trace the increase in size of ocean-going vessels in the 20th century 266–267

Recount the story of the American merchant marine down to the World Wars. Indicate the effect of the wars on American shipbuilding. Show by statistics the part played by American ships in carrying American import and export cargoes 267–268

Of what importance were rivers in ancient and medieval commerce? 268

Review the most important canal building projects of modern times in France and England 268

In what canal building plans was George Washington interested? By what different means were his purposes later realized? . . 268

In what way did the War of 1812 influence the United States as to the internal improvement policy? 269

Show why Federal expenditure for rivers and harbors could be renewed and enlarged after the Civil War 269

Of what economic importance was the Erie canal? 269–270

Trace the history of canal development in Canada 270

State the main features of the Saint Lawrence power-navigation project 270

By whom was the Suez canal constructed? State its dimensions and original cost. Name the largest stockholder in the canal company 271

Name the two men to whom the chief credit for the Panama canal construction is due. Describe the course of the canal. What is its height above sea level in Gatun lake? What was the total cost of the canal? . . 271

Point out the remarkable growth of railroad building in the United States between 1865 and 1910. What was the track mileage of railroads in the United States in 1920? in 1930? 272

What advantage did the North and the South realize from railroads in the Civil War? . . 272

Summarize the main facts as to the distribution of railway mileage among the various states 272

When and where was the first railway placed in operation in Canada? Enumerate, with important dates, the chief Canadian railway projects. Outline the relations of the Canadian government with Canadian railroads 272

In what four types of service is the electric preferable to the steam locomotive? . . . 274

When and where was the first streamlined train put into service? 274

Give the dates of the introduction of horse car service in various American cities; of the introduction of cable lines; of elevated roads. In what chief cities of the world have subways been constructed? 275

What year marks the beginning of commercially practicable electric railways? 275

Trace the history of highway building in the United States 276

Who invented the idea of aircraft driven by a propeller with rotating blades? 277

LABOR RELATIONS

Name two advantages which employers ordinarily have over employees in a test of collective strength 279

On what grounds is governmental intervention in labor relations justified? 279

What was the crime called which persons before 1840 committed when they organized to improve their working conditions? 279

Distinguish between a simple boycott and a secondary boycott 280

List five methods sometimes employed as means of breaking strikes 280

What are "yellow-dog contracts"? 280

When was the first labor injunction granted by a Federal court? 280

Before they were forbidden by law, what were three successful methods of defeating the right of employees to organize? 280

What two reasons stand out in explaining the effectiveness of the Wagner act? 281

Wherein do "unfair labor practices" under the Taft-Hartley act differ from those forbidden under the Wagner act? 281

List four kinds of strikes which may get the strikers into trouble under the Taft-Hartley act 281

In what way are strikers in a stronger position if the strike is caused by unfair labor practices of an employer than if it is caused merely for the purpose of securing better working conditions? 282

What is the difference between closed shop and union shop? 282

If an employee is expelled from a union having a union-shop contract, what are the consequences if (1) the reason is nonpayment of dues? (2) the reason is breaking union rules? 282

If an employer discharges an employee because he is a member of a union, what is the employer ordinarily required to do by the labor board to make amends? 283

What is a unit for bargaining? Name three kinds of bargaining units 283

What special standing in law has a labor union which is selected as bargaining agent by the majority of employees in an appropriate bargaining unit? 283

By what token can one distinguish between voluntary arbitration and compulsory arbitration? between arbitration of rights and arbitration of interests? 285

Tell the difference between a craft union and an industrial union 286

Give an example of a typical jurisdictional dispute between craft unions; between a craft union and an industrial union . . . 286

When did the earliest strike take place in America having as its object an increase in wages? 286

What is the oldest national trade union in America? 286

Give four advantages of collective bargaining on an industry-wide basis 286

Why is each of the following dates significant in the history of child labor legislation in the United States: 1836, 1918, 1922, 1938? . . 287

Does the Fair Labor Standards act limit the number of hours that may lawfully be worked? 287

How does technological unemployment differ from cyclical unemployment? 288

Name three devices for socializing the cost of mechanical progress 288

Name the law by which Congress takes responsibility for promoting full employment 288

MARKETING

Define Marketing as it may be viewed by a sociologist, an economist, a businessman, a consumer 289

Discuss the role of Marketing from the standpoint of its counterpart in other historical and contemporary societies 289

Characterize the society of the United States, and show the effects of social factors upon the manner in which marketing is carried on. 290

Why is a distinction made between the primary and secondary aspects of the marketing task? 291

Illustrate the fact that the services or processes required in marketing are a "function" of the marketing task 292

Explain and illustrate what is meant by a "market" 292

What economic contributions are made through the performance of marketing? 292

Expand the discussion given any one of the marketing functions 293

Distinguish between the processes of wholesaling and retailing 294

What is the difference between a marketing function and a marketing functionary? . . 294

From a management viewpoint, how would you describe a marketing establishment? . . . 294

Trace the effect upon any type of retailing establishment of 1) evolving internal man-

agement policies and 2) external environmental influences 296

Account for the diversity of types of wholesaling establishments 296

Define and explain the significance of the "marketing mix." 298

Explain in general terms the philosophy underlying the marketing legislation of the 20th
century 298

INSURANCE

State the real function of insurance. Define
life insurance 303

Indicate the extent of modern business uses of
life insurance 303

In what vital respect does life insurance differ
from other forms of insurance? What is the
purpose of a mortality table? 303

Distinguish between "net premium" and
"gross premium." What is meant by the
term "participating" applied to an insurance policy? 304

Explain the term "reserve" 304

State the methods taken by insurance companies to protect themselves against undesirable risks 304–305

Who may be the beneficiary of an insurance
policy? 305

Name four leading types of life insurance
policies. Upon what does the amount of tne
premium mainly depend? State the difference between an ordinary whole life policy
and a limited-payment whole life policy.
Distinguish between these types of policies
and the endowment policy. 305

Compare term insurance and whole life insurance in respect to certain advantages and
disadvantages of each 305–306

What are the objections to paying insurance to
beneficiaries in lump sum? State some advantages of the life income plan . . . 306–307

Explain the phrase "cash or loan value" . . 307

What is "paid-up insurance" and "extended
insurance?" 307

Outline the purpose and the methods of industrial insurance 307

Point out changes that have been made in the
methods of fraternal insurance 307

What is the purpose of health and accident insurance? How many working days are said
to be lost annually in the United States
through illness? 308

State some of the principal features of accident
policies; of health insurance 308

Define employers' liability insurance. How
are employers' premium payments adjusted? 308

State the three legal doctrines which formerly
operated to prevent an employee from securing compensation for injuries 309

What is the purpose of the workmen's compensation laws? State some of the provisions
of these laws 309

Give the estimated value of property in the
United States protected by fire insurance.
What is the computed amount of annual
fire insurance premiums? 309

Point out the importance of fire and marine
insurance in our system of trade and industry 309

Explain the personal character of the fire insurance contract; the nature of the indemnity
provided under the contract 309–310

What classes of persons may insure against loss
by fire? 310

Trace the development of the standard policy
of fire insurance in America 310

Discuss the meaning and consequences of coinsurance 310

Enumerate the classes of bonds issued by
bonding companies. Define title insurance.
What is the purpose of credit insurance?. . 311

INVESTMENTS

Define investment. Point out, by example, a
difference between an investor and a speculator 315

Summarize the characteristics of a true investment 315

Give two illustrations to show how the yield of
an investment in stocks or bonds is determined 315

Enumerate some classes of securities and outline the special advantages of each 316

State six attributes of a good investment.
What are the three major tests? 316

Classify public bonds. 316

What are municipal bonds? Upon what conditions does the value of a state bond depend? State some tests of the desirability of
county and city bonds 316

State the relations which should exist between
value, income, operating expenses, and
interest charges in order to make the following securities desirable: railroad; public
utility; industrial 316

Explain three tests of the soundness of a railroad security 316

Enumerate the types of securities issued by
public utility companies 316

State some advantages enjoyed by these companies 317

Why is the average investor advised to exercise unusual precaution in purchasing
industrial securities? 317

What proportion should the amount of a real
estate mortgage bear to the conservative
value of the property? Which are preferable, mortgages on residence property or
mortgages on business buildings? 317

Point out the effect of taxation upon investment income 317

By what conditions are stock prices determined? What determines bond prices? Indicate the most favorable time to buy stocks;
bonds 317

Enumerate some characteristic marks of
fraudulent investment offerings 318

Why are United States savings bonds so
popular? 318

MONEY AND BANKING

Point out the practical relations between production and distribution on the one hand
and price and profit on the other. 319

Give a definition of money. 319

Why has gold been so generally used as money?
What is its chief use today? 319

What four functions does money serve in commerce? Describe the use of money as a
medium of exchange; as a standard of value;
as a store of value; as a standard of deferred
payment 319

How is the general level of prices measured? . 320

What establishes the value of money? From
whom does the true demand for money
come? What is the supply of money? . . . 320

Illustrate the reasons for rise and fall of prices
by stating the conditions governing the
variations in the price of wheat 320

What is meant by saying that a country is on the gold standard? 321

How many times has the dollar been devalued in the course of American history? When? 321

Does the supply and demand for money determine the rate of interest? If not, what does? 322

Tell the meaning of the term "managed currency." How is such "management" accomplished? 322

Explain the importance of balance of payments in international trade 323

In what way is the retirement of Federal Reserve notes assured when the need for their issuance is past? 323

Is there any difference between legal tender and lawful money? If so, what? 324

Whose property are the funds deposited in a bank? 324

Are demand deposits or time deposits more satisfactory to a bank? Why? 324

What is the maximum amount to which each bank account may be insured by the Federal government under present law? 325

From what kind of bank would one normally expect to borrow $5,000 for five years to finance the purchase of a home? 325

What three chief qualifications of prospective borrowers are considered by bankers before granting a loan? 325

State some of the common rules governing the time limit and other conditions of commercial bank loans 325

Tell two advantages which banks obtain from rediscounting of loans, as allowed in the Federal Reserve system 325

What are some of the differences between national banks and state banks? 325

For what purpose was the Federal Reserve system created? What significant change was made in 1936? Why? 325

Name four means by which the Federal Reserve board may influence the use of credit. 326

What is meant by open-market operations of the Federal Reserve banks? 326

By what device of law is the independence of the Federal Reserve board strengthened as against the executive branch of the government? 326

Name six agencies through which the Federal government extends credit to citizens. When was the first one established? . . . 327

BUSINESS, BANKING, AND LEGAL TERMS

State two meanings of the term acceptance. Explain the use of a trade acceptance. . . 329

What is accommodation paper? 329

Discuss the application of the term "accrued interest" 329

What is the function of an actuary? of an agent? 329

Define the following: amortization; arbitrage; assessed valuation 329

State two uses of the term assessment . . . 329

Define assets 329

What is an audit? 330

Discuss the phrase "balance of trade" . . . 330

State the true nature of a bank balance; the meaning of bank discount 330

Describe the work of a bank examiner . . . 330

Discuss bankruptcy 330

What is meant by the term "bank statement"? 330

Explain the following terms: bear; bear panic; bear raid; bids and offers . . .330–331

What is a bill of exchange? 331

What are the chief points of difference between a "straight bill of lading" and an "order bill of lading"? 331

Define bills payable; bills receivable 331

What is a blanket mortgage? 331

Explain the phrase "bonded debt" 331

Indicate the effect of the action implied in the phrase "books closed" 331

Define book value 331

What is a broker's function? 331

In financial parlance, what is a bull? a bull market? 331–332

Account for the phrase "callable bonds". . . 332

What is a call loan? 332

Distinguish two meanings of the term "call" 332

How do cartels operate? 332

How does a cashier's check differ from an ordinary check? 332

Explain the meaning of the term "certificate of deposit" 332

Is a certified check a direct obligation upon a bank? 332

What property rights are conveyed by a chattel mortgage? 332

Why should checks be presented promptly for payment? 333

Describe the procedure of a clearing house. . 333

What is a collateral loan? a collateral note? 333

Outline the service rendered by commercial agencies 333

Why has commercial paper attained such high favor among banks? 333

Explain the term "common stock" 333

When does a broker become responsible for the sale price of goods handled on "consignment"? 334

How is the word consols, applied to certain British securities, accounted for? 334

In what ways is the term "controlling interest" employed? 334

In financial usage, what is a corner? 334

Explain the term "coupon bonds" 334

When is a person dealing in securities said to "cover"? 334

What is the American Stock Exchange? . . 334c

Distinguish between a quitclaim deed and a warranty deed 334

Point out several meanings of the term discount 335

Define dividend; dollar exchange; domestic exchange 335

In what ways does double taxation come about? 335

How is the term draft now applied in the United States? 335

Point out the particular effect of an anomalous endorsement; of a restrictive endorsement; of a special endorsement 336

Discuss the liability of an endorser 336

Define the following: exchange; excise; face value 336

What is a fiscal year? How is the term "fixed charges" applied? 337

Explain the effect of a foreclosure 337

Is the use of a "gold" clause in a bond an effective safeguard to bondholders against devaluation of the currency? 337

What is the principal use of gold certificates? 337

Where in the U.S is the largest "gold reserve" depository located? 337

Indicate the rank of good will among business assets 337

How many parties must there be to a transaction in order to permit a true guarantee? . 338

Explain the term hedging. 338

What is a holding company? 338

Define the term income; income tax. Explain how there may lawfully be double income taxation. 338

Indicate the origin of the term indenture . . 338

For what purpose are interim certificates issued? 338
Describe the function of an investment banker. 338
Enumerate three possible effects of a court judgment 339
Describe the process called "kiting" 339
Discuss legal investment 339
By what authorities in the United States is a legal rate of interest fixed? 339
What is a letter of credit? Name the two classes of such instruments. Explain how letters of credit are drawn and used . . . 339
What is a lien? 340
Discuss limited partnership. What is liquidation? 340
Define manifest. What must a manifest show? 340
What is a margin as applied in market trading? What governmental agency has the authority to set margin requirements in so far as they are dependent on bank credit? . . . 340
Explain the term "matched order." 340
Point out the important characteristics of a mechanic's lien 340
By what authorities are money orders issued? Point out the advantages of these orders . . 341
Discuss the nature of a mortgage and some important legal provisions in respect to mortgages 341
When is a check or other similar instrument negotiable? 341
What is a note? an option? 341
Explain the legal application of the principle implied in the popular term "outlawed" . 341
What does the word overdrawn, used in reference to a bank account, really mean? . . . 341
What is the meaning of the phrase "payable to bearer?" 342
Explain "parity prices" 341
To what things does the term "personal property" apply? 342
Explain the operation of a pool in stock transactions. What is the status of pools under the law? 342
What is a power of attorney? 342
Point out the essential quality of preferred stock. Discuss some special features and provisions in respect to this type of stock . 342
Explain the term premium 342
What is a promissory note? 342
What is the business of a promoter? 342
Explain the procedure referred to as protest . 343
Define proxy; put 343
Outline the process known as pyramiding . . 343
Discuss rate of exchange 343
What constitutes real property? 343
Discuss the practice of rebate and the legislation directed against it 343
For what purposes is a receiver appointed? . 343
Explain the term "registered bonds" 343
For what purposes does a corporation maintain a reserve? 343
Define scrip 344
Indicate the claims involved in a second mortgage against property 344
Define the following: seigniorage; sellers' option; selling short 344
Point out the status of silver certificates in the United States currency system 344
What is a sinking fund? 344
Define sterling; sterling exchange 344
What is represented by the capital stock of a corporation? 344
Explain the stock dividend 345
What is the purpose of a stop-loss order? . . 345
Indicate the effect of an order to stop payment on a check 345
Define subpœna 345
Point out some effects of the registry of a trade-mark 345

State the functions of trust companies. . . . 345
What is the function of a trustee under a will? under a corporate mortgage? 346
What is underwriting? Explain the origin of the term and the present use of it 346
Define unearned increment 346
Under what act were United States notes first issued? When were they first redeemable in gold? 346
Define upset price; voucher; wash sales; watered stock 346

AGRICULTURE

Discuss the beginnings of prehistoric agriculture 347
By whom was agriculture developed in medieval Europe? 347
To what are the two greatest improvements in modern agriculture said to be due? 347
Enumerate the cultivated products raised by Indians in America before the European settlement 348
Compare colonial agriculture in the South with that of the North 348
Trace the early development of cotton raising in America 348
At what dates were cattle and hogs brought to Florida? to Canada and Virginia? 348
Outline the crop regions of the United States. 348
What measures were taken for the relief of American agriculture in 1933? 351
What are some of the principal features of the Agricultural Ajustment Act of 1938? . . . 351
What sciences are now included under the term horticulture? 354
What fruit in North America leads in quantity and value of production? Name the three flowers that lead in commercial production. 354
What state ranks first in production of asparagus? of cabbages? of celery? of sweet corn? of watermelons? 355
Name the three leading field crops of Canada on the *basis of value*. Which province leads in *yield* of wheat produced? of oats? of potatoes? of barley? of hay and clover? In what province is flaxseed an important crop? . . 355
Discuss the value of land drainage 356
In what state is the greatest amount of capital invested in drainage enterprises? 356
In what country of the world is irrigation most extensively practiced? 357
What is the total number of irrigated farms in the United States? the total area? 358
Define forestry. Enumerate several valuable characteristics of forests 359
Summarize the history of Federal Government control of forests in the United States. 359
What states have more than 100,000 acres each of state forests? Give the total area of state forests; of national forests 359–360
In what ways has intensive agriculture led to destructive erosion of the soil? Give four methods of combating the damage . . .359–361

ANIMAL INDUSTRY, MINING

Name, in order, the chief swine producing countries of the world; the leading sheep producing countries. 361
What countries lead in the raising of horses? Where is the world's greatest horse and mule market located? Name four other draft animals 361
Name the chief beef exporting countries. Name two leading breeds of beef cattle; of dairy cattle 362

Indicate by figures the commercial importance of the poultry raising industry   361

State the average annual per capita consumption of meat in the United States   362

Distinguish between a vaccine and an antitoxin. Under what conditions are these substances prepared in the United States? Describe the preparation of one kind of each .   362

Indicate the use and value of insulin   362

State the total value of products of animal industry in Canada in a recent year. Which province ranks first in this industry? . . .   363

Discuss the relative importance of mining among American industries   370

Classify mining products   370

What is the value of the annual mineral production in the United States? State approximately the number of people engaged in the mining industry.   370

INVENTIONS

Explain the action of the air brake   373

Define airplane. How are airplanes usually classified?   373

To what flying machines is the term airship applied? When was the first successful dirigible built? Indicate the extent to which rigid dirigibles have been used commercially. What is a "Blimp"?   374

Outline the chief features of construction and operation in present-day automobiles . . .   374

Who, probably, should be called the inventor of the gasoline automobile? Who made the first commercially manufactured car? What make of automobile was the first to be sold in the United States? 374–375

Explain the action of the magnetic compass.   375

Describe the use of the Sperry compass . . .   375

Explain the meaning of the phrase "boxing the compass"   375

Distinguish between the linotype and the monotype machine 375, 376

What is the meaning of the term dynamo-electric machine?   376

To what uses is the electron tube applied? . .   376

Describe two characteristics of a rotating gyro-top wheel 376–377

Outline the action of a four-cycle internal combustion engine. What are the special features of the Diesel engine?   377

Distinguish between the simple microscope and the compound microscope   378

Explain the means by which the effect of continuous vision and motion is produced in moving pictures   378

Give figures which indicate the extent and importance of the moving picture industry. Where was the first moving picture studio located? 378–379

Explain the principle of the phonograph. How are commercial records produced? . .   379

Summarize the services of several men to the development of modern photography. What means are used to produce photographs in natural colors?   380

What scientists, by their discoveries, laid the foundation for modern systems of radio-telegraphy? 380–381

In what year was the first transatlantic wireless message sent?   381

How does the process of radiotelephony differ from that of radiotelegraphy?   381

Describe the operation of the chain stitch sewing machine; of the lock stitch machine. Discuss the invention of the sewing machine and various improvements upon it . . .   382

Which is more efficient, the reciprocating steam engine or the turbine? 382–383

Explain the operation of the telegraph. Point out several improvements that have enlarged its usefulness. Discuss the question as to who invented the telegraph   383

Who invented the telephone?   383

Describe the means by which pictures may be transmitted over telephone lines   384

Who invented the modern typewriter? . . .   384

ENGINEERING AND BUILDING

Enumerate the chief branches of engineering .   387

Outline the work of the mechanical engineer .   387

Indicate the importance of electrochemical engineering   387

Illustrate the magnitude of the work done by United States military engineers   389

Name and give the dimensions of several famous European aqueducts. Describe the Catskill aqueduct; the Los Angeles aqueduct   389

Summarize the history of bridge building. Describe the following types of bridges: truss; suspension; arch; cantilever. What is a bascule? 389–390

Explain the use and action of canal locks . .390–391

Discuss the various types and uses of dams. How high is the Hoover dam and where is it located? 391–392

Give the names of three of the first locomotives used commercially in America. Enumerate three of the chief improvements in locomotive building   392

What is the greatest speed attained by a locomotive? State the average life of a locomotive   392

Describe the usual methods of securing adequate foundations for skyscrapers . . .392–393

Explain how each floor of a skyscraper is made to carry its own wall   393

For what purpose were the oldest known tunnels used? What special method of rock excavation did the Romans understand? . .   393

State some of the difficulties under which Simplon tunnel was constructed. Describe methods of tunneling in soft ground. Where is the largest tunnel in the world?   394

MANUFACTURING

Discuss the literal and the actual meaning of the term manufacturing   395

What was the outstanding feature of the Industrial Revolution? Describe the organization of the cloth industry in England before 1780   395

Indicate the nature of four inventions in the textile industry in the latter part of the 18th century   396

Enumerate the industrial advantages enjoyed by England in the 19th century   396

Outline the geographic distribution of Germany's industrial plants   397

What is the most important branch of French manufacturing? Name its chief centers . .   397

Enumerate the chief manufactured products of Switzerland; of Scandinavia; of Czechoslovakia   397

Narrate the story of the expansion of industry in colonial New England. Where and by whom was the first blast furnace set up in the colonies?   400

Describe the beginnings of the textile industry in America. Point out the early influence of railroads on American manufacturing . . .   400

Enumerate 10 important groups of American manufacturing industries. Name the cities each of which produces more than one per cent of American manufactures   401

Where are the chief centers of the American cotton industry? 402

Indicate by statistics the growth of cotton manufacturing in the South 402

What are the chief principles of management involved in mass production? Tell two industries which exemplify it. 402

TECHNOLOGY:

HOW THINGS ARE MADE

By what means is the light of an arc lamp produced? What is a flaming arc? 407

Explain the action of baking powder in dough. 407

What is bell metal? By what is the characteristic tone of a bell determined? 407

Name three of the first books printed from movable types. Describe the preparation of electrotypes. What are signatures in bookmaking? 408

To what operation in bookmaking is the term casing-in applied? 409

To what products is the name bread applied? Why is the dough kneaded? Outline the changes which take place in the loaf during the process of baking 409

Describe early methods of making bricks. Outline the modern process 409–410

Enumerate the processes involved in making butter. Describe the effect of the processes of souring and ripening; the effect of churning. What is renovated butter? 410

Describe the making of pearl buttons 410

Summarize the early history of submarine cables. Describe the structure of a submarine cable. How are cable messages sent and received? 410–411

Describe the production of celluloid 411

Why was portland cement so named? How is it prepared? Why does cement set? . . . 411

From what source is chocolate obtained? . .411–412

Enumerate the by-products secured in modern production of coke 412

Point out some of the advantages of concrete as a structural material 412

Outline the process of obtaining cork. Enumerate several uses of the material . . .412–413

Point out the characteristic that makes cotton so satisfactory for spinning 413

How is mercerized cotton produced? absorbent cotton? 413

Describe the production and uses of various grades of cottonseed oil. Enumerate several valuable cottonseed products 413–414

Name some natural products formerly used as dyes. Explain the term "coal-tar dyes". . 414

Discuss simple fire extinguishers 414

What is a fireless cooker? 414

Distinguish between Graham flour and whole wheat flour 414–415

Describe several kinds of artificial gas. . . . 415

Outline the process of preparing gelatin . . . 415

Name the principal ingredients of glass. Describe the manufacture of plate glass; of window glass 415–416

From what sources is glucose derived? Compare glucose and sugar as to sweetness and healthfulness 416

In what industries is glycerin a by-product? 416

Describe the process of preparing gold leaf . 416

State the composition of gunpowder. Describe the type of explosives which now are used instead of ordinary gunpowder . .416–417

Explain the working of a hot-air furnace in heating a building. Compare the costs of various common heating systems 417

Which part of a raw skin is used for leather? Name the three methods of changing the skin to leather. From what skins is chamois produced? For what purpose is morocco leather especially valued? 418

Outline the process of preparing flax fibers for the manufacture of linen. State two tests for distinguishing linen from cotton fabric . 419

What are three principal methods of illumination by electricity? 419

How is raw linseed oil produced? To what characteristic is its value for waterproofing and for inks attributable? 419–420

Of what materials is luminous paint composed? What is radiolite? 420

Describe some early types of matches. What dangerous practice in matchmaking was made virtually impossible by law in 1912?. 420

How is the use of the abbreviation "d." as used in classifying nails explained? 421

Trace the history of the manufacture and use of needles 421

Discuss the composition and some of the important characteristics and uses of nitroglycerin 421

Why does nylon feel cool to the skin? . . .421–422

Describe the preparation of oleomargarine. How may one easily distinguish oleomargarine from butter? 422

Of what three elements does the vehicle of paint consist? Name the substances commonly used to make up the vehicle. What are the chief pigments used? 422

Point out the origin of the word paper. Where is paper chiefly produced today? 422

Distinguish between mechanical pulp and chemical pulp for paper making. Outline the process of producing paper by the Fourdrinier machine; the process of coating paper 422

Outline the modern process of manufacturing pins 422

Define porcelain. Of what materials are the various types of it made? 423–424

Distinguish between stoneware and porcelain. Describe the process of working the prepared clay into forms on the potter's wheel . . . 424

Describe the process of making raisins . . . 425

From what source is rubber obtained? What is vulcanization? 425

Tell, in general terms, how rayon is made . . 425

Describe the method by which Oriental rugs are woven 425–426

What designs are commonly used in Chinese rugs? By what characteristics may a Bokhara rug be distinguished? 426

By whom was the weaving of rugs and carpets introduced into Europe? 426

Describe the process of obtaining the silk fiber from the cocoons 427

Outline the chemical process involved in soap making. Name the alkalies and fats that are commonly used in soap manufacture . . . 427

Describe the special processes and ingredients used in making the following: floating soaps; toilet soaps; shaving soap. How does soap clean? 427–428

Discuss the sources of starch. Outline the process of producing starch from corn . . . 428

Describe the production of sugar from sugar cane; from sugar beets 428–429

How is maple sap secured and manufactured into sugar? 429

Explain the principle of the thermos bottle . 429

Enumerate several uses of water glass. . . . 430

State the chief difference between wool and other textile fibers. What is a fleece? . . . 430

BIBLIOGRAPHY

The literature covering the general field of economics and its many special divisions is very large and is constantly growing. Because of the current study and interest in the subject, new publications and revisions of texts are constantly in demand, particularly in the field of world economics, international trade, and labor relations. A carefully selected list of books both of popular and of scientific interest is here presented.

GENERAL WORKS

Behr, Michael R., and Nelson, Dennis L.—Economics: A Personal Consumer Approach
Reston '75

Edel, Matthew—Economics and the Environment
Prentice-Hall '73

Eells, Richard, and Walton, Clarence—Conceptual Foundations of Business, 3d ed. . . . *Irwin '74*

Fabrycky, W. J., and Thuesen, G. J.—Economic Decision Analysis . . . . . *Prentice-Hall '74*

Friedmann, John—Urbanization, Planning, and National Development . . . . . *Sage '73*

Galbraith, John Kenneth—The New Industrial State . . . . . . *Houghton-Mifflin '71*

Ghelardi, Robert—Economics, Society, and Culture: God, Money, and the New Capitalism
Delacorte '76

Harte, N. B.—The Study of Economic History
Frank Cass '71

Loebl, Eugene—Humanomics . *Random House '76*

McNee, Robert B.—A Primer on Economic Geography . . . . *Random House '71*

Samuelson, Paul—Economics, 10th ed.
McGraw-Hill '76

Schlossberg, S., and Sherman, F.—Organizing and the Law . . . . *Bureau of National Affairs '71*

Schneider, Harold K.—Economic Man; The Anthropology of Economics . . . . *Free Press '74*

Spencer, Milton H.—Contemporary Economics
Worth '71

Turkel, Louis (Studs)—Working . . *Pantheon '74*

Weisskopf, Walter A.—Alienation and Economics
Dutton '71

COMMERCE AND TRANSPORTATION

Ellsworth, P. T., and Leith, J. Clark—The International Economy, 5th ed. . . . *Macmillan '75*

Farris, Martin T., and McElhiney, Paul T., eds.—Modern Transportation; Selected Readings, 2d ed. . . . . *Houghton-Mifflin '73*

Gunston, Bill—Transportation: Problems and Prospects . . . . *Dutton '72*

Pegrum, Dudley Frank—Transportation: Economics and Public Policy, 3d ed. . . . *Irwin '73*

Pisar, Samuel—Coexistence and Commerce; Guidelines for Transactions between East and West
McGraw-Hill '70

Quandt, Richard E., ed.—The Demand for Travel: Theory and Measurement . . . . *Heath '70*

William, E. W., Jr.—The Future of American Transportation . . . . . . *Prentice-Hall '71*

MARKETING

Boone, Louis E., and Johnson, James C.—Marketing Channels . . . *General Living Corp. '73*

Corey, E. Raymond—Industrial Marketing: Cases and Concepts . . . . . . *Prentice-Hall '76*

Cundiff, Edward W.; Still, Richard R.; and Govoni, Norman A. P.—Fundamentals of Modern Marketing . . . . *Prentice-Hall '76*

Enis, Ben M.—Marketing Principles: The Management Process . . . . *Goodyear '74*

Enis, Ben M., and Cox, Keith K.—Marketing Classics . . . . *Allyn and Bacon '69*

Fisher, Lawrence—Industrial Marketing: An Analytical Approach to Planning and Execution
Brandon/Systems '70

Gist, Ronald R.—Marketing and Society
Holt, Rinehart, and Winston '71

Heskett, James L.—Marketing . . . *Macmillan '76*

Rothberg, Robert R.—Corporate Strategy and Product Innovation . . . . *Free Press '76*

West, Christopher—Marketing on a Small Budget
Wiley '75

INSURANCE, INVESTMENTS, MONEY, AND BANKING

Bracker, Lewis A., and Wagner, Walter—The Trouble with Wall Street . . *Prentice-Hall '72*

Goldsmith, Raymond William—Financial Structures and Development *Yale University Press '69*

Hallman, Victor, and Rosenbloom, Jerry S.— Personal Financial Planning . . *McGraw-Hill '75*

Hendrickson, Robert A.—The Future of Money
Prentice-Hall '70

Jones, J. P.—The Money Story . . . *Drake '73*

Mehr, Robert I., and Neumann, Seev—Inflation, Technology, and Growth; Possible Long-Range Implications for Insurance . . *Indiana Univ. '72*

Mowbray, Albert H.; Blanchard, Ralph H.; and Williams, C. Arthur, Jr.—Insurance; Its Theory and Practice in the United States, 6th ed.
McGraw-Hill '69

Pfeffer, Irving, and Klock, David R.—Perspectives on Insurance . . . . . . *Prentice-Hall '74*

Renwick, Fred B.—Introduction to Investments and Finance . . . . *Macmillan '71*

Riegel, Robert; Miller, Jerome S.; and Williams, C. Arthur, Jr.—Insurance Principles and Practices: Property and Liability, 6th ed.
Prentice-Hall '76

Ritter, Laurence, and Silber, William—Principles of Money, Banking, and Financial Markets
Basic Books '74

AGRICULTURE, FISHERIES, AND MINING

Cameron, Eugene N., ed.—The Mineral Position of the United States, 1975–2000
Univ. of Wisconsin '73

Hallett, Graham—The Economics of Agricultural Policy . . . . . . *Augustus M. Kelley '68*

Hickling, C. F.—The Farming of Fish
Pergamon '68

McDivitt, James Frederick, and Manners, Gerald—Minerals and Men . . . . . *Johns Hopkins '74*

Mellor, John Williams—The Economics of Agricultural Development . . . . . . *Cornell '69*

Royce, William F.—An Introduction to the Fishery Sciences . . . . *Academic Press '72*

Temple, John—Mining; An International History
Praeger '73

Wilcox, Walter; Cochrane, W. W.; and Herdt, R. W.—Economics of American Agriculture
Prentice-Hall '74

INVENTIONS AND ENGINEERING

Abernathy, David, and Knipe, Wayne—Ideas, Inventions, and Patents; An Introduction to Patent Information . . . . *Pioneer Press '73*

Beakley, George C., and Chilton, Ernest G.—Design; Serving the Needs of Man
Macmillan '74

Beakley, George C., and Leach, H. W.—Engineering: An Introduction to a Creative Profession, 2d ed. . . . . *Macmillan '72*

Bowker, Albert H., and Lieberman, Gerald J.—Engineering Statistics, 2d ed. . *Prentice-Hall '72*

Clarke, Arthur Charles—Profiles of the Future; An Inquiry into the Limits of the Possible, rev. ed. . . . . *Harper & Row '73*

Graham, A. Richard—An Introduction to Engineering Measurements . . . . . *Prentice-Hall '75*

History

CONTENTS GUIDE

	Page		Page
American Flags	469	Republican Party	472
American History	441	Revolutionary War	450
American History Dictionary	479	Roman Emperors	590
American History Outline	502	Rulers of England	530
Ancient Cities	599	Rulers of France	563
Bibliography	726	Rulers of Germany	568
Bishops and Popes of Rome	644	Rulers of Russia	593
British Commonwealth of Nations	528	State History Outline	466
British History	517	Territorial Growth of the	
Canadian History	531	United States	456, 466
Canadian Provinces Development	536	Treaties:	
Civil War	460	United States	499
Colonial Wars	447	World	668
Democratic Party	470	Vice Presidents of U.S.	476
Governors-General of Canada	534	War of 1812	455
Latin American History	541	Wars, Important	720
League of Nations	622	War with Spain	464
Mexican War	457	World Court	623
Peoples of the World	601	World History—	
Prehistoric and Atomic Dating	440	Countries, alphabetical	547
Presidents of the United States	474	World History Dictionary	641
Presidential Elections	478	World History Outline	672
Prime Ministers of Canada	534	World War I	611
Questions, Review	722	World War II	624

Picture Guide: The Acropolis at Athens—Pictures of Historic Europe—View of Earth as Seen by the Astronauts of the Apollo 8 U.S. Space Mission.

The southern Bavarian Alpine peak, Zugspitze, highest point in Germany, rises 9,721 feet above sea level. (*German Natl. Tourist Office*)

View of Stockholm, showing the Old Town, from which the capital originated about 700 years ago. (*Courtesy Swedish National Travel Office*)

European Scenes: Chenonçeaux, one of the most famous of French chateaux. The foundations were laid in 1515 and in 1535 the estate became royal property, serving as a residence of Francis I. In 1559, Mary Queen of Scots spent her honeymoon here with Francis II, son of Catherine de' Medici. Constructed in a style that is transitional between Gothic and Renaissance, the castle spans the river Cher, 21 miles southeast of Tours. Chenonçeaux was extensively restored during the 19th century, and is now the property of the French nation. During the tourist season, the chateau and its grounds are illuminated at night.

The Acropolis at Athens. *Crowned by the* **Parthenon (opposite),** *the Acropolis, or High City, was fortified in the 6th century B.C. By the time of the Golden Age of Pericles, magnificent civic buildings thronged the first democratic city-state to appear in history. The Acropolis was the center of Athenian government, as well as the historic heart of all Greece. A triumph of architecture, the Parthenon was both a temple to the goddess Athena and the treasury of the Delian League, of which Athens was the leading power.*

APOLLO 8 EARTH VIEW—*This spectacular view of the rising Earth greeted Apollo 8 Astronauts as they rounded the far side of the Moon on their first orbit, Dec. 24, 1968. On Earth, 240,000 miles distant in space, the sunset terminator (lower profile) bisects the Continent of Africa. (NASA)*

History

INTRODUCTORY

THE word history is sometimes used to mean all that has happened in the past. In this sense we speak of the history of the earth, of rocks, or of plants, as well as of the history of man. In the narrower sense, however, history is an account of the actions and the fortunes of mankind. Such an account must be based upon reliable records which can be understood and interpreted by the writers of history. The records may be in the form of buildings, products of art, manufactured objects, or writings. They may even be institutions, language, or survivals of customs.

Unfortunately, it has been the exception for people to try consciously to hand down to their successors information about their own day. It often happens that certain records are preserved by the merest chance, while others, which would have been much more valuable, are lost. These conditions, it will be seen, make it a very difficult task to obtain a true picture of a past age, to recover the habits and the customs of a society, to trace the effects of its actions upon later times, and to understand the motives and the feelings of people who ceased to live many years or even centuries ago. Yet these are the things which the writers of history aim to do. To accomplish their purpose, historians have worked out an elaborate science of evidence. The more successful historians have also brought to bear upon the task consummate gifts of art and of understanding.

The Use of History. To study history is to live over again this story of the past, to meet familiarly great men and notable women, and to see the outcome of their actions more clearly than the actors saw it themselves. It is to have at one's disposal authentic facts about the past. More than this, the reading of history enlarges our experience, and enables us to judge of present issues and to forecast the future of situations through our knowledge of similar situations in the past. For these reasons, history is a study of the utmost importance for every one, and especially for citizens of a democracy, in order that they may help to determine public policies and actions.

The Task of the Historian. The first requisite for all sound historical writing is the careful establishment of facts. This object is attainable only if the historian has full knowledge of the sources of information in regard to the period to be described. Furthermore, he must possess the gift of critically estimating the value of his sources according to the rules of historical evidence. We look to him also for interpretation of movements and of events.

To this task the historian must bring an insight into the motives which actuate men in various situations. He needs a power of discernment in state affairs and a due appreciation of the parts which economic, social, and religious interests play in human affairs. Moreover, the historian should keep himself free from considerations of self-interest, that his interpretation may be objective, reasonable, and as free from bias as is humanly possible.

Earlier Historians. Such demands have not always been met. The earliest historian was probably Herodotus, but he had not learned to test his sources critically. However, Thucydides, another Greek historian, showed a spirit so scientifically rigorous that his work has seldom been equaled. During the middle ages, histories were seldom more than chronicles, devoid alike of artistic form and of scrupulous care for fact. With the Renaissance and in early modern times an interest in genuine history was roused by controversy over facts connected with religion. The histories in that period were written, however, by people who were familiar with religious wars and with struggles between dynasties, and who were acquainted only with a royalist form of government. They failed to understand records of democratic institutions in the past or to estimate justly social and economic changes in their own day.

Modern Writing of History. In more recent times a different problem has confronted the historian. Broadening interests in his readers have made it necessary for him to treat more aspects of life, and this means that for the history of the past more material must be collected. In the present also an extraordinarily great amount of material is being produced, largely because of the wide use of the printing press. The result is that sifting and selection of material has become one of the chief tasks of the historian. In fact, the increasing complexity of the historian's work has proceeded to such a point that no one man is equal by himself to the task of writing a comprehensive history of even a short period. All great histories now are corporate undertakings.

Divisions of History. In treating of history, an arbitrary division is commonly made into three periods,—ancient, medieval, and modern.

Ancient history deals with the course of the Eastern and Western civilizations up to 476 A. D., the year in which the last Roman emperor of the West was deposed. The civilizations of the East included Babylonia, Elam, Assyria, Mesopotamia, Egypt, Palestine, Phœnicia, Persia, India, China, and Japan; those of the West were Greece, Carthage, and Rome. India, China, and Japan, though having a historical past corresponding to the period we call ancient, are less intimately connected with European civilization and so are usually treated separately.

The history of the medieval period takes up the story of civilization at the fall of Rome. Throughout the course of a thousand years, it traces the gradual development of the old world into the new. Beginning with the almost complete cessation of governmental authority and of learning, it proceeds to describe the growth and power of Christianity, to narrate the rise of the feudal system, and to reveal the origin of the states which developed into the various nations of today.

Modern history may be said to begin with the time of the invention of printing and with the discovery of America. It is largely the story of the internal development and of the outward expansion of nations, together with their conflicts.

These divisions have been found useful, but they should not be allowed to obscure the fact that in reality history is continuous, and that, in particular, European and American history exhibits an unbroken chain of development in culture and ideas from the dawn of civilization to the present.

The Study of History. For various reasons, the history of certain periods or nations may be more attractive or more enlightening to the reader than that of other times and peoples. This fact has led to the placing of a certain emphasis on those eras which show the growth of political power, or which reveal a high development of art, of learning, and of culture. Some ages are of especial interest because we see in them the unfolding of religious ideas or the spread of democratic views and practices; or they may gain significance from the sheer force of great personalities which they produced.

The Hebrews.—In the history of the Hebrews we follow the evolution of an ethical religious faith and the rise of a conception of a just and universal god.

Greece.—The history of Greece in the 5th century B. C. shows a people so inspired by an ideal of freedom as to defy a despotic empire of much greater power. This too was a period prolific in inventions, rich in literature and in art—a period which has had something to teach to every nation.

Rome.—The history of Rome, on the other hand, from the Punic wars to the widest extent of the Empire, shows the overmastering power of organization. It describes a time in which was built up a system of law that underlies the legal customs of Western Europe and of Latin America.

The Crusades.—Next come the Crusades. Though the military result was the defeat of the Christian nations and a diminution of their prestige, yet the enterprise widened the horizon of the people of Western Europe, and began for a second time to unite the destinies of Europe and Asia.

The Renaissance.—After the Crusades, we arrive at the period of the Renaissance—the rebirth of literature, art, philosophy, and science. Allied to this was the Reformation, from which dates the origin of the Protestant Church.

The Commonwealth.—One of the most instructive periods is that of the struggle between Parliament and the Stuart monarchs in England during the 17th century. It was in this period that the power of Parliament was first made paramount over the authority of the king.

The Modern World.—Finally, we see history take a new direction as a result of the growth of knowledge and the heightening of the sense of individual human worth, which had been going on ever since the time of the Renaissance. The widespread conviction of the value of personality led to a growth of democratic sentiment and to the overthrow of absolute forms of government.

The increase of knowledge led to inventions which profoundly influenced the course of history. First, the introduction of machinery broke the chains that bound man to the soil; efficient means of manufacture, travel, communications promised an era of plenty to replace the tyranny of scarcity. But the new industrial organization did not come easily. Accompanying social injustices created unrest that led in Russia and China to revolution and tyranny and in other countries to more gradual but far-reaching changes to make the lot of the common man more secure.

At the same time the war-making power of individual nations grew apace. The more advanced built up empires at the expense of the weaker in Africa and elsewhere. Then came two worldwide wars, the bloodiest in history, leaving two giant powers with their allies confronting each other—Russia and the United States. Former empires dissolved; less advanced nations became independent under the shield of an international organization—the United Nations. Meanwhile the character of war itself was transformed by the application of atomic energy to a potential destructiveness from which the imagination of the world shrank in horror. Finally, science's gift of plenty and of control over disease led to a rapid increase in the world's population which, unless controlled, would darken the world's future with ominous portent.

PREHISTORY AND ATOMIC DATING

Dating is basic to history. Until recently, the accurate placing of events in their time sequence could seldom extend back before the use of writing, which was invented between 3500 and 3000 B.C. But with the announcement in 1947 by Dr. Willard F. Libby of an "atomic clock" which could pinpoint many events as early as 60,000 years ago, a new era dawned in our knowledge of prehistory.

The Carbon-14 Method. This method depends on the fact that the isotope of carbon with atomic weight 14, which exists in the atmosphere, is radioactive at a level that is believed to have been uniform until man-made atomic explosions came on the scene. All living matter appropriates some of this carbon-14. After the death of the organism, the carbon-14 begins to lose its radioactivity at a uniform rate. In 5730 years (within an accuracy of 40 years), it is reduced by half; one-half of the remainder (i.e., one-fourth of the original) is lost in the next 5730 years; finally, after about 60,000 years, it is too small to be measured accurately. The measurement is made by refined geiger counters, and from the count can be computed the age of organic materials associated with early man—skeletons, charcoal, ivory, etc. Accuracy is within 1 to 10%.

The Potassium-Argon Method. Inorganic material can sometimes be dated for millions of years by this method, which depends on the uniform rate of decay of a radioactive isotope of potassium. In this way, it has been shown that a manlike creature who could make cutting tools lived 1,750,000 years ago in Tanganyika, East Africa.

Neanderthal and Cro-Magnon Man. It is now known that Neanderthal Man inhabited Eurasia long before the last ice age and that he managed to survive it. A skeleton of such a man was found in Iraq dating back 43,000 years. This race lived by hunting, and its weapons and implements were fashioned with a view to both utility and beauty. It disappeared in Europe as the taller and more intelligent race of Cro-Magnon man became dominant, the ancestor of the modern Europeans.

This latter race was in its prime as the last ice age retreated, from about 18,000 B.C. It is to them that we owe the world's earliest paintings and wall carvings, those found in many caves of Spain and southern France, hearth ashes in which have been dated at around 13,000 B.C.

The Agricultural Revolution. A turning point in human development came when the uncertainties of the chase were replaced by the relative security of agriculture and domestication of food and draft animals. Wealth could thereafter be stored, a necessary base for political society. The first agricultural village, found in Iraq, has been dated at 7000 B.C. Agriculture reached England about 2300 B.C.

The Bronze Age. Before about 6000 B.C., man relied almost exclusively on stone and bone for weapons and implements. But then in Egypt and Mesopotamia bronze (copper and tin alloy) made its appearance. Its use spread slowly. By about 1900 B.C., a race in Spain known as the "beaker folk" made articles of bronze and spread them widely through Europe. The bronze age is believed to have been an era of sea-faring more extensive than any until the 15th century A.D.

America before Columbus. The earliest trace of man in the New World is charcoal from Lewisburg, Texas, which has been dated at 33,000 B.C. Mammoths were being hunted by men in Arizona as early as 10,000 B.C. A thousand years later, 9000 B.C., we find evidence of the farthest advance of the ice cap near Milwaukee, Wis. Copper was being mined in Isle Royal, Mich., in 2000 B.C., and was traded as far south as Florida. The first year of the Mayan calendar was about 613 B.C.

AMERICAN HISTORY

THE discovery and the colonization of the American continent were immediate consequences of the intellectual movements of the Renaissance and of the political and economic conditions of Western Europe at the close of the 15th century. Europe, by that time, had fairly passed from the middle ages to the modern period. With equal truth it may be said that the creation of the United States of America was one of the first great results of the growth of liberal political thought in Western Europe during the 17th and 18th centuries. A brief survey of the European conditions of these periods is, therefore, a necessary preliminary to the study of American colonial and national history.

European Background of American History. The Renaissance, which had created a new world of literature, painting, sculpture, and architecture, had also prepared the way for scientific discovery. Western Europe was thus made ready to enter upon an era of search for new modes of living and for new lands. The movement toward geographic discovery found its enthusiastic and inspiring apostle in Prince Henry of Portugal.

At the same time, the opening of the modern period was signalized by the appearance of national states—England, France, and Spain being the first to rise from the disorder of medieval feudalism. The emergence of these countries from long periods of war left many adventurous spirits free to engage in voyages of exploration. The ranks of the merchant adventurers, too, were swelled, and the demands of commercial enterprises gave impetus to the search for a new route to the Indies, whence came the goods for the most profitable traffic of the times. Not only were the Western merchants chafing under the large tolls taken by the Italian cities, but the Ottoman conquests had resulted either in the imposition of ruinous exactions upon commerce or in the practical closing of the ancient overland trade routes to the East.

Another important influence was due to the fact that, in England particularly, the 16th century saw a very large increase in population. The industrial and agricultural methods of the time, which had changed but little in many centuries, were proving inadequate to provide for the needs of the people. Moreover, a land system that restricted land ownership to a few was becoming irksome to the common people. These conditions caused thousands to welcome an opportunity for life in a new country.

From Imperialism to Popular Government. The questions as to the character and the rights of the state and as to its relation to the lives and happiness of the people occupied the attention of many European thinkers in the 17th and the 18th century. Moreover, these same centuries had seen in Europe the struggle among the powers to unite large areas into imperial states. But the governing classes and the "benevolent despots" of Europe remained generally indifferent to the intellectual movement of the period, while, among the political leaders in the American colonies, this liberal thought found hospitable minds. The political mission of the united colonies in 1776 was to withdraw from the arena of imperial rivalry, and to initiate a movement which should endow with modern liberal meanings the ideas of the state and of political union of states. The realization of this ideal continues to be the task of the American people.

Early Voyages of Discovery. In the latter half of the 15th century, Portuguese sailors attempted the sea route around the Cape of Good Hope. Numerous scholars, however, had come to believe that the earth was round and that, consequently, the Indies could be reached by sailing directly westward from Europe. The credit for putting these theories to a practical test belongs to Christopher Columbus, a Genoese sailor.

After years of fruitless endeavor to gain a hearing for his proposals, Columbus at length appealed to Isabella, the Spanish queen, through her interest in Christianizing the natives of heathen lands. With her aid, he finally secured three small ships and money with which to fit out his first expedition. Toscanelli, an Italian geographer, probably supplied Columbus with a map, on which Japan was represented in a position about 2500 miles west of the Canary islands. This error of distance was fortunate, for it is doubtful that Columbus could have found the men or the means for an undertaking which was likely to involve a longer time and greater danger than the voyage down the west coast of Africa.

Thus equipped with ships, and thoroughly acquainted, through years of study, with the scientific knowledge of geography and navigation that his age afforded, Columbus sailed westward from Palos, Spain, on August 3, 1492. On October 12, the explorers sighted land, probably one of the Bahama islands, which they called San Salvador. In the belief that they had found the East Indies, they took possession of San Salvador, Hispaniola (Haiti), and other islands in the name of the king of Spain. The report carried home by Columbus in 1493 prompted the sailors of other nations to make similar attempts to reach the East. He himself made three more voyages, in 1493, 1498, and 1502, touching at length the northern coast of the continent of South America. But the significance of his discovery was not appreciated until after his death.

The Portuguese redoubled their efforts, and in 1498 Vasco da Gama actually reached India, following the eastward route, by way of the Cape of Good Hope. Henry VII of England, who had refused the offer of Columbus to sail under the English flag, commissioned John Cabot, another Genoese, to set out in search of a new westward route to the Indies. Cabot sailed from Bristol in 1497, and reached the coasts of Labrador and Newfoundland. England, however, lacked money and ships to follow up the discoveries of John Cabot and his son Sebastian, and American exploration was left for the time to Spain.

In 1513 Balboa crossed the Isthmus of Panama and discovered the Pacific Ocean. Magellan, in 1520, entered the Pacific through the strait, which now bears his name, at the southern end of the American continent, sailed up the west coast of South America, and thence westward to the Philippines, where he met his death. One of his ships, however, finally reached Spain by way of the Cape of Good Hope, thus completing the first circumnavigation of the globe. Magellan had reached the goal in Asia toward which Columbus had sailed, and which he believed he had gained.

Exploration. During the early part of the 16th century, Spain was without a rival in the exploration of America. In 1513 Ponce de León visited Florida. While Cortés and Pizarro were gathering fabulous wealth in Mexico and Peru, other Spaniards, inspired by the hope of similar fortune, led expeditions into the country which now forms the southern part of the United States. De Soto marched inland from Florida and explored the country westward to the Mississippi river and the present state of Arkansas. About the same time, Coronado, in search of the rich cities of Cibola, led an expedition northward from the west coast of Mexico as far as the present state of Kansas. Within the latter half of the century, Spaniards visited points on the Pacific coast northward to the Strait of Juan de Fuca.

Meanwhile, French ambitions had been aroused. In 1493-94, Pope Alexander VI had confirmed to Spain possession of all new lands to the westward of a meridian drawn 370 leagues west of the Cape Verde islands, and to Portugal similar discoveries east of that line. Ignoring this division, the French king, Francis I, sent an Italian sailor, Verrazano, westward across the Atlantic. He explored the coast in the neighborhood of the present harbor of New York. Ten years later (1535), Jacques Cartier found the entrance to the St. Lawrence river, and sailed up that stream until his further progress was stopped by the rapids which were later called Lachine, or Chinese. Charmed by the beauty of the situation, he gave the name Mount Royal to the eminence which now crowns the city of Montreal.

In the opening years of the reign of Queen Elizabeth, English merchants and sailors, stirred to emulation by the commercial monopoly enjoyed by Spain, and, being in religious and political conflict with that power, began to think of possessing the New World. Their activities took two directions: (1) the search for a passage to India around the northern shore of America; (2) a direct attack on Spanish commerce in the Caribbean. The most valuable immediate results of English attempts to find the northwest passage were the discovery and the exploration of Hudson bay, in whose tributary land basin the powerful Hudson's Bay Company gained its first foothold upon the American continent.

The harrying of Spanish commerce was carried on most effectively by Francis Drake. In 1577 Drake, who had already played the pirate with great success, passed through the Strait of Magellan, took several rich prizes from the Spanish fleets on the west coast of America, and put in at a harbor north of the bay of San Francisco for repairs. Thence he continued his voyage of three years by way of the Cape of Good Hope, around the world to England and to the prize of knighthood (1580).

During this same period, persistent efforts toward more permanent possession and colonization of the New World were made by Englishmen. In 1578, Sir Humphrey Gilbert attempted to colonize Newfoundland. His first expedition failed to reach America, but a second, in 1583, entered St. John's harbor, Newfoundland. The colonists became discouraged, however, and soon returned to England. Sir Walter Raleigh, under a charter obtained from Queen Elizabeth I in 1584, made three attempts to settle a colony on Roanoke island, off the coast of that part of Virginia which later was included in North Carolina. All three of his attempts failed, largely because supplies could not be sent from England.

The failures of Gilbert and Raleigh proved that the founding of colonies was too expensive a venture for individuals. Further attempts at settlement were postponed until after the close of the wars with Spain in 1604.

The French, meanwhile, had followed up the explorations of Cartier on the St. Lawrence river. The greatest of the French explorers in the 16th century was Champlain, who pushed boldly westward from Quebec into the interior. He initiated that movement of French missionaries and settlers which at length planted a line of missions, forts, and settlements, stretching from the St. Lawrence west and south through the Mississippi valley to New Orleans.

Colonization. Nevertheless, while their leaders were the boldest and most successful explorers of the time, most of the Frenchmen who came to the New World were little interested in real colonizing. They ignored the advantage which early French discoveries on the middle Atlantic coast would have given them, and pressed back into the interior along the line of the St. Lawrence river. As the Spaniards in the South sought for wealth in the mines, so the Frenchmen in the North developed the fur trade, penetrating very early as far west as Lake Superior and north to Hudson bay.

French colonial government, moreover, was despotic. This governmental policy and the dearth of suitable colonists lost the New World to France.

The French claims, which at the opening of the 17th century stretched from the latitude of Philadelphia to that of Quebec, overlapped those of the English. But the only French settlements of importance were made at Port Royal, the present city of Annapolis, Nova Scotia (1604), and at Quebec (1608).

Frenchmen were, however, the first to attempt settlements within the present territory of the United States. In 1562 a group of Huguenots settled at Port Royal on the coast of what is now known as the state of South Carolina. Upon the failure of this colony, they planted another on the St. Johns river in Florida in 1565. The Spanish retaliated by founding St. Augustine in the same year and by then destroying the French colony.

The Spaniards were able rapidly to conquer large and rich territories in Mexico and in South America. Their policy of exploitation reduced to slavery many of the natives, whom they used in working the mines. However, an important feature of Spanish colonization is the fact that Spanish settlers intermarried with the natives and produced a mixed race of people who proved themselves capable of a culture which rivaled that of Spain itself. They built cities, with parks and churches and notable public buildings. They established universities and encouraged literature; the first printing press in North America was set up in Mexico. But the government of the Spanish colonies was military, under governors who carried out instructions from the despotic home government in Spain. Under Spanish rule, neither democracy nor representative government appeared.

The English victory over the Spanish *Armada* in 1588 had so checked the growth of Spanish power that, while Spain was able to keep her colonies in Mexico and South America, she was not able to extend settlements into the northern territory which she had already explored. Moreover, this territory did not appeal to the Spaniards, because it did not appear to be rich in mineral wealth. At the beginning of the 17th century, therefore, the settlement of the eastern coast of North America, between Florida and Nova Scotia, approximately the present Atlantic coast of the United States, was left to the English and the Dutch.

In 1609 Henry Hudson, sailing under the Dutch flag, discovered and explored the Hudson river, and in 1613 a Dutch trading company established a post on the site of the city of New York, calling it New Amsterdam. In 1621 the Dutch West India Company secured the right to colonize in territory adjoining New Amsterdam and the Hudson river. The company granted large estates to patroons, who were given feudal rights over whatever settlers they chose to send out. These settlements remained under Dutch control until 1664, when they were surrendered to the English. Meanwhile, a colony of Swedes and Finns was established at Fort Christina on the present site of Wilmington, Delaware, in 1638, but this territory was seized by the Dutch in 1644, and it passed later, with the other Dutch holdings, to England.

England in the Seventeenth Century. English colonization of America was profoundly influenced by the political and the religious conditions dominant in England in the 17th century. Following the brilliant reign of Elizabeth I, which ended in 1603, came the period of the Stuart kings, interrupted by Cromwell and the Commonwealth from 1649 to 1660. The leading political movement of the century arose out of the demand of the middle classes to be heard in affairs of government. It resulted in the temporary overthrow of the Stuarts in 1649 and in the effectual restriction of royal power through the revolution of 1688-89. In the domain of religion, the Puritan movement gathered strength until it controlled the established church of England during the Cromwellian period and, after the Restoration of 1660, maintained itself in the Nonconformist churches, which secured toleration and political privilege after the revolution of 1688-89. The Puritan and Cavalier migrations to America reflect the influence of these great struggles.

Motives for Colonization. A desire to outdo the Spaniard had been the motive of English explorers in the 16th century. The attempts of such men as Gilbert and Raleigh to establish colonies had been prompted by mixed patriotic, commercial, and religious motives. When, after some disastrous experiments, it became clear that colonization was a business for companies of men who could supply large capital, the commercial motive became supreme. After 1660, the influence of this incentive became noticeable in the grants of territory for commercial purposes, especially in connection with the Carolinas (1663) and, to a less extent, with Georgia and Pennsylvania. It is worthy of note, however, that the religious ideal of Christianizing the natives was never quite lost.

London and Plymouth Companies. In 1606 a group of London merchants formed a company of two divisions,—one called the London Company, the other, the Plymouth Company. Their purpose was to colonize the coast of America between the Spanish claims on the south and the French claims on the north. The London Company was granted a tract of land 100 miles along the coast and extending inland 100 miles, located somewhere between Cape Fear (Carolina) and the Hudson river. The Plymouth Company had a similar grant somewhere between the Potomac and Maine. The result was that the country lying between the Potomac and the Hudson, in which the grants overlapped and which was to go to the company that should first occupy it, was avoided by both companies. The London Company planted a settlement at Jamestown in 1607, and in 1620 the Pilgrims settled at Plymouth, within the Plymouth Company's grant.

Virginia Colonial Government. The first charter granted to the London Company, giving them the privilege of making settlements in Virginia, divided the powers of government between the king and the company, or the proprietors, as the company was called. It conferred no privileges of self-government on the colonists, although it did grant them the privileges of Englishmen, which meant jury trial, the right of habeas corpus, and free speech. The colony at Jamestown was really a great plantation. The colonists were servants and employees of the company. All cultivation of the soil was done in common. Products went into the company's storehouse, from which food and clothing and other articles needed by the settlers were issued to them, and such products as might find ready sale in England were taken for shipment. The profits from these sales went to the members of the company who had invested in the enterprise.

Some changes in the charter were made in 1609 and in 1612. The government was placed in the hands of the company. The first governor was Sir Thomas Dale, a soldier who ruled the colony with an iron hand from 1611 to 1616. Severe martial law was in force during this time, and Dale's governorship was known as the "time of slavery." Whatever his faults of undue severity, Dale maintained order in the colony and made one very important change in the government. This was the allotment of three-acre plots to private holders in 1614.

First Representative Assembly. The year 1618 brought the chief power in the London Company into the hands of Sir Edwin Sandys and the earl of Southampton. These men were Puritans and bitter opponents of King James I and his Stuart policies. They seized the opportunity to grant a larger measure of freedom to the colonists. In 1618 they issued a charter, or contract, and appointed Governor Yeardley to carry out this contract in the colony. The new governor abolished the system of common industry and granted 100-acre tracts to free immigrants. Then he formed an assembly made up of representatives from each plantation. In this act of Governor Yeardley, we see the beginning of representative government in America.

The date of the first meeting of the assembly, or House of Burgesses, as it came to be called, was July 30, 1619. This assembly soon fell into the ways of the English Parliament. It sat for six days and did most of its work in committees. It passed laws, which today would be called "blue laws," against drunkenness, gambling, absence from church, and excess in fine clothing. Although the governor possessed veto power, there was no occasion for its use. But the most important act of the Virginia assembly was that of 1624, which asserted the right of the assembly to control taxation. This right was reasserted upon the appointment of later governors.

The Founding of Maryland. The settlement of the colony of Maryland was due to the enterprise of a Catholic gentleman, George Calvert. Calvert had secured from King James in 1623 a title to Newfoundland, but his attempt to plant a colony there failed on account of the harsh climate of the island. He then petitioned for territory farther south, and Maryland was granted to him. In 1633, after his death, the title was confirmed to his son, Cecil Calvert, second baron of Baltimore. This charter made the baron really a constitutional king over the settlers in the new colony, but it provided for a representative assembly to be composed of freeholders, or freemen.

The Maryland assembly proved to be as progressive and tenacious as the House of Burgesses in Virginia. In 1635 it passed a code of laws, which Calvert vetoed. In 1638 the assembly rejected a code of laws which Calvert presented to it for acceptance; by 1650 it had won the right to initiate legislation.

The most notable feature of the Maryland government was its provision for religious toleration. Catholics were at this period severely persecuted in England, but Calvert secured for his colony the privilege of toleration. An act of the assembly, passed in 1649, declared that all persons professing belief in Jesus Christ should not be molested nor discountenanced for their religion. Although this act excluded Jews, it was far in advance of English practice or that of other English colonies.

New England. The Plymouth Company, formed by gentlemen in the west of England, attempted in 1607 to plant a colony at the mouth of the Kennebec river, but the venture was a failure, and for several years this company did nothing. Then some of its members formed the Council for New England. They did not send out colonists, but granted lands to individuals who would undertake to make settlements. Their policy, however, was unsuccessful. Only seven little settlements were made before 1630, the chief one being at Salem.

The Settlement of Plymouth. Meanwhile, a little band of Separatists,—Puritans who had withdrawn from the Church of England and, because of persecution, had settled at Leyden,—became desirous of leaving Holland and finding more favorable conditions under the English flag. Through the influence of the Puritan members of the London Company, these people secured a grant of land from that company and also obtained a loan of several thousand pounds from a company of London merchants. After many delays, 102 persons embarked on the *Mayflower* at Plymouth, England, in September 1620. Driven out of their course by autumn storms, they landed in America at a point to which Captain John Smith had already given the name of Plymouth. But Plymouth was outside the London Company's territory, and, consequently, the Pilgrims' grant of land was of no value. In this situation, 41 members of the company joined in signing an agreement known as the Mayflower Compact. This agreement bound the signers to co-operate in providing such government as might be necessary for the colony. The next year (1621) they secured a grant from the Council for New England.

The agreement of the Plymouth colonists with the London merchants provided that industry should be carried on in common for seven years. Supplies were to be sent out from London each year. After two years' trial, Governor Bradford found that the system of common industry was not working well, and he therefore granted parcels of land to individuals for temporary use. Under this new arrangement the colony began to prosper. In 1627 the term of agreement with the London merchants expired. Bradford and a few others assumed the debt of the colony, on condition of being allowed a monopoly of the fur trade. It took them fourteen years to repay the loan.

During the first few years of the Plymouth colony, government was carried on by an assembly which was virtually a town meeting. But as other settlements were formed near by, the need of a different legislature became insistent, and in 1636 a representative assembly was first convened. It provided the first written code of laws in the portion of America that later became the United States. As in other colonies, the franchise was not conferred even upon all freemen. An act of 1671 provided that a voter must give evidence of upholding the orthodox faith. During all this time, the colony of Plymouth had no charter, nor was it ever recognized by the home government. Probably this condition was due to the disturbed state of affairs in England. In 1691, the colony was annexed to Massachusetts.

Colony of Massachusetts Bay. The first settlements around Massachusetts bay were due to the activity of the Dorchester Company, made up of west of England men, who were interested in the fishing trade. A station was established at Cape Ann in 1623, largely through the influence of John White, a member of the company, to provide a home for the extra crews necessary on the fishing vessels. The settlement was moved to Salem in 1628. The Massachusetts Bay Company was formed, and in the following year a large body of settlers was added to the group already at Salem. The danger to English Puritanism, which appeared now in the policy of Charles I, brought a number of the members of the Massachusetts Bay Company to make the famous Cambridge Agreement, by which they secured control of the company and agreed to transfer the charter and all the government of their colonies to America. In this way the commercial company became an organized government and the promoter of the great Puritan migration.

The Puritan Migration. In the course of the next eleven years, during which period no Parliament was summoned in England, 25,000 selected English colonists were transferred to New England at a cost of about $4,000,000. The leader of this movement was John Winthrop. With a company of 900 he came to Massachusetts in 1630. In this year six new towns were founded in the neighborhood of Massachusetts bay. In 1640, when Parliament was again summoned in England, many colonists returned to the mother country, and New England received very few immigrants until after the American Revolution (1775–82).

Colonial Conditions. In the early years of the 17th century, glowing accounts of the climate and productiveness of the region of English settlement had been carried back to England, and all the early colonists, including the Pilgrims who landed at Plymouth, had visions of rapid rise to wealth. It took but a few years to dissipate these visions and to teach the colonists that they were dealing with a country of greater extremes of climate than they had known in England, and a land whose soil yielded returns only to labor. John Smith, the restless soldier and explorer, when he was president of the council at Jamestown in 1608-09, grappled sternly with this problem. He enforced regulations as to industry and social organization which probably saved the colony from utter extinction within the first three years of its existence.

While the colonists in New England at first drew some profit from the fur trade, they soon learned that the prosperity of the colonies was dependent upon the utilization of the fisheries and upon the cultivation of the soil. They learned from the Indians how to raise Indian corn, or maize, the food which saved the lives of the Pilgrims in the first difficult years of the settlement at Plymouth. Raleigh had brought back to England from Virginia the first tobacco which he had secured from the Indians. The growing of tobacco was for many years discouraged by the London Company, but it formed the basis of the wealth of the colonists in Virginia, as the cultivation of maize gave them their staple food.

The severe climate in New England came near proving fatal to the first settlements. Half of the first company of 102, who landed at Plymouth in the winter of 1620, died before spring. The colony of Jamestown in Virginia was planted on low, unhealthful ground, and in the first year two-thirds of the immigrants perished. It is said that for twenty years each new body of immigrants lost one-half their number within the first season.

Popular Government in New England. The charter of the Massachusetts Bay Company provided that eighteen assistants, freemen of the corporation, should be elected each year, to carry on the government with the governor, but only twelve of the elected assistants came to the colony. These men were all of the rank of English gentlemen and had been made magistrates before leaving England. According to the charter, four general courts were to be held each year for the making of laws. At first, the magistrates—the governor and the assistants—themselves constituted this court. Very soon after the first settlements were made, however, a movement arose for the extension of political power. A group of about 100 settlers demanded a share in the lawmaking, and a considerable number of new freemen were admitted to the corporation. In 1634 a delegation composed of men from each of eight towns met in Boston and asked to see the charter. Out of this action came representative government for the colony. The charter, they found, granted the lawmaking power to the whole body of freemen. The next step was taken by the towns in sending delegates to represent them in the general court. Furthermore, the freemen demanded voting in the general court by ballot instead of by a show of hands. Thus the ballot was introduced into American politics.

It is important to remember that there were in the colony five classes of people: (1) gentlemen, who were addressed as Master; (2) skilled artisans and freeholders, usually addressed as Goodman; (3) unskilled laborers, addressed by their given names; (4) servants; (5) slaves. The three lowest classes were never admitted to political citizenship, while, of the first two, only those who were approved church members were given the franchise.

During the 17th century, about one-fourth of the adult males in the colony of Massachusetts bay could vote. The struggle between the freemen and the assistants continued until, in 1644, the general court was divided into two houses, the Upper House of the Assistants, the Lower House of the Deputies. This was the first two-chamber legislature in America.

Town Government. Meanwhile, new machinery of local government was being contrived in the villages or towns. In these towns the people did not live on widely separated farms or plantations as they did in Virginia, but the houses were grouped closely together in the village, around which lay the farms. The town meeting came into use first in Dorchester and Watertown in 1633. It was a clumsy and often a slow means of government, but it proved to be the greatest of all schools of political liberty. All residents of the town might attend the town meeting and speak, but only the "inhabitants," that is, the gentlemen, artisans, and freeholders, might vote. Usually, the possession of a certain amount of property was necessary to entitle one to vote in the town meeting. Outside the pale of the governing classes, there was a lower class of "cottagers," made up of strangers and day laborers, to whom the town meeting had not given any rights.

This form of town government became characteristic of New England, and was perhaps the most significant contribution of that section to the practice of government in the United States, just as the county organization was the peculiar contribution of the southern colonies. As the town meeting developed through its appropriateness to the needs of people who lived close together and farmed small areas of land, so the county government flourished in the circumstances arising from the custom of farming large plantations and from the consequent separation of homes in Virginia.

Massachusetts Laws. The colony of Massachusetts did not have a written code of laws until 1641, when, after several years of deliberation, the Body of Liberties was drawn up and adopted by the general court. The government of the colony, while it came gradually to provide a considerable degree of political freedom, never allowed religious liberty. The founders of the colony intended to provide a place where they could practice their own forms of religion and develop a "City of God" after their own pattern. They were acting consistently with their principles when they expelled from the colony Roger Williams and Anne Hutchinson, with their followers.

Rhode Island. Roger Williams opposed the union of church and state as it was practiced in the colony of Massachusetts, and Anne Hutchinson questioned the authority of some of the ministers. Williams escaped to the Narragansett Indians and later founded the colony of Rhode Island. His great purpose was to prove that a colony could be governed successfully while complete religious freedom was allowed to all its citizens. In this experiment he succeeded, being fortunate in getting encouragement both from the Long Parliament in 1644 and from Charles II after the Restoration.

Connecticut. As the founding of Rhode Island was a protest against the lack of democracy in religion in the colony of Massachusetts, so the founding of Connecticut was a protest against the aristocratic tendencies in Massachusetts politics. The inhabitants of Watertown, Dorchester, and Newtown had been leaders in the first opposition to the oligarchy set up by the assistants at the founding of the colony. In 1635, citizens of these towns began the first of those westward migrations which were to mark the next two centuries of American history. They moved into the Connecticut valley and established the towns of Hartford, Wethersfield, and Windsor. In 1639, they drew up a document which may be called the first written constitution in America, the Fundamental Orders. The new colony still maintained control of the churches, but in politics it was far more democratic than the mother colony. Voting was not restricted to church members, but was regulated by the towns until, in 1659, the general court declared that no one could be made a freeman or allowed to vote unless he possessed property to the value of 30 pounds.

New England Confederation. The next stage in the political history of New England was marked by the formation of the New England Confederation in 1643. This provided for a firm and perpetual league of the colonies of Massachusetts, Connecticut, New Haven, and Plymouth. With the restoration of the Stuarts in England in 1660, a new period of colonial history began, which was marked by efforts of the English government to draw the growing colonies into closer relations with the home government. Charles II organized a colonial department under various names. This was a wise act of statesmanship, but it aroused the colonists to greater insistence upon their right of popular government.

British Colonial Policies. During the thirty years from 1660 to 1690, several important changes occurred in the situation of the American colonies. The Dutch and Swedish possessions, which had separated the two large English settlements, were brought under English control, the wealthy colony of Pennsylvania was founded, and the Carolinas, including the territory which later became the colony of Georgia, were added to the English domain. By the year 1690, therefore, England controlled the entire coast from the Penobscot river in the North to the Savannah in the South. During these thirty years the population of the colonies increased from 60,000 to 250,000. Under the advice of his Council for Foreign Plantations, the policy of Charles II took two forms.

Navigation Acts. First came the passage of the Navigation acts, which were designed to hold the trade of the colonies for the mother country. Such a trade policy was in accord with the practices of all the nations of the time, and the English methods were far less oppressive than those of Spain or of France. The first Navigation act provided that all trade with the colonies should be carried in either English or colonial vessels. This was a positive benefit to New England, for it gave the first impetus to the great New England industry of shipbuilding. A later act restricted imports. All goods imported by the colonists had to pass through English ports. This requirement gave rise to smuggling. It is estimated that in the year 1700 one-third of the trade at the port of New York was in smuggled goods.

Colonial Charters. The second part of the policy of Charles II was concerned with controlling more closely the colonies already in existence. It is interesting to note that, in spite of the tyrannical character of the Stuart government in England, very liberal charters were granted to the heretofore unauthorized governments of Connecticut (with New Haven) and Rhode Island. On the other hand, there was continual trouble between the English government and Massachusetts, arising chiefly from the unwillingness of that colony to tolerate churches other than Puritan. So many complaints were made about this denial of civil and religious rights, that Charles sent a commission, in 1664, to hear appeals from the colonial courts. The authority of the commissioners was recognized in Connecticut, Rhode Island, and Plymouth, but the magistrates of Boston forbade recognition of the commissioners, and they were forced to leave the colony without hearing any appeals whatever. Matters dragged on until the year 1684, when the highest English court declared the Massachusetts charter of 1629 forfeited.

Consolidation of Colonies. The next move of the English government was to consolidate New England into one province. This was done by James II, who appointed Sir Edmund Andros governor-general of New England. Andros was already proprietor of New York and New Jersey, and these colonies were consolidated with New England. James struck out of the new charter all provision for any representative government, and made the governor virtually a despot. What would have been eventually the result of continuing this policy we can only imagine, for within three years the revolution of 1688 occurred in England, and in 1689, upon the accession of William III to the English throne, the colonists revived their old governments. The people of Boston and near-by towns seized the fort in the harbor and imprisoned Andros. In 1691

Massachusetts was given a new charter, which provided, among other things, that all Protestants should have religious freedom and that the franchise should be based upon a property qualification. These were important changes from the earlier government of the colony. Maine, Plymouth, and Nova Scotia were included in what was now the royal province of Massachusetts.

Cavalier Migration. During this same period the government of Virginia was subjected to important changes. Between 1650 and 1670 the colony grew rapidly and became very prosperous. A royalist immigration set in, which raised the population of the colony from 15,000 to 40,000. This was the second great colonial migration of the century. Virginia became the land of the Cavaliers. At this time the Lee family, the Masons, and the Washingtons came to Virginia, — families which were later to furnish great leaders of the Revolution. Berkeley was again appointed governor, and the colonial democracy, which had been growing in power, was changed into an oligarchy made up of the governor and a council entirely subservient to him. Under this influence, the franchise was restricted to freeholders, and for a long period even they were practically disfranchised, because, between 1660 and 1676, Berkeley permitted no election for his Cavalier assembly.

Struggles for Popular Government. The local government units in Virginia had been counties and parishes. The parish rendered such social service as taking care of the poor, and sometimes even punished minor offenses. Until 1645 the parish vestry meeting had been opened to all free white males, but in that year the parishes began to elect vestrymen. Berkeley, however, made the vestrymen's office a life position, providing that vacancies were to be filled by the vestrymen themselves. County affairs had been managed by a county court, which was a meeting of all free white males. Under Berkeley, this court was displaced by a board of eight justices, appointed by the governor. Along with these changes went serious abuses in taxation and expenditure. At the same time, Berkeley's government failed to protect the frontier against the Indians.

Out of this situation grew the uprising known as Bacon's Rebellion. As a result of this movement, some of the worst abuses introduced by Berkeley were corrected, but the aristocratic organization in both colonial and local government became permanent in Virginia. In 1686, however, the House of Burgesses, in opposition to Governor Effingham, insisted upon its right to levy taxes in spite of any veto by governor or king. This right was confirmed by William III.

The Carolinas. In response to the interest which some of his courtiers had shown in colonization, Charles II, in 1663, granted to eight proprietors the colony of Carolina. The grant, as amended in 1665, included territory between the parallels of 29° and 36° 30′ north latitude. In the case of this colony, the expected returns from trade were realized. Government of the colony, however, under various methods, including the famous plan drawn up by John Locke, proved difficult. At length, the proprietors were willing to sell their rights to the crown. In 1729 the territory was reorganized into two royal provinces, North Carolina and South Carolina; thus the more democratic northern part of the original colony was separated from the more aristocratic southern portion.

The Colony of Pennsylvania. Pennsylvania was founded as a proprietary colony, but the proprietor, William Penn, a man of large wealth and of great influence at the English court, was a friend to popular government. He had already aided some of his Quaker friends to organize the colony of New Jersey. In 1681 he received a charter for a new colony. This charter provided for religious toleration, for appeal from the colonial courts to the king, and for the right of the colonists to tax themselves. From the first, the population of Pennsylvania differed from that of the other colonies in being at least one-third non-English. It contained large settlements of German Mennonites, Moravians, Amish, and Dunkards, besides some Swedes and Dutch.

Thanks to the wise dealing of Penn, the colony was free from Indian troubles, and the large resources of English and Welsh Quakers saved it from the biting poverty that the other colonies had experienced. Nevertheless, its political history for a number of years was stormy. At length, a new charter was granted in 1701. This has been called one of the most important of American governmental documents, for it was the first written constitution to provide for its own amendment. Under this charter a single house assembly was organized, which could be dissolved only by its own vote.

Government in New York. In the matter of popular government, the colony of New York was distinctly behind its neighboring colonies. During the period of Dutch rule, there was no self-government in the colony except what was insisted upon by English settlers on Long Island. They demanded a measure of self-government from the Dutch director, Stuyvesant, in 1653, but, before any important action was taken, the colony fell into the hands of the English. King Charles gave the province to his brother James, duke of York, with arbitrary power. The insistence of the English towns on Long Island compelled the introduction of a representative assembly in 1682, though the governor of New York still retained more power than the governor in any other of the colonies.

Growth of Population. The period from 1690 to 1760 in America was one of very remarkable growth in wealth and population. At the beginning of this period, the total population of the colonies, including Georgia, was about 250,000; at the end of the period, about 1,600,000. It has been noted already that Pennsylvania had in the beginning a large German population. Many of these Germans had been driven from their homes in South Germany by religious persecution. After 1683, a great many Huguenots, exiled from France by the persecutions of Louis XIV, came to the English colonies. Most of them settled in the Carolinas, but many historic names indicate their presence in the northern colonies also. Among such names are those of Paul Revere, the hero of Lexington, and Peter Faneuil, the builder of Faneuil Hall.

Another large element of the 18th century immigration was made up of the so-called Scotch-Irish, who between 1730 and 1750, it is said, came to America at the rate of 12,000 a year. They settled principally in what was then the back country of Virginia and Pennsylvania. Later, they were in the van of migration across the mountains into the territory of Kentucky and Tennessee. It has been remarked that these people, descendants of Saxon English who had lived for centuries in the Scottish lowlands, were the first of the American colonists to turn their faces away from the Old World, thus marking the real beginnings of America.

Contest for the Continent. During this period, Spain still held a strip of territory in Florida and along the coast of the Gulf of Mexico, and her missionaries were beginning their settlements on the coast of California. She was, however, clearly out of the race for control of the North American continent. The struggle for this lay between England and France. At the close of the 17th century, the English held a narrow domain between the Appalachian mountains and the Atlantic coast and a district around Hudson bay. The French were in control of the St. Lawrence valley. In 1682, moreover, the intrepid La Salle, after having made the long journey from Lake Ontario southwest to the mouth of the Mississippi, had taken possession of the Mississippi valley for the French king, Louis XIV,

Remote and Immediate Causes: (1) The Colonial wars in America were incidents in the general European wars which involved England and France upon opposite sides. (2) They were immediately occasioned by the unavoidable struggle of the two nations to control the continent of North America.

Historic Name	Chief Battles	Leaders English	Leaders French	Victor	Results
King William's War, 1689–97.	Schenectady, Feb. 8, 1690 . .	Colonists	Iberville	French	War terminated by Treaty of Ryswick (1697), each side retaining the territory held prior to the war. French retain Quebec. The "Five Nations" subdued.
	New Eng'nd Massacres, March 1690–97	Colonists	Frontenac	French	
	Siege of Quebec, April 1690 .	Phipps	Frontenac	French	
	Attacks on the "Five Nations," 1693–97	Indians	Frontenac	Indians	
Queen Anne's War, 1702–13.	Deerfield Massacre, Feb. 29, 1704	Colonists	Indians	Indians	Settled by Treaty of Utrecht. Hudson Bay and its borders, Acadia and Newfoundland. ceded to England by France.
	Haverhill Massacre, Aug. 29, 1708	Colonists	Hertel		
	Conquest of Nova Scotia, 1710	Nicholson	Subercase	English	
King George's War, 1744–48.	Capture of Louisburg, June 17, 1745	Pepperell	Ducham-bon	English	Louisburg was returned to the French by the Treaty of Aix-la-Chapelle, Oct. 7, 1748.
French and Indian War, 1754–63.	Surrender of Fort Necessity, July 4, 1754	Washington	Villiers	French	In 1763, by the Treaty of Paris, France ceded to England, Canada and all her possessions lying east of the Mississippi river; to Spain, New Orleans and all her possessions west of the Mississippi. The transfer from the French to the British of the posts between the Great Lakes and the Ohio river led to a war with the Indian tribes, in which the leading figure was Pontiac. The French and Indian war convinced the colonists of the necessity of union.
	Expedition against Fort Duquesne, July 9, 1755 . . .	Braddock	Beaujeu	French	
	Deportations of Acadians, June 16-17, 1755.				
	Capture of Louisburg, July 26, 1758	Amherst	Drucour	English	
	Capture of Fort Duquesne, Nov. 25, 1758	Forbes	?	English	
	Capture of Fort Niagara, July 1759	Johnson	D'Aubry	English	
	Capture of Fort Ticonderoga, July 26, 1759	Amherst	Bourla-maque	English	
	Capture of Quebec, Sept. 13, 1759	Wolfe	Montcalm	English	

naming it Louisiana. The contest began in the way of peaceful penetration, but the Indians were frequently stirred up by both sides, and between 1689 and 1763 four wars were fought by the contending parties. At length, by the treaty of 1763, at the close of the French and Indian war, France lost Canada and, consequently, her line of outposts in the Mississippi valley. After this event, England's position in America was to depend entirely upon her treatment of the colonies.

Movement toward Self-Government. The defeat of the French in Canada removed from the colonies all feeling of dependence upon England for protection against any foreign power. They were free to insist upon their rights. But, apparently oblivious of this fact, England, in her colonial policy, blundered continuously and stupidly, until the patience of the colonists was exhausted and American independence became a fact. These blunders in the policy of England are clearly revealed in the two fields of industry and politics.

English Restriction on Industry. First, the development of industry in the colonies occasioned several restrictions which were designed to eliminate colonial competition with England. In 1696, colonists were forbidden to export any woolen manufactures. Later acts limited the fabrication of iron products. Even when these restrictions were not burdensome, they gave rise to irritation and to the suspicion that the English government did not look with favor upon the rise of a free people in America.

Political Control. The most important movements of the 18th century, however, were those concerned with the form of colonial government and the control of taxes. The English Board of Trade, which had taken the place of Charles II's Council for Foreign Plantations, found many things to criticize in the conduct of the colonists. The Navigation laws were evaded; smuggling, as well as trade with pirates, was a general practice; and the colonies were notably careless in provision for their own defense. In 1701 a proposal was introduced in Parliament to unite all the colonies in one province. This aroused great opposition in America, and the bill was never passed. Steady progress was made, however, in converting the colonies into royal provinces. Only Connecticut and Rhode Island, at the outbreak of the Revolution, possessed the privilege of electing all branches of their governments. On the whole, in spite of the attempt at greater royal control, and notwithstanding increases in the authority of royal governors, the colonial assemblies maintained their rights of taxation and even somewhat enlarged them. They used without stint their power over the governor through their control of his salary. It was the custom to make the fixing of the governor's salary the last business of the legislative session, a practice which proved effective in preventing a governor from vetoing bills.

Colonial Life. Life in the English colonies during the latter part of the 17th century and during the 18th exhibited great variety in customs and industry. This diversity was due, in the first place, to the variant native characteristics of the different groups of people who made up the colonies, and, in the second place, to the wide range of conditions of soil and climate. In the South, industry was almost entirely agricultural. Tobacco raising was the chief occupation of the people upon large plantations worked by slaves. The Virginia plantation was an industrial unit in itself, and the product of the plantation, mostly tobacco, was loaded on ships at the plantation wharf and sent to England. The ships brought back supplies of various kinds, but most of the clothing and the simpler utensils of the workers on the plantations were made in the plantation shops. Each great farm had its blacksmith and woodworking shops. The mistress of the plantation supervised the spinning and weaving and the preparation and preserving of food.

In the middle colonies, such as Pennsylvania, foodstuffs were raised, and the German colonists maintained, upon a small scale, many industries, including the manufacture of linen, pottery, and clothing. New England was the real district of the small farm, although its two most characteristic industries were fishing and shipbuilding. New Englanders also carried on a rich trade with the other colonies, and indeed with all parts of the world. The possession of water power to operate sawmills enabled them to build up a particularly large trade in lumber.

Slaves and Servants. There were negro slaves in all the colonies, though in New England most of the labor was free. The middle colonies had a large number of white bond servants, some of whom had sold their time to the extent of from four to seven years as the price of the voyage to America, while others were convicts who had been transported from England. While some of these convicts were of an undesirable class and made much trouble in the colonies, the severe English laws caused the "transportation" of many persons who proved themselves good citizens. One of these, a convicted thief, later became attorney-general of Virginia, and it is said that most of the tutors and teachers in Maryland, just before the Revolution, had come to America under sentence for offenses against English law.

Education. Education in most of the colonies was sadly neglected. Although parents were required by law to have their children taught the rudiments of knowledge, many of them lacked the ability and the time to carry out these requirements. In some parts of the colonies, church schools were established. The wealthy planters of the South employed private tutors for their families. At the very beginning of their history, Massachusetts and Connecticut had established school systems, but the work of these schools was severely limited by the primitive conditions of life and by the poverty of many settlements. The most important service of these early institutions in New England was the preservation of the ideal of an educated citizenship. Nine colleges were established in the colonies in the 17th and the 18th century, up to the period of the Revolution.

Questions of Taxation. The close of the wars with France left the English government with a serious financial problem on its hands. The cost of the wars had been heavy. It seemed that the colonists, who were highly prosperous and had scarcely any public debt, should help to carry the load. Unfortunately for the English government, however, the antagonism of the colonists had already been aroused when, in 1755, the writs of assistance came into use. These were warrants by which an English officer might search any house or place of business, merely upon suspicion that the owner had been trading with the French and furnishing them with supplies. The prevalence of such trade was not denied, but the colonists were alive to the danger which lay in the use of general search warrants. In 1761, when application was made to the superior court of Massachusetts for renewal of the writs of assistance in that colony, James Otis, the advocate-general, resigned his office and opposed the granting of the writs. He lost his case, but his argument opened the whole question of Parliamentary government of the colonies.

The Sugar Act. In 1733 a sugar act had been passed as a part of the Navigation laws, whose purpose was to restrict colonial trade to England. The colonists had never seriously objected to these Navigation laws, and many of the acts had been helpful. But now, in 1764, a new sugar act was passed, not as a trade law, but as a means of taxing the colonies for revenue. The act laid a tax upon sugar imported from the French West Indies, and the tax was made so heavy as practically to stop this very profitable trade of the New England and middle colonies. The tax did not, however, affect the southern colonies, and, therefore, it was not a means of unifying the sentiment of the colonists, as the Stamp act, passed in 1765, proved to be.

The Stamp Act. The English government insisted that it must have revenue and proposed the stamp tax method in 1764, giving the agents of the colonies a year to propose some other means of raising money. But the absence of any general government or central authority in the colonies, as well as the great differences of sentiment among the colonists themselves, made any counter proposal impossible. Protests were sent to the English ministry from all the colonies, but without producing any effect. The law was enacted in March 1765. Opposition to the sugar act had been based upon its interference with trade; it resulted in actual money loss to the colonists. The stamp tax ushered in a new era of opposition, for now the colonists contended against the principle of the tax. They were not concerned with the immediate money burden placed upon them, but with the possible future use of such a tax, if once they permitted the English government to impose it.

Opposition to England. Several of the colonial assemblies passed resolutions, condemning the Stamp act and asserting their right to be taxed only by a body in which they were represented. The most forcible of these resolutions were introduced by Patrick Henry in the Virginia assembly, when he used the expressions, "Cæsar had his Brutus, Charles I his Cromwell, and George III— may profit by their example." At the invitation of the Massachusetts assembly, the Stamp Act Congress met in New York, October 7, 1765. This congress drew up a petition to the British government, together with a statement of the rights and liberties of the colonists. The society of the Sons of Liberty was organized for the purpose of compelling people to comply with the agreements not to import British goods. It was at first a secret society, but later it became public and very effective.

The Townshend Acts. So intense was the opposition that, in 1766, a new ministry secured the repeal of the Stamp act, with the provision, however, that Parliament still retained its authority to tax the colonies. In 1767 the prime minister, Townshend, secured the passage of a series of acts which placed duties on several articles of import into the colonies, among which glass, paper, and tea were included. Previous attempts at taxation had been justified by the plea that money was needed to protect the colonies. The proceeds of the Stamp act had been pledged beforehand for this purpose. Now, however, the revenue from the Townshend duties was to be used for the payment of colonial governors and judges. This proposal struck at the very heart of the independence of colonial assemblies, because the principle was well recognized, that the governor and judge served the party who appointed and paid them. Trials for evasion of the Townshend acts were to be held in courts of admiralty without juries. This again was a violation of a cherished principle in colonial government.

Further Provocation and Controversy. Throughout the three years during which the Townshend acts remained in force, the opposition of the colonists, through their legislatures and by mob violence, never ceased. In 1769 Parliament provided by a treason act that a colonist accused of treason should be taken to England for trial. The assembly of Virginia, which had not been seriously affected by the Townshend acts themselves, was aroused by this violation of the principle of jury trial. It adopted unanimously a resolution condemning both the Townshend laws and the treason act. This was followed by agreements among the colonies not to import merchandise from England until the objectionable acts were repealed. Fuel was added to the flames by the sending of troops to Boston in 1768, to aid the governor in maintaining order. The immediate result of this attempt to overawe the colonists was a settled hostility between citizens and soldiers, which resulted in the Boston Massacre of 1770.

Committees of Correspondence. The revenue collected under the Townshend acts amounted to about one-tenth of the cost of collecting it. On the day of the Boston Massacre, Lord North moved the repeal of these acts, except that providing a tax on tea. The tea tax was kept as a mark of the supremacy of Parliament. During the next two years, the British ministry persisted in various arbitrary orders which interfered with the liberties of the colonial legislatures. The assemblies protested, and the governors dissolved them. The result was the organization of provisional governments. Under the leadership of Samuel Adams, the towns of Massachusetts organized town committees of correspondence in 1772. Virginia in the following year took a further step, prompted thereto by the incident of the *Gaspee*. English officers had attempted to arrest some Rhode Islanders, suspected of burning the revenue ship *Gaspee*, and to take them to England for trial. On March 12, 1773, the Virginia House of Burgesses appointed a committee for intercolonial correspondence and invited the other colonies to take similar measures.

Boston Tea Party and the First Congress. Meanwhile, the English government attempted to force upon the colonists the tea of the British East India Company. The duty on tea was lowered to such a point that the company could sell it to the colonists more cheaply than they could buy smuggled tea. Under this arrangement, large cargoes were sent to the American ports. At Charleston, South Carolina, the tea was seized and stored. At New York, Annapolis, and Philadelphia, the authorities were compelled to send the tea ships back to England. But a group of the people of Boston held the famous "tea party," when large quantities of tea were thrown from the East India ships into the harbor.

To punish the Bostonians, the English government passed the Boston Port bill in 1774, closing the port to all commerce. This was deemed as harsh a blow as could be delivered to any commercial, maritime town. But the result was that food and supplies were poured in from all parts of the colonies, the merchants of Salem offered Boston merchants the use of their wharves, and the committees of correspondence in the colonies immediately proceeded to consider means of redress. The House of Burgesses in Virginia set apart June 1, 1774, on which day the port bill became effective, as a day of fasting and prayer. The governor dissolved the assembly two days later, but the burgesses met at a tavern, and recommended an annual congress of delegates from all the colonies to consider their united interests. On August 1, at Williamsburg, they appointed delegates to such a congress. Other colonies took similar action, some in the regular assemblies, but many of them in irregular meetings of legislators or citizens. Thus the members of the First Continental Congress were chosen to meet at Philadelphia on September 5, 1774.

Self-Government. English authority had now broken down in the colonies. The colonists were governing themselves through agencies which were really revolutionary legislatures and committees. Actual independence, however, was not yet considered, and the congress which had been called was to be only an informal conference. This was its actual character. Its most important act was to recommend agreements among the colonies neither to import nor to export English goods. This recommendation and others were considered and adopted by the revolutionary bodies in the various colonies. Before its adjournment, the First Continental Congress arranged for calling a second congress to meet in May 1775, if the grievances of the colonies had not been redressed before that time.

Concord and Lexington. Most of the members of the First Continental Congress, in common with the majority of the people in the colonies, believed that a peaceful settlement of the difficulties with England was possible, but, before the second congress met, trouble had broken out in Massachusetts and war had become a fact. The leaders in Massachusetts had organized a revolutionary body called the Provincial Congress, within which was created a committee of safety. This committee, among its varied activities, organized a body of militia called minutemen.

General Gage, who was in command of the British garrison at Boston, planned to arrest John Hancock and Samuel Adams, the leaders of the patriots. For the purpose of seizing the two men and also of destroying some military stores of the patriots at Concord, a force of 800 men was sent out from Boston on the night of April 18, 1775. Warning of this movement was carried through the countryside by Paul Revere and other riders, and, when the British appeared at Lexington on the morning of April 19, they found a small body of minutemen drawn up on the village green. Seven of the patriot force were killed and nine were wounded by the fire of the British troops. Later in the morning, the minutemen made a stand at the North bridge at Concord. The British were forced to retreat, and during the day the militia took revenge in harassing the British column on its march from Concord back to Boston. In this running fight, 273 British and 93 Americans were killed. The result of the day's conflict was to encourage the people in the other colonies to drive out their governors and to proceed more rapidly with the formation of revolutionary congresses and conventions.

The Second Congress. When the Second Continental Congress, composed of representatives from all of the thirteen colonies, met in Philadelphia on May 10, 1775, it had to set about the business of organizing for war. The congress had no formal authority from the colonies, but depended altogether upon their general good will and assent. It must be remembered that the Revolutionary War was not a struggle of united colonists in America against a united England, but rather, in reality, a civil war in the colonies, both sides having sympathizers in the mother country. It is estimated that at least one-third of the colonists were Tories or Loyalists, while many of the other two-thirds were only half-hearted in their support of resistance to English authority. Nevertheless, the Second Continental Congress ordered the colonies to be put into a state of defense, organized a post office, voted to raise an army, appointed George Washington commander in chief, and began to consider Franklin's proposal of a federal constitution.

Bunker Hill. Massachusetts, however, had acted without authority from Congress. Twenty thousand militia laid siege to the British in Boston. Patriots intrenched themselves on Breed's Hill, near Bunker Hill, June 17, 1775, but were driven out by the British. This battle of Bunker Hill, however, was really a victory for the colonists, since it showed that they could fight the British regulars and inflict severe losses upon them. Washington took command of the force of militia intrenched around Boston, and in the early spring of 1776 he fortified Dorchester Heights and compelled the British force of 10,000 to leave the city. Meanwhile, General Montgomery and Benedict Arnold led two small detachments of troops into Canada, but they failed to get the support of the Canadians.

The story of the Revolution from this time forward has two phases. The military history is made up of a long series of conflicts on sea and land, with but few important pitched battles. The civil history is concerned with the struggle of the various colonies to maintain their new governments, to suppress or expel the Tories, and to agree upon a plan of union.

REVOLUTIONARY WAR

Contributing Causes: Unjust Legislation; Taxation without Representation; Infringements of the Rights of the Colonists by Great Britain.

CAMPAIGNS	Chief Battles	AMERICAN		BRITISH		Victor	Results
		Leaders	Troops	Leaders	Troops		
Contest for control of Boston.	Lexington and Concord, April 19, 1775 . . .	Parker . . } Heath . . }	500	Smith . . } Lord Percy }	1,700	Amer.	British besieged in Boston after battle of Bunker Hill. Howe and his army evacuate Boston March 17, 1776, leaving guns and supplies.
	Bunker Hill, June 17, 1775.	Prescott . } Warren . }	1,500	Gage . . .	2,500	Brit.	
	Dorchester Heights, Mar. 4, 1776	Washington } Thomas . }	2,500	Howe . . .	10,000	Amer.	
American invasion of Canada.	Ticonderoga, May 10, 1775.	Ethan Allen	83	Delaplace .	48	Amer.	Ticonderoga captured. Fruitless siege of Quebec. Ethan Allen captured. Invaders dispersed.
	Montreal, Nov. 12, 1775 .	Montgomery	2,000	Carleton . .	?	Amer.	
	Quebec, Dec. 31, 1775 . .	Arnold . . .	900	Carleton . .	1,200	Brit.	
Attack on Charleston.	Fort Moultrie, June 28, 1776	Moultrie . .	435	Clinton . .	?	Amer.	British abandon the attack and sail for New York.
Struggle for control of the City of New York and for New Jersey.	Long Island, Aug. 27, 1776.	Sullivan . } Putnam . }	5,000	Howe . . .	20,000	Brit.	Americans forced across the Hudson. British occupy New York City. American forces inspired to renewed efforts. British forces evacuate New Jersey.
	Harlem Heights, Sept. 15, 1776	Washington.	12,000	Howe . . .	25,000	Brit.	
	White Plains, Oct. 28, 1776.	Washington.	1,400	Howe . . .	4,000	Brit.	
	Fort Washington, Nov. 16, 1776	Magaw . . .	3,000	Howe . . .	5,000	Brit.	
	Trenton, Dec. 25, 1776 .	Washington.	2,400	Rall	1,600	Amer.	
	Princeton, Jan. 3, 1777 .	Washington.	5,000	Mawhood .	1,200	Amer.	
British attempt to control the Hudson and to divide the colonies. Burgoyne's invasion from the north.	Ticonderoga, July 6, 1777.	St. Clair . .	2,500	Burgoyne. .	7,500	Brit.	Americans control the Hudson valley, New York, and New England. Burgoyne's surrender, Oct. 17, 1777, marks the turning point of the war.
	Oriskany, Aug. 6, 1777 .	Herkimer. .	800	St. Leger . .	1,200	Amer.	
	Bennington, Aug. 16, 1777.	Stark . . .	2,000	Baum . . .	1,200	Amer.	
	Fort Stanwix, Aug. 22, 1777	Arnold . .	800	St. Leger . .	?	Amer.	
	Bemis Heights, or Stillwater, Sept. 19, 1777 .	Gates . } Lincoln . } Arnold . . }	2,500	Burgoyne. .	6,000	Amer.	
	Bemis Heights, Oct. 7, 1777	Gates . . } Arnold . . }	8,000	Burgoyne. .	5,000	Amer.	
British attack on Philadelphia.	Brandywine, Sept. 11, 1777.	Washington.	11,000	Howe . . .	17,000	Brit.	Howe's army enters and occupies Philadelphia during the winter.
	Germantown, Oct. 4, 1777.	Washington.	10,000	Howe . . .	15,000	Brit.	
British retreat from Philadelphia, begun June 18, 1778.	Monmouth, June 28, 1778.	Washington.	12,000	Clinton . .	10,000	Amer.	British return to New York.
Indian massacres.	Wyoming, July 4, 1778 .	Zeb. Butler .	400	Butler . . .	1,100	Brit.	
	Cherry Valley, Nov. 11, 1778	Alden . . .	?	Butler . . } Brant . . }	800?	Brit.	
Expedition for control of the Western frontier.	Kaskaskia, July 4, 1778 .	Clark . . .	200	Indians. . .	?	Amer.	Americans establish claim to possession of the Northwest.
	Vincennes, Feb. 14, 1779 .	Clark . . .	170	Hamilton . .	500	Amer.	
Campaign for control of the South by British.	Savannah, Dec. 29, 1778 .	R. Howe . .	900	Campbell . .	2,000	Brit.	Georgia reduced to submission. .
	Savannah, Oct. 9, 1779 .	Lincoln . .	4,500	Prevost. . .	2,500	Brit.	
Battle for control of the Hudson.	Stony Point, July 15, 1779.	Wayne . . .	1,200	Clinton . .	600	Amer.	Continental army encouraged.
Naval operations.	*Bon Homme Richard* and *Serapis*, Sept. 23, 1779 .	J. Paul Jones		Pearson . .		Amer.	
American expedition against the Indians.	Newtown (Elmira, N. Y.), Aug. 29, 1779	Sullivan . .	5,000	Johnson . } Brant . . }	1,500	Amer.	"Six Nations" weakened.

CAMPAIGNS	Chief Battles	AMERICAN		BRITISH		Victor	Results
		Leaders	Troops	Leaders	Troops		
Campaigns for control of the South; conflict in North and South Carolina.	Charleston, May 12, 1780.	Lincoln . .	3,700	Clinton . .	9,000	Brit.	British in possession of the South.
	Camden, Aug. 16, 1780 .	Gates . . .	3,000	Cornwallis .	2,000	Brit.	
	King's Mountain, Oct. 7, 1780	Shelby . . ⎱ Sevier . . ⎰	1,000	Ferguson . .	1,100	Amer.	
	Cowpens, Jan. 17, 1781 .	Morgan . .	900	Tarleton . .	1,100	Amer.	British forced to retire towards Charleston. Americans in control of the South.
	Guilford Court House, March 15, 1781 . . .	Greene. . .	4,400	Cornwallis .	2,200	Brit.	
	Hobkirk's Hill, April 25, 1781	Greene. . .	940	Rawdon . .	900	Brit.	
	Eutaw Springs, Sept. 8, 1781	Greene. . .	2,000	Stuart . . .	2,500	Amer.	
Invasion of Virginia.	Siege of Yorktown; surrender, Oct. 19, 1781 .	Washington ⎰ Rochambeau ⎱ De Grasse ⎰ (navy) ⎰	20,000	Cornwallis ⎰ Graves ⎱ (navy) ⎰	8,000	Amer.	Surrender of Cornwallis. Contest terminated.

Result of War: Preliminary treaty of peace signed at Paris, November 30, 1782. Final and definitive treaty signed at Versailles, September 3, 1783, by which the United States were formally acknowledged by Great Britain to be free, sovereign, and independent. United States territory extended from the Atlantic to the Mississippi, from Florida to Canada.

Independence. Sentiment in favor of independence was crystallized during the spring of 1776 by the publication of Thomas Paine's pamphlet entitled *Common Sense.* Virginia's convention, which met on May 6, 1776, instructed its representatives to move in the Continental Congress for a declaration of independence.

Following instructions, Richard Henry Lee, on June 7, 1776, moved that the united colonies should be free and independent states. The first vote, taken on July 1, showed nine states in favor; on the following day twelve voted yes, and the declaration was adopted on July 4. The delegates from New York did not vote, because they had no instructions from the provisional congress of that colony. New York's approval was given on the 9th of July. On August 2 the official copy was signed by the members of the Congress who were present.

State Constitutions. In reality, the colonies had been acting independently even before the declaration of independence. After the battle of Lexington, several colonies applied to the Congress for advice. The Congress advised New Hampshire to set up such a government as seemed necessary "during the continuance of the present dispute between Great Britain and the colonies." In May 1776, a general resolution was adopted, advising the colonies to form governments for themselves whenever the old government had broken down. Virginia adopted its constitution in June 1776. The first part of this Virginia constitution was a bill of rights, the first document of its kind drawn up in America. This became a model for the bills of rights in the later state constitutions. It stated the rights of man as general principles, rather than as particular privileges, such as that of self-taxation. Jefferson placed similar statements in the Declaration of Independence.

Provisions of First State Constitutions. Several characteristics of these constitutions deserve notice. Some of them were made under the impression that the colonies would remain under the rule of England, but they were all republican in form. They provided for an executive, who was called either governor or president, and for courts and legislatures. The legislatures, however, were given large powers of control over both the executive and the judiciary. Nearly every constitution contained a bill of rights. Several of them had no provision for amendment, although today this is regarded as one of the most important parts of a constitution. All maintained some sort of religious discrimination. Throughout the colonies, the suffrage for local elections was made more general than it had been, but the privilege of voting was still restricted in some way in all the colonies. The most democratic provisions permitted only taxpayers to vote.

Officeholding and Voting. Nor did the privilege of voting carry the privilege of holding office, at least in respect to colonial offices. In North Carolina, to be elected governor, it was required that a man must own real estate to the value of 1000 pounds. In Massachusetts, a member of the lower house of the general court had to own at least 1000 pounds in real estate or 200 pounds in other property; a senator, three times as much. Most of these constitutions were drawn up and adopted by conventions or congresses in the colonies. In Massachusetts, a referendum was demanded, and it was not until 1780 that the constitution of that state was adopted. The mechanics of New York City, who were largely of New England descent, demanded a referendum in New York, but none was ever held.

Military Movements. Meanwhile, the military campaigns were dragging on under most discouraging conditions for Washington and his little army. From the first, the colonies were unwilling to enlist troops for long service. Consequently, the number of troops at Washington's command varied considerably from time to time. The Continental Congress proved weak and undependable in its provision of funds and supplies. This was due in part to the very nature of a government which had no central authority. Washington was continually subject to interference and slights, which he bore with an admirable patience and self-control. He never had more than 40,000 men under arms at one time, and his forces often dwindled to four or five thousand. This condition persisted in a country that might with ease have put 300,000 men in the field. On the other hand, the British had hired 30,000 Hessians for service in the colonies. Both sides enlisted the Indians, but the British had the greater number of them in their service, because both the Iroquois in New York and the Indians of the West recognized that the colonists were their real enemies.

Following the evacuation of Boston in the spring of 1776, the British were defeated in an attempt to take the city of Charleston, South Carolina. In this battle, Sergeant Jasper, by his rescue of the colors of Fort Moultrie, began his brave and romantic career. In August, however, the British landed an army of 25,000 men on Long Island, and the Americans were compelled to withdraw after severe defeats in the battles of Long Island and White Plains. It appears that only the heroic work of Robert Morris, who raised funds on his private credit to supply the army, prevented the collapse of the Revolution at this point. Washington was able to encourage the patriots by his victories at Trenton and Princeton in the early winter.

In the spring of 1777, the British planned to divide the colonists by bringing a force under General Burgoyne from Canada down Lake Champlain and the Hudson, to be joined by General Howe. Burgoyne advanced and issued very boastful proclamations, but the colonists rallied from all sides. General Howe embarked from New York in August 1777, to attempt the capture of Philadelphia. He defeated Washington at the battle of Brandywine in September. Washington, however, in addition to keeping Howe occupied around Philadelphia, sent men north to Schuyler, who was obstructing Burgoyne's progress, while a body of patriots under General Herkimer defeated a British expedition from Canada at the battle of Oriskany on August 6. Burgoyne was thus deprived of expected help from the West, and, as Clinton failed to move up the Hudson to meet him, while the farmers of Vermont, New Hampshire, and Massachusetts rose to attack him, he was compelled to surrender his entire force at Saratoga in October 1777. This defeat of Burgoyne is generally reckoned as the turning point of the Revolution, because it aroused in the French government sufficient confidence in the colonial cause to prompt the aid which came from France in the next year.

French Alliance. During the winter of 1777, Washington's troops endured great suffering at Valley Forge, while the British held the capital, Philadelphia. Benjamin Franklin secured a treaty of alliance with France early in 1778, and the coming of French forces compelled the English to evacuate Philadelphia. Washington pursued them across New Jersey, but by treachery he was prevented from completely defeating them at Monmouth, and they succeeded in regaining their base at New York City.

War in the South. The war was now transferred in the main to the southern colonies, and became largely a series of raids against towns and countrysides, directed by colonial Loyalists who were familiar with the country. The patriots, Marion and Sumter, maintained a vigorous guerrilla warfare. General Gates was defeated by the British at the battle of Camden in August 1780, but the battle of King's Mountain was won in October by the settlers from west of the mountains.

Surrender of Cornwallis. In 1781 General Nathanael Greene was put in command of the American forces in the South. Cornwallis withdrew into Virginia, and was besieged at Yorktown by Greene and Lafayette. A French fleet blockaded Chesapeake bay and prevented re-enforcements from reaching Cornwallis. Washington, with a French force under Rochambeau, went to the aid of Greene, and Cornwallis was compelled to surrender his whole army, October 19, 1781. His capitulation virtually ended the war.

Efforts at Confederation. The effort to secure a formal union of the states began almost as soon as the Second Continental Congress met, and a plan was at length drawn up and proposed under the title of Articles of Confederation. The ratification of these articles was not completed until 1781, the chief cause of the delay being the questions which arose over the disposition of the western lands. While the war was going on, along the Atlantic seaboard, important events were happening in the West, which affected the negotiations for peace and the whole history of the country thereafter.

Occupation of Western Lands. The territory west of the Allegheny mountains, as far as the Mississippi, formerly in the hands of the French, had come into British possession by the treaty of 1763. After the war with Pontiac in 1763-64, the British government had proclaimed this section closed to settlement and reserved for the Indians. Detroit was made the seat of government for the region. The principal French settlements were at Vincennes on the Wabash river and at Kaskaskia on the Mississippi. The town of Pittsburgh had been founded on the site of Fort Pitt shortly after the close of the French and Indian war. Frontiersmen of Scotch-Irish and of German blood, together with some Huguenots, ignored the British proclamation and crossed the mountains into the western wilderness. In 1774, Parliament, by the Quebec act, united to the Province of Quebec all the region between the Ohio river and the Great Lakes, thus indicating that new colonies were not wanted in that territory.

Kentucky Pioneers. Just as the Revolution was breaking out, Daniel Boone blazed the pack trail, known as the "wilderness road," through the Cumberland gap into Kentucky, and a little later Boonesboro and Harrodsburg were founded. People of this region petitioned Congress to admit them as a fourteenth state of the Confederation, but Virginia organized the country south of the Ohio in 1776 as Kentucky county. Farther south, the Watauga settlement was made, in a region included in North Carolina's western claims.

During the next few years, the frontier was subjected to the horrors of Indian warfare, in spite of the efforts of Congress to placate the Indians. The Iroquois in New York were finally subdued by General Sullivan in 1779.

George Rogers Clark. In 1778-79, George Rogers Clark led a notable expedition down the Ohio river and into the Illinois country, where he took the towns of Kaskaskia. Cahokia, and Vincennes. enlisting the aid of the French residents. Clark had been commissioned by Virginia, and that state now erected the territory between the Ohio and the Mississippi and the Great Lakes into the county of Illinois.

The Confederation. The Articles of Confederation went into effect on March 1, 1781. Congress then proceeded to authorize the survey of the western territory by the Land act of 1785, and the Ordinance of 1787 provided for the government of the Northwest Territory. The disputed lands south of the Ohio river were soon formed into the states of Kentucky and Tennessee.

Despite the late date for the adoption of the Articles of Confederation, Congress, under the necessity of providing for war, had long been acting on the assumption that the articles would certainly be ratified; the executive and judicial offices had already been organized.

Treaty of Peace. It now fell to the United States to conclude a treaty of peace with England. Benjamin Franklin, John Adams, John Jay, and Henry Laurens were appointed to conduct the negotiations. They were instructed, in accordance with the alliance of 1778, to take no step without the approval of the French government, but, when it appeared that the French, owing to Spanish influence, did not desire to make boundary concessions west of the Appalachians, the American envoys agreed to ignore their instructions. As a consequence, they secured a very favorable treaty, which was signed in preliminary form, November 30, 1782. The final treaty was completed in 1783. The United States of America was at last recognized by Great Britain as independent.

Weakness of the Confederation. Very soon the serious weaknesses of the Confederation began to appear. Congress was merely a body of delegates elected by the legislatures of the states. It possessed no adequate powers for dealing with foreign nations; it had no real authority over the people themselves; it could not control commerce either between the states or with foreign countries. Moreover, Congress had no adequate means of raising funds to carry on its work. And, finally, amendment of the Articles of Confederation proved impossible.

Need for Strong Central Government.
Washington and other leaders saw the conditions clearly, and urged provision for a stronger government. Not only was the power of Congress at a low ebb, but the rapid changes in state governments had in some cases weakened the authority of the law within the states themselves. The conditions in many places could be described only as anarchy. Both the Confederation and the states were deeply in debt. Both had issued paper money to the extent of many millions of dollars, which had so depreciated that, at the end of the war, one specie dollar would purchase a thousand dollars in the continental currency. In 1786, delegates from several states met at Annapolis to consider questions of common interest. One result of this meeting was a call for the states to elect delegates to a convention for the purpose of revising the Articles of Confederation. All the states except Rhode Island finally sent delegates.

The Constitutional Convention. The convention met in Philadelphia in May 1787. Its members represented the ablest men in America, including such leaders as Benjamin Franklin, Alexander Hamilton, William Patterson of New Jersey, James Wilson of Pennsylvania, John Jay, George Washington, and James Madison. Of these men, Madison probably did the most to secure agreement among the sharply divided parties in the convention. Three great difficulties presented themselves: (1) adjustment of the interests of the small and the large states; (2) treatment of slavery; (3) control over commerce. No more thorough discussion of the fundamentals and details of a great instrument of government has ever occupied the minds of legislators than that which was conducted in Philadelphia between May 25, 1787 and September 17 following, when the Constitution was signed by 39 of the original 55 members of the convention.

Compromises. A series of compromises had made possible the framing of the new constitution. (1) The differences between the small and the large states were reconciled by giving to all the states equal representation in the Senate, and by apportioning membership in the House of Representatives according to the population of each state. (2) The slavery compromise provided that the slave trade should not be prohibited before the year 1808 and also that, in the apportionment of representation and direct taxes according to population, five slaves should count as three free persons. (3) In respect to commerce, Congress was empowered to lay duties upon imports and to regulate interstate commerce, but was forbidden to levy taxes upon exports.

Ratification. There remained the difficult task of getting the Constitution ratified by the states. Its supporters went out to work for its ratification, under the name of Federalists. To their opponents the name Antifederalists was applied. Alexander Hamilton, James Madison, and John Jay published in New York newspapers a series of articles in defense of the Constitution, signed "Federalist." Their discussion was very influential in the campaign which was waged with great bitterness, especially in Massachusetts, Virginia, and New York. The assent of nine states was necessary to adoption, and New Hampshire ratified as the ninth state, May 23, 1788. Others followed, Rhode Island finally in 1790. Certain objections urged by the Antifederalists were removed by the adoption of the first ten amendments (1791), which added to the Constitution a bill of rights.

Population. A glimpse at the diversities of population and at the conditions of intercourse and industry in the United States about the year 1790 helps one to understand some of the difficulties which threatened the new union, as well as the elements of strength which promised well for it. In 1790 the total population of the United States was 3,930,000, excluding 80,000 Indians. Sixty thousand of the inhabitants were free negroes and 700,000 were slaves. In all the states, the English race was predominant. About 300,000 Scotch-Irish were scattered throughout the colonies, chiefly on the frontier. New York had a small Dutch population. Most of the 175,000 Germans lived in Pennsylvania and in the great valley to the southward. There was a small Huguenot group in the Carolinas. Nine-tenths of the people lived in the country. Philadelphia was the largest city, with about 42,000 people, and Louisville on the Ohio river was the town farthest west.

Agriculture. Some changes in agriculture had taken place since the middle of the 18th century. The most valuable crop in 1790 was wheat. Rice was becoming an important crop in the South. Cotton was not yet extensively raised, because of the great expense in the employment of hand labor to separate the fiber from the seed. This situation was changed by Whitney's invention of the cotton gin in 1793. Cotton growing then became profitable.

Manufactures. By the year 1800, manufacturing had increased considerably in the middle and northern states. Philadelphia exported about 300,000 barrels of flour a year. In New England the spinning and weaving industries had not yet developed. There was no power loom in America until 1814, when one was set up at Waltham, Massachusetts, by F. C. Lowell.

Commerce. Large numbers of New Englanders were engaged in the China and East India trade. American inventors had begun to show the ability for which they later became famous. John Fitch ran a steamboat on the Delaware river in 1787. Communication between the colonies was difficult because of the lack of good roads, but between 1790 and 1800 many roads were built from the East across the mountains, and in the eastern parts of the colonies numerous turnpikes or stone roads were constructed. A few canals were built, but, for the most part, such improvements in the means of communication and transport were left to later years.

Culture. The Revolution was followed by rapid extension of education. The Northwest Ordinance had made provision for popular education in the Northwest Territory before that great area had any English inhabitants. This act reflected the interest in education that was general in the colonies. The University of North Carolina, the first state institution of its kind, was founded in 1795. There was as yet no American literature, but several artists, notably John S. Copley and Gilbert Stuart, were very successful. Their work enables us today to be familiar with the faces of most of the leaders of the Revolutionary era. Throughout the states, there were to be found numerous private residences and public buildings of excellent architecture, which perhaps constitute America's best contribution to art, previous to the 19th century.

Political Ideas. The assertions about the rights of men, which had been found in many of the state constitutions and had been put into the Declaration of Independence, were widely discussed, and out of this discussion grew a more humane spirit in the treatment of workers and criminals. In politics, most of the state governments were still aristocratic, though the influence of the Western communities and of Vermont, in which manhood suffrage prevailed, was beginning to make itself felt.

Religion. The moral and religious life of the 18th century in the colonies cannot be said to have been of a high order. After the Revolution, the churches of America began to organize in forms appropriate to the new national life. In 1785 the first general convention of the Protestant Episcopal Church was held. The Methodist Episcopal Church was organized in 1784. The first diocese of the

Roman Catholic Church was established with the appointment of Bishop Carrol (Baltimore) in 1789. In the same year, the Presbyterian synods united in a general assembly of the Presbyterian Church. The Congregational churches in New England had no general government, and they were nearly all supported by taxation. These and several other denominations enjoyed religious freedom, and within a few years the states removed most of the religious qualifications formerly required for voters and officials. In this matter the Federal Constitution had been in advance of the states.

The New National Government. The first presidential election was held in 1788. George Washington was the unanimous choice for president, and John Adams was elected vice president. Congress, meeting in New York City, was organized on April 6, 1789, with Frederick Muhlenberg of Pennsylvania as speaker of the House. The committees of the House of Representatives were at first elected, but after 1790 the speaker was instructed to appoint all committees, and he retained this power until 1911. Washington was inaugurated as president on April 30, 1789. Congress created three executive departments: (1) the department of state; (2) the war department; (3) the treasury department. The office of attorney-general was created and also that of postmaster-general. Washington then formed the chiefs of the departments, with the attorney-general, into an advisory body which came to be called the president's cabinet. He originated the cabinet meeting.

The secretary of the treasury was Alexander Hamilton, and to him is due much of the credit for the successful organizing of the government. He succeeded in maintaining the confidence of the business world by insisting upon the honorable payment of the government's obligation in full, not in depreciated currency. To Hamilton also is to be attributed the plan of chartering the Bank of the United States. The discussion upon this proposal brought about the first clash between Hamilton, who believed in a strong central government, and Jefferson, who argued against what he thought to be an unwarranted extension of the Federal authority. Out of this dispute was to grow within a few years the division of the people into two great parties, the Federalists and the Republicans or Democratic-Republicans.

Foreign Difficulties. The outbreak of the French Revolution brought Washington's administration face to face with a serious foreign problem. Many Americans wanted the United States to support France against the other European powers. The French minister, Genet, violated the privileges of his office by attempting to force Washington into calling an extra session of Congress. Washington stood firmly for neutrality, and issued a proclamation which made it clear that the United States would not take sides. Trouble arose also with England over the rights of American vessels on the high seas, and Congress was on the point of declaring war. Washington, however, sent John Jay to England to negotiate a treaty, by which war with England was averted. In 1795 a treaty with Spain opened the mouth of the Mississippi River to navigation by American boats.

The Presidency of John Adams. With the retirement of Washington, real party struggles began in the United States, but the system of election then in vogue put the two leading presidential candidates into office at once, making the Federalist, Adams, president and the Democratic-Republican, Jefferson, vice president. John Adams was the first president to occupy the White House at Washington (1800).

The new administration was beset with foreign troubles. France had been resentful over the Jay treaty with Great Britain, and the French government warned the American minister, Charles C. Pinckney, to leave Paris. President Adams tried to arrive at an understanding with the French government, but the only result was a demand for bribes. This demand was refused, and for a time America and France were virtually at war. Bonaparte, however, soon came into power in France, and a treaty of peace was negotiated in 1800. The French behavior gave rise to the passage of the Alien and Sedition acts in Congress in 1798. The enforcement of these acts intensified the conflict between the Federalists and the Republicans.

Jefferson's Administration. The most important result of this political situation was the so-called revolution of 1800, when the Republican (Democratic-Republican) candidates, Thomas Jefferson and Aaron Burr, were elected president and vice president respectively. The dispute in this election led to the passing of the 12th amendment, requiring that president and vice president be voted for separately.

Jefferson's administration is notable for two things: (1) the personal influence of the president in the direction of greater democracy in government; (2) the remarkable foresight which he displayed in connection with the purchase of the Louisiana territory and its exploration by Lewis and Clarke. His second term as president was troubled by the conspiracy of Aaron Burr and by the stoppage of American trade, due to the European war measures. Jefferson believed that if American foodstuffs and exports were cut off from Europe, the belligerents would be compelled to make peace. He proposed the Embargo act, with the main result that American ships were tied up at their wharves and American commerce seemed strangled, although Europe did suffer to some extent by the policy.

The War of 1812. Ever since the signing of the Treaty of Paris in 1783, the policy of Great Britain toward American shipping had occasioned friction between the two governments. As the war between Napoleon and the allies dragged on, American commerce was robbed under Napoleonic decrees and English orders in council. The failure of such retaliatory policies as the Embargo act of 1807 and the Nonintercourse acts of 1809 and 1810 became clear, and there grew up in Congress a strong party which favored war against Great Britain. This hostile feeling was intensified by British impressment of American seamen.

The Republican party drew much of its strength from the West, and many Westerners believed it would be easy to strike at England through Canada, although the United States maintained but a small regular army, and had made no provision for a larger one. Finally, war was declared on June 18, 1812. At first the American forces were defeated on land, but American ships won brilliant victories at sea. The year 1813 was less favorable to the American ships, although Perry's victory on Lake Erie opened the way for a campaign in western Canada. In 1814 the British seized Astoria in Oregon, burned public buildings in the city of Washington, and made an attack upon Baltimore. The Americans failed in an attempt to invade Canada, but Andrew Jackson successfully defended his position at New Orleans against the British forces under General Pakenham.

The war had brought no especial credit to either side, but English shipowners were impatient at their losses, and their influence prompted the English government to make a favorable treaty with America. Within the United States, the war had been made the occasion of party conflict. When President Madison called for state troops, Federalist New England refused to send them. The climax of this opposition to the government was the Hartford Convention, the action of which was virtually a threat to withdraw from the Union. But just before the report of this convention was issued, the treaty of peace had been signed at Ghent, December 24, 1814.

Causes, direct and remote: England's asserted right to search American vessels; Impressment of American seamen; Inciting of Indian hostilities by British agents; Blockades and other arbitrary practices under the British orders in council; Neglect on the part of England to transfer to the United States the posts on the western frontier.

Campaigns	Chief Battles	American Leaders	Troops	British Leaders	Troops	Victor	Results
On the Canadian frontier.	Fort Dearborn, Aug. 15, 1812	Heald	67	Indians	1,300	Ind.	Americans surrender to British and abandon Michigan territory. Ends first attempt to invade Canada.
	Detroit, Aug. 16, 1812	Hull	1,400	Brock	1,300	Brit.	
	Queenston Heights, Oct. 13, 1812	Van Rensselaer	1,100	Brock	1,500	Brit.	
Harrison in the Northwest and Perry on Lake Erie.	River Raisin, Jan. 22, 1813	Winchester	900	Proctor	1,100	Brit.	Americans regain Michigan territory. British and Indian alliance broken. Tecumseh slain. British fleet on Lake Erie annihilated.
	Fort Meigs, May 5, 1813	Harrison	1,100	Proctor	2,200	Amer.	
	Fort Stephenson, Aug. 2, 1813	Croghan	160	Proctor	391	Amer.	
	Naval Battle of Lake Erie, Sept. 10, 1813	Perry	54 guns	Barclay	63 guns	Amer.	
	The Thames, Oct. 5, 1813	Harrison	3,500	Proctor Tecumseh }	1,700	Amer.	
Lake Ontario and Niagara frontier.	York, April 27, 1813	Pike	1,600	Sheaffe	600	?	Americans convinced that their troops could successfully cope with trained veterans of Europe.
	Fort George, May 27, 1813	Chauncey	4,500	Vincent	2,500	?	
	Sackett's Harbor, May 29, 1813	Brown	650	Prevost	800	Amer.	
	Stony Creek, June 6, 1813	Winder Chandler }	1,400	Vincent	750	Brit.	
	Beaver Dams, June 24, 1813	Boerstler	600	Kerr Brant }	500	Brit.	
	Crystler's Farm, Nov. 11, 1813	Wilkinson	2,000	Morrison	1,000	Brit.	
	Chippewa, July 5, 1814	Brown	3,200	Riall	2,500	Amer.	
	Lundy's Lane, July 25, 1814	Brown	3,100	Drummond	3,500	?	
	Fort Erie, Aug. 15, 1814	Gaines	2,400	Drummond	3,600	Amer.	
	Fort Erie, Sept. 17, 1814	Brown	3,000	Drummond	4,000	Amer.	
Prevost attempts to invade New York via Lake Champlain.	Plattsburg, Sept. 11, 1814	Macomb	2,000	Prevost	13,000	Amer.	British retreat, leaving northern frontier clear for remainder of the war.
	Lake Champlain, Sept. 11, 1814	MacDonough	14 vessels 86 guns	Downie	16 vessels 92 guns	Amer.	
Destruction of Washington; attack on Baltimore.	Bladensburg, Aug. 24, 1814	Winder	6,000	Ross	5,000	Brit.	Washington abandoned to the British. British retire to Halifax.
	Fort McHenry, Sept. 13, 1814	Armistead	3,200	Ross	5,000	Amer.	
Jackson's victory at New Orleans.	New Orleans, Jan. 8, 1815	Jackson	5,500	Pakenham	10,000	Amer.	British withdraw.

ON THE SEA

Location	Date	American Vessels	Commanders	British Vessels	Commanders	Victor
Off Newfoundland	Aug. 13, 1812	Essex	Porter	Alert	Langharne	Amer.
Off Massachusetts Bay	Aug. 19, 1812	Constitution	Hull	Guerrière	Dacres	Amer.
Off North Carolina	Oct. 18, 1812	Wasp	Jones	Frolic	Whinyates	Amer.
Off Canary Islands	Oct. 25, 1812	United States	Decatur	Macedonian	Carden	Amer.
Off Brazil	Dec. 29, 1812	Constitution	Bainbridge	Java	Lambert	Amer.
Off Demerara	Feb. 24, 1813	Hornet	Lawrence	Peacock	Peake	Amer.
Off Massachusetts coast	June 1, 1813	Chesapeake	Lawrence	Shannon	Broke	Brit.
Off English Channel	Aug. 14, 1813	Argus	Allen	Pelican	Maples	Brit.
Off Maine coast	Sept. 5, 1813	Enterprise	Burrows	Boxer	Blythe	Amer.
At Valparaiso	Mar. 28, 1814	Essex	Porter	Phoebe Cherub }	Hillyar Tucker }	Brit.
In English Channel	June 28, 1814	Wasp	Blakeley	Reindeer	Manners	Amer.
Off Africa	Sept. 1, 1814	Wasp	Blakeley	Avon	Arbuthnot	Amer.
At Fayal, Azores	Sept. 26, 1814	Gen'l Armstrong	Reid	Plantagenet Carnation Rota }	Floyd Bentham Somerville }	?
Off Long Island	Jan. 15, 1815	President	Decatur	Endymion Pomone Tenedos Majestic }	Hope Lumly Parker Hayes }	Brit.
Off Madeira	Feb. 20, 1815	Constitution	Stewart	Cyane Levant }	Falcon Douglass }	Amer.
In South Atlantic	Mar. 23, 1815	Hornet	Biddle	Penguin	Dickenson	Amer.

Results of War: The independence of the United States was definitely insured. Respect for American seamen was fully established. Treaty of Ghent terminated war, Dec. 24, 1814, but did not definitely settle questions of its cause. Owing to lack of facilities for transmission of news, the battle of New Orleans and some naval battles were fought after date of signing the treaty of peace.

Territory	Year Acquired	How Acquired	Occasion of Acquisition	Area in Square Miles	Cost
Original Thirteen States, including claims in the Northwest Territory	1783	. . . . . .		892,135	
Louisiana Territory. .	1803	Purchase . .	Negotiations for Purchase of New Orleans. French Offer.	827,987	$15,000,000
West Florida	1810–13	Occupation .	Boundary Dispute	13,435	
Florida	1819	Cession, indemnity	Settlement of Border Troubles	58,666	5,000,000
Texas	1845	Annexation .	Petition of Republic of Texas	389,166	
Oregon Territory . .	1846	Treaty . . .	Settlement of Boundary Dispute	286,541	
Mexican Cession . . .	1848	Cession, indemnity	Close of Mexican War	529,189	15,000,000
Gadsden Purchase . .	1853	Purchase . .	Boundary Dispute	45,535	10,000,000
Alaska	1867	Purchase . .	Pacific Coast Interest in Alaska Fisheries. Russian Offer	590,884	7,200,000
Midway Islands . . .	1867	Annexation .	Fitness for Coaling Station		
Hawaiian Islands. . .	1898	Annexation .	Petition of Hawaiian Government	6,449	
Guam	1898	Annexation .	Close of Spanish War	210	
Palmyra Island . . .	1898	. . . . . .	Obtained with Hawaii		
Puerto Rico	1898	Cession . .	Close of Spanish War	3,435	
Philippine Islands . . (Now Independent)	1898	Cession, indemnity	Close of Spanish War	114,400	20,000,000
Samoan Islands . . .	1899	Annexation .	Treaty with Germany and Great Britain	58	
Add. Philippine Islands	1901	Indemnity .	Boundary Adjustment	68	100,000
Canal Zone	1903	Lease . . .	Canal Construction and Control	436	{ 10,000,000 250,000 annually
Virgin Islands	1917	Purchase . .	Need of Naval Base	149	25,000,000

The Monroe Doctrine.

In European affairs, after the close of the Napoleonic wars, there was much unrest and domestic discord, which directly affected the United States chiefly through immigration. But to the southward, throughout the American continent, there was a general movement of revolution in the Spanish colonies, tending toward the establishment of independent republican states. During the administration of President Monroe, Canning, the English prime minister, had suggested that England and the United States should join in preventing the annexation of any American state to Spain, France, or Portugal. The president responded to this suggestion with the famous Monroe Doctrine.

A New National Period.

With the close of the War of 1812, a new period opened in American history. This era was to be marked by several notable features: (1) the expansion of United States territory in the West; (2) the beginnings of the slavery dispute; (3) the tariff question; (4) the rise of new political parties; (5) the rise of humanitarian and educational societies and movements.

Expansion.

In 1800 the western boundary of the United States was the Mississippi river, access to which from the sea was still controlled by Spain. The western half of the Mississippi valley was claimed by France. Within a few years, New Orleans had passed from Spain to France and from France, together with Louisiana, to the United States. Settlers poured into the valley of the Ohio and began to fill up the Northwest. Ohio was admitted as a state in 1803. The expedition of Lewis and Clark revealed the greatness of the Western country, and John Jacob Astor, a New York merchant, by establishing his trading post at Astoria, began competition in the fur trade with the Hudson's Bay Company.

Both Great Britain and the United States claimed the territory now included in the states of Washington and Oregon. The planting of Indian missions in the valleys of the Columbia and Willamette rivers was followed before 1840 by an immigration of United States citizens. Spain still held the California coast and territory now known as New Mexico and Arizona. The increasing travel, incident to the immigration from all sections of the East into the Mississippi valley, necessitated further building of roads and canals. By the year 1825 the Erie canal was finished from Albany to the Niagara river. The Cumberland road from Maryland westward through Wheeling and Columbus to St. Louis was built about the same time. After 1812, steamers began to appear on the Western rivers.

Slavery.

The settlement of the Western country raised at once the question of the extension of slavery. In the Northwest Territory, slavery was forbidden by the Ordinance of 1787, but this prohibition did not extend to the vast lands of the Louisiana Purchase, out of which new states would be formed. The consequent dispute reached its first crisis in 1819 with the discussion over the admission of Missouri, the first state to be formed out of the Louisiana Purchase. The immediate result was the passage of the Missouri Compromise, by which a line was drawn across the Louisiana Purchase, north of which there were to be no slaveholding territories and no slaveholding states except Missouri.

From this time, slavery was a sectional question between the North and the South. States were admitted in such an order as to maintain a kind of balance between the two forces. The general growth of humane sentiment throughout the country gave rise to the formation of antislavery societies and encouraged an increasing agitation of the question. Abolition societies were at first general in both the North and the South, but about the year 1830 those in the South disappeared, and the societies in the North were largely increased in membership and vigor. The second great crisis came in 1850, when the question of admitting California and New Mexico arose. Following the resulting compromise, came the famous Kansas-Nebraska bill.

New Parties.

Politically, the period from 1815 to 1860 saw the break-up of the old party alignment of Federalists and Republicans and the formation of new parties. From 1800 to 1828 the government was in the hands of the Republicans (Democratic-Republicans), who gradually, under the stress of expansion and war, adopted the policies of the Federalists to such an extent that the Federalist party disappeared. The administration of Monroe was known as the "era of good feeling." As a matter of fact, it was a time of factional strife.

At the close of Monroe's administration, several candidates for the presidency were put into the field by various means. Nominations were made by some of the state legislatures; other nominations were made by small political groups. John Quincy Adams, now a Republican, although he had begun his political life as a Federalist, was elected. He represented the old aristocratic line of presidential succession.

New Political Elements. Several conditions in the country contributed to the development of new parties. First, the growth of the West, with its democratic ideas and its popular organization of local government, gave rise to a political group which looked with suspicion on the growing financial interests of the East. In the second place, there had taken place in all the states, since the formation of the Union, a wide extension of the suffrage, which had brought into the ranks of voters the growing class of mechanics in Eastern cities and towns. Moreover, the close of the period of wars in Europe left the industries and commerce of the United States open to a new competition. This situation gave rise to the demand for higher tariffs to protect "infant industries." Upon this question the southern states, which were mainly agricultural, the middle states, in which factories had grown up, and the New England states, interested chiefly in shipping, were divided. And, finally, the question of slavery, in its various phases, was more and more frequently injected into political contests, until, linked with the question of state rights, it finally became the ruling issue in American politics.

Political Leaders. Political organizations were being developed in the states during this period, particularly in New York and Pennsylvania, and these contributed to the general uncertainty of politics during the decade from 1830 to 1840. Several notable leaders came to the front. Henry Clay early became the champion of the protective tariff under the name of the "American system." Daniel Webster at first opposed, and then favored, the tariff. John C. Calhoun of South Carolina, in the beginning a friend of the tariff, soon changed to opposition and became the great exponent of the nullification idea. Andrew Jackson, who belonged by birth to the so-called "poor whites" of the Carolinas, had gone to Tennessee as a young man and had gained prominence in politics and in the military operations of the War of 1812. During the administration of John Quincy Adams, he became the leader of the opposition and of the democratic movement. He was looked upon as the man of the people, and the combination of the South and West elected him president in 1828. His is the first administration controlled by the Democratic party.

The Presidency of Jackson. The two great issues of Jackson's administration were the question of the United States bank and the question of the right of states to nullify tariff acts. He attacked the bank as an instrument of dangerous commercial monopoly and succeeded in destroying it as a government institution. On the question of nullification, he took the position that the Federal Union must be preserved. The tariff which had aroused the opposition of South Carolina was modified, and this issue disappeared. It was in connection with this discussion upon the question of a state's right to nullify Federal acts that the great debate between Daniel Webster of Massachusetts and Senator Hayne of South Carolina took place in 1830. Webster was from this time recognized as the great champion of Federal supremacy.

The Whigs. Between 1830 and 1840 several political groups drew together into a party which took the name of Whigs. They became strong enough to elect William Henry Harrison in 1840 over Martin Van Buren, the Democratic candidate, who had served one term as president. Harrison died very soon after his inauguration, and the vice president, John Tyler, of Virginia, who was not in reality a Whig, began a stormy administration.

Texas and Mexico. The most important issues of the period between 1840 and 1850 grew out of the expansion of the United States toward the west and south. Party strife became especially bitter because of the relationship of this expansion to the Monroe Doctrine and to the extension of slavery. A strong demand arose for the annexation of territory belonging to Mexico, which was now independent of Spain.

A considerable number of Americans had moved into Texas and had set up an independent state in which slavery was legal. A treaty of annexation was proposed in 1844, but it was rejected by the Senate. In the election of that year, Clay was the Whig nominee, opposed to annexation, and James K. Polk was the Democratic nominee, in favor of annexation. Polk was elected. As a consequence, just before the close of Tyler's administration, Texas was annexed by joint resolution of Congress.

In 1846 President Polk settled with England the boundary of the Oregon country and thus completed the adjustment of the boundary between Canada and the United States. Several exploring expeditions, such as that led by John C. Frémont in 1842–45, had been sent by Americans into California, and President Polk was determined that not only Texas but also the remaining Mexican territory north of the line of the Rio Grande, should be taken for the United States. He finally ordered General Taylor to advance into the disputed territory north of the Rio Grande, where Taylor's forces were attacked by the Mexicans. In a message

MEXICAN WAR

Causes: (1) Dispute over the western boundary of Texas; (2) The desire of the United States government to annex the Mexican territory, southwest of the boundary fixed by treaty in 1819, which included the present states of Arizona, Nevada, Utah, New Mexico, and California, with parts of Wyoming and Colorado.

CAMPAIGNS	Chief Battles	AMERICAN		MEXICAN		Victor	Results
		Leaders	Troops	Leaders	Troops		
Along the Rio Grande.	Palo Alto, May 8, 1846	Taylor	2,000	Arista	6,000	Amer.	
	Resaca de la Palma, May 9, 1846	Taylor	2,200	Arista	6,800	Amer.	
	Monterey, Sept. 20–24, 1846	Taylor	6,600	Ampudia	10,000	Amer.	
	Buena Vista, Feb. 23, 1847.	Taylor	5,000	Santa Anna	20,000	Amer.	
Expedition from Vera Cruz to the City of Mexico.	Vera Cruz, March 10–25, 1847	Scott	12,000	?	?	Amer.	The Treaty of Guadalupe Hidalgo added 522,568 sq. mi. of territory to the United States, awarding to Mexico payment of $15,000,000. Rio Grande made boundary between Texas and Mexico.
	Cerro Gordo, April 18, 1847	Scott	8,500	Santa Anna	12,000	Amer.	
	Contreras, Aug. 20, 1847.	Scott	4,500	Valencia Santa Anna }	19,000	Amer.	
	Churubusco, Aug. 20, 1847.	Scott	7,300	Santa Anna	25,000	Amer.	
	Molino del Rey, Sept. 8, 1847	Scott	3,500	Santa Anna	10,000	Amer.	
	Chapultepec, Sept. 12–13, 1847	Scott	7,500	Bravo	4,800	Amer.	

to Congress, May 11, 1846, Polk declared that a state of war existed, and Congress passed a declaration of war. The campaign of the American troops was entirely successful. Mexico ceded New Mexico and California and gave up all claim to Texas.

New States and Slavery. These western additions of territory had been reckoned as valuable chiefly for their furs, but the discovery of gold in California revealed far greater wealth in the new territory than anybody had hoped to find there. In 1849, immigrants began to pour into California, and the question of its admission to the Union as a state came to the fore in the administration of Zachary Taylor, who was elected as the Whig candidate in 1848. He encouraged the Californians to adopt a constitution, and determined to bring California into the Union. The miners, who were working with their own hands, declared against slavery in the new constitution.

In 1849 the Union consisted of fifteen slave states and fifteen free states. There was no slave territory ready to be admitted. The annexation of California would give the free states a majority in the Senate. This situation led to the Compromise of 1850, urged by Henry Clay, "the great pacificator." Under this compromise, California came into the Union as a free state, while New Mexico and Utah were organized as territories with the privilege of determining whether they would be slave or free.

Continuance of the Slavery Issue. The Compromise of 1850 failed to settle the great dispute which was gradually dividing the North from the South, and which was raising to national importance an issue in respect to which neither the Democratic nor the Whig party took a decided position. In the election of 1852, Franklin Pierce of New Hampshire, the Democratic candidate, was elected. President Pierce's first step was in pursuit of a policy looking to the annexation of Cuba. This project was viewed with great favor in the South, because Cuba was a rich slave territory. But the scheme failed, largely because of the rise of the Kansas and Nebraska difficulty over slavery. The Missouri Compromise of thirty years before had forbidden slavery in the territory out of which Kansas and Nebraska were to be formed. Stephen A. Douglas, one of the greatest debaters of the day, supported the theory of squatter sovereignty, virtually embodied in the Kansas-Nebraska bill, which would give the settlers in the territories the right to decide whether or not they would have slavery. Settlers from both North and South poured into the country in dispute, and civil war broke out.

The Republican Party. Out of this discussion over the Kansas-Nebraska bill came the new alignment of parties under the names of Republicans and Democrats. In the election of 1856, the Republicans, whose candidate was John C. Frémont, were defeated by the Democrats, and James Buchanan became president. Far more significant than the outcome of this election, however, was the political contest and great debate between Douglas and Lincoln in 1858. The two men were candidates for the senatorship from Illinois. Douglas won the election, but Lincoln had compelled him to announce his Freeport Doctrine, which cost him the support of Southern Democrats. This series of debates was largely influential in making Lincoln the Republican candidate for president in 1860.

Social Movements, 1820–1860. In order to comprehend thoroughly the course of events which, in the period succeeding the War of 1812, gradually brought the states to the verge of civil war, we must take account of the remarkable contemporary growth of enthusiasm for humanitarian and religious reforms in America. The churches in this period began their extensive missionary efforts in the West and in foreign countries. The circuit rider was a common and important figure on the frontier.

The Sunday school movement for the education of poor children, which had begun in England, was adopted in America. American missions were started in the Hawaiian islands, in Asia, and in Africa. The churches began also to emphasize social duties and to found many schools and academies. In the Eastern cities, trade-unions began about 1830 to call attention to the cruel conditions of labor for both adults and children in the factories of New England and of the middle states.

Aside from these organized movements, many individual reformers arose, who spent their lives in efforts for better social conditions. Dorothea Dix brought about the establishment of public asylums for the insane. The treatment of prisoners in jails and penitentiaries was generally brutal at the beginning of the 19th century. In 1830 the Eastern penitentiary at Philadelphia marked a great advance in this respect by providing separate cells for prisoners. The harsh laws against poor debtors were modified also in the course of this period.

The great vice of Americans in the colonial period and throughout the early years of the republic was drunkenness. Agitation for reform of drinking customs gave rise to temperance societies in Boston in 1824; in 1840 the Washingtonian societies began in Baltimore the more widespread movement for temperance. The first state prohibition law was adopted in Maine in 1846.

About 1830 the woman's rights movement began. Its first fruits were seen in the founding of good schools and academies for girls. In 1833 Oberlin college opened its doors to women. The demand for woman suffrage was part of this movement, but it was not to attain success for nearly a hundred years.

The idea of popular education was growing. The mechanics' organizations in Eastern cities protested against the prevalent idea of pauper schools to educate the children of those who could not afford private instruction. About 1830 the policy of a general public school system supported by taxation began to gain favor. This entire educational movement was enlarged and vitalized through the lecture tours of such intellectual leaders as Ralph Waldo Emerson and Edward Everett, and by the establishment of "circulating" libraries in many small towns throughout the country.

Economic Progress. American industry had been progressing by leaps and bounds during this period. The great cotton and woolen mills grew up in New England; coal and iron had been discovered in the neighborhood of Pittsburgh; and the beginnings of the giant steel industry were made. Many inventions of labor-saving machinery appeared between 1830 and 1860. By the invention of his reaper in 1831, Cyrus McCormick made possible a revolution in methods of farming. Railroads were built on lines running westward from the Atlantic seaboard and, to a less extent, southward from the Potomac and Ohio rivers. Canals were constructed by states and by private companies. The foundations of many large individual fortunes were laid through the granting of land for railroad building and by the rapid growth of cities. Industry received a severe check in the panic of 1837, but business organization was greatly strengthened through the economic lessons taught by this disaster.

Immigration. The era under review was also a time of great increase in immigration. Between 1820 and 1840, about 600,000 people came from the Old World and were scattered over all sections of the country. Most of the immigrants were English, Scotch, and Irish. After the unsuccessful revolutionary movement of 1848 in Germany, a large German immigration began, which included many highly educated and able men, such as Carl Schurz. Famine conditions in Ireland sent more than a million Irishmen to America between 1845 and 1855. Immigrants of these groups furnished the labor with which cities, roads, canals, and factories were built, and they occupied much of the new farming land in the West.

The South. Most of this industrial development took place in the North and West, where the laborer was free. In the South, the main change from colonial conditions was the abandonment of much of the worn-out tobacco land of the East and the movement of planters into the black belt of the Carolinas, Georgia, Alabama, and Mississippi, for the raising of cotton. Cotton was the one staple Southern crop, and so much of the land was given up to its production that the South had to draw its food supplies in large amounts from the North.

South and North. Thus, at the opening of the war of secession, the Southern states were behind the North in industrial development and in population. When the crisis came, Maryland, Delaware, Kentucky, and Missouri—all slaveholding states—remained in the Union, and many of the people of eastern Tennessee—descendants of the early English pioneers, and opponents of slavery—were loyal. The South, therefore, entered the war with about 9,000,-000 people as opposed to 22,000,000 in the North. It is estimated that the South had 1,300,000 white men available for military service, while the North had 5,500,000, about half of whom were foreign born. The Southern society was aristocratic, and its leaders were generally highly educated men. In the North, democracy, together with popular education, had become more general.

The Election of 1860. The controversy over the Dred Scott decision, the constitutional struggle in Kansas, and the Lincoln-Douglas debates helped to weld together various elements into the new Republican party, as the party of opposition to slavery. Between 1859 and 1861 this party had a small majority in the House of Representatives, but the Senate was strongly Democratic. In February 1860, Jefferson Davis, senator from Mississippi, introduced in the Senate a number of resolutions, which were passed. They declared for the protection of slavery by Congress, for the suppression of abolitionist agitation in the North, and for the sovereignty of the states. This action was interpreted as a notice that the election of an antislavery president would be the signal for possible withdrawal of the Southern states from the Union.

The Democratic party met in a convention at Charleston, South Carolina, in April 1860, and divided upon the policy of extending slavery. A second convention, held at Baltimore, nominated Douglas, while the extreme Southern Democrats nominated John C. Breckinridge, who was at that time vice president. A Constitutional Union party, made up of Southern and Northern Whigs, nominated John Bell of Tennessee. The Republican party, meeting at Chicago in May, nominated Abraham Lincoln.

Lincoln and Secession. Lincoln was elected, although he received a minority of the total popular vote. The Republicans had a majority in every Northern state except California, Oregon, and New Jersey. On the day after the national election, steps were taken in South Carolina to call a secession convention. By unanimous vote, this convention, on December 20, 1860, declared South Carolina no longer a part of the Union. Before the first of February 1861, six other states—Mississippi, Florida, Alabama, Georgia, Louisiana, and Texas—had followed the example of South Carolina. In the month of February, a convention of delegates from six states drew up a provisional constitution for the Confederate States of America, and elected Jefferson Davis president and Alexander H. Stephens vice president. Preparations for war began immediately. Southern citizens resigned their civil and military offices under the United States government, thus demoralizing, to a large degree, the Union army and navy.

The sentiment in the North during these months was divided. Strong pressure was brought by such leaders as Horace Greeley in favor of acquiescing in the action of the Southern states and of recognizing the independent Confederacy. Lincoln was inaugurated on March 4, 1861, and his inaugural address stated clearly his position. He declared himself opposed to interference with the institution of slavery in the states where it existed, but he expressed equal determination to maintain the Union unbroken, and he clearly stated his belief in the utter unwisdom of secession. Lincoln had already lent his aid to efforts at reconciliation, but these efforts had failed, and he now placed upon the South the responsibility for war.

Opening of the War. On April 12, 1861 the Confederate forces began the bombardment of Fort Sumter in Charleston harbor. On April 15, Lincoln issued his call for 75,000 volunteers. The president's stand in his inaugural address and his action in calling for recruits for the army crystallized sentiment in the North as well as in the South. North Carolina and Virginia, Tennessee and Arkansas joined the Confederacy. The two sides stood 22 Union states and 11 Confederate. There was a general belief in the North that the conflict could be ended with one blow. But this opinion reckoned without the gallant spirit and unanimous determination of the Southern people. To the Southern mind, loyalty to the state came first. This ingrained belief accounts for the action of such men as Alexander H. Stephens and Robert E. Lee. Stephens fought against secession in Georgia, but, when once the majority of his fellow citizens of that state had decided against him, he threw in his influence with them. Robert E. Lee, a Virginian, was an officer in the army of the United States and was offered command of the Union armies, but, when Virginia decided for secession, he remained true to his state.

The Opposing Forces. Both sides misjudged and underestimated each other's powers. The men of the South were accustomed to outdoor life, to the use of firearms, and to the management of horses. Their leaders had been trained in their own military schools and at West Point. The South could put a larger proportion of its white men into service, because the labor on the plantations would be done by the slaves. On the other hand, the North had less of military spirit than the South; a larger proportion of its white population was engaged in the labor of farming and in factories. Moreover, its labor at home had to be done by freemen, and, therefore, a smaller proportion could be spared for military service. As a matter of fact, during the war, about nine men out of every ten in the South served in the army, while in the North one man out of two bore arms at some period of the war. Both sides had to put forth tremendous efforts to equip and maintain armies and navies. One very great advantage the North possessed; namely, its factories and its developed resources in coal and iron. Added to this was the wide distribution of labor-saving machines on the farms, without which it is doubtful whether the North could have maintained itself throughout the war. One other advantage was that, in the decade between 1850 and 1860, railroad lines had been completed, which bound together the Mississippi valley and the Atlantic seaboard, thus directing the products of the Western farms toward the East, rather than toward the South.

The Siege of the South. The military problem of the war was simple. The Southern armies had to protect a border running from the Potomac river westward across the mountains through Tennessee to the Mississippi river. In order to succeed, they had also to keep communications open through their ports for the shipment of their cotton and for the importation of food supplies and arms. The first task of the Northern army and navy was to draw a line around the Confederate states and, by means of the armies on the north and west and the navy on the south and east, to isolate the Confederacy from the outside world. In the second place, the Northern armies had to invade the South and defeat the Southern forces on their own territory.

At first, a blockade of the Southern ports was impossible, for the Federal government had only twelve ships at its disposal. But it had shipyards, and blockading squadrons were rapidly gathered until an effective blockade was secured. Cotton was piled up on the wharves of Southern ports, where it became valueless, and food and medicines grew scarce.

War in the West. The northern frontier of the Confederacy was well protected by the mountains of western Virginia, Kentucky, and Tennessee. There were strongly fortified points on the Kentucky and Tennessee rivers and along the Mississippi. But several railroad lines penetrated southward from the Potomac in the East and from Louisville, on the Ohio, in the West. The campaigns of the Northern armies were determined by these approaches. The first three years of the war were consumed by a stubborn struggle in the West for control of the Mississippi and of the railroad lines leading southward into Georgia and Alabama. This struggle was finally won by the Union armies through the capture of Vicksburg and the defeat of General Bragg at Chickamauga and Chattanooga in the summer and fall of 1863.

War in the East. In the East, the better fortune of war was with the Confederate armies commanded by General Lee, until their defeat at the battle of Gettysburg. General Grant was placed in command of the army of the Potomac in the spring of 1864, and for a year the war settled down to a contest between the armies of Lee and Grant in Virginia. The Northern losses were terrific and discouraging. Lee handled his army in masterly fashion, and he surrendered at Appomattox, April 9, 1865, only after his resources in men and equipment were exhausted. The material resources of the South had been seriously crippled by the march of Sherman from Atlanta to Savannah in the fall and winter of 1864.

Reconstruction. Lincoln's diplomacy had already laid the basis for wise reconstruction to follow the war, but his assassination removed the only man who could lead wisely in this process. Andrew Johnson, who became president, lacked the tact and skill to carry out Lincoln's policy, although he set himself to the task. Under Lincoln's plan, the Southern states were viewed as never having been outside the Union. Governors were appointed for the states which recognized the conditions laid down by the president for the restoration of government. Conventions in these states adopted new constitutions, elected legislatures and governors, and ratified the 13th amendment, which abolished slavery. Civil government was then declared to be fully restored.

CIVIL WAR OR WAR OF SECESSION

Causes: (1) The conflict between the North and the South upon the question of slavery; (2) The state rights controversy, involving the right of secession; (3) The lack of understanding between the North and the South, due to differences of economic development.

CAMPAIGNS	Chief Battles	UNION		CONFEDERATE		Victor	Results
		Leaders	Troops	Leaders	Troops		
Opening conflicts.	Fort Sumter, S. C., April 12–14, 1861	Anderson . .	75	Beauregard .	?	Confed.	Both sides realize the seriousness of the conflict and prepare for a long war.
	First Battle of Bull Run (Manassas), Va., July 21, 1861	McDowell .	18,000	J.E.Johnston } Beauregard }	22,000	Confed.	
	Ball's Bluff, Va., Oct. 21, 1861	Baker . . .	1,700	Evans . . .	1,600	Confed.	
Western campaigns, 1862. To close the northern frontier in Kentucky and Tennessee; to control the Mississippi; to open routes of invasion into the South.	Mill Spring, Ky., Jan. 19-20, 1862	Thomas . .	4,000	Crittenden .	4,000	Union	
	Ft. Henry, Tenn., surrender, Feb. 6, 1862 . . .	Grant . . } Foote(navy) }	20,000	Tilghman. .	4,000	Union	
	Ft. Donelson, Tenn., surrender, Feb. 14–16, 1862.	Grant . . } Foote(navy) }	20,000	Pillow . . } Floyd . . } Buckner . }	14,000	Union	
	Shiloh (Pittsburg Landing), Tenn., April 6-7, 1862	Grant . . } Buell. . . }	38,000	A.S.Johnston } Beauregard }	40,000	Union	
	Island No. 10 (Miss. river), surrender, April 7, 1862.	Pope . . } Foote(navy) }	?	Mackall . .	6,000	Union	Union troops in control of the upper Mississippi and of the Tennessee river.
	Corinth, Miss., Oct. 3-4, 1862	Rosecrans .	20,000	Van Dorn } Price. . . }	22,000	Union	
	Perryville, Ky., Oct. 8, 1862	Buell. . .	54,000	Bragg . . .	68,000	Union	
Eastern campaigns, 1862. First contest for capture of Richmond. Peninsular campaign.	Yorktown, Va., siege, April 5–May 3, 1862 .	McClellan .	110,000	J. E. Johnston	50,000	Union	
	Williamsburg, Va., May 5, 1862	McClellan .	110,000	J. E. Johnston	50,000	Union	
T. J. (Stonewall) Jackson's Valley campaign	McDowell, Va., (now W. Va.), May 8, 1862 . .	Schenck . .	2,600	Jackson . .	?	Union	
	Fair Oaks (Seven Pines), Va., May 31–June 1, 1862	McClellan .	51,000	J. E. Johnston	42,000	Union	
	Seven Days' Battles before Richmond, Va., June 25–July 1, 1862 .	McClellan .	92,000	Lee	80,000	Confed.	McClellan retreats to Malvern Hill.

CAMPAIGNS	Chief Battles	UNION		CONFEDERATE		Victor	Results
		Leaders	Troops	Leaders	Troops		
Shenandoah Valley campaign.	Second Battle of Bull Run, Va., Aug. 28–30, 1862 .	Pope . . .	65,000	Lee . . . } Jackson	54,000	Confed.	Union armies fail in attempt to capture Richmond.
First Confederate invasion of the North.	Antietam (Sharpsburg), Md., Sept. 16-17, 1862 .	McClellan .	75,000	Lee	40,000	Union	Lee's invasion of the North defeated.
	Fredericksburg, Va., Dec. 13, 1862	Burnside . .	116,000	Lee	78,000	Confed.	
Coast and Harbors campaign.	Hampton Roads, Va., *Merrimac* and *Monitor*, March 9, 1862	Worden . .	?	Buchanan . .	?	Union	
Effort to blockade the Southern ports.	New Orleans, La., surrender, April 29, 1862 . .	Farragut (navy) } Butler (army)	11,000	Mitchell (navy) } Lovell (army)	?	Union	Effective blockading of Southern commerce assured.
Western campaigns, 1863. For control of the Mississippi and to open the way for invasion to Atlanta. J. H. Morgan's raid across the Ohio ended at Salineville, July 26, 1863.	Murfreesboro (Stone River), Tenn., Dec. 31, 1862–Jan. 2, 1863 . .	Rosecrans .	43,000	Bragg . . .	37,000	Union	
	Vicksburg, Miss., surrender, July 4, 1863 . . .	Grant . . } Porter (navy)	75,000	Pemberton .	40,000	Union	
	Port Hudson, Miss., July 9, 1863	Banks . . .	13,000	Gardner . .	6,000	Union	
	Chickamauga, Ga., Sept. 19-20, 1863	Rosecrans. } Thomas .	57,000	Bragg . . .	71,000	Confed.	Complete control of the Mississippi and of the approaches to Atlanta by Union forces.
	Battle of Chattanooga, Lookout Mountain, Missionary Ridge, Tenn., Nov. 23–25, 1863 . . .	Grant . . } Sherman . } Thomas .	60,000	Bragg . . .	40,000	Union	
Eastern campaign, 1863. Second Confederate invasion of the North, "High Tide of the Confederacy."	Knoxville, Tenn., siege, Nov. 17–Dec. 4, 1863 .	Burnside . } Sherman .	12,000	Longstreet .	20,000	Union	
	Chancellorsville, Va., May 1–4, 1863	Hooker. . .	60,000	Lee	40,000	Confed.	Lee's second attempt to invade the North fails.
	Gettysburg, Pa., July 1–3, 1863	Meade . . .	93,000	Lee	70,000	Union	
Western campaign, 1864-65. To break the industrial power of the South. Sherman's march through Georgia and the Carolinas.	Battles before Atlanta, Ga., July 20, 22, 29, 1864 Capture of Atlanta, Sept. 2, 1864.	Sherman . .	(max'm) 112,000	J.E.Johnston } Hood . . }	(max'm) 71,000	Union	Resources of the Confederacy exhausted. J. E. Johnston surrenders to Sherman at Durham Station, N. C., April 26, 1865.
	Savannah, Ga., surrender, Dec. 21, 1864	Sherman . .	60,000		?	Union	
Eastern campaigns, 1864-65. Final struggle for control of Richmond. The Valley campaign.	Battle of the Wilderness, Va., May 5–7, 1864 . .	Grant . . .	(max'm) 116,000	Lee	(max'm) 61,000	?	
	Spottsylvania Court House, Va., May 8–18, 1864	Grant . . .	66,000	Lee	?	?	
	Opequon (Winchester), Va., Sept. 19, and Fisher's Hill, Va., Sept. 22, 1864	Sheridan . .	(max'm) 43,000	Early . . .	(max'm) 20,000	Union	Fall of Richmond, April 2, 1865.
	Cedar Creek, Va., Oct. 19, 1864	Sheridan . .	31,000	Early . . .	13,000	Union	Complete defeat of the Confederate armies through exhaustion of man power and supplies. Capital of the Confederacy in Union hands. Lee surrenders at Appomattox C. H., April 9, 1865.
	Cold Harbor, Va., June 3, 1864	Grant . . .	103,000	Lee	78,000	Confed.	
	Petersburg, Va., June 15–18, 1864	Grant . . .	(max'm) 110,000	Lee	(max'm) 66,000	Confed.	
	Siege of Petersburg and Richmond, June 22, 1864–April 2, 1865 . .	Grant . . .	(max'm) 124,000	Lee	(max'm) 57,000	Union	
	Five Forks, Va., March 31, 1865	Sheridan . .	?	Pickett. . .	?	Union	

Results of the War: The institution of slavery was abolished within the United States. The Union was preserved, and the supremacy of the Federal government over the states was established.

Congressional Policies. Congress, however, was jealous of the power of the president, and a large Northern element became alarmed at the speedy restoration of the Southern states. In 1865 Congress ignored the work of the president and proceeded to treat the Southern states as rebel territory. This movement was led by Charles Sumner, who was determined at all hazards to do justice to the Negro, and Thaddeus Stevens, who was equally determined to establish Republican power in the South through the command of Negro votes. The 14th amendment was passed, and ratification of this was made a condition of the admission of states to the Union.

Then began, in 1867, the passage of a series of reconstruction acts. The former Confederacy was divided into five military districts. The commanders of these districts had supervision of elections. The result was to bring into power a large, ignorant Negro vote. Anarchy and misgovernment grew throughout the South. The legislatures, without competent leadership and largely influenced by the "carpetbaggers" and "scalawags," made enormous appropriations of money and laid heavy taxes, the proceeds of which were largely wasted by irresponsible adventurers. Enormous state debts were piled up. Most of the taxpaying classes were disfranchised, a condition which intensified the general disturbance.

Restoration of the South. The result of thus displacing Lincoln's moderate diplomacy by an arrogant Congressional scheme of reconstruction was to provoke a countermovement on the part of the Southern whites. This movement was prevented from using legal means of redress, and therefore such organizations as the Ku-Klux Klan were resorted to. During the administration of President Grant, the arbitrary means necessary to maintain Southern Republican and Negro influence became more and more distasteful to the president and to the country. Political rights were restored to all save a few ex-Confederates in 1872, and after the election of 1876 President Hayes withdrew the military forces that had been in control of the elections. The abuses which had attended the Ku-Klux Klan subsided, and white rule was established in all the Southern states.

Impeachment of President Johnson. The conflict between Congress and President Johnson grew more and more intense, until impeachment proceedings were brought against the president in 1868. He was acquitted, though by a very narrow margin, and the country was saved this dangerous precedent of removing a president because he disagreed with Congress.

The Presidency of Grant. The most important feature of Grant's first term was an agreement with England for the settlement of the Alabama claims. President Grant was unfortunate in his selection of officials, but he himself was a vigorous foe of abuses, such as the passing of private pension and relief bills and the wholesale removing of civil officers, a practice which had begun in Jackson's time. He secured a civil service act in 1871, but three years later Congress cut off appropriations for its enforcement, and so destroyed its effect. President Grant's second term was a period of humiliation on account of the inefficiency and corruption revealed in the government. Congressmen and officials were found to have been involved in frauds in connection with Indian affairs, in the financing of the Union Pacific railway, and in the Whisky Ring. One result of these revelations was the appearance of a Democratic majority in the House of Representatives in 1874.

Contested Election of 1876. The presidential election of 1876 proved to be a critical event in American history. On the morning after the election, a Democratic victory was announced by newspapers of both parties, but "carpetbagger" govern-
ments were still in control in Louisiana, Florida, and South Carolina. From these states and from Oregon, rival electors secured credentials, which threw doubt upon the election. The matter was finally referred to an electoral commission of fifteen, which decided all contests by a strictly party vote in favor of the Republicans. Historians generally remark the notable restraint which characterized the people of the United States in this trying situation. The peaceable settlement of the election dispute furnishes a strong assurance of the strength of popular government.

The New Industrial Period. The ten years following the Civil War constituted a period of very rapid commercial and industrial growth throughout the country. It is true that the South had been ruined and devastated by the war, but one of the most admirable features of American history is the heroic manner in which the Southern people returned after defeat to take up the work of rebuilding their homes and industry and of maintaining their civilization. They still had the soil which produced large cotton crops. Soon Northern and foreign capital began to flow in. This made possible the development of water power by which cotton mills could be operated. Alabama possesses large deposits of iron and coal, and the larger use of these resources in manufacturing was begun. Thus a new industrial era was introduced in the South.

The Northern states had developed industrially and commercially under the stress of war necessities. Railroad building had been pushed westward, initiated by the chartering of the Union Pacific in 1862.

Banking and Currency. This was a period of change in banking conditions, through the extension of the national banking system and the organization of trust companies. Large amounts of money became available for investment in land' and for savings in the form of savings bank deposits and of life insurance. Soon after the Civil War, also, a period of speculation set in, which contributed to the bringing on of the panic of 1873. The problem of national currency was difficult after the Civil War, for the greenbacks, or paper money, which had been issued, depreciated in value when the government would not redeem them in gold. But from the government surplus a sum was gradually accumulated in the treasury to redeem the greenbacks, and what is called resumption of specie payment was begun in 1879. About the same time, a demand arose in the West for the restoration of silver coinage, which had been discontinued by act of Congress in 1873. An act providing for a limited coinage of silver was passed in 1878.

Invention and Discovery. The discovery of oil and the invention of new processes for making steel gave rise to the great organizations for producing these two commodities. The inventive genius of Americans, which has been noted before, produced a multitude of new inventions and processes, especially in electricity. The system of making machine parts of standard dimensions led to the specialization and division of labor. The wonders of all this tide of invention and discovery gave occasion for the exposition of 1876 in Philadelphia, where thousands of people saw for the first time the wealth of their own country and of foreign lands. This was also the era of the invention of the telephone and of the rapid extension of the telegraph.

The organization of capital into large units was followed by organizations of labor and by contests between employers and employees, which led to serious disturbances, such as the railroad strike of 1877.

Immigration, which had been checked during the Civil War, was largely increased. Immigrants from Asia as well as from Europe were received. Chinese laborers by the thousand were employed on the new railroads of the West. In 1879, however, a policy of Chinese exclusion was initiated.

Garfield and Civil Service. The election of 1880 placed James A. Garfield in the White House. The Democratic candidate, General Hancock, was supported by the "solid South," the first occasion of a united Southern Democratic vote. Garfield was shot by a half-crazed office seeker, and died September 19, 1881. The vice president, Chester A. Arthur, succeeded to the presidency, and in 1883 a civil service act was passed, which provided for the classified service and for competitive examinations. President Arthur began the enforcement of this act.

Cleveland and the Tariff. In the election of 1884 the Republican candidate, James G. Blaine, was defeated by Grover Cleveland, who became the first Democratic president since Buchanan. Blaine was opposed by the "Mugwumps," the reform element in the Republican party. Cleveland extended the scope of the classified civil service in the face of intense opposition within his own party. He also aroused antagonism by his vetoes of pension bills and of bills for public buildings and for rivers and harbors which he deemed extravagant. His message of December 1887 brought the tariff forward as the dominant issue. A high tariff had been imposed during the Civil War and many of its rates remained even after revision in 1883, the revenue resulting in a surplus accumulating in the national treasury,— an encouragement to extravagance. The real issue was not so much a matter of rates as of policy, whether the tariff should be for protection or primarily for revenue.

The Presidency of Harrison. Cleveland raised the issue of a lower tariff, or a tariff for revenue only, in the campaign of 1888. The Republicans responded by a platform which declared for high protection as a party policy. The Democrats were defeated, and Benjamin Harrison was elected president with a Republican majority in both houses of Congress. Appropriations for pensions were greatly enlarged, as were expenditures for public buildings, and the building of a new navy was carried forward. In October 1890, the McKinley tariff was passed, which raised some duties, but provided a large free list and arranged for reciprocity treaties with foreign nations.

Second Administration of Cleveland. Under the new tariff, prices on many commodities suddenly rose, and, in 1892, in a campaign waged over the tariff issue, Grover Cleveland was again elected president,—this time with a majority in both houses of Congress during the first two years of his term. Cleveland's second administration was an era of hard times. Government revenues dropped. There were many commercial failures throughout the country, and in the West a new movement for free coinage of silver arose. The Democratic Congress passed a new tariff act, which President Cleveland refused to sign, because it contained so many protective duties. Congress also passed an income tax law, which, in 1895, the supreme court declared unconstitutional. A notable feature of Cleveland's second administration was the stand taken by the president and his secretary of state, Richard Olney, upon the Venezuelan boundary question, in maintaining that the interests of the United States under the Monroe Doctrine were involved in Great Britain's refusal to arbitrate. In the election of 1896 the Democratic party was split on the silver question, and William McKinley, the Republican candidate, was elected by a large plurality over the Democratic candidate, William J. Bryan.

Cities. The period from 1860 to 1885 brought before the American people a new set of problems. One serious question was that of city government, rendered more acute by the growth of large cities in the period following the Civil War. With the opportunities for private gain at the expense of the community, corruption was rife in city governments. The infamous Tweed Ring in New York plundered that city of millions of dollars. Since 1890 much has been done to provide efficient systems of city management.

Trusts and Trade-Unions. The second great problem which appeared in this time grew out of the organizing of so-called trusts for the control of certain industries, forming monopolies and able, at their pleasure, to extort high prices and rates. Control of these evils in connection with the railroads began with the Interstate Commerce act of 1887. In 1890 the Sherman Antitrust law was passed. Closely related to the rise of huge industrial combinations of capital were questions connected with the rapid growth of the labor unions and with increasing agitation for the improvement of working conditions.

Immigration. In the last quarter of the 19th century, a marked change came about in respect to the nationalities and the numbers of immigrants who came to America. About 1880, they began to come from southern and central, rather than from northern, Europe. A large number of French Canadians also came into the New England states. Numerous laws were passed, beginning in 1885, to prevent the immigration of "contract labor," paupers, the insane or disabled, or anarchists. Nevertheless, the number of immigrants admitted kept increasing until, in 1907, and again in 1914, it reached its maximum of well over a million.

World Power. The administration of President McKinley was marked by the outbreak of the war with Spain. The most important question which arose out of this short conflict concerned the disposition of the Philippine Islands. The country was sharply divided over the policy of retaining the islands,—one group favoring it, the other opposing such an "imperial policy." In the end, the Philippines were retained under the control of the United States. Another outcome of the war with Spain and the consequent acquisition of the Philippines, together with the annexation of the Hawaiian islands, was the rise of the United States as a world power, with important territorial interests in the Pacific, bringing United States troops into the Boxer Rebellion in 1900 in China.

The New West. No feature of the history of the United States since the Civil War is more important than the building up of the Middle West, the Southwest, and the Far West. During the Civil War a new policy of homesteading was adopted, and after the close of the war great numbers of ex-soldiers took advantage of this act to settle beyond the Mississippi and the Missouri. Gradually, the land was taken up as far as the Rocky Mountain slopes. Several military campaigns were necessary to settle Indian difficulties, as white settlement encroached upon Indian lands. Cattle raising became the great industry upon the plains of the West and Southwest, while the states immediately west of the Mississippi rapidly became the vast granary of the nation.

Several railroad lines were soon completed to the Pacific coast, and a steady tide of migration followed these lines into California, Oregon, and Washington. Out of these newly settled sections, new states were formed after 1888, the last being New Mexico and Arizona in 1912. The settlement of the West opened up new and large sources of wealth. Mines of lead and silver were discovered in the Black hills and in Colorado; large copper deposits were opened in Montana; and the vast forests of the Pacific coast were made available.

Presidency of Theodore Roosevelt. After the assassination of President McKinley, the vice president, Theodore Roosevelt, came into the presidency. Roosevelt was a courageous and outspoken leader in affairs, a man of large experience in city, state, and national government. He increased the classified civil service list until it included about half the civil employees of the government, and during his

WAR WITH SPAIN

Causes: (1) Disorders in Cuba under Spanish rule; (2) Destruction of the battleship *Maine* in Havana harbor.

CAMPAIGNS	Chief Battles	AMERICAN		SPANISH		Victor	Results
		Leaders	Troops	Leaders	Troops		
In the Philippines.	Manila Bay, May 1, 1898.	Dewey . .	(navy)	Montojo . .	(navy)	Amer.	
	Siege of Manila, July 31–Aug. 13, 1898	Merritt . Dewey }	11,000	Jaudenes. .	13,000	Amer	Treaty of peace by which Cuba was freed from Spain; Puerto Rico, Guam, and the Philippines were ceded to the United States. The United States paid to Spain $20,000,000.
		Aguinaldo (insurgents)	12,000				
In Cuba.	El Caney and San Juan Hill, June 30, 1898 . .	Shafter . Wheeler . Lawton . Kent . . }	6,600 8,000	Linares . . Toral . . .	500 4,200	Amer.	
	Santiago Harbor, July 3, 1898	Sampson. Schley . . }	(navy)	Cervera . .	(navy)	Amer.	

administration the consular service was improved by the application of the merit system and by the more general appointment and promotion of experienced men. Roosevelt probably represented the people at large more completely than any president since Jackson, and he acted upon that theory. He used his influence to settle a great coal strike in 1902, and he took an active interest in the direction of prosecution for violations of the Sherman Antitrust act and of other laws dealing with corporations.

Progressive Measures. Probably the most far-reaching influence of the Roosevelt administration is the impulse that the president gave to the conservation of national resources in forests, water power, and other natural forms of wealth. The diplomatic negotiations and the beginning of actual construction in connection with the Panama canal form part of the achievements of Roosevelt's administration. Two very important enlargements of government activity belong to this period: (1) the giving of greater powers to the Interstate Commerce Commission; (2) the extension of government control over the preparation of food products, through what are known as the pure food laws.

Foreign Relations. In international affairs, President Roosevelt brought about the Treaty of Portsmouth between Russia and Japan in 1905. In 1907–09 a fleet of United States battleships made a cruise around the world. American naval prestige was heightened by this demonstration. United States delegates to the Hague Conference in 1907 exerted their influence strongly in favor of proposals for world peace. The president also gave some important applications to the Monroe Doctrine, which he interpreted as implying for the United States a kind of police power in the Western world.

The Presidency of Taft. On the expiration of Roosevelt's second term, William H. Taft was elected president. Mr. Taft came into the presidency with a party divided into two sharply opposed factions,—the progressives, who were strong supporters of the policies urged by Roosevelt, and the conservatives, who were definitely opposed to these policies. The first task of the new administration was the revision of the tariff. The conservative elements of both parties combined to pass the Payne-Aldrich tariff, and Mr. Taft gave the act his approval, thereby alienating progressive Republicans.

Mr. Taft, nevertheless, by his executive orders and through encouragement of legislation, did much to enforce the conservation policy. To this administration belong also the establishment of the parcel post and the postal savings system. Many treaties of arbitration were negotiated, and the constitutional amendments providing for the Federal income tax and for direct election of senators were submitted to the states by Congress. In 1912, the "standpat" Republicans nominated Mr. Taft, while the progressive Republicans, or Progressives, nomi-

nated Theodore Roosevelt, for president. The Republican vote was thus split, and the Democratic candidate, Woodrow Wilson, was elected.

Wilson's Administration. President Wilson's first term was occupied with legislation upon three principal matters: (1) the tariff,—Congress was called in a special session, and the Underwood tariff, intended to produce revenue and to discourage monopoly, was passed in October 1913; (2) banking, —the discussion of this question resulted in the formation of the Federal Reserve banking system; (3) control of corporations,—the president secured the passing of a law which provided for the Federal Trade Commission, and also the Clayton Antitrust act. Mr. Bryan, as secretary of state, initiated an enlarged program of arbitration treaties.

In 1913, the 16th amendment to the Constitution, authorizing an income tax, and the 17th amendment, providing for the election of United States senators by direct vote, were ratified by the states.

World War I. In 1914 World War I broke out. The United States government took a position of strict neutrality. Nevertheless, without any adequate preparation, it was being surely drawn into the circle of the war. Germany's decisive act in the matter was the declaration of unrestricted submarine warfare, January 31, 1917. On April 6, 1917, the United States declared war. At the end of the war, the Versailles Treaty was rejected through a deadlock between the president and the Senate, centering on the question of the League of Nations. See *World War I*.

Constitutional Amendments. In January 1919 the 18th amendment to the Constitution, forbidding the manufacture and sale of intoxicants for beverage purposes, was ratified. In 1920 the 19th amendment, granting equal suffrage to men and women, became a part of the fundamental law of the nation. Of these amendments, the former occasioned ceaseless controversy. A rising tide of opposition bore fruit in 1933 with its repeal by the ratification of the 21st amendment. By the 20th amendment, ratified also in 1933, the presidential and Congressional terms begin in the January following elections.

The Presidency of Harding. In 1920 the Republican candidate, Warren G. Harding, was elected on the issues of oppositions to the League of Nations and "return to normalcy."

Prominent among the achievements of the new administration was the provision for a bureau of the budget. The first general budget was submitted to Congress by President Harding on December 5, 1921. In the same year an international conference was called to consider limitation of armaments. It met at Washington, November 12, 1921. See *Washington Conference*. A treaty of peace with Germany was signed in Berlin on August 25, 1921. President Harding died suddenly on August 2, 1923. Vice President Calvin Coolidge succeeded him.

Coolidge's Administration. The first months of this administration were clouded by irregularities in connection with the leases of the Teapot Dome oil properties. Coolidge was reelected in 1924. Features of his administration were the refunding of the Allied war debts; a measure in 1924 restricting immigration to 150,000 annually; and the multilateral Kellogg treaty of 1928, renouncing war as an instrument of national policy.

Herbert Hoover. Coolidge was succeeded in 1929 by another Republican, Herbert Hoover. He was successful in negotiating a naval limitation treaty with England, Japan, France, and Italy. A serious economic depression, beginning in 1929, was in no way helped by the Smoot-Hawley upward revision of the tariff and little mitigated by measures establishing a Federal Farm Board and the Reconstruction Finance Corporation. In 1932, his Democratic opponent, Franklin D. Roosevelt, promising a "new deal," was elected by a landslide.

The New Deal. Roosevelt's inauguration coincided with a collapse of the banking system. Receiving extraordinary powers from Congress, he speedily effected changes touching every aspect of economic life. To meet the emergency, he initiated measures for caring for the needy, halting bankruptcies, and increasing employment. These were followed by changes designed to guard against recurrence of such crises. Among them were efforts to reopen the channels of foreign trade by reciprocal tariff concessions, taxation policies to prevent concentration of wealth, policing the securities markets, and establishment of a program of social security. The Republican party, opposing these changes and the general trend toward the centralization of national power, was decisively defeated in 1936, its candidate carrying only two states.

The supreme court had declared unconstitutional some of the new deal measures for controlling agriculture and manufacturing. Roosevelt's proposal for conditional enlargement of the supreme court failed in Congress, but changes in the court (between 1937 and 1941 seven of the nine justices died or retired) resulted in more favorable decisions. The presidential campaign of 1940 resulted in the unprecedented election of President Roosevelt for a third term by an electoral vote of 449 to 82 for his Republican opponent, Wendell L. Willkie.

World War II. At the outbreak of the war in Europe in September 1939, the president issued the usual proclamations of neutrality, although both public opinion and the administration were strongly favorable to the Allies. The stringent Neutrality act of 1937 was amended, November 3, 1939, to the advantage of Great Britain and France, allowing sales of munitions on a "cash and carry" basis.

The course of the war in the Atlantic, the danger from Axis influence in Latin America, and above all the fall of France in July 1940, emphasized the nation's weakness in the face of modern war. In January 1940, President Roosevelt asked for nearly two billion dollars for national defense, and special taxes were levied to meet it. Congress passed acts in September 1940 calling out the national guard and reserves and increasing the regular army. A conscription act called men between 21 and 36 into service for one year's training. Arms production was speeded up. The principle of a two-ocean navy was put into operation.

From the beginning the United States adopted a policy of conference and cooperation with Canada and the Latin American nations. In August 1940, the United States and Canada set up a Permanent Joint Board of Defense. Conferences at Panama in September 1939 and at Havana in July 1940, arranged for common action of the American nations. They laid out neutrality zones adjoining the American continent, and would not permit a transfer of other American colonies to non-American powers.

Measures for Defense. Acting on the assumption that American interests lay with the victory of the Allies, and wishing to promote that victory by "measures short of war," President Roosevelt, in September 1940, transferred 50 over-age destroyers to Great Britain, in return for leases of sites for naval and air bases in the Atlantic.

Congress, on the president's recommendation, passed in March 1941 the "Lend-Lease Act," authorizing the president to transfer to other countries, whose defense he regarded as vital to the defense of the United States, war materials and other commodities under arrangements providing for their return or "recompense." The United States was to be an "Arsenal of Democracy." Naturally only a small part of the articles "lent" would ever be returned. By the end of hostilities, the United States in 1946 had loaned goods and munitions amounting to $50,692,000,000, and received in return something over $10 billion.

After the invasion of Denmark, the United States assumed control of Greenland and sent troops to Iceland. The "neutrality patrol" of our coasts was extended. All these transactions involved clashes with the Axis submarine blockade.

Other defense measures included the registration of aliens; the closing of German and Italian consulates to check espionage and propaganda; and the freezing" of the assets of Axis and Axis-occupied countries. Embargoes were laid on the export of war materials required for the national defense.

The War and War Measures. When war came with the Japanese attack on Pearl Harbor, December 7, 1941, it fused the nation into an unprecedented unity of purpose. Japan's allies, Germany and Italy, immediately declared war, and their declarations were answered in kind. The draft age was extended, and 11 million men were drawn into the armed forces. Despite heavy initial losses the navy's strength was tripled. The national debt, on February 15, 1946, reached a peak of $279,496,760,104.49, or $1991.52 per capita.

The special commissions already existing were enlarged and new ones created: the war production board (WPB), organizing production; the war manpower commission (WMC); and the war labor board (WLB), regulating labor and wages; and, with the same purpose of preventing inflation, the office of price administration (OPA) tried to hold down prices, and administered the rationing system. And, as the overlapping and duplication inseparable from piecemeal legislation appeared, the Office of War Mobilization and Rehabilitation (OWMR) was created in 1944 in an attempt to co-ordinate their activities. The number of government employees increased from 932,000 in 1939 to approximately three million in 1945. American production increased phenomenally, supplying America and her allies. (For the military history, see *World War II*.)

President Roosevelt was reelected for a fourth term in 1944, with an electoral vote of 432 to 90 for the Republican candidate, Thomas E. Dewey.

War's End and After. President Roosevelt died on April 12, 1945, and was succeeded by the vice president, Harry S. Truman. But without regard to changes in Washington, the war moved on to a victorious conclusion. In May came the surrender of Germany. On August 14, 1945, President Truman announced to the nation the unconditional surrender of Japan. The latter was hastened by the destruction of two Japanese cities, Hiroshima and Nagasaki, by two atomic bombs, this first use of which constitutes a great divide in the history of warfare.

Under pressure of public opinion, American forces were rapidly repatriated and demobilized. This move created an opportunity for Russia, of which it made the most under Stalin's ambition to spread communism and Russian power throughout the world.

The United States played a leading part in the formation, at San Francisco in 1945, of the United Nations, an organization in which hopes were placed for prevention of future wars. Almost at once it

Name of State or Territory	Origin and Meaning of Name	Date of Admission or Acquisition	Settlement*			Area in Square Miles	Population When Admitted or Acquired
			Where	When	By Whom		
Alabama	Indian—Thicket Cutters. Erroneously thought to mean, "Here We Rest."	1819	Mobile Bay	1702	French	51,609	127,901
Alaska	Indian—Al-ay-ek-sa, meaning Great Country	1867	Kodiak	1783	Russians	590,884	126,661
Arizona	Indian—Place of Little Springs	1912	Tucson	1776	Spanish	113,909	204,354
Arkansas	From a tribe of Indians	1836	Arkansas Post	1685	French	53,102	97,574
California	First used in a Spanish romance, 1510	1850	San Diego	1769	Spanish	158,693	92,597
Canal Zone	Strip of land bordering Panama Canal	1904	Panama	1519	Spanish	436	......
Colorado	Spanish—Red, or Colored	1876	Auraria	1859	Americans	104,247	39,864
Connecticut	Indian—Long Tidal River	1788†	Windsor	1633	English	5,009	237,946
Delaware	Named for Lord Delaware	1787†	Wilmington	1638	Swedes	2,057	59,096
District of Columbia	From poetic name of United States	1791	Georgetown	1695	Scotch and Irish	69	......
Florida	Spanish—Flowery	1845	St. Augustine	1565	Spanish	58,560	87,445
Georgia	Named for George II	1788†	Savannah	1733	English	58,876	82,548
Guam	Spanish Guajan—Juan	1898		1688	Spanish	210	......
Hawaii	Hawaii—Big Island	1898	Honolulu	1820	Americans	6,449	109,020
Idaho	Indian—Gem of the Mountains	1890	Cœur d'Alene	1842	Americans	83,557	88,548
Illinois	Indian—The People	1818	Kaskaskia	1700 ?	French	56,400	55,211
Indiana	Indian's Ground	1816	Vincennes	1727	French	36,291	147,178
Iowa	Indian—Drowsy Ones	1846	Dubuque	1833	Americans	56,280	192,214
Kansas	From a tribe of Indians	1861	Leavenworth	1854	Americans	82,276	107,206
Kentucky	Indian—Prairie. Not "Dark and Bloody Ground."	1792	Boonesboro	1775	English	40,395	73,677
Louisiana	Named for Louis XIV	1812	New Orleans	1718	French	48,523	76,556
Maine	The Main Land	1820	Saco, Monhegan	1622 ?	English	33,215	298,335
Maryland	Named for Queen Henrietta Maria	1788†	St. Mary's	1634	English	10,577	319,728
Massachusetts	The Place of Great Hills	1788†	Plymouth	1620	English	8,257	378,787
Michigan	Indian—Great Water or Lake	1837	Sault Ste. Marie	1668	French	58,216	212,267
Minnesota	Indian—Cloudy Water	1858	St. Paul	1838	Americans	84,068	172,023
Mississippi	Indian—Great River, or Father of Waters	1817	Biloxi	1699	French	47,716	75,448
Missouri	Indian—Great Muddy	1821	St. Genevieve	1735	French	69,674	66,586
Montana	Spanish—A Mountain	1889	Yellowstone River	1809	Americans	147,138	142,924
Nebraska	Indian—Shallow Water	1867	Bellevue	1847	Americans	77,237	122,993
Nevada	Spanish—Snow-covered	1864	Genoa	1850	Americans	110,540	42,491
New Hampshire	Hampshire, England	1788†	Portsmouth	1623	English	9,304	141,885
New Jersey	Named in compliment to the governor of Jersey Island	1787†	Elizabethtown	1617	Dutch	7,836	184,139
New Mexico	Mexitl, Aztec war god	1912	San Gabriel	1598	Spanish	121,666	327,301
New York	Named for the duke of York	1788†	New York	1613	Dutch	49,576	340,120
North Carolina	Named for Charles II	1789†	Albemarle Sound	1653	English	52,712	393,751
North Dakota	Indian—Allied	1889	Pembina	1859	Americans	70,665	190,983
Ohio	Indian—Beautiful River	1803	Marietta	1788	Americans	41,222	45,365
Oklahoma	Indian—Land of Red Men	1907	Guthrie (Land rush)	1889	Americans	69,919	1,414,042
Oregon	Spanish—Wild Marjoram	1859	Astoria	1811	Americans	96,981	52,465
Pennsylvania	Latin—Penn's Woodland	1787†	Chester	1638	Swedes	45,333	434,373
Puerto Rico	Spanish—Rich Port	1898	Pueblo Viejo	1508	Spanish	3,435	813,937
Rhode Island	Rhodes, an island in the Ægean Sea	1790†	Providence	1636	English	1,214	68,825
Samoan Islands, Tutuila and Manua	From Sa-ia-moa, meaning Sacred to Moa	1899		1830	English	58	5,000‡
South Carolina	Named for Charles II	1788†	Ashley River	1670	English	31,055	393,751
South Dakota	Indian—Allied	1889	Southeast part	1859	Americans	77,047	348,600
Tennessee	Indian—Cherokee Indian Town, Tennassee	1796	Watauga	1769	Americans	42,246	35,691
Texas	Indian—Hello, Friend	1845	San Antonio	1692	Spanish	267,339	212,592
Utah	Indian—Mountain Dwellers	1896	Salt Lake City	1847	Americans	84,916	210,779
Vermont	French—Green Mountain	1791	St. Anne	1665	French	9,609	85,425
Virgin Islands	Named in honor of St. Ursula and her companions	1917	St. Croix	1625 ?	Dutch and English	149	26,051
Virginia	Named for Elizabeth, the Virgin Queen	1788†	Jamestown	1607	English	40,815	747,610
Washington	Named for George Washington	1889	Columbia River	1811	English	68,192	357,232
West Virginia	From Virginia	1863	Berkeley County	1726-7	Americans	24,181	442,014
Wisconsin	Indian—Meaning unknown	1848	Green Bay	1745	French	56,154	305,391
Wyoming	Indian—The Plain	1890	Cheyenne	1867	Americans	97,914	62,555

* Exact dates and places of first permanent settlements are frequently difficult to determine; authorities differ.
† Dates of ratification of the Constitution by the Thirteen Original States.   ‡ Estimate.

became apparent that this institution was powerless before a split among the most powerful nations. Russia and the United States were now the two greatest powers and the world's history was played out within the framework of their antagonism for succeeding decades.

Russian Advances. Russia's power lay in its messianic promises of a better social order reinforced by the Communist party, a close-knit secret organization of converts in every land, who had allegiance only to the Russian head of the party. The members were trained to take advantage of social disorders and seize political power. The strategy worked where the Russian army was already occupying the country, as in Poland, Rumania, Bulgaria, Albania, Hungary, and Yugoslavia. Its presence on the border permitted the takeover of Czechoslovakia in 1948. Greece was threatened. There were strong communist parties in Italy and France and weaker ones in other countries.

The American defense and counter attack against Communism took three chief forms—the so-called Truman doctrine of containment, the Marshall Plan for restoring western Europe's strength, and a system of military alliances.

The Truman Doctrine. In 1947, President Truman set forth, and Congress implemented, the policy of supporting free peoples who are resisting attempted subjugation by armed minorities or by outside pressures. Applied first to combat communist pressure in Greece and Turkey, this strategy was enlarged in 1949 by Truman's so-called "Point Four" policy of supplying economic and technical aid to underdeveloped countries.

The Marshall Plan. This plan grew out of a proposal made in a speech at Harvard University in June 1947 by General George C. Marshall, then secretary of state. He proposed that the countries of Europe as a unit survey their resources and find out what they could do toward reconstruction. The United States then would decide what it could provide in long-term loans or gifts to meet these needs.

Russia refused to participate and forbade her satellites to do so. But Great Britain and France called the Conference of European Economic Co-operation at Paris in July 1947. Sixteen countries were represented, and a program of rehabilitation needs was drawn up.

In April 1948, Congress accepted the program and appropriated $5,300 million for the first year's work. It was administered initially by an agency known as the Economic Co-operation Administration. With this fructifying assistance, Europe's rich human and technical resources sufficed to bring western Europe within a few years to a level of prosperity never before known. The communist, non-participating states lagged far behind, and the communist gospel lost its appeal in the more advanced nations.

The Marshall Plan and the Truman doctrine set the pattern for a continuing program of foreign aid, sometimes economic and sometimes military, administered, since 1961, by the Agency for International Development. The idea spread to other nations. Leading European nations formed an organization with similar purpose, and this was enlarged in 1961 to include the United States and Canada, with Japan, Yugoslavia, and Finland as associate members. Finally Russia also was prompted to institute aid programs.

The Western Alliance. The need for a military alliance against Russia became apparent immediately after the war. Under armistice terms, Germany was to be occupied jointly by American, Russian, British, and French troops, each within a separate zone. Berlin itself was likewise zoned. But the controlling body was paralyzed by Russian intransigence, obviously aimed at forcing western withdrawal. The Russian-occupied territory became the satellite state of East Germany, whose territory isolated Berlin but through which access

NEGRO POPULATION BY STATES

State	1950	1960	1970
Alabama	979,617	980,271	908,247
Alaska	(*)	6,771	8,911
Arizona	25,974	43,403	53,344
Arkansas	426,639	388,787	357,225
California	462,172	883,861	1,400,143
Colorado	20,177	39,992	66,411
Connecticut	53,472	107,449	181,177
Delaware	43,598	60,688	78,276
Dist. of Col.	280,803	411,737	537,712
Florida	603,101	880,186	1,049,578
Georgia	1,062,762	1,122,596	1,190,779
Hawaii	2,651	4,943	7,573
Idaho	1,050	1,502	2,130
Illinois	645,980	1,037,470	1,425,674
Indiana	174,168	269,275	357,464
Iowa	19,692	25,354	32,596
Kansas	73,158	91,445	106,977
Kentucky	201,921	215,949	241,292
Louisiana	882,428	1,039,207	1,088,734
Maine	1,221	3,318	2,800
Maryland	385,972	518,410	701,341
Massachusetts	73,171	111,842	175,817
Michigan	442,296	717,581	991,066
Minnesota	14,022	22,263	34,868
Mississippi	986,494	915,743	815,770
Missouri	297,088	390,853	480,172
Montana	1,232	1,467	1,995
Nebraska	19,234	29,262	39,911
Nevada	4,302	13,484	27,762
New Hampshire	731	1,903	2,505
New Jersey	318,565	514,875	770,292
New Mexico	8,408	17,063	19,555
New York	918,191	1,417,511	2,166,933
North Carolina	1,047,353	1,116,021	1,137,664
North Dakota	257	777	2,494
Ohio	513,072	786,094	970,477
Oklahoma	145,503	153,084	177,907
Oregon	11,529	18,133	26,308
Pennsylvania	638,485	852,750	1,016,514
Rhode Island	13,903	18,352	25,338
South Carolina	822,077	829,291	789,041
South Dakota	727	1,114	1,627
Tennessee	530,603	586,876	631,696
Texas	977,458	1,187,125	1,419,677
Utah	2,729	4,148	6,617
Vermont	443	519	761
Virginia	734,211	816,258	865,388
Washington	30,691	48,738	71,308
West Virginia	114,867	89,378	73,931
Wisconsin	28,182	74,546	128,224
Wyoming	2,557	2,183	2,568
Total	15,044,937	18,871,831	22,672,570

* Not available.

to Berlin was guaranteed by the armistice terms. In April 1948, the Russians blocked the road, rail, and water routes to Berlin. The western allies backed away from opening them by force but conducted a massive "air-lift" by means of which the city was supplied with necessities. The Russians withdrew the blockade.

The immediate fruit of this incident was the formation of the North Atlantic Treaty Organization by 12 nations, which organized a military and naval force to defend each and all of them against aggression. See *North Atlantic Treaty*.

Communist Challenge in Asia. After Japan surrendered in 1945, it was occupied by American forces under General MacArthur. In 1949, the Communist party obtained control of continental China, driving out the president, Chiang Kai-shek, whom the United States had supported during the war and subsequent to it. Chiang Kai-shek set up his government in Taiwan (Formosa); an American fleet was directed to resist an attack against it, and the United States gave it extensive military aid.

Korea, a possession of Japan before the war, was occupied in the north by Russian troops and in the south by Americans. In 1950, the North Koreans invaded South Korea without warning and in great force. Eventually they were driven back. The defensive operation was technically a police action by the UN, but the U.S. carried most of the burden.

As in Europe, the answer to Communist aggression was an alliance, and the U.S. entered into the Southeast Asia Collective Defense Treaty in 1954 with Britain, Australia, New Zealand, the Philippines, France, Pakistan, and Thailand.

The postwar change of British, French, and Dutch colonies in southeast Asia to independent nations created troubled waters in which Communist and American influences confronted each other. Most of the new states were established peaceably with no Communist takeover, but Viet-Nam, made up of former French dependencies, was the theater of a long, costly war, in which Communist foes drove out the French. The U.S. intervened and the territory was divided between Communist North Viet-Nam and the state of South Viet-Nam.

Economic Expansion. The transition from war to peace was relatively smooth. The millions demobilized from the armed forces were readily absorbed into employment since pent-up demands for goods supported rapid industrial expansion. The cuts in defense spending were less than had been expected. Russian and later Chinese aggressiveness made it clear that the world had entered a period of cold war, with the U.S. as the acknowledged champion of non-Communist nations. America supplied most of the strength of the North Atlantic Treaty Organization.

The character of war itself had changed since the advent of the atom bomb. Money was poured into nuclear projects and the first hydrogen bomb was exploded as a test in 1953. Until 1949, the U.S. had an atomic monopoly, but when Russia exploded its first bomb in that year, U.S. efforts in atomic weaponry were speeded to the utmost. Then, after Russia electrified the world by orbiting the first artificial satellite in 1957, billions of dollars were voted toward achieving leadership in space.

Perhaps the chief cause of the postwar industrial buildup in the U.S. was the unprecedented amount of money and effort spent on research in nearly every area of life. New miracle drugs unlocked means of prolonging life; new products were developed and older ones improved and put to new uses; many human heart transplants were made following the first successful transplant to Dr. Philip Blaiberg, a dentist in South Africa. Finally, electronic computers were developed that were capable of performing mechanically innumerable operations.

Economic Problems. These developments did not come about without inflation and other dislocations. As price controls were removed, prices rose. In 1945 and 1946, strikes affected most of the large industries. In 1946, with quick congressional approval, Truman seized the railroads to prevent a work stoppage. The general effect was an increase in wages of about 18 per cent in the two years, while consumer prices rose about 20 per cent.

Further inflation came with the outbreak of the Korean War in 1950; U.S. consumer prices rose by 8 per cent, but for the next decade they were relatively stable, increasing by about 12 per cent.

When Dwight Eisenhower succeeded Truman in 1953, federal expenses were cut back, and a mild recession followed. Other recessions followed later, but none was as severe as those earlier in the century. Remedies devised under the New Deal and elaborated later appeared to have had their effect.

In Eisenhower's second term, a new problem arose—a steady loss of gold, on which the currency is based. This was due to the excess of U.S. spending abroad over purchases made at home, the main items of such expense being foreign aid, foreign investments abroad (chiefly in the expanding economies of western Europe), and a phenomenal increase in American travel abroad. Yet the balance of trade continued favorable. Measures begun by Eisenhower and continued by his successors, along with co-operation by other countries, appeared to have stabilized the situation by 1964.

Communist Spy Scare. The struggle with communism abroad was accompanied by a spy scare at home. The Federal Bureau of Investigation, with little publicity, brought about conviction in a number of cases. Congressional committees had for many years held public hearings in which charges were given the widest publicity against individuals without the safeguards customary in the courts. They led to a few convictions, most notably that of Alger Hiss, found guilty of perjury in denying that he, when an official in the State Department, had given data from the Department's files to a Russian agent. But the name most prominent during the espionage hearing was that of Sen. Joseph R. McCarthy (R., Wis.). His charges of treason against high and low finally led to his downfall in 1954. The Senate found him guilty of contempt in connection with investigation of charges brought against him by the Army.

Desegregation. On May 17, 1954, the Supreme Court ruled that segregation in public schools was unconstitutional and decreed that desegregation be effected with all reasonable speed. The Court made it clear that it considered the Constitution forbade discrimination because of race in all legal rights and privileges. Thereafter, for the first time Negro leaders took the initiative in demanding rights denied them because of race, and their demands were backed up by the federal government. Resistance was threatened in parts of the South, but at Little Rock, Ark. and elsewhere it disappeared in the presence of federal troops. In some places organized boycotts of stores or public transportation were used to force desegregation. On restaurants that excluded Negroes, pressure was brought through "sit-ins." Segregationists resorted to all possible legal means in return, and there was sporadic violence. But slow, relentless pressure worked toward gradual elimination of discrimination. A Civil Rights Act was passed in 1964. In ensuing years came Black Power groups, violence and riots in ghettoes in major cities, and the assassination of the Negro leader Rev. Martin Luther King, Jr. on April 4, 1968. The response of city, state, and federal government to these problems was increased welfare activities, and the issues of Negroes vs. whites became a campaign issue in the election of 1968, with third-party presidential candidate George Wallace as an outspoken champion of "law and order" in the troubled cities.

Eisenhower's Administration. With Eisenhower as their candidate, the Republicans came to power in 1952. The nation had already evinced a more conservative mood, and Eisenhower's policies accorded with the mood. Nevertheless, many measures dating from the New Deal era were expanded. Social security benefits were increased. Minimum wages were raised. Under Eisenhower also the Department of Health, Education and Welfare was created; Congress voted to participate with Canada in building the St. Lawrence Seaway; coastal states were granted title to submerged lands along their borders with the right to obtain oil from them; a public housing measure was passed; and aid for agriculture took the form of a soil bank. Alaska and Hawaii were admitted as states. A 79-nation agreement on atoms for peace was approved.

Eisenhower was the first president affected by the constitutional amendment of 1951 that barred a third term. The republicans nominated Richard M. Nixon, who lost a close election in 1960 to Democratic nominee John F. Kennedy.

Kennedy and Johnson. The outstanding event of the Kennedy administration was the confrontation of Russia over the installation in Cuba of Russian missiles capable of carrying atomic warheads. Castro had seized power in Cuba in 1959. He declared himself a Communist and invited Russian aid. Air reconnaissance in 1962 revealed long-range missiles in Cuba. Kennedy, seeing that the balance of power would thus shift to Russia, ordered a military blockade of Cuba on Oct. 22, 1962, warning Russia that an atomic missile fired from Cuba would bring massive retaliation against the U.S.S.R. Premier Khrushchev withdrew the missiles.

Kennedy's policies favoring closer political union among western European countries as a stronger bulwark against Communism were balked in early 1963 when French President De Gaulle prevented Britain's entrance into the common market. Some of Kennedy's domestic policies were also blocked when Congress refused to pass (1) a Medicare bill to have Social Security funds provide medical care for the aged, (2) stronger civil rights legislation, and (3) federal aid for education. But he succeeded in obtaining a new aid program for Latin America (the Alliance for Progress), and the Peace Corps to train volunteers to aid underdeveloped nations. President Kennedy's career was cut off when, on Nov. 22, 1963, he was shot and killed in Dallas, Tex.

Vice President Lyndon B. Johnson succeeded to the presidency, achieving further goals of the Kennedy program—Medicare, civil rights legislation, large-scale federal aid to education. He also secured the establishment of two new cabinet posts—for Urban Affairs and for Transportation. Calling for a war against poverty, he envisaged a program to realize what he called the Great Society. Meanwhile, aid to South Vietnam grew into a costly war of a novel type, and its prosecution was pushed vigorously despite wide domestic criticism. The close of the Johnson Administration was marked by a halt in the bombing of North Vietnam and by increased stress on peace talks.

Nixon and Watergate. The 1968 election issues reflected persisting problems—student violence, strikes, the unpopular Vietnam war, and the overall issue of civil rights, marked by riots and by the assassination of Martin Luther King, Jr.

In 1968 Richard Nixon defeated Hubert Humphrey for the presidency; in 1972 he was re-elected by a landslide over George McGovern. U.S. participation in the Vietnam war ended. Yet inflation and unemployment remained major concerns. Nixon continued the detente with Russia and negotiated a truce in the Middle East warfare. In 1973 he made a state visit to Communist China, which was then recognized by the U.S. and joined the UN. In the same year Spiro Agnew resigned the vice presidency, after he had failed to contest charges of income-tax evasion. To counter rising inflation, Nixon vetoed a series of congressional acts, impounded committed funds, and tried economic controls.

In Nixon's second term the Watergate affair came to a head. Burglary and wiretaps of the Democratic headquarters were revealed and congressional inquiries continued in 1973–74. Members of Nixon's staff were tried and presidential tape recordings were aired. Congress then formed a committee to probe the question of impeachment. Citing White House privilege, tapes were withheld. The Supreme Court ruled against the action and further evidence was bared. Nixon then admitted acts of omission. On Aug. 9, 1974, he resigned, the first U.S. president to do so.

Ford as President. Gerald R. Ford, who had been appointed to replace Spiro Agnew, succeeded Nixon in the White House. Ford continued Nixon's foreign policy, retaining Henry Kissinger as Secretary of State. With inflation as the foremost concern, Ford held a series of economic-planning meetings. He appointed Nelson Rockefeller as vice president, granted full pardon to former president Nixon, and extended limited amnesty to resisters of the Vietnamese war. In the 1974 elections Ford campaigned vigorously for Republican candidates for office. In 1975 refugees were airlifted from South Vietnam as the threat from the North increased. Then the North Vietnamese victory ended the war in Asia. In the same year Ford announced his candidacy for the 1976 elections, and survived unhurt in a series of attempted assassinations.

The elements of the final design of the American flag were already in common use in the colonies. The red and white stripes were in the Dutch flag which flew over New Netherlands from 1609 to 1664. The Great Union flag, raised Jan. 1, 1776, on Prospect Hill, Somerville, Mass., followed the design of a British merchant marine flag—13 alternating red and white stripes for the 13 colonies with a union in which appeared the crosses of St. George and St. Andrew on a blue field. Contemporary prints show no stars before 1780.

The Stars and Stripes. After the declaration of independence, the design of stars and stripes, known as the Betsy Ross flag, was presented to the Congress for consideration. On June 14, 1777, the Continental Congress passed the following resolution: "Resolved, That the flag of the United States be thirteen stripes, alternate red and white, that the union be thirteen stars, white in a blue field, representing a new constellation."

On January 15, 1794, Congress, in order to adapt the flag to the new number of states, 15 after the admission of Vermont and Kentucky, enacted "that from and after May 1, 1795, the flag of the United States be fifteen stripes, alternate red and white and the union be fifteen stars, white in a blue field." In 1818 the number of stripes was reduced to the original number, and Congress ordered that the number of stars should correspond to the number of states, a star to be added on the 4th of July next following the admission of a new state.

Various arrangements of the stars were used at different times. On July 4, 1960, the 50-star flag was officially raised on Independence Hall, Philadelphia.

The name of *Old Glory* was given by Captain William Driver of Salem, Mass., in 1831 to an American flag preserved in the Smithsonian Institution, Washington. It has 24 stars and an anchor.

Instruction in the symbolic and historical meanings of the flag is part of the work of every American school. The first recorded raising of the flag over a school, now so general a custom, took place on Catamount hill, Colrain, Mass., in May 1812. A monument marks the site of the old log schoolhouse. June 14, the anniversary of the Congressional adoption of the stars and stripes, is widely observed as Flag Day. The following pledge, first suggested by Francis Bellamy, in 1892, adopted by Congress December 22, 1942 and amended in 1954 by adding the words "under God," is a part of school program and Flag Day exercises:

"I pledge allegiance to the flag of the United States of America and to the Republic for which it stands, one Nation under God, indivisible, with liberty and justice for all."

Bunker Hill Flags. As early as the year 1737, a recognized flag of the New England colonies had a blue field with a white union quartered by a red cross. Such a flag, with the addition of a green pine tree in the upper inner quarter of the union, was carried at the battle of Bunker Hill.

Flag of Lexington and Concord. In the fight at Concord and Lexington, Captain Nathaniel Page, of the Bedford Minutemen, carried a maroon-colored flag, upon which was the motto *Vince Aut Morire*, meaning "Conquer or Die." This flag is preserved in the town of Bedford, Mass., and is known as the Bedford flag.

Rattlesnake Flags. The device of a rattlesnake, usually represented coiled and ready to strike, was popular with the American colonists just before the Revolution. The flag of the Culpepper Minutemen carried this symbol, together with the two inscriptions—"Don't Tread on Me" and "Liberty or Death." It appeared also on a yellow banner presented to Congress by Col. Gadsden on Feb. 8, 1776.

Crescent Flags. In the southern colonies, during the early part of the Revolution, a blue flag, having in its upper inner corner a white crescent, was popular. The first use of this design as a distinctively American emblem is credited to Colonel William Moultrie, who hoisted a crescent flag over Fort Johnson, on James island, South Carolina, September 13, 1775. The crescent flags sometimes bore the word "Liberty" in white letters.

Pine Tree Flags. The design of a green pine tree was a favorite emblem in colonial New England. The Sons of Liberty are said to have unfurled on Harvard College campus in 1770 a plain red flag, upon which later a green pine tree design was sewed. On some New England flags, the tree had a serpent coiled around the trunk. Below the design were the words "Don't Tread on Me," and above was the inscription "An Appeal to Heaven."

Flag of Philadelphia Light Horse. It is believed that this flag was carried by the troop that escorted General Washington from Philadelphia to New York, in June 1775, when he was on his way to take command of the army at Cambridge. The banner, now in possession of the Philadelphia City Cavalry, has a canton of thirteen stripes, alternating blue and silver.

The Continental Flag. This name is applied to the Grand Union flag described in the first paragraph of this article. It was the first use of the 13 alternating stripes of white and of red.

The Betsy Ross Flag. This was the first flag combining the stars and stripes. It contained thirteen five-pointed stars arranged in a circle on a blue field. This is said to have been the design authorized for the official flag by the Continental Congress, June 14, 1777. The design was produced by a committee of Congress, consisting of General Washington, Robert Morris, and Colonel George Ross, with the assistance of Betsy Ross.

The Bennington Flag. This banner was unique among Revolutionary flags. It was made of homespun linen; its union was nine stripes in depth instead of seven; its stars were seven-pointed instead of five-pointed, and they were arranged in an arch rather than in a circle. It was probably made near Bennington and carried into the battle of Bennington by Nathaniel Fillmore, August 16, 1777.

Eutaw Flag. A crimson banner with a romantic history, presented in 1780 to Colonel William A. Washington by Miss Jane Elliott, of South Carolina, whom he later married. It was carried in the battles of Cowpens and Eutaw Springs. Mrs. Washington later presented this flag to the Washington Light Infantry of Charleston, S. C.

Flag of the Bon Homme Richard. It is said that some young women of Portsmouth, N. H., made this flag for Captain John Paul Jones from pieces of their silk gowns. The name of the *Bon Homme Richard* attaches to this flag because of the fact that it was the ensign of that ship in the famous battle with the *Serapis*, September 23, 1779, when Captain Jones captured the *Serapis*, although he lost his own unseaworthy vessel. When the *Bon Homme Richard*, riddled with shot, sank beside the *Serapis*, the flag was still flying at her masthead.

Commodore Perry's Flag. This flag, flown at the battle of Lake Erie, September 10, 1813, contained the words of the dying Lawrence, "Don't give up the ship," which have become the watchword of the American navy.

Flag of Fort McHenry. The flag which waved over the American defenses during the British bombardment on the night of September 13, 1814, inspired the writing of the "Star-Spangled Banner." The pattern of this flag, fifteen stripes and fifteen stars, is that authorized by Congress in 1794.

THE DEMOCRATIC PARTY

The Democratic party had its origin coincidently with the beginning of the republic. Thomas Jefferson was its first leader and spokesman. The elements of the party existed when the Constitution was adopted. Its earliest representatives were opponents of the Constitution, who objected that the government was being centralized and that it was organized to favor the privileged classes. Calling themselves "Antifederalists" at first, they were known by 1792 as the Democratic-Republican (or "Republican") party.

This party was made up of men who, like Jefferson, were theoretical believers in the rights of the people, and of those without wealth or position, many of whom had previously been disfranchised. Jefferson stated their principles as follows: ". . . to maintain the will of the majority. We believed that man was a rational animal endowed by nature with rights and with an innate sense of justice; and that he could be restrained from wrong and protected in right, by moderate powers confided to persons of his own choice, and held to their duties by dependence on their own will."

Early Power and Principles. The "Republican" party opposed the Federalists. In 1792, it carried Congress and numerous local elections, but did not oppose Washington for his second term as president. In 1797, it received 68 electoral votes in comparison with the Federalists' 71, and Jefferson became vice president. The party opposed the Alien and Sedition laws of 1798 as dangerous assertions of power by the central government. It elected Jefferson president and Burr vice president in 1800, and re-elected Jefferson in 1804.

The "Republican" party ceased to oppose the Constitution after the first ten amendments were made. However, it continually opposed such extensions of Federal power as were construed by Chief Justice John Marshall to be constitutional.

The elections of 1808 and 1812, when Madison was elected president, indicated general acceptance of the "Republican" party. The Federalist party nearly disappeared in most of the states, and it ceased to exist as a national body after its futile opposition to the War of 1812. At the close of that conflict, the country was in a strong financial condition. The "Republicans" accepted the idea of a national government, and the former Federalists generally acted with the only party now in existence. Monroe was elected president in 1816 and again in 1820; John Quincy Adams, a former Federalist, was elected in 1824.

The Democratic Party of Jackson. Up to this period in American history, nearly every one elected to conspicuous public office, no matter what his belief in the rights, powers, and privileges of the common people, had been a man of wealth, education, and family. From some of the newer districts, however, especially of the West, men who owed little to such advantages had come to Congress. In 1828, Andrew Jackson, a man of this style, was elected to the presidency. His followers were first called "Jackson men" and then "Democrats." Democracy was no longer a theory, but was exemplified. Although the principles of Jefferson continued to be followed, the agents were new.

Jackson, re-elected in 1832, put down nullification, secured a lowering of the tariff, and destroyed the Bank of the United States. Van Buren, his trusted friend, followed him in the presidency. But, in 1840, after the panic of 1837 had occasioned widespread dissatisfaction with the Democrats, William Henry Harrison, the representative of a new party, the Whigs, was elected.

Democrats and Whigs. Until 1856 the Democrats and Whigs contested the elections. There was no sharp sectional division, but everywhere there were Democratic districts alongside the more conservative or aristocratic regions which voted Whig. In principle, the Democrats opposed high tariffs and Federal aid for internal improvement. After 1840 the Democratic party definitely aligned itself as opposed to interference with slavery.

The Divided Party. The slavery question finally overshadowed all others. It caused a split in Democratic ranks in 1848, when Lewis Cass became the regular Democratic candidate, while antislavery Democrats joined with the Free Soilers in supporting Van Buren. In the years from 1852 to 1856, the same issue broke up the Whig party. The new opposition party was called Republican. It drew most of its supporters from the North and West; the Democratic party was strongest in the South.

In 1860 the Democratic party had two candidates, one Northern, one Southern. The Republicans won. The Southern states seceded, but the ensuing Civil War resulted both in the preservation of the Union and in the destruction of slavery. At the end of the struggle, the Northern Democrats were weak and discredited; the Southern Democrats were disfranchised. Not until 1874 was there much chance of victory. In that year the party won in the Congressional elections. In 1876, it won a popular victory for the presidency, but was not awarded the electoral votes by the electoral commission.

Cleveland and Bryan. In the 1880's, the question of civil service reform and of reform of the tariff became prominent. In 1884, the Democrats won, largely on these issues. They received a large Republican vote, dubbed "Mugwump," made up chiefly of men who feared and disliked Blaine and approved Cleveland's record on civil service. Cleveland was the victor. He was defeated in 1888 only to be elected again in 1892. In his second term came financial depression.

Dissatisfaction with the capitalists, moneyed interests, banks, and railroads was rife among large sections of the people. Free coinage of silver was seized upon as a method of relief. The silver men, under the lead of William Jennings Bryan, captured the Democratic party and won most of the Western states as well as the South. But the conservatives or standpatters, especially in the East, went solidly into the Republican party. The term "sound money" won for the Republicans in 1896.

By 1900, the Spanish American war had been fought, and the demand for the retention of the Philippines was so strong that the anti-imperialistic and free silver platform of the Democrats carried but few states. In 1904, the Democrats swung to a conservative candidate, but the progressive measures adopted by the Republicans gave Roosevelt the victory, and the success of their policy carried the country again in 1908.

Wilson to Carter. From 1908 to 1912, the progressive element revived among Democrats, and the Republicans were divided. In the 1912 election, the Republicans split, and Wilson won. In the close 1916 contest he was re-elected, his second term marked by U.S. entry into World War I and the ensuing Peace Treaty. The war's end left wide unrest and the Democrats lost in 1920. The Republicans rode the wave of prosperity in the 1920's, but with the depression the country turned to the Democrats, electing Franklin D. Roosevelt in 1932. Re-elected three times, he led the U.S. through great social and economic reforms and the critical era of World War II. Though losing control of Congress, the party won with Truman in 1948 but lost to Eisenhower in 1952 and 1956. Eight years of conservative Republican leadership were followed by the 1960 election of John F. Kennedy, whose championship of a "new frontier" policy ended with his assassination in 1963. His successor, Lyndon Johnson, with party strength in Congress, pursued like aims, enlarging them under his "great society" slogan. The problems of civil rights and the Vietnam war continued as major issues into the campaign year of 1968, with Johnson announcing he would not seek another term. The Democratic convention in Chicago was marked by unprecedented antiwar violence and the Democrats, with Hubert Humphrey as candidate, lost the election by a narrow margin. The old Democratic coalitions took second place to the "new Democrat" at the 1972 convention—new rules provided for the seating of more women, young people, and minorities. With the party split, candidate George McGovern, hindered by a reputation of "indecisive radicalism," lost the 1972 election by a landslide.

A major issue in the 1976 presidential campaign was the restoring of trust and confidence in the federal government. Democrat Jimmy Carter, the first major-party candidate from the Deep South since 1848, won the election by a narrow margin.

Democratic Principles. In all its history, the party has stood for the rights of the people. It opposed the "rich, the well-born, and the able" in Washington's time; it advocated extension of the suffrage; it opposed the manufacturers and the bankers. It was strong on the frontier and on the farms and among the mechanics. When it became associated with the slave interests, it had an aristocratic element that came to dominate the party. After the Civil War, the party reverted to its old principles, although with a tendency to adopt radical proposals in opposition to the Republicans.

The Democratic party throughout most of its history opposed a loose construction of the Constitution. Its leaders felt that those in control of capital would find the Federal government easier to influence than the numerous state governments. Consequently they opposed enlargement of Federal power, a result most easily secured through a loose interpretation of the language of the basic law. In the party's first years, its leaders could see no justification for a national bank, for protective tariffs, or for government interference with state functions. The party believed also in states rights, although it was not willing to go as far as nullification in 1832.

On the other hand, the Democratic party, under strong leaders, has been vigorous in its national policy. Jefferson, having purchased Louisiana, found the leaders of his party in Congress prepared to surpass him in a broad construction of the Constitution to justify an act not expressly provided for. Jackson, faced by the threat of nullification in South Carolina, declared: "The Federal Union, it must and shall be preserved." Cleveland and Wilson were strong leaders in national policies. Democrats, like Dix, Douglas, Logan, Palmer, and McClellan, emphatically repudiated secession, and fought for the Union. Finally, Franklin D. Roosevelt went beyond all earlier leaders of either party in finding ways for the central government to handle problems of national importance.

The Party Constituency. In the course of its history, the constituency of the party has changed. There have always been in its ranks, among the wealthy and among men of position, the theoretical or doctrinaire democrats, like Jefferson himself and Gallatin. But the frontier developed men of character who were democratic by nature. Up to the Civil War practically all the immigrants who had escaped from autocracy in Europe were Democrats by instinct. The cities ceased to be controlled by merchants and bankers, and elections were carried by the votes of the masses.

Several changes are notable in the period since the Civil War. The South became reliably Democratic except in the Appalachian Mountain region. However, notwithstanding the tradition of a "solid South," fundamental differences over states rights and other issues have sometimes arisen between the Northern and Southern branches of the party. In Congress the Democratic members, having been regularly re-elected, have acquired a seniority that has entitled them to many important committee chairmanships. Thus they have usually been more powerful and influential than their more numerous Northern colleagues. In other parts of the nation the makeup of the Democratic party has depended upon local, and to some extent economic, conditions. While losing something of its hold on the conservative Southern members, the party has gained strength through increased support and activity among labor groups. The economically discontented have seemed to look to the Democratic party for relief, and most third parties of the period have eventually been absorbed by the Democrats—as Greenbackers, Populists, and, more recently, Progressives.

THE REPUBLICAN PARTY

The Republican party has been, since 1854, one of the two chief political parties in the U.S. It developed out of the political and territorial disputes concerning slavery. This question had forced one of the compromises in the formation of the Constitution, but did not appear as a political issue so long as free states and slave states were evenly balanced in the Senate. In 1819, the question of the admission of Missouri arose, because Missouri comprised a part of the new Louisiana territory and, although in the region far enough north to be included in the free states, was proposing to come in as a slave state.

Rise of the Slavery Issue. By Clay's compromise of 1820, Missouri was admitted as a slave state, but slavery was not to exist in the territories north of its southern border. This compromise remained in force for 34 years. In the meantime, abolition societies had grown up in the North, a Free Soil party had been formed to prevent the extension of slavery into the territories. The Democratic party, under the control of its Southern portion, was definitely committed to noninterference with slavery in the states. The Whig party was divided, its main body holding to the compromises secured by its great leader, Henry Clay.

In 1854 the Missouri Compromise was broken by the Kansas-Nebraska act, which proposed squatter sovereignty for the territories north of the line laid down in 1820 as the dividing line between slave and free regions. The slavery party was strengthened by the Dred Scott decision of 1857.

The opponents of the Kansas-Nebraska act were the Free Soilers, the Northern Democrats, and the Northern Whigs. The Free Soil party, though small, had been fighting for opposition to slavery. The Northern Whigs belonged to a national party which had for years refrained from agitating the slavery question, until the Kansas-Nebraska act seemed to repudiate the act of Henry Clay, and to arouse the long suppressed antislavery feeling of the North. The anti-Nebraska Democrats could not accept a betrayal of the compact of 1820, in favor of the slaveholding aristocracy of the South. Their number was increased in 1858 by anti-Lecompton Democrats who protested against forcing the Lecompton constitution on Kansas. Later, the American or Know-Nothing party of the 1850's, which had not been long in existence, and was found chiefly in free states, dissolved. These elements united to form a new party.

The New Party. The Republican party sprang up simultaneously in different states. The founding date is June 1854; the place, Jackson, Mich. It entered the 1854 Congressional campaign, elected a plurality in the House, and, by combining with the American party, elected the speaker of the House. Republican strength was in the north Atlantic and north central states.

In the 1856 presidential campaign the Republicans nominated Frémont for president, and won New England, New York, and the West—114 votes; but Buchanan carried Pennsylvania and the South —174 votes. In the 1858 senatorial campaign in Illinois, Lincoln and Douglas debated the slavery question; with the result that a break between the Northern and the Southern Democrats became inevitable. In 1860, the Republicans, instead of nominating a radical antislavery man, turned to Lincoln. The Democrats split, and the remnant of the Whigs nominated a candidate. Lincoln secured 180 votes against 123 for all others.

War and Reconstruction. The Civil War broke out almost immediately. Lincoln said the North would fight for the preservation of the Union. The War Democrats supported him, while the abolitionist element in the Republican party tried to urge more rapid action against slavery; the Peace Democrats favored no action. The Republican party was essentially the antislavery party, but it needed the support of the former Democrats. In 1864 it called itself the Union party, and the War Democrats continued with the party in the reelection of Lincoln. The vote was 212 for Lincoln to 21 for McClellan. Lincoln's assassination resulted in Johnson's succession; the extreme antislavery element of the Republicans controlled Congress for four years and opposed the president. Three Civil War amendments to the Constitution were passed, and the control of the Southern states was placed under Northern troops. In 1868 Grant was elected president by the Republicans.

By 1872, the liberal element in the Republican party had become restive under the domination of the extremists, and they broke away, nominating Horace Greeley for president. The Democrats also nominated Greeley, but the vote was 286 for Grant to 63 for his opponent. In 1873, however, came a business panic, and there were political and financial irregularities in Grant's administration, so that the Republicans lost Congress in 1874.

The 1876 presidential election was disputed. The electoral commission declared Hayes elected by one vote over Tilden. The liberal administration was opposed by the Stalwarts. In 1880 the latter desired Grant for a third term; the fight in the convention resulted in the nomination of Garfield, a 'dark horse,' who was elected, 214 to 155, but was assassinated a few months after his inauguration.

Tariff and Civil Service Issues. Arthur succeeded, and during his term the tariff and civil service became important issues. By this time the Southern states had become solidly Democratic.

In 1884, the weakness occasioned by the certain loss of the South to the Republicans was aggravated by the movement within the party of those who favored an exponent of civil service reform in the person of Cleveland. The Republican position favoring a high tariff for protect on of American industries was alienating a considerable number of voters. The result was that the Republicans lost Congress in 1882 and the presidency in 1884. Blaine was defeated by Cleveland, 182 to 219.

During the next twelve years, when economic and industrial questions were prominent, it was claimed that the Republican party was in the hands of the moneyed classes, including the banks, the railroads, Wall Street, and the manufacturers. In the West, the Farmers' Alliance entered politics, and then the People's party, later called the Populists, arose. These drew votes away from the Republicans. The presidential elections varied. In 1888, Harrison defeated Cleveland, 233 to 168, largely on the issue of the tariff; but in 1892, Cleveland again became president.

Free Silver. In 1893 came a financial depression which, being charged to the Democratic tariff, gave Congress to the Republicans in 1894. Between the election of 1894 and that of 1896, the question of free silver came to the fore as the summing up of the prevailing economic discontent. There were free silver advocates in both parties. The Democrats declared in favor of free and unlimited coinage of silver at the ratio of 16 to 1. The Republicans were not extreme advocates of gold as a single standard, but became known as the "sound money" men, and attracted the conservative economic elements. The Silver Republicans voted with the Democrats. The Gold Democrats nominated a ticket of their own. Republican McKinley won.

During McKinley's term, the gold standard was adopted, and the Spanish American war was fought. Out of the war there arose a new issue of imperialism, the main question being the retention of the Philippines, which the Republicans favored. The Republican and the Democratic candidate of 1896 ran again in 1900, and McKinley won. As a result of the alignment of the parties in 1900, the Republicans became the "standpat," almost reactionary, party.

Conservatives and Progressives. Upon the assassination of McKinley, Roosevelt succeeded to the presidency, and in 1904 he was elected president over Parker. In Roosevelt's term the liberal element of the party was in control, and the Republicans favored measures providing for government regulation of industry and demanding the "square deal." In 1908, Taft was elected president. During his term, the policies pursued with respect to the tariff and conservation of natural resources indicated that the "old guard," "standpat," reactionary element had again secured control of the party. In 1912, the two elements, progressive and conservative, split. The conservatives nominated Taft; a newly formed Progressive party nominated Roosevelt. Wilson, the Democratic nominee, was elected.

World War I broke out in 1914. In 1916, the **Republicans and Progressives united again, but** Wilson defeated Hughes. After the war, the Republicans came into · power again in 1920. Under Harding, Coolidge, and Hoover, the country pursued a relatively isolationist policy, restricting immigration and raising tariffs. It was a period of prosperity followed by depression; the presidency passed to the Democrats in 1932. The years 1932 to 1952 brought economic and social progress and the U.S. emerged as the most powerful nation in a world shattered by World War II. In a mood to consolidate, the nation elected Republican Eisenhower, who served until 1961. John F. Kennedy, elected in 1960, was assassinated in 1963. Lyndon B. Johnson succeeded him and served another full term.

Republican Principles. From Civil War days the Republican party supported a broad construction of the Constitution, but it abruptly reversed its position in 1936. Favoring centralized power in an era when this meant high tariffs, an imperialistic foreign policy, and federal aid for railroads, water-ways, and reclamation, the party declared for states rights when the federal government, under Franklin D. Roosevelt, introduced a program declared by Republicans to mean interference with private initiative and ruinous taxation on business.

In general, the Republican party has been a party of the North and West. The "solid South" is normally Democratic because of Civil War memories, although the Republicans won some successes there in 1928, 1952, and 1956.

Until 1964, the Republican party antagonized the South by sponsoring civil rights legislation. That year the party chose Barry Goldwater, senator from Arizona, who had opposed such legislation and five Southern states voted to make him president.

In 1968, after narrowly defeating Hubert Humphrey, Richard Nixon became the first president since Zachary Taylor in 1848 to begin his first term with opposition control in both houses. Nixon was re-elected in 1972, capturing the majority of votes in every state except Massachusetts and Washington, D.C. The reputation of the Republican party suffered during the latter years of the Nixon administration—as a result of the Watergate scandal Nixon resigned and several cabinet members resigned or were indicted; Vice President Agnew had resigned earlier because of income-tax evasion charges. Gerald Ford, who had been appointed vice president in 1973, became president in 1974 when Nixon resigned. Like Nixon, Ford faced a Democratic-dominated Senate and House. His major concerns included restoring trust in the federal government and restoring the integrity of the Republican party. Ford was defeated by a narrow margin in the 1976 election.

COMPARATIVE PARTY STRENGTH IN CONGRESS

| Congress | President | DEMOCRATS | | REPUBLICANS | | OTHER PARTIES |
		Senate	House	Senate	House	A.L., American Labor: F-L., Farmer-Labor; H, House; Ind., Independent; Pop., Populist; Pg., Progressive; Proh., Prohibition; S, Senate; Soc., Socialist; Vac., Vacancy.
50th	1887–1889	Cleveland . . .	37	169	39	152	Ind., H, 4
51st	1889–1891	Harrison	37	161	45	169	
52d	1891–1893	Harrison	39	235	47	88	Ind., S, 2. Farmers' Alliance, H, 9
53d	1893–1895	Cleveland . . .	44	218	37	127	Ind., S, 4; H, .11
54th	1895–1897	Cleveland . . .	39	104	43	248	Ind., S, 6; H, .7
55th	1897–1899	McKinley . . .	34	130	47	202	Silver and Pop, S, 8; H, 25
56th	1899–1901	McKinley . . .	26	159	50	189	Silver and Pop, S, 10; H, 8
57th	1901–1903	McKinley . . .					
		Roosevelt. . . .	29	151	53	198	Pop. and Ind., S, 8; H, 8
58th	1903–1905	Roosevelt. . . .	33	178	57	208	Union Labor, H, 2
59th	1905–1907	Roosevelt. . . .	32	136	58	250	
60th	1907–1909	Roosevelt. . . .	31	166	60	220	
61st	1909–1911	Taft	32	175	60	214	Unionist, H, 1
62d	1911–1913	Taft	42	227	49	162	Soc., H, 1
63d	1913–1915	Wilson	51	290	45	127	Progressive, H, 18
64th	1915–1917	Wilson	55	230	41	201	Pg., H, 5. Ind., H, 1. Soc., H, 1
65th	1917–1919	Wilson	51	209	42	212	Pg., S, 1; H, 3. Soc., H, 1. Ind., H, 2
66th	1919–1921	Wilson	47	190	49	240	Ind., H, 2. Proh., H, 1
67th	1921–1923	Harding	37	132	59	300	Soc., H, 1
68th	1923–1925	Harding, Coolidge	42	206	53	223	F-L., S, 1; H, 1. Soc., H, 1. Ind., H, 1
69th	1925–1927	Coolidge	39	183	56	247	F-L., S, 1; H, 3. Soc., H, 2
70th	1927–1929	Coolidge	47	195	48	237	F-L., S, 1; H, 2. Soc., H, 1
71st	1929–1931	Hoover	39	165	55	268	F-L., S, 1; H, 1
72d	1931–1933	Hoover	47	216	48	218	F-L., S, 1; H, 1
73d	1933–1935	Roosevelt . . .	59	313	36	117	F-L., S, 1; H, 5
74th	1935–1936	Roosevelt . . .	69	322	25	102	Pg., S, 1; H, 7. F-L., S, 1; H, 3. Vac., 1
75th	1937–1938	Roosevelt . . ·.	76	334	16	88	Pg., S, 1; H, 8. F-L., S, 2; H, 5. Ind., S, 1
76th	1939–1940	Roosevelt . . .	69	262	23	170	Pg., S, 1; H, 2. F-L., S, 2; H, 1. Ind., S, 1
77th	1941–1942	Roosevelt . . .	66	268	28	162	Pg., S, 1; H, 3. F-L., H, 1. Ind., S, 1; H, 1.
78th	1943–1944	Roosevelt . . .	59	222	36	208	Pg., S, 1; H, 2. F-L., H, 1. A.L., H, 1
79th	1945–1946	Roosevelt, Truman	56	243	39	190	Pg., S, 1; H, 1. A.L., H, 1
80th	1947–1948	Truman	45	188	51	246	A.L., H. 1
81st	1949–1950	Truman	54	275	42	162	A.L., H. 1
82d	1951–1952	Truman	49	235	47	199	Ind. 1
83d	1953–1954	Eisenhower . . .	46	211	47	221	Ind., S, 1; H, 1. Vac., S, 1; H, 2
84th	1955–1956	Eisenhower . . .	49	231	47	203	Vac., H. 1
85th	1957–1958	Eisenhower . . .	49	233	47	201	Vac., H. 1
86th	1959–1960	Eisenhower . . .	66	279	34	152	Vac., H. 6
87th	1961–1962	Kennedy	65	262	35	175	
88th	1963–1964	Kennedy, Johnson	66	256	34	179	
89th	1965–1966	Johnson	68	295	32	140	
90th	1967–1968	Johnson	64	248	36	187	
91st	1969–1970	Nixon	59	245	41	191	Vac., H. 3
92d	1971–1972	Nixon	54	254	45	180	Vac., S. 1; H. 1
93d	1973–1974	Nixon, Ford . .	57	240	43	192	Vac., H. 3
94th	1975–1976	Ford	62	291	38	144	Ind., S. 1; Conservative 1
95th	1977–	Carter	61	292	38	143	Ind., S. 1

| NAME | BORN | | PARENTS | | Paternal Ancestry |
	When	Where	Father	Mother	
1. George Washington	Feb. 22, 1732	Bridge's Creek, Va.	Augustine	Mary Ball	English
2. John Adams	Oct. 30, 1735	Quincy, Mass.*	John	Susanna Boylston	English
3. Thomas Jefferson	Apr. 13, 1743	Shadwell, Va.	Peter	Jane Randolph	Welsh
4. James Madison	Mar. 16, 1751	Port Conway, Va.	James	Nelly Conway	English
5. James Monroe	Apr. 28, 1758	Westmoreland Co., Va.	Spence	Eliza Jones	Scotch
6. John Quincy Adams	July 11, 1767	Quincy, Mass.*	John	Abigail Smith	English
7. Andrew Jackson	Mar. 15, 1767	Waxhaw Settl'nt, S.C.†	Andrew	Elizabeth Hutchinson	Scotch-Irish
8. Martin Van Buren	Dec. 5, 1782	Kinderhook, N. Y.	Abraham	Maria Hoes	Dutch
9. William H. Harrison	Feb. 9, 1773	Berkeley, Va.	Benjamin	Elizabeth Bassett	English
10. John Tyler	Mar. 29, 1790	Charles City Co., Va.	John	Mary Armistead	English
11. James K. Polk	Nov. 2, 1795	Mecklenburg Co., N.C.	Samuel	Jane Knox	Scotch-Irish
12. Zachary Taylor	Sept. 24, 1784	Orange Co., Va.	Richard	Sarah Strother	English
13. Millard Fillmore	Jan. 7, 1800	Summer Hill, N. Y.	Nathaniel	Phebe Millard	English
14. Franklin Pierce	Nov. 23, 1804	Hillsborough, N. H.	Benjamin	Anna Kindreck	English
15. James Buchanan	Apr. 23, 1791	Stony Batter, Pa.	James	Elizabeth Speer	Scotch-Irish
16. Abraham Lincoln	Feb. 12, 1809	Nolin Creek, Ky.	Thomas	Nancy Hanks	English
17. Andrew Johnson	Dec. 29, 1808	Raleigh, N. C.	Jacob	Mary M'Donough	English
18. Ulysses S. Grant	Apr. 27, 1822	Point Pleasant, Ohio	Jesse Root	Hannah Simpson	Scotch
19. Rutherford B. Hayes	Oct. 4, 1822	Delaware, Ohio	Rutherford	Sophia Birchard	Scotch
20. James A. Garfield	Nov. 19, 1831	Orange, Ohio	Abram	Eliza Ballou	English
21. Chester A. Arthur	Oct. 5, 1830	Fairfield, Vt.	William	Malvina Stone	Scotch-Irish
22. Grover Cleveland	Mar. 18, 1837	Caldwell, N. J.	Richard F.	Anna Neal	English
23. Benjamin Harrison	Aug. 20, 1833	North Bend, Ohio.	John Scott	Elizabeth Irwin	English
24. Grover Cleveland	Mar. 18, 1837	Caldwell, N. J.	Richard F.	Anna Neal	English
25. William McKinley	Jan. 29, 1843	Niles, Ohio	William	Nancy C. Allison	Scotch-Irish
26. Theodore Roosevelt	Oct. 27, 1858	New York City, N. Y.	Theodore	Martha Bullock	Dutch
27. William H. Taft	Sept. 15, 1857	Cincinnati, Ohio	Alphonso	Louise M. Torrey	English
28. Woodrow Wilson	Dec. 28, 1856	Staunton, Va.	Joseph R.	Jessie Woodrow	Scotch-Irish
29. Warren G. Harding	Nov. 2, 1865	Corsica, Ohio	George T.	Phebe E. Dickerson	Scotch-Dutch
30. Calvin Coolidge	July 4, 1872	Plymouth, Vt.	John C.	Victoria J. Moor	English
31. Herbert Hoover	Aug. 10, 1874	West Branch, Iowa	Jesse Clark	Hulda R. Minthorn	Germ.-Swiss
32. Franklin D. Roosevelt	Jan. 30, 1882	Hyde Park, N. Y.	James	Sara Delano	Dutch
33. Harry S. Truman	May 8, 1884	Lamar, Mo.	John Anderson	Martha Ellen Young	Eng. Scotch-Ir.
34. Dwight D. Eisenhower	Oct. 14, 1890	Denison, Texas	David J.	Ida Elizabeth Stover	Penn. German
35. John F. Kennedy	May 29, 1917	Brookline, Mass.	Joseph P.	Rose Fitzgerald	Irish
36. Lyndon B. Johnson	Aug. 27, 1908	Near Stonewall, Tex.	Samuel E.	Rebekah Baines	Eng.-Scotch
37. Richard M. Nixon	Jan. 9, 1913	Yorba Linda, Cal.	Francis A.	Hannah Milhous	Scotch-Irish
38. Gerald R. Ford	July 14, 1913	Omaha, Neb.	Leslie King	Dorothy Gardner King	English
39. Jimmy Carter	Oct. 1, 1924	Plains, Ga.	James Earl	Lillian Gordy	Scotch-Irish

PRESIDENTS OF THE

| NAME | Married | Wife's Name | CHILDREN | | Inaugurated | Residence When Elected | Age Inaugurated |
			Boys	Girls			
1. George Washington	1759	Mrs. Martha Custis	..	..	1789	Mt. Vernon, Va.	57
2. John Adams	1764	Abigail Smith	3	2	1797	Quincy, Mass.	61
3. Thomas Jefferson	1772	Mrs. Martha Skelton	..	6	1801	Monticello, Va.	57
4. James Madison	1794	Mrs. Dorothy Todd	..	..	1809	Montpelier, Va.	57
5. James Monroe	1786	Eliza Kortwright	..	2	1817	Oakhill, Va.	58
6. John Quincy Adams	1797	Louisa C. Johnson	3	1	1825	Quincy, Mass.	57
7. Andrew Jackson	1791	Mrs. Rachel Robards	..	..	1829	Hermitage, Tenn.	61
8. Martin Van Buren	1807	Hannah Hoes (Goes)	4	..	1837	Kinderhook, N. Y.	54
9. William H. Harrison	1795	Anna Symmes	6	4	1841	North Bend, O.	68
10. John Tyler	1813 / 1844	Letitia Christian / Julia Gardiner	3 / 4	4 / 2	1841	Williamsburg, Va.	51
11. James K. Polk	1824	Sarah Childress	..	..	1845	Nashville, Tenn.	49
12. Zachary Taylor	1810	Margaret Smith	1	3	1849	Baton Rouge, La.	64
13. Millard Fillmore	1826 / 1858	Abigail Powers / Mrs. Caroline McIntosh	1 / ..	1 / ..	1850	Buffalo, N. Y.	50
14. Franklin Pierce	1834	Jane Means Appleton	3	..	1853	Concord, N. H.	48
15. James Buchanan	....	Unmarried	..	..	1857	Wheatland, Pa.	65
16. Abraham Lincoln	1842	Mary Todd	4	..	1861	Springfield, Ill.	52
17. Andrew Johnson	1827	Eliza McCardle	3	2	1865	Greenville, Tenn.	56

*Formerly a part of Braintree. † Jackson stated that he had been told this was his birthplace. Some authorities give Mecklenburg county, N. C.

Father's Business	Educational Advantages	Early Vocation	Politics	Profession	Religious Connections	NAME	
Planter	Common School	Surveyor	Fed.	Planter	Episcopalian	Washington.	1
Farmer	Harvard College, 1755	Teacher	Fed.	Lawyer	Unitarian	Adams.	2
Planter	Entered College, William and Mary	Lawyer	Rep.	Lawyer	Liberal	Jefferson.	3
Planter	Princeton College, 1771	Lawyer	Rep.	Lawyer	Episcopalian	Madison.	4
Planter	Entered College, William and Mary	Lawyer	Rep.	Politician	Episcopalian	Monroe.	5
Lawyer	Harvard College, 1787	Lawyer	Rep	Lawyer	Unitarian	Adams, J. Q.	6
Farmer	Self Taught	Lawyer	Dem.	Lawyer	Presbyterian	Jackson.	7
Farmer	Academy	Lawyer	Dem.	Lawyer	Reformed Dutch	Van Buren.	8
Statesman	Entered Hampden-Sidney College	Medicine	Whig	Army	Episcopalian	Harrison.	9
Jurist	College, William and Mary, 1807	Lawyer	Dem.	Lawyer	Episcopalian	Tyler.	10
Farmer	University of North Carolina, 1818	Lawyer	Dem.	Lawyer	Methodist‡	Polk.	11
Planter	Common School	Soldier	Whig	Army	Episcopalian	Taylor.	12
Farmer	Public School	Tailor	Whig	Lawyer	Episcopalian	Fillmore.	13
Farmer	Bowdoin College, 1824	Lawyer	Dem.	Lawyer	Episcopalian	Pierce.	14
Merchant	Dickinson College, 1809	Lawyer	Dem.	Lawyer	Presbyterian	Buchanan.	15
Farmer	Self Taught	Farmer	Rep.	Lawyer	Liberal	Lincoln.	16
Sexton	Self Taught	Tailor	Rep.	Politician	Liberal	Johnson.	17
Farmer	West Point Military Academy, 1843	Tanner	Rep.	Army	Methodist	Grant.	18
Merchant	Kenyon College, Ohio, 1842	Lawyer	Rep.	Lawyer	Methodist	Hayes.	19
Farmer	Williams College, 1856	Teacher	Rep.	Lawyer	Disciples	Garfield.	20
Clergyman	Union College, 1848	Teacher	Rep.	Lawyer	Episcopalian	Arthur.	21
Clergyman	Common School	Teacher	Dem.	Lawyer	Presbyterian	Cleveland.	22
Farmer	Miami University, Ohio, 1852	Lawyer	Rep.	Lawyer	Presbyterian	Harrison.	23
Clergyman	Common School	Teacher	Dem.	Lawyer	Presbyterian	Cleveland.	24
Iron Manfr.	Entered Allegheny College	Lawyer	Rep.	Lawyer	Methodist	McKinley.	25
Merchant	Harvard, 1880	Publicist.	Rep.	Publicist	Reformed Dutch	Roosevelt.	26
Lawyer	Yale, 1878	Lawyer	Rep.	Lawyer	Unitarian	Taft.	27
Clergyman	Princeton, 1879	Lawyer	Dem.	Teacher	Presbyterian	Wilson.	28
Physician	Attended Ohio Central College	Editor	Rep.	Publisher	Baptist	Harding.	29
Farmer	Amherst College, 1895	Lawyer	Rep.	Lawyer	Congregationalist	Coolidge.	30
Blacksmith	Stanford University, 1895	Engineer	Rep.	Engineer	Quaker	Hoover.	31
Capitalist	Harvard, 1904	Lawyer	Dem.	Lawyer	Episcopalian	Roosevelt.	32
Farmer	Kansas City School of Law, 1923-25	Business	Dem.	Pub. service	Baptist	Truman.	33
Mechanic	West Point Military Academy, 1915	Soldier	Rep.	Army	Presbyterian	Eisenhower.	34
Capitalist	Harvard, 1940	Reporter	Dem.	Legislator	Roman Catholic	Kennedy.	35
Farmer	S. W. Tex. State Teachers College, 1930	Secretary	Dem.	Legislator	Disciples of Christ	Johnson.	36
Storekeeper	Whittier College, 1934; Duke, 1937	Lawyer	Rep.	Legislator	Quaker	Nixon.	37
Businessman	U. of Michigan, 1935; Yale, 1941	Lawyer	Rep.	Legislator	Episcopalian	Ford.	38
Farmer	U.S. Naval Academy, 1946	Navy	Dem.	Farmer	Baptist	Carter.	39

UNITED STATES—TABLE II

Served as President	Died	Age at Death	Cause of Death	Place of Death	Place of Burial	
7 yr., 10 m., 4 d.	1799	67	Acute laryngitis	Mt. Vernon, Va.	Mt. Vernon, Va.	1
4 yr.	1826	90	Natural decline	Quincy, Mass.	Quincy, Mass.	2
8 yr.	1826	83	Chronic diarrhœa	Monticello, Va.	Monticello, Albemarle Co., Va.	3
8 yr.	1836	85	Natural decline	Montpelier, Va.	Montpelier, Orange Co., Va.	4
8 yr.	1831	73	Natural decline	New York City	Originally, N. Y. Removed, 1858, to Hollywood Cemetery, Richmond, Va.	5
4 yr.	1848	80	Paralysis	Hall of Congress, Washington, D. C.	Unitarian Church, Quincy, Mass.	6
8 yr.	1845	78	Dropsy	Hermitage, near Nashville, Tenn.	Hermitage, near Nashville, Tenn.	7
4 yr.	1862	79	Asthma	Kinderhook, N. Y.	Kinderhook, N. Y.	8
1 m.	1841	68	Pleurisy	White House, Washington, D. C.	North Bend, Ohio.	9
3 yr., 11 m.	1862	71	Bilious attacks, with bronchitis	Ballard House, Richmond, Va.	Hollywood, Richmond, Va.	10
4 yr.	1849	53	Chronic diarrhœa	Nashville, Tenn.	Nashville, Tenn.	11
1 yr., 4 m., 5 d.	1850	65	Cholera morbus and typhoid fever	White House, Washington, D. C.	Near Louisville, Kentucky.	12
2 yr., 7 m., 26 d.	1874	74	Paralysis	Buffalo, N. Y.	Forest Lawn, Buffalo, N. Y.	13
4 yr.	1869	64	Dropsy and inflammation of stomach	Concord, N. H.	Minot Cemetery, Concord, N. H.	14
4 yr.	1868	77	Rheumatic gout	Lancaster, Pa.	Woodward Hill Cemetery, Lancaster, Pa.	15
4 yr., 1 m., 11 d.	1865	56	Assassinated	Washington, D. C.	Oak Ridge Cemetery, Springfield, Ill.	16
3 yr., 10 m., 19 d.	1875	66	Paralysis	Greenville, Tenn.	Greenville, Tenn.	17

‡ Baptized on death bed by minister of Methodist Episcopal Church, South. His wife was a member of the Presbyterian Church, which he sometimes attended with her.

Name	Married	Wife's Name	Children Boys	Children Girls	Inaugurated	Residence When Elected	Age Inaugurated
18. Ulysses S. Grant	1848	Julia Dent	3	1	1869	Washington, D. C.	46
19. Rutherford B. Hayes	1852	Lucy Ware Webb	7	1	1877	Fremont, Ohio	54
20. James A. Garfield	1858	Lucretia Rudolph	4	1	1881	Mentor, Ohio	49
21. Chester A. Arthur	1859	Ellen Lewis Herndon	1	1	1881	New York City	50
22. Grover Cleveland	1886	Frances Folsom	2	3	1885	Buffalo, N. Y.	47
23. Benjamin Harrison. {	1853 / 1896	Caroline Lavinia Scott / Mary Scott (Lord) Dimmick	1 / ..	1 / 1 }	1889	Indianapolis, Ind.	55
24. Grover Cleveland	....	(See above)	..	..	1893	New York City	55
25. William McKinley	1871	Ida Saxton	..	2	1897	Canton, Ohio	54
26. Theo. Roosevelt {	1880 / 1886	Alice Lee / Edith Carow	.. / 4	1 / 1 }	1901	Oyster Bay, N. Y.	42
27. William H. Taft	1886	Helen Herron	2	1	1909	Cincinnati. Ohio	51
28. Woodrow Wilson {	1885 / 1915	Ellen Louise Axson / Mrs. Edith Bolling Galt	.. / ..	3 / .. }	1913	Princeton, N. J.	56
29. Warren G. Harding	1891	Florence Kling	..	..	1921	Marion, Ohio	55
30. Calvin Coolidge	1905	Grace A. Goodhue	2	..	1923	Northampton Mass.	51
31. Herbert Hoover	1899	Lou Henry	2	..	1929	Stanford Univ., Cal.	54
32. Franklin D. Roosevelt	1905	Anna Eleanor Roosevelt	4	1	1933	Hyde Park, N. Y.	51
33. Harry S. Truman	1919	Bess Wallace	..	1	1945	Independence. Mo.	61
34. Dwight D. Eisenhower	1916	Mamie Geneva Doud	2	..	1953	New York City	62
35. John F. Kennedy	1953	Jacqueline Bouvier	2	1	1961	Boston, Mass.	43
36. Lyndon B. Johnson	1934	Claudia Alta "Lady Bird" Taylor	..	2	1963	Near Stonewall, Tex.	55
37. Richard M. Nixon (3)	1940	Patricia Ryan	..	2	1969	New York City	56
38. Gerald R. Ford	1948	Elizabeth Bloomer Warren	3	1	1974	Grand Rapids, Mich.	61
39. Jimmy Carter	1946	Rosalynn Smith	3	1	1977	Plains,Ga.	52

VICE PRESIDENTS OF THE

Name	Born When	Born Where	Parents Father	Parents Mother	Paternal Ancestry	Educational Advantages
1. John Adams (1, 5)	1735	Quincy, Mass.	John	Susanna Boylston	English	Harvard, 1755.
2. Thomas Jefferson (1)	1743	Shadwell, Va.	Peter	Jane Randolph	Welsh	Wm. and Mary, 1762.
3. Aaron Burr	1756	Newark, N. J.	Aaron	Esther Edwards	English	New Jersey, † 1772.
4. George Clinton (2, 5)	1739	Little Britain, N. Y.	Charles	Elizabeth Denniston	English	Academy.
5. Elbridge Gerry (2)	1744	Marblehead, Mass.	Thomas	Elizabeth Greenleaf	English	Harvard, 1762.
6. Daniel D. Tompkins (5)	1774	Scarsdale, N. Y.	Jonathan G.	Sarah Hyatt	English	Columbia, 1795.
7. John C. Calhoun (3, 5) (2 terms)	1782	Abbeville Dist., S.C.	Patrick	Martha Caldwell	Scotch-Irish	Yale, 1804.
8. Martin Van Buren (1)	1782	Kinderhook, N. Y.	Abraham	Mary Hoes	Dutch	Kinderhook Acad.
9. Richard M. Johnson	1781	Bryant's Station,Ky.	Robert	Jemima Suggett	English	Transylvania.
10. John Tyler (4)	1790	Greenway, Va.	John	Mary Armistead	English	Wm. and Mary, 1807.
11. George M. Dallas	1792	Philadelphia, Pa.	Alexander J.	Arabella M. Smith	Scotch-Eng.	New Jersey, † 1810.
12. Millard Fillmore (4)	1800	Summerhill, N. Y..	Nathaniel	Phebe Millard	English	Public School.
13. Wm. Rufus King (2)	1786	Sampson Co., N. C.	William	Margaret Devane	Irish-Hug'n't	Univ. of N. C. 1803.
14. John C. Breckinridge	1821	Lexington, Ky.	John C.	Mary C. Smith	Scotch	Centre, 1839.
15. Hannibal Hamlin	1809	Paris, Me.	Cyrus	Anna Livermore	English	Hebron Acad.
16. Andrew Johnson (4)	1808	Raleigh, N. C.	Jacob	Mary McDonough	English	Self-taught.
17. Schuyler Colfax	1823	New York City	Schuyler	Hannah Stryker	Eng.-Dutch	Public School.
18. Henry Wilson* (2)	1812	Farmington, N. H.	Winthrop*	Abigail Witham	Scotch-Irish	Academy.
19. William A. Wheeler	1819	Malone, N. Y.	Almon	Eliza Woodward	English	Vermont.
20. Chester A. Arthur (4)	1830	Fairfield, Vt.	William	Malvina Stone	Scotch-Irish	Union, 1848.
21. Thomas A. Hendricks(2)	1819	Zanesville, O.	John	Jane Thomson	Sc'h-Hug'n't	Hanover, Ind., 1841.
22. Levi P. Morton	1824	Shoreham, Vt.	Daniel O.	Lucretia Parsons	English	Shoreham Acad.
23. Adlai E. Stevenson	1835	Christian Co., Ky.	John T.	Eliza Ewing	Scotch-Irish	Centre.
24. Garret A. Hobart (2)	1844	Long Branch, N. J.	Addison W.	Sophia Vanderveer	Eng.-Hug'n't	Rutgers, 1863.
25. TheodoreRoosevelt(1,4)	1858	New York City	Theodore	Martha Bullock	Dutch	Harvard, 1880.
26. Charles W. Fairbanks	1852	Unionville Center, O.	Loriston M.	Mary A. Smith	English	Ohio Wesleyan, 1872.
27. James S. Sherman (2)	1855	Utica, N. Y.	Richard U.	Mary F. Sherman	English	Hamilton, 1878.
28. Thomas R. Marshall(5)	1854	N. Manchester, Ind.	Daniel M.	Martha A. Patterson	English	Wabash, 1873.
29. Calvin Coolidge (1, 4)	1872	Plymouth, Vt.	John C.	Victoria J. Moor	English	Amherst, 1895.
30. Charles Gates Dawes	1865	Marietta, O.	Rufus R.	Mary Beman	English	Marietta, 1884.
31. Charles Curtis	1860	N. Topeka, Kans.	Oran A.	Helen Pappan	Kaw Indian	Public School.
32. John Nance Garner (5)	1868	Red River Co., Tex.	John N.	Sarah	English	Public School.
33. Henry Agard Wallace	1888	Adair Co., Ia.	Henry A.	May Brodhead	Scotch-Irish	Iowa State Coll.
34. Harry S. Truman (1, 4)	1884	Lamar, Mo.	John A.	Martha Ellen Young	Eng.-Sco.-Ir.	Kans. City Law Sch.
35. Alben William Barkley	1877	Graves Co., Ky.	John W.	Electa Smith	Eng.-Sco.-Ir.	Marvin,Emory Coll.
36. Richard M. Nixon (1, 5)	1913	Yorba Linda, Cal.	Francis A.	Hannah Milhous	Scotch-Irish	Whittier College.
37. Lyndon B. Johnson(1,4)	1908	Near Stonewall, Tex.	Samuel E.	Rebekah Baines	Eng.-Scotch	S.W. Tex. State T. C.
38. Hubert H. Humphrey	1911	Wallace, S. D.	Hubert H.	Christine Sannes	Eng.Sc. Wel.	Univ. of Minnesota.
39. Spiro T. Agnew (3, 5)	1918	Baltimore, Md.	Theodore S.	Margarate A.	Greek	Univ. of Baltimore.
40. Gerald R. Ford	1913	Omaha, Neb.	L. King (6).	Dorothy G. King	English	Univ. of Mich.. Yale.
41. Nelson A. Rockefeller	1908	Bar Harbor, Me.	John D., Jr.	Abbe Green Aldrich	Ger.-Eng.	Dartmouth.
42. Walter F. Mondale	1928	Ceylon, Minn.	Theodore S.	Claribel Cowan	Norwegian	Univ. of Minn.

* Born Jeremiah Jones Colbath, son of Winthrop Colbath; changed his name to Henry Wilson. † Now Princeton.
(1) Vice presidents thus marked were later elected president (Adams, Jefferson, Van Buren, Roosevelt, Coolidge, Truman, L. Johnson., Nixon) (2) These vice presidents died while in office (Clinton, Gerry, King, Wilson, Hendricks, Hobart, Sherman).
(3) Resigned from office (Calhoun, Agnew, and Nixon). (4) Succeeded to the presidency at death of president. (Tyler, Fillmore,

Served as President	Died	Age at Death	Cause of Death	Place of Death	Place of Burial	
8 yr.	1885	63	Cancer of the tongue	Mt. McGregor, N. Y.	Riverside, New York City.	18
4 yr.	1893	70	Neuralgia of heart	Fremont, Ohio	Fremont, Ohio.	19
6½ m.	1881	49	Assassinated	Elberon, Long Branch, N. J.	Lake View Cemetery, Cleveland, Ohio.	20
3 yr., 5½ m.	1886	56	Bright's disease	New York City	Rural Cemetery, Albany, N. Y.	21
8 yr.	1908	71	Heart failure.	Princeton, N. J.	Princeton, N. J.	22
4 yr.	1901	67	Pneumonia	Indianapolis, Ind.	Crown Hill Cemetery, Indianapolis, Ind.	23
4 yr., 6 m., 10 d.	1901	58	Assassinated	Buffalo, N. Y.	Cemetery, Canton, Ohio.	25
7 yr., 5 m., 20 d.	1919	60	Embolism	Oyster Bay, N. Y.	Young's Memorial Cemetery, Oyster Bay, N. Y.	26
4 yr.	1930	72	Hardening of arteries	Washington, D. C.	Arlington National Cemetery.	27
8 yr.	1924	67	General breakdown	Washington, D. C.	Washington, D. C.	28
2 yr., 4 m., 30 d.	1923	57	Apoplexy	San Francisco, Cal.	Marion, Ohio.	29
5 yr., 7 m., 1 d.	1933	60	Coronary thrombosis	Northampton, Mass.	Plymouth, Vt.	30
4 yr.	1964	90	Intestinal hemorrhage	New York, N. Y.	West Branch, Iowa	31
12 yr., 1 m., 8 d.	1945	63	Cerebral hemorrhage	Warm Springs. Ga.	Hyde Park, N. Y.	32
7 yrs., 9 m., 8 d.	1972	88	Natural decline	Kansas City, Mo.	Independence, Mo.	33
8 yr.	1969	78	Coronary thrombosis	Washington, D. C.	Abilene, Kans.	34
2 yrs., 10 m., 2 d.	1963	46	Assassinated	Dallas, Tex.	Arlington National Cemetery	35
5 yrs., 1 m., 29 d.	1973	64	Coronary thrombosis	San Antonio, Tex.	Stonewell, Tex.	36
5 yrs., 6 m., 20 d.						37
2 yrs., 5 m., 11 d.						38
						39

UNITED STATES

Profession	Politics	Served as Vice President		Died	Place of Burial	
		Length of Time	Administration of			
Lawyer	Fed.	7 yr., 10 mo., 4 d. (1789–1797)	Washington	1826	Quincy, Mass.	1
Lawyer	Rep.	4 yr. (1797–1801)	Adams, John	1826	Monticello, Va.	2
Lawyer	Rep.	4 yr. (1801–1805)	Jefferson	1836	Princeton, N. J.	3
Politician	Rep.	4 yr. (1805–1809)	Jefferson	1812	Washington, D. C.	4
		3 yr., 1 mo., 16 d. (1809–1812)	Madison			
Politician	Rep.	1 yr., 8 mo., 19 d. (1813–1814)	Madison	1814	Washington, D. C.	5
Lawyer	Rep.	8 yr. (1817–1825)	Monroe	1825	New York City.	6
Lawyer	Rep.	4 yr. (1825–1829)	Adams, J. Q.	1850	Charleston, S. C.	7
		3 yr., 9 mo., 24 d. (1829–1832)	Jackson			
Lawyer	Dem.	4 yr. (1833–1837)	Jackson	1862	Kinderhook, N. Y.	8
Lawyer	Dem.	4 yr. (1837–1841)	Van Buren	1850	Frankfort, Ky.	9
Lawyer	Dem.	1 mo. (1841)	Harrison	1862	Richmond, Va.	10
Lawyer	Dem.	4 yr. (1845–1849)	Polk	1864	Philadelphia, Pa.	11
Lawyer	Whig	1 yr., 4 mo., 5 d. (1849–1850)	Taylor	1874	Buffalo, N. Y.	12
Lawyer	Dem.	1 mo., 14 d. (1853)	Pierce	1853	Selma, Alabama.	13
Lawyer	Dem.	4 yr. (1857–1861)	Buchanan	1875	Lexington, Ky.	14
Lawyer	Rep.	4 yr. (1861–1865)	Lincoln	1891	Bangor, Maine.	15
Politician	Rep.	1 mo., 11 d. (1865)	Lincoln	1875	Greenville, Tenn.	16
Journalist	Rep.	4 yr. (1869–1873)	Grant	1885	South Bend, Ind.	17
Politician	Rep.	2 yr., 8 mo., 18 d. (1873–1875)	Grant	1875	Dell Park, Natick, Mass.	18
Lawyer	Rep.	4 yr. (1877–1881)	Hayes	1887	Malone, N. Y.	19
Lawyer	Rep.	6 mo., 15 d. (Mch. 4–Sept. 19, 1881)	Garfield	1886	Albany, N. Y.	20
Lawyer	Dem.	8 mo., 21 d. (Mch. 4–Nov. 25, 1885)	Cleveland	1885	Indianapolis, Ind.	21
Banker	Rep.	4 yr. (1889–1893)	Harrison	1920	Rhinebeck, N. Y.	22
Lawyer	Dem.	4 yr. (1893–1897)	Cleveland	1914	Bloomington, Ill.	23
Banker, Lawyer	Rep.	2 yr., 8 mo., 17 d. (1897–1899)	McKinley	1899	Paterson, N. J.	24
Publicist	Rep.	6 mo., 10 d. (Mch. 4–Sept. 14, 1901)	McKinley	1919	Oyster Bay, N. Y.	25
Lawyer	Rep.	4 yr. (1905–1909)	Roosevelt	1918	Indianapolis, Ind.	26
Lawyer	Rep.	3 yr., 7 mo., 26 d. (1909–1912)	Taft	1912	Utica, N. Y.	27
Lawyer	Dem.	8 yr. (1913–1921)	Wilson	1925	Indianapolis, Ind.	28
Lawyer	Rep.	2 yr., 5 mo. (1921–23)	Harding	1933	Plymouth, Vt.	29
Banker	Rep.	4 yr. (1925–1929)	Coolidge	1951	Evanston, Ill.	30
Lawyer	Rep.	4 yr. (1929–1933)	Hoover	1936	Topeka, Kans.	31
Lawyer	Dem.	7 yr., 10 mo., 17 d. (1933–1941)	Roosevelt	1967	Uvalde, Tex.	32
Editor	Dem.	4 yr. (1941–1945)	Roosevelt	1965	Des Moines, Ia.	33
Pub. serv.	Dem.	2 mo., 23 d. (1945)	Roosevelt	1972	Independence, Mo.	34
Lawyer	Dem.	4 yr. (1949–1953)	Truman	1956	Paducah, Ky.	35
Lawyer	Rep.	8 yr. (1953–1961)	Eisenhower			36
Lawyer	Dem.	2 yr. 10 m. 2 d. (1961–1963)	Kennedy	1973	Stonewell, Tex.	37
Pharmacist	Dem.	4 yrs. (1965–1969)	Johnson			38
Lawyer	Rep.	4 yrs., 8 mo., 21 d. (1969–1973)	Nixon			39
Lawyer	Rep.	8 mo. (247 d.) (1973–1974)	Nixon			40
Banker	Rep.	2 yrs., 1 mo., 1 da. (1974–1977)	Ford			41
Lawyer	Dem.		Carter			42

A. Johnson, Arthur, T. Roosevelt, Coolidge, Truman, L. Johnson).
(5) Elected as vice president two terms (Adams, Clinton, Tompkins, Calhoun, Marshall, Garner, Nixon, Agnew). (6) Ford was christened Leslie King, Jr., for his natural father, but was then given the name of his stepfather.

Showing the States Carried by Each Party Since 1888

R, Republican; D, Democratic; P, Populist; Pr., Progressive; S., States Rights; A., American Independent.

STATE	1888	1892	1896	1900	1904	1908	1912	1916	1920	1924	1928	1932	1936	1940	1944	1948	1952	1956	1960	1964	1968	1972	1976
Alabama	D	D	D	D	D	D	D	D	D	D	D	D	D	D	D	S	D	D	D	R	A	R	D
Alaska																			R	D	R	R	R
Arizona							D	D	R	R	R	D	D	D	D	D	R	R	R	R	R	R	R
Arkansas	D	D	D	D	D	D	D	D	D	D	D	D	D	D	D	D	D	D	D	D	A	R	D
California	R	D a	R f	R	R	R	Pr j	D	R	R	R	D	D	D	D	D	R	R	R	D	R	R	R
Colorado	R	P	D	D	R	D	D	D	R	R	R	D	R	D	D	D	R	R	R	D	R	R	R
Connecticut	D	D	R	R	R	R	D	R	R	R	R	D	D	D	R	R	R	R	D	D	R	R	R
Delaware	D	D	R	R	R	R	D	R	R	R	R	D	D	D	R	R	R	R	D	D	R	R	D
Dist. of Columbia																				D	D	D	D
Florida	D	D	D	D	D	D	D	D	D	D	D	R	D	D	D	D	R	D	R	D	R	R	D
Georgia	D	D	D	D	D	D	D	D	D	D	D	D	D	D	D	D	D	D	D	R	A	R	D
Hawaii																			D	D	D	R	D
Idaho		P	D	D	R	R	D	D	R	R	R	D	D	D	D	R	R	R	R	D	R	R	R
Illinois	R	D	R	R	R	R	D	R	R	R	R	D	D	D	R	R	R	R	D	D	R	R	R
Indiana	R	D	R	R	R	R	D	R	R	R	R	D	D	R	R	R	R	R	D	D	R	R	R
Iowa	R	R	R	R	R	R	D	R	R	R	R	D	D	R	R	R	R	R	D	D	R	R	R
Kansas	R	P	D	R	R	R	D	D	R	R	R	R	D	D	R	R	R	R	D	D	R	R	R
Kentucky	D	D	R g	D	D	D	D	D	R	R	D	D	D	R	R	D	R	R	D	R	R	D
Louisiana	D	D	D	D	D	D	D	D	D	D	D	D	D	D	D	S	D	R	D	R	A	R	D
Maine	R	R	R	R	R	R	D	R	R	R	R	R	R	R	R	R	R	R	R	D	D	R	R
Maryland	D	D	R	R	D h	D i	D	D	R	R	R	D	D	D	R	R	R	R	D	D	D	R	D
Massachusetts	R	R	R	R	R	R	D	R	R	R	R	D	D	D	R	R	R	R	D	D	D	D	D
Michigan	R	R b	R	R	R	R	Pr	R	R	R	R	D	D	R	D	R	R	R	D	D	R	R	R
Minnesota	R	R	R	R	R	R	Pr	R	R	R	R	D	D	D	D	D	D	R	D	D	D	R	D
Mississippi	D	D	D	D	D	D	D	D	D	D	D	D	D	D	D	S	D	D	D	R	A	R	D
Missouri	D	D	D	R	R	R	D	D	R	R	R	D	D	D	R	D	R	R	D	D	R	R	D
Montana		R	D	D	D	D	D	D	R	R	R	D	D	D	D	R	R	R	D	D	R	R	R
Nebraska	R	R	R	R	R	R	D	D	R	R	R	D	D	R	R	R	R	R	D	D	R	R	R
Nevada	R	P	D	D	R	D	D	D	R	R	R	D	D	D	D	D	R	R	D	D	R	R	R
New Hampshire	R	R	R	R	R	R	D	R	R	R	R	R	R	D	R	R	R	R	D	D	R	R	R
New Jersey	D	D	R	R	R	R	D	R	R	R	R	R	D	D	R	R	R	R	D	D	R	R	R
New Mexico							D	D	R	R	R	D	D	D	D	D	R	R	D	D	R	R	R
New York	R	D	R	R	R	R	D	R	R	R	R	D	D	D	R	R	R	R	D	D	R	R	D
North Carolina	D	D	D	D	D	D	D	D	D	D	D	R	D	D	D	D	D	D	D	D	R	R	D
North Dakota		P c	R	R	R	R	D	R	R	R	R	D	D	R	R	R	R	R	R	D	R	R	R
Ohio	R	R d	R	R	R	R	D	D	R	R	R	D	D	D	R	R	R	R	D	D	R	R	R
Oklahoma							D	D	R	D	R	D	D	D	D	D	R	R	R	D	R	R	R
Oregon	R	R e	R	R	R	R	D	R	R	R	R	D	D	R	R	R	R	R	D	D	R	R	R
Pennsylvania	R	R	R	R	R	R	Pr	R	R	R	R	R	D	D	R	R	R	R	D	D	R	R	D
Rhode Island	R	R	D	R	R	R	D	R	R	R	R	D	D	D	D	D	D	R	D	D	D	R	D
South Carolina	D	D	D	D	D	D	D	D	D	D	D	D	D	D	D	S	D	D	D	R	R	R	D
South Dakota		R	D	R	R	R	Pr	R	R	R	R	D	D	R	R	R	R	R	R	R	R	R	R
Tennessee	D	D	D	D	D	D	D	D	R	D	R	D	D	D	D	D	D r	R	R	D	R	R	D
Texas	D	D	D	D	D	D	D	D	D	R	R	D	D	D	D	D	R	R	D	D	D	R	D
Utah			D	R	R	R	D	D	R	R	R	D	D	D	D	D	R	R	R	D	R	R	R
Vermont	R	R	R	R	R	R	R	R	R	R	R	R	R	R	R	R	R	R	R	R	D	R	R
Virginia	D	D	D	D	D	D	D	D	D	D	D	R	D	D	D	D	R	D	D	D	R	R	R
Washington		R	D	R	R	R	Pr	D	R	R	R	D	D	D	D	R	R	R	D	D	R	R	D
West Virginia	D	D	R	R	R	R	D	R k	R	R	R	D	D	D	D	R	D	R	D	D	D	R	D
Wisconsin	R	D	R	R	R	R	R	R	R	P l	R	D	D	D	R	D	R	R	R	D	R	R	D
Wyoming		R	D	R	R	R	D	D	R	R	R	D	D	D	R	R	R	R	R	D	R	R	R

a Dem., 8; Rep., 1. b Rep., 9; Dem., 5. c Rep., 1; Dem., 1. d Rep., 22; Dem., 1. e Rep., 3; Pop., 1. f Rep., 8, Dem,. 1.
g Rep., 12; Dem., 1. h Dem., 7; Rep., 1. i Dem., 6; Rep., 2. j Prog., 11; Dem., 2. k Rep., 7; Dem. 1. l Dem., 11; S., 1.

DICTIONARY OF AMERICAN HISTORY

THE following section deals with topics in the history of the American people, both in regard to the nation's development at home and in regard to its relations with other peoples. Some of these topics have already received mention in the article on the history of the United States but are here treated with greater completeness than is possible in the continuous narrative. The majority of the items, however, are concise accounts of parties, events, and other phases of national life which have not received specific mention in the connected narrative of the country's history, being reserved for a more adequate treatment in special articles.

Abolitionists. The Northern group active from 1830 to 1850 which advocated the immediate emancipation of slaves without compensation to their owners. In 1832, William Lloyd Garrison, publisher of the militant journal *Liberator*, organized with his associates the New England Antislavery Society, which became the American Antislavery Society in 1833. The purpose of this organization was to establish antislavery societies throughout the country and to spread antislavery propaganda. Such activities aroused intense antagonism in both the North and South, and, as a result, meetings were often broken up, Garrison was mobbed, and Lovejoy, a leading abolitionist, was killed. In 1840 the Society split: the radical group followed Garrison, while the conservative group formed the Liberty party, whose purpose was to bring the national government under the control of those opposed to slavery.

Air Force, United States. Prior to the Armed Services Unification Act of 1947, the U.S. Army and the U.S. Navy each operated its own air force. That of the Army, originating in 1907 as the aeronautical division of the Signal Corps, had developed through two world wars as a combat and later a bombing arm of decisive importance. That of the Navy became the Navy's initial striking force and participated in anti-submarine service. After unification, the Navy retained operational planes, including those from aircraft carriers, and the Marine Corps likewise retained operational planes. The Army was restricted mainly to helicopters. All other air operations were centralized under the Air Force.

The Air Force comprises the regular, reserve, and national guard divisions. It is organized into three operational commands, with 17 supporting commands. The operational commands are: the air defense command, responsible also to the joint U.S.-Canada joint defense agency; the strategic air command, which operates long-range bombers based at home and abroad, intercontinental guided missiles, and missile interceptors; and the tactical air command, which operates fighters, bombers, and troop carriers. The strength of the Air Force in 1966 consisted of between 15,000 and 16,000 aircraft and personnel of over 800,000.

The Korean War was the first war in which the newly organized Air Force took part, operating chiefly from bases in Japan.

Alabama Claims. A series of claims for indemnity made upon Great Britain by the United States, based upon alleged failure of Great Britain to observe certain obligations of international law. These claims arose chiefly from damages inflicted by vessels in the Confederate service, which vessels had been fitted out or built in English waters. The history of the Confederate cruiser *Alabama* is typical of the more flagrant cases. This vessel was built at Birkenhead, England, and, although the attention of the British government was repeatedly called to suspicious circumstances, "No. 290," as the ship was called, sailed July 29, 1862, without register or clearance papers. After taking on equipment in the Azores from two English vessels, she assumed the name *Alabama* and began her famous career of destruction. She is said to have destroyed 70 vessels, before being sunk by the *Kearsarge*, June 19, 1864.

The determination of the extent to which the government of Great Britain was responsible for the damage inflicted by the *Alabama* and other vessels of similar history was the most important problem of diplomacy resulting from the Civil War. By the Treaty of Washington, 1871, the *Alabama* claims were submitted to the decision of five arbitrators,—one named by England, one by the United States, and one each by the king of Italy, the emperor of Brazil, and the president of Switzerland. The arbitrators met at Geneva, December 15, 1871, and, on September 14, 1872, signed the final award. By unanimous vote, England was adjudged responsible for the depredations of the cruiser *Alabama* and, in full satisfaction of this and all other claims, was directed to pay an indemnity of $15,500,000.

Alamo, Defense of the. In the year 1835, the people of Texas, then a department of the Republic of Mexico, revolted against the Mexican government. Their ultimate purpose was annexation to the United States. In 1836, Santa Anna, with an army of several thousand, undertook to crush the revolution. For a time his campaign was successful. It was the heroic defense of the old fort of the Alamo, at San Antonio, by 183 Texans under W. B. Travis, that inspired the people to successful efforts at resistance. The little band endured a siege of thirteen days. When all but six of the garrison had been killed, the Mexicans took the place by storm, and the survivors were shot by order of Santa Anna. The war cry of Texas became "Remember the Alamo."

Alaska Boundary Commission. A commission of six jurists appointed under the treaty of 1903 to determine the eastern boundary of the Alaska "Panhandle." The boundary was admitted to be ten marine leagues from the sea. Canada claimed that the distance should be measured from a straight line from headland to headland; the United States, that the boundary should follow the windings of the coast. A majority decision, rendered October 20, 1903, supported the United States contention.

Alaska Highway. A road from Dawson Creek, B. C., about 250 miles west of Edmonton, Alta., to Whitehorse, Y.T., and thence to Fairbanks, Alaska, on the east of the Rocky Mountains. Between March and November 1942, it was built as a war measure by the United States Army Engineers under an agreement between the United States and Canada to give a land route to Alaska. Its cost was $138,-000,000; its length, 1523 miles. Before 1946 it was called Alcan Highway. In April 1946 the Canadian portion, 1221 miles, was turned over to Canada.

Alaska Purchase. By a treaty between the United States and Russia, in 1867, the latter power surrendered all her possessions on the continent of North America, approximately the present great territory of Alaska, together with the Pribilof islands, in consideration of a payment of $7,200,000.

Albany Regency. The first well organized American political machine. A coterie of Democrats who, from 1820 to 1854, exercised a controlling influence over the politics of the State of New York, and had consequently considerable power in national politics. Their headquarters were at Albany. Chief among this regency were Martin Van Buren and W. L. Marcy.

Alien and Sedition Acts. A series of four acts passed by the Federalist party in Congress in 1798, after the publication of the "X Y Z" letters. The Alien acts (1) raised the residence period for naturalization from five to fourteen years, (2) authorized the president for two years to order out of the country any aliens he might judge dangerous, (3) authorized the president to expel from the country citizens of any nation with which the United States might be at war. The Sedition act provided penalties of fine and imprisonment for combining to oppose governmental measures and for any false, scandalous, or malicious writing against the government or its high officials, with intent to bring them into disrepute. A few prosecutions took place under this Sedition act. These acts provoked the first assertions of the doctrine of state rights. See *Virginia and Kentucky Resolutions.*

Amana (*ăm′à-nà*) **Society.** A religious community established in 1855 at Amana, Iowa, in which all land and factories were owned by the community, which practiced certain principles of communism. The chief interest of the community was the religious society, which was founded by Eberhard Gruber in Württemberg in 1714. The community was reorganized as a joint stock company in 1932.

America. This name was first applied, with little warrant, to the continental regions of the western hemisphere by Martin Waldseemüller, a young geographer at Saint-Dié, a town in the Vosges mountains. In a Latin work, *Cosmographiæ Introductio*, which Waldseemüller edited in 1507, he used the name America in honor of Amerigo (Americus) Vespucci, whose narrative of the latter's voyages of discovery to the New World Waldseemüller had read. "Because Americus discovered it," wrote the geographer, "it ought to be called the land of Americus, or America."

America, Discovery of. According to the Norse sagas, the discovery of America should be placed to the credit of the vikings who made five expeditions to the coast between 985 and 1011, the first being that of Eric the Red, who settled in Greenland in 986, and the most famous that of Thorfinn Karlsefne, about 1007. Madoc, a Welsh prince, is said to have established a colony in the Western world in 1170. A Norse expedition penetrated into western Minnesota, leaving an inscription dated 1362 on a stone which was discovered in 1898. But the discovery that opened the continent to colonization was made by Columbus in 1492.

America Act. An act passed by the British Parliament in 1775, consolidating all the previous penal acts relating to the American colonies. It declared that all American vessels were lawful prizes, and that all Americans captured in them, or elsewhere, could be forced to take service against America. Commissioners were appointed to receive the submission of the revolted colonies, but no provisions were made for the redress of grievances.

American Antislavery Society. See *Abolitionists.*

American Customs Act. An act passed by the British Parliament in 1764, levying customs duties on goods imported into the American colonies. These duties were to be levied for the benefit of England, and the proceeds thereof were to be paid into the English treasury. The assertion of this right to tax the colonies for the benefit of the mother country was a main cause of the Revolutionary War.

American Party. Name adopted in 1854 by a faction of the Whigs who sought to crush the power of the foreign-born in politics, particularly through opposition to the Irish and to the Roman Catholic Church. From about 1835 there had been an organized movement aimed at keeping Roman Catholics out of public office. The early "Native American" movement, which later passed into the "Know-Nothing" movement, was occasioned by the political ascendancy of certain foreign groups in Eastern cities. The so-called American party was formed by the merging of the "Know-Nothings" with a faction of the Whigs. In 1855 the American party swept the elections in New York, Massachusetts, Rhode Island, Connecticut, and New Hampshire, and elected a number of its candidates in other states. In 1856 the party nominated Millard Fillmore for president and Andrew Jackson Donelson for vice president. These nominees were adopted by the Whig party as its candidates. Among the provisions in the platform of the American party were such declarations as the following: "Americans must rule America"; "Native-born citizens should be selected for all state, Federal, and municipal offices." A further provision of the platform was that a residence of 21 years should be required for citizenship in the United States. In 1860 the American party virtually dissolved, and the major part of its members joined the Constitutional Union party.

American Protective Association, "A. P. A." A secret organization formed in 1887. Its avowed purpose was to curb the political power of the Roman Catholic Church, to keep Catholics out of public office, and to protect the public school system from subversion by the Roman Church. The society fell into desuetude soon after its organization. It has, however, been revived in various parts of the country from time to time and has endeavored to make itself felt in local elections in some of the larger municipal centers. At times it has been also a factor in state and national elections.

American System. The name applied to the policies advocated by the National Republicans under Clay from 1829 to 1833. Primarily, it designated the policy of a high protective tariff; but it was extended to include the establishment of a national bank and the construction of internal improvements by the Federal government, particularly the construction of national highways.

Annapolis Convention, The. A small conference which met at Annapolis, September 11, 1786, and was attended by delegates from five states, New York, New Jersey, Pennsylvania, Delaware, and Virginia. The meeting was originally suggested for discussion of matters relating to roads for commerce and to uniform duties on imports, but the members found it necessary to consider the entire subject of the weakened Confederation. As a result, they issued a call for a meeting of delegates from all the states, to be held at Philadelphia in the following May. This action brought about the Constitutional Convention of 1787.

Antifederalists. The "small states" party which opposed the adoption of the Constitution, taking their name from their opposition to the group which favored adoption. The Antifederalists became the party of state rights, and consistently opposed the expansion of the powers of the Federal government. After the adoption of the Constitution, this party merged into the Republican, or, as it was later called, the Democratic-Republican, party, under the leadership of Jefferson and Madison.

Anti-Imperialists. The political group which, after the close of the Spanish war in 1898, opposed the retention of the Philippine Islands by the United States. They maintained that holding this territory or any other, on the terms contemplated by the treaty with Spain, would be a violation of the principles and institutions of the United States. The leading figures in this group were Senator George F. Hoar of Massachusetts, Republican, and Senator Arthur P. Gorman of Maryland, Democrat. After the ratification of the treaty which provided for the acquisition of the Philippines, those who sympathized with the antiannexation view organized the Anti-Imperialist League, embracing numerous societies throughout the country, whose purpose was to secure the early recognition of Philippine independence.

Antimasonic Party. A third party which exercised considerable power in state and in national elections from 1828 to 1840. One William Morgan, a resident of Batavia, N. Y., who announced in 1826 that he was about to publish the secrets of the Masonic order, was said to have been abducted and murdered. The popular indignation over the reported outrage crystallized in 1827 into a political organization opposed to the election of Masons to office.

In the State of New York the party polled a very strong vote in 1830, and in 1831 the movement had spread so far throughout the country that a national nominating convention was called to meet in Philadelphia,—the first meeting of its kind in the United States. The convention named an Antimasonic candidate for the presidency, but his decisive defeat in 1832 marked the end of the movement as a national party. In various states, however, the party continued to exercise a definite influence until 1840.

Anti-Nebraska Men. Whigs and Democrats who in 1854 were opposed to the repeal of the Missouri Compromise and to the extension of slavery to the territories. This group had a large part in forming the Republican party. See *Kansas-Nebraska Bill*.

Antirent Riots. Disturbances attending the movement in New York to abolish certain survivals of feudal land tenure which persisted in the 19th century on the so-called patroon estates along the Hudson river, which were owned by the Van Rensselaers and other families of Dutch origin. The tenants banded together in 1839 to resist the collection of arrears of rents and of other perquisites due the estate owners. A state of virtual rebellion existed in 1844 and 1845. For some years tenants commanded sufficient votes to make them a force in the legislature, but their real victory was due to a decision of the court of appeals in 1852, which declared that agreements of sale entailing the feudal obligations to which the tenants objected were illegal. Settlements between landlords and tenants were accordingly effected, so that the titles to the land were placed on the same basis as that on which land titles elsewhere in the county rested. See *Patroons*.

Antisaloon League. A nonpartisan organization formed in 1893. The purposes of the league were to spread propaganda and to exert a united nonpartisan influence at elections within the major political parties, in order to bring about the eradication of the saloon and the ultimate suppression of the manufacture and sale of intoxicating liquor. After the enactment of prohibition laws in the states, and particularly after the adoption of the 18th amendment, the Antisaloon League constituted itself a private committee of citizens seeking to aid the authorities in securing the proper enforcement of the prohibition laws.

Anti-Snappers. Supporters of Grover Cleveland, who in 1892 withdrew from the regular state convention of the Democratic party in New York. They held a separate convention and chose delegates to the Democratic national convention to contest the seats of the delegates from the regular state convention, all of whom were opposed to the presidency of Cleveland. See *Snappers*.

Army, United States. The military history of the United States goes back to the establishment of the volunteer militia before the Revolutionary War. In 1775, Washington took command of the militia of several states, and, finding himself plagued by problems of discipline, short-term enlistments, and a generally loose organization, he urged the formation of an army directly under the authority of Congress and with an enlistment period of several years. On July 14, 1775, Congress had passed the first legislation ordering the formation of such a force. However the Continental Army was always lacking in strong discipline, and its numbers rarely exceeded 30,000 at any time.

In 1802 the Military Academy at West Point was established for the training of officers. The first national militia law was passed by Congress in 1792. It remained in force until 1903, when it was supplemented by the National Defense act of 1916, which reorganized the National Guard.

In the War of 1812, neither the small force of regulars nor the much larger body of volunteers registered many notable successes. The Indian wars

and the Mexican war were fought by a combination of regulars, volunteers, and militia. The regular army was small, numbering 67,000 just before the Civil War. Following the war, detachments of regulars, operating from frontier military posts, carried out campaigns against the Indians. The Spanish-American War demanded a rapid increase in the number of fighting men, and, since a legal question prevented the sending of National Guard troops abroad, the regular army was heavily supplemented by volunteers until it totaled 281,000.

In 1916 the National Defense Act raised the peacetime force to an unprecedented high of 259,000 men. After war was declared on April 6, 1917, Congress raised this figure to 713,000. The passage of the Selective Service Act provided 67 per cent of the World War I army. The dangerous shortage of officers was partly relieved by the establishment of both short-term training camps and the ROTC program in colleges and universities. After the war, the 1918 army of 3,710,563 was reduced to 260,000.

World War II and After. The growing threat of war in 1940 led Congress to pass the first peacetime selective service act, and, by calling National Guard units into active duty, an army of 1,500,000 was raised by 1941. Reorganization of the War Department placed George C. Marshall, chief of staff, at the head of the Army Ground Forces, the Army Air Forces, and the Army Service Forces. The need to keep as many men as possible at home for industrial work led to the formation of the Women's Army Corps. At its peak strength in May 1945, the army numbered 8,291,336 men and women. In the first nine months after victory, over 6,000,000 of these were released.

After World War II, the National Security Act of 1947 made the Air Force a separate branch and combined the Army, Navy, and Air Force under the Department of Defense. The Korean War saw an army of 600,000 in June 1950 mobilized to a force of 1,500,000 while General MacArthur carried out delaying tactics in the Far East.

After 1949, the United States entered into anti-Communist agreements with fifty nations, a situation which necessitated a strong peace-time army and a new kind of strike-back force in the event of enemy atomic attack. Obsolete equipment was replaced by lighter, air-transported weapons and materials. In 1961, the army instituted the Reorganization Objective Army Division (ROAD), which provided fighting forces suitably tailored to the demands of various terrain, missions, and foes. Special training was given in guerilla and psychological warfare.

A large-scale reorganization in 1962 set up the following commands: (1) Army Materiel Development and Logistic Command (MDLC); (2) Army Combat Developments Command (ACDC); (3) Continental Army Command (CONARC); and (4) the Army components of unified commands (including overseas commands). Overall control of the army is held by the Department of the Army under the Department of Defense. The Secretary of the Army, a civilian, is the head of the Department of the Army. Army headquarters are at the Pentagon in Washington, D.C.

In 1966, over 50 per cent of the Army's total combined strength was in overseas theaters. Two new military commands were created in 1965: the Army Intelligence Command at Fort Holabird, Maryland, and the Military Traffic Management and Terminal Service, at Washington, D.C. New weapons were developed which included a lightweight rifle that permits individual soldiers to carry twice the ammunition, and the Sheridan weapon system armed with the Shillelagh guided missile.

The war in Viet-Nam saw modifications designed to free troops from restrictions of terrain by substituting transport and armed helicopters for trucks and tanks.

Bacon's Rebellion. The armed uprising in Virginia in 1676 against the arbitrary, "special privilege" rule of Governor Berkeley. Its immediate occasion was the governor's failure to authorize protection of the plantations from Indian attacks. Nathaniel Bacon, a young planter, took matters into his own hands, raised a force, and punished the Indians. Berkeley was forced to call a new assembly, which passed several acts, known as Bacon's Laws, restoring a degree of representative government. The death of Bacon robbed the movement of leadership. Berkeley took so fiendish a revenge in executions that Charles II recalled him in disgust.

Barbary War. From the 16th to the 19th century the Barbary states—Morocco, Algiers, Tunis, and Tripoli—carried on systematic piracy and levied blackmail upon the powers that wished to trade in the Mediterranean. The United States paid several millions in tribute and for ransom of prisoners. Finally, in 1815, Commodore Decatur with his fleet forced Algiers, Tunis, and Tripoli to give up all claims to payments from the U.S. and to release Christian prisoners of all nationalities.

Barnburners. A name given by their opponents, the Hunkers, to the antislavery faction of the Democratic party in New York from 1844 to 1848. The name has reference to the faction's indifference to all issues but slavery, which suggested the conduct of the man who is said to have burned his barn to rid it of rats. This faction opposed James K. Polk, the party's presidential candidate in 1844, and in 1848 they nominated for president Van Buren, who was later nominated by the Free-Soil party.

"Battle above the Clouds," The. Popular name given to a part of the battle of Chattanooga, November 23-24-25, 1863. While General Hooker's troops were ascending the slopes of Lookout mountain on the 24th, a fog hung over them, concealing the battle from the view of troops in the valley.

Bay of Pigs. In April 1961 anti-Castro exiles attempted to invade Cuba by landing on Girón Beach in the Bay of Pigs. A U.S. Senate investigation revealed that the invasion had been planned since May 1960 by the U.S. Central Intelligence Agency. The agency trained, financed, equipped, and supervised the invasion. The Bay of Pigs invasion failed, and the U.S. had to give Cuba approximately $53 million worth of food and medicine for the release of the invasion survivors.

Bering Sea Controversy. The question as to the right of Canadian sealers to capture seals in Bering Sea (known as pelagic sealing), after being long in dispute, was submitted to arbitration in 1892. The right to conduct land sealing on the Pribilof islands had been leased by the United States to the North American Commercial Company. Pelagic sealing by Canadians and other nationalities involved killing of females and young. This threatened extinction of the seal herd. To prevent this calamity, the United States asserted a claim to the right to control all sealing in Bering Sea. In 1893 the arbitrators decided against this claim, and declared Bering Sea to be open ocean. But, as authorized by the terms of the reference, they made the following regulations: (1) all sealing within sixty maritime miles of the Pribilof islands to be forbidden; (2) a closed time for seals to be established; (3) all sealing vessels to be licensed. These regulations proved worthless. In 1898 Americans were forbidden by law to do pelagic sealing. Finally, in 1911, the U.S., Britain, Russia, and Japan agreed to suspend sealing for a period of fifteen years.

Bicentennial Year. The United States celebrated its 200th birthday in 1976 with a variety of activities. Many of the celebrations focused on the ethnic heritages of different groups of Americans. Throughout the year, the Freedom Train, a traveling exhibition of American culture and history, visited over 200 cities. A wagon train traveled across the country from Oregon to Valley Forge, Pa., where it was met on July 3 by President Ford. The highlight of the July Fourth celebration was a voyage of 16 tall sailing ships up the Hudson River past New York City.

Bill of Rights, The. The name given to the first ten amendments to the Constitution, which restrict the power of the Federal government with respect to certain rights of the individual citizen and of the separate states. Precedent for this statement of "rights" was found in the Bill of Rights presented by Parliament to William and Mary in 1689. Similar declarations of rights are attached to the constitutions of most of the states of the Union.

Black and Tans. About 1892–96, this name was applied to Southern Republicans who believed in giving to the Negro an equal opportunity with the whites in holding party and political office. They were opposed by the Lily-white Republicans.

Black Hawk War. Two short campaigns in 1831-32 in Illinois. Black Hawk, chief of the Sac Indians, after his tribe had ceded their lands to the United States and moved west of the Mississippi, returned and began massacres of white settlers. He was captured in August 1832. Abraham Lincoln was a captain of militia in the campaign.

Black Republicans. Name applied by Democrats to members of the newly created Republican party during the years immediately preceding the Civil War, by reason of the new party's apparent solicitude for the interests of the Negro race. Those who thus contemptuously applied the name distinguished the new Republican party from the old Republican or Democratic-Republican party, which had been the predecessor of the Democratic party.

Black Warrior Case. An incident which almost brought war between the U.S. and Spain in 1854. A U.S. vessel was seized at Havana, Cuba, for alleged violation of customs regulations. The ship and cargo were confiscated despite the protest of the U.S. consul. The U.S. demanded restoration of the property. Hostilities were avoided by the disavowal by Spain of the acts of the Havana officials and by payment of the value of the ship and its cargo to the owners. The case acquired importance from its connection with attempts of filibusters to force the annexation of Cuba to the U.S.

Bloody-Shirts. A term applied after the Civil War to those Northerners who, prompted by petty political motives, persisted in denouncing Southerners as traitors to their country, and who, in political parlance, thus sought to keep alive the Southern issue by "waving the bloody shirt."

Blue Laws. Laws which seek to regulate the moral conduct of individuals in the community. Blue was the color adopted by the Scotch Covenanters in the 17th century in England, and it became also the Whig color. The term blue was applied to those who decried the licentious freedom of the Restoration period, and to Puritans in general. In New England it came to be attached to certain rigorous laws, passed at various times and in different colonies, for the regulation of religious and personal conduct. The "blue laws of Connecticut" became proverbial. The title seems to have attached to the earliest code of the colony of New Haven (about 1640).

Blue Light Federalists. Applied first to Federalists, and later to all New Englanders who were opposed to the war with England in 1812. The term originated from the charge that blue light signals had been flashed by Federalists at New London in 1813 as a warning to the British, when Commodore Decatur was trying to escape through the blockade.

Bonus Army (Bonus Expeditionary Force). In the summer of 1932 more than 12,000 World War I veterans, led by Walter W. Waters, marched on Washington, D.C. Congress had voted in 1924 on adjusted compensation certificates payable in 1945. The marchers, who had to be dispersed by the army, demanded immediate payment of wartime-service benefits.

Booth's Conspiracy. A conspiracy headed by John Wilkes Booth, at the end of the Civil War, having for its object the assassination of the president, the vice president, and members of the cabinet. President Lincoln was shot by Booth on April 14, 1865, and on the same date Seward, the secretary of state, was wounded by Payne, another of the conspirators. Booth was shot while in hiding. Four of the other conspirators were hanged, the rest being sentenced to various terms of imprisonment.

Border Ruffians. The name applied in Kansas before the Civil War to the lawless element, coming largely from Missouri, which menaced the settlers from the North and attempted to prevent the establishment of a free state government.

Border States. Before the Civil War, this name was applied to the five slave states—Delaware, Maryland, Virginia, Kentucky, and Missouri—bordering on the free states.

Boston Massacre. A conflict of citizens and British soldiers on March 5, 1770, in which five persons were killed and six were injured. The affair grew out of quartering soldiers on the townspeople for purposes of intimidation. Blame attaches to the government that made the trouble possible. John Adams and Josiah Quincy volunteered as counsel for the soldiers at their trial. Two were given light punishment, the others were acquitted.

Boston Port Bill. An act passed by the British Parliament in 1774, closing the custom house and port of Boston. It was a measure of retaliation for the action of the inhabitants in preventing the importation of tea by the British East India Company.

Boston Tea Party. The American colonists had determined not to pay the tea duty imposed by Parliament. On December 16, 1773, the tea ships of the British East India Company, which were lying in Boston harbor, were boarded by a party of men disguised as Indians, who threw into the harbor the entire cargo of the three ships, 342 chests of tea, valued at about £18,000.

Bounty Jumping. During some periods of the Civil War, the government paid "bounties" to volunteers. Unprincipled men would enlist, go to the front and serve long enough to get the "bounty money," and then desert, afterward re-enlisting under assumed names, thus getting another "bounty." Such men were called "bounty jumpers."

Braddock's Defeat. The utter rout of the combined English and colonial forces under General Edward Braddock by a small body of French and Indians near Fort Duquesne, July 9, 1755. The defeat was due to Braddock's refusal to adopt the methods of frontier warfare, with which he was unfamiliar. English losses were nearly 900 out of 1400. Washington accompanied Braddock as an aide, and he, with Virginia troops, saved the remnant of the retreating army from massacre.

Brown vs. Board of Education. A milestone in American public education came on May 17, 1954, when the Supreme Court ruled in this case that racial segregation in public schools was unconstitutional. In making the decision, the Court unanimously held that the "separate but equal" doctrine established in the case of *Plessy vs. Ferguson* in 1896 had no place in public education because separate educational facilities were inherently unequal.

Buck Stove and Range Case. A case on which, from 1906 to 1940, reliance was placed for limiting action of labor unions in industrial disputes. In 1906 the American Federation of Labor, acting in conjunction with the striking employees of the Buck Stove and Range Company, placed on a widely circulated "unfair list" the names of all retailers who sold the company's stoves. The company brought action in the federal courts to enjoin the federation from circulating the list. The injunction was granted on the ground that the federation's action was a "secondary boycott," that is, a boycott not of the company itself, but of those who dealt with the company. A series of decisions in 1940-41 by the Supreme Court declared the advertising of a labor dispute to be under the protection of the free speech guarantee of the Constitution.

Bucktails. Applied to members of the Tammany Society during its early years, by reason of the buck's tail worn in the hat as a part of the costume of members of the society. The term was later applied to all opponents of Governor Clinton's canal project in New York, since the Tammany men constituted the most aggressive of these opponents.

Bull Moose. Nickname applied to the Progressive party in 1912, the name originating from Theodore Roosevelt's remark upon one occasion: "I feel as fit as a bull moose." The bull moose was taken up as the emblem of the party, and the party itself came to be called the "Bull Moose party."

Busing. The compulsory transfer of public school students in order to achieve racial balance. Busing became a major political issue after the passage of the Civil Rights Act in 1964. Although Congress prohibited the use of federal funds to finance busing, federal courts continued to order desegregation plans for school systems in both the North and the South. While many of these orders were followed without incident, some—most notably in Boston and Louisville—met violent resistance.

Butternuts. Northerners who sympathized with the South during the Civil War. The term was suggested by the "butternut" color of the Confederate uniform.

Canadian Fisheries Question. A long-standing dispute between Canada and the U.S., dating from the treaty of peace of 1783, which recognized American fishing rights off the coast of Canada, to 1871, when a treaty was signed at Washington giving the two countries reciprocal rights. Canada maintained that her fisheries were more valuable than those off the American coast. In 1877 a commission, which met at Halifax, awarded Canada and Newfoundland $5,500,000 as compensation. The U.S. abrogated the reciprocity treaty in 1885. The question was settled by an arbitration board appointed by the Hague Tribunal in 1910.

Cannonism. The term applied by Progressive Republicans in 1910-12 to the arbitrary methods of Joseph G. Cannon in his use of the great power of the speaker of the House of Representatives. The Progressives accused him of giving committee appointments only to members who agreed with him, thus directing legislation in the interests of a few.

Carpetbaggers. A term applied to Northern politicians who, after the Civil War, went to the Southern states with no more baggage than a carpetbag, and, by fraud and manipulation of the votes of the newly enfranchised Negro, obtained control of several state governments. Through misgovernment by these carpetbaggers, some of the Southern states were run deeply into debt.

Chinese Exclusion Acts. In 1881 a treaty with China gave the United States power to "regulate, limit, or suspend" immigration of Chinese laborers. Successive acts suspended such immigration from 1882 to December 1943, when the existing act was repealed. The naturalization of Chinese already in the United States was permitted, and new immigrants were admitted on a quota basis, 105 in a year.

Civil Rights Act of 1964. Passed by Congress on July 2, 1964, the act was designed to ensure and protect the constitutional rights of black citizens. Its key provisions barred unequal application of voting-registration requirements, outlawed discrimination in most public places, and established a community-relations service to mediate disputes. The act also authorized the U.S. Attorney General to file suit against segregated schools and other city- or state-owned facilities, and permitted the federal government to cut off funds from any discriminatory program.

Clintonians. Followers of the Clinton family, who, together with the Livingston and the Schuyler families, controlled the government of the State of New York from 1777 to 1827. This group formed a powerful support for the Democratic-Republican or Antifederalist party, which secured the election of Jefferson to the presidency in 1800. George Clinton was elected vice president of the United States in 1804. His nephew, DeWitt Clinton, leading a Republican faction opposed to the Virginian domination of the party, was nominated for the presidency in 1812 and, with Federalist support, unsuccessfully opposed Madison.

Compromise of 1850. The name given to a group of bills passed by Congress in 1850. These measures were modifications of the omnibus bill proposed by Henry Clay. They contained the following provisions: (1) The admission of California as a free state; (2) the organization of Utah and New Mexico, with the question of slavery left to the people of those territories; (3) payment of $10,000,000 to Texas for her claims to portions of New Mexico; (4) prohibition of the slave trade in the District of Columbia; (5) a more drastic fugitive slave law.

Confiscation Acts. During the Civil War, two so-called Confiscation acts were passed by Congress, the first in 1861, and the second in the following year. Under the first act, all property of rebels, used in furthering the rebellion, was subjected to forfeiture or confiscation by the federal government, the proceeds thereof to be used to support the Northern armies. By the act of 1862, the penalty of confiscation was extended to cover all property, including slaves, of rebels and of traitors to the Union. Although the validity of the Confiscation acts was never questioned in the courts, they probably were unconstitutional as violative of Article I, Section IX (III), which forbids the passing of bills of attainder and of *ex post facto* laws.

Congress, Meeting Places of. The First Continental Congress met at Philadelphia in 1774, continuing in session from September 5 to October 26. The Second Continental Congress met at Philadelphia on May 10, 1775; this Congress continued as the national government until 1781. With the ratification of the Articles of Confederation in that year, it became the Congress of the Confederation. From 1775 to 1785 the Congress convened ten times in eight different places, as follows:

Philadelphia, May 10, 1775–December 12, 1776.
Baltimore, December 20, 1776–March 4, 1777.
Philadelphia, March 4, 1777–September 18, 1777.
Lancaster, Pa., September 18, 1777–September 27, 1777.
York, Pa., September 30, 1777–June 27, 1778.
Philadelphia, July 2, 1778–June 21, 1783.
Princeton, N. J., June 30, 1783–November 4, 1783.
Annapolis, Md., November 26, 1783–June 3, 1784.
Trenton, N. J., November 1, 1784–December 24, 1784.
New York, January 11, 1785–November 4, 1785.

Its later sessions in New York were held as follows:

November 7, 1785–November 3, 1786.
November 6, 1786–October 30, 1787.
November 5, 1787–October 21, 1788.

From this time until March 1789, the Confederation Congress was kept alive by the occasional attendance of a few members. The last entry in the journal, March 2, 1789, records the presence of Mr. Philip Pell, from New York.

The first Congress under the Constitution met in New York, March 30, 1789. On June 28, 1790, an act was passed which provided that, from the year 1800, the capital should be established on the Potomac River, at a point between the mouth of the East Branch and that of the Connogocheague. In the intervening ten years the Congress met in Philadelphia. The first session in Washington was opened on November 17, 1800.

Conscience Whigs. A name applied about 1850 to members of the Whig party in New England who felt so strongly upon the subject of the moral evils of slavery that they were willing to sacrifice political office and the interests of their party rather than violate the dictates of their consciences by sanctioning the extension of slavery into federal territory. Together with the Democratic "Barnburners" of New York, the Conscience Whigs formed the nucleus of the Free-Soil party, which developed into the Republican party.

Constitutional Union Party. Remnant of the old Whig party, composed largely of Southerners who favored conciliation upon the slavery issue. In 1860 this party nominated an independent national ticket headed by John Bell of Tennessee and by Edward Everett of Massachusetts, upon an evasive platform of adherence to "the Constitution and the Union" and law enforcement.

Consumerism. Consumerism includes those methods or policies instituted to protect the consumer (buyer) in direct or indirect contacts with manufacturers, sellers, and advertisers. This is accomplished by legislative controls, voluntary controls, or consumer-organization influence. Consumerism evolved largely during the 1960s and 1970s because of the complexity and growth of industry and business.

Conway Cabal. A petty intrigue against Washington in 1777-78. It was headed by Horatio Gates, Charles Lee, Thomas Mifflin, James Lovell, and Thomas Conway. Their object was to put Gates in Washington's place. They succeeded in having Gates made president of the board of war in November 1777. But his acts were so inefficient that he was soon removed, and the cabal broke up.

Copperheads. A scornful term applied by Northerners during the Civil War to fellow Northerners who sympathized with the Confederacy and were suspected of secretly aiding the South. The allusion suggested in the name was to the venomous copperhead snake. Some of the partisans of the peace policy wore badges of heads cut from copper cents. Their leader was Clement L. Vallandigham, Congressman from Ohio, 1853–63. Lincoln banished him to the South.

Cotton Whigs. "Old-line" Whigs who preferred to have their party side-step the question of slavery rather than to endanger the integrity of their party and of the Union. They were accused of failing to take a stand in opposition to slavery because of their personal interest in fostering the cotton trade. See *Conscience Whigs*.

Countervailing Legislation. The series of acts passed by Congress at the close of the War of 1812, discriminating against British shipping and commerce because of the injuries inflicted upon American shipping by the British navigation acts.

Credit Mobilier (*mô-bēl'yĕr*). The "inside" construction company formed in 1867 by a group of the leading stockholders of the Union Pacific Railroad Co. The latter company had received from the U.S. government, in land grants and loans, far more than the cost of the railroad to be built from Omaha to California. The Credit Mobilier was used by the manipulators of the Union Pacific to construct the road at an excessive cost. In this way, both the railroad and the government were defrauded. The participation of government officials in the profits of this scheme was the occasion of one of the greatest scandals in American political history.

Crime of '73. The characterization given by the free silver advocates to the demonetization of silver by Congress in 1873. It was alleged that the provision in the act of 1873, which omitted silver from the freely coined metals, was passed surreptitiously and with the design of injuring the farmer and debtor classes of the West and of the South. In fact, no silver had been brought to the mint for coinage for more than twenty years before the act was passed. In providing that silver should no longer be freely coined, therefore, Congress was merely repealing a provision which had been a dead letter for many years. See *Free Silver Movement*.

Custer's Last Fight. The battle of the Little Big Horn, June 25, 1876. General George A. Custer, in command of a cavalry regiment of 600 men, had been sent in advance of the main body of United States troops in pursuit of Sitting Bull and his band. In the belief that he was attacking only a part of the Indian force, Custer divided his regiment and, with 260 men, attacked the Indian center. Instead of encountering 1000 Indians he found himself surrounded by 5000. The general and every man in his troop were killed. One Indian scout attached to the force is said to have escaped. The field is marked by marble monuments.

Danbury Hatters' Case. The popular name of a case on the strength of which, from 1908 to 1941, boycotts of interstate manufacturers by labor unions were held illegal. The United Hat Makers' Union, supported by the American Federation of Labor, declared a boycott of the products of a firm of hat manufacturers in Danbury, Connecticut, who insisted on maintaining an open shop. The action of the union was declared by the supreme court in 1908 to be a violation of the Sherman Antitrust act. The Clayton act, in 1914, declared that, if workmen entered into combinations to further their interests by lawful means, such combinations should not be regarded as unlawful. In 1941, the supreme court, in the case of U. S. v. Hutcheson, decided that this law made the earlier ruling untenable.

Dark Horse. One who has not been prominently in the public eye as a candidate, but who is brought forward at the psychological moment as a compromise candidate when a nominating convention has reached a deadlock. Often a so-called "dark horse" is in fact the candidate who has been the favorite of the party manager from the beginning, but for strategic purposes has been held in reserve. Presidents Polk, Pierce, Hayes, Garfield, and Harding were all "dark horse" candidates.

Dartmouth College Case. A celebrated case, in regard to which the supreme court in 1819 handed down a decision, declaring that charters given to private corporations were contracts and, as such, inviolable. The decision also demonstrated for the first time the method by which the sovereignty of the individual states could, through the supreme court, be limited by the Federal Constitution.

The legislature of New Hampshire had attempted to take the control of Dartmouth college out of the hands of the trustees chosen according to its charter and to intrust the college to other trustees chosen by the legislature. The original trustees brought suit against the officers of the new board of trustees, who had obtained possession of the college property. The case for the regularly appointed trustees was argued by Daniel Webster before the supreme court, which decided for the inviolability of the charter. Since this decision, it has been the custom for the states, in granting charters, to insert clauses reserving to the legislature the right of amendment.

Democratic-Republican Party. The name given to the party, at first called Republican, founded by Thomas Jefferson soon after the adoption of the Federal Constitution. The party inherited from the Antifederalists their opposition to a strong centralized government and set its face against the broad-constructionist and nationalist tendencies of Hamilton. Its members sympathized strongly with the French revolutionists and, like them, glorified the rights of man.

The party succeeded in having Jefferson elected to the presidency in 1800. It continued to hold power until 1828, but departed so far from the principles of its founders that after 1816 there was no longer any apparent difference between its position and that of its former opponents, the Federalists, who had long ceased to exist as a separate group. In 1828 the Democratic-Republicans split into two parts: one, under the leadership of Andrew Jackson, called the Democratic party; the other, under the leadership of Clay, which took the appellation of National Republicans. The Democratic party has continued until the present day, but the National Republican party dissolved after the defeat of its ticket in 1832. This Republican party must not be confused with the Republican party which was formed in 1854 on quite different issues and which still exists.

Deseret (dĕz'ẽr-ĕt), **The State of.** The name is from the *Book of Mormon* and means "land of the honeybee." A convention of Mormons in 1849 organized an independent state with this name. Congress refused them recognition and in 1850 organized the territory under the name of Utah.

Dixiecrats. Popular name of Southern Democrats who revolted from the Democratic party because of President Truman's stand against racial discrimination. They formed a splinter party of their own called the States Rights party. Their presidential candidate carried four states in the 1948 election.

Donkey, Democratic. Popular symbol of the Democratic party. It was originated by Thomas Nast in a cartoon published January 15, 1870.

Dorr's Rebellion. An insurrection in Rhode Island, headed by Thomas W. Dorr, 1841-42, having for its object the extension of the suffrage, which, according to the charter of 1663, was restricted to holders of real estate and to their eldest sons. Dorr, chosen governor by an irregular election, seized the statehouse at Providence. His forces, however, were dispersed, and he himself was tried for treason and sentenced to life imprisonment. In 1845 he was released. The movement resulted in the adoption, in 1842, of a constitution providing for extended suffrage.

Doughfaces. A name used by John Randolph in 1820 in reference to the Northerners in Congress who voted with the South on the Missouri Compromise. It was taken up and applied by abolitionists to Northerners with Southern sympathies during the decades preceding the Civil War.

Draft Riots. An outbreak in New York City in 1863, occasioned by resistance to the drafting of New Yorkers into the Union army. The mob held possession of the city for four days, the absence of the militia at the front having left only the police available for the protection of the city. It is estimated that more than 1000 persons were killed, and that damage of $1,500,000 was done.

Dred Scott Case. A case of notable importance in American history, decided in 1857 by the supreme court of the United States. Dred Scott, a negro, claimed that, having lived with his owner in a free state, he could not legally be sold back into slavery on his master's death. The action was first brought in the state circuit court of St. Louis county, Missouri, and was later carried to the supreme court. The supreme court decided against Scott, and it was further laid down that he had no standing before the court, as no person who had been a slave, or was the descendant of a slave, could claim rights of citizenship. After the decision, Scott, having been transferred to a new owner, was freed. The utterances of the court with respect to these points were received in the North as challenges from the slave power, and they did much to hasten the war.

Drys. A name popularly applied to members of the Prohibition party, and later to persons of any political affiliation who advocated the prohibition or restriction of the manufacture and the sale of intoxicating liquor.

El Caney (ĕl kä-nā'). A small town located four miles northeast of Santiago de Cuba. It was made famous during the Spanish American war. On July 1, 1898, a force of about 4500 Americans fought a sharp battle here with a force of about 525 Spaniards. The American troops were commanded by General Lawton, while the Spaniards were under the command of General Vara del Rey. The Spanish force was thoroughly intrenched and desperately resisted the attacks of the Americans. The battle was finally won by the American force, the casualties amounting to more than 400 on each side. The battlefield is now a public reservation owned by the United States.

Elephant, Republican. Symbol of the Republican party, originated by Thomas Nast in a cartoon published November 7, 1874.

Emancipation Proclamation. A first proclamation was issued by President Lincoln on September 22, 1862, announcing that on the first of the following January "all persons held as slaves within any state or designated part of a state the people whereof shall then be in rebellion against the United States, shall be then, thenceforward, and forever free"; and that on that day he would, by proclamation, "designate the states and parts of states, if any, in which the people thereof" should be in "rebellion against the United States." The final emancipation proclamation was issued January 1, 1863.

Embargo Act. An act of Congress, passed December 22, 1807, forbidding any ship to sail with cargo from an American port to any foreign port. It was a reply to the English orders in council and to the Napoleonic decrees, which made lawful prizes of American ships on the high seas. These threatened to destroy American commerce. The embargo, however, served only to bring distress at home. The act was replaced in 1809 by a Non-intercourse act applying only to France and England.

Equal Rights Party. A faction which arose within the Democratic party of New York in 1835. This group opposed the granting of special privileges and exemptions to state banks and to other corporations, in many of which the regular or Tammany leaders of the Democratic party were personally interested. The Equal Rights men were also called "Locofocos." See *Locofocos*.

Era of Good Feeling. The period of Monroe's administration (1816–24), during which there was a truce between Republicans and Federalists. The latter party's doctrines had been adopted in large part by the Republicans (Democratic-Republicans).

Faneuil (*făn''l*) **Hall.** The famous market house and hall in Boston, built and given to the city in 1742 by Peter Faneuil. During the Revolutionary period it was the meeting place of the patriots and came to be called "the cradle of American liberty." In 1805 the hall was enlarged to a capacity of 3000 people. Here the great speakers of the country have been heard, from the days of Webster and Wendell Phillips to our own time.

Farmers' Alliance. A national organization for the bettering of agricultural conditions through social and legislative activity. The first state organization of societies out of which the alliance grew is credited to Texas in 1876. Similar organizations were developing about the same time in the Southern, Western, and Central states. The earlier activity of these alliances was chiefly nonpolitical. In 1887, however, the National Farmers' Alliance was formed, and its energies were directed into political channels, its chief strength being in Kansas and Nebraska. An agreement with the Knights of Labor in 1889 resulted in the formation of the National Farmers' Alliance and Industrial Union. The political phases of this movement were soon transferred to the Populist party. The Farmers' Alliance ceased to be political, but has survived as an agricultural organization. It joined in the Farmers' National Congress of 1914, as a body of about three million farmers.

Federalists. The party of Alexander Hamilton and John Marshall, which favored the creation of a strong national government and urged the adoption of the Federal Constitution. The party drew its supporters from the commercial classes, who looked for a strong government to afford greater security to person and property than the discarded Confederation had supplied, and from other farsighted, patriotic groups, who desired a government that would command international respect and fair treatment. The strength of the party lay mainly in the large states—Massachusetts. New York, Pennsylvania, and, for a time, Virginia. The smaller states feared that they would be eclipsed by the overwhelming influence of the large states in the new Union.

The Federalists were in control of the national government for 12 years—from 1789 to 1801. The death of Alexander Hamilton in 1804 robbed the party of its only great political leader, and its disintegration speedily set in. The Democratic-Republicans, however, during a supremacy which lasted for the next two decades, appropriated the main Federalist principles. The supreme court, too, under the influence of Chief Justice Marshall, continued, until his death in 1835, to exert a dominant nationalist influence in keeping with the principles that had been upheld by the Federalist party. Thus the Federalists, by means of their influence both in the legislature and in the judiciary, impressed themselves deeply on the early history of the country and determined the direction of its subsequent development toward a strongly centralized Federal government.

Federal Republicans. A name applied at different times to two different groups: (1) the followers of George Clinton in New York, who, in 1787, organized to oppose the adoption of the Constitution; (2) the supporters of President Monroe who had formerly been Federalists.

Fiat (*fī'ăt*) **Money Party.** Another name for the Independent National or Greenback party organized in 1874. See *Free Silver Movement, Greenbackism, Greenback Party*.

Fifty-Four Forty or Fight. Slogan of those Americans who from 1842 to 1846 demanded that the boundary line between American and British territory in the Northwest be established at 54° 40′. This was the southern boundary of Alaska, agreed to by Russia and by the United States in 1824. The phrase is ascribed to Senator William Allen of Ohio. The line was in fact established at the 49th parallel to a point in the Strait of Georgia, thence through the Haro canal and the Juan de Fuca strait to the Pacific.

Finality (*fī-năl'ĭ-tĭ*) **Men.** A term applied by abolitionists to those Northerners who, in the decade before the Civil War, sought to avert the pending danger to the Union by a "conspiracy of silence" upon the question of slavery. The group received the name in allusion to its contention that the Compromise of 1850 constituted a final solution of the slavery question.

Fire Eaters. The extreme supporters of slavery and of state rights in the South were so called by their political opponents before the Civil War.

Five Nations, The. The five tribes of Indians who formerly ranged the east coast of America, along the Hudson, and as far south as the Delaware. They were always on the English side in the wars with France. The designation included the Mohawks, Oneidas, Onondagas, Cayugas, and Senecas. See *Six Nations*.

Force Bill. The popular name given to several acts of Congress applying to the South: (1) a bill of March 2, 1833, to enforce the tariff law which had been challenged by nullification acts in South Carolina; (2) acts passed in 1870 and 1871 authorizing the president to use troops to protect election places in the South; (3) the Lodge Election bill providing for efficient enforcement of United States election laws, passed by the House July 2, 1890 but defeated in the Senate.

Bunker Hill Flag 1775

Continental Flag 1776

Betsy Ross Flag 1777

Stars and Stripes

Bennington Flag 1777

Flag of the Bon Homme Richard 1779

Flag of Fort McHenry 1814

"Old Glory" Flag 1831

American Flags

Medal of Honor
Navy

Medal of Honor
Army

Distinguished
Service Cross

Navy Cross

Distinguished
Service Medal
Army

Brevet Medal
Marine Corps

Legion of Merit

Distinguished
Flying Cross

Distinguished
Service Medal
Navy

Purple Heart

Soldier's Medal

Principal
DECORATIONS
of the U. S. Armed Forces

Navy - Marine Corps
Medal

Bronze Star
Medal

Air Medal

Distinguished
Service Medal
Merchant Marine

Silver Star

Mariner's Medal

HISTORIC AMERICA

Independence Hall. The Declaration of Independence was signed here July 4, 1776. (*Philadelphia Convention & Tourist Bureau*)

On July 8, 1776, the Liberty Bell rang the news of the Declaration of Independence. (*Philadelphia Convention & Tourist Bureau*)

The Alamo, San Antonio, scene of the fatal battle in the war of Texas for liberation from Mexico. Called the "Cradle of Texas Liberty," the fort was besieged by a Mexican force of 5,000 for 13 days before the garrison of 187 Americans was wiped out. (*Photograph courtesy of Texas Tourist Division*)

From INDIANS OF THE UNITED STATES by Clark Wissler.
Copyright © 1940, 1966, by Doubleday & Company, Inc.
Reprinted by permission of the publisher.

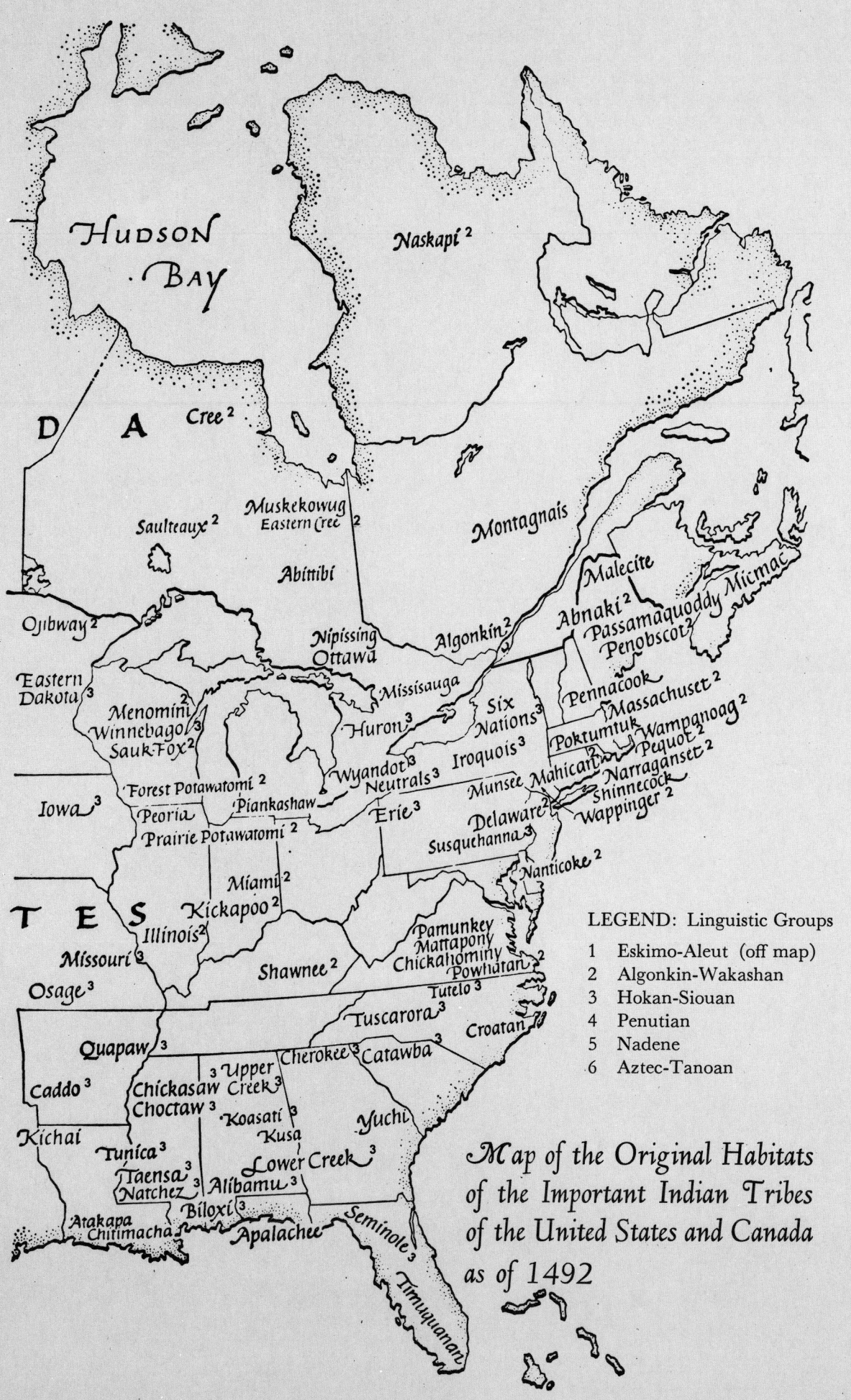

HUDSON BAY

Naskapi [2]

D A

Cree [2]

Saulteaux [2]   *Muskekowug Eastern Cree* [2]   *Montagnais*

Abittibi   *Malecite*

Abnaki [2]   *Passamaquoddy Micmac* [2]
Penobscot [2]

Ojibway [2]   *Nipissing Ottawa*   *Algonkin* [2]   *Pennacook*

Eastern Dakota [3]   *Missisauga*   *Massachuset* [2]

Menomini [2]   *Six Nations* [3]   *Poktumtuk Wampanoag* [2]
Winnebago [3]   *Huron* [3]   [2] *Pequot* [2]
SaukFox [2]   *Mahican* [3]   *Narraganset* [2]

Forest Potawatomi [2]   *Wyandot* [3]   *Iroquois* [3]   *Munsee* *Shinnecock*
Neutrals [3]   *Delaware* [2]   *Wappinger* [2]

Iowa [3]   *Peoria*   *Piankashaw*   *Erie* [3]

Prairie Potawatomi [2]   *Susquehanna* [3]

Miami [2]   *Nanticoke* [2]

T E S   *Kickapoo* [2]

Illinois [2]   *Pamunkey Mattapony Chickahominy*   **LEGEND: Linguistic Groups**

Missouri [3]   *Shawnee* [2]   *Powhatan* [2]   1 Eskimo-Aleut (off map)
2 Algonkin-Wakashan
Osage [3]   *Tutelo* [3]   3 Hokan-Siouan
4 Penutian
Tuscarora [3]   *Croatan*   5 Nadene
6 Aztec-Tanoan

Quapaw [3]   *Cherokee* [3]   *Catawba* [3]

Caddo [3]   [3] *Upper Creek* [3]   *Map of the Original Habitats*
Chickasaw
Choctaw [3]   *Koasati* [3]   *of the Important Indian Tribes*
Kusa   *Yuchi*
Kichai   *of the United States and Canada*
Tunica [3]   *Lower Creek* [3]
Taensa [3]   *as of 1492*
Natchez [3]   *Alibamu* [3]
Biloxi [3]
Atakapa   *Seminole* [3]
Chitimacha   *Apalachee*

Timuquanan

PRIMITIVE FISHING AND HUNTING IMPLEMENTS—The Eskimos who made the tools just below crossed the Arctic from Alaska to Greenland. Their chipped flint tools echo an Asian heritage. The Dorset Eskimos, who came next, followed the seasons to hunt seal, walrus, caribou, birds, and fish. Their artifacts include harpoons, spears, flint and slate tools, bone needles, adzes, and carved wood, ivory and antlers. The Thule Culture, third major stage of Eskimo archaeology, also originated in Alaska, ranging eastward to Greenland and Labrador. Unlike their predecessors, Thule Eskimos hunted whales, using elaborate harpooning gear. (*Canadian Dominion Bureau of Statistics*)

Artifacts representing three cultures—Pre-Dorset, Dorset and Thule—that successively inhabited the Canadian Arctic from about 2500 B.C. to recent Eskimo culture of the eighteenth century

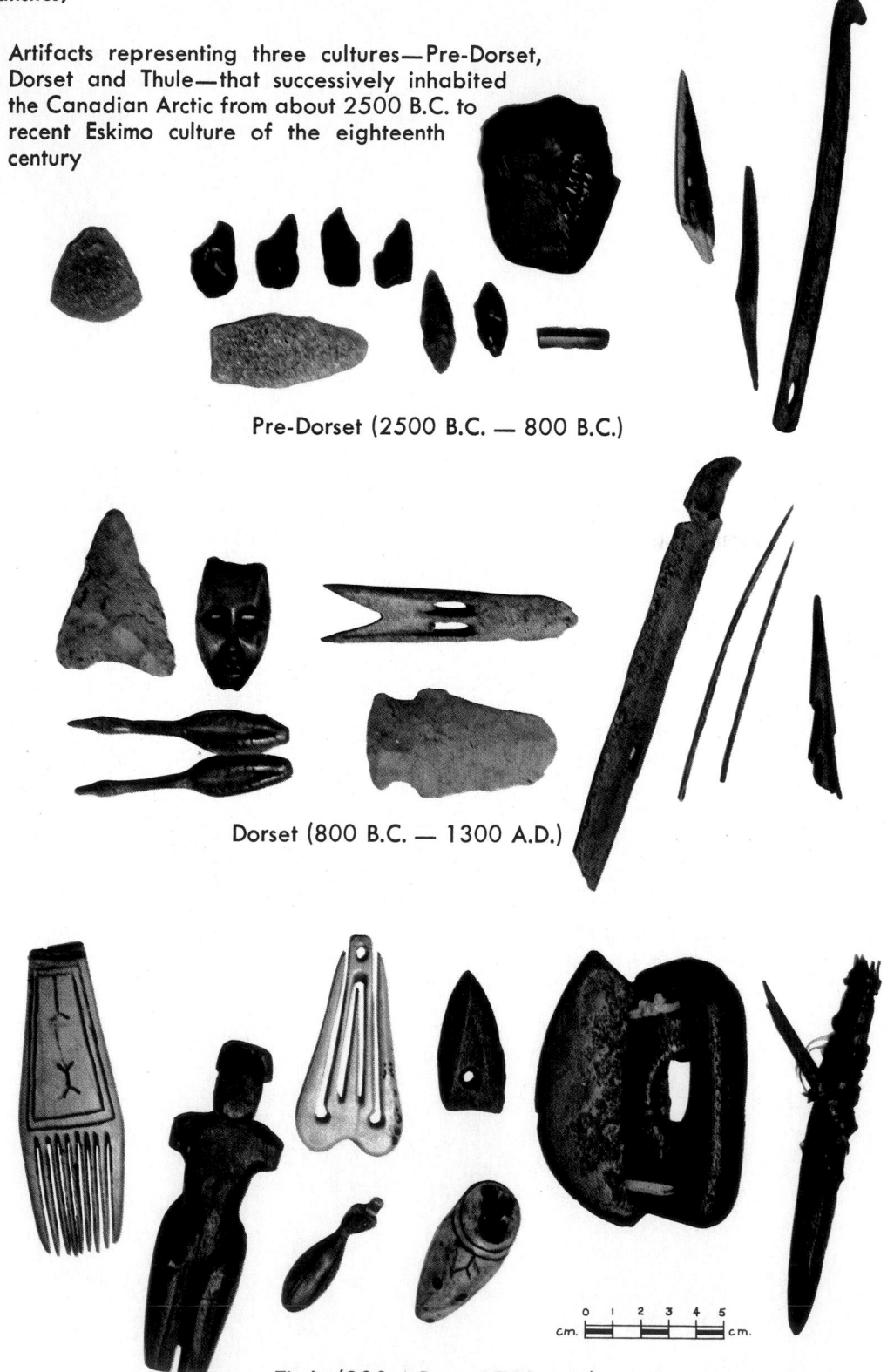

Pre-Dorset (2500 B.C. — 800 B.C.)

Dorset (800 B.C. — 1300 A.D.)

Thule (900 A.D. — 1750 A.D.)

Fort Duquesne (*dōo-kān'*). A colonial fort on the present site of Pittsburgh, at the junction of the Allegheny and Monongahela rivers. The work was begun in 1754 by a party of Virginians sent out by Governor Dinwiddie. They were driven away by French and Indians before completing the fort. It was then finished by the French and named *Du Quesne*. After being burned by the French in 1758, it was rebuilt by the English and named Fort Pitt. Only a blockhouse now remains, preserved by the Daughters of the American Revolution.

Fort Niagara. A masonry fort built by the French governor Vandreuil in 1725-27 at the mouth of the Niagara river, on the American side. Fort Niagara was the most important French military station and trading post on the Great Lakes. The English leader Sir William Johnson captured it in 1759 and there negotiated treaties with numerous Indian tribes. The Wyoming and Cherry Valley expeditions set out from this fort during the Revolutionary War. The British relinquished it to the United States by the Treaty of 1783, but actual evacuation was delayed until 1796. Canadian forces held it in the War of 1812 from December 19, 1813, until March 27, 1815. Through the activities of a patriotic association, a beginning was made in 1928 toward restoring the fort in its original form from plans preserved in archives at Paris, France.

Fort Sumter. A brick-walled fortification built on a shoal in the narrowest part of the harbor of Charleston, South Carolina. When that state seceded, December 20, 1860, this fort was in process of completion. Guns were being mounted, but no garrison had been assigned to it. On December 26, 1860, Major Anderson, expecting an attack, transferred his 75 men from Fort Moultrie to Fort Sumter. On April 12, 1861, the attack came in a bombardment from the other harbor batteries; on the 14th, Anderson and his little garrison, whose supplies were exhausted, evacuated the place. Not a man had been killed on either side during this engagement, which opened the Civil War.

Four Freedoms. In his annual message of January 6, 1941, President Roosevelt announced as essentials of the post-war world "four essential human freedoms": freedom of speech and of expression; freedom of worship; freedom from want, secured to the world by economic understandings; freedom from fear, secured by limitation of armaments to prevent aggression.

Freeport Doctrine. Called also "Freeport heresy." The proposal, advocated by Stephen A. Douglas in his debate with Lincoln at Freeport, Ill., in 1858, was that any territory had the right to stamp out slavery by "unfriendly" police laws. It was suggested that this policy would in time do away with the institution of slavery.

Free Silver Movement. An agitation, supported by the farmers and the silver mining industry, for the free minting of silver with a fixed valuation of sixteen ounces of silver for one of gold.

The Bland-Allison act of 1878 provided for the coinage of silver dollars in a limited amount, and in 1890 by the Sherman act the purchases of silver were increased and treasury certificates were issued against the silver acquired. In 1893, however, the further purchase of silver was stopped. In 1900, by the Gold Standard act, the coinage of the country was established on a gold basis. The agitation died down as a result of an increase in general prosperity.

In the earlier stages of the free silver movement its supporters were not confined to any one party, but in 1891 the Populist party was organized mainly for the purpose of furthering the policy. In 1896 and in 1900 the Democratic party espoused the cause and were joined by the Populists in the support of their presidential candidate, William J. Bryan. He attained to national prominence as the champion of free silver. He was defeated, however, in both elections, and with the passage of the Gold Standard act in 1900 the movement ceased to be a political issue.

Free-Soil Party. A party organized in 1840 by the amalgamation of the Liberty party with Antislavery or Conscience Whigs of New England and Antislavery Democrats, or Barnburners, of New York, upon a platform of opposition to the extension of slavery. By nominating Van Buren, an old-line Democrat, for president in 1848, the new party lost the support of many Antislavery Whigs who otherwise would have joined its ranks. By 1856 the Free-Soil party had practically disintegrated, and the remnant of the party was ready to join with the now swelling number of Antislavery Whigs and Antislavery Democrats of the North, to form the new Republican party, which represented the principles for which the Free-Soilers had stood.

Fries's (*frēs'ĕz*) **Rebellion.** An uprising in Pennsylvania, led by a man named Fries. It was a protest against the tax placed by the Federal government, in July 1798, on slaves and real estate. It was sometimes called the "Window Tax War" because houses were assessed according to the size and number of their windows. President Adams called out troops to suppress the rioters, who, at Bethlehem, had forced a United States marshal to release prisoners. Fries and other leaders were captured. In 1800 President Adams proclaimed an amnesty for all who had participated in the "rebellion."

Fugitive Slave Laws. The fugitive slave law of 1793, amended in 1818, failed to accomplish its purpose because its enforcement was left to the states. Free states refused to carry out the provisions of the law. In the Compromise of 1850 a new law was included, which made it the duty of Federal officers to capture and to return to their owners all fugitive slaves. The slave was denied jury trial, and a citizen who refused to aid an officer was declared guilty of treason. Attempts to enforce the provisions of this act served to arouse more intense opposition in the free states, and its repeal was demanded by the Republican party. The law, which had thus become a leading immediate cause of the Civil War, was repealed in 1864.

Full Dinner Pail. Campaign slogan adopted by the Republican party in 1900 and used occasionally in national campaigns since that time. It symbolized the promise of employment and a fair wage for the laborer, and the outlook of industrial prosperity for the country under a Republican administration.

Gadsden Purchase. The United States purchased from Mexico, for $10,000,000, about 45,000 square miles now forming the southern part of Arizona and New Mexico. This was known as the Gadsden Purchase. It was negotiated by James Gadsden while he was United States minister to Mexico in 1853. This transaction gained immediate importance from the fact that the treaty accompanying it settled questions of boundary and Mexican damage claims, which grew out of the provisions of the Treaty of Guadalupe Hidalgo (1848).

Gag Rules. The name applied to the series of rules adopted by the House of Representatives during the period from 1836 to 1844 to prevent reception of antislavery petitions. John Quincy Adams fought this policy as a violation of the Constitution and finally won his long battle in 1844.

Geneva Award. The decision of the board of five arbitrators appointed by the United States, Great Britain, Italy, Switzerland, and Brazil, in the matter of the Alabama claims. This tribunal met in Geneva, December 15, 1871. In the final award, signed September 14, 1872, allowance was made for an indemnity of $15,500,000, to be paid by Great Britain to the United States. This decision greatly strengthened the principle of arbitration as a means of settling serious international differences. See *Alabama Claims.*

Goldbugs. A nickname applied by the Free Silver partisans in the campaign of 1896 to Democrats and Republicans who favored the single gold monetary standard. See *Free Silver Movement*.

Gold Democrats. "Sound money" Democrats, largely from the Eastern states, who were opposed to the free coinage of silver, and who bolted the regular Democratic national convention in 1896, when William J. Bryan was nominated on a free silver platform. Under the name of the National Democratic party, the Gold Democrats nominated a national ticket of their own, with John M. Palmer for president and Simon Buckner for vice president. The party disappeared upon the passage of the Gold Standard act in 1900.

Grandfather Clauses, The. This name was popularly applied to certain clauses written into the constitutions of some Southern states, providing that certain educational tests for voters should not apply to white persons whose fathers or grandfathers were voters before the year 1867. The effect of the literacy tests was to decrease the black vote, while the "grandfather clause" prevented a corresponding decrease of the white vote.

Grand Old Party. Characterization given by Republican campaign orators to the Republican party in 1880. It was abbreviated to Gop in the Cincinnati *Gazette* in 1884. Thereafter G. O. P. became the accepted abbreviated form.

Grangers. See *Patrons of Husbandry*.

Greenbackism. A term applied to the doctrine of those who, in the decades following the Civil War, opposed the deflation of the large and unredeemable paper issues of government notes (greenbacks) and advocated the further inflation of the currency. The amount of the notes issued had reached the total of half a billion dollars, but was subsequently considerably reduced. The supporters of the doctrine organized the Independent National or Greenback party in 1874 and, in 1878, succeeded in having a law passed in Congress, which provided that the amount of government notes should not be reduced beyond the point which it had reached at that time. The amount of outstanding government notes stood then at $346,681,016, and, through the renewal of worn-out notes, remained at the same figure. The notes were made redeemable in gold in 1879.

Greenback Labor Party. The name of the party formed in 1878 by the merging of the Greenback party with certain labor groups, who had much in common with the Greenback party, particularly a belief in the desirability of an inflated currency. In 1880 the Greenback Labor party nominated James B. Weaver for president, and in 1884 it nominated Benjamin F. Butler. The party soon disintegrated, many of its members joining the Populist party, organized in 1891.

Greenback Party. The popular name of the Independent National party, which held its first national convention at Indianapolis in 1874. In 1876 it nominated Peter Cooper for the presidency. The party opposed further retirement of the greenback or paper money issue, which had been authorized during the Civil War but was not redeemable in gold. Hoping thereby to increase the price of farm products, they even advocated the further inflation of the currency. In 1878 the party incorporated with itself certain labor groups and took the name of the Greenback Labor party.

Green Mountain Boys. An organized band of settlers in Vermont, formed in 1773 to resist the encroachments of the New Yorkers, who claimed Vermont as part of the colony of New York under the charter of Charles II. At the head of a regiment of Green Mountain Boys, Ethan Allen made his effective demand for the surrender of Fort Ticonderoga "in the name of the Great Jehovah and the Continental Congress," May 10, 1775.

Half-Breeds. The name applied in 1877 to President Hayes and those Republicans who supported him in his policy of withdrawing troops from the South, thus permitting Democratic officials to take office. The suggestion in the epithet was that the followers of the president were not "full-blooded" Republicans. The term was applied later (1880) to the New York Republicans who failed to support Senator Conkling.

Halifax Fishery Commission. A commission appointed in 1877 to assess the compensation to be awarded to the British-American colonies, in return for the recognition of American fishing rights in colonial waters. Canada was awarded $4,500,000 and Newfoundland $1,000,000.

Hampton Roads Conference. A conference held on February 3, 1865, on board the ship *River Queen* in Hampton Roads, between President Lincoln and representatives of the Confederacy, with the object of bringing about a suspension of hostilities. The conference was barren of results.

Hard-Shell Democrats. See *Hunkers*.

Hartford Convention. A secret convention of prominent members of the peace party in New England, who, in 1814, objected to the energetic prosecution of the war with England. The chief proposals of the convention involved such amendment of the Constitution as would diminish the control of Congress over questions of peace and war.

Hawley-Smoot Tariff Act. Signed by President Hoover on June 17, 1930, this act increased tariff rates on the average by about 20 per cent, the largest increases being on agricultural products. By a so-called flexible tariff provision, the president was empowered, on the recommendation of a tariff commission, to increase or decrease rates on individual commodities by a maximum of 50 per cent.

Hay-Herran Canal Treaty. A treaty between the United States and Colombia, signed January 22, 1903. By this treaty, the United States was to secure a strip of territory six miles wide along the route of the canal, against a payment to Colombia of $10,000,000 and an annual subsidy. This was granted on a lease for a hundred years, renewable at the option of the United States. Colombia failed to ratify the treaty, and within a few months the independent Republic of Panama was set up.

Haymarket Square Riot. On May 4, 1886, a rally was held at Haymarket Square in Chicago to protest the killing of several striking workers by police the day before. Police attempted to disperse the crowd and a bomb was thrown, killing seven policemen. Eight anarchists were tried for the crime. The only evidence presented against them was their radical political beliefs, but they were nevertheless found guilty. Four were hanged and one committed suicide. The remaining three men were pardoned by the governor of Illinois in 1893.

Hearst Party. See *Independence League*.

"Higher Law," Seward's. A speech delivered by William H. Seward during the debates on the Compromise of 1850 is referred to as Seward's "higher law" speech. He used the following words: "The Constitution devotes the domain to union, to justice, to defense, to welfare, and to liberty. But there is a higher law than the Constitution, which regulates our authority over the domain, and devotes it to the same noble purpose." The South interpreted this to mean that the Constitution, which recognized slavery as existing, was set aside by this "higher law."

Homestead Act. The first of a series of acts and amendments, which made up the national homestead law, was passed by Congress in 1862. This act provided that a tract not exceeding 160 acres of unappropriated portions of the public domain should be given to any head of a family who would live on the tract for five years and improve it. The provisions of the law extended also to any person 21 years of age, who was a citizen of the United States or had filed declaration of his intention to become a citizen. Within ten years, 28 million acres were "homesteaded" under this act. Later laws permitted withholding of grants and all unappropriated land was withdrawn from settlement in 1935.

House Committee on Un-American Activities. A congressional committee established in 1938 to conduct investigations into and hearings on the activities of Nazi, Fascist, Communist and other organizations termed "Un-American" in character. The committee reached its peak between the end of World War II and the early 1950's. The committee hearings were characterized by badgering of uncooperative witnesses and by little regard for due process. In 1975 the House abolished the committee.

Hunkers. A contemptuous name of uncertain origin applied by the Barnburners to the proslavery section of the Democratic party in New York from 1844 to 1848. They supported the party's presidential candidate, James K. Polk, in 1844, and after his election they received most of the offices. After 1848 this section was called the Hard-Shell Democrats or merely the Hards. See *Barnburners.*

Icarian (*ĭ-kā'rĭ-ăn*) **Community.** A communistic society founded by Cabet, a Frenchman, in 1849, after the plan set forth in his novel *Voyage en Icarie.* The community was first established in Texas, but later migrated to Illinois and then to Iowa, where it continued to exist until about 1895.

Impeachment of President Johnson. As a result of his long quarrel with Congress, the House presented articles of impeachment against Johnson in 1868. The special charge voted upon in the Senate was that the president had tried to remove Secretary Stanton, contrary to the Tenure of Office act passed by Congress over the president's veto. The impeachment failed for lack of one vote.

Impressment and Search. Impressment was forcible recruiting for the English navy. Search was the right, claimed by England after the Revolution, to stop American ships and search their crews for English deserters or English citizens liable to naval service. Frequently, Americans were thus impressed along with the real deserters. This practice was one of the occasions of the War of 1812.

Independence League. A political organization initiated by William Randolph Hearst in 1905 in New York City. It extended also for a brief period to Boston, Chicago, and San Francisco. Out of it grew the national Independence party, sometimes called the Hearst party, which held a national convention at Chicago in 1908. Its program called for government ownership of public utilities and other radical reforms.

Independent National Party. An official name adopted by the Greenback party in 1876, when it placed in the field an independent national ticket, headed by Peter Cooper for president.

Indian Population of Early America. As a result of the archeological researches of H. J. Spinden and others, it would appear that the Indian population reached its maximum about A.D. 1200, with a total of from 50 to 75 million, although the peak of population in Mexico and Central America was attained about A.D. 550. After Europeans arrived in America, a rapid depopulation took place, chiefly as a result of the introduction of smallpox and measles. In the West Indies the aborigines were virtually exterminated.

Industrial Workers of the World (IWW). A militant industrial labor union founded in Chicago in 1905. Its purpose was to organize all workers into "one big union," dedicated to the maxim "an injury to one is an injury to all." At its peak in 1912, the IWW numbered about 100,000 members, the bulk of whom worked in Western mining, lumber, and agricultural industries. The union won a few battles, but failed to organize in the Eastern industrial centers. During World War I, IWW membership declined drastically. Some notable "Wobblies" were Eugene V. Debs, William Haywood, Jack London, Joe Hill, and Helen Gurley Flynn.

Insurgents. Progressive Republicans in Congress who, during the second administration of Theodore Roosevelt and the administration of Taft, rebelled against the methods of Speaker Cannon and the control of legislation by conservative Republican leaders in Congress. They sought to secure the enactment of progressive measures looking to the more effective government regulation of railways and "big business." The House insurgents were successful in bringing about a drastic change in the rules, depriving the Speaker of many powers.

Integration of Schools. In a decision striking at school segregation, the U.S. Supreme Court on Oct. 30, 1969, ordered immediate end to the operation of dual state school systems for Negroes and whites. The ruling replaced the 1955 order that integration proceed "with all deliberate speed."

Intolerable Acts. A name often applied to four (sometimes five) acts of Parliament, passed in 1774, in retaliation for the destruction of tea in Boston harbor, December 1773: (1) The Boston Port Bill, which closed the port of Boston; (2) the Regulating Act, which virtually abolished the charter of Massachusetts; (3) the Quebec Act, extending the boundary of Quebec to the Ohio River; (4) an act providing that officers or soldiers accused of murder should be tried in England or in some colony other than that in which the murder had been committed; (5, sometimes included) an act compelling citizens to give supplies to the soldiers quartered among them.

Ironclad Oath. The oath required by Congress from 1862 to 1871 for federal officeholders. It was designed to exclude from office any possible enemy of the Union, and received its name because of its very stringent character. After the close of the war, this oath was required of officeholders in the "reconstructed" states.

Jacksonian Democracy. A term applied to an ideal of popular government to which Andrew Jackson gave expression and which he applied during his presidential term. To its hostility toward aristocracy of all kinds the ideal adds a belief in the capability of the common people to rule by direct participation in government. The election of Jackson in 1828 was regarded as a triumph for this democratic ideal. It had become politically effective for the first time, through the strong sentiment of equality prevalent in the South and the West, and by reason of the general extension of the suffrage in the East, whereby citizens who did not own property were given a direct voice in government.

Jackson Men. Supporters of Andrew Jackson for the presidency during the so-called period of "personal politics" in the U.S., 1822–1828. During this period there was but one recognized national political party—the Democratic-Republican party —and such political divisions as existed were based merely upon adherence to one leader or another.

Jackson-Vanik Trade Bill Amendment. The Jackson-Vanik amendment, aimed at preserving human rights, is part of the 1975 Trade Reform Act. At the time of its passage, it was directed at the U.S.S.R. The amendment denies most-favored-nation status to any Communist country that does not allow free emigration.

Jeffersonian Democracy. A term applied to an ideal of popular government advocated by Jefferson. The ideal was based upon faith in the political wisdom of the common people, who could be relied upon to choose those of ability to rule for them. Jeffersonian democracy recognized a natural aristocracy of ability. With it was associated an advocacy of a broad sovereignty for the individual states and of a restricted province for the federal government.

Jeffersonian Republican. A term used to designate the member of the Republican or Democratic-Republican party founded by Thomas Jefferson in the last decade of the 18th century.

Jim Crow. The system of practices, laws and customs enforcing segregation of Negroes. In the early 19th century it was the name of a dance. The phrase comes from an old song and had gained currency by 1880. In some states Jim Crow laws required public segregation of the races. After the postwar end of segregation in the armed forces, Supreme Court rulings, the Civil Rights Act of 1964 and the end of school segregation in 1969–70, such laws were invalidated.

John Brown's Raid. The seizing of the U. S. arsenal at Harpers Ferry, Va., by John Brown and a company of 22 men, October 16, 1859. The purpose of the raid was to start a slave insurrection. But the slaves did not respond. Brown was captured by U. S. Marines under Colonel Robert E. Lee. He was tried in a Virginia court, convicted of murder and treason, and hanged. Although Brown's whole enterprise was madly fanatical and utterly failed of its immediate aim, yet it did serve his ultimate purpose of furthering the fight against slavery.

Jones & Laughlin Case. A case, decided by the supreme court April 12, 1937, which established the validity of the National Labor Relations act as applied to manufacturing. By ruling that interruption in operations of a business whose raw materials and finished products cross state lines interferes with interstate commerce, the decision radically enlarged the authority of Congress.

Kansas Border Warfare. The armed conflict between slavery and free state settlers in Kansas in 1856. The Kansas-Nebraska bill put into the hands of the settlers the decision as to slavery in the territory. Immigrants poured into the country from both North and South. Rival governments were set up. Elections for the proslavery government were fraudulently carried by raiders from Missouri. In the murder and open warfare that followed, about 200 lives were lost. President Pierce supported the proslavery legislature and broke up the free state government, July 4, 1856.

Kansas-Nebraska Bill. An act of Congress, May 30, 1854, by which Kansas and Nebraska were admitted to the Union as territories. This act was a breach of the Missouri Compromise, as it left to each of the new territories the settlement of the question of slavery within its borders.

King Philip's War. The name given to the series of battles and Indian massacres in New England in 1675–76. The conflict was precipitated by the slaying of an Indian interpreter who had revealed to the Plymouth authorities a plot to exterminate the white settlers. The Indians who, at the instance of King Philip, a son of the great sachem, Massasoit, killed the informer were executed. This action provoked Indian retaliations, which grew into a terrible series of atrocities. The war ended with the killing of King Philip at Bristol, August 12, 1676.

Kitchen Cabinet. The name given by their political opponents to the unofficial advisers of President Andrew Jackson, 1829–37. Among these men, whose influence with the president was believed to be greater than that of his official advisers in the cabinet, were Amos Kendall, Isaac Hill, and General Duff Green.

Knights of the Golden Circle. A secret political order organized shortly before the Civil War. It was composed of Northerners with proslavery sentiments. It was suspected during the war of secretly aiding, and of negotiating with, the Confederacy. In 1863 the order was dissolved, and its members reorganized, first as the order of American Knights, and later as the Sons of Liberty. At the close of the war a number of the leaders of the order were convicted of treason for their part in the Northwest conspiracy, an attempt to disrupt the North by organizing a confederacy in the Northwest.

Its name has reference to a slaveholding empire which the order hoped to set up, centering in Havana and including the territory within a "golden circle" which should have a radius of 1200 miles.

Know-Nothings. A name given to the members of a secret political organization which had as its purpose the exclusion from political offices of Catholics and of foreign-born citizens. The name arose from the usual reply of members to inquiries about the nature or aims of the organization, "I know nothing about it." The movement, rising soon after 1840, became prominent in 1852, and, being joined in 1854 by a large part of the Northern Whig party, the organization assumed the name of the American party. It held a national convention in 1856 but disintegrated as a national party in the controversies over the slavery question, although in separate states it continued to be a force until 1860.

Koszta Incident. A dispute between Austria and the U.S. in 1853. Koszta, a Hungarian with U.S. papers issued in 1850, was seized at Smyrna by Austrian officers. Instructed by the U.S. minister at Istanbul, Captain Ingraham of the *St. Louis* demanded and received his surrender. Austria called for satisfaction, but Secretary of State Marcy held that Koszta was a U.S. citizen and Congress decorated Capt. Ingraham.

Ku Klux Klan. A secret society formed in the South in 1865–66 to check the threat of Negro supremacy. It terrorized Negroes and white "carpetbaggers" and became so flagrant that Congress acted against it in 1871. The name is from the Greek *kyklos* ("circle" or "society"). The Ku Klux Klan, Inc., was founded in 1915 at Atlanta, Ga. Largely a national underground movement in the years that followed, the Klan continued sporadic violence through the 1960's.

Labor Party. The first American labor party of national scope, the Labor Reform party, or National Labor Reform party, as it was later called, was organized in 1869 as an outgrowth of the National Labor Union. The party inveighed against both major parties as dominated by the capitalist class, and called upon laborers to unite behind a party of their own which would enact legislation favorable to the laborer. The party advocated a protective tariff imposing a tax on the importation of luxuries only, and also advocated a national, legal tender, paper currency issued by, and under the control of, the national government as the basic currency of the country. In 1872 the National Labor party nominated Charles O'Connor, of New York, as its candidate for president. The party polled comparatively few votes at this election, and in 1878 merged with the Greenback party to form the Greenback Labor party.

Lewis and Clark Expedition, The. The exploring expedition conducted by Meriwether Lewis, private secretary to President Jefferson, and by Captain William Clark into the Oregon country. The success of this expedition furnished a part of the basis for the claim of the United States to the Oregon territory. The enterprise was due primarily to Jefferson's keen scientific interest in determining the extent and character of the country west of the Mississippi. One of his first acts upon becoming president was to secure from Congress an appropriation for such an exploration. The explorers left River Dubois, near St. Louis, May 14, 1804, and reached the mouth of the Columbia river on November 15, 1805. Beginning the return journey on March 23, 1806, they arrived at St. Louis on September 23 in the same year.

Liberal Republicans. A party which appeared in 1872, caused by a schism in the Republican party. The new party favored removing political disabilities from those who had favored the South in the Civil

War and advocated conciliation rather than force in dealing with the defeated states. The ticket adopted was chosen also by the Democrats, but it was defeated, and the party dissolved.

Liberty Bell. This famous bell, cast in England in 1752 for the Pennsylvania statehouse, was injured in transport and its tone ruined. It was recast in Philadelphia in 1753 with the inscription "Proclaim Liberty throughout the land unto all the inhabitants thereof." On July 8, 1776, it was rung to announce the first public reading of the Declaration of Independence. While the British occupied Philadelphia, the bell was hidden in the Zion Reformed church at Allentown, Pa. It was broken while tolling the death of Chief Justice Marshall, July 8, 1835. Since 1854 it has been in the hall of the old statehouse.

Liberty, Equality, Fraternity. This watchword of the French Revolution is ascribed to Antoine F. Momoro (1756–94). Its first official use goes back to 1793, when householders were invited to have painted on their facades a slogan containing these words.

Liberty Party. The name given to a new national party, formed in 1840 by the more conservative abolitionists, who refused to adopt the extreme position of the Garrisonians. Their purpose was to bring about by political means the abolition of slavery in all territory under the jurisdiction of the national government. This party merged with the Free-Soilers in 1848 and with the Republicans in 1856.

Lincoln-Douglas Debates. A series of joint debates to which Abraham Lincoln challenged Stephen A. Douglas in 1858. Lincoln was the Republican candidate for the Senate in Illinois; Douglas, the Democratic candidate. Lincoln's position was antislavery; Douglas championed the Popular Sovereignty doctrine, and won the senatorial election However, Lincoln's conduct of this discussion helped to make him president.

Little Giants. Political followers of Stephen A. Douglas, who had been nicknamed the "Little Giant," because of his short stature and because of his great mental and oratorical powers.

Locofocos (lō′kō-fō′kōs). The nickname given in 1835 to members of the Equal Rights faction of the Democratic party in New York, and later to members of the Democratic party itself. At a meeting in Tammany Hall, October 29, 1835, the Tammany men withdrew, turning off the gas as they left. The Equal Rights party, however, were supplied with candles and "locofoco" matches. The meeting proceeded, and from that time the faction was dubbed the "Locofocos."

Lost Colony. The name applied to a colony of 121 persons sent out by Sir Walter Raleigh from England under John White, which settled on Roanoke Island July 22, 1587. White, who went back to England for supplies, returned in 1590 after unavoidable delays only to find no trace of the colony except the word "Croatan" carved on a tree, a name designating an Indian tribe. Virginia Dare, granddaughter of White, was born in the colony August 18, 1587, the first child of English parents to be born in America.

Louisiana Purchase. In 1803 the United States purchased from France the (then) city of New Orleans and the territory west of the Mississippi, extending to the eastern spurs of the Rocky mountains and to the British frontier on the North. The price paid was $15,000,000.

Lynch Law. On the western frontier in and after 1819, lynch law was the substitution of irregular trials for due process of law. It is now regarded as mob rule and an act of summary execution without the form of a trial. The origin of the name is uncertain. Charles Lynch of Virginia, who flogged Tories during the Revolution, is said to have named the practice. Another explanation is that the Carolina Regulators about 1770 whipped offenders on Lynch's creek.

McKinley Tariff Act. The high protective tariff act passed by Congress in 1890. William McKinley, as chairman of the Ways and Means committee, was chief sponsor for the bill. It fixed import duties at an average of 49 per cent. Its novel feature was a "reciprocity" provision. See *Reciprocity*.

Marches on Washington. *1963.* The "Freedom March," largest mass protest in U.S. history, occurred Aug. 28, 1963, when more than 200,000 people of all races and creeds, representing both North and South, held a civil rights meeting at the Lincoln Memorial. The nonviolent protest represented efforts of Negro leaders and civil rights groups to make clear the scope of civil discontent and to draw support for desegregation and the right to work. A climax of the meeting was a march of some 50,000 protesters, half of them white, in support of the "jobs and freedom" campaign. The keynote speech was given by Martin Luther King, Jr.

1968. The "Poor People's March," planned by Martin Luther King before his assassination, began in Memphis on May 2, led by Rev. Ralph Abernathy, successor to Dr. King as head of the Southern Christian Leadership Conference. The campaign started in Washington on May 17 with the dedication of "Resurrection City," built to house some 3000 demonstrators. Programs included meetings with officials and protests to federal agencies to demonstrate the plight of the poor in the U.S. The aim was to secure increased welfare, housing, food, medical care and jobs. Coming in the midst of riots and nationwide tension, the brief campaign was not regarded as successful in attaining its ends.

Mason and Dixon's Line. The boundary line fixed between the colonies of Pennsylvania and Maryland in 1767; so called from the two English surveyors, Charles Mason and Jeremiah Dixon, who determined the line, thereby ending a. longstanding controversy between the two colonies. Later, this line was regarded as the boundary between the free states and the slave states.

Mayflower. The 180-ton ship that carried the Pilgrims, first colonists of New England, to America. The ship, chartered from a London owner, left Southampton Aug. 5, 1620, with the *Speedwell*, which proved unseaworthy, and both ships put into Plymouth, with the *Mayflower* sailing alone on Sept. 17. The original plan had been to reach the mouth of the Hudson, but the captain of the *Mayflower* set his course for Cape Cod and the first landing was near the site of Provincetown. After exploration, the site of the present Plymouth was chosen for settlement. The Plymouth landing was on Dec. 21, 1620, and is celebrated on Forefathers' Day, Dec. 22. According to the passenger list, given by Gov. William Bradford, 102 persons, including 2 children born at sea, arrived in the *Mayflower*. While at Provincetown harbor, 41 of the men signed the agreement on the government of the colony that is known as the Mayflower Compact. The names were:

Alden, John	Hopkins, Stephen
Allerton, Isaac	Howland, John
Allerton, John	Lister, Edward
Billington, John	Margeson, Edmond
Bradford, Wm.	Martin, Christopher
Brewster, Wm.	Mullins, William
Britteridge, Richard	Priest, Degory
Brown, Peter	Ridgedale, John
Carver, John	Rogers, Thomas
Chilton, James	Soule, George
Clarke, Richard	Standish, Miles
Cook, Francis	Tilley, Edward
Crackston, John	Tilley, John
Doty, Edward	Tinker, Thomas
Eaton, Francis	Turner, John
English, Thos.	Warren, Richard
Fletcher, Moses	White, William
Fuller, Edward	Williams, Thomas
Fuller, Samuel	Winslow, Edward
Gardiner, Richard	Winslow, Gilbert
Goodman, John	

Mecklenburg Declaration. A document resembling in its phraseology the Declaration of Independence, and dated May 20, 1775, supposed to record the action of a body of citizens of Mecklenburg county, North Carolina, in declaring their independence of Great Britain. Historians regard this document as having been written from memory some time after the event it purports to record. The generally accepted facts are that, on the occasion of a militia muster at Charlotte, May 31, 1775, the citizens present, having heard of the conflict at Lexington and Concord, adopted a vigorous set of patriotic resolutions. In effect, they declared all civil and military commissions void and set up a local administration to serve "until laws shall be provided for us by Congress." A copy of this notable document, known as the Mecklenburg Resolves, was sent to England, where it is preserved.

Medicare. Medicare is a U.S. health insurance program, approved by Congress in 1965, available to persons 65 years and older and to disabled persons who have received Social Security benefits for two years. It assists in paying hospital, post-hospital, and physician's costs, and certain other medical expenses.

Middle of the Roaders. Populists who refused to merge with the Democratic party in 1896, preferring to "keep to the middle of the road" as a separate political organization. See *Populist Party.*

Minuit's Purchase of Manhattan. Peter Minuit (1580–1638) was governor of the Dutch settlements in North America, known as New Amsterdam, from 1625 to 1631. Some time between July and September 1626, he negotiated with Indian chiefs on Manhattan Island for the purchase of the entire island for merchandise valued at about $24.

Minutemen. The organization of provincial militia in Massachusetts in 1775. They were under the orders of the Committee of Safety, and were so called because they were supposed to be ready to march at a minute's notice. Minutemen met the British at Lexington, April 19, 1775.

Missouri Compromise. An agreement between the slavery and antislavery parties in 1820. The act passed by Congress in 1820, admitting Missouri to statehood, determined that, west of the Mississippi River, slavery should be lawful only south of 36° 30′ north latitude, except in Missouri. This arrangement was maintained until 1854, when it was violated by the admission of Kansas and Nebraska as territories, with the right to decide the slavery question for themselves.

Modoc (*mō'dŏk*) **War.** The conflict between U.S. troops and the Modocs, a warlike tribe of northern California Indians, in 1872—73. Their chief, "Captain Jack," was captured and hanged. Part of the tribe were allowed to remain in California; the rest, about 150, were sent to Indian Territory.

Monitor and Merrimac. These armored Civil War ships met in decisive combat at Hampton Roads, Va. The *Merrimac* was a wooden U.S. frigate, rebuilt and named the *Virginia* by the Confederates. Covered with iron plates, it bore an iron prow for ramming enemy ships and was expected to break the blockade of Southern ports. The *Monitor* was a new type of vessel, built low, with nothing above deck but smokestacks and a gun turret. It was the North's reply to the challenge of the *Merrimac.* The two craft engaged on March 9, 1862. The Confederate ship was so badly damaged by the *Monitor's* shells that it withdrew to Norfolk. The battle left the blockade intact and demonstrated the superiority of ironclads over wooden warships.

Monroe Doctrine. A statement of policy in President Monroe's message to Congress in 1823, to the effect that the United States could not regard with indifference any further territorial expansion on the part of European powers on the American continent. The occasion for the pronouncement was the suspected intention of the Holy Alliance to intervene on behalf of Spain in its struggle with its colonies. The doctrine was broadened in later interpretations.

Moon Landings. Apollo 11—the first U.S. lunar-landing mission—carried the first astronauts to reach the moon, land, and return to earth. Civilian Neil Armstrong (in command), Air Force Col. Edwin Aldrin, Jr., and Air Force Lt. Col. Michael Collins were launched from Cape Kennedy (Canaveral), Fla., July 16, 1969. On July 20, in the lunar module *Eagle,* Armstrong and Aldrin landed on the moon. The two spent 21 hours, 36¼ minutes on the surface, with a 2¼-hour stay outside the *Eagle.* They rejoined Collins in the orbiting command module *Columbia,* and then splashed down in the Pacific on July 24, to complete the historic flight.

This mission was followed by five other successful U.S. lunar landings: The Apollo 12 mission, launched November 14, 1969, landed on the moon November 19; Apollo 14, launched January 31, 1971, landed February 5; Apollo 15, launched July 26, 1971, landed July 30; Apollo 16, launched April 16, 1972, landed April 20; and Apollo 17, launched December 7, 1972, landed December 11. The Apollo program, which ended after the Apollo 17 mission, landed twelve astronauts on the moon. See *Space Exploration.*

Morgan's Raid. The expedition of Confederate Gen. John H. Morgan, with 2400 men, into Indiana and Ohio, July 2–26, 1863. Morgan, ordered by Gen. Bragg to destroy railways and public works at Louisville, exceeded orders and crossed the Ohio into Indiana from Brandenberg, Ky., July 8–9. Union Gen. Hobson pursued him and local militia blocked his force. Near Pomeroy, Ohio, Morgan tried to cross the Ohio, but was attacked and lost a third of his men. A second try to cross was checked after many of the raiders escaped into Kentucky. Morgan, with the last third of his force, started northeast. He was finally captured, with a few troops, near New Lisbon.

Mormons. A sect founded in 1830, at Fayette, N.Y., by Joseph Smith, the son of a Vermont farmer. The Mormons moved westward and, after several years' wanderings, settled on Great Salt Lake in 1847, under the leadership of Brigham Young. Their advocacy of polygamy was for a long time a bar to the admission of Utah to the Union, but the enforcement of the Edmunds Act of 1882 led to the formal abandonment of polygamy as a tenet by the Mormons in 1890, and Utah was admitted to statehood in 1896.

Mossbacks. The name given during the Civil War to men who hid themselves in swamps and elsewhere to avoid conscription for the Southern army. The fancy was that they would stay hidden till the moss grew on their backs. The name was later applied to extreme conservatives in politics.

Mountain Meadows Massacre. The massacre by Indians, under alleged Mormon leadership, of a party of 140 emigrants, who were crossing Utah on their way to California in 1857. Only 17 children were spared. They were distributed among Mormon families, but were restored to relatives by the U. S. government. The leader of the band, J. D. Lee, an Indian agent, was executed for the crime in 1877.

Mugwumps. A name applied by Blaine supporters to those who, in 1884, supported Cleveland, the Democratic candidate for president, owing to his advocacy of civil service reform. The word later came to be applied to independent voters. It had been used ironically as early as 1832 to mean a person of superior views. In Eliot's Indian Bible the original *mugquomp* meant "big chief" or leader.

Mulligan Letters. A series of letters written by James G. Blaine to a business associate, Warren

Fisher. It was alleged that these letters proved Blaine's share in some corrupt railroad transactions. The letters were presented to a congressional committee by James Mulligan, a clerk employed by Fisher. Blaine obtained possession of the letters, and in a dramatic defense before the House of Representatives, June 5, 1876, read parts of them. He defied the committee to compel him to give them up. The suspicion engendered by the incident was used effectively against him in the campaigns of 1876 and 1884.

National Association for the Advancement of Colored People (NAACP). Mainly Negro, but with many white members, the NAACP works for civil and political rights, an end to segregation, the right to work and freedom from violence and intimidation. It was formed in the wake of lynchings of two Negroes in Springfield, Ill., when Mary Ovington, a white social worker, called a conference on Negro rights. Among participants were Jane Addams, William Dean Howells and John Dewey. The conference led to the NAACP's founding in 1910. W.E.B. Du Bois, one of the founders, rejected Booker T. Washington's gradualism for demands for immediate equality. Most early action was against lynching. Since World War II, the NAACP has worked for integrated education and voters' rights. Continuously advocating nonviolent protest. by the 1970's it had some half-million members.

Nationalists. Those who, during the period preceding the adoption of the Federal Constitution, favored the creation of a strong national government resting upon proportionate representation, possessing broad national powers, and acting directly upon individuals rather than upon or through the state governments. Their policy was adopted by the Federalist party and was supported by the supreme court decisions in the early decades of the nation's existence. This doctrine of centralization was carried further under the name of the New Nationalism and the New Deal. See *Federalists, New Deal, New Nationalism.*

Navy, U.S. The Navy began on Oct. 13, 1775, when Silas Dean, John Adams and John Langdon were appointed by the Continental Congress to outfit two ships for service against the British. Although the *Bonhomme Richard* under John Paul Jones claimed a spectacular victory over the *Serapis*, the Continental Navy never had more than 64 ships and had disappeared by 1785.

Attacks against ships by North African Barbary pirates led Congress in 1794 to authorize building of frigates—of these, the *Constitution* and *United States* were the most powerful of the time. In 1798 the Navy Department was established under Sec. Benjamin Stoddard. The pro-Navy policies of Adams were curtailed by Jefferson in 1801.

U.S. naval victories in the War of 1812 were spectacular but few. British blockade sealed the Atlantic coast, but the Navy achieved two great victories—by Commodore Perry on Lake Erie in 1813 and by Commodore Macdonough on Lake Champlain in 1814.

During the Civil War, under Secretary of State Welles, the Union Navy grew to 800 ships. Commanded by Admiral Farragut, the Navy blockaded the South, seizing key ports. The most famous battle was between the Confederate *Merrimac* and the *Monitor*, in which the Union ship used to great advantage the first revolving turret.

In 1896, with completion of the *Indiana, Oregon* and *Massachusetts*, steel battleships became standard. Construction continued rapidly under Theodore Roosevelt. However, by 1911 the U.S. was in third place, behind the British and German navies.

In World War I, the main tasks of the Navy were antisubmarine warfare, transport of troops and supplies, and mine-laying. After the war, the Washington Arms Conference (1921–22) curtailed shipbuilding and indifference to increased naval spending did not end until 1934, when Carl Vinson

of the Naval Affairs Committee obtained increases of strength.

World War II found the Navy somewhat prepared, due to legislation by Vinson in mid-1940 authorizing a 70 percent increase. A force of 284,000 men and officers in 1941 grew to more than three million by 1945. Changes in warfare during the war included the formation of the carrier task force, improvement in handling supplies, and use of amphibious vessels. The Navy's prime tasks were antisubmarine warfare, landing troops, and the recovery of the Pacific. In 1947, the Navy became one of the three divisions of the Department of Defense.

The U.S. fleet consists of aircraft carriers, cruisers, destroyers, battleships, patrol ships, minecraft, amphibious craft, and auxiliaries. Carriers permit the extension of power far inland, as in Vietnam, or engagement of a distant, unseen fleet, as at Midway. The first nuclear vessel, the submarine *Nautilus*, was built in 1955. In 1959, the *George Washington* was commissioned, the first submarine capable, without surfacing, of launching atomic missiles.

By 1970, carriers were largely withdrawn from Vietnam and moved to other strategic areas. Supporting naval operations increased, however, in the Mekong Delta and on many rivers. In addition to tactical operations, the Navy had to respond to Soviet naval challenges in the Mediterranean and the Sea of Japan. The Navy also engages in extensive oceanographic research.

New Deal. A term used of the political and economic program sponsored by President Franklin D. Roosevelt. Suggested by the title of a book, *A New Deal*, published by Stuart Chase in 1932, the term came into wide use in the electoral campaign of that year. The New Deal signified, in its broadest aspects, a change in the accepted function of the Federal government, no longer merely an arbiter, but an active agent to guide economic activities.

Its principal measures adopted were: 1. relief of the destitute by providing work at a living wage; 2. adjustment of agricultural production in line with demand; 3. strengthening the bargaining power of labor; 4. limiting cut-throat competition carried on with the help of sweat shops and child labor; 5. insurance of bank deposits; 6. protection of investors against market manipulation; 7. taxation policies designed to decrease concentration of wealth; 8. extension of the use of electric power at low rates partly by direct competition through publicly owned plants and partly by policing utility holding companies to prevent exaction of unduly high rates; 9. conserving natural resources by discouraging wasteful use of land and its products; 10. encouraging balanced commerce with foreign nations by mutual tariff concessions; 11. safeguarding neutrality by licensing export of munitions; 12. regulating the use of credit to check deflation and inflation; 13. control of the dollar's value in foreign exchange with a view to stabilizing domestic prices; 14. provision of old age pensions and unemployment compensation.

New Nationalism. Name given to the views advanced by Theodore Roosevelt in 1910 and 1911 with respect to the powers of the Federal government. According to this doctrine. the government is looked upon, not as one of limited, delegated powers, but as a sovereign government possessing jurisdiction over all matters with respect to which the Federal government can act more effectively than the states. The field in which these powers were to be immediately exercised was in the national regulation of all corporations doing interstate business. Associated with the theory as to the national scope of the powers of the Federal government was a system of reforms which included the graduated income and inheritance taxes, conservation of natural resources, revision of the banking system, direct primaries. and a strong army and navy. The so-called New Nationalism became a central feature of the platform of the Progressive party.

New Orleans, Battle of. An engagement, January 8, 1815, between the British forces under General Pakenham and the Americans under General Andrew Jackson. The Americans, 5500 in number, were well commanded and thoroughly intrenched at Chalmette, below the city. They repulsed the attack of 10,000 British troops, inflicting a loss of 2000. The battle took place after the signing of the peace treaty at Ghent. Means of communication were slow, and the news of the signing of the treaty in December had not reached America.

Nonintercourse Act. An act passed March 1, 1809, forbidding all commerce with France and Great Britain. It was part of a scheme of retaliation against French and British interference with American ships. Enforcement proved impossible.

Nullification, Right of. A constitutional principle asserted by the Southern states before the Civil War, to the effect that "a state under the Constitution retained the right to judge for itself the extent of the powers vested in the Federal government." Under this so-called right of nullification, it was further maintained that if, in the opinion of any state, the Federal government had exceeded its constitutional powers, such state could itself declare that act to be inoperative, and nullify its effect within the borders of that state. The right was first asserted in the Kentucky Resolutions of 1799. The climax of the discussion and also the virtual abandonment of the principle came in 1832 in connection with the protest of South Carolina against the tariff bill passed in that year. The outcome of this contest, which was virtually compromised, left doubtful the decision upon the principle of nullification. However, after 1832 in the Southern states the more fundamental doctrine of state sovereignty displaced the nullification doctrine, until the entire discussion was terminated by the Civil War.

Old Ironsides. A popular name for the 44-gun U. S. frigate *Constitution*. This famous ship was launched October 21, 1797; took part in three bombardments of Tripoli in 1805; in 1812, escaped from a British squadron in July, defeated the frigate *Guerrière* in August, and captured the *Java* in December; took the *Picton* with a convoy in 1814 and the *Cyane* and *Levant* in 1815. She was reported unseaworthy in 1828, but her proposed dismantling was prevented through popular sentiment aroused by O. W. Holmes's "Old Ironsides." Rebuilt in 1833, she was in active service till 1855 and was then used as a training ship, being again partially rebuilt in 1877; crossed the Atlantic for the last time in 1878; and was stored at the Boston Navy yard in 1897. In 1927-30, she was reconditioned in order to be converted into a U. S. Navy museum afloat.

Omnibus Bill. A name applied to bills covering several different matters, to be voted upon as a whole. The most noted of such bills in American history is that reported out by a compromise committee of the U. S. Senate on May 8, 1850.

Ordinance of 1787. An act of the Congress of the Confederation making provision for the government of the Northwest Territory, providing for religious toleration and popular education, and forbidding slavery in the territory.

Panama Canal Commission. The board of engineers and officials appointed to govern the Canal Zone and to construct the Panama canal. The commission was first organized in May 1904 with Major General Whitfield Davis as chairman. After disagreements and change of plans, Theodore P. Shonts was made chairman of a reorganized body. In 1907 a new commission was formed with Lieutenant Colonel George W. Goethals as chairman. It was abolished when the canal was completed in 1914.

Pan-American Congress. A congress of the various states of North, of South, and of Central America, organized by James G. Blaine during the term of office of President Harrison, and held at Washington in 1890. Similar congresses were held in 1901 at the City of Mexico, in 1906 at Rio de Janeiro, in 1910 at Buenos Aires, in 1923 at Santiago,

in 1928 at Havana, in 1933 at Montevideo, and in 1938 at Lima. Conferences of foreign ministers to deal with the conditions created by World War II were held at Panama, September 1939; at Havana, July 1940; and at Rio de Janeiro, January 1941.

Pan-American Highway. A projected road planned in 1925 at Buenos Aires by the first Pan-American Highway Congress to connect Circle, Alaska with Puerto Montt, Chile, a distance of 19,000 miles. From 1930, the United States offered to pay two-thirds of the cost of sections through Central America. A 3142-mile section connecting Laredo, Tex., and Mexico City was opened in 1963.

Pan American Union. The organization formed in 1890 and called the International Union of the American Republics changed its name in 1910 to the Pan American Union. More recently, at a conference held at Bogota, Colombia, in 1948, a new body with the same membership took the name of the Organization of American States (OAS). The new organization designated the Pan American Union as its General Secretariat. An expanded program of activities was announced, centering in three main branches: The American Economic and Social Council; The Inter-American Council of Jurists; and The Inter-American Cultural Council.

Patrons of Husbandry. A fraternal organization called The National Grange of the Patrons of Husbandry, formed in 1867 for the promotion of agricultural interests in the United States. Between that date and 1876, when the society reached its zenith, the number of lodges or "granges" increased from 90 to 19,000. *Grange* means "farm," and the members of the society are known as Grangers. The discussion of political questions was strictly forbidden at their meetings, but, as the organization grew in strength, its members became a considerable political force.

Patroons. A Dutch term meaning "patron" or "protector." It was popularly applied to certain large landholders under Dutch West India Company grants of 1629 and 1640. The grants really gave to any good citizen of the Netherlands feudal authority over large tracts of land bordering the seacoast or navigable streams, on condition of settlement with a colony of fifty or more. Some of the estates thus created along the Hudson river were held until the middle of the 19th century.

Payne-Aldrich Tariff. The law enacted by Congress August 5, 1909, providing a comprehensive system of taxes on imports. The bill was attacked by its opponents as operating to raise import duties rather than to lower them, contrary to what was deemed to be the public demand.

Pearl Harbor. Large American naval base near Honolulu, Hawaii. A surprise attack on Pearl Harbor by the Japanese, Sunday morning, December 7, 1941, brought the United States into World War II as a belligerent. Two battleships and three destroyers were sunk, other vessels were damaged, about 500 planes were destroyed on the ground, and 2897 men were killed or wounded, all by air attacks launched from Japanese aircraft carriers. This was the greatest naval disaster in American history.

Pentagon Papers. Excerpts from a top-secret Pentagon study of the origins and role of the U.S. in the Vietnam conflict, published by the *New York Times* and several other newspapers in the summer of 1971. The publication added to popular feeling against American involvement in the war. The papers were taken from files in the Pentagon by Daniel Ellsberg, an economist and former government advisor. In the trials that followed, the Supreme Court held that the First Amendment protected newspapers from prior restraint by the government. Ellsberg was brought to trial but was freed in 1973. In the process of his trial improper acts were committed on the part of the government and finally all charges against Ellsberg were dropped.

Peonage (pē'ŏn-áj) **Act.** The law passed by Congress in 1867, forbidding peonage in the states and territories. Peonage is a kind of slavery under which a person is held in debt to another and is forced to labor to pay the debt.

"Permanent" Generals. During war officers and men of the United States Army (Regular Army) may be given temporary higher rank in the Army of the United States, that is, the Army as expanded for war purposes. Only four such commissions have been made permanent—those of Grant, Sherman, Sheridan, and Pershing.

Personal Liberty Party. An organization formed in New York and Pennsylvania in 1887 to secure the repeal of laws requiring Sunday closing of saloons by voting on candidates of the regular parties according to their position on this question.

Philippine Insurrection. The outbreak of Filipinos against U.S. authority. Manila was attacked Feb. 4, 1899, and fighting continued until the capture of the rebel leader, Emilio Aguinaldo, by Gen. Frederick Funston in March 1901.

Pilgrim Fathers. The name applied to the band of English Separatists who became the first colonists of New England. They belonged to a group of dissenters who had previously emigrated to Leyden, in Holland. Preferring to be under the English flag, they founded the settlement of Plymouth, in New England, in 1620. Early New England writers referred to them as "pilgrims and strangers on the earth," and before the end of the 18th century the name Pilgrims had come to signify the original Plymouth colonists.

Platt Amendment. Regulations passed by Congress, March 2, 1901, for the government of Cuba. The Cubans agreed to make no compacts with foreign powers contrary to U.S. interests, to keep their debt within reason, to cede lands for U.S. naval stations, and to maintain sanitary conditions in ports. The U.S. was given the right of occupation to maintain order. In 1934 the agreement was abrogated.

Plessy vs. Ferguson. Homer Plessy, a New Orleans Negro, attempting to ride in a white railway car, was arrested, then convicted. Plessy appealed the Louisiana decision to the Supreme Court. In 1896, Justice Henry Brown, writing the opinion, called the enforcement of "separate but equal" accommodations a "reasonable" use of power. He declared that the 14th Amendment was not meant "to abolish distinctions based on color, or to enforce social as distinguished from political . . . equality." Justice John M. Harlan dissented, stating, "The judgment . . . will, in time, prove to be quite as pernicious as the decision made by this tribunal in the Dred Scott case." The doctrine of separate but equal accommodations continued in effect until overturned by civil rights legislation in 1954 ordering desegregation of schools.

Pony Express. By changing horses every 10 miles, Pony Express riders carried mail between St. Joseph, Mo., and Sacramento, Cal. (some 2000 miles) in 8 days—2 weeks less than by normal means. Begun in April 1860, the Express lasted until telegraph communication between East and West was established in October 1861—then the service was gradually abandoned.

Popular Sovereignty. The doctrine, championed by the Northern element of the Democratic party, and particularly by Stephen A. Douglas, during the period from 1850 to 1854, that the settlers of each Federal territory should determine for themselves whether slavery should be permitted in that territory and also whether that territory should be admitted to the Union as a free or as a slave state. The policy was derisively termed "squatter sovereignty" by its opponents, because, in practice, it left the question of slavery to be decided by "squatters," that is, by individuals who rushed to the territory and took up a temporary residence there for the single and express purpose of affecting the slavery issue within that territory.

The Democratic party, from 1852 to 1856, advocated popular sovereignty as a solution of the slavery question so far as it related to the territories, and the Kansas-Nebraska act embodied an attempt to put that policy into practice. It was upon this issue that Lincoln and Douglas squarely met in the senatorial contest in Illinois in 1858. The Dred Scott decision, rendered by the supreme court in 1857, held, in effect, that the doctrine of popular sovereignty was unconstitutional; that it was beyond the power of Congress and of the government of any territory to exclude slavery from its limits. Despite this decision, however, the Democratic party continued to insist upon that principle as the solution of the slavery question in its relation to the territories, and the doctrine did not disappear from American politics until the problem of slavery itself was wiped out by the Civil War.

Populist Party. The popular name for the People's party, organized in 1891, which drew its support largely from the earlier Farmers' Alliance, from the Greenback party, and from the Union Labor party. The principal policy advocated by the party was the expansion of the currency, especially by the free coinage of silver. This was part of a revolt against the alleged advantages enjoyed by the financiers of the East, by the railroads, and by the capitalists generally. It was expected that the free coinage of silver would offset these advantages by increasing the prices of farm products and by making it easier for farmers to obtain money.

In 1892 the People's party carried four states: Colorado, Nevada, Idaho, and Kansas. In 1894 the party polled nearly two million votes in the Congressional elections. In 1896, however, the Democratic party adopted the chief item of the Populists' program, the unlimited coinage of silver, and the Populists indorsed William J. Bryan, the presidential candidate of the Democratic party. Rather than fuse entirely with the Democrats, however, a majority of the Populists, accepting the name "Middle of the Road" Populists, voted to nominate a vice presidential candidate of their own. After the defeat of Bryan, the Populist party split into the Fusionists, who favored co-operation with the Democrats and with the "Middle of the Road" branch. After the election of 1900, when Bryan, as the candidate for the Democratic party and the Fusion Populists, was again unsuccessful, increasingly conservative control of the Democratic party led the Fusionists to seek union with the "Middle of the Road" Populists. The united party put a presidential candidate in the field in 1904 and again in 1908, but, in the latter year, polling only 29,100 votes the party ceased to exist. See *Free Silver Movement*.

Privateers. Privately owned armed vessels that by government permission warred on hostile shipping. Permission was by "letters of marque" during the Revolution and the War of 1812, with American privateers inflicting heavy damage on British shipping.

Progressive Party. Organized in 1912 as a result of the split in the Republican party between the conservative, "standpat," group and the more liberal or progressive members of the party. The immediate occasion of the formation of the Progressive party was the success of the old-line leaders in controlling the convention party machine and in renominating Taft for the presidency, to the exclusion of Roosevelt. The principles advocated by the Progressive party were fundamentally similar to those which the insurgent group in Congress had advocated during the Roosevelt and Taft administrations. These policies included a greater measure of government control of the railroads and large industrial combinations, a radical reduction of the tariff, adoption of the direct primary, and the initiative and referendum, as well as the application of the recall both to officials and to judicial decisions.

The Progressive party nominated Theodore Roosevelt for president and Senator Hiram Johnson, of California, for vice president. In the election which followed, the Progressive party polled nearly one million more votes than the Republican party, and its candidates received 88 electoral votes, as against 8 for the Republican ticket. The split in the Republican party enabled the Democratic candidates to win in the election, the combined popular vote of the Republican and Progressive parties exceeding by nearly 1½ million the vote cast for the Democratic. With the return of its leader, Theodore Roosevelt, to the Republicans in 1916 the party rapidly disintegrated.

Prohibition Party. The national Prohibition party was organized in 1869 upon a platform advocating the prohibition of the manufacture and sale of intoxicating liquor except for religious and medicinal purposes. In 1872, the party nominated candidates for president and vice president. The party polled its largest presidential vote in 1892, when John Bidwell, of California, received 271,000 votes.

Puritans. The name applied to the group of people within the Established Church of England, in the 16th and 17th centuries, who disapproved of certain usages and ceremonies derived from the Roman Catholic Church, and being used in the Church of England. Because of their purpose to "purify" the English Church by eliminating these customs, *Puritan* was applied to this party.

Among the Puritans, some groups, called Separatists, withdrew from the state church and set up independent congregations. One group left England and settled in Holland in 1609, whence a number emigrated to America, founding in 1620 the colony at Plymouth. These colonists were later known as Pilgrims.

The persecution of the Puritans by the Stuart kings drove most of them out of the Established Church. Many left England altogether. Among these were the Puritans who, in 1630 and later, settled the Massachusetts Bay Colony.

Quebec Act. An act passed by the British Parliament in 1774 to provide for the government of Canada, which had come under British authority by the Treaty of Paris in 1763. In this act, three features aroused the attention of the thirteen English colonies: (1) The act extended the boundaries of Quebec to include the territory between the Ohio river and the Great Lakes, westward from the Allegheny mountains to the Mississippi; (2) It established French civil law in the province; (3) It withheld from the inhabitants such representative government as existed in the English colonies. The English colonists regarded the act as a blow at their free institutions. It was consequently a factor in the Revolutionary War.

Quids (*kwĭds*). Followers of John Randolph, of Virginia, in Congress, who opposed the policies of the Jeffersonian administration and favored Monroe over Madison to succeed to the presidency. They were the first "third party" in the United States and were called quids from the phrase *tertium quid*, "a third thing," because they supported neither the administration forces nor their Federalist opponents.

Race Riots. Conflicts between races have always been a more or less major issue in the U.S. The 1863 "Draft Riots" in New York were among the worst, with some 1000 killed. Outbreaks occurred, in order, in 1866, 1868 and 1871 in Tennessee, Louisiana and Mississippi. The 1878 Colfax Massacre in Grant Parish, La., resulted in more than 600 Negro dead. Between 1900 and 1908, rioting marked New Orleans, La.; Springfield, Ohio; Brownsville, Tex.; and Atlanta, Ga. East St. Louis, Ill., in 1917 saw martial law declared, with from 40 to 200 estimated Negro deaths. Chester and Philadelphia had wartime riots in 1918. The "Red Summer" of 1919 followed, with conflicts in Washington, Chicago, Texas and Arkansas. Tulsa riots in 1921 counted 21 white and 60 Negro dead. Riots in Detroit in 1942–43 were followed by outbreaks in Harlem. Tennessee and Alabama had riots in 1946. Then, as civil rights came to the fore in the 1950's, serious riots recurred in Tennessee, Mississippi and Florida. The year 1964 brought riots in Harlem, Rochester, Chicago, Philadelphia, and New Jersey cities. The major 1965–66 riots in Los Angeles' Watts area were followed by outbursts in Cleveland's Hough ghetto in 1967, as well as in other cities. A climax came in 1968 after the assassination of Martin Luther King, Jr., with riots of disaster proportion in 125 U.S. cities.

Rag Baby. During the currency expansion agitation of the late 70's, this term was applied by the "sound money" advocates to the greenbacks, the government fiat currency issued during the Civil War. The term originated in cartoons by Thomas Nast in *Harper's Weekly* in 1876.

Rainbow Division. The 42d Division of the American Expeditionary Force in World War I. The 42d consisted of National Guard troops from most of the states—hence its name. The last units of the division reached France on Dec. 7, 1917. At Chateau-Thierry, St. Mihiel and the Argonne, the 42d served with great distinction.

Readjusters. The name of a faction of the Democratic party in Virginia, formed in 1878. Its main issue was that of a readjustment of the state debt by means of refunding at 3 per cent.

Red Herring. Originally a herring cured by smoking, used in English hunting practice to train dogs. "To drag a red herring across the trail," became used later in political argument for the practice of raising an obscure issue to draw attention away from a more important one.

Rosenberg Case. In 1950 Ethel Greenglass and Julius Rosenberg were accused of giving agents of the U.S.S.R. information concerning U.S. atomic weapons and military matters. The Rosenbergs were found guilty under the Espionage Act of 1917. The case was appealed to the U.S. Supreme Court and protests against the convictions were organized in the U.S. and Europe. The Rosenbergs were executed on June 19, 1953—the first U.S. civilians to be given the death sentence for espionage.

Rum, Romanism, and Rebellion. Used by Rev. Samuel Burchard to describe the Democratic party, at a banquet given Oct. 30, 1884, in honor of James G. Blaine, Republican candidate for president. Blaine repudiated it, but the phrase was used to draw away Irish Catholic votes.

Sacco and Vanzetti Case. In April 1920, a shoe factory in South Braintree, Mass., was robbed and two guards were killed. Nicola Sacco, a shoemaker, and Bartolomeo Vanzetti, a fish peddler, were charged with the crime. The two men were convicted not on hard evidence, but largely on the basis of their anarchist political beliefs. In 1925, another man confessed to the crime but the judge declined to reopen the case. Despite a world-wide outcry, the governor of Massachusetts refused to intervene and the two men were executed in 1927.

Salary Grab. Popular name for an act of Congress of March 4, 1873, which made the salary increase for members of Congress, provided in the general salary act of March 3, effective for the preceding two years. Popular indignation was so intense that both acts were repealed.

Salem Witchcraft. An outbreak of superstition occurred in Salem, Mass., in 1692. In the summer of that year, 19 persons were convicted and executed on the charge of witchcraft. The belief was that some evil influences in the colony were responsible for certain military and political disasters. In 1689, Cotton Mather had published his study of the symptoms of two girls upon whose testimony an Irish laundress in Boston had been convicted of witchcraft and executed.

Sand Lotters. Anti-Chinese and anti-capitalist agitators in California in 1887–89 so called because their regular meeting place was a sand lot in San Francisco. The movement, led by Denis Kearney, was known as Kearneyism.

San Juan (*săn hwän'*) **Arbitration.** The question as to the ownership of the island of San Juan, lying between Vancouver and the American coast, arose out of the wording of the Treaty of Ghent in 1814, by which instrument the middle of the channel between Vancouver and the mainland was fixed as the boundary. San Juan being in the middle of the channel, the question of ownership was a doubtful one. Emperor William I of Germany, acting as arbitrator in 1872, decided in favor of the United States.

Scalawags. Nickname applied by Southerners to Southern whites who, like the Northern carpetbaggers after the Civil War, were willing to use the Negro vote to gain political office and political spoils for themselves.

Secession, Ordinance of. The declaration issued by South Carolina, December 20, 1860, dissolving its union with the United States. The other Southern states followed with similar declarations.

Sedition Act. See *Alien and Sedition Acts.*

Seminole (*sĕm'ĭ-nōl*) **War, The.** The longest and most severe conflict between United States forces and the Indians. In 1835, the Seminoles under their chief, Osceola, refused to cede lands in Florida and to remove to Indian Territory. The war continued until 1842, when the Indians were completely subdued. In 1843, about 4000 were removed to form one of the five nations in Indian Territory. A few of the tribe fled to the Everglades, and there still maintain themselves, unconquered.

Separatists. This was the name which attached to the more radical and democratic groups of Puritans in England, during the reigns of Elizabeth and James I. In obedience to their belief that the English Church had not gone far enough in Protestantism, they withdrew, as many more moderate Puritans were forced later to do, and set up their own independent congregations. To the Separatists belonged the congregation of Scrooby, in Nottinghamshire, some of whom became the Pilgrims of Plymouth. See *Mayflower, Pilgrim Fathers, Puritans.*

Seward Whigs. Members of the Whig party in New York who approved the conduct of Seward, when, as United States senator, he came out flatly in opposition to any further extension of slavery and opposed the Compromise of 1850. This group joined the ranks of the Republican party soon after its formation. See *Silver Grays.*

Sharecropping. A system of farm tenancy in the South that arose from the plantation system after the Civil War. Sharecroppers supplied human farm labor, with land and equipment supplied by the landowners. After harvest, the cropper would receive a share of the receipts and from that would pay his debt to the owner for money and supplies advanced during the year. Once widespread among the poor of the rural South, the system was reduced by decreases in cotton cultivation and by farm mechanization.

Shays's Rebellion. A rising in Massachusetts, in 1786-87, headed by an ex-officer named Daniel Shays, in protest against the increasing burdens of court fees, lawsuits, and imprisonment for debt. It was part of the general unrest of the times, due to weaknesses in state governments and in the Confederation. At the head of 1100 men, Shays attacked the Springfield arsenal, December 25, 1787, but his forces were repulsed and scattered. Minor outbreaks occurred in the course of several following months, but the unrest gradually died down. A general amnesty was extended to the leaders. Shays himself was pardoned.

Sheridan's Ride. The famous ride of General Philip H. Sheridan, from Winchester, Va., to Cedar Creek. His army had been surprised and routed, October 19, 1864. When the news reached him, he rode the distance of twenty miles, rallied his retreating forces, and attacked and defeated the Confederates under General Early. This exploit is celebrated in a stirring poem by T. B. Read.

Sherman Silver Act. An act of Congress, passed in 1890, by which the treasury was obliged to purchase, at market price, 4½ million ounces of silver monthly. Treasury notes payable in coin were to be issued against this silver. The act was repealed in 1893.

Sherman's March. The famous march of General William T. Sherman, during the Civil War, through the state of Georgia from Atlanta to Savannah. His purpose, in which General Grant concurred, was to complete the invasion of the South by destroying the sources of Confederate supplies. Before starting on his march, Sherman ordered the evacuation of Atlanta and burned the city. The army left a wide swath of devastation over the entire distance of 300 miles. Sherman entered Savannah on December 23, 1864. This campaign, which really ended only with the surrender of General Johnston at Durham Station, N. C., on April 18, 1865, combined with Grant's victory over Lee to end the Civil War.

Silver Purchase Act. The purpose of this act of 1934 was to increase the proportion of silver to gold in the monetary stock of the country to one-fourth of the whole, an object never attained. Under the act the Treasury was required to pay for newly mined domestic silver 64.64 to 77.58 cents per ounce; against a market price of 35.3 to 42.5 cents. Amendments in 1939 fixed the price at 71.11 cents. The procedure was a mild inflationary factor.

Six Flags over Texas. The history of Texas, 1) as a colony, 2) as a republic, and 3) as a state, is commemorated by a "theme" park established in 1961 midway between Dallas and Fort Worth. Historical exhibits illustrating the successive periods, together with replicas of the flags themselves, recall the sovereignty of France, Spain, and Mexico, in that order, the independent republic (1836-45) with its "lone star" symbol, the admission of Texas as a state in 1845, and its continuance under the Stars and Stripes except for the interval 1861-65 when the state, having seceded along with other southern states, was represented by the Stars and Bars of the Confederacy.

Six Nations, The. The name by which the Iroquois Indian confederacy was known after the Tuscaroras were united with the original "five nations" in 1722. The confederacy or league was first formed about 1570 among the tribes occupying territory now in northern and northeastern New York. In it were included the Mohawks, Oneidas, Onondagas, Cayugas, and Senecas. The name Iroquois was given them by French explorers. They called themselves "the people of the long house." They extended their authority southward to the Susquehanna and to the Ohio, westward to Lake Michigan, and northward over Upper Canada. The league, which superseded the tribal organization, was a true federal union, providing for a central council at Onondaga and for independence of the tribes in local affairs.

Because of the mistaken policy of the early French explorers, the Iroquois became partisans of the English. During the Revolution the league was neutral, but the tribes, with the exception of the Oneidas and some of the Tuscaroras, sided with the British. Chief Brant, at length, led the Mohawks and Cayugas into Canada, whither parts of the other tribes also went. The Canadian government gave them reservations.

The Iroquois in the United States are now on reservations in New York, except part of the Oneidas in Wisconsin and some Senecas in Oklahoma.

Sixteen to One. A phrase expressive of the ratio at which silver and gold were to be valued by the mint under the bimetallic system, or free coinage of both silver and gold, advocated by the Free Silver men. See *Free Silver Movement.*

Snappers. Machine Democrats in New York who convened at a "snap" convention in 1892 at the call of "Boss" Hill, and who picked a solid anti-Cleveland delegation to the Democratic national convention. See *Anti-Snappers*.

Social Democrats. Original name of the present Socialist party, organized in 1897 by Eugene V. Debs. The ultimate aim of the party was the abolition of the capitalist system by peaceful means, its program resting flatly upon the economic doctrines of Karl Marx. In 1900, with Debs as its candidate for president, it received the support of most of the members of the Socialist Labor party.

Socialist Labor Party. The name adopted in 1877 by an organization to promote an economic rather than a political program. It adopted a platform of opposition to the capitalist system, and advocated, among other reforms, immediate government ownership and operation of all basic industries, and an elastic paper currency issued and controlled by the government. In 1892, it designated its first national ticket, and has placed in nomination candidates for president and vice president at every election since that time, although it has never polled any considerable number of votes.

In 1900 most of the members of the party joined the ranks of the Social Democratic party, the present Socialist party. The more radical members of the Socialist Labor group, however, continued their separate organization, maintaining their identity as distinct from the Socialist party upon a more thoroughgoing adherence to the Marxian doctrines of economic and social revolution. The Socialist Labor party holds the view that the abolition of private property can be achieved only as a result of the class war predicted by Marx and through the economic revolution which is to follow in its train. The 1928 platform of the party declared that the desired revolution is to be effected by constitutional means.

Socialist Party. The party formed in 1900 by the union of the Social Democratic party and most of the members of the Socialist Labor party. The party has advocated, in addition to state ownership of public utilities and of basic industries, the initiative, referendum, and recall, and a strict limitation of the power of the courts, particularly with respect to declaring laws unconstitutional. This party has nominated a national ticket at each presidential election since 1900, Eugene V. Debs being its candidate for president five times. Norman Thomas was nominated six times between 1928 and 1948. He was the leading spokesman for American socialism.

Solid South. A phrase used to express the consistency of the Southern states in their support of the Democratic party. It appears to have been first applied during the presidential campaign of 1876.

Sons of Liberty. A society of Americans, which arose in New York and Connecticut in 1765, and pledged to work for liberty in the American colonies. After the close of the Revolution, the members became part of the Tammany Society.

Southern Christian Leadership Conference (SCLC). Founded in 1957, with Martin Luther King, Jr., as its first president, the SCLC is a "nonsectarian coordinating agency" for individuals and groups seeking improved civic, economic, cultural and religious conditions through "non-violent direct mass action." Its programs have included boycotts, lectures, forums, voter registration drives, marches and demonstrations at local, state and national levels. The SCLC is interracial, with supporters coming from all religions.

Spoils System, The. Popular name for the practice, inaugurated by Andrew Jackson, of turning out officeholders of a preceding administration and of filling their places with political friends. In 1820 a bill had been passed by Congress which provided that many Federal offices should automatically become vacant at the end of a four-year term. The purpose was to provide against "bureaucracy." President Adams (1825–29) made only twelve removals during his term. But this law and the constitutional powers of the president gave Jackson and the new Democratic party a convenient means for punishing enemies and rewarding friends.

Spoliation Claims, French. Claims of American merchants and shipowners against the United States government for damages inflicted by French privateers in 1798-99, when the two countries were virtually at war. No indemnity was ever obtained from France. But descendants of the original claimants continued to press their demands until 1885. At that time the matter was referred to the court of claims, which awarded $4,800,000 in satisfaction of damages.

Squatter Sovereignty. The principle of leaving the slavery question in a state or territory to the decision of the settlers. It was first applied to the districts acquired from Mexico in 1848, on their admission to the Union as territories. It was afterward extended, in spite of the Missouri Compromise, to Kansas and Nebraska in 1854.

Stalwarts. New York Republicans, led by Senator Conkling, who were opposed to President Garfield in 1881 on the question of civil service reform. Guiteau, the assassin of Garfield, was a Stalwart, and gave as his reason for the crime that he could see no other way to bring about a reunion of the Republican party. The word had come into political use early in the presidency of Hayes, to designate those Republicans who opposed his policy in the Southern states. See *Half-Breeds*.

Stamp Act. An act passed by the British Parliament in 1765, for the purpose of raising revenue from the colonies. It was even more unpopular in America than was the American Customs act, and it proved almost impossible to enforce. It was repealed in 1766.

Standpat Policy. A phrase used to describe the general conservative attitude of the regular or old guard wing of the Republican party in Congress, particularly during the second administration of President Roosevelt and during the administration of President Taft. The term is supposed to have originated in a declaration of Senator Mark Hanna in 1900, to the effect that the Republican party should "stand pat" upon the high protective tariff plank.

Strict Constructionists. A general name applied to all those who advocated a narrow construction of the powers granted to the Federal government by the Constitution. The Antifederalists, the Jeffersonian Republicans, the State Rights men, and the Southern Secessionists were all strict constructionists, believing in a minimum of Federal authority and activity and in a maximum of state rights.

Student Nonviolent Coordinating Committee (SNCC). Founded in 1960, the SNCC organizes student groups engaged in "direct action" protests. Membership is drawn from students on both Negro and white colleges throughout the U.S. The SNCC has been widely active in promoting voter registration and in integrating public facilities. It seeks the development of political understanding and civic participation and has taken "antiauthoritarian" stands on diverse social and political issues.

Tammany Hall. A New York city political organization, founded in 1789 as the Society of St. Tammany by William Mooney, and named for the Delaware Chief Tamanend, famous for his virtues and wisdom.

The society, under the guidance of Aaron Burr, took an interest in politics, and in 1798 threw in its lot with the Democratic-Republicans as opposed to the Federalists and was mainly instrumental in carrying New York for Jefferson in 1800. It later identified with the national Democratic party, which succeeded the Democratic-Republican party, and has since claimed to represent New York city Democrats.

Tammany's influence rested on charitable activities and advantages its friends might expect when it was in power. Before 1830 it supported a pure Americanism, but with extension of the vote and the rise of immigration, it came to identify its interests with the foreign-born; its control of the foreign vote and its strong organization made it a dominant force.

In 1872 William Tweed, "boss" of Tammany, was convicted of stealing millions from the city. The resulting unpopularity made Tammany relax its controls for a time. Later revelations also brought reverses, but Tammany has usually recovered power.

Tariff for Revenue Only. Tariff policy advocated by the Democratic party during the period of the tariff controversy from 1876 to 1912. Under this policy, taxes on imports were to be levied only for the purpose of raising revenue to meet the expenses of the government, as distinguished from the Republican policy of a protective tariff, the chief purpose of which was to promote American industry by barring or handicapping foreign competition.

Teapot Dome. Oil fields named the Teapot Dome, near Casper, Wyo., were reserved by President Wilson in 1915 for naval use and transferred to the Interior Department in 1921. In Harding's term, Interior Secretary Albert Fall leased the fields to private interests without competitive bids. Inquiry by Sen. T.J. Walsh led to prosecutions and Fall and other involved officials resigned. The trials lasted into Coolidge's term and the Supreme Court in 1927 found the leases fraudulent and ordered restitution of the lands.

Thirteen States. The thirteen American colonies which became the original thirteen states of the Union were New Hampshire, Massachusetts, Connecticut, Rhode Island, New York, New Jersey, Delaware, Pennsylvania, Maryland, Virginia, North Carolina, South Carolina, and Georgia.

Tippecanoe and Tyler Too. Refrain of a campaign ballad composed by A. C. Ross, which became the campaign slogan of the Whigs in the picturesque national campaign of 1840. The Whig candidates in that election were William H. Harrison, who had been nicknamed "Tippecanoe" from the battle in which he first gained national fame, and John Tyler.

Tories. The party in colonial politics which supported the authority of the English king and of the royal government. After the Revolution the Tories disappeared as a political party. Some of those who had belonged to it emigrated to Canada, where they were known as the United Empire Loyalists, while others returned to England. The rest joined the Nationalists, and later the Federalists, who favored a strong central government.

Treaties of United States. The following list includes the most important treaties and agreements between the United States and foreign powers. Besides these major pacts, the United States has entered into many treaties with the Indians. It is also a party to many international agreements upon matters of commerce and trade, as well as to treaties providing for international arbitration. See *Treaties* under *Dictionary of World History*.

1782-83 Treaty of Paris. The treaty with Great Britain which terminated the Revolutionary War and recognized the independence of the United States. The treaty recognized the rights of United States fishermen in Newfoundland waters; it also provided that the Mississippi river, at that time the western boundary of the United States, should be open equally to British and to American navigation. A preliminary agreement was signed at Paris, November 30, 1782. The definitive treaty was signed, also at Paris, on September 3, 1783. The American negotiators were Benjamin Franklin, John Adams, John Jay, and Henry Laurens.

1794 Jay's Treaty. The treaty between Great Britain and the United States negotiated by John Jay. It provided for the withdrawal of British military posts south of the Canada boundary in the Northeast, and settled certain boundary and financial questions. The assertion in the treaty that a neutral flag did not protect enemy merchandise, as well as its vague recognition of the right of search, aroused opposition. Only Washington's personal influence secured its ratification, June 24, 1795.

1795 Treaty with Spain. An agreement which provided for free navigation of the Mississippi, with privilege of deposit at New Orleans, and established a boundary between the U. S. and the Spanish possessions on the south.

1803 Louisiana Treaty. The treaty with Napoleon which provided for the purchase of the Louisiana territory. The acquirement of the area included in the purchase price of $15,000,000 more than doubled the area of the United States. See *Louisiana Purchase*.

1814 Treaty of Ghent. A treaty between Great Britain and the United States. It provided (1) for the restoration of all territory seized during the war, except certain islands near Passamaquoddy bay, the disposition of which was referred to a commission; (2) for a commission to settle boundary lines between the United States and Canada; (3) for co-operation between the United States and Great Britain in suppressing the slave trade.

1817 Rush-Bagot Convention. Between Great Britain and the United States. It restricted the building, arming, and use of naval vessels on the Great Lakes.

1818 Convention with Great Britain. This agreement provided for fishing rights off Newfoundland and Labrador, for establishing the boundary line between Canada and the United States, from Lake Superior to the Rockies, on the parallel of 49°, and joint occupation of Oregon.

1819 Treaty with Spain. By this treaty, Spain surrendered all claim to West Florida and ceded East Florida. The United States gave up all claim to Texas and agreed to pay to American citizens, claims against Spain to the amount of $5,000,000.

1842 Webster-Ashburton Treaty. The treaty with Great Britain which settled the question as to the boundary between Maine and Canada.

1846 Oregon Boundary Treaty. Negotiated with Great Britain. This treaty settled the question of the boundary between Canada and the United States, from the Rocky mountains westward. The dividing line was fixed at the 49th parallel.

1848 Treaty of Guadalupe Hidalgo. A treaty between the United States and Mexico at the close of the Mexican war. It provided for the cession to the United States of New Mexico and California, in return for a cash payment of $15,000,000. The United States also took over the debts of Mexico to American citizens, amounting to about $3,250,-000. The territory acquired by the United States included the present states of Arizona, Nevada, Utah, New Mexico, and California, with parts of Wyoming and Colorado.

1850 Clayton-Bulwer Treaty. A treaty between Great Britain and the United States, providing for joint control of a canal to connect the Atlantic and the Pacific by the Nicaragua or any other route. The treaty stipulated that neither party should erect fortifications on the line of the canal, nor assume any sovereign rights over any portion of Central America. Abrogated by the Hay-Pauncefote Treaty in 1901.

1854 American-Japanese Treaty. Also called Perry's Treaty. A treaty negotiated between the shogun, for Japan, and Commodore Perry, on behalf of the United States, in 1854, by which Japan opened the ports of Yokohama, Kobe, Nagasaki, and Hakodate to foreign commerce. Foreigners had been excluded from Japan for 216 years before this date, with the exception of the Dutch, who, however, were strictly confined to their factory at Deshima.

1868 Burlingame Treaty. The treaty of the United States with China which first provided for recognition of international law by China. It stipulated certain important reciprocal privileges for the signatories.

1871 Treaty of Washington. A treaty negotiated with Great Britain. It provided for arbitration of the Alabama claims, the San Juan (Vancouver) boundary question, British Civil War claims, and the Nova Scotia fisheries dispute.

1898 Treaty of Paris. The treaty with Spain which terminated the Spanish American war. It provided for the independence of Cuba and for the cession of the Philippines, Guam, and Puerto Rico to the United States. The United States paid to Spain, under the treaty, $20,000,000.

1901 Hay-Pauncefote Treaty. A treaty signed November 18, 1901, between Great Britain and the United States, with respect to the Panama canal. This treaty abrogated the Clayton-Bulwer Treaty of 1850. It maintained the general principle of neutralization of the canal, but the United States alone was charged with the maintenance of its neutrality. General rights of control and fortification were left undefined. The U.S. reserved the right to maintain a force along the line of the canal for protective purposes. It was not required to keep the canal open in time of war.

1903 Hay-Bunau-Varilla Convention. A treaty between the U.S. and Panama, in lieu of the Hay-Herran convention between the U.S. and Colombia (1903). It provided that the U.S. should guarantee the integrity of Panama, and that, for a cash payment of $10,000,000 and annual payments of $250,000, the U.S. should receive full sovereignty over a strip of land 10 miles wide across the isthmus, within which the interoceanic canal should be constructed.

1921 Peace Treaty with Germany. This provided for peace relations, reserving to the U.S. any rights and advantages which would have accrued under the Treaty of Versailles, and recognizing that the U.S. was not bound by any provisions of that treaty relating to the League of Nations.

1921 Four-Power Pacific Treaty. A treaty negotiated at Washington with England, Japan, and France. It provided for diplomatic adjustment of disputes occasioned by possessions of these powers in the Pacific.

1922 Five-Power Armament Treaty. A treaty negotiated with England, Japan, France, and Italy. It provided for limitation of naval armaments.

1923 North Pacific Fisheries Treaty. The first convention made directly by Canada with the United States. It provided measures for the preservation of the halibut fisheries in the north Pacific Ocean.

1924 "Twelve-Mile Limit" Treaty. A treaty negotiated with Great Britain extending the right of search on British ships suspected of carrying liquor. By international law, the authority of United States officers extends three miles from the coast. By treaty, this zone was increased to an hour's sailing distance from the coast.

1945 United Nations Treaty. On July 28, 1945, the Senate ratified, by a vote of 89 to 2, the Charter of the United Nations, framed by the San Francisco conference.

1949 North Atlantic Treaty. This treaty, the foundation of the North Atlantic Treaty Organization (NATO), is a security alliance for mutual defense between the U.S., Britain, Canada, France, Belgium, the Netherlands, Luxembourg, Norway, Denmark, Iceland, Italy, and Portugal.

1951 Pacific Security Pact. This mutual security treaty between the United States, Australia, and New Zealand was signed at San Francisco, September 1, 1951.

1952 Japanese Peace Treaty. Ratified by the Senate March 29, 1952, this treaty formally ended the state of war declared December 7, 1941, and restored Japan's sovereignty. Treaty signed at San Francisco September 8, 1951, by the United States and 48 other nations.

1954 Southeast Asia Collective Defense Treaty. Initiated by the U.S. and aimed at preventing aggression, this treaty was signed at Manila, P.R., September 8, 1954, by the U.S., Britain, France, Australia, New Zealand, Philippine Republic, Thailand, and Pakistan.

1972 SALT I Pacts. The first phase of U.S.-Soviet disarmament negotiations ended with pacts limiting U.S. and Soviet antiballistic missiles and freezing offensive ballistic missiles on both sides at current levels for up to five years.

1973 Vietnam Cease-Fire Agreement. Signed on January 28, the agreement allowed for U.S. disengagement from the Vietnam conflict, ending the longest war in American history.

Trent Affair. In 1861, Captain Wilkes of the United States sloop *Jacinto* intercepted the British steamer *Trent* at sea and removed two Confederate envoys, Mason and Slidell, who were accredited to France. The two men were released, January 1, 1862, on the protest of the British government. Secretary Seward held the British demand to be a recognition of the U.S. doctrine which denied the right of search.

Turner, Nat. Leader of the most famous slave uprising in U.S. history—Nat Turner's Rebellion. Born a slave in Southampton, Va., in 1800, Turner was a fiery preacher who believed he was divinely inspired. He led a group of rebelling slaves who killed the Joseph Travis family Aug. 21, 1831. Securing arms and enlisting other slaves, the band of about 30 ravaged the area, killing more than 50 people. Some 3000 armed whites gathered and wholesale slaughter of Negroes followed. On Aug. 25 the revolt collapsed and Turner fled. Six weeks later he was captured and hanged at Jerusalem, Va., on Nov. 11.

Tuscarora (*tŭs′kà-rō′rà*) **War.** The conflict waged between the Tuscarora Indians and the white settlers on the Roanoke river and Pamlico sound in North Carolina. An expedition made up of colonial troops and friendly Indians defeated the hostile Indians in a battle, January 28, 1712. The remnant of Tuscaroras migrated to New York State.

Tweed Ring. A group of politicians, led by William M. Tweed, "boss" of Tammany Hall, who in 1871 were shown to have defrauded New York City of millions of dollars. The disclosures were by the *New York Times, Harper's Weekly,* and a so-called Committee of Seventy.

Underground Railroad, The. Popular name applied to the system used by Northern abolitionists before the Civil War, to aid the escape of fugitive slaves. More than 3000 people had a part in the system, and between 1830 and 1860 at least 60,000 slaves escaped by this route.

Union Labor Party. A party organized in 1886 by members of the newly developing trade-unions. A national ticket was nominated in 1888. Successor of the Greenback Labor party, it favored a national greenback currency with free coinage of silver, state ownership of transportation lines, no monopoly of land, woman suffrage, a graduated income tax, and arbitration in labor troubles.

Union Party. Organized in 1936, this party consisted of followers of Francis Townsend, advocate of old-age pensions; followers of Father Charles Coughlin, who proposed ending the privilege of banks to issue notes; and the remnant followers of Huey Long, populist Louisiana senator assassinated in 1936. The party's 1936 presidential candidate was Rep. William Lemke, who promoted a plan to replace existing farm mortgages by low-interest government mortgages.

Union Savers. Group of Northerners who, during the pre-war slavery agitation, placed the preservation of the Union above the question of slavery. They were willing to permit slavery to be extended to the territories, if that would preserve the Union. Henry Clay and Stephen A. Douglas were typical leaders of this group. See *War Democrats.*

United Labor Party. Organized in 1886 as a result of an independent labor movement. In New York City, with Henry George as its candidate for mayor on a single tax platform, the party came close to scoring a notable victory. Most of the members of this party joined the People's or Populist party.

Valley Forge. A village on the Schuylkill River, 24 miles west of Philadelphia, famous for the heroic conduct of Washington, Baron Steuben, and the American army of 11,000 men in the winter of 1777-78. The troops suffered from lack of food and clothes. A fifth of the army, influenced by the glamour of life among the well-fed British in Philadelphia and by the apparent weakness of Congress, deserted. But the large majority of the troops endured their hardships nobly.

Venezuela Boundary Arbitration. In January 1895, Venezuelan troops crossed the Cuyuni River into British Guiana, and hoisted the Venezuelan flag in territory which had been in dispute since 1814. The British issued an ultimatum, whereupon Venezuela appealed to the U.S. to intervene, in support of the Monroe doctrine. President Cleveland, under authority of Congress, appointed a U.S. commission to examine the boundary question. The commission concluded its work when Britain and Venezuela agreed in February 1897 to submit to arbitration, which confirmed most of the British claims.

Vinland or Wineland. The name given to the region on the American continent visited by Norsemen early in the 11th century. The leaders cited in the sagas were Leif and Thorfinn, who is said to have founded a colony that survived three years. It was described as having vines and trees.

Virginia and Kentucky Resolutions. These were passed by the Republican legislatures of the two states in 1798 and 1799 to protest the Federal Alien and Sedition acts. Virginia's resolution asserted the duty of the states to *interpose* when the central government exercised dangerous power. Kentucky's resolution of 1799 declared *nullification* by the sovereign states to be proper in such a case.

Voting Rights Act of 1965. This act suspended literacy and other voter-qualification tests; it authorized the appointment of federal voting examiners to register blacks; and it provided for the federal government to initiate court suits to bar poll taxes as a voting requirement.

War Democrats. Members of the Democratic party in the North who, at the outbreak of the Civil War, pledged the national government their cooperation in the war and the effort to preserve the Union. In 1864, many of these Northern Democrats combined with the Republicans, who, in that year and following years, adopted the name of the Union or National Union party.

Wars, American. Since 1775 the U.S. has engaged in the Revolution, War of 1812, Mexican War, Civil War, Spanish War, two World Wars, the Korean war, and the Vietnam war. In addition, the Army was used in the Whisky Insurrection (see below). During most of the 19th century there was almost constant fighting with the Indians. The Army intervened in Mexico in 1916. The Navy fought minor wars against France in 1798–99 and the Barbary pirates in the early 19th century.

Watauga Articles. The Articles of Association drawn up in 1772 by the settlers on the Watauga, a headwater of the Tennessee River. The settlers, who had come from Virginia in 1769, drew up in articles the first written constitution "ever adopted west of the mountains, or by a community of American-born freemen." These articles established religious freedom and manhood suffrage. A court of 13 representatives, one from each fort, was chosen. In turn, they chose a commission of 5 to manage the colony's affairs.

Watergate. The most extensive political scandal in American history began with the arrest of five men on June 17, 1972. The five broke into Democratic national headquarters at the Watergate offices in Washington, D.C. Then began a slow and difficult uncovering of a web of political espionage, sabotage, and conspiracy. The results exposed illegal campaign contributions, irregularities in handling large sums of money, wiretapping, burglary, invasion of civil rights, perjury, cover-ups, and abuse of presidential power. When President Richard Nixon was forced to resign on August 9, 1974, the affair was still not final because of the far-reaching implications of the scandal.

It was due largely to John J. Sirica, chief judge of the U.S. District Court for the District of Columbia, that the affair was exposed. Not satisfied that all the facts had been uncovered during the trial of the seven original defendants, Sirica urged that a Congressional inquiry be undertaken. The Senate Select Committee on Presidential Campaign Activities was formed, headed by Sam Ervin, Jr. As evidence mounted to implicate officials high in the Nixon administration, the President continued to deny any knowledge of or guilt in the affair. Cabinet members, White House aides, and presidential advisers were indicted. Most were found guilty, others resigned. Nixon was implicated, but because of the pardon by President Ford after Nixon resigned, the full extent of his role could not be exposed through the courts.

A special prosecutor, Archibald Cox, was appointed by the U.S. Attorney General to conduct an investigation into the affair. Although promised cooperation from the White House, Cox was refused when he tried to subpoena presidential tapes as evidence. Cox was then dismissed by executive order. Nixon refused to submit the tapes to Cox's successor, Leon Jaworski, and to the Senate committee. This brought Nixon into direct conflict with the courts; his actions were seen as an abuse of presidential privilege. The U.S. Supreme Court ruled that Nixon must submit the tapes. In an opinion by Chief Justice Warren E. Burger, the court stated that the assumption of absolute executive privilege would "upset the constitutional balance" of government and "gravely impair the role of the courts." President Nixon released the tapes on August 5. The tapes contradicted repeated assertions that he had neither known nor approved the affair. As the House of Representatives continued with impeachment proceedings, Richard Nixon announced his resignation on August 8, 1974. He was the first U.S. president to resign from office.

Whigs. The Whigs among the colonists included those who sought greater authority for the colonial assemblies. With the end of the Revolution, the Whigs split into two groups; some joined the Federalists and others the Anti-federalists, later the Democratic-Republican party.

In 1834, *Whig* came into use again, adopted by a party of various elements, including the former members of the National Republican party. Led by Henry Clay, this party opposed the Democrats under Andrew Jackson. The new Whig platform centered on a protective tariff, national internal improvements, and a national bank. In 1840 the Whigs elected Harrison and Tyler. They were successful again in 1848, when Taylor and Fillmore were elected. With the Whig failure to oppose slavery, the party strength waned. By 1860 the Whigs had practically dissolved.

Whisky Insurrection. A serious rising in western Pennsylvania in 1794, caused by the authorities' attempt to suppress illicit distilling, then rife in the region. Some 6,000–7,000 insurgents took arms. The outbreak was suppressed after 15,000 militia had been called out.

Wilmot Proviso. An amendment to the bill for the purchase from Mexico in 1846 of California and New Mexico, which by Mexican law were "free" territory. Proposed by David Wilmot of Pennsylvania, the amendment provided that neither slavery nor involuntary servitude should ever exist in the territory. Passed by the House, the amendment was defeated in the Senate. It is important as a statement of antislavery principle and as an issue around which the free-state and slave-state struggle was waged for several years.

Woman's Rights Party. A group that nominated a presidential ticket in 1884 with Belva Lockwood for president and Marietta Stow for vice president, on a platform of women's political equality with men. In 1888 the party again named a ticket, with Lockwood for president and Alfred Love for vice president.

Wounded Knee. On February 27, 1973, approximately 200 supporters of the American Indian Movement took control of Wounded Knee on the Ogalala Sioux Reservation in South Dakota. The AIM supporters wanted Senate investigations of Indian problems, including investigations of treaties between the U.S. and Indian nations and of the Bureau of Indian Affairs. An agreement, providing for talks between Sioux representatives and government officials, was signed by Indian leaders and federal representatives on April 5, 1973.

Wyoming Massacre. During the Revolution, in 1778, the settlement in the Valley of Wyoming, Pa., was attacked by British soldiers, with a band of Seneca Indians and some Tories who had been expelled from the valley. Most of the area's men were in the field under Washington. The remaining settlers had taken refuge in Forty Fort, near Wilkes-Barre. Some 400, mostly old men and boys, opposed the British forces of 1100. Losing two-thirds of their men, the settlers surrendered.

X Y Z Mission. A U.S. mission sent to France in 1797. Demands were made on them for bribes to the French officials. In the report of the U.S. commissioners to Congress, the initials X, Y, Z were used for the real names of the French agents.

Yemassee War. A series of Indian outbreaks in South Carolina in 1714–15. In its course several hundred settlers were killed. The Yemassees were driven into Florida, then Spanish territory.

From the Discovery of America by Columbus to the Settlement of Jamestown—1492–1607

1492	Columbus sails from Palos, Spain, and discovers West India islands.	1534	Jacques Cartier enters Gulf of Saint Lawrence.
1493	Columbus, on his second expedition, founds town of Isabella on the island of Haiti.	1535	Cartier ascends Saint Lawrence river to Montreal. Lima founded by Pizarro; Buenos Aires, by Mendoza.
	Cattle first brought to America.	1540	Coronado discovers the Grand Canyon of the Colorado and the Pueblos of New Mexico.
1494	Columbus discovers Jamaica.		California coast explored by Spaniards.
1497	John Cabot discovers the North American continent, probably Labrador.	1541	De Soto discovers the Mississippi.
1498	Columbus, on his third voyage, discovers mainland of South America.		Santiago de Chile founded.
	Sebastian Cabot explores Atlantic coast, Labrador to Carolina.	1548	La Paz founded.
		1549	Bahia established as capital of Brazil.
1499	Voyage of Amerigo Vespucci to coast of Venezuela.	1562	Jean Ribault explores coast of Florida.
1500	Cortereal explores Labrador and Newfoundland.	1565	Saint Augustine, Florida, founded by Menéndez.
	Cabral touches coast of Brazil, and claims the country for Portugal.	1567	Caracas and Rio de Janeiro founded.
	Amazon river discovered.	1572	Drake makes a voyage to South America.
1502	Columbus, on his fourth voyage, explores Panama coast.	1576	Frobisher, searching for northwest passage, discovers Frobisher's straits.
1504	French fishermen reach the banks of Newfoundland.	1583	Sir Humphrey Gilbert takes possession of Newfoundland.
1511	Velásquez subjugates Cuba; Havana founded.	1584	Raleigh's first expedition lands in Virginia.
1513	Florida discovered by Ponce de León.		First book printed at Lima, Peru.
	The Pacific Ocean discovered by Vasco de Balboa.	1585	John Davis discovers Davis strait.
1516	Solis discovers Rio de la Plata.		English settlers left on Roanoke island.
1517	Cordova rediscovers Yucatan.	1586	Sir Francis Drake visits Roanoke Inlet; burns Saint Augustine.
1519	Hernando Cortés lands in Mexico; Panama settled.	1587	Virginia Dare, first English child born in America.
1520	Magellan sails through the Strait of Magellan.	1590	English settlement at Roanoke island disappears.
1521	Cortés captures the City of Mexico.	1602	Bartholomew Gosnold discovers Cape Cod.
1524	Verrazano explores Atlantic coast northward from Cape Fear.		San Diego bay discovered.
1525	Pizarro explores coast of Peru.	1603	Martin Pring explores New England coast. Champlain's first voyage up the Saint Lawrence river.
1526	Cabot explores in South America for Spain.	1604	Founding of Port Royal (Annapolis), Nova Scotia.
1527	Spaniards, under Narváez, land in Florida.	1605	De Monts takes possession of Maine.
1533	Cuzco conquered by Pizarro.		
	Lower California discovered by Jiminez.		

From the Settlement of Jamestown to the Declaration of Independence—1607–1776

	BRITISH AMERICA	FRENCH AMERICA	SPANISH AMERICA
1607	English settlement at Jamestown. First settlement in Maine; lasted one year.	1608. Champlain settles Quebec.	
1609	Second charter of Virginia. Henry Hudson discovers Hudson river.	1609. Champlain discovers Lake Champlain.	
1610	The "starving time" in Virginia.	1610. Discovery of Hudson bay. French Jesuits settle at Port Royal.	1610. León, Nicaragua, established at present site.
1612	Third charter of Virginia, including Bermudas.	1612. Champlain, lieutenant governor of Canada.	
1613	French settlement at Mt. Desert island; destroyed by Virginians.		1613. Dutch settle Demerara.
1614	Fort built by Dutch at Manhattan. Captain John Smith explores New England coast.		
1615	Dutch build Fort Orange (Albany).	1615. Champlain and Le Caron visit the Huron country.	
1619	First colonial assembly in Virginia. Dutch ship brings first slaves to Virginia.		
1620	First women brought to Virginia. Pilgrims land at Plymouth, Mass. Peregrine White, first white child born in New England.		
1621	Death of John Carver, first governor of Plymouth colony; succeeded by William Bradford. Treaty between Plymouth colony and Massasoit. Dutch West India Company founded.	1621. Acadia granted to Sir Wm. Alexander, as Nova Scotia, by James I. Newfoundland granted to Lord Baltimore.	
1622	Settlement at Portsmouth and Dover, N. H.		
1623	First settlement on Manhattan island.		
1624	Lord Baltimore founds a colony at Ferryland, Newfoundland.		1624. The Dutch capture Bahia.
			1625. The Spanish and Portuguese retake Bahia.
1627	Governor Bradford and associates assume debt of Plymouth colony to London merchants.	1627. Colony of Quebec given to the Hundred Associates.	
1628	Settlement at Salem under John Endicott as governor.	1628. The English take possession of Port Royal.	
1629	The company of Massachusetts bay organized.	1629. Sir David Kirke captures Quebec.	
1630	Settlement of Charlestown and Boston; John Winthrop, governor.		1630. The Dutch capture Pernambuco.
1632	Lord Baltimore receives the grant of Maryland.	1632. Richelieu obtains restoration of Canada and Acadia.	Discovery of silver at Cerro de Pasco.
1634	English Catholics settle at Saint Marys, Maryland.		

From the Settlement of Jamestown to the Declaration of Independence—1607–1776—Con.

	BRITISH AMERICA	FRENCH AMERICA	SPANISH AMERICA
1635	First English settlement of Connecticut.	1635. Death of Champlain.	
1636	Roger Williams settles Rhode Island.	1639. Jesuit mission at Ste. Marie.	
1637	Pequot war begins in Massachusetts.	Ursuline convent established	
1638	Swedes settle Delaware; Harvard College founded; New Haven settled.	at Quebec.	
		The French attempt a settlement at Green Bay, Wisconsin.	
1639	Printing press established by Stephen Daye at Cambridge, Mass.	1642. Montreal founded.	
	First constitution of Connecticut.	1644. Iroquois attack Montreal.	
1643	New England Confederation formed.	1649. Iroquois massacre of Huron Indians.	
1644	Indians massacre 300 colonists in Virginia.		
1647	Peter Stuyvesant comes to New Amsterdam as governor.	1659. Laval, first bishop of New France.	1662. Dutch give up Brazil.
1652	Mint established in Boston. Coinage of "Boston shillings."	1660. Dollard's defense of the Long Sault.	1663. Grant of Guiana by Charles II to Lord Willoughby.
1655	Delaware brought under Dutch rule.	1662. French West India Company grant.	
1656	Quakers arrive in Boston; persecuted.	1663. Canada a royal province.	
1662	Connecticut charter granted.	1668. Marquette establishes mission at Sault Sainte Marie.	1665. Saint Augustine pillaged by English buccaneers.
1663	Patent for Carolina colony granted by Charles II.	1669. La Salle sails down the Ohio to Louisville.	
	Rhode Island charter granted.	Father Allouez begins a mission at Green Bay.	
1664	New Amsterdam surrendered to the English; name changed to New York.	1672. Count Frontenac, governor of Canada.	1671. Danes occupy Saint Thomas.
1669	Fundamental Constitutions of Carolina.		
1670	South Carolina settled; Charleston.	1673. Marquette and Joliet discover the Mississippi.	
	Hudson's Bay Company founded.	Fort Frontenac built.	
1671	Mackinac island founded.	1679. La Salle launches the *Griffin* on Niagara River and sails to southern end of Lake Michigan.	
1675	King Philip's war in Massachusetts.		
1676	Nathaniel Bacon's rebellion in Virginia.		
1680	New Hampshire made separate colony.	1680. Discovery of the Mississippi by Hennepin.	
1681	William Penn receives charter for Pennsylvania.	1682. La Salle descends the Mississippi to the Arkansas, and names the valley Louisiana.	
1682	Founding of Philadelphia.		
1683	First assembly in New York under English rule.	1685. La Salle in Texas.	1685. Dampier, English buccaneer, sacks León.
1684	Charter of Massachusetts forfeited.	1689. Iroquois capture Lachine.	
1686	Andros governor of New England.	1691. Nova Scotia retaken by the French.	
1689	Andros deposed; former governments resumed.		
	King William's war breaks out.		
1690	French and Indian massacre of settlers at Schenectady, Salmon Falls, and Casco.		
	Colonial congress called in New York.		1693. Gold mining begins in Brazil.
1691	New charter for Massachusetts (Plymouth and Maine included).		1697. France secures western half of Haiti from Spain.
1692	Salem witchcraft.		1698. Scotch attempt a settlement on Isthmus of Panama.
	College of William and Mary founded.	1699. French colony under Iberville at Biloxi, in Louisiana.	
1701	Philadelphia incorporated as a city.	1702. Biloxi colony moved to Mobile.	
	Yale College founded.	1710. Port Royal captured by English fleet.	1711. French capture Rio de Janeiro.
1702	Queen Anne's war breaks out.		1719. French capture Pensacola.
1711–12	Tuscarora Indian war in Carolina.	1713. Hudson Bay, Nova Scotia, and Newfoundland ceded to England.	1723. Pensacola restored to Spain.
1714–15	Yamassee Indian war in Carolina.	1718. New Orleans founded.	1726. Spaniards establish themselves at Montevideo.
1729	North and South Carolina separated; become royal provinces.	1729. Massacre of French at Natchez by Indians.	1740. Governor Oglethorpe attacks Florida.
1732	First stage between Boston and New York.	1745. Louisburg falls to New England and British troops.	1750. Treaty between Spain and Portugal marking boundaries in South America.
1733	Settlement of Georgia.	1748. Louisburg restored to France.	
1744	King George's war breaks out.	1749. Fort Rouille (Toronto) built.	
1750	First theater opened in New York.	1754. Halifax founded.	
1753	George Washington sent by Virginia to the Ohio region.	1755. French defeat Braddock near Fort Duquesne.	1759. Royal edict expelling Jesuits from Brazil.
1754	Albany Congress.	1758. English capture Louisburg.	1763. Florida ceded to Great Britain.
	French and Indian war begins.	1759. Quebec surrenders to the English.	French Guiana colonized.
1755	Braddock defeated at Fort Duquesne.	1760. Montreal surrendered to the British.	Rio de Janeiro made capital of Brazil.
	Battle of Lake George.	1762. Louisiana ceded to Spain.	1766. Large colony of Acadians arrive in Louisiana.
1758	Fort Frontenac surrendered to English.	1763. Nova Scotia and Canada ceded to the British.	1767. Jesuits expelled from Spanish America.
1759	Battle of Quebec—Wolfe and Montcalm killed.	1764. English settle in New Brunswick.	1768. Revolt of the French against Spanish rule in Louisiana.
1761	James Otis argues against writs of assistance in Massachusetts.		1769. Spanish missions established in California; San Diego settled; San Francisco bay discovered.
1763	Pontiac's war begins.		
1765	Delegates of the colonies assemble in New York to resist the Stamp act.		
1766	Stamp act repealed.		
1767	Parliament passes Townshend revenue acts.		
1768	British troops arrive in Boston; selectmen refuse quarters for them.		1773. Santiago, Guatemala, destroyed by an earthquake.
1770	Boston Massacre.	1774. Passage of the Quebec act.	1776. Paraguay placed under the jurisdiction of Buenos Aires.
1772	Destruction of the *Gaspee*.		
1773	Tea thrown overboard in Boston harbor.		
	Virginia appoints committees of correspondence.		
1774	Boston Port bill.		
	The Continental Congress adopts a declaration of rights.	1775. Gen. Montgomery captures Montreal and Saint John.	
1775	Beginning of the Revolutionary War with the battle of Lexington.	Death of Montgomery at Quebec and failure of American campaign.	Buenos Aires made capital of the viceroyalty.
	Battle of Bunker Hill.		
	Washington commander in chief.		
1776	First Union flag unfurled at Cambridge. British evacuate Boston.		

FROM THE DECLARATION OF INDEPENDENCE TO THE ADOPTION OF THE CONSTITUTION—1776–1789			
UNITED STATES	CANADA	SPANISH NORTH AMERICA	SOUTH AMERICA
1776 Declaration of Independence adopted by Congress at Philadelphia.			
1777 Landing of Lafayette at Charleston. Battles of Princeton, Brandywine. British army occupies Philadelphia. Surrender of Burgoyne at Saratoga. Washington at Valley Forge.			1777. Treaty of San Ildefonso, establishing Spanish and Portuguese boundaries in South America.
1778 Treaty of alliance with France. British Evacuate Philadelphia. Battle of Monmouth.	1778. Frederick Haldimand, governor of Canada. *Montreal Gazette* published.		
1779 War in the South. British overrun South Carolina. Stony Point captured by Wayne. Paul Jones gains naval victory over the British off the coast of Scotland.	1779. Library founded at Quebec.	1779. Baton Rouge captured from the British.	
1780 Benedict Arnold bargains treasonably to surrender West Point. Major André hanged as a spy. Battle of King's Mountain, S. C.	1780. Coteau du Sack canal built.		1780. Insurrection of Peruvians under Amaru.
1781 Battles of Cowpens, Guilford Court House, and Eutaw Springs. Cornwallis surrenders at Yorktown. Articles of Confederation ratified. Bank of North America established.			1781. The English admiral Rodney takes possession of Guiana.
1782 Holland recognizes the independence of the United States. Preliminary peace signed at Paris.	1782. United Empire Loyalists settle in Nova Scotia.		1782. France takes Guiana from England.
1783 Denmark, Sweden, Spain, and Russia recognize the United States. Treaty of peace signed with Great Britain.	1783. Saint John, N. B., founded. Kingston founded. United Empire Loyalists settle in Upper Canada.		1783. Dutch colonies restored to Holland. Spain regains Florida from England.
1784 Connecticut and Rhode Island adopt slave emancipation measures. New Hampshire constitution anti-slavery.	1784. Province of New Brunswick formed.	1784. Island of Saint Bartholomew transferred to Sweden.	
1785 Jefferson appointed minister to France; John Adams to Britain.			
1786 Daniel Shays's rebellion. Annapolis Convention.			1786. Pacifications of the Negroes and tribes in Dutch Guiana.
1787 Constitutional Convention assembles at Philadelphia; adopts constitution. Ordinance for Northwest Territory.	1788. King's College, Windsor, Nova Scotia, founded		
1789 **George Washington,** president; John Adams, vice president. First Congress meets in New York. First tariff bill passed.	1789. Sir Alexander Mackenzie discovers Mackenzie River.	1789. Settlers from North Carolina arrive in Louisiana.	
1790 Indian war in Northwest Territory. Census enumeration ordered.			
1791 Bank of the United States established. Vermont admitted as a state.	1791. Quebec divided into Upper and Lower Canada.	1791. Negroes of Haiti revolt against France.	
1792 Corner stone of White House laid. Kentucky admitted as a state. Decimal system of coinage adopted. First mint established at Philadelphia.	1792. First parliaments of Upper and Lower Canada meet.	1792. First refined cane sugar made in Louisiana.	
1793 **Washington re-elected;** receives all electoral votes. Whitney invents the cotton gin. Corner stone of United States Capitol laid by Washington. Political parties assume names of Republican and Federalist.	1793. Slavery Abolition act passed in Upper Canada.		
1794 First ships of U.S. Navy authorized. Whisky insurrection in Pennsylvania. Jay's Treaty with England.	1794. Jay's Treaty provides agreements relative to commerce, navigation, and boundary. York founded.	1794. Refined sugar produced on commercial scale.	
1795 Antirent troubles in New York.		1795. Maroon war in Jamaica. France secures Spanish portion of Haiti.	
1796 Tennessee admitted as a state. Washington's Farewell Address.			1796. Guiana again in British possession.
1797 **John Adams,** president; Thomas Jefferson, vice president. X Y Z mission to France.	1797. York (Toronto) becomes capital of Upper Canada.		1802. The Dutch resume possession of British Guiana
1798 Alien and Sedition laws passed. Commerce with France suspended. Naval conflict results.	1798. Northwest Fur Company completes canal at Sault Sainte Marie.		1803. British Guiana finally acquired.
1798-99 Virginia and Kentucky Resolutions.			1806. Miranda's expedition against Caracas.
1799 Death of George Washington.			
1800 Capital removed from Philadelphia to Washington.			1806-07. Argentina repels two British attacks.
1801 **Thomas Jefferson,** president; Aaron Burr, vice president. Congress establishes the District of Columbia. Tripoli declares war against U.S.			1808. Royal family of Portugal arrive in Brazil. 1809. Ecuador makes unsuccessful attempt to secure independence.
1803 Louisiana purchased for $15,000,000. Ohio admitted as a state.			

From the Adoption of the Constitution of the United States to the Close of the Civil War—1789–1865			
UNITED STATES OF AMERICA	**CANADA**	**SPANISH AND FRENCH NORTH AMERICA**	**SOUTH AMERICA**
1804 Burr kills Hamilton in a duel.	1803. Slavery illegal in Lower Canada.	1801. Louisiana transferred to France by Spain.	1810. Movement for independence begins in Argentina and in Chile.
1805 **Jefferson re-elected;** George Clinton, vice president.		Toussaint L'Ouverture founds republic of Santo Domingo.	
1807 Embargo act passed. Fulton's steamboat *Clermont* steams from New York to Albany.		1803. French quit Haiti.	1811. Paraguay declares its independence.
1808 Importation of slaves prohibited.	1809. Steamer *Accommodation* arrives at Quebec from Montreal.	1808. Rebellion against France in Santo Domingo.	Venezuela proclaims its independence.
1809 **James Madison,** president; George Clinton, vice president. Embargo act repealed.			New Granada declares independence. Spanish defeated in Uruguay.
1811 Trading posts first established among the Indians. Battle of Tippecanoe with Indians. First steamboat on the Ohio.	1812. Sir George Prevost, governor. Capture of Detroit by General Brock.	1810. Mexican revolt begins under Hidalgo.	1812. Great earthquake in Caracas. Battle of Tucumán. San Martín begins his revolutionary career.
1812 Louisiana admitted as a state. War declared against Great Britain. American successes at sea: *Constitution* defeats *Guerrière*; *Wasp* defeats *Frolic*; *United States* defeats *Macedonian*; *Constitution* defeats *Java*. Canada invaded unsuccessfully.	Battle of Queenston Heights; Americans defeated; Brock killed. Red River settlement, led by Lord Selkirk.		1813. Bolivar begins his military career in New Granada.
1813 **Madison re-elected;** Elbridge Gerry, vice president. Perry captures the English fleet on Lake Erie. Battle of the Thames.	1813. York (Toronto) captured and burned by Americans. American fleet defeated on Lake Ontario.	1813. Mexico declares independence.	1814. Chile temporarily reconquered by Spain. Montevideo captured by the revolutionary army of Buenos Aires.
1814 Battle of Lundy's Lane. British capture and burn Washington. Hartford Convention opposes war.	Americans defeated at Chrystler's Farm. Buffalo burned by British.	1814. Provisional constitution formed for Mexico. Spain receives Santo Domingo from France.	French Guiana restored to France by Portugal.
1815 Jackson defeats the British at New Orleans. Peace Treaty with Britain ratified. Algerian war. Decatur negotiates Treaty.	1816. Half-breeds assault Fort Douglas in Red River settlement.		1815. Brazil becomes a kingdom. 1816. Buenos Aires declares its separation from Spain. Francia made perpetual dictator of Paraguay.
1816 Second Bank of the United States chartered. The *Ontario*, first steamboat on Great Lakes. Indiana admitted as a state. American Colonization Society formed; founds Liberia (1822).			1817. Chileans defeat Spanish. Bolivar leads another revolt in New Granada.
1817 **James Monroe,** president; Daniel D. Tompkins, vice president. Mississippi admitted as a state. Seminole war.	1817. First bank note issued at Montreal.	1817. Unsuccessful insurrection in Mexico ends.	1818. Chileans declare independence; O'Higgins, supreme director.
1818 Illinois admitted as a state. Pensions to Revolutionary soldiers.	1818. United States and Great Britain make agreement to limit war vessels on Great Lakes.		1819. New Granada and Venezuela form Republic of Colombia. Bolivar, president.
1819 The *Savannah*, the first transatlantic steamship. Alabama admitted as a state. Florida purchased by the United States from Spain. Maine separated from Massachusetts.			1820. Revolt in Peru.
1820 Maine admitted as a state. Missouri Compromise bill passed.	1820. Earl of Dalhousie, governor.		1821. San Martín, protector of Peru.
1821 **Monroe re-elected;** Tompkins, vice president. Missouri admitted as a state. Andrew Jackson appointed governor of Florida.	1821. McGill College founded.	1821. Mexico becomes independent of Spain. Santo Domingo revolts from Spain. Costa Rica independent.	1822. Brazil declares its independence. Pedro I, emperor. Ecuador joins Colombia.
1822 Independence of Spanish South American states recognized. Gaslight introduced into Boston.		1822. Mexico, an empire under Iturbide. Costa Rica united to Mexico.	1824. Bolivar, dictator of Peru. Ayacucho, last battle in wars of independence.
1823 President Monroe proclaims the "Monroe Doctrine."	1826. Canada Company chartered.	1823. Federation of Central American states.	1825. Argentine constitution decreed.
1824 General Lafayette visits U.S. Protective Tariff law.	Bytown (now Ottawa) founded.	1824. Federal republic proclaimed for Mexico.	Upper Peru, independent, takes the name of Bolivia.
1825 **John Quincy Adams,** president; John C. Calhoun, vice president. Treaty with Russia ratified. Erie Canal finished.		1826. First survey for Nicaragua ship canal.	1826. Callao, last Spanish stronghold, surrenders.
1827 First railroad in United States built at Quincy, Mass.	1827. King's College founded at York.	Panama congress.	1827. Independence of Uruguay.
1828 "Tariff of Abominations."		1827. Expulsion of Spaniards from Mexico decreed.	1829. Venezuela separates from New Granada.
1829 **Andrew Jackson,** president; John C. Calhoun, vice president.	1829. Welland Canal from Port Dalhousie to Port Robinson completed.		
1830 Webster and Hayne speeches on "nullification" in Senate. First steam railroad for passengers opened at Charleston, S. C.			1830. Death of Bolivar. Ecuador separates from Colombia.

	FROM THE ADOPTION OF THE CONSTITUTION OF THE UNITED STATES TO THE CLOSE OF THE CIVIL WAR—1789–1865—CON.			
	UNITED STATES OF AMERICA	CANADA	MEXICO, CENTRAL AMERICA, AND WEST INDIES	SOUTH AMERICA
1831	The *Liberator* established by William Lloyd Garrison. First national nominating convention (Antimasonic).	1832. Newfoundland obtains a colonial legislature.	1833. Santa Anna, president of Mexico.	1831. Revolution in Brazil. Dom Pedro abdicates. 1832. Charles Darwin visits Patagonia.
1832	Black Hawk war. Nullification in South Carolina. United States Bank bill vetoed.			
1833	**Jackson re-elected;** Martin Van Buren, vice president. Bank deposits removed from the National Bank.	1833. Constitutional government in Newfoundland.		
1834	Whig party first takes its name.		1836. Texas declares her independence. Spain and Mexico sign a treaty.	
1835	Seminole war begins.			1835. Rosas becomes supreme ruler in Argentina.
1836	Massacre at the Alamo, Texas. Arkansas admitted as a state. Sam Houston elected president of Texas.	1836. First railway in Canada opened.		
1837	**Martin Van Buren,** president; Richard M. Johnson, vice president. Great commercial panic. Morse system of telegraphy patented. Michigan admitted as state.	1837. Papineau and Mackenzie rebellion.	1838. Mexico declares war against France. Slavery abolished in British West Indies.	1836. Confederation of Peru and Bolivia under Santa Cruz. Dissolved, 1839.
1838	*Great Western* and *Sirius* cross the Atlantic.	1838. Canadian rebellion suppressed.		
1839	Vulcanized rubber patented by Goodyear.	1839. Issuance of Lord Durham's report on Canada.	1839. Termination of the Mexican-French war. Dissolution of Central American Confederation.	1839. Dissolution of Confederation of Peru and Bolivia.
1841	**William H. Harrison,** president; John Tyler, vice president. Harrison dies April 4; **John Tyler,** president.	1840. Upper and Lower Canada reunited.		1840. Death of Francia in Paraguay. Spain acknowledges Ecuador's independence.
1842	Dorr's rebellion in Rhode Island. Webster-Ashburton Treaty with England signed.	1841. First Parliament of Canada meets at Kingston.	1841. Santa Anna, dictator of Mexico.	1842. Independence of Argentine Republic recognized by Spain. Republic established in Paraguay.
1843	Bunker Hill monument dedicated.	1843. McGill University, Montreal, opened.		
1844	Morse telegraph completed from Baltimore to Washington.	1844. Toronto *Globe* first published.	1844. Dominican Republic set up by revolt from Haiti.	1844. López, president of Paraguay. Spain acknowledges Chilean independence.
1845	**James K. Polk,** president; George M. Dallas, vice president. Florida admitted as a state. United States Naval Academy established at Annapolis. Texas admitted as a state. Petroleum discovered near Pittsburgh.			1845. England and France blockade Buenos Aires, pending civil war. Venezuela's independence recognized by Spain.
1846	Mexican war begins. Wilmot Proviso. Smithsonian Institution established. Oregon Treaty with Great Britain. Iowa admitted as a state. Howe patents sewing machine.	1846. Earl of Cathcart, governor.	1846. Gen. Mejía of Mexico issues proclamation of hostility to the United States; War with United States.	1846. Civil war period of 15 years begins in Ecuador. Spain recognizes Bolivian independence. 1847. Slavery prohibited in New Granada.
1847	Settlement on Great Salt lake, Utah, founded by the Mormons.			
1848	Gold discovered near Colonia, Cal. Peace signed with Mexico; Acquisition of New Mexico and California. Wisconsin admitted as a state. Corner stone of Washington monument laid.	1848. Responsible government established.	1848. Peace between the United States and Mexico; treaty of Guadalupe Hidalgo.	1848. Belzu, president of Bolivia; liberal policy.
1849	**Zachary Taylor,** president; Millard Fillmore, vice president. Gold rush to California begins.		1849. Soulouque, emperor of Haiti.	1849. First export of guano from Peru.
1850	Death of President Taylor, July 9; **Millard Fillmore,** president. California admitted as a state. Clayton-Bulwer Treaty with Great Britain signed. Fugitive Slave bill passed. Clay's compromise bills passed.	1850. Riots in Montreal; Parliament House burned.	1850. Cuba invaded by American filibusters under López. Spain acknowledges independence of Costa Rica and Nicaragua.	1850. Steamship line from Brazil to Europe inaugurated. Jesuits expelled from New Granada.
1851	Vigilance committee organized in San Francisco.		1851. Second invasion of Cuba; López shot.	1851. Manuel Montt, president of Chile.
1852	Mint authorized at San Francisco. Deaths of Henry Clay and Daniel Webster.	1852. Laval University chartered.		1852. Slave trade suppressed in Brazil.
1853	**Franklin Pierce,** president; Wm. Rufus King, vice president. Gadsden Purchase.		1853. Santa Anna again president of Mexico.	1853. Rosas defeated in Argentina.
1854	Treaty with Japan. Kansas-Nebraska bill approved. Ostend Manifesto issued.	1854. First petroleum wells bored. Clergy reserves abolished. Seignioral land tenure abolished.	1854. Carrera proclaimed president for life in Guatemala.	1854. Buenos Aires separates from Argentine confederacy. First railway in Brazil. Slavery abolished in Venezuela.
1855	Completion of Panama railroad.		1855–60. Central America invaded by American filibusters under Walker.	
1856	Civil strife in Kansas. First Republican national convention.	1855. Suspension bridge at Niagara Falls opened.		
1857	**James Buchanan,** president; J. C. Breckinridge, vice president. Dred Scott decision. Great financial panic in United States. First state agricultural college established at Lansing, Mich.	1856. Grand Trunk railroad opened. Allan steamship line established.	1857. Mexican constitution established.	1857. Linares, president in Bolivia; in office four years.

FROM THE ADOPTION OF THE CONSTITUTION OF THE UNITED STATES TO THE CLOSE OF THE CIVIL WAR—1789–1865—CON.

	UNITED STATES OF AMERICA	CANADA	MEXICO, CENTRAL AMERICA, AND WEST INDIES	SOUTH AMERICA
1858	Minnesota admitted as a state. Second treaty with China signed. First message over Atlantic cable. Lincoln-Douglas debates in Illinois.	1858. Ottawa made the capital. Decimal system of coinage adopted.	1858. Mexican constitution annulled by church party. Civil war in Mexico. Haiti, a republic.	
1859	Oregon admitted as a state. John Brown's raid.		1859. Juárez of Mexico confiscates church property.	1859. Buenos Aires reunited to Argentine confederacy.
1860	South Carolina passes ordinance of secession from the Union. Morrill high tariff bill passed.	1860. Prince of Wales visits Canada.		1860. Revolutions and insurrections prevail in Uruguay for next thirty years.
1861	**Abraham Lincoln,** president; Hannibal Hamlin, vice president. Secession of Miss., Fla., Ala., Ga., La., Tex., Va., N.C., Ark., Tenn. Attack on Fort Sumter. Kansas admitted as a state. Southern states form a confederacy. McCellan commander in chief. Mason and Slidell taken from British ship.	1861. Gold found in Nova Scotia. CONFEDERATE STATES OF AMERICA 1861. Jefferson Davis, president; A. H. Stephens, vice president.	1861. Juárez, president of Mexico. Mexican troubles with England, France, and Spain. Dominican Republic united to Spain.	1861. Pérez, president of Chile. In Bolivia, beginning of period of anarchy and loss of prestige. Mosquera, president in New Granada. New Granada becomes United States of Colombia.
1862	Slavery abolished in District of Columbia. Treaty with Great Britain for suppression of slave trade. Law to prevent polygamy in the territories. Greenbacks first issued.	1862. Capture of New Orleans by Farragut and Butler. Battle of Fair Oaks. Battles before Richmond. Battle of Fredericksburg. Battle of Murfreesboro.	1862. Macdonald, premier.	1862. England and Spain disapprove Mexican monarchy for Maximilian.	1862. General Mitre becomes president of Argentine Republic. The younger López elected president of Paraguay.
1863	Emancipation proclamation. W. Va. admitted as a state. Battle of Gettysburg. Draft riots in New York.	1863. Battle of Chancellorsville. Siege of Vicksburg. Battle of Chickamauga. Battle of Lookout Mountain.		1863. Mexico occupied by the French. Spain acknowledges independence of Guatemala.	1863. Falcon, president of Venezuela.
1864	Fight between *Kearsarge* and *Alabama*. Fugitive Slave law repealed. Premium on gold, 285 per cent. Nevada admitted as a state. President calls for 800,000 volunteers. Modoc Indian war begins.	1864. Grant's Virginia campaign. Battles of Wilderness, Spottsylvania, Cold Harbor. Atlanta campaign. Capture of Mobile. Sherman's march to the sea.	1864. Confederates in Canada plan raids.	1864. Maximilian, emperor of Mexico.	1864. Paraguayan war.
1865	**Lincoln reelected;** Andrew Johnson, vice president. Hampton Roads Conference. President Lincoln shot, April 14; **Andrew Johnson,** president, April 15. Thirteenth amendment passed, prohibiting slavery.	1865. Confederate Congress adjourns *sine die*. Richmond evacuated by Confederates. Lee surrenders at Appomattox, April 9. Johnston, Morgan, Taylor, and Kirby-Smith surrender. Jefferson Davis captured.	1865. Quebec Resolutions favoring confederation of provinces passed in Quebec legislature.	1865. United States protests against French occupation of Mexico. Insurrection in Jamaica. Spain withdraws from Santo Domingo. Spain recognizes independence of Salvador. Carrera dies in Guatemala.	1865. Agassiz makes scientific expedition up the Amazon. American congress at Lima, Peru. Treaty between Brazil, Uruguay, and Argentina against Paraguay. Four years' war follows. Religious toleration begins in Chile. Chile declares war against Spain.
1866	Civil Rights bill passed over president's veto. Atlantic telegraph completed. Shoshone Indian war begins.	1866. Invasion of Canada threatened by Fenians.	1866. Napoleon III agrees with United States to withdraw French troops from Mexico.	1866. Spaniards bombard Valparaíso, Chile. Bolivia cedes territory to Chile.

FROM THE CLOSE OF THE CIVIL WAR, 1865, TO THE PRESENT TIME			
UNITED STATES OF AMERICA	CANADA	MEXICO, CENTRAL AMERICA, AND WEST INDIES	SOUTH AMERICA
1867 Nebraska admitted as a state. Alaska transferred by Russia to the United States. Reconstruction acts passed over president's veto.	1867. British North America act forms Dominion of Canada. Dominion Day, July 1. Lord Monck, first governor-general. New Parliament at Ottawa.	1867. Maximilian, Miramón, and Mejía tried in Mexico and shot. Republic re-established in Mexico.	1867. Bolivia cedes territory to Brazil.
1868 President Johnson impeached, tried, and acquitted. Readmission of Southern states to representation in Congress begins. Burlingame Treaty with China signed. Fourteenth amendment adopted.	1868. Agitation against confederation in Nova Scotia. Fenian raid repelled. Sir John Young, governor-general.	1868. Insurrection of Creoles in Cuba; beginning of ten years' war. Santo Domingo treaty for annexation to U. S.	
1869 **U. S. Grant,** president; Schuyler Colfax, vice president. Union Pacific and Central Pacific railroads opened for traffic. Financial panic in New York.	1869. Newfoundland refuses to join the Dominion. Hudson's Bay Co. territory purchased by Dominion.	1869. Filibusters again attack Cuba; repelled.	1869. Asunción occupied by allied troops of Argentina, Brazil, and Uruguay.
1870 Northern Pacific railroad begun. Fifteenth amendment ratified.	1870. Rupert's Land made the Province of Manitoba.	1870. Continual insurrections in Cuba.	1870. Guzmán Blanco begins 20 years of power as real ruler of Venezuela. First Peruvian railway opened.
1871 Legal Tender act declared constitutional "Tweed Ring" in New York exposed. Great fire in Chicago. Treaty of Washington signed with Great Britain.	1871. British Columbia united to the Dominion. Uniformity of currency established.	1871. Juárez, president of Mexico. Present constitution of Costa Rica drawn up.	1871. Brazilian law passed for gradual emancipation of slaves.
1872 Geneva award of $15,500,000 made to the United States. Great fire in Boston; loss $80,000,000. Modoc war in California.	1872. Lord Dufferin, governor-general.	1872. Death of Juárez in Mexico.	1873. Defensive alliance of Peru and Bolivia, against Chile.
1873 **Grant re-elected,** Henry Wilson, vice president. Credit Mobilier investigation by Congress. One-cent postal cards issued. Financial panic sweeps entire country.	1873. Prince Edward Island joins the Dominion.	1873. Slavery abolished in Puerto Rico.	1874. Treaty between Bolivia and Chile about Atacama and the nitrate deposits.
1875 Act authorizing the resumption of specie payments, beginning January 1, 1879.	1875. Icelanders settle in Northwest Territories.		1876. Venezuela renounces papal authority. Beginning of Daza's notorious dictatorship in Bolivia.
1876 Massacre of Custer's troops by Sitting Bull. Centennial exposition at Philadelphia. Colorado admitted as a state. Electoral commission appointed.	1876. Intercolonial railway opened from Quebec to Halifax.	1877. Porfirio Diaz, provisional president of Mexico.	
1877 **Rutherford B. Hayes,** president; William A. Wheeler, vice president. Great railroad strike. "Molly Maguires" hanged in Pennsylvania. War with the Nez Percés Indians.	1877. Canadian fisheries award by Halifax commission.		
	Edison announces his phonograph.	1878. Marquis of Lorne, governor-general. Second premiership of Sir John A. Macdonald begins.	1878. Surrender of insurgent government in Cuba.	1878. President Hayes decides El Chaco boundary question in favor of Paraguay.
1878 Bland Silver bill passed over president's veto. Electric lighting introduced by Edison. First telephone exchange established.			1879. War of the Pacific, between Chile on one side and Peru and Bolivia on the other.
1879 United States government resumes specie payment. Women permitted to practice before United States courts. French Atlantic cable laid.	1879. Industrial exhibition at Ottawa. 1880. Royal Canadian Academy of Arts founded.	1880. Manuel Gonzáles, president of Mexico.	1880. Buenos Aires made the capital of Argentina. Spain acknowledges Paraguay's independence.
1880 Immigration treaty with China.	1881. Contract for Canadian Pacific railway ratified. Last British soldiers leave the Dominion.		
1881 **James A. Garfield,** president; Chester A. Arthur, vice president. President Garfield shot, July 2; **Chester A. Arthur,** president, September 20. International Cotton exposition at Atlanta, Ga.			1881. Lima occupied by the Chileans. United States mediates in boundary dispute between Chile and Argentina. Spain recognizes Colombia's independence.
1882 Star Route trails begin. War with the Apache Indians. Chinese Exclusion act passed.	1882. Northwest Territory beyond Manitoba divided into Assiniboia, Saskatchewan, Alberta, and Athabaska.	1882. Heureux, president of Dominican Republic. In power 17 years.	
1883 Northern Pacific railroad completed. Opening of the Brooklyn bridge. Pendleton Civil Service act passed.	1883. Standard time adopted. Marquis of Lansdowne, governor-general.	1883. Ancient city discovered in Sonora, Mexico.	1883. Peace treaty signed by Chile and Peru.
1884 Great floods in the Ohio valley. Financial crises in New York.		1884. Porfirio Diaz, president of Mexico.	
1885 **Grover Cleveland,** president; Thomas A. Hendricks, vice president. Apache war in New Mexico. World's industrial exposition at New Orleans.	1885. The Riel insurrection in Northwest.	1885. Concessions to the Nicaragua Canal company granted by Nicaragua.	1884. Treaty between Chile and Bolivia.
1886 Railroad strikes and anarchistic riots. Silver certificates authorized. Bartholdi's Statue of Liberty unveiled.	1886. Fisheries dispute with United States. City of Vancouver founded.	1886. Slavery abolished in Cuba.	1886. Balmaceda, president of Chile. Colombia becomes a centralized republic.

FROM THE CLOSE OF THE CIVIL WAR, 1865, TO THE PRESENT TIME—CON.			
UNITED STATES OF AMERICA	**CANADA**	**MEXICO, CENTRAL AMERICA, AND WEST INDIES**	**SOUTH AMERICA**
1887 Interstate Commerce Commission created.	1887. Great railway bridge at Lachine completed.		Politico-religious struggles begin.
1888 Chinese immigration further restricted.	1888. Lord Stanley, governor-general.		1888. Slavery totally aboli hed in Brazil.
1889 **Benjamin Harrison,** president; Levi P. Morton, vice president. Johnstown flood. Pan-American congress meets in Washington. North and South Dakota, Washington, and Montana admitted as states. Oklahoma opened for settlement.	1889. Northwest Territories given responsible government. 1890. Dominion Commons passes a resolution of loyalty to Great Britain.		1889. Revolution at Rio de Janeiro; emperor banished; republic declared. 1890. First Brazilian congress meets. Great financial crisis in Argentina.
1890 Idaho and Wyoming admitted as states. People's party convenes at Topeka, Kansas. McKinley tariff goes into effect. Sioux war; Sitting Bull killed.	1891. Canadian Pacific railway completed. First Pacific mail steamer arrives at Vancouver from Yokohama.		1891. Civil war in Chile; Jorge Montt becomes president. Brazilian republican constitution adopted. Fonseca, president.
1891 Lynching of Italians in New Orleans. National People's party organized.			Mutiny and insurrections. Peixoto becomes president.
1892 Bering Sea dispute referred to arbitration.	1892. Dominion discriminates against United States in use of Welland Canal.		
1893 **Grover Cleveland,** president; Adlai E. Stevenson, vice president. Columbian exposition, Chicago. Chinese Exclusion bill approved. Great financial depression. Silver Purchase act repealed.	1893. Canal tolls arranged with U. S. Earl of Aberdeen, governor-general. Bering Sea arbitration.	1893. Zelaya elected president of Nicaragua (to 1910).	1893. Insurrections in Argentina. Naval revolt in Brazil.
1894 Wilson tariff bill passed. Coal and railroad strikes. Republic of Hawaii recognized. New treaty with Japan.	1894. Intercolonial Congress opened at Ottawa.	1894. Spain recognizes independence of Honduras.	1894. Moraes, president of Brazil.
1895 Free silver movement. Special message of the president on the Venezuelan question.	1895. First exhibition in Northwest opened at Regina.	1895. Cuba, in rebellion, demands autonomy from Spain. Weyler issues *reconcentrado* order in Cuba.	1895. Naval revolt in Brazil suppressed. Venezuela boundary dispute with England.
1896 Treaty with the Choctaw Indians. Utah admitted as state.	1896. Sir Wilfrid Laurier, Liberal, premier.		
1897 **William McKinley,** president; Garret A. Hobart, vice president. Universal postal congress meets in Washington. Strikes among coal and iron miners. Dingley tariff bill goes into effect.	1897. School question settled in Manitoba. Commission for Yukon gold region appointed.	1897. Weyler recalled from Cuba; Blanco appointed captain general.	1897. Venezuela ratifies boundary treaty with Great Britain.
1898 City government of Greater New York inaugurated. War with Spain. Admiral Dewey destroys tne Spanish fleet at Manila. Naval battle at Santiago; destruction of Cervera's fleet. Treaty of Paris: United States acquires sovereignty over Puerto Rico and the Philippines. Annexation of Hawaii.	1898. Great influx of miners to Yukon gold region. Earl of Minto, governor-general. Joint high commission meets at Quebec to settle difficulties between Canada and U. S.	1898. United States battleship *Maine* blown up in Havana harbor. Invasion of Cuba and Puerto Rico by United States. 1898–1902. Cuba temporarily governed by the United States war department.	1898. Chile and Peru adopt convention in Tacna-Arica controversy. Campos Salles, president of Brazil; financial reforms. First Latin American scientific congress at Buenos Aires.
1899 Aguinaldo foments Philippine war. First Philippine commission named. General Wood, governor of Cuba.	1899. Adjournment of the joint high commission.		1899. Venezuelan boundary award. Castro in power in Venezuela.
1900 Civil government established in the Philippines under act of Congress. Galveston flood and hurricane. Civil government in Alaska. American forces sent to China.	1900. Great fire in Ottawa. Liberal ministry retains power.	1900. Mexican drainage canal completed.	Revolution in Colombia begins. Pando, a liberal, in power in Bolivia.
1901 **McKinley, re-elected;** Theodore Roosevelt, vice president. Platt amendment relating to Cuban independence passed. President McKinley shot at Buffalo, N. Y., Sept. 6; **Theodore Roosevelt,** president, September 14. Cuban autonomy granted.	1901. Toronto exhibition opened.	1901. Cuban constitution adopted. Second international American conference, in City of Mexico.	1901. War declared between Venezuela and Colombia. Riesco, a liberal, president of Chile.
1902 President recommends Panama Canal purchase. Civil government established in the Philippines. Decision of United States supreme court in Northern Securities case.	1902. Canadian-Australian cable laid. Treaty between Newfoundland and United States.	1902. Revolution in Santo Domingo. Eruption of Mt. Pelée, Saint-Pierre.	1902. End of revolution in Venezuela. Civil war in Colombia ended. Boundary award on dispute between Argentina and Chile.
1903 Department of commerce and labor. Pacific cable completed. Alaskan boundary dispute decided. Hay-Bunau-Varilla canal treaty with Panama.	1903. Bill providing for new transcontinental railway passed.	1903. West Indian hurricane destroys many lives.	1903. Hay-Herran canal treaty rejected by Colombia. The Republic of Panama proclaimed.
1904 Commercial treaty with China. Arbitration treaty with France. Great fire in Baltimore. Louisiana Purchase exposition at Saint Louis.	1904. Earl Grey, governor-general.		1904. Hague Tribunal awards payments from Venezuela to European powers.

From the Close of the Civil War, 1865, to the Present Time—Con.

	United States of America	Canada	Mexico, Central America, and West Indies	South America
1905	**Theodore Roosevelt,** president; C. W. Fairbanks, vice president.	1905. Provinces of Alberta and Saskatchewan created.	1905. U. S. establishes financial protectorate over Dominican Republic.	
1906	Destruction of San Francisco by earthquake and fire. Interstate Commerce act. Second occupation of Cuba by U. S.	1906. British preferential tariff debated.	1906. Mexican agreement with U. S. on boundary and irrigation.	1906. Pan-American conference, at Rio de Janeiro. Earthquake at Valparaíso.
1907	Pure Food law becomes effective. Jamestown exposition opened. Oklahoma admitted as a state. Financial panic.	1907. Miners' strikes; anti-Asiatic riots in Vancouver.	1907. Central American conference at Washington.	
1908	General arbitration treaty with France. Conference of governors at the White House, to discuss conservation.	1908. Tercentenary held at Quebec.		1908. Railroad, Guayaquil to Quito, completed.
1909	**William H. Taft,** president; James S. Sherman, vice president. Payne-Aldrich tariff. Alaska-Yukon-Pacific exposition. Peary discovers north pole.	1909. Unusual immigration from the United States begins. Railway development.	1909. Meeting of presidents Taft and Diaz at El Chamizal. Gómez, president of Cuba. U. S. troops withdrawn.	1909. Boundary treaty between Brazil and Peru.
1910	Commerce court created. Postal savings banks established.	1910. Laurier's naval defense bill accepted by Parliament.	1910. President Diaz re-elected.	1910. Hermes da Fonseca, president of Brazil.
1911	Trust trials before United States supreme court; dissolution of Standard Oil company ordered. Arbitration treaties with Great Britain and France.	1911. Duke of Connaught, governor-general. Reciprocity with the U. S. defeated. Borden, Conservative, premier.	1911. Diaz forced to resign. Francisco I. Madero, president.	1911. "Bolivian Congress" of representatives from different South American states.
1912	Formation of Progressive party. Arizona and New Mexico admitted as states.	1912. Conservative emergency naval bill defeated.	1912. Insurrection in Mexico.	1912. Railroad across Andes completed.
1913	Parcel post established. Sixteenth amendment adopted. **Woodrow Wilson,** president; Thomas R. Marshall, vice president. Seventeenth amendment adopted. California anti-alien land law. Underwood-Simmons tariff law. Glass-Owen currency law.	1913. Unusual prosperity throughout the Dominion. Notable extension of rural free delivery system.	1913. Madero, president of Mexico, forced to resign. Madero is assassinated. Huerta, leader of insurrection in Mexico.	1913. Brazil: Coffee valorization dispute settled with United States. Ex-President Roosevelt visits South America.
1914	Neutrality of United States in European war proclaimed. Nicaragua canal treaty negotiated. Federal Reserve banks established.	1914. Death of Lord Strathcona. *Empress of Ireland* sinks.	1914. Revolution in Haiti. United States troops at Vera Cruz.	1914. "A. B. C." conference concerning Mexico. Panama Canal opened to traffic.
1915	Federal trade commission. Pan-American financial conference at Washington. Naval advisory board established. Government railroad in Alaska begun.	1915. Canada sends troops and supplies to Europe.	1915. Carranza recognized president of Mexico.	1915. South American delegates at third Pan-American scientific congress, Washington.
1916	Philippine Independence bill. Military expedition in Mexico. National Guard mobilized. Purchase of Danish islands approved. Workman's Compensation act. Eight-hour Railway Wage law. Canal treaty with Nicaragua ratified.	1916. Duke of Devonshire, governor-general. Prohibition legislation in all provinces.	1916. United States lands marines in Santo Domingo. Villa's raid on Columbus, New Mexico.	1916. Ramón Valdéz chosen president of Panama. Irigoyen elected president of Argentina.
1917	Diplomatic relations with Germany severed. **Wilson re-elected;** T. R. Marshall, vice president. Senate adopts cloture rule. Congress declares war on Germany. Selective Conscription bill. Navy greatly increased. Government takes over railways.	1917. Woman suffrage granted, in limited form. Conservatives win election. Terrific explosion wrecks Halifax. Compulsory military service.	1917. Cuba declares war on Germany. Guatemala, Honduras, Haiti, and Nicaragua end diplomatic relations with Germany.	1917. Brazil declares war on Germany. Argentina, Bolivia, Ecuador, Peru, and Uruguay sever relations with Germany. Guerra elected president of Bolivia.
1918	Federal fuel administration. War Finance Corporation bill. Daylight Saving bill. Man power registration exceeds 23,000,000. Two million American troops overseas. Severe influenza epidemic. American troops in Rhenish Prussia.	1918. Dominion troops win distinction at second battle of the Somme, Quéant, Drocourt, Bourlon Wood, Cambrai, Douai, Valenciennes, and Mons.	1918. Guatemala, Nicaragua, Costa Rica, Honduras, and Haiti declare war on Germany. Mexico severs diplomatic relations with Cuba.	1918. Brazil gives Allies interned German ships. Railroad strike in Argentina. Territorial dispute between Peru and Chile revived.
1919	Death of Theodore Roosevelt. President Wilson heads American delegation to Peace Conference. Prohibition amendment ratified. Peace Treaty and League of Nations rejected by Senate.	1919. Premier Borden represents Dominion at Peace Conference. Death of Laurier.	1919. Mexico and Cuba resume diplomatic relations. Tension over foreign concession in Mexico.	1919. General strike in Argentina. Brazil excludes German banks.
1920	Woman Suffrage amendment ratified. Republican victory in presidential election. Army reorganized. Railways returned to private management.	1920. Arthur Meighen, Conservative, becomes premier. Prohibition an issue in the provinces.	1920. Carranza assassinated. General Obregon becomes president. Downfall of Cabrera in Guatemala.	1920. In Argentina, the Radicals win in elections. Irigoyen, president. Alessandri, president of Chile.

	FROM THE CLOSE OF THE CIVIL WAR, 1865, TO THE PRESENT TIME—CON.			
	UNITED STATES OF AMERICA	CANADA	MEXICO, CENTRAL AMERICA, AND WEST INDIES	SOUTH AMERICA
1921	**Warren G. Harding,** president; Calvin Coolidge, vice president. Congress restricts immigration. Agricultural *bloc* in Congress. Washington Conference meets. Peace Treaty with Germany ratified.	1921. Defeat of Conservatives. W. L. M. King premier. Opening of Queenston hydroelectric plant.	1921. Zayas declared president of Cuba. United States plans withdrawal from Santo Domingo.	1921. Saavedra, president of Bolivia.
1922	Four Power Pacific Treaty ratified by the United States. General coal strike. Supreme court declares Federal child labor law unconstitutional. Fordney-McCumber tariff law. Lincoln memorial temple at Washington dedicated.	1922. Coal strike. United Farmers party controls legislatures in Ontario, Alberta, and Manitoba.	1922. Nicaragua, Honduras, and Salvador renew treaty of peace with United States. Growth of labor organizations in Mexico.	1922. Peru and Chile submit Tacna-Arica dispute to arbitration by President Harding. Brazilian centennial exposition at Rio de Janeiro.
1923	Last American troops withdrawn from the Rhine. Great Britain refunds debt to the United States. First nonstop airplane flight across continent, from New York to San Diego. Death of President Harding; **Calvin Coolidge,** president, August 5.	1923. First treaty between Canada and U. S. signed; trade treaty with Italy. Murray, premier of Nova Scotia for 27 years, resigns.	1923. Crowder first ambassador from U. S. to Cuba. U. S. recognizes Obregon government in Mexico.	1923. Pan-American conference at Santiago, Chile. Peru and Chile present Tacna-Arica controversy before the arbiter, President Harding.
1924	Death of Woodrow Wilson. Lease of oil lands by Navy department cancelled by government. Jap immigrants excluded. United States navy fliers encircle globe. Soldier bonus bill passed.	1924. Liquor treaty with the United States ratified. Strike of postal employees.	1924. Calles elected president of Mexico. U. S. troops withdrawn from Dominican Republic.	1924. Constitutional curb placed on power of presidency in Chile. Insurrections in Brazil suppressed.
1925	**Calvin Coolidge,** president; Charles G. Dawes, vice president. Scopes "Evolution Trial" attracts world-wide attention. Italy and Belgium fund debts to the United States. Postal rates increased.	1925. Defeat of Liberal party. Premier retains office, governing with help of Progressives. United Church of Canada formed.	1925. Costa Rica announces intention of withdrawing from League of Nations.	1925. Revolution in Ecuador. Boundary dispute among Brazil, Colombia, and Peru settled through U. S. arbitration.
1926	Senate votes adherence to World Court but with unacceptable reservations. North pole reached by U. S. navy airplane from Spitzbergen. Sesquicentennial Exposition, Phila.	1926. First minister to the U. S. Liberal government elected. W. L. M. King premier.	1926. Chamorro dictator, Nicaragua. Church properties seized by Mexican government.	1926. Brazil blocks entry of Germany into League of Nations.
1927	Disastrous floods in Mississippi valley and in northern New England states. Lindbergh flies alone from New York to Paris. Federal Radio Commission appointed. Execution of Sacco and Vanzetti arouses protests.	1927. Canada elected to League of Nations Council. Canada protests U. S. order classifying as imigrants Canadian commuters to U. S. cities.	1927. Mexico seizes petroleum lands. Civil war in Nicaragua; U. S. supervises elections. Cuba elected to Council of League of Nations.	1927. Chile nitrate industry faced with crisis due to new processes of nitrogen fixation. Deportation of radicals from Chile.
1928	Mississippi flood control bill passed. President-elect Hoover makes tour of South America. Notable expansion in air transportation.	1928. Canada establishes diplomatic relations with France and Japan.	1928. Pan-American conference, Havana. Obregon, pres. of Mexico, slain; Portes Gil, pres.	1928. Paraguay-Bolivia dispute over Chaco.
1929	**Herbert Hoover,** president; Charles Curtis, vice president. Senate ratifies Paris pact. Naval increase voted by Congress. Census and reapportionment bill. Federal farm board established. Stock market panic.	1929. Canadian rum runner *Im Alone* sunk by U. S. coast guard under circumstances resulting in diplomatic protests.	1929. Rebellion suppressed in Mexico; church-state conflict compromised. Insurrection in Haiti suppressed by U. S. marines.	1929. Tacna-Arica dispute settled amicably, Tacna going to Peru and Arica to Chile.
1930	Admiral Byrd returns from Antarctic. London conference provides for Anglo-American naval parity. Hawley-Smoot tariff bill enacted.	1930. Conservative government elected on tariff increase issue; R. B. Bennett premier.	1930. Mexico severs diplomatic relations with Soviet Russia; Ortiz Rubio president. Revolution in Dominican Rep.	1930. Revolutions in Brazil, Peru, Argentina, Bolivia, due to economic crises. Vargas seizes Brazil presidency.
1931	Depression and bank failures. Moratorium on war debts for one year.	1931. Welland ship canal opened. Westminster statute, legalizing Canadian independence.	1931. Revolution in Salvador. Mexico joins League of Nations.	1931. Revolutions in Panama, Chile, Peru, Ecuador, Paraguay.
1932	Reconstruction Finance Corporation established to aid credit. St. Lawrence waterway treaty with Canada negotiated.	1932. Ottawa conference for imperial economic unity.	1932. Rodriguez president of Mexico; Mexico resigns from League of Nations.	1932. Chaco war between Paraguay and Bolivia resumed. Alessandri regime begins in Chile.

FROM THE CLOSE OF THE CIVIL WAR, 1865, TO THE PRESENT TIME—CON.

	UNITED STATES OF AMERICA	CANADA	MEXICO, CENTRAL AMERICA, AND WEST INDIES	SOUTH AMERICA
1933	**Franklin D. Roosevelt,** president; John N. Garner, vice president. All banks closed for 10 days; deposit insurance established. Gold standard suspended. New Deal—N R A, A A A, T V A established. "Lame duck" and prohibition repeal amendments ratified.	1933. Newfoundland accepts British control of finances. Royal commission recommends establishment of central bank for Canada.	1933. Revolution in Cuba; Machado driven out; Grau San Martin president.	1933. Revolution in Uruguay. Colombia-Peru dispute over Leticia. Pan-American conference at Montevideo.
1934	Dollar revalued. Securities exchange regulation begun. First reciprocal trade agreement with Cuba. Severe drought and dust storms.	1934. Dionne quintuplets born. Relief and recovery laws passed.	1934. Mendieta president of Cuba. Cardenas president of Mexico.	1934. Brazil adopts new constitution. Contreras president of Venezuela.
1935	Supreme Court holds N R A codes unconstitutional. Social Security act passed. Reserve Board's control over banking system enlarged. National labor relations act.	1935. Bank of Canada opened. "Social credit" government elected in Alberta led by Aberhart.	1935. General strike in Cuba.	1935. Brazil and United States sign reciprocal trade treaty. Unsuccessful revolt in Brazil. Truce ends Chaco war.
1936	A A A declared unconstitutional; soil conservation act substituted. Labor movement splits, C. I. O. unions being suspended from A. F. of L. Inauguration of trans-Pacific airplane mail service to Manila. President Roosevelt re-elected.	1936. Liberal government elected. W. L. Mackenzie King premier. Reciprocal trade agreement with the United States.	1936. Pres. Gomez of Cuba impeached, succeeded by Bru. Batista, controlling army, exercises power.	1936. Pan-American conference at Buenos Aires, Monroe Doctrine tending to become "common front" policy.
1937	**Franklin D. Roosevelt,** president; John N. Garner, vice president. Ohio-Mississippi floods, more than a million homeless. President seeks enlargement of Supreme Court; plan defeated. Supreme Court upholds social security act and Wagner labor law.	1937. Supreme court invalidates trade and social insurance acts. Commission appointed to study possible changes in constitution. Alberta's social credit government admits failure.	1937. Cardenas renews drive to create "democracy of workers" in Mexico; assumes control over oil industry. Batista of Cuba announces three-year plan of economic and social reconstruction.	1937. Bolivia reinstates constitution of 1880; seizes foreign oil concessions.
1938	Japan attacks American gunboat, *Panay,* in Chinese waters.	1938. Reciprocal trade agreement with United States extended.	1938. Mexico seizes foreign oil properties to enforce court decision growing out of labor dispute.	1938. Chaco dispute finally settled. Aguirre, president of Chile; forms "popular front" government.
1939	"Cash and Carry" neutrality act. Neutrality proclamations. Government Reorganization act.	1939. Declaration of war against Germany; establishment of training centers for British war aviators.	1939. Declaration of Panama for safety zone for neutral shipping.	1939. Venezuela-U. S. trade pact. German warship *Graf Spee* sunk at Montevideo.
1940	Defense measures: bases leased in British possessions; enlargement of army and navy; conscription act. President Roosevelt re-elected for a third term.	1940. King government re-elected. Earl of Athlone governor-general.	1940. Act of Havana forbidding transfer of colonies. Camacho, president of Mexico.	
1941	**Franklin D. Roosevelt,** president; Henry A. Wallace, vice president. "Lend-Lease" act for aid to Britain. Pearl Harbor attacked; war declared on Japan, Germany, and Italy.	1941. Joint defense measures with U. S. planned. War declared against Japan.	1941. Nine republics declare war against Japan. Mexico cooperates with United States for defense.	
1942	Philippines taken by Japan. Battles of Coral Sea and Midway. Americans attack the Solomons; join in invasion of North Africa.	1942. Conscription for overseas service. Dieppe raid.	1943. French West Indies capitulate.	1942. Conference at Rio de Janeiro. All countries except Argentina and Chile sever diplomatic relations with Axis powers. Brazil declares war on Germany and Italy.
1943	Americans in Sicily and Italy. Victories in Southwest Pacific.	1943. Regulations for manpower control.	1944. Dr. Grau San Martin elected president of Cuba.	
1944	Americans invade Normandy; liberate France and Belgium. Ardennes attack: "Battle of the Bulge;" last German offensive. Philippines invaded. Japanese Navy smashed at Leyte.	1944. Conflict over applying overseas conscription.		1943. Revolutions in Argentina and Bolivia.
1945	**Franklin D. Roosevelt,** president; Harry S Truman, vice president. Manila retaken. Death of President Roosevelt. **Harry S Truman,** president, April 12. Americans invade southern France; advance into Germany. United Nations conference at San Francisco; U. S. ratifies charter. Iwo Jima and Okinawa taken. First use of atomic bomb. Surrender of Japan. Americans occupy Japan and southwestern Germany.	1945. King government re-elected. 1946. Viscount Alexander of Tunis, governor-general. Loan to Britain of $1,250,000,000.	1945. Inter-American conference at Mexico City. Act of Chapultepec. 1946. Mexico elects Miguel Alemán president to succeed Camacho.	1945. Vargas deposed in Brazil. 1946 Juan Perón elected president of Argentina. Revolution in Bolivia; Enrique Herzog elected president.
1946	Winston Churchill's "Iron Curtain" speech at Fulton, Mo. Rapid conversion of industry to peacetime basis; removal of controls. Philippines become independent. Atom bomb tests at Bikini.	1946. Exposure of "spy ring" within the government, giving information to Russian agents. Wartime controls lifted.	1946. Mexico elects Alemán president to succeed Camacho.	1946. Peron, president of Argentina, moves toward dictatorship. Revolution in Bolivia, President Villaroel murdered.

From the Close of the Civil War, 1865, to the Present Time—Con.

	UNITED STATES OF AMERICA	CANADA	LATIN AMERICA	
1947	U. S ends intervention in China. Taft-Hartley labor bill passed. "Marshall Plan" for economic rehabilitation of Europe begun. Army, navy, and air force merged in unified department of defense. Beginning of McCarthy agitation.	1947. President Truman visits Canada; warmly received at Ottawa. Peace treaties with Italy, Rumania, Hungary, Finland.	1947. Mexico completes payments for U.S. oil properties expropriated in 1938.	1947 Bolivia and Argentina make arbitration treaty. Argentina and Chile lay claim to Antarctic lands.
1948	U.S. and British "Airlift" relieves Russian blockade of Berlin. Russian spy activities exposed in U. S.	1948. Question of "dollar exchange" causes limitation of trade with U. S.	1948. Disputed election and civil war in Costa Rica leaves Figueres in power.	1948. Communist movements in Brazil and Chile lead to outlawing the party.
1949	**Harry S Truman,** president; Alben W Barkley, vice president. U.S. recognizes Israel and Jordan. North Atlantic Treaty Organization. Russian explosion of atomic bomb.	1949. Newfoundland admitted as tenth province.	1949. United States grants de facto recognition to new government in San Salvador.	1949. Paraguay's president, after five months in office, is ousted in a coup.
1950	National Science Foundation created President's action entering Korean war against Communist aggression supported by Congress.	1950. Death of Mackenzie King. 1951. Defense program of Canada to fulfill obligations under UN charter.	1950. A convention for the settlement of claims between U.S. and Panama approved by Panama.	1950. President of Chile makes good will tour of the U.S.
1951	XXII Amendment to Constitution limiting president to two terms. President removes MacArthur from command in Korean war.		1951. President Arnulfo Arias of Panama deposed.	1951. Argentine government suppresses independent newspaper, *La Prensa*.
1952	Japanese peace treaty ratified by Senate; also West German peace contract. Puerto Rico becomes commonwealth. U.S. detonates first hydrogen bomb.	1952. Vincent Massey first native-born Canadian, Governor-General.	1952 Mexico elects Adolfo Ruiz Cortines president, to succeed Alemán.	1952. Following revolution, Bolivia nationalizes tin mines.
1953	**Dwight D. Eisenhower,** president; Richard M. Nixon, vice president. New executive department of Health, Education, and Welfare established. Korean truce proposal adopted.	1953. Liberal party of Prime Minister St. Laurent wins general election.	1953. British West Indies agree to federate under British Commonwealth.	1953. Brazil ratifies military aid pact with US and others for defense of Hemisphere.
1954	U. S. and Britain allocate first fissionable material to world atomic project. U. S. Air Force Academy established. Supreme Court holds that racial segregation in schools is forbidden by constitution. First atomic submarine, *Nautilus*.	1954. U. S. joins Canada in building St. Lawrence Seaway and Power project. 1955. Canada and U.S. extend defensive radar net.	1954. Guatemala's Pro-Communist President Arbenz ousted; succeeded by Col. Castillo Armas.	1954. President Vargas of Brazil forced by the army to retire. Commits suicide.
1955	Congress gives President Eisenhower mandate for defense of Formosa. Merging of AFL and CIO.	1956. By Ottawa declaration Canada reserves right to act independently of U. S. and Britain.	1955. President Jose Remon of Panama assassinated. 1956. Economic integration of Central American countries agreed upon by their representatives.	1955. President Peron of Argentina deposed by junta.
1956	Congress adopts "soil bank" measure. U. S supports UN demand for cease fire in Suez area. Declaration establishing Organization of American States.	1957. Canada provides troops for U.N. police force to control Suez area. Conservative party wins election; Diefenbaker premier.	1957. Honduras repels invasion by Nicaraguans. Army takes over control of Haiti. Guatamala's election voided by army.	1956. Juscelino Kubitschek becomes president of Brazil; lifts press censorship. 1957. Economic woes exploited by Communist agents but with little success.
1957	**Dwight D. Eisenhower,** president; Richard M. Nixon, vice president. First underground atomic explosion set off in Nevada. Troops used to integrate school in Little Rock, Ark.	1958. Conservative party wins sweeping victory in elections.	1958. Mateos elected president of Mexico. Federation of ten British colonies in West Indies.	1958. Venezuela elects Betancourt president.
1958	Explorer I is first U.S. satellite to be orbited. U.S. submarine *Nautilus* passes North Pole under Arctic ice cap.	1959. St. Lawrence seaway opening.	1959. Castro seizes power in Cuba.	1959. Anti-U.S. riots in Bolivia.
1959	Alaska and Hawaii admitted to the Union as 49th and 50th states.	1960. Government tightens control of corporations controlled by non-Canadians.	1960. Castro seizes foreign property in Cuba; makes trade agreements with Russia and China.	1960. President Betancourt averts threatened revolution in Venezuela.
1960	Civil Rights Act passed. Polaris-missile submarines permitted to use base in Scotland.		1961. President Trujillo of Dominican Republic assassinated.	1961. Alliance for Progress launched.
1961	**John F. Kennedy,** president; Lyndon B. Johnson, vice president. U.S. Peace Corps established. American-backed invasion of Cuba fails at Bay of Pigs.	1961. Refusal to observe trade boycott of Cuba; surplus wheat sold to Russia and China.	1962. Russian missiles installed in Cuba; U.S. forces their removal by blockade. Cuba expelled from O.A.S. Jamaican independence from Britain.	1962. President Frondizi of Argentina ousted by military coup. Venezuelan revolts crushed. Peruvian government seized by military group.
1962	First U.S. manned orbital flights. Kennedy forces removal of Russian missiles from Cuba. President compels steel industry to rescind price increase; stock prices drop but later resume rise. Supreme Court outlaws prayers in schools.	1962. Canadian dollar devalued. General election results in loss of majority status by Conservatives.		
1963	Civil-rights march of 200,000 in Washington. Limited nuclear-ban treaty negotiated with Russia and Great Britain. President Kennedy assassinated.	1963. Lester Pearson premier as Liberals win in close election. U.S. nuclear warheads accepted for defense.	1963. Dominican president Bosch ousted; U.S. and O.A.S. intervene to forestall a Communist takeover.	1963. Leoni elected president of Venezuela; Communist disorders quelled. Argentina cancels oil contracts.

FROM THE CLOSE OF THE CIVIL WAR, 1865, TO THE PRESENT TIME—CON.

	UNITED STATES OF AMERICA	CANADA	LATIN AMERICA	
1964	**Lyndon B. Johnson,** president. Stepped-up fighting in Viet-Nam. Earthquake in Alaska. Supreme Court establishes rule of equal representation for Congressional elections. Medicare act passed. Federal law against racial discrimination in registration and voting.	1964. Treaty with U.S. for joint development of Columbia river project. Extremists in Quebec agitate for independence.	1964. Anti-American demonstrations in Panama. Organization of American States votes sanctions against Cuba.	1964. Brazil's president is deposed by Branco. Bolivia's government overthrown by the military.
1965	**Lyndon B. Johnson,** president; Hubert H. Humphrey, vice president. Orbital rendezvous of space ships.	1965. Liberal government under Lester B. Pearson returned to power.	1965. Cuba permits refugee airlift to US. New Panama pact over canal.	1965. Branco tightens hold on Brazil. Bolivian revolt suppressed.
1966	Both diplomatic peace moves and warfare in Viet-Nam intensified. Transportation Department set up.	1966. Rail strike settled by new law. Wheat sales to Communist China.	1966. Barbados becomes independent.	1966. Brazil under dictatorial powers.
1967	Three astronauts die in first U.S. space tragedy.	1967. Centennial for nation's founding.		1967. Constitutional changes in Uruguay.
1968	Over half million U.S. troops in Viet-Nam. North Korea seizes US intelligence ship *Fueblo.* Riots in major cities follow assassination of Negro leader Martin Luther King, Jr. Robert F. Kennedy assassinated. Johnson ends bombing of North Viet-Nam; Paris peace talks begin. *Pueblo* crew released and returned to US. Apollo 8: first manned moon fligh.	1968. Pearson receives vote of confidence. Pierre Trudeau succeeds Pearson. Seaway strike imperils shipping. Army, Navy, and Air Force unified. Medicare begins.	1968. Two U.S. aides slain in Guatemala. $2 billion program to keep Mexican economy growing. Student riots in Mexico City; Army moves in; 49 killed. Earthquake in Mexico City; 4 dead. Olympic Games held in Mexico.	1968. Brazil faces power struggle. Peru: Pres. Terry ousted by Army; Gen. Velasco new president; earthquakes kill 16. Uruguay: Strikes force martial law.
1969	**Richard M. Nixon,** president; Spiro T. Agnew, vice president. Apollo 11 lands first men on moon. Apollo 12 marks second moon landing. Paris Vietnam peace talks stalemated. Defense appropriations bill passed, authorizing antiballistic missile (ABM) project and other weapons systems and research. Anti-war demonstrations continue across US.	1969. Nuclear Non-Proliferation Pact signed. Police strike in Montreal; crime wave results. Strikes in Toronto, Quebec, and other cities.	1969. NY Gov. Rockefeller, on presidential Latin American mission, is met by anti-US riots.	1969. Brazil: Terrorists kidnap US Ambassador Elbrick; later exchange him for freed political prisoners. Pres. da Costa e Silva dies; junta seizes power.
1970	Apollo 13 moonshot fails, crew returns safely to Earth. Supreme Court sets deadline for school integration. US faces crises in Laos and Cambodia. Mail, air and truck strikes cause stoppages in many US cities. Supreme Court decrees national vote for 18 year olds.	1970. Steel strike is settled. Canada claims Arctic regions. Separatists kidnap, then kill Canadian official Laporte; British official Cross is released; Trudeau invokes wartime emergency measures.	1970. Costa Rica elects Figueres president. Guatemala: Arana elected president. OAS convenes El Salvador-Honduras peace talks. Soviet nuclear submarines rendezvous in Cuban waters. Mexico City opens new, computerized subway system.	1970. Gen. Medici becomes president of Brazil. World's Fair for 1972 planned for Rio. Earthquake strikes Peru.
1971	Apollo 14 mission completes third US landing on the Moon. Apollo 15 fourth Moon landing, first use of mobilized lunar vehicle.	1971. Red China and Canada establish diplomatic relations.	1971. Haiti: Dictator Duvalier dies, replaced by his son.	1971. Terrorist kidnappings of foreign officials continue throughout Latin America. Allende, first popularly elected Marxist president in Western Hemisphere, nationalizes foreign properties in Chile. Argentine army seizes power. Gen. Lanusse replaces Levingston as president.
1972	US troops in Vietnam cut to 70,000. Pres. Nixon schedules summit trips to Peking and to Moscow. US peace offer rebuffed by Hanoi. West Coast dock strike ties up shipping. Federal Election Campaign Act of 1971 requiring full disclosure of campaign funds takes effect.	1972. US Pres. Nixon plans Canadian trip to discuss US-Canada trade issues.	1972. Ecuador seizes US fishing boats. Latin American narcotics smuggling to US becomes major problem.	1972. Allende faces economic crises. Brazil plans first nuclear power plant.
1973	US forces leave Vietnam; draft ends. Pentagon Papers trial dismissed. Agnew resigns vice presidency—Gerald Ford appointed to replace him. Watergate probe reveals illegal acts by the Nixon Administration.	1973. Canada and Cuba sign pact to outlaw highjacking. Canada ends role in four-nation Control Commission in Vietnam.	1973. Argentina's Juan Peron returns after 18 years in exile, takes over again as president. Brazil's Gen. Geisel elected president.	1973. Chilean junta takes power. Pres. Allende dies in takeover.
1974	Richard Nixon resigns, conceding acts of omission as President. **Gerald Ford** becomes 38th President. Nelson Rockefeller is appointed 41st Vice President of the US. Inflation, recession, unemployment reach new national peaks.	1974. Trudeau is re-elected—survives budget-policy crisis. Unemployment at 14-year top. Canada supplies material for India's nuclear test: then suspends supply in protest over use. Quebec rules French sole official language for Province.	1974. Landslide in Colombia kills 200. Argentina: Peron dies; widow, Isabel Peron succeeds to presidency. Honduras hurricane leaves 5000 dead. Mexican oil strikes are reported.	1974. Brazil: nuclear pact signed with West Germany. Peruvians seize US mining firm's assets. Venezuela nationalizes oil and iron industries.

FROM THE CLOSE OF THE CIVIL WAR, 1865, TO THE PRESENT TIME—CON.

	UNITED STATES OF AMERICA	CANADA	LATIN AMERICA	
1975	US airlifts South Vietnamese refugees. North Vietnamese victory ends war. US ship Mayaguez is seized by Cambodia. Ford orders action—Mayaguez retaken. Soviet Soyuz and US Apollo are linked in joint space mission. European Security Conference pact signed. Secretary of State Kissinger achieves Egyptian-Israeli interim peace pact. Gerald Ford announces his candidacy for 1976 election—escapes series of attempted assassinations. New York City faces major financial difficulties. Senate investigates CIA and FBI past procedures. Justice William O. Douglas retires from Supreme Court; replaced by John Paul Stevens.	1975. Oil and natural gas sales to US cut. North American defense agreement is renewed. Atlantic ports closed to Soviet fishing fleets; but third major wheat sale is made to USSR. Postal workers stage a 43-day strike.	1975. Cuban–US trade embargo is eased. Mexico reports added oil discovery. Cuba sends troops to fight in Angolan civil war. Cuba holds 1st Communist Party Congress.	1975. Bolivian miners stage strike. Velasco regime is overthrown in Peru —Gen. Bermudez takes over government. Surinam, formerly Dutch Guiana, becomes independent. Honduras military group deposes General Lopez. Argentine Pres. Isabel Peron is asked to resign.
1976	Busing continued in US schools in efforts to reach racial integration. Military draft registration ends. Women accepted into US service schools. US fishing limits extended to 200 miles. Pres. Ford asks Congress for $135 million to fund vaccine injections for anticipated swine flu epidemic. USSR purchases $400 million in US grain. Congress votes permanent committee to oversee CIA activities. Idaho's Teton Dam on the Snake River bursts—leaving 11 dead. Supreme Court rules capital punishment constitutional. US celebrates national Bicentennial on July Fourth. Viking 1 and 2 explore surface of Mars. Over 100 people die in the Big Thompson River flood in Colorado. MIT scientists report construction of synthetic bacterial gene. Candidates Ford and Carter stage first national TV presidential campaign debate in 16 years. US Episcopal Church approves ordination of women as priests. Democrat Jimmy Carter wins US presidential election. Americans win five Nobel prizes. Swine-flu vaccinations suspended—linked to paralytic disease.	1976. Prime Minister Pierre Trudeau visits Cuba. Canada posts record budget of $41.25-billion. $320-million, 520-mile pipeline opens between Sarnia and Montreal to lessen East Canadian dependency on imported oil. Canada posts trade surplus of $1.13 billion. US and Canada sign accord to stabilize wheat prices. Olympic games held in Montreal. Separatist party candidate Rene Levesque becomes Quebec provincial premier.	1976. Venezuela completes nationalization of oil. Major new oil fields found in Brazil. Junta deposes Gen. Rodriguez Lara in Ecuador. British witness testifies to torture of political prisoners in Chile. UN and OAS urge Chile to end torture. Earthquake in Guatemala leaves more than 22,000 dead; 74,000 injured; more than 1 million left homeless. Cuba adopts new constitution by referendum: socialist programs continued. Lockheed and other US firms are involved in widespread bribery in Latin America.	1976. Armed forces overthrow Isabel Peron in Argentina. Gen. Videla becomes president. Bordaberry ousted in Uruguay, replaced by Vice Pres. Alberto Demicheli. US bans arms aid to Uruguay for alleged torture and violations of human rights. Lopez Portillo elected president of Mexico in landslide victory. Mexico floats peso, ending 22 years of fixed parity with US dollar. Aparicio Mendez becomes president of Uruguay. Brazilian inflation rate reaches highest point since 1964 at 46%.
1977	**Jimmy Carter,** president. Walter Mondale, vice president. Pres. Carter pardons Vietnam war draft evaders. Record cold and natural gas shortages in Eastern US. Many schools and industrial plants are closed. Drought plagues Western US. Pres. Carter initiates energy-planning policy. Other proposals: tax revision, welfare reform, increased conservation, government reorganization, arms accord with USSR, human-rights support by US. Pres. Carter ends ban on American travel to Vietnam, North Korea, Cambodia, and Cuba. Leonard Woodcock leads first official US visit to Hanoi for talks on US armed forces members missing in action in Vietnam war. Pres. Carter attends economic summit conference in London; gives CIA director authority over all intelligence budgets; and names new FBI director, Frank M. Johnson, Jr. Budget Director Bert Lance forced to resign because of possible misconduct while occupying top positions at two Georgia banks.	1977. Prime Minister Trudeau visits US. Quebec Premier Levesque declares Quebec independence inevitable. Canada and US agree to build trans-Canada pipeline that will carry natural gas from Alaska to the lower 48 states.	1977. Chilean inflation hits 174% over 1976; 1975 rate was 340%. Mexican Pres. Lopez Portillo visits US, meets Pres. Carter. US makes overtures to Cuba for improved relations. Ban on American travel to Cuba lifted by Pres. Carter. Argentina, Guatemala, El Salvador, and Uruguay act to reject US aid in response to Pres. Carter's stand on human rights.	1977. Brazilian coffee prices quadrupled over 1976 levels, at $4 per pound. Brazilian government, angered at US probe of human-rights abuse, rejects $50 million in US aid credits. Brazil also gives notice of dissolving the 1952 US-Brazilian military assistance pact. Brazil plans to buy nuclear-fuel plant from W. Germany. Panama's chief of government Omar Torrijos and Pres. Carter sign Panama Canal Treaty that would gradually give control of the canal to Panama by the year 2000 and would guarantee neutrality of the canal.

PRIME MINISTER	PARTY	TERM	PRIME MINISTER	PARTY	TERM
Robert Walpole*	Whig	1721–1727	Edward George Geoffrey Smith Stanley (Earl of Derby)	Tory	1858–1859
Robert Walpole (Earl of Orford)	Whig	1727–1742	Henry John Temple (Viscount Palmerston)	Liberal	1859–1865
Spencer Compton (Earl of Wilmington)	Whig	1742–1743	John Russell (Earl Russell)	Liberal	1865–1866
Henry Pelham	Whig	1743–1754	Edward George Geoffrey Smith Stanley (Earl of Derby)	Conservative	1866–1868
Thomas Pelham-Holles (Duke of Newcastle)	Whig	1754–1756	Benjamin Disraeli	Conservative	1868
William Cavendish (Duke of Devonshire)	Whig	1756–1757	William Ewart Gladstone	Liberal	1868–1874
Thomas Pelham-Holles (Duke of Newcastle)	Whig	1757–1762	Benjamin Disraeli (Earl of Beaconsfield)	Conservative	1874–1880
John Stuart (Earl of Bute)	Tory	1762–1763	William Ewart Gladstone	Liberal	1880–1885
George Grenville	Whig	1763–1765	Robert Arthur Talbot Gascoyne-Cecil (Marquis of Salisbury)	Conservative	1885–1886
Charles Watson-Wentworth (Marquis of Rockingham)	Whig	1765–1766	William Ewart Gladstone	Liberal	1886
William Pitt (Earl of Chatham)	Coalition	1766–1767	Robert Arthur Talbot Gascoyne-Cecil (Marquis of Salisbury)	Conservative	1886–1892
Augustus Henry Fitzroy (Duke of Grafton)	Whig	1767–1770	William Ewart Gladstone	Liberal	1892–1894
Frederick North (Lord North)	Tory	1770–1782	Archibald Philip Primrose (Earl of Rosebery)	Liberal	1894–1895
Charles Watson-Wentworth (Marquis of Rockingham)	Whig	1782	Robert Arthur Talbot Gascoyne-Cecil (Marquis of Salisbury)	Conservative	1895–1902
William Petty (Earl of Shelburne)	Whig	1782–1783	Arthur James Balfour	Conservative	1902–1905
William Henry Cavendish Bentinck (Duke of Portland)	Coalition	1783	Sir Henry Campbell-Bannerman	Liberal	1905–1908
William Pitt (the Younger)	Tory	1783–1801	Herbert Henry Asquith	Liberal	1908–1915
Henry Addington	Tory	1801–1804	Herbert Henry Asquith	Coalition	1915–1916
William Pitt (the Younger)	Tory	1804–1806	David Lloyd George	Coalition	1916–1922
William Wyndham Grenville (Lord Grenville)	Whig	1806–1807	Andrew Bonar Law	Conservative	1922–1923
William Henry Cavendish Bentinck (Duke of Portland)	Tory	1807–1809	Stanley Baldwin	Conservative	1923–1924
			James Ramsay MacDonald	Labor	1924
			Stanley Baldwin	Conservative	1924–1929
Spencer Perceval**	Tory	1809–1812	James Ramsay MacDonald	Labor	1929–1931
Robert Banks Jenkinson (Earl of Liverpool)	Tory	1812–1827	James Ramsay MacDonald	Coalition	1931–1935
George Canning	Tory	1827	Stanley Baldwin	Coalition	1935–1936
Frederick John Robinson (Viscount Goderich)	Tory	1827–1828	Stanley Baldwin (Earl Baldwin of Bewdley)	Coalition	1936–1937
Arthur Wellesley (Duke of Wellington)	Tory	1828–1830	(Arthur) Neville Chamberlain	Coalition	1937–1940
Charles Grey (Earl Grey)	Whig	1830–1834	Winston Leonard Spencer Churchill	Coalition	1940–1945
William Lamb (Viscount Melbourne)	Whig	1834	Winston Leonard Spencer Churchill	Conservative	1945
Sir Robert Peel	Tory	1834–1835	Clement Richard Attlee	Labor	1945–1951
William Lamb (Viscount Melbourne)	Whig	1835–1841	Winston Leonard Spencer Churchill	Conservative	1951–1952
Sir Robert Peel	Tory	1841–1846	Sir Winston Leonard Spencer Churchill	Conservative	1952–1955
John Russell (Lord Russell)	Whig	1846–1852	Sir (Robert) Anthony Eden	Conservative	1955–1957
Edward George Geoffrey Smith Stanley (Earl of Derby)	Tory	1852	(Maurice) Harold Macmillan	Conservative	1957–1963
George Hamilton Gordon (Earl of Aberdeen)	Peelite	1852–1855	Sir Alec Douglas-Home	Conservative	1963–1964
			(James) Harold Wilson	Labor	1964–1970
			Edward Heath	Conservative	1970–1974
Henry John Temple (Viscount Palmerston)	Liberal	1855–1858	(James) Harold Wilson	Labor	1974–1976
			(Leonard) James Callaghan	Labor	1976–

*Walpole is considered the first British prime minister. Earlier the sovereign had attended sessions of the ministers. With Walpole, the office of chief minister was unified in one central position.
**Assassinated.

THE COMMONWEALTH OF NATIONS

THE name Commonwealth of Nations designates the group of nations, states, colonies, protectorates, and administrative areas which acknowledge the sovereign of Great Britain either as titular head of their governments or as a symbol of their free association as independent members of the Commonwealth. The nucleus of the group is the United Kingdom of Great Britain (England, Wales, Scotland) and Northern Ireland. The Commonwealth evolved from what was known as the British Empire, a power complex based on exploration, settlement, and conquest over a period of more than 300 years.

The Period of Commercial Foundations. The first stage of the empire, from the annexation of Newfoundland in 1583 to the treaty of Paris in 1763, is marked by the predominance of commercial interests. The challenge of English private interests to the Spanish monopoly of the New World resulted in the occupation of some West Indian islands, and the establishment of colonies on the North American coast. In the 17th century England competed with the French for the fishing industry and the fur trade in America. In Asia she struggled unsuccessfully with the Dutch for the trade of the East Indies, but the East India Company laid the foundation for English control of India.

At the opening of the 18th century, France had superseded Spain and the Netherlands in the contest and remained England's chief colonial rival. Out of the consequent struggle, which was ended by the Treaty of Paris in 1763, England won supremacy in India and in North America.

The attempt to tighten political and commercial control over the colonies, in the face of their own economic and political growth, brought friction with the American colonies. This was accentuated by a new feeling of distinct nationality. The result was the American Revolution (1775–1783).

From Empire to Commonwealth. Despite the loss of the American colonies, the empire continued to grow. In America, Canada and the West Indian Islands remained. Possessions in India expanded. In the Napoleonic wars, areas of commercial and strategic significance were added. Exploration and colonization in Australia, New Zealand, and especially in Africa brought expansion of the empire to its greatest extent. Finally, a number of areas were added as a result of victory in World War I.

But the spirit of colonial independence which had resulted in the loss of the American colonies operated powerfully in those colonies which had a preponderantly British or European population. In the 19th and early 20th century, Canada, Australia, New Zealand, and South Africa, along with Newfoundland and the Irish Free State, obtained a large measure of self-government and were later accorded "dominion status." Finally, a new form of association took place when, in 1931, the Statute of Westminster declared that Great Britain and the six self-governing dominions were "equal in status in no way subordinated to one another." They were independent in foreign as well as in domestic affairs but united by common allegiance to the British crown and by their culture and traditions. Of the six, the Irish Free State and South Africa subsequently became republics and withdrew; Newfoundland was absorbed as a province of Canada.

After World War II the spirit of colonial independence overleaped racial bounds, and peoples of nearly every stage of economic and cultural development demanded immediate freedom. India, in 1947, was the first of the former dependencies to remain within the commonwealth despite adoption of a republican form of government. The number of such independent members multiplied since practically all the emancipated states elected membership. See the tabulation *Commonwealth of Nations*.

ENGLAND

The British Isles have not been successfully invaded since the Norman Conquest of 1066 A. D., but their early history records a series of settlements by peoples from the continent of Europe. The earliest belong to the age of tradition. Before the Christian era, migrations of tall, fair-haired people largely displaced the aboriginal inhabitants of the islands. One migration brought over a bronze-using folk, probably the ancestors of the Gaels of Scotland and Ireland; another introduced the Brythonic, iron-using race, who gave their name to Britain and occupied the southern part of what is now England, when Cæsar's legions landed in 55 B. C. Greek travelers and traders are supposed to have visited Britain as early as the 4th century B. C., linking its trade with the Greek colony of Massilia (Marseille). The invasion by the Romans is the first of which a written record exists.

Germanic Tribes Invade Roman Britain. Roman generals and governors extended Roman authority until Agricola, by the year 84 A. D., completed a line of forts between the Forth and the Clyde as a barrier against the Caledonians. Roman colonists settled in the island, built towns around their military camps, connected these with roads, and introduced Roman law and civilization. Christianity likewise spread to this remote province. With the decline of the empire, however, the Roman legions were withdrawn to the continent, and the Britons were unable to defend themselves against the inroads of the barbarians from the North. They are said to have appealed for help to the Saxons, Angles, and Jutes, who lived along the North Sea to the south of Denmark. The response of these German folk developed into the Germanic invasion and settlement of Britain. The Anglo-Saxon chronicles date the principal migration at 449 A. D.

The Jutes were the first to form a settlement, taking possession of part of Kent and the Isle of Wight; but the more extensive conquests of the Saxons in the South and of the Angles in the North gave these two folk the lead. The struggle for occupation continued 150 years; at the end of that time the entire southern part of Britain, with the exception of Strathclyde, Wales, and West Wales (Cornwall), was in the hands of the new German kingdoms.

Before the common struggle with the Britons was settled, the small German kingdoms were at war with one another. In the middle of the 6th century, the West Saxons defeated the Jutes, who were pressing westward from Kent. The West Saxons, turning north, were probably faced by the Angles, already in possession in the valley of the Ouse, and so were diverted westward. They occupied the Severn valley. Meanwhile, in the North and the East, the Angles were making a slow advance. They formed three kingdoms: Mercia, in the upper valley of the Trent; Bernicia and Deira, together called Northumberland, or the country north of the Humber. These kingdoms, with those of the East Saxons, South Saxons, and Jutes, are sometimes called the Saxon Heptarchy; but they never formed such an organization as this name would indicate.

Christianity Established in Kent. While the Saxons and Angles, in the 6th century, were still struggling with the Britons, the men of Kent enjoyed a more settled life and carried on intercourse with the Latinized Gauls of the continent. Toward the end of the century, their king, Ethelbert, had become overlord of all the other kings south of the Humber. He had married a Christian wife, Bertha, daughter of a Frankish king. In 597 came Augustine and a band of Roman missionaries, sent by Pope Gregory. The legal and political changes immediately consequent upon the adoption of Christianity in the Germanic kingdoms in Britain were not great, but there began a more intimate relation with the continent and its Christian civilization. The introduction of Christian learning and culture, the formation of a written vernacular, and the fusion of the small kingdoms into a single large kingdom may be credited to the influence of the Roman clergy.

Upon the death of Ethelbert, the overlordship that he had maintained passed to the Anglian kings of the North. Northumbria had come under the influence of the Church, through first the Irish, and then the Roman, missionaries, and in the Northumbrian monasteries learning flourished. By the 7th century, the Church had regained all the Saxon kingdoms, which had previously all but obliterated the traces of the earlier British Church. Egbert of Wessex, before his death in 839, united the English kingdoms under his overlordship and may be considered the first king of England.

Danish Incursions. The land, meanwhile, was kept in a state of disturbance by the repeated incursions and attacks of the Danes. About half a century after Egbert's unification of the kingdom, the Danes acquired the mastery of nearly the whole of England. But the genius of Alfred the Great overcame the Danes at Ethandun (878). Guthrum, their king, embraced Christianity, acknowledged the supremacy of the English king, and received a strip of land including Northumbria on the east coast and known as the Danelaw. The two immediate successors of Alfred, Edward (899–925) and Athelstan (925–940), the son and the grandson of Alfred, both vigorous and able rulers, had in turn to direct their arms against these Danes of the Danelaw. The reigns of the next five kings, Edmund, Edred, Edwig, Edgar, and Edward the Martyr, are remarkable chiefly for the influence exerted by Dunstan, who was counselor to Edmund, minister of Edred, treasurer under Edwig, and virtual ruler during the reigns of Edgar and his successor. It was possibly due to Dunstan that from the time of Athelstan until after the death of Edward the Martyr (979) the country had comparative rest from the Danes.

During the 10th century many changes were altering the character of early English government. A feudal system was beginning to appear; the king's authority increased; the folkland was being taken over as the king's personal property; the nobles by birth, or ealdormen, were becoming of less importance in administration than the nobility of thegns, the officers of the king's court. Ethelred (978–1016), who succeeded Edward, was a minor. The government was feeble, and, no united action being taken against the Danes, their incursions became more frequent and destructive. Animosities between the English and the Danes who had settled among them became daily more violent, until a general massacre of the latter took place in 1002. The following year Svend invaded the kingdom with a powerful army and assumed the crown of England. Ethelred was compelled to take refuge in Normandy; though he afterwards returned, he found in Canute an adversary no less formidable than Svend. Ethelred left his kingdom to his son Edmund, who displayed great valor but was compelled to divide his kingdom with Canute. When Edmund died in 1016, the Danes succeeded to the sovereignty of the whole.

Canute (Knut), who espoused the widow of Ethelred that he might reconcile his new subjects, obtained the name of Great, not only on account of his personal qualities, but from the extent of his dominions, since he was master of Denmark and Norway as well as of England. In 1035 he died, and in England the reigns of two other Danish kings, Harold and Harthacnut, lasted till 1042, after which the English line was again restored in the person of Edward the Confessor.

The Norman Conquest. Edward was a weak prince; in the latter years of his reign, he had far less real power than his brother-in-law Harold, son of the great earl Godwine. On Edward's death in 1066, Harold accordingly obtained the crown. He found,

however, a formidable opponent in the second cousin of Edward, William of Normandy, who instigated the Danes to invade the northern counties, while he landed in the South. Harold vanquished the Danes and, hastening southward, met the Normans at Senlac, near Hastings. Harold and his two brothers fell, October 14, 1066, and William (1066–87) immediately claimed the crown as lawful king of England. He is known in history as William I, the Conqueror. For some time he conducted the government with great moderation; but, being obliged to reward those who had assisted him, he bestowed the chief offices of the government upon Normans and divided among them a great part of the country. The consequent revolts of the native English were quickly crushed, continental feudalism in a modified form was established, and the English Church came under Norman influence through Lanfranc, archbishop of Canterbury.

At the death of the conqueror in 1087, his desire to have the strongest-willed of his sons rule England resulted in bestowing the throne upon William Rufus. The eldest son, Robert, was given the duchy of Normandy, while the third son, Henry, received a sum of money. The character of William II was vicious, and his rule in England, an unscrupulous tyranny. When, in 1100, he was found dead in the New Forest, with an arrow through his body, he was buried without funeral rites. He was succeeded by his younger brother, Henry, who set out to undo the evils of the previous reign. He allied himself with the English by marrying Eadgyth, or Matilda, a descendant of English kings. He subdued the Norman barons and wrested Normandy from his brother Robert. Henry's power being secured, he entered into a dispute with Anselm, the primate, and with the pope, concerning the right of granting investiture to the clergy. He supported his quarrel with firmness and brought it to a not unfavorable issue. In 1135 he died in Normandy, leaving behind him only a daughter, Matilda.

By the will of Henry I, his daughter Matilda, wife of Geoffrey Plantagenet, count of Anjou, was declared his successor. But Stephen, son of the count of Blois and of Adela, daughter of William the Conqueror, raised an army in Normandy, landed in England, and declared himself king. After years of civil war and bloodshed, an amicable arrangement was brought about, by which it was agreed that Stephen should continue to reign during the remainder of his life, but that he should be succeeded by Henry, son of Matilda and the count of Anjou. Stephen died in 1154, and Henry Plantagenet ascended the throne with the title of Henry II, the first of the Plantagenet, or Angevin, kings. A larger dominion was united under his sway than had been held by any previous sovereign of England, for at the time when he became king of England he was already in possession of Anjou, Normandy, and Aquitaine.

Beginnings of Constitutional Government. Henry II found far less difficulty in restraining the license of his barons than in abridging the special privileges of the clergy, who claimed exemption. not only from the taxes of the state, but also from its courts, and who were supported in their demands by the primate Becket. The king's wishes were formulated in the Constitutions of Clarendon (1164), which were first accepted and then repudiated by the primate. The assassination of Becket by the king's followers placed the king at a moral disadvantage in the struggle; after his conquest of Ireland (1174) he submitted to the Church and did penance at Becket's tomb. Henry contrived to associate the people of England with his new plan of government. The system of frankpledge was revived, trial by jury was sanctioned by the Assize of Clarendon, and the system of itinerant justices, twelve justices on circuit from the king's court, employed by Henry I, was revived. To lessen the power of the nobles he granted charters of incorporation to towns, freeing them from all obligation to any but himself, thus laying the foundation of a burgher or town class in society.

Richard I, called Cœur de Lion, who in 1189 succeeded his father, Henry II, spent most of his reign away from England. Having gone to Palestine to join in the Third Crusade, he proved himself an intrepid soldier. Returning homeward in disguise through Germany, he was made prisoner by Leopold, duke of Austria, but was ransomed by his English subjects. In the meantime, John, his brother, had aspired to the crown, and hoped, by the assistance of the French, to exclude Richard from his right. Richard's presence for a time restored matters to some appearance of order; but, having undertaken an expedition against France, he received a mortal wound at the siege of Châlus in 1199.

The reigns of Henry II and Richard were marked by an improved government. The kingdom became more orderly; the collection of taxes, more regular. The Church also was in large measure subject to royal control. The towns grew in wealth, and the merchant guilds became powerful. English churchmen promoted learning; in 1186 there were at Oxford faculties in several branches of study. The work of government and the law courts had made a demand for "clerks," that is, men skilled in writing and in law.

Magna Charta. At the death of Richard, John was at once recognized as king of England, and he secured possession of Normandy; but Anjou, Maine, and Touraine acknowledged the claim of Arthur, son of Geoffrey, second son of Henry II. On the death of Arthur, while in John's power, these four French provinces were lost to England. John's opposition to the pope in electing a successor to the see of Canterbury led to the pope's placing the kingdom under an interdict in 1208. On account of the disturbed condition of the nation, John was at last compelled to receive Stephen Langton as archbishop and to accept England as a fief of the papacy (1213). His exactions and misgovernment had equally embroiled him with the nobles. In 1213 they refused to follow him to France, and, on his return, defeated, they at once took measures to secure their own feudal rights and to limit the prerogatives of the crown. King and barons met at Runnymede, and, on June 15, 1215, the great charter (Magna Charta) was signed. It was speedily declared null and void by the pope, and war broke out between John and the barons, who were aided by the French king. In 1216, however, John died, and his turbulent reign was followed by the almost equally disturbed period of Henry III. Up to this time, the barons and the organized townspeople had entrenched themselves in a body of liberties, but no favor was shown the poor. Every town was surrounded by the miserable hovels of the poverty-stricken. It was to minister to these that the Franciscan friars came from Italy in the 13th century.

During the first years of the reign of Henry III, the ability of the earl of Pembroke, who was regent until 1219, retained the kingdom in tranquillity; but, when Henry assumed the reins of government in 1227, he showed himself incapable of ruling. The charter was three times reissued in a modified form, and new privileges were added to it, but the king took no pains to observe its provisions. The struggle over money grants, long maintained in the great council, henceforward called Parliament, reached an acute stage in 1263, when civil war broke out. Simon de Montfort, who had laid the foundations of the House of Commons by summoning representatives of the shire communities to the Mad Parliament of 1258, had by this time engrossed the sole power. He defeated the King and his son Edward at Lewes in 1264, and in his famous Parliament of 1265 he still further widened the representation of the people by summoning to it burgesses from the boroughs as well as knights from the shires. The escape of Prince Edward, however, was followed by the battle of Evesham (1265), at

which Earl Simon was defeated and slain; the rest of the reign was undisturbed.

On the death of Henry III, in 1272, Edward I succeeded without opposition. From 1276 to 1284, he was largely occupied in the conquest and annexation of Wales, which had become practically independent during the barons' wars. In 1292, Balliol, whom Edward had decided to be rightful heir to the Scottish throne, did homage for his kingdom to the English king; but when, in 1294, war broke out with France, Scotland also declared war. The Scots were defeated at Dunbar (1296), and the country was placed under an English regent; but the revolt under Wallace (1297) was followed by that of Bruce (1306), and the Scots remained unsubdued.

The First Perfect Parliament. The reign of Edward was distinguished by many legal and legislative reforms, such as the separation of the king's court into the court of exchequer, the court of king's bench, and the court of common pleas. The passage of the statute of mortmain forbade the gift of land to clergy, because they paid no feudal dues. In 1295 the first "perfect parliament" was summoned, the clergy and barons by special writ, the commons by writ to the sheriffs directing the election of two knights from each shire and two burgesses from each borough. Two years later the imposition of taxation without consent of Parliament was forbidden by a special act, De Tallagio non Concedendo. The English constitution, in outline, was now complete. The great aim of Edward, however, to include England, Scotland, and Wales in one kingdom proved a failure, and he died in 1307, on an expedition against Robert Bruce.

Edward II made a feeble attempt to carry out his father's last and earnest request to prosecute the war with Scotland, but his army was constantly unsuccessful. At length, in 1314, it received at Bannockburn a defeat from Robert Bruce, which insured the independence of Scotland. The king proved incapable of ruling his baronage; and his consort, a woman of intrigues, joined in the confederacy against him, which resulted in his imprisonment and death in 1327.

Edward III and the French War. The reign of Edward III was as brilliant as that of his father had been the reverse. His main projects were directed against France, the crown of which he claimed in 1328. The victory won by Edward at Crécy (1346), the capture of Calais (1347), and the victory of Poitiers (1356) ultimately led to the Peace of Bretigny in 1360, by which he received all the West of France, on condition of renouncing his claim to the French throne. Before the close of his reign, however, these advantages were all lost, save for a few principal towns on the coast.

A Period of Political and Social Disorder. Edward III was succeeded in 1377 by his grandson Richard II, son of Edward the Black Prince. In 1379 an unjust and oppressive poll tax brought outstanding popular grievances to a head; 100,000 men, so accounts say, under Wat Tyler, marched toward London (1381). Wat Tyler was killed while conferring with the king, but the prudence and courage of Richard appeased the insurgents. Despite his conduct on this occasion, Richard was deficient in the vigor necessary to curb the lawlessness of his nobles. In 1398 he banished his cousin, Henry Bolingbroke; on the death of the latter's father, the duke of Lancaster, Richard unjustly appropriated his cousin's patrimony. To avenge the injustice, Bolingbroke landed in England, during the king's absence in Ireland, and, at the head of an army of malcontents, compelled Richard to surrender. Richard was confined in the Tower, and despite the superior claims of Edmund Mortimer, earl of March, Henry was appointed king (1399), the first of the house of Lancaster. Richard was, in all probability, murdered early in 1400.

The continued struggle of Parliament to retain control of taxation marked the constitutional side of the reign of Edward III. In 1341 the two houses of Parliament separated, the knights going with the burgesses into a lower house, or House of Commons. Social conditions in this period displayed marked contrasts in the distribution of wealth. On the one hand, the spoils of the French wars brought new luxuries to the nobles and upper classes. Larger and more comfortable houses were built, and the churches became more richly ornamented. On the other hand, the laborers had small share in this gain. When, after their ranks had been thinned by the Black Death, they attempted to secure higher wages, Parliament passed the Statute of Laborers, fixing wages at the old rate.

The manner in which the duke of Lancaster, now Henry IV, acquired the crown rendered his reign turbulent, but the vigor of his administration quelled every insurrection. The most important—that of the Percies of Northumberland, Owen Glendower, and Douglas of Scotland—was crushed by the battle of Shrewsbury (1403). During the reign of Henry IV, the government acquired a legal sanction for burning heretics, under the act *de haeretico comburendo*, passed in the second year of his reign. The act was directed chiefly against the Lollards, as the followers of Wiclif now came to be called. Henry died in 1413, leaving his crown to his son, Henry V, who revived the claim of Edward III to the throne of France in 1415 and invaded that country. The disjointed councils of the French rendered their country an easy prey; the victory of Agincourt was gained in 1415; and, after a second campaign, a peace was concluded at Troyes in 1420, by which Henry received the hand of Katherine, daughter of Charles VI. He was appointed regent of France during the reign of his father-in-law and, on the latter's death, was declared heir to his throne. The two kings, however, died within a few weeks of each other in 1422, and thus, at the age of nine months, the infant son of Henry became king of England and France.

English Defeat in France. England during the reign of Henry VI was subjected, in the first place, to all the confusion incident to a long minority, and afterwards to all the misery of a civil war. Henry allowed himself to be managed by anyone who had the courage to assume the conduct of his affairs, and the influence of his queen, Margaret of Anjou, a woman of uncommon capacity, was of no advantage either to himself or to the realm. In France (1422–53), the English forces lost ground and were finally expelled, Calais alone being retained. The withdrawal was the triumph of an attack begun by the heroic and inspired Joan of Arc, now Saint Joan of Arc since her canonization at the end of World War I. A rebellion under Jack Cade in 1450 was suppressed, only to be followed by more serious trouble. In that year, Richard, duke of York, the father of Edward IV, began to advance his pretensions to the throne which had been so long usurped by the house of Lancaster.

Wars of the Roses. The wars which resulted, called the Wars of the Roses, from the fact that a red rose was the badge of the house of Lancaster and a white one that of the house of York, lasted for thirty years, from the first battle of St. Albans, May 22, 1455, to the battle of Bosworth, August 22, 1485. This period, marked by the rapacity of the great landholders and by ferocious cruelty in the conduct of war, is, in some respects, the darkest in English history. A callous materialism, that found no place for the enthusiasms of Renaissance culture and despised the printing press, ruled the land. Henry VI was twice driven from the throne, in 1461 and in 1471, by Edward of York, whose father had previously been killed in battle in 1460. Edward of York reigned as Edward IV from 1461 till his death in 1483, with a brief interval in 1471. He was succeeded by two other sovereigns of the house of York,—first his son Edward V, who reigned for eleven weeks in 1483, and then his brother Richard III, who reigned from 1483 till 1485. Richard was defeated and slain on Bosworth field by Henry Tudor, of the house of Lancaster, who then became Henry VII.

Henry VII was at this time the representative of the house of Lancaster, and, in order at once to strengthen his own title and to put an end to the rivalry between the houses of York and Lancaster, he married, in 1486, Elizabeth, the sister of Edward V and heiress of the house of York. His reign was disturbed by insurrections attending the impostures of Lambert Simnel (1487), who pretended to be a son of the duke of Clarence, brother of Edward IV, and by the pretensions of Perkin Warbeck (1488), who affirmed that he was the duke of York, younger brother of Edward V; but neither of these disturbances attained any magnitude. The king's worst fault was his avarice, which led him to employ in schemes of extortion such instruments as Empson and Dudley. His administration throughout did much to increase the royal power and to establish order and prosperity. He died in 1509.

Henry VIII; The Reformation. The authority of the English crown, which had been so much extended by Henry VII, was, by his son Henry VIII, exerted in an exacting and capricious manner, though always for national and not merely for selfish ends. The most important event of the reign was undoubtedly the breach with Rome; though this had its official origin rather in Henry's personal caprice and in his relations with the court of Spain than in his conviction of the need of ending the pope's authority in England. Henry had been espoused to Catherine of Spain, the widow of his elder brother, Arthur, who died very shortly after marriage. Henry tired of his queen, who bore him no male heir, and became enamored of one of her maids of honor, Anne Boleyn. He had recourse to the pope, therefore, to dissolve a marriage which had at first been rendered legal only by a papal dispensation; but, failing in his desires, he broke entirely with the Holy See. In 1534 he got himself recognized by act of Parliament as supreme head of the Church of England. He died in 1547 while his court was sharply divided upon the question of further ecclesiastical and doctrinal changes.

In spite of adverse conditions and the lack of Renaissance enthusiasm in England, the new learning had secured a foothold in Oxford. Colet became a leader in the study of Greek. Out of this movement came Tyndale's translation of the New Testament. Thomas More founded St. Paul's School in 1510 to give boys an education in the spirit of the new learning. His criticism of the cynical policy of Henry VIII moved him to write his *Utopia*.

Henry was married six times and left three children, each of whom reigned in turn. These were: Mary, by his first wife, Catherine of Aragon; Elizabeth, by his second wife, Anne Boleyn; and Edward, by his third wife, Jane Seymour. Edward, who reigned first, with the title of Edward VI, was nine years of age at the time of his accession, and he died in 1553, when he was only sixteen. His short reign, or rather the government of the earl of Hertford, afterward duke of Somerset, who was appointed regent, was distinguished chiefly by the success which attended the measures of the Protestant reformers. The intrigues of Dudley, duke of Northumberland, caused Lady Jane Grey to be declared Edward's successor; but her reign, if it could be so called, lasted only a few days. Mary, daughter of Henry VIII, was placed on the throne, and Lady Jane Grey and her husband were both executed. Mary, a zealous Catholic, seems to have wished for the crown chiefly to restore papal authority. Persecution of the Protestant reformers drove many for safety to Geneva, to Holland, and to Scotland. Political motives had induced Philip of Spain to marry her; but she could never prevail on her subjects to allow him any share of power. She died in 1558.

Reign of Elizabeth I. Elizabeth, who succeeded her half-sister Mary, was attached to the Protestant faith, and she found little difficulty in re-establishing it in England, accomplishing her end partly by the relentless persecution of Catholics. Having concluded peace with France (1559), Elizabeth set herself to promote the confusion which prevailed in Scotland, to which country her cousin Mary Queen of Scots had returned from France in 1561. Mary was forced to seek asylum under Elizabeth's protection (1568) and, after many years' imprisonment, charged with plot and intrigue, was sent to the scaffold (1587). As a powerful Protestant nation and as a rival of Spain in the New World, England drifted into conflict with that country. The dispersion of the *Armada* (1588) by the English fleet under Howard, Drake, and Hawkins was the most memorable event of an era which first revealed the energy and daring of English seamanship.

Elizabeth's reign was for England a period of unprecedented commercial enterprise. Town industries increased, land that had been enclosed for pasture was turned back to grain production; the food and dwellings of the people improved. Imposing manor houses, often built in the form of the letter E, were erected by the more wealthy landowners. These had chimneys and glass windows, which were novelties. Many might be compared to the palaces of the Italian cities for luxury in service and appointments. Along with material prosperity, came a rich, spontaneous, original literature which of itself makes the Elizabethan era immortal.

The Stuart Struggle with Parliament. Elizabeth was succeeded in 1603 by James VI of Scotland and I of England, son of Mary Queen of Scots and Darnley. His accession to the crown of England in addition to that of Scotland began the union of the two nations. His dissimulation, however, ended in his satisfying neither of the discontented church parties,—the Puritans and the Catholics; and his insistence on his prerogative made his reign an unseemly struggle between the crown and the people. His extravagance kept him in constant disputes with Parliament, which would not grant him the sums he demanded and compelled him to resort to monopolies, loans, benevolences, and other unparliamentary methods. The nation at large, however, continued to prosper through the whole of this inglorious reign. Colonial enterprises in America marked a new departure in trade and in empire building.

Charles I, who succeeded James in 1625, inherited his father's exalted ideas of royal prerogative; his marriage with a Catholic, his arbitrary rule, and his unparliamentary methods of raising money provoked bitter hostility. Under the guidance of Laud and Strafford, partisanship grew inflamed in both Church and State. Civil war broke out at last in 1642 between the king's party and that of the Parliament. The royal government was overthrown, and in 1649 Charles was beheaded.

Cromwell and The Commonwealth. A commonwealth, or republican parliamentary government, was now established, in which the most prominent figure was Oliver Cromwell. Mutinies in the army among Fifth-monarchists and Levellers were subdued by Cromwell and Fairfax; and Cromwell, in a series of masterly movements, subjugated Ireland and gained the important battles of Dunbar and Worcester. At sea, Blake had destroyed the Royalist fleet under Rupert and was engaged in a struggle with the Dutch under Van Tromp. But, within the new government, matters had come to a deadlock. A dissolution of Parliament was necessary, yet Parliament shrank from dissolving itself, and in the meantime the reform of the law, a settlement with regard to the Church, and other important matters remained untouched. In April 1653, Cromwell cut the knot by forcibly ejecting the members and putting the keys of the house in his pocket. From this time, he was practically head of the government, which was vested in a council of ten.

An attempt at a nominated parliament—the Little, or Barebone's Parliament—failed. The council then promulgated England's only written constitution, the Instrument of Government, under which, in December 1653, Cromwell was installed Lord Protector of the Commonwealth of England, Scotland, and Ireland. With more than the power of a king he controlled the confusion at home and made his government respected abroad. Cromwell died in 1658, his son Richard was a failure, and a year of uncertainty and unrest made England long for security under the old forms.

The Stuart Restoration. Charles II, son of Charles I, was called to the throne by the Restoration of 1660. He came without conditions, but he had learned the lessons of the Civil war. He took complete advantage of the popular reaction against the narrowness and intolerance of Puritanism; later, he even endeavored to carry it to the extreme of establishing the Catholic religion. The promises of religious freedom made by him in the declaration of Breda, before the Restoration, were broken by the Test and Corporation acts, and by the Act of Uniformity, which drove two thousand clergymen from the Church and created the great dissenting or nonconformist movement of modern times. The reaffirmation of the principle of habeas corpus, however, was a most praiseworthy step in the advance of the liberty of the subject.

The society of the court of Charles II was notoriously corrupt and profligate. This condition was reflected in the drama and literature of the period following the Restoration. Commercially, however, this was a prosperous time. More colonies were established in America, and English seaports grew upon the new trade thus built up. Country life remained dull, but London attracted the county families by its gaiety. The coffeehouses of London answered the purpose of informal clubs, promoting a more general political and literary discussion. The Royal Society was founded in 1660. England was hospitable to such foreign painters as Van Dyck, but her own architects designed her buildings, such as the new St. Paul's cathedral. In politics, this period saw the rise of the Whig and Tory parties. Macaulay, in his *History of England*, Chapter III, gives a description of this era; it is one of the most graphic delineations to be found in his writings.

The Revolution of 1688. As Charles II left no legitimate issue, his brother, the duke of York, succeeded him as James II (1685–89). The king's zealous support of Roman Catholicism and his attempts to force the Church and the universities to submission provoked a storm of opposition. Seven prelates were brought to trial for seditious libel, but they were acquitted amid general rejoicing. The whole nation was prepared to welcome any deliverance, and in 1688 William of Orange, husband of James's daughter Mary, was invited to come to England. James fled to France; and a convention settled the crown upon William and Mary. Annexed to this settlement was a declaration of rights, circumscribing the royal prerogative by depriving the king of the right to exercise dispensing power, or to exact money, or to maintain an army without the assent of Parliament. This placed the right of the British sovereign to the throne upon a purely statutory basis. A toleration act, passed in 1689, allowed nonconformists their own chapels and freedom of church worship.

An armed opposition to William lasted for a short time in Scotland but ceased with the fall of Viscount Dundee, the leader of James's adherents; though the struggle was prolonged in Ireland, it was brought to a close before the end of 1691. The following year saw the beginning of the national debt, the exchequer having been drained by the heavy military expenditure. A bill for triennial parliaments was passed in 1694, the year in which Queen Mary died. For a moment after her death, William's popularity was in danger, but his successes at Namur and elsewhere in the campaigns against Louis XIV, with the obvious exhaustion of France, once more confirmed his power. The Treaty of Ryswick followed in 1697, and the death of James II in exile in 1701 removed a not unimportant source of danger. Early in the following year William also died, and, by the Act of Settlement, Anne succeeded him.

Party and Cabinet Government. Several significant changes in politics and finance belong to William's reign. The Whig Junto, formed to stabilize the House of Commons, was the beginning of the "cabinet." The refusal of Parliament to renew licensing acts in 1695 freed the press from censorship. The great accumulations of capital in London brought about the founding of the Bank of England in 1694.

The closing act of William's reign had been the formation of the Grand Alliance, between England, Holland, and Austria, against Louis XIV. Queen Anne's rule opened with the successes of Marlborough at Blenheim (1704) and Ramillies (1706). Throughout the earlier part of her reign, Marlborough practically ruled the kingdom, the duchess of Marlborough, Sarah Jennings, being the queen's most intimate friend and adviser. From 1707 the history of England becomes the history of Great Britain, the Act of Union passed in that year having merged the parliaments and realms of England and Scotland into a single state. This has proved to be one of the most successful political experiments ever tried.

The wars with France ended in the Treaty of Utrecht in 1713, by which the British right of sovereignty over Hudson Bay Territory, Newfoundland, Acadia, Minorca, and Gibraltar was acknowledged, and the foundation of Great Britain's imperial and colonial power was securely laid. The remainder of Queen Anne's reign was distracted by the never-ending altercations of Whigs and Tories. She died on the 1st of August 1714, and with her ended the line of the Stuarts. The period is notable for the practice of securing skillful controversial writers for both government and opposition. Dean Swift was the ablest Tory writer, Addison the ablest Whig.

At the death of Anne, George I, elector of Hanover, descended from Elizabeth, daughter of James I, ascended the throne of Great Britain, according to the Act of Settlement. The Whigs under this prince regained in the national councils that superiority of which the Tories recently deprived them. Their extreme measures to destroy Tory power provoked retaliation. In 1715 the earl of Mar in Scotland and the earl of Derwentwater in England raised the standard of rebellion and proclaimed the Chevalier St. George, the "Old Pretender," king. But the insurrection, feebly supported by the people, was soon suppressed.

In 1716 the Septennial act was passed, making Parliament of seven instead of three years' duration. In 1720 occurred, after a phenomenal growth, the collapse of the South Sea Company. From this date until 1742 the government was in the hands of Sir Robert Walpole, the first of modern premiers, leading the cabinet and chiefly responsible for its acts. Walpole had great sagacity, prudence, and business ability, and could manage dexterously the king, Parliament, and the people alike. It is true that in the case of Parliament he achieved this by undue influence in elections and a scandalous use of bribery. But the power he thus acquired was, for the most part, wisely used. The failure of the war with Spain, into which he had reluctantly entered, drove him from office, and in 1742 his long ministry came to an end. In 1743, George II, frightened at the danger to Hanover, drew Great Britain into the wars between France, Prussia, and Austria, regarding the succession of the emperor Charles (War of the Austrian Succession). George himself fought at the head of his troops at Dettingen (1743), where he obtained a complete victory over the French. This victory was balanced later on, however, by the defeat at Fontenoy (1745).

The Young Pretender. A fresh attempt was made, while the war was in progress, to restore the Stuart family to the throne. Charles Edward, son of the Old Pretender, having been furnished by France with a small supply of money and arms, landed in the West Highlands in 1745 and was joined by a considerable number of the people. Marching southward with 1500 Highlanders, his forces increasing as he advanced, he entered Edinburgh without opposition; having defeated Sir John Cope near Prestonpans, he marched into England. Finding himself disappointed of expected succors from France, and the English Tories, contrary to his expectations, keeping aloof, he commenced his retreat into Scotland, closely pursued by the king's troops, whom he again defeated at Falkirk. With this victory his good fortune terminated. The duke of Cumberland arrived from the continent and put himself at the head of the forces which were destined to check the rebels. At Culloden, near Inverness, the Young Pretender was completely defeated. After lurking for six months amid the wilds of Inverness-shire, he at length, with much difficulty, escaped to France.

Eighteenth Century Life. During this period came notable changes in religion, philosophy, art, and literature. The 18th century is the Augustan or Classical age, with common sense, skepticism, and a belief in natural law as its chief traits. But, before the middle of the century, a reaction against the skeptical spirit set in. Butler defended Christianity in his *Analogy*. John Wesley led the evangelical religious movement, called Methodism, among the common people. The life of the times was realistically portrayed in the drawings of Hogarth. Fielding and Richardson created the modern, middle class, sentimental novel.

The War of the Austrian Succession, which was the cause of hostilities between the French and the British in India and America as well as in Europe, was terminated by the Treaty of Aix-la-Chapelle in 1748. During most of this period, Pelham and his brother, the duke of Newcastle, had been the ruling ministers; and in their hands the conduct of government reached, for modern times, a very low level of morality and statecraft.

The Seven Years' War. The French, uneasy at the growing colonial power of Great Britain, began after 1748 a determined effort against the British colonies and possessions in North America and in the East Indies. In 1756 fighting became general in the Seven Years' war. Austria and France were allied on the one side, and Prussia and England on the other. The advantage at first lay everywhere with France. But a great war minister, William Pitt, retrieved these early defeats. In 1758 the British made themselves masters of Louisburg, uncovering the approach to the Gulf of St. Lawrence, while the attack made by Wolfe on Quebec in 1759 was completely successful and gave Britain the mastery in Canada. In the same year the British and their allies defeated the French at Minden in Prussia. In the East Indies, the French were even less successful than in America. Clive's victory at Plassey (1757) and Coote's at Wandewash (1760) secured British ascendancy in the East. These successes, together with the naval victories of Hawke and Boscawen, made England the greatest of maritime and colonial powers.

On the accession of George III in 1760, hostilities were still carried on, generally to the advantage of the French as far as the theater of war in Germany was concerned, but still more to their loss in the other quarters of the world; and this notwithstanding the fact that Spain had now joined her forces to those of France. At length the success of the British arms induced France and Spain to accede to terms, and the hard-fought war ended by the Treaty of Paris in 1763. The French relinquished their possessions in North America; Minorca was restored to Britain; in the East Indies, the French got back their factories and settlements, on condition that they should maintain neither forts nor troops in Bengal; Cuba and Manila were resigned to the Spaniards.

The American Revolution. The close of the Seven Years' war ushered in a new and critical period in the history of the British Empire. The expenses of this war, which had been undertaken partly for the defense of the American colonies against the French, brought the amount of the national debt to more than 132 million pounds. It seemed to the British government to be just that the Americans should be taxed to assist in the payment of the interest. The Americans did not deny the justice of the claim, but replied that if they were to be taxed they had a right to be represented in Parliament, in order that, like other British subjects, they might be taxed only with their own consent. Grenville, then the prime minister, stood to his purpose, however, and introduced a bill for imposing certain stamp duties in the American colonies. The Americans protested and resisted; partly by the influence of the great Pitt, who had steadily opposed the measure, the act was repealed. On the illness of Pitt, now Lord Chatham, in 1767, Townshend became premier and revived the project of taxing the colonies indirectly by imposing duties on tea.

In 1770, Lord North, as Townshend's successor, set himself to carry out his scheme. The result was that in 1775 the thirteen colonies were in a state of rebellion, and a war began, in which both France and Spain joined the revolted colonies. The end was recognition of the independence of the United States. On the American side of this struggle, the great name is that of George Washington. On the British side, the war was unskillfully conducted; though some successes were gained, these were more than counterbalanced by such losses as the capitulation of Burgoyne at Saratoga (1777) and of Cornwallis at Yorktown (1781). Against France and Spain, the British could show such successes as that of Admiral Rodney off Cape St. Vincent (1780), the brilliant defense of Gibraltar by General Eliott (1779–82), and Admiral Rodney's victory over the French fleet in the West Indies (1782). The war closed with the Treaty of Versailles in 1783. Britain finally acquired several West Indian islands; Spain recovered Florida and Minorca; France secured Pondicherry and Chandernagore in India.

Industrial and Political Progress. In England, far-reaching changes were at the same time making their influence felt. In politics, freedom to criticize the king and the government and freedom to report and discuss Parliamentary debates in the press were being recognized. The way was thus prepared for Parliamentary reform. The latter part of the 18th century was a period of great economic progress. Population increased rapidly. Agricultural experiments were carried on; improved methods of farming were introduced; intelligent cattle breeding was undertaken. The invention of the steam engine and of labor-saving machinery brought about those great changes in management of industry, in factory production, and in the relation of labor to capital, known as the Industrial Revolution.

From 1783 to 1801, the government of Great Britain was directed by William Pitt, the younger son of Lord Chatham, who when only 24 years of age was made first lord of the treasury and chancellor of the exchequer. The affairs of Ireland and India and the impeachment of Warren Hastings were among the first subjects that occupied the attention of Pitt's ministry. In 1782, Ireland had been accorded legislative independence. There were thus two separate parliaments in the British Isles until 1800, when Pitt, who had in the interval experienced some of the difficulties arising out of two separate parliaments, contrived their union. Great Britain and Ireland became the United Kingdom, the two houses of lords and houses of commons being merged into the Imperial Parliament.

The Napoleonic Wars. In 1789, the French Revolution began. For a time there was in England general approval of this movement; but as the revolutionaries proceeded to extremes there was a reaction in English feeling, of which Edmund Burke became the exponent. The execution of Louis XVI was followed by the French declaration of war against Great Britain, on February 1, 1793. With one brief interval, the war lasted till 1815. At first, Britain co-operated with Prussia and Austria against France, and successes were gained on sea and on land. Later, the armies of the French Republic were everywhere victorious on the continent. In 1797 Britain stood alone in the conflict and indeed soon found a European coalition formed against her. The war was now largely maritime, and the naval success of Jervis off St. Vincent and of Duncan off Camperdown were followed by the victory of Nelson in Aboukir bay and of Abercromby at Alexandria.

In 1798, a rebellion in Ireland had to be crushed. Peace with France was made in 1802 by the Treaty of Amiens, only to be broken by another declaration of war in 1803, as the ambitious projects of Napoleon became evident. In spite of the efforts of Pitt, who died in 1806, in the way of forming and supporting a new coalition against France, the military genius of Napoleon swept away all opposition on land, though the naval victory of Trafalgar (1805) established England's supremacy on the seas.

Napoleon, who had assumed the title of emperor of the French in 1804, was now virtually the ruler of Europe. He put forth his Berlin Decree (1806), prohibiting all commerce with Great Britain wherever his power reached, set his brother Joseph on the throne of Spain, and occupied Portugal. But the spirit of resistance had now taken deep root in the British people; in 1808, troops were sent into Spain under Sir John Moore, and a year later Wellington, then General Wellesley, landed in Portugal. Then began that famous series of successful operations, the Peninsular war, which drove back the French into their own country and powerfully aided to undermine the fabric of Napoleon's empire.

The other chief European powers having united, Paris was occupied in 1814, Napoleon was deposed and exiled to Elba, and Louis XVIII was placed on the throne of France. Escaping in 1815, Napoleon appeared once more in the field with a large army. Wellington and Blücher hastened to oppose him, and at Waterloo his long career of conquest ended in a crushing defeat. The restoration of Louis followed, and Napoleon was sent to the island of St. Helena. Of her conquests, Britain retained Tobago, St. Lucia, Mauritius, the Cape of Good Hope, Demerara, Essequibo, Berbice, Helgoland, and Malta. Ceylon and Trinidad had been gained in 1802, and Britain emerged from this long struggle with a very great increase of territorial possessions and political importance.

Political and Economic Reform. After the termination of the wars with Napoleon, many things concurred to make a troublous era in the home administration. The new burden of debt which the wars had left on the nation, the bad harvest of 1816, a government which had no idea but that of absolute resistance to all reforms—all these contributed to increase popular discontent. The result was a strong Radical agitation, accompanied often by serious riots throughout the country, more especially in the large towns, and loud demands for reform in Parliament and in the system of representation. The death of George III and the accession of George IV in 1820 made little change in this respect. From 1822 a succession of able statesmen, Canning, Peel, and Huskisson, gave the government a more liberal turn and did much to satisfy the popular demands. The Catholics were admitted to Parliament; political restrictions on Dissenters were removed; and, in the face of a determined opposition, Earl Grey carried the Reform bill of 1832, which gave large manufacturing towns a representation in some proportion to their importance, practically transferring the basis of political authority from the upper to the middle classes. Similar changes affected all local government. The next great public measure was the abolition of negro slavery in every British possession in 1833. Even more important was the factory act of 1833, which began the correction of abuses in the factory system by limiting the hours of labor for women and children.

William IV died June 20, 1837, and was succeeded by Victoria. The year following is notable as that in which the Chartists began their movement for radical reform, which continued, with popular meetings, presentations of monster petitions, and occasional tumults, till 1848. This same period saw the struggle of the Anti-Corn-Law League (of which Cobden and Bright were the leaders), which was finally successful when Sir Robert Peel, the leader of the Tory party, himself proposed the repeal of the corn duties (1846). The principle of free trade had further success in the repeal of the navigation laws and in the general repeal of import duties made during Lord Aberdeen's ministry (1853).

The Crimean War. In 1852-53, dissension arose between Russia and Turkey, regarding the rights of the Latin and Greek Christians to access to the "holy places" in Palestine. The emperor of Russia, aiming at the possession of Constantinople and finding the concessions made to French devotees a sufficient pretext for war, sent Prince Menshikov to Constantinople to demand redress. Not being satisfied with the response secured, he declared war on Turkey in October 1853. On the plea that it was impossible to leave Russia a free hand in dealing with Turkey or in extending her influence in the Balkans, France and Great Britain formed an alliance against Russia in 1854. A joint invasion of the Crimea followed; Russia was defeated, and peace was signed in 1856 at Paris.

Immediately after the Crimean War came the mutiny of the sepoys in India. In 1858, sovereignty over the East India Company's possessions was transferred by Parliament to the crown. Wars with China (1857 and 1860) opened up five new Chinese ports to trade.

Extension of Suffrage. In 1867, Parliament passed the second Reform bill,—a measure establishing the principle of household suffrage. The act, by extending the franchise to the factory wage earner, made England politically democratic; and it has profoundly influenced all subsequent English history. Disraeli, who soon became official leader of the Conservative party, sought to attach the new voters to the Conservative interest by making the crown and the Church popular, and by a spirited foreign policy. But the next year put the Liberals in power. In 1869, Gladstone passed a bill for the disestablishment of the Irish Church. In 1870, an Irish land bill, for improving the relations between landlord and tenant, became law; and a national system of public elementary education for England was started. Early in 1874, Gladstone dissolved Parliament, and, a large Conservative majority being returned, Disraeli again became premier. His politics followed the lines of the new imperialism, with its interests in India, Africa, and the Near East. The Ashantee war, begun the previous year, ended early in 1874.

In 1876 the title, Empress of India, was added to the titles already held by the queen. During the Russo-Turkish war of 1877-78, Britain remained neutral; but she took an important part in the settlement by the Congress of Berlin and acquired from Turkey the right to occupy and administer Cyprus. Then followed war in Afghanistan, war with the Kafirs of Zululand, and a brief war with the Boers of the Transvaal.

Gladstone and Irish Home Rule. In 1880 Gladstone again became premier. By this time the Irish Nationalists in the House of Commons formed a third party, under the lead of C. S. Parnell. This party worked for Home Rule. Parliament passed another land act for Ireland (1881); an act for putting down crime in Ireland (1882), under which Parnell was arrested and imprisoned in Kilmainham jail; a third reform bill equalizing the borough and county franchise (1884)—all important. The intervention of Britain in Egypt led to the bombardment of Alexandria in July 1882 and the sending of an army into Egypt to quell rebellion. A rising in the Sudan caused British troops to be dispatched to Suakin; but another force, sent by way of the Nile to relieve General Gordon at Khartoum, arrived too late for its object, and the Sudan was abandoned temporarily. For a brief period Lord Salisbury was premier in 1885; but in February 1886 he made way for Gladstone. In April, Gladstone proposed the first Home Rule bill, a bill which would establish a separate Irish legislative body. Against this a determined opposition was organized, and the bill was thrown out on its second reading. This gave rise to the Unionist party, which left the Liberals for the Conservatives. The Liberal remnant was mainly Radical and Irish.

Conservative-Unionist Government. A general election followed, in which the new Unionists and Conservatives had a great majority. The Conservative-Unionist party assumed office, with the marquis of Salisbury as head. A criminal law amendment act for Ireland (1887) and a local government act for England (1888) were passed. In 1887 the golden jubilee of the queen was celebrated. The Liberals won in the elections in 1892, Gladstone acting as premier until his retirement, when Lord Rosebery became premier. In 1895 Lord Salisbury, with the Conservative-Unionists, was returned to power. October 11, 1899, war was declared by the Boers of the Transvaal and Orange Free State, who hoped to destroy British paramountcy in South Africa; these states were annexed to the empire in 1900 and made part of the Union of South Africa in 1909. In 1900, a new Parliament was elected, with a slightly increased Conservative majority. Victoria died January 22, 1901, and was succeeded by Edward VII.

In 1902, on Lord Salisbury's retirement, the new ministry was reconstituted, with A. J. Balfour as premier. The Balfour ministry came to grief over Chamberlain's protective tariff controversy. It was succeeded in 1905 by a Liberal ministry headed by Sir Henry Campbell-Bannerman, who, at his death in 1908, was succeeded by Mr. Herbert Asquith.

The Conservative-Unionist, or, more briefly, the Unionist, party, which went out of office in 1905, had, with the slight interval of Liberal government from 1892 to 1895, been in power continuously since 1886. It inaugurated the Irish Land Purchase system, designed to do away with landlords in Ireland by advancing purchase money to peasants to enable them to buy outright the full title to their farms. Peasant proprietorship began a new era in Ireland's economic and social history. The ominous rivalry with Germany indirectly ended the Unionist government, for Mr. Chamberlain's protective tariff, which split the party, cut too deeply across the old free trade prejudices. The Unionists, nevertheless, had already formed the Anglo-Japanese alliance (1902) and had entered into the *Entente Cordiale* with France (1904).

Liberal Government. The Liberal government that came into office in 1905 drew its support from a strong intellectual radical element (Fabian Socialists, etc.) with its views of the "social uplift," discountenanced during the long Unionist ascendancy, also from the new Labor Party, and from the Irish Nationalists. It had to satisfy these three groups and to watch the threatening course of world politics.

The new Radicalism showed itself first in the act for old age pensions paid by the state (1908),—a controversy which marks the end of the Victorian school of Liberalism and the victory of the younger radical thinkers. Lloyd George, as chancellor of the exchequer, next (1909) framed a budget destined to have important consequences. It embodied a new scheme of taxation bearing heavily upon the "unearned" incomes of the well-to-do. When the House of Lords rejected this budget, a grave constitutional crisis was reached. For years Liberals and Radicals had resented the privileged hereditary position of the Peers and their indifferent rejection of popular measures passed by the Commons. But this was the first case of an entire budget being annulled. A general election (1910) gave popular endorsement to the rejected budget, which the Lords accordingly passed. They then, to ward off the impending crisis, put forward plans which would have modified the composition and privileges of their own house. But the government was bent upon a more radical constitutional alteration. Soon after the death of King Edward (1910) and the accession of George V, Parliament was dissolved, and a general election, largely on the House of Lords question, once more returned the Liberals to office. The Parliament act of 1911 followed,—passed by the Lords only when it was known that the king was prepared to create enough peers to assure its passage. Henceforth, if any measure passed the Commons in three successive sessions, it would become law regardless of the contrary vote of the Lords; at the same time, the duration of Parliament was reduced from seven to five years.

The bill for the disestablishment of the Church in Wales became law in 1914, without the consent of the Lords, after passing the Commons for the third time. The question of women's franchise was settled by the fourth Reform bill of 1918. With certain exceptions, women over thirty years of age were given the Parliamentary vote—a later act enabled them to sit in Parliament—while, by the same bill, the franchise for men approximates to manhood suffrage. At the same time, the Education bill made full time attendance at school compulsory to the age of 14, with compulsory continuation work until the age of 18. The further development of the views of the radical school will probably come from the Labor party, numerically already very strong, and comprising professional men as well as wage earners in its ranks.

Irish Home Rule. It required the new procedure of the Parliament act of 1911 to secure an Irish Home Rule bill. A measure passed the Commons for the third time, in 1914, and became law without the consent of the Lords. Certain counties in Ulster actually prepared for civil war rather than have the measure come into force. When World War I began, the enforcement of the act was suspended, and subsequent events caused it to lapse altogether. The war proved a most troublesome and chaotic period for Ireland, bringing to the surface all the latent antagonism between the two races. A further Home Rule bill, recognizing two separate parts and two separate governments for Ireland, was passed in 1920; but this was generally disregarded. The position of the Nationalists, who still hoped for favorable concessions from the Imperial Parliament, was complicated by the political program of the Sinn Fein, demanding an independent Irish Republic completely detached from the United Kingdom and from the empire. Late in 1921 Lloyd George succeeded in framing a "treaty" which the Imperial Parliament approved. The treaty, on the part of Great Britain, recognized the Irish Free State—the inclusion of the Ulster counties was left to their own consent—and the new Free State was to acquire the status of a self-governing dominion, analogous to that of Canada, within the empire. The treaty was ratified by the Irish representative assembly, the Dail Eireann, January 7, 1922.

The Approach of War. The rivalry with Germany took the direction (1) of a competition in naval armament, and (2) a diplomatic understanding with a group of powers which together should outbalance the Triple Alliance of Germany, Austria, and Italy. The naval competition had begun before 1905; but the victory of the Japanese fleet over the Russian in the battle of Tsushima in that year had demonstrated the advantage of the long range gun. The British admiralty at once laid the keel of the first modern dreadnought, a ship of high speed, with a few guns only and those of the largest caliber. Germany followed suit and took up the challenge which drove both powers to a naval program of overreaching dimensions.

To the alliance with Japan and the entente with France was added (1907) an understanding with Russia. This completed the diplomatic edifice intended to outmatch the German alliance. The main German objective, of which the Constantinople to Bagdad railway was a part, would have given the Central Powers a wide belt of influence and exclusive economic exploitation extending from the North Sea through the Balkan states and Asia Minor to the Persian Gulf, and impinging upon both Russian and English interests in western and central Asia. On the other hand, the French design of rounding out an empire in northwestern Africa by an inclusion of Morocco aroused German resentment. From either quarter, a reason for war might have come.

The annexation of Bosnia and Herzegovina by Austria (1908) found Russia not yet sufficiently recovered from the war with Japan to make this a crucial issue. The annexation was a diplomatic victory for the Central Powers; but it increased the tension between the two rival groups. The sending of the German gunboat *Panther* to Agadir in 1911 brought England at once to the diplomatic support of France, and Germany had to be content to leave France a free hand in Morocco, accepting territorial compensation elsewhere in Africa. The war of Italy against Turkey for territory in North Africa left the two groups of powers undisturbed. But the Balkan wars seemed to tell on the whole against the diplomatic prestige of the German group; and they left Serbia strengthened with Russian support against Austria's advance. While the memory of this diplomatic setback was fresh, the heir to the Austrian throne was assassinated at Sarajevo by Serbian nationalists. This event seemed to Germany to involve a further loss of prestige unless avenged by the complete humiliation of Serbia.

While Russia was mobilizing for the support of Serbia, England tried to have the impending conflict localized, and then to have it made the subject of a general European conference. Failing both, the full implications of the understanding with Russia and with France had to be met. When Germany declared war against Russia and then against France, England took the occasion of the violation of Belgian neutrality to enter the lists against Germany, and World War I had begun.

World War I. England's contribution to the combined operations of the Entente against the Central Powers and their allies was primarily naval. She resisted successfully, although with fearful loss of mercantile tonnage and food supply, the German submarine blockade of the British Isles. Her navy maintained to the end the counter blockade of all the maritime approaches of the Central Powers—a task which the adherence of Italy to the Entente in 1915 made the easier—thus cutting off all sea-borne war supplies and foodstuffs for the enemy. The naval battle of Jutland, the only large open engagement between the two high seas fleets (1916), ended in the safe withdrawal of the German squadrons to cover, whence they never emerged till the surrender after the armistice. After Turkey had joined the Central Powers, with Bulgaria, the attempt to force the Dardanelles, preparatory to taking Constantinople with the army quartered at Gallipoli, was foiled by the Turkish land batteries (1915). But Turkey was despoiled of most of her empire. England successfully defended the Suez canal and Egypt (severed definitely from the Turkish empire and declared a British possession, 1914), secured Jerusalem, and gained Mesopotamia. See *World War I.*

Inter-War Period. After the Treaty of Versailles the government was faced by problems of demobilization, debt finance, and unemployment. Within the Empire, the Dominions, including Eire (Irish Free State), were given an equal status with Great Britain, extending to foreign relations, and India received a new constitution. Lloyd George was compelled to resign in 1922, when Greece, whose claims he had supported, was overcome by Turkey. A Conservative government succeeded, first under Bonar Law and later under Stanley Baldwin.

In 1923 a Labor government under Ramsay MacDonald held office for 10 months, Baldwin being returned to power again at the end of the year. The Labor government was returned to power in 1929 and was succeeded in October 1931 by a coalition government, preponderantly Conservative, led by Ramsay MacDonald.

A system of preferential tariffs within the empire was adopted in 1932. The Conservatives won the election of 1935, Baldwin serving as prime minister until 1937. He was succeeded by Neville Chamberlain.

Edward VIII, who had succeeded George V in January 1936, abdicated in December because the Cabinet objected to his proposed marriage with Mrs. Wallis Simpson. He was succeeded by a younger brother, crowned May 12, 1937, as George VI.

Abroad, England had been a leading supporter of the League of Nations and the limitation of armaments. The rising military strength of Germany under its totalitarian government, together with the aggressive policy of Japan and Italy, forced a change in 1936 to a rearmament program. Even after the Italian conquest of Ethiopia and the German annexation of Austria, England followed a policy of appeasement, climaxed by the Munich agreement in September 1938, which allowed Germany to take over the Sudeten lands of Czechoslovakia. England and France then guaranteed the integrity of Poland against German attempts to regain Danzig and the Polish Corridor. Russia signed a ten-year non-aggression pact with Germany with a secret agreement to divide Poland. Germany invaded Poland on September 1, 1939, and Britain and France declared war two days later.

World War II. After the fall of France in 1940, Churchill succeeded Chamberlain as prime minister. He rallied the nation in the face of disaster in Europe against the aggressive might of Hitler's Germany. Churchill's friendship with the American president, Franklin D. Roosevelt, and his close co-operation established a lasting policy of solidarity which became the backbone of the resistance to Russian aggressive moves after the war.

Social Changes. Churchill's war ministry was unseated in July 1945, and the Labor party took control with Clement Attlee as prime minister. The new government in the next three years nationalized the Bank of England, the coal and electrical industries, the railroads and canals, and finally the steel industry. It also established a system of state medicine. This ambitious policy undertaken after a war which had decimated foreign trade and cut deeply into national resources led to economic crisis. Britain was forced to contract its commitments for military support of Greece and Turkey against Russian encroachments, these responsibilities being taken over by the U.S. Its mandate over Palestine was resigned to the UN in 1948.

Transformation of the Empire. The postwar world was a world of social and political ferment. The British government was faced with demands, often accompanied by violence, for immediate independence. By agreement with the dependencies and by enabling acts, the government granted independence first to Ceylon, India, and Pakistan; then, in the 1950's and 1960's, to nearly all the other dependencies. Rhodesia occasioned the most serious problem since the Rhodesian white rulers would not guarantee rights to the natives on which the British insisted. It accordingly made a unilateral declaration of independence which Britain did not recognize.

Conservative Administration. Most of these changes were carried out under Conservative leadership, which in 1951 returned Churchill to the helm. The steel industry was denationalized, but other innovations of the Labor government were untouched.

George VI died Feb. 6, 1952, and his daughter was crowned Elizabeth II on June 2, 1953.

Anthony Eden succeeded Churchill in 1955. The next year Egypt nationalized the Suez Canal, controlled by the British and the French but due to revert to Egypt in 1968. Their communication with the Orient thus threatened, Israel attacked, conquering in six days all Egyptian territory east of the canal, and England and France bombed canal defenses and landed troops; but all withdrew on pressure of world opinion. Eden resigned and was succeeded in early 1957 by Harold Macmillan.

Relations with Europe. Britain rejected an invitation to adhere to the Treaty of Rome, which founded the "European Common Market" in 1957. Macmillan later sought admission, but was blocked by France in early 1963. Macmillan resigned that year and was succeeded by Alexander Douglas-Home, who lost a close election in 1964 to Harold Wilson and his Labor Party. Wilson resolutely attacked mounting economic problems. Believing that Britain's future demanded integration with Europe, early in 1967 he reopened negotiations for joining the Common Market. This was blocked again by France's veto later that year, one month after the pound had been devalued from $2.80 to $2.40. A stern austerity program followed, and the standard of living declined during 1968. A gold crisis forced the 7 nations of the London gold pool to disband in 1968.

Wilson was prime minister from 1964–70. Money problems, unemployment, and lagging economic growth led to an austerity program in the late 1960's. In 1970 Conservative Edward Heath became prime minister. The Arab oil boycott forced the government to set a 3-day work week in 1973, and the situation grew worse when coal miners struck. On the positive side, Britain joined the European Common Market in 1973. Inconclusive elections in 1974 brought Wilson's return to power. Through 1975, the trade deficit, inflation, and unemployment all increased. Wilson resigned in April 1976, and was replaced by the Labor Party leader, James Callahan. The new prime minister faced critical economic problems as the pound sterling plunged to $1.57 (U.S. dollars) in October.

Britain also faced problems in Northern Ireland, where conflict between the Protestants and the Catholic minority had continued since the state's creation in 1920. Fighting between 1968 and 1975 took more than 1,000 civilian lives. In the 1970's, England experienced widespread bombings in its urban centers by Irish terrorists. While negotiations failed to end hostilities, British troops attempted to keep order in Northern Ireland.

Scotland was known to the Romans as *Caledonia.* The Romans, from 80 A.D., held parts of the lowlands. After their departure in 410 the country was occupied by the Picts, the Scots in the west, originating in Ireland, the Britons in the southwest, and the Angles in the southeast.

Early Scottish Kings. In 844 the Scots and Picts were united under Kenneth MacAlpin. The new kingdom, called *Scotland,* absorbed the Britons, and by the victory of Carham (1018), over Canute's forces, gained the district of Lothian. The line of Kenneth MacAlpin ruled until 1290, except for the reign of Macbeth (1040–57). The Norman Conquest of England and the marriage of Malcolm III with Margaret, a Saxon princess, tended to bring in the English language and Norman-English institutions.

English Suzerainty Begun. The English kings since Athelstan had made vague claims of suzerainty over Scotland. In 1173, William the Lion of Scotland, after his defeat in Northumbria, was forced to become a liegeman of Henry II. This

English suzerainty, however, was relinquished by Richard Cœur de Lion in 1188.

From 1214 to 1285, under Alexander II and Alexander III, Scotland once more experienced a long period of national progress and prosperity. Alexander III was succeeded by his eight-year-old granddaughter, Margaret, in 1285. The child queen dying suddenly, the vacant throne was disputed among many rivals. Between two of these claimants, John of Baliol and Robert Bruce, Edward I was appointed arbiter. He decided in favor of Baliol, which decision implied once again suzerainty over Scotland.

In 1296, Edward defeated Baliol, who had chafed against his position as vassal, and forced him to abdicate, appointing a governor to administer the Scottish kingdom.

Wallace and Bruce. The Scots under Wallace rose in rebellion and won a decisive victory over the English at Stirling in 1297. The following year Edward again invaded Scotland, and at Falkirk the Scottish forces, after a brave but futile resistance, were broken. Wallace was later betrayed, and after a mock trial was condemned and executed, August 23, 1305.

Soon, however, another champion of the cause of Scotland was found in Robert Bruce, who, in 1314, at Bannockburn, drove the English into headlong flight and thus freed his country from foreign dominance. Bruce reigned fifteen years as Robert I of Scotland. After a period of civil war, his son, David II, gained the throne in 1342.

Rise of Stuart Dynasty. David died childless, and a new line of Scottish kings began in the person of Robert II, son of Marjorie (daughter of Bruce) and the high steward, from which hereditary office the new dynasty took its name. He was succeeded in 1390 by his son Robert III, and, on the death of the latter in 1406, James I became king, under the regency of the duke of Albany. Internal strife among his turbulent barons led to James's being held captive in England for eighteen years. He was subsequently liberated and crowned at Scone in 1423.

James I proved a capable and gifted monarch, but unfortunately he was assassinated at Perth in 1437, being succeeded by his young son, James II. After a long minority, James assumed the reins of government and showed signs of being a firm and prudent ruler. He was, however, accidentally killed in 1460, and was succeeded by his son James III, who was slain in 1488 at the battle of Sauchieburn. James IV, son and successor of James III, in 1503 married Margaret, daughter of Henry VII of England. When Henry VIII, in 1509, ascended the English throne, border troubles broke out between him and James IV, resulting in the defeat and death of the latter at Flodden Field (1513).

Mary Queen of Scots. James V, son of James IV, became king in 1513. He made war in turn on England and was defeated at Solway Moss in 1542, dying a few days later on December 14 at Caerlaverock Castle. He was succeeded by his infant daughter, pitifully famous in Scottish history as Mary Queen of Scots. Her unfortunate marriage with Lord Darnley, a worthless ingrate, lost her the support of the Reformed party in Scotland.

He was murdered, and Mary married Bothwell, who was suspected of complicity in the crime. A rebellion forced her to abdicate in favor of her infant son who, in 1567, became King James VI, with the earl of Moray as regent. After a thwarted attempt to regain her throne, Mary fled to England, where Elizabeth detained her as a state prisoner. As the head of the Catholic party and the next heir to the throne, Mary became the center of a series of plots against the queen, and Elizabeth finally ordered her execution. She was beheaded in Fotheringay Castle in 1587.

Union of Scotland and England. On the death of Elizabeth, James VI, as nearest heir, succeeded to the English throne in 1603 as James I of England, with the title of King of Great Britain, France, and Ireland. James I died in 1625 and was succeeded by his son Charles I, whose reign was marked by foreign wars and religious dissensions, which resulted in his execution, January 1, 1649. Six days later the Scots proclaimed his son, Charles II, king and invited him to Scotland. On two occasions he was defeated by Cromwell's troops, the second being at Worcester (1651), where his army was completely annihilated. In 1660 Charles was restored to the throne in Scotland and England. Charles II was succeeded at his death in 1685 by his brother James VII of Scotland and II of England. The Revolution of 1688 drove James from his kingdom and in 1689 placed on the throne William and Mary, who were succeeded by Anne in 1702.

Coalescence of Parliaments. Already a spirit of alienation was rife in Scotland, due to commercial jealousy of England. To prevent a more serious estrangement between the two countries, the Scottish and English parliaments in 1707 passed an act by which the two governments were amalgamated into one ruling body.

Subsequent history has shown that the Scottish people have been in no way fallible in the intuition that guided them to the acceptance of a political arrangement which has brought to them such lasting peace and prosperity.

WALES

The early inhabitants of Wales were a mixed race of Celtic and pre-Aryan peoples. They are largely represented in the small, dark, dolichocephalic (long-headed) types, still to be met in the coal valley districts of southern Wales. These "small dark" Welshmen, as they are known today, probably represent an early migration of Mediterranean peoples along the Atlantic coast. Their own name for themselves was *Cymri*, "men of the same country," in contrast to the Saxon invaders, who called them Welsh (Wälsch) or foreigners.

The Roman Occupation. The Romans, under Ostorius Frontinus and Agricola conquered Wales by 78 A.D. They received a veneering of Roman culture and were so far reconciled to Roman rule that their defense was left largely in their own hands. After the departure of the Romans, however, they reverted to their clan system and Celtic culture, with the addition of Christianity

Saxons and Normans. The Saxon invasion cut off the Welsh from their kinsmen to north and south. Against the Saxon kings they fought with varying success. The Norman kings, after 1072, allowed their barons to carve out feudal domains as they could in Wales, and by the end of the next century these "Marcher Lords" had occupied most of the level ground in the Severn valley and on the southwest coast, but they were less successful in the mountains.

Subjugation by Edward I. The princes of the house of Llewelyn attained some degree of unity among the clans, and had some success against the English. The last of them made the mistake of defying Edward I, who invaded Wales (1276–84) and conquered it. He divided the former Welsh lands into shires, and built castles to secure control. Wales, with its mixture of native clans, royal domain, and Marcher lordships, was far from stabilized, and even became an element of discord in English politics. In 1403, Owen Glendower, with Harry Hotspur, rose in rebellion against Henry IV, but was defeated.

Incorporation in England. In 1485 Henry VII, himself of Welsh stock, began a reorganization, which was completed by Henry VIII with the amalgamation of Wales with England. Local government was established on the English model, and Welsh members sat in the English parliament. The Welsh became and remained loyal adherents to the English crown, but they have always maintained their spirit of individual nationality, which in great measure has been kept alive by the preservation of their native tongue.

THE COMMONWEALTH	Political Designation	Form of Government	Executive Authority	Area in Sq. Miles
MEMBERS*				
England ⎫Great ⎫Great	United Kingdom . .	Constitutional Monarchy	King through ministry	50,331
Wales ⎬Britain ⎬Britain				8,016
Scotland ⎭ ⎬and Nor.	. . . .			30,405
Northern Ireland ⎭Ireland		Responsible	Chief executive . . .	5,462
Isle of Man		Representative	Governor	211
Channel Islands		Representative	Lt. Governor . . .	75
Australia, 1931	Commonwealth . .	Parliamentary Democracy	Gov.-Gen.thr.ministry	2,967,900
Bahamas, 1973	Commonwealth . .	Part. Representative . .	Governor	5,353
Bangladesh, 1972	Republic	Parliamentary Democracy	President	55,126
Barbados, 1966	State	Parliamentary Democracy	Gov.-Gen.thr.ministry	166
Botswana, 1966	Republic	Part. Representative . .	President	222,000
Canada, 1931	Dominion	Parliamentary Democracy	Gov.-Gen.thr.ministry	3,851,809
Cyprus, 1961	Republic	Representative	President	3,572
Fiji, 1970	Dominion	Representative	Prime Minister . . .	7,055
Gambia, 1965	Republic	Parliamentary Democracy	President	4,467
Ghana, 1957	Republic	Military	Head of State . . .	92,100
Grenada, 1974	Republic	Parliamentary	Gov.-Gen.thr.ministry	133
Guyana, 1966	Republic	Representative	President	83,000
India, 1947	Republic	Parliamentary	Prime Minister . . .	1,266,602
Jamaica, 1962	Republic	Part. Representative . .	Gov.-Gen.thr.ministry	4,244
Kenya, 1963	Republic	Part. Representative . .	President	224,961
Lesotho, 1966	Republic	Constitutional Monarchy	King through ministry	11,720
Malawi, 1964	Republic	Parliamentary	President	45,747
Malaysia, 1963	Federation	Constitutional Monarchy	Head of State . . .	127,316
Malta, 1964	Republic	Mixed Democracy . . .	Governor	122
Mauritius, 1968	State	Parliamentary	Gov.-Gen.thr.ministry	787
Nauru, 1968†	Republic	Parliamentary Democracy	President	5,263
New Zealand, 1931	Dominion	Parliamentary Democracy	Gov.-Gen.thr.ministry	103,736
Nigeria, 1960	Republic	Military	Head of State . . .	356,669
Papua New Guinea, 1975 . .	State	Parliamentary Democracy	Gov.-Gen.thr.ministry	426,840
Seychelles, 1976	Republic	Representative	Governor	107
Sierra Leone, 1961	Republic	Representative	President	27,925
Singapore, 1965	Republic	Representative	President	227
Sri Lanka, 1948	Republic	Part. Representative . .	President	25,332
Swaziland, 1968	Kingdom	Constitutional Monarchy	King	6,704
Tanzania, 1961	Republic	Part. Representative . .	Gov.-Gen.thr.ministry	364,943
Tonga, 1970	Kingdom	Constitutional Monarchy	King	270
Trinidad and Tobago, 1962 . .	Republic	Representative	Gov.-Gen.thr.ministry	1,980
Uganda, 1962	Republic	Military	Head of State . . .	91,452
Western Samoa, 1970	State	Parliamentary	Head of State . . .	1,097
Zambia, 1964	Republic	Part. Representative . .	President	290,586
ASSOCIATED STATES				
Antigua	Assoc. St.	Part. Representative . .	Gov. thr. ministry .	170
Dominica	Assoc. St.	Part. Representative . .	Gov. thr. ministry .	290
St. Kitts—Nevis—Anguilla‡ . .	Assoc. St.	Part. Representative . .	Gov. thr. ministry .	153
St. Lucia	Assoc. St.	Part. Representative . .	Gov. thr. ministry .	238
St. Vincent	Assoc. St.	Part. Representative . .	Gov. thr. ministry .	150
DEPENDENCIES				
Europe				
Gibraltar	Colony	Representative	Governor	2.30
Africa				
British Indian Ocean Territory . .	Colony	. . . .	Commissioner . . .	29
St. Helena and dependencies§ . . .	Colony	Part. Representative . .	Governor	47
Asia and Oceania				
Brunei‖	Protected Sultanate .	Constitutional Monarchy	Sultan thr. ministry	2,226
Hong Kong	Colony	Part. Representative . .	Governor	403
Pacific Islands (British)				
Gilbert Islands	Colony	Representative	High Com's'n'r . .	5,700
New Hebrides	Condomin. with Fr. .	. . . .	Governor	102
Solomon Islands	Colony	Part. Representative . .	Governor	10,983
Pitcairn Island	Colony	Representative	Governor	2
Tuvalu	Colony	. . . .	Commissioner . . .	9.5
Western Hemisphere				
Belize, 1976	Dominion	Part. Representative . .	Governor	8,867
Bermuda	Colony	Representative	Governor	21
Falkland Islands and dependencies# .	Colony	Part. Representative . .	Governor	4,618
West Indies				
Cayman Islands	Colony	Part. Representative . .	Governor	100
Montserrat	Colony	Part. Representative . .	Governor	39.5
Turks and Caicos Islands	Colony	Part. Representative . .	Governor	166
British Virgin Islands	Colony	Part. Representative . .	Governor	59
Antarctica				
British Antarctic Territory	Colony	. . . .	High Commissioner	600,000

* With date of membership.   † Special member—has the right to attend Commonwealth meetings and activities, but not to attend meetings of Commonwealth heads of government.   ‡ Anguilla is administered as a dependent territory.   § Dependencies: Ascension and Tristan da Cunha.   ‖ Brunei ceased to be a protected state in 1971.   # Dependencies: South Georgia and South Sandwich Islands.   ** No permanent civilian population.

Accession		Foreign Trade millions, U.S. dollars		Population	Capital	The Commonwealth
Method	Date	Imports	Exports			
						MEMBERS
		. . . . .	. . . . .	46,018,000	⎫	England
Conquest	1283			2,731,000	⎬ London . . .	Wales
Political union . . .	1603, 1707	46,233	32,988	5,228,963	⎭	Scotland
Conquest, settlement	1172, 1494	. . . . .	. . . . .	1,536,065	Belfast	Northern Ireland
Purchase	1827	. . . . .	. . . . .	49,743	Douglas . . .	Isle of Man
Thro' duke of Norm'dy	1066	. . . . .	. . . . .	125,240	St. Peterport .	Channel Islands
Settlement	1788–1828	6,802	9,389	13,339,000	Canberra . . .	Australia
Settlement	1609	1,906	1,444	197,000	Nassau . . .	Bahamas
Treaty	1972	331	263	74,990,000	Dacca	Bangladesh
Settlement	1625	169	54	244,000	Bridgetown . .	Barbados
Conquest	1885–1895	75	42	661,000	Gaborone . . .	Botswana
Settlement, conquest	1627–1763	31,639	32,177	22,479,000	Ottawa	Canada
Annexation	1914	409	153	641,000	Nicosia . . .	Cyprus
Cession	1874	204	79	560,000	Suva	Fiji
Treaty, cession . . .	1807	31	25	510,000	Banjul	Gambia
Treaty, cession . . .	1672	823	755	9,607,000	Accra	Ghana
Cession	1763–1783	43	11	106,219	St. George's .	Grenada
Conquest, cession . .	1803–1814	258	268	774,000	Georgetown . .	Guyana
Conquest, cession . .	1612–1857	4,800	3,900	586,266,000	New Delhi . .	India
Conquest, cession . .	1655–1670	936	632	1,998,000	Kingston . . .	Jamaica
Cession	1905	1,026	603	12,912,000	Nairobi . . .	Kenya
Conquest	1884	32	5	1,016,000	Maseru . . .	Lesotho
Treaty, cession . . .	1891	184	119	4,900,000	Lilongwe . . .	Malawi
Treaty, cession . . .	1785, 1918	4,400	4,500	11,700,000	Kuala Lumpur	Malaysia
Annexation, treaty . .	1814	357	134	298,000	Valletta . . .	Malta
Conquest, cession . .	1810–1814	157	132	872,000	Port Louis . .	Mauritius
Conquest	1914	7	10	7,561	Nauru	Nauru
Settlement, treaty . .	1840	3,700	2,400	3,027,000	Wellington . .	New Zealand
Settlement, purchase	1861–1900	2,730	9,560	61,219,000	Lagos	Nigeria
Annexation, mandate .	1884, 1920	. . . . .	. . . . .	2,650,000	Port Moresby .	Papua New Guinea
Treaty	1814	. . . . .	. . . . .	60,000	Victoria . . .	Seychelles
Purchase from chiefs	1787	158	132	2,707,000	Freetown . . .	Sierra Leone
Settlement	1819	8,300	5,800	2,219,000	Singapore . .	Singapore
Treaty, cession . . .	1796–1815	624	434	13,679,000	Colombo . . .	Sri Lanka
Treaty	1894	60	70	478,000	Mbabane . . .	Swaziland
Conquest, cession . .	1918, 1890	448	321	14,763,000	Dar es Salaam	Tanzania
Protectorate	1900	5	3	100,000	Nukualofa . .	Tonga
Conquest, cession . .	1797, 1802	777	692	1,062,000	Port of Spain .	Trinidad and Tobago
Protectorate declared	1894	213	327	11,172,000	Kampala . . .	Uganda
Mandate	1920	. . . . .	. . . . .	155,000	Apia	Western Samoa
Conquest	1889	532	1,100	4,751,000	Lusaka . . .	Zambia
						ASSOCIATED STATES
Settlement	1632	. . . . .	. . . . .	76,840	St. Johns . . .	Antigua
Conquest	1759	. . . . .	. . . . .	74,300	Roseau . . .	Dominica
Settlement	1623	. . . . .	. . . . .	61,150	Basseterre . .	St. Kitts—Nevis—Anguilla
Treaty	1814	. . . . .	. . . . .	112,000	Castries . . .	St. Lucia
Treaty	1783	. . . . .	. . . . .	100,427	Kingstown . .	St. Vincent
						DEPENDENCIES
						Europe
Conquest	1704	. . . . .	. . . . .	27,650	Gibraltar . . .	Gibraltar
						Africa
Treaty	1965	. . . . .	. . . . .	**	. . . .	British Indian Ocean Territory
Settlement	1659	. . . . .	. . . . .	5,000	Jamestown . .	St. Helena
						Asia and Oceania
Conquest	1888	. . . . .	. . . . .	155,900	Bandar Seri Begawan . .	Brunei
Treaty, cession . . .	1842	. . . . .	. . . . .	4,302,600	Victoria . . .	Hong Kong
						Pacific Islands (British)
Colony	1892–1915	. . . . .	. . . . .	58,000	Tarawa . . .	Gilbert Islands
Treaty	1906	. . . . .	. . . . .	93,000	Vila	New Hebrides
Cession	1893	. . . . .	. . . . .	190,600	Honiara . . .	Solomon Islands
Cession	1898	. . . . .	. . . . .	124	Adamstown .	Pitcairn Island
Colony	1892–1915	. . . . .	. . . . .	5,817	Funafuti . . .	Tuvalu
						Western Hemisphere
Settlement	1638	. . . . .	. . . . .	130,000	Belmopan . . .	Belize
Settlement	1612	. . . . .	. . . . .	54,000	Hamilton . .	Bermuda
Treaty, cession . . .	1771	. . . . .	. . . . .	2,000	Stanley . . .	Falkland Islands
						West Indies
Conquest, treaty . .	1655	. . . . .	. . . . .	11,500	Georgetown .	Cayman Islands
Settlement	1632	. . . . .	. . . . .	12,400	Plymouth . .	Montserrat
Settlement	1678	. . . . .	. . . . .	5,800	Cockburn Town	Turks and Caicos Islands
Cession	. . . . .	. . . . .	. . . . .	12,000	Road Town .	British Virgin Islands
						Antarctica
Settlement	1834	. . . . .	. . . . .	**	Stanley . . .	British Antarctic Territory

History

NAME	LINEAGE	Period of Reign		Birth	Death
		A. D.	A. D.	A. D.	A. D.
ANGLO-SAXON KINGS					
Egbert	First King of all England	827	839	775?	839
Ethelwulf	Son of Egbert	839	857	....	858
{ Ethelbald	Son of Ethelwulf	857	860	....	860?
{ Ethelbert	Second son of Ethelwulf	860	866	....	866?
Ethelred I	Third son of Ethelwulf	866	871	....	871
Alfred the Great	Fourth son of Ethelwulf	871	899	849	899
Edward the Elder	Son of Alfred	899	925	870?	925
Athelstan	Eldest son of Edward	925	940	895?	941
Edmund I	Brother of Athelstan	940	946	923	946 or 8
Edred	Brother of Edmund I	946	955	....	955?
Edwy	Son of Edmund I	955	959	939?	959
Edgar	Second son of Edmund I	959	975	943?	975
Edward the Martyr	Son of Edgar	975	978	961?	978
Ethelred II	Half-brother of Edward	978	1016	968	1016
Edmund Ironside	Eldest son of Ethelred	1016	1017	989	1017
DANISH KINGS					
Canute	By conquest and election	1017	1035	995	1035
Harold I (Harefoot)	Son of Canute	1035	1040	....	1040
Hardicanute	Another son of Canute	1040	1042	1019	1042
SAXON KINGS					
Edward the Confessor	Son of Ethelred II	1042	1066	1004	1066
Harold II	Brother-in-law of Edward	1066	....	1022	1066
NORMAN KINGS					
William I	Second cousin to Edward the Confessor; conquest	1066	1087	1027	1087
William II	Third son of William I	1087	1100	1056	1100
Henry I	Youngest son of William I	1100	1135	1068	1135
Stephen	Third son of Stephen, Count of Blois	1135	1154	1105	1154
THE PLANTAGENETS					
Henry II	Son of Geoffrey Plantagenet by Matilda, d. of Henry I	1154	1189	1133	1189
Richard I, the Lion-hearted	Eldest surviving son of Henry II	1189	1199	1157	1199
John	Youngest son of Henry II	1199	1216	1166	1216
Henry III	Eldest son of John	1216	1272	1207	1272
Edward I	Eldest son of Henry III	1272	1307	1239	1307
Edward II	Eldest surviving son of Edward I	1307	1327	1284	1327
Edward III	Eldest son of Edward II	1327	1377	1312	1377
Richard II	Son of the Black Prince, eldest son of Edward III	1377	1399	1366	1400
HOUSE OF LANCASTER					
Henry IV	Son of John of Gaunt, fourth son of Edward III	1399	1413	1367	1413
Henry V	Eldest son of Henry IV	1413	1422	1387	1422
Henry VI	Only son of Henry V	1422	1461	1421	1471
HOUSE OF YORK					
Edward IV	His grandfather was Richard, son of Edmund, fifth son of Edward III	1461	1483	1441	1483
Edward V	Eldest son of Edward IV	1483	....	1470	1483
Richard III	Younger brother of Edward IV	1483	1485	1452	1485
HOUSE OF TUDOR					
Henry VII	Son of Edmund, eldest son of Owen Tudor, by Katharine, widow of Henry V; his mother was great-granddaughter of John of Gaunt	1485	1509	1457	1509
Henry VIII	Only surviving son of Henry VII	1509	1547	1491	1547
Edward VI	Son of Henry VIII by Jane Seymour	1547	1553	1537	1553
Mary I	Daughter of Henry VIII by Katharine of Aragon	1553	1558	1516	1558
Elizabeth I	Daughter of Henry VIII by Anne Boleyn	1558	1603	1533	1603
HOUSE OF STUART					
James I	Son of Mary Queen of Scots, granddaughter of James IV and Margaret	1603	1625	1566	1625
Charles I	Only surviving son of James I (executed)	1625	1649	1600	1649
Commonwealth and Protectorate {	Oliver Cromwell, Lord Protector	1649	1658	1599	1658
	Richard Cromwell, third son of Oliver, Lord Protector	1658	1659	1626	1712
Charles II	Eldest son of Charles I	1660	1685	1630	1685
James II	Second son of Charles I	1685	1689	1633	1701
William III and	Son of William, Prince of Orange, by Mary, daughter of Charles I	} 1689	1702	1650	1702
Mary II	Eldest daughter of James II	} 1689	1694	1662	1694
Anne	Second daughter of James II	1702	1714	1665	1714
HOUSE OF HANOVER					
George I	Son of Elector of Hanover, by Sophia, daughter of Elizabeth, daughter of James I	1714	1727	1660	1727
George II	Only son of George I	1727	1760	1683	1760
George III	Grandson of George II	1760	1820	1738	1820
George IV	Eldest son of George III	1820	1830	1762	1830
William IV	Third son of George III	1830	1837	1765	1837
Victoria	Daughter of Edward, fourth son of George III	1837	1901	1819	1901
HOUSE OF WINDSOR *					
Edward VII	Son of Victoria	1901	1910	1841	1910
George V	Son of Edward VII	1910	1936	1865	1936
Edward VIII	Son of George V	1936	1936†	1894	1972
George VI	Son of George V	1936	1952	1895	1952
Elizabeth II	Daughter of George VI	1952	....	1926	....

* Adopted in place of Saxe-Coburg by George V, July 1917 † Accession, January 20; abdication, December 10.

CANADA

After the voyages of the Norsemen, Bjarni Herjulfson and Leif Ericson, in the 10th century, when, as related in the Norse sagas, they probably explored much of the east coast of Canada, no European for five centuries left evidence of setting foot on the American continent. Impelled by his own surmises as to the longitude of the east coast of Asia, and also by news of the landfall of Columbus, John Cabot, in 1496, obtained a commission from King Henry VII of England for a westward voyage of discovery under the English flag. In the spring of 1497 Cabot sailed from Bristol; on June 24 he sighted land, possibly Cape Breton island. His discovery furnished a ground for England's later claim to North American territory. The English did not follow up the advantage offered by the later explorations of John Cabot and his son Sebastian, doubtless because the reports about the new found land confuted John Cabot's boast that the wealth of Asia should flow into the port of London.

First Explorations and Settlements. By the early 16th century, French fishermen, among others, began to frequent the codbanks off Newfoundland. By sailing around the northern extremity of Newfoundland they discovered the Straits of Belle Isle, and became aware of the vast body of water into which the straits led. It was Jacques Cartier, a sailor of St. Malo in Brittany, who discovered this body of water to be the gulf of a great river, and with this discovery the story of Canadian exploration really begins. In 1534 Cartier sailed into the Gulf of St. Lawrence and took possession of its shores in the name of the French king. On a second voyage, in 1535-36, he ascended the St. Lawrence as far as the rapids by the island of Montreal. Following Cartier, attempts were made by the French to plant colonies along the coast of Acadia and the shores of the Gulf of St. Lawrence (Canada). The penetration and occupation of this latter region awaited the genius and devotion of Samuel Champlain. Champlain made his first voyage to the St. Lawrence in 1603; he began the first permanent settlement at Quebec in 1608. His activities during the next twenty years left an indelible impress upon the fortunes of the French in Canada. To him is due the discovery of Lake Champlain (the link between the St. Lawrence and the Hudson) as well as of Lake Ontario, and the establishment of a trading post at Montreal. But Champlain committed the French to an alliance with the Algonquin and Huron Indians against the more powerful confederacy of the Iroquois, who thus became the allies of the English both in war and in the fur trade. To this alliance is due in some measure the failure of the French to hold their empire in North America.

The conversion and the civilizing of the Indians were undertaken in earnest by the Jesuit fathers, who began their great mission on their arrival in Quebec in 1625. Many suffered martyrdom when their converts, the Hurons, were practically exterminated by the vengeful Iroquois. The Jesuit fathers shared in the exploration of the interior of the continent, where many a distant mission center attests their pious labors; they made the Church the most powerful influence in shaping the history of New France in the 17th and the 18th century.

Government of New France. To correct the abuses attending the early government and commerce of the colony, Richelieu, in 1627, organized the Hundred Associates, a company that controlled New France and enjoyed a monopoly of the fur trade until 1663. In that year Louis XIV constituted Canada a royal province. Its civil government was administered by a governor, an intendant, who was usually a lawyer, and a council. These were all appointed by the crown; no trace of representative government ever appeared in New France, nor, it may be added, was any Huguenot or heretic ever permitted to settle. Sturdy French peasants were encouraged to migrate from France; they brought with them the traditions of the seignioral system of land tenure, which was used in Canada as the basis of land grants.

Large tracts of uncleared land, called seigniories, were bestowed upon seigniors, who thus formed a landed noblesse. The seigniors held their estates by the "tenure of fealty and homage"; they enjoyed social leadership and judicial powers over the tenant farmers under them. The farmers, or habitants, received from their seignior a tenure resting upon payment of small annual rentals in money or in produce, together with the customary seigniorial dues. The seigniories, sometimes called côtes, usually had the bank of a river for a base line. Each habitant received a rectangular strip of land running from the river into the woodland behind. The houses, one to each rectangular strip, were built close to the river front; the village bore the appearance of a single line of houses placed at wide intervals instead of a cluster of cottages grouped around a church, as in the European manor or seigniory. Since each habitant was expected to divide his land fairly among his children, the original rectangular farm became subdivided into mere ribbons of land, such as are to be seen today in the St. Lawrence valley. The system with its seigniorial dues survived in Lower Canada (Quebec) until 1854, when, by a statute of that year, seigniorial rights were terminated and seigniorial dues commuted.

English and French Rivalry. In 1689, with the beginning of the world-wide struggle between England and France for maritime and commercial supremacy, the wars of the French and the English colonies for the control of America were opened in earnest. The warfare was carried on by means of cruel, merciless border raids, in which the Indians shared. The Treaty of Utrecht in 1713 gave England Acadia (now the provinces of Nova Scotia and New Brunswick) and recognized the English title to Newfoundland and to Hudson Bay Territory. For the next forty years the French tried to hold the interior country of the Lakes and the Mississippi valley, and to confine the English to the Atlantic seaboard. English pioneers from Virginia and Pennsylvania, pushing west to the Ohio, were checked at the Alleghenies by forces of the French and of the Indians friendly to them. The Iroquois for long held the balance of power, seeing their own safety in the rivalry of the two contending white nations. The Seven Years' war, commencing in the Ohio valley in 1756, turned at the start in favor of the French, until the fall of Louisburg in 1758, and the capture of Quebec by Wolfe in 1759 put an end to French power in America. Canada, as well as all the territory between the Alleghenies and the Mississippi, was given to England by the Treaty of Paris (1763).

An area comprising the portion of the St. Lawrence valley already settled by the French Canadians was erected at the close of the war into the province of Quebec, the Ohio valley and beyond being administered separately as an Indian reservation. The ill-advised attempt to introduce English law and English courts among the French of the new province of Quebec provoked so much discontent that in 1774 the Quebec act restored the old French civil law, at the same time virtually establishing the Roman Catholic Church. Both have helped to perpetuate the French language, which with English is recognized as an official language in the country. The Quebec act also extended the area of the province to include the Indian reservation, which became the Northwest Territory of the United States after the Treaty of 1783. The delimitation of the various portions of the long boundary between Canada and the United States from the Northeast Boundary of 1783, through the adjustment of the 49th parallel, to the Alaska Award of 1903, has been an example of arbitration and treaty negotiation in international disputes.

Growth of the Provinces. The Continental Congress at the outbreak of the American Revolution tried to secure the adherence of the French Canadians of Quebec; but these remained neutral during the struggle. After the independence of the thirteen colonies had been acknowledged, thousands of loyalists—known later as United Empire Loyalists—assisted by the English government, found asylum in Nova Scotia and Quebec. Those who settled in Nova Scotia, being refused adequate representation in the provincial assembly, which had been instituted in 1758, petitioned for a separate government. For them the province of New Brunswick was formed out of the western part of Nova Scotia in 1784. Those taken to Upper Quebec were settled in the vicinity of Lake Ontario. Between them and the French Canadians in the lower part of the province, differences in language, in religion, and in law provoked an estrangement which seemed to make impolitic the further inclusion of the two races under one provincial government. By the Canada act, or the Constitutional act of 1791, Quebec was divided: the French-speaking province took the name of Lower Canada; Upper Canada, with its English-speaking loyalist pioneers, began its separate history under Governor Simcoe. Public land was offered to pioneers upon terms which soon raised their number to 30,000. York, later Toronto, grew up as the center of industry and commerce.

In both provinces, to a governor responsible only to the Colonial office, and to a council appointed by the governor, was added by the Constitutional act an elective assembly. The governor and council together had no means of controlling the assembly; nor had the assembly any means of making the governor and council responsible to its wishes or to the wishes of the people of the province. This fatal adjustment of constitutional machinery precipitated the long struggle for responsible government—a struggle that did not end until provincial assemblies acquired a position and procedure similar to that enjoyed by the British House of Commons.

Expansion and Union. The defense of Canada in the War of 1812 was the first general or "national" venture of the four unrelated provinces; it bore with special hardship, however, upon Upper Canada. At the same time the exploration of the great Northwest, the prairies and the Rocky mountains, as well as the Pacific coast, by Mackenzie and Vancouver, gave the first glimpses of a "national" domain. Lord Selkirk founded the Red River settlement, the beginning of the province of Manitoba, in 1812. Immigration, likewise the concern of all the provinces, had begun to increase through the work of land companies and colonization societies which brought in more than 150,000 people before 1833. But no "national" policy was possible until the issue of responsible government was settled. The question inflamed the politics of both Canadas until, in 1837, the *Patriotes* under L. J. Papineau, in the lower province, and the Reformers under W. L. Mackenzie, in the upper province, set up the flag of revolt. The armed insurrections, slight enough in themselves, were easily suppressed, but they served to direct the attention of the British government to the two difficulties under which the Canadas labored; namely, race friction and irresponsible rule. The government took the momentous step after 1837 of dispatching to Canada as high commissioner the earl of Durham, well known for his great wealth and for his radical opinions. The statesmanlike report, which he and his secretaries prepared, exposed clearly the impolicy of continuing the irresponsible rule of governor and council.

Durham allowed himself to form an adverse judgment upon the special claims of the French Canadians, and he fancied that he could devise a political expedient to bring about their ultimate Anglicization. To this end he proposed the union of the two provinces, carried out by the Union act in 1841. The plan to obliterate the distinctiveness of the French could not in the nature of things be successful, for the inclusion of both races into a single union government merely intensified their mutual hostility, and in the end forced the two races apart, to come together again on the basis of confederation instead of union.

The Union, however, achieved responsible government. To the Assembly of the new government, Upper and Lower Canada each was to send an equal number of representatives, regardless of any differences in the population. While, at the outset, this device served to protect the interests of the English-speaking minority, in the end it turned to their disadvantage when the balance of population stood in their favor. An executive council, or cabinet, chosen by the governor from the Council and the Assembly, made the constitution parliamentary in form. But cabinet responsibility to the Assembly was not actually settled until 1849, when the governor, Lord Elgin, acting in the full spirit of Durham's report, signed a bill granting compensation for losses of property in the rebellion in Lower Canada,—a bill acceptable to the French and to the Reformers, who together had a majority in the Assembly, but extremely distasteful to the "Tories." The signing of this bill marks the supremacy of the Canadian Assembly in its control of the executive. For his action Lord Elgin was stoned at Montreal by a "Tory" mob, which also set fire to the Parliament house. Mob violence prompted the removal of the capital to Bytown, renamed Ottawa, on the Ottawa river, which has since remained the capital.

Confederation. The impracticability of the Union, as seen in the Parliamentary deadlock, and the apprehension that Canada might be involved in the American Civil War, led in 1864 to a convention of delegates from all the provinces, who met in Quebec to confer upon a confederation. Under the guidance of such statesmen as John A. Macdonald, Charles Tupper, George Brown, George E. Cartier, D'Arcy McGee, and others, known as the Fathers of Confederation, a set of resolutions was adopted, which served as the basis of the British North America act passed by the Imperial Parliament in 1867. By this act, the provinces of Upper and Lower Canada, of Nova Scotia, and of New Brunswick were formally confederated into the Dominion of Canada. Newfoundland preferred not to enter the Confederation, but in 1948 decided upon union with the Dominion. Upper Canada became Ontario; Lower Canada took the name of Quebec.

The federal constitution provides for a governor-general, a privy council, a Senate, and a House of Commons; the system of executive and legislative procedure follows the English Parliamentary model. In contrast to the Constitution of the United States, the British North America act, in view of the state rights controversy in the United States, accords to the provinces certain specific and explicit rights only, reserving to the Federal government all the general and residuary rights and prerogatives of sovereignty.

Unifying the Dominion. To give the Dominion its continental scope from ocean to ocean and to unify its widely separated parts was the task of Canadian statesmen in the two decades following 1867. In 1869 the Dominion acquired by purchase from the Hudson's Bay Company its title to the Northwest Territories. Thus the prairies, hitherto guarded as an exclusive preserve for the Indian fur trade, were thrown open to settlers and proved to be among the richest wheat yielding areas of the continent. Railways were to bind together all these distant outlying parts. New Brunswick and Nova Scotia had been influenced to consent to confederation by an agreement, incorporated in the British North America act, to unite them with Quebec and Ontario by a railway. This promise was fulfilled by the completion of the Intercolonial railway in 1876. After the Oregon boundary had been settled, the Hudson's Bay Company procured the creation of Vancouver island into a crown colony. On the mainland, owing to the discovery of gold in 1856, New Caledonia became a crown colony in 1858, under the name of British Columbia. The union of the two crown colonies under the latter title came in 1866. British Columbia joined the Confederation in 1871. Prince Edward Island agreed to enter the Confederation in 1873.

A serious difficulty in taking over the Northwest was raised by the half-breed and Indian revolt of 1869-70, led by Louis Riel. The trouble arose over the half-breeds' fear that their holdings under the Hudson's Bay title might be disregarded. The disturbance subsided when the new province of Manitoba was taken into the Confederation.

Sir John A. Macdonald headed the first federal cabinet after confederation (1867-73). In this administration, the outstanding disputes between the Dominion and the United States were settled by arbitration or negotiation. The issues involved the Newfoundland and east coast fisheries, the adjustment of the 49th parallel on the Pacific coast, and the losses due to the Fenian raids of 1866 and 1870-71. Macdonald took the first steps toward the construction of the transcontinental railway; but a scandal connected with campaign funds subscribed by a company seeking the charter brought his resignation. The Liberal leader, Alexander Mackenzie, formed a new ministry.

As leader of the Conservative opposition, Macdonald found it opportune to champion the "National Policy" of protection for Canadian industries; in 1878 he was returned to office on this platform. He led the Conservative government from that year until his death in 1891. A protective tariff was established, and, largely as a direct consequence, the Dominion secured the right to negotiate directly her own commercial treaties with foreign states. The first transcontinental railway, the Canadian Pacific, was completed late in 1885. Two others, the Grand Trunk Pacific and the Canadian Northern, later consolidated in the Canadian National system, have been built since. As the Canadian Pacific was being completed, Louis Riel led a second revolt of half-breed settlers in the Saskatchewan valley. This outbreak, easily suppressed by a military force, served to direct public and newspaper attention to the Northwest Territories. Settlers poured in, brought by the railway, and the Territories received representation at Ottawa. The two provinces of Saskatchewan and Alberta were constituted in 1905.

After the death of Sir John A. Macdonald, several Conservative ministries followed in rapid succession. Then the general elections of 1896 brought the Liberals into office under Sir Wilfrid Laurier.

National Development. The period of Liberal government which lasted for fifteen years proved to be a time of rapid economic development, accompanied by signs of a very distinctive national spirit. The sending of a contingent to South Africa during the Boer war showed this. The Laurier government lowered duties on some manufactured goods and instituted a British preference, but still retained the principle of adequate protection for Canadian industries. In 1903 the Alaska boundary dispute and questions relating to the joint use of the Great Lakes and other boundary waters were settled with the United States. The Imperial government left Canada free to reach an agreement with Japan in 1907, upon the restriction of Japanese immigration into the Dominion. Reciprocity with the United States became a major political issue in 1910. Previously, in 1854, the two countries began a reciprocity agreement which continued until the United States abrogated it in 1866. In 1911 the Laurier government took the question to the country at a general election and was defeated. The Conservatives under Sir Robert Borden formed a ministry.

Canada in World War I. In 1912 the Borden government had proposed to contribute three dreadnaughts to the imperial navy at a cost of $35,000,000, as Canada's share of imperial defense. The measure was defeated by the Liberals in the Senate, who wanted an exclusively Canadian navy. But when war came Canada responded instantly.

Inter-War Period. The Borden government, which piloted Canada through the war, was defeated in 1921 due partly to dissatisfaction over tariff policies. A new Farmers', or Progressive, party joined forces with the Liberals, whose leader, W. L. Mackenzie King, controlled Parliament until 1930. The Conservatives, in power from 1930 to 1935, raised tariffs and established a central bank, the Bank of Canada. Mackenzie King was back as premier in 1935.

Early in the century, nearly all the provinces had passed laws to prohibit the manufacture and sale of liquor. Most of these were repealed after World War I. In 1924, the United Church of Canada was formed, consisting of Methodist, Presbyterian, and Congregational communions. In 1926, a minister to Washington was appointed. It was largely due to Canadian insistence that the Statute of Westminster was passed in 1931 by the British parliament, the measure which granted independence to Canada and certain other British dominions within the cooperative framework of the British Commonwealth of Nations. Direct diplomatic relations were established with foreign countries. Governors-general were appointed only on recommendation of the Canadian government. A law creating Canadian citizenship was enacted in 1945.

World War II. On Sept. 10, 1939, Canada declared war on Germany; war with Italy followed in 1940 and with Japan in 1941. A Permanent Joint Board of Defense was set up in 1940 to co-operate with the U.S. in hemisphere defense. The National Resources Nationalization Act declared all property to be at the government's disposal and all manpower to be subject to conscription for home defense. In 1942, over Quebec's opposition, conscription for overseas service was authorized; but soldiers went overseas only with their consent. At war's end, about 40 per cent of men of war age were in the armed forces. Casualties, 104,925 (41,371 dead); cost, $20 billion.

Canada played a prominent role also in the UN. Its foreign minister made the original suggestion that ripened into the North Atlantic Treaty Organization in 1949. In the same year Newfoundland became Canada's 10th province. Military forces went to Korea in 1950.

Postwar Canada. The potentialities of atomic warfare drew Canada and the U.S. closer together militarily. A defensive warning system was jointly built and manned in the far north. This association and the influence of the U.S. in other areas of Canada's economy stirred Canadian fears of U.S. domination. After 20 years of power, Canada's Liberal Party was defeated in 1957 by the Progressive conservatives and John Diefenbaker. Failure to complete an agreement to accept weapons from the U.S. brought a formal protest from Washington in 1963. This precipitated a political crisis and a new election; Lester Pearson and the Liberals won.

In 1967 Canada celebrated the 100th anniversary of its federation by holding an international exposition (Expo '67) in Montreal. Relations with France were strained that year when the French statesman Charles de Gaulle, speaking in Montreal, urged Quebec to seek independence. Pearson, 71, decided to retire and in April 1968, the Liberals selected Pierre Elliott Trudeau as his successor. By 1970, Quebec separatists' acts of terrorism had increased, climaxed by the kidnapping of a Canadian official who was later released. As a result, Trudeau invoked wartime emergency measures. Canada emerged from the shadow of the U.S. as Trudeau traveled to Red China in 1970. Plagued with high unemployment, labor unrest, and inflation, Canada moved toward closer ties with the European Economic Community, increased trading with Japan, and became less reliant on the U.S. The Olympic games were held in Canada for the first time in 1976 at Montreal.

Name	Title While in Office	Born	Parents — Father	Parents — Mother
Sir Charles Stanley	4th Vis. Monck, G. C. M. G.	1819	C. J. K. Monck, 3d Viscount	Bridget Willington
Sir John Young	1st Lord Lisgar, G. C. M. G.	1807	Sir William Young	Lucy Frederick
Frederick T. H. T. Black-wood	Earl of Dufferin, K. P., K. C. B., G. C. M. G., 1st Marquess of Dufferin and Ava	1828	Price Blackwood, 4th Baron Dufferin	Helen Sheridan
John Douglas S. Campbell	The Marquess of Lorne, K. T., G. C. M. G., 9th Duke of Argyll	1845	George S. Campbell, 8th Duke of Argyll	Elizabeth, dt. 2d Duke of Sutherland
Henry C. K. Fitz-Maurice	The 5th Marquess of Lansdowne, G. C. M. G.	1845	Henry Fitz-Maurice, 4th Marquess of Lansdowne	Emily Jane, dt. Comte de Flahault
Frederick A. Stanley	Lord Stanley of Preston, G. C. B., 16th Earl of Derby	1841	Edward Geoffrey, 14th Earl of Derby	Emma, dt. of 1st Baron Skelmersdale
John C. Gordon	The Earl of Aberdeen, K. T., G. C. M. G., 1st Marquess of Aberdeen and Temair	1847	George J. J. Gordon, 5th Earl of Aberdeen	Mary Baillie
Gilbert J. M. K. Elliot	The 4th Earl of Minto, G. C. M. G.	1845	William H. Elliot, 3d Earl of Minto	Emma, dt. of Sir T. Hislop Bart.
Albert H. G. Grey	The 4th Earl Grey, G. C. M. G.	1851	Charley Grey, 2d son 2d Earl Grey	Mary, dt. 1st Baron Ponsonby
Arthur Connaught	Field Marshal His Royal Highness the 1st Duke of Connaught, K. G.	1850	H. R. H. The Prince Consort	H. M. Queen Victoria
Victor C. W. Cavendish	The 9th Duke of Devonshire, K. G., G. C. M. G., G. C. V. O.	1868	Lord Edward Cavendish, 3d son 7th Duke Devon	Lady Blanche, dt. 6th Earl of Carlisle
Julian H. G. Byng	General the 1st Lord Byng of Vimy, G. C. B., G. C. M. G., M. V. O.	1862	George S. Byng, 2d Earl of Strafford	Hon. Harriet, dt. 1st Baron Chesham
Freeman Freeman-Thomas	The 1st Lord Willingdon of Ratton, G. B. E., G. C. S. I., G. C. I. E.	1866	Frederick Freeman Thomas	Mabel, dt. of 1st Viscount Hampden
Vere Brabazon Ponsonby	The 9th Earl of Bessborough	1880	Edward Ponsonby, 8th Earl of Bessborough	Blanche Vere
John Buchan	1st Baron Tweedsmuir	1875	Rev. John Buchan	Helen Masterton
Alexander A. F. W. A. G. Cambridge	1st Earl of Athlone	1874	Duke of Teck	Princess Mary Adelaide
Harold R. L. G. Alexander	Viscount Alexander of Tunis	1891	James, 4th Earl of Caledon	Lady Elizabeth Graham Toler
Rt. Hon. Vincent Massey	. . . .	1887	Chester D. Massey	Anna Vincent
Georges Philias Vanier	. . . .	1888	Philias Vanier	Margaret Maloney
Daniel Roland Michener	. . . .	1900	Edward Michener	Mary Edith Roland
Jules Léger	. . . .	1913	Ernest Léger	Alda Beauvais

PRIME MINISTERS OF CANADA SINCE

Name	Born — When	Born — Where	Parents — Father	Parents — Mother	Religious Connection	Educational Advantages
Sir John A. Macdonald	1815	Glasgow, Scotland	Hugh	Helen Shaw	Anglican	Grammar School, Kingston, Ontario
Alexander Mackenzie	1822	Logierait, Scotland	Alexander	Mary Fleming	Baptist	Parish School
Hon. Sir John A. Macdonald (2d term)	1815	Glasgow, Scotland	Hugh	Helen Shaw	Anglican	Grammar School, Kingston, Ontario
Sir J. J. C. Abbott	1821	St. Andrews, Que.	Joseph	Harriet Bradford	Anglican	McGill University
Sir J. S. D. Thompson	1844	Halifax, Nova Scotia	John S.	Charlotte Pottinger	Roman Catholic	Academy, Halifax
Sir Mackenzie Bowell	1823	Rickinghall, England	John	. . . .	Methodist	Printer's Apprentice
Sir Charles Tupper, Bart.	1821	Amherst, Nova Scotia	Charles	Miriam Lockhart	Baptist	Edinburgh University
Sir Wilfrid Laurier	1841	St. Lin, Quebec	Carolus	Mariette Martineau	Roman Catholic	L'Assomption College, McGill University
Sir Robert L. Borden	1854	Grand Pré, Nova Scotia	Andrew	Eunice Laird	Anglican	Academy, Horton, Nova Scotia
Arthur Meighen*	1874	Anderson, Ontario	Joseph	Mary Meighen	Presbyterian	Toronto University
W. L. Mackenzie King†	1874	Kitchener, Ontario	John	Isabel Mackenzie	Presbyterian	Toronto, Chicago, and Harvard Universities
Richard B. Bennett	1870	Hopewell, N. B.	Henry	Henrietta Stiles	United	Dalhousie University
Louis Stephen St. Laurent	1882	Compton, Quebec	J. B. Moise	Mary Broderick	Roman Catholic	St. Charles Coll. Laval Univ.
John Diefenbaker	1895	Grey County, Ontario	Wm. Thomas	Mary Bannerman	Baptist	University of Saskatchewan
Lester B. Pearson	1897	Toronto, Ont.	Rev. Edwin A.	Annie S. Bowes	United	Univ. Toronto, Oxford
Pierre Elliott Trudeau	1919	Montreal	Charles	Grace Elliott	. . . .	Brebeuf College and Univ. of Paris

*Besides the term of office here indicated, Meighen was premier from July 13, 1926, following the resignation of Mackenzie King.

Educational Advantages	Profession	Date Married	Wife's Name	Date of Appointment	Date of Assuming Office	Date of Death
Trinity College, Dublin	Lawyer	1844	Elizabeth	June 1, 1867	July 1, 1867	Nov. 29, 1894
Eton, Oxford	Lawyer	1835	Adelaide Dalton	Dec. 29, 1868	Feb. 2, 1869	Oct. 6, 1876
Eton, Oxford	Diplomatist	1862	Harriot Hamilton	May 22, 1872	June 25, 1872	Feb. 12, 1902
Eton, St. Andrews, Cambridge	Author, Historian	1871	H. R. H. Princess Louise, 4th dt. Queen Victoria	Oct. 5, 1878	Nov. 25, 1878	May 2, 1914
Eton, Oxford	Statesman, Administrator	1869	Lady Maud Hamilton, dt. 1st Duke of Abercorn	Aug. 18, 1883	Oct. 23, 1883	June 3, 1927
Eton	Army	1864	Lady Constance, dt. 4th Earl of Clarendon	May 1, 1888	June 11, 1888	June 14, 1908
St. Andrews and Oxford	Statesman, Administrator	1877	Hon. Ishbel Marjoribanks, dt. 1st Baron Tweedmouth	May 22, 1893	Sept. 18, 1893	Mar. 7, 1934
Eton, Cambridge	Statesman, Administrator	1883	Mary, dt. Gen. Hon. Charley Grey	July 30, 1898	Nov. 12, 1898	Mar. 14, 1914
Harrow, Cambridge	Statesman, Administrator	1877	Alice Holford	Sept. 26, 1904	Dec. 10, 1904	Aug. 29, 1917
Royal Military Academy, Woolwich	. . . . . .	1879	H. R. H. the Princess Louise, 3d dt. H. R. H. Prince Frederick Charles of Prussia	Mar. 21, 1911	Oct. 13, 1911	Jan. 16, 1942
Eton, Cambridge	Statesman, Administrator	1892	Lady Evelyn Fitz-Maurice, dt. 5th Marquess of Lansdowne	Aug. 19, 1916	Nov. 11, 1916	May 6, 1938
. . . .	Army	1902	Marie, dt. Hon. Sir Richard Moreton	Aug. 2, 1921	Aug. 11, 1921	June 6, 1935
Eton, Cambridge	Administrator	1892	Hon. Marie Adelaide, dt. 1st Earl of Brassey	Aug. 5, 1926	Oct. 2, 1926	Aug. 12, 1941
Harrow, Cambridge	Lawyer	1912	Roberte de Neuflize, dt. Baron Jean de Neuflize	Feb. 9, 1931	Apr. 4, 1931	Mch. 10, 1956
Glasgow, Oxford	Publisher, Author	1907	Susan Charlotte, dt. Hon. Norman Grosvenor	Mar. 27, 1935	Nov. 2, 1935	Feb. 11, 1940
Eton, Sandhurst	Statesman, Soldier	1904	Princess Alice, dt. Duke of Albany	April 3, 1940	June 21, 1940	Jan. 16, 1957
Harrow, Sandhurst	Army	1931	Lady Margaret Diana Bingham	July 31, 1945	April 12, 1946	June 16, 1969
Toronto, Oxford	Diplomat	1915	Alice Stuart (d. 1950)	Jan. 24, 1952	Feb. 28, 1952	Dec. 31, 1967
Loyola Coll., Laval Univ.	Army	1921	Pauline Archer	Aug. 1, 1959	Sept. 15, 1959	Mch. 5, 1967
Oxford, Univ. of Alta.	Lawyer	1927	Norah Evangeline	April 4, 1967	April 17, 1967	
Valleyfield, U. of Montreal, U. of Paris, McGill U.	Diplomat	1938	Gabrielle Carmel	Oct. 5, 1973	Jan. 14, 1973	

CONFEDERATION (1867)

Profession	Date Married	Wife's Name	Party Connection	Appointed	Resigned	Died	Place of Death
Lawyer	1843 1867	Isabella Clark (d. 1857) Agnes Bernard	Conservative	July 1, 1867	Nov. 6, 1873	1891	Ottawa, Ontario
Stonecutter	1853	Helen Neil (d. 1852) Jane Sym	Liberal	Nov. 7, 1873	Oct. 16, 1878	1892	Toronto, Ontario
Lawyer	1843 1867	Isabella Clark (d. 1857) Agnes Bernard	Conservative	Oct. 17, 1878	June 6, 1891 (Died)	1891	Ottawa, Ontario
Lawyer	1849	Mary Bethune	Conservative	June 16, 1891	Dec. 5, 1892	1893	Montreal, Quebec
Lawyer	1871	Annie Affleck	Conservative	Dec. 5, 1892	Dec. 12, 1894 (Died)	1894	Windsor Castle, England
Journalist	1847	Harriet L. Moore	Conservative	Dec. 21, 1894	April 27, 1896	1917	Belleville, Ontario
Physician	1846	Frances Morse	Conservative	May 1, 1896	July 8, 1896	1915	Bexley Heath, England
Lawyer	1868	Zoe Lafontaine	Liberal	July 11, 1896	Oct. 6, 1911	1919	Ottawa, Ontario
Lawyer	1889	Laura Bond	Conservative	Oct. 10, 1911	July 10, 1920	1937	Ottawa, Ontario
Lawyer	1904	Isabel Cox	Conservative	July 10, 1920*	Dec. 29, 1921*	1960	Toronto, Ontario
Publicist	. .	. . . .	Liberal	Dec. 29, 1921†	Aug. 7, 1930†	1950	Kingsmere, Quebec
Lawyer	. . .	. . . .	Conservative	Aug. 7, 1930	Oct. 14, 1935	1947	Dorking, England
Lawyer	1908	Jeanne Renault	Liberal	Nov. 15, 1948	June 17, 1957	1973	Quebec, Que.
Lawyer	1929 1953	Edna May Brower (d. 1951) Olive Freeman Palmer	Progressive Conservative	June 21, 1957	April 22, 1963	. . .	. . . .
Teacher	1925	Elspeth Moody	Liberal	April 22, 1963	April 6, 1968	1972	Ottawa, Ont.
Law Professor	1971	Margaret Sinclair	Liberal	April 6, 1968	. . . .	. . . .	. . . .

until September 14, 1926. †Reappointed October 15, 1935, and served until November 15, 1948.

DEVELOPMENT OF THE PROVINCES OF CANADA—TABLE I

Province	Origin and Meaning of Name	Area Square Miles	Early Settlements Where	When	By Whom	First Separate Gov't	Entered Confederation
Alberta	In honor of H.R.H., Princess Louise Alberta, dt. of Queen Victoria, wife of marquis of Lorne, governor-general of Canada.	255,285	Ft. la Jonquière (Now Calgary) / Ft. Athabaska	1752 / 1778	Sieur de Niverville / Peter Pond	1882	1905
British Columbia	Devised and chosen by Queen Victoria (1858). "Columbia" on many old maps of this region.	355,855	Nootka	1788 / 1789	Capt. Meares / Martinez	1858	1871
Manitoba	From Indian *Manito-Wabo*, meaning "narrows of the Great Spirit," from wind rushing through the narrows.	251,832	Ft. York (Nelson) / Ft. Saint Charles / Ft. Rouge	1686 / 1732 / 1736	Hudson's Bay Company / } Sieur de la / } Verendrye	1870	1870
New Brunswick	In honor of English royal family, originally of German line of Brunswick-Luneburg.	27,985	Sainte Croix / Port Royal	1604 / 1605	Sieur de Monts / Sieur de Monts	1784	1867
Newfoundland	First called *Terra Nova*, New Land; Newfoundland appears about 1620.	42,734 (Labrador, 110,000)	Ferryland	1638	Sir David Kirke	1728	1949
Northwest Terr's: ** / Keewatin / Franklin / Mackenzie	From geographical location. / Cree for "north wind." / After Sir John Franklin. / After Sir Alexander Mackenzie.	1,309,682	. . . .	. . . . .	. . . .	1876 / 1882 / 1895 / 1895	
Nova Scotia	New Scotland.	21,428	Port Royal (Annapolis, 1710)	1605	Sieur de Monts	1710† 1713‡	1867
Ontario	After Lake Ontario,—Iroquois and Huron for "the beautiful or the great lake."	407,262	Ft. Rouille (Now Toronto) / Ft. Frontenac	1749 / 1673	French traders / Frontenac	1791	1867
Prince Edward Island	In honor of duke of Kent, Edward Augustus, father of Queen Victoria.	2,184	Port la Joie (Charlottetown)	1713	Acadians	1769	1873
Quebec	In Algonquin, Kebec means "narrowing of the waters," referring to narrowing of the Saint Lawrence at the present city of Quebec.	594,434	Tadousac / Quebec	1600 / 1608	Chauvin and Pont-Grave / Champlain	1760† 1763‡	1867
Saskatchewan	From the river Saskatchewan. Cree for "rapid river."	251,700	Ft. Cumberland / Ft. Chipewyan	1774 / 1788	Samuel Hearne / R. Mackenzie	1882	1905
Yukon	From Yukon river. Yukon is an Indian term for "the river."	207,076	Dawson	1896	Gold seekers	1898	

DEVELOPMENT OF THE PROVINCES OF CANADA—TABLE II

Province	Original Territory or District from which Derived	Population Entering Confederation ††	Pop. 1941	Pop. 1951	Pop. 1961	Pop. 1971	* Largest City and Capital
Alberta	Formerly Alberta and part of Athabaska, Saskatchewan, and Assiniboia, districts of original N. W. Territories.	73,022 (1901)	796,169	939,501	1,331,944	1,627,874	Edmonton.
British Columbia	Vancouver island and New Caledonia (British Columbia after 1858) joined in 1866.	36,247 (1871)	817,861	1,165,210	1,629,082	2,184,621	Vancouver. Victoria.
Manitoba	Red River Settlement.	25,228 (1871)	729,744	776,541	921,686	988,247	Winnipeg.
New Brunswick	Part of Acadia; later, county of Sunbury, Nova Scotia.	252,047 (1861)	457,401	515,697	597,936	634,557	Saint John. Fredericton.
Newfoundland	Separately settled for fisheries.	325,000	320,101 (1945)	361,416	457,853	522,104	St. John's.
Northwest Terr's: ** / Keewatin / Franklin / Mackenzie	Prince Rupert's Land and Hudson's Bay Co's Territory.	. . . . . .	12,028	16,004	22,998	34,807	Administered from Ottawa. Land Office at Fort Smith.
Nova Scotia	A portion of Acadia	330,857 (1861)	577,962	642,584	737,007	788,960	Halifax.
Ontario	Formerly Upper Canada, part of old province of Quebec.	1,396,091 (1861)	3,787,655	4,597,542	6,236,092	7,703,106	Toronto.
Prince Edward Island	Formerly Isle Saint Jean, attached to Acadia.	94,021 (1871)	95,047	98,429	104,629	111,641	Charlottetown
Quebec	A portion of "Canada" under French rule before 1760.	1,111,566 (1861)	3,331,882	4,055,681	5,259,211	6,027,764	Montreal. Quebec.
Saskatchewan	From parts of Saskatchewan, Athabaska, and Assiniboia, districts of old Northwest Territories.	91,279 (1901)	895,992	831,728	925,181	926,242	Regina.
Yukon	Part of old Northwest Territories	27,219 (1901)	4,914	9,096	14,628	18,388	Dawson. Whitehorse.

* Where but one name is given, it indicates both the largest city and the capital; elsewhere, the second name is that of the capital. † Military rule. ‡ Province. ** Provisional districts. †† Figures in parenthesis indicate date of census.

AUSTRALIA

The Australian continent was not known to Europeans until after the Portuguese and the Dutch developed trade with the East Indies. The earliest maps of this region of the globe show a blank space where Australia actually lies. But gradually portions of the west coast were sighted and were added piece by piece to the map.

Dutch mariners made the principal additions to the world's knowledge of the continent in the 17th century. But the Dutch never made an attempt to utilize their knowledge either for settlement or for commercial purposes. The most important of the Dutch voyages was that of Tasman, who in 1642 discovered Van Diemen's Land, now called Tasmania. He also discovered New Zealand, but believed it to be part of a great southern continent.

The voyage which directed the attention of the English to the possibilities of Australia was that of James Cook in 1770. Cook discovered the entire eastern coast of the continent. He had with him the botanist, Sir Joseph Banks, who was able to speak with authority on the potentialities of the country.

First Settlements. Prior to the separation of the American colonies from the British Empire, it had been the practice to send convicted persons to that quarter of the globe. But after 1776 that policy was no longer possible. As transportation was the punishment imposed for a long list of offenses, it became necessary to find some other place to which convicts might be sent. The British government determined to use New South Wales for this purpose. The first settlement was made at Port Jackson, where the city of Sydney was founded under the command of Captain Arthur Phillip in 1788.

The settlement at Sydney provided quite sufficient accommodation for the convicts who were sent out from Great Britain, but the activities of French explorers in Australian waters generated the fear that rival settlements would be formed, and this fear led to the establishment of the first subsidiary colonies in other parts of the continent. Tasmania was occupied in 1803. Settlements were founded in what is now the state of Victoria, and in Western Australia in 1827. Fear of French rivalry was the motive in each of these cases.

Exploration and Industry. Meanwhile, the continent was completely mapped. The southern coast was discovered by Captain Matthew Flinders in 1802, and the same navigator was the first to circumnavigate Australia (1803). Flinders also made the first complete map of the continent, and he it was who gave to it the name Australia.

Inland exploration was mainly promoted by the necessity of finding pasture for sheep and cattle. John Macarthur, a military officer with a genius for improving the breed of domestic animals, imported some merino sheep and crossed them with Indian varieties. He produced a sheep bearing a fleece superior to any which British cloth weavers had known before. Sheep breeding became from about the beginning of the 19th century the principal Australian industry. In search of pasture land, explorers found a way over the extremely difficult barrier of the Blue mountains, rising like a wall at the back of Sydney, in 1813. Thence, extending their researches still farther towards the center of the continent, explorers opened up the watershed of the Murray and Darling rivers, and revealed the richness of the territory of Victoria.

The most important of these inland journeys of exploration were those of Oxley, who opened up the regions watered by the Lachlan and the Macquarie (1817-18); of Hume and Hovell, who explored the country south of the Murray to Port Phillip (1824); of Allan Cunningham, who crossed the Liverpool Range and discovered the Darling Downs, thus making possible the settlement of Queensland (1827); of Charles Sturt, who explored the great rivers Darling and Murray (1828–30); of Mitchell,

who found the rich western plains of Victoria (1836); and of J. McDouall Stuart, who crossed the continent from south to north, and set the flag upon the central point of the vast expanse of the interior (1862).

As the first phase of Australian settlement was the convict phase, and the second the pastoral, so gold was the third. Important discoveries of the precious metal were made in 1851-52, at Ballarat and Bendigo. Enormous yields were obtained. In later years the gold discoveries of Western Australia proved to be exceedingly rich. In 1900, one-fourth of the world's gold production came from Australia. During the last half of the 19th century, this industry acted as a powerful magnet for immigration. Subsequently the value of gold production fell as mines were exhausted, but a population base was left which supported a rapid development of industry.

Colonial Government. The form of government was in the beginning necessarily despotic. But the convict system came to an end when the number of free settlers, attracted by the conditions of life in Australia, outnumbered the involuntary exiles. The transportation system was abolished in 1852, but, at the request of Western Australia, was revived for a few years to provide that state with labor.

From first to last, the convict system brought about 150,000 persons to Australia. Many of these were transported for offenses which would be considered comparatively trivial under the more humane criminal laws of a later age. Very many were youths under twenty-one, who were transported under the theory that their removal from a contaminating environment, together with the provision of opportunities for starting life afresh in a new country, would be morally salutary. There were a few thousand political prisoners, victims of the Irish rising of 1798, of the Chartist troubles of the 19th century, and of disturbances connected with the Industrial Revolution; some thousands also were transported under the extremely harsh game laws of the 18th and early 19th centuries.

The total number transported was small, however, in proportion to those who came voluntarily, attracted to Australia by the conditions of life and work in this country, or assisted to immigrate by the governments of the states, or lured by the richness of the gold fields. Demands for self-government were made from about 1820. A popular element was introduced into the government from 1823, and this element was extended from time to time, until, in 1855, the British government resolved to confer full responsible government upon the Australian colonies. They were thus equipped with legislatures elected by the people and with ministries responsible to these legislatures.

The Commonwealth. The six colonies of Australia which existed under responsible government were New South Wales, the oldest of the group, founded 1788; Tasmania, founded 1803; South Australia, founded to demonstrate the soundness of Wakefield's colonization principles in 1836; Victoria, colonized originally by "Squatters," in 1835, but not recognized as a separate colony till separated from New South Wales in 1851; Western Australia, colonized in 1829; and Queensland, which was proclaimed as a separate state in 1859.

These colonies maintained each a separate political existence and often the rivalry between them was acute. However, it was realized by thoughtful men that the separateness of these communities, scattered over a continent consisting of 2,900,000 square miles, was a source of weakness to Australia as a whole, and a federation movement was started quite soon after responsible government was inaugurated. Discussion educated the public as to the gain to be attained by union; and, as the outcome of several tentative efforts, a Federal convention in 1897-98 drafted a constitution which was accepted by the people of all the states, and was passed as an act of the Imperial Parliament in 1900. That act established the Commonwealth of Australia.

Lord Hopetoun (afterward Lord Linlithgow) was appointed the first governor-general of the new commonwealth. In March 1901, the members of the first Parliament under the new constitution were elected, and the Parliament was opened by the Prince of Wales on May 9 following.

Contemporary Australia. The policy of Australia under the Commonwealth has been directed toward (1) controlling immigration from Asian and Pacific areas and promoting immigration from Britain, Canada, and the U.S.; (2) developing Australian industries by means of tariff protection; (3) strengthening the defense of the country; (4) providing for the settlement of differences between capital and labor, by means of a court of conciliation and arbitration; (5) strengthening the ties with the British Commonwealth of Nations.

Australia gave whole-hearted support in World War I. From its first decades the Commonwealth had adopted the policy of building up an Australian-controlled navy. This was now placed under imperial control, while over 300,000 Australian troops fought on the various fronts. The "Anzacs" at Gallipoli won undying fame.

World War II and After. Australia followed Great Britain in declaring war on Germany. A National Security act gave the government almost unlimited control over persons and property for war purposes. Australian troops served in Libya, Greece, and Malaya, and the navy was increased. Equally important was the development of the manufacture of munitions, tanks, and planes. Australia had from the first apprehended danger from Japan, and her declaration of war on December 9, 1941, was followed by redoubled efforts. Australia became a base for American troops. Australian forces participated in the fighting in the Solomons and on New Guinea. After the war, the nation became a member of the Southeast Asia Treaty Organization (SEATO) and made a defensive military pact with the United States in 1951.

Robert G. Menzies was prime minister from 1939 until 1966, except for 1941 to 1949, when the Labor party was in power. Under his leadership, the chief objective in Australia's foreign policy was vigorously pursued—co-operation with the Anglo-Saxon nations to contain Communist China and to avert other threats to the country's integrity. Under the Labor government, social security measures were enlarged, but rising inflation and unemployment caused a major crisis. In 1975, the governor general withdrew the commission of Prime Minister Edward Whitlam, the first time the crown had ever removed an elected prime minister.

NEW ZEALAND

The discovery and the naming of the two islands now included in the self-governing dominion of New Zealand is credited to the Dutch navigator, Tasman (1642). So far as is known, no other white man visited the country until Captain Cook arrived in 1769. He made several later visits and mapped the islands. In 1814, the Reverend Samuel Marsden established a mission in the Bay of Islands. Under this influence, the natives, the Maoris, began rapidly to adopt the outward forms of Christianity. At the same time, however, their intertribal wars were made more destructive through their use of firearms in place of the clubs and spears they had used before the coming of Europeans. It is estimated that their numbers were decreased by one-fourth within the following twenty years. Between 1830 and 1840, a comparatively peaceful period, large numbers of the Maoris accepted Christianity.

Colonization. Systematic emigration from Europe to New Zealand began in 1839. The first company of English settlers reached Wellington in January 1840, and the English government took formal possession of the islands in the same month. In spite of difficulties with the Maoris and with the home government, the colony, under the leadership of the governor, Sir George Grey, made substantial progress during the next ten years. In 1852 the colonists were granted self-government, and in 1856 the first responsible government came into power.

Several years of war with the Maoris followed, and the settlements in the North Island made little progress. At length, about 1871, a policy of conciliation toward the natives was adopted, provision was made for their education, and they were given representation in the colonial parliament. This peaceful policy ushered in a period of advance in industry and public improvements. Meanwhile, agriculture and sheep raising had made great strides in the South Island.

Political Development. The era of political progress for which New Zealand is famous began with the year 1877. Previous to that year, political power had been in the hands of the landholding and professional classes, under a limited franchise. Under the leadership of Sir George Grey, a popular, democratic party brought about the organization of a national system of public education. This has been developed until New Zealand has a national university with four co-operating colleges and a system of public schools in which elementary education is free and compulsory for children from 7 to 14 years of age. In the secondary and the special schools, the payment of fees is required for advanced instruction. The university is an examining body and conducts no courses of instruction.

In 1890, manhood suffrage was adopted, and, in the year 1893, women were given the ballot. The growth of industries other than farming and grazing gave rise to a notable series of legislative acts for the control of land and public utilities, and for the settlement of labor disputes. This legislation attracted world-wide attention. In 1891 the land tax system was adopted, which lays a tax upon the land rather than on improvements. In 1892 the government began the policy of buying large estates and leasing them for long periods in parcels of 2000 acres or less. Arbitration of labor disputes was made compulsory in 1894. Old age pensions were introduced in 1898, and a minimum wage law was passed in 1899. The leader in these liberal policies was Richard Seddon, a Lancashire mechanic, who was premier from 1893 to his death in 1906. The government of New Zealand has owned the railroads since 1870, and the policy of public ownership and operation has been extended to telegraphs and telephones, and to other utilities of public concern, such as coal mines. Co-operative production and marketing are popular and successful in the dominion.

After a period of greater conservatism in social legislation, the Parliament of New Zealand in 1938 provided for health insurance and extended the country's earlier measures of socialism by taking over the steel industry.

New Zealand troops did notable service in World War I in Egypt and at Gallipoli, and on the western front. After the war, the government assisted several thousand returned soldiers to settle on farms. In September 1939 New Zealand declared war on Germany. Like Australia the Dominion feared possible Japanese encroachments. The government introduced conscription of men and property and sent 157,000 men to the imperial army.

INDIA

There is no authentic political history of India previous to the expedition of Alexander the Great into the Punjab in 327 B. C. Seleucus, Alexander's successor in Syria (312–280), maintained a limited authority in the Punjab and established relations with Chandragupta, ruler in the Ganges valley, whose dynasty established Buddhism in India. The

Greek influence left a deep mark upon the art and science of India. In the 7th and again in the 8th century the Moslems invaded northern India, but they were driven out by the Hindus in 750. Their great invasion, led by Sultan Mahmud of Ghazni, Turkish ruler of Afghanistan, occurred late in the 10th century. In the 12th century, the Afghan Moslems rose to power, and, about the beginning of the 13th century, Delhi became the Mohammedan capital of India. In 1398 the great Mongol conqueror, Timur, or Tamerlane, invaded India, and, in 1526, Baber, a descendant of Timur, established there the Mogul Empire, which, enlarged and consolidated by Akbar the Great (1556–1605), lasted until 1857. The consequence of these invasions is that India is peopled by races speaking 222 different languages and practicing the rites of innumerable religious sects.

Beginning of Western Trade. In 1498 India was first visited by Vasco da Gama. From 1500 to 1600 the Portuguese had a monopoly of Indian trade, but they aroused a religious struggle of Christian against Mohammedan, and their power declined. In the beginning of the 17th century the Dutch and English drove the Portuguese entirely from the field, and during the 17th century they were rivals, but gradually the Dutch withdrew from the mainland to the East Indian islands. The French, in the 18th century, secured great influence in southern India, but in 1761 their power was broken.

The British East India Company. The first English trading post was established at Surat (1612–14). For more than a hundred years the British were in India simply as traders, but the decay of the Mogul Empire necessitated military action in self-defense. From the year 1750, a series of conquests by Britain placed nearly all India under their sway. In 1773, by act of the British Parliament, the three provinces, or presidencies of Madras, Bombay, and Bengal were placed under the administration of a governor general, and Calcutta was made the seat of a supreme court of judicature.

India under British Sovereignty. In 1858 the direct sovereignty of India and the powers of government hitherto held by the East India Company were vested in the British crown. From that time the history of India was marked by slow development in industry and agriculture, extension of education, more settled control of the frontiers, and provision for a wider native share in government. Agitation for self-government and for ultimate independence increased in those provinces under direct British rule. The princes of the numerous small states strongly favored continued British suzerainty. In World War I India supported the Empire.

Thereafter pressure for independence was intensified. In 1917 the Montagu-Chelmsford reforms provided a rather shadowy legislature, elected by about 3 per cent of the population. During the decade of 1920–30, native protests took the form chiefly of a noncooperative movement, headed by Mohandas Gandhi. In 1937 several years' work by a British commission resulted in a new constitution, creating a federation still under British control.

During World War II the defense of India was hampered by the refusal of Indian leaders to cooperate, and their demand for immediate independence. At the close of the war the British government, in fulfillment of its promises, set up an interim government to draft a constitution and announced its intention of withdrawing from India by June 1948. Religious differences between the Hindu, or All-India Congress party, and the Moslem League interposed serious obstacles to agreement, but in June 1947 both parties at last accepted a plan for partition into Hindu India and Moslem Pakistan, and the two dominions were proclaimed August 15, 1947. The process of organizing them was marred by religious rioting and by the movement of some eight million refugees between the two countries. In 1948 Mohandas Gandhi was assassinated.

The Republic. Under a constitution adopted in 1950, India became a sovereign democratic republic but remained a member of the Commonwealth of Nations. The president acts on advice of the prime minister, who is thus the most powerful official. The first occupant of this post was Jawaharlal Nehru, leader of the Congress party.

Nehru regarded Pakistan with a hostile eye. He refused to permit an election in Kashmir to determine its adherence to one country or the other, as recommended by the United Nations. Declaring India leader of the neutralist nations, he refused military aid from the United States as a bulwark against Communist China and, when Pakistan accepted such aid, concentrated troops on the Pakistani border. Former French possessions in China were taken over by agreement and the Portuguese colony of Goa was taken by force.

In 1962, China invaded India's northern outposts and routed the Indian defenders. India called on the West and Russia for assistance but did not declare war. The Chinese, however, in 1963 evacuated part of the ground taken. Nehru died in 1964 and was succeeded by Shastri. In the latter's brief administration occurred an inconclusive war with Pakistan over Kashmir. He died after agreeing to a truce negotiated by the Russians. His successor was Indira Gandhi, daughter of Nehru.

Internally, India launched ambitious five-year plans to modernize production with some aid from Russia but much more from the United States. The problems were stupendous—rapidly increasing overpopulation, concentrated land ownership, religious hostility, inertia, and difficulty of communication because of numerous languages. A beginning was made toward introducing methods of birth control.

In June, 1975, Indira Gandhi was accused of election irregularities and her administration was threatened. She declared a state of emergency and assumed wide powers. Censorship was imposed, many people were arrested on political grounds, freedom of speech and assembly were restricted, and the court's authority was diminished. In October, a law was passed allowing the government to suspend the right of habeas corpus and hold prisoners arbitrarily for two years. By 1976, estimates were that some 176,000 dissidents had been jailed.

Before the 1977 parliamentary election Indira Gandhi ended censorship and released political prisoners. Her party lost the election; she lifted the state of emergency and then resigned. Morarji Desai became India's prime minister.

SRI LANKA (CEYLON)

Vijaya, a prince from the valley of the Ganges, invaded Ceylon in 543 B.C. and established a dynasty. The island was called Lanka in early Sanskrit works, but Vijaya called it Sinhala, and the colonists he brought from the neighboring mainland of India took the name of Sinhalese or Singhalese. In the reign of King Tissa (307 B.C.), Buddhism was made the state religion, and the famous sacred bo tree was planted (288 B.C.). After several centuries of conflict with invading Malabars, another notable era in the history of Ceylon began in 1155 A.D. with the reign of Parakrama, famed for the monuments of architecture he left behind him.

In 1505 the Portuguese reached Ceylon, and gradually conquered the coastal lowlands. In 1638 the Dutch invaded the island, and conquered the Portuguese after a 20-year struggle. Both were seeking a monopoly of the cinnamon trade. In 1796 the English took it from the Dutch, desiring mainly the naval base of Trincomalee. The island was ceded to England in 1802. In 1815 the English completed their occupation by conquering the Kingdom of Kandy, in the central highlands. The chief features of recent history have been the rise of the coffee industry, its subsequent fall, and the substitution of tea and rubber. In 1946 the island received a new constitution; and, on February 4, 1948, it became an independent republic.

OTHER COMMONWEALTH MEMBERS

The countries below became members after 1950. See also table of *British Commonwealth of Nations.*

Bangladesh. This former eastern province of Pakistan won the majority of seats in the 1971 election for the Pakistan national assembly. When their demand for greater autonomy was denied, the province declared itself an independent country. Pakistani troops occupied the province and subdued the revolt in bloody fighting. Late that year Pakistan began war with India, whose troops subsequently defeated the occupation forces in Bangladesh. In December, India recognized the independent People's Republic of Bangladesh.

Cyprus. This island in the Mediterranean Sea played a key role in the Bronze Age by reason of its copper mines, its name being the Greek word for copper. The Iron Age saw its decline. Egypt conquered it about 1500 B.C. and subsequently it was ruled by Persia, Greece, Rome, the Moslems, the Crusaders, and Turkey. England annexed it in 1878 and made it a colony in 1914. From the 1930s, Cyprus has been plagued by strife between the Greek inhabitants and the Turkish inhabitants, the former being a four-to-one majority. By agreement among Britain, Greece, and Turkey, Cyprus became an independent republic in 1960. In 1963, proposed changes in that agreement provoked violence between the two factions on the island. During the next ten years, frequent attempts by UN negotiators failed to resolve the conflict and sporadic fighting continued. In 1974, a coup instigated by the ruling Greek military junta attempted to overthrow Cyprian President Makarios. Turkish troops invaded and quickly gained control. In 1975, a Turkish Cypriot Federated State was proclaimed. Makarios' death in 1977 heightened the turmoil in Cyprus; solutions seemed in the distant future.

Gambia. This former crown colony at the extreme western tip of Africa became independent in 1965 as a parliamentary democracy.

Ghana. Freed of colonial status in 1957 and becoming a republic in 1960, Ghana at first followed a pro-Communist policy under the leadership of its first president Nkrumah. His term was extended for life by parliament. In 1966, however, while he was visiting China, a military group seized power. The name Ghana is adopted from a monarchy that ruled the middle Niger region for 1000 years.

Guyana. This former British colony on the north coast of South America was explored by Raleigh in the 1500s. It was ruled alternately by the Dutch, English, and French until treaties of 1814–15 confirmed it as a British colony. About one-third of the population are descendants of fugitive Negro slaves. Most of the remainder are of East Indian descent from laborers imported in the 1880s. Independence was granted in 1966.

Jamaica. Formerly a colony in the West Indies, Jamaica became independent in 1962. The island was discovered by Columbus in 1492 and was under Spanish rule until 1655. The Spanish exterminated the aboriginal Arawak Indians, and Negro slaves were imported. The English took Jamaica by force of arms, and their title was confirmed by treaty in 1670. A charter for trading in slaves made Jamaica one of the world's largest slave markets. Its wealth, based on sugar and slavery, grew apace but suffered after emancipation of the slaves in 1833.

Kenya. A country of eastern Africa, Kenya emerged from colonialism in 1963 and became a republic in 1964. Subject to Arabs from the 8th century and the British from 1887, it was opened by the latter to European settlement in 1903, its climate being suitable. East Indian settlers, however, soon outnumbered the European. Its first constitution after independence made separate constituencies of the different races, but in 1964 the republic left power in the hands of the Negroes, who were vastly in the majority. In 1965, the opposition party disbanded, leaving a one-party government.

Lesotho. This country of southern Africa was transformed from the British protectorate of Basutoland into an independent state in 1966. The population is divided among eight tribes.

Malawi. Formerly the British protectorate of Nyasaland, Malawi, located in south central Africa, was granted independence under a parliamentary democracy in 1964. By popular vote it became a republic in 1966.

Malaysia. This federation of former British dependencies in southeast Asia was formed in 1963. It originally included Singapore, which, with a predominantly Chinese population, withdrew peacefully in 1965. Indonesia waged an undeclared war on it in 1964–66 but without significant result.

Malta. The parliamentary democracy of Malta was granted independence in 1964. By treaty, British military forces were to remain in the island for ten years. Historically, Malta's position in the Mediterranean Sea rendered it a strategic point throughout recorded history. Occupied by the Phoenicians until the 8th century B.C., it was controlled successively by the Greeks, Carthaginians, Romans, Arabs, and Knights of St. John. The latter held it from 1530 to 1798, when Napoleon took it over for France and lost it to England by treaty in 1814. At a critical point in World War II, it was the sole British point of defense in the Mediterranean, having survived over 3000 air raids.

Nigeria. A former British colony, this African country became independent in 1960 under a parliamentary form of government. A 1966 military coup by one tribal group was followed by a counter-coup led by troops of another tribal group. After thousands of Ibo tribesmen were massacred, the eastern part of the country seceded in 1967, calling itself Biafra. A bloody 30-month civil war followed, resulting in the reunification of Nigeria under Gen. Gowon as a compromise head of state. Gowon's government was overthrown in 1975; military rule continued.

Sierra Leone. Acquired by England in 1787 as a home for Negro waifs in London and later used as a sanctuary for slaves rescued from slave ships, Sierra Leone became independent in 1961. It is governed as a parliamentary democracy.

Singapore. This Asiatic island state joined by a causeway to the extreme south of the Malay peninsula was granted self-government in 1957. It joined Malaysia in 1963 and withdrew in 1965. By agreement, Britain retained there its chief naval base in the Far East.

Tanzania. A republic of southeast Africa formed in 1964 from two former British dependencies, Tanganyika on the mainland and the island of Zanzibar. Tanganyika had attained independence in 1961 and Zanzibar in 1963. A one-party socialist state led since the beginning by President Julius Nyerere, Tanzania has been a leader in efforts to end colonial control and to unify Africa.

Uganda. An inland state of eastern Africa, Uganda became independent in 1962 and a republic in 1963. The problem of national unity was complicated by tribal rivalries, four tribes being recognized as monarchies federated with the central government. In 1967, Uganda adopted a republican constitution and the four kingdoms were abolished. In 1971, General Idi Amin seized power in a military coup. Amin's methods of rule have alienated many world governments.

Zambia. Formerly the British protectorate of Northern Rhodesia, Zambia was from 1953 until 1963 a part of the Federation of Rhodesia and Nyasaland. Zambia became an independent republic in 1964, electing Kenneth Kaunda as its first president. Under him, the country began nationalizing foreign-controlled mining interests and other businesses. In 1972, Kaunda signed a new constitution based on one-party rule.

LATIN AMERICA

THE term Latin America is applied to the American countries lying south of the United States because the language and cultures of these countries are mainly of Latin origin—particularly Spanish and Portuguese. This section brings together histories of all these states, including Mexico in North America, the republics of Central America, and the independent countries of the West Indies.

The prehistory of Latin America is much richer than that of North America, although its inhabitants are believed to have come via North America from Asia. While the aborigines of North America had barely passed beyond the hunting stage in their economy when Columbus discovered America, inhabitants of the regions from Mexico southward to Peru had developed advanced arts and skills, enabling them to build roads, erect elaborate buildings, work gold and silver, and establish highly organized political societies. They had no iron, cattle, or horses. In Mexico the Mayans, alone among New World inhabitants, developed a written language and a calendar, which goes back more than 2000 years. See *American Indians*.

After Columbus, the Spaniards quickly conquered the ruling Indian peoples, seeking primarily metallic wealth but also the conversion of the Indians to Christianity. They won control of the West Indies, later disputed with the English, French, and Dutch, and of the mainland from the Rio Grande to the extreme south, except for a portion that later became Brazil. Portugal obtained it. These rulers of Latin America discouraged or forbade immigration from countries other than their own, although Negro slaves were brought in from Africa to work in mines and on sugar plantations. Feudalism long continued to dominate economic and personal relations. Political absolutism died a slow death. Roman Catholicism remained almost the sole religion. The Spanish, however, partly because they were fewer, did not drive out the Indians. They intermarried with them extensively, so that today the Indian strain is predominant in many parts of the continent.

Spanish rule in America lasted 300 years without serious disturbances. But the American and French revolutions, with the decline of Spanish power in Europe, encouraged the spirit of independence throughout all Latin America.

Argentina. The land now called Argentina was first explored in 1516, but no systematic settlement was undertaken until 1580, when Buenos Aires was established. Argentina is an extensive fertile plain (pampas) backed by the Andes Mountains on the west. The Spanish at first occupied only the fringes of the great pampas, where vast herds of cattle maintained themselves, descendants of animals introduced by the earliest settlers. The aboriginal Indians continued to live in the plains. There was little admixture with the European settlers, and Argentina's population is still overwhelmingly of European origin.

Independence. During the next two centuries, immigration was gradual, but many educated liberals fled from oppression in Spain to the colonies on the Plata and the seeds of independence were sown by books and papers smuggled from France and England. In 1776 the Viceroyalty of Buenos Aires was formed including the present states of Argentina, Paraguay, Uruguay, and Bolivia.

In 1816 a congress at Tucuman proclaimed the independence of the United Provinces of Rio de la Plata. But the union was weak, and years of anarchy followed, relieved by the strong and progressive work of Rivadavia, secretary of the government of Buenos Aires, in founding schools, building public works, and promoting commerce. During this time,

however, forces from Argentina aided Chile and Peru to free themselves from Spain, and a war with Brazil resulted in the independence of Uruguay. In 1835 Juan Manuel de Rosas became dictator, and until 1852 his power was absolute. With stern cruelty he maintained a measure of order in Buenos Aires, the other provinces going their own ways, but his tyranny drove many of the industrial and educated classes into exile in Uruguay and Chile. Finally, a concerted effort of men of all the provinces, aided by Brazilian forces, overthrew De Rosas, and in 1853, the Argentine Republic was formed.

A New Period of Progress. Immediately, the old jealousy between Buenos Aires and the other provinces broke out, and personal rivalries of military leaders added to the political confusion. A five years' war with Paraguay drew heavily on the resources of the nation; but the leadership of President Mitre strengthened the national spirit.

From a very early period, Argentina has had a large and influential class of liberal, cultured citizens. Education in all grades has received generous government support. The entire school system was reorganized in 1916.

During the late 19th century Argentina was ruled by conservative landholders, who drove off the Indians and used the great plains to raise cattle, wheat, and corn. Argentina had an extensive trade with England in foodstuffs and the aristocrats of beef supported a truly regal life on their great estates. New immigrants arrived, mostly from Italy and Spain. By the end of the century, demands for wider voting rights were pressed, and in 1912 compulsory manhood suffrage was introduced.

Argentina under the presidency of Irigoyen remained neutral in World War I although German submarines sank Argentine shipping. Neutrality paid off in prosperity. Reforms followed; the government reorganized the university system so as to favor less wealthy students but had its troubles with the rising labor movement.

In 1943 the Army took over and the next year Juan Peron, an army colonel with experience in Italy, became dictator. He organized the workers into a striking force which, allied with the army, kept him in power for a decade. He attempted to remain neutral in World War II but, when it became evident that Germany must lose, Argentina entered the war. Peron was elected president in 1946.

Peron's ambitious projects, which were aimed at making Argentina a world power, bankrupted the country and led to his fall in 1955. The Argentine economy had a slow recovery, plagued by economic, social, and political upheaval. Provisional governments, caretaker governments, nullified elections, and governments verging on dictatorships succeeded each other in rapid succession.

In 1972 Juan Peron returned to Argentina and the following year, 18 years after he was sent into exile, he was again inaugurated as president, with his wife Isabel as vice president. When Peron died in 1974 his wife Isabel succeeded him as president. In 1976 a military junta led by General J. R. Videla ousted Isabel Peron and declared martial law.

Bolivia. The territory included in Bolivia was conquered by Pizarro in 1538. He and his successors subdued the Indians so thoroughly that no uprising occurred until 1780. The usual Spanish policy of compelling the Indians to work in the mines rapidly reduced their numbers. From 1809 to 1824 a bloody struggle for independence was waged, and in the latter year the Spanish army was defeated by a Colombian force under General Sucré. On August 6, 1825 the independence of Upper Peru, as the country was then called, was declared, and the Republic of Bolivia was organized five days later. A constitution, drafted by Bolivar, the Liberator, was adopted in 1826.

Since 1827 the history of Bolivia has been a story of chronic civil war. In that period it has had many presidents and dictators. War with Chile, ended by treaty in 1884, robbed Bolivia of its Pacific seacoast and rich mineral deposits. In 1904, however, by a new agreement, Bolivia obtained access to the coast through Chilean territory and the right to establish customhouses at certain ports. A dispute with Paraguay over title to the Gran Chaco led to a bloody three-year war, which ended in 1935 with Paraguay in possession. Arbitration in 1938 gave Paraguay three-fourths of the disputed territory, reserving to Bolivia her rights of transit to the sea. Despite the fascist leanings of its government following a revolution in 1936, Bolivia broke off diplomatic relations with the Axis powers in 1942 and received aid from the United States in return for its tin. In 1952 a military junta seized the government, making Dr. Paz Estenssoro president. He was ousted in 1964, and the military again took over, headed by Rene Barrientos, who was killed in an air accident in 1969. Bolivia had three presidents in the next two years. The third, Juan Jose Torres, was overthrown in a virtual nationwide civil war in 1971 and was succeeded by Hugo Banzer.

Brazil (bra-zil'). The name of this South American country is derived from a Portuguese word, *braza*, meaning "live coal," in reference to the color of its dyewoods, the first cargo of which was taken to Portugal in 1503 by Amerigo Vespucci. He had been sent by the king of Portugal to take possession of the territory discovered by both a Spaniard, Pinzón, and a Portuguese commander, Cabral, in 1500. Vespucci, in 1503, left a small garrison at a point which he named *Todos os Santos*, "All Saints." Portugal was occupied with her Indian and African trade, however, so the settlement of Brazil was left to private grantees to whom were given large areas, called captaincies, with fifty leagues of seacoast each. Much trouble was encountered in dealing with the natives.

The supposed poverty of Brazil spared her from the commercial rivalries of the next 150 years. In 1649 the Brazil Company of Portugal successfully repelled the encroaching Dutch West India Company. About the beginning of the 18th century, diamonds and gold were discovered in the South and West, and labor was withdrawn from the growing sugar industry, to the detriment of the country. Slaves were, at this period, brought in from Africa.

Independence.—In 1789 an unsuccessful attempt was made to free the country from Portugal. Independence came finally as an indirect result of the French Revolution; for, in 1807, when Napoleon threatened Portugal, the prince regent, afterward King John, with the royal family, fled to Brazil. John opened Brazilian ports and brought in workmen and manufacturers from northern Europe and England. In 1821 he returned to Portugal, leaving his son, Dom Pedro, in Brazil. The latter proclaimed the independence of Brazil in 1822 and became constitutional emperor, but he lost his popularity, abdicated, and returned to Portugal in 1831. In 1840 his son, then fourteen years old, was declared of age, and in the following year as Dom Pedro II took possession of the throne, which he held until 1889. In that year a peaceful revolution exiled the emperor, and a provisional government was set up under Fonseca. In 1891 a national congress proclaimed the United States of Brazil, with Fonseca as first president.

Many difficulties faced the new government, the most serious being the disorder attending the final freeing of slaves, and several attempts were made during the period from 1890 to 1900 to restore the monarchy.

In World War I Brazil declared war on Germany, and her navy co-operated with the United States. In World War II she also declared war, and sent a contingent to the Italian front. During this time Vargas was ruling as a benevolent dictator, since the constitution he proclaimed in 1937 had not been put into effect. In May 1945, he proclaimed an election, to be held the following December, and in this election Gaspar Dutra, a moderate "rightist," was chosen president. Elected again in 1950, Vargas encountered strikes, inflation, and other troubles, and in 1954 he committed suicide. Juscelino Kubitschek, elected in 1956, was followed in 1961 by Janio Quadros, who resigned within a year and was succeeded by Joao Goulart. The latter, leaning toward Communism and helpless before inflation, was driven out in 1964 by Gen. Castello Branco, whom Congress elected to fill out Goulart's term. Congress subsequently extended his term to 1967, when he was succeeded by Artur da Costa e Silva, former war minister. Emilio G. Medici, former chief of the National Intelligence Service, was chosen to replace him in 1969. In 1974 Ernesto Geisel, brother of Brazil's war minister, was inaugurated as president, the fourth military man to hold the office since the armed forces seized power in 1964.

Chile. Central Chile was a part of the Peruvian empire of the Incas which the Spaniards overthrew. Valdivia pacified the civilized area in 1540 but the southern part of the country occupied by the heroic Araucanians resisted until the mid 19th century.

Chile, like Argentina, was a neglected portion of the Spanish Empire. The central portion lies in a series of very fertile valleys in the lofty Andes which run the length of the country. The Spaniards settled down to live off the labor of the Indians as feudal lords in a geographic paradise.

When Napoleon took over Spain (1808) the Chileans, like the other Latin Americans, were ripe for revolt. Spanish troops from Peru repressed overt revolt for a time, but, with the help of the Argentine Jose de San Martin, and the Chilean refugee Bernardo O'Higgins, they achieved independence in 1818. A period of internal revolution followed.

By 1833, control rested securely in the hands of the feudal-type landowning class, which continued to govern under a constitution superficially like that of the United States but with property qualifications for voting. In the war of the Pacific, 1879–84, Chile conquered from Bolivia and Peru desert territory in the north, containing rich nitrate and guano deposits—natural nitrates which contributed much to Chilean prosperity.

In 1920, economic difficulties brought political trouble. Chile's market for fertilizers was undermined by the process discovered and used by the Germans in World War I, whereby nitrates were made from atmospheric nitrogen. About the same time Chile's copper exports came into competition with metal from vast new sources in the Congo, and prices fell sharply. Chilean miners resisted the resulting economic misery by violent action and political force. The result was a new constitution of 1925 which included the social laws connected with the modern industrial state—pensions, minimum wages, social insurance, and the like. President Alessandri was the leader in this move. The world-wide depression of the 1930's, coupled with Chile's special economic difficulties, led to political chaos.

In the 1940's, began a long struggle to raise the standard of living and thus avoid the disasters of a dissatisfied working force. Chile has made valiant attempts to industrialize, to create a fishing fleet, to break up estates, to provide land for family-sized farms. All these efforts have been largely nullified by the birth rate, which creates mouths to feed faster than production can fill them.

As in most Latin American countries, the governments have tended to pay attention chiefly to the cities. The small communities have little power in taxing or spending and are largely indifferent to politics.

In 1970 Salvador Allende became the first freely elected Marxist president in the Western Hemisphere. He began a program of agrarian reform, urban redevelopment, and moved to nationalize foreign-owned banks and companies. His election is regarded as the most significant development in Latin America since Castro's accession in Cuba. In 1973, the Popular Unity government of Allende was overthrown by a military junta. Augusto Pinochet became president and Allende allegedly committed suicide rather than surrender. Pinochet dissolved the national congress, banned all political activities, and suspended most civil liberties.

Colombia. In 1499 Ojeda and Vespucci explored the north coast of Colombia, and, after Balboa's discovery of the Pacific, settlements were rapidly made on the Isthmus of Panama and along the west coast. Until the beginning of the 19th century this territory was a Spanish possession, known as New Granada. In 1810 the colony revolted, become independent in 1819, and joined with Venezuela and Ecuador, under Bolivar, the Washington of South America, to form the Republic of Colombia. This union broke up on the death of Bolivar in 1830. The Republic of New Granada was formed in 1831. Civil wars followed, until, in 1863, eight states formed a federal union as the United States of Colombia. This was changed in 1886 into a centralized republic, with the former "states" as provinces. But this policy was unpalatable to the Liberals. A succession of rebellions and civil wars ensued; the most serious resulted in the independence of the province of Panama.

The issue at stake in this conflict was the policy of the government toward the disposal of the rights of the French canal company in Panama. This company had offered its rights to the United States for $40 million. A new congress, in August 1903, rejected the Hay-Herran treaty, which provided for construction of the canal by the United States. In November, Panama declared its independence, thus taking the canal question out of Colombia's hands. In 1921, the United States Senate ratified a treaty which awarded to Colombia $25 million. In 1930, the first Liberal president since 1886 was elected in the person of Enrique Herrera. By plebiscite in 1957, it was provided that, until 1974, a Conservative and a Liberal president should alternate each four years. In 1970 Misael Pastrana Borrero, Conservative, was elected to a four-year term, the last under the 1957 agreement of party alternation. Alfonso Lopez Michelsen, a Liberal, was elected in 1974.

Costa Rica. A Central American republic lying just north of Panama. The Spanish province of Costa Rica was established in 1540. For 250 years it was reckoned the poorest of Spanish possessions, a condition due to the inroads of Indians and buccaneers. Within the last century it has made great advance in industry and education. Independence of Spanish rule was declared in Costa Rica on Sept. 15, 1821. From 1824 to 1839 it formed part of the Central American union. Since 1839 it has been an independent state. The president is elected for four years. Costa Rica is primarily agricultural, and, by a system of limited holdings, land tenure is almost universal. Country schools provide instruction in rural industry. Daniel Oduber Quiros was elected president in 1974.

Cuba (kū′bȧ). Discovered by Columbus in 1492, the island of Cuba was first settled by the Spanish at Baracoa. Rich in resources and regarded as the "Key of the New World," Cuba was for centuries in constant danger from pirates. Havana was burned in 1528 and in 1556. In 1762, the English took Havana, but the Treaty of Paris in the next year restored it to Spain.

The early 19th century was a period of prosperity in the island, and the Cubans remained loyal to Spain, while other colonies fell away. But, as soon as the great value of her fertile soil was apparent, Cuba began to feel the strong impact of Spanish policy. The captains general were, by the decree of 1825, given absolute power over the lives and property of Cubans. From the rebellion of 1829, through the slave insurrection in 1844 and the Ten Years' war (1868–78), to 1895, the story of Cuba is one of revolts and reprisals.

War with Spain.—The insurrection begun in 1895 gained formidable proportions by 1898. The United States battleship *Maine*, while on a visit, was blown up in Havana harbor, February 15, 1898, and, on April 19, the Congress of the United States adopted resolutions declaring Cuba independent. War with Spain began at once. Cervera's Spanish fleet was destroyed at Santiago de Cuba, July 3, and Santiago and its large army were surrendered on July 17. The leading military events of the war, so far as Cuba was concerned, were the fights at El Caney and San Juan, the battle at Santiago, and the destruction of Cervera's fleet. From 1898 to 1902, the island was under United States military governors. Financial reforms were introduced, a free school system was organized, the island was freed from yellow fever.

Independence.—A constitutional convention assembled in November 1900 and adopted a constitution providing for a republican form of government. Thereupon, the United States Congress authorized the transfer of the government to the people of Cuba but subject to the Platt amendment, a treaty dated May 20, 1902, providing for American intervention in case of civil disorder, American occupation of certain naval stations, and prohibition of treaties impairing Cuban independence.

The country is largely dependent on a single crop, sugar. Production was carried on in large estates under semi-feudal conditions. The United States government intervened five times in all, ruling through provisional governors. In 1934, the Platt amendment was abrogated by the American government. In 1933, Fulgencio Batista, chief of staff of the army, rose in power and was president from 1940 to 1944. In 1952, he ousted the elected president and governed until the end of 1958, when he fled the country before the power of guerrilla forces led by Fidel Castro.

Communist Dictatorship.—Castro, turning on the United States as the supporter of Batista, nationalized the industries, expelled Americans, and promised a bright future under revolutionary social and economic reforms. The United States cancelled its sugar purchases and placed an embargo on trade. Cuba's dearth of resources opened the way for Russian assistance. This was supplied in huge amount, particularly in weapons. Money was supplied also to spread Castro's type of communism in Latin America. In 1961, an attempt by Cuban refugees, with some American aid, to invade Cuba was defeated by Castro at the Bay of Pigs.

When it was learned by reconnaissance in 1962 that Cuba had long-range missiles capable of carrying atomic warheads, the American president, Kennedy, with full support of the Organization of American States and NATO powers, imposed a blockade and, by threat of atomic war, compelled Russia to remove the missile installations.

Dominican (dȯ-mǐn′ǐ-kȧn) **Republic** or **Santo Domingo** (sän′tō dȯ-mǐng′gō). A state formed in 1844 by separation of the Spanish or eastern section of the island of Haiti from the Republic of Haiti. In 1861 Spain took possession of her former colony, but in 1863 she gave it up in the face of a revolt. The republic has since maintained a troubled existence. In 1907 an agreement between the Dominican

Republic and the United States was ratified, under which the latter undertook to collect the customs revenues, assist the Dominican government to maintain peace, and act as intermediary between the republic and its foreign creditors. In 1916, after a series of revolutionary outbreaks, American marines were landed on the island in force, and United States naval and marine officers took charge of the executive posts of the government. Toward the end of 1922, the military governor installed a provisional native government. In 1925 the United States forces were withdrawn, but customs were to be collected by an American-appointed commissioner until the Dominican debts were paid.

The United States military government left a constitutionally elected government behind it when it withdrew. In 1930 Raphael Trujillo was elected president and remained in charge of the country as dictator. After 31 years of oppression he was assassinated May 27, 1961.

The elimination of the dictator opened the door to a struggle among successors and an upheaval of popular aspiration. A succession of caretaker governments held on until a constitutionally elected president, Juan Bosch, was installed in December 1962. Bosch was responsive to the demand for reform but proved too weak to control the opposing groups, one demanding expensive social services and the other fearing the loss of their advantageous position. An army group displaced him less than a year after he took office. In April 1965, a revolt was launched allegedly to restore him to office, although he did not participate but left the country. Fearing a repetition of the Cuban episode of 1958, when Castro seized power and then turned to Communism, the United States intervened to stop the fighting and referred the matter to the Organization of American States. The latter voted to step in and sent troops to keep order until a legal election could be held. Under a new constitution, Joaquin Balaguer was elected president in 1966 and re-elected in 1970 and 1974.

Ecuador (ĕk′wȧ-dôr′). After the Spanish conquest of the Inca dominions, the kingdom of Quito remained under Spanish rule from 1533 to 1822. It achieved its independence by the battle of Pichincha, May 22, 1822. The territory was incorporated into the Republic of Colombia, on the disruption of which, in 1830, it became an independent republic under the name of Ecuador. But a series of civil broils among rival political leaders and wars with neighboring states ensued, lasting, almost without intermission, for more than twenty years. Since 1850 the political struggles have been continuous and bitter. Outstanding features have been the conservative dictatorship of Garcia Moreno, 1860-75; and the Liberal ascendancy of Alfaro, 1895-1911, during which the church was disestablished. A new constitution was adopted in 1945. The first conservative-oriented administration in 61 years was that of Enriquez, elected in 1956. Velasco Ibarra was elected president in 1960, but a military group took control from 1963 to 1966. After an interim government until 1968, Velasco again was elected president. He suspended the constitution in 1970 and the military party regained control in 1972.

French Guiana. An overseas department of France on the Atlantic coast of South America east of Dutch Guiana. The first settlement made by the French at Cayenne in 1636 was abandoned in 1653. Ten years later a new company took over the venture, but development was slow in the face of Portuguese attacks. Complaints about the deadly effects of the climate made by political prisoners sent to the colony late in the 18th century gave the place an evil reputation. The English and Portuguese seized the colony in 1809, but it was restored to France in 1815. From 1854 to 1946 Guiana had a notorious penal colony for habitual criminals and those sentenced to hard labor. In this period the worst offenders were confined to Devil's Island.

Guatemala. The Central American republic which borders Mexico on the south. From 1524 to 1821 it was a Spanish possession. After a brief period of union with the Mexican empire, its independence of all powers was declared in 1823, and a union was effected with the other new republics of Central America. In 1839 Guatemala seceded from this union and assumed the name Republic of Guatemala on March 21, 1847. Its history has been marked by a series of long dictatorships: Carrera, 1842-65; Cabrera, 1898-1920; and Ubico, 1931-44. The constitution of 1945 provided for democratic rule and the socialist Jacobo Arbenz was elected president. His wide reforms brought his downfall in 1954 when Castillo Armas, with U.S. help, took power. He was assassinated in 1957 and military juntas ruled until 1965. The following year, Cesar Mendez was elected president under a new constitution, but constitutional guarantees were suspended in 1968. Elections were held in 1970 and 1974.

Hispaniola (Haiti). This island was discovered and named Santo Domingo by Columbus in 1492. The inhabitants were rapidly exterminated by warfare and by the heavy labor imposed by their Spanish masters, who soon began to import Negroes from Africa. French adventurers occupied part of the island early in the 17th century, and the Treaty of Ryswick (1697) assigned the island to France. In 1789, the freedmen of the island began a movement for equal political rights. The French National Assembly granted their request, but a struggle ensued with the landlords, aided by the English.

At this juncture, Toussaint L'Ouverture took command of the freedmen's forces and drove English and Spanish alike from the island. The French government made him governor. Later, at Napoleon's orders, he was deposed and at length taken prisoner to France. In 1804, Haiti, under General Dessalines, proclaimed its independence. In 1844 the Spanish section of the island set up a separate government, as the Dominican Republic. The later history of Haiti has been a long series of rebellions and revolutions. In 1915, violent disturbances led to intervention by the United States. Under a treaty of that year, the control of customhouses and of a native constabulary, to continue for 10 years, later increased to 20, was given to the United States. Civil government was restored in 1930; the country had prospered under American control, but disliked it. Four years later American personnel was withdrawn with the exception of a fiscal representative. Constitutions were promulgated in 1950 and 1957, but government continued to be constitutionally irregular. In 1957 Dr. Duvalier became president. In 1964 he promulgated a constitution which made him president for life. When he died in 1971, his son Jean-Claude Duvalier succeeded him as president for life.

Honduras. This republic is the second largest of the Central American states. On its shores, near the present Cape Honduras, Columbus made a landing in 1502. The conquest of the country was completed by Cortés, who came there from Mexico in 1525. For three centuries the land suffered the usual fate of exploitation under Spanish rule. In 1821, after a successful revolt, Honduras became a part of the Mexican empire. It joined the Central American Confederation in 1823, and became independent in 1839. From 1849 to 1863, it shared in a union with Salvador and Nicaragua. The later history of the republic has been marked by frequent revolutions; those of 1910-11 were the occasion of intervention by the United States. The United States intervened also at the time of a threatened revolution in 1934; acted as a mediator in a boundary dispute with Guatemala in 1928; and in 1937 in a similar dispute with Nicaragua. A new constitution was adopted in 1957. Dr. Jose Ramon Morales was elected president but was deposed. Gen. Lopez Arellano was made president in 1965. In 1971 Ramon Ernesto Cruz was elected president. Former President Lopez, who was not eligible for reelection in 1971, seized power in a bloodless coup in 1972. Since then government has been by decree. A military junta deposed Lopez in 1975.

Mexico. Ancient Mexican tradition tells of the passage of numerous tribes from the north to the south across the country and of the establishment of powerful states by some of these peoples. In this shadowy procession the accomplishments of two tribes, the Toltecs and the Aztecs, stand out boldly. The Toltecs, in the course of their migrations, are said to have reached Tulacingo, a little north of the City of Mexico, early in the 8th century. They appear to have been a commercial people who built great cities. Apparently, their government extended its authority over a large territory. Other kindred races shared the land of Mexico with the Toltecs, and all were skillful workers in textiles and metals. They possessed elaborate religious systems, the ceremonies of which centered around many vast temples.

The Aztecs.—After some 400 years, disaster in the shape of civil war and disease overtook the Toltecs. Their traditions and culture were preserved by the Texcocan people, whose city, Texcoco, situated on the lake of the same name, became the most famous center of culture in the later Aztec empire. In government, the Aztecs were the real successors of the Toltecs. They established their capital of Tenochtitlan, or Mexico, "the place of Mexitli," their war god, in the 14th century. The superior ability of their kings brought all central Mexico under the Aztec authority. It was this empire, ruled over by Montezuma (Moctezuma) II, that the Spanish adventurers met with in the beginning of the 16th century.

Cortés, led on by a dream of vast wealth, landed at Vera Cruz in 1519 and started on his daring march toward the Aztec capital. On the way, he recruited a native army from various states tributary to the Aztecs and contrived to so impress the emperor, Montezuma, that he was received into the royal palace. In 1520 he made Montezuma his prisoner. The death of the monarch and the desecration of their shrines roused the Mexicans to an attack on the little band of Spaniards. For a time Cortés and his followers were in desperate straits, but they rallied, and, on August 13, 1521, they captured the City of Mexico. From that event dates the Spanish rule in Mexico, which continued to the year 1821.

Mexico under Spanish Rule.—The governors and viceroys of New Spain gave to Mexico a government which, in its tyranny, was not very different from the system to which they had been accustomed. The zeal of the churchmen stamped out the horrible practices that had attended the old Aztec worship; but, unfortunately, the system of exploiting the natives destroyed much that was valuable in their ancient culture. Mexico, however, became the most prosperous and progressive of Spain's colonies. The government encouraged settlement, built roads and harbors, and established schools and a university. But the restriction of trade and agriculture, to avoid all competition with Spain, and the enslaving of the natives were evils that far outweighed the good in Spanish government.

Independence.—The revolt which led to Mexican independence was really opened by the patriot priest, Hidalgo, of Dolores, in 1810. He was defeated and executed, but, in 1821, under General Iturbide, the Spanish power was finally broken. For a brief period Iturbide ruled as emperor. Then followed many years of turmoil, during which the general, Santa Anna, exercised a predominant influence. During his ascendancy, Texas was lost in 1836, and in the war with the United States (1846–47) New Mexico and California were also lost.

The evils of constant internal warfare were overshadowed for a time when, in 1861, England, France, and Spain sent a fleet to Vera Cruz to compel a settlement of Mexico's foreign debt. This was followed by the French military expedition which placed Maximilian on the throne as emperor of Mexico. Diplomatic warning from the United States, in support of the Monroe Doctrine, moved France to withdraw her troops. Maximilian was captured by revolutionary forces and executed.

The Presidency of Diaz.—The next important period in Mexican history is that covered by the administration of Porfirio Diaz. Except for the presidency of Gonzales (1880–84), Diaz ruled Mexico as a sort of benevolent despot from 1876 to 1911. Diaz reformed the government, introducing an adequate tax system with modern methods of accounting which largely prevented dishonesty among officials. He encouraged public improvements, railroads, and manufactures, and developed the educational system of the country. But numerous abuses, incident to long holding of power by a small group of men, led to severe criticism and active opposition to the Diaz régime. He was compelled to resign in 1911.

Revolution and Reform.—A period of disorder in Mexico was ushered in by the withdrawal of Diaz. Rival leaders kept the country in a state of civil war. The presidency of Madero was brief. His successor, Huerta, assumed a defiant attitude toward the United States over a demand for reparation for the arrest of American sailors at Tampico in 1914. This led to an attempt at mediation by the "A B C powers," Argentina, Brazil, and Chile, which produced no result. Meanwhile, various revolutionary and bandit forces were active, chiefly those of Carranza and Villa. Raids by the latter's troops into American territory led to the sending of a punitive expedition into Mexico under General Pershing in 1916.

A constituent assembly, in 1917, directed by Carranza, ushered in a new epoch for Mexico. It radically revised a former constitution dating from 1857. The earlier constitution had decreed the separation of church and state. The new one sought to make the separation effective by nationalizing all ecclesiastical property, limiting the number of priests, abolishing monastic orders, and forbidding public religious demonstrations. It provided also for expropriating large landed estates to be divided among small farmers or given to communal villages.

Enforcement of the constitution awaited the presidency of Obregon in 1921 and of his successor Calles, in 1924. Calles, though in retirement after 1928, wielded the real power until exiled by President Cardenas in 1936.

The land program was the first to be put into operation. Then in 1926 the laws against the church began to be enforced, arousing intense bitterness. The government wished to nationalize church property and secularize education. A "Six-Year Plan," looking toward a cooperative economic system, was adopted in 1934. In March 1938, Cardenas announced the expropriation of all oil properties owned by foreign companies, which had defied the new laws. Gustavo Diaz Ordaz became president in 1964 and was succeeded in 1970 by Luis Echeverria Alvarez. Under him, Mexico asserted its independence from economic ties to the U.S. and became associated with the European Economic Community. In 1976, Echeverria's finance minister, Jose Lopez Portillo, won the presidential election.

Nicaragua (*nĭk'ȧ-rä'gwȧ*). The largest Central American republic. The coast of Nicaragua was discovered by Columbus in 1502. Until 1821 the country was a Spanish dependency, but in that year it declared its independence. It formed part of the

United Provinces of Central America from 1823 to 1839, when it again assumed independence. Nicaragua was the scene of constant war until 1860 when William Walker, a self-proclaimed dictator, was shot. Then followed a long period of peace, broken only in 1893 by a factional struggle for the presidency. In 1909 Zelaya, president since 1894, was forced to resign. From 1909 to 1933, U.S. attempts to maintain order resulted in constant interventions, opposed by local factions. In 1916, the U.S. was given the right to build an interocean canal. Since 1963, government officials have been directly elected for 4-year terms by secret ballot. After the Constituent Assembly started its discussions on a new Constitution in 1972, Anastasia Somoza Debayle, president since 1967, resigned, yielding power to a triumvirate which ruled until 1974. In that year, Somoza was again elected president.

Panama (*păn'ȧ-mä'*). Since 1513, when Balboa discovered the Pacific Ocean, Panama, the link between North and South America, has been of great importance as a possible trade route. This made its union with Colombia, during both the Spanish era and later, very insecure. In 1855, Panama was made a self-governing state dependent upon Colombia. It gained its independence in 1903, and immediately negotiated a treaty with the U.S. for the construction of the Panama Canal. In 1964, when students rioted over display of flags in the Canal Zone, both diplomatic relations and negotiations for a new treaty with the U.S. were ruptured; in 1967, three new treaties were negotiated but not ratified by the two countries. In 1968, a military junta ousted Arias and suspended the constitution. A new constitution was approved in 1972 and Omar Torrijos was voted military ruler for six years.

Paraguay (*păr'ȧ-gwā*). The territory included in this South American republic was first explored by Sebastian Cabot in 1526. A fort was built on the site of the present capital city of Asunción in 1536. The most notable feature of the Spanish period is the management of the country by the Jesuits from 1609 to 1768. Their mission communities, or *reductions*, were centers of education for the Guaranies, or native Indians. After the overthrow of the Spanish government in 1811, the state was governed by a triumvirate until 1816, when José Gaspar Francia made himself dictator. He ruled until 1840, maintaining a policy of national isolation. Carlos López established another dictatorship in 1844. He was succeeded by his son, Francisco López, whose territorial ambition plunged Paraguay into a war with Argentina, Brazil, and Uruguay. When the war closed in 1870, Paraguay had lost nearly half a million of its population. Following a war with Bolivia over the Gran Chaco, in 1932-35, Paraguay received 70 per cent of the disputed area under an arbitration award in 1938. Alfredo Stroessner, president since 1954, was re-elected in 1973.

Peru (*pĕ-rōō'*). A republic on the west coast of South America. Authentic history of this country begins with the coming of the Spaniards under Pizarro in 1531. They found the land of the Incas engaged in a war between rival chiefs and took advantage of this situation to establish Spanish authority. The conquerors at once began to seize vast quantities of gold and silver and to enslave the natives for work in the mines.

After the first few years of Spanish control, no serious uprising of the Indians occurred until 1780. This rebellion was crushed with great cruelty. The Viceroyalty of Peru included at first all of Spanish South America, but in 1718 New Granada was separated from it, and in 1776 the Viceroyalty of Rio de la Plata was formed, including most of Argentina, Paraguay, Uruguay, and Bolivia.

Independence.—A movement for separation from Spain was started in 1820 under the leadership of General San Martin. Independence was declared at Lima, July 28, 1821. After several years of conflict, the Peruvians, led by General Bolivar,

succeeded in defeating the Spanish forces. A constitution was adopted in 1828.

A dispute over the possession of the rich mineral territory of Tarapaca and the provinces Arica and Tacna brought on war with Chile in 1879. The Peruvians were defeated, Chile annexed Tarapaca and Peru ceded Tacna and Arica to Chile for ten years. In 1929 Tacna was assigned to Peru and Arica to Chile.

Recent political history has consisted largely of revolutions, with the dictatorships of Leguia (1919-30) and Benavides (1933-39). President Bustamante y Rivero was deposed in 1948 by a military junta. Turmoil ensued, but in 1956 free elections were held. After further turmoil in 1963, Fernando Terry was made president.

By 1968, a military junta permitted new elections and Terry, a moderate, again became president. However, the economy continued to decline and a junta headed by Gen. Velasco seized power and nationalized U.S. oil properties. Velasco was deposed in 1975 by Gen. Francisco Morales.

Salvador, El (*säl'vȧ-dōr'*). The smallest and most thickly populated of Central American republics. In El Salvador, as in Guatemala, the native Indian blood still predominates. From 1524 until 1821 El Salvador was part of the vice-royalty of Guatemala. Following union with Mexico and with the other Central American states, it became independent in 1839. It is largely agricultural, depending heavily on coffee with its uncertain market. It has therefore been subject to severe economic dislocations, which in turn caused political crises. A liberal constitution was adopted in 1950, based on universal suffrage. It was abolished in 1962 by army leaders who had assumed power in 1960. Col. Adalberto Rivera became president in 1962. Under Rivera a new constitution was established, income taxes were instituted and the currency stabilized. Col. Fidel Sanchez was president from 1967 to 1972. In 1969 El Salvador waged a brief war with Honduras. Mediation by the Organization of American States helped to end the fighting and in 1970 a demilitarized zone was established. In 1972 Arturo Armando Molina was elected president for five years.

Surinam. Formerly Dutch Guiana, Surinam lies just east of Guyana. It was first settled by the English in 1652, but in 1667, by the Treaty of Breda, it was transferred to the Dutch. By the same treaty, New Amsterdam (New York) passed to the English. Surinam gained independence in 1975.

Uruguay (*ū'rōo-gwā*). This South American republic lies east of the Uruguay river and north of the river Plata. The district was known in Spanish times as the *Banda Oriental*, and the official title of the state is *Republica Oriental del Uruguay*, or "Eastern Republic of Uruguay." The native Indians prevented settlement by Europeans until 1624, when the first permanent colony was founded on the Rio Negro. The Portuguese claimed the territory and made numerous settlements, but they were compelled to give way to the Spaniards.

Independence.—An English fleet captured the city of Montevideo in 1807 but gave it up after the failure of their attack on Buenos Aires. The people of Uruguay joined the Argentinians in their revolt against Spain in 1810, and the Spanish forces were driven from Montevideo in 1814. Brazil took advantage of Uruguayan weakness following this struggle and annexed the country. A number of patriotic leaders took refuge in Buenos Aires, watching for an opportunity to drive the Brazilians out. Their opportunity came in 1825, and by 1828 the Brazilian forces were finally defeated. The republic was organized in 1830. By a constitutional amendment adopted in 1951, which abolished the presidency, executive power was vested in a bipartisan national council of 9 men. In 1966 Uruguay returned to the presidential system. Juan Maria Bordaberry began a five-year term in 1972.

Venezuela (*věn'ĕ-zwē'là*). A South American republic lying east of Colombia and bordering the Caribbean Sea. The name, meaning "little Venice," was given to the country probably on account of the pile dwellings built by the natives on Lake Maracaibo, which suggested Venice to the early explorers. These natives were living in a savage state when Columbus sailed along the coast in 1498. Settlers were very early attracted to the coast islands by the pearl fisheries, and by 1520 several Spanish colonies had been established on the mainland by Franciscan and Dominican monks. In 1731 most of the territory now known as Venezuela was placed under the authority of a captain general and all of it was so governed after 1777.

Independence.—The first serious revolt against Spanish rule occurred in 1797, but it failed, as did others in the first decade of the 19th century. A Venezuelan congress met and declared independence on July 5, 1811. Several years of intermittent conflict between republican and royalist forces ensued, and it was not until Oct. 8, 1823 that the royalists finally surrendered. During this period, Simon Bolivar, a young Venezuelan aristocrat, launched his great scheme for a Colombian republic, in which Venezuela was included. Venezuela withdrew from the union in 1829, and in 1830 formed an independent republic with its capital at Caracas.

Political Difficulty.—After some years of peace, civil war broke out in 1846 between the Liberal and Conservative parties, which lasted almost continuously until 1870. Since that time several revolutions have marked the transfer of power from one party or dictator to another. Slavery in the republic was abolished in 1854. Two disturbing incidents in the later history of Venezuela took on international importance. The long-standing boundary dispute with Great Britain reached a critical stage in 1886, when the British fortified the mouth of the Orinoco. Settlement by arbitration was secured, at the insistence of the United States, in 1899. The despotic conduct of Cipriano Castro, who secured control of affairs as president in 1900, brought on a blockade of Venezuelan ports by Germany, England, and Italy in 1903, to force payment of Venezuelan indebtedness in Europe. This matter was submitted to the Hague Tribunal and settled in favor of the European claimants in 1904.

Recent Events.—In line with nearly a half century of dictatorships, including particularly those of Gomez and Contreras, was the ten-year rule of Marcos Perez Jimenez, which was overthrown by a military junta in 1958. Chosen at a regular election in that year was Romulo Betancourt. Despite efforts to overthrow him financed from Cuba, he was succeeded in 1964 after a regular election by Raul Leoni. Betancourt introduced agrarian reforms, raised taxes to improve education, and set up a government oil company to compete with foreign oil companies, the aim being to raise the standard of living and combat inequities. Carlos Andres Perez began a five-year term as president in 1974. He had been the candidate preferred by foreign oil firms. Perez did not feel it urgent to recognize Cuba as his predecessor, Rafael Caldera, had attempted to do.

WORLD HISTORY

The following section brings together accounts of the origin and progress of existing sovereign states not previously considered, as well as accounts of ancient and medieval states and countries. Topics of such particular historical importance and interest as to demand special treatment are discussed further on in the Dictionary of World History. These include accounts of parties, treaties, alliances, congresses, and especially such notable events as affected at once the history of several countries.

There are several additional sections designed for maximum assistance to the user. Immediately after the alphabetic account of countries referred to above is a dictionary of ancient cities that history has buried, from Jericho to Pompeii. A section on Peoples of the World sets forth what is known of man's prehistoric ancestors and the divisions of mankind on the basis of physical and other characteristics. Besides extensive articles on World War I and World War II there is a chart of World History.

The political natures and the governmental organizations of existing states are discussed in the department of Government. Geographical characteristics and relations of countries, which so notably affect the history of nations, will be found in the department of Geography, while, for commercial and industrial facts and conditions which help to determine the course of history, the reader is referred to the department of Economics.

ABYSSINIA (ETHIOPIA)

Abyssinia (*ăb'ĭ-sĭn'ĭ-à*) was, until 1936, one of the three independent states of Africa, the others being Egypt and Liberia. In that year it was conquered by Italy and made an Italian colony in a freshly proclaimed New Roman Empire. The official title, Ethiopia, reverts to the name of the country of which it anciently formed a part, the modern name Abyssinia being a corrupt Portuguese form of the Arabic word *habash* or *habeshi* meaning "mixture," applied in reference to the diverse tribes of the country. Abyssinia had never been subject to any foreign power until its conquest by Italy. Early traditions and some features of the language, known as Amharic, indicate contact with the Jews, and the Queen of Sheba is supposed to have ruled the land in Solomon's time. In the 4th century, Christianity was introduced, and a bishop, called in the Abyssinian tongue, *Abuna Salamah*, "our father of peace," was consecrated by the patriarch of Alexandria. This original Coptic church rite has been maintained. The abuna is appointed by the Coptic church at Alexandria and shares authority with the native head of the monastic orders.

In the 6th century, the Abyssinians conquered the Yemen, a district of Arabia on the Red Sea, opposite Abyssinian territory, and ruled it as a province for 60 years until it was lost to the Mohammedans, shutting off Abyssinia from the outer world. Up to the 19th century Abyssinia was known only through a few explorers. An English punitive expedition in 1868 left it unchanged. An Italian attempt at conquest was defeated in 1896. Abyssinia became a member of the League of Nations in 1923, but League protests and attempted sanctions did not prevent the Italian conquest in 1936.

Prior to the Italian conquest, the government of Abyssinia was feudal, with the emperor, or negus, at the head and governors in charge of the nine provinces. Menelek, who reigned from 1889 to 1913, was one of the strongest rulers. Under his authority, boundary treaties were concluded with England, a bank was established, a line of railroad between the Gulf of Aden and his capital, Addis Ababa, was begun (completed in 1917). Haile Selassie became emperor in 1928. He took refuge in England in 1936, but, in the early months of 1941, English expeditions overcame the Italians and restored Haile Selassie.

Under his rule the country advanced economically and technologically, but the progress was slow. Health and educational standards were greatly improved, and foreign agricultural experts helped to modernize farm production. Haile Selassie held almost complete control until a military junta led by Gen. Teferi Benti ousted him in 1974. Many of the emperor's supporters were executed and Selassie died in 1975.

AFGHANISTAN

Afghanistan (*ăf-găn'ĭ-stän'*), a small Asiatic country, called by the natives Khorassan, lies between Iran and western Pakistan. It was conquered by Alexander the Great in the 4th century B.C. In the succeeding centuries this land was the prey of many conquerors. Islamic conquests were responsible for establishment of their religion in the region. Sometimes existing as a group of petty states, sometimes the center of great empires, and at other times dismembered among rival monarchies, Afghanistan first attained an independent status about the middle of the 18th century under Ahmed Shah. This status was precariously maintained, thanks in part to the rivalry of the Russian and British empires. In 1838, the British intervened to combat Russian influence with the Afghan ruler Dost Mohammed. The latter was deposed but, after ten years of conflict, returned to the throne on a basis friendly to the British.

In 1901, the British government acknowledged the independence of Afghanistan, which was reaffirmed by definite treaty in 1921. After World War II, Russia made territorial demands on Afghanistan but, under pressure of western powers, settled for a minor boundary rectification. A process of westernization, at times resisted with violence, had been going on for two decades. In 1952, a five-year plan for economic development was announced, and this was succeeded in 1962 by a second such plan. Many new manufacturing industries were established, partly by the government and partly by private investment, some of it from abroad. Russia and the United States granted assistance in this program. In 1973, a military coup led by Mohammad Daoud overthrew King Zahir Shah. The constitution was abolished and Daoud became head of state, ruling by decree.

ALBANIA

A part of the Turkish Empire until 1912, Albania received independence as a result of the Balkan wars. After a declaration of its independence on November 28, the separate existence of the Albanian government was approved on December 20 by a conference of ambassadors held in London. An international commission was appointed to control the Albanian finances for a period of ten years. The crown was accepted by Prince William of Wied. He arrived in Durazzo, then capital of Albania, on March 7, 1914, but, at the outbreak of World War I, he left the country.

On June 3, 1917, Albania was proclaimed independent under Italian protection, and its complete independence was recognized on July 2, 1920. From 1925 to 1928 Albania was a republic. In 1928 its president, Ahmed Beg Zugu, became king, under the title of King Zog. In April 1939 Italian troops invaded Albania and annexed it. King Zog fled. Albania was invaded by the Greeks, and regained by the Germans, but popular resistance continued, and by the end of 1944 the Germans were driven out. In 1945 a provisional government was established under Enver Hoxha. The Communists, gaining control, proclaimed a republic in 1946.

ALSACE-LORRAINE

Alsace-Lorraine (*ăl-săs' lô'răn'*) is the name applied to the combined portions of Alsace and Lorraine, which, after the war of 1870, the German government organized under a single imperial administration. The cession secured by Germany included all of the historic French province of Alsace, except the district around Belfort, and about one-fourth of the old province of Lorraine, a district rich in iron and including the fortified city of Metz.

Until their incorporation in the kingdom of France, the histories of these provinces had been quite distinct. The name Lorraine is derived from Lotharingia, the kingdom of Charlemagne's grandson Lothair. French Lorraine represented a district known in early medieval times as Upper Lorraine, which had been separated from Lower Lorraine— now part of Belgium and the Netherlands—in the middle of the 10th century. Though tributary to the Holy Roman Empire, Upper Lorraine became more and more closely related to France. Ruled by the dukes of Lorraine until the 18th century, it was then for a time in the possession of Stanislas, ex-king of Poland. At his death in 1766, it passed under the sovereignty of France.

Alsace, a territory lying in the upper Rhine valley, has been, throughout its history, disputed territory. The Romans, on entering Gaul, found this district inhabited by Celtic tribes. The Celts in time were supplanted by the Teutons, and the whole territory gradually came under German sway. From the 7th century, Alsace was governed by petty princes and other dignitaries, later by the dukes of Swabia, and finally by the Habsburgs. Between the years 1648 and 1697, Alsace became partly incorporated with France and was subsequently taken through force of arms by Louis XIV. Accordingly, by the Treaty of Ryswick, 1697, it came entirely under the dominion of France.

The French government made intermittent efforts to amalgamate the Teutonic element in Alsace with that of the French. But it was not until the Revolution that the German and the French peoples of the province were drawn close together in sentiment and sympathy—all classes of the German population becoming thoroughly reconciled to French rule.

In 1790, in the process of reorganization of the realm of France in departments, Alsace was divided into the departments of Haut Rhin and Bas Rhin, while Lorraine was distributed among three— Moselle, Meurthe, and Vosges. The cession to Germany included Bas Rhin, most of Haut Rhin, the department of Moselle, and portions of Meurthe and Vosges. For administrative purposes, Germany divided Alsace-Lorraine into three civil districts— Lower Alsace, Upper Alsace, and Lorraine. Members of the legislative body, 58 in number, were elected by popular suffrage. But, at heart, the people in general were strongly opposed to the change in government. More than 150,000 proclaimed their adherence to France, and of this number no less than 50,000 chose exile rather than become German subjects.

For nearly half a century, the possession of Alsace-Lorraine by Germany had been a source of the keenest bitterness and resentment to the French. Neither had this sentiment grown less intense, nor had the loyalty of the people of Alsace-Lorraine became less devoted at the outbreak of World War I. By the Treaty of Versailles, in 1919, Alsace and Lorraine were returned to France. They were taken back by Germany on the fall of France in 1940, and reorganized as a part of the Reich, Lorraine becoming the Westmark, but on the defeat of the Axis were regained by France.

ANATOLIA

Anatolia (*ăn'ā-tō'lĭ-à*), a name of Greek derivation, meaning sunrise, or eastern land, was anciently applied to Asia Minor, the land east of the Ægean Sea. Under the Eastern Empire, it designated one of the three Phrygian provinces. It is still used in a popular sense to designate this region, now territory of Turkey. The western part of this land, along the Ægean coasts, was the home of early Greek civilization. Here, in the 6th century B. C., arose the famous kingdom of Lydia, ruled by Crœsus. Persia extended its sway to the Ægean, to be superseded by the Macedonian power. Numerous states which arose after the death of Alexander, including the powerful realm of Pontus, succumbed to the advance of Rome in the 2d and the 1st century B. C. The power of the Eastern, or Byzantine, Empire in Asia Minor was shattered by the Turkish attacks begun in the 11th century A. D. Since 1453 the land has been ruled by Ottoman Turks. After the close of World War I, the Turkish Nationalist movement fixed its political center at Ankara in Anatolia.

ANDORRA

Andorra is one of the two oldest and smallest republics in the world, the other being San Marino in Italy. It consists of 6 parishes in the diocese of the Spanish bishop of Urgel, lying in the valleys of the eastern Pyrenees, between France and Spain. Within its 175 square miles of territory, about 5000 people live, 1000 in the capital, Andorra. Charlemagne is said to have rewarded the little state for its help during his campaigns against the Moors by declaring it independent. Similar independence was enjoyed in feudal times by the people of many valleys of the Pyrenees. Fortunately for Andorra, the suzerainty over this territory was, in 1278, divided in perpetuity between the counts of Foix and the bishops of Urgel. The rights of the house of Foix descended to the French crown, and hence Andorra is now under the protection of the government of France and the bishop of Urgel.

ARABIA

The peninsula of Arabia has never been a political unit, although the recently established kingdom of Saudi Arabia embraces nearly all the territory. At a very early period, it was settled by two groups of Semitic people, one of which occupied the South, the other the North. The people of the South adopted a settled, agricultural life more readily than the northern tribes, and are said to have maintained a kingdom, perhaps that of Yemen, for 2000 years. It was a period of Semitic migrations eastward into Mesopotamia and northward into Syria. Since Roman power affected only portions of the North, many Christian sects took refuge in Arabia, where they preserved valuable ancient manuscripts. Found in a convent on Mt. Sinai was the oldest known Bible (4th century), which is antedated only by sections of the Dead Sea Scrolls.

With the coming of Mohammed arose the brilliant historic period of the Arabs. From the 7th to the 15th century they swept out in conquest, established many centers of civilization, and contributed to the progress of science and art among the Western nations. But their homeland was still a group of petty states around the interior of the peninsula.

In 1517 the Turks subdued Hejaz and Yemen on the Red Sea coast. Oman, on the Persian Gulf, maintained independence except during the 16th century, when for a time it was subject to Portugal. Its later history has been turbulent. It is now independent.

In 1916 the Grand Sherif of Mecca, or "Keeper of the Holy Places," proclaimed the independence of Hejaz and assumed the title of king. His troops co-operated with British forces in Syria and penetrated northward as far as Damascus. The king of Hejaz aspired to rule all Arabia but was conquered in 1924 by Ibn Saud, sultan of the Nejd. Saud captured also Jebel Shammar and created the sultanate of Hejaz and the Nejd, renamed Saudi Arabia in 1932. It was later extended to include almost the entire peninsula from the Red Sea to the Persian Gulf. See *Saudi Arabia, Arabians.*

ARMENIA

As a state, Armenia first appears in history in the 6th century B. C., when the Armenian people were freed by Tigranes from the rule of the Assyrians and the Medes. About the beginning of the 2d century B. C., the division of Armenia into Armenia Major, east of the Euphrates, and Armenia Minor, west of the Euphrates, was made. The former was ultimately divided between Turkey, Persia, and Russia. The latter became Turkish territory in 1541.

Nationalist movements in Armenia led to cruel repressions and massacres, none of which exceeded in barbarity the "deportations" by the Turks during World War I. Armenian independence was recognized by the Allies in 1920. On April 2, 1921, Armenia declared itself a Soviet republic. From 1922 to 1936, it formed part of Transcaucasia, a federated state of the Soviet Union. Armenia itself was then given the status of a federated state. See *Armenians.*

ASSYRIA

In ancient history, we hear of Assyria first as a northern province of the Babylonian Empire in the 19th century B. C. It grew in power until about 1100 B. C., when its king, Tiglath-Pileser I, taking advantage of Babylonian troubles with Arabian invaders, made himself master of the empire. After his death, the realm fell apart. In 745 B. C. an adventurer, Pul, who had been a gardener, seized the reins of authority and, as Tiglath-Pileser II, established the strongest empire the world had yet seen. He originated the organization of provinces, to take the place of the earlier principalities.

Sargon II, the next great king, used the favorite plan of the Assyrians for subduing rebellious people, when he carried the tribes of Northern Israel into captivity, 722-723 B. C. Sennacherib, son of Sargon, in the course of extending his power westward, met disaster in a siege of Jerusalem, celebrated in Byron's poem beginning, "The Assyrian came down like a wolf on the fold." His son Esarhaddon conquered Egypt in 672 B. C. But the murderous cruelty and oppressive taxation of this great empire roused hatred among its subject peoples. Egypt and Babylon revolted, the Scythians invaded from the north, and finally the Medes and Babylonians conquered Nineveh, the capital, the very site of which was forgotten until recent years. See *Assyrians.*

AUSTRIA

The history of Austria is chiefly the history of the house of Habsburg. When Rudolf of Habsburg became emperor of Germany, Ottokar, king of Bohemia and duke of Austria, Styria, and Carinthia, refused to take the oath of allegiance. The emperor succeeded in dispossessing Ottokar of his fiefs (1278) and subsequently conferred them on his own sons (1280). Thus the dynasty of Habsburg was founded.

In the first half of the 16th century, Duke Ferdinand of Austria was elected king of Hungary by one party; John Zapolya of Transylvania was elected by another. After several wars, in which John was supported by the Turks, Ferdinand came out victorious and united Hungary to Austria. Possessed of a large territory, fertile and densely peopled, the house of Habsburg was for several centuries the richest and most powerful family in Europe. But humiliations came with Napoleon. Driven out of Germany, the emperor Francis assumed, August 11, 1804, the title of emperor of Austria.

After the fall of Napoleon, Austria was restored to its former size, and under the administration of Metternich it also regained its prestige in European politics. But its internal weakness became apparent, first by the revolution of 1848, when only the support of Russia prevented the whole fabric from falling to pieces; again, after the battle of Sadowa, 1866, when, for the second time, it was driven out of Germany and lost its hold on Italy. The empire was then constituted as a double state—Austria and Hungary. In 1878 the administration of Bosnia and Herzegovina was given to Austria. In 1882 the dual kingdom entered into the Triple Alliance with Germany and Italy. Thereafter, the policy of the Habsburg rule became more and more identified with the Hohenzollern ambition for world domination. In 1908 Austria annexed Bosnia and Herzegovina in defiance of Russia. With Germany's support in 1913, Austria, by securing a protectorate over Albania and by denying Serbia access to the sea, prevented the Balkan allies from realizing the fruits of their victory over the Turks.

Francis Ferdinand, Austrian heir apparent, was assassinated at Serajevo, June 28, 1914. Accusing Serbia of complicity, Austria demanded that Serbia punish the accomplices and suppress anti-Austrian influence. Rejecting Serbia's reply, Austria invaded Serbia, thereby beginning World War I. Following the utter defeat of the Austrian armies by the Italian forces in October 1918, Austria-Hungary, on Nov. 3, signed terms of truce equivalent to military surrender. On Nov. 11, Charles I abdicated his throne, thereby ending more than 600 years of Habsburg rule. The Republic of Austria was proclaimed on Nov. 12, 1918. A constitution was adopted in November 1920.

The Treaty of Versailles dismembered Austria-Hungary and left Austria a small inland state. Grave economic depression ensued. As Germany became stronger after her defeat in World War I, she pursued a policy looking toward union with Austria. Austrian opinion was divided, and violence soon led to a dictatorship and a new constitution declaring Austria a Christian, German federal state on a corporative foundation. But Hitler found grounds for taking over the country in 1938.

At the end of World War II in 1945, Austria was occupied by the allied powers. After ten years of delaying tactics, Russia finally agreed to a treaty of peace, which was ratified July 27, 1955. Austria became an independent republic pledged to military neutrality. Political or economic unity with Germany was forbidden. Although officially neutral, the country continued to be strongly oriented toward the west.

BABYLONIA

At two periods the territory of Babylonia, located in the lower valley of the Tigris and Euphrates, was the center of an empire with the city of Babylon as its capital. The first Babylonian empire was organized from the Mesopotamian states by Hammurabi about 2000 B. C. About 1500 B. C. this empire in its growth came into conflict with Egypt, and later with the increasing power of its rival, Assyria. But the city of Babylon continued to be a center of political power and culture until the 8th century B. C., when it fell before the Assyrians.

The second Babylonian empire arose about 625 B. C., when the people rebelled against Assyrian tyranny and divided the Assyrian dominions with the Medes. This state lasted until 538 B. C., when the Persians captured Babylon. Within this period falls the brilliant reign of Nebuchadnezzar, who rebuilt Babylon with great magnificence and extended his power beyond the bounds of the first empire. In his reign the city of Jerusalem was sacked and many Jews were carried off as captives to Babylon. See *Sumerians*.

BARBARY STATES

The Barbary States were the North African lands of Morocco, Algeria, Tunis, and Tripoli. The name Barbary is derived from the Berbers, who were the earliest known inhabitants of the territory. In the 10th and the 9th century B. C. the Phoenicians colonized northern Africa, their principal city being Carthage. Their state was conquered and the city of Carthage destroyed by the Romans in 146 B. C. North Africa formed one of the most prosperous provinces of the Roman Empire, and the extensive ruins of great Roman towns and public works are still to be seen in many places. With the decline of the empire, a state of anarchy ensued, and the Vandals found the country an easy prey. The first tide of Mohammedan conquest swept over the country in 647. The Arabs mingled with the Berbers, and the combined races advanced into Spain, where they were known as Moors.

After the expulsion of the Moors from Spain, the fugitives settled on the African coast, and the states there formed became the home of piracy. Spain in the 16th century and France in the 17th made vigorous war on these Barbary pirates, but with little success. During the 18th century all the Christian states were paying tribute to the heads of the Barbary States, which were either independent or nominally under the government of the Turkish sultan. In 1815 the United States forced Algeria, Tripoli, and Tunis to cease attacks on American shipping. England took similar action in 1819.

The French established control of Algeria in 1847, of Tunis in 1881, and the greater part of Morocco in 1912, the latter two being protectorates while Algeria was administratively a part of France. Italy conquered Tripoli and Cyrenaica in 1912 and united them into one colony as Libya. By treaty in 1912, Spain obtained control over part of Morocco. The French, Italian, and Spanish dependencies became independent after 1950.

BAVARIA

Bavaria, the second largest state of the former states, and since 1934 an administrative unit, of Germany, has long been famous for its literature, art, and music. Its name is derived from the Latin *Boiarii*, the name given to the Germanic tribe that seized the land of the Boii (Bohemia) and drove out the Celtic people of the present Bavarian territory. These Celts were subject to Rome from 15 A. D. to the fall of the Western Empire. The Franks overran the country about the 6th century, and Charlemagne later made it part of his empire. In 1180 an imperial grant placed the count of Wittelsbach in power, and descendants of that family ruled as counts, dukes, and kings until the establishment of the republican Free State of Bavaria in 1918.

Bavaria sided with Napoleon against Austria, and in 1805 he made it a kingdom, a dignity which the king, by adroit changing of sides in 1813, managed to retain. In 1818 a constitution was adopted, but King Louis I was more interested in rebuilding and embellishing his capital, Munich, than in promoting popular liberty. His policy, followed by his successors, made Munich one of the most beautiful cities of Europe and enriched it with art and scientific collections. The year 1848 brought an uprising of the citizens of Munich, who demanded further political reform. Louis abdicated, and his son, Maximilian, acceded to the demands of the people.

In 1866 Bavaria sided with Austria, and after the Prussian victory she was compelled to cede territory to Prussia and form an alliance. This alliance as well as national feeling placed her by the side of Prussia against France in 1870 and brought her into the German Empire. After the collapse of Germany in 1918 a radical government was formed under the leadership of Kurt Eisner, an Independent Socialist.

After the assassination of Eisner by a reactionary army officer, the inability of any one group to maintain a government resulted in a period of great disorder. At length, with the military aid of the central German government, the city of Munich was wrested from the extremists. A moderate coalition government secured the adoption of a new constitution in August 1919.

Further difficulties arose over disarming the "home guards," but Bavaria became a part of the German Republic. In November 1923 Munich was the scene of an unsuccessful revolt which brought Adolf Hitler into prominence. At Munich, September 30, 1938, was signed the agreement by which England, France, and Italy allowed Germany to take the Sudeten lands from Czechoslovakia. See *Germany*.

BELGIUM

The name of this heroic little country comes from that of a division of the ancient Roman province of Gallia Belgica, of which modern Belgium includes only a small part. Throughout the middle ages this name, of which the French form is *Belgique* and the Flemish, *Belgie*, was used locally for the southern provinces of the Netherlands, which remained loyal to Catholicism and Spain when the northern Netherlands attained independence, in 1579, as the United Provinces. This territory, on account of its strategic military position and its agricultural, industrial, and commercial wealth, has been coveted and fought for by all the nations of western Europe. Its history has been colored by the rivalry of the Germanic and Celtic peoples who have occupied it, by their religious differences, and by the conflict of the agricultural interests of the South with the commercial interests of the North.

A Province of Spain and Austria. The earlier history of Belgium belongs to the story of Flanders and the Netherlands in the middle ages. After the successful revolt of the United Provinces in 1579, the duke of Parma diplomatically retained the Belgic provinces for Spain, but the oppressive and bigoted measures of the Spanish government put a blight upon the flourishing industries of the country and drove artisans and merchants to England and to the Dutch Republic. Grass grew in the once busy streets of Ghent and Bruges. From 1598 to 1633, under Archduke Albert and his wife Isabel, daughter of Philip II of Spain, the country was officially independent, but in 1633 it reverted to Spain, and, as the Spanish Netherlands, entered upon a long period of disaster. It was the pawn in the wars of the 17th century. As the battlefield of contending armies, it justified its name, the "cockpit of Europe." France seized much of its territory, and the closing of the Scheldt river to shipping in 1648 shut its cities out from the ocean and commerce.

A brief respite from disaster came when the Bavarian elector, Maximilian Emanuel, an able and enlightened ruler, was made governor in 1692. He endeavored to revive commerce by the building of canals to take the place of the Scheldt river. But at the opening of the 18th century the insatiable ambition of Louis XIV again made the country a battle ground. Louis's desire to annex Belgium was thwarted by the successful campaigns of the English, Dutch, and Austrians, under Marlborough, and the Peace of Utrecht in 1713 gave the country to Austria. For a century it was known as the Austrian Netherlands.

The Belgians were jealous of their local liberties, especially of the right of their own assemblies, or "states," to levy or approve taxes, and the Austrians for a time found their new subjects difficult to rule. But a liberal policy was maintained, first by the archduchess Mary Elizabeth and later by Charles of Lorraine, Austrian governors. The latter was known as the "Good Governor" for his efforts in enlarging the canal system, in developing agriculture, and in providing for education. Among other institutions, he founded the Academy of Science.

Belgian Independence. The victorious armies of the French Revolution brought the Belgians into the Republic in 1794, and until the fall of Napoleon in 1814 they were governed as French people. In 1815 the Congress of Vienna joined the country to Holland in the Kingdom of the Netherlands, a union which, in view of the commercial power of Holland and the industrial resources of Belgium, would seem wise. But the conflicting temper and interests of the two peoples at once became evident. Differences arising from history, religion, and language could not be settled. In spite of real progress and prosperity in this period under the rule of the Dutch king, the Belgians found grievances in the large number of Dutch officeholders, in the regulations set up for education, and in the government's policy of religious toleration. Liberal and Clerical parties joined in a demand for separate administration of the Belgian provinces. This was finally granted, but not until the extremists had forced a national revolt in 1830.

In 1831, with the approval of a conference of the Powers, called in London, the Belgians adopted a constitution providing for a Senate and a Chamber of Deputies, a ministry responsible to the legislature, and a king with restricted powers. Leopold of Saxe-Coburg was elected king of the Belgians. Belgium was made, by treaty among the powers, an independent, neutral state. Holland, however, withheld assent until 1839, when a final settlement of boundaries was effected.

Political and Economic Progress. The great confidence placed by the people in King Leopold carried Belgium through the revolutionary period of 1848 without disturbance, that year being marked only by an extension of the franchise by lowering the property qualification of voters. This question of the franchise continued to share with the question of public education the first place in Belgian politics. In 1899 the system of proportional representation was put in force. But great inequalities in the suffrage still remained. In 1919 the Parliament ordered elections on a "one man, one vote" basis, and the new Parliament was required to legalize this system of election.

Belgium, in the 19th century, rapidly grew into an industrial country, and about 1886 Socialism became a political force. Frequent strikes led to extension of the suffrage already referred to and to the passing of much progressive legislation, providing, among other things, for industrial councils of employers and workmen, for regulating hours of labor, for old age pensions, and for better education.

At the death of Leopold I in 1865 his son was proclaimed king as Leopold II. The new king was a shrewd business man and an able administrator. His influence was strong in extending Belgian trade, but his chief accomplishment was acquiring the Belgian Congo, or Congo Free State. He was succeeded in 1909 by his nephew, Albert I.

The World Wars. On Aug. 2, 1914, Germany demanded free passage of German troops through Belgium to attack France. Belgium refused, and a German invasion began in direct violation of Germany's treaty agreement of 1839. Belgian forces, bravely contending, were defeated and compelled to retreat. On Aug. 20 the Germans took Brussels, levying upon it a war tax of $40 million. The city of Louvain was burned, Aug. 27. Ghent and other cities were in turn occupied. On Oct. 8 Antwerp fell. Hundreds of thousands of refugees found shelter in England, Holland, France, and America.

The army continued to fight heroically in the Allied lines, while the patriotism of the king and the loyalty of the people were unwavering. Finally, in the autumn of 1918 the invaders were forced to withdraw. On Nov. 22 King Albert re-entered Brussels at the head of the victorious army, and Belgium was proclaimed a free and independent nation. The Treaty of Versailles in 1919 abrogated the neutrality treaties of 1839 and provided for new agreements to take their place. The government formed a defensive alliance with France. King Albert was killed by a fall while rock-climbing, February 17, 1934, and his son succeeded him as Leopold III. In October 1936, Belgium proclaimed her neutrality. Nevertheless, she was invaded and occupied by the Germans in 1940. King Leopold became a German prisoner, while the cabinet retreated to England and set up a government in exile there. The king's role in the war lost him popular favor. He abdicated in 1951 and was succeeded by his son Baudouin. Belgium became a member of the Common Market at its organization in 1957.

In 1960, Belgium, with little preparation, granted independence to its large, rich colony in Africa, the Congo. Chaos followed. Finally the United Nations sent a special military force to keep order.

Brittany is the medieval and popular modern name applied to the district in the northwest peninsula of France, now included in the departments of Finistère, Côtes-du-Nord, Morbihan, Ille-et-Vilaine, and Lower Loire, called in ancient times *Armorica*, meaning "upon the sea." The Romans subdued this territory in 51 B. C. In the 5th century, Celtic people, fleeing before the Anglo-Saxon invasion of Britain, settled a large part of the peninsula. From the name of these people, Britons, came the names Brittany for the country and Bretons for the people. They built up a powerful aristocracy and fought off both Frankish kings and Norman dukes. In the 12th century, however, Conan IV, duke of Brittany, called on Henry II of England for help against rebellious Breton nobles. Henry forced Conan to give his daughter in marriage to Henry's son Geoffrey, who thus became duke of Brittany. But a French line soon succeeded this dynasty, and in 1532 Brittany was annexed to France. The Bretons, however, retained many special rights until the French Revolution.

BULGARIA

The modern kingdom of Bulgaria occupies virtually the territory of the ancient Roman province of Mœsia. In the 4th and 5th centuries A. D., a Slavic people invaded this district, and about a century later came the Bulgars, a people related to the Huns. A mingling of Bulgars and Slavs took place, and these racial elements have since been supplemented by mixture with neighboring peoples. About the middle of the 9th century, Christianity was introduced into the state, which had been growing into power. In addition to religious faith, the Bulgarians in this period borrowed many cultural elements from the Greeks, some of which they later transmitted to Russia.

In the 12th and 13th centuries, the Bulgarian state rose to great power, only to be surpassed by Serbia as the leading Slav state, and to fall a prey to the Ottoman Turks in the latter part of the 14th century. Not until the last quarter of the 19th century did Bulgaria again have a distinct national existence.

A revolt in 1876 against the crushing tyranny of the Turk was put down with the barbarously cruel measures known as the "Bulgarian atrocities." This was the occasion of the Russo-Turkish war of 1877–78, out of which Bulgaria emerged as an autonomous principality, tributary to Turkey. In 1885, through a revolution, Eastern Rumelia was united to Bulgaria. Prince Alexander abdicated in the following year, and in 1887 Prince Ferdinand of Coburg was elected by the people. In spite of opposition on the part of the European powers, Ferdinand, with the aid of his minister, Stambulov, so strengthened his power that, in 1896, he was recognized as prince of Bulgaria.

Under the rule of Ferdinand, the Bulgarian state made rapid progress in economic growth and in military power. In the midst of political disturbances in Turkey in 1908, Ferdinand proclaimed the independence of the Bulgarian kingdom. In 1912 Bulgaria made common cause with her former enemies—Serbia, Montenegro, and Greece—against the Turk, but lost the greater part of her gains in the Second Balkan war. In 1915 Bulgaria entered World War I on the side of the Central Powers, and again suffered heavy losses.

Bulgaria was forced by the Axis powers into World War II, but changed sides when invaded by Russia in 1944. Two years later, September 8, 1946, the boy king, Simeon II, was deposed, and Bulgaria became a republic. The peace treaty, signed February 10, 1947, promised free elections and a democratic government, but in the following months the Communists gained control, suppressed all other political parties, executed their leaders, and set up a Communist régime under Russian control.

Burmese tradition suggests the immigration of a people from the northwest, about 2000 years ago, who conquered the earlier inhabitants and set up a kingdom. When European traders first entered the country, in the 15th century, the kings of Ava, who traced descent to the early Buddhist rulers of India, were supreme. Toward the close of the 16th century, power passed to the kings of Pegu, a southern capital, but the French and English, who began trading at the delta of the Irrawaddy, early in the 18th century, found a weak government. In 1753–54, Alompra, a village chief of Ava, made himself master of Burma and founded a peculiarly bloodthirsty and cruel dynasty.

England gained control of southern Burma in 1853, by the annexation of Pegu. In 1885 the British deposed King Thebav, and in 1886 Burma became a part of the British Empire. It was made a province of India in 1895; a separate colony, with partial self government, in 1937. It was overrun by the Japanese in 1942. The British returned in 1945 but Burmese dissatisfaction led the British government to offer them independence, which was granted January 4, 1948. Burma established a republic and chose to remain outside the British Commonwealth of Nations.

CHINA

Chinese tradition carries the story of civilization in eastern Asia back to about the year 2852 B.C. The historical period, however, begins in 841 B.C. during the rule of the Chou dynasty (1122-256 B.C.).

The long period of the Chou kings was distinguished by remarkable progress in literature and the arts. It was during the reign of the Chou dynasty that Confucius lived (551-479 B.C.). Luxury and war had brought the Chinese people to a low ebb of moral and political life. The teachings of this great sage, with those of his older contemporary, Lao Tzu, and those of Mencius, a disciple of Confucius, who lived in the 4th and 3d centuries B.C. (372-289), are represented as an unavailing protest against the decay of their times.

The Chou dynasty fell into anarchy and was supplanted by the Ch'in, from which comes the name of China. The Ch'in dynasty abolished feudalism and built the Great Wall, but was short-lived. The Early and Later Han dynasties followed (206 B.C.-220 A.D.). During this period intercourse with Rome began and Buddhism was introduced.

The Golden Age. After a long series of divisions and civil wars, the great T'ang dynasty arose (618-907 A.D.). The empire was extended as far west as the Caspian Sea. Embassies came from Persia, from Tibet, from Annam, and from Japan. Nestorian missionaries introduced Christianity. The Arabs brought in Mohammedanism. The Chinese capital became a center of international influence. Commerce flourished, literature was encouraged, and the invention of printing from movable blocks gave a great impetus to bookmaking. It was the golden age of Chinese poetry and painting. The Sung period (960-1278) was distinguished for its philosophical speculation.

The Mongols, led by Genghis Khan, invaded China and ruled from 1280 to 1368. Marco Polo has described the glorious reign of Kublai Khan. His successors were unequal to the task of ruling so great an empire and soon lost the throne. Dramatic writing characterized the literature of the period.

The Manchus; Relations with the West. The Ming dynasty succeeded. Under its sway modern intercourse with Europe began. The Portuguese discovered the route via the Cape to the Far East and arrived in China in 1516. The Ming dynasty was replaced in 1644 by the Manchus. The mark of their mastery was the requirement that Chinese men should wear the queue. The Manchus adopted the language and general customs of the people they ruled. Russian aggression was stopped. By the treaty of 1689 they were compelled to leave the Amur valley.

Gifts sent to the court by Western potentates were considered as tribute, and the refusal of the representatives of these powers to perform the kowtow, as China's tributaries did, was regarded as insubordination. To the Europeans, this was an arrogant assumption of superiority, and it was met by an overbearing attitude upon their part.

Growth of Trade; Treaties with Western Powers.
In spite of the political friction, trade at Canton flourished. The British East India Company enjoyed the largest share of it. This company was dissolved in 1834. Opium smuggling constituted a good part of the foreign trade. The attempt to suppress this smuggling, added to other causes of friction, brought on war with Great Britain.

The treaty of peace of 1842 and the commercial treaty of 1843 opened five ports to foreign trade and limited Chinese import and export duties to 5 per cent *ad valorem*. The first American treaty, that of 1844, provided definite arrangements for the exercise of extraterritorial jurisdiction.

The seizure of a Chinese vessel in 1856 by the Chinese, on the charge that acts of piracy had been committed by some of the crew, was the occasion of further trouble with Great Britain, for the vessel had had a British charter and was still flying the British flag. This, with the repeated refusal of the Chinese to revise the treaties and to redress various other grievances, brought on the second war with Great Britain, in which the French joined. It resulted in the revision of the treaties, the legalizing of the opium traffic, diplomatic representation at Peking, and the toleration of Christianity.

The Taiping rebellion had meanwhile been in progress. It was suppressed in great part by the "Ever Victorious Army," which was organized and led by the American general, Frederick Townsend Ward, and, after he had been killed in battle, was commanded for a short time by Charles George Gordon—whence his sobriquet of "Chinese Gordon."

In 1868 the United States entered into a treaty with China to encourage Chinese immigration. It was supplemented in 1880 by another permitting the suspension of labor immigration. In 1894 China agreed to a suspension for ten years. In 1904 China refused to extend the period, and Congress voted to make the exclusion of Chinese immigrants perpetual.

War with Japan.
In 1894 Japan forced a war upon China over the control of Korea. China was defeated, and by the treaty of Shimonoseki she recognized the independence of Korea and ceded to Japan the Liaotung Peninsula, Formosa, and the Pescadores. Russia, Germany, and France protested against the Japanese holding of Liaotung and compelled its restoration to China, but they proceeded to take advantage of China's revealed weakness to press their own claims to compensation for their intervention. Russia obtained railway rights in Manchuria; Germany added to her claim that of compensation for the murder of two missionaries and secured the lease of Kiaochow; Russia then demanded and obtained further compensation in the lease of a portion of Liaotung; France secured Kwang-chow Wan; and Britain, to preserve the balance of power, obtained the lease of Weihaiwei and the enlargement of her Hongkong colony.

The Boxer Rising.
The United States took the position of insisting upon an "open door," or equality of opportunity, in these spheres of interest. The aggressive attitude of the European powers brought on the "Boxer" rising, which at first was a movement directed against the Manchu government because of its supineness, but subsequently was converted into an antiforeign rising.

The suppression of this disturbance brought about a few progressive changes in Chinese administration, which were given further impetus by the Japanese victory over Russia in 1905. Large numbers of Chinese students were sent to Japan, to Europe, and especially to the United States, whose remission of a portion of her share of the Boxer indemnity each year, as it was being paid, provided an annual fund for the American education of Chinese.

The Republic.
In 1911 a dispute over the building of a railway by means of a foreign loan was the immediate cause of the revolt that swept the Manchus out of power in 1912. Dr. Sun Yat Sen, who had long worked for this result, became provisional president of the government set up in the South in January 1912. In March, a reconciliation of the North and the South was effected, and Yuan Shih-kai was elected to the office of president.

Yuan's government was republican only in name, and the division between the North and the South grew more pronounced. A threatened establishment of a new monarchy with Yuan as emperor was prevented in 1915 by the warning of Japan. Yuan Shih-kai died in 1916, and Li Yuan Hung became president. The Parliament, which had been dissolved by Yuan Shih-kai, was reassembled.

China during the First World War.
Meanwhile, during World War I, Japan, assisted by Great Britain, had taken up the task of eliminating the Germans from Shantung. She pushed her expedition beyond the limits of German occupation and forced demands on China, the acceptance of which gave Japan virtual control over the valuable province of Shantung. In 1917, at the invitation of the United States, China broke off diplomatic relations with Germany and declared war.

A secret treaty between Chinese and Japanese militarists had alarmed the Parliament, which for a time refused to declare war. This led to an overthrow of the cabinet and an attempt by a Manchu general to re-establish the Manchu dynasty. Parliament was dissolved, but a portion reassembled at Canton and set up an opposition government. The dynastic movement was suppressed within six days. Representatives of the Canton faction and of the recognized government united in a refusal to sign the Versailles treaty, because it gave to Japan the territorial and economic rights formerly enjoyed by Germany in Shantung. The Shantung question was, at length, satisfactorily adjusted by a treaty between China and Japan signed during the Washington Conference, 1921-22.

The Years of Chaos.
The authority of the republic set up in 1912 was recognized only as far as its armies kept control, and this area changed with the fortunes of warfare and intrigue against regional war lords. Among the latter were Chang the so-called Christian general, and Feng, the War Lord of Manchuria. Sun, leader of the central government, in 1923 called in Russian political and military advisers, who organized labor and peasant unions and schooled them in communistic and antiforeign doctrines. Its social institutions already weakened by western influence, China was ripe for the new ideas. The nationalist armies found opposition melting before them and by 1927 had restored its authority in the southern region.

Sun had died in 1925, and his aide Chiang Kai-shek succeeded to the command. The latter found his Russian collaborators arrogating political powers. At Hangkow in 1927 he turned on them, drove them out, and had large numbers of their communist followers massacred. Meanwhile a rival general had seized Peking, and Chiang set up a new government at Nanking.

Japanese Aggression.
The rival generals tended to close ranks when Japan in 1931 used its preponderant military power to drive the Chinese forces out of Manchuria. In 1932, it set up in Manchuria

a puppet state named Manchukuo and placed at its head the last emperor of China, Pu Yi. A defensive alliance was made between Japan and Manchukuo. China appealed to the League of Nations, which condemned Japan.

China's response was a trade boycott against Japan. Japanese forces then took a portion of Shanghai and also occupied a considerable territory south of the puppet state of Manchukuo. In 1937, the Japanese determined to eliminate the government of Chiang and establish one more favorable to its interests. Although there had been no declaration of war, Japanese armies invaded China at many points, capturing Peking, all the port cities, and many inland ones, including Nanking. Chiang removed his capital to Hankow, but this also was captured the next year, and Chiang established his government in the western city of Chungking.

World War II and the Communists. In 1941, Japan entered World War II on the side of Germany. China received extensive British and American aid in the form of war materials, advisers, and organizers of guerrillas resistance. The decisive moves were made elsewhere, but the result was that Japanese forces in China surrendered and Manchuria was restored to Chinese sovereignty.

With the end of World War II, a struggle that had begun before the war reasserted itself. The Communist forces of Mao Tse-tung, consolidated in the northern province of Yenan and toughened by the war, now began to move against Chiang.

When Japan surrendered in 1945, the armies of the Communists obtained most of the Japanese war material. American military aid to Chiang Kai-shek often ended in the hands of the communists as Chiang's supporters deserted him. Finally, in 1949, the last of the national government's forces took refuge in Taiwan. On Sept. 9, 1949, the People's Republic of China was proclaimed with its capital in Peking. In effect, there now were two Chinas: one, communist, on the mainland; the other, nationalist, on the island of Formosa.

The People's Republic. The U.S. position resulted from the theory that the Chinese Communist leaders Mao Tse-tung and Chou En-lai were tools in a Soviet-directed takeover.

Two developments, which began in 1950, served to widen the gap in Sino-American relations. In June 1950, Russian-equipped North Korean troops invaded South Korea. As U.S. forces under Gen. Douglas MacArthur began to drive the invaders from South Korea, China grew restive. Traditionally, Korea had been a buffer between China and Japan. With U.S. forces (now joined by other United Nations troops) advancing, China took action. Communist Chinese "volunteers" defeated the South Korean army and halted the UN army at the 38th geographic parallel. The ensuing stalemate finally ended in 1953, when a truce was declared.

This show of force by the Chinese Communists led the U.S. to sign a treaty with the nationalist Chinese government in Taiwan.

Also in 1950, China had made an alliance with Russia. Until 1960, the People's Republic of China received Soviet aid. The Chinese began a broad Soviet-style program of industrialization. But China and Russia disagreed on the goals in international Communism. China favored armed aid of the revolutionary movement abroad, while Russia wanted peaceful competition between the socialist and capitalist systems. Sino-Soviet relations deteriorated. When China asked for more aid, Russia severed relations. Soviet exports and machinery were withdrawn and, by 1964, China's industrial revolution was almost at a standstill. Vast quantities of grain had to be imported.

Yet the People's Republic continued to develop its military capabilities. When the U.S. and Russia agreed to a nuclear-test-ban treaty in 1963, China refused to sign. The first Chinese hydrogen bomb was exploded in 1967.

In 1966, Mao Tse-tung launched a "great proletarian cultural revolution." It turned into a long, bloody turmoil as the Red Guard (Maoist youth) became uncontrollable. Their excesses subsided in 1968 under the influence of Premier Chou En-lai.

Increased diplomatic communications with other nations paved the way for recognition of the Communist regime as the legitimate government of China. In 1971 the UN voted to admit the Peking government and expel Taiwan. After President Nixon's trip to mainland China in 1972, China and the U.S. issued a statement acknowledging only one China, with Taiwan forming a part of it. Peking pledged tolerance for Taiwan if the island would agree to peaceful coexistence.

Mao Tse-tung and Chou En-lai died in 1976, leaving no appointed successors. A struggle developed between radical party leaders, led by Mao's wife, Chiang Ch'ing, and more moderate party leaders. A moderate, Hua Kuo-feng, became Party Chairman in October and Chiang Ch'ing was arrested for conspiracy to assassinate Hua.

Nationalist China. In Taiwan, Chiang Kai-shek's nationalist government had built up a relatively prosperous nation. Taiwan (Formosa), 110 miles off the China coast, had been taken by Japan in 1895, but returned to China in 1945, after World War II. The President of the "Republic of China," Chiang Kai-shek, also headed the Kuomintang (Nationalist Party). Taiwan's prosperity waned after U.S. support ceased and the mainland People's Republic was accepted by the UN as China's only legal government.

CORSICA

The Mediterranean island of Corsica received its first civilized colonists in a body of Phocaeans from Ionia, who founded the town of Alalia in 560 B.C. These people were followed by the Etruscans, the Carthaginians, and then the Romans, who established their power in the island about the middle of the 2nd century B.C. In the early Christian centuries, Rome banished political offenders to Corsica. After the decline of Rome, the island was invaded by Goths, Vandals, Lombards, Franks, and Moors.

To counteract the feudal anarchy which engulfed the country, a kind of republic, called the Terra di Comune, was set up in the north part of the island in the 11th century. This federation of parishes continued to exist until the French Revolution. Pisans, Genoese, and Aragonese fought for the island during the next four centuries.

From 1568 until 1729, Corsica, exhausted by war, was peaceful under Genoese control. After another period of disturbance and a bold attempt at independence led by the most famous hero of Corsican freedom, Pasquale Paoli, France completed a conquest of the island in 1770. Paoli led another revolt in 1793, which was followed by a British occupation of two years. Under Bonaparte, French authority was again asserted.

CRETE

From about 2800 B.C. this large island south of Greece was the seat of the highly developed Minoan civilization, named after a legendary lawgiver, Minos. About 1500 B.C. the island established control over the sea as far as Sicily to the west and Canaan to the east. The people possessed a system of writing that was derived from early Greek.

In early historical times, Crete was conquered by a Greek race and had a government much like Sparta's. It became a great slave market and was a resort for pirates until the Romans conquered it in 67 B. C. The Saracens took it in 823 A. D. Held later by the Venetians, by the Turks from 1669, and claimed by the Greeks since 1830, the island has had a history of oppression and massacre. In 1912 it was recognized as part of Greece. A Cretan, Venizelos, was Greek's ablest statesman during World War I. The island was seized by the Germans in an air-borne invasion in 1941, but guerrilla warfare continued until the final surrender of the occupation troops in 1944.

CZECHOSLOVAKIA

The socialist republic of Czechoslovakia (*chĕ K'ô-slô-vä′kĭ-a*) in central Europe first became a nation after the fall of Germany and Austria-Hungary in 1918. It was formed from four provinces of Austria-Hungary: Bohemia, Moravia, Slovakia, and Austrian Silesia. Bohemia and Moravia had been independent before absorption by Austria-Hungary. The first president, T. G. Masaryk, had helped organize Czech forces abroad to aid the Allies and had gained Allied recognition of the new state. In 1935 Edward Benes succeeded him. Under these two, a democratic regime was maintained amidst totalitarianism and the Little Entente was formed to protect the independence of smaller nations.

In 1937, a minority, the Sudeten Germans, with Hitler's support, demanded independence. Appealed to by Czechoslovakia, Britain and France were unwilling to challenge Germany. At Munich in 1938, to avoid war, they agreed to the partition of Czechoslovakia and a German takeover followed.

In 1945 the country was freed by U.S. and Russian forces and Benes resumed office. Trusting to Russian good faith, he allowed Communist infiltration and in 1948 they took over the country, making it a Russian satellite. Benes resigned in June, succeeded by Klement Gottwald. Antonin Novotny became president in 1957 and was party leader until 1968. That year a liberalization movement swept the country. Novotny lost power to Alexander Dubcek, who declared he would democratize the nation. Gen. Svoboda became president and Oldrich Cernik premier, forming a cabinet pledged to liberalization and economic reform. Russia brought pressure on the new government to desist and the year was marked by student riots and workers' protests against the U.S.S.R. In July Soviet-bloc forces invaded and occupied Prague, proceeding to force the submission of Dubcek's regime and a return by the Czechs to Communist orthodoxy.

Bohemia (*bô-hē′mĭ-à*). A former crownland of the Austro-Hungarian empire. The name means "home of the Boii," but this Celtic tribe occupied the country for only a short time at the beginning of the Christian era, being driven out or killed by the German Marcomanni. In the 6th century, the territory was occupied by a Slavic people, the Czechs, who were converted to Christianity during the 9th century. Various houses of princes and kings ruled these Czechs, until, under Ottokar II, reigning from 1253 to 1278, the kingdom of Bohemia became a powerful state, extending from the Elbe to the Adriatic. It fell before Emperor Rudolf of Habsburg, and became a crownland of the Austro-Hungarian empire.

In 1348, Emperor Charles IV founded the University of Prague, the first in the old German Empire. Under his successor, Wenceslas, the religious movement led by John Huss and Jerome of Prague took place. After 1526, when Ladislas II, king of both Bohemia and Hungary, lost his life in the battle with the sultan Soliman at Mohács, Bohemia became a possession of the house of Habsburg. It was a center of the Reformation struggle, and the bloodiest battle-ground of the Thirty Years' war.

Moravia (*mô-rā′vĭ-à*). A district conquered by the Slavs in the 6th century A. D. In the 9th century the Moravian princes formed a powerful kingdom, Great Moravia, but the Magyar invasions reduced this territory. In 1029, Moravia was united to Bohemia, and in 1526 it came into the hands of the Austrian monarchs. The country was almost depopulated during the Thirty Years' war.

All of the districts included in Czechoslovakia had been subject to a determined policy of Germanization pursued by the Austrian government, but in the 18th century, in Bohemia and Moravia, a movement arose for the revival of the Czech language. This developed into a political movement for independence in the 19th century.

DENMARK

Upon the Danish peninsula there are many remains which indicate the presence of man in the early Stone age. Norse sagas contain more or less mythical traditions of the movements of tribes in very early ages, but very little is certainly known of Danish affairs before the 9th century A. D. Probably about the 2d century the coast islands had become the home of the Angles, Saxons, and Jutes, who, in the 5th century, began their invasion of Britain, leaving their former territory to the Danes. The latter, in the following centuries, formed parts of the roving bands of Northmen. The monk Ansgar preached Christianity in Denmark in the 9th century, but the conversion of the country took place in the 10th century only after a bitter struggle between adherents of the old and the new faith. King Gorm the Old is said to have been a determined enemy of the Christians.

Svend (Sweyn) I (985 or 986-1014) was the first Danish king to exercise his power in England. Canute, his son, was the great king of both England and Denmark. His death in 1035 was followed by a period of internal dissensions and external wars, which weakened the country and brought about the introduction of a feudal system whence sprang a powerful nobility.

Reigns of the Waldemars. Waldemar I (1157-82), by the help of his minister, Bishop Absalon, subjugated the Wends and forced them to accept Christianity. During the time of Canute VI and in the early part of the reign of Waldemar II, the conquest of Denmark extended so far into German and Wendic lands that the Baltic was little more than an inland Danish sea. Envy and resentment on the part of the German princes, together with the perfidious conduct of his vassals, served to rob Waldemar II of these brilliant conquests. However, this period of the Waldemars was a time of great internal prosperity. National resources were developed, education spread, a vigorous middle class appeared, guilds were founded, and the yeomen were independent.

But the death of Waldemar in 1241 was followed by a century of misrule and inglorious decadence of the authority of the crown. Under Waldemar's great-grandson, Waldemar III (1340-75), Denmark made a quick but transient recovery of the conquests of the older Waldemars, and a system of national law was framed so as to form one thoroughly exhaustive and comprehensive code. This strong monarch revived the Danehof as a popular assembly and sharply curbed the power of the nobles. His daughter, the great Margaret (1375-1412), first as regent for her only and early lost son, Olaf, and later as sole monarch, ruled Denmark, Sweden, and Norway with such consummate tact and with so light yet firm a hand that, for once in the course of their history, the three rival Scandinavian kingdoms were content to act in harmony. Margaret's successor, Erik, for whose sake she had blended the three sovereignties into one, undermined her glorious work with fatal rapidity and was finally deposed by the nobles. The short reign of his nephew, Christopher of Bavaria, is notable for the ascendancy of the nobles and the oppression of the peasants to the point of serfdom.

The Oldenburg Kings. The Danes, on the death of Christopher in 1448, again exercised their long dormant right of election to the throne, and chose for their king Christian of Oldenburg, a descendant of the royal Waldemar family. As Christian I, he founded the Oldenburg line of Danish kings, which continued unbroken until the death of Frederick VII in 1863. Christian was at the same time elected duke of Schleswig and Holstein, and the resulting combined rule became the source of the later Schleswig-Holstein troubles. The insane tyranny of the otherwise able and enlightened Christian II cost him his throne. Denmark chose his uncle, Frederick I, as king, and Sweden became independent under Gustavus Vasa. Christian III (1534-59). in whose reign Protestantism was established, united the Schleswig-Holstein duchies in perpetuity to the crown. But he and his successor, Frederick II, made trouble by partitioning the duchies among members of their families.

Christian IV (1588-1648) was one of the ablest of Danish rulers. His liberal policy was, however, cramped by the nobles, through whose supineness Denmark and Norway lost some of their provinces to Sweden. During the reign of his son and successor, Frederick III, the last of the old Danish provinces on the eastern side of the sound were lost to Sweden (1658-60). The national abasement which followed led to the rising of the people against the nobles in 1660 and the surrender of the supreme power into the hands of the king. But the common people reaped little benefit from the autocracy they had thus set up. The abolition of serfdom was delayed until the reign of Christian VII. In 1797 it was begun, although the process was not completed until twenty years later. In 1804 the serfs were liberated in the duchies of Schleswig and Holstein.

During the period of the Napoleonic wars, Denmark's attempt to remain neutral brought her into disastrous conflict with England in the battle of Copenhagen (1801), which entailed the loss of her fleet, and in the destructive bombardment of Copenhagen (1807). Her subsequent alliance with Napoleon brought about the loss of Norway by the Peace of Kiel in 1814. After 1830 the discontent and animosity of the Danish and German peoples of Schleswig and Holstein increased and in 1848 broke out into open warfare. The disturbance came to an end in 1851 without settling the difficulty.

Parliamentary Government. Meanwhile, agitation for parliamentary government brought about the adoption of a new constitution in 1849. This provided for a national assembly composed of an upper house, or *Landsthing*, and a lower house, or *Folkething*. The 38 members of the upper house were partly to be appointed by the king, the 114 members of the lower house, elected by the people. But the Germans and other continental powers who had joined in the settlement of the royal succession in 1851 looked upon the new government as too democratic. Repeated futile attempts were made to arrange a constitution that would operate for Denmark and the duchies of Schleswig and Holstein. The matter was finally settled when Prussia and Austria took the duchies in 1864, after Christian IX had come to the throne.

After 1864 Danish history was for a number of years marked by the struggle for supremacy between the Landsthing and the Folkething. The political struggle centered from the first around the question of the control of financial measures. From 1874 to 1894 Estrup, the Conservative premier, was able to maintain his position. However, after his retirement the Radical party gained power. In 1913, after the accession of Christian X (1912), the Folkething narrowed somewhat the king's power and granted suffrage to women. Under the constitutional charter of 1915, universal and equal suffrage was established and also a system of proportional representation.

The first half of the 20th century saw remarkable developments in agriculture and commerce. Manufacturing was still of minor importance. In World War I Denmark was neutral. In World War II it was occupied by the Germans and remained under their control until King Christian's authority was restored at the German surrender.

After World War II, a co-operative movement in agriculture greatly increased farm production and industrialization grew significantly. Lacking abundant natural resources, the country has been plagued by economic difficulties caused by import surpluses. Denmark joined the European Economic Community (the Common Market) in 1973. Frederick IX reigned from 1947 until 1972 when he was succeeded by Queen Margrethe II.

EASTERN (BYZANTINE) EMPIRE

Constantine the Great, before his death in 337 A. D., divided the administration of the Roman Empire among his three sons and two nephews. In 395, at the death of Theodosius, this division of administration became a permanent division of the empire into East and West. Arcadius became emperor of the East, with his capital at Byzantium, or Constantinople. This Eastern Empire maintained itself for nearly 1000 years after the fall of the Roman power in the West. Such survival was made possible, despite weak frontiers, by the vast wealth at the command of the Eastern emperors, their strong armies, their despotic government, and the almost impregnable position of the city of Constantinople.

The greatest of the Eastern emperors was Justinian, who ruled from 527 to 565. His most notable work was the codifying of the Roman law. Before his death, his realm reached from Spain to the eastern end of the Black Sea and practically commanded all the shores of the Mediterranean, making it again a "Roman lake."

But the following centuries formed a period of almost continuous struggle against Slavs and other barbarians on the north and west, and Persians, Arabs, and Tatars on the east. In the 11th century the reigning emperor appealed to the Western Christians for help, and their answer was the First Crusade. After the Third Crusade, jealousy of the trade and wealth of Constantinople caused the knights of the Fourth Crusade to attack the Christian city instead of the Moslems and divide its diminished lands among Venetians, Genoese, and other Western peoples. After the crusaders had quarreled over their spoils for half a century, the Eastern throne was established again under the family of the Palæologi, the last of whom, Constantine, died heroically defending his capital against the final, irresistible onslaught of the Turks in 1453.

EGYPT

Egypt's fertile delta of the Nile was, after the Euphrates River bed, the earliest cradle of civilization. Barley was domesticated at least as early as 5000 B. C., and its cultivation, supplemented by the use of metals, formed the economic and technological base for the rise of cities. Furthermore, Egypt invented a written language (hieroglyphics, meaning "sacred writings"). Its ships made interchange of goods and ideas from the older Asian cultures possible. Warring cities evolved into what became the world's earliest empire.

Egypt's history begins with Menes, who reigned probably about 3400 B. C. He consolidated the whole Nile valley into a kingdom, with its capital at Memphis, in Lower Egypt. The next thousand years formed a period of rapid development of civilization. About 3000 B. C. King Cheops erected the Great Pyramid, and later kings followed his example, in building pyramids, temples, and tombs. From about 2400 to about 2000 B. C. the country was ruled by a new line of pharaohs, whose capital was Thebes, in Upper Egypt. This period is called the Middle Kingdom or, by some, the Feudal age. It was a time of foreign conquest, of extended commerce, and of the development of great economic works, such as the irrigation systems and the canal from the Nile to the Red Sea. The Egyptian power reached into Ethiopia and Syria.

The Empire. About the year 2000 B. C. bands of roving invaders from Arabia established themselves in Egypt, and their chiefs at last ruled the land, from a capital in the delta of the Nile, as the Hyksos, or Shepherd Kings. They are said to have introduced the horse into Egypt. It was during this period that the Hebrews, in a time of famine in Syria, came to Egypt. However, the native monarchs of Thebes drove out the foreigners about 1600 B. C., and for about 500 years maintained a powerful military state. They made conquest of Syria and even had a short period of rule in Babylon. Thus came about the first contact of the two ancient civilizations of Egypt and Mesopotamia. Syria and northern Arabia became the routes of travel and commerce. The last and greatest of the strong pharaohs of this period was Rameses II, who waged war against the Hittites and finally made an alliance with them. Rameses was an ardent patron of architecture, and Thebes in his reign is said to have been the most magnificent city of the age, by reason of its wealth of statuary and the splendor of its temples.

Decline of Egyptian Power. About 1300 B. C. the power of Egypt steadily declined, until in 672 it became subject to Assyria. Early in this period, the Hebrews returned to Canaan, escaping from a weak pharaoh. After twenty years of Assyrian rule, Psammetichus, an aggressive leader of foreign blood, restored the independence of Egypt. His greatest service was in opening the country to travelers and colonists. Greeks thronged to his capital of Sais, and the treasures of Egyptian civilization were passed on to the new nations of the north and west. In the reign of his successor, Necho, about 600 B. C., Egyptian sailors are credited with having sailed around the coasts of Africa.

The Ptolemies. In 525 B. C. Persia conquered Egypt and ruled it until Alexander in 332 B. C. established his Greek empire. Egypt now became a Greek state, many Greeks having been already settled in the country, and the Egyptians were treated as an inferior race. Alexandria was founded as the new Greek capital. On the death of Alexander, his general, Ptolemy, took possession of the throne and became the first ruler of a Greek dynasty that for 300 years made Egypt one of the chief kingdoms of the world. The Ptolemies were magnificent patrons of arts and letters. Theocritus, Callimachus, Euclid the geometrician, the astronomers Eratosthenes and Aratus, with many others, flourished under their rule. But, while the Alexandrian Greeks managed to keep down the native Egyptians, they were themselves sinking under the Romans. Ptolemy Auletes, "the Flute Player" (81–51 B. C.), went to Rome to ask help against his subjects, and the famous Cleopatra maintained her power only through her personal influence with Julius Cæsar and Mark Antony.

Roman Rule. On the defeat of Mark Antony by Augustus, 30 B. C., Egypt became a province of Rome. It was still a Greek state, and Alexandria was the chief seat of Greek learning and science. On the spread of Christianity, the old Egyptian doctrines lost their sway. Now arose in Alexandria the Christian catechetical school, which produced Clement and Origen. The sects of Gnostics united astrology and magic with religion. From the school of Alexandria emerged such neoplatonic philosophers as Plotinus and Proclus. Monasteries were built throughout Egypt, Christian monks took the place of the pagan hermits, and the Bible was translated into Coptic.

Mohammedan Conquest. On the division of the Roman Empire, in the time of Theodosius, into the Western and the Eastern Empire, Egypt became a province of the latter and sank deeper and deeper in barbarism and weakness. It was conquered in 640 A. D. by the Saracens under Caliph Omar. As a province of the caliphs it was under the government of the celebrated Abbassides, Haroun-al-Raschid and Al-Mamun, and that of the heroic sultan Saladin. The last dynasty was, however, overthrown by the Mamelukes (1250); and

the Mamelukes in their turn were conquered by the Turks (1516-17). The Mamelukes made repeated attempts to cast off the Turkish yoke, and had virtually done so by the end of the 18th century. The French conquered Egypt in 1798 and held it till 1801, when they were driven out by the British.

On the expulsion of the French, a Turkish force under Mehemet Ali Bey took possession of the country. Mehemet Ali was made pasha and administered the country vigorously, greatly extending the Egyptian territories. At length he broke with the Porte, and, after gaining a decisive victory over the Ottoman troops in Syria, in 1839, was acknowledged by the sultan as viceroy of Egypt, with the right of succession. Mehemet Ali died in 1849. He was succeeded by his grandson Abbas, who, murdered in 1854, was succeeded by his uncle Said, son of Mehemet. Under his rule, railways were opened and the cutting of the Suez canal was commenced. After Said's death, Ismail Pasha, a grandson of Mehemet Ali, obtained the government in 1863. His administration was vigorous but extravagant, and brought the finances of the country into disorder. In 1866, he obtained a royal license from the sultan, granting him the title of khedive. In 1879 he was forced to abdicate, under pressure of the British and French governments, and was replaced by his son Tewfik.

British Control. In 1882 the "national party" under Arabi Pasha revolted and forced the khedive to flee. On July 11, a British fleet bombarded Alexandria and restored the khedive, and Arabi's forces were totally crushed at Tel el Kebir on September 13. A rebellion in the Sudan, under the leadership of Mohammed Ahmed, the so-called mahdi, now gave the government trouble. In 1883 the mahdi's forces annihilated an Egyptian force under Hicks Pasha in Kordofan. British troops dispatched to Suakin inflicted two severe defeats on the mahdi's followers. The British cabinet resolved to abandon the Sudan; General Gordon was sent to effect the safe withdrawal of the garrisons (1884). However, the mahdi's forces were strong enough to shut the general up in Khartoum for nearly a year. He perished (January 1885) before the relief expedition could reach him.

In World War I, Egypt was declared a British protectorate mainly because of the strategic importance of the Suez canal, the corporate owner of which was controlled by Britain and France. British troops prevented a Turkish attempt to invade Egypt and block the canal traffic.

Independence Regained. After the war, in 1922, the British government approved a policy of making Egypt an independent state. The ruler was proclaimed king. In 1936, under a treaty of alliance, the British abandoned their extraterritorial courts in Egypt and obtained the right to keep a military force to guard the canal until the canal should revert to Egypt in 1968.

In 1949, Egypt led other Arabic states in an attempt to crush the newly formed republic of Israel, but the invaders were decisively defeated by the Israeli army.

In 1952, the ruling sultan was forced to abdicate by a military uprising led by Gamal Abdel Nasser. A republic was declared the next year with General Naguib its first president and premier. In 1954, he was ousted by Nasser, who announced a broad program of economic reforms. In 1956, the British were persuaded to withdraw their military forces from the canal, and a few months later Nasser nationalized the canal, announcing that profits would be used to build a dam on the Nile at Aswan.

The British and French reacted by bombing Egyptian forces along the canal, and Israel, in a six-day lightning campaign, conquered all Egyptian territory east of the canal. Then, pursuant to a resolution of the United Nations, armed forces of these three powers were withdrawn, and a special

United Nations force was set up to keep peace on the Israeli-Egyptian border.

The United Arab Republic (consisting of Egypt and Syria in federation with Yemen) was formed in 1958. Syria and Yemen withdrew in 1961, but Egypt retained the name. Nasser continued to aspire to lead the Arab world. He accepted Russian arms and aid in building the Aswan Dam, the first stage of which was opened in 1964. Egypt closed the Gulf of Aqaba to Israel on May 22, 1967, and war broke out on June 5. By June 9 the Israeli forces had defeated the combined Arab armies and occupied strategic lands in Egypt, Syria and Jordan. Egypt severed relations with the U.S. and Britain, and Russia immediately began to help rebuild Egypt's military forces.

In 1970, President Nasser died and was succeeded by Anwar Sadat. War broke out again between Egypt and Israel in October 1973. Egyptian forces attempted to regain the Sinai peninsula while other Arab countries attacked from the east. The crisis almost brought both the U.S. and the U.S.S.R. into the conflict. After two weeks of fighting, a cease-fire was established. Extensive "shuttle diplomacy" by U.S. Secretary of State Henry Kissinger helped to win concessions from both sides in a 1975 agreement that seemed to achieve a period of stability, the first step toward a permanent settlement. After the October war, Egypt's relations with the Soviet Union deteriorated while relations with the U.S. improved. The Suez Canal was reopened in June, 1975.

FINLAND

Finland lies on the northwest border of Russia. Finnish tribes of unknown origin, were conquered by the Swedes in the mid-12th century. In 1809 Finland was annexed to Russia as a grand duchy, but was allowed self-rule. During the late 19th century, the Finns revived their own language and developed the state along democratic lines. Finland was, however, subjected to a Russification policy in 1897. After the Russian Revolution of 1917, Finland declared its independence. Civil war ensued between the Red Guards, siding with the Russian Bolsheviks, and the White Guards, supported by farmers and the upper class. The White Guards won, with German assistance, and set up a republic.

In 1939 Finland refused a "mutual assistance" treaty with Russia. After heroic resistance, Finland was forced to accept peace terms that included ceding Viborg and the Karelian peninsula and the establishment of Russian bases on the Gulf of Finland. These were retaken during World War II when the Russians were under German attack. In 1944, however, Russia recovered these cessions, along with the Petsamo area, and an armistice was signed. The 1947 Treaty of Paris confirmed other terms of the armistice—a 50-year lease for a Russian base on the Porkkala peninsula and reparations of $300 million. In 1948, a treaty of friendship was signed, extended another 20 years in 1970. The Soviet Union returned Porkkala in 1956.

FIUME

This city, on the Adriatic Sea where Italy borders on Yugoslavia, kept these two countries at dagger's point immediately after World War I. It was declared independent by treaty in 1920 with commercial rights guaranteed to both countries. Fascist-inspired violence toppled the government in 1922, but Italy ceded it to Czechoslovakia in 1924. After World War II it was incorporated in Yugoslavia.

FLANDERS

Flanders was a medieval country of Europe, which comprised the present provinces of East and West Flanders in Belgium, the southern part of the province of Zealand in the Netherlands, and parts of the departments of Nord and Pas-de-Calais, in France. It included Ghent, Bruges, Ypres, Douai, Lille, cities which became powerful through their textile manufacture trade and won a large measure of independence from their feudal lords. From the 10th to the 14th century these occupations provided economic strength but generated industrial strife between artisans and merchants. In the 1370's the workers of Ghent established a species of social utopia. Attacked by the king of France, the city held out for six years before being subdued. In 1392 Flanders passed under the power of Burgundy.

FRANCE

The history of France begins with the peoples who dwelt in Gaul long before the Christian era. The principal element of the French nation is Celtic. The Celts appear to have entered from the north and to have absorbed the scattered tribes. Although the Gauls had a developed civilization when Caesar began his conquests (58–51 B. C.), they soon became in language and in institutions as Roman as the Italians. Colonists from Italy, however, affected the Gallic population chiefly in the South.

Rise of the Capetian Dynasty. With the barbarian invasions, Roman Gaul fell away from the Empire and became a group of warring kingdoms. The Franks under Clovis were relatively few in number. So were the Goths and the Burgundians. These tribes were soon assimilated by the older population. When the Frankish empire, which Charlemagne (768–814) had created, fell to pieces in the 9th century, France in the narrower sense took its beginnings under the Capetian dynasty, the first of whose kings, Hugh Capet, was consecrated in 987. The Carolingian empire had fallen because it did not rest upon the solid foundation of an organized administration, an imperial revenue, and a law valid throughout its borders. For them had been substituted varying codes of local or tribal law, a meager income from landed estates, and a body of officials bound to their chiefs mainly by ties of personal loyalty. What is called "feudal anarchy" was coming into existence. The great dukes and counts of Flanders, Burgundy, Aquitaine, Brittany, and Normandy recognized Capet's nominal right to the usual feudal services, but held themselves independent in their own territories. The chief task of the kings from the time of Hugh to the reign of Charles VIII (1483–98) was to strengthen the royal power and unify the realm of France.

Several forces aided the kings in their task. One was the Church, which, in its canon law, reflected the old Roman ideal of universality, and in its principle of authority, the notion of an effective royal power. Another influence in the same direction was the towns, which began to grow strong with the revival of trade in the 12th century. The Crusades also helped, stimulating a feeling of unity in a common cause. The crusades against the Albigenses in southern France during the reign of Philip Augustus (1180–1223) weakened the nobles of that region and enriched the monarchy. It was the same king who, in his wars with King John of England, annexed Normandy and other important fiefs which had belonged to the English crown. Later kings also, by marriage alliances, war, intrigue, and by purchase, added to the domain, until this included practically all of the kingdom of France.

Philip Augustus allied himself with the lawyers and the clergy against the nobles. His jurists applied the principles of the old Roman law and provided for appeals from local to royal courts. His grandson Louis IX, or St. Louis, embodied in all his acts so high an ideal of justice that his very name grew to be a symbol of kingly authority. In 1302 a States-General was summoned by Philip IV, including delegates from the "good towns" along with the clergy and the nobles. Originating at the same time as the English Parliament, this assembly failed to develop into a strong representative body.

Medieval Civilization in France. The development of royal power by no means sums up French activity in the middle ages. The breakdown of feudalism carried with it the freedom of the rural classes from serfdom as well as the growth of a flourishing body of merchants and artificers in the towns. Agricultural methods were primitive, but the peasant acquired more permanent tenant rights and began to show that love for the soil which has ever been one of the corner stones of French prosperity. Industry was organized under a guild system which lasted until the Revolution. Artistic skill and creative genius found its noblest manifestations in the cathedrals of Paris, Chartres, Amiens, and Reims, in great town halls and palaces of justice, not to forget the castles of wealthy nobles and the dwellings of merchant princes. A literature arose, first in the Latin tongue, afterward in French. Universities were organized, and Paris took its place as a center of light and learning.

England and France at War. The work of medieval civilization in France was menaced and marred by the Hundred Years' war, a struggle between the English heirs of the Angevin empire and their French rivals. It arose out of a disputed succession, after the death of the three sons of Philip IV without male heirs. A curious survival of Frankish times, the so-called Salic law, was given a new meaning by designing intriguers in order to exclude the daughters of the late kings. From this time forward it became the rule in France that succession was strictly in the male line. Accordingly, the throne passed to Philip VI of Valois, a nephew of Philip IV. But Edward III of England claimed the throne through his mother, a daughter of Philip IV. In reality, the conflict grew out of economic rivalries in Flanders and of the desire of the French kings to seize the fiefs which the English kings still held in France.

The Hundred Years' war was rendered illustrious by battles, Crécy (1346), Poitiers (1356), and Agincourt (1415), in which English bowmen proved more than a match for French knights; by the career of Bertrand du Guesclin, who reduced the English possessions to a few coast towns; and by the heroic conduct of Joan of Arc. Joan, when the English had again overrun the country and had conquered all the region north of the Loire, saved Orleans, conducted Charles VII to Reims for his coronation, and drove the English from half a dozen provinces, only to be captured and burned as a heretic and sorceress at Rouen. Shortly after the death of Joan, the duke of Burgundy, who had been driven into the arms of the English by the murder of his father in a factional struggle, made terms with Charles VII and assisted him in driving the English armies from the country. When the war ended in 1453 Calais alone remained under English control. The devastation of the land by armies and by partisan bands had been terrible. Hundreds of villages were reduced to heaps of ruins, haunted by wild animals. The monarchy, however, emerged stronger than before. The work of consolidating the royal domain went on rapidly under Louis XI, so that when he died the only great independent fief was Brittany. His successor, Charles VIII, secured that province by marriage and completed his father's work by creating a thorough military organization.

Expansion of French Power. The campaigns of Charles VIII in Italy marked the beginning of the French policy of expansion abroad, and the reign of Francis I (1515–47) brought into France from Italy the inspiration of the Renaissance. A new era of art and architecture began, rivaling that of the middle ages. This development, again, was retarded by the religious wars, partly a consequence of the Reformation, partly due to factional conflicts between the powerful house of Guise and Protestant nobles and princes. At this time the real ruler was not one feeble monarch after another,

but their mother Catherine de' Medici, widow of Henry II, who made up in unscrupulousness what she lacked in strength. After the massacre of St. Bartholomew (1572), the leadership of the Huguenots passed to Henry of Navarre, a Bourbon prince who came to the throne in 1589 as Henry IV. On the principle that "Paris was well' worth a Mass," Henry became a Catholic, thus pacifying his Catholic subjects. Then, in 1598, he issued the Edict of Nantes, which granted religious freedom to the Protestants.

With the religious question settled in such a way as to insure quiet at home and also to encourage the Protestant German states in their contest with the Habsburgs, Henry and his minister, Sully, set about the military and administrative strengthening of the crown, with the purpose of making France the first power in Europe, but in the midst of his work he was struck down by an assassin. Several years of regency under Marie de' Medici and a period of personal rule under Louis XIII followed. The States-General met in 1614 for the last time before 1789. In 1624 Cardinal Richelieu took direction of affairs; during the next sixteen years he crushed the Protestant political power and all Catholic oligarchical tendencies, hopelessly divided the German states, and made France a united nation with a highly centralized government. Cardinal Mazarin continued Richelieu's work and left to Louis XIV the machinery of the personal despotism which that monarch wielded for more than half a century. The policy of all the great French kings since the days of Hugh Capet could be carried no further than the absolutism of the Grand Monarch.

Reign of Louis XIV. With the financial genius of Colbert, the engineering skill of Vauban, the organizing gifts of Louvois, and the military talent of Turenne at his command, Louis was able to secure enormous revenue, to build magnificently, and to wage war splendidly. France advanced her frontier northward and eastward by annexations in the Netherlands, by the conquest of Alsace, and the seizure of Franche-Comté. French explorers and traders in America and India laid the foundations of a great colonial empire. In the arts of civilization, France achieved the leadership of Europe. Domestic and public architecture flourished. Poetry and the drama were adorned by the names of Corneille, Racine, and Molière; prose, by those of Bossuet, La Rochefoucauld, and Saint-Simon. But excessive taxation depleted the resources of the people, unprovoked wars set all the powers of Europe against France, and the bigotry and prodigal luxury of king and court sapped the moral foundations of the national life. Louis XIV left to his infant great-grandson, Louis XV, a decaying power.

The Eighteenth Century. The long and disastrous reign of Louis XV, intelligent, but nonchalant and corrupt, culminated in the loss of Canada and the abandonment of India. The discredit of the government abroad made more insistent the demands for reform at home. The great books of the period belong to the literature of criticism and revolution. Authority in State and Church was undermined. Writers like Montesquieu, Voltaire, Diderot, Rousseau, and Turgot were establishing new principles in public law and social economy. Even the monarchy began to take on the characteristics of a benevolent despotism, and it made belated efforts to correct a vicious system of taxation in which the burden rested mainly upon the industrious peasantry. To break down the dead wall of privilege, a Henry IV was needed, but the successor of Louis XV was his weak-willed, half-educated grandson, the unfortunate Louis XVI. He had no lack of able advisers in such finance ministers as Turgot, Necker, and even Calonne, but he had not the persistence of character to push through their schemes against the opposition of the privileged classes. If the country was to be saved from bankruptcy it was essential to abolish exemptions from taxation and to demand its proper share from every form of wealth. Upon Calonne's advice, an assembly of the notables was called in 1787, but this body, composed of privileged persons, was frightened at the thought of thoroughgoing reform. At last the king summoned the States-General and recalled Necker, in whom the public had great confidence.

The Revolution. The States-General, which met at Versailles on May 5, 1789, was composed of members elected by the three orders,—nobility, clergy, and commons. The *cahiers*, or "statements," drawn up by each order, gave promise of speedy agreement upon governmental reform, but the nobles and the higher clergy were opposed to the demand of the commons that all three orders should sit together and vote individually. A long deadlock ensued. After a majority of the clergy and many of the nobles had gone over to the side of the third estate, the king intervened with a declaration aimed at the preservation of the distinction between the three orders. Within four days he was obliged to yield and to sanction the union of all the orders in a single National Assembly. Influenced by the reactionary court nobles, he dismissed Necker. He also called several regiments to the neighborhood of Paris and Versailles. Popular suspicion credited the government with a plan to dissolve the National Assembly.

On July 12 Paris rose, and two days later a mob forced the surrender of the Bastille, a royal fortress and prison which seemed to symbolize the despotism of the old régime. Similar scenes of violence spread over France. This strengthened the hands of the reform party in the Assembly and intimidated their opponents. In a night session, on August 4, nobles, clergy, and commons seemed to vie with one another in renouncing every form of privilege. A few days later the Assembly drew up its famous Declaration of the Rights of Man and the Citizen, proclaiming the new gospel of human equality. The king believed the Assembly was going too far, and he determined to check its career with a royal veto. Again he summoned troops to protect himself against an outburst of popular violence. The result in October was the same as that in July. This time a mob led by several thousand women streamed out to Versailles, brought the royal family to Paris, and compelled the king to take up his residence in the Tuileries.

The National Assembly. In the period from October 1789 to June 1791, the National Assembly, also called the Constituent Assembly, carried through constructive reforms which lie at the foundation of modern French life. The country was redistributed into departments, and a uniform system of local government introduced. New courts with a more liberal mode of procedure protected innocence and reduced the expenses of justice. Landed property was freed from feudal dues, and peasant ownership was promoted. The taxes characteristic of the old régime gave place to a new system which distributed the burden fairly. Here the Assembly's fault was failure to secure prompt collection, with the consequence that revenues steadily failed. A more serious mistake was the attempt to reorganize the Church and to free it from papal control. This followed the confiscation or nationalization of the vast ecclesiastical landed estates, in the hope that by their sale the country could be saved from bankruptcy. The plan of issuing land scrip, or assignats based upon the proceeds of the expected sales, led to inflation, which multiplied the difficulties of the government, especially after 1792.

The king was forced to accept the changes which the Assembly made in the Church, but his conscience was so troubled that he lent himself to schemes of counter-revolution. In this pass of affairs, the king and queen made the fatal error of trying to escape from Paris to the frontier, where a zealous royalist, the Marquis de Bouillé, was in command of the army. They were arrested and brought back. This episode gained importance for two reasons: it confirmed popular suspicion of the king's disloyalty to the Constitution; it gave impetus to a hitherto slow movement toward republicanism.

The Legislative Assembly. The National Assembly adjourned on September 30, 1791, to give place to the Legislative Assembly provided for in the Constitution. But, in an excess of disinterestedness, the members passed a "self-denying ordinance," which declared all members of the Constituent Assembly ineligible for membership in either the new Legislative Assembly or the ministry. The new body, therefore, which met on October 1, was made up of inexperienced men and was subject to the vagaries of doctrinaire leaders and the sway of undisciplined groups among its members.

The evils arising from this lack of statesman-like counsel in the government were increased by the rise of two radical clubs, the Jacobins and the Cordeliers. To these were added a group of ambitious, unpractical republicans in the Assembly, the Girondists. France was still monarchist; the French people did not desire a republic. But radicalism, spurred by the spirit of self-seeking and rivalry, was rapidly moving toward the destruction of the monarchy without being able to provide a stable government to take its place.

On the other hand, the king and the queen were plotting with the émigrés, or royalists who had fled from the country, and Austria had joined with Prussia during the summer of 1791 in a threat of intervention. The Assembly declared war against Francis II of Austria on April 20, 1792. This also involved Prussia by virtue of the alliance between Francis and Frederick William II. Only Robespierre and a few others opposed the move on the ground that war never helped democracy. But the tide of national feeling was running high, and the Jacobins proclaimed the conflict to be one of democracy against autocracy. When, in the late summer, the Prussian army crossed the French frontier, a manifesto was issued which confirmed this Jacobin view. The manifesto demanded the restoration of Louis XVI to complete liberty of action, under penalty of the sack and ruin of Paris. The Jacobins had their reply ready. They engineered a popular uprising, established a Revolutionary Commune in place of the regular city government, and made an assault on the palace of the Tuileries, compelling the king to take refuge in the hall of the Legislative Assembly. Intimidated by this new revolution, the Assembly, reduced to a third of its numbers, called a convention to draft a constitution on republican lines, and proclaimed universal suffrage. A ministry was elected, of which the leading member was Danton. But it was the Commune rather than the national government that seemed to control the course of events. It signalized its bloody career by permitting its Committee of Surveillance to organize a massacre of political prisoners, nobles, and priests. The butchery went on for four days, and more than a thousand persons perished.

The Convention. On September 20 the Convention, the third of the revolutionary assemblies, which was to last for three years, or until October 26, 1795, began its work. On the same day the army of Prussia was defeated at Valmy, more by its own failure to press home its attack than by the strength of the French armies.

The Convention must be recognized as one of the great governmental bodies of history. The bitter party rivalry between Girondists and Jacobins, resulting in the expulsion of the former, the execution of the king, the Terror with its especial ferocity in Lyons and the Vendée—these are incidents in the defensive and constructive work of that body. Terrible as were these excesses, tragic as was the fate of Madame Roland, the Girondist leader, of Danton, the vigorous compromiser, and of Robespierre, the austere fanatic, such things have not been confined to France of the Revolution.

The first act of the Convention was to declare unanimously that "royalty is abolished in France." Thus almost furtively was the French Republic ushered in. Constitution making was postponed by the bitter struggle between the Girondists, who represented the provinces, and the Jacobins, whose main strength was in Paris. Supported by the Commune, the Jacobins won. The invasion of the Austrian Netherlands and the menace to Holland alarmed the English. The execution of Louis XVI served as the occasion for an outbreak of war, not only with England, but also with Holland and Spain. Soon all Europe seemed united against the regicide republic. The Vendean peasants rose in behalf of king and Church. The Convention met the encircling perils by decreeing universal military service and by organizing a government under a committee of public safety. The opposition was cowed by the threat of trial before a revolutionary tribunal, from whose judgments there was no appeal. Such was the machinery of administration until the danger was past.

The Commune of Paris, led by Marat, forced the Convention to expel the Girondists; they retaliated by arousing a revolt in the departments. The Jacobin Convention hastily prepared a constitution so generous in its democratic provisions that the country ratified it by an overwhelming vote. This took the heart out of the revolt. Having served this purpose, the constitution of 1793 was never put into effect. France had need of a strong government, which was already provided for in the committees and the widely distributed and highly organized Jacobin clubs. The Committee of Public Safety became supreme; its members toiled tremendously. Their method was the appeal to fear, to impress by startling and ruthless action. Carnot raised and equipped a dozen armies, aggregating 750,000 men. Every commander, watched by representatives of the Convention on mission, had the alternative of victory or the guillotine. Under this stimulus, superhuman feats were accomplished. The armies were everywhere victorious against the allies, and civil war was stamped out at home.

Meanwhile, in affairs of peace the Convention wrought greatly. It gave France the metric system of weights and measures; it began the work of codifying the law; it planned an elaborate system of popular education; it created or enlarged many institutions, such as the Polytechnic School of Paris, the Museum of the Louvre, and the National Library. The Convention also devised a new calendar.

The revolutionary tribunal in Paris became increasingly the instrument of the violent elements of the Commune. The success of the Commune, which was wholly antichristian, attained its climax when it set up at Paris in 1793 the worship of Reason. Robespierre condemned this move and a few months later urged the worship of the Supreme Being as the only democratic religion. To enforce this virtuous régime, he seized control of the Tribunal and would have used it to destroy his political enemies, a corrupt group which discredited the Revolution. These men combined to bring about his fall and execution. The power of the Jacobins dwindled, and the Convention in 1795 drew up a new constitution.

The Rise of Napoleon Bonaparte. This third constitution of the Revolution placed the Republic in the hands of property holders, who alone could vote, thus striking a blow at the power of the Paris mob. The Convention added supplementary decrees, in accordance with which two-thirds of the new legislature should be chosen from the membership of the Convention itself. This provoked strong protests, especially in Paris. The conservative elements of the National Guard, with the aid of many royalists, planned an attack upon the Convention. Its defense was undertaken by Barras, one of its members, and he called to his aid an artillery officer, General Napoleon Bonaparte, who had won distinction at the siege of Toulon. Bonaparte turned his cannon upon the advancing insurgent columns, saved the Convention, and at the same time inaugurated a great career.

The time was auspicious for Napoleon. The Terror had robbed France of her natural leaders. The constitution of 1795 provided for a legislative body of two houses, the Council of Five Hundred and the Council of Elders. The executive power was lodged in the Directory composed of five men. Such extreme division of power, with its consequent weakness of decision, made Napoleon's opportunity. After four years of troubled history, the Directory and the Councils reached the verge of collapse. During these same years Napoleon had become the most renowned military commander in Europe. Dispatched to northern Italy in the struggle with Austria, he had won an astonishing series of victories and in 1797 had negotiated the Peace of Campo Formio. One of the consequences was the application in Italy of the French program of reform and the beginnings of the *Risorgimento*. In 1798 he was sent to Egypt, and the luster of Oriental conquest added to his name, although Nelson's destruction of the French fleet at the battle of the Nile deprived France of the fruits of the enterprise. Napoleon now left his army and returned to France. With the opportune and dramatic aid of his brother Lucien, president of the Council of Five Hundred, he executed his famous *coup d'état* in 1799. He dictated a new constitution which provided for three consuls (himself to be first consul with power to initiate all legislation), a tribunate to discuss bills, and a legislative body to vote them.

The Concordat. Now opened the period of the Consulate, a period of reorganization,—administrative, financial, and social. An efficient local government in the departments was put under the control of prefects. The taxes were collected and a bank of France was established. A civil code summed up the legal gains of the citizen during the Revolution, reconciling the new law with the older principles of French jurisprudence. By a concordat the schism, which had vexed the Catholic population since 1791, was brought to an end. New victories over Austria led to the Peace of Lunéville, and even Great Britain saw the necessity of agreeing to a treaty at Amiens in March 1802. All that lacked was political liberty, for the First Consul soon assumed the attitudes of a dictator. With the creation of the Consulate for Life in 1802, France, though still a republic in name, was in fact a monarchy. Two years later Napoleon was declared emperor of the French.

Napoleon, Emperor. Meanwhile, war broke out again with England, which country Napoleon could not reach across the channel. In 1805 the coalition of England, Russia, and Austria was formed against him. He struck at Austria, won the battle of Austerlitz, and dictated the Peace of Pressburg. He then organized the Confederation of the Rhine and destroyed the Holy Roman Empire. In 1806, at Jena and Auerstädt, the Prussian armies crumbled before the French, but the battle of Eylau, February 1807, was a disaster, only partially retrieved by the victory at Friedland in June. Napoleon was satisfied to make the Treaty of Tilsit with Alexander of Russia. England alone remained to be dealt with. The victory of Trafalgar in 1805 had left her supreme on the sea. Napoleon attempted to reach her through his Continental System, that is, by excluding her trade from continental ports and by attacking Portugal, an ally of England, through Spain. But here he went too far in attempting to reduce Spain also. Although he unseated an unpopular Bourbon monarch, he aroused national sentiment which he found unconquerable. This new power of national feeling was in the end the conqueror's undoing.

Leaving Spain hastily when Austria declared war in 1809, he again brought that power to her knees and dictated the Treaty of Vienna. England still was unconquered, even though her industries were feeling the effect of the continental blockade. In 1809 Napoleon was at the height of his career, but the anticlimax was approaching. The Russian campaign in 1812, ending in disaster and retreat, the battle of Leipzig in October 1813, which was a decisive defeat—these were the signals for the defection of the German states. On March 31, 1814 the allies entered Paris, and Louis XVIII was placed on the throne, reckoning himself to be in the 19th year of his reign, king "by the grace of God." He went too far, however, in ignoring the Revolution and Bonaparte, and the people were soon ready to receive their "emperor" again. But the battle of Waterloo sealed his doom. The Congress of Vienna, which had rearranged the states of Europe, trying vainly to forget the Revolution and Napoleon, had already come to a close.

The Restoration. Under Louis XVIII some beginnings toward a liberal government, such as periodical elections, annual voting of the budget, and liberty of the press, were made. But a reaction set in under Charles X, who attempted a *coup d'état* in 1830. He was defeated, and Louis Philippe of the house of Orleans was placed on the throne, with the title "King of the French," instead of "King of France." During his reign, manufacturing industries grew beyond precedent, and the power of the working classes was thereby increased. Socialist doctrines were widely taught, although they were opposed by the ministry. But Guizot, the prime minister, erred by governing with too little regard for popular movements.

Revolution and the Second Empire. The storm broke in February 1848. The king abdicated and went into exile in England, and a provisional government was compelled by the workmen of Paris to establish "national workshops" and to guarantee employment. The experiment, never sincerely undertaken, turned out to be merely a scheme for occupying the unemployed, which drained the national treasury. When the National Assembly suddenly closed the shops, Paris was thrown into the hands of mobs of idle, half starved workmen, demanding "bread or lead." The terrible "June days" of 1848, when the military crushed the revolt with great severity, left an evil influence in the labor problem of France. But the peasants of the provinces were not in sympathy with the Paris workmen, and conservative republicans were able to put a new constitution in force. A single chamber legislature and a president, to be chosen by popular vote, were provided for. The election made Louis Napoleon president of the second French Republic.

The new president was a nephew of Napoleon I. In 1832 he had put forward his claims to the throne of France, but, not meeting with encouragement, he had then retired to England. In 1840 he made a second attempt to seize the crown, but this time he was captured and shut up in a fortress, whence he escaped to England. He continued, however, to ingratiate himself with the people by posing as a democrat. On the eve of the election of 1848, he adroitly offered himself as the champion of the working classes, the middle classes, and the army. Elected by an overwhelming majority, he set to work at once to arouse enthusiasm for a restored empire. The Assembly refused to aid him, and on December 2, 1851, the anniversary of the battle of Austerlitz, he dissolved that body. A special election gave him a large vote of approval for this *coup d'état*. Another vote in 1852 approved a decree of the Senate making him emperor.

From 1852 to 1860 Napoleon III wielded a despotic rule, largely through the magic of his name. Yet during this period France made great industrial and scientific advance. Railroads were built, the city of Paris was modernized with broad streets and avenues, and institutions of charity and education multiplied. Little of this is to be credited to the emperor. His one real service to France was the acquisition of Nice and Savoy, and this was the outcome of Cavour's adroit use of Napoleon in driving the Austrians out of Italy. His weakness and indecision allowed a more liberal policy of government after 1860 but left France an easy prey to the Prussians in 1870.

Fall of Napoleon III. The Franco-Prussian war grew out of Napoleon's schemes for annexations on the northeastern frontier of France and Bismarck's conviction that only through a German triumph over the French Empire could the unification of Germany be assured. Bismarck seized the occasion of a dynastic controversy apropos of the succession to the crown of Spain to provoke the struggle. French armies crumbled before the German attack, the emperor was made prisoner, and the Empire collapsed like a house of cards. Bismarck, by the Treaty of Frankfort, May 10, 1871, forced France to cede Alsace and Lorraine to Germany and to pay an indemnity of one billion dollars.

The Third Republic. In this crisis, as in 1793 and 1848, Paris was the center of a radical movement, that of the "Communards." National Assembly, sitting at Versailles, suppressed the Commune after a bloody second siege.

The National Assembly then proceeded to the work of framing a constitution. The republican minority gained time and gathered strength against the divided royalists, until they were able to set up the Third Republic in 1875. An unsuccessful attempt to check republican tendencies led to President Mac-Mahon's resignation in 1879. A strong anti-clerical movement led France in 1905 to abrogate the Concordat of 1801 and effect separation of church and state.

Economic and Political Growth. In spite of the seemingly crushing burden of the war indemnity of 1871, France speedily cleared the obligation. The Third Republic was a period of large development in French industries and commerce. In 1870, French colonial possessions were limited to Algeria, the Senegal region, and some small stations on the Gulf of Guinea in Africa, besides a settlement in Cochin China. These were extended until France controlled an area about twenty times as large as her home area in Europe.

After the Franco-Prussian war the army had been reorganized upon the principle of universal military service. In 1913, following upon large German military preparations, France made feverish efforts to strengthen her army. Within a few months, French territory was invaded and Europe was plunged into a prolonged war, fought chiefly on French soil. See *World War I*.

After the war, French policy was concerned mainly with (1) the problem of security against a renewal of German attack on the Rhine frontier; (2) enforcement of the reparation provisions of the Treaty of Versailles; (3) alliances with the new small states of central Europe; (4) development of French interests in Morocco and the Near East.

In 1922 Prime Minister Poincaré seized the Ruhr and held it for three years as security for reparations payments. Poincaré's successors had to meet a rapid trend toward financial collapse through currency inflation, aggravated by expensive wars in Syria and Morocco.

Aristide Briand, in the next five years, secured somewhat better relations with Germany. Then came the depression. It brought an end of reparations, it brought the Hitler dictatorship in Germany, and, finally, in 1936, the "popular front" administration of Leon Blum, with its labor disorders.

After 1939 the German danger overshadowed all

else. France acquiesced in the annexation of Austria and Czechoslovakia. When Germany invaded Poland, France and Britain declared war, Sept. 3, 1939.

World War II. With the armistice of June 22, 1940, France withdrew from the war, completely defeated. By the terms of the armistice, the Germans occupied northern France, Paris, and the western coast. A government under Marshal Pétain and Pierre Laval, at Vichy, collaborated with Germany. Meantime a "Free French" government, headed by Gen. Charles de Gaulle, had been organized in London and recognized by the Allies. On the invasion of France, the Committee proclaimed itself the Provisional Government and was accepted by the people. French troops took part in the invasion and occupation of Germany. France became a member of the United Nations, with a seat on the Security Council. Pétain was condemned to life imprisonment, and Laval and others executed.

Ascendancy of De Gaulle. The hero of the new France was De Gaulle. He dedicated himself to removing the political causes of French weaknesses under the third Republic and to restoring France's former glory.

In 1946 a new constitution was adopted, the basis for the Fourth Republic, but De Gaulle was opposed to it because it did not provide for a strong executive power. He went into retirement. Several ministers succeeded each other, struggling with reconstruction problems and with the revolt of the French colonial empire. Although participating in the North Atlantic Treaty Organization and contributing forces to it so as to contain Russian threats to Europe, France poured most of her strength into Vietnam in Asia and Algeria in Africa. Vietnam, with communist aid, drove the French out after a bloody struggle. In Algeria, which had a large French population, hostilities led to negotiations for independence, which the French army leaders opposed. France seemed near civil war in 1958. Political

leaders turned to De Gaulle, who consented to become premier, but insisted on a free hand for a stated time. He then peaceably subdued the insubordinate army leaders, and persuaded the country to adopt a new constitution, the basic law for the Fifth Republic, under which he became president.

He next transformed the French empire into a commonwealth—the French Community—offering each dependent territory a choice: incorporation as a department of France, or independence within or without the Community. Algeria and several others chose independence within.

Under the new constitution, the government controlled credit and taxation, directed the flow of investment, and promoted a rapid buildup of wealth. The franc was stabilized. Exploding an atom bomb in 1960, France became the fourth nuclear power. France also led in forming the Common Market, based on the 1957 Treaty of Rome. De Gaulle, however, in 1963, blocked its expansion by barring Britain. By a pact with West Germany, he sought to end traditional Franco-German enmity; and, seeking leadership in Europe, he opposed U.S. policies. Re-elected in 1965, he withdrew from NATO (though insisting that France remained an ally) and attempted direct negotiations with Russia.

By summer of 1968, however, civil and economic disobedience threatened. Students rioted and commerce was halted by a general strike. De Gaulle pledged reform and set new elections—from which he again emerged in strength.

Pompidou Government. De Gaulle lost a vote of confidence in 1969 and resigned. His candidate, Georges Pompidou, succeeded him and De Gaulle died in 1970, the last of the great Allied World War II leaders. Pompidou, who died in 1974, followed De Gaulle's policies in the face of continuing unrest and student violence. The franc, defended so long by De Gaulle, was finally devalued. In May of 1974, Valery Giscard d'Estaing, formerly Pompidou's minister of finance, was elected president.

RULERS OF FRANCE

NAME	LINEAGE	Period of Rule		Birth	Death
		A. D.	A. D.	A. D.	A. D.
	THE OLD FRANKISH KINGDOM				
	THE MEROVINGIANS				
Clodian	King of the Salian Franks	428?	448	?	?
Meroveus	Founder of the Merovingian dynasty	448	456	411?	456
Childeric I	Son of Meroveus; king of the Franks	456	481	?	481
Clovis I	Son of Childeric I	481	511	466?	511
	THE KINGDOM IN FOUR PARTS				
Childebert I	Son of Clovis I; king of Paris	511	558	495	558
Thierry I	Son of Clovis I; king of Austrasia	511	534	?	534
Clodomir	Son of Clovis I; king of Orleans	511	524	?	524
Clothaire I	Fourth son of Clovis I { king of Soissons	511	558		
	{ sole king	558	561	497	561
	SECOND DIVISION OF THE KINGDOM				
Charibert {	King of Paris	561	567	?	567
Guntram } Sons of }	King of Orleans and Burgundy	561	593	?	593
Chilperic I } Clothaire I }	King of Neustria at Soissons	561	584	?	584
Sigebert I (	King of Austrasia at Metz	561	575	?	575
Childebert II	Son of Sigebert I; king of Austrasia and Burgundy	575	596	570	596
Clothaire II	Son of Chilperic I; sole king	613	628	584	628
Dagobert I	Son of Clothaire II; sole king	628	638	602	638
Clovis II	Son of Dagobert I	638	656	633	656
Dagobert II	King of Austrasia	656	679	652	679
Clothaire III	King of Neustria	656	670	652?	670?
Childeric II	Son of Clovis II; sole king	670	673	?	673
Thierry III	Son of Clovis II; king of Burgundy	673?	691	652?	691
Clovis III	King of Neustria	691	695	681	695
Childebert III	King of Neustria	695	711	?	?
Dagobert III	King of Neustria	711	715	699	715
Chilperic II	Son of Childeric II	715	720	?	720
Thierry IV	Son of Dagobert III	720	737	712?	737
Childeric III	Son of Chilperic II; deposed by Pepin the Short	742	752	?	755
	THE CAROLINGIANS				
Pepin the Short	Son of Charles Martel	752	768	714?	768
Charlemagne, or Charles the Great	Son of Pepin the Short	768	814	742	814
Louis I, le Débonnaire	Son of Charles the Great	814	840	778	840
Charles the Bald	Younger son of Louis I, le Débonnaire	840	877	823	877
Louis II	Son of Charles the Bald	877	879	846	879
Louis III	Son of Louis II	879	882	863	882

NAME	LINEAGE	Period of Rule		Birth	Death
		A. D.	A. D	A. D.	A. D.
Charles the Fat	Son of Louis the German	882	888	832?	888
Count Eudes (Odo)	Elected king at Compiègne	888	893	857?	893
Charles III, the Simple	Son of Louis the Stammerer	893	923	879	929
Raoul (Rudolf of Burgundy)	Elected king by the nobles	923	936	?	936
Louis IV	Son of Charles III, the Simple	936	954	921?	954
Lothair	Son of Louis IV	954	986	941	986
Louis V	Son of Lothair	986	987	966?	987

THE KINGDOM OF FRANCE
HOUSE OF CAPET

NAME	LINEAGE	Period of Rule		Birth	Death
Hugh Capet	Son of Hugh the Great	987	996	939?	996
Robert II	Son of Hugh Capet	996	1031	971?	1031
Henry I	Son of Robert II	1031	1060	1011?	1060
Philip I	Son of Henry I	1060	1108	1052?	1108
Louis VI, the Fat	Son of Philip I	1108	1137	1078?	1137
Louis VII	Son of Louis VI	1137	1180	1120?	1180
Philip II, Augustus	Son of Louis VII	1180	1223	1165	1223
Louis VIII	Son of Philip II, Augustus	1223	1226	1187	1226
Louis IX, or St. Louis	Son of Louis VIII	1226	1270	1215?	1270
Philip III, the Bold	Son of Louis IX	1270	1285	1245	1285
Philip IV, the Fair	Son of Philip III	1285	1314	1268	1314
Louis X	Son of Philip IV	1314	1316	1289	1316
Philip V, the Tall	Second son of Philip IV	1316	1322	1293	1322
Charles IV, the Fair	Youngest son of Philip IV, the Fair	1322	1328	1294	1328

HOUSE OF VALOIS

NAME	LINEAGE	Period of Rule		Birth	Death
Philip VI of Valois	Son of Count Charles of Valois	1328	1350	1293	1350
John the Good	Son of Philip VI	1350	1364	1319	1364
Charles V, the Wise	Son of John II	1364	1380	1337	1380
Charles VI	Son of Charles V	1380	1422	1368	1422
Charles VII, the Victorious	Son of Charles VI	1422	1461	1403	1461
Louis XI	Son of Charles VII	1461	1483	1423	1483
Charles VIII	Son of Louis XI	1483	1498	1470	1498
Louis XII	A descendant of the younger son of Charles V	1498	1515	1462	1515
Francis I	Son of Charles, count of Angoulême	1515	1547	1494	1547
Henry II	Son of Francis I	1547	1559	1519	1559
Francis II	Eldest son of Henry II	1559	1560	1544	1560
Charles IX	Second son of Henry II	1560	1574	1550	1574
Henry III	Third son of Henry II	1574	1589	1551	1589

HOUSE OF BOURBON

NAME	LINEAGE	Period of Rule		Birth	Death
Henry IV	Son of Antoine de Bourbon, king of Navarre	1589	1610	1553	1610
Louis XIII	Son of Henry IV	1610	1643	1601	1643
Louis XIV	Son of Louis XIII and Anne of Austria	1643	1715	1638	1715
Louis XV	Great-grandson of Louis XIV	1715	1774	1710	1774
Louis XVI	Grandson of Louis XV	1774	1792	1754	1793

REVOLUTIONARY PERIOD

NAME	LINEAGE	Period of Rule		Birth	Death
National Convention	September 21, 1792—October 26, 1795	1792	1795		
Directory nominated	October 27, 1795—November 10, 1799	1795	1799		

THE CONSULATE

NAME	LINEAGE	Period of Rule		Birth	Death
Bonaparte				1769	1821
Cambacérès	Elected by the Elders and the Five Hundred	1799	1804	1753	1824
Lebrun				1739	1824
Bonaparte	Elected consul for life	1802			

THE EMPIRE

NAME	LINEAGE	Period of Rule		Birth	Death
Napoleon I (Bonaparte)	Crowned emperor, December 2, 1804	1804	1814	1769	1821

THE RESTORATION

NAME	LINEAGE	Period of Rule		Birth	Death
Louis XVIII	Brother of Louis XVI; proclaimed April 11, 1814.	1814	1824	1755	1824
Charles X	Younger brother of Louis XVIII; deposed 1830	1824	1830	1757	1836

HOUSE OF ORLEANS

NAME	LINEAGE	Period of Rule		Birth	Death
Louis Philippe	Son of Philippe Egalité; abdicated 1848	1830	1848	1773	1850

THE SECOND REPUBLIC

NAME	LINEAGE	Period of Rule		Birth	Death
Louis Napoleon	Nephew of Napoleon I; elected president	1848	1852	1808	1873

THE SECOND EMPIRE

NAME	LINEAGE	Period of Rule		Birth	Death
Napoleon III (Louis Napoleon)	Elected emperor; deposed 1870	1852	1870	1808	1873

THE THIRD REPUBLIC

NAME	LINEAGE	Period of Rule		Birth	Death
Louis Adolphe Thiers	Elected president	1871	1873	1797	1877
Marshal MacMahon	Elected president	1873	1879	1808	1893
Jules Grévy	Elected president	1879	1887	1807	1891
M. F. Sadi Carnot	Elected president	1887	1894	1837	1894
Jean Casimir-Périer	Elected president	1894	1895	1847	1907
François Félix Faure	Elected president	1895	1899	1841	1899
M. Emile Loubet	Elected president	1899	1906	1838	1929
Clément Armand Fallières	Elected president	1906	1913	1841	1931
Raymond Poincaré	Elected president	1913	1920	1860	1934
Paul Deschanel	Elected president, served Feb. 18–Sept. 16	1920	1920	1856	1922
Alexandre Millerand	Elected president, September 23, 1920	1920	1924	1859	1943
Gaston Doumergue	Elected president, June 13, 1924	1924	1931	1863	1937
Paul Doumet	Elected president, May 13, 1931	1931	1932	1857	1932
Albert Lebrun	Elected president, May 11, 1932; April 5, 1939	1932	1940	1871	1950
Henri Philippe Pétain	Chief of state, July 11, 1940	1940	1944	1856	1951

Heads of Provisional Government: Charles De Gaulle (1890-1970) rec. Oct. 23, 1944; Felix Gouin (1884-) elec. Jan. 23 1946; Georges Bidault (1899-) elec. June 24, 1946.

NAME	LINEAGE	Period of Rule		Birth	Death
	THE FOURTH REPUBLIC	A. D.	A. D.	A. D.	A. D
Vincent Auriol	President, Jan. 16, 1947	1947	1954	1884	1966
René Coty	President, Jan. 1954	1954	1959	1883	1962
	THE FIFTH REPUBLIC				
Charles de Gaulle	President, Jan. 1959	1959	1969	1890	1970
Georges Pompidou	President, June 15, 1969	1969	1974	1911	1974
Valery Giscard d'Estaing	President, May 27, 1974	1974		1926	

GEORGIA

As an independent kingdom in the Caucasus, Georgia, with occasional periods of submission to Turkish and also to Persian power, maintained its existence from the death of Alexander the Great (323 B. C.) to 1801, when it was annexed by Russia. After the Russian revolution, in 1918, Georgia declared its independence but, in 1920–21, under pressure from Russia, became a socialist soviet republic.

GERMANY

German history, perhaps better than that of any other country, exemplifies the conflict between internal dissension and the centralizing trend of human governments. In Roman days the country was inhabited by numerous tribes. one of which, the Cherusci, under their Roman-trained prince Arminius, drove the Roman invaders permanently back to the Rhine in the great battle of the Teutoburg Forest, 9 A.D. With the fall of the Roman Empire came a general westward movement of the German tribes, from which the Franks emerged as the dominant power. Charlemagne (Karl the Great, 768-814) ruled to the Atlantic, the Pyrenees, the Po, the Raab (Hungary) and the Elbe. The Franks were now Christians, and Charlemagne was crowned by Pope Leo III on Christmas Day 800 as Emperor of the Romans. This unity under Charlemagne saved European civilization, but it was premature, and his empire disintegrated under his weaker successors before racial and local separatism and new invasions.

Founding of a German State. German history proper begins with the Treaty of Verdun, 843, in which Charlemagne's grandsons partitioned his empire, conceding to Lewis the German the lands east of the Rhine. For the first time a German prince ruled German-speaking tribes. But unity was a different matter. The feudal system made rapid advances under weak rulers, and there were serious internal disturbances, which were terminated only under the Saxon Henry I (919–936), called the Fowler, a born statesman and warrior, who established peace within the realm, and did much to insure it against foes from without, defeating the Magyars in 933.

Henry had established a federated state, anticipating German history by a thousand years. His son Otto I (936–973) the Great, increased the number of the German princes and the power of the prelates, but the latter turned against his successors in the struggle with the Papacy. Still more fateful was his attempted expansion into Italy, and his coronation in 962 by the Pope as head of the Holy Roman Empire. The power which might have united Germany was frittered away in Italian expeditions, and the imperial crown became a curse to the German kings and people. Otto's first Italian expedition, indeed, gave opportunity for a rebellion in Germany and a dangerous Magyar invasion. But the German people united, 955, to crush it in a battle near Augsburg.

The history of subsequent reigns is largely a reaping of the evil harvest sown by Otto's misguided policies, a record of civil strife and of fruitless and often ignominious conflicts with Italian princes and the popes. The memorable scene at Canossa in 1077, when for three days the emperor Henry IV begged for admission to the pope's presence, has become one of the bywords of history. The struggle over the investitures, settled by the compromise Concordat of Worms in 1122, ended in an empty victory for the emperor.

The Hohenstaufens. One of the most interesting epochs in German history is the period of the Hohenstaufens (1138–1254), two of whom, Frederick I, called Barbarossa, or Redbeard, who died in 1190 by drowning while on a crusade, and Frederick II, his grandson, were among the most brilliant of German kings. It was the golden age of the minnesingers and other court poets, and marked a revival of culture which anticipated the Renaissance, while there were remarkable ideas of religious tolerance in Walther von der Vogelweide and Wolfram von Eschenbach. The Wartburg castle and many splendid cathedrals prove the wealth and good taste of the time. It was then that the cities made their great growth, partly owing to Barbarossa's policy, and the famous Hansa was only one of many leagues of cities.

Important political changes took place. Prussia was conquered for Christianity by the Teutonic Order. The German kings, straining for world empire, lost control of Poland, Denmark, Burgundy, Prussia, and Schleswig-Holstein. Power passed more and more into the hands of the German princes, seven of whom now came to form the electoral college, which chose the successive emperors. These rulers, requiring powerful support for their foreign ventures, increased the control of the nobles, repressed the cities, and thus retarded for generations the development of a united nation.

The Habsburgs. Coming to power with the election of Rudolf in 1273, thus ending the Great Interregnum, the Habsburgs pursued similar policies. Ambitious more for themselves than for Germany, they did erect a powerful Austrian dynasty, but the fortunes of Germany sank under Frederick III (1440–93), who lost all influence at home and abroad. Wars raged unchecked across the land, the worst being a 4-year struggle between a league of cities and a group of princes, whose victory was disastrous to German unity.

Frederick's son Maximilian I (1459–1519), crowned in 1486, gave the Empire an authority unfelt for centuries. Germany remained feeble, but by inheritance and marriage, Maximilian was one of Europe's most powerful princes. His reign marked the end of the Middle Ages. Gunpowder and the rise of mercenaries destroyed feudalism. The discovery of America, printing, the revival of learning —these changed the face of the world. And the medieval relation of State and Church was about to undergo the fiery trial of the Reformation.

The Reformation; Thirty Years' War. Outwardly, the struggle began in Germany when Luther nailed to the church door at Wittenberg his 95 theses against the indulgences; inwardly, it had long been preparing, and was doubtless inevitable. The religious schism soon invaded the field of politics, and the princes were divided, the Protestants forming the Schmalkaldic League. The hostility maintained toward the League by Charles V (1520–58), Maximilian's brilliant grandson, finally led to his crushing victory over it at Mühlberg in 1547; but the movement went on. The Peace of Augsburg (1555) secured freedom of worship; sectarian friction produced the strife of the Counter Reformation under Rudolf II (1576–1612); both parties prepared for war. A dispute over the succession to the throne of Bohemia precipitated the most devastating conflict Europe had known since the middle ages—the Thirty Years' war.

Germany suffered most. Plundering armies crossed and recrossed her; industry and trade were crippled; she lost three-fourths of her population, and the remainder were crushed by taxes; the solid middle classes were wiped out; the empire disintegrated. In the final peace, Switzerland, the Netherlands, Alsace, and other territory left the empire, which had fallen apart into a loose confederation of petty states.

The Rise of Prussia. It was reserved for Prussia to weld the fragments into a new and more powerful state. In the 15th century a Hohenzollern had received the March of Brandenburg; a series of able descendants gradually built up a considerable province. Prussia's greatness, however, begins with Frederick I; he laid the foundations of the military system, and saved the money to run it. His son, Frederick the Great (1740–86), had the genius to employ his heritage, and the ambition to increase it. No sooner had he ascended the throne than he advanced a claim of the house of Brandenburg to the Silesian principalities, and when Maria Theresa (1740–80) of Austria—which had tried to weaken Prussia's growing power—rejected the claim, he promptly seized the disputed territory. This seizure was confirmed, after the War of the Austrian Succession (1741–45) had ended in the recognition of Maria Theresa's husband, Francis I, as emperor, in the Peace of Dresden (1745). But Austria was still resentful, and the issue was finally fought out in the Seven Years' war (1756–63), in which Frederick's extraordinary military genius triumphed over apparently irresistible coalitions. Prussia was now a military power of the first rank, and in the foundation of the Princes' League (1785) assumed for the first time a leadership in German affairs.

This initial movement toward a union of the North German states was halted for many years by the French Revolution and the Napoleonic wars. Divided, Germany was an easy prey for the conqueror and lay helpless before him until 1813, when the war of liberation, in which Russia, Austria, and England participated, finally terminated his sway in the great battles at Leipzig and Waterloo (1815).

At the Congress of Vienna (1815) a German Confederation was formed, with Austria as president of the federal diet. Constant agitation for the recognition of popular sovereignty, encouraged by the Parisian revolutions of 1830 and 1848, led to constitutional government in several German states, and to the attempt to set up a federal constitution. The crown of the empire was indeed offered to Frederick William IV of Prussia, but on condition that the Prussian state should be broken up into its several provinces. To this the interests of Prussia were utterly opposed, and the entire plan met with shipwreck.

Founding of the German Empire. Enmity to Austria had already borne fruit in her exclusion from the new constitutional state; and when, after the Schleswig-Holstein campaign of 1864, Prussia and Austria could not agree on the partition of the acquired territory, the step to armed conflict was not great. Hence the war of 1866, in which Austria was decisively defeated, and which resulted in the formation of the North German Confederation. Neither Austria nor the South German states were members, but the latter had formed with Prussia a secret offensive-defensive alliance. The time was nearly ripe for a closer union of the German states, and it was a sudden political crisis that made it possible. The war of 1866 had brought Germany and France near to the breaking point, for the insensate ambition of Napoleon III saw a threat to his power in the imminent union of the German peo-

ple. A point of honor, arising out of the disputed succession to the Spanish throne, led to a declaration of war in 1870, in which, however, Napoleon found himself opposed both by the North German Confederation and by the South German states, whereas neither Austria nor Italy was ready for war. The struggle was brief, and in 1871 William I of Prussia was proclaimed German emperor.

Industrial and Social Progress. Germany now entered upon a long period of peaceful growth, marked at the same time by extraordinary industrial activity. France had been compelled to pay as indemnity the enormous sum—as it was then considered—of five billion francs; and the investment of this money in Germany resulted in a fever of speculative enterprise in every direction. At the same time there were profound social changes going on. The rise of the industrial magnate had done two things: it had weakened the power of the old landed gentry (Junker); and it had developed a new class, the proletariat. Thence originated the spectacular rise to power of the Socialists, who, despite measures designed to limit their voting strength, rapidly grew to such proportions as a political party that they had to be seriously reckoned with. Only the astute policy of Bismarck, the "iron chancellor," prevented grave disturbances. His plan was, essentially, to steal the thunder of the Socialists by putting into effect the reforms which they advocated.

International Rivalry. It was not hard to suggest to this newly self-conscious nation an ideal of military prominence, if not of world domination, and such a program appealed to the young kaiser, William II, who ascended the Prussian throne in 1888. Gradually the entire foreign policy was shaped along lines of power and military action. The army was steadily strengthened, its organization improved; presently a navy came to the fore. And the German people approved, for they were convinced that their national life was threatened.

The European situation had indeed grown more and more tense. The Triple Alliance (1882), between Germany, Austria, and Italy, was balanced in 1892 by a similar understanding between France, which wanted revenge for the loss of Alsace-Lorraine (1871), and Russia, which had become estranged from Germany. The age-long desire of Russia to play a dominant rôle in the Balkans and to gain control of Constantinople threatened to force a conflict with Austria, which would bring in Germany.

Meanwhile, Great Britain also had been drifting into the hostile camp. In the year 1884 Germany had inaugurated a colonial policy which eventually led to the development of a large navy. In this step England saw a menace and a challenge which she could not ignore. The lifeblood of England is overseas commerce; her food is largely imported in ships; a naval blockade could starve her out in three months. Vainly she attempted to secure Germany's consent to a halt in the race of armaments. And Germany's attitude toward the efforts for international peace, signalized by the Hague Conferences, served to strengthen the suspicion that she was bent upon war. In another respect also Germany had crossed the lines of English policy. William II had cultivated the friendship of Turkey with a view to securing valuable concessions in Asia, the fruit of which was to be the famous "Berlin to Bagdad" railway, with its allied plans that threatened to imperil British interests in the Orient.

It was natural, then, that England should begin to feel a community of interest with France, one of the first fruits of which was the agreement of 1904 with respect to Morocco. Germany felt in this a blow at her commercial interests there, and forced the conference at Algeciras (1906) to grant her recognition as the price of peace. But Europe had now heard the rattling of the German sword, and plot and counterplot followed on each other's heels. The next dispute that threatened the peace of Europe arose from the annexation of Bosnia and Herzegovina by Austria in 1908. Serbia protested, and Russia supported the protest, but finally withdrew her opposition, feeling herself weakened by the disastrous war with Japan (1906), and hence not yet ready to try conclusions with the powerful military machine of Germany. Nevertheless, she remained secretly unreconciled, and proceeded on her part with military preparations.

World War I. By this time Germany had become the most efficient military power the world had ever seen. Such was the situation when, in June 1914, the Austrian heir apparent and his wife were assassinated in the streets of the Bosnian capital. Within two months the enmities of western Europe had burst forth into conflict and produced the then-greatest war of history. (See *World War I.*)

The German Republic. One of the most dramatic events attending the armistice was the German revolution of November 9, 1918. The disaffection on Germany's "home front," as von Hindenburg called it, had reached the point of open rebellion. The kaiser, forced to abdicate, fled to Holland, and within a short time every hereditary ruler in Germany had abdicated or been deposed. A temporary government provided for a constituent convention, which drew up a democratic constitution. Two armed attempts were made by communist groups to establish a socialist commonwealth similar to that in Russia. These were the so-called Spartacan revolts in Berlin and a communist revolt in Munich, all in the early months of 1919. They were ruthlessly suppressed, and the constitution was adopted on July 31, 1919.

There were two attempts by monarchist partisans to overthrow the democracy. Under the leadership of Kapp, in 1920, this group held Berlin for five days but was defeated by means of a general strike. In 1923, a similar insurrection broke out in Bavaria, led by Erich von Ludendorf and a young Austrian named Adolf Hitler. The leaders were captured, and Hitler was imprisoned.

Friedrich Ebert was the first president of Germany. His policy, pursued also after his death in 1925 by his successor, Paul von Hindenburg, was directed toward a peaceful defeat of the Versailles treaty by combined sabotage and conciliation.

Reparations Problem. The peace treaty fastened on Germany the payment of large annual sums as reparations. The result was a runaway inflation. The Allies declared Germany in default, and French troops, in January 1923, seized the Ruhr valley. Germany then refused all payments. The deadlock was broken by the Dawes plan, named from Charles G. Dawes, the American chairman of the commission framing it. The amount of the annuities was fixed, and the French left the Ruhr in 1925. Four years later a new arrangement fixed also total reparations. In 1931 came the depression, and the Allies cancelled their claims.

Nazi (*nä'tsè*) **Rule.** Hitler, having failed in the revolt of 1923, proceeded to organize a political party (Nazi) from the extremists of the right and the discontented middle class. It was anti-communistic and ultra-nationalistic. Its power grew phenomenally, and Hitler was a close rival of Hindenburg for the presidency in 1932.

Appointed chancellor in 1933, Hitler seized the opportunity of a fire in the Reichstag to ask for dictatorial power to suppress the Communists, who were accused of causing the fire. Receiving the powers sought, Hitler proceeded to establish a totalitarian state, suppressing all other parties. His policy aimed at aggrandizement abroad and was based on glorification of the Nordic race. Aspects of this policy involved persecution of the Jews and the encouragement of a revised form of Protestantism, based on old Teutonic myths.

Under Hitler's leadership, Germany ignored the disarmament clauses of the Versailles treaty, withdrew from the League of Nations, and proceeded to build up her military might. One immediate aim of German foreign policy remained union with Austria, although consideration of Italian jealousy and of French opposition counselled delay in its realization. The method used in seeking control of Austria and other countries was to foster the organization of a Nazi party, which, with German help, was expected eventually to obtain the reins of power. This technique facilitated the acquisition of both Austria and Czechoslovakia in 1938–39. France and Britain agreed, in a conference at Munich, to Germany's taking over a part of Czechoslovakia. But when the remainder was taken over contrary to agreement and Poland was next attacked in 1939, these countries declared war on Germany in the face of a German-Russian non-aggression treaty.

World War II. During the first three years of the war, Germany was everywhere victorious. She conquered Poland, Denmark, Norway, Holland, Belgium, France, and the Balkans. But Britain remained unsubdued. Then in 1941, Hitler threw his armies against Russia, penetrating as far as the Volga and the Caucasian oil fields, but failed to take Moscow or Leningrad. The United States entered the war in late 1941. In 1942, the tide turned. Defeated at Stalingrad and in North Africa, the German armies everywhere gave ground. In 1944, Germany itself was invaded. She fought to the end against hopeless odds until Hitler committed suicide and the armies surrendered. See *World War II.*

The Two Germanies. After the war Germany was divided into two parts: East Germany, which had been occupied by Russian armies, became a satellite of Russia; West Germany, which had been occupied by American, British, and French troops, became a federal republic in 1949. Under its first chancellor, Konrad Adenauer, West Germany became a member of NATO and a participant in the Common Market. Trade and industry grew at a phenomenal rate.

By 1955, all foreign controls were removed from West Germany except in West Berlin, where the new constitution was in abeyance. The Russians had tried to drive the western powers from the city in 1948–49 by cutting off supplies, the city being surrounded by East German territory, but a gigantic airlift defeated the move. Berlin remained an outpost of defense against Russia. Germans by the millions migrated to the west, the tide increasing after a revolt in 1953 was swiftly suppressed. Finally, in 1961, the East German government erected a wall between the two zones in Berlin.

Adenauer resigned in 1963, and was succeeded as chancellor by Ludwig Erhard, belonging to the same political party, the Christian Democrats. He had been economic minister under Adenauer and was given much of the credit for Germany's postwar economic resurgence. He looked to integration with other western powers as the best hope for eventual reunion with East Germany.

Erhard was succeeded in 1966 by Kurt Kiesinger, who moved to establish ties with Eastern Europe. During his term, U.S. and British troops in West Germany were reduced in number.

Willy Brandt, elected as West Germany's first Social Democrat chancellor in 1969, moved still further to close the gap between East and West, pursuing a policy of reconciliation with the Communist nations. He has been described as the first West German politician to accept the full consequences of Germany's defeat in World War II, and sought to shape a unifying course in the arena of European politics. For his efforts in the area of detente with Eastern Europe, Brandt received the 1971 Nobel Peace Prize. Throughout the next three years, his popularity declined somewhat as he faced multiple domestic and foreign policy problems. Then in 1974, a member of Brandt's personal staff, Günter Guillaume, was arrested as an agent for East Germany. The scandal forced Brandt's resignation. He was succeeded as chancellor by Helmut Schmidt, another leading Social Democrat.

Name	Lineage	Period of Rule		Birth	Death

CAROLINGIAN EMPERORS

Name	Lineage	A. D.	A. D.	A. D.	A. D.
Louis the German	Son of Emperor Louis I. He is regarded as the founder of the German Empire	843	876	804?	876
	Kingdom divided on death of Louis the German.				
Charles the Fat	Son of Louis the German; sole king through death of his brothers, Carloman and Louis; crowned emperor 882	876	887	832	888
Arnulf of Carinthia	Illegitimate son of Carloman; elected by the nobles	887	899	850?	899
Louis the Child	Son of Emperor Arnulf	899	911	893	911

HOUSE OF FRANCONIA

Conrad I	Duke of Franconia, elected king of Germany	911	918	?	918

HOUSE OF SAXONY

Henry I, the Fowler	Son of the duke of Saxony	919	936	876	936
Otto the Great	Son of Henry I; crowned emperor 962	936	973	912	973
Otto II	Son of Otto I	973	983	955	983
Otto III	Son of Otto II	983	1002	980	1002
Henry II, the Saint	Son of Henry the Quarrelsome of Bavaria	1002	1024	972?	1024

SALIAN OR FRANCONIAN EMPERORS

Conrad II	Crowned emperor 1027	1024	1039	990?	1039
Henry III	Son of Conrad II	1039	1056	1017	1056
Henry IV	Son of Henry III	1056	1106	1050	1106
Henry V	Son of Henry IV	1106	1125	1081	1125

HOUSE OF SAXONY

Lothair II	Crowned emperor 1133	1125	1137	1060?	1137

THE HOHENSTAUFENS

Conrad III	Duke of Franconia	1138	1152	1093	1152
Frederick I, Barbarossa	Nephew of Conrad III; crowned emperor 1155	1152	1190	1121?	1190
Henry VI	Son of Frederick Barbarossa; crowned emperor 1191	1190	1197	1165	1197
Otto IV ⎰Double	Son of Henry the Lion; crowned emperor 1209	1198	1215	1174	1218
Philip of Swabia ⎱Election		1198	1208	1177?	1208
Frederick II	Son of Henry VI; crowned emperor 1220	1215	1250	1194	1250
Conrad IV	King of Germany, not emperor	1250	1254	1228	1254
An Interregnum		1254	1273		

HOUSE OF HABSBURG

Rudolf I	Son of Albert IV, count of Habsburg	1273	1291	1218	1291

HOUSE OF NASSAU

Adolphus	Elected king of Germany and deposed	1291	1298	1252?	1298

HOUSE OF AUSTRIA

Albert I	Eldest son of Rudolf I	1298	1308	1250?	1308

HOUSE OF LUXEMBOURG

Henry VII	Son of the count of Luxembourg, crowned emperor 1312	1308	1313	1262	1313

HOUSE OF BAVARIA

Louis IV ⎰Double	Son of the duke of Bavaria	1314	1347	1286?	1347
Frederick the Fair ⎱Election	Son of Albert I; minority choice	1314	1330	1286?	1330

HOUSE OF LUXEMBOURG

Charles IV	Son of John of Luxembourg; crowned emperor 1355	1347	1378	1316	1378
Wenceslas	Son of Charles IV; elected king of Romans 1376, deposed from German throne	1378	1400	1361	1419

HOUSE OF PALATINATE

Rupert	Elector of the Palatinate	1400	1410	1352	1410

HOUSE OF LUXEMBOURG

Sigismund	Son of Charles IV; crowned emperor 1433	1411	1437	1368	1437

HOUSE OF HABSBURG

Albert II	Son-in-law of Sigismund	1438	1439	1397	1439
Frederick IV	Son of Ernest, duke of Austria; crowned emperor (Frederick III) 1452	1440	1493	1415	1493
Maximilian I	Son of Frederick IV	1493	1519	1459	1519
Charles V	Son of Philip of Burgundy	1519	1556	1500	1558
Ferdinand I	Younger brother of Charles V	1556	1564	1503	1564
Maximilian II	Son of Ferdinand I	1564	1576	1527	1576
Rudolf II	Son of Maximilian II	1576	1612	1552	1612
Matthias	Younger son of Maximilian II	1612	1619	1557	1619
Ferdinand II	Son of Charles, duke of Styria	1619	1637	1578	1637
Ferdinand III	Son of Ferdinand II	1637	1657	1608	1657
Leopold I	Second son of Ferdinand III	1658	1705	1640	1705
Joseph I	Son of Leopold I	1705	1711	1678	1711
Charles VI	Son of Leopold I	1711	1740	1685	1740

HOUSE OF BAVARIA

Charles VII	Elector of Bavaria	1742	1745	1697	1745

NAME	LINEAGE	Period of Rule		Birth	Death
	HOUSE OF LORRAINE	A. D.	A. D.	A. D.	A. D.
Francis I	Son of Leopold, duke of Lorraine	1745	1765	1708	1765
Joseph II	Son of Francis I	1765	1790	1741	1790
Leopold II	Third son of Francis I	1790	1792	1747	1792
Francis II	Son of Leopold II	1792	1806	1768	1835
	THE CONFEDERATION OF THE RHINE	1806	1815		
	THE GERMAN CONFEDERATION	1815	1866		
	THE NORTH GERMAN CONFEDERATION	1866	1871		
	THE HOUSE OF HOHENZOLLERN				
William I	Second son of Frederick William III of Prussia	1871	1888	1797	1888
Frederick III	Son of William I	1888	....	1831	1888
William II	Son of Frederick III and grandson of William I	1888	1918	1859	1941
	GERMAN REPUBLIC				
Friedrich Ebert	Chosen provisionally, later elected president	1918	1925	1871	1925
Paul von Hindenburg	Elected president	1925	1934	1847	1934
Adolf Hitler	Führer and Chancellor	1934	1945	1889	1945
Konrad Adenauer	Chancellor (West Germany)	1949	1963	1876	1967
Ludwig Erhard	Chancellor (West Germany)	1963	1966	1897	1977
Kurt Georg Kiesinger	Chancellor (West Germany)	1966	1969	1904	
Willy Brandt	Chancellor (West Germany)	1969	1974	1913	
Helmut Schmidt	Chancellor (West Germany)	1974		1918	

GREECE

The history of Greece is the story of a group of tiny states which grew up as independent units and resisted to the end any plan of federation among themselves. Consequently, Greece never became a military power which could present a united front to the world, and her greatness did not lie in the field of political organization. Yet, despite the serious menace of foreign invaders and devastating wars between the states themselves, these states maintained their independence long enough to produce literature, philosophy, art, and architecture.

The Coming of the Hellenes. Greece was occupied by the Hellenes, an Indo-European people, at some time after 2000 B. C. They came as undeveloped tribes in search of homes, and immediately demolished an earlier civilization which had flourished in the prehistoric period, established themselves as masters of the entire peninsula, and made it their home henceforth, while the earlier occupants were entirely driven out or annihilated. This was probably accomplished by a gradual process covering several hundred years; for the Hellenic people comprised different groups, who may be supposed to have swept down into the peninsula in successive waves. These groups were closely related to one another but showed different characteristics. They were known in later times, when the Greeks were reconstructing their own ancient history, as Achæans, Æolians, Dorians, and Ionians, and, with the development of the Hellenic civilization, the special characteristics of each group produced a distinctive culture.

The Hellenes, thus established in a permanent home, began immediately to display the vigor and aggressiveness of a virile race. They soon spread over the neighboring islands of the Ægean, and then passed over these as by stepping-stones to the western coast of Asia Minor and to Crete. The sea was their highway and they became essentially a seafaring people. They developed a vigorous commerce and were ultimately competing for markets with the Phoenicians, whose powerful colony, Carthage, was dominant for a time in the West.

Greek Colonization. There followed a period of colonization which cannot be defined as to its beginning, but it was over by the end of the 6th century B. C. The colonies were founded as private enterprises by groups who were led to leave their native homes, sometimes through dissatisfaction with political conditions, sometimes through lack of land or by economic distress; they were not in the first instance commercial enterprises. The colonies thus established became independent units, but each maintained a close association with the mother state.

In this way colonies were sent to the shores of the Black Sea, to Egypt, to southern Italy, and to Sicily. A few of the important Greek colonies were: Byzantium (modern Constantinople), founded by Megarians in 660 B. C.; Naucratis, "Mistress of Ships," in Egypt, founded by Milesians about 640 B. C.; Cyrene on the northern coast of Africa, founded by Therans about ten years later; Syracuse in Sicily, founded by Corinthians in the 8th century B. C.; and Croton in southern Italy, founded by Achæans about 700 B. C. These and many other colonies were trading centers for Greek commerce.

The large cluster of colonies established in southern Italy gave a distinctive character to this district, which was called by the Romans *Magna Græcia*. This was to the Greeks a land of promise and opportunity such as the American "great West" has been. Here wealth was accumulated in great abundance, and the colony of Sybaris came to be spoken of as typifying extravagance and luxurious living. It was from these particular colonies that the first gleams of Greek culture began to reach the vigorous Roman people, and hence came the mellowing influence which was destined to make over the Roman character and bring about Rome's willing acknowledgment of the supremacy of Greece in the world of the spirit.

Greek Division and Unity. The segregation of the Greeks into tiny political units was brought about, first and chiefly, by the character of the people themselves and, secondly, by the nature of the country in which they settled. The Greek was by instinct strongly individualistic, thoroughly devoted to the interests of his family and immediate community, but inclined to be jealous and suspicious of those not so closely connected with him, even though they might be Greeks like himself. He was also ready to defend his own views, with prolonged argument if necessary, and unwilling to let any other man do his thinking for him. The land of Greece, on the other hand, with its endless succession of mountains and narrow valleys, each with a limited area of arable land, made isolation natural and easy, and strongly encouraged—indeed, almost made inevitable—the formation of small units which came to have a sense of independence and self-sufficiency.

Yet the centrifugal tendency was not the only one at work. The Greeks were led by a sort of national pride to designate all who were not Greeks as "barbarians," or people without the pale. This term was at first used without the reproach now attaching to the word, but it soon came to have a distinct suggestion of inferiority, and finally it indicated downright contempt. Then the songs of Homer, which were known and sung throughout Greece, strongly encouraged the same feeling; for in them the Greek states were represented as fighting together against a foreign power. Furthermore, the religious worship of the Greeks was, broadly speaking, the same; and so they came together at stated intervals to honor special divinities in great festivals which assumed a national character. Such festivals were held at Olympia and at Nemea, in honor of Zeus, at Delphi, in honor of Apollo, and at the Isthmus, in honor of Poseidon. While these festivals were going on, it was customary to observe a religious truce throughout Greece. Mention may also be made of a council or league of several states in northern Greece, called the Amphictyonic League, which met primarily to discuss and settle questions pertaining to religious matters, and which naturally fostered a close bond of sympathy between all the participating states.

The City-State. The political unit throughout Greece was the *polis*, or "city-state," an independent organization composed usually of the inhabitants of a single small town. Occasionally, a town associated neighboring villages with itself in a small federation; this was done by Athens with the country villages of Attica, and by Sparta with those of Laconia. The population of these city-states was astonishingly small, and this characteristic remained one of the determining factors in Greek political development. The typical city-state of early times was ruled by a king, and this was doubtless the only form of government known in Greece during several centuries, after the tribal organization was outgrown and before the time when the record of Greek history commences, about the 8th century B. C.

At this time we find a state of political unrest prevalent throughout the land, for the reigning families were being overthrown in many of the states. The power was being taken over by small groups of nobles, or by individuals who succeeded for a time in getting sufficient support to maintain themselves supreme; in the former case the government came to be called an *oligarchy*, in the latter, a *tyranny*. Many of the tyrants were men of real ability and proved to be excellent rulers.

The spirit of political unrest, however, did not always lead to violence. In some states men of conspicuous wisdom and integrity were designated to draw up and codify a new system of laws. Such a service was rendered by Draco, and later by Solon, at Athens, and by Pittacus at Mytilene. This, of course, implies that writing was by this time in common use throughout Greece. The alphabet had been adopted from the Phœnicians at some time after 1000 B. C.

Government in Athens. The fortunes of the city-state of Athens may be considered typical of what was taking place throughout Greece prior to the end of the 6th century B. C. The early Athenian monarchy was gradually transformed into an aristarchy, which finally gave place to a pure democracy. This was accomplished as follows: First, the king's power was curtailed by the introduction of two new magistrates, the *polemarch* and the *archon*, elected by the people. Later, the kingship became elective, and six new magistrates were added, making the "nine archons." Meanwhile, unfavorable economic conditions were causing distress among the common people. The introduction of money to replace the old system of barter produced serious disturbance in the economic development of Athens, as it did in all Greece. The first coinage is said to have come into the Greek world from the wealthy kingdom of Lydia in Asia Minor in the 7th century B. C. This and other causes brought about a situation which demanded a remedy, and Draco was appointed an extraordinary legislator (*thesmothetes*) and commissioned to draw up a new code of laws. This he did in 621 B. C., but the penalties imposed by his laws for wrongdoing were so severe that it was found difficult to use his code; in later times an Athenian orator said that Draco's laws were written in blood, not in ink.

About thirty years later Solon was chosen to perfect the work of Draco. He undertook his task with a statesman's skill and was remarkably successful. By his social legislation he relieved the poor of their unbearable burdens, and by his political reforms he erected the framework of the Athenian democracy, making the people the sovereign power of the state, with complete control over all their executives, and giving all free men some degree of right as citizens.

The Athenian democracy, however, was not even yet fully established. Party strife continued, and Pisistratus, a popular and successful general, backed by the discontented element of the population, was able to grasp the supreme power. He proved himself a wise and able ruler; for he kept the form of the constitution laid down by Solon, while holding the guiding power in his own hands. The diversity and importance of the various enterprises carried on by Athens during his rule bear testimony to his tireless activity. Among these, may be mentioned the re-editing of the poems of Homer, the foundation of a huge temple of Olympian Zeus,—which had to await the wealth of a Roman emperor to bring it to completion,—the establishment of the great annual festival of "Dionysus in the City," in which tragedy, one of the richest fruits of the Greek genius, was performed, and the prosecution of successful military operations on the Hellespont.

The rule of Pisistratus was carried on by his sons after his death, until the tyranny was brought to an end, with the help of Sparta, in 510 B. C., and the descendants of Pisistratus were forever debarred by law from the rights of citizenship. Athens now began her career as a democracy, first modifying the constitution of Solon by the reforms of Cleisthenes, which provided for a new and more satisfactory grouping of the citizens.

Sparta and Other States. The other states had meanwhile been working out practicable constitutions, each in its own way. In contrast to the pure democracy finally achieved by Athens, a constitution of a strangely mixed character was adopted in Sparta. Here there were two hereditary kings, holding office for life, and a board of five ephors, elected annually; these ephors exercised most of the important civil functions which had belonged to the kings, and represented the common people as against the nobility. The senate or *Gerusia*, however, was composed of nobles and naturally represented the interests of that class. The Spartans had grown to be a conservative people devoted to a strict military discipline—in fact, a military state composed of a limited number of free warriors imposed upon a larger number of serfs or *helots*. The strictness of the Spartan discipline, which has become proverbial, did indeed produce a remarkably efficient corps of fighting men, but it repressed rather than encouraged the free development of the individual citizen.

Thus, by the end of the 6th century B. C., all the Greek states had passed through the period of political readjustment, and, temporarily at least, tyrannies were at an end. The period under discussion had witnessed notable achievement in many fields of activity. There had been great commercial expansion, as noted above, with marked progress in local industry, and real achievement in architecture and in literature. Indeed, the Greeks had by this time attained a high level of culture which marked them out as a peculiarly gifted people.

Religious Conceptions. The Greek had been wrestling also with the problems of life as expressed in his religion. The old anthropomorphic gods of Homer, whose writings were to the Greeks almost sacred, were little better than humans and had ceased to fulfill the ideal of an awakening age, and a more spiritual interpretation of godhead than that found in Homer was coming to be adopted by thoughtful men. Yet the outward form of the old polytheistic religion remained, with its temples, its priests, and its ritual worship.

A widespread yearning for immortality is evidenced by the prominence of societies which gave promise of this boon to mortals. The Eleusinian

Mysteries, a kind of Passion Play of the sorrows of Demeter, were open to all, even the humblest. Here great numbers found comfort in the hope of salvation and purification from the sins of the world. There was also the Orphic Sect, of widespread influence, and, in southern Italy, Pythagoras had founded his brotherhood.

On the other hand, many had been turning to seek a rationalistic explanation of the universe, as a protest against the mysticism of such bodies as the Orphic Sect. This movement grew up in Ionia in Asia Minor, and it was here that Greece was saved from the tyranny of religion interpreted by a priestly class. Beginning with crude speculations upon the nature of the material composition of the world, and progressing very slowly at first, a succession of serious and able men prepared the way for the great achievement of Greek philosophy in the 5th and the 4th century B. C. Thales, the pioneer of this movement, proposed that water is the primary element of all things.

Athens, Sparta, Thebes. At the beginning of the 5th century B. C., the important Greek states were related as follows: Sparta, with her wonderfully efficient army and her iron discipline, was unquestioned leader in the Peloponnesus, having come to overshadow Argos, whose ancient importance was waning. This pre-eminent position of Sparta placed her automatically at the head of a kind of league of Peloponnesian states. Even Athens, as we have seen, was indebted to Sparta for deliverance from her tyrants, and was for a time strongly under her influence. Athens, at the head of the federation of the villages of Attica, had outstripped her nearby rivals and held a secure and easily defended position as a sea power. The rival of Athens on the north was Thebes, the dominant power in Bœotia.

Persian Wars. At this time a new age dawned on Greece. The expanding Persian power was turning toward European conquest. Meanwhile the Athenians had sent aid to the Ionian cities in Asia Minor during a revolt against Persian rule. With this revolt crushed, Darius planned to punish Athens. His first expedition, in 492 B. C., was destroyed by storms, but two years later he sent a fleet and an army across the Ægean, which landed on the plain of Marathon, about twenty-five miles distant from Athens. His forces were guided by Hippias, son of Pisistratus, former tyrant of Athens. The Greeks, remembering the terrible Persian punishment of Asiatic cities, were panic-stricken. But Miltiades, who was familiar with Persian methods of warfare, roused their courage by his confident plans for meeting the invader, and under his leadership the Greek citizen-soldiers, with their spears, broke the attack of the Persian bowmen. The Persians fled, leaving 6000 dead on the field, while the Greek loss was only about 200. The grateful Athenians, who had borne the brunt of the battle almost without assistance, raised a memorial mound, which may still be seen on the field of Marathon.

Ten years passed, and Xerxes, son of Darius, in 480 B. C., entered Greece with an army of overwhelming size, accompanied by a great fleet. Sparta, on this occasion, stood solidly with Athens, and the Persian advance was opposed at strategic points on land and sea. Treachery, however, enabled Xerxes to enter the pass of Thermopylæ—but only over the dead bodies of the heroic Leonidas and his loyal band of Spartans. Athens was burned. But the Athenians, wisely advised by Themistocles, had built a navy, and in the strait of Salamis they crushed the Persian fleet. The next year, 479 B. C., the remnant of Xerxes' army was defeated by the Greek spearmen at Platæa. Never again did a Persian army enter Greece. In the West also, the year 480 B. C. saw the Hellenic world freed from an Asiatic menace through the overwhelming defeat of the Carthaginians by the Greeks of Syracuse.

The generous co-operation of Athens and Sparta ceased, unfortunately, as soon as the danger was passed, and the old spirit of jealous rivalry again manifested itself. The Spartans looked with apprehension upon the energetic preparations of Athens to meet another possible emergency; sullen distrust and mutual suspicions prepared the way for the internecine struggle which was destined to ruin the fairest city of Greece.

The Athenian Empire. The Athenians, led by Themistocles, rebuilt their city with strong fortifications and improved and protected the harbor of the Piræus. Next, in order to secure complete protection against the menace of Persia, they organized the Confederacy of Delos, whose guiding spirit was Aristides, known as "The Just." This was a union of Athens with the Greek cities of Asia Minor and the Ægean islands and was at first a purely co-operative league. Its name arose from the fact that its treasury was located on the island of Delos under the protection of Apollo. The allies at first contributed ships, with which Cimon, son of Miltiades, freed the entire Asia Minor coast from Persian control, as far as the mouth of the Black Sea. Under his leadership, Athens gradually brought the states of the league into the position of dependencies, while maintaining friendship with Sparta. In 454 B. C. the transfer of the treasury to Athens marked the beginning of the Athenian "empire." But Cimon's policy of co-operation with Sparta was unpopular with the radical, democratic party at Athens, and he was ostracized.

At this period most of the offices of the Athenian democracy were filled by lot; hence the men selected were often inefficient. But the ten generals were elected by the votes of the people, an arrangement which gave a single powerful man his opportunity to direct the state. For about thirty years this position in the Athenian state was maintained by Pericles. His supremacy coincided with the most brilliant era of Athenian culture, though this period was marred by the first of those contests with Sparta which finally resulted in the complete ruin of Athenian political power.

The Periclean Age. Pericles' ambitious plan of establishing an Athenian land empire led to conflict with Sparta, and after years of fruitless struggle the so-called Thirty Years' Truce, in 445 B. C., restored the *status quo*. Both sides were exhausted. Meanwhile Athens had carried on a disastrous campaign against the Persians in Egypt. The next fifteen years in Athens are known as the Periclean age. Commerce brought the wealth of the world to the port of the Piræus. Tribute from allied and subject cities filled the public treasury. Rich citizens and the state lavished money without stint upon festivals and public buildings. Sculptors and architects of genius were employed to raise statues and temples in honor of the gods and of great men, and to express in marble the beauty and dignity of the human form. Contests and public prizes stimulated poets and dramatists. The democracy, by opening offices to all save the poorest citizens, encouraged a keen interest in politics. Schools flourished, oratory became a fine art, and the sophists, disturbers though they were, challenged the skill of the cleverest by the subtleties of their art of dialectics. Athens had become the center of Greek culture, and her influence extended far beyond the limits of Greece.

The Fall of Athens. But the other cities of Greece were jealous and hostile, and in 431 B. C. the truce of 445 B. C. was broken. The armies of Sparta, Thebes, and Corinth, with their allies, entered Attica and devastated the country about Athens. The people who were thus driven within the city were stricken with a plague due to crowded, unsanitary conditions. Pericles fell a victim to the disease, and Athens, lacking capable leadership, was thrown into confusion. The war continued for ten years. Athens managed to maintain control of the sea, and in 421 B. C. a truce of fifty years was arranged. But this peace failed to settle any real issue or to check the brutal passions that the war had aroused.

At this stage of affairs, Alcibiades, a high-spirited young man of remarkable ability, rose to power as champion of those opposed to the peace party in Athens. He incited the Athenians to undertake an expedition against the Corinthian city of Syracuse in Sicily, 415 B. C. But Alcibiades, who sailed as a general with the expedition, found himself recalled to Athens to answer a charge of impiety. He promptly deserted to Sparta. By his advice a Spartan general and a few troops were sent to Syracuse. The Athenian fleet and army were annihilated, 413 B. C., and the Spartans, who had been making annual invasions of Attica during the early years of the war, now definitely locked her within her walls by occupying the fortress of Decelea, a few miles to the north. For ten years the city held out, though forced to see her flourishing farms devastated and to import all supplies by sea. At length, in the battle of Ægospotami, 405 B. C., the entire Athenian fleet was captured or destroyed by the Spartans, and Athens, faced by starvation, surrendered. Her fortifications were leveled, and she was forced to recognize the supremacy of Sparta. After enduring a reign of terror carried out under Spartan protection, her democratic constitution was again restored, but her strength was broken.

Sparta and Thebes. There followed a dreary period of negotiations with Persia, both Athens and Sparta bidding in turn for an alliance which would gain the support of Persian gold. The King's Peace, 387 B. C., gave Greek leadership to Sparta. She had won her final battle with Athens by means of Persian funds, under the guise of champion of the free Greek cities. Now she revealed her purposes by overturning every democratic government and establishing in each state an oppressive and irresponsible Spartan governor supported by a garrison of Spartan soldiers. On a fateful night, a young Theban noble entered Thebes with a band of followers, killed the leaders of the oligarchic party, and forced the Spartan garrison to an ignominious surrender. Pelopidas and his friend, Epaminondas, thus challenged Sparta and made Thebes, for a few years, supreme in Greece. Epaminondas, who gave evidence of possessing a high type of statesmanship, was killed at the battle of Mantinea in 362 B. C.

It is worth noting that, even during the stress of her life-and-death struggle with Sparta, Athens had still been able to continue the work on the noble buildings which crown her acropolis. The shameless mismanagement of Athenian affairs after the death of Pericles had been subjected to the biting satire of Aristophanes, the dramatist, and the sophists had been ably and fearlessly met by the challenge of Socrates The story of the nations was being completed by Herodotus the very year in which Pericles succumbed to the plague, and Thucydides was engaged in setting forth in his history the lessons of the Greek wars while the greatest of them was actually in progress. In the years after the war, Plato, a pupil of Socrates, wrote of the ideal city-state, but he failed to see the larger problem of statesmanship, the union of cities. Isocrates, understanding the weakness of the Greek policies, pleaded for united action against the foreigner, and Xenophon endeavored to rouse Greek patriotism through his story of the Ten Thousand. But Greece was not to see political unity realized until her many quarreling states were welded into a dependency by the Macedonian power.

Alexander the Great. Macedonia, peopled by a race which was Greek in language as well as in blood, had been slowly assimilating the culture of its southern neighbors since the period of the Persian wars. In 360 B. C., Philip, a man of Greek education and military experience, came to the throne. He at once adopted a policy of Macedonian expansion. The battle of Chæronea in 338 B. C. gave him control of all Greece except Sparta. Death cut short his ambitious plan of invading Persia, but he left to his son Alexander a remarkable body of trained and devoted councilors and officers. Alexander, however, coming to the throne at the age of twenty, was soon to display a genius that outshone them all. He had been taught by Aristotle, who not only instructed him in history and science but also fired his imagination with the vision of a world empire resting on the firm basis of Greek culture and Greek traditions and headed by Macedonia.

In 334 B. C., after crushing a rebellion at Thebes, Alexander crossed the Hellespont and began the march which was to make his dream a reality. During the next twelve years he led his armies along the ancient highways of Asia, subjugating the cities which had been seats of civilization from hoary antiquity. He conquered Egypt, where he founded the great city of Alexandria, and penetrated the trackless desert as far as the shrine of Ammon, in order to win assurance from the god himself that he was, in very truth, son of Ammon; here he stood on the confines of the Carthaginian empire. His eastward march carried him into India, and only the restlessness of his army drew him back from the valley of the Ganges. In Babylon he made his capital with the magnificence of an Eastern potentate, and in that ancient city of the marshes, fever struck him down. He had brought Greek culture to the East; the Hellenistic age, which he ushered in, saw this culture thriving in many flourishing cities, from his own Alexandria in Egypt to the central plains of Asia.

The Greco-Roman World. But, if this age Hellenized the East, it also Orientalized the West. Oriental ideas of religion and statecraft found their way into the thinking and practice of the Greeks and of the Romans as well; for, although Alexander did not march into the West, Rome had long been under the spell of Greek influence. The religious cults of the Egyptian Isis and the Persian Mithra became widely popular in the Roman world, which was soon to include Greece among its provinces. Likewise, the Romans became acquainted with the notion of the divine character and right of kings, which may be traced to Alexander's practice of having himself proclaimed the son of Zeus. This may have seemed to him necessary in order to sustain his great authority, but it must be said that his assumption of divine right alienated loyal followers from him and, in the end, proved disastrous to his plans.

The death of Alexander destroyed the last hope of a unified Greek empire. Within a generation the vast realm he had conquered was divided among three of his generals. Macedonia and Greece fell to Antigonus; Syria, to Seleucus; and Egypt, to Ptolemy. One more attempt was made by a group of states in the Peloponnesus to assert Greek independence. But this Achæan League, as it was called, though led by able and patriotic men, was only partially and temporarily successful. For 150 years, under the Ptolemies, Alexandria was the center of that later widespread Greek civilization known as Hellenism. Here the Hebrew Old Testament was translated into Greek. The Museum of Alexandria was in effect a great state university. The schools of Alexandria were rivaled by those of Pergamum and of Rhodes; but it was an age of scholarship rather than of creative activity.

The strife and internal weakness of the Greek kingdoms left by Alexander gave Rome an opportunity to extend her power over all the East and to hammer the Greco-Roman world into a stable empire, a realm of Greek culture and Roman law.

Modern Greece. Greece was merged in the Eastern or Byzantine Empire when the Roman world was divided and, after the fall of Constantinople in 1453, it became a part of the Turkish empire. From the 4th century B. C. until 1821, when the Greeks rose in revolt against the Turkish power, they were at no time a free people. During the 18th century an intellectual revival had taken place in Greece, and this had aroused national pride and brought about a restoration of the Greek language. This revival of the national consciousness of Greece had stirred the interest of enlightened people in all the nations of the West. England, France, and Russia finally intervened; by the treaty of Adrianople in 1829 Greek independence was acknowledged by Turkey, and guaranteed by the three powers. In 1833 Otto of Bavaria became king.

Otto was deposed in 1862; in the next year a brother of the Danish king succeeded him as George I. In the same year a new constitution established a legislature, the *Boule*, elected by universal suffrage. In 1881 Greece gained Thessaly, but lost a part by the Turkish war of 1897. King George was assassinated in March 1913.

World Wars and After. At the outbreak of World War I, the Greek prime minister, Venizelos, supported the cause of the Allies against the wishes of King Constantine, whose sympathies favored Germany. Venizelos was compelled to resign, Oct. 7, 1915. In October of 1916 he set up a provisional government at Saloniki, which was recognized by the Allies. After great pressure on the part of the Allies, Constantine abdicated on June 11, 1917, and his son Alexander ascended the throne. Venizelos now brought Greece officially into the war on the side of the Allies. The Treaty of Sèvres, which was never fully ratified, gave to Greece important accessions of territory. Venizelos, however, defeated at the polls, left the country. On King Alexander's death, Constantine was recalled. This act estranged the Allies, who consented to a revision of the Treaty of Sèvres. Constantine took the field to enforce against the Turks the favorable arrangements previously agreed to, but was defeated.

Greece was obliged to sign the humiliating peace of Lausanne in 1923, by which Turkey recovered her control of Istanbul and the Anatolian coast of the Ægean. Over 1,500,000 Greeks were expelled from Turkey and settled in Greece. Constantine was forced to abdicate a second time. His successor, George II, was later compelled to leave the country and, on May 1, 1924, a republic was proclaimed. A royalist movement, however, slowly gathered force and, after a futile revolt led by Venizelos, it succeeded in re-establishing the monarchy in 1935. George II returned to the throne. The next year power was seized by a military group under John Metaxis. Greece was forced into World War II by an Italian attack in 1940. She was conquered by the Germans the next year and liberated by the British in 1944.

George II was recalled in 1946. Revolts broke out led by leftists and aided by neighboring Communist regimes. The Greek government faltered and Britain announced it could no longer help. Greece then appealed to the U.S. and Congress voted $250 million in aid. At the same time, Yugoslavia fell out with the Communist bloc and stopped infiltrating guerrillas into Greece. Order was soon re-established. George II was succeeded in 1947 by Paul I, who was followed by his son, Constantine II, in 1964.

In the 1960's Greece hovered on the verge of war with Turkey over control of Cyprus, whose Greek population wanted union with Greece. Constantine's reign was also marked by continuing internal crises and by 1968 he and Premier Papandreou were forced to flee by the military junta that seized control of the country and formed a new government and constitution. The Greek colonels who ran the country were headed by George Papadopoulos. Most civil liberties were suspended and thousands of dissidents were jailed. In June 1973, Papadopoulos abolished the monarchy and proclaimed himself head of a new Greek republic. In November, he was deposed by another military junta. Their rule lasted until the abortive attempt to topple Cyprian President Makarios in 1974. The debacle caused the military's downfall and former premier Constantine Caramanlis (1955–1963) returned from exile to head the country again. Elections in November made Caramanlis premier under a new constitution and re-

jected a reinstitution of the monarchy. In reaction to U.S. support of the fallen junta and the alleged U.S. favoritism toward Turkey, Greece dropped out of NATO in 1974.

GREENLAND

The discovery of Greenland is credited to the Norwegian, Eric the Red, who is said to have spent three years on the coast of the country (982–985). Within the next few years, several Norwegian settlements were made. These colonies had originally a republican organization but they fell under the authority of the Norwegian kings about the middle of the 13th century. Christianity had already been established about the year 1000. During the 15th and 16th centuries, Greenland disappeared from history, and, in 1585, the explorer John Davis found only Eskimos on the coast. After a lapse of 150 years, Hans Egede, a Norwegian clergyman, established a Lutheran mission settlement near Godthaab, under the authority of the king of Denmark. Greenland, like Iceland, was left in Danish hands at the separation of Norway and Denmark in 1814.

In consequence of the invasion of Denmark by Germany, the United States in 1941 assumed temporary control of Greenland to prevent any transfer or hostile use by the colony. In 1951 a Danish American agreement for the common defense of Greenland was concluded. Two years later Greenland was made an integral part of Denmark with the same rights of self-government with other divisions of the country.

Holland. See *Netherlands*.

HOLY ROMAN EMPIRE

The Roman Empire succeeded the republic and began its history with the rule of Augustus Cæsar in 29 B. C. After the death of Theodosius the Great in 395 A. D., the Western Roman Empire was separated from the Eastern, sometimes called the Byzantine, or Greek, Empire. The Eastern Roman Empire lasted until the fall of Constantinople in 1453 A. D.; the Western had come to an end as early as 476 A. D. In the year 800, Charlemagne at Rome inaugurated anew this Western empire as the Holy Roman Empire and was crowned as its first emperor by Leo III. After the extinction of the Carolingian line, there ensued a period of feudal disturbance, when the empire existed only in name. The title of emperor was, however, again given substance by Otto I, king of the East Franks. At the invitation of the pope, he entered Italy with his victorious armies, and at Rome in 962 was crowned emperor. In the reign of Henry IV (1056–1106) began the momentous contest for supremacy between the emperors and the popes.

On the death of Henry V in 1125, the imperial office became elective, the first elected emperor being Lothair II. In 1356, the emperor Charles IV promulgated the Golden Bull, which determined the imperial electors.

In 1273 Rudolf, the first emperor of the house of Habsburg, was elected, and from 1438 the succeeding emperors belonged to this house. Not until 1806, when the Empire was broken up by Napoleon, did Francis II relinquish his title as emperor of the Holy Roman Empire. See *Austria, Italy, Spain.*

HUNGARY

The Magyars, an Asiatic people of Turanian race, allied to the Finns and the Turks, dwelt in what is now southern Russia before they descended, under Arpád, into the plain of the Danube, toward the end of the 9th century, and conquered the whole of Hungary and Transylvania. During the first half of the 10th century their invasions and incursions spread terror throughout Germany, France, and Italy; but at length their total defeat by Otto I of Germany put an end to their maraudings, and under their native Arpád dynasty they settled down to learn agriculture and the arts of peace. Stephen I (997–1038) was the first who was successful in extending Christianity generally among the Hungarians; and he was rewarded with a crown from Pope Sylvester II and the title "apostolic king" (1000). Stephen encouraged learning and literature, and under him Latin became the official language of the government.

About the end of the 11th century the boundaries of Hungary were extended by the conquest of Croatia, Slavonia, and Dalmatia. In the 12th century the Hungarians first attained, through French connections, a certain refinement of life and manners. About the middle of the 13th century, King Bela induced many Germans to settle in the country, which had been depopulated by Mongol invasions. With Andrew III (1290–1301) the male line of the Arpád dynasty ceased, and the sovereignty now became dependent upon an electorate. Charles Robert of Anjou was the first to be thus chosen (1309). Louis I (1342–82) added Poland, Red Russia, Moldavia, and a part of Serbia to his kingdom.

Decline of the Kingdom. From the accession of Sigismund, elected emperor of the Holy Roman Empire, dates the beginning of the decline of Hungary. His reign (1387–1437) was marked by the Turkish invasion and the Hussite war. He nevertheless introduced various reforms and founded an academy at Buda. Matthias Corvinus (1458–90), surnamed the Great, combining the talents of diplomatist and general, proved successful against his enemies at home and abroad. He was an ardent patron of learning, and he founded a university at Pest.

During the early 16th century, domestic troubles and the rapacity of the magnates brought the power of Hungary to a low pass, and the battle of Mohács (1526) reduced a part of the country to a Turkish province. The rest was left to the opposing claims of Ferdinand of Austria and John Zapolya. Eventually, with the aid of the Protestants, the quarrel was settled in favor of Ferdinand, who was proclaimed king of Hungary. In 1687 the sovereignty was made hereditary and remained until 1918 under the scepter of the Habsburgs. In 1686 Leopold I took Buda and recovered most of Hungary and Transylvania from the Turks. In 1723 Charles VI, by a decree known as the Pragmatic Sanction, secured from his several hereditary states their promise of allegiance at his death to his daughter, Maria Theresa. In this way the Hungarian crown passed to the female descendants of the house of Habsburg. Charles died in 1740, and the loyalty of the Hungarians to his daughter was at once proved by the support they gave her in her struggle against the encroachments of Frederick of Prussia and the insidious designs of France.

Movement for Independence. Despite the War of the Austrian Succession, Maria Theresa did much for the improvement of Hungary, particularly in the founding of schools and colleges. Her son and successor, Joseph II (1780–90), tried to break down all the ancient Magyar institutions of self-government. Opposition to this policy was increased by his edict of 1784, making German the official language. However, on the advent of the French Revolution and during the wars that ensued, the Hungarians once more played a prominent part in support of the Habsburg crown. Leopold II (1790–92) had revived the power of the Hungarian diet. But the Revolution had given an impetus to ideas of national and popular rights, which the Hungarians, long stifled under the Germanic traditions and tendencies of their rulers, were among the first to feel. For a time, Francis I and Metternich stood stiffly out against all concessions, and tried to govern by pure absolutism, but they ended by summoning a new diet in 1823, controlled by Magyars.

Successive diets made new demands for religious equality, suffrage, and abolition of privileges. The Austrian government responded by imprisoning Deak, Kossuth, and other leaders, but the diet of 1839 forced their release and other concessions. The revolution of 1848 in Austria drove out Metternich and gave new force to the Magyar struggle.

The Dual Empire. Prince Metternich fled to London and the court at Vienna made concessions but planned reprisals. In December 1848 the Austrian army, reinforced by the Slav dependencies of Austria, renewed the war. The Hungarians held their own, and the Austrians, in despair, called on Russia for assistance. The Hungarian revolt was cruelly suppressed, but a constitutional agitation continued, and, after her defeat at Sadowa, in 1866, Austria, facing a nation as strong as herself, was compelled to make terms. In 1867 Hungary became an equal partner in the empire; the emperor and empress were crowned king and queen of Hungary.

The dualism of the Austrian empire was thus finally constituted. But Hungary itself was made up of people of several races, the Slavs constituting more than half of the population, although the Magyars, or rather the Magyar nobles, alone held political power. About 1875 this ruling class began a policy of "Magyarizing" the entire state through manipulating the suffrage laws and insisting on the universal use of the Magyar language. Until the outbreak of World War I, this policy was a source of increasing bitterness among the Hungarians.

Hungary in the World Wars. At the opening of World War I Hungary followed Austria and Germany. In the collapse of 1918 the Slav population went to the new states, Czechoslovakia and Yugoslavia; the Rumanians, with over a million Magyars, to an enlarged Rumania; leaving Hungary practically a Magyar state, with about half its former area.

In November 1918, Hungary proclaimed the Hungarian People's Republic, with Count Karolyi as provisional president. This government lasted until March 1919, when a soviet administration, under Bela Kun, was set up. A socialist government succeeded the soviet, and after an interim of seven months, Admiral Nicholas Horthy was elected regent, March 1, 1920, by the National Assembly. A "party of Unity," under Stephen Bethlen, succeeded in stabilizing the political situation. In 1921 Charles IV, former emperor of Austria and king of Hungary, attempted unsuccessfully to regain the throne.

In World War II Hungary was forced to side with the Axis powers. She recovered some of her territory, lost to Rumania and Yugoslavia, joined Germany in her wars against Yugoslavia and Russia, and declared war against the United States, December 13, 1941. Upon invasion by the Russians in 1944, her government was taken over by the Germans, but Russia occupied the country. A provisional anti-German government made an armistice with Russia. A republic was established November 1, 1945, after elections which had given a majority to a non-Communist Small Land Owners party. Under Communist pressure the economic situation grew steadily worse, and inflation ran rife. Hungary signed a peace treaty, prepared by the Allies, in February 1947.

In May the Communists holding key positions in the ministry discovered a "conspiracy against the government," implicating the leaders of the Small Land Owners party. The premier, Ferenc Nagy, was forced to resign. With Russian connivance and support, a Soviet regime was set up. February 1, 1949, Hungary was declared a "People's Republic." In 1956 a popular revolt against the government flared into revolution, which was suppressed with the aid of Russian tanks and troops. Russian control was further evidenced by Hungary's execution of former premier Nagy and other patriots, announced in 1958. The Soviets placed Janos Kadar at the head of the party. Although loyal to the U.S.S.R., his regime cautiously liberalized social and economic life in Hungary. Under a new economic plan introduced in 1968, Hungary has become much more consumer-oriented than other Eastern European countries.

ICELAND

Though the Culdees, an ancient order of Irish monks, are said to have settled in Iceland as early as 795 A. D., it was not until between 870 and 930 that Iceland was discovered and colonized by the Norsemen or Scandinavian vikings. The earliest immigrants came in three successive movements,— from Norway, then from the Norse kingdom of Dublin, the Orkneys, and the Hebrides, and, latest, again from the kingdom of Norway. Christianity established itself about the year 1000.

In the beginning the government of Iceland was a species of aristocratic republic made up of small landowners whose laws were framed and sanctioned by a national assembly called the *Althing*, which met once a year in summer time. But, between the years 1262 and 1271, a period of internecine strife brought the island under the sway of the Norwegian kings. From 1280, Iceland, through the union of the Scandinavian crowns, became a dependency of the Danish crown, though it was not until 1381 that it was constituted such by law.

This medieval period under foreign rule saw a sad decline in the spirit and enterprise of the Icelandic people. The Black Plague decimated the population. Ancient arts and crafts perished, and song and story languished. The Reformation kindled anew the intellectual life of the country, but this wrought little change in the economic state of the people. Moreover, throughout the 16th and 17th centuries the island was the prey of pirates and buccaneers. In the 18th century plagues of smallpox, famines, and volcanic eruptions caused the death of about a fourth of the population.

When Norway was separated from Denmark in 1814, Iceland remained a dependency of the latter kingdom, but eventually was granted home rule and virtual independence. On Germany's invasion of Denmark in 1940, the Icelandic parliament took charge, and, in 1944, Iceland, again a republic, formally separated from Denmark. For protection, Iceland has permitted U.S. troop bases, despite vigorous protests from the Soviet government.

INDONESIA

The former Netherlands East Indies, a part of the Malay archipelago, including the islands of Java, Sumatra, Borneo, Celebes, and many others, became the United States of Indonesia, December 28, 1949.

Two-thirds of the population is centered in Java. The first Europeans to settle in Java were the Portuguese in 1511. They were driven out by the British and Dutch in 1595. Then the Dutch evicted the British. The Dutch East India Company, organized in 1602, conquered the islands, and governed them until the Company was dissolved in 1798. From 1916 until the Japanese conquest in 1942 the islands were ruled by the Netherlands home government. Following the Japanese surrender in 1945, the Dutch returned, but the Indonesians declared their independence, and for more than four years there was recurrent fighting between Dutch and Indonesian forces. Finally, at a conference held at the Hague in November 1949, it was agreed that complete sovereignty should be transferred to the Republic of Indonesia. Indonesia's self-chosen president, Sukarno, issued a decree in 1960 enabling him to control the political parties.

Under his rule, the economy drifted into disorder but was saved by massive aid from the United States and Russia. In 1965, leftist groups attempted a coup, but it was put down by military forces under the leadership of General Suharto. The subsequent purge of Communists left thousands dead. Suharto became president in 1968 and was reelected, running unopposed, in 1973.

Iran. See *Persia*.

IRAQ

Modern Iraq covers approximately the territory of ancient Mesopotamia. The ancient name means "between the rivers" of the Euphrates and Tigris. Mesopotamia, "the cradle of civilization," was the site of mankind's earliest civilization. Here were invented the first form of writing (cuneiform script) going back beyond 3500 B.C., the wheel, the division of the day into twelfths, the earliest irrigation works, the smelting of iron, and the development of astronomy and mathematics. These inventions followed the so-called agricultural revolution, which is placed at least as early as 7000 B.C., and the political development which was thereby made possible.

The earliest known inhabitants were the Sumerians. The country was conquered successively by the Amurru, the Akkadians, the Kossites, the Hittites, the Babylonians, and the Assyrians. Later came the Persians, Greeks, Romans, Parthians, and the Sassanids, the last named ruling from 226 to 637 A.D., when the Arabs conquered the country. Their capital, Baghdad, founded in 762, became the world's chief center of learning and art. In 1259, the Mongolian prince Jenghis Khan utterly destroyed Baghdad and ruined the canal system. The country lay a desert for nearly 700 years.

The British army occupied Mesopotamia in World War I and set up a state called Iraq, which was declared a British mandate by the League of Nations. Iraq promptly revolted and set up a monarchy with Faisal I as the first king. In 1945, Iraq joined the Arab League of Egypt's Nasser, but withdrew in 1958 after a revolution in which the king, Faisal II, was killed. A republic was declared. First aligned with the western powers, Iraq later accepted arms from Russia. It discussed political union with Egypt and Syria, but the proposals failed. Various coups followed. Then, in 1968, Gen. Ahmed Hassan al-Bakr took power along with the councils of the leftist, nationalistic Baath party, which established a police state.

The year 1925 was a landmark in Iraq's history. Oil was discovered that year, and Iraq became one of the world's leading producers of oil. The revenues were applied toward modernization and also to build irrigation works.

IRELAND

The early history of Ireland rests on narrative songs entirely oral until the middle of the 7th century A.D. The story teller (*fili*) held a position of high honor, having received long training and being customarily in the pay of the kings and nobles.

Before the Christian era, Ireland was divided into five kingdoms, or "fifths," and later into seven, sometimes called the heptarchy. Petty kings owed fealty to the seven kings, and they in turn owed fealty to a high king. This feudal organization differed from that on the European continent in that subordinates were less easily replaced, their power being based on family descent and the loyalty of their followers.

Christianity and St. Patrick. Although there were a few Christian societies in Ireland before 432 A.D., when St. Patrick was sent there by Pope Celestine, St. Patrick was the founder of Christianity in the island. He organized these communities and converted most of the rest, having won the protection of the high king Tara. Schools and monasteries were founded. In the next three centuries, Latin manuscripts were copied and illustrated, scholars from abroad studied in Ireland, and Irish missionaries spread Christianity in England and every land in Europe.

Invasion of the Danes. But the progress of civilization was checked at the close of the 8th century by the invasions of the Danes, who left destruction and ruin behind them wherever they went. After 200 years of this marauding, the Danes were completely overthrown in 1014 at the battle of Clontarf by Brian Boroihme, who paid the price of victory with his life.

Anglo-Norman Period. Henry II was the first English king to attempt to control Ireland. Beginning in 1172 he invaded the land and for two centuries the Irish were subjected to almost constant plunder and persecution. The next century saw the conquest by the Irish of their conquerors. The descendants of the Anglo-Norman knights who ruled in Erin became more Irish than the Irish themselves and English influence by the dawn of the 16th century seemed on the wane.

The Tudor Period. Trouble began again when Henry VIII repudiated the authority of the papacy. The clergy and people of Ireland could not be won from Rome. Immense properties of the Church were confiscated, much of it given to the nobles to pay them for their allegiance to the English crown. Queen Mary began the practice, continued by the later Tudor rulers, of driving out the Irish to provide land for English colonization.

In the reign of Elizabeth, a series of rebellions took place under Shawn O'Neill, Desmond, and Hugh O'Neill, earl of Tyrone. After ten years' fighting, Hugh O'Neill was defeated in 1603, and the whole of the island passed into the hands of the English. No less than 600,000 acres of land belonging to Irish chieftains were divided among English colonists.

The Stuarts and Cromwell. James I, the first Stuart king (1603–25), continued the policy of confiscation, making Ulster County a home for Protestant settlers and permanently dividing the country religiously. Under Charles I, continued confiscation resulted in another general rising, called by the British "the massacre of 1641," when thousands of the new settlers lost their lives.

In 1649 Cromwell landed with 10,000 troops and quelled all rebellion. At Drogheda, he put to the sword 2000 Irish soldiers who formed the garrison. It has been said that 20,000 Irish were deported and 40,000 fled the country. Under Charles II confiscations ceased and some 600 land owners had their lands restored.

William of Orange. In the English revolution of 1688, the Catholics of Ireland rallied to the side of James II, while the Protestants supported William of Orange. William crossed over to Ireland in 1689 and defeated the Irish forces under James at the battle of the Boyne. The English Parliament decreed that one million acres of land should be divided among the Protestants. All Irish trade with the English colonies was prohibited, and commerce and industries, including the great woolen trade which had been built up by Irish Protestants, were crushed. Thus it was that the best elements of the country were forced to emigrate.

The Act of Union. The British government under Pitt now decided to unite the English and Irish parliaments. To effect this, $8 million was spent in bribing and in buying up the petty boroughs which held the majority of the seats in the Irish House of Commons. The Act of Union was accordingly proclaimed in 1801.

George III refused to sign a measure introduced by Pitt to emancipate the Catholics of Ireland; thereupon the Catholic Association was inaugurated and, under the leadership of O'Connell, forced the government to bring in an emancipation bill which received the assent of George IV on the 13th of April, 1829. Following this victory, O'Connell founded an association for the repeal of the Union. The government, fearing sedition, suppressed the association.

In 1847–48 Ireland was stricken by an appalling famine due to the failure of the potato crop. The British government distributed relief but on a piteously inadequate scale. It is estimated that over 1,500,000 persons died of starvation, while another 1,000,000 emigrated, chiefly to Canada and the United States.

In 1864 a conspiracy originating with the Fenians, having as its object the separation of England and Ireland, was discovered and likewise suppressed by the British government.

From this time onward there were two views taken among British politicians regarding Ireland, one favoring coercion, the other supporting a policy of conciliation. Gladstone, in 1869, disestablished the Protestant Episcopal Church of Ireland, but he was unable to carry the whole of the Liberal party with him on his Home Rule bill of 1886. Again, in 1892, with a small majority of forty, he failed to force his second Home Rule bill through an antagonistic House of Lords.

In August 1914, World War I broke out. Asquith was now prime minister. He had been elected on a Home Rule platform and had succeeded in placing his Home Rule bill on the statute book. But Ulster had to be reckoned with. Four of the Ulster counties opposed the Act and threatened armed resistance. The government, thus intimidated, showed signs of vacillation, and it was arranged that the act should not come into force until the termination of the war.

Sinn Fein's Proclamation. Meanwhile, two great forces had long been silently leavening the life of the Irish people socially and intellectually. One of these forces was the Gaelic League, whose main object was the rejuvenation of the national language and the popularizing of all things Gaelic. The other was that of Sinn Fein (*shĭn făn*), a revolutionary society of young Irish intellectuals. The Sinn Fein, in Easter week of 1916, rose in rebellion against England and proclaimed Ireland a republic.

Irish Free State. After a week of fighting in Dublin, the republican army was defeated. The Sinn Fein party turned to guerrilla tactics and terrorism; it and its opponents, the Black and Tans, chiefly from Northern Ireland, engaged for over two years in an undeclared civil war. At the general election of 1918, the Sinn Fein party swept the country and set up a parliament (Dail Eireann), declared to be for all of Ireland. At length a truce was declared and the British government, on December 6, 1921, signed a treaty in which Ireland, exclusive of Ulster, was given the status of a free state in the British Commonwealth. Northern Ireland had already been given a parliament but remained an integral part of the United Kingdom of Great Britain and Northern Ireland.

Eamon De Valera, who had been president of the de facto republic, would not accept the treaty. He placed himself at the head of the extremists and waged a civil war against the constitutional party, which lasted until 1923. By 1924, political prisoners were released, and the government, headed by Cosgrave, made marked progress toward a better day. The process of land distribution, begun in 1870 by the British government, was completed in 1931.

End of British Tie. The election of 1932 brought De Valera to power as president. His first moves were to abolish the oath of allegiance to the sovereign of the Commonwealth and refuse to continue payments due to Great Britain for land purchases made by it. Tariff war followed. Ensuing economic stress and internal dissention led to a gradual abandonment of this policy.

In the election of 1937, De Valera was returned to power as prime minister. By the same election, he secured a new constitution declaring the country an independent republic under the Irish name of Eire. During World War II, Eire remained neutral. After the war, in 1949, it withdrew from the Commonwealth, although not under the leadership of De Valera, who had been defeated in the elections of 1948. He served again as prime minister, however, in 1951–53 and 1957–59. He had the Sinn Fein organization outlawed when it advocated direct action to take over Northern Ireland, and interned members who resisted. He was elected president in 1959 for a seven-year term. During the 1960's, substantial progress was made toward industrialization for the first time in Ireland's long history. Eire supplied troops to the United Nations for several police actions, including the Congo.

Israel. See *Palestine*.

ITALY

The history of ancient Italy is the story of Rome down to 476, when Odoacer, the strongest of the German generals in Italy, having deposed the boy-emperor Romulus Augustulus, made himself master of the western half of the Roman Empire. In 493, however, he was overthrown by Theodoric, leader of the invading Ostrogoths (East Goths), a powerful and able man who established himself as king and ruled until his death in 526. The strong and statesmanlike policy of Theodoric seemed to promise order and the preservation of the remnants of ancient Italian civilization. But, just after his death, Justinian succeeded to the throne of the Eastern Empire, and he sent his general, Belisarius, to conquer the Goths. They were so completely defeated that they withdrew from Italy.

The Lombard Supremacy. After the death of Justinian (565), his successors at Constantinople were unable effectively to protect their reconquest of the Western Empire. In 568 they lost a great part of it to the invading Lombards, who poured from the north over the Alps into the plain of northern Italy, which still bears the name of Lombardy. Originating from near the Baltic, these barbarians, unlike the Ostrogoths, had had little intercourse with the Empire and were consequently far less civilized. Their leader, Alboin, who came to a violent end in 573, was in no way comparable to Theodoric. Though the Lombards overran the North and strips of territory down the center of Italy without meeting serious resistance, they lacked military and administrative capacity to complete the conquest of the peninsula. Their kingdom, which endured two centuries (568-774), consisted of a loose confederation of over thirty duchies which the central authority at Pavia was too weak to weld together.

The period of the Lombard domination is noteworthy for the rise of the power of the papacy, especially in the time of Gregory the Great, bishop of Rome from 590 to 604, under whom was begun the conversion of the heathen Germanic tribes who had conquered Britain. The term "pope" (father), formerly the title of every Christian bishop, came to be applied exclusively to the successor of St. Peter; and as the bond between Rome and the Eastern Empire gradually weakened, the people of Rome came to look for protection more and more to the pope as their temporal as well as spiritual ruler.

The final rupture between Constantinople and Rome occurred following a rebellion in Italy, supported by the pope, against the image-breaking decree promulgated by the emperor Leo III in 726. In this strife the Lombards intervened in the hope of completing their conquest of Italy. They captured Ravenna and the coast cities that had been held by the Eastern Empire, and threatened Rome; but their king, Liutprand, out of deference to Pope Gregory II, desisted from an attempt on the city, and even presented the pope with some conquered towns, thus laying the foundation of papal temporal sovereignty.

Overthrow of the Lombards. From this time on, the popes worked steadily and successfully to undermine the Lombard power. In 754, ten years after Liutprand's death, Pope Stephen II crossed the Alps and appealed in person to Pepin, the first king of the Franks of the Carolingian line, for aid against the Lombard king, Aistulf, who was threatening Rome. In requital for being anointed king of the Franks by the pope, Pepin twice made war on Aistulf, forcing him to surrender his conquest of the

same coast cities that had been taken 26 years before by Liutprand, and handing them over to the pope.

Twenty years later, Pepin's son Charles, known to history as Charlemagne, for a personal grudge against Desiderius, then king of the Lombards and his own father-in-law, and in response to an appeal from the pope, led his army into Italy and made an end of the Lombard rule. In view of his great power in Italy, Gaul, and Germany, it seemed very natural and wise that the pope, on Christmas Day in the year 800, should crown him emperor of the Romans. This act, however, was to bring Italy little good, as it was the origin of frequent and far-reaching struggles between emperors and popes over supremacy of authority. For a time Italy found herself in close relationship with northern Europe, but the Treaty of Mersen in 870 established her once more as the Kingdom of Italy, and for many centuries this ancient land, the center of the Christian Church, was the battle-ground of her own jealous cities and of contending foreign armies. Southern Italy and Sicily were overrun by the Byzantines, Lombards, and Saracens, until the Normans drove them out in the 11th century and established the rich and strong Kingdom of the Two Sicilies.

In 962 Otto the Great, who had subdued the rebellious Lombards in the North, was crowned emperor, and later the rise of the Norman power in the South, the strengthening of the papal states, and the growth of the city-states, such as Florence and Venice, practically displaced the imperial authority. The northern Italian cities formed the Lombard League and successfully opposed the attempts of Emperor Frederick Barbarossa (reigned 1152-90) to establish his authority over their local affairs.

Italian City-States. These Italian cities were usually governed by an oligarchy composed of the wealthier citizens. They were continually at war with each other. But, in spite of all their disorder, they grew rich and powerful. Venice and Florence achieved rank among the important states of Europe. In the 14th and the 15th century, Italian cities became the centers of the revival of art and learning known as the Renaissance.

At the beginning of the 14th century the kingdom of Naples occupied southern Italy, the papal states extended in a diagonal band across the center of the peninsula, and the North was divided among the city-states. The greatest of these were Venice and Florence. Most of the cities fell at one time or another into the control of despots. Venice was a city of merchants, ruled by an aristocracy; Florence was a republic, but its government came to be directed by the family of the Medici. Rome was governed by the popes, and after the return of the papacy from Avignon (1417) they rebuilt the city and employed the greatest artists and architects of the time to adorn their capital with splendid buildings, paintings, and sculptures.

Period of Foreign Rule. The latter years of the 15th century mark the beginning of the long series of struggles of France, Spain, and Germany in the peninsula. Naples and Sicily were in the hands of the Spanish kings of Aragon. Charles VIII of France determined to seize the Spanish territory and, if possible, unite Italy under his authority. But, after a campaign in which he lost but one battle, he was compelled to withdraw. His successors, Louis XII and Francis I, endeavored to extend the French power in Italy, and protracted warfare ensued, especially between Francis I and the emperor Charles V, in which Francis I was repeatedly worsted. By the Peace of Cambrai in 1529 the Habsburgs secured a grip upon Italy that was not broken until the establishment of the Kingdom of Italy in the 19th century. The most important result of these campaigns, however, was the revelation of the treasures of Italian learning and art to the northern nations.

In the course of the struggle between France and Austria in the 17th century and the early part of the 18th, the house of Savoy secured Sardinia, and the duke of Savoy took the title of king of Sardinia. From the growth of this power in Piedmont sprang the modern national strength of Italy.

Napoleon in Italy. After the French Revolution, the French armies entered Italy and drove the Austrians out of the North, leaving them, however, in possession of Venice, where the ancient republican government was destroyed. The French set up the Cisalpine, Ligurian, Roman, and Parthenopean republics. But the democratic movements which were thus encouraged received sharp repression from Napoleon when he was firmly in power. He took for himself the iron crown of Lombardy and gave Naples to his brother Joseph and later to Joachim Murat. Rome became part of the French Empire. After the fall of Napoleon, the Congress of Vienna restored, with few changes, the 18th century order.

Struggle for Italian Freedom. The despotisms maintained in Italy by Austria and the Holy Alliance met with continued opposition from patriotic Italians. The ideal of a unified and independent Italy gained more and more adherents. The strong movement toward the realization of this ideal began in 1831, when Charles Albert, King of Sardinia, began steps to liberate Italy. Pope Pius IX introduced reforms in the papal states, and several other states secured constitutions in 1848. Failing in a campaign against the Austrians in Lombardy, Charles Albert abdicated in favor of his son, Victor Emmanuel II. Meanwhile, the people of Rome, led by Mazzini and Garibaldi, had abolished the temporal rule of the pope and set up a republic. This was overthrown by the French. The kingdom of Sardinia, now under a liberal constitution, became the rallying point for the party of United Italy. The statesmanship of Cavour (1810–61), the prime minister of Sardinia, secured attention to the claims of Italy in the Congress of Paris in 1856.

In 1858 Cavour secured the aid of Napoleon III in an attempt to drive the Austrians from Lombardy. After the victories of Magenta and Solferino (1859), Napoleon suddenly weakened and signed the preliminary treaty of Villafranca. However, in spite of Napoleon's lapse, Piedmont had acquired Lombardy. Soon the duchies of Tuscany, Parma, and Modena, and the papal state of Romagna united with Piedmont. On April 2, 1860 a parliament of the enlarged kingdom met at Turin.

On May 5, 1860 Garibaldi, whose name was worth an army, embarked from Genoa with a thousand men for the conquest of Sicily and Naples. This was one of the most audacious and brilliant exploits of modern history. On September 6 Garibaldi, with a few companions, entered Naples by rail. The king had fled. Victor Emmanuel entered the city on Nov. 7. On the 18th of February 1861 a parliament representing all Italy, except Venetia and Rome, met at Turin, and the title of king of Italy was bestowed on Victor Emmanuel. Austria, crippled by her disastrous war with Prussia in 1866, was forced to yield Venice to Italy in that year, and when, in 1870, the French, at war with Prussia, withdrew their garrison from Rome, the sole support of the temporal rule of the popes was gone, and Italy could at last claim the Eternal City for her capital.

The Kingdom of United Italy. Many serious problems confronted the new state. The people, more than 75 per cent of whom were illiterate, had to be educated. A compulsory education law was passed in 1877, and since that time the percentage of illiteracy has been largely reduced. In 1881 and again in 1912 the suffrage was greatly extended; in 1920 it was made universal for men and women. Relations with the pope were difficult. The Law of Papal Guarantees, passed in 1871, gave the pope sovereignty over certain parts of the city of Rome and an annual grant of money. This arrangement was never accepted by the pope in its original form. In 1882 Italy joined the Triple Alliance.

In 1885 Italy embarked upon a colonial policy and became involved in a disastrous war with Abyssinia. Popular discontent increased under heavy taxation. In July 1900 King Humbert was assassinated; Victor Emmanuel III succeeded.

Great increase of population and consequent emigration to other countries turned the attention of the Italian government to the acquisition of colonies. In 1912, after a war with Turkey, Italy acquired Tripoli and twelve Ægean islands. She long looked upon the region around the city of Trent, Trieste, and Istria as properly Italian territory, *Italia Irredenta*, or "unredeemed Italy." On the outbreak of World War I, Italy remained neutral until May 1915, when she entered the war on the side of the Allies. By the Treaty of St. Germain her territory was greatly enlarged at the expense of Austria.

Fascist Rule. The years 1920-21 were marked by conflicts between communist and nationalist groups. The latter, known as Fascisti, seized power in 1922, under the leadership of Benito Mussolini.

Dictatorial power was conferred on Mussolini. He established a form of modified capitalism which he described as a corporative state, Fascism. Mussolini made peace with the Vatican in 1929, yielding to the papacy the sovereignty over Vatican City.

In 1935–36 Italy conquered Ethiopia, in defiance of League of Nations sanctions, and assisted the insurgents in the Spanish civil war, 1936–39.

Before World War II, Mussolini made an alliance with Hitler's Germany. After Germany had conquered France, he brought Italy into the war to join in what he thought was the kill. But it turned out otherwise. See *World War II*.

The Republic. When the allies entered Rome, the king retired and formally abdicated in May 1946. In a popular referendum, held in June, 54 per cent of the people voted for a republic, which came into effect by a new constitution in 1948.

After World War II, Italy was plagued by unemployment and civil dissension. The Communist party tried to win power but, under the influence of the Vatican and the U.S., the country turned to the West and joined NATO. In 1957, it became a member of the European Common Market.

Mariano Rumor became premier in 1968, succeeding Aldo Moro. Student strikes, civil disturbances, and a series of government crises, often concerning factional fighting between the Socialists and the Christian Democrats over the status of the Communist party, brought the collapse of the Rumor government. Emilio Colombo, sworn in in 1970, promptly began a program of anti-inflation measures and social reforms to aid Italy's threatened economy. Succeeding governments of Giulio Andreotti, Rumor, and Moro failed to meet the growing economic and political crises. In the 1976 national elections, the Communist party made wide gains. No majority existed in parliament, so Andreotti formed a weak minority government while Communists headed many of the legislative committees. By August of 1976, the Communist party controlled the local government of every major Italian city.

JAPAN

Early Japanese history is interwoven with myths and legends. Tradition says that Jimmu Tenno set up his government near the present Kyoto in 660 B. C. Modern historians place the event about the beginning of the Christian era. Koreans were the civilizers of Japan. Confucianism is thought to have been introduced about 415 A. D.; Buddhism, in 552. In 604 the earliest Japanese laws were written in Chinese. The government was modeled upon that of China.

Medieval Government. From the middle of the 8th century onward, the country was governed by military families or by armed monastic communities, whose heads exercised a regency, while the emperor, often a minor, was a mere figurehead.

Near the end of the 16th century, Nobunaga attempted to subjugate the armed Buddhist communities. He was assassinated. Hideyoshi followed and established peace. About 1600, Iyeyasu established a feudal government, known as the Tokugawa Shogunate, with its capital at Yedo, the present Tokyo. Nominally, the shogun was appointed by the emperor, but the emperor could not remove or punish him, so long as the shogun's family possessed the power. On the other hand, the shogun sometimes removed and exiled an emperor.

Early Relations with Western Nations. It was during the 16th century, too, that Europeans made their first acquaintance with Japan. Mendez Pinto, a Portuguese, was shipwrecked on the coast of Japan in 1542. This led to a visit by St. Francis Xavier in 1549. Thousands of Japanese became Christians. Missionaries and merchants of various nationalities followed the Portuguese. Much rivalry was created. Religious jealousy mingled with political intrigue and the strife of feudal clans. Hideyoshi, moved in part, perhaps, by the fear of foreign domination, sought to banish the missionaries. The attempt failed, and in 1596 the authorities, in order to terrify the Christians, seized several of them, together with a number of missionaries, and crucified them at Nagasaki. This persecution led to a rebellion of the Christians, which was punished in 1606 by an edict forbidding the exercise of the Christian religion. Another Christian conspiracy in 1611 brought about the expulsion of the missionaries in 1614. In 1636 an edict excluding all foreigners and prohibiting all intercourse with foreign countries was issued.

Commercial Treaties. In 1852 the American government, in order to secure the protection of American sailors shipwrecked on the coasts of Japan, and in the hope of opening ports where American vessels might obtain supplies, sent Commodore Perry to Japan to attempt to establish treaty relations. He arrived in Japan in July 1853 and delivered the president's letter to the shogun. In February 1854 he returned for a reply, and in March that year signed the treaty that opened Shimoda and Hakodate to the use of American vessels. A commercial treaty between the two countries was signed in 1858. The example of the United States was followed by other countries.

The signing of the treaties by the shogun provided a rallying cry for the clans that opposed the Tokugawa Shogunate. A civil war was followed in 1867 by the restoration of the emperor to real power and by the removal of the capital from Kyoto to Tokyo in 1868.

Modern Progress. In 1871 feudalism was abolished. Western laws and military organization were introduced. Teachers from America and Europe were invited to establish schools. A constitution was proclaimed in 1889, and the first Parliament assembled in 1890.

The extraterritorial jurisdiction enjoyed by foreign powers over their nationals resident in Japan was surrendered in 1899. Tariff autonomy was not fully recovered until 1911. These two accomplishments were perhaps aided by Japan's triumph over China in the war of 1894–95.

Russian intrigue in Korea led in 1904 to war with Russia, which secured for Japan a protectorate over Korea and the transfer to herself of Russian leases of railways and ports in southern Manchuria, together with certain mining rights. In 1910 Japan annexed Korea.

Japan in World War I. During World War I, Japan, assisted by Great Britain, expelled the Germans from Kiaochow, leased territory in China, and took possession of the former German rights in the province of Shantung. These rights were eventually relinquished to China by treaty in 1922.

World War I gave Japan also a mandate over the islands north of the equator, formerly belonging to Germany. The mandate was not recognized by the United States until the Treaty of Yap was signed on February 11, 1922, in which Japan acknowledged certain American rights in Yap.

Recent Developments. The Anglo-Japanese defensive alliance of 1902 was replaced in 1922 by an agreement between the United States, Great Britain, France, and Japan to respect one another's rights in their insular possessions in the Pacific. In 1924 the Japanese Diet abolished the dual nationality of Japanese born in foreign lands, thereby removing a serious objection in certain countries to Japanese immigration.

A serious earthquake, resulting in great loss of life and enormous destruction of property occurred September 1, 1923. The emperor, Hirohito, succeeded to the throne on Dec. 25, 1926. The first parliamentary election under a new manhood suffrage act was held in 1928.

In 1931, Japan began a career of expansion by attacking Manchuria, and turning it into a puppet state, called Manchukuo. Further aggressions on northern China followed, including the seizure of Peiping. From 1937 to 1940 Japan conquered, without a formal declaration of war, a half million square miles of China, including its six largest cities. All this was pursuant to the policy of establishing in Asia a "co-prosperity sphere," which aimed eventually at driving out the Europeans. The government believed that an opportunity offered when Hitler's Germany proposed an alliance in 1936. In 1940, Japan attacked Germany's enemies in Asia, chiefly the dependencies of Great Britain, and in a surprisingly short time overran all southeastern Asia. Then Japan suddenly attacked Hawaii and wiped out most of the American fleet. For the turning of the scales against Japan and her final defeat, see *World War II*.

Japan surrendered formally and unconditionally September 1, 1945. Complete authority now passed to the Allied Supreme Commander, General Douglas MacArthur, and the Allies began a complete reorganization of Japan. Emperor Hirohito abjured the myth of his divine origin and that of his race. The old feudalism and the modern monopolistic industrialism were attacked. The power of the ruling classes was broken, and their leaders excluded from office or brought to trial as "war criminals." Parliament was summoned and a new constitution was prepared and promulgated November 3, 1946. On September 8, 1951, a treaty of peace was signed by Japan and the representatives of 48 countries at San Francisco. Japan again became a sovereign nation April 28, 1952.

Postwar Japan amazed the world by the speed with which the people adapted themselves to their new situation. Democratic government took root. Agricultural productivity, following on land reform, radically reduced the need for imports. Although without iron ore, Japan broke into the front rank of steel producers and became the world's largest shipbuilder. Relying on American protection, Japan was able to spend comparatively little on armaments since its new constitution forbade it to engage in war.

THE JEWS

The word *Jew*, derived from *Judah*, designates the Hebrew people as a religious group, a church, in contrast to the terms Israel and Israelites, which designate them as a national group. The Hebrew people, like all the kindred Semites, were cradled in the Arabian desert. They migrated thence in small tribal groups between the 15th and 12th centuries B. C. and settled in Palestine. In this movement, Moses and Joshua were the main figures. Moses led a few small tribes forth from Egypt, where they had been dwelling, federated them with other small tribes of the desert, established for them the worship of Yahwe, founded certain legal institutions that became the nucleus of the later Israelite law code, and settled his followers in southern Palestine. Joshua was the leader of another group of tribes that settled in the central part of Palestine.

The Early Kingdom of Israel. There the Israelite tribes encountered powerful enemies, especially the Philistines. After a century-long struggle with them, Israel finally triumphed about 1000 B. C., chiefly through the able leadership of David. This struggle welded the originally independent tribes into one compact nation with many national traditions. Among these was the tradition of the descent of all the Israelite tribes from one common ancestor, Abraham, and his descendants, Isaac and Jacob. Many stories and traditions about these prehistoric figures are recorded in the book of Genesis. Some may possess a basis of historic truth. Furthermore, the figures of Moses and Joshua have been enveloped in legend until the true story of these men and their times is not definitely known by historians.

Israel's recorded history begins with the entrance of the tribes into Palestine. But we tread firm historical ground only when we reach the time of David. After his conquest of the Philistines, David subdued the surrounding nations. His empire was consolidated by his son Solomon. A rebellion of the northern tribes, provoked by taxation, after Solomon's death in 932 B. C., divided his realm into the Northern and Southern kingdoms, called Israel and Judah respectively.

Northern and Southern Kingdoms. The Northern Kingdom lasted until 722 B. C., when the Assyrians destroyed the capital, Samaria, and deported a considerable number of people. These mixed eventually with other Eastern nations and disappeared. Tradition speaks of them, though incorrectly, as the Ten Lost Tribes. The Southern Kingdom endured until overthrown by the Babylonians in 586 B. C. Many of the people were carried away to exile in Babylonia, while others, among them the prophet Jeremiah, fled to Egypt.

The Prophets. But, while Israel's national existence was brief and ill-starred, during this period the beginning of Israel's chief contribution to human civilization was made. Amos, Hosea, Isaiah, Jeremiah, and their fellow-prophets gave to the old tribal and national religion a significant reinterpretation. They conceived of Yahwe as Creator of the entire universe, the loving Father of mankind; all men, God's children, therefore, they regarded as brothers, forming one human family. They denounced idolatry, immorality, and social injustice, and proclaimed that above all else God desires that men do justice, love mercy, and walk humbly with Him. They thus established ethical monotheism, a universalistic conception of both God and man, and justice and love as the basic forces of human conduct.

The Return from Exile. Cyrus, founder of the Persian empire, permitted the exiles in Babylonia to return to Palestine in 536 B. C., undoubtedly for political reasons. But only a comparatively few did so, and that no longer as an independent nation, Israel, but solely as a religious community. Henceforth they are known as Jews. Under Ezra and Nehemiah, Judaism was definitely established. From 536 B. C. on, the Jews of Palestine were successively vassals of Persia, Alexander the Great, Egypt, and Syria. During this entire period, with the exception of the short reign of Alexander, increasing oppression was their lot.

The Dispersion. Finally, in 166 B. C., under the Maccabees, they revolted against Syria, and through marvelous heroism against tremendous odds they regained independence and set up their own kings, the Asmonean dynasty. But this new independent Jewish state was short-lived. It crumbled with the conquest of Syria by Pompey in 63 B. C. For a while it continued as a Roman vassal under a semi-Jewish dynasty, Herod and his successors. During this period Jesus of Nazareth lived and worked and Christianity arose. Finally, in 70 A. D., after a heroic but fruitless defense, the Romans under Titus captured Jerusalem, destroyed the Temple, massacred thousands of Jews, and sold other thousands as slaves throughout the world. A heroic attempt to regain independence under Bar-Cochba in 132-135 A. D. failed miserably. Hadrian completed Titus's work of dispersion.

During the next two centuries the interest of the Jews remaining in Palestine centered in their religion. About the year 200 the *Mishna*, an extensive legal code, was compiled, and about 330 the *Palestinian Talmud*. At nearly the same time Constantine closed the great rabbinical schools.

Since the Babylonian Exile a large Jewish population had flourished in Babylonia. This now became the chief center of Jewish life and thought. There the *Babylonian Talmud* was compiled about 550. Under the Mohammedan rulers the lot of the Jews improved materially.

The Jews in Europe. But, with the decadence of Mohammedan power in the East, the center of Jewish life gradually shifted to Europe, particularly to Spain, where Jews attained great influence in both learning and commerce, and occasionally even became royal counselors. In southern Russia in the 7th century the entire Tatar kingdom of the Chazars was converted to Judaism. During this period Jewish scholars translated much of Arabic literature into European languages, thus giving Arabic science and philosophy to Europe.

The religious zeal and bigotry fostered by the Crusades reacted unhappily upon the Jews. Increasing oppression became their lot. They were successively banished from England, France, Spain, Portugal, and many of the small German states. However, Italy, Poland, Turkey, and especially Holland granted them refuge. Cromwell finally permitted them to return to England. In Holland, Baruch Spinoza, the Jew, laid the foundations of modern philosophy. In many cities of Italy, however, and of other countries to which Jews were admitted, ghettoes were established—districts where Jews were required to dwell and out of which they might pass only if wearing a distinctive garb. See *Ghetto*.

The French Revolution and the rise of liberalism had a tendency to dissolve anti-Jewish animus. Since that time, waves of anti-Semitism have swept over parts of Europe.

Anti-Semitism. The characteristic of more recent anti-Semitism is that it is based less on religious considerations than on national, racial, and economic ones. This turn was first given as a result of a pamphlet published in 1873 by a Hamburg journalist, *Jewry's Triumph over Germanism*. This book attributed to international Jewry a severe economic depression that followed three years after Germany's triumph over France. The book had a great influence throughout central Europe and Russia. Anti-Jewish political parties were formed in several countries.

The movement was gradually discredited in Germany. In France it did not survive the Dreyfus Affair as a political factor. See *Dreyfus Affair*. In Russia, it exploded in the pogrom of Easter, 1881.

The second wave of anti-Semitism likewise took its rise in Germany. Hitler rose to power in the 1930's by fanning the flames of German nationalism and pride of race, the chief enemies of which he declared were the twin evils of Jewry and Communism. His ascendency brought laws which deprived Jews of civil and political rights. He then began a systematic extermination of all persons of Jewish origin. An estimated 5 million were put to death before Hitler's overthrow in 1945.

The Jews in America. In the 17th century, Jews sought in North America a refuge from European persecution. The first notable migration was that of a group from Brazil to New Amsterdam, in 1654, while that colony was under Dutch rule. In 1658, a few Jews settled in Newport, R. I., under the conditions of religious toleration which prevailed in that colony. There were Jewish settlements in other colonies before the Revolution.

Zionism. In general this was a plan to establish an autonomous Jewish state in Palestine. It had a twofold source, the ancient dream of a restored Israel and the need of an asylum for oppressed Jews. The Zionist Organization was founded in 1897, under the leadership of Theodore Herzl.

Balfour Declaration. On November 2, 1917, Lord Balfour issued the following statement on behalf of the British government: "His Majesty's government view with favour the establishment in Palestine of a national home for the Jewish people, and will use their best endeavours to facilitate the achievement of this object, it being clearly understood that nothing shall be done which will prejudice the civil and religious rights of existing non-Jewish communities in Palestine or the rights and political status enjoyed by Jews in any other country."

A mandate for Palestine was assigned to Great Britain after World War I, and, in 1923, effect was given to the Declaration. See *Palestine*.

JORDAN

This Arab state, included in the British mandate of Palestine, was given a separate administration under Emir Abdullah in 1923. Britain recognized its independence in 1946 and the Emir became King Abdullah ibn Hussein of the Hashemite Kingdom of Jordan. When Israel declared its independence in 1948, Jordan became the battleground for the war in which the Arab League tried but failed to crush Israel. A truce agreement gave Old Jerusalem to Jordan and designated eastern Palestine as an asylum for Palestinian Arabs. Annexation of this area with its million refugees by Egypt and Jordan created many problems. Abdullah was assassinated by a League member in 1951. His son Talal, mentally ill, was deposed and Talal's son became Hussein II in 1952. Considered pro-Western, Hussein was frequently in dispute with his Arab neighbors. In 1958 he turned from Britain to the U.S. for financial aid. The Arab League urged Hussein to a sterner attitude toward Israel, culminating in the 1967 Arab-Israeli war. Defeat brought Jordan the loss of Old Jerusalem and the territory west of the Jordan River. Throughout 1968 serious clashes continued between Israel and Jordan-based guerrillas. In 1970, Palestinian refugees attempted to take power but were defeated and confined to a few camps in the north. Jordan was only briefly involved in the 1973 Arab-Israeli War and continued good relations with the U.S.

KOREA (CHOSEN)

Tradition carries the story of the Asiatic country of Korea (*kô-rē'à*) back to about 1122 B. C., when Ki-tse is said to have founded a state. The first authentic date marks the annexation of the country to China in 108 B. C. About 960 A. D. a period of great prosperity and progress began, which continued for several centuries. Art, religion, literary forms, and governmental methods were borrowed from China. In 1392 Buddhism was displaced in favor of Confucianism. In the 16th century the Japanese, led by Hideyoshi, the Japanese regent, occupied much territory for a time, being driven out finally by Chinese forces. Early in the 17th century the rising Manchu power overran the country and exacted tribute, which was afterward paid annually to the Manchu rulers of China until 1894.

Until very recently, most of our scanty knowledge of Korea was obtained from the narratives of Dutch sailors who were wrecked on the Korean coast in 1653 and detained in the country some years. For Korea was determined to seclude herself from the world.

From 1835 till 1860, several French missionaries contrived to find shelter, and, in spite of persecutions, the Christian community, founded in the 18th century, continued to increase. In 1864 a reactionist was made regent, and he encouraged persecution of Christians.

In 1876, however, Korea made a treaty with Japan, and, later on, through Admiral Shufeldt, with the United States,—followed by others with England, Russia, France, Germany, and Italy. After Japan's victory over China, in 1895, Korea's independence was recognized by both powers. In 1907, pursuant to the recognition of Japan's interests by the Treaty of Portsmouth, Korea practically passed under a Japanese protectorate and in 1910 was annexed to that empire, under the ancient name of Chosen. In 1945 it was taken from Japan, and was promised ultimate independence. The Americans occupied southern Korea up to 38°; the Russians, the north. As a result of disagreements between the two powers, two governments were set up in 1948, a Communist government and a republic under U.S. protection. See *Korean War*.

LEBANON

Owing to its cross-roads position, Lebanon enjoyed a flourishing trade with neighboring countries as early as the 13th century. Lying between Israel and Syria, with which it was formerly combined, Lebanon was made a republic under French mandate after World War I, and was recognized as an independent state in 1941. The constitution of the country provided for governmental separation along religious, or "confessional," lines. The Maronite Catholics controlled the presidency, the army, and a majority in parliament while the Moslems remained second-class citizens. The situation was complicated by the influx of Palestinian refugees and the establishment in Lebanon of the main base of the Palestine Liberation Organization (PLO). By 1975, Moslems made up 60 percent of the population. The country experienced strife in 1958, when American troops landed to help restore order, and in 1969, when war was narrowly averted. In 1975, full-fledged civil war erupted as Moslems and the PLO tried to gain more control. As the fighting escalated, other Middle Eastern countries became involved. The Moslems received support from Iraq and Egypt while Israel aided the Christians. In late 1976, Syria, which had tried to help in negotiations, invaded Lebanon to crush the PLO and to gain influence in the eventual resolution of the civil war.

LIBERIA

Liberia is an independent Negro republic on the west coast of Africa. It had its origin in the plan of the American Colonization Society, founded in 1817, to colonize free Negroes from the United States. The name is derived from the Latin word *liber*, meaning "free." Settlement of the territory acquired by the Society began in 1822, and in 1838 a government called the Commonwealth of Liberia was organized. The independent Republic of Liberia was established in 1847. Only persons of Negro blood may become citizens. Liberia declared war on Germany in 1917, and again in 1942. She has permitted the United States to establish military bases in her territory.

LIBYA

The former Italian colony of Libya on the Mediterranean coast of North Africa has been a coveted prize for the last 2000 years. It was dominated successively by Carthage, Rome, the Vandals, Islam, the Ottoman Empire, and, from 1911 until World War II, by Italy. The British and French then held control until it was declared an independent federal kingdom in 1951 under King Idris I, pursuant to resolutions passed in the United Nations. Idris ruled until 1969 when he was deposed by a military junta led by Muammar al-Qaddafi. Under the new leadership, foreign oil interests were nationalized and Libya became a leader in efforts to unify the Arab world.

LIECHTENSTEIN

Liechtenstein (*lĭк′tĕn-shtĭn*) is a principality lying between Austria and Switzerland. It consists of territory which came into the possession of the house of Liechtenstein at the beginning of the 18th century, and it was made a principality by the emperor Karl VI in 1719. From 1815 to 1866 it formed part of the German Confederation. Later it was practically a dependency of Austria, but in 1918 the Diet resolved to establish independence.

LUXEMBOURG

Luxembourg (*lŭk′sĕm-bûrg*) is a grand duchy bordering France, Belgium, and Germany. It was made a duchy within the German Empire by Charles IV in 1354. In 1814 it was raised to a grand duchy under the king of Holland but passed to the duke of Nassau in 1890. It was included in the German Confederation from 1815 to 1866. The Treaty of London in 1867 declared Luxembourg neutral territory and guaranteed its independence. It was overrun by the Germans in 1914, but regained its independence in 1919. On May 10, 1940, the Germans again occupied it, and Grand Duchess Charlotte took refuge in Canada. It was liberated by American troops in September 1944.

MALAGASY (MADAGASCAR)

This island off the southeast coast of Africa was given its name Madagascar by Marco Polo, although he did not actually visit the island. Diaz disembarked there in 1500. France made it a protectorate in 1885. The last native monarch was Queen Ranavolona III, who was deposed in 1895, and the island became a French colony. Despite some abortive efforts to secure independence, the island remained under French rule until 1958. In that year a referendum was held under French auspices, and the people chose independence within the French Community. By a constitution adopted in 1959, it became the Republic of Malagasy.

Mesopotamia. See *Iraq*.

MONACO

Smallest state in the world, the principality of Monaco (*mŏn′-à-kō*) occupies a strip of Mediterranean coast about two miles long and not more than three-fifths of a mile wide at any point. On the landward side, the country is entirely surrounded by France. Italian is the language spoken, but finances and custom privileges are under French control. As a winter resort, and especially as a gambling center, Monaco is world-famous. Income from the gambling concession and from the issuance of postage stamps has provided most of the revenue.

Politically, Monaco has a long history of independence, or near-independence, dating back to the 14th and 15th centuries, when it was ruled by the Genoese family of Grimaldi. Albert I, who reigned from 1889 to 1922, changed Monaco from an absolute to a limited monarchy in 1911. His grandson, Prince Rainier III, became ruler in 1949.

MOROCCO

This country was held by the Romans under the name of Mauretania. It was taken by the Vandals in the 5th century A.D. The Arabs conquered it about 700 A.D. and imposed the Mohammedan religion upon the native Berbers. Morocco later became independent under a Berber dynasty and extended its power as far east as Egypt, conquered Spain, and penetrated deep into France until checked by Charles Martel in 732 A.D. These Moors, as they were generally known in Europe, were driven from Spain in the early 13th century. Morocco was one of the so-called Barbary states until the 20th century. Spain held a portion of the territory from 1860. In 1894, an American citizen Ion Perdicaris was seized and held for ransom by Raia-Uli, a Moroccan chief. He was released after American and European pressure. France held most of Morocco as a protectorate from 1912 to 1956,

when Morocco was recognized as an independent country. Under a constitution adopted in 1962, it became a limited monarchy.

THE NETHERLANDS

The northern European kingdom popularly called Holland. Originally, the name, meaning "low countries," applied to all the territory now included in Holland, Belgium, and northeastern France. Julius Cæsar found this country peopled by the Frisii in the north, the Batavi in the center along the lower Rhine, and the Belgæ in the south. Cæsar brought the Gallic Belgæ into subjection to Rome, but the Germanic tribes of the Batavi and the Frisii resisted Roman conquest somewhat longer. They finally made peace and were recognized as allies. The low-lying territory of the Batavi between the Waal and the Rhine, known as the "island of the Batavians," was long an important outpost of the empire. Batavian soldiers served in Roman armies and formed a large part of the Prætorian guard. By the end of the 3d century, when the Franks began their inroads, the Batavi, as well as the other tribes within the Roman frontier, had become Romanized. But the Frisii, or Frisians, allied with the Saxons, held the seacoast from the Scheldt to the Ems in defiance of the Franks, until the time of Charlemagne. They resisted Christianization as well as Frankish conquest, and their conversion was more the result of armed compulsion than of missionary zeal.

The division of Charlemagne's empire in 843 gave the part of the Netherlands east of the Scheldt river to Lothair, to be known as Lothair's kingdom, or *Lotharii Regnum*, whence comes the name Lorraine. It finally passed to the East Frankish power, and in 953 Otto the Great transferred it to Bruno, archbishop of Cologne. Bruno divided his lands into Upper and Lower Lorraine, giving the charge of the latter to Godfrey of Verdun. This territory, difficult of access, far removed from both French and German seats of government, but open to the ravages of the Northmen on its rivers and coast line, now became for two centuries the scene of pirate raids and petty dynastic struggles.

Rise of Free Cities. At the close of the 11th century, stable government began in these feudal states, and then the Crusades opened a new era. The soldiers of the Netherlands distinguished themselves with a valor equal to that which had made their ancestors famous in Roman times. New avenues of trade were opened up, and the cities of the Low Countries began their wonderful growth in industry and commerce. Free cities and communes, governed by burgomasters and sworn councilors, flourished as practically self-governing republics. This development was slower in the North than in the South. The charters of the free cities of Holland and Zealand date from the 13th century, while those of the communes of Flanders date from the 12th. The latter also came earlier into conflict with the dukes of the great Burgundian power. In the 15th century the house of Burgundy brought all the Netherlands under its control; but lack of statesmanship wrecked the promising schemes of Duke Charles the Bold, and in 1477 the marriage of his daughter Mary to Maximilian of Austria threw the Netherlands into the power of the Habsburgs.

Period of Spanish Rule. In February 1477, the provinces secured Mary's signature to the Great Privilege, a charter confirming their political rights and local liberties. Her grandson, who in 1519 became emperor as Charles V, was born and brought up in the Netherlands, and his policy, administered first through his aunt, Margaret, and later through his sister, Mary, was moderate and progressive. But the notable spread of Protestantism, especially in the northern provinces, moved him to severe measures of restraint. His son, Philip II, a thorough Spaniard, who lacked sympathy with the Netherlands, used every means at his command to suppress both civil and religious liberty. By the year 1566 the most violent passions had been aroused, and fanatical mobs, called iconoclasts or "image breakers," spread ruin among the churches and religious houses. In 1567 Philip sent the duke of Alva to curb the disturbance with Spanish and Italian troops. Six years of pitiless, bloody severity served to bring him the curses of the Netherlands as well as the disfavor of Philip. He resigned in 1573.

The most important result of Alva's rule was the revolt of the northern, Protestant provinces under the leadership of William of Orange. Their struggle for independence is one of the most splendid episodes in history. Again and again they cut their dikes and flooded hard-won land to baffle the foreign troops. The University of Leyden is a memorial founded in 1574 by the province of Holland in honor of the deliverance of the city of Leyden, accomplished by the help of a great flood over the broken dikes. In 1576 the southern provinces, terrified by the outrages of the mutinous Spanish troops, joined with the northern provinces in the Pacification of Ghent. But the policy of Alessandro Farnese won the southern, Catholic provinces back to Spain, and in January 1579 Holland, Zealand, Utrecht, Gelderland, Friesland, Overyssel, and Gröningen bound themselves together in the Union of Utrecht, thus founding the modern state of the Netherlands.

Independence of Dutch Republic. William, called "the Silent," was murdered in 1584, but the struggle was continued by his son, Maurice of Nassau, stadholder of Holland and Zealand. The merchants of these two provinces had prospered and achieved a Dutch supremacy in trade, which continued through the 17th century. They had no other thought but that of independence. In 1609 a twelve years' truce was concluded with Spain, but not until the close of the Thirty Years' war was the independence of the United Provinces finally recognized. During this time the Union was a confederacy of sovereign states, among which Holland was leader. In 1651 the office of stadholder was abolished, and the head of the Union was called the grand pensionary. For twenty years this office was held by the statesmanlike John de Witt; but in 1672, when Louis XIV attacked the Netherlands, the prince of Orange, afterward William III of England, was made stadholder and captain general.

The Kingdom of the Netherlands. During the 18th century the United Netherlands, or Dutch Republic, played a secondary rôle among the nations, and internal government with the old machinery was becoming more and more difficult when the French Revolution broke out. In 1795, under French direction, the Batavian Republic was organized on the wreck of the United Netherlands. In 1806 Napoleon made the country a kingdom, and in 1810 he incorporated it in the French Empire. The Congress of Vienna united it with Belgium in the Kingdom of the Netherlands, but the Belgians withdrew in 1830.

The people of the United Netherlands, under their old republican, stadholder system of government, had been pioneers in many features of modern democracy. The ideas of a written constitution and a state-supported school system are rightly credited to them. Religious toleration made the Netherlands the refuge for the persecuted of all nations in the 17th century. The rights of the provincial states and the States-General had been jealously guarded. The Fundamental Law of 1815, however, quite in the spirit of the Congress of Vienna, provided for a constitutional monarchy in which the king was more powerful than the Parliament, or States-General, which could not originate or amend legislation.

The Dutch maintained their neutrality in World War I under difficult conditions. In World War II they were less fortunate. The Germans invaded the country in May 1940. The queen and ministers escaped to England and carried on from there. (See *World War II*).

Queen Wilhelmina returned in May 1945. On September 4, 1948, she abdicated the throne, and was succeeded by her daughter, Princess Juliana of Orange and Nassau. Queen Juliana, born in 1909, is married to Prince Bernhard, who received the title of Prince of the Netherlands on her accession.

NORWAY

Like the other Scandinavian peoples, the Norwegians have a long legendary story preserved in sagas. But the authentic history of Norway begins in the latter part of the 9th century A. D. in the time of Harold Fairhair, who united the petty tribal kingdoms under his authority and died about 933. This was the period of the Norse sea rovers. Contact with the more civilized peoples of Europe resulted in the establishment of Christianity in Norway in the 10th and the 11th century. Olaf the Saint, who was a zealous apostle of the new faith, ruled the turbulent chieftains from 1015 to 1028. He was slain in 1030 in war with rebellious subjects who invited Canute of Denmark and England to come to their aid. Olaf's son, Magnus I, recovered the throne from Canute's son Svein in 1035, and henceforth, till 1319, Norway was governed by native kings.

Union with Sweden and Denmark. During this period the country was prosperous. The small landholders gained political control, and Norse colonies were established in Iceland and Greenland. The death of Hakon V in 1319, without male heirs, threw the election of a new king into the hands of the National Assembly, who, after many discussions, made choice of Magnus VII of Sweden, the son of Hakon's daughter. He was in turn succeeded by his son Hakon and his grandson Olaf V, who, having been elected king of Denmark in 1375, became ruler of the sister Scandinavian kingdoms on the death of his father in 1380. This young king, who exercised only a nominal sway under the guidance of his mother, Queen Margaret, heiress of Waldemar IV of Denmark, died without issue in 1387. Margaret's love of power and capacity for government brought about her election to the triple throne of the Scandinavian lands, and from this period till 1814 Norway continued united with Denmark.

While Norway shared in the general fortunes of Denmark, it retained its own constitutional mode of government and exercised its right of electing its monarchs. After a time, like the sister kingdom, it agreed of its own free will to relinquish this privilege in favor of hereditary succession to the throne. The Napoleonic crisis may be said to have severed this union, which had existed for more than 400 years; for Denmark, after having given unequivocal proofs of adhesion to the cause of Napoleon, was compelled, after his defeat, to purchase peace at the cost of sovereignty over Norway. Crippled in her resources and almost bankrupt, she saw herself constrained to sign the Treaty of Kiel in 1814, by which it was stipulated by the allied powers that she should resign Norway to Sweden, receiving in return, by way of indemnity, some portion of Swedish Pomerania and the island of Rügen, which were subsequently exchanged with Prussia for Lauenburg.

Union of Norway and Sweden. The Norwegians, having refused to admit the validity of the Treaty of Kiel, nominated Prince Christian, heir presumptive to the throne of Denmark, as regent and subsequently king of Norway. This nomination was made by the Constitutional Assembly, which also drew up a constitution based on the French constitution of 1791. These measures found, however, neither supporters nor sympathizers among the other nations. With the sanction of the great allied powers, Charles John Bernadotte, crown prince of Sweden, led an army into Norway and, after taking Frederikstad and Frederikshald, threatened Christiania. Norway, being utterly destitute of the means necessary for prosecuting a war, accepted union with Sweden on the basis of equality of the two kingdoms. Norway retained self-government.

Independence of Norway. The growth of parliamentary government brought about a desire on the part of the parliaments of both Sweden and Norway to control the king's selection of ministers and his foreign policy. This condition kept alive Norwegian impatience with the union. Besides, Sweden was aristocratic, while Norway was strongly democratic. In spite of the royal veto the Norwegian parliament abolished the orders of nobility in that country. Meanwhile, Norway became prosperous and developed a large commerce. This led to demand for a separate consular service. After several years of dispute, the Norwegians declared the union with Sweden dissolved in 1905. Their decision was confirmed by the Treaty of Karlstad. Prince Charles of Denmark became king of Norway as Haakon VII.

The World Wars. Norway remained neutral and fairly prosperous during World War I. In World War II the Germans invaded Norway in April 1940, and conquered it after a stiff resistance. They set up a puppet government under Vidkun Quisling, which most of the people resisted. The great merchant fleet and all other resources outside of the kingdom were put at the service of the Allies. On June 7, 1945, King Haakon returned amid popular rejoicing.

PALESTINE

Previously to the 16th century B.C., it appears that Palestine was subject to the power of Babylon. Babylonian culture persisted even when the territory was mastered for a time by the Amorites. Early Egyptian records disclose the fact that the peoples of Canaan, as Palestine was at that time called, had commercial relations with Egypt. Canaan was conquered by the Egyptian king, Thothmes III, in the first half of the 15th century B.C.

The period of Egyptian supremacy was interrupted for some time by the inroads of the Hittites from the north. About 1350 B.C., however, the power of Egypt was again dominant in Canaan. It was within the following two centuries that the country was subjected to invasion by the Israelites.

For a brief period in the 10th century B.C., the entire land of Canaan, with some adjacent territory, was brought under the power of the independent kingdom of Israel and was ruled by David and by his successor, Solomon. The subsequent division of the realm between northern Israel and Judah left the land an easy prey to the Assyrian and the Babylonian empire. The northern kingdom fell in 722 B.C., and the southern, Judah, in 586 B.C. The inhabitants of the latter kingdom, known as Jews, were taken as captives to Babylon. Being permitted by Cyrus, the Persian, to return in 536, they became the nucleus of a small Jewish community.

The conquests of Alexander, at the end of the 4th century B.C., brought a strong Greek influence to bear on the country. After the death of Alexander, Palestine passed first under the control of the Ptolemies of Egypt, and, later, in 197 B.C., it came into the power of Antiochus of Syria. In 168 B.C., the Jews, led by the Maccabean princes, threw off the tyranny of the Syrian ruler and set up an independent state extending throughout southern Palestine from the river Jordan to the sea.

In 63 B.C., internal strife opened the way for intervention and conquest by the Romans. A revolt of the Jews in 66-67 A.D. resulted in the destruction of Jerusalem (70 A.D.). A second rebellion, in 132-135 A.D., terminated in the final dispersion of the people.

For a brief period in the early part of the 7th century, Palestine was under Persian control. In 636, Jerusalem surrendered to Mohammedan armies under Omar.

Toward the end of the 11th century, Palestine became the goal of the crusaders, who, in 1099, established in the Holy Land the Latin kingdom of Jerusalem. This kingdom lasted barely a century. The country remained in the hands of Mohammedan powers until it was conquered by Allied troops in 1918, and assigned as a mandate to Great Britain.

Britain held out hope of a Jewish homeland in Palestine. The Jewish Zionist organization fostered immigration, especially from Nazi persecution, but the Arabs bitterly opposed it. British proposals for partition were rejected. In 1948 Britain resigned its mandate and withdrew. Jewish leaders promptly proclaimed Israel independent. Arab forces invaded from all landward sides. The UN proposed dividing Israel into an Arab and a Jewish state. Meanwhile, Israeli forces drove back the Arabs and conquered 50 per cent more territory than allotted to it by the UN. An armistice ensued, but the Arabs refused to make a peace treaty.

Despite Arab economic boycotts, Israel, led by Premier Ben-Gurion, grew rapidly. In 1950 the "law of return" gave every Jew the right to enter as an immigrant. The Jewish population increased from 130,000 in 1930 to 2,700,000 by 1968. Loans from the U.S. and indemnities paid by West Germany were used to develop the country.

When Egypt seized the Suez Canal in 1956, the Israelis drove them from the territory east of the canal, but withdrew when the UN raised a special force to guard the Egyptian border. In May 1967, Egypt had the UN force withdrawn, then closed the Gulf of Aqaba to Israel. Attacking on June 5, Israel defeated the combined Arab forces in 6 days. The UN arranged a cease-fire but no peace treaty. Frequent skirmishes continued in 1968, but Israel, awaiting direct Arab negotiations, held on to the Golan Heights in Syria, the entire west bank of the Jordan, the Gaza Strip, and the Sinai Peninsula.

In addition to the Israeli-occupied Arab territory, a main obstacle to peace was the plight of the Palestine refugees. Displaced by the creation of the Israeli state, as many as 2 million Palestinians had been living since 1948 in camps in adjacent Arab nations. Arab nations refused to absorb the people, claiming that it would imply recognition of Israeli sovereignty, while Israel claimed that it was Arab aggression that had caused the problem. Attempting to regain their homeland, refugees began terrorist activities in the 1950s. By the late 1960s, most of the refugee groups had consolidated into the Palestine Liberation Organization (PLO) led by Yasir Arafat. Recognized by many countries as a government in exile, the PLO considered itself the "third front" (with Syria and Egypt) in the fight against Israel.

Plagued by Palestinian terrorist activities, Israel nevertheless felt militarily secure after the 1968 war. But a surprise attack by Egyptian and Syrian forces in October 1973 dealt a severe blow. Only with massive U.S. military aid were the Israeli forces able to repel the attack. After two weeks of fighting, the Israeli army had regained lost ground and was advancing on Cairo when pressure from the U.S. and the Soviet Union produced a cease-fire. By the 1975 Sinai agreements, a large UN buffer zone was created between Israel and Egypt, and U.S. aid was guaranteed to Israel. Although the threat from Egypt had been lessened, Israel still had many problems. Golda Meir, prime minister since 1969, resigned in 1974 and was replaced by Yitzhak Rabin. Rabin resigned as his party's candidate in the 1977 election because of illegal personal bank accounts in the U.S. Manachem Begin became prime minister. He faced spiraling inflation and widespread dissatisfaction caused by the large amount spent on national defense. The solution to the Palestine question remained unanswered and Syria still threatened from the north. See *Jews.*

PARTHIA

Parthia is the name of the ancient empire of the Parthians, a people related to the Mongols. Their original territory lay to the southeast of the Caspian Sea. They were conquered by Cyrus the Great of Persia in the 6th century B.C., but in 250 B.C. they revolted. From that time the empire of Parthia was rapidly extended as far as the Euphrates and Indus. It successfully repelled Roman attacks until 217 A. D., when, after the battle of Nisibis, both sides were ready to make peace. In 226 the Parthian empire, weakened by factional conflicts, passed to the Persian dynasty of the Sassanidæ.

PERSIA (IRAN)

The ancient Persians were an Aryan people who occupied territory to the east of the Persian Gulf and were for a time subject first to Assyria and then to Media. In 553 B. C., under the leadership of Cyrus the Great, they revolted against the Medes. Three years later the union of the Persians and Medes began the Persian empire.

The Reign of Cyrus. Cyrus pushed the boundaries of his domain westward to the Mediterranean and the Ægean coasts, eastward almost to the Indus. He subdued Babylonia and Lydia. The return of the exiled Jews to Palestine was part of his scheme to have loyal colonists on the western borders of his empire. His successor, Cambyses (529–522 B. C.), brought Egypt within his control, and Darius the Great (521–486 B. C.) added Macedonia and Thrace in Europe and the Punjab in India to the Persian dominions. Darius organized the civil government under satraps, or governors, thus separating the civil from the military authority in each province. He built splendid roads, the most important of which, the Royal Road from Susa, the capital, to Sardis in Lydia, was 1500 miles long.

Greco-Persian Wars. But the "great king," with his formidable masses of soldiery, met a new type of foe when he attempted to push his conquests farther into Europe. The Athenians, realizing the danger in the Persian advance, gave aid to the Ionian cities of Asia Minor in a revolt (499–493 B. C.). Darius crushed this rebellion and then set out to punish the Athenians. But at the battle of Marathon in 490 B. C. the Greeks, under Miltiades, gave the Persian forces a defeat that sent them back to Asia. Ten years later, Xerxes bridged the Hellespont with boats and built a canal through the promontory of Mt. Athos. Treachery alone gave his troops access to Greece through Thermopylæ, but the Greek fleet practically destroyed the Persian fleet in the strait between the island of Salamis and Attica. A land battle at Platæa and a naval engagement at Mycale, in 479 B. C., forced the final withdrawal of the Persians from Greece.

After Alexander's Conquest. One hundred and fifty years later the Persian empire yielded to Alexander, and at his death in 323 B. C. the greater part of it came under the family of the Seleucidæ. The Parthians ruled it for a time, until the dynasty of the Sassanidæ restored a large degree of Persian power about 226 A. D. This new Persian kingdom was long the chief foe of the Byzantine Empire. In the 7th century the Mohammedan conquests engulfed Persia; between the 11th and the 16th century the land was held by various dynasties of the Seljuk Turks and the Mongols. From 1501 to 1722 the Sufi dynasty, a native Persian family descended from the ancient Sassanidæ, ruled Persia. In the 18th century an Afghan dynasty ruled Persia.

Modern Persia. Modern relations with Russia and Britain began in the 19th century, and the conflict of foreign interests injured Persia's development. In 1906 the first national assembly met and a short-lived constitution was granted.

An Anglo-Russian treaty in 1907 divided Persia into three "spheres of influence," the north to be Russian, the southeast, English, the remaining section to be neutral. The finances of the country were chaotic, and in 1911 Mr. Morgan Shuster, an American, was selected to take control. His vigorous administration of eight months resulted in his dismissal under pressure from Russia. Anarchy increased, and at the opening of World War I, although Persia was neutral, German agents fomented uprisings. A British force was organized in 1916, which did much to restore order.

In 1919 Persia made a favorable treaty with Great Britain. In 1921 she repudiated it, and made a more favorable treaty with Russia. A constituent assembly, in 1925, placed the government in the hands of a hereditary shah. In 1935 the name Persia was officially changed to Iran.

In World War II Iran became important as a corridor through which Britain and the U. S. could send munitions to Russia. Iranian oil deposits were also significant. By the Tehran agreement, Britain, Russia, and the U. S. guaranteed the independence of Iran.

In 1946, the Russians attempted a takeover by setting up a puppet regime in the Azerbaijan region, but it was forcibly driven out. In 1951, under the leadership of Mossadegh, the legislature voted to take over the Anglo-Iranian oil industry, which provided a large proportion of governmental revenue. This led to a break of diplomatic relations with Britain and a cessation of oil exports. After three years, Mossadegh's party was overthrown, and a new contract was made with foreign oil companies. Shah Mohammed Reza Pahlavi, who assumed the throne in 1941, regained full control after Mossadegh's downfall. The Shah's programs of evolutionary reform, called the "white revolution," have slowly modernized the country. Iran again nationalized foreign oil interests in 1973 and has been a leading member of the Organization of Petroleum Exporting Countries (OPEC).

PHILIPPINE REPUBLIC

The Republic of the Philippines occupies a group of islands, lying off the eastern coast of Asia, extending from Formosa to Borneo. Discovered by Magellan in 1521, they remained a Spanish colony for over three centuries, and then became an American dependency for nearly 50 years. In 1933 an act of Congress provided for their independence, after a ten-year transition period, as the Philippine Commonwealth. On July 4, 1946, the islands, with Manuel A. Roxas as their first president, became independent, although closely connected by treaties and economic relations with the United States.

Immediately after independence, the government was confronted by jungle warfare conducted by partisans of the Communist party, and this was put down only after several years of conflict. In 1957, under President Carlos Garcia, the Communist party was outlawed. During the early 1960's, the Philippine Republic was a leader in the efforts to unify the countries of the Southeast Asia area.

Ferdinand Marcos was elected president in 1965. With an increase in guerrilla activity, martial law was imposed in 1972. Under a new 1973 constitution, Marcos appointed himself prime minister. Martial law continued into 1976 with wide opposition.

PHOENICIA

Phoenicia comprised a strip of land about 120 miles long and hardly more than 12 miles wide, between the Lebanon mountains and the eastern shore of the Mediterranean. The Phoenicians were probably a Semitic people related to the Hebrews.

Our earliest acquaintance with Phoenicia comes through records of Egyptian control from 1600 to 1300 B. C. The city of Sidon then became powerful and withstood the advance of the Israelites. Tyre assumed leadership about 1250 B. C. and held it for nearly 400 years. Hiram, king of Tyre, furnished Solomon with ships, workmen, and building materials.

The forests of Phoenicia supplied excellent wood for shipbuilding, and its coast furnished good harbors. Under these conditions, with the smallness of the country, the Phoenicians became the greatest sailors and traders of the ancient world. They supplied ships to Egypt, and Phoenician vessels and sailors made up the sea forces with which Darius and Xerxes attacked Greece. It is probable that there were Phoenician colonies on the Ægean islands as early as 1500 B. C. By 1100 B. C. Phoenician ships had passed Gibraltar, and the coasts of Europe and Africa were dotted with colonies and trading posts.

Phoenician traders brought tin from Cornwall in England, silver from Spain, linen from Egypt, and copper from Cyprus. Phoenician mechanics knew how to work the metals skillfully and how to dye cloth in the purple hue so highly prized among the ancients, while Phoenician scholars gave to the Western peoples a simplified alphabet.

Assyria broke the power of Tyre in the 9th century B. C. Control by Egypt and Babylon followed, and under the Persians Tyre became important again as the center of their sea power. After a siege in 332 B. C., in which Alexander captured Tyre, the history of Phoenicia ended.

POLAND

Poland was an important kingdom of Europe, with its capital at Krakow from about 1320 to the reign of Sigismund III (1587–1632), when it was removed to Warsaw. At the period of its greatest extent, previous to 1660, it had an area of about 375,000 square miles, extending northward to the Baltic Sea and the Gulf of Riga, westward to Brandenburg, southward to Hungary and almost to the Crimea, and eastward throughout most of the basin of the Dnieper.

Poland was a state of much influence and promise until it was weakened by serious factional troubles in the 18th century and fell a prey to the more powerful neighboring states of Russia, Prussia, and Austria. In 1772, 1793, and 1795 occurred the three successive partitions of Poland whereby all the territory of the kingdom was divided among these three great powers.

At the outbreak of World War I in 1914, about six-sevenths of this area was comprised in Russia, including Russian Poland, Lithuania, Volhynia, and a major part of Little Russia, Livonia, and Courland. The portion of Poland which belonged to Austria comprised the crownland of Galicia. The portion belonging to Prussia comprised Posen, West Prussia, and Ermland, in what is now known as East Prussia.

In November 1918 the independence of Poland was proclaimed at Warsaw, and the powers signatory to the Treaty of Versailles guaranteed the independence of the new state, within the limits of the 18th-century Polish Commonwealth. The success of Polish claims at the Paris peace conference was due in no small part to the diplomacy of the pianist Paderewski, who became the first prime minister. Poland attacked Russia in 1919 but in turn was invaded in 1920 by Russian forces, which were turned back with French aid when near Warsaw. The Treaty of Riga, in October 1920, terminated hostilities and increased Poland's territory by about one-third at the expense of Russia. An insurgent Polish army seized Vilna, the capital of Lithuania, in 1920. It later withdrew, but the city was reoccupied by Poland in 1922 after a plebiscite favorable to Poland and was awarded to her in 1923 by the League of Nations. A republican constitution was adopted in 1921. General Pilsudski, the hero of the war with Russia, made himself dictator in 1926. On his death in 1935 a new constitution was adopted. World War II, which began with Hitler's invasion of Poland in 1939, resulted first in a new partition by Germany and Russia, and second, in a partially reconstituted Poland, augmented by a slice of East Prussia but existing since 1945 as a Soviet satellite.

Wladyslaw Gomulka came to power in 1956, in the wake of bloody strikes in Poznan. Gomulka denounced Stalinism and bettered relations with the Catholic church. In 1968, there was a wave of antisemitism, in which 15,000 Jews were driven into exile. By the end of 1970, economic crises, riots in Baltic cities, and strikes suppressed by police in Gdansk and elsewhere, forced Gomulka's resignation and brought to power Edward Gierek, a close follower of the Soviet line. Gierek and U. S.

President Ford exchanged visits in 1974 and 1975. The ensuing negotiations helped to better U. S.-Polish relations.

PORTUGAL

The Portuguese people are descended originally from the ancient Iberians, who occupied the country when Carthaginian and Greek settlers appeared on the west coast of the Iberian peninsula. The Romans conquered the country, and they were followed by the Visigoths and the Moors.

At the end of the 11th century, Portugal, then called Portucalia from the old Roman name of Oporto, *Portus Cale*, was an obscure fief of the kingdom of León. In 1095 Alfonso VI gave this fief to Henry of Burgundy, one of the northern adventurers who came to Spain to fight the Moors. Henry extended the boundaries of his realm, and his son, Alfonso I, became the first king of Portugal. Within the next two centuries, despite wars with the Moors and opposition from the pope, the boundaries of the kingdom were extended to their present limits, and Portugal became a power in Europe. The 13th century saw the end of war with the Mohammedans, and an era of prosperity and organization of government began in the 14th century. King Ferdinand, who came to the throne in 1367, was successful in correcting the abuses of the corrupt court and making war with Spain. On his death in 1383, the legitimate Burgundian line ended. In 1385 John I was chosen by the Cortes. His reign is notable for beginning the series of explorations inaugurated by his son, Henry the Navigator.

The voyages of Portuguese sailors led to the building of a great commercial empire. Portugal secured possession of Madeira and the Azores, a part of Morocco, the Cape Verde islands, and the Guinea Coast. At the close of the 15th century, Vasco da Gama discovered the route to India by way of the Cape of Good Hope. The opening of the 16th century saw the establishment of Portuguese settlements in Brazil, India, Malacca, and the Sunda islands. Portugal then ranked as one of the strongest European states. But her decline was at hand, and was hastened by policies of bigoted oppression and tyranny at home and in the colonies. The Jews, who controlled the wealth of Portugal, were expelled, and other emigration weakened the state. In 1580 Philip II became king of Portugal, and the country was the victim of his imperial schemes.

Portugal's friendship with England brought her into the wars following the French Revolution. In 1807, at the approach of Napoleon, the regent, Prince John, transferred his government to Brazil. He returned to Portugal in 1821, although he had reigned as king of Portugal and Brazil since 1816.

The 19th century was a period of almost continual struggle between the party of absolute monarchy and the friends of constitutional government. The reign of Carlos I, which began in 1889, was a period of demoralization. He and his son, the crown prince, were assassinated in Lisbon, Feb. 1, 1908. Prince Manuel came to the throne, but in 1910 he was deposed. A republican government was then set up, which survived several stormy crises but was at length overthrown by a military *coup d'état* in 1926.

In 1932 Oliveira Salazar became premier and soon after assumed dictatorial powers. Portugal remained neutral in World War II but joined NATO after the war. Salazar retained firm control over the affairs of Portugal until 1968, when he became ill and was forced to resign. He was succeeded by Marcello Caetano who continued Salazar's policies. In 1974, a bloodless military coup ended more than 40 years of civilian dictatorship and 2 years later the first free parliamentary elections in over half a century took place. Ramalho Eanes was elected president and he appointed Mario Soares premier. A new constitution which committed future governments to socialist principles was also adopted in 1976.

PROVENCE

Provence (*prŏ'väNs'*) is the district of south-eastern France which corresponds roughly to the ancient Roman province, *Provincia Romana*, whence the name. This province was organized in the 2d century B. C., after the Greek city of Massilia (Marseilles) had appealed to the Romans for protection against the invading Ligures. In the first four Christian centuries the province was the seat of a rich and cultured life which centered at Arles and Marseilles. Many interesting remains of this Roman period, such as the theater at Arles, are still preserved. Provence was the field of the conflict between Cæsar and Pompey, and between the Franks and the Saracens. It became a part of France under Louis XI. In the 12th and the 13th century Provence was the seat of a splendid poetic literature, and the Provençal dialect still persists, in both speech and writing.

Rhodesia. See *Government and Politics*.

ROME

The Roman Empire was built on the foundation of a strong local state in Italy. The geography of the peninsula and its ethnographic condition in the early period would scarcely have led us to predict a united Italy. The peninsula is not compact, but long and narrow. The Alps with their many easy passes set up no barrier to the north; a long coast line and frequent harbors along the southern coasts tempted immigrants from overseas. When recorded history begins, then, we are not surprised to find Italy occupied by six or seven peoples of entirely different racial stocks. The most important of these peoples were the Italians, who had entered the peninsula by a land route, and the Greeks and Etruscans, who had come by sea. The Etruscans held north central Italy; the Italians, the central and southwestern part of the peninsula; while the Greeks settled along the southern coast. The factors which gave unity to Italy and in the end made Rome mistress of the Western world were: the sturdiness of the Italic peoples; the strength of their compact political organization, when pitted against the lack of political unity which their principal rivals, the Greeks and Etruscans, showed; the convenient position of Rome near the center of the peninsula and on a navigable river; and the position of the broad fertile strip of Italy west of the Apennines, with the more important harbors on the western coast.

The Latin People. The people who were to build the Roman state were tribes of Indo-European stock, who very early descended through the Alpine passes into the valley of the Po and thence spread into the highlands of the East and the plains of the West and South. The tribes who occupied *Latium*, or the "flat lands" to the south of the Tiber, were the Latins, a hardy race. They were neighbors of the Etruscans, who lived north of the Tiber. From these people the Latins acquired many of the arts of civilization, but they were at the same time forced to defend themselves against the encroachments of the Etruscans and against the Sabines, a highland people in the upper valley of the Tiber. Perhaps it was this situation which brought about the formation of the Latin League, a union of several settlements whose peoples met annually at the town of Alba Longa, where there was a temple of Jupiter. His worship brought the tribes together.

At a ford of the Tiber, near the Palatine mount, was an ancient market, where the Latin peasants came to purchase the wares of the Etruscan merchants. Here the rude Latins had their first glimpse of the civilization and industry of the East, for the Etruscans did business with Greek and probably with Phœnician merchants. By this route too the alphabet may have come to the Latins, as they learned to spell out the accounts and invoices of traders. The earliest settlement to which we may

properly give the name Rome was made on the Palatine and the neighboring hills, with its stronghold on the Capitoline. Recent excavations carry the foundation of the city back to a very early date; the Romans fixed 753 B. C. as the year of its founding, and they dated events from that year. The population of the early city was probably made up of Latins, Etruscans, and Sabines, but the Latins predominated.

The Early Latin Republic. For a time this Latin state was ruled by kings, assisted by a council of old men (*senes*), or a senate, but toward the close of the 6th century B. C. the monarchy was displaced by a republic. At the head of the state were two consuls, elected for a year. In an emergency, supreme power was sometimes granted to a single official, who was called a dictator. The two annually elected officials were chosen from among the patricians, as the governing class was called, and they did not treat the plebeians, or common people, fairly. With the establishment of the republic, therefore, began a struggle on the part of the plebeians to compel the patricians to grant them a share in the government. This contest lasted for more than two centuries. The first step in the progress of the plebeians was the election of tribunes of the people. The persons of these officers, ten of whom were elected annually, were declared inviolate, and they were given the power of vetoing any act of a magistrate that seemed to bear too hard upon a citizen. A long step toward securing the rights of the average citizen was taken in 449 B. C., when the laws, which previously had been known to the priests only, were codified, engraved on twelve bronze tablets, and set up in the Forum where they could be read by anyone. In course of time, these laws were developed into a system which has proved one of the richest legacies left to the world by the Romans.

By the middle of the 3d century B. C., the plebeians had won the right to hold the highest offices of the state and had attained equality with the patricians before the law. The republic was really what the words *res publica* implied,—an "affair of the people." Yet the popular assembly never had the right of discussion. It could only vote *yes* or *no* upon measures proposed by the magistrates; debate was reserved to the Senate, which, throughout the period of the republic, in the main, guided the state wisely.

Besides the tribunes and consuls, ancient Rome had also prætors, who served as judges; quæstors, who had charge of the treasury; and censors, whose business it was originally to take a census of the people and assess the taxes. The office of censor grew in importance, and after a time the censors assumed the power of expelling senators for immorality and of depriving citizens of their votes because of misconduct. These offices are interesting, not only for their original character in the republic, but also because the Roman emperors acquired their power by assuming the functions of some of them, and because the old Roman titles appear frequently in modern history, as in France and in the Latin states of South America.

Growth of the Roman State. The task of the Senate and the consuls in the growing Roman state was not an easy one. While the struggle for democracy within the republic was going on, constant warfare was the price of safety from attacks by the Etruscans and the neighboring highland tribes. In the midst of all this, the Gauls, in the early part of the 4th century, captured and burned the city of Rome. But when this danger had passed, the Roman armies pursued the business of conquest until, by the year 338 B. C., when Greece was surrendering her freedom to Philip of Macedon, Rome was supreme in Latium and had extended her power over southern Etruria. The beginning of the 3d century B. C. saw her victory over the Samnites in the South, and, in 264 B. C., Roman arms had triumphed over the Greek cities in the extreme

South, or Magna Græcia. Italy was united, from the Strait of Messina on the south to the Arno and Rubicon rivers on the north.

Citizenship and Colonies. A new problem in government now presented itself to the Romans. The idea of citizenship was at this time confined to residence in Rome or the nearby territory. All elections were held in the city, and election days were numerous. Consequently, even those who held Roman citizenship but lived at a distance from Rome found attendance upon elections impossible. It thus came about that, even while Roman conquests were confined to Italy, elections and legislation were controlled by the Roman populace. This defect in the Roman system was never wholly corrected, and it led to grave evils. It might have been remedied by the introduction of a representative system. This concession, however, the city of Rome was unwilling to make. But immediate trouble was avoided by allowing the conquered peoples to manage their own local affairs, and by demanding only that they should furnish soldiers for the Roman armies in time of war. The loyalty of the new territory in Italy was secured by the planting of Latin and Roman colonies at various points. The Latin colonists were mainly poor plebeians and veterans who wanted their own farms. Although possessing the private rights of Roman citizens, they had not yet acquired the right to vote and hold office, whereas these rights and privileges were possessed by the members of the Roman colonies, who were able to exercise political power by going to Rome. Both classes of colonies, however, were loyal to Rome and served to spread Roman customs and the Latin language throughout Italy. Moreover, what was quite as important as anything else, the agricultural development of the land was assured through these farmer settlements.

These colonies were connected by splendid roads, which served both as a means of rapid military movements and, since they were free to the public, as arteries of trade and routes of travel. In later centuries this admirable system of roads was extended throughout the empire, from Britain to Asia Minor, and so well were the highways built that many stretches of them are even now in good condition. By such means, the people of Italy were brought to feel their national unity, even though they belonged to many separate tribes and spoke widely differing dialects and languages.

The long wars which had resulted in making Rome mistress of Italy had developed the Roman citizen army into a military machine of wonderful efficiency. The basis of it was the legion, in which all citizens from 17 to 46 years of age were liable to service. Added to this was a body of auxiliaries, recruited from the subject states. The severe discipline of these troops, their open order of fighting, and the skillful use of reserves carried the Roman standards to victory.

Rome and Carthage. Such was the preparation of the Roman state for its life and death struggle with its greatest rival, the commercial Carthaginian power. The first stage of this long contest was the fight for Sicily, begun in 264 B. C. The Romans remedied their one weakness, lack of sea power, by building a navy, with which in 241 B. C. they won a complete victory. During the next twenty years they prepared for a second contest by subjugating the Gauls in the Po valley and by seizing Sardinia and Corsica, while the Carthaginians were making good their losses by developing the resources of Spain. In the summer of 218 B. C. the Carthaginian commander, Hannibal, carried the war into Italy by successfully leading his army from Spain through Gaul and over the Alps. At first the rapid movements of this great captain took the Romans by surprise. They appointed Quintus Fabius Maximus dictator. He earned the title of "delayer" through his policy of

avoiding a direct conflict until he could drill his troops. The Romans were impatient of delay, and the new consuls of 216 B. C., yielding to the popular demand for speedy action, joined battle with the numerically inferior force of Hannibal at Cannæ. They were disastrously defeated, and 35,000 of the 50,000 men who made up their army were killed or captured. For nearly fifteen years Hannibal maintained himself in Italy with forces inferior to those of the Romans, but he failed to arouse the Italians to revolt, and when, in 202 B. C., he was summoned to Africa, which Publius Scipio had invaded after driving the Carthaginians from Spain, he was defeated on the field of Zama. Carthage became a dependent ally of Rome, and Rome's political supremacy was assured.

But Carthage still remained a dangerous rival of Rome. For fifty years the Romans watched the city's growth and then determined to destroy it. In 146 B. C., after a heroic defense of three years, an adopted grandson of the conqueror of Zama carried out the order of the Senate to burn the city and declared its site accursed.

The difficult task of subjugating Spain was completed in 133 B. C., and all of the peninsula except the mountainous northwest part became gradually and thoroughly Romanized; a few years later the strip of southern Gaul, or France, which connects Italy with Spain, was made Roman territory. In 121 B. C., Rome had conquered Italy and the adjacent islands of Sicily, Sardinia, and Corsica, southern Gaul, Spain, and northern Africa. In other words, she was mistress of the western Mediterranean. In the eastern Mediterranean, Rome became involved in quarrels with Macedonia and Syria in the early part of the 2d century, and by 133 B. C. she had annexed Macedonia and the western portion of Asia Minor.

Economic Problems. As the domain of the republic became imperial in extent, it appeared that the old plan of making allies and citizens of conquered tribes, which had worked so well in Italy, was difficult to apply on distant and barbarous frontiers. Rome, therefore, began the policy of making provinces of the conquered lands outside of Italy, and of requiring them to pay tribute. The result was that these provinces were, in many instances, treated as mere opportunities for plunder. But the consequences of the vast influx of wealth from this new territory to Rome were even more disastrous for the city than for the provinces. The gulf between the rich, to whom the power and wealth of conquest went, and the citizen farmers, who fought the battles, became wider. Cheap wheat from the new provinces flooded the market of Italy, and the small farmer was forced to sell his land to the great landholder who could work it with slaves. These landless folk flocked to Rome, and they, with the quickly enfranchised slaves, who had been brought in great numbers to Italy as a result of the long wars, made up the Roman mob which was to be for centuries a constant menace to the peace of the city. Thus, while the richer classes of Italy were appropriating the wealth of the Mediterranean world and assimilating the culture of Greece, a difficult social problem arose in the state.

The Gracchi. The first serious attempt to meet this situation was made by the tribune Tiberius Gracchus, in 133 B. C. He proposed that the government should reclaim from the great landlords a part of the public lands and divide it into small holdings to be given to poor citizens. He even wanted to use public funds to stock these little farms. Tiberius at length secured the passing of a law covering these points, but the violent means used by him, added to the hatred aroused by his plan among the rich landholders, brought about his assassination and the repeal of the measure. Ten years later, Gaius Gracchus, the younger brother of Tiberius, was elected a tribune of the people. The means he took to carry out the reforms which he had in mind combined good and bad elements. His first move was to secure a law permitting sale of grain from the public storehouses to citizens at half the market price. This led directly to plain charity and disaster. but it gave Gaius the political support of the needy. He then projected a system of roads and began a policy of establishing colonies of poor citizens in the provinces. Here were the beginnings of wise policies, but the next measure proposed, although equally wise, proved his undoing. He wanted to bestow citizenship upon the people of the Latin colonies. But the Roman populace saw in this a possible curtailment of their privileges. They refused to re-elect him to the tribunate, and he was killed in an ensuing riot.

The Movement toward Monarchy. The work of the Gracchi had begun the revolution that was finally to make one man supreme in the Roman state. One element of weakness in their plans lay in their entire dependence upon the fickle, ignorant, selfish Roman populace. Later, men with trained legions at their command were able to master the mob and use it for their own purposes.

At the beginning of the 1st century B. C. the struggle between the aristocracy and the democracy centered around Marius and Sulla. Marius was of peasant birth, but his military ability, signalized in his victory over Jugurtha in Africa, in 105, and over the Germans, in 102 B. C., gave him great influence with the people. Sulla was a noble, who won his early military honors in the Social war (90-88 B. C.), a contest through which all Italians won Roman citizenship. Later he carried on a successful war against Mithridates in Syria. While he was in the East, the democratic faction, under Marius, was supreme in Rome, where it carried out a campaign of terror against the aristocrats. Marius died suddenly, and Sulla returned to defeat the democrats and wreak a bloody vengeance on their leaders. He ruled as "Perpetual Dictator" for three years.

The next stage in the march of the Roman state toward monarchy was marked by the ascendancy of Pompey, a friend of Sulla. He had won military laurels in Spain, in campaigns against the Mediterranean pirates, and in the final subjugation of Mithridates. He annexed Syria to the Roman domain and returned to Rome in 62 B. C. Three other men were also to be reckoned with in Rome. They were men of different types. Cicero was the leading lawyer of his day, champion of the Senate and of the traditions of the republic. Julius Cæsar was a young politician, popular with the masses because of his oratory and his lavish expenditure for public shows. When his own fortune was exhausted, the wealthy Crassus came to his aid. Cæsar and Crassus made a private compact with Pompey, known as the First Triumvirate. They were masters of Rome. But Cæsar was more daring and able than his colleagues, and fortune favored him. While he was engaged in the conquest of Gaul, Crassus met defeat at the hands of the Parthians at Carrhæ in Mesopotamia.

Julius Cæsar. Pompey, fearful of Cæsar's ambition for despotic power, now sided with Cicero and the Senate. Cæsar was summoned to return to Rome without his army; his reply was the crossing of the Rubicon with his troops. Taken unawares, Pompey, with what forces he could collect, withdrew to Greece. Cæsar, after a brief campaign in Spain, followed and defeated him at Pharsalus in 48 B. C. Two years sufficed to subdue revolts in Egypt, Asia, and Africa. In 46 B. C., Cæsar returned to Rome. He now began a series of wise political and economic reforms. He struck at the worst abuses of public charity, reformed the system of tax collection, planned foreign colonies for landless Italians, and began the extension of

Roman citizenship. But his political and personal enemies formed a conspiracy against him and brought about his death in 44 B. C.

The Rise of Octavius. Then followed a desperate struggle for power between the senatorial party, led by Cicero, Brutus, and Cassius, and the opposition, under the Triumvirs,—Antony, Octavius, and Lepidus. The battle of Philippi, in 42 B. C., put an end to the hopes of the senatorial oligarchy and the republicans. Of the three new masters of the Roman world, Lepidus, a weak man, quickly dropped out of sight; Antony was defeated at Actium, and the reins of power came into the hands of Octavius. But Octavius took care that the old governmental forms should be preserved. The Senate gave him the title of *Augustus*, "the majestic"; he called himself *Princeps*, "the first citizen"; his command of the army carried the title of *Imperator*, "commander." Here are the origins of modern royal titles, to which we may add Octavius' family name of *Cæsar*. Augustus, as he is known, held the tribunate, which gave him large authority in Rome, and he had the proconsul's power on the frontiers and in the provinces. In this way the new government was linked with the old.

The Early Empire. The reigns of Augustus and his successors to the year 180 A. D. cover the period of the Early Empire, the time of Rome's greatness. Except on the frontiers of the empire, the reign of Augustus was a period of general peace. The emperor gave his personal attention to the problems of ruling. He made the Rhine the boundary of the empire on the north; the Euphrates, on the east. He built splendid structures in Rome; he constructed long stretches of roadway in the provinces; and he made life and property more secure throughout the empire.

With few exceptions, the emperors of the first two centuries were able men, great builders, and strong administrators. The list includes Claudius, Vespasian, Trajan, Hadrian, and Marcus Aurelius. In the reign of Claudius the conquest of Britain was begun, a difficult task, which was not completed until the end of the 1st century A. D., after which time, for 300 years, Britain was a Roman province. Vespasian rescued the Roman state from the anarchy which threatened after the death of Nero. During his reign, his son Titus captured Jerusalem, 70 A. D. Trajan, one of the so-called "good emperors," pushed the frontiers of the empire to their extreme limit, but his conquest of the Tigris-Euphrates valley was abandoned by Hadrian, who found the difficulties of administration too great in so distant a province. With the reign of Marcus Aurelius, the philosopher-emperor, the barbarians began to show the growing strength that was at last to break through the Roman barriers.

Civic Life in the Empire. But the real story of this great period is to be read in the traces of Roman life that still remain in all parts of the wide territory that became the home of the Roman citizen. Massive and beautiful ruins of cities in Syria, in Dalmatia, in Africa, Spain, France, Germany, and England testify to a wealthy and luxurious civilization that appropriated the traditions and genius of its predecessors in sculpture and architecture. The rich commerce which sustained this civilization entered splendidly improved ports and passed over a vast system of paved roads. In hundreds of free, self-governing cities a vigorous political life developed, which left to medieval and modern times a lasting tradition of free local government. In these cities the industries were carried on largely by free workmen who were organized in guilds. Art and literature were cultivated, and the Latin language became the common tongue of the Western world. Roman law was supreme and became the basis of the modern legal systems of western Europe. With all this greatness, however, there grew up the

ROMAN EMPERORS

NAME	LINEAGE	Period of Rule		Birth	Death
		B. C.	**A. D.**	**B. C.**	**A. D.**
THE CÆSARS					
Augustus (Octavian) . . .	The title of Augustus conferred by the Senate .	27	14	63	14
Tiberius	Stepson of Augustus	A. D. 14	37	42	37
Caligula	Youngest son of Germanicus, nephew of Tiberius	37	41	A. D. 12	41
Claudius	Son of Drusus, stepson of Augustus	41	54	B. C. 10	54
Nero	Adopted son of his stepfather Claudius.	54	68	A. D. 37	68
Galba	Was proclaimed emperor	68	69	B. C. 5	69
Otho	Was proclaimed emperor	69	. . . .	A. D. 32	69
Vitellius	Was proclaimed emperor	69	. . . .	15	69
Vespasian	Was proclaimed emperor	69	79	9	79
Titus	Son of Vespasian	79	81	41	81
Domitian	Second son of Vespasian	81	96	51	96
THE FIVE GOOD EMPERORS					
Nerva	Was proclaimed emperor	96	98	32	98
Trajan	Adopted son of Nerva	98	117	53	117
Hadrian	Nephew of Trajan	117	138	76	138
Antoninus Pius	Adopted son of Hadrian	138	161	86	161
Marcus Aurelius Antoninus	Nephew and adopted son of Antoninus Pius . .	161	180	121	180
THE PERIOD OF MILITARY DESPOTISM					
Commodus	Son of Marcus Aurelius	180	192	161	192
Pertinax	Was proclaimed emperor	193	. . . .	126	193
Didius Julianus	Was proclaimed emperor	193	. . . .	?	193
Septimius Severus	Was proclaimed emperor	193	211	146	211
Caracalla	Son of Septimius Severus	212	217	188	217
Macrinus	Was proclaimed emperor	217	218?	164	218
Elagabalus	First cousin of Caracalla	218	222	205?	222
Alexander Severus	Cousin of Elagabalus, by whom he was adopted .	222	235	205	235
Maximin	Was proclaimed emperor by his soldiers on the Rhine	235	238	?	238
Gordianus I	Was elevated by insurgents in Africa	238	. . . .	158	238
Gordianus II	Son and associate of Gordianus I	238	. . . .	192	238
Pupienus and Balbinus . .	Were appointed by the Senate	238	. . . .	?	238
Gordianus III	Grandson of Gordianus I	238	244	224?	244
Philip	Murdered Gordianus III and usurped the throne	244	249	?	249
Decius	Was proclaimed emperor by the army	249	251	?	251
Gallus	Was elected emperor by Senate and soldiers . .	251	253	?	253?
Æmilianus		253	. . . .	208?	254
Valerian		253	260	?	269
Gallienus	Son of Valerian	260	268	?	268
Claudius II		268	270	214	270
Aurelian	Was designated by Claudius	270	275	212	275
Tacitus	Was chosen by the Senate	275	276	200	276
Florian	Was proclaimed emperor	276	. . . .	?	?
Probus	Was chosen by the army	276	282	?	282
Carus	Was elevated to throne by soldiers	282	283	222	283
Carinus and Numerian	{ Elder son of Carus . . . . { Son of Carus . . . . }	283	284	? ?	285 ?
Diocletian and Maximian . . .	{ Was proclaimed emperor by the army } { Was made Augustus by Diocletian . . . . }	284 } 286 }	305	245 ?	313 310
Constantius I	Nephew of Claudius II { Had been Cæsars under	305	306	250?	306
Galerius	the Augusti, Diocletian and Maximian }	305	306	?	311
Constantine the Great . .	Eldest son of Augustus Constantius I	306	337	274	337
Constantine II	{ Eldest son of Constantine the Great . . . . }		340	312?	340
Constans	{ Youngest son of Constantine the Great . . . }	337	350	320?	350
Constantius II	{ Second son of Constantine the Great . . . . }		361	317	361
Julian the Apostate . . .	Cousin of Constantius II, was proclaimed emperor by his soldiers	361	363	331	363
Jovian	Was elevated to the throne by the army	363	364	332	364
ROMAN EMPERORS OF THE WEST		**A. D.**	**A. D.**	**A. D.**	**A. D.**
Valentinian I	Was proclaimed emperor by the army	364	375	321	375
Gratian	Son of Valentinian I	375	383	359	383
Valentinian II	Son of Valentinian I	375	392	372	392
Theodosius the Great . .	Was called by Gratian to share the { In the East empire . . . . { In East and { West	379 } 392 }	395	346	395
Honorius	Second son of Theodosius	395	423	384	423
Valentinian III	Grandnephew of Valentinian II	425	455	419?	455
Maximus	By force of arms	455	. . . .	395?	455
Avitus		455	456	?	456
Majorian	Was elected by Ricimer	457	461	?	461
Severus	Was raised to imperial dignity by Ricimer . . .	461	465	?	465
Anthemius	Was made emperor through influence of Leo I . .	467	472	?	?
Olybrius	Was made emperor by Ricimer	472	473	?	?
Glycerius	Was proclaimed emperor	473	. . . .	?	?
Nepos	Was proclaimed emperor by order of Leo I . . .	474	475	?	480
Romulus Augustulus . . .	Son of Orestes	475	476	?	?

Augustulus was deposed and banished by Odoacer, who thus put an end to the line of Western Roman emperors.

social, political, and religious evils that accompany the rise of a luxury-loving society. Wealth was concentrated in the hands of a few. Cities grew at the expense of the country, and their citizens were divided into the very rich and the very poor.

The Later Empire. The period of the Later Empire extends from the year 180 to the year 395, when, on the death of Theodosius, the empire was divided. The first half of this period was marked by civil wars provoked by the strife of rival claimants for the imperial throne. Emperors were made and unmade by the legionaries from Rome or the provinces. This internal trouble was made more serious by the constant attacks of the northern barbarians and the Persians. Diocletian (284–305 A. D.) undertook to reorganize the government. He associated with himself a trusted officer, Maximian. Each was called *Augustus* and had all the honors of emperor. Diocletian ruled the East; Maximian, the West. Each *Augustus* selected a younger associate, or *Cæsar*, to aid him. The civil and the military authority were separated, and the empire was divided into more than one hundred provinces. By these means, Diocletian hoped to hold in check ambitious aspirants for the throne. His system prolonged the existence of the empire, but along with it went absolutism and all the old strife as to the succession.

Constantine, a man of ability in war and statecraft, became sole master of the empire in 324. He made his reign of thirteen years memorable by the recognition of Christianity and by moving his capital to the ancient Greek town of Byzantium, which became Constantinople, or the "city of Constantine." Both of these acts were founded upon good reasons of state. Byzantium was a better military center than Rome from which to repel the barbarian attacks, and it was well adapted to connect the eastern and western halves of the empire.

The death of Constantine, however, was the signal for another period of disorder in the empire. The barbarians were crowding in along the Danube and the Rhine, and the interests of the eastern and western parts of the empire were driving Rome and Constantinople farther apart. The slave system and childlessness sapped the vitality of the population. The Roman armies lacked free men. Expenses of government increased faster than revenues. The Roman Empire faced bankruptcy.

Rise of Christianity. Christianity, the latest of the religious faiths to come out of the East, in its principles and practice was not in perfect harmony with the religious and social conditions of the time. The Christians refused to worship the emperor or to share in any of the customary pagan rites. Their conduct brought many years of persecution until at last the emperor Constantine himself accepted Christianity. Slowly the new faith triumphed inside the empire over the old paganism and the newer Oriental faiths, such as the popular cult of Mithra. Christian missionaries had made converts among the Germans, so that the Roman world passed to their hands with less disturbance than otherwise would have occurred.

Germanic Invasions; Fall of Rome. A peaceful mingling of Romans and Germans was going on along the Danube, when the Huns suddenly appeared. The Germanic Visigoths were allowed refuge on the Roman side of the Danube. Here Roman officials robbed and persecuted them until they revolted. At the battle of Adrianople in 378 A. D. they overthrew the emperor Valens and his legions. They had now learned their power, and after the death of Theodosius in 395 the great Gothic invasion of Greece and Italy began. In 410 the Goths captured the city of Rome itself. Four years earlier a vast body of Germans had crossed the Rhine. A few years later (429–439) the Vandals conquered North Africa, and by the middle of the century the Angles and Saxons were masters of

Britain, while the Franks controlled Gaul. The Huns were beaten back at the battle of the Mauric plains in 451 by a union of Romans and Germans. But in 455 the Vandals sacked the city of Rome. The government of the West by the Romans was now a thing of history. German officers made and unmade puppet emperors. The last claimant to the imperial throne was the boy, Romulus, nicknamed *Augustulus*, "the little Augustus." He was dethroned, and the German troops made Odoacer king. The date of his accession is sometimes taken to mark the end of the Roman Empire in the West, but no line can be drawn to mark the end of the old world and the beginning of the new. The new rulers of Italy, of Gaul, and of Spain still thought of their authority as coming from Rome. Roman law was followed, and the Latin language was still spoken for many centuries throughout the West.

RUMANIA

Rumania (*rōō-mā′nǐ-à*) is a kingdom of southeastern Europe, bordering on the Black Sea. In ancient times this country was peopled by the Dacians, who were conquered by Trajan about 101 A. D. Roman colonists were introduced, and Dacia was made a Roman province in 106. As an outpost of the empire, Dacia was for several centuries a battleground of invading barbarians. Toward the end of the 13th century the principality of Wallachia was founded, and about the middle of the 14th century, Moldavia. In the 16th century both of these principalities were forced to acknowledge Turkish sovereignty. In 1861 they were united under the ancient name of Rumania. Prince Alexander John Cuza was chosen as head of this union. He introduced several reforms, but his despotic methods forced his abdication in 1866. Prince Charles of Hohenzollern was then elected. The independence of Rumania was recognized by the Congress of Berlin in 1878, and in 1881 the country was made a kingdom. Rumania is an agricultural country, with rich soil and fine grazing lands. Ownership of land has been one of its political problems.

Rumania took no part in the first Balkan war in 1912-13, but she secured additional territory through the second Balkan war of Serbia, Greece, and Rumania against Bulgaria. In 1914 Ferdinand became king on the death of his uncle. Rumania was drawn into World War I on the side of the Allies, and defeated. She was compensated at the peace with territory taken from Russia and Hungary.

King Ferdinand died in 1927. His son Carol had renounced his claim to the throne, which was conferred on Carol's infant son Michael. Carol seized the throne in 1930. In 1940, Rumania was forced to cede Bessarabia and northern Bukovina to Russia, a part of Transylvania to Hungary, and southern Dobruja to Bulgaria. Carol was again deposed in 1940. Prince Michael was proclaimed king with a pro-German ministry, and Rumania joined the Axis powers, sent contingents to the German army invading Russia, and occupied Odessa. When the Russian counterattack reached Rumania, in August 1944, Rumania promptly changed sides, and a pro-Communist government took office. It was recognized by Great Britain and the United States on promises of free elections and liberty of speech and press. These promises were not kept and the protests of the two countries were disregarded. Rumania signed her peace treaty, September 15, 1948, receiving back the territory she had formerly seized from Hungary, but not that taken by Russia. King Michael abdicated, December 30, 1947, under Communist pressure, and a "People's Republic" was proclaimed. By 1948 Rumania was completely under Russian control, economically and politically. The opposition was liquidated, and an attack on the Catholic Church began.

By 1958, the Rumanian government had persuaded the Russians to withdraw all Russian troops from Rumania. In 1966, Rumania boldly urged decentralization of power in eastern Europe.

The story of Russia begins with the coming of the Norseman, Rurik, with a body of followers, to Novgorod in 862 A. D. The Norsemen, or Varangians, set up an orderly government among the warring Slavic tribes and, moving southward to Kiev, opened the country to trade and to the influence of Mediterranean civilization. By the middle of the 10th century, the Norsemen and the Slavs had become thoroughly united. One must not, however, judge that the Norsemen were more than a very small minority. Their influence helped the formation of early Russia, and even named the country, but the native race and culture always predominated. Under Vladimir the Great, Russian authority was extended in all directions. Vladimir was converted to Greek Christianity, and in 988 he and his followers were baptized.

The Tatar Conquest. During the next two centuries, Russia was a field of conflict among petty states. The land was therefore an easy prey to the Mongols in the 13th century. Despite the heroic resistance of the Russian princes, the superior numbers and generalship of the Mongols enabled them to take complete mastery of Russia in 1238. This Tatar conquest cut Russia off from contact with the Western nations of Europe for 300 years; the Renaissance and the Reformation, which remolded the rest of Europe, she did not share in. The conquerors appear to have been content to exact tribute from Russia. They did not interfere seriously with the language or customs of the Russians, but nevertheless they introduced many Oriental elements into Russian life.

The 14th century saw the rise of the principality of Muscovy, with its capital at Moscow. This state attained a position of supremacy among the Russians in the 15th century, and the grand prince, Ivan the Great (1462–1505), united the rival principalities and threw off the Tatar yoke. Under his son, Ivan the Terrible, the boyars, or nobles, were reduced to submission, western Siberia was conquered, and trade with England was opened up. Ivan took the title of czar. After the death of his grandson, Feodor, a long period of strife resulted in the choice of Czar Michael Romanov, the first of the dynasty that ruled until 1917.

Peter the Great; Catherine II. Modern Russian history begins with the accession of Peter the Great in 1689. He was a man of restless energy, and he attempted to modernize and Westernize Russia by main force. He enlarged his territory, built a new capital, Saint Petersburg, on land taken from the Swedes, and introduced Western industry and customs. After Peter's death, his schemes fell into abeyance until the vigorous and unscrupulous Catherine II came to the throne in 1762. In her reign of more than thirty years, she improved governmental methods, encouraged modern industry, and established schools. She directed the division of Poland and secured the Crimea from Turkey.

Extension of Russian Power. Czar Alexander I (1801-25) opened his reign by freeing the serfs in the Baltic provinces, but he later receded from his liberal position. In 1807 Alexander made the famous Treaty of Tilsit with Napoleon, in consequence of which he was able to take Finland from Sweden in 1809 and to wrest much territory from Turkey. The reign of his successor, Nicholas I (1825-55), was marked by the beginnings of the liberal movement in Russia and by a succession of wars with Turkey. Russian defeat of the Turkish fleet at Navarino in 1827 aided materially the cause of Greek independence. In 1832, after crushing a revolt in Poland, Nicholas began a policy of repression in that country.

Reform; Reaction; Nihilism. The liberal reform movement in Russia received great encouragement from the early policies of Alexander II (1855-81). Serfdom was abolished in 1861. Reforms in the administration of justice were introduced. But the period of vast extension of Russian power in Asia was marked by reaction at home. The government's repressive measures provoked nihilist activity. Alexander was killed by a bomb, March 13, 1881. His son, Alexander III (1881-94), pursued a reactionary policy. Repression of liberals and persecution of the Jews in Russia accompanied imperial policies in Asia. Nicholas II (1894-1917) continued the blind policy of his father. Intervention in the Chinese-Japanese war (1894-95) gave Russia possession of Port Arthur, and absorption of Manchuria followed the Boxer troubles of 1900.

Meanwhile, the large increase of manufacturing in Russia had been adding new elements to the revolutionary forces. The workers learned from Western factory managers and superintendents the superior conditions of their class in other countries. The government had tried to meet this rising tide of revolution by various kinds of paternalistic laws and by stirring up hatred between races in the empire. The trouble reached a climax in 1904 and 1905. The crushing defeat of Russian armies and fleets by Japan had clearly revealed the corruption of the government. In the midst of a series of strikes and riots, a congress of delegates from the zemstvos, or provincial assemblies, met in Petrograd and formulated demands for political and industrial reform. Bloody repression led to an outbreak of strikes in all industrial centers.

The Duma. At length, on October 30, 1905, the czar issued a manifesto which announced the speedy establishment of a representative assembly, the Duma, and real participation of the people in the government. But this announcement was immediately followed by a reign of terror, in which the people, and especially the Jews, were made to feel the iron hand of the autocracy. The first Duma met in the Winter Palace at Saint Petersburg on May 10, 1906. But this body and its successors found the imperial government unprepared to further any genuine reform. The following years, up to 1914, formed a period of virtual deadlock between the reactionary court party and the liberals, who were, by changed electoral laws, virtually excluded from even the Duma.

Upon the outbreak of war in the summer of 1914, the Russian people rallied to the support of the government. For a time the government held out promises of progressive reform, but military successes were accompanied by reactionary programs. When, in the summer of 1915, the government stood in need of popular support, a large progressive party in the Duma demanded a ministry responsible to that body. This demand was answered by a proroguing of the Duma.

Evidence of the same government corruption and traitorous intrigue that had been so disastrous in 1904-05 now began to accumulate. At the same time, the people, providing war supplies and hospitals through their zemstvos and municipal organizations, were learning their strength. The inevitable result was revolution, which broke out in 1917. The czar abdicated, and a government by an executive committee of the Duma was attempted.

The Bolsheviki. A temporary government under Alexander Kerensky, a socialist, was wrecked by the extreme radicals, or Bolsheviki, led by Nicolai Lenin and Leon Trotzky. In November 1917, the All-Russian Congress of Workmen's and Soldiers' Delegates made Lenin the premier, and Trotzky the foreign minister, of the Soviet Republic. On March 3, 1918, Lenin's envoys signed a peace with Germany at Brest-Litovsk. The Bolshevik government was set up at Moscow, and Trotzky, with his armies, proceeded to the task of suppressing rebel-

NAME	LINEAGE	Period of Rule		Birth	Death
	HOUSE OF RURIK	A. D.	A. D.	A. D.	A. D.
Ivan III, the Great	Grand Duke of Moscow	1462	1505	1440	1505
Vasily IV	Son of Ivan. the Great	1505	1533	?	?
Ivan IV, the Terrible	Son of Vasily IV, assumed title of czar	1533	1584	1530	1584
Feodor I	Son of Ivan, the Terrible	1584	1598	1557	1598
Boris Godounov	Brother-in-law of Feodor, was elected to the throne	1598	1604	1552	1605
Demetrius	Usurped the throne (The "Time of Troubles")	1604	1606	?	1606
Zuiski (Vasily V)		1606	1610	?	?
An Interregnum		1610	1613		
	HOUSE OF ROMANOV				
Michael Romanov	Unanimously elected czar	1613	1645	?	1645
Alexis	Grandson of Czar Michael Romanov	1645	1676	1629	1676
Feodor II	Eldest son of Alexis	1676	1682	1656	1682
Ivan V and Peter the Great	Half brothers, sons of Alexis. Sophia Alexeyevna, sister of Ivan, ruled as regent	1682	1689	1666	1696
Peter the Great	Son of Alexis	1689	1725	1672	1725
Catherine I	Was married to Peter the Great in 1711	1725	1727	?	1727
Peter II	Grandson of Peter the Great	1727	1730	1715	1730
Anna	Daughter of Ivan V	1730	1740	1693	1740
Ivan VI	Grandnephew of Anna	1740	1741	1740	1764
Elizabeth	Daughter of Peter the Great	1741	1762	1709	1762
Peter III	Grandson of Peter the Great	1762		1728	1762
Catherine II	Wife of Peter III	1762	1796	1729	1796
Paul I	Son of Peter III	1796	1801	1754	1801
Alexander I	Son of Paul I	1801	1825	1777	1825
Nicholas I	Third son of Paul I	1825	1855	1796	1855
Alexander II	Son of Nicholas I	1855	1881	1818	1881
Alexander III	Son of Alexander II	1881	1894	1845	1894
Nicholas II	Son of Alexander III	1894	1917	1868	1918
	FEDERAL SOVIET REPUBLIC				
Nicolai Lenin	President Council of People's Commissars	1917	1924	1870	1924
Joseph Stalin	Gen. Sec. Communist Party; premier 1941	1922	1953	1879	1953
Georgi Malenkov	Premier	1953	1955	1902	
Nikolai Bulganin	Premier	1955	1958	1895	1975
Nikita Khrushchev	Premier; First Sec. Communist Party	1958	1964	1894	1971
Leonid Brezhnev	First Secretary Communist Party	1964		1906	
Alexi Kosygin	Premier	1964		1904	

lion. The avowed purpose of the Bolsheviki to support propaganda for the proletariat revolution in other countries led the Entente Allies and the United States to maintain troops in Russia, to support various anti-Bolshevik movements, and to refuse to trade with the Russians. Eventually all the anti-Bolshevik enterprises collapsed.

The government of Russia was dominated by the personality of Lenin until his death in 1924. Private property and the right to trade were at first abolished by decree, enforced through terrorism by the notorious *cheka*. The peasants, however, who had recently seized the land, had no intention of relinquishing it and refused to raise surplus grain to be confiscated by government agents. Economic maladjustment and widespread famine ensued and led to a so-called new economic policy. Trade was permitted to individuals, but the government remained the chief property holder and trader.

The Third International. Russia's foreign relations were based on the theory of world revolution, the Bolshevik party regarding itself as a branch of the so-called Third International. This organization, formally founded at Moscow in 1919, aimed at fomenting movements in every country that might lead toward a dictatorship of the proletariat. After Lenin's death, Russia continued to foment revolution abroad but greater emphasis was placed on economic development at home. Trotzky, who opposed such temporizing, was exiled and eventually murdered in Mexico, where he had sought asylum.

The revolution introduced drastic social changes, notably a new marriage code based on equality of men and women. Education became universal; students were provided with state support through college and technical school.

Five-Year Plans. In 1928 began a process momentous for Russian life. Under the dominating influence of Joseph Stalin, who had become absolute dictator, the first of several five-year plans of industrialization was initiated. This embraced both agriculture and manufacturing. With a combination of propaganda and ruthless compulsion, individual farming was transformed into large cooperative or state enterprises, huge factories were built, sources of power were developed, and transportation facilities were constructed. The standard of living, however, remained painfully low by western standards.

Such drastic changes entailed suppression of many civil rights, such as freedom to leave the country, and freedom to choose jobs without government consent. Private business was practically abolished. The strain of the process engendered opposition but recalcitrants were "liquidated" in numbers estimated in the millions. Nevertheless, Russia succeeded in building up an image before the world of a country proceeding from a primitive to an advanced economy at one stride.

As Germany under Hitler's dictatorship prepared a war of conquest, Stalin appeared to side with the West. But in early 1939 he and Hitler made an agreement to divide Poland and lay out respective fields of influence. When Hitler began World War II later that year, Russia remained neutral but ready to seize any advantage. In 1942, Hitler attacked Russia, apparently taking Stalin by surprise, and penetrated as far as Moscow and the Caucasus. But with prompt and extensive Western aid, the Russian army rallied. It eventually conquered half of Germany, joining forces with the Western armies. See *World War II*.

Stalin led his allies to believe that he favored a permanent peace settlement, but actually he directed his policy craftily but ruthlessly toward fomenting worldwide communist revolutions, with Russia as the beneficiary. Bulgaria, Rumania, Hungary, Poland, the Baltic states, Yugoslavia, and East Germany became satellites by direct army control, and Czechoslovakia followed in 1948. China, having been taken over by a communist government, was made an ally.

In 1950, Stalin gave the word to have the communistic government of North Korea take over the non-communistic southern half. But here the United Nations with United States initiative and military power stepped in and administered a decisive check. Yugoslavia meanwhile had gotten rid of Russian army personnel and asserted a measure of independence under its communist dictator, Tito. Stalin failed in attempts to tame Tito.

Stalin died in 1953; his successors, chiefly Khrushchev, slowly relaxed governmental tyranny.

The postwar period was one of rapid, forced industrial development in Russia, with emphasis on heavy industry and military might. The secret of nuclear weapons was soon mastered so that Russia faced America as one of the world's two giant military powers. It forged ahead in prestige by being the first to launch a space satellite. Throwing energy and money into subversive activities abroad and particularly in the numerous new nations that emerged with the dissolution of western empires, it did its utmost to achieve its dream of world preeminence.

But here also Russia was decisively checked. Western Europe, with initial economic aid from the United States, grew rapidly in power and dwarfed Russia and its satellites in economic well-being. Economic aid to emerging nations from the Western powers bested Russian efforts at subversion, even when Russia began to imitate the West in advancing economic aid to them. In the 1960's, the Chinese-Russian alliance began to crack, the two powers hurling insults at each other and competing for the allegiance of new nations. In 1962, Russia made the error of arming Cuba with weapons capable of using atomic warheads. The United States forced their removal by threat of war. Finally, Russia was faced with a food crisis. Agriculture lagged and industrial growth slowed down. In 1964, Khrushchev was deposed and was succeeded by Brezhnev as head of the Communist Party and by Kosygin as premier.

The new government instituted some basic modifications of the old order. The concepts of profit and of supply and demand entered the picture. Efforts began for winning consent from satellites in place of rule by naked force. Talk of world revolution was replaced by that of the need for peace and economic progress.

SAN MARINO

The little independent state of San Marino (*sän mä-rē′nō*), lying in the Apennines near the Adriatic coast in northeastern Italy, is the smallest republic in the world and claims to be the oldest independent state in Europe. The city of San Marino is said to have been founded in the 4th century. In 1631 Pope Urban VIII formally acknowledged the independence of the state, which has an area of about 38 square miles. Undisturbed by Napoleon, its sentimental interest probably saved it from union with Italy in 1860-61.

SAXONY

The name of Saxony was anciently applied to the entire northwestern district of Germany, extending from the Zuider Zee to the present neighborhood of Cassel and Magdeburg. By scattering the Saxons, who resisted bitterly, and by bringing in Frankish colonists, Charlemagne finally subdued the country. In the 10th century, Duke Henry of Saxony became king of Germany, and his son, Otto the Great, was crowned Roman emperor. The territory of Saxony was frequently changed during the following centuries. In 1485 the domain was divided between Elector Ernst and Duke Albert, the latter becoming the founder of the royal house of Saxony, which ruled until 1918. Frederick Augustus III was made king by Napoleon, and Saxony became the scene of Napoleon's struggle with the allies in 1813. In the Austro-Prussian war of 1866 Saxony sided with Austria and was compelled at the close of the war to join the North German Confederation and thus became part of Germany.

SIAM (THAILAND)

Siam (*sī-ăm′*). Its authentic history begins with the year 1350, when the old capital, Ayuthia, was founded. After a Burmese conquest, Siamese forces were rallied by a Chinese leader, Phya Tak, on whose death in 1782 the present dynasty came to the throne.

Under King Mongkut, who came to the throne in 1851, the development of Siam as a modern state began. Between 1855 and 1865, the principal foreign powers obtained the right by treaty to trade in Siam under a 3 per cent tariff, and they established their own extraterritorial courts there. In 1920-26, these courts were abolished by agreements, and the tariff was replaced by a most favored nation clause. Siam was an absolute monarchy until 1932, when King Prajadhipok granted a constitution. Siam changed its official name to Thai in 1939. A military group seized power in 1959 allegedly to combat communist inroads. Various military leaders ruled along with the king until 1973, when a parliament was elected and a prime minister was appointed. During the Vietnam war, the U. S. used Thailand for military bases and supported Thai troops. In 1976, a military junta again took control.

SICILY

Recorded history of the island of Sicily begins with the establishment of the Greek city of Naxos in 735 B. C. This, with other Greek colonies established in the course of the following two centuries, became the center of thriving commerce. From the year 536 B. C. until the period of the Punic wars, Greeks and Carthaginians contended for mastery in the island. In 210 B. C., however, Sicily became the first of the Roman provinces. During the middle ages, Goths, Byzantines, and Saracens in succession held sway. At length, in the year 1090, the Normans made conquest of the land, and Roger II became king of Sicily in 1130. From the close of the 13th century until the Treaty of Utrecht in 1713, Sicily was ruled by princes of Aragon and by the Spanish crown. In 1734, under Don Carlos, the Kingdom of the Two Sicilies arose, uniting Naples and Sicily under a Bourbon dynasty. Garibaldi's bold expedition in 1860 opened the way for the union of Sicily with the kingdom of Italy in 1861.

SOUTH AFRICA

The republic of South Africa consists of four provinces plus South West Africa, which is treated as a province although claimed by the United Nations as trusteed territory. The early history of each is treated separately below.

Cape of Good Hope. The oldest province is Cape of Good Hope, which was first settled by the Dutch in 1642. It remained under the control of the Dutch East India Company until 1795, when it was captured by the English. The British forces evacuated it in 1803 pursuant to the Treaty of Amiens but reoccupied it in 1805 to prevent its capture by the French. England's possession was confirmed by treaty in 1814. Its area was enlarged by annexations later in that century. The colony was granted responsible government in 1872.

Natal. Discovered in 1497 by Vasco da Gama, Natal was settled by the English in 1824 and later by the Dutch Boers ("farmers") from Cape of Good Hope. The Boers declared themselves independent, but the British reclaimed the territory in 1843.

Orange Free State. Boers from Cape of Good Hope in 1835–36 settled in what became the Orange River Colony after the British seized it in 1848. England recognized its independence as the Orange Free State in 1854.

Transvaal. This territory also was settled by Boers from Cape of Good Hope, in 1836–37. England controlled it at first but recognized its independence in 1852 as the Transvaal republic; then resumed control in 1877 because of its financial difficulties and hostilities with the natives. There was a revolt in 1880, after which the Transvaal was granted independence as the South African Republic. The discovery of rich gold and diamond mines brought a great influx of English settlers, who were far from welcome by Paul Kruger, president of the Transvaal. Incidents of growing seriousness led to the Boer war against England, in which the other provinces joined, 1899–1902. The Boers were eventually defeated. In 1910, the four provinces were united and granted self-government as the Union of South Africa.

During World War I, South Africa supplied troops for European service and also for campaigns against the Germans in Africa. It conquered German South West Africa and was granted a mandate over it by the League of Nations after the war. This course was followed under the first premier, Louis Botha, and his successor, Jan Smuts, under whom South Africa played a prominent part in the British Commonwealth. Under Smuts also, South Africa participated in World War II. Thereafter he was defeated at the polls by Herzog, leader of the National party on a platform of strict racial segregation, known as *apartheid*. In 1961, under a new constitution, South Africa became a republic. Since other members of the British Commonwealth opposed its racial policies, South Africa withdrew from the Commonwealth.

Meanwhile, in respect to South West Africa, then a trusteed territory under the UN, South Africa resisted efforts of the UN to hold it to account. It extended its policies of racial segregation there and treated the territory as a province. Under a new name, Namibia, the country was slated for independence by 1978.

Under the racial policy, only white citizens may sit in Parliament. Black inhabitants have no civil rights in white South Africa and only a few rights in territories reserved for them. These territories, according to government plans, would eventually be autonomous all-black states still under economic control of South Africa. The first such state, Transkei, was set up in 1963. South Africa's policy of white supremacy made it the target of vituperation by black nations in Africa and by most other countries committed to racial equality. On the other hand, its example encouraged Rhodesia to adopt a similar policy. South Africa's prime minister, H. F. Verwoerd, the architect of the racial policy, was assassinated in 1966 and was succeeded by B. J. (John) Vorster.

In the 1970's, as more of Africa came under black rule, the days of exclusive white power in South Africa seemed numbered. The rising anger of blacks within the country produced riots and terrorism in 1976. By 1978, South Africa seemed sure to be surrounded by hostile nations. The government faced either major reforms or armed insurrection.

SPAIN

The original inhabitants of the Spanish peninsula, which was known to the Greeks and Romans as Hispania or Iberia, were probably a primitive race called Iberians. Upon these a host of Celts are supposed to have descended from the Pyrenees. The two races mingled and formed the mixed nation of the Celtiberians. About the middle of the 3d century B. C. the Carthaginians, deprived by Rome of their trading posts in Sicily and Sardinia, began to develop Iberia as a source of wealth and soldiers, and an extensive tract of territory was brought under subjection to Carthage by Hamilcar Barca, who is said to have founded the city of Barcelona.

Roman, Gothic, and Moorish Rule. The Romans had driven the Carthaginians from the peninsula in 206 B. C., and the country was erected into a Roman province. From this time until the end of the 2d century A. D., the condition of Spain was eminently prosperous. Everywhere throughout the country, Roman towns sprang up, and numerous aqueducts, bridges, and amphitheaters were built. Spain was for three centuries the richest province of the Roman Empire. Its fertile grainfields fed the imperial city, and its mines yielded enormous wealth. Many of the leading men of the later empire, in politics, military life, and literature, were natives of Spain.

In 409 A. D. hordes of barbarians, Alans, Vandals, and Suevi, crossed the Pyrenees and swept over the peninsula. About 412 the Visigoths invaded the country as agents of the weakened Roman government. After the fall of the Western Empire they maintained a show of authority with a monarchy organized in imitation of the Roman system. But they fell an easy prey to the Mohammedan invasion, and in 711–714 the Moors obtained mastery of nearly the whole of Spain. Under the Ommiad dynasty Spanish civilization far surpassed that of other European states. Systems of irrigation made a garden out of desert areas. Learning and literature were highly developed in great universities.

Castile and Aragon United. In 1031, however, the realm split into several small kingdoms, and the Christian kings of Castile, Aragon, and Navarre quickly took advantage of the divisions among the Moors to break their power. Ferdinand II, the last sovereign of Aragon, married Isabella, queen of Castile, in 1469. By the conquest of Granada in 1492 and that of Navarre in 1512, they united all the states of Spain under their joint rule.

It was under the auspices of the united kingdoms of Castile and Aragon, and especially under the protection of Queen Isabella, that Columbus started on his voyages of discovery, which laid the foundation for Spain's vast empire in the three Americas.

The kingdoms of Castile and Aragon had developed in the direction of constitutional government, with much power in the hands of the estates of the realm, or the Cortes. But Ferdinand and Isabella used the Cortes and other councils for their own purposes. At the great Cortes of Toledo in 1480 far-reaching reform and organization of the government were undertaken, the Inquisition was firmly established, and oppressive measures were adopted against the Jews. The free growth of industry, religion, and national life was checked by a vast system of taxation, supervision, and espionage.

Period of the Empire. At the death of Ferdinand in 1516, all Spain came under the single rule of his daughter Juana, called "the mad." But her son, the Habsburg Charles I, who in 1519 became emperor as Charles V, seized the throne, and Spain was dragged into the great scheme for aggrandizing the house of Austria. Charles V gave little attention to Spain, except as it served to supply him with treasure out of the newly acquired American territories. He even acknowledged the claim of the Cortes to the right of granting taxes, although he got what he wanted by bribery. Under his son, Philip II, the country was the victim of the worst vices of a bigoted absolutism. Its resources were exhausted in futile wars with every power of Europe. Spanish ships and soldiers won glory at the battle of Lepanto against the Turks, but the Protestant Netherlands were lost, the *Armada* was destroyed, and oppressive taxation served only to pile up disaster.

In 1680, the royal orders and laws relative to the Spanish colonies in America were compiled in the famous *Recopilación de las leyes de Indias,* "Laws of the Indies," a system of laws admirable so far as it went, and remarkably enlightened in its day. The system fundamentally failed, however, in looking upon the American possessions as a vast estate, closed to all the world and exploited only by Spain under a régime of the narrowest overlordship and the most exclusive of monopolies.

A Period of Decline. The reigns of Philip III and Philip IV witnessed a fearful acceleration in the national decline. That of Charles II was still more unfortunate, and his death was the occasion of the War of the Spanish Succession. Philip V was the first of the Bourbon dynasty who occupied the throne of Spain. Under Charles III (1759–88) an industrial revival began. But, even though "enlightened," Charles III was a despot, and no sound national growth could come from his policy.

During the inglorious reign of Charles IV (1788–1808), a war broke out with Britain, which was productive of nothing but disaster to the Spaniards; and, by the pressure of the French, another arose in 1805 and was attended with similar ill success.

Charles's eldest son ascended the throne as Ferdinand VII. Forced by Napoleon to resign all claims to the Spanish crown, Ferdinand became a prisoner of the French, and Joseph, the brother of the French emperor, was declared king of Spain and the Indies. But before this time an armed resistance had been organized throughout the country. The various provinces elected juntas, or councils, and it was their business to administer local rule. The Supreme Council of Seville declared war against Napoleon and France in 1808. England made peace with Spain, recognized Ferdinand VII as king, and sent an army to aid the Spanish insurrection. After many bloody campaigns the French were driven from the country.

Efforts toward Liberal Reform. The Cortes in 1812, during the absence of Ferdinand, had adopted a liberal constitution, but on his return this was abolished and the old abuses restored. But the struggle against tyranny, already on the road to success in her New World colonies, had now really begun in Spain. A revolution in 1820 formulated a remarkably liberal constitution, but a French invasion suppressed the movement. The only reform which survived was the abolition of the Inquisition.

The next hundred years was a continual struggle between the advocates of a liberal, constitutional government and the adherents of the old absolutist and clerical party. Of the latter group, the extremists were the Carlists who, on the death of Ferdinand VII in 1833, supported Don Carlos in opposition to Isabella, for whom Queen Maria Christina was ruling as regent. Civil war broke out and the Carlists were defeated. The absolutists then aligned themselves with the queen regent and later with Queen Isabella.

The attempt to enforce an absolutist government provoked further liberal agitation, and in 1868 Isabella was compelled to flee from the kingdom. A liberal monarchical constitution was formulated, and in 1870 Amadeus, duke of Aosta, was induced to take the crown. But the chief supporter of the new government, Prim, had been assassinated, and after a troublous reign the king abdicated in 1873. A republic was declared with Castelar as president. But he displeased the radicals. After his resignation Alfonso XII, son of Isabella, became king.

A measure of parliamentary government was attained, but its effectiveness was rendered futile by a compromise whereby Liberals and Conservatives were to alternate in power as a matter of form rather than in response to public opinion.

Coming of the Republic. Alfonso XIII came to the throne in 1902, and during his reign Spain was neutral in World War I. A serious revolt of the Riff tribes in Spanish Morocco, however, revealed grave weaknesses in the army and the government. Misrule and industrial disturbances culminated in a military revolt, led by General Primo de Rivera. He made himself dictator, with the king's aid, and ruled from 1923 until 1930.

General Berenguer succeeded Rivera in 1930 and arranged for general elections. In March 1931, he was forced to resign; election plans were canceled; and, on April 13, a group headed by Niceto Zamora declared Spain a republic. King Alfonso fled from the country, and Zamora issued a call for the election of a constitutional convention. Elections were held on June 29. The republican form of government received popular ratification. A new constitution was drawn up and adopted. The church and state were separated; women were enfranchised.

The Republican regime, though victorious in the election of 1936, encountered opposition from the Church, the army, and the land-owning groups. A rebellion ensued, leading to civil war. In this struggle the Republicans received aid from France and Russia and were opposed by Germany and Italy. Britain and the U.S. maintained a nonbelligerent status. In 1939 the government forces were defeated, and a corporate state headed by General Francisco Franco was established. During World War II Spain remained neutral, but favored the Axis.

Consolidating its power through execution and imprisonment, the Franco regime established a repressive state-controlled society that lasted until his death. Although the political institutions had a progressive appearance, Franco himself held complete power. One of his last acts was to reestablish the monarchy and in November 1975, Juan Carlos I became king. The king declared an amnesty for most political prisoners, introduced bills to provide for considerable changes in the Francoist system, and appointed a new premier to guide Spain's transition to democracy. A legislative election—Spain's first free election in 41 years—in 1977 endorsed the new premier's government.

SUDAN

On January 1, 1956, the Sudan proclaimed its independence, and Great Britain and Egypt hauled down their flags in Khartoum, after jointly administering the Anglo-Egyptian Sudan for more than half a century by virtue of an agreement signed by the two governments in 1899. Early in 1953 an Anglo-Egyptian agreement guaranteed the Sudanese the right to determine whether they should join Egypt or become completely independent. A further agreement signed at Cairo in December 1955 provided a plebiscite to determine the country's future. But the Sudanese did not wait for this; they proclaimed a republic on January 1, 1956.

SWEDEN

When Sweden first appears in history, the country was inhabited by numerous politically separate tribes. The two principal groups were the Goths and the Swedes. Ingiald Hrada, the last ruler of the old royal family, sought to establish a single government. Erik Edmundsson acquired the sovereignty of the whole of Sweden about 829. Efforts to introduce Christianity were made, but it was not until the year 1000 that Olaf Skottkonung, the Lapp king, was baptized.

Growth of Swedish Power. The murder of Erik in 1160 by the Danish prince, Magnus Henriksen, who had made an unprovoked attack upon the Swedish king, was the beginning of a long series of troubles. In 1389 the throne was offered by the Swedish nobles to Margaret, queen of Denmark and Norway, who threw an army into Sweden, defeated the Swedish king, Albert of Mecklenburg, and, by the Union of Calmar, in 1397, brought Sweden under the same scepter with Denmark and Norway. In 1523 Sweden emancipated itself from the union with Denmark, which had become hateful to the Swedes, and rewarded its deliverer, the young Gustavus Vasa, by electing him king. Gustavus Vasa, on his death in 1560, left to his successor a hereditary and well-organized kingdom, a full exchequer, a standing army, and a well-appointed navy. Sigismund, grandson of Vasa, who had been elected king of Poland through the influence of his Polish mother, was compelled in 1599 to resign the throne to his uncle Charles, who was crowned as Charles IX in 1604. He renewed the policies of his great father, Gustavus Vasa, developing the power of the burghers at the expense of the aristocracy.

The deposition of Sigismund gave rise to the Swedo-Polish War of Succession; on the death of Charles IX in 1611, his son, the great Gustavus

Adolphus, found himself involved in hostilities with Russia, Poland, and Denmark. The young king soon concluded treaties of peace with his northern neighbors and placed internal affairs in order. Although he ranks as one of the greatest military commanders of his age, the extraordinary number of benefits which he conferred on the administrative system of Sweden entitles him to still greater renown as the benefactor of his native country.

After the death of Gustavus, his great minister, Oxenstierna, ably directed the government during the minority of Christina, his daughter. Sweden became the leading power of northern Europe. The reign of Christina, however, was disastrous. Charles X was occupied in wars against Poland and Denmark. The southern Swedish provinces, Danish up to that time (1658), were acquired by him. The long rule of his son, Charles XI (1660–97), was characterized by success abroad and the augmentation of the regal power. The military genius of Charles XII brought the climax of Swedish power, but his vast schemes of conquest left the country overburdened with debt. The male line of the Vasas expired with his death in 1718. His sister and her husband, Frederick of Hesse-Cassel, were called to the throne by election. During their reign the government was really in the hands of the nobles, who were divided into rival factions,—the Hats, or French party, and the Caps, or Russian party.

Union of Sweden and Norway. The weak Adolphus Frederick of Holstein-Gottorp, who was called to the throne on the death of Frederick in 1751, did little to retrieve the evil fortunes of the state; but his son, Gustavus III (1771–92), skillfully recovered the lost power of the crown. Gustavus IV was forcibly deposed in 1809 and obliged to renounce the crown in favor of his uncle, Charles XIII. The dominant party in Sweden, in order to win the favor of Napoleon, elected General Bernadotte to the rank of crown prince. Sweden's steady support of the allies against the French emperor, secured to her the promise of Norway, which, however, resulted in a purely personal union of the two kingdoms. Under the administration of Bernadotte, who in 1818 succeeded to the throne as Charles XIV John, the united kingdoms of Sweden and Norway made great advances in material prosperity and in political and intellectual development. Although the nation at large entertained very little personal regard for their alien sovereign, his son and successor, Oscar (1844–59), and his grandsons, Charles XV and Oscar II, so identified themselves with their subjects that the Bernadotte dynasty secured the loyal affections of the Swedish people.

Sweden, a Separate Kingdom. In the latter part of the 19th century serious difficulty arose between Norway and Sweden, owing to the desire of the former for a consular service of her own. In 1905 the two nations separated, and Oscar II continued monarch of Sweden until his death, December 8, 1907, when he was succeeded by his oldest son, Gustavus V. In 1909 manhood suffrage was introduced for elections to the lower house of the Parliament. Now there is in Sweden, as in Denmark and in Norway, universal and equal suffrage. During the World wars, Sweden maintained a neutral position.

From 1932 to 1976, Sweden was governed by the Social Democratic party, either alone or in coalition. The country established itself as the prime example of the mature, stable welfare state, and, by the 1970's, its people had the highest standard of living in the world. But rising taxes coupled with a decline in growth and trade produced widespread dissatisfaction and a victory for a conservative coalition in the 1976 elections.

SWITZERLAND

When the Romans began their conquest of Gaul (about 58 B. C.), they found in the Alpine territory two peoples, the Helvetians and the Rhætians. The country was conquered and connected with Italy by roads, and it became the center of a flourishing trade. About 400 A. D. the barbarian invasions brought the Burgundians and Alemanni into the country. They in turn were subdued by the Franks. The Burgundians accepted Christianity about the end of the 5th century, but the Alemanni retained their paganism until the 7th century.

After the downfall of the kingdom of Burgundy, the entire country fell to the control of Germany and so became a part of the Holy Roman Empire. Switzerland remained a stronghold of feudalism for several centuries. Under the rule of the dukes of Zähringen in the 12th century, the Swiss towns grew very prosperous, and in the 13th century, when the Habsburgs were the most powerful among the princes of the country, many of the towns and some of the cantons obtained imperial charters of liberties. The three forest cantons, Uri, Schwyz, and Unterwalden, formed a league in 1291 to resist the tyranny of the Habsburgs. Allied with Zurich, the confederation won the battle of Morgarten in 1315, thus securing their independence from Austria. The cantons of Glarus and Zug joined the confederation, which, with this added strength, defeated the Austrians at Sempach in 1386 and at Näfels in 1388. Early in the 15th century the cantons took the offensive, and a series of conflicts with Austria and Burgundy enlarged their territory and won them recognition from the states of Europe. In 1516 an alliance was concluded with France, which lasted until the French Revolution. During these two centuries Switzerland was rent by civil and religious dissension. Swiss independence was formally confirmed by the Peace of Westphalia in 1648.

The 18th century was a period of remarkable advance in Swiss agriculture and industry. Swiss scientists and scholars became famous. But the old struggle between the privileged aristocracy and the growing democratic element of the population continued. In 1798, under French direction, the Helvetic Republic was organized. This was changed to a confederation of cantons by Napoleon in 1803. A period of quiet and prosperity followed, and the Congress of Vienna in 1814-15 recognized the independence of the Swiss and guaranteed the perpetual neutrality of their state.

The 19th century was a period of steady advance in Swiss economic and political life. The confederacy and the cantons in 1848 finally became purely republican. Later revisions of the constitution have enlarged the powers of the central government, improved the educational system, and strengthened the machinery of the democracy. The Swiss use the initiative and referendum.

In the World wars Switzerland maintained her neutrality, kept her army on a war footing, and served as a refuge for wounded prisoners and exiles.

TURKEY

The name commonly applied to the Ottoman empire and the republic which succeeded it. In the Turkish language, *Turk* means "a rustic or clown" and is applied to the Turkomans of central Asia. The ruling people of the Ottoman empire called themselves Osmanli, from a chieftain, Osman or Othman, who established himself in western Asia Minor at the beginning of the 14th century. This Osman and his followers were the decendants of emigrants from central Asia, who, nearly a hundred years earlier, had sought safety among the Seljuk Turks from the advance of the Mongol conqueror, Genghis Khan. The Seljuks granted the newcomers land in Phrygia and converted them to the faith of Islam. But the Seljuk power declined, and the new Ottoman state rose in its place.

Ottoman Conquests. The first expansion of the Ottomans was westward. They mastered all the northwest coast of Asia Minor and crossed into Europe, where they seized Gallipoli and Adrianople. They closed steadily in on the Roman Empire of the East, until it had shrunk, in 1400, to the city of Constantinople and the small neighboring district of Thrace, Macedonia, and part of Greece. In 1389 the Turks had broken the Serbian power at the battle of Kossovo and had then made conquest of Bulgaria. They were now the first military power in Europe; their disciplined Janizaries, inspired by fanatic zeal, were irresistible. Macedonia, Hungary, and Greece were rapidly conquered, and in 1453 the city of Constantinople, deserted and weakened through the commercial jealousy of Western Christians, fell before the Mohammedan onslaught. The Turks moved their capital from Adrianople to Constantinople and proceeded to consolidate their European dominion. The Tatar khan of the Crimea became a vassal of the sultan. Albania, which had long held out, was at last subdued, and before the close of the 15th century the conquest of Otranto gave the Ottomans a foothold in Italy. Only Montenegro remained unconquered.

Selim I (1512–20) led the Ottoman arms in triumph through Syria to Persia, into Egypt, and down the western border of Arabia, where he assumed the power of the caliphs at Mecca. Under his successor, Solyman the Magnificent '1520–66', the height of the Ottoman power was reached. In his reign Belgrade was taken (1521), the island of Rhodes was captured (1522), the Hungarian power was broken at the battle of Mohács (1526), and in 1529 Vienna was besieged, a large part of Hungary being made a Turkish province. Algeria had already become tributary to the sultan, and Tripoli was taken in 1561. The Turks ruled the Mediterranean.

Decline of Turkish Power. But Western Christendom was now thoroughly alarmed. The pope, Venice, and Spain formed a Holy League, and, although Cyprus had fallen into the hands of the Turks, their sea power was broken by the defeat of Lepanto, off the coast of Greece. The decline of the Ottoman empire dates from this, the greatest naval battle the world had witnessed since the time of the Romans and Carthaginians. The rise of the Persian power checked the Ottoman advance in the East. The Polish monarch, John Sobieski, in 1683 turned back the Moslem force from Vienna, and in 1695 Peter the Great took up the Russian contest with Turkey, which was to last, with varying fortune, until World War I. In 1774 Russia secured the Crimea and other Tatar lands on the Black Sea; she was granted free navigation of Turkish waters and also a protectorate over Moldavia and Wallachia. The 19th century was a period of steady loss of territory. In 1854 only the intervention of England and France, who feared Russia, saved the Turks from being driven out of Europe. They were again saved from Russian destruction by the Congress of Berlin in 1878.

The Treaty of Paris in 1856, by which the Western Powers guaranteed the integrity of Turkey, was followed by the sultan's proclamation of civil rights to all races and creeds in the empire, and in 1876 a parliamentary constitution was proclaimed. But the real Turkish policy of persecution and massacre of non-Moslem peoples was carried out. The slaughter of Christians in Lebanon in 1860 and the Armenian atrocities in 1895-96 aroused angry but empty protests, significantly barren in results.

The Young Turks. At the opening of the 20th century, Turkey was rent by disorders and revolts in Europe and Arabia. In 1908 the Young Turk party, headed by men who had studied in Western universities, proclaimed the restoration of the constitution of 1876. In 1909 Sultan Abdul Hamid was deposed and Mohammed V was enthroned. But this widely-heralded "reform" movement proved to be only a transfer of tyranny from one group to another. The extermination of all peoples other than Ottomans within the empire soon appeared as the real policy of the Young Turks. Armenian atrocities before and during World War I appear as the characteristic conduct of the Turkish government toward non-Moslems. The Balkan wars of 1912-13 materially cut down Turkish territory in Europe. Italy in 1912 seized Tripoli, in Africa.

World War I. World War I revealed Turkey as the tool of Germany. Turkish troops successfully repelled Allied attacks on the Dardanelles, but the army, despite German leadership, was disastrously beaten in Palestine and Mesopotamia.

The Treaty of Sèvres between the Entente Allies and Turkey was signed on August 10, 1920. The terms left to the Turks in Europe only Constantinople and a small neighboring territory. Smyrna was placed under Greek control; Konia, given to Italy; and Cilicia, assigned to France. Armenia and Kurdistan were declared independent.

The Republic. This treaty was never ratified by Turkey. A strong nationalist movement began, led by Mustapha Kemal Pasha. A government was set up at Ankara (Angora), which demanded modification of the treaty. When Constantine was recalled to the Greek throne in December 1920 the Allies agreed to a settlement more favorable to Turkey. Greece dissented but, in August 1922, suffered defeat by the Turks. Kemal demanded restoration of Smyrna, Istanbul, and Thrace east of the Maritza river, which he obtained by the treaty of Mudania, Oct. 11, 1922. With their prestige enhanced by victory, the Nationalist leaders abolished the office of sultan. A new constitution was adopted. Turkey became a republic with Kemal as the first president. Ankara was made the capital, and the name of Constantinople was changed to Istanbul.

Kemal proceeded to modernize Turkey. Polygamy was forbidden. The law of the Koran was replaced by a civil code. The wearing of the fez, with its religious associations, was prohibited. Education was secularized. Arabic letters were replaced by the Latin alphabet. Railroad building and irrigation projects were undertaken and state-sponsored industries were initiated. Kemal died in 1938.

Turkey joined NATO in 1953 but the country has generally taken a neutral position in most conflicts, including the Arab-Israeli wars. Its military forces did invade Cyprus in 1974 when the Greek junta attempted to overthrow the island's government. As a result, relations became strained with the U. S.

UKRAINE

The soviet republic of Ukraine (ū'krān) includes a large territory which, before World War I, was divided between Russia and Austria. The history of this area as a distinct and, at times independent, state dates back to the 9th century, when the city of Kiev was made the center of a government. After the Tatar invasions of the 13th century, the country was for 200 years a part of the Lithuanian state. In the 16th century it was incorporated with Poland, but in the middle of the 17th century the Ukrainians revolted from the Polish power, and, by the Treaty of Pereyaslavl, the greater part of Ukraine was joined to the territory of the Muscovite czars. The western portion of Ukraine passed later to Austria. After the close of World War I, both Russian and Austrian Ukraine declared their independence. A union of the two was effected in 1919, and in 1920 a soviet government was established. It joined the Russian Soviet Union in 1923. In 1945 the union of the Ukraine was completed by the Czechoslovak cession of Carpatho-Ruthenia to Russia.

VATICAN CITY

The state of Vatican City, occupying almost 109 acres within the city of Rome, was created in 1929 when Pius XI and Mussolini, dictator of Italy, signed the Lateran Pacts. The Italian constitution of 1947, reaffirmed the Vatican independence. For almost 1000 years, the papacy, or Holy See, had held extensive possessions known as the Papal States. By 1870, these possessions, including Rome, had been annexed to the kingdom of Italy. A unilateral settlement, granting the pope the use of the Vatican and an annuity, was declined until 1929, when Italy recognized the Vatican's sovereignty and the papacy accepted compensation for its lost possessions.

The southern European state of Yugoslavia (*yōō'gō-släv'ĭ-à*) was constituted in December 1918 by the union of Serbia with certain Croatian, Slovenian, and other Slav provinces of the former Austro-Hungarian empire. In March 1921, Montenegro joined the new state. A constitution, which provided for a limited monarchy, was put into effect on June 28, 1921. It was suspended in 1929 by King Alexander, who made himself dictator. In 1931, he promulgated a new constitution, but it left him still with supreme power in matters of state. King Alexander was murdered at Marseilles in 1934; his minor son, Peter, became king.

In World War II, Yugoslavia at first leaned toward Germany. Its government was overthown in March 1941, and the Nazis promptly occupied the country. An underground army under Jozip Tito skillfully pinned down large German forces during the war. It cleared the country of the invaders in 1945 and declared Yugoslavia a people's republic with Tito as prime minister. Under a constitution of 1953, Tito served as president and, by amendment in 1963, was made president for life. Under his leadership, Yugoslavia's soviet-type government followed policies at variance with Russia's. Stalin tried to replace him but failed partly because of Western economic assistance. With a modified form of communism, he maintained a neutral position between East and West.

Serbia (*sĕr'bĭ-à*). From the 7th to the 11th century the Serbs enjoyed virtual self-government in the Roman province of Mœsia in the northwestern part of the Balkan peninsula. When the Byzantine government attempted to place some restrictions on them, they revolted under their grand shupon, or patriarch, Michael, who took the title of king and made a successful fight for independence. By the middle of the 14th century the Serbian empire included Bosnia, Albania, Macedonia, Thessaly, and part of Bulgaria, and reached to Attica and the Peloponnesus. But the Serbian power fell before the Turks, who completed their conquest in 1459. The independence of Serbia was recognized by the Congress of Berlin (1878), and in 1882 it became a kingdom.

In 1893 Alexander I came to the throne. He began at once to assume the role of autocrat. This policy exasperated the liberal party. On June 11 the king, the queen, and about fifty others were assassinated. As king the government chose Peter, grandson of Kara George, a patriot who had led an unsuccessful revolt against the Turks.

Serbian national ambitions now brought the country into frequently strained relations with Austria and Turkey. Through the Balkan wars (1912-13) Serbia doubled her territory. But Serbian hatred of Austria was increased by the refusal of the latter to allow Serbia a port on the Adriatic. On June 28, 1914, Archduke Ferdinand, heir to the Austrian throne, was assassinated in Bosnia by Serb nationalist conspirators. This event touched off World War I.

Montenegro (*mŏn'tĕ-nē'grō*). Formerly a principality on the eastern shore of the Adriatic Sea, and united to the Serbian kingdom from 1159 to 1356. After the defeat of the Serbs by the Turks at Kossovo in 1389, the Montenegrins, in their mountain fastnesses, began in turn their long struggle with the same enemies. In 1484 Ivan the Black withdrew with his people to the mountain village of Cetinje, founded a monastery, and created a bishopric. In 1696 the offices of prince and bishop, or *vladika*, were combined under the title of vladika. The last and greatest ruler to hold this title was Peter II (1830-51). Danilo I took the title of prince. In 1878 the independence of Montenegro was recognized by the Treaty of Berlin. On Nov. 29, 1918 the National Skupshtina deposed King Nicholas, who had reigned since Aug. 28, 1860, and a decision was made to unite Montenegro with Serbia.

In the course of the centuries, the various races and tribes of the world's population have shifted from region to region, and, as a result, many cities, once busy and prosperous, have become as so many desert places of the earth.

Most of the cities described below are today no longer existent. In the case of others, their sites are occupied by villages or small towns of little importance.

Antioch (*ăn'tĭ-ŏk*). This ancient capital of the Greek kings of Syria, on the Orontes, 21 miles from the sea, was built by Seleucus Nicator about 300 B. C. and named for his father. As a point of trade exchange between the caravans from the East and the Mediterranean shipping from the West, it became wealthy, and both Greeks and Romans so adorned it with public buildings that it was called the "Queen of the East." Here the disciples of Jesus were first called Christians. The modern Antioch, or Antakieh, is a small city with but little manufacturing and trade.

Baalbec (*băl'bĕk*), "City of Baal," the sun god, called Heliopolis by the Greeks. A ruined city on the slope of the Antilibanus mountains, about forty miles northwest of Damascus. It was a very ancient center of sun worship, and in Greek and Roman times it became the site of a great temple of the sun, built by Romans about 150 A. D. Pillaged by Arabs, Tatars, and Turks, and ruined by earth quakes, the city survives merely as a small village.

Babylon (*băb'ĭ-lŏn*). The ancient capital of Babylonia. The name probably means "gate of the gods." Already in existence in the time of Sargon, about 2800 B. C., the city grew in importance until Hammurabi made it his capital, about 2100 B. C. It was several times destroyed and rebuilt. Nebuchadnezzar enlarged it and brought it to its greatest splendor. Excavations in several mounds and villages, mostly on the east bank of the Euphrates, have recently revealed this city of Nebuchadnezzar (605-562), as well as scanty remains of earlier periods.

Byblos (Compare the word Bible). Now a village of 1000 called Jebeil, its former importance is shown by rich archaeological discoveries. Phoenician writing from the tomb of King Ahiram (1100 B.C.) is among the earliest known alphabetical inscriptions. Pottery fragments link Byblos with Babylonian and Persian civilizations.

Carthage (*kär'thåj*). An ancient Phoenician city in northern Africa, near the site of the modern Tunis. Probably it was originally founded in the 9th century B. C. as a trading post for Tyre and Utica. It grew in commercial power, extending its authority westward to the Atlantic and establishing trade in Sardinia, Gaul, Spain, and Britain. Conflict with Rome arose in the 3d century B. C. and, after the three Punic wars, it was utterly destroyed in 146 B. C. It was rebuilt by Augustus, and was for several centuries a great Roman city. Recent excavations by French archeologists have revealed important remains dating from the earliest period of the city, which throw much light upon its culture.

Corinth. An ancient city of Greece, situated between the gulfs of Corinth and Ægina. It became proverbial for its luxuries and pleasures. Its fountains, statues, theaters, and other buildings were of a design which created the order of architecture known by its name. The Romans destroyed the city in 146 B. C., but Julius Cæsar rebuilt it in 46 B. C. St. Paul addressed his *Epistles to the Corinthians* to a Christian community which formed in Corinth under his ministrations. New Corinth was built on a site three miles distant, after an earthquake had destroyed the old city in 1858.

Ephesus (*ĕf'ê-sŭs*). The origin of this Ionic city of Asia Minor is lost in mythology. It was situated in Lydia, near the mouth of the river Cayster, at the western end of a great Asiatic trade route. Under the Romans, it was the capital of the Province of Asia and a prosperous trade center. Its greatest fame arose from its temple of Diana. St. Paul spent three years in the city, and the church of Ephesus was important in early Christian history. Several times destroyed and rebuilt, it sank to small importance in the middle ages. Recent excavations have uncovered the Roman city.

Gaza (*gā'zà*). An ancient Syrian town, situated near the seacoast, about fifty miles southwest of Jerusalem. The ancient city, which Herodotus regarded as equal in importance to Sardis, was a border fortress and a commercial center because of its position at the junction of trade routes between Egypt, Arabia, and Syria. The earliest notice of the place is in the Tel-el-Amarna letters, one of which was written by the local governor to his superiors in Egypt. The Israelite king, Hezekiah, held Gaza for a short time, but surrendered it to Assyria. It withstood a siege of five months by Alexander the Great. In 96 B. C. it was totally destroyed by Alexander Jannæus. Aulus Gabinius rebuilt the city on a new site in 57 B. C., the old location being spoken of as Desert Gaza. Gaza was famous for the long and bitter struggle to substitute Christianity for the local worship of *Marna*, "Lord." In 402, the new faith triumphed. The modern town is called Ghuzzeh.

Herculaneum (hĕr'kṵ-lā'nê-ŭm). A Roman city, situated about five miles southeast of Naples. In the eruption of Vesuvius, 79 A. D., it was buried under volcanic mud and lava. The site was forgotten, until in 1738 the digging of a well in the village of Portici uncovered its ancient theater.

Jericho. The oldest known city. It occupied what is now Ariba in Jordan, six miles northwest of the Dead Sea. Extant walls were built there about 6800 B.C., more than 5500 years before the city was captured from the Canaanites by the Israelites under Joshua.

Memphis (mĕm'fĭs). A city of ancient Egypt, said to have been built by Menes, first king of Egypt. It was for a time the capital of Egypt, and, in the 6th century B. C., the chief commercial city. In the 7th century A. D., it was destroyed by the Arabs. The site of its ruins is the village of Metrahineh, twelve miles south of Cairo.

Mycenæ (mi-sē'nê). An ancient Greek city, on a steep hill six miles northeast of Argos. It was the home of Agamemnon before the Trojan war. Excavations begun by Schliemann in 1876 have revealed, through the relics recovered, the life of the period of Greek civilization called Mycenean, dating from before 1600 B.C.

Nineveh (nĭn'ê-vĕ). One of the ancient capitals of Assyria, first made important by Sennacherib, 705–681 B. C. It was destroyed about 606 B. C. by Babylonians and Medes. The site of the city is the present village of Kuoyinjik, opposite Mosul. Excavations by Layard and later explorers have uncovered splendid palaces, temples, and libraries in the mounds of this district.

Palmyra (pȧl-mĭ'rȧ), "City of Palms." A ruined city situated in an oasis of the Syrian desert, about 140 miles northeast of Damascus. It was enlarged by Solomon in the 10th century B. C. as an outpost of the kingdom of Israel. It is most famous as the residence of Zenobia, "Queen of the East," in whose reign the city was besieged and destroyed by Aurelian, 273 A. D.

Pergamum (pĕr'gȧ-mŭm). A city of Asia Minor, on the north bank of the Caicus, fifteen miles from the sea, the site of the modern Bergama. From the beginning of the 3d century B. C., it was famous for its library, second only to that of Alexandria, for its architecture, and for its manufacture of tapestries and pottery. Parchment (*Pergamenta Charta*) derives its name from the city. The church at Pergamum was one of the seven addressed in the Book of Revelation.

Persepolis (pĕr-sĕp'ô-lĭs), "City of the Persians." The capital of ancient Persia, most famous under Darius and Xerxes. The citadel was destroyed by Alexander about 330 B. C., but the rest of the city was important for two centuries more. The ruins of Persepolis, in the mountain-rimmed plain near the junction of the Kur and Polvar rivers, are among the most extensive and important remains of the ancient world.

Pompeii (pŏm-pā'yē). The ancient city, about twelve miles southeast of Naples, destroyed in the eruption of Vesuvius, 79 A. D. At this time it was covered by ashes and pumice in such a way that the entire city was preserved almost intact. For two centuries it had been a favorite sea-coast resort for the Romans.

Sardis (sär'dĭs). The ancient capital of Lydia, in Asia Minor. Through its market place flowed the river Pactolus. Once the center of a rich trade, and the residence of Crœsus, nothing remains on its site today but a village and some mounds. Recent excavations conducted by Americans have uncovered a great temple of Artemis, of the 4th century A. D.

Sidon (sī'dŏn). "Fishingtown." One of the chief commercial cities of ancient Phœnicia, situated on the coast midway between Tyre and Beirut. It is now called Saida. Many allusions to the city are found in Homer and in the Old Testament. It was famous for its manufacture of glass, linen, and purple dye. Many notable remains of the city's splendor have been found, among them a collection of sarcophagi from the best period of Greek art.

Susa (soo'sȧ). A city, originally under Babylonian rule, which came under Persian authority in the time of Cyrus and was made a splendid capital. From Susa to Sardis, in Asia Minor, ran a royal road, 1500 miles in length. In the middle ages the city was still noted for its manufacture of sugar. It is mentioned in the Old Testament as Susa or Shushan, in connection with Esther and Daniel. From the ruins of the place, which lie in southern Iran about fifty miles west of Shuster, many inscriptions and remains of ancient art and building have been recovered.

Tarsus (tär'sŭs). An ancient city of Asia Minor, in Roman times the capital of the province of Cilicia. Some traditions ascribed its foundation to the Assyrian king, Sardanapalus. It was, however, very early colonized by Greeks, and Greek writers speak of it as an important and wealthy city. The situation of Tarsus, on the river Cydnus, placed it in the path of armies of conquest from the time of Cyrus to the ages of Alexander and the Cæsars. Under the Romans, the inhabitants of Tarsus enjoyed Roman citizenship and the city rivaled Alexandria as a center of culture. St. Paul proudly claimed it as his native city. After its capture by the Saracens in 640 A. D., it lost its former importance. Modern Tarsus is but a small town in the Turkish province of Adana.

Thebes (thēbz). Egypt. A city, about 350 miles southeast of the modern city of Cairo, which was the capital of ancient Egypt between the 16th and 12th and, again, in the 7th century B. C. It fell into insignificance later, and an earthquake, in 27 B. C., completed its ruin. Its remains, recently discovered near the villages of Karnak and Luxor, bear witness to its former magnificence and splendor, and include colossal statues, palaces and tombs of kings, and temples sacred to Ammon and to other gods. The most notable recent discovery near Thebes was the uncovering of the tomb of Tutankhamen, in the valley of the Tombs of the Kings. See *Egypt*.

Thebes. Greece. A city of Bœotia, probably one of the earliest centers of population in Greece. It owed its chief importance throughout its history to its strength as a fortress. Tradition ascribed the building of the first citadel, the Cadmeia, to Cadmus. In the 6th century B. C. the Thebans adopted a hostile attitude toward the Athenians. The outbreak of the Persian wars found them on the side of Sparta, but their ruling aristocracy soon went over to the Persians. In the Peloponnesian war Thebes fought on the side of Sparta, but in the early part of the 4th century B. C. the two cities were almost continuously at war with each other. At length, under the leadership of Epaminondas and Pelopidas, Thebes attained for a short period (371–362) to the position of the chief power in Greece, but speedily lost it after the death of Epaminondas. The resistance of the Thebans to the Macedonian and the Roman power brought severe reprisals upon the city. It sank into an insignificance relieved only by a transitory prosperity in the 11th and 12th centuries A. D., and was finally destroyed by the Catalans in 1311.

Troy. A city on the coast of Asia Minor, about three and a half miles from the Dardanelles. Troy was the most famous city of Greek legend, having been celebrated in the first instance by Homer in the *Iliad* as the prize of the Trojan war. The site is now known as Hissarlik. In 1870, Schliemann began a series of excavations there, which have revealed the remains of nine successive settlements made upon the spot. The sixth one is believed to be the city described by Homer, on account of the similarity of its remains to those found at Mycenæ. The other settlements range from a village of the Stone age to a Greco-Roman town which rose into prominence after 334 B. C. This last town passed under Roman protection in 189 B. C. and was honored as the city from which came Æneas, a reputed ancestor of the Romans. In 1306, the Turks plundered the city, which, since that time, has lain in ruins.

Tyre. The famous city of ancient Phœnicia. It attained its greatest glory under Hiram, in the 10th century B. C. It was celebrated by ancient poets for the beauty of its scenery, and its harbors were among the wonders of the world. The basis of its commerce, which reached all countries, was its dyed woolens. This trade it continued, though in diminished volume, until the 16th century A. D., when the discovery of the sea route to the East diverted trade from its old courses. A small town, called Sûr, now occupies the ruins of the ancient city.

Ur (ûr). The Bible story of Abraham mentions Ur of the Chaldees as the Mesopotamian home of the patriarch. The site of this ancient city bears the modern name of Mughair, meaning pitch-built and given in allusion to the large quantities of pitch which were used in the construction of its earliest buildings. The city, which stood about 140 miles southeast of Babylon, was the chief center of the worship of the moon god Sin. The ruins of the famous zikkurat, or stage tower, still rise impressively above the surrounding plain.

Recent excavations have revealed successive reconstructions of walls and temples, made in various periods from the 30th to the 4th century B. C. The earliest remains, however, which are of unbaked clay bricks, indicate Sumerian construction antedating by many centuries the year 3000 B. C. Conspicuous among the reconstructions is that carried out by Nebuchadnezzar, in which the early form of the temple of Sin was, for the first time, radically altered. The historical record of the city is now complete from about 2300 B. C. to about 400 B. C., when, under Persian rule, Zoroastrianism displaced the city's ancient religious cult and effected the destruction of its temples.

PEOPLES OF THE WORLD

The known origins of man begin some two million years ago. Progress toward the man of today (*Homo sapiens*) was slow, but ever increasing in tempo. Many strains and varieties lived in the remote past, but elements of many of these have blended and united to yield modern man—one genus, one species. Modern man has divided further from his fellows in three ways. The first of these is linguistic; there are approximately 2500 languages spoken in the world today and thousands of others have become extinct. The second type of human difference is cultural, lying in the different ways in which each human group solves those problems general to all mankind or special to each because of its environment or recent history. It is harder to divide similar cultures than similar languages, but the number of distinct cultures is close to that for languages.

The third difference between human populations is a physical, or, more accurately, a genetic difference. This is commonly called *race*. There are far fewer races than there are languages or cultures; the largest recent classification lists 34 races, the smallest six. None of these includes all human populations, some being too small and others too heterogeneous.

These three elements of differentiation—race, language, and culture—are not definitely linked to each other; they vary with surprising independence. Peoples close in language may be different in culture (as the French and Rumanian); those close in culture may be different in language (as the Finns and the Swedes); and most racial groups cross both linguistic and cultural barriers. Racial differences between peoples do not imply in any sense cultural or psychological differences. Rather, they are based on known genetic differences in fairly minor characteristics, such as the relative frequency of each of the blood-group types. The articles which follow are divided into prehistoric and historic peoples. The historic peoples, although going back to prehistoric times, are those existing in historic times and usually to the present day.

PREHISTORIC PEOPLES

For over 150 years man has been unearthing the physical and cultural remains of his ancestors. Evidence ranges from scattered surface finds to caves and garbage heaps (middens) through the more highly developed settlements and in some cases into huge ceremonial centers or cities. Altogether, for most areas of the world prehistorians have at least a good general knowledge of man's prior cultures and the general series of patterns of man's development. Detailed knowledge exists as to several of the richer areas of only several thousands of years' antiquity. Such knowledge is based on many disciplines but particularly on the application of atomic research. See *Prehistory and Atomic Dating*.

Almost all prehistoric men belonged to one of three large taxonomic groups, *Australopithecus*, *Homo erectus*, and *Homo sapiens*, though each of these may be further subdivided. Physical anthropologists have shown that the major diagnostic trait of man (all members of the family *Hominidae*) is his adaptation to permanently erect posture. This freed the hands from locomotion so that tool using could become much more important, and this in turn fostered the evolution of the larger, more complex brain. This latter development was very slow and was completed only in the last 15 minutes of a 12-hour day representing man's total time on earth.

Until the end of the Pleistocene epoch, some ten to fifteen thousand years ago, man remained a hunter using flaked or chipped stone tools and living in small nomadic bands. Prior to this time, man had changed physically from something very close to an erect ape to man as we know him now. Then, about 10,000 years ago, in advantageous areas began the inventions that led to the atomic age.

The first step was the domestication of plants and, in some areas, animals. This led to a settled life in which a major portion of the people could be freed from having to raise their own food. Population grew rapidly with economic specialization, village life, then civilization, and finally cities and nations. Civilization was characterized by huge public buildings, by centralization of religion and government, and by development of the arts and sciences.

The following articles describe in alphabetical order some of the better known prehistoric populations of the Old World. In the New World, there was no known human habitation prior to 25,000 years ago.

Australopithecus. Sometimes erroneously called "man-apes," this is a large group of the earliest men. They are variously cited as a separate genus or sub-genus of the human family, the *Hominidae*, though one member may be placed within the genus *Homo*. They are most widely known in late form from South Africa, but the earliest two strains, *Homo habilis* (6 specimens) and *Zinjanthropus boisei* (3 specimens) come from Dr. Louis Leakey's work in the Oldowan Gorge of Tanzania. Tools are associated with each of these. In 1967, Harvard University's Professor Bryan Patterson reported the discovery in Kenya of the lower portion of a human humerus, the large bone of the upper arm. The specimen dates from 2,500,000 years ago, the very beginning of the Pleistocene epoch. As such, this is the earliest known specimen of man. Known only as Kanapoi Hominid One (KH1), from the dry wash where it was found, it can be classed as an early form of Australopithecine.

Most members of the Australopithecine group fall into one of two categories. One, often labeled *Paranthropus*, tends to be large, robust, and have huge molars, prominent brow-ridges, and a sagital crest. Zinjanthropus belongs to this group. The second group tends to be smaller, have normal teeth, small brow-ridges, and to be generally more modern. *Homo habilis* belongs in this group, as does the later *Australopithecus africanus*. It is impossible to assign the Kanapoi specimen to one or the other definitely. Compared to modern man, both were small and had small cranial capacities, 500 to 800 cc. as opposed to 1300 to 1600 cc. Yet all were upright in posture, and one strain, possibly *Homo habilis*, may well have given rise to later forms of man. The probable time span of these early humans was from two million to almost 500,000 years ago.

Cave Men, or **Cave Dwellers.** This is a misnomer. Early man lived in caves all over the world. There is no one such group.

Cro-Magnon Man. This is the generic name for the *Homo sapiens* population of Europe, whose first appearance comes around 25,000 years ago and who bear Upper Paleolithic tool traditions. The name is taken from a French cave, where remains of five persons were discovered in 1858. Dr. Theodosius Dobzhansky classified Cro-Magnon and all of his cousins as *Homo sapiens cosmopolitans*, the last prehistoric race of *Homo sapiens* and a major ingredient in all modern peoples. Cro-Magnon man lived in Europe and North Africa, used blade tools, inhabited caves, but had many different cultures, though all were hunters. They were modern men in all respects and of modern size and cranial capacity.

Heidelberg Man. This name is given to a group on the basis of a single specimen of a lower jaw discovered in 1907 near the city of Heidelberg, Germany. The jaw is clearly human and fits well into the classification of *Homo erectus*, the second stage in the major lines of mankind. The most probable date is late second glacial period, possibly about 360,000 years ago. This is the only known specimen of *Homo erectus* from Europe.

Homo Erectus. This is the taxonomic name given to a widely spread but relatively homogeneous human population. It represents the "second stage" in the development of man, following on *Australopithecus*. All members of this group were larger than their ancestors, their brow-ridges were large, their limb-bones bent, and their cranial capacity ranged from around 900 cc. to 1200 cc. All were tool users, some may have mastered fire. Their geographic distribution covers the whole of the Old World—Java man in southeast Asia, Peking man in eastern Asia, Heidelberg man in Europe, Atlanthropus in northern Africa, and Chellean III man in eastern Africa. Their distribution in time is open to some doubt. Some authorities place the last of the *Homo habilis* specimens in *Homo erectus*, yielding a date of before 1 million years ago. Others place Java Man IV, 800,000 years ago, as the first of this genus. Most experts see the end of this genus *per se*, at about the time of Peking man, 450,000 years ago; a few differ, and see the genus as continuing until almost 50,000 years ago in Rhodesia man and Solo man.

Homo Habilis. A very early yet somewhat modern strain of man. (See *Australopithecus*).

Homo Sapiens. This taxonomic name is given to all modern men, but it can be traced back 250,000 years or a little more. This is the third stage of man's development, after *Australopithecus* and *Homo erectus*. *Homo sapiens* is taller, slimmer-boned, has less brow-ridge and more forehead, and has a larger cranial capacity than any of his forebears. Generally speaking, the cranial capacity of *Homo sapiens* is over 1250 cc. Included in this group are the Pre-Neanderthaloids, the Neanderthals, Cro-Magnon, and all modern derivative strains.

Java Man. He is sometimes called *Pithecanthropus erectus*, more recently *Homo erectus javanensis*. He was a prototype of the *Homo erectus* form of man, having a cranial capacity of 900 + cc. to 1100 cc., taller and heavier than the australopithecines, with heavy brow ridges, bent limb bones, and a large ridge on the back of the skull. Known specimens spanned the time from the first to the end of the second glacial periods, some 700,000 to 500,000 years ago. There is some evidence of continuation of descent from Java man to the contemporary inhabitants of Australia and perhaps New Guinea.

Kanapoi Hominid. The name given in 1967 to the earliest discovered human fossil specimen. See *Australopithecus*.

Neanderthal Man. This group covers many local strains of men who lived from just before to nearly the end of the fourth glacial period. Centered in western Europe, they ranged through North Africa and far into Asia. They were characterized by the Mousterian tool tradition, a combination of the two major tool-making techniques (flaking and core-biface) which preceded them. Neanderthal man gives our first secure evidence of formal religion, seen in their regular burial practices. These people appear to many to be "throwbacks," in that they had large, bent limb bones, massive eye ridges, and generally "primitive" characteristics. Some experts hold these people to be a local adaptation to the onset of the last (4th) glacial period; others suggest an amalgamation of *Homo erectus* and *Homo sapiens* types. Whichever is correct, Neanderthal man and the Mousterian culture which characterizes him disappeared during the Gottweig interstadial, a recession of the Würm (4th) glaciation. Only in Israel is there any possible evidence of intermixture between Neanderthal and Cro-Magnon, and even this is based on a very small number of specimens.

Peking Man. This name refers to the remains of over 40 individuals found in the lower cave at Choukoutien near Peking. Peking man is now usually referred to as *Homo erectus pekinensis*, showing the clear affiliation to Java man. He is clearly a first cousin to Java man, though he postdates his Java cousin, having lived around 450,000 years ago. At the Choukoutien cave there was a scorched hearth, which gives Peking man first honors to date as a user of fire.

Pre-Neanderthaloids. This is the name given most often to the earliest known members of *Homo sapiens*. As a group they are massive and primitive in appearance than the "classic" Neanderthals, who came after them. Dr. T. Dobzhansky classes this group as *Homo sapiens presapiens*, the first known race of modern man. Two specimens, *Steinheim* from Germany and *Swanscombe* from England, lived a quarter of a million years ago during the second interglacial period. The other specimens were also found in Europe, but lived during the third interglacial period between 100,000 and 70,000 years ago. Some of the better known finds in this group are *Ehringsdorf* from Germany, *Fontechevade* from France, *Saccopastore* from Italy, and *Krapina* from Yugoslavia.

Rhodesia Man. An almost complete skull and other bones were found at Broken Hill, Rhodesia, in 1921 as part of a mining operation. The bones are peculiarly massive, the skull having the largest brow ridges of any fossil specimen. Rhodesia man dates from the middle of the fourth glacial period, perhaps 25,000 years ago. This specimen is most likely an African representative of Neanderthal man.

Solo Man. Eleven skulls, with some legbones, discovered in Java between 1931 and 1933 are collectively known as Solo man. All the faces had been cut off, and all but two of the brain cases were broken open at the base. Almost certainly, these eleven persons served as dinner for someone else. Morphologically, they lie intermediate in grade between *Homo erectus* and *Homo sapiens*. They are almost certainly descendents of Java man and ancestors of the contemporary, aboriginal population of Australia. They probably date from approximately 50,000 years ago.

Zinjanthropus. The name means "nutcracker man" and is applied to a very early hominid, almost certainly not ancestral to modern man. See *Australopithecus*.

HISTORIC PEOPLES

Afghans. The primarily pastoral and recently sedentary peoples of the Afghan Mountains and the eastern Iranian Plateau. Probably related to the *Aryan* invaders of India, the Afghans inhabit the gateway from the West to the East, the Khyber Pass entry into Pakistan. Indo-European in speech and Islamic in religion, the Afghan tribes are noted for their bravery and prowess in the arts of war. They are of tall stature, medium complexion, and aquiline feature, and are especially remarked for their full, flowing beards.

Albanians. The name is most properly applied to the speakers of Albanian, in and of itself a separate family within the Indo-European stock. Dwellers of the southwest coast of the Balkan peninsula, the Albanians exhibit a tenacity for their own customs in spite of the many centuries of exposure to Greek, Italian, and Turkish influence. Even in the late 1960's, Albania's government chose to align itself with the Chinese Communist regime, although surrounded by Russian satellites, Titoist Yugoslavia, and free Greece. The state of Albania contains over 1.5 million people, but perhaps as many as one half million more Albanians live in eastern Greece, southern Italy, and Sicily. Though nominally allied in "The Peoples Republic of Albania," these peoples are largely governed today, as they have been for centuries, by local chieftains ruling over their kinsmen. They are predominantly Islamic in religion, though 20 per cent are Greek Orthodox and 10 per cent are Roman Catholic.

Algerians. These are citizens of Algeria, but the term is more widely applied to the culturally and racially heterogeneous population of former French Algeria. Specifically, they are French colonists in Algeria, as opposed to *Berbers* and *Arabs*. These three groups aim at establishing a national identity, Islamic by religion, north African by alliance, and French by influence.

AMERICAN INDIANS

Thinking he had circled the globe, Christopher Columbus gave the name Indians to the inhabitants of the New World. It is generally believed that the first of their ancestors were travelers who, about 25,000 years ago, went from Asia to North America across Bering Strait, then a land bridge between the continents. Groups came, settled, and moved on, eventually populating the whole continent. As far south as the tip of Chile, remains have been radiocarbon dated at more than 8000 years ago. Not much is known about these early people save that they were hunters. At Folsom, New Mexico, one of the stone points found was embedded in the bones of a bison. Radiocarbon dating established that these hunters lived 10,000 years ago.

North American Indians. Many of the inhabitants of North America lived by hunting and gathering for thousands of years, improving their technology and the beauty of their crafts. On the West Coast, food was boiled by dropping very hot stones into water-tight baskets in which acorn meal was cooked. In the Ozarks and elsewhere, Indians learned to cultivate the local plants, among them beans, squash, and corn, which spread north from Mexico between three and five thousand years before the time of Christ. Pottery-making was also learned, perhaps by accident as someone left a clay-covered basket too long in the fire.

Other natives of America are known for their building; great apartment houses or pueblos still stand in New Mexico and at Mesa Verde in Colorado, built in the 12th and 13th centuries A.D. Great earthworks or mounds for temples or houses may be seen in the Ohio and Mississippi valleys, built by Hopewell people and their descendants in the 14th through the 16th centuries A.D. Had Columbus traversed the continent, he would have met with great variety.

Linguists have perhaps best been able to group the various American Indian tribes. In 1891 J. W. Powell separated more than 50 different families, later arranged by Edward Sapir into six major groups of language stocks: Eskimo-Aleut, Algonkin-Wakashan, Hokan-Siouan, Penutian, Nadene, and Aztec-Tanoan. Many groups are now widely separated, while others are geographic and cultural neighbors, sharing some words and many customs. Work by Morris Swadesh has revealed additional linguistic relationships which may link peoples to specific waves of migrations across Bering Strait those many years ago.

Indians of the Arctic Region. Far to the north live the Eskimos and the Aleuts, the latter inhabiting the westernmost islands of Alaska. Known for their ability to endure the Arctic climate, these people used skin boats and dog sleds to hunt seal and other sea mammals; caribou were also hunted, particularly in Alaska. Among the products of Eskimo technology which have found their way into present-day use are the fur parka, toggle fasteners, kayak, snow goggles, and soapstone carving, all well executed.

Woodland Peoples. In the Eastern United States and Canada lived woodland peoples, including the Algonkin and most of the New England and Atlantic Coastal tribes, such as the Powhatan, of whom Pocahontas is well known. Also included were the Ojibway, Menomini, Winnebago, Potawatomi, and Shawnee, all speakers of the Algonkin-Wakashan stock. Others were Hokan-Siouan speakers, such as the Six Nations (Seneca, Cayuga, Onondaga, Oneida, Mowhawk, and later Tuscarora) and the Iroquois, plus the Choctaw, Chickasaw, Creek, Cherokee, and Seminole among others. Among these peoples the languages were not always mutually intelligible; hand signs or pictographs often served as a means of communication between groups. In the northern part of the woodland area, hunting and fishing formed the major way of life, giving way to the cultivation of maize, squashes, melons, beans, and tobacco towards the south.

Women did most of the cultivation, while men hunted and built houses. These varied in shape from the tipi of the north to the circular wigwam or long domed structure of New England and the Middle Atlantic states (the Iroquois Long House, for example) to the rectangular thatched-roof house of the southeast. Most were framed of wood or saplings, covered with bark mats, thatch, or, in the western part of the area, by hides. Deer provided meat and clothing, and in the south plant fibers were also used. Pottery was known. Most containers and utensils were made of wood, bark, or basketry; other implements and weapons were of stone and bone. Around the Great Lakes, the gathering of wild rice provided sustenance where corn was not easily grown. Birchbark canoes and snowshoes in winter were frequently seen. Here too flourished the secret Midewiwin, or Grand Medicine Society, with its esoteric medicine bundles and ritual communication with the supernatural. Medicine societies among the Iroquois centered on curing rituals; members of the False Face Society wore grotesque wooden masks while performing a ritual to drive away evil spirits.

In the south, the Natchez of the Lower Mississippi were met by De Soto and other early explorers. The Natchez were famed for their worship of the sun and for the distinction among them of nobles and commoners. Later, some of them even emulated the colonists and owned slaves. A Cherokee named Sequoya deserves his fame, for he adapted the alphabet to the Cherokee language, then taught it to his people. Within a year (1820-21), the Cherokee were a literate nation.

Plains Indians. On the plains and prairies the way of life was very different from that in the woodland areas. Most inhabitants were speakers of the Hokan-Siouan languages, merging with Penutian speakers such as the Nez Percé; the Algonkin speaking Blackfoot and Cree; and the Cheyenne and Arapaho. Deer, antelope, and herds of buffalo provided material for housing (tipis were covered with skins), clothing (especially decorated robes), and food for many. Before the advent of horses in the 17th century, buffalo were stalked on foot. Baggage was placed in a skin bundle on poles harnessed to the back of a dog; this "travois" was later pulled by horses. Wild plants supplemented the game supply, but corn was not grown, nor did they make pottery. The advent of the horse increased their mobility, however. Since prestige was counted not only by quantity of horses but by bravery, raids for horses and to "count coup" (gallop in, touch the enemy, and return unharmed) became a way of life.

The Sun Dance was a ceremony shared by many plains tribes. Modified in form (without the self torture of aboriginal times), this rite is still held. There were clubs and societies for a variety of purposes, including the maintenance of law and order. Associated with them were ritual paraphernalia, songs, and dances. In the 1880's the Ghost Dance became popular among the plains Indians. Pressures of westward expansion, a depleted supply of buffalo, and reservation life combined sparked a reaction characterized by frenzied dances, the belief in communication with ghosts, and in a Messiah who would lead the Indians back to the good old days. In time it subsided, but its influence can be seen in the Native American Church.

Indians of the Plateau. Living in the forests and grasslands, these Indians shared the plains customs but in a different environment. Foods included wild roots, which were also cooked into loaves; and berries, which were also dried. Salmon were caught by spears or nets, the surplus being dried or smoked. Many of these peoples, such as the Palouse, Nez Percé, the Cayuse, and Molale, were Penutian speakers, and some, such as the Spokan, Flathead, and Pend d'Oreilles, were speakers of the Algonkin-Wakashan stock.

Great Basin Indians. The Shoshoni, Ute, Paiute, California Kern River, and Mono were speakers of the Aztec-Tanoan stock. An inland sea thousands of years ago, the great basin is now largely semidesert, making subsistence difficult. Small game and a sparse but great variety of wild plants, roots, and acorns provided subsistence where they were available. Brush shelters or windbreaks provided housing. Early observers watched these people digging roots and contemptuously named them the Diggers, yet they could live where their observers could not. These peoples, especially the Paiute, were good basket makers, and their works are prized in museum collections.

Indians of Southwest. The main inhabitants of the southwest (the states of Arizona, New Mexico, southern Colorado, and Utah) are two groups: the pueblo Indians and the southern Athapascans. The pueblos, while speakers of the Aztec-Tanoan languages, are further separated, one group living along the Rio Grande and the other in the western mesas. Languages and customs differ among these peoples. Pueblo dwellers live as did their remote ancestors, in apartment-house villages of adobe bricks. Corn is a staple crop, and orchards are now grown, as is cotton for clothing. Each pueblo village has its own distinctive style of pottery. Supernatural beings or gods, especially in the western pueblos, are called *kachinas.* Wooden dolls are carved to represent them, and at ceremonies they are impersonated by masked dancers. Among the Hopi, the Snake Dance is perhaps the most spectacular of the rites. Much of the ritual is secret, but on the last day performers assemble in the village plaza and dance with rattlesnakes, each for a time with one in his mouth.

Sharing the ecology, but by no means the way of life, are the Apache and the Navaho, Nadene-speaking Athapascan neighbors of the pueblo Indians. Geronimo was a well known Apache leader whose raids put fear into the frontier. The Apache were semi-nomadic, living in wickiups—brush or hide covered dwellings in the mountains. The Navaho, like the Apache, were hunters, but more sedentary, and they kept gardens. Their houses are called hogans, built of stout interlocked poles covered with mud. Later hogans were hexagonal in shape, built up like a log cabin. After 1800, the Navaho and some Apache extensively developed sheep herding. Sheep provide not only food, but pelts for bedding, cash sales, and wool for the weaving of fine blankets. Navaho work in silver and turquoise is also excellent.

West Coast Peoples. California is considered a single area of high diversification, but little is known of many of its peoples; they often became extinct or merged with neighbors before careful tribal records were kept. The last survivor of the Yahi, the southernmost Yana tribe, wandered into civilization in 1911; he died in 1916 (see ISHI, by Theodora Kroeber). These Indians hunted deer and small game, caught salmon, gathered roots and vegetables. Acorns were a staple food and were prepared in a number of ways.

The area known as the Northwest Coast extended from northern California to British Columbia and southeastern Alaska. Language stocks included the Algonkin-Wakashan (Yurok, Kwakiutl), Penutian (Chinook), and Nadene (Haida, Tlingit). These peoples lived in plank houses; a large carved totem pole often stood in front, representing the clan of the house owner. They hunted sea mammals and fished from long fire-hollowed boats. They had social classes, and raided neighbors for plunder and slaves. Chiefs vied with each other by giving "potlatch" feasts in which the host destroyed as many blankets, furs, copper plates, and shells as he could afford; the larger the destruction the greater the prestige of the chief. This was a form of conspicuous consumption not unlike the "keeping up with the Joneses."

RECENT CHANGES IN INDIAN LIFE

As the American continent became populated by Spanish, French, English, and finally American settlers, conflict often became a way of life, ultimately changing the aboriginal Indian ways or eradicating them.

A good many tribes in the east moved westward before the frontier, a process often repeated as white settlements extended. Wars on the plains and in the southwest were bitterly fought as late as the 1880's, and raids continued long after. Only the Seminole in Florida never actually conceded defeat. Government dealings with the Indians were by treaties until 1878; after that by Congressional enactment. Gradually most Indians were settled on reservations, where they often met disease, famine, and ill treatment by unsympathetic agents. In 1887 Indian land was authorized for individual rather than tribal allotment; remaining land was sold. As a result, Indian lands estimated at 138 million acres in 1887 dwindled to 47 million in 1934, when a new policy was adopted. Population also declined. An aboriginal population estimated at 1,153,000 was reduced to 269,388 by 1901; by 1937 it had climbed to 337,366; and by 1960, it had reached 552,228. Tribal lands were also stabilized; individuals wishing to sell their allotments would do so to the tribe, in return for stock, thus halting the alienation of the Indian lands.

Supervision of Indian welfare is the duty of the Office of Indian Affairs, created in 1832. Many Indians served gallantly in World War II, but returned as heroes who could not vote. Citizens by act of Congress in 1924, they could not vote in some states until 1948.

In 1946 the Indian Claims Commission was established. Most of the claims brought against the government have been for insufficient payment for lands taken in the past.

There is still great variety in the life of the Indians of the United States. Some tribes, such as the Navaho, are collectively wealthy, although individuals may be poor; other tribes are relatively poor. Oil and uranium ores discovered on tribal lands have provided great wealth for some tribes. Sources of income are equally varied for individuals, and many skilled workers earn good wages; a number of industries have established factories near reservations to the mutual advantage of both the Indians and the industries.

In Canada, Indians were settled on reservations pursuant to treaties which called for distribution for each individual of a certain amount of money and provisions. They were regarded as wards of the government. In 1950, this system was superseded. Under the Indian Act of that year, Indians are citizens with voting and contractual rights and are liable to pay taxes. They are eligible for the social services open to all citizens. The department of citizenship and immigration is charged with looking after their interests both off and on reservations, these totaling 2265 covering nearly 6 million acres. The organizational unit is known as a band, of which there are 559. These are treated as municipalities for administrative purposes. Land in the reservations may not be sold without the department's consent. Indians are encouraged but not pressured to become integrated economically with the rest of the population, and about one-fourth of their numbers no longer live on reservations. The population, which had shown a decline prior to 1940, approximately doubled in the next 25 years to about 200,000.

INDIANS OF THE UNITED STATES

STATE	Area of Indian Lands Acres	Population 1970*
Alaska		51,528**
Arizona	19,224,717	95,812
California	666,817	91,018
Colorado	666,533	8,836
Florida	60,574	6,719
Idaho	817,659	6,687
Iowa	3,386	2,992
Kansas	35,678	8,672
Michigan	26,872	16,854
Minnesota	652,746	23,128
Montana	6,454,953	27,130
Nebraska	75,958	6,624
Nevada	1,127,171	7,933
New Mexico	7,153,109	72,788
New York		28,330
North Carolina	56,849	43,487
North Dakota	1,036,292	14,369
Oklahoma	2,844,431	97,731
Oregon	1,736,794	13,510
South Dakota	5,864,604	32,365
Texas		18,132
Utah	1,693,160	11,273
Washington	2,739,830	33,386
Wisconsin	445,443	18,924
Wyoming	2,013,409	4,980
All Other States	9,427	83,883
Total	55,406,412	827,091

* Source: *U. S. Bureau of the Census*
** Includes total of 28,078—Aleuts (5,755) and Eskimos (22,323).

INDIANS OF CANADA

PROVINCE	Area of Indian Lands Acres	Population 1966*
Alberta	1,603,475	25,396
British Columbia	817,754	44,260
Manitoba	522,575	31,009
New Brunswick	37,671	3,905
Nova Scotia	25,404	4,189
Ontario	1,556,437	50,608
Prince Edward Island	2,741	401
Quebec	188,143	25,083
Saskatchewan	1,224,111	31,297
Territories	6,796	8,088
Total	5,985,107	224,236

* Source: *Canada Year Book*

Central and South American Indians. In Central and South America, native civilizations arose to vie with those of Egypt and Mesopotamia. The key to such civilizations was the domestication of maize (corn). Recent excavations in the Valley of Mexico show that squash-and-gourd agriculture was practiced at 7000 B.C. and that maize was first domesticated about 5000 B.C. in Mexico. Writing was developed in Mexico, though it is not readable today beyond dates, numbers, and the names of gods. South America never developed writing, though the civilizations of the Andean highlands developed a very adequate substitute, the *Quipu*. This looked like a string mop, made with colored strands knotted at intervals. These colors and knots were mnemonic devices used by professional "memory experts," the tax recorders of South American civilization. In many parts of both Central and South America, civilization brought central government, state religions, organized trade, and most notably monumental architecture. These peoples included Mayans, Toltecs, Zapotecs, and Aztecs of Mexico, and the Kechuan and Chibchan peoples of South America. They moved from localized village agriculture, to the development of ceremonial centers with temples, marketplaces, and palaces, and to a final stage in Central America of full-fledged cities of hundreds of thousands of occupants.

First American Civilization. As part of the development of the ceremonial center and the later city, there was also great specialization of trades, crafts, and even professions. Pottery and metallurgy became stable occupations. Classes of priests, astronomers, architects, and masons took on new importance. Trade was established between cities. In South America thousands of miles of guarded toll roads were built to protect the traveler from marauding natives. In Mexico and Guatemala, special laws were passed protecting the merchant and traveler. Gradually, in each area local government gave way to ever larger political entities. Finally, in Central America, the warlike *Aztecs* captured the reins of government of the most important Valley of Mexico. In South America, the *Incas* occupied the same position as a dominant, ruling class. While both centers of civilization had developed highly sophisticated arts and sciences, they were deficient in the art of war and were subdued and eventually subjected by Europeans with firearms and cannon.

Many legacies of these early American civilizations exist today, in items used and words spoken: tomato, potato, tobacco, quinine, hammock, hurricane, maize, chocolate, coca (and cacao and cocaine), and atlatl (Nahua for spearthrower). Yet many more people lived in these areas who never did participate in the great civilizations or were only partly influenced by them. Further, as the leaders of the civilized nations and tribes were killed or imprisoned by the Europeans, the commoner members of these groups drifted off again into village agriculture, often as tenants with European landlords. As such they lost many of the traditions of their ancestors, particularly those related to civilized and urban life.

Central and South America today are a patchwork of aboriginal peoples, once-civilized peoples now less than such, and various combinations of each of these and European immigrants. In general, all may be classified as *Indios* (Indians, never civilized or driven from civilization), *Mestizos* (a mixture of Indian and Spanish, in culture or ancestry, often local businessmen), and *Ladinos* (those who claim Spanish descent, often erroneously).

Angles. A tribe which left northern Germany in the 5th century A.D. and established a settlement in eastern England. They gave their name in Germanic form to the country, England, and, in Latinized form, to the locality in which they settled—East Anglia.

Arabians or **Arabs.** The former name refers properly to the peoples of the Arabian peninsula, particularly the nomadic tribes such as the Bedouin. Arab is a more general term, referring to speakers of the Arabic tongue who are of Mediterranean racial stock. The Arab world of today extends from Morocco in the west to Oman in the east, from central Sudan in the south to Syria in the north. The Arab world displays many cultural variations, but they all look upon the Arabians proper as the ultimate example of an Islamic and Arab people. It was from stock such as the Bedouin tribesmen that Mohammed came, the prophet and founder of the Islamic religion. In Arabia lies the city of Mecca, birthplace of Mohammed and Holy City to the 500 million Moslems of the world, yet the Arabian peninsula has only twenty million natives. In the northern regions of Arabia, within the country of Iraq, the world's first civilizations developed.

The descendants of these civilizations became united in the Mohammedan religion during the 7th and 8th centuries A.D. This new Moslem civilization not only kept alive many of the discoveries of their own ancestors, but also much of the knowledge of the Greeks. A good deal of this knowledge filtered back into Europe during the Middle Ages and had a profound effect on the development of philosophy. Arab soldiers, traders, and missionaries greatly expanded Arab influence and spread Islam throughout the northern half of Africa and through southern Asia as far as Indonesia, primarily from the 9th through the 14th century A.D. After a decline of 600 years, into semi-colonialism, the Arabs after World War II achieved independence as a number of nations above which Arabic unity hovered as an unrealized ideal.

Armenians. Speakers of the Armenian language, a separate division of the Indo-European stock, Armenians inhabit the area of Russia bordering on the eastern frontier of Turkey. The Armenian-speakers conquered and occupied this region several centuries B.C. and then interbred with the Turkic inhabitants.

The Armenians vie with the Ethiopians for the title of earliest Christian state, the Armenian Church having been founded in 301 A.D. by Gregory the Illuminator. Originally attached to the Eastern Rite of the Catholic Church, the Armenian Church broke off in 451 A.D. Today, for political reasons, the Patriarch of the Church resides in Turkey. In the past few centuries, many Armenians have espoused the Roman Catholic faith.

After an initial stable period, the Armenians have seldom been free from political domination by the Persians, Turks, and Russians. Armenia had one brief year of independence in 1919, when the Armenian Republic was declared after the fall of Czarist Russia, but it was soon incorporated into Soviet Russia. Prior to World War I, the Turkish government had set about the deliberate annihilation of the Armenians; the soviet domination was somewhat milder. As a result of such persecution, many Armenians left the area of their nativity and spread through parts of Europe, North Africa, and the Americas. In these areas they won recognition as businessmen, bankers, and teachers. The population of Soviet Armenia is approximately two million; but half that number of Armenians live in other countries.

Aryans. This name properly refers both to the invaders of India about 2000 B.C. and to the speakers of the Indo-Aryan family of the Indo-European stock. Sometimes Aryan is used to distinguish the Hindi speakers of India from the Urdu, Tamil, etc. Aryan is misused when applied to any racial group, though Hitler's Germany gave the term much local popularity; there is no Aryan race.

Assyrians. The Semitic speakers of the Assyrian Empire of the upper Tigris River in the region of modern Syria. The political domain began about 1600 B.C. and reached its height in the 7th century B.C. This was one of many tribal empires of the Middle East, and was contemporary with the Judaic peoples in the time of the Old Testament.

Aztecs. The name of the ruling tribe in the Valley of Mexico at the time of Spanish contact and for several hundred years before. The origins of the Aztecs are obscure, but they were a highland people speaking Nahua, a branch of Uto-Aztecan and ultimately Macro-Penutian, the largest stock of New World languages. Aztec is derived from *Aztlan*, meaning heron-place; the Aztecs were then the "heron clan." When the Spaniards came, seven major cities were united in the Aztec confederacy, but they controlled much more of Mexico than the area they occupied.

When first seen by Cortez, the Aztec capital of Tenochitlan was a magnificent city, with huge public buildings, wide highways, and a complex of canals. They had highly skilled engineers, architects, astronomers, masons, potters, and artists. They had highly developed the domestication of maize, which provided most of their sustenance. The Spaniards overthrew the government, confiscated the precious metal, and, with equal determination, extirpated their religion, which involved worship of naturalistic deities and the presentation of human and other sacrifices to these gods. The Aztecs ruled over the final, militaristic phase of Mexican culture, beginning with the Mayas. Today's descendants of the Aztec phase of Mexican culture still live in the Valley of Mexico, and many villagers do not yet speak Spanish.

Babylonians. The people of the great Mesopotamian civilization of Babylon, which flourished from approximately 2300 to 538 B.C. The first codification of human laws was handed down by the Babylonian king, Hammurabi, in the 20th century B.C.

Bantus. Generically, the several hundred tribes of South and Central Africa who speak languages of the Bantu family. These people occupy almost one third of the African continent. They are noted as cattle breeders, though the animals are usually kept as wealth, while basic subsistence comes from agriculture. Many Bantu tribes are noted for military skill. One tribe, the Zulu, in the early 19th century seized an empire larger than that of Napoleon.

Basques. The inhabitants of the Western Pyrenees mountains. They are distinct in race, language, and culture from the French and Spanish, between whom they live.

Outwardly, they do not appear to be different from their neighbors, but in terms of the blood-group genes used by modern biologists to distinguish race they are very different. Most notable is the fact that they have no gene for blood type B, and they are the only human population in which the frequency of the gene for Rh negative blood is over 50%. This difference in race is strengthened by the fact that their language is unrelated to any other known language. They are believed to be the modern descendants of a very early European population, probably fifteen thousand or more years old.

The Basques are a proud people, still adhering to their own customs. They largely rule themselves, holding their own elections, and, well into the 20th century, collecting their own taxes and paying their own police force. In return, they paid an annual levy to the Spanish government. They are noted as herders, though they farm as well. Basque herders moved with the expansion of sheep herds across the western United States in the 19th century, and many are still to be found there today. Many more, perhaps 200,000, moved to South America.

Today small enclaves of Basques are to be found throughout the Americas, in North Africa, and in many parts of western Europe, as well as in their homeland. Around 750,000 still live in the Pyrenees, predominantly on the Spanish side. Perhaps another 300,000 live elsewhere.

Bedouins. See *Arabians*.

Belgae. The northernmost group of Celtic tribes which inhabited ancient Gaul. The Belgæ occupied the country between the Seine, Marne, and Moselle rivers and the ocean, which includes modern Belgium, together with portions of Holland and northern France. Some of the Belgæ settled in Kent and Sussex in southern Britain. In 57 B.C., Julius Cæsar conquered the Belgæ in a long, hard campaign, though part of the tribes revolted later. According to Cæsar, the Belgæ were the bravest of all the Gauls.

Belgians. The name applied to natives or citizens of Belgium, but not the name of a distinct race. Southern Belgians, for the most part, are Walloons, and northern Belgians are Flemish. See *Walloons, Flanders*.

Berbers. A people of North Africa whose ancestors inhabited the same region for perhaps 20,000 years. Mediterranean in race, they speak a language of the Hamitic branch of the Afroasiatic stock, thus ultimately being related to the semitic-speaking peoples of the modern and ancient worlds. Indeed, it was from the ancient Egyptians that they received first domesticated plants and animals, and later their metals. They have withstood many colonizations of North Africa, but only the expansion of Islam left a lasting effect, and today they are all Mohammedan and show many marks of Arab influence. A few even speak Arabic instead of Berber.

Today they are primarily pastoralists scattered around settled farmers of other origins. They are still noted for their ability in working metals. They are divided into 29 groups or tribes, though tribal organization is weak and government is by a democratic council at the community level. Their numbers today exceed 8,000,000.

Bohemians. See *Czechs*.

Boii. A Celtic people who emigrated from trans-alpine Gaul into Italy, where they occupied the old seat of the Umbrians, between the Po and the Apennines. In 283 B.C., the Boii were defeated by the Romans at the Vadimonian lake, and thereafter they prolonged their resistance to Roman arms through numerous campaigns, especially in support of Hannibal, but sometimes single-handed, till their complete defeat by Scipio Nasica in 191 B.C. They were subsequently compelled to recross the Alps, and they dwelt for more than a century in a part of modern Bohemia, which derives its name from them. They were ultimately exterminated by the Dacians. See *Bohemia*.

Bretons. About the 6th century B.C., the Celts of Gaul invaded Britain and, coalescing with the Iberians, founded the states later overthrown by the Romans. Upon the invasion of the Anglo-Saxons between the 5th and 6th centuries A.D., the British Celts who fled from England to avoid the Saxon domination crossed to the northwest of France and founded the Celtic state of Brittany, then called Armorica. These Celts are the direct ancestors of the modern Bretons, whose language is closely allied to the Welsh and the now extinct Cornish languages. It is spoken by over 1¼ million persons. Of its four dialects *León* is the purest and *Cornuallais* the most widely spread. See *Brittany*.

Britons. A people, largely of Celtic origin, who inhabited England at the time of Julius Cæsar's visit. They had a highly developed druidic religion. Young men in Gaul who wished to be priests were sent to Britain to be educated.

Bulgars. An Asiatic race akin to the Huns. When first known, they were nomadic horsemen, fierce and barbarous, who migrated westward behind the Huns. In the 4th century A.D., they conquered the region between the Volga and the Urals. Later they formed a state north of the Black Sea. In the 7th century, they menaced Constantinople. Settling down, they gave their name to the region now known as Bulgaria.

Burmese. Inhabitants of Burma or speakers of one of the dialects of the Burmese language. Burmese constitutes a separate branch of the Sino-Tibetan stock, which also contains Chinese, Tibetan, and many other languages of southeast Asia. Racially as well they are similar to the Thai, southern Chinese, and others in southeast Asia. The Burmese people are highly developed agriculturalists, raising cereal grains along the drainage of the Irawaddy River and its tributaries. This river complex really constitutes Burma, as the borders of the country lie in the high mountains and open coast surrounding the rivers. The Burmese are strongly Buddhist, and the country abounds in shrines and temples. They have had a constitutional government since their separation from British rule in 1947. U Thant, a Burmese Prime Minister, was appointed Secretary General of the United Nations in 1961. The nation has over 25 million people.

Bushmen. A modern stone-age people of the South African desert. A branch of the Khoisan linguistic stock, the Bushmen are the descendants of peoples who have inhabited the southern portions of Africa for tens of thousands of years. They are nomadic hunters, living on the edge of survival. They were pushed from the plains into the desert by the expansion of the Bantu peoples less than 2000 years ago. See *Bantu*.

Catalans or **Catalonians.** The people inhabiting Catalonia, the northeastern division of Spain. They extend northward over the Spanish boundary into France, and their language, called Catalan, is distinct from both the Provençal of southern France and the Castilian of Spain. Castilians can understand the speech of Portuguese more easily than that of Catalans, and the rapid enunciation of the Catalan adds to the difficulty.

Caucasian. This term is usually used to refer to the so-called "white" or "European" race, though most modern anthropologists hold that such an inclusive racial category is almost meaningless. European peoples of today are divided into several separate races which grade into neighboring races outside of Europe. "Caucasian" was originally used in the belief that the peoples of the Caucasus mountains were the most typical representatives of the "race." It is to these peoples that the term is best applied, though as a linguistic term. There are some 4 million people who speak languages of the Caucasian stock, which is not related to Indo-European. Of these the best known is Georgian, in which written records go back some 1000 years.

Celts. A vague term which names the large group of peoples, of mixed race but using a common language, whose early home, about 1000 B.C., was in the upper valleys of the Rhine and the Danube. From this center they spread west, south, and east. One branch became the Galatians of Asia Minor; another, the Gauls of western Europe. In Italy, as early as the 4th century B.C., they made large settlements in the valley of the Po, a region from which afterward came Virgil, Catullus, and other men of note in Latin letters. In the East, they served as mercenaries in Africa and Asia. They were known to the ancients by many different names, and there seem to have been two distinct physical types among them, one tall and fair, the other short and dark. On the continent, the Celts succumbed to Roman and Germanic conquest. At the present day, they are represented most conspicuously by the Irish, the Welsh, and the Highland Scotch.

Chinese. In common use, the name of the inhabitants of the country of China but more properly referring also to the many Chinese-speaking peoples in China and scattered throughout the world. Racially, the peoples of China show many gradations from the burly, dark-skinned peoples of the north to the rather slight, light-skinned peoples of the south. The northerners appear to be most like their Manchurian and Mongolian neighbors, but the southerners are much more like the Thai or Malay. Except for small areas, one or another of the many dialects of Chinese is spoken throughout the realm. But these are often not mutually intelligible, so the Mandarin dialect serves as a common tongue for all educated Chinese. For over 2000 years up to the beginning of the 20th century, the major emphasis on Chinese life was upon the extended family and the clan; the major value was filial piety. An individual had very little freedom until he became a grandparent and head of his family group. The lessons of the past were regarded of more importance than the doubtful future. This is especially a tenet of the Confucian religion which dominated Buddhist and Taoist religions in classical China. Until this century, government was in the hands of local administrators appointed by the Imperial Court, the first of which predates 1800 B.C. The Chinese are noted for their acumen in business and commerce, and their commercial communities exist in most countries and all continents, though Hong Kong, Singapore, and Macao are the largest.

The impact of western civilization has been great, though turmoil has characterized this nation since the overthrow of the last Manchu dynasty in 1911. The value placed by the classical Chinese on family and on the past have made transition to the modern world difficult. The effort to industrialize has been sped up by the Communist government which took over rule from the Nationalists in 1949. Many of the latter followed their leader, Chang Kai-shek, to form a second Chinese nation on the island of Formosa (Taiwan). Estimates give over 800 million Chinese on the mainland, over 12 million on Formosa, and some 5 million scattered elsewhere.

Circassians. The name applied to people inhabiting the northwestern part of the Caucasus. Their name for themselves is *Adighe;* the Turks and Russians call them *Tcherkasses,* or "brigands." Both Circassian men and women are noted for physical beauty, and many Circassian girls entered Turkish harems. After the Russian conquest of their territory in 1864, several hundred thousand of them emigrated. Among the upper classes, Mohammedanism is the chief religion; among the lower classes, this is mixed with vestiges of earlier religions.

Copts. Followers of the Coptic rite of the Christian faith. They began by translating the scripture into Egyptian and other native languages of northeastern Africa, and broke from the mother Church in the 5th century. Egypt, Nubia, and Ethiopia all had large numbers of the Coptic faith. In the former two, the persecutions of Byzantium and the propagation of Islam almost erased the Coptic faith. Today there are perhaps 25,000 Egyptian Copts under the Patriarch of Alexandria, and the Sudan (Nubia) has far fewer. However, in Ethiopia the Coptic Church is the official state church and is independent of the Egyptian. See *Egypt, Ethiopia.*

Cossacks. The inhabitants of the southern and eastern frontiers of Russia. The most important of these communities were those of the Dnieper and the Don. Until the reign of Catherine II, they retained a certain degree of independence with a kind of democratic government, at the head of which was their "hetman." In lieu of taxes, they supplied the Russian empire with a most valuable military force of cavalry and scouts. In 1918 the Cossacks proclaimed a Republic of the Don, but they were later overrun by the Soviet forces.

Croatians. A southern Slavic people whose language differs but slightly from that of the Serbians, with whom they are commonly grouped as Serbo-Croatians. The Croatians are most numerous in Croatia, Slavonia, Dalmatia, and Bosnia, former provinces of the Austrian empire and now included in Yugoslavia.

Czechs. A northern group of the Slavic peoples who were living in Bohemia, Moravia, and Austrian Silesia as early as the 5th century. Their struggle against Habsburg tyranny started the Thirty Years' war. After the French Revolution they began a revival of their literature, a movement which became political in 1848. The Czechs united in 1918 with their neighbors, the Slovaks, to form the republic of Czechoslovakia.

Danes. A northern European tribe which, in the 5th century A.D., drove the Saxons and the Angles from Jutland and from the adjacent islands. Most of them remained in the country which has become Denmark, but others settled in England in the 9th and the 10th century.

Dorians. A race of people in ancient Greece who are believed to have come from the north and conquered the Peloponnesian peninsula before 1000 B.C. In Sparta, the leading Doric state, the conquerors held the subject population in rigorous servitude. Thence arose the conception of the Dorians as aristocratic and warlike in temper as opposed to the Ionian peoples, among whom the leading state was Athens, the extreme exponent of democracy.

Dravidians. The non-Aryan people who inhabit the southern part of India and Ceylon. They occupied the country before the coming of the Aryans. Their languages, of which there are more than a dozen, constitute a single group. Some of the tribes are of a very low type of civilization, but the Tamils and Telugus have attained a high culture and produced excellent literature and architecture. The religion of the Dravidians varies from rude nature worship to a borrowed Islamism or Hinduism.

Egyptians. The ancient Egyptians spoke a language of the Hamitic branch of the Afro-Asiatic stock. To them the world owes one of its two oldest centers of civilization and one of its two earliest written languages. Egyptians lost their national independence to the Romans in 30 B.C. With the spread of Islam in the 8th and 9th centuries, they almost all abandoned Coptic Christianity and adopted the Mohammedan faith and with it their own version of Arabic, a Semitic language of the same stock. In physical type, they are of the Mediterranean race. See *Copts, Egypt.*

Eskimos. The inhabitants of Arctic America, from the Bering Straits to Greenland. They were the last native people to enter the New World and show many similarities to the peoples of northeastern Siberia.

Ethiopians. The many and varied peoples of the country of Ethiopia. There are over 80 separate languages in Ethiopia, though all belong to either the Hamitic or the Cushitic branches of the Afro-Asiatic stock. The people grade from dark-skinned Mediterranean in the northeast to Sudanic in the west and to East African in the south. Culturally, most fall into three main groups. First are the Amhara and related peoples of the north. These are Coptic Christians, and they claim descent from the Queen of Sheba. They have ruled the north for many years and all of Ethiopia for the last hundred years. Second are the Gallas, several groups of pastoral peoples inhabiting the plains of the central, western, and southern regions. They are primarily Mohammedan, though some are pagans, and are noted warriors. Lastly, there are the highland agriculturalists of the western and southern regions; these are almost wholly pagan. See *Copts.*

Etruscans. An early people who inhabited Italy north of the Tiber, but whose culture and language were distinct from those of other Italian peoples. By some they are thought to have come from Asia Minor; by others, from Africa. They developed a considerable commerce and art, and at one time conquered Rome. The inscriptions left by them have not yet been deciphered.

Fellahs or **Fellahin.** The name by which the settled agricultural peoples of the Arab world are known, in contrast to the wandering Bedouin. It is more often applied to a class of agricultural laborers or peasants in Egypt and the Middle East.

Filipinos. The Malay inhabitants of the Philippine Islands. The earliest occupants of the islands are thought to have been the Negritos, or pygmy Negroes, about 25,000 of whom are still found in the interior of Luzon. At some remote period there occurred a series of Malay migrations. These immigrants scattered over the islands in small groups with different dialects and local customs. Like their modern descendants, such as the Igorots, they were headhunters and warriors. In the northern highlands of Luzon, some of them developed a remarkable system of irrigated mountain terraces for the cultivation of rice. Probably they brought with them a knowledge of ironworking.

Later Malay migrations brought the people represented by the three most important tribes of the present time, Visayans, Tagalogs, and Ilocanos, to whom the name Filipinos is often restricted. Of these, the Tagalogs, who are the most numerous of the inhabitants of Manila, central Luzon, and Mindanao, are the most highly civilized group. The Moros of the southern islands are Mohammedan Malays who followed the other migrations. Since the beginning of the Spanish occupation of the Philippines, intermarriage of Filipinos with Spaniards, Chinese, and Mexicans has produced a large group of mixed ancestry, called *mestizos,* who are the leaders in government and business. See *Philippines.*

Finns. The inhabitants of Finland and neighboring parts of Russia. They are linguistically related to the Hungarians and Estonians, as well as to the Lapps and other native Siberian peoples. Physically, they are northwestern European blended with northeastern European. The former probably came with the conquest of Finland by the Swedes in 1157, which also brought Christianity to the Finns. Though less than 5 million in number, they wrested independence from Russia in 1917, and have given the world the music of Jean Sibelius and their own classic epic, *Kalevala,* from which Longfellow borrowed the meter for his *Hiawatha.* See *Finland.*

Franks. A group of Germanic tribes which from the 3d century A.D. were allied with the Romans and, after the overthrow of the Empire, conquered Gaul. The Franks established a kingdom there under Clovis and gave their name to the country which we now call France.

Frisians. An ancient Germanic people who inhabited the extreme northwest of Germany between the mouths of the Rhine and Ems. They were subjected to the Roman

power under Drusus and were later subdued by the Franks. On the division of the Carlovingian empire, their country was divided into West Frisia (West Friesland) and East Frisia (East Friesland). The language of the Frisians is closely akin to the Anglo-Saxon. Our knowledge of the old Frisian is derived from certain collections of laws, called the "Asegabuch," composed about 1200. Modern Frisian is split into many dialects, but the greater part of its literature is written in West Frisian.

Gauls. See *Celts.*

Goths. A powerful German people who originally dwelt on the Prussian coast of the Baltic at the mouth of the Vistula. They later migrated to the south. About the beginning of the 3d century we find them separated into two great divisions: the Ostrogoths, or Eastern Goths; and the Visigoths, or Western Goths. The meaning of *Goth* is said to be "nobly born."

Gypsies. The English name for a series of wandering tribes of Europe and later of the Americas. They call their language *Romany,* and its basic words are linked to the Indo-Iranian family of Indo-European. Blood group analysis also suggests an Indian origin. Protected only in Scotland, the Gypsies have been persistently blamed for anything happening in their vicinity, from theft to witchcraft. In language and culture, each Gypsy group shows many traits of the host country in which it lives.

Hamites. Once used as a racial term (the descendants of Ham, son of Noah), this term refers more appropriately to the speakers of the languages of the Hamitic family of the Afro-Asiatic stock. As such, Hamites would include Berbers, Ancient Egyptians, Amharas, and others. See *Berbers, Egyptians, Ethiopians.*

Helvetii or **Helvetians.** An ancient Celtic people, who, in the 1st century B.C., lived in the country between the Rhone and Rhine rivers and between the Jura mountains and the Rhaetian Alps. Their territory was somewhat smaller than modern Switzerland. Cæsar opposed their migration into Gaul and drove them back into their mountains, with great slaughter. In the reign of Vitellius they were again mercilessly attacked. After this they disappeared from history.

Hindus. The name is commonly applied to all the inhabitants of India, but it properly indicates only the Aryan people of the north central portion of the peninsula. At a very early period, this people descended into India from the northwest and crowded the inhabitants, known as the Tamils, toward the south. The religion of the Hindus is the ancient Brahmanism, which dates from the period of the *Vedas.*

Hittites. This people appears in history at 2000 B.C. in central Asia Minor. Their language is classed by some as belonging to the Indo-European group, by others as a sister tongue derived from an older common source. The Hittite military empire competed with the Egyptian and Assyrian until its fall around 1200 B.C.

Hottentots. A people of South Africa, physically and linguistically related to the Bushmen though showing some admixture with the Bantus. It was from the latter that the Hottentot acquired cattle. The territory of the Hottentot has been much reduced, first by the Bantus and then by the Dutch settlers.

Huns. A people, probably of western Asian origin, who are first noticed in history about 375 A.D., when they moved westward into the Danube valley. A half century later they became the terror of Europe. Under their vigorous leader, Attila, whose boast it was that grass never grew again where his horse's hoofs had trod, they swept across the Rhine, burning and devastating. Their host included conquered Ostrogoths and many other tribes. The Romans and their allies, the Visigoths, Burgundians, and Franks, met and defeated the Huns at the battle of Châlons in 451. Within a few years they withdrew to Asia or mixed with their conquered tribes, leaving only their name as the synonym for barbarous cruelty.

Incas. A civilized people formerly inhabiting the highlands of Peru, Bolivia, and Ecuador. They were subjugated and almost exterminated by the Spaniards in the 16th century. Our knowledge of the people is derived mainly from accounts left by their conquerors. Like all other South American peoples, they had no written records. Their language survives, however, as *quechua,* which is spoken by several million people.

Inca builders showed a rare skill in the cutting and fitting of stone for their buildings, which were often of immense size although they had neither iron nor wheels. They were skilled also in the working of precious metals. They excelled in road building. From about 1100 to 1400 A.D., they built up an extensive empire.

Indians. See *American Indians, Hindus, Dravidians.*

Iranians. The settled Persian-speaking peoples of modern Iran, as opposed to the Kurdish tribesmen. See *Kurds.*

Irish. The name applied generally to the people of Ireland. In the population of the island, however, are included three physical types: (1) a short, dark-haired type, representing the primitive race; (2) a taller, blond type, representing the Tuatha De Danaan (tribe of the goddess Danu) of Irish tradition; (3) the Celtic, which is the dominating Irish type of the present day, representing that of a people who conquered the island probably within historic times.

Israelis. The population of the state of Israel. People of the Jewish faith, though of many races and nationalities, have added their numbers to the indigenous peoples of Israel. They number close to 3 million, and include 8 per cent Moslems and approximately 7 per cent other religions.

Japanese. The dominant population of the Japanese Islands, as opposed to the *Ainu,* the remnants of the aboriginal inhabitants. The Japanese speak a language unrelated to any other in the world, though in their writing they make frequent use of Chinese characters. Racially, they belong with the Koreans and Mongols, members of the classic mongoloid race.

Kazak. These are the nomads of the central Asian steppes, together with the Kirghiz and Kalmucks. All claim descent from Ghengis Khan. The Kazak and Kalmucks were horsemen exclusively; the Kirghiz also used the Yak. All were noted as fearless warriors. Today all have been to a large extent made farmers on Soviet or Chinese collective farms. The Kazak and Kirghiz are primarily Mohammedan; the Kalmuck exhibit Buddhist influence.

Kurds. A primarily nomadic people of Indo-Iranian language and physical type who live in Iraq, Iran, Turkey, and Afghanistan. They live their own lives, paying little attention to the rules of the country in which they live. They have a thin veneer of Mohammedan religion.

Lapps. The reindeer breeders of Arctic Scandinavia. They are closely related to the Finns, though lacking the industrial and political development of the latter. Nominal Christians, they still follow their older, Shamanistic religion.

Lithuanians and **Letts.** Peoples speaking languages of the Baltic family of Indo-European. Lithuanians are similar in culture to the Latvians and Estonians, but are historically of different origin. Alternately under domination from west or east, these two peoples and their Baltic neighbors have preserved their cultural independence.

Lombards. A Germanic people, originally from the region of the lower Elbe River. Not very numerous but of distinguished valor, they played an important part in the early history of Europe. The name may have been given with reference to their long beards. About the 2d century A.D., they seem to have begun to leave their original district and to have fought their way south and east till they came in close contact with the Eastern Roman Empire on the Danube and adopted an Arian form of Christianity. After having been for some time tributary to the Heruli, they raised themselves upon the ruins of their power and of that of the Gepidæ, shortly after the middle of the 6th century, to the position of masters of Pannonia and became one of the most wealthy and powerful nations in that part of the world. Under their king, Alboin, they invaded and conquered the northern and central parts of Italy (568–572). The conversion of the Arian Lombards to the orthodox faith was brought about by the policy of Gregory the Great and the zeal of Theodolinda, wife of Authari and subsequently of his successor, Agilulf (590–615). Charlemagne put an end to the Lombard kingdom in 774.

Magyars. The ancestral people of Hungary, whose descendants make up perhaps about two-thirds of the country's present population. They are of the same origin as the Finns, Hungarian being the other major branch of the Finno-Ugric linguistic stock. Western Asia is the most likely point of origin of the Magyars.

Malasians or **Malays.** The physically and linguistically related peoples of the Malayan peninsula and of the islands of Sumatra, Borneo, and Indonesia generally. Though of similar origin in southeast Asia, these people display marked cultural diversity. Speaking languages of the Malayan branch of the Macro-Malayopolynesian stock, they are also related to almost all of the Pacific Islanders.

Manchus. The Mongol or Tartar people who overran China in the 12th century and again in the 17th century. They established the dynasty which ruled China until their overthrow in 1911. They made the wearing of the *queue,* or single pigtail, mandatory for the Chinese as a sign of subjection to Manchu authority. See *China, Chinese, Tatars.*

Maoris. The native Polynesian people of the Islands of New Zealand. Unlike other Polynesians, the Maoris were once principally hunters, stalking the huge wingless bird, the Moa. These huge birds were hunted to extinction before the first European arrived at New Zealand, by which time the Maoris had returned to agricultural pursuits. To a great degree, the Maoris have kept pace with the progress of New Zealand.

Masai. These are a very tall, Sudanic speaking people of Kenya. Living by herding vast numbers of cattle, the Masai are noted warriors, lion hunters, and athletes. The majority of them have chosen to ignore the blandishments of 20th century civilization and steadfastly follow their traditional nomadic life.

Mayas or **Mayans.** A group of related peoples in southern Mexico and Guatemala. In pre-Columbian times, the Mayas had achieved a highly developed civilization, but since the conquest most have remained peasants under the domination of Spanish descendants.

The ancient Mayas had developed the arts and sciences to a degree unknown elsewhere in the New World. Their system of writing, as yet only partly understood, served as a basis for later Mexican writing. They erected many monumental buildings, especially temples. They had invented the cipher (zero) long before its use in Europe. Corn (maize) was almost certainly first cultivated by these people. The height of Mayan civilization lasted from perhaps 1000 B.C. to 1000 A.D., after which the Mayas came under the domination of the Toltecs. See *Toltecs.*

Minoans. Taken from the name of their legendary king Minos, this is the name given to the people of the Mediterranean island of Crete, especially during the period of their dominance in the area about 2500 to 1000 B.C. The language of the early Minoans does not seem to have belonged to the Indo-European group, but they later spoke a form of Greek. Some experts believe that a fragment of the Minoan population left Crete after its power had failed and established the five Philistine cities which oppressed the Biblical Hebrews.

Mongolians. This term used to apply to all Asiatic races and often American Indians as well. This was a mistaken application as there is far more diversity among Asian races than had been thought. Today the term is best applied racially to the "classic mongoloid" peoples, the Mongols themselves, the Koreans, and the Japanese.

Mongols. The native peoples of Mongolia, now politically divided into two states, Inner and Outer Mongolia. Most Mongols are nomadic herders, gathered into local bands under tribal chieftains. The Mongols produced two famous conquerors—Genghiz Khan and his grandson Kublai Khan. The former established a brief empire which extended from eastern Asia to the gates of Vienna; the latter established the first Manchu dynasty in China. Today, approximately 5 million Mongols live in western China, the eastern Soviet Union, and in the independent Republic of Outer Mongolia. The latter switched its primary allegiance from Communist China to Russia in the mid-1960's.

Moors. The people of Morocco, where the Arab conquerors of the 7th century mixed with the natives of the Roman province of Mauretania. The Spaniards designated as Moors the invaders of Spain in the 8th century, and the term was loosely extended to all Mohammedans of northern Africa. See *Morocco, Spain.*

Moravians. A Slavic people which in the 6th century displaced Germanic tribes in the valley of the Morava River, south of Silesia. In the mild climate of their district, they have a wide variety of agricultural products, and their flocks produce a fine quality of wool. In religion they are mostly Roman Catholic. After World War I, they were included in the republic of Czechoslovakia. See *Moravia.*

Negritos. The name, meaning "little negroes," has been applied to the small statured, frizzly-haired populations of Southeast Asia and the off-shore islands. India, Malaysia, the Philippines, and New Guinea all have such populations, and the Andaman Islands have only them. They are normal in all aspects save their stature. Their origins is still obscure, though probably of great antiquity. See *Filipinos.*

Negroes. This term has had many meanings. Coming from the Spanish and Portuguese *negro,* it stems from the Latin *niger,* black or dark. It was applied as early as the 15th century by the Portuguese to the dark-skinned peoples of Africa. Later it was extended to all people with some African ancestry. Thus applied to all sub-Saharan Africans and their descendants, the term is notably incorrect.

Traditionally, anthropologists have classified most of the peoples of the world in accordance with inherited physical characteristics as Negroid (dark-skinned), Caucasoid (white), and Mongoloid (yellow).

Negroid racial stock, in general, falls under two main subdivisions: African Negroids and Oceanic Negroids, inhabiting the Melanesian islands of the Pacific. A minor group, pygmy Negritos, inhabit areas of the Pacific.

In popular usage, Negro has had different meanings in different places. Throughout the United States, persons who are known to have a Negro ancestor are generally considered Negroes, even though their skins may be white. Some dark-skinned peoples—the aborigines of Australia and some ethnic groups of India—are not typified as Negroid; they include Negroid mixtures, but they are considered Caucasoid. In Latin America and some other areas, physical characteristics are considered of less importance than social or economic status.

The continent of Africa has several differing races, such as the Bantu, Forest Negroes, Sudanic, East African, and others. The New World populations with African ancestry also have many European ancestors and are typically distinct from any native African populations. The term Negro has more meaning when applied to the colored populations of North America, although it then cannot be applied to another human population. When used for people of African ancestry, the term becomes sociological and psychological, rather than clearly descriptive of physical category.

The black peoples first encountered by the Portuguese were well-organized kingdoms of West Africa, such as the Ashanti, the Dahomey, and the Yoruba of the Gold Coast and Nigeria. Such peoples were known to the ancient Hebrews and Egyptians. Slavery had been an active institution from these early ages and persisted into modern times. The slave trade was to become uneconomical with the expansion of trade and the spread of industrialization. But with the opening of the New World, a highly profitable slave trade was developed. The slave trade was the source of the Negroes of the New World. Slaves were brought to the Western Hemisphere to replace the Indian workers of Latin America who had been decimated by the Spanish. Negroes were also imported in large numbers to provide labor for the plantations of North America.

These African slaves, primarily Forest Negroes, were brought in large numbers to the Americas from the 16th to the 18th century. Those in South America were afforded some human rights through the Church; they were allowed the sacraments and families were treated as inseparable. In North America, the slave was little more than property. The entire pattern of southern agriculture was tied to slave labor. In some areas slaves were well treated, in others their treatment was brutal. From the earliest days the Negro slaves sought freedom, which finally became legally effective in the middle and late years of the 19th century in the various nations of America—in the United States after the Civil War and the passage of the 13th Amendment in 1866; in Brazil in 1871; in Puerto Rico in 1873; and in Cuba in 1880.

By 1860 there were some 4,400,000 Negroes in the United States, of whom only 400,000 were free citizens. At present, there are about 25 million Negroes in the United States; some 30 million in Latin America; 125,000 in Europe; and about 35,000 in Canada.

The 13th and 14th amendments to the U. S. Constitution gave the Negro nominal rights, but they were seldom given actuality except in the few years immediately following the Civil War. In spite of the strides taken by a few individuals, major advancement to full citizenship for the American Negro did not really begin until the mid-1950's with the several decisions of the Supreme Court against segregation, first in the schools and then in other places and accommodations.

Since World War I the Negro population of America has been leaving the South, seeking new occupational opportunities in the North and West. Here, too, they met antagonism and prejudice, which gradually yielded to legal pressure and changing attitudes.

The Negro has left his own particular mark upon American culture. While many Negroes have made major contributions to the arts and sciences, jazz music and the spiritual are uniquely American idioms, deriving principally from American Negro traditions.

Normans, Northmen, or **Norsemen.** The sea rovers from Scandinavia who, in the early Middle Ages, ravaged the coasts of England, Germany, and France and established themselves in various parts of western Europe and Russia. They were called Danes in England, where they gained a foothold in the 9th century, after having made settlements in Ireland. In the 11th century, Canute and two successors ruled England for about 25 years.

Meanwhile, other bands had settled in northern France and compelled the French king to give his daughter in marriage to Rollo, their chieftain. Rollo embraced Christianity and became Robert, first duke of Normandy. The name Norman is usually restricted to these settlers in France, who assimilated the culture, language, and religion of the Frankish kingdom. William, Duke of Normandy, led the Normans into England in 1066 and was known thereafter as William the Conqueror. Norman nobles also became rulers in southern Italy and in Sicily. Norsemen are believed the first Europeans to visit North America.

Parsees or **Parsis.** The modern followers of Zoroastrianism, which was the ancient religion of Persia. They are popularly called "fire worshipers," but to this designation they strongly object, since the fire to them is simply one of the emblems of the power of their god Ormuzd. Their beliefs have changed somewhat since ancient times, but they are still scrupulously careful about purification.

After the Mohammedan invasion of Persia in the 7th century, several bands of Zoroastrians emigrated to India, and from these have sprung the Parsi communities of present-day India. They are most numerous in the vicinity of Bombay. They are leaders among Oriental peoples in education.

Philistines. A Semitic-speaking people of the Middle East. Mentioned in the Old Testament as a neighboring people to the Israelites, today few Philistines still exist, living primarily in Israel and secondarily in Jordan.

Picts. The early inhabitants of the northern part of Great Britain. They were called Caledonians by the Romans, the name Picts being given later because of their custom of painting the skin. The origin of this people is uncertain. They carried on continual warfare with the Romans, who built long walls to keep them out of the southern provinces. In the 7th century the Saxons came into conflict with them. After their conversion to Christianity, their king Angus MacFergus ruled all Scotland for a period in the early part of the 8th century. About the beginning of the 9th century, they disappeared as a separate people, leaving no literature and but scanty traces of their language.

Polynesians. The name applied to the inhabitants of the eastern Pacific Islands from New Zealand in the southwest to Hawaii in the northeast. All are physically similar and speak similar languages. Polynesia was the last area of the Pacific to be occupied in historic times, these peoples having settled there in the first few centuries A.D.

The origins of the Polynesians lie in Southeast Asia or Indonesia, to whose original occupants the Polynesians are far closer than they are to the Micronesians or Melanesians. The Polynesian peoples are sailors of renown and good fishermen, but their basic staples are tree and root crops. The exception to this pattern were the Maoris, who spent several centuries as hunters of a bird, the Moa. Polynesian contact with South American civilizations certainly did occur, and even perhaps with the civilizations of Mexico. However, no significant immigration from the New World occurred, as shown by evidence of language, race, and culture.

Pygmies. The term applied to a number of widely varied human populations. Pygmy is best applied to the small-statured, frizzly-haired peoples of the Congo rainforests of Africa, as opposed to the Negrito populations of southeast Asia. The African pygmy lives in symbiotic relationship with the surrounding peoples. He exchanges his hunted meats for many more calories of agricultural products. Each side gets what it wants.

Two theories of pygmy origin conflict. One states that the pygmies are a very old population, having inhabited the Congo area for tens of thousands of years. The other proposes that they are a late adaptation to crowding and reduced food supply. In either case, the pygmy is very unlike the small-statured populations of Asia. See *Negrito.*

Rumanians. A people of mixed race who, since the 12th century, have occupied the territory north of the lower Danube and the slopes of the Transylvanian Alps. Most of them now live in Rumania, although there are scattered communities throughout the Balkans. They speak a Romance language which closely resembles the Latin. Scholars now believe that the Roman colonists of the Province of Dacia, established along the lower Danube by Trajan, withdrew to the Illyrian coast before the inroads of barbarians but later re-entered the Danube country, preserving their Latin speech in spite of mingling with Slavic, Greek, and Turkish peoples. See *Rumania.*

Samoans. The Polynesian people of the Samoan Islands. See *Polynesians.*

Saracens. A name derived from an Arabic word meaning "rise." It was applied in the 1st century A.D. to a tribe in northwestern Arabia. Later, the name was used by medieval writers to designate all Mohammedans.

Saxons. A Germanic people first heard of in the 2d century A.D. as inhabiting what is now southern Denmark. They migrated southward, subdued all northwestern Germany, and invaded the Roman Empire. In the 5th century they invaded Normandy, and, in that and the next century, many settled in England. The Saxon strain is very prominent in the modern population both of Germany and of England.

Scots. Scotland takes its name from a group of Gaelic invaders, called Scots or Dalriads, who came from Ireland in the 3d or the 4th century A.D. The strongest of the earlier inhabitants were the Picts, also a Celtic people. The Angles, or English, early established a kingdom in southern Scotland, and Scandinavian immigrants were mingled with these people of the Lowlands as well as with the Highlanders. In many parts of North and West Scotland, known as the Highlands, a Gaelic tongue is spoken; the dialect of the South and East Lowlands is a mixture of English and Scandinavian speech. See *Picts*; *Scotland.*

Scythians. An ancient nomadic warrior people, famous as horsemen and bowmen, who inhabited what is now southwestern Russia. Herodotus and other Greek writers describe this wandering tribe as living in tent-covered wagons. They were conquered by neighboring tribes and disappeared from European history in the 2nd century B.C. The name Scythian was later used loosely for any northern and central Asiatic tribes.

Semites. Properly referring to the speakers of the Semitic family of the Afro-Asiatic stock, Semite is more often applied to any people of the Middle East and, most restrictively and inaccurately, to persons of the Jewish faith. The Semitic peoples are those who speak Arabic or Hebrew today, though in ancient times the group included the Sumerians, Babylonians, Assyrians, and many other of the ancient civilized peoples of the Middle East. See *Arabs, Israelis.*

Serbians or **Serbs.** The group of southern Slavic peoples who occupy the former kingdom of Serbia and neighboring lands of Croatia, Bosnia, and Dalmatia. They joined with the Croats and Slovenes in 1918 to form the Kingdom of Yugoslavia. The term Serbo-Croatian is frequently used to include the Serbs and Croats, who differ only slightly in language. The Croats are Roman Catholics, while the Serbs are mostly of the Greek Catholic faith. An interesting national characteristic of the Serbs is the love of all classes for their legends, ballads, and romances about old national heroes. See *Croatians, Yugoslavia.*

Sicilians. The earliest known inhabitants of Sicily were the Siculi, who gave their name to the island. In historic times, Phoenicians, Greeks, Romans, Saracens, Normans, Germans, French, and Italians have at different times ruled and colonized Sicily. The Sicilians have long had an unenviable reputation for turbulence and violence, a temper probably the result of centuries of backward economic and social conditions due to the repeated struggles of many nations for possession of the island.

Singhalese or **Ceylonese.** The native peoples of the island of Ceylon, off the Indian coast. The Singhalese language is derived from Hindi, the Indo-European language of India. But there are many other languages spoken on Ceylon, notably of the Tamil group from eastern India. The people of Ceylon display much of the racial diversity of India and Pakistan, whence most of its peoples came.

Slavs. This term refers to the speakers of the Slavic languages—Russian, Serbo-Croatian, Czech, Bulgarian, and Polish plus many smaller languages. It is also used to refer to the peoples of the Northeastern European race, sometimes called Slavic. Probably originating near the Baltic, the Slavs seem to have had two major migrations. One, about the 4th century A.D., took many of these people down to and along the Danube Valley and across the mountains to the Adriatic. A second migration was to the east, where they displaced other peoples and founded the nucleus of the many Russian peoples.

Slovaks. The Slavic people who for several centuries maintained an independent kingdom on the south side of the Carpathians and in the 9th century formed the basis of the Moravian state. Conquered by the Magyars, many of them became scattered over Hungary. After World War I they united with the Czechs in the republic of Czechoslovakia. The Slovak dialect possesses numerous very beautiful popular songs, many of which have been collected and published. See *Czechs, Czechoslovakia.*

Slovenians or **Slovenes.** The Slavic people who, from the 6th century, have lived in the southern districts of the former Austrian empire, reaching to the Adriatic. Most of them have been included in Yugoslavia. They possess in their language some of the earliest Slavic writings. Their name is a survival of the ancient name for Slavs. It probably means "speaking," or "those who speak," as the ancient Slavs called foreigners "the dumb," that is, those not speaking the Slavic language.

Sumerians. The citizens of the world's first known civilization, dating from before 4000 B.C. In the fertile crescent of the Tigris and Euphrates rivers, ancient Sumeria developed food production, monumental architecture, a central state and religion, and a high degree of skill in the arts and sciences. The first writing and the first use of metals came from the Sumerians.

Syrians. The name is often used as a generic term for all peoples of the eastern Mediterranean. The ancient Syrians were the descendants of the Phoenicians. Mixed with other peoples, they were primarily Mohammedan in faith in the Middle Ages. The modern Syrians are even more mixed in background, having incorporated Roman and Crusader, Arab and Turk, Greek and Egyptian, Frenchman and Kurd. The republic of Syria today is strongly pan-Arab in orientation. The coastal Syrians are noted for their commercial enterprise, though a nomadic, herding life prevails in the interior.

Tatars or **Tartars.** The true Tatars appear to have been a tribe of Mongols who lived in the 9th century along the upper Amur River in Asia. They later formed part of the horde led by Genghis Khan, and the name came to be applied to all Mongols. Their fierceness is said to have given rise to the notion that they came from Tartarus, Latin for hell; hence the familiar name for them, Tartars. See *China, Mongols.*

Toltecs. An Indian tribe of Mexico, dominant in central Mexico before the Aztecs from the 9th to the 13th centuries. They are known primarily from archaeological discoveries and no equation to living Indians is regarded as reliable. Their most famous ruins are the constellation of temples and other monumental buildings at Teotihuacan, in the Valley of Mexico. Here the Pyramid of the Sun is the largest human structure yet excavated. See *Mexico, Mayans, Aztecs.*

Vandals. A people, closely related to the Goths. whose early home was along the southern shore of the Baltic Sea. During the first four Christian centuries, they moved southward and then westward into Gaul. They swept through Spain in the 5th century and established a kingdom in northern Africa, thence invading Italy. They were overthrown in 534 by the troops of Justinian under Belisarius. Later, they were converted from Arianism to the orthodox Catholic faith. Their reputed cruelty and destructive methods in warfare gave us the word vandal.

Vietnamese. The various peoples of North and South Viet-Nam, diverse in language and culture. Annamite and Chinese dialects are prevalent in the north, Vietnamese and French in the south. The people range from the simple Montaignard tribesmen of the interior to the highly educated, French speaking elite of Saigon. The Vietnamese are primarily Buddhist, with a large Roman Catholic minority.

Visigoths. The West Goths, who, at the first approach of the Huns in the Danube valley in the 4th century, were allowed by the Romans to settle in Roman territory south of the Danube. Having learned their power in battle with the Roman legions, they moved westward through Greece to the valley of the Po. In 410 they conquered and plundered the city of Rome, sparing the churches at the command of Alaric, their young leader. After his death in southern Italy, they moved into Gaul and northern Spain, founding a Visigothic kingdom with its capital at Toulouse. Under their king Theodoric, they aided in defeating Attila and the Huns in 451. But the Franks drove them from Gaul in 507. They re-established themselves in Spain, with a capital at Toledo. When the Arabs invaded and seized the greater part of Spain in the 8th century, the Visigoths retired to the mountains and founded the modern states of Spain and Portugal.

Walloons. The modern descendants of the ancient Belgae mentioned by Cæsar, occupying the southern part of Belgium and some districts in France. Their mother tongue is a French dialect. The name Walloons, which means "strangers," was given them by the Dutch, when in 1567 large numbers of the Protestant population fled to Holland. From there, a company of them emigrated to America in 1624, settling on the Hudson near Albany and on the Delaware near Gloucester, N.J. They were the first white people to till the soil of New Netherlands. See *Belgians, Belgium.*

Welsh. The Celtic people of Wales. They are the descendants of the Brythonic Celts who occupied Britain when the Anglo-Saxons entered the island. They are most closely related to the Celtic people of Brittany. See *Bretons, Wales.*

Zulus. A Bantu people who now occupy a district in the northeast part of Natal, South Africa. They are chiefly herdsmen, but they also raise crops of millet, corn, sweet potatoes, and tobacco. They are of fine physical build and are formidable soldiers. Their dwellings are thatched and plastered huts of beehive form, which they arrange in a circular group, or kraal, with their cattle in the center. At the beginning of the 19th century, they controlled a large part of southeast Africa by means of a splendid military organization. They maintained their independence until 1883–84, when the British annexed their territory.

WORLD WAR I

The immediate occasion of the World War of 1914–18 was the assassination of a Habsburg prince in a remote city of Austria-Hungary, but the real causes lay far deeper, and reached far back into the past. The century-long rivalry of French and Germans, the aspirations of united Germany for a position as a world power, her fear of the pressure of the Russian glacier, ever crowding west and south, the commercial rivalry of Great Britain and Germany, the unrest of the smaller states and of racial minorities,—all had contributed to set up stresses and strains which were sure to fracture the thin crust of international peace when the occasion arose.

There had been other world wars, such as the Seven Years' war of 1756–63, or the Napoleonic wars, but in sheer magnitude the war of 1914–18 dwarfed all that had gone before. In the end it embattled twenty-eight nations, embracing more than nine-tenths of the entire population of the globe.

German Pre-War Policy. Racial rivalry was one of the causes of the war, and in its earliest phase the conflict was a clash of Pan-German and Pan-Slavic aspirations in the region of the Balkans. But the World War was more than a conflict of Teuton and Slav. Germany, united under the house of Hohenzollern and allied to the Habsburg empire of Austria-Hungary, controlled Central Europe. The Germans had gained that position by war, and it was natural that they should think that war was a paying business. Yet, mighty as was Germany's power, the Germans were not content with their position in the world. To spread German "kultur" and German rule became the ardent desire of millions of Germans. Many writers emphasized Germany's need for expansion to furnish an outlet for German population and energies. Not a few openly proclaimed that this expansion must be obtained by conquest. Great efforts even were made to prevent German emigrants to other countries forgetting their loyalty to their Fatherland.

Alliances with other powers were builded to strengthen the German position. The Dual Alliance of 1879 with Austria-Hungary was broadened in 1882 into the Triple Alliance by the inclusion of Italy. Unfortunately Bismarck's policy of a good understanding with Russia was neglected. Much attention was paid to cultivating friendly relations with Turkey, and this policy proved fruitful. Geographical factors counted here. Germany in a general war would be exposed to attack from both east and west. Whether for attack or for defense, she must be ready to strike hard and swiftly in either direction. For this reason the German army must be made— and was made—the strongest in Europe.

French and German Antagonism. It had been a principle of French policy since Louis XIV to keep Germany disunited and helpless; and German particularism and rivalries had helped her opponents. In the Franco-Prussian war of 1870–71 Germany had become united and had inflicted a humiliating defeat on France. Ever since that conflict her people had dreamed of revenge and of regaining their lost provinces of Alsace-Lorraine. The increasing population of Germany and the static population of France was also making Germany increasingly dangerous should she, as some Germans wished, attack France again. France needed allies; hence the Dual Alliance.

Germany and Great Britain. In the last analysis, the rivalry that had developed between these two peoples arose out of the fact that one was already what the other wished to become. The British had entered early into the work of Empire building, and had arrived. The Germans entered the race very late. Having already acquired all that she desired, Great Britain coveted nothing that Germany possessed, but in course of time she came to have an uneasy feeling that Germany was becoming a menace to her position in the world. The development of German industry was cutting into British markets; the increase of her commerce and merchant marine was making her a dangerous rival in world trade. The open declarations of hostility by some Germans tended to deepen British distrust. Worst of all was the increase in the German navy. For Great Britain, control of the sea-routes by her own navy was vital; Germany, Great Britain thought, was under no such necessity. Great Britain increased her navy accordingly.

Fear of Germany had already brought about an important diplomatic revolution. For centuries Great Britain and France had been rivals, but common dread of Germany led, about 1904, to the forming of the *Entente Cordiale* between the two nations. In 1891, as a makeweight against the Triple Alliance, France and Russia had formed the Dual Alliance. Differences between Great Britain and Russia were now composed, for Germany seemed to have become a greater danger to the Empire than Russia, and the *Entente Cordiale* was broadened into the Triple Entente. The Entente powers said their purpose was purely defensive; the Germans called it an "encirclement" and grew restive. These alliances meant a balance of power, and to that extent made for peace; on the other hand they made it inevitable that, if war ever began, all would be drawn in.

The Balkan Problem. In 1909 Austria-Hungary, without consulting the other interested powers, annexed Bosnia and Herzegovina, former Turkish provinces over which she had held a protectorate since 1878. These provinces were largely Serb in population, so Austria-Hungary's action was a blow to the desires of the Serbians for national unity. In 1912 and 1913 came the Balkan wars. The result was a great increase in the territory and strength of Serbia, although the creation of Albania cut her off from the Adriatic. Serbia had the sympathy and support of Russia, who had never lost sight of her old desire to control Constantinople (Istanbul) and the Straits. A general European war was narrowly averted by the efforts of Great Britain and Germany, but Teutonic prestige in the Balkans suffered, and the hostility of Austria-Hungary and Serbia increased.

The Immediate Occasion of the War. On June 28, 1914, Archduke Francis Ferdinand, heir apparent to the Habsburg monarchy, and his morganatic wife, were assassinated while on a visit to Sarajevo, the capital of Bosnia. The murderers were Habsburg subjects of Serbian blood. Later investigations showed that the plot had been formed in Serbia by a powerful Pan-Serbian secret society, the Narodna Odbrana, and included some Serbians, one a member of the Serbian general staff. Count Berchtold, the Austrian premier, thought he saw the opportunity to settle scores with Serbia once and for all. The German government rashly promised to support Austria-Hungary, unfortunately without knowing the details or full extent of Berchtold's plans. On July 28 the Austrian government dispatched to Serbia an ultimatum demanding reparation and suppression of the Pan-Serbian movement in a form which meant Austrian intervention in Serbian domestic affairs. An answer was demanded within forty-eight hours.

From the outset the dangerous possibilities of the situation were apparent in the European chancelleries, and the Great Powers, especially England, were at work to prevent war, or at least to localize it. Germany, whose influence at Vienna was the greatest, was hampered by the "blank check" she had already given, and her efforts to restrain Austria came too late. The Serbian reply conceded almost everything, in form, but it made no difference. Austria-Hungary rejected her answer, broke off diplomatic relations, and on the 28th declared war.

Now the effect of the alliances began to appear. Along with it came the influence of the general staffs in Russia, Germany, and France, none of whom wished to lose the advantage of speedy mobilization. But mobilization meant war. Russian interests could not allow Serbia to be crushed. On July 26 she began premobilization measures; on July 29 she mobilized against Austria-Hungary. Germany could not allow Austria-Hungary to be defeated. On July 31, she demanded that Russia cease her war preparations and peremptorily asked France to state her position. On August 1, Germany declared war against Russia, and France ordered mobilization. On August 3 Germany declared war against France. On August 2 Sir Edward Grey assured France of the assistance of the British fleet in the North Sea and the Channel.

British doubts were resolved by the German invasion of Belgium. German military strategy had long planned, in the event of a war on two fronts, an overwhelming attack upon France before Russia could mobilize. But the Franco-German frontier was strongly protected by nature and art, and military opinion had long foreshadowed a movement through Belgium by one side or the other. Belgium's neutrality had been guaranteed by treaties, but the German government pleaded a "state of necessity." On August 2 they demanded the right to cross Belgium, alleging that France intended to march through the country, and offering guarantees and indemnity. Belgium replied (August 3) that she would defend her neutrality, and King Albert appealed for aid to Great Britain.

On August 4 Sir Edward Grey sent an ultimatum to Berlin demanding that Germany should immediately promise to respect the neutrality of Belgium. The German chancellor Bethman-Hollweg expressed regret that Great Britain should go to war "just for a word . . . just for a scrap of paper," but he refused to give the promise.

Comparison of the Combatants. In area the Entente Powers were very much superior to the Central Powers; in population and wealth about double. On land, Germany had an army of 5,400,000, war strength, splendidly organized; the Russian army was about equal, but poorly organized; the French, somewhat less but on a par with Germany. Austria-Hungary's army of 3,600,000 was much less efficient than Germany's. The armies of the smaller powers were insignificant in comparison. Great Britain's regular army amounted to 137,000 men, besides territorials and colonial forces. The Central Powers possessed an immense military advantage because their position, while it exposed them to attack on two sides, enabled them to fight on interior lines.

The German navy was greatly superior to the combined forces of France and Russia, but Great Britain brought into the conflict the mightiest fleet ever built up to that time. For many years it had been her policy to maintain a navy superior to that which any two powers combined could bring against her. Furthermore the combined fleets of France and Russia were much superior to that of Austria-Hungary, but the Russian fleets were bottled up in the Baltic and Black Sea.

The Invasion of Belgium and France. The best chance for the Central Powers to win was to make the war a short one, getting a decision before the superior naval strength of the Allies and the inevitable blockade could do their work. The German high command, therefore, planned to throw an immense army against France through Belgium and Luxemburg, the latter also a neutral state, and crush her before Russia could be ready. To the Austro-Hungarian forces and to a few German army corps was left the task of holding the eastern front.

The first German troops to enter Belgium crossed the frontier on August 3. Their objective was the city of Liége, whose forts commanded the railway lines that must be used in any invasion of France

from the northeast. The German heavy artillery broke the ring of forts, and Liége fell on the 7th. The Germans pushed on to the heart of Belgium. Brussels was captured on the 20th and the main Belgian army moved north to defend Antwerp. Detaching a small force to keep the Belgians in check, the main German army moved south to the French frontier.

The French meanwhile had attempted a generally unsuccessful invasion of Aisace and Lorraine. The strength of the movement through Belgium had been underestimated by General Joffre, the French commander in chief, and the forces along the Belgian border were inadequate, though reinforced by two British army corps under the command of Field Marshall Sir John French. The defenses of Namur were crushed by the German 42-centimeter howitzers, and by the 23d of August the invaders had won control of the passages over the Meuse and Sambre.

The French around Charleroi were forced back. The little British army around Mons held back the German right wing under General von Kluck until the 24th. Then, outnumbered and outflanked, the corps commanders, Generals Haig and Smith-Dorrien, began a stubborn retreat. The Germans pursued with unprecedented rapidity, making use of motor transport.

On August 27 it was announced that the French government had been reconstituted on a war basis. General Galliéni was appointed governor of Paris, and preparations for a siege were hurriedly made. On the 30th a German airplane dropped bombs upon the city. The government was hastily removed to Bordeaux, and a large part of the civil population fled, but French morale continued good.

Meanwhile the French and British armies on the northern front fell back southward, pivoting on the great fortress of Verdun—swinging back upon Paris like a door. On the 17th the German right was within 17 miles of Paris, but, instead of stopping to besiege the city, the Germans turned southeastward after their true objective, the retreating Allied armies.

First Battle of the Marne. The French retreat had been calculated strategy on the part of General Joffre, who was determined to fight the decisive battle on ground of his own choosing. Von Kluck's movement to the southeast (ordered by von Moltke, the commander in chief) had exposed his right flank to an attack from Paris. Urged by Galliéni, Joffre now halted his retreat, and, on September 5, the Allied armies, on a front of 180 miles from Paris to Verdun, turned upon the invaders and began the battle of the Marne. The French efforts were directed to defeating and rolling up the German right wing under von Kluck, which was now over-extended, and had been weakened by the withdrawal of troops for the eastern front; that of the Germans, to breaking through the French center. In defending his exposed flank against Galliéni's attack (at a critical moment, that general commandeered all the taxicabs in Paris to bring out his reserve) von Kluck opened a gap between the First and Second armies. The French broke through, and the Germans were forced to retreat. The battle of the Marne stopped the first German drive, and, as the event proved, decided the war. The German retreat was skillfully conducted, with small losses, and their army now took position behind the river Aisne.

The fighting now moved north. The Germans had already taken Maubeuge; they now attacked Antwerp. The "Big Bertha's" (42-centimeter howitzers) smashed through the defenses, and on October 9 the city surrendered. Their next move was toward Dunkirk and Calais. They were opposed by a mixed force of British and colonial troops, the remains of the Belgian army under King Albert, and French reinforcements, the whole commanded by General Ferdinand Foch. The Allies won this "race to the sea" by a narrow margin. When, after six weeks of desperate fighting the battle died down, they still held a small corner of southwestern Belgium.

The battle in the west now resolved itself into a warfare of trenches, each side holding a front of more than 400 miles from Switzerland to the North Sea. Until almost the end of the war, this condition of stalemate was to continue.

First Battles on the Eastern Fronts. Meanwhile, great events had been taking place on the eastern front. Although the main Teutonic effort had been in the west, the Austro-Hungarians massed about a million men in Galicia and undertook an invasion of Poland from the southwest.

But the Russians managed to mobilize their forces more rapidly than had generally been considered possible. Under the skilled generalship of the Russian commander in chief, the grand duke Nicholas, immense forces were hurled against the Austrians in Galicia, while by way of diversion in favor of hard-pressed France, two armies totaling about 250,000 men undertook an invasion of East Prussia.

For a time the Russians carried all before them. The Germans were defeated at Gumbinnen, and the Russians ravaged the country. To hold the Russians in check, several army corps were hastily detached from the western front and were hurried to meet the Muscovites. This was a serious military blunder, since the presence of these troops on the Marne might have changed the result.

To command the German forces in East Prussia a new general was selected, General Paul von Hindenburg, a veteran of the wars of 1866 and 1870. The new leader had made a careful study of the country which he was now called upon to defend, and he enjoyed the assistance of a capable chief of staff, General von Ludendorff. On August 26 began what is generally known as the battle of Tannenberg. Von Hindenburg's plan was masterly, resembling that of Hannibal at Cannæ. After four days of fighting, the Russians attempted to retreat, but they were hopelessly involved in a labyrinth of lakes and swamps, and their army was almost annihilated.

Meanwhile a vast and complicated conflict was being fought out in southern Poland and Galicia. Here the outnumbered Austro-Hungarians were badly defeated. Lemberg was captured; by September 16 the Russians claimed to have taken 250,000 prisoners, besides immense quantities of supplies and cannon. Siege was laid to Przemysl, and Hungary was in danger.

The blow dealt Austria-Hungary at this time was a staggering one and might have proved fatal had not the Germans rendered aid. Von Hindenburg advanced through Silesia into Poland, while the Austrians moving forward from Krakow succeeded in raising the siege of Przemysl. By a sudden dash the Germans almost captured Warsaw. Again assuming the offensive, the Russians drove von Hindenburg back toward Silesia and the Austrians to Krakow and again laid siege to Przemysl. To effect a diversion in behalf of their western allies, the Russians also attempted a new invasion of East Prussia. In November another German attempt to take Warsaw failed, and another attempt to relieve Przemysl was foiled. In February 1915 von Hindenburg concentrated about 200,000 men in East Prussia and fell like a thunderbolt upon the inferior Russian army. In this conflict, known as the battle of the Masurian Lakes, the Russians were almost annihilated and suffered losses almost equal to those at Tannenberg. He followed up this victory by an invasion of Poland from the north, but after bitter fighting was repulsed.

Meanwhile the Russians had continued to besiege the great fortress camp of Przemysl in Galicia. Repeated Austrian efforts to relieve the fortress were foiled. On March 22 the fortress surrendered. The prisoners taken numbered over 119,000, the greatest number that had ever surrendered at one time in warfare. The grand duke Nicholas followed up this great victory by a drive designed to capture the passes of the Carpathians.

On the Seas. As was generally expected by naval experts, the control of the high seas was immediately seized by the Entente Allies. German and Austrian merchant ships either sought safety in home ports or in those of neutral powers or were captured by the enemy. In the Mediterranean the Austrian navy took refuge in home ports on the Adriatic, while the German protected cruiser *Breslau* and the giant battle cruiser *Goeben* managed to evade French and British pursuers and steamed up the Dardanelles and through the Sea of Marmora to Istanbul, where they played an important part in bringing Turkey into the war on the Teutonic side.

Just before the war began, the main British battle fleet had assembled at Spithead for maneuvers. The admiralty had held them there and had them ready at the critical moment. The German fleet retired behind the fortified island of Helgoland, and there, protected by mine fields and heavy guns of their land forts, they were safe from attack.

At the outbreak of the war, German naval vessels scattered in various parts of the world at once began to prey upon Allied commerce. The most famous of these, the *Emden*, in three months captured over a score of merchant ships. On November 9, 1914, while attempting to destroy a wireless station on one of the Cocos islands, she was destroyed by a much more powerful Australian cruiser, the *Sydney*.

The largest German fleet outside of European waters was the Pacific squadron, commanded by Admiral von Spee. It consisted of the armored cruisers *Scharnhorst* and *Gneisenau*, the light cruisers *Dresden*, *Nürnberg*, and *Leipzig*, and an armed liner. After destroying a number of allied vessels, they met, off Coronel, Chile, on November 1, a British squadron of two armored cruisers and two lighter ships. The British commander, Vice Admiral Sir Christopher Cradock, decided to give battle. The two British cruisers, the *Good Hope* and *Monmouth*, were sunk; the other two vessels escaped in the darkness. The British admiralty hurriedly sent a powerful British squadron southward, under the command of Vice Admiral Sturdee. This squadron, two battle cruisers, two armored cruisers, and some lighter cruisers, met the German squadron off Port Stanley, in the Falkland islands. Only the *Dresden* escaped; she was destroyed later in neutral waters near the island of Juan Fernandez.

Events in the North Sea. The British grand fleet was based on Scapa Flow, in the Orkneys; the German, as has been said, on Helgoland. Each wisely refused to attack the other in its fortified base. It was the British policy to keep the German fleet off the high seas, meantime preserving their own fleet for the defense of Great Britain; it was the German policy to whittle down the superior British fleet, if possible, by floating mines, Zeppelins, and U-boat attacks until they could risk a fleet action.

This policy of attrition at first had some success. The Germans sowed floating mines, illegal by international law, but later the Allies adopted the same practice. One British dreadnaught, the *Audacious*, (October 27, 1914), some smaller warcraft, and many merchant vessels were sunk in this way. The Zeppelins were practically useless. But the submarines were more effective. Their greatest success was on September 22, 1914, when three British cruisers, the *Aboukir*, *Cressy*, and *Hogue*, were sunk by one submarine, the *U-29*, commanded by Captain Lieutenant Otto Weddingen.

The first important naval battle of the war took place on August 28, 1914, in Helgoland Bight, the German losses amounting to three light cruisers and a destroyer.

In November and December the Germans raided the English coast without material results. In January a German raiding squadron met a superior British force and lost the armored cruiser *Blücher*. It soon became evident that the policy of whittling down would not succeed. British dockyards were building ships faster than the Germans could sink them.

The Allied Blockade. Meantime the Allies sought to make use of their sea power to cut off the communications of the Central Powers with the rest of the world. The right of blockade was well established under international law, provided a real and not a "paper" blockade was maintained. But with their own ports closed the Central Powers were still able to carry on trade with Switzerland, Holland, and Denmark, and with Norway and Sweden across the Baltic. The quantity of goods directly obtainable in this way was comparatively small, but an effort quickly developed to use the neighboring neutral states for transshipment from other countries.

At first the Entente powers did not attempt to exclude all goods, but limited their efforts to certain "contraband" articles of distinctly warlike nature. Early in the war, however, they began to extend the list of contraband articles, and to seize them even when consigned to a neutral port. International law on this point was not so clear, but they could cite the practice of the United States during the Civil War.

Food, by international law, was only "conditionally" contraband, that is, if destined for the armed forces. With that excuse a German raider sank an American sailing ship, the *William P. Frye*, carrying a cargo of grain consigned "to order" at British ports which were fortified naval bases. Late in January 1915, the German government took all supplies of grain and flour under government control and established a rationing system. This gave their enemies a pretext for declaring all food contraband.

On October 2, 1914, Great Britain announced that she would lay mines in designated areas in the North Sea. A month later she declared the whole sea a military area, and warned neutral vessels against entering it without stopping at a British port for sailing directions.

On February 4, the German Government announced that, by way of retaliation against the English policy, all waters around the British Isles would be treated as within the "zone of war," and that "all enemy merchant vessels encountered in these waters will be destroyed, even if it will not always be possible to save their crews and passengers."

Neutrals protested against this decree, but the Germans persisted in their course, and sank several vessels, including the *Lusitania*. An extended controversy followed, and Germany for a while modified her policy, but without yielding on the principle.

On March 11, 1915, by way of retaliation for the German submarine decree, the British government issued an order in council establishing a virtual blockade of Germany, though the word "blockade" was not used. Thenceforth all goods of every kind were to be kept out of Germany, and neutral goods destined for Germany, if not contraband, were, when seized, to be purchased by the captors instead of confiscated. All German goods, wherever found, were to be confiscated.

Their control of the high seas enabled the Allies to conquer the German colonies. Japan declared war on Germany on August 23, 1914, and a Japanese expedition, aided by a small British contingent landed in Shantung and captured the German fortress of Tsing-Tao (November 7, 1914). Japanese warships also captured the Caroline Islands and other German possessions in that region, while Australasian forces took German Samoa, New Guinea, and other islands in that part of the world. In Africa the French and British speedily overran Togoland and, by February 1916, completed the conquest of Kamerun. In South Africa dissatisfied Boers attempted a revolt against British rule but were soon put down. An expedition from South Africa, led by Premier Botha, with General Jan C. Smuts as second in command, invaded German Southwest Africa and conquered it. In German East Africa more resistance was encountered, and a small German force managed to hold out until the end of the war.

Turkey Enters the War. As a part of the "Drang nach Osten," the eastward movement exemplified by the Baghdad railway, German diplomatic influence had been steadily increasing at Istanbul. The German cruisers *Breslau* and *Goeben* had been allowed to take refuge there under the special permission required by the treaties of 1856 and 1879. Instead of expelling or interning them the Turkish government "purchased" them, against the protest of the Entente powers. The German officers and crew continued to man the ships. Many of the Turks and some members of the cabinet desired to remain neutral, but they were overborne by the pro-German party, headed by Enver Pasha, the minister of war. When, in October, the *Breslau* and *Goeben* raided the Russian ports on the Black Sea, the Entente powers announced a state of war with Turkey. Five months later, Great Britain and France agreed to Russian control of Istanbul and the straits at the end of the war.

Warfare with Russia in the Transcaucasus region began immediately and continued with varying fortunes. Early in February 1915 a Turkish attack on the Suez canal was defeated but the canal continued to be in some danger for two years longer.

The Gallipoli Campaign. The importance of opening the Dardanelles and Bosporus and reestablishing communication with southern Russia was obvious to good strategists everywhere, but the Allies delayed fatally. They blockaded the Dardanelles, but Earl Kitchener, with his eyes on the western front, underestimated the importance of sending the necessary land forces. The navy destroyed the forts at the mouth of the Dardanelles on February 19, but an attack on the main defenses at the Narrows, a month later, cost the British three ships.

At last the Allies decided to send a land force, after further delays had given the Turks and Germans time to strengthen their defenses. Hoped-for aid from Russia and Greece was prevented by the German drive against Russia and the refusal of the pro-German King Constantine to bring Greece into the war. Not until April 25 was the first landing attempted, and then the 45,000 troops used, mostly "Anzacs" (Australian-New Zealand Army Corps) could do little more than seize and hold positions near the tip of Gallipoli peninsula. When in May a German submarine sank two battleships, the navy became of less assistance. After further delays more troops were sent, but no important gains resulted. For many weeks the troops held on, suffering from disease and the enemy fire. A last effort in August, after heavy reinforcements had arrived, failed to reach the key positions. A new landing at Suvla Bay resulted only in immense losses, with no material gains.

The Allies held their positions for months longer, until the conquest of Serbia and the entrance of Bulgaria on the German side, gave the Central Powers a clear road to Istanbul and no hope of opening the straits remained. At the end of 1915 the Allied positions were abandoned. This campaign cost the Allies more than 230,000 men.

Italy Declares War. Italy had refused to join her partners in the Triple Alliance in 1914, alleging that Germany and Austria-Hungary were the aggressors. The old hatred of Austria still persisted and with it the desire to "redeem" the Italian-speaking regions of the Dual Monarchy. Both sides bid for Italian support, and the Allies bid higher. In April the secret Treaty of London with the Entente powers promised to Italy the Trentino, Trieste, South Tyrol, and other territory and concessions, and the next month Italy declared war. Italy brought to the Entente a navy more powerful than Austria's and an army of 1,200,000 trained men with considerable reserves. In their attack upon Austria the mountainous character of the frontier country was against them. Their main movement against Trieste was checked at the Isonzo river, and they made no great progress in the next two years.

The Great Drive against Russia. In the campaign of 1915, the Teutonic leaders, accepting the defensive in the west, launched a great offensive in the east, designed to free Austrian Galicia, to conquer Russian Poland, to destroy the Russian army, and thus to eliminate Russia from the war.

On May 2 General von Mackensen broke through the Russian lines on the Dunajec river in Galicia. Far inferior in artillery, the Russians were unable to check him. In a few weeks von Mackensen retook Przemysl and Lemberg and practically all of Austrian Galicia, together with immense quantities of booty and hundreds of thousands of prisoners.

Meanwhile, in the north, von Hindenburg had taken Libau and had overrun a large part of Courland. Poland was now like a nut in the grasp of a giant nutcracker. Russians were aided by great fortresses such as Ossowetz, Novo Georgievsk, and Ivangorod; but they were handicapped by their lack of artillery, shells, and other munitions. The war had already shown that infantry, no matter how brave, was practically helpless against an enemy that enjoyed a great superiority in artillery. After suffering enormous losses, Grand Duke Nicholas, in order to save his whole army from capture, was forced to evacuate Poland. Warsaw was occupied by the victors on August 5, and the fortress of Novo Georgievsk fell on August 20. After an unsuccessful attempt to make a stand on a line running through Brest-Litovsk, Osowiec, and Kovno, the great retreat had to continue. Grand Duke Nicholas was transferred to the Caucasus, where he was successful against the Turks, and the czar himself assumed nominal command, the real direction, however, being exercised by General Alexieff. The Teutons took Vilna, but their efforts to capture Dvinsk and Riga were foiled by stiffening Russian resistance. The Russians even launched an offensive in Galicia and checked the Germans in that quarter.

The Conquest of Serbia and Montenegro. The Teutonic victories over Russia made a profound impression, particularly in the Near East. In October 1915 Bulgaria threw in her lot with the Central Powers and attacked Serbia from the rear. Greece remained neutral. A strong army under General von Mackensen invaded Serbia from the north, recaptured Belgrade, and drove the Serbians southward. The allies of Serbia procrastinated as usual, and, too late, landed an army at Saloniki. Late in October the Bulgarian and Teutonic armies joined hands in eastern Serbia, and both Serbia and Montenegro were speedily conquered.

Through the conquest of Serbia the Teutons opened a way by which to aid hard-pressed Turkey, and trains loaded with munitions were soon running to Istanbul. With Istanbul under their control, the Teutons hoped to break through to Suez and the Persian Gulf, but that hope was never realized.

On the western front the deadlock that had begun after the repulse of the Germans in Flanders continued throughout 1915. In the second week of March, an attack on Neuve Chapelle, preceded by a heavy bombardment, in which more shells were fired than in the whole of the Boer war, resulted in slight success, and the loss of almost 13,000 men.

Poison Gas and Air Warfare. In an offensive against the British lines near Ypres, April 22, 1915, the Germans for the first time made use of poison gas. It had a momentary success, but the Germans failed to make the most of their advantage, partly by not fully understanding how much the gas had done, partly because of the gallant resistance of a Canadian division. The use of poison gas was denounced as illegal, but the Allies soon adopted it; improvements in technique were made by both sides, and it became an accepted feature of the war.

Aerial warfare also began. The German Zeppelins, or dirigible balloons, made raids on the English coast towns and finally, on the last night of May, reached London and dropped nearly a hundred incendiary bombs. The Germans claimed substantial damage to military objectives from these raids; the British said that only civilian lives and property suffered.

The use of airplanes expanded with astounding rapidity. New types were developed. Within a few months there were fighting planes, bombing planes, observation planes, —a type for each kind of work. By far the most important use to which planes were put was observation, spying out the enemy's movements and directing artillery fire. Later the planes were armed, and real battles were fought in mid-air.

The Deadlock on the Western Front. During the greater part of the campaign of 1915 the French and British attempted no great offensives but confined their efforts to what Marshal Joffre called "nibbling." In April the French failed at the St. Mihiel salient, south of Verdun. In May they had more success at "The Labyrinth," near Arras, but the method was costly out of proportion to results. One reason for this comparative inaction was the scarcity of munitions, particularly high explosive shells. The new technique of intensive artillery preparation before an attack, introduced by the Germans, entailed an expenditure of ammunition undreamed of in the past and not fully appreciated by the Germans themselves, much less by their opponents.

Late in September the British and French began the most serious offensive they had yet undertaken. They attacked a sector in Champagne, a second in Artois, and a third near Ypres after a fierce cannonade, or "drum fire," in places continued for 72 hours. Gas was also used. On the morning of September 25 the Allies delivered assaults in great force in each sector, and for days a bloody confusion of attack and counter-attack followed. Ultimately a little ground was gained but the main German lines held. The total German losses were estimated by the French at 120,000; the Allied losses probably exceeded those of the Germans.

The Drive against Verdun. At the beginning of the campaign of 1916 the Germans again turned their main attention to the western front. With the purpose of "bleeding France white," by drawing the French reserves to one point and destroying them, they launched late in February a tremendous offensive against the great armed camp of Verdun. Their first attacks made substantial gains, but General Joffre and his advisers decided to hold the place at any cost, partly because to lose it would have a depressing effect upon Allied morale.

For months thereafter the bitter battle continued. Hundreds of thousands fell on each side; week after week the Germans forged slowly forward against the bitterest resistance of the French, whose watchword was "They shall not pass." Early in July, the Germans got within a thousand yards of Fort Souville, the key to the French position, only three miles from Verdun. But the British advance on the Somme forced them to withdraw many troops and the fighting gradually diminished. In the following October and December, General Nivelle recaptured almost all the ground that had been lost.

The Battle of Jutland. On the last day of May the main fleets of Great Britain and Germany at last met in battle. On that day, both fleets were in the North Sea to the west of Jutland, neither knowing of the other. Shortly after two o'clock the advance squadron of the German fleet under Vice Admiral von Hipper met a heavier British squadron under Admiral Beatty, and turned back to the main fleet, sixty miles to the south. Beatty pursued, signalling to his main body, seventy miles to the north. In the running fight which followed, the British lost two battle cruisers, the *Indefatigable* and *Queen Mary*. On sighting the German fleet, Beatty turned back north to draw the Germans into conflict with the grand fleet under Admiral Jellicoe, which was hastening to his support. The Germans lost a battle cruiser, the *Luetzow*, in the pursuit. About 6 P. M. the main British fleet came up. Another British battle cruiser was sunk in the first clash but von Scheer saw he was outmatched. By skillful maneuvering he mystified the British admiral and, before the enemy could close in upon him, escaped in the darkness.

Both sides claimed the victory. The Germans had inflicted heavier losses on a superior fleet, six British capital ships against two of their own,—but the British could better afford it. On the other hand, the British retained command of the sea, and the Germans never ventured another battle.

Only seven days after the battle of Jutland, the British armored cruiser *Hampshire*, which was carrying Secretary of War Kitchener to Russia, struck a German mine off the coast of one of the Orkney islands, and all on board except eleven men perished. Kitchener's tragic death created a great impression.

The Italian and Russian Fronts in 1916. In the middle of May 1916, the Austro-Hungarians launched in the Trentino a great offensive which they hoped would result in their breaking through into the Lombard plain, Milan, and taking Venice and enveloping of the Italian main army along the Isonzo front. Their first attack, on May 15, was very successful and was so competently followed up that by the end of May they had taken two or three hundred cannon and over 30,000 prisoners, and the whole Italian army was in peril.

Once more, however, the Russians made an effective diversion in favor of their hard-pressed western allies. Under the leadership of General Brussilov, the Russians on June 2 attacked along the southern half of the eastern front. They broke Austrian lines and took the great fortress of Lutzk and Dubno. The whole Austrian line in the east crumbled, Bukowina was overrun, and 100,000 prisoners were captured. The Dual Monarchy had to suspend its drive against Italy and withdraw troops from that front to meet the victorious Muscovites. Germany also had to slacken her own offensive against Verdun. The Russians were held in check before Lemberg and Kovel after enormous losses on both sides.

Thanks to this opportune Russian diversion, the Italians were able to regain most of the ground they had lost. Early in August they captured Gorizia, but there their success ended, and the virtual deadlock along the Isonzo continued.

The Battle of the Somme. The British army in France had now grown to over seventy divisions, well-trained, fully equipped, and organized. Under the command of General Sir Douglas Haig, it was now ready for an offensive movement. On June 24 the British artillery began a terrific bombardment of the German lines and continued it until the morning of July 1, when British and French infantry attacked on a front of over twenty miles in the region of the Somme river. The British objective was Bapaume; the French, Peronne. Both were successful in taking the first lines, but resistance stiffened as they advanced. On the first day of the attack the British lost 60,000 men, and advanced half a mile.

To pound unceasingly was the Allied policy; the Germans brought up thousands of reserves for resistance and counterattack. Aloft, the opposing aircraft fought for the control of the air, a necessity in so flat a country for directing artillery fire. The surface for miles was transformed into a barren wilderness of shell craters. In an attack on September 15 the British for the first time made use of "tanks,"—armored cars mounted on caterpillar tractors. The smaller tanks were armed only with machine guns; the larger ones, with small pieces of artillery also. The tanks proved able to move through barbed wire entanglements, to cross trenches, to push down walls and even trees, and were especially helpful in destroying machine gun "nests." They proved, on the whole, successful, and assumed greater and greater importance as the war progressed.

Late in November the coming of wet, wintry weather brought the battle to a close. The Allies had gained something less than seven miles on a twelve mile front; they had not gained the break-through for which they had hoped. This gain had cost the British 420,000 men; the French, nearly 200,000. The German loss may have been as great.

The Defeat of Rumania. Meanwhile Rumania had entered the war on the side of the Entente. She was promised the Banat, Transylvania, and other territory, in much of which the population was largely Rumanian. On August 28, 1916, she declared war on Austria-Hungary, and hostilities with the other Central Powers soon followed. After some initial Rumanian successes, the armies of the Central Powers, led by Generals von Mackensen and von Falkenhayn, attacked Rumania from the north, west, and south, captured the capital, and overran two-thirds of the country, while an Allied force remained immovable at Saloniki. Russian reinforcements finally checked the invaders, at a line running along the lower Sereth river, and thence northeastward to the Carpathians.

The Rumanian fiasco created much dissatisfaction in Allied countries, and was instrumental in bringing about cabinet changes in both France and Great Britain. In the latter country the Liberal cabinet under Asquith had declared the war. The Conservatives had supported them, but early in 1915 had demanded a share in power as well as in responsibility, and a coalition cabinet had been formed. Now the feeling grew that Asquith was too careful of the rights of the citizen and lacked the energy necessary for a war premier. He retired and was succeeded by David Lloyd George. In France similar conditions brought about, after some friction, the appointment of "the Tiger," Georges Clemenceau, as a premier in November 1917. In the field Joffre retired at the end of the year; he was succeeded by General Nivelle, the defender of Verdun.

Peace Discussions. Toward the end of 1916 proposals for peace came forward from two quarters. On December 12 the German government announced its willingness to enter into peace negotiations. On December 18, President Wilson, in a note framed before the German proposal appeared, asked the belligerents to state the terms on which peace might be concluded. The replies to both propositions showed that no agreement was yet possible. On January 22, President Wilson explained his position to the Senate, saying that there must be a "peace without victory," since "only a peace between equals can last"; and favoring a League of Peace to secure the fulfillment of such a treaty.

The United States Enters the War. In the United States, especially in the northeast, popular sympathy had been generally with the Allies from the beginning. German policies toward the United States, even before the war, had been irritating; the old feeling against England was weakening; and France had been our traditional ally. At the outset of the war President Wilson, following our accepted policy, had issued a neutrality proclamation and had repeatedly protested against both British and German violations of international law. American feeling, however, especially in the West and Middle West, was against any participation in a European war, and Wilson was re-elected in 1916 under the campaign cry, "He kept us out of war."

The submarines brought matters to a crisis. Wilson had protested against the German war zone of February 1915. After the sinking of the *Lusitania* and later the *Sussex*, with the loss of American lives, his position held such prospects of vigorous action that, in May 1916, the German government agreed not to sink merchant vessels without warning, provided the United States held Great Britain also to "strict accountability." On January 31, 1917, the German high command suddenly announced that it would resume unrestricted submarine warfare against any merchant ships found in "barred zones" around the British Isles, along the Atlantic coast of France, and in the Mediterranean. The United States was permitted, under certain restrictions, to send one ship a week to Falmouth in southern England. President Wilson's answer was the breaking off of diplomatic relations with Germany, on February 3.

The unrestricted submarine warfare continued. On February 26, President Wilson announced that he deemed it desirable for the United States to adopt an attitude of "armed neutrality," and asked for authority to arm American merchant ships. This was obviously a step toward war. The same day word reached Washington of the loss of three Americans on the British ship *Laconia*. A few days later an intercepted dispatch was published which showed that Zimmerman, the German foreign minister, was seeking to stir up Mexico and Japan against the United States in the event of war with Germany. A bill empowering the president to arm merchantmen, and making appropriations for that purpose, passed the House by 403 to 13, but Senator La Follette and other opponents of war defeated it by a filibuster in the Senate. The president then found authority, under an act of 1797, for placing naval guns and crews on merchant ships. Congress was called to meet in special session on April 16, a date later advanced to April 2.

Meantime the submarines had been working great havoc. In February the Germans claimed the sinking of 781,000 tons of shipping; the British admitted 490,000. The peak was reached in April, with the loss of nearly a million tons. Then, with the adoption of the convoy system, due largely to Lloyd George, the Allies began to get the upper hand. American ships were among those lost.

On April 2, President Wilson appeared before Congress and delivered a war message. He stated that the recent course of the German government constituted a "warfare against mankind." Armed neutrality had proved ineffectual, and he asked Congress to recognize that war had been thrust upon the United States by the acts of the German government. He requested the necessary steps to force the German government to terms and end the conflict. Resolutions to that effect passed the Senate on the night of the 4-5th of April by a vote of 82 to 6 and the House on the early morning of the 6th by a vote of 373 to 50. The same day, the president signed the resolutions, and America and Germany were formally at war.

Relations with Austria-Hungary had long been strained, and in September 1915 the United States had demanded and secured the recall of Constantine Dumba, the Austro-Hungarian ambassador, for attempting to stir up strikes in American munition factories. Diplomatic relations were severed by the dual monarchy on April 8, but war was not formally declared until the 7th of the following December, the declaration being made by the United States. Turkey severed relations on April 17, but a state of war was never declared. Diplomatic relations between the United States and Bulgaria were continued throughout the conflict.

American Preparations. America's entry into the conflict greatly heartened the Entente Powers. Furthermore, it encouraged several other nations, such as China, Brazil, Panama, Cuba, and Bolivia, to break relations with Germany or to declare war against her.

Within less than three weeks after the declaration of war Congress appropriated seven billion dollars for war purposes. Subsequently other immense appropriations were made. A policy of advancing loans to our Allies was at once adopted, and by the close of hostilities about eight billion dollars had been so advanced. In May, Congress passed and the president signed a Selective Service bill, and under this and subsequent extensions all male persons not alien enemies, between the ages of 21 and 45, were required to register. After exemptions, about 3,000,-000 soldiers and sailors were obtained. Some hundreds of thousands, also, volunteered.

To obtain money with which to conduct the war, Congress enacted special tax legislation and authorized the issuance of certificates of indebtedness, war savings certificates, better known as thrift stamps, and government bonds. By far the largest sum was realized from the sale of bonds, of which five great issues were floated, the first on May 14, 1917. The four liberty loans aggregated $14,000,000,000, at rates varying from $3\frac{1}{2}$ to $4\frac{1}{4}$ per cent. A fifth, called the victory loan, for $4,500,000,000, was floated soon after the armistice. All were oversubscribed.

The country now had to prepare for war. Between April 5, 1917, and June 30, 1919, 35 billion dollars were expended, which was several billions more than had been spent for all purposes from the beginning of the Revolution down to 1917. Of this sum, however, nine billions were advanced to our allies in the conflict.

Work of the American Navy. Shortly before the United States entered the war, Vice Admiral William S. Sims was sent to England to arrange cooperation of American naval forces with those of the Allies. On his arrival in London he found the British much depressed over the submarine situation. The American navy took over the work of patrolling a large part of the Atlantic, thus freeing British ships for use in home waters, and from May on destroyers and other craft were sent abroad. In December 1917 a squadron of four dreadnoughts (a fifth was later added) was sent over under command of Rear Admiral Hugh Rodman and joined the British Grand Fleet. Two other battleships in the early summer of 1918 began operations from a base in Ireland. An immense amount of work was done in convoying ships across the Atlantic and through the war zone.

The greatest loss suffered by the American navy during the war was the sinking of the armored cruiser *San Diego*, which struck (July 1918) a German mine laid by a submarine off Long Island. One destroyer, the *Jacob Jones*, was sunk (December 6, 1917) by a submarine in European waters. Other destroyers and smaller vessels were sunk or damaged, and a large number of armed merchant vessels and transports were lost. In return we captured one submarine and probably sank others.

American Troops sent to France. The American regular army, on April 1, 1917, numbered only 128,000 men. The French government, however, urged that at least a few American troops should be sent to France as speedily as possible, for the sake of the effect on Allied morale. To command the overseas force the president selected Major General John J. Pershing. General Pershing and his staff sailed from New York late in May. Late in June the first contingent of troops landed at St. Nazaire, whence they were transferred to training bases in Lorraine.

The Western Front in 1917. During the first two months of 1917 the French and British made preparations for a grand offensive. General von Hindenburg who in the previous summer had succeeded von Falkenhayn, forestalled them by withdrawing to a shorter and stronger zone of defense, the Hindenburg line, laying waste the country behind him. Although the conditions had changed, the offensive was not given up. On April 9 the English launched a great attack about Lens and Arras. Canadian troops carried the important Vimy Ridge, and more gains were made at less cost than in the battle of the Somme: but the German lines still held. On April 16, the French, under Nivelle, attacked in front of Reims. They gained some initial successes, but their losses were severe, even resulting in mutinies among the French troops. General Nivelle was succeeded by General Pétain, with General Foch as his chief of staff.

Again in June the British launched another attack in Flanders. They took Messines Ridge, after the explosion of a gigantic mine, and bitter fighting continued through the summer. In the fall British operations in the low ground about Passchendaele literally bogged down in the swampy terrain, though a part of Passchendaele Ridge was taken. The French meanwhile had recovered sufficiently to make another drive with some success, near Soissons, and drove the Germans from the Chemin des Dames.

The Russian Revolution. Unintelligent despotism, universal corruption, and radical intrigue were doing their work in Russia. In March a revolution broke out, which resulted in the deposition of the czar and the establishment of a republic. Moderate revolutionists who favored continuing the war at first managed to control, but the Soviets, or councils of workmen's and soldier's delegates, who desired more radical measures and a speedy peace, constantly increased in power. German secret agents took advantage of the situation. The republican government, headed by Kerensky, inspired the army to a last effort. In July an offensive was launched in Galicia; successful at first, it turned into a disgraceful rout. The Germans occupied Riga and Odessa. For a time Kerensky held power as a virtual dictator, but in November the radical revolutionists, or Bolsheviki, under Lenin and Trotzky, seized control. They not only carried through a complete economic and social revolution but, on December 15, 1917, signed an armistice, and, in the following March, the humiliating treaty of Brest-Litovsk.

The breakdown of Russia enabled the Germans, even in 1917, to concentrate most of their forces on the Western front. Large forces of men and guns were transferred to Flanders to hold the British in check and a grand drive was prepared against Italy.

The Italian Disaster. During the spring, summer, and early fall the Italians had continued to make slow progress on the Isonzo. On October 24 the Austro-Hungarians and some German divisions launched a sudden offensive. German shock troops broke through the Italian lines in the region of Caporetto and drove them westward in disastrous rout. Venice and Milan were in grave danger; the whole of the Lombard plain was threatened. General Diaz, who succeeded General Cadorna, rallied the Italians behind the Piave river, and the arrival of French and British reinforcements helped to save the situation. A German attack from the Trentino, to turn the Piave line, was finally checked.

The Italian defeat had, however, been a major disaster; northeastern Italy was overrun; and the enemy had taken a quarter of a million prisoners, about 2500 guns, and vast stores of munitions. The Italian situation continued to be grave until near the end of the war.

Partly to prevent the Germans from sending any more troops against the Italians, the British Third Army under General Byng, on November 20, launched a sudden attack on the German lines in front of Cambrai. A great number of tanks were used to break through the barbed wire entanglements and destroy machine gun nests. The British got within three miles of Cambrai, but had not sufficient reserves with which to follow up the success. On November 30 the Germans restored their lines by a powerful counterattack and recovered about a third of the ground lost. The main importance of the battle was that it demonstrated the possibilities of tanks.

Campaign in Mesopotamia (Iraq) and Palestine. The Allied hope of victory in 1917 had not been realized. In some important fields of action their arms had met with disaster, and only in Iraq and Palestine could they point to really notable successes. Late in 1914 an expedition, composed mainly of troops from India, had landed at the head of the Persian gulf, and managed to fight its way in November 1915 almost to Baghdad. At Ctesiphon,

however, it met superior forces and had to retreat down the Tigris river to Kut-el-Amara, where, despite the efforts of a relieving army, it was forced to surrender (April 29, 1916). In the following December the relieving army, commanded by General Maude and increased to over a hundred thousand men, again assumed the offensive in Iraq, recaptured Kut-el-Amara, and after decisive victories entered the city of Baghdad, March 11, 1917.

Meanwhile the British had encouraged the Arabs in Arabia to revolt against the Turks. Thomas Edward Lawrence, a young British archeologist, organized and led the Arab tribes. Utilizing their methods of desert warfare, he made them an invaluable auxiliary force.

In March 1917 a British army pushing northward from the Isthmus of Suez defeated a Turkish force near the ancient city of Gaza. In October General Sir Edmund Allenby took command and began an active campaign, and in December, for the first time since the Crusades, the flag of a Christian nation floated over Jerusalem.

In Greece, also, affairs had taken a turn more favorable to the Allies. Former Premier Venizelos and Admiral Condouriotis began a revolutionary movement in Crete and established a provisional government, which won over other islands and most of the Greek fleet, and entered the war on the side of the Entente. In June 1917, the Allies compelled King Constantine to resign in favor of his second son, Prince Alexander. Venizelos became premier, and Greece was brought into the war.

The Great German Offensive of 1918. During the winter of 1917-18 both Teutonic and Allied leaders made pronouncements with regard to peace, but their views as to terms differed so widely that it was clear that the war must go on. Meanwhile the Germans made preparations to launch a stupendous blow which they hoped would bring them victory before America could take a real part in the war. With forces released by the collapse of Russia, they were now equal to the Allies on the Western front. The place selected for the offensive was in the region between Arras and La Fere, at the point of junction of the French and British lines. At five o'clock on the morning of March 21 the Germans began a terrific bombardment on a front of about sixty miles.

After four hours the infantry moved forward to the attack. The British, outnumbered five to one at the point of attack, were unable to withstand the blow. The Fifth British Army was practically cut to pieces. In a few days the Germans had regained practically all the territory they had lost. At one time it seemed probable that the Germans would be able to separate the British from the French and to defeat each in detail. France was in greater danger than at any time since the battle of the Marne. Paris was subjected to repeated air raids and was bombarded by super-guns concealed in the forest of St. Gobain at the unheard-of distance of 74 miles.

But the British Third Army under Byng held like a wall before Arras, containing the flood on the north, while hastily gathered French forces, after bloody fighting, dammed it on the south. The French and British joined hands once more, and the Germans, worn out by their gigantic efforts, failed to reach the vitally important town of Amiens.

On April 9, Ludendorff and Hindenburg delivered another great blow against the British lines in Flanders. The Germans broke through a portion of the line held by a Portuguese division, took the Passchendaele and Messines ridges, Armentieres, and Kemmel Hill, and threatened Ypres. There was grave danger that the whole British army might be hurled back in irretrievable disaster upon the Channel, but British fighting qualities and French reenforcements once more brought the assailants to a pause.

Foch Becomes Commander in Chief. From the Allied point of view the German offensive had been productive of at least one good result. Hitherto in the war their activities had been greatly hampered by lack of united command. A Supreme War Council had been created. But this was not enough. On March 27, in the midst of the first German offensive, British and French representatives met and gave the supreme command to Ferdinand Foch. On the next day General Pershing tendered his forces to Foch, and ultimately the great Frenchman became generalissimo of all the Allied armies on all fronts.

At the time Pershing made his tender there were less than 370,000 American troops in Europe, of whom about half were noncombatants. American participation in the fighting had been almost wholly confined to meeting petty German raids. The First Division was now sent to the active front near Montdidier, and, at the urgent request of the French and British leaders, great efforts were concentrated upon bringing more American troops over. During the war only 396 American soldiers were lost as a result of submarine activities.

The Final German Efforts. On May 27 the Germans launched a new offensive on a thirty-mile front between Reims and Soissons. The Allies were taken by surprise, and with comparatively slight losses the Teutons recaptured the Chemin des Dames Ridge and drove a deep salient to the river Marne, taking great numbers of prisoners and guns.

On the day after the Germans launched this offensive, the American First Division under Major General Bullard captured the town of Cantigny near the apex of the Amiens salient. This was the first considerable operation in which American troops were engaged, but the Second and Third divisions were now sent to the Marne front in the Chateau-Thierry region and helped to bring the German drive to a pause. In fighting for Belleau Wood a brigade of marines won great distinction. Meanwhile, French troops in the region of Compiegne had defeated with great slaughter a German effort to connect the Marne salient with that driven toward Amiens.

By July 1 the Germans claimed to have captured, since the launching of their March offensive, 191,454 unwounded prisoners and over 2000 cannon, but they had failed to obtain the decisive victory they had hoped to win. Owing to the rapid arrival of American troops, the "rifle strength" of the Allies on the western front had passed that of the Germans.

The scene of the last German attack was the Reims salient, on a great front from Chateau-Thierry almost to the Argonne Forest. But the Allied leaders divined the German plan and concentrated great numbers of troops and guns to meet it. When the attack came on the morning of July 15, the Allies, by using a "yielding defense," stopped the German drive in most places after inflicting great losses. Some German divisions forced their way over the river Marne, but on the sector held by the American Third and Twenty-eighth divisions determined counter-attacks speedily hurled the assailants back across the river. By the end of the third day of battle it was evident that the drive was doomed to failure.

The Allies Assume the Offensive. The time had come for which Foch had long been waiting. At dawn of the 18th he attacked the western side of the Marne salient. The American First and Second divisions participated in the initial attack, and others were soon thrown into the fight. There was no preliminary artillery preparation, but the troops charged behind a rolling barrage and were aided by many tanks. The surprise was complete. The Allies advanced eight miles. The salient was no longer tenable, and the Germans retreated over the Vesle river, with heavy losses.

On August 8 a new offensive was launched against the salient projecting toward Amiens. The Canadian army formed the center of this attack and made a greater advance on the first day than was accomplished by any other army on the western front in the campaign of 1918.

"To make war is to attack" had long been General Foch's maxim. He followed up these initial successes and by the middle of September the Germans had been driven back virtually to the old Hindenburg Line, from which they had launched their offensive in the spring.

In these operations American troops fighting with the French and British armies played a glorious part, and General Pershing with a newly organized army performed a notable exploit by taking the St. Mihiel salient northeast of Verdun. Careful preparations were made, and an army of about 600,000, including some French troops, was concentrated for the purpose. The attack was made on September 12. The Germans, already withdrawing, were caught in the act; they lost 16,000 prisoners and the salient was wiped out. In the two months since the middle of July the Germans had lost nearly half a million men. In the words of Pershing: "The Allies found they had a formidable army to aid them, and the enemy learned finally that he had one to reckon with."

Bulgaria and Turkey Beaten. In late September the Allied army in the Balkans began a sudden offensive northward from Saloniki. In a few days the lines of the enemy were broken, and Bulgaria, threatened with annihilation, signed (September 30) an armistice which was practically an unconditional surrender. Bulgaria's withdrawal from the war isolated Turkey. The dual monarchy was attacked from the south.

On September 19, General Allenby launched a blow at the Turkish army in Palestine and in a few days practically annihilated it, taking 75,000 prisoners and 360 cannon. The victors took Damascus, and in the middle of October they reached Aleppo and cut the Berlin to Baghdad railway, thereby isolating the Turkish army in Iraq, which on October 30 surrendered to the British army under General Marshall. On the same day the Turkish government bowed to the inevitable and withdrew from the war.

The Battle of the Hindenburg Line. In the last days of September the Allies on the western front began an epic assault on the Hindenburg Line. Belgian, British, and French troops under King Albert took the offensive in Flanders, British and French armies thundered against the zone of defenses in front of St. Quentin and Laon, and a great American army, aided by French troops on their left, began a drive down the valley of the Meuse river. The German lines were broken; Dixmude, Lens, Armentieres, and the great city of Lille were taken; and in the middle of October the Germans evacuated the Belgian coast.

Meanwhile, British, Canadian, and Australian troops, aided by the 30th and 27th divisions of Americans, steadily battered their way through the immensely strong zone of defenses in front of Cambrai and St. Quentin. Tanks and artillery were used in great profusion, and defensive works were taken that had once been considered impregnable. In the second week of October, Haig's forces finally burst through the German system of defenses and took Cambrai and St. Quentin.

In front of the Americans and French in the region of the Meuse lay the rugged Argonne Forest and three German zones of defense. The Germans were not expecting an offensive in this quarter, and at first their lines were lightly held. An initial attack was made on September 26. The French forces, operating on the west side of the Argonne Forest, made good progress the first day; on the east side the Americans advanced in places for six or seven miles, but strong resistance encountered at Montfaucon and elsewhere prevented them from breaking completely through the first zone of defense, and assaulting the second, before the Germans could bring up reserves. The attack was continued the next two days against increasingly strong resistance, due to the arrival of German re-enforcements; Montfaucon and other strong points were taken, and in the three days about 10,000 Germans were captured.

Thus began the bloodiest battle in American history, a conflict comparable to that in the Wilderness in Civil War days, but on a larger scale and much more prolonged. Both sides constantly threw fresh divisions into the fray, and every day bitter but confused fighting took place. German machine-gunners fought for every foot of ground and exacted a heavy toll from the Americans, most of whom were taking part in their first great battle. The American losses were enormous, but the troops from beyond the seas fought with a dogged determination to win through at any cost. By October 10, with French assistance, they had cleared the Argonne Forest of the enemy. The great obstacle before them now was the powerful German line known as the Kriemhilde Stellung.

By the end of October the Americans were through the Kriemhilde zone of defense, and on November 1 the final advance was begun. The third German line, the so-called Freya Stellung, was incomplete, and it was mastered with comparative ease. On November 6 the Rainbow Division reached a point on the Meuse opposite Sedan. The Americans had now attained their objective—the railways running through Sedan and Mezieres. In the words of General Pershing: "The strategical goal which was our highest hope was gained. We had cut the enemy's main line of communications, and nothing but surrender or an armistice could save his army from complete disaster."

The total number of Americans engaged in the Meuse-Argonne offensive has been estimated at 631,-000, the French at 138,000, making a total of 769,-000. The Germans had less than 400,000. In the battle the Americans had taken 16,059 prisoners and 468 guns; their own losses in killed, wounded, and missing exceeded 100,000. During the whole campaign the Americans captured about 44,000 prisoners and 1400 guns. In all, 2,034,000 American soldiers reached France, and of these 1,390,000 saw more or less active service at the front. In all, 29 divisions took part in active combat service.

The Americans were undoubtedly the decisive factor in winning victory; without their aid the war might have been lost. It should be remembered, however, that they came in at the end, when the enemy had been worn down. Even in the campaign of 1918 the French and British losses were much heavier than those of the Americans, and each of them captured more prisoners and guns.

Great credit is also due to the Canadians. Their troops performed some of the most brilliant exploits of the whole war, and no other soldiers were more dreaded by the Germans.

They broke through the Hindenburg Line between Queant and Drocourt. In this victory and the one near Amiens mentioned above their casualties were numerous but were exceeded by the number of prisoners which they captured. On Oct. 9 they took Cambrai and on Nov. 2, Valenciennes. A few hours before the armistice became effective, Canadian troops entered Mons, from which the British expeditionary force had begun its retreat before the on-pouring flood of Germans in the last week of August 1914.

In the whole war nearly 600,000 Canadians, 7 per cent of the population, served in the army, nearly all by voluntary enlistment. The financial cost was met largely by internal popular loans, amounting in all to $2,202,762,250 and subscribed for by well over a million persons. At the same time, special taxes were imposed calculated to retire these extraordinary loans and maintain the country's credit. Nearly 1000 ships were built during the war in Canadian shipyards for Canada or her allies. The losses in men during the war were approximately equal to those of the United States. The Canadian army captured 45,000 prisoners and re-

took 130 towns. A Canadian aviator, Colonel William Avery Bishop, of Ontario, was credited with 72 official victories, a record exceeded by only one German and one French aviator.

On October 24 General Diaz's army assumed the offensive in the Trentino and along the Piave river against the Austro-Hungarians. The Austrian army was broken and demoralized; three hundred thousand prisoners were taken. Revolutions broke out in Hungary and Austria, and the emperor Charles, the last of the Habsburgs, was forced to abdicate. On November 3, military representatives of the falling dual monarchy signed in the field an armistice that amounted practically to a complete capitulation.

The War Ended. With her last ally gone, Germany stood alone, facing a world of determined enemies. Before the end of September the German high command had realized that peace must be made, and, on October 4, Prince Maximilian of Baden, who had recently become imperial chancellor, sent to President Wilson a request for an armistice. Exchange of notes continued for more than a month; meanwhile the German armies were driven back, and the allies of Germany retired from the conflict. On the last day of October a mutiny began in the German fleet. In a few days uprisings took place in Berlin and elsewhere. Emperor William and the crown prince fled to Holland. On November 8 German representatives met Marshal Foch and other Allied representatives in a railway car near Rethondes, and, at five o'clock on the morning of the 11th, signed an armistice to take effect six hours later.

In the negotiations leading up to the armistice, the Germans had agreed to accept as a basis for peace the program set forth by President Wilson in an address to Congress on January 8, 1918, and in later pronouncements, particularly in a speech of September 27. In his address of January 8 the president had stated fourteen points which he considered essentials. These included "open covenants of peace openly arrived at" and no secret diplomacy in the future; freedom of the seas in both peace and war; reduction of armaments; evacuation of all territory conquered by the Central Powers, with reparation and restoration of Belgium, Serbia, etc.; Alsace and Lorraine to be returned to France; readjustment of the frontiers of Italy along lines of nationality; an independent Poland; and the formation of an association of nations to safeguard the independence and territorial integrity of both great and small states. The European allies of the United States had, however, reserved complete freedom of action on the matter of "the freedom of the seas" and had insisted that the sweeping stipulation that "invaded territories must be restored as well as evacuated" must be interpreted to mean "that compensation will be made by Germany for all damage done to the civilian population of the Allies and their property by the aggression of Germany by land, by sea, and by the air." In addition to these terms, the Germans were required by the armistice to surrender 5000 cannon, 25,000 machine guns, 1700 airplanes, all the German submarines, and practically all their above-water navy. All of Germany west of the Rhine was to be occupied by Allied troops, a neutral zone ten kilometers wide was to be drawn on the east bank, and the Allies were to have bridgeheads east of the river at Mayence, Coblenz, and Cologne.

Treaty Negotiations. The opening session of the Peace Conference was held at Versailles, near Paris, on January 18, 1919. Representatives of all the Allied nations were present, but the decisions were made by the leaders of the five chief powers.

The document containing the terms fixed upon for Germany was delivered to the German delegates on May 7. In Germany it was considered a "monstrous document," but the victors would consent to only a few modifications, and the vanquished, being powerless to resist, were obliged to accept it, the actual signing taking place on June 28, the fifth anniversary of the assassination of the archduke Francis Ferdinand. Under it Germany gave up all her colonies, ceded Alsace and Lorraine to France and a small strip of territory to Belgium, and consented that the Sarre (Saar) Basin, with its rich iron and coal mines, should be internationalized for fifteen years, after which the inhabitants were to be given the right to decide as to their future. Plebiscites were to be held in Schleswig, Silesia, and parts of East Prussia to determine the future political affiliation of these regions, and the port of Danzig was to be internationalized. The German army was to be reduced to 100,000 men; the German navy, to six battleships, six light cruisers, and some smaller vessels. The fortifications of Helgoland were to be destroyed, and the Kiel canal must be opened to all nations. Germany accepted responsibility for all damages done to the Allies and their peoples and agreed to reimburse civilians for their losses and to restore the devastated regions in Belgium, France, and elsewhere. She also agreed to the trial of the kaiser and other Germans accused of offenses against international morality and the laws of war.

Subsequently it was found difficult to enforce all the provisions of the treaty, and some modifications were made. The claims for reparations were scaled down, and comparatively little was collected. Holland refused to give up Wilhelm II and but few of the others accused were ever brought to trial.

Treaties were later concluded with Bulgaria, Austria, and Turkey. Bulgaria was compelled to surrender territory and to pay an indemnity. Parts of the old dual monarchy were ceded to Italy, Rumania, and Poland; Hungary and Czechoslovakia were recognized as independent republics; the regions chiefly inhabited by Yugoslavs were united with Serbia and Montenegro into a greater Serbia, — the Kingdom of the Serbs, Croats, and Slovenes. Of Austria proper there remained only about 32,000 square miles, with a population of 6,000,000 or 7,000,000, chiefly of German blood. A republican form of government was adopted.

The Turkish treaty reduced the domains of the sultan to Istanbul and a small region round about it and to part of Asia Minor. An international force was to be maintained at Istanbul, and the Dardanelles and the Bosporus were neutralized. Arabia was to be independent; Iraq and Palestine were to be under British control; Thrace and the region about Smyrna, under that of Greece; and France and Italy were given spheres of influence in Syria and Anatolia respectively. The mandate over Armenia was offered to the United States, but Congress declined it.

Russian and Turkish Affairs. Unfortunately the conference was unable to bring peace everywhere to a distracted world. At the time of the signing of the German treaty a score of other wars, or conflicts amounting to a state of war, were still raging. For example, Poland was fighting the Ruthenians, the Ukrainians, the Germans, the Yugoslavs, and the Russian Bolshevists.

In Russia the Allies lent assistance to the opponents of the Bolshevists, but all counter-revolutionary movements ultimately failed. The Bolshevist regime, dedicated to an experiment in communism on a scale never before witnessed, consolidated its position as a class dictatorship by means of a Revolutionary court and the army. It survived widespread famine and acute industrial disorganization.

Turkish Nationalists refused to accept the terms imposed upon their country, and one of their leaders, Mustapha Kemal, assembled a large army in Asia Minor. Allied jealousies also complicated the Turkish situation. The main burden of opposing the Nationalists was assumed by the Greeks, who overran Thrace in the summer of 1920, and in 1921 conducted a successful offensive against the Nationalists in Asia Minor, but in 1922 the Greeks were defeated and driven out of Asia Minor. The Turks subsequently, by the Treaty of Lausanne (July 1923), obtained much more favorable terms.

America Rejects the League of Nations. In the United States a bitter political struggle developed over the peace treaty. To be ratified, the treaty had to receive a two-thirds majority in the Senate. A majority of the Senate were Republicans, and in that body, as well as among the people at large, there existed a great deal of hostility toward President Wilson. Special objection was made to Article X of the Covenant, which bound members of the League "to respect and preserve as against external aggression the territorial integrity and existing political independence of all members of the League." In an effort to win popular support for the treaty and the League, President Wilson set out (September 1919) on a tour of the country, but on the way back from the Pacific coast he had an apoplectic stroke and was forced to return to Washington, where for months he was confined to the White House unable to attend to any but the most urgent public business. Meanwhile the Senate adopted a number of reservations to the Covenant, including one which provided that the United States assumed no obligation to use its military or naval forces or otherwise aid to enforce Article X unless Congress should by act or joint resolution so direct. In defense of this reservation its supporters pointed to the constitutional clause that provides that only Congress can declare war. All attempts to secure ratification of the treaty, with or without reservations, failed (November 1919, March 1920). The Senate also refused to ratify an agreement by which the United States and Great Britain bound themselves to go to the assistance of France in case of unprovoked attack by Germany. A joint resolution declaring the war at an end was passed by both houses, but the president vetoed it (May 27, 1920). Under Harding's administration a treaty embodying many of the terms of the Versailles Treaty but omitting the League of Nations Covenant was negotiated with Germany and was ratified by the Senate. On November 11, 1921, exactly three years after the close of hostilities, the two governments exchanged ratifications.

Results of the War. Three famous royal houses, the Romanovs, the Habsburgs, and the Hohenzollerns, were swept from their thrones. King Ferdinand of Bulgaria and King Constantine of Greece also lost their crowns. Monarchy, as a system of government, disappeared in Germany; the various states set up republican forms, which united into a new German republic, with Socialist tendencies, but keeping the old name of the Reich.

The Habsburg dominions were broken into fragments. Three republics—Hungary (later declared a monarchy), Austria, and Czechoslovakia—arose from the ruins, while portions were incorporated with Italy, Rumania, Poland, and Yugoslavia. Germany lost Alsace-Lorraine to France, a small district to Belgium, part of Schleswig to Denmark, large territories in the east to Poland, and all of her colonies, amounting to more than a million square miles. Bulgaria lost territory, and of the once vast dominions of the sultan nothing remained save a small tract of land about Istanbul and part of Asia Minor. Heavy indemnities were saddled upon all the vanquished peoples.

Russia, which entered the war on the side of the Entente but withdrew from the conflict before victory was won, underwent a social and economic revolution, which set off a train of events destined to lead to a still more terrible war of worldwide extent 20 years later. On her western border new states were created or old ones were restored: Finland, Estonia, Lithuania, and Poland—all republics.

The victors enlarged their territorial domains, but the condition of many of them was little better than that of the vanquished. All that took a real part in the conflict emerged from it bearing immense burdens of debt. Russia and Germany found it necessary to repudiate their national currencies. Hungary and Austria were in scarcely less difficult situations. Even France and Italy failed to stabilize their currencies until these had dwindled to a mere fraction of their pre-War values. Great Britain was least affected financially, but her economic recovery was slow and halting.

The net result of the disorganization and economic losses of the chief belligerents was a shift in balance of strength from Europe to America. The United States became a creditor nation instead of a debtor nation. Governmental debts alone due from European nations to the United States totaled approximately 10 billion dollars. According to agreements negotiated with the individual debtor governments, these amounts were to be paid off in a period of about 60 years. The Allied powers expected to obtain the funds for payment from the indemnity imposed on Germany. Only a small fraction was ever paid.

LEAGUE OF NATIONS

During World War I, the necessity for an association of nations, to settle controversies threatening the peace of the world, was voiced at frequent intervals. Premier Asquith of Great Britain made one of the first official utterances to this effect. President Wilson, in Number 14 of his famous "Points," appealed for a "league of nations." Thus, the delegates to the Peace Conference at Paris in 1919 were generally receptive to such a plan, and several brought concrete suggestions.

Organization. The Covenant of the League of Nations was adopted by the conference April 28, and became binding, upon the powers ratifying the treaty with Germany, on January 10, 1920. The Covenant provided an organization designed to embrace eventually all independent states and self-governing dominions. The organization consisted of three parts: a Council; an Assembly; and a permanent secretariat.

The Council. The Council was composed of representatives of the British Empire, Russia, France, Italy, and nine (originally four) other member nations, elected by the Assembly for three-year periods, three being chosen each year. The Covenant provided places for the United States, Germany, and Japan as permanent members of the Council. Germany and Japan resigned from the League and the United States never joined. The Council met at least annually to deal with any matter affecting the peace of the world. Its first meeting was held January 16, 1920.

The Assembly. The Assembly was made up of representatives of nations which were members of the League. It had power to deal with any matter within the sphere of action of the League, or affecting the peace of the world. Each power was en-

titled to at most three delegates but to only one vote. Seven members of the British Commonwealth of Nations were regarded as distinct powers, each with one vote in the Assembly. At the seat of the League, in Geneva, Switzerland, the Assembly held annual meetings, opening on the first Monday of September.

The Secretariat. The secretariat of the League was established at the headquarters of the League in the city of Geneva. In consisted of the secretary general and the necessary staff of secretaries and advisers.

Program of the League. The nations which were members of the League agreed to respect and preserve, as against external aggression, the territorial integrity and existing political independence of all members. They were further pledged to submit, either to arbitration or to inquiry by the League, any disputes likely to lead to a rupture of friendly relations.

The Covenant also provided for the registration, with the permanent secretariat, of all treaties between states; for issuing commissions to administer territory under mandate; and for the taking over by the League of all international bureaus, with the consent of the states establishing them. The Covenant provided also for the establishment of the Permanent Court of International Justice at The Hague. Amendments to the Covenant could take effect only when ratified by all members of the League represented in the Council and by a majority of the members whose representatives composed the Assenbly.

Member Nations. At the first meeting of the Assembly, November 15, 1920, 42 states were members of the League. Its largest membership was 57, in 1934; first and last 63 nations have been members. At the beginning of 1942, the League nominally included 45 nations: Afghanistan, Argentina, Australia, Belgium, Bolivia, Bulgaria, Canada, China, Colombia, Cuba, Czechoslovakia, Denmark, Dominican Republic, Ecuador, Egypt, Eire, Estonia, Ethiopia, Finland, France, Great Britain, Haiti, Greece, India, Iran, Iraq, Latvia, Liberia, Lithuania, Luxembourg, Mexico, Netherlands, New Zealand, Norway, Panama, Poland, Portugal, Rumania, South Africa, Sweden, Switzerland, Thäi, Turkey, Uruguay, and Yugoslavia. Of these Denmark, Finland, France, and Rumania had given notice of withdrawal; Belgium, Luxembourg, Netherlands, Norway, Greece, Czechoslovakia, and Yugoslavia were under the military control ot the Axis powers; Estonia, Latvia, and Lithuania were absorbed in Russia, and Poland was divided between Russia and Germany. Ethiopia had been conquered by Italy and reconquered by Great Britain.

CASUALTIES IN THE UNITED STATES ARMY AND NAVY DURING WORLD WAR I

CAUSE OF DEATH	FOREIGN			DOMESTIC			GRAND TOTAL		
	Officers	Enlisted Men	Total	Officers	Enlisted Men	Total	Officers	Enlisted Men	Aggregate
Killed in action	1,618	35,193	36,811	....	5	5	1,618	35,198	36,816
Died of wounds received in action	603	13,108	13,711	1	44	45	604	13,152	13,756
Died of disease	609	23,091	23,700	1,037	37,369	38,406	1,646	60,460	62,106
Died of accident	355	2,203	2,558	357	1,535	1,892	712	3,738	4,450
Drowned	17	308	325	13	372	385	30	680	710
Suicide	60	237	297	75	598	673	135	835	970
Murder or homicide	6	152	158	13	146	159	19	298	317
Executed	.....	11	11	....	24	24	.....	35	35
Other causes	1	120	121	2	154	156	3	274	277
Totals	3,269	74,423	77,692	1,498	40,247	41,745	4,767	114,670	119,437
Total wounded	7,292	190,657	197,949	....	.....	.....	7,292	190,657	197,949
Grand total died and wounded *	10,561	265,080	275,641	1,498	40,247	41,745	12,059	305,327	317,386

CASUALTIES IN THE NAVY AND MARINE CORPS: Killed in action, 3129; Died of disease, 6600; Wounded in action, 10,789. The Marine Corps lost 2707 killed in action; the Navy, 422.

* Note.—The figures given in the above table represent the latest available government statistics. As in the case of casualty statistics of other wars, however, they are subject to correction in detail.

Sixteen former members had withdrawn: Albania, Brazil, Costa Rica, Chile, Germany, Guatemala, Honduras, Hungary, Italy, Japan, Nicaragua, Paraguay, Peru, Salvador, Spain, and Venezuela. Russia was expelled, December 1939. Austria was annexed to Germany. The United States and Saudi Arabia had never been members.

The United States and the League. President Wilson, who represented the United States at the Peace Conference, was an active promoter of the League, and, by his insistence, the Covenant was made an integral part of the Treaty of Versailles, fixing the conditions of peace with Germany. Upon his presentation of this treaty to the Senate for ratification, serious objections were raised. The most important of these were: (1) the impairment of the fundamental principle of American foreign policy known as the Monroe Doctrine; (2) the guarantee to respect and preserve against external aggression the territorial integrity and existing political independence of all members of the League. This provision, embraced in Article X, was declared by President Wilson to be the "heart of the Covenant" and incapable of amendment without destroying the purpose of the instrument. Reservations embracing these and some minor points were framed by the Senate, and the ensuing deadlock between the president and the Senate led to the rejection of the entire treaty.

The Work of the League. Among the political undertakings of the League were the government of the Saar basin through an international commission, the protection of Danzig, the regulation of traffic on the Danube, the supervision of a corridor giving Bulgaria access to the Ægean Sea at Kavala, Greece, and the settlement of a number of geopolitical problems.

Conspicuous failures of the League to prevent conflicts include Japan's refusal to desist from "aggressive" action against China in 1931 and Italy's defiance of economic sanctions invoked after an "aggressive" warfare against Ethiopia in 1935-36. The League was helpless in the face of Germany's seizure of Austria in 1937, of Czechoslovakia in 1938, and of Danzig and Poland in 1939.

Dissolution. The League ended with World War II. A meeting at Geneva in September 1939 delegated authority for League activities for the duration of the war to a Supervisory Committee. A small part of the Secretariat remained at Geneva, while important nonpolitical branches were moved to Princeton university, Montreal, and Washington. On April 8, 1945 the last Assembly met at Geneva. Ten days later the League voted its dissolution, transferring its material property to the United Nations.

MANDATES

Politically, the term "mandate" was devised by the Peace Conference of 1919, as a system of trusteeship for the government and development of dependent peoples wrested from the possession of Germany and from the Ottoman empire.

On May 16, 1919, the Paris Conference agreed to allot to Great Britain, German East Africa; to the Union of South Africa, German Southwest Africa; to New Zealand, German Samoa; to Australia, German New Guinea, the Bismarck archipelago and adjoining islands; and to Japan, the former German islands north of the equator, with the exception of the Island of Nauru, which was allotted to Great Britain. At this same meeting, Great Britain and France agreed to divide the German colonies of Togoland and Cameroon between them. This was accomplished, July 10, 1919.

An allocation of territories of the Ottoman empire was accomplished at the conference of San Remo, April 18 to 25, 1919, where the representatives of Great Britain and France agreed that the former power should receive Iraq and Palestine, and the latter, Syria and Lebanon. A subsequent agreement, at Paris, December 23, 1920, transferred a portion of Syria to the British mandate of Palestine, and France received, as a consideration, a share in oil land concessions in Iraq, and other advantages.

PERMANENT COURT OF INTERNATIONAL JUSTICE (WORLD COURT)

The establishment of an international court for the adjudication of disputes between nations was provided for by the Peace Conference of 1919. Such a tribunal had already been proposed by Elihu Root in 1907. An arrangement in 1910 to which the United States, France, Germany, and Great Britain were parties was stopped by the World War. Pursuant to Article XIV of the Covenant, the Council of the League, early in 1920, appointed a committee of jurists to formulate a plan or organization. With some modifications, this plan was adopted by the Assembly of the League of Nations, December 13, 1920.

Organization. The Court consists of 15 members, elected for terms of nine years by the Assembly and Council of the League of Nations from a list of names nominated by the panels of jurists from which members are appointed to the Permanent Court of Arbitration at The Hague.

Jurisdiction. For trial of international disputes, the court is open to members of the League and to states mentioned in the annex to the Covenant of the League. States ratifying its constitution may recognize as compulsory the jurisdiction of the court in any or all of the following classes of legal disputes: (a) the interpretation of treaties; (b) questions of international law; (c) the existence of any fact which, if established, constitutes a breach of international obligations; (d) reparation for such a breach. Over 45 nations, including Great Britain, France, Italy, and Japan, accepted this compulsory feature.

The court, in making its awards, was to apply the principles of international conventions, international law, general principles of law recognized by civilized nations, and, as a subsidiary means of determining the rules of international law, the teachings of the most highly qualified publicists of various nations. A majority of the court might render a decision. The court was empowered to render advisory opinions.

The Permanent Court of International Justice was dissolved by the last Assembly of the League of Nations. It was replaced, and its work continued by the International Court of Justice, organized at the Hague, April 18, 1946, under the charter of the United Nations.

REPARATIONS

Under the Treaty of Versailles a commission was set up to fix the amount of the reparation payments to be made by Germany and to determine its division among the recipients. A definite assessment was finally made on April 21, 1921, at London. It amounted to about 32 billion dollars.

The first plan for collection proved impossible. Under the Dawes plan of 1924 and the Young plan of 1929, the total was finally scaled down to 8.806 billion dollars, as of September 1, 1929. Payments were to be spread over 59 years. In July 1931 a one-year moritorium was granted; no payments were made thereafter. The amount actually paid under all the plans was about $4,470,300,000.

BANK FOR INTERNATIONAL SETTLEMENTS

This bank was created under the Young plan to handle the reparation funds. It was in addition to provide facilities for international financial operations. It was organized in May 1930 with headquarters at Basel, Switzerland. Its directors are named by the central banks of the leading countries. It cannot issue currency or make loans to governments. It may, however, hold gold reserves for central banks, thus reducing the need for shipments and acting as a clearing house.

WORLD WAR II

As compared with World War I, World War II was more nearly a universal war. It was also much more complex. Many of its issues grew out of World War I but many others did not. Both wars might be regarded as phases of a continuing struggle to determine by whom the world should be controlled.

Such struggles had been going on from the beginning of history, but the advances of the last century in the means of transportation and communication and in the mechanization of production made it possible to correlate activities of armed forces on a global scale. They also made war potentially more decisive, for the victor would control the means necessary for any resistance, present or future, and the vanquished would be powerless. The rapidly increasing population of the world added an element of urgency.

Comparison between the Two Wars: The Line-Up. In both wars Germany was the leading antagonist against an alliance of other powers. She had as allies in World War I Austria-Hungary and later Bulgaria and Turkey. In World War II, Germany, enlarged by portions of the old Austria-Hungary, was joined by Italy and Japan. She also had the more or less reluctant assistance of four satellite states—Finland, Hungary, Rumania, and Bulgaria. Early conquests gave her control of the resources, human and material, of Norway, Denmark, France, Belgium, The Netherlands, Poland, Yugoslavia, Greece, and part of Russia.

Great Britain and France were leading powers against Germany at the opening of both wars. In World War I Russia was an ally from the first, but she did not enter World War II until attacked in mid-1941. As the war enlarged, however, the alliance against Germany embraced also the United States, China, the nations originally non-belligerent which Germany had conquered, and a number of countries of Latin America, the most active of which was Brazil.

Geography of the War. World War I was waged almost exclusively in Europe, though operations were carried on to some extent also in Africa, in southwestern Asia, and on the high seas. With World War II, besides the primary conflict in Europe, eastern Asia and the Pacific became a major theater of warfare; Africa was involved from the equatorial lakes to the Mediterranean; Australia was attacked; even the Americas found their outlying shores and islands within the zone of conflict. Air power made war on the oceans more widespread and intense.

Weapons and Methods. These and other contrasts were due to radical developments in weapons and methods of their use, particularly the airplane, the tank, and electrical devices.

Airplanes.—Airplanes during World War I had been used chiefly as the "eyes" of the land forces; combat had been incidental to their major use, and bombing raids were few. During World War II, they constituted a fighting force without which no army or navy could achieve victory. The airplane and glider were also developed for the transport of troops to hostile islands or behind enemy lines.

Still more revolutionary was the use of airplanes to destroy entire cities, wiping out large sections of a nation's production and transport facilities. The airplane above all other weapons brought civilians into the center of warfare, for in such raids little discrimination of "military objectives" could be made.

The airplane also greatly altered the form of naval warfare. By means of aircraft transported on carriers battle fleets were enabled to concentrate striking power against opponents long before ships came within range of each other.

Tanks.—The caterpillar tractor, already used in agriculture and industry, was applied to armored motor vehicles in World War I. Such bullet-proof tanks broke down the advantage which the machine gun had given to the defense. In World War II the tank was given heavier armor and heavier guns,

which made it extremely formidable despite development of anti-tank guns. Above all, its speed was increased. Tanks moving at forty miles an hour were fortress and cavalry combined. Land and amphibious truck transportation and the equipping of ordnance with self-propulsion vastly increased mobility.

This superior mobility made World War II predominantly a war of movement. Conflicts of tank divisions became a feature of most battles. Add to this the immense numbers of troops employed, and a single battle might cover a terrain hundreds of miles in extent. Whereas in 1815 the battle of Waterloo, fought within an area less than three miles square, decided the fate of Europe, in 1940 the battle of Flanders, with a battle line a hundred miles long, was merely one phase of an operation extending from the North Sea to the Pyrenees.

Electrical Devices.—Radio communication, in its infancy in World War I, was a necessity of World War II. Only by means of radio signals could the movements of airplanes, tanks, and motorized troops be co-ordinated. Radio beams directed air raids. "Radar," a newly developed electrical instrument, permitted detection with amazing accuracy. Electrical sighting devices were used for bombing and anti-aircraft guns, for naval guns, and torpedoes.

Importance of Productive Facilities. World War I marked a real departure from previous wars in the extent to which the decision turned on the manufacturing ability of the participants and of the nations which could be counted on to supply them. The greater ascendancy of machinery in World War II made the ability to produce and supply such machinery an indispensable element of success. This brought the factory into the battle line, for the destruction of the factory and its civilian worker became as necessary and almost as desirable as the destruction of a field force. In the airplane was found an ideal weapon for that purpose. Protection against an air raid is difficult, retaliation is much easier. But the airplane can only strike and destroy, it cannot capture and carry away. So sheer destruction became more than ever before a dominant feature of war. The phrase "total war" began to be used, implying that every element of a nation's life and energies must be employed for victory. The civilian at home was a participant as truly as the soldier in the field—and therefore equally open to attack.

Psychology and Economics. On both sides psychological weapons were used with new skill. "Wars of nerves" played on the popular fears and uncertainty by radio, leaflets, and press reports. Economic threats and trade agreements were used to bring under control smaller countries, especially those with useful natural resources.

Causes of the War: The Heritage of World War I. Two main groups of causes combined to bring about World War II. First were questions inherited from World War I: the desire of Germany to regain her lost territory and prestige; the desire of the winning powers to hold their gains; the dissatisfaction of some of them with their share of the spoils; and the fear by the new national governments created after the war of losing their independence, particularly in view of the frequent existence of dissatisfied minorities within their borders.

Causes of the War: The Conflict of Ideologies. Before the war and in its early stages, an ideological conflict, cutting across national lines, appeared as a prominent factor. As the war went on, this element was pushed into the background by rising national feeling and power politics. With the end of the war, the ideological conflict showed signs of revival, but on different lines: a leftward tendency within the western European democracies, and signs of divergence between them and communist Russia.

Communism. The Russian revolution represented the first large scale application of Marxian socialism. The absolute control of the individual it involved was the antithesis of the individual freedom which was the ideal of democratic nations. A government based on control from the top and by the Communist party professed to attend a future return to individual freedom, but that future was distant. One reason was the belief of the leaders in a future struggle with capitalistic countries. To prepare for the struggle they worked for the extension of the party to other countries, enlisting party members abroad, and training them, for action in the party interest, even against their own country

Anti-Communism. The natural result was agitation and organization against Communism. This feeling helped Mussolini and Hitler. Hitler was aided also by the economic depression, a powerful factor in bringing about other dictatorships after 1930. The peoples were willing to follow any leader who promised to help them. This internal social conflict helped also to paralyze the resistance of small countries to the possible danger from Fascism. Pacificism also played a part. But the German leaders were not pacifists. See *Germany*, *Hitler*, *Adolf*, *Anti-Semitism*.

The Axis and the Anti-Comintern Pact. In 1935 and 1936 Germany and Italy developed a common policy based on opposition to communism as embodied in the Russian-controlled Third Communist International (Comintern) and also to democratic governments and their principles. Both nations, moreover, asserted their need of expansion to relieve their growing populations. This understanding, popularly referred to as the Rome-Berlin Axis, met a sympathetic response from Japan.

On November 25, 1936, Japan and Germany signed the Anti-Comintern pact, ostensibly providing for consultation and cooperation against the Communist International but directed also against the democratic governments. Other powers which might feel themselves threatened were invited to join. Italy joined the next year and was followed two years later by Manchukuo, Hungary, and Spain. The agreement was to last for five years. On its expiration in 1941, it was renewed at Berlin, and seven other governments adhered: Bulgaria, Croatia, Denmark, Finland, Rumania, Slovakia, and the Nanking government of China, while the Vichy government of France endorsed its principles.

Beginnings of the War. It is part of the complexities of World War II that no one date can be confidently fixed on for its outbreak. There is rather a series of dates on which different stages of the war began.

Of the dates which might be selected, the most important are:

September 1, 1939, when Germany invaded Poland, thus bringing France and Great Britain into the war;

June 22, 1941, when Germany attacked Russia;

December 7, 1941, when Japan attacked the United States.

There are, however, several earlier dates, marking the stages of its approach, when hostilities were begun which preluded or merged into the general war. These dates are:

September 18, 1931, when Japan occupied Mukden and began the conquest of Manchuria, which it erected into the puppet state of Manchukuo;

July 7, 1937, when Japan attacked China proper, thus beginning a war which later became an integral part of the larger global war after Japan had attacked the United States and Great Britain;

October 1935, when Italy began the conquest of Ethiopia in an attempt to build up her African empire;

July 17, 1936, when a conservative party rebellion against the left-wing government of Spain provided an opportunity for the Fascist powers to set up a government favorable to their cause;

March 12, 1938, when Germany occupied Austria;

October 1, 1938, when Germany took over the Sudetenland from Czechoslovakia.

Expansion by Italy and Japan. Beginning with 1935, the axis powers, either by war or other politico-military techniques, expanded their territories. Italy conquered Ethiopia in 1935-36. When the League of Nations attempted to enforce sanctions Italy resigned, as Germany and Japan had done the year before. In April 1939, Italy overran Albania, which was erected into a separate kingdom under the king of Italy.

Japan had seized Manchuria in 1931 and the northern provinces of China in 1935. In 1937, she entered upon an undeclared war with China. By 1939 she was in control of the coastal regions and of most of the large cities, and had set up a puppet government at Nanking. But the Chinese under Chiang Kai-shek still held out in the interior.

The Spanish Civil War. As the Balkan Wars had been a prelude to the First World War, so the Spanish Civil War preceded the second. It had started in appearance as a revolt of the conservative army leaders, representing the monarchical and clerical tradition of old Spain, against the Republican government. The communist wing of the Republicans gained control and was supported by Russia to the end, while the Insurgents, quickly assuming Fascist forms and principles, received men and munitions from Germany and Italy. Great Britain, France, and the United States pursued a policy of non-intervention which operated decisively against the Government. The war ended in 1939 with the triumph of the Insurgents under General Franco and the establishment of a totalitarian government bound by close ties to the Axis.

German Expansion. In 1935 a plebescite in the Saar District, in accordance with the Treaty of Versailles, resulted in a ten-to-one vote in favor of reunion with Germany. Germany was now showing her intention of disregarding all the restrictive clauses of the treaty. In 1936 she reintroduced conscription and began to rearm. The Rhineland was again occupied by German troops and fortified while France and Britain looked on. They remained silent. Hitler then turned to Austria. The government of that country was now a practical dictatorship under Chancellor Schuschnigg after the Socialist party had been suppressed. Schuschnigg made a gesture of resistance by calling for a plebescite, whereupon Hitler, on March 12, 1938, moved German troops into Austria and occupied the country. A vote taken under German auspices showed a heavy majority for union. Austria became the *Ostmark*.

The Munich Pact. Czechoslovakia came next. The Versailles treaty had included in that country border districts largely populated by Germans—the Sudeten lands. These claimed to be treated unfairly by the Czechs, appealed to Hitler for aid, and threatened revolt. The Czech government appealed to France, England, and Russia for assistance. A crisis threatened which might result in a European war. Premier Chamberlain averted the immediate danger by flying to a conference with Hitler at Berchtesgaden. England and France advised Czechoslovakia to submit, and with Mussolini's help, persuaded Hitler not to use force. The final adjustment was made at Munich, September 29-30. The parties were, in addition to Hitler and Mussolini, Neville Chamberlain and Edouard Daladier, premier of France. Russia was ignored. Czech territory with more than fifty per cent of German population was taken over by the Reich. Final determination of the boundary was to be made by a commission of the four powers and Czechoslovakia.

The Fruits of "Appeasement." Chamberlain's action was generally approved in England. Hitler had promised at the time of the Munich pact, to respect the independence of Czechoslovakia, and had said that Germany had no further territorial claims in Europe, but he made no opposition when Hungary and Poland took parts of the weakened state and when Slovakia demanded autonomy. In March 1939, on the occasion of trouble in Slovakia, Hitler moved troops into Bohemia and Moravia. and declared them a protectorate of the Reich. Slovakia became independent, but under German control. Great Britain, France, Russia, and the United States, refused to recognize the new status. In March 1939 also, Memel, with a large German population, was yielded by Lithuania. All these additions to the Reich were justified by the Germans as reclamations of territory unjustly taken from them in World War I.

Germany, Poland, and Russia. Hitler now turned to Danzig and the Polish corridor. The corridor, cutting off East Prussia from the rest of Germany, had been created to give Poland an outlet to the sea; a large part of its population was German. Danzig, German from its foundation, had been made a free city under the League of Nations with guarantees for German and Polish commercial rights. Near it, the Poles had built their own seaport of Gdynia. Hitler was now demanding that Danzig be returned to the Reich with guarantees for Polish commercial rights and that Germany be given an extraterritorial corridor across the corridor. Poland refused, and the deadlock continued for several months.

One reason for the delay was the position of Russia. Great Britain had already declared, on March 31, that she would support the Poles against any action which threatened their independence. France was committed to the same policy. But Russia was the only power which could give Poland real military assistance against a German attack.

Russia had formerly cooperated with Great Britain and France, fearing Nazi policies. The western powers had ignored her in the Munich agreement. Now Britain and France asked her support for Poland. Stalin, now the real ruler of Russia, negotiated with both sides. At last, on August 20, 1939, he signed a trade treaty with Germany and, four days later, a ten-year non-aggression pact.

Stalin gained by this treaty the time which Russia needed to strengthen her army and defenses against a possible German attack. He also divided the western powers, setting Great Britain and France against Germany. The price he received was a free hand with the Baltic states and Poland. The immediate effect was to free Germany from any fear of an attack from the east, and to cut off Poland from any effective military assistance.

The news of the German-Russian alliance burst upon the world like a thunderbolt. But if Hitler expected it to deter the British and French from going to war, he was disappointed. Neville Henderson, the British ambassador, made it clear that Great Britain would fight if Poland was attacked.

At the last moment Germany put forward proposals for a peaceful settlement, but the Poles were given no opportunity to consider or hardly to understand them. On September 1, the German armies invaded Poland. For two days longer the British and French governments, without success, continued to urge withdrawal of the troops and a conference. On September 3, at 11 A.M., Great Britain declared war; six hours later France followed her example.

Great Britain was followed in its declaration of war by most of the British dominions. Australia and New Zealand declared war simultaneously; Canada settled a constitutional question without raising it by delaying her declaration of war until her parliament had acted on September 10. South Africa, after some deliberation and a change of ministry from General Herzog to General Smuts, severed diplomatic relations on September 5. Eire, refusing to follow the other dominions, remained neutral.

The Polish War. Poland had no natural frontier defense. The surface of the country was generally level, dry at that time of year, ideal terrain for mechanized armies. The industrial district was near the German border. To defend this open country the Poles had about 600,000 men and 900 planes.

The Poles hoped to delay the Germans in western Poland, and on the line of the Vistula, until the fall rains and the English and French armies in the west could come to their relief. The German plan was a double "pincers" movement. Two armies converged on Warsaw from East Prussia and Pomerania; two others, cutting off the industrial district, and outflanking the Vistula line, converged upon Warsaw from the south and southwest. Germany used most of her first line troops, almost a million men. General von Brauchitsch was commander in chief, General von Bock led the northern army, and General von Rundstedt, the southern.

It was the German plan which succeeded. The Poles were driven back in the north and west and were outflanked in the south. The rains did not come. The Germans made abundant use of mechanized troops, but a great part of their success was due to air power. Their overwhelming air force crushed the Polish air defense at the first onslaught, broke up the mobilization by attacking concentration points, especially in eastern Poland, bombed Warsaw and other cities, and kept the Germans fully informed of Polish troop movements. On September 5 the Germans were within 40 miles of Warsaw, on the 6th the southern army entered Krakow, by the 14th the Germans were closing in on Warsaw itself. The western army was cut off; the only hope of the eastern army was to make a last stand in the marshes on he eastern border.

Poland's deathblow came from Russia. On September 17 Russian troops, "to protect Russian interests and the White Russian and Ukrainian minorities," entered Poland and occupied the eastern half, as far as Brest-Litovsk and Lemberg (Lvov), with little resistance. Half a million Polish troops were captured. Warsaw held out until the 27th.

Danzig, the occasion of the trouble, had, meantime, announced its union with the Reich.

President Moscicki and the Polish government fled to Rumania, thence to France, and ultimately to London. They organized a government which Great Britain, France, and the United States continued to recognize as the legitimate Polish government.

Germany and Russia now divided Poland—its fourth partition—on the general lines of the Bug and San rivers, the "Curzon line." Russia received the larger territory, but the smaller population. Her share was mostly annexed to the Soviet Republics of White Russia and the Ukraine, with which its population was racially connected. Germany left the part around Warsaw for the Poles, and prepared the rest for German occupation. The price the Germans paid was 43,000 casualties, 10,000 killed.

Defensive Attitude of Allies. France and Britain had declared war, but in neither country was the mental attitude propitious for victory. England was trusting to her seapower and her blockade; France, to her fortifications. In England Chamberlain, a competent peace minister, was not the man to conduct a war. In France, the administration was weakened by personal rivalry and party politics. In both countries pacifist feeling was strong. Both countries were thinking first of defense. Germany, schooled by her years of adversity under the Versailles treaty, and forced by her disarmament to start from scratch, could take advantage of changes in technique to develop a new army and a new type of war, the *Blitzkrieg*.

British and French Preparation. Great Britain had introduced compulsory military service in May 1939; now the draft was extended to men twenty to forty-one. The "territorials" (militia) were increased. Air raid precautions were taken and a rationing system was set up. France was more advanced in preparations. The Chamber in May had given Daladier "full powers" for national defense. Very early in the war a joint war council was established to co-ordinate operations.

Strength of the Opposing Forces. On paper the armies were not very unequal. Germany had potentially six million men, 160 divisions. Against these England could bring about four million men, 600,000 being in the regular army. France had 765,000 regulars, with 4,250,000 reserves. The German army, however, was at home. and could be used there. The British and French armies had the areas of their empires to cover.

In naval strength, especially in capital ships, the Allies had an overwhelming advantage, but the Germans were strong in submarines. In the air the Germans had 11,000 planes against the Allies' 8,000, and superior facilities for replacement.

Maginot and Siegfried Lines. In the hope of preventing such an invasion as they had suffered in 1914, the French had constructed their great Maginot line, so called from the war minister who had initiated its construction. This was a continuous fortification from Switzerland to the Belgian border. It cost $150,000,000, and was believed impregnable against assault or siege. Unfortunately, it was not continued along the Belgian border. Over against it, the Germans were hastily building the Siegfried line, or Westwall, a zone of disconnected but supporting redoubts, 30 miles wide.

When Poland was attacked, the French manned the Maginot line, but failed to use their time to strengthen the defenses on the Belgian border. They made only futile demonstrations against the German reserves in the Siegfried line. A British expeditionary force of 350,000 men, under General Viscount Gort, took over a sector near Luxembourg in December. General Maurice Gamelin, commanding the French army, was made commander in chief of the Allied armies. The British Admiralty directed the navies.

First Stages of the War at Sea. Naval warfare was begun at once by Britain on the lines of World War I. The battle fleet was concentrated at Scapa Flow and in the Firth of Forth. A strict blockade was established. Control ports were set up at strategic points, and the usual friction with neutral powers began.

The Germans at once began a counter-blockade. They had about 50 submarines and were building more. They sent them out to prey upon enemy commerce and sank 785,000 tons of shipping, neutral as well as allied, in the first four months. The British met the attack with some success by using the convoy system. Both sides laid mines.

German submarines sank two British capital ships but only one real ship action occurred, the sinking of the *Graf Spee*. She was driven into Montevideo, Uruguay, by three British cruisers, and scuttled in the River La Plata.

Russia Moves on the Baltic. As soon as the treaty with Germany was signed, Russia began to move on the Baltic with German approval. Her aim was to regain control of the Baltic states—Finland, Estonia, Latvia, and Lithuania, which had become independent in 1919. In September and October 1939 she obtained treaties of "mutual assistance" which gave her military control of the eastern end of the Baltic. Then the Communist parties within the states acted, and in July 1940 Latvia, Estonia, and Lithuania were admitted to the Soviet Union.

The Finnish War. Finland, however, was stronger and less complaisant. She refused Moscow's demands for a cession of territory at the head of the Gulf of Finland. On November 30, Russia invaded the country, alleging the necessity of defending Leningrad from attacks by or through Finland.

The key to the Finnish defense was the Mannerheim line, across the Karelian isthmus, from Viborg (Viipuri) on the Gulf to Lake Ladoga. To defend these works and the long eastern boundary General Mannerheim had 225,000 trained troops and a militia force of about 100,000.

For two months the Finns repulsed the Russians from the Mannerheim line and threw back attacks around Lake Ladoga and along their eastern frontier, though the Russians took Petsamo in the north. The weather, exceptionally severe, was on their side, and the Russian troops were second-rate and poorly led. In February the Russians sent better commanders with more troops, bringing their force up to

800,000, and broke through the Mannerheim line

The Scandinavian countries, though traditionally suspicious of Russia, gave Finland no open assistance. Fearing German reprisals, they refused passage to British and French troops.

On March 12, a treaty was signed at Moscow by which Finland gave up Viborg and the Karelian isthmus, leaving her defenseless in that quarter. The cession of Hango and its islands completed Russian control of the Gulf of Finland.

The Norwegian War. Norway, Sweden, and Denmark had hoped to maintain their neutrality in this war, as in the last. Sweden alone succeeded.

Norway lay between the two belligerents. The Germans alleged that her neutrality had been invaded by the British seizure of a German prisonship in Norwegian waters, and by British mine-laying in the route of ships bringing iron ore from Narvik. Under pretext of protecting Norway and Denmark from Allied invasion, the Germans themselves invaded these countries on the night of April 9, 1940. They promised the territorial integrity of both countries in the future.

Denmark could not resist, and King Christian advised his people to make no opposition. But outside the continent, Iceland declared its independence, and received a British garrison; Greenland turned to the United States for support; and the British occupied the Faroe Islands.

In Norway the German attack was directed against Oslo, and the western ports of Bergen, Trondheim, Narvik, and Stavanger. The attacking force numbered about 25,000, later increased fourfold. Norway had about 15,000 trained soldiers, and no air force to speak of. Oslo was taken, but the king, ministry, and parliament escaped.

Most of Norway's wealth, population, and resources are concentrated south of Trondheim, in the coast towns, and the two river valleys, Ostendal and the Godbrandsdal. The Germans had already seized the coast towns. They now fanned out from Oslo up the river valleys, meeting brave but inadequate resistance. The Allied troops sent to assist Norway were too few and came too late. By early June the Norwegian army had surrendered and the Allies were forced to withdraw.

By this success the Germans had made secure their ore supplies from the Swedish mines, clinched their hold on Sweden, blocked any chance of attack from the north, and secured bases for sea and air operations against Britain.

King Haakon, his family and ministers escaped to England. Since the Storting had authorized him to act from outside Norway, his continued to be the only legal government. The gold reserve had been sent to England, and the Norwegian merchant marine obeyed his orders. The Germans set up a government of Nazi sympathizers, headed by Vidkun Quisling, which met determined resistance, active and passive. See *Quisling*.

The Norwegian fiasco brought about the fall of the British cabinet headed by Chamberlain. He was succeeded by Winston Churchill, who told the Commons, quoting Garibaldi, "I have nothing to offer you but blood, toil, tears, and sweat."

The Invasion of the Netherlands. Scarcely had Winston Churchill taken office when he had to meet a new German attack on the Continent. On the morning of May 10 the Germans, without a formal declaration of war, poured over the borders of the Netherlands and Belgium.

Unlike Norway, both countries were ready for and expecting an attack. Both had counted on holding their defense lines until help should come from Great Britain and France. Both countries had insisted on their neutrality to the last, and no Allied troops were in either country when the invasion came.

The Germans crushed the Dutch resistance in the north of Holland and cut off relief from the south. Air power, with the use of parachute troops, and the fifth column, partly of pro-German Netherlanders, wrecked the Dutch resistance. Airfields were seized, Rotterdam was bombed, the Dutch army, under General Winkleman, fought bravely, but was forced to surrender May 14.

On May 13th Queen Wilhelmina with her ministers left the Hague for England on a British cruiser and she continued to govern the Dutch colonial empire from London. They had brought with them the Dutch gold reserve and control over the great Dutch merchant marine, which was largely still at sea. The Germans organized in Holland, as in Norway, a government of Dutch Nazis.

The Battle of Flanders. This name is given to the fighting in Belgium and northern France between the German frontier and the Channel ports. On the morning of May 10 the German army swept into Belgium.

In this quarter Belgium was defended by Liège and its forts,. the fortified line of the Albert canal, and the supposedly impassable ground of the Ardennes Forest. To defend these the Belgians had mobilized perhaps 800,000 men. General Gamelin had assumed that this line would delay the Germans for four or five days, giving the Allied forces time to establish themselves on the line of Antwerp-Louvain-Namur for defense or counterattack. Accordingly, on the first news of the German invasion, the British expeditionary force and three French armies left their defensive positions in northern France and moved north into Belgium.

But the Germans moved too rapidly. They attacked Fort Eben Emael, north of Liège, and crossed the Albert canal on the first day of their advance. On the second day they had taken or destroyed the defenses of Liège. The Albert canal defenses gave way entirely, perhaps through treachery, and the invaders were passing the Ardennes, threatening the right flank of the Allies moving north.

The French Ninth Army under General Corap was to occupy the defenses along the Belgian border, but the Germans struck it before it got fairly into position. The Ninth Army disintegrated. Sedan was taken, and with it the bridge over the Meuse, which, for reasons never fully explained, had not been destroyed. The rout of Corap's army opened a gap fifty miles wide in the French line, and through it the invaders poured, heading westward to the sea.

The Allied forces in Belgium now met the main German advance in a confused struggle. In a tank battle near Gembloux the French fought creditably, but were outnumbered. Meanwhile the German air force operated in the rear of the Allied army, bombing the advancing reserves, the railways, and concentration points. The Allies found their movements handicapped by the crowds of fleeing civilians, panic-stricken by the planes which swept over them and machine-gunned them as well as troops. On the 17th Brussels, whence the Belgian government had already removed to Ostend, was occupied by the Germans, and Namur was taken. On the 18th the Germans entered Antwerp. The plan for a second line of defense had broken down.

Meantime the Nazi southern column was driving west across northern France. It passed the Aisne and Oise rivers and swept down the Somme valley. On the 20th it had reached Cambrai, the scene of the Battle of the Somme in 1916. On the 21st the Germans entered Amiens, which they had just failed to reach in 1918. The same day they reached Abbeville, at the mouth of the Somme.

It was now evident that the French high command had made a terrible mistake in the movement north. The Belgian army, the British Expeditionary Force, and the remnants of three French armies, the First, Seventh, and Ninth, were pressed by the Germans from the north and east, the advance of the southern column had cut them off from the main French army. Their only source of supply was the Channel ports, which were being bombed by the German air force, while the German mechanized columns, having turned north, were attacking from Arras and driving along the coast. Boulogne was taken on the

28th, and fierce fighting began near Calais. The Allies were now pressed back into a rough crescent around Dunkirk, with the Belgian army forming the north wing.

There was still hope if they could break through to the south, and such a movement, co-ordinated with a French attack from that quarter, would put the long, thin German salient in grave peril. General Weygand, who had replaced Gamelin in command of the French army, began to mass troops near Amiens for such a movement.

Any chance for the forces cornered in Belgium vanished when, on the morning of May 28, the Belgian army was surrendered by King Leopold, who declared that his army was starving and out of ammunition. The Belgian surrender exposed the right flank of the British. They could do nothing but fall back upon Dunkirk, the only port left in their hands. With them were a few Dutch troops and the remains of the French armies, about 400,000 men in all.

Dunkirk. The evacuation of the British army from Dunkirk was the one bright spot in the gloomy picture of disaster. The nearly 400,000 men in the town and its environs were crowded into an ever narrowing space by unceasing attacks, under fire from the German batteries, and bombed at times by the German airplanes. Military experts estimated that possibly 25 per cent of them could be rescued. British cruisers and destroyers fought off German submarines in the Channel. British and French aircraft, helped by cloudy weather. struggled with enemy planes above the town, and for a few days kept qualified control of the air. The British garrison in Calais fought to the last man to gain time.

Meantime every available craft on the opposite coast, merchant ships, tugboats, ferryboats, fishing boats, pleasure craft, river steamers, was called into service to assist the navy and the army transports in bringing the cornered troops to safety.

While the rearguard fought desperately on the hills around the town, this nondescript transport fleet took off the soldiers, dropping from the ruins of the shattered piers or wading out in long lines into the shoal waters from the beaches. Loaded to the gunwale, they steamed off for the English coast— and came back for more. The Admiralty estimated that 222 naval vessels and 665 other craft, besides French naval and private vessels took part in the embarkation. For three days and nights the evacuation went on. When the Germans finally forced their way through the town, 335,000 men, more than three-fourths of the Allied force were in England. All their heavy arms and equipment were lost.

The Germans now held all the Netherlands and Belgium, with a strip of northern France, including the Channel ports. The Dutch and Belgian armies were non-existent. The British Expeditionary Force had been driven off the Continent, and three French armies had been cut to pieces. In all the Allies had lost not far from a million men, including the larger part of their mechanized forces. The price the Germans paid, according to their own statements, was 10,252 dead, 42,523 wounded, and 9,463 missing.

The Collapse of France. The German army now turned southward. General Weygand was attempting to form a new line on the Aisne and Somme, but his troops had lost confidence in their commanders. Nevertheless, the Germans admitted losses of 17,000 killed and 68,000 wounded before the armistice.

The Germans now threatened Paris from two directions—from Rouen on the west and from the Marne on the east. The French government retired to Tours and later to Bordeaux. On June 13, Paris was proclaimed an "open city" and evacuated; the Germans entered it the next day without resistance. Verdun fell on the 15th, and the impregnable Maginot line lost its significance; Weygand withdrew a part of its garrison to a new line he was attempting to form on the Loire; the rest surrendered.

Italy, thinking the end was in sight, declared war on June 10, 1940. She made some slight advances in the Alps and on the southern coast, but her action made very little difference.

On June 16 defeatist elements in the French cabinet forced out Premier Reynaud. He was succeeded by Marshal Pétain, now controlled by a fascist group. The new government ignored its promise to make no separate peace, gave up its opportunity to retreat to Africa and carry on the war from there, and on June 17, asked for an armistice. It was signed on June 22; fighting ceased on June 25. The Germans staged the signing in the same railroad car, and at the same spot, Rethondes, where Germany had received the armistice terms of 1918.

Under the armistice the Germans occupied Paris, the northern industrial districts and the west coast. The Italian border, the Mediterranean naval bases, and certain African districts were to be demilitarized. The French navy was concentrated and disarmed; the army demobilized; German and Italian prisoners were released. French communications and trade passed under German control. Pétain set up his government for unoccupied France at Vichy.

Control of Colonies. All five of the conquered countries had dependencies which remained out of German control. On Spitsbergen, Norway's arctic coal-mining settlement was destroyed by an Anglo-Norwegian expedition in September 1941, and the population was removed. A later German attempt to occupy the islands was destroyed. The action of the Danish colonies has been described. The Dutch colonies obeyed the queen and her government in London; Belgian Congo, the ministers of the captive King Leopold.

The French colonial empire was divided. Indo-China passed into the hands of a watchful and aggressive Japan. North Africa and West Africa, with Madagascar, obeyed the Vichy French government, as did the West Indies. One of the younger French generals, Charles de Gaulle, fled to London at the armistice and organized there the French National Committee, the "Free French" government, which was recognized by Britain. This government was recognized by French Equatorial Africa, French Cameroon, and some of the Pacific dependencies. In September 1940, with British assistance, he made an unsuccessful attempt to take Dakar, in French West Africa. In May and June 1941, Syria and Lebanon were forcibly occupied by British and Free French troops.

The Siege of Britain. After the fall of France Britain alone seemed to stand between Hitler and complete victory. There is some evidence that he expected her to yield and delayed his attack. But Britain had in Winston Churchill a leader who refused to acknowledge defeat. The British set to work with feverish haste to transform their country into an armed camp. The government was given absolute power over persons and property. Potential "fifth columnists" were imprisoned.

Whether an invasion was actually attempted was never made known, but there is considerable evidence that a large scale rehearsal met with disaster. At any rate, the German attempts to "soften" Britain by air attack definitely failed.

After a period of comparative quiet following the French armistice, German air attacks became more intense and frequent. They culminated on August 15, when wave after wave of planes swept over England, ranging as far north as Scotland. The British claimed to have brought down 180 planes on this occasion and 185 during a raid on London on September 15. No raid at this time was participated in by as many as 500 planes. Losses of this proportion appeared ruinous, although the British air strength, technically superior but much inferior numerically, had been whittled down to dangerously low levels. At any rate, daylight raids were abandoned.

The Germans then turned to night raids and, for 13 consecutive nights in September, did terrible damage to London, striking Buckingham Palace, the British Museum, and the Houses of Parliament.

Outlying cities like Birmingham and Coventry, harbors like Southampton and Bristol were attacked. At Coventry, on the night of November 14, an intensive raid showered bombs on the city for ten and a half hours. At the end of the year, official figures showed 23,081 killed and 32,296 wounded as a result of the raids.

The Royal Air Force retaliated with raids upon German cities. The striking force of their air power steadily grew until the blows they struck dwarfed anything the Germans had attempted.

At sea the British blockade still made itself felt in the Axis countries, though severely handicapped. The German counter-blockade at sea became more effective and caused serious losses in 1941 and 1942.

Two incidents of naval warfare may be mentioned in this connection. While the French armistice only provided for its internment, the British had always feared the acquisition of the French fleet by Germany. On the refusal of the squadron at Oran, in Algeria, to surrender or proceed to the West Indies, the British attacked it and destroyed its most important ships, July 3, 1940. In May 1941, the new German battleship *Bismarck* sank the *Hood*, the largest of the British battle fleet, in an encounter near Greenland. A few days later, other units of the British navy, assisted by aircraft, sank the *Bismarck*.

Italy in the War. The entry of Italy into the war at a time calculated to bring her "in on the kill" greatly broadened the area of the war. Italy's African territory was extensive—Libya in Africa and Italian East Africa, consisting of Eritrea, Italian Somaliland, and Ethiopia. Across the Adriatic was her subject kingdom of Albania. Between them lay the Mediterranean, where Italy menaced also the "lifeline" of the British Empire, the route by Suez to India. Italy hoped to make the Mediterranean an "Italian lake" and to increase her African possessions at the expense of the British and the French.

Italy brought to the Axis battle line an army of perhaps 1,500,000, including native troops, and varying greatly in quality. She had about 3000 available planes. Her navy was weak in capital ships but strong in smaller craft. Her natural resources were limited.

Italy gained some initial successes in Somaliland but the British soon came back. An imperial force, partly South African, took the coast colonies and brought back Haile Selassie to Ethiopia. The main Italian army surrendered on May 19, 1941; the last remaining force, in November.

The war in North Africa showed a series of alternations of fortune. In September 1940, Marshal Graziani with 280,000 troops pushed 70 miles into Egypt. Egypt did not declare war, leaving its defense to the British. In December, the British general, Sir Archibald Wavell, attacked the Italians with 100,000 men, mainly Australians and New Zealanders, and by February 1941 had taken over 100,000 prisoners, occupied all Cyrenaica, and completely destroyed the Italian army as a fighting force.

A large part of the British force was now withdrawn to aid in the defense of Greece. In consequence the British were forced back to their Egyptian bases by the German General Rommel, Graziani's successor, but they still held the fortified port of Tobruk. Receiving reinforcements, the British again advanced in November and drove the Italians, now strengthened by German tank troops, to the borders of Tripoli. After desultory fighting, Rommel, with some reinforcements, advanced again in May 1942, and by the middle of July had recaptured Tobruk, invaded Egypt, and was threatening the British base at Alexandria and the Suez canal. In this fighting, tanks, some of them American, played a great part, being well adapted to deal with the distances and the desert terrain.

In the Mediterranean the Italians for a time closed the Suez canal route to India, and bombed Malta, unsuccessfully. On the other hand the British severely damaged the Italian navy in engagements at Tarano and off Cape Matapan.

The Balkan War. On October 28, 1940, Italy suddenly attacked Greece, striking from Albania. To everyone's surprise the small Greek army, of 150,000 men, not only repulsed the Italians, but advanced into Albania.

In the spring of 1941 Germany turned her military power toward the Balkans. Her diplomacy already had prepared the way. Hungary and Rumania were now under German control, and Rumania had been forced to return much of her gains of 1919 to Hungary, Bulgaria, and Russia. King Carol had abdicated in September 1940, and a Fascist government took his place. On November 23, 1940, Rumania signed the Axis pact. Bulgaria did the same. Turkey remained neutral, signed non-aggression treaties with both sides, and refused to be drawn in by either. In Yugoslavia the pro-German regent, Prince Paul, on March 20, accepted the German "new order." On the 27th the Serbian party staged a revolution which put his nephew, King Peter, on the throne, and repudiated the treaty.

Yugoslavia had about 550,000 men, poorly organized and equipped. They were assisted by the Greeks, and by an English contingent of 60,000 from Africa. The German army of 550,000, massed in Bulgaria, struck east and south. On April 9, Saloniki was taken. On April 17, the main Yugoslav army, attacked from the east and north, surrendered. Belgrade was taken.

The Germans now advanced on the Anglo-Greek army defending the Greek peninsula. On the 24th the Greek army in the west, about 220,000 men, capitulated. From the 11th to the 24th Australians and New Zealanders successively defended positions on the lines of Mt. Olympus and Thermopylae, but the increasing German pressure made further resistance impossible. About 45,000 of the British forces were evacuated from Megara and other ports, abandoning large amounts of equipment. By May 1 the Germans had conquered Yugoslavia and Greece. In the last days of May, a German attack, conducted almost entirely by air-borne troops, conquered Crete. The British lost six naval vessels from air attacks while defending it and about half of their garrison of 27,000 men.

The Axis powers now controlled the Balkan peninsula, with the important exception of Turkey. They controlled also most of the islands and had secured a base for operations in the Middle East. Yugoslavia fell apart into its original elements, while Italy and Hungary took large areas. Bulgaria took parts of Macedonia and Thrace from Greece, Serbia received a puppet government at Belgrade, but many of the Serbs continued a resistance in the mountains which took on the character of organized warfare. This resistance increased in importance as the war went on.

It was at this time that the British and Free French seized Syria and Lebanon to forestall a German march to India. German intrigue in Iraq brought prompt repressive action by Britain. A year later, a similar situation in Iran led to joint Russian and British occupation of Teheran.

The position of Italy was unenviable. Germany had saved her in North Africa and in the Balkans, and her price was entire subordination. German troops and officials in large numbers moved in.

The Atlantic Charter. The triumph of German arms in southeastern Europe was followed by a pause in which the anti-Axis world breathlessly awaited hints of the direction in which new blows would fall. At this point the leaders of the two great English-speaking nations met to provide a statement of the principles about which all nations opposed to the "New Order" of the Axis might rally.

Framed by President Roosevelt and Premier Churchill at a meeting on naval vessels "somewhere in the Atlantic" in August 1941, the statement was given the name of the Atlantic Charter. It was a statement of post-war aims despite the fact that the United States was not formally at war.

The Charter contained eight points: (1) The United States and Great Britain seek no aggrandizement, territorial or other; (2) they desire no territorial changes except with the approval of the peoples concerned; (3) they pledge themselves to further self-determination and the restoration of self-government; (4) to secure to all, victors and vanquished, access on equal terms to trade and raw materials; (5) the fullest collaboration of all nations in the economic field; (6) after the destruction of "Nazi tyranny," a secure and lasting peace, with freedom from fear and want; (7) enabling all men to traverse the seas without hindrance; (8) to secure the abandonment of force, for which, pending the establishment of a wider system of general security, "the disarmament of aggressor nations is essential." At an Inter-Allied Conference in London, September 24, twelve governments pledged adherence to the Charter. The term United Nations was applied to the signatories.

The Russian War. The war took a new turn on June 22, 1941, when Hitler suddenly hurled the full force of his armies against Russia. Hitler alleged that Russia was treacherously preparing to attack him when engaged elsewhere.

Military experts gave Russia six weeks to last. Expert opinion, however, both German and other, has seldom so completely underestimated the power of a nation. Russia had used the two-year respite secured by the German treaty to speed the construction of a war machine comparable technically with that of Germany. She alone among German foes had a first-class tank and air force. The industrial development required to support a large-scale war had been speeded with an astonishing energy. The world assumed that Russia under a communistic government lacked efficiency; an earlier "purge" extending throughout the army had raised doubts as to the loyalty of the people to their rulers. When the cloud of secrecy partly lifted, it was found that the "fifth column" in Russia had been completely eliminated; not only the army but the civilian population was trained and keyed to fight with a tenacity which for the first time was to halt the German legions.

Germany put into the field against Russia an army of 160 divisions, perhaps 2,400,000 men, increased as the war went on. Besides these Hitler had, like Napoleon, contingents from his subject nations, Italians, Slovakians, Rumanians, and Magyars; and the Finnish army in the north. Russia, though not fully mobilized, could put 2,000,000 men into the field, later increased to 4,000,000.

The plan of the war was simple. An advance on a 2,000 mile front, from the Baltic to the Black Sea, with all the German military technique, met by a "defense in depth" along the same line, withdrawing as necessary to preserve their fighting forces, and leaving "scorched earth" behind them. The German objectives were Leningrad in the north, Kiev and Odessa in the south, and Moscow in the center.

On the outbreak of the war, Winston Churchill forestalled any attempt by Hitler to assume leadership of an anti-communist crusade by accepting Russia immediately as a full ally. President Roosevelt pledged all possible aid. On July 13 a formal treaty of alliance was concluded between Great Britain and Russia, succeeded a year later by a 20-year pact for military and economic cooperation, within the framework of the Atlantic Charter.

The Anglo-Russian treaty of 1942 was signed on May 28. It consisted of two parts, one relating to the war and the other to post-war relations.

Under Part I, each nation pledged full military aid to each other and promised to refuse to enter negotiations for a separate peace with Germany or any of her satellites in Europe.

Under Part II, both parties accepted the principles of the Atlantic Charter. Specifically they renounced territorial aggrandizement. They also promised non-interference with the internal affairs of other states and co-operation in seeking the security and economic advancement of the two nations.

In the north the Germans attacked Leningrad from the south and west. The Finns, under General Mannerheim, retook Viborg and Karelia and threatened the city from the north. The siege of Leningrad, thus begun, lasted for 30 months.

The central armies under Marshal von Bock met with stubborn resistance from Marshal Timoshenko's forces. They took Smolensk July 16, and stopped there for a time.

In the South General Rundstedt's armies, with Magyar and Rumanian contingents, overran Bessarabia and Galicia; while one army group pressed along the Black Sea, another turned north toward Kiev. Odessa was passed by and left to the Rumanians; it fell on October 16. By the middle of August, the Russians were forced across the Dnieper, where they blew up the famous Dnepropetrovsk dam. Kiev fell in the last weeks of September. The southern German columns pressed on to the Crimea and the industrial region of the Donets basin, taking Kharkov on October 24 and Rostov on November 22. The Russians were "trading space for time." In spite of heavy losses, they kept their armies largely intact.

Meantime the struggle for Moscow, under Hitler's personal supervision, was renewed in the central sector. In October the Germans were within a hundred miles of the city on the north and south, and Stalin sent the government offices to Kuibeshev (Samara) on the Volga. Some German units approached within 37 miles of the city. Against the advice of his generals, Hitler ordered Moscow taken at any cost. A final assault was made in mid-November. It failed.

The Russian winter closed down. Unexpectedly the Russians attacked in the south, retaking Rostov and Kerch. The Russian armies advanced farther north also but were unable to take any of the numerous fortified "hedgehog" points on which the German army relied for defense.

Russia in 1942; Stalingrad. In the spring of 1942, the Germans, paying less attention to Leningrad and Moscow, concentrated their forces in the south. Their general aim was to gain the manufacturing and food-producing districts of southern Russia and to destroy the Russian armies. Their specific objective was threefold: to reach the Volga and cut the north and south lines of communication by rail and river; to acquire the oil wells of the Caucasus; and by holding the northern Caucasus to cut off the supplies which were reaching the Russians by the Persian Gulf.

With about two million men at his disposal, Marshal von Bock moved into the lower Don valley. He occupied the Donetz basin, but the Russians under Timoschenko avoided encirclement. Rostov was retaken on July 24, and the way was open southwest to the Caucasus and northwest to the Volga. The advance into the Caucasus reached the seaport of Novorossisk and the Maikop oil fields. Driving through the northern foothills of the Caucasus, the Germans reached Mozdok on August 24. But the Russians held them back from the more important Grozny and Baku oil fields, and winter stopped further advance.

The northern drive reached Stalingrad, a leading industrial city on the west bank of the Volga, and began its attack on August 31. For four months the siege continued. Stalingrad was bombed by planes and heavy artillery into a rubbish heap, in which Germans and Russians fought from ruined house to ruined house. It was estimated that the Russians lost 6000 men each day but they took 2000 Germans with them. Reinforcements from the eastern provinces crossed the Volga under fire.

In late November, the Russians struck back and inflicted on Germany a major disaster which marked the turning point of the Russian war. Two flanking movements across the Volga to north and south cut the German supply lines. The Germans were forced to abandon the army besieging Stalingrad. In January 1943, the Russians claimed the destruction or capture of 22 divisions, 330,000 troops, with their commanding generals.

Japan and the Far East. When the war broke out in 1939, Japan had for two years been engaged in an undeclared war with China. She was meeting stubborn resistance from General Chiang Kai-shek's forces in western China and from guerilla bands in the east. Great Britain and the United States were unofficially supporting General Chiang Kai-shek and the Chungking government, whose chief line of supply was the Burma Road from Rangoon.

In the European war, Japan, ruled by its military class, was in natural sympathy with the Axis powers. On September 27, 1940, she signed a defensive treaty with Germany and Italy, under which each of these powers would come to the assistance of any one of their number attacked by a third power not already at war with it. It was obviously aimed at the United States.

With the fall of France Japan seized her opportunity to get control of French Indo-China. She was now in position to menace the American Philippines and the British possessions in Malaya, as well as the Netherlands Indies to the south. Her move fitted into a policy pursued since 1930, when Manchuria was invaded, the ultimate objectives of which involved establishment of a "New Order" in Eastern Asia.

With Great Britain in a death-grapple in Europe, opposition to Japan fell to the United States. Both sides professed a desire for peace and continued negotiations up to and beyond the moment when war began. But peace could endure only if one or the other side abandoned its objective—the "New Order" on the side of Japan and an "open door" economic policy for other nations on the part of the United States.

On November 26, 1941, Secretary of State Hull gave Japan a final and definite statement of the American position. Hull proposed: a multilateral pact guaranteeing non-aggression in eastern Asia; that Japan should withdraw her troops from French Indo-China; that she should cease her opposition to the Chungking government in China. In return he offered a reciprocal trade agreement and the removal of the "freezing" restrictions on Japanese credit. On Sunday afternoon, December 7, the Japanese envoys handed to Secretary Hull a memorandum charging the United States and Great Britain with "imperialistic exploitation" in that region and with maliciously opposing Japan's efforts for peace and order. The memorandum proposed that the United States, in agreement with Japan, should send no more forces into the western Pacific, restore commercial relations as before the "freezing," supply Japan with oil, and cease support of China. When these things were done, Japan agreed to withdraw its forces from Indo-China.

As the Japanese envoys were presenting the memorandum, news arrived that a Japanese air force, which must have taken weeks in preparation, had attacked the American naval base at Pearl Harbor.

America at War. Up to this point, American opinion on entering the war had been divided. The attack on Pearl Harbor instantly brought about the closing of ranks in preparation for what was recognized as a life-and-death struggle.

On President Roosevelt's recommendation, Congress declared war on Japan the next day, December 8. Japan's Axis partners, Germany and Italy, declared war on the United States December 11, and Congress at once reciprocated. At a Congress which met at Rio de Janeiro January 15, 1942, all Latin-American nations suspended diplomatic relations with the Axis powers except Argentina and Chile. Nine countries, the Central American and island republics, had already declared war. Hungary and Bulgaria declared war on the United States, December 13; in July 1942, the United States declared war on Hungary, Bulgaria, and Rumania.

Premier Churchill promised that, in the event of an American declaration, Britain would follow. Her declaration slightly preceded that by the United States.

Britain had sufficient reason, for Japan had simultaneously attacked Hong Kong and moved into Thai. Thai capitulated at once, and the Japanese entered Malaya. At the same moment Japan struck at the Philippines, where for six years General Douglas MacArthur had been training the Filipino army. With command of the sea and air and superior equipment, the trained Japanese forces landed on Luzon and pushed toward Manila, resisted but not stopped by the island forces. MacArthur abandoned Manila December 27 and declared it an open city, concentrating his troops in Bataan peninsula, across Manila Bay. The Japanese nevertheless bombed Manila. MacArthur's Americans and Filipinos held out in Bataan, keeping Japanese forces estimated at 300,000 fully occupied, until April 8, 1942, when what were left of Bataan's 36,000 defenders surrendered. Corregidor fortress was taken May 5, and Japan held the Philippines. Before the surrender of Bataan, General MacArthur had been ordered to Australia to take command in the western Pacific. General Jonathan M. Wainwright succeeded him, and conducted the defense until he was forced to surrender.

The attack on Pearl Harbor gave the Japanese temporary control of the Pacific. Five American battleships were sunk or put out of action, 3 battleships, 3 cruisers, and 8 other vessels were damaged, and 240 planes were destroyed; airfields were wrecked; about 3000 were killed and wounded. For the moment it was impossible to maintain American outposts against the Japanese; Guam was taken at once; Wake three weeks later, after considerable damage to the attacking fleet; Midway held out. Japanese submarines appeared on the west coast, but did no serious damage. On February 1, an American task force inflicted heavy damage on the Japanese bases in the Gilbert and Marshall islands.

Meanwhile the Japanese armies had been victorious on the Asiatic mainland. Hong Kong fell on Christmas Day. The Japanese were already attacking Malaya, and the British slowly retreated southward toward Singapore. The battleship *Prince of Wales* and the battle cruiser *Repulse*, recently sent to aid in its defense, were sunk December 10 by Japanese torpedo bombers. Singapore had been made impregnable from the sea, but not from the land side. It fell February 17.

The conquest of the Malay peninsula gave the Japanese the world's chief source of tin, one of the two chief sources of rubber, and the greatest British naval base in the Far East, on which all Allied plans for Pacific warfare had centered.

Already Japanese sea and air forces had been raiding the East Indies. Before the fall of Singapore, they had occupied Sarawak, in Borneo, had a footing in Celebes, had taken the Amboina naval base, and were attacking Sumatra. The small Dutch army and navy with the American Asiatic squadron and a few British ships resisted bravely. In a week of fighting in Macassar Strait at the end of January Dutch and American sea and air forces sank nearly half of a large Japanese fleet, but Java was occupied three weeks after the fall of Singapore, and the American-Dutch fleet was destroyed in a battle in the Java sea.

With the Dutch East Indies in their hands, the Japanese now controlled the second major source of rubber. By occupying the oil fields they cut off the Allies from their nearest supply of oil.

Australia was now faced with the danger which had been its nightmare for 60 years. The Commonwealth had already made preparations, but the arrival of an American expeditionary force was welcome. The Japanese had taken Rabaul in New Britain in January and had occupied positions in the Solomon islands. They had made landings in New Guinea and were bombing Port Moresby in that island and Darwin in Australia. In April they began concentrations at their bases. On May 4 their fleet,

moving south in the Coral Sea, met the American fleet, which had been watching them. The battle which followed set a precedent in naval warfare in that the contending ships never saw nor fired on one another; it was a battle of aircraft. In the next four days the Japanese lost 2 aircraft carriers, 7 cruisers, and 5 destroyers, sunk or damaged, with other vessels, 23 in all. The Americans lost the carrier *Lexington* and two smaller ships.

The Japanese had turned north upon Burma, not only to occupy it, but to cut the Burma Road, the supply line of China. In spite of desperate British resistance, they reached Lashio, its southern terminus, at the beginning of May. By early June, when the rains stopped further progress, they were threatening Assam. Beyond Assam lay India, where the demands of Gandhi and the Indian Native Congress for immediate independence were hampering British defense.

The Japanese check in the Coral Sea may have contributed to greater activity in the North Pacific. On April 17 American carrier-based aircraft—from "Shangri-La," President Roosevelt explained,—dropped bombs on Tokyo and Yokohama. Admiral Nimitz, expecting some Japanese attack, had centered his defense on Midway Island. On June 3 patrol planes picked up a Japanese force of about 80 vessels, including transports, heading toward the island. Their purpose appeared to be an attack on Midway or possibly on Pearl Harbor itself. An American carrier force farther north was notified and hastened to the scene. Meantime the land based airplanes from Midway attacked and inflicted considerable damage. Carrier-based planes from the Japanese fleet bombed Midway; the damage, though serious, was not disabling. As the Japanese turned to retreat the next morning, the American carrier fleet came up and pursued them. In a three-days running fight, again entirely by airplanes, four Japanese carriers and two heavy cruisers were sunk; three battleships and ten other vessels were sunk or damaged. The American carrier *Yorktown*, and one American destroyer were sunk, the latter by a submarine. The American loss was 92 officers and 215 men. Japanese casualties were estimated at 4800.

The battle of Midway Island was the turning point in the Pacific war. Thereafter the initiative was in the hands of the United Nations.

The Invasion of Africa. The late summer of 1942 marked the height of Axis success. The Germans had driven the Russians back to the Volga and entered the Caucasus; in Africa, Rommel was threatening the British hold on Egypt; Japanese conquests had reached Burma and New Guinea and threatened India and Australia. Against this could only be set the damage by Allied air raids, the improvement in the submarine situation, and the growth of production in the United States. With the autumn of 1942 the scales began to tip in favor of the Allies.

Toward midnight on November 7, radios announced that American and British forces had successfully invaded northwest Africa. A fleet of 850 ships under British naval escort at 1 A.M. on November 8 had landed American and British battalions near Oran and Algiers; a few hours later other American forces, moving directly across the Atlantic, reached Casablanca, in Morocco. At dawn, parachute troops flown directly from England landed and siezed the airfields. There was little resistance, most vigorous at Casablanca. Algiers surrendered on the evening of the 8th, Oran the next day, and Casablanca on the 11th. The Americans had less than 2000 casualties. Sixteen ships were sunk, including five transports, but most of the men were rescued. The expedition was directed by Lieutenant-General Dwight D. Eisenhower.

In four days the Allies had gained possession of all French North Africa except Tunisia. The operation presented a political as well as a military problem. It happened that Admiral Jean Francois Darlan, commander of all French forces and Pétain's designated successor in the Vichy government of France, was in Algiers at the time of the invasion. Darlan, after negotiations with General Eisenhower, on November 11 ordered the French troops to cease firing and proclaimed a provisional government for North Africa aligned with the United Nations with himself as chief of state. French West Africa, including the important port of Dakar, accepted the new regime. The recognition of Darlan, whom the Free French regarded as dyed in the treasonable colors of Vichy, excited alarm among those who feared compromise with the Nazis. The plan was said to be temporary and was adopted to save lives and time.

The problem was somewhat simplified when, on Christmas eve, Darlan was assassinated by a young French national. Darlan's recently organized imperial council chose General Henri Giraud, who had made good his escape from France with American aid, as high commissioner and commander in chief.

De Gaulle controlled most of the rest of the French empire. To achieve a measure of unity, he was accepted as co-chairman with Giraud in a committee of national liberation, which superseded the imperial council. Soon eclipsing Giraud, De Gaulle purged the administration of pro-Vichy elements and became the recognized French leader.

Repercussions in France. The Allied seizure of North Africa was answered by Hitler's cancellation of the armistice with France and the sending of German troops into the unoccupied section. Pétain disavowed Darlan's action and removed him from office. On November 17, he transferred his powers to Hitler's tool, Laval.

Meanwhile most of the French fleet lay at the great naval base of Toulon, immobilized under the armistice. On the morning of November 27, the Germans sent troops to seize them. The commanders, under orders of their admiral, at once proceeded to scuttle the ships while French troops on guard kept off the Germans. About nine-tenths of the fleet was destroyed. A few submarines escaped to Africa.

With Morocco and Algeria secured, a race began for Tunisia. This race the Allies lost. In spite of the efforts of sea and air forces, the Germans under General von Arnim poured men and munitions across the narrow straits from Sicily into Tunis and the naval base of Bizerta, overwhelmed the French garrisons there, and occupied the coastal plain behind the ports of Sfax and Gabes.

Montgomery and Rommel. Meantime, at the other corner of the Mediterranean, the British Eighth army, now commanded by General Sir Bernard Montgomery, faced Rommel's Germans and Italians at El Alamein between the sea and the soft sands of the Qattara depression. Montgomery had been reinforced to 200,000 men, with 1000 tanks and other munitions. Rommel also received reinforcements and had about 140,000 men and 500 tanks.

Montgomery moved first. On October 22, the British artillery began blasting a way through the opposing lines. Two weeks later Rommel's forces were in full retreat. Tanks were half the battle in this desert warfare, and Rommel lost half of his, besides 600 planes and 9000 prisoners. The mechanized German force retreated along the coast road, abandoning several divisions of Italian troops, who surrendered gladly. Tobruk was retaken on November 13. On the 20th, Rommel gave up Benghazi. He had now lost 75,000 men. With the German Afrika Corps, he made a stand at El Agheila, 560 miles west of his initial position.

El Agheila, on the border of Tripolitania, had been the limit of previous British advances. For three weeks Montgomery reorganized his transport and brought up supplies. Then, on December 13, he struck again, and two days later Rommel was again in retreat. Tripoli was abandoned January 23. Rommel, with about half his original force, made his final stand on the Mareth line, the border fortifications of Tunisia. He had conducted a masterly retreat of 1500 miles from his position in Egypt. He had left about half of his original force. His purpose was now to support General von Arnim's forces in Tunisia.

Tunisia. Tunisia is an irregular quadrilateral, washed on the north and east by the Mediterranean. The northwestern part is mountainous, one ridge running out into the promontory of Cape Bon. In the southeast is a broad coastal plain. The important military objectives were Tunis and Bizerta on the north coast, held by the Germans, who held also the coastal plains and the coast towns.

The Allied forces held a generally north and south line in western Tunisia. On February 24 the Germans struck in the south at the Americans holding the Kasserine Pass. Inexperienced and outnumbered, the Americans were driven back about 28 miles but recovered the lost ground by the beginning of March. On March 20, the Eighth army launched an attack on the Mareth line, while the Americans and British to the north increased their pressure. A New Zealand corps under Montgomery's command outflanked the Mareth line. On April 7 American patrols made contact with units of the Eighth army. Under the combined attack Rommel was forced to retreat north nearly to Cape Bon.

From the beginning of the movement the sea and air forces of the Allies had been watching and attacking the Axis transport. On April 5 a smashing attack on the aerodromes of Sicily and Italy crippled the Axis air force, and continuous bombing cut their communications with Sicily. A combined assault by the ground forces followed. The Axis line was broken by a tank attack. On the 7th the Americans entered Bizerta, and the British entered Tunis at almost the same time. A part of the enemy, trapped between them, surrendered on May 9. The remainder were driven into the Cape Bon peninsula and surrendered the next day. The captured troops numbered some 252,000, besides large quantities of equipment. They included General von Arnim but not General Rommel, who had been previously ordered to Italy to direct the defense there.

By this campaign the German plan to join forces with Japan by taking the Suez canal was ruined. In its place, a line of attack on southern Europe was opened up for the Allies. The route to the Japanese war by the Suez canal was now open to the Allies.

The Collapse of Italy. The Allied army was now poised on the tip of Africa, ready to strike at "Fortress Europe." The air forces began the work by bombarding the fortified islands between Africa and Italy and the supply bases in Italy itself. On the morning of July 10 a fleet of 2000 vessels of all sizes landed 150,000 British, Americans, and Canadians on the south and east coasts of Sicily. There was very little resistance, for the enemy had expected them in the west of the island, and clouds of parachute troops the night before had seized the principal airfields.

Sicily is, for the most part, a mass of mountains culminating in Mt. Etna at the northeast corner. There the narrow strait of Messina separates it from Italy. The British Eighth army moved up the east coast, took Syracuse, and, on the 19th, was stopped at Catania just south of Mt. Etna by stiff German resistance. The Canadians moved forward in the center. The American Seventh army, under command of General George Patton, was nearer the region where the defenders were prepared and met more opposition at first. From Agrigento (Girgenti) it advanced inland. Americans and Canadians reached Enna, in the center of the island, on the 21st, and resistance in the west practically ceased. The Americans pushed through to the north coast, taking 100,000 prisoners and much undamaged war material. They had throughout overwhelming air support. The Germans fought stubbornly, but the Italians were more willing to surrender. From Palermo the Americans turned east to outflank the German position at Catania. By the end of the month the whole enemy force was crowded into the northeastern corner of the island between Mt. Etna and the sea. On August 5 the British took Catania, on the 17th resistance ceased in Messina, and Sicily was conquered. Some of the garrison escaped, but about 200,000 were captured.

The losses in Sicily brought about a revolution at Rome. On July 25 King Victor Emmanuel requested Mussolini's resignation and appointed Marshal Badoglio premier. The new government soon began secret negotiations with the Allies. After an attempt to make terms, the Badoglio government surrendered unconditionally September 8, handing over most of the fleet. About the same time, Mussolini, who had been taken into custody by the new government but rescued by a daring German raid and taken to northern Italy, was set up by the Germans as a puppet ruler. Italian liberals, meanwhile, led by Count Carlo Sforza and Benedetto Croce, demanded that the king abdicate in favor of his young grandson. The Allies recognized the Badoglio government, which declared war on Germany October 13. The king and Badoglio were safe behind the Allied lines.

Mussolini's retirement had taken everyone by surprise—including the Allies. The Germans rushed 19 divisions into northern Italy and proceeded to strengthen their position there and at Rome despite Italian opposition. They had two powerful advantages: Most of the Italian army was in garrisons under control of the Germans; and 200,000 Italians, laboring in Germany, were hostages. As the king and Badoglio played for time, the Allies acted. On September 3, the British Eighth Army landed in Calabria and advanced with little opposition. On the 8th, the American Fifth Army under Lieutenant General Mark Clark landed near Naples. It was vigorously opposed by German forces in readiness to meet the landing and escaped disaster at the Salerno beachhead only by concentration of all available air and sea support. Meantime the British took Bari and the important airfields of Foggia. Their left made contact with the Americans on the 17th, and the advance up the peninsula continued. On the 30th the Americans entered Naples.

The Germans were now in complete control of northern and central Italy, and the beginning of 1944 found them struggling fiercely with the Allies on the so-called Gustav line extending across the peninsula from Piscara to Cassino. On January 22 a surprise landing by the Fifth Army within a few miles of Rome threatened the entire German army south of that point. Skilful German defense in a rugged terrain, however, delayed the fall of Rome for nearly six months.

The Gustav line was finally broken and on June 5 the Allies entered Rome. A repetition of the German tactics of delay, taking every advantage of favorable terrain, slowed down the Allied advance again. By the end of the year, the Allies, reinforced by French and Brazilian contingents, had taken Florence and Pisa, but were still struggling on the southern edge of the Po valley. Italy was now becoming, however, a secondary theater, mainly important for its effect on greater operations elsewhere.

Russian Victories of 1943. In the campaign of 1943, the Russians drove the German army from the Volga to the former Russian boundary, recovering over 300,000 square miles of territory.

Russian successes began with the encirclement and destruction of the German armies besieging Stalingrad. This success was followed by new offensives which retook Rostov and Kharkov in February. The Germans saved their men, however, and a month later retook Kharkov. The Germans in the Caucasus were cut off.

To the west of Moscow the Russians had taken Velikye Luki in December, and were breaking into a German salient at Rzhev. Farther north they partially relieved Leningrad in January, but the Germans still clung to their positions within artillery range of the city. The Russians claimed that the Germans, in the winter campaign, had lost 850,000 men killed and wounded, and 344,000 prisoners.

The Germans started their last offensive in July. It was soon stopped, and they began a slow withdrawal, closely followed by the Russians, but the skill of the German "strategic retirement" prevented heavy losses. The Russians now retook Kharkov—

its fourth change of hands—and recovered the Donets basin. By October they had retaken the Caucasus, and were entering the Crimea.

The Germans may have expected to hold the line of the Dnieper, but did not succeed. The Dnepropetrovsk dam was recovered. Kiev was taken November 7. Before the end of the year the Russians were across the Dnieper in many places, aiming for the vital Odessa-Warsaw railway.

In the center, advancing from Moscow, they took Smolensk, and had reached the old Polish border in January. In the north Leningrad was completely freed and Novgorod retaken.

While carrying out this sustained and gigantic offensive, Stalin planned sagaciously for the future. A 20-year treaty was signed with the friendly government-in-exile of Czechoslovakia. Grounds for suspicion in the West were weakened by dissolution of the Comintern and by recognition of the Greek Orthodox Church. Stalin, however, refused to recognize the unfriendly Polish government-in-exile located at London and made clear Russia's intention to keep territory which Poland took from Russia in 1920.

The Ukraine Recovered. The Russian activity now centered in the Ukraine. The Germans on the lower Dnieper were encircled, and some ten divisions, over 100,000 men were taken. Kherson, on the Black Sea, surrendered. The Russians passed the Dniester, and the boundary river Pruth. By the end of March they were attacking Czernowitz (Cernauti) in Rumania. Odessa was retaken on April 10, and Sevastopol a month later. The Russians announced that in the spring campaign the Red army had liberated 16,000 square miles of territory, and had killed or captured 500,000 of the enemy.

Poland and the Satellites. As the ground dried and military operations became possible, the Russians were again in motion. By July the Germans were pushed back to Minsk and the Polish border. In central Poland the Red army reached the Vistula in mid-July and attacked Warsaw, but there the advance was halted. In August an insurrection of the Polish underground broke out in Warsaw and held a part of the city for several weeks, but the Russians gave no assistance, and the Poles were forced to surrender. The Russians asserted that the uprising was premature and uncoordinated with Russian plans; the Poles charged betrayal.

For the time the main Russian effort was directed to the south. Lwow (Lemberg) was taken on August 17. On August 22 the Russians took Jassy, and the next day Rumania asked for an armistice, surrendered, and two days later declared war on Germany. The Russians nevertheless advanced across Rumania, occupied Bucharest, the Ploesti oil fields, and Constanta and the Black Sea coast. It was now Bulgaria's turn. Bulgaria had maintained a formal peace with Russia, but now Russia declared war on Bulgaria, entered the country on September 8, and occupied Sofia five days later. Bulgaria made peace with Russia, and declared war on Germany, opening the way to Yugoslavia and Greece. The German forces in these countries withdrew as best they could. Marshal Tito and the Partisans in Yugoslavia joined forces with the Red army. They entered Belgrade on October 14. Greece was liberated by the British, who had been landing forces since September and had pushed north with almost no resistance. By November Greece was free.

Red armies were already pressing forward in other quarters. They passed the prewar boundary of Hungary early in October. Admiral Horthy asked for an armistice, and the Germans took possession of the country. The Russian advance drove the Germans back beyond the Tisza and Lake Balaton and began the siege of Budapest, which fell in early 1945, while other Russian forces were entering Slovakia. In the north, the Baltic provinces were also falling. In July and August Lithuania had been conquered. By the end of September Estonia was cleared, and the Russians were in Riga and attacking East Prussia. Finland was forced to agree to terms, returning to the boundaries of 1940. The Germans in Finland retired to northern Norway. The Red army followed and the Germans gave up Finnmark, laying waste the country as they retreated.

The Invasion of France. The part taken by Russia in the war led to repeated intimations from Russia and demands in Britain and the United States for the opening of a "second front" in order to deliver the decisive blow of the war. At the beginning of 1944, preparations were in progress for such an invasion, the nature and magnitude of which were unprecedented in the history of warfare.

Meanwhile the aerial offensive from British bases against Germany and the occupied countries rose to a terrible crescendo. The Ruhr valley was wrecked. A raid on Cologne in May 1942 in which 1130 planes took part was called the greatest air raid in history, but it was surpassed by later attacks which demolished Hamburg, a large part of Berlin, and numerous other cities. The Rumanian oil fields and Sofia, in Bulgaria, were likewise visited. Skilfully directed air assault on German aircraft factories in February 1944 was credited with so crippling German air power that Allied supremacy in the skies was never seriously challenged thereafter.

Among pre-invasion devices experimented with was the commando raid, undertaken by small parties which did the greatest possible damage to a definite objective and retreated with what information they could acquire about defenses. The most elaborate of these was the raid on Dieppe, August 19, 1942. It was carried out by 5000 Canadians with British, American, and French contingents, 10,000 in all. The Canadians lost 67 per cent of their men. The experiment was not repeated.

The most serious obstacle to invasion at first was the submarine, but by mid-1943 it was definitely eliminated as a factor. In 1942, about 7,000,000 tons of Allied shipping were sunk. In late 1943 almost as many German submarines as Allied ships were sent to the bottom. Moreover, Allied shipping was growing at the rate of more than half a dozen ships a day.

In preparation for the attack on "Fortress Europe," General Dwight D. Eisenhower was appointed Supreme Allied Commander in Western Europe. General Sir Bernard L. Montgomery commanded the British ground forces; Lieutenant General Omar P. Bradley, the American; Admiral Sir Bertram Ramsay was naval commander. To oppose them the Germans had assigned command to Field Marshal Rommel and General von Kluge.

Meanwhile the Germans on their side were preparing new secret weapons, the most formidable of which was the robot bomb, propelled from a ramp to travel great distances and fall with terrific explosive force. In the months immediately after the invasion of Europe began, London suffered damage or destruction of a large proportion of its buildings through this weapon.

On "D-Day," June 6, 1944, the Anglo-American expeditionary force struck the French coast in the most gigantic amphibious operations ever undertaken. Supporting 3200 transports and landing craft were 800 fighting ships. Some 8000 Allied planes held control of the air. Three divisions of airborne troops preceded the landing craft and held off the enemy; the warships shelled the shore fortifications. The Americans landed at the foot of the Cotentin peninsula, while the British struck farther west toward Caen, holding between them some 30 miles of the Normandy beaches. Initial losses were heavy enough, but less than had been expected. Within a week the beachheads were secure against counterattack. Then the Americans turned against Cherbourg, while the British around Caen protected their flank. Cherbourg was taken by the end of June, and its port facilities were soon available.

Three weeks of "hedgerow war" followed; the British holding off the Germans around Caen, the Americans struggling inland, until the capture of St. Lo on July 18 placed them in position for a breakthrough. Another American army, the Third, commanded by Lieutenant General George S. Patton, was now in operation. Its armor overran Brittany, then, turning, swept east across France through Tours and Orleans. Paris was entered on August 25. The German Seventh Army attempted a counterattack but was driven, wholly disorganized, across the Seine. The British and Canadians followed them eastward along the coast. In the first days of September they crossed Belgium and entered the Netherlands, taking Antwerp and Breda. The Americans swung north to western Belgium and Luxembourg. In late September a daring attempt by parachute troops to secure a position at Arnheim, beyond the lower Rhine, was unsuccessful, but the Americans took Aachen in October against desperate resistance.

Meantime another American force had made a landing, August 15, on the southern coast of France between Nice and Cannes. Taking Marseilles and Toulon, they pushed up the Rhone valley, meeting little resistance. The French "Forces of the Interior," whose time had now come, rose all over France. A part of the German army of occupation escaped through the Gap of Belfort; more surrendered. The American and French armies, crossing the Vosges mountains at Belfort, joined the northern armies on the Rhine. By the end of October France and Belgium were liberated. The Germans had suffered a terrible but not yet fatal disaster. Over 800,000 of their troops had passed into Allied prison camps.

Anglo-American Assault on Germany. Steady Allied advances into the deep defenses of the Siegfried line were interrupted in December 1944 by a strong German counterattack into Belgium and Luxembourg. Massing three armies in this area and favored by weather conditions which kept down the stronger American air force, the Germans drove through the Ardennes 50 miles into Belgium. General Eisenhower concentrated his defenses at the northern and southern flanks. The heroic resistance of an American division at Bastogne and prompt counterattacks from north and south brought the Germans to a halt. They were forced back to their original lines and beyond. The "Battle of the Bulge," while costing the Allies 40,000 casualties, was estimated to have brought the Germans losses of several times this number.

The Allied pressure against the German lines culminated in several breakthroughs in late February 1945, and the German army was soon in full retreat beyond the Rhine, destroying bridges as they retired. The Americans entered Cologne on March 7; the next day, seizing a bridge at Remagen before it could be destroyed, they began to pour troops across the river for an advance into central Germany.

The War in the Pacific. The Japanese drive in the summer of 1942 had carried them to the Solomon Islands and New Guinea. Both positions threatened Australia. In the easternmost islands of the Solomon group, the fine harbor of Tulagi, with an airfield on the neighboring island of Guadalcanal, offered a base for attacks on New Caledonia and the supply line from the United States. Behind and supporting both was the air and naval base under construction at Rabaul on New Britain. One thousand miles to the north was Japan's "Pearl Harbor," Truk.

The first Japanese attack was on Port Moresby in southern New Guinea. In July, the Japanese made a landing at Buna, farther down the coast. Two attempts to take Port Moresby failed.

In August the American and Australian navies took the offensive and attacked the Japanese positions in the eastern Solomons. Tulagi was taken and held. American marines landed on Guadalcanal August 7 and seized the almost completed airfield. Around this airfield, renamed Henderson Field, American and Japanese were locked for months in the most crucial struggle of the campaign, the final outcome of which was destined to be decided by the naval and aerial conflict.

On the night of August 8, a Japanese air force attacked the Allied fleet and sank four heavy cruisers—the American *Quincy*, *Astoria*, and *Vincennes*, and the Australian *Canberra*, but did not reach the transports. In October, November, and December, the Japanese renewed their attacks, first to reinforce their men and, as the great battle gradually turned against them, to evacuate their troops. In October, Vice Admiral William F. Halsey was placed in command of the operations. In a final Japanese assault in November, officially called the battle of Guadalcanal, the Japanese lost two battleships, four cruisers, six destroyers, and eight transports with other vessels, 28 in all, and an estimated 40,000 men. Allied losses were two cruisers and seven destroyers. By January 1943, the fighting around Guadalcanal was practically over. The Americans renewed their offensive, slowly drove the Japanese from the middle Solomons, and at the beginning of 1944 had made lodgments on New Britain and were closing in on the principal base at Rabaul.

On January 31, 1944, the Americans struck Japan's Marshall islands. Within a few days this outpost of the Japanese Empire was taken. The Gilbert islands had already been occupied in November 1943 in a swift but costly three-day assault.

Meantime General MacArthur was taking personal charge of the offensive on the northern coast of New Guinea. Buna and Gona were taken in December 1942. In March 1943, a Japanese transport fleet attempting to reinforce Lae, was caught by land-based aircraft in the Bismarck sea. All twelve transports and their escort were sunk, with an estimated loss of 40,000 men. In September Salamaua and Lae were captured, and the Japanese were driven from eastern New Guinea.

In the Aleutians, the Japanese had made lodgments on Attu and Kiska islands after the battle of Midway. In May Attu was taken. Kiska was later evacuated, and the Aleutians were clear.

"Island Hopping" Stage. With the Gilbert and Marshall islands and eastern New Guinea in their hands, the American forces in the Pacific moved westward on two lines, converging on the Philippines. General MacArthur's Southwest Pacific command worked along the coast of New Guinea. Admiral Nimitz and the fleet continued their conquest of Micronesia. Sea, land, and air forces co-operated.

By such means the American and Australian forces, with assistance from the fleet, took Hollandia and later Biak island in New Guinea. By August, MacArthur was at the tip of the island, and the Japanese left behind were negligible. In September he occupied Morotai and neutralized Halmahira in the sea between New Guinea and the Philippines.

Meanwhile the fleet had been moving westward. The Carolines, with the fabulously strong base at Truk, was the next objective. Truk was repeatedly bombed until it was temporarily harmless. Halsey's Third fleet assisted MacArthur's advance and carried out carrier-based bombing raids as far as Luzon.

On June 14, 1944, marines were put ashore in the Marianas within range of Japan itself. The danger brought out a Japanese naval force, which was defeated with heavy loss by Admiral Spruance. Saipan resisted for several weeks; in August the recapture of near-by Guam was announced. The Palau islands were taken in September. Admiral Halsey extended his activities to Formosa and the Ryukyu islands, but the Japanese fleet avoided an action.

Return to the Philippines. The way was now clear for the invasion of the Philippines. General MacArthur, with 600 ships and 250,000 men, landed on Leyte island, in the middle of the group, on October 17. The initial resistance was slight, but apparently the Japanese determined to make their fight for the Philippines there, for reinforcements were sent—not all of them arrived—and three Japanese task forces converged on Leyte October 25 to destroy the American transports. The Third and Seventh fleets met them off the eastern coast in the Second Battle of the Philippine Sea. One task force was destroyed, the others were driven off with 24 vessels sunk, including at least three battleships and four carriers, and 33 others damaged. The American loss was one carrier and five smaller ships. Fighting in Leyte continued into December. Meanwhile the Americans occupied near-by Samar and Mindoro.

The occupation of Mindoro cleared the way to Luzon. In early January 1945, a fleet of 800 ships steamed through the Sulu sea and landed at the head of Lingayen Gulf, where the Japanese had landed three years before. A series of air raids upon Formosa prevented opposition from that quarter. The Japanese resistance was surprisingly light; on February 6 MacArthur entered Manila.

On the mainland the Japanese had better fortune. By occupying the line of the Peiping-Hankow railway, they cut Free China in two. On the other hand they lost ground in Burma, where the British entered Mandalay on March 8, 1945. About the same time a Chinese army took Lashio, the old terminus of the Burma road.

Earlier Conferences. As it became apparent that the unexpected power of Russian arms and the potentially crushing weight of American materials and forces spelled doom to Germany in a military sense, hope of escape turned to dividing the Allies. This hope was effectively cut off by inter-Allied conferences and agreements. January 14-24, 1943 Roosevelt and Churchill with their military advisers met at Casablanca, Morocco. "Complete agreement" was reached for the "intensive prosecution of the war in 1943."

Another conference, at Quebec, between Roosevelt, Churchill, and King, prime minister of Canada, August 20-24, was preceded by meetings of British and Canadian officials and followed by a visit of Churchill to Washington. T. V. Soong, Chinese foreign minister, also attended. Decisions were reached on military movements and the political issues.

Decisions of the highest importance were made by the Moscow conference, October 18-30, between the three secretaries, Hull, Eden, and Molotov.

Its communiqué recognized the importance of collaboration for carrying on the war, making peace after it, and determining the treatment of "Hitlerite Germany."

Russia naturally could not participate in conferences regarding the war with Japan. For this purpose President Roosevelt, Premier Churchill, and Generalissimo Chiang Kai-shek met at Cairo (November 22-26). They committed their nations to the restoration of Japanese conquests, including Formosa and Manchuria, and the future independence of Korea.

The fifth of these conferences followed almost immediately. It was signalized by the presence of Marshal Stalin, who at last met President Roosevelt and Premier Churchill at Tehran, Iran, November 28-December 1, 1943. Their declaration stated that they had "concerted their plans for the destruction of the German forces," and "no power on earth could prevent" Germany's overthrow.

Later Conferences and Postwar Plans. President Roosevelt and Premier Churchill met in a second conference at Quebec, September 11-16, 1944, dealing chiefly with questions relating to the war in the Pacific. A more important conference was held at Yalta, in the Crimea, February 4-11, 1945, where Marshal Stalin met the two Western leaders. At this conference, plans for the defeat, occupation, and control of Germany were settled. Preliminary plans were made for a world peace organization to be further considered by an assembly of the United Nations, called for April 25, 1945, at San Francisco.

Another class of conferences, of larger membership and limited scope, dealt with postwar problems. The International Monetary Conference, held at Bretton Woods, N. H., July 1-23, 1944, proposed the establishment of an international monetary fund and of an International Bank of Reconstruction and Development to stabilize currency, prevent inflation, and promote reconstruction after the war. The International Security Conference, at Dumbarton Oaks, Washington, D. C., June 21-October 7, 1944, participated in by representatives of the United States, Great Britain, and Russia, and later China, formulated a plan for a world organization to preserve peace. The Pan-American Conference at Mexico City in March 1945 put forward a similar plan for the Americas, the Act of Chapultepec. An International Aviation Conference at Chicago January 1-5, 1945, agreed upon some features of the control of civil international aviation.

The Western Front. The American crossing of the Rhine at Remagen was inadequate, and led into a terrain where an advance could easily be contested. A successful advance could only be made over the Baltic plain. This was soon remedied. While General Hodges' First Army enlarged its bridgehead and threatened the Ruhr district, General Patton's Third Army drove down the Moselle valley to Coblenz; reaching it March 17, they trapped the German armies still east of the Rhine. Farther south the Seventh Army advanced toward Karlsruhe, pocketing the Germans in the Saar basin. In the north, Marshal Montgomery's British and Canadian armies forced a passage at Wesel on March 23, and drove north and northeast, the British toward Bremen and Hanover, the Canadians along the Dutch border, trapping the enemy forces who remained in Holland. The Germans were unable to hold the line of the Wesel against the British and American armies. Bremen and Hamburg were taken, the Allies pressed on to the Elbe, and by mid-April their advance had passed it, but was held back to avoid possible collision with the Russians. The Germans pocketed behind them in the Ruhr valley, upwards of 300,000, surrendered on April 19th.

While the British were overrunning the northern plain the American Third Army had reached the Main valley and entered Frankfort. The Seventh Army, crossing near Karlsruhe, approached Nuremberg, and the First French army entered Germany farther south. It was the part of the Third Army, noted for its rapidity of movement, to cut off southern Germany, and forestall the rumored intention of the Nazi leaders to retire into the mountains of Bavaria for a final stand. This was done by mid-April. The Third Army took Leipzig on the 19th, and pressed on into Czechoslovakia. Farther south the Seventh Army, with the French on their right flank, occupied the Bavarian cities, Nuremberg, Augsburg, and Munich (April 30). On April 26 Russian and American forces met at Torgau in Saxony.

Meantime the air forces were in constant action, assisting the ground forces and bombing industrial centers and communication lines. Berlin was continually under fire. The Germans retaliated with a new secret weapon, the V-2 rocket bomb, causing great damage in London and southern England.

The Final Russian Victory. On January 12, 1945, Stalin ordered a grand offensive, designed to destroy the German armies in the east. Beginning with a drive upon Krakow, it extended to East Prussia on the north, and Silesia on the south. Warsaw was taken in passing, and Poland overrun, as the Germans drew back to the Oder, their last line of defense. The southern column, crossing the Oder, attacked and surrounded Breslau, and deprived Germany of its industrial district of Silesia. The central column, under General Zhukov, drove through Poland toward Berlin. The Oder was crossed in force near Berlin, but before delivering its principal blow at the German capital, the Russian army secured its northern flank. By the beginning of March, the Russians had sliced up northeastern Germany. Konigsberg and Danzig resisted until April; Stettin, the seaport of Berlin, until April 27; and the Russians moved down the Baltic coast as far as Rostock.

In the south, the Red army, by the end of March, had cleared Hungary of the Germans, taken Bratislava in Slovakia, and were entering Austria. Vienna

was attacked on April 6, and surrendered on the 13th. Farther north another army, passing around besieged Breslau, was entering Saxony to meet the Americans at Torgau.

Thus the stage was set for the climactic attack on Berlin itself. On April 15 the final drive began. The Soviet armies converged upon it from three sides. On the 25th, Berlin was completely surrounded. Foot by foot, Russian tanks and infantry fought their way into the doomed city, while from the housetops to the subways the garrison and armed citizens contested their advance. On May 2, the last resistance ended.

The End of Adolf Hitler. Adolf Hitler remained in Berlin to the last. On May 1, Grand Admiral Karl Doenitz announced over the Hamburg radio that the Fuehrer had fallen that afternoon. The exact circumstances of his death were not stated and later stories were conflicting but it is probable he committed suicide. Dr. Goebbels, propaganda minister, committed suicide at about the same time. Of the other Nazi leaders, Marshals Goring and Von Rundstedt were captured earlier by the Americans. Himmler, the hated chief of the police, was captured and committed suicide. Ribbentrop was arrested later. Admiral Doenitz announced that Hitler, a few days before, had designated him as his successor.

The Surrender of Germany. For the new Fuehrer nothing was left but surrender. While the German field armies continued to fight fiercely against the Russians, they seemed quite willing to surrender to the Anglo-American forces in the west. The army in Italy had signed articles of surrender on April 29. On May 4, Marshal Montgomery received the surrender of the German forces in the Netherlands, Denmark, and Northwest Germany. The next day, two German armies in Austria surrendered to General Devers. Admiral Doenitz accepted the situation. On May 7 his representatives surrendered to General Eisenhower, at his headquarters at Reims, the entire armed forces of the Reich. The surrender was formally announced on the morning of the 8th by President Truman and Premier Churchill. A few hours later the final articles of surrender to Russia were signed at Berlin by Marshal Zhukov and Marshal Keitel. So the European war officially ended, five years, eight months, and six days after the invasion of Poland.

The End in Italy. On April 10, the Allied armies, long stalled on the edge of the Po valley, launched their final offensive. Bologna, the primary objective, fell on the 21st, and resistance began to weaken as the allies pushed northward. Genoa and Milan fell to the Americans on the 29th, and Venice to the British. Realizing that the American advance in Germany left them no refuge there, and threatened by a flank attack from France, the German commanders opened negotiations for a surrender. The capitulation was signed at Naples on the 29th, becoming effective on May 2d, and northern Italy, with the adjacent Austrian territory, passed to the Allies.

Even before the surrender the end had come for Benito Mussolini. Attempting to escape to Switzerland, he was arrested by Italian partisans, given a "trial," and shot, at a village near Lake Como.

The Occupation of Germany. The Third Reich came to an end on May 23, when Admiral Doenitz and his officers, who had been carrying on an administration, under Allied supervision, were put under arrest. Germany was now without a government. In its place was military control by the Allies.

In pursuance of the arrangements made at Yalta, Germany was to be divided into four zones of military occupation. The Russians took charge of most of Germany beyond the Elbe. The Americans were to occupy southern Germany, with lines of communication through the British zone in the northwest and along the North Sea. France occupied the regions adjoining the upper Rhine. A central council, with its seat at jointly-occupied Berlin, was to co-ordinate the administration of the four zones.

The Potsdam Conference. The further disposition of the conquered Reich was decided at a conference held at the old royal Prussian palace of Potsdam, July 17 to August 2, 1945, between President Truman, Premiers Churchill and Attlee and Marshal Stalin. It was announced that German life was to be reorganized. Army and navy were to be abolished and war production, actual or potential, to be eliminated. Reparations in kind were divided on a basis which gave the largest share to Russia. Eastern Germany was divided between Russia and Poland. Poland's western boundary was not fixed, but the country west of the Oder was placed under Polish administration. The conference also created a Council of Foreign Ministers, to meet at the respective capitals.

For the trial and execution of the war criminals, among whom were included the surviving Nazi leaders, an International Military Tribunal was set up at Nuremberg, September 1945. On October 1, 1946, the verdicts were pronounced. Goring, Keitel, Jodl, Von Ribbentrop, and eight others were sentenced to death; seven others to terms of imprisonment. The other liberated countries were already dealing with their own "collaborators." France imprisoned Petain, and executed Laval and others. Norway executed Quisling. The Netherlands and Belgium took similar action.

The Fall of Japan. In the United States rejoicing at the end of the war with Germany was tempered by the realization that another war was still to be won. The bulk of our troops in Europe had now to be transferred to the Pacific.

With the reconquest of the Philippines and the occupation of the Marianas islands, Japan's outer ring of defenses had fallen. The next attack was made on the inner line. It began at the little island of Iwo (Iwojima) in the Volcano group. The first landing was made on February 18, but the island was not completely occupied until March 18, at a cost of 20,000 casualties, including 4000 dead.

The next point of attack was Okinawa, in the long chain of the Ryukyu (Nansei) islands, between Formosa and Japan. On April 1 the Tenth army, under General S. B. Buckner, landed. The landing was made and the northern portion of the island occupied with little resistance, but on the hilly and strongly fortified southern tip the Japanese garrison of over 100,000 made a desperate resistance. Marines and infantry advanced foot by foot over rugged hills in the hardest fighting yet seen in the Pacific. Repeated attempts to relieve the island were beaten off. Constant "suicide" attacks on the American fleet sunk or damaged nearly 100 vessels. Okinawa fell on June 22. Its capture cost the Americans 39,000 casualties. The 11,000 dead included Gen. Buckner.

The war now came home to Japan. Large sections of Tokyo, Osaka, and Nagoya had been destroyed by long-range bombers based on the carrier *Hornet*. The Japanese navy had been driven from the sea, and a sea and air blockade was cutting off supplies from the Japanese conquests in the south. What was left of the fleet was destroyed in its harbors. The navy came into action, assisted by a British squadron, and through July the Third fleet ravaged the coasts with carrier-based planes, and even naval gunfire. City after city was reduced to ruins, industrial centers were destroyed and transportation wrecked. On August 6, the first atomic bomb fell.

For some years the problem of the "splitting of the atom" and the release of atomic energy for man's use had occupied the minds of physicists. For three years American, British, and Canadian scientists, with some assistance from European exiles, had been working on a mysterious "Manhattan Defense Project." Its reported cost was $2 billion, but the result was the splitting of the uranium atom (already accomplished) in such a way that its force could be controlled and used as an explosive. On July 16 the first successful experiment was made near Alamogordo, N. M. The first atomic bomb used in warfare was dropped upon the city of Hiroshima, and an area of 4½ square miles, 60 per cent of the city, was wiped out of existence. Two days later another bomb was dropped upon the seaport of Nagasaki.

In January 1945, Russia had given the required twelve months notice of the end of her non-aggression treaty with Japan. At Potsdam the Russians had promised to engage in the Asiatic war within three months after the surrender of Germany. On August 8 Russia declared war, and her armies swept into Manchuria and Korea. Meantime in the south Japan was losing. The British capture of Rangoon on May 4 completed their conquest of Burma. The Burma road was again open. The Chinese, with American assistance, were taking the offensive.

Already at Potsdam the Japanese had put out peace feelers through Russia, then a neutral, and had received a very definite choice between unconditional surrender and "total destruction." With the Russian entry, it also gave opportunity for the "saving of face" so dear to the oriental mind. On August 10, the Japanese emperor made Switzerland a qualified proposal of surrender, "ever anxious," as he later explained, "to advance the cause of world peace, and with a view to saving mankind the calamities to be imposed by further continuance of the war." At 7 P.M. August 14, President Truman announced that Japan had surrendered unconditionally.

End of World War II. On September 1 (September 2, by Tokyo time) on the U. S. battleship Missouri, in the harbor of Tokyo, General MacArthur, as Supreme Allied commander, accompanied by representatives of the Allied powers, received the formal surrender of Japan.

So the war ended, six years to a day after the German invasion of Poland; 3 years, 8 months, and 25 days after the Japanese attack on Pearl Harbor. America had paid for its victory with 1,058,000 casualties; 248,000 killed. Canada lost 36,000 killed, out of 101,000 casualties. Great Britain and the other dominions, 300,000 killed, with total casualties of 1,132,000.

On September 8, 1951, forty-eight nations signed a peace treaty with Japan at San Francisco. Russia and her satellites refused to sign. Although stripped of her former empire, Japan regained full sovereignty, and became eligible for United Nations membership.

Also at San Francisco, a Pacific defense pact was signed by the United States, Australia, and New Zealand, and another defense pact by the United States and the Philippines. At the same time still another security treaty was concluded between the United States and Japan authorizing the stationing of U.S. armed forces in and around Japan to deter armed attack upon that country. All these treaties were ratified by the United States in March 1952.

The San Francisco Conference. In pursuance of the recommendations of the Dumbarton Oaks and Yalta conferences, delegates from 51 nations met at San Francisco, April 25, 1945, to frame a "charter" for an organization of nations to maintain peace.

The charter was framed and adopted June 26, 1945, and submitted for ratification to the member nations. The United Nations came into being October 24, 1945, when Soviet Russia deposited with the United States Department of State the twenty-ninth instrument of ratification. See *United Nations*.

The Cold War. This term is applied to the conflict of policy originating in World War II between Communist Russia on the one hand and, on the other, the United States and other nations opposed to Communism. Basically it was due to Russia's belief in her destined role to spread Communism throughout the world.

During the war, Stalin, the Russian ruler, astutely obtained agreements from his allies favorable to extension of Russian power or ignored unfavorable agreements when in a position to do so. The first example relates to Germany.

Division of Germany. On September 12, 1944, it was agreed that Germany, when defeated, would be occupied in separate zones by Russia, Great Britain, and the United States and that it would be ruled by a joint council of the commanding officers. Berlin, although falling within the Russian zone, the largest of the three, was similarly divided into zones; corridors of access were provided for the other allies, later including France. The Russian commandants refused to co-operate in the council. The Western allies authorized a popularly elected government to take over in their sectors. The Russians responded by recognizing a soviet regime in East Germany. Berlin was similarly divided.

The second example relates to the countries of Eastern Europe and the Far East. It was agreed in 1945 that, after liberation from the Germans and Japanese, free elections should be held to establish governments in Poland, Rumania, Yugoslavia, Hungary, Czechoslovakia, and Korea. No free elections were held except in Czechoslovakia. Russia's alter ego, the Communist party, set up soviet regimes in those countries it reconquered, although this process was delayed in Czechoslovakia until 1947, when subversion and military threats had done their work. The Communist party set up a soviet regime also in the northern half of Korea, which the allies had agreed Russia might occupy.

Russia attempted in 1946 to force the Western powers from western Berlin by blocking surface traffic through the corridors. The reply was a massive air-lift of supplies to Berlin. Russia reopened the corridors to Berlin. Two years later, the North Atlantic Treaty Organization (NATO) was agreed to for combatting Russian expansion in Europe.

World-Wide Competition. Blocked in Europe, Russia turned next to Asia, where the cause of Communism had been enormously strengthened by adherence of China after the party leader Mao Tse-tung had overthrown the Nationalist Government in 1949. In June 1950, Communist North Korean forces invaded South Korea without warning. The United Nations authorized resistance, of which the main burden was carried by the United States. After three years of war, in which China also intervened, the North Korean Communists were confined again to their zone.

The above aspects of the cold war resembled, from the anti-Communist viewpoint, a fire-fighting operation. Another aspect, beginning shortly after World War II, had the character of fire prevention. The strength of Russia lay chiefly in the Communist party, with branches throughout the world, which was ready to fan discontent and take over control when the ruling hands faltered. Countermeasures dictated strengthening the rulers and proffering means to reduce discontent.

Rivalry Based on Aid. Greece was the first example. When Great Britain saw herself unable to continue support of Greece in the face of Communist-inspired disorders, the United States stepped in with military and economic aid. From this beginning rose the Marshall Plan, suggested by Gen. George C. Marshall, of sparking rebirth of prosperity by gifts and loans. The idea worked brilliantly in the countries of Europe, already rich in skilled manpower. The influence of those who preached revolution as the gateway to paradise steadily waned.

However, among the underdeveloped nations of Africa, Asia, and South America, the contest was less one-sided. One legacy of World War II was a passion for independence among countries that had been colonies and protectorates of more powerful nations. The Western powers had been the principal colonizers. Hence they were the targets of those who demanded independence. Even where there was no colonial tie, as with Latin American nations and the United States, the charge of economic and political exploitation was raised against them. Russia and later China sought to capitalize on this revolu-

tionary movement by encouraging revolt and promising economic aid, covertly with a view to eventual establishment of Communist states. Russia's own repression of her satellite states was ignored by native leaders who sought Russia's aid against their "colonialist oppressors." In countries already independent, the United States normally supported the administration in power to suppress Communist subversion; the opposition therefore tended to label America as an imperialist power.

A key conflict arose in Egypt in 1956. The United States offered aid to build the high Aswan Dam. When Egypt's ruler, Nasser, accepted aid from Russia also, America's offer was withdrawn. Nasser then took possession of the Suez Canal in advance of the time its cession to Egypt had been promised by Britain and France. Israel seized the opportunity to attack Egypt because of its blockade of Israeli shipping. Britain and France intervened with air power. Russia threatened to support Egypt with atomic weapons. The United States declined a confrontation. Britain and France withdrew. Likewise, America remained quiescent when East Germany, Poland, and Hungary revolted and were reconquered by Russia.

The Crises. The next confrontation was not declined. Russia took advantage of a revolution in Cuba which brought Castro to the top—anti-American and pro-Communist. Russian launching sites for intermediate missiles capable of carrying atomic warheads were installed, as revealed by American air surveillance. President Kennedy declared a partial blockade of Cuba, warning Russia that the first missile firing from Cuba would bring massive retaliation against Russia and that any hostile move to take over Berlin would be met. Premier Khrushchev of Russia backed away, promising to withdraw the missiles from Cuba.

This was the turning point in the cold war. Thereafter, Russia signed a treaty for limiting nuclear tests, as proposed by the United States and Britain. Hostility to the West gradually decreased, under both Khrushchev and his successors. One factor was the increasing hostility toward China, whose claims to leadership split the Communist party in nearly all countries.

Newly independent countries became disillusioned with Russian and Chinese promises. Above all, the United States demonstrated its determination to withstand Communist encroachment by armed support of South Viet-Nam.

The Korean War. When Japan surrendered in 1945, the United States war department set the 38th parallel in Korea as the line to the northward of which the Russians would receive the surrender of Japanese troops, while the Americans did the same in the area south of the line. It was a temporary measure, but the Russians made a closed frontier of the parallel.

In November 1947, the UN created a commission to arrange and supervise elections in Korea, with a view to forming a United Korean government. Russia had held aloof from the proceedings of the commission, and the Red regime in North Korea, calling itself "The Democratic People's Republic of Korea," barred UN officials and refused to participate in the elections. Despite this, elections were held in May 1948 in the American occupation zone, and delegates to a national assembly chosen. The assembly adopted a constitution, and elected Dr. Syngman Rhee president of the new republic, which was promptly recognized by the United States. In December the General Assembly of the UN also recognized it as the legitimate government of Korea. In 1948–49 Soviet and American forces were withdrawn from North and South Korea, respectively.

The Red Invasion. On June 25, 1950, Russian-armed North Korean forces crossed the 38th parallel in a surprise attack which the less well equipped South Koreans were unable to turn back. At an emergency meeting of the Security Council a resolution was passed that same day stigmatizing the attack as an aggression and calling on the North Koreans to cease hostilities and withdraw to the 38th parallel. All United Nations members were asked to assist in carrying out the resolution. Thanks to the Soviet Union's boycott of the Security Council, its representative was not present to veto the resolution.

On June 27th, President Truman stated to Congress that the invaders from North Korea had disregarded the United Nations order to withdraw and that, as assistance had been asked, he had ordered our air and sea forces to give the Korean troops cover and support.

Collective Action. Aid was quickly forthcoming. American planes went into action June 28th. On the 30th the first United States ground troops landed at Pusan from Japan. The Security Council on July 7th passed a resolution for a unified command under the United States for all United Nations forces in Korea. President Truman was asked to designate the commander. The following day he named General of the Army Douglas MacArthur commander in chief, and authorized him to use the flag of the United Nations.

Meanwhile, the Reds, who had taken Seoul within the first few days of fighting, were pressing their offensive vigorously and successfully, pushing the South Koreans before them as they drove down the peninsula. For more than two months there was a series of delaying actions and retreats, until all Korea, save for a relatively small beachhead at Pusan, was in Communist hands.

Then came the counteroffensive. A successful amphibious landing was made at Inchon, the port of Seoul, which was soon taken. The troops broke out of the Pusan beachhead, putting the North Koreans to flight. The allies reached the 38th parallel October 1. The pursuit of the Reds then continued to the Yalu river on the Manchurian border.

Communist China Enters the War. The end was in sight, but the situation changed with the entry of Communist China into the war. In November, powerful Chinese Red forces compelled a United Nations retreat, and it was not until January 1951 that the "Chinese herdes" were finally stopped on a line 75 miles south of the 38th parallel. On February 1 the General Assembly of the United Nations branded the Chinese Communist government aggressors. In February the United Nations took the offensive. Seoul, which had fallen to the Communists in January, was retaken March 15th.

On April 11th General MacArthur was relieved of his command by President Truman, who replaced him with General Matthew B. Ridgway. The end of the first year of the war found United Nations troops well north of the 38th parallel. By this time, 16 nations, besides the Republic of Korea, had forces in the field, but the brunt of the fighting had been borne by the United States.

The Truce Negotiations. In June 1951 Malik of Russia proposed a cease-fire agreement, and on July 10 protracted negotiations began between representatives of the United Nations, Communist China, and North Korea. Although agreement was reached on many points, the negotiations after being dragged out for more than a year finally bogged down over the question of what to do with the thousands of Chinese and North Korean prisoners who were unwilling to return home. The Allies declared that they would not send anybody back to a Communist country who did not wish to go, while the Communists were equally firm in insisting that all prisoners should be returned. On October 8, 1952 further talks were indefinitely postponed.

Following the death of Josef Stalin early in 1953, the Communist attitude toward this problem changed. At the suggestion of General Mark Clark, who succeeded General Ridgway as UN Commander in April 1952, an agreement was made and carried out for the exchange of sick and disabled prisoners. The Communists then agreed that they would not insist on the repatriation of all prisoners, and when further details had been settled, the armistice after just over two years of negotiations was finally signed at Panmunjom, July 27, 1953.

Collective Achievement. By fighting the Communists to a standstill in Korea the United States and the United Nations achieved what they set out to do when they entered the war. They stopped an unwarranted Communist attack on a free country.

In repelling the Reds, men from many nations fought side by side with the armed forces of the Republic of Korea—men from Australia, Belgium, Colombia, Canada, Ethiopia, France, Greece, Luxembourg, the Philippines, the Netherlands, New Zealand, Thailand, Turkey, Union of South Africa, the United Kingdom, and the United States.

Cost in Casualties. The thirty-seven months of fighting cost the United Nations forces more than 455,000 casualties in men killed, wounded, and missing. Of this number about 72,500 died. The heaviest losses were those suffered by the armed services of South Korea, with 300,000 casualties, including about 45,000 killed.

Statistics of United States losses, as announced by the Department of Defense, totalled 142,177, including 25,604 killed in action, 103,492 wounded, 8529 missing, 12,219 captured, and 2433 previously reported captured or missing and since returned to duty. Enemy battle casualties were put at 1,540,000, including 120,000 taken prisoner.

VIETNAM WAR. This war stemmed from French Indochina's war of liberation from France, which was disastrously defeated in 1954. In a conference of Vietnamese and interested nations at Geneva, it was agreed that, until 1956, control of North Vietnam should go to Communist-oriented leaders, with the South to be controlled by an anti-Communist group. An election, set for 1956 to choose a national government, was never held.

North Vietnam supported the Communist Viet Cong party in the South in its efforts to overthrow the government. South Vietnam called on the U.S. for military advisers to aid in pacifying the country.

The Viet Cong, directed and later assisted by North Vietnam, waged guerrilla warfare against the South, soon controlling most of the countryside. U.S. military aid was then sought by the South and was granted.

With U.S. aid, Viet Cong lines were thinned, underground forts cleared, and villagers now supplied intelligence to South Vietnam and U.S. troops. Hanoi, though not directly attacked, was largely depopulated for fear of bombing. Meanwhile, Red China could not promise aid because of internal commotion.

By 1968 U.S. bombings of the North were limited and the Paris peace talks between the U.S. and North Vietnam were begun; later, U.S. bombings were halted. In the following year came the first reduction of U.S. forces in Vietnam and the peace talks were expanded. North Vietnam's leader, Ho Chi Minh, died during the year, but the course of the war and the negotiations continued.

In 1970 U.S. forces entered Cambodia to clear Viet Cong "sanctuaries," captured arms caches, and later withdrew. The peace talks went on in Paris; the U.S. continued troop withdrawals and held to a policy of increasing South Vietnam's takeover of operations.

The U.S. made one last attempt to win the war in 1972, bombing the Hanoi-Haiphong area and mining Northern ports. Then, late in the year, secret talks suggested that peace was near and U.S. troops were reduced. In 1973, President Nixon halted all U.S. military operations in Vietnam. Later, American prisoners of war were released. U.S. participation officially ended, but fighting continued between the North and South until 1975. when North Vietnam won a conclusive victory.

DICTIONARY OF WORLD HISTORY

THE following section deals with topics of world history which do not specifically concern the United States. These topics as a rule have respect to countries whose histories are to be found in the preceding sections. The topics are of such a nature, however, that they can be dealt with more satisfactorily in separate articles. In some cases, this situation is due to the fact that the topic concerns several countries; in other cases, an adequate treatment of a certain phase of a national history would be impossible without unduly interrupting the connected narrative of the country's development. Such topics have therefore received special treatment in accordance with their importance.

Abbassides, The (*ă-băs'ĭ-dēz*). The most famous dynasty of Mohammedan caliphs, taking its name from Abbas, the uncle of Mohammed. This family reigned in Bagdad from 750 until 1058, when the temporal power as monarchs was taken from it, though for 200 years following this date the caliphs were recognized as the spiritual heads of Islam. The greatest glory of the dynasty was the reign of Haroun-al-Raschid, 786–809, the contemporary and admirer of Charlemagne. The wealth and luxury of this period are celebrated in many stories of the *Arabian Nights*. Haroun-al-Raschid became a prince of romance, and Bagdad a synonym for courtly splendor. In the following reign, science and philosophy which enriched Europe were cultivated. But underneath the splendid surface were poverty and injustice which weakened the state and made it an easy prey to the invader. In 1258 the Abbassides were driven out of Bagdad by the Mongols, who burned the city. From 1258 to 1517 the Abbassides maintained a limited power in Egypt, when the last of the line was taken captive by the Turkish sultan, Selim I. See *Egypt*.

A. B. C. Powers. An expression which came into general use about 1914-15, to designate the group of three principal South American powers, Argentina, Brazil, and Chile. In the former year, these powers joined in a diplomatic effort to mediate in the difficulties between Mexico and the United States. In 1915, they concluded among themselves a group of treaties of peace and arbitration. See *Argentina*, *Brazil*, *Chile*.

Abdication. The renunciation of an office. Strictly this term is applied to the giving up of crown and authority by sovereign rulers of states, or by occupants of the papal throne. Various influences have prompted historic abdications. Sometimes the only motive has been the desire of the monarch to escape the cares of state; more often, however, compulsion, rebellion, or conquest has rendered such an act imperative. It is worthy of note that, though despotic or absolute monarchs are free to hand over the cares of state to another at any time they will, the situation is different in a limited monarchy. The king of England, for example, cannot lawfully abdicate without the consent of Parliament, the government of that country being in the nature of a constitutional contract between king and people.

In the following list are enumerated most of the important abdications recorded in history, including those due to the World Wars.

Diocletian 305
Maximian 305
Richard II of England 1399
Amadeus VIII of Savoy 1449
Charles V of the Holy Roman Empire 1556
Christina of Sweden 1654
Augustus of Poland 1706
Philip V of Spain 1724
Victor Amadeus II of Sardinia 1730
Stanislaus Leszczynski (of Poland) 1735
Poniatowski Leszczynski (of Poland) 1795
Charles Emmanuel II of Sardinia 1802
Charles IV of Spain 1808
Louis Bonaparte of Holland 1810

Napoleon . . . . 1814 and 1815
Victor Emmanuel I of Sardinia 1821
Charles X of France 1830
William I of the Netherlands 1840
Ferdinand of Austria 1848
Ludwig of Bavaria 1848
Louis Philippe of France 1848
Charles Albert of Sardinia 1849
Amadeus of Spain 1873
Alexander of Bulgaria 1886
Milan I of Serbia 1889
Dom Pedro of Brazil 1889
Hsuan-Tung, emperor of China 1912
Nicholas II of Russia 1917
William II, emperor of Germany 1918
King of Württemberg . . . . November 10, 1918
King of Saxony . . . . November 11, 1918
Grand Duke of Oldenburg . . . . November 11, 1918
Charles, emperor of Austria . . . . November 12, 1918
Prince of Reuss . . . . November 12, 1918
Grand Duke of Saxe-Weimar . . . November 13, 1918
Prince of Waldeck-Pyrmont . . . . November 14, 1918
Duke of Anhalt . . . . November 14, 1918
King of Bavaria . . . . November 16, 1918
Grand Duke of Baden . . . . . . November 17, 1918
Duke of Saxe-Coburg . . . . . . November 17, 1918
Grand Duke of Mecklenburg-Schwerin November 17, 1918
Constantine of Greece, June 12, 1917, and Sept. 27, 1922
Alfonso XIII of Spain . . . . April 14, 1931
Prajadhipok of Siam . . . . March 2, 1935
Edward VIII of Great Britain. . . . December 10, 1936
Victor Emmanuel III . . . . May 9, 1946
Michael of Rumania . . . . December 30, 1947
Wilhelmina of the Netherlands . . . . . Sept. 4, 1948
Leopold III of Belgium . . . . July 16, 1952
Farouk I of Egypt . . . . July 26, 1952

Popes who have abdicated:

Marcellinus 308
Liberius 366
Benedict IX 1044
Gregory VI 1046
St. Celestine V 1294
Gregory XII 1415

Abencerrages (*à-bĕn'sĕ-rā'jĕz*). This celebrated family of Moors held pride of place among Oriental races as being of pure Arab descent. They were famous in Granada in the 15th century and figured prominently in Spanish romance, especially in the many accounts given of their massacre by the Zegris, inveterate rivals of that period. Accused by the latter of an intrigue against Abdallah, king of Granada, the Abencerrages were decoyed into the Alhambra, where 36 of their number were slain.

Achæan (*à-kē'ăn*) **League, The.** This confederacy of Greek city-states of the Peloponnesus has been called "the most remarkable federal union in history before the founding of the United States of America." About 280 B. C. four little towns on the south shore of the Gulf of Corinth revived an ancient confederacy that had been destroyed by the Macedonian conquerors. Soon other towns joined in driving out the Macedonian tyrants. Within a few years the league included most of the cities of the Peloponnesus in its federal assembly, in which all citizens of the cities who chose to attend had a voice and a vote. For a hundred years, in spite of the narrow aristocratic power allowed by the character of the assembly, the league gave good government to its citizens. It was finally dissolved after the capture and destruction of Corinth by the Romans in 146 B. C. See *Greece*.

Adscriptus Glebæ (*ăd'skrĭp'tŭs glē'bē*). This Latin phrase means "bound" or "attached to the soil." An adscript was, in feudal times, a serf. He was regarded as an implement or chattel on his master's estate and in this sense belonged, or was attached to, the land. So true was this, that, on the transfer of an estate from one ownership to another, the new owner claimed as a right the serfs who were working on the estate at the time.

Afrikander. The Dutch name for African. Commonly used of native whites of Dutch or Huguenot ancestry in South Africa.

Albigenses (ăl'bĭ-jĕn'sēz). A name given to a sect also called Catharists, or "the pure," which taught a Manichean dualism, the conflict of two principles, good and evil. Triumph of the "good" was sought through extreme asceticism. The center of the heresy was in Languedoc, and it took its name from the city of Albi. In an endeavor to suppress the heresy, Innocent III sent legates in 1203 to southern France. One of them was assassinated and the pope organized a crusade against the Albigenses. Its leader was Simon de Montfort, and he and his followers seemed chiefly anxious to conquer rich estates in the South. The final result was to bring southern France under royal control.

Algeciras Conference. Prior to 1905, France carried on a policy of "peaceful penetration" in Morocco. In that year Wilhelm II of Germany visited Tangier and promised to uphold Moroccan independence. Peace being threatened, a conference of leading European powers was called at Algeciras in 1906. Aided by British influence, France's claims were upheld, and a mixed French and Spanish police force was set up.

When native disturbances occasioned the French seizure of Fez in 1911, the Germans protested and sent the warship *Panther*. This was known as the Agadir affair. In subsequent negotiations, France won from Germany recognition of her Morocco claims, ceding in return extensive territories in the Congo. Germany nevertheless considered herself humiliated and increased her army, thereby augmenting the suspicions which culminated in World War I.

Allied Debts. World War I and the readjustments immediately ensuing left the various Allied countries in debt to the United States to the amount of about 10.338 billion dollars, of which Great Britain owed 4.277 billion and France, 3.405 billion. Great Britain was a creditor to other Allies to the extent of about 7.270 billion dollars, and France had advanced to others about 2.775 billion dollars. The United States was thus the largest creditor; Great Britain was second, being owed about 3 billion more than her debt to the United States. On August 1, 1922, the British government announced that it would cancel all debts to it and reparation claims over and above what were required to meet its payments to the United States. The American government refused to admit any connection between reparations and Allied debts.

The British debt to the United States was funded in 1923, payments to be made over a period of 62 years. Most of the other debtor countries followed, the interest charges and installments being adjusted to their estimated capacity to pay. Payments were made regularly until 1931, when a world-wide financial crisis led President Hoover to propose a moratorium, subsequently ratified, on all Allied debts and German reparations. No more reparations were paid. After the moratorium most debtor countries defaulted immediately. Great Britain made one complete payment and two "token" payments. Finland alone continued to make her small payments due.

Amphictyonic (ăm-fĭk'tĭ-ŏn'ĭk) **League, The.** This name means "league of neighbors." In ancient Greece, before 500 B. C., there were several such leagues formed for the protection of various shrines and temples. The chief of these was the Delphic Amphictyony, or "The Amphictyonic League," which included in its council delegates from all the important states and represented a religious union of the Greek people. Its original purpose was the care of the temple at Delphi; but its council also laid down rules for more humane warfare, for instance, forbidding the cutting off of a town's water supply in war or peace. This was a first step in international law. The Amphictyonic League continued to exercise great religious and political sway as late as the 3d century A. D. See *Greece*.

Annus Mirabilis, "Wonderful Year." A phrase applied to various noted years in history. It gave the title to Dryden's poem, in which are commemorated the two English victories over the Dutch in 1666 and the Great Fire of London in the same year.

Armada, The. A Spanish word, meaning "armed force," but applied especially to the great naval expedition sent against England by Philip of Spain in 1588 and decisively defeated by the English fleet and the storms of the North Sea. Philip's purpose was three-fold: to suppress English Protestantism, to stop English piracy in Spanish America, and to prevent English aid from reaching the rebellious Netherlanders. When, after long delays in storms, the vast Spanish fleet appeared in the English channel, it numbered 120 ships, carrying 20,000 soldiers and 8000 sailors, besides the galley slaves. But Philip, whose policy suppressed invention in his own dominions, had failed to reckon with the superior intelligence of the Englishmen and also with their patriotism. Catholic and Protestant had united in a supreme effort to build up the depleted English navy. The Spanish ships, built after an old, high, unwieldy type, to carry many soldiers for fighting at close quarters, were no match for the new English vessels, built to sail swiftly and to carry heavier guns. The English commanders, Lord Howard, Drake, Hawkins, and Frobisher, allowed the *Armada* to pass Plymouth, July 21, 1588. Then, with a favoring southwest wind, they followed, and, in a series of sharp attacks at long and short range, so harried and crippled the Spaniards that on the 27th of July they anchored off Calais. Here eight fire ships were sent into the midst of the unwieldy floating castles, and they were compelled to put to sea. On the following day, off Gravelines, the helpless *Armada* was riddled by English shot. The wind rose to a storm which drove pursuers and pursued northward past the coasts of Holland, where the waiting prince of Parma saw his hope of transporting his army to England vanish. The Spanish admiral, the duke of Sidonia, himself utterly unpracticed in seafaring, saw his only chance of escape around the north of Scotland. Storm and wreck followed him into the Atlantic. Of the "invincible *Armada*" but 54 battered hulks were finally anchored in Santander bay. See *England*.

Armenian Massacres. By the Treaty of Berlin in 1878, the sultan of Turkey promised reforms in the government of Armenia; but these promises were not kept, and revolutionary movements arose among the oppressed people. In 1895 the Kurds, called in to police the country, carried on brutal massacres. Protests by England, France, and Russia were ignored. In 1909 at Adana and in Cilicia and northern Syria 30,000 Armenians were killed. It is estimated that, between April 1915 and January 1922, through a Turkish policy of extermination, nearly a million Armenians were massacred. See *Turkey, World War I*.

Assassins or **Hashisheens.** A fanatical military order instituted in Persia about 1090 by Hassan ben Sabah. They migrated to Syria and settled in the mountains of Lebanon, whence the name of their chief, who was known as "the Old Man of the Mountain." The secret murders they committed, in obedience to this chief, made them notorious. Their religion was a mixture of Mohammedanism, Judaism, and Christianity. They believed the Holy Spirit dwelt in their leader, and so they obeyed his orders as coming direct from God. For two centuries they were the terror of the surrounding nations. They fought, 50,000 strong, against the crusaders and became a formidable obstacle to the success of the Christian armies. They were at length overcome by the sultan Bibars in 1272.

Austrian Succession, War of. In 1740 Charles VI, Habsburg emperor, died without male heirs. Frederick II (the Great) seized Silesia. Other countries hastened to help divide the Austrian realms. Maria Theresa, daughter of Charles, loyally supported by her subjects and later aided by England and Holland, succeeded in preventing any losses of territory besides Silesia. Out of this war, ended by the Peace of Aix-la-Chapelle in 1748, grew the rivalry of Prussia and Austria in Germany and that of England and France in America. See *Pragmatic Sanction*.

Avignon (à′vē′nyôn′) **Captivity.** The period of 70 years during which the popes were forced to reside at Avignon, on the southeastern border of medieval France. The influence of the French kings in the affairs of the papacy seemed so predominant that, when the Hundred Years' war broke out, England distrusted the popes as tools of the enemy. This humiliating sojourn lasted from the papacy of Clement V, 1309, until that of Gregory XI, 1377. It is known also as the Babylonian Captivity, the period of exile approximating to that of the Jews in the time of Nebuchadnezzar.

Babington Plot. A plot set on foot in 1585 by a number of young Catholic noblemen at court, acting, it is alleged, under the instructions of a Jesuit named Ballard. Letters secured by Walsingham, secretary of state and head of the secret service, were said to have proved Mary Stuart's complicity in the plot. Babington and his companions were condemned to death, Mary also being subsequently tried and executed for her part in this conspiracy

Baghdad Pact. What came to be known as the "Baghdad Pact" originated as a mutual defense treaty signed February 24, 1955 by Turkey and Iraq. Later that year the alliance was joined by Great Britain, Pakistan, and Iran, in that order. The United States, though not a member, co-operated with the organization's economic and military committees. Earlier Turkey had tried unsuccessfully to interest Egypt and other Arab states in forming a pro-western security system. Russia exerted strong pressure to prevent countries from joining. Designed to be somewhat like NATO as a warning to aggressors and a protector of small nations, the Baghdad Pact has been less effective because of cross-purposes among its members, as in the case of the Cyprus and Suez disputes, and because of a generally confused situation in the Middle East. It suffered most from the 1958 *coup d'etat* in Iraq which overthrew the pro-western government of that country.

Balaklava (bä′lä-klä′và). The name of this little Russian seaport in the Crimea is famous because of two exploits of British troops in the battle of Balaklava, Oct. 25, 1854. A brigade of heavy cavalry, in a brilliant charge, repulsed a huge mass of Russian horsemen. More famous is the charge of the brigade of light cavalry, "the light brigade." A vague order to retake some guns was misunderstood, and the brigade, under Lord Cardigan, rode against the very center of the Russian army. Few escaped from the ensuing slaughter. "It is magnificent," said a French officer, "but it is not war."

Balance of Power. The name at first given to that relation of European states in which no one country is strong enough to threaten the safety of its neighbors. From the close of the religious struggle of the Thirty Years' war in 1648 to World War I, 1914–18, the chief concern of European diplomacy was the maintaining of the "balance of power." The advocacy of disarmament aims at bringing about an adjustment of power, not only among the sovereign states of Europe, but also among those throughout the rest of the civilized world, so that no one state can be in a position to menace or dominate another. See *Disarmament*.

Balkan League, The. An alliance formed in 1912 by Bulgaria, Serbia, Greece, and Montenegro for the purpose of action against Turkey. It lasted barely a year, being broken in the bloody dispute which arose among the allies after their complete defeat of the Turk in 1913. See *Greece, Turkey*.

Barmecides. A wealthy Persian family who furnished viziers to Haroun-al-Raschid and to former caliphs of Baghdad; so called from their founder Barmek. Jaffar became the favorite vizier of the caliph, and, by his magnificent services

and patronage of the arts, reflected great glory on his master's reign. Through jealousy or suspicion or both, Jaffar fell into disgrace with Haroun-al-Raschid, who put him to death in 802, together with nearly all of the Barmecide family.

Bashi-Bazouks (bắsh′ĭ-bà-zōōks′). Irregular troops or volunteers attached to the Turkish army and noted for their wildness and cruelty. As a rule, they are mounted and serve for their maintenance without pay; this deficiency, however, they rectify by acts of pillage. Their services are also used by the municipal authorities, who often detail them to escort travelers wishing to explore the country. Such services are by no means inexpensive, as the Bashi-Bazouks expect not only to be fed well, but to be rewarded generously. Their uniform being that of tatterdemalions, they are called *Bashi-Bazouks*, which signifies "disorderly appearance."

Bastille (bàs-tēl′), **Destruction of the.** The famous fortress of the Bastille once flanked the city gate of St. Antoine, Paris. Its construction was begun, under Charles V, by the provost Hugh Aubriot in 1370 and was completed in 1382. It became in a short time a prison of state and held within its walls, among other illustrious victims, such men as Jacques d'Armagnac, "The Man with the Iron Mask," Voltaire, and Lally-Tollendal. Its terrors reached their climax during the ministry of Richelieu, 1624–42. In the reign of Louis XI, cages of iron had been built, and the vaults beneath the towers, being on a level with the water in the moat, were the object of especial dread. For the populace, the Bastille stood as the symbol of royal despotism.

Louis XVI, June 23, 1789, had declared certain recent acts of the third estate of the National Assembly to be unconstitutional. He sent Brézé, his master of ceremonies, to bid the members withdraw from the hall of the Convention. Mirabeau, a French noble who had been chosen a deputy by the third estate, exclaimed with passion, "Go tell your master we are here by the will of the people and shall leave only at the point of the bayonet!" A few days later foreign mercenaries appeared in Paris. The Assembly sent to the king, demanding their removal. Louis replied by dismissing Necker, a minister favorable to reform and trusted by the people. Camille Desmoulins, a young journalist, announced the news in public on July 12. Paris was all aflame. Two days later, July 14, the populace, re-enforced by companies of French Guards, attacked the ancient monument of tyranny. De Launay, the commander, offered to surrender. When the doors of the fortress were thrown open, the mob seized him and a few of the Swiss Guards and murdered them. The heads of De Launay and Major de Losme of the Swiss were mounted on pikes and carried about the city. The walls of the grim fortress were later pulled down, so that not "one stone was left upon another." The fall of the Bastille is one of the most dramatic events in modern history. Its anniversary is celebrated in France as the chief national holiday and as the day when a new era of liberty dawned for the people and an end was put to the *ancien régime*. It is interesting to note that Lafayette sent the key of the fortress to George Washington "because the principles of America it was that opened the Bastille." This relic may still be seen at Mt. Vernon.

Bath, Order of the. An order of knighthood, founded by Henry IV in 1399. From the time of Charles I it lapsed, until revived by George I in 1725 as a military order, which it remained until 1845. It was then established on its present basis with a military and a civil division.

BATTLES OF THE WORLD, DECISIVE

1. Marathon, Sept., 490 B. C. A small Greek army, commanded by Miltiades, defeated a much larger Persian force. The Persians were compelled to retreat into Asia.

2. Syracuse, 413 B. C. The besieged Syracusans turned upon and almost completely destroyed the invading Athenian forces.

3. Arbela, Oct. 1, 331 B. C. The Greeks, led by Alexander the Great, defeated the Persian armies of Darius and overthrew the Persian power.

4. Metaurus, 207 B. C. The Carthaginians, led by Hasdrubal, the brother of Hannibal, were defeated by the Romans under the command of Marcus Livius and Claudius Nero.

5. Teutoburg. 9 (?) A. D. The Roman legions, led by Varus, were defeated by the Germans under Arminius. This victory freed Germany permanently from the Roman power.

6. Châlons, 451 A. D. The Romans and their allies, the Visigoths, led by Aëtius, defeated the Huns and their Ostrogoth and other allies, led by Attila, compelling them to retire into Pannonia.

7. Tours, 732 A. D. The Franks under Charles Martel, won a great victory over the invading hosts of the Saracens, led by Abderrahman. This conflict, which checked the Mohammedan invasion of western Europe, is known also as the battle of Poitiers.

8. Hastings, October 14, 1066. The Norman invaders defeated the Saxons. King Harold of England lost his life, and the kingdom passed to William, duke of Normandy.

9. Orleans, May 8, 1429. The siege of Orleans by the English was raised by the French, led by Joan of Arc. This victory insured the final defeat of the English invaders of France.

10. Defeat of the Spanish Armada, July 20–29, 1588. The Spanish fleet was almost completely destroyed by the British fleet and by severe storms.

11. Blenheim, Aug. 13, 1704. The French and Bavarians were defeated by the English under the duke of Marlborough, aided by their allies led by Prince Eugene.

12. Pultowa, July 8, 1709. Charles XII of Sweden was completely defeated by the Russians under Czar Peter the Great.

13. Quebec, Fall of, Sept. 17, 1759. After an extended siege and after the battle on the Heights of Abraham, where the English under Wolfe defeated the French under Montcalm, the French surrendered the city.

14. Saratoga Oct. 7, 1777. The British army under General Burgoyne was utterly defeated by the Americans. The entire force was surrendered on Oct. 17 to the American commander, General Gates.

15. Valmy, Sept. 20, 1792. The French forces, commanded by Kellermann, defeated the Prussians, commanded by the duke of Brunswick.

16. Waterloo, June 18, 1815. Napoleon and his French forces were finally defeated by the British and their allies under the duke of Wellington

17. Gettysburg, July 1–3, 1863. The Confederate troops under Lee were defeated by the Federals under Meade. Confederate invasion of the North was proved impossible.

18. Vicksburg, The Fall of, July 4, 1863. The capture of this stronghold by Grant, in command of the Federal army, gave command of the Mississippi to the North and cut the Confederacy in two. The Confederate general, Pemberton, surrendered after a long siege.

19. Sedan, Sept. 1, 1870. Defeat of the French forces by the Germans compelled the surrender of the French army in Sedan and of Emperor Napoleon III.

20. Tsushima, or The Sea of Japan, May 27–28, 1905. The Japanese, under Admiral Togo, destroyed Rojestvensky's Russian fleet, establishing Japanese sea-power.

21. The Marne, First Battle of, Sept. 6–9, 1914. The British and French armies checked the German advance, and with it the German hope for a speedy victory.

22. Jutland, May 31, 1916. The defeat of the German fleet confirmed British control of the sea.

23. Stalingrad, Aug. 1942–Jan. 1943. The Russian resistance at Stalingrad on the Volga, and the destruction of the German army besieging it, was the turning-point on the eastern front.

24. Normandy, June 6–July 18, 1944. The landing and establishment of the Anglo-American armies on the Norman coast made possible the liberation of France and the invasion of Germany.

25. Philippine Sea, Second Battle of, Sept. 25, 1944. The defeat of the Japanese fleet off Leyte ruined Japan's sea-power, and left her open to invasion.

Bayonne (*bȧ'yŏn'*) **Decree.** Napoleon's decree of 1808, ordering the seizure of all vessels under the American flag found in French ports, claiming that since all American vessels were held at home by the Embargo Act, these were English vessels in disguise.

Belgian Congo. Formerly Congo Free State and, since 1960, the Congo Republic. It owed its existence largely to Leopold II, king of the Belgians. In 1876, Leopold, in co-operation with several European governments, formed the International African Association, to promote the exploration and colonization of Africa. He employed Henry M. Stanley to explore the Congo region, and Stanley was active in founding stations, and making treaties with the native chiefs. After several powers, including the United States, had recognized the independent Congo Free State, the Berlin Conference of 1885 declared it neutral, and open to the trade of all nations, with Leopold as its personal sovereign. Governmental abuses, which arose under this régime, aroused international protest. From 1908, until it gained its independence in 1960, it was a Belgian colony.

Belgian Neutrality Treaty. The Treaty of London, 1839, signed by Austria, Belgium, France, Great Britain, Prussia, and Russia, guaranteed the perpetual neutrality of Belgium. This neutrality being threatened by the Franco-Prussian war in 1870, the belligerents signed special agreements with Great Britain to respect Belgian neutrality. In 1914 Germany was charged with violating the treaty obligation. The agreement was abrogated by the Treaty of Versailles in 1919.

Benelux. A term applied to an economic agreement made in 1947 between Belgium, the Netherlands, and Luxembourg aiming at full economic and monetary union for all three countries.

BISHOPS AND POPES OF ROME

The word pope is derived from an ecclesiastical Latin word *papa*, meaning "father," applied in the early Christian centuries as a term of respect to clergy of high rank, especially bishops. By the 5th century, the title had come to be applied almost altogether to the bishop of Rome, and from the 11th century it has been claimed exclusively for him as the sovereign pontiff of the Roman Catholic Church.

Primarily the pope, as the successor of Saint Peter, is the bishop of Rome. The actual predominance of Rome over other episcopal sees was, as early as the 1st century, acknowledged by the then universal church. This supremacy, through a gradual process extending over several centuries, grew and expanded with the natural development of the Christian Church. The council of Chalcedon in 451 accepted as authoritative the profession of faith proposed by Leo I. The pontificates of Gregory the Great (590–604), Gregory VII (1073–85), and Innocent III (1198–1216) mark important stages in the growth of the papal power.

Electors. Early accounts of elections indicate that for several centuries the right of choosing bishops and the early popes was shared by both the clerical and the lay members of the Christian community of Rome and of its neighboring territory. After the election had come to be a concern of the entire Church, the possession of the right was restricted, until at length, in the 12th century, it came to be confined to the college of cardinals. The pope is now elected by a body known as the conclave, which includes all cardinals of the world. The creation of 24 new cardinals in 1953 brought the sacred college to 70. Pope John XXIII created 10 new cardinals bringing the total to 90 in 1962. In 1968, the sacred college comprised 109 members.

The Conclave. The word conclave signifies a room which may be locked, and is often applied to the apartments in which the papal electoral body meets, as well as to the assemblage itself. The cardinals are required to live in entire seclusion from the outside world during the period necessary to secure the election of a new pope. After the death of a pope, a portion of the Vatican adjoining the Sistine Chapel is walled off and divided into apartments of three or four rooms each where the cardinals live. Each may be accompanied by a secretary and a servant, who are called conclavists.

Method of Election. The conclave opens officially the evening of the fifteenth day after the pontiff's death. On the morning of the sixteenth day, the cardinals assemble for the actual balloting in the Sistine Chapel. The voting is by secret ballot, and for an election a two-thirds plus one vote is required.

Two ballots are taken each day, in the morning and in the evening, until an election is secured. After each ballot, the votes are burned. If no election has taken place, damp straw is mixed with the paper, and the resulting dark smoke, the famous *sfumata*, from the chimney, informs the people waiting outside that a new pope has not yet been chosen. When the new pope has been chosen, the paper ballots alone are burned without the straw and a white almost invisible smoke from the chimney notifies the populace that the pope at last has been elected.

Installation. When a candidate has received the necessary two-thirds vote plus one, the doors of the chapel are opened. Upon formal inquiry by the presiding dean as to whether the newly chosen pontiff is willing to accept the burden of the papacy, the pope-elect duly declares his assent and announces the name by which he desires to be known. He is then clothed in the papal vestments, and receives the first homage of the cardinals. Following this ceremony occurs the public announcement of the election. On the election of Pius XI in 1922, this proclamation, for the first time since 1870, was made from the gallery of Saint Peter's. The pope's jurisdiction begins with his election, but he dates his pontificate from the following Sunday or holyday upon which the formal coronation takes place.

The following list contains the names, with the dates of their pontificates, of the pontiffs who have occupied the chair of Saint Peter. The list will be found especially valuable for reference in connection with the study of the various periods of European history.

Pontiff	Pontificate	
	First Century	
	A. D.	A. D.
1 Saint Peter		67(?)
2 Saint Linus	67	79(?)
3 Saint Anacletus	79	90(?)
4 Saint Clement I	90	99(?)
	Second Century	
5 Saint Evaristus	99	107(?)
6 Saint Alexander I	107	116(?)
7 Saint Sixtus I	116	125(?)
8 Saint Telesphorus	125	136(?)
9 Saint Hyginus	136	140(?)
10 Saint Pius I	140	154(?)
11 Saint Anicetus	154	165(?)
12 Saint Soter	165	174
13 Saint Eleutherius	174	189
14 Saint Victor I	189	198
15 Saint Zephyrinus	198	217
	Third Century	
16 Calixtus I	217	222
17 Urban I	222	230
18 Saint Pontian	230	235
19 Saint Anterus	235	236
20 Saint Fabian	236	250
21 Cornelius	251	253
22 Saint Lucius I	253	254
23 Saint Stephen I	254	257
24 Saint Sixtus II	257	258
25 Saint Dionysius	259	268
26 Saint Felix I	269	274
27 Saint Eutychianus	275	283
28 Saint Caius	283	296
	Fourth Century	
29 Saint Marcellinus	296	304
30 Saint Marcellus I	308	309
31 Saint Eusebius	309 (310)	
32 Saint Miltiades	311	314
33 Saint Silvester I	314	335
34 Saint Mark	336	
35 Saint Julius I	337	352
36 Liberius	352	366
37 Saint Damasus I	366	384
38 Saint Siricius	384	398
39 Saint Anastasius I	398	401

Pontiff	Pontificate	
	Fifth Century	
	A. D.	A. D
40 Innocent I	402	417
41 Saint Zosimus	417	418
42 Saint Boniface I	418	422
43 Saint Celestine I	422	432
44 Saint Sixtus III	432	440
45 Saint Leo I, "The Great"	440	461
46 Saint Hilarius	461	468
47 Saint Simplicius	468	483
48 Saint Felix III	483	492
49 Saint Gelasius I	492	496
50 Anastasius II	496	498
	Sixth Century	
51 Saint Symmachus	498	514
52 Saint Hormisdas	514	523
53 Saint John I	523	526
54 Felix IV	526	530
55 Boniface II	530	532
56 John II	533	535
57 Saint Agapetus I	535	536
58 Saint Silverius	536	538(?)
59 Vigilius	538(?)	555
60 Pelagius I	556	561
61 John III	561	574
62 Benedict I	575	579
63 Pelagius II	579	590
	Seventh Century	
64 Saint Gregory I, "The Great"	590	604
65 Sabinianus	604	606
66 Boniface III	607	
67 Saint Boniface IV	608	615
68 Saint Deusdedit	615	618
69 Boniface V	619	625
70 Honorius I	625	638
71 Severinus	638	640
72 John IV	640	642
73 Theodore I	642	649
74 Saint Martin I	649	655
75 Saint Eugenius I	654	657
76 Saint Vitalianus	657	672
77 Saint Adeodatus	672	676
78 Donus	676	678
79 Saint Agatho	678	681
80 Saint Leo II	682	683
81 Saint Benedict II	684	685
82 John V	685	686
83 Conon	686	687
	Eighth Century	
84 Saint Sergius I	687	701
85 John VI	701	705
86 John VII	705	707
87 Sisinnius	708	
88 Constantine	708	715
89 Saint Gregory II	715	731
90 Saint Gregory III	731	741
91 Saint Zacharias	741	752
92 Stephen III	752	757
93 Paul I	757	767
94 Stephen IV	768	772
95 Adrian I	772	795
	Ninth Century	
96 Saint Leo III	795	816
97 Stephen V	816	817
98 Paschal I	817	824
99 Eugenius II	824	827
100 Valentine	827	
101 Gregory IV	827	844
102 Sergius II	844	847
103 Saint Leo IV	847	855
104 Benedict III	855	858
105 Saint Nicholas I	858	867
106 Adrian II	867	872
107 John VIII	872	882
108 Marinus I	882	884
109 Saint Adrian III	884	885
110 Stephen VI	885	891
111 Formosus	891	896
112 Boniface VI	896	
113 Stephen VII	896	897
114 Romanus	897	
115 Theodore II	897	
116 John IX	898	900
	Tenth Century	
117 Benedict IV	900	903
118 Leo V	903	
119 Christopher	903	904
120 Sergius III	904	911

Pontiff	Pontificate	
Tenth Century—Con.	A.D.	A.D.
121 Anastasius III	911	913
122 Lando	913	914
123 John X	914	928
124 Leo VI	928	
125 Stephen VIII	928	931
126 John XI	931	936
127 Leo VII	936	939
128 Stephen IX	939	942
129 Marinus II	942	946
130 Agapetus II	946	955
131 John XII	955	964
132 Leo VIII	963	965
133 Benedict V	964	
134 John XIII	965	972
135 Benedict VI	973	974
136 Benedict VII	974	983
137 John XIV	983	984
138 Boniface VII	984	985
139 John XV	985	996
140 Gregory V	996	999
Eleventh Century		
141 Silvester II	999	1003
142 John XVII	1003	
143 John XVIII	1003	1009
144 Sergius IV	1009	1012
145 Benedict VIII	1012	1024
146 John XIX	1024	1032
147 Benedict IX	1032	1045
148 Gregory VI	1045	1046
149 Clement II	1046	1047
150 Damasus II	1048	
151 Saint Leo IX	1049	1054
152 Victor II	1055	1057
153 Stephen X	1057	1058
154 Benedict X	1058	1059
155 Nicholas II	1059	1061
156 Alexander II	1061	1073
157 Saint Gregory VII	1073	1085
158 Victor III, Blessed	1087	1087
159 Urban II, Blessed	1088	1099
Twelfth Century		
160 Paschal II	1099	1118
161 Gelasius II	1118	1119
162 Calixtus II	1119	1124
163 Honorius II	1124	1130
164 Innocent II	1130	1143
165 Celestine II	1143	1144
166 Lucius II	1144	1145
167 Eugenius III, Blessed	1145	1153
168 Anastasius IV	1153	1154
169 Adrian IV	1154	1159
170 Alexander III	1159	1181
171 Lucius III	1181	1185
172 Urban III	1185	1187
173 Gregory VIII	1187	
174 Clement III	1187	1191
175 Celestine III	1191	1198
Thirteenth Century		
176 Innocent III	1198	1216
177 Honorius III	1216	1227
178 Gregory IX	1227	1241
179 Celestine IV	1241	
180 Innocent IV	1243	1254
181 Alexander IV	1254	1261
182 Urban IV	1261	1264
183 Clement IV	1265	1268
184 Gregory X	1271	1276
185 Innocent V, Blessed	1276	
186 Adrian V	1276	
187 John XXI	1276	1277
188 Nicholas III	1277	1280
189 Martin IV	1281	1285
190 Honorius IV	1285	1287
191 Nicholas IV	1288	1292
192 Saint Celestine V	1294	
193 Boniface VIII	1294	1303
Fourteenth Century		
194 Benedict XI	1303	1304
195 Clement V	1305	1314
196 John XXII	1316	1334
197 Benedict XII	1334	1342
198 Clement VI	1342	1352
199 Innocent VI	1352	1362
200 Urban V, Blessed	1362	1370
201 Gregory XI	1370	1378
202 Urban VI	1378	1389
203 Boniface IX	1389	1404

Pontiff	Pontificate	
Fifteenth Century	A.D.	A.D.
204 Innocent VII	1404	1406
205 Gregory XII	1406	1415
206 Alexander V	1409	1410
207 John XXIII*	1410	1415
208 Martin V	1417	1431
209 Eugenius IV	1431	1447
210 Nicholas V	1447	1455
211 Calixtus III	1455	1458
212 Pius II	1458	1464
213 Paul II	1464	1471
214 Sixtus IV	1471	1484
215 Innocent VIII	1484	1492
216 Alexander VI	1492	1503
Sixteenth Century		
217 Pius III	1503	
218 Julius II	1503	1513
219 Leo X	1513	1521
220 Adrian VI	1522	1523
221 Clement VII	1523	1534
222 Paul III	1534	1549
223 Julius III	1550	1555
224 Marcellus II	1555	
225 Paul IV	1555	1559
226 Pius IV	1559	1565
227 Saint Pius V	1566	1572
228 Gregory XIII	1572	1585
229 Sixtus V	1585	1590
230 Urban VII	1590	
231 Gregory XIV	1590	1591
232 Innocent IX	1591	
233 Clement VIII	1592	1605
Seventeenth Century		
234 Leo XI	1605	
235 Paul V	1605	1621
236 Gregory XV	1621	1623
237 Urban VIII	1623	1644
238 Innocent X	1644	1655
239 Alexander VII	1655	1667
240 Clement IX	1667	1669
241 Clement X	1670	1676
242 Innocent XI	1676	1689
243 Alexander VIII	1689	1691
244 Innocent XII	1691	1700
Eighteenth Century		
245 Clement XI	1700	1721
246 Innocent XIII	1721	1724
247 Benedict XIII	1724	1730
248 Clement XII	1730	1740
249 Benedict XIV	1740	1758
250 Clement XIII	1758	1769
251 Clement XIV	1769	1774
252 Pius VI	1775	1799
Nineteenth Century		
253 Pius VII	1800	1823
254 Leo XII	1823	1829
255 Pius VIII	1829	1830
256 Gregory XVI	1831	1846
257 Pius IX	1846	1878
258 Leo XIII	1878	1903
Twentieth Century		
259 Pius X	1903	1914
260 Benedict XV	1914	1922
261 Pius XI	1922	1939
262 Pius XII	1939	1958
263 John XXIII	1958	1963
264 Paul VI	1963	

* By some historians regarded as anti-pope.

Black Death. One of the most famous and most destructive plagues of history. Spreading westward from Asia, it swept away from one-third to one-half the population of Europe in the years 1347–50. The disease was named from the black spots that appeared on the bodies of those afflicted. It may have been similar to what is now called "bubonic plague."

Black Hole of Calcutta. A small cell, intended for two or three men, in the East India Company's citadel, Fort William. The story told by the commandant, J. Z. Holwell, is that the subahdar of Bengal, who stormed the fort, June 20, 1756, had his guards drive all the white inmates of the fort, 146 in number, into this almost airless room where they were left overnight to die of suffocation. Only 23 were alive in the morning.

Black Shirts. A name applied to the members of the Fascist party in Italy, by whom the black shirt was worn as a party badge.

Boers (*boorz*). The Dutch colonists in South Africa. Boer is a Dutch word meaning peasant or farmer. The Boers first settled in Cape Colony in 1652. Through a century and a half of pioneer life, these people maintained a stern type of Calvinistic faith which intensified their severe exclusiveness. Besides, they firmly believed in their right to enslave the native peoples. When the colony was finally ceded to Great Britain in 1815, the policies of the new government in respect to the natives roused the opposition of the Boers. In 1835 they started the Great Trek, or migration, to the Orange River district, where they settled in the Orange Free State. Later, a large body moved beyond the Vaal, where they organized the Transvaal Republic. Here, under the presidency of Paul Kruger, elected in 1883, they maintained a stubborn independence until the victory of the British in the Boer war. After that time, through the statesmanship of such men as Lord Milner, General Botha, and General Smuts, the reconciliation of Boers and English progressed rapidly inside South Africa.

Botany Bay. A small inlet on the coast of New South Wales, where the first convict establishment was formed in 1788. Later in the same year the penal settlement was removed to Port Jackson, but the name Botany bay was constantly used, generically, for the convict settlements in Australia. Captain Cook, in 1770, gave the bay its present name on account of the many strange plants he found there.

Bourbon Family. Members of this royal line have governed France, Spain, the Two Sicilies, Lucca, and Parma. The family is traced to Robert of Clermont, youngest son of Louis IX, but the name comes from Louis, duke of Bourbon, who died in 1341. French kings of this house were Henry IV, Louis XIII, XIV, XV, XVI, XVII, XVIII, and Charles X.

Boxer Uprising. The patriotic, antiforeign demonstration in China in 1900 led by the Chinese secret society called "The Fist of Righteous Harmony" or, popularly, "Boxers." The outbreak was precipitated by the foreign occupation of Chinese ports,—Kiaochow by Germany, Port Arthur by Russia, Weihaiwei by England, and Kwang-chow by France. The government failed to control the insurgents, and the warships of the powers, except the United States, intensified the antiforeign feeling of the Chinese by bombarding the forts at Taku. The foreign legations at Peking were besieged, and finally a relief force of Japanese, Russian, British, French, German, and American troops, commanded by Count Waldersee, advanced on the capital and relieved the legations on August 14. The 9th regiment, United States army, suffered heavy losses, including its colonel and several other officers. Military operations continued until the spring of 1901. An indemnity of $333,000,000 was imposed on China by the allied powers, the United States and various other countries later resigning claim to their shares. See *China*.

Boycotting. A system of reprisals organized in 1880 by the Land League in Ireland in return for the harsh treatment of tenants by landowners and their agents. It took its name from one Captain James Boycott, a landlord of Mayo. The victim of boycotting was cut off from the social and commercial life of the community, being permitted neither to buy nor to sell, and those attempting to deal with him were treated in like manner.

Brest-Litovsk (*brĕst'lyĕ-tôfsk'*), **Treaty of.** The treaty of peace concluded March 3, 1918, between Germany and the Bolsheviki, by which Germany was to gain control of Finland, the Baltic provinces, Lithuania, Poland, and the Ukraine, and direction of Russian industry. Although never enforced, it enabled the Germans to transfer troops to the western front at a critical moment of World War I.

Buccaneers. An association of sea rovers formed about 1525, to harry the Spanish possessions in South America and prey upon their commerce. They were of various nationalities, but chiefly English and French, their most famous leaders being Montbars, known as the Exterminator, and Henry Morgan, afterwards Sir Henry and deputy-governor of Jamaica. Under the latter leader they crossed the isthmus and sacked the city of Panama in 1671, and for years they paralyzed the Spanish trade, both in the Caribbean Sea and in the Pacific. They ceased to exist as an association early in the 18th century, but some of them continued careers of indiscriminate piracy for many years longer. The name is said to be derived from *buccan*, which in the Caribbean islands meant to dry meat on a frame, or *buccan*, over smoke. The early French adventurers adopted this custom.

Bulgarian Atrocities. A rising of the Mohammedan inhabitants of Bulgaria, assisted by the Bashi-Bazouks, or Turkish Irregulars, against the Christians in 1876. Thousands of Christians were massacred. Turkey refused redress, and Russia consequently declared war in the following year.

Burgundy. The name is derived from the Burgundians, a Teutonic people who settled in eastern Gaul in the 5th century. In 1361 the duchy of Burgundy, of which the chief town was Dijon, became a possession of the French crown. It was conferred upon Philip the Bold. He and his vigorous descendants enlarged their territories until, in the 15th century, Burgundy was one of the most important European states, controlling the rich territories and cities of the Low Countries, now Holland and Belgium. Duke Charles the Bold successfully maintained his position against the scheming Louis XI, until he was slain at the battle of Nancy in 1477. The Burgundian realms were then divided between France and Austria, since the Habsburg Maximilian had married Mary, daughter and sole heir of Charles.

Cahiers de Doléances (*kȧ'yȧ' dĕ dô'lā'ȧɴs'*). "Documents of Grievances." These documents contained representations of grievances and demands made by the people. They were signed and laid before the king of France in 1789 by the deputies of the States-General. The principal demands were: suppression of the sale of public offices; the abrogation of judicial power claimed by the owners of certain hereditary estates, who acted as resident magistrates; the repeal of the gabelle, an iniquitous tax on salt; the abolition of the corvée, which exacted free labor from the peasant on the part of the landowner; the suppression of the militia ballot; religious toleration; and better conditions for the clergy.

Caliphate of Cordova. The powerful western dynasty of caliphs. After the decisive battle of Tours in 732, Cordova became the capital of Moorish Spain. Abderrahman, one of the family of Ommiad caliphs of Damascus, who had escaped the massacre inflicted on his house by the rival Abbassides, founded there a new caliphate. Under this powerful dynasty, the caliphate of Cordova became, in culture, wealth, and splendor, the formidable rival of the Abbasside caliphate at Baghdad. This division in the world of Islam relieved Europe from the threat of Mohammedan conquest. See *Abbassides, Arabs, Moors, Spain*.

Canossa. The castle of Matilda of Tuscany, where Gregory VII was staying when the emperor Henry IV made a pilgrimage to Italy, in 1077, to make his submission to the pope, who had excommunicated him. He was treated in the most humiliating fashion by Gregory, who left him for three days in the snow in the courtyard of the castle before consenting to receive him. Hence arose the proverbial expression "Go to Canossa," meaning surrender to the claims of the Church. See *Germany*.

Capetian Dynasty. The remarkable line of kings who ruled France from the election of Hugh Capet in 987 to the fall of Louis Philippe in 1848. The real father of the line was Robert the Strong, said to have been the son of a butcher in Paris. He and his son Odo held the Northmen back from Paris and central France. Odo was chosen king in 887, and in 987 his grandnephew Hugh was made king when the Carolingian line had died out. The name *Capet* comes from Hugh's custom of wearing an abbot's *cape*. The first break in the direct line of descent came with the accession of Philip VI (of Valois) in 1328. The houses of Valois, Bourbon, and Orleans were branches of the Capetian family. See *France*.

Carolingian or **Carlovingian Dynasty.** The second dynasty of the Frankish kings. The name is derived from the Latin *Carolus* (Charles), the name of Charles Martel or of Charles the Great. The first king of the line was Pepin the Short, son of Charles Martel, who deposed the Merovingian king in 751. Charles the Great, or Charlemagne, the greatest of the family, reigned from 768 to 814. The line died out with Louis V in 987. See *France*.

Catacombs. Underground galleries of intricate pattern used, particularly by the early Christians in Rome, as places of burial, of religious worship, and of refuge during persecutions. Catacombs had been employed as burial places by the Etruscans some eight centuries before the Christian era. Roman noble families and Jews in Rome also made use of them. Their greatest development, however, was due to the Christians.

These labyrinthine passages, often one above the other, with many interconnecting branches and blind alleys, are from 30 to 50 feet underground, descent being provided by stairways. In width about three to four feet and twelve feet in height, they honey-comb the environs of Rome, encircling the city at a distance of a mile or two outside the city walls. Their total length is estimated to exceed 750 miles in some 75 separate units. Chambers or chapels were constructed at intervals, their walls being frequently ornamented with paintings of sacred subjects. The dead were placed in recesses excavated in the side walls of the passages and were closed in with slabs sealed with cement. Some two million corpses are estimated to have been so interred. Burial in the catacombs ceased with the sack of Rome by the Goths in 410 A. D. Their existence was forgotten from the 12th century until their accidental rediscovery in 1578. Catacombs have been discovered also in Syracuse, Alexandria, and other communities of the Mediterranean region.

Cavaliers. Royalist sympathizers in England and in the American Colonies during the reigns of Charles I and Charles II. See *Roundheads*.

Cawnpore or **Cawnpur, Massacre of.** The massacre by Nana Sahib of the English garrison in Cawnpore, during the Indian mutiny of 1857. The garrison had surrendered under a pledge of being permitted to retire unharmed. Of those massacred, 560 were women and children. See *Sepoy Mutiny*.

Chaldea (*kăl-dē'à*). The most ancient name of the territory in the lower Tigris and Euphrates valley, practically identical with Babylonia. About 2800 B. C. it became the center of an empire under Sargon, king of Accad. His power extended into the northern Mesopotamian valley and westward to the Mediterranean, but after his death this empire broke up. New Arabian invaders entered Chaldea and made Babylon their capital. They continued to spread Chaldean culture, traditions, and the cuneiform (wedge-shape) system of writing over all western Asia.

Chartist Movement, The, or **Chartism.** A radical reform movement in England in the period from 1838 to 1848. The name arose from the National or People's Charter drawn up by a group of members of Parliament and workingmen, which demanded universal suffrage and salaries for members of Parliament. The causes of the movement were the failure of the Reform bill of 1832 to include the working classes in its benefits and the terrible misery and want among these classes. The movement continued, with various attempts to secure Parliamentary action and with frequent riots, until 1848, when some improvements in working conditions and a period of cheaper food following the repeal of the corn laws robbed it of its strength. See *England*.

Children's Crusade. This tragic incident of the period of the Crusades has been the theme of sober history and of legend. The facts are established that thousands of children and youths—their numbers being estimated at from 50,000 to 90,000—inspired apparently by the crusading spirit of the times, left their homes in the year 1212 and marched in many bands toward the Mediterranean ports of embarkation for the Holy Land. The leaders in France and Germany were two peasant boys. Some of the bands were accompanied by a few older persons, who in most cases appear to have preyed upon the children rather than to have protected them. The fate of the young crusaders is obscure. Some returned sadly to their homes, but many lost their lives. Some are said to have been lost at sea; others, sold into slavery.

Cinque (*sĭngk*) **Ports.** The ancient name of five English Channel ports, Sandwich, Dover, Hythe, Romney, and Hastings, to which later two more, Winchelsea and Rye, were added. *Cinque* is the Old French word for "five." These towns were granted certain independent privileges by the early Norman kings, in return for which their chief service was to furnish ships and sailors to the king, England having no regular navy before the reign of Henry VII (1485–1509).

Clan-na-Gael (*klăn'nà-gāl'*). An Irish secret society, an offshoot of the Fenians, formed in 1881. It was composed of the extreme physical force men among the Fenians and was known also as the United Brotherhood. See *England, Fenians, Ireland*.

Cockpit of Europe. The name given to Belgium on account of the numerous important battles which have been fought there. See *Belgium*.

Code Napoleon. The code of law issued by Napoleon in 1804. It was based on the old French law, with such alterations as had been rendered necessary by the Revolution, and on certain new provisions, introduced by Napoleon, notably those relating to the law of succession and to the marriage law. For the purpose of this codification, which remains the law of France, he called to his councils the most eminent French lawyers, irrespective of party,—among others Tronchet, Cambacérès, Portalis, and Roederer.

Code of Justinian. The systematic body or code of Roman law prepared by a commission of lawyers appointed by the emperor Justinian (527–565). This code, called the *Corpus Juris Civilis*, or "Body of Civil Law," became the basis of nearly all modern European legal systems. Its principles influenced the common law of England, which has prevailed also in the United States. See *Rome*.

Commune, Paris. An outbreak of the extreme revolutionary party in Paris in 1871 (March 18–May 27), after the National Assembly, which met at Bordeaux, had agreed to peace with the victorious Germans, ceding Alsace and Lorraine, and had decided to transfer its sittings to Versailles rather than to Paris. The radical Parisians accused the Assembly of being monarchist and of the design of overthrowing the republic constituted the September previous. Among the revolutionaries were leading socialists and representatives of the *Internationale*. One of the leading projects was to grant autonomy to the communes, or city governments, uniting them by a loose tie to the central government. Thiers, who had been chosen head of the executive in the new government, reorganized the army and prepared to capture Paris. The Germans still occupied the forts on the northern side of the city, for the Peace of Frankfort was not signed until May 18. In the struggle that followed, neither side gave quarter. The *Communards* even put to death the hostages they had seized, including the archbishop of Paris. Thousands of those who were captured by the national troops were shot without a trial.

Communist Party. Political party, organized in nearly all countries in the 20th century, which differs from most political parties in its objective of taking over the government, appropriating for the state the means of production, and establishing a "dictatorship of the proletariat." The parent of such parties was the Bolshevik party, which seized power in Russia in 1919. See *Bolshevism.*

Communist parties outside of Russia owed their origin largely to the inspiration and later to the direction and control by the Communist International (Comintern), organized in 1919 by the Russian Communist party. The Comintern's influence was based on social discontent in each country and on the appeal of its program to persons in those countries who saw in it a quick means of getting rid of social injustices. Its evangelic appeal seduced numerous gifted persons, whom missionaries of the International were quick to entrap and to enlist in efforts to undermine their own governments.

Party members were sworn to blind obedience to orders, and orders came from the head of the Comintern. Obedience was enforced, where possible, by terroristic methods. Detection was made difficult by the device of isolating members in small "cells" to prevent their acquaintance with more than a few others. The aim was to infiltrate the government itself in each nation while exploiting discontents and spreading disorders until an opportunity came for taking over political control.

In 1943, the Comintern was declared dissolved by Russia to disarm the suspicions of its allies in World War II. But its greatest successes were to come. Czechoslovakia was taken over by the party's usual methods in 1948. China embraced communism the same year, succumbing to methods learned in Russia, although the leaders later adopted governmental methods of their own which led to estrangement from Russia. Finally, in 1958, Cuba's Communist party took advantage of Fidel Castro's revolution to win control of the government through Castro and his aides.

In most countries, however, the tactics of the Communist party were completely futile; the bulk of the citizens were deaf to its appeal, particularly when they saw the type of society to which its program led in Russia; arrest and conviction of members for espionage revealed the party's unscrupulous methods to the public; in many countries membership in the Communist party was made unlawful. In the United States much the same effect was produced by court rulings that the party is an agency of a foreign government and hence subject to a 1950 law requiring registration.

Tactics of the Communist party produced little success among the emerging nations of Africa or among the Arab nations. Egypt, for example, while accepting Russian armaments, suppressed the party. In nearly all countries the party was weakened by the schism between Russia and China, partisans of the two countries forming factions which tended to paralyze concerted action.

Concert of Europe. A diplomatic term long applied to the idea of European powers acting as a unit. Such a concert of princes was set up after the Congress of Vienna in 1815. This broke down before the rise of national ambitions. The ideal expressed in the phrase is a vague foreshadowing

of a league of nations. See *Congress of Vienna; France;* also *Concert of Powers.*

Concordat (kŏn-kôr′dăt), **French.** An agreement entered into in 1801, but abrogated in 1905, between Napoleon and the pope, providing for the re-establishment of the French Catholic Church, which had been disrupted during the Revolution. Roman Catholicism was declared to be the religion of the majority of the French nation. It was agreed, among other provisions, that bishops were to be nominated by the government, but consecrated by the pope. The nomination of parish priests was vested in the bishops, the government having a right of veto. The state undertook to see that adequate stipends were provided for the clergy, to replace the ancient revenues which had been confiscated during the Revolution. See *France.*

Concordat of Worms. The agreement reached in 1122 between the German emperor, Henry V, and the pope upon the old dispute over the appointment and investiture of bishops. It provided that bishops should be elected by the clergy and consecrated by the pope, but that the emperor might veto any election, since he was to invest the bishop with the episcopal lands. See *Germany.*

Condottieri (kŏn′dŏt-tyär′ē). Soldiers of fortune who hired themselves out to the various petty states of Italy during the wars of the 14th and the 15th century. Their contests came to be bloodless, because each side wanted only to take prisoners for the sake of ransom money to be exacted.

Confederation of the Rhine. A league of German states, at first chiefly southern but finally including all, save Prussia and Austria, with Napoleon as "protector," formed in 1806. These states were permitted to absorb many of their smaller neighbors by a process known as "mediatization." They withdrew from the Holy Roman Empire, which then came to an end. Together with the "secularizations" in 1803, which destroyed the independence of 112 ecclesiastical, city, and other small states, the annexations of 1806 marked the beginning of unification in Germany. The Confederation was broken up in 1813 by the defeat of Napoleon at Leipzig. See *France, Germany.*

Congress of Berlin. A congress held at Berlin in 1878, after the conclusion of the Russo-Turkish war. The outcome of the congress was a treaty which modified the terms of the Treaty of San Stefano. Rumania, Serbia, and Montenegro were made independent states, Montenegro also obtaining a port on the Adriatic. The northern portion of Bulgaria was made a self-governing state, under the suzerainty of the Porte, and the southern portion, known as Eastern Rumelia, remained Turkish territory, but under a Christian governor. Austria was to administer Bosnia and Herzegovina; Rumania returned a portion of Bessarabia to Russia, while, in Asia, Turkey ceded Ardalian, Kars, and Batum to Russia. The action of the congress prevented the formation of a strong Slav state in the Balkans and kept Russia out of the Mediterranean. It is of this treaty that Lord Beaconsfield used the famous phrase "We have brought back peace with honor." In 1909 Great Britain, Germany, France, and Russia consented to Austria's annexation of Bosnia and Herzegovina. See *World War I.*

Congress of Vienna, The. The congress of all the sovereigns of Europe, called after the fall of Napoleon by the four powers allied against him. It met in Vienna in November 1814, and completed its work in June 1815, after the final defeat of Napoleon at Waterloo. The general purpose of the congress was to restore all "legitimate" princes and kings, as nearly as possible, to the power they enjoyed before the French Revolution. The interests and desires of nations and peoples had no place in the plans of this great reactionary congress. All republics, old and new, except Switzerland, were given to monarchs. The 12 states of Italy and the 38 of Germany were restored to their old ruling families. Holland, with Belgium unwillingly added.

was made the Kingdom of the Netherlands. Territory west of the Rhine, taken from France, was divided between Bavaria and Prussia. To Austria went Venice in exchange for Belgium. Russia took the kingdom of Poland and also secured Finland from Sweden, which as compensation received Norway (formerly Danish). Prussia, with half of Saxony and land west of the Rhine as her share of the spoils, was set on the road to German leadership. England obtained some colonial territory, including Cape Colony and Ceylon.

The congress took forward-looking action in declaring against the slave trade and holding that navigable rivers flowing through or between different countries should be open to all commerce. It also guaranteed the neutrality of Switzerland.

Conservatives, English. One of the two great political parties of Great Britain. This party has usually been regarded as opposed to radical change or innovation of any character in government, and particularly to the liberal, socializing movements which seek to increase the political power of the masses to ameliorate their conditions, and to mitigate the effects of the uneven distribution of wealth. The party has in the past drawn most of its strength from the so-called "landed aristocracy," and other landed interests of England. It is the direct successor to the Tory party of the 18th and early 19th centuries, the name Conservative having been substituted for the older name Tory soon after the Reform act of 1832. Although the Conservative has traditionally been regarded as the party of reaction, yet it has known how to adapt itself to deep-going changes in the nation. Under Disraeli in 1867 and Salisbury in 1884, it extended the franchise to the great mass of the English people. Under Macmillan in the mid-20th century, it extended social security measures begun by the Liberal and Labor parties and guided the country through the transition from the head of an empire to the leader of a commonwealth of nations.

Constitutions of Clarendon. A body of 16 regulations drawn up at the Great Council summoned by Henry II of England to meet at Clarendon in 1164. These regulations were intended to settle points in dispute between king and clergy. They specified, among other things, that clergy accused of civil crime should be turned over to the civil courts for punishment. Archbishop Thomas Becket refused to sign the document. After Becket's murder, Henry, in 1172, seeking reconciliation with the pope, renounced the Constitutions. But some of their provisions remained in force as permanent gains to the civil power in England. See *England*.

Corn Laws. English laws regulating grain imports. In 1815, in the midst of agricultural and industrial depression following the end of the Napoleonic wars, a Parliament made up of landowners passed a law forbidding the importation of corn (wheat) unless the price should rise to 80 shillings a quarter. The price, however, went down. This law was amended from time to time, to provide heavy import duties whenever the English harvest was good, in order to keep prices up. In 1838 an Anti-Corn-Law League was organized, which worked for the repeal of the corn laws. No action was secured until, under the stimulus of the Irish famine in 1845-46, a repeal bill introduced by the prime minister, Sir Robert Peel, was passed in 1846. This act is an important incident in the long controversy between protectionists and free traders. See *Chartist Movement, England, Ireland*.

Corvée (kôr'vā'). Enforced labor on the roads and other public works, exacted from the French peasants before the Revolution. Distinction should be made between the "royal" corvée, which exacted from 8 to 40 days of labor on the high roads, and the "seignioral" corvée, or services claimed by the lords. The latter had nearly disappeared by the 18th century.

Coup d'Etat (kōō dā'tà'). There is no English equivalent for this term. It means the sudden overthrow of government by force and the consequent seizure of state and power. (1) The most remarkable example of this in history is the *coup d'état* of Napoleon I. The government of France from 1795 to 1799 was known as the Directory. It had proved corrupt and incompetent. Napoleon, now the idol of France by reason of his successful campaigns, saw his opportunity. With the aid of Abbé Sieyès, a statesman who planned a change in the constitution, Napoleon overthrew the Directory on the 18th of Brumaire (November 9, 1799). The plan of Sieyès was adopted but with drastic amendments dictated by Napoleon. Napoleon was chosen first consul and given the substance of power, his two colleagues being merely consultative. In 1802 he was made consul for life and on May 18, 1804, was proclaimed emperor of the French.

(2) Half a century later a similar *coup d'état* was made by Louis Napoleon Bonaparte, nephew of Napoleon I. Louis conceived the idea that he had a right to rule over France. The revolution of 1848 gave him the opportunity of offering his services to that country. He knew the name he bore was one to conjure with. He became a candidate for the presidency and was elected with an overwhelming majority in December of the same year. He had taken an oath to uphold the Republic. On Dec. 2, 1851, he broke this oath. In the early hours of the morning he had the civil and military leaders who might prove obstacles to his plans arrested. These were afterwards imprisoned or exiled. He next proclaimed martial law throughout France and instituted a plebiscite. The French people were to register their vote on the question of the re-establishment of the imperial dignity. The people proved willing to make the experiment, and on Dec. 2, 1852, Louis Napoleon Bonaparte, having skillfully maneuvered his *coup d'état*, was proclaimed emperor of France under the name of Napoleon III.

Curfew. From *couvre feu*, meaning "cover fire." The famous enactment of William the Conqueror, ordering all persons in the country districts to be in their houses, with all lights extinguished, by eight o'clock in winter and by sunset in summer. It was presumably designed to prevent secret meetings and conspiracies directed against the king among the Saxon element of the population.

Danzig (Gdansk). This Baltic port of Poland was long a free city. It was annexed by Russia in 1793. After World War I, it was made a free city to provide Poland with access to the Baltic Sea. Hitler opened World War II in 1939 by invading Danzig. In 1945, under the Potsdam agreement between Russia, the United States, and Britain, it passed to Poland. The Poles changed its name to Gdansk.

D-Day. The opening day of a military operation, from which other days are reckoned,—D-day+1, D-day+2, etc. Notably, the day of the Allied invasion of Normandy, June 6, 1944.

Declaration of London. A set of rules formulated by an international conference at London in 1909, designed to govern the naval prize court established at The Hague in 1907. The Declaration was never accepted by a sufficient number of nations to put it in force. At the outbreak of World War I, Great Britain announced that the Declaration would be adhered to by the Allies. But under the stress of actual war conditions the provisions of the Declaration were disregarded.

Declaration of Paris. A formal statement of rules governing naval warfare, drawn up by the powers that signed the Treaty of Paris in 1856 after the close of the Crimean war. These rules abolished privateering; established the protection of enemy goods, except contraband, by a neutral flag, the protection of neutral goods, except contraband, by an enemy flag; and declared that blockades, to be binding, must be effectively maintained by naval force. The U.S., not having a strong navy, maintained that in war she would be dependent upon privateers, and did not adopt the declaration.

Detente. Detente is a French word meaning the relaxation of tension. During the Nixon administration, 1972, detente was used to describe the U.S. foreign policy toward the U.S.S.R.—an end to the Soviet-American rivalry and the beginning of peaceful coexistence between the two superpowers. Since that time detente has become an international term for cooperation between nations.

Divine Right. The patriarchal theory or doctrine that neither kings nor their heirs for any reason whatsoever can forfeit their right to the throne and to the obedience of their people. Under this theory, the king is the direct representative of God and can do no wrong. This doctrine was promulgated and reached its climax in England in the Stuart times, but it was set aside at the accession of William III as king of Great Britain and Ireland in 1688.

Domesday Book. A book containing a written synopsis in Latin of the census of the population, lands, and livestock of England, compiled under the direction of William the Conqueror and completed in 1086. The work forms the most valuable existing source of facts about early English history.

Draco, Laws of. In the latter part of the 7th century B.C., the people of Athens, suffering under the unjust administration of justice by the ruling class of nobles, demanded a written code. An Athenian named Draco was employed to draw up such a body of laws. The severity of these laws gave rise to the saying that the Draconian code was written, "not in ink, but in blood."

Drang nach Osten. A German phrase meaning "push toward the East." It was originally applied to the eastward extension of German power over Slavic and Baltic territory. Its most important meaning, however, was the steady extension of German and Austrian influence in the Balkans and in Asia Minor which brought on World War I.

Dreyfus (*drā′füs′*) **Affair.** The imprisonment and persecution of Alfred Dreyfus, member of a wealthy Jewish family and an officer on the general staff of the French army. He was charged in 1894 with revealing military secrets to a foreign government, condemned, and sent to Devil's Island for life. New evidence was discovered in 1896, pointing to another officer, Esterhazy, as the real traitor. A new court-martial in 1899 again condemned Dreyfus, but this time to only ten years' imprisonment. President Loubet gave him a full pardon. The Court of Cassation reviewed the case in 1906, declared the court-martial verdict in error, and Dreyfus was restored to the army and promoted.

Druids (*drōō′ĭdz*). The powerful order of priests and judges who ruled the Celtic peoples of Gaul, Britain, and Ireland. The druids gathered youths about them for oral instruction, as they never committed their secret lore to writing. The oak and the mistletoe were sacred among the druids, and their ceremonies were frequently performed in oak groves. They used their influence against the Romans, but they were finally driven to the island of Anglesey and subdued in A.D. 78.

Dual Monarchy. The name used to describe the organization of the empire of Austria-Hungary from 1867 to 1918. The two states stood on a plane of complete equality, the emperor of Austria being king of Hungary. Although each had its own parliament, there was a joint ministry of three departments—foreign affairs, war, and finance.

Dukhobors (*dōō-ᴋŏ-bŏrz′*). A Russian religious sect, founded about the middle of the 18th century at Kharkov. Their principal tenet is that Christ was only human, not divine, and that at certain periods He reappears in mortals. They reject the need of rulers, priests, or churches, and have no confession, images (*icons*), or marriage ceremonies. They are opposed to all violence and refuse to make use of the labor of animals. Driven out of Russia, many of the Dukhobors emigrated to western Canada. Conflict with authorities led part of this group to migrate to Paraguay.

Eastern Question. A name given to the political problems raised by the gradual dissolution of the Turkish Empire in Europe from about 1822 to 1922. Russia aimed to secure Constantinople (Istanbul). She fought two wars for it. In the first (Crimean, 1853-56), she was defeated by France and England. After the second (Russo-Turkish, 1877-78), while victorious, she was balked by the other powers. German ascendancy in Turkey began in 1889 and ended when the two nations suffered defeat in World War I. The prize of Istanbul went to none of the great powers. It remained Turkish, but was placed under control of an international commission. This commission's control ceased in 1936.

East India Company, British. "The Governor and Company of merchants trading to the East Indies," chartered in 1600, became in time incorporated with several other important companies and in 1660 was known as "The United Company of Merchants Trading to the East Indies." It is usually referred to as the British East India Company.

In 1612 it obtained from the rajah of Delhi the privilege of establishing a factory at Surat. By a charter of Charles II in 1661, it was empowered to sign treaties, make peace or war with infidels, erect fortifications, acquire territory, and exercise civil jurisdiction. In 1668 it secured a grant of the Island of Bombay, and in 1675 established a factory in Bengal which paved the way to the foundation of Calcutta. A dispute with the rajah of Tanjore in 1749 resulted in a series of territorial acquisitions which became the nucleus of the British Empire in India. A board of control was eventually set up by Parliament in 1784, and in 1858 the company gave over the reins of government to the British crown. See *England, India.*

East India Company, Dutch. A company formed by the union of several small trading companies, March 20, 1602. The government granted it a charter, by which it was given the monopoly of trade on the farther side of the Strait of Magellan and of the Cape of Good Hope. It was also given the right to establish factories, build fortresses, employ soldiers, and make alliances in the name of the states-general. In 1619 it established the colony of Batavia in Java; within less than half a century it became the principal trading power in Ceylon, Sumatra, and Borneo, and possessed flourishing colonies in South Africa. In 1795 the company became insolvent, and its territories were handed over to the state.

Elamites (*ē′lăm-īts*). The ancient people who inhabited the plateau and plain east of the lower Tigris and north of the Persian Gulf. The name is derived from the Assyrian word for "highlands." The race to which they belonged is not known. They maintained a long struggle against the Babylonians and Assyrians. The latter finally subdued the Elamite state in 642 B.C. Later references to Elam are uncertain, the word sometimes meaning Persia.

Electors. In the Holy Roman Empire, a body of German princes, originally seven in number, with whom, from the 13th to the beginning of the 19th century, rested the election of the emperor.

Emancipation Act. For many years the English courts of law strongly held that slavery should not be allowed to exist in any part of the British dominions and that in tolerating it the prestige of England suffered. Two of the greatest pleaders in the cause of the slave were Sir Thomas Buxton and Zachary Macaulay, father of the historian. In 1833, Colonial Secretary Stanley came into office. A man of great ability and ardent temperament, he set to work to master the details of this crying injustice. In the space of three weeks he introduced into Parliament a bill for the complete abolition of slavery, which was immediately passed. All children under six and those born after the passing of the act thenceforward were free. All others ceased to be slaves, but were to remain as apprentices to their masters for a period of twelve years. The slave owners were indemnified for their loss in the sum of $100,000,000. Though they showed dissatisfaction with this amount, they were forced to accept it. The system of apprenticeship proved, after four years, to be unsatisfactory and so was abandoned. See *Slavery.*

Emigrés (*ā'mē'grā'*). The name given to the French aristocracy, or, more accurately, to the partisans of the *ancien régime,* or royalists, who were forced to fly from France during the French Revolution. The émigrés, in order to crush the Revolution, appealed to other European powers to send armies into France. For this, the Legislative Assembly and the Convention passed measures of reprisal against the émigrés, whereby their lands and estates became forfeit to the Republic. The term has been applied also to those who fled the Russian and other revolutions in the 20th century, particularly if they belonged to the aristocracy.

Entente Powers or **Triple Entente** (*äN'täNt'*). England, France, and Russia, who, before the opening of World War I, had concluded an *entente* or "understanding" among themselves with respect to a common defensive attitude toward the Triple Alliance,—Germany, Italy, and Austria. This Triple Entente was not an alliance. It was composed of two "ententes." The first was negotiated in 1904 between England and France, in order to bring to an end controversies chiefly in relation to Egypt and Morocco. The second was between England and Russia, in 1907, and centered in Asiatic questions, marking out for the two powers spheres of interest in Persia. France was already bound to Russia by a military alliance. For this reason, when Germany declared war against Russia in 1914, France was necessarily involved. The obligations of England, on the other hand, were principally moral. See *Triple Alliance, World War I.*

Estonia. This Baltic province of Russia enjoyed a period of independence between World War I and World War II. Prior to 1920, it was ruled successively by Danes, Germans, Swedes, and Russians. In 1940 Russia concluded with it a treaty of "mutual assistance," the implementation of which extinguished Estonia's independence. The Germans held it briefly in World War II.

Fabian Society of Socialists. One of the most important socialistic societies in England, organized in London in 1884. It derives its name from Fabius, the Roman general, who hoped to conquer "by delaying," and supports meliorative tendencies rather than revolution.

Fascism (*fash'iz'm*). A former political party and governmental regime of Italy. Founded by Benito Mussolini at Milan in 1919, the movement was inspired by an exalted patriotism. Its members banded themselves together to crush communistic outbreaks and other disruptive factors in Italian life. Its expanding influence enabled Mussolini, at the head of his armed followers, to take control of the Italian parliament on October 28, 1922. The party's control of the government was maintained by drastic action. It came to an end with Italy's defeat in World War II. The term was generalized to describe movements seeking to safeguard the capitalistic system by establishment of a corporate state.

Fashoda (*fä-shō'dä*) **Question.** Commercial and colonial jealousies between France and England in 1898 led to a French general's hoisting of the French ensign over Fashoda, which Great Britain regarded as within her particular zone of influence. English armies had for two years been engaged in a campaign against the Khalifa for the recovery of the Sudan. Their commander, General Kitchener, invited Marchand to withdraw. Marchand refusing, the matter was referred to London and Paris. France acquiesced in the wishes of England. On April 8, 1904, an agreement was signed between the two countries, each acknowledging the other's rights in Morocco and in Egypt. This friendly understanding came to be known as the *Entente Cordiale.* See *Entente Powers.*

Fenians. The members of an Irish revolutionary society, started in Paris in 1848. Their avowed object was the fomenting of disturbances in Ireland, to make the government of that country by England impossible. The leader was James Stephens. The Fenians in the United States attempted raids into Canada in 1866, 1870, and 1871. In 1867 a general rising in Ireland was planned. These projects were all anticipated or promptly suppressed.

Feudalism. The system of land tenure and personal relationships prevailing throughout Europe especially from the 9th to the 13th century. Its activating cause was the need of protection, which could no longer be secured by governmental authority. The base of the structure was the fief, a body of land which a tenant held from his lord who protected him in return for certain feudal services, such as aid in war. The tenant was thus also a vassal. The lord exercised judicial and many other rights over his tenants, who often became virtually his subjects. The tenant might also, if holding a large tract of land, grant parts of it to others, who would be his tenants and vassals and to whom he stood in the relation of lord.

Field of the Cloth of Gold. The meeting place of Henry VIII and Francis I in the valley of Ardres on the border of the territory of Calais. This meeting in 1520 was arranged by Francis to detach Henry from his Spanish alliance. The name arose from the magnificence of the display on both sides. No political result followed.

Fifth Column. A term used to describe persons ready to cooperate with an aggressor against the country of which they are citizens or residents. It obtained currency from a remark of General Franco, Spanish insurgent leader, as he was advancing in 1939 on Madrid with four converging columns in the final action of the Spanish civil war. He declared that he was attacking with four columns outside the city and with a "fifth column" within the city.

Flagellants (*flăj'ĕ-lănts*). A sect which appeared in Europe during the middle ages, notably in Italy in 1360, and in Hungary and other countries during the terror occasioned by the Black Death in 1348. They looked upon scourging as the only means of avoiding divine punishment for sin. See *Black Death.*

Flodden Field. Name of a battle fought near the hamlet of Flodden in Northumberland, Sept. 9, 1513, between the Scots and the English, in which the Scottish king, James IV, was defeated and slain by the earl of Surrey.

Franco-Prussian War. The conflict between France and Prussia in 1870-71. The immediate occasion of the war was the election of a Hohenzollern prince to the throne of Spain. The chief military events were the siege of Metz and the siege of Strasbourg, in August and September 1870; the fall of Sedan on September 1, 1870; and the siege of Paris, September 19, 1870 to January 28, 1871. After the fall of Sedan, a republic was proclaimed at Paris, and a provisional government undertook the defense of the city. The close of the war saw the founding of the new German Empire. See *Alsace-Lorraine, France, Germany.*

Francs-Tireurs (frăn'tē'rŭr'). As the name implies, an independent band of "free-shooters," composed of French peasants who at first fought alone a guerrilla warfare against the Germans in the Franco-Prussian war of 1870. When captured, they were usually shot by the enemy as brigands. Later in the campaign they were organized by the French military authorities and used as a corps of detached light troops engaged in forays, skirmishes, and such minor actions.

Freedom of the Seas. This phrase means, in general, the right of the ships of any nation to free use of the highways of the sea. In particular it has come to mean: (1) that the jurisdiction of a government extends to a distance of three nautical miles beyond its coast line and no farther; (2) that neutral ships are not liable to capture on the high seas by belligerents in time of war; (3) that, in time of war, private property, unless contraband or destined for a blockaded port, is not liable to seizure. See *World War I.*

Free Imperial Cities. Certain towns in Germany that owed allegiance to no sovereign prince except the emperor. They exercised sovereign powers within their own limits and sent representatives to the Imperial Diet. In 1790 they were 51 in number. Until the dismemberment of the German Empire at the close of World War I, Lübeck, Bremen, and Hamburg still retained the privilege of sending representatives to the Reichstag and the Bundesrath. Bremen and Hamburg continued each to be a "free state and city."

Fronde (frŏNd). The name given to the civil war which broke out in France, 1648–53, between the party of the court (Anne of Austria and Mazarin) and the parlement of Paris. The Fronde originated in the deplorable financial policy of Mazarin and passed through two phases. The first was known as the Old Fronde, in which the parlement, allied to Condé and Cardinal de Retz, played the principal rôle. The most notable incidents under its short régime were the arrest of Counselor Broussel, the setting up of barricades by the people of Paris, and the withdrawal of the court to Saint Germain. During the second phase, with the title of the Young Fronde or Fronde des Princes, Condé, Beaufort, and Madame de Longueville, with the secret support of Spain, gave battle to the royal troops under Turenne at Bléneau and Porte St. Antoine. Turenne proved superior on both occasions, and the revolt was crushed in 1653. The Old Fronde lasted from 1648 to 1649; the Young Fronde, from 1649 to 1653. The word *fronde* means a "sling," used sometimes by the small boys of Paris against the police. The adversaries of Mazarin had been called *frondeurs*, or "slingers."

Geneva Conventions. Agreements made by representatives of European powers at Geneva, beginning in 1864, by which more humane regulations were adopted covering wartime sick and wounded. The 26 signing nations agreed to respect the wounded, the neutrality of hospitals, and other humanitarian rules. In 1868, a second conference extended these principles to naval warfare. These early agreements, were closely linked with the founding of the International Red Cross. Extensive revisions occurred in 1906 and 1907. In 1929, and again in 1949, further agreements were signed for the protection of civilian victims of war. By 1949, 59 nations had signed the articles. During the Korean conflict, all the powers involved declared themselves bound by the conventions, whether signing the agreements or not.

Germany, Unification of. The North German Confederation, which embraced the 22 states north of the river Main, was the work of Bismarck. The inclusion of the south German states was yet necessary to the perfect unification of Germany. Since Napoleon III was known to be averse to this plan, Bismarck deemed a war with France a necessary contingency. In this instance, it would seem "the wish was father to the thought," for on July 5, 1870, the rest of Europe woke to the fact that France and Prussia were at war. Germany emerged as victor from the series of campaigns. While the war was being waged, negotiations had been carried on between Prussia and the south German states. Accordingly, treaties were signed and the confederation widened so as to include all the German states. Thus was brought about the complete unification of Germany, and Bismarck's lifelong dream was realized. Berlin became the capital of a federal empire, and on Jan. 18, 1871, in the royal palace of Versailles, William I was proclaimed emperor of Germany.

Golconda. A ruined city in the Nizam's dominions, seven miles northwest of Hyderabad. It is celebrated for its fortress and for the mausoleums of its ancient kings. The diamonds cut and polished in Golconda were once world renowned. From 1512 it was the seat of a powerful government until it was taken by Aurungzebe in 1687 and made a Mogul province. See *Moguls.*

Golden Bull (**Germany**). So called from the golden seal with which it was stamped. The Golden Bull was an imperial edict issued in 1356 by the emperor Charles IV, which fixed the form and places of the imperial election and coronation. It also determined the privileges and duties of the electors. This electoral constitution continued unaltered until the extinction of the Holy Roman Empire in 1806.

Good Parliament. A Parliament of Edward III which met in 1376. The Commons refused to grant supply till an account of receipts and expenditures had been placed before them. Edward's brother Lancaster sought to intimidate the Parliament but failed. The Commons secured a new Council, from which Lancaster was debarred and in which William of Wykeham was included. They then proceeded to impeach, before the House of Lords, Lyons and Latimer on the charge of embezzlement of the king's revenue. Both were sentenced to imprisonment on the charge. These two cases form the first instance of the accusation of political offenders by the Commons before the House of Lords.

Guelphs (gwĕlfs) and **Ghibellines** (gĭb'ĕl-ĭnz). The names of two celebrated political factions in the Middle Ages. The Guelphs were the popular party in Italy, and ranged on the side of the pope. The Ghibellines formed the imperial and aristocratic party, and were opposed to the Guelphs. In 1140 the two factions engaged in civil war, in which the Guelphs were defeated in the battle of Weinsberg.

Guillotine. Although decapitation by means of a falling weighted knife was a mode of punishment used by some European countries in Medieval times, it is commonly associated with France and the Reign of Terror. The instrument used for this purpose during the French Revolution gets its name from a well-meaning physician, Dr. Guillotin, who wished to make the process of execution swift and comparatively painless. The historical case of Marie Antoinette and the fictional incident climaxing Dickens' *Tale of Two Cities* have made the guillotine stand out as a dramatic symbol for the cruelty of the time.

Gunpowder Plot. This was a plot engineered by a Catholic named Robert Catesby, in 1604, to blow up king, lords, and commons at the opening of Parliament. Both the Catholics and the Puritans of the time had appealed to James I for better treatment. They were being fined for recusancy, that is, for refusing to attend the services of the established form of worship. James remitted the fines for recusancy, but banished the Catholic priests from London. Thereupon, Catesby determined upon destroying the powers that dealt so harshly with his coreligionists. He communicated his plans to Guy Fawkes, a cool and intrepid soldier in Flanders. Fawkes favored them and came to England. By accident, the conspirators found that a cellar ran beneath both houses of Parliament. Into this they managed to convey barrels of gunpowder, and the mine was laid for the second session of Parliament on Nov. 5, 1605. However, the plot was doomed to failure. One of the conspirators in fear betrayed the secret, and Fawkes was seized in the very act of setting the fuse to the powder. He, with those of his companions who were captured, was forthwith executed, and the persecution of the Catholics waxed stronger than before. See *England*.

Habeas Corpus Act. The Latin term is an injunction, meaning "Have thou the body" (in court). The act was passed by the Parliament of England during the reign of Charles II, 1679. The "habeas corpus" is a common law writ, or mandate, issued by a judge on the petition of some friend of an accused person detained in prison or in any other way deprived of liberty. It calls upon the jailer to bring such a person actually into court at a specified time, in order that his case may be examined and judgment passed. Moreover, any accused person held in prison too long without a hearing can claim a writ of habeas corpus to be issued in his behalf, in order to force his accusers to show cause why he should be detained longer in custody. The habeas corpus acts of the United States and of Canada follow lines similar to those of the English statute.

Hague Peace Conferences. Meetings of representatives of leading nations of the world, to consider means for arresting the danger of war and for mitigating the burdens of armaments. Two conferences have been held at The Hague in Holland. The first was convened, at the suggestion of Czar Nicholas of Russia, in 1899. It formulated regulations for more humane conduct of warfare and established an international tribunal to which nations might submit their disputes for arbitration. The second Hague Conference met in 1907, at the suggestion of the United States. This Conference enlarged somewhat the work of the first Conference. But neither body was able to adopt any resolution either for disarmament or for limiting of armaments.

Hanseatic League. A federation of northern German cities, formed in the 13th century for mutual protection and assistance, particularly in trade. The immediate cause of this famous and powerful organization was the insecurity of trade routes. The princes and states of the time were unable to afford protection against the pirates and robbers on sea and land. The alliance of the towns of Hamburg and Lübeck, about the middle of the 13th century, is regarded as the beginning of the confederacy, to which the name *Hansa*, meaning "league," was later applied. The organization at the height of its prosperity, in the 14th and 15th centuries, included about ninety cities and towns. It passed out of existence about the middle of the 17th century. See *Venice and the Hanse*.

Hearth Money. A tax laid in England on hearths. It was first levied in 1663. Each hearth in every house that paid church and poor rates was taxed at the rate of two shillings. This tax, known also as chimney money, was repealed in the reign of William and Mary, 1689.

Hegira or **Hejira** (*hĕj′ĭ-rȧ*). An Arabic word meaning "departure." It is used to designate the flight of Mohammed from Mecca to Medina in 622. Mohammed sought to persuade his countrymen to forsake idolatry. They rose in anger against him, and he was forced to flee for his life to Medina. The Mohammedan calendar is dated from this flight, as that of the Christians is dated from the birth of Christ. See *Arabia, Arabians*.

Heptarchy. A government of seven rulers; a union of seven territories. In Saxon times in England seven small kingdoms or principalities were established, known as Northumbria, East Anglia, Mercia,

Kent, Sussex, Essex, and Wessex. The number of these tribal divisions was not constant. Feuds and struggles between rival princes at times merged one principality into another. Egbert, who was king of the West Saxons, 802–839, is said to have made himself Bretwalda or overlord of the British. It was this, no doubt, that gave the 16th century historians the idea that the seven Angle and Saxon kingdoms were really a monarchy ruled by one supreme king; hence they introduced the word *heptarchy* into their writings to convey this conception. Though the designation is questionable, it seems to have been preserved as a matter of convenience. See *England*.

Hindenburg Line. A system of elaborate entrenchments on the western front in World War I. It was established by Hindenburg, commander in chief of the German field forces, after the fighting on the Somme in 1916. These entrenchments took approximately the shape of a crescent whose arc swept from the North Sea, between Nieuport and Westende, until it reached the banks of the Aisne river on the south. At the northern horn of the crescent stood what was known as the "*Wotan*" *line*, the middle of the crescent was occupied by the "*Siegfried*" *line*, and at the southern horn was placed the "*Albrecht*" *line*.

The Allied front opposed to the Hindenburg line was divided into three sections: a British front from the North Sea to the Oise river, a distance of 125 miles; a French front from the Oise to Verdun, about 150 miles; and an American front from Verdun to the Swiss frontier—the latter known as the Lorraine front. The supposedly impregnable German defense was first penetrated by Australian troops, May 3, 1917. On September 29, 1918, the Siegfried line was broken at the famous tunnel sector, near Cambrai, by American troops acting with British and Australian forces. See *World War I*.

Hinterland Doctrine. After the explorations of Livingstone and Stanley, Africa no longer remained an "unknown land." Upon various pretexts, European powers appropriated large areas to themselves. Germany, to make secure and to enlarge her new acquisitions, enunciated in 1883 a doctrine by which the possession of a stretch of coast line carried with it the right to the territory lying inland. This doctrine maintained that no other country could annex such territory.

Hittites. A people primarily of Indo-European stock. Their original home was in central Asia Minor, whence they gradually pushed southward, invading Babylonia about 2000 B. C. and conquering northern Mesopotamia, Syria, and Palestine. In the 14th century B. C., they were driven from Palestine by the Egyptians, with whom, after an indecisive battle at Kadesh in Syria, they concluded a treaty, the oldest written treaty in history. Hittite dominion over Syria lasted until the 8th century B. C., when this country too was conquered by Assyria. A century later they had disappeared from history. Little was known about the Hittites until quite recently. Excavations, begun by Winckler, a German scholar, in 1905, at Boghaz-Köi on the Halys river, the site of the ancient Hittite capital, yielded about 10,000 baked clay tablets, with writing practically identical with Babylonian cuneiform, but in an unknown language. The key to this was discovered by Hrozný, a Czechoslovakian Assyriologist, in 1915.

Hohenstaufen Dynasty. The line of emperors who ruled Germany from 1138 to 1254. They were distinguished for patronage of commerce and the arts. The greatest of the family were Frederick Barbarossa (1152–90) and Frederick II (1215–50).

Hohenzollern Family. A family of German princes tracing descent from Thassilo, count of Zollern, who, in the 8th century, founded a castle on the Zollern hill in the Swabian Alps. In 1415 Frederick VI of the younger line of Hohenzollern was made elector of Brandenburg. He thus became the founder of the former royal house of Prussia. See *Germany, World War I.*

Holy Alliance. An alliance formed between Russia, Austria, and Prussia in September 1815, by which the three sovereigns undertook that for the future their policy, both domestic and foreign, should be guided solely by the precepts of the Christian religion. In reality, it was regarded by those powers who were asked for their approval as a huge farce and one of dubious taste. But the name was too good to be ignored; and Russia, Austria, and Prussia came to be known as the "holy allies." The alliance aimed at stemming the tide of political liberty, set flowing by the French Revolution. The threatened interference of this alliance in the quarrel between Spain and her American colonies provoked the enunciation of the Monroe Doctrine in 1823. See *Monroe Doctrine.*

Holy Sepulcher, Knights of the. Members of a military order whose founding was traditionally ascribed to Godfrey de Bouillon, one of the leaders of the First Crusade His followers were the first to enter Jerusalem when it was captured by storm in 1099, and he was named ruler of the city. Actually, however, the order goes back only to 1496, when it was instituted by Pope Alexander VI to help guard the pilgrims who, in great numbers, visited the Holy City. Although Jerusalem was ruled by the Turks, Christian pilgrims were not unwelcome as tourists who spent money. But there were plenty of hazards against which protection was needed.

Hudson's Bay Company. A British joint-stock association chartered in 1670 by Charles II. It was given vast tracts of territory and exclusive trade rights throughout what is now Canada. It engaged exclusively in the skin and fur trade with the North American Indians. The company spread a chain of forts and trading posts from the Atlantic to the Pacific and exercised complete legislative and executive power within these precincts. By the Indians it was looked upon as more powerful than any nation. It played a prominent part in the disputes between the United States and Great Britain over the northwest boundary. In 1869 it sold its territorial rights to the Dominion of Canada, but it still operates as a trading company. See *Canada.*

Huguenots (*hū'gĕ-nŏts*). The name given to the French Protestants in the 16th and the 17th century. Huguenot is said to be derived from the German word *Eidgenoss*, a "confederate by oath," or perhaps from the name of Hugues, one of their leaders. Under Francis I and his successors, the Huguenots were welded together in a kind of politico-religious unity. Under Condé and Admiral Coligny they fought several wars against the Catholics. When, by the revocation of the Edict of Nantes, they were deprived of religious liberty, they left France in vast numbers. Thousands of them emigrated to England, Holland, and other Protestant countries. Many settled in America, especially in South Carolina.

Hundred Years' War. The name given to the series of wars between England and France from 1337 to 1453, due in part to the claim of the English kings to the French throne. The English won three great battles,—Crécy, 1346, Poitiers, 1356, and Agincourt, 1415,—but finally lost all their French possessions except Calais, which they retained till 1558.

Hussites. The followers of John Huss, a native of Bohemia and rector of the University of Prague, 1402-03. The writings of Wiclif had attracted him, and he spread the Wiclifite doctrine among the people. He attacked the abuses of the clergy and expressed opposition to the pope's supremacy. Alexander V excommunicated him, but this sentence failed to quench his ardor. He was finally cited before the Council of Constance, which condemned him as a heretic in 1415. The emperor Sigismund, who had granted Huss safe-conduct, violated his word and allowed him to be burned at the stake.

The flames that burned Huss set all Bohemia on fire. The Hussites looked upon him as a national hero and made his martyrdom the signal for rebellion against the Holy Roman Empire. Under the leadership of John Ziska, they began a long series of wars against Sigismund and his successors, which came to an end only in the year 1471. A part of the Hussites returned at length to the Catholic faith. From those who remained Protestants the groups of Bohemian Brethren and Moravian Brethren later developed.

Hustings. The name of a court of limited jurisdiction which at one time sat in London. Before the English Ballot act of 1872, this court was the place where members of Parliament were usually nominated, the method of nomination being by a speech made from the platform of the court. From this custom, the term "hustings" came to be applied to any stump speech or organized canvassing for votes in a political campaign.

Imperial Federation. The policy within the British Empire of closely uniting the mother country and the colonies for defense and trade, while at the same time maintaining the self-governing character of each colony. The Imperial Federation League was formed in 1884, and in 1897 the practice of holding conferences of prime ministers and delegates from the colonies in London was begun. The united action of the colonies at the outbreak of war in 1914 is pointed out as a result of this policy.

Inquisition. Tribunals established in the middle ages and in still later times, for the seeking out and for the punishment of heretics, were designated by this name. The condemnation of heretics was entrusted to the Lombard bishops in 1183 by the Council of Verona, which may be said to have laid the foundation of the Inquisition. If a heretic refused to renounce his heresy, the ecclesiastical authorities handed him over to the civil authorities to be dealt with. This institution was first put into effect in Languedoc against the Albigenses. It then spread, little by little, over the Christian world. In France, however, it played a small part. Spain and Italy were the countries in which the majority of cases were brought before the papal inquisitors. Used during its earlier stages against secret Judaism and secret Mohammedanism, it served also to repress all those who dissented from Catholic doctrine.

Viewed in the eyes of the 20th century, the Inquisition was the most intolerant, biased, and unjust institution in history. In view of the intimate union of Church and State, however, which formerly existed, heresy was naturally regarded as a crime punishable by the State and with the severe penalties then customarily inflicted on criminals of every type. The number of those put to death by the inquisitorial courts has often been exaggerated. The sentences passed by the courts tended in later centuries to take the form of excommunication.

Iron Curtain. This phrase became current after Winston Churchill used it in an address delivered at Fulton, Mo., in March 1946. He referred to the barrier of secrecy and intimidation with which Soviet Russia had shut off herself and her satellites in Eastern Europe from the West.

Italia Irredenta (*ē-täl'yä ēr'rā-dĕn'tä*). A name meaning "unredeemed Italy." It was applied after 1870 to Trieste and the Trentino, territories mainly Italian in population but under Austrian rule. The peace treaty of 1919 gave these territories to Italy.

Italy, Unification of. Italy was being torn to pieces by conflicting political parties, each of which sought to bring about her unification in its own especial way. In 1849 Victor Emmanuel succeeded to the throne of Sardinia. The unification of Italy was also his dream. He chose Cavour, one of the most distinguished statesmen of Europe, to be his prime minister. Cavour set to work to bring about the realization of his master's vision. In 1854 the Crimean war broke out, and at once Cavour signed an alliance with France and England and sent troops to their aid. In 1859 Victor Emmanuel managed to bring about a war with Austria. France came to his aid and helped to defeat the Austrians at Magenta. Lombardy was then ceded to Victor Emmanuel by Austria. In 1860 Parma, Modena, and Tuscany declared for the expulsion of their respective rulers and for annexation to the kingdom of Sardinia, which accordingly was brought about. The Romagna repudiated the temporal rule of the pope and in due course was joined to Sardinia. The Two Sicilies, the Marches, and Umbria next followed. In 1861 Victor Emmanuel declared himself king of Italy. In 1866 he joined Prussia in a new war against Austria and secured Venetia. In 1870 the complete union of Italy was effected by the taking of Rome, the last of the papal territories. See *Italy.*

Jacobins (*jăk'ō-bĭnz*). The most famous of the political clubs of the French Revolution, so called because originally its members met in a Jacobin monastery. They were the most radical of all the revolutionists. The political party of which the Jacobins were members was the Mountain. From its use at this period, the name Jacobin has come to denote any extreme radical wing of politics.

Jacobites (*jăk'ō-bīts*). A name given to the adherents of James II after his forced abdication, and in general to the supporters of the claim of the Stuarts after the revolution of 1688. See *England.*

Jameson Raid. Various causes led up to this notorious raid. The uitlanders, or foreigners, at work in the gold mines of the South African Republic, sought equal rights of citizenship with the Boers. The Boers, in turn, suspected British control, north and west of the Transvaal, and likewise rejected the British claim of suzerainty. Rhodes, premier of Cape Colony, planned to place the Dutch states under British rule, and connived at a conspiracy of the uitlanders to raid Johannesburg. To this end he sent troops under Jameson to take that city. The Boers routed the invaders, captured Jameson, and handed him over to the British authorities, who, disclaiming the raid, sentenced Jameson to six months' imprisonment: See *South Africa.*

Janizaries (*jăn'ĭ-ză-rĭz*). A military force established in the 14th century by the Turkish sultan Orkhan and further developed by Amurath I. They were recruited from Christian youths captured in war, who were brought up in Mohammedan faith and trained to arms. It was their boast that they had never fled in battle.

Jingoes. The nickname given in England to the supporters and enthusiasts of Lord Beaconsfield, who sent a fleet to Turkish waters to oppose Russia's advance on Constantinople in 1878. Originally a jocular oath, "By Jingo" came into popular vogue when used by "The Great Macdermott" in a famous music hall song.

Junius, Letters of. This remarkable series of political letters, to the number of 69, were written under the mysterious pen name of "Junius," and appeared at intervals between Jan. 21, 1769, and Jan. 21, 1772, in the pages of the *Public Advertiser,* the most popular newspaper in Great Britain at the time. Masterly in style, they attacked all the leading characters of the government, not excepting royalty itself. The authorship of the "Letters of Junius" has been attributed to no fewer than 50 different persons, but it is now generally accepted that they were written by Sir Philip Francis.

Junkers (*yŏong'kĕrz*). The name applied to the arrogant class of Prussian landowning nobility. From their feudal ideals, the Prussian army officer took his peculiar haughty air of superiority.

Jutland, The Battle of. The decisive naval engagement of World War I, fought in the North Sea on the night of May 31–June 1, 1916. The English losses were 6014 killed and drowned and 674 wounded. The German losses were reported to be 3076, of which number 2000 were drowned. But the German navy undertook no further action during the war chiefly because of the destruction of morale resulting from this battle.

Ket's Rebellion. During the reign of Edward VI, the gentry had enriched themselves at the expense of both the clergy and the poor, whose claims had been contemptuously set aside. A tanner named Ket raised the standard of rebellion on Mousehold hill near Norwich, and commanded his followers to pull down the enclosures on all estates. The earl of Warwick, supported by German and Italian mercenaries, quelled the rising with great slaughter. Ket, with several other leaders, was captured and hanged.

Knights Templars. A military and religious order founded at Jerusalem in 1118 for the protection of pilgrims and for the protection of the Holy Sepulcher. It was confirmed by Honorius II in 1128. The members took their name from the site of Solomon's temple, on which their headquarters were located. They were bound by vows of chastity and poverty. After the conquest of Palestine by the Saracens, the Knights Templars spread over Europe and received donations in wealth and lands. They soon became a great political power; consequently, their enemies accused them of heresy and other crimes. Finally the order was proscribed by Clement V in 1312, and its property was confiscated.

Kulturkampf (*kŏol-tōor'kämpf'*). "Battle for civilization." The name given by Virchow to the struggle between the German government and the Catholic Church which arose about 1870. Bismarck regarded the Catholic Church and its Center party as an anti-national influence, and the contest within the Church over papal infallibility embittered the feeling. The Jesuits were expelled, and the so-called Falk or May laws, 1873–75, resulted in the suppression of religious orders. Most of these laws were repealed in 1878–87, when Bismarck wished the support of the Catholics against socialism.

Labor Party, British. This party was organized in 1906. In 1923, with passive support from the Liberals, it took over the government, under J. Ramsay MacDonald as premier, but fell when Liberal support was withdrawn the next year. The weakness of the Liberals made it the leading opposition party. It returned to power again in 1929, but a financial crisis forced it to yield to a National ministry, mainly Conservative, in 1931. Its leaders entered Winston Churchill's war ministry in 1940. At the general election of 1945 it returned under Clement Attlee and carried out policies of a definitely socialistic character until defeated in 1951.

During the next decade the party was rent by dissention between policies of the left and right, championed respectively by Aneurin Bevin and Hugh Gaitskell. Death having removed these leaders, Harold Wilson led the party to victory at the polls in 1964, although his majority was small and was only slightly increased when he appealed to the country again in 1966.

In 1970 Conservative Party leader Edward Heath won an unexpected victory over Labor leader Harold Wilson. Beset by labor problems and increased unemployment in 1974, Heath failed to win support for a coalition government and Wilson again won the election. The new Prime Minister named the first minority government since 1929.

Laissez Faire (*lĕ'sā' fâr'*). A phrase used in economics to deprecate any sort of governmental interference in trade, commerce, or manufactures. The expression in full, *Laissez faire, laissez aller,* means that anyone should be allowed to make what he likes and as he likes, without minute government regulations.

Land League. This Irish organization was founded in 1879 by Michael Davitt, a member of the British Parliament and a bitter opponent of English rule in Ireland. In October of the same year, Parnell was elected its president. The League became a powerful weapon aimed at the rack-renters as the landlords of that period were called. Its main objects were the reduction of the rents of small farmers and tenant-laborers. It was met by truculent and stubborn opposition on the part of the landlords. Agrarian crimes followed, and the league was suppressed in 1881. By the Wyndham act of 1903 most of the claims insisted on by the Land League were granted. See *England, Ireland.*

Last Battle. The battle of Culloden, 1746, between Charles Edward, the Young Pretender, and the duke of Cumberland; so called by reason of its being the last battle fought on British soil.

Latvia. This Baltic province of Russia, inhabited chiefly by Letts, had a period of independence beginning in 1919. It had previously been known as Courland, which from about 1260 to 1560 was part of a federal republic organized by the Knights Templars among the Baltic provinces. For the next 135 years it was a duchy tributary to Poland. Then, in 1795, it was subject to Russia. Its modern period of independence came to an end when, in 1940, Russia occupied it pursuant to a secret agreement with Hitler. The United States refused to recognize the occupation.

Legitimists. The supporters of the claims of the elder branch of the Bourbon dynasty to the throne of France. As partisans of Charles X, king of France (1824–30), and of his family, they were known as Carlists. On the death of the Comte de Chambord, last of the French Bourbons, most of the Legitimists gave their adhesion to the Orleans branch, a few only, who were called *Blancs d'Espagne,* choosing to transfer their allegiance to the Spanish claimants represented by the family of General de Bourbon. See *Spain.*

Letters of Marque. A license or commission granted by a government to a private individual, to fit out an armed vessel for the purpose of cruising at sea as a privateer and capturing the enemy's ships and merchandise. Such acts were formerly not regarded as piracy. Letters of marque were condemned and abolished by the powers that signed the Treaty of Paris in 1856, and they are no longer recognized by civilized powers. See *Declaration of Paris.*

Lettres de Cachet (*lĕt'r' dĕ kȧ'shĕ'*). Letters, or warrants, bearing the royal seal. Before the French Revolution, French monarchs often issued such letters, containing arbitrary orders for the imprisonment, without trial, of certain persons who might be regarded as obnoxious to the court. These warrants were used also to protect family honor or to discipline unruly sons like the Comte de Mirabeau.

Liberals, British. With the transformation of English political parties and political institutions that accompanied the important political and industrial reforms of 1832 and the period that followed, the Whigs, the more progressive English party, gradually assumed the name Liberals, and the Tories, the name Conservatives. The Liberals have traditionally been the party of peace, anti-imperialism, free trade, and social reforms. See *Whigs, Conservatives.*

Liberal Unionists. Faction of the Liberal party in England, which, under the leadership of Joseph Chamberlain, refused to support Gladstone's Irish Home Rule bill in 1886 and formed an independent group which finally merged into the Conservative party.

Liberum Veto (*lĭb'ĕ-rŭm vē'tō*). In the ancient diet, or state assembly, of Poland, before any measure of legislation could be passed, complete unanimity among the members was required. Any one member could veto any proposition under discussion and so prevent its passage into law. This extraordinary right was called the *liberum veto.*

Lithuania. This Baltic province of Russia enjoyed a period as an independent republic from 1920 to 1940. In the 11th century, the Lithuanians were tributary to Russia, but under Ringold and his successors, in the 13th century, they became independent. Eventually the Lithuanian power extended southward to the Black Sea. In the 14th century, by a royal marriage, Poland was united with Lithuania. A closer political union was effected in 1569. In the late 18th century, when Poland was partitioned, Lithuania was divided between Russia and Prussia.

Lithuania declared its independence in 1918, and a constitution was adopted in 1920 making it a democratic republic. Pursuant to a secret treaty between Russia and Germany in 1939, Russia occupied Lithuania the following year. This occupation was not recognized by the United States.

Little Entente. A name applied to the series of agreements among Czechoslovakia, Yugoslavia, Rumania, and Poland, which followed the convention signed on August 13, 1920, between the first two of these powers. Edward Benes, foreign minister of Czechoslovakia, was the leading spirit of the Entente. Its purpose was mutual protection and it served powerfully to support the interests of France against those of Germany. It opposed consistently the union of Austria with Germany. Its power was broken when Germany occupied Austria and later Czechoslovakia without France coming to its assistance.

Locarno Treaties. At Locarno, Italy, on October 5, 1925, representatives of Great Britain, France, Italy, Belgium, Germany, Poland, and Czechoslovakia met for the purpose of insuring mutual security from war. As a result, the Rhine Security Pact was agreed to by Germany, Great Britain, France, Italy, and Belgium. It bound the signatories to accept the existing frontiers established by the Versailles treaty and to the demilitarization of the Rhineland, a provision subsequently repudiated by Germany. Germany and France, and Germany and Belgium undertook not to attack each other, but to submit possible disputes to conciliatory bodies.

Lollards. A nickname given to the followers of Wiclif about the year 1381. Calling themselves "poor preachers," they attacked the abuses of the wealthy religious orders and some of the most vital teachings of the Church. In the reign of Henry V, 1414, a plot against the life of the king was traced to some of the Lollards, and as a consequence many of them were hanged or sent to the stake. Those who escaped were forced to live in the larger cities, where they are reputed to have paved the way for the reformed doctrines in the reign of Henry VIII.

Long Parliament. The fifth parliament of Charles I, which assembled Nov. 5, 1640. In 1653, reduced to 60 members, the Rump, it was turned out by Cromwell. It was recalled in December 1659, and dissolved itself March 16, 1660.

Mad Parliament. The Parliament held in 1258 to settle the differences between Henry III and his barons, and so called, in derision, by the adherents of the king. It drew up the Provisions of Oxford, by which an advisory council of fifteen was to meet twelve representatives of the barons thrice a year for consultation. This plan operated until the rising of the barons in 1263, under Simon de Montfort.

Madras (*mȧ-drȧs'*) **Mutiny.** This mutiny, among the officers in the Madras army of the East India Company, arose from the action of the directors, who sought to deprive the officers of certain perquisites which had been looked upon as rights. Sir George Barlow made an appeal to the sepoys, who took the side of the authorities, so that the officers were forced to submit. Twenty-one of the ringleaders were punished, the rest of the mutineers being allowed to resume their duties.

Maffia (*măf'fĕ-ä*). An Italian secret society which attains its ends by assassination and murder. The murder of Notarbartolo, deputy of Palermo, in 1899, forced the Italian government to institute a close investigation, which led to the temporary suppression of the maffia in Italy. Many atrocities in the United States, notably in New Orleans in 1890, have been traced to the activities of this ruthless gang. Its strength is said to have been broken through the conviction, in 1928, of 214 members of the organization in Italy.

Magdeburg, Sack of. The Thirty Years' war (1618–48) began in Germany with the rising of the Protestant nobility against the emperor Matthias, a Catholic. Henceforward, it might be said, religion was made a pretext in Europe for incessant warfare, in which neither side gave quarter to the other. An instance of this ruthless fighting was the sack of Magdeburg in 1629, when nearly the entire population of this Protestant town was put to the sword by the troops under the Austrian general Tilly.

Magna Charta (*măg'nà kär'tà*). The great charter which the English barons forced King John to grant at Runnymede, June 15, 1215. It was an amplification of a previous charter granted by Henry I a century before, and included certain rights and privileges, which in the course of time had come into existence. It was the foundation of the personal liberty of the English people. It limited the feudal obligations of the barons and others toward the crown, restricted the powers of sheriffs and other legal officers, and gave an accused person the right to be tried by his peers.

Mahdi. The last *imam*, or spiritual leader of the faithful, expected by the Mohammedans. This title has been taken by several leaders of Moslem sects, notably by Mohammed Ahmed, who in 1885 captured Khartoum and put to death General Gordon, who was then Egyptian governor of that region.

Majuba Hill. Gladstone, in 1880, had denounced the annexation of the Transvaal by the English government under Disraeli. But, before he could alter the government's policy, the Boers rose in revolt and defeated a detachment of British troops at Majuba hill, Feb. 7, 1881. The name became a battle cry of the English, during the Boer war of 1899–1902.

Mamelukes. A corps of Turko-Egyptian cavalry formed originally from slaves who had been sold by Jenghis Khan to the Egyptian sultan in the 13th century. Becoming powerful, they established their own government by appointing one of their leaders sultan in 1251. This government was overthrown by Selim I of Turkey, who took Cairo, their capital, by storm in 1517. The Mamelukes, however, remained attached to the Egyptian army until 1811. They were defeated by Bonaparte at the battle of the Pyramids in 1798. See *Egypt*.

Manchukuo (*măn'choo'kō'*). A state erected under Japanese suzerainty in 1932 out of the Chinese territory formerly known as Manchuria. Ex-emperor Hsuantung of China was made regent as Henry Pu-Yi. Ostensibly to protect Japanese investments and rights under various "secret treaties," the Japanese army seized this territory in 1931, the population of which is over 90 per cent Chinese. Active economic development of the country began at once with Japanese capital. After World War II, Russia took control and returned it to China pursuant to a treaty of 1950.

Mandarins. The term is properly applied only to officials called *kwan* by the Chinese. There were nine grades of kwan, and a distinguishing colored button or stone set in the hat was worn by each to denote the particular grade to which the wearer belonged. The word probably comes from the Sanskrit and signifies "a counselor."

Mestizos (*mĕs-tē'zōz*). In Spanish America and in the Philippines, this name is applied to persons of mixed blood; especially the offspring of a European or person of European stock and an East Indian, a Negro, a Malay, or other person of dark non-European stock. Often in the Philippine Islands, the term is applied to those of Chinese and native blood.

Métayage (*mĕ-tā'yàj*). The system of cultivating land for a share of its yield, carried out in France before the days of the Revolution. The tenant was supplied with stock, seed, and implements, receiving in return for his labor one-half of the produce. This system was once common in England, and it is still found in Italy and in certain districts of the United States.

Mississippi Bubble. A speculative scheme projected by John Law in Paris about 1717. Well known in the financial world as an ardent advocate of paper money, Law in 1716 founded the Banque Générale and began to carry out his views regarding this form of currency. So successful was he, at first, that the French government granted him control of the trade with Canada and the Mississippi country. For a while his "system" prospered and large fortunes were made. But the overissue of paper money proved his undoing; this, together with government hostility, brought about the inevitable collapse, which left France on the verge of bankruptcy and thousands of families ruined.

Mogul. The word is the same as *Mongol*. The moguls, or "great moguls," were the descendants and successors of the Mongol conqueror, Timur, or Tamerlane. They ruled India from 1526 to 1765, when their power was subordinated to English authority. See *India*.

Molly Maguires. Members of a secret society in Ireland, formed in 1843 to intimidate law officers and prevent the service of writs. Their name came from an Irish rebel leader in 1641, and from the fact that they wore women's attire as a disguise. A similar Irish association was organized in the coal districts of Pennsylvania against the mine owners in 1854, which, after a series of many crimes, was at length vigorously suppressed in 1877.

Moros (*mō'rōz*). A group of Mohammedan Malays inhabiting the southwestern part of the Philippines, chiefly the Sulu archipelago and the islands of Palawan and Mindanao. Their social and legal customs are interpretations of the *Koran*. Polygamy and slavery were formerly established customs among them, and their piracy was long a source of trouble. After the United States took over the islands, a Moro province was organized, education was introduced, slavery was abolished, and the natives were disarmed.

Mountain (**La Montagne**). A name given to the extreme revolutionary faction in the National Convention during the French Revolution. It was so called because the Jacobins, with Robespierre and Danton at their head, occupied the upper tiers of seats at the left in the Convention. The "mountain" came to an end soon after the fall of Robespierre in 1794.

Nantes, Edict of. This name designates the law of Henry IV in France which, in 1598, gave a measure of religious freedom to the French Protestants, or Huguenots. They received liberty of conscience, full civil rights, permission to meet for worship in certain places, and provision by the government of 100 places of safety. The privileges enjoyed by the Huguenots under the Edict of Nantes were under constant attack by the Catholic majority. Churches built in places not specified in the Edict were destroyed. At length, in 1685, Louis XIV revoked the law, and all civil rights and religious liberties were withdrawn from the Huguenots. Approximately 400,000 migrated to other countries. French

Protestantism was again accorded tolerance at the time of the Revolution.

Nations, Battle of the. The battle of Leipzig, Oct. 16, 17, 18, 1813. Five nations were represented. The armies of France met the combined forces of Prussia, Russia, Austria, and Sweden. The battle was followed by the retreat of the French, under Napoleon. See *France.*

Naval Limitation. On July 11, 1921, the Congress of the United States, by an amendment to the naval appropriations bill, authorized President Harding to arrange for an international conference upon limitation of armaments. The president, on August 11, 1921, issued formal invitations to Great Britain, France, Italy, Japan, and China; later, to Belgium, the Netherlands, and Portugal. The conference assembled in Washington on November 12, 1921, and terminated its deliberations on February 6, 1922.

Agreement upon any limitation of military armaments proved impossible, and restriction of naval forces was virtually confined to placing limitations upon the building of capital ships. Seven treaties embodied the results of the work of the conference. Of these the most important were:

1. A *Five-Power Naval Treaty*, by which the capital ship strength of the United States and Great Britain was fixed at 525,000 tons each, that of Japan at 315,000 tons, that of France and Italy at 175,000 tons each.

2. A *Nine-Power Treaty*, with reference to Chinese affairs. This treaty was signed by representatives of the United States, Great Britain, Japan, France, Italy, Belgium, the Netherlands, Portugal, and China. It provided essentially for recognition of the territorial integrity of China and for an open-door policy in respect to economic rights and privileges.

The Washington Conference set a precedent in naval limitation by agreement. This precedent was followed in the London naval arms conference of 1930, where the battleship tonnage of the United States and that of Great Britain were further reduced to about 460,000 and Japan's to 290,000. Limitation agreements were extended also to cruisers and other classes of ships.

By 1937, the results of the Washington conference had largely been erased. The territorial integrity of China was ignored in Japanese aggression that resulted, among other gains, in erecting the puppet state of Manchukuo in 1932. The Japanese refused to renew the London agreement on any terms short of naval parity with the United States and Great Britain, and these powers refused to accede to terms demanded. The United States, Great Britain, and France agreed to a conditional limitation of the caliber of guns used on certain types of ships. The essential failure of agreement in any large sense, however, ushered in a period of rearmament that cast its shadow over the entire international horizon.

Nihilists. Members of a great revolutionary party organized in Russia as early as 1818, to whom the term "nihilists" was first applied in 1860 by Turgenev, the Russian novelist. Originating as a protest against serfdom, the movement found a leader and theorist in Mikhail Bakunin (1814–76), who advocated the overthrow of governmental authority so that an uncoerced communism might take its place. It was, in fact, a philosophical anarchism, which was to bear strange fruit in the 20th century.

The Russian government sought to crush the movement with an iron hand, many persons being imprisoned or exiled to Siberia. Reprisals on the part of the nihilists followed, culminating in the assassination of Alexander II in 1881. For many years after this event, nihilists and anarchists conducted their propaganda and operated from abroad, chiefly in France and Switzerland. They made common cause with communist underground leaders, such as Lenin and Trotzky. But when the latter seized the right moment in 1919 to take over the Russian government, it became apparent that aboli-

tion of governmental authority was the last thing sought by the new leaders. Nihilists and anarchists were more ruthlessly suppressed in the new Russia than they had been under the czars. See *Bolshevism.*

Nîmes (*nĕm*), **Pacification of.** The proclamation of an edict at Nîmes in 1629, confirming the religious freedom of the Huguenots who had been defeated the previous year at the siege of La Rochelle. While it endorsed the Edict of Nantes, it left the Huguenots a powerless and unarmed political party, without rights or privileges as citizens. As a result, the Huguenot League in a short time was disbanded.

"No Bishop, No King." Utterance credited to James I, in criticism of the self-governing organization of the Presbyterian and Independent churches. The phrase involves recognition of the kinship between revolt against the authority of an established head of the church and revolt against the authority of a single monarch in the state. Events proved the truth of James's prophesy. The democratic organization of Presbyterian and Independent churches gave substance and currency to the principle of self-government, which, carried over into the organization of the state, resulted in the English Revolution of 1649, the decapitation of Charles I, and the founding of the English Commonwealth. The later Revolution of 1688 and the American Revolution were likewise, in no inconsiderable degree, the product of the democratic spirit fostered by the self-governing organization of the Independent churches.

Noche Triste (*nō'chä trĕs'tä*). The "mournful" or "disastrous night" of June 30, 1520, when the Spanish conquerors of Mexico were well-nigh annihilated. On the death of the friendly disposed chieftain Montezuma, Cortés, fearing violence from the natives, decided to withdraw secretly from Mexico City. His intentions, however, had been anticipated; for he and his troops were met by the natives at the pass of Tlacopan. A terrible slaughter followed, in which the Spaniards lost 450 of their own men together with 4000 Indians who fought with them as allies. Most of the rich plunder they had secured and the costly treasures given them by Montezuma were sunk in the lake and never after recovered. See *Mexico.*

Normandy. The district of northern France, bordering on the English channel, and now included in the departments of Seine-Inférieure, Eure, Orne, Calvados, and Manche. The name Normandy comes from the Normans, or Northmen, who conquered the territory in the 10th century. In 1066 William II, duke of Normandy, became William I of England and united the two realms. The French regained Normandy in 1204 and held it until 1417. Then the English recovered it and maintained their authority until 1450, when Charles VII finally seized it for the French. Small remnants of the old province, the Channel islands, still belong to England. In them much of the old customary law of Normandy is in force, and many of the people continue to speak the old Norman French tongue. See *England, Normans.*

North German Confederation, The. This union of all the German states north of the river Main was formed in 1867, after the close of the Austro-Prussian, or Seven Weeks', war. It was Bismarck's creation. A legislature of two houses, the Bundesrath and the Reichstag, was provided for. The members of the Bundesrath were appointed by the sovereigns of the states, and Prussia had 17 out of the total of 43 votes. The members of the Reichstag were elected by the people. The Confederation gave way, in 1871, to the German Empire. See *Germany.*

Olympiad (*ô-lĭm'pĭ-ăd*). In ancient Greece, the interval of four years between successive celebrations of the Olympic games. Said to have been used first by the historian Timæus as a unit for computing time. The year 776 B. C., when Corœbus won the foot race, was taken as the first year of the first Olympiad. The use of this system ceased with the abolition of the Olympic games in 394 A. D.

Open-Door Policy. The arrangement with respect to Chinese commerce, supported by general consent rather than by special treaties of the nations, under which all nations should be allowed to trade in China upon equal terms. The policy was opposed to that of special "spheres of influence." The United States made this the cornerstone of its policy toward China early in the 20th century. The policy became meaningless when Japan sought to conquer China in 1937 and remained so after China was taken over by the Communists in 1948.

Opium War. This war (1840–42) between Great Britain and China was precipitated by the attempt of the Chinese government to stop the importation of opium, which was being smuggled into China by British merchants. It ended in the Treaty of Nanking, by which Hongkong was ceded to Great Britain, while Canton, Amoy, Foochow, Nangpo, and Shanghai were opened as treaty ports, thus giving a free hand to the opium merchants for their illegal traffic. See *China*.

Orangemen. A secret politico-religious society founded by Ulster Protestants in 1795 to uphold Protestant ascendancy against Catholic influence in the government of Ireland. Lodges or branches of this society are to be found throughout the British Empire and in many parts of the United States. The name was given them by the Catholics of Ireland on account of the Protestant support of the cause of William III, prince of Orange, in the revolution of 1688.

Ordeal, Trial by. This ancient method of determining the guilt or innocence of a person by putting him to painful or dangerous tests was supposed to be under divine control and intervention. It formed a part of judicial procedure in Europe as late as the 13th century. One of the severest of these tests was that by which the accused person was forced to walk blindfolded over red-hot plowshares. If he escaped injury, he was adjudged innocent. Other kinds of trial by ordeal were those by battle, by water, and by the drawing of lots. Such trials were condemned by the Church in 1215 and were abolished in England in the same year, with the exception of the ordeal by battle.

Orders in Council, 1807. These were specific orders made in Council and promulgated by the British government, as a reply to Napoleon's Berlin Decree, establishing a blockade on the continent. They prohibited any neutral from trading directly with France or with her allies. All goods were to be landed in England for the payment of duty and were then to be re-exported according to English regulations. These orders had an especially serious effect on American commerce, and the irritation they caused was, without doubt, one of the chief causes of the War of 1812. See *Berlin Decree*.

Organizer of Victory. The popular title of Lazare Nicolas Marguerite Carnot, noted French statesman, strategist, and scientist, whose services as war minister (1793–95) were marked with great distinction and success. He became governor of Antwerp in 1814 and was minister of the interior under Napoleon in 1815. He was born at Nolay, Burgundy, France, May 13, 1753, and died at Magdeburg, Prussia, Aug. 2, 1823.

Outlawry. In early days, outlawry was a declaration of hostility by the community against one who defied its constituted authority. The goods of such a person were forfeit, and he was liable to be killed at sight. Later, it became a mere process by which the criminal was brought within the jurisdiction of the courts. After the 13th century the wanton killing of the outlaw was forbidden. Outlawry in this sense is now practically abolished in England and is completely obsolete in the United States. The term is also used to express the process of making a particular act or course of conduct unlawful, either by legislation, by judicial interpretation, or, in the case of nations, by treaty.

Oxford Group. A semi-religious but informal movement founded by Frank N. D. Buchman while an undergraduate at Oxford University in 1921. The name was first applied by the press of South Africa in 1928. The professed purpose of the movement is "to solve personal, national, and international problems by bringing men and women everywhere back to the basic principles of the Christian faith, enhancing all their primary loyalties."

Without organization, membership, subscriptions, or definite creed, the movement rapidly obtained adherents in nearly all countries of the world, particularly among the middle and upper classes, and was accorded recognition by leading figures in many governments. Adopting the slogan of "moral rearmament" in 1938, the leaders of the movement sought by spread of its principles to stem the rising tide of national hostilities. Buchman was born at Pennsburg, Pa., in 1878.

Oxford Movement. This was a movement to counteract the liberalism and rationalism toward which the clergy of the Church of England, at the time, were tending. It originated at Oxford university in 1833 in an endeavor to bring the Anglican Church back to the principles of the early Christianity of the Fathers. Its fundamental principles were laid down in a series of ninety pamphlets known as "Tracts for the Times." These tracts, contributed mainly by Newman, Pusey, Froude, and Isaac Williams, set forth the necessity of a visible church with sacraments and theological dogmas, and they supported the contention that this church is based upon unbroken apostolic succession and includes the Anglican Church. Tract No. 90, written by Newman, declared that the Thirty-nine Articles might be so interpreted as to be consistent with the doctrines of the Council of Trent. It caused a great sensation among the Anglican bishops and was condemned by them in 1841. Newman, with several other leading tractarians, thereupon entered the Church of Rome.

Panama Scandal. The estimate for the building of the Panama canal was given by De Lesseps, the French engineer, as $169,000,000. The French Panama Company was accordingly formed, shares were taken rapidly throughout France and elsewhere, and the work was begun in 1881. In 1889 the company declared itself bankrupt, and an investigation followed. It was found that of the 54 miles only 12 had been finished, and that no less than $260,-000,000 had been expended. The directors of the company, including De Lesseps and his son, were tried and found guilty,—some of bribery, others of misuse of the company's funds. This great scandal was called by the Parisians *La Lessive du Panama*— "the Panama dirty linen." In 1904, the United States acquired by purchase the rights of the French company and undertook to build the canal. See *Colombia, Panama Canal*.

Pan-Germanism. A movement in Germany which developed in 1894 into the Pan-German League. The purposes of the league were stated in 1903 as (1) the strengthening of German national self-consciousness, (2) the education of German youth in German ideals, (3) the uniting of all Germans wherever they resided, (4) the furthering of German colonization.

Pan-Slavism. A Russian movement having for its ideal the confederation of all the Slavic nations under the leadership of Russia. The natural conflict of this policy with the designs of Turkey and those of Germany had much to do with precipitating World War I.

Paris Pact. This treaty, known also as the Briand-Kellogg peace treaty, grew out of an original proposal of April 1927 by Aristide Briand, foreign minister of France, that France and the United States should agree mutually to outlaw war as a means of settling their disputes. Secretary of State Frank B. Kellogg proposed that the treaty be multilateral. This proposal was accepted. The pact was signed in Paris on August 27, 1928, by representatives of the following fifteen nations: United States, France, Great Britain, Germany, Italy, Japan, Irish Free State, Canada, Australia, New Zealand, South Africa, India, Belgium, Czechoslovakia, and Poland. All other nations were invited to be adherents.

By this pact, the contracting parties condemn recourse to war for the solution of international controversies and renounce it as an instrument of national policy in their relations with one another. They further agree that the settlement of all disputes arising among them shall never be sought except by pacific means. An important effect of this agreement is to confer on all signatory governments the legal right to express an opinion on any incident which threatens war. The exercise of this right involves consultation. In general, aggressive wars thereafter were carried on without official declaration.

Partition of New World, Papal. Pope Alexander VI, in order to prevent disputes between the Spaniards and the Portuguese in regard to their discoveries in the East Indies and the West Indies, established, in 1493, a line of demarcation which was to serve as a permanent division between the claims of the two rival powers. The pope had already confirmed Portugal in her claims to the islands and countries of Africa which she had discovered. Spain asked for a similar confirmation of her claims in the West. Accordingly, the pope drew upon the map a line from the north to the south pole, at a distance 100 leagues west of the Azores, and decreed that the newly discovered lands west of that line should belong to the Spaniards, and those east of it to the Portuguese. Portugal, however, proved dissatisfied with this arrangement, and, by the Treaty of Tordesillas in 1494, another line 370 leagues west of the Cape Verde islands was substituted. By the new adjustment, Portugal eventually obtained possession of Brazil.

The authority claimed for the partition was a document which later was found to be a forgery but at the time was generally regarded as authentic. This was the so-called Donation of Constantine, purporting to be a grant by the Emperor Constantine (324-337 A. D.) to the Pope of temporal dominion over Rome and the states of the West. The document was proved to have been fabricated in Rome in the 8th century.

Patricians and Plebeians. The two classes of citizens in ancient Rome. The struggles of the plebeians to gain social and political rights mark the early history of the republic. The patricians were the descendants or adopted members of the original ruling *gentes* or "clans." The heads of these clans were called *patres*, or "fathers," hence the word "patricians." The plebeians, from *plebs*, or "multitude," were mostly small landowners of the country near Rome. See *Rome*.

Peace Corps. An agency of the United States government established in 1961 to train and support persons dedicated to improving the lot of underdeveloped peoples throughout the world. Established by President Kennedy March 1, 1961, and made permanent by Congress the following September 21, the corps is authorized to send enlistees abroad only on the invitation of the host nation for specific projects. Enlistees must be at least 18 years of age and serve for two years, including a period of intensive training. They receive a subsistence allowance and $75 a month at the end of their service. Emphasis is on training native personnel to carry on the projects worked on, which cover agriculture, engineering, education, sanitation, community development, and many others.

Peace of Portsmouth. The peace treaty which closed the Russo-Japanese war was signed at Portsmouth, N. H., September 5, 1905. The envoys of Japan and Russia had been brought together through the mediation of President Theodore Roosevelt. The treaty provided for (1) a Japanese guardianship of Korea, (2) evacuation of Manchuria by both powers, (3) transfer of Russian rights at Port Arthur to Japan, (4) division of the Manchurian railway between Japan and Russia.

Peasant War, The Great. The most important of a series of peasant uprisings in the 16th century. This revolt spread, in 1525, from the southern Black Forest through Austria, Alsace, and the lower Rhine. At first, the peasants were under the leadership of Götz von Berlichingen, who finally deserted them. He was succeeded by an Anabaptist fanatic named Münzer, who, with vast numbers of his admirers, played the leading part in this most bloody insurrection. After issuing a manifesto, in which they set forth their demands, they finally proclaimed a community of goods. None of their demands was granted. Münzer was captured at Frankenhausen and was executed. The rebellion, quelled with unheard-of cruelty, left the peasants in a worse condition than they were in before.

Peking, Treaty of. This treaty, signed Oct. 24, 1860, by China, Great Britain, and France, ratified that of Tientsin, made two years previous. It also imposed upon the Chinese the payment of a large indemnity for insults offered to the plenipotentiaries on their way to Peking. Moreover, it stipulated that Christianity was to be tolerated, that the Chinese tariff should be revised, and that, in the future, ambassadors should reside in Peking.

Peninsular War, The. Sometimes called the War of Spanish Independence. A series of campaigns conducted from 1808 to 1814 by the English, Spanish, and Portuguese against the French forces in Spain. The English general, Wellington, had succeeded in driving the French from Spain at the time of Napoleon's abdication, April 6, 1814. See *England, France, Spain.*

Pericles (*pĕr'ĭ-klēz*), **The Age of.** The period in the 5th century B. C. in which Athens reached its highest point of achievement in democratic government, in literature, and in art. The era takes its name from Pericles, who from about 461 to 429 was the most influential leader in Athens. Some historians reckon this entire period as the age of Pericles; others restrict the term to the fifteen years, 445–431, when Pericles was sole ruler of the Athenian democracy. During this latter period Pericles brought about the adornment of Athens with statues and public buildings, including the Parthenon and other structures on the Acropolis, which reflect the greatest glory upon his age. See *Greece.*

Personal Union. Where two countries are united, not organically or politically, but through the person of their common ruler, their relation is a personal union. Such was the union of England and Scotland from 1603 to 1707. Other instances are the following: From 1815 until 1831 the czar of Russia was king of Poland; the king of the Netherlands was also grand duke of Luxembourg (1814–90); the king of Denmark was, for several centuries, duke of Schleswig and Holstein; in 1920, Iceland ceased to be a Danish posession, and had the status of a personal union by electing the king of Denmark as her king until she became a republic in 1944.

Peter's Pence. Voluntary contributions sent from all over the world by members of the Catholic Church, for the use of the pope. It serves not only as maintenance of the papal household, but also for the multitudinous expenses of the Vatican, a great portion of these funds going to the support of Catholic missions abroad. Peter's pence dates its origin to Offa, king of Mercia, in the 8th century, and had then for its object the establishment and the upkeep of a Saxon college in Rome.

Physiocrat. A follower of the 18th century school of economic thought which maintained that land is the sole source of national prosperity, and that wealth itself consisted of nothing more than raw materials and other products of the soil. The farmer, under the physiocratic doctrine, was the only productive worker in the state; the merchant, capitalist, and town laborer were in large measure looked upon as parasites who added nothing at all to the total production of the state. The founder of this school of thought was a Frenchman, François Quesnay.

A corollary of the central principle of the physiocratic theory was that all revenues required by the state should be derived from a single, direct tax upon the land—that being the only true resource of the nation. Likewise, the *laissez-faire* doctrine was approved, according to which the state should not interfere with the natural economic and social evolution of the community.

Plantagenets (*plăn-tăj'ĕ-nĕts*). The ruling house in England from the accession of Henry II in 1154 to the accession of Henry VII in 1485. Matilda, daughter of Henry I, married Geoffrey, count of Anjou, and Henry II was the child of this marriage. Geoffrey, it is said, usually wore in his cap a sprig of broom, or *plante de genêt*, whence arose the name.

Poland, First Partition of. By a mutual arrangement in 1772, between Catherine of Russia, Maria Theresa of Austria, and Frederick of Prussia, the following division of Poland was made: Russia received the eastern part of Lithuania; Austria, East Galicia and Lodomeria; Prussia, Polish Prussia (except Danzig, Thorn, and Ermeland) and the Netze district.

Poland, Second Partition of. At the close of the Polish civil war in 1793, Russia and Prussia invaded Poland and extorted new cessions. Russia took the remaining part of Lithuania, together with Volhynia and Podolia; Prussia took Danzig, Thorn, and the whole of Great Poland. In addition to this, Russia forced the Poles to a *treaty of union*, by which the former received: (1) free entry for her troops into Poland; (2) the conduct of all future wars; (3) the right of confirming all foreign treaties made by Poland. All this ruthless treatment and appropriation led to the famous revolution in Poland the following year, under the leadership of Kosciusko. See *Lithuania, Poland*.

Poland, Third Partition of. The remaining territories of Poland were divided between Prussia, Austria, and Russia in 1795, after the defeat of Kosciusko. By the three partitions, the following increase of territory had been acquired:

Russia, 181,000 sq. mi., 6,000,000 inhabitants
Austria, 45,000 sq. mi., 3,700,000 inhabitants
Prussia, 57,000 sq. mi., 2,500,000 inhabitants.

Popes. See *Bishops and Popes of Rome*.

Popish Plot. In August 1678, there appeared in England an adventurer of the name of Titus Oates, who sought to make profit out of the prevailing distrust of the English people for Charles II. Oates had adopted various religions and had actually been a Jesuit lay brother in Spain, where he had been expelled by that society for drunkenness and worse. He announced the existence of a great "popish plot," which proved to be a tissue of lies and absurdities. Nevertheless, the populace was more than inclined to believe him. Shortly after his "revelations," Sir Edmund Berry Godfrey, before whom Oates had made his depositions, was murdered. All London became inflamed, and the Catholics were at once accused of the crime. A new test act was hurriedly passed, excluding all Catholics

from Parliament, and five Catholic peers were sent to the Tower. Coleman, secretary to the duchess of York, was tried for treason and was executed.

Pragmatic (*prăg-măt'ĭk*) **Sanction.** An edict upon important state business, issued by the head of the state and formerly regarded as an unchangeable part of the fundamental law of a country. The most important of such papers in European history is that published in 1713 by the Holy Roman emperor, Charles VI. Having no son, Charles VI, by this instrument, settled his dominions on his daughter Maria Theresa. He induced most of the European sovereigns to guarantee it; but Charles Albert, elector of Bavaria, the next heir to his dominions, refused. This caused the War of the Austrian Succession after the death of the emperor in 1740. Bavaria finally acknowledged the pragmatic sanction in the Peace of Füssen (1745). See *Austrian Succession, War of; Hungary*.

Prague, Peace of. The name applied to two important treaties. (1) A treaty signed in 1635, to which the various sovereign states of Germany were parties. By it the following provisions were made: The elector of Saxony was to receive Lusatia, and his son August, the archbishopric of Magdeburg for life. The hereditary right of Austria to Bohemia was to be recognized and Pomerania given to the elector of Brandenburg. Certain ecclesiastical estates, confiscated before the Convention of Passau and now at the disposal of the emperor, were to be retained by the present possessor forever. Common cause was to be made in driving out the Swedes from Germany, and religious freedom was to be allowed to Lutherans alone. (2) The treaty between Prussia and Austria, Aug. 23, 1866. It closed the Seven Weeks' war. Austria recognized the dissolution of the German Confederation, the reorganization of Germany to the exclusion of Austria herself, and the annexations contemplated by Prussia. See *Germany*.

Pride's Purge. The name given to the act of Colonel Pride and his troopers, who forcibly ejected from the House of Parliament, in 1648, the Presbyterian majority of the Long Parliament, who favored reconciliation with the king, Charles I. The remaining sixty members, army sympathizers, came to be known as the Rump Parliament. See *Rump Parliament*.

Primogeniture (*prī'mô-jĕn'ĭ-tŭr*). The law or custom, still in force in Great Britain, by which all real estate descends to the oldest son. The custom derives historical importance from its effect upon succession to the throne or to titles of nobility.

Quietists. A body or sect of religious mystics, whose system was based on the withdrawal of the mind from all worldly matters and its constant employment in the passive contemplation of God and His attributes. This system was first set forth by Miguel de Molinos, a Spanish priest living in Rome. His views were opposed by the Jesuits, and he was condemned by the inquisition. About 1680 Quietism came into vogue among certain devotees in France, under the guidance of Madame Guyon.

Quisling. Term used in World War II to characterize those who, in the countries conquered by Germany, aided the invaders, and took part in governments formed by them on Nazist principles. It derived from Major Vidkun Quisling, an officer in the Norwegian army, who used his position to aid the invasion, and was placed at the head of a German-controlled government. Quisling was executed after the war as a traitor.

Reconcentrados. The noncombatants of the rural districts of Cuba during the rebellion of 1895–98. General Weyler forced them to leave their homes and concentrated them in camps, where many died as a result of government neglect.

Red River Rebellion. A rising, in 1869, of the half-breed settlers in the valley of the Red River of the North, as a protest against the transfer of this settlement to the new province of Manitoba. The rebels, led by Riel, became a serious menace. Sir Garnet Wolseley was sent against them the following year and succeeded in quelling the insurrection. Riel escaped, but, leading a later rebellion in 1885, he was captured and executed.

Reformation, The. The name applied to the religious movement in the 16th century, to which the Protestant Church traces its origin. As a result of this revolution, several European states renounced their adherence to the Roman Catholic Church and adopted some form of Protestant belief and organization. John Huss of Bohemia and John Wiclif in England, who belong to the 14th century, are regarded as forerunners of the Reformation, but Germany was the scene of the first decisive action. Here the movement began in 1517 with Martin Luther's attack on what he called the sale of indulgences. He was excommunicated and in 1521 placed by the Diet of Worms under imperial ban. Other leaders of the revolt on the continent were Zwingli in Zurich and Calvin in Geneva. In England, the direct separation from the Roman Church was brought about by Henry VIII. In its main phases, the Reformation movement was virtually completed by the end of the 16th century.

Reform Bills, English. The Reform bill of 1832 provided for more equitable representation of boroughs and towns in Parliament and extended the suffrage. Its provisions as to redistribution and the franchise, however, still left the larger share of political power in the hands of the landowning classes. The Reform bill of 1867, introduced by Disraeli, provided further extension of suffrage, so that workingmen in large towns were given the ballot. The third Reform act of 1884 gave suffrage to counties on the terms given to boroughs in 1867, and so divided constituencies that, with few exceptions, but one member of Parliament is now elected by each constituency. See *England*.

Regicides. The name given by the supporters of Charles I to the members of the high court of justice, before whom the king was arraigned on the charge of treason and by whom he was found guilty and was sentenced to death in 1649. See *England*.

Renaissance or **Renascence, The.** The name signifies the period of transition, in western Europe, from the middle ages to modern times. With the meaning "re-birth," it is associated with the brilliancy of Petrarch and that of the classic scholars of the 14th century in Italy, where it led to great advances in expressional painting and sculpture and to a return to classical design and form in architecture. The glorious works of such men as Michelangelo, Brunelleschi, Leonardo da Vinci, Raphael, Correggio, Titian, and others testify to what heights this movement rose toward the end of the 15th and early in the 16th century.

The renewal of relations between Italy and Constantinople, due to the menace of Turkish advance at the close of the 14th century, brought the Byzantine scholars, with the literature of Greece, into Italy, and further stimulated the free spirit of the Renaissance in the culture of art and letters, which spread rapidly throughout the rest of Europe. Such momentous events, too, as the invention of printing, the discovery of America and of the sea route around Africa, added a new impetus to this great revival and conduced to wonderful expansion in every branch of trade, industry, and commerce.

Reptile Fund. A name given in Germany to a Prussian fund, held as indemnity for the deposed king of Hanover, the interest on which fund was payable to the king for the loss of his sovereign rights. A part of this fund, it was said, was diverted by Bismarck to subsidize certain journals in the interest of the government.

Revolution of February 1848. The French Revolution which overthrew the government of Louis Philippe, drove him into exile, and established the Second Republic. Its effects were felt in other countries in Europe; for risings followed quickly in Germany, Italy, Belgium, and elsewhere.

Rhodesia. This former colony of Great Britain in southeastern Africa declared its independence unilaterally in 1965. The declaration was rejected by Great Britain, which imposed economic sanctions.

Rhodesia, previously known as Southern Rhodesia, had been a member of the Federation of Rhodesia and Nyasaland from 1953 until 1963, when the federation foundered on the rocks of racial discrimination and the white settlers' fear of expropriation by the Negro majority. The other members became the independent states of Malawi and Zambia, while Rhodesia reverted to self-governing status under a constitution approved by Britain and the Rhodesian electorate. This constitution pledged enlargement of the political rights of the Africans, who outnumbered the whites by about 28 to 1.

The premier, Ian Smith, in 1965 in effect nullified the constitution by this declaration of independence and aligned his country's policy with that of the contiguous republic of South Africa in providing for white supremacy.

Riel's Rebellion. This was a rising of Indian half-breeds in Saskatchewan, Canada, in 1885. They were led by Louis Riel, who had been at the head of a similar rebellion, which took place in the valley of the Red River of the North in 1869. It was suppressed by the Canadian militia under Middlelow, Riel being captured and executed. See *Red River Rebellion.*

Riff. This mountainous district adjacent to Spanish Morocco in northwestern Africa was the scene of repeated attacks by natives under Raisuli against Spanish outposts prior to 1921. In that and the following year, Abd-el-Krim threatened Spain's hold over the protectorate. In 1925, Abd-el-Krim attacked French Morocco, but after initial successes was driven into the Spanish zone and in 1926 was forced to surrender.

Romanovs (rô-mä′nŏfs). The reigning family in Russia from the accession of Michael Feodorovich Romanov, founder of the family, in 1613, to the deposition of Nicholas II in 1917. Through the grandmother of Michael, the family is connected with the line of Rurik, the Scandinavian ruler of Novgorod in the 9th century.

Roundheads. Nickname given to the Anti-Royalist party in England during the period of the Civil War and the Commonwealth, so-called because of their Puritan custom of wearing the hair closely cut, as distinguished from the Cavalier habit of wearing the hair in long flowing locks. The Roundheads were the immediate precursors of the Whigs, as the liberal party in English politics. The term was also sometimes applied to members of the Whig party by their opponents.

Rump Parliament. The name given to the 60 members of the Long Parliament left sitting after "Pride's purge." Having been expelled by Cromwell in 1653, they were recalled to the House in May 1659, their number now reduced to 42, and again turned out in October. Recalled two months later, they were forced by Monk, in the succeeding year to receive the excluded members, and the Rump, as such, came to an end. See *Pride's Purge.*

Rye House Plot. A plot hatched in 1683 by the Whigs to kill Charles II and the duke of York. It owed its name to a farmhouse in Hertfordshire, the supposed meeting place of the conspirators. Lord Russell and Algernon Sidney, said to be the ringleaders, were tried and executed.

Ryswick, Treaty of. A treaty signed at a village of this name near The Hague, Sept. 21, 1697, between France on the one side and England, Holland, and Spain on the other. Its chief provisions were: (1) France acknowledged William III as king of England and Anne his lawful successor, thus abandoning the cause of James. All conquests in Catalonia were restored to Spain as well as those in the Spanish Netherlands, with the exception of 82 places. (2) The Dutch restored Pondicherry in India to the French, receiving commercial privileges in return. (3) England and France mutually restored conquests in America. The treaty was ratified a month later by the emperor Leopold, when France ceded all the annexed territories except Alsace and restored to the duke of Lorraine most of his dominions. See *England*.

Salic Law. A code of laws relating to crimes, civil injuries, and inheritance of estates among the Salian or Merovingian Franks. It was compiled, probably, toward the end of the 5th century. By the Salic law, "no portion of Salic land shall come to a woman; but the whole inheritance of the land shall come to the male sex." The reason for this exclusion was, it is said, that certain military duties attached to the possession of land at that time. By the arbitrary application of this law to the succession to the crown, women were excluded from the throne of France in the 14th century; and it is in this sense that the term "Salic law" is commonly used. In medieval France great fiefs were held by women, and the "law" would have had no application to the royal domain and the crown, save for intrigues which followed the death of the sons of Philip IV without male issue. The same principle was successfully used by Philip of Valois, who became Philip VI. It was partly involved in his conflict with Edward III of England and in similar conflicts in Spain from 1714 to 1830. See *England, France, Hundred Years' War.*

Sanctions. A term applied to penalties that could be imposed under terms of the League of Nations Covenant against a nation officially declared an aggressor. They could be economic, involving partial or complete trade boycotts, or military, involving armed force. Economic sanctions were applied ineffectively against Italy in 1935-36 as penalty for an aggressive war against Ethiopia.

Sanctuary. The protection afforded to criminals, debtors, and others, from the ordinary operation of the law, by reason of the sacred character of the place to which they fled, such as a church or abbey. From the days of Constantine, in many Catholic countries, certain churches were set aside and privileged as asylums for those escaping from the hands of justice. In England down to the Reformation, any person who sought refuge in such a place was immune from the law—except in the case of sacrilege or treason—if, within forty days, he showed signs of repentance and expressed his willingness to go into exile. Sanctuary for crime was abolished by James I; but sanctuaries for debtors continued to exist in and around London till 1697, the most noted of these being that of Whitefriars, near the Temple, which claimed this privilege to a much later date. The Abbey of Holyrood in Scotland still retains the right of giving sanctuary; but, since the abolition of imprisonment for debt, the need for seeking it no longer exists.

San Salvador. A little island of the Bahama group, West Indies, known also as Watling's island. This probably is the island upon which Columbus made his first landing in the New World, October 12, 1492, and to which he gave the name of San Salvador.

Sans-Culottes (*sănz'kū-lŏts'*). Literally, "without breeches." An opprobrious name given by the aristocrats during the French Revolution to the advanced republicans and to the Paris mob in general, who stormed the Bastille. It appears to have been a name willingly assumed, as many of the revolutionaries had, in contempt, discarded the knee breeches affected by the royalists and now wore trousers as a mark of differentiation.

Saragossa (*sä'rà-gŏs'à*). A city of northeastern Spain, situated on the Ebro river. It rises picturesquely on a fertile plain, a cluster of castles and palaces. Saragossa was one of the first Spanish cities to adopt Christianity. In 1808-09 the French besieged the city, which resolutely resisted, the siege costing 60,000 lives. The citadel was formerly the palace of the kings of Aragon and the headquarters of the Inquisition.

Sardinia, Kingdom of. An old-time dynasty, restored in 1720, when Austria ceded Sardinia to the duchy of Savoy. It comprised principally Savoy, Piedmont, and the island of Sardinia, and became the nucleus of the present kingdom of Italy. King Charles Albert, being defeated in a war with Austria in 1848-49, abdicated in favor of Victor Emmanuel. Cavour was then appointed premier. He sought for and achieved the unification of Italy. Emilia, Tuscany, the papal states, and Naples were, in turn, annexed in 1860, and in the following year Victor Emmanuel assumed the title of king of Italy. See *Italy.*

Sassanidæ (*să-săn'ĭ-dē*) or **Sassanids** (*săs'à-nĭdz*). A strong Persian dynasty named from Sassan, the grandfather of Ardeshir, or Artaxerxes, the founder of the dynasty. In 226 Ardeshir overthrew the Parthian rule. He revived the Zoroastrian religion, and began the extension and strengthening of his realm which was continued by his successors. The last of the line, Isdegerd III, was defeated by the caliph Omar in 641 at the battle of Nehavend, and in 651 was murdered. The caliphs thereafter ruled Persia. See *Parthia, Iran.*

Scapa Flow. An enclosed water area in the Orkneys, off the north coast of Scotland, between the islands of Mainland and Hoy. Scapa Flow became of note during the World War of 1914–18 as the base of the British fleet. In 1919, it was the scene of the scuttling of the German fleet, which lay anchored there after its surrender to the Allies.

Schism (*sĭz'm*) **of the East, The Great.** Called also the Eastern Schism. The severance of the Greek from the Roman Church in the 9th century. It began by a dispute over what is known as the *Filioque* clause, inserted in the Nicene Creed in 589, affirming that the Holy Ghost proceeds from the Father *and the Son.* The Greek theologians raised doctrinal difficulties on this point and denied such procession of the Holy Ghost. In this way a bitter and endless controversy arose between the two great churches. To this dispute was added the high-handed action of the emperor Michael III in 857, who intruded Photius into the see of Constantinople in place of Ignatius, the rightful patriarch, thereby overriding the papal jurisdiction. Still further differences arising between Pope Leo IX and Patriarch Michael Cerularius in 1054, the Greeks were at length cut off from communion with the Church of Rome.

Schism of the West, The Great. After the return of the papal court from Avignon to Rome and the death of Gregory XI (1378), an Italian was elected his successor as Urban VI. The French cardinals refused to acknowledge him and named Clement VII as their choice. This scandal of two rival popes lasted nearly forty years. It was finally quelled in 1417 by the deposition of no less than three phantom popes and the election of Martin V. It is known as the Great Schism of the West.

Schleswig-Holstein Question. From 1386, when the two duchies, Schleswig and Holstein, came under one government, to 1850, their political relations formed a vexed question. Schleswig was mostly Danish in population; Holstein, mostly German. Holstein was a member of the German Confederation, Schleswig was not. The Germans in Schleswig sought to induce the Danes to enter the

Confederation; but the latter resented such attempts and in 1863 declared Schleswig incorporated in Denmark. In the quarrel that ensued, Bismarck saw the means of possible aggrandizement for Prussia and for later differences with Austria. He invited Austria to co-operate with him in settling the Schleswig-Holstein entanglement. War was declared by the two powers against Denmark, which, being defeated, was forced to cede the two duchies to her joint conquerors. These, in turn, now disputed as to the disposition of their spoils. This was the opportunity for which Bismarck had planned. Accordingly, in 1866, he forced Austria into war. It took but seven weeks for Prussia to overthrow her unyielding rival; as a result the duchies of Schleswig and Holstein were annexed and incorporated in the Prussian kingdom. After World War I, a plebiscite provided for by the peace treaty gave North Schleswig to Denmark, South Schleswig and Holstein to Germany. See *Denmark, Plebiscite, World War I.*

Scutage, "Shield Money." This was a tax first levied by Henry II in 1159. The owner of every knight's fee or shield (*scutum*) was obliged to pay a sum of money known as scutage, or escuage, in lieu of personal service. The feudal vassals were bound to but forty days' foreign service, whereas Henry needed a standing army in Europe to defend his continental possessions against the king of France. By this levy, he was enabled to hire mercenaries abroad, and the vassals were saved from taking part in quarrels in which they took no interest.

Seleucidæ (*sĕ-lū'sĭ-dē*). The dynasty of kings descended from Seleucus who, after the death of Alexander, came into possession of the satrapy of Babylon in 323 B. C. He assumed the kingship of territory reaching from the Euphrates to the Indus and later conquered Syria and Asia Minor. The later kings of the dynasty gradually lost power and territory until the last, Asiaticus, was conquered by Pompey in 64 B. C.

Sepoy Mutiny, The. A mutiny among the native soldiers of India against their British officers in 1857. India was governed at the time by the British East India Company. The mutiny was suppressed, but it resulted in the transfer of the administration of India to the British Crown. This bloody conflict was popularly believed to have been caused by the refusal of sepoys, or native soldiers, to use cartridges that were greased with pork or beef fat, the muzzle-loading rifles requiring the soldier to bite off the end of the cartridge. But this was only incidental. There was evidently a carefully laid plot, with powerful influence behind it. The revolt spread through the greater part of India, the principal leader being Nana Sahib, rajah of Bithoor. His grievance was that the East India Company, which virtually ruled India, had stopped the pension that was granted to his family and had refused to let him, an adopted son, inherit lands. Among the other leaders was the ranee, or princess, of Jhansi, who appeared in the field at the head of two mutinous regiments. She fought ferociously and was killed at Gwalior in the last great battle. There were sieges at Lucknow, Bithoor, Cawnpore, Gwalior, Delhi, and at other towns; and there were fearful massacres by the natives, with terrible vengeance by the British. Two generals, Lawrence and Havelock, died in the war. Sir Colin Campbell, general in chief, defeated Nana Sahib at Cawnpore and then, with increased forces, conquered the other bands of mutineers, destroyed many forts, and disarmed the people. More than 1,300,000 arms were surrendered. See *East India Company, British; India.*

Serfs, Russian. Formerly, nine-tenths of the agricultural land of Russia was owned by the imperial family and by the Russian nobility. It was tilled by the millions of people known as serfs, whose condition was little better than that of slaves. They were attached to the soil by what was known as seignioral prescriptive right, that is to say, they were bound to cultivate the land for the owner, from the fact that they were born or lived on the estate.

Alexander II began in 1859 to free the crown serfs. In 1861 he issued an edict of emancipation which abolished serfdom throughout the empire and won for him the title of "Czar Liberator." But it brought neither peace nor prosperity. The peasants found that they were worse off than in pre-emancipation days and were paying the landlords, through the state, more than the land given them was worth. The following fifty years saw the steady growth of unrest and dissatisfaction, ending in the most appalling tragedies that modern times have ever witnessed. See *Russia.*

Sevastopol (*sĕ-vàs'tô-pôl*). A seaport in southern Russia, on the Black Sea. The town submitted to a memorable siege in the Crimean war of 1854-55, being beleaguered by the British, French, and Turks for eleven months, the Russians finally yielding. Sevastopol was virtually created anew after the ruin wrought by the conflict. In World War I it was a Russian naval base, and its occupation by the Bolsheviki marked the end of the Czarist resistance. In World War II it was taken by the Germans, after a long and heroic defense, in July 1942; and retaken by the Russians in May 1944.

Seven Years' War. One of the most important wars, in its far-reaching effects, of the 18th century. It was waged (1756-63) between Frederick the Great of Prussia and the allied forces of Austria, France, Russia, Saxony, and Sweden. Frederick received naval and financial aid from England and had the support of Hanoverian troops. In 1762 Peter III of Russia made alliance with Frederick and supported him until the end of the struggle. The war was waged, not only in Europe, but also in India and America, where it was known as the French and Indian war. It was concluded by the Peace of Paris, which left the British triumphant in America and in India and raised Prussia to the rank of a first-class power.

Shantung (*shän'tŏŏng'*). This historic province of China embraces an area of about 56,000 square miles in the peninsula lying between the Gulf of Chihli and the Yellow Sea. Here live approximately 26 million people in one of the most densely populated districts of the world. Shantung is famous as the birthplace of the Chinese sages, Mencius and Confucius. The loftiest mountain in the province, Tai-shan, near the western boundary, has for centuries been a sacred place of pilgrimage.

The Boxer rebellion centered in Shantung. In 1897-98, Germany secured a lease of the port of Kiaochow, with some inland territory and valuable mining concessions in this province, as indemnity for the killing of German missionaries. Early in World War I, Japan seized Kiaochow, and by the Treaty of Versailles she was confirmed in the possession of all rights and concessions which Germany had held. To this arrangement China refused to subscribe, and, by a treaty negotiated at Washington in 1922, Japan agreed to surrender these privileges to China. Japanese forces were withdrawn from Shantung in December 1922. See *China, World War I.*

Shimonoseki (*shē'mô-nō-sà'kĕ*), **Treaty of.** The Chinese, defeated by Japan in the Chinese-Japanese war and alarmed for the safety of Peking, agreed to make peace and signed the Treaty of Shimonoseki, April 17, 1895. By the terms of this treaty, China ceded Port Arthur, the Liaotung peninsula, the island of Formosa, and the Pescadores islands to Japan, agreeing to pay also an indemnity of about $300,000,000. Moreover, China recognized the independence of Korea. But Japan was, in the end, deprived of the most coveted fruits of her victory. She was forced, by Russia, France, and

Germany, to surrender the Liaotung peninsula on the ground that Japanese possession of Port Arthur would be a menace to the peace of the Far East. See *China, Japan, Russia.*

Siberia. This region, occupying most of Asiatic Russia and covering an area of nearly 4,000,000 square miles, was inhabited by Tatars and Turks before its partial colonization and conquest by Russia in the 17th century. The Russians agreed in 1689 by the Treaty of Nerchinsk with China, not to occupy territory beyond the Amur River, that is, in the present Manchuria. In 1710, Peter the Great began the practice of exiling political offenders to Siberia, and the country became notorious for its prison camps both under the monarchy and later under Communist rule.

About the middle of the 19th century, the eastward movement of Russian power was resumed. The Amur River was established as the boundary with China in 1847. In 1860, Vladivostok on the Sea of Japan was founded. The Trans-Siberian railway was begun in 1891 to link this port with European Russia. Penetration into Manchuria was checked by the Russo-Japanese War in 1905.

Under the Soviet Russian government, Siberia was divided into a number of separate political units. The government began intensive development, founding new cities, and developing new industries. By 1960, the population of the region was over 24,000,000, about three times that of 40 years earlier. Siberia contains 90 per cent of Russia's coal resources, 80 per cent of its water power, 65 per cent of its iron ore, and 50 per cent of its known oil and gas reserves.

The intensive development of Siberia before World War II had, as one objective, the strengthening of Russian defense against Germany. This purpose was fulfilled in that the German conquest of the greater part of European Russia in 1941 and 1942 did not paralyze Russia's war production. The arrival of military reserve forces from Siberia is believed to have saved Moscow from capture, and production from east of the Ural Mountains contributed heavily to the western advance of its armies in 1943 to 1945.

Sicilian Vespers. A massacre of French people in Palermo, Sicily, which began at the hour of Vespers on Easter Tuesday 1282 as a popular uprising against the Norman French ruler of Sicily, Charles I. The latter had imposed heavy taxes in preparation for war against the East Roman Empire. Peter III of Aragon, in Spain, took advantage of the rising which had driven Charles I from Sicily and established Spanish rule in the island.

Sikhs (*sēks*). A religious sect constituting the greater part of the population of the Punjab in India. The sect, founded about 1500 by Nanak Shah, professes belief in the unity of the Godhead and in human brotherhood. The name *sikhs* means "disciples." They were organized into a military force by Guru Govind in the latter part of the 17th century, for defense against the Mohammedans and various other religious groups. This force was called the *khalsa*, and every member received the title of *singh*, meaning "lion," hence "noble." Overcome by the Mohammedans after the death of Guru Govind (1708), the sikhs lived in separate communities until they were united under Ranjit Singh in 1792. As a military organization they were crushed by the British in 1849, but they later proved a valuable asset to the British army.

Silesia. A region in central Europe, now lying partly in Poland and partly in Czechoslovakia, which played a prominent role for over 800 years in the political and military struggles of Europe. Occupied by Slavic tribes before 1000 A.D., it was incorporated for a time in the kingdom of Poland and, about 1150, was divided into two semi-independent dukedoms of Upper Silesia and Lower Silesia. The rulers invited German settlers, who introduced weaving industries and developed Silesia's rich mineral resources of coal, iron, and

lead. In 1241, Henry II, Duke of Lower Silesia, turned back a Mongol invasion at the battle of Liegnitz.

Central political power was weakened by the practice of dividing feudal estates among the heirs, and protection was sought from Bohemia against Teutonic military orders and other assailants. Silesia was in the orbit of the Habsburg monarchs before the Thirty Years' War (1618–48) and suffered devastation in this struggle. Maria Theresa, ruler of Austria, lost Lower Silesia and most of Upper Silesia to Prussia in 1748. What remained went to Czechoslovakia after World War I, while the German portion, after a plebiscite in 1920, was divided between Germany and Poland. Poland got all the German share after World War II.

Slavery. The system of holding certain persons as the property of other persons to whose will they are wholly bound. Slavery was practiced among all ancient peoples, and in Christian Europe the slave trade did not begin to decline until the 13th century. In the 16th, 17th, and 18th centuries, both Christians and Mohammedans engaged in the African negro slave trade. The Portuguese landed the first shipment of negro slaves to the New World in Santo Domingo in 1503. The first shipload of slaves brought into the British American colonies arrived at Jamestown in 1619.

Great Britain abolished slavery in her colonies in 1833, Sweden took similar action in 1846, France in 1848, Holland in 1859, the United States in 1863, Brazil in 1871, Puerto Rico in 1873, and Cuba in 1880.

Solon, Laws of. In 594 and 593 B. C. Solon, already famous as poet, philosopher, and general, was made archon of the city of Athens, with power to make new laws and to remodel the government. In the first year of his archonship, Solon made several changes in the laws relating to property: (1) Tenants were given full ownership of land which they had tilled for nobles; (2) All debts were canceled; (3) Athenians enslaved in Attica were freed; (4) Enslavement of Athenians was made illegal; (5) The amount of land to be owned by any one person was limited. In his second year Solon created a senate, enlarged the assembly, introduced coinage, required each father to teach his son a trade, and restricted the public appearance of women. See *Greece.*

South Sea Bubble. A financial scheme which was launched in 1711 and which collapsed in 1720. The national debt of England had been causing anxiety to politicians. Accordingly, a bill was passed, enabling those to whom the nation owed money to take shares in the South Sea Company, in place of their claims upon the nation. All classes were under the delusion that the wealth of Spanish America, with which the company proposed to trade, was so enormous that they would be enriched beyond expectation. The madness of speculation spread like an epidemic. Landlords, clergymen, and widows hastened to invest their savings in the South Sea Company. But Spain's refusal to enter into commercial relations with England had rendered the privileges of the company worthless. The result was disaster, which brought appalling distress to thousands of impoverished families in England. See *England.*

Spanish Succession, War of the. A war (1702–14) arising out of disputes regarding succession to the Spanish crown. Charles II of Spain, dying childless, left by will the whole of his dominions to Philip of Anjou, the grandson of Louis XIV of France. Louis, setting aside the Treaty of Partition, which he had made with William III, chose to follow out the will and proceeded to support the claims of his grandson. The Grand Alliance of England, Holland, and the Holy Roman Empire was thereupon formed to oppose his designs. A series of bloody campaigns ensued, lasting nearly ten years. Marlborough fought in Flanders, while Archduke Charles overran Spain. The war came to an end with the Treaty of Rastatt and Baden in 1714, by which Philip was recognized as king of Spain, under the title of Philip V.

Sphere of Influence. A somewhat elastic term indicating rights claimed by a foreign state over a region with which it has economic or cultural ties. The relationship is not official like a protectorate but is chiefly a matter of custom or implied agreement.

Star Chamber, Court of. So called from decorations on the ceiling of an apartment in the royal palace of Westminster in England. It is first mentioned in 1398 as an established institution. Judicial functions were performed there by the king's councilors in cases not within the jurisdiction of other courts or if the power of the parties was sufficient to overawe jurors in other courts. There were no jurors in the Star Chamber and hearings were open. Cases were often tried there by the desire of the parties but normally the king determined which cases should be heard. The death penalty was never inflicted. In the period of the Civil War against Charles I, this court naturally was used to punish the king's enemies. In 1641, it was abolished by the Long Parliament under Cromwell. The hostility of the Parliamentary party to the court succeeded in attaching to it an odium in later ages which it never had earlier.

States-General (France). The name given to the legislative assembly in France, before the Revolution, consisting of the nobles, clergy, and commons. It is said to have been first summoned in 1302 by Philip the Fair. Sessions were rare, and none were summoned between 1614 and 1789.

Sublime Porte. The name adopted by Western nations to designate the Turkish government at Constantinople. In allusion to the ancient Eastern custom of administering justice at a gate of a city or of a palace, the Ottoman rulers referred to their court as "the lofty gate." The equivalent Turkish phrase was translated into French, the language of diplomacy, and hence into English as Sublime Porte.

Submarine Warfare. The indiscriminate and inhumane use of the submarine, or U-boat, as an instrument of warfare by Germany was a main cause of America's entering World War I. The German navy under von Tirpitz began, January 31, 1915, to destroy without warning British merchant and cargo ships. This policy was followed by the war zone decree of February 4, 1915, and reached its full development on May 7, 1915, when the passenger vessel *Lusitania* was sunk with a loss of 114 American lives. Owing to the protests of the United States, Germany later made some pretense of curbing the activities of the U-boats, but on February 1, 1917, began sinking all ships found within the waters around the Allied countries.

In World War II, the scope of submarine warfare was greatly expanded. Larger submarines with much greater cruising ranges were built. Germany relied heavily on this arm for victory after the United States entered the war, and in 1942 it was estimated that over 7,000,000 tons of Allied shipping was lost through the U-boats.

In the following year, however, the submarine menace to the Allies was practically eliminated by a combination of moves, including provision of "air umbrellas" over convoys, improved methods of detection, and use of special types of boats to track down submarines and destroy them by depth bombs.

In 1954 the launching of the world's first atomic-powered submarine, the U.S. *Nautilus*, marked the beginning of a new era in submarine development. From January 1955 to February 1957, the *Nautilus* completed 60,120 nautical miles at sea without refueling, of which 34,500 miles was submerged travel. It would take three million gallons of oil to equal the *Nautilus'* charge of U-235 weighing only a few pounds. In "Operation Magellan," 1960, the U.S. Navy's largest nuclear submarine, the *Triton*, circumnavigated the globe in 84 days, remaining submerged the entire time.

Suttee (*sŭ-tē'*). A Hindu woman who cremates herself on the funeral pile of her husband; also the act of cremation itself. This dread custom is now practically obsolete in India, having been made illegal by the British government in 1829, under Lord William Bentinck.

Taiping (*tī'pĭng'*) **Rebellion.** A rebellion instigated in southern China, in 1850, by Hung-siu-tsuen, who pretended he was divinely inspired to overthrow the Manchu dynasty and to set up in its place the *Taiping Chao*, or "Great-Peace" dynasty. He promulgated a vague form of Christianity, in which God was called the "Heavenly Father," and Christ, the "Heavenly Elder Brother." Discarding the queue, the insurrectionists went with unshaven heads and flowing locks and were known as the "long-haired rebels." They made many daring attacks on different cities, but were at length overcome in 1864 by forces under the command of Charles George Gordon, known afterwards as Chinese Gordon. See *China*.

Tatar or **Tartar Invasion.** Russia, located on the borders of Asia, fell an easy prey to the Tatars, or Mongols, of the East. In 1237 the successors of Jenghis Khan swept resistlessly over the Russian lands. In a short time the greater part of the country was in their hands, and, after subjugating the people, they obliged them to pay tribute and to furnish soldiers for the Tatar armies. For 250 years the Tatars ruled Russia and to some extent "orientalized" it; but they did not interfere with the religion, laws, and customs of her people. Toward the end of this period, in 1462, Russia under Ivan the Great found herself strong enough to throw off the Mongol yoke. See *Mongols, Russia*.

Terror, Reign of. That period of the French Revolution, between September 1793 and July 1794, when fear was an instrument of government. France was then battling a coalition of all Europe and was at the same time torn by bitter civil strife. The dominant party, of which Robespierre was the best-known member, believed itself justified in obtaining unity of action by literally destroying the opposition. The revolutionary tribunal and the guillotine were the instruments. The government was, however, not responsible for all the atrocities which characterized the time. The deeds of a Carrier at Nantes or of a Fouché at Lyons shocked even Robespierre himself. In Paris about 3000 persons were executed, and no fewer than 15,000 perished in other parts of France. See *France*.

Terrorists. The extreme revolutionary mob of Paris in 1848. Imbued with advanced socialistic ideas, they sought to end their real and imaginary wrongs by the spoliation of the rich. They refused to work and proceeded to set up a revolutionary government at the Hôtel de Ville, but they were overpowered by the garde mobile.

Teutonic Knights. A military and religious order, similar to that of the Templars, established at Acre in 1190 as a brotherhood of German crusaders. It became a political rival of the Knights Templars and Hospitalers, excelling them in lands and riches and winning great prestige in its conquest of the heathen Prussians. The order was dissolved by Napoleon in 1809, but up to a recent period a branch of it existed in Austria, as a semireligious knighthood, devoted especially to ambulance service. See *Germany*.

Thirty Years' War. A war which began in 1618 in which Protestant nobles sought to replace a Catholic Holy Roman emperor, Ferdinand, with a Calvinist, Frederick. For the next 30 years, central Europe was devastated by rival armies living by indiscriminate plunder. The leading generals on the Catholic side were Tilly and Wollenstein, while Gustavus Adolphus of Sweden for the Protestants revealed military genius of a high order. France, Spain, and England engaged also in the struggle, in which motives of national advantage vied with religious partisanship. The war was brought to a close by the Peace of Westphalia in 1648. Germany is said to have lost one-third of its entire population from the sword, fire, and starvation.

Thugs. A fraternity of religious fanatics in India who worshiped the goddess Kali, to whom it had long been the custom to make bloody sacrifices. From plunder of the property of their victims, murdered by strangling, the thugs derived their support. They were suppressed by the British government in 1830–40.

Tiers Etat (*tyâr′ zā′tȧ′*). In France, the "third estate," or that portion of the nation which was not included in the nobility nor in the clergy. It included the landholding peasantry. In the last States-General (1789) they struggled fiercely for power equal to that of the two privileged classes of nobles and clergy. The "third estate" succeeded at length in reorganizing all the deputies of the three orders as a single National Assembly. They had 600 deputies, equal to the number for the other two orders together, so that with the aid of the minor clergy and the liberal nobles they now took the lead. See *France.*

Tilsit, Treaty of. A treaty between France on the one side and Russia and Prussia on the other. Napoleon and Alexander met on a raft on the river Memel, June 25, 1807. Napoleon dictated the terms, according to which (1) the grand duchy of Warsaw was created out of parts of Prussia; (2) a part of Prussia was ceded to Russia; (3) Danzig was made free; (4) the region on the left bank of the Elbe was ceded to Napoleon; (5) the Confederation of the Rhine was recognized, and Joseph, Louis, and Jerome Bonaparte were acknowledged as kings of Naples, Holland, and Westphalia respectively; (6) Prussian harbors were closed to the British, the Prussian army was reduced to 42,000 and Prussia was to pay large indemnities and be reduced to a second-rate power. See *France, Russia.*

Toleration Act. An act passed in 1689, during the reign of William and Mary, by which Protestant dissenters from the Church of England were given the legal right to worship publicly in their own chapels. They were, however, bound to take the oaths of supremacy and allegiance and to repudiate the doctrine of transubstantiation. See *England.*

Tories, British. After the English revolution of 1688-89, two distinct parties with opposite political views came into existence—the Whigs and the Tories. The Whigs stood for the supremacy of Parliament as against the authority of the king, and for a more liberal, more democratic view of social, economic, and public questions. The Tories, on the other hand, stood for the continuance of the broad royal powers of the Stuart monarchs. When, after a long period of Whig supremacy, George III placed Lord North in power in 1770, the Tory principle of the supremacy of the king in the choice of ministers was put into effect. The period from 1783 to 1794 saw the Tories in power, led by Pitt, and opposed to the landholding group of Whigs. From 1794 until 1830, the Tories and the great Whig landowners were generally united in opposition to popular reform. In 1830, the name Conservative was suggested as a substitute for Tory and was generally used after 1832.

Torres Vedras (*tôr′rĕsh vä′dräsh*), **Lines of.** The fortifications which extended from near the old town of Torres Vedras to the banks of the Tagus. The Anglo-Portuguese armies under Wellington defended these lines against the French led by Masséna, during the winter of 1810-11, and checked their advance toward Lisbon. The longest of the three lines of defense, protecting 500 square miles of territory, measured 29 miles.

Treaties. Treaties are formal written agreements between independent states, with reference to political, commercial, or territorial relations, or other matters of common concern. The constitution and laws of each state determine what authorities shall negotiate treaties. The following are the most important treaties recorded in medieval and modern times. See *Treaties of United States.*

843 Treaty of Verdun. Between Lothair, Louis, and Charles the Bald. It divided Charlemagne's empire among these three grandsons of Charlemagne. To Louis was given the land east of the Rhine; to Charles, the country west of the Rhone and the Meuse; to Lothair, the strip between, including most of Italy.

911 (?) Treaty of St. Clair-sur-Epte. Between Rollo the Northman and Charles the Simple of France. The Northmen were granted a permanent possession of territory along the Seine, later known as Normandy, and feudal sovereignty over Brittany.

1122 Concordat of Worms. Between the emperor (Henry V) and the pope (Calixtus II). It settled by compromise the dispute over investitures.

1183 Peace of Constance. Between Frederick Barbarossa and the Lombard cities. The emperor renounced all royal privileges and rights in the cities, and acknowledged their right to raise armies and to manage their own local affairs. The cities recognized the overlordship of the emperor by an annual money payment.

1360 Brétigny. Between England and France. Closed first period of Hundred Years' war. Edward III renounced claim to French crown, and received sovereignty over Aquitaine, Ponthieu, Guisnes, and Calais.

1397 Union of Calmar. Between Denmark, Sweden, and Norway. United the three kingdoms under Queen Margaret of Denmark.

1420 Peace of Troyes. Between England, France, and Burgundy. Henry V of England married Katherine, daughter of Charles VI of France, and became regent and heir to the French throne.

1466 Second Peace of Thorn. Between Poland and Teutonic Knights. West Prussia and Ermeland were ceded to Poland. The Knights retained East Prussia as a Polish fief.

1508 League of Cambrai. Between Pope Julius II, Emperor Maximilian, Louis XII of France, and Ferdinand of Spain, against Venice.

1529 Peace of Cambrai. Between Francis I and Charles V. Called *Paix des Dames* because negotiated by Margaret of Austria and Louise of Savoy. Francis paid two million crowns and gave up claim to Italy, Artois, and Flanders. Charles temporarily gave up claim to Burgundy and released the French princes, held as hostages since 1526 (Peace of Madrid).

1552 Convention of Passau. Provided for free exercise of religion by adherents of the Confession of Augsburg until the next diet.

1555 Peace of Augsburg. Granted to the territorial princes and the free cities, adhering to Augsburg Confession, freedom of worship and right to introduce the Reformation in their territories.

1576 Pacification of Ghent. Treaty between the provinces of the Netherlands, whereby they united to drive the Spaniards from the country.

1579 Union of Utrecht. The seven northern Netherlands provinces united and declared their independence of Spain.

1632 Treaty of St. Germain. Between France and England. Canada, Acadia, and New France were ceded to France.

1648 Peace of Westphalia. Between France, Sweden, and the Estates of the Empire. Closed the Thirty Years' war.

1659 Peace of the Pyrenees. Between France and Spain. France received some territory. Louis XIV married Maria Theresa, eldest daughter of Philip IV of Spain. She renounced all claim upon her Spanish inheritance, in consideration of a dowry of 500,000 crowns to be paid by Spain. England received the town of Dunkirk by this peace.

1660 Peace of Copenhagen. Between Denmark and Sweden. Denmark surrendered the southern part of the Scandinavian peninsula.

1667 Treaties of Breda. Between England, Holland, France, and Denmark. France was given Acadia; England received Antigua, Montserrat, and English St. Christopher's; Holland retained Surinam; England, New Amsterdam. The treaty provided that goods brought down the Rhine could be shipped to England in Dutch vessels.

1668 Peace of Aix-la-Chapelle. The formation of the Triple Alliance forced Louis XIV to sign this peace, thereby ending his war with Spain. Burgundy was restored to Spain by Louis in return for 12 fortified frontier towns.

1678-79 Peace of Nimwegen. A series of treaties: between Holland and France; Spain and France; the emperor (Holy Roman Empire), France, and Sweden; Holland and Sweden; France and Denmark; Denmark and Sweden. Holland received its entire territory back on condition of neutrality. Spain and France exchanged large cessions of territory.

1679 Peace of Saint-Germain-en-Laye. Between Louis XIV and the elector of Brandenburg. The elector surrendered his Pomeranian conquests to Sweden.

1686 League of Augsburg. Signed by the emperor, the kings of Spain and Sweden, the electors of Bavaria, Saxony, and the Palatinate. Directed against Louis XIV of France.

1697 Peace of Ryswick. Between France and the allied powers,—England, Spain, Holland, and the Holy Roman Empire. Two treaties, providing, among other things, for general restoration of conquests, recognition of William III as king of England and of Anne as his successor. France was given permanent possession of Alsace.

1699 Peace of Karlowitz. Between Turkey and the allies,—Austria, Poland, and Venice. Turkey and Austria divided the territory of Hungary and Transylvania. Venice received Morea (the Peloponnesus).

1713 Peace of Utrecht. Between France and the allies,—England, Holland, Savoy, Prussia, and Portugal. Ended the War of the Spanish Succession. The separate treaties recognized the Protestant succession in England and provided for separation of the crowns of France and Spain. England received Gibraltar, and Sicily was given to Savoy.

1714 Peace of Rastatt and Baden. Between France and the emperor and the Holy Roman Empire. A separate peace by which Austria received the Spanish Netherlands.

1718-19 Quadruple Alliance. Between Great Britain, France, the emperor, and Holland. Designed to maintain the Peace of Utrecht. Spain was forced out of Sicily and Sardinia; Savoy exchanged Sicily for Sardinia.

1721 Peace of Nystad. Between Sweden and Russia. Cession of some territory on the part of Sweden. Russia restored Finland and paid indemnity.

1738 Peace of Vienna. Between France and Austria. Ended the War of the Polish Succession. Provided for French possession of Lorraine; for cession of Naples and Sicily from Austria to Spain; for French guarantee of the Pragmatic Sanction.

1742 Peace of Breslau. Between Maria Theresa of Austria and Frederick II of Prussia. Closed First Silesian war. Frederick withdrew from alliance against Maria Theresa; he received Upper and Lower Silesia from Austria.

1748 Peace of Aix-la-Chapelle. Between Austria supported by Holland and England, and Prussia, associated with France and Spain. Silesia was confirmed to Prussia; the Pragmatic Sanction was sustained in Austria.

1763 Peace of Paris. Between Great Britain, France, Spain, and Portugal. Canada was ceded to Great Britain by France; Florida to England by Spain; Louisiana to Spain by France (treaty of 1762). This peace, with the Treaty of Hubertusburg, closed Seven Years' war.

1763 Treaty of Hubertusburg. Between Austria and Prussia. Ratified Treaty of Breslau.

1774 Treaty of Kutchuk-Kainardji. Between Turkey and Russia. Brought Tatars under Russian influence; gave Russia a powerful position on the Black Sea.

1783 Treaty of Versailles. Between Great Britain, France, and Spain. Great Britain ceded Tobago to France and Florida to Spain.

1795 Peace of Basel. Between France and Prussia and between France and Spain. France was given temporary possession of the left bank of the Rhine, which Prussia, in secret treaty, agreed should be permanent.

1797 Treaty of Tolentino. Between the pope and the French Republic. The pope ceded the Romagna, Bologna, and Ferrara.

1797 Treaty of Campoformio. Between France and Austria. Provided for convening of Congress of Rastatt. Gave France the Austrian Belgian provinces and most of the left bank of the Rhine. Austria received Venice and other territory.

1797-99 Congress of Rastatt. Between France and the Holy Roman Empire. Fruitless negotiations.

1801 Concordat. Between Napoleon I and Pius VII. Provided that French bishops and archbishops should be appointed and supported by the government and confirmed by the pope.

1801 Peace of Lunéville. Between France, Austria, Spain, and the Holy Roman Empire. The Empire virtually abolished. Treaty of Campoformio confirmed. Left bank of Rhine given to France. Louisiana ceded to France by Spain.

1802 Treaty of Amiens. Between Great Britain, Holland (the Batavian Republic), France, and Spain. England surrendered all conquests to France; Spain ceded Trinidad to England; Holland ceded Ceylon to England.

1805 Treaty of Pressburg. Between France and Austria. Austria made large cessions to France and to the kingdom of Italy, recognizing Napoleon as king of Italy. Bavaria and Württemberg recognized as kingdoms.

1805 Treaty of Schönbrunn. Between Napoleon and Prussia. Prussia ceded Cleves, Ansbach, and Neuchâtel to France, on the promise of receiving Hanover in exchange.

1807 Peace of Tilsit. Treaties between France and Russia, and between France and Prussia. Provided large cessions of territory and payment of indemnities by Prussia, and for alliance between France and Russia.

1809 Peace of Vienna. Between Napoleon and Francis I of Austria. Signed at Schönbrunn. Austria ceded 32,000 square miles of territory.

1814 Peace of Kiel. Between Denmark, Sweden, and England. Denmark surrendered Norway. Sweden ceded western Pomerania and Rügen to Denmark. England retained Helgoland.

1814-15 Peace of Paris. Between France and the Coalition. By the treaty of 1814 France retained her general boundaries of 1792, paid no indemnities, and retained captured art treasures. By the treaty of 1815, she was reduced to her boundaries of 1790, an indemnity of 700 million francs was exacted, and art treasures were reclaimed. Louis XVIII made king.

1829 Peace of Adrianople. Between Russia and Turkey. Russian conquests in Turkey surrendered. Recognition by Turkey of the independence of Greece.

1839 Treaty of London. Between Great Britain, Austria, France, Prussia, Russia, and the Netherlands. Regulated position of Belgium (neutralized) in international law.

1842 Treaty of Nanking. Between Great Britain and China. Closed the Opium war. Hongkong ceded to England. Several treaty ports opened.

1856 Treaty of Paris. Between Russia, Turkey, England, France, Sardinia, Austria, and Prussia. Ended the Crimean war. Declaration signed with respect to privateering, blockades, and contraband.

1859 Treaty of Zürich. Between Austria and France and Sardinia. Sardinia received the greater part of Lombardy. Italy was to be a confederation under the honorary presidency of the pope. Treaty provisions soon overridden.

1860 Peace of Peking. Between China and the Western Powers. Ratified the Treaty of Tientsin (1858) and imposed indemnity on China.

1865 Convention of Gastein. Between Prussia and Austria. Provided for control of the duchies of Schleswig and Holstein.

1866 Peace of Prague. Between Prussia and Austria. Closed the Austro-Prussian (Seven Weeks') war. Austria separated from reorganized Germany. Prussian territory largely increased. Venice ceded to Italy.

1871 Convention and Preliminary Treaty of Versailles. Between France and Germany. Provided for cession of Alsace and German Lorraine to Germany and for payment of large indemnity by France.

1871 Peace of Frankfort-on-Main. Final settlement which ended the Franco-Prussian war.

1878 Treaty of San Stefano. Between Russia and Turkey. Closed Russo-Turkish war. Provided for large cessions of Turkish territory to Montenegro, Serbia, Rumania, Bulgaria, and Russia.

1878 Treaty of Berlin. Between Great Britain, Germany, France, Austria, Russia, Turkey. Called to consider Eastern Question. Declared inoperative most of the terms of San Stefano.

1882 Triple Alliance. Between Austria, Germany, and Italy.

1891 Dual Alliance. Between Russia and France. Served to counterbalance the Triple Alliance, formed by Germany, Austria, and Italy.

1895 Treaty of Shimonoseki. Between Japan and China. China acknowledged independence of Korea and ceded Formosa, the Pescadores, and Liaotung peninsula to Japan, besides paying a large indemnity. Cession of Liaotung later exchanged for larger indemnity.

1902 Anglo-Japanese Treaty. A defensive alliance between Japan and Great Britain. Provided mutual aid in case of attack by more than one outside power.

1905 Treaty of Portsmouth. Between Japan and Russia. Russia acknowledged Japan's paramount interest in Korea; transferred lease of Port Arthur to Japan. Both powers were to evacuate Manchuria and restore it to China.

1907 Triple Entente. Treaty between England and France in 1904; between England and Russia in 1907. A diplomatic understanding which developed into the alliance of 1914.

1912 Treaty of Lausanne. Between Italy and Turkey. Closed Turco-Italian war. Tripoli was ceded to Italy.

1913 Treaty of London. Between Balkan states and Turkey. Provided for restriction of Turkey to Constantinople and small adjoining territory. Redistributed conquered Balkan territory.

1913 Treaty of Bucharest. Between Balkan states. Ended second Balkan war. Serbia, Greece, Rumania, and Turkey enlarged at expense of Bulgaria.

1918 Treaty of Brest-Litovsk. Between Germany and Russia. Ended hostilities between the two countries.

1919 Paris-Versailles Treaty. Between the Entente Allies and Germany. Marked the close of World War I. Provided for cession of Alsace and Lorraine to France. Indemnity imposed on Germany.

1919 Treaty of St. Germain. Between Entente Allies and Austria. Provided for reduced Austrian boundaries.

1921 Four-Power Pacific Treaty. Between the United States, Japan, Great Britain, and France.

1922 Five-Power Treaties. Between the United States, Great Britain, France, Japan, and Italy, providing for the limitation of naval armaments. See *Washington Conference.*

1922 Nine-Power Treaties. Between the United States, Great Britain, France, Japan, Italy, Holland, Belgium, China, and Portugal, providing for adjustment of Chinese tariffs and for the open-door policy in China. See *Washington Conference.*

1923 Treaty of Lausanne. Between Turkey and Greece, Great Britain, France, Italy, and Rumania, defining limits of Turkish territory.

1925 Locarno Treaties. Between France, Germany, Great Britain, Belgium, and Italy, demilitarizing the Rhineland and providing for peaceful settlement of disputes; between Germany, Czechoslovakia, and Poland.

1928 Pact of Paris. Between 15 leading nations as original signatories, most other nations later adhering. Renounced war as an instrument of national policy in dealing with parties to the treaty.

1945 United Nations Treaty. The United States and fifty other nations accepted the charter of the U. N.

1949 North Atlantic Treaty. Anti-Communist pact signed by Belgium, Britain, Canada, Denmark, France, Holland, Iceland, Italy, Luxembourg, Norway, Portugal, and the United States. Greece and Turkey became members in 1951 and West Germany in 1955.

1954 Western European Union. Fifteen nations sign accords in Paris, including Britain and the U. S., providing for restoration of German sovereignty, limited rearmament, and its admission to NATO; also autonomy for Saar and stronger supreme command.

1957 European Economic Community. Signed at Rome, agreement created "common market" for members setting schedule for customs union and envisaging monetary, economic, transport, and eventual political union. Original members: France, Italy, West Germany, Belgium, Holland, Luxembourg.

Triple Alliance. In 1879 Germany and Austria formed an alliance by which they bound themselves "to lend each other reciprocal aid with their whole military force and to conclude no peace, except conjointly and in agreement." It was aimed particularly against Russia and, in a lesser degree, against France. In 1882 Italy became a party to this alliance, which then became known as the Triple Alliance. In 1915 Italy declared the alliance dissolved, holding Germany and Austria to be aggressors in the hostilities of 1914.

Trojan War. A conflict between the ancient Greeks and the people of the city-state of Troy, on the coast of Asia Minor. Concerning this war, only the vague traditions and hero tales found in the Homeric poems have survived. Modern excavations on the site have disclosed a ruined city of the 12th century B. C., which is generally presumed to be the city to which Homer's *Iliad* refers.

The city is said to have been captured by the stratagem of the "Trojan horse." This was a huge wooden horse in which a company of Greeks belonging to the besieging army was concealed. The main Greek army pretended to withdraw. The Trojans took the horse inside the city walls. The troops concealed in the horse, emerging at night, opened the gates to the Greek army and the city was sacked.

Tyrol or **Tirol** (*tĭr'ŏl*). An Alpine district which was formerly a crownland of Austria. By the peace treaty of 1919 the northern part of the district was included in Austria as North Tyrol, while the southern part was given to Italy.

Ukase (*û-kās'*). In Russia, under the monarchy, the public proclamation, or edict, of the czar, bearing the imperial seal and having the force of law. The whole system of Russian government was based on such absolutism.

Ulster Massacre. Repressive measures against the Catholics and the influx of fresh colonists from England, to oust the Irish more completely from the land, led to this fateful massacre in 1641. The Irish, impatient of promised amelioration, attempted to seize Dublin. This plot being frustrated, they turned savagely on the English and Scottish colony in Ulster and put to death, indiscriminately, many thousands of the inhabitants. See *Ireland.*

Ultramontanes. Formerly this term applied to the members of a schismatic body, for instance, those of the Gallican Church who were opposed to papal supremacy. It is now used to designate any party that upholds the papal claim to temporal power, such as the Catholic party in Germany under Doctor Windthorst during the Kulturkampf. See *Kulturkampf.*

Union Jack. The national ensign of Great Britain and Northern Ireland. It is composed of the red cross of St. George on a white field (England), the white X-shaped cross of St. Andrew on a blue field (Scotland), and the red X-shaped cross of St. Patrick on a white field (Ireland). The application of the term "Union Jack" to the national ensign, or Union flag, is an extension of its use by sailors to signify a small flag of like design used as a signal flag, and also flown at the bowsprits of men-of-war and from the mainmast by an admiral of the fleet. Usage, however, seems to have sanctioned the misnomer.

Utrecht, Treaty of. A treaty signed in 1713 between Louis XIV and the allies, England and Holland, at the close of the War of the Spanish Succession. By its terms, Spain and the Indies were to remain under Philip V, who renounced all claim to the throne of France. Sicily was to go to the duke of Savoy, who was to be known as king of Sicily; Naples, Milan, and the Netherlands were to be given to Charles VI; the Dutch were allowed to garrison the southern frontier of the late Spanish Netherlands; France recognized Anne and the Protestant succession in England. The greatest beneficiary of the treaty was England. She retained Gibraltar, Minorca, and in America acquired Hudson Bay territory, Nova Scotia, Newfoundland, and the French part of St. Christopher in the West Indies. Spain also granted her the right of importing slaves into the Spanish colonies and of sending goods to Panama for the Spanish colonists. See *England.*

Vassalage. In the middle ages, the tie between the tenant and the lord from whom he held his land or estate was known as vassalage. Every holder of land was the vassal of some lord. The vassal owed to his lord civil and sometimes military services, also payments of money. In return for such services the lord was bound to protect the life and property of his vassals—in those days no trivial undertaking. All below the king, down to the lesser knights, were regarded as vassals and owed fealty to their immediate superiors.

Vendée, Wars of the. At the period of the French Revolution, the western district of France called La Vendée, with neighboring territories, was inhabited chiefly by a peasant population, among whom the ideas of the Revolution found little acceptance. When, in 1793, a conscription was decreed throughout France, the Vendéan peasants, fond of their old institutions, rose in revolt. Some of the émigrés took advantage of the ensuing conflict to land in France. By the end of the year 1793, however, the republican armies had suppressed the revolt. A policy of conciliation was then followed until the last remnants of the uprising were quelled in 1796. See *Emigrés, France.*

Vikings. Scandinavian sea warriors, sometimes called Norsemen, who harried the coasts of northern and western Europe and the British isles from the 8th to the 10th century and in some places made permanent settlements. Their first recorded expedition was on the coast of Dorsetshire, England, in 789. Their usual method was to make sudden raids on a coast in the summer. After a few seasons, they prepared for a more permanent conquest by "wintering" in the district. By 842 half of Ireland had submitted to the Vikings. Danish Vikings came close to conquering all of England but were defeated by King Alfred. After 897, they settled down and were eventually assimilated in the English population. In France, Vikings besieged Paris for a year (885). In 911, the French king, Charles III, ceded to their chieftain Rollo a region thereafter known as Normandy, where they were quickly assimilated into the French culture.

In this same period, Swedish buccaneers made their way south as far as Constantinople and established rule over market towns on the way. They were known by the conquered Slavs as Rus, which is the origin of the name Russia.

The Viking raids, together with the Moslem conquests to the south of Europe, were the principal factor in converting the continent to an agricultural society insulated for generations from the rest of the world. See *Normans.*

Villafranca, Armistice of. After the defeat of Austria by Piedmont and France at Solferino and Magenta, Napoleon III, without consulting his ally, concluded a truce with Austria. By the terms it was agreed: that Lombardy should be ceded to Piedmont; that Austria was to retain Venetia; that the Italian states were to form a federation; and that the rulers of Tuscany and Modena were to be returned to their duchies. The disloyalty of Napoleon toward his ally, as it appeared in this action, caused the indignant resignation of Cavour. The terms of the armistice were never enforced. Nor indeed were the people of Italy prepared to observe them, as they were determined that nothing should prevent them from reaching their goal, which was the unification of Italy. See *Italy.*

Waldenses. The followers of Peter Waldo, who was a Lyons merchant about 1160. Though they did not seek to set up a new religion, they objected to certain doctrines of the Church, such as the Mass and the praying to saints. They advocated the charity and the poverty of the Apostles and held that the Bible was the only guide to the religious life. They spread from France through many countries in Europe, but exerted no great influence as reformers. They survived much persecution and are still to be found as a Protestant sect in Italy and in other parts of Europe.

Wergild (*wûr'gĭld'*). Among the Anglo-Saxons and other Teutonic races, the money compensation that had to be paid by a murderer to the relatives of his victim in order to avoid a blood feud, or vendetta. Acceptance of the wergild was at first optional, then it became compulsory. Later, it could not be demanded, nor the feud waged, the slayer being left to public justice.

Westminster Confession. The confession of faith framed by Presbyterian and Calvinistic divines at the Westminster Assembly, whose sessions lasted from 1643 to 1649. The confession was mainly an exposition of the Calvinistic doctrine.

Westphalia, Treaty of. This treaty, signed in 1648 by France, Sweden, and Germany, put an end to the Thirty Years' war. It provided that each reigning prince should be free to choose Catholicism, Lutheranism, or Calvinism as the religion of his subjects. In Germany, Protestantism was recognized as the state religion, but provision was made for equal representation of Catholicism in the German diet. The independence of Holland and Switzerland was acknowledged; France acquired Alsace; Sweden secured Bremen, North Pomerania, and Stettin. This treaty virtually ended the period of religious wars in Europe.

Whigs, English. One of the two great English parties from the English Revolution of 1688 until about 1835, when the name Liberals gradually replaced the name Whigs. The Whigs were the anti-Court, anti-Clerical party as distinguished from the Tories who tended to support the old privileges of the king and clergy. From 1714 to 1761, the Whigs were continuously in power, and it was during this period that the cabinet system of England developed into its present form. The Whigs displaced the Tories in 1830 and carried through the reform measures of that period. See *Tories.*

Witenagemot (*wĭt'ĕ-nȧ-gĕ-mōt'*). In Anglo-Saxon times, the king sought the advice and consent of a body of thegns, nobles, bishops, and abbots, which was known as the *Witenagemot,* or "Assembly of Wise Men." This assembly served as a court of appeal, and, within certain limitations, it could elect or depose a monarch. After the Norman Conquest it still continued to meet under the name of the Great Council, and in the reign of Henry III became transformed into a national parliament representing the people.

Worms, Diet of. An assembly held at the city of Worms in 1521, before which Luther was summoned to answer the accusation of heresy made against him. He refused to retract any of his writings or teachings and was ordered to return to Wittenberg to await the imperial edict. The elector of Saxony, who feared for Luther the fate of Huss, had him conducted in secret to the castle of Wartburg, where he spent a year in translating the New Testament. He then returned to Wittenberg, where he died 24 years later.

Young Italy. A society of enthusiastic Italian republicans led by Giuseppe Mazzini. Formed in 1831, the organization reached the climax of its activity in the unsuccessful invasion of Savoy, under Mazzini, in 1834. This society served, not only to inspire Italian patriotism, but also to arouse the youth of other European nations to progressive political ideals.

Zollverein (*tsôl'fĕr-īn'*). A union of German states for the purpose of establishing and maintaining uniform rates of duty on imports from foreign countries and of free trade among themselves. It was inaugurated under the auspices of Prussia in 1834. The growth and success of this economic system contributed much to the political unification of Germany.

In the preceding pages, the stories of the rise and progress of he states and nations of the world are recounted at some length. Moreover, many special topics, including notable movements, parties, periods, and events of international importance, are treated succinctly in the Dictionary of World History. To complete this plan, and still further to unify the treatment of the subject, the entire course of world history is graphically presented in the following comparative summary of outstanding facts in the story of mankind. The chronological outline histories of the nations are arranged in parallel columns in order to facilitate the attainment of *comparative view* that is so important in the study of history.

Progress in civilization and in political and social development has not been uniform among the nations. In a comparative chart, the occasional long blank spaces in a column, parallel with other quite crowded columns, are instructive. They frequently mark the shallows and the backwaters in the stream of history, telling a story of the persistence of primitive culture, of political stagnation, or of subordination to foreign invaders.

Besides being a convenient source of information, this chart furnishes a study plan for fixing in the memory *related* events and dates, thus supplementing the preceding historical narratives. In this connection, two features especially distinguish this plan: (1) The entries in the column of Arts of Civilization summarize, in its varied phases, the advance of human culture; (2) the distinctive character of modern history since 1815 finds emphasis in the column of International Affairs.

A similar chart, covering the history of the United States and the other American nations, will be found at the close of the section devoted to American history.

PREHISTORIC MAN IN EUROPE

About 50,000 years ago EARLY STONE AGE	Beginning of 3d warm period. Climate grows warm.	Men are hunters. They know the use of fire.	First stone tools. Use of the first hatchet. Flint chipped by pounding.
MIDDLE STONE AGE	Beginning of 4th glacial period. Climate grows cold. Reindeer are plentiful.	Men are still hunters. They begin to live in caves. Clothing of skin sewed with bone needles. Cave walls decorated with drawings. Dead buried under family hearth.	Flint tools sharpened by pressing along edge with hard bone. Ivory tools. Weapons of bone, wood, and flint. Bone whistles.
LATE STONE AGE About 10,000 B. C. Period Begins	Beginning of 4th warm period (which includes present time).	Men hunt; women learn to plant seed and to harvest. Wooden dwellings along streams. Pile dwellings in Swiss lakes. Agriculture leads to permanent settlements. Towns. Primitive commerce. Wars among communities. Rise of nomad tribes, herdsmen, in country east of the Danube.	Polished flint and stone tools. Tools ground on whetstones. Earliest use of the plow. Pottery made.
Period closes about 3000 B. C.	Metals (copper) discovered, probably in peninsula of Sinai, as early as 4000 B. C.; introduced in southeastern Europe about 3000 B. C.; in Britain about 2000 B. C. Bronze age begins.		

FROM EARLIEST RECORDS TO THE EIGHTH CENTURY B. C.

B. C.	ASIA	EUROPE	EGYPT
4000	Sumerians in Babylonia. Cuneiform writing in use.		4241. Solar calendar adopted; earliest dated event in history. 4000. By this date copper tools and hieroglyphic writing were in use. Before 3500, Egyptians had an alphabet of 24 letters. 3400. Two kingdoms of Upper and Lower Egypt united. 3400–2400. "Old Kingdom" period; capital at Memphis. 3050 (about). Earliest stone masonry.
3000	By this time, the Sumerians had built a civilized state in Babylonia.	3000 (about). Ægeans use metal tools and weapons. Rise of Cretan civilization.	3000–2500. Age of pyramid building. 3000. Book of the Dead already venerable. Egyptians have seagoing ships. Great progress in woodworking, paper making, weaving, glassmaking, metal working, pottery, and painting. Portrait sculpture.
3000 (about)	Canaanites settling in Palestine. Nineveh a trading city.		
3050–2750 (about)	Age of Sumerian city-states in Babylonia.		
2800 (about)	Sargon I builds a strong Babylonian kingdom (Akkad).		
2500	Parent people of Indo-Europeans living on steppes east of Caspian Sea. They have the horse, domestic oxen, and wheeled carts.	2200. Egyptian influence in Crete.	
2150 (about)	Hammurabi makes Babylon the center of a powerful state.		
2000 (about)	Hittites (in Asia Minor) use hieroglyphic writing. Light-skinned Indo-Europeans settle in the Punjab. Establishment of Vedic culture. Barbarian Kassites from the East conquer Babylonia. They introduce the horse, the training of which they learned from Indo-European tribes of the North.	2000 (about). Indo-Europeans in the Balkan peninsula. Bronze and copper in use in Norse countries. 1700. Cretan influence in Greece.	2000. Egyptian mathematics well developed. 2000–1500 (about). Feudal Age in Egypt. 1800 (about). The Hyksos gain control of Egypt. 1700 (about). Horse introduced. Cliff tombs. Oldest libraries found in tombs of nobles.

B. C.	FROM EARLIEST RECORDS TO THE EIGHTH CENTURY B. C.—CON.		
	ASIA	**EUROPE**	**EGYPT**
1600 (about) 1400 (?) 1400 (about) 1200 (about) 1140–1040 (about) 1025 (about) 1010–975 1000 (about) 975–935 (about) 935 10th Century 860–825	Feudal system extended throughout China. Hindu kingdoms established on the Ganges. Hebrews and Arameans settle in Syria and Palestine. Exodus of Hebrews from Egypt, led by Moses. Era of the Judges in Israel. Reign of Saul in Israel. Reign of David; kingdom of Israel at its zenith. Ionians settle in Asia Minor. Phœnicians become powerful. Reign of Solomon in Palestine. Israel divided into northern kingdom (Israel) and southern kingdom (Judah). Alphabet, without vowel signs, in use by Phœnicians. Shalmaneser II, a great warrior, reigns in Assyria and makes conquests in western Asia. He defeats Ahab, king of Israel, and his allies in battle of Karkar (854).	1600–1100. Cretan (Ægean) civilization at its height. 1200. Rise of Mycenæ and Tiryns in Greece. 1193–1184. Conquest and destruction of Troy. 1100–750 (about). Homeric Age in Greece, Asia Minor, Ægean islands. 900–700. Greek epic poetry is at its zenith. Age of Homer. 820 (?). Lycurgus introduces many reforms in Sparta.	Development of literature and government, religion, and ideas of social justice and kindness. 1580–1150. Egypt a world power. Period of the New Kingdom. Development of monotheism in religion. 1180–1050. Decline of the New Kingdom. 926. Shishak, king of Egypt, invades Palestine. 814 (?). Carthage founded.

B. C.	FROM THE EIGHTH CENTURY B. C. TO THE GRECO-PERSIAN WARS, ABOUT 490 B. C.				
	ARTS OF CIVILIZATION	**JUDAH**	**ISRAEL**	**ASIA AND AFRICA**	**EUROPE**
8th Cent. 776 763 700 (about) 700–460 621	Coinage in Lydia. Period of the great writing prophets in Judah and Israel. Olympic games. Beginning of first Olympiad. A solar eclipse recorded in this year; it determines dates in Assyrian chronology. Writing common among the Greeks. Lyric poetry flourishes in Greece. Spherical form of the earth and true cause of lunar eclipses taught by Thales, who also discovered the electricity of amber. Draconian code formulated.	740–701. Period of the ministry of Isaiah. 728–697. Hezekiah, king; abolishes idolatry; makes alliance with Egypt. Sennacherib invades Judah. His army destroyed by pestilence. 697–642. Manasseh, king; carried to Babylon; afterward restored to throne. 622 (about). Religious reform. Prophet Jeremiah. 621. Book of Deuteronomy discovered at Jerusalem.	782–741. Reign of Jeroboam II. Period of Amos and Hosea. 734–732. Pekah, king of Israel, is deposed and slain. Hoshea appointed in his place. 722. Samaria taken by the Assyrians. End of the kingdom of Israel. 705. Sennacherib, king of Nineveh. 660. First mikado of Japan, named Jimmu Tenno. 657. Byzantium founded. 624. Greeks from Thera found a new colony in Libya, named Cyrene.	745. Pul, or Tiglath-Pileser II, seizes the throne of Assyria. 732. Damascus taken by Tiglath-Pileser. 722. Sargon II, king of Assyria, takes Samaria and carries the Ten Tribes into captivity. 681. Babylon and Nineveh are united under Esarhaddon. **EGYPT** 660 (about). Psammetichus, king of Egypt. Memphis becomes the capital.	753. Building of Rome (legend). 734. Syracuse and Corcyra are founded by the Corinthians. 721. Sybaris founded in Magna Græcia by Achæans. 678. Argæus, first king of Macedon. 665. First naval battle recorded in history, between the Corinthians and Corcyræans. 645. Second Messenian war in Greece. 629. Periander rules Corinth.

B. C.	FROM THE EIGHTH CENTURY B. C. TO THE GRECO-PERSIAN WARS, ABOUT 490 B. C.—Con.				
	ARTS OF CIVILIZATION	JUDAH	BABYLONIA	EGYPT	EUROPE
610	Pharaoh Necho begins a canal between the Mediterranean and Red Sea. Many lives lost in the attempt. He also sent out a Phœnician fleet which circumnavigated Africa.	609. Battle of Megiddo. Judah subject to Egypt. 605. Battle of Carchemish; Judah subject to Babylon.	606. Nineveh a second time destroyed. 605. Nebuchadnezzar defeats Necho of Egypt; invades Judea. Battle of Carchemish.	609. Pharaoh Necho, king of Egypt.	
6th Cent.	Taoism, a system of philosophy, founded in China by Lao Tzu. Written laws in existence in Crete.				600 (about). Foundation of Massilia (Marseille).
594	Solon's code supersedes that of Draco in Athens.			589 (about). Pharaoh-Hophra, king of Egypt.	594. Solon, archon of Athens.
586?	Pythian games established at Delphi.	586. Captivity of Judah completed. Jerusalem destroyed. Jews carried to Babylon. Prophet Ezekiel.			
582?	Establishment of Nemean games in Greece.				
578	Money coined at Rome by Servius Tullius. (Legend)		573. Nebuchadnezzar takes Tyre.	569. Amasis, king of Egypt, makes alliance with Greece.	578. Servius Tullius, king of Rome. (Legend)
		PERSIA		568. Egypt invaded by Nebuchadnezzar.	600–500 (about). Etruscans supreme in Italy.
			562. Crœsus, king of Lydia, subjects Asia Minor.		
557	Gautama Buddha is born.	558. Persian Empire founded by Cyrus.	556–539. Nabonidus rules in Babylon.		
551 (about)	Era of Confucian philosophy in China.	546. Cyrus conquers Lydia. 539. Cyrus takes Babylon. 537. Jews returned to Palestine; Zerubbabel, leader. 529. Death of Cyrus; Cambyses, king of Persia.			**ROME, ETC.** 534–510. Tarquin the Proud, king. 530. Cadiz built by the Carthaginians.
			GREECE 527. Pisistratus dies.		
525–456	Æschylus, greatest of the Greek tragic poets; won thirteen contests; defeated in 468 by Sophocles.	525. Cambyses conquers Egypt and makes it a Persian province. Psammetichus, last king of Egypt. 522–486. Darius I, king of Persia. 516. Second temple at Jerusalem completed. 508 (about). Darius conquers the Punjab.		525. Egypt becomes a Persian province. **MACEDONIA**	
500 (about)	Voyage of Hanno, a Carthaginian, down west coast of Africa.		510. Followers of Pisistratus expelled; democracy established at Athens.		509 (about). The Tarquins expelled from Rome. Patrician commonwealth established. Brutus and Collatinus, first consuls. Roman treaty with Carthage.
500–406	Tragedy flourishes at Athens.				
5th Cent.	Use of water clock in Greece. Hippocrates begins development of medical science.	499 (about). The Ionians revolt and burn Sardis. 494. The Persians destroy Miletus.		498. Alexander I rules in Macedonia.	496. Romans win battle at Lake Regillus. 494. Tribunes of the people chosen. 491. Coriolanus banished.

B. C.	From the Battle of Marathon to the Death of Alexander the Great—B. C. 490–323				
	Arts of Civilization	Persia	Greece	Macedonia	Rome, Etc
		490. Darius sends an army into Greece. 486. Xerxes, king of Persia. 481. Expedition of Xerxes into Greece; destroys Athens.	490. Battle of Marathon. Persians under Datis defeated (Sept. 12). 483. Aristides banished. 480. Battle of Thermopylæ. Battle of Salamis and defeat of Persians. 479. Battle of Platæa; Persian fleet destroyed at Mycale. 478–477. Themistocles rebuilds Athens. 477. Sparta assumes conduct of war.		486. Agrarian riots at Rome; the patricians kill Spurius Cassius. 480. Carthaginians defeated. Hamilcar killed in battle.
477	Death of Buddha; first Buddhistic council held at Rajagriha.				
469	Socrates born.	465. Xerxes assassinated. Artaxerxes I, king. 458. Ezra arrives at Jerusalem.	461. Pericles impresses himself upon Greek affairs. 457–455. Sparta wars on Athens.		460 (about). Cincinnatus, consul. 458 (about). Cincinnatus, dictator.
456	Æschylus dies at Gela in Sicily. The Secular games instituted at Rome.		456. Long walls of Athens completed.	454. Perdiccas II reigns in Macedonia.	450 (about). Laws of the 12 tables.
446	Herodotus, the historian, in Athens.	445. Nehemiah comes on a mission to Jerusalem. Walls of Jerusalem rebuilt by Nehemiah.	446. First Peloponnesian war ended.		
438	The Parthenon completed at Athens.		431. Second Peloponnesian war begun.		
429	Birth of Plato.		429. Death of Pericles.		
427	Aristophanes produces first comedy at Athens.		415. Expedition against Syracuse. 413. Expedition ends in failure. 411. Athens governed by the "400." Alliance of Sparta with Persia. 409. Capture of Byzantium by Athenians. 404. Surrender of Athens and end of war.	413. Archelaus, patron of learning, seizes the throne and kills Perdiccas.	413. Egypt regains independence.
399	Death of Socrates.	401. Cyrus the Younger defeated. Retreat of the 10,000 under Xenophon.		399. Archelaus murdered. The Illyrians invade Macedonia. 394–370. Reign of Amyntas.	
390	Inauguration of Capitoline games at Rome.	387. Greek cities of Asia made tributary to Persia.			390. Rome destroyed by the Gauls.
383	Birth of Demosthenes.				
377	Second Buddhistic council assembles at Vesali.				376. War between patricians and plebeians. Lucius Sextus, first plebeian consul.
			371. Battle of Leuctra. Predominance of Thebes. 362. Battle of Mantinea; death of Epaminondas; end of Theban power. Decline of Greek city-states.	359. Philip II, king; institutes the Macedonian phalanx; defeats the Athenians. 356. Philip II conquers Thrace and Illyria. Birth of Alexander the Great.	371. Curule magistrates appointed. 367. Licinian laws passed after ten-year struggle; patricians and plebeians are granted equal rights.
354	Demosthenes makes his first appearance in public in an affair of state.				

B. C.	FROM THE BATTLE OF MARATHON TO THE DEATH OF ALEXANDER THE GREAT—B. C. 490–323—CON.				
	ARTS OF CIVILIZATION	PERSIA	GREECE	MACEDONIA	ROME, ETC.
351	Demosthenes delivers the first of his orations, known afterward as "Philippics."				348. Commercial treaty between Rome and Carthage.
347	Plato dies.				
344 (about)	The philosophers, Zeno and Epicurus, flourish.	344. Aristotle visits Mytilene.		341. War against the Athenians.	343. Samnian war; continued fifty-three years.
			339. War with Macedonia.	338. Athenians and Thebans defeated at Chæronea.	340. War with the Latins. They obtain rights of Roman citizens.
		336. Darius III, king.	336. Philip slain. Thebes destroyed.	336. Alexander the Great succeeds to the throne.	337. First plebeian prætor.
			335. Greeks conquered by Alexander the Great.	335. Alexander the Great conquers Greeks and leads army against Persians.	
		334. Alexander the Great invades Persia.		334. Alexander the Great invades Persia; defeats Darius at the Granicus.	
				333. Battle of Issus.	
				332. Egypt conquered by Alexander; Alexandria built.	332. Roman treaty with Alexander of Epirus.
		331. Battle of Arbela.			
		330. Darius III murdered. Alexander founds the Grecian, or Macedonian, monarchy.	330. Æschines, the orator, banished.	327 Alexander invades India.	
323	Aristotle founds Lyceum in Athens.		324. Demosthenes banished.	323. Ptolemy I restores the independence of Egypt. Alexander the Great dies in Babylonia.	

B. C.	FROM THE DEATH OF ALEXANDER THE GREAT TO THE ROMAN CONQUEST OF CARTHAGE AND CORINTH—B. C. 323–146				
	ARTS OF CIVILIZATION	ROME, ETC.	MACEDONIA	GREECE	ASIA MINOR, SYRIA, JUDEA, INDIA, CHINA	EGYPT, CARTHAGE
322	Demosthenes dies at Calauria; Aristotle dies at Chalcis.	321. Roman army surrenders to the Samnites.				
		319. Samnites defeated at Luceria.	319. Cassander assumes the throne of Macedon.	319. Polyperchon succeeds Antipater.	320 (about). Founding of empire of Magadha in India.	320 (about). Ptolemy I, called Soter, makes a military expedition into Palestine; takes Jerusalem.
				318 (about). Birth of Pyrrhus II, greatest hero of his time.		317–275. Wars between the Sicilian Greeks and the Carthaginians.
				317. Demetrius Phalereus governs Athens.		
				315 (about). Cassander rebuilds Thebes.	315 (about). Maurya dynasty founded in India by Chandragupta.	
312	Appian Way begun by Appius Claudius.	312. War with the Etruscans.			312. Seleucus I retakes Babylon and restores its independence.	
300 (about)	Euclid, the celebrated mathematician, writes on geometry. The Indian epic *Ramayana* composed.			294. Demetrius murders King Alexander and seizes throne of Macedon.	301. Battle of Ipsus, Alexander's empire divided anew into four parts: Syria, Macedon, Greece, Egypt.	
		287. Law of Hortensius, by which the decrees of the people had the force of those of the senate.	288. Lysimachus, king of Thrace, subdues Macedonia.			

B. C.	FROM THE DEATH OF ALEXANDER THE GREAT TO THE ROMAN CONQUEST OF CARTHAGE AND CORINTH—B. C. 323–146—CON.					
	ARTS OF CIVILIZATION	ROME, ETC.	MACEDONIA	GREECE	ASIA MINOR, SYRIA, JUDEA, INDIA, CHINA	EGYPT, CARTHAGE
285 (about)	Science and literature flourish at the Museum of Alexandria. The work of translating the Hebrew Scriptures into Greek for the Jews at Alexandria is begun. Era of bucolic poetry. Theocritus writes his famous idyls.	280. Pyrrhus in Italy. 280–275. The Tarentine war. 275. Pyrrhus defeated by the Romans at Beneventum; date of Rome's supremacy.	281. Pyrrhus of Epirus aids Tarentum in Italy. 274. Pyrrhus invades Macedonia, defeats Antigonus, and is proclaimed king. 272. Antigonus restored.	280. The Achæan League formed. 278. Invasion by the Gauls, who are routed by the Greeks at Delphi.	285. The Scythians invade Bosporus. 281. Antiochus Soter succeeds Seleucus in Syria. 278. Settlement of Gauls in Asia Minor. Later they became the Galatians.	285. Ptolemy Philadelphus, king of Egypt. 283. Death of Ptolemy Soter. 276. A Carthaginian fleet defeats Pyrrhus of Epirus.
270	Epicurus, the philosopher, dies.					
269 (about)	Silver money first coined at Rome.	266. Rome mistress of all Italy. 264. First Punic war begun.	268. Second incursion of the Gauls.	268. Athens taken by Antigonus.		
263	Aristarchus teaches that the earth moves around the sun.		250. Parthia revolts from Macedon.	255. Athens joins the Achæan League.	260. Asoka, the king of Magadha, brings northern India beneath his rule.	
246 (?)	The building of the Great Wall of China begun under the emperor Chi Hwang-ti.	241. End of first Punic war.			246 (?). Chi Hwang-ti first autocratic emperor of China; destroys feudalism and extends empire to its modern limit. 246. Death of Antiochus II. 226. Seleucus III, king of Syria.	246. Ptolemy Euergetes subdues Syria.
224 (about)	Archimedes makes known his discoveries in mechanics.	225. The Gauls repulsed in Italy.			223. Death of Asoka, king of Magadha. 222. Antiochus the Great, king of Syria.	221. Ptolemy Philopator, king.
		219. Hannibal takes Saguntum and crosses the Alps. 218. Second Punic war. Hannibal defeats the Romans at the Ticinus and the Trebia. 216. Varro at Cannæ totally defeated by Hannibal.	220. Philip V assists the Achæans against the Ætolians. 217. Philip V makes peace with the Ætolians at Naupactus.	220. The Social war begins, between Achæan and Ætolian leagues.	219. War between Antiochus and Ptolemy. 217. Ptolemy defeats Antiochus at Raphia.	
213	Burning of the books by Chi Hwang-ti, the Chinese emperor.	214. First Macedonian war.	214. Alliance of Philip and Hannibal.			
206	Revival of classics and general learning in China.	206. Carthaginians driven out of Spain.		206. Spartans defeated at Mantinea.	206. Founding of Han dynasty of China.	205. Ptolemy Epiphanes, king.
204	Death of Livius Andronicus who translated the *Odyssey*; first of Latin dramatic writers.	202. Hannibal defeated by Scipio at Zama in Africa. End of war.				

B. C.	FROM THE DEATH OF ALEXANDER THE GREAT TO THE ROMAN CONQUEST OF CARTHAGE AND CORINTH—B. C. 323–146—CON.					
	ARTS OF CIVILIZATION	ROME, ETC.	MACEDONIA	GREECE	ASIA MINOR, SYRIA, JUDEA, INDIA, CHINA	EGYPT, CARTHAGE
204—con.	The Great Wall of China completed.	201. Second Macedonian war. 190. Rome shatters power of Syria.	201. Second war with Rome. 197. Philip V defeated at Cynoscephalæ.	198. Achæan League makes first treaty with Rome. Achæans and Spartans join the Romans against Macedon.	198. Jews assist Antiochus in expelling the Egyptian troops from Jerusalem. 190. Scipio Africanus defeats Antiochus at Magnesia. 187. Antiochus killed. Syria becomes temporarily a Roman province.	198. Egypt loses her Syrian possessions.
					SYRIA / **JUDEA**	
184	Death of Plautus, foremost among the early Roman writers of comedy.		179. Reign of Perseus.		187. Seleucus IV, king.	182. Ptolemy Philometor, king. 175. Cato's embassy to Carthage.
169	Death of Ennius, first of the great Roman epic poets.		171. Third war with Rome.		175. Antiochus IV, king. 170. Jerusalem plundered by Antiochus Epiphanes.	
166	Book of Daniel probably written in this year.		168. Perseus defeated at Pydna.	167. Romans enter Achæa.	168. Jews persecuted by Antiochus; the temple of Jerusalem defiled. 165. Judas Maccabeus expels the Syrians. 161. Treaty with Romans.	
156 (about)	Paper made in China.					150. Massinissa defeats the Carthaginians.
149	Death of Cato the Censor, historian and economist.	149. Third Punic war begins. 146. Conquest of Carthage and Corinth. Greece annexed to the Roman Empire.	146. Macedonia becomes a Roman province.	146. Corinth destroyed by the Romans. Greece becomes a Roman province under the name Achæa.		146. Carthage destroyed by the Romans. Ptolemy Physcon becomes sole king of Egypt.

B. C.	FROM THE ROMAN CONQUEST OF CARTHAGE AND CORINTH TO THE BIRTH OF CHRIST—B. C. 146–4				
	ARTS OF CIVILIZATION	ROME, ETC.	SYRIA	JUDEA	EGYPT, CARTHAGE
		133. Spain becomes a Roman province. 123. Caius Gracchus, tribune, endeavors to follow out constitutional reforms advocated by his brother; is killed. 113. First great migration of the German nations.	139–129. Antiochus VII, king.	135–105. John Hyrcanus reigns as prince and high priest in Jerusalem.	130. Physcon driven from his throne for cruelty.
104	A new calendar is adopted in China on the calculations of Ssu-ma Ch'ien; the Chinese date their chronology from this epoch.	102. Battle of Aquæ Sextiæ. Marius defeats Teutones. 101. Battle of Vercellæ. Marius defeats the Cimbri. 100. Birth of Julius Cæsar.		104. War with Egypt.	107. Alexander I, king of Egypt.
91	First comprehensive history of China written by Ssu-ma Ch'ien.	91–88. Social war in Italy.			

B. C.	FROM THE ROMAN CONQUEST OF CARTHAGE AND CORINTH TO THE BIRTH OF CHRIST—B. C. 146–4—CON.				
	ARTS OF CIVILIZATION	ROME, ETC.	SYRIA	JUDEA	EGYPT, CARTHAGE
88	Texts of Buddha transferred to Pali writing in Ceylon.	88. War with Pontus. 82. Sulla defeats Marius and is created dictator. 64. Syria becomes a Roman province. 63. Cicero, consul. Catiline's conspiracy detected and suppressed by Cicero. 60. First triumvirate,—Pompey, Crassus, and Cæsar. 59. Cæsar, consul.	66. Mithridates, the Parthian emperor, defeated by Pompey. 64. Syria passes under Rome.	63. Judea a Roman province.	81. Alexander II, king of Egypt. 80. Ptolemy Auletes, king.
55	Death of Lucretius Carus, poet and philosopher.	55. Cæsar passes the Rhine, defeats the Germans and Gauls, and invades Britain. 53. Crassus defeated and killed in Parthia. 51. Cæsar completes conquest of Gaul, which becomes a Roman province. 49. Civil war between Cæsar and Pompey. Pompey defeated; Cæsar, dictator. 48. Battle of Pharsalus—Pompey defeated by Cæsar. Death of Pompey in Egypt.			55. Auletes restored. 51. Cleopatra driven from throne of Egypt.
47	Library at Alexandria said to have been destroyed.	47. Cæsar takes Alexandria and conquers Egypt.			47. Cleopatra, with her brother, Ptolemy XV, on throne of Egypt. 46. The African war.
45	Cæsar reforms the calendar by introducing the solar for the lunar year.	44. Cæsar assassinated. Antony, master of Rome. 43. Second triumvirate,—Octavius Cæsar, Mark Antony, and Lepidus 42. Battle of Philippi; defeat and death of Brutus and Cassius.			
39 (?)	Pollio founds first public library at Rome.	31. Battle of Actium. Antony defeated. Octavius, master of Roman world. 27. Titles of Augustus and Emperor conferred on Octavius for ten years.			31 Defeat at Actium. 30. Suicide of Antony and Cleopatra. Egypt passes to Rome.
		19. Conquest of Spain completed. Death of Virgil. 15. Austria and other territory conquered by Drusus is added to the Empire.			
8	Calendar corrected by Augustus.	4 or 6 (about). Birth of Christ.			

A. D.	FROM THE BIRTH OF CHRIST TO THE FALL OF ROME—B. C. 4–A. D. 476		
	ARTS OF CIVILIZATION	DEVELOPMENT OF CHRISTIANITY	THE ROMAN EMPIRE
		29. Crucifixion of Jesus.	6. Romans abandon Germany. 14. Augustus dies at Nola; is succeeded by Tiberius as emperor. 29. Agrippina banished. 37. Tiberius succeeded by Caligula, noted for his profligacy. 41. Claudius, emperor.
46	Birth of Plutarch, Greek biographer and moralist.	44–66. Judea under the Roman procurators. 47–48. Paul's first missionary tour; into Asia Minor.	46. Thrace becomes a Roman province. 47. The Romans subjugate southern Britain. 48. Claudius orders a census to be taken.
50 (about)	Development of realistic sculpture in Rome.	49–52. Paul's second missionary tour; reaches Athens and Corinth. 52–56. Paul's third missionary tour; long residence at Ephesus. 59 or 60. Paul a prisoner in Rome. 64 or 65. Martyrdom of Paul and Peter. 70. Destruction of Jerusalem by Titus.	49. He expels the Jews from Rome. Builds a camp on the site of London. 51. Caractacus, king of the Britons, is brought to Rome in chains. 54. Nero, emperor; a profligate and tyrant. 61. Revolt of the Britons under Queen Boadicea. 64. Nero sets fire to Rome; accuses Christians. 68. Galba, emperor. 69. Otho, emperor. Vitellius defeats Otho. Vespasian defeats Vitellius. 70. Vespasian, emperor.

A. D.	FROM THE BIRTH OF CHRIST TO THE FALL OF ROME—B. C. 4–A. D. 476—CON.		
	ARTS OF CIVILIZATION	DEVELOPMENT OF CHRISTIANITY	THE ROMAN EMPIRE
75	Vespasian undertakes the building of the Colosseum.		
78	Era of Shalivahana, or Shaka, in India.		78. Agricola, governor of Britain; completes conquest as far north as Scottish Highlands.
			79. Titus, emperor.
	Jurisprudence flourishes.		Pompeii and Herculaneum destroyed by Vesuvius.
	Forum built.	95. Persecution of the Christians by Domitian.	81. Domitian, emperor.
	Pillar of Trajan, and Baths.		96. Nerva, emperor.
	Bridge built over the Danube.	107. Persecution by Trajan.	98. Trajan, emperor; Roman Empire at its greatest extent.
	Silver Age of Roman literature.	118. Persecution by Hadrian.	117. Hadrian, emperor; makes a journey through the provinces; visits Britain and builds there a wall from the Tyne to Solway Firth; builds a wall from the Rhine to the Danube.
130 (about)	Great buildings of Palmyra.	134. Heresy of Marcion.	
	The Pantheon built at Rome.		138. Antoninus, emperor.
		150. Canon of Scriptures fixed about this time.	145–152. Antoninus defeats the Moors, Jews, and Brigantes.
			Antoninus partly stops the persecution of the Christians.
166 (?)	Apuleius writes the *Golden Ass*, one of the earliest romances.		161. Marcus Aurelius, emperor.
			166. Very destructive Asiatic plague in the empire.
			191. Rome nearly destroyed by fire.
			193. Septimius Severus, emperor. A vigorous ruler. Emperors (to 284) appointed by the army.
			194. Septimius Severus besieges Byzantium.
		202. Persecution under Severus.	208. Severus builds the wall of Severus in Britain.
			226. Artaxerxes begins the new kingdom of Persia.
		235. Persecution under Maximinus.	232. Persian war.
		250. Persecution of the Christians.	240 (about). The Franks appear in history.
			248. Celebration of 1000th anniversary of the founding of Rome.
			253–268. Goths invade Asia Minor and Greece.
			261. Sapor, the Persian, takes Antioch.
		262. Paul, bishop of Samosata, denies the divinity of Jesus Christ.	264. Alliance with Odenathus, king of Palmyra, who is succeeded by his wife Zenobia, who reigns with the titles of "Augusta" and "Queen of the East."
			270. Aurelian, a great warrior, becomes emperor.
			271. Aurelian defeats the Alemanni.
		272. Persecution of Christians under Aurelian.	272. Zenobia conquers Egypt.
			273. Aurelian reduces Palmyra and takes Queen Zenobia prisoner.
			274. Franks, Spain, and Britain reduced to obedience.
			275. Aurelian killed near Byzantium.
			276. Great wall around Rome completed.
		277. The emperor Probus expels the Germans from Gaul.	
		283 (about). Religious ceremonies multiplied.	284. Diocletian, emperor.
		Pagan rites imitated by the Christians.	
		296. Monks in Spain and Egypt.	296. Diocletian divides the empire among four assistant rulers.
		303. Persecution under Diocletian.	
305 (about)	Constantine's Basilica built at Rome.	311. Galerius recognizes Christianity.	305. Diocletian and Maximian resign the empire to Constantius and Galerius.
		313. Edict of Milan proclaims religious toleration.	
		325. Council of Nicæa.	324. Constantine the Great, first Christian emperor.
			330. Founding of Constantinople.
			337. Death of Constantine; accession of his three sons to the empire.
		339. Persecution of Christians in Persia.	364. Death of Jovian; accession of Valentinian and Valens, under whom the empire is divided.

			WESTERN EMPIRE	EASTERN EMPIRE
			364. Valentinian, emperor.	364. Valens, emperor.
		373. Bible translated into Gothic language.	368. The Picts and Scots invade Britain, but are defeated by Theodosius.	
		Death of Athanasius.	375. Valentinian gains victory over the Germans.	
				376. Hungary, ancient Pannonia, invaded by the Huns, from whom it is named.
		379. Prerogatives of the Roman See much enlarged.		379. Theodosius the Great becomes emperor; a zealous supporter of Christianity.

FROM THE BIRTH OF CHRIST TO THE FALL OF ROME—B. C. 4–A. D. 476—CON.

A. D.	ARTS OF CIVILIZATION	DEVELOPMENT OF CHRISTIANITY	WESTERN EMPIRE	EASTERN EMPIRE
382	St. Jerome revises the Latin version of the New Testament at Rome.	381. Second general Council of Constantinople. 384. Symmachus pleads in the Roman Senate for paganism against St. Ambrose. 392. St. Chrysostom, patriarch of Constantinople.	388. St. Patrick taken captive to Ireland by Niall of the Nine Hostages. 392. Theodosius becomes sole emperor of the East and West.	388. Theodosius defeats Maximus, the tyrant of the Western Empire.
394	Olympian games abolished.		394. Final division of empire between the sons of Theodosius. 401. Europe overrun by the Visigoths. 406–409. Vandals allowed to settle in Spain and Gaul. 410. The Goths under Alaric sack and burn Rome. 412. Rise of the Vandal power in Spain. 413. Burgundian kingdom begun near the Rhine.	408. Theodosius II, a child, emperor. 410. Honorius abdicates his kingship of Britain.
420	St. Jerome dies, after completing translation of the Bible (Vulgate).	416. The Pelagian heresy condemned.	420. The Franks form a kingdom, under Pharamond, on the lower Rhine. 425. Valentinian III, emperor.	414. Regency of the emperor's sister, Pulcheria. 420. Persian war. 425. University of Constantinople organized.
426	St. Augustine of Hippo publishes his famous work *De Civitate Dei,* "The City of God."	431. Third general Council at Ephesus. 432. St. Patrick preaches the Gospel in Ireland. 435. Nestorianism prevails in the East.		
450	Establishment of Buddhism in Burma.	443. The Manichean books burned in Rome. 447. Eutyches asserts the existence of only one nature in Jesus Christ. 451. Fourth general Council at Chalcedon.	439. The Vandals, under Genseric, form Kingdom of Africa, take Carthage, and plunder Italy. 449–455. Arrival of Saxons in Britain. 451. Battle of Châlons. Attila driven back east of Rhine. 452. City of Venice founded. 455. Rome plundered by Vandals. 458. Franks, under Childeric I, conquer as far as the Loire and take Paris.	442. Thrace invaded by Attila. 450. Marcian, emperor. 457–461. War with the Goths. 457–484. Peroz rules in Persia.
473	Topography of Japan written for the first time by Ki no Tsuno no Sukune.	465–476. Oligarchy of the bishops of Rome, Constantinople, Alexandria, Antioch, and Jerusalem. The Church now begins to assume a political aspect.	466–483. The Visigoths under Eric establish their kingdom in Spain. 476. Odoacer, king of the Heruli, takes Rome and founds a short-lived kingdom lasting fourteen years. With him ends the Roman Empire and ancient history in Europe.	474. Zeno, emperor; a turbulent reign marked by debauchery and conspiracies.

FROM THE FALL OF ROME TO THE DIVISION OF THE WESTERN EMPIRE—A. D. 476–843

A. D.	ARTS OF CIVILIZATION	THE EASTERN EMPIRE	GREAT BRITAIN AND IRELAND	ITALY AND THE CHURCH	FRANCE
	FIFTH CENTURY				
		477. A rising in Constantinople.	477. Saxons win foothold in Sussex. Followed by other Saxons (Wessex and Essex) and by Angles.	482. Christians persecuted by the Vandals.	481. Clovis I, founder of the French monarchy. 486. Battle of Soissons gained by Clovis.
493	Theodoric gives new impetus to architecture in Italy. Beautiful buildings at Ravenna.	488. Theodoric, chief of the Ostrogoths, invades Italy.	491. Capture of Anderida by Ella, king of the South Saxons.	493. Italy conquered by Theodoric, chief of the Ostrogoths.	

A. D.	FROM THE FALL OF ROME TO THE DIVISION OF THE WESTERN EMPIRE—A. D. 476–843—CON.				
	ARTS OF CIVILIZATION	THE EASTERN EMPIRE	GREAT BRITAIN AND IRELAND	ITALY AND THE CHURCH	FRANCE
			495. Beginning of the kingdom of Wessex, under Cerdic and Cymric.		496. Clovis baptized. Christianity introduced into France.
	SIXTH CENTURY				
524 (about)	Cassiodorus (490–580), in his library and monastery, encourages learning. *Consolations of Philosophy* by Boethius.	503–505. War with Persia.	520. Battle of Mt. Badon. West Saxons defeated by Britons.	510. Boethius becomes consul at Rome. 524. Boethius put to death by Theodoric. 526. Death of Theodoric.	510. Clovis makes Paris his capital.
531	Khosru I, king of Persia, great patron of learning.	527. Justinian I begins a brilliant reign over the Eastern, or Byzantine, Empire. 528. Belisarius, the famous general, defeats the Persians.		529. Order of the Benedictine monks instituted at Monte Cassino, near Naples.	
532	The Christian era proposed and introduced by Dionysius, a monk. Completion of Justinian's code. Manufacture of silk introduced from China into Europe by monks.	533. Belisarius defeats the Vandals in Africa. 534. Belisarius takes possession of Africa, Sardinia, and Balearic Isles. 535. Belisarius subdues Sicily. 536. Belisarius takes Naples and Rome.			534. Burgundy conquered by the Franks.
537	Church of Santa Sophia at Constantinople completed. Alexander of Tralles, a noted physician, teaches prevention of disease as important part of physician's work. St. Benedict establishes his "rule," enjoining both labor and prayer. The Benedictines begin important work in agriculture and industry.	548–553. Italy governed by Greek Exarchs. 552. Narses overthrows Totila. End of Ostrogothic kingdom. 558. A plague extends over Europe and Asia and lasts about fifty years. 570. Birth of Mohammed.	547. Ida, king of Bernicia. 552. Cymric, king of West Saxons, captures Sorbiodunum. Master of Salisbury plain. Union of Celtic tribes, under name of Cymry, or Comrades. 593. Ethelbert, king of Kent, gains the ascendancy.	536. Italy conquered by Belisarius, for Justinian. 539. Milan ravaged by the Goths. 568. Italy conquered by the Lombards. 590. Gregory the Great, bishop of Rome. Beginning of the papacy. 597. St. Augustine, goes as missionary to Britain; made first archbishop of Canterbury.	536. Ostrogoths surrender their possessions in Gaul to the Franks. 557. Church of St. Germain des Prés built at Paris. 558. Clothaire I, king; unites Franks into a kingdom. 561. Clothaire dies; kingdom again broken up into petty states.
	SEVENTH CENTURY				
600	First code of English laws drawn up by Ethelbert. Literature and learning fostered in English abbeys of Whitby and Glastonbury. Rise of Mohammedanism. Islamism and the power of the caliphs established in the East. In the caliphs were united the highest spiritual and regal authority.	602. Invasion of the Persians. 610. Heraclius takes Constantinople, kills Phocas, the emperor, and makes himself king. 614. Jerusalem taken by the Persians. 622. The Hegira, or Mohammed's flight, from Mecca to Medina. 632. Death of Mohammed.	600 (about). St. Paul's church founded by Ethelbert of Kent. St. Peter's (1050, Westminster Abbey) founded by Sebert of Essex. 626. Edwin of Northumbria, overlord of English kingdoms.	608 (about). The Pantheon of Rome dedicated to Christianity. 625–640. Churches of Jerusalem, Antioch, and Alexandria lost to the Christian world by the sweep of Mohammedanism.	613. Clothaire II, king. Franks again united under one king. 630 (about). Dagobert I builds the church of St. Denis, the sepulture of the French kings.
633 (about)	Isidore of Seville encourages learning in the West.	636. Omar, caliph, takes Jerusalem.	664. Synod of Whitby; triumph of Roman over Celtic Church.		

A. D.	FROM THE FALL OF ROME TO THE DIVISION OF THE WESTERN EMPIRE—A. D. 476–843—CON.				
	ARTS OF CIVILIZATION	THE EASTERN EMPIRE	GREAT BRITAIN AND IRELAND	ITALY AND THE CHURCH	FRANCE
633 (about)– con.	Arts and crafts encouraged by Dagobert I, Frankish king. Appreciation of art and literature preserved in Ravenna.	673. Siege of Constantinople by the Saracens, whose fleet is destroyed by the Greek fire of Callinicus. 680. First kingdom of Bulgaria founded. 698. Carthage destroyed by the Saracens, and the north coast of Africa subjugated.	673. First English church council at Hertford. 688–726. Ine, king of Wessex.	680. The sixth general Council called at Constantinople.	687. Pepin d'Heristal, mayor of the palace.
	EIGHTH CENTURY	709. North Africa subdued by the Saracens. 711. Saracens cross over to Spain.			714. Charles Martel, mayor of the palace.
	Charlemagne's schools provide for women as well as men. Charlemagne founds hospitals. Three great scholars of the 8th century: Bede, John of Damascus, Vergilius of Salzburg.	717. Leo III, emperor. 718. The Saracens invest Constantinople, by land and sea. City saved by Greek fire. 746–747. A plague in Constantinople.	735. Death of the Venerable Bede.	726. The emperor Leo forbids image worship. 751. The pope dethrones Childeric, king of France, by a papal decree.	725. Charles Martel subdues Bavaria. 732. Charles Martel defeats the Saracens at battle of Tours. 751. End of Merovingian line of French kings. Pepin the Short, first of the Carolingian line.
	Golden period of learning in Arabia under Caliph Haroun-al-Raschid and Caliph Al-Mamun. Foundation of schools in monasteries and cathedrals by Charlemagne.	755–775. Constantine V wars with the Bulgarians. 762 (about). Caliph Al-Mansur builds Baghdad and makes it his capital. 783. The Empire makes peace with the Arabs.	757. Offa of Mercia begins his reign. 787. First recorded invasion of the Danes—the sea kings and vikings.	754. Pepin aids Pope Stephen III against the Lombards. 756. Donation of Pepin. Foundation of Papal States. 787. Seventh general Council of Nicæa.	771. Charlemagne becomes sole ruler of Franks.
	NINTH CENTURY				
	Agriculture and horticulture encouraged by Charlemagne; both flourish in Spain under the caliphs. Rapid growth of feudal system.	812. Peace between Michael I and Charlemagne. 816. A council condemns the worship of images.	815–823. Egbert, king of Wessex, conquers the Britons in Cornwall.	800. Charlemagne reforms the Church. Many bishoprics founded.	800. Charlemagne founds the new Western Empire and is crowned at Rome, emperor of the Romans. 801. Charlemagne receives an embassy from Haroun-al-Raschid. 814. Death of Charlemagne. His son, Louis the Pious, succeeds him.
827 (about)	Arabian geographers calculate size of earth. John Scotus Erigena, great scholar of the century.	827. Arabia begins conquest of Sicily. 829. Theophilus, emperor.	827. The Anglo-Saxon kingdoms acknowledge Egbert, king of Wessex, as suzerain or overlord. 839. Death of Egbert, king of the West Saxons, who had become overlord of the other kingdoms. Ethelwulf, king. About this time, Kenneth MacAlpin unites Picts and Scots in one kingdom.	827–865. Christianity carried to Denmark and Sweden.	840. Louis the Debenair dies; his three sons fight for the possession of the kingdom. 841–844. The Northmen take Rouen and Nantes and advance to Toulouse.
	Venetians become a great merchant people. Architecture encouraged in Venice. St. Mark's cathedral built.	842. Theodora restores image worship.			843. Treaty of Verdun. Charles I, king of France. Louis I, king of Germany. Lothair, king of Italy.

A. D.	FROM THE DIVISION OF THE WESTERN EMPIRE TO THE NORMAN CONQUEST OF ENGLAND—A. D. 843–1066			
	ARTS OF CIVILIZATION	ITALY AND THE CHURCH	EASTERN EMPIRE	THE BRITISH ISLES
		844. Ignatius, patriarch of Constantinople. 846. The Saracens destroy the Venetian fleet and besiege Rome. 850. Persecution of the Christians in Spain.	844 (about). Decline of the caliphate begins. Frequent wars between the Greeks and the Saracens.	851. Danes capture and sack Canterbury and London. 855. Danes begin to settle in England.
		860. The False Decretals brought to Rome.		
866 (about)	Bible translated into Slavonian.	866. Schism of the Greeks begins. 869. Eighth Council at Constantinople.	866. Synod of Constantinople. Break between Eastern and Western Church. 867. Basil inaugurates the Macedonian dynasty.	866–870. Danish conquest of Northumbria.
	Alfred gives great encouragement to literature and learning in England; founds schools; codifies English law.			871. Alfred the Great becomes king of Wessex.
		877. Arabs take Syracuse.		878. Alfred defeats the Danes. Treaty of Chippenham. Danes retain eastern and northern England.
882	First mention of episcopal school at Paris,—later became university.		886. Leo VI, emperor.	886. Danes surrender London to Alfred.
	The Moors in Spain promote architecture and adorn their cities with rich buildings.		890. Southern Italy subject to the Greek Empire. Seat of power at Bari.	
	Cordova, in Spain, becomes famous as a center of science, learning, industry, and commerce.	911 (about). The Normans in France embrace Christianity.	907. Russian expedition under Oleg against Constantinople.	899 (?). Edward the Elder succeeds Alfred. At his death in 925 he was overlord of all the kingdoms.
	The figures of arithmetic brought into Europe by the Saracens.	921 (about). The Bohemians adopt Christianity.	919. Romanus, general of the fleet, usurps the empire and rules with his three sons.	
	Linens and woolens manufactured in Flanders.			925. Athelstan, king.
932	Printing in use in China. Confucian Canon printed.			
	Hroswitha, the nun at Gandersheim, writes comedies to counteract evil influence of classical plays.		941. Romanus gains a naval victory over the Russians.	937. Athelstan defeats the northern king at Brunanburh. 943. Malcolm I, king of Scotland.
		955. Baptism of Olga; conversion of Russia to Christianity. 959. St. Dunstan, archbishop of Canterbury, attempts to reform the Church. 962. Otto crowned emperor of the Romans by Pope John XII. Holy Roman Empire of the German Nation.	959. Emperor Romanus II. 966. Miecislas, king of Poland, becomes a Christian. 969. The Fatimites subjugate Egypt.	955. Dunstan, abbot of Glastonbury, rises to great power.
980	Birth of Avicenna, Arabic writer on medicine.			984. Renewed Danish invasions.

A. D.	FROM THE DIVISION OF THE WESTERN EMPIRE TO THE NORMAN CONQUEST OF ENGLAND—A. D. 843–1066				
	FRANCE	GERMANY	SPAIN	RUSSIA	LESSER COUNTRIES
		843. Louis I, king.			
845	Northmen take Rouen and sack Paris.				
847	Defense against the inroads of the Northmen occasions the Edict of Mersen, which required every man to have a feudal lord.	847. Raid of the Northmen up the Elbe as far as Hamburg. 855. Louis II becomes king.	850 (about). Under Abderrahman II and his successors, caliphate of Cordova enters period of weakness.		
857	Charles the Bald and Lothair II unite against the Northmen.				
858	Louis of Germany makes war on Charles and Lothair, and is defeated.	860. Peace between Louis and Charles of France.		860. Russian campaign against Constantinople. 862. Rurik the Northman, grand duke of Novgorod.	860. Gorm unites Jutland and the Danish Isles and becomes king of Denmark. 861 (about). Iceland discovered.
			866. Alfonso the Great becomes king of Asturia, the Christian monarchy in Spain, afterward called León.		
870	Lorraine divided between France and Germany by Treaty of Mersen.		873. Sancho Iñigo, count of Navarre.		872. Harold, first king of Norway. 874. Northmen colonize Iceland.
876	First settlement of Northmen in France.	876. Charles the Fat, emperor 882–888.			
879	Louis III and Carloman reign jointly.	881. Treaty of Elslan with the invading Danes.			
885	Paris besieged by Northmen; city defended by Count Odo; Charles the Fat buys off the besiegers.	887. Arnulf, emperor.			889 (about). Arpád lays the foundation of Hungary.
898	Charles III, sole king.	899. Invasion by the Hungarians.	905. Kingdom of Navarre founded. 910. Kingdom of León founded by Garcia.	907. Oleg invades the Greek Empire.	
911	The Northmen, under Rollo, establish themselves in Normandy.	911. Conrad I, king. Carolingian dynasty becomes extinct. 919. Henry the Fowler, king.	912. Abderrahman III begins to reign in Cordova, introducing the golden age of Arabian power in Spain.		
923	Civil wars.				
936	Louis IV, son of Charles the Simple, king.	936. Otto the Great becomes king. 950. Bohemia annexed.	939. Ramiro, king of León, defeats the Moors at Simancas.		933. The union of the two Burgundies, forming the kingdom of Arles, which lasted a century. 951. Decay of Saracen power begins. 955. Otto overcomes the Hungarians on the Lech.
954	Louis confers the dukedoms of Burgundy and Aquitaine on Hugh the Great.		955. Sancho I, king of León.	957. Swatoslav, king of Russia.	
		962. Beginning of the Holy Roman Empire. Crowning of Otto. 978. Otto at war with Lothair.	976. Hisham II, caliph of Cordova.	980. Vladimir the Great, the first Christian ruler.	
986	Louis V, last of the Carolingians.				

A. D.	FROM THE DIVISION OF THE WESTERN EMPIRE TO THE NORMAN CONQUEST OF ENGLAND—A. D. 843–1066—CON.			
	ARTS OF CIVILIZATION	ITALY AND THE CHURCH	EASTERN EMPIRE	THE BRITISH ISLES
997	Venice under the doges dominates the Mediterranean and with Genoa rises to great importance in commerce.	989. Greek Christianity propagated in Russia by Vladimir. 993. First canonization of saints. 999. Hungary becomes a fief of the Church.	996. War with Bulgaria.	994. Olaf Trygvasson and Svend attack London.
	ELEVENTH CENTURY Firdousi, the Persian Homer, flourishes (940?–1020). Great activity in the repairing and rebuilding of churches. Rise of the Romanesque style of architecture. Foundation of University of Salerno; a famous medical school was chief department. Teachers in this school, famous surgeons. Both women and men admitted.	1024. John XIX, pope.	1001. Invasion of India by Mahmud of Ghazni. 1018. Bulgaria reduced to a Grecian province.	1002. Massacre of the Danes in England. 1002–14. Brian Boroihme, sole ruler of Ireland. 1005. Scotland ruled by Malcolm II. 1013. Danes, under Svend, become masters of England. 1016. Edmund Ironside fights six battles with Canute, king of the Danes, with whom he divides the kingdom. Edmund dies, leaving Canute sole ruler.
	Truce of God, forbidding warfare on certain days and at certain seasons, an effort toward peace in this disturbed century.			1034. Duncan, king of Scotland. 1040. Macbeth murders Duncan and usurps the throne.
	Lanfranc and Queen Matilda famous for their establishment of hospitals. Anselm, great scholar of this century.	1041. Normans establish power in Apulia. 1049. Leo IX, the first pope to keep an army. 1054. Excommunication of the patriarch of Constantinople and the Greeks. 1059. Quarrel between the popes and the German emperors. Robert Guiscard, duke of Apulia.	1042. First invasion of the Seljuk Turks. 1043. The Russians invade Thrace with 100,000 men and are repulsed by the Greeks. 1054. Theodora, last of the Macedonian dynasty. 1058. Supremacy of the Seljuk Turks.	1042. The Saxon line restored under Edward the Confessor. 1051. William, duke of Normandy, visits England. 1066. Harold II, king, killed at the battle of Hastings. William the Conqueror, king. End of the Anglo-Saxon line.

A. D.	FROM THE NORMAN CONQUEST OF ENGLAND TO THE FALL OF THE EASTERN EMPIRE—A. D. 1066–1453			
	ARTS OF CIVILIZATION	ITALY AND THE CHURCH	EASTERN EMPIRE	THE BRITISH ISLES
	Margaret of Scotland, wife of Malcolm III, does much to refine manners and secure justice for the poor.	The papacy at the height of its power. College of Cardinals founded by Nicholas II for the election of the popes. 1073. Quarrel of Pope Gregory VII (Hildebrand) with the emperor Henry IV. 1074. Celibacy of the clergy decreed at a council summoned by Pope Gregory VII. 1075. The pope sends legates to the various courts of Europe. 1077. Submission of Henry IV to the pope at Canossa.	1071. Emperor Romanus IV defeated and taken prisoner by the Turks. Turks seize Asia Minor; Normans take Bari, last Greek possession in Italy. 1074. Syria and Palestine subdued by Melek Shah.	1070. Lanfranc, archbishop of Canterbury. 1071 (about). Feudal system introduced. 1075. Rebellion of the Norman earls against William.

A. D.	FROM THE DIVISION OF THE WESTERN EMPIRE TO THE NORMAN CONQUEST OF ENGLAND—A. D. 843–1066—CON.				
	FRANCE	GERMANY	SPAIN	RUSSIA	LESSER COUNTRIES
987	Hugh Capet, king, and founder of the Capetian line of French kings.				
996	Robert II succeeds his father on the throne.		999. Alfonso V, king of León.		994. Svend I of Denmark invades England.
1000	The end of the world expected; consequent religious excitement.	1002. Henry II, emperor.			1000 (about). Hungary a kingdom under its first hereditary king, St. Stephen.
				1015. Death of Vladimir.	1014. Canute II, king of Denmark.
					1017. Canute supreme in England.
				1019. Yaroslav rules Russia.	
		1024. Conrad II, first of the Franconian line.	1020 (about). Rise of burgher class.		
1031	Henry I, king.		1031. Ommiad dynasty ends with death of Hisham III of Cordova.		1028. Norway conquered by Canute. Danish ascendancy.
1034	Burgundy annexed.		1033. Sancho the Great of Navarre constitutes Castile a kingdom.		
		1039. Henry III becomes emperor.	1035. Ramiro I, king of Aragon.		
		1041. Henry III defeats the Bohemians and Hungarians. Truce of God proclaimed.			
		1054. Henry III causes his son, Henry, to be proclaimed king of the Romans. This title was applied for several centuries to the emperor's eldest son.		1054. Russia violently dismembered. Civil wars and great distress.	1055. The Turks reduce Bagdad and overturn the empire of the caliphs.
1066	William, duke of Normandy, claims the crown of England and wars on Harold to obtain it.				

A. D.	FROM THE NORMAN CONQUEST OF ENGLAND TO THE FALL OF THE EASTERN EMPIRE—A. D. 1066–1453				
	FRANCE	GERMANY	SPAIN	RUSSIA	LESSER COUNTRIES
					1067. Polish conquests in Russia.
					1069. Olaf III, king of Norway.
					1070. Bergen, Norway, built.
1073	Maine conquered by William, king of England.	1073. Revolt of the Saxons.	1072. Alfonso VI, king of Castile and León.		
			1074–99. Time of Rodrigo Díaz, "the Cid."		
1079	Birth of Abélard.	1077–80. Civil war in Germany.			

A. D.	FROM THE NORMAN CONQUEST OF ENGLAND TO THE FALL OF THE EASTERN EMPIRE—A. D. 1066–1453—CON.			
	ARTS OF CIVILIZATION	ITALY AND THE CHURCH	EASTERN EMPIRE	THE BRITISH ISLES
	Omar Khayyam, poet-astronomer of Persia, corrects the calendar.	1084. Triumph of Henry IV over Gregory. The order of the Carthusians instituted by Bruno. 1095. Peter the Hermit preaches against the Turks. 1096. The First Crusade.	1081. Alexius I (Comnenus), emperor. 1082. Robert Guiscard invades the empire and defeats Alexius. 1084. After the capture of Jerusalem by the Turks, the Christian pilgrims are insulted and oppressed, which gives rise to the Crusades. 1099. Jerusalem taken by Godfrey. Battle of Ascalon and defeat of the Turks. 1104. Battle of Acre. 1109. Tripoli taken by crusaders.	1087. William invades France and is killed at Mantes. 1093. Malcolm III of Scotland invades England and is slain near Alnwick castle. 1100. Henry I, king of England, unites the Normans and Saxons. 1107. Henry's quarrel with Anselm ended.
1118	Knights Templars instituted. Scholastic philosophy reaches a high point under Abélard. Age of cathedral building. Rise of the Gothic style. Colleges of theology, philosophy, and law at Paris. Woolen manufactories established in England.	1123. First Lateran, or ninth general, Council. 1127. Pope Honorius II makes war against Roger, king of Sicily 1139. Second Lateran, or tenth general, Council. Senate revived in Rome. 1147. The Second Crusade. 1154. Pope Adrian IV, an Englishman. 1167. Rome taken by Frederick Barbarossa. League of Lombard cities formed. 1172. Grand Council of Venice formed. 1178. Renewed activity of the Waldenses, forerunners of Protestantism. 1179. Third Lateran, or eleventh general, Council. Waldensian teaching forbidden. 1189. The Third Crusade.	1118. John Comnenus reforms the manners of his people. 1124. Tyre taken by crusaders. 1143. Manuel Comnenus, emperor. 1171–74. War between Venice and the Eastern Empire. Venetians keep their commercial privileges. 1175. Saladin founds the Sultanate of Egypt. 1185. Dynasty of the Comneni overthrown.	1124. David I promotes civilization in Scotland. 1154. Henry II, king of England; also possessed more than half of France. 1155–64. Ascendancy of Thomas Becket, archbishop of Canterbury. 1170. Becket assassinated at the instigation of Henry II. 1171. Henry invades Ireland. 1188. Collection of the Saladin Tithe. Beginning of taxation on movable goods. 1189. Richard I engages in the Third Crusade. 1193. John attempts to seize the crown in the absence of Richard.

A. D.	FROM THE NORMAN CONQUEST OF ENGLAND TO THE FALL OF THE EASTERN EMPIRE—A. D. 1066-1453—CON.				
	FRANCE	GERMANY	SPAIN	RUSSIA	LESSER COUNTRIES
		1080. Henry degrades the pope and triumphs.			
		1090–1100. The popes continue their struggle against the Empire.	1085. Toledo taken from the Moors by Alfonso. 1094. Pedro I, king of Navarre and Aragon. 1095. Conquest of Valencia by the Cid.		1084. Bohemia made a kingdom by Henry IV of Germany. 1090. Sicily taken from the Saracens by Roger the Norman.
1096	Many French noblemen take part in the First Crusade.				
1100 (about)	Rise of the troubadours in Provence.			1100 (about). Many ephemeral principalities contend for supremacy in Russia.	
			1104. Alfonso I, king of Navarre and Aragon.		
1108	Abbé Suger, minister to Louis VI of France.	1111. Henry V enters Italy and compels the pope, who is his prisoner, to crown him. 1114. Henry V marries Matilda of England.			
			1118. Alfonso captures Saragossa.		1119. Charles the Good becomes count of Flanders.
		1125. Lothair II opposed by Conrad and Frederick, duke of Swabia. 1138. Dissensions of the Guelphs and Ghibellines break out.			
1147	Louis VII joins the Second Crusade.		1139. Battle of Ourique. Alfonso, duke of Portugal, defeats Saracens and Moors and becomes first king of Portugal.	1147. Moscow founded.	1139. Pope Innocent compelled to recognize the kingdom of Sicily and southern Italy, under Roger. 1150–1162. Erik the Saint, king of Sweden; Christianity introduced.
		1152. Frederick Barbarossa, emperor of Germany and Italy.			
			1157. Castile and León divided.		
1159	War with the English.			1158. Riga on the Baltic founded.	
1170	Rise of the Waldenses.	1169. Frederick's son, Henry, crowned king of the Romans. This title afterward implied the right to the imperial throne. 1174. Frederick's fifth expedition into Italy. 1176. Frederick defeated at the battle of Legnano.	1169. Towns send representatives to the Cortes of Castile.	1169. Final overthrow of Kiev.	1167. League of the Italian cities. 1171. Saladin, sultan of Egypt, extends his dominions; conquers Syria, Assyria, and Arabia.
		1183. The Peace of Constance reestablishes the independence of the Italian republics.	1188. Alfonso IX, king of León.		1187. Saladin directs all his efforts against the crusaders; takes Jerusalem.
1190	Philip Augustus, one of the leaders of the Third Crusade.	1190. Henry VI, emperor, and king of Italy.			1191. Battle of Ascalon. Saladin defeated. 1193. Death of Saladin.

A. D.	FROM THE NORMAN CONQUEST OF ENGLAND TO THE FALL OF THE EASTERN EMPIRE—A. D. 1066–1453—CON.			
	ARTS OF CIVILIZATION	ITALY AND THE CHURCH	EASTERN EMPIRE	THE BRITISH ISLES
	Period of the troubadours in France; the minstrels in England; minnesingers in Germany.	1202. The Fourth Crusade. Constantinople taken.	1204. The crusaders plunder Constantinople.	1199. John, king of England.
		1215. Fourth Lateran Council, against the Albigenses. 1217. The Crusade of Andrew II of Hungary.		1215. Magna Charta signed at Runnymede. 1216. Henry III, king.
1222	University of Padua founded.			
	Architecture, and arts and crafts flourish in western Europe.	1226. The Lombard League renewed to resist Frederick. 1228–1270. Fifth, Sixth, and Seventh crusades.		
1229	University of Cambridge, England, founded. Rise of strong guilds of artisans.	1229. Papal troops defeat Frederick's army and occupy the mainland part of the Kingdom of the Two Sicilies.	1229. Frederick II occupies Jerusalem, which is ceded to the Christians by the sultan of Egypt.	1236. Henry marries Eleanor of Provence.
1239 (about)	Coal mining begun at Newcastle-upon-Tyne.			
1250 (about)	Roger Bacon describes principle of the telescope.	1243. Struggle of Pope Innocent IV with Emperor Frederick.		1254. Knights of the shires in Parliament. 1258. Famous "mad" Parliament at Oxford.
	Literature and science flourish in Spain under Alfonso the Learned.	1267. Dominion of Italy passes to the pope. 1274. Fourteenth general Council at Lyons.	1261. Emperor Michael Palæologus recovers Constantinople.	1265. First regular Parliament. Civil war. 1272–1307. Reign of Edward I.
1280	Institution of the three great courts of law in England.			1276. War between England and Wales. 1283. England and Wales united.
			1288 (about). Osman establishes an independent rule in the north of Asia Minor.	1291-92. Robert Bruce and John Balliol contend for the crown of Scotland.
	Cimabue, the first of modern painters at Florence. Roger Bacon makes many scientific discoveries.	1296. Struggle of the Church with France. Bull *Clericis Laicos* forbids ecclesiastics to pay taxes to the civil power.	1299 (about). Osman invades Nicomedia; establishes the Ottoman empire.	1296. Scotland submits to England. 1297. Scotland rebels. War between England and Scotland follows.
	FOURTEENTH CENTURY			
1300 (about)	Beginning of the Renaissance or revival of learning. Indian spinning wheel introduced into Europe. Knives made in England at Sheffield.			
1301	Duns Scotus becomes professor of theology at Oxford.	1303. Papal power declines.	Genoese control trade of Black Sea.	
				1304. Scotland conquered by Edward I. 1306. Robert Bruce proclaimed king of Scotland. War with England continued.
		1309. Seat of the popes transferred to Avignon. 1311. General Council at Vienna. 1312. Knights Templars condemned by the Council of Vienna.		1314. Bruce defeats the English at Bannockburn, June 24.

A. D.	FROM THE NORMAN CONQUEST OF ENGLAND TO THE FALL OF THE EASTERN EMPIRE—A. D. 1066–1453—CON.				
	FRANCE	GERMANY	SPAIN	RUSSIA	LESSER COUNTRIES
1204	Normandy reunited to France.				1206 (about). Jenghis Khan subdues the north of China.
1207	Albigensian crusade begun.		1212. The Christians gain the battle of Las Navas de Tolosa.		
1214	Battle of Bouvines.	1215. Frederick II, crowned emperor.	1217. Ferdinand, king of Castile.		1216 (about). Tartary overrun by Jenghis Khan.
1223	Louis VIII conducts crusade against the Albigenses.			1224. Mongolian invasion, known as the "Golden Horde."	1222. Hungarian liberty assured by charter of Andrew II.
1226	Louis IX, king.	1226. Frederick grants Prussian territory to Teutonic Knights.			
		1230. Teutonic Knights begin to settle in Prussia.	1230. Castile and León united by Ferdinand III, who takes large territory from the Moors.	1237. Second Mongolian invasion. Moscow burned. 1238. Russian independence overthrown by the Tatars. Khan of Kiptchak, grand duke.	
1248	Louis IX leads the Sixth Crusade.	1250. Conrad IV, emperor.	1250–1282. Alfonso the Learned, king of León and Castile.		1241. Mongolian invasion of Europe under Batu Khan.
					1258. Mongols overthrow caliphate of Bagdad.
1270	Louis IX sets out on the Last Crusade.	1273. Rudolf, emperor, founds house of Habsburg.	1274. Crown of Navarre passes to France.	Khan of Kiptchak wields strong rule in Russia.	1267 (about). Kublai Khan builds Peking and makes it his capital.
1276	France at war with Castile.				
1294	English fiefs in France declared forfeited.	1291. League of Swiss cantons formed.	1291. James II, king of Aragon.		1290. Wenceslas, king of Bohemia, takes Cracow.
1297	Invasion of Flanders.	1298. Adolphus, emperor, deposed and Albert I enthroned.	1296. Ferdinand IV, king of Castile. Period of anarchy.		1299 (about). Foundation of the Ottoman empire.
				1300. Kremlin built.	
1302	First convocation of the States-General in France.				
1304	War with Flanders.				
		1308. Henry of Luxemburg, emperor. 1309. Swiss Confederacy recognized by the emperor.			1307. Swiss republic founded.
1315	Edict for the enfranchisement of slaves.	1314. Louis of Bavaria and Frederick of Austria contend for the crown.	1312. Alfonso XI, king of Castile and León.		

A. D.	FROM THE NORMAN CONQUEST OF ENGLAND TO THE FALL OF THE EASTERN EMPIRE—A. D. 1066–1453—CON.			
	ARTS OF CIVILIZATION	ITALY AND THE CHURCH	EASTERN EMPIRE	THE BRITISH ISLES
1318	Dante completes *Divina Commedia*; dies 1321.			
			1321. Civil war in the Eastern Empire between the emperor and his grandson.	
			1326. Orkhan, sultan of the Turks, makes Brusa his capital.	1328. Peace. Independence of Scotland.
1340	Chaucer, father of English poetry, born in London.	Struggle in Rome between the Colonna and the Orsini.		1337. Struggle for the French crown begins.
1340 (?)	Coal used in iron smelting in Belgium.			1346. Battle of Crécy.
1347	First recorded importation of wheat into England.	1347. Democracy in Rome under Rienzi, last of the tribunes.		1348. The plague of the Black Death sweeps over Europe, lasting four years.
1352	Library of St. Mark's in Venice, founded by gifts from Petrarch.	1354. Rienzi killed; papal dominion restored.	1355. John Palæologus, emperor.	1356. Edward, the Black Prince, wins the battle of Poitiers.
			1373. Treaty with Amurath, the Ottoman emperor.	1376. Death of the Black Prince.
		1377. Papal court reestablished at Rome; end of the "Babylonian Captivity."		
		1378. Schism of the West; Pope Urban VI acknowledged in England; Clement VII in France, Spain, and Scotland.		1381. Peasants' Revolt.
				1385. The Scots, assisted by France, invade England.
			1389. Bajazet, sultan of the Turks.	
1400 (about)	Wood engraving.			1399. Henry IV, king. House of Lancaster begins.
1400	Chaucer dies.			
1401	Bank of Barcelona (earliest existing) founded.		1402. Bajazet defeated and made prisoner by Timur at the battle of Angora.	1406. James I, king of Scotland.
		1409. The Council of Pisa.		
		1414. Council of Constance.		1414. Henry V claims the French crown.
		1415-16. Huss and Jerome burned for heresy.		1415. Henry V gains the battle of Agincourt.
		1417. Schism of the West ended by election of Pope Martin V.	1419. The Portuguese explore the Madeira Islands under the patronage of Henry the Navigator.	1422. Death of Henry V. Accession of Henry VI. War with France.
			1425. Emperor John VII visits Italy to obtain help against the Turks.	
1436	First public library in Italy, at Florence; gift of Niccolo Niccoli.			
			1444. Vladislas, king of Poland, defeated and killed by the Turks.	1444. Truce with France.
1447	Vatican library founded.	1447. Congress by which the liberties of the German Church are compromised.		1445. Marriage of Henry to Margaret of Anjou.
1450 (about)	Gutenberg invents printing with metal types.		1448. Constantine XI, last of the Greek emperors.	
1450	The Renaissance, at first a literary revival, now extends to art in general, particularly architecture, which is influenced throughout central and western Europe.		1453. Siege and capture of Constantinople by the Turks, ending the Eastern Empire.	1450. Insurrection of Jack Cade. Richard, duke of York, claims the throne.

A. D.	FROM THE NORMAN CONQUEST OF ENGLAND TO THE FALL OF THE EASTERN EMPIRE—A. D. 1066–1453—CON.				
	FRANCE	GERMANY	SPAIN	RUSSIA	LESSER COUNTRIES
1316	Philip V succeeds by virtue of the Salic law, now first established.	1322. Frederick of Austria defeated.		1318. Finland invaded by Russians.	1319. The oligarchy of Venice established.
1337	War with England.		1340. Moors defeated near Tarifa.		1336. Timur (Tamerlane) born at Kesh, Tartary.
				1346. Novgorod at height of its commercial importance.	
1356	King John defeated and taken prisoner at Poitiers.	1356. Promulgation of the Golden Bull.			1355. Establishment of the Ottomans in Europe.
1360	John regains his liberty; cedes much territory to England.		1365. War between Navarre and France.		1369. Timur makes Samarkand the capital of his new empire.
1380	Charles VI, king.	1378. Wenceslas, king of Bohemia, emperor.		1380. Tatar war. Dimitri Ivanovitch checks Tatars at the Don.	
1382	Defeat of the Flemings at Roosebec. Victory of nobles over the cities.			1382. Moscow burned.	
1386	Fruitless attempt to invade England.	1394. The emperor imprisoned at Prague.		1395. Timur invades Russia. Russia under the Mongol Tatars until 1480.	1389. Swiss force the Habsburgs to make a truce. 1398. Invasion of India by Timur.
		1400. Rupert, Count Palatine, emperor.			
1410	Civil war between Orleans and Burgundy.	1411. Sigismund, king of Hungary, emperor.	1406. John II, king of Castile.	1410. Battle of Tannenberg. Poles and Lithuanians defeat Teutonic Knights.	
1415	French defeated by the English at Agincourt.		1416. Alfonso V, king of Aragon and Sicily.		
1422	Henry VI, proclaimed at Paris, king of France and England.				1419–27. The Hussite war in Bohemia.
1429	Orleans saved by Joan of Arc. Charles VII crowned at Reims.			1429. Founding of Solovetski monastery on White Sea.	
1431	Joan of Arc burned.				
		1438. Albert II, first emperor of the house of Habsburg.			1437–38. Rise of Portugal.
1453	End of the Hundred Years' War.	1453. Austria made a hereditary duchy by Emperor Frederick III.			

A. D.	FROM THE FALL OF THE EASTERN EMPIRE TO THE CLOSE OF THE THIRTY YEARS' WAR—A. D. 1453–1648				
	ARTS OF CIVILIZATION	ITALY AND THE CHURCH	GREAT BRITAIN	GERMANY	SPAIN AND PORTUGAL
1460 (about)	Copperplate engraving.	1458. The French rule in Genoa. 1463. War of Venice with the Turks.	1455. Wars of the Roses begin. 1461. Edward IV, king. House of York.	1462. Civil war in Germany.	1454. Henry IV, king of Castile.
1474	First book printed in England by Caxton.	1469. Lorenzo de' Medici succeeds Piero at Florence. 1471. Sixtus IV, pope.	1470. Henry VI restored by Warwick; dies 1471.		1469. Marriage of Ferdinand of Aragon with Isabella of Castile.
1477	Watches made at Nuremberg.		1475. Edward IV invades France; signs seven year truce with Louis XI.	1477. Marriage of Maximilian and Mary of Burgundy.	1479. Union of Castile and Aragon.
1488	Bartholomew Diaz, a Portuguese, discovers the Cape of Good Hope.		1483–1485. Richard III, king.		1491. Conquest of Granada by Spaniards.
1492	Discovery of America by Columbus begins era of discovery.	1492. Alexander VI, pope.	1492. Henry VII invades France.	1493. Maximilian I, emperor.	1492. The Jews are expelled from Spain. 1498. Vasco da Gama reaches India via Cape of Good Hope.
1500 (about)	Clocks first used in astronomy.	1504. Naples annexed to the Spanish crown. Julius II, pope.	1509. Henry VIII, king.		
1506	First stone laid for St. Peter's church at Rome.				
		1513. Pope Leo X, patron of literature and the arts.	1512. War with France. 1513. Battle of Flodden; James IV of Scotland killed. 1515. Wolsey, chancellor and cardinal.	1512. Maximilian divides the empire into 10 administrative circles.	
1516	Juan Diaz de Solis discovers the river La Plata; declares the country Spanish possession.			1517. Beginning of the Reformation; Luther's theses at Wittenberg. 1519. Charles V, emperor.	1516. Charles, king of all Spain and the Netherlands. (As emperor, Charles V.)
1520	Fernando Magellan navigates the straits between Tierra del Fuego and Patagonia.	1520. Pope Leo X excommunicates Luther. 1525. Spanish ascendancy by the victory of Pavia.	1520. Francis I of France and Henry VIII meet on the Field of the Cloth of Gold near Guînes.	1521. Diet of Worms. 1525. German Peasants' war. 1529. Turks invade Germany; besiege Vienna.	1525. Charles V defeats French and Italians at Pavia.
1530 (about)	"Saxony" flax wheel in Nuremberg.		1531. The English clergy acknowledge Henry as head of the Church.		
1533	Flax growing ordered by law in England.		1534. Henry excommunicated by the pope.		
		1540. Order of Jesuits founded by Loyola. 1545. Council of Trent. 1550. Julius III, pope.	1544. Invasion of France. 1547. Formal establishment of Protestantism. Edward VI, king.	1542–54. War with France.	1540. Lisbon, the market of the world.
1547	First China orange tree brought to Europe by Portuguese. Rude carriages used in France.			1552. Treaty of Passau secures religious liberty to the Protestants. 1553. Michael Servetus, Spanish philosopher, burned at Geneva. 1556. Charles V abdicates.	
			1553. Mary, queen of England. 1554. Lady Jane Grey executed. 1555. Persecution of the Protestants. 1558. Elizabeth, queen. Rise of the Puritans.		

A. D.	FROM THE FALL OF THE EASTERN EMPIRE TO THE CLOSE OF THE THIRTY YEARS' WAR—A. D. 1453–1648				
	FRANCE	RUSSIA	SCANDINAVIA	OTTOMAN EMPIRE	LESSER COUNTRIES
1461	Louis XI, king.	1462. Ivan III founds czardom of Muscovy.		1456. War with Hungary. 1460. Greece subjected to the Turks.	1454. Poland's independence confirmed by diet of Petrekin. 1458. Hungary vigorous under Matthias Corvinus. 1466. Prussia a fief of Poland. 1468. Uzun Hassan, master of Persia.
1474	War between France and Burgundy.	1472. Ivan marries Sophia, niece of the Greek emperor.	1470. Sten Sture, regent of Sweden.		
1477	Artois and Burgundy united to France.	1479. Great invasion of the Tatars. 1480. Power of the Tatars overthrown.	1481. Hans, king of Denmark, partially acknowledged in Sweden.	1480. Otranto taken. 1481. Bajazet II, sultan.	1485. Matthias of Hungary takes Vienna.
1491	Brittany united to the crown.				
1498 1499	Louis XII, king. Conquest of Milan.				1499. Swiss independence acknowledged by the Empire. 1506. Poland under Sigismund the Great.
1510	Council of Tours.		1513. Christian II, king of Norway and Denmark.	1512. Accession of Selim I. 1514. Persians defeated; Kurdistan added to the empire. 1517. Selim conquers Egypt.	
1515	Francis I invades Italy.				
1521	Long conflict with the Habsburgs begins.		1520. Christian, king of Sweden. 1523. Gustavus Vasa, king of Sweden. Union of Calmar dissolved.	1520. Solyman the Magnificent, sultan. 1526. Invasion of Hungary. 1529. Invasion of Germany. Siege of Vienna.	1519–21. Spaniards, under Cortés, conquer Mexico.
1525	Francis defeated and taken prisoner at Pavia.				
		1533. Accession of Ivan the Terrible.			1533. Pizarro conquers Peru.
1547	Henry II, king; Catherine de' Medici, queen.	1547. Ivan the Terrible takes the title of Czar.		1551. Tripoli taken.	1545. Mines at Potosi discovered.
					1556. Akbar raises the Indian empire to its greatest splendor.

A. D.	FROM THE FALL OF THE EASTERN EMPIRE TO THE CLOSE OF THE THIRTY YEARS' WAR—A. D. 1453-1648—CON.				
	ARTS OF CIVILIZATION	ITALY AND THE CHURCH	GREAT BRITAIN	GERMANY	SPAIN AND PORTUGAL
1562	Tusser's *Five Hundred Points of Husbandry*.	1559. Termination of French wars in Italy.			
				1564. Maximilian II, emperor.	1564. Settlement of the Philippines.
					1567. Duke of Alva, governor of the Netherlands.
		1569. Florence becomes capital of grand duchy of Tuscany.	1568. Mary Queen of Scots takes refuge in England and is made captive by Elizabeth.		
		1570. The Catholics and Huguenots sign a treaty of peace at St. Germain.			1571. Battle of Lepanto. Turks defeated by the Holy League under John of Austria.
					1572. Crown of Poland becomes elective.
1576	Martin Frobisher, an Englishman, sets out to explore a northwest passage to India.			1576. Rudolf II, king of Bohemia and Hungary, emperor.	
1580	Coarse white paper made in England.				1580. Portugal passes under Spanish dominion.
1582	Pope Gregory XIII reforms the calendar, changing Oct. 5 to Oct. 15.	1585. Pope Sixtus V restores the Vatican library.	1587. Execution of Mary Queen of Scots.		
1588	First English work on shorthand published by Doctor Timothy Bright.		1588. Spanish *Armada* destroyed.		
1600	Gilbert generates electricity by rubbing substances other than amber.		1600. British East India Company chartered.		
			1603. Union of England and Scotland under James I. Tudor dynasty in England ends.		
1608	Telescopes manufactured in Holland.		1605. Guy Fawkes's plot to blow up Parliament.	1608. Protestant union under Frederick the Elector.	
1609–18	Kepler announces laws of planetary motions.				1609. Expulsion of the Moors.
1614	Lord John Napier invents system of logarithms.				
1616	William Harvey, famous physician, demonstrates the circulation of the blood.		1618. Sir Francis Bacon, lord chancellor.	1618. Thirty Years' War begins.	
	Death of Shakspere, April 23.		1620. Pilgrims sail in *Mayflower*.	1620. Battle of Prague.	1621. Dutch war.
			1625. Charles I, king.		1625. Naval war with England.
		1626. St. Peter's dedicated.	1627. War with France.		
				1628. Victories of Wallenstein.	
				1632. Battle of Lützen.	
1635	French Academy of Arts and Sciences founded at Paris.		1638. Abolition of the episcopacy in Scotland; publication of the National Covenant.		
	First Irish theater opened at Dublin.				
1639	Transit of Venus first recorded by Horrocks.				
			1640. Short Parliament. Long Parliament.		1640. Portugal regains independence.
1641	Descartes enunciates his system of philosophy.	1641. War between Pope Urban VIII and the Italian princes.			
1642	Van Diemen's Land and New Zealand discovered by Tasman, a Dutchman.		1642. Civil war and revolution.		

A. D.	FROM THE FALL OF THE EASTERN EMPIRE TO THE CLOSE OF THE THIRTY YEARS' WAR—A. D. 1453–1648—CON.				
	FRANCE	RUSSIA	SCANDINAVIA	OTTOMAN EMPIRE	LESSER COUNTRIES
1562	Religious liberty granted to the Huguenots. Huguenot wars.		1560. Eric XIV, king of Sweden. 1563. Seven Years' War between Sweden and Denmark begins.	Military power of the Turks at its greatest height under Solyman. 1566. Selim II, emperor.	1566. The Compromise, a league of nobles against the Inquisition in the Netherlands.
1572 1574 1576	Massacre of St. Bartholomew. Henry III, king. The Catholic League.	1571. Russia devastated by the Tatars and Moscow burned. 1578. Alliance of Sweden and Poland against Russia.	1570. Peace of Stettin.	1571. Turks defeated at battle of Lepanto. 1574. Amurath III, emperor.	1579. Beginning of the republic in Holland.
1588 1589 1590 1598	Revolt of Paris. House of Bourbon begins with Henry IV. Siege of Paris raised by the Spaniards. Edict of Nantes— toleration granted to the Protestants.	1598. Boris Godounov begins a new dynasty.	1588. Christian IV, king of Denmark.	1589. Revolt of the Janizaries. 1595. Power in Hungary declines; revolt of Wallachia.	1585. Persia acquires great power under Abbas the Great. 1601. Portuguese expedition reaches Australia. 1605. Jehangir, Mogul emperor of India. 1609. First envoy of the British East India Company sent to India.
1610 1614	Assassination of Henry IV. Louis XIII, king. Last assembly of the States-General before French Revolution.	1613. Michael Feodorovich, czar, founds the house of Romanov.	1611. Gustavus Adolphus, king of Sweden. War between Sweden and Denmark. 1617. Sweden dominates the North.	1620. War with Poland.	
1624 1627 1638	Ministry of Cardinal Richelieu begins. War with England over the Huguenots. Invasion of Spain.	1632. War with Poland.	1632. Christina, queen of Sweden; Oxenstierna, regent.	1638. Final and greatest expedition against Persia.	1639. Great naval victory of the Dutch admiral, Van Tromp, over the Spanish fleet in the Downs. 1640. Madras, India, founded.
1640 1642	Turin taken by the French. Death of Richelieu.				

A. D.	FROM THE FALL OF THE EASTERN EMPIRE TO THE CLOSE OF THE THIRTY YEARS' WAR—A. D. 1453–1648—CON.				
	ARTS OF CIVILIZATION	ITALY AND THE CHURCH	GREAT BRITAIN	GERMANY	SPAIN AND PORTUGAL
1643	The barometer invented by Torricelli.				1643. The colonies of New England form a union.
1647	Society of Friends founded by George Fox.	1647. Revolt of Naples under Masaniello.	1648. Second civil war.	1648. Peace of Westphalia. End of Thirty Years' War. The balance of power in Europe practically established by this treaty.	

A. D.	FROM THE CLOSE OF THE THIRTY YEARS' WAR TO THE BEGINNING OF THE FRENCH REVOLUTION—A. D. 1648–1789				
	ARTS OF CIVILIZATION	ITALY AND THE CHURCH	GREAT BRITAIN	GERMANY	SPAIN AND PORTUGAL
1650	First coffeehouse in England.		1649. Commonwealth under Cromwell. 1652. War with Holland. 1653. Cromwell, lord protector.		
				1658. Leopold I, emperor.	1654. Brazil recovered from the Dutch.
			1660. Charles II, king. Restoration of Stuarts.		1660. Portugal makes alliance with England.
1662	Coffee introduced into France.				
1663	First newspaper in England, *Public Intelligence.*				
1667	First designs drawn for Gobelin tapestry.		1666. Great fire in London. St. Paul's rebuilt by Sir Christopher Wren.		
1669	British East India Company first import tea.		1668. Triple Alliance of England, Sweden, and Holland against France.		
				1674. War of Austria and France.	1673. War with France to protect Holland.
		1676. Messina revolts in favor of the French; blockaded by the Dutch and Spanish fleets.	1678 (about). Rise of the Whigs and Tories. 1679. Habeas corpus act passed.		
1681	Canal of Languedoc completed.			1680. Part of Alsace seized by France.	
1684	Newton announces theory of gravitation.		1685. James II, king.	1683. Siege of Vienna by the Turks and Hungarians. 1687. Joseph I, king of Hungary.	
			1688. Revolution.		
		1689. Alexander VIII, pope.	1689. William III, king, and Mary II, queen.		1689. Revolt in Catalonia in favor of France.
1690	Manufacture of paper for writing and printing encouraged by law in England.	1693. Battle of Marsaglia.	1690. Battle of the Boyne. James defeated. 1694. Bank of England chartered.	1690. Joseph I elected king of the Romans.	1691. Incursion of the French into Aragon.
1696	Hoste writes on science of shipbuilding.		1697. Peace of Ryswick.	1697. Victory of Prince Eugene over Sultan Mustapha at Zenta.	
1698	Linen manufacture established in northern Ireland.			1701. Prussia made a kingdom. Hohenzollern dynasty established.	1700. Philip V, king of Spain.
		1702. Battle of Luzzara between French under Vendôme and the Imperialists.	1702. Queen Anne. War against France and Spain. 1704. Gibraltar taken by English.		
		1706. French driven from Italy by Prince Eugene.			1705. Barcelona taken by the allies.

A. D.	FROM THE FALL OF THE EASTERN EMPIRE TO THE CLOSE OF THE THIRTY YEARS' WAR—A. D. 1453-1648—Con.				
	FRANCE	RUSSIA	SCANDINAVIA	OTTOMAN EMPIRE	LESSER COUNTRIES
1643	Louis XIV, king.	1645. Era of progress begins with reign of Czar Alexis.	1645. Peace between Sweden and Denmark.	1645. War with Venice.	
1648	Wars of the Fronde.				1648. Independence of the Republic of the United Provinces.

A. D.	FROM THE CLOSE OF THE THIRTY YEARS' WAR TO THE BEGINNING OF THE FRENCH REVOLUTION—A. D. 1648-1789				
	FRANCE	RUSSIA	SCANDINAVIA	OTTOMAN EMPIRE	LESSER COUNTRIES
1649	Siege of Paris.				
1653	Mazarin enters Paris in triumph.	1654. Russian victories in Poland.			1653. John de Witt, grand pensionary of Holland.
1659	Peace of the Pyrenees.		1657. War between Denmark and Sweden. 1660. Peace of Copenhagen and Oliva.	1657. Leopold I of Germany becomes king of Hungary. 1661. War with Austria.	1661. Bombay ceded to England.
				1663. Invasion of Hungary. 1664. Germans win the battle of St. Gotthard.	
1667	War with Spain over possession of the Spanish Netherlands.				
1672	War with Holland.	1671. The Cossacks subjugated.		1672. Invasion of Poland.	1674. Sobieski, king of Poland.
1678	Peace with Holland and Spain restores tranquillity to Europe. France the most formidable power in Europe.	1682. Ivan and Peter, czars.	1680. Diet of Stockholm.	1678. First war with Russia. 1682. War with Austria. 1683. Defeat at Vienna.	
1685	Revocation of the Edict of Nantes.				
1688	Louis declares war against the Empire and the United Provinces.	1689. Peter the Great, czar.		1687. Revolution in Constantinople, Soliman II, sultan. 1689. Recovery of Belgrade from the Austrians.	1689 (about). Mogul power at its height in India.
			1693. The king of Sweden declared absolute.		1695. Brussels bombarded by the French.
1697	General Peace of Ryswick between France and the Allies.		1697. Charles XII begins to reign.		
1702	Invasion of Holland. Revolt of the Camisards (Protestants).	1700. Peter the Great wars with the northern powers. 1703. Petrograd founded.	1700. Defeat of the Russians at Narva. 1702-08. Charles XII sweeps Poland and Russia.	1699. Peace of Karlowitz. The Ottoman power broken. 1703. Mustapha II deposed by the Janizaries.	
1704	Defeat at Blenheim.		1705. Denmark joins Russo-Polish alliance.		1704. Stanislas I, king of Poland.

A. D.	FROM THE CLOSE OF THE THIRTY YEARS' WAR TO THE BEGINNING OF THE FRENCH REVOLUTION—A. D. 1648–1789—CON.				
	ARTS OF CIVILIZATION	ITALY AND THE CHURCH	GREAT BRITAIN	GERMANY	SPAIN AND PORTUGAL
		1707. All Spanish possessions in Italy abandoned.	1707. Act of union of England and Scotland. First united Parliament of Great Britain meets.		
1710	First "self-acting steam engine" patented by Thomas Newcomen.		1713. Peace of Utrecht. England acquires large American possessions. 1714. Accession of George I. Beginning of the house of Hanover.	1711. Charles VI, emperor.	
		1718. Sicily invaded by the Spanish.	1720. South Sea Bubble.	1718. Quadruple Alliance against Spain.	
1721	Inoculation for small-pox introduced into England.				
1731	An early book on farming: Tull's *Horse-Hoeing Husbandry.*	1730. Clement XII, pope.	1727. George II, king of England.	1725. Alliance of Spain and Austria. 1733. War of the Polish Succession.	1725. Alliance with Austria.
1735	Linnæus publishes his *Systema Naturæ.*		1739. War with Spain.	1740. War of the Austrian Succession. Maria Theresa succeeds to the hereditary states.	1734. Conquest of Sicily and Naples by Don Carlos.
1747	Franklin announces single fluid theory of electricity.	1744. Italy invaded by the French and Spaniards. 1746. French and Spaniards driven from Lombardy.	1745. The Young Pretender in Scotland.	1745. Francis I, husband of Maria Theresa, emperor.	1746. Ferdinand VI, king of Spain.
1752	Franklin demonstrates identity of electricity and lightning.		1760. Accession of George III. 1763. Peace of Paris.	1756. Seven Years' War—Austria and France against Prussia and England.	
1767	Hargreaves builds a spinning jenny.				1767. Jesuits expelled from Spain.
1769	Arkwright builds a spinning mill.				
1773	First regular academy for deaf-mutes (in Great Britain) opened in Edinburgh.	1773. Jesuit order suppressed.	1775. War with the American colonies. 1776. British army takes possession of New York. Hessians hired for service in America. City of London remonstrates against American war.	1778. War of the Bavarian Succession. Bavaria seized by Germany.	
1780	Sunday schools organized at Gloucester, England, by Robert Raikes.				
1781	Watt first patents a double steam engine.		1781. Surrender of Cornwallis at Yorktown.		
1782	Montgolfier successfully uses heated air balloons.		1783. Treaty of Versailles with United States. 1786. Impeachment of Warren Hastings.		
1787	Society for the Suppression of the Slave Trade founded.				1788. Charles IV, king of Spain.

A. D.	FROM THE CLOSE OF THE THIRTY YEARS' WAR TO THE BEGINNING OF THE FRENCH REVOLUTION—A. D. 1648–1789—CON.				
	FRANCE	RUSSIA	SCANDINAVIA	OTTOMAN EMPIRE	LESSER COUNTRIES
		1708. Revolt of the Cossack Mazeppa. Charles XII of Sweden invades Russia. 1709. Charles is defeated at Pultowa.		1710. The sultan declares war on Russia.	
1713	Peace of Utrecht— perpetual separation of the crowns of France and Spain.		1714. Charles returns to Sweden.		
1715	Louis XV, king (Regency till 1723).	1716. Finland conquered.		1717. Turks lose Belgrade.	1715. Treaty of Antwerp with Austria. "Barrier Treaty."
1718	The Quadruple Alliance against Spain.	1720. Treaty of Stockholm between Sweden and Russia.	1718. Charles invades Norway and is killed at the siege of Frederikshald.		
1724	Congress of Cambrai.	1721. Peter assumes the title "Emperor of all the Russias." 1725. Catherine I, empress. 1726. Alliance with Austria.	1721. Peace of Nystadt between Sweden and Russia.	1723. Turks and Russians attempt to dismember Persia.	1724–32. Jesuits expelled from China.
1733	The Polish succession involves France in war.	1730. Death of Peter II, last of the male line of Romanovs.	1730. Christian VI, king of Denmark.	1734. Turks driven from Persia by Nadir Shah.	1733. Frederick Augustus II, king of Poland. 1739. India invaded by Nadir, shah of Persia, who takes Delhi.
1744	War with England and Austria.		1742. Swedes driven out of Finland.		
1747	War with Holland.			1745. Defeat of the Turks at Kars.	1746–49. Hostilities between the French and English in India.
1760	Loss of all Canada.				1756. Calcutta taken by the nabob of Bengal.
1764	Dissolution of Jesuit order.	1762. Catherine II reigns.			1765. Establishment of the English in India. 1766. Power of the Mamelukes revived in Egypt under Ali Bey.
1770	Marriage of the Dauphin to Marie Antoinette.	1768. War with the Ottoman empire. 1772. First partition of Poland. 1773. Revolts of the Cossacks.	1772. Despotism reestablished in Sweden by Gustavus III.		
1774	Louis XVI, king.				1774. Warren Hastings, first governor-general of India.
1776 1778	Franklin in Paris. Alliance with America.				
				1783. The Crimea annexed to Russia.	
1789	The States-General meets at Versailles.	1787. War with the Turks.		1787. Disastrous war with Austria and Russia.	

A. D.	FROM THE BEGINNING OF THE FRENCH REVOLUTION TO WORLD WAR I—1789–1914				
	ARTS OF CIVILIZATION	ITALY AND THE CHURCH	GREAT BRITAIN	GERMANY	SPAIN AND PORTUGAL
1792	First use of gas for illuminating.		1792. Canada divided by Britain into Upper and Lower Provinces.	1792. War with France.	
		1796–97. Napoleon's Italian campaign.	1793. First coalition against France.	1797. Napoleon's Austrian campaign.	
1798	Invention of lithography.	1798. Roman Republic proclaimed by the French.	1798. Nelson destroys French fleet at battle of the Nile.		
			1799. Second coalition against France. 1801. Union of England and Ireland.		
1802	Wedgwood's photographic experiments.	1802. Napoleon, president of the Italian Republic.			
1803	Fulton's steamboat *Clermont* operated on the Seine.		1803. Successful war in India.		
		1805. Napoleon crowned king of Italy.	1805. Napoleon defeated at Trafalgar.	1805. Battle of Austerlitz.	1805. Battle of Trafalgar.
				1806. Confederation of Rhine. End of Holy Roman Empire.	
		1808. Rome annexed by Napoleon to the Kingdom of Italy.		1809. Peace of Vienna.	1808. Madrid taken by the French. Joseph Bonaparte, king.
			1812. War with the United States.	1812. Austria in alliance with France against Russia.	1812. Battle of Salamanca.
1814	Steam cylinder printing press first used for *London Times*.	1814. Fall of Napoleon. Kingdom ceases.			1814. Ferdinand VII restored.
			1815. British defeated at New Orleans. Wellington victorious at Waterloo.	1815. Congress of Vienna.	
	ARTS OF CIVILIZATION	INTERNATIONAL AFFAIRS	GREAT BRITAIN	PRUSSIA	AUSTRIA
		1815. Congress of Vienna. Holy Alliance. Abolition of slave trade.	1816. Bombardment of Algiers. The Dey compelled to abolish slavery.		
		1818. Great Lakes Anglo-American naval agreement.		1818. The Zollverein policy initiated.	
1819	S. S. *Savannah* makes the first trip across Atlantic. Electromagnetism discovered.		1820. Accession of George IV.		
1822	Hieroglyphics deciphered by Champollion.	1821. Conference of monarchs at Laibach.			
1824	Inland navigation stimulated in the United States.	1823. Proclamation of Monroe Doctrine.	1823. Catholic Association formed in Ireland.		
1825	Steam navigation on the Rhine. Vast increase in periodical literature. First passenger railway, Stockton to Darlington, England.		1826. England and Russia sign agreement for settlement of Greek question.	1826. Austria and Prussia oppose English-Russian mediation in Greece.	
1827	Improved cylinder printing press, *London Times*, 5000 impressions per hour.	1827. Treaty of nations with respect to Greece. 1828. Independence of Uruguay.	1828. Wellington ministry. Irish disturbances. 1830. William IV, king.		
1831	Reaper invented. Dynamo electric machine.	1831. Belgian independence and neutrality agreed to by the powers.	1832. Reform bills passed. 1834. Difficulties with China. Robert Peel, premier.	1834. Zollverein includes most of the German states.	1831. Austria interferes in Italian affairs. 1835. Ferdinand I, emperor.

A. D.	FROM THE BEGINNING OF THE FRENCH REVOLUTION TO WORLD WAR I—1789–1914				
	FRANCE	RUSSIA	SCANDINAVIA	OTTOMAN EMPIRE	OTHER COUNTRIES
1789	National Assembly adopts Declaration of the Rights of Man.				
1792	War with Germany. France declared a republic.		1792. Gustavus III assassinated. Gustavus IV, king.		
1793	Reign of Terror.	1793. Second partition of Poland.			
1795	Napoleon Bonaparte commands army.	1795. Final partition of Poland.			1794. Polish revolt at Cracow.
1796	War in Italy.	1796. Unsuccessful war with Persia.			
1797	Napoleon in Austria.				
1798	Expedition to Egypt.			1798. Turkey joins coalition against France.	1798. Swiss revolution. Helvetian Republic declared.
1799	Swiss campaign.				
1800	Battle of Marengo.				
1802	Napoleon made consul.	1801. Alexander, czar.	1801. Denmark and Sweden accede to the alliance between England and Russia.		
1803	War with England.			1803. Insurrection of Mamelukes at Cairo.	
1804	Napoleon I, emperor of the French.				
1805	Battle of Austerlitz.	1805. Russia joins the coalition against France.			
1807	War with Russia. Invasion of Portugal.	1807. Treaty of Tilsit.	1808. Finland invaded by the Russians.		1806. Louis Napoleon, king of Holland. 1807. Duchy of Warsaw formed.
1809	Battle of Wagram.		1809. Charles XIII, king of Sweden.	1809. Russians defeated at Silistria.	
1810	Continental peace except with Spain.				
1812	Russian campaign.	1812. Invasion by Napoleon. Moscow burned.		1809–12. War with Russia.	1812. American war with England.
1814	Allies enter Paris. House of Bourbon restored; Louis XVIII, king.		1814. Union of Sweden and Norway as two kingdoms under one monarch.	1814. Malta falls to England.	
1815	Napoleon defeated at Waterloo; abdicates; banished to St. Helena.	1815. The Holy Alliance formed.			1815. William I, king of the Netherlands.

	FRANCE	SPAIN AND PORTUGAL	ITALY AND GREECE	RUSSIA	LESSER COUNTRIES
		1816. Union of Portugal and Brazil.	1816 Kingdom of Two Sicilies restored.	1815. Poland united to Russia.	1816. Lord Amherst's unsuccessful mission to China.
1818	France joins the Holy Alliance.	1817. Slave trade abolished.			1818. The Mahratta power completely overthrown in India by the British.
			1821. Austrian invasion of Italy. 1822. Greek revolution. Declaration of Independence.		
1824	Charles X, king.	1823. Constitutional movement in Spain crushed.			
			1825. Death of Ferdinand IV of Naples, after reign of 66 years.	1826. Nicholas I crowned at Moscow. War against Persia.	1826. Missolonghi taken by the Turks. Athens taken by the Turks.
1830	Revolution and abdication of Charles X. Louis Philippe, king. Algiers taken by the French.			1830-31. Polish insurrections.	1830. Polish struggles for nationality begin.
1831	Abolition of hereditary peerage in France.	1833. Isabella II, queen of Spain. 1834. The Carlist war.	1832. Kingdom of Greece founded.	1832. Poland made part of empire.	1831. Leopold I, king of the Belgians. 1833. Portugal, a constitutional monarchy.

A. D.	FROM THE BEGINNING OF THE FRENCH REVOLUTION TO WORLD WAR I—1789-1914—CON.				
	ARTS OF CIVILIZATION	INTERNATIONAL AFFAIRS	GREAT BRITAIN	PRUSSIA	AUSTRIA
1837	Morse patents his telegraph. Wheatstone's telegraph patented in England.	1839. Dutch and Belgian boundary dispute settled.	1837. Difficulties in Canada. Victoria, queen.		1838. Commercial treaty with England.
1842	Ether as an anesthetic.		1840-42. War with China over the opium trade.	1840. Frederick William IV, king.	
1844	First telegraphic message, Washington, Baltimore.				
1845	Gutta-percha used.				
1846	Howe's sewing machine patented.	1846. Oregon boundary treaty.	1846. Repeal of the corn laws.		1846. Austria takes possession of Kracow.
1847	Great canal from Durance to Marseille completed.		1846-47. Severe famine in Ireland.		
1848	Girard College opened.	1848. Treaty of Guadalupe Hidalgo between Mexico and United States. Revolutionary disturbance in Europe.	1848. Civil war in Ireland. Habeas corpus act suspended.	1848. Insurrection in Berlin.	1848. Revolution in Hungary and Austria. Francis Joseph, emperor.
1849	Magnetic clock invented by Doctor Locke of Cincinnati.		1849. Punjab annexed to England.	1849. The king declines the imperial crown.	1849. New constitution promulgated.
1850	Tubular bridge in Anglesey, England. Woman's Rights convention at Worcester, Mass.		1850. The war in Lahore ended.	1850. Treaty of peace with Denmark. New constitution for Prussia.	
1851	Railway between Moscow and Leningrad opened. Cable across the English Channel.	1851. International exhibition at London.			1851. Louis Kossuth sentenced to death at Pest.
1853	First Norwegian railway opened.				
1854	First railway in Brazil.	1854. Commercial treaty between the United States and Japan. France, England, Sardinia, Russia, Turkey in Crimean War.	1854. Crimean War. Treaty of alliance with France.	1854. Treaty with Austria, offensive and defensive.	1854. Alliance with England and France.
1855	Panama railway completed. Bessemer's steel process patented.				
1856	Submarine telegraph laid from Cape Breton to Newfoundland.	1856. Close of Crimean War. Treaty of Paris.	1856. British fleet bombards and partially destroys Canton, China.		1856. Hungarians granted amnesty.
1857	Peabody Institute founded at Baltimore.		1857. Rebellion in India begins. King of Delhi proclaimed sovereign of India.		
1858	*Great Eastern* launched. Boston Public Library opened.	1858. Laying of Atlantic cable.			
1859	Storage, or secondary, battery.	1859. India and England connected by telegraph.			1859. War with France and Sardinia. Peace after battle of Solferino.
1860	Ammonia absorption ice machine.				
1861	Passenger elevator.		1861. Death of Prince Albert.	1861. William I, king.	1861. New constitution for the Austrian monarchy.
1863	Abolition of slavery in the U. S. Pneumatic pianoforte player (first to strike keys by pneumatic pockets).	1864. Convention (International) for telegraph to U. S. Geneva convention (Red Cross).		1862. Bismarck, premier. 1864. War with Denmark.	1864. Alliance with Prussia against Denmark.
1865	Antiseptic surgery.		1865. Fenian outbreaks in Ireland.		
1866	Open-hearth steel process.	1866. Atlantic telegraph completed. Latin union begun.		1866. Prussia wars on Austria; annexes Hanover.	1866. War with Prussia and Italy.

A. D.	FROM THE BEGINNING OF THE FRENCH REVOLUTION TO WORLD WAR I—1789–1914—CON.				
	FRANCE	SPAIN AND PORTUGAL	ITALY AND GREECE	RUSSIA	OTHER COUNTRIES
1836	Insurrection attempted by Louis Napoleon at Strasbourg.	1836. The monasteries in Spain dissolved.			
1838	Death of Talleyrand.				
					1839. Turkey at war with Egypt.
					1840. William I abdicates as king of Holland.
		1841–42. Insurrection in Barcelona.			1842. Insurrection in India.
1844	War with Morocco.		1843. King Otto of Greece compelled to accept a constitution.	1844. Emperor visits England.	
		1846. Marriage of Isabella to the Duke of Cadiz. Civil war in Portugal.			1847. Soulouque, president of Haiti.
1848	Abdication of Louis Philippe, and a republic proclaimed. Louis Napoleon, president. Bloody insurrection in Paris.		1848. Rising of the great Italian cities in revolution. Roman republic proclaimed.		1848. Holland receives a new constitution. Hungary given an independent ministry.
			1849. Victor Emmanuel, king of Sardinia.	1849. Russia aids Austria in subduing Hungary.	
1850	Jerome Bonaparte, marshal of France. Death of Louis Philippe.			1850. Harbor of Sebastopol completed.	1850. Death of Emperor Tau-Kwang of China. Battle of Idstedt, Denmark. Outbreak of Taiping rebellion.
1851	Louis Napoleon elected president for ten years (coup d'état).	1851. Death of Godoy, "prince of peace."			1851. Discovery of gold in Australia.
1852	Louis Napoleon declared emperor as Napoleon III.			1853. War begins with Turkey.	1852. Buenos Aires taken by the liberating army.
1854	Crimean War. Allies victorious at Inkerman.	1854. Military insurrection under O'Donnell.	1854. Sardinia takes part in the Crimean War.	1854. War with France and England. Siege of Sebastopol. Battle of Balaklava.	War between Turkey and Montenegro.
				1855. Alexander II, emperor.	1855. Santa Anna abdicates the presidency of Mexico.
1856	Peace with Russia.			1856. Evacuation of the Crimea.	
					1857. Mexican constitution promulgated.
				1858. Partial emancipation of the serfs.	1858. Massacre of Christians in Turkey. Suez railroad completed.
1859	War of France and Sardinia against Austria.	1859. War with Morocco.	1859. War between Austria and Italy.		
1860	Commercial treaty with England. Savoy and Nice surrendered to France by Sardinia. Colonial expansion in West Africa.	1860. Defeat of the Moors.	1860. Sicily and Naples annexed to Sardinia.		
			1861. Victor Emmanuel, king of Italy. Death of Cavour.	1861. Emancipation of serfs completed.	1861. Canton restored to the Chinese by the French and English.
1863	The French occupy Mexico.		1862. Insurrection in Greece.		
1864	Maximilian proclaimed emperor of Mexico.	1864. Rupture with Peru.	1864. Ionian Isles made over to Greece.	1864. Emigration of Caucasian tribes into Turkey.	1864. Nanking, China, taken by Gordon for the Imperialists. End of Taiping rebellion.
1865	Death of Proudhon. Bismarck visits Napoleon.	1865. Dispute with Chile. 1866. Military revolt led by General Prim.	1865. Florence made capital of Italy. 1866. Austrian war. Venetia made part of Italy.	1866. Inauguration of trial by jury.	1866. Valparaiso bombarded by Spanish fleet.

A. D.	FROM THE BEGINNING OF THE FRENCH REVOLUTION TO WORLD WAR I—1789–1914—Con.				
	ARTS OF CIVILIZATION	INTERNATIONAL AFFAIRS	GREAT BRITAIN	PRUSSIA	AUSTRIA
		1867. International exposition at Paris.	1867. Passage of Reform bill.	1867. First parliament of the North German Confederation.	1867. Autonomy for Hungary announced. Emperor crowned king of Hungary.
1868	First practical typewriting machine.	1868. Burlingame Treaty (United States and China). Suez canal formally opened.	1870. Irish Land act passed.	1870. War with France.	1870. Concordat with Rome suspended.
1869	French Atlantic telegraph completed.				
1870	Railway from Calcutta to Bombay. Mount Cenis tunnel boring completed.			GERMANY	
1873	Japan adopts European calendar.	1871. Treaty of Washington between United States and Great Britain.		1871. William I, of Prussia, emperor. 1874. Kulturkampf laws against Catholics.	1871. New German Empire recognized.
1876	Exposition at Philadelphia. Telephone invented by Bell.	1875. Formation of International Bureau of Weights and Measures.	1875. Purchase of Suez Canal shares from khedive of Egypt.		
1877	Four cycle gas engine invented.		1877. Queen Victoria proclaimed empress of India.		1878. Occupation of Bosnia and Herzegovina.
1879	Edison's incandescent electric lamp.	1878. Congress of Berlin.			
1882	Tuberculosis bacillus isolated. Hydrophobia bacillus isolated.	1882. Triple Alliance formed. 1883. International society founded for protection of industrial property.	1882. Control of Egypt secured.	1882. German Colonial Society founded.	
1884	Rotary steam turbine.				
1885	Linotype machine. Revised version of the Old Testament published.	1885. International exhibition at Antwerp. 1887. Convention of Bern. International copyright agreement. 1890. Anti-slave trade agreement.	1885. Khartum captured by the Mahdi. Death of Gordon. 1887. Queen's jubilee.	1888. Frederick III, William II, emperors. 1890 Bismarck dismissed.	
1888	Pasteur discovers cure for hydrophobia.		1889. Great labor strikes. 1890. Stanley returns from Africa.		
1891	Carborundum.	1891. Renewal of Triple Alliance.			
1892	Color photography.		1892. Gladstone's fourth premiership.		
1893	Electrical measurements established.	1893. Exposition at Chicago. 1894. War between China and Japan.	1893. Bering Sea arbitration. 1894. Manchester ship canal opened.	1893. Anti-Jesuit law repealed.	1894. Commercial treaty with Russia.
1895	Lick refracting telescope made by Clark. Discovery of X-rays.			1896. New civil code completed.	1896. Archduke Karl Ludwig, heir to the throne, dies.
1898	Reform edict issued in China. Discovery of radium.	1897. Universal postal congress. 1898. Pope offers mediation in Cuba.	1897. Queen's diamond jubilee celebrated. 1898. Irish local government bill passed. Death of Gladstone.	1898. Emperor visits Jerusalem.	1898. Assassination of the empress.
1900	Opening of the Elbe and Trave canal, Germany.	1899. First Hague conference. "Open door" policy for China declared by U. S.	1899. The Boer war in South Africa begins. 1901. Death of Victoria; Edward VII king.	1900. Abolition of Roman law. New civil code goes into effect.	1900. Marriage of Francis Ferdinand.
1902	First wireless message across the Atlantic.	1902. Venezuelan claims of European powers arbitrated.	1902. Japanese alliance. End of Boer war.		1902. Triple Alliance renewed.
1903	Completion of the Pacific cable.	1903. Canal treaty with Panama.	1903. King visits Italy, Portugal, and France.		
1904	New York subway opened.		1904. Younghusband enters Tibet.		
1905	Power plants erected at Niagara Falls. Simplon tunnel.	1905. Norway and Sweden separate. 1906. Algeciras conference.	1906. Militant agitation for woman suffrage begun.	1905. Moroccan intervention.	1905. Treaty with Germany.
1907	*Lusitania's* first voyage.	1907. Second Hague conference.	1908. Asquith, prime minister. Old Age Pension act passed.	1907. William II in London.	1907. Universal suffrage bill. 1908. Bosnia and Herzegovina acquired.
1909	Discovery of north pole announced.				
1910	Woman's suffrage movement grows.				
1911	Amundsen discovers south pole.	1911. Atlantic fisheries dispute between U. S. and Great Britain settled by Hague Tribunal. Agadir affair.	1911. Coronation of George V.	1911. Moroccan disagreement.	1911. Austria increases army.
1912	*Titanic* disaster. Scott at south pole.		1912. Minimum wage bill.		
1913	Wireless messages across Atlantic.				

A. D.	FROM THE BEGINNING OF THE FRENCH REVOLUTION TO WORLD WAR I—1789-1914—CON.				
	FRANCE	SPAIN AND PORTUGAL	ITALY AND GREECE	RUSSIA	OTHER COUNTRIES
		1867. Death of Marshal O'Donnell. 1868. Queen deposed.	1867. Garibaldi and the Papal States. Second attempt to take Rome.	1867. Russian America (Alaska) sold to the United States.	1867. City of Mexico evacuated by French. Execution of Maximilian in Mexico. Egypt declared by the sultan to be a separate sovereignty.
1870	New liberal constitution approved by a plebiscite. War with Prussia.	1870. Amadeus, king of Spain.			
1871	Capitulation of Paris. Peace ratified.	1871. Sagasta, minister.	1871. Rome made capital of Italy.	1871. Telegraph between Russia and Japan.	1871. Abolition of Feudalism in Japan.
1874	Endeavor to establish monarchy.	1874. Alfonso XII, king. 1875. Civil war.			
1876	Large republican gains in elections.				
				1877. War against Turkey.	
1879	Jules Grévy, president.		1878. Humbert, king. Leo XIII, pope.	1878. Spread of nihilism.	1878. Montenegro, Serbia, and Rumania, independent.
1881	Protectorate over Tunis.	1881. Sagasta, minister.		1881. Alexander III, czar.	1882. Beginning of Pan-Islam movement in Turkey.
1883	Madagascar occupied.				
1884	War with China.				
1885	Death of Victor Hugo.		1885. War with Abyssinia.	1885. Kronstadt canal opened.	
1887	Boulanger incident. Military scandals.		1887. Failure of Abyssinian expedition.	1887. Czar forbids real estate holding by foreigners.	
1890	War with Dahomey.	1890. Castillo, premier.		1890-92. Famine throughout the country.	1890. First Japanese parliament opened.
1892	Panama scandals.				
		1893. War with Morocco.	1893. Pope's jubilee (Leo XIII).		
1894	Casimir-Périer, president. Dreyfus tried; imprisoned.			1894. Nicholas II, czar.	1895. Federation act of Australia approved. 1896. Jameson raid in South Africa.
			1896. Peace with Abyssinia.		
1897	Fashoda Incident.	1897. Assassination of Castillo.			1897. Turko-Grecian war.
1898	Review of Dreyfus case.	1898. Spanish-American war.		1898. Port Arthur leased from China.	1898. Hawaii annexed to U. S. Wilhelmina, queen of Holland.
1899	Loubet, president.		1900. Victor Emmanuel III, king.	1901. Tolstóy excommunicated.	1900. Outbreak of the Boxers in China. 1901. Submission of China to the allied powers.
		1902. Alfonso XIII, king.			
1903	Dreyfus declared innocent.		1903. Accession of Pope Pius X. 1904. General strike in Italy.	1904. War with Japan. 1905. Constitution granted. 1906. First Russian Duma opens.	1903. Peter I, king of Serbia.
1907	French occupation of Morocco.	1908. Manuel II, king of Portugal.	1907. Italo-Argentine treaty.		
					1909. Abdication of Abdul Hamid II.
1910	Railway strike suppressed.	1910. Portugal a republic.	1910. New Greek constitution. 1911. Italo-Turkish war.	1910. Cholera epidemic. 1911. Treaty of 1832 abrogated by U. S.	1910. Japan annexes Korea. 1911. Diaz overthrown in Mexico.
1912	Morocco made a protectorate.	1912. Franco-Spanish treaty.	1912. Balkan war.	1912. Russia increases navy.	1912. China a republic. War in the Balkans.
1913	M. Poincaré, president.		1913. Constantine, king of Greece.	1913. Serf class abolished.	1913. Balkan war closes.

A. D.	FROM THE BEGINNING OF WORLD WAR I, 1914, TO THE PRESENT TIME				
	ARTS OF CIVILIZATION	INTERNATIONAL AFFAIRS	GREAT BRITAIN	GERMANY	CENTRAL EUROPE
1914	First important use of airplanes in warfare.	1914. World War. Panama canal opened.	1914. Irish home rule bill passed. War with Germany.	1914. War with Russia, France, Belgium, England, Serbia.	1914. Assassination of Francis Ferdinand and wife.
1915	Voice transmitted by wireless telephone from Arlington, Va., to Honolulu, 4900 miles.	1915. Belgian relief under commission directed by Herbert Hoover.	1915. War continues. New coalition ministry.	1915. Germany declares waters around British Isles war zone. War with Italy.	1915. Przemysl taken by Russians. Italy wars on Austria-Hungary.
1916	Marseille-Rhone canal completed. Alaskan railway building.	1916. United States sends peace note to warring nations.	1916. Compulsory military service bill. Lloyd George, prime minister.	1916. Siege of Verdun fails. Rumania conquered.	1916. Charles I succeeds Francis Joseph.
1917	Food production increased in belligerent countries by public instruction and control.	1917. United States enters World War.	1917. Imperial war cabinet.	1917. Use of submarines increased.	1917. German-Slav dissension.
1918		1918. Central Powers collapse; Armistice.	1918. Suffrage granted to women.	1918. Treaty of Brest-Litovsk with Russia.	1918. Breakdown of the dual monarchy.
1919	Airplane flight across Atlantic.	1919. Paris Peace Conference.		1919. Ebert elected president.	1919. Treaty of Saint Germain.
1920	Notable progress in flood protection projects in United States.	1920. Versailles Peace Treaty in effect. League of Nations holds first meetings.	1920. Continued industrial disturbances. Rebellion in Ireland.	1920. Industrial unrest. Communist uprising.	1920. Czechoslovakia in defensive alliance with Jugoslavia forms nucleus of Little Entente.
1921	Great extension in use of radio. Second Simplon tunnel completed. Michelson measures diameter of two stars.	1921. Continued difficulties over reparations payments. Arms conference meets at Washington.	1921. Imperial Conference of Premiers at London. Establishment of Irish Free State approved by Parliament.	1921. Ludendorff conducts reactionary militarist campaign.	1921. Rumania joins Little Entente, which prevents ex-Emperor Charles from regaining throne of Hungary
1922	Radio broadcasting daily feature in many cities. Einstein relativity theory confirmed by solar eclipse observations in Australia.	1922. Washington Conference adopts several treaties. First meeting of World Court. Peace treaties between U. S. and Germany and Hungary.	1922. Gandhi, in India, imprisoned for sedition. Irish Free State established. Independence of Egypt recognized. Premier Lloyd George resigns.	1922. Treaty of Rapallo with Russia. Foreign minister Rathenau assassinated. Germany in default of reparations payments.	1922. Swiss reject capital levy. Anthony Svehla, an Agrarian, becomes premier in Czechoslovakia. Hungary abolishes secret voting.
1923	Holland-Java wireless service, 7500 miles. First transcontinental air mail service inaugurated by United States. Insulin treatment for diabetes.	1923. Treaty between Yugoslavia and Italy over Dalmatia. Turkish-Allied Treaty of Lausanne. Naval Limitation treaties ratified.	1923. Bonar Law succeeded by Stanley Baldwin as premier. War debt to United States funded. Development of great naval base at Singapore announced.	1923. Part of Rhineland occupied by France. Chancellor Cuno succeeded by Streseman. The mark continues to fall in value.	1923. Czechoslovakia and Rumania sign a defensive military treaty. Legitimists plot to restore Habsburgs to Hungarian throne.
1924	U. S. navy fliers encircle globe.	1924. Dawes Reparations Plan accepted by the powers concerned.	1924. Labor government in power; after defeat, is succeeded by Conservative government under Baldwin.	1924. Evacuation of Ruhr by French. Currency stabilized.	1924. Czechoslovakia concludes treaties of amity with Italy and France.
1925	Discovery by Millikan of cosmic rays. Body of Tutankhamen disinterred. Discovery of phototelegraphy.	1925. Locarno treaties for replacement of war by arbitration among European powers ratified.	1925. Government restores gold standard of currency. Coal mine operators subsidized to avoid strike over wage cut.	1925. President Ebert's death followed by election of Hindenburg.	1925. Deportation of Germans from Polish Upper Silesia and of Poles from German portion.
1926	North Pole reached by airplane and dirigible. Production of "Coolidge" rays.	1926. Arms traffic treaty signed by 32 nations at Geneva.	1926. General strike called to support miners, who struck on withdrawal of government subsidy to coal mines.	1926. Germany admitted to League of Nations. Neutrality Treaty with Russia.	1926. General Pilsudski overthrows Polish government with the help of the army; makes himself dictator.

A. D.	FROM THE BEGINNING OF WORLD WAR I, 1914, TO THE PRESENT TIME				
	FRANCE	SPAIN AND PORTUGAL	ITALY AND GREECE	RUSSIA	OTHER COUNTRIES
1914	War with Germany, Austria, Turkey. Battle of the Marne. Battle of the Aisne.	1914. Spain and Portugal neutral in European war.	1914. Italy proclaims her neutrality.	1914. War with Germany, Austria, Turkey.	1914. Chinese parliament dissolved. Japan seizes Kiaochow.
1915	War continues. War with Bulgaria.	1915. Revolution in Portugal. Spanish cabinet resigns.	1915. Italy at war with Austria, Germany, Turkey, Bulgaria.	1915. Evacuation of Warsaw. War with Bulgaria.	1915. Allies attack Dardanelles. Massacre of 800,000 Armenians. Bulgaria makes war on Serbia.
1916	$15,000,000 loan from New York financiers. Siege of Verdun successfully resisted.	1916. Portugal seizes Austrian and German vessels.	1916. Italians capture Gorizia. Provisional government in Greece.	1916. Russians capture Erzerum; Brusilov advances.	1916. Allies withdraw from Dardanelles. Rumania at war with Teutonic powers.
1917	Battle of the Somme.	War on Portugal declared by Germany.	1917. King Constantine of Greece abdicates.	1917. Monarchy ended. Soviet Republic established.	China again a republic. Denmark ratifies sale of Danish West Indies to the United States.
1918	Foch, generalissimo.				
1919	Electoral reform act.	1919. Spain joins League of Nations.	1919. D'Annunzio enters Fiume.	1919. Bolshevists defeat all invaders.	1919. Paderewski ministry in Poland.
1920	Serious railroad strike. Fiftieth anniversary of Republic. Millerand elected president.	1920. In Portugal, former king, Manuel II, renounces claim to the throne.	1920. *Greece:* Constantine recalled by plebiscite. *Italy:* Strong agrarian and socialist movements.	1920. Bolsheviki defeat General Wrangel. Attempted invasion of Poland repelled.	1920. *Turkey:* Treaty of Sèvres signed. Nationalist movement in Asia Minor.
1921	Briand, prime minister, succeeding Leygues. France supports Turkey against Greece in the Near East.	1921. Spanish troops defeated in Morocco. Premier Dato assassinated.	1921. *Italy:* Fascisti movement against the socialists. *Greece:* King Constantine leads Greek army against Turks in Asia Minor.	1921. Breakdown of Bolshevist industrial scheme. Famine conditions widespread.	1921. Non-co-operation movement under Gandhi in India. Mining and oil rights exempted from government appropriation in Mexico. Famine in China.
1922	Poincaré succeeds Briand as premier. Stinnes-Lubersac agreement for handling reparations payments in materials.	1922. Moors on the Riff coast resist Spanish troops successfully. Portugal has nine ministries within the year.	1922. Greeks defeated. Fascisti under Mussolini seize government in Italy. Pope Benedict XV succeeded by Pius XI.	1922. Commercial treaties with Germany and Italy. Conflict between the government and the Church.	1922. Civil war in China. Japan completes evacuation of Shantung province. Turkish National Assembly at Angora deposes the sultan. Poland takes Vilna from Lithuania.
1923	French and Belgian troops occupy the Ruhr valley. Pacific and Naval Limitation treaties ratified.	1923. Spanish campaigns in Morocco. Rivera becomes dictator of Spain.	1923. Violent eruption of Mt. Etna. Fascist reorganization of army, under General Diaz.	1923. American relief commission terminates work. Diplomatic differences with Great Britain adjusted.	1923. Memel assigned to Lithuania by council of ambassadors. Li Yuan Hung, president of China, compelled to resign.
1924	Poincaré defeated. Succeeded by Herriot, who adopts more conciliatory tone in international relations.	1924. Continued hostilities in Spanish Morocco.	1924. Greece made a republic. Fiume annexed to Italy by agreement with Yugoslavia.	1924. Lenin dies and is succeeded by Stalin. Trotzky loses power in government.	1924. Turkish government abolishes the caliphate and declares for a republic. Disastrous earthquake in Japan.
1925	France wars with native tribes in Morocco and Syria. Financial difficulties occasion several ministerial crises.	1925. General Rivera assumes title of premier, relinquishing that of dictator. General growth of prosperity.	1925. Pangalos seizes Greek premiership. Marked economic recovery of Italy under Fascist direction.	1925. Treaty with Japan, by which Japan withdrew troops from northern Sakhalin.	1925. Chinese tariff autonomy granted. Tacna-Arica plebiscite commission headed by General Pershing.
1926	French victorious over Riff tribesmen. Poincaré forms national government; balances the budget.	1926. Rivera proclaims end of parliamentarianism. Republican régime in Portugal overthrown.	1926. Attempted assassination of Mussolini. Greece returns to constitutional government.	1926. Communistic practices greatly modified to secure co-operation of peasants.	1926. General Chang in China seizes Peiping. Poland and Rumania sign 5-year mutual guarantee treaty.

A. D.	FROM THE BEGINNING OF WORLD WAR I, 1914, TO THE PRESENT TIME—CON.				
	ARTS OF CIVILIZATION	INTERNATIONAL AFFAIRS	GREAT BRITAIN	GERMANY	CENTRAL EUROPE
1927	Transatlantic radio-telephone service. Television demonstrated. First solo transatlantic flight, by Lindbergh.	1927. Poland-Lithuania break averted through League of Nations.	1927. Rupture of trade relations with Russia. Britain recognizes independence of Iraq.	1927. Continued progress in industrial expansion; leads in forming international trusts.	1927. Serious labor riots in Vienna suppressed. Treaty between Yugoslavia and France.
1928	Turkey adopts Latin alphabet. Louvain library dedicated. Invention of teletypesetter.	1928. Signing of Paris Pact for outlawing war. Bolivia-Paraguay war postponed through League and Pan-Amer. Conference.	1928. Continued depression in Coal mining industry. Simon Commission on Indian home rule.	1928. Government upheld in general election; chancellor advocates union with Austria.	1928. Polish elections strengthen Pilsudski. Peasant party wins power in Rumania.
1929	Byrd leads Antarctic expedition; flies over South Pole. *Graf Zeppelin* flies around world.	1929. Young Plan supersedes Dawes Plan for final settlement of reparations problem.	1929. First election under universal adult suffrage. Labor party wins plurality. MacDonald premier.	1929. Serious Communist riots in Berlin suppressed by police.	1929. King of Yugoslavia becomes dictator.
1930	International bank begins operations.	1930. Naval disarmament conference in London.	1930. "Civil disobedience" riots in India. Unrest in Egypt.	1930. Occupation of German territory by Allies terminated.	1930. Monarchists and Socialists in Hungary endanger public peace. Carol seizes throne of Rumania.
1931	Rapid progress in discovering the nature of atoms and of celestial bodies.	1931. Year's moratorium on German reparations and Allied debts granted.	1931. Gold standard suspended. Coalition government under MacDonald introduces tariff.	1931. Plans for customs union with Austria abandoned under pressure. Bruening chancellor.	1931. Yugoslavia adopts new constitution.
1932	Zuider Zee reclamation dike in Holland completed. Pontine marshes in Italy reclaimed.	1932. Lausanne conference puts virtual end to German reparation payments. World-wide economic crisis spreads unemployment and discontent.	1932. Imperial Economic Conference at Ottawa promotes economic cohesion of Empire. Irish Free State in tariff war with Great Britain.	1932. Hindenburg re-elected president. Hitlerites gain in power.	1932. Hungary and other countries default on foreign debt payments.
1933	Century of Progress Exposition, Chicago. Lindberghs fly 30,000 miles visiting 21 countries.	1933. World Economic Conference at London meets; disbands without results.	1933. De Valera president of Irish Free State; abolishes oath of allegiance. Constitution for India announced.	1933. Hitler made dictator; Nazi rule. Withdrawal from League of Nations.	1933. Austria, under Dolfuss, resists German attacks; Socialist party crushed. Union of Little Entent.
1934	U. S. naval squadron flies from west coast to Hawaii.	1934. Japan ends naval limitation agreement.	1934. Progress in economic recovery.	1934. Hindenburg dies. Anti-Jew decrees. Party purged by assassinations. Rapid build-up of armed forces.	1934. Dolfuss assassinated by Nazis. Schussnigg chancellor of Austria.
1935	Trans-Pacific air service begun — San Francisco to Manila.	1935. England, France, and Italy meet in conference at Stresa to discuss peace problems.	1935. Stanley Baldwin, prime minister. Silver Jubilee of King George V. Conciliatory policy toward Italy reversed.	1935. Saar returns to Germany. Naval Treaty with Britain. Hitler renounces Treaty of Versailles.	1935. Death of Pilsudski. Polish treaties with Russia and Germany.
1936	Hoover dam completed. Launching of the *Queen Mary*. Zeppelin inaugurates trans-Atlantic service. Great Lakes Exposition, Cleveland, Ohio.	1936. Sanction policy against Italy fails. Fascist and Communist powers clash in Spain. League declares Italy aggressor in Ethiopian war.	1936. Deaths of King George V and Rudyard Kipling. Edward VIII king; abdicates. George VI succeeds. Eire abolishes Governor Generalship. Egypt independent.	1936. Aids Spanish rebels. Alliance with Japan. Sends troops into demilitarized Rhine zone.	1936. Economic penetration by Germany. Continued friction in Austria with Nazi Partisans.

A. D.	FROM THE BEGINNING OF WORLD WAR I, 1914, TO THE PRESENT TIME—CON.				
	FRANCE	SPAIN AND PORTUGAL	ITALY AND GREECE	RUSSIA	OTHER COUNTRIES
1927	Trade treaty with Germany. Treaties of arbitration with Yugoslavia and Rumania.	1927. Rivera summons national assembly; it acts in advisory capacity only.	1927. Italian treaty with Albania. Italian electoral laws increase power of Mussolini.	1927. Defeat of revolutionary efforts in Europe and China.	1927. Continued civil war in China. Financial panic in Japan; Hirohito crowned emperor.
1928	Poincaré returned to power by large majority. France on gold standard.	1928. American and British loans for stabilizing exchange.	1928. Italian parliament replaced by Fascist controlled chamber. Venizelos again premier of Greece. Italo-Greek treaty of friendship.	1928. Stalin succeeds in banishing opponents; Five-year plan for economic progress begun.	1928. Albania becomes kingdom. Famine in China; Chiang Kai-shek becomes president.
1929	Death of Marshal Foch. Tardieu becomes premier.	1929. Attempted revolution suppressed.	1929. Temporal power of Pope restored by Mussolini.	1929. Trotzky exiled. War with China averted.	1929. China enacts first national tariff. Tacna-Arica dispute settled.
1930	Briand urges formation of United States of Europe.	1930. Spanish dictator, Rivera, resigns. Berenguer becomes premier.	1930. Italian naval rivalry with France. Turco-Greek treaty of friendship.	1930. Rapid progress in economic plan and extension of "collective" farms.	1930. Renewed civil war in China. Greece and Turkey, after exchange of population, sign treaty of friendship and arbitration.
1931	Doumer president. Death of Briand. Laval premier; visits President Hoover.	1931. Republic in Spain; Alfonso XIII flees; church and state separated.	1931. Controversy between Italy and Vatican; temporary suppression of Catholic organizations in Italy.	1931. Rapid industrialization during five-year plan. Socialization of agriculture. Populace controlled by terrorism.	1931. Japan seizes Manchuria.
1932	Tardieu premier. Herriot premier, defeated on issue of war debt payments to U. S.	1932. Catalonia made autonomous within Spain. Jesuits expelled from Spain.	1932. Amnesty for political prisoners in Italy. Greece defaults on foreign debt payments.	1932. Non-aggression treaties with France and Poland. Food crisis with widespread distress.	1932. Japan takes and relinquishes Shanghai; establishes Manchukuo.
1933	Several premiers defeated on budget proposals for meeting deficit.	1933. Portugal ends dictatorship; resumes constitutional government. Spain disestablishes Catholic church.	1933. Italy negotiates 4-power pact with Britain, France, Germany on arms, economic interests.	1933. Non-aggression treaties with nine countries. Relations with U. S. resumed.	1933. Japan resigns from League of Nations.
1934	Financial scandal compromises officials.	1934. Conservatives gain in Spanish Cortes.	1934. Italy plans abolition of Chamber.	1934. Communist control legalized.	1934. Japan moderates militant attitude. Turkey enfranchises women.
1935	Laval premier. Deflation by decree as depression makes itself felt.	1935. Political crisis in Spain.	1935. Civil war in Greece. Italy invades Ethiopia.	1935. Closer relations with Great Britain.	1935. Threatened Chino-Japanese conflict in North China; Japanese seize Chahar.
1936	Blum premier. Popular front government. Alliance with Russia. Munitions manufacture nationalized. Autonomy granted to Syria, a mandated territory.	1936. Liberals win. Conservatives rebel, supported by Fascist powers, Italy and Germany.	1936. Italy conquers Ethiopia; aids Spanish rebels. New Roman Empire proclaimed. Greece goes Fascist, a dictatorship being set up under Gen. Metaxas.	1936. Adopts constitution democratic in form. Alliance with France. Stalin removes opponents by treason trials.	1936. Chinese resistance to Japan hardens. Japanese pro-army cabinet defeated; refuses to resign. Turkey remilitarizes the Dardanelles.

A. D.	From the Beginning of World War I, 1914, to the Present Time—Con.				
	ARTS OF CIVILIZATION	INTERNATIONAL AFFAIRS	GREAT BRITAIN	GERMANY	CENTRAL EUROPE
1937	Automatic landing device for airplanes introduced. Paris Exposition. Construction of solar heat collector for power. Two longest span bridges in the world opened at San Francisco.	1937. Unrestricted armaments race. Belgium returns to status of neutral state, cutting tie with France and England. Patrol of Spanish coast by ships of 27 nations to prevent outside aid to either party.	1937. Tariff reductions within empire. Chamberlain succeeds as prime minister. Coal mines nationalized, effective in 1942. Federal constitution for India effective. New constitution adopted by Irish Free State (Ireland).	1937. Rapprochement with Italy and enlargement of influence among central European nations.	1937. Balkans in move to curb outside intrigue. Yugoslavia signs 5-year treaty of friendship with Italy.
1938	Production of practical lightweight Diesel engine announced.	1938. Munich conference: Britain and France abandon Czechoslovakia to Germany.	1938. Parleys with Ireland for settlement of pending controversies. Chamberlain returns from Munich with prophesy of "peace in our time."	1938. Austria and Czechoslovakia taken.	1938. Czechoslovakia seized by Germany.
1939	New York and San Francisco expositions. First year of commercial air traffic in U. S. without fatal accident.	1939. Political influence of League of Nations in eclipse. World War II begins.	1939. Declaration of war against Germany.	1939. Danzig taken. Poland conquered and divided with Russia. Alliance with Russia.	1939. Poland conquered by Germany and Russia.
1940	Laboratory method devised for release of atomic energy.	1940. Tokyo joins Rome-Berlin axis. International Labor office removed to Montreal.	1940. Churchill premier. Army driven from France; German invasion threatened; terrific aerial raids. Conquest of Italian East Africa.	1940. Conquest of Norway, Lowlands, France.	1940. Germany takes control of Hungary, Bulgaria, Rumania; gains access to Black Sea.
1941	Grand Coulee dam completed. War needs cause improvement in aircraft.	1941. Atlantic Charter promulgated by Roosevelt and Churchill.	1941. Reverses in Greece; huge shipping losses; alliance with Russia; war against Japan.	1941. Conquest of Yugoslavia and Greece. War declared on Russia and U. S.	1941. German domination complete.
1942	Announcement of radar detection device. Use of penicillin.		1942. Loss of Malaya, Singapore, Burma.	1942. Advance into Russia; N. Africa to Egypt.	
1943		1943. Conferences at Casablanca, Quebec, Moscow, Cairo, Tehran.	1943. Victories in N. Africa and Italy; submarines beaten.	1943. Driven from N. Africa; defeat in Russia; cities ruined.	1943. Yugoslav patriots battle Germans.
1944	Development of rocket planes.	1944. Dumbarton Oaks agreement on draft of international charter.	1944. Invasion of Normandy. V-bomb attack on England.	1944. Germans defeated in Italy, France and Poland. Americans cross Rhine.	1944. Rumania and Bulgaria desert Germany. Yugoslavia and Greece freed.
1945	Atomic bomb tested at Los Alamos; used at Hiroshima. First use of atomic energy.	1945. Crimean Conference at Yalta. Potsdam Conference. UN Charter framed.	1945. British in northern Germany. Germany surrenders. Attlee (Labor) succeeds Churchill.	1945. Berlin taken by Russians. Germany occupied by Allies.	1945. Poland and Czechoslovakia liberated. Austria, Hungary occupied.
1946	Radar signals reflected from moon.	1946. League of Nations dissolved. First General Assembly of U. N.	1946. Bank of England nationalized.	1946. Nuremburg trials of war criminals.	1946. Poland: pro-Russians in power. Austria: 4-power military rule.
1947	Baruch (U. S.) plan for atomic control fails through Russian opposition.	1947. Marshall plan proposed.	1947. Coal railways and electrical industries nationalized.	1947. Moscow conference on German and Austrian treaties fails.	1947. Communists seize Bulgaria and Hungary.
1948	Hale 200-inch reflecting telescope.	1948. U. N. admits Burma. Britain, France and Benelux nations unite for defense.	1948. National Health Service act. Burma independent.	1948. Russians blockade Berlin by land. "Airlift" supplies city.	1948. Communist coup gains control of Czechoslovakia.

A. D.	FROM THE BEGINNING OF WORLD WAR I, 1914, TO THE PRESENT TIME—CON.				
	FRANCE	SPAIN AND PORTUGAL	ITALY AND GREECE	RUSSIA	OTHER COUNTRIES
1937	Checks German penetration of Morocco. Blum resigns after having been refused extraordinary fiscal powers. Chautemps succeeds as premier.	1937. Civil war continues. Portugal aids rebels.	1937. Italo-British treaty on Mediterranean fleet. Italy joins pact with Germany and Japan to combat Communism.	1937. Treason purge extends to army command and throughout every department of life. First popular election held for legislators.	1937. Chinese Communists grow in power. Japan seizes Peiping, Shanghai, Nanking.
1938	Enlarged armament program. Daladier premier. Policy of appeasement toward Germany.	1938. Government and rebel forces struggle, success varying.	1938. Closer relations with England and Germany enhance power of Italy in Mediterranean.	1938. First meeting of national legislature.	1938. Chinese resist Japanese invasion, using guerilla warfare.
1939	War against Germany in aid of Poland.	1939. Spanish government forces conquered. Franco dictator.	1939. Italy declares neutrality in War of 1939.	1939. Alliance with Germany; bases obtained from Baltic states. Poland divided with Germany. War on Finland.	1939. Japan exerts pressure to drive nationals of other countries from captured Chinese cities.
1940	Defeat by Germany; two-thirds of country occupied; Pétain chief of state.	1940. Spain hovers between neutrality and affiliation with axis powers.	1940. Italy declares war on France; attacks Greece and British Africa; disastrous defeats.	1940. Finland cedes territory; three Baltic states incorporated.	1940. Stalemate in China; United States obtains 8 bases in British America.
1941	German pressure to force cooperation. "Free French" in Africa and Syria.	1941. Germany seeks passage to Gibraltar.	1941. Greece conquered by Germany. Italy under Germans.	1941. Germany at war; takes Odessa, Kiev; fails at Moscow, Leningrad.	1941. Japan attacks United States.
1942	Laval in power.		1942. Allies take Libya.	1942. Germans reach Don.	1942. Japan takes Philippines, Singapore; defeated at Coral Sea, Midway.
1943	Germany completes occupation; fleet scuttled; DeGaulle rises in power.	1943. Portugal permits British bases in Azores.	1943. Allies invade Italy; peace with Allies, war with Germany.	1943. Germans retreat to Dnieper.	1943. Japan defeated in Solomons, New Guinea.
1944	Liberation from Germany. De Gaulle assumes leadership.	1944. Franco maintains power.	1944. Rome taken. Germans driven into north Italy.	1944. Germans driven from Russia.	1944. Japan gains in China; loses Guam, Saipan. Fleet ruined at Leyte.
1945	Constituent assembly meets. Petain, Laval, prosecuted.		1945. Germans in northern Italy surrender. Mussolini killed.	1945. Russia occupies Berlin and east Germany.	1945. Japan loses Iwo Jima and Okinawa. Atomic bomb at Hiroshima. Japan surrenders.
1946	DeGaulle resigns. Gouin succeeds. First proposed constitution rejected; second, adopted.	1946. U. N. recommends that its members withdraw diplomats from Madrid.	1946. Peace treaty. Victor Emmanuel III abdicates. Italy votes for a republic.	1946. New 5-year plan. Russian control of Dardanelles opposed by Turkey.	1946. Japan under Allied Supreme command. Civil war in China. Philippines independent.
1947	Fourth Republic inaugurated Auriol president. DeGaullists win local elections.	1947. Franco gets majority in plebiscite.	1947. U. S. gives to Greece, Turkey $400,000,000 for defense against Communism.	1947. Russia in general opposition to Western powers.	1947. U. S. gives up attempt to mediate in China. Civil war continues with Communist gains.
1948	Queille succeeds Schuman. Political strikes continue.		1948. DeGasperi carries elections against Communists.	1948. Russian blockade of Berlin met by airlift.	1948. Korea: two gov'ts set up; north and south. State of Israel set up.

A. D.	FROM THE BEGINNING OF WORLD WAR I, 1914, TO THE PRESENT TIME—CON.				
	ARTS OF CIVILIZATION	INTERNATIONAL AFFAIRS	GREAT BRITAIN	GERMANY	CENTRAL EUROPE
1949	U. S. bomber circles globe in 94 hours in first non-stop flight.	1949. U. N. mediates truce between Palestine and Egypt.	1949. Britain, U.S., Canada, France, Belgium, Netherlands, Luxembourg, Norway, sign North Atlantic pact.	1949. Marshall Plan production goals in Western Germany retarded by lack of capital.	1949. Hungarian Communist court convicts Cardinal Mindszenty of treason.
1950	National Science Foundation for basic research created.	1950. U.N. calls North Korea to cease invasion of South Korea.	1950. Labor party wins general election by narrow margin. India independent.	1950. May day calm as 500,000 Berliners defy communism.	1950. The U. S. breaks diplomatic relations with Bulgaria.
1951	Single-engine American plane flown over North Pole.	1951. U. N. declares Communist China committed aggression in Korea.	1951. Nationalization of steel industry. Conservatives win general election.	1951. West Germany approves Schuman plan.	1951. Archbishop Beran of Czechoslovakia banished.
1952	Successful hydrogen weapon test by United States.	1952. Korean peace talks blocked by Communist China and Soviet Union.	1952. King George VI died. Elizabeth II proclaimed queen. Atom bomb exploded.	1952. West Germany granted independence.	1952. Yugoslav forces equipped by U.S.
1953	First ascent of Mount Everest.	1953. Armistice ends Korean War.	1953. Elizabeth II crowned.	1953. Adenauer re-elected as chancellor.	1953. Tito elected first president of Yugoslavia.
1954	First atomic submarine, US Nautilus.	1954. Geneva conference arranges armistice in Indo-China.	1954. World tour of the queen and the Duke of Edinborough.	1954. Problem of German rearmament discussed.	1954. Yugoslavia, Greece, Turkey sign defense pact.
1955	Salk anti-polio vaccine proves successful.	1955. Warsaw pact of defense by Communist states in Europe.	1955. Churchill succeeded by Anthony Eden.	1955. West Germany becomes NATO member.	1955. Peace treaty with Austria by great powers.
1956	International Atomic Energy Agency approved by 82 nations.	1956. Egypt seizes Suez. Britain, France, Israel attack Canal zone; then withdraw.	1956. Greek riots in Cyprus and Suez crisis unsettle government.	1956. Organization of West German army begins.	1956. Revolts in Poland, Hungary crushed by Soviets.
1957	First satellites, Russia's Sputniks I and II.	1957. European Market Treaty signed in Rome.	1957. Eden succeeded by Macmillan. Hydrogen bomb exploded.	1957. Saar is reunited to West Germany.	1957. Repression in Hungary continued.
1958	U.S. launches satellite, Explorer I.	1958. Common Market begins.	1958. Macmillan visits leading capitals to urge easing of cold war.	1958. Russian demand to make Berlin "Free City" rejected.	1958. Polish subservience to Russia is slowly mitigated.
1959	Russian Lunik II and III reach moon.	1959. Greece, Turkey, and Britain agree on constitution of Cyprus.	1959. Conservatives under Macmillan win election.	1959. German Social Democrats abandon Marxism.	1959. Massive exodus from East to West Germany.
1960	Polaris missile launched from submerged craft.	1960. Seventeen new African states independent.	1960. Britain leads new European Free Trade Association.	1960. Trade agreement between East and West Germany.	
1961	First manned spacecraft orbit the earth, Russian Vostok I and II.	1961. UN secretary killed while seeking truce in Congo.	1961. Government decides to seek entry into the Common Market.	1961. Adenauer reelected.	1961. East Germans wall off West Berlin.
1962	Widening application of computing machines.				
1963		1963. Limited ban on nuclear tests agreed to; China, France refuse to sign.	1963. Entry to Common Market vetoed by France. Home succeeds Macmillan.	1963. Treaty of co-operation with France. Adenauer succeeded by Erhard.	
1964	U.S. missile to moon transmits excellent photographs.	1964. UN crisis over Russian and French nonpayment of assessments compromised.	1964. Harold Wilson prime minister.		1964. Increase of independence in Russian satellites.

A. D.	FROM THE BEGINNING OF WORLD WAR I, 1914, TO THE PRESENT TIME—CON.				
	FRANCE	SPAIN AND PORTUGAL	ITALY AND GREECE	RUSSIA	OTHER COUNTRIES
1949	Georges Bidault becomes premier.		1949. Italy signs North Atlantic pact.	1949. Russia forms Council to oppos Marshall Plan.	1949. Communists take over China. Indonesia independent.
1950	Schuman proposes merger of French-German coal, steel industries.	1950. U. S. votes Spain $62,500,-000 under Marshall plan.	1950. Holy Year draws many visitors to Italy.	1950. Shooting down of un-armed U. S. plane over Baltic.	1950. King Leopold of Belgium resumes throne, but abdicates Sept. 7, 1951.
1951	Official visit of President Auriol to U. S.		1951. Communists lose in elections.	1951. U.S., Britain, France, and Russia meet in Paris.	
1952		1952. Spain and Portugal form joint front against Soviet.	1952. Conservatives win Greek election. Soviets veto Italy's admission to U.N.	1952. New central committee supersedes the Politburo.	1952. King Farouk of Egypt abdicates when army seizes power.
1953	Coty elected president.	1953. Spain grants U.S. air and naval base rights.	1953. De Gasperi's government falls.	1953. Death of Stalin.	1953. Egypt a republic under Nasser. Shah of Iran regains power.
1954	French defeat in Indo-China ends French rule.	1954. Spanish rioters demand cession of Gibraltar by Britain.	1954. Italy and Yugoslavia agree on control of Trieste.	1954. Russian objection to German rearmament.	1954. India recognizes Chinese control of Tibet.
1955	Algeria revolts against French rule.	1955. Spanish economy bolstered by U.S.	1955. Gronchi is elected president of Italy.	1955. Malenkov succeeded by Bulganin.	
1956	Franco-British intervention in Egypt balked by Russia and U.S.	1956. Spain recognizes independence of Morocco.	1956. British-Greek dispute over Cyprus.	1956. Revolts in Poland and Hungary suppressed.	1956. Nasser first president of Egypt. Sudan, Morocco, Tunisia become independent.
1957	Algerian war intensified. UN urges settlement.	1957. Franco introduces reforms.			1957. Ghana independent.
1958	De Gaulle premier; Fifth Republic formed. French Community inaugurated.	1958. Total of U.S. aid to Spain reaches over $800 million.	1958. Roncalli is elected pope as John XXIII.	1958. Khrushchev achieves power; pushes foreign aid program.	1958. Egyptian partisans try to take over Iraq and Lebanon.
1959	De Gaulle introduces drastic reforms.			1959. Soviet leadership challenged by China.	1959. South African racial segregation policy continued.
1960	Franc devalued 99 per cent and stabilized.		1960. Pope summons first council since Council of Trent.	1960. U.S. espionage plane over Russia downed.	1960. Chaos in Congo; UN sends troops.
1961	Revolt of French army in Algeria suppressed.	1961. Portugal loses Goa to India; suppreses Angola revolt.		1961. Russia explodes largest atomic bomb.	1961. South Africa withdraws from Commonwealth.
1962	Algeria independent. Presidency made elective by popular vote.		1962. Pope convenes Second Vatican Council to reconsider some doctrines of Church.	1962. After installing missile bases in Cuba, Russia removes them under U.S. atomic threat.	1962. China invades northern India; then withdraws. Organization of African Unity formed
1963	Progressive withdrawal from NATO.		1963. Paul VI becomes pope; continues Vatican II.		1963. Army in South Vietnam takes over.
1964	Effort to weaken dollar by converting to gold.		1964. Aldo Moro prime minister of Italy.	1964. Khrushchev ousted.	1964. Bombing of bases in North Vietnam begun by U.S. China explodes A-bomb.

A. D.	FROM THE BEGINNING OF WORLD WAR I, 1914, TO THE PRESENT TIME—CON.				
	ARTS OF CIVILIZATION	INTERNATIONAL AFFAIRS	GREAT BRITAIN	GERMANY	CENTRAL EUROPE
1965	First "space walks" by Russian and U.S. astronauts.		1965. Drastic plan adopted for economic expansion.		
1966	First soft landing on moon by Russian and U.S. space ships.	1966. NATO moves to Brussels. U.S. and Russia pledge no use of weapons in space.	1966. Rhodesia's white supremacy policy rules out recognition of independence.	1966. Erhard replaced by Kiesinger.	1966. Yugoslavia, Rumania, and Czechoslovakia compromise their Marxist economies.
1967	Evidence of 2½ million years as human race's antiquity.		1967. Renewed bid for entry into Common Market. Pound devalued.		
1968	U.S. Apollo 8 makes first manned flight to the moon. S. Africa is scene of first human heart transplant.	1968. North Korean patrol seizes U.S. *Pueblo.* International gold crisis.	1968. Rhodesia executes reprieved Africans. British austerity continues; immigration is curtailed.	1968. West Berlin under pressure. Yugoslavia and West Germany reopen diplomatic relations.	1968. Rumania quits Communist Conference. Russian invasion crushes liberal Czech regime.
1969	US Apollo 11 lands first men on the Moon. Historic flight followed by Apollo 12.	1969. Vietnam Peace Talks stalemated in Paris. US reduces forces in Vietnam. US to return Okinawa to Japan.	1969. Religious strife persists in Northern Ireland. British forces maintain uneasy peace in civil rights conflict.	1969. West Germany moves nearer two-party system; Christian Democrat Kiesinger elected, then challenged and defeated by Social Democrat Willy Brandt.	1969. Czechs return to Communist orthodoxy following Soviet invasion; Dubcek ousted; Husak succeeds.
1970	Apollo 13 Moon mission fails, but returns safely.	1970. Russian missiles installed at Suez sites, despite Mideast truce.	1970. Edward Heath Prime Minister, takes steps to denationalize industries.	1970. Brandt moves to close gaps between East & West.	1970. Gomulka resigns in wake of Polish crises.
1971	Apollo 14 completes mission for third Moon landing. US and USSR launch unmanned spacecraft on flights to Mars. Human Growth Hormone (HGH) is synthesized. Apollo 15 fourth US Moon landing. USSR Astronauts in space platform set new record—some 24 days in orbit—but are found dead on return.	1971. Soviets test naval missiles with range of 5000 miles. US withdraws more forces from Vietnam.	1971. Britain adopts decimal currency, retains pound and pence as units.	1971. West Germany restricts arms sales to Greece and Portugal.	1971. Gierek takes power in Poland, promises conservative regime.
1972	USSR makes first soft landing of unmanned spacecraft on Mars.	1972. US Pres. Nixon holds summit meetings with Red Chinese.	1972. Britain enters European Economic Community. Civil War worsens in Northern Ireland.	1972. East and West Germany sign accords to ease access between the two states.	1972. Polish Communist 6th Congress opens under Party Chief Gierek.
1973	US Skylab-Apollo space-station missions completed safely. Europe: Eleven nations create joint space agency.	1973. US-Red China open liaison missions. Russia's Brezhnev US visit marks easing in US-USSR relations. US military role in Vietnam comes to official end.	1973. Bahamas independent. Britain disputes Iceland's claim to 50-mile coastal fishing waters.	1973. East and West Germany establish normal relations; both apply to enter UN.	1973. Czech-West German treaty restores relations, nullifies 1938 Munich pact. Rumanian Pres. Ceausescu is first leader in east Europe to visit West Germany.

A. D.	FROM THE BEGINNING OF WORLD WAR I, 1914, TO THE PRESENT TIME—CON.				
	FRANCE	SPAIN AND PORTUGAL	ITALY AND GREECE	RUSSIA	OTHER COUNTRIES
1965	De Gaulle reelected to presidency.		1965. Vatican Council backs religious liberty.	1965. Food crisis.	1965. Brief war between India and Pakistan.
1966	World tour by De Gaulle to court Russia and gain status for France.	1966. Easing of censorship and some relaxation of dictatorship in Spain.		1966. Move toward introducing profit incentives; softening of Cold War.	
1967	Initiative in moderating East-West tension.	1967. Spanish people approve new constitution.	1967. Pope sets up first synod of bishops.		1967. Chaos in China. Israeli & Arabs at war.
1968	De Gaulle loses majority in Parliament. Students riot in Paris. De Gaulle survives political crises.	1968. Students protest college closings. Caetano succeeds ill Salazar as premier of Portugal.	1968. U.S. resumes diplomatic relations. Constantine in exile. Greek military junta retains control; new constitution voted.	1968. USSR moves fleet into Mediterranean. Soviets quell uprisings in Czechoslovakia and Poland.	1968. Viet Cong attack South Vietnamese.
1969	De Gaulle resigns, succeeded by Pompidou. Franc devalued.	1969. Franco names Prince Juan Carlos as his successor. Guerrilla warfare continues in Portuguese colonies.	1969. Strikes stall Italian industry. Greek junta continues in power.	1969. Russia-US negotiate arms limitations.	1969. Golda Meir succeeds Lev Eshkol as Israeli premier. Tensions with Arab states persist. North Vietnam leader Ho Chi Minh dies.
1970	Death of De Gaulle, last of World War II Allied leaders.	1970. Franco commutes death sentences of Basque terrorists. Former premier Salazar dies in Lisbon.	1970. Italy and Red China agree to establish diplomatic relations.	1970. USSR lands lunar vehicle on Moon.	1970. Pakistan typhoon is worst disaster of century. Some 300,000 dead.
1971	France and West Germany plan accord on retrials of war criminals.	1971. Spain cracks down on leftists, suspends right of habeas corpus.	1971. Italy legalizes divorce.	1971. Soviets commute sentences of Jewish hijackers.	1971. Prime Minister Indira Gandhi dissolves Indian Parliament, sets national election for new legislature. Civil War in Pakistan: Secessionist East Pakistanis are crushed by Karachi forces.
1972	French and Algerians settle dispute on Algerian nationalization of French oil interests.	1972. Madrid announces third 4-year plan for economic development.	1972. Leone is elected sixth president of Italy. Greek Premier announces release of political prisoners.	1972. Soviets complete world's largest hydro-electric plant. Russia buys huge amounts of US grain.	1972. India defeats Pakistan in brief war. Bangladesh established. Red China joins UN, Nationalist China expelled.
1973	France holds atom test in Pacific.	1973. Bishops of Spain call for mutual independence of Church and State.	1973. Referendum in Greece abolishes monarchy, creating new parliamentary republic.	1973. USSR signs contract to supply gas to US.	1973. War breaks out between Egypt-Syria and Israel.

A. D.	FROM THE BEGINNING OF WORLD WAR I, 1914, TO THE PRESENT TIME—CON.				
	ARTS OF CIVILIZATION	INTERNATIONAL AFFAIRS	GREAT BRITAIN	GERMANY	CENTRAL EUROPE
1974	US Skylab III sets new space record: 84 days in orbit of the earth.	1974. World crisis in energy and food.	1974. Heath fails to win liberals' support. Harold Wilson returned.	1974. Brandt resigns on exposure of spy on his staff. Helmut Schmidt elected.	1974. Czechs sign accord with West Germans voiding Munich Pact of 35 years ago. Yugoslavs adopt 4th constitution since World War II.
1975	Soviet Soyuz—US Apollo link in joint mission in space.	1975. North Vietnamese victory ends war in Asia. Egypt and Israel sign interim peace accord in Mideast. 33 nations sign European security pact, recognizing European borders at end of World War II.	1975. Parliament outlaws Irish Republican Army in move against terrorism. First referendum in British history favors continuance in European Economic Community.	1975. West Germany grants long-term credit to East Germany. Travel is eased between the two states.	1975. Rumania signs 5-year agreement with US, to cooperate in science and technology.
1976	US Viking I and II search for life on planet Mars. First supersonic jet transport flights made by French-British Concorde.	1976. Death of Mao Tse-tung, Chinese Communist leader. China-Japan sign pact declaring formal end to World War II. Southeast Asia Treaty Organization disbanded.	1976. British Prime Minister Wilson resigns—succeeded by Labor Party's James Callaghan. Worst drought in Britain's history forces strict conservation. Mass peace rallies in Northern Ireland—but fighting is continued.	1976. Helmut Schmidt elected again as West German Chancellor. Pact signed with Poland.	1976. Crash of Yugoslav and British planes— 176 killed. Yugoslavs imprison Soviet spy. Netherlands' Prince Bernhard involved in Lockheed graft scandal. Sweden's Social Democrats lose in national elections.
1977	US begins testing of space shuttle. New dating technique, more advantageous than carbon-14 dating, in developmental stages in US.	1977. Major nations call for worldwide human rights. Ocean spills cause environmental concern. Terrorist attacks—bombings, assassinations, kidnappings, skyjackings—on industrial nations.	1977. 200-mile fishing limit put into effect. $3.9 billion loan acquired from International Monetary Fund. Elizabeth II's Silver Jubilee held.	1977. East Germany imposes visa requirements between West Berlin and East Berlin.	1977. Czech dissidents protest suppression of human rights.

A. D.	FROM THE BEGINNING OF WORLD WAR I, 1914, TO THE PRESENT TIME—CON.				
	FRANCE	SPAIN AND PORTUGAL	ITALY AND GREECE	RUSSIA	OTHER COUNTRIES
1974	Pompidou dies; Giscard d'Estaing is elected President. Voting age lowered to 18. Labor laws liberalized, taxes raised—but strikes persist as economy continues decline.	1974. Caetano's overthrow ends dictatorships in Portugal dating from 1926. Leftist military junta takes power. Series of governments fail to resolve crises. Uprisings in African colonies bring them independence.	1974. Italy in crisis; borrows $2 billion from West Germany. Greece: Military dictatorship collapses; monarchy is rejected. Turkey seizes Cyprus.	1974. US–USSR detente continues. Soviets advance space program in cooperation with US. Shortfall of crops adds to demand for US grain.	1974. India: Inflation, famine, government crises—yet India successfully completes first nuclear tests.
1975	France re-enters European currency bloc. Gold price raised. National postal strikes stall mail.	1975. Spanish government executes terrorists as Free Europe protests reprisals. Franco dies: Juan Carlos I becomes king.	1975. Greece signs cease-fire with Turkey after Cyprus invasion. With Constantine Caramanlis as prime minister, Greece adopts new constitution.	1975. USSR–US–Japan agree to cooperate in developing Soviet natural gas fields. Red Chinese–Soviet tensions are eased. Soviet stages its largest fleet maneuvers in Pacific.	1975. North Pakistan earthquake—5000 dead. India becomes 11th nation to launch a space satellite. Indira Gandhi survives election crises. Govt. controls, censorship imposed. Israel-Egypt sign interim peace pact. Egypt reopens Suez. Australian Prime Minister dismissed by Governor-General Kern.
1976	Premier Chirac resigns and is succeeded by Raymond Barre. First woman general is appointed. Controversial sales of nuclear plants to Pakistan and South Africa.	1976. Nationwide strikes occur in Spain. US-Spain sign defense pact. Portuguese approve new constitution: elect parliament. President Antonio Ramalho appoints Mario Soares prime minister.	1976. US-Greek pact renews military base agreement. Communist Party make significant gains in Italian elections.	1976. 25th Communist Party Congress convened under Leonid Brezhnev. Premier Kosygin visits Middle East. Egypt ends Treaty of Friendship with USSR.	1976. Chinese Premier Chou En-lai dies. Hua Kuo-feng succeeds Mao as party chairman. Earthquake in Tangshan kills an estimated 655,000. Gandhi gains more power in India and imprisons rivals. North and South Vietnam united. Civil wars fought in Angola and Lebanon. Hundreds die in S. Africa riots.
1977	Government releases terrorist Abu Daoud. President Giscard d'Estaing's political party changes name to Republican. France's last colony in Africa, the Territory of Afars and Issas, becomes an independent state—Djibouti.	1977. Spain continues liberalization, frees Communist head. First free election in 41 years in Spain endorses Premier Adolfo Suarez Gonzalez.	1977. Italy passes liberal abortion law.	1977. Dissidents led by Sakharov, appeal to US for help. Leonid Brezhnev replaces Nikolai Podgorny as president—becoming first to hold both this position and that of party chief. USSR develops anti-satellite interceptor (ASAT) that can track and destroy spacecraft.	1977. Increased guerrilla warfare in Rhodesia as Geneva talks fail. Food riots in Egypt. India's Prime Minister Gandhi replaced by Morarji Desai. Dutch-US 747s collide in worst accident in aircraft history—more than 570 killed. Menachem Begin elected Israeli premier. Civil war between Ethiopia and Eritrea continues. Teng Hsiao-p'ing becomes China's vice premier. Cypriot leader Makarios dies.

TIME	NAME AND RESULTS	LEADING BATTLES	CHIEF LEADERS
B. C. 2750	Triumph of Semitic invaders over people of the Mesopotamian valley.	. . . .	Sargon of Accad.
2200	Amorite kings conquer Babylon, Sumer, and Accad.		
1600	Egyptians make conquest of western Asia.		
14th to 12th century	Hittites and Hebrews conquer and occupy the Asiatic realms of the Egyptians.		
1300–1000	Greeks conquer the Ægean lands.	Siege of Troy.	
13th century	Hittite empire overthrown by Indo-European invaders.		
750–700	Assyrian kings become masters of western Asia.	. . . .	Sargon II.
606	Assyrian empire overthrown by the Chaldeans.		
550–525	Persian Conquests. Persia supreme in western Asia and in Egypt.	. . . .	Cyrus; Cambyses.
500–479	Greco-Persian Wars. Greece successfully resists Persian invasion.	Marathon; Thermopylæ; Salamis; Platæa; Mycale.	Miltiades; Leonidas; Themistocles; Pausanius; Xerxes; Darius.
431–404	Peloponnesian War. Athens conquered by Sparta.	Mytilene; Platæa; Sphacteria; Amphipolis.	Pericles; Alcibiades; Lysander.
343–290	Samnite Wars. Romans conquer Samnites.	Caudine Forks; Sentinum.	Fabius Maximus; Gaius Pontius.
334–323	Wars of Alexander the Great. Greek forces conquer Persia and Egypt.	Granicus; Issus; Arbela.	Alexander the Great; Darius.
264–146	Punic Wars. Romans destroy Carthage.	Ticinus; Trebia; Thrasymenus; Cannæ; Metaurus; Zama.	Fabius; Scipio; Hannibal.
200–146	Greco-Roman War. Greece subdued by Rome.	Cynoscephalæ; Pydna.	Flaminius; Æmilius Paulus; Mummius; Perseus.
112–106	Jugurthine War. Romans conquer Numidia.	Muthul; Cirta.	Jugurtha; Metellus; Marius.
90–88	Roman Social War. Right of Roman citizenship granted the Italian allies.	. . . .	Sulla.
88–65	Mithridatic Wars. Mithridates, king of Pontus, defeated.	Chæronea; Orchomenus.	Lucullus; Pompey; Sulla; Mithridates; Archelaus.
73–71	Gladiatorial War. Gladiators defeated.	Petelia.	Spartacus; Crassus.
58–51	Gallic War. Gauls conquered by Cæsar.	Bibracte (Autun); Alesia (Alise Sainte-Reine).	Cæsar; Ariovistus; Vercingetorix.
50–31	Roman Civil War. Roman Empire established.	Pharsalus; Thapsus; Munda; Philippi; Actium.	Cæsar; Pompey; Brutus; Cassius; Antony; Augustus.
A. D. 70	Jewish-Roman War. Jerusalem taken; temple destroyed.	Siege of Jerusalem.	Titus.
101–106	Dacian War. Country beyond Danube conquered.	. . . .	Trajan; Decebalus.
400–493	Barbarian Wars. Teutonic hordes capture Rome, ravage Italy, and displace Roman emperors.	Sack of Rome; East Gothic kingdom set up.	Alaric; Genseric; Attila; Theodoric.
709–1492	Saracen Conquests. The Saracens occupy northern Africa and Spain; defeated in France; driven from Spain.	Xerez; Tours; Tarifa; Granada.	Musa; Tarik; Charles Martel; Cid Campeador.
1095–1291	The Crusades. Christians capture Palestine and set up the feudal kingdom of Jerusalem, but are finally repulsed.	Siege of Jerusalem; Acre.	Godfrey of Bouillon; Conrad III; Louis VII; Frederick II; Philip Augustus; Richard the Lion-Hearted; Louis IX; Edward I; Saladin.
13th century	Mongol Conquests, from southern Russia eastward to China.	Wahlstatt.	Batu; Henry the Pious.
1337–1453	Hundred Years' War. England lost all her possessions in France except Calais.	Crécy; Calais; Poitiers; Agincourt.	Edward III of England; Edward the Black Prince; Henry V of England; Joan of Arc.
1386–1388	Austro-Swiss War. Independence of Switzerland.	Sempach; Näfels.	Arnold von Winkelried; Leopold of Austria.
1419–1436	Hussite War. Religious toleration secured.	Deutsch-Brod; Böhmisch-Brod.	John Ziska; Sigismund.
1455–1485	Wars of the Roses. House of York supplants that of Lancaster on English throne.	St. Albans; Bloreheath; Wakefield; Towton; Barnet; Tewksbury.	Richard, duke of York; Edward, duke of York; Earl of Warwick; Queen Margaret; Henry VI.
1526–1565	Mogul Conquest of India.	Panipat; Talikota; Sikri.	Baber; Akbar; Vijayanagar.
1562–1598	French Civil Wars. Edict of Nantes, Protestant toleration.	Dreux; St.-Denis; Jarnac; Moncontour; Ivry.	Duke of Anjou; Henry III; Henry IV; Prince de Condé.
1567–1609	Spanish-Netherlands War. Independence of the Netherlands achieved.	Zutphen; Nieuport; various sieges and naval conflicts.	William of Orange; Maurice of Nassau; Duke of Alva; Alexander Farnese, duke of Parma.
1616	Invasion of China by Manchu Tatars.		
1618–1648	Thirty Years' War. Religious freedom secured in Germany.	Dessau; Leipzig; Lech; Lützen; Nördlingen.	Gustavus Adolphus; Wallenstein; Tilly; Turenne.

Time	Name and Results	Leading Battles	Chief Leaders
1642–1653	English Civil War. English Commonwealth established.	Edgehill; Marston Moor; Naseby; Worcester.	Prince Rupert; Fairfax; Charles I: Cromwell.
1700–1709	Swedish-Russian War. Defeat of Charles XII.	Narva; Pultowa (Poltava).	Charles XII of Sweden; Peter the Great.
1701–1714	Spanish Succession. French and Spanish crowns disunited. Protestant succession in England.	Blenheim; Ramillies; Turin; Oudenarde; Malplaquet.	Duke of Marlborough; Prince Eugene; Marshals Tallard and Villars.
1740–1748	Austrian Succession. Many previous treaties affirmed; Maria Theresa, empress of Austria.	Dettingen; Fontenoy; Piacenza.	Marshal Saxe; George II of England; Duke of Cumberland.
1756–1763	Seven Years' War. Prussia gains high rank as military state.	Prague; Kolin; Rossbach; Minden; Torgau; Freiberg.	Marshal Daun; Frederick the Great.
1775–1783	American Revolutionary War. The United States achieve their independence.	Bunker Hill; Saratoga; Monmouth; Yorktown.	Washington; Greene; Burgoyne; Cornwallis; Clinton; Howe; Lafayette; Gates.
1789–1799	French Revolution. Bourbons defeated. Republic established, *coup d'etat* of Bonaparte.	Valmy; Jemappes; Wattignies; Lodi; Arcole.	Kellerman; Dumouriez; Jourdan; Moreau; Bonaparte.
1800–1815	Napoleonic Wars. France advances to the first place in Europe, and falls with Napoleon.	Marengo; Trafalgar; Austerlitz; Jena; Eylau; Friedland; Wagram; Leipzig; Waterloo.	Napoleon; Wellington; Nelson; Blücher; Alexander I; Francis I; Frederick William III; Ney.
1812–1815	War of 1812. The United States entirely independent of Britain.	Lake Erie; New Orleans.	Perry; Cockburn; Ross; Jackson; McDonough.
1821–1829	War for Greek Independence. Greece independent of Turkey.	Missolonghi; Navarino.	Kanaris; Byron; Ibrahim Pasha; Marco Bozzaris; Ypsilanti.
1846–1848	Mexican War. United States-Mexico boundary fixed.	Buena Vista; Cerro Gordo; Capture of Mexico City.	Taylor; Scott; Santa Anna.
1854–1856	Crimean War. Independence of Turkey. Peace of Paris.	Alma; Balaklava; Inkerman; Malakov.	Lord Raglan; St.-Arnaud; Prince Menshikov; Canrobert.
1859–1861	Italian War. Victor Emmanuel becomes king of united Italy.	Magenta; Solferino; Castelfidardo; Gaëta.	Napoleon III; Victor Emmanuel; Francis Joseph; Garibaldi.
1861–1865	American Civil War. Abolition of slavery; preservation of the Union.	Bull Run; Shiloh; Seven Days; Antietam; Murfreesboro; Chancellorsville; Vicksburg; Gettysburg; Chickamauga; Chattanooga; Atlanta; Wilderness.	McClellan; Grant; Sherman; Sheridan; Jackson; Thomas; Lee; J. E. Johnston; Meade.
1866	Seven Weeks' War. Prussia defeats Austria, unifies Germany.	Langensalza; Königgrätz (Sadowa).	Benedek; William I; von Moltke.
1870–1871	Franco-Prussian War. Paris taken and Alsace and Lorraine added to German Empire.	Wörth; Gravelotte; Sedan; Metz; Capture of Paris.	William I; von Moltke; Frederick; Frederick Charles; Napoleon III; MacMahon; Bazaine.
1877–1878	Russo-Turkish War. Rumania, Serbia, and Montenegro become independent of Turkey. Treaty of Berlin.	Shipka Pass; Kars; Plevna.	Grand Duke Nicholas; Gurko; Skobelev; Totleben; Osman Pasha; Mukhtar Pasha.
1894–1895	Chinese-Japanese War. Indemnity to Japan; Korean independence.	Occupation of Korea by Japanese; Port Arthur; Weihaiwei.	Prince Oyama; Prince Arisugawa; Prince Komatsu.
1898	Spanish-American War. End of Spanish rule in America; Cuba independent; U. S. takes Puerto Rico and Philippines.	Manila Bay; Santiago; San Juan; El Caney.	Dewey; Schley; Sampson; Montojo; Cervera; Shafter; Toral.
1899–1902	South African War. Annexation of Transvaal and Orange River colony to British Empire.	Kimberley; Ladysmith; Mafeking; Pretoria.	Joubert; De Wet; Botha; De la Rey; French; White; Buller; Kitchener; Roberts.
1904–1905	Russo-Japanese War. Mutual concessions, confirmed by Treaty of Portsmouth.	Yalu; Liaoyang; Shaho; Siege of Port Arthur; Mukden; Battle of the Japan Sea.	Kuropatkin; Linevitch; Prince Oyama; Kuroki; Togo; Rojestvensky; Nogi; Oku.
1911–1912	Turco-Italian War. Tripoli ceded to Italy.	Bengazi; Derna; Tobruk; Hodeida.	Aubry; Enver Bey; Farrabelli.
1912–1913	Balkan Wars. Turkey loses much territory in Europe.	Scutari; Saloniki; Lule-Burgas; Monastir; Adrianople.	Putnik; Savov; Kleomenes; Hassan Tahsi; Enver Bey.
1914–1918	World War I. Downfall of the Romanov, Hohenzollern, and Habsburg dynasties. Establishment of several new republics. Defeat of Central Powers.	Liege; Marne; Tannenberg; Ypres; Gallipoli; Verdun; Jutland; Somme; Vimy Ridge; Caporetto; Erzerum; Chateau-Thierry; St. Mihiel; Argonne; Samaria.	Foch; Joffre; Pétain; French; Haig; Jellicoe; Allenby; Pershing; Cadorna; Brusilov; Hindenberg; Ludendorff; Mackenson.
1937–1945	Chinese-Japanese war. Japanese driven from China.	Japanese invasion and occupation of eastern China.	Chiang Kai-shek; Noboyuki Abe.
1939–1945	World War II. Defeat of Axis powers.	Poland; Finland; Norway; Flanders; France; North Africa; Coral Sea; Midway; Stalingrad; the Solomons; Italy; Normandy; the Ardennes; Germany.	Pétain; Alexander; Wavell; Montgomery; Göring; von Runstedt; Rommel; Marshall; MacArthur; Nimitz; Eisenhower; Patton; Zhukov; Vatutin.
1946–1954	French-Viet Minh War. Defeat of French. Geneva Conference divides Vietnam.	Dienbienphu.	Ho Chi Minh, Giap; Navarre.
1950–1953	Korean War. UN stops Communist aggression.	Pusan, Inchon, North Korea, 38th Parallel.	Rhee; MacArthur, Ridgway; Nam Il, Kim Il Sung, Lin Piao.
1961–1975	Vietnamese War. Communists support North Vietnam; US backs South Vietnam. Cease-fire ends US military involvement. Sporadic fighting in Indochina continues. North Vietnamese victory ends war.	Gulf of Tonkin, Khe Sanh, Dak To, Pleiku, Danang, Mekong, Tet Offensive, US bombing of Hanoi.	Ho Chi Minh, Pham Van Dong; Westmoreland, Abrams; Khanh, Huang, Ky, Thieu.

REVIEW QUESTIONS

Give three reasons why every one should read and study history 439

How do we derive our knowledge of the life of primitive man? 439

Outline the particularly notable characteristics of the history of the Hebrew people; of the Greeks; of the Romans 440

Explain the carbon-14 method of dating . . . 440

AMERICAN HISTORY

Why is a study of the European background of American history important? 441

What nation initiated the voyages of discovery and exploration in the 15th century? 441

Describe the equipment and the preparations of Columbus for his first voyage to the west. Name three other great discoverers of this period 441

Recount the efforts of Gilbert and Raleigh to colonize North America 442

Who first led the French into the interior of the North American continent? What source of wealth attracted French enterprise in the North? State two weaknesses of French colonization policies in America 442

Summarize the history of Dutch exploration and colonization in North America 442

Colonial Period

Account for the English Puritan and Cavalier migrations to America 442–443

Describe the first organization and management of the Virginia colony. Recount the events which led up to the assembling of the first House of Burgesses 443

Describe the early activities of the Plymouth Company in New England. What was the policy of the Council for New England? . . 443

Recount the conditions under which the Pilgrims settled at Plymouth in 1620. What is the Mayflower Compact? 443–444

How many colonists came to New England in the Puritan migration? Who was the leader of this movement? 444

Explain how representative government and the ballot were introduced in New England . . 444

Account for the rise of the town meeting in New England and for the prevalence of the county form of government in Virginia . . . 444–445

Under what circumstances and with what purpose did Roger Williams found Rhode Island? 445

State three important provisions contained in the first charter of Pennsylvania. How did this colony differ from the others? 446

Discuss the growth of population in America from 1690 to 1760. From what countries did immigrants come? 446

State two restrictions placed by England upon colonial industry 447

Describe Virginia plantation life in the 18th century. What were the industries of the middle colonies? of New England? . . 447–448

Revolutionary Period

Account for the efforts of England to impose taxes on the colonies after 1763 448

What was the purpose of the sugar act of 1764? Why did New England oppose the sugar act? Upon what basis was opposition to the stamp tax founded? 448

Why was the tea tax retained by Parliament when the Townshend acts were repealed? . . 448

Why may the battle of Bunker Hill be called an American victory? 448

What pamphlet issued in the spring of 1776 crystallized sentiment for independence? Who moved in Congress on June 7, 1776 that the united colonies should be independent? 451

Recount the chief military events of 1776. What notable service did Robert Morris render to the American cause? 451–452

Explain the importance of the surrender of Burgoyne at Saratoga in 1777. Who secured the treaty of alliance with France in 1778? . . 452

State the immediate results of Daniel Boone's pioneering in Kentucky; of George Rogers Clark's expedition into the Illinois country . 452

From 1789 to 1861

Analyze the composition and the distribution of population in the colonies in 1790. Cite two facts which illustrate the development of American manufacturing from 1800 to 1814. 453

State two important acts of Washington in respect to foreign policy 454

Summarize the notable features of Jefferson's administration 454

In what way was the question of slavery connected with the settlement of the West? How did the question affect the admission of states? 456

What were the two great issues of Jackson's administration? 457

Who was the first Whig president? 457

What was the immediate occasion of the Mexican war? State the results of this conflict. 457–458

What discovery occasioned the great migration to California? Under what compromise was California admitted as a state? 458

How did the Lincoln-Douglas debates affect the political fortunes of the candidates? . . 458

Discuss the character of the immigration into the United States between 1820 and 1855. What events in Europe caused notable migrations to America? 458–459

Which of the Southern states was the first to secede from the Union? What other states seceded before February 1861? 459

Outline Lincoln's position as stated in his inaugural address of March 4, 1861 459

What event opened the War of Secession? Indicate the number of states on each side . 459

State the military problem of the Civil War. 459–460

What were the decisive battles of the war in the West? Who were the commanding generals in the final struggle in Virginia? 460

From the Civil War to the Present Day

Outline the reconstruction policy of Lincoln. . . 460

Outline the Congressional policy. 462

Discuss the rebuilding of Southern industry after the Civil War 462

Enumerate several inventions that occasioned reorganization of manufacturing and of business in the decade before 1880 462

Characterize the city problems that arose in America between 1860 and 1885. 463

Discuss the restriction of immigration in the period from 1880 to 1914 463

State the causes and the results of the war with Spain 463–464

Under what circumstances did Theodore Roosevelt come into the presidency in 1901? With what preceding president is he compared in respect to popular influence? 463–464

How was the Republican party divided during the presidency of Taft? 464

What were the three principal subjects of legislation in Wilson's first term? What two amendments were ratified in 1913? 464

Why did America enter World War I? . . . 464

What part did the United States play in World War II? 465

Where was the earliest settlement in the territory which is now the state of Florida? 466

From what source was the design of the stripes in the American flag derived? When was the design of stars and stripes adopted as the national flag? State the actions of Congress with respect to the flag in 1794 and 1818 . . . 469

Who was the first leader and spokesman of the Democratic party? What other names were very early applied to this party? Of what groups of people was the party composed? . 470

What political conditions gave rise to the Republican party? Of what party elements was the party composed at first? 472

DICTIONARY OF SUPPLEMENTAL TOPICS IN AMERICAN HISTORY

What were the Alabama claims? How were they settled? 479

Narrate the story of the defense of the Alamo. 479

State the main issue in the Alaska boundary controversy. How was the dispute settled? . 479

When, from whom, and for how much did the United States purchase Alaska? Why was the Alaska Highway built? 479

What was the occasion of the Alien and Sedition acts? Summarize their chief provisions . 479

Who is credited with first applying the name America to the New World continent? Name three men who are said to have visited America before Columbus 479

How did the feudal patroon system of the Dutch settlements give rise to the Antirent riots in New York? 481

Tell briefly the story of Bacon's rebellion 481–482

Name an English precedent for the Bill of Rights embodied in the first ten amendments to the American Constitution 482

Explain the designation Black Republicans. Outline the story of the *Black Warrior* case. 482

Define the phrase "blue laws." Account for the use of blue in this connection. Is there any justification for the phrase "blue laws of Connecticut"? 482

Tell the story of Booth's conspiracy . . . 482–483

When did the Boston Massacre occur? What two patriots volunteered to defend the soldiers at their trial? 483

Where and when did the engagement known as Braddock's defeat take place? 483

Cite the five provisions of the Compromise of 1850 484

Account for the use of the nickname Copperheads during the Civil War. Who were the Cotton Whigs? 484

Characterize the Credit Mobilier as to its origin and purpose 484

What is meant by Crime of '73? 484

Recount the story of Custer's last fight . 484–485

Explain the political expression, "dark horse." 485

By whom was the State of Deseret organized? 485

Explain the occasion of the draft riots in New York City in 1863 485

In what year did Nast originate the Republican Elephant symbol? 486

What was the Era of Good Feeling? 486

What were the Five Nations? 486

Explain the historical interest attaching to Fort Sumter 487

What are the Four Freedoms? 487

Explain the term Free Silver movement . . . 487

Outline the main features of the Geneva award. Indicate the importance of this decision in general international relations 487

What were the Grandfather Clauses? 488

To what doctrine is the name Greenbackism applied? 488

Who were the Green Mountain Boys? What dispute occasioned their organization? . . . 488

Why was the Hampton Roads Conference held? 488

Who were the members of the Hartford Convention? What did this meeting propose? . 488

When was the first Homestead act passed by Congress? In what year were settlement rights withdrawn? 488–489

State the reason for the impeachment of President Johnson; the result of the proceedings. 489

What were the Intolerable acts? 489

When was the so-called ironclad oath established? State the purpose of its application. 489

Distinguish between Jeffersonian democracy and Jacksonian democracy 489

Explain the meaning of Jeffersonian Republican. 489

Tell the story of John Brown's raid on Harpers Ferry. Estimate the effect of the raid. . . 490

What events precipitated King Philip's War? . 490

Outline the history of the Know-Nothing movement 490

Recount the history of the Ku-Klux Klan. Whence is the name derived? 490

Tell the story of the Liberty Bell 491

Explain the origin of the political nickname Locofocos 491

State the general extent of the Louisiana Purchase. What price was paid for this domain? 491

Explain the origin of the name Mason and Dixon's Line. What historical interest attaches to this boundary? 491

Narrate the leading facts about the historic voyage of the *Mayflower* in 1620. How many persons arrived at Plymouth on this vessel? 491

For what price did the island of Manhattan change ownership in 1626? 492

Discuss the early history of the Mormons . . 492

Explain the origin and the historical application of the term mossbacks. To whom was the nickname Mugwumps applied? 492

Characterize the career of the navy in the War of 1812 493

How did the term New Deal originate? . . . 493

Describe the principal change in the rôle of government sought by President Franklin D. Roosevelt in the New Deal 493

Who sponsored the "new nationalism"? . . . 493

Who were the generals in command at the battle of New Orleans? How does this battle illustrate the value of modern means of communication? 494

Who were the patroons? State the nature of the grants which they received 494

What is peonage? 494

What is meant by "Permanent Generals"? . . 495

Account for the historic name Pilgrim Fathers. 495

When was the Prohibition party organized? State the principal part of its platform . . 496

Tell the story of the Salem witchcraft delusion . 496

Explain the application of the political nickname Scalawags 497

Explain: solid South; Sons of Liberty; spoils system 498

Summarize the history of Tammany Hall. 498–499

Name the original thirteen states 499

Who were the Tories in the American colonies? What became of them after the Revolution? 499

What was the Tweed Ring? 500

What was the Underground Railroad? 500

For what is Valley Forge famous? 500

Explain the name Vinland 500

In how many major wars has the United States been involved? 501

ENGLAND

Trace the evolution of the British Empire into the Commonwealth of Nations 517

Indicate the character of the Roman occupation of the island. What is said to have prompted the migration of Saxons, Angles, and Jutes to Britain? 517

State the occasion and some effects of the introduction of Christianity into Kent . . . 517–518

Characterize the reign of William the Conqueror 518

Explain how the family of Plantagenet came to the English throne 518

What means did Henry II use to lessen the power of the nobles? 518–519

State the events which led up to the signing of Magna Charta. Why did the barons demand this charter of liberties? 519

For what purpose did the Franciscan friars come to England in the 13th century? 519

Recount the events leading up to Simon de Montfort's famous Parliament of 1265 . . 519

By what means did Henry VII gain the throne? 520

What was the most important event of the reign of Henry VIII? State the notable work done by Colet; Tindale; More 520

What was the most notable naval event of Elizabeth's reign? Characterize the economic progress of this period in England. For what other development is the era notable? . . . 521

Explain the downfall of Charles I 521

What kind of government was established after the execution of Charles I? Outline the career and achievements of Cromwell 521

By what right did George I come to the English throne? What party came into power in his reign? Who was the Old Pretender? . . . 522

What are said to have been the chief traits of 18th century life in England? Name a religious leader, an artist, and a novelist . . . 522

Indicate the territorial increases of the British Empire through the Napoleonic wars . . . 523

What important change in the relation of England to India took place in 1858? 524

In what year did Gladstone introduce the first Irish Home Rule bill? 524

When was woman suffrage adopted in England? 525

What was Britain's part in World War II? Under whose leadership? What changes occurred after the war? 526

CANADA, AUSTRALIA, INDIA

When did John Cabot make the first discovery that furnished a basis for England's claim to North American territory? 531

Indicate the importance of Champlain's work of exploration and colonization. Why is he held, in some measure, responsible for the failure of the French in North America? . . 531

Describe the character of the early government of New France. Explain the seigniory . . . 531

Discuss the territorial expansion of Canada and its increase of population before 1833 . . . 532

In what year was the union of Upper and Lower Canada accomplished? Who, as governor, settled the question of the responsibility of the cabinet to the Assembly? 532

Who became the Liberal premier in 1896? How long did the Liberal government continue in power? State the main policies and the chief events of this period 533

Discuss the effect of World War I upon the status of Canada 533

To what extent did Canada participate in World War II? 533

Through what commercial enterprises was Australia first made known to Europeans? . 537

Who discovered Tasmania and New Zealand? 537

By whom was the name Australia originated? 537

What motive prompted most of the early inland exploration of Australia? Name the most famous of the inland explorers 537

Tell the story of the establishment of the Commonwealth of Australia 537

Why did World War II bring Australia closer to the United States? 538

With what event does authentic history in India begin? Indicate two fields of Indian culture that were influenced by the Greeks 539

Name the dates and leaders of the principal invasions of India by Asiatic peoples. State three consequences of these invasions . . . 539

In what year did Vasco da Gama first visit India? How did England gain Indian trade supremacy? 539

LATIN AMERICA

When and by whom was the site of the present capital of Argentina first settled? 541

Tell the story of the dictatorship of Juan Manuel de Rosas. In what year was the Argentine Republic formed? 541

How did Brazil gain her independence? How was her government changed to a republic? Discuss President Vargas. 542

State the cause and the results of Chile's war with Peru and Bolivia 542

What explorers opened the way for the settlement of Colombia? 543

In what words did Columbus describe the island of Cuba? 543

Recount the history of Haiti, down to 1789. Describe the work of Toussaint L'Ouverture. 543

Recount the story of the conquest of Mexico . . 545

Recount the main achievements of President Diaz. Who were the chief Mexican leaders between 1911 and 1920? Give two important provisions of the constitution of 1917 . . . 545

In what year did Panama become independent? 546

In what political condition did the Spaniards find the Incas of Peru in 1531? Indicate the original extent of the viceroyalty of Peru, and its divisions in the 18th century? . . . 546

Account for the use of the name Venezuela. What form of wealth first attracted settlers to Venezuela? Who early established colonies in Venezuela? 547

CHINA, CRETE, EGYPT

To what period before Christ does Chinese tradition carry the story of civilization? When does the historical period begin? . . 552

Under what circumstances did the Chou dynasty begin? 552

When was the golden age of Chinese poetry and painting? 552

When did the Mongols rule China? Who was their principal leader? 552

Describe the policies of the Manchus toward foreigners 553

In what year were the Manchus swept out of power? Who became the first president of the Chinese republic? 553

How did the People's Republic of China arise? 554

Explain the application of the term Minoan to early Cretan history. Indicate the ancient commercial and naval importance of Crete . 554

By what peoples has Crete been governed within historic times? 554

At about what date was the Great Pyramid erected? by what monarch? Characterize the civilization of the Middle Kingdom . . 556

When, and under what leader, did the Saracens conquer Egypt? At what period did the French hold the country? 557

FRANCE, GERMANY

In what century, and under what dynasty, did the kingdom of France "in the narrower sense" begin? What was the task of the French kings, down to the time of Charles VIII? 558

Describe the membership of the States-General summoned in 1302 558

Characterize the work of Cardinal Richelieu and Cardinal Mazarin. What kind of government was wielded by Louis XIV? 559

Enumerate the reforms effected by the National (Constituent) Assembly 562

Describe the career of the Revolutionary Commune 561

Describe the circumstances that brought Napoleon Bonaparte to the front. Why was the time auspicious for him? By what steps did Napoleon become emperor? 561

Tell the story of the fall of Napoleon III 562

What disasters befell France in World War II? 563
With what event does the history of Germany properly begin? 565
Characterize the reign of Frederick III as to its effect upon Germany. What dispute occasioned the Thirty Years' war? 565
Describe the social changes that took place in Germany after 1871 566
Discuss the expansion and fall of Germany under Hitler. 567

GREECE, IRELAND, ITALY

Point out the most important contributions that Greek states made to civilization . . . 569
Describe the conquest of Greece by the Hellenes. Name the four historic groups of this people 569
What caused early Greek colonization? . . . 569
Compare the Spartan with the Athenian government 571
Who was the pioneer of Greek philosophy? . . 571
Explain the occasion of the Persian wars. For what exploits are the following places famous: Marathon? Thermopylæ? Salamis? Platæa? 571
Describe the Confederacy of Delos. For what is the Periclean age famous? 571
Tell the story of the downfall of Athens, 431-405 B. C. 571-572
When did Greece become independent of Turkey? What part did Greece take in the Balkan wars? in the World wars? . . . 572-573
Under what names was Ireland known to early classic writers? 575
State the effects of the Danish invasions . . . 575
Describe the effects of the policy of William of Orange in Ireland 576
In what year were the British and Irish parliaments united? Who led the movement for emancipation of Catholics? 576
Describe the Sinn Fein organization. Outline the story of the conflict in Ireland, 1915–18. 576
Who established the Ostrogothic kingdom in Italy? By whom were the Goths driven out of Italy? 577
Describe the character of the Italian citystates. Name the greatest of them 577
Characterize the Sicilian expedition led by Garibaldi. When did Rome become the capital of Italy? 578
What part did Italy play in World War II? . 578

JAPAN, ROME, RUSSIA

Upon what model was the government of Japan organized, about 604? Who established a feudal government, or shogunate? . 578
State the occasion and the results of Commodore Perry's expedition to Japan 579
Summarize Japan's part in World War II . . 579
Name the three most important peoples of Italy at the beginning of recorded history. Who were the Latin people? 587
Describe the conditions which gave rise to the founding of the city of Rome 587
With what rival state did Rome wage wars in the 3d and 2d centuries B. C.? Name three noted commanders in these conflicts 588
Outline the reorganization of government undertaken by Diocletian. State two memorable acts of Constantine. 591
Describe the conditions that led up to the great Gothic invasion of Greece and Italy . 591
How did the Tatar conquest affect Russia? . 592
For what share in Russian history are the following notable: Ivan the Great? Ivan the Terrible? Michael Romanov? 592
Outline the achievements of Peter the Great and Catherine II 592
Who was the moving spirit behind the "fiveyear plan" inaugurated in Russia in 1928? 593
What part did Russia take in World War II? 593

SPAIN, TURKEY, YUGOSLAVIA

Discuss the Carthaginian occupation of Spain. Describe the condition of Spain under Roman rule. Recount the most important features of the reign of Ferdinand and Isabella . . . 595
Who first proclaimed the Spanish republic? . 596
Discuss the Civil War and Franco's dictatorship 596
Outline the steps by which the Ottoman Turks became the first military power in Europe . 597
What defeat broke the sea power of the Turks? 597
Summarize the career of the Turkish Nationalist movement. Who led this movement? . . . 598
When and from what territories was Yugoslavia constituted? 599

WORLD WAR I

What were the causes, immediate and more remote, of World War I? 611
Compare the strength of the combatants at the opening of the war 612
In what respects was the battle of the Marne among the decisive battles of the world? . . 612
How did von Hindenburg become a national hero? 613
How was poison gas introduced? how did airplanes develop? 615
State the result of the battle of Jutland . 615–616
What was the effect on the war of the Russian Revolution? 618
When and where was the armistice with Germany signed? 620
Summarize the provisions of the treaty signed June 28, 1919 by the Allies and Germany. 620–621
State several governmental and territorial changes in Europe, resulting from the war. 621–622

WORLD WAR II

Compare the two World Wars as to extent, weapons, and method 624
What part was played by communism? . . . 624
What was the Munich Pact? 625
Why did Great Britain and France declare war? 626
Describe the siege of Britain 629
Trace the course of the Russian war in 1941–42 630–631
Trace the course of the war in the Pacific and the Far East 631–632
Trace the movements of the Allied armies in the West from Normandy to the Rhine . . 635
What caused the surrender of Japan? 638

DICTIONARY OF WORLD HISTORY

Tell the story of the *Armada* 642
Recount the circumstances that occasioned the destruction of the Bastille 643
Name the so-called decisive battles fought since the year 1800. 644
What were the chief uses to which the catacombs of Rome were put? 648
Tell the story of the Children's Crusade. . . . 648
What is the "domesday book"? 651
Who were the Guelphs and the Ghibellines? . 653
When was the English Habeas Corpus act passed? State the meaning of the act . 654
Who were the Lollards? Account for the name Long Parliament; for Mad Parliament . . 657
Describe trial by ordeal 660
Explain the so-called "papal partition of the world." 661
When was the Peace Corps founded? What was its purpose? 661
Explain the historical application of the term Renaissance 663
For what events in the Crimean war and the World Wars is Sevastopol famous? 665
Recount briefly the history of the so-called South Sea Bubble 666
What was the "Trojan Horse?" 670

BIBLIOGRAPHY

While not forming in any sense an exhaustive list of history readings, this bibliography represents a selected library of authoritative and readable works upon the histories of important nations and geographical regions, and upon world history in its different periods. For perspective on the entire field of human history, the reader is referred to Arnold J. Toynbee's *A Study of History* (available in abridged form) and to *The Outline of History* by H. G. Wells. Books which furnish background for an understanding of history may be found under fiction, biography, geography and other classifications.

ANCIENT HISTORY

Bibby, Geoffrey—Four Thousand Years Ago.
Knopf '61
Bourne, Frank C.—A History of the Romans.
Heath '66
Breasted, J. H.—History of Egypt . . . *Scribner*
Carrington, Richard—A Million Years of Man.
World '65
Ehrich, Robert W., ed.—Chronologies in Old World Archaeology . . . . *U. of Chicago Pr. '66*
Heurtley, W. A.—A Short History of Greece, from Early Times to 1964 . . . . . . *Cambridge '65*
Jastrow, M.—The Civilization of Babylonia and Assyria. . . . . *Lippincott*
Laistner, Max L. W.—The Intellectual Heritage of the Early Middle Ages. . . . . . *Octagon '66*
Lindsay, Jack—A Short History of Culture, from Pre-history to the Renascence. . . . *Fawcett '66*
Osborn, H. F.—Man of the Old Stone Age.
Scribner
Parkes, Henry B.—Gods and Men; the Origins of Western Culture . . . . *Knopf '59*
Pfeiffer, Charles F.—Ancient Israel from Patriarchal to Roman Times; a Study Manual.
Baker Bk. '65

AMERICA

Brock, William R.—The Character of American History. 2nd ed. . . . . *St. Martin's '66*
Dorf, Philip—Concise History of the United States.
Oxford '65
Eaton, Clement—A History of the Old South. 2nd ed. . . . . *Macmillan '66*
Frederickson, George M.—The Inner Civil War; Northern Intellectuals and the Crisis of the Union . . . . *Harper '65*
Hart, A. B., ed.—The American Nation Series.
Harper
Krout, John Allen—United States since 1865 15th ed. . . . . *Barnes & Noble '65*
Miers, Earl S.—Our Fifty States . . . *Grosset '61*
Morison, Samuel E.—The Oxford History of the American People . . . . *Oxford '65*
Morris, Richard B., ed.—Encyclopedia of American History. Updated, rev. . . . . . *Harper '65*
Muzzey, D. S.—Our American Republic. New ed.
Ginn '66
Nevins, Allan and Commager, Henry S.—A Short History of the United States. rev. . *Knopf '64*
Potter, David M.—Eight Issues in American History; Views and Counter-views.
Scott, Foresman '66
Tate, Merze—The United States and the Hawaiian Kingdom; a Political History . . . . *Yale '65*
Wissler, Clark—Indians of the United States. Rev. by L. W. Kluckhohn. . . . *Doubleday '66*
Wright, Edmond, ed.—Causes and Consequences of the American Revolution . . . . *Quadrangle '66*

LATIN AMERICA

Blakemore, Harold—Latin America . *Oxford '66*
Fagg, John E.—Cuba, Haiti, and the Dominican Republic . . . . *Prentice '65*
McKown, Robin—The Story of the Incas; Mightiest Empire of the Early Americas.
Putnam '66
Smith, Robert F., ed. Background to Revolution; the Development of Modern Cuba . *Knopf '66*

BRITAIN AND CANADA

Bradley, A. G.—The Making of Canada. . *Dutton*
Burton, Elizabeth—The Pageant of Elizabethan England . . . . *Scribners '62*
Churchill, Sir Winston—History of the English-Speaking Peoples. Arr. by Henry S. Commager
Dodd '65
Creighton, D. G.—History of Canada; Dominion of the North . . . . *Houghton Mifflin '58*
Thornton, A. B.—The Habit of Authority; Paternalism in British History . *U. of Totonro Pr. '66*

EUROPE

Cheney, Edward P.—European Background of American History, 1300–1600 . . . . *Ungar '66*
Daniell, Albert Scott—World War II; and Illustrated History . . . . *Verry '66*
Hughes, Henry S.—Contemporary Europe; a History. 2nd ed. . . . . *Prentice '66*
Trevor-Roper, Hugh Redwald—The Rise of Christian Europe. . . . . *Harcourt '65*

FRANCE AND GERMANY

Cairns, John Campbell—France . . . *Prentice '65*
Corban, Alfred—A History of Modern France. New ed. rev., enl. . . . . *Braziller '65*
Pinson, K. S.—Modern Germany. 2nd ed.
Macmillan '66
Shirer, William L.—The Rise and Fall of the Third Reich . . . . *Simon & Shuster '60*
Strauss, Franz Josef—The Grand Design; a European Solution to a German Reunification.
Praeger '66

ITALY AND SPAIN

Bertrand, L.—The History of Spain . . *Appleton*
Prescott, William H.—The Portable Prescott: The Rise and Decline of the Spanish Empire.
Viking '66
Salbadori, Massimo—Italy . . . . *Prentice '65*
Whelpton, Eric—A Concise History of Italy.
Roy '65

RUSSIA

Habberton, William—Russia; the Story of a Nation . . . . *Houghton '65*
Oliva, Lawrence Jay, ed.—Russia and the West from Peter to Khrushchev . . . . . *Heath '65*
Rieber, Alfred J. and Nelson, Robert C.—A Study of the USSR and Communism . . *Putnam '64*
Teall, Kaye (Moulton)—From Tsars to Commissars; the Story of the Russian Revolution.
Messner '66

ASIA

Bain, Chester Arthur—History of the Far East. 4th ed. . . . . *Littlefield, Adams '65*
Clyde, Paul Hibbert—The Far East. 4th ed.
Prentice '65
Fitzgerald, Charles Patrick—A Concise History of East Asia . . . . *Praeger '66*
Griffis, W. E.—The Mikado's Empire . . *Harper*
Hitti, Philip K.—A Short History of the Near East.
Van Nostrand '66
Meskill, John Thomas, ed.—The Pattern of Chinese History . . . . *Heath '65*
North, Robert C.—Chinese Communism.
McGraw '66
Schwarz, Walter—The Arabs in Israel.
Faber & Faber '66

AFRICA

Davidson, Basil—A Guide to African History. Rev., ed. by Haskel Frankel . . *Doubleday '65*
Hatch, John Charles—Africa Today—and Tomorrow; an Outline of Basic Facts and Major Problems. 2nd rev. ed. . . . . . . *Praeger '65*

GENERAL

Coblentz, S. A.—Ten Crises in Civilization.
Follett '65
McLellan, David S.—The Cold War in Transition.
Macmillan '66
Stavrianos, L. A., ed.—The Epic of Modern Man; a Collection of Readings . . . . *Prentice '66*

Government

CONTENTS GUIDE

	Page		Page
Agencies and Commissions, Federal	749	Dependencies, U.S.	757
Amendments to the Constitution	737	Executive Dept., U.S.	739
Articles of Confederation	730	Federal Government,	
Bibliography	840	United States	739
Cabinet Officers:		Government and Politics,	
Attorneys-General	745	History of	727
Postmasters-General	748	Judicial Dept., U.S.	740
Secretaries of:		Legislative Dept., U.S.	739
Agriculture	746	Local Government	757
Commerce	747	Municipal Government	757
Defense	744	Political Terms and Institutions	
Health, Education and		Dictionary	805
Welfare	747	Popular and Electoral Vote	762
Housing and Urban		Presidential Voting Records	761
Development	747	Questions, Review	833
Interior	746	Recall, The	757
Labor	747	Referendum and Initiative	754
State	743	State Government	752
Transportation	747	Limitations on Legislative	
Treasury	745	Powers	753
Civil Service, State	756	Tabulated Data	759–760
Congress, U.S.	740	Supreme Court Justices	751
Constitution, The	733	United States Government	729
Continental Congress	730	World Governments—	
Declaration of Independence	729	Countries, alphabetical	765

Picture Guide: The World Trade Center in New York City—The United Nations Building—Views of Historic Washington, D.C.

Historic Washington Buildings—Right, Monument to George Washington, First President of the United States. The 555-foot obelisk rises near the Potomac River, between the Capitol and Lincoln Memorial. Designed by Robert Mills in 1836, the monument was begun in 1848. Completed in 1884, it was dedicated in 1885. Above, the Jefferson Memorial to the third U.S. President. It was completed in 1941 and dedicated in 1943 on the 200th anniversary of Thomas Jefferson's birth. It was designed by John Russell Pope in the classical style Jefferson admired. (*Photographs courtesy U.S. Department of the Interior*)

The White House—Official residence of the President of the United States. The presidential mansion was designed by the Irish-American architect James Hoban. The cornerstone was laid in 1792 and the building was completed in 1800. British troops set fire to the structure in 1814, destroying the interior; Hoban supervised the reconstruction, which was completed in 1817. White paint had been used to cover the blackened exterior in 1817, and from that time the building was known as the White House—the name was made official in 1902. The view above is of the north portico, which forms the main entrance. (*Courtesy of the White House*)

Government

INTRODUCTORY

IT may be useful to distinguish between the art of politics and the science of politics. The art, ideally, is the practice of government so that it accords with justice, so that the dignity and the effectiveness of institutions are maintained and good and able men are kept in control of public affairs. The science of politics analyzes and elaborates the theory of the state and examines the various types of public administration, past, present, and proposed. The two things flow into each other. The fields of "morals and legislation" tend to become closely united. It has been a common conception, from the time of Hobbes to the present day, that the state creates morals or standards of conduct; that what the state decides and commends is ethically right. But there is a different view; namely, that there is a Moral Order higher than any human laws, higher than the state itself, by which all acts of authority are to be judged. This, in the final analysis, was the ethical issue in World War I and subsequent wars.

Need for Government. There is a widespread disposition, by no means of recent origin, to question the usefulness of the state. To the anarchist, laws are a stumbling block and a stone of offense, and, to radical reformers generally, governments are institutions for the exploitation of the many by the few. But a scientific canvass of society in its various stages, from savagery to civilization, reveals the certain fact that, however much governments have been and still are associated with acts of oppression, there is no escape from human ills in anarchy. Mankind, without a common authority, is predatory. Society released, as occasionally happens, from the respect and dread of government, promptly exhibits the most violent and terrible tendencies. Imperfect as governments are, discriminating in their bestowal of advantages as they too frequently are, nevertheless they are the safeguard and security for the advantages of life. The sentimental philosophers of the 18th century imagined a natural state enjoyed by savage peoples, in which the blessings of simplicity and freedom were attained. Modern study of primitive society reveals no such happy "state of nature," but everywhere a cramped and cruel savage existence in which life is never free from danger and the human mind seldom released from terror.

History of Political Philosophy. The science or philosophy of politics is one of the richest fields of human inquiry. It possesses a great and classical literature. Its scope and its form of reasoning were first clearly developed by the Greek philosopher, Aristotle, whose *Politics* lies at the base of subsequent discussion. Aristotle's studies were limited to the Greek "city-state," which, to his mind, represented the highest attainment of human freedom and law. His method was concrete and inductive. He collected hundreds of city-state constitutions, compared their provisions, and deduced general principles. The state, to Aristotle, was not a Utopia such as that imagined by Plato, but it was an actual institution realized in hundreds of examples throughout the Ægean and Mediterranean seas. No writer has stated better, or in fewer words, the purpose of civilized society. "The state," says Aristotle, "comes into existence, that man may live. It continues, that man may live well." "Good life," in all its rich and noble expressions, is the aim and object of the state.

Centuries after Aristotle, another political philosopher, the Italian statesman Machiavelli, examined the city-states of his own day, with results that offer startling contrasts. Machiavelli's political studies are embraced in two works. The first, called *The Prince*, is a discussion of the sinister principles whereby the Italian despot of that day maintained himself in power. The other, *The Discourses*, which is a far nobler and more suggestive work, examines the principles whereby a republic may endure.

A century later comes the period where national governments rise above feudal conditions. The king attains an absolute power and destroys the independence of the nobles. This monarchical movement met with opposition. In England it was overthrown by revolution. Out of the struggles of the period came several notable works, the most influential one being *The Leviathan*, by Thomas Hobbes, who attempted to justify monarchical absolutism by the theory of a "social contract" between subjects and kings.

Later, in the 18th century, John Locke, in his two treatises on civil government, turns the doctrine of the social contract against the monarchists, laying the basis for the "right of revolution" in the abusive exercise of a power which monarchs have contracted to use with justice and discretion. "Men are," said Locke, "by nature all free, equal, and independent." Only by free consent does man enter into the obligations of society, resigning his natural rights to a public authority in return for benefits which, if not satisfactorily conferred, he is at liberty to end. Misrule by a monarch, in Locke's view, not only justifies rebellion but makes it inevitable. Locke powerfully affected the minds of the English colonists in America, and some of his actual language appears in the Declaration of Independence. The revolutionary ideas of Locke were put into a winged form by Rousseau, whose *Social Contract* contributed incalculably to the French Revolution and has remained to the present day an inspiration to political revolt.

Latin America. Particularly in the countries of South and Central America, the example of the American revolution against Great Britain exerted a powerful influence. Country after country threw off the Spanish yoke and adopted a republican form of government modeled after that of the United States and incorporating such ideas as bicameral legislatures, the legal separation of powers between legislative, executive, and judicial departments, commitment of executive office to a president popularly elected for a fixed term, and the constitutional guarantees of civil and political rights.

Independence and an attempt at self-government has not always brought stability to Latin-American countries, for several reasons. In the first place, the people lacked political experience. During the entire period of her empire, Spain never established or permitted a representative legislature in any of her American colonies, but instead built a tradition of strong executive authority with centralized initiative and direction. On this account conditions in the newly-freed nations were favorable for an occasional military coup or other form of revolt unseating a president and creating at least a temporary dictatorship. A second reason was the lack of a middle class to bridge the gap between an oligarchy of rich citizens and a mass of destitute illiterate people. Finally, and perhaps the root cause, was an economic system with origins in feudalism which tended to perpetuate the inequalities. Latin American countries differ greatly in the extent to which they still suffer from this unfortunate political heritage. They are all affected by two newer influences: international advice and assistance to make their economies more efficient, as exemplified by the Alliance for Progress, and the efforts of Communist powers to persuade them that the road to plenty is through the dictatorship of the proletariat. Cuba exemplified the latter.

Early Asiatic Revolutions. In Asia, the constitutional movement made its way from Europe to Turkey in 1908, Persia in 1909, and China in 1911. Absolute monarchies were overthrown or limited by constitutional enactments and by the introduction of representative institutions. Pressure was building up in India for self-government and the rejection of British rule.

Governments and World War I. World War I brought to the surface much that had been germinating in secret. The empires of Central Europe and Russia disappeared. Through the disintegration of monarchical states, the number of nations increased.

Among other effects produced in these European states by World War I was a widening of democracy. The war had given an illustration of the possible power of governments over economic systems, which was reflected by the drift toward socialism in many constitutions. The New World felt these influences of the war much less than did Europe.

Rise of the New Autocracy. World War I and its after-effects led to a crisis in human government on a colossal scale. As early as 1848, Karl Marx issued the "Communist Manifesto," a landmark in an underground revolutionary movement based on the belief that the ills of an industrial society could be cured only if the laboring class seized power. War-shattered Russia proved ripe for application of the idea and fell under the spell and power of one of its ablest protagonists, Lenin. He established the first dictatorship of the proletariat with himself as dictator. Unlike tyrants of earlier ages, he had a program of social transformation for his country and all other countries as well. This program was pushed by a party organized publicly in Russia and secretly in other countries.

Predictably, the party's success in Russia and the threat it presented elsewhere struck terror in the hearts of rulers of other lands, particularly in countries seriously weakened by the war. Ostensibly to combat the new threat, Mussolini in Italy in 1922 and Hitler in Germany in 1933 overthrew their constitutional governments and assumed autocratic power with the assistance, in each case, of a party acting outside the law. In these two countries constitutional government was restored after their defeat in World War II, but the Russian influence was widened after that struggle, and a number of adjacent European countries fell within Russia's orbit as satellites. Finally, in 1949, a revolution in China brought that country also under a totalitarian regime dedicated to the doctrines of Karl Marx.

Twilight of the Empires. The unsettling effects of World War II, combined with the accelerating unification of the world by radio, television, and air travel, bore harvest in an almost universal demand for independence by peoples long subject to the control of other nations. A measure of its success appears in the fact that the United Nations, organized immediately after the war with 51 members, had by 1969 admitted a total of 126 new members, nearly all being countries which achieved independence after the war. Furthermore, in contrast with experience in earlier ages, all but two achieved their independence without warfare, the exceptions being Algeria and Viet-Nam.

The proliferation of new states offered a field day for the competing political ideals of constitutional government and the newer programs of Communist dictatorships. In general the new governments tended to adapt to their use the political institutions of their former rulers but usually chose republics on the American or French models. Their cultural and economic ties were usually retained, often with formal affiliation, as in the British Commonwealth or French Community. As in Latin America, however, the harsh realities of their economic life forced compromises, and many dictators appeared. But the Communists had a minimum of success in securing their adherence.

Some of the more forward-looking leaders of the new nations sought to advance their power collectively by federation. Egypt attempted to form an Arab super-state under the title of the United Arab Republic, but failed to achieve permanent success. Under the leadership of Ghana, an Organization of African Unity was formed by 30 countries in Addis Ababa in 1963 looking toward cooperative action.

Social Ideals in Politics. Parallel with the evolution of formal political development throughout the world, and speeded up by competition with the Communist revolution, has progressed a vast social movement designed to increase the well-being of the masses of the people and to secure a wider distribution of the proceeds of industry.

The free play of individual initiative, which theoretically accompanied modern democracy, is no longer permitted by even the most democratic governments. It is limited by a vast amount of "social legislation" supported by taxation, by organizations of workmen and employers, and by various forms of cooperation. Even governmental planning, the key operation under Communist rule, is resorted to and applied by means of differential tax rates and by credit policies with the objective of achieving the optimum economic growth.

Internationally, there has been a parallel development. By means of credit, technical assistance, and outright gifts, the better developed nations have sought to stimulate the economic progress of those nations emerging from more primitive economies. The motive has been partly to achieve political influence but partly also to forestall social disorder and the attendant dangers of warfare.

Politics and History. In thought, politics is often associated with history. But while history is, largely, the record of political activities, the two subjects differ widely in scope and in method. History surveys the past. The historian has the advantage of adequate accumulations of materials. He studies episodes and movements that are completed. He may separate himself from the partisanship and emotions of the time he describes. The student of politics does not have these advantages. He is dealing, primarily, not with the past, but with the present and with the future. His mind must be incessantly occupied with the morrow. Political sense comprises not only good judgment of actual events, but prescience for the future. Politics is not static, but dynamic; political forces are constantly altering, finding new directions, and attaining new balances. Institutions tend to constant change. The activity of the lawmaker is incessant. The materials for the study of politics thus constantly become obsolete and remain incomplete and unsatisfactory. Practical considerations of the highest importance, none the less, demand constant fresh examination of governments and policies and require the training of special faculties of the mind.

The Department of Politics of this work is divided into three parts. The first deals with the government of the United States, Federal, state, and local. In the second part are described the governments of foreign states, while the third part is composed of a dictionary of political terms and institutions.

THE UNITED STATES OF AMERICA

THE United States arose through the union of thirteen of the colonies of Great Britain in North America into a new nation under a federal form of government. This union was brought about by successive stages of development, after experiences with several forms of concerted action, and by a common protest and resistance to acts of the British king and Parliament.

Intercolonial Assemblies. This common resistance found expression in several intercolonial assemblies, first in the Stamp Act Congress (1765), which met at New York, was attended by delegates of nine colonies, and adopted a declaration of "rights and grievances," a petition to the king and a memorial and a petition to the House of Lords; second, by the First Continental Congress (1774), called by Massachusetts and Virginia and attended by delegates from all the colonies except Georgia. This Congress passed resolutions called the "Association" binding the colonies in a far-reaching boycott of British trade.

Independence of Colonies. The Second Continental Congress assembled after warfare had actually begun. It recruited a Continental army to resist the British forces, and appointed George Washington commander in chief. On July 4, 1776, it declared the independence of the colonies from Great Britain, and, in the absence of any more effectual organization, united the efforts of the colonies for the prosecution of the war until the adoption of the Articles of Confederation in 1781. The original Declaration of Independence is on display at the National Archives Exhibition Hall, Washington, D. C.

DECLARATION OF INDEPENDENCE

THE UNANIMOUS DECLARATION OF THE THIRTEEN UNITED STATES OF AMERICA, IN CONGRESS, JULY 4, 1776.

When, in the course of human events, it becomes necessary for one people to dissolve the political bands which have connected them with another, and to assume, among the powers of the earth, the separate and equal station to which the laws of nature and of nature's God entitle them, a decent respect to the opinions of mankind requires that they should declare the causes which impel them to the separation.

We hold these truths to be self-evident—that all men are created equal; that they are endowed by their Creator with certain inalienable rights; that among these are life, liberty, and the pursuit of happiness. That to secure these rights, governments are instituted among men, deriving their just powers from the consent of the governed; that, whenever any form of government becomes destructive of these ends, it is the right of the people to alter or to abolish it, and to institute a new government, laying its foundation on such principles, and organizing its powers in such form, as to them shall seem most likely to effect their safety and happiness. Prudence, indeed, will dictate that governments long established should not be changed for light and transient causes; and, accordingly, all experience hath shown, that mankind are more disposed to suffer, while evils are sufferable, than to right themselves by abolishing the forms to which they are accustomed. But when a long train of abuses and usurpations, pursuing invariably the same object, evinces a design to reduce them under absolute despotism, it is their right, it is their duty, to throw off such government, and to provide new guards for their future security. Such has been the patient sufferance of these colonies; and such is now the necessity which constrains them to alter their former systems of government. The history of the present king of Great Britain is a history of repeated injuries and usurpations, all having in direct object the establishment of an absolute tyranny over these states. To prove this, let facts be submitted to a candid world.

He has refused his assent to laws the most wholesome and necessary for the public good.

He has forbidden his governors to pass laws of immediate and pressing importance, unless suspended in their operations till his assent should be obtained; and, when so suspended, he has utterly neglected to attend them.

He has refused to pass other laws for the accommodation of large districts of people, unless these people would relinquish the right of representation in the legislature—a right inestimable to them, and formidable to tyrants only.

He has called together legislative bodies at places unusual, uncomfortable and distant from the repository of their public records, for the sole purpose of fatiguing them into compliance with his measures.

He has dissolved representative houses repeatedly, for opposing with manly firmness, his invasions on the rights of the people.

He has refused, for a long time after such dissolutions, to cause others to be elected; whereby the legislative powers, incapable of annihilation, have returned to the people at large for their exercise; the state remaining in the meantime, exposed to all the dangers of invasion from without and convulsions within.

He has endeavored to prevent the population of these states; for that purpose obstructing the laws for the naturalization of foreigners; refusing to pass others to encourage their migration hither, and raising the conditions of new appropriations of lands.

He has obstructed the administration of justice, by refusing his assent to laws for establishing judiciary powers.

He has made judges dependent on his will alone for the tenure of their offices, and the amount and payment of their salaries.

He has erected a multitude of new offices, and sent hither swarms of officers, to harass our people and eat out their substance.

He has kept among us, in times of peace, standing armies, without the consent of our legislatures.

He has affected to render the military independent of, and superior to, the civil power.

He has combined with others to subject us to a jurisdiction foreign to our constitutions and unacknowledged by our laws; giving his assent to their acts of pretended legislation:

For quartering large bodies of armed troops among us;

For protecting them, by a mock trial, from punishment for any murders which they should commit on the inhabitants of these states;

For cutting off our trade with all parts of the world;

For imposing taxes on us without our consent;

For depriving us, in many cases, of the benefits of trial by jury;

For transporting us beyond seas, to be tried for pretended offenses;

For abolishing the free system of English laws in a neighboring province, establishing therein an arbitrary government, and enlarging its boundaries, so as to render it at once an example and fit instrument for introducing the same absolute rule into these colonies;

For taking away our charters, abolishing our most valuable laws, and altering, fundamentally, the forms of our governments;

For suspending our own legislatures, and declaring themselves invested with power to legislate for us in all cases whatsoever.

He has abdicated government here, by declaring us out of his protection, and waging war against us.

He has plundered our seas, ravaged our coasts, burned our towns, and destroyed the lives of our people.

He is at this time transporting large armies of foreign mercenaries, to complete the works of death, desolation, and tyranny, already begun with circumstances of cruelty and perfidy scarcely paralleled in the most barbarous ages, and totally unworthy the head of a civilized nation.

He has constrained our fellow citizens, taken captive on the high seas, to bear arms against their country, to become the executioners of their friends and brethren, or to fall themselves by their hands.

He has excited domestic insurrection among us, and has endeavored to bring on the inhabitants of our frontiers the merciless Indian savages, whose known rule of warfare is an undistinguished destruction of all ages, sexes, and conditions.

In every stage of these oppressions we have petitioned for redress in the most humble terms: our repeated petitions have been answered only by repeated injury. A prince whose character is thus marked by every act which may define a tyrant is unfit to be the ruler of a free people.

Nor have we been wanting in our attentions to our British brethren. We have warned them, from time to time, of attempts by their legislature to extend an unwarrantable jurisdiction over us. We have reminded them of the circumstances of our emigration and settlement here. We have appealed to their native justice and magnanimity and we have conjured them by the ties of our common kindred, to disavow these usurpations, which would inevitably interrupt our connections and correspondence. They, too, have been deaf to the voice of justice and of consanguinity. We must, therefore, acquiesce in the necessity which denounces our separation, and hold them as we hold the rest of mankind—enemies in war—in peace, friends.

We, therefore, the representatives of the United States of America, in general Congress assembled, appealing to the Supreme Judge of the world for the rectitude of our intentions, do, in the name, and by the authority of the good people of these colonies, solemnly publish and declare that these united colonies are, and of right ought to be, free and independent states; that they are absolved from all allegiance to the British crown, and that all political connection between them and the State of Great Britain is, and ought to be, totally dissolved; and that, as free and independent states, they have full power to levy war, conclude peace, contract alliances, establish commerce, and to do all other acts and things which independent states may of right do. And for the support of this declaration, with a firm reliance on the protection of Divine Providence, we mutually pledge to each other our lives, our fortunes and our sacred honor.

The foregoing declaration was, by order of Congress, engrossed, and signed by the following members:

JOHN HANCOCK.

New Hampshire

JOSIAH BARTLETT,   MATTHEW THORNTON.
WM. WHIPPLE,

Massachusetts Bay

SAML. ADAMS,   ROBT. TREAT PAINE,
JOHN ADAMS,   ELBRIDGE GERRY.

Rhode Island, etc.

STEP. HOPKINS,   WILLIAM ELLERY.

Connecticut

ROGER SHERMAN,   WM. WILLIAMS,
SAM'EL HUNTINGTON,   OLIVER WOLCOTT.

New York

WM. FLOYD,   FRANS. LEWIS,
PHIL. LIVINGSTON,   LEWIS MORRIS.

New Jersey

RICHD. STOCKTON,   JOHN HART,
JNO. WITHERSPOON,   ABRA. CLARK.
FRAS. HOPKINSON,

Pennsylvania

ROBT. MORRIS,   JAS. SMITH,
BENJAMIN RUSH,   GEO. TAYLOR,
BENJA. FRANKLIN,   JAMES WILSON,
JOHN MORTON,   GEO. ROSS.
GEO. CLYMER,

Delaware

CÆSAR RODNEY,   THO. M'KEAN
GEO. READ,

Maryland

SAMUEL CHASE,   THOS. STONE,
WM. PACA,   CHARLES CARROLL OF
        CARROLLTON.

Virginia

GEORGE WYTHE,   THOS. NELSON, JR.,
RICHARD HENRY LEE,   FRANCIS LIGHTFOOT LEE,
TH. JEFFERSON,   CARTER BRAXTON.
BENJA. HARRISON,

North Carolina

WM. HOOPER,   JOHN PENN.
JOSEPH HEWES,

South Carolina

EDWARD RUTLEDGE,   THOMAS LYNCH, JR.,
THOS. HEYWARD, JR.,   ARTHUR MIDDLETON.

Georgia

BUTTON GWINNETT,   GEO. WALTON.
LYMAN HALL,

The Continental Congress. The defects of the Continental Congress as an agency for united effort were serious and were early apprehended. It rested on no constitution and commanded no support except as a revolutionary body. Its members represented the colonies from which they came, and voted under instructions, each state having one vote. The states regarded themselves as independent and able to disregard Congress when it appeared to their interest to do so.

The same session that produced the Declaration of Independence provided also a committee to draw up a plan for a better union. A committee was appointed which produced the Articles of Confederation, the first constitution of a united America. Nearly five years passed, however, before, on March 1, 1781, these articles became effective. The Congress did not adopt the committee's report until November 15, 1777. Eleven states ratified within a year following, but Delaware withheld ratification until 1779, and Maryland until 1781.

Articles of Confederation. As the precursor of the Constitution of the United States, the Articles of Confederation is a political document of first interest. As its name indicates, it provided for a "confederation," not for a "federal" government. It left the independence and the "sovereignty" of the thirteen states unimpaired (Article II). The states delegated certain powers to the national government; but, in spite of the use of the word "perpetual" in the document, they undoubtedly regarded themselves as possessing the right to withdraw if they desired.

The government created dealt only with the states. It could not act upon the individual. As in the Continental Congress, each state possessed one vote, and could send a number of "delegates," not less than two nor more than seven. These delegates the state chose and compensated in any desired manner (Article V). Action under the really important powers granted to the Congress required the assent of nine states to be effective (Article IX, 6th paragraph). The government created consisted only of the Congress, a single chamber body. A "president" was authorized (Article IX, 5th paragraph) to serve not "more than one year in any term of three," but he was simply a presiding officer. Executive functions were intrusted to "committees" of which a great number were eventually created. During recess a "Committee of the States," with one representative from each state, was authorized. To it was delegated a limited control.

The Congress had no independent power to enforce its measures. It was dependent upon the states for all resources and for troops; it had no courts nor officers to enforce its laws. Nevertheless, the government here created was an advance toward actual national union, and it furnished an experience essential to the final production of the constitution. The document in its entirety follows:

ARTICLES OF CONFEDERATION OF THE UNITED STATES OF AMERICA.

TO ALL TO WHOM THESE PRESENTS SHALL COME, WE THE UNDERSIGNED DELEGATES OF THE STATES AFFIXED TO OUR NAMES, SEND GREETING.

Whereas the delegates of the United States of America in Congress assembled did on the 15th day of November in the year of our Lord 1777, and in the second year of the independence of America agree to certain Articles of Confederation and perpetual union between the States of New Hampshire, Massachusetts Bay, Rhode Island and Providence Plantations, Connecticut, New York, New Jersey, Pennsylvania, Delaware, Maryland, Virginia, North Carolina, South Carolina and Georgia, in the words following, viz.

ARTICLES OF CONFEDERATION AND PERPETUAL UNION BETWEEN THE STATES OF NEW HAMPSHIRE, MASSACHUSETTS BAY, RHODE ISLAND AND PROVIDENCE PLANTATIONS, CONNECTICUT, NEW YORK, NEW JERSEY, PENNSYLVANIA, DELAWARE, MARYLAND, VIRGINIA, NORTH CAROLINA, SOUTH CAROLINA, AND GEORGIA.

ARTICLE I. The style of this confederacy shall be "The United States of America."

ARTICLE II. Each state retains its sovereignty, freedom and independence, and every power, jurisdiction and right, which is not by this confederation expressly delegated to the united states, in Congress assembled.

ARTICLE III. The said states hereby severally enter into a firm league of friendship with each other, for their common defense, the security of their liberties, and their mutual and general welfare, binding themselves to assist each other, against all force offered to, or attacks made upon them, or any of them, on account of religion, sovereignty, trade, or any other pretense whatever.

ARTICLE IV. The better to secure and perpetuate mutual friendship and intercourse among the people of the different states in this union, the free inhabitants of each of these states, paupers, vagabonds, and fugitives from justice excepted, shall be entitled to all privileges and immunities of free citizens in the several states; and the people of each state shall have free ingress and regress to and from any other state, and shall enjoy therein all the privileges of trade and commerce, subject to the same duties, impositions and restrictions as the inhabitants thereof respectively, provided that such restriction shall not extend so far as to prevent the removal of property imported into any state, to any other state of which the owner is an inhabitant; provided also that no imposition, duties or restriction shall be laid by any state, on the property of the United States, or either of them.

If any person guilty of, or charged with treason, felony, or other high misdemeanor in any state, shall flee from justice, and be found in any of the united states, he shall upon demand of the Governor or executive power, of the state from which he fled, be delivered up and removed to the state having jurisdiction of his offense.

Full faith and credit shall be given in each of these states to the records, acts and judicial proceedings of the courts and magistrates of every other state.

ARTICLE V. For the more convenient management of the general interest of the united states, delegates shall be annually appointed in such manner as the legislature of each state shall direct, to meet in Congress on the first Monday in November, in every year, with a power reserved to each state, to recall its delegates, or any of them, at any time within the year, and to send others in their stead, for the remainder of the year.

No state shall be represented in Congress by less than two, nor by more than seven members; and no person shall be capable of being a delegate for more than three years in any term of six years; nor shall any person, being a delegate, be capable of holding any office under the united states, for which he, or another for his benefit receives any salary, fees or emolument of any kind.

Each state shall maintain its own delegates in any meeting of the states, and while they act as members of the committee of the states.

In determining questions in the united states, in Congress assembled, each state shall have one vote.

Freedom of speech and debate in Congress shall not be impeached or questioned in any court, or place out of Congress, and the members of Congress shall be protected in their persons from arrests and imprisonments, during the time of their going to and from, and attendance on Congress, except for treason, felony, or breach of the peace.

ARTICLE VI. No state without the consent of the united states in Congress assembled, shall send any embassy to, or receive any embassy from, or enter into any conference, agreement, alliance or treaty with any king, prince or state; nor shall any person holding any office of profit or trust under the united states, or any of them, accept of any present, emolument, office or title of any kind whatever from any king, prince or foreign state; nor shall the united states in Congress assembled, or any of them, grant any title of nobility.

No two or more states shall enter into any treaty, confederation or alliance whatever between them, without the consent of the united states in Congress assembled, specifying accurately the purposes for which the same is to be entered into, and how long it shall continue.

No state shall lay any imposts or duties, which may interfere with any stipulation in treaties, entered into by the united states in Congress assembled, with any king, prince or state, in pursuance of any treaties already proposed by Congress, to the courts of France and Spain.

No vessels of war shall be kept up in time of peace by any state, except such number only, as shall be deemed necessary by the united states in Congress assembled, for the defense of such state, or its trade; nor shall any body of forces be kept up by any state, in time of peace, except such number only, as in the judgment of the united states, in Congress assembled, shall be deemed requisite to garrison the forts necessary for the defense of such state; but every state shall always keep up a well regulated and disciplined militia, sufficiently armed and accoutred, and shall provide and have constantly ready for use, in public stores, a due number of field pieces and tents, and a proper quantity of arms, ammunition and camp equipage

No state shall engage in any war without the consent of the united states in Congress assembled, unless such state be actually invaded by enemies, or shall have received certain advice of a resolution being formed by some nation of Indians to invade such state, and the danger is so imminent as not to admit of a delay, till the united states in Congress assembled can be consulted: nor shall any state grant commissions to any ships or vessels of war, nor letters of marque or reprisal, except it be after a declaration of war by the united states in Congress assembled, and then only against the kingdom or state and the subjects thereof, against which war has been so declared, and under such regulations as shall be established by the united states in Congress assembled, unless such state be infested by pirates, in which case vessels of war may be fitted out for that occasion, and kept so long as the danger shall continue, or until the united states in Congress assembled shall determine otherwise.

ARTICLE VII. When land forces are raised by any state for the common defense, all officers of or under the rank of colonel, shall be appointed by the legislature of each state respectively by whom such forces shall be raised, or in such manner as such state shall direct, and all vacancies shall be filled up by the state which first made the appointment.

ARTICLE VIII. All charges of war, and all other expenses that shall be incurred for the common defense or general welfare, and allowed by the united states in Congress assembled, shall be defrayed out of a common treasury, which shall be supplied by the several states, in proportion to the value of all land within each state, granted to or surveyed for any person, as such land and the buildings and improvements thereon shall be estimated according to such mode as the united states in Congress assembled, shall from time to time, direct and appoint.

The taxes for paying that proportion shall be laid and levied by the authority and direction of the legislatures of the several states within the time agreed upon by the united states in Congress assembled.

ARTICLE IX. The united states in Congress assembled, shall have the sole and exclusive right and power of determining on peace and war, except in the cases mentioned in the sixth article—of sending and receiving ambassadors—entering into treaties and alliances, provided that no treaty of commerce shall be made whereby the legislative power of the respective states shall be restrained from imposing such imposts and duties on foreigners, as their own people are subjected to, or from prohibiting the exportation or importation of any species of goods or commodities whatsoever—of establishing rules for deciding in all cases, what captures on land or water shall be legal, and in what manner prizes taken by land or naval forces in the service of the united states shall be divided or appropriated—of granting letters of marque and reprisal in times of peace—appointing courts for the trial of piracies and felonies committed on the high seas and establishing courts for receiving and determining finally appeals in all cases of captures, provided that no member of Congress shall be appointed a judge of any of the said courts.

The united states in Congress assembled shall also be the last resort on appeal in all disputes and differences now subsisting or that hereafter may arise between two or more states concerning boundary, jurisdiction or any other cause whatever; which authority shall always be exercised in the manner following. Whenever the legislative or executive authority or lawful agent of any state in controversy with another shall present a petition to Congress, stating the matter in question and praying for a hearing, notice thereof shall be given by order of Congress to the legislative or executive authority of the other state in controversy, and a day assigned for the appearance of the parties by their lawful agents, who shall then be directed to appoint by joint consent, commissioners or judges to constitute a court for hearing and determining the matter in question: but if they cannot agree, Congress shall name three persons out of each of the united states, and from the list of such persons each party shall alternately strike out one, the petitioners beginning, until the number shall be reduced to thirteen; and from that number not less than seven, nor more than nine names as Congress shall direct, shall in the presence of Congress be drawn out by lot, and the persons whose names shall be so drawn or any five of them, shall be commissioners or judges, to hear and finally determine the controversy, so always as a major part of the judges who shall hear the cause shall agree in the determination: and if either party shall neglect to attend at the day appointed, without showing reasons, which Congress shall judge sufficient, or being present shall refuse to strike, the Congress shall proceed to nominate three persons out of each state, and the secretary of Congress shall strike in behalf of such party absent or refusing; and the judgment and sentence of the court to be appointed, in the manner before prescribed, shall be final and conclusive; and if any of the parties shall refuse to submit to the authority of such court, or to appear or defend their claim or cause, the court shall nevertheless proceed to pronounce sentence, or judgment, which shall in like manner be final and decisive, the judgment or sentence and other proceedings being in either case transmitted to Congress, and lodged among the acts of Congress for the security of the parties concerned: provided that every commissioner, before he sits in judgment, shall take an oath to be administered by one of the judges of the supreme or superior court of the state, where the cause shall be tried, "well and truly to hear and determine the matter in question, according to the best of his judgment, without favor, affection or hope of reward": provided also that no state shall be deprived of territory for the benefit of the united states.

All controversies concerning the private right of soil claimed under different grants of two or more states, whose jurisdictions as they may respect such lands, and the states which passed such grants are adjusted, the said grants or either of them being at the same time claimed to have originated antecedent to such settlement of jurisdiction, shall on the petition of either party to the Congress of the united states, be finally determined as near as may be in the same manner as is before prescribed for deciding disputes respecting territorial jurisdiction between different states.

The united states in Congress assembled shall also have the sole and exclusive right and power of regulating the alloy and value of coin struck by their own authority, or by

THE UNITED STATES CAPITOL, WASHINGTON, D.C. Combining classic and Renaissance design, the Capitol faces East in the section of Washington called Capitol Hill — 97 feet above the Potomac. The Capitol's length is 751 feet, 4 inches; its width 350 feet. The overall height is 307 feet, 6 inches. Topping the dome is a statue of Freedom. On September 13, 1793, the cornerstone was laid by George Washington. The wings, finished in 1811, were partially burned in 1814 by British forces attacking the city. In 1827 the central building was completed; the present dome, as pictured here, was finished in 1865. The original architect was William Thornton; his designs were later modified by Henry Latrobe and Charles Bulfinch.

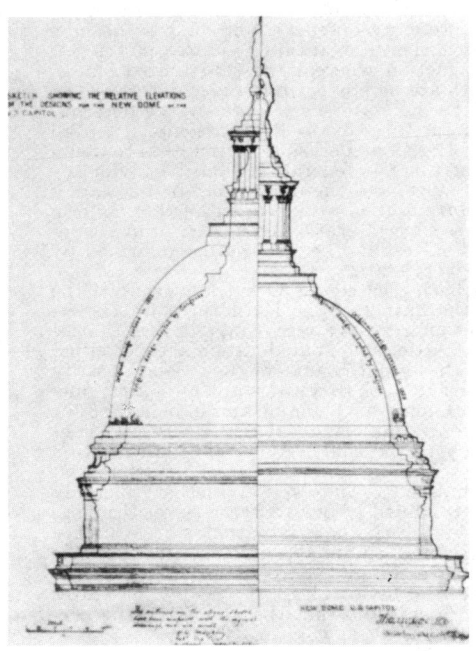

ARCHITECT'S MODEL. Architect Thomas Walter's sketch in 1860 shows him judging elevation and profiles.

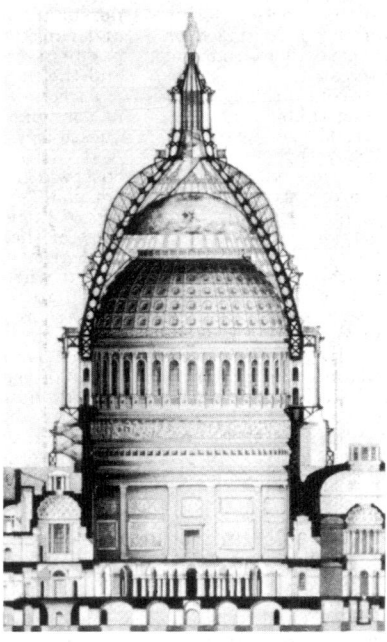

SKETCH OF NEW DOME. Architect projects conception to show relation to total structure.

THE DOME EVOLVES. Drawing of the dome as accepted.

THE DOME NEARS COMPLETION. In this picture a huge stone column is about to be hoisted into place on the Senate side.

THE CAPITOL, 1861. Less than a month after Lincoln was inaugurated the first time, the Civil War broke out and troops were called to protect the Capitol. Statuary for the Senate pediment and troops drilling on the east lawn were all part of the Capitol scene this May day of 1861.

that of the respective states—fixing the standard of weights and measures throughout the United States—regulating the trade and managing all affairs with the Indians, not members of any of the states, provided that the legislative right of any state within its own limits be not infringed or violated—establishing and regulating post offices from one state to another, throughout all the united states, and exacting such postage on the papers passing through the same as may be requisite to defray the expenses of the said office—appointing all officers of the land forces, in the service of the united states, excepting regimental officers—appointing all the officers of the naval forces, and commissioning all officers whatever in the service of the united states—making rules for the government and regulation of the said land and naval forces, and directing their operations.

The united states in Congress assembled shall have authority to appoint a committee, to sit in the recess of Congress, to be denominated "A Committee of the States," and to consist of one delegate from each state; and to appoint such other committees and civil officers as may be necessary for managing the general affairs of the united states under their direction—to appoint one of their number to preside, provided that no person be allowed to serve in the office of president more than one year in any term of three years; to ascertain the necessary sums of money to be raised for the service of the united states, and to appropriate and apply the same for defraying the public expenses—to borrow money, or emit bills on the credit of the united states, transmitting every half year to the respective states an account of the sums of money so borrowed or emitted—to build and equip a navy—to agree upon the number of land forces, and to make requisitions from each state for its quota, in proportion to the number of white inhabitants in such state; which requisition shall be binding, and thereupon the legislature of each state shall appoint the regimental officers, raise the men and clothe, arm and equip them in a soldierlike manner, at the expense of the united states; and the officers and men so clothed, armed and equipped shall march to the place appointed, and within the time agreed on by the united states in Congress assembled: But if the united states in Congress assembled shall, on consideration of circumstances judge proper that any state should not raise men, or should raise a smaller number than its quota, and that any other state should raise a greater number of men than the quota thereof, such extra number shall be raised, officered, clothed, armed and equipped in the same manner as the quota of such state, unless the legislature of such state shall judge that such extra number cannot be safely spared out of the same, in which case they shall raise, officer, clothe, arm and equip as many of such extra number as they judge can be safely spared. And the officers and men so clothed, armed and equipped, shall march to the place appointed, and within the time agreed on by the united states in Congress assembled.

The united states in Congress assembled shall never engage in a war, nor grant letters of marque and reprisal in time of peace, nor enter into any treaties or alliances, nor coin money, nor regulate the value thereof, nor ascertain the sums and expenses necessary for the defense and welfare of the united states, or any of them, nor emit bills, nor borrow money on the credit of the united states, nor appropriate money, nor agree upon the number of vessels of war, to be built or purchased, or the number of land or sea forces to be raised, nor appoint a commander in chief of the army or navy, unless nine states assent to the same: nor shall a question on any other point, except for adjourning from day to day be determined, unless by the votes of a majority of the united states in Congress assembled.

The Congress of the united states shall have power to adjourn to any time within the year, and to any place within the united states, so that no period of adjournment be for a longer duration than the space of six months, and shall publish the journal of their proceedings monthly, except such parts thereof relating to treaties, alliances or military operations, as in their judgment require secrecy; and the yeas and nays of the delegates of each state on any question shall be entered on the journal, when it is desired by any delegate; and the delegates of a state, or any of them, at his or their request shall be furnished with a transcript of the said journal, except such parts as are above excepted, to lay before the legislatures of the several states.

ARTICLE X. The committee of the states, or any nine of them, shall be authorized to execute, in the recess of Congress, such of the powers of Congress as the united states in Congress assembled, by the consent of nine states, shall from time to time think expedient to vest them with; provided that no power be delegated to said committee, for the exercise of which, by the Articles of Confederation, the voice of nine states in the Congress of the united states assembled is requisite.

ARTICLE XI. Canada acceding to this Confederation, and joining in the measures of the united states shall be admitted into, and entitled to all the advantages of this union: but no other colony shall be admitted into the same, unless such admission be agreed to by nine states.

ARTICLE XII. All bills of credit emitted, moneys borrowed and debts contracted by, or under the authority of Congress, before the assembling of the united states, in pursuance of the present Confederation, shall be deemed and considered as a charge against the united states, for payment and satisfaction whereof the said united states, and the public faith are hereby solemnly pledged.

ARTICLE XIII. Every state shall abide by the determinations of the united states in Congress assembled, on all questions which by this Confederation is submitted to them. And the articles of this Confederation shall be inviolably observed by every state, and the union shall be perpetual; nor shall any alteration at any time hereafter be made in any of them; unless such alteration be agreed to in a Congress of the united states, and be afterwards confirmed by the legislatures of every state.

And whereas it hath pleased the Great Governor of the World to incline the hearts of the legislatures we respectively represent in Congress, to approve of, and to authorize us to ratify the said Articles of Confederation and perpetual union. Know ye that we the undersigned delegates, by virtue of the power and authority to us given for that purpose, do by these presents, in the name and in behalf of our respective constituents, fully and entirely ratify and confirm each and every of the said Articles of Confederation and perpetual union, and all and singular the matters and things therein contained: And we do further solemnly plight and engage the faith of our respective constituents, that they shall abide by the determinations of the united states in Congress assembled, on all questions which by the said Confederation are submitted to them. And that the articles thereof shall be inviolably observed by the states we respectively represent, and that the union shall be perpetual.

In witness whereof we have hereunto set our hands in Congress. Done at Philadelphia in the State of Pennsylvania the ninth day of July in the year of our Lord, 1778, and in the third year of the independence of America.

On the part and behalf of the State of New Hampshire.

| JOSIAH BARTLETT, | JOHN WENTWORTH, JUN., August 8, 1778. |

On the part and behalf of the State of Massachusetts Bay.

JOHN HANCOCK,	FRANCIS DANA,
SAMUEL ADAMS,	JAMES LOVELL,
ELBRIDGE GERRY,	SAMUEL HOLTEN.

On the part and behalf of the State of Rhode Island and Providence Plantations.

| WILLIAM ELLERY, | JOHN COLLINS. |
| HENRY MARCHANT, | |

On the part and behalf of the State of Connecticut.

ROGER SHERMAN,	TITUS HOSMER,
SAMUEL HUNTINGTON,	ANDREW ADAMS.
OLIVER WOLCOTT,	

On the part and behalf of the State of New York.

| JAS. DUANE, | WILLIAM DUER, |
| FRAS. LEWIS, | GOU'R MORRIS. |

On the part and behalf of the State of New Jersey.

| JNO. WITHERSPOON, | NATH'L SCUDDER, November 26, 1778. |

On the part and behalf of the State of Pennsylvania.

ROBT. MORRIS,	WILLIAM CLINGAN,
DANIEL ROBERDEAU,	JOSEPH REED,
JONA BAYARD SMITH,	July 22, 1778.

On the part and behalf of the State of Delaware.

JOHN DICKINSON,	THOS. M'KEAN,
May 5, 1779,	February 12, 1779.
NICHOLAS VAN DYKE,	

On the part and behalf of the State of Maryland.

| JOHN HANSON, | DANIEL CARROLL, |
| March 1, 1781, | March 1, 1781. |

On the part and behalf of the State of Virginia.

RICHARD HENRY LEE,	JNO. HARVIE,
JOHN BANISTER,	FRANCIS LIGHTFOOT LEE.
THOMAS ADAMS,	

On the part and behalf of the State of North Carolina.

JOHN PENN,	JNO. WILLIAMS.
July 21, 1778,	
CORNS. HARNETT,	

On the part and behalf of the State of South Carolina.

HENRY LAURENS,	RICHARD HUTSON,
WILLIAM HENRY DRAYTON,	THOS. HEYWARD, JUN.
JNO. MATTHEWS,	

On the part and behalf of the State of Georgia.

JNO. WALTON,	EDW'D LANGWORTHY.
24th July, 1778,	
EDW'D TELFAIR,	

CONSTITUTION OF THE UNITED STATES

The unsatisfactory character of the union effected by the Articles of Confederation became increasingly apparent during the period of its existence. The Congress had no power to raise money by taxation. It could borrow, issue paper money, and make requisitions on the states; but the use of these ineffective powers only added to the financial difficulties and lowered the public credit. Congress sought the right to levy tariff duties, but the opposition of one or more states defeated this amendment.

The Constitutional Convention. The increasing gravity of American affairs, the growing probability of disruption, gradually convinced the people of the states of the need of a "more perfect union." A group of talented statesmen, led by Washington, Madison, Hamilton, and Franklin, worked unceasingly to this end, and in 1787 their labors were rewarded by the convention which met at Philadelphia in May and framed the Constitution of the United States.

Seventy-three delegates in all were appointed by the states, but only fifty-five ever attended. The average number present was from thirty to thirty-five, nearly all thoroughly experienced in public affairs and representative of the varying views of the states, while among them were a group of men distinguished for greatness of character and for political sagacity. Moreover, all were practical men, interested in effective forms of government, rather than in theoretical expedients. They were interested also in the protection of those ancient civil rights for which their race had contended for centuries, rather than in vague conceptions of political felicity.

Organization of Convention. The convention organized on May 25, and George Washington was unanimously chosen president. It adjourned on September 17. The convention met behind closed doors. It imposed a bond of secrecy on its members as to the differences and disputes which divided them, and this obligation of protecting the reputation of all concerned was never violated.

The journal of the convention was not published until 1818, when Congress so ordered. Nearly all that is known of the debates and adjustments of this meeting is derived from a private journal kept by Madison and first published in 1840. But it is apparent that no body of men intrusted with a comparable responsibility ever labored with greater disinterestedness and patriotism or strove in greater loyalty to bring the different views which separated them into a common agreement and workable plan.

The First Constitution. The Constitution, which is the first of modern constitutions in point of time, is easily the first also in the praise it has evoked and in the confidence of those who live under it. It may also be said that no political instrument ever framed embodies a more remarkable series of contributions to government or has exerted a wider influence on the subsequent history of states.

Among the institutions given original form in the Constitution are (1) Federal government, subsequently initiated in such widely different states as the Dominion of Canada, the Swiss Confederation, the German Empire, the Mexican and Argentine republics, and the Commonwealth of Australia; (2) the Senate, with its principle of equality of representation of member states as contrasted with a House of Representatives based on population; (3) the office of president, a plan of government which contrasts with ministerial or parliamentary executive as one of the two predominant types of national administration; (4) the supreme court, with its august and remarkable power of judicially interpreting the provisions of the Constitution itself, and of declaring void national or state legislation in conflict with the Constitution; (5) the creation of a sphere of constitutional liberty inviolable by government and protected by judicial power; (6) the creation of complete freedom of movement and of commerce within the union of states, subject only to Federal control.

Character of the Constitution. The Constitution is remarkable for the brevity and for the exactness of its language. While it is an instrument based on experience in government, extending over a long period of colonial and revolutionary statesmanship, its original character justifies the eulogy of Gladstone, that it is "the most wonderful work ever struck off at a given time by the brain and purpose of man."

In spite of the expansion of the United States since 1787 and the growth of the American people, the amendments to the Constitution have been relatively few and have little altered its original character as the first plan of the government. These amendments are 25 in number; their character and dates of adoption are as given below.

Ratification of Constitution. The Constitution was signed on September 17, 1787, by all members present except Mr. Gerry of Massachusetts and Mr. Mason and Mr. Randolph of Virginia. The president of the convention transmitted it to Congress and Congress on September 28 directed it to be "transmitted to the several legislatures in order to be submitted to a convention of delegates chosen in each state by the people thereof, in conformity to the resolves of the convention."

The Constitution was ratified by the thirteen original states in the following order:

Delaware, December 7, 1787, unanimously.
Pennsylvania, December 12, 1787, vote 46 to 23.
New Jersey, December 18, 1787, unanimously.
Georgia, January 2, 1788, unanimously.
Connecticut, January 9, 1788, vote 128 to 40.
Massachusetts, February 6, 1788, vote 187 to 168.
Maryland, April 28, 1788, vote 63 to 12.
South Carolina, May 23, 1788, vote 149 to 73.
New Hampshire, June 21, 1788, vote 57 to 46.
Virginia, June 25, 1788, vote 89 to 79.
New York, July 26, 1788, vote 30 to 28.
North Carolina, November 21, 1789, vote 193 to 75.
Rhode Island, May 29, 1790, vote 34 to 32.

The original document is on display at the National Archives Exhibition Hall, Washington, D. C.

Amendment of the Constitution. The Constitution (Article V) provides the method of its amendment. The initiative may come either from Congress by a two-thirds vote of both Houses, or by the applications of the legislatures of two-thirds of the states. An amendment thus legally proposed becomes a part of the Constitution when three-fourths of the states have ratified it. This ratification may be given either by the legislatures of the states or by conventions called for this purpose. The dates and circumstances occasioning the amendments are as follows:

Articles I–X were declared in force December 15, 1791.

The Constitution, as originally submitted, contained no code of fundamental civil rights. To make unequivocal the retention by the people or by the states of powers not expressly conferred upon the national government, these ten amendments were enacted by the first Congress and submitted to the states.

Article XI was declared in force January 8, 1798.

Article XII altered in some particulars the method of choosing the president and the vice president. It was ratified by all the states except Connecticut, Delaware, Massachusetts, and New Hampshire, which rejected it. It was declared in force September 25, 1804.

Article XIII, the emancipation amendment, was ratified by 31 of the 36 states; rejected by Delaware and Kentucky; not acted on by Texas; conditionally ratified by Alabama and Mississippi. Proclaimed December 18, 1865.

Article XIV, the reconstruction amendment, was ratified by 23 northern states; rejected by Kentucky,

Delaware, Maryland, and 5 southern states; and not acted on by California. New Jersey, Ohio, and Oregon withdrew ratification. The 5 southern states subsequently ratified under pressure. Proclaimed July 28, 1868.

Article XV, Negro citizenship amendment, was not acted on by Tennessee; rejected by California, Delaware, Kentucky, Maryland, New Jersey, and Oregon. It was ratified by the remaining 30 states; New York rescinded its ratification January 5, 1870. Proclaimed March 30, 1870.

Article XVI, income tax amendment, was ratified by 39 states. It was proclaimed February 25, 1913.

Article XVII, providing for the direct election of senators, became *de facto* a part of the Constitution on its ratification by the last of the required number of states on April 8, 1913.

Article XVIII, the prohibition amendment, had on January 16, 1919, been ratified by 36 states, and on January 29, 1919, was formally proclaimed to take effect on January 16, 1920. Connecticut and Rhode Island alone failed to ratify.

Article XIX, the equal suffrage amendment, was adopted between June 10, 1919, and August 19, 1920, by three-fourths of the states, and proclaimed in effect August 26, 1920.

Article XX, the "lame duck" amendment, had been ratified by 39 states by February 6, 1933, when it was proclaimed valid.

Article XXI, repealing the prohibition amendment, article *XVIII*, was ratified by the 36th state, Utah, on December 5, 1933, and was immediately proclaimed valid.

Article XXII, limiting presidential terms of office to two. Went into effect February 26, 1951.

Article XXIII, enabling the District of Columbia to choose presidential electors on the same basis of representation as the states. Went into effect April 3, 1961.

Article XXIV, forbidding disqualification for voting which is based on failure to pay any poll or other tax. Became effective January 23, 1964.

Article XXV, providing for succession to presidency and vice presidency. Became effective February 10, 1967.

CONSTITUTION OF THE UNITED STATES

PEAMBLE.—We, the people of the United States, in order to form a more perfect Union, establish justice, insure domestic tranquillity, provide for the common defense, promote the general welfare, and secure the blessings of liberty to ourselves and our posterity, do ordain and establish this Constitution for the United States of America.

ARTICLE I

SECTION I. All legislative powers herein granted shall be vested in a Congress of the United States, which shall consist of a Senate and House of Representatives.

SECTION II. 1. The House of Representatives shall be composed of members chosen every second year by the people of the several states, and the electors in each state shall have the qualifications requisite for electors of the most numerous branch of the state legislature.

2. No person shall be a representative who shall not have attained to the age of twenty-five years, and been seven years a citizen of the United States, and who shall not, when elected, be an inhabitant of that state in which he shall be chosen.

3. Representatives and direct taxes shall be apportioned among the several states which may be included within this Union, according to their respective numbers, which shall be determined by adding to the whole number of free persons, including those bound to service for a term of years, and excluding Indians not taxed, three-fifths of all other persons. The actual enumeration shall be made within three years after the first meeting of the Congress of the United States, and within every subsequent term of ten years, in such manner as they shall by law direct. The number of representatives shall not exceed one for every thirty thousand, but each state shall have at least one representative; and until such enumeration shall be made, the state of New Hampshire shall be entitled to choose 3; Massachusetts, 8; Rhode Island and Providence Planta-

tions, 1; Connecticut, 5; New York, 6; New Jersey, 4; Pennsylvania, 8; Delaware, 1; Maryland, 6; Virginia, 10; North Carolina, 5; South Carolina, 5; and Georgia, 3. See *Article XIV., Amendment.*

4. When vacancies happen in the representation from any state, the executive authority thereof shall issue writs of election to fill such vacancies.

5. The House of Representatives shall choose their speaker and other officers; and shall have the sole power of impeachment.

SECTION III. 1. The Senate of the United States shall be composed of two senators from each state, chosen by the legislature thereof, for six years; and each senator shall have one vote (Superseded by the 17th Amendment).

2. Immediately after they shall be assembled in consequence of the first election, they shall be divided as equally as may be into three classes. The seats of the senators of the first class shall be vacated at the expiration of the second year, of the second class at the expiration of the fourth year, and of the third class at the expiration of the sixth year, so that one-third may be chosen every second year; and if vacancies happen by resignation, or otherwise, during the recess of the legislature of any state, the executive thereof may make temporary appointments until the next meeting of the legislature, which shall then fill such vacancies.

3. No person shall be a senator who shall not have attained to the age of thirty years, and been nine years a citizen of the United States, and who shall not, when elected, be an inhabitant of that state for which he shall be chosen.

4. The vice president of the United States shall be president of the Senate, but shall have no vote, unless they be equally divided.

5. The Senate shall choose their other officers, and also a president pro tempore, in the absence of the vice president, or when he shall exercise the office of president of the United States.

6. The Senate shall have the sole power to try all impeachments. When sitting for that purpose, they shall be on oath or affirmation. When the president of the United States is tried, the chief justice shall preside: and no person shall be convicted without the concurrence of two-thirds of the members present.

7. Judgment in cases of impeachment shall not extend further than to removal from office, and disqualification to hold and enjoy any office of honor, trust, or profit under the United States; but the party convicted shall nevertheless be liable and subject to indictment, trial, judgment, and punishment, according to law.

SECTION IV. 1. The times, places, and manner of holding elections for senators and representatives shall be prescribed in each state by the legislature thereof; but the Congress may at any time by law make or alter such regulations, except as to the places of choosing senators.

2. The Congress shall assemble at least once in every year, and such meeting shall be on the first Monday in December, unless they shall by law appoint a different day.

SECTION V. 1. Each House shall be the judge of the elections, returns, and qualifications of its own members, and a majority of each shall constitute a quorum to do business; but a smaller number may adjourn from day to day, and may be authorized to compel the attendance of absent members, in such manner, and under such penalties as each House may provide.

2. Each House may determine the rules of its proceedings, punish its members for disorderly behavior, and, with the concurrence of two-thirds, expel a member.

3. Each House shall keep a journal of its proceedings, and from time to time publish the same, excepting such parts as may in their judgment require secrecy; and the yeas and nays of the members of either House on any question shall, at the desire of one-fifth of those present, be entered on the journal.

4. Neither House, during the session of Congress, shall, without the consent of the other, adjourn for more than three days, nor to any other place than that in which the two Houses shall be sitting.

SECTION VI. 1. The senators and representatives shall receive a compensation for their services, to be ascertained by law, and paid out of the treasury of the United States. They shall in all cases, except treason, felony, and breach of the peace, be privileged from arrest during their attendance at the session of their respective Houses, and in going to and returning from the same; and for any speech or debate in either House, they shall not be questioned in any other place.

2. No senator or representative shall, during the time for which he was elected, be appointed to any civil office under the authority of the United States, which shall have been created, or the emoluments whereof shall have been increased, during such time; and no person holding any office under the United States, shall be a member of either House during his continuance in office.

SECTION VII. 1. All bills for raising revenue shall originate in the House of Representatives; but the Senate may propose or concur with amendments as on other bills.

2. Every bill which shall have passed the House of Representatives and the Senate, shall, before it become a law, be presented to the president of the United States; if he approve he shall sign it, but if not he shall return it, with his objections, to that House in which it shall have originated, who shall enter the objections at large on their journal, and proceed to reconsider it. If after such reconsideration two-thirds of that House shall agree to pass the bill, it shall be sent, together with the objections, to the other House, by which it shall likewise be reconsidered, and, if approved by two-thirds of that House, it shall become a law. But in all such cases the votes of both Houses shall be determined by yeas and nays, and the names of the persons voting for and against the bill shall be entered on the journal of each House respectively. If any bill shall not be returned by the president within ten days (Sundays excepted) after it shall have been presented to him, the same shall be a law, in like manner as if he had signed it, unless the Congress by their adjournment prevent its return, in which case it shall not be a law.

3. Every order, resolution, or vote to which the concurrence of the Senate and House of Representatives may be necessary (except on a question of adjournment) shall be presented to the president of the United States; and before the same shall take effect, shall be approved by him, or being disapproved by him, shall be repassed by two-thirds of the Senate and House of Representatives, according to the rules and limitations prescribed in the case of a bill.

SECTION VIII. The Congress shall have power:

1. To lay and collect taxes, duties, imposts, and excises, to pay the debts and provide for the common defense and general welfare of the United States; but all duties, imposts, and excises shall be uniform throughout the United States.

2. To borrow money on the credit of the United States.

3. To regulate commerce with foreign nations, and among the several states, and with the Indian tribes.

4. To establish an uniform rule of naturalization, and uniform laws on the subject of bankruptcies throughout the United States.

5. To coin money, regulate the value thereof, and of foreign coin, and fix the standard of weights and measures.

6. To provide for the punishment of counterfeiting the securities and current coin of the United States.

7. To establish post offices and post roads.

8. To promote the progress of science and useful arts by securing for limited times to authors and inventors the exclusive right to their respective writings and discoveries.

9. To constitute tribunals inferior to the supreme court.

10. To define and punish piracies and felonies committed on the high seas, and offenses against the law of nations.

11. To declare war, grant letters of marque and reprisal, and make rules concerning captures on land and water.

12. To raise and support armies, but no appropriation of money to that use shall be for a longer term than two years.

13. To provide and maintain a navy.

14. To make rules for the government and regulation of the land and naval forces.

15. To provide for calling forth the militia to execute the laws of the Union, suppress insurrections, and repel invasions.

16. To provide for organizing, arming, and disciplining, the militia, and for governing such part of them as may be employed in the service of the United States, reserving to the states respectively, the appointment of the officers, and the authority of training the militia according to the discipline prescribed by Congress.

17. To exercise exclusive legislation in all cases whatsoever, over such district (not exceeding ten miles square) as may, by cession of particular states, and the acceptance of Congress, become the seat of the government of the United States, and to exercise like authority over all places purchased by the consent of the legislature of the state in which the same shall be, for the erection of forts, magazines, arsenals, dockyards, and other needful buildings.

18. To make all laws which shall be necessary and proper for carrying into execution the foregoing powers, and all other powers vested by this Constitution in the government of the United States, or in any department or officer thereof.

SECTION IX. 1. The migration or importation of such persons as any of the states now existing shall think proper to admit, shall not be prohibited by the Congress prior to the year one thousand eight hundred and eight, but a tax or duty may be imposed on such importation, not exceeding ten dollars for each person.

2. The privilege of the writ of habeas corpus shall not be suspended, unless when in cases of rebellion or invasion the public safety may require it.

3. No bill of attainder or ex post facto law shall be passed.

4. No capitation, or other direct, tax shall be laid, unless in proportion to the census or enumeration hereinbefore directed to be taken (Changed by the 16th Amendment).

5. No tax or duty shall be laid on articles exported from any state.

6. No preference shall be given by any regulation of commerce or revenue to the ports of one state over those of another: nor shall vessels bound to, or from, one state be obliged to enter, clear, or pay duties in another.

7. No money shall be drawn from the treasury, but in consequence of appropriations made by law; and a regular statement and account of the receipts and expenditures of all public money shall be published from time to time.

8. No title of nobility shall be granted by the United States: And no person holding any office of profit or trust under them, shall, without the consent of the Congress, accept of any present, emolument, office, or title, of any kind whatever, from any king, prince, or foreign state.

SECTION X. 1. No state shall enter into any treaty, alliance, or confederation; grant letters of marque and reprisal; coin money; emit bills of credit; make anything but gold and silver coin a tender in payment of debts; pass any bill of attainder, ex post facto law, or law impairing the obligation of contracts, or grant any title of nobility.

2. No state shall, without the consent of the Congress, lay any imposts or duties on imports or exports, except what may be absolutely necessary for executing its inspection laws: and the net produce of all duties and imposts, laid by any state on imports or exports, shall be for the use of the treasury of the United States; and all such laws shall be subject to the revision and control of the Congress.

3. No state shall, without the consent of Congress, lay any duty of tonnage, keep troops, or ships of war in time of peace, enter into any agreement or compact with another state, or with a foreign power, or engage in war, unless actually invaded, or in such imminent danger as will not admit of delay.

ARTICLE II

SECTION I. 1. The executive power shall be vested in a president of the United States of America. He shall hold his office during the term of four years, and, together with the vice president, chosen for the same term, be elected as follows.

2. Each state shall appoint, in such manner as the legislature thereof may direct, a number of electors, equal to the whole number of senators and representatives to which the state may be entitled in the Congress: but no senator or representative, or person holding an office of trust or profit under the United States, shall be appointed an elector.

3. The electors shall meet in their respective states, and vote by ballot for two persons, of whom one at least shall not be an inhabitant of the same state with themselves. And they shall make a list of all the persons voted for, and of the number of votes for each; which list they shall sign and certify, and transmit sealed to the seat of the government of the United States, directed to the president of the Senate. The president of the Senate shall, in the presence of the Senate and House of Representatives, open all the certificates, and the votes shall then be counted. The person having the greatest number of votes shall be the president, if such number be a majority of the whole number of electors appointed; and if there be more than one who have such majority, and have an equal number of votes, then the House of Representatives shall immediately choose by ballot one of them for president; and if no person have a majority, then from the five highest on the list the said House shall in like manner choose the president. But in choosing the president, the vote shall be taken by states, the representation for each state having one vote; A quorum for this purpose shall consist of a member or members from two-thirds of the states, and a majority of all the states shall be necessary to a choice. In every case, after the choice of the president, the person having the greatest number of votes of the electors shall be the vice president. But if there should remain two or more who have equal votes, the Senate shall choose from them by ballot the vice president (Superseded by the 12th Amendment).

4. The Congress may determine the time of choosing the electors, and the day on which they shall give their votes; which day shall be the same throughout the United States.

5. No person except a natural born citizen, or a citizen of the United States, at the time of the adoption of this Constitution, shall be eligible to the office of president; neither shall any person be eligible to that office who shall not have attained to the age of thirty-five years, and have been fourteen years a resident within the United States.

6. In case of the removal of the president from office, or of his death, resignation, or inability to discharge the powers and duties of the said office, the same shall devolve on the vice president, and the Congress may by law provide for the case of removal, death, resignation, or inability, both of the president and vice president, declaring what officer shall then act as president, and such officer shall act accordingly, until the disability be removed, or a president shall be elected.

7. The president shall, at stated times, receive for his services, a compensation, which shall neither be increased nor diminished during the period for which he shall have been elected, and he shall not receive within that period

any other emolument from the United States, or any of them.

8. Before he enter on the execution of his office, he shall take the following oath or affirmation:—

"I do solemnly swear (affirm) that I will faithfully execute the office of President of the United States, and will, to the best of my ability, preserve, protect, and defend the Constitution of the United States."

Section II. 1. The president shall be commander in chief of the army and navy of the United States, and of the militia of the several states, when called into the actual service of the United States; he may require the opinion, in writing, of the principal officer in each of the executive departments, upon any subject relating to the duties of their respective offices, and he shall have power to grant reprieves and pardons for offenses against the United States, except in cases of impeachment.

2. He shall have power, by and with the advice and consent of the Senate, to make treaties, provided two-thirds of the senators present concur; and he shall nominate, and by and with the advice and consent of the Senate, shall appoint ambassadors, other public ministers and consuls, judges of the supreme court, and all other officers of the United States, whose appointments are not herein otherwise provided for, and which shall be established by law: but the Congress may by law vest the appointment of such inferior officers, as they think proper, in the president alone, in the courts of law, or in the heads of departments.

3. The president shall have power to fill up all vacancies that may happen during the recess of the Senate, by granting commissions which shall expire at the end of their next session.

Section III. He shall from time to time give to the Congress information of the state of the Union, and recommend to their consideration such measures as he shall judge necessary and expedient; he may, on extraordinary occasions, convene both Houses, or either of them, and in case of disagreement between them, with respect to the time of adjournment, he may adjourn them to such time as he shall think proper; he shall receive ambassadors and other public ministers; he shall take care that the laws be faithfully executed, and shall commission all the officers of the United States.

Section IV. The president, vice president, and all civil officers of the United States shall be removed from office on impeachment for, and conviction of, treason, bribery, or other high crimes and misdemeanors.

ARTICLE III

Section I. The judicial power of the United States, shall be vested in one supreme court, and in such inferior courts as the Congress may from time to time ordain and establish. The judges, both of the supreme and inferior courts, shall hold their offices during good behavior, and shall, at stated times, receive for their services, a compensation, which shall not be diminished during their continuance in office.

Section II. 1. The judicial power shall extend to all cases, in law and equity, arising under this Constitution, the laws of the United States, and treaties made, or which shall be made, under their authority;—to all cases affecting ambassadors, other public ministers and consuls;—to all cases of admiralty and maritime jurisdiction;—to controversies to which the United States shall be a party;—to controversies between two or more states;—between a state and citizens of another state;—between citizens of different states;—between citizens of the same state claiming lands under grants of different states,—and between a state, or the citizens thereof, and foreign states, citizens, or subjects.

2. In all cases affecting ambassadors, other public ministers and consuls, and those in which a state shall be party, the supreme court shall have original jurisdiction. In all the other cases before mentioned, the supreme court shall have appellate jurisdiction, both as to law and fact, with such exceptions, and under such regulations as the Congress shall make.

3. The trial of all crimes, except in cases of impeachment shall be by jury; and such trial shall be held in the state where the said crimes shall have been committed; but when not committed within any state, the trial shall be at such place or places as the Congress may by law have directed.

Section III. 1. Treason against the United States, shall consist only in levying war against them, or in adhering to their enemies, giving them aid and comfort. No person shall be convicted of treason unless on the testimony of two witnesses to the same overt act, or on confession in open court.

2. The Congress shall have power to declare the punishment of treason, but no attainder of treason shall work corruption of blood, or forfeiture except during the life of the person attainted.

ARTICLE IV

Section I. Full faith and credit shall be given in each state to the public acts, records, and judicial proceedings of every other state. And the Congress may by general laws prescribe the manner in which such acts, records, and proceedings shall be proved, and the effect thereof.

Section II. 1. The citizens of each state shall be entitled to all privileges and immunities of citizens in the several states.

2. A person charged in any state with treason, felony, or other crime, who shall flee from justice, and be found in another state, shall on demand of the executive authority of the state from which he fled, be delivered up, to be removed to the state having jurisdiction of the crime.

3. No person held to service or labor in one state, under the laws thereof, escaping into another, shall, in consequence of any law or regulation therein, be discharged from such service or labor, but shall be delivered up on claim of the party to whom such service or labor may be due.

Section III. 1. New states may be admitted by the Congress into this Union; but no new state shall be formed or erected within the jurisdiction of any other state; nor any state be formed by the junction of two or more states, or parts of states, without the consent of the legislatures of the states concerned as well as of the Congress.

2. The Congress shall have power to dispose of and make all needful rules and regulations respecting the territory or other property belonging to the United States; and nothing in this Constitution shall be so construed as to prejudice any claims of the United States, or of any particular state.

Section IV. The United States shall guarantee to every state in this Union a republican form of government, and shall protect each of them against invasion; and on application of the legislature, or of the executive (when the legislature cannot be convened) against domestic violence.

ARTICLE V

The Congress, whenever two-thirds of both Houses shall deem it necessary, shall propose amendments to this Constitution, or, on the application of the legislatures of two-thirds of the several states, shall call a convention for proposing amendments, which, in either case, shall be valid to all intents and purposes, as part of this Constitution, when ratified by the legislatures of three-fourths of the several states, or by conventions in three-fourths thereof, as the one or the other mode of ratification may be proposed by the Congress; provided that no amendment which may be made prior to the year one thousand eight hundred and eight shall in any manner affect the first and fourth clauses in the Ninth Section of the First Article; and that no state, without its consent, shall be deprived of its equal suffrage in the Senate.

ARTICLE VI

1. All debts contracted and engagements entered into before the adoption of this Constitution, shall be as valid against the United States under this Constitution, as under the Confederation.

2. This Constitution, and the laws of the United States which shall be made in pursuance thereof; and all treaties made, or which shall be made, under the authority of the United States, shall be the supreme law of the land; and the judges in every state shall be bound thereby, anything in the Constitution or laws of any state to the contrary notwithstanding.

3. The senators and representatives before mentioned, and the members of the several state legislatures, and all executive and judicial officers, both of the United States and of the several states, shall be bound by oath or affirmation, to support this Constitution; but no religious test shall ever be required as a qualification to any office or public trust under the United States.

ARTICLE VII

The ratification of the conventions of nine states, shall be sufficient for the establishment of this Constitution between the states so ratifying the same.

Done in convention by the unanimous consent of the states present the seventeenth day of September in the year of our Lord one thousand seven hundred and eighty-seven, and of the independence of the United States of America the twelfth. In witness whereof we have hereunto subscribed our names,

GO: WASHINGTON—
Presidt. and Deputy from Virginia

New Hampshire	*New Jersey*
JOHN LANGDON	WIL: LIVINGSTON
NICHOLAS GILMAN	DAVID BREARLEY
	WM. PATERSON
Massachusetts	JONA: DAYTON
NATHANIEL GORHAM	
RUFUS KING	*Pennsylvania*
	B. FRANKLIN
Connecticut	THOMAS MIFFLIN
	ROBT. MORRIS
WM. SAML. JOHNSON	GEO. CLYMER
ROGER SHERMAN	THOS. FITZSIMONS
	JARED INGERSOLL
New York	JAMES WILSON
ALEXANDER HAMILTON	GOUV. MORRIS

Delaware
GEO: READ
GUNNING BEDFORD JUN
JOHN DICKINSON
RICHARD BASSETT
JACO; BROOM

Maryland
JAMES MCHENRY
DAN OF ST. THOS. JENIFER
DANL. CARROLL

Virginia
JOHN BLAIR—
JAMES MADISON JR.

North Carolina
WM. BLOUNT
RICHD. DOBBS SPAIGHT
HU WILLIAMSON

South Carolina
J. RUTLEDGE
CHARLES COTESWORTH
PINCKNEY
CHARLES PINCKNEY
PIERCE BUTLER

Georgia
WILLIAM FEW
ABR. BALDWIN

Attest WILLIAM JACKSON,
Secretary

AMENDMENTS TO THE CONSTITUTION
* *Date when declared ratified by a sufficient number of states.*

ARTICLE I
Congress shall make no law respecting an establishment of religion, or prohibiting the free exercise thereof; or abridging the freedom of speech, or of the press; or the right of the people peaceably to assemble, and to petition the government for a redress of grievances.

ARTICLE II
A well regulated militia, being necessary to the security of a free state, the right of the people to keep and bear arms, shall not be infringed.

ARTICLE III
No soldier shall, in time of peace, be quartered in any house, without the consent of the owner, nor in time of war, but in a manner to be prescribed by law.

ARTICLE IV
The right of the people to be secure in their persons, houses, papers, and effects, against unreasonable searches and seizures shall not be violated, and no warrants shall issue, but upon probable cause, supported by oath or affirmation, and particularly describing the place to be searched, and the persons or things to be seized.

ARTICLE V
No person shall be held to answer for a capital, or otherwise infamous crime, unless on a presentment or indictment of a grand jury, except in cases arising in the land or naval forces, or in the militia, when in actual service in time of war or public danger; nor shall any person be subject for the same offense to be twice put in jeopardy of life or limb; nor shall be compelled in any criminal case to be a witness against himself, nor be deprived of life, liberty, or property, without due process of law; nor shall private property be taken for public use, without just compensation.

ARTICLE VI
In all criminal prosecutions the accused shall enjoy the right to a speedy and public trial, by an impartial jury of the state and district wherein the crime shall have been committed, which district shall have been previously ascertained by law, and to be informed of the nature and cause of the accusation; to be confronted with the witnesses against him; to have compulsory process for obtaining witnesses in his favor, and to have the assistance of counsel for his defense.

ARTICLE VII
In suits at common law, where the value in controversy shall exceed twenty dollars, the right of trial by jury shall be preserved, and no fact tried by a jury shall be otherwise re-examined in any court of the United States, than according to the rules of the common law.

ARTICLE VIII
Excessive bail shall not be required, nor excessive fines imposed, nor cruel and unusual punishments inflicted.

ARTICLE IX
The enumeration in the Constitution, of certain rights, shall not be construed to deny or disparage others retained by the people.

ARTICLE X
The powers not delegated to the United States by the Constitution, nor prohibited by it to the states, are reserved to the states respectively, or to the people.
* *The first ten amendments (Bill of Rights) were declared in force December 15, 1791.*

ARTICLE XI
The judicial power of the United States shall not be construed to extend to any suit in law or equity, commenced or prosecuted against one of the United States, by citizens of another state, or by citizens or subjects of any foreign state.
* *January 8, 1798*

ARTICLE XII
The electors shall meet in their respective states, and vote by ballot for president and vice president, one of whom, at least, shall not be an inhabitant of the same state with themselves; they shall name in their ballots the person voted for as president, and in distinct ballots the person voted for as vice president, and they shall make distinct lists of all persons voted for as president, and of all persons voted for as vice president, and of the number of votes for each, which list they shall sign and certify, and transmit sealed to the seat of the government of the United States, directed to the president of the Senate;—the president of the Senate shall, in the presence of the Senate and House of Representatives, open all the certificates and the votes shall then be counted; —the person having the greatest number of votes for president, shall be the president, if such number be a majority of the whole number of electors appointed; and if no person have such majority, then from the persons having the highest numbers not exceeding three on the list of those voted for as president, the House of Representatives shall choose immediately, by ballot, the president. But in choosing the president, the votes shall be taken by states, the representation from each state having one vote; a quorum for this purpose shall consist of a member or members from two-thirds of the states, and a majority of all the states shall be necessary to a choice. And if the House of Representatives shall not choose a president whenever the right of choice shall devolve upon them, before the fourth day of March next following, then the vice president shall act as president, as in the case of the death or other constitutional disability of the president. The person having the greatest number of votes as vice president, shall be the vice president, if such number be a majority of the whole number of electors appointed, and if no person have a majority, then from the two highest numbers on the list, the Senate shall choose the vice president; a quorum for the purpose shall consist of two-thirds of the whole number of Senators, and a majority of the whole number shall be necessary to a choice. But no person constitutionally ineligible to the office of president shall be eligible to that of vice president of the United States. **September 25, 1804*

ARTICLE XIII
1. Neither slavery nor involuntary servitude, except as a punishment for crime whereof the party shall have been duly convicted, shall exist within the United States, or any place subject to their jurisdiction.
2. Congress shall have power to enforce this article by appropriate legislation. **December 18, 1865*

ARTICLE XIV
1. All persons born or naturalized in the United States, and subject to the jurisdiction thereof, are citizens of the United States and of the state wherein they reside. No state shall make or enforce any law which shall abridge the privileges or immunities of citizens of the United States; nor shall any state deprive any person of life, liberty, or property, without due process of law; nor deny to any person within its jurisdiction the equal protection of the laws.
2. Representatives shall be apportioned among the several states according to their respective numbers, counting the whole number of persons in each state, excluding Indians not taxed. But when the right to vote at any election for the choice of electors for president and vice president of the United States, representatives in Congress, the executive and judicial officers of a state, or the members of the legislature thereof, is denied to any of the male inhabitants of such state, being twenty-one years of age, and citizens of the United States, or in any way abridged, except for participation in rebellion, or other crime, the basis of representation therein shall be reduced in the proportion which the number of such male citizens shall bear to the whole number of male citizens twenty-one years of age in such state.
3. No person shall be a senator or representative in Congress, or elector of president and vice president, or hold any office, civil or military, under the United States, or under any state, who, having previously taken an oath, as a member of Congress, or as an officer of the United States, or as a member of any state legislature, or as an executive or judicial officer of any state, to support the Constitution of the United States, shall have engaged in insurrection or rebellion against the same, or given aid or comfort to the enemies thereof. But Congress may by a vote of two-thirds of each House, remove such disability.
4. The validity of the public debt of the United States, authorized by law, including debts incurred for payment of pensions and bounties for services in suppressing insurrection or rebellion, shall not be questioned. But neither the United States nor any state shall assume or pay any debt or obligation incurred in aid of insurrection or rebellion against the United States, or any claim for the loss or emancipation of any slave; but all such debts, obligations, and claims shall be held illegal and void.
5. The Congress shall have power to enforce, by appropriate legislation, the provisions of this article. **July 28, 1868*

ARTICLE XV

1. The right of citizens of the United States to vote shall not be denied or abridged by the United States or by any State on account of race, color, or previous condition of servitude.

2. The Congress shall have power to enforce this article by appropriate legislation. *March 30, 1870

ARTICLE XVI

The Congress shall have power to lay and collect taxes on incomes, from whatever source derived, without apportionment among the several states, and without regard to any census or enumeration. *February 25, 1913

ARTICLE XVII

The Senate of the United States shall be composed of two senators from each state, elected by the people thereof, for six years, and each senator shall have one vote. The electors in each state shall have the qualifications requisite for electors of the most numerous branch of the state legislatures.

When vacancies happen in the representation of any state in the Senate, the executive authority of such state shall issue writs of election to fill such vacancies: Provided, that the legislature of any state may empower the executive thereof to make temporary appointments until the people fill the vacancies by election as the legislature may direct.

This amendment shall not be so construed as to affect the election or term of any senator chosen before it becomes valid as part of the Constitution. *May 31, 1913

ARTICLE XVIII

1. After one year from the ratification of this article the manufacture, sale, or transportation of intoxicating liquors within, the importation thereof into, or the exportation thereof from the United States and all territory subject to the jurisdiction thereof, for beverage purposes, is hereby prohibited.

2. The Congress and the several states shall have concurrent power to enforce this article by appropriate legislation.

3. This article shall be inoperative unless it shall have been ratified as an amendment to the Constitution by the legislatures of the several states, as provided in the Constitution, within seven years from the date of submission hereof to the states by the Congress. *January 29, 1919

ARTICLE XIX

1. The right of citizens of the United States to vote shall not be denied or abridged by the United States or by any state on account of sex.

2. Congress shall have power, by appropriate legislation, to enforce the provisions of this article. *August 26, 1920

ARTICLE XX

1. The terms of the president and vice president shall end at noon on the 20th day of January, and the terms of senators and representatives at noon on the 3d day of January, of the years in which such terms would have ended if this article had not been ratified; and the terms of their successors shall then begin.

2. The Congress shall assemble at least once in every year, and such meeting shall begin at noon on the 3d day of January, unless they shall by law appoint a different day.

3. If, at the time fixed for the beginning of the term of the president, the president elect shall have died, the vice president elect shall become president. If a president shall not have been chosen before the time fixed for the beginning of his term, or if the president elect shall have failed to qualify, then the vice president elect shall act as president until a president shall have qualified; and the Congress may by law provide for the case wherein neither a president elect nor a vice president elect shall have qualified, declaring who shall then act as president, or the manner in which one who is to act shall be selected, and such person shall act accordingly until a president or vice president shall have qualified.

4. The Congress may by law provide for the case of the death of any of the persons from whom the House of Representatives may choose a president whenever the right of choice shall have devolved upon them, and for the case of the death of any of the persons from whom the Senate may choose a vice president whenever the right of choice shall have devolved upon them. *February 6, 1933

ARTICLE XXI

1. The 18th article of amendment to the Constitution of the United States is hereby repealed.

2. The transportation or importation into any state, territory, or possession of the United States for delivery or use therein of intoxicating liquors, in violation of the laws thereof, is hereby prohibited.

3. This article shall be inoperative unless it shall have been ratified as an amendment to the Constitution by conventions in the several states, as provided in the Constitution, within seven years from the date of the submission thereof, to the states by the Congress. *Dec. 5, 1933

ARTICLE XXII

1. No person shall be elected to the office of the President more than twice, and no person who has held the office of President, or acted as President, for more than two years of a term to which some other person was elected President shall be elected to the office of the President more than once. But this article shall not apply to any person holding the office of President when this article was proposed by the Congress, and shall not prevent any person who may be holding the office of President, or acting as President, during the term within which this article becomes operative from holding the office of President or acting as President during the remainder of such term.

2. This article shall be inoperative unless it shall have been ratified as an amendment to the Constitution by the legislators of three fourths of the several states within seven years from the date of its submission to the states by the Congress. *February 26, 1951

ARTICLE XXIII

1. The District constituting the seat of government of the United States shall appoint in such manner as the Congress may direct:

A number of electors of President and Vice President equal to the whole number of Senators and Representatives in Congress to which the District would be entitled if it were a State, but in no event more than the least populous State; they shall be in addition to those appointed by the States, but they shall be considered, for the purpose of the election of President and Vice President, to be electors appointed by a State; and they shall meet in the District and perform such duties as provided by the twelfth article of amendment.

2. The Congress shall have power to enforce this article by appropriate legislation. *April 3, 1961

ARTICLE XXIV

1. The right of the citizens of the United States to vote in any primary or other election for President or Vice President, for electors for President or Vice President, or for Senator or Representative in Congress, shall not be denied or abridged by the United States or any State by reasons of failure to pay any poll tax or any other tax.

2. The Congress shall have power to enforce this article by appropriate legislation. *January 23, 1964

ARTICLE XXV

1. In case of the removal of the President from office or of his death or resignation, the Vice President shall become President.

2. Whenever there is a vacancy in the office of the Vice President, the President shall nominate a Vice President who shall take office upon confirmation by a majority vote of both houses of Congress.

3. Whenever the President transmits to the President pro tempore of the Senate and the Speaker of the House of Representatives his written declaration that he is unable to discharge the powers and duties of his office, and until he transmits to them a written declaration to the contrary, such powers and duties shall be discharged by the Vice President as acting President.

4. Whenever the Vice President and a majority of either the principal officers of the executive departments or of such other body as Congress may by law provide transmit to the President pro tempore of the Senate and the Speaker of the House of Representatives their written declaration that the President is unable to discharge the powers and duties of his office, the Vice President shall immediately assume the powers and duties of the office as acting President.

Thereafter, when the President transmits to the President pro tempore of the Senate and the Speaker of the House of Representatives his written declaration that no inability exists, he shall resume the powers and duties of his office unless the Vice President and a majority of either the principal officers of the executive departments or of such other body as Congress may by law provide transmit within four days to the President pro tempore of the Senate and the Speaker of the House of Representatives their written declaration that the President is unable to discharge the powers and duties of his office. Thereupon Congress shall decide the issue, assembling within forty-eight hours for that purpose if not in session. If the Congress, within twenty-one days after receipt of the latter written declaration, or, if Congress is not in session within twenty-one days after Congress is required to assemble, determines by two thirds vote of both houses that the President is unable to discharge the powers and duties of his office, the Vice President shall continue to discharge the same as acting President: otherwise, the President shall resume the powers and duties of his office. *February 10, 1967

ARTICLE XXVI

1. The right of citizens of the United States, who are eighteen years of age or older, to vote shall not be denied or abridged by the United States or any state on account of age.

2. The Congress shall have the power to enforce this article by appropriate legislation. *July 5, 1971

THE FEDERAL GOVERNMENT

THE LEGISLATIVE DEPARTMENT

THE CONGRESS

Consisting of both the Senate and the House of Representatives as coordinate bodies.

DURATION.—The term of each Congress is for two years, beginning January 3 of the odd years.

REGULAR SESSIONS.—Annual, beginning at noon on January 3.

SPECIAL SESSIONS.—At the call of the president.

MEMBERSHIP.—Each House is the judge of the elections and qualifications of its own members.

The Senate

NUMBER.—Two senators from each state.

ELECTED.—By direct vote of the people.

TERM.—Six years; one-third of the Senate being elected every two years.

ELIGIBILITY.—Citizen of the United States nine years; resident of state; minimum age, 30 years.

SALARY.—$57,500 per year.

PRESIDENT OF THE SENATE.—The vice president of the United States.

POWERS OF THE SENATE.—

Confirms or rejects nominations of the president.

Ratifies or rejects treaties with foreign powers.

Elects president *pro tempore* of the Senate, and its other officers.

Elects vice president of the United States if regular election fails.

Acts as a court for the trial of impeachments.

The House of Representatives

NUMBER.—Four hundred thirty-five members. *

ELECTED.—By voters of congressional districts.

TERM.—Two years—the entire House being elected every two years.

ELIGIBILITY.—Citizen of the United States seven years; resident of the state; minimum age 25 years.

SALARY.—$57,500 per year; the speaker, $75,000 per year.

POWERS OF THE HOUSE OF REPRESENTATIVES.—

Elects its speaker (presiding officer) and its other officers.

Elects president of the United States if the regular election fails.

Prosecutes impeachments before the Senate.

Originates all bills for raising revenue.

---

*There are besides a resident commissioner from Puerto Rico and delegates from the Virgin Islands, the District of Columbia, and Guam who have the right to take part in floor discussions and to vote in the committees to which they are assigned, but they cannot vote on the floor of the House.

THE EXECUTIVE DEPARTMENT

THE PRESIDENT

HOW ELECTED.—In several steps as follows:

State electors are chosen at a general election held on the Tuesday following the first Monday of November of every fourth year, the number of electors of each state being equal to the number of senators and representatives to which the state is entitled in Congress. The date of the election was fixed by act of Congress in 1845.

The electors meet in their respective states on December 15 and vote by ballot for president and vice president; at the same time they make certificates of their vote and transmit the same to the president of the Senate.

The Senate and the House of Representatives meet jointly and count the votes of the state electors, when, if there is an election, the president of the Senate declares who are elected president and vice president.

In case there is no choice by the state electors, the president is elected by the House of Representatives from the three candidates who received the most electoral votes for president, in which election the vote is taken by states, each state having but one vote, and a majority of all the states being necessary to a choice.

TERM OF OFFICE.—Four years, from January 20.

ELIGIBILITY.—A natural born citizen; resident of the United States 14 years; minimum age, 35.

SALARY.—$200,000 a year.

POWERS AND DUTIES OF THE PRESIDENT.—

Commander in chief of the armed services.

Receives representatives of foreign governments.

Communicates with Congress by message.

Approves (signs) or disapproves (vetoes) acts of Congress. See *Law, Enactment of.*

Calls and adjourns special sessions of Congress.

Makes treaties with advice and consent of the Senate.

Appoints public officers with the advice and consent of the Senate.

Commissions public officers of the United States.

Grants reprieves and pardons for offenses against the United States.

The Vice President

HOW CHOSEN.—Elected by state electors the same as the president; or by the Senate, in case there is no choice by the state electors. Vacancy filled by nomination by president, confirmed by a majority vote of both houses.

TERM AND ELIGIBILITY.—Same as for president.

SALARY.—$75,000 a year.

THE PRESIDENTIAL SUCCESSION.—In case of the removal, death, or resignation of the president, the vice president takes the president's place; in case of the president's disability, the vice president serves as acting president during the period of the president's disability. If presidency and vice presidency are both vacant, the order of succession to the presidency is (1) speaker of the House, (2) president pro tempore of the Senate, (3) heads of executive departments in order given below, each being subject to constitutional requirements of eligibility.

The Executive Departments

DEPARTMENT OF STATE.—Has charge of foreign affairs.

TREASURY DEPARTMENT.—Has charge of fiscal affairs.

DEPARTMENT OF DEFENSE. — Has charge of the national defense forces: army, navy, and air force.

DEPARTMENT OF JUSTICE.—Has charge of the legal affairs of the government.

DEPARTMENT OF THE INTERIOR.—Has charge of domestic affairs, including public lands, pensions.

DEPARTMENT OF AGRICULTURE.—Has charge of agricultural affairs, etc.

DEPARTMENT OF COMMERCE.—Has charge of domestic and foreign affairs relating to commerce, transportation, supervision of Weather Bureau, etc.

DEPARTMENT OF LABOR.—Has charge of labor affairs and naturalization.

DEPARTMENT OF HEALTH, EDUCATION AND WELFARE.—Has charge of public health service, office of education, social security administration.

DEPARTMENT OF HOUSING AND URBAN DEVELOPMENT.—Has charge of public housing, mortgage insurance, planning for city development and transportation.

DEPARTMENT OF TRANSPORTATION.—Has charge of safety and promotion in air, rail, highway, and pipe line transportation, but not navigation.

U.S. POSTAL SERVICE.—Formerly a cabinet-level department, in 1971 it was made a government-owned, independently operating, nonprofit corporation within the executive department.

The Cabinet

MEMBERS.—Heads of the executive departments.

APPOINTMENT.—By the president with the advice and consent of the Senate.

SALARY.—All cabinet members, $66,000 annually.

THE JUDICIAL DEPARTMENT

JUDGES OF THE UNITED STATES COURTS

APPOINTMENT.—By the president with the advice and consent of the Senate.

TENURE OF OFFICE.—During life or good behavior; but may retire on full salary at 70 and 10 years' service or 65 and 15 years' service.

THE SUPREME COURT OF THE UNITED STATES

MEMBERS.—One chief justice; eight associate justices.

SALARIES.—Chief justice, $75,000; associate justices, each, $72,000.

TERMS OF COURT.—One each year, beginning on the second Monday in October.

ORIGINAL JURISDICTION.—In all cases affecting ambassadors, ministers, and consuls, and in all cases in which a state is a party.

APPELLATE JURISDICTION.—In cases of law and equity where the inferior courts have original jurisdiction, with such exceptions and regulations as Congress has made.

THE CHIEF JUSTICE.—Presides over the Senate when it sits as a court of impeachment for the trial of the president.

INFERIOR COURTS

JURISDICTION:

In cases between citizens of different states.

In cases in which the United States is a party.

In cases of admiralty and maritime jurisdiction.

In trials for crimes against the United States; but the trial of crimes must be by jury, and must be held in the state where the crime was committed.

Appeals to the Supreme Court may be had in all cases of law and equity, with such exceptions and regulations as Congress has made.

United States Circuit Courts of Appeals:

Organized in 1891 to relieve the United States Supreme Court in appellate cases.

NUMBER.—One in each of the ten judicial circuits and one in the District of Columbia.

SALARIES.—$57,500 annually.

MEMBERS.—Three judges: the chief justice, or the associate justice assigned to the circuit, or any circuit or district judge within the circuit, is competent to sit.

United States District Courts:

NUMBER OF DISTRICTS.—One or more in each state and territory. At present there are ninety judicial districts within the United States and the District of Columbia.

SALARIES.—$54,500 annually.

United States Territorial Courts:

NUMBER.—One each in Puerto Rico, Guam, the Virgin Islands, and the Canal Zone.

JURISDICTION.—The same as district courts and, except in Puerto Rico, many local matters.

SALARIES.—$54,500 annually.

United States Court of Claims:

JURISDICTION.—Claims against the United States, including those referred to it by Congress.

MEMBERS.—One chief justice and four associate justices.

SALARIES.—$57,500 annually.

United States Court of Customs and Patent Appeals:

JURISDICTION.—Cases involving appeals from customs duties and from the patent office.

MEMBERS.—One chief justice; four associate justices.

SALARIES.—$57,500 annually.

United States Customs Court:

JURISDICTION.—Civil actions arising under the tariff laws.

MEMBERS.—One chief justice; eight associate justices.

SALARIES.—$54,500 annually.

United States Tax Court:

JURISDICTION.—Tax-related cases and judgments on retirement plans.

MEMBERS.—Sixteen justices who elect a chief judge.

SALARIES.—$54,500 annually.

CONGRESS

All legislative power granted by the Constitution is intrusted to the "Congress of the United States," which consists of a Senate and a House of Representatives.

The Senate. To the Senate is given the power of ratifying nominations of the president to public office. The Constitution specifically mentions judges of the Supreme Court and "ambassadors, other public ministers and consuls" for appointment "with the advice and consent of the Senate." The Senate, however, is never formally consulted. It has no right of nomination, but it does at times reject the president's appointments, though rarely in the case of heads of executive departments or "cabinet positions."

Foreign treaties are made "by and with the consent of the Senate, provided two-thirds of the Senators present concur." These two special powers associate the Senate with the president in the determining of foreign policy and in the guidance of foreign relations. Yet this responsibility for foreign policy has been sparingly and rather negatively exercised by the Senate.

The president is considered to have the sole right of negotiating with representatives of other nations and the Senate has never received either foreign delegates or communications. The president does not formally consult the Senate upon foreign relations, though he generally seeks to maintain touch with Senate opinion through its committee on foreign affairs. The president retains complete control of a treaty until he delivers it to the Senate, and he may even then withdraw it. He is not bound to disclose to the Senate correspondence with foreign states, or even to give information within his possession. For these reasons the president, rather than the Senate, generally determines foreign policy, though subject to the severe limitation of having his treaties rejected. The president also has repeatedly conducted foreign negotiations through "personal representatives," unconfirmed by the Senate, or he may himself negotiate personally and directly, as did President Wilson at Paris.

It may also be noticed that, through the treaty ratifying power, the Senate, with the president, may end war and conclude peace, though only Congress can declare war. For the trial of impeachments, the Senate sits as a judicial body, a concurrence of two-thirds of the members present being necessary for conviction. (Article I, sec. 3, par. 6). The chief justice presides at the impeachment trial of a president.

The vice president of the United States is the constitutional presiding officer of the Senate, but a president *pro tempore* is chosen from among the senators. In presidential elections, if no person receives a majority of votes of the electors, the vice president is chosen by the Senate. The salary of all senators is $57,500 per year.

The House of Representatives. The House of Representatives, likewise, has special powers. It alone can vote impeachment and prosecute the trial of an impeached officer. It alone can initiate bills for raising revenue, though such measures are frequently totally altered by the Senate. In case of a failure of a presidential election to give a majority of electors for one person, the House of Representatives is empowered to select the president by ballot, each state casting one ballot. The salary of members of the House of Representatives is $57,500 per year; the Speaker of the House receives $75,000.

Powers of Congress. Other than as above stated, the two houses possess equality in legislation. The Constitution limits this legislative faculty, however, to expressly defined fields.

To provide for the raising and disbursement of revenue.

To borrow money; to coin money and to regulate its value; and to fix the standard of weights and measures.

To regulate foreign and interstate commerce.

To declare war, and to maintain an army and a navy.

Some Presidential Addresses to Joint Sessions in Recent History

FIRST SINCE ADAMS. President Wilson, shown before Congress in 1914, became first President since 1800 to deliver his messages to Congress in person.

TWENTIETH AMENDMENT. President Roosevelt addresses the 73d Congress on January 3, 1934. This was the first Congress to meet under the terms of the Twentieth Amendment which set the opening day of each session of Congress on January 3 of each year and the date of Presidential inaugurations on January 20 of every fourth year.

STATE OF THE UNION. President Truman gives his state of the Union Message to a Joint Session of Congress on January 5, 1949. Senator Kenneth McKellar (left), President Pro Tem of the Senate and House Speaker Sam Rayburn are seated behind the President.

HERBERT HOOVER TAKES OFFICE. Statesman and humanitarian is sworn into Presidency, March 4, 1929, not to be followed by a Republican until 1953.

WHITE HOUSE CHANGES HANDS. President Herbert Hoover and President-elect Franklin Delano Roosevelt on drive to inaugural, March 4, 1933.

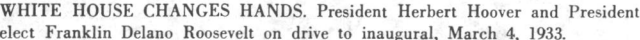

AGE OF ACTION BEGINS. Newly sworn President Roosevelt lifts heart of Nation with first inaugural speech (1933) that attacked deep national despondency.

THREE GREAT AMERICANS. President Roosevelt, Speaker Rayburn, Senate Leader Barkley drive to Capitol (1941) for FDR's third inauguration.

FOURTH TERM INAUGURAL. Address delivered from South Portico of the White House (January 20, 1945). War strain shows in President Roosevelt's face.

THE GOVERNMENT OF THE UNITED STATES

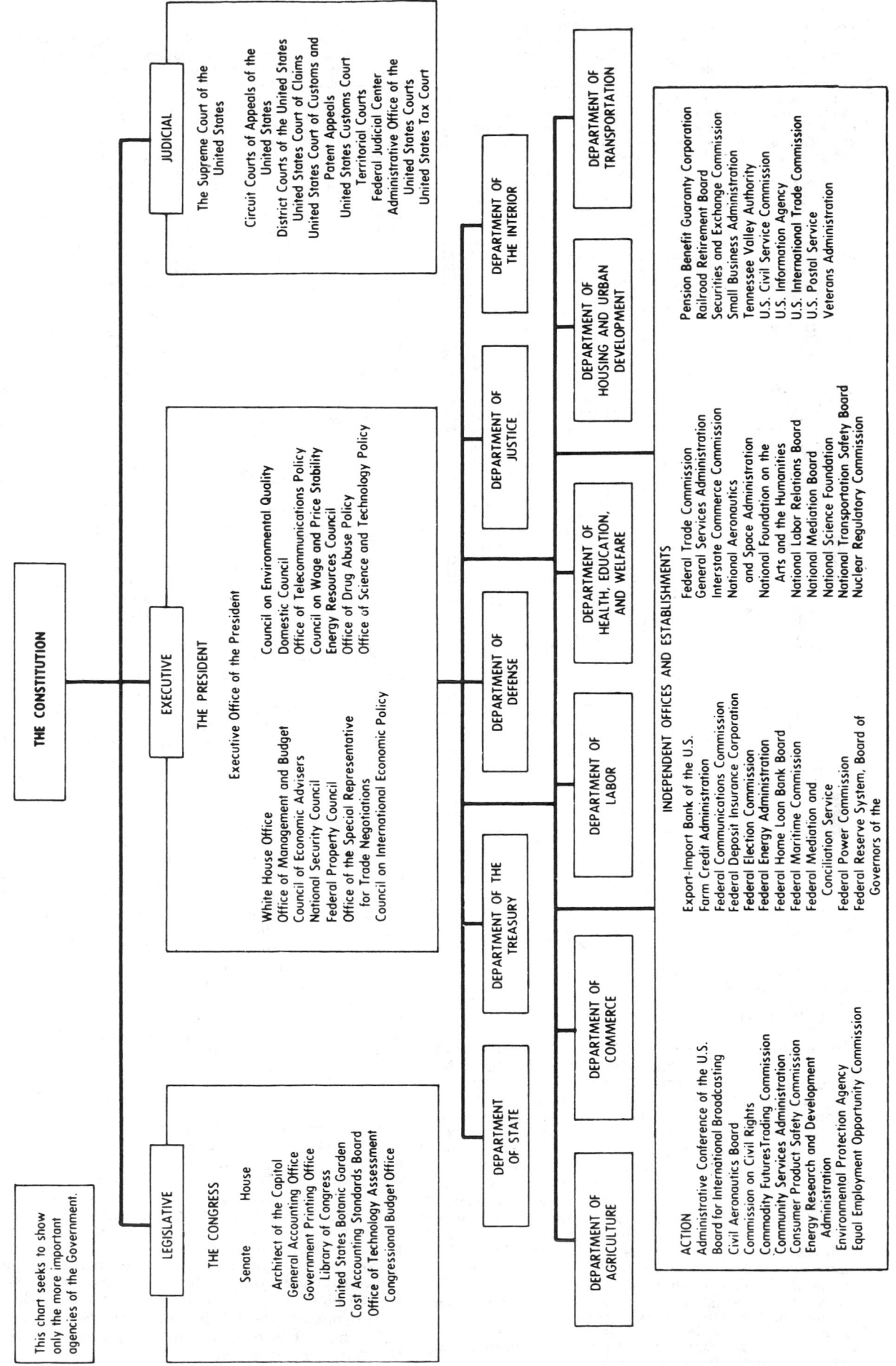

This chart seeks to show only the more important agencies of the Government.

THE CONSTITUTION

LEGISLATIVE

THE CONGRESS

Senate   House

Architect of the Capitol
General Accounting Office
Government Printing Office
Library of Congress
United States Botanic Garden
Cost Accounting Standards Board
Office of Technology Assessment
Congressional Budget Office

EXECUTIVE

THE PRESIDENT

Executive Office of the President

White House Office
Office of Management and Budget
Council of Economic Advisers
National Security Council
Federal Property Council
Office of the Special Representative
    for Trade Negotiations
Council on International Economic Policy

Council on Environmental Quality
Domestic Council
Office of Telecommunications Policy
Council on Wage and Price Stability
Energy Resources Council
Office of Drug Abuse Policy
Office of Science and Technology Policy

JUDICIAL

The Supreme Court of the United States

Circuit Courts of Appeals of the United States
District Courts of the United States
United States Court of Claims
United States Court of Customs and Patent Appeals
United States Customs Court
Territorial Courts
Federal Judicial Center
Administrative Office of the United States Courts
United States Tax Court

DEPARTMENT OF STATE

DEPARTMENT OF THE TREASURY

DEPARTMENT OF DEFENSE

DEPARTMENT OF JUSTICE

DEPARTMENT OF THE INTERIOR

DEPARTMENT OF AGRICULTURE

DEPARTMENT OF COMMERCE

DEPARTMENT OF LABOR

DEPARTMENT OF HEALTH, EDUCATION, AND WELFARE

DEPARTMENT OF HOUSING AND URBAN DEVELOPMENT

DEPARTMENT OF TRANSPORTATION

INDEPENDENT OFFICES AND ESTABLISHMENTS

ACTION
Administrative Conference of the U.S.
Board for International Broadcasting
Civil Aeronautics Board
Commission on Civil Rights
Commodity FuturesTrading Commission
Community Services Administration
Consumer Product Safety Commission
Energy Research and Development Administration
Environmental Protection Agency
Equal Employment Opportunity Commission

Export-Import Bank of the U.S.
Farm Credit Administration
Federal Communications Commission
Federal Deposit Insurance Corporation
Federal Election Commission
Federal Energy Administration
Federal Home Loan Bank Board
Federal Maritime Commission
Federal Mediation and Conciliation Service
Federal Power Commission
Federal Reserve System, Board of Governors of the

Federal Trade Commission
General Services Administration
Interstate Commerce Commission
National Aeronautics and Space Administration
National Foundation on the Arts and the Humanities
National Labor Relations Board
National Mediation Board
National Science Foundation
National Transportation Safety Board
Nuclear Regulatory Commission

Pension Benefit Guaranty Corporation
Railroad Retirement Board
Securities and Exchange Commission
Small Business Administration
Tennessee Valley Authority
U.S. Civil Service Commission
U.S. Information Agency
U.S. International Trade Commission
U.S. Postal Service
Veterans Administration

To establish post offices and post roads.
To enact patent and copyright laws.
To enact uniform naturalization and bankruptcy laws.
To provide for the punishment of crimes against the U.S.
To establish courts inferior to the supreme court.
To provide for organizing and calling out the militia.
To admit new states into the Union.
To provide for the government of the territories.
To exercise exclusive jurisdiction over the District of Columbia, public lands and buildings, forts and navy yards.
To enact all laws necessary and proper for carrying into execution all the powers vested by the Constitution in the government of the United States.

SPEAKERS OF THE HOUSE

NAME	State	Born	Died	Congress	Years
F. A. Muhlenberg	Pa.	1750	1801	1	1789–91
Jonathan Trumbull	Conn.	1740	1809	2	1791–93
F. A. Muhlenberg	Pa.	1750	1801	3	1793–95
Jonathan Dayton	N. J.	1760	1824	4, 5	1795–99
Theo. Sedgwick	Mass.	1746	1813	6	1799–01
Nathaniel Macon	N. C.	1758	1837	7–9	1801–07
Joseph B. Varnum	Mass.	1750	1821	10, 11	1807–11
Henry Clay	Ky.	1777	1852	12, 13	1811–14
Langdon Cheves	S. C.	1776	1857	13	1814–15
Henry Clay	Ky.	1777	1852	14–16	1815–20
John W. Taylor	N. Y.	1784	1854	16	1820–21
Philip P. Barbour	Va.	1783	1841	17	1821–23
Henry Clay	Ky.	1777	1852	18	1823–25
John W. Taylor	N. Y.	1784	1854	19	1825–27
Andrew Stevenson	Va.	1784	1857	20–23	1827–34
John Bell	Tenn.	1797	1869	23	1834–35
James K. Polk	Tenn.	1795	1849	24, 25	1835–39
R. M. T. Hunter	Va.	1809	1887	26	1839–41
John White	Ky.	1805	1845	27	1841–43
John W. Jones	Va.	1791	1848	28	1843–45
John W. Davis	Ind.	1799	1859	29	1845–47
Robert C. Winthrop	Mass.	1809	1894	30	1847–49
Howell Cobb	Ga.	1815	1868	31	1849–51
Linn Boyd	Ky.	1800	1859	32, 33	1851–55
Nathaniel P. Banks	Mass.	1816	1894	34	1855–57
James L. Orr	S. C.	1822	1873	35	1857–59
Wm. Pennington	N. J.	1796	1862	36	1859–61
Galusha A. Grow	Pa.	1823	1907	37	1861–63
Schuyler Colfax	Ind.	1823	1885	38–40	1863–69
James G. Blaine	Me.	1830	1893	41–43	1869–75
Michael C. Kerr	Ind.	1827	1876	44	1875–76
Samuel J. Randall	Pa.	1828	1890	44–46	1876–81
Joseph W. Keifer	Ohio	1836	1932	47	1881–83
John G. Carlisle	Ky.	1835	1910	48–50	1883–89
Thomas B. Reed	Me.	1839	1902	51	1889–91
Charles F. Crisp	Ga.	1845	1896	52, 53	1891–95
Thomas B. Reed	Me.	1839	1902	54, 55	1895–99
David B. Henderson	Iowa	1840	1906	56, 57	1899–03
Joseph G. Cannon	Ill.	1836	1926	58–61	1903–11
Champ Clark	Mo.	1850	1921	62–65	1911–19
Fred. H. Gillett	Mass.	1851	1935	66–68	1919–25
Nicholas Longworth	Ohio	1869	1931	69–71	1925–31
John N. Garner	Tex.	1868	1967	72	1931–33
Henry T. Rainey	Ill.	1860	1934	73	1933–34
Joseph W. Byrnes	Tenn.	1869	1936	74	1935–36
Wm. B. Bankhead	Ala.	1874	1940	74–76	1936–40
Sam Rayburn	Tex.	1882	1961	76–79	1940–47
Joseph W. Martin, Jr.	Mass.	1884	1968	80	1947–49
Sam Rayburn	Tex.	1882	1961	81–82	1949–53
Joseph W. Martin, Jr.	Mass.	1884	1968	83	1953–55
Sam Rayburn	Tex.	1882	1961	84–86	1955–61
John W. McCormack	Mass.	1891	....	87–91	1962–70
Carl Albert	Okla.	1908	....	92–94	1971–76
Thomas P. O'Neill	Mass.	1912	....	95–	1977–

Interpreted Powers. The practice of legislation has grown and taken on new aspects through the felt necessity of extending the scope of the national government. The supreme court has usually given a liberal interpretation to these powers, especially to the power to regulate interstate commerce and to enact needed laws to carry into execution the powers vested by the constitution in the national government. The court having decided, however, that the Constitution did not give the power to levy a direct tax on incomes, the 16th amendment was adopted in 1913, giving Congress this right.

Limitations on Powers of Congress. The Constitution limits Congress to powers expressly conferred. It also forbids Congress to:

Suspend the writ of habeas corpus unless, in case of rebellion or invasion, the public safety so requires.
Pass any bill of attainder or ex post facto law.
Lay any direct per capita tax, other than an income tax, without apportionment among the states according to population.

Lay any tax or duty on articles exported from any state.
Give any preference to the ports of one state over those of another.
Grant any title of nobility.
Create a new state within the jurisdiction of another state or out of its territory, without the consent of the state.
Make any law respecting the establishment of religion or prohibiting its free exercise.
Abridge the freedom of speech or of the press.
Forbid the right of peaceable assembly.
Forbid the right of petition.
Pass any law for the quartering of soldiers in private houses, without the consent of the owners, in time of peace.
Pass any law providing for unreasonable searches and seizures, or for the issue of warrants without the usual judicial process.
Infringe the right to keep and bear arms.
Pass any law providing for the holding of a person for a capital or otherwise infamous crime, unless on presentment and indictment of a grand jury, except in cases arising in the land or naval forces or in the militia when in actual service in time of war or public danger.
Pass any law that would subject a person to being twice put in jeopardy of life or limb or deprive him of life, liberty, or property, without due process of law.
Pass any law taking private property for public use without just compensation.
Pass any law denying or abridging the right of citizens of the United States to vote, by reason of race, color, sex, or previous condition of servitude.
Assume or pay any debt or obligation incurred in aid of rebellion or insurrection against the United States, or to pay any claim for the loss of slaves.
Pass any law denying the rights of an accused person to a speedy and public trial by a jury of the locality where the crime is committed, to be informed of the nature and cause of the accusation against him, to be confronted with the witnesses against him, and to compel witnesses to testify in his favor, and to have the assistance of a counsel.
Pass any law forbidding jury trial for suits at common law, where the value in controversy exceeds twenty dollars.
Pass any law requiring excessive bail or imposing excessive fines or cruel and unusual punishments.

These prohibitions apply to the power of Congress in legislating for the Union. It will be noted that they refer explicitly to Congress, not to the states. However, the 14th amendment does place certain restrictions on the states. See *State Rights*.

Enactment of a Law. The process of making laws is long and complex. An understanding of the essential steps in it, however, is necessary for an intelligent grasp of newspaper accounts of the progress of legislation.

Of the numerous steps which a measure may have to pass through before becoming a law, the 16 listed below are the most important. For the sake of simplicity, it will be assumed that the typical bill here traced through Congress originates in the House of Representatives, although all bills except those relating to appropriations may originate also in the Senate. If the Senate acts first on a measure, the rôles of the houses as described here will be reversed. Here are the principal steps:

1. A bill is introduced by an individual Congressman. This step may be preceded by a message from the president recommending action. The message is ordinarily referred to a committee, the chairman of which introduces a bill embodying the proposals. (See *Congressional Committees.*)

2. The bill is referred for study to a standing committee of the House, designated by the speaker.

3. The committee, if it so decides, may take testimony regarding the measure from spokesmen for interested groups, these hearings usually including executive officers of the government.

4. The committee may then report the bill back to the House, with or without amendments and with or without recommendation for enactment. If the committee takes no action, the bill is said to die in committee. The House may, however, discharge the committee from further consideration of the bill and so place the bill on the legislative calendar.

5. If passed, the bill is sent to the Senate.

6. There it is referred to a committee, as in the House.

7. The Senate committee may, at its discretion,

Inside the House

JAMES MADISON. In 1789, during the first of his four terms in the House, Madison introduced legislation which subsequently became the Bill of Rights of our Constitution. His rise to the Presidency in 1809 made him the first of sixteen Presidents in U.S. history who have served in the House of Representatives.

JOHN RANDOLPH. Sometimes reckless, often audacious, usually sarcastic, and always flamboyant, this fiery orator served 14 colorful terms in the House of Representatives and 2 years as a Senator. He was an early chairman of the Ways and Means Committee.

ELBRIDGE GERRY. Member of Continental Congress, signer of Declaration of Independence, and Delegate to the Constitutional Convention, Gerry is representative of the early patriots who rendered distinguished service in the House.

A Historical Sampling of the Men and Events That Have Made It Great

SAM HOUSTON. He served two terms as a Member from Tennessee before going to Texas to win enduring fame.

BATTLE FOR SPEAKER. The majority party's candidate usually wins the Speakership election, but occasionally a serious contest develops. This sketch depicts a two month battle in the Thirty-fourth Congress when Speaker Nathaniel Banks was elected on the 133d vote.

JOHN QUINCY ADAMS. Two years after his Presidency, Adams was elected to the House, where he rendered 17 years of the most distinguished service of his career. Articulate, industrious, and honorable, he was dubbed "Old Man Eloquent" by his colleagues. In 1848 he was stricken on the floor of the House and died.

DAVY CROCKETT. This frontier politician served three terms in the House before riding off to Texas. Under this engraved likeness he has written, "I leave this rule for others when I am dead: Be always sure you are right, then go ahead."

report the bill for favorable action, with or without changes, or it may substitute another bill already before it or an entirely new bill on the subject.

8. If the Senate approves the bill as it came from the House, it goes to the president for his signature. If defeated in the Senate, the bill is dead, barring a reconsideration. The third possible action is approval in amended form.

9. In this last case, the bill goes back to the House, which may accept the amendments, thus making it ready for the president's signature.

10. If the House refuses to accept the Senate amendments or makes others which the Senate refuses to accept, the bill "goes to conference." This means that the measure is submitted to a group consisting of 3 or 5 members of the House and the same number of members of the Senate, each panel appointed by the presiding officer of the house represented. The duty of conferees is to reconcile differences in the bill as approved by the two houses.

11. If no agreement is reached, the bill is said to "die in conference." Otherwise the conferees report their agreement to both houses, and the report is either sent back for further efforts or is accepted.

12. When the conference report is accepted by both houses, the bill goes to the president.

13. The president may sign the bill, usually after consultation with his advisers. It then becomes a law, and is classified by the secretary of state as public or private, and is given a number.

14. The president may fail to sign the bill after he has had it for ten days, exclusive of Sundays. In that case, it becomes law without his signature, except in one circumstance, which is described below under *Pocket Veto*.

15. The president may return the bill to Congress with a veto.

16. Congress may then repass the bill by two-thirds majorities in both houses. If this is done, the bill becomes law without the president's signature. If either house fails to override the veto by this majority, the bill is dead.

Pocket Veto. This term is popularly applied when the president withholds for ten days his approval of a bill and Congress adjourns before the end of the ten days. Under these circumstances, the bill dies without having been specifically vetoed.

Congressional Committees. These bodies form bottle-necks, as it were, by which the vast majority of bills are kept from consideration by Congress, only those regarded as the most important being allowed to pass through. It is by these committees also that the only genuine study in Congress is made of the need and probable effect of the prospective laws.

Representation of the political parties on committees is in approximate proportion to their strength in Congress. The chairman of each committee is always a member of the majority party. It is for this reason that few laws are ever enacted which have not the support of the party in power.

The most powerful committees include the appropriations committee, which handles measures for spending money, and the ways and means committee, which deals with tax bills. Measures from these committees have the right of way at all times. The power to give preferential places on the calendar to other bills rests with the committee on rules. The so-called steering committee is made up of leaders of the majority party only. Its purpose is to hasten legislation favored by the party in power.

Kinds of Congressional Action. Bills are measures which, on approval, become acts. Resolutions represent Congressional action of a "nonlegislative" character. Senate resolutions and House resolutions require action by one house only. Concurrent resolutions require approval by both houses but not by the president. Joint, or public, resolutions require the same procedure as bills. They are frequently indistinguishable from bills except in form and name.

General Accounting Office. The GAO is an independent non-political agency within the legislative branch. Created in 1921, the GAO assists Congress in its legislative responsibilities, audits the federal government, and makes recommendations for more efficient government.

Library of Congress. Established in 1800, it is the foremost library of the U.S. and functions as a research service for the federal government.

THE PRESIDENT

The president of the United States is the highest representative of the nation. Elected by the voters of all the states for a fixed term of years, he is largely independent of Congress, the courts, and sectional demands. In spite of the theory of separation of powers, in accordance with which the constitution-makers created the office, the president has immense influence over legislation and is generally held responsible for the work of Congress.

The president's influence springs from his power of veto; from his constitutional practice of submitting recommendations to Congress; and from his influence as the molder of public opinion. His power of appointment, with his ability to distribute "patronage" among members of Congress, serves to keep the members who are of his party in accord with his policies.

The National Leader. While dependent on his party for nomination and support, he is the recognized national leader of his party and frequently dominates its views and controls its organization. He is, moreover, the head of the entire national administration. Members of Congress, the president, and the vice president are the only elected officers of the U. S. All others are appointed by the president or by heads of departments under his control. The president's removal power extends to nearly all offices, except the judicial or quasi judicial.

Powers. The president is the commander in chief of the armed services, with the right to determine their employment and to dispatch armed forces upon foreign missions. While Congress alone can legally declare war, the president has repeatedly, of his own authority, used the armed services for military action and for territorial incursion. After the Vietnam war, however, the Wars Power Act was passed by Congress, thus limiting the president's military powers somewhat. On his will and judgment, more even than on the attitude of Congress, seems to rest the momentous decision of peace and of war. By his direction the attorney general undertakes judicial investigations and prosecutions. These may be suspended or abandoned by the president's direction. He may grant pardon to persons convicted for offenses against the U. S. or those under investigation for past offenses, and amnesty to political prisoners or to those in rebellion. He may commute or suspend sentences after conviction or during the trial. He may fill a vacancy in the vice presidency subject to Congressional ratifications.

Cabinet. The cabinet meets solely to advise with the president and may not with propriety assemble without his presence. Its views are purely consultative and in no manner bind his freedom of decision. He may at any time direct the action of the head of a department, and in the field of foreign relations frequently does so, and may alter or reverse a department's decision.

Disability. The president remains in office, irrespective of the attitude of Congress or of the support of the nation, until the end of his term, or until his death in office. In case of his disability, the vice president serves as acting president. Rules for determination of disability and its termination are set forth in the 25th amendment.

Place of Power. The official actions of the president need not be taken at the national capital. He may exercise any power at any place within the country or while abroad.

Jimmy Carter—39th President of the United States. Former Georgia Governor Jimmy Carter became President on January 20, 1977. In a close election, Carter defeated Gerald R. Ford, the Republican candidate. Walter F. Mondale, Carter's running mate, became the 42nd U.S. Vice President.

Impeachment. Impeachment is the only way of removing a capable president from office. Impeachment charges are brought by the House of Representatives and are tried by the Senate. A two-thirds vote of the Senate is necessary for conviction. There have been two impeachment proceedings initiated by Congress against presidents. The first, against Andrew Johnson in 1868, failed by one vote in the Senate. The second, against Richard Nixon in 1974, ended after he resigned.

The President and Judiciary. Prior to the Watergate scandal of 1972–74, it was believed that federal courts could not issue writs against the president nor could his actions be judicially reviewed. However, Chief Justice Warren Burger in a Supreme Court decision handed down on July 24, 1974, declared: "Neither the doctrine of separation of powers, nor the need for confidentiality of high-level communications, without more, can sustain an absolute unqualified presidential privilege of immunity from judicial process under all circumstances." Although the Supreme Court's decision was unprecedented, wide-ranging conclusions could not be drawn from it because of the special circumstances surrounding the decision.

Authority in Crises. During war time, the president becomes virtually a national dictator, concentrating in his office the strength and the will of the nation. However, while Congress and the nation have given unreserved support and authority to the president during war, they have limited him in the arrangement of peace.

Magnitude of Power. Reviewing the office of president in the light of other national executives, it is probably correct to say that it exceeds most other modern offices in the breadth of its powers and in the respect which it commands. Since the term of Washington, it has steadily grown in independence and in influence. Although the power of the presidency has increased over the years, it might be noted that any attempts to make the office all-powerful and encompassing have been checked by the legislative and judicial branches.

THE EXECUTIVE DEPARTMENTS

These are 11 in number, all established by acts of Congress. The department heads constitute the president's cabinet. The departments with dates of establishment are: State (1789), Treasury (1789), Interior (1849), Justice (1870), Agriculture (1889), Commerce (1903), Labor (1913), Defense (1947), Health, Education and Welfare (1953), Housing and Urban Development (1966), Transportation (1966). Except for the attorney general, heads are called "secretary."

Heads of Departments. The departments have from one to several assistant secretaries and a chief clerk. They are divided into bureaus and divisions, each with a single head known as "director" or "commissioner," "chief," etc. Subject always to his subordination to the president, who appoints and may at any time remove him, and who is politically responsible for his official acts, a department head directs the entire service under him; appoints and removes subordinate officials; issues "regulations" governing the administrative work; and decides disputes or controversies arising from the actions of his subordinates.

In many cases the decision of the department head is final, though in others there is appeal to the president. The list of bureaus and of other divisions as fixed by statute is given in a tabulated form below, together with the list of department heads and the years of their service. There is no department corresponding to the ministry of dependencies in other governments. The Department of the Interior supervises the Virgin Islands, Guam, and Samoa. The Canal Zone is under army direction.

DEPARTMENT OF STATE

The secretary of state, in event of the death of the president, is fourth in the line of presidential succession. Thus far, no secretary of state has been called to fill this place. All treaties are negotiated by the secretary of state, who often conducts the discussions in person, through interviews with foreign representatives. The secretary, under the direction of the president, is charged with the duties of correspondence with ministers and consuls of the United States, and with representatives of foreign powers accredited to the United States. He is charged also with negotiations of whatever character relating to foreign affairs.

He and his staff represent the U.S. in over 50 international organizations (such as the United Nations and the Organization of American States) and at various international conferences. His primary functions are to execute current U.S. foreign policy and to make recommendations on future action. As the most important cabinet officer, the secretary is a member of the National Security Council. He is also custodian of the treaties made with foreign states, and of the laws of the U.S. The modern Department of State has been relieved of virtually all domestic duties.

SECRETARIES OF STATE

PRESIDENTS	Cabinet Officers	Residences	Appointed
Washington	Thomas Jefferson	Va.	1789
Washington	Edmund Randolph	Va.	1794
Washington	Timothy Pickering	Mass.	1795
Adams	Timothy Pickering	Mass.	1797
Adams	John Marshall	Va.	1800
Jefferson	James Madison	Va.	1801
Madison	Robert Smith	Md.	1809
Madison	James Monroe	Va.	1811
Monroe	John Quincy Adams	Mass.	1817
J. Q. Adams	Henry Clay	Ky.	1825
Jackson	Martin Van Buren	N. Y.	1829
Jackson	Edward Livingston	La.	1831
Jackson	Louis McLane	Del.	1833
Jackson	John Forsyth	Ga.	1834
Van Buren	John Forsyth	Ga.	1837
Harrison	Daniel Webster	Mass.	1841
Tyler	Daniel Webster	Mass.	1841
Tyler	Hugh S. Legaré	S. C.	1843
Tyler	Abel P. Upshur	Va.	1843
Tyler	John C. Calhoun	S. C.	1844
Polk	James Buchanan	Pa.	1845
Taylor	John M. Clayton	Del.	1849
Fillmore	Daniel Webster	Mass.	1850
Fillmore	Edward Everett	Mass.	1852
Pierce	William L. Marcy	N. Y.	1853
Buchanan	Lewis Cass	Mich.	1857
Buchanan	Jeremiah S. Black	Pa.	1860
Lincoln	William H. Seward	N. Y.	1861
Johnson	William H. Seward	N. Y.	1865
Grant	Elihu B. Washburn	Ill.	1869
Grant	Hamilton Fish	N. Y.	1869
Hayes	William M. Evarts	N. Y.	1877
Garfield	James G. Blaine	Me.	1881
Arthur	F. T. Frelinghuysen	N. J.	1881
Cleveland	Thomas F. Bayard	Del.	1885
B. Harrison	James G. Blaine	Me.	1889
B. Harrison	John W. Foster	Ind.	1892
Cleveland	Walter Q. Gresham	Ill.	1893
Cleveland	Richard Olney	Mass.	1895
McKinley	John Sherman	Ohio	1897
McKinley	William R. Day	Ohio	1898
McKinley	John Hay	Ohio	1898
T. Roosevelt	John Hay	Ohio	1901
T. Roosevelt	Elihu Root	N. Y.	1905
T. Roosevelt	Robert Bacon	N. Y.	1909
Taft	Philander C. Knox	Pa.	1909
Wilson	William J. Bryan	Nebr.	1913
Wilson	Robert Lansing	N. Y.	1915
Wilson	Bainbridge Colby	N. Y.	1920
Harding	Charles E. Hughes	N. Y.	1921
Coolidge	Charles E. Hughes	N. Y.	1923
Coolidge	Frank B. Kellogg	Minn.	1925
Hoover	Frank B. Kellogg	Minn.	1929
Hoover	Henry L. Stimson	N. Y.	1929
F. D. Roosevelt	Cordell Hull	Tenn.	1933
F. D. Roosevelt	Edward R. Stettinius	N. Y.	1944
Truman	Edward R. Stettinius	N. Y.	1945
Truman	James F. Byrnes	S. C.	1945

SECRETARIES OF STATE—Con.

Truman . . .	George C. Marshall . .	Pa.	1947
Truman . . .	Dean G. Acheson . .	Md.	1949
Eisenhower	John Foster Dulles . .	N. Y.	1953
Eisenhower	Christian A. Herter . .	Mass.	1959
Kennedy . .	Dean Rusk	N. Y.	1961
Johnson . . .	Dean Rusk	N. Y.	1963
Nixon	William P. Rogers . .	Md.	1969
Nixon	Henry A. Kissinger . .	Mass.	1973
Ford	Henry A. Kissinger . .	Mass.	1974
Carter . . .	Cyrus R. Vance . . .	N.Y.	1977

DEPARTMENT OF DEFENSE

The National Military Establishment was created July 26, 1947, to unify the armed forces. Formerly, military control had been divided between the War Department, created in 1789, and the Department of the Navy, created in 1798. These two were merged to become the Department of Defense, headed by the secretary of defense. Subordinate to him in separately organized departments are the secretaries of the army, navy, and air force. The Department of Defense is responsible for providing military forces to deter war and to ensure the security of the country. It provides civilian oversight of the armed forces while working closely with the joint chiefs of staff. Its central headquarters is the Pentagon.

SECRETARIES OF WAR

PRESIDENTS	Cabinet Officers	Residences	Appointed
Washington .	Henry Knox	Mass.	1789
Washington .	Timothy Pickering . .	Mass.	1795
Washington .	James McHenry . . .	Md.	1796
Adams . . .	James McHenry . . .	Md.	1797
Adams . . .	Samuel Dexter . . .	Mass.	1800
Adams . . .	Roger Griswold . . .	Conn.	1801
Jefferson. . .	Henry Dearborn . . .	Mass.	1801
Madison. . .	William Eustis	Mass.	1809
Madison. . .	John Armstrong . . .	N. Y.	1813
Madison. . .	James Monroe	Va.	1814
Madison. . .	William H. Crawford .	Ga.	1815
Monroe . . .	John C. Calhoun . . .	S. C.	1817
J. Q. Adams .	James Barbour . . .	Va.	1825
J. Q. Adams .	Peter B. Porter . . .	N. Y.	1828
Jackson . . .	John H. Eaton	Tenn.	1829
Jackson . . .	Lewis Cass	Ohio	1831
Jackson . . .	Benjamin F. Butler . .	N. Y.	1836
Van Buren. .	Joel R. Poinsett . . .	S. C.	1837
Harrison. . .	John Bell	Tenn.	1841
Tyler	John Bell	Tenn.	1841
Tyler	John C. Spencer . . .	N. Y.	1841
Tyler	James M. Porter . . .	Pa.	1843
Tyler	William Wilkins . . .	Pa.	1844
Polk	William L. Marcy . . .	N. Y.	1845
Taylor . . .	George W. Crawford .	Ga.	1849
Fillmore . .	Charles M. Conrad . .	La.	1850
Pierce . . .	Jefferson Davis . . .	Miss.	1853
Buchanan . .	John B. Floyd	Va.	1857
Buchanan . .	Joseph Holt	Ky.	1861
Lincoln . . .	Simon Cameron . . .	Pa.	1861
Lincoln . . .	Edwin M. Stanton . .	Ohio	1862
Johnson. . .	Edwin M. Stanton . .	Ohio	1865
Johnson. . .	U. S. Grant (ad in) . .	Ill.	1867
Johnson. . .	Lor. Thomas (ad in) .	Del.	1868
Johnson. . .	John M. Schofield . .	N. Y.	1868
Grant . . .	John A. Rawlins . . .	Ill.	1869
Grant . . .	William W Belknap . .	Ia.	1869
Grant . . .	Alphonso Taft	Ohio	1876
Grant . . .	James Don. Cameron .	Pa.	1876
Hayes . . .	George W. McCrary . .	Ia.	1877
Hayes . . .	Alexander Ramsey . .	Minn.	1879
Garfield . . .	Robert T. Lincoln . .	Ill.	1881
Arthur . . .	Robert T. Lincoln . .	Ill.	1881
Cleveland . .	William C. Endicott . .	Mass.	1885
B. Harrison .	Redfield Proctor . . .	Vt.	1889
B. Harrison .	Stephen B. Elkins . .	W. Va.	1891
Cleveland . .	Daniel S. Lamont . . .	N. Y.	1893
McKinley . .	Russell A. Alger . . .	Mich.	1897
McKinley . .	Elihu Root	N. Y.	1899
T. Roosevelt .	Elihu Root	N. Y.	1901
T. Roosevelt .	William H. Taft . . .	Ohio	1904
T. Roosevelt .	Luke E. Wright . . .	Tenn	1908
Taft	J. M. Dickinson . . .	Tenn.	1909
Taft	Henry L. Stimson. . .	N. Y.	1911
Wilson . . .	Lindley M. Garrison .	N. J.	1913
Wilson . . .	Newton D. Baker . . .	Ohio	1916

SECRETARIES OF WAR—Con.

PRESIDENTS	Cabinet Officers	Residences	Appointed
Harding . .	John W. Weeks. . . .	Mass.	1921
Coolidge . .	John W. Weeks. . . .	Mass.	1923
Coolidge . .	Dwight F. Davis . . .	Mo.	1925
Hoover . . .	James W. Good . . .	Ill.	1929
Hoover . . .	Patrick J. Hurley. . .	Okla.	1929
F. D. Roosevelt	George H. Dern . . .	Utah	1933
F. D. Roosevelt	Harry W. Woodring . .	Kansas	1936
F. D. Roosevelt	Henry L. Stimson . .	N. Y.	1940
Truman . . .	Henry L. Stimson . .	N. Y.	1945
Truman . . .	Robert P. Patterson .	N. Y.	1945
Truman . . .	Kenneth C. Royall . .	N. C.	1947

SECRETARIES OF THE NAVY

PRESIDENTS	Cabinet Officers	Residences	Appointed
Adams . . .	Benjamin Stoddert . .	Md.	1798
Jefferson. . .	Benjamin Stoddert . .	Md.	1801
Jefferson. . .	Robert Smith	Md.	1801
Jefferson. . .	Jacob Crowninshield .	Mass.	1805
Madison . .	Paul Hamilton	S. C.	1809
Madison . .	William Jones	Pa.	1813
Madison . .	B. W. Crowninshield .	Mass.	1814
Monroe . . .	B. W. Crowninshield .	Mass.	1817
Monroe . . .	Smith Thompson . . .	N. Y.	1818
Monroe . . .	Samuel L. Southard .	N. J.	1823
J. Q. Adams .	Samuel L. Southard .	N. J.	1825
Jackson . . .	John Branch	N. C.	1829
Jackson . . .	Levi Woodbury. . . .	N. H.	1831
Jackson . . .	Mahlon Dickerson . .	N. J.	1834
Van Buren .	Mahlon Dickerson . .	N. J.	1837
Van Buren .	James K. Paulding . .	N. Y.	1838
Harrison. . .	George E. Badger . .	N. C.	1841
Tyler	George E. Badger . .	N. C.	1841
Tyler	Abel P. Upshur . . .	Va.	1841
Tyler	David Henshaw . . .	Mass.	1843
Tyler	Thomas W Gilmer . .	Va.	1844
Tyler	John Y. Mason	Va.	1844
Polk	George Bancroft . . .	Mass.	1845
Polk	John Y. Mason	Va.	1846
Taylor . . .	William B. Preston . .	Va.	1849
Fillmore . .	William A. Graham . .	N. C.	1850
Fillmore . .	John P. Kennedy . .	Md.	1852
Pierce . . .	James C. Dobbin . . .	N. C.	1853
Buchanan . .	Isaac Toucey	Conn.	1857
Lincoln . . .	Gideon Welles	Conn.	1861
Johnson . . .	Gideon Welles	Conn.	1865
Grant . . .	Adolph E. Borie . . .	Pa.	1869
Grant . . .	George M. Robeson . .	N. J.	1869
Hayes . . .	Richard W. Thompson .	Ind.	1877
Hayes . . .	Nathan Goff, Jr. . . .	W. Va.	1881
Garfield . . .	William H. Hunt . . .	La.	1881
Arthur . . .	William E. Chandler .	N. H.	1882
Cleveland . .	William C. Whitney. .	N. Y.	1885
B. Harrison .	Benjamin F. Tracy . .	N. Y.	1889
Cleveland . .	Hilary A. Herbert . .	Ala.	1893
McKinley . .	John D. Long	Mass.	1897
T. Roosevelt .	John D. Long	Mass.	1901
T. Roosevelt .	William H. Moody . .	Mass.	1902
T. Roosevelt .	Paul Morton	N. Y.	1904
T. Roosevelt .	Charles J Bonaparte .	Md.	1905
T. Roosevelt .	Victor H. Metcalf. . .	Cal.	1906
T. Roosevelt .	Truman H. Newberry .	Mich.	1908
Taft	George von L. Meyer .	Mass.	1909
Wilson . . .	Josephus Daniels . . .	N. C.	1913
Harding . .	Edwin Denby	Mich.	1921
Coolidge . .	Edwin Denby	Mich.	1923
Coolidge . .	Curtis D. Wilbur . .	Cal.	1924
Hoover . . .	Charles F. Adams . .	Mass.	1929
F. D. Roosevelt	Claude A Swanson . .	Va.	1933
F. D. Roosevelt	Charles Edison . . .	N. J.	1940
F. D. Roosevelt	Frank Knox	Ill.	1940
F. D. Roosevelt	James Forrestal . . .	N. Y.	1944
Truman . . .	James Forrestal . . .	N. Y.	1945

SECRETARIES OF DEFENSE

PRESIDENTS	Cabinet Officers	Residences	Appointed
Truman . . .	James Forrestal	N. Y.	1947
Truman . . .	Louis A. Johnson . . .	W. Va.	1949
Truman . . .	George C. Marshall . .	Pa.	1950
Truman . . .	Robert A. Lovett . . .	N. Y.	1951
Eisenhower .	Charles E Wilson . . .	Mich.	1953
Eisenhower .	Neil H. McElroy . . .	Ohio	1957
Eisenhower .	Thomas S. Gates, Jr. .	Pa.	1959
Kennedy . .	Robert S. McNamara .	Mich.	1961
Johnson . . .	Robert S. McNamara .	Mich.	1963
Johnson . . .	Clark M. Clifford . .	Mo.	1968
Nixon . . .	Melvin R. Laird . . .	Wis.	1969

SECRETARIES OF DEFENSE—Con.

Nixon	Elliot L. Richardson	Va.	1973
Nixon	James R. Schlesinger	Va.	1973
Ford	James R. Schlesinger	Va.	1974
Ford	Donald H. Rumsfeld	Ill.	1975
Carter	Harold Brown	Cal.	1977

The Secretaries appointed since consolidation are:

Army. Kenneth Royall, 1947; Gordon Gray, 1949; Frank Pace, 1950; Robert Stevens, 1953; Wilbur Brucker, 1955; Elvis Stahr, 1961; Cyrus Vance, 1962; Stephen Ailes, 1964; Stanley Resor, 1965; Robert Froehlke, 1971; Howard Callaway, 1973; Martin Hoffmann, 1975; C. L. Alexander, 1977.

Navy. Jno. Sullivan, 1947; Fran. Matthews, 1949; Dan Kimball, 1951; Robt. Anderson, 1953; Chas. Thomas, 1954; Thos. Gates, 1957; Wm. Franke, 1959; Jno. Connally, 1961; Fred Korth, 1961; Paul Nitze, 1963; Paul Ignatius, 1967; Jno. Chafee, 1969; Jno. Warner, 1972; J. W. Middendorf, 1974.

Air Force. S. Symington, 1947; Thos. Finletter, 1950; Harold Talbott, 1953; Don. Quarles, 1955; Jas. Douglas, 1957; Dudley Sharp, 1959; Eug. Zuckert, 1961; Harold Brown, 1965; Robt. Seamans, 1969; Jno. McLucas, 1973; Thos. Reed, 1975.

DEPARTMENT OF THE TREASURY

The secretary of the treasury is charged by law with the management of the national finances. He prepares plans for the improvement of the revenues and for the support of the public credit, including the issuing of government bonds and treasury certificates; superintends the collection of customs and the internal revenue, including income taxes and taxes on tobacco and other commodities or articles; directs the forms of keeping and rendering public accounts and of making returns; grants warrants for all moneys drawn from the treasury. This department also handles the planning, construction, and maintenance of public buildings. It coins metallic money and engraves and prints the paper currency. An annual estimate of revenues and expenses of the government is prepared by the treasury department for presentation to Congress by the president.

SECRETARIES OF THE TREASURY

PRESIDENTS	Cabinet Officers	Residences	Appointed
Washington	Alexander Hamilton	N. Y.	1789
Washington	Oliver Wolcott	Conn.	1795
Adams	Oliver Wolcott	Conn.	1797
Adams	Samuel Dexter	Mass.	1801
Jefferson	Samuel Dexter	Mass.	1801
Jefferson	Albert Gallatin	Pa.	1801
Madison	Albert Gallatin	Pa.	1809
Madison	George W. Campbell	Tenn.	1814
Madison	Alexander J. Dallas	Pa.	1814
Madison	William H. Crawford	Ga.	1816
Monroe	William H. Crawford	Ga.	1817
J. Q. Adams	Richard Rush	Pa.	1825
Jackson	Samuel D. Ingham	Pa.	1829
Jackson	Louis McLane	Del.	1831
Jackson	William J. Duane	Pa.	1833
Jackson	Roger B. Taney	Md.	1833
Jackson	Levi Woodbury	N. H.	1834
Van Buren	Levi Woodbury	N. H.	1837
Harrison	Thomas Ewing	Ohio	1841
Tyler	Thomas Ewing	Ohio	1841
Tyler	Walter Forward	Pa.	1841
Tyler	John C. Spencer	N. Y.	1843
Tyler	George M. Bibb	Ky.	1844
Polk	Robert J. Walker	Miss.	1845
Taylor	William M. Meredith	Pa.	1849
Fillmore	Thomas Corwin	Ohio	1850
Pierce	James Guthrie	Ky.	1853
Buchanan	Howell Cobb	Ga.	1857
Buchanan	Philip F. Thomas	Md.	1860
Buchanan	John A. Dix	N. Y.	1861
Lincoln	Salmon P. Chase	Ohio	1861
Lincoln	William P. Fessenden	Me.	1864
Lincoln	Hugh McCulloch	Ind.	1865

SECRETARIES OF THE TREASURY—Con.

Johnson	Hugh McCulloch	Ind.	1865
Grant	George S. Boutwell	Mass.	1869
Grant	Wm. A. Richardson	Mass.	1873
Grant	Benjamin H. Bristow	Ky.	1874
Grant	Lot M. Morrill	Me.	1876
Hayes	John Sherman	Ohio	1877
Garfield	William Windom	Minn.	1881
Arthur	Charles J. Folger	N. Y.	1881
Arthur	Walter Q. Gresham	Ind.	1884
Arthur	Hugh McCulloch	Ind.	1884
Cleveland	Daniel Manning	N. Y.	1885
Cleveland	Charles S. Fairchild	N. Y.	1887
B. Harrison	William Windom	Minn.	1889
B. Harrison	Charles Foster	Ohio	1891
Cleveland	John G. Carlisle	Ky.	1893
McKinley	Lyman J. Gage	Ill.	1897
T. Roosevelt	Lyman J. Gage	Ill.	1901
T. Roosevelt	Leslie M. Shaw	Ia.	1902
T. Roosevelt	George B. Cortelyou	N. Y.	1907
Taft	Franklin MacVeagh	Ill.	1909
Wilson	William G. McAdoo	N. Y.	1913
Wilson	Carter Glass	Va.	1918
Wilson	David F. Houston	Mo.	1920
Harding	Andrew W. Mellon	Pa.	1921
Coolidge	Andrew W. Mellon	Pa.	1923
Hoover	Andrew W. Mellon	Pa.	1929
Hoover	Ogden Mills	N. Y.	1932
F. D. Roosevelt	William H. Woodin	N. Y.	1933
F. D. Roosevelt	Henry Morgenthau, Jr.	N. Y.	1934
Truman	Henry Morgenthau, Jr.	N. Y.	1945
Truman	Frederick M. Vinson	Ky.	1945
Truman	John W. Snyder	Mo.	1946
Eisenhower	George M. Humphrey	Ohio	1953
Eisenhower	Robert B. Anderson	Texas	1957
Kennedy	Douglas Dillon	N. Y.	1961
Johnson	Douglas Dillon	N. Y.	1963
Johnson	Henry H. Fowler	Va.	1965
Nixon	David M. Kennedy	Ill.	1969
Nixon	John Connally	Texas	1971
Nixon	George P. Shultz	Ill.	1972
Nixon	William E. Simon	N. J.	1974
Ford	William E. Simon	N. J.	1974
Carter	W. Michael Blumenthal	Mich.	1977

DEPARTMENT OF JUSTICE

The attorney general is head of the Department of Justice and chief law officer of the government. He directs and controls a large force of attorneys and marshals, not only in the office at Washington, but also in the 85 judicial districts into which the United States and the territories are divided. He furnishes opinions and interpretations of the laws for the guidance of the president and the heads of executive departments. In the performance of this last duty he may approve and adopt the opinions of his subordinates except upon questions involving the construction of the Constitution, but upon such questions he must give his own opinion. Immigration and naturalization laws, federal prisons and paroles, are administered by this department. The department of justice conducts a bureau of narcotics and dangerous drugs; also a bureau of investigation (F.B.I.) (est. 1908) to secure evidence against crimes that violate federal laws and to assist states and localities in law enforcement.

ATTORNEYS GENERAL

PRESIDENTS	Cabinet Officers	Residences	Appointed
Washington	Edmund Randolph	Va.	1789
Washington	William Bradford	Pa.	1794
Washington	Charles Lee	Va.	1795
Adams	Charles Lee	Va.	1797
Jefferson	Levi Lincoln	Mass.	1801
Jefferson	Robert Smith	Md.	1805
Jefferson	John Breckinridge	Ky.	1805
Jefferson	Cæsar A. Rodney	Del.	1807
Madison	Cæsar A. Rodney	Del.	1809
Madison	William Pinkney	Md.	1811
Madison	Richard Rush	Pa.	1814
Monroe	Richard Rush	Pa.	1817
Monroe	William Wirt	Va.	1817
J. Q. Adams	William Wirt	Va.	1825
Jackson	John McP. Berrien	Ga.	1829
Jackson	Roger B. Taney	Md.	1831

ATTORNEYS GENERAL—Con.

Presidents	Cabinet Officers	Residences	Appointed
Jackson	Benjamin F. Butler	N. Y.	1833
Van Buren	Benjamin F. Butler	N. Y.	1837
Van Buren	Felix Grundy	Tenn.	1838
Van Buren	Henry D. Galpin	Pa.	1840
Harrison	John J. Crittenden	Ky.	1841
Tyler	John J. Crittenden	Ky.	1841
Tyler	Hugh S. Legaré	S. C.	1841
Tyler	John Nelson	Md.	1843
Polk	John Y. Mason	Va.	1845
Polk	Nathan Clifford	Me.	1846
Polk	Isaac Toucey	Conn.	1848
Taylor	Reverdy Johnson	Md.	1849
Fillmore	John J. Crittenden	Ky.	1850
Pierce	Caleb Cushing	Mass.	1853
Buchanan	Jeremiah S. Black	Pa.	1857
Buchanan	Edwin M. Stanton	Ohio	1860
Lincoln	Edward Bates	Mo.	1861
Lincoln	James Speed	Ky.	1864
Johnson	James Speed	Ky.	1865
Johnson	Henry Stanbery	Ohio	1866
Johnson	William M. Evarts	N. Y.	1868
Grant	Ebenezer R. Hoar	Mass.	1869
Grant	Amos T. Ackerman	Ga.	1870
Grant	George H. Williams	Oreg.	1871
Grant	Edwards Pierrepont	N. Y.	1875
Grant	Alphonso Taft	Ohio	1876
Hayes	Charles Devens	Mass.	1877
Garfield	Wayne MacVeagh	Pa.	1881
Arthur	Benjamin H. Brewster	Pa.	1881
Cleveland	Augustus H. Garland	Ark.	1885
B. Harrison	William H. H. Miller	Ind.	1889
Cleveland	Richard Olney	Mass.	1893
Cleveland	Judson Harmon	Ohio	1895
McKinley	Joseph McKenna	Cal.	1897
McKinley	John W. Griggs	N. J.	1898
McKinley	Philander C. Knox	Pa.	1901
Roosevelt	Philander C. Knox	Pa.	1901
Roosevelt	William H. Moody	Mass.	1904
Roosevelt	Charles J. Bonaparte	Md.	1906
Taft	George W. Wickersham	N. Y.	1909
Wilson	James C. McReynolds	Tenn.	1913
Wilson	Thomas W. Gregory	Texas	1914
Wilson	A. Mitchell Palmer	Pa.	1919
Harding	Harry M. Daugherty	Ohio	1921
Coolidge	Harry M. Daugherty	Ohio	1923
Coolidge	Harlan F. Stone	N. Y.	1924
Coolidge	John G. Sargent	Vt.	1925
Hoover	William D. Mitchell	Minn.	1929
F. D. Roosevelt	Homer S. Cummings	Conn.	1933
F. D. Roosevelt	Frank Murphy	Mich.	1939
F. D. Roosevelt	Robert H. Jackson	N. Y.	1940
F. D. Roosevelt	Francis Biddle	Pa.	1941
Truman	Thomas C. Clark	Tex.	1945
Truman	J. Howard McGrath	R. I.	1949
Truman	J. P. McGranery	Pa.	1952
Eisenhower	Herbert Brownell, Jr.	N. Y.	1953
Eisenhower	William P. Rogers	N.Y.	1957
Kennedy	Robert F. Kennedy	Mass.	1961
Johnson	Robert F. Kennedy	Mass.	1963
Johnson	Nicholas Katzenbach	Pa.	1965
Johnson	W. Ramsey Clark	Tex.	1967
Nixon	John N. Mitchell	N. Y.	1969
Nixon	Richard G. Kleindienst	Ariz.	1972
Nixon	Elliot L. Richardson	Va.	1973
Nixon	William B. Saxbe	Ohio	1974
Ford	Edward H. Levi	Ill.	1975
Carter	Griffin Bell	Ga.	1977

DEPARTMENT OF THE INTERIOR

The secretary supervises public business relating to domestic welfare; oversees surveying and mapping of the country; improvement of national parks; land reclamation; construction of large dams and disposal of their power. The department has supervision of Indian affairs: educational, hygienic, and relief activities on reservations; also with supervising insular affairs, fisheries, and biological surveys. It controls appropriations for agricultural colleges and mechanical institutions in the states and territories, and for certain hospitals and charitable institutions in the District of Columbia. The secretary supervises conservation of oil resources and collects information on minerals and mining.

SECRETARIES OF THE INTERIOR

Presidents	Cabinet Officers	Residences	Appointed
Taylor	Thomas Ewing	Ohio	1849
Fillmore	Thos. M. T. McKennan	Pa.	1850
Fillmore	Alexander H. H. Stuart	Va.	1850
Pierce	Robert McClelland	Mich.	1853
Buchanan	Jacob Thompson	Miss.	1857
Lincoln	Caleb B. Smith	Ind.	1861
Lincoln	John P. Usher	Ind.	1863
Johnson	John P. Usher	Ind.	1865
Johnson	James Harlan	Iowa	1865
Johnson	Orville H. Browning	Ill.	1866
Grant	Jacob D. Cox	Ohio	1869
Grant	Columbus Delano	Ohio	1870
Grant	Zachariah Chandler	Mich.	1875
Hayes	Carl Schurz	Mo.	1877
Garfield	Samuel J. Kirkwood	Iowa	1881
Arthur	Henry M. Teller	Colo.	1882
Cleveland	Lucius Q. C. Lamar	Miss.	1885
Cleveland	William F. Vilas	Wis.	1888
B. Harrison	John W. Noble	Mo.	1889
Cleveland	Hoke Smith	Ga.	1893
Cleveland	David R. Francis	Mo.	1896
McKinley	Cornelius N. Bliss	N. Y.	1897
McKinley	Ethan A. Hitchcock	Mo.	1898
T. Roosevelt	Ethan A. Hitchcock	Mo.	1901
T. Roosevelt	James R. Garfield	Ohio	1907
Taft	Richard A. Ballinger	Wash.	1909
Taft	Walter L. Fisher	Ill.	1911
Wilson	Franklin K. Lane	Cal.	1913
Wilson	John Barton Payne	Ill.	1920
Harding	Albert B. Fall	N. M.	1921
Harding	Hubert Work	Colo.	1923
Coolidge	Hubert Work	Colo.	1923
Coolidge	Roy O. West	Ill.	1928
Hoover	Ray L. Wilbur	Cal.	1929
F. D. Roosevelt	Harold L. Ickes	Ill.	1933
Truman	Harold L. Ickes	Ill.	1945
Truman	Julius A. Krug	Wis.	1946
Truman	Oscar L. Chapman	Colo.	1949
Eisenhower	Douglas McKay	Ore.	1953
Eisenhower	Frederick A. Seaton	Nebr.	1956
Kennedy	Stewart L. Udall	Ariz.	1961
Johnson	Stewart L. Udall	Ariz.	1963
Nixon	Walter J. Hickel	Alaska	1969
Nixon	Rogers C. B. Morton	Md.	1970
Ford	Rogers C. B. Morton	Md.	1974
Ford	Stanley Hathaway	Wyo.	1975
Ford	Thomas S. Klepp	N. D.	1975
Carter	Cecil Andrus	Idaho	1977

DEPARTMENT OF AGRICULTURE

The secretary directs all public business relating to agricultural industry. He administers laws on marketing, subsidizing, and insurance of crops, also on land use and surpluses. The department engages in research and information services. It works to control plant and animal diseases and to improve crops and livestock. It provides weather reports, crop reports and estimates, and forest services and grants credits to farmers on crops, farms, and co-operatively constructed rural electrification projects.

SECRETARIES OF AGRICULTURE

Presidents	Cabinet Officers	Residences	Appointed
Cleveland	Norman J. Colman	Mo.	1889
B. Harrison	Jeremiah M. Rusk	Wis.	1889
Cleveland	J. Sterling Morton	Nebr.	1893
McKinley	James Wilson	Ia.	1897
T. Roosevelt	James Wilson	Ia.	1901
Taft	James Wilson	Ia.	1909
Wilson	David F. Houston	Mo.	1913
Wilson	Edwin T. Meredith	Ia.	1920
Harding	Henry C. Wallace	Ia.	1921
Coolidge	Henry C. Wallace	Ia.	1923
Coolidge	Howard M. Gore	W. Va.	1924
Coolidge	W. M. Jardine	Kans.	1925
Hoover	Arthur M. Hyde	Mo.	1929
F. D. Roosevelt	Henry A. Wallace	Ia.	1933
F. D. Roosevelt	Claude R. Wickard	Ind.	1940
Truman	Clinton P. Anderson	N. M.	1945
Truman	Charles F. Brannan	Colo.	1948
Eisenhower	Ezra T. Benson	Utah	1953
Kennedy	Orville Freeman	Minn	1961
Johnson	Orville Freeman	Minn	1963
Nixon	Clifford M. Hardin	Nebr.	1969
Nixon	Earl L. Butz	Ind.	1971
Ford	Earl L. Butz	Ind.	1974
Carter	Bob Bergland	Minn.	1977

DEPARTMENT OF COMMERCE

The secretary of commerce is charged with the promotion of the commerce of the U.S. and with its manufacturing, shipping, fishing, and transportation interests. He investigates the organization and management of corporations engaged in interstate commerce (except railroads), and enforces laws to protect life and property on the water. The department also supervises the National Bureau of Standards, Patent Office, Coast and Geodetic Survey, Weather Bureau, and Bureau of the Census. The divisions gather and distribute information and encourage standardization in manufacture. The department has charge of setting rates and making regulations of the Civil Aeronautics Board (CAB). Since 1966, the safety functions of the CAB have been delegated to the Department of Transportation.

SECRETARIES OF COMMERCE *

PRESIDENTS	Cabinet Officers	Residences	Appointed
T. Roosevelt .	George B. Cortelyou .	N. Y.	1903
T. Roosevelt .	Victor H. Metcalf. . .	Cal.	1904
T. Roosevelt .	Oscar S. Straus	N. Y.	1906
Taft	Charles Nagel	Mo.	1909
Wilson . . .	William C. Redfield . .	N. Y.	1913
Wilson . . .	Joshua W. Alexander .	Mo.	1919
Harding . .	Herbert C. Hoover . .	Cal.	1921
Coolidge . .	Herbert C. Hoover . .	Cal.	1923
Coolidge . .	William F. Whiting. .	Mass.	1928
Hoover . .	Robert P. Lamont . .	Ill.	1929
Hoover . . .	Roy D. Chapin . . .	Mich.	1932
F. D. Roosevelt	Daniel C. Roper . . .	S. C.	1933
F. D. Roosevelt	Harry Hopkins	Iowa	1939
F. D. Roosevelt	Jesse Jones	Tex.	1940
F. D. Roosevelt	Henry A. Wallace . . .	Iowa	1945
Truman . . .	Henry A. Wallace . .	Iowa	1945
Truman . . .	W. Averell Harriman .	N. Y.	1946
Truman . . .	Charles W. Sawyer . .	Ohio	1948
Eisenhower .	Sinclair Weeks . . .	Mass.	1953
Eisenhower .	Frederick H. Mueller .	Mich.	1959
Kennedy . .	Luther H. Hodges . .	N. C.	1961
Johnson . . .	Luther H. Hodges . .	N. C.	1963
Johnson . . .	John T. Connor . . .	N. J.	1965
Johnson . . .	Alexander B. Trowbridge	N. J.	1967
Johnson . . .	Cyrus R. Smith . . .	Tex.	1968
Nixon . . .	Maurice H. Stans . .	N. Y.	1969
Nixon . . .	Peter G. Peterson . .	Neb.	1972
Nixon . . .	Frederick B. Dent . .	S. C.	1973
Ford	Frederick B. Dent . .	S. C.	1974
Ford	Rogers C. B. Morton .	Md.	1975
Ford	Elliot L. Richardson .	Mass.	1975
Carter . . .	Juanita M. Kreps . . .	N. C.	1977

* Prior to 1913, Secretaries of Commerce and Labor.

DEPARTMENT OF LABOR

The secretary of labor is charged with fostering, promoting, and developing the welfare of wage earners, improving working conditions, and advancing opportunities for employment. He administrates and assists in the enforcement of the Fair Labor Standards Act. He takes the initiative in seeking cooperation with state legislatures for protecting labor's welfare. He also gathers and publishes data on labor conditions abroad. He makes available information on the cost of living and the extent of employment and pay rolls in industry and trade. The department is charged also with conduct of the national employment offices.

SECRETARIES OF LABOR

PRESIDENTS	Cabinet Officers	Residences	Appointed
Wilson . . .	William B. Wilson . .	Pa.	1913
Harding . .	James J. Davis	Pa.	1921
Coolidge . .	James J. Davis	Pa.	1923
Hoover . . .	James J. Davis	Pa.	1929
Hoover . . .	William N. Doak . . .	Va.	1930
F. D. Roosevelt	Frances Perkins . . .	N. Y.	1933
Truman . . .	Lewis B. Schwellenbach	Wash.	1945
Truman . . .	Maurice J. Tobin . . .	Mass.	1948
Eisenhower .	Martin P. Durkin . .	Ill.	1953
Eisenhower .	James P. Mitchell . .	N. J.	1953
Kennedy . .	Arthur J. Goldberg . .	D. C.	1961
Kennedy . .	W. Willard Wirtz . .	Ill.	1962
Johnson . . .	W. Willard Wirtz . .	Ill.	1963

Nixon . . .	George P. Shultz . .	Ill.	1969
Nixon . . .	James D. Hodgson . .	D. C.	1970
Nixon . . .	Peter J. Brennan . .	N. Y.	1973
Ford	John T. Dunlop . . .	Cal.	1975
Ford	Willie J. Usery . . .	Ga.	1976
Carter . . .	F. Ray Marshall . . .	Texas	1977

DEPARTMENT OF HEALTH, EDUCATION AND WELFARE

The secretary of this department supervises the extension work of the Public Health Service in the field of medical research and in the maintenance of hospitals. Through the Office of Education, information is collected on all matters pertaining to education, and funds are allotted which are made available by Congress in federal aid to education. The department also has oversight of the Social Security Administration.

HEW SECRETARIES

PRESIDENTS	Cabinet Officers	Residences	Appointed
Eisenhower .	Oveta Culp Hobby . .	Tex.	1953
Eisenhower .	Marion B. Folsom . .	N Y.	1955
Eisenhower .	Arthur S. Flemming .	Ohio	1958
Kennedy . .	Abraham Ribicoff . .	Conn.	1961
Kennedy . .	Anthony J. Celebrezze .	Ohio	1962
Johnson . . .	Anthony J. Celebrezze .	Ohio	1963
Johnson . . .	John W. Gardner . . .	N. Y.	1965
Johnson . . .	Wilbur J. Cohen . . .	Md.	1968
Nixon . . .	Robert H. Finch . . .	Cal.	1969
Nixon . . .	Elliot L. Richardson .	Va.	1970
Nixon . . .	Caspar W. Weinberger .	Cal.	1973
Ford	Caspar W. Weinberger .	Cal.	1974
Ford	David F. Mathews . .	Ala.	1975
Carter	Joseph A. Califano, Jr.	D. C.	1977

DEPARTMENT OF HOUSING AND URBAN DEVELOPMENT

The secretary of this department supervises agencies which insure mortgages, coordinates programs of agencies having major impact on community development, including local transportation. The secretary also serves as chairperson of the board of directors of the New Community Development Corporation.

HUD SECRETARIES

Presidents	Cabinet Officers	Residences	Appointed
Johnson . . .	Robert C. Weaver . . .	D.C.	1966
Nixon . . .	George Romney	Mich.	1969
Nixon . . .	James T. Lynn	Ohio	1973
Ford	James T. Lynn	Ohio	1974
Ford	Carla A. Hills	Cal.	1975
Carter . . .	Patricia R. Harris . . .	D. C.	1977

DEPARTMENT OF TRANSPORTATION

The secretary supervises safety and promotion in aviation, highways, railways, pipe lines, and has jurisdiction over the U. S Coast Guard and the Bureau of Roads. National transportation policies and programs are developed in this office.

SECRETARIES OF TRANSPORTATION

Presidents	Cabinet Officers	Residences	Appointed
Johnson . . .	Alan S. Boyd	Florida	1966
Nixon . . .	John A. Volpe	Mass.	1969
Nixon . . .	Claude S. Brinegar . .	Cal.	1973
Ford	Claude S. Brinegar . .	Cal.	1974
Ford	William T. Coleman, Jr.	Pa.	1975
Carter . . .	Brock Adams	Ga.	1977

U.S. POSTAL SERVICE

Government In 1970 the Post Office Department was made a government-owned, independently operated, self-supporting corporation within the executive branch, ending Congressional authority over the system. The U.S. Postal Service, as it is now called, has an 11-man board of governors; 9 are appointed by the president with approval of the Senate. Those 9 select a 10th, who becomes postmaster general; those 10 select the 11th, who is deputy postmaster general. The postmaster general is no longer a cabinet-level position.

POSTMASTERS GENERAL

PRESIDENTS	Cabinet Officers	Residences	Appointed
Washington .	Samuel Osgood . . .	Mass.	1789
Washington .	Timothy Pickering . .	Mass.	1791
Washington .	Joseph Habersham . .	Ga.	1795
Adams . . .	Joseph Habersham . .	Ga.	1797
Jefferson . .	Joseph Habersham . .	Ga.	1801
Jefferson. . .	Gideon Granger . . .	Conn.	1801
Madison . .	Gideon Granger . . .	Conn.	1809
Madison . .	Return J. Meigs, Jr. .	Ohio	1814
Monroe . . .	Return J. Meigs, Jr. .	Ohio	1817
Monroe . . .	John McLean	Ohio	1823
J. Q. Adams .	John McLean	Ohio	1825
Jackson . . .	William T. Barry . .	Ky.	1829
Jackson . . .	Amos Kendall	Ky.	1835
Van Buren .	Amos Kendall	Ky.	1837
Van Buren .	John M. Niles	Conn.	1840
Harrison. . .	Francis Granger . . .	N. Y.	1841
Tyler	Francis Granger . . .	N. Y.	1841
Tyler	Charles A. Wickliffe .	Ky.	1841
Polk	Cave Johnson	Tenn.	1845
Taylor . . .	Jacob Collamer . . .	Vt.	1849
Fillmore . .	Nathan K. Hall . . .	N. Y.	1850
Fillmore . .	Samuel D. Hubbard. .	Conn.	1852
Pierce . . .	James Campbell . . .	Pa.	1853
Buchanan . .	Aaron V. Brown . . .	Tenn.	1857
Buchanan . .	Joseph Holt	Ky.	1859
Buchanan . .	Horatio King.	Me.	1861
Lincoln . . .	Montgomery Blair . .	Md.	1861
Lincoln . . .	William Dennison. . .	Ohio	1864
Johnson . . .	William Dennison. . .	Ohio	1865
Johnson . . .	Alexander W. Randall	Wis.	1866
Grant . . .	John A. J. Creswell . .	Md.	1869
Grant . . .	James W. Marshall . .	Va.	1874
Grant . . .	Marshall Jewell. . . .	Conn.	1874
Grant . . .	James N. Tyner . . .	Ind.	1876
Hayes . . .	David McK. Key . .	Tenn.	1877
Hayes . . .	Horace Maynard . . .	Tenn.	1880
Garfield . .	Thomas L. James . .	N. Y.	1881
Arthur . . .	Timothy O. Howe . .	Wis.	1881
Arthur . . .	Walter Q. Gresham . .	Ind.	1883
Arthur . . .	Frank Hatton	Ia.	1884
Cleveland . .	William F. Vilas . .	Wis.	1885
Cleveland . .	Don M. Dickinson . .	Mich.	1888
B. Harrison .	John Wanamaker . .	Pa.	1889
Cleveland . .	Wilson S. Bissell . .	N. Y.	1893
Cleveland . .	William L. Wilson . .	W. Va.	1895
McKinley . .	James A. Gary	Md.	1897
McKinley . .	Charles Emory Smith .	Pa.	1898
Roosevelt . .	Charles Emory Smith .	Pa.	1901
Roosevelt . .	Henry C. Payne . . .	Wis.	1902
Roosevelt . .	Robert J. Wynne . . .	Pa.	1904
Roosevelt . .	George B. Cortelyou .	N. Y.	1905
Roosevelt . .	George von L. Meyer .	Mass.	1907
Taft	Frank H. Hitchcock. .	Mass.	1909
Wilson . . .	Albert S. Burleson . .	Tex.	1913
Harding . .	Will H. Hays.	Ind.	1921
Harding . .	Hubert Work	Colo.	1922
Harding . .	Harry S. New	Ind.	1923
Coolidge . .	Harry S. New	Ind.	1923
Hoover . . .	Walter F. Brown . . .	Ohio	1929
F. D. Roosevelt	James A. Farley . . .	N. Y.	1933
F. D. Roosevelt	Frank C. Walker . . .	N. Y.	1940
Truman . . .	Robert E. Hannegan .	Mo.	1945
Truman . . .	Jesse M. Donaldson .	Ill.	1947
Eisenhower .	Arthur E. Summerfield	Mich.	1953
Kennedy . .	J. Edward Day	Cal.	1961
Kennedy . .	John A. Gronouski . .	Wis.	1963
Johnson . . .	John A. Gronouski . .	Wis.	1963
Johnson . . .	Lawrence F. O'Brien .	Mass.	1965
Johnson . . .	Wm. Marvin Watson .	Tex.	1968
Nixon . . .	Winton M. Blount . .	Ala.	1969
Nixon . . .	Elmer T. Klassen . .	Maine	1971
Ford . . .	Elmer T. Klassen . .	Maine	1974

THE EXECUTIVE OFFICE OF THE PRESIDENT

By the authority of the Reorganization Act of 1939, various agencies were placed in the office of the president. Since then other agencies have been established within the office by legislation, executive order, and reorganization plans. These councils play a close advisory role to the president on policy decisions and have grown in importance. Some of the most significant are listed and described below.

The Office of Management and Budget (OMB), formerly the Bureau of the Budget, was established by a reorganization plan of 1970. Headed by a presidential appointee, it helps to manage, prepare, and supervise the federal budget and performs management duties that cross depa tmental lines. It is the president's vehicle for making the government more efficient and economical.

The Council of Economic Advisors was established in the executive office by the Employment Act of 1946 and consists of three members appointed by the president with the advice and consent of the Senate. Its primary functions are to analyze the national economy and world economic developments and to advise the president on economic policy.

The National Security Council was established by the National Security Act of 1947, the act which also created the Central Intelligence Agency. An executive director, appointed by the president as his assistant for national security affairs, presides over the council which consists of the president, the vice president, and the secretaries of state and defense. The council integrates domestic, foreign, and military policies relating to the national security.

The Central Intelligence Agency (CIA) functions by an executive order of 1976 and is overseen by the National Security Council and other presidential advisory boards. Its purpose is to collect foreign intelligence and to coordinate and evaluate the foreign intelligence activities of the federal government. It has no internal security functions. The director of the CIA is appointed by the president with the advice and consent of the Senate.

The Domestic Council was established by a reorganization plan of 1970. It consists of presidential assistants, cabinet members, and agency heads whose primary interest is in domestic affairs. The council coordinates domestic policy, makes policy recommendations to the president, and reviews established domestic programs.

The Energy Resources Council was created by an executive order of 1974. It consists of an executive director, cabinet members, and various agency heads whose concerns include energy. Its main function is to develop an overall energy policy for the president. It is also charged with coordinating energy policy matters in the various agencies concerned with energy in the federal government.

The Council on Environmental Quality was established by the National Environmental Policy Act of 1969. It consists of three members appointed by the president with the advice and consent of Congress. The council develops and recommends to the president policies which could further environmental quality. It reviews and analyzes government programs affecting the environment and is the administrator of the environmental impact statement process.

The Council on Wage and Price Stability was established by an act of 1974 as amended by an act of 1975. It consists of an assistant to the president for economic policy; the secretaries of agriculture, commerce, labor, and the treasury; and the director of the OMB. Its main function is to monitor the economy with respect to such key indicators as wages, costs, productivity, profits, and prices. It also reviews federal programs to find which are inflationary.

FEDERAL AGENCIES AND COMMISSIONS

Outside of the executive departments, a large number of functions of the government are entrusted to boards, agencies, and commissions. Created by Congress and operating in conjunction with the executive branch, these bodies nevertheless have a large measure of freedom in performing tasks assigned to them.

In addition to the work of the major commissions, federal affairs are carried on by numerous bodies known variously as administrations, agencies, authorities, boards, bureaus, committees, corporations, councils, offices, and systems. Some are chiefly advisory, but all have far-reaching powers within the controls exercised by the legislative and executive branches to which they are responsible.

From time to time, Congress has granted presidents the power to reorganize, combine, or abolish various executive agencies—such actions being final unless reversed by Congress within a limited period.

Some of the most important agencies include those below. Additional agencies are treated in other parts of this volume as shown in the index. They include: the Federal Deposit Insurance Corporation, Federal Reserve Board, National Labor Relations Board, National Mediation Board, and the Securities Exchange Commission. See the index also for the Tennessee Valley Authority.

Action was created by a reorganization plan of 1971. Its authority is provided by the Peace Corps Act of 1961 and the Domestic Volunteer Service Act of 1973. Action provides centralized coordination and administration of domestic and international volunteer activities sponsored by the federal government. Some of the organizations under the jurisdiction of Action are: The Peace Corps, volunteers who work overseas; VISTA (Volunteers in Service to America), volunteers who work in the U.S.; and RSVP (Retired Senior Volunteer Program), citizens of 60 years or older working in their own communities.

The Civil Service Commission was created by a special act of 1883 as the central personnel agency of the executive branch. Its main purpose is to recruit, examine, train and promote employees on the basis of ability, regardless of their race, religion, sex, political influence, or any other nonmerit factors. The Commission also ensures that the government provides various services to employees.

The Consumer Product Safety Commission was established by an act of 1972. The CPSC protects the public against unreasonable risks of injury from consumer products, evaluates the comparable safety of products, develops uniform safety standards for products, works to minimize conflicting state and local regulations, and researches and investigates the cause of and works for prevention of product-related deaths, illnesses, and injuries. The CPSC also conducts educational programs and has the authority to ban hazardous products.

The Energy Research and Development Administration was established by the Energy Reorganization Act of 1974 and was activated in 1975 by an executive order. ERDA was created to reorganize and consolidate federal activities relating to research and development of the various sources of energy. Its overall purpose is to increase the productivity of the national economy and strengthen its international trade position by demonstrating the commercial feasibility and practical applications of the extraction, transmission, and utilization of energy from various sources.

The Environmental Protection Agency was established in the executive branch as an independent agency by Reorganization Plan No. 3 of 1970. Its mandate is to mount a coordinated attack on environmental pollution in cooperation with state and local governments. The EPA has authority to control and reduce pollution in areas of air, water, solid waste, pesticides, noise, and radiation.

The Federal Communications Commission was created under an act approved June 19, 1934.

Its duty is to supervise, and guard the public interest in, interstate communications, including: radio, television, cable TV, telegraph, and telephone. It was given additional authority in 1962 to regulate communications satellites. The FCC licenses broadcasting stations, assigns wavelengths, and issues rules regarding the fairness doctrine, political broadcasting, and fair competition.

The Federal Power Commission was created by the Federal Water Act of 1920, originally to license hydroelectric developments on navigable streams. Its authority was later enlarged to include regulation of interstate transmission of electricity, sale and purchase of properties by utility companies engaged in interstate commerce, interstate aspects of natural gas industries, and the construction of interstate pipeline facilities. Its principal concern is that consumers have adequate supplies of gas and electricity at reasonable rates.

The Federal Trade Commission was created by an act of Sept. 26, 1914, and organized as an independent administrative agency in 1951. It supervises and regulates corporations or persons engaged in interstate commerce other than those under the jurisdiction of the Interstate Commerce Commission. The foundation underlying all its duties is to prevent the free enterprise system from being stifled by monopolies or restraints on trade, or corrupted by deceptive trade practices. Among its principal functions are: to prevent corporate mergers that would lessen competition, to enforce the Fair Packaging and Labeling Act and the Truth in Lending Act, and to make available information to interested parties.

The General Services Administration was established by the Federal Property and Administrative Services Act of 1949. It manages all the government's properties and records, supervises the construction and operation of buildings, and distributes supplies. Among the bureaus that are under the GSA are the Automated Data and Telecommunications Service, the Federal Preparedness Service, and the National Archives and Records Service.

The Interstate Commerce Commission was created by the Interstate Commerce Act of 1887. Its powers were broadened by later legislation such as the Elkins Act of 1903, the Hepburn Act of 1906, the Mann-Elkins Act of 1910, the Panama Canal Act, the Motor Carrier Act of 1935, and the Transportation Acts of 1920, 1940, and 1958.

The ICC has the power to regulate interstate surface transportation, including trains, trucks, buses, inland waterway and coastal shipping, freight forwarders, oil pipelines, and express companies. Its mandate is to ensure that the public obtains the full measure of all transportation services to which it is entitled with rates that are fair and reasonable.

The National Foundation on the Arts and the Humanities was created by an act of 1965. The Foundation consists of the National Endowment for the Arts, the National Endowment for the Humanities, and the Federal Council on the Arts and the Humanities. The Federal Council consists of 14 members including the two endowment chairmen and coordinates the activities of the two endowments and related programs of other federal agencies.

The Nuclear Regulatory Commission was established by the Energy Reorganization Act of 1974. All of the licensing and related regulatory functions previously assigned to the Atomic Energy Commission were transferred to the NRC. The commission makes rules and sets standards for the licensing of persons and companies to build and operate nuclear reactors and to own and use nuclear materials. The commission also inspects the activities of persons and companies licensed to ensure that the safety rules of the commission are not violated.

Smithsonian Institution. This institution "for the increase and diffusion of knowledge," was created by act of Congress in 1846 in accordance with the will of James Smithson, of England, who in 1826 bequeathed his property to the United States government for the purpose. It is governed by a Board of Regents consisting of the Chief Justice of the Supreme Court, the Vice-President of the U. S., three Congressmen, three Senators, and six private citizens. The executive head is the Secretary of the Smithsonian Institution. It carries on its functions by means of sponsoring scientific research and exploration, the publication of books and periodicals, and the collection and exhibition of objects of scientific, historical, and artistic interest.

The original building, the "Old Smithsonian," was completed at Washington, D. C., in 1855 under the direction of the first Secretary, Joseph Henry.

The United States International Trade Commission was established by the Trade Act of 1974. It formerly was the United States Tariff Commission, created by an act of Sept. 8, 1916. Its main purpose is to furnish studies, reports, and recommendations involving international trade and tariffs to the President, the Congress, and other government agencies. The Trade Commission was given broad powers of investigation relating to: customs laws of the U. S. and foreign countries, the volume of importation in connection with domestic consumption and production, conditions relating to competition of foreign industries with U. S. industries, and all other factors affecting competition between articles manufactured in the U. S. and imported ones.

Veterans Administration. This establishment represents a consolidation of all government agencies affecting war veterans. Formed under authority of an act passed in 1930, it supervises the payment of pensions and disability allowances to veterans and their relatives, administers war risk insurance, the hospitalization, medical care, and vocational rehabilitation of veterans, and has charge of the payment of adjusted compensation certificates.

THE FEDERAL JUDICIARY

The Constitution (Art. III) provides that the judicial power of the U. S. shall be vested in one Supreme Court and inferior courts established by Congress and that all Federal judges shall hold office during good behavior, with compensation that may not be diminished during their term of office.

Organization. Congress in 1789 passed a judiciary act providing for the organization of the Supreme Court, with a chief justice and five associate justices. Later laws were revised and codified in the act of March 3, 1911. Since 1863 the court has consisted of a chief justice and eight associate justices. The annual salary of the chief justice is $75,000 and of the associate justices, $72,000.

Two attempts, one in 1802 and the other in 1866, made by Congress to reduce the size of the court by enacting that the next vacancy occurring should not be filled, were repealed before the vacancies occurred.

District courts of the United States increased from 13, in 1789, to 89 in the 50 states by 1976. In addition, there is one in Washington, D. C., and one in Puerto Rico. All district courts are entirely within the boundaries of single states, with some states having as many as four districts. Each district court has from 1 to 27 district judgeships; and in districts where there are more than one, the judge senior in commission who has not reached his 70th birthday acts as chief judge. Usually one judge hears a case, but in some circumstances three judges may sit. The judges hold office provided by Article III, Section 1 of the Constitution.

Since their first organization the Supreme Court and the district courts have remained practically unchanged. The system of circuit courts, however, has varied at different times. At present it has the form of eleven circuit courts of appeals. Each court is formed of a member of the United States Supreme Court, designated as circuit justice, and several circuit judges, who are frequently appointed from among the United States district judges. No more than three judges usually sit at a single hearing. These courts were created to relieve the Supreme Court from its excessive burden of appealed litigation. They hear most cases of appeals from the district courts, and, except in a narrow range of cases, their decisions are final.

Constitutional Jurisdiction. The Constitution fixes the jurisdiction of the Federal courts and limits it to:

Cases arising under the Constitution.
Cases under Federal laws and treaties.
Cases affecting ambassadors, ministers, and consuls.
Cases in admiralty and maritime jurisdiction.
Cases in which the United States is a party.
Controversies between states; between citizens of different states; or by a state against the citizens of another state.
Cases between U.S. citizens and foreign states, citizens, or subjects.
Cases between citizens of the same state claiming lands under grants of different states.

The Constitution limits the court's appellate power by making it subject to exceptions and regulations determined by Congress. Congress has never attempted to use this power.

In cases affecting ambassadors, public ministers, and consuls, and in cases in which the state is a party, the Supreme Court has "original jurisdiction." Other cases before the Supreme Court come to it on appeal from the district courts, where the evidence is taken. It is thus rare for the Supreme Court to take evidence, its business being interpretation of the law and listening to arguments thereon.

A unique feature of the United States courts is their practice of passing upon the constitutionality of both congressional and state legislation. The Constitution (Art. VI, clause 2) provides: "This Constitution and the laws of the United States which shall be made in pursuance therewith, and all treaties made or which shall be made under the authority of the United States, shall be the supreme law of the land; and the judges in every state shall be bound thereby, anything in the constitution or laws of any state to the contrary notwithstanding."

It follows naturally that the Supreme Court and other Federal courts have been called upon to determine whether certain laws were in harmony or in conflict with the "supreme law of the land." This power was exercised very sparingly in the first 70 years of American history. Up to 1861, only three Federal laws had been invalidated by the court. By 1936, out of some 24,300 laws passed by Congress, 65 were declared unconstitutional. This judicial determination of constitutionality is a feature original with the American tradition.

Critics have contended that some of the court's decisions have encroached on the functions of legislation. The power of enforcing its own interpretation of the Constitution has placed the court in a position to determine, within limits, how wide Federal powers are. Under John Marshall's 34 years as chief justice a broad interpretation was given to Federal powers, provided they were clearly derived from the Constitution. In the present century this tendency was carried further, although with a temporary reversal in 1935-36, when numerous economic laws of the Roosevelt administration were declared invalid. A statute of 1937 provided that one-man Federal courts might not enjoin enforcement of laws on the ground of unconstitutionality and that, when injunctions were issued on this ground, appeal might be taken direct from district court to Supreme Court. The Supreme Court and other Federal courts limit their pronouncements on state legislation to the question of whether it is in harmony with the Federal Constitution, laws and treaties.

A majority opinion only among the justices of the Supreme Court participating is necessary to a decision. The decision presenting the majority view is prepared and signed by a member of the court designated by the chief justice. A justice holding the majority view, but upon other grounds than those expressed in the opinion of the court, may offer a "concurring decision." A dissenting justice may submit a "dissenting opinion." In voting on a final decision, the youngest judge in point of service votes first, followed by the next youngest, and so on, with the chief justice voting last.

The Court of Customs and Patent Appeals. This court, established in 1909, consists of five judges appointed by the president for life. It reviews decisions of the board of general appraisers on collection of customs duties and decisions of the patent office.

United States Customs Court. The court was established as the Board of United States General Appraisers by an act of 1890 and was made the United States custom court by an act of 1926. The court has exclusive jurisdiction of civil actions involving the tariff laws. It also has the authority to exclude merchandise from entry into the U.S. The court consists of a chief judge and 8 associate judges; not more than 5 of whom can belong to any one political party.

United States Territorial Courts. In accordance with its authority to govern the territories, Congress has established district courts in the territories of Puerto Rico, Guam, the Virgin Islands and the Canal Zone. Except in Puerto Rico, where the court operates in the same way as a U.S. district court, these courts have jurisdiction over many local matters.

United States Tax Court. This court was created originally as the United States Board of Tax Appeals by the Revenue Act of 1924 and was subsequently changed to its present name and status by the Tax Reform Act of 1969. The court has jurisdiction over cases involving underpayments or overpayments in income, estate, gift, and personal holding company surtaxes as determined by the commissioner of internal revenue.

Court of Claims of the United States. The court was established by an act of February 24, 1855, with general jurisdiction over all claims upon the United States government, except pension claims, and, since 1915, except claims growing out of the Civil War. The court consists of seven judges, the concurrence of four being necessary to a decision. Where the court finds for the complainant, judgment is entered against the United States payable out of the public treasury.

JUSTICES OF THE SUPREME COURT*

Name	Term	Yrs.	Born	Died
John Jay, N. Y.	1789–1795	6	1745	1829
John Rutledge, S. C.**	1789–1791	2	1739	1800
William Cushing, Mass.	1789–1810	21	1733	1810
James Wilson, Pa.	1789–1798	9	1742	1798
John Blair, Va.	1789–1796	7	1732	1800
Robert H. Harrison, Md.	1789–1790	1	1745	1790
James Iredell, N. C.	1790–1799	9	1751	1799
Thomas Johnson, Md.	1791–1793	2	1732	1819
William Paterson, N. J.	1793–1806	13	1745	1806
John Rutledge, S. C.**	1795–1795	..	1739	1800
Samuel Chase, Md.	1796–1811	15	1741	1811
Oliver Ellsworth, Ct.	1796–1800	4	1745	1807
Bushrod Washington, Va.	1798–1829	31	1762	1829
Alfred Moore, N. C.	1799–1804	5	1755	1810
John Marshall, Va.	1801–1835	34	1755	1835
William Johnson, S. C.	1804–1834	30	1771	1834
Brockholst Livingston, N. Y.	1806–1823	17	1757	1823
Thomas Todd, Ky.	1807–1826	19	1765	1826
Joseph Story, Mass.	1811–1845	34	1779	1845

Name	Term	Yrs.	Born	Died
Gabriel Duval, Md.	1811–1835	25	1752	1844
Smith Thompson, N. Y.	1823–1843	20	1767	1843
Robert Trimble, Ky.	1826–1828	2	1777	1828
John McLean, Ohio	1829–1861	32	1785	1861
Henry Baldwin, Pa.	1830–1844	14	1779	1844
James M. Wayne, Ga.	1835–1867	32	1790	1867
Roger B. Taney, Md.	1836–1864	28	1777	1864
Philip P. Barbour, Va.	1836–1841	5	1783	1841
John Catron, Tenn.	1837–1865	28	1786	1865
John McKinley, Ala	1837–1852	15	1780	1852
Peter V. Daniel, Va.	1841–1860	19	1785	1860
Samuel Nelson, N. Y.	1845–1872	27	1792	1873
Levi Woodbury, N. H.	1845–1851	6	1789	1851
Robert C. Grier, Pa.	1846–1870	23	1794	1870
Benj. R. Curtis, Mass.	1851–1857	6	1809	1874
John A. Campbell, Ala.	1853–1861	8	1811	1889
Nathan Clifford, Me.	1858–1881	23	1803	1881
Noah H. Swayne, Ohio	1862–1881	20	1804	1884
Samuel F. Miller, Iowa	1862–1890	28	1816	1890
David Davis, Ill.	1862–1877	15	1815	1886
Stephen J. Field, Cal.	1863–1897	34	1816	1899
Salmon P. Chase, Ohio	1864–1873	9	1808	1873
Edwin M. Stanton	1869–1869	4d.	1814	1869
William Strong, Pa.	1870–1880	10	1808	1895
Joseph P. Bradley, N. J.	1870–1892	22	1813	1892
Ward Hunt, N. Y.	1872–1882	10	1811	1886
Morrison R. Waite, Ohio	1874–1888	14	1816	1888
John M. Harlan, Ky.	1877–1911	34	1833	1911
William B. Woods, Ga.	1880–1887	7	1824	1887
Stanley Matthews, Ohio	1881–1889	8	1824	1889
Horace Gray, Mass.	1881–1902	21	1828	1902
Samuel Blatchford, N. Y.	1882–1893	11	1820	1893
Lucius Q. C. Lamar, Miss.	1888–1893	5	1825	1893
Melville W. Fuller, Ill.	1888–1910	22	1833	1910
David J. Brewer, Kan.	1889–1910	21	1837	1910
Henry B. Brown, Mich.	1890–1906	16	1836	1913
George Shiras, Jr., Pa.	1892–1903	11	1832	1924
Howell E. Jackson, Tenn.	1893–1895	2	1832	1895
Edward D. White, La.**	1894–1910	16	1845	1921
Rufus W. Peckham, N. Y.	1895–1909	14	1837	1909
Joseph McKenna, Cal.	1898–1925	27	1843	1926
Oliver W. Holmes, Mass.	1902–1932	30	1841	1935
William R. Day, Ohio	1903–1922	19	1849	1923
William H. Moody, Mass.	1906–1910	4	1853	1917
Horace H. Lurton, Tenn.	1909–1914	5	1844	1914
Charles E. Hughes, N.Y.**	1910–1916	6	1862	1948
Edward D. White, La.**	1910–1921	11	1845	1921
Willis VanDevanter, Wyo.	1910–1937	27	1859	1941
Joseph R. Lamar, Ga.	1910–1916	6	1857	1916
Mahlon Pitney, N. J.	1912–1923	11	1858	1924
Jas. C. McReynolds, Tenn.	1914–1941	27	1862	1946
Louis D. Brandeis, Mass.	1916–1939	23	1856	1941
John H. Clarke, Ohio	1916–1922	6	1857	1945
William H. Taft, Conn.	1921–1930	9	1857	1930
George Sutherland, Utah	1922–1938	16	1862	1942
Pierce Butler, Minn.	1922–1939	17	1866	1939
Edward T. Sanford, Tenn.	1923–1930	7	1865	1930
Harlan F. Stone, N. Y.**	1925–1941	16	1872	1946
Charles E. Hughes, N.Y.**	1930–1941	11	1862	1948
Owen J. Roberts, Pa.	1930–1945	15	1875	1955
Benjamin N. Cardozo, N.Y.	1932–1938	6	1870	1938
Hugo L. Black, Ala.	1937–1971	34	1886	1971
Stanley F. Reed, Ky.	1938–1957	19	1884	
Felix Frankfurter, Mass.	1939–1962	23	1882	1965
William O. Douglas, Conn.	1939–1975	36	1898	
Frank Murphy, Mich.	1940–1949	9	1890	1949
James F. Byrnes, S. Car.	1941–1942	1	1879	1972
Robert H. Jackson, N. Y.	1941–1954	13	1892	1954
Harlan F. Stone, N. Y.**	1941–1946	5	1872	1946
Wiley B. Rutledge, Jr., Iowa	1943–1949	6	1894	1949
Harold H. Burton, Ohio	1945–1958	13	1888	1964
Frederick M. Vinson, Ky.	1946–1953	7	1890	1953
Thomas C. Clark, Texas	1949–1967	18	1899	1977
Sherman Minton, Ind.	1949–1956	7	1890	1965
Earl Warren, Cal.	1953–1969	16	1891	1974
John M. Harlan, N. Y.	1955–1971	16	1899	1971
William J. Brennan, Jr., N.J.	1956–	..	1906	
Charles E. Whittaker, Mo.	1957–1962	5	1901	1973
Potter Stewart, Ohio	1958–	..	1915	
Byron R. White, Colo.	1962–	..	1917	
Arthur J. Goldberg, Ill.	1962–1965	3	1908	
Abe Fortas, Tenn.	1965–1969	4	1910	
Thurgood Marshall, Md.	1967–	..	1908	
Warren E. Burger, Minn.	1969–	..	1907	
Harry A. Blackmun, Ill.	1970–	..	1908	
Lewis F. Powell, Va.	1971–	..	1907	
William H. Rehnquist, Ariz.	1971–	..	1924	
John Paul Stevens, Ill.	1975–	..	1920	

* Names of Chief Justices appear in bold face.
** Served as Justice and also Chief Justice.

STATE CAPITOLS

A traditional American spirit is preserved in the clean lines of Delaware's capitol at Dover.

A. Ken. Pfist

Functional design for practicality and classic lines for beauty distinguish Oregon's capitol at Salem.

Oregon State Highway Department

Towering above the prairie landscape, North Dakota's new state building at Bismarck accentuates the modern skyscraper design.

A wooded background suggesting the "Green Mountain State" frames Vermont's classic capitol at Montpelier.

Vermont Development Commission

Kentucky's capitol at Frankfort is placed far back in a landscaped setting that enhances its beauty.

Dept. of Public Relations, Frankfort, Ky.

Santa Fe, the only state capitol built in the Territorial style, based on Spanish colonial architecture. The tower rises 105 feet.

New Mexico Tourist Bureau

AMERICAN STATE GOVERNMENT

The United States of America is a federal union of fifty commonwealths, or "states." It has been defined as "an indestructible union of indestructible states." Two classes of government are created or recognized by the Constitution: the national or "federal" government; and the state governments. Back of both of these governments is the nation, with its political sovereignty in the entire people.

State government is older than the federal government, which was created by the bestowal upon it of powers previously existent in the states. These powers are definitely prescribed by the federal Constitution. All powers not given to the federal government are reserved to the states. This constitutional arrangement gave to the modern world its first expression of "federalism."

Federal Expansion. The tendency of successful federal government is to augment gradually the scope and the authority of the national government as against the state governments. This tendency is observable in America. The theory that sovereignty still existed in the states and not in the national government was extinguished by the outcome of the Civil War, 1861–65. The existence of complete free trade between the states, as guaranteed by the Constitution, has built up an industrial organization within the United States that recognizes no state boundaries or lines. Transportation and commerce have become largely "interstate." The population moves unhindered from state to state, while domicile with political rights is a matter of automatic transfer of residence. These and other considerations have constantly tended to extend the federal government and to strengthen its control over industry and transportation on a national scale.

Concurrent Powers. The result of this process at times has seemed to menace the original character of the state governments. Nevertheless, while the activity of the national government is more impressive and of much more interest to the average citizen of the United States, the authority of the state government comes closer to his person, to his business, and to his home. The field of administration exercised by the state embraces the establishment and control of local and municipal government, of public instruction (except so far as it is assisted and consequently influenced by federal grants or subventions), and of public health (except where the federal government may exercise authority in the case of national epidemic). It embraces also the care of dependents and defectives; the construction of highways and other communications; private law, including domestic relations, inheritance, rights of property, contracts; the exclusive control of corporate industry (except where it takes on an interstate character); the punishment of criminals; and the protection of public order.

In this last and important field the president may, on request of the governor of a state, apply the power of the national government. In cases where interstate commerce has suffered interference or the movement of the United States mails has been stopped by violent acts, the president has dispatched United States troops and placed localities under military control without application of the governor, and even in the face of his protest. While generally the police powers exercised by the Federal government and by the state governments are distinct fields, they are frequently used in collaboration.

Furthermore, in about 1906 the state governments took on new vigor, which expressed itself in a large variety of social and industrial legislation, in the creation of new administrative agencies, and in movements to reorganize and strengthen state administration.

But during World War I, power shifted once again to the federal government as the states be-

came mere executors of federal policy. Afterwards, even though two-thirds of the states went on record in favor of the League of Nations, the U.S. Senate failed to ratify the treaty. The prosperity of the 1920s further demoralized any attempts to pass progressive legislation in the states. When the Great Depression struck in 1929, even the richer states could not afford to meet the demand. Everyone turned to the federal government and Roosevelt's New Deal to pull the country out of the crisis. Since that time, government in the United States has continued to become much more centralized.

Interstate Compacts. With the permission of Congress states may enter into treaties or compacts for dealing with common problems. Compacts have been authorized by Congress for concerted action on such matters as use of water from a common river, limitation of petroleum production, and regulation of labor standards. They have been found more satisfactory when involving one definite arrangement, as in a boundary agreement, but less so when used as a substitute for unified authority in meeting a complex problem.

STATE CONSTITUTIONS

The written constitutions of the American states are older than the federal Constitution. They are, in fact, an American political invention. They grew out of the colonial charters of the period of English sovereignty. They assumed their typical form during the Revolutionary War, 1775–1783. They still bear the marks of their origin and of the political theory of that day. A century and a half of growth has occasioned an extraordinary number of changes and recastings of these organic acts, without radically altering their general type.

Upon the outbreak of the Revolutionary War in 1775, the Continental Congress, a body formed by representatives of the thirteen American colonies which were united in revolution, recommended to these colonies the adoption of new constitutions, to take the place of the governments which had existed under British royal authority. Certain colonies adopted this suggestion in the following order: New Hampshire, South Carolina, Virginia, New Jersey, Delaware, Pennsylvania, North Carolina, and Maryland. Virginia was the first state to devise a constitution with a complete frame of government and with a code of popular rights.

None of these new constitutions was "popularly ratified." Massachusetts, by its constitution of 1780, inaugurated a further step. An assembly elected for that sole purpose framed the constitution, which was then submitted to the suffrage of the people of the commonwealth. Thereby was initiated the practice of popular ratification of constitutions, now the representative procedure.

Some 144 state constitutions have been prepared and put into execution during the history of American state government. Each of the 50 American states is governed by such an organic act. Louisiana, in the course of its history, has had 11 constitutions, the last effective from 1975.

Admission to Statehood. "Admission to the Union" is an action taken by the Congress under one of its most important constitutional powers. With the exception of the 13 original states, Texas, Vermont, Maine, West Virginia, and California, all of the states, before admission, were territories governed under acts of Congress. The territories were not members of the Union. Their people had no constitutional political rights and did not participate in national elections. "Admission" of a territory to statehood, however, was admission to full equality with all other states. Congress, when it judged the time ripe for the admission of a territory as a new state, by an "enabling act," authorized an election for the purpose of drafting a constitution.

This action, if satisfactory, led to the admission by Congress into the Union. Congress, more than once, by legislation, has prescribed conditions under which a given territory should be admitted to statehood. as, by the suppression of polygamy in the case of Utah. Such limitations, however, imposed by the Federal government, become invalid as soon as the state is admitted to the Union.

Arizona was admitted to statehood in 1912 only after removing from its proposed constitution, at the insistence of the president and the Congress of the United States, a provision for the recall of judges. Immediately after admission into the Union, however, the state of Arizona exercised its right to replace this provision in its constitution. The dates of the original ratifications of the Federal Constitution and of admission of states since the formation of the Union, in 1789, are given in the table entitled *United States, Historical Statistics.*

Amendments to State Constitutions.

Three procedures exist for the amendment of a state constitution, two being operative in the great majority of states. These are (1) amendment on proposal of the legislature; (2) amendment by a constitutional convention; and (3) amendment by popular initiative. In addition, Florida's constitution authorizes the use of a constitutional commission to initiate constitutional changes and to submit them directly to the electorate. The oldest and most generally utilized method of amendment is by a proposal of the legislature.

The Legislative Proposal.

Differing conditions attend the legislative proposal: (1) that it must be passed by two successive legislatures (in Delaware this procedure enacts the amendment); (2) passage by an extraordinary majority—two-thirds or three-fifths vote of all members elected; (3) limitations as to the number of amendments proposed at one time, or the frequency with which the same amendment can be passed. In all states but Delaware the proposal, having passed the legislature, is submitted to popular ratification.

In most states a majority of votes cast ratifies the amendment and makes it a part of the constitution. Nebraska and Hawaii require a majority of those voting on the measure, provided votes cast in favor are not less than 35 per cent of the total votes cast at the election; New Hampshire requires two-thirds of those voting thereon; and Tennessee requires a majority of citizens voting for governor. A majority of all votes cast at the election is required in 3 states—Illinois, Minnesota, and Wyoming. In amendments concerning certain elective franchise and education matters, New Mexico requires approval by three-fourths of all electors voting in the state and two-thirds voting in each county.

Constitutional Conventions.

Constitutional conventions or extraordinary legislative bodies, popularly elected for the purpose of revising the constitution, are the usual method where a *general revision* of the constitution is sought. In most states the proposal to call a constitutional convention is submitted to popular vote, and in 14 states—Alaska, Connecticut, Hawaii, Illinois, Iowa, Maryland, Michigan, Missouri, Montana, New Hampshire, New York, Ohio, Oklahoma, and Rhode Island—the constitution requires that such a proposal be submitted regularly at the conclusion of a certain interval of years. In Georgia, Louisiana, Maine, South Carolina, and Virginia, the legislature may call a convention without popular approval. In 9 states—Arkansas, Indiana, Massachusetts, Mississippi, New Jersey, North Dakota, Pennsylvania, Texas, and Vermont—there is no provision for calling a constitutional convention.

Popular Initiative.

Amendment by popular initiative is now authorized in Arizona, Arkansas, California, Colorado, Florida, Illinois, Massachusetts, Michigan, Missouri, Montana, Nebraska, Nevada, North Dakota, Ohio, Oklahoma, Oregon, and South Dakota. The petition must be signed by a definite number of voters or by a number equal to a certain percentage (3 to 15) of the total vote cast for some state officer at the last preceding election. Once the signatures are verified, the measures are submitted to the people at the next general election. In Massachusetts the popularly initiated amendment must receive the approval of at least one-fourth of all members of two successive legislatures and the legislature may submit a competing or substitute measure.

Popular Ratification.

The practice of referring to popular ratification constitutions framed or revised by a convention has steadily grown. The early constitutions, except in New Hampshire and in Massachusetts, were not submitted to the people, but from 1784 to 1840 all such constitutions were submitted except in the cases of Delaware, Minnesota, and Arkansas.

During the Civil War period the practice was against submission. Between 1870 and 1890 there was a return to the pre-war practice and all constitutions drafted by conventions were submitted to popular ratification. From 1890 to 1910, of eleven constitutions adopted, five were popularly ratified. Since 1910, many new constitutions or important revisions have been effected by constitutional conventions, and, in almost all cases, these constitutions were popularly ratified.

CONSTITUTIONAL LIMITATIONS UPON THE POWERS OF STATE LEGISLATURES

By the Constitution of the United States, all legislative powers not expressly bestowed upon the national Congress are reserved to the states. Thus no enumeration of the powers of a state legislature is necessary in a state constitution. "All residuary legislative power" being implied, the only original restraint is that state laws must not conflict with the Constitution of the United States, with the laws of Congress, or with United States treaties.

The early state constitutions were framed at a time of great popular confidence in elected legislatures. Gradually, however, as legislatures were tempted into passing unrepresentative legislation or yielding to corrupt influences, restrictions upon the powers of legislatures were introduced by amendments to state constitutions. Louisiana in 1845 and Iowa in 1846 adopted constitutional provisions that forbade "special legislation." The constitution of Michigan (1847) and that of California (1849) contained similar restrictions on the legislature.

Special Municipal Laws.

The purpose of these changes was to prohibit the legislatures from appropriating money or conferring other benefits upon private individuals or corporations. In 1850-51, the states of Ohio and Indiana prohibited state legislatures from passing special laws for municipalities. This action was to remedy a growing abuse of interfering with municipal government and even of penalizing cities in the interests of partisan politics.

The movement initiated by Ohio became general, particularly in western and southern states. Five-eighths of the states have adopted constitutional provisions that no special law shall be enacted where a general law can be made applicable. In the New England states alone are the legislatures generally free to enact laws applying to a particular person, city, town, or other corporation.

Legislative Freedom.

Undeniably, the process of placing fetters upon state legislatures was carried too far and resulted in denying to state legislatures a discretion which was properly theirs and which would be to the interest of state government to exercise. A movement became apparent to restore to state legislatures a freedom which nearly a century of constitutional amendment largely destroyed. The adoption by many states of the legislative referendum created a popular check upon vicious legislation and legislative favoritism, while the legislatures themselves became more powerful.

STATE LEGISLATURES

In all American states excepting Nebraska, which voted to adopt the unicameral legislature in 1937, the legislative power is intrusted to a representative body consisting of two chambers and usually known as the state legislature, or general assembly. In Massachusetts and in New Hampshire it is called the general court. The bicameral or two-chamber plan has been adopted in American states in obedience to the "theory of checks and balances," one house halting and correcting the wrong or impulsive action of the other. In all states the "upper" and uniformly smaller body, being elected for a longer term and with sometimes a higher age qualification for its members, is called the Senate. The larger or more popular house in all but four states is called the House of Representatives; in the others it is called the Assembly.

Qualifications. In all states the qualifications for voting for both houses are the same. The "aristocratic" character of the electors of the upper house long ago disappeared. Among the qualifications for election, certain states require a higher age for the Senate (sometimes 30 years) than for the lower house (18 to 25 years). Residence in the state for a prescribed term before election to the legislature is a usual condition, as is residence in the district from which a member is chosen. This last requirement has the result of increasing the representative's responsibility to his constituency, since, if defeated by unpopularity in the district in which he resides, he cannot without change of residence stand for election in another. Federal officeholders are generally ineligible, as are paid officials of the state, with certain customary exceptions (notaries, national guard officers, soldiers, etc.).

Organization and Legislation. State constitutions usually provide that the lieutenant governor or vice governor shall be the presiding officer of the Senate, and provisions have been introduced into many constitutions regarding the procedure of legislation, the publication of bills, etc. Other than these, both houses are free to organize themselves in their own way. The American system of legislative committees everywhere prevails. Members of either house have an almost unlimited privilege of introducing bills, which, after being read by title, are referred to the appropriate committee for examination. The unrestrained practice of introducing bills results in legislatures being burdened, at each session, with bills which cannot be properly examined or discussed.

The interest felt by members in the passage of their bills and the political reputation made or lost by the success or failure of such measures leads to the practice of members supporting one another's projects in return for support of their own, and results in the loading of American statute books with ill-digested, unwise, and practically undebated laws.

Another embarrassment to American state legislation is the mass of detail written into statutes, the effort of the legislator being to cover every possible assumed contingency. These provisions, being frequently purely theoretical and not based upon experience with the measure, usually require a large amount of amendment or alteration by subsequent legislatures with resulting delays and embarrassments in their enforcement.

Distrust of state legislatures and apprehensions felt as to radical action by them led, in many states, to constitutional provisions limiting the frequency of legislative meetings and the duration of their proceedings. The earlier practice of annual meetings of legislatures gave way to biennial legislatures.

After World War II, this process was reversed. Legislatures became more important as the matters before them became more complex. In most states, the legislatures were reestablished as coequal to the executive branch.

The design of the United States gave each state exclusive jurisdiction over many aspects of laws and regulations, creating a diversity to counteract the authority of the central government. But too many differences would tend to discourage free passage by people and commerce. In 1890, the National Conference of Commissioners on Uniform State Laws was established to advise state legislatures on areas in which a uniformity of codes would be desirable. States are under no compulsion to adopt the uniform acts. The institution has drafted legislation in such diverse areas as criminal extradition procedure, motor vehicle laws, commercial codes, and divorce laws.

Legislative Bureaus. A device to avoid defects of drafting, duplication, and other bad features of state legislation was the creation of offices providing legislative staff services, diversified and multilayered with full-time, year-round personnel. In some states, they are organized as joint, nonpartisan agencies, and in others, as partisan committees that work through party leadership. Experts within each bureau advise legislators on such matters as bill preparation, legal authority, and policy analysis. All 50 legislatures have staffs to review and analyze budget and fiscal actions of their states. The staff services also help to provide continuity between sessions.

Legislative Councils. Led by Kansas and Michigan in 1933, a number of states established legislative councils with paid staffs to study, plan for, and prepare legislative proposals in advance of the sessions. They usually consist of legislators only, but may include administrative officers.

Members of state legislatures receive compensation for their services; but this compensation varies greatly in different states, as may be seen from the table *Tabulated Data on State Governments.*

REFERENDUM AND INITIATIVE OF LAWS

The original sole competence of legislatures to enact laws has been modified in 39 states by the adoption of the "legislative referendum" and in 21 states by the "legislative initiative." These modifications of "representative government" are Swiss devices and were first adopted in America as joint measures by the state of South Dakota in 1898. While usually associated, the two institutions are unlike in spirit, the referendum being a conservative practice, the initiative, radical.

A referendum of constitutional measures, as stated above, dates from the early Revolutionary constitutions. The practice is old, also, of requiring local bond issues and exceptional fiscal measures to be ratified by voters of state, county, school district, or city. But, since the example of South Dakota, the practice has spread of giving to the people the right of annulling an act of the legislature or of originating laws to be submitted to popular judgment either without legislative consideration, "direct initiative," or together with a similar measure proposed by the legislature in its place, "indirect initiative."

The referendum of a law is accomplished by securing signatures to a petition to suspend the operation of the act and to submit it to popular judgment as expressed at a general election. The number of signatures required is usually 5 per cent of the votes of the state. Such a petition must be signed and submitted to the secretary of state for verification within a certain period (usually 90 days) following the adjournment of the legislature. States possessing referendum procedures only are Florida, Georgia, Illinois, Iowa, Kansas, Kentucky, Maryland, New Hampshire, New Jersey, New

Mexico, New York, North Carolina, Pennsylvania, Rhode Island, South Carolina, Vermont, Virginia, and Wisconsin.

The states possessing both initiative and referendum are Alaska, Arizona, Arkansas, California, Colorado, Idaho, Maine, Massachusetts, Michigan, Missouri, Montana, Nebraska, Nevada, North Dakota, Ohio, Oklahoma, Oregon, South Dakota, Utah, Washington, and Wyoming. The number of signatures required to place an initiative measure on the ballot ranges from 3 per cent of the votes cast in the last general election for governor in Massachusetts to 15 per cent of the voters in the last general election in Wyoming. Most states require from 8 to 10 per cent of the votes cast for some state official in the last election.

In each state where initiative and referendum occur, a majority of the popular vote is required to enact a measure. Idaho stipulates that the majority must be equal to the majority of total votes cast for governor at such an election. Massachusetts requires the majority to be equal to 30 per cent of the ballots cast in the election.

In a number of states that possess initiative, a still higher requirement exists for the initiative of a constitutional amendment. Alaska, Idaho, Maine, Utah, Washington, and Wyoming make no provision for the popular initiative of a constitutional amendment.

THE GOVERNOR

The executive power in all American states is intrusted to a governor. The office, both in its functions and in its title, is an inheritance from the colonial period. The Revolution substituted the practice of popular election of the governor for that of appointment. In all states the governor is directly elected by the qualified voters, for a definite term.

Qualifications. Among the qualifications for election as governor frequently provided by state constitutions are American citizenship, previous residence in the state of from 1 month in Rhode Island to 10 years in Missouri. The minimum age is usually thirty, but in some states the candidate must only be a qualified voter. In eight states, the governor is not eligible for re-election. The term varies from 2 years (4 states) to 4 years (46 states).

Authority of Governor. As the period of early state constitution making showed a confidence in legislatures, so it exhibited a marked distrust of executive or gubernatorial authority. This prejudice survived the entire first century of the history of state governments. In no state had the governor an administrative power over state affairs comparable to that of the president over national administration. The executive departments were entrusted to officers popularly elected and independent of the governor's control. It was thus impossible to hold the governor responsible for the general conduct of the state's business and equally impossible for him to enforce a consistent policy throughout the state administration. The governor seldom had the power of appointment of state or local officials, nor the right to remove for negligence, inefficiency, or malfeasance. Beginning with the second decade of the present century, however, came a movement to enlarge the authority of the governor over state administration. One proposal was that of the so-called "short ballot," whereby a governor alone would be elected, other state officials being generally his appointees. More recently, in many states radical reorganization has been effected, both by constitutional amendment and by legislation. State services have been centralized, or organized in departments, with the suppression of numerous independent boards and commissions. The department heads are made appointable and removable by the governor, and in some states now sit with the governor as an administrative and advisory "cabinet." There has been an increase in the number of officials holding office at the pleasure of the governor rather

than for fixed terms. One of the most radical of such measures was that passed in Iowa in 1933 centralizing financial control in the hands of the governor. A somewhat similar measure was passed in New Jersey the same year. The trend has been toward lengthening the governor's term.

On the political side, the position of governor is an honorable and conspicuous one. His influence in state and national politics is great, and tends to increase. It is from the class of successful state governors that strong presidential candidates are usually derived. The dignity and the influence of the position are sufficient to attract, as candidates for the office, able and representative citizens. Nevertheless American state administration remains generally "decentralized" in contrast to the national administration.

The Veto Power. Although the office of governor was originally conceived as entirely distinct from the legislative power, the "doctrine of separation of powers" being generally avowed by American state constitutions, the governor has come to possess a great influence over the legislature and its legislation. This has been accomplished in several ways. First, by the bestowal upon the governor of the veto power.

In the earlier state constitutions, the veto power was generally absent, but, by successive amendments, it has been created until now it exists in all states except North Carolina. Only four state constitutions withold the governor's right to veto a constitutional amendment. Furthermore, in 43 states the governor may exercise a veto on any item in an appropriation bill. Since most states require a two-thirds vote in both the House and Senate to override a veto, this provision enables the governor practically to determine the state's budget, and places upon him the responsibility of defeating riders to appropriation bills. Public opinion in American states, furthermore, has come to require the governor to frame and press upon the legislature at each session an "administrative program."

Influence on Legislation. The influence possessed by the governor over legislatures, not only by the importance of his position, but by his power of vetoing bills in which members are interested and by reason of his leadership in the party, gives a special character to what are called "administrative measures" or bills proposed or supported by him, and it is hardly too much to say that the governor is today judged quite as much for the legislation which he secures as for his general conduct of the state's executive business.

A governor, faced with an unwilling legislature, frequently goes directly to the people of the state, and, through interviews or radio addresses, organizes the force of public opinion to bear upon the legislature to favor measures upon which he has staked his political reputation. These practices, while they have contradicted the theory of the separation of powers, undoubtedly have introduced into American state government a necessary authority and have enabled the voters of the states to hold the government to a closer responsibility.

The Power to Pardon. Another important power of the governor is that of pardon. This power may be classified in its several forms as the power to "commute" a sentence or reduce it below the punishment fixed by a court, the power to "pardon" or entirely free a person from the consequences of guilt, the power to grant "reprieves" or postpone sentence, and the power to remit fines and forfeitures.

In 32 states the sole power of pardon, except in cases of treason or impeachment, resides in the governor; in 29 states the governor alone has the power to commute sentence. In 41 states he has the sole power to grant reprieves and in 22 states the sole power to remit fines and forfeitures. In 12 states the governor has the power to pardon, when acting with his council, or on the recommendation of a board of pardons; in 9 states he similarly exercises the power of commuting sentence; and in 6 states he similarly exercises the power of remitting fines and forfeitures. In 6 states, however (Connecticut, Florida, Idaho, Nevada, New Jersey, and Utah), the pardoning power resides exclusively in a board of pardons.

The power of remitting fines or forfeitures is less frequently confided to the governor, and 21 states by constitutional provision entirely prohibit its exercise.

STATE OFFICERS

Besides a governor and a lieutenant governor (in 38 states), the usual officers are a secretary of state (all states), an attorney-general (all states), a treasurer (all states except New York), an auditor or comptroller (all but 3 states), and a superintendent of public instruction (all states). These are usually popularly elected at the same time and for the same term as the governor. In a few cases the secretary of state (Delaware, Maryland, New Jersey, New York, Pennsylvania, Texas, Virginia), or the superintendent of public instruction (7 states), is appointive by the governor, while in a few states (Maine, New Hampshire, New Jersey, Tennessee) one or more of these officers may be elected by the legislature. In 8 states the school superintendent is elected by a board of education. Other usual officers are the adjutant general of the national guard or state militia, of which the governor is the commander in chief, and a surveyor-general, or a registrar of lands.

As stated above, by recent legislation in a few states, the heads of departments now constitute a "cabinet" of the governor. Usually, however, they perform their duties independently of him and may even represent political parties other than that with which the governor is affiliated.

Nearly all other state offices have been created, not by the constitution, but by legislation, and have come into existence gradually as the state has assumed added responsibilities or taken private professions and certain classes of business under its control.

Types of Administration. Several types of administration have been adopted to discharge new forms of state business: (1) the "*ex officio* board," composed of the governor, secretary of state, the attorney-general, an executive officer, and frequently other members; (2) the "lay board," a corporation of citizens, unsalaried, and usually appointed by the governor for fixed terms, with the power to choose the executive of a state institution (educational, penal, charitable, etc.), and to direct its conduct; (3) a "bureau type" where a branch of administration is intrusted to a single directive head (commissioner of insurance, banks, corporations, etc.); (4) the "commission type" where public business is intrusted to a salaried board whose members are considered technically qualified or expert administrators and who have a joint or "collegiate" responsibility (public service commissions, boards of control, etc.).

Boards and Commissions. Practically all states have public service commissions, charged with regulating public utilities. Admission to the practice of certain professions is secured in most states only after examination and certification by boards composed of selected representatives of these professions (law, medicine, dentistry, pharmacy, architecture, public accounting). The number of these offices, boards, and commissions has multiplied to an astonishing degree, many states having over 100 such bodies. The system has obvious disadvantages; viz., duplication of expense, overlapping functions, absence of responsibility, and undue independence of common administrative authority.

Reorganization of state administrations to assure simplicity, efficiency, economy, and responsibility is a perennial problem of American government. Because the citizens of a state are already obliged to meet growing demands from federal and local governments, the raising of state income is increasingly difficult. And yet, the states have many long-term commitments as well as unpredictable expenditures. In fiscal 1966, for example, the estimated revenue from state and local sources was $85 billion. From time to time different state administrations have made serious efforts to reduce expenses. Sometimes overlapping services have been consolidated into fewer departments, sometimes commissions have been organized to operate independent of executive control, and hence comparatively free from political pressure. In some instances central purchasing agencies and bureaus of audit and investigation have been added. In recent years such matters peculiar to the states have been discussed at Governors' Conferences.

Some forms of reorganization have increased, instead of limiting, the power of the governor. The aim has been to make him the head of the state administration as the president is of the federal government, with power to appoint and remove heads of departments and directors in charge of administrative services. Such reorganization has been accomplished by constitutional amendment where necessary, or by legislation. In some states the governor has control of the budget, as in California, New York, Iowa, and New Jersey. In Iowa the spending agencies must submit quarterly estimates to the governor, who is empowered to cut allowances not covered by prospective revenue income.

CIVIL SERVICE

One consideration operating against the "short ballot" and the enlargement of the governor's control of state administration is fear of the misuse of this power to reward political adherents and to create "political machines." The number of employees in certain states is large (202,000 in New York). The unrestricted power to employ and to dismiss so great a force undeniably offers opportunities for serious abuses. While the power to appoint department staffs is legally vested in the heads of the offices, the actual choice may be made by party leaders or "bosses" regardless of the efficiency of the service. Public service has become highly specialized and can be well discharged only by trained and conscientious officials holding office for considerable terms and free from the disturbing vicissitudes of party contests.

Tenure of Office. As in the Federal service, so in the state, including local and municipal administration, advocates of civil service reform have sought to secure laws establishing a "merit system" for public office with security of tenure for competent and faithful public servants. The movement, however, has not met with wide success, and, as yet, no state has adopted a general standard for determining the fitness of aspirants to all offices, local as well as state.

Civil service laws provide for general coverage in 30 states and apply to selected departments in the other 20 states. Federal requirements provide that state employees handling federal funds must be chosen by civil service procedures. The usual method of administering a civil service system is by a commission, which is given power to "classify" the public positions, fix qualifications for each grade of employment, hold examinations to determine fitness, certify "eligibles" to the appointing power, keep official service records of employees, and in some cases to try or investigate charges of unfitness. Civil service laws usually declare public positions open on equal conditions to both men and women.

THE RECALL

The recall has been defined as "a special election to determine whether an official shall be superseded before the ordinary expiration of his term." It is in use in 13 states: Alaska, Arizona, California, Colorado, Idaho, Kansas, Louisiana, Michigan, Nevada, North Dakota, Oregon, Washington, and Wisconsin. In 8 of the states, all elected officials are subject to recall, while in the other 5 judges are exempt (Idaho, Kansas, Louisiana, Michigan, and Washington). The most common requirement for the number of signatures on a recall petition is 25 per cent of the voters in the last general election in the jurisdiction affected. In each state where a recall election might occur, a majority vote recalls the official.

LOCAL GOVERNMENT

The organization of local government (county, township, district, municipality) is entirely a function of the states. Local government serves two purposes: (1) the need of the state for agencies in conducting its administration and enforcing its laws in the subdivisions of the state; (2) the need of communities for organization to satisfy local or community needs. Theoretically, a county may be considered a local agency of the state and a town or city a community organization for determining and supplying its own public wants; but actually state and local activities overlap, or merge and separate in response to an altering social order.

Education, public health, charities, and communications are likely to command the interest of both the state and the town. Justice and preservation of public order are clearly state, not local, functions; but the American practice of "decentralizing" public authority and a prejudice for local self-government have influenced the state usually to leave these essential services to be performed by judges and peace officers locally elected and responsible only to the people of the locality.

Division into Counties. All of the 50 states are divided into counties (in Louisiana called "parishes"). Within the counties (largely rural in character), cities and towns exist as incorporated municipalities. There are more than 3000 counties in the United States, the average number for each state being more than 60. But Delaware has only 3 counties, Rhode Island has 5, while Texas has 254. In New England, county government is mainly limited to the administration of justice, though the county may be a unit of senatorial representation. Elsewhere, it is the usual unit for maintaining roads and bridges, for poor relief, for school administration, and in some states for health supervision and for agricultural aid.

County Government. County government is organized according to no general principle. Outside of Connecticut, Rhode Island, and Georgia, there is an elective board of commissioners or supervisors, with powers, in southern and western states, to assess county taxes, to care for county property, to maintain highways and roads, and to conduct county institutions. In addition, the usual officers are the judge or judges of the county or "superior" court, the sheriff, the attorney, the clerk, the recorder of deeds and other instruments, the assessor of taxes, the collector of taxes, the school superintendent, the health officer, etc. The term of office varies from two to six years.

There is an absence of any responsible head for the county administration and usually county officers are subject to a little or to no state supervision. Removal power is rarely placed in the hands of the governor.

MUNICIPAL GOVERNMENT

In 1970, the population of standard metropolitan areas in the U.S. was about 140,626,400. The metropolitan area is considered to be the urban area around and including each important city of about 50,000 or more.

City government in the United States follows no accepted plan. Three chief forms are found: the mayor and council plan with separation of executive and legislative functions; the "commission" plan; and the "city manager" plan. The first is the most common. The mayor is popularly elected and may be given a veto over legislation of the council and a large control over city offices. Earlier practice was to divide the council into two chambers.

Commission Form of Government. The commission plan had its origin in Galveston in 1901. It has been adopted in all parts of the Union but particularly in Pa., N. J., Ill., Kans., Okla., and Tenn. Pennsylvania, in 1913, made commission government compulsory for all cities of the third class. Cities of largest population which have employed this form are Newark, N. J., New Orleans, La., Jersey City, N. J., Portland, Ore., St. Paul, Minn., Oakland, Cal., Omaha, Nebr., Birmingham, Ala., Memphis, Tenn., San Antonio, Tex., Dallas, Tex., Houston, Tex., Des Moines, Iowa, Trenton, N. J., Salt Lake City, Utah, Reading, Pa., Spokane, Wash. Under this plan both executive and legislative functions are entrusted to a commission, usually of five. They are popularly elected and are chosen, not by districts, but "at large," though not necessarily all at the same election. This commission employs the city officials and directs the entire administration. In some instances it appoints a city manager, as explained below.

City Manager Plan. This plan was first tried in Staunton, Va., in 1908. Dayton, Ohio, in 1913, was the first large city to adopt it. Between that date and 1945, approximately 450 American cities altered their charters or ordinances to provide for city managers. The maximum number of adoptions, 53, occurred in 1921. In addition to these American cities, 17 cities in Canada and 2 in New Zealand have adopted the plan. Under this plan the elected city council or commission engages a manager who is the head of the entire municipal administration and confines its attention to determining policies, raising revenue, making appropriations, and supervising the administration of the manager.

Municipal Charters. Municipal governments under the American legal system have only those powers and functions which are specifically given them by their charters or by statutes. Originally a city was incorporated and provided with a charter by an act of the legislature. This practice has been altered in two ways: first, by the provision of standard types of city government (corresponding to populations of different sizes or "classes") laid down in "general laws"; and, secondly, by allowing city populations to frame their own charters, which, when ratified by the legislature, become effective.

"Municipal home rule" is now provided for by the constitutions of 31 states and by statute in 8 states. In many of these states minimum population requirements exist for eligibility, ranging from 2,000 to 10,000. Others allow a choice of a few specified forms of governments. Home rule is intended to give communities greater freedom and authority in the structure of their government and in matters primarily of local concern.

DEPENDENCIES

The Spanish American war of 1898 brought new responsibilities which made the United States one of the principal "colonial powers" of the world. The chief scene of hostilities was Cuba, and that island was conquered from Spain in 1898. Puerto Rico and the Philippines were ceded outright by Spain to the United States by the treaty of Paris, ratified in 1899. The acquisition of the right to build the Panama Canal, with other responsibilities also, flowed from the war and resulted in practical acquisition of the Canal Zone although Panama retained the right to fly its flag there beside the American flag.

The liquidation of the American "colonial empire" began early. Cuba was given its freedom in 1903, subject to the right of American intervention in case of civil disorder—a right which was exercised a number of times before its abrogation in 1934. A naval base on the island was also retained.

The Philippines was granted independence in two steps. By the first, in 1934, the Philippines became a "dominion" for a ten-year transitional period. The period expired during World War II, which had the effect of postponing the final step until 1946. It then became an independent republic.

Puerto Rico. After a period of military rule, a liberal government was created for the island of Puerto Rico, which was modified by the Organic Act of Congress of 1917. This act granted American citizenship to the people of Puerto Rico. Legislative power is vested in two houses, a Senate of 29 members and a House of Representatives of 54 members. These are elected partly from districts and partly at large. The franchise is possessed by all citizens, and no property qualifications may be imposed. The governor, who ruled with an executive council of department heads, was appointed by the president.

In August 1947 the Organic Act was amended in response to long continued demands from the island. By the new law the governor is elected for a term of four years, beginning in August 1948, by the Puerto Rican people. The governor now appoints the department heads. The president appoints the auditor and a co-ordinator of federal agencies. The new constitution drafted by the people of Puerto Rico was approved by Congress July 3, 1952. It made Puerto Rico a commonwealth.

The judiciary consists of a United States District judge and a supreme court of 9 justices, appointed by the governor. There are also 11 superior courts, 39 district courts, and justices of the peace.

Puerto Rico has a resident commissioner in Washington who has a voice but not a vote in the House of Representatives.

Virgin Islands. The Virgin Islands, formerly known as the Danish West Indies, were purchased by the U.S. from Denmark in 1917 for $25 million. At first all governing powers were vested in the governor. Legislative power is now vested in a single-chamber legislature composed of 15 senators popularly elected for 2-year terms from the two districts of St. Croix and St. Thomas-St. John. Until 1970 the governor was appointed by the president; he now is elected. Suffrage is extended to residents who are U.S. citizens over 18. The islands are supervised by the Department of the Interior.

Canal Zone. By treaty with Panama, ratified 1904, the United States acquired title to the Canal Zone, a strip 10 miles wide, with use and control of waters and islands at each end of the canal for purposes of construction, maintenance, or defense of the canal. See *Panama*. This interoceanic strip is, by act of Congress of 1912, placed under the control of the president, who commits its administration to a governor, who is an army officer. Negotiations were under way in 1976 to draw up a new treaty between the United States and Panama.

Guam. The largest island of the Ladrones or Marianas group, ceded to the United States by Spain in 1898. It is an important strategic outpost, an air and naval base, and a communications center.

Its affairs were formerly administered by the Navy Department, a naval officer acting as governor; but by executive order of President Truman the civil administration was placed in charge of the Department of the Interior, the transfer being completed in June 1950. A month later U. S. citizenship was granted to the inhabitants.

Until 1970 the governor was appointed by the U.S. president; presently, he is elected by the residents of Guam to a 4-year term. There is a single-chamber Guamanian Congress elected by permanent residents. Its powers are largely advisory; however, a veto of the governor may be overridden, and an appeal taken directly to Washington. There is a court of appeals, with an island court; a justice court; and a police court, without juries.

Guam was captured by the Japanese in December 1941, but was retaken by United States forces in July 1944. The capital and port of entry, Agana, was totally destroyed during World War II, but has since been rehabilitated.

Samoa. American Samoa, the principal island of which is Tutuila, was acquired by the United States through a tripartite treaty with Great Britain and Germany, November 14, 1899, whereby the other two countries renounced claims over this part of the Samoan islands. America had been in the islands, however, since 1872, when the harbor of Pago Pago was purchased from a native king. Since 1951 this dependency has been supervised by the Department of the Interior, with a civilian governor. Before that it was controlled by the Navy Department and a naval officer was governor. A bicameral legislature with advisory powers chosen by the Samoans was established in 1948. There are district and magistrates courts, and a High Court with a chief justice, who is an American civilian; all other judges are natives. Native lands may not be sold to foreigners.

Pacific Islands. A number of small islands in the Pacific ocean are important in naval defense and for trans-Pacific aviation. These are:

Midway and *Kure* islands, 1,200 miles northwest of Hawaii, claimed by the U.S. since 1867; under the control of the Navy Department.

Wake Island, midway between Hawaii and Guam; formally claimed in 1900 and under the control of the Federal Aviation Agency. The island serves as an important commercial aviation base.

Johnston and *Sand* islands, known as the Johnston Atoll, were annexed by the U.S. in 1858 and are under the jurisdiction of the Navy Department.

Kingman reef, on the direct route to Samoa; annexed by the U.S. in 1922 and under the Navy Department.

Palmyra Island, administered by the Interior Department.

Howland, *Jarvis* and *Baker* islands, near the equator, were assigned to the Interior Department in 1936.

Corn Islands, leased to the U.S. in 1916 for a period of 99 years by Nicaragua.

Canton and *Enderbury* islands, controlled jointly by the U.S. and Britain. They formerly were used for aviation purposes but now are uninhabited.

Caroline, *Marianas*, and *Marshall* islands, known as Micronesia, were formerly a Japanese mandate and are now a U.S. trusteeship under the UN. In 1976 the Northern Marianas became a commonwealth of the U.S.

Protectorates. During the first three decades of the 20th century, the United States acquired protectorates, official or unofficial, over Cuba, Panama, Haiti, Dominican Republic, and Nicaragua. These relationships were largely abrogated by treaty revision or withdrawal of troops during the administration of President Roosevelt beginning in 1933. The United States returned the Ryukyu Islands, including Okinawa, to Japan on May 15, 1972. The islands had been under the jurisdiction of the United States since 1952.

STATE	Capital	SIZE OF LEGISLATURE		TERM OF MEMBERS (YRS.)		Frequency of Session	Limit of Regular Session*	Salaries of Members for Regular Session Exclusive of Travel Allowance
		Sena's	Repre's	Sena's	Repre's			
Alabama	Montgomery	35	105	4	4	Annual	30 L	$10 per diem
Alaska	Juneau	20	40	4	2	Annual	None	$14,720 per annum
Arizona	Phoenix	30	60	2	2	Annual	None	$6,000 per annum
Arkansas	Little Rock	35	100	4	2	Biennial	60 C	$2,400 per biennium
California	Sacramento	40	80	4	2	Annual	None	$21,120 per annum
Colorado	Denver	35	65	4	2	Annual	None	$15,200 per biennium
Connecticut	Hartford	36	151	2	2	Annual	{ Odd June / Even May }	$11,000 per biennium
Delaware	Dover	21	41	4	2	Annual	June 30	$9,000 per annum
Florida	Tallahassee	40	120	4	2	Annual	60 C	$12,000 per annum
Georgia	Atlanta	56	180	2	2	Annual	{ Odd 45 L / Even 40 L }	$7,200 per annum
Hawaii	Honolulu	25	51	4	2	Annual	60 L	$12,000 per annum
Idaho	Boise	35	70	2	2	Annual	60 C	$10 per diem
Illinois	Springfield	59	177	4	2	Annual	None	$20,000 per annum
Indiana	Indianapolis	50	100	4	2	Annual	{ Odd 61 L / Even 30 L }	$6,000 per annum
Iowa	Des Moines	50	100	4	2	Annual	None	$16,000 per biennium
Kansas	Topeka	40	125	4	2	Annual	{ Odd none / Even 90 C }	$35 per diem
Kentucky	Frankfort	38	100	4	2	Biennial	60 L	$25 per diem
Louisiana	Baton Rouge	39	105	4	4	Annual	60 L	$50 per diem
Maine	Augusta	33	151	2	2	Annual	None	$3,850 per biennium
Maryland	Annapolis	47	141	4	4	Annual	90 C	$25,000 per biennium
Massachusetts	Boston	40	240	2	2	Annual	None	$25,376 per biennium
Michigan	Lansing	38	110	4	2	Annual	None	$19,000 per annum
Minnesota	St. Paul	67	134	4	2	Biennial	120 L	$16,800 per biennium
Mississippi	Jackson	52	122	4	4	Annual	90C †	$16,200 per biennium
Missouri	Jefferson City	34	163	4	2	Annual	{ Odd J. 30 / Even M. 15 }	$16,800 per biennium
Montana	Helena	50	100	4	2	Biennial	90 L	$31.60 per diem
Nebraska a	Lincoln	49 Legislators;		4 year	term	Annual	{ Odd 90 L / Even 60 L }	$9,600 per biennium
Nevada	Carson City	20	40	4	2	Biennial	60 C	$60 per diem
New Hampshire	Concord	24	400	2	2	Biennial	None	$200 per biennium
New Jersey	Trenton	40	80	4	2	Annual	None	$10,000 per annum
New Mexico	Santa Fe	42	70	4	2	Annual	{ Odd 60 C / Even 30 C }	$40 per diem
New York	Albany	60	150	2	2	Annual	None	$23,500 per annum
North Carolina	Raleigh	50	120	2	2	Biennial	None	$9,600 per biennium
North Dakota	Bismarck	51	102	4	2	Biennial	60 L	$5 per diem
Ohio	Columbus	33	99	4	2	Annual	None	$35,000 per biennium
Oklahoma	Oklahoma City	48	101	4	2	Annual	90 L	$19,920 per biennium
Oregon	Salem	30	60	4	2	Biennial	None	$11,616 per biennium
Pennsylvania	Harrisburg	50	203	4	2	Annual	None	$31,200 per biennium
Rhode Island	Providence	50	100	2	2	Annual	60 L	$5 per day, 60 days
South Carolina	Columbia	46	124	4	2	Annual	None	$175 per diem
South Dakota	Pierre	35	70	2	2	Annual	45 L	$5000 per biennium
Tennessee	Nashville	33	99	4	2	Biennial	30 L	$12,481 per biennium
Texas	Austin	31	150	4	2	Biennial	90 L	$14,400 per biennium
Utah	Salt Lake City	29	75	4	2	Annual	140 C	$25 per diem
Vermont	Montpelier	30	150	2	2	Biennial	None	$150 per week
Virginia	Richmond	40	100	4	2	Annual	{ Odd 30 C / Even 60 C }	$10,950 per biennium
Washington	Olympia	49	98	4	2	Biennial	60 C	$7,600 per biennium
West Virginia	Charleston	34	100	4	2	Annual	60 C	$9,600 per biennium
Wisconsin	Madison	33	99	4	2	Annual	None	$35,686 per biennium
Wyoming	Cheyenne	30	62	4	2	Annual	{ Odd 40 L / Even 20 L }	$15 per diem

a One-chamber legislature.   * Abbreviations: L—Legislative days; C—Calendar days; J.—June; M.—May
† Except 125 C in Gubernatorial election years.

| GOVERNOR | | HIGHEST COURT | | | | | Electoral College d (Inc. 3 for Dist. Col.) Total, 538 | STATE |
Term (Yrs.)	Salary	Name	How Chosen	Number of Judges	Term of Judges	Salaries of Judges		
4	$28,955	Supreme Court	Elected	9	6 years	$33,500	9	Alabama
4	50,000	Supreme Court	Elected e	5	10 years	52,992	3	Alaska
4	40,000	Supreme Court	{ App. by Gov. with } { consent of Council }	5	6 years	37,000	6	Arizona
2	10,000	Supreme Court	Elected	7	8 years	31,189 / 34,024c	6	Arkansas
4	49,100	Supreme Court	Elected e	7	12 years	57,985 / 61,609c	45	California
4	40,000	Supreme Court	Elected e	7	10 years	35,000 / 37,500c	7	Colorado
4	42,000	Supreme Court	{ By Governor and } { General Assembly }	6	8 years	36,000 / 40,000c	8	Connecticut
4	35,000	Supreme Court	{ Governor, con- } { firmed by Senate }	3	12 years	42,000 / 42,500c	3	Delaware
4	50,000	Supreme Court	Elected	7	6 years	40,000	17	Florida
4	50,000	Supreme Court	Elected	7	6 years	40,000	12	Georgia
4	46,000	Supreme Court	{ Governor with } { consent of Senate }	5	10 years	45,000 / 47,500c	4	Hawaii
4	33,000	Supreme Court	Elected	5	6 years	30,000	4	Idaho
4	50,000	Supreme Court	Elected	7	10 years	50,000	26	Illinois
4	37,000	Supreme Court	Elected	5	10 years	38,100	13	Indiana
4	40,000	Supreme Court	Elected e	9	8 years	36,000 / 37,000c	8	Iowa
4	35,000	Supreme Court	Elected e	7	6 years	32,500 / 35,000c	7	Kansas
4	35,000	Supreme Court	Elected	7	8 years	31,500	9	Kentucky
4	50,000	Supreme Court	Elected	7	10 years	50,000	10	Louisiana
4	35,000	Supreme Judicial Court	{ App. by Gov. with } { consent of Council }	6	7 years	36,000 / 37,500c	4	Maine
4	25,000	Court of Appeals	Elected	7	15 years	44,100 / 45,200c	10	Maryland
4	40,000	Supreme Judicial Court	{ App. by Gov. with } { consent of Council }	7	To age 70	40,738 / 42,236c	14	Massachusetts
4	45,000	Supreme Court	App. by Gov. . . .	7	8 years	43,500	21	Michigan
4	41,000	Supreme Court	Elected	9	6 years	36,000 / 40,000c	10	Minnesota
4	43,000	Supreme Court	Elected	9	8 years	26,000 / 27,000c	7	Mississippi
4	37,000	Supreme Court	Elected	7	12 years	36,500	12	Missouri
4	30,000	Supreme Court	Elected e	5	8 years	27,000 / 28,000c	4	Montana
4	25,000	Supreme Court	Elected	7	6 years	35,500	5	Nebraska
4	40,000	Supreme Court	Elected	5	6 years	35,000	3	Nevada
2	34,070	Supreme Court	{ App. by Gov. with } { consent of Council }	5	To age 70	34,060 / 34,268c	4	New Hampshire
4	60,000	Supreme Court	{ App. by Gov. with } { consent of Senate }	7	b	48,000 / 50,500c	21	New Jersey
4	35,000	Supreme Court	Elected	5	8 years	32,000	4	New Mexico
4	85,000	Court of Appeals	Elected	7	14 years	60,575 / 63,143c	41	New York
4	38,500	Supreme Court	Elected	7	8 years	38,000 / 39,000c	13	North Carolina
4	18,000	Supreme Court	Elected	5	10 years	32,000 / 33,500c	3	North Dakota
4	50,000	Supreme Court	Elected	7	6 years	40,000 / 43,500c	25	Ohio
4	42,500	Supreme Court	Elected e	9	6 years	30,000	8	Oklahoma
4	38,500	Supreme Court	Elected	7	6 years	35,200	6	Oregon
4	60,000	Supreme Court	Elected	7	10 years	50,000 / 52,500c	27	Pennsylvania
2	42,500	Supreme Court	Elected by Leg. . .	5	Life	33,000 / 34,000c	4	Rhode Island
4	39,000	Supreme Court	Elected by Leg. . .	5	10 years	36,000 / 41,000c	8	South Carolina
4	27,500	Supreme Court	Elected	5	8 years	28,000	4	South Dakota
4	50,000	Supreme Court	Elected e	5	8 years	39,330 / 41,830c	10	Tennessee
4	65,000	Supreme Court	Elected	9	6 years	45,600 / 46,100c	26	Texas
4	35,000	Supreme Court	Elected e	5	10 years	30,000	4	Utah
2	36,100	Supreme Court	{ Governor with } { consent of Senate }	5	6 years	29,900 / 31,200c	3	Vermont
4	50,000	Supreme Court of Appeals	Elected by Leg. . . .	7	12 years	41,300 / 48,300c	12	Virginia
4	42,150	Supreme Court	Elected	9	6 years	39,412	9	Washington
4	35,000	Supreme Court of Appeals	Elected	5	12 years	32,500	6	West Virginia
4	44,292	Supreme Court	Elected	7	10 years	42,462 / 48,000c	11	Wisconsin
4	37,500	Supreme Court	Elected e	5	8 years	32,500	3	Wyoming

b Seven years with re-appointment for life.   d Equals, for each state, number of Congressmen plus 2 U.S. Senators.
c Chief justice.   e Initially appointed by Governor; then run in election.

PRESIDENTIAL VOTING RECORDS 1960-1976

STATE*	Population 21 and over 1960 Census	Population 18 and over 1970 Census	1960 Election Votes Cast	1964 Election Votes Cast	1968 Election Votes Cast	1972 Election Votes Cast	1976† Election Votes Cast	1976† Per cent of Eligible Voters Voting
Alabama	1,834,000	2,209,500	570,225	454,318	1,038,929	1,006,111	1,149,000	46.0
Alaska	124,000	180,523	60,762	55,136	80,816	95,219	88,000	37.9
Arizona	732,000	1,126,925	398,491	467,882	470,540	622,926	731,000	47.0
Arkansas	1,043,000	1,267,072	428,509	527,429	606,368	651,320	763,000	50.7
California	9,660,000	13,317,162	6,506,578	6,818,738	7,106,072	8,367,862	7,598,000	49.7
Colorado	1,031,000	1,433,248	736,236	766,378	807,499	953,884	1,040,000	58.7
Connecticut	1,591,000	2,010,750	1,222,883	1,216,890	1,310,468	1,384,277	1,360,000	61.5
Delaware	267,000	351,003	196,683	200,765	212,235	235,516	235,000	58.3
Dist. of Col.‡	569,000	531,070	—	191,373	170,578	163,421	153,000	29.7
Florida	3,088,000	4,677,168	1,544,176	1,763,031	2,187,805	2,583,283	2,959,000	46.8
Georgia	2,231,000	2,944,208	733,349	1,038,303	1,234,173	1,174,772	1,432,000	42.4
Hawaii	348,000	493,932	184,705	206,931	236,205	270,274	287,000	47.9
Idaho	372,000	449,339	300,450	290,771	288,922	310,379	336,000	59.3
Illinois	6,281,000	7,318,353	4,757,409	4,632,955	4,530,616	4,723,236	4,613,000	59.8
Indiana	2,778,000	3,353,376	2,135,360	2,071,080	2,113,197	2,125,529	2,176,000	59.8
Iowa	1,664,000	1,849,439	1,273,810	1,180,085	1,161,379	1,225,944	1,271,000	63.2
Kansas	1,322,000	1,500,224	928,825	830,913	855,515	916,095	946,000	58.7
Kentucky	1,764,000	2,103,244	1,124,462	1,038,874	1,044,495	1,067,499	1,150,000	48.4
Louisiana	1,804,000	2,253,419	807,891	891,356	1,114,689	1,051,491	1,309,000	51.7
Maine	581,000	648,201	421,767	381,527	382,742	417,042	477,000	64.3
Maryland	1,845,000	2,540,666	1,055,349	1,119,019	1,279,193	1,353,812	1,385,000	48.4
Massachusetts	3,245,000	2,813,406	2,469,480	2,206,177	2,306,091	2,458,756	2,519,000	60.4
Michigan	4,580,000	5,623,713	3,318,097	3,188,163	3,222,384	3,489,727	3,626,000	57.8
Minnesota	2,001,000	2,423,484	1,541,887	1,543,387	1,497,955	1,741,652	1,921,000	70.6
Mississippi	1,171,000	1,373,145	298,171	412,756	652,035	645,963	745,000	48.2
Missouri	2,696,000	3,123,629	1,934,422	1,694,646	1,798,672	1,855,803	1,928,000	57.6
Montana	389,000	441,284	277,579	277,336	257,885	317,603	317,000	61.2
Nebraska	858,000	976,002	613,095	554,053	510,103	576,289	592,000	54.8
Nevada	175,000	318,589	107,267	133,068	151,031	181,766	194,000	45.9
New Hampshire	373,000	483,470	295,761	288,826	297,190	334,055	338,000	58.9
New Jersey	3,861,000	4,783,319	2,773,111	2,788,042	2,875,518	2,997,229	2,933,000	56.9
New Mexico	501,000	609,784	311,107	326,010	325,492	386,241	407,000	52.8
New York	10,881,000	12,359,629	7,291,079	7,012,056	6,711,587	7,165,919	6,398,000	49.6
North Carolina	2,557,000	3,320,975	1,368,556	1,437,586	1,567,011	1,518,612	1,662,000	43.2
North Dakota	355,000	391,411	278,431	241,003	247,428	280,514	289,000	66.9
Ohio	5,839,000	6,913,720	4,161,859	3,960,927	3,946,122	4,094,787	4,067,000	54.5
Oklahoma	1,416,000	1,721,096	903,150	931,587	943,086	1,029,900	1,088,000	56.1
Oregon	1,073,000	1,393,702	776,421	758,726	808,517	927,946	1,010,000	61.1
Pennsylvania	7,100,000	7,945,807	5,006,541	4,604,993	4,575,382	4,592,106	4,576,000	54.2
Rhode Island	540,000	646,696	405,535	376,472	370,873	415,808	389,000	60.1
South Carolina	1,266,000	1,635,353	386,688	530,757	669,201	673,960	788,000	40.8
South Dakota	392,000	424,587	306,487	287,788	278,152	307,415	298,000	63.5
Tennessee	2,093,000	2,595,712	1,051,792	1,147,257	1,238,404	1,201,182	1,463,000	49.4
Texas	5,534,000	7,194,167	2,311,084	2,577,990	3,076,233	3,471,281	3,939,000	46.3
Utah	468,000	636,423	374,709	401,811	423,035	478,476	521,000	66.6
Vermont	231,000	287,564	167,324	162,804	161,080	186,947	181,000	55.3
Virginia	2,313,000	3,058,033	771,449	1,040,867	1,363,115	1,457,019	1,645,000	46.6
Washington	1,718,000	2,249,395	1,241,572	536,591	1,170,152	1,470,847	1,363,000	53.7
West Virginia	1,083,000	1,162,818	837,781	783,860	752,005	762,399	741,000	57.9
Wisconsin	2,354,000	2,834,088	1,729,082	1,685,899	1,689,570	1,852,890	2,083,000	64.9
Wyoming	190,000	212,392	140,782	136,226	126,045	145,570	155,000	58.3

* The Voting Rights Act of 1965 temporarily suspended literacy tests and other voter-qualification devices nationwide. The ban became permanent in 1975. The Voting Rights Act was amended in 1970 to include a ban on long residency requirements for voting in presidential elections and a provision for a 30-day residency requirement, which was upheld by the Supreme Court the same year. In 1972 the Supreme Court ruled lengthy residency requirements for state and local elections unconstitutional and suggested a 30-day residency requirement. Every state requires that voters be U.S. citizens. The Twenty-sixth Amendment to the Constitution ratified in 1971 lowered the minimum voting age to 18 for all federal, state, and local elections. † Unofficial.
‡ The Twenty-third Amendment to the Constitution ratified in 1961 extended presidential suffrage to the District of Columbia.

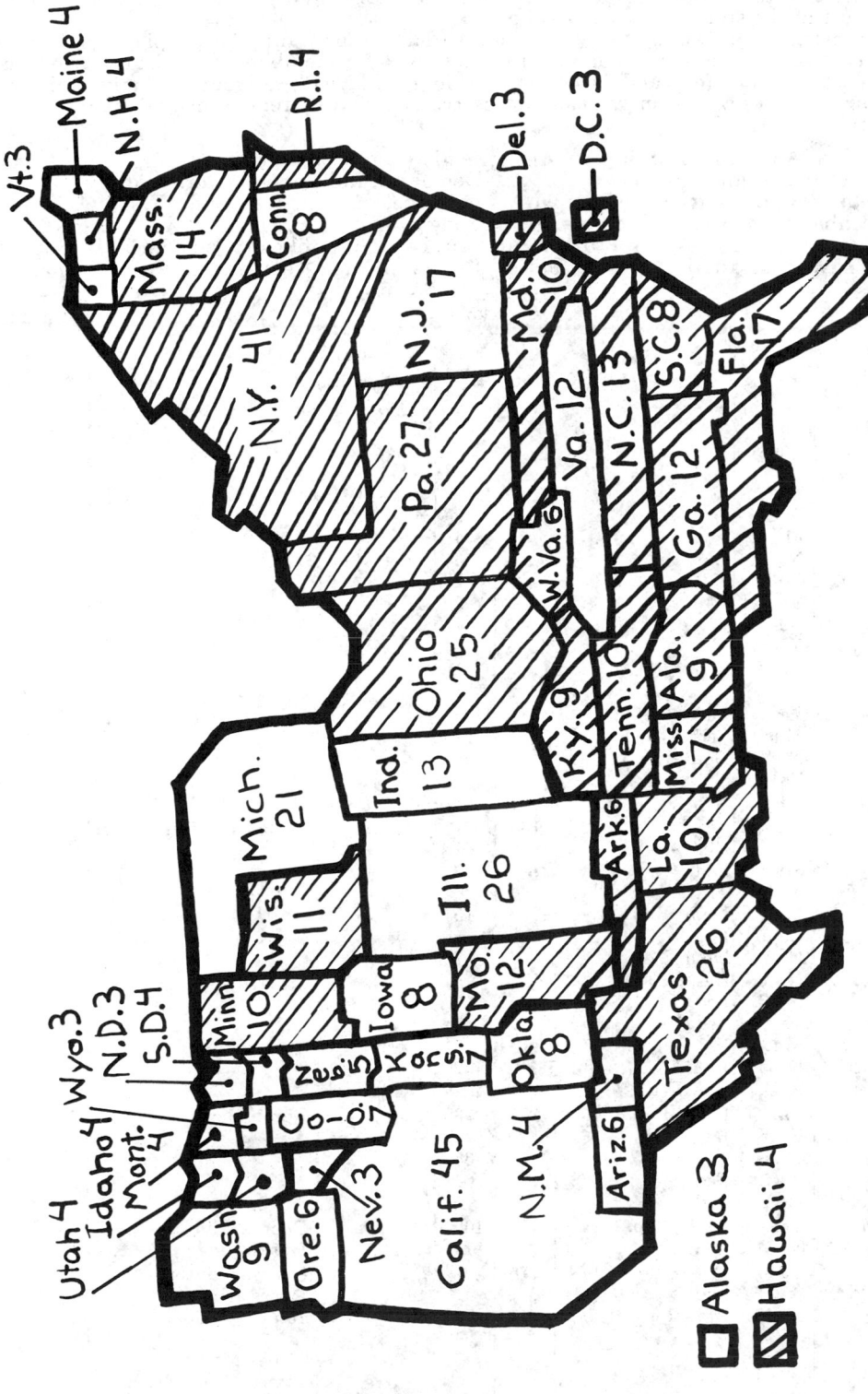

U.S. Presidential Election Map—1976. In this map, the 50 states have been sized in relation to their populations. To win the election, 270 electoral votes were required. The Republican candidate, Gerald Ford, received 240 votes. One elector from the state of Washington cast his vote for non-candidate Ronald Reagan, a symbolic gesture made after the contest had already been decided. The winner, Democratic candidate Jimmy Carter, received 297 votes. The states shaded with diagonal lines cast their electoral votes for Carter.

□ Alaska 3
▨ Hawaii 4

POPULAR AND ELECTORAL VOTE FOR PRESIDENT AND VICE PRESIDENT
FROM 1789 TO THE PRESENT

Strictly speaking, there is no popular vote for president and vice president; the people vote for electors, and those chosen in each state meet therein and vote for the candidates for president and vice president. Each state has as many electors as it has Representatives and Senators, plus 3 electors from Washington, D.C., making a national total of 538. The number of each state's representatives is determined by the decennial census and the ratio of the state's population to the country as a whole. The first House of Representatives in 1790 had 65 members. Since 1912 the total membership in the House has been 435. The record of any popular vote for electors prior to 1824 is so meager and imperfect that a compilation would be useless. In most of the states, for more than a quarter century following the establishment of the government, the state legislatures "appointed" the presidential electors, and the people therefore voted only indirectly for them, their choice being expressed by their votes for members of the legislature. In this tabulation, only the electoral vote for candidates for president and vice president in the first nine quadrennial elections appears. In a few instances, candidates receiving an extremely insignificant number of votes have been omitted.

ABBREVIATIONS: Amer., American; Antimas., Antimasonic; Cm., Communist; Const. Un., Constitutional Union; D. or Dem., Democrat; D. & L. R., Democrat and Liberal Republican; Dem.-Rep., Democratic Republican; Far.-L., Farmer-Labor; Fed., Federalist; F. S., Free Soil; F. S. D., Free Soil Democrat; Gr'b., Greenback; Ind., Independent; Indep., Independence; L., Labor; Nat. Rep., National Republican; P., Populist; Prog., Progressive; Pro., Prohibition; Rep., Republican; Soc., Socialist; Soc. Dem., Social Democrat; Soc. L., Socialist Labor; St. R., States' Rights; Temp., Temperance; U. L., Union Labor.

YEAR	Presidential Candidates	State	Party	States Voting	Total Vote	Electoral Vote	Popular Vote	Name	State	Electoral Vote
								CANDIDATES FOR VICE PRESIDENT		
1789*	George Washington	Va.	. . . .	10†	73	69	. . . . .	John Adams	Mass.	34
	John Adams	Mass.	. . . . . .			34				
	John Jay	N. Y.	. . . . .			9				
	R. H. Harrison . .	Md.	. . . . .			6				
	John Rutledge . . .	S. C.	. . . . .			6				
	John Hancock . . .	Mass.	. . . . . .			4				
	George Clinton . .	N. Y.	. . . . . .			3				
	Samuel Huntington	Conn.	. . . . .			2				
	John Milton	Ga.	. . . . .			2				
	James Armstrong .	Ga.	. . . . . .			1				
	Benjamin Lincoln .	Mass.	. . . . . .			1				
	Edward Telfair . . .	Ga.	. . . . . .			1				
	Vacancies††		. . . . .			4				
1792	George Washington	Va.	Fed. . . .	15	135	132	. . . .	John Adams	Mass.	77
	John Adams	Mass.	Fed. . . .			77				
	George Clinton . .	N. Y.	Dem.-Rep.‡			50				
	Thomas Jefferson .	Va.	. . . . .			4				
	Aaron Burr	N. Y.	. . . . .			1				
1796	John Adams	Mass.	Fed. . . .	16	138	71	. . . . .	Thomas Jefferson . .	Va.	68
	Thomas Jefferson .	Va.	Dem.-Rep.			68				
	Thomas Pinckney .	S. C.	Fed. . . .			59				
	Aaron Burr	N. Y.	Antifed. .			30				
	Samuel Adams . . .	Mass.	Dem.-Rep.			15				
	Oliver Ellsworth . .	Conn.	Fed. . . .			11				
	George Clinton . .	N. Y.	Dem.-Rep.			7				
	John Jay	N. Y.	Ind.-Fed. .			5				
	James Iredell . . .	N. C.	Fed. . . .			3				
	George Washington	Va.	Fed. . . .			2				
	John Henry	Md.	Ind. . . .			2				
	S. Johnston	N. C.	Ind.-Fed. .			2				
	C. C. Pinckney . .	S. C.	Ind.-Fed. .			1				
1800	Thomas Jefferson .	Va.	Dem.-Rep.	16	138	73§	. . . . .	Aaron Burr	N. Y.	73
	Aaron Burr	N. Y.	Dem.-Rep.			73§				
	John Adams	Mass.	Fed. . . .			65				
	C. C. Pinckney . .	S. C.	Fed. . . .			64				
	John Jay	N. Y.	Fed. . . .			1				
1804	Thomas Jefferson .	Va.	Dem.-Rep.	17	176	162	. . . . .	George Clinton . . .	N. Y.	162
	C. C. Pinckney . .	S. C.	Fed. . . .			14	. . . . .	Rufus King	N. Y.	14
1808	James Madison . .	Va.	Dem.-Rep.	17	176	122	. . . . .	George Clinton . . .	N. Y.	113
	C. C. Pinckney . .	S. C.	Fed. . . .			47		Rufus King	N. Y.	47
	George Clinton . .	N. Y.	Ind.-Rep.			6	. . . . .	John Langdon . . .	N. H.	9
	Vacancy					1				
								James Madison . .	Va.	3
								James Monroe . . .	Va.	3
1812	James Madison . .	Va.	Dem.-Rep.	18	218	128	. . . . .	Elbridge Gerry . . .	Mass.	131
	De Witt Clinton . .	N. Y.	Fusion . .			89	. . . . .	Jared Ingersoll . . .	Pa.	86

* Prior to 1804 each elector was entitled to vote for two candidates for president. The candidate receiving the greatest number of votes was declared elected, while the candidate receiving the next highest vote was declared vice president.

† Three states not voting. New York legislature failed to agree on electors; N. Carolina and Rhode Island had not ratified the Constitution.

‡ The Democratic-Republican (also called Republican) party was the predecessor of the present Democratic party.

†† "Vacancies" means electors absent or not voting.

§ As there was no election the choice was decided by the House of Representatives.

Vice President and President of the Senate

The Vice President, who is constitutionally designated presiding officer of the Senate, is a unique figure in our government. He is the only official with duties both in the executive and legislative branches. For many years the Vice President was not much more than "the man in the wings" waiting to fill the void should a vacancy occur in the presidency.

Since Harry Truman's presidency, however, the role of the Vice President has been steadily expanded.

The Constitution states the key role of the President of the Senate as follows: "The Vice President of the United States shall be President of the Senate, but shall have no vote, unless they be equally divided."

THOMAS JEFFERSON, Virginia, presided over the Senate (1797) as Vice President, under John Adams, and was elected third President of the United States.

JOHN ADAMS, Massachusetts, a Federalist, first President of the Senate and Vice President (1789); second President of the United States.

AARON BURR, New Jersey, was Jefferson's Vice President (1801), an able but disturbed politician, whose duel with Hamilton, and sad decline ruined his place in history.

GEORGE CLINTON, New York, Vice President (1805) in Jefferson's second term, (an Uncle of the better known De Witt Clinton), a member of the Continental Congress in 1775–76; served also as Vice President under James Madison.

ELBRIDGE GERRY, Massachusetts, was vice President (1813) under James Madison. A signer of the Declaration of Independence, later elected Governor of Massachusetts.

DANIEL D. TOMPKINS, New York, Vice President (1817) under James Monroe. Tompkins was Governor of New York and one of the founders of the New York Historical Society; re-elected with Monroe in 1820.

JOHN C. CALHOUN, South Carolina, Vice President (1825) under John Q. Adams. One of the south's great statesmen. Re-elected Vice-President 1828 on the Jackson ticket.

MARTIN VAN BUREN, New York, was Vice President in the Jackson administration (1833) when Calhoun resigned on his election to the Senate. Succeeded to Presidency 1837.

RICHARD M. JOHNSON, Kentucky, Van Buren's Vice President (1837), soldier and Senator, voted into Vice-Presidency by the Senate, because regular candidates failed of majority of electoral votes.

JOHN TYLER, Virginia, Harrison's Vice President (1841), Representative and Senator, Governor, succeeded to Presidency on Harrison's death, was subject of the spirited campaign slogan: Tippecanoe and Tyler, too.

GEORGE M. DALLAS, Pennsylvania, James K. Polk's Vice President (1845), Van Buren's Minister to Russia; President Pierce's minister to Great Britain; one time Mayor of Philadelphia.

MILLARD FILLMORE, New York, Zachary Taylor's Vice President (1849) succeeding him to the Presidency when Taylor died, fought in the Civil War on Union side, prominent in state and national politics.

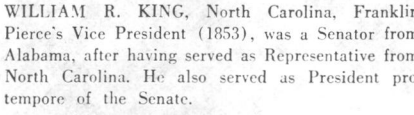

WILLIAM R. KING, North Carolina, Franklin Pierce's Vice President (1853), was a Senator from Alabama, after having served as Representative from North Carolina. He also served as President pro tempore of the Senate.

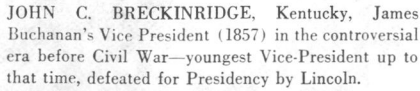

JOHN C. BRECKINRIDGE, Kentucky, James Buchanan's Vice President (1857) in the controversial era before Civil War—youngest Vice-President up to that time, defeated for Presidency by Lincoln.

POPULAR AND ELECTORAL VOTE FOR PRESIDENT AND VICE PRESIDENT FROM 1789 TO THE PRESENT—Con.

763

United States

YEAR	Presidential Candidates	State	Party	VOTE				CANDIDATES FOR VICE PRESIDENT		
				States Vot- ing	Total Vote	Elec- toral Vote	Popular Vote	Name	State	Elec- toral Vote
1816	James Monroe . . .	Va.	Rep. . . .	19	221	183	. . . . .	D. D. Tompkins . .	N. Y.	183
	Rufus King	N. Y.	Fed. . . .	. .	. .	34	. . . . .	John E. Howard . .	Md.	22
	Vacancies	. .	. . . .	. .	. .	4	. . . . .	James Ross	Pa.	5
1820	James Monroe . . .	Va.	Rep. . . .	24	235	231	. . . . .	D. D. Tompkins . .	N. Y.	218
	John Q. Adams . .	Mass.	Ind.-Rep.	. .	. .	1	. . . . .	Richard Stockton . .	N. J.	8
	Vacancy.	. .	. . . .	. .	. .	. .	. . . . .	Daniel Rodney . . .	Del.	4
1824	John Q. Adams . .	Mass.	⎫	24	261	84§	108,740	John C. Calhoun . .	S. C.	182
	Andrew Jackson . .	Tenn.	⎬No party	. .	. .	99§	153,544	Nathan Sanford . .	N. Y.	30
	Henry Clay	Ky.	⎪	. .	. .	37	47,136	Nathaniel Macon . .	N. C.	24
	W. H. Crawford . .	Ga.	⎭	. .	. .	41	46,618	Andrew Jackson . .	Tenn.	13
	Vacancy.	. .	. . . .	. .	. .	. .	. . . . .	. . . .	. .	1
1828	Andrew Jackson . .	Tenn.	Dem. . .	24	261	178	647,286	John C. Calhoun . .	S. C.	171
	John Q. Adams . .	Mass.	Nat. Rep.	. .	. .	83	508,064	Richard Rush . . .	Pa.	83
								William Smith . . .	S. C.	7
1832	Andrew Jackson . .	Tenn.	Dem. . .	24	288	219	687,502	Martin Van Buren .	N. Y.	189
	Henry Clay	Ky.	Nat. Rep.	. .	. .	49	530,189	John Sergeant . . .	Pa.	49
	John Floyd	Ga.	Ind.-Dem.	. .	. .	11	. . . . .	Henry Lee	Mass.	11
	William Wirt . . .	Md.	Antimas. .	. .	. .	7	. . . . .	Amos Ellmaker . .	Pa.	7
	Vacancies	. .	. . . .	. .	. .	2	. . . . .	William Wilkins . .	Pa.	30
1836	Martin Van Buren .	N. Y.	Dem. . .	26	294	170	762,978	R. M. Johnson . . .	Ky.	147
	Wm. H. Harrison. .	Ohio	Whig. . .	. .	. .	73	⎫	⎧Francis Granger . .	N. Y.	77
	Hugh L. White. . .	Tenn.	Whig. . .	. .	. .	26	⎬736,250	⎨John Tyler	Va.	47
	Daniel Webster . .	Mass.	Whig. . .	. .	. .	14	⎭	⎩William Smith . . .	Ala.	23
	W. P. Mangum . .	N. C.	Ind. . . .	. .	. .	11				
1840	Wm. H. Harrison. .	Ohio	Whig. . .	26	294	234	1,275,016	John Tyler	Va.	234
	Martin Van Buren .	N. Y.	Dem. . .	. .	. .	60	1,129,102	R. M. Johnson . . .	Ky.	48
	James G. Birney . .	N. Y.	Liberty	. .	. .	. .	7,069	L. W. Tazewell . .	Va.	11
								James K. Polk . . .	Tenn.	1
1844	James K. Polk . . .	Tenn.	Dem. . .	26	275	170	1,337,243	George M. Dallas .	Pa.	170
	Henry Clay	Ky.	Whig . .	. .	. .	105	1,299,062	T. Frelinghuysen . .	N. J.	105
	James G. Birney . .	N. Y.	Liberty	. .	. .	. .	62,300	Thomas Morris . .	Ohio	
1848	Zachary Taylor . .	La.	Whig. . .	30	290	163	1,360,099	Millard Fillmore . .	N. Y.	163
	Lewis Cass	Mich.	Dem. . .	. .	. .	127	1,220,544	Wm. O. Butler . . .	Ky.	127
	Martin Van Buren .	N. Y.	F. S. . . .	. .	. .	. .	291,263	Chas. F. Adams . .	Mass.	
1852	Franklin Pierce . .	N. H.	Dem. . .	31	296	254	1,601,474	William R. King . .	Ala.	254
	Winfield Scott . . .	N. J.	Whig. . .	. .	. .	42	1,386,580	Wm. A. Graham . .	N. C.	42
	John P. Hale . . .	N. H.	F. S. D. .	. .	. .	. .	155,825	George W. Julian . .	Ind.	
1856	James Buchanan . .	Pa.	Dem. . .	31	296	174	1,838,169	J. C. Breckinridge. .	Ky.	174
	John C. Fremont .	Cal.	Rep. . . .	. .	. .	114	1,341,264	Wm. L. Dayton . .	N. J.	114
	Millard Fillmore . .	N. Y.	Amer. . .	. .	. .	8	874,534	A. J. Donelson . . .	Tenn.	8
1860	Abraham Lincoln .	Ill.	Rep. . . .	33	303	180	1,866,452	Hannibal Hamlin . .	Me.	180
	J. C. Breckinridge .	Ky.	Dem. . .	. .	. .	72	849,781	Joseph Lane	Ind.	72
	Stephen A. Douglas.	Ill.	Dem. . .	. .	. .	12	1,376,957	H. V. Johnson . . .	Ga.	12
	John Bell	Tenn.	Const. Un.	. .	. .	39	588,879	Edward Everett . .	Mass.	39
1864	Abraham Lincoln .	Ill.	Rep. . . .	36	314	212	2,216,037	Andrew Johnson . .	Tenn.	212
	Geo. B. McClellan .	N. J.	Dem. . .	. .	. .	21	1,802,237	G. H. Pendleton . .	Ohio	21
1868	Ulysses S. Grant . .	Ill.	Rep. . . .	37	317	214	3,015,071	Schuyler Colfax . .	Ind.	214
	Horatio Seymour .	N. Y.	Dem. . .	. .	. .	80	2,709,615	F. P. Blair, Jr. . . .	Mo.	80
	Not counted . . .	. .	. . . .	. .	. .	23				
1872	Ulysses S. Grant . .	Ill.	Rep. . . .	37	366	286	3,597,132	Henry Wilson . . .	Mass.	286
	Horace Greeley . .	N. Y.	D. & L. R.	. .	. .	‖	2,834,125	B. Gratz Brown . .	Mo.	47
	Charles O'Conor . .	N. Y.	Straight D.	. .	. .	. .	29,489	John Q. Adams . .	Mass.	
	James Black . . .	Pa.	Temp. . .	. .	. .	. .	5,608	John Russell	Mich.	
	Thos. A. Hendricks	Ind.	Ind.-Dem.	. .	. .	42	. . . . .	Geo. W. Julian . . .	Ind.	5
	B. Gratz Brown . .	Mo.	Dem. . .	. .	. .	18	. . . . .	A. H. Colquitt . . .	Ga.	5
	Others	. .	. . . .	. .	. .	3	. . . . .	. . . .	. .	
	Not counted . . .	. .	. . . .	. .	. .	17	. . . . .	. . . .	. .	
1876	Ruth'd B. Hayes .	Ohio	Rep. . . .	38	369	185	4,033,768	Wm. A. Wheeler . .	N. Y.	185
	Samuel J. Tilden . .	N. Y.	Dem. . .	. .	. .	184	4,285,992	T. A. Hendricks . .	Ind.	184
	Peter Cooper . . .	N. Y.	Gr'b. . . .	. .	. .	. .	81,737	Samuel F. Cary . .	Ohio	
1880	James A. Garfield .	Ohio	Rep. . . .	38	369	214	4,449,053	Chester A. Arthur. .	N. Y.	214
	Win'd S. Hancock .	Pa.	Dem. . .	. .	. .	155	4,442,035	Wm. H. English . .	Ind.	155
	James B. Weaver .	Iowa	Gr'b. . . .	. .	. .	. .	307,306	B. J. Chambers . .	Tex.	
1884	Grover Cleveland. .	N. Y.	Dem. . .	38	401	219	4,911,017	T. A. Hendricks . .	Ind.	219
	James G. Blaine . .	Me.	Rep. . . .	. .	. .	182	4,848,334	John A. Logan . . .	Ill.	182
	John P. St. John . .	Kans.	Pro. . . .	. .	. .	. .	133,825	William Daniel . . .	Md.	

§ As there was no election the choice was decided by the House of Representatives.
‖ Owing to the death of Horace Greeley the Democratic electors scattered their vote.

YEAR	Presidential Candidates	State	Party	States Voting	Total Vote	Electoral	Popular Vote	Candidates for Vice President	State	Electoral
1888	Benjamin Harrison	Ind.	Rep.	38	401	233	5,440,216	Levi P. Morton	N. Y.	233
	Grover Cleveland	N. Y.	Dem.			168	5,538,233	A. G. Thurman	Ohio	168
	Clinton B. Fisk	N. J.	Pro.				249,907	John A. Brooks	Mo.	
1892	Grover Cleveland	N. Y.	Dem.	44	444	277	5,556,918	A. E. Stevenson	Ill.	277
	Benjamin Harrison	Ind.	Rep.			145	5,176,108	Whitelaw Reid	N. Y.	145
	James B. Weaver	Iowa	People's			22	1,041,028	James G. Field	Va.	22
1896	William McKinley	Ohio	Rep.	45	447	271	7,035,638	Garret A. Hobart	N. J.	271
	William J. Bryan	Nebr.	Dem. }			176	6,467,946	{ Arthur Sewall	Me.	149
	William J. Bryan	Nebr.	People's }					{ Th. E. Watson	Ga.	27
1900	William McKinley	Ohio	Rep.	45	447	292	7,219,530	Theo. Roosevelt	N. Y.	292
	William J. Bryan	Nebr.	Dem. & P.			155	6,358,071	A. E. Stevenson	Ill.	155
	John G. Woolley	Ill.	Pro.				209,166	Henry B. Metcalf	R. I.	
	Eugene V. Debs	Ind.	Soc. Dem.				94,768	Job Harriman	Cal.	
1904	Theodore Roosevelt	N. Y.	Rep.	45	476	336	7,628,834	Charles W. Fairbanks	Ind.	336
	Alton B. Parker	N. Y.	Dem.			140	5,084,491	Henry G. Davis	W. Va.	140
	Eugene V. Debs	Ind.	Soc.				402,400	Benjamin Hanford	N. Y.	
1908	William H. Taft	Ohio	Rep.	46	483	321	7,679,006	James S. Sherman	N. Y.	321
	William J. Bryan	Nebr.	Dem.			162	6,409,106	John W. Kern	Ind.	162
	Eugene V. Debs	Ind.	Soc.				420,820	Benjamin Hanford	N. Y.	
1912	Woodrow Wilson	N. J.	Dem.	48	531	435	6,286,214	Thos. R. Marshall	Ind.	435
	William H. Taft	Ohio	Rep.			8	3,483,922	Nicholas M. Butler	N. Y.	8
	Theodore Roosevelt	N. Y.	Prog.			88	4,126,620	Hiram W. Johnson	Cal.	88
1916	Woodrow Wilson	N. J.	Dem.	48	531	277	9,129,606	Thos. R. Marshall	Ind.	277
	Chas E. Hughes	N. Y.	Rep.			254	8,538,221	Chas W. Fairbanks	Ind.	254
	A. L. Benson	N. Y.	Soc.				585,113	G. R. Kirkpatrick	N. J.	
1920	Warren G. Harding	Ohio	Rep.	48	531	404	16,152,200	Calvin Coolidge	Mass.	404
	James M. Cox	Ohio	Dem.			127	9,147,353	Franklin D. Roosevelt	N. Y.	127
	Eugene V. Debs	Ind.	Soc.				919,799	Seymour Stedman	Ill.	
1924	Calvin Coolidge	Mass.	Rep.	48	531	382	15,725,016	Charles G. Dawes	Ill.	382
	John W. Davis	W. Va.	Dem.			136	8,385,586	Charles W. Bryan	Neb.	136
	Robert LaFollette	Wis.	Prog.			13	4,822,856	Burton K. Wheeler	Mont.	13
1928	Herbert Hoover	Cal.	Rep.	48	531	444	21,392,190	Charles Curtis	Kans.	444
	Alfred E. Smith	N. Y.	Dem.			87	15,016,443	Joseph T. Robinson	Ark.	87
	Norman M. Thomas	N. Y.	Soc.				267,420	James H. Maurer	Pa.	
1932	Franklin D. Roosevelt	N. Y.	Dem.	48	531	472	22,821,857	John N. Garner	Tex.	472
	Herbert Hoover	Cal.	Rep.			59	15,761,841	Charles Curtis	Kans.	59
	Norman M. Thomas	N. Y.	Soc.				884,781	James H. Maurer	Pa.	
1936	Franklin D. Roosevelt	N. Y.	Dem.	48	531	523	27,752,309	John N. Garner	Tex.	523
	Alfred M. Landon	Kans.	Rep.			8	16,682,524	Frank R. Knox	Ill.	8
	Norman Thomas	N. Y.	Soc.				187,342	George A. Nelson	Wis.	
	Earl Browder	Kans.	Cm.				80,096	James W. Ford	Ala.	
1940	Franklin D. Roosevelt	N. Y.	Dem.	48	531	449	27,245,422	Henry A. Wallace	Iowa	449
	Wendell L. Willkie	N. Y.	Rep.			82	22,333,801	Charles L. McNary	Ore.	82
	Norman Thomas	N. Y.	Soc.				116,796	Maynard C. Kreuger	Ill.	
	Roger W. Babson	Mass.	Pro.				58,674	Edgar V. Moorman	Ill.	
	Earl Browder	Kans.	Cm.				49,028	James W. Ford	Ala.	
1944	Franklin D. Roosevelt	N. Y.	Dem.	48	531	432	25,602,505	Harry S. Truman	Mo.	432
	Thomas E. Dewey	N. Y.	Rep.			99	22,006,278	John W. Bricker	Ohio	99
	Norman Thomas	N. Y.	Soc.				80,518	Darlington Hoopes	Pa.	
1948	Harry S. Truman	Mo.	Dem.	48	531	304	24,045,052	Alben W. Barkley	Ky.	304
	Thomas E. Dewey	N. Y.	Rep.			189	21,896,927	Earl Warren	Cal.	189
	J. Strom Thurmond	S. C.	St. R.			38	1,168,687	Fielding L. Wright	Miss.	38
	Henry A. Wallace	Iowa	Prog.				1,137,957	Glen Taylor	Ida.	
	Norman Thomas	N. Y.	Soc.				95,908	Tucker P. Smith	Mich.	
1952	Dwight D. Eisenhower	N. Y.	Rep.	48	531	442	33,927,549	Richard M. Nixon	Cal.	442
	Adlai E. Stevenson	Ill.	Dem.			89	27,311,316	John J. Sparkman	Ala.	89
1956	Dwight D. Eisenhower	N. Y.	Rep.	48	531	457	35,575,420	Richard M. Nixon	Cal.	457
	Adlai E. Stevenson	Ill.	Dem.			73*	26,033,065	Estes Kefauver	Tenn.	73*
1960	John F. Kennedy	Mass.	Dem.	50	537†	303	34,221,531	Lyndon B. Johnson	Texas	303
	Richard M. Nixon	Cal.	Rep.			219‡	34,108,474	Henry Cabot Lodge	Mass.	219‡
1964	Lyndon B. Johnson	Texas	Dem.	50	538	486	42,328,350	Hubert H. Humphrey	Minn.	486
	Barry M. Goldwater	Ariz.	Rep.			52	26,840,650	William E. Miller	N. Y.	52
1968	Richard M. Nixon	N. Y.	Rep.	50	538	302	31,785,480	Spiro T. Agnew	Md.	302
	Hubert H. Humphrey	Minn.	Dem.			191	31,275,166	Edmund S. Muskie	Me.	191
	George C. Wallace	Ala.	Am. Indpt.			45	9,906,473	Curtis E. LeMay	Cal.	45
1972	Richard M. Nixon	Cal.	Rep.	50	538	520‡	47,168,963	Spiro T. Agnew	Md.	520‡
	George S. McGovern	S. D.	Dem.			17	29,169,615	Sargent Shriver	Md.	17
	John G. Schmitz	Cal.	Am. Indpt.				1,080,541	Thomas J. Anderson	Tenn.	
1976	Jimmy Carter	Ga.	Dem.	50	538	297	40,828,587	Walter F. Mondale	Minn.	297
	Gerald R. Ford	Mich.	Rep.			240‡	39,147,613	Robert Dole	Kans.	241
	Eugene J. McCarthy	Minn.	Indpt.				751,728	William Clay Ford	Mich.	

* One elector pledged to vote for the Democratic candidate voted for a noncandidate.   † Fourteen unpledged electors voted for a noncandidate.   ‡ One elector pledged to vote for the Republican candidate voted for a noncandidate.

WORLD GOVERNMENTS

THIS section on World Governments comprises the accounts of all independent states, other than the United States of America, which are recognized as possessing "sovereignty." The usual test of sovereignty is the recognized conduct of foreign affairs through fully accredited diplomatic agents. Nearly all sovereign states are members of the United Nations, but such membership is not a test of sovereignty. Some old and powerful nations are not members, and some constituent republics of the Soviet Union are members.

Earlier Forms of Government. The earliest form of political organization goes back to the tribe, which itself is an extended form of the family. The chief held absolute power. When hunting as the means of subsistence gave way to agriculture and husbandry, it was possible to store the means of subsistence, initially in the form of grain, cattle, and land. These constituted wealth, and usually the control of wealth spells power. Cities then for the first time became possible with a multitude of new activities—industry, trade, better weapons, and organized armies. Writing was invented initially to keep records of wealth but soon was utilized to strengthen control by the more powerful. Kings succeeded chiefs of the earlier tribal ages. More powerful cities extended their power over their weaker neighbors, thus creating empires which rose and fell with the fortunes of war. The king held power of life and death over his subjects and, in general, was the source of all law. Such was the picture in the parts of the world where the early civilizations arose on the Nile and the Tigris. These spread through southwestern Asia and northeastern Africa and made their way into southeastern Europe over a period of several thousand years.

Toward the Modern Age. Beginning in the 5th century B.C., came a so-called Golden Age. In the city states of Greece, the power of the kings was first broken, authority was shared by wider groups, and ultimately resided in the ordinary citizen in the leading cities of the Greek world. In the same general period, Rome developed a constitutional system which, while less radically democratic than that of Greece, was better able to perpetuate itself. Political ideas from the two peoples, gaining prestige with the Roman conquest of Greece and most of the rest of the then known world, established the forms and much of the vocabulary of government which prevails today.

Actually, there was an "iron-age" interlude between the period of Greco-Roman political thought and practice and that of the modern world. The Roman empire was succeeded by over a thousand years of a resurgent feudalism, which in turn was succeeded by a period of absolute monarchies. Cities again grew up, and the earlier evolution from absolutism to democracy was essentially repeated in Europe from the 16th to the 19th century.

As intimated above, our language of government is dominated by words which have come down from Greece and Rome. From Greece, for example, we have the terms monarchy (rule by one person), aristocracy (rule by the upper class), and democracy (rule by the common people). From Rome the terms republic (rule by elected officials under constitutional forms), empire (wide-spread control through military strength), and senate (legislative body originally of more experienced citizens).

Realities Behind the Forms. In seeking to understand the nature of the government of any country, it is necessary to look behind the terms used to describe them. There are several reasons for this.

First, many governments have evolved from one type to another without changing the language describing them. For example, Great Britain and Sweden are monarchies, but real control lies, not with the monarch, but with the ordinary citizen; these countries are no less democratic than many other democracies and much more so than many governments which are called democracies.

Second, many so-called democracies are so designated because of what their leaders hope they will become rather than because of what they are. For example, some newly independent African countries call themselves democratic republics even though they may still be ruled by an oligarchy of tribal chieftains or by a dictator. In practice, their ruler may ignore the constitutional forms which were based on ideas learned from democratic European states or from the United States of America.

Third, the 20th century has witnessed the rise of a number of governments which have democratic republican constitutions but which operate their institutions by means of one party, and the party is governed by rules entirely outside the constitution. This party manipulates the institutions so that the ordinary citizen has no effective choice in selecting his rulers. Russia and China are outstanding examples.

It thus appears that, while the constitutions are the forms of government, the way a nation is actually governed depends on the experience and character of the people who rule and are ruled. A people which, over a long period of time, has developed the habit of individual liberty tempered by self-restraint in respecting the liberty of fellow citizens can govern itself well even under a constitution which does not guarantee civil rights, whereas a people without such a habit of liberty is apt to be governed tyrannically despite an elaborate bill of rights in its constitution. Canada, for example, has no bill of rights in its fundamental law, apparently not having felt the need for a formal guarantee of what was customarily enjoyed. A recent law corrects the oversight. On the other hand, the Russian constitution has an elaborate bill of rights, which serves as a hope rather than a reality.

It may be said that, at best, constitutions show the legal framework within which a country is actually governed and that, at worst, they set up a legal standard which hopefully may some day be attained.

Present-Day Status of Nations. The 20th century has witnessed a vast expansion in the number of independent nations. In 1907, 48 states were invited to send representatives to the Second Hague Conference, and this was considered the number of the "family of nations" at that time. The number of nations was increased by World War I. Following World War II, there were, in 1951, 60 members of the United Nations, with over a dozen others awaiting admission or which chose not to be members. The next two decades saw an unexampled proliferation of states as the peoples of Asia and Africa threw off the political yoke of their former masters.

This section contains accounts of the governments of more than one hundred states. Three of these states have two governments each—China, Germany, and Korea—and each claims that it alone is able to represent the entire country. A description of both governments is given in each such case. Summaries indicate the time and manner in which each state became independent and set forth the main points in its formal framework of government based on an examination of the constitution. Where the realities of government differ markedly from its form, this also is indicated. The reader is enabled thereby to understand better the day-to-day political happenings in these states, the importance of which, in today's closely knit world, readily overleaps national boundaries and affects the interests of all.

AFGHANISTAN

ANDORRA

From the time it was unified by invaders from Iran in the 18th century, Afghanistan was a kingdom. In 1922 a constitution added a parliament consisting of a senate and a national assembly, both with limited powers. The constitution of 1965 established the full constitutional monarchy. Then, in 1973, a coup by the army deposed the king. A military committee declared a republic and elected its leader president. In the absence of a constitution, government was by presidential decree.

Afghanistan forms a mountain barrier between Russia and India. Invaders such as Alexander the Great and Tamurlane crossed the region to conquer India. The defense of the Khyber Pass, called the gateway to Asia, was long regarded as the major task of Indian and British armies.

Following wars in 1839 and 1842, British-Afghan relations were governed by treaty. The war of 1880 led to British control of Afghan foreign relations. British and Russian rival interests were adjusted in 1907 by a treaty that also defined their interests in Iran and Tibet. In 1918 the treaty was denounced by the Soviet regime. A British mission then effected a treaty in 1921 restoring British predominance. After World War II and the independence of India, Afghanistan followed a neutral policy between the conflicting interests of the East and West.

ALBANIA

Ruled for 450 years by the Turks, Albania was set up as an independent state in 1912 but was conquered by Italy and Germany in World War II. On their defeat, Albania again became independent in 1945, when the Albanian Labor Party, a branch of the Communist party, established Albania as a people's republic. The ruling body both of the state and the party is the Politburo, with 11 full members and 4 candidate members. In addition, there is a People's Assembly of deputies, one for each 8000 inhabitants, elected for 4-year terms, the candidates are selected by the party. In the rift between Russia and China in the 1960s, Albania sided with China.

ALGERIA

After 132 years of French rule, Algeria became an independent republic in July 1962. A national assembly met in September and elected Ferhat Abbas president and Ben Bella prime minister. A constitution was issued in 1963. It provided for a one-party (the National Liberation Front) government. Also in 1963, a national assembly elected for 5 years by universal vote, with candidates designated by the National Liberation Front. The party also designated a candidate for president of the republic, to be elected by popular vote. The assembly, led by its president and cabinet, was to pass legislation. If the assembly censured the policy of the president of the republic, the assembly's president could take over the latter's duties. In the 1963 national elections, Ben Bella, the sole candidate, was elected president of the Democratic People's Republic of Algeria.

In 1965 a military coup, led by Col. Houari Boumedienne, overthrew the government and set up a revolutionary council with Boumedienne as the head. The constitution of 1963 was suspended.

A new constitution, approved in 1976, provided for a national assembly to be elected every five years and a president with a renewable six-year term. The president would be head of state, commander in chief of the armed forces, and head of national defense and would have the authority to appoint a vice president and prime minister.

Boumedienne was reelected in 1976 and a 261-member national assembly was elected in 1977.

A small, neutral "republic" on the Franco-Spanish frontier. It is a surviving specimen of the semi-independence of feudal lordship, possessed in medieval times by many valleys of these mountains. It is governed by a council of 24 members elected for 4 years by men over 25 years old. A first and a second "syndic" are chosen by the council as presiding officers and executives of the republic. The state is under the joint suzerainty of the Spanish bishop of Urgel and the president of France, as successor to the Bourbon kings. Andorra pays nominal tribute to France and to the bishop.

ANGOLA

Angola is an independent country—bounded by Zaire, Zambia, and South West Africa—on the Atlantic coast in the Congo region. The area was discovered in 1482 and was the site of the first European colonies in Africa. The Portuguese settled the region in 1491 and founded Luanda as their main city in 1575. Portuguese rule continued for nearly five centuries. The spread of black African nationalism led to guerrilla warfare in Angola in 1961. Facing its own internal problems, Portugal declared Angola autonomous in 1972, but the fighting there continued through the revolution in Portugal in 1974. On January 15, 1975, the three competing Angolan liberation groups signed an agreement under which Angola, the last major European colony in Africa, would gain independence on November 11. Terms calling for a temporary coalition in Luanda proved ineffective as civil war raged in 1975 among the rival factions. Two distinct governments were formed. In Luanda, the Popular Movement declared its leader, Agostinho Neto, president. The other two factions, the National Front and the Union for Independence, announced their own joint government. With Soviet aid and troops from Cuba, Neto's group assumed military control. On February 11, 1976, the People's Republic of Angola under Neto was admitted to the Organization of African Unity as its 47th member. Other countries, including the nine nations of the European Community, also recognized Neto's government. Yet with internal problems and wide unrest, guerrilla warfare in the new nation continued.

ARGENTINA

Argentina arose out of the Spanish viceroyalty of La Plata. In 1816 a congress at Tucuman proclaimed the Argentinian provinces an independent republic; but, the union was weak and years of anarchy followed. Juan Manuel de Rosas became dictator in 1835; he governed until 1852. The Argentine Republic was formed in 1853 and a constitution was issued. A new constitution was drafted in 1949 by the Peron government. Juan Peron had become president in 1946. He remained president until he was deposed in 1955. While in exile Peron maintained his influence in Argentina, and in 1973 he was reelected president, with his wife as vice president. Isabel Peron became president after her husband's death in 1974. She was deposed in 1976 by a military junta, and Jorge Rafael Videla assumed the presidency.

The present constitution, adopted in 1957, follows generally the liberal constitution of 1853 but gives the central government greater control over the economy. It resembles the constitution of the U.S., particularly in its union of the provinces of the country into a federal republic. These provinces are 22, besides one federal district, Buenos Aires. The provinces, like the American states, elect their own legislatures and governors and have jurisdiction over provincial affairs. Powers not granted to the nation are retained by the provinces, but the federal government has more powers than those granted by the U.S. constitution.

Executive Organization. Under the theory of separation of powers, the federal government is divided into executive, legislative, and judicial departments. Executive authority is conferred on a president, who occupies the position of an independent executive.

In addition to the usual powers of an American executive, the president of Argentina makes all appointments to federal offices without the limitation of senatorial confirmation, except in the appointment of magistrates of courts, diplomatic representatives, and higher officers of the army, where the advice and consent of the senate are required.

The Congress. The federal legislative authority is vested in a congress composed of a senate and a chamber of deputies, which meet in regular session annually beginning on May 1. The 46 senators are elected by the legislatures of the 22 provinces and by a special body of electors in the federal district.

Deputies are elected by the people in electoral districts of 85,000 inhabitants or a major fraction thereof each, with a minimum of 2 for each province. The term is 4 years, half of the chamber being renewed every 2 years.

AUSTRALIA

By the end of World War II Australia had become an economically successful industrialized nation, with a greater importance in international relations. The Labor government, in power from 1941 to 1949, had enacted broad welfare legislation. The population had increased more than 60 per cent since the war, mostly through government-encouraged immigration. After 23 years of Liberal-Country government, marked chiefly by anti-Communist internal and foreign policies, together with a closer alliance with the U.S., the Labor party came to power again in 1972. Under Prime Minister Edward Gough Whitlam, the government ended the military draft, withdrew forces from Vietnam, established ties with Asian nations including Communist China, ended the death penalty, set the voting age at 18, and established representation for aborigines. However, inflation at 20 per cent a year, unemployment higher than in depression years, and government problems including cabinet-level scandals, brought Australia its worst crisis in history. In November 1975, the governor general removed Whitlam from office—the first time the crown had ever removed an elected prime minister. Whitlam was replaced by John Fraser, heading a Liberal-Country care-taker government. In the following December elections, Fraser won the greatest coalition majority in Australia's history.

AUSTRIA

Following World War I the dual monarchy of Austria-Hungary was dismembered by the Treaty of Versailles into Austria, Czechoslovakia, Hungary, and Yugoslavia. In 1918 Austria became a republic and continued as an independent state until forcibly annexed by the German Reich in 1938. After the liberation of Austria by the Allies in 1945, the republic was reestablished but, the country was under occupation by the United States, Britain, France, and the U.S.S.R. until May 1955.

Under its constitution of 1945, Austria is a federal republic with some features of a parliamentary democracy. The president is elected for a 6-year term by universal suffrage, voting being compulsory. He may serve a maximum of 2 terms. He appoints the chancellor and, with the latter's recommendations, the other ministers, who may not be members of the assembly. The national assembly is elected for a 4-year term by universal suffrage. The senate

is chosen by the state legislatures by proportional representation as to parties.

AZORES

The Azores, an archipelago of 3 island groups, is in the North Atlantic Ocean approximately 900 miles west of Portugal. Under the constitution of 1832, the islands were grouped into 3 administrative districts, which were later granted limited autonomous administration. In the free elections for the Portuguese constituent assembly (April 25, 1975), Azoreans voted overwhelmingly for the Popular Democratic and Socialist parties, giving the Communists only 2 per cent of their vote. Resistance toward the leftist central government in Lisbon appeared soon after the Popular Democrats and Socialists withdrew from the Lisbon government. A small independence movement, the Azores Liberation Front (FLA), arose in opposition to a Communist takeover in Lisbon and announced the establishment of a government in exile. In August 1975, the Lisbon government established a governing commission (the general junta) for the entire archipelago. A transitional legislation was to be enacted until the constituent assembly in Lisbon could draft a new constitution. While the FLA and many Azoreans favored complete independence from Portugal, the Lisbon government planned to grant the islands greater regional autonomy with an elected assembly of deputies. Regional elections in the Azores were held on June 27, 1976, with the Popular Democrats, who supported broad autonomy, earning a decisive victory. Nevertheless, the newly appointed president of Portugal warned against the secessionist movement.

BAHAMAS

The Bahamas became independent in 1973, ending three centuries of British rule. Of the 700 islands in the group, 30 are populated. The capital is Nassau, on the island of New Providence. Under the new constitution, power rests in the prime minister, senate, and house of assembly. The Bahamas became the 33rd member of the Commonwealth of Nations and a member of the UN in 1973.

BAHRAIN

The Arab sheikhdom of Bahrain, an archipelago in the Persian Gulf, was long a British protectorate. This ended with a treaty of friendship with Britain in 1971. The Arab dynasty had been in power since 1782. A council of state was formed in 1970 to administer the country; the council was replaced in 1971 by a cabinet. In 1972 a constituent assembly drafted a constitution, which was issued the following year. A national assembly with a 4-year term met in 1974. The head of state is the hereditary emir, or sheikh. Bahrain joined the UN in 1971. Its largest city and capital is Manama.

BANGLADESH

This nation was formerly the eastern province of Pakistan. It achieved independence in 1971 and became known as the People's Republic of Bangladesh. Under the constitution of 1972 the president is directly elected for 5-year terms. The legislature is a one-chamber national assembly of 300 members directly elected for 5-year terms by citizens over 18. For the first 10 years of the republic 15 extra women members will be elected by parliament to the national assembly. The country has been under martial law since a coup in 1975.

BARBADOS

An island in the Caribbean, Barbados is an independent democracy within the Commonwealth.

The head of state is the sovereign of England, represented by a governor-general. The head of government is the prime minister. Parliament, a bicameral legislative body, has a house of assembly, with 24 members elected popularly for 5-year terms, and a senate of 21 members, 12 appointed by the governor-general on the prime minister's recommendation, 2 on the advice of the opposition, and 7 as representatives of various social and racial groups. Barbados became independent and joined the United Nations in 1966.

BELGIUM

In its present form, Belgium was established in 1830 under a guarantee of neutrality by Austria, Russia, Britain, and Prussia. By the constitution, leadership of the state is vested in the king. While the government is conducted by ministers responsible to Parliament, the king exerts large influence on national policy. He may convoke, prorogue, and dissolve Parliament. Parliament consists of a Chamber of Deputies and a Senate. The Chamber of Deputies is composed of 212 members but not more than one to each 40,000 population. They sit for 4 years.

The provinces, representing one-time separate principalities, have a considerable degree of autonomy which is recognized by the constitution. Each has a provincial assembly chosen by the qualified electorate. The head of the provincial administration is a governor, appointed by the king.

The real Belgian local autonomy, however, is expressed in the "communes," the towns. In the Belgian kingdom, there are some 2672 communes. They are governed according to a common plan and are under one municipal law.

The Belgian nation is composed of two distinct European peoples, the Flemish and the Walloons. The Flemish occupy the northern portion of Belgium; in speech (Flamand) and in physical appearance they are akin to the Dutch. The Walloons are a darker, less phlegmatic race who speak French.

BELIZE

Belize, formerly British Honduras, is located on the Caribbean coast of Central America, bordered by Mexico and Guatemala. A new constitution was drawn up in 1954, and a nationalist group came to power. The constitution of 1961 called for extended autonomy; full internal self-government was achieved on January 1, 1964. Universal suffrage was granted to those over 21. The colony has since pushed to achieve gradual independence from British rule. Unfortunately, increased border disputes with Guatemala, which claims the territory, have prevented Great Britain from granting Belize independence. On December 8, 1975, the UN General Assembly passed a resolution sponsored by Britain and some 60 other nations calling for Belize's right to self-determination and independence, and for the preservation of the colony's territorial integrity.

In 1970 Belmopan was built as the new capital and seat of government. The country's name was changed to Belize on June 1, 1973. The government consists of a 2-chamber national assembly with an 18-member house of representatives elected by universal adult vote and an appointed senate of 8 members. The cabinet is headed by the premier. The cabinet and premier, who exercise executive power, are responsible to the legislature, which can remove them through votes of no confidence. Cabinet ministers are members of the majority political party and hold seats in the national assembly concurrent with their cabinet posts. Elections are held at least every 5 years. A British crown-appointed governor is responsible for defense, foreign affairs, security, and civil service employment.

Members of an independent judiciary also are appointed by the British crown.

BENIN (DAHOMEY)

Benin has been under French influence since the mid-19th century, as a kingdom and later as the French colony of Dahomey. Self-governing since 1958, it achieved full independence on August 1, 1960. Five military coups, interspersed with short-lived civilian regimes, followed. After the fifth coup, on October 26, 1972, Major Mathieu Kerekou established military control. He abolished the presidential council and the assembly. In December 1974 President Kerekou declared Dahomey a "Marxist-Lenin State," and began nationalizing banks, oil companies, and other businesses. On November 30, 1975, the name of the country was changed to Benin.

The president, assisted by a council of ministers, directs the country. A 67-member national council provides policy direction. The central government administers the country through department heads and prefects appointed by the president. The judicial system, based on the French code, is headed by a supreme court. Local courts administer either African tribal law or Moslem law. A member of the Organization of African Unity, Benin joined the UN in 1960.

BHUTAN

A constitutional monarchy since it gained independence in 1949, this Buddhist kingdom in the eastern Himalayas is guided in foreign relations by India. The king's subjects may dismiss him by a vote of no confidence, and he would be replaced by the next in line of royal succession. The king rules with 3 ministers and must maintain the confidence of the assembly, a unicameral body of 140–200 members nominated by the villages for 3-year terms.

BOLIVIA

The revolution against Spain was initiated 1809–10 in the territory of Bolivia, then known as Upper Peru. After independence in 1824, the Bolivians met with representatives of Argentina to determine whether or not they would join that country. They unanimously voted to remain a separate nation under the style of the "Republic of Bolivia," the name being taken from Simon Bolivar, liberator of South America. The independence of the republic was proclaimed on August 26, 1825. The territory claimed for the new republic was that which, under Spanish authority, was subject to the Audiencia of Charcas.

Bolivia has experienced many constitutional changes—1829, 1831, 1834, 1836 (a confederation with Peru, dissolved in 1839), 1841, 1843, 1851, 1861, 1880. In 1964 a constitution of 1961 was abrogated in favor of an earlier constitution of 1947. A new constitution was adopted in 1967. In 1969 military rule was established and the national congress dissolved. The country presently is being ruled by presidential decree.

BOTSWANA

The British protectorate of Bechuanaland became the independent African Republic of Botswana in 1966. A constitutional democracy, its chief of state is the president, who also is chief executive and commander-in-chief of the armed forces. The present constitution, effective as of 1965, provides for a national assembly of 36 members—32 elected directly, 4 appointed by the president and attorney general. An advisory house of chiefs consists of 8 principal chiefs and 4 subchiefs. Botswana is a member of the British Commonwealth.

BRAZIL

The United States of Brazil is a federal republic, comparable in area to the U.S. It was a dependency of Portugal from the time of its discovery in 1500 until 1822, except for a period of 60 years, 1581-1640, during which Portugal was united to Spain.

Brazil was the seat of the Portuguese government and the residence of the royal family from 1807 to 1821. On the return of the Portuguese royal family to Portugal, a national congress assembled in Brazil and chose Pedro, the king's son, as "Perpetual Defender of Brazil." In the same year, Pedro proclaimed the independence of Brazil and was chosen constitutional emperor. Brazil remained an empire until 1889, when Pedro II was dethroned and the imperial family was exiled. The decree of banishment against the family was repealed August 6, 1920.

The Republic. A republican constitution bearing a close resemblance to the U.S. Constitution was adopted in 1891. It was in effect until 1930, when the union was saved at the cost of civil war. A new constitution was adopted in 1934, the chief alteration being the large powers granted to the federal government to control economic activities. These powers included the right to regulate industry, to nationalize banks and insurance companies, and to take over any industry, subject to payment of compensation. The constitution was altered again for greater centralization in 1937 and in 1946. A revision of the constitution in 1969 granted the president almost absolute power.

The union is divided into 22 states, a federal district, and 4 federal territories. Each state is self-governing with its own constitution, legislature, and judicial system.

By the constitution of 1969, the president and vice-president are elected to 5-year terms by an electoral college of members from the national congress and delegates from the state legislatures. The president appoints state governors and city mayors. Under the "institutional act" written into the 1969 constitution, the president may revoke the rights of citizens and recess congress.

There are 17 departments of government: agriculture, air, army, communications, education, finance, foreign affairs, health, industry and commerce, interior, justice, labor, mines and energy, navy, transportation and public works, and welfare and social security.

The legislative branch consists of a senate and a chamber of deputies, both of which are elected by compulsory vote of literate citizens over 18. The senate has 66 members—3 from each state, elected to 8-year terms. The chamber of deputies is composed of 1 deputy for each 300,000 inhabitants, with a minimum of 7 per state and 1 per territory. They are elected to 4-year terms.

The judicial system consists of a supreme court, whose justices are appointed by the president and approved by the Senate; federal courts; federal courts of appeal; and special courts which handle military, labor, and electoral cases. The state judicial system resembles the federal system.

Frontier Settlements. The frontiers of Brazil adjoin the territory of every other South American state except Ecuador and Chile. Boundary disputes with the Guianas were settled by negotiation and arbitration in 1901, 1904, and 1906.

The boundary between Brazil and Venezuela was settled in 1905, after a long period of negotiations, and the demarcation was made by a mixed commission in 1914. In 1872, Brazil and Paraguay signed a treaty whereby the title to Brazilian territory north of the Rio Apa was determined. The boundary with Argentina was settled by an arbitral decision by the president of the United States in 1895. The Brazilian contention was sustained. A remaining boundary difficulty between Brazil, Peru, and Colombia was settled by agreement at Washington, March 4, 1925.

In boundary negotiations with Uruguay, Brazil, by a treaty of 1851, secured rich territory that, by a treaty of 1777, had been admitted to belong to Spain. In this case, as in others, Brazil was able to acquire territories beyond those fixed during the period of Spanish domination. Thus, by means of a series of remarkable negotiations and awards, there was ended the long competition between Spain and Portugal that began in 1493, when the bull of Pope Alexander divided between those two countries the discovery and the conquest of the world.

BULGARIA

Bulgaria, long a subject territory of Turkey, obtained autonomy in 1878 by the Treaty of Berlin, which ended the Russo-Turkish War. In 1885 Rumelia, the Bulgar-inhabited province south of the Balkan Mountains, obtained union with Bulgaria. In 1908, during a revolution in Istanbul, Bulgaria declared complete independence, and its reigning prince, Ferdinand, of the house of Saxe-Coburg-Gotha, proclaimed himself king of the Bulgarians. By the second Balkan War, 1913, Bulgaria lost territory to Rumania. In World War I it suffered further losses, but by treaty in 1924 regained an outlet to the Aegean. After World War II it retained the southern Dobruja, ceded by Rumania in 1940.

The first constitution of Bulgaria was adopted in 1879, and amended in 1893 and in 1911. At the end of World War II, Bulgaria, which had joined the Axis powers, was at the mercy of Russia. The monarchy was abolished by popular vote, and a constitutional convention set up a people's republic under a constitution of 1947.

A new constitution was adopted in 1971. Under it a single-chamber national assembly is elected to a 5-year term by direct universal vote of citizens over 18. All candidates, however, are nominated by the Fatherland Front, of which the executive body, or politburo, exercises the ultimate power in the state although it is not mentioned in the constitution. The assembly elects the council of state, which is the highest organ of the state.

BURMA

Under British influence or rule since about 1610, the Union of Burma became an independent republic in 1948 following a 1947 treaty with Britain. All ties with the British Commonwealth were severed.

A constitution was adopted providing for a president with a term of five years. The president was elected by the parliament, consisting of a chamber of deputies and a chamber of nationalities. The supreme court was the court of final appeal. Its members were appointed by the president with the approval of parliament.

Constitutional rule was suspended by the military during 1958–60 and again in 1962. General Ne Win overthrew the elected government of U Nu, replacing it with a revolutionary council. The parliament and state councils were dissolved. A new constitution was approved by referendum in 1973. Military control was ended in 1974 and Burma became a single-party socialist republic. Elections to the new people's assembly were held and Ne Win became president. The assembly then elected a council of ministers for foreign and national affairs.

BURUNDI

German military occupation ended in Burundi in 1919 when Burundi became part of the UN territory Ruanda-Urundi administered by Belgium. Burundi was granted independence in 1962, and in 1966, following 51 years of monarch rule, Burundi was declared a republic. In 1974 the country's first constitution was approved. Its provisions include a one-party system. The party defines and controls the actions of the government and judiciary. The party's leader, the secretary-general, is elected by the absolute majority of the party's national congress. He is president and prime minister for a renewable 7-year term. The president appoints and dismisses ministers and defines their duties. Legislative power is vested in the president; all members of government are responsible to him. The president also is commander of the armed forces. The social and economic development of the republic and its citizens is controlled by the government.

Burundi is bounded on the east and southeast by Tanzania, on the north by Rwanda, on the west by Zaire, and on the southwest by Lake Tanganyika.

CAMBODIA

Cambodia was under French rule and protection from 1863 until 1953, when a constitutional monarchy led by Prince Sihanouk was formed. Growing civil strife was fed by economic difficulties, Communist guerrilla infiltration, and increasing involvement with the Vietnam war. In 1970 Sihanouk was deposed in a bloodless coup by pro-Western General Lon Nol; the Kingdom of Cambodia became the Khmer Republic under a new constitution. The next five years were marked by intensified insurgent activity by the Khmer Rouge (Communist-supported) factions led by Khieu Samphan and joined by pro-nationalist supporters of Sihanouk. The Khmer Republic fell and Lon Nol fled in April 1975. The Khmer Rouge, using Sihanouk as titular head, approved a new constitution in late 1975 and held a national election in March 1976, forming a 250-member national congress. Kieu Samphan was named chief of state. Despite the constitutional election, Cambodia has been listed among the "not free" nations of the world.

CAMEROON

This republic is a federation dating from 1961, formed by two provinces, East Cameroon and West Cameroon. In 1972, by national referendum, the United Republic of Cameroon was proclaimed.

The constitution provides for a president as head of state. The president is assisted by a cabinet of 24 ministers and 4 deputy ministers. The 120-member national assembly consists of representatives from East Cameroon and from West Cameroon. The first federal elections took place in 1964. The president is nominated by a congress of the republic's only political party and is elected for a 5-year term. In 1975 the position of a prime minister responsible to the president was established. In 1976 Cameroon was described as "partly free."

CANADA

Canada was originally a French settlement ceded to England in 1763. The portion colonized by the French, known as Lower Canada, and Ontario, or Upper Canada, which was inhabited by British settlers, were united in 1867 with two other British colonies—Nova Scotia and New Brunswick—to form the Dominion of Canada. To this union were subsequently admitted, as provinces of the federation, Manitoba (1870), British Columbia (1871), Prince Edward Island (1873), Alberta and Saskatchewan (1905), and Newfoundland (1949). The Yukon and Northwest Territories are governed by commissioners appointed by the federal government.

The early British colonial policy in America was to reserve executive power to a proprietary, or royal, governor, while granting local legislative power to a representative assembly. The laws of the colonies were subject to the approval of the governor and of the home government. After the separation of the colonies composing the United States, the desire for self-government in Canada led to continuous difficulty with the royal governors and even to local rebellion. In 1838, when political relations in Canada had reached a deadlock, the British government sent out a commission of inquiry headed by Lord Durham, who recommended the recognition of self-government in the Canadian colonies and the formation, in each colony, of a ministry that would be politically responsible for the legislature and not to the British government. This principle was adopted. The governor, or representative appointed by the British crown, became the nominal representative of imperial authority, while a "premier" responsible to the local Parliament became the actual head of government.

When 4 colonies confederated in 1867, a form of government was established by the British North America act, which, with many amendments, forms the basis of the Canadian constitution. The constitution does not exist as a formal document. It includes much which is not in the original act and its amendments, such as the role of the cabinet based on custom and a bill of rights, adopted by the Canadian Parliament as a law in 1960. The most important amendment of the basic British act was the Westminster statute of 1931, which provides that the British Parliament may not legislate for Canada except on the specific authorization of the Canadian Parliament. A law of 1947 created Canadian citizenship; previously Canadians had been known as British subjects. Queen Elizabeth II of Great Britain was declared queen of Canada by Canadian law.

Federal and Provincial Powers. The following subjects are specifically enumerated as reserved to the national Parliament:

Amendment of the constitution, except regarding legislative authority of the provinces, schools, use of French and English languages, and duration of Parliament.
The public debt and property.
The regulation of trade and commerce.
The raising of money by any mode or system of taxation.
The borrowing of money on the public credit.
Postal service.
The census statistics.
Militia, military and naval service, and defense.
The fixing of, and providing for, the salaries and allowances of civil and other officers of the government of Canada.
Beacons, buoys, lighthouses, and Sable Island.
Navigation and shipping.
Quarantine, and the establishment and maintenance of marine hospitals.
Seacoast and inland fisheries.
Ferries between a province and any British or foreign country, or between two provinces.
Currency and coinage.
Banking, incorporation of banks, and the issue of paper money.
Savings banks.
Weights and measures.
Bills of exchange and promissory notes.
Interest.
Legal tender.
Bankruptcy and insolvency.
Patents of invention and discovery.
Copyrights.
Indians and lands reserved for the Indians.
Naturalization and aliens.
Marriage and divorce.
The criminal law, except the constitution of courts of criminal jurisdiction, but including the procedure in criminal matters.
The establishment, maintenance, and management of penitentiaries.
Such classes of subjects as are expressly reserved from the provincial legislatures.

The powers expressly bestowed upon the provincial legislatures are as follows:

The amendment of the provincial constitution, except as regards the office of the lieutenant governor.
Direct taxation for provincial purposes.
Borrowing of money on sole credit of the province.
The organization of the provincial administration.
The management or sale of provincial lands.
Reformatory prisons.
Hospitals, asylums, and charitable institutions other than marine hospitals.
Municipal institutions.
Local excises.
Provincial works, including railways, canals, telegraph systems, shipping lines.
The incorporation of stock companies.
Solemnization of marriage.
Definition of property and civil rights within the province.
Administration of justice, including provincial courts.
Imposition of punishments for enforcing provincial laws.
In general, all matters of a merely local nature.

Both the federal and provincial governments may legislate on immigration, education, and social welfare. However, an attempt to restrict oriental immigration by British Columbia was invalidated by the national government. The organic law permits the provinces to conduct education but provides also for protection of the educational rights of minorities in the different provinces.

Governor-General. The crown is represented in Canada by a governor-general, a Canadian citizen chosen by the crown on the advice of the prime minister. Originally, the governor-general was assisted by a privy council, chosen from the royal family, former prime ministers and other high officials, and the current cabinet. The privy council, however, never meets but its function is carried on by the cabinet, which is responsible to the House of Commons. The term of the governor-general is not fixed but usually lasts from 4 to 7 years.

Parliament. The federal Parliament consists of two houses—a Senate and a House of Commons. A senator must be at least 30 years of age, a natural born or naturalized Canadian subject, possess at least $4,000 in excess of liabilities, be a resident of the province for which he is appointed, and, in the case of Quebec, he must either be a resident of the district which he represents or hold the qualifying amount of real property therein. Senators are nominated for life by the governor-general, but their actual selection rests with the Canadian prime minister. The Senate consists of 104 members, 24 from Ontario, 24 from Quebec, 10 from Nova Scotia, 10 from New Brunswick, 4 from Prince Edward Island, 1 from the Yukon Territory, 1 from the Northwest Territories and 6 from each of the following: Manitoba, British Columbia, Alberta, Saskatchewan, Newfoundland. The total number may not exceed 104.

The House of Commons consists of 264 members elected by universal suffrage from the provinces roughly in proportion to their populations. Its term is 5 years unless it is dissolved earlier. When it first meets, the leader of the dominant party assumes the office of prime minister, while the leader of the other or next strongest party is the leader of the opposition. The prime minister chooses a cabinet of 15 to 30 ministers, practically always from the House but not necessarily so. If the prime minister is defeated on a crucial issue in the House, he may resign or advise the governor-general to dissolve the House. The governor-general may persuade him or the leader of another party to attempt to form a cabinet having the confidence of the House, or he may dissolve the House and call for a new election.

Legislation. Bills originate in either house, except finance bills, which may originate only in the House of Commons. The Senate may reject a finance bill but not amend it. Most bills are initiated by the House. While the position of a senator is a highly privileged one, senators have never played a political role comparable to that of the members of the House of Commons and are seldom offered seats in the cabinet.

Courts. Judges in Canada are appointed and paid by the federal government to hold office for life or during good behavior. The supreme court of Canada receives appeals from the provincial courts and questions may be referred to it by the governor-general in council. A ruling may thereby be obtained on the constitutionality of any law without the delay and expense of litigation. Judgments of the supreme court are final. Policing powers throughout the entire nation are in the hands of the Royal Canadian Mounted Police.

Provincial Governments. The powers of provincial governments have already been noted. Each of the nine provinces has its own parliament and administration. With the exception of Quebec, the legislature consists of a single chamber. A lieutenant governor, appointed by the governor-general, represents the federal union, but actual government is in the hands of a premier and provincial ministers responsible to the provincial parliament.

CAPE VERDE ISLANDS

The Cape Verde Islands, an independent island republic, is an archipelago of 10 islands and 5 islets in the Atlantic Ocean some 400 miles west of Africa. The former Portuguese colony was made an overseas province in 1951. During the 1960s nationalist movements opposed Portuguese control. Following continued fighting and demonstrations, Portugal promised to grant Cape Verde independence. A transitional government was established on December 30, 1974.

The Cape Verde Islands became independent on July 5, 1975, ending over 500 years of Portuguese rule. The newly elected national assembly, which was to write the nation's constitution, chose a president and premier for the parliamentary republic. The U.S. extended recognition to Africa's 44th independent nation. Cape Verde established diplomatic relations with the U.S.S.R. and China; became a member of the Organization of African Unity on July 18, 1975; and was granted full membership to the UN General Assembly on September 16, 1975.

CENTRAL AFRICAN EMPIRE

This country was organized by France as a territory in 1894 and became an independent republic in 1960, remaining within the French Community. In December 1976 Jean-Bedel Bokassa, president-for-life, declared that the republic would become an empire ruled by a parliamentary monarchy, and that he would be known as Emperor Bokassa I. The Central African Empire is a member of the UN.

CHAD

Chad was part of French Equatorial Africa until 1960 when it became an independent republic, remaining within the French Community. Relations with France, however, have been strained. Chad did not attend the three French-African conferences (1973, 1974, 1975) and, in October 1975, following an order from the Chadian government, French troops were removed. The withdrawal ended 78 years of French military presence in Chad. In April 1975 President Tombalbaye was killed during a military coup. The constitution was suspended and the civilian government replaced by a nine-member military council with a president (Felix Malloum) and a vice president. The council established four commissions to supervise all government functions. The commissions covered control of financial matters, revision of the statutes of public service, economic and social services, and a military commission. There was an assassination attempt on President Malloum in 1976 on the first anniversary of the coup.

Chad was admitted to the UN in 1960. It is in northern Africa, bordered by Libya, Sudan, the

Central African Republic, Cameroon, Nigeria, and Niger.

CHILE

The republic of Chile arose from the Spanish captaincy-general of the same name. On September 18, 1810, the inhabitants of Chile deposed the Spanish authorities and created a provisional government. The Spanish fought to retain this province, and it was not until 1818 that Chile became free.

The Chilean constitution of 1833 was long the oldest constitution in force in South America. For decades a stable and effective government was maintained through the active participation in politics of an upper class strongly united by family associations. A new constitution came into effect in 1925, substantially altering the form of government and tending to vest more power in the president of the republic. The chief executive was elected by direct popular vote. Under the constitution of 1925 legislative power was vested in the congress, composed of a senate and a chamber of deputies.

After a military takeover in 1973, the national congress was dissolved although the constitution of 1925 is still basically in effect.

CHINA

Politically there are two Chinas—Mainland China, calling itself a people's republic, and the National Republic of China, occupying the island of Formosa (Taiwan).

China is the oldest political society in the world. The last imperial dynasty ruled from 1644 to 1911. Its emperors followed a policy of isolation from the rest of the world. They governed from Peking through a bureaucracy recruited through a competitive examination system, the governor of each province, while having wide powers, being subject to transfer or demotion at the word of the emperor. Within each province, authority was confided principally to direct magistrates, beneath whom the ancient social and family-oriented life of town and farming village functioned with a minimum of interference and with a maximum of individual freedom. Society was essentially democratic, there being no aristocracy beyond a few Manchu nobles and no privileged class except educated officialdom open to all. Caste was nonexistent.

This society was ill prepared to cope with a world in which isolation was no longer possible. The inexorable pressure of traders backed by governments with radically superior weapons forced concession of territories. The ferment of western ideas undermined the traditional bases of Chinese society. The dynasty fell and was succeeded in 1912 by a republic unable to function in the ensuing chaos created by rival "war lords," who were provincial governors maneuvering for power. In 1928, under the leadership of Chiang Kai-shek, the *Kuomintang* ("Nationalist party") established a government at Nanking. It was essentially a party government, in which the central executive committee of the party appointed the members of five councils to carry on the government. Three of these councils administered respectively the executive, legislative, and judicial functions. A fourth determined qualifications for holding public office, and the fifth exercised powers of impeachment and auditing. The head of the party was the president of the republic and commander of the army.

Russian trained Communists had controlled the party until Chiang Kai-shek expelled them by a bloody purge in 1927. But they continued to oppose the government, which was beset also by Japanese aggression before and during World War II. The Communists, under the leadership of Mao Tse-tung, obtained control of 5 northern provinces and, by dint of arms and promises of economic reforms, succeeded by 1949 in driving the nationalist government to Formosa, where its independence was protected by the United States.

The people's republic of China was proclaimed in September 1949. Mao Tse-tung, who had been the authoritative leader and theoretician of the Communist movement since 1938, was elected chairman of the new central committee. Mao began a program against corruption, waste, and bureaucracy. He issued a five-year plan providing for large-scale industrialization and collectivization of agriculture. A reign of terror against landlords and Kuomintang officials existed for several years. Under the constitution of 1954 Mao became the chairman of the people's republic of China and of the national defense council.

By 1956 about 83 per cent of all Chinese peasants were on collective farms. Mao had recognized as early as 1925 the potential role of the peasant in a cultural revolution. The farms were economic institutions under county administration. Economic conditions, however, did not improve—by 1957 there was so much criticism of the government's economic policies that Mao had to impose police rule. In 1958 he established communes under party control.

By his own request Mao was not reelected head of state in the 1959 elections, but he remained the government's chief policy planner and chairman of the Chinese Communist party. In 1966 Mao began an intense campaign (the Great Proletarian Cultural Revolution) to impose upon the people of China a disciplined society, under complete control of the party. He put a tight grip on art, literature, and culture, ending individual creativity. Mao taught the Chinese to be committed totally to the revolution and to China. He strongly opposed anyone with capitalist ideas. The revolution, which was marked by violence, ended in 1969 and was followed by a period of moderation.

Mao died in September 1976. Although he was not considered a great administrator, he was China's greatest leader. He had installed in the Chinese people a sense of pride and purpose, and he had helped to make China an emerging superpower.

Mao Tse-tung was one of the 12 founding members of the Chinese Communist party. Another member of this group, Chou En-lai, had become China's premier and minister of foreign affairs. He was Mao's chief of staff. He administered the government and tried to balance the party's two factions—the radicals and the moderates (pragmatists). He brought order to the economy after the cultural revolution of 1966, and he was the Chinese official responsible for reconciliation between the U.S. and China. Chou died in January 1976.

Communist China. Under a constitution adopted in 1954, the National People's Congress is the highest organ of state authority. It is composed of deputies elected for a 4-year term by provinces (one deputy for each 800,000 population), by cities directly under federal authority (one for each 100,000), by national minorities (150 deputies), by the armed forces (60 deputies), and by overseas Chinese (30 deputies). It has a permanent standing committee, which convenes the Congress, conducts elections, interprets the laws, adopts decrees, and supervises the work of the government, or state council. The highest judicial organ is the supreme people's court. The people's procurator-general's office has the responsibility of seeing that the laws are strictly observed by government institutions and officials. All judges serve for 4-year terms. The Congress may be regarded as mere democratic trappings, since real power resides in the party. The constitution of the party is secret, but control over the personnel and action of the various governmental bodies is complete.

The constitution provides for state ownership of the means of production but recognizes also co-operative ownership by workers, individual ownership, and capitalist ownership, the latter two being temporary until absorbed by collective or co-operative ownership.

Nationalist China. Like that of Communist China, the government of Nationalist China is a one-party system. The president, elected for a 6 year term, is the head of the party. There are also a vice president and a prime minister. The government claims rule not merely over the island of Formosa, to which its effective authority is confined, but over all of China, whereas Communist China considers Formosa as one of its provinces. The administration of island affairs is in the hands of a governor, whereas the national government controls the army.

Nationalist China, unlike Communist China, encourages private ownership of property on a wide basis. Its program for developing small independent farms stands out as a conspicuous success and resulted in rapid increase in food production. The government invests directly in the development of industry.

COLOMBIA

Upon the revolt of Spanish America from Spain, a republic was formed by the union of the "viceroyalty" of New Granada, the "captaincy-general" of Venezuela, and the "presidency" of Quito. This united state was called Great Colombia, and a government was formed, based upon a constitution adopted in 1821. Venezuela withdrew from this state in 1829, forming a separate republic, and Ecuador seceded in 1830. The remaining territory reorganized as the Republic of New Granada, with a constitution adopted February 29, 1832. A new constitution was formed in 1843 and another in 1853. The constitution of 1858 transformed the former centralized government into a federal form, composed of 8 states, styled the "Granadan Confederation."

Colombia remained a federal republic modeled upon that of the United States, with a corresponding measure of independent authority accorded to the 8 states of which it was composed, until the revolution of 1885. This brought about a new centralized government designated by the constitution of August 4, 1886, as "The Republic of Colombia." This act is the basis of the present fundamental law. By this constitution, the independence of the states was suppressed and they were transformed into "departments," with governors appointed by the president of the republic. The state of Panama protested against this suppression of its sovereignty, which action later became a ground for the justification of secession. Colombia is an example of a state (New Zealand being a second) which, having experimented with the federal principle, returned to centralized government. In the case of Colombia, it may be said that federation was not based, like that of the United States or Switzerland, upon a former independence of political units.

Balanced Parties. From 1953 to 1962, the government was controlled by the army. Thereafter the constitution of 1886 was reinstated with important modifications effective until 1974. While there is universal suffrage, the elections are so arranged that members of each of the two legislative bodies are equally divided between the Liberal party and the Conservative party. Presidents belonging to each of these parties must alternate in office.

The house of representatives consists of one member for each 90,000 inhabitants or a major fraction thereof. The senate has one member for each 190,000 inhabitants or a major fraction thereof. Each department elects an equal number of members of each party with an alternate for each member. If the rule respecting population results in an odd number of members from a department, one more is added. The terms are for 4 years. Senators

are limited to those who have held certain high offices, university professors of 5 years' standing, and members of a profession requiring a university degree. While members of both houses may introduce bills, they are prepared by a council of state, members of which are chosen by congress from lists submitted by the president.

The president, elected for a 4-year term, appoints a cabinet, equally divided between the two parties. It is the channel of communication between him and congress. The cabinet may introduce legislation and advise him on approving or objecting to legislative acts. The president has a limited veto; he must promulgate a law repassed over his objection by both houses. The president appoints the governors of the departments (provinces). There is no vice president, but each two years congress elects a "designate" who assumes the duties of the president in the event of the latter's "absolute default." Such designate must belong to the same political party as the president.

Other provisions, all inserted into the constitution of 1886 in later years, include the following: Women shall have the same political rights as men, the minimum voting age for both being 21; the right to strike, except against the government, is guaranteed subject to regulatory laws; public aid is a function of the state; at least 10 per cent of the general budget of expenditures must be used for the support of public education.

Each of the 17 departments in which Colombia is divided is headed by a governor appointed by the central government and responsible to it. Each has also an elective assembly with power to regulate elementary and secondary education and charitable establishments, to regulate and encourage industry, and to deal with matters of land settlement, roads, and canals. Each elective assembly can create or abolish municipalities. The mayor of each municipality is the agent of the governor of the department. By this system of executive control, power is exerted in a highly centralized form with little participation by the individual citizen.

COMORO ISLANDS

A former French dependency, the Republic of the Comoros was established July 6, 1975. The French took possession of Mayotte in the Comoro Islands in 1843 and established a protectorate in 1886. The islands became a French colony in 1912 and a territory with representation in the French parliament in 1947. The present government was established in August 1975, after a coup in the capital city of Moroni. Governmental power is vested in a 12-member national executive council headed by the chief of state and the prime minister. Local government is conducted on each of the four main islands by district assemblies. Besides the supreme court of appeal, there are lower courts and 16 courts of Moslem law. Pending adoption of a constitution, legislative functions are performed by the national executive council. The Comoro Islands were admitted to the Organization of African Unity and to the UN in 1975.

CONGO (BRAZZAVILLE)

This country, becoming independent of France in 1958 but adhering to the French Community, established a republican form of government. A 1963 constitution provided for a national assembly elected by universal suffrage and a president chosen by an electoral college composed of members of the national assembly and regional and local legislative bodies.

Another constitution, adopted in 1973, was suspended in 1977. The national assembly was replaced by an 11-member military committee; local government was dissolved. The Congo has only one legal political party.

COSTA RICA

The population consists largely of descendants of white colonists. The present constitution, adopted in 1949, is a revision of the earlier constitution of 1871.

The legislative power is confided to a single body called the legislative assembly composed of deputies chosen for 4 years in the proportion of one for each 25,214 inhabitants. Voting is compulsory for all men under 70. All citizens are entitled to vote, the minimum age being 18 for married men and teachers, 20 for other men, and 21 for women. Deputies may not serve for consecutive terms. The state pays electoral expenses of political parties up to 2 per cent of the national budget. The assembly meets annually, on May 1, for a session of 60 days and may be called in extra session by the executive. In addition to possessing national legislative authority, the assembly appoints the justices of the supreme court, whose terms are for 8 years but are automatically renewed unless the assembly decides otherwise by a two-thirds majority. The assembly, moreover, may hear charges against the president and may order his trial before the supreme court of justice.

During the recess of the assembly, a "permanent commission" of five deputies continues in session, with the powers of interpreting laws in case of doubt, of preparing and putting in order unfinished business, of suspending the constitutional guarantees, and, at the request of the executive power, of passing urgent decrees. It may also be consulted by the executive on matters of importance.

The president and two vice presidents are elected for 4-year terms by universal suffrage. The candidate with the highest number of votes is elected, provided he polls at least 40 per cent of the vote. Otherwise a second election is held. The president appoints his ministers and, through them, may introduce bills in the assembly. He has a limited right of veto, which may be overridden by a two-thirds vote of the assembly.

The territory of Costa Rica is divided for administration into provinces, cantons, and districts. In each province are a governor, appointed by the president, and his agent. In the chief town of each canton is a municipal council with powers fixed by law. Under this somewhat conservative constitution, Costa Rica has enjoyed political stability.

CUBA

Cuba was the last of the Spanish dependencies in the Western Hemisphere to become independent and the only one in whose independence the U.S. played a role. By the Treaty of Paris, in 1898, Spain relinquished sovereignty over Cuba, then occupied by American forces, and the U.S. expressed its resolution to leave Cuba to the political control of the Cubans. Nevertheless, by act of Congress, the U.S. attached strings to Cuba's independence. (See *Platt Amendment.*)

A new constitution was adopted in 1940. It included provisions for a semiparliamentary government. When Batista seized power in 1952, he dissolved congress and the political parties; he was the only candidate in the election of 1954. Castro assumed the position of premier in 1959. He worked to establish a socialistic society and a government consisting of the Cuban Communist party and patterned after the Communist countries. At that time there were no elections. Rule was by decree issued by the premier. By such decrees, a program of collectivization was put into effect.

Property of foreign corporations was confiscated, cattle and tobacco land was nationalized, and sugar and other agricultural land was turned over to cooperatives. Banks and industrial enterprises were nationalized. Castro declared allegiance to the Communist party in 1961; Russian, Chinese, and other Communist advisers were invited to assist in the collective reorganization of Cuba.

The first congress of the Cuban Communist party met in December 1975. Cuba's first five-year plan was introduced. A new constitution was drafted in 1975 and approved by a national referendum in February 1976. It proclaimed a socialist state and the Communist party the major force in Cuba. Elections are held every five years for members of the national assembly. The assembly elects a council of state which consists of a president, a first vice president, five vice presidents, and 24 other members. The council president is chief of state and head of the government. Assembly sessions are open to the public unless national interest is at stake. Legislation can be introduced by the state labor union, other mass organizations, or individuals with proposals signed by 10,000 citizens. Cubans also can exercise power through smaller popular assemblies. All citizens over 16 are eligible to vote. There is freedom of expression, religion, the press, speech, as long as the goals and principles of the government and society are not opposed. The state controls the press and communications.

CYPRUS

This republic, formerly a British crown colony, became independent in 1960 under an agreement (Zurich-London) by Britain, Greece, and Turkey following years of terrorism as one party favored union with Greece while the Turkish minority (about 20 per cent) opposed. The constitution reflects this division, Greek Christians versus Turkish Moslems.

It provides that the president has to be a Greek Cypriot, elected separately by his community, and the vice president a Turkish Cypriot, elected separately by his community. Both have veto powers over foreign affairs, security, and defense. Legislative power is exercised by the house of representatives, whose 50 members must be 35 Greeks and 15 Turks. This body has no jurisdiction over matters of religion, education, and other communal affairs. Such matters are dealt with by two separate bodies—a Greek communal chamber and a Turkish communal chamber. The members of the former are elected by Greek communes, those of the latter by Turkish communes. Each commune determines how many representatives it will send. Public employees must be in the approximate proportion of 70 Greek to 30 Turkish at all levels.

An attempt to amend the constitution in 1963 was resisted by the Turkish Cypriots and led to hostilities and intervention by the UN. Turkish Cypriots withdrew from the house of representatives in protest. In July 1974 Cypriot army insurgents led by Greeks staged a coup and overthrew President Makarios, who fled to Britain. He returned to the presidency in December. Later in July Turkish troops invaded Cyprus; Greek troops mobilized on the Greek border. The Turkish troops occupied 40 per cent of the northern part of Cyprus, forcing Greek Cypriots to move south as refugees. By UN resolutions attempts were made to have all foreign troops withdrawn from Cyprus. In February 1975, a Turkish Cypriot Federated State was proclaimed in northern Cyprus. Makarios' death in 1977 added another crisis to the unrest in Cyprus as hostilities continued. Cyprus is a member of the Commonwealth of Nations.

CZECHOSLOVAKIA

Czechoslovakia became an independent republic in 1918 upon the dismemberment of Austria-Hungary. Germany absorbed it in 1938–39. It was restored to independence in 1945 with close political and economic ties to Russia, with whose help Communist party members seized control of the government in 1948. A popular democratic constitution was adopted. In 1960 this was replaced by a new constitution on the Russian model declaring the country a socialist republic. It is described as a unitary state of two Slav nations, the Czechs and the Slovaks, possessing equal rights.

By 1968 there was a strong trend toward liberalization. The movement for political and economic reform brought the overthrow of the pro-Soviet leaders. Their place was taken by the reform group led by Alexander Dubcek. Within months U.S.S.R. troops forcibly occupied Czechoslovakia. Dubcek was ousted and a pro-Moscow leadership under Gustav Husak was established. In the process purges and trials were held and 50,000 fled abroad seeking asylum. By 1970 a 20-year treaty of friendship with the Soviets was signed.

In 1973–74 Czechoslovakia and West Germany signed an agreement that annulled the Munich Pact of 1938, which had given the Sudeten region to Nazi Germany. The event signaled closer ties with Western Europe, but also marked 25 years of Communist rule in Czechoslovakia.

In 1976 the main features of the 1960 constitution remained in effect. The federal assembly consisted of the dual chamber of nations (with 75 Czech and 75 Slovak delegates elected by their own national councils) and the chamber of the people, with 200 deputies elected by national vote of those over 18. The governing body is the presidium, or Communist politburo, under the party secretary general.

DENMARK

The three Scandinavian countries have at periods been united. In 1381 Denmark and Norway united under a common sovereign, separating in 1814.

Denmark is a limited monarchy. The present constitution, which is a modern version of the constitution of 1849, was signed June 5, 1953. By its terms the legislative power is vested jointly in the king (or queen) and parliament. The executive power is held by the king. He appoints the prime minister and presides over the cabinet, which handles new bills and important measures. Parliament consists of a single chamber composed of 179 members, 135 of whom are elected by proportional representation. An additional 40 seats are divided among the various political parties to equalize the representation. The Faroe Islands and Greenland, which have equal status with other parts of the kingdom, have 2 representatives each. Parliament is elected for 4 years and meets annually, but may be dissolved earlier by the king. Suffrage is universal; the voting age is 21.

The king can neither make war nor sign peace treaties without the consent of parliament. Under certain circumstances the constitution permits the transfer of some sovereign powers to international organizations, if approved by five-sixths of the parliament members or a plebiscite majority. Since 1953, women may succeed to the Danish throne.

There is a supreme court at Copenhagen, with a chief justice and 14 associates. The established church is the Evangelical Lutheran Church, of which the king must be a member. Its officers have no part in politics and dissenters have complete religious freedom.

Denmark is divided into 14 counties, each of which is subdivided into districts, and the districts are divided into parishes. Each urban municipality has a mayor and council.

DJIBOUTI

The Republic of Djibouti is located between Somali and Ethiopia at the southern entrance of the Red Sea. Formerly the Territory of the Afars and the Issas, a French colony for 115 years, Djibouti became independent in 1977 following a national independence referendum and assumed the name of its capital. A constituent assembly of 33 Issas and 30 Afars was chosen by a general election. The president of Djibouti named a premier, who appointed a cabinet. The new republic is a member of the Arab League, OAU, and UN.

DOMINICAN REPUBLIC

This country occupies the eastern section (approximately two-thirds) of the West Indian island Hispaniola. The western third of the island is the French-speaking Republic of Haiti. Hispaniola, discovered by Columbus in 1492, was part of the Spanish empire until 1795 when it fell under French rule. The eastern portion of the island eventually returned to Spanish rule and became independent in 1821. In 1844 the Dominican Republic was founded and a constitution approved. The country's first elections were held in December 1962. The following year a new constitution was proclaimed. After the civil war of 1965, the constitution was suspended and a provisional government with rule by decree was established. In November 1966 a new constitution was adopted.

It provides for a president elected by direct vote to a 4-year term. In case of death, disability, or resignation, the president is succeeded by the vice president. There are 12 secretaries of state, a judicial adviser with secretary-of-state rank, and 2 ministers in charge of departments. Citizens can vote at 18, or younger if they are married.

The Dominican Republic's history has been one of recurrent dictatorships, bankruptcy, and periodic financial and military intervention by the U.S.

ECUADOR

Ecuador, located in northwestern South America, is bounded by Colombia on the north, Peru on the east and south, and the Pacific Ocean on the west. The Galapagos Islands, 600 miles west of the mainland, are also part of Ecuador.

The territorial boundaries of Ecuador are still in part unsettled. In 1894, a three-party treaty, between Ecuador, Colombia, and Peru, was submitted for arbitration to the king of Spain. The congress of Ecuador, however, failed to ratify the treaty. In 1904, Ecuador and Peru again submitted their disputes to the king of Spain. A commission was appointed, but no award was given. A boundary treaty with Colombia was signed in 1916, and a delimitation of the frontier was completed in 1919 by a joint commission. In the Treaty of Rio in 1942, Peru was given over half of Ecuador's Amazonian territories after a conflict between the two countries. In 1961, Ecuador denounced this treaty and the issue remains unsettled.

Ecuador, founded by Spain, became a republic within the federation of Gran Colombia in 1822. Ecuador declared independence in 1830.

Ecuador has been plagued with government disorder. A military coup overthrew the government in 1963—a military junta was established and the 1946 constitution suspended. This junta was ousted in 1966 and a civilian government was formed. The following year a new constitution was adopted, and in 1968 elections for president and congress were held. The president assumed dictatorial powers in 1970. He was deposed in 1972 and another military government was established. In 1974 the government suspended all elections and political activity. A 3-man military junta took control of the government in 1976 and martial law was imposed. The military government announced that the country eventually would be returned to constitutional rule.

EGYPT

The modern independence of Egypt dates from 1922 when England recognized the sovereignty of its former protectorate but retained certain defense rights and control of the Suez Canal. Under a treaty of alliance in 1936, these rights were to be relinquished in 1956; however, Egypt abrogated the treaty in 1951. Egypt was ruled as a limited monarchy from 1923 until 1952 when a military uprising compelled the king to abdicate; a republic was declared in 1953. In 1956, under the leadership of Nasser, a republican constitution was adopted by referendum, with Nasser as the first president. Later that year he seized the Suez Canal. From 1958 to 1961 Egypt was united with Syria and Yemen to form the United Arab Republic.

Under a new constitution issued in 1964, a national assembly is elected for a 5-year term by public secret ballot. One-half of the members must be workers or farmers; 10 may be appointed by the president. The president is nominated by the national assembly; the nominee's name is submitted to the electorate in a referendum. A majority of votes makes him president for a 6-year term. If he does not receive a majority, a new nominee is submitted. The president may appoint and remove one or more vice presidents. He also appoints the prime minister and other ministers who form the cabinet. The cabinet is the supreme executive and administrative organ of the state; it may submit bills to the general assembly. Bills, when passed, are subject to a limited veto by the president; a two-thirds majority in the assembly overrides the veto. The assembly may pass a vote of no confidence in any minister, in which case, the minister must submit his resignation. It is not stipulated that the president must accept the resignation. The president may dissolve the assembly and call for new elections. Islam is the religion of the state and the socialist system is its economic foundation. The constitution may be amended on proposal of one-third of the members of the general assembly if the proposal receives a two-thirds majority.

With the death of Nasser in 1970 and the naming of Anwar Sadat as president and military governor general, Egypt's foreign policy changed. Egypt expelled Russian advisers and began to negotiate with France and England. When President Nixon visited Egypt in 1974, diplomatic relations between the U.S. and Egypt were restored after a 7-year lapse. In 1975, Egypt reopened the Suez Canal and broke off a treaty of friendship with Russia. Egypt's move toward a more pro-West, anti-Communist stance was strengthened by the invitation of the U.S. to join the Middle East peace talks. Egypt's domestic problems continue to grow. Overpopulation, a floundering economy, and a 25 per cent yearly inflation rate have led to labor unrest—numerous riots have been reported between workers and the government.

EIRE

A 1921 treaty gave Ireland, exclusive of Ulster (Northern Ireland), the status of a free state in the Commonwealth of Nations. It became the Irish Free State in 1922 and was renamed Eire in 1937. Northern Ireland, which had been given a parliament in 1920, remained an integral part of the United Kingdom. Eire's charter of government established a republic with no organic link with Great Britain. Its parliament exercises jurisdiction in 26 of Ireland's 32 counties.

The legislature consists of 2 houses, the assembly (Dail) and senate (Seanad), which meet annually for a maximum term of 7 years. The senate consists of 60 members, 11 nominated by the prime minister, 6 elected by the universities, and the remaining 43 elected from 5 panels of candidates representing the following vocations: art and literature; agriculture and allied interests; labor, whether organized or not; industry, including banking and finance; and public administration and social services. Membership of the assembly is fixed by law from time to time subject to a rule that there shall be 1 member for each 20,000 to 30,000 of the population but at least 3 members from each constituency.

The president is elected for a 7-year term by direct vote of the people under a proportional representation plan. He must be an Irish citizen at least 35 years of age. Candidates for the presidency, except former presidents, must be nominated by at least 20 members of parliament (Oireachtas) or by not less than four county councils.

The president is assisted by a cabinet. Its 7 to 15 members must have been elected to parliament. Parliament selects the prime minister, who is head of the cabinet. The prime minister selects the other members, of whom the vice prime minister and those in charge of the department of finance must be members of the assembly.

A fourth governmental body, known as the council of state, is provided, its function being to give advice to the president. Members include the prime minister, the vice prime minister, chief justice, president of high court, chairman of the senate, ex-presidents, past incumbents of the first 3 of the posts named, and a maximum of 7 other members appointed by the president.

The president may, but is not required to, dissolve the assembly if the prime minister loses his majority in the house. He may convene either house on the advice of the council of state. His messages to the people must receive the prior approval of his cabinet. His signature is required before a bill passed by parliament becomes law. He is commander of the army.

There is no vice president. If the president is incapacitated or absent from the country, his duties are taken over by a commission consisting of the president of the high court, the prime minister, and the chairman of the senate.

EQUATORIAL GUINEA

Equatorial Guinea consists of mainland territory and offshore islands in the Gulf of Guinea. It has been independent from Spain since 1968, having gained this status after numerous appeals to the UN. After elections, the president takes office for a 5-year term; he is also minister of foreign affairs. The constitution, adopted in July 1968, set up a unicameral national assembly of 35 members, also with 5-year terms.

ETHIOPIA

This ancient kingdom in northeast Africa resisted European colonization until 1936 when it was conquered by Italy. Italy's occupation ended in 1941. After World War II the former Italian colony of Eritrea was added to Ethiopia, giving it an outlet on the Red Sea.

The emperor of Ethiopia granted a constitution in 1931. A new constitution was issued in July 1974. It was in effect for only a short time before a military coup suspended the constitution and deposed Emperor Haile Selassie, who had ruled for 58 years, in September 1974.

Ethiopia is ruled by the Dergue, a military administrative council composed of 60–70 members elected by the armed forces. The Dergue consists of three bodies: congress, a central committee, and a permanent committee. The chairman of the Dergue is the head of state and the chief of government. Real power lies within an inner circle of military officers.

Ethiopia is a founding member of both the UN and the Organization of African Unity.

FIJI

Fiji, a possession and dependency of Great Britain from 1874, was granted increasing measures of self-government during the 1960's, and attained complete independence as a nation in October, 1970. Governmental authority is vested in an elected House of Representatives, a Prime Minister, and a Governor-General, who represents the Sovereign of England in Fiji, as Fiji is a member of the Commonwealth.

FINLAND

Finland, formerly a province of Russia, became independent in 1917, first as a kingdom. In 1919, a republic was established.

According to the constitution of 1919, government belongs to the people, who are represented by a Parliament of 200 members elected for 4-year terms by universal suffrage with proportional representation. Voters must be over 21 years of age. The executive power is vested in a president, who is chosen for a term of 6 years by an electoral college elected by the citizens. The president supervises the administration, conducts foreign relations, and is commander in chief of the army. Foreign treaties, as well as the decision of peace and war, require the ratification of the Chamber. The president may initiate legislation and may dissolve the Chamber; he exercises the pardoning power and presides over the council of state, or cabinet of ministers, when present. He has a suspensive veto on legislation, during which suspensive period the president may request the counsel of the supreme court or of the supreme administrative court. If a measure is then not approved, it may become a law only after its re-enactment without alteration by a newly elected Chamber.

The constitution provides that the decisions of the president, except for supervising administration and for directing the "arraignment of ministers," must be countersigned by a minister; that ministers must decline counter signature if the president's action is contrary to the fundamental law; and that the council of ministers must enjoy the confidence of the Chamber.

The supreme court is established by the constitution; trial courts, by legislation. A supreme administrative court, which is a tribunal of last resort on questions of administrative law, is established by the constitution. Both the supreme court and the supreme administrative court have the right to address the president on the subject of necessary legislation.

While the president is intrusted with the enforcement of laws, a "solicitor" supervises the enforcement of laws in court and other proceedings. In county district courts, the jurors are 12 farmers owning property, but the judge decides the case unless the jurors are unanimously opposed, in which event their decision prevails.

FRANCE

The government of France since the Revolution has undergone many fundamental changes. Its present government, established in 1958, is known as the Fifth Republic. Republican government was first established in the wake of the revolution of 1791, but the monarchical idea died hard; an emperor and several kings succeeded. The Second Republic was established in 1848 when Louis Philippe abdicated. The Third Republic, established in 1871 after the deposition of Napoleon III, lasted until after World War II. It was succeeded by the Fourth Republic in 1947 and finally by the Fifth Republic in 1958.

The comparative instability of government in France may be explained in part by the fact that France failed to achieve national unity until many centuries after England was first unified under its Saxon kings. Hence there was not such a long experience of popular rights slowly acquired and jealously guarded. Under the Third Republic

in its later years and under the Fourth Republic, parties in the legislature grew so numerous that it became more and more difficult to form a stable administration. The Fifth Republic was formed because the government was paralyzed in the face of an army revolt over a war in Algeria. The ministry called on Charles De Gaulle to take the helm. He consented on condition that he be given a free hand for a stated period and be allowed to carry to the voters his proposal for a new constitution. His new constitution was adopted by over 80 per cent of the voters in France and its overseas dependencies in a referendum held September 28, 1958.

Administration. Much that is fundamental in French government is contained in earlier laws which have survived constitutional changes. Particularly is this the case with administrative laws, which have undergone little change since their enactment under Napoleon in 1800.

For administrative purposes, France is divided into districts called "departments," 95 in number. The departments are arbitrary divisions, approximately equal in area and in population and have no relation to the historic provinces, such as Normandy, Picardy, Champagne, or Gascony, which the French Revolution erased as political subdivisions. The departments are all named after physical features, such as rivers and mountains.

Each department is subdivided, for convenience of administration, into two or more *arrondissements*. In each department and in each arrondissement a town is designated as the seat of administration and is called the "chief place." In each chief place is a public building, the seat of local government, called the "prefecture" or "subprefecture."

The Prefect. The entire public administration, national and local, within the department, is in charge of a trained official called the prefect, who is appointed and directed by the minister of the interior and who is never a native of the department whose affairs he directs. The prefect reports, not alone to the minister of the interior, but to the other ministers of the government whose local interests he superintends. In the arrondissements, subprefects assist the prefect. To further aid and counsel this important official, there is the prefectural council, composed of 3 or 4 trained functionaries who, presided over by the prefect, constitute an administrative court to hear complaints against public actions, to adjust taxation, to examine departmental and communal budgets, and to settle questions of jurisdiction.

General Council. To supply a measure of local representation, there is a departmental assembly, or local legislature, called the "general council," which consists of from 17 to 67 members, according to the size of the department. This council is elected by the people of the department for a term of 6 years, one-half elected each 3 years. The general council meets at least twice a year, its most important tasks being to examine the departmental budget and the rates, and to audit the economic conduct of the prefectural government. Within the arrondissements is a lesser territorial subdivision, the "canton," which has no administrative significance but is the jurisdiction of the justice of the peace and is an election district for the general council.

Communes. The entire territory of France is comprised in municipal organizations called "communes," the number exceeding 36,000. They vary greatly in size and in population. All, except Paris, are governed under a single brief code, the municipal law of 1884. Each commune has a municipal council composed of from 10 to 36 members, elected by universal suffrage for 4 years by "general ticket," and a mayor elected by the municipal council, who may be assisted by one or more aides called "adjoints." All serve without pay. The position of mayor is highly honorable, has been filled by many statesmen of distinction, and is sometimes held by one trusted individual for many years.

The mayor has large powers, not only as a local official, but also as the agent of the national government for all its interests within the commune. He controls the local police and, like the prefect above him, may issue police ordinances covering a wide field. For the enforcement of laws and for the maintenance of public order, he is responsible, not to the government or the inhabitants of the commune, but to the prefect of the department. Against excessive or illegal actions of the mayor, appeal may be had to the prefectural council and from that court an appeal is made to the highest administrative court, the council of state at Paris.

The Council of State. This body, historically a heritage from the "ancient regime" but reformed by Napoleon, in recent decades has developed as the supreme administrative court into a regulatory organ of administration of the first importance. Its decisions form a legal corpus known as the administrative law. It is the capstone of a system of centralized administration which has been found equally serviceable under empire, monarchy, or republic.

The Executive. The Fifth Republic, unlike its predecessors, gives the president very wide powers. He is elected for a term of 7 years. The constitution originally provided that he should be chosen by an electoral college of national and local representatives totaling about 80,000. In 1962, however, the constitution was amended to provide for direct universal suffrage in presidential elections. Overseas departments and territories may participate but not, as originally, states which are bound to France merely as members of the French Community. Campaigning is strictly regulated by national and local electoral control commissions. Campaigns may begin only after the official list of candidates is published and must cease on the Friday before the Sunday on which the election is held. Two hours of radio and of television time is allotted to each candidate in an order determined by lot. The display of posters is likewise strictly regulated. If no candidate receives a majority of the votes on the first election day, a second election is held on a Sunday following shortly thereafter. Those candidates who wish may withdraw, and the two others who received the highest number of votes on the first election day are placed on the ballot.

The president has exclusive powers and powers shared with the prime minister. In his own right, he chooses the prime minister, dissolves the Assembly, may address the Assembly (but not the nation without the prime minister's consent), may request opinions as to constitutionality from the constitutional council, 3 of whose 9 members he appoints, and assumes emergency powers in a crisis. He may also veto laws by withholding his assent. Although the prime minister and other ministers, chosen by him, are responsible to Parliament, they may not be members of Parliament. The president can compel their acceptance by Parliament by threatening to dissolve the Assembly. He presides over the council of ministers, on whose advice he issues orders either pursuant to law or in fields excluded from the competency of the legislature.

The Legislature. Parliament comprises two houses—the National Assembly and the Senate. The National Assembly is elected by universal suffrage of all citizens over 21. Elections are held on two successive Sundays. In the first balloting, a majority of all votes cast is necessary to election; in the second, a plurality suffices. The membership is 552, elected for 5-year terms, which may be reduced if the Assembly is dissolved earlier.

The Senate is composed of 302 members elected indirectly by universal suffrage for 9-year terms, one-third being renewed each 3 years. They are chosen by an electoral college composed of municipal councilmen and a smaller number of specially elected deputies under a system favoring small city and rural areas. The total electoral college numbers about 120,000.

Bills may originate in either house or in the president's council of ministers. The budget and money bills may originate only in the council, all of whose bills have precedence in that they may not be amended. No assemblyman or senator may introduce a bill which increases or decreases budgeted expenditures. If the budget is not voted with a prescribed limit, the president may put it into effect by decree. If a bill passed by one house is defeated by the other, it may again be taken up by the first house and sent to the second. If no agreement can be reached, the prime minister may refer it to a joint committee, whose bill is again submitted to both houses. If again defeated, the president may ask the Assembly to cast the deciding vote. Treaties must be ratified by the Assembly, and their provisions may override domestic laws.

The constitution defines two fields of rule making —one reserved to Parliament and the other to the president, with the residual powers exercised by the president through executive orders. Hence disputes may arise whether a measure falls within the reserved powers of Parliament or whether it does not and therefore may be the subject of an executive order. A constitutional council is set up to determine such disputes and other matters of constitutionality. It consists of former presidents and 9 appointed members—3 by the president and 3 by each of the two houses. It may be required to give an opinion within a month on questions submitted by the president, the prime minister, or the chairman of the Assembly or the Senate.

The French Community. In the referendum for adoption of the constitution of 1958, it was participated in, not only by metropolitan France, but by all French dependencies. French dependencies were permitted, in the same referendum, to choose among three options: (a) to retain their present status, (b) to become overseas departments of France, and (c) to become autonomous member states of the French Community. One state, Guinea, voted not to accept the constitution and became automatically independent. Twelve states voted to be members of the Community. Although this entailed French citizenship, French control of foreign policy, defense, and money, and appointment of a head of state by Paris, each state adopted its own constitution modeled in general on that of France.

In 1960, the constitution of 1958 was amended so as to provide for complete independence of the states. Membership in the Community then became a matter of negotiation between France and the newly independent state. Some made such agreement before admission to the United Nations; most of them after admission. All of them concluded special agreements with France covering trade and economic assistance. Their relationship to France became analogous to that between Great Britain and the other members of the British Commonwealth.

GABON

This republic was proclaimed in 1960. A president is the chief executive officer, chosen for a 7-year term by universal suffrage. An absolute majority is requisite, by means of a run-off election if necessary. The president names a vice president, to whom he may delegate most powers and who serves temporarily in case of the president's incapacity or death in office. Legislative power is vested primarily in a unicameral National Assembly, whose members are elected for 5-year terms by universal suffrage. The president, however, may also initiate legislation to be passed by the Assembly. He has a limited power of veto.

FOREIGN HIGHLIGHTS

Located in the capital city of Jerusalem, Israel, Yad Vashem (Memorial Shrine) is dedicated to the memory of the Nazi victims of the world.

Left A store house in Rotorua, New Zealand, reserved for the food eaten by the native priests (tohunga) of the Maori people, is a striking example of the intricate wood carving for which these people are noted.

New Zealand Consulate General

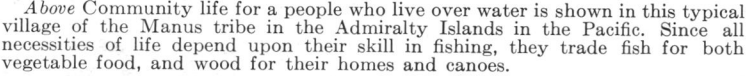

Above Community life for a people who live over water is shown in this typical village of the Manus tribe in the Admiralty Islands in the Pacific. Since all necessities of life depend upon their skill in fishing, they trade fish for both vegetable food, and wood for their homes and canoes.

Right The Buddha of Wat Doi Suteb, Chiengmai, Thailand, is made of brick stucco and is heavily gilded. The approach to the wat (temple) is through columns of pines festooned with orchids. Thailand has about 16,000 temples.

Left Residents and tourists alike enjoy outstanding plays and light operas presented at the beautiful O'Keefe Centre for the Performing Arts in Toronto, Canada.

Below left Cape Town, a vigorous modern city, reflects the wealth of South Africa's valuable exports—gold and wool. Shown here is Heerengracht, one of the city's main thoroughfares.

Photo *SATOUR*

Below The Palace and the meticulously sculptured Gardens at Queluz, Portugal make this a popular sight-seeing spot for tourists.

Photo *Sni-Yan*

Above Like numerous other cities, London's expansion program includes many modern buildings as shown on both banks of the Thames.

Left The American Embassy in Tel-Aviv, Israel, is one of the most modern buildings in that city.

WORLD CITIES

Bermuda's laws are made in the Parliament Buildings, Hamilton, in the foreground.

Midan al Tahrir ("Liberation Square") in Cairo, Egypt.
UAR Tourist Office

A typical Buddhist temple in Bangkok, Thailand.

Paris's Arc de Triomphe commemorates the victories of Napoleon. It is 160 feet high and 147 feet wide.
French Govt. Tourist Office

The Secretariat Buildings in New Delhi, India, with a portion of the Council Chamber at the right.

GAMBIA

Gambia is a small country on the west coast of Africa. It became a republic within the British Commonwealth in 1970. Parliament has 32 popularly elected members, 4 chiefs elected by chiefs in assemblies, and a speaker and deputy speaker appointed by the governor general.

GERMANY

No country in modern times has had such a long tortured governmental evolution as has Germany. No important country is still faced with so many governmental problems not yet soluble.

First, Germany was not even a political entity until 1871, when Prince Bismarck created a monarchical state under the leadership of Prussia, with a strong militaristic bent. Defeated in World War I, Germany turned to a democracy and operated under a constitution framed at Weimar in 1919. This constitution was not proof against subversion by Hitler, who converted the government into a personal dictatorship. Precipitating Germany into World War II, Hitler in effect delivered his country into the hands of victors, who, dividing in the hour of victory, cut his country into two parts under two governmental systems of opposite and conflicting character. There are now a West Germany under a democratic constitution and an East Germany under a Communist regime.

The Germany of 1871 was made up of 25 states: 4 kingdoms, Prussia, Bavaria, Saxony, and Württemberg; 18 lesser principalities, grand duchies, and mark-graviates; and 3 "free cities," Hamburg, Lubeck, and Bremen, survivors of the old "Hanseatic League" of German trading cities. The states retained their own interior administration, generally monarchical, except in the free cities.

First German Constitution. Under the first constitution, the federal government comprised a legislature consisting, first, of an elective body, the *Reichstag*, or Imperial Diet, of 397 members chosen by popular election on the basis of universal manhood suffrage.

The upper house was a unique institution, the heritage of earlier German diets, and was called the *Bundesrat*, or "Federal Council." It was composed of 61 representatives of the federated states, of which Prussia had 17. These members were the appointees of the governments represented and were usually high ranking members of these governments, under whose instructions they acted. The Bundesrat had predominant powers. It initiated practically all legislation, and no bill could be considered by the Reichstag without the consent of the Bundesrat. It took cognizance of the failure of any state to execute imperial laws and could sanction the employment of armed force to coerce a state into obedience. It was presided over by the imperial chancellor, who was the head of the national administration and controlled all its political departments. This official was the personal choice of the German emperor and was responsible to him alone.

The imperial chancellor was usually prime minister of Prussia as well and head of the government of that predominant state. Bismarck established the principle that other imperial ministers, foreign affairs, finance, war, navy, etc., were responsible to the chancellor and must report to the emperor through him. The emperor was the king of Prussia.

The Weimar Constitution. Germany's defeat in 1918 brought about the emperor's abdication and the disappearance of the monarchies in all the states. Each state held a constitutional convention and adopted a democratic constitution. Germany became a union of republics. This form of state government was a requirement under the federal constitution of Weimar.

The new German constitution established a universal, equal, direct, and secret franchise of male and female voters and a system of proportional representation. All states acquired popularly elected diets or assemblies. The conduct of government was entrusted to a commission or "cabinet" of ministers. The chairman of this body bore the title of "president" or "premier."

The Reichstag, or popular legislative chamber, was elected on most liberal suffrage conditions. The former Bundesrat reappeared as an imperial senate, the *Reichsrat*, in which the states were represented roughly in proportion to population. The "cabinet," composed of the chancellor and of ministers, required the support of the Reichstag. The constitution guaranteed equality before the law; freedom of religion, of speech, and of the press; and abolished all class privileges of whatever kind.

The president of the empire was elected by the whole German people for a term of 7 years. He had the unusual power of ordering a referendum of laws which did not command his approval or of proposed laws on which the chambers disagreed. While most executive acts had to be performed through ministers responsible to the Reichstag, the president commanded the armed forces of the Reich and might declare martial law or a "state of siege." Finally, he might dissolve the Reichstag and order a new election. The president might be removed from office by vote of the people on proposal of the national legislature.

Nazi Rule. On March 23, 1933, the principal provisions of the Weimar constitution were set aside by vote of the Reichstag, which entrusted complete dictatorial powers to Adolph Hitler, leader of a new National Socialist party, abbreviated as Nazi. Hitler immediately placed governors in control of the individual states and empowered them to appoint state premiers who were to pick their own cabinets. The cabinets were made independent of the state legislatures, being responsible solely to the national dictator. These legislatures were later dissolved.

All law-making activities were centered in a cabinet of 16 members headed by Hitler, who adopted the title of *Führer* ("Leader") and Chancellor. His office carried with it supreme authority, or "leadership," in the army, all civil offices, and party activities. The cabinet promulgated laws and could alter the constitution.

Hitler created what he called a totalitarian state, in which all labor unions were dissolved and factory councils representing employers, workers, and the party took their place. Farmers were forbidden to mortgage or sell their land; they could get credit only from the state. Labor battalions of youth under government control were organized. Education was "unified" by seeing to it that teachers and textbooks were in accord with the party doctrine. An attempt was made to unify the churches under state direction, with an infusion of Teutonic mythology. A ministry of propaganda was organized to create and lead public opinion. Anti-Semitic laws discriminated against the Jews, who were almost eliminated from Germany by mass murder.

Division of Germany. When Germany surrendered unconditionally in World War II, there was no government with which the victorious powers could deal. The country was divided into four zones of military government and occupation. Russia occupied Eastern Germany to the upper Elbe; the United States, the south, including most of Bavaria and Württemberg, Hesse, and Hesse-Nassau; Great Britain, the northeastern section, including the Ruhr, Hamburg, and Bremen; and France, an area along the upper Rhine. Berlin was occupied by the four powers jointly, and the four Allied commanders in chief formed a control council with supreme authority.

Russia systematically blocked action in the control council, which broke up by 1948. In the zones controlled by the United States, Great Britain, and France, German states drafted a constitution which could be valid within the framework of the occupation statute. It was adopted by a German parliamentary council on May 8, 1949, and was promulgated as the constitution of the German Federal Republic.

The Russians meanwhile set up a state in their zone of control, and their administrative functions were transferred in 1950 to the provisional government of the German Democratic Republic.

Berlin was similarly divided, two separate municipalities being formed. East Berlin was part of East Germany, and West Berlin, although cut off from West Germany by 70 miles of intervening East German territory, was claimed as part of West Germany.

German Federal Republic. The constitution, promulgated and approved by voters in the Western occupation zone in 1949, became effective March 15, 1955. A convention was signed with the Western allies by which West Germany would have full authority over its internal and external affairs, with reservations relating to stationing armed forces in Germany and also to the status of Berlin and to questions relating to unification and the final peace settlement.

The constitution provides that it applies to Berlin and is to be put into force in the Eastern zone upon the latter's accession. While freedom of speech, press, and organization is guaranteed, this freedom is limited so as to exclude the enemies of a free, democratic basic order.

The legislature consists of a Federal Diet (*Bundestag*) and a Federal Council (*Bundesrat*). Members of the Diet are elected for a 4-year term by universal suffrage. The Council consists of members of the governments of the constituent republics, each sending at least 3 but as many as 5 if the population is over 6,000,000.

A president is chosen for a 5-year term by an electoral college consisting of members of the Diet and an equal number elected by the diets of the constituent republics. The president can succeed himself only once. The president nominates a chancellor who must be elected by the Diet, and the chancellor selects ministers for appointment by the president. The Diet may elect a new chancellor, an act which is equivalent to a vote of no confidence in the incumbent chancellor, and the president must appoint the new chancellor. If the chancellor proposes a vote of confidence and this is defeated, the president may, on the chancellor's proposal, dissolve the Diet unless a new chancellor has been elected within 21 days.

Bills may be introduced into the Diet by individual members or by members of the cabinet. Bills introduced by the latter may be on the cabinet's initiative or they may be bills passed by the Council and turned over to the cabinet to send to the Diet with cabinet recommendations. Bills passed by the Diet go to the Council, which may veto but not amend them. This veto may be overridden by the Diet—a simple majority veto by a majority vote and a two-thirds majority veto by a two-thirds vote. The president has no veto power. But appeal may be made against a bill to a federal constitutional court, whose members are appointed half by the Diet and half by the Council. Members of these bodies may not be appointed to the court.

The president may be impeached for willful violation of the law on a two-thirds vote of either legislative body. Trial is before the federal constitutional court. The place of the president, however, in the German constitutional scheme, is inferior to that of the chancellor, who speaks as head of the government.

West Germany is divided into 11 states (*Länder*), each of which has a government parallel to that of the federal republic. The states include the western section of the city of Berlin.

German Democratic Republic. The constitution of East Germany was promulgated in 1950. The constitution makes it a crime to boycott democratic organizations and to manifest religious or racial hatreds. Estates of over 100 hectares are forbidden, such estates being dissolved and redistributed without compensation. Private monopolistic organizations aiming at increase of profits by control of prices, production, and markets are prohibited.

The supreme legislative body is the People's Chamber, its 500 members being elected for 4-year terms by universal suffrage of those over 18 years of age. Candidates are limited to those nominated by the Communist party. The Chamber may be dissolved before the end of its term on its own resolution, by referendum, or on a vote of no confidence. Under an amendment of 1960, the Chamber elects, not a presidium headed by a president, as before, but a council of state, consisting of a chairman, 6 deputy chairmen, 16 members, and a secretary. The council is authorized to issue decrees with the force of laws and to interpret the laws.

The Chamber elects also a cabinet, headed by a prime minister, one of whom is charged with the duty of economic planning, in which he has the assistance of the economic council. The real power, however, lies with the politburo of the Communist party, which consists of 14 full members and 9 candidate members. Its secretary is the key man in the government.

GHANA

Ghana was formerly under British rule as the Gold Coast colony and trusteed territory of Togoland. It was granted independence in 1957 and, in 1960, became a republic within the British Commonwealth. Kwame Nkrumah was the republic's first president.

A military coup was staged in 1972, resulting in the establishment of a military regime and the suspension of the 1969 constitution. In October 1975 a supreme military council was established as the administrative and legislative body. It consists of a chairman (the head of state) and six other members appointed by virtue of service appointments. The national redemption council is a subordinate body of the military council; it also is directed by the head of state. Members are appointed by virtue of their service appointments in the government and armed forces. For administrative functions commissioners have been named to head the various ministries. Ghana is divided into nine regions; each region is administered by a regional commissioner, who is an army officer.

GREAT BRITAIN

The United Kingdom of Great Britain and Northern Ireland adopted its present title in 1920, when southern Ireland (Eire) was separated from the kingdom. Northern Ireland is represented in the British Parliament as an integral part of the kingdom and it also has its own local government under a governor and parliament.

Great Britain is the oldest political society in Europe and the oldest kingdom in the world, if one excepts the 11-year interruption of the Cromwellian period. When one of the feudal lords of France, William of Normandy, conquered England in 1066, it was already a unified monarchy. Wales was conquered in 1283 and incorporated in the kingdom about 1500. The thrones of England and Scotland were combined in 1707 by the Act of Union, when their parliaments were combined into a single legislature.

Great Britain was the cradle of democracy in the modern world. There, over a period of 800 years, a struggle between ruler and people resulted in the representative institutions which have given it the title of mother of parliaments. This long political experience enabled it to adapt itself to social and economic changes without the bloody revolutions such as France and Russia passed through. Unlike practically all other countries Great Britain does not have a formal constitution. Its frame of government is based on acts of Parliament passed in the course of many centuries

Seat of Government. Adjoining the ancient city of London is Westminster, which was chosen as a residence by the Norman kings and is the seat of British government. Here are "Whitehall Street" and "Downing Street," with the residence of the prime minister; Westminster Hall and Abbey; and the modern houses of Parliament. The British sovereign lives at Buckingham palace or other royal residences, or at Windsor castle on the Thames, 21 miles from London. From this latter ancient residence of British sovereigns, Edward VII adopted in 1917 the family name of House of Windsor.

The British Monarchy. The monarchy, which was firmly established on a national basis by William the Conqueror and by his successors, attained its greatest power and influence under the Tudors, Henry VII, Henry VIII, and Queen Elizabeth I; but their successors, the Stuart kings, aiming at an absolutism attained elsewhere in European kingdoms, were summarily checked by Parliament, which beheaded Charles I and expelled James II.

The long conflict between king and Parliament for state control resulted in the complete supremacy of Parliament and the reduction of the sovereign to a symbol of national loyalty and to a position of simple influence. "The king rules but does not govern." All crown powers are exercised in his name by ministers who are no longer his choice but who are a committee of members of Parliament, dependent upon the House of Commons for continuance of office.

Ministers. There are some 43 high officials known as ministers, selected by the prime minister, the actual leader of the majority in the Commons. The chief ministers are the lord president of the council and minister for science; the lord chancellor, who presides over the House of Lords and over the supreme court of judicature and is a general minister of justice; the chancellor of the exchequer, who is the financial minister; 4 secretaries of state—first, foreign affairs, home affairs, and commonwealth relations and colonies; the first lord of the admiralty; the president of the boards of trade; the ministers of defense, transport, education, health, labor, and agriculture and fisheries; the secretary for Scotland; and the attorney-general. Several offices—lord president of the privy council, the first lord of the treasury, lord of the privy seal, and the chancellor of the Duchy of Lancaster—have become sinecures; they are usually taken by the prime minister and by members left free of administrative duties, or "without portfolio."

Of these ministers, a minor group constitutes, with the prime minister, the "cabinet." The cabinet determines policies, settles the budget and financial schemes for submission to Commons, institutes practically all legislation, and takes responsibility at all times before Parliament for the conduct of government. A refusal of the House of Commons to follow the cabinet's lead or to enact its measures results either in the immediate resignation of the ministry or in "an appeal to the country," that is, the dissolution of the Commons and an election of a new House.

Parliamentary Government. This historically established organization for conducting the government has given to the world the widely imitated institution of "parliamentary," "responsible," or "ministerial" government, as distinguished from "presidential government" wherein the chief executive has a tenure independent of the legislative or parliamentary body.

The British Parliament consists of the House of Lords and of the House of Commons. The members of the Commons are elected for a term of 5 years or until a dissolution of the House. A member need not, and seldom does, reside in his "constituency." The House of Lords has a membership of about 1,118 and includes the archbishops of Canterbury and York; bishops of the English Church; and "peers" created by the sovereign on recommendation of the prime minister, comprising, in order of rank, dukes, marquises, earls, barons, and "life peers."

Down to 1911, the Lords had a legislative position comparable with the Commons, except in initiation of financial legislation. Its opposition to legislation demanded by the Commons could be overcome only by the threat to create enough new peers favorable to the law to "swamp the Lords." In 1832, this threat was effectual in securing the passage of the "Reform act" and was used in 1911 to pass the "Parliament act" whereby the supremacy of the Commons is recognized. Under this act, if the Commons passes an act in three successive sessions within an interval of not less than two years, it may become a law without the consent of the Lords. No "money bill" may be denied assent by the Lords, and the "speaker" of the Commons is the final judge of whether or not any certain act is a money bill. The king must give assent to every bill of Parliament. To refuse would be an unconstitutional act; in fact, it would be an act of revolution.

Sovereignty. The "King, Lords, and Commons" legally have complete sovereign powers; no political act is beyond their competence. They can legally alter, in any particular, the constitution of Great Britain and her dependencies. Until the passage of the Statute of Westminster in 1931, they had the theoretical right to legislate for the self-governing dominions also.

The constitution of Great Britain consists of a great number of separate acts, as well as of established practices which can be altered only by Parliament itself. These acts have never been codified or reduced to a single charter, and in this sense the British constitution is "unwritten." Since it can be changed by Parliament itself, it is spoken of as "flexible" as distinguished from "rigid" or "written" constitutions.

Previously to 1832, suffrage in Great Britain was restricted to the aristocratic and land-owning class. By the "Reform acts" of 1832, 1867, and 1884, it was successively extended, and, by the "Representation of the People act" of 1918, full manhood suffrage was realized, and the vote was given to women 30 years of age. By the "Equal Franchise act" of 1928, women were admitted to complete equal suffrage with men. The voting age is 21, with residential qualifications. Voting has for many years been carefully protected by a Corrupt Practices act. Thus, under the forms of a monarchy, Great Britain, now almost the last remaining kingly government of consequence, has become in fact one of the most democratic of countries. The families of the nobility, however, continue to exercise a leadership and an influence found today in few other countries.

Local Government. For purposes of local government, England and Wales are divided into 62 "administrative counties" and 87 county boroughs. Northern Ireland is divided into 6 administrative counties and 2 boroughs. County government is ordered by the Local Government act of 1888, which provides elective councils to supervise local government and to appoint the county officials. Its chief responsibilities are for local communications, education, asylums, and police. In Scotland, local government is the responsibility of the Scottish development department, set up in 1962.

English boroughs or towns before 1835 were close corporations, governed largely in the interests of a narrow body of "freeholders." By the Municipal Corporations act of that year, a systematic and more liberal form of city government was introduced, whereby the borough council became the city administration. This body acts through committees and employs city officials who, while relatively few in number, are chosen for experience and qualifications. The most unusual of these is the "clerk." While conforming to a general type, the powers of boroughs are expressly given by charters or by acts of Parliament, and the latter body is constantly importuned to extend the functions of boroughs. Nearly all so-called "private bills" are of this character.

The "mayor" of an English town is in no sense the head of its administration. The office, usually held for one year, is important in a social and a civic sense, and frequently imposes upon the occupant considerable expenditure for entertainment and for representation of the borough.

London. The government of London must be described separately. At its center is the ancient "City of London." This is still an "unreformed" English borough, governed by a close corporation of "councilmen" and "aldermen." The "lord mayor of London" is the presiding head; he resides in "Mansion House" and is an important civic figure in British life. Surrounding the city is the county of London, made up of 28 boroughs with district governments; but the London County council, created in 1888, has definite general powers over the whole area. The "Metropolitan Police Area" includes London county and extends over adjacent territory for nearly 700 square miles. To the metropolitan police is entrusted the public order of this central part of England. This highly trained force, with its headquarters at New Scotland Yard, is directly under the home secretary of Great Britain.

GREECE

Until 1967 Greece was a constitutional monarchy under a charter adopted in 1952, designating it as a crowned democracy. The reign of Constantine II, who became king in 1964, was marked by crises and he was forced to flee on Dec. 14, 1967, after a rightist junta seized power.

The Greek parliament had been dissolved before the April 1967 coup in preparation for parliamentary elections scheduled for May, but which were never held. Parliament remained dissolved. Col. George Papadopoulos was named premier and another officer was appointed "regent" to replace the king. In December 1967 and February 1968 the officers of the junta resigned their commissions and formed a "civilian" cabinet. A new constitution was drafted to be voted on by the people in September 1968. Greek voters approved the new charter submitted by the junta to replace that of 1952. The new constitution went into effect in November 1968. A new cabinet was named in December and Papadopoulos was confirmed as premier.

Civilian control of the government resumed on July 23, 1974, and the present constitution was adopted June 7, 1975. Under the new charter, the president is elected by a two-thirds majority of the legislature to a 5-year term. He has the power to appoint cabinet members and the premier, to dissolve parliament, and to veto legislation. He can also declare martial law and rule by decree for as long as 30 days without the approval of parliament.

The legislature is a single-chamber body of 300 members elected to 4-year terms by direct universal vote. The judiciary consists of a supreme court and lower courts. The 1975 constitution also changed the formal name of Greece to the Hellenic Republic.

GRENADA

Located in the Caribbean Sea, Grenada occupies the southernmost island of the Windward chain. Grenada was granted self-government in 1967 as part of the British West Indies Associated States. Following a constitutional conference in London, Grenada became independent within the British Commonwealth on February 7, 1974. It is a parliamentary state on the British model. The legislative branch consists of a 13-member senate and a 15-member house of representatives. House members are elected every five years by universal vote, while the senate is appointed by the governor general, who as part of the executive branch, is appointed by the ruler of England. The majority party in the house of representatives forms the government, and its leader becomes prime minister, the head of state. Divided into six parishes and one dependency (Carriacou), Grenada is served by a regional supreme court.

GUATEMALA

Guatemala achieved independence in 1821 and became a republic with an elected president in 1944. The constitution of 1956 extended suffrage to all men and all literate women, the minimum age being 18. Voting was compulsory for the literate and optional for the illiterate.

A new constitution became effective in 1966. The head of government remained the president, elected every 4 years. Under him is the cabinet, the council of state consisting of 14 members from the three branches of government, and the national congress, a body of 55 members elected by universal suffrage for 4-year terms. The country is divided into 22 departments, each administered by a governor appointed by the president. Municipalities elect their own mayors and councils.

Since the late 1960s Guatemala has suffered terrorism from both the left and right. Following the kidnapping and execution by leftists of the West German ambassador in 1970, a state of siege was declared and constitutional guarantees were revoked.

GUINEA

The former French Guinea decided in a referendum in 1958 to separate itself from the French Community and later the same year proclaimed itself an independent "democratic, secular, and social republic." A National Assembly, whose members are elected by universal suffrage on a national list for a 5-year term, has sole and unlimited power to legislate. The president is popularly elected for a 7-year term. He names the cabinet from Assembly members, and they are responsible to him, but he is responsible to the Assembly and must promulgate all laws passed by it. He has no power of veto.

GUINEA-BISSAU

Discovered by Nuno Tristao in 1446, Guinea-Bissau is located on the west coast of Africa and was formerly known as Portuguese Guinea. It became a separate colony in 1879 and an overseas province in 1951. In the 1960s the Party for the Independence of Guinea-Bissau waged war against the Portuguese troops and formed their own government. When the Independence party, then controlling most of the country, adopted a constitution in 1973, Portugal decided to give it recognition. On September 10, 1974, Guinea-Bissau became a republic. The Independence party remained the sole political group. The people elect the national assembly, which carries out legislative functions. The assembly members, who serve 3-year terms, elect the council of state. The 15-member council of state serves in an executive capacity, and elects its own presiding officer, who heads the government and is aided by a commissioner of foreign affairs.

GUYANA

Formerly British Guiana, Guyana is an independent South American cooperative republic within the Commonwealth. Its head of state is the British sovereign, represented by a president. The head of the government is the prime minister. The present constitution came into effect in 1966. The legislative body is a unicameral national assembly of 53 members, elected on the basis of proportional representation.

Originally a French colony, Haiti became independent in January 1804. The constitution and laws of the government purported to construct a republic after the French model. In practice, the government for more than a century was a military despotism in the hands of the president.

The constitution of 1964 provides for a single-chamber legislature of 58 deputies known as the legislative chamber. Its members are elected for 6-year terms by majority vote in "primary assemblies." They may be reelected indefinitely. This body meets also as the national assembly for purposes such as declaration of war, consideration of treaties, revision of the constitution, and as a high court. The chamber may be dissolved by the president in case of serious disagreement with him. New elections are then held.

The president alone has the power to introduce money bills in the chamber. He has a limited veto, which can be overridden by a two-thirds majority. If he fails to approve a bill before the chamber adjourns, the bill retains its status when the next session begins. The president is assisted by a cabinet responsible to him, although the members may appear in the legislature to support measures of the president. He appoints the justices of the supreme court, who have life tenure. Local government is carried on by communal councils chosen for 6-year terms.

The president also holds life tenure. Francois Duvalier was elected president in 1961. In 1964, in accordance with a constitutional change, he was named president for life. After his death, in 1971, he was succeeded as life president by his son, Jean-Claude Duvalier, whom he had nominated.

HONDURAS

Honduras revolted against Spain with the other Central American provinces in 1824. In 1838 Honduras adopted its own constitution which has been revised repeatedly. After a 1972 coup the congress was suspended; the country was then governed by decree.

HUNGARY

The Hungarian Republic of Workers and Working Peasants is the designation adopted in 1949 by the Communist government of Hungary, which was set up under Russian pressure after World War II. The country had been established as an independent nation after World War I. It was ruled as a regency for a vacant monarchy until World War II, when, having joined with Germany, it shared in the debacle of the Axis and was occupied by Russian troops. A rebellion in 1956 was crushed with Russian help, leaving the government unchanged in form but with a perceptibly wider latitude under its Russian tutelage.

The governing party is known as the Hungarian Socialist Workers' Party. The first secretary of the party is also the prime minister and effective ruler of the state. Parliament consists of about 340 deputies, all nominated by the party and elected for 4-year terms. A presidential council exercises legislative power between sessions of Parliament and can annul legislation if deemed unconstitutional or detrimental to the working people. As is the custom in Communist governments, however, such bodies are under the control of the politburo of the party, whose president is usually the first secretary of the party. Parliament normally gives a unanimous assent to measures which the politburo proposes through the prime minister and first secretary of the party.

Although the constitution recognizes the right of private property if it does not violate the public interest, the chief means of production are in the hands of the state and of party-controlled co-operatives.

From 930 to 1264, Iceland was an independent republic. It was joined to Norway in 1264 and with Norway came under the rule of Danish kings in 1381. It so remained until December 1, 1918. By the act of Union of November 30, 1918, it was recognized as a sovereign state in personal union with Denmark through the monarch. This act was to expire in 1943, and Icelandic opinion was against its renewal. On the invasion of Denmark by the Germans, Iceland was occupied by British troops, who later were replaced by Americans. On May 17, 1941, Iceland declared its complete autonomy under an elected regent. Formal separation from Denmark took place June 17, 1944.

The present constitution of Iceland was adopted on May 18, 1920, but was radically amended in 1934 and 1944. The executive power is exercised in Iceland by a president, elected for a 4-year term. He is assisted by a cabinet appointed by him but responsible also to the legislature, or *Althing*, which can impeach cabinet members before a special tribunal for parliamentary impeachment, the *Landsdomur*. The Althing consists of 2 chambers with a total of 60 members elected by proportional representation for 4-year terms. Upon assembling, it selects 20 members for the upper house, while the remaining 40 form the lower house. The two sit together to vote on bills approved by one House and disapproved by the other, a two-thirds majority being required for affirmative action. Budget bills form an exception, a majority being sufficient for adoption.

The president has no direct veto power. If he disapproves a bill, it nevertheless becomes law but must be submitted to a referendum, the outcome of which determines whether it continues as a law or is struck down.

The president's tenure of office may be cut short by a plebiscite held pursuant to a resolution approved by a three-fourths majority of the Althing. In the period between the resolution and the plebiscite, presidential powers are performed as though the presidency were vacant by a committee of the prime minister, speaker of the united Althing, and the chief justice of the supreme court. If the plebiscite rejects the resolution, the Althing must be dissolved and a new election held.

INDIA

India became independent in 1950 after having been part of a British colony for nearly a century, and part of a British dominion since 1947. In 1947 British India was divided into the two nations of India and Pakistan. Each country remained a member of the British Commonwealth of Nations.

In 1976 India was a union of 22 states and 9 territories. Each state and territory is governed by an official named by the president. The president is elected by a body of all elected members of the parliament. A vice president heads the upper house of the two-chamber parliament. The vice president is elected by the two houses and assumes presidential power if the president is unable to act from illness or other cause.

The parliament consists of the upper council of states and the lower house of the people. Council members are chosen partly by the elected members of the state legislatures, with one-tenth appointed by the president from among the more prominent citizens of India. The house consists of not more than 500 members, nearly all elected by popular vote.

The Indian constitution was passed by the constituent assembly in 1949 and became effective in January 1950. The constitution incorporated features of the systems of the United Kingdom, the U.S., and other Western democracies. By 1976 some 30 amendments had been made to the charter. The union of Indian states is more centralized than that of the U.S. and the rights of states are more limited. In basic human rights the constitution outlawed the old Hindu system of "untouchable" castes; it also prohibited double jeopardy under law and discrimination. Freedom of speech and assembly were guaranteed. The supreme court was empowered to decide on all questions of constitutionality.

The power to form government policy and establish an administrative cabinet is assigned to the prime minister. India's third prime minister, Indira Gandhi, was elected in 1966. She is the daughter of Jawaharlal Nehru, the first Indian prime minister. Her regime was marked by continuing problems of politics and economics.

On June 26, 1975, a state of emergency was declared and Prime Minister Gandhi assumed broad and arbitrary powers. Threats to national security and increasing domestic unrest were cited as reasons for the declaration of the emergency. Political arrests were made and many constitutional rights were suspended, including freedom of speech and assembly. The press was subjected to censorship by a constitutional amendment of January 1976. The courts were forbidden to challenge constitutional amendments and laws passed by parliament; citizens were barred from appealing against restrictions of their rights.

Although a group was formed to oppose emergency rule, opposition for the most part remained underground and unorganized. In 1976 it was reported that some 175,000 political dissidents were in jail. In June 1976, the parliament extended the government's right to hold prisoners for two years without a charge being made against them.

In October 1976 the parliament met for the consideration of further revisions of the constitution. Proposed amendments would increase executive powers once more and would further restrict the powers of the courts. The supreme court was slated to lose its authority to question the substance of legislation—in effect it would be able to pass only on legislative procedures. Yet it was also expected that Prime Minister Gandhi might lift some emergency powers and carry out the long-delayed election process. Many in India felt that emergency rule was necessary in view of national problems. The government had achieved some success in controlling black-market activities and the economy was considered to be improving.

In January 1977 elections were at last scheduled for March. Censorship was ended and political prisoners were freed, among them a former national official, Morarji Desai. Desai then headed a coalition opposed to Indira Gandhi. Supported by popular resentment of sterilization to control population and the forced relocation of slum-dwellers, Desai achieved the greatest turnout of voters in history. After 11 years as head of state, Gandhi saw her party defeated, ending 20 years of control. Gandhi lifted the state of emergency imposed 21 months before and then resigned. Morarji Desai, at 81 and after 19 months in prison, became prime minister, promising restoration of civil liberties and a policy of nonalignment with any foreign power.

INDONESIA

Before Indonesia was recognized as an independent republic in 1949, it had been a colonial empire under the Netherlands since 1809 after nearly 200 years of prior rule by the Dutch East India Company. In World War II, it was conquered by Japan, upon whose defeat in 1945 the territory was formally restored to the Netherlands. However, a nationalistic uprising in Java, Madura, and Sumatra took over those islands from the Japanese. The Indonesian republic was proclaimed with Sukarno as president. Hostilities with the Dutch continued intermittently until 1949, when the Netherlands transferred sovereignty to Indonesia. A constitution adopted that year was superseded in 1950 by

another, which Sukarno abrogated by decree in 1959 in order to reinstate the original revolutionary constitution of 1945. By so doing, he made himself practically dictator.

In 1966, army officers and Indonesian Communists forced Sukarno to name Suharto as head of the army. The following year, Sukarno was stripped of power and Suharto became president—the Communist party was then outlawed. Sukarno died in 1970.

The constitution of 1945 provides for six organs:

(1) The People's Congress, which is declared to represent the entire nation. To it is entrusted establishment of national policy and the election of the president. It meets once each 5 years. As to its membership, manner of selection, and term of office, the constitution is silent.

(2) The executive consists of the president and vice president, who serve for 5-year terms and may be re-elected. The president is assisted by a council of ministers chosen by himself and responsible to him alone. He is commander in chief of the army. He is invested also with legislative power, but his legislative measures must be ratified by the legislature. The president has an absolute veto over measures passed by the legislature. He may legislate by decree in an emergency, subject to later ratification.

(3) The unicameral legislature, known as Council of Representatives, which assembles once a year. It is appointed in part by local administrations or functional groups and partly by members representing political parties. However, the president issued a decree in 1960 enabling him to control political parties and, on recommendation of the supreme court, to dissolve them.

(4) A supreme advisory council, or council of state, which has the duty of advising the president on his request and may also submit proposals to him.

(5) The supreme court, which is independent of the government. The constitution is silent on how justices are appointed and on their tenure of office. Different codes of law govern Indonesians, Europeans, and foreign Orientals.

(6) The state controlling council, which accounts for public funds. It is independent of the legislature but makes recommendations to it.

IRAN

This Moslem constitutional monarchy was formerly known as Persia, with a long history as a powerful state both in ancient times and for some centuries in the Christian era. In the past it was able to dominate adjacent territory in periods of strength and yet was open to invasion from northern steppes and western plains in times of weakness. Its modern history is a record of decay, at least until the discovery of extensive oil deposits there in the 20th century. This and its location next to the U.S.S.R. gave it a certain key importance in the national rivalries and the emergent independence of the Arab nations.

Until 1906, Iran was an absolute monarchy. A constitution granted by the shah, or king, in that year, with subsequent amendments, provided for a national consultative assembly of 136 members. Presently, the assembly has 268 members elected to 4-year terms. The constitution also provided for a senate of 60 members, half appointed by the shah and half elected. The senate was constituted for the first time in 1950. The shah may dissolve either or both houses at any time.

The country is divided into 14 provinces, 6 governor-generalships, 151 governorships, and 459 districts. Provinces are divided into counties, each under a governor. The counties are divided into districts and groups of villages, each with its governing official. All the above officials are appointed by the central government. Individual villages, however, have a head man chosen locally.

In 1975 the two-party system was dissolved and a one-party system established. The National Political Resurrection Movement was then formed.

IRAQ

Freed from Turkish rule during World War I, Iraq was assigned as a mandate to Great Britain by the League of Nations and continued as such until 1922. Britain then recognized it as an independent state and concluded with it a treaty of protection. A constituent assembly in 1924 enacted an organic law establishing a limited monarchy and a responsible government. In 1958 an army group overthrew the monarchy and, in an interim constitution, declared Iraq to be an independent, sovereign, Islamic republic but forming an integral part of the Arab nation. Another military revolution terminated the adherence of Iraq to the Arab Federation. The rulers promulgated in 1964 a new interim constitution, which was to be superseded by a permanent republican constitution within three years.

The 1964 constitution provides in effect for a military dictatorship or oligarchy. The manner of choosing the president is not defined, but, in the event his office becomes vacant, his successor must be a member of the national council of the revolutionary command, a body which is not defined in the constitution. The successor is elected in a joint session of the members of this body, the cabinet, and the national defense council, another body not defined by the constitution. The president appoints the prime minister and other members of the cabinet and, with them, lays down the general policy of the state. Both the president and members of the cabinet must be of Iraqui parents from a family resident in Iraq since 1900 A.D., of Ottoman citizenship, and, if married, must have wives with Arab parents and grandparents.

Under a constitutional amendment announced by the prime minister in late 1964, a Consultative Assembly was set up, the members being appointed by a "republican decree" to represent the provinces in proportion to population, one member for each 70,000 to 100,000 inhabitants. The cabinet ministers are *ex officio* members. Its function is to draw up a permanent constitution and to take part in legislation in the interim.

IRELAND. See *Eire*, *Great Britain*.

ISRAEL

The republic of Israel came into existence on May 14, 1948, when the British mandate over Palestine given by the League of Nations in 1922 was relinquished. The United Nations set up boundaries between Israel and its Arabic neighbors, a move which touched off a war in which the Arabic states tried to conquer Israel, but the latter defeated them and enlarged its territory beyond the limits set by the United Nations.

Israel, like Great Britain, has no written constitution. Its frame of government follows the British model in making the legislature supreme, the president having no more power than the British monarch, but the British system is extensively modified by "basic laws," which are expected eventually to form the basis of a written constitution.

The one-chamber legislature, known as the *Knesset*, adopted the name and size of the Jewish governing body of about 2000 years earlier. Members are elected for a 4-year term, which may be cut short by dissolution voted by the Knesset itself. They are elected by universal suffrage of inhabitants over 18 on a nation-wide system rather than by local constituencies. The method of election is unique. Each political party nominates candidates in a priority determined by the party. Voters cast ballots for a party, not a candidate. The number of members of each party seated in the legislature is determined by the proportion of the total vote cast for that party. Thus, if a party is entitled to seat 15 members, the 15 party candidates having the highest priority are seated. Under this sytsem, it is not expected that any one party will have a clear majority; hence the government is a coalition of parties.

The president is elected by the Knesset for a 5-year term by majority vote and may be removed by a three-fourths vote. He has no veto power but is required to sign all bills adopted. It is his function to select the prime minister, usually the leader of the party with the largest representation in the legislature. The prime minister chooses his cabinet, which may include non-members of the legislature. The latter may sit in the Knesset but without the right to vote. If the cabinet resigns or is, in effect, ousted by a vote of no confidence, the legislature is then required to dissolve itself, and a new election is held.

Civil and religious judges are appointed by the president on the recommendation of a nominating committee. There is no provision for courts to pass on the constitutionality of acts, but merely on their legality. Apart from statutes, Israeli law is based on English common law, Hebraic law, and Moslem law, the last being due to the fact that the country was ruled by Moslems for over 1200 years. The courts are required to accord complete procedural equality of the citizen and the government.

Local government is exercised by municipal corporations, local councils, and regional councils, members of which are popularly elected for 4-year terms. They operate under by-laws and with revenue sources approved by the minister of the interior.

A fundamental law provides that every Jew is entitled to come to Israel as an immigrant.

The organization known as the Jewish Agency has played a principal part in the establishment of social, political, and economic bases that are fundamental to the state of Israel. The agency has continued its role in organizing and maintaining immigration from the Jewish communities of the world.

Another organization, called the Malben, provides services for immigrants to Israel who are sick, handicapped, or advanced in age.

A national insurance law, which came into effect in 1954, administers pensions for the aged, insurance for survivors of broken families, compensation for work-connected injuries or disabilities, maternity insurance, family allotments, and unemployment compensation payments.

ITALY

Italy, now a republic, was once the center of the Western world's political authority under the Roman Empire and again the religious center of Western civilization in the religious union of the Roman Catholic Church. For centuries it was broken into fragments and subjected to foreign domination. It became a unity as a modern state only in 1861, when the king of Sardinia was proclaimed "king of Italy" by the first Italian Parliament. The remainders of the provinces of Mantua and Venetia were added in 1866. In 1870 Rome was entered by Italian troops, the last remnant of the papal states was incorporated in the kingdom, and the "temporal power" of the pope was suppressed.

The Monarchy and Fascism. Under the monarchy the Italian constitution was the fundamental law granted March 4, 1848, to the Kingdom of Sardinia. Around this nucleus Italy was united, and it was adopted as the constitution of the new kingdom. This constitution vested executive power in the sovereign, who was to exercise it through ministers responsible to him. Legislative power resided in the king and a two-chamber legislature.

Under the leadership of Benito Mussolini, the Fascist party seized the government on October 22, 1922. The king accepted Mussolini as prime minister, and the government was gradually transformed. The constitution was not repealed, but much was added.

The dominant feature of the government was the control by the Fascist party which numbered about 5 per cent of the population. The Fascist Grand Council named by the leader (*Il Duce*) might choose his successor. The prime minister and his cabinet issued decrees and executed them. The only other law-making body was the National Council of Corporations. The former Parliament remained but without power.

With the fall of Mussolini the Fascist party was abolished. The king resumed his functions, which, after the taking of Rome, he delegated to Prince Humbert.

When the allies entered Rome, the king retired and formally abdicated in May 1946. In a popular referendum in June, 54 per cent of the people voted for a republic, which came into effect by a new constitution in 1948.

The constitution describes Italy as a "democratic republic founded on work." At the head of the government is a president elected by a joint session of the two houses of Parliament, and 3 additional delegates from each region. His term is 7 years, and he must be 50 years old. He has power to dissolve Parliament, except during the last 6 months of his term. There is no vice president. The speaker of the Senate serves in the event of temporary disability of the president. If the office becomes vacant, the speaker of the Chamber of Deputies orders a new presidential election.

Parliament is made up of the Chamber of Deputies and the Senate. The deputies, one for each 80,000 inhabitants, are elected by direct universal vote and serve 5 years. The senators are elected for 6 years from the regions, one for each 200,000 people, but at least 6 from each region except Aosta, which has one. Besides these, the president, who is himself a senator for life, can appoint 5 life senators from men eminent in science or arts.

The president appoints the prime minister and, on the latter's recommendation, other cabinet ministers. They need not be members of Parliament. The cabinet and prime minister can be forced out of office only by a direct vote of lack of confidence, not by a mere defeat of their measures.

Bills may be introduced by members of Parliament, by members of the cabinet on the president's authorization, by councils of the regions, and by popular referendum on a bill proposed by at least 50,000 voters. A bill approved by both houses goes to the president for approval. If he disapproves, the bill is sent back to Parliament. If it is again passed by both houses, it becomes law.

Italy has the usual system of local and higher courts and courts of appeal. The constitution creates a constitutional court with power to pass upon the constitutionality of laws, decide cases between regions, and try impeachment cases.

Administratively, the country is divided into 19 regions, some of them, as Sicily and Sardinia, partly autonomous; each has a council and executive. The regions are subdivided into provinces, and the provinces are divided into communes, each with its own elective councils. The national Parliament may dissolve the regional councils on specified grounds and arrange for new elections. Laws passed by regional councils must be approved by the president of the republic, who may refer it to the constitutional court for validity or to Parliament on questions of policy.

Roman Catholicism is the state religion, but other religions are tolerated. Civil marriage is allowed, and divorces may be granted. Titles of nobility are no longer recognized, but those granted before 1922 may be used as part of the name.

The constitution may be amended by proposals passed by both houses of Parliament and passed again in 2 successive sessions at intervals of not less than 3 months. Thereafter the proposal must be again approved by an absolute majority of all members in each house. The republican form of government is not subject to amendment.

After 25 years of Fascist rule and five years of war, Italy was plagued by unemployment and civil dissension. Vatican and U.S. aid under the Marshall Plan helped Italy through its postwar troubles. Italy also became a member of NATO. By the Treaty of Rome in 1957, Italy became a partner in the European Common Market.

The Christian Democrats have been in power since World War II, but in recent years, the Italian Communist party has been making major gains at the polls. The Communist party has taken advantage of the country's worst and longest recession since the war. In the June 1976 national elections, the Communists gained their most important parliamentary role since the formation of the republic.

Relations with the Pope. The occupation of the city of Rome by Italian troops in 1870 and the making of this city the capital of the Kingdom of Italy suppressed the temporal powers of the pope. The papacy was unreconciled to this loss. Improved relations between the "Vatican" and "Quirinal," effected by the Fascist administration, led to the signing, on February 11, 1929, of 3 treaties whereby the Italian government recognized the full independent sovereignty of the pope over the City of the Vatican.

Italia Irredenta. The unification of Italy, 1861–70, did not succeed in uniting to the kingdom the entire population subject to Austria. Considerable territory remained 'unredeemed." Italy entered World War I with the object of securing these territories under guarantees from the Allies through a treaty signed at London in 1915 with Great Britain, France, and Russia. The political situation was altered at the end of the war by the disintegration of the Austro-Hungarian Empire and by the demands of the kingdom of Yugoslavia. As a result Italy secured only some strategic points on the Dalmation coast. After World War II, by the treaty of 1947, Italy lost to Yugoslavia all its territory east of the Adriatic. Trieste, with its surrounding territory, was made a free port under the jurisdiction of the United Nations but subsequently with jurisdiction divided between Italy and Yugoslavia. Italy's frontier with France was "rectified," and the Dodecanese Islands were ceded to Greece.

Former Colonies. Before World War II Italy had a considerable colonial empire in Africa. The first acquisitions, in 1885, were Eritrea, on the Red Sea, and Italian Somaliland, on the Indian Ocean. Italian Libya, on the Mediterranean Sea, was taken from Turkey by conquest in 1911. Italian Somaliland was enlarged by the cession of a part of Kenya by Great Britain in 1924. Ethiopia was conquered and annexed in 1936. Albania was annexed in April 1939. Ethiopia was liberated by the British in 1941. Albania had driven out the Germans and set up a provisional government by the end of 1944, and in 1946 was proclaimed a republic. Eritrea was federated with Ethiopia in 1952.

IVORY COAST

Formerly a French territory, Ivory Coast voted in 1958 to become independent and remain outside the French Community. Under a constitution adopted in 1960, it declared itself a republic. It has a National Assembly of about 65 members elected by universal suffrage for a 5-year term from a one-party slate. There is a popularly elected president, who also serves for 5 years. He is the chief executive officer and may initiate legislation in the Assembly. In the event of his death in office, the president of the Assembly names a successor from that body. Laws become effective 15 days after transmittal to the president, who, however, may within the period return them to the Assembly for reconsideration or submit them to a referendum of the people.

JAMAICA

Jamaica, independent since 1962 and a member of the British Commonwealth, is a constitutional democracy with a government modeled on that of Great Britain. Parliament consists of a governor-general as representative of the sovereign, a Senate of 21 members, and House of Representatives of 45 to 60 members.

The House of Representatives is elected by universal suffrage for a 5-year term. The leader of the majority party is prime minister. Members of the Senate are appointed by the governor-general, 13 on the advice of the prime minister and 8 on the advice of the leader of the opposition. The governor-general has powers of veto, in which he may be advised by a privy council of six members whom he selects, two being present or former office holders.

JAPAN

According to Japanese records, Japan is an ancient monarchy, dating from the emperor Jimmu Tenno (B.C. 660). In the 16th century, when foreign intercourse began through the Dutch and the Portuguese, Japanese civilization had acquired its characteristic forms. Government was organized in a feudal system. The territory was divided among great lords, *daimyos*, possessing military retainers, *samurai*, and owing allegiance to the emperor at Kyoto but virtually independent and frequently at war with one another. Actual central power was exercised in the emperor's name by a succession of rulers called the shoguns. By one of these, in the early part of the 17th century, foreign intercourse, which at first had been welcomed, was prohibited and Japan remained closed to the outside world until the arrival of the American naval mission under Commodore Perry in 1853.

The "opening" of Japan was followed by the overthrow of the "shogunate," the restoration of the emperor, and the introduction in 1868 of a new period of progress called the era of Meiji or enlightenment. From that began a process of "Westernization" by means of which Japan transformed itself from feudalism to modern industrialism without such bloody revolutions as occurred when France, Russia, and China passed through a similar transformation.

A constitutional movement followed upon the "restoration." The feudal daimyos surrendered their powers; experiment began with quasi representative institutions. A constitution was promulgated in 1889, and in 1890 the first Imperial Diet, or representative legislature, convened.

The Meiji Constitution. By this constitution the emperor was sovereign, of divine descent, his person sacred. He both governed and legislated. He was apt to be guided by a small body of councilors, the *Gen Ro*, elder statesmen, who had no constitutional status but very great influence.

The Diet was composed of a House of Peers and a House of Representatives. The peerage was reorganized with European grades and titles. A law of 1925 diminished the number of peers in the upper branch and admitted a number of commoners selected by the emperor. At the same time, universal manhood suffrage was introduced. The lower house was elected for 4-year terms.

In theory, government was by a responsible ministry, but the Diet could not control the budget, the ministers of war and navy must be officers in service, and the privy council, an elderly and conservative body, could effectively oppose the ministry. This central government showed German influence. The local government was rather on the French model, with prefectures, districts, and towns governed by appointed officers, and controlled from above. Finally, the industrial revolution had created a group of influential families, the *Zaibatsu*, who controlled the economic life of Japan and influenced its politics.

Rise and Fall of the Empire. A long period of imperial expansion followed in the course of which Japan acquired Formosa, Korea, the southern half of Sakhalin, Port Arthur, and, as mandates after World War I, the former German Pacific islands north of the equator. In 1931, Japan seized Manchuria and conquered much of China. She began World War II by challenging the United States as a world power and quickly overran British, Dutch, French, and American dependencies in southeast Asia, proposing to organize them into a "co-prosperity sphere." Then came defeat, loss of the empire, and a new form of government.

The New Constitution. Under the terms of surrender in August 1945, Japan was allowed to retain her emperor but without his claim to divine authority. A constitution adopted in 1948 declares that the "emperor shall be the symbol of the state and of the unity of the people, deriving his position from the will of the people with whom resides sovereign power." All his governmental powers must be exercised on the advice and approval of the Diet, over whose acts he has no power of veto. In this respect, he resembles the British monarch. The Shintu religion is disestablished.

Testimony to Japan's reversal of its military past is the unique provision of the constitution by which Japan renounces war and forbids the maintenance of land, sea, and air forces. This is to be understood in the light of the umbrella which the strength of the United States held for her protection in the post-war period.

The sole lawmaking body is the bicameral Diet. The House of Representatives is elected by universal suffrage for 4 years, unless sooner dissolved. The House of Councilors is elected for 6 years, one-half retiring every 3 years. Laws require the consent of both houses, but the lower house may overrule the upper by a two-thirds vote. The prime minister is chosen by the Diet. He and a majority of his colleagues must be members. The cabinet is responsible to the House of Representatives. If it loses their confidence it must resign, or dissolve the House and order new elections.

The supreme judicial body is the supreme court. Judges of the supreme court are appointed by the cabinet and must, on their appointment and every 10 years thereafter, receive popular approval. The independence of judges is guaranteed, but they may be impeached. The supreme court may pass on the constitutionality of a law. The Diet alone may levy taxes and make appropriations. Local public entities elect their own assemblies and generally manage their own affairs.

The constitution guarantees civil rights, including freedom of speech, religion, assembly, collective bargaining, and academic teaching. Marriage is to be based on equal rights of the sexes in property rights, domicile, and divorce.

The constitution can be amended by a two-thirds vote of each house of the Diet and must be ratified by popular vote.

JORDAN

The kingdom of Jordan, formerly a part of the British mandated territory of Palestine, became independent by a treaty with Britain in 1946. Under the constitution of 1952, it is designated as the Hashemite Kingdom of Jordan. The king has an unusually large measure of control over the government. He appoints the 30 members of the upper house of parliament and designates its president. Members serve for 8-year terms. The king appoints the prime minister and other ministers and may dismiss them. The king may dissolve the lower house—the council of representatives—and thereby bring about another election, this 60-member body being elected by male suffrage. The king's veto of bills may be overridden by a two-thirds majority of each house. He appoints and may dismiss judges. The constitution may be amended by two-thirds vote in each house but cannot become effective without the king's signature.

KENYA

The former British East Africa, Kenya became independent in 1963 under an interim charter of 1963. At the end of 1964, the government declared itself a republic within the British Commonwealth. Legislative power resides in Parliament, consisting of a Senate and a House of Representatives. Members of the Senate elected by universal suffrage from districts for a term of 6 years. Members of the House are popularly elected in part, from 110 to 130 constituencies, and these members choose other members, numbering 10 per cent of those popularly elected.

The president, who must be a member of the House, is chosen by the elected members of the House. The president chooses ministers from both houses and appoints a vice president from ministers who are elected members of the House. Bills introduced into Parliament require his prior consent.

KOREA

Korea was a kingdom from 668 A.D. until it was annexed by Japan in 1910. It was freed in 1945 by Russian and American forces, who divided it for military convenience at the 38th parallel of latitude.

North Korea. Under the constitution of 1972 a supreme people's assembly is elected every 4 years by universal suffrage. The assembly elects a premier who is the official head of government. In effect, the country is ruled by the Korean Workers' (Communist) party which elects a central committee. The central committee appoints the ruling politboro. The secretary-general of the party serves as president and head of state.

South Korea. The South Koreans, in 1948, adopted a republican constitution under which the elected president ruled without a cabinet. North Korea invaded the country in 1950, but was driven back by UN forces, chiefly U.S. and South Korean troops. Under a 1972 constitution the president is given wide powers. He is elected to a 6-year term by a national council for unification, which is elected by direct popular vote. The president may be re-elected for a limit of 3 consecutive terms. One-third of the members of the national assembly are appointed by the president; the others are popularly elected. The national assembly consists of no more than 250 members.

KUWAIT

From 1899 until 1961 this oil-rich monarchy was under the protection of Britain. A constitution was then proclaimed in 1963. Its provisions included the establishment of a 50-member national assembly, the members of which are to be elected. The ruler of Kuwait is the amir. There is also a crown prince, prime minister, and deputy ministers for information, foreign affairs, and oil production. Kuwait joined the Arab League in 1961.

LAOS

Formerly a part of French Indo-China, Laos became a constitutional monarchy in 1947 and an independent sovereign state within the French Union in 1949. In 1973 an agreement was signed ending the war which the Royal Lao government and the Communist Pathet Lao had been fighting since 1953 and establishing a coalition government. In 1975, following Communist victories in Cambodia and Vietnam, the Pathet Lao took control of the entire country. A 264-member people's congress voted to end the 600-year-old monarchy and proclaimed a people's democratic republic. The Pathet Lao control the provincial administration with orders coming from the central committee. There is a president, prime minister, and 4 deputy prime ministers. Political disorders continue.

LEBANON

The republic of Lebanon was for 20 years after World War I a mandated territory of France. It was granted independence in 1941, and in 1944 powers formerly exercised by France were transferred to the Lebanese government. Lebanon became a member of the UN and of the Arab League.

The republic's first constitution, which has been amended, was adopted in 1926 when Lebanon was still under the French mandate. The executive branch consists of a president and a prime minister, with a cabinet appointed by him. There also is a single-chamber legislature, elected by universal adult vote, and an independent judiciary. An electoral law allocates deputies according to the religious distribution of the population. According to the constitution the president is to be a Maronite Christian, the prime minister a Sunni Moslem, and the speaker of the chamber a Shia Moslem. There are distinct religious divisions in Lebanon's political, geographic, and social structures.

A civil war erupted in Lebanon in April 1975. Despite the religious compromise proposed in the constitution, Lebanon's government has been unable to handle the problems created by a multi-religious society. Also there have been increased tensions and military confrontations resulting from the Arab-Israeli conflict.

LESOTHO

Formerly the British protectorate of Basutoland, Lesotho is surrounded by the Republic of South Africa. A constitutional monarchy, it has a government headed by a prime minister. In 1965 the constitution set up a bicameral parliament consisting of a national assembly, with 60 elected members, and a senate with 22 chiefs and 11 other members appointed by the king. Lesotho became independent and joined the UN in 1966.

LIBERIA

This republic on the west coast of Africa was founded July 26, 1847. A constitution was adopted the same year. The country is still governed under this constitution, with a few amendments, although the actual government is far from extending throughout the entire country, the vast majority of the population continuing under tribal rule.

Liberia is almost alone among modern countries in requiring ownership of real property as a qualification for voting. For the hinterland, possession of a hut is sufficient. The constitution in general is modeled on that of the United States. The president and a vice president are elected directly by popular vote of qualified citizens over 18 for an 8-year term. The president has a limited right of veto over bills passed by Congress, which can be overridden by a two-thirds vote of each house. The constitution authorizes removing from office those in authority who become oppressors, but the manner of doing so is not prescribed. The president is assisted by a cabinet chosen with the advice and consent of the Senate.

Congress consists of (1) a Senate of 18 members elected for 6-year terms, but 3 or 4 of the members must run for re-election each 2 years and (2) a House of 71 members elected for 4-year terms. Two senators are elected from each county, while the number of congressmen elected from each county is roughly proportional to its population except that each of the three provinces in the hinterland is entitled to one only.

LIBYA

The Kingdom of Libya comprises the former Italian colony of Libya. For centuries it was under the rule of the Turkish Ottoman Empire until the Italians occupied it in 1911. During World War II the administration of Libya was taken over by Britain and France, the British controlling the provinces of Tripolitania and Cyrenaica, the French that of Fezzan. In 1949 the UN stated that Libya should become a sovereign country by 1952. A constitution was adopted, and in December 1951, King Idris I, who had been recognized in 1949 as Amir of Cyrenaica, proclaimed the country's independence. Before 1963, Libya had been a federal state consisting of three provinces, each administered by a governor. In April 1963 the federal system was abolished and comprehensive unity declared. The king was deposed by a group of army officers in September 1969. Some of the officers established the revolutionary command council. The 10-member council rules Libya with the assistance of a cabinet, which is mainly civilian. There is a chairman of the council and a prime minister. The country is divided into 10 divisions, each administered by a commissioner.

LIECHTENSTEIN

This Alpine principality of 65 square miles is a hereditary monarchy, succession being in the male line only. There is a Diet of 15 members, elected by universal suffrage. Voting is direct and election is by proportional representation. An administrator for the state is appointed by the prince. There is a high court.

From 1867 to 1918, the principality was dependent on Austria, but the Diet proclaimed the complete independence of the state in 1918. Nevertheless, by treaty of 1920, Switzerland took over its diplomatic representation and administration of its postal and telegraph systems. In 1923, it was incorporated in the Swiss customs union.

LUXEMBOURG

This constitutional monarchy, known as a grand duchy, bordering on France, Belgium, and Germany, was given its rank as a principality by the Congress of Vienna in 1815. By the Treaty of London (1867), it was neutralized and its integrity and its independence were guaranteed. But, having been invaded and occupied by German armies in 1914, it abandoned neutrality and aligned its policies with Belgium.

The monarchy is heritable by either male or female heir. The present constitution is that of 1868 with later amendments. In 1919, universal suffrage was introduced with proportional representation of parties in the legislature.

The unicameral legislature, the Chamber of Deputies, consists of about 55 members elected for 5-year terms, barring prior dissolution of the Chamber. The grand duke has no veto power over bills, but he may dissolve the Chamber. He is assisted by a cabinet of members appointed by him, who may not be members of the Chamber. They may, however, introduce bills in behalf of the grand duke and may be called into attendance by the deputies. The grand duke is assisted also by a council of 21 members appointed by him for life. The legislature may also call on the council for advice on legislation. Local government is by popularly elected community councils headed by a mayor appointed by the grand duke. In order to amend the constitution, it is necessary for the Chamber to so resolve, whereupon it is dissolved, and a new Chamber is elected. This body, with at least three-fourths of its members present, must uphold the proposal by a two-thirds vote in order to make it valid.

MALAGASY (MADAGASCAR)

This former French colony is a member of the French Community. In October 1958 Madagascar was proclaimed a republic and became known as the Republic of Malagasy. A second republic, the Malagasy Democratic Republic, was proclaimed in December 1975. Malagasy was admitted to the UN in September 1960. It is located off the southeast coast of Africa.

The constitution of 1959 provided for a national assembly, senate, president, and ministers; however, the government was dissolved in May 1972, and in October, a provisional constitution was declared. A national military directorate was created in February 1975. In June of the same year, the military directorate was terminated, and the supreme revolutionary council formed. Didier Ratsiraka was declared president and head of the council. A socialist state was established; Ratsiraka nationalized banks, insurance companies, and movie theaters. The council, composed of 9 members, is the policy-making body of the government and supervises the activities of government ministers. In a referendum in December 1975 voters supported the Ratsiraka regime, gave him the power to rule by decree for 18 months, approved a 7-year term for the leader, and approved a new constitution. In January 1976 Ratsiraka was sworn in as president of the Malagasy Democratic Republic. He then appointed a premier.

MALAWI (NYASALAND)

Malawi, formerly the British protectorate of Nyasaland, became an independent state within the British Commonwealth on July 6, 1964. It had been granted self-government in February 1963. Hastings Kamuzu Banda was sworn in as prime minister, and a cabinet and parliament were created. On July 6, 1966, Malawi was declared a republic within the Commonwealth and Banda sworn in as the first president. The president is head of government and of the Malawi Congress party. Banda became president for life on July 6, 1971—a constitutional amendment in 1970 established the new position. The functions and authority of the presidency have increased since 1970. Banda assumed some cabinet posts in 1972 and 1976 and took control of the press and communications in 1973. A 12-member cabinet was appointed in 1976. Malawi is a one-party republic. Parliament is composed of 60 elected members and 15 nominated members. The country is divided into 3 regions and 24 districts, each administered by a district commissioner. Malawi lies along the western and southern shores of Lake Malawi in southern Africa.

MALAYSIA

A "federal constitutional monarchy" formed from 13 former British dependencies. Nine of them had become independent in 1957 as the Federation of Malaya, each being ruled by a hereditary sultan. To this federation were added two former British Straits Settlements (Penang and Malacca). Singapore with Sarawak and North Borneo adhered until 1965, when Singapore withdrew, claiming to take Sarawak and North Borneo with it. The official religion is Moslem.

Under a constitution adopted in 1963, the "monarch," known as the supreme head of the federation, and a deputy to act in his absence are chosen for 5-year terms by a conference of rulers, consisting of the heads of the federated states. He, with the deputy, must be a head of a state and on election relinquishes his rule over the state, except that part of it relating to religious matters.

Parliament consists of a Senate and House of Representatives. The Senate consists of members elected by each state legislative assembly and members appointed by the federal head of state for their distinction and their capability of speaking for minorities and the aborigines. The term of office is 6 years. Parliament may, by majority vote, provide for election of all senators by popular vote. The Senate is not subject to dissolution. The House consists of members elected by universal balloting from the different states roughly in proportion to their population.

The supreme head of state appoints the prime minister, who is responsible to the House, and also the other ministers on the prime minister's recommendation.

MALDIVE ISLANDS

There are 2000 islands in this Indian Ocean group, 220 of them inhabited. Except briefly in 1953, the islands were a sultanate until the establishment of republican government by the constitution of 1968. A president, elected for a 4-year term heads the government. Election to the unicameral legislature is by popular vote—there are 54 members. The islands became independent and joined the UN in 1965. British rights to an airbase in the islands expire in 1986.

MALI

Formerly the territory of the French Sudan, the Republic of Mali became independent in September 1960. It is in the western portion of north Africa. The constitution of 1960 provided for a national assembly of 70 members elected by universal vote for a 5-year term and a president elected by the assembly. In November 1968 the president was overthrown by a bloodless military coup. A liberation committee took control of all political and administrative functions, and Yoro Diakite assumed the position of president. In September 1969 Moussa Traore replaced Diakite as chief of state and head of the government. A new constitution was approved by popular vote in June 1974. It stated that the liberation committee would define national policies and supervise the government for the next five years. It also provided for the election by universal vote of a president and the establishment of a national assembly and a single political party.

MALTA

This strategic Mediterranean island has been victim to economic strain and political unrest since the withdrawal of British forces—completed in 1969. Malta became a republic in 1974 within the Commonwealth. The ruler of England, represented by a governor-general, is head of state, while the government is headed by a prime minister. The single-chamber house of representatives has 55 members, elected for 5-year terms. Malta's constitution became effective in 1964.

MAURITANIA

A former French territory which became an independent Islamic republic in 1960, electing to remain within the French Community. The president, who must be of the Islamic faith, is elected by universal suffrage for a 5-year term, as are also members of the National Assembly. The president as well as assemblymen can initiate bills in the legislature. He appoints the ministers. He can exercise a suspensive veto of bills by sending them back for reconsideration within 15 days but otherwise must promulgate them.

MAURITIUS

This Indian Ocean island is a parliamentary state within the British Commonwealth. The head of state is the British sovereign, represented by a governor-general. The single-body legislature has a speaker and members elected to 5-year terms by universal vote.

MEXICO

Mexico is a federal republic with a constitution modeled on that of the United States but with a number of modifications directed toward avoidance of abuses in its history since its independence from Spain in 1821. Rivalry between imperial and republican proponents took the form of frequent civil war until the adoption of a liberal republican constitution in 1857, which was temporarily in eclipse during 1864–67, an emperor, Maximilian, having been imposed by French power. Mexico's liberator, Diaz, held the presidency continuously from 1876 to 1911, when he was overthrown. A new constitution was adopted in 1917 designed to prevent a long rule, such as that of Diaz, and to break up the landed aristocracy upon whose power Diaz depended.

The national government is entrusted to a president and a bicameral legislature—Senate and House of Representatives. The Senate consists of 60 members, 2 from each state and the federal district, elected by universal suffrage for 6-year terms. The House consists of one deputy for each 170,000 inhabitants. Deputies are chosen for 3-year terms. No member of Congress may succeed himself. Bills may originate from either house and also from the president and from state legislatures. The president may veto a bill but the veto may be overridden by a two-thirds vote of both houses. Suffrage may be exercised by citizens who are 18 or older and have an honest means of livelihood.

The president is elected by universal suffrage for a 6-year term. If the office becomes vacant in the first 2 years, Congress elects an interim president and calls a new election for a president to complete the term. A vacancy in the last 4 years is filled by a new president elected by Congress for the balance of the term. The president has sole discretion in the choice and dismissal of his cabinet. In no case may a president serve more than one term.

There is a supreme court of 27 members appointed by the president and subject to Senate approval within 10 days.

Ownership of land is restricted to Mexican citizens or to foreigners only if they agree to be bound therein as citizens. No commercial company may own rural real estate. Electric power may be developed and distributed only by the federal government. Religious institutions are forbidden to own land.

MONACO

A tiny principate which, except for a small strip of Mediterranean coast, is entirely surrounded by French territory. The state is the private possession of the prince, and was governed autocratically until January 7, 1911, when a constitution was granted. This constitution was suspended in 1959 by the prince and was replaced in 1962 by another which recognizes the hereditary monarchy, although the reigning prince renounced his "divine right" to rule. A legislature of two houses is provided—the National Council of 18 members and the Communal Council of 16 members, both elected by universal suffrage.

Representation on a popular basis is accorded to Monaco, La Condamine, and Monte Carlo, the three "communes" which comprise the principate. Public revenue and the income of the prince are derived almost entirely from the concessions to gambling establishments.

MONGOLIA

The Mongolian People's Republic won independence from China in 1921 with Russian help, and is now a Soviet satellite. It has a one-party system with an elected assembly meeting at least every 3 years; 30 members form an executive committee, which selects a presidium of 7 as an interim body. A cabinet of 10 ministers chosen by the executive committee governs. The political leader is the secretary of the Communist party; the head of state is chairman of the presidium. Mongolia's present constitution dates from 1960.

MOROCCO

Prior to 1956, what is now the constitutional monarchy of Morocco was, from 1912, divided into a French protectorate and a British protectorate, the area of Tangiers being from 1923 an international zone. The ruler was a sultan. Its independence was recognized in 1956, and the sultan, Mohammed V, changed his title to king. While retaining the supreme religious authority which was his as sultan, he planned to share his political authority under a constitution framed by himself. His son, Hassan II, submitted a constitution to referendum by universal suffrage in 1962, and it was approved by an overwhelming majority.

The crown descends in the male line. The king appoints the prime minister and other members of the cabinet and may dismiss them. He presides over meetings of the cabinet, the supreme court, and the supreme council for national reconstruction and planning. The legislature consists of a Chamber of Representatives and a Chamber of Councilors. Representatives are elected by universal suffrage for a 4-year term. Councilors are elected for a 6-year term, one-half renewable each 3 years, by an indirect method. Two-thirds are chosen by an electoral college consisting of town, provincial, and county councils; the remaining third are elected by chambers of commerce, industry, arts and crafts, and delegates from labor unions. Only members of the electoral college, chambers of commerce, or unions are eligible.

MOZAMBIQUE

Mozambique is located on the southeastern coast of Africa. Vasco da Gama discovered Mozambique in 1498; it was first colonized in 1505. In 1951 Mozambique became an oversea province of Portugal.

With the rise of the black African nationalist movement, Eduardo Mondlane founded the Front for the Liberation of Mozambique in 1962. Operating from headquarters in Tanzania, the independence movement began to wage guerrilla warfare in 1964. Mondlane was assassinated in Dar es Salaam in 1969, and leadership was passed on to his assistant, Samora Moises Machel. In 1972 Mozambique became an overseas state of Portugal.

In April 1974 a military coup overthrew the Portuguese regime. After a decade of fighting between guerrillas and Portuguese troops, a transitional Portuguese-Liberation Front government, led by Joaquim Chissano, was established in September 1974.

On June 25, 1975, after 470 years of Portuguese colonial rule, the People's Republic of Mozambique achieved full independence. Machel became the country's first president. The one-party state, dedicated to Marxist-Maoist ideology, was to be ruled by central, political, and military committees, with the liberation front supreme over both the government and army. The black administration called for the nationalization of land, the establishment of collective farms, and the eradication of tribalism, regionalism, and racism.

Mozambique was admitted to the UN and the Organization of African Unity, and established diplomatic relations with the U.S. Since independence, groups have been formed in opposition to the country's austerity program and its many economic problems persist.

NAURU

Called Pleasant Island by its American discoverers in 1798, Nauru was renamed when annexed by Germany in 1888. It was administered by an Australian-New Zealand-British mandate after World War I. The island is now a republic, headed by a president elected by the legislature and assisted by a 4-man cabinet. The 18 members of the unicameral assembly are popularly elected. In 1968, when Nauru became independent, the natives rejected Australian protection and political direction in foreign affairs.

NEPAL

This Hindu constitutional monarchy owes its long history of independence largely to its rugged terrain in the Himalaya mountains between China and India. Prior to 1951, the king was a puppet, and the country was ruled arbitrarily by a hereditary prime minister belonging to the Rama family. In that year, the power of this family was broken and the king established his authority. He proclaimed a constitution in 1951 under which there was an elected Congress and a cabinet. In 1959, the king dissolved Congress and assumed sole leadership. Three years later, he promulgated a new constitution, which, however, he may revoke in an emergency.

The constitution of 1962 provides for a National Congress, partly indirectly elected and partly appointed. There are 112 elected members, their electors being zonal congressmen elected by district congressmen, who in turn are elected by village and town congresses, recognized as the basic units of democracy. Appointed members of the National Congress comprise 23 representatives of professional organizations and university graduates, and royal nominees not exceeding 15 per cent of the elected members.

NETHERLANDS

The Dutch nation arose in the 16th century by the revolt of the provinces of the "low countries" against Spain. In 1579, the provinces of Holland, Zealand, Utrecht, Gelderland, Groningen, Friesland, and Overyssel joined to form the 'United Netherlands" under the prince of Orange as governor, or *stadthouder*. The remaining provinces were resubjected to Spanish authority and experienced a different fortune. In 1830, they united to form the present kingdom of Belgium.

In 1815, the Netherlands was reconstituted as a sovereign state and was raised by action of the "great powers" to the rank of a kingdom. The constitution was promulgated in 1814, was revised in 1815 after the addition of the Belgian provinces, in 1840 after their secession, in 1848, and 10 times thereafter. In 1917 an electoral reform act provided for universal suffrage and for proportional representation.

The royal succession is the direct male line of descent from Prince William of Orange. In default of male heirs, the female heir becomes queen.

The legislative body is known as the States General and comprises a First Chamber of 75 members elected by the provincial legislatures for a term of 6 years, one-half retiring each 3 years, and of a Second Chamber of 150 members, chosen for 4 years by citizens of both sexes above 18 years of age on a system of proportional representation. Voting is compulsory. Both men and women of the age of 25 are eligible for election to the States General. Initiation of laws is restricted to the government and to the Second Chamber, the First Chamber having power only to approve or to reject but not to amend. The sovereign may dissolve either or both chambers, in which case a new election must take place within 40 days and the first session be held within 3 months.

Government is conducted by the sovereign and by a council of ministers, one of whom is appointed president of the council. There is also a "state council" of 16 members, appointed by the sovereign. The sovereign presides over this council, which has consultative participation in both legislative and executive matters.

The Provinces. The 11 provinces of which the Netherlands is composed are North Brabant, Guelders, South Holland, North Holland, Zealand, Utrecht, Friesland, Overyssel, Groningen, Drenthe, and Limburg. They have a large autonomy and (subject to the veto of the sovereign) a local legislative power which is exercised through assemblies, "the provincial states," chosen for 4 years by the same electors as choose the national second chamber. These bodies meet twice annually, and in the intervals between sessions they are represented by permanent commissions, or "deputed states," of 6 members, who administer the affairs of the provinces and oversee the execution of the laws. A commissioner appointed by the sovereign presides over both the provincial states and the deputed states, and in the latter body has a deciding vote.

The Dutch "communes," or municipal corporations, number over 1100 and are governed by councils chosen by the same electors, residents in the commune, as choose the national Second Chamber. The by-laws of the council are subject to the veto of the sovereign. The municipal budgets and all proposals to alienate municipal property must receive the approval of the provincial states.

Further central control is exercised through the mayor, who is a state as well as a municipal officer. The police are under his authority, and he has a suspensive veto on resolutions of the council for 30 days, during which time the provincial states must be advised. The municipal executive power is intrusted to the mayor and to a commission of aldermen, 2 to 7 in number, elected by the council. This commission is a body analogous to the "college of echevins" of the Belgian commune.

Dutch civil and criminal law is based on the Roman law and reflects its principles. Trial by jury is unknown. There are a high court of the Netherlands (court of cassation), 5 courts of appeal, 19 district tribunals, and 62 cantonal courts. The cantonal courts deal with minor offenses and have one judge each. All judges, 3 in number for appeal and district courts and 5 for the high court, are appointed by the sovereign for life. They can be removed only by a decision of the high court. There are also juvenile courts, presided over by one judge unless the penalty may be 6 months or more of imprisonment, in which case there are 3 judges.

Colonies. Previous to World War II, the Netherlands possessed a vast colonial empire, the acquisition of which dated from the 17th century. But in 1965 its overseas territories included only Surinam, or Dutch Guiana, on the northeast coast of South America and the Netherlands Antilles in the Caribbean Sea, comprising two groups of three small islands each, about 500 miles apart.

The Netherlands Antilles is constitutionally the equal of the Netherlands, the Dutch sovereign being represented by a governor. The latter is assisted by a cabinet responsible to the legislature of 22 members elected for a 4-year term by universal suffrage. The country consists of the Windward Islands (Curaçao, Aruba, and Bonair) and the Leeward Islands (St. Eustatius, Saba, and part of St. Martin). Each island has control of its own affairs, but in the common interest sends elective representatives to the *Staten* (legislature). The governor has charge of the colony's external affairs, while the executive power in general internal matters is vested in the cabinet responsible to the legislature.

NEW ZEALAND

This constitutional monarchy was from 1840 until 1852 a British colony. In the latter year it was granted responsible government. As a self-governing dominion it formed part of the British Empire and later the British Commonwealth of Nations, as the latter organization was defined in the British Statute of Westminster Act of 1931. Nevertheless, New Zealand was slow in accepting its role as an independent country within the Commonwealth. It adopted this Act in 1947.

New Zealand does not have a formal constitution. Its mode of government rests on ordinary laws which may be repealed as such, with the exception of 6, which by their terms can be repealed only by a three-fourths majority. Of these 6, 3 relate to the formation of electoral districts, one provides for a secret ballot, one fixes the term of Parliament at 3 years, and the last fixes voting age at 21. Women were first permitted to vote in 1893.

The monarch of New Zealand is the British monarch, who, when not in New Zealand, functions through a governor-general appointed by the British crown on the advice of its New Zealand ministers. The governor-general is assisted by an executive council, a body consisting of the prime minister and 14 other cabinet members. He is not necessarily bound by its advice but, if he disagrees, refers the matter promptly to the crown. Parliament consists of the governor-general and the General Assembly of 80 members elected by universal suffrage for a 3-year term unless dissolved earlier. Four members must be of the Maori race from Maori election districts. Members of the cabinet must be members of the majority party in the Assembly. Orders-in-council (executive orders) are issued by the executive council pursuant to or in conformity with laws, but the Assembly acts as a watchdog over them through a statutes revision committee, which is charged with the duty of calling the Assembly's attention to orders which appear to trespass on individual liberties, to make unexpected use of statutory authority, or to require clarification. The Assembly may bring about the resignation of the cabinet by passing a resolution of no confidence or rejecting a vital proposal of the government, but this does not necessarily entail dissolution of the Assembly, this being in the discretion of the governor-general.

In addition to the hierarchy of regular courts, New Zealand has a court of arbitration concerned with awards and general orders governing wage determinations and employment in industry.

NICARAGUA

In 1971 congress voted to dissolve the constitution of 1962; a constituent assembly was formed in 1972 to draw up another constitution. A new constitution was adopted in 1974. It calls for a president to be elected directly by universal vote. Neither he nor any relative of his may run for re-election. The president chooses his own ministers—they cannot be members of congress. The 1974 constitution provides for a two-chamber national congress with a 30-member senate and a 70-member chamber of deputies.

NIGER

The republic of the Niger, formerly a part of French West Africa, became independent in 1960. It voted to adhere to the French Community. In April 1974, after a military coup, the president was overthrown, the constitution suspended, and the national assembly dissolved. A military assembly with Lt. Col. Seyni Kountche as president was formed to assume the government. In 1976 Kountche added civilians to the assembly.

NIGERIA

Nigeria became independent in 1960 after more than half a century of British rule. It is a republican federation of 12 states. In 1966 the government was overthrown by the army; the constitution was suspended. After another coup in 1975 and the assassination of the head of state in 1976, moves were made toward civilian rule. A 26-member federal executive council, consisting of civilians and military officers, was formed; local elections were held.

NORWAY

By the Congress of Vienna, 1814, Norway was united to Sweden under the sovereignty of the Swedish king. The union was personal in the monarch, each country retaining its own nationality, government, and laws. On June 7, 1905, Norway declared this union dissolved, and an accord to this effect was signed with Sweden in October 1905. Public opinion in Norway, to a certain extent, inclined toward a republic; but reasons of policy appear to have prevailed over the naturally democratic instincts of the Norwegians, and, by a plebiscite, the throne was offered to Prince Carl of Denmark, who took the title of Haakon VII. The constitution of Norway is that which has existed since May 17, 1814, with a number of amendments. The executive power resides in the king, who acts through ministers responsible to the Norwegian parliament. Before 1913, the king had a qualified veto over legislation. In that year it was made suspensive, that is, a measure passed by three successive parliaments formed by separate elections becomes law without the royal assent.

The national legislature, called the *Storthing*, is elected by universal suffrage of all Norwegians over 21 years of age. The election of the Storthing, which numbers 150 members, takes place every fourth year, is direct, and according to proportional representation. Upon assembling, each Storthing divides itself into two bodies, one called the *Lagthing*, composed of one-fourth of the membership. The remainder form the *Odelsthing.* These two bodies ordinarily act as separate houses; but, in the case of disagreement, they meet in a joint session and a final decision is reached by a majority of two-thirds of the voters. An amendment to the constitution in 1913 gave to ministers the right to sit in the Storthing, but without a vote.

For local government, the country is divided into 20 districts; 2 of them, the cities of Oslo and Bergen, are urban, and 18 of them are rural counties, or *fylker.* The chief executive, or *fylkesmann*, is appointed by the crown. Districts are governed by elective councils with a membership of from 13 to 85, while the administration is conducted by an administration council chosen from among the representatives. In local government, women with property qualifications gained the vote and the right to representation in 1901. In 1910, their suffrage became the same as that of men.

Justice is administered by 106 district courts with 5 higher tribunals and a supreme court, all of which handle both civil and criminal cases. Criminal cases may be tried with or without a jury.

Dependencies. These include the Spitzbergen Archipelago, acquired in 1920, and Jan Mayen Island in the Arctic Ocean; Bouvet and Peter I islands, in the Antarctic; and a section of the Antarctic continent southeast of the Falkland Islands, ownership of which was claimed in January 1939.

OMAN

The Sultanate of Oman (formerly Muscat and Oman) was renamed on August 9, 1970. Conquered by the Portuguese in 1508, Oman revolted in 1650. Except for a period of Iranian invasion (1741–43), it has remained independent. The Sultanate of Muscat and Oman signed a treaty of friendship with Britain in 1798 and with the U.S. in 1833.

On July 23, 1970, the son of the reigning sultan staged a successful coup. Oman is a monarchy with no constitution, no legislature, and no legal political parties. The sultan is the supreme ruler, assisted by a cabinet. The country is divided into 10 regions. Local governors work through tribal authorities. The judicial system is based on Islamic law. The courts are administered by judges whom the sultan appoints. In remote areas, the law is based on tribal custom. Oman is a member of the Arab League and was admitted to the UN in 1971.

PAKISTAN

Before independence came in 1947, Pakistan was under British colonial rule, as a part of India. In 1956 it was proclaimed an Islamic republic within the Commonwealth of Nations. In 1970 the capital was moved from Karachi to Islamabad, West Pakistan, a new city built for the purpose.

Direct general elections were held for the first time on December 7, 1970. The Awami League won 149 seats out of 243, and immediately announced their goal of greater independence from East Pakistan.

Martial law was imposed in East Pakistan after disturbances in Decca. On March 25, 1971, Civil war erupted in East Pakistan when 70,000 troops of Pakistan's central government (in West Pakistan) launched widespread attacks. They were attempting to crush East Pakistan's growing nonviolent movement for self-rule. On April 1, the government of newly independent East Pakistan, now called Bangladesh (Bengali Homeland), proclaimed its sovereignty. Pakistan emerged a much smaller and weaker nation. In 1972, Pakistan withdrew from the Commonwealth of Nations.

Martial law, in effect in West Pakistan since 1958, when Marshall Khan established his military regime, was discontinued in April 1972. A new constitution—Pakistan's third in 25 years—went into effect in April 1973. Proclaiming Pakistan a federal Islamic republic, the constitution established the offices of prime minister and president and a two-chamber parliament. The upper chamber of parliament, the senate, was to have 63 members elected by the provincial assemblies. The lower chamber, the national assembly, was to consist of 200 directly elected men and women, plus 10 seats to be filled only by women.

The first election under civilian rule was held in March 1977. Election fraud was suspected, however, and opposition among the political parties threatened civil war. The army assumed control of the government in July. The 1973 constitution was to remain in effect and elections and civilian rule were scheduled.

PANAMA

The republic of Panama owes its independence to the United States. From 1821 until 1903, it was a part of Colombia. When the latter country rejected a proposed treaty with the United States for construction of a canal across the Panama isthmus within Colombian territory, the department of Panama declared its independence and was recognized 10 days later by the United States, which guaranteed the independence and internal order of the new republic of Panama. This guarantee was part of a treaty providing for construction of the Panama Canal and payment to Panama of a lump sum and later annuities. The annuity was originally $250,000 but was increased to $430,000 in 1936 and to $1,930,000 in 1955.

At Panaman request, the United States in 1936 withdrew its guarantee of independence. The original treaty excluded Panama from exercise of any sovereign rights in the Canal Zone, but, on the theory that this did not extinguish theoretical sovereignty, it was agreed that the Panaman flag might be displayed along with the American flag in areas under civilian control. An incident involving the tearing down of the American flag sparked a demand in 1962 for renegotiation of the treaty between Panama and the United States.

Colombia protested the action of the United States in supporting the independence of Panama in 1903 and refused recognition of Panama until 1914, when it agreed to extend recognition only if the United States paid it $25,000,000. A treaty so providing was ratified by the United States Senate in 1921, and diplomatic relations between Colombia and Panama were established in 1924.

The first constitution of Panama was adopted February 13, 1904. It was replaced by the constitution of 1946, which provided for a legislative national assembly with members elected for 4-year terms. Executive power was entrusted to a president elected by direct universal vote for a 6-year term. The assembly chose two vice presidents, and the president named a cabinet to assist him. The 7 provinces of Panama were administered by elected governors.

In 1968, after 11 days in office, President Arnulfo Arias was deposed. The assembly was suspended and replaced by a military-civilian coalition with power vested in General Omar Torrijos. In 1972 a new assembly of 505 members was popularly elected. Its members approved a new constitution calling for the indirect election of a president, vice president, and legislative council—but executive control was assigned to Torrijos for a transitional term of 6 years.

The laws dating from the period of union with Colombia were replaced in 1917 by new civil and criminal codes. Under these codes, capital punishment is prohibited. Foreigners are prohibited from mingling in politics and may be ejected from the country for criticism of public offices or institutions. The laws relating to mining, industry, and exploitation of land are favorable to foreign investment.

PAPUA NEW GUINEA

Papua New Guinea covers the eastern half of the island of New Guinea and includes many offshore islands, among them New Britain, New Ireland, and Bougainville. Papua New Guinea shares the island of New Guinea with the Indonesian province of Irian Jaya. Just north of Australia, most of Papua New Guinea has been a protectorate of that country since 1906, under mandates from the League of Nations and the UN. It achieved independence September 16, 1975, and became the 142nd member of the UN. A member of the Commonwealth of Nations, the country is governed by an elected assembly of 100 members, a prime minister and his cabinet, and a governor general who represents the sovereign of England. Papua New Guinea is divided into 19 districts. The capital is Port Moresby.

PARAGUAY

The republic of Paraguay, like Bolivia, is an inland country, possessing no seaboard on the South American coast. The country was settled by Jesuit missionaries. Paraguay, formerly part of the Spanish viceroyalty of La Plata organized in 1776, declared independence on August 10, 1811. A revolutionary government was established under two "consuls," but it rapidly dissolved into a dictatorship, which continued until 1870. Under the last period of dictatorship, Paraguay was involved in struggles with Brazil, Argentina, and Uruguay, which were ruinous in loss of life and territory.

The constitution of November 25, 1870, completely reorganized the government. It remained nominally in force until 1936, when a military clique seized the government. A strongly authoritarian constitution was adopted by popular approval in 1940. This was replaced by a new constitution in 1967.

By the 1967 constitution executive power is entrusted to a president chosen by popular vote for a term of 5 years; a vacancy is filled by the parliament. The president appoints his own cabinet and can govern by decree during parliamentary recess through the council of state, which is composed mostly of members from the government and armed forces. The president also has been granted wide powers to use in an emergency. A clause forbidding reelection of a president was removed by a constituent assembly in 1977. This was done to allow the reelection of Gen. Alfredo Stroessner, who seized power in 1954 and began a fifth term as president in 1973.

Legislative power is vested in a two-chamber parliament. There is a 30-seat senate and a 60-seat chamber of deputies. Two-thirds of the seats in each chamber are given to the majority party while the other one-third is distributed proportionately to the remaining minority parties according to the votes cast. All citizens over 18 are eligible to vote. Voting is compulsory.

At the head of the judicial system is a supreme court of 5 justices, appointed by the president and council. There also are chambers of appeal, lower courts, and justices of the peace. The attorney general handles all state legal matters.

By law the country is divided into two sections, the eastern, "Oriental" (east of the Paraguay River), and the western, "Occidental" (west of the Paraguay River). The Oriental section is divided into 15 departments. The departments are administered by officials appointed by the central government. The Occidental section is under military government.

PERU

The republic of Peru arose from the viceroyalty of Peru, which in the Spanish colonial period was considered the ranking kingdom of the New World. Here Spanish prestige and authority were more strongly entrenched than elsewhere. It was not until 1821 that Spanish authority was overthrown.

Peru became an independent republic July 28, 1821. The most recent constitution of Peru went into effect on April 9, 1933. It provided for a congress composed of a senate and a chamber of deputies. Political disturbances in 1936 led to a suspension of the constitutional government until November 14, 1939. Then a constitutional regime was restored but with amendments which tended to increase the power of the executive.

In 1968 a military junta took control of the government; congress was suspended. Rule presently is by decree. The government has stated that the existing constitution will be revised before new elections are held.

PHILIPPINES

The Republic of the Philippines came into existence on July 4, 1946. The Philippine Islands, discovered by Ferdinand Magellan in 1521, were a colony of Spain from 1565 to 1898, when they became a dependency of the U.S. after the Spanish-American War. The U.S. Congress granted the Philippines the status of a self-governing commonwealth in 1934. After a 10-year transitional period and a delay because of World War II, the Philippines achieved full independence.

The first constitution was adopted in 1935, modeled on that of the U.S. A new constitution ratified on January 17, 1973, has not yet been put into effect. Martial law was declared on September 23, 1972, by President Ferdinand Marcos, because of increasing violence on the islands. Virtually all legislative functions have been suspended and President Marcos's term has been extended indefinitely. Marcos announced in January 1976 that martial law would be in effect until at least 1980.

The constitution of 1973 called for a parliamentary system with a president as head of state and a prime minister as chief executive. Both are elected from and by a universally elected national assembly. Members of the assembly serve 6-year terms. The judicial system consists of a supreme court and lower courts. All judges are appointed by the president. The constitution also called for changing the name of the Philippines to Maharlika (a Tagalog word meaning "noble").

POLAND

Poland was a state of much influence and promise until it was weakened by serious factional troubles in the 18th century and fell prey to the more powerful neighboring states of Russia, Prussia, and Austria. In 1772, 1793, and 1795 occurred the three successive partitions of Poland whereby all the territory of the kingdom was divided among these three great powers. Napoleon, in return for military support, promised to reconstruct an independent Poland, but accomplished little.

After having been extinguished as an independent state by the partitions, Poland was reunited and was raised again to the rank of an independent state by World War I. The independence of the country was proclaimed and a provisional constitution was declared in 1918. Elections for a constituent assembly were held in 1919 and a constitution was finally adopted in 1921.

A new constitution was adopted in 1935 which provided for a high degree of centralization under the personal authority of a president.

The People's Republic of Poland was set up in 1947 under effective Russian control. During World War II, Poland was conquered by Germany, and a government in exile was recognized by Great Britain and the United States. When the German army was driven out by Russia, the latter set up and recognized a committee of national liberation. These were merged after the war, and an election was held while the Russians still occupied the country. The Communist party was swept into power, and it promptly set up a Communist-type government.

The present constitution, adopted in 1952, offers the unusual example of a republic without a president, his place being taken by a council of state.

The constitution declares that Poland is a people's democracy based on an alliance between the working class and the working peasants. The highest organ of state authority is the *Seym*, whose members are elected by universal suffrage for 4-year terms, one member for each 60,000 inhabitants. In practice, the candidates are selected by the Communist party, one candidate for each seat. It passes laws and exercises control over other organs of the state and adopts the national economic plans.

The Seym chooses a council of ministers, whose duty it is to guide the work of the Seym, present the economic plans, and also to insure the execution of laws and protection of public order. The members may be removed by the Seym and, between sessions, by the council of state.

The executive power lies, as already stated, with the council of state, the members of which are elected by the Seym from among its members. They consist of a president, 4 vice presidents, a secretary, and 9 other members. The council of state lays down universally binding interpretations of the laws and may issue decrees having the force of law when the Seym is not in session. It has treaty-making powers and the power to proclaim martial law or military mobilization. It also exercises ultimate control over the local people's councils.

People's councils are elected in towns, districts, and other minor subdivisions of the country, those in smaller subdivisions being subject to those in the larger subdivision of which they are parts. Each people's council acts through a presidium. Their function is to insure the maintenance of public order and watch over the observance of the people's rule of law. In other words, they form the mechanism by which the authority of the state makes itself felt.

There is a supreme court whose judges are appointed for 5-year terms by the council of state.

PORTUGAL

One of the great European monarchies of medieval and early modern times, Portugal has been a recognized state since the 12th century. Except for a period of Spanish rule from 1580 to 1640, Portugal was a kingdom until 1910. On October 5, 1910, the Independent Republic of Portugal was proclaimed.

Following a military revolt in 1936, Marshal Antonio Carmona became president, a position he held until 1951. In 1932 Antonio de Oliveira Salazar became premier. Until 1968, Salazar dominated political life in Portugal, reducing the presidency to a figurehead status. Under a constitution adopted in 1933, Portugal's government remained stable until 1974.

On April 25, 1974, a coup led by the Armed Forces Movement seized power, ending more than 40 years of civil dictatorship. A transitional government was then established.

Two years after the armed forces coup, the first free parliamentary election in 50 years took place, on April 25, 1976. A 265-seat assembly was elected, the Socialist party capturing 107 seats. A new constitution committed the government to socialist policies. General Antonio Ramalho Eanes was elected president on June 27, 1976, and he appointed Mario Soares premier. Under the new constitution, the president held the power to name a premier and his cabinet, to veto legislation, and to dissolve the assembly.

The once-vast Portuguese colonial empire has all but disappeared. In 1974, Guinea-Bissau (formerly Portuguese Guinea) was granted independence; in 1975, Angola, the Cape Verde Islands, Mozambique, and Sao Tomé and Principe became independent. Portugal planned to grant independence to Macao and other lesser territories by 1978.

QATAR

Under British protection until 1971, Qatar is a sheikdom in the Persian Gulf region, bounded by Saudi Arabia and the United Arab Emirates. There is a minister of foreign affairs, but no legislature. The capital and chief port is Doha (population 120,000). The area of the peninsular country is some 4,250 square miles; the total population is estimated at 180,000. Qatar has a treaty of friendship with Great Britain.

RHODESIA

Located in the southern part of Africa, Rhodesia was for many years the British dependency of Southern Rhodesia. In 1965 Rhodesia unilaterally declared itself independent, thus blocking England's intent to guarantee eventual black majority rule. The new government—controlled by the white minority, estimated at under 5 per cent of the over 6 million inhabitants—was led by Prime Minister Ian Smith. The legislative assembly consisted of 50 members elected by the white inhabitants and 15 members elected by the black population. Threatened by UN sanctions and international boycotts, Rhodesia's position has remained critical.

Negotiations continued through the 1970s between Rhodesian and British officials. In 1971 Ian Smith actually initialed an agreement for ultimate majority rule, but he later disavowed it. Black nationalists started to mount armed resistance; in December 1971, guerrilla war began along the Zambian and Mozambique borders to the north and east. The balance of power shifted in favor of the blacks in 1974 when the Portuguese revolution led to the independence of Mozambique and Angola. The two new Marxist governments became involved directly in the struggle and provided safe bases for nationalist guerrillas. Its supply routes to the ocean cut off by hostile black nations, the Rhodesian government began to depend heavily on the white-ruled Republic of South Africa for trade and arms.

Fearing a major war and Soviet interference, as in the Angolan civil war, U.S. Secretary of State Kissinger began "shuttle diplomacy" between Rhodesia and black leaders in September 1976. After 12 days of intense negotiations, an agreement seemed to have been accepted by both sides. The plan called for a compromise transitional government with black majority rule by 1978. The interim administration would consist of a 4-man council of state, composed of two whites and two blacks, with one of the whites serving as chairman. Under that council would be a council of ministers, which was to have a black majority and a black "first minister." The army and police would be controlled by the whites and the new constitution would be constructed inside Rhodesia by the interim government. Black leaders then reconsidered and rejected the plan, claiming it would legalize the existing racist structures of power. In late 1976, Ian Smith, the presidents of the 5 "front line" countries (Zambia, Tanzania, Mozambique, Botswana, and Angola), and black Rhodesian leaders met in Geneva, Switzerland, under the auspices of the British. Although March 1, 1978, was established as the target date for independence under majority rule, Smith continued to promote a plan for a multiracial government.

In Rhodesia the black nationalists were divided into at least 6 feuding factions. Who would gain power would depend on whether a peaceful transfer could be negotiated. All nationalists had agreed that the new country would be renamed Zimbabwe, after an ancient African civilization that once thrived in the area.

RUMANIA

Rumania is a people's republic, after having been a monarchy from the time of its liberation from Turkish rule in 1877 until 1947. Russia occupied Rumania in 1944. In the election of 1946, the Communist party won control of the government and drew up a draft constitution on Soviet lines. Most of the industries were immediately nationalized, and no move was made without Russian consent. A new constitution was adopted in 1952, which affirms the role of the Rumanian Workers' Party as the "leading political force."

The constitution declares that Rumania is a people's republic of working people of town and country. It sets forth a foreign policy of alliance with the Soviet Union. Power of the people is said to be exercised through the Grand National Assembly and the people's councils, the latter being called the political foundation of the republic. Social ownership of the means of production is decreed, either in the form of state property or in the form of co-operative-collective property. The land, it is stated, belongs to those who till it. Private property is recognized only in the form of a plot of land and household on a collective farm, a small shop where the owner alone works, or a sector of residual capitalism scheduled for eventual liquidation.

The legislative power resides in the Grand National Assembly elected for a 5-year term of universal suffrage, one deputy for each 40,000 inhabitants. The assembly has the power to amend the constitution. It establishes national economic plans. Its laws become effective when signed by the president and secretary of its guiding body, known as a presidium. There is no direct veto power. However, the presidium, accountable to the assembly, has very wide powers, which extend to interpreting the laws, annulling orders of the executive department on the ground of non-conformity with the law, appointing the military commander in chief, ratifying treaties, and ordering mobilization.

The assembly appoints also the highest executive organ of the state, namely, the council of ministers. This body is accountable to the assembly if in session; otherwise to the presidium. It adopts measures to carry out the economic plans and to maintain public order, directs the organization and raising of the military forces, and gives guidance in foreign relations.

RUSSIA

The vast territorial extent of Russia, amounting to one-seventh of the land surface of the globe, combines with the strength of the Russian people, more numerous than any other white nation, to make it one of the greatest political factors in the world. The Russian stock excels in physical vitality and in intellectual vigor, but was held for centuries in an oppressed state, illiterate and without freedom of opportunity.

Imperial Russia. For centuries, and even within the present century, the government was despotic. The emperor, or czar, bore the title of "autocrat of all the Russias." Legislation was by imperial decree, or *ukaz*. The imperial power was administered by a great bureaucracy, established by Peter the Great and divided into a hierarchy of classes, at the top of which ministers and political competitors contended for the favor of the court and for position and power. Corruption and inefficiency, at times moderated by a strong-willed ruler or by the abilities of a talented minister, permeated the organization.

Constitutional progress was contending with bureaucracy and reaction when World War I broke out in 1914. In a gesture of liberality, the czar in 1905 granted a constitution which set up an elective body, the Duma, but it was powerless to affect national policy. Meanwhile revolutionary pressure grew underground, led by embittered exiles waiting for an opportunity to overthrow the government.

The Revolution. The opportunity came during World War I, in which Russian defeats led to the rise of a liberal government set up by the Duma in 1917. The czar abdicated. But this government was overthrown shortly by a more radical party bearing the standard of dictatorship of the proletariat. It announced that Russia thereafter would be governed as a socialist state with the government owning the means of production. Under the ruthless leadership of Lenin, Russia thus established the first Communist government. It was based on the gospel of Karl Marx, a German who lived in England to write his famous *Das Kapital*. This work purported to show that, under capitalism, the rulers appropriated the fruit of the labor of the ruled and that the latter could enjoy what they had produced only by overthrowing the system and substituting their own dictatorship. So began the world's most bloody revolution.

Looked at in the perspective of half a century, it would appear that Russia, an economically backward nation which had scarcely shared at all in the industrial and technological revolution, had taken this costly step to catch up quickly. Its economic success was striking. After World War II, it towered militarily over all other countries of the world except the United States. From the standpoint of government, it perfected the one-party system by which a constitution ostensibly providing democratic control could be operated by a party subject to autocratic control.

Constitution of 1920. A government, federal in form, was established with the definite purpose and hope of adding to the union as new states such countries as should establish "dictatorships of the proletariat." It was known as the Union of Soviet Socialist Republics (U.S.S.R.) and consisted at first of 5 separate republics. These were later increased to 16.

A Supreme Soviet (Council) of the U.S.S.R. was set up to legislate for the country, representatives being chosen by local "soviets." Class enemies were disfranchised, including those employing others for profit and all monks and priests. Moreover, the basis of representation gave five times as much weight to each city voter as to a rural voter. Control of the machinery of government was assured through party discipline, the decisions of greatest importance usually being made first in party councils and later ratified by elective assemblies, both in the U.S.S.R. and in the constituent republics. A uniform system of secret courts and of espionage served also to make control absolute in the hands of the ruler. This control was used to wipe out the remains of feudalism and capitalism and to replacing them by a system of production for use rather than for private profit. After a period of trial and error, the picture which emerged was somewhat as follows:

A supreme economic council determines what probably can be produced by industries of national importance, taking into account both raw materials, labor, and demand, as well as national welfare. The task of production is then allotted among plants, which are operated by corporations owned by the government. Wages and prices are fixed with a view to having consumption balance production. Profit and loss are absorbed by the government. A somewhat similar pattern is followed for industries of regional or local importance, the smaller political divisions operating them at their own risk and for their own profit. These industries are integrated with national plans through control of credit.

Constitution of 1936. Ostensibly on the assumption that the Russian people had become accustomed to the new system and would continue to operate it, a democratic constitution was announced in 1936, based on universal, secret suffrage.

Corresponding to a Congress there is a Supreme Soviet, consisting of two chambers—the Soviet of the Union and the Soviet of Nationalities. The Soviet of the Union is popularly elected, one deputy to each 300,000 of the population. The Soviet of Nationalities, like the United States Senate, is intended to give equal representation to separate states irrespective of their population. Each state, or "union republic," sends 25 deputies, each "autonomous republic" sends 11, each "autonomous province" sends 5, and each national area sends 1. The deputies to the Council of Nationalities are directly elected by the voters within these constituencies. Both chambers have equal legislative rights. In case of failure to reach agreement on a bill after reconciliation efforts of an interchamber committee and resubmission to the chambers, the Supreme Council must be dissolved and a new election must be held. The term of office is 4 years.

The two chambers in joint session elect a presidium of 33 members, including a president, 16 vice presidents, a secretary, and 15 members. This body is declared responsible to the Supreme Soviet, but it has very broad powers. It issues decrees, convenes the Supreme Soviet, interprets the laws, and may annul as invalid orders of the highest executive body, the council of ministers. The council of ministers is appointed also by the Supreme Soviet. It exercises the function, not only of administration, but the economic planning on which ultimately the strength and development of the country depend.

The supreme court justices are elected by the Supreme Council for 4-year terms. Other judges are elected by the people for 3-year terms.

Individual republics have similar forms of government. Federal law is paramount in all cases of conflict of authority.

Behind and parallel to the constitutional government is the organization of the Communist party, the real seat of power, whose supreme organ is the Soviet Union Party Congress. This body, made up of delegates from provincial congresses, elects the central executive committee, which in turn elects a secretariat of 5 members. One of these, the general secretary, is the real head of the party. This Secretariat controls legislation and foreign policy, though the formal action is taken by the state administration, all of whose organs are headed and controlled by party members. Party discipline is rigorously enforced.

Property Rights. These are of three kinds—public, co-operative, and private. Means of industrial production and most property necessary to public services are owned by the government, either federal, state, or local. These include the bulk of the dwelling houses in cities and industrial localities. Means of agricultural production and property used in providing certain services in common are owned by co-operatives. Individuals may own property provided it is not used to exploit the labor of others. Trading for profit is forbidden. Individual houses and lots, household equipment, and other personal property fall within the permissible limits of individual ownership.

Bill of Rights. Citizens are guaranteed the right of remunerative work, of reasonable leisure, of education, and of support and medical care when unable to work. Guaranteed also is freedom of conscience, of speech, of the press, of assembly, of street processions, and of organization. Unlawful search, seizure, and arrest are forbidden. Women are given equal status with men. On all alike rest the duties of performing social obligations, safeguarding public property, and serving in the armed forces of the republic. Asylum is provided for foreigners persecuted for defending workers' interests, for their scientific activity, or for their struggle for national liberation.

The constitution may be amended by a two-thirds vote of both chambers of the Supreme Soviet.

Foreign Relations. At the beginning of the Soviet regime, Russia practically declared war upon all governments adhering to the capitalistic system. As an instrument of propaganda, the "Third International" was established at Moscow in the spring of 1919. Propagandists were sent abroad through the countries of Europe, America, and Asia. After China established a Communist government in 1949 and subsequently challenged Russia's leadership in the Communist party, the effect of such propaganda weakened—partly because of the rivalry and partly because of the practical demonstration in other nations that the fruits of labor can be distributed broadly without autocratic control by government. Russia's growing economic well-being finally asserted its influence for preferring peace.

RWANDA

Rwanda was established as an independent republic in 1962 from part of a former trusteed territory of Belgium. A legislative council formed in 1961 declared the government a republic following a referendum in which a majority voted to abolish the monarchy. It has a 47-member Assembly elected by universal suffrage for a 4-year term and a president similarly chosen for 4 years. The president names the vice president with the Assembly's consent.

SALVADOR, EL

El Salvador became an independent republic in 1839, when the Central American Federation was dissolved. A constitution first proclaimed in 1824 was repeatedly modified. In 1945 the constitution of 1886, repealed in 1939, was reinstated with some alterations. This constitution was replaced in 1950 by a new one which, in turn, was succeeded by the constitution of 1962. There is universal suffrage for election of a single-chamber legislature whose members are elected for 2-year terms, one member for each 38,000 inhabitants. The president is popularly elected for a 5-year term and may not succeed himself. He is assisted by a cabinet of 10 ministers.

SAN MARINO

Lying within Italy, San Marino is known as the world's smallest and oldest republic—founded about A.D. 350. Its neutrality violated by both sides in World War II, from 1945 to 1957 it was ruled by a Communist-Socialist coalition but is now anti-Communist. The legislature is a council of 60 members elected for 5-year terms by popular vote. The council elects 10 members to its administrative council of state. There is no prime minister, but two council members are appointed as regents every six months.

SAO TOME AND PRINCIPE

The Democratic Republic of Sao Tome and Principe gained independence from Portugal on July 12, 1975. The island group was discovered by Pedro Escobar and Joao Gomes in 1471. To colonize them, the Portuguese sent convicts and others expelled from Portugal. Slaves were brought from Angola to work on plantations—slavery existed until the 1950s. Sao Tome and Principe, with the islands of Pedros Tinhosas and Rolas, became an overseas province of Portugal in 1951; Portuguese citizenship was granted its inhabitants in 1961.

In 1972 the Movement for the Liberation of Sao Tome and Principe was formed under Manuel Pinto da Costa. After the 1974 military coup in Lisbon, Portugal began negotiations with the movement, agreeing in November to recognize the islands' independence on July 12, 1975. A provisional government, with Da Costa as president, was established, pending the adoption of a constitution. Portugal appointed a minister and a high commissioner to help the new government. The government consisted of a president, a prime minister, and a cabinet of 10 ministers. Sao Tome and Principe joined the UN in September 1975.

SAUDI ARABIA

This kingdom embracing almost the entire Arabian peninsula was formally established in 1926, when Ibn Saud, sultan of the Nejd, conquered Hejaz and joined these two mid-peninsular territories.

Government takes the form of a feudal autocracy although a constitution was issued in 1926 and subsequently amended. The religious law of Islam is the common law of the kingdom. It is administered by religious courts. The constitution provided also for setting up a consultative Legislative Assembly and municipal councils consisting of tribal officials and notables nominated or approved by the king. In 1958, a so-called cabinet system was instituted but the king retained the power to name the members.

SENEGAL

Senegal became an independent republic in 1960, having chosen in 1958 to sever its ties with France, its former ruler, but to remain within the French Community. It has a president and a National Assembly of 80 members elected by universal suffrage for 4-year terms. The president is assisted by ministers and secretaries of state, who are chosen by him and may not be members of the Assembly.

SEYCHELLES

A 90-island archipelago in the Indian Ocean, the Republic of Seychelles (SAY-SHELL') gained full independence in June 1976. It was originally settled by the French in 1794 before passing to the English in 1814 as a result of Napoleon's defeat. Seychelles was a British crown colony from 1903 until limited self-government was granted in 1970. The 1976 constitution provides for a president as head of state, a premier as head of the government, and a single-chamber national assembly of 42 members elected for 5-year terms. Seychelles became a full member of the British Commonwealth of Nations at independence and was admitted to the UN in September 1976.

SIERRA LEONE

After 174 years of British rule, Sierra Leone became an independent African democracy and a member of the British Commonwealth in 1961. In 1971, after a succession of military coups, a new constitution was adopted. The nation was declared a republic, with executive power assigned to the president as head of state and commander of the armed forces. Elected through the assembly, the president serves a 5-year term. He is assisted by a cabinet of ministers for domestic and foreign affairs. The judicial system consists of a supreme court and local courts following native tribal law. Internal government is based on the authority of "paramount chiefs" of tribes.

SINGAPORE

The world's fifth largest port, Singapore is the largest Chinese community outside the mainland; however, it has an anti-Communist republican government. A former British colony, it was given internal self-government in 1959. Singapore achieved full independence in 1965 and entered the British Commonwealth. A 1970 constitution provides for a one-chamber parliament of the members elected by popular vote of citizens over 21. Parliament is responsible for the election of the president, who is the chief of state. A prime minister assists the administration.

SOMALI REPUBLIC

A republic formed in 1960 through the union of territories formerly under the control of Britain and Italy. A constitution was adopted in 1960. In 1969 military forces took control of the government. The parliament was dismissed, the constitution suspended, and the supreme court dissolved (later reinstated). A supreme revolutionary council was formed to administer the country. The council appointed 14 civilian secretaries of state.

SOUTH AFRICA

The Republic of South Africa includes the provinces of Natal, the Cape of Good Hope, the Transvaal, and the Orange Free State. South Africa also controls the territory of South West Africa.

The head of the republic is the state president, elected to a 7-year term by the electoral college. The electoral college consists of the senate and the house of assembly and is presided over by either the chief justice or a judge of appeal designated by the chief justice. The state president selects the prime minister and other ministers to form a cabinet. He has the authority to summon, adjourn, and dissolve parliament.

Legislative power is vested in the parliament, composed of the state president, house of assembly, and senate. Members of the house of assembly serve for 5 years and are chosen from electoral divisions in the provinces and South West Africa (Namibia). A member of the house of assembly must be a white South African citizen, a resident of the republic for a minimum of 5 years, and qualified as a voter. The senate consists of members nominated by the state president-in-council and of members elected from the provinces and South West Africa. A senator must be a white South African citizen, at least 30 years of age, a resident of the republic for a minimum of 5 years, and qualified as a voter in one of the provinces. A senator's term of office is 5 years. Parliament must meet at least once a year.

In each province there is an administrator, appointed by the state president-in-council for 5 years, and a provincial council. The administrator is chairman of the provincial council. The council, which is elected by the same system as members of parliament, elects a 4-member executive committee. The provincial committee and council have the authority to handle local matters.

Pretoria is the seat of government; Cape Town is the seat of legislature.

SOUTHERN YEMEN

See *Yemen, Republic of (South)*.

SPAIN

The kingdom of Spain was formed in the latter part of the 15th century by the union of a number of monarchies and by conquest of the southern part of the peninsula from the Moors. Under Charles V and Philip II, the ancient rights of these kingdoms and certain representative institutions which they possessed were suppressed and the basis for absolute monarchy was laid.

The modern constitutional history of Spain begins in 1808; it was followed by a period of civil conflict between liberal and reactionary forces, within which period Spain for a brief time, 1873–74, was a republic. The Bourbon family, under Alfonso XII, was restored at the beginning of 1875. This dynasty ruled until April 14, 1931, when King Alfonso XIII was driven from the throne. Spain was proclaimed a republic, a constituent *Cortes* was elected on June 28, and a new constitution was adopted on December 9 of the same year.

Republican Constitution. The constitution of 1931 provided for a democratic republic, with separation of church and state. Legislative power was exercised by a single-chamber Cortes, its members elected by universal suffrage on the basis of proportional representation. The president was elected for a 6-year term.

Corporate State. In 1936, by a coalition of leftist parties, the Cortes removed the incumbent president and elected a successor. Rightist parties organized a rebellion under the leadership of Gen. Francisco Franco, who, after 3 years of civil war, established a Fascist-type dictatorship with himself as chief of state and head of the Falangist party. In 1947, Franco announced that Spain would become a monarchy with him as head of state and that, on his death, a king or regent should be nominated by a two-thirds vote of the regency council and approved by a two-thirds vote of the Cortes. Embodied in a law of succession, this proposal was ratified in a popular referendum by an overwhelming majority.

The constitution of 1942 provided for a 441-member Cortes. By a national referendum in 1966 various regulations of the constitution were consolidated and partly modified to form the "Organic Law of the Spanish State." This law explains the executive powers of the head of state (king) and those of the premier. The head of state directs the government through a council of ministers. In case of absence or illness of the head of state his func-

tions are performed by the heir to the throne—if over 30 years of age—or by the regency council. The premier is to be chosen by the head of state from 3 recommendations submitted by the council of the realm. The premier's term of office is 5 years, although he can be removed by the head of state on proposal of the council of the realm.

The council of the realm consists of 16 members; the president of the council is its chairman. There also is a national council composed of 1 elected councillor for each province, 40 councillors appointed by the head of state, 12 elected by the Cortes, 6 appointed by the premier, and a secretary-general appointed by the head of state.

The Cortes consists of the members of government; the national councillors; the presidents of the supreme court of justice, the supreme military tribunal, the court of exchequer, the national economic council, and the council of the realm; 150 representatives of the trade unions; representatives of the municipalities and provincial councils; 100 deputies elected by the heads of families; and some 30 other representatives.

Roman Catholicism is established as the state religion. The church and the national government cooperate in matters of common interest.

In local government, municipalities manage their affairs through councils elected by heads of families. Each province has a sole administrator.

Juan Carlos I, grandson of Alfonso XIII, became king in 1975, succeeding Franco as head of state. Spain was faced with problems of political and economic unrest—strikes and violence occurred increasingly. Abroad, Spanish troops left the Sahara colonial territory under pressure from Arab states. In Spain, there were continued movements for amnesty for political prisoners. Unemployment remained high and wages low.

Promoting economic and political reform, Juan Carlos appointed a new premier, Adolfo Suarez Gonzalez, in July 1976. Suarez was to guide Spain in its transition to democracy.

A legislative election was held in June 1977—Spain's first free election in 41 years. Premier Suarez and his political party won wide approval. The premier announced a new constitution would be drafted.

Of Spain's once vast colonial empire, there remain only vestiges. The Canary and Balearic islands are treated administratively as a part of Spain. A protectorate over part of Morocco was relinquished to the kingdom of Morocco in 1956. The colonial empire, however, left the impress of Spanish institutions over wide areas, particularly in the Americas.

SRI LANKA (CEYLON)

Sri Lanka occupies the island of Ceylon in the Indian Ocean. It was invaded by the Portuguese in 1505, the Dutch replaced them by 1658, and the British took power in 1796. Ceylon became a crown colony in 1815 and a dominion in 1948. A 1956 agreement called for British withdrawal by 1962, but Ceylon remained in the Commonwealth of Nations. The 1972 constitution established the republic as an independent parliamentary democracy on the British model. The name Sri Lanka (great and beautiful island) was adopted at the same time. There is now a single-chamber national assembly with combined legislative and executive functions. Of its members, 151 are elected and 6 are appointed. The prime minister and his council of ministers are responsible to the assembly, whose members serve for 6 years. The president, appointed by the prime minister, serves for 4 years. Local administration in each of the 22 districts is by an agent of the central government. As a Commonwealth member, Sri Lanka observes an international affairs accord with Britain.

SUDAN

The Sudan obtained independence in 1956 from the British-Egyptian dominion previously controlling it. Sudan operated under a provisional republican constitution until 1958, when the army seized power. From 1964 to 1968 the provisional constitution was again in effect. Following the resignation of the president in 1969, a 10-man revolutionary council took over the government and military rule was reestablished. A constitution adopted in 1973 placed executive power in the president and his appointed cabinet. The president also may appoint one-tenth of the 250-member people's assembly. The three southern provinces are largely independent from the central government. This southern region is governed by a president who also is a national vice-president. It has a 60-member regional people's assembly.

SURINAM (DUTCH GUIANA)

In 1975, after more than 300 years as the Netherlands colony of Dutch Guiana, Surinam became an independent South American state. Holland had received the territory from Britain in 1667 in exchange for the island of Manhattan. At the time of independence, a new constitution was adopted for Surinam by its 39-member parliament. The 1975 charter provided for the new office of a president of the state. National problems persisted among the racially mixed population. Political power was a source of rivalry between the numerically close populations of Creoles (of African ancestry) and those of Asian Indian descent. Before independence, large numbers of the Asians, as Dutch colonial citizens, had sought jobs and welfare in Holland. After independence, the new Surinamese government sought the return of the emigrants.

SWAZILAND

The last British protectorate to gain independence (1968), Swaziland is a constitutional monarchy within the British Commonwealth. It is linked economically by a customs union with South Africa. In 1973 the king assumed supreme power, revoked the constitution, dissolved parliament, and banned all political activity. He appointed a royal constitutional commission to draw up a new constitution, but has not yet accepted its proposals.

Swaziland is divided into 4 districts governed by district commissioners.

SWEDEN

Sweden has long been the seat of constitutional system. The representative legislature *Riksdag* came into existence in the 16th century. Between 1680 and 1718, however, during the period of Sweden's prominence as a military power, the monarch became well-nigh absolute. This was followed by a period of legislative dominance.

In 1973 parliament approved a new constitution replacing the one adopted in 1809. It reduced the king to a mere figurehead, lowered the voting age to 18, and guaranteed citizens the right to hold demonstrations.

Since World War I, the general progress in democracy has affected the Swedish constitutional system. By a constitutional change, a foreign affairs committee of the Riksdag, with which the government consults on international affairs, is elected each year. The Riksdag is a one-chamber parliament of 349 members directly elected to 3-year terms by all men and women over 18. Election to the Riksdag is proportional. Three hundred and ten members are elected from 28 voting districts, while the remaining 39 members are elected from a nationwide pool.

The kingdom is divided into 24 administrative provinces or counties, in which the administration is confided to a governor in Stockholm. Each province has a legislative assembly whose members are elected directly by voters on the principle of proportional representation. Absentee voting is permitted; a husband may carry his wife's sealed ballot to the polls, and a wife, that of her husband. Soldiers, seamen, fishermen, and employees of railroads, ports, customs, and pilot services may vote by post. There is an optional referendum, or plebiscite, which may be ordered on important matters if the government and the Riksdag concur in believing it advisable.

The supreme court of Sweden has a constitutional status, while courts of appeal and district courts of first instance are organized by laws. The supreme court is authorized to render an interpretation of the law, if requested by the government.

SWITZERLAND

The "Swiss Confederacy" is the oldest republic of Europe and the first European state to adopt a federal form of government adapted from the American plan. This country is also the originator of several widely adopted democratic institutions and is an example of how peoples of different race (French, German, and Italian), of different speech, and of different religious belief may form a completely harmonized nation.

The country is composed of states or "cantons." Alliances and unions between certain of these small states date from the 13th century; but it was not until 1848 that the existing union, under a true federal form of government, was achieved. This constitution was revised in 1874 and was added to by several later amendments. The central government is complete and adequate, and certain of its powers are exercised directly upon the people and upon the territory of the whole country. The cantons, however, are protected in free exercise of their local jurisdictions by the constitution. Sovereignty undoubtedly resides in the whole nation; the union is thus a federation and not a confederacy, as its official title might imply.

The national legislative power is conferred on the Federal Assembly, which consists of two chambers. The upper house, like the American Senate, represents the separate states and is called the Council of States. It is composed of 44 members, 2 from each canton. The mode of their election, their term of service, and their remuneration are left to the cantons. The more popular house, or National Council, consists of about 200 deputies chosen by direct vote, one for each 22,000 of the population. Members of the National Council are paid from the federal treasury. Their term is 4 years. All Swiss citizens over 20 years of age are entitled to vote.

Referendum and Initiative. Switzerland has made fuller experiment of direct or popular legislation than has any other country. There is a national "referendum" of federal legislation, which is (a) obligatory for all amendments to the constitution and (b) optional upon petition of 30,000 voters or upon the demand of 8 cantons on more important acts of legislation. Perhaps the most striking instance of the exercise of this right was the proposal to enter the League of Nations, which was submitted to the voters in May 1920 and approved by a popular vote of 414,000 to 322,000. Switzerland did not apply for membership in the United Nations. An initiative procedure for amendments of the constitution on petition of 50,000 voters was adopted in 1891.

Commission Executive. Strong democratic prejudices prevented the makers of the Swiss constitution from entrusting the executive power to a single person like the American president. In place of a presidency or a ministry, there exists a commission of 7 members, who are chosen by the Federal Assembly for a 3-year term and are usually re-elected if competent. This commission is called the Federal Council. It is responsible to the Assembly for its conduct of affairs, and its dispositions may be overruled. Besides administering, it prepares legislative acts to be submitted to the Assembly. Each member is charged with the administration of a separate department—political (foreign affairs), interior, justice and police, military, finance and customs, national economy, and posts and railways. However, responsibility is collegiate, and matters of importance are considered "in commission."

Each year the Federal Assembly designates one member of the federal council to serve as "Swiss president." He becomes thereby the representative of the state at home and abroad and oversees the conduct of the business of the executive commission. He is ineligible for re-election for a consecutive term. A vice president is elected at the same time as the president and, by custom, succeeds to the chief office. While this institution of "commission executive" might be inapplicable to republics differently situated, its practice has commended itself to the Swiss nation.

There is a federal court. The judges and their alternates are appointed for a 6-year term by the Assembly. This court decides cases of conflict of jurisdiction between federal and cantonal authorities, cases between cantons, and private complaints based on violation of constitutional or treaty rights. It also has jurisdiction in certain cases between the federation and individuals.

Cantonal Government. The 22 cantons differ interestingly in the form in which their democratic character is politically exhibited. Five are small mountain states and are genuine democracies. There is no representative legislature, but laws are enacted by a popular assembly, even meeting by custom in the open field.

The other cantons have local unicameral legislatures usually called the grand council or the cantonal council. All but one of these cantons (Freiburg) has either the obligatory or optional referendum. In all cantons the executive power is entrusted to a commission of 5 or 7 members known as the administrative council or the small council. At the head of each commission is a president and a vice president

The larger cantons are divided into administrative districts or are organized in communes. Each canton has its own judicial system, comprising justices of the peace, district courts, and a superior court. There may be also special courts of commerce and industrial courts, on which sit representatives of employers and workmen. Within the jurisdiction of the cantons are such matters as poor relief, public health, labor protection, agricultural improvement, primary schools, maintenance of religious worship, citizenship, and naturalization. Proportional representation is established in several of the larger cantons.

Switzerland is a country of guaranteed neutrality by action of the "great powers" in 1815, and neutrality as well as independence is enjoined by the Swiss constitution. This status does not limit the republic in taking measures to safeguard its security, and the Swiss, always a people of high military spirit, are completely organized in a citizen army.

Switzerland has for centuries extended asylum to political and religious exiles, and is the home of a number of international associations, including the Red Cross Society and the Postal Union. The League of Nations had its seat in Geneva.

The Syrian republic was formerly a province of the Turkish Empire, and from 1920 until its independence in 1943, was a French mandate under the League of Nations. While under the mandate, Syria set up a republican form of government with a one-house legislature. In 1958 Syria and Egypt joined to form the United Arab Republic as a hoped-for nucleus of a federation of all Arab states. Three years later, the government was overthrown and the union with Egypt was dissolved. In 1964 a provisional constitution was adopted. Although the constitution was republican in form, the government was not a representative government but was operated by a few individuals.

A permanent constitution was approved by plebiscite in 1973. The president is chief of state and head of the government. Elected for a 7-year term, he has the power to dissolve the legislature and to appoint and dismiss the vice-president. The constitution made permanent the people's council whose 173 members are nominated by presidential decree. The constitution protects personal and religious freedoms and declares the economy socialist.

TANZANIA

Tanzania is a federation formed in 1964 from Tanganyika and Zanzibar, each part having a republican form of government. Tanganyika emerged from colonial status under Britain in 1961 and in 1962 became a republic within the British Commonwealth. Zanzibar became independent of Britain in 1963 under a monarchy, which was overthrown in 1964 to become a people's republic. The president is head of state and commander-in-chief of the armed forces. The first vice-president of Tanzania is the president of Zanzibar; the second vice-president and prime minister is the head of the national assembly. The national assembly is composed of 193 members: 96 elected from Tanganyika, 10 appointed from both Tanganyika and Zanzibar, 15 elected by the national assembly, 20 regional commissioners, 32 members from the Zanzibar revolutionary council, and 20 members from Zanzibar appointed by the president.

THAILAND

Thailand, formerly Siam, was an unlimited autocracy until 1932, when a revolutionary group seized the government. The king then ruled as a constitutional monarch. In 1939 the name of the country was changed to Thailand. The 1932 constitution was replaced by a new constitution in 1946 which lasted a little over a year. A military revolution in 1947 led to extensive revisions in 1949. The army again took control in 1951 and restored the constitution of 1932, which was in effect until 1958.

In 1959 an interim constitution was established by decree. Its principal feature was the formation of a constituent assembly appointed by the king to draft a permanent constitution, the governing of the country meanwhile being carried on by a council of ministers appointed by the king.

In 1969 the first general elections in 11 years were held under a new constitution. The government formed consisted of a prime minister, cabinet, and house of representatives. The constitution was suspended in 1971 when a military group took control. The military government was forced to resign in 1973 and a national convention enacted a new constitution in 1974. In 1975 a house of representatives was elected and a senate was appointed by the interim premier. The coalition government formed consisted of a prime minister and cabinet. New elections in 1976 moved the government to a more leftist situation. Later that year, a military junta again seized control.

TOGO

Togo became an independent republic in 1960. It was a German colony from 1894 until World War I, after which it was a trusteed territory. The UN relinquished its trusteeship after the citizens of Togo had voted, in 1956, to join the French Community as an autonomous republic. When its president was murdered in 1963, a new president was appointed and a strongly centralized government was established with a national assembly elected every 5 years. In 1967, asserting that civil war was at hand, the army chief Etienne Eyadema led a bloodless coup. Although he promised elections shortly, four months later Eyadema named himself president and defense minister of a largely military state. The government was reorganized in 1975. Togo was one of the prime forces behind the 1975 economic union of 15 countries—The Economic Community of West African States. Along with Nigeria, it has major responsibility to steer the organization.

TONGA

Tonga became an independent constitutional monarchy on June 4, 1970. It was a British protectorate from 1900–1970, thereafter remaining a member of the Commonwealth. The Sovereign, a Privy Council, and a Cabinet headed by the Prime Minister constitute the executive authority of Tonga, and the partly elected Legislative Assembly is the legislative branch of government.

TRINIDAD AND TOBAGO

This constitutional parliamentary democracy was granted independence from Great Britain in 1962, remaining a member of the British Commonwealth. Its constitution provides for a House of Representatives of 36 elected members and a Senate of 24 appointed members—13 appointed on the advice of the premier, 4 on the advice of the leader of the opposition in the House of Representatives, and 7 from religious, economic, and social bodies considered important by the premier. The appointments are made by the governor-general.

TUNISIA

Tunisia, a former French protectorate, declared itself a republic in 1957. Under a constitution adopted in 1959, the president, who must be a third-generation Tunisian of Islamic faith, is elected by universal suffrage for a five-year term. A National Assembly of 90 members is similarly elected at the same time, under a one-party system. The president may introduce into the Assembly bills which have precedence over other bills. He must promulgate within 15 days measures passed by the Assembly but may send them back for reconsideration, in which case they require a two-thirds majority. He names the ministers who assist him in governing. He may succeed himself three times.

TURKEY

The republic of Turkey was established in 1924. The country is what remained of the former Turkish Empire with capital at Istanbul, then known as Constantinople. After World War I the sultan was deposed by a nationalist leader Kemal Pasha, and a constitution was adopted in 1921 which vested both legislative and executive power in a Grand National Assembly. Three years later the country was declared a republic. In 1960, the army under a national union committee overthrew the government and submitted to a referendum a new constitution, which was adopted July 9, 1961.

The sovereign power is vested in the Grand National Assembly, which is composed of a National Assembly and a Senate. The National Assembly consists of 450 members elected for 4-year terms by all citizens, women as well as men, over 23 years of age. The Assembly may decide to hold new elections before the end of the 4-year term. The Senate is composed of 185 members elected by universal suffrage, 15 members appointed by the president of the republic, and 15 *ex officio* members, including past presidents and the members of the national unity committee. Except for *ex officio* members the term of office is 6 years, one-third being elected every second year.

The president is elected for a 7-year term by the Grand National Assembly from among its members sitting in joint session. A two-thirds majority is required to elect on the first two ballots, thereafter a simple majority is sufficient.

The president appoints from members of the Grand National Assembly a prime minister, who recommends other ministers to be appointed by the president from that body or from those eligible to be elected to it. The ministers present the governmental program to each chamber and may ask for a vote of confidence in the Assembly. If a ministry is unseated within 18 months by a vote of lack of confidence and thereafter incurs a third such vote, the prime minister may ask the president to dissolve the assembly and call for a new election, the ministers meanwhile being replaced by new, provisional appointees.

UGANDA

This republic became independent of British rule in 1962 and was admitted to the British Commonwealth. The constitution originally provided for a governor-general, but in 1963 it was amended to substitute a president as the chief executive, thereby making the country a republic. A coup in 1966 resulted in a new government and constitution. When that government was overthrown by army troops led by Idi Amin in 1971, a military government was established. Amin dissolved the parliament and assumed all legislative powers, assisted by a council of ministers whom he appointed. Political parties were banned and political activities outlawed. Noncitizen Asians were expelled. Amin began a program of purges, took over privately owned land, nationalized the copper mines, and introduced the death penalty for economic crimes. Most professional workers left the country or were expelled. To relieve the crisis, Amin instituted two policies in 1975: a compulsory labor program and a settlement plan that moved urban unemployed to farmland. In 1976 Amin was named president for life.

Uganda's judicial system consists of a high court, presided over by a chief justice, and lower courts. In 1973 military courts were authorized to try cases of violent or subversive crimes.

Britain severed ties with Uganda in 1976—the first time a relationship with a member of the Commonwealth was ended.

UNION OF SOVIET SOCIALIST REPUBLICS
See *Russia.*

UNITED ARAB EMIRATES

Formed in 1968, this union consists of seven sheikhdoms, or emirates. Formerly called the Trucial States, or Trucial Oman, with Bahrain and Qatar, they made up the Persian Gulf States. Britain administered their defense and foreign relations from the 19th century until 1971, when British forces withdrew. Each state has a feudal government, under a hereditary emir. The states are: Abu Dhabi, Ajman, Dubai, Fujairah, Ras al-Kaimah (which joined in 1972), Sharjah, and Umm al-Qaiwain. Shiekh Zaid, of Abu Dhabi, became president in 1971. With rising oil reserves, he made the union a power in the Arab world.

UNITED KINGDOM See *Great Britain*.

UPPER VOLTA

Upper Volta became an independent republic in 1960, remaining within the French Community. In 1966 Sangoule Lamizana overthrew the existing government, dissolved the national assembly, and suspended the constitution. He imposed military rule until 1970, when a new constitution was adopted. In 1974 the army resumed power; the constitution was again suspended and political activities were banned. Lamizana replaced the national assembly with a national council having only advisory function. Although the 65-member council had to include 12 soldiers or veterans, 11 rural representatives, and 8 trade union members, all were appointed by the president. Because of increasing conflict between unions and the military government, Lamizana announced a new largely civilian council in 1976, and promised a new constitution.

Upper Volta's judicial system includes a supreme court with constitutional, judicial, administrative, and fiscal chambers; a high court of justice; a court of appeals; and 4 lower courts. Since 1967 a special tribunal under the minister of justice hears cases involving national security.

URUGUAY

The Republic of Uruguay became independent of Spanish and Portuguese claims in 1828. Its first constitution, 1830, provided a centralized form of republican government. In 1919 a new constitution, designed to avoid dictatorship, divided executive power between a president and an administrative council, both elected by the people but for different terms. A constitution adopted in 1951 abolished the presidency entirely, and all executive power was vested in a 9-member bipartisan national council. Uruguay returned to the presidential system in 1966. Dissolving congress in 1973, the president ruled by decree until June 1976, when he was overthrown by the army. Uruguay was then ruled by a national council consisting chiefly of military men. In July 1976 the council named a president with limited powers for a 3-year term.

VATICAN CITY

Vatican City became an independent sovereign state in 1929 when the Holy See and Italy signed the Lateran Pacts. The smallest state in the world, it is an elected absolute monarchy. Its constitution, adopted in 1929, names the pope, who is head of the church, as head of state. The pope, elected on the death of his predecessor by a two-thirds majority of the College of Cardinals, has full legislative, executive, and judicial powers. He appoints and can remove all members of the various committees or Congregations to which he delegates authority. There is no legislature and there are no elections. During a vacancy in the papacy, the College of Cardinals assumes authority.

Vatican City has its own flag, seal, stamps, and money. Citizenship is granted to permanent residents and is lost when that residency is ended. Vatican City is pledged to political neutrality between governments. It is not a member of the United Nations, although it maintains official observers there.

VENEZUELA

In 1829 Venezuela seceded from the republic of Colombia and formed a separate republic to include the territory of the former "captaincy-general" of Venezuela. Its first constitution was proclaimed in 1830.

Under the constitution adopted in 1961, executive authority is vested in a president chosen by direct popular vote for a 5-year term. He may not serve an additional term until 10 years after his first term.

The legislative authority is vested in a congress composed of a senate and a chamber of deputies. Two senators are popularly elected from each of the 20 states and the federal district for 5-year terms, and ex-presidents also serve as senators. Deputies are popularly elected from districts none of which may have more than one per cent of the population. The term is 5 years. Suffrage is universal and compulsory for all citizens over 18.

Bills may be introduced into either house by legislative committees, by any three or more legislators, by the president, and by 20,000 or more voters. If a bill passed by one house is amended by the other, the differences are resolved in joint session. If the president disapproves of a bill, it may be passed over his veto by a two-thirds vote in joint session. If his objection is on constitutional grounds, the bill is submitted to the supreme court, whose decision must be made within 10 days. Members of the supreme court are chosen by congress for 9-year terms, one-third being renewed each 3 years.

Venezuela is composed of 20 states, 2 territories, and a federal district. They are autonomous, politically equal, and exercise residual powers not assigned to the federal government.

VIETNAM

Vietnam is part of former French Indochina. The French were defeated by troops under Communist leadership in 1954, when an agreement was reached at Geneva dividing control of the country. The north was under Communist control; the south was controlled by an anti-Communist party. The agreement called for a general election in 1956 in all Vietnam to determine its governmental status. The election was not held and guerrilla warfare broke out. When the French left, the U.S. lent support to the government of South Vietnam.

In North Vietnam, a Chinese-type Communist government was set up in 1960 calling itself a people's democracy. Ho Chi Minh was the first head of state, continuing until his death in 1969.

In South Vietnam, a republican constitution was adopted in 1956 with a president and a national assembly, both popularly elected. In 1961 the president was granted emergency powers to combat Communist encroachment. Two years later he was overthrown by a military group and the constitution was in abeyance as civil disorder and war with the north continued. U.S. aid was stepped up, as the war continued, to a peak in 1969 of 543,000 troops. In 1973 a ceasefire agreement was signed in Paris and U.S. troops were withdrawn. On April 30, 1975, South Vietnam was defeated by North Vietnam; a year later on April 25, 1976, the first national elections since 1946 were held. The Socialist Republic of Vietnam was officially declared reunited on July 2, 1976, after 22 years of separation.

A 492-member national assembly was elected by universal vote of citizens 18 and over. The 1976 election results showed 249 deputies from the north and 243 from the south. All candidates were selected by the Communist party. The assembly chooses a president, a premier, and 30 cabinet members. Real power lies with a 10-member politburo chosen from the Communist party. Vietnam is a member of the UN.

WESTERN SAMOA

This South Pacific island group became independent in 1962, after having been controlled by Germany, the United States, and New Zealand, which still handles Western Samoa's foreign affairs. There is a unicameral legislature of 45 members, most of whom are chiefs of family or tribal groups. The head of state is a chief; the first was elected in 1962 to serve for life—his successors will be elected by the legislature for 5-year terms.

YEMEN ARAB REPUBLIC

Yemen Arab Republic fell under the rule of the Turkish Empire in the 16th century. The withdrawal of Turkish forces in 1918 allowed Iman Yahya to gain control. In 1958 Yemen joined the United Arab Republic as one of the United Arab States. In 1962 it became an Independent Islamic Arab republic.

A constitution adopted in 1970 established a government headed by a presidential council whose chairman served as the head of state. The council, a policy-making organ, appointed a prime minister, who selected a cabinet. The constitution also provided for a consultative council responsible for legislative functions. After a military coup in 1974, a command council suspended the constitution and the consultative council. The prime minister and his cabinet continued in office. Since then the consultative council has been reestablished, but the constitution remained suspended.

The Yemen Arab Republic is divided into 7 provinces, each headed by a governor or commander of armed forces. The provinces are subdivided into districts. Provincial and district officials are responsible to the central government. The judicial system is based on Islamic religious law. The Yemen Arab Republic is a member of the Arab League and the UN.

YEMEN, REPUBLIC OF (SOUTH)

British control of Southern Yemen began in 1839. Control of the territory was handed over by the British to the National Liberation Front on November 30, 1967. Its name was changed to the People's Democratic Republic of Yemen in December 1970.

Under the 1970 constitution executive authority is vested in a 3-member presidential council. The chairman of the council serves as chief of state. The prime minister, also a member of the presidential council, serves as the head of government and is responsible to the legislature. The legislative branch is the 101-member people's supreme council. The council is appointed by the supreme general command to represent the party, professional groups, and trade unions. Yemen is divided into 6 governates, each headed by a centrally appointed official. The governmental structure also includes a 7-member political bureau and a 31-member central committee. The judicial system is composed of a supreme court, a court of appeal, and magistrate's courts. In some areas, Islamic law and tribal customs are applied. The Republic of Yemen is a member of the Arab League and the UN.

YUGOSLAVIA

Yugoslavia was proclaimed a republic in November 1945; its first constitution was adopted in 1946. The 1963 constitution changed the name of the country to the socialist Federal Republic of Yugoslavia—composed of the socialist republics of Bosnia and Herzegovina, Crna Gora (Montenegro), Croatia, Macedonia, Serbia, and Slovenia. Every citizen over the age of 18 was given the right to vote.

A new constitution was issued in 1974. It strengthened the power of the central government and of the Communist party. It provided for greater political and economic control by workers through factory councils. The constitution stated that national and regional legislatures would be composed of workers and other nonprofessional politicians elected from factories and other economic units. The Communist party would provide guidance to the legislators. President Josip Broz-Tito would remain president for life and would be replaced by a collective presidency of 9 rotating members. Tito, president since 1953, is president of the Communist League of Yugoslavia.

ZAIRE

A Belgian colony from 1885, Zaire (formerly the Congo) was granted independence in 1960 under a parliamentary constitution. Within a week of independence the army mutinied; political infighting and rebellion swept the country. In November 1965, Lt. General Joseph Mobutu, commander of the national army, seized control of the government and declared himself president. For two years rebellions continued, but since late 1967 Zaire has had political stability and internal peace. In 1967 Mobutu founded the Popular Movement of the Revolution, a political party that has since become the sole political arm of the government. The same year Mobutu proposed a constitution which was approved by popular vote.

The name of the Congo was changed to the Republic of Zaire (ZY-EAR) in October 1971. In 1966 the name of the capital had been changed to Kinshasa from Leopoldville. The people were required to replace their Christian or foreign names with African ones.

New constitutional changes were made in August 1974 that resulted in a strong centralized presidential government. The president of the Popular Movement is automatically president of Zaire and presides over the political bureau, the party congress (which meets every 5 years), and the executive, judicial, and legislative councils. The president makes all major appointments, commands the armed forces, and can declare war and conclude treaties. Except for Mobutu, whose term is for life, presidents are to be elected for 5-year terms, renewable only once. Under the president is the 20-member political bureau whose decisions immediately become law. The legislative council, with some 200 members, drafts laws as directed by the president. Council members are to be chosen by the electorate from a slate. Voting is compulsory for all over 18.

ZAMBIA

The Republic of Zambia was formed in 1964 from the former British protectorate of Northern Rhodesia after the latter had acquired independence from the Federation of Rhodesia and Nyasaland. This federation, formed in 1953, was dissolved in 1963; it also had included Malawi (formerly Nyasaland) and Southern Rhodesia. Zambia remained a member of the British Commonwealth.

The legislative assembly has 10 nominated members and 125 members elected by universal vote for a 5-year term. The first president was appointed by the legislative assembly but his successors are elected by the people for a 5-year term. The vice-president is appointed by the president. The 1972 constitution provided for one-party rule.

POLITICAL TERMS AND INSTITUTIONS

THE study of the governments of the world today is facilitated by the scientific definition of political ideas and by increasingly accurate descriptions of forms of political organization. An acquaintance with these general conceptions and facts is necessary to comprehension of any nation's history and government. This dictionary presents, with brief and authoritative treatment, a large number of the most important of such institutions and terms. They are discussed in respect to their general forms and meanings and also with regard to particular developments and usages in different countries. Significant features of American political life are given especial attention.

This section therefore has a threefold value. It supplies a convenient reference dictionary of political terms. Further, it supplements the articles upon the history and the governments of the world, adding more complete treatment of special topics than could be given in those articles. Finally, it furnishes a valuable means for comparative study of political ideas and practices prevailing in different countries.

Absolutism. A form of government in which the supreme power of the state is vested in a person who rules unlimited by constitutional laws.

Admiralty (ăd'mĭ-răl-tĭ). The branch of the law which treats of civil and criminal cases arising on the high seas. In the United States, admiralty jurisdiction is vested by the Constitution in Federal courts.

In England, admiralty denotes that department of the government which has jurisdiction over the naval forces and over all merchant vessels flying the British flag.

Air Zone. Air space above the territory and waters of belligerents. In international law, air zone is regarded as a field for military combat.

Alderman. A member of a municipal body, either popularly elected or "co-opted," that is, added by choice of the municipal council.

Allegiance. Obligation of obedience and loyalty on the part of a citizen toward his country. An alien is under obligation of temporary and partial allegiance to a country in which he is a resident, and thereby is bound to obey its laws and answer the summons of its duly constituted authorities. The term is also used broadly to designate the relation of loyalty and support which one has assumed toward any institution, party, movement, or leader.

Ambassador. See *Diplomatic Representation.*

American's Creed. See *Creed, The American's.*

Amnesty (ăm'nĕs-tĭ). An act of government granting exemption from criminal prosecution and punishment. It often extends to a class or group. It differs from pardon in being granted before rather than after conviction.

Anarchism. A social doctrine which advocates the abolition of all governmental authority, to the end that the individual may be free to realize his desires and aspirations without legal restraint.

Apportionment. See *Representation.*

Appropriation. Restriction to a specific purpose of money voted by a legislative body. In England traces can be found as early as the Fourteenth century, but it did not become the established practice until the Seventeenth. In the United States it is prescribed by the Constitution (Art. I, sec. 9). Historically it has been an important means of controlling the executive.

Arbitration. A method of settling disputes between nations by referring the matters in question to an arbitral authority for decision. Sometimes this authority is an individual, as the head of a state; at other times it is a board, a court, or a special arbitral tribunal. International practice of arbitration has been much advocated in America.

Among important arbitrations to which the United States has been a party are the Geneva Award, 1872, which settled American claims upon Great Britain; the Venezuela Boundary Dispute of 1897; and the Bering Sea Arbitration of 1893. The United States has treaties providing for arbitration with many states. See *Hague Tribunal.*

Arbitration of Industrial Disputes. Continued struggle between employers and employees in the development of modern industry has occasioned repeated resort to arbitration to settle labor disputes and to terminate deadlocks, injurious not only to those concerned but to the public as well. Many states have established public boards of industrial arbitration without providing for compulsory resort to them.

In New Zealand, and later in New South Wales and in West Australia, laws have been passed compelling submission of industrial disputes to arbitration and providing state arbitral machinery.

In the state of Kansas, a compulsory arbitration act was passed in 1920, and a court of arbitration was created. This legislation was upheld by the state courts; but, in June 1923, the United States supreme court decided that the power accorded this court to fix wages is in conflict with the 14th amendment and is therefore unconstitutional.

Aristocracy. A term used by the Greek philosopher, Aristotle, to denote government by the best qualified. He recognized the tendency of such a form to degenerate into government by the corrupt or the wealthy, to which debased type he applied the name "oligarchy." Aristotle contrasted aristocracy with "monarchy" on the one hand and "democracy" on the other, and since his time these have remained fundamental political conceptions.

The term "aristocracy" is applied also to the nobility and gentry of states with monarchical institutions, and so, by analogy, to those people who assume superior qualities or social standing.

Army of the United States. See *National Defense.*

Attainder. The extinction, by an act of a legislative body, of all civil rights of a person, and his sentence to death, without hearing or other judicial process. The Parliament of England passed many such acts, particularly during the 15th and 16th centuries. Bills of attainder are expressly prohibited by the Constitution of the United States and by most of the state constitutions.

Bills of "pains and penalties" of the British Parliament resembled bills of attainder, but they imposed lesser punishment than death.

Autocracy. A form of government in which political power is absolute and unlimited. This form of monarchy reached its greatest pretensions in Europe in the 18th century. It generally disappeared in the 19th century. Among the great European powers, Russia was the last to adhere to it, and the title of "Autocrat of all the Russias" was held by the czar until the abdication of 1917.

Ballot. See *Voting.*

Belligerency (bĕ-lĭj'ĕr-ĕn-sĭ). The status whereby regularly organized fighting forces become entitled to the protection of the laws and usages of war. The Hague Convention of 1899, which codified international rules of warfare, provided that troops, to be entitled to these privileges, must be part of the military organization of a recognized "belligerent"; must be commanded by properly commissioned officers; must wear distinctive uniform; must carry arms openly and not be guilty themselves of conduct contrary to the usages of war among civilized nations. Among recognized rights of belligerents are: the right of surrender or of capture rather than death upon the field; trial by court-martial before execution, and humane treatment as prisoners of war.

Belligerency is an official recognition withheld from mere rebels or insurgents, who may be treated without regard to the laws and usages of nations.

Bicameral (bĭ-kăm'ĕr-ăl) **System.** That form of legislature which consists of two separate chambers or houses, the concurrence of both ordinarily being essential to the enactment of legislation. A one-chamber legislature is known as a *unicameral* system. The bicameral system is found in the United States in both Federal and all state governments, with the exception of Nebraska. More than half the national legislatures in Europe are bicameral, the remainder being unicameral. In state, provincial, and local government, single chambers are the rule in Mexico and Canada.

The bicameral system is traced to the influence of the English bicameral Parliament, which, for reasons that were accidental rather than deliberate, early organized into a House of Lords and a House of Commons.

In the American state, the bicameral Congress harmonized the conflicting purposes of the framers of the Constitution, the Senate representing the states, with equal representation, and the House of Representatives, the nation, on the basis of population.

Elsewhere than in federal government, the two-chamber legislature is usually justified merely as a check upon hasty, ill-considered legislation.

Bill of Rights. An English act of Parliament of 1689, entitled "an act declaring the rights and liberties of the subject, and settling the succession to the crown." After reciting the abdication of James II and the vacancy of the crown, the act declares the ancient rights and liberties of Englishmen: (1) that it is illegal for the king to attempt to suspend laws without the consent of Parliament; (2) that levies of taxes without grant of Parliament are illegal;

(3) that subjects have the right freely to petition the king; (4) that the raising or keeping of a standing army within the kingdom in time of peace, unless it be with the consent of Parliament, is against the law; (5) that Protestant subjects may bear arms suitable for their defense and as allowed by law; (6) that the elections of members of Parliament shall be free; (7) that freedom of speech and debate or of proceedings in Parliament shall not be impeached or questioned outside of Parliament; (8) that excessive bail shall not be required, nor excessive fines imposed, nor cruel and unusual punishments inflicted; (9) that a person accused of crime shall be entitled to a trial by impartial jurors; (10) that grants of the fines and forfeitures of accused persons before conviction are illegal; and (11) that Parliament shall be frequently convened.

These so-called "rights of Englishmen" expressed in definite form those limitations upon the royal prerogative to which Englishmen believed they were entitled under the customs and common law of the realm. Next to Magna Charta, the Bill of Rights of 1689 is regarded as the most important constitutional document in English history. The accession of William and Mary was made dependent upon its recognition. From this fundamental statement, similar bills have been framed in the course of constitutional development in many countries.

The American colonists held to the principle of these limitations upon the power of the crown, and their revolution rested in part upon the alleged violation of them. The first ten amendments of the Federal Constitution constitute the so-called "American bill of rights," several repeating the language of the English law. (See *Constitution of the United States*.) Similar constitutional guarantees have been incorporated in the constitutions of every American state.

In 1789, the French National Assembly adopted the famous "Declaration of the Rights of Man and of the Citizen" which, more theoretical than its English predecessor, has enjoyed scarcely less influence in the progress of revolution against autocratic government.

Bloc. A French word, meaning "mass" or "group," somewhat recently introduced into political parlance, to mean an association of legislative members or of political workers of different parties, formed to support a certain measure or ministry.

One of the most famous of such combinations was the so-called "Blue-Black bloc," a union of Conservatives (blues) and Clericals (blacks) in the German Reichstag, especially between 1894 and 1907, in which latter year a new bloc was created, that of the Conservatives and the Liberals.

The term has been introduced into American politics through the union of members of Congress pursuing certain agrarian policies in what is called the "agricultural bloc."

Blockade. The closing or blocking of entrance to the ports of a belligerent country by hostile naval forces to shut out neutral commerce and to prevent the entrance of supplies or re-enforcements. A blockade, to be valid in international law, must be officially declared by a belligerent against the ports of another belligerent; must be officially called to the attention of neutral powers; and must be effective.

During World War I, the British, by their naval control, practiced a blockade upon German ports by proclamation rather than by the close patrol of war vessels. This system was extended to ships bound for the ports of neutral countries contiguous to the central European powers, or with which they were able to maintain communication.

Bolshevism (*bŏl'shĕ-vĭz'm*). A term derived from the Russian *bolshestvo*, meaning "majority"; hence bolshevik, plural, bolsheviki. Bolshevism is the radical extreme of Marxian socialism. It accepts the doctrine of Karl Marx, that an irreconcilable antagonism exists between the propertied class, or bourgeois, and the propertyless workers, or proletariat. It invites as inevitable and necessary the "class war," the object of which is the destruction of all classes except the proletariat, in whose interest and by whom future society will be organized with a view to production for use rather than for private profit.

Bolshevists differ from more moderate socialists by the literal interpretation they give to Marx's phrases. By the "class war," they mean actual warfare. They repudiate peaceful measures, especially parliamentary action, and advocate and employ violence for the immediate and complete attainment of the "revolution." They hold the political achievements of the last century and a half—political freedom, representative government, etc.—to be deceptive and illusory "bourgeois triumphs" inimical to the proletariat, since they have strengthened and extended the power of the propertied class.

The philosophy of Karl Marx, which was essentially "determinist," taught that the evolution of capitalistic society into communism is inevitable, through the process of the rich becoming richer and fewer in number, while the poor become poorer and more numerous. This irresistible

development would go on until the overwhelming mass of mankind would be reduced to the class of proletarians, when capitalism would be "mature" and incapable of resisting its "capture" by the propertyless.

Envisioned as steps in the process were the organization of workers into unions, teaching them to act in concert, and periodic social distress arising from economic depressions. The Marxian analysis of capitalism held that the urge for profitable markets would precipitate "imperialist" wars, and that the resulting disorganization would lend opportunities for the proletariat to seize power. With each nation refashioned on a socialist pattern, Marx held, a world federation of co-operating republics would be possible.

BOLSHEVIST POLICY IN RUSSIA. The collapse of Russia in 1917 afforded the Bolshevists an opportunity to seize the power of the state, to destroy the opposition ("counter-revolutionists"), and to establish a communistic society on a gigantic, national scale. (See *Russia*.) The form of government set up to replace the constitutional and representative system was that of "soviets" (committees of propertyless workmen and soldiers) to which soviets or councils all power was attributed. (See *Soviet*.) All property was seized; all trading or commerce was penalized; all persons became the operatives or fellow laborers of the soviet state, which assigned to each individual or to his group its definite task and fixed the output or production required. An elaborate system of accounting and of control of industry was created. Severe penalties were visited upon recalcitrant bodies of laborers and upon peasant communities which failed to deliver the required production to the Soviet state.

The plan came near to being wrecked by the refusal of peasants to part with their produce. For a time the government compromised with a system of private profit. Then in 1927 began a ruthless effort to collectivize farming. State farms and co-operative farms were organized, many of them of enormous size, and the most improved types of machinery were used to work them. Private property was permitted to the extent of allowing each farmer to own enough land and animals to supply his own needs.

Other compromises with a rigorous communism were made by permitting different pay for different types of work and allowing individuals to accumulate property as long as this was not accomplished by using the labor of others to make profit. Five-year plans of national development were undertaken and carried through with a success that made Russia a rival of other great industrial states. The nation continued to advance economically throughout the great depression which plagued the rest of the world in the years following 1929.

RELATION TO OTHER NATIONS The attitude of the Bolshevists at first was to expect a world-revolution within a short time. To bring this about they organized the "Third International" at Moscow in March 1919. Briefly successful Bolshevist revolutions were effected in several German states and in Hungary. These movements were ruthlessly suppressed. Definitely anti-Communist governments were set up in Italy and later in Germany. Meanwhile the attitude of Bolshevists toward the world revolution was modified. Aggressive propaganda was gradually discarded and peace abroad was cultivated. Instead of struggling for revolution directly, the government proposed to demonstrate in Russia the advantages of organizing economic life not for private profit but for public welfare.

This policy was changed in 1939, when Soviet Russia, in alliance with Germany, absorbed the Baltic states. After World War II the expansion continued, with the reappearance of the Comintern as the Cominform, and the capture by the Communists (the term now used) of the governments of countries bordering on Russia in Europe and Asia, and the organization of Communist parties, directed from Moscow, in other countries.

Bonus. Money paid in addition to a stated compensation. A bonus system, while common in private employment, is rare in public service and usually is adopted only when a sudden rise in prices recommends a temporary increase of government pay.

In the United States the term was used after World War I to describe payments by the national and state governments to former soldiers, as "adjusted compensation." Under the national measure, passed in 1924, over President Coolidge's veto, about four billion dollars was paid. After World War II most states granted bonuses to veterans.

Boodle. Money used in bribing public officials or in improperly influencing elections. The term also signifies plunder, or wealth improperly secured by officials through abuse of public office. It is said that the word "boodle" is derived from a Dutch colonial term meaning estate or inheritance.

Boss System. A term used in the United States to describe the method by which professional politicians, or "bosses," control nominations and elections to public office, and secretly direct the policy and conduct of government, particularly in states and municipalities.

The boss exercises power through a well organized "machine" of partisan workers who seek petty public office in exchange for services at primaries and elections. He frequently controls the candidates, whom his machinery elects, in their exercise of office. Thus the boss system has been aptly termed "invisible government."

The boss system has had its greatest development in the United States where frequency of elections and the number of elective officials overtax the interest of the average citizen.

Direct primaries, the initiative, the referendum, and the recall have been tried as methods of taking from the professional politician his pernicious power.

Bounty. A grant of land or money by the government to private individuals to reward services or encourage activities deemed of public benefit.

After the Civil War, large bounties in public land were given to the transcontinental railway companies to encourage the rapid extension of their lines and to hasten the development of the West.

Bounties frequently take the form of subsidies to owners of private merchant vessels, a flourishing merchant marine being regarded as a needed naval auxiliary in time of war.

Valuable bounties of land or money have often been given to induce enlistment in the military forces of a country, or to reward military service in time of war.

Brainwashing. The compulsory substitution of one body of political principles by another body through indoctrination or oppression, especially mental torture.

Budget. A detailed statement of the estimated expenditures and revenues for the ensuing fiscal period, submitted to the legislature by an officer responsible for the financial administration of the government. In England, where the budget system has been most completely developed, the chancellor of the exchequer prepares the budget showing the receipts from every source and the expenditures of each department for the year then expiring, together with estimated expenditures for the coming year, and a scheme of taxation for meeting such expenditures.

In the United States, satisfactory budget systems have come much later. American legislatures were long reluctant to let the executive branch of the government propose how moneys should be raised and spent. In 1921, Congress enacted a budget law whereby a director of the budget prepares, under the direction of the president, a budget for submission to Congress. California, New York, and many other states have entrusted similar powers to their governors. In 1933-34, the United States began the practice of dividing the budget into two parts, one showing estimates of current expenditures and income, the other, of sums chargeable to capital or other extraordinary outlays.

Absence of a budget results in waste, duplication of expense, and extravagance in appropriations. From the same cause follows lack of businesslike correlation between the raising and expending of revenues, and the absence of a definite responsibility for the financial administration of the government. See *Logrolling.*

Bureaucracy (*bū-rō′krå-sĭ*). Government by an elaborate system of administrative departments and officials, the lower functionaries subordinate in all matters to the higher. A bureaucracy generally tends to become unwieldy and laborious in its operation, through the absence of discretion in any but the higher officials. This produces "red tape" or over-systematization. Bureaucracy may exhibit also a tendency to disregard individual rights and to engage in arbitrary acts, but its most frequently charged defects are its rigidity, conservatism, and spirit of routine.

Cabinet Government. The form of government such as that of Great Britain, which is composed of a group of ministers, collectively called the "cabinet." Usually members of the cabinet are chosen from the leaders of the majority party of the Parliament or legislative body, and they are collectively responsible to that majority for the general policies and conduct of the government. As a rule, each member is the head of an administrative department.

Under systems of parliamentary government, the cabinet retains office only so long as it commands the support of the legislature.

Where there is more than one chamber in the national legislature, the dominant chamber, as the House of Commons in England or the Chamber of Deputies in France, is the one upon whose support the cabinet rests. Upon an adverse vote of that chamber on a material matter, the cabinet resigns.

Cabinet government, which is called also "parliamentary" or "responsible" government, differs fundamentally from "presidential" government as found in the United States. Here the president is the actual executive head. The cabinet is responsible, not to Congress, but to him.

The president is responsible to the nation for his policies and his administration. Members of his cabinet are merely his advisers and subordinates.

Throughout Europe and in the British "dominions," cabinet government, responsible to a Parliament, has become nearly universal, but, almost without exception, the republics of the western hemisphere have followed the example of the United States, choosing their executives for a fixed term and making them independent of congressional direction.

Campaign, Political. Organized effort by a political party or group to secure the election of a particular candidate or list of candidates to political office. In the United States, formerly, the political campaign was marked by spectacular parades, campaign songs and slogans, immense gatherings of enthusiastic throngs, and by other devices calculated to arouse partisan interest and enthusiasm. More recently, however, political campaigns have been carried on principally by printed appeals, particularly through the medium of the daily newspaper.

In most American states, "direct primaries" or nominations by "primary elections" have taken the place of local and state nominating conventions. This has reduced party influence in political campaigns and has made them largely personal. It has at the same time doubled the effort necessary to secure election, as a candidate must compete at the polls twice, once for the nomination of his party and again for election to office. This system necessitates a large appeal to voters through the mails, by the circulation of personal appeals and "campaign literature," and has had the result of introducing a large element of expense not previously known.

Caucus. A meeting or conference of members of a political party or group to determine upon the candidate or policy to be supported in an election or other political contest. The term is American and is said to be derived from the Indian "kaw-kaw-was," meaning to counsel or confer.

A person entering a caucus is usually held to be honorably bound to accept the decision of the caucus, even though it be adverse to himself or to his views. He may, however, refuse to "caucus" with other members of his party or affiliation, thereby preserving independence of action and choice.

Census. An official enumeration of the population of a country, sometimes including also a tabulation of its industries and resources. In the Western world, the census is of Roman origin. In the time of Augustus, it was extended to the whole empire. The modern system, directed by the government, originated in Sweden in the 17th century. It was then adopted by France. No census was taken in Great Britain until 1800. Modern census-taking, however, may be considered to have originated in the United States. The Constitution provides that a national census shall be taken every ten years. The original purpose was to provide a basis for the periodical reapportionment of members of the House of Representatives, but the scope of the census has been extended to include the securing of data upon racial, religious, social, and economic conditions.

Charter. A grant from a sovereign or other superior authority to an individual, a company, or a territorial division, authorizing the exercise of certain functions or the enjoyment of certain privileges. In England, the crown often granted special charters to authorize individuals to exercise powers of government. Thus charters were granted to the proprietors who established colonies in America. Other colonies received direct charters from the crown empowering the people of the colonies to organize colonial governments. Similar "chartered companies" were created for extending British rule in Africa.

In the United States, charters may be granted for the creation of either public corporations or private corporations. The charter of a public or municipal corporation is today generally in the form of an act of the legislature, pursuant to which the corporation is organized, and which prescribes its form of organization and the powers which it may exercise. As a result, in England and America, municipalities have only such powers as are specifically enumerated in their charters or are bestowed by general laws. Incorporation is extensively used in the United States to create departments of government to carry on specific enterprises, the government owning all the stock. Examples are the Port Authority of New York and the Tennessee Valley Authority.

In the case of private corporations, it was the practice until about 1860 for legislatures to pass special acts for each private corporation created, and an act constituted the charter of the company in precisely the same manner as in the case of the public or municipal corporation. However, with the growth of the corporate form of business organization, the need of a special enactment for each private corporation burdened legislatures with private bills and led to political abuses. As a result, constitutional or legislative provisions were adopted in nearly all states, providing for the organization of private corporations under general incorporation laws.

Child Labor Legislation. See *Social Legislation.*

Chinese Exclusion. See *Immigration Legislation.*

Citizenship. The relation of an individual to his state, by which he owes obedience and loyalty, and in turn receives protection. The term as now used does not necessarily include the possession of political rights. Thus minors and women are citizens regardless of their right to vote.

In the United States, there is generally a dual citizenship: that of the nation and that of the particular state of which one is a resident. By express provision of the 14th amendment, as well as by the common law, any person born in the United States, of American parentage or of alien parents temporarily resident in the United States and therefore subject to its jurisdiction, is a citizen of the United States. Persons born of American parents on the high seas, or while such parents are temporarily resident abroad, are also citizens by birth. Children of diplomatic representatives of the United States, temporarily resident in a foreign land, are likewise citizens.

Citizenship in two different countries at the same time is technically possible and frequently occurs. Thus the laws of some countries provide that a citizen by birth ever continues to be a citizen of that country and cannot divest himself of allegiance. If such an individual becomes naturalized in another country, both his native country and the country of naturalization may then claim from him the duties of citizenship. Whether he is to be regarded as a citizen of one country or of the other may depend upon whether the question arises within the territory of the old citizenship or the new. See *Naturalization.*

City Government. Frequently spoken of as "municipal government." Legally, a city is an agent created by government for a definite local area, primarily for the satisfaction of local needs. In European countries generally, outside of Great Britain, and in some non-European countries, city government is also the agent of the state for the local administration of national affairs, and the chief executive of the city is responsible not only to the city government for the conduct of its interests, but also to the national government, whose agent he is. See *France.*

MUNICIPAL AUTHORITY. In Europe, city governments seldom enjoy autonomy or complete "home rule" but are subjected to supervision from higher branches of administration. This supervision usually applies to such matters as approval of municipal budgets, the granting of franchises and particularly to the exercise of the police power wherein the city is regarded as an agent of the state, discharging state functions. In Great Britain, and to an even larger degree in the United States, city governments are autonomous, free to vote moneys, incur indebtedness, grant public franchises, and engage in municipal undertakings without superior administrative sanction or direction. It is a fundamental principle, however, of British and also of American law that a city government has no inherent or "implied powers" but can legally undertake only those activities enumerated in its charter or sanctioned by general laws. (See *Charter.*) In Great Britain, city government powers are altered or enlarged by acts of Parliament in what are called "private bills."

In Great Britain and in the United States, the courts may be invoked to restrain a city government from undertaking activities not specifically granted by law. In the countries of continental Europe, the range of the activities of municipalities is not exactly fixed by law; but a city, subject to superior administrative approval, is presumed to be competent to assume any undertaking for the better satisfaction of local needs.

In the United States and likewise in Great Britain, city government is usually confined to urban areas where the population is sufficiently dense to require that service which cities are organized to supply. The public needs of rural regions are taken care of by county government, the jurisdiction of which extends also over the cities. This leads to a certain duplication of public service within American cities, and, in a few instances, notably San Francisco, California, it has led to the creation of a special combined "city and county government."

STATE CONTROL. In the United States, originally, state legislatures possessed complete power over city governments and could alter their charters at any time or subject them to special laws and administration. Abuse of this legislative power led to constitutional limitations upon state legislatures, forbidding them to pass special laws affecting municipalities. Furthermore, in a number of American states the freeholders or citizens of a city are permitted to frame and to adopt a special charter embodying their own choice of the principles of municipal government, and this charter, when ratified by the legislature, becomes the legal basis of city government.

City Planning. The orderly laying out of a city into industrial, mercantile, and residential sections, and the organization of its streets, parks, and public buildings, so as to obtain the maximum of convenience, health, and beauty.

The Roman cities were laid out on the "checkerboard plan" with streets at right angles and with a central square or plaza on which the principal public buildings fronted. During the Middle Ages such orderly layouts largely disappeared in much of Europe as cities were destroyed or decayed and a primary objective became defense against outside enemies. Protective walls were more important than convenient streets and sanitation.

Although the Roman system had survived in Spain and was followed in Spanish cities in the New World, it was not until the 18th and 19th centuries that advanced principles of city planning were adopted elsewhere. Philadelphia was laid out on the checkerboard plan. Later, in Europe, the central portions of Vienna and Paris were reconstructed at great expense to achieve impressive beauty, and wide boulevards replaced the ancient walls. In Paris, avenues radiating from central plazas provided vistas and shortened diagonal travel distances. Washington, D.C., was laid out on this plan with broad streets and beautiful parks.

By the mid-20th century, motor-car traffic and parking problems compelled drastic modifications in the large cities. Resort was had to roads passing above and below the street level with complicated ramps and interchanges, a system in which Stockholm and Los Angeles led the way. One interchange in Stockholm accommodates traffic on five different levels. In some cities, reconstructed after their destruction in World War II, certain central areas are reserved for pedestrians. See *Zoning Ordinances.*

Civic Center. The more important buildings of a municipality grouped together within an area conveniently accessible from all parts of the city form a civic center. By such grouping, an impressive architectural scheme is made possible and the transaction of public business is facilitated. See *City Planning.*

Civil Rights and Liberties. Civil rights are those explicitly conferred upon the citizens, subjects, or residents of a state by positive law, the enjoyment of such rights being secured by action of the state itself. Political rights, likewise conferred by law, are normally confined to citizens and include voting in public elections, holding office, serving on juries, etc. So-called "natural rights" are purely theoretical and have interest for the political scientist mainly because of their influence on revolutionary or reform movements or after they have been converted into civil rights embodied in positive law.

GROWTH OF MODERN RIGHTS. As a matter of fact, civil rights as they exist in the Western world have been defined mainly by actual struggles of governed peoples for greater freedom against arbitrary authority, and they represent practical achievements in this direction. (See *Bill of Rights.*) The original home of most civil rights recognized in modern law was England; thence these liberties were carried to America by English colonists and there received an expansion and an emphasis through the American Revolution. From the United States these ideas were carried to France and there, by the French Revolution, were restated in the form in which they have been communicated to most peoples of the world.

CIVIL LIBERTY IN AMERICA. American protection of civil rights was first incorporated in the Constitution in 1791 by amendments I to IX. After the Civil War, amendments XIII and XIV were adopted, the first in 1865 abolishing slavery and the second in 1868. The latter affirmed citizenship of all persons born in the United States and forbade states to make laws abridging the privileges or immunities of citizens. The purpose of these amendments was to erase the discriminatory after-effects of slavery, but this purpose was far from being realized.

Nearly a hundred years later, the Civil Rights Act of 1964 was adopted with the broad purpose of preventing political and economic discrimination based on race, color, religion, sex, or national origin. Article XIX (1920) had forbidden political discrimination based on sex. The new law widened this protection and extended protection also to religious and national-origin minorities. Specifically, discrimination was forbidden in registration and voting rights, in administration of government-financed projects, in employment, in schools, and in establishments serving the public, such as restaurants.

Enforcement is by the courts through civil suits by individuals, in which suits the government may intervene. The act sets up a Civil Rights Commission to investigate discriminatory practices and a Community Relations Service to assist in solving problems of discrimination. It undercuts discriminatory literacy tests by states for registration to vote by providing, among other things, that completion of the sixth grade is presumption of literacy.

CONSTITUTIONAL PROTECTION. The United States has undoubtedly given a wider legal protection, particularly to the rights of property, than has any other country of the world. The Constitution, furthermore, has made these rights inviolable, not only by executive officers, but even by Congress or by legislatures. This condition has come about through the supremacy of constitutional law over national or state legislation and through the practice of the courts, and particularly of the Supreme Court of the United States, in refusing to enforce statutes judged to be at variance with the Constitution. A vast body of judicial decisions defining and protecting civil rights has been developed by the courts of the United States and of the states.

Civil Service. This term includes, in its broadest sense, all positions under the government, Federal, state, and municipal, outside of the army and navy. Commonly, however, it is limited to administrative or executive positions, particularly to those that are appointed and are protected by legal safeguards against demotion or dismissal.

Beginning with the inauguration of President Jackson in 1829, for many decades the public service in the United States suffered from the carrying out of certain so-called "democratic" theories of government. The first of these was that public administration was not an expert function, but could be fitly discharged by any citizen, even though inexperienced and untrained. The second was the theory of "rotation in office," which demanded the frequent transfer of public position from one individual to another, on the theory that the right to hold office should be enjoyed by the largest possible number of citizens. It was further supposed that continuous employment led to neglect, indifference, and discourtesy on the part of public officials.

CIVIL SERVICE REFORM. These generally accepted political views, to which was added also the theory of "spoils" (See *Spoils System*), long deprived American government of an efficient body of public servants and resulted in a loss of efficiency and in the corruption of politics. An office-seeking class grew up, whose purpose was to control politics, national and state, for the purpose of securing office and using its power for private advantage. This experience, while discreditable to American politics, nevertheless prevented the development of an overbearing or autocratic official class. (See *Bureaucracy*) After the Civil War, active effort was begun to secure "civil service reform," or the placing of employment under the national government upon a "merit basis," open to all candidates, irrespective of party or religious affiliation. This movement was emphasized by the assassination in 1881 of President Garfield by a disappointed office-seeker.

The act of 1883 grouped Federal employees into three classes: (1) classified or competitive; (2) unclassified; (3) excepted and noncompetitive. The classified or competitive positions were to be filled by examinations under the direction of a "civil service commission" of three members appointed by the president with the approval of the Senate. Preference was given to persons "honorably discharged from military or naval service by reason of disability, wounds, or sickness incurred in the line of duty." Furthermore, a person holding a position in the competitive or classified civil service could not be dismissed without first being notified of the charges against him and given an opportunity to reply in writing. Since the enactment of this law, the class of competitive positions has steadily increased; and the proportion of unclassified and noncompetitive positions has diminished. Statutes similar to the act of Congress have been adopted in certain states, and similar provisions have been made by numerous cities.

Classified. Confidential government information which for reasons of national security cannot be divulged except to authorized persons.

Cloture or **Closure Rule.** Used in parliamentary bodies to close debate upon a bill or proposal, by moving "the previous question." The motion is made "that the question be now put"; and, in the event that this motion carries, the matter under discussion is immediately put to vote, without further debate. The term has its origin in the *clôture* (klô′tür′) of the French parliament.

In the British House of Commons, a modified form of the closure was adopted in 1882. The United States Senate is one of the few great legislative bodies which long refused to incorporate the closure in its rules of procedure. A minority in that body, by occupying the floor in continuous discussion and maneuvering, was, and still is, able to delay the passage of a bill until the emergency disappears, or the session comes to a close. This procedure is called "filibustering." In March 1917, the Senate adopted a closure rule, which somewhat controls filibustering. On the other hand, the absence of the closure rule prevents the majority from imposing a "gag rule" on the minority and permits a freedom of debate.

Coalition. An alliance of persons, parties, or states. The term coalition has been used repeatedly in European history to designate a league of states for offensive or defensive purposes.

Its more common use at the present time refers to the union of parties and to a government built upon such a coalition. The necessity for "coalition governments" arises in many countries through the fact that in their legislatures there are a number of parties or groups, and no one party possesses sufficient strength to form a government that will command the support of a majority of the legislature; hence an alliance or coalition of party elements is indispensable to the formation of a government.

During World War I and II, in order to present a united front for the prosecution of the war and to utilize, without distinction of party, the best statesmanship available, in most of the belligerent countries a party truce was declared and a coalition government was formed.

Cold War. A conflict between nations which does not involve the use of armed forces in combat, but is conducted by means of political and economic pressure and propaganda; a war of nerves.

Collectivism. A theory of economic and social organization in which all "productive capital" would belong to the community, and the share of each individual would be determined by the value or social utility of his contribution to the social income. Collectivism is practically synonymous with the generally accepted concept of socialism. See *Socialism* and *Bolshevism*.

Commission Government. A type of administration widely used in Great Britain and in America, whereby executive and sometimes legislative and judicial or quasi-judicial functions are entrusted to a number of individuals forming a board or "college." The theory of commission government is that responsibility for all decisions and directive action rests in the group, not in any one individual, and that all members of the group are officials with expert knowledge, presumably giving their entire time to the service of the office. In these respects, commissions differ from boards, which, in the United States, are frequently used as the legal governing bodies of institutions and are composed of laymen managing the public business through an executive appointed by and responsible to the board. Where, as frequently happens, a commission is given an ordinance or legislative power or the power of judicial review, such government represents an abandonment of the popular theory of "separation of powers."

Well-known types of commission government in England are the admiralty lords, who administer the British Navy, and formerly the lords of the treasury, although this commission has now become obsolete and its functions are exclusively exercised by another official, the chancellor of the exchequer. In the United States, the Interstate Commerce Commission, the Civil Service Commission, and public utility commissions in several states represent commission government. One of the most notable instances was the Philippine Commission of 1900-1907, which was vested, first by the president and subsequently by Congress, with the powers of governing and legislating for the Philippine Islands. In 1901, following the flood which destroyed the city of Galveston, Texas, the government of that municipality was entrusted to a commission of five citizens. The success of this experiment led to the general adoption in the United States of the so-called "commission plan of city government." See *Commission Form of Government*.

At times, in British and in American practice, an executive office ordinarily consigned to a single minister or public official may be entrusted to a group, in which case the office is said to be "placed in commission." Such a body created for one single purpose, either temporary or permanent, is in English practice described as an "*ad hoc* commission."

Common Law. The body of rules, principles, and forms of judicial proceedings which, while not enacted in statutes, have been immemorially recognized and enforced by the courts of England and by the courts of those countries which inherited their systems of jurisprudence from England. Thus it is distinguished from "statute law" or enactments of Parliament or state legislatures.

The common law is frequently used to mean English law, as distinguished from Roman or "civil law," which was revived and put into force on the continent of Europe at the beginning of the Renaissance period. In England, by reason of the king's courts, the common law at that time was making such progress as successfully to hold the field against the Roman law revival.

In some American states, only those principles and rules of the common law which were recognized before the 4th year of James I, when Virginia was settled, are regarded as having been carried over to the United States; but in most states the common law, together with certain fundamental statutes, as it existed at the time of the American Revolution, is regarded as forming a part of the law of such states.

Communism (kŏm′ū-nĭz′m). A system of social and economic organization in which property is owned by the state or group, to be shared in common or to be distributed among members of the community equally or in proportion to their respective needs. In communism, there is practically a complete abolition of the notion of private property; the property of each is truly the property of all. Thus communism goes much further than either collectivism or socialism, which proposes to bring all "productive capital," such as land, factories, mines, and railways, under public ownership. See *Bolshevism*.

Communism as thus described has been tried by small communities in Europe and America, but with little permanent success. The term has now become appropriated to the Bolshevist Marxist Socialism as developed in Soviet Russia by Lenin, Trotsky, and Stalin, and the political parties affiliated with it in other countries. See *Bolshevism.*

Concert of Powers. An understanding between the major European states for the enforcement of treaty provisions, for the maintenance of peace, for the control of minor states and peoples within the European system, and for the solution of Near Eastern problems. The concert may be said to have arisen about 1828. The "Great Powers" were, at the time of its origin, Britain, France, Russia, Austria, and Prussia.

The concert was broken in 1854 by the Crimean War, and again in 1871. The most imposing exhibition of the concert was the Congress of Berlin of 1878, which composed the affairs of the Balkans and the Ottoman Empire, reaffirming the sovereignty of Turkey in European possessions. Its arrangements gave Europe peace for an entire generation, and were not broken until 1908, when Austria-Hungary annexed Bosnia and Herzegovina. The concert was destroyed by the outbreak of World War I in 1914.

Congressional Record. The Constitution, Article I, Section 5, states, "Each house shall keep a journal of its proceedings, and from time to time publish the same, excepting such parts as may, in their judgment, require secrecy." The proceedings of the House and Senate are published daily when Congress is in session in the *Congressional Record.*

Conscription. The compulsory enrollment of citizens or inhabitants of a country for filling its military forces. Also called "the draft" or "compulsory military service."

While compulsory military service is of ancient date, the French Revolution initiated the plan of commanding the entire manpower of the nation for national defense. The National Assembly in 1792 decreed the *levée en masse.* While this hurried assembling of untrained men proved ineffective, it led to the practice of vast drafts upon the able-bodied men of the nation for the Napoleonic wars.

EUROPEAN SYSTEMS. The system of compulsory training of all able-bodied young men originated in Prussia, after the overwhelming defeat of that country by Napoleon in 1806. Napoleon limited the standing army of Prussia to a force numerically ineffective. Prussia met this condition by the brief but thorough training of this limited number of men and by their prompt retirement into a reserve, which could be "mobilized" or called to the colors at any crisis and would thereby many times augment the limited standing army. Out of this incident have come the modern systems of compulsory training which, before World War I, had been adopted by most European countries and Japan.

In Germany, the system was carried out in the most thorough way. Theoretically, all men were trained for appropriate duty in time of war and were classified into several categories: those undergoing active training; those in a first reserve, to be immediately mobilized on the threat of war, each man joining an assigned battalion or other unit; a *landswehr,* or second reserve, of older and less active men; and finally a *landsturm,* composed of men in middle life no longer judged capable of front-line duty, but serviceable for duty on lines of communication, for garrison duty, and for home guards. Great Britain had at times practiced unsystematic "impressment" of men for the army and navy, depending generally on voluntary enlistment. World War I forced her to the Conscription Act of 1916. Peacetime conscription was begun in May 1939, and there was rigorous conscription in World War II.

AMERICAN CONSCRIPTION. The United States has four times resorted to conscription and involuntary enlistment. During the Civil War, the Northern states, in 1862, the Southern states earlier, adopted compulsory enlistment. On the entrance of the United States into World War I in April 1917, a selective draft act was passed by Congress which required the enrollment for military duty of all men between 21 and 31, the act being subsequently extended to include all men between 18 and 45. From these a selective draft was made for active service. September 16, 1940, the Selective Training and Service Act authorized the first peacetime draft in American history. It provided for the induction of males between 21 and 36 to be trained for one year for national defense in the Western Hemisphere. By later enactment the time and area of service were extended. Men from 20 (later 18) to 65 were required to register, and men up to 45 were liable to induction, except certain officials and clergymen. But men in certain key industries, men with dependents, or physically disabled, might be deferred. Provision was made for conscientious objectors. The selection was made by local boards on the basis of a lottery conducted after the first registration, and contested cases might be taken to appeal boards. In June 1948 the Selective Service Act was revived. It lasted until the American disengagement from Vietnam in January of 1973. At that time the U.S. converted to all-volunteer armed forces.

Conservation. The term applied to the policy of government regulation of the use and development of the natural resources of the country so as to prevent their rapid and wasteful exhaustion by private ownership. Conservation further aims to provide a systematic development of such resources in the interests of the general public and for the benefit of later generations. See *Public Lands Policy.*

Constitution. A constitution is a fundamental or "organic law," upon which the government of a nation rests. To be theoretically complete, a constitution should provide a structure of government; an enumeration of civil rights and liberties (See *Civil Rights and Liberties*); and a provision for its own amendment. The amending provision has special significance, since it may be assumed to disclose the sovereign power within the state; for that power which is above the constitution, and which may alter or repeal it, may fairly be regarded as the "legal sovereign."

The modern practice of adopting "written" or "rigid" constitutions as a basis for national or state government is of American origin and is one of the political achievements of the nation that has been generally borrowed the world over. The earliest constitutions of this typical form were those adopted by the American states, when, by the Declaration of Independence in 1776, they ceased to be colonies of Great Britain. These were followed in 1789 by the Constitution of the United States. (See *Constitution of the U.S.*) Nearly every government in the world today rests upon a written constitution, either granted by a monarch or framed by a national convention.

Great Britain has what is called an "unwritten constitution," in that a large part of it is not in written or statute form, but is a matter of practice. Furthermore, the various statutes underlying the government of the realm have never been codified or unified in a single document; also, it is a fundamental principle of the English constitution that it can be changed in any respect by a simple act of Parliament. In this sense, no act of Parliament is more fundamental or organic than any other. This character gives to the British constitution a flexibility not possessed by that of the United States.

The period of active constitution-making in Europe began with the French Revolution, when numerous constitutions were devised, many of them on highly theoretical lines, and a number successively put into operation. From Europe, the revolutionary movement passed back to the Spanish colonies of America, where an active process of constitution-making arose, greatly influenced by the constitutional forms of the United States.

Following the revolution of 1848, European countries generally attained constitutions or fundamental laws limiting monarchical power and increasing the political participation of the people. A new and extremely active period of constitution-making followed the end of World War I in 1918, when many new states came into existence and when older constitutions were subjected to radical revision.

Consul. A representative of a government in a foreign country, particularly for commercial purposes and for the aid and protection of its citizens abroad. The duties of a consul include the making of reports on commercial conditions in the country to which he is assigned, various services in connection with the landing of vessels at foreign ports, the relief and protection of citizens of his country in times of distress or disturbance, and other duties, even including those of a diplomatic character in the absence of an ambassador or a minister.

For the judicial functions exercised by consuls, see *Extraterritoriality.*

Contraband. Primarily, articles sent from a neutral to a belligerent country in time of war for military and naval use. Under generally recognized laws of war, such merchandise may be seized and confiscated if taken upon the high seas or within enemy territory. Ordinarily, confiscation follows the judgment of a prize court, in which the neutral owner may have the right to appear and to defend his title and interest. Formerly, the list of articles generally recognized as contraband was limited, and embraced mainly arms and military supplies. World War I, however, so completely engaged the entire resources of the belligerent nations that it led to a great expansion of the list of contraband goods. At present it would be difficult to say what is not contraband in time of war.

Convention, Political. A gathering of party adherents or delegates for the purpose of selecting candidates for public office, for declaring their body of political principles or "platform," and for organizing party administration.

Political conventions were a relatively late development of American democracy. In the early decades of the Union, candidates were nominated in various ways, a caucus of members of the same party in Congress usually choosing the national candidates. After 1832, the national political convention became the accepted method of nominating candidates for president and vice president.

In the states, it was formerly the universal practice to hold not only state conventions for nominating candidates for state offices, but county conventions and local primaries. The place of these conventions in American political life has been greatly reduced in recent years by primary election laws. The national party convention, however, meeting once in four years, shortly preceding the presidential election, continues to be a political institution of first importance, although almost entirely unrecognized by federal laws. Each party, by its own rules, determines how delegates shall be chosen and how the business of the conventions shall be conducted. Election as a delegate to a national convention is an eagerly sought distinction, and, preceding and during the days of their meeting, such conventions overshadow other matters of national interest. The greater part of the time during which a national convention meets is usually devoted to the nomination of, and the successive ballotings for, candidates for the presidency and the vice presidency. This is accomplished by a majority vote of all delegates present. The Democratic party adopted this rule in 1936 after having, since the party's origin in 1832, required a two-thirds vote for nomination.

Besides nominating its presidential candidates, the convention adopts a party platform and, before adjournment, chooses the national committee, made up of one representative from the party organization in each state. The national committee has great power over the organization in the period between conventions.

Corporate Campaign Contributions Legislation. In January 1975 a U.S. federal election campaign-funding reform bill became effective. The bill, signed into law in October 1974, was intended to eliminate improper and excessive influence by large campaign contributors. This action was taken due to the campaign-funding abuses revealed during the Watergate investigations. The bill placed ceilings on contributions by individuals and by organizations and prohibited cash contributions over $100. Individual contributions to all federal candidates and their organizations were limited to $25,000 in any election year; to any one presidential candidate, $1,000; and to any one Congressional candidate in any one election (primary, runoff, or general election), $1,000. Organization contributions to presidential candidates were limited to $5,000 and to Congressional candidates, in each election, $5,000. The bill also provided for: public financing of presidential primaries and elections; spending ceilings for presidential and Congressional campaigns; establishment of a six-member commission to supervise the enforcement of the law; and the reporting, by presidential and Congressional candidates, of all contributions and expenditures.

Corporate State. A term applied to such governments as those established by the Fascists in Italy and the Nazi party in Germany. Totalitarian is sometimes used as a synonym. The idea behind the word is that the nation consists of one class, or body (Latin *corpus*, "body"), and not two classes, the workers and exploiters, as the Marxian Socialists contend. Implied in the word also is the absence of political parties, all those except the ruling one being suppressed.

Court Martial. See *Military Law.*

Creed, The American's. Written by William Tyler Page, Clerk of the U. S. House of Representatives, in 1917, and adopted and promulgated by the Government's Committee on Publication. Accepted by the House of Representatives, on behalf of the American people, April 3, 1918.

De Facto Government. A government actually exercising governing power in a particular territory, irrespective of its legal authority. *De facto* government is distinguished from *de jure* government, the latter being a government which exists by legal right or by international recognition.

Democracy. Democracy signifies popular government. It has been defined in Lincoln's phrase, "government of the people, by the people, and for the people." It is distinguished from monarchy, in which the head of the state is a king or prince, and from aristocracy, or government by a privileged or superior group. None of these words is used with entire consistency or exactness in political writings. By democracy is sometimes meant direct popular government rather than government by chosen representatives, and a distinction is then drawn between a democracy and a republic. Few of the new countries established as republics after World War II were democracies.

The word democracy is used also to indicate not only a government which is immediately or ultimately controlled by popular opinion or by the majority of the people, but also one in which society is distinguished by an absence of privileged and aristocratic classes. The theory of democracy rests upon an assertion of the worth of the ordinary man and woman and upon a confidence in the good judgment and moral rectitude of common people; upon the belief that if unwise or wrong action prevails for a time, in the long run the common sense of the bulk of society will recognize and correct the evil. Democracy further rests upon the conviction that the interests of all classes are better served when they are politically controlled by all classes rather than by a single class.

Diplomatic Representation. Diplomacy is the art and the practice of international negotiation. In the early history of Europe, such negotiations were intrusted to special heralds, ambassadors, or missions. The system of keeping diplomatic representatives resident in the important countries with which they had friendly relations was first practiced by the Italian city-states and particularly by Venice.

Such representatives are of different ranks; by the Treaty of Aix la Chapelle, 1818, they were classified in the following four grades: (1) ambassadors, including papal legates and *nuncios*; (2) envoys extraordinary and ministers accredited directly to the sovereign; (3) ministers resident; (4) chargés d'affaires. The first three grades are accredited to the head of the state; the fourth, to the minister having charge of foreign relations. Consuls, when charged with a diplomatic mission, rank with the chargés d'affaires.

EMBASSIES. "Embassies" are established between nations whose mutual interests are of importance; elsewhere the diplomatic office is usually a "legation."

In 1976 the U.S. had embassies to 136 countries. These states, also maintaining embassies at Washington, were as follows: Afghanistan, Algeria, Argentina, Australia, Austria, Bahamas, Bahrain, Bangladesh, Barbados, Belgium, Benin, Bolivia, Botswana, Brazil, Bulgaria, Burma, Burundi, Cameroon, Canada, Central African Empire, Chad, Chile, China (People's Rep.), China (Taiwan), Colombia, Costa Rica, Cyprus, Czechoslovakia, Denmark, Dominican Rep., Ecuador, Egypt, El Salvador, Ethiopia, Fiji, Finland, France, Gabon, The Gambia, German Democratic Rep., Germany (Fed. Rep. of), Ghana. Greece, Grenada, Guatemala, Guinea, Guinea-Bissau, Guyana, Haiti, Honduras, Hungary, Iceland, India, Indonesia, Iran, Ireland, Israel, Italy, Ivory Coast, Jamaica, Japan, Jordan, Kenya, Korea, Kuwait, Laos, Lebanon, Lesotho, Liberia, Libya, Luxembourg, Madagascar, Malawi, Malaysia, Maldives, Mali, Malta, Mauritania, Mauritius, Mexico, Morocco, Mozambique, Nauru, Nepal, Netherlands, New Zealand, Nicaragua, Niger, Nigeria, Norway, Oman, Pakistan, Panama, Papua New Guinea, Paraguay, Peru, Philippines, Poland, Portugal, Qatar, Rumania, Rwanda, São Tomé and Principé, Saudi Arabia, Senegal, Seychelles, Sierra Leone, Singapore, Somalia, South Africa, Spain, Sri Lanka, Sudan, Surinam, Swaziland, Sweden, Switzerland, Syria, Tanzania, Thailand, Togo, Tonga, Trinidad and Tobago, Tunisia, Turkey, U.S.S.R., United Arab Emirates, United Kingdom, Upper Volta, Uruguay, Venezuela, Western Samoa, Yemen, Yugoslavia, Zaire, Zambia.

The terms "embassy" and "legation" are used also for the residence or buildings of the minister and the staff. The official residence of an ambassador is known as an "embassy"; that of a minister, as a "legation."

DIPLOMATIC CREDENTIALS AND PRIVILEGES. A diplomatic agent is usually accompanied by an official suite which may include counselors, secretaries, attachés from the army or navy, commercial attachés, interpreters, etc. A diplomatic representative carries a recommendation called a "letter of credence" and also, usually, a "letter of instructions" conferring full powers for the closing and the signing of a treaty, and a special passport. On arrival in the country to which he is accredited, he is accorded an official reception by the head of the state, if he is ranking in one of the first three classifications, and by the foreign minister if he is a chargé d'affaires. A diplomatic representative is accorded certain immunities and privileges which extend to members of the household and suite. These include inviolability of person and residence—an assault committed upon him is an injury to his nation and must be correspondingly compensated for (See *Extraterritoriality.*)—exemption from local jurisdiction; and exemption from taxes on personal property or official residence. From the immunity of a diplomatic representative has arisen the "right of asylum" or of taking shelter in a legation.

It is a general principle that a diplomatic representative must be acceptable to the state to which he is sent, or, if his conduct becomes objectionable, that he may be sent home. This is usually done by the formality of furnishing passports. (See *Persona Non Grata.*) Diplomatic relationship is always terminated on the outbreak of war, and it may also be broken off as a protest threatening war.

The act of accrediting a diplomatic representative to a government is equivalent to recognition of that government, so that, where recognition is withheld, countries intrust the preservation of their interests to a representative of lower grade than an ambassador or minister or to a personal representative. See *Personal Representative.*

Direct Legislation. A term used to describe the enactment of law by popular vote rather than by representative legislative bodies. Direct legislation has been frequently practiced by local communities, from the Greek cities down to New England town meetings. In certain of the Swiss cantons, it still exists in the form of popular meetings for legislative enactments. It was in Switzerland also that the modern method of direct legislation by organized balloting arose. Thence, in the form of the popular proposal of laws (initiative) and the popular ratification or rejection of laws (referendum), the institutions of direct legislation have spread to other countries and particularly to the United States.

In another form, however, direct legislation in America is older than in Switzerland, that is, in the direct vote of the people upon constitutional or organic laws, which originated in Massachusetts in 1780.

Due Process of Law. The federal Constitution, in both the 5th and 14th amendments, and all state constitutions, contain provisions protecting the individual against the deprivation of "life, liberty, or property without due process of law."

The due process clause of the 5th Amendment operates as a limitation upon the action of the federal government only. But the similar provision, which was added to the Constitution by the 14th Amendment in 1869, expressly protects every American citizen against the unlawful infringement of his life, liberty, or property by the action of any state. The latter provision of the federal Constitution, although originally intended as a means of safeguarding the independent status of the Negro, has been construed by the courts as operating to the benefit of every citizen of the United States whatever his race or color. This clause has been the basis upon which the Supreme Court of the United States has declared unconstitutional numerous acts of state legislatures, particularly laws limiting freedom of contract.

Fundamentally, due process of law is merely that judicial procedure "which hears before it condemns, which proceeds upon inquiry, and renders judgment only after trial." As developed by the courts, however, the phrase has come to have a broader significance. It appears to signify the protection under the law of every individual against arbitrary and unreasonable acts of the executive and legislative branches of the government.

Elder Statesman. A retired statesman who because of his experience in public affairs is sometimes called upon to give unofficial advice on current issues, especially to government officials.

Electors, Presidential. The framers of the Constitution of the United States believed that the direct popular election of the president was both impractical and undesirable. They therefore provided for an indirect election of the president and the vice president by special electors, who were intended to be a select body of individuals possessing a broader acquaintance with men and a better understanding of national issues than the ordinary voter. The Constitution provides that each state shall appoint "in such manner as the legislature thereof may direct" a number of electors equal to the state's quota of senators and representatives in Congress.

The electors chosen in the manner provided by each state legislature were thereafter to meet in their respective states and to cast their ballots for two persons. Since the adoption of the 12th Amendment, in 1804, each elector is required to designate his choice for president and for vice president. Electors meet in each state on the first Monday after the second Wednesday in December to cast their ballots. The vote thus taken is transmitted to the president of the Senate, who, on January 6 in the presence of both houses of Congress, opens the certificates and counts the ballots from all states.

The choice of the president and the vice president by electors as thus provided has become largely a matter of form. Since 1800, the electors have generally followed the dictates of the parties to which they have belonged. Electors are expected, as a matter of course, to cast their ballots for the regular party nominees although they are not legally required to do so. A vote for a particular elector is in effect a vote for the party's nominees. In some states, however, the names of the party nominees with or without electors' names appear on the ballot.

Embargo. An order or act of a country, prohibiting vessels or merchandise from leaving its ports. The purpose of an embargo, ordinarily, is to injure another country by depriving it of its usual commerce. Where the embargo applies only to the vessels or goods of a country's own citizens, it is a "civil embargo." Where the prohibition applies also to the vessels of a foreign state against whom the embargo is particularly directed, it is a "hostile embargo." Where the embargo applies to the vessels and goods of all nations found within the ports of a country, it is an "international embargo."

Eminent Domain. The pre-eminent right of the sovereign to all of the property within its jurisdiction, by virtue of which it may appropriate any of such property, howsoever owned, to public uses. A limitation upon this right, fixed or implied in all constitutional governments and expressly incorporated in the Constitution of the United States and in the constitutions of all of the states, is that private property shall not be taken for public use without compensation.

Among the public uses for which the power of eminent domain is most frequently exercised are the creation of streets, parks, forts, docks, and public buildings. The right may be delegated by the state to public service corporations, such as railroads, telephone and telegraph companies, or corporations serving the public with water, gas, electricity, and similar utilities, which are regarded as quasi governmental functions.

Expatriation. See *Naturalization*.

Export Tax. The Constitution of the United States (Article I, Section 9) provides that "no tax or duty shall be laid upon articles exported from any state." This limitation upon the federal government does not deprive it of the power of declaring an embargo or of otherwise regulating exports, nor does it deprive Congress of the power of imposing a tax on income derived from exports. Trade between the United States and its insular possessions, such as Puerto Rico, has been held not to be foreign commerce; but a tax laid by Congress upon such trade is not prohibited by this section of the Constitution.

The Constitution (Article I, Section 10) also prohibits the states from levying any duties on exports or imports, except such as are necessary for the execution of its inspection laws, and then only subject to the control of Congress. The effect of this provision has been to deter the states entirely from such legislation and to maintain complete free trade between states of the Union.

Ex Post Facto Law. Retroactive legislation which makes punishable an act which was lawful when committed or imposes for an unlawful act a more severe punishment than was provided by law at the time the act was committed, or otherwise retroactively affects, to his material disadvantage, the position of one accused of a crime.

The Constitution of the United States forbids both the federal government and the governments of the states from passing any *ex post facto* legislation.

Extradition. The surrender of a fugitive from justice by one country or state to the authorities of another. Nearly all civilized countries have entered into treaties with one another providing for the extradition of persons who have committed specified crimes in one country and have then fled to another. Common limitations in these treaties are that the duty of a nation to surrender such a fugitive shall not extend to its own citizens and that persons extradited shall be tried only for the crime specified in the request for extradition. A further limitation which the United States has inserted in its treaties is that it shall not be compelled to give up persons charged with political offenses.

Extradition between nations is effected by a request of the state or foreign office of one nation upon the state or foreign office of the other. The Constitution of the United States contains an express provision requiring every state to extradite, upon demand of another state, any fugitive from justice (Article IV, Section 2). In extradition among the states of the Union, there are no limitations with respect to the character of the crime or the citizenship of the person whose extradition may be sought. A requisition signed by the governor of the state from which the accused has fled is addressed to the governor of the state in which the accused is found, and, if honored by the latter, the person is surrendered. Not infrequently, however, a governor refuses to surrender an alleged fugitive from justice, on the ground that he will not receive a fair trial in the state where he is indicted. And, although the Constitution is mandatory with respect to delivering up offenders to sister states, the Supreme Court has refused to compel the extradition of a fugitive whose surrender a governor has denied.

Extraterritoriality (ĕks′trȧ-tĕr′ĭ-tō′rĭ-ăl′ĭ-tĭ). An immunity from its general jurisdiction granted by a state to the representatives or subjects of another state within its own territory. Such immunity extends, by the practices of international law, to sovereigns sojourning in an official capacity in a foreign country. The sovereign and his retinue are exempted from civil and criminal jurisdiction and from police and administrative regulations, as well as from the payment of taxes and from the performance of other duties imposed upon ordinary residents. A similar exemption is accorded by all nations to the diplomatic representatives of other states accredited to them. (See *Diplomatic Representation*.) Any foreign army within the territorial limits of a state, with that state's permission, is free from its jurisdiction, and, when a foreign vessel of war, without inconvenience to a state, enters or remains within its maritime jurisdiction, the vessel and the crew are ordinarily accorded an immunity from local jurisdiction.

Extraterritoriality may have, furthermore, a much wider scope. It was customary for European nations, in negotiating treaties of commerce with Oriental countries and in arranging for the residence of their citizens within these countries, to obtain for their citizens rights of extraterritoriality. By these treaties, foreign citizens are triable, not by the courts of the country in which they reside and travel, but by courts of their own government, usually of a consular character.

In Japan, the right of consular jurisdiction, with other privileges for American citizens, was obtained in the treaty negotiated by Commodore Perry in 1858. This action was followed by similar concessions to other Western nations. Following the reorganization of Japan, that country zealously sought the abolition of these extra-territorial rights, which were properly considered prejudicial to her sovereignty, and, after the modernization of her courts and codes of law, extraterritoriality was relinquished by all foreign states from July 1899. Similar rights existed in China, where the United States in 1906 created the "United States Court of China," with jurisdiction over its own nationals. Great Britain had a similar court, established in 1865. In 1943 these countries relinquished their extraterritorial rights by treaties, and Sweden and Belgium took similar action.

Favored Nation Clause. A provision found in treaties between practically all modern countries. It assures to the citizens of a foreign state all such privileges within the territory of another state as may at any time be accorded to the citizens of the "most favored nation."

Favorite Son. A person who is politically popular in a particular locality, large or small. Local candidates who have the backing of their state delegations at presidential nominating conventions are known as favorite sons. The vote for them is usually complimentary, but there is always the hope that in case of a deadlock the favorite son will be chosen.

Federalism. A system of government wherein the political powers of the state are constitutionally distributed between the national government and the local governments of member units which are called "states," "provinces," "cantons," etc. Federal government is distinguished from "unitary" or "centralized" government. In centralized government, the whole authority is vested in the central or national structure; local governments have no constitutional independence or autonomy, but are vested with functions by act of the central government itself and are subordinate to the central government.

The term federal refers to the government, not to the "state." It is politically incorrect to speak of a "federal state," or of a "divided sovereignty" in the state, since sovereignty, by its philosophical conception, is divisible.

A federal government or a "federation" differs from a "confederacy" or a "confederation" in that it is actually the government of a sovereign state, whereas a confederation is a union of states in which sovereignty or state independence resides in the member states themselves The one is a "perfect union;" the other, a league. In a confederation, the member states reserve the power of withdrawing from the union, and their consent must be implied or assumed to actions taken by the confederate government. A federal government is an "indissoluble union" which can be disrupted only by successful rebellion or revolution. The authority of the government in a federation is direct upon the citizens of all member units, and allegiance is primarily to the federal union and secondarily to the member units.

The United States of America is the first federation in the modern sense. Its success is attested by its long history and by the development of other federations, largely inspired by the American Union. See *Argentina, Australia, Brazil, Canada, Mexico, Switzerland, Union of South Africa, Venezuela.*

A federal government usually arises out of the union of previously independent states or governments and the creation of a new national government through this union. The act of union preserves as separate local governments the unit members of which have merged. Usually the powers bestowed upon the federal government are specified and enumerated, all others being reserved to the states or provinces. In the case of the Canadian federation, however, the reverse principle holds, where the provinces have enumerated powers.

The federal principle has been applied also in countries having elements with strong local attachments and presenting differences of type. The chief example is Russia, where autonomy was granted to diverse regions, yet without sacrificing central authority over national policies.

Fellow Traveler. Originally a person who, though not actually a member of the Communist party, was in sympathy with its principles and willing to co-operate with it.

Filibuster. One who engages in an unlawful military expedition into a foreign country. The word is derived from the Spanish *filibustero* which, besides connoting a "freebooter," is used also as a term of contempt for a seditious plotter.

In parliamentary slang, "filibuster" is used to designate measures employed to prolong debate and to prevent a vote. See *Closure Rule.*

Franchise Tax. A tax either upon the privilege or franchise granted by a state to a corporation empowering it to act as a legal body, or upon a special franchise granted to a public-service corporation permitting the use of the public streets or other public places for the business of the corporation.

States cannot impose a tax upon the general franchise of a corporation created by the Federal government. Nor can any state impose upon a corporation, organized under the laws of another state, a tax which is calculated upon the entire capital stock of the corporation, the courts holding that this constitutes an attempt to tax property not within the jurisdiction of the state.

Franking Privilege. A privilege possessed by members of Congress, as well as by members of other branches of the Federal government, of sending official mail free of charge.

Free City. The early states of the Mediterranean and Ægean seas were "city-states." Political life was confined to the urban community; the surrounding land, usually of limited extent, was subordinate and tributary to the city. Such were the ancient Greek states, and such in the beginning was Rome. The development of medieval commerce and manufacture again brought the city to the front, and the Italian cities, such as Venice, Florence, and Genoa, became free and independent states. In the north, the Flemish and Baltic cities, and also those of the Rhineland, attained comparable freedom of government, although nominally each was under the sovereignty of some greater political authority.

These free cities frequently leagued together in a confederacy or "hanse," for mutual protection and defense of commercial rights. The most famous of these associations was the Baltic or Teutonic Hanse, under the head of Lubeck. The development of nationalities broke up these leagues and brought the free cities under national authority. Three,—Lübeck, Bremen, and Hamburg,—retained their freedom as members of the second German Empire. The Treaty of Versailles created two free cities, Danzig and Fiume. Fiume was absorbed by Italy in 1924; Danzig by Germany in 1939. In January 1937, Hamburg became "Hansa City, Hamburg," and Lübeck was annexed to Prussia. See *Hanseatic League* and *Venice and the Hanse.*

Freedom of Contract. Political and economic thought at the close of the 18th century and at the beginning of the 19th century favored the complete freedom of the individual, both to employ labor and to accept employment, without interference from the state or coercive influence of other individuals. Economic teaching held that attempts on the part of public authority to limit industrial or commercial competition interfered with the law of supply and demand and violated fundamental personal rights.

Changed industrial relations and the sufferings and abuses arising from unrestrained competition have revealed the necessity of considerable limitation of the so-called right to freedom of contract. This right, although specifically protected by the United States Constitution, has always been regarded as subject to the "police power"—the regulation or limitation of actions in the interest of public health, safety, and morals. Much of the social legislation of the 20th century, limiting hours of labor, prescribing working conditions, and fixing minimum wages, has met with the objection that it infringes freedom of contract. In most instances, such legislation has been upheld by the supreme court of the United States as within the police power of the states or the commerce power of the nation.

The conception of the police power has undergone marked extension, and the once unchallenged right to sell one's labor in the dearest market or to hire at wages and terms that take no care for the safety, health, or comfort of the employed has been greatly abridged. Freedom of contract between employer and employed has further been restricted by the growth of labor unions and by the practice of collective bargaining. See *Social Legislation.*

Freedom of Religion. The first amendment to the United States Constitution and similar provisions in state constitutions guarantee freedom of worship as a fundamental right. This right, however, does not permit the individual to engage in practices which are regarded as inimical to the health, morals, or safety of the state.

Thus bigamy may be made a crime and may be punished as such, even though plural marriage be a tenet of a particular faith. A person is not excused from compulsory military service because his religious faith forbids bearing arms. A state may make it a crime for a parent to refuse to obtain medical attention for a child because of religious conviction that bodily ills can be cured only by religion.

Freedom of Speech. Freedom of speech and of the press was one of the established rights of Englishmen; it was transported to America by English colonists and is protected by the United States Constitution.

This right in ordinary times extends to the free criticism of the government itself, and even to advocacy of revolution. Justice Holmes, in the case of *Abrams* vs. *United States,* said:

"We should be eternally vigilant against attempts to check the expression of opinions that we loathe and believe to be fraught with death, unless they so imminently threaten immediate interference with the lawful and pressing purposes of the law that immediate check is required to save the country."

Picketing and use of handbills in labor disputes have been protected by the supreme court as an exercise of the right of free speech.

The right, however, is not without limitation. Criticism that unduly hinders the government in the performance of its proper functions has been held by the same jurist to be illegal and punishable. "The question in every case is whether the words used are used in such circumstances and are of such a nature as to create a clear and present danger that they will bring about the substantive evils that Congress has a right to prevent. It is a question of proximity and degree. When a nation is at war, many things that might be said in time of peace are such a hindrance to its effort that their utterance will not be endured so long as men fight, and that no court could regard them as protected by any constitutional right." (*Schenck* vs. *United States*).

The historical origin of this guarantee was as one of the moral and legal weapons used in the fight against absolute monarchy. Subsequent events have shown that the right can be maintained only when the existing social and political order is firmly established and felt to be in no danger. For this reason transition stages between contrasting regimes are marked by the suppression of this right.

Free Port. An area at a gateway of foreign trade which a government permits to remain outside tariff walls. Goods may be brought there from abroad without payment of duty, this being levied only when the commodities pass from the free port to other parts of the country.

Advantages include the possibility of avoiding tariff payments in processing materials brought from abroad into commodities to be sold abroad. Free ports make possible also displays of foreign merchandise for inspection of importers, without payment of tariff duty.

The United States Congress in 1933 authorized the establishment of free ports. The first to be set up was in Staten Island at New York, N. Y., where an area of 78 acres is devoted to the purpose.

Free Trade. See *Tariff*.

Functional Representation. A plan for representation in political bodies, based upon occupational or class groups rather than upon territorial units or electoral districts. Functional representation is an old institution, and parliamentary development sprang from the assembling of representatives of the different classes of medieval society. These representatives at first sat in separate bodies and deliberated and voted apart. Constitutional development in western Europe, however, has tended to draw these classes together into single chambers and to obliterate occupational divisions.

In the United States, parties have been composed of people of all walks of life. Neighborhood interests and local and sectional attachments have been the potent influences in stirring people to political activity.

As government has become more and more closely associated with economic controls, however, voters have tended to divide according to their economic interests. This explains the rise of labor parties, Socialist parties, agricultural blocs, and similar political groups that speak for economic classes. The tendency has increased in democratic countries since World War I, but actual elections continue on a local basis, with few exceptions.

The most extreme form of functional representation was found in Fascist Italy, where 22 separate councils combined in the National Council of Corporations each represented workers and employers in one division of industry. Legislation by this body, however, related mainly to industrial questions.

Fusion. A coalition or combination of political parties or groups for the purpose of defeating another party or group; e.g., of Republicans and independent Democrats in New York City against Tammany Hall or of Republicans and Democrats against socialist candidates.

Geopolitics. The application of the study of geographical influences to the determination of political objectives. Based on the geographic studies of Ratzel in Germany and Mackinder in England, it was applied in its German form *Geopolitik* by Haushofer to justify German expansion and to indicate the political and military strategy dictated by geography. It teaches that space and the contents of space determine everything. A central idea is that of the "Heartland" (eastern Europe) and the advantage over maritime empires given its possessors by improvements in air and land transportation.

Gerrymander (gĕr'ĭ-măn'dĕr). A form of political sharp practice, whereby electoral districts are so laid out that the party in power will possess a majority of votes in as many of them as possible.

The practice has produced districts of very eccentric appearance, one of which, attributed to Governor Gerry of Massachusetts in 1812, being likened to a salamander, was wittily dubbed a "gerrymander"; hence the name.

Government Ownership. This term is usually applied in America to the acquisition and operation, by a state or municipality, of public utilities, such as railroads, street railways or bus lines, telephone and telegraph systems, and gas, water, and electric companies.

The impetus toward public acquisition of such properties usually comes from the belief that companies having a monopoly interest in them are charging excessive rates. Public control of rates is frequently difficult because involving long and expensive litigation. Commissions set up to regulate rates are often felt to adopt a neutral attitude instead of being spokesmen for consumers. In many cases also there is the added fact that the local company is controlled and managed by a holding company subject to the authority of a different state.

A new influence toward public ownership of power properties was introduced in 1933, when the Tennessee Valley Authority was set up as a government corporation. Its policy is to sell power to municipalities owning their own distribution systems and to take measures insuring efficient operation of those systems. Such projects were declared "yardsticks" of power costs. The government lent money at low rates also to many local authorities to build or purchase their own facilities for generation and distribution of power. See *Municipal Ownership*.

Habeas Corpus, Writ of. In English and in American law, a writ issued by a court of justice, commanding the person to whom the writ is directed to bring before the court the body of a person detained or in custody. Failure to appear with the person of a prisoner places an officer in "contempt of court" and makes him liable to the summary imposition, by the court, of fine or other punishment. The court, once the prisoner is brought into its presence, determines whether he is being legally held and may, after due examination, set him at liberty, release him upon bail, or recommit him to prison.

The writ of habeas corpus is an ancient one in English law, antedating Magna Charta. It had the constant support of Parliament against efforts of English kings to set it aside, and was strengthened by repeated legislative acts. It was brought to America by English colonists.

The Constitution of the United States (Article I, Section IX, Par. 2) provides that "the privilege of the writ of habeas corpus shall not be suspended unless, when in cases of rebellion or invasion, the public safety may require it." The weight of learned opinion holds that the suspension of the right must be accomplished by act of Congress; but President Lincoln, during the Civil War, by executive action suspended the privilege over extensive territory. His act was subsequently ratified by Congress. See *Habeas Corpus Act*.

The constitutions of all American states contain provisions safeguarding the privilege of habeas corpus, analogous to the provision of the Federal Constitution. A state court cannot issue a habeas corpus for the discharge of a person held in the custody of the Federal government. Four states—Mass., N. H., R. I., and S. C.—provide in their constitutions that the privilege of the writ may be suspended by the state legislature. (See *Martial Law*.) The writ of habeas corpus has been carried wherever the common law has been established.

Hague Peace Conferences. Two international conferences of modern states have been held that are known by the place of their assembly, the city of The Hague, which is the capital of the Netherlands. The first was proposed by Czar Nicholas II of Russia, and met in 1899 on the invitation of the czar and the queen of the Netherlands. In a circular note of August 12, 1898, issued by the Russian government, the objects of the conference were suggested to be "the maintenance of general peace and a possible reduction of excessive armaments." Twenty-seven states took part in this conference.

RESULTS OF FIRST CONFERENCE. The deliberations of this conference resulted in three "conventions," three "declarations," and six "resolutions." The first convention was for "pacific settlement of international disputes." This provided for a permanent court of arbitration at The Hague, a permanent administrative council, made up of the diplomatic representatives of the signatory powers to The Hague, and an international bureau, acting under the direction of this council. The second convention dealt provisionally with the laws and customs of warfare on land. The third convention sought to adapt maritime warfare to the principles expressed in the Geneva Convention of August 24, 1864. The declarations sought to prohibit, for a period of five years, the use of projectiles or explosives discharged from balloons; the use of asphyxiating or poisonous gases; and the use of expanding or "dumdum" bullets in warfare.

The second conference was first proposed by President Roosevelt in 1904, but his proposal was withdrawn in order to allow the czar of Russia the privilege of calling the second conference as he had called the first. This met from June 15 to October 18, 1907. The following states, to the number of 44, were represented: Argentine Republic, Austria-

Hungary, Belgium, Bolivia, Brazil, Bulgaria, Chile, China, Colombia, Cuba, Denmark, Dominican Republic, Ecuador, France, Germany, Great Britain, Greece, Guatemala, Haiti, Iran, Italy, Japan, Luxembourg, Mexico, Montenegro, Netherlands, Nicaragua, Norway, Panama, Paraguay, Peru, Portugal, Rumania, Russia, El Salvador, Serbia, Siam, Spain, Sweden, Switzerland, Turkey, United States, Uruguay, Venezuela. It will be observed that, with the exception of two Central American states, Costa Rica and Honduras, the two African states of Ethiopia and Liberia, and the Central Asian monarchy of Afghanistan, the representation included practically all states then recognized as independent. Delegates from Korea, which by the Treaty of Portsmouth had recently passed under the control of Japan, failed to secure seats.

ACTS OF THE SECOND CONFERENCE. This conference adopted a series of conventions, the first providing means for the peaceful settlement of international disputes and altering in certain respects the measures proposed by the first conference. The second limited the employment of force for the recovery of duties due from the citizens of one country to the citizens of another, and the third defined the procedure for the opening of hostilities in the event of war; and ten conventions which in a measure modified the laws of war on land and at sea. These conventions and declarations were only in part ratified by the participating nations, different countries excepting from the ratification of different measures.

Inasmuch as it was not contemplated that they would become effective between belligerents unless all belligerents were ratifying parties, the rules which sought to regularize the conditions of war and to mitigate its severities were completely disregarded in World War I. This was particularly noticeable in the case of the conventions forbidding bombardment of unfortified towns by naval forces, the laying of automatic submarine contact mines, the discharge of explosives from air vessels, the use of poisonous gases, and the respect for private property in warfare.

However, the war department of the United States, following this conference, revised its regulations governing the conduct of its armies in the field so as to include the provisions of the Hague Conference, thereby presumably making incumbent upon the officers and men of its own forces compliance with many of these principles. The extreme measures followed by all belligerents in World War I and the development of a public opinion that the severities of warfare cannot be softened without a prolongation of the struggle have probably rendered inapplicable the measures of the Hague Conference in this field.

Hague Tribunal. A standing court of arbitration created by the first Hague Peace Conference. Such a tribunal was proposed at the conference by the representative of the British government. The government of the United States had also specifically instructed its delegates to labor for such a court. In a convention signed at this conference, the nations agreed "to use their best efforts to ensure the pacific settlement of international differences" and, with this object in view, to undertake the organization of a "permanent court of arbitration." By the plan then devised, each signatory state nominated four jurists for a six-year period. These jurists constituted a panel, from which judges were to be selected to sit in arbitration.

The first case to be tried before this tribunal was one submitted by the United States and Mexico for the adjustment of a contention that followed the settlement of the Mexican war and was known as the "Pious Fund of the Californias." The award was made October 14, 1902, and was accepted by both governments. Three other awards were made by the Hague Tribunal, before the meeting of the second Hague Conference in 1907. This latter conference made some changes in the organization of the court and provided an alternative procedure called "arbitration by summary procedure."

Helsinki Accord. A non-binding agreement, formally known as the Conference on Security and Cooperation in Europe, and signed by 35 nations (all of the European nations, except Albania, plus the United States and Canada) on August 1, 1975. The pact has four major sections. The first section recognizes the permanence of post-war boundaries, calls for the notification of major military maneuvers to all participating nations, and asks for nonintervention in internal affairs, among other provisions. The second section requests economic, scientific, and environmental cooperation between participating nations. The third part, a human rights provision, asks the signature nations to "respect human rights and fundamental freedoms," including: the right to leave and enter countries on family visits, access to foreign publications, and improved conditions for journalists working abroad. The fourth section simply states the time and place of the next meeting.

Home Rule. Local self-government or the administration of home or local affairs in a part of a state by the people of that section. In British history, the phrase refers particularly to autonomous government for Ireland. In American politics, it is used mainly to express municipal autonomy, granted either by placing constitutional limitations upon state legislatures in favor of municipal governments or by a system of authorizing the citizens of a municipality to frame their own charter of government.

Immigration Legislation. Laws designed to exclude, limit, or select immigrants entering one country from a foreign country.

The power of a state to deny admission of a foreigner to its territory is an undoubted right under international law, and has been exercised in all times. Complete exclusion of foreigners and denial of free intercourse with foreign nations has, however, been treated as an act of unfriendly or hostile character, and against it nations have applied forceful methods. In this manner the foreign exclusion policy imposed upon China by the Manchu Dynasty was broken through by European nations, even at the cost of war; and in 1854 the United States, by a naval demonstration under Commodore Perry, coerced the government of Japan into abandoning its policy of nonintercourse with foreigners, which had been in force for nearly 250 years. In 1904 the British sent an armed mission into the "forbidden land" of Tibet and compelled the government at Lhasa to modify its exclusion policy.

These instances, however, in no way affect the political principle that a state possesses unlimited power, except as modified by treaty, to decide what classes of foreigners shall become immigrants and settlers. Serious diplomatic difficulties, however, may arise, as, for example, between the United States and Japan, when immigration legislation is not uniform with respect to all races and nations.

IMMIGRATION TO AMERICA. The extraordinary migrations of peoples from Europe and Asia to the Americas, Australasia, and Africa during the last hundred years, not as colonists but as immigrants to countries already politically established, is one of the noticeable and far-reaching phenomena of the present economic age. The United States, as the country which has received these immigrants in greatest numbers, has experienced the greatest perplexity over the problems they create.

Immigration into the United States has passed through several phases. Previously to 1880 the immigration was almost exclusively from peoples of northern Europe, whence the original settlers of the United States had come. After that date, immigration from northern Europe declined, and that from southern Europe and from Russia rapidly increased. This so-called "new immigration" produced a change in the American attitude toward unlimited immigration. Until World War I, the immigration laws were designed only to exclude certain undesirable classes, including feeble-minded, insane, epileptics, sufferers from certain contagious or loathsome diseases, paupers, criminals, prostitutes, polygamists, anarchists, and those convicted of, or admitting, crimes or misdemeanors "involving moral turpitude." The importation of labor under contract was also forbidden.

RESTRICTION OF ASIATIC IMMIGRATION. In addition, Asiatic immigration had been restricted, first, by the Chinese Exclusion act of 1882, re-enacted in 1892 and in 1902, whereby all immigration from China, except students, merchants, and a few other classes, was forbidden. In December 1943, the exclusion law was repealed, and Chinese were placed on the same footing as other immigrants. After 1900, when Japanese immigration into California became notable, an exclusion league was organized in that state and agitation was commenced to secure legislation forbidding the admission of Japanese. In 1907, when an immigration bill restricting the admission of Japanese and Korean laborers was introduced into Congress, the president secured in its place Congressional authority to suspend Japanese and Korean labor immigration coming from our insular possessions or from Canada or from Mexico. An agreement was made between the president of the United States and the government of Japan—the so-called "gentlemen's agreement"—whereby the latter government undertook to limit, by the refusal of passports, the entrance of laborers into the United States.

GENERAL LIMITATION OF IMMIGRATION. In 1924 Congress passed an act which reduced annual immigration to 2% of the number of foreign residents living in the U.S. in 1890. The Immigration and Naturalization Act of 1952 (McCarran-Walter Act) removed race as a barrier to entry, but barred anyone who held "membership in or affiliation with subversive organizations." In 1965, the Immigration and Nationality Act provided for a total permissible immigration of 120,000 yearly from independent countries of the Western Hemisphere and 170,000 from all other countries, but not over 20,000 from any one country. Seven preference categories were set up: four to reunite relatives of U.S. citizens, two to encourage skilled and professional workers, and one for political refugees. In 1975, some 131,000 Vietnamese refugees were admitted to the U.S. under this last category.

Impeachment. A form of criminal procedure, involving charges and trial, by a legislative body against those in high office. Impeachment differs from attainder in being a judicial, not a legislative, measure. It originated in England through the bringing of charges by the House of Commons against oppressive acts of officials of the crown. The House of Lords, as the highest judicial body of England, judged the complaints pressed by the Commons. The right of the Commons to impeach whomsoever it will, has been recognized, though the practice has fallen into disuse in Great Britain for more than a century, the system of responsibility of ministers to the House of Commons having made impeachment unnecessary.

The earliest instances are the impeachment of Lord Latimer in 1376 and of Pole, earl of Suffolk, in 1386. The last British impeachments were those of Warren Hastings, 1788-1795, and Lord Melville, 1806.

The institution of impeachment was adopted by the framers of the United States Constitution, which provides that the president, the vice president, and all civil officers of the U.S. shall be removed from office "on impeachment for and conviction of treason, bribery, and other high crimes and misdemeanors." The penalty upon conviction, however, is confined to removal from office and to disqualification to hold any office of honor, profit, or trust under the U.S.

Impeachment charges are brought by the House of Representatives and are tried by the Senate. If the president of the U.S. is impeached, the chief justice of the U.S. Supreme Court presides at the trial; otherwise, the vice president presides. A two-thirds vote of the Senate is necessary for conviction. There have been nine cases of impeachment of federal officials and three convictions. The most famous impeachment trial was that of President Johnson in 1868, who failed conviction by one vote.

Members of Congress are not subject to impeachment, but they may be expelled from either chamber by a two-thirds vote of its members. Impeachment of state officials is provided for in most state constitutions, the procedure being modeled upon the federal system. In 1913 a governor of New York was impeached and was convicted on the charge of misappropriating campaign funds. In this case, the crime was committed before election to office.

Inauguration Day. The day when a chief executive of a nation, state, or city assumes office.

The Continental Congress, upon the ratification of the Constitution of the United States in 1788, provided that states should choose presidential electors on the first Wednesday in January 1789; that these should choose the first president and the first vice president on the first Wednesday in February; and that the new Congress should assemble in New York on the first Wednesday in March. The first Wednesday in March was the 4th, and, although President Washington was not inaugurated until April 30, the date March 4th, following a presidential election, continued to be inauguration day until changed in 1933 by the 20th Amendment to January 20th.

Industrial Court. See *Arbitration of Industrial Disputes.*

Initiative of Laws. A procedure whereby proposals of law may originate in the petition of private citizens. This measure is frequently associated with another procedure, the referendum of laws, but, as stated elsewhere, it differs from the referendum in being a radical device.

Before the adoption of the popular initiative, projects of law came from two recognized sources: (1) In countries having parliamentary or cabinet governments, they usually are initiated by ministers; and in the United States, where presidential government exists, they may originate in "executive measures" recommended to the attention of Congress by the president or to state legislatures by governors. (2) Measures arise in the legislatures themselves, either by the action of single members or by the work of committees or commissions. Under the operation of the popular initiative, a project of law may be originated by anyone, and, a sufficient number of petitioners in behalf of the measure having been obtained, the proposal goes either to the legislature under an obligation to pass upon it, or to the popular judgment as expressed in a general election. The second practice is the one common in the U.S.

Among the objections to the popular initiative are the following: It affords opportunity for the proposal of eccentric legislation. It frequently encumbers the electoral ballot with an undue number of complicated and doubtful measures that confuse and embarrass the electoral mind. Where there is indifference or inertia of the voters, it may lead to the enactment of laws by minorities of the voting population. As a procedure, it affords no opportunity for the improvement of a bill by discussion preceding enactment, a most important parliamentary step in the proper shaping of legislation. In American states, where the practice exists of recognizing the popular enactment as superior to the legislative will, it imposes additional impediments upon legislatures and tends to bring into doubt and confusion the constitutional laws of the state.

The popular initiative was adopted by the American people from the example of Switzerland and exists by constitutional provision in 21 American states. See *Referendum and Initiative of Laws.*

Injunction, Writ of. The name for a judicial process under English law, whereby a party is "enjoined" or commanded by the court to refrain from doing some particular thing described in the writ. While injunction is properly a restraining order, it may be used to prevent persons from interrupting the normal continuance of things, as the flow of water or the movement of trains.

In the United States, the writ is issued both by federal and by state courts. It has been issued at the instance of the president, to prevent organized obstruction of interstate commerce and, particularly, of the movement and delivery of mail. It has been used to prevent labor unions and other organizations, when on strike, from interfering with the property and interests of employers. Leaders of such organizations, disobeying the writ, have been arrested by order of the court. Laws attacked as unconstitutional have frequently been enjoined from enforcement by lower courts so as to be nullified in their effect until ruled on by the Supreme Court.

Criticism against the use of writs of injunction has resulted in two types of restrictions in their use by federal courts. In 1932, an act was passed by Congress forbidding issuance of injunctions in labor disputes except under carefully defined conditions, such as actual evidence of prospective damage. In 1937, Congress forbade injunctions against the government on the ground of a law's unconstitutionality unless issued by a three-judge court, one member being a justice of the circuit court of appeals.

International Labor Organization. A specialized agency of the United Nations since 1946, the International Labor Organization was established in 1919 as part of the Treaty of Versailles. The agency was designed to encourage social justice, to improve labor and living standards, to promote the adoption of labor legislation, and to support economic and social stability. The ILO won the 1969 Nobel Peace Prize for its pre-World War II activities to further world peace and for its involvement in population and unemployment problems.

Delegates from each member nation number four, all appointed by the government. Two represent the government, one represents employers, and one speaks for organized labor. Member nations of the League of Nations automatically became members of the body; other nations may join. Delegates convene yearly for decisions on agenda prepared by the International Labor Office, a committee of 32 delegates of the organization. Recommendations, requiring a two-thirds vote for adoption, take the form chiefly of draft conventions. Delegates of member nations are required to bring the proposed conventions, or treaties, before bodies of their own countries competent to conclude treaties. If ratified, the treaties become binding between the ratifying nations. Limitation of work hours and measures for the protection of women and children from exploitation have been among the conventions ratified.

The United States, by action of Congress in 1935, became affiliated as the 62d member. Relations between the ILO and U.S. weakened as the ILO became more political, more anti-West. In 1975 the U.S. issued a required two-year notice of intent to withdraw. Two years later, after much debating within the country, the U.S. formally withdrew from the ILO—the first U.S. resignation from a UN agency.

Interstate Commerce. The Constitution of the United States empowers the federal government to regulate commerce "with foreign nations and among the several states." It also forbids states to impose specified burdens on the commerce of other states. These provisions, as interpreted by the Supreme Court, are the foundation of Congressional power to rule economic activities in the U.S.

The Court has interpreted commerce to include interstate transportation and communication. It has also extended the definition of commerce to mean all that directly affects commerce between states, thereby enlarging federal authority to cover many intra-state railroad rates, business practices, and price fixing that impede the interstate shipment of goods.

For many years Congress was unable to regulate manufacture and production generally, these processes being held to be wholly intra-state. By the *Jones* and *Laughlin* decision on April 11, 1937, however, the Supreme Court ruled that practices which threatened to interrupt production destined for interstate commerce were subject to federal control.

Intervention. The interference by one state in the affairs of another sovereign state by force or by the threat of force. Even when hostilities are avoided, intervention can with difficulty be distinguished from an act of war, since it is the coercion by one nation of the will of another by acts of violence or by menace of violence. Except where a right of intervention has been conceded by one state to another during the existence of certain crises, as is the case with certain Latin-American countries and the United

States, it is difficult to find "legal" justification for the numerous acts of intervention with which the history of states is filled. Justification must be based upon political or moral grounds, among which the most important are: to ward off imminent danger to the intervening state or to its citizens; to end a condition of violence, anarchy, or oppression, repellent to the instincts of humanity; to preserve a balance of power and to prevent the aggrandizement of the influence of a rival state. This last ground of intervention in the past has been the frequent occasion of European wars.

Modern instances of intervention, on one or another of the above grounds, are the allied intervention in China, 1900, to rescue, from the Boxers, legations and nationals under siege; the intervention of the United States to end Spanish rule and warfare in Cuba in 1898; American intervention in Cuba in 1906 in compliance with the terms of the Platt amendment (See *Cuba*); and further American interventions in Santo Domingo, Haiti, Nicaragua, Panama, and Mexico.

Intervention in the past has been so frequently employed upon trivial and unjustifiable pretexts that a doctrine of "nonintervention" has developed, particularly associated with the name of the English Liberal, Richard Cobden, 1804–1865. Cobden's political platform was "free trade and no intervention." Noninterventionists hold that the sanctity of a state is so great and the right of a people to settle their internal affairs so sacred that intervention can never be justified on any grounds whatever, and that for one state to employ force against another to end revolution, misrule, or violations of the rights of its own nationals, is without possible moral justification.

Such extreme views are at the basis of the "anti-imperialistic" movement in the United States, which found political expression in the platform of the Democratic party in 1900, when imperialism was declared to be the "paramount issue." The Platt amendment was abrogated in 1934. The purpose in part was to establish confidence, throughout the New World, in the pacific intentions of the United States and so to pave the way toward international agreements for the restriction of warfare.

It is difficult at times to distinguish intervention from an undeclared war. The operations which led to Japan's taking of Manchuria from China in 1931 and Italy's conquest of Ethiopia in 1935-36 began as drastic forms of intervention. In neither case was there a declaration of war.

Lobbying. The practice of importuning legislators for the passage or defeat of pending legislation. Many large well-organized groups of the population which hope to obtain benefits, or fear disadvantages, from legislation maintain "contact men" or "legislative departments" for the purpose of influencing legislation.

Among the methods used are:

1. Cultivating members of Congress or state legislatures.

2. Observing and reporting to voters the action of individual legislators on the object sought by the lobby, the purpose being to add to, or detract from, the legislator's popular support. Legislators may or may not be questioned on their attitude in this process.

3. Creating an impression in the minds of the legislators that there is a large popular demand for the measures advocated. This may take the form of having large numbers of letters and telegrams sent to legislators, urging enactment of the measures. In other cases, "marches" on the capitol are organized.

The practice has been abused and has frequently been made the means of bribery and of corruption. To protect themselves, legislatures have enacted antilobby measures, such as prohibiting the presence of lobbyists on the floor of legislative halls, or in their anterooms. The Public Utility act of 1935 requires that all persons seeking to influence legislation on public utilities must register and report monthly on the interests for whom they are acting, the amount of money received for the purpose, and the manner in which it was spent.

Properly controlled, the practice of lobbying may be legitimate and may even prove an assistance to a legislature struggling with a mass of proposed legislation. The preferred procedure for advocates or opponents of bills is to appear before committees of the legislature and in open session to state their case and disclose the groups for whom they are speaking.

The term is derived from the word lobby, meaning a cloakroom or antechamber, wherein the so-called lobbyist is supposed to exert important influence upon the members of the legislature.

Logrolling. A system of bargaining among members of a legislative body, whereby one member, by giving his support to other members' measures, obtains the support of others for a measure in which he or his constituency is interested. Logrolling has been carried to its highest point in American legislatures, facilitated, as it is, by the practice of allowing members to introduce bills without limit.

Logrolling is connected especially with "pork barrel" legislation, or with bills appropriating moneys for local improvements and for interests without reference to state or national policy. See *Pork Barrel*.

Majority. A number greater than half of a total number. In deliberative bodies or elections, a number greater than half the votes cast, or, in another sense, the excess of that greater number over the remainder of the total. The term "majority" is sometimes loosely used to designate the number of votes received by a candidate, or by one of several candidates, in excess of the vote of his nearest competitor; but this relation is properly termed a "plurality."

An "absolute majority" means, in common usage, the number greater than half of all voting, or of all present whether or not voting, or of those entitled to vote.

Majority Leader. The leader of the majority party in a legislative body as in the U. S. Senate or in the House of Representatives.

Marine Corps. Marines, or, as they are sometimes popularly called, "soldiers of the sea," are a military organization serving under the navy department. In the United States, they constitute a distinct corps under the secretary of the navy. Originally they were introduced into the British navy to enforce discipline over the sailors. Their employment, however, has been continued for other reasons. Marines are favored in the United States navy because of their extreme serviceability for guard duty and ceremonies aboard ships, for the defense of naval property ashore, and as landing parties from war vessels for the protection of life and property in foreign countries in times of disturbance.

They have been used especially by the United States government in foreign intervention. Forming a part of the navy and transported aboard warships, they exceed all other land forces in mobility, while their frequent employment for police or protective duty makes their use on foreign soil less likely to be misconstrued as an act of war than would the landing of elements of a regular army.

Martial (*mär′shăl*) **Law.** Martial law must be distinguished from "military law" and "military government." While the statement is often made that "martial law has been declared" in some city or district in the United States, this does not mean the substitution of military for civil authority, which, under the American system of constitutional guarantees, cannot take place except during an actual state of war. The phrase does not correspond to what is elsewhere called "suspending constitutional guarantees" or "declaring a state of siege." In these latter cases, civil government is actually suspended, and civil authority gives place to military.

In the United States the activity of troops, either state or national, in time of civil disturbance, means no more than that the military forces have been called into action to uphold the authority of the president or of the governor of the state and to enforce his orders. Government remains civil, but acts through military organization because the ordinary administration is unable to cope with the situation. The employment of troops is not to wage war but to keep peace. In preserving life and property, troops may resist violence, even to the point of taking life, but their responsibility in such cases is not different from that of civil officers. Arrests may be made, but as measures of precaution, not for the infliction of punishment by military courts.

Undoubtedly, a state of domestic insurrection may be so serious as to justify strong measures by troops, but the authority for their employment remains with the civil head. Civil courts are not superseded nor is civil law abrogated unless action to suspend the guarantees of civil liberty is taken by Congress, or by the legislature of a state, as is permitted in a few state constitutions.

Mayor. The chief executive of a British or an American city, corresponding to the French "maire" or the German "burgomaster." See *France* and *Germany*.

In addition to administrative powers, the mayor in certain countries possesses the authority of a local magistrate; and in continental states generally he has a legislative or "ordinance" power. Outside of British and American states, he is almost invariably an agent of the national government as well as the head of municipal administration.

In Great Britain, the mayor is the presiding officer of the city council and possesses no greater legislative authority than any member. He is the official representative of the municipality and as such occupies a position of high honorary and social distinction. In the United States, under the older and more customary form of municipal government, the mayor has a veto over the legislation of the council and may have extraordinary power in budget matters. See *City Government*.

Merit System. The appointment of persons to positions in the civil service of the city, state, or nation for reasons of fitness shown in competitive examinations, rather than as a means of payment for political services to the party in power.

Military Government. Government, in either domestic or foreign territory, under army or navy commanders.

Under the constitutional system of the United States, military government is set up by order of the president as commander in chief of the army and navy of the United States. The president may prescribe such administration for domestic territory in rebellion, for foreign territory occupied in time of war by the forces of the United States, or for territory recently acquired by conquest or treaty. The president may also set up military government within or over foreign territory in which the United States has intervened, with army or navy force.

Subject to the president's authority, such government may employ the widest types of administration, may pass laws, and may create courts. While normally resorted to in time of war or during hostilities, such government may continue after peace has been secured and is legal until altered by act of Congress.

Over territory outside of the Union, such government is not limited by the prohibitions of the Constitution. Trial by jury need not be established. In such a case, to use a popular expression, "the Constitution does not follow the flag."

Military Law. Military law must be distinguished from martial law. As this term is used in England and in America, it means those laws and regulations which apply to soldiers and sailors, assure the discipline of armies and fleets, and are enforced not by civil courts, but by military tribunals, or "courts-martial."

In the United States, on the outbreak of the Revolutionary War, the Continental Congress issued a series of rules modeled upon English regulations, which were reissued September 30, 1776, and have been frequently revised. This code is known as the "Articles of War." They prescribe a series of offenses and infractions of discipline to which military officers and men are subject and which may be visited by various penalties, including death for certain offenses in time of war. A person becomes subject to military law upon accepting an appointment or commission or upon enlisting in, or being called or drafted into, the army or navy. He is ordinarily free from this jurisdiction upon discharge or upon the termination of his commission or appointment.

Liability to military law in no way lessens the liability of a soldier or sailor to the civil and the criminal law of the nation or state. It simply subjects him to a double jurisdiction, one as a citizen, the other as a soldier or sailor. Being thus subject, he may be tried twice and punished twice, that is, by both civil and military authority, without constitutionally being placed twice in jeopardy for the same offense.

Military law is usually enforced through military courts or "courts-martial." These consist of boards of officers, convened, by order of the president or a military commander, for the trial of such cases as may be submitted to them. The sentences of these courts have no effect until they are approved by the authority convening the court, or by the president of the United States.

A "summary court" consists of a single officer for the trial of minor infractions of soldierly behavior, punishment being limited to penalties not greater than one month's confinement or detention, loss of two-thirds of one month's pay, or both.

A "general court-martial" consists of a board of officers, not less than five in number, of rank appropriate to the rank of the accused, if an officer. It possesses jurisdiction over every offense triable under the Articles of War, and has power to impose a sentence of dishonorable dismissal, or of death.

Minority Leader. The head of the minority party in a legislative body as in the U. S. Senate or in the House of Representatives.

Modus Vivendi (*mō'dŭs vĭ-vĕn'dī*). A temporary arrangement between the governments of two countries, pending the settlement of relations by a formal treaty.

Monarchy. That form of government in which, actually or theoretically, political authority is vested in a single ruler who represents the sovereign power of the state.

Monarchy is intimately connected with the principles of "divine right" and those of "legitimacy," the latter theory maintaining that royal power can be derived only by legitimate succession from a previous ruler through blood or recognized connection. In the legitimist conception, there is at a given time only one person in the world lawfully entitled to any given throne, and the right of this person cannot be affected or taken away by Parliament, popular will, or revolution.

Legitimate monarchy is to be distinguished from the "imperialist" conception, in which a Cæsar or a Napoleon rises to a position of monarchical authority by military triumphs and by the devotion of the people or of the army. In this institution, the right to rule is derived from the unprecedented services of an individual to the nation, rather than from legitimate succession or through the claim of divine ordination.

There may further be distinguished the seizure of supreme power by a civil or a military leader and its maintenance by the ruthless suppression of opponents. Such were the "tyrants" of the Greek city-states, the "despots" of Italian cities, and the "dictators" of Spanish America.

LIMITATION OF MONARCHY. While, in theory, monarchy is an absolute power of government, practically all monarchies tend to become, or have become, limited or constitutional. In the first place, monarchies are usually limited by the presence of a nobility who may contend with the king, as the English nobles did with King John at Runnymede. Corporations arise, such as the medieval towns, which secure concessions of rights, subsequently to be tenaciously defended against royal prerogative. The religious power or organization enters, usually supporting the pretensions of the monarchy, but frequently opposing it in defense of its own sacred position.

In Europe, monarchy attained its highest pretensions in the 18th century, when the "benevolent despots" of France, Spain, Austria, Prussia, and Russia claimed and nearly succeeded in exercising unlimited power. In England, these same claims had been defeated in the 17th century by the English revolution and by the strength of the British aristocracy. These circumstances gave rise to British constitutional monarchy. The French Revolution largely destroyed popular support of unlimited monarchy and brought into force the conception of government resting upon popular will. Throughout the 19th century, however, monarchy played a leading part in European governments. It rose again in esteem, partly through the success of the British system of parliamentary government and the exercise of all crown powers by ministers responsible to a representative body, and partly through the achievements of monarchical government in unifying Italy and Germany. After 1871, for an entire generation, republican government in Europe appeared to make little progress except in France and in Switzerland.

World War I swept away many monarchical governments, and republicanism appeared dominant; but economic and political unrest produced in many countries dictatorships hardly to be distinguished from monarchy in fact. In 1977, the monarchical governments of Europe were Great Britain, Belgium, Norway, Sweden, Denmark, the Netherlands, Luxembourg, Monaco, Liechtenstein, and Spain.

Monopoly. This is the right, or the power, so to dominate the market for a commodity that a higher price may be exacted than would prevail under free competition.

Since the monopolies granted by kings under royal charters, the leading forms have been: patent rights; local franchises for public utility companies; and more or less informal combinations of producers. The first two forms are provided for by law as being in the public interest. The third is a defense that has arisen more or less spontaneously against destructive competition. Opinion differs regarding its advantages to the public.

TRUST. This term is used popularly to describe industrial combinations, whether they operate through private agreements, mergers, acquisition of competing concerns by a holding company, influence over policy by investment banks, interlocking directorates, or numerous other devices. Their power lies partly in their ability to supply a large proportion of the market and to make it difficult for new producers to obtain credit or materials so as to enter the market. The advantage to their sponsors lies in the ability to prevent demoralization of prices through competition, production normally being cut when demand falls off. Their danger from the consumers' viewpoint is that they have the power to increase prices above a reasonable level. A more recent criticism is that, by holding up some prices when others, lacking such support, are being readjusted to lower levels in a depression, they choke off demand in certain fields and so prevent a speedy return of the idle to employment.

From a social viewpoint, benefits of "trusts," or concentration of control in industry, include low cost production through large buying power, and economies in selling, financing, standardization, and management. Dangers include lack of flexibility, possibilities of withholding from buyers the benefits of economies brought about, and the concentration of power in hands not responsive to considerations of public interest.

ANTI-TRUST LAWS. The Sherman act of 1890, the first of these statutes in the United States, prohibited all combinations in restraint of interstate and foreign trade. The Supreme Court interpreted this law to prohibit "unreasonable" restraint of trade and made the illegality of a combination depend on the proportion of the industry it represented.

The Clayton act of 1914 legalized certain activities of trade associations outlawed under the earlier act and forbade acquisition of the shares of one company by another if a tendency toward monopoly resulted. Acquisition of assets, however, was not forbidden. A federal trade commission was established in the same year to investigate and prosecute unfair competition.

These laws did not prevent concentration of industrial control from marching steadily on. The government temporarily changed its attitude in 1933 and permitted combinations in the form of "codes" under the National Recovery Act, industries being required in return to increase wage rates and abstain from opposing the organization of employees. After the Supreme Court declared this act unconstitutional, administrative policy returned to a stricter enforcement of antitrust laws.

Monroe Doctrine. An important declaration of policy made by President Monroe in a message to Congress, December 2, 1823, in which the president declared "that the American continents, by the free and independent condition which they have assumed and maintained, are henceforth not to be considered as subjects for future colonization by any European powers." The message called attention to what the president considered to be the difference between the political system of the monarchies of Europe and that of America, and stated that any attempt on the part of these European monarchies to extend their system to any portion of the Western Hemisphere would be regarded as dangerous to the peace and safety of the United States.

The doctrine, at the time, accomplished its purpose of warning the Holy Alliance, composed of European powers, from intervening to overthrow the independence of the newly arisen Spanish American republics, and it has since been repeatedly appealed to by successive presidents, though not until 1896 was it formally noticed by Congress. Following the "Venezuela incident" of that year, in which the American government interfered to stop what it regarded as encroachments of the British government upon territorial rights of Venezuela, the policy was overwhelmingly endorsed by the American nation and by both the great political parties.

The Monroe Doctrine is not, as is sometimes supposed, a principle of international law. It is in fact directly opposed to a fundamental principle of international law; namely, that a state may dispose of its own territory to another state without hindrance, for the Monroe Doctrine would probably be invoked to prevent the cession of an American possession by a weak state to a stronger one. The Monroe Doctrine is simply an American policy, never directly admitted by European nations until it found mention, though not a satisfactory mention, in the Covenant of the League of Nations. As a policy, it accorded with a deep, though undefined, American resolution to liquidate the possessions of European states in the New World and to prevent the political issues of the Western continents from being determined at the capitals of Europe.

Under some presidents, this policy has approximated the claim of a protectorate over Latin-American countries and as such was deeply resented. Under Franklin D. Roosevelt's administration a new turn was given to it. In multilateral trade treaties negotiated in 1936-37 at Buenos Aires, he sought to make the Doctrine a policy of all American states, pledged to oppose aggression from outside and to minimize conflicts among themselves by prompt consultation when threats to peace arose.

Mugwump. A celebrated political cartoon picturing the independent voter as having his mug on one side of the fence and his wump on the other.

Municipal Ownership. The civic possession of certain properties, as streets, bridges, ferries, parks, and sewage systems, is well-nigh indispensable to urban life. Only in rare instances, and then to the prejudice of city life, are such necessities as these privately owned. In most cities, water supply is now municipally owned. Other public utilities, such as street railways and lighting systems, are either privately or municipally owned. In Europe, they are generally the property of the city and are operated by its employees. In the United States, more frequently, they are privately owned, but are controlled, with respect to service and rates, by their franchises, by ordinances of the city government, or by state public utility commissions.

The question of private ownership and operation of public utilities in cities has been one of the most important and the most perplexing problems of American government. A franchise for such a utility carries with it the creation of a virtual monopoly privilege and the right of eminent domain; it also presents, if unrestrained, the opportunity for maintaining extortionate rates for service. As such, it is a privilege that has been eagerly sought, bitterly contested for, and frequently corruptly acquired. See *Government Ownership.*

In the United States, municipal governments do not generally engage in several kinds of services, such as public pawnshops, municipal orchestras, opera houses, etc., which are common in Europe. In America, great attention has been given to parks and to public playgrounds. The scope of municipally owned activities can hardly be settled by any theoretical principles. In each country and in each community, it is a matter for practical decision.

National Convention. Since 1832, in the United States, candidates for president and vice president have been nominated at national conventions especially convened for that purpose once in four years.

The national convention is not the creature of the law. It is an extra-legal party meeting, and its membership, machinery, and procedure are determined by party rules.

The rules of the Democratic and Republican parties provide for the selection of two delegates from each congressional district, and for four delegates at large from each state. An amendment to the rules of the Republican party, which was passed in 1916, limits full representation in the national convention to those congressional districts having a Republican enrollment of at least 7500 voters. To the Republican party convention, delegates are chosen in the same manner as that in which congressmen are nominated in the several districts. The Democratic party leaves the method of selecting delegates to the party organization of each state.

CONVENTION PROCEDURE. The chairman of the national committee, who has been chosen at the preceding national convention, initiates the proceedings of the convention. He is succeeded by a temporary chairman chosen by the convention. The convention committees, the most important being the committee on credentials and the committee on rules, are then chosen, the delegation from each state choosing one member for each committee.

The report of the committee on credentials, affecting contested seats, is then presented to the convention as a whole, which either approves and adopts the report in its entirety, or votes upon each contested seat separately. In the Republican convention, under the ruling of Senator Root, in 1912, every person entered upon the temporary roll of the convention by the national committee, even though his own right to sit in the convention is contested, is eligible to vote with respect to the seating of any other contested delegate. See *Convention, Political.*

National Defense. This term is used to describe the established provisions of a state for protecting its rights and territory, particularly from foreign invasion or aggression. Some such provision has ever been regarded as indispensable for national existence and security. The preamble to the Constitution of the United States declares that one object of the Union is to "provide for the common defense."

The type of defense establishment varies greatly with different states, generally according to their size, their frontiers, their geographical security, their traditional friendships and enmities, and the aims of their foreign policies. The main reliance may be naval, as in the case of Great Britain, or, at an earlier date, of Holland; or it may be land forces. In the main, four types of armies have been relied upon by states for the attainment of their military policies: (1) professional armies; (2) mercenary troops; (3) "militia," or organizations of citizens trained in time of peace, and volunteer forces raised in case of emergency; (4) forces prepared by universal or general military training.

PROFESSIONAL ARMIES. The first, that of a professional army recruited voluntarily, was the general reliance of European states down to the French Revolution. Great Britain, throughout her history, has relied almost entirely upon professional armies, except where she has employed mercenary troops or has subsidized foreign troops in common wars. In World War I, an army conscription bill was not enacted by the British Parliament until 1916. A professional army may be brought to the highest state of proficiency, and, for a country possessing overseas responsibilities which have to be guarded, it is a well-nigh indispensable element in the national plan of defense.

MERCENARY ARMIES. Mercenary armies have been employed in all times, and their use has frequently been notorious, as in the case of the mercenary bands that infested Italy in the 16th century, or in the employment of German troops by Great Britain against the American colonists in the Revolutionary War. Their use has been unsparingly condemned by practically every serious student of the art of politics or of war.

VOLUNTEER FORCES. The third, the method of volunteer forces raised in time of emergency, has been the traditional policy of the United States. Reliance upon hastily raised troops, while a congenial policy to a people little troubled by threat of war, has proved again and again in American history to be ineffective from a military standpoint, and frightfully wasteful of life and treasure. The highly technical character of modern warfare, the variety of war matériel, the extreme expenditure of munitions, and especially the need of trained officers to take command of levies of troops, have rendered obsolete and indefensible a reliance upon extemporized volunteer forces.

UNIVERSAL TRAINING. Some system of general training of all young men for military duties appears at once the most satisfactory, as it is the most just and the most democratic, of all plans of defense. It recognizes the duty of protection of nation and civilization as a common duty, from which no man of suitable age or physique may properly be exempted. It imposes the hardships and sacrifices of warfare upon all classes of society alike, and puts at the disposal of a nation its full resource of man power without the demoralizing effects of discrimination and bounties. That such a policy is now endorsed by the American people is evidenced by the draft legislation of Congress of 1917 and by the National Defense act of 1916 and of 1920.

This latter legislation gives the country a policy of national defense and a prospective complement of forces adequate for any probable emergency. Under this act, the army of the United States is formed of three components: (1) the "regular army," a small standing body of professional soldiers whose duties are to man the coast defenses, garrison overseas possessions, care for the stores, ordnance, fortifications, camps, and other military property, supply a limited mobile body of troops as a first element for defense and, through its officer and noncommissioned officer personnel, furnish instruction to the national guard, organized reserves, reserve officers' training corps in colleges and schools, and citizens' training camps. (2) The second component is the "national guard," organized in such a manner that each state is charged with the responsibility of maintaining, in times of peace, certain units of citizen soldiers, which may be combined into a number of army divisions and corps. (3) Third, the "organized reserves," comprising officers and men of training, so developed as to form the "cadres" or skeleton structures of additional divisions, which, within a few months' time after a declaration of war, could be raised to full strength, armed, equipped, and trained for the field.

THE NATIONAL GUARD. The national guard, with the regular army, constitutes the first line of defense and is to be so officered, equipped, and trained as to approximate, in its organization and performance of duty, the standards of the regular army. The national guard in each state is, moreover, under the orders of the governor of the state, and constitutes a constantly ready force at his command for the execution of the law and for the maintenance of public order. It may, by order of the president of the United States, be called into the Federal service to repel invasion, to suppress insurrection, or to enforce the laws of the Union.

Naturalization. A term given in law to the acquisition of citizenship in a country other than that in which one has been a citizen or a subject.

The act is necessarily voluntary on the part of the person acquiring naturalization, and must have the consent of the state in which citizenship is acquired. The consent of the state whose citizenship is renounced is not necessary to the act, and may even be refused. The act of severing citizenship is called "expatriation." It is a renunciation, by formal action, of the rights and obligations of citizenship therein. If the act of renunciation is not recognized by the state in which citizenship was formerly held, it may happen that two states may claim the same citizen or subject. See *Citizenship*.

AMERICAN NATURALIZATION. The United States has given great attention to naturalization of foreigners who seek permanent residence in this country. Prior to 1942, the procedure consisted of two steps—a declaration of intention to become a citizen filed two or more years after arrival and a petition for naturalization filed at least three years later. Moreover, citizenship was available only to members of the white and Negro races.

The law was extensively revised in 1942 to simplify procedure and for other purposes. All racial bars were removed. The same rules apply to men as to women. The essential requirements now are as follows:

1. The applicant must be at least 18 years of age and have had legal residence in the United States for at least five years. The residence period is reduced to three years for the wife or husband of a citizen.

2. He must apply to a federal court, signing the application in his own handwriting and (with certain exceptions for older people) be able to read, write, and speak words in ordinary use in the English language.

3. He must attest by two credible citizen witnesses that he has been, for the qualifying period, a person of good moral character, attached to the principles of the constitution, and well disposed to the good order and happiness of the United States. Naturalization is denied to anyone who, in the prior ten years, was a member of a subversive organization unless he was under 16 at the time or became a member under duress. Those excluded because of lack of good moral character include habitual drunkards, adulterers, polygamists, gamblers, violators of criminal law, those convicted of murder, those who have spent 180 days or more in prison, and those who gave false testimony to obtain a benefit under the immigration law.

4. He must demonstrate to the court's satisfaction a knowledge and understanding of the fundamentals of the history of the United States and of its principles and form of government.

When these tests are met, the applicant waits 30 days and then takes the oath of allegiance to the United States before the court and receives his "certificate of citizenship."

The oath of allegiance is as follows:

"I hereby declare, on oath, that I absolutely and entirely renounce and abjure all allegiance and fidelity to any foreign prince, potentate, state or sovereignty, of whom or which I have heretofore been a subject or citizen; that I will support and defend the Constitution and laws of the United States of America against all enemies, foreign and domestic; that I will bear arms on behalf of the United States when required by the law; that I will perform noncombatant service in the armed forces of the United States when required by the law; that I will perform work of national importance under civilian direction when required by the law, and that I take this obligation freely without any mental reservation or purpose of evasion; so help me God."

In many states the public school system now offers special instruction for aliens desiring to prepare for the citizenship examination, and the practice of making the oath of citizenship a formal ceremony is becoming common.

Neutrality. The status of a nation taking no belligerent part in a conflict between other nations, but preserving friendly relations with both or all.

By international law, citizens of a neutral nation may trade freely with a belligerent, even to the extent of furnishing arms and munitions. Such goods, however, may be seized as "contraband of war," and neutral merchant vessels are subject to "visit and search" by war vessels of the belligerent states to determine the presence of contraband in their cargoes.

A nation, to remain neutral, must be strictly impartial in the assistance which it or its citizens afford. It may not permit its territory to be used as a refuge for troops of belligerent nations, nor as a means of transit for them, nor for the recruiting of troops. Its ports may be used by the war vessels of belligerents only for a limited number of days, and that use is restricted to the making of repairs or to the securing of supplies indispensable to the continued voyage of the belligerent vessel. Similar obligations bind the neutral state with respect to the use of its territory for purposes of communication by telegraph, by cable, or by radio, and, while private citizens may freely sell their wares to a belligerent state, a nation may not dispose of its naval vessels or of war matériel to a belligerent during the actual period of the war, without violating neutrality.

A legislative attempt was made in 1935 to safeguard American neutrality in foreign wars by directing the president to forbid sales of arms or loans to warring nations and warning American citizens against trade and travel. In 1939 the law was changed to allow the sale of arms, to be paid for and transported by the purchaser ("cash and carry"). American citizens were forbidden to travel in belligerent countries or on their ships, or to extend credits to such countries. American ships also were forbidden to enter combat areas.

The neutrality of some states has been guaranteed by treaty. Examples are Belgium before World War I and Austria after World War II.

Nihilism (nĭ′hĭ-lĭz′m). A term given to Russian radicals who refused to recognize the validity of existing institutions, social, political, or religious. The word was first used in this sense by the novelist Turgéniev in his *Fathers and Sons*, published in 1862.

The movement, which at first centered in student communities, was highly rationalistic and materialistic. It regarded religion, family life, private property, and even public administration as obstacles to the free development of the individual and of rational society. The movement had philosophical points of contact with anarchism. The repressive action of the Russian bureaucracy led to acts of retaliation and terrorism by the Nihilists, the most sensational being the assassination of the czar Alexander II in 1881.

The word is frequently applied in the United States to all "terrorists," or to those who use the assassination of officials to intimidate the government.

Oligarchy (ŏl′ĭ-gär′kĭ). A government in which the power of the state is held by a few, as opposed to the many. It is distinguished from an aristocracy only as being a corrupt form. Of all forms of government—democratic, aristocratic, or monarchic—an oligarchy has generally been condemned as the worst, its members invariably being led to exercise their power in their own interest, unrestrained by such consideration as is felt by a king for his people, or by the traditional sentiments of honor and public responsibility that may characterize an aristocracy under the phrase, "noblesse oblige." Oligarchies have frequently been associated with the seizure of governments by violence, chicanery, fraud, or by monetary power.

Ombudsman. The title of a Swedish officer whose duty it is to hear complaints of citizens against the government. He may explain that the complaints are baseless or, if they are well founded, may use his authority to have responsible officials correct the situations complained of. The office was established in Sweden in 1809. Some other jurisdictions have copied it.

Open Door Policy. The preservation of opportunity for foreign trade in a country, on a basis of fair and equal competition for all nations. Open door policy means also that, in the development of economically backward countries, all foreign nations shall have an equal opportunity to offer the services of their credit and their technical experts, and to obtain concessions for transportation construction or for mineral development upon equal terms.

The term "open door" seems to have been first used by Admiral Lord Charles Beresford in 1899. Secretary Hay adopted it in 1900 in stating the policy of the United States toward China in opposing the aggression of other nations, particularly Japan.

Open Town or **Open City.** A term applied to a city or town which has been formally declared undefended and open to the enemy. The approach to the town must be open, all troops withdrawn, and fortifications dismantled. Such a town may be occupied, but not bombarded nor destroyed. The immunity apparently does not extend to military installations such as arsenals within the town nor to railway yards, and other facilities in its suburbs. Paris, Manila, and Rome were declared open cities in World War II.

Pacifism (păs'ĭ-fĭz'm). An attitude of convinced opposition to war. Pacifists vary in their programs from those who, like Tolstoy, teach a doctrine of pure non-resistance to those who, admitting the justice of defense for the individual and the nation, deplore and oppose all forms of preparation for national defense.

Most pacifists are temperamentally optimistic with regard to human nature and the willingness of nations to compromise. The weakness of this type of pacifism lies in the failure properly to appreciate that the forces of cupidity and inherited antipathy are very powerful in human society and that a sense of the rights of a people is rapidly impaired by a knowledge that it lacks the resolution to defend those rights.

Another school of pacifists takes the view that the profit system is the mainspring of aggressive warfare. Socialists, who advocate production for use instead of profit, claim an end of imperialistic wars as a central merit of their proposals. Likewise the guiding principle of actual and proposed legislation to ensure neutrality, as placed before the United States Congress, has been limitation of profits from war and from preparation for war.

Pair. When legislators who are opposed to each other on a particular measure agree that the vote of one shall cancel the other, it is called a pair, and neither votes. The agreement does not affect the result. It is usually resorted to when one or both has to be absent.

Pan-Americanism. A term produced by newspaper discussion of the international American Conference at Washington in 1889 and 1890. It is the doctrine that the states of the American hemisphere possess certain common interests and institutions not generally shared by the peoples of the Old World, and that these should be the basis of a common understanding and of common political and commercial actions among these American states. Such an idea is involved in the Monroe Doctrine. To give effect to the ideas, the first International American Conference met at the call of Secretary Blaine at Washington in 1889-90. Including one in 1937, eight such conferences have been held. A special one for discussion of peace machinery in the New World was called at Buenos Aires in 1936 at the instance of President Franklin D. Roosevelt.

American advocacy of the Monroe Doctrine has at times advanced the sense of Pan-American unity, and at other times has awakened in Central and South America a sense of irritation and of concern. A considerable body of writers exists in several countries of Spanish inheritance, who assert that the cultural affiliation of those countries is with Europe rather than with the United States.

Pardoning Power. The existence of an executive power of remitting the consequences of a conviction is an almost necessary provision of government. The power frequently is invoked to mitigate the severity of the law, to assume a responsibility which is beyond the competence of a court, to recognize an alteration in conditions taking place subsequent to conviction or in view of new evidence, or to recognize good behavior or reformation of character in a person who has endured a portion of his sentence. Under monarchical government, such power resides in the king, who is the fount both of grace and of justice. The development of constitutional government has transferred this authority to ministers, as to the home secretary in the British government.

In the United States, the pardoning power is constitutionally vested in the president, and, by state constitutions generally, though not invariably, in the governor. A pardoning power usually exists in the legislative branch unless, as frequently under the American system, it has been limited or denied by the Constitution.

Party Platform. A document issued by party leaders or by a party convention, setting forth the principles and the measures for which the party stands and upon which it purposes to make its appeal for the support of the electorate.

Party Whip. A member of a legislative chamber assigned by party leaders to the task of rounding up members of the party to insure their vote on important measures and to hold them in line with party policy. In the British House of Commons, the whips may act as tellers at a "division" of the chamber when important votes are taken. They have other responsible functions of keeping track of sentiment on public matters, of arranging patronage, and, in general, of promoting party solidarity.

It is customary in England for the whips of the party in power to be appointed to the ministerial offices of "junior lords of the treasury," which offices are now sinecures.

The term whip is often used in the United States to designate party leaders in Congress.

Passport. A certificate of identity granted by a government, authorizing the holder to leave the country he is in or to enter a foreign country, and requesting for him safe and free passage and all lawful aid and protection. Passports are issued by the foreign office of a government, or by its diplomatic agents resident abroad.

In the United States, passports may be obtained by applying to the "passport bureau" of the department of state. It is customary for passports to be "viséd" by the representative of the foreign country to which it is proposed to go, in order that any difficulties may be met and surmounted before departure from the home country.

Paternalism. A policy whereby the state assumes to enter into and to regulate the activities of individuals in their social and industrial life. The early part of the 20th century, and to a less degree the latter half of the 19th century, have been marked by an extension of the activities and functions of government, directly opposed to the policy of the 18th century in Europe, which was dominated by the doctrine of "laissez faire," or noninterference by the state. See *Social Legislation.*

Patronage. Places in the government employ at the disposal of persons elected to political office. The term is also broadly used to cover contracts, franchises, and other public favors turned over to preferred individuals or localities by those in power. See *Civil Service.*

Peonage (pē'ŏn-ȧj). A form of servitude in which a laborer is compelled against his will to remain in the service of his creditor or employer. Peonage arises out of a contract whereby a debtor undertakes to serve a creditor until a debt or an advance of money or goods is paid, or it may result from the operation of law upon mere nonpayment of a debt. The word is derived from the Mexican term "peon," in which country peonage is a long established institution.

Amendment XII to the Constitution, which prohibited "slavery or involuntary servitude except in punishment of crime," made peonage unlawful. Congress, by a law enacted March 2, 1867, further provided that "the holding of any person to service or labor known as peonage is abolished and forever prohibited in the territory of New Mexico or in any other territory of the United States." The law further made the holding of anyone in peonage punishable as a crime.

Personal Representative. Heads of governments have long followed the practice of sending special and often secret agents to secure information abroad and even to negotiate treaties with foreign states. Inasmuch as the Constitution of the United States requires the consent of the Senate to the appointment of ambassadors, other public ministers, and consuls, the conduct of official relations with a foreign government by a personal representative of the president, unconfirmed by the Senate, would seem to be of doubtful constitutionality, and the practice has met with criticism and congressional opposition. Nevertheless, on numerous occasions the president of the United States has dispatched personal representatives on diplomatic missions.

President Washington, in October 1789, sent Gouverneur Morris to England to negotiate a commercial treaty, without having his appointment confirmed by the Senate. Several hundred such representatives, in all, have been dispatched by different presidents. Well-known examples are the mission of Nicholas Trist to Mexico in 1847 to negotiate a treaty of peace; of James H. Blount to Hawaii in 1893 to end a revolutionary movement of Americans against the Hawaiian monarchy; of John Lind and several other representatives to Mexico; and of Edward M. House to Europe by President Wilson. Trist was authorized by President Polk practically to order the American army and navy to cease active hostilities against Mexico. Blount was endowed by President Cleveland with "powers paramount" to those of the American minister at Hawaii. Lind was sent to force the retirement of President Huerta from the head of the Mexican government.

A survey of the instances in which personal representatives, rather than diplomatic agents confirmed in their appointments by the Senate, have been used by the presidents of the United States reveals the following purposes for which they have been employed: to make special reports on conditions prevailing in foreign countries; to reopen relations with countries with which diplomatic relations have been broken; to interfere in the internal affairs of countries disturbed by revolution; and to negotiate treaties.

The motives that have led to such appointments are the advantages of secrecy, of expedition, and of the opportunity of avoiding a compromising situation in case of failure. Against them may be directed all the arguments in favor of open diplomacy and the constitutional privilege of the Senate to participate in developing the foreign policy of the government and of confirming the appointment of agents through which the promises of the government are expressed and the obligations of the nation are created.

Persona Non Grata (pĕr-sō′nȧ nŏn grā′tȧ). A term applied to a diplomatic representative who is not acceptable personally to the government to which it is proposed to send him. All countries reserve the privilege of refusing to receive any representatives accredited to them who are thus unacceptable, or to cancel for cause acceptance of such envoys.

Pigeonholing. The laying aside of a bill or other matter by a legislative committee, presumptively for future consideration, but in fact with the intent of allowing the bill to die through failure to act upon it; also similar action by an executive, where such action is equivalent to a veto.

Plebiscite (plĕb′ĭ-sĭt). In ancient Rome, a "plebiscitum" was the enactment of a law by the assembly of the "plebs" or common people.

In modern politics, the term plebiscite is given to an expression of the popular will, taken in various forms and for various purposes, such as an alteration in the form of government, change of rulers, or the transfer of territory from one sovereignty to another. The last purpose is of great modern interest, because of numerous provisions, in the treaties that followed World War I, for the holding of plebiscites to ascertain the preference of peoples for the sovereignty of one state or another.

This application of the principle of self-determination arose during the period of the French Revolution, when a plebiscite of the inhabitants of Avignon was taken before the transfer of that city and adjacent territory from the sovereignty of the pope to that of the French republic. The practice was soon abused and discredited.

The plebiscite again came into use in the period 1848 to 1870, especially in the process of the unification of Italy. A plebiscite of the inhabitants of Nice and Savoy accompanied their cession by Piedmont to France. In 1877 a plebiscite was taken of the inhabitants of the island of Saint-Barthelemy in the West Indies, before the transfer of that island from Sweden to France, and again upon the separation of Norway from Sweden in 1905.

The following plebiscites were provided for in the peace settlements following World War I: Allenstein and Marienwerder, districts in East Prussia; Eupen and Malmedy, small districts or "kreisen" on the border of Prussia and Belgium; Upper Silesia; Klagenfurt, lying between Austria and Serbia; Northern Schleswig; and the Saar Basin. These have all been held, resulting in the retention of Allenstein and of Marienwerder by Germany; the cession of Eupen and of Malmedy to Belgium; the division of Upper Silesia between Poland and Germany; and the retention of Klagenfurt by Austria. By a plebiscite the Saar, which was under French control for 15 years, was returned to Germany in 1935.

A plebiscite was provided also for the district of Teschen, in dispute between Poland and Czechoslovakia, but this was abandoned in favor of a diplomatic settlement ratified by the powers.

Plurality. The number of votes received by a successful candidate in excess of the number cast for the next highest candidate for the office. In the election of public officials, the law may be so framed that a plurality only may elect. In such a case, if there are more than two candidates, it may happen that a candidate is elected even though he fails to obtain a majority of the total number of votes cast. See *Majority*.

Police Power. A general term that expresses the fundamental power vested in every state to limit and to regulate the exercise of private rights in the interest of public health, public morals, public safety, and the general welfare of the community.

Under this power, it has been held that a state may absolutely prohibit the sale of intoxicating liquor (*Mugler* vs. *Kansas*) or of cigarettes (*Austin* vs. *Tennessee*), as intrinsically harmful to the health of the community. It has also been held to be within the scope of the police power of the state to prohibit the manufacture of a commodity, such as oleomargarine, which readily lends itself to fraud upon the public (*Powell* vs. *Pennsylvania*).

Under the police power, a state, or, when properly authorized, a municipality, may prohibit within a particular locality the manufacture of bricks, the maintenance of livery stables, public laundries, billboards, public garages, coal yards, slaughterhouses, and the erection of buildings of more than a prescribed height, and may impose any other regulations which are reasonably calculated to secure the public welfare while not unreasonably interfering with the liberty of the individual.

Laws limiting the hours of labor for women and children, prescribing the conditions under which factories shall operate, laws regulating the relative rights of landlord and tenant, as well as those prescribing regulations for buildings used as tenements, are other instances of the exercise of police power. With the growing complexity of society and with the greater interdependence of individuals and classes, the theory of the police power has been extended far beyond the narrow confines to which it once was thought to be limited. Thus antitrust laws, although directly interfering with the liberty of contract, and statutes prohibiting the sale or use of trading stamps, have been upheld (*National Cotton Oil Company* vs. *Texas*; *Tanner* vs. *Little*). Zoning ordinances designed merely to promote the æsthetic interest and general welfare of the community are constitutional exercises of the police power (*Lincoln Trust Company* vs. *Williams Building Corporation*).

In the last analysis, whether an act is within the police power of the state depends upon a judicial balancing of interests—that of the individual in the unlimited use of his property and the unrestrained pursuit of his own inclinations on the one hand, and that of the rest of the community and of the state on the other.

Populism. Term applied to the series of reforms advocated by the People's or Populist party in the United States. Chief among these reforms were the free coinage of silver at the ratio of 16 to 1, the creation of a national paper currency to replace the national bank notes, stringent government regulation of railroads and of monopolies, and a general policy of legislation directed against the alleged control of the government by financial interests.

Pork Barrel. A term applied in the United States to appropriation bills for federal expenditures in various parts of the country. So termed because each congressman secures his "piece of bacon" to bring back to the "folks at home." See *Logrolling*.

Pourparler (pōōr′pär′lā′). An informal, preliminary conference of representatives of different groups, factions, or countries, looking to a formal agreement settling disputed questions between the parties.

Preferential Voting. See *Proportional Representation*.

President Pro Tempore of the Senate. One of the members of the Senate elected by that body to preside over the Senate during the absence of the vice president, who is normally the constitutional presiding officer. Should there be a vacancy in the office of vice president, the president pro tempore would preside regularly.

Pressure Group. Advocates of a cause who bring pressure to bear on lawmakers by lobbying or other means to compel passage of legislation they favor. They also use propaganda to convert public opinion to their views to add to the pressure, or to bring about a change in public policy. See *Lobbying*, *Propaganda*.

Primary. A preliminary election, held by voters of a party to determine the party's candidates for office. When carried out by a legally prescribed election and as a substitute for local meetings or conventions, it is generally termed the "direct primary."

In the "nonpartisan primary," all aspirants to office, regardless of political affiliation, enter the primary election, and members of all parties are eligible to vote. The two candidates receiving the highest number of votes for any office are regarded as nominated, and these two then compete against each other in the final election.

Prime Minister. A term applied to the head of a ministry, particularly in Great Britain and in member states of the British Commonwealth. He is called also "the premier." In France, he is legally termed "the president of the council of ministers."

Privileges and Immunities of Citizens. The 14th Amendment to the Constitution of the United States provides that "No state shall make or enforce any law which shall abridge the privileges or immunities of citizens of the

United States." These privileges and immunities are incidents of federal citizenship. They include the right to protection of life, liberty, and property on the high seas and in foreign countries; the right peaceably to assemble and petition the federal government for redress of grievances; the right of habeas corpus; the right to use the navigable waters of the United States; the right to hold office under the federal government; and the rights secured to citizens of the United States by treaties with foreign nations.

Article IV, Sec. 2, of the Constitution provides that "Citizens of each state shall be entitled to all privileges and immunities of citizens in the several states." These rights include protection of life, liberty, and property under state law; the right to sue in the state courts; the right to engage in any lawful business; and the right to acquire and to devise or bequeath property. See *Civil Rights and Liberties.*

Prize Courts. Tribunals of a belligerent state, established for the purpose of adjudicating the title to property captured by its citizens on the high seas, and of examining the nationality of such property.

Prohibition. Governmental action which prohibits by law the manufacture and the sale of intoxicating liquors except for medicinal or sacramental uses. In the United States, the first state prohibition law was enacted in Maine in 1851. Between that date and 1920, nearly half of the states, at various times, enacted laws prohibiting or strictly limiting the manufacture and sale of liquor. The 18th Amendment to the United States Constitution (in force January 16, 1920) made illegal the manufacture and sale of liquors containing more than one-half of one per cent of alcohol. The ensuing 13 years provided a working test of the policy. The prohibition, fairly effective at first, became less so as time went on. Bootlegging of liquor on an unprecedented scale diverted large sums of money to criminal elements of the population. These and other considerations led, in 1933, to the adoption of the 21st Amendment to the Constitution, repealing the earlier one but giving Congress power to prevent transportation of liquor into states where its sale is illegal.

Propaganda. This term is used to describe any means of instilling or promoting ideas favorable to a cause or organization, particularly in the field of politics. Usually, this is accomplished by indirect or incidental means, as by suggestion, insinuation, or by more or less subtle appeals to prejudice. If the propaganda is sufficiently clever, the victim is led to think that he has arrived independently at impressions that have been introduced into his mind by someone else. Propaganda may be conveyed by news articles, plays, motion pictures, or even in conversation. The word itself has a respectable origin, in the sense of missionary work. Its evil repute comes from its political use in spreading half truths by illicit methods.

Proportional Representation. Any one of a variety of plans designed to give minority parties or groups representation in a legislative body, in proportion to the relative strength of each minority group as shown in elections; frequently called also "minority representation."

Such a plan was first tried on a national basis by Denmark in 1854 and was successfully adopted by Belgium in 1899.

HISTORY OF THE MOVEMENT. Proportional representation was discussed and advocated for both national and local elections for about 60 years preceding World War I, but, before 1914, it was adopted only for the choice of national representatives, by several smaller states, as Denmark in part, Belgium, Sweden, Bulgaria, Serbia, and Portugal.

During World War I, the system was adopted by Holland and was extended in Denmark. It appears in most of the new postwar constitutions; Germany, Austria, Czechoslovakia, Jugoslavia, Danzig, Greece, Poland, Esthonia, Latvia, Lithuania, and Bulgaria. France adopted it in 1919 but in 1927 returned to the uninominal system. In Switzerland, it was adopted nationally by an initiative proposal in 1918.

PLANS IN USE. Of the several plans, the following may be mentioned:

(1) The "limited vote" plan. Each constituency or district elects several representatives, but each voter therein casts a ballot for a number of candidates, less than the number of seats to be filled, giving his vote but once to any one candidate. A minority, by limiting its nominees, may be large enough to elect one or more candidates. This system was applied to certain constituencies in England in 1867 but was abolished in 1885.

(2) The "cumulative vote" plan. Each voter has as many votes as there are places to fill, but he may cast all his votes for one candidate or may distribute them between candidates, as he chooses. Here again, a minority party, by limiting its nominees, may elect. This device was used for election to the legislative council of Cape Colony before the Union of South Africa was formed. English school board

elections also have used this system, and the state of Illinois employs it to elect its House of Representatives.

(3) The "single vote" plan. In each constituency, though there may be more than one place to fill, each voter is allowed to cast his ballot for one member only. Minorities, by this plan, may elect if they confine nominations to the number of candidates their voting strength represents. Japan has used this system since 1900, and her experience shows that quite close approximations to the results of more elaborate methods of proportional representation may be obtained.

(4) The "single transferable vote," known as the "Hare system." First used in Denmark in 1855 and adopted in 1909 by the Union of South Africa. Each voter indicates on the ballot his first, second, third, etc., choice. A "quota" determining the number of votes necessary for election is obtained by dividing the total number of votes by one more than the number of places to be filled and by adding one to this number. When all the first choices are counted, if a candidate is found to have the quota, he is elected. If there are surplus votes, they are transferred by various methods under various systems to other candidates as indicated by the ballot. The Hare system of preferential and proportional representation has been adopted in a few cities of the United States and Canada.

(5) The "list system." Lists of candidates are nominated by political organizations or groups of voters. Each voter has as many votes as there are places to be filled, but he may not "cumulate" them. The number of votes registered by a group or party is used to determine the number of elective candidates of the group. There are various ways of apportioning seats under this system, but the most widely copied is "the d'Hondt system" in Belgium, known from its originator. It may be made clear by illustration. Suppose an election for 5 seats, and 4 party lists obtain 24,000, 11,000, 9000, and 3000 votes, respectively. These figures are then divided by two, with results of 12,000, 5500, 4500, 1500; by three, with results of 8000, 3666+, 3000, 1000; if necessary by four, and so on. As there are 5 seats, the 5th largest of the figures thus obtained (in this case 8000) becomes the "quotient." By dividing the party votes by this quotient, we obtain the number of seats to which each party is entitled; namely, 3, 1, 1, and 0.

Protective Tariff. See *Tariff.*

Protectorate. A country or territory under the political control and protection of another. A protectorate invariably represents some restriction upon the foreign relations of the country, and may extend to complete control of them. Usually foreign authority is exercised also over the financial affairs and obligations of the protectorate. A nation claiming or exercising such protection becomes responsible to other nations for the protectorate's regard of international obligations, and the tendency is to go even further and admit responsibility for internal order and well-being.

Protocol (*prō′tô-kŏl*). A preliminary agreement between two or more countries, intended to form the basis of a more formal and complete treaty.

Public Lands Policy. Over two-thirds of the total area of the United States, including Alaska and consisting of over 1,800,000,000 acres, has at some time been the property of the nation. The development of this vast public domain into farms and homes, privately owned, has been one of the most important policies of the American government, and its carrying out has profoundly influenced the development of American society. Of this original domain, there remains about 400,000,000 acres, mostly arid or otherwise unfit for settlement. The rest has been distributed.

The Constitution gave to Congress the right to dispose of public lands, and under this power Congress has developed a public land policy, which, however, has taken several different forms. In the beginning it was believed that the sale of these lands would produce a considerable revenue and, among other common benefits, would extinguish the public debt. Accordingly, large tracts were sold to companies for subdivision and speculation. After 1800, small tracts were sold to settlers on credit. In 1820, a system of cash sale was adopted, the minimum price being reduced from $2.00 to $1.25 an acre. Public land was frequently occupied by settlers in advance of government surveys, and without negotiation with government agents. These settlers, known as "squatters," came to be recognized as having prior claims to the acquisition of lands which they had improved.

HOMESTEAD POLICY. The policy of using the public domain to encourage national development received complete recognition in the "homestead law" of 1862. This act permitted any head of a family to secure 160 acres, or a quarter section of land, by residing on it for five years. Amendments changed the law so as to extend the privilege to any person 21 years of age or older who was a citizen or had declared his intention to become a citizen.

For homesteads in certain arid regions, Congress extended the acquirable tract to 320 acres, without the necessity of residing on the land. On other tracts, designated as "grazing lands," the law permitted the acquisition of 640 acres. An act passed in 1878, and in 1892 made applicable to all public lands, allowed the outright purchase of 160 acres of unappropriated nonmineral land unfit for cultivation but valuable for timber or stone, at a minimum price of $2.50 an acre.

LAND GRANTS TO STATES. The government has also granted public lands to states, to individuals, and to corporations, for specific purposes. Previously to 1850, one section out of each 36, within a state, was granted to it by the national government for support of education. Since 1850 the amount has been doubled. In 1860 the "Morrill act" granted each state an amount of land for the support of a college of agriculture and mechanic arts. This measure forms the basis of a large number of western state institutions. Extensive grants of land were made to the soldiers of the Revolutionary and Mexican wars, as compensation for their military service. To encourage the building of railways, particularly the transcontinental systems, Congress granted large areas of public land along the lines of these railways through undeveloped country, such grants amounting to more than 155 million acres.

CONSERVATION. The "Desert Land act," as amended in 1891, enabled settlers to obtain 320 acres by bringing the land under irrigation within three years' time and expending not less than one dollar an acre for improvements. The government has undertaken also the reclamation of arid and swamp lands.

In the 20th century a conservation policy has been defined, designed to preserve the remaining public domain from wasteful exploitation. Under this policy, the timber, the minerals, and the surface of the lands are disposed of separately, and water power sites have been withheld from entry.

Congress also granted authority to the president to withdraw the public domain from private acquisition and to create extensive reservations, either as "forest reservations" or as "national parks." Nearly 200 million acres are included in forest reservations in the West.

All unappropriated land was withdrawn from settlement by an executive order in 1935 signed by President Franklin D. Roosevelt. This move was in accord with recommendations of a national resources committee which the president had commissioned to report on the best use of land and other natural resources. Among the points made by the committee was the fact that much land unfit for cultivation was nevertheless being tilled. Farmers so engaged, who required public relief for their support, were given aid in acquiring better land elsewhere through the agency of a federal resettlement administration. At the same time an extensive land-purchase program was carried out, the land so acquired being reforested or otherwise used as appeared desirable.

Public Ownership. See *Government Ownership, Municipal Ownership, Socialism.*

Punishments, Cruel and Unusual. The English Bill of Rights 1688 contained a provision, forbidding the infliction of "cruel and unusual punishments." This provision has been incorporated in the Constitution of the United States, in the 8th Amendment, and in the constitution of nearly every American state.

"Cruel and unusual punishments" within these provisions are such punishments as are revolting to the civilized mind, or involve torture and lingering death. However, a punishment wholly disproportionate to the crime committed may, under some circumstances, constitute a "cruel and unusual punishment."

Recall. A process for removing an elective official from office before the expiration of his term. This method is entirely distinct from impeachment, as the latter is applicable only in case of gross malfeasance or breach of trust. The recall is initiated by a petition signed by a designated percentage of the electorate. Within a certain period after the filing of the petition, a recall election is held, in which the official against whom the recall is directed is compelled to contest for the office with one or more candidates who have been nominated to replace him.

Recall of Judicial Decisions. A process whereby the decision of a court declaring any law unconstitutional may be submitted to a popular referendum initiated by petition, and, in the event that the popular vote is favorable to the law, the court decision is disregarded and the law is enforced notwithstanding. The incorporation of such a provision in the United States Constitution would be tantamount to providing a special method of amendment by a mere majority vote.

Colorado is the only state where the recall of judicial decisions has been adopted, with specific limitations.

Reciprocity. An arrangement between two or more countries whereby each admits the exports of the other duty free, or at rates more favorable than those applied to similar importations from other countries.

Reciprocity provisions were incorporated in the American Tariff act of 1890. The method of making them effective was to empower the president to impose higher duties on certain imported articles if the foreign countries from which they came should appear to have imposed, upon products of the United States, duties which might be deemed to be "reciprocally unjust or unreasonable." See *Tariff.*

Red Tape. An expression signifying official formality and delay. It owes its origin to the red tape usually employed in tying up public documents. The phrase is said to have been first used in this sense by Lord Minto in 1775.

Referendum of Laws. (See also *Direct Legislation.*) A constitutional procedure whereby a measure enacted by a legislature may be subjected to the judgment of the people before becoming effective.

The referendum has been closely associated with the initiative of laws; but the two procedures differ in character, the referendum being conservative in its nature, and the initiative, radical. The referendum, as well as the initiative, in its modern use, has been most highly developed and employed by Switzerland, and it was from this country that the influence came which lead to the adoption of these procedures for ordinary legislation in American states.

The referendum may be "optional" or "obligatory." An optional referendum occurs when a legislature provides that a measure shall not become effective until approved by the voters of the jurisdiction affected. In this form, the referendum was common in the United States even before 1898, the year when the popular referendum of statutory laws was adopted by South Dakota, and was applied particularly in such matters as county division and creation of bonded indebtedness.

Under the obligatory use of the referendum, a law is suspended, usually for 90 days, to provide an opportunity for the voters to scrutinize the measure and by petition of a certain number, to compel its reference to popular judgment at a general election. There may be exception of certain law, called "emergency measures," such measures usually requiring for passage an extraordinary majority of votes in the legislature.

Besides the "popular" referendum of laws, recent constitutions have provided other means whereby legislation may be submitted to the judgment of the voters. In Sweden, by a constitutional enactment, there is a referendum of laws if the government and the national legislature concur in its submission.

The popular referendum has made no progress in the Latin American republics, but in some of these countries, according to an old practice, acts of the government are referred to the councils of the municipalities for approval.

There appears to be a growing practice to except certain measures of the legislature from the operation of the referendum. The constitution of the state of Massachusetts, the last American state to adopt the referendum, exempts from its operation a large group of subjects.

In the United States, 39 states have adopted the referendum in some form.

The referendum is a popular safeguard against hasty or corrupt action of legislatures. In the United States its adoption was distinctly encouraged by distrust of state legislatures. This dissatisfaction, at an earlier period of constitutional amendment, took the form of placing in the state constitutions a wide variety of limitations upon the legislative power. The substitution of the referendum for this precaution would seem to recommend the repeal of many existing constitutional limitations which now unduly limit and embarrass the work of state legislatures. See *Referendum and Initiative of Laws.*

Representation. This is the device by which a citizen participates in government by proxy through an elected representative. Representation is direct when the citizen may vote for the candidate; it is indirect when he helps elect a body which in turn may vote for the candidate.

Direct representation in most countries is arranged so that electorates for each candidate have approximately the same population; hence the vote in each electorate is considered to have the same weight. It is to preserve this principle that Congress reapportions Congressional districts after the taking of a census. This does not apply to the Senate, to which each state elects two senators regardless of the state's population.

In 1964, the Supreme Court ruled that the clause of the Constitution guaranteeing equal protection of the law requires apportionment of both houses of bicameral state legislatures on a population basis. It held that the analogy of the United States Senate does not permit election of one state senator from each county regardless of population. This decision had the effect of ending a situation in which a disproportionate weight was given to rural districts as compared with urban districts.

Republic. A political community in which government is exercised, not by a monarch or hereditary rulers, but by and for all the people through their representatives. The term derives from the Latin words *res publica* ("commonwealth"), which was applied to Rome when the kings were expelled and elected officials were entrusted with the welfare of the state. Its use survived to describe Rome's government long after the emperors took over power from elected representatives.

The word has been applied to the aristocratic government of the medieval Italian cities. When the United States rid itself of the power of the British monarch, it followed the Roman example of calling itself a republic. Each non-monarchical government of France has so designated itself. The Latin American countries, after throwing off the yoke of Spain and Portugal, proclaimed themselves republics. The Communist governments of the 20th century without exception called themselves republics. The same is true of all the new states arising after World War II whenever they rid themselves of monarchical institutions.

It is obvious from the above that a republic is not necessarily a democracy, in which effective control is exercised by the majority of the people. Some political writers have tended to equate the two terms, and this fact has doubtless had an influence when newly independent countries chose political titles. Many of the Communist countries, in their excessive claims to popular sovereignty, call themselves republics.

A national monarch may be an impressive and useful symbol of strength, unity, and devotion, and, under such a guise, monarchy in all ages has appealed to popular admiration and has commanded intense devotion. The conception of a republic, in which the central personal leader is lacking or is transitory, undoubtedly calls for higher political development and is successful only by the display of higher popular political capacity.

Republicanism rejects not only kingship, but hereditary caste, class privileges, and hereditary distinctions. The price of this repudiation and of the refusal of these great rewards to political ambition is the frequent inability of republics to command and to keep in the public service the highest talent of the nation.

Residence. Legally, the place where one habitually resides or sleeps. Residence differs from "domicile" in that the latter term generally designates a more permanent attachment to a particular place, and includes the intention of remaining in that place indefinitely, while residence may connote a less permanent habitation. One may possess two residences, but he can have but one domicile, at any particular time. In the U.S., voting privileges and eligibility to office usually are limited to one place of residence.

Retroactive Legislation. A law made to apply to acts performed or to conditions existing prior to its enactment.

Revolution, Right of. The right of the people to revolt against the established government whenever that government becomes tyrannical or fails to afford public satisfaction.

This right was particularly asserted by such writers as Locke in England (1689), by Rousseau in France, and by Thomas Paine during the American Revolution. The Declaration of Independence, in which the ideas and even the language of Locke are used, is based on the assertion of this right.

The right of revolution is particularly opposed to the doctrine of legitimacy of royal rule or of "divine right."

Rider. A measure, the passage or executive approval of which seeming doubtful, is "tacked on" to a bill which is assured of passage, such as an appropriation bill, in order that the doubtful measure may "ride in" on the strength of the main bill.

This device is frequently effective in the federal government of the United States because of the inability of the president to veto a part of a bill, without invalidating the whole. In many states, however, the governor is now given the power to veto part of a bill and to ratify the remainder.

Right and Left. In legislative bodies of continental European countries generally it is the fixed habit of the conservative groups and parties to seat themselves on the right hand of the president or speaker, and of the liberal or radical elements to seat themselves on the left. The terms have thus come to be used as indicative of conservative and radical position on political matters; and, with the differentiation of positions within the group, the expressions "extreme right" or "extreme left," etc., have come into vogue. Thus the socialist party, which is always a left group, is divided into "right and left wings" according to the moderate or the revolutionary character of the group. The term "center" is used for middle parties or groups.

Roll Call. If one-fifth of the members present of either house of Congress wishes a record of the yeas and nays on a particular measure, a roll call vote showing how each member voted must be taken and published in the *Congressional Record*.

Roorbach or **Roorback.** A libel, or falsehood of a defamatory nature, used for political ends. The word had its origin in the presidential election of 1844, when a forgery of this nature was published to the detriment of James K. Polk. It was supposed to be an extract from the *Travels of Baron Roorbach*, but was later traced to G. W Featherstonhaugh's *Tour*, whence the malicious statement had been drawn by a newspaper writer, William Linn.

Sabotage (*să′bô′tăzh′*). The wanton destruction of the property of employers by laborers, or the practice of various means to slow down or stop production, to damage machinery, to discourage employers, and to make capitalism unproductive. As a resort for the enforcement of labor demands, it is a substitute for the strike. As stated by an advocate, "it means to strike but stay on the pay roll." It is particularly advocated by the revolutionary element among the working class as a means to end private ownership of productive capital.

The modern practice of sabotage arose among the radical French labor circles known as "syndicalists" (See *Syndicalism*.), and the term is derived from the supposed practice of a French workingman of throwing his wooden shoe, *sabot*, into moving machinery, thereby causing wanton damage.

Sabotage, or the destruction of private property, began to be advocated and practiced in the United States about 1910, particularly by members of the "Industrial Workers of the World." (See *I.W.W.*) It was advocated also during the first years of World War I by sympathizers with Germany, as a means of stopping the production of munitions furnished to the Allies. During World War I and immediately thereafter, legislation, called "syndicalist laws," was passed by many American states, severely punishing the practice of sabotage and even making it a crime to advocate such doctrines.

Satellite. A country which is under the political and economic domination of a stronger power.

Scratching. The practice, by American voters, of marking out from a party ballot one or more of the regularly nominated candidates. It is the opposite of voting a "straight ticket."

Sectionalism. The advocacy of measures or policies designed to promote the interests of a particular section rather than the good of the country at large.

Self-Determination. The principle or proposal that every distinct people or nation ought to have the right to determine the question of its independence, its form of government, and its political destiny. The phrase appears to have originated in the "Manifesto to the Proletariat" adopted by the conference of antinationalist socialists, held at Zimmerwald, Switzerland, in September 1915. This manifesto summoned the propertyless workers of Europe to a battle for peace "without annexations or war indemnities." Neither whole nations nor separate sections of nations were to be forcibly incorporated into states. "The right of self-determination of peoples," it declares, "must be the indestructible foundation of the creation of national relations." The Zimmerwald conference was attended by Lenin and by other Russian socialists, and among the early declarations of the Bolshevik revolutionary government in Russia was a pronouncement for "no annexations, no indemnities, self-determination of peoples."

Stated in a broad way, this declaration would seem to be equivalent to the principle of "government with the consent of the governed." On some such understanding, the principle of self-determination was championed by President Wilson in his proposals for world peace, preceding the entry of the U.S. into World War I, and particularly in his program presented to the Paris Peace Conference. In President Wilson's mind it was associated with a league to maintain the rights of peoples and with the probable reduction of certain great states into a number of minor sovereignties. In Paris the phras became a shibboleth leading to demands by numerous peoples for national independence. Its practical result was seen in the dissolution of the Austro-Hungarian Empire and in the emergence of new states, such as Poland, Estonia, Latvia, Lithuania, Czechoslovakia, and Ruthenia, and particularly in the declarations of independence of numerous small republics within the area of the former Russian Empire. The phrase also had great influence on political movements in Ireland, Egypt, Persia, the Ottoman Empire, and elsewhere.

DIFFICULTIES OF APPLICATION. In spite of the glamour attending a declaration seemingly so democratic, the principle is difficult of application and may even lead to political reaction. Much depends upon what constitutes a small nation or people with the presumptive right to separation and self-government. Peoples are not wholly independent, economically, politically, or morally, especially where they have previously been united under a common sovereignty. Dissociation inevitably carries with it the repudiation of certain obligations involving hardship, injustice, and, almost inevitably, economic injury to all parties. Particularly has it led to the setting up of new economic barriers, where freedom of trade and movement formerly existed, to the stimulation of animosities, and to a particularism dangerous to political unity and stability. Political progress, according to one well established ideal, is toward the uniting of the human family into larger political units, with a consequent suppression of national prejudices, rivalries, and retaliations, either political or economic. The multiplication of small states, in this point of view, must be regarded as a backward step. For the great nations, particularly when composed of peoples presenting local differences, united under some form of federal government or empire, the principle is a disintegrating one, dangerous to their existence. Strictly applied, the right of self-determination would have justified the separation of the Southern Confederacy from the American Union, or the division of any state on grounds satisfactory to the seceding portion.

Senate. The upper legislative chamber in the Congress of the United States and in each of the 50 states of the Union except Nebraska; also a similar body with the same name in a number of other modern governments.

The happy agreement in the American constitutional convention to give to all the states equal representation in the Senate made possible the acceptance of the Federal Constitution. This feature has been successfully copied in the "senates" of other federal governments, including Canada, Australia, South Africa, Mexico, and Argentina, in the Union of Soviet Socialist Republics (Russia), and in the Swiss "Council of States."

In a large number of other governments, American and European, which are not federal, the upper chamber of the national legislature has been given the name of Senate. The list includes France, where in 1875 a Senate was added to the National Assembly; Belgium under the constitution of 1831; and, more recently, Italy and Cuba.

It is the general practice, following the American provision, to set a higher age qualification for eligibility to a senate, to fix a longer term than for the lower house, and to renew the senate by degrees, thus giving it a continuous life and a slowly altering membership. The net effect is believed to be to increase the conservative character of the government.

Senatorial Courtesy. A custom whereby the president, in making nominations to Federal offices, is expected to consult the United States senators from the state in which the vacancies exist before submitting nominations to the Senate for confirmation. Where the senators are of a different political party from the president, the custom is not applicable.

Separation of Powers. A principle of government which sharply separates the executive, legislative, and judicial branches of the government, confining each to its special sphere and making each independent of the other two.

The principle was enunciated by the French political writer Montesquieu in his *Spirit of the Laws*, and was, actually, a misapprehension of the British constitution as it existed in the 18th century. To the supposed separation of powers and the "checks" upon arbitrary action which it secured, Montesquieu attributed the security of English freedom.

The theory of Montesquieu was much regarded by the founders of independent government in America and by them the separation of powers was proclaimed as an indispensable element of free government. Many state constitutions endeavor specifically to apply it and to make it mandatory. The constitution of the state of Massachusetts, of 1780, declares: "In the government of this commonwealth the legislative department shall never exercise the executive and judicial powers or either of them; the executive shall never exercise the legislative and judicial powers or either of them; the judicial shall never exercise the legislative and executive powers or either of them, to the end that it may be a government of laws and not of men."

As a matter of fact, the precise principle never existed in England and has not been truly realized in the United States. The president and the state governors participate actively in legislative programs and exercise a veto over laws. Courts have been intrusted with numerous executive functions, and, by judicial interpretation, they expand or nullify legislation. In the commission type of government, the theory is entirely abandoned.

Serfdom. A status of personal servitude whereby the peasant is deemed bound to the soil upon which he is born, and is required to perform certain services and to give to his lord a certain proportion of the yield of the land. On the other hand, the peasant may legally be entitled to the protection of his lord and to certain assistance, and may have rights to his holding of which he may not arbitrarily be dispossessed.

Serfdom is closely connected with the institution of feudalism. It existed generally on the continent of Europe until the close of the 18th century. The French Revolution suppressed it in France and in other countries to which the Revolution extended. In Prussia it was ended by the edict of Stein in 1807. In Russia it continued until the emancipation of the serfs by the czar Alexander II in 1861. Until the reform of the landholding system in 1871, Japan had a feudal form of society, in which the status of the tiller of the soil resembled European serfdom. Its last traces in England disappeared in the reign of Queen Elizabeth.

Single Tax. A principle of taxation, advocated by Henry George in his work *Progress and Poverty*, published in 1879, whereby all increase in the value of land would be appropriated by the state as a substitute for other taxes. The principle rests upon the theory that the appreciation of value of unimproved land is an "unearned increment" due to the growth of society itself, and not to the exertions or investments of the owner. Thus the owner justly may be deprived of this increased value by land taxation sufficiently heavy to absorb it.

The theory has attracted less attention in the United States than in Great Britain, where vast private estates held in an unimproved condition invite the application of the doctrine. It has been sparingly applied in certain cities of the United States and Canada.

Smuggling. Illicit importing of goods into a country without submitting them to the customs authorities or paying legal import duties.

Social Contract. The theory that the state originates in a contract between individuals, whereby the freedom and the equality of the "state of nature" are surrendered for the advantages of state protection and authority.

The theory fills a large place in the history of political philosophy, particularly in the writings of Hobbes, Locke, and Rousseau. Thomas Jefferson and many of the political thinkers of the time of the American and French revolutions rested their governmental doctrines upon this theory of the origin of the state, and from it deduced their justification of the right of revolution, or of dissolving the social compact.

As a historical explanation of the origin of political society, the social contract theory is rejected by modern students of government.

Socialism. A social program whereby private ownership of land and of all other "productive capital" would be extinguished in favor of ownership by the state.

The present-day orthodox theory of socialism is that expounded by Karl Marx, particularly in his work *Capital*, published in 1872, although the essential ideas were expressed in the *Communist Manifesto* issued in 1848 by Marx and Engels.

The distinctive feature of Marxian Socialism is the doctrine that the socialist state will arise inevitably out of the evolution of modern industrialism. Marx predicted a progressive and inescapable concentration of the means of production in the hands of the few, until there would remain but a few capitalists, or bourgeois, on the one side and the rest of the community of propertyless workers, or proletariat, on the other. The so-called "middle class" would entirely disappear. When this stage had completely evolved, modern industrialism would be "mature," and revolution, either peaceful or bloody, would be inevitable. The masses would take from the capitalists control of the means of production and would operate them in the interest of the community. The socialist state would arrive.

ECONOMIC CRISES. The chief impetus toward the transition is held to be economic crises, or depressions. Their recurrence is represented as inevitable under capitalism. From the Socialist point of view, these crises serve the double purpose of speeding up the concentration of "productive capital" in the hands of the few and creating active discontent in the involuntary idle. These results are expected to lead to a demand that society should plan its production so as to use the services of all who wish to work.

Half a century after the death of Karl Marx, Socialism passed from the realm of political theory to a testing laboratory, so to speak. That is to say, it was adopted by Russia. Its evolution there did not follow the sequence predicted by Marx, since capitalism was much less advanced there than in many other countries.

SOCIALISM AND THE NATION. Orthodox socialism repudiates national allegiance in favor of loyalty to the "proletariat of all lands." It views the modern state as the buttress of capitalism and as the means for "imperialistic aggressions" in favor of the capitalist class. In World War I, while the socialist parties generally supported the governments of their respective countries, an extreme international wing in each belligerent state repudiated the war aims of its nation and even sought its defeat or overthrow. A so-called "Third International," with headquarters at Moscow, directs the policy of those working in separate nations for the realization of Socialist aims.

To Marx is due also an "economic interpretation of history" in which all human activity and social development are held to be controlled by economic motives and causes.

Social Legislation. Under this term is embraced a wide variety of measures designed to protect terms of employment and to improve the general well-being. Modern legislation of this character followed the rise of the factory system in England and in Continental Europe and the industrial inventions which revolutionized industry in shops, mines, and transportation.

LEGISLATION IN ENGLAND. During the first decades of the 18th century, there prevailed a doctrine of *laissez faire*, or complete abstention of government from interference in the conditions of employment and in the relations between employer and laborer. Such interference was held to be an unwarranted trespass upon the freedom of employment and of labor and an unwise disturbance of the law of supply and demand. Factory and mining conditions, however, became so deplorable as to lead, in 1802, to the beginnings of English social legislation, the first law, regulating the labor of "bound" children. Such legislation was at first confined to the protection of the health, safety, and morals of children and women. In 1842, a working day in excess of 10 hours for women and children was prohibited. The English example was followed in many other industrial countries toward the end of the 19th century, and the program was vastly expanded in the 20th century.

LEGISLATION IN AMERICA. In the United States, laws have been passed for the protection of the laborer from the following hazards of employment: dangerous gases, acids, and dusts, poisonous and nonpoisonous; harmful bacteria and micro-organisms; compressed or rarefied atmospheres; improper lighting; extremes of temperature and of humidity; and excessive physical or mental strain. Many laws have been designed to prevent accidents both to employees and to the public, and to require the installation of provisions for safety in dangerous employments, such as mining. Child labor is limited or prohibited in most states. Federal laws prohibiting employment of children having been ruled invalid by the Supreme Court, a constitutional amendment was submitted to the states in 1924 which would empower Congress to regulate or prohibit the employment of persons under 18 years of age. It was not ratified, but the situation was saved when the Supreme Court held that the child labor restrictions in the Fair Labor Standards Act of 1938 were constitutional.

OLD AGE PENSIONS. These are of two kinds—aid for the needy aged and annuities based on the employment history of the individual. The first kind is a contribution to be matched by states and paid on a non-discriminatory basis to indigent persons over 65 years old. These are the assistance grants paid out of federal and state appropriations and are distinct from the Social Security insurance programs financed by taxes. (*See Social Security.*)

UNEMPLOYMENT COMPENSATION. The Federal government does not directly administer this program. Its part is to collect a pay roll tax and to hand the proceeds, less administrative expenses, over to States for carrying out their own programs provided these programs meet the standards laid down in the Federal law as interpreted by a social security board. Those who have been employed for a minimum period and then lose their jobs are entitled to unemployment compensation for a limited number of weeks. Details differ from state to state. Funds are raised by an impost on pay rolls of employers.

Provision is made also for Federal contribution to states on a matching basis for aid to dependent children and for child welfare. This includes support for needy mothers with children to support. Each state program must be mandatory and uniform in all districts as a condition of receiving Federal contributions.

THE MINIMUM WAGE. Legislation has also been passed establishing the "minimum wage" that may legally be paid in certain industries. The theory of a minimum wage is that it corresponds to the lowest compensation which will afford a livelihood that is not destructive to health and to self-respect.

Social Security. Legislation to insure workers against the hazards of industrial life was first enacted by Germany, a law of 1883 providing for sick benefits. Such benefits have been widened in many countries to include compulsory accident insurance, unemployment compensation, aid for dependent children and invalids, and old age pensions.

A landmark in social legislation in the United States was the enactment, August 14, 1935, of a comprehensive Social Security law providing for old age pensions, unemployment insurance, and aid for dependent children and the blind. Under this act, a wage earner contributes part of his or her earnings in the form of a tax (5.85 per cent or more, according to schedule), which is matched by an equivalent payment made by the employer. In return the worker is entitled to receive upon retirement at age 65 or total disability a monthly benefit based on his average earnings over a given period. Until he reaches age 72, a retired person receiving Social Security benefit is allowed to supplement his income by earnings up to $2400, or slightly more with

some benefits withheld. After he passes age 72, no limit is placed on his supplementary earnings.

From time to time following the passage of the original Social Security Act, Congress has broadened its coverage to include different classes of employed persons like farm owners and farm hands, household workers, and self-employed persons such as professional people engaged in different lines of activity. Men and women are permitted to retire at 62 with reduced benefits. The law has operated under the Department of Health, Education and Welfare.

MEDICARE. This is a program of health insurance for persons over 65 years of age. As adopted in 1965, it consists of hospital insurance and medical insurance. Hospital insurance is financed entirely from social security taxes. It pays most of the cost of hospital service. Medical insurance is voluntary and is financed half from social security taxes and half by a fee withheld from recipients of federal old age pensions.

Sovereignty. The ultimate or supreme political authority in the state. In a democracy, sovereignty is vested in the people; in an absolute despotism, it is in the monarch.

Soviet (*sō'vyĕt'*). Russian term for a council or deliberative body; used particularly with reference to the village, city, county, and provincial councils, composed of deputies elected by the workmen, soldiers, and peasants, which form the basis of the Russian Soviet government and constitute the governing bodies of the local districts. See *Russia.*

Speaker of the House. The presiding officer of the U. S. House of Representatives elected from its own membership. The Speaker may vote but generally does so only to break a tie. He is first in line after the Vice President in order of succession to the presidency.

Sphere of Influence. A "sphere of influence" or a "sphere of interest" is a region, frequently the territory of another recognized state, within which some foreign power claims a position of preponderant or "special interest." The conception arose in the "partition of Africa" by the European states, which followed rapidly after 1884. In these settlements, which were partly arranged at the Berlin Conference of 1884-85, the entire seaboard of Africa, not already possessed, was distributed as colonial possessions or protectorates among the European states, particularly Great Britain, France, Belgium, and Germany. In addition, the interiors or "hinterland" covered by the coastal possessions were declared to be "within the sphere of influence" of these particular states. The agreement aimed to establish rights of subsequent penetration and development over areas of Africa which the colonizing powers were not at the moment prepared to occupy effectively.

Subsequently the conception was applied to China, where vast areas of that country were more or less definitely accorded by one European power to another as a sphere in which economic and political preference was recognized. The foreign country claiming a sphere in China endeavored to maintain a claim of exclusive or preferential opportunity in railroad building, in mineral development, and even in financial and political affairs. Such claims disappeared everywhere after World War II.

Splinter Group. A group which has seceded from a larger parent political organization.

Stampede. A break in the balloting at a nominating convention, when the great majority of the delegates desert the candidates whom they have hitherto supported, and rush to the support of the candidate who appears likely to be the nominee.

State, The. The word "state" is popularly used to denote a country, such as France. It is used also, both popularly and legally, to designate the constitutent parts of the United States, as, the state of Ohio. In this latter sense, the word is applied to the parts of the commonwealth of Australia, as, the state of Queensland.

As used in political science, the term "state" implies a body of people organized for government within a definite territory, and possessing a degree of independent authority within that area. Theoretically, the state is the corporate being or legal person which, under the above conditions, is acknowledged as the supreme source of law. The distinguishing attributes of such a state are sovereignty with respect to its own affairs and independence with respect to other states. The political state is thus to be distinguished from the territory over which it is sovereign and from the government through which it operates. Political scientists generally agree that the state is constituted by the will of the people who share in the making of laws and the choosing of officials.

Modern political thought recognizes that both sovereignty and independence are never actually absolute, but always relative, even in the greatest states. Further it is conceded that a sovereign state may delegate certain functions without impairing its sovereignty. These two considerations justify the application of the word "state" to the constituent units of a larger state, where, as in Australia and in the United States, a federal form of government exists. By virtue of the constitutions of these countries, the individual commonwealths share in the sovereignty of the general state while retaining, in the spheres of their peculiar interests, a measure of sovereignty.

State Judiciary. In the United States, each state maintains its own judiciary, comprising courts of merely local jurisdiction in counties and municipalities and courts of various higher grades. Each state system includes courts of general civil and criminal jurisdiction as well as special tribunals for certain types of cases. Some of the courts exercise both judicial and large administrative functions, the practice varying rather widely in different states.

The law administered in a state court is, in general, that of the state statutes, the Federal statutes, and the English common law adapted to American conditions. In Louisiana, the civil law is based upon French and Spanish precedent. A state court is bound by the Federal Constitution and by the constitution of its particular state. Some judges and justices are appointed, but the general state practice is to elect judges. In state courts of general jurisdiction a jury is employed, a unanimous verdict being usually necessary.

The following summary represents, in general, the organization of the state judicial systems:

1. *The lowest grade of courts,*—(1) the justice's court, held by a justice of the peace, who may be a town, township, or county officer; (2) municipal courts (under various names) in towns and cities, presided over by judges or magistrates, who are officers of the municipality; (3) the county court, held by a judge who is, in some states, a county official and, in others, a state officer.

2. *The intermediate grade of tribunals,*—known variously as district, superior, and circuit courts. The judges of these courts are state officers, elected or appointed, either for the entire state or for particular districts. Under whatever name, these are the principal trial courts of the state. In a few states, another court, sometimes called "supreme court," either takes the place of the circuit court or is intermediate between that court and the highest tribunal of the state.

3. *The highest tribunal, or court of last resort.*—In most of the states, this is called the supreme court; in others, it is termed court of appeals, court of errors, or court of errors and appeals. The opinions rendered by this court are held to be of binding authority in the lower courts of the state.

SPECIAL CLASSES OF COURTS. (1) *Court of Probate.*—Generally, this name is applied to the court having charge of the probate of wills, the administration of estates, and the supervision of orphans. In New York and New Jersey, it is called the surrogate's court. In Georgia, the old ecclesiastical term "ordinary" is applied to the judge of probate. In Pennsylvania, Delaware, and Maryland, the name "orphans' court" is used.

(2) *Court of Common Pleas.*—Originally, in England the term "common pleas" applied to cases arising between subjects, as distinguished from those to which the crown was a party. In the United States, the name has been retained in New Jersey, Pennsylvania, Delaware, Ohio, Missouri, and Kentucky for courts whose jurisdiction is limited to a district made up of one or more counties.

(3) *Court of Quarter Sessions.*—This name arose originally from the quarterly sessions held by English justices of the peace. In Pennsylvania, a court under this title has some important administrative functions.

(4) *Juvenile Courts.*—These are sometimes called children's courts. Their jurisdiction includes cases of dependent, neglected, and delinquent children. Generally, the upper age limit is 16 years, although in some states it is 18 or even 21 years. These courts endeavor to correct the conditions responsible for a child's wrongdoing rather than merely to determine punishment for an offense.

State Rights. The field of independent action enjoyed by states in the American Union. The discussion of the exact character and scope of these rights has played a great rôle in the constitutional history of the United States. The framers of American government were divided between those who sought a strong national government and those who jealously defended state rights. Among the most extreme of state claims, advocated after the formation of the Union, were the doctrine of "nullification," or the right of a state to nullify national legislation which it might judge inconsistent with the Constitution, and the doctrine of "secession," or the right of a state to withdraw at will from the Union. These doctrines were lost by the issue of the Civil War.

GROWTH OF FEDERAL POWER. There has been a natural and almost inevitable tendency for the Federal power to grow. This growth has been contributed to by decisions of the supreme court of the United States, which during long and important periods of its history was disposed to interpret the Constitution in favor of Federal jurisdiction. But the main factor operating to enhance the power and importance of the national government has been the extraor-

dinary integration of the American people as a nation, the predominance of their national loyalty and interest over state and local feeling, and the binding together of all sections of the country by economic attachments.

This economic unity, which was happily provided for by the Constitution when it assured freedom of trade between the states, has made necessary an ever-increasing authority of the Federal government over economic affairs. This is particularly evident in its control of interstate commerce, which has been defined by the Supreme Court to include intrastate action merely affecting commerce in almost any degree.

The 14th amendment extended the authority of the national government to the protection of life, liberty, and property, while the 15th amendment, enfranchising the colored race, and the 19th amendment, guaranteeing political rights to women, largely removed from the decision of the states the determination of the rights and privileges of citizenship. The 16th amendment, conferring upon Congress the right to levy taxes upon incomes, diverted a source of public revenue of increasing interest to state taxation. In recent years, Congress has passed a number of appropriations providing for the distribution of sums of money among the states in aid of education, agriculture, and other projects, provided additional appropriations are made by the states and a national policy is followed in their expenditure. These sums of money, appropriated out of the national treasury for objects belonging exclusively to state government, have had an undoubted tendency to bring further under Federal control matters constitutionally reserved to the state.

PRESENT STATUS. The continuous growth of the power, service, and repute of the national government, while highly gratifying from many standpoints, has undoubtedly an unfortunate effect upon the vitality and activity of state governments, and prejudices popular interest in their conduct. Thus the question of state rights emerges anew in American politics, and it is now representative, not of the aims of those who desire to deny or to reduce the necessary powers of the Federal government, but rather of the purpose of those who feel the necessity of preserving an actual distinction between the scope of the national government and the functions which properly and necessarily, under a federal system, are reserved for state governments. Interest in state rights in this sense is no longer represented by party lines. While the Democratic party originally was a strong "state rights" party, since the Civil War, Democratic presidents, hardly less than Republican, have by their actions augmented the national control. And some of the American statesmen who are today most sensitive to the need of preserving state rights are members of the Republican party.

Statute of Limitations. A law which prescribes a definite limit of time within which a legal right or remedy must be prosecuted by action in the courts, or thereafter be barred. Such laws are intended to protect the individual against stale demands, when, from lapse of time, death of witnesses, failure of memory, or other causes, the true situation may be obscured.

The periods prescribed by statutes of limitations vary in the different states, and differ in the same state for different kinds of claims. Under the laws of most states, rights in regard to property must be asserted within twenty years or be barred by the continuous "adverse occupation" of another.

Steam Roller. A term descriptive of the manner in which the faction in control of a political convention or legislative body may force through a slate or program previously determined upon. The use of the "steam roller" at the Republican convention of 1912, through the control of the national committee, gave the term and the procedure wide publicity.

Steering Committee. An informal committee in each house of Congress, dominated by the leading members of the majority party in the body, which determines the order in which business shall be taken up by the house. In the House of Representatives, the steering committee is practically synonymous with the committee on rules, which is vested with the power of reporting a special rule placing any important measure ahead of ordinary business.

Still Hunt. A secret campaign on behalf of or against a candidate for office. The phrase is used also to designate secret propaganda against a particular candidate.

Straight Ticket. See *Scratching.*

Straw Vote. An informal, unofficial canvass of political votes, taken prior to a regular election, for the purpose of determining the direction of political sentiment.

Syndicalism (*sĭn'dĭ-kăl-ĭz'm*). A labor organization originating in France which has for its aim the destruction of the state and the organization of society by trade-unions ("syndicats"). The organization upon which syndicalists depended for the accomplishment of their aims was the

"General Confederation of Labor" (*Confédération Générale du Travail*, commonly known as the "C. G. T."), founded in 1895 and attaining a final form of organization in 1902. This was a national association of revolutionary labor unions.

THE SYNDICALIST PROGRAM. Syndicalism differs from socialism and the extreme form of socialism, or bolshevism, in that it entirely repudiates the state. In this respect it approaches anarchism. Syndicalism, however, adopts as a central principle the distinctive socialist doctrine of the "class war." It has developed certain tactics and policies which have been adopted also by bolshevism. These tactics completely repudiate political activity or "parliamentary action" and substitute for them methods of industrial warfare, commonly called in America "direct action." These include the boycott, sabotage, and the "general strike." By the general strike is meant such an organization of industrial labor, embracing all crafts and industries, and so general and synchronous a cessation of labor therein as to completely paralyze industrial production and the supply to communities of the necessities of life. By so general a strike, syndicalists aim to throw existing society into chaos, to overthrow the state, and to gain social power for the federation of industrial workers.

Syndicalism came into prominence in the great French railway strike of 1910, which was broken by the action of the French minister Briand, who arrested the strike committee, mobilized the army reserves, including strikers, and replaced striking workingmen by soldiers under military discipline.

As stated above, syndicalism differs fundamentally from socialism and communism, with which it is frequently confused, by the fact that these latter social programs have in mind the realization of a "great state" devoted not only to political objects, but also to owning and operating all productive capital, controlling the activities of all individuals, and thereby becoming the common employer.

INFLUENCE OF SYNDICALISM. World War I and the repressive action of the French government upon all revolutionary movements shattered French syndicalism, and, since the rise of bolshevism in Russia, revolutionary elements have turned toward the program of this socialist party rather than toward the program of syndicalism. The influence of its theory, however, is traceable in other movements than the above, and particularly in "guild socialism," which, like syndicalism, views with alarm that exaggeration of the state which pure socialism would produce, and proposes to organize society in a decentralized form around industrial groups or "guilds."

Tariff. The word is used in America in two senses: (1) It is used to describe any schedule of charges, but particularly rates for the shipment of goods by public-service corporations, or other services afforded the public. Such charges at the present day are usually controlled by the government, either through the interstate commerce commission or by public utility commissions in the states. (2) Tariff is used to designate the scale of customs duties imposed upon foreign products entering home territory. It is in this second sense that the term "the tariff" is used politically in the United States.

Broadly speaking, a tariff is devised either "for revenue only" or "for the protection of home industry." As a means of raising revenue, tariffs have been employed by nearly all governments. This form of taxation has the advantage of being "indirect." It falls upon the people in higher prices paid for such articles as they purchase and thus avoids the difficulty and the irritation arising from the collection of "direct taxes"; it is relatively easy of administration, being collected at the frontiers at certain designated points where customhouses are established; and, in the case of a highly industrial or commercial people, it may be productive of a very great revenue.

PROTECTION. A "protective tariff" rests upon different principles. It is devised not solely nor mainly for revenue, but rather as a means of building up national manufactures or other forms of production in the face of foreign competition which, if given free entry, would endanger the native industry. It is upon this basis that American tariffs have been largely framed. The effect of such tariffs is undoubtedly to bring profit to certain interests and to certain sections of the country at the cost of the purchasing public generally. Defenders of the protective system, however, urge the desirability of developing all reasonably profitable industries and forms of products as a means of bringing a nation to its highest point of economic development and of making it self-sufficient, particularly in the event of war and blockade.

RECIPROCAL TRADE AGREEMENTS. These are pacts, authorized by Congress in 1934, between the United States and other nations for the reciprocal lowering of tariffs. The policy is based on the belief that protective tariffs adopted by many nations against one another's goods have the effect of choking trade and production to the disadvantage of all. These agreements extend to other nations the advantages given each nation signing a pact, but with the proviso that these other nations may be barred from the benefits if they refuse to enter into similar agreements after a reasonable time or if they discriminate against American products. The adoption of this policy in America came at a time when trade barriers had been raised to unprecedented heights and when commerce and industry throughout most of the world had dropped to less than half their volume of five years earlier.

FREE TRADE. Opponents of protection, or "free traders," take the broad view that the modern world is, or should be, organized internationally for industrial production. Under such a system each country would produce mainly those things which, because of its resources or its situation, it can produce most cheaply, and would purchase elsewhere, in the cheapest markets of the world, other necessities and luxuries of life. Thereby, it is argued, we should avoid the waste through excessive cost to the consumer, occasioned by an artificially stimulated domestic production of goods that can be acquired abroad more cheaply.

Taxation. Taxes are general compulsory contributions of wealth, levied upon natural persons or upon corporations, to defray the expenses of government. They are inseparable from all governments and are a part of the price paid for protection and for the advantage of society. While taxes are general in the sense that they affect all persons and all classes of society, there have been and are many exceptions to their universal payment. These take the form of "exemptions." In European feudal society, the nobility, the clergy, and their properties were untaxed. Even in democratic countries, like the United States, it is usual to exempt from the payment of certain direct taxes persons possessing small incomes or small properties. Ex-soldiers or veterans of certain wars are frequently granted tax exemptions. Taxation may take the form of money payments or of personal services, such as labor on roads or public works.

KINDS OF TAXES. Taxes may be classified as "direct" and "indirect." The former embrace contributions of money or service directly furnished by those upon whom the tax is imposed. Indirect taxes take the forms of customs duties, "excises," or taxes on articles of luxury or common use, and government monopolies, where the state reserves the exclusive sale of a product at a price advantageous to the public revenue. The most common and lucrative form of direct tax is the property tax, which may be levied upon land or "real property" or upon movables or "personal property."

Other forms of indirect imposts are the sales tax and the payroll tax. The most widely used form of the sales tax in America is that imposed on gasoline. The principal argument advanced against sales taxes is that they fall with disproportionate weight on those least able to bear them. The payroll tax has been used to pay the costs of social security legislation, on the ground that insurance against uncertainty in employment is properly accounted as one of the costs of doing business.

Two forms of taxation which have become extremely important are "inheritance taxes," or "death dues," and "income taxes." Under the former tax, the state appropriates a certain proportion of the estate of a deceased person before the balance is distributed among his heirs. In the second form of taxation, the state regularly collects a proportion of the gross or the net income of a person or of a corporation. Not only are these last two types of taxes, in certain cases, made to yield large revenues, but they have a definite social effect in limiting the accumulation of private fortunes and their succession. Usually the amount appropriated by the government increases rapidly with the size of the fortune or income.

INCOME TAX IN AMERICA. In 1894, the Congress of the United States imposed a federal income tax, which was declared unconstitutional by the Supreme Court in 1895. This decision led to the adoption of the 16th Amendment, empowering Congress to lay and to collect taxes on income without apportionment among the several states. The federal income tax became an immensely valuable resource to the government. The states also have made use of this source of income.

As applied to corporations, the income tax has been used as an instrument of governmental policy. By making the rate higher for larger incomes, an advantage is given to smaller corporations. Similarly, by assessing a higher rate when larger proportions of earning are retained instead of being distributed in profits, money is forced out to individuals where, if the individuals are wealthy, it may be taxed at the very high rates imposed on large personal incomes. This device is aimed against concentration of wealth.

Tax Dodging. The practice of avoiding payment of taxes. A means frequently employed by people of wealth is that of acquiring a nominal or actual residence in a small town or village where taxes are light, or in another state, in order to avoid the heavy personal property taxes which they would bear if legal residents of the city in which their interests are actually centered.

Tenure of Office Act. The United States Constitution, while making the president the general appointive authority to positions in the federal service, is silent upon the method of removing such officers. In 1789, during the session of the first Congress, the question of whether the president could remove such officers without the consent of the Senate was raised, and at that time, after some discussion, it was recognized that the power of removal rested in the president.

In 1867, however, Congress passed, over the president's veto, an act known as the "Tenure of Office act," which aimed to prevent the president from removing federal officials without the consent of the Senate. President Johnson disregarded this law, holding it to be unconstitutional, and his conduct was the basis for charges of impeachment.

In 1869, the act was in part repealed, and the remaining provisions of the act were repealed in 1887. A decision by the Supreme Court in 1926 supported the president's right to remove appointees of executive departments when the term of appointment is not fixed by law. Removal of a member of an independent agency, however, appointed for a definite number of years was ruled beyond the president's authority by a decision in 1934.

Theocracy (thē-ŏk′ra-sĭ). A form of government in which God is viewed as the supreme civil ruler, and in which government is conducted by a priesthood claiming the representation of Deity and enforcing laws supposed to be divinely inspired.

Third Parties. The American system of government, as well as the British, is considered to function properly only where two great parties divide the political field and contend for the possession of the government. So-called "third" parties have often been formed, but in the United States they have had brief existence. They have from time to time served the purpose of organizing support for new or neglected policies to the point where they have been adopted by either or both of the major parties. The Prohibition party, the Populist party, and the Progressive party are examples of this result.

Third Term. Before the adoption of the 22d Amendment to the United States Constitution in 1951, there was no limitation to the number of terms a president could serve. The example set by Washington, who refused to consider a third term, established a precedent which was followed until it was shattered by President Franklin D. Roosevelt, who was elected to a third term in 1940, and to a fourth term in 1944.

In 1880, a strong movement within the Republican party sought the nomination of Grant for a third term, but was unsuccessful. Again, in 1912, the question of the third term arose when Theodore Roosevelt sought nomination after having occupied the presidency 7½ years. In this case the third term would have been separated from previous executive position by an interval of four years. This fact, in many minds, removed possibilities of danger.

Other nations which have adopted the institution of the presidency have in some cases limited eligibility to a single term. In Mexico, where the right to indefinite re-election was secured by President Diaz, the principle of "no re-election" has been made constitutional both for national and for state executives.

Three-Mile Limit. By general recognition, it has become a principle of international law that the territorial sovereignty of a nation bordering on the high seas is not limited to its shores at low tide, but extends out into the seas a distance of three marine miles. This understanding among nations permits a country to enforce its domestic laws within this limit and has proved of much practical value. The distance of three miles was settled upon at a time when this was regarded as the extreme possible range of guns. Owing to the difficulty experienced by the United States in preventing the landing of contraband liquor from the sea, the British government consented to an exercise of American jurisdiction over British shipping up to a distance of twelve miles from the coast. Although the three-mile limit is still being used in parts of the world, in recent years numerous nations, including the United States, have adopted a 200-mile limit.

Town Meeting. An assemblage of all of the voters or qualified inhabitants of a town, held annually for the purpose of electing administrative officials of the town and of passing upon all important legislative matters.

The town meeting, since colonial times, has been the chief organ of local government in New England. It is an example of direct popular government in its simplest form. When the community, however, reaches the proportions of a city, some form of representative government becomes essential, and many towns in New England have abandoned the town form of government.

Treason. The Constitution of the United States provides: "Treason against the United States shall consist only in levying war against them, or in adherence to their enemies, giving them aid and comfort. No person shall be convicted of treason unless on the testimony of two witnesses to the same overt act or on confession in open court. The Congress shall have power to declare the punishment of treason, but no attainder of treason shall work corruption of blood or forfeiture except during the life of the person attainted." (Art. III, Sec. 3).

The purpose of these provisions was to provide a clear definition of this crime in place of the broad and elastic interpretation given to it by English courts and to limit punishment to the actual offender.

Treason may be committed against any state of the Union as well as against the United States. The limitations given above are not limitations upon the states, but most state constitutions contain similar provisions.

Treaty-Making Power. This power is quite universally recognized as an executive function. The president of the United States is vested with the power "by and with the advice and consent of the Senate to make treaties, provided two-thirds of the senators present concur." Negotiations leading to the making of a treaty are carried on exclusively by the president, usually acting through the State Department. Congress has invariably refused to receive foreign missions or representatives and has not even a constitutional right of being informed of the progress of negotiations. As a means of assuring the Senate's ratification, it is the preferable practice for the president to appoint members of the Senate upon commissions of negotiation, particularly peace negotiations.

Trial by Jury. The United States Constitution, 6th Amendment, provides: "In all criminal prosecutions the accused shall enjoy the right to a speedy and public trial by an impartial jury of the state and district wherein the crime shall have been committed." The 7th Amendment provides: "In suits of common law, where the value in controversy shall exceed twenty dollars, the right of trial by jury shall be preserved, and no fact tried by a jury shall be otherwise re-examined in any court of the United States than according to the rules of the common law." Likewise in all the state constitutions, there are provisions which insure trial by jury to those accused of crime and to litigants in civil actions, the right being generally limited to those cases in which trial by jury was assured at the time of the adoption of the particular constitution.

Trial by jury, unless otherwise constitutionally provided, means trial by a jury of twelve persons of the jurisdiction in which the case is tried, who are impartial and who have been chosen by impartial officials, and who are sworn to render a verdict according to the evidence and the law.

An essential feature of "trial by jury" is that the jury shall proceed under the guidance and instructions of the court, and that only questions of fact upon which there can be a reasonable difference of opinion shall be submitted to the jury. It is the duty of the presiding judge to "instruct the jury" as to its verdict. He may even take the case out of the jury's hands if the situation so demands.

Alongside the common law courts of England, which decided criminal and civil controversies with the aid of a jury, there grew up a system of "equity" jurisprudence, under which cases were determined by the chancellor as the representative of the king. In this field of equity jurisprudence, the right to trial by jury did not exist at the time of the adoption of the United States Constitution and the early state constitutions, and therefore is not guaranteed by them.

Civil and criminal cases of minor importance, by custom, are tried before justices with summary power, and in these cases the right of trial by jury does not exist unless expressly provided by law.

A grand jury is a body of 12 to 23 members which, in some jurisdictions must bring in a formal indictment before certain types of cases can be tried. It may act on information of prosecutor, witnesses, or its own members.

Ultra Vires (ŭl′tra vī′rez). A Latin phrase meaning "beyond powers." It is used of an act beyond the authority vested in a public or private corporation exercising functions limited by law or charter.

Unicameral System. See *Bicameral System.*

Unit Rule. A practice followed at nominating conventions which permits the majority of a state delegation to decide how the delegates shall vote as a unit.

Unwritten Law. General principles of justice, which, together with the customary rules of law and of procedure of courts in medieval England, formed the basis of the unwritten or "common law" of England and of those countries that have inherited their law from England. The term is used in contrast to the "written" or statute law passed by the legal legislative authority. The unwritten law exists in a vast and ever growing body of judicial decisions in which its principles are expounded and applied by courts.

In a popular and sensational sense, "unwritten law" is used to express a moral justification for illegal acts, like murder under excessive provocation. This so-called "unwritten law" is entirely without legal foundation, but juries in the United States have been influenced by its appeal to find for the accused in direct disregard of positive law.

Veto. Executive refusal to approve an action, particularly a legislative enactment. The word "veto" comes from the Roman practice of conferring the same power upon two magistrates, as on the consuls, either of whom by pronouncing the word *veto*, "I forbid," could negative the action of the other.

In the constitutional development of Europe, a veto power was assumed to reside in the king, particularly as against acts of Parliament. As late as the Stuart kings of England, the monarch retained and frequently exercised the power of refusing assent to acts of Parliament, and royal assent is still nominally given. Every statute takes the form of an act of the king, but the assumption of the king's powers by ministers and the responsibility of these ministers to the House of Commons have made the royal veto an anachronism. The last employment of the royal dissent was by Queen Anne in 1707. Today, a British monarch's refusal to subscribe to a statute of Parliament would be an act of revolution.

VETO POWER. The American colonists were thoroughly familiar with the veto power, as this right was exercised constantly in the name of the king by their colonial governors. It was thus adopted by them in the Constitution of the United States as a presidential power. In bestowing it upon the president, the framers of the Constitution intended to set up another of those "checks and balances" which the political theory of the time recommended. It was also felt that a president's veto was needed to protect the executive department against usurpation by the legislative. The veto, however, was not made absolute; it can be overridden by a two-thirds vote of each house of Congress.

In the early decades of the American republic, the veto power was sparingly employed by the president. It was very boldly used, however, by President Jackson, and its exercise in recent decades has become common. President Cleveland used it unsparingly to defeat private bills. The disposition today is to associate the president with congressional legislation and to hold him, as well as Congress, responsible for all legislation which he may not disapprove.

The veto power has also been finally conferred upon every state governor except in North Carolina, and, in a number of states, it may extend to items of a bill and particularly to items in an appropriation bill.

In American city charters which bestow legislative power upon a council and executive power upon a mayor, the veto power is usually given to the mayor.

The veto power has been provided generally in the constitutions of those countries adopting presidential government. Sometimes it takes the form of a "suspensive veto," whereby the executive simply returns the bill to the legislature for reconsideration. In states where the initiative and the process of framing laws is in the hands of the executive, the veto power has no significance.

The term is often, though inaccurately, applied to the procedure in the Security council of the United Nations, where any one of the five permanent members is able to defeat a motion by voting against it.

Visa (vē′zȧ; vê-zä′). See *Passport.*

Voting. Voting is the formal expression of opinion or of choice, either upon some question submitted for decision or upon the election of officers or representatives. In a democratic government or society, voting is almost an essential institution for determining the will of the majority. It may, however, be expressed in a variety of ways: orally, or *viva voce*, either with or without a "call of the roll"; by some physical manifestation, as, by rising, or by a "show of hands"; by ballot.

Early forms of balloting consisted in dropping a small object, like a pellet or ball, into urns, or other receptacles; hence the word "ballot," meaning "a little ball." Balls of different colors, as white and black balls, have been and still are used to express affirmative or negative decision; from this practice comes the expression, "to blackball." For political purposes at the present time, however, a ballot is a written or printed expression of the will or choice of the voter.

In political elections, practically all countries have experienced difficulty in providing balloting machinery that would be simple, inexpensive, and protected from fraud or intimidation. In the United States, voting systems have been greatly abused down to recent decades. Agitation for an official secret ballot commenced about 1882. In 1888, Massachusetts adopted a form of ballot called, from its place of origin, the "Australian ballot," the principle of which rapidly spread until today nearly every state has some such system. In most states voting machines, in which the voter records his choice by pressing a lever, have come into use. The main objects are secrecy, to protect the voter from intimidation and to discourage bribery, and a fair count and return of the vote.

Similar forms of voting have now been adopted by many European countries.

SHORT BALLOT. One of the mistakes of the democratic theory in America has been to make elective too many nonpolitical administrative offices. This results in cumbering ballots with so large a number of offices and names as to make a judicious selection impossible to the ordinary voter. A wise reaction has occurred in favor of the appointment of administrative officials so that the voters' responsibility is limited to the selection of a few important executive and legislative representatives. This is the principle of the "short ballot."

PLURAL VOTING. The democratic theory would seem clearly to limit one man to one vote in any election, on the principle that all persons and all classes should have identical political weight in all decisions. In Prussia, before World War I a system of "three-class voting" existed, whereby electors were divided into three categories, each of which represented equal taxpaying power. Each class then chose one-third of the representation. This system is imitated in Japan. The democratic movement in Germany, which triumphed at the conclusion of World War I, has abolished this system in that country. In Belgium, before World War I, a system of plural voting prevailed, whereby two and even three votes were given to citizens possessing unusual qualifications. This system was abolished in the electoral reformation after World War I. In Great Britain, under certain circumstances, a voter may vote for two parliamentary representatives, one in the district of residence, the other in some other district in which he may have exceptional qualifications.

COMPULSORY VOTING. The lethargy or indifference of the electorate is one of the most serious problems of democracy. Certain countries have endeavored to solve it by obliging qualified electors to vote, under penalties for abstaining. Compulsory voting was introduced into Belgium by constitutional amendment in 1893, the penalty for the first offense being a reprimand from the justice of the peace or a fine of from one to three francs, and, for subsequent delinquency, a penalty amounting to as much as the deprivation of the right of suffrage for ten years.

ABSENTEE VOTING. State legislatures in the United States have repeatedly made provisions whereby citizens absent from the state on military duty have had their votes taken at important elections. Certain American states allow all voters absent from their town or election district, but within the state, to cast their votes in another electoral district. Vermont passed such a law in 1896; Kansas in 1901 provided that railway employees might vote by mail, and in 1911 extended this privilege to all voters. Among other states with similar laws are North Dakota, South Dakota, Nebraska, Minnesota, Missouri, Colorado, Iowa, Michigan, Montana, Oregon, Wisconsin, Washington, Wyoming, Virginia, Utah. In Sweden, a husband may deliver his wife's vote in a closed envelope, and a wife that of her husband. In other elections in the same country, soldiers, absent seamen and fishermen, employees of railways, ports, customs, and pilot service, may vote by mail. Absentee voting is legalized also in Australia, New Zealand, Norway, and in some of the Swiss cantons.

War. War is an act of violence inflicted by one people or nation upon another people or nation, in order to compel compliance with its will.

Coercive measures that fall short of actual employment of force and the infliction of damage and destruction are not war. Recognized "measures short of war" include: severance of diplomatic relations; "embargo," or the detention of ships in port; "reprisals," which may take the form of the seizure of property or the death of the citizens of another state, and even such extreme steps as the occupation of enemy territory and "pacific blockade," or the stoppage of communication with a country by arrest of shipping. Such measures as these last may become actual warfare, although war has neither been declared nor been legally recognized. Among such cases may be cited the German blockade of Venezuela in 1902 and the American occupation of Vera Cruz, Mexico, in 1914.

War may be carried on upon the land, upon the sea, or upon both elements at the same time. From the warfare of Rome upon Carthage to World War II, superior sea power, or the domination of ocean communication by one belligerent, has been demonstrated to be a factor of immense influence upon the prospects of victory. The actual decision, however, must almost of necessity be gained by the victory of land forces and by the destruction of the enemy's power of armed resistance. With the great advance in aerial warfare, "control of the air," or the power to deny another enemy the employment of aircraft, is recognized as a paramount and perhaps a decisive factor in future wars.

It has long been the continued effort of supporters of international law and of humanitarian principles to confine the practices of warfare to the armed forces of the belligerents. But modern warfare is waged upon a scale so much vaster and with so much greater intensity of resolution that the undoubted theory of present day warfare is that it is a contest between the entire populations and resources of the belligerent nations. The object of warfare today, therefore, is not only the destruction or capture of the enemy's armed forces, but also the embarrassment, the injury, and the depression of the enemy's civil population to such a degree that its will for resistance may be broken.

DECLARATION OF WAR. War dates from the first act of hostility and may precede a formal declaration. The declaration of war itself may take various forms, including formal advice to the enemy government, a general proclamation of hostilities, or the declaration of a blockade of the enemy's territory.

The decision to end peaceful negotiation and to embark upon war is without doubt the most weighty and the most terrible responsibility that a government may have. In the past, the power of decision usually has been vested in the sovereign or in the executive branch of government. By the constitution of the former German Empire, the final decision rested with the kaiser. But more and more the development of the sense of responsibility in governments has tended to place this decision in a representative legislative body. This is specifically done by the Constitution of the United States, which recognizes Congress alone as capable of making a declaration of war. In spite of this constitutional provision, however, it must be recognized that the issue of peace and of war rests more with the president than with Congress. The president, by his conduct of negotiations, by the movement or employment of the armed forces, practically may commit the nation to war in advance of the authorization of Congress. Congress alone, nevertheless, has the power to furnish the vast supplies of money and men whereby a war of magnitude can be waged. A similar situation exists in the British government, where, although the war-declaring power is a crown prerogative exercised by the ministry, no British government today would embark upon war without the assured or expressed support of the House of Commons. This was sufficiently indicated in the last days of August 1914, preceding Great Britain's entrance into World War I.

The confiding, to the executive branch of government, of so momentous a responsibility as the issue of war or peace springs from the necessity of prompt decision and the instant employment of war measures. The opening actions of modern warfare have an extreme, if not a decisive, influence upon the outcome. These actions embrace rapid mobilization of troops, the seizure of strategic or defensible positions, the sudden and, if possible, unexpected destruction of the enemy's forces, and the seizure of the "initiative." It is for these reasons that such an extreme proposal as the requirement of a national plebiscite, in place of an executive or legislative decision, might delay a nation in the employment of its military strength until the enemy had gained insuperable advantages.

RESTRICTIONS ON WARFARE. Since the time of the great jurist Grotius, the legal thought of the modern world has been consistently occupied with efforts to abate the severities and inhumanities of warfare. Numerous authoritative writings and repeated conferences of European nations have been directed to this end. Particularly was this the object sought in the agreements reached at the second Hague Conference. The practices of armies and navies in World War I, however, disregarded most of these conventions. Extreme supporters of vehement warfare have laid stress upon the expediency and justification of severity as the policy most likely to shorten war and to bring an enemy to the acceptance of peace. It must be clearly seen, however, that ruthless measures may weaken more than they may aid the nation employing them. This they do by the sacrifice of neutral sympathy, by the weakening of the moral quality of the people employing them, and by the strengthening of the passion of resistance in the people against whom they are employed.

RIGHT TO MAKE WAR. Justification for warfare is a matter of wide differences of view which must be weighed from moral rather than from legal considerations, although international law writers have attempted to define acts legally warranting hostility, which are termed "casus belli." Opinion varies from the view that war may be engaged in only as an unavoidable act of national self-defense, to the view that war is but a "continuation of politics," a reenforcement to the aims of statesmen and diplomatists where these efforts are unduly obstructed or delayed. This was the view advocated by extreme partisans of war, both political and military, in Germany before World War I.

"The right to wage war" has long been recognized as one of the essential attributes of a sovereign state. In certain cases, however, this right has been surrendered by treaty, as in the case of Switzerland and of Belgium before 1914. Japan renounced war by its constitution of 1946.

Warfare, however it must be deplored, appears to spring not more from the ignoble passions of a people than from its noble qualities—from its national pride and high spirit; from its quickness to feel injustice and wrong; and from a moral preference for the sufferings and losses of warfare rather than for the acceptance of injustice and oppression.

The prospects of future avoidance of war, as a practical matter, would seem to lie less in the establishment of leagues and treaty engagements than in the general diffusion of sympathy and understanding between nations, and in the cultivation, particularly among the greater peoples, of patience, restraint, and spirit of concession. Such a spirit has the strongest possible support from considerations of the devastation entailed in atomic warfare, which constitutes what has been called a balance of terror.

Welfare State. A state which by its social legislation shows its concern for the well being of the people in such matters as health, old age pensions, unemployment insurance, child welfare, etc., and gives direction and support to such programs.

Whip. *See Party Whip.*

Whitewash. The exoneration of officials accused of misconduct, without a sincere attempt by the investigation committee to uncover the real facts or to punish the offenders.

Wirepulling. A term used to describe the secret means whereby political bosses control legislation and political appointments.

Woman Suffrage. During the colonial period, women in Massachusetts and Virginia who possessed the necessary property qualifications were at times permitted to vote. However, under all of the state constitutions adopted during the Revolution, voting was restricted to male citizens, except in New Jersey, where women voted until an act of the legislature in 1807 expressly limited the suffrage to "white male citizens."

The woman's suffrage movement in the United States began about the middle of the 19th century. In 1848 the state of New York passed a law, soon adopted by other states, which permitted married women to hold and to dispose of property. This was the beginning of a series of laws which ultimately extended full civil rights to women.

In 1869 were formed both the National Woman's Suffrage Association and the American Woman's Suffrage Association. The latter sought suffrage for women through amendments to state constitutions, while the National Woman's Suffrage Association sought it through Federal amendment. In 1890 the two associations merged into the National American Woman's Suffrage Association.

The first victory of the American suffragists was in 1869 in the territory of Wyoming, where women were granted full and equal suffrage. The territory of Utah followed in 1870. In 1890, when Wyoming was admitted as a state, its state constitution provided woman suffrage, and Wyoming thereby became the first state in which equal political rights were extended to women. The suffrage was granted to women in Colorado in 1893; in Idaho and Utah in 1896; in Washington in 1910; in California in 1911; in Kansas, Oregon, and Arizona in 1912; in Alaska in 1913; in Nevada and Montana in 1914; in New York in 1917; and in Michigan, South Dakota, and Oklahoma in 1918. In 1917 women obtained the right to vote in primaries in Arkansas; in 1918 they obtained a similar right in Texas. In certain other states, the right to vote for president was granted.

Finally, in the fall of 1918, a resolution to amend the Constitution by providing that "the right of citizens of the United States to vote shall not be denied or abridged by the United States or any state on account of sex" was passed by the House of Representatives by the necessary two-thirds vote. It was twice defeated in the Senate and was not passed until the special session called by President Wilson in 1919. The amendment was ratified by the necessary 36 states in 1920.

Suffrage was extended to women in Finland in 1906, and in Norway and Denmark in 1907. By 1936, it had been granted in more than two-thirds of all countries in the world. In some of these countries, however, women were under legal disabilities in holding public office. Enfranchisement of women appears to follow with the evolution of society from a feudal and agricultural stage to the industrial stage.

Zoning Ordinances. Ordinances passed in American cities, dividing the municipal territory into zones or districts of several kinds, as residence zones, business zones, industrial zones, unrestricted zones, and definitely limiting the uses to which property in these districts may be devoted. The purpose of these ordinances is to insure health, beauty, and convenience in the geographical development of the city. Doubt has existed as to the power of legislatures or their agents, the municipalities, to enact such laws; but recent decisions of the courts have upheld them as within the police power of the state.

REVIEW QUESTIONS

Distinguish between the art and the science of politics 727

Criticize the 18th century idea that savage peoples enjoyed an ideal freedom 727

Compare Aristotle's idea of a state with that of Plato. What, in Aristotle's view, is the object of the state? 727

Discuss the contributions made to political philosophy by Machiavelli and Bodin. Through what ideas did John Locke influence the American colonists? 727

Point out some political movements produced by World War I 728

State some of the political problems of the present day. Differentiate politics from history 728

THE UNITED STATES

Name two intercolonial assemblies, with the date of each, previous to the assembly which declared American independence . . . . .

What general reason for the issuance of the Declaration of Independence is set forth in the first paragraph of the document? . . . 729

From what source are governments said to derive their just powers? 729

Enumerate ten facts set forth in the declaration as proof of the purpose of the king of Great Britain to establish a tyranny in America. 729

By what title are the signers of the declaration described? By what authority do they affirm the declaration to be issued? 729-730

Whose name headed the list of signers of the declaration? 730

Enumerate the defects of the Continental Congress as an agency of government. When were the Articles of Confederation adopted by Congress? When were they finally ratified? 730

For what kind of united government did the Articles of Confederation provide? Of what body did the central government consist? . 730

By what title did the members of the Congress refer to themselves in the heading of the Articles of Confederation? 730

In what words is the confederation described in Article III? What purposes of the union are enumerated? 730

To how many delegates in the confederation Congress was each state entitled? to how many votes? 731

How many delegates were elected to the Constitutional Convention of 1787? How many attended the sessions? Characterize the membership of this body 733

Enumerate the six institutions which were given original form by the Constitution. For what two characteristics of form is the Constitution remarkable? Quote Gladstone's judgment about the Constitution 733

Upon what date was the Constitution signed? Name the nine states that first ratified it . . 733

What methods of amendment are provided by the Constitution? How have amendments actually been proposed and adopted? . . 733

For what reason were the first ten amendments proposed and adopted together? . . 734

Give the dates upon which the several amendments became effective 734

Who, according to the preamble of the Constitution, established that frame of government? Enumerate the purposes of the Constitution, as stated in the preamble. . . . 734

What article of the Constitution of the United States provides for the taking of the decennial census? 739

Of what two houses does Congress consist? State the length of the term of each Congress. Upon what date do the regular sessions of Congress begin? By whom are special sessions called? 739

How many United States senators are elected from each state? By whom are they elected? State the length of a senator's term. Who are eligible for election to the Senate? . . . 739

Outline the powers of the Senate 739

By whom are members of the House of Representatives elected? for what term? Who is eligible for election to the House? . . . 739

Outline the powers of the House of Representatives 739

Summarize the method of electing the president of the United States. State the eligibility requirements of the office 739

Enumerate the powers and duties of the president 739

Who elects the vice president when the state electors fail to make a choice? What is the salary of the vice president? State the order of succession to office, in case of the removal, death, resignation, or inability of the president 739

Enumerate the executive departments of the government. Summarize the particular field of each. What is the salary of cabinet members? 739

By whom are judges of United States courts appointed? What is their term of office? . . 740

How many members constitute the supreme court? Summarize the field of the supreme court's original and appellate jurisdiction. What especial function, outside the court, attaches to the chief justice? 740

Over what classes of cases do the inferior courts have jurisdiction? What judges are competent to sit in a circuit court of appeals? . 740

How many United States district courts are there? State the jurisdiction of the United States court of claims 740

Point out how the Senate is associated with the president in the direction of foreign relations. What customs and practices indicate the extent of the president's power in foreign affairs? Indicate the Senate's peculiar function with respect to war and peace. What body only can declare war? 740

Compare the importance of membership in the Senate with that of membership in the House. 740

State the fields to which the legislative powers of Congress are limited by the Constitution. 740

Enumerate the acts which are at present forbidden to Congress by the Constitution. In what field of legislation may Congress overstep these prohibitions? 741

Tell three ways in which Congressional committees influence legislation 742

How does a bill become an act? Is the President's approval necessary for a concurrent resolution of Congress? For a public resolution? 741-742

From what powers and practices does the president derive his great influence over legislation? 742

What is the function of the cabinet? 743

Discuss the question of the disability of a president. Is the president limited as to the place where he may officially act? 743

Point out the appointive powers of the president that make him the real head of the national administration. Indicate the extent of his power through the army and the navy and through the department of justice. . 742-743

Discuss the authority of the president in respect to war and peace. Discuss the growth of the power of the presidency and the maintenance of the integrity of the office by those who have occupied it 742-743

Enumerate the functions of the secretary of state with respect to treaties; presidential elections; laws and resolutions of Congress. 743

Is the secretary of defense a civil or a military officer? Summarize his duties 744

What secretaries of war served under two successive presidents? Name the secretaries of war who later became presidents. Under what president was Jefferson Davis secretary of war?. 744

Summarize the duties of the secretary of the treasury in respect to government finance; in respect to other functions of government. 745

Outline the duties of the attorney-general. Upon what questions must he give his own opinion? What president appointed five different attorneys-general? 745

Outline the duties of the secretary of the interior in relation to parks; to conservation of natural resources 746

When was the first secretary of this department appointed? Under what president was Carl Schurz secretary of the interior? . . 746

What is the title of the head of the Federal postal service? Indicate the scope of his powers of appointment. Outline his other functions 748

Name the postmaster-general who served under three presidents 748

Outline the duties of the secretary of agriculture. By what president was the first secretary of agriculture appointed? 746

State the general field of action of the secretary of commerce. Enumerate some of his specific duties 747

What are the general duties of the secretary of labor? Summarize his special powers and duties. When was the first secretary of labor appointed? 747

Enumerate the functions of the secretary of the navy. Is he a civil or a military officer? 744

In what year was the first secretary of the navy appointed? 744

What president appointed six different secretaries of the navy? 744

Discuss the Department of Defense 744

Enumerate the functions of the civil service commission. 749

What Federal body assigns wave frequencies for radio broadcasting stations? When was this body established?. 749

Describe two duties with which the Federal power commission is charged. What act does it aid in administering?. 749

State the composition of the Federal trade commission. What are the duties of this body? What is its chief purpose?. 749

By what acts have the powers of the interstate commerce commission been defined and enlarged? How many members constitute the commission? Indicate the range of the powers of this body 749

When was the Smithsonian institution created? Who made it possible? For what purposes was it created? 750

State the purposes of the veterans administration 750

When were the United States supreme court and district courts organized? From what year does the present system of circuit courts date? What is the function of the circuit courts? 750

From what provision of the Constitution do the United States courts derive their power to pass upon the constitutionality of laws?. 750

What proportion of the supreme court must agree to a decision? Explain "concurring decision"; "dissenting opinion." Name the chief justices of the United States. . . 751

American State Government

What two classes of government are recognized by the Constitution? What authority stands back of these governments? . . . 752

Point out the influences that have tended toward the extension of the field of the Federal government's activity 752

Outline the field of state administration. Discuss the relation of the Federal and state governments in the protection of public order 752

What states of the Union never held the status of territories? 752

State the first step in admitting a territory to statehood 752–753

Enumerate the existing methods of amending state constitutions 753

For what purpose is the constitutional convention generally used? By what authority may a constitutional convention be called? 753

In what states is amendment by popular initiative now authorized? Point out some restrictions attending the use of this procedure 753

Summarize the history of popular ratification of state constitutions 753

Indicate the extent of the state legislative field under the Federal Constitution. Why have numerous state constitutions limited the powers of legislatures? Discuss the movement for greater legislative freedom 753–754

Describe the general form of legislative body adopted in American states. By what names are the body and its parts known? 754

Discuss the qualifications for membership in the legislative houses 754

Who is usually the presiding officer of a state senate? 754

Point out several ways in which state legislatures are overburdened and embarrassed by too great a volume of legislative projects . 754

Discuss the use of the referendum and the initiative in state legislation. Indicate by statistics the extent to which these plans have been used 754–755

State the qualifications required for election as governor 755

Account for the small degree of authority attached to the office of governor. What is the relation of the "short ballot" to gubernatorial power? Estimate the present status of the governor's office in American politics. 755

Discuss the effect of the veto power in gubernatorial influence upon legislation. What are "administrative measures" in state legislation? 755

Explain the nature and the extent of the governor's pardoning power in various states 755–756

Describe the several important types of administration in vogue in the states. Criticize the system of boards and commissions. 756

Name some states which have recently reorganized their administrations. What are the functions of the California board of control? 756

In what states are civil service laws now in force? Point out the usual powers of a civil service commission 756

What is the recall? Summarize the provisions governing its use in various states. 757

Point out the two purposes served by local government. Indicate some types of public service in which the interests of the state and those of the locality overlap 757

Indicate the proportion of the population of the United States which is classed as "urban." Name the three chief plans of American city government 757

In what city was the commission plan first used? Name several important cities now governed by commissions. Describe the essential features of the plan. Indicate its merits 757

Name some important cities which operate the "city manager" plan of government. Point out the function of the manager . . . 757

Describe the government of Puerto Rico . . 758

How is the governor of Puerto Rico chosen? 758

What representation have Puerto Rico and the other dependencies at Washington? . . . 758

How are the Virgin Islands governed? . . . 758

Under what authority is the Panama Canal Zone administered? 758

How was American Samoa obtained? How is it governed? 758

What smaller Pacific islands does the United States own? Why are they significant? What islands are held in common with Great Britain? What as trustees? 758

What state has the greatest number of members in its house of representatives? . . . 759

In what states are the judges of the highest state court chosen by the governor and legislature? in what states, by the legislature? 760

WORLD GOVERNMENTS

State a generally recognized test of "sovereignty." Discuss membership in the United Nations as a test of sovereignty 765

How did the change from hunting to agriculture produce a revolution in governmental forms? 765

How did the Middle Ages lead to a repetition of the evolution from absolutism to democracy? 765

What governmental ideas does the world owe to the Greek city states? 765

Give two reasons why many so-called democracies are not democratic. Can a monarchy be a democracy? 765

Show by examples the use of Greek and Roman terms in describing forms of government. 765

Illustrate by numbers the proliferation of new nations after World War II 765

What form of government does Afghanistan have? 766

What role did Albania play in the ideological rift between Russia and China? . . . 766

Illustrate one-party government by pointing to procedures in Algeria 766

By what body is Andorra governed? What two individuals act as its suzerains? . . . 766

What role did Portugal play in the political history of Angola? How has black nationalism affected Angola? 766

Summarize the political history of Argentina down to 1852. Compare the general provisions of the Argentine constitution with those of the United States constitution. What historic difference led to giving larger powers to the federal government? 766

Of what states and territories is Australia composed? What officer and legislative bodies constitute the federal government? Point out a likeness between the Australian government and that of the United States . . 767

Austria—Cameroon

Following World War I Austria-Hungary was dismembered into what countries? After the liberation of Austria in 1945, Austria was occupied by what countries until 1955? Explain the structure of Austria's federal government 767

What country rules the Azores? What influence has Communism had in the political history of the Azores? 767

In what year did the Bahamas become independent? Name the more powerful positions in that nation 767

How did Bahrain gain independence from Britain? What method is used to fill the head of state position? 767

Bangladesh formerly was the eastern province of what country? In the Bangladesh constitution what provision applies only to women? 767

Describe Britain's political relationship with Barbados. How many chambers does the parliament of Barbados have? 767

Summarize the king's role in the government of Belgium. How is the provincial government structured? Name the two distinct groups of people living in Belgium . . . 768

Britain's colony of Belize is claimed by what other country? Can the premier or cabinet of Belize be removed before the completion of a term? 768

Before independence what country controlled Benin? What was Benin's former name? In what year did it become independent? . 768

What form of government rules in Bhutan? What is the most prominent religion in Bhutan? 768

From what country did Bolivia gain independence? Describe the political situation in Bolivia 768

In Botswana who is the most powerful government official? Does Botswana have any political ties with Britain? 768

How is Brazil's president elected? What is the minimum voting age? What power does Brazil's federal government have over state finances? 769

What is Bulgaria's highest organ of the state? What is the Fatherland Front? How many chambers comprise the national assembly? . 769

What influence has the military had in Burma? Is Burma a member of the Commonwealth? 769

In 1919 Burundi became part of what UN territory? Discuss Burundi's one-party system. How extensive is the party's control? 770

Summarize Cambodia's political history following French rule 770

Outline the constitution of Cameroon. From what provinces was this nation formed? . 770

Canada—China

During the early colonial period of Canada, what was Canada's relationship with the British government? What is the legal basis of Canada's constitution? What is the importance of the 1931 Westminster statute to the British North America Act? Is the queen of Britain also the queen of Canada? 770

In what manner is the British crown represented in Canada? The federal parliament of Canada consists of how many chambers? What are the eligibility requirements for members of parliament? Describe the powers of the provincial governments . . 771

Cape Verde was a colony of what country for 500 years? How was the transition to self-rule conducted? 771

The Central African Empire became independent of France in what year? Is it still a member of the French Community? . . . 771

Chad was a part of what French colony until 1960? What are Chad's ties with France? Explain the military's authority in Chad and the status of Chad's constitution . . 771

In what year did Chile become independent? When was the first constitution of Chile adopted? Describe the power structure under that constitution. What changes have occurred since then? 772

836

Government

Describe the former imperial system of government in China. What factors brought about its fall? Characterize the government that arose in 1912 and the one established in 1928 772

Trace the steps that led to the division between Communist China and Nationalist China. What was the territorial division? . 772

Describe the Cultural Revolution in China and the period following it. Outline the powers of the National People's Congress. How are its members chosen? Where does the real power lie in China? 772

State one similarity and basic difference between the two governments of the two Chinas. Contrast their claims of territorial authority 773

Colombia—France

What countries comprised Great Colombia? Summarize the political history of Colombia to 1886. Name some of the more recent provisions to the 1886 constitution 773

Explain how power is divided between the two political parties in Colombia. Describe the functions of the house of representatives and those of the senate. Discuss the departmental governments 773

When did the Comoro Islands become a French colony? When did the islands become a republic? What is the major federal government body, and the major local government body? 773

When was the Congo granted independence from France? How long are the terms of national assembly members? How are they chosen? Describe the process by which a bill becomes law 773

Discuss the voting requirements in Costa Rica. How are the president and vice president elected? Legislative power in Costa Rica is divided among how many bodies? Explain the judicial system 774

By what treaty did Spain relinquish sovereignty over Cuba? After Batista, what kind of government and society did Castro try to impose? What were his methods? As a result of the 1976 constitution, what is the major political party in Cuba? . . . 774

Discuss the operations of Cuba's national assembly and the ways legislation can be introduced to the assembly. Explain the policies of the federal government toward the press and other forms of communication 774

Cyprus was a colony of what country? What are the two major divisions reflected in the constitution. How does this affect the executive and legislative branches of government. What were the events leading up to the formation of a Turkish Cypriot federated state in Northern Cyprus? 774

Summarize the political history of Czechoslovakia until 1960. Describe the reform movement of 1968 and the eventual outcome. Outline the structure of the federal government 775

What are the three Scandinavian countries? What type of government rules Denmark? In what year were women first permitted to succeed to the throne? 775

Describe the relation between the Dominican Republic and Haiti. How long is the president's term? 775

The territorial boundaries of Ecuador are in dispute—discuss this. Describe the role the military has played in Ecuador's recent history 775

What countries formed the United Arab Republic? Egypt's 1964 constitution provided for a national assembly. What was one of the provisions concerning the members. How is the president of Egypt chosen? 776

What are Eire's ties with Britain? Outline the requirements for members of the legislative branch of the federal government. What are the requirements for president? How does the council of state participate in government? In the absence of the president, what procedure is followed? . . . 776

When did Equatorial Guinea gain independence? What country ruled Equatorial Guinea? 776

Following World War II what former colony of Italy was added to Ethiopia? Why? What is the Dergue? 776

How many years was Fiji a possession or dependency of Britain? What is the make-up of the federal government? 777

The parliament of Finland contains how many members? How can a bill become law over the veto of the president? Who supervises the enforcement of law in court? 777

When was the Fifth Republic of France established? Give the dates of the preceding four republics. State some reasons for the political instability of France as compared to Britain 777

Describe the office of prefect in France; the role of the general council; the manner of government in the communes; the power of mayors 777

Indicate the powers granted to the president of France under the Fifth Republic. Describe the procedures by which a bill becomes law and by which a treaty is ratified. In 1958 what options were given to members of the French Community? 778

Gabon—Israel

When did Gabon become a republic? How is the president elected? 778

Outline the federal government of Gambia . 779

Describe the upper house under the first German constitution and under the Weimar constitution. Discuss the federal government and the totalitarian state under Hitler's control 779

Summarize the steps that resulted in Germany being divided into two countries after World War II. Compare the legislative bodies of East Germany and West Germany 779

What are the functions of the supreme military council in Ghana? 780

What is the status of the monarch in Great Britain? Give the titles of three of Great Britain's chief ministers. Name the two chambers of the British parliament. Describe the system of local government . . 781

List the powers of the president of Greece. According to the 1975 constitution, what is the formal name of Greece? 782

The government of Grenada is patterned after the government of what country? How is the head of state chosen? 782

Explain the literacy regulation in regard to voting in Guatemala. Who is the departmental head in each of Guatemala's 22 departments? 782

Guinea was a colony of what country? What individual or body has sole and unlimited power to legislate? 782

Explain Portugal's role in the history of Guinea-Bissau 782

What are Guyana's ties with Britain? . . . 782

How many years is the term of Haiti's president? Describe the president's legislative authority 783

In what year did Honduras revolt against Spain? 783

What influence did Russia have on Hungary following World War II? Discuss the Hungarian government's policy concerning ownership of property 783

How may the term of Iceland's president be cut short by political action? 783

What position in India has the authority to form government policy and establish an administrative cabinet? Who was the first person to occupy this position? 784

Name the six organs of the Indonesian government 784

What is the former name of Iran? Iran's modern history was a record of decay until what discovery? 784

Summarize Iraq's political history since World War I. What form of government exists in Iraq? 785

Israel's government is patterned after the government of what country? How are the president, prime minister, and Knesset chosen? 785

Italy—Morocco

How is the president of Italy elected? By whom, other than legislators, may bills be introduced into parliament? What subject is excluded from possible amendments to the Italian constitution? 786

In the Ivory Coast how do bills become law? Who succeeds the president in the event of the president's death? 787

When did Jamaica become independent? How is the prime minister chosen? 787

Describe the role of the emperor and the elder statesmen under the Japanese constitution prior to World War II. Specify two striking innovations in the Japanese constitution as adopted after World War II . . 787

Detail several powers of the king of Jordan . 788

How are the nonelected members of Kenya's house of representatives chosen? 788

Compare the procedure of electing government officials in North Korea with the procedure in South Korea 788

How many members comprise the national assembly of Kuwait? What is the title of Kuwait's ruler? 788

Who controls the government of Laos? . . . 788

How does the Lebanese constitution seek to keep in check the rivalry between religious sects? 788

Lesotho was the protectorate of what country? What was its former name? 788

The constitution of Liberia is modeled on that of what country? Name two requirements for voting 788

What is the major ruling body in Libya? . . 789

Can women succeed to the throne of Liechtenstein? 789

Can women succeed to the throne of Luxembourg? How is the constitution amended? . 789

What form of government exists in Malagasy? 789

How many major political parties are there in Malawi? What was Malawi's name while a British protectorate? 789

Who is the supreme head of Malaysia? What is the official religion? 790

When did Mali become independent? 790

Who is the head of state in Malta? Who is the head of government? 790

The president of Mauritania must be of what religion? Who can initiate bills in the legislature? 790

How many chambers comprise the legislature of Mauritius? 790

Characterize the Mexican constitution of 1917. What are the qualifications for voting? In what way is land ownership restricted? . . 790

What is unusual about the ownership of land and public revenue in Monaco? 791

What are Mongolia's ties with the U.S.S.R.? . 791

From 1912 to 1956 Morocco was divided into two protectorates of what two nations? What kind of federal government rules in Morocco? 791

Describe the system of electing members to the states general of the Netherlands. Outline the authority of a municipal corporation's mayor 792

Nicaragua's president is allowed to serve for how many terms? 793

Describe the federal government of Niger . . 793

How influential is Nigeria's army in government affairs? 793

Can a bill become law in Norway without the king's approval? How did women's right to vote differ from that of men from 1901 to 1910? 793

What is the basis of Oman's judicial system? Who appoints the judges? 793

Before independence in 1947 Pakistan was under the colonial rule of what country? By what means did Bangladesh become a nation? 793

What role did the United States play in the independence of Panama? 794

Papua New Guinea is governed by an elected assembly of how many members? 794

Summarize the political history of Paraguay preceding the 1967 constitution. Describe how the president is chosen and the authority of the president 794

Peru became an independent republic in what year? 794

The Philippines became a dependency of the United States after what war? How much influence does the United States have in the government of the Philippines? 795

Who interprets Poland's laws and has treaty-making powers? 795

What important event occurred in Portugal in April 1976? 795

Characterize the legislature of Qatar 795

Discuss the relationship between Great Britain and Rhodesia 796

Rumania had what type of government until 1947? Rumania has a foreign policy of alliance with what major country? 796

Russia—Sweden

Describe the system of government in the former imperial Russia. Review the course taken by the Russian Revolution. What is the relationship of the Communist party to the Russian government. Name five rights guaranteed to individuals under the Russian constitution; three duties that are demanded 796

How are Rwanda's president and vice president chosen? 798

El Salvador became an independent republic in 1839 when what federation was dissolved? 798

What authority has the Communist party in San Marino's government? 798

Until 1975 Sao Tome and Principe was under the rule of what country? 798

What is the common law of Saudi Arabia? . 798

Is Senegal a member of the French Community? 798

When did Seychelles become independent? . . 798

In Sierra Leone who is commander of the armed forces? 798

Singapore's parliament has how many chambers? 798

Somali Republic was formed in 1960 from territories formerly under the control of what countries? 798

South Africa is comprised of what areas? . . 798

838

Government

How was the Spanish kingdom formed? With what date does the modern constitutional history of Spain begin? 799

What type of government was set up as a result of the Spanish Civil War of 1936–1939? 799

How is the membership of the Cortes chosen?. 799

Indicate the extent of the powers of the king of Sweden. To whom are the ministers responsible? Discuss democratic trends in the government since World War I 800

Switzerland—Zambia

State the outstanding facts about the government of Switzerland 800

Discuss the relation of the Swiss cantons to the central government. Why is the Swiss title of "Confederacy" a misnomer?. . . . 800

Point out the use of referendum and initiative in Switzerland 800

Describe the functions of the Swiss commission executive. How is the Swiss president chosen? What are his functions?. 801

How was Syria's union with Egypt dissolved?. 801

Of what two parts is Tanzania formed? . . . 801

When did Thailand cease to be an unlimited autocracy? 801

How are members of the Senate of Trinidad and Tobago selected? 802

What religious qualification must the president of Tunisia meet? 802

Review the historical events that led up to the establishment of a republic in Turkey. . . 802

What educational qualification must the president of Turkey meet? What is the extent of his veto power over legislation? 802

How is the president of Venezuela elected? . 803

Explain the historical reason for the division of Vietnam into two parts 803

Trace the course of Yugoslavia from its establishment as an independent republic in 1918 to its establishment as a people's republic in 1946 804

Who selects the vice president of Zambia?. . 804

POLITICAL TERMS AND INSTITUTIONS

Define absolutism; admiralty; air zone . . . 805

Indicate two uses of the word allegiance. . . 805

Distinguish between amnesty and pardon . . 805

Enumerate some important examples of international arbitration. 805

Name some states that have passed compulsory arbitration laws 805

Discuss the applications of the term aristocracy; of autocracy 805

State the rules adopted at The Hague in 1899, governing the recognition of belligerent rights 805

What is a bicameral system of legislature? Name an American state having a unicameral legislature. 805

To what English document is the name Bill of Rights applied? State the rights and liberties of Englishmen that are summarized in this document. Compare this declaration with later similar state papers 805–806

Define the political term bloc. Point out its application in America 806

What is a blockade? State the conditions governing a valid blockade 806

Trace the derivation of the term bolshevism. State the relation of the theory of bolshevism to the doctrines of Karl Marx; its relation to other nations 806

What was the bonus? 806

Describe the "boss" system 807

Define the term budget. Discuss the use of the budget system in England and in the United States 807

State the chief dangers in a bureaucracy. . . 807

Outline the chief features of cabinet government. What other names are applied to this system? 807

Explain the political use of the word caucus. Trace the development of the census as a governmental activity 807

Discuss the granting of charters by the government in England and in the United States . 807

Define citizenship. Show how a person may be a citizen of two different countries at the same time 808

What is the legal status of a city? Discuss the extent of municipal authority, especially in Great Britain and the United States . . . 808

Point out some changes in the relations of American state governments to cities . . . 808

Define city planning. Point out some defects in the American "checkerboard" plan of laying out cities. What is a civic center? . 808

Contrast civil rights with natural rights. Discuss the growth of modern rights. Point out the provisions for the maintenance of civil liberty in America 808–809

State the applications of the term "civil service." From what two theories did public service in the United States long suffer? Describe the general provisions of the Civil Service act of 1883 809

Discuss the parliamentary device known as the closure rule. Describe the procedure known as filibustering 809

Explain the theory of commission government. Distinguish the character of a commission from that of a board 809

What is the meaning of the term "common law"?. 809

Describe the chief features of communism. .809–810

Illustrate the meaning of the phrase "concert of powers" 810

Define conscription. Where did compulsory military training originate? When has the United States used conscription? 810

State the purposes of conservation 810

What three parts are necessary to a theoretically complete constitution? Indicate the extent to which the example of the United States in adopting a written constitution has been followed by other states 810

Outline the duties of a consul 810

Define the term contraband. Indicate the effect of the World Wars upon the extent of the list of contraband goods 810

Discuss the American practice of holding political conventions. Summarize the work of a national party convention 810–811

Recite the American's Creed 811

Distinguish between *de facto* and *de jure* government. 811

Differentiate the fundamental meaning of democracy from that of monarchy and that of aristocracy. Discuss the present meaning of democracy 811

Define diplomacy. Enumerate the grades of diplomatic representatives. To what countries does the United States accredit embassies? Explain the uses of the words "embassy" and "legation" 811

To what immunities and privileges is a diplomatic representative entitled? 811

Explain, with examples, the practice of direct legislation 811–812

Explain the purpose of the framers of the Constitution in providing for presidential electors. Outline the procedure of the electors. Contrast their present function with that intended by the Constitution 812
Distinguish two kinds of embargo 812
What is the right of eminent domain? State a limitation upon this right in the United States. For what purposes is the right most frequently exercised? 812
State some limitations that have been placed upon the practice of extradition. Outline the procedure followed in extradition among the states of the Union 812
Discuss extraterritoriality 812–813
Define federalism. Illustrate the nature of this form of government by comparison with other forms 813
What is a franchise tax? 813
Define the franking privilege 813
Describe the free city as it has existed at various periods of history 813
Point out the recent change in political and economic thought with reference to freedom of contract 813
Indicate the provisions of the United States Constitution with respect to freedom of religion and freedom of speech. Point out some limitations of the right of free speech 813–814
Are there any free ports in the United States? If so, where? 814
Define the political term fusion; gerrymander. 814
Discuss the practice of government ownership. 814
What is a writ of habeas corpus? 814
When was the first Hague Peace Conference held? Summarize the results of the conference 814
By whom was the second Hague Peace Conference called? Discuss the acts of this conference 814–815
Outline the history of the establishment and the work of the Hague Tribunal 815
Explain the meanings of the term "home rule" 815
Explain impeachment. State the earliest instance of the process. Outline the procedure in cases of impeachment in the United States. 815
What is the object of the International Labor Organization? 815
What is meant by the phrase "initiative of laws"? 816
Define the term "writ of injunction." Discuss the use of this writ in the United States . . 816
State the nature of intervention. Outline the circumstances under which intervention has been justified 816–817
Tell three ways in which modern lobby practitioners seek to influence legislation . . . 817
Describe the origin and indicate the value of the marine corps 817
Explain the significance of the term "martial law," as used in the United States 817
Define merit system 817
Outline the possible uses of military government under the constitutional system of the United States. Give an illustration of such uses 818
What is meant by the term "military law?" By whom is military law enforced? 818
Discuss modern limitations of monarchy . . 818
Give one reason for the rise of monopoly, two benefits attributed to it, and three dangers inherent in it 818
Outline the history of the application of the Monroe Doctrine 819
Discuss the policy of municipal ownership of public utilities 819
Enumerate the four types of armies relied upon by various states for national defense. Discuss the comparative values of these

forces. Analyze the composition of the army of the United States 819–820
Define naturalization. Outline the procedure required for American naturalization . . . 820
Define neutrality. Point out the essential obligations of a state which desires to maintain neutrality 820
Why is oligarchy so universally condemned? . 820
Discuss the significance of the open door policy in international affairs 821
Define pacifism and point out the chief principles of the doctrine 821
In what officials, in the United States, is the pardoning power vested? 821
Explain the phrase *persona non grata* 822
Indicate the nature and the development of the police power 822
Characterize the various forms of primary elections 822
Enumerate several privileges and immunities of citizens of the United States. . . .822–823
Outline the history of prohibition legislation in the United States 823
Define propaganda 823
State the purpose of the election plans known as proportional representation. Describe the principal plans that are in use 823
Summarize the early history of the public lands policy in the United States. Describe the main features of the policy since 1862 . .823–824
Explain the meaning of the phrase "recall of judicial decisions" 824
Distinguish between the optional and the obligatory referendum. Discuss the use of the referendum in various countries. . . . 824
Discuss the various historical conceptions of a republic. State an arbitrary general definition of this form of government. Show the modern tendency of republics to supersede monarchies 825
Point out the meanings of the terms "right" and "left" in legislative bodies. 825
Define sabotage. Trace its origin. 825
Discuss the signification of the term self-determination. State some difficulties in the application of the principle 825–826
State the theory upon which the principle of the single tax rests 826
Explain the theory of the state known as the social contract 826
Give a general definition of socialism. What is the distinctive feature of Marxian socialism? 826
Are economic crises looked on by Socialists as advantageous to their cause or disadvantageous? 826
Discuss the rise and progress of modern social legislation 827
Define the term soviet 827
Enumerate the state courts of the lowest grade; of the intermediate grade. What is the purpose of the juvenile court? 828
Summarize the early history of the state rights controversy. Outline the growth of Federal power. What is the present status of the state rights question? 828
What is the purpose of a statute of limitations? 828
Explain the following: steam roller; steering committee; straw vote 828
Explain the program of syndicalism . . .828–829
State two meanings of the word tariff. What are reciprocal trade agreements? 829
Describe several modern kinds and forms of taxes 829
Explain the phrase "three-mile limit" 829
What is a town meeting? 829
State the general meaning of the expression "trial by jury"; "unwritten law" 829
Outline the principle of the short ballot . . . 831
With whom does the power of declaring war rest in the United States? 832
Review the history of the woman suffrage movement in the United States 832

BIBLIOGRAPHY

Reflecting the wide range of material dealing with politics and government, the following list contains, in addition to encyclopedias and yearbooks, a variety of specific works useful to the student and the general reader. Books in the latter group cover different phases of organic and constitutional law, political philosophy, the evolution of constitutions and party systems, the machinery of government, practical politics.

ENCYCLOPEDIAS, YEARBOOKS, AND OTHER REFERENCE WORKS

Adams, G. B. and Stephens, H. M.—Select Documents of English Constitutional History.
Macmillan

American Statesman Series (biographies). *Houghton*
Book of the States (annual).
Council of State Governments

Burchfield. L.—Student's Guide to Materials in Political Science . . . . *Holt*

Mallory, Walter H.—Political Handbook and Atlas of the World. (Pub. for Council on Foreign Relations.) . . . *Harper '66*

McLaughlin, A. C. and Hart, A. B.—Cyclopedia of American Government. . . . . *P. Smith*

Moore, J. B.—A Digest of International Law.
U. S. Gov't. Printing Office

Municipal Year Book; an authoritative resumé of activities and statistical data of American cities (annual).
Chicago. International City Managers Association

Munro, W. B.—A Bibliography of Municipal Government in the United States.
Harvard Univ. Press

Richardson, J. D.—Messages and Papers of the Presidents . *New York. Bureau of Nat'l Literature*
Statesman's Year Book—(annual).
Macmillan & Co., Ltd.

Thorpe, F. N.—The Federal and State Constitutions, Colonial Charters and other Organic Laws of the States, Territories and Colonies, now or heretofore forming in the United States of America. (1492–1908.) . *U. S. Gov't. Pt'g. Office*
Whitaker's Almanac—(annual).
London. Whitaker, 13 Bedford Square, W.I.C.

POLITICAL HISTORY, THEORY AND PRACTICE

Akzin, Benjamin—States and Nations.
Doubleday '66
Bliven, Bruce—The World Changers . . . *Day '65*
Easton, David, ed.—Varieties of Political Theory.
Prentice '66
Ebenstein, William—Great Political Thinkers: Plato to the Present . . . . . . *Rinehart '56*
Fried, Robert C.—Comparative Political Institutions . . . . *Macmillan '66*
Johnson, Samuel A.—Essentials of Political Science.
Barron's '66
Mill, John Stuart—Utilitarianism, Liberty, and Representative Government . . . . . *Dutton*
More, Sir Thomas—Utopia, tr. and introd. by Paul Turner . . . . *Penguin '66*
Swindler, William F.—Magna Carta; Legend and Legacy . . . . *Bobbs '65*
Thornton, A. P.—Doctrines of Imperialism.
Wiley '65
Viorst, Milton—The Great Documents of Western Civilization . . . . *Chilton '65*
Wiseman, Herbert V.—Political Systems.
Harper '66

UNITED STATES GOVERNMENT

Anderson, William and Others—Government in the Fifty States. Rev. ed . . . . *Holt '60*
Baker, Gordon E.—The Reapportionment Revolution . . . . *Random '65*
Burns, James M.—Government by the People; the Dynamics of the American National Government. 6th ed . . . . *Prentice '66*
Canham, Edwin D.—The Ethics of United States Foreign Relations . . . *U. of Mo. Pr. '66*

Cleveland, Harlan—The Obligations of Power; American Diplomacy in Search of Peace.
Harper '66
Davids, Jules—The United States in World Affairs.
Harper '65
Glib, Corinne Lathrop—Hidden Hierarchies; the Professions and Government . . . *Harper '66*
Havens, Murray C.—The Challenges to Democracy; Consensus and Extremism in American Politics.
U. of Texas '65
Higgins, Marguerite—Our Vietnam Nightmare.
Harper '65
Kallenbach, Joseph E.—The American Chief Executive; the Presidency and the Governorship.
Harper '66
Kennan, George F.—Realities of American Foreign Policy . . . . *Norton '66*
Ladd, Everett C., Jr.—Negro Political Leadership in the South . . . . *Cornell '66*
McConnell, Grant—Private Power & American Democracy . . . . *Knopf '66*
Odegard, Peter H.—American Government; Documents and Readings . . . . . . *Holt '61*
Perkins, Dexter—The Evolution of American Foreign Policy. 2nd ed . . . . . . *P. Smith '66*
Raphael, Jesse S.—Governmental Regulation of Business . . . . *Free Pr. '66*
Reidy, Joseph W.—Strategy for the Americas.
McGraw '66
Scott, Andrew M.—Congress and Lobbies; Image and Reality . . . . . . *U. of N. C. Pr. '66*
Sindler, Allen P.—Political Parties in the United States . . . . *St. Martin's '66*

FOREIGN GOVERNMENTS

Dutt, Vidya Prakash—China and the World; an Analysis of Communist China's Foreign Policy (rev.) . . . . *Praeger '66*
Emerson, Rupert and Kilson, Martin, eds.—The Political Awakening of Africa . . . *Prentice '65*
Lacouture, Jean—Vietnam; between Two Truces. Tr. from French . . . . *Random '66*
Merkl, Peter H.—Germany; Yesterday and Tomorrow . . . . *Oxford '65*
Neumann, Robert G.—European and Comparative Government . . . . *McGraw '60*
Rose, Richard, ed.—Studies in British Politics.
St. Martin's '66
Scalapino, Robert A., ed.—The Communist Revolution in Asia . . . . *Prentice '65*
Ulam, Adam B.—The Bolsheviks; the Intellectual and Political History of the Triumph of Communism in Russia . . . . *Macmillan '65*
Whitaker, Arthur P.—Nationalism in Contemporary Latin America . . . . *Free Pr. '66*

INTERNATIONAL RELATIONS

Dean, Arthur H.—Test Ban and Disarmament; Path of Negotiation . . . . . . *Harper '66*
George, Margaret—The Warped Vision; British Foreign Policy, 1912–1939 *U. of Pittsburgh '65*
Halpern, A. M., ed—Policies Toward China; Views From Six Continents . . . . . . *McGraw '66*
Lanyi, George A., ed.—Crisis and Continuity in World Politics . . . . *Random '66*
Middleton, Drew—The Atlantic Community; a Study in Unity and Disunity . . . *McKay '65*
Padelford, Norman J. and Lincoln, George A.—The Dynamics of International Politics *Macmillan '62*
Perkins, Dexter—America's Quest for Peace.
Indiana U. Pr. '62
Steele, A. T.—The American People and China.
McGraw '66
Stoessinger, John G. and McKelvey, Robert G.—The United Nations and the Super-Powers;United States-Soviet Interaction and the United Nations.
Random '66
Wood, Bryce—The United States and Latin American Wars, 1932–1942 . *Columbia U. Pr. '66*
Zartman, I. William—International Relations in the New Africa . . . . *Prentice '66*

Education

CONTENTS GUIDE

	Page
Bibliography	924
Childhood Education, Early	918
Colleges and Universities	898
Curriculum Studies	883
Defectives, Education of	915
Educational Foundations	912
Educational Measurements	873
Educational Reformers	854
Educational Societies	913
Education in America	848
Education in United States	890
Elementary School	893
English Educational System	886
Expansion in American Education	861
Federal Funds for Education	905
French School System	885
German School System	884
High Schools	895
History of Education	843
Illiteracy	889
Intelligence Tests	874
Job Analysis	883
Junior College	900

	Page
Laboratory Studies	882
Medieval and Modern Education	845
Parent-Teacher Associations	914
Professional Schools	902
Psychology, Experimental	869
Public High School Growth	866
Public School System	890
Questions, Review	922
Radio and TV in Education	917
Religious Education	916
Russian Educational System	888
School Buildings	911
School Districts	892
School Finance	903
School Surveys	882
School Systems of Foreign Countries	884
Science of Education	869
Special Types of Schools	915
Television in Education	917
Textbooks	917
University Extension	901
Vocational Education	907

Picture Guide: Students at Work in a Library—New Library Buildings—Contemporary Campus Architecture in the U.S.

New Libraries Contribute to Public Education. Top: Scottsdale Public Library Civic and Cultural Center, Scottsdale, Arizona. Lower left: Madison Public Library, Madison, New Jersey. Lower right: San Lorenzo Public Library, Alameda County Library System, California. Each of these recent and varied examples of functional architecture expresses contemporary community-service approaches to continuing public needs for information, education, research, and recreation.

Contemporary Campus Architecture. Top left: The United States Air Force Academy Chapel, Colorado Springs, Colorado—Architects: Skidmore, Owings and Merrill. Top right: The book tower of the library at Emory University, Atlanta, Georgia—essential to library science courses. Bottom: Crown Hall, Illinois Institute of Technology, Chicago, Illinois—Designed by architect Ludwig Mies van der Rohe, who died in 1969. (*Photographs on this page and overleaf courtesy of the particular institutions.*)

Education

"Knowledge is of two kinds. We know a subject ourselves or we know where we can find information upon it."—James Boswell, in *The Life of Samuel Johnson*

Primitive peoples and societies in earlier stages of civilization had no institution such as the school we know today. They did, indeed, give their youth preparation for adult life, but this training was through imitation of the older members of the family or tribe; the process of education was in no way separated from the life of the group.

Specialized Education. The first demand for a definite type of education, which appeared as civilization advanced and as the earlier type of education became inadequate, was the demand for religious training. Primitive tribes often organized rituals at the time the boy became a candidate for admission to adult society, and through these rites initiated him into the secrets of tribal religion. Special education of the girls was never as fully organized as the education of boys.

Secular Education. As civilization became more complex, special bodies of knowledge accumulated, which were not religious in character and could not be transmitted through simple imitation.

Throughout the history of educational systems, the transmission of literary material has been one of the main functions of the school. The result was that the content of the course of study in schools of all grades was largely literary. Training for industry and instruction in the ordinary practices of social life were, even in modern times, left largely to the family or given lower priority in the educational structure. Then, in the 1970s came a movement for greater emphasis on career/vocational education. At the same time, increasing attention was paid to the education of those with learning/behavioral disabilities.

Education and the Government. What originated as the practice of the privileged has gradually come to be the general practice of the community. Schools have been brought together under teachers trained to handle large groups and thus relieve parents of the necessity of individual training or private tutoring.

All modern nations have educational laws of more or less complete scope, and enforce these laws so as to provide, with a high measure of certainty, that no child shall lack training in the fundamentals necessary for social interchange.

For example, it is unacceptable in society that any considerable number of persons be unable to read. Reading is necessary so that there may be ready communication between a government and its citizens.

Likewise, modern society cannot be carried on unless its members can count and perform accurately the simpler calculations needed for commerce and trade. Society has provided by law that every child attend organized school long enough so that it should be possible to learn the basics of common subjects such as reading, writing, and arithmetic.

In the United States, the goals of the schools, what is taught and how, and who teaches it, are all decided by two types of forces: lawfully constituted authorities and informal groups of citizens exercising independent power and influence.

Education is a constitutional responsibility of all fifty states. It is one of the powers reserved for the states, rather than for the federal government. Yet education is not mentioned in the Constitution of the United States. No record can be found in the debates of the Constitutional Convention that education was ever considered to be of little more than remote concern to the federal government at the time the Constitution was written.

Yet by the year 1820, of the twenty-three states in existence, thirteen had constitutional provisions and seventeen had provisions by statute regarding public education. All but two of the states had either constitutional or statutory provisions, and nine of the early states had both. Today, all states of the union have firm mandates in regard to public education. The general note is set in the Illinois constitution: "The General Assembly shall provide a thorough and efficient system of free schools, whereby all children of this State may receive a good common school education."

With the early spread of public education, provisions for compulsory attendance and public tax support of the schools became important. Beginning with Massachusetts in 1852 and including Mississippi in 1918, all forty-eight states had enacted laws for compulsory education. Similarly, Alaska and Hawaii have enacted such provisions.

In 1812 New York was the first of the states to pass a law establishing public schools. In 1820 New Jersey provided for the education of poor children and for all children in 1838. In 1821 Delaware and Ohio authorized taxes for public education; Illinois followed suit in 1825. Then, by about 1850, every state in the North had established publicly supported education. Thus, step by step, tax support and compulsory attendance became essential in the establishment of public schools.

The laws of the states in general came to require the establishment and support of "common schools." Yet there remained areas of doubt that common schools included secondary schools. In 1874 the Michigan Supreme Court noted:

> We content ourselves with the statement that neither in our state policy, in our constitutions, or in our laws, do we find the primary school districts restricted in the branches of knowledge which their officers may cause to be taught, or the grade of instruction that may be given, if their voters consent in regular form to bear the expense and raise the taxes for the purpose.

The keynotes of the passage lie in the concepts of freedom of the school districts and consensus of the voters in favor of such taxes. Decisions of this kind established that local boards of education had the authority to establish schools, to set their levels of instruction, and to apply state minimum standards to all schools. The decisions also authorized the levying of taxes to support schools, even if state law did not provide specifically for such schools and levels of instruction.

Two types of levies are commonly used. Bond issues in considerable amounts provide capital to purchase land, to build new schools, to make additions to existing buildings, or to purchase major plant equipment. Operating levies, when lesser expenditures are called for within a given period, provide funds for administration and for the salaries (or salary increases), as well as the retirement programs and fringe benefits of teachers, secretaries, and other workers. Operating levies also cover funds needed for maintenance and repair of schools, as well as purchase of textbooks, learning-center materials and equipment, and other continuing needs.

Nonpublic School Relations. As the public school system expanded, there came the concept that nonpublic schools should be eliminated. At length, this question brought a United States Supreme Court decision. In the Oregon case of 1925, the court affirmed that the statute requiring all children to attend public schools only was unconstitutional. That is, the state holds the right to examine and regulate private schools in a reasonable manner, but it does not have the right to abolish such nonpublic schools.

There arose further the idea that the states may exercise certain supports of nonpublic schools. The principle is contained in the "child benefit" theory. In 1947 the United States Supreme Court stated that the use of tax money for transportation of any school pupil, public or private, was constitutional. As time went on, many states have provided textbooks, audiovisual equipment, and other materials and services to nonpublic schools under legal sanctions. Thus, it can be stated that while schools may not require pupils to take part in religious observances on the basis of separation of church and state, yet some cooperation between religious groups and the public schools is constitutional.

Continuing Issues. In 1955 the Brown Case brought the decision that racially segregated schools were unconstitutional. This ended the long-held doctrine of "separate but equal" schools. The decision did not bring an immediate end to the problems of civil-rights issues in the schools. In the years that followed, busing, or the transportation of white and nonwhite children across district boundaries, was used to promote social integration.

With growing inflation in the 1970s, a further problem was the financial support of schools. The issue was: What part of the public resources—federal, state, and local—should be allotted to education. The chief concern lay in the sources, control, and allocation of such funds. The forthcoming responses were threefold. First came a flow of federal revenues, depending chiefly on individual and corporate income taxes, and increasingly, but not totally, directed to areas of dense population and low income. There were also changes in the allotment of state funds, dependent largely on income and sales taxes. The principle underlying both changes was that of "revenue sharing" on the basis of need. At local levels—to cover increased costs of buildings, school supplies, and teacher salaries—real estate taxes were increased across the United States. Since such taxes are subject to public approval in most cases, there came a reluctance to approve such measures by vote. The results were that in some parts of the nation deficit financing, or the use of funds borrowed against future revenues, had to be undertaken for the operation of public schools. By 1977 the issue came to a head in Cleveland, Ohio, when local courts approved the closing of schools for lack of funds. In response, federal courts ordered that the schools remain open and that deficit financing be applied.

The social and individual need for adequate education is clear. The relative powers of the levels of government—federal, state, and local—are generally resolved and are also subject to legal recourse, ending with the United States Supreme Court. Equality of education remains a problem, as does the issue of financial support and its control. The solutions remain to be found in the two houses of the national Congress, the fifty legislatures of the states, and the varying structures of hundreds of thousands of local communities and school districts.

U.S. and European Schools. A study of the schools of the United States will bring out characteristics that most Americans do not know to be unique. It is thus proper to note the major fact that the schools of the United States have factors that could appear only in a democratic system.

European Universities. The schools of Europe began to take on their present forms during the late medieval period. In Spain the Moors had established a system that included universities as early as A.D. 715. These served as models for other universities established in other parts of Europe.

The first of such institutions was a law school at Bologna, Italy, chartered in 1158. The scholar Irnerius had succeeded in translating the codes of law of the northern Italian cities. He lectured on these codes to students who came from all parts of Europe to prepare to maintain their places as members of the ruling classes of their nations. This was the beginning of the medieval universities.

Preparatory Schools. In connection with these centers of learning, there grew up in the provinces preparatory schools, where boys who would attend the universities learned the Latin language, necessary to understand the university lectures. These lower schools had to get their teachers from the only educated class then in existence, the clergy. The Church, therefore, exercised an overall influence throughout the educational scheme.

The preparatory schools, like the universities, received only boys from the upper classes of society. They were schools for the aristocracy, not for the common people.

Common Schools. Schools for the ordinary working people were not organized until much later. Such schools grew up in part under the control of the Church. There were so-called cathedral schools, gradually organized at the great centers of population, within the cathedrals themselves, for the training of boys who were to serve in the choir. The boys assigned to such service were the sons of the common families. They had to be trained in reading and music to take part in the Church services. A little arithmetic was often added to other areas of teaching. The catechism was also taught. Indeed, the clergy commonly taught the catechism to all the people in connection with Church services. Catechism classes became the nuclei of schools that were in no way related to the higher schools.

These religious schools were gradually extended, and at the time of the Reformation, the Protestant leaders saw the importance of religious instruction for all children. They therefore organized schools in connection with their religious centers.

Dual European System. From the sources described, it can be seen why Europe developed two distinct types of schools—one for the aristocracy and one for the ordinary people.

Early Division in America. American practice differed from that of Europe. Originally, the schools of the United States were so organized that there was a common school for the ordinary people and a higher school for the clergy. When Harvard College was first organized in Massachusetts, it was intended for the upper classes, that is, for boys who were to enter the ministry. A preparatory school in connection with Harvard was organized as the Boston Latin School. Like Harvard, it was not meant for the ordinary boys (or girls) of Boston, but was a classical school of preparation for college.

The common schools that grew up in Massachusetts and the other colonies were semireligious institutions with much simpler courses than that of the Latin school. The reading matter used in the common schools consisted of the catechism and extracts from the Bible. As described in the early statutes of the Massachusetts colony, the schools were for training children in reading, so that they might come into direct contact with the Scriptures.

The dual system thus begun in early colonial days broke down in time, because the small groups of migrating families that moved westward toward the frontier were becoming more and more democratic in spirit and organization and did not want to maintain the distinctions common in Europe between privileged classes and the ordinary people. The villages that grew up in Massachusetts and Connecticut maintained only a single school. In part, this was due to the direct expense of maintaining schools. In larger measure, it came about through the absence of distinction between the different classes of people in these small communities.

After the single school system was begun in the villages of the colonies, it was natural that it should expand along lines that would maintain the democratic character of the original organization. When the communities prospered and were able to set up higher schools, these also were open to all classes of young people. The result has been that in the United States both the common schools and the higher schools have been organized with a unit plan of education—for all the people.

HISTORY OF EDUCATION

THE practices of modern schools can be understood only in the light of history. Enough has been said in the introductory section to make it clear that the administrative units of modern American and European schools are descended directly from earlier forms of organization which grew up in various nations in response to the needs of the special types of civilization cultivated by these nations. But we may go much further than was indicated in the introduction. The details of instruction, including the materials in the course of study and the methods of classroom instruction, are dependent in all educational systems on the traditions which have come down from earlier times. Striking examples of this fact can be seen in the high respect in which the classics are held in American higher schools. This pre-eminence of the classics can be understood only when reference is had to the educational traditions of Europe. Furthermore, the methods of teaching in American and European schools are alike while the methods of Oriental schools are of a wholly different order.

In treating the history of education, it becomes necessary to draw a distinction between the school as an institution and certain personal influences which from time to time have appeared and have operated to reform institutional practices. The school as an institution tends to be conservative. Once its practices are established, it is natural for each succeeding generation of teachers to follow the examples of those who trained them. Progress or change in methods of teaching and in the courses of study usually depends on the vigorous efforts of some reformer who sees the inappropriateness for a later period of the educational procedures which have been brought down from an earlier age.

Reformers are seldom able to overcome altogether the conservatism of established institutions. The history of education is accordingly the account of a series of compromises between new ideas of what ought to be done and traditional practices which are thoroughly established.

For the purposes of our treatment, it is legitimate to treat in separate subdivisions first the institutions which have appeared in various countries at different times, and second the reformers who have labored to improve these institutions.

EDUCATIONAL INSTITUTIONS

Ancient systems of education must be understood as parts of the religious and governmental organization of the nations to which they belonged. Numerous glimpses into the educational system of Egypt are given by passages in the Old Testament. It is recorded that Moses was trained in all of the wisdom of the Pharaohs. This means that Moses, as a member of the royal family, was given the benefit of such knowledge as the governmental officials and priests of the day were able to accumulate and transmit.

Egyptian Education. Moses was in this respect absolutely separated from the other Hebrews, who, as slaves, enjoyed no privileges of education whatsoever. Moses was a member of the ruling class. His associates were the priests and princes. The priests had a body of knowledge which the common people did not possess. A curious and striking illustration of this can be given in the fact that these priests apparently knew enough about the science of optics to project from concave reflectors images of people on the walls of their temples and on the columns of smoke which rose from their altars. The projected images appeared to the common people like apparitions of their gods. The priests who knew how to make these projections are not to be charged with insincerity. They, undoubtedly, regarded these scientific secrets as gifts from the Deity, given them for the purpose of maintaining their control over the common people. They transmitted their knowledge of optics and other sciences, such as

astronomy and architecture, to the rulers of the nation and to the members of their own priestly class, the training of princes and of novices for the priesthood being an important part of the work of every clerical community.

The educational system of Egypt was thus strictly a religious and royal institution carried on through the priests. The records show that schools for the young noblemen were organized in the palaces. Here discipline was severe and flogging was common. Instruction dealt largely with good manners, with ethical and political principles, and with such sciences as the priests and other teachers could command. The measurement of land was one subject taught. This was especially important in view of the necessity of relocating property after the inundations of the Nile. The boys were also taught swimming and gymnastics.

Greek Education. Greek education was of a somewhat different type. There had been developed in the Greek states a form of government which called for participation on the part of all the members of the aristocracy. Public debates among the members of the aristocracy were the common form of procedure in arriving at public decisions. Anyone who wanted to be a leader in the state must accordingly be prepared to speak in public and to maintain himself in an argument with his contemporaries. Training in rhetoric was, therefore, essential to the youth of the Greek states, and we find that special teachers of this subject exercised great influence in public affairs. Socrates (469–399 B. C.) was charged with having corrupted the youth of the land by the special form of logic and debate which he inaugurated. He was a philosopher and a teacher. He gathered about him a group of the younger men, taught them morals, and prepared them for participation in public life. Following his example, Plato (429–347 B. C.) and Aristotle (384–322 B. C.) conducted training classes for the young men of the aristocracy. The records of the sayings and teachings of these philosophers constitute a major contribution to European intellectual life. Again we must recognize the fact that these teachers were not connected with any public institution, but were influential because they gave a special type of training which was needed by the upper classes to maintain their social and political positions.

There was another important aspect of Greek education; it consisted in physical training in preparation for participation in the great national Olympic games. The Greeks prized perfection of bodily development most highly. They celebrated this perfection in the plastic art which still remains the wonder of the world. The youth of Greece were trained to run and to participate in other forms of physical exercise, and thus to perfect their bodies. In this way they were prepared to become formidable soldiers when they grew to be men. The prizes awarded at the Olympic games were regarded as great civic honors and were eagerly contested for by the young men fr m all the Grecian states.

Although the institutions which grew up among the Greeks were not perpetuated in the later periods of European education, the writings and teachings of the Greek philosophers exercised an enormous influence, furnishing in no small measure the materials which were used in all the higher schools of medieval and modern Europe. Thus the writings of Aristotle were the basis of scholastic education. The system of logic laid down by him was perfected until it became the chief subject of attention on the part of scholars.

The University of Alexandria. A part of the Greek influence came into Europe indirectly through the University of Alexandria where many **great** scholars worked. It was here that Euclid formulated about 300 B. C. the system of geometry which set forth in the form of strict Aristotelian syllogisms the principles of land measurement which had been developed in Egypt and Greece. The Euclidean geometry which is still taught in our modern schools is a combined product of Greek and Egyptian education.

In theology as well as in the mathematical sciences, the influence of the University of Alexandria and the Greek schools was strong. Plato as well as Aristotle was accepted by many of the medieval scholars as an authority on matters of government and philosophy. His theory of the state which included a definition of education has been cited even in modern times as a proper basis for social organization. Plato was one of the authorities much studied in Alexandria and his doctrines were there worked over into a system of religious dogma.

Chinese Education. If we go to the Orient and consider the development of education in China, we find something which is a cross between the type of education found in Egypt and that which appeared in Greece. The great philosopher and teacher of China, Confucius (551–478 B. C.), laid the foundation for the political system of the Chinese state. His writings came to be of the greatest importance to anyone who intended to share in the government of China. Hence, the educational system of China centered about the writings of Confucius, and the young men of the country sought to make themselves masters by a process of merely memorizing all the maxims laid down by the great teacher.

There was a peculiar difficulty in the transmission of the maxims of Confucius, because the written language of the Chinese is clumsy and requires the very highest degree of specialization in order that the student may learn to read. Chinese written symbols were never simplified into a single alphabet, as were the written symbols of the Greeks. Each Chinese word is represented by a separate symbol. The labor of learning to read is, therefore, very considerable.

In recent years the Chinese schools have undergone a radical change through the stimulus of European and American models. The old formal scholastic training in Confucianism has rapidly given way. Since the People's Republic of China was formed, education has been designated as a responsibility of the provisional government under the general control of a Ministry of Education and Culture in the central government. Schools are organized at three levels: primary, secondary, and the University. In 1952 a standard five-year primary school was introduced. Children enter this school at seven years of age. Secondary education covers a period of six years and is divided into junior and senior secondary education with three years in each section. Technical and vocational schools are organized also. A 5-3-3-4 plan of organization is in effect with all students completing secondary education, eligible for the University. However, only a few of the secondary school graduates attend the University. In 1952 there were approximately 49 million children in primary schools, 3 million in secondary schools, and 220 thousand students enrolled in institutes of higher education.

Education in India. There has been a long tradition for education in India. When Europe was in the infancy of its culture, the Universities of India were flourishing and their scholars were respected throughout the then-known world.

In the past two hundred years English schools served as models for the schools of India, and Western ideas permeated education. After 1947 India engaged in a nation-wide attempt to develop education. There now is a central ministry whose main function is to plan, guide, and co-ordinate education for the entire country. An attempt is made to provide free schools at the primary and secondary levels for all children who want to attend them. At present, more than 24 million pupils are enrolled in primary and secondary schools, and approximately 400,000 students attend institutions of higher education. Education at the primary and secondary levels is financed by the State government, local bodies, and private organizations. Higher education is financed by private groups, the state, and the central government.

The entering age for primary schools is usually six years. The medium of instruction in the primary school is usually the mother tongue or the regional language. Secondary education has two stages: the middle school and the high school. The middle school follows the primary school and the length varies from two to four years. Subjects of the middle school, generally, are: the mother tongue, English, mathematics, geography, history, hygiene, nature study, classics, drawing, music, modern Indian languages, and physical training. The medium of instruction in some states is English and in others hindi or the regional language. The medium of instruction in most universities is English. Arts are most common in the University although science, technology, and professional subjects are gradually becoming more popular.

Roman Schools. The Roman boy of the earliest period was educated by his father. After 300 B. C. he was generally educated by a Greek slave. When the Roman state came into ascendancy and conquered the European provinces, Greece was gradually breaking up, and in 146 B. C. she became a conquered state. Learned Greeks came to Rome, in many instances as slaves of rich families. These learned Greeks were able to read; they knew the ancient literature of their race, and had some equipment in scientific knowledge. The Roman aristocracy was made up chiefly of warriors. There was, at the outset, no Roman literature to compare with the perfection of the writings of Homer and the other Greeks. The Greek slave was, therefore, a great asset in the Roman home. He took the boy in hand and gave him a type of knowledge which the father did not possess. From time to time, groups of families united in employing some especially competent Greek to instruct their boys.

Apparently, from the records, the boys in the Roman state were not especially eager to take on the training which the learned Greeks were prepared to offer them. Like the boys of all generations—but it seems in an unusual degree—the Roman boys were unruly and disorderly. Furthermore, from the conditions that have been described, it will be seen that the course of study which could be offered by the Greek was hardly suited to the taste and the future activities of most of the Roman boys. We have here one of the first examples of an imported education.

There were other forms of education in Rome, especially the military types of training. The boys were prepared for the army by strenuous physical exercises and by games, through which they were made vigorous in body and skillful in the use of all sorts of weapons. Physical education was, therefore, an important part of the training of the Roman youth. As contrasted with the Greek physical education, it aimed less at æsthetic development, and sought more to produce powers of resistance.

Charlemagne's Palace School. With the disintegration of the Roman state, Europe broke up into a number of half-civilized nations and tribes. As any one of the rulers in the early medieval period succeeded in enlarging his state and solidifying his government, he was compelled to set up some of the institutions of civilization. The most notable example of the establishment of a school in these early days is to be found in the Palace School of Charlemagne. Charlemagne had conquered a very large part of the western countries of Europe. He employed an English monk named Alcuin (735–804) to conduct a school which was attended by his sons and by the other princes of the royal group.

Alcuin prepared material for this school, and we have some curious examples of the textbooks which were used at that time. One of these is an arithmetic. The numbers were all expressed in Roman numerals. It is not easy to carry on the more complex arithmetical operations if one uses Roman numerals. For example, if one tries to state a problem in multiplication in these numerals, one will readily see the difficulty that was encountered by Alcuin and his pupils. Take the problem, XXVII multiplied by XLIV; the multiplication thus expressed suggests no regularity of relations between the different numbers. As a matter of fact, Alcuin found it necessary to devise an elaborate system of addition which would give the results that the modern boy, who has the advantage of the Arabic numerals, can readily work out according to the modern multiplication tables. Alcuin gave the princes of Charlemagne's court, in spite of the difficulties which he encountered, the best training in arithmetic and in letters that his broad knowledge could command.

It is probably true also that at about this period some of the art and wisdom of the Arabs, who came into Europe by way of Spain, began to influence the intellectual life of the European nations. At all events, it is certainly true that, after the withdrawal of the Moors from Spain, literature and the sciences of mathematics and medicine developed more rapidly than they had in earlier years, and that schools of the higher type, referred to in the introduction as medieval universities, began to develop.

MEDIEVAL AND MODERN EUROPEAN SCHOOLS

The latter period of medieval education in Europe exhibits a number of different kinds of schools. There were the schools for knights, in which the younger members of the aristocracy learned to ride and hunt and to carry on the arts of war; there were medieval universities, which were schools of law, medicine, and theology. Later, various reform movements arose within and without the Church, yielding in many cases organized systems of education.

Jesuit Schools. Notable among the later systems of this type were the Jesuit colleges which flourished for centuries and are influential even in modern times, especially in Roman Catholic countries. These schools were maintained by the religious order established by Loyola, who was born in 1491. They were highly organized, with a carefully planned course of study designed not only for the training of novices who were to enter the religious order but also for the training of boys of the better families, who were to be governors and military leaders. The course of study always included liberal quantities of the Latin language, which was in universal use among the educated classes in the medieval period.

Latin. The Latin language had a unique place in medieval Europe, and the whole history of European education revolves around this subject. Not only was Latin taught because of its utility as a medium of communication, but it was the bearer to the medieval world of the older and vastly influential Roman civilization, which dominated the religious, legal, and military organization of every European state. The great cultural movement known as the Renaissance can be understood only when it is remembered that the nations of northern Europe were very dependent for their culture upon the art and literature of an earlier age.

The enthusiasm for the study of Greek and Latin during the 14th and 15th centuries reflects the dependence of the northern European nations upon the culture of the South. There are many indications that the intellectual awakening of the northern nations was accomplished by devoted study on the part of the clergy, as well as on the part of those who had literary tastes and who were not satisfied with the intellectual life provided by the Church. In a poem entitled "The Grammarian's Funeral," Browning has given a picture of the enthusiasm of the Renaissance for knowledge of Greek and Latin. The Grammarian is pictured as an old man who has

devoted himself in his later years to the arduous studies necessary to master the Greek language. He had gathered about him a group of enthusiastic students, who, in the poem, are represented as following their master to his grave and celebrating in this ceremony their appreciation of the intellectual world which his studies had opened up to them.

The Classical Traditions. Classical and theological subjects were the chief studies in the higher schools of Europe. The establishment of the classical course was so complete that, throughout all of the later generations of European civilization, this course has been the characteristic feature of the higher schools. For example, in England it is only within recent years that the modern languages have had any adequate attention. In Germany, it required the personal influence of the former kaiser Wilhelm II to give standing in the higher schools to subjects other than the classical languages. The best higher schools of Europe today are still devoted to the classical traditions, and the classical languages have been brought over to the United States as important elements of the high school and college curriculum.

Secondary Education and the Classics. What is true of the universities is true of the schools which prepare students for the universities. Such schools are commonly called, following the French terminology, secondary schools. This term has come to have very general use. We speak of the American high school as a secondary school. In like fashion we speak of the French *lycée* and the German *Gymnasium* as secondary schools.

The development of secondary schools in Europe was first a succession of efforts to organize instruction in the classical languages, afterwards a slow growth of additional subjects, such as mathematics, and, at length, science and the modern languages. The various periods of this development are characterized by recurrences of enthusiasm for the content of Greek and Roman culture. The enthusiasm for the classics degenerated from time to time into mere attention to the grammatical and rhetorical forms of Latin authors. The periods of devotion to the content of classical culture are called periods of humanism.

There was a period, for example, during which the teachers of Latin were more interested in the use of a vocabulary and a style copied from Cicero than in the facts of Roman life or the facts of Greek culture. Formalism in expression dominated this period. It made very little difference what were the subjects of discourse so long as most of the phrases were of the Ciceronian type.

After each period of interest in form, there came a period of interest in the content of that which was read. For example, in Germany in the latter part of the 18th century the intellectual leaders of the nation, such as Goethe (1749–1832), Herder (1744–1803), and their contemporaries, rebelled against instruction in the mere forms of expression and inaugurated a reform which is known as "neo-humanism." This neo-humanism sought to find serenity and balance of life in a revival of Greek art and an imitation of Greek literature.

Similar alternations of interest in form and content have marked the whole history of the study of the classics. Even in modern times this same contrast appears. There are some teachers who defend Latin today on the ground that it is a perfected form of expression; while there are others who point out that a study of the classics is justified only in the degree in which it makes students acquainted with the experiences of earlier and highly developed nations.

New Secondary Subjects of Instruction. The later periods of secondary education have been complicated by the fact that many new subjects have been developed and are demanding a place in the scheme of education. The natural sciences developed rapidly after the 17th century, and it has become increasingly important in modern times for every student who is going to be a leader in social and political life to know something of the natural sciences. Within the last century, the scope of scientific inquiry has vastly increased through the development of the biological as well as of the physical sciences. Commercial and industrial life have been modified and reorganized through the influence of these sciences, with the result that a higher education is altogether incomplete if it does not include a generous amount of training in natural science. Moreover, within the last two generations, the social sciences have been added to the natural sciences, and it has become apparent that in a complex society, such as that in which we live, it will be necessary, even in the lower schools, to give instruction in economics and the theory of government.

Among the purely literary subjects, also, there has been competition. Modern languages and the culture of modern nations, as well as the earlier civilizations of Rome and Greece, have come to be important for students. Secondary schools have accordingly adopted modern languages into their curriculum, and in some instances the effort has been made to substitute the modern for the ancient languages.

Slow Change in Traditions. Whatever have been the changes in the curriculum and in the organization of the secondary schools, these institutions have maintained their place in Europe as entirely separate from the schools for the common people. Thus, in England there are a number of famous and ancient endowed schools which still continue to train the aristocracy and still maintain the traditions of the medieval educational system. These schools are called "public schools." This name was adopted in the early history of such institutions as Rugby, Winchester, and Eton, because these schools differed from the tutorial system that was practiced in many of the homes of the aristocracy. Furthermore, it was common for the patrons who endowed these schools to give certain scholarships and to permit bright boys from among the common people to enjoy the advantages of a special education without cost to themselves. The institutions are not public in the sense in which free schools are public. Indeed, all European secondary schools charge a tuition. Furthermore, the so-called public schools of England continue to give a formal, classical course of study. It is the traditional theory of these English schools that, by studying Greek and Latin, boys can acquire the type of mental concentration and moral discipline necessary to make them competent officers in the army and satisfactory members of the civil service corps.

It has been the contention of many reformers, on the other hand, that the same ends could be much more advantageously attained if science and modern literature were substituted for the classics. Such a substitution, it is argued, would provide mental discipline and, at the same time, give the information necessary for intelligent participation in the activities of modern society. One writer whose essays have been a very large influence in promoting reform in English and American education in the direction of science and modern literature is the philosopher Herbert Spencer (1820–1903). His essays on education, published in 1861, were a vigorous attack upon the traditional classical system and a powerful plea in favor of science in secondary education.

The English municipalities have in recent years contributed to the reorganization of secondary education by establishing a new type of higher schools. These schools are known as municipal secondary schools. They are maintained by the industrial cities of England, such as Liverpool, Leeds, Birmingham, and Sheffield, and they give instruction in the sciences that are necessary for the maintenance of the industries in these various centers. They are open also, on a much more liberal scale than are the traditional schools, to the boys of the cities who are going into the industries and commercial life.

European Universities and Scholasticism. The European university has been from the first typically a professional school. At the outset, as was indicated in the introduction, each university center had its characteristic course. It was a school of theology or a school of medicine or a school of law. Later each institution set up a number of branches. The branches which were most common were those which have been mentioned, namely, theology, law, and medicine. There was also a general branch, known as the philosophy division of the university, in which a miscellaneous collection of literary and scientific subjects was provided. In this division of the university most of the new developments have taken place.

The universities of the medieval period were the homes of so-called "scholasticism." This word is often used as a term of reproach, from the point of view of modern educational thinking. It is commonly implied that scholasticism means mere formalism in thinking, as a substitute for productive originality.

There is ground for this notion that scholasticism was altogether formal. The common type of instruction was that which emphasized logical forms. The Aristotelian syllogism was the pattern which was adopted for all thinking. A science of logic was cultivated to the exclusion of interest in any real facts. The scholastics often debated purely artificial questions with a view to increasing their critical knowledge of the possible uses of the syllogism. Given certain premises for an argument, it made no difference to them whether the argument was practically productive or not. They merely wanted to make sure that the consequences of the premises assumed were carefully worked out. History tells of debates, between great leaders in this scholastic period, which continued day after day, and the debater who received the highest academic awards after one of these debates was the logician who was most competent in the use of syllogistic forms and in the exercise of criticism which attached to these forms.

While, however, there is ample ground for the statement that scholasticism was excessively formal, it should not be overlooked that this period devoted to the study of logic was of great significance in the development of the power to think in fine distinctions. The scholastics created, in the languages which they developed, an instrument for a later type of discriminating scientific thinking.

They also established the practice of research, that is, they set aside a group of people whom society was prepared to support for the purpose of developing an intellectual life which had no immediate practical bearings. There has always been some prejudice on the part of practical people against university organization, because it has been felt that the universities are in many instances remote from practical life; but the later history of higher institutions has shown that it is altogether to the advantage of society that science be cultivated for its own sake. The scholastics furnished the example which has been followed in later academic organization, and developed communities where intellectual life was pursued, first of all for its own sake and secondarily for the applications of science and letters to the needs of civilization.

Academic Freedom. One of the great struggles carried on in the universities of Europe was the contest for academic freedom. The patrons who supplied resources for the maintenance of universities tried from time to time to dominate the thinking of the teachers in these institutions. Great theological controversies sometimes arose in the universities. It will be remembered that Luther was in the University of Wittenberg when he first made his attack upon the theological doctrines which became the issues of the Reformation. Political issues also arose from time to time when some ruler objected to the teachings of those who were connected with the universities. But from the earliest periods it was the contention of the universities that the teacher must be entirely free to follow the truth wherever he sees it, and the tradition has finally come to be thoroughly established that universities are to be free from any outside control.

English Academic Social Life. The English universities, in addition to the establishment of the right of the teacher to think freely, developed a social life of the most intense sort. One of the reasons why American students under the Rhodes scholarships find it advantageous to go to Oxford in England is that they are brought into close contact with a group of students who, during their university lives, are intimately associated in the dining halls and living quarters of the colleges of that university.

The English universities go so far in their emphasis on social life that they are hospitable to students who pursue their studies with such leisure that they are called mere "pass students." It is not uncommon for members of the wealthier classes to look upon the university life chiefly as a social opportunity. As distinguished from the "pass students" there are "honor students" who are looking forward to professional or academic careers which require rigorous scholarly preparation. It has been suggested by students of American higher institutions that a similar distinction to that made in English universities might advantageously be adopted in this country. It is asserted that there would then be a frank recognition of what is now in fact the true condition. It would relieve college authorities also of the necessity of living under the shadow of the pretense that all American students are hard-working scholars.

American Colleges. As compared with the European universities, the American college is a somewhat detached institution. It does not aim to give professional training, but is higher in its scholastic requirements than the secondary schools. We shall have occasion later to discuss more fully the development of this unique American institution, but it is to be noted here that the American college is in part borrowed from the English university. It is the social life of the American college which is frequently emphasized when one attempts to describe its relation to its students and its importance in our educational system.

Common Schools as Missionary Enterprises. The European school for the common people was in all of its earlier stages a missionary enterprise. As indicated in the introduction, the common school began as a result of the desire on the part of the Church authorities to train choir boys or to give general religious instruction to the common people. Luther and his colleagues in the Reformation recognized the importance of making the common people independent in their religious faith. Luther's translation of the Bible is a clear indication of his desire that they should have access to the means of religious independence. The training of the people to read the Bible was quite as important as the making of the translation. We find, therefore, that the leaders of the Reformation were in favor of schools and exercised their influence in the direction of the development of schools on a large scale for the common people.

What is true of the Reformation applies also to the efforts of later religious sects which developed in Europe and England, and it is true also in the Roman Catholic Church from which these various bodies separated. A few illustrations will serve to indicate the character of these movements for the establishment of mission schools for the common people. One of the most noted of these institutions was the school established at Halle by Francke (1663–1727). In 1695, Francke, who had had a broad academic and theological training, established in a suburb of the city in which he lived an evangelical organization which conducted as one of its major enterprises an orphan asylum and training school for teachers.

Francke was a member of the sect known as the Pietists. This religious group held to certain austere doctrines with regard to human nature, not unlike the doctrines held later by the Puritans. They believed that all children are born with an evil nature inherited from Adam and Eve and that it is necessary to change this nature by the most rigorous discipline, if the child is to be saved from eternal damnation. The rigor of Francke's discipline is illustrated in the following statement which he makes about children's play:

"Play must be forbidden in any and all of its forms. The children shall be instructed in this matter in such a way as to show them, through the presentation of religious principles, the wastefulness and folly of all play. They shall be led to see that play will distract their hearts and minds from God, the eternal Good, and will work nothing but harm to their spiritual lives. Their true joy and hearty devotion should be given to their blessed and holy Savior and not to earthly things, for the reward of those who seek earthly things is tears and sorrow."

In France, the common school was promoted by the activities of the religious order known as the Christian Brothers. This was an order of monks, founded in 1684 by Jean Baptiste de la Salle (1651–1719), which devoted itself to the betterment of the poor children of the country by giving training in the rudiments of knowledge to the boys and girls of the common people. The rule of the schools conducted by this order was that both pupils and teachers should keep silent throughout all of the day. Corporal punishment was common. The curriculum consisted in the rudiments of reading, writing, arithmetic, and religion.

In England, similar movements were carried forward, and led to the organization of schools which were, as will be seen by their very name, efforts on the part of philanthropic organizations to provide for the poorer people. The common schools of England were known as "pauper schools" or as "ragged schools." They were supported by various societies, such as the British and Foreign Missionary Society, and the Society for Bettering the Conditions and Increasing the Comforts of the Poor. A number of interesting experiments in the conduct of cheap schools were made under the auspices of these societies.

The so-called "monitorial" system was developed under the auspices of the society first mentioned above. In 1797, Dr. Andrew Bell (1753–1832) had suggested that the older boys in the orphan asylums could be used as instructors for the younger boys. At about the same time, Joseph Lancaster (1778–1838) organized a school in which a series of gradations was introduced, by which the teacher could come into direct contact with the older pupils, who in turn carried to the lower classes the instruction which they received from their teacher. Each child was provided with a knapsack in which he kept such books and material as he needed. A huge room was fitted with benches on which the children could sit, and in this way the teacher sometimes was able to take care of 1000 children.

The Lancastrian movement, as it is called, is of special interest because it was brought to New York and contributed to the early stages of development in American education. It provided one great advantage over schools which had preceded it. It compelled the grading of the children. The older groups, who were more mature and able to take instruction directly from the teacher, constituted the upper grades, and the younger children were organized in groups of different levels to receive instruction from these monitors.

Common Schools under Civil Patronage. A second type of development, acquaintance with which is of the greatest importance for an understanding of the history of common schools in Europe, is that which flourished first in Germany. Here, the rulers of political states very frequently united with the Church authorities in maintaining schools for the training of the common people. The advantages of this combined action soon began to make themselves apparent in both the economic and the political life of the state. The taking over of the function of education by the political government was an innovation which ultimately exercised very great influence in the life of the nation.

In 1763, at the close of the Seven Years' war, Frederick the Great (1712–86) gave this general movement of state education a great impetus by issuing what is known as *The General School Regulation*. This order established for the first time the principle of compulsory attendance on the part of the children. It also provided that the teachers who conducted the schools should be specially trained for their duties and adequately compensated, and that the state would assume responsibility for this compensation. A policy of religious tolerance also was proclaimed in the *Regulation*. It is to be noted that religious instruction was not eliminated from the school curriculum by this proclamation of tolerance, but it was provided that families of different types of religious affiliation should be allowed to receive in public institutions the type of religious training which conformed to their beliefs.

The *Regulation* of Frederick drew the most violent opposition from the clergy and from many people who had come to think of the schools as strictly religious institutions, but it marked the beginning of a new era in educational matters. Because of their adequate support and strong organization, the Prussian schools have been the model for all other European school systems; and in many respects they furnish also the pattern for American schools.

The Influence of Prussian Schools. The direct influence of these Prussian schools on the other systems of Europe can be traced through a report which was prepared in 1833 by a French commissioner named Cousin (1792–1867). The French schools, as indicated in an earlier paragraph, were first maintained by religious orders, but at the time Cousin made his report there was great interest in the organization of public support for schools which should admit children of all classes. Cousin went to Prussia, and made an exhaustive report on the organization and course of study of the common schools. This report was widely distributed in France. It was translated into English, and had a large influence in England and the United States in bringing about a new type of organization of public schools.

The Prussian school for the common people had at this time come to be a school which took charge of the children from six to fourteen years of age. It is interesting to comment on the reason for the adoption of fourteen years of age as the upper limit for school attendance. The original practice in German schools was to leave to the pastors the decision as to when children were mature enough to leave the school and be confirmed in the Church. Pastors gradually found that the age of fourteen was approximately the age at which they could approve the conclusion of the training course in the schools and could admit children to the Church. Throughout the civilized world, compulsory education laws have been passed, following the example of these German pastors in setting the age of fourteen years as that at which common school training is regarded as completed. Many of the reforms which are being suggested at the present time in American school organization will be more clearly understood if it is remembered that the upper limit of the common school was thus determined through a European organization which is in fact wholly different in character from the common school of the United States.

The secular organization of education in Germany prepared the way for a modern development which has been of great importance. These schools were among the first to be supplemented by a system of industrial education. The secular ruler was naturally much interested in the economic welfare of his people. Accordingly, he was willing to provide for the training of children in the trades.

The tendency to provide practical education was further powerfully re-enforced by the writings of some of the educational reformers who will be discussed in another section.

EDUCATION IN AMERICA

The educational system of America, during the Colonial period, was in part an imitation of the European system. Three grades of schools were to be found in the American colonies. There was, first of all, the highest institution, or college. The three institutions of this type which have exercised the greatest influence in American education are Harvard (founded in 1636), Yale (founded in 1701), and Princeton (founded in 1746). These institutions were organized by the clergy for the purpose of training boys to become members of their own profession. Closely connected with the colleges were the Latin grammar schools. These were modeled on the European secondary schools which administered a classical course of study and accepted pupils of the better social grades from the families which could afford to pay tuition. Finally, there was a common school which in its organization was influenced from the beginning by the European people's school.

Local Control of American Schools. The American common school differed from the European school in that it was from the outset an expression of the desire on the part of the American colonies to develop a type of intellectual freedom not prevalent in Europe. There are two further characteristics of the American common school which have distinguished it from its European predecessors. In the first place, the school was, from the beginning, controlled by local authority. Communities were indeed compelled by early legislation in the colonies to maintain an educational institution of some kind for the young people, but the details of organization were left to the communities.

We find that there was the greatest variety in the method of controlling these schools. In New England the town meeting determined the policy of the school. It set the salary of the teacher, and very frequently went so far as to select the teacher, although it commonly delegated supervision of the school to a trustee or to a committee. This committee often included the pastor of the church and one or more of the leading citizens.

The southern colonies differed from the New England colonies in their attitude toward education. To these southern colonies, especially to Virginia, had come Englishmen who brought with them the traditions of the English aristocracy. They usually lived on plantations so large that their neighbors were far removed, and the demand for any community life was, accordingly, much reduced. Virginia, therefore, did not have any town meeting which could control the school, and, because of the great distances between families having children of the same social level, schools were not organized. The young people were sent from the Virginia plantations back to England for their education, or they were trained by tutors at home.

In New York, the Dutch company which had large concessions sometimes provided schools as part of the inducement to immigrants to settle its lands. In Pennsylvania, William Penn (1644–1718) saw the importance of providing education for the children as a part of the general scheme of social organization. In these cases, however, the schools were left to the control of the community to a degree unknown in the European countries.

American Schools, Reading Schools. A second distinguishing fact about American schools is that they were reading schools. Instruction in the European schools was given orally by a teacher who was professionally trained and authorized to instruct the children. The colonies, unprovided with skilled teachers and unable to equip these teachers

This Bicentennial exhibit at the Center of Science and Industry in Columbus, Ohio, features talking wax replicas of all the **American Presidents.** A recorded message with a biographical sketch and a famous quote by each president is heard on pressing a button on the panel directly in front of the exhibit. *(Photo courtesy COSI, Columbus, Ohio)*

This antique doll display at COSI features **dolls of early America.** The first dolls were brought to America by William Penn in 1699, although they were not called *dolls* until around 1750. In the American Colonies they were called "little ladies." Early American dolls were made of wood, china, wax, or bisque, a type of earthenware. The dolls pictured here are made of bisque. *(Photo courtesy COSI, Columbus, Ohio)*

These exhibits show the early American **spinning wheel** being used. The spinning wheel, used for making thread from cotton, flax, and wool fibers, was introduced to Europe from India in the 14th century. The spinning wheel arrived in America in the 17th century. Spinning was usually done by young women and from this comes the word "spinster." *(Photo courtesy Center of Science and Industry, Columbus, Ohio)*

with any technical preparation for their work, were satisfied to conduct schools as best they could, employing anyone to teach who could be secured for the relatively small wage which the community was able to provide. But there was one ambition which prompted the organization of the schools, especially in the New England colonies. It is clearly expressed in the preamble of the school laws of these colonies. A quotation from the school law of Connecticut, adopted in 1650, and resembling very closely the early law of Massachusetts, adopted in 1647, will make clear the purpose of the colonies in establishing their first common schools.

"It being one chief project of that old deluder, Satan, to keep men from a knowledge of the Scriptures, as in former times, keeping them in an unknown tongue, so in these latter times, by persuading them from the use of tongues, so that at least, the true sense and meaning of the original might be clouded by false glosses of saint-seeming deceivers; and that learning may not be buried in the grave of our forefathers," (the court decreed that whenever a township increased to fifty householders they should employ some one) "to teach all such children as shall resort to him, to write and read."

The influence of this legislation has been of great importance in the American schools. Throughout our history, emphasis on reading has controlled the form of organization of all classroom instruction. Reading books have been provided, in contrast to the oral instruction which is typical of European schools. The method of instruction has included preparation of lessons at home out of books, and the recitation has been from the first the typical form of classroom exercise in these schools.

Industrial Training. There was one further ambition in the minds of the New England colonists as to the training of their young people. It is expressed in the statute adopted at about the same time as that quoted above. This second statute aimed to provide training in industry for all of the children. The statute is as follows:

"All parents and masters do breed and bring up their children and apprentices in some honest lawful labor, or employment, either in husbandry or some other trade profitable for themselves and the commonwealth, if they will not nor cannot train them up in learning, to fit them for higher employment, and if any of the selectmen, after admonition by them given to such masters of families, shall find them still negligent of their duty . . . the said selectmen, with the help of two magistrates, shall take such children or apprentices from them, and place them with some masters for years, boys until they come to be twenty-one, and girls to eighteen years of age complete."

This statute did not exercise any large influence, because it did not provide adequate administrative machinery for enforcement. It is not until a relatively late period in the history of American education that industrial training reappears as an important part of the system.

Early Methods of Paying for Schools. In the matter of support, there was great variety of practice in the different colonies and in the different grades of schools. In the main, it may be said that higher education was never free, and in many instances the elementary schools were supported in part by payments made by the pupils. There was practically no full community support of schools until long after the establishment of the present Federal government of the United States. Indeed, as late as 1873, the last of the Northern states to abandon pupil payment was still receiving some support for the teacher from so-called "rate bills" paid by the pupil. Even in colonial times, however, partial support of the school out of the community treasury had begun. Accordingly, common schools have been from the first, so far as the public could make them so, free schools.

Early Schools and Lack of Organization. By way of negative statement, it may be pointed out that the early colonial schools were not graded. They were one-teacher schools, and in the form of their organization were of the type known even in modern times as "the district school." The teacher

organized such classes as he or she was able to conduct, and the pupils were distributed according to their various abilities in the different subjects. The school term was often very short. Sometimes, the school year was divided into a winter term and a summer term; the latter was attended by the younger children, and the former by the older children. The original school laws of the northern colonies very frequently prescribed 4 to 21 as the ages for attendance on school. Later the European model of closing the elementary schools to students at about 14 years of age came to be adopted, but the original plan of American school organization was at once loose and comprehensive.

Early Schools, Religious but Secular. The schools of the American colonies were secular; that is, they were set up by the law of the colonies and were governed by the community rather than by the church. They were at first, however, religious in the content of their teaching. The reading books were full of quotations from the Bible and the catechism. The religious content of instruction reflects the main interest of the community. Nevertheless, the control and organization were secular. The consequence of this has been that, in modern times, the separation of the public school and the Church has been complete, and religious teaching has gradually disappeared.

The development of parochial schools in this country reflects the desire on the part of certain religious bodies to control, more completely than is possible in the public schools, the religious and moral education of their children.

Schools in the Early National Period. Between the Colonial period and the present, there is a pronounced break in the history of American schools. The Revolutionary War left the colonies in many cases financially weak and detached from the sources of their earlier social life and traditions. The Constitutional Convention, which established the national government, did not include education as one of the matters to be dealt with by the new Federal government. There was in fact so much disagreement between the practices of the northern and the southern colonies in matters of school organization that it was deemed wiser to leave schools to local control. The tendencies toward decentralized organization which appeared in the colonies thus became a part of the national policy. It was not until the middle of the last century that the Federal government made any provision for the consideration of educational problems. In 1867 an office of education was established, first as an independent department and in 1868 as an office of the department of the interior. This office, however, has no authority of any kind whatsoever over the schools in the different states. It is merely an agency for collecting information. The fact that the Federal Constitution does not mention education leaves the control of public schools to the states.

Since, during the early years of American history, the states were busily engaged in developing the material resources necessary for the life of the people, education was carried on in a somewhat irregular fashion, in accordance with the plans which had been set up during the Colonial period; but it was very meager. The United States office of education has estimated that in 1800 the average American citizen was not receiving more than 82 days of schooling in his lifetime. Many communities had no schools, sometimes because families were so isolated, and sometimes because teachers could not be found. The educational situation during the first decades of American national life was wholly chaotic.

A Typical Report. A report prepared by the committee which visited the schools of Taunton, Massachusetts, in 1801 throws so much light on the general situation early in the last century that parts of it may be quoted as exhibiting the conditions common at that time:

"The committee chosen by the town to inspect the schools beg leave to report their situation and examination . . . " January 6th, 1801. Your committee visited a school kept in Rueben Richmond's house instructed by Mrs. Nabby Williams of 32 scholars. This school appeared in an uncultivated state the greater part of the scholars.

"On the 26 of Feb. visited Mrs. Nabby Williams' school the second time and found that the scholars had made great proficiency in reading, spelling, writing and some in the grammar of the English language.

"On Nov. 10th, the committee visited and examined two Schools just opened: one kept in a school house, near Baylies works, of the number of 40 scholars, instructed by Mr. Philip Lee. This School we found to have made but small proficiency in reading, spelling and writing, and to be kept only six or seven weeks; upon inquiry why it should be taught no longer, we were informed that the ratio of school money for this School was and had been usually expended in paying the Master both for his service and board, and in purchasing fire wood which is contrary to the usual custom of the town.

"The other School, visited the same day, was kept near John Reed's consisting of the number of between 30 and 40 Scholars instructed by Mr. William Reed; This School, being formed into regular classes, appeared to have made a good and pleasing proficiency in reading, spelling, writing, some in arithmetic and others in the Grammar of the English language. This School's share of school money is expended to pay the Master for his service only, so that the School will be continued three months.

. . . . .

"Feby. 26th, visited Mr. Dean's School 2 time, the Scholars were crowded into a small room, the air was exceedingly noxious. Many children were obliged to tarry at home for want of room and though the school was kept only a few weeks they were deprived of its advantages. A want of books was the complaint. The committee were anxiously desirous that this evil might have a remedy and were of opinion it may be easily done. The Scholars appeared to increase in knowledge & claim our approbation.

"March 5th, visited two schools, one kept at Mr. Aaron Pratt's of the number of 30 scholars, instructed by Mr. Philip Drown. This school appeared quite unimproved and uncultivated in reading and spelling, some of them did better in writing.

"This uncultivated state did not appear to be from a fault in the children but, as your committee were informed, from the disadvantage of having had masters illegally qualified for their instruction; of which class is their present master unauthorized by law."

Beginnings of State Supervision. Shortly after the appearance of Cousin's report, the English translation of which was distributed in this country in 1835, a movement was started in Massachusetts and the other New England states and in Ohio—the first state to be organized out of the Northwest Territory—for a better organization of common schools. In 1837, the state of Massachusetts organized a state board of education and appointed as secretary of this board Horace Mann (1796–1859). In the meantime, Connecticut was moving in the same direction, and in 1838 appointed Henry Barnard (1811–1900) secretary of the state board of education. Ohio, under the influence of a group of organized educators in the city of Cincinnati, appointed a state superintendent of schools in 1837.

These were the beginnings of state supervision of public education. The local districts had found it impossible to give proper training to teachers, and even the selection of teachers, when left to local authorities, was carried on in a fashion that frequently led to complete failure in school organization. The state now began to assert its rights to insure good schools by establishing normal training classes and by compelling the various communities to employ teachers who had the approval of the state department and to submit to supervision by a central state authority.

Beginnings of Compulsion of Pupils. After the organization of state boards of education, came the movement to control attendance through the exercise of central state authority. In 1852, Massachusetts passed a compulsory educational law which differed from the earlier laws adopted in this country, in that it not only compelled communities to provide schools but also compelled pupils to attend school. The other states in rapid succession followed

the example of Massachusetts,—the District of Columbia in 1864, Vermont in 1871, and other states later. It was not, however, until the '80's that even the most advanced compulsory educational laws began to be enforced. Since that time, compulsory education has been the accepted practice in the Northern states. The Southern states have been much slower in adopting compulsory education. Indeed, until after the Civil War the South had practically no public school system. It was not until very recently that the last Southern state adopted compulsory education, and in many cases the laws which are now in force are relatively weak.

The situation in the South is seriously complicated because this section of the country, in its effort to deal with this matter, maintained two school systems—one for the whites and one for the Negroes. The Southern states are handicapped also because of lack of resources, with the result that most of the developments in common school education have been slower in the Southern than in the older Northern states of the country.

Segregation. On May 17, 1954, the Supreme Court of the United States handed down its historic decision that public school segregation laws are unconstitutional because they violate the Fourteenth Amendment, which guarantees equal protection of the laws to all American citizens.

The decision, which was unanimous, overruled the case of Plessy *vs.* Ferguson, decided in 1896, which held that the states could provide "separate but equal" schools for white and Negro children. On this point Chief Justice Earl Warren said:

"We conclude that in the field of public education the doctrine of 'separate but equal' has no place. Separate educational facilities are inherently unequal. . . Today, education is perhaps the most important function of state and local governments."

Some 21 states in the North and South with segregation laws are affected by the decision, but the court left open for later determination the question of how and when the ban should be enforced.

Grading and Better Organization. As soon as the state boards of education began to deal with the problems of school organization, there appeared a tendency to grade the pupils better and to provide more definite courses of study for the common school. There was great interest during the decades between 1830 and 1850 in the example of Prussia. Many of the leading educators of this country visited the Prussian schools. Calvin Stowe (1802–86) of Cincinnati was compensated by the state legislature of Ohio for preparing a report highly favorable to the Prussian common school. Mann and Barnard also visited Germany and reported vigorously in their state documents on the virtues which they had observed in those schools.

There was also going forward in Europe a series of reforms, which will be referred to in later sections, under the stimulation of the writings of Pestalozzi (1746–1827) and Rousseau (1712–78). These reform movements in Europe were brought to America during the early years of the century, and encouraged the better arrangement of the course of study and the improved organization of the pupils.

Furthermore, there were growing up during the middle of the last century a number of municipalities which could afford to maintain better schools than those which had been possible in the rural districts prior to 1840. All these influences were operative at about the time that state departments were organized. The result in point of organization was that the common school of the United States took on its present form as an eight-year graded school during the decade between 1840 and 1850. The graded school has not yet entirely superseded in all parts of the country the native district school; but, in the main, the district school has disappeared, and the eight-year elementary school is the typical form.

In the South, where resources were meager, a seven-year school was adopted after the Civil War, as the typical organization of the elementary grades. In New England, there are some exceptional school systems which conduct a nine-year elementary school. These departures from the rule, however, merely go to emphasize the importance of the general movement which resulted in the eight-year organization of elementary education.

Academies and Union Schools. Parallel with the development of common schools and of state control in these schools, was the development of secondary education. The early years of the 19th century saw the establishment of numerous private academies. There had grown up also in some of the larger communities in Massachusetts and in the other states so-called union schools, which offered a higher grade of education than did the common district school. There emerged slowly out of this development of secondary education an institution which did not begin to appear in any large numbers until after the Civil War, but which is one of the unique creations of the American educational system, namely, the public high school.

Characteristics of the Public High School. The public high school differs from the secondary schools of Europe in that it follows the elementary school. As has been shown in earlier paragraphs, the common school of Europe is separate from the secondary school. In this country, the high school takes the graduates of the eighth grade and continues their training through a period of four years. Furthermore, the American high school is free, the cost of maintenance being paid by the community in the same way in which the community pays for the maintenance of elementary education.

The high school began to flourish after 1870, and its history from that date has been one of phenomenal growth. Statistics in regard to this development will be presented in a later section. The curriculum in these schools began as a classical course modeled closely after that of the secondary schools of Europe, but in this respect also there has been a tremendous expansion in the years since 1870. The modern American high school offers a very wide range of courses and makes numerous adjustments to the students who enter the institution.

In 1893, a committee of the National Education Association, known as "The Committee of Ten," rendered a report on the organization of the high school curriculum, which defined the practice in these schools in a way which has been of the greatest influence in determining the development of the institution. Since that date, the high schools of the United States have followed a fairly uniform path. There is in recent years some indication that the standard pattern will undergo a modification in the direction of an expansion of its lower and upper grades; but the high school, as a typical institution in American life and altogether different in its organization and character from any secondary institution to be found in Europe, may be said to have been finally established in the early '90's.

City Superintendencies. One other line of development in American public educational systems may be commented on briefly. The cities of the United States have gradually developed a complex organization for the control and supervision of schools. In 1837, the cities of Buffalo, New York, and Louisville, Kentucky, each appointed a school officer known as a superintendent of schools. In 1839, Saint Louis, Missouri, and Providence, Rhode Island, did the same. Since that time it has become altogether common for the larger and even the smaller cities to support such a supervisory officer. Today, cities commonly organize their school systems under separate charters granted them by the state, and these independent school districts confer on their chief educational executive various powers and duties which differ greatly from city to city and are still in most cases in process of complete definition. The main fact for us to notice at this time is that a group of technical officers has been created for

the management of the larger school systems of the country. In some instances these officers have had jurisdiction over both the elementary and the high schools. In other cases their jurisdiction has been limited to the elementary schools.

With the appearance of the graded elementary school, the high school, and the modern system of organization presided over by a superintendent, the modern American school system may be said to be launched.

Normal Schools. Standing somewhat apart from the elementary and high schools of the country are the institutions which provide the teachers for the elementary schools, namely, the normal schools. During the early periods of American education no special provision was made for the training of teachers. It was assumed that anyone who was educated was competent to take care of little children and to give them appropriate instruction. Indeed, during the Colonial period and the Early National period, it was altogether common to assume that very little training was necessary for any adult to qualify as a school-teacher. Accordingly, the public esteem for the pedagogue was relatively slight, and the social and literary traditions of our people have reflected the attitude that the teacher is an individual who cannot succeed in the competition of the business or professional world and is therefore assigned to the trivial task of caring for little children.

A different tradition grew up in Europe, especially after the development of a group of followers who attempted to put into practice the principles of some of the educational reformers. The school established by Francke in Halle became a center for the training of teachers, and the old castle at Yverdun, where Pestalozzi gathered about him a group of followers, became a center for educational reform in a new and important sense. These schools devoted much attention to the training of teachers, and set the example which in Europe and America has led to the organization of special institutions for this purpose.

The first moves in the United States for the training of teachers were in New England and New York. In 1823, the Reverend Samuel R. Hall conducted classes for the training of teachers in Concord, Vermont, and afterwards in Andover, Massachusetts. In 1827, James Carter opened at Lancaster, Massachusetts, a normal institution which he conducted privately. At about this same time Governor Clinton recommended to the legislature of New York state the establishment of a seminary for the education of teachers. Governor Clinton was especially interested in developing through such an institution the monitorial system which had been imported to this country with the Lancastrian schools. It was, however, the European influence which ultimately led to the development of normal schools as public institutions. The publication of Cousin's report in 1835, together with the enthusiasm of Mann and Barnard and Charles Brooks for German education, led to the acceptance in 1839 by the legislature of Massachusetts of a gift of $10,000 to be devoted to the establishment of a normal school. This school was opened at Lexington, Massachusetts, in the town hall, with one teacher and three pupils. From this date, normal schools were established in the various Northern states, as follows:

1839 Massachusetts (1st)	1854 Massachusetts (4th)
1839 Massachusetts (2d)	1854 Rhode Island
1840 Massachusetts (3d)	1855 New Jersey
1844 New York	1857 Illinois
1849 Connecticut	1859 Pennsylvania
1849 Michigan	1860 Minnesota

The normal schools thus established were supported by the states. In later years some of the large city systems have found it necessary to supplement the state normal schools by city training schools for teachers. Conspicuous examples of such institutions are to be found in New York City, Philadelphia, Saint Louis, and Cleveland. In some cases the state normal school is located in a city, and serves the double purpose of a state normal school and a city training school. Examples of this type are to be found in Montclair, New Jersey; in New Britain, Connecticut; and in Milwaukee, Wisconsin.

The curriculum of the normal school ordinarily consists of a review of the subjects taught in the elementary school, such as arithmetic and spelling. This review is intended to prepare teachers to give instruction in these subjects. There are also courses entitled "methods," which deal with the best modes of presenting the various school subjects. Finally, there are certain general professional subjects, such as psychology and history of education. These strictly professional subjects are treated in a great variety of ways. Sometimes the psychology is of a general type, corresponding closely to the ordinary academic treatment of this subject. In some cases the effort is made to apply psychology directly to the study of the school subjects. The history of education has been very largely a history of the theory of education, and has been not infrequently replaced in recent years by more practical studies of classroom management and of the school laws of the state in which the student is preparing to teach.

Teachers' Colleges. The normal school has usually been a highly independent institution, its character being determined by its president and faculty. In some instances the normal school has taken on the character of a people's college. This is especially true in the Western states where no other institution of higher learning is easily accessible from the section of the state in which the normal school is located. In recent years, normal schools have been transforming themselves into teachers' colleges and have extended their curriculum from two years, which has traditionally been the length of the normal school training, to four years.

Most of the Western normal schools are permitted by their charters to give degrees, and many of them have taken advantage of this provision. More than one hundred normal schools of the country are at the present time classified as teachers' colleges. The curriculum ordinarily covers four years, the first two years being devoted to the typical normal professional training, but including a liberal amount of general training; the last two years being in many cases given largely to general training like that provided in the ordinary college.

Colleges. American colleges were originally established, as was pointed out in an earlier paragraph, for the purpose of training the clergy. The first of these institutions was Harvard which was founded in 1636. This institution was an imitation of Emmanuel college in Cambridge, England. William and Mary followed in 1693. Yale was established by a group of Congregational ministers in 1701. The charter granted to Yale, like that granted to Harvard, indicates a desire to uphold and propagate the Christian Protestant religion. Both charters express also the wish that the youth of the country may be instructed in the arts and sciences and may through the blessing of God be fitted for employment in both church and state.

The University of Pennsylvania claims 1740 as the date of its origin. This institution has special significance because it grew out of a somewhat more secular motive than the earlier institutions. About 1740 Benjamin Franklin published a pamphlet entitled *Proposals Relating to the Education of Youth in Pennsylvania*. Soon after its appearance 24 public-spirited citizens of Philadelphia took over the charter and property of a charity school established in 1740, and organized an academy largely, though not wholly, on the lines suggested by Franklin. The University of Pennsylvania, chartered in 1755 as the "College, Academy and Charitable School of Philadelphia," was built on this foundation. Its curriculum, including history and civil and international law, went beyond the original curriculum of most American colleges. In 1746 Princeton was founded; in 1754 King's college in New York, afterwards known as Columbia university.

These institutions were followed in late years by a group of public foundations. Perhaps the most famous—and certainly one of the most influential—of these, was the University of Virginia, which was established in 1817, when Thomas Jefferson was elected rector of the board of an institution which had been in existence as an academy since 1803. The board authorized in 1817 the purchase of a farm of 200 acres near Charlottesville, Virginia. The corner stone of the building of the so-called Central college was laid in October of the same year. Jefferson was very eager to have this institution adopted by the legislature as the state university. The example thus set has been of great influence in determining the practices of communities which in later years have developed, especially throughout the Central and Western states of the country, state-supported institutions.

The early colleges were by no means large institutions. As late as 1815, Harvard graduated a class of 66; Yale, of 69; Princeton, of 40; Williams, of 40; Pennsylvania, of 15; and the University of South Carolina, of 37. It was not until after 1820 that the rapid development of American colleges began.

Denominational Colleges. During the decade between 1820 and 1830 a large number of institutions were established, especially by the independent religious denominations, which began to feel the necessity of providing themselves with trained ministers to carry on the work of their churches. So vigorous has been the energy of churches in setting up these institutions of higher learning, that they may be said to have dominated the development of American higher education, in spite of the efforts of Jefferson and of later organizers to bring higher institutions under the control of the state. The statement has been made that, of the 750 institutions of higher learning in the United States and Canada nominally termed colleges, at least two-thirds were originally under the control of religious denominations.

College Graduates and the Professions. The purposes of colleges can be clearly defined in terms of the professions taken up by their graduates. For many years after the founding of Harvard the largest percentage of its graduates went into the ministry. During the early years, more than 70 per cent of all the graduates entered this profession. Later the profession of law became important, and, finally, medicine, engineering, and the modern profession of business took their places, both in society in general and in the colleges, along with the ministry.

A bulletin published in 1912 by the United States bureau of education has canvassed the gradual change in the character of professional choices by college graduates, and summarizes the whole matter as follows. Between 1642 and 1780 the ministry was the chief profession for which the colleges prepared. Up to 1720, the percentage of graduates entering this profession was somewhat more than fifty. After this time a rapid decline is shown in the number of graduates entering the ministry, and in 1780 the percentage fell to about twenty. The percentage of graduates entering that profession during the last period of the 19th century was only five and nine-tenths. Though surpassed by law between 1780 and 1820 in the number of college graduates entering, the ministry again led between 1820 and 1840. It is significant of the final decline of the interest among college students in preaching, that at the close of the 19th century the ministry is overtopped by teaching, commercial pursuits, law, and medicine.

During the first century of higher education in this country, training for law received scant attention, inasmuch as the governing class came directly from England, where they received their legal training. Between 1745 and the period of the Revolutionary War there was a slight increase. This increase was greatly accelerated immediately after the Revolution by reason of the change in government, which removed the English-trained lawyers and created a demand for lawyers trained in American institutions. Law, accordingly, was in the ascendancy in the colleges during the early part of the 19th century, and once more between 1840 and 1885, perhaps because of litigations growing out of the Civil War. For a hundred years after the Revolution the law attracted a greater percentage of graduates than any other profession except the ministry. At the close of the century, however, it is surpassed by teaching and commercial pursuits.

Before 1705 medicine was an extremely variable profession. From 1705 to 1745 the percentage of college students entering medicine is approximately seven, rising to about twelve per cent from 1745 to 1780. While law was attracting many college graduates after the Revolutionary War, medicine fell off slightly, with an average percentage between 1781 and 1805 of about nine. Since 1850 this average has been further reduced by the growth of teaching and the commercial pursuits, with the result that this profession closed the century with an average of only six and six-tenths per cent of the graduates of colleges, a lower percentage than that of any other five-year period since 1735. Medicine has been the most constant of all the professions.

Recent Changes in Professions. Within one hundred years the profession of teaching has grown from about one-twentieth to about one-fourth of the graduates of colleges. Previously to 1835 it was outnumbered by the ministry, law, and medicine, but after this date the curve for medicine is lower. Since 1880 the line for teaching has crossed that of the ministry, and since 1890 that of law. At present it is the dominant profession into which college graduates go with business as its closest competitor.

The general trend of the curve for college graduates entering commercial pursuits since 1825 has been upward. At present, the commercial group takes approximately ten per cent of the graduates, and is exceeded only by the group of teachers. The general rise of this curve is one of the most striking facts brought out by a study of the colleges, and one to which too little attention has been given.

The profession of engineering scarcely appears until after 1825. Its rise from that time until the present time has been steady. At present, the profession has attained a percentage of about nine. A larger proportion of the graduates of the collegiate departments of institutions maintaining special engineering schools enter this profession, but the aggregate percentage is kept down by the small colleges, only a very small percentage of whose graduates, as a rule, pursue this vocation. At the present time, many liberal arts colleges which do not offer engineering as a course in the curriculum have arrangements with engineering schools. These arrangements enable the student to enroll in "pre-engineering" courses which have credits transferable to co-operating engineering schools.

In spite of the comparatively large number of agricultural courses, farming does not attract and never has attracted a very large number of college graduates; the present percentage is about two. The rapid development of the land-grant colleges, however, has greatly stimulated enrollments. Although the number of graduates entering agricultural pursuits is increasing, it is not increasing so rapidly as the number entering other professions.

Prior to 1830, the profession of letters did not take more than one per cent of the graduates. Between 1830 and 1855 the percentage rose from one to two per cent, and by 1885 it had touched its maximum of three and three-tenths per cent. Many men do not adopt the pen as a means of livelihood until comparatively late in life, and the result is that this series of records stops before the date at which a number of the more recent college graduates can have qualified for inclusion in this group.

Degrees granted by institutions of higher learning in 1950–51 and 1969–70 indicate the change in tendency in major fields of study:

Field of Study	1969–70		1950–51	
	Men	Women	Men	Women
Agriculture	9,896	494	8,924	118
Architecture	3,736	181	2,556	88
Biological Sciences	32,268	12,104	6,725	2,072
Business and Commerce	105,219	9,328	52,320	5,917
Computer Science	1,813	196	. . .	. . .
Education	73,841	155,649	18,898	32,633
Engineering	59,735	438	41,386	87
English and Journalism	25,531	44,508	9,513	9,095
Fine and Applied Arts	17,609	22,565	2,487	3,119
Foreign Languages	8,537	19,247	1,597	2,671
Forestry	2,371	18	. . .	. . .
Geography	3,204	821	. . .	. . .
Home Economics	363	9,963	55	7,848
Law	17,772	799	13,926	412
Library Science	1,212	5,737	. . .	. . .
Mathematics	22,362	11,788	4,311	1,442
Philosophy	5,839	1,261	2,333	321
Psychology	20,657	14,402	4,836	2,983
Religion	10,318	2,526	3,329	135
Social Science	107,172	60,686	4,722	2,339
Trade and Ind. Training	4,392	20	. . .	. . .

Source: *Statistical Abstract of the United States.*

Growth of Colleges. The development of colleges during recent years has been extremely rapid. The following summary from a bulletin of the United States Office of Education shows this development during the last five decades:

During the 50-year period 1889–90 to 1939–40 the total number of administrative and instructional staff members at institutions of higher education increased more than eightfold, from 15,809 to 131,552. In 1941–42 the number stood at 134,137, which was 8.48 times the 1889–90 figure. The number of women members of staffs increased more than twelvefold, from an estimated 3,105 in 1889–90, to 37,886 in 1941–42. In 1889–90, women constituted 19.6 per cent of college and university faculties; in 1939–40, 28.1 per cent, and in 1941–42, 28.2 per cent.

Since 1890, and possibly an earlier date, enrollment of students in higher education has been steadily on the increase, not only in absolute numbers, but also in proportion to the total population of the country, and in proportion to the total number of persons of college age (18-21 inclusive). In 1889–90, the enrollment of 156,756 was 0.25 per cent of the total population and 3.04 per cent of the population 18-21 years of age. The enrollment increased steadily until the economic depression period of the thirties, when it suffered a temporary setback. It quickly rallied from this loss, and increased to about 1939–40. The outbreak of the war in Europe soon started another decrease.

In 1941–42, the nonmilitary resident college enrollment was 1,398,981, which was 1.07 per cent of the estimated population of the nation, and 15.66 per cent of the nonmilitary population 18-21 years of age.

Expenditures increased from $377,903,377 in 1929–30 to $572,465,437 in 1941–42.

Since the close of hostilities of World War II in 1945, college enrollment has increased by leaps and bounds. Approximately 2,000,000 students were enrolled during 1946–47, and an additional 475,000 students were turned away because of lack of college facilities.

In 1966 the enrollment in college and professional schools in the United States reached seven million students. This is an increase of approximately 350 per cent over the college enrollment of 1946.

Along with the development of educational institutions, there have appeared from time to time educational theorists and writers who have exercised an influence upon the course of subsequent school organization, through their criticisms of existing practices and their suggestions of new types of organization which should be set up. In general, it may be said that these educational reformers reflect the thinking of their times only indirectly. Usually they are significant in the history of the world because they recommend radical departures from tradition and from ordinary views about education. In many instances they have been teachers who have seen from their experience the fallacy of existing methods and have, therefore, thought out new modes of school organization. Very frequently their suggestions are so far removed from the possibilities of realization that the reform suggested is nothing but a theory. Even in such instances, however, the extreme theory has often operated to modify existing methods, and, while the plan proposed by the reformer has never been fully achieved, the modifications which have been attained have been sufficiently radical to justify his efforts.

In a few instances the writings of the educational reformer have led to the organization of a group of disciples who have carried his ideas into effect. Sometimes, indeed usually, the disciples have not followed exactly in the steps of their masters. For example, when Froebel developed the philosophical plan for the training of little children, which led to the organization of the kindergarten, he set in operation a movement which, especially in recent times, has developed in directions other than those implied in his suggestions. The kindergarten has had an independent history reaching far beyond the writings and immediate teachings of its founder. At the same time there can be no doubt that Froebel's writings were the source and original inspiration of the whole movement. The question has arisen within the kindergarten group from time to time whether Froebelian doctrines should be adhered to closely, or should be accepted as mere suggestions of a general type of thinking to be worked out by practical teachers who have to deal with the training of little children. In the course of this discussion, kindergartners have separated into conservative and radical groups.

Similarly, various groups of modern educators have attempted to interpret the general ideas which were laid down by Herbart. In many instances, these interpreters have been in disagreement with each other, but have expressed full acknowledgment of their dependence upon the original teachings of Herbart.

In considering, therefore, the life and writings of any reformer, it is necessary, first, to refer briefly to the conditions under which he did his work. It is then essential to summarize his views on education. Finally, it is important to estimate, as far as possible, the type of influence which he exerted on subsequent periods.

Socrates (469–399 B. C.). One of the earliest educational reformers was Socrates, the Greek philosopher who lived in the 5th century B. C. He was a teacher of morals, logic, and political philosophy; and he attempted to lead the young men of Athens to a clearer conception of their duty to the state, to their parents, and to their associates. His fundamental belief was that knowledge leads to virtue.

His system of teaching consisted in a series of questions which, step by step, followed up any assertion made with regard to any fundamental matter of conduct. The so-called Socratic method consists in drawing out from the individual the necessary consequences of any statement made by him. The teacher is not supposed to contribute directly any information; his business is to stimulate the student to think for himself and to be thoroughly critical of every conclusion at which he arrives.

Socrates did his teaching in a small state in which the young men to whom he appealed were members of the aristocracy which governed the state. The effect of his teaching was to spread broadcast among these young aristocrats skepticism in regard to contemporary practices and forms of social thinking and organization. So influential was this skepticism that in many instances the followers of Socrates became political radicals who sought, not only to criticize existing governmental policies, but to modify them in actual legislation and in the interpretation given to the laws of the state and to the customs of their times.

At length, aroused by the radical tendencies of Socrates' followers, the conservative party in Athens brought about his execution as a false teacher.

Socrates never wrote out any of his own views with regard to the state. It was his followers who gave expression to his doctrines. The writings of Plato and Aristotle, therefore, have been among the chief vehicles through which the influence of Socrates has been brought to the modern world.

Plato (429–347 B. C.). Plato wrote on philosophy, on social subjects, and on government, developing ultimately a general theory of the state. This theory distinguishes between the different classes of society, and defends the general position, which he borrowed from Socrates, that knowledge and clear thinking are the only possible bases of good conduct. Practical writers have sometimes criticized Plato by pointing out that knowledge is not always immediately expressed in action. A man may think clearly on social matters and yet not be just in his social behavior. Plato, on the other hand, emphasized very explicitly the relation between knowledge and action, and devoted his writings and teachings to the development of this theory.

Plato's doctrine of the state distinguishes between the slaves who are to carry on the ordinary activities necessary to provide society with the necessities of life, the warriors who are to defend the state, and the philosophers who through meditation develop a system of laws and practices which shall embody all of the principles of justice.

His influence was very great over a large group of followers, whom he taught in the school which he founded and called the Academy. Here he taught not only his system of philosophy but the higher branches of mathematics, which he deemed an important part of the mental equipment of youth.

Plato's writings and teachings were accepted in the later medieval period as the chief authority on educational organization.

He divides higher education into four main branches—arithmetic, geometry, astronomy, and music. This subdivision of the subjects of instruction, known in the medieval period as the quadrivium, was long the basis of study of the school curriculum. Plato's discussion emphasizes, not only the importance of these particular subjects, but also the necessity of developing a unity and symmetry of thought which can be arrived at only by mastering the full round of the curriculum.

Plato was an idealist—an ardent advocate of the æsthetic and the moral in education. He was especially congenial to the religious leaders of the medieval period and to the later thinkers who, in the Renaissance, sought to restore Greek culture with all its artistic accompaniments.

Aristotle (384–322 B. C.). Aristotle was a much more practical and scientific teacher than was Plato. He was the instructor of Alexander the Great, and in later life he received from his royal pupil many additions to his materials of knowledge. It is said that Alexander sent to Aristotle, from all parts of the world into which he carried his expeditions, samples of the things which he found. He sent, for example, actual specimens of strange animals, with the result that the science of zoology developed in Aristotle's hands. In like fashion, other natural sciences were opened up by Aristotle because of the breadth of material which he found available.

Aristotle organized the Lyceum as a place where he trained the young legislators and statesmen of Athens. It became a center of research in biology, history, and the science of government. Aristotle developed numerous systems of knowledge which were of great influence during the medieval period, and his discussions on the nature of the mind were the bases of the psychology and of much of the theology of this time. He formulated the principles of logic, which were taken over to the great school at Alexandria and were later utilized by Euclid in the formulation of geometry. Through geometry the Aristotelian logic was carried into the medieval schools and became the most important subject of higher education in Europe, both in the medieval and in the early modern period. The disputes of the scholastics are based upon the principles of this logic.

Aristotle advocates the beginning of education when the child is seven years of age. He mentions and evaluates the various subjects to be taught, namely, reading and writing, gymnastics, music and drawing. He lays great stress on physical training and on reading and music.

Aristotle's theories about education were much less completely formulated than were those of Plato. He contributed new content for education rather than new methods of giving instruction.

Quintilian (35–100? A. D.). Quintilian was a teacher of rhetoric in Rome. He formulated a theory of education for the orator, which became the classic of subsequent organization of training in language and letters during the medieval and modern periods. Quintilian may be regarded as the father of classical education. In his day classical education meant, of course, the transfer of Greek learning to Roman soil. He pointed out quite explicitly that the study of Greek is not so important in its content as in the training which it gives to the young orator.

Quintilian wrote his educational works late in life, after a period of successful experience as a teacher of Roman boys. It was his theory that the proper training of the orator must begin with infancy. He therefore devotes much of his writing to the theory of training the child from infancy up. He wrote a series of books entitled *De Institutione Oratoria*, in which he gave in great detail the methods of literary training. For example, he discussed the teaching of writing, and advocated teaching the forms of letters by requiring the child to trace letters which had been written for him. He afterwards discussed in equally great detail the method of teaching Greek grammar and the methods of teaching literary style. Quintilian favored also, as had Plato, the teaching of geometry and music as parts of a liberal education. He discussed the matter of corporal punishment, and advocated an abandonment of frequent floggings, on the grounds that the child's individuality must be respected.

Quintilian's influence in formulating the modern classical curriculum is perhaps greater than that of any other single writer.

Alcuin (735–804). Alcuin has been mentioned in the earlier paragraphs. He was educated in the Cathedral of York in England, and came to the continent as educational adviser of Charlemagne. In this capacity he exercised a great influence, not only over the princes who which were his pupils, but in the political matters with which his master was always engaged. His influence was felt in the more vigorous and systematic organization of education and of the intellectual side of civilization wherever his pupils went.

Anselm (1033–1109). Anselm has been called the father of scholasticism. He was archbishop of Canterbury in England. For a time he did his work in the monastery of Bec, which he made the chief center of learning in western Europe. His teachings were chiefly upon religious doctrines. His fundamental principle was that Christianity can be founded on stable grounds only if reason guides. He trained his followers, therefore, to cultivate methods of correct and vigorous thinking. From Bec there issued, as a result, the most vigorous disputants of the age.

Peter Abelard (1079–1142) was the most famous teacher of the 12th century. Like all teachers of that day he was trained for theology, and his fame rests in large part upon his ability as a disputant on theological topics. He was an opponent of William of Champeaux, whom he seriously worsted in theological debate. He became a hermit in Champagne but hundreds of students flocked to him and were influenced by his liberal and spirited teachings. He is one of the important forerunners of the school of theology which afterwards became the great University of Paris. Much of the teaching which he did in his early years was at Notre Dame in Paris.

Saint Thomas Aquinas (1225–1274). Aquinas was undoubtedly the greatest and most influential philosopher of the middle ages. He adopted the method of teaching which later came to be universal in European universities, namely, the so-called commentary. He read Aristotle's works to his students and followed the reading by critical comments. This method is reflected in the lecture method of instruction which is common today in all higher institutions of learning in Europe and America.

Aquinas was a voluminous writer on theological and philosophical topics. His writings, like his oral methods of teaching, have exercised a lasting influence. No single authority has contributed more to the fixed teachings of the Roman Catholic Church and its schools than Aquinas.

Erasmus (1466 1536) was one of the leaders in the Northern Renaissance. He was educated in the schools of the Brethren of the Common Life in France and later was himself a teacher of the classics in various parts of Europe, and the author of many of the textbooks used in the teaching of Latin. He was the author of several treatises on education. In these he points out the importance of beginning education early and developing the powers of the child in the natural order. He also maintains that it is the business of the Church and state to see that there is an adequate number of properly qualified teachers. He himself exemplified throughout his life devotion to the profession which he thus aimed to promote in these writings. He was at home in all parts of Europe because of his command of the classical languages and is said to have been known in all of the schools of his time and during the century following his life.

Martin Luther (1483–1546). Luther was the father of the Reformation in Germany. The essentials of Luther's teaching were independence of religious belief and reliance on individual faith. Luther championed the cause of the common people and by his writings strove to improve the intellectual condition of his fellow citizens. He and his followers, like many of his lay and clerical contemporaries, were friendly to the classics, but he advocated the establishment of vernacular schools for the common people. He combated vigorously the pseudo-science of astrology.

The main subject of Luther's interest was religious teaching, and he is regarded as the pioneer of Protestant household instruction. His influence has undoubtedly been of prime importance in keeping in the curriculum of the common schools of Germany, even though they are under secular control, instruction in religion.

Ignatius Loyola (1491–1556). Loyola was a Spanish youth brought up in the court of Ferdinand and Isabella. He was wounded while engaged in military operations against the French. During the period of his convalescence he read certain religious treatises and resolved to give his life to the Church.

He became the leader in a movement for reform within the clergy. With a number of his followers, he founded, under a charter granted by Pope Paul III, the Order of Jesus, which has been throughout its history a teaching and missionary order.

The object of the order is described as "The progress of souls in good life and knowledge of religion, the propagation of faith by public preaching, spiritual exercises, and works of charity, and particularly the instruction of youth and ignorant persons in the Christian religion."

In the accomplishment of this purpose, the order established schools and colleges, and developed the so-called *Ratio Studiorum*, or plan of studies, which prescribed a rigid training in the classics and in religion. Latin and Greek were the backbone of the curriculum, but science and mathematics were also included. Where the order undertook missionary enterprises, the scope of the curriculum was enlarged to include instruction in the vernacular and in rudimentary subjects. The characteristic of all the teaching was its systematic and carefully planned organization.

Ignatius Loyola was not a reformer in the sense that he revolted against earlier ideals; he aimed rather at realizing ideals for which the Church already stood. His companion Peter Canisius strove to check the progress of Luther's social and religious teaching in Germany. Loyola's labors gave to the Catholic Church the order which continued to exert great influence over its educational activities. See *Jesuits*.

Johannes Sturm (1507–1589) was a German educator of the extreme classical type. He was educated in the school of the Brethren of the Common Life at Liege. His chief work was carried on in the Gymnasium at Strasbourg. He was a rigid disciplinarian and a devoted classicist. He was an organizer of large ability and, by virtue of the fact that he wrote extensively on methods of education and organization of secondary education, his influence spread to other cities and to other countries. The modern organization of the German gymnasium is to be attributed in very large measure to the influence of the school which he conducted in Strasbourg.

Roger Ascham (1515–1568) wrote after 1563 an educational work entitled *The Schoolmaster*. It is one of the most representative Renaissance writings in England. It is full of a liberal spirit and exhibits a large interest in physical education as well as intellectual training. In this book Ascham describes the method of teaching Latin which is known as the method of double translation. The Latin author is to be translated first into English and afterward to be translated back again into Latin. Ascham's book on schoolteaching is interesting, not merely because of the liberal reforms he suggested in teaching, but also because of its literary style and because of the insight which it gives into the social and political life of the day in which he wrote.

Francis Bacon (1561–1626) was an English philosopher, statesman, and man of letters. He was one of the brilliant group that gathered around Queen Elizabeth. He advocated the development of science through observation and direct contact with objects, as distinguished from the acceptance of statements made by writers of books.

His educational influence is general rather than specific. He inaugurated the period of sense-realism. His methods of scientific investigation were indeed much less productive than those of some of his contemporaries, but his writings were of such an impressive character as to attract the attention of readers and to give prestige to his theory that education should be based on direct observation.

John Amos Comenius (1592–1670). Comenius, or Komensky if the Bohemian form of his name is used, ushered in the change in attitude which came naturally after the long period of formal classical education. He was interested in making knowledge concrete and definite. He criticized the schools in the most severe terms, pointing out that they dealt in words rather than in useful forms of knowledge. He characterized the schools as "the slaughterhouses of the mind where ten or more years are spent in learning what might be acquired in one." "They are," he said, "places where minds are fed on words." These criticisms he made because of his experiences in the gymnasium in Prerau and his observation of the attitude of his fellow pupils in that and other schools which he attended.

He began his work as an educational reformer by preparing new materials for the teaching of Latin. He selected the names of common objects and arranged this selected vocabulary in simple sentences which the pupils could understand. Later he added to the concreteness of his teaching by preparing a pictorial encyclopedia called *Orbis Pictus*, in which lists of words are given. Each word is defined and accompanied by an illustration.

In order to change the practices of the schools, he organized a school at Sarospatak, near Tokay. Here, he made education thoroughly interesting to his pupils by instruction that was concrete rather than abstract.

He is to be described as the father of realism in modern education. He ushered in a period in which education was to cease being austere and remote and was to become sympathetic and helpful to the pupil, interesting and congenial to the child's native tendencies.

John Locke (1632–1704). Locke was one of a group of essayists who wrote on education, though their chief interests were in other matters. He was an English philosopher who spent his time and energy chiefly in discussing the issues of philosophy. His great work is his *Essay Concerning Human Understanding*. This, together with his political writings, gave him an influential position among the serious readers of his day.

His book entitled *Thoughts on Education* is a protest against too close devotion to books and bookish knowledge. He would have the young English gentleman, on whom his "thoughts" are concentrated, travel and become acquainted with things rather than merely learn languages.

Locke was a modern realist in every sense of the word. He belonged to a period when natural science was flourishing in England. His philosophical system was realistic in its interests, and he was thus one of the early advocates of a new type of education which breaks away from the severely classical traditions of an earlier period.

Jean Jacques Rousseau (1712–1778). Rousseau wrote at a time when education was dominated by the idea that the younger members of the court of France must be trained in the social arts which would make them acceptable in court life. The strictly court type of training which had been evolved was not primarily a system for the training of the intellects of the pupils. It was a course in manners. The breach between the common people, who had to work, and the aristocracy, who idled about the court and cultivated artificial manners, was daily growing wider; and Rousseau, as he wrote on education, was writing also on political issues.

Indeed, his two great works deal, one with political theory, the other with the theory of the training of the individual. We may, perhaps, gain a better view of his educational theory by referring first to his chief political essay, entitled the *Social Contract*. Rousseau held, in this essay, that the rights of the sovereign arise from the consent of society. In a primitive state men are at war with one another, but seeing that war is destructive they come together and form a group, agreeing each in his turn to surrender some of his individual rights to the group as a whole. The social contract thus formed is held to be the basis of civilized government. Rousseau's doctrine of the social contract was a powerful influence in the French Revolution. It has been said that this book helped more than anything else to precipitate the Revolution.

On the side of individual training, Rousseau held that all of the false institutions which have grown up in modern society must first be eliminated if the individual is to come to the full development of his powers and personality. He wrote a book entitled *Emile*, in which he expressed his educational doctrines in the form of a life history of a boy who is supposed to have been properly educated. This book begins with the famous statement that all things are good as they come from the hand of the Creator. It is man who has destroyed the natural goodness of everything. Rousseau advocates, therefore, a return to nature. The boy who is to be properly educated must be taken away from association with society. He must never see a book until he is sufficiently mature to escape all the evil consequences which result from the use of books. Freed, in this way, from contact with society and books, the child must wander in the woods and open country and gather up knowledge which will satisfy his natural curiosity. In order that this boy may have the advantage of such knowledge as the race has accumulated, he is to be accompanied by a sympathetic tutor whose business it is merely to help him answer the spontaneous questions which arise in his mind. After the child has reached a certain stage of maturity, he should be led to see the importance of cultivating some type of skill which, in case of necessity, will provide him in later life with the means of livelihood. Still later, he may be brought back into the society from which he has been separated during the earlier period, and may now be introduced to books and men. He will be able to adjust himself to the social conditions which he thus encounters, because of the intelligence and the strength of physique which he has cultivated through his early training.

Rousseau's *Emile* was so fascinatingly written that it was accepted by Europe as a philosophy of life as well as a scheme of education. His teachings have also been of influence in subsequent generations where the general principle of the return to nature has seemed most attractive to those who are critical of modern society and the modes of life which modern education has developed. There are constant references to Rousseau's doctrine of education in such modern theories as that developed by Madame Montessori.

In many quarters of Europe, immediately following the appearance of his book, the education of children was organized on the free plan suggested by Rousseau. Not only were children taken out into the open fields and woods, but mature individuals attempted to give themselves a freedom of life and a detachment from the difficult problems of modern society by accepting Rousseau's doctrine as a philosophy of life.

From the nature of the case, Rousseau's teachings did not lead to the organization of a school system or a group of teachers. His writings tended, however, to modify the practice of existing schools in the direction of greater freedom and the recognition of natural impulses of children.

Johann Basedow (1723–1790). Basedow is the educational reformer of the post-Reformation period who is to be compared in general character with Comenius of the pre-Reformation era. Basedow, like Comenius, conceived of education as an appeal to the natural interests of children. He sought to promote nature study and contact with objects.

He devoted himself assiduously to the preparation of suitable textbooks for use in schools. In order to secure the funds for the preparation and publication of these books, he made an appeal to men of property for a public subscription and received a generous response. His movement was termed from this time on Philanthropinism.

The influence of Rousseau is very marked in the writings of Basedow. His motto was, "everything according to nature." A description of the new type of school which he established is given by Herr Schummelas as follows:

"I have just come from a visit with my father to the Philanthropin, where I saw Herr Basedow, Herr Wolke, Herr Simon, Herr Schweighauser, and the little Philanthropinists. I am delighted with all that I have seen, and hardly know where to begin my description of it. There are two large white houses, and near them a field with trees. A pupil—not one of the regular scholars, but of those they call Famulants (a poorer class, who were servitors)—received us at the door, and asked if we wished to see Herr Basedow. We said 'Yes,' and he took us into the other house, where we found Herr Basedow in a dressing gown, writing at a desk. We came at an inconvenient time, and Herr Basedow said he was very busy. He was very friendly, however, and promised to visit us in the evening. We then went into the other house, and inquired for Herr Wolke."

By him they were taken to the scholars. "They have," says Fred, "their hair cut very short, and no wigmaker is employed. Their throats are quite open, and their shirt-collar falls back over their coats." Further on he describes the examination. "The little ones have gone through the oddest performances. They play at 'word-of-command.' Eight or ten stand in a line like soldiers, and Herr Wolke is officer. He gives the word in Latin, and they must do whatever he says. For instance, when he says *claudite oculos*, they all shut their eyes; when he says *circumspicite*, they look about them; *imitamini sartorem*, they all sew like tailors; *imitanini sutorem*, they draw the waxed thread like the cobblers. Herr Wolke gives a thousand different commands in the drollest fashion.

"Another game, 'the hiding game,' I will also teach you. Some one writes a name, and hides it from the children— the name of some part of the body, or of a plant, or animal, or metal—and the children guess what it is. Whoever guesses right gets an apple or piece of cake. One of the visitors wrote *intestina*, and told the children it was a part of the body. Then the guessing began. One guessed *caput*, another *nasus*, another *os*, another *manus*, *pes*, *digiti*, *pectus*, and so forth, for a long time; but one of them hit it at last. Next, Herr Wolke wrote the name of a beast, a quadruped. Then came the guesses: *leo*, *ursus*, *camelus*, *elephas*, and so on, till one guessed right—it was *mus* Then a town was written, and they guessed Lisbon, Madrid, Paris, London, till a child won with St. Petersburg. They had another game, which was this: Herr Wolke gave the command in Latin, and they imitated the noises of different animals, and made us laugh till we were tired. They roared like lions, crowed like cocks, mewed like cats, just as they were bid."

Johann Heinrich Pestalozzi (1746–1827). Pestalozzi is one of the world's greatest educational reformers. He was born in Zurich, Switzerland, and did his work in the little Alpine republic, but his influence has spread to every civilized country on the globe.

He was in temperament and behavior erratic and unsystematic. He failed to hold together the schools which he founded, and so far as his personal affairs were concerned he was always unfortunate. But in his insight into the needs of the common people, in his sympathy with children, and in his genius for devising methods of teaching, he is one of the foremost leaders of modern times.

After drifting from one enterprise to another, Pestalozzi wrote and published in 1781 the work on which his fame chiefly rests, a book entitled *Leonard and Gertrude*. In this book the author gives first a picture of the deplorable condition of a poor family in a Swiss village. The picture shows how the family lacked all the comforts of life and all prospects of securing even the barest living necessities. In the midst of these squalid conditions, the brave mother, Gertrude, takes up the task of teaching her children. Gertrude turns out to be such a genius in getting her children to carry on the simple industrial and domestic activities to which she directs their attention that, through their co-operation, she relieves the condition of the family and ultimately the poverty of the whole village.

Gertrude's method is that of organizing the children's activities and at the same time instructing them in the intelligent comprehension of all that is about them. She reads to them as they work. The language of her school concerns itself with the commonplace facts of everyday life, and yet it raises these facts to the level of understood and clearly explained matters. The moral tone of the home and of the village is raised through this intellectual clarification of the facts of life. Skill which is cultivated at the same time that minds are trained makes it possible for the children to develop comfortable and wholesome surroundings.

Pestalozzi's message came as a great inspiration to an age which was impoverished by wars and by the lack of trained workers in industry. All over Europe the effort was put forth by rulers and religious leaders to bring the common people up to the level described in *Leonard and Gertrude*.

His teachings were brought to America and were eagerly accepted, especially at the normal school at Oswego, N. Y. Under the leadership of its principal, Edward Austin Sheldon (1823–97), this school became a great center for the dissemination of the doctrine of sense training, observation, and the cultivation of practical knowledge.

Charles Maurice Talleyrand-Périgord (1754–1838) was a French statesman. To his influence may be attributed the compact organization of the educational system of France. Napoleon adopted the suggestions which he made with regard to the organization of the educational system, and made it in this way a part of the public policy of France. To Talleyrand himself the organization of the educational system was a mere side issue. He was engaged in important diplomatic and political missions at different times during his life and seems not to have been seriously interested in carrying out the reforms which he had suggested in his writings. His personal influence, therefore, is relatively slight, although his statesmanship appears in the organization which he suggested and which was adopted by the French state.

Johann Friedrich Herbart (1776–1841). Herbart was a German philosopher and teacher. He was the first educational reformer to enunciate clearly the idea that education must be organized on the basis of carefully ascertained scientific principles. There are two sciences, he pointed out, on which education must be based—psychology and ethics. The first supplies an analytical account of the nature of the human mind which is to be educated; the second works out the social goals toward which educational systems must direct their efforts.

Herbart had experience as a tutor of boys in the home of the governor of Interlaken, and he was thoroughly acquainted with the sciences on which he proposed to base education. Indeed, his occupation was that of professor of philosophy in various German universities.

The system of psychology of which he was author stimulated the empirical studies of the last century which resulted in the establishment of laboratories for the development of an experimental and physiological science. The system was not in itself especially productive for education. The pedagogical writings of Herbart seem to have grown more out of his practical experience than out of his system of psychology.

Herbart laid great stress on the importance of arousing the pupils' interests and then extending these interests in many directions, until there should result what he calls many-sidedness of interest.

Herbart's doctrine of apperception is another of his leading contributions to educational theory. All experiences, in order to be clear, must be introduced into the learner's experience in such a way as to be fully assimilated.

In order that ideas may be apperceived, teachers must have a regular method of getting ideas into the pupil's mind. The method involves five steps, which are known as formal steps because they can be adopted as the proper form for any content whatsoever. These steps are preparation, presentation, assimilation, generalization, and application. Put in other words, the experience of the pupil must be so marshaled that the mind is ready to take in the new idea. This must then be presented in clear form.

The mind must have time to receive the idea and put it into its proper relations. The mind must then contemplate it until the general nature of the new idea is recognized. Finally, the mind must carry over what it has absorbed into all productive new relations or applications.

Herbart's influence has been very great in America. Through the school at the University of Jena in Germany, over which Professor Wilhelm Rein (1847–1929) for many years presided, a great many Americans, notably Charles DeGarmo and Frank and Charles McMurry, were introduced to Herbartianism. They have been prolific writers on educational methods.

Friedrich Froebel (1782–1852). Froebel was the founder of the kindergarten. He was powerfully influenced on the one side by Pestalozzi, whose school at Yverdun he visited for a period, and on the other side by the idealistic philosophy of Schelling and Fichte.

Unlike Pestalozzi, he was not especially interested in the practical aspects of human training, but he was absorbed in the attempt to bring into complete harmony the inner experience of the child and the natural world in which the child lived. Prompted by his idealistic philosophy, he sought to bring about this harmonizing of the inner and outer worlds by finding the universal principles in nature and exposing the child to these at the earliest possible age.

There is much mysticism in Froebel's thinking and writing. This fact has led to confusion in the development of the institution which he founded. Indeed, it has permitted a certain sentimentalism to come into the kindergarten, which has tended to inhibit the careful study of children and their needs.

Froebel's Principles.—A number of extracts from Froebel's writings will serve to bring out the leading principles of his educational philosophy:

"A life of more than thirty years with nature, often, it is true, falling back and clouded for great intervals, has taught me to know this, especially the plant and tree world, as a mirror, I might say, an emblem of man's life in its highest spiritual relations; so that I look upon it as one of the greatest and deepest conceptions of human life and spirit when in Holy Scripture the comparison of good and evil is drawn from a tree. Nature, as a whole, even the realms of crystals and stones, teaches us to discriminate good from evil; but, for me, not so powerfully, quietly, clearly, and openly as the plant and flower kingdom.

"The child . . . perceives in the ball the general expression of each object as well as of itself (the child) as a self-dependent whole and unity . . . so the child likes to employ himself with the ball, even early in life, in order to cultivate and fashion himself, though unconsciously, through and by it, as that which is his opposite and yet resembles him.

"The cube is to the child the representative of each continually developing manifold body. The child has an intimation in it of the unity which lies at the foundation of all manifoldness and from which the latter proceeds.

"The pleasure with which the children play these games and others of a similar kind may therefore have its ground in a presentiment of what is symbolic and significant in them. May not their delight in these encircling movements, for example, spring from the longing and the effort to get an all-round or all-sided grasp of an object? . . . I am convinced that the exalted and often ecstatic delight of children in their simple movement plays is by no means to be explained through the exertion of mere physical force—merely bodily activity. The true source of their joy is the dim premonition which stirs their sensitive hearts that in their play there is hidden a deep significance; that it is, in fact, the husk within which is concealed the kernel of a living spiritual truth.

"Experience and history, too, teach that men truly and effectively promote human welfare much more by what they put forth from themselves than by what they may have acquired. Every one knows that those who truly teach, gain steadily in knowledge and insight . . . Again, to learn a thing in life and through doing is much more developing, cultivating and strengthening than to learn it merely through verbal communication of ideas. Similarly, plastic material representation in life and through doing, united with thought and speech, is by far more developing and cultivating than the merely verbal representation of ideas

"The young growing human being should, therefore, be trained early for outer work, for creative and productive activity . . . play, building, modeling are the first tender

NOTABLE COLLEGES

Above Timothy Dwight College, Yale University, New Haven, Connecticut. One of the numerous colleges on the campus which serve as dormitories for male students.

Above Chapel at Duke University in Durham, North Carolina. The university was founded in 1838.

Right Taylor Gate at Vassar College, Poughkeepsie, New York. An institution for women, Vassar was founded in 1861.

Below Hoover Tower at Stanford University, California. This building, named for former president Herbert Hoover, a Stanford alumnus, contains the Hoover Institute and the Library on War, Revolution, and Peace. The university was founded in 1885.

Below Striking in its modern architectural design, the Kresge Auditorium of the Massachusetts Institute of Technology, located in Cambridge, Massachusetts, combines simplicity with efficiency.
MIT Office of Public Relations

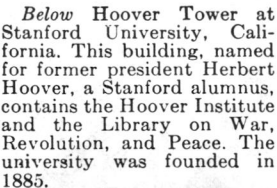

Below Dunster House of Harvard University in Cambridge, Massachusetts. This house is one of the seven dormitories for the students. Harvard is one of the country's oldest educational institutions and was founded in 1636.

Mark Hopkins

Horace Mann

AMERICAN EDUCATORS

Mary McLeod Bethune
Culver Pictures, Inc.

Rev. Theodore M. Hesburgh, C.S.C.

James B. Conant

David Starr Jordan

John Dewey

John W. Gardner
Los Angeles Times

blossoms of youth . . . Every child, boy and youth, whatever his condition or position in life, should devote daily at least one or two hours to some serious activity in the production of some definite external piece of work. It would be a most wholesome arrangement in schools to establish actual working hours similar to the existing study hours; and it will surely come to this.

"A universal and comprehensive plan of human education must, therefore, necessarily consider at an early period singing, drawing, painting, and modeling; it will not leave them to an arbitrary, frivolous whimsicalness, but treat them as serious objects of the school. Its intention will not be to make each pupil an artist in some one or all of the arts, but to secure to each human being full and all-sided development, to enable him to see man in the universality and all-sided energy of his nature, and, particularly, to enable him to understand and appreciate the products of true art.

"This school (he said) will be based on the interdependence of doing and thinking, representation and knowledge, art, and science . . . on the student's personal efforts in work and expression, making these again the foundation of all genuine knowledge and culture. Joined with thoughtfulness, these efforts become a direct medium of culture; joined with reasoning, they become a direct means of instruction, and thus make of work a true subject of instruction."

Thomas Arnold (1795–1842) was head master of Rugby for 14 years, from 1828 to 1841. During this period he exercised on the organization of secondary education in England an influence which was of the greatest importance. He assumed in an intimate way the social and intellectual leadership of Rugby. He contributed very largely to the establishment of the type of discipline which has come to be regarded as characteristic of the English so-called public schools. He was in favor of classical studies but he also provided, in the curriculum of his school, for modern history and modern languages and mathematics. In all these subjects he maintained the highest standards of scholarly exactness. The integrity of his character and the great influence which he exercised over the boys who attended Rugby is reflected in Thomas Hughes's *Tom Brown's School Days*. The influence of his methods of administration spread to the other schools of England.

Horace Mann (1796–1859). Mann was the first secretary of the state board of education in Massachusetts. In this position he exercised an enormous influence during the critical period of reconstruction which brought into being the American graded elementary school as a substitute for the older district school.

Mann was an indefatigable worker and a prolific writer. His annual reports deal with all kinds of problems, such as illiteracy, school buildings and sanitation, the training and employment of teachers, methods of teaching, methods of local school control, and public financing of education.

He was greatly impressed by the organization of German schools, and advocated the conservative importation of some of the practices which he observed there. He pointed out fearlessly the faults which he found in existing schools and suggested many reforms.

His criticisms aroused much animosity among the schoolmasters, especially those in the Boston schools, and brought him into sharp controversies. However, he was able to secure the establishment of the first normal school to have a continuous existence in his country. He modified the district school; he greatly improved public respect for education; and he fundamentally changed the methods of teaching in the schools.

Henry Barnard (1811–1900). Barnard was successively the head of the school systems of Connecticut and Rhode Island. He was also the editor of the *American Journal of Education*, which during the period of its publication in the middle of the last century was one of the leading factors in bringing about far-reaching reforms in American education. With Mann, Stowe (1802–86), and others, Barnard labored for the more definite organization of instruction, especially in elementary schools. He visited the schools of Europe, helped to acquaint

American educators with the teachings of Pestalozzi, and contributed through his administrative activities to the improvement of elementary education.

Herbert Spencer (1820–1903). Herbert Spencer conceived early in his career the idea of preparing a comprehensive statement of the philosophy of the world. In order to develop this complete system of philosophy he began with an investigation of biological science, and from this point progressed through a study of society and its nature and of the individual and his nature to a treatment of the problems of ethics, or human conduct. Spencer laid the foundation for sociology and the modern studies of society. In the course of his inquiry he naturally came upon the problems of educational organization.

He found the English higher schools devoted to classical training, which had been traditional throughout the medieval and modern periods, on the theory that, through this type of training, the discipline of the mind can be secured more effectively than by any other means. Against this classical scheme of education Spencer rebelled. His interest in the sciences was so keen that he defended scientific training as superior to classical training for all purposes, even for the discipline of the mind. His discussion of education was embodied in four essays which were published in 1861 and have been widely read. They were perhaps more effective in the United States than in England, because in this country the classical tradition was less firmly established.

The first of Spencer's educational essays was entitled *What Knowledge is of Most Worth?* His answer to the question is that scientific knowledge is much more significant than any training in mere letters. In the course of his discussion he mercilessly criticized existing schools as utter failures in preparing children for the practical duties of life. Especially he points out that in such important matters as preparation for parenthood the school curriculum is silent. Science, he contends also, is even more useful than the classics for the discipline of the mind.

The second essay lays down the proper principles of *Intellectual Education*, such as progression from the simple to the complex and from the concrete to the abstract. The third of his essays is on moral training, and expresses the general view that punishment is justified only when it follows the pattern of nature and gives the child the training which will improve his adaptation to the world about him. The fourth essay advocates a better physical training for pupils.

Spencer's essays have done much to promote the development of the modern scientific curriculum in American high schools and colleges. His influence has also been large in the development in higher institutions of the social studies, such as sociology and political science.

William Torrey Harris (1835–1909). Harris contributed to educational reform through his work in the city of Saint Louis, where he was for years superintendent of schools, and in the Federal bureau of education where, during the later years of his life, he was commissioner.

In Saint Louis he introduced the kindergarten, reorganized the elementary schools and their curriculum, set up an eight-year graded system in the elementary schools, and promoted secondary education.

In the bureau of education, he elaborated the reports and laid the foundation for the most complete system of school statistics published by any government.

In his contributions to education, Harris labored to accomplish three great purposes. The first was to psychologize education. Along with other leaders in the school world, he showed the futility of the old-time psychology, with its so-called "faculties of the mind," and demonstrated the worth of the new. His second purpose was to establish faith in the school as an institution having sociological functions and value. In the *Report of the Committee of Fifteen* he discussed four bases for the correlation of studies: (1) the logical order of topics and studies; (2) the symmetrical whole of studies in the world of human learning; (3) psychological symmetry; (4) the pupil's natural and spiritual environment. His final purpose was to place education upon an enduring foundation. He subjected the whole field to critical analysis, interpreting and justifying the school and assigning to it its proper place in the scheme of institutional life.

Alfred Binet (1857–1911). Binet was a French psychologist and director of the laboratory of physiological psychology at the Sorbonne. Prior to 1905, he had made numerous investigations of the deficiencies exhibited by children in the course of their development. At this date he was asked by the school authorities of Paris to undertake the study of children in the public school systems, for the purpose of detecting the various forms of mental deficiency which interfered with school work. He devised a series of tests, with the co-operation of Thomas Simon. These tests have been very widely used in Europe and in the United States as a means of determining the intellectual possibilities of children. The characteristic of these tests is that they are arranged in such a way as to determine the intellectual age of the child. By a series of trials, Binet assembled those tests which should be passed by a child three years of age if he is entirely normal in his mental development. Other series were developed for other ages, so that it is possible by means of this scale to compare any given child with other children of his chronological age. Various revisions of the Binet scale have been made by Terman and others who have taken up the work, especially in the United States.

Granville Stanley Hall (1846–1924). Hall was an American psychologist and writer on education. In 1881 he established at Johns Hopkins university one of the earliest psychological laboratories in the United States. He was the chief leader in the child study movement. In 1888 he became president of a university established in Worcester, Massachusetts, and named after its chief patron, Clark university. This institution was devoted entirely to graduate work, and, during the first two decades after its establishment, developed chiefly research in education under Hall's personal leadership. Hall was a severe critic of formalism in the schools. He advocated the abandonment of the ordinary types of teaching in the primary grades and a substitution, for the academic training in those grades, of physical education and observation of natural objects.

For the higher schools, he advocated a complete reorganization of the curriculum on the basis of studies he made of the adolescent period. His most influential work is a treatise on *Adolescence*, in which he describes this period as a distinct phase in the child's development, analogous to the periods of evolution which have led from time to time to the production of new species in the animal kingdom. The great emphasis which Hall laid upon the fundamental change which comes with the adolescent period in human life made him one of the chief exponents of the doctrine of periodicity in education.

During the later years of his presidency at Clark university, Hall's influence distinctly diminished, because of the lack of scientific methods in his work and the development in other quarters of more productive lines of educational research.

Charles William Eliot (1834–1926). Eliot became president of Harvard college in 1869. He found a conservative institution devoted chiefly to classical instruction. He reconstructed the college and transformed it into a great university.

Among his most notable educational reforms is the development of an elective system. Through this system, which has now become universal in American colleges and high schools, a student can so select subjects of study as to give himself the specific training which he needs for the calling in life which he intends to take up.

Eliot also labored for the enlargement of the college curriculum. He brought about the introduction of a great variety of subjects. The result is that a college is no longer the home of a small group of selected students who are intending to enter the learned professions,—it is the resort of all classes.

As the chairman of the Committee of Ten of the National Education Association, Eliot contributed to the organization of the American high school.

He retired at seventy years of age from the active presidency of Harvard, universally recognized as the Nestor of American education.

John Dewey (1859–1952). Dewey is first of all a teacher of philosophy. His contributions in the fields of logic and ethics have been of major importance in determining the trend of current thinking. His philosophical system is characterized by its devotion to the accomplishment of practical ends. Thus, in his theory of logic he points out that it is the solution of problems which in all cases stimulates human intellectual effort. In the field of ethics he has shown himself to be interested in practical social reforms of all types. Especially has he emphasized the influence of industrial and economic life on human conduct.

In the field of education he has been an untiring critic of formalism of every type. He began by objecting to the type of reading matter which is taken up in the schools, where very frequently words are substituted for fruitful ideas. Teachers, he points out, have been content to carry children through many series of exercises which have no meaning to the children themselves. Education ought to deal with the living interests of children and ought to use books only when children, of their own initiative, see the importance of going to this source of information.

In order to make concrete his educational doctrines, Dewey established a school which was entirely unconventional in its form of organization and in its practice. In this school the ordinary forms of discipline were abandoned, and the children were allowed freedom to ask questions as they occurred to them and to move about without restraint in seeking materials with which to answer these questions. For example, the children were given opportunity to cook their own meals, in order that they might come into contact with practical problems of social institutions. They were, for the same reasons, given training in the woodworking shop and in the garden.

Charles Hubbard Judd (1873–1946). Through energetic use of his outstanding abilities as teacher, orator, writer, and college administrator, Judd became one of the most influential leaders in American education. He was trained to be a psychologist, and during the early years of his professional career he taught psychology and completed many renowned researches in that subject. During his later years his interest shifted to education. He believed that the problems of education could be attacked scientifically, and he became the nation's greatest protagonist of the scientific movement in education. In his classroom instruction he insisted that his students buttress their opinions with objective data and that they meet the highest standards of scholarship in every other manner.

Most of his professional career was spent at the University of Chicago where he was professor and head of the department of education from 1909 until he retired in 1938. He served at least one term as president of several nationally prominent educational organizations. He was a remarkably effective platform orator and was more frequently than any other educator of his generation called upon to address professional and lay groups in all sections of the United States. He was the author of numerous books and of many other works on psychology and education.

RECENT EXPANSION IN AMERICAN EDUCATION

Since 1870, American education has expanded so rapidly that a special section may with propriety be devoted to the discussion of this period. Furthermore, it is possible to make very exact statements with regard to this development because the United States Office of Education has kept careful statistical records of the various phases of educational activity in the country. Our knowledge of educational institutions prior to 1870 is based largely on the facts that are known with regard to certain typical educational institutions. Subsequently to this date a full body of statistics is available.

INCREASE IN AVERAGE SCHOOLING

One of the striking facts about education in the United States is the large numbers of the population who attend school. In 1975 nearly 61 million people 3 to 34 years of age were enrolled in U.S. schools. Almost 31 million were in elementary school, 16 million in high school, and 10 million in college. More than $89 million was spent on education in the United States in 1973. The number of persons attending college for four or more years has tripled since 1940. The number of college degrees conferred has jumped from 499 thousand in 1950 to almost 1.5 million in 1974.

The significance of these figures may be pointed out in the following terms. As late as 1840 the American school taught the ordinary pupil practically nothing but "the three R's." The school term was very short, and attendance was very irregular. The result was that ordinary people got preparation for adult life chiefly through the domestic activities they encountered as children in the home and in which they participated to a greater or less extent. Since that date the average schooling demanded for intelligent participation in the commercial and industrial activities of ordinary life has been increasing more rapidly than in any other period in the world's history. The use of machinery in all phases of life and the rapid expansion of transportation are some of the important economic causes that have developed this situation. The school may be said to have contributed in some measure to this general change in the character of public life; in some degree it has merely followed the development of civilization and has endeavored to prepare young people for participation in commerce and industry.

Each U.S. census since 1940 has gathered statistics on the amount of schooling completed by the adult population of each state. The data found in census reports are extremely significant. They show the cumulative effect of mass education in recent years by the median of 12.3 years of school completed by the population 25 years of age or older in 1975 as compared with only 8.4 for this age group of the population in 1940.

Reading. Whatever is assigned as the cause of the development of the school, it is altogether clear from an examination of the facts that instruction has come to be in recent years a very much more important part of the individual's life than it was in

SCHOOL ENROLLMENTS

Age	1960 Number Enrolled	1960 Per cent Enrolled*	1965 Number Enrolled	1965 Per cent Enrolled*	1970 Number Enrolled	1970 Per cent Enrolled*	1975 Number Enrolled	1975 Per cent Enrolled*
Total, 5–34 years .	46,300,000	—	53,800,000	—	58,900,000	—	58,900,000	—
Male	24,200,000	60.0	28,100,000	63.5	30,600,000	62.6	30,500,000	57.7
Female	22,000,000	52.8	25,700,000	56.0	28,300,000	55.5	28,400,000	52.6
3–4 years	—	—	900,000	10.6	1,500,000	20.5	2,100,000	31.5
5–6 years	6,400,000	80.7	7,000,000	84.4	7,000,000	88.3	6,600,000	94.7
7–13 years	25,600,000	99.5	27,500,000	99.4	28,900,000	99.2	26,100,000	99.3
14–17 years	10,200,000	90.3	13,000,000	93.2	14,800,000	94.1	15,700,000	93.6
18–19 years	1,800,000	38.4	2,900,000	46.3	3,300,000	47.7	3,800,000	46.9
20–24 years	1,400,000	13.1	2,400,000	19.0	3,400,000	21.5	4,100,000	22.4
25–34 years	800,000	3.6	1,000,000	4.4	1,500,000	6.0	2,600,000	8.5

Source: U.S. Department of Commerce, Bureau of the Census.

SCHOOL EXPENDITURES, SOURCE OF FUNDS

	Total (in billion of dollars) 1960*	1970	1973	1974	1975	Per cent 1970	1975
Elementary/Secondary†	18.0	45.5	57.8	63.3	68.5	100.0	100.0
Public	15.9	41.0	52.1	57.1	61.8	90.1	90.2
Federal	0.7	3.3	4.7	4.6	5.5	7.3	8.0
State	5.6	16.3	20.5	22.7	24.7	35.8	36.1
Local	9.5	21.3	26.8	29.7	31.5	46.8	46.0
Other	0.1	0.1	0.1	0.1	0.1	0.2	0.1
Nonpublic	2.1	4.5	5.7	6.2	6.7	9.9	9.8
Higher Education‡ . .	6.7	24.7	31.4	35.0	40.2	100.0	100.0
Public	3.8	15.8	20.7	23.2	26.8	64.0	66.7
Federal	0.5	2.4	3.1	3.4	3.8	9.7	9.5
State/Local	1.8	7.1	9.9	11.2	13.2	28.7	32.8
Other	1.5	6.3	7.7	8.6	9.8	25.5	24.4
Nonpublic	2.9	8.9	10.7	11.8	13.4	36.0	33.3
Federal	0.5	1.7	2.0	2.1	2.3	6.9	5.7
State/Local	§	0.2	0.3	0.4	0.4	0.8	1.0
Other	2.4	7.0	8.4	9.3	10.7	28.3	26.6

Source: U.S. Department of Commerce, Bureau of the Census. * Years refer to the end of school year. † Includes kindergartens and publicly financed nursery schools. ‡ Includes institutions granting degrees, offering degree-credit courses, or offering nondegree occupational curriculums. § Less than $50 million.

the middle of the last century. A concrete illustration of this is to be found in the changes which have taken place in respect to the ability of the common man to read and write.

Since the invention and the development of printing, reading has become the greatest intellectualizing agency in the world, and, thanks to the schools, the people of the United States have become the most avid readers in the world. According to N. W. Ayer's *American Newspaper Annual and Directory*, more than 22,130 different newspapers and magazines were published in the United States in 1964. This number far exceeds that of any other country; in fact, it approximates one-third of the periodical publications of the whole world. There are few homes in the United States that do not subscribe for at least one newspaper and for at least one magazine.

Some of the more important reasons for the tremendous development in periodical publication and circulation in the United States are stated as follows by the author of a special census report on newspapers and magazines:

"This sketch of the rise and development of the American newspaper has now reached the period of time which marks the commencement of the third and present era in its history. It is not possible to assign the beginning of this era to any particular year or event, its coming being due to a variety of causes, which may be enumerated in the following order: First, the establishment of the penny press; second, the development of railroads as a means for the distribution of newspapers, the transmission of news reports, and the reduction of heavy postage rates; third, the discovery of telegraphy, and its immediate application to the purposes of journalism; and fourth, but not less important than other causes, the improvements of the printing press, which have rendered it possible to print large editions of newspapers in a short time."

Writing. Before commenting on the significance of these facts for education, it will be well to include in our discussion certain statistics which show that the more general use of reading has been accompanied by an equal demand for the mastery of the second of "the three R's," namely, writing.

A very definite knowledge of the extent to which writing has gained ground as a common art in the last three-quarters of a century can be obtained from an examination of the statistics of the post office. If we take all of the money paid for letter postage in 1843 and assume that it was spent for the cheapest letter that could be forwarded through the mails, it will be found that the average letter writing of each inhabitant of the United States during the full year amounted to less than four letters of one sheet each. This estimate is altogether extravagant, because the lowest letter postage of that date, namely, 6 cents, would carry only one sheet of paper within a radius of 30 miles. If letters went more than 30 miles, or were made up of more than one sheet, the cost was greater, reaching a maximum at 400 miles or more, when each sheet cost 25 cents. Letters sent at rates of postage higher than the minimum would reduce the average computed. It is fair to assume, therefore, that letter writing in 1843 was not a common practice.

Other facts of the same import are as follows: In 1840 the revenue of the post office for all classes of mail was 27 cents a year for each inhabitant of the United States. This amount had not doubled in 1870, when it was 49 cents. It rose to the point where in 1890 it was $0.97; in 1900, $1.34; in 1910, $2.43, and in 1946 more than $5. Not all of this was for letters, but the figures show that reading and writing are much more commonly used today than a generation ago. This conclusion is overwhelming when account is taken of the steady reduction of rates which until recently characterized the history of the post office.

Overcoming Illiteracy. Such statistics emphasize the fact that our modern life is utterly dependent on means of communication. This social fact is not merely an external material fact; it has to do with human habits and human education. It has to do with the common expectations of life. Not very far back in the history of this nation writing was not thought of as essential to the practical equipment of a man. Indeed, if we consider only the most highly authentic figures on this matter, we find that, in 1880, 17 per cent of our population could not write or read. Back of this date, the statistics are largely matters of speculation, but it is certain that the percentage increases rapidly. We find, for example, in a message of Governor Campbell to the legislature of Virginia in 1839, the statement that "almost one-quarter part of the men applying for marriage licenses were unable to write their names." If we go a little farther back, the fraction of illiterates undoubtedly puts in the majority those who did not command the art of writing.

The attitude of modern society is such that a percentage of illiteracy even as high as that of 1880 is wholly intolerable. Today no man willingly admits that he cannot read or write. The expectation of the nation is that all its members are to go to school long enough to be part of a common social whole which is held together by written and printed means of communication.

With regard to reading, modern expectations are even more far-reaching than are those with regard to writing. Public signs are used on every hand, on the assumption that all who make use of the streets will be able to follow written directions. The man who cannot read can hardly take care of himself in a crowded city.

Inadequacies of Early Schools. If one stops to translate these various expectations into definite terms regarding education, one begins to realize that the modern school has a task which the old-fashioned school with its simple expectations never faced. The school of 1840, with its brief period of contact with the pupils, with its untrained teachers, with its meager supply of books, and with its inadequate schoolrooms, was not in most cases a place where the type of fluent reading and writing demanded by modern society could be imparted.

Such statements about the schools of the last century can be abundantly verified by reference to contemporary literature. Thus, in 1838 Horace Mann, in his second report to the Massachusetts board of education, wrote:

"I have devoted especial pains to learn, with some degree of numerical accuracy, how far the reading, in our schools, is an exercise of the mind in thinking and feeling, and how far it is a barren action of the organs of speech upon the atmosphere. My information is derived, principally, from the written statements of the school committees of the respective towns,—gentlemen who are certainly exempt from all temptation to disparage the schools they superintend. The result is, that more than eleven-twelfths of all the children in the reading-classes, in our schools, do not understand the meaning of the words they read; that they do not master the sense of the reading-lessons; and that the ideas and feelings intended by the author to be conveyed to, and excited in, the reader's mind, still rest in the author's intention, never having yet reached the place of their destination."

The major part of the report from which the foregoing passage is taken is devoted to a discussion of the reasons for this deficiency in reading ability. Mann finds that one important reason for the failure of pupils of that day is to be found in the emphasis laid on formal spelling and mere pronunciation. A quotation from a later part of the report reveals the practices of that time and also one important reason why instruction in reading was ineffective. The quotation is as follows:

"Another device to fill vacuity by pouring in vacuity, is this:—a book is prepared, in which the spelling and reading lessons alternate. First come a few columns of words, and then a page of apothegms and synopses of universal truths, not occupying, perhaps, more than a line each; some one word in the spelling columns being incorporated into each of these short sentences. The force of the reasons against the preceding mode is but little abated when applied to this. This motley company of sentences repels all interest on the part of the learner. Topics more alien from each other, and more bewildering to the mind, could not be found, if one were to stick a pin through all the leaves of a book, and then to read continuously all the sentences through which the puncture was made. As many-colored and diverse-shaped objects, flitting swiftly before the eye, will make no stable impression upon the retina; so a multitude of incongruous ideas and feelings, trooping hurriedly before the mental vision, can leave no enduring traces of outline, aspect or quality upon the mind. A rapid succession of discordant images will inflict distraction upon the mind of an adult;—how much more certain are they to do it upon that of a child! The power of passing abruptly from one subject of thought to another, without mental disturbance, requires long habit and familiarity with the matters presented. Children can have neither.

"Another reason is to be found in the inappropriate character of the reading exercises offered to children.

"And yet, in many of the reading-books now in use in the schools, the most pithy sayings of learned men; the aphorisms in which moralists have deposited a life of observation and experience; the maxims of philosophers, embodying the highest forms of intellectual truth, are set down as First Lessons for children;—as though, because a child was born after Bacon and Franklin, he could understand them of course. . . . Using incomprehensible reading-books draws after it the inevitable consequence of bad reading."

Shortly before Horace Mann wrote his second report on reading, an educational event of major importance had occurred in the Middle West. William Holmes McGuffey, a professor of ancient languages in the small college of Miami at Oxford, Ohio, had published the earliest volumes of the series of Readers that were to make his name a household word throughout the country for more than three quarters of a century. His First Reader and Second Reader appeared in 1836, and the Third and Fourth Readers in 1837. The Fifth and Sixth Readers, which are really anthologies of good literature, were published originally as *"The Rhetorical Guide,"* having been prepared by William's brother, Alexander McGuffey. They were added to the series to round out the McGuffey line and to include instruction in such subjects as Articulation, Inflection, and Accent and Emphasis. In their beginning William McGuffey's Readers were the outgrowth of experiments in a private school that he conducted at his home in Oxford. Because the selections studied represented not only high literary quality but also a wholesome ethical tone, the Readers exerted a cultural and social influence that is an important part of the American heritage.

Demand for Reading Ability. Other passages might be quoted from the second Mann report, but perhaps enough has been repeated to indicate the fact that in the middle of the last century the pupils who went out from the schools were not fluent, intelligent readers. The expectations of society with regard to the attainments of the individual were slight, and the use of the art of reading in after life was correspondingly meager.

It would, of course, be out of keeping with the facts to assert that defects of the kind described by Horace Mann made no serious difference in the lives of men and women in 1840. But such a statement is much more nearly true of that time than would be a statement that today we can look with complacency on the crudities of our treatment of reading in the schools. In 1840 average citizens were called on very little to read. Their political affiliations were fairly direct; they usually voted for representatives whom they knew. Their correspondence was very light; and the contacts of daily life were simple. It is not unqualifiedly true that it made no difference whether men and women could read or not, but it is true that they used the art very little in ordinary routine.

In contrast with all these facts, are the expectations of modern society. Today everyone must read if they are to share in the life of their times. There has been an enormous increase in the amount of attention given to education.

GENERAL EXPANSION

From 1870 to 1920, the number of schoolhouses more than doubled. Since 1920, the number has constantly decreased, due primarily to the merging of one-room schools with other schools. While the number of one-room schools was decreasing, the number of school districts also was decreasing. In 1931 there were 127,422 school districts in the United States. By 1955 this number had been reduced to 54,859; by 1973, 16,730. Although the number of public elementary schools also is declining (104,427 in 1955; 65,070 in 1973), the number of public secondary schools remains relatively constant (26,046 in 1955; 25,906 in 1973). Expenditure per student is increasing: $108 in 1929; $388 in 1955, $1,364 in 1973. The median number of school years also is increasing.

During the years of economic depression in the 1930's, school attendance showed a decline owing to the falling birth rate. But the increase in the birth rate immediately before and after World War II shattered all previous enrollment records, and enrollments continue to increase. The present decreasing birth rate, however, is expected to cause a drop in school attendance. In 1965 approximately 31 million people 3 to 34 years old attended school; this figure increased to 61 million in 1975. The projected enrollment for 1984 is 56.4 million.

The U.S. Office of Education reports: "The United States has gone a long way toward providing universal elementary and secondary education for its citizens. While regulations differ somewhat from one jurisdiction to another, it may be said in general that free public education is available to all and that school attendance is compulsory between the ages of 7 and 16." In 1975 approximately 99 per cent of the persons 7 to 13 attended school; 94 per cent for 14 to 17 year olds. The median number of school years completed was 12.3. Some 45 per cent of high school graduates were enrolled in college. Almost 14 per cent of the people 25 years old and over had attended four or more years of college.

ANNUAL COST PER COLLEGE STUDENT*

Year	Total Cost†		Tuition and Required Fees	
	Public	Private	Public	Private
1965	$ 950	$1,907	$243	$1,088
1970	1,205	2,533	324	1,534
1975	1,708	3,592	503	2,290

Source: U.S. Department of Commerce, Bureau of the Census. * Annual estimated cost per full-time resident degree-credit student at universities, 4-year colleges, and 2-year colleges. † Includes tuition and required fees, and board and dormitory fees.

Region and State	Public Schools, 1974			Nonpublic Schools, 1971		Institutions of Higher Education, 1974‡	
	Elementary*	Secondary†	Elementary, Secondary	Elementary*	Secondary†	Public	Private
New England	4,562	1,163	45	1,034	405	75	165
Maine	720	130	10	71	36	4	14
New Hampshire . . .	362	83	20	81	32	10	15
Vermont	340	58	12	38	19	6	14
Massachusetts.	1,927	585	0	477	193	31	87
Rhode Island	324	64	3	108	30	3	10
Connecticut	889	243	0	259	95	21	25
Middle Atlantic	8,245	2,607	381	3,297	850	140	326
New York	3,099	1,145	192	1,476	420	80	179
New Jersey	2,052§	425§	0	604	163	28	33
Pennsylvania	3,094	1,037	189	1,217	267	32	114
East North Central . . .	12,604	4,397	251	3,511	627	160	273
Ohio	3,149	1,019	1	703	149	33	71
Indiana	1,469	526	177	373	51	6	39
Illinois	3,385	1,123	73	1,053	172	50	87
Michigan	2,907	1,111	0	700	170	42	46
Wisconsin	1,694	618	0	682	85	29	30
West North Central . . .	7,813	3,471	6	1,533	303	122	170
Minnesota	1.180	632	6	401	61	26	31
Iowa	1,293	696	0	254	46	18	37
Missouri	1,544	715	0	432	89	22	51
North Dakota	495	299	0	46	12	9	3
South Dakota	678	222	0	75	18	6	10
Nebraska	1,478	398	0	181	45	13	14
Kansas	1,145	509	0	144	32	28	24
South Atlantic	8,237	2,860	681	1,325	486	229	211
Delaware	139	50	11	43	15	3	4
Maryland.	991	311	35	266	95	25	22
District of Columbia . .	135	54	2	49	33	3	14
Virginia	1,237	473	81	206	80	36	34
West Virginia	950	348	0	43	15	15	10
North Carolina	1,430	479	122	142	53	56	43
South Carolina	814	344	32	128	30	23	24
Georgia	1,121	335	343	94	49	31	31
Florida	1,420	466	55	354	116	37	29
East South Central . . .	3,613	1,444	610	698	285	81	110
Kentucky.	1,123	358	0	217	48	8	28
Tennessee	1,320	370	73	118	38	19	43
Alabama	516	287	537	197	76	30	21
Mississippi	654	429	0	166	123	24	18
West South Central . . .	5,992	3,610	212	900	257	127	91
Arkansas	716	476	0	58	14	8	11
Louisiana	843	384	211	322	105	12	11
Oklahoma	1,179	701	1	45	12	26	14
Texas	3,254	2,049	0	475	126	81	55
Mountain.	3,671	1,544	39	456	116	81	32
Montana	641	198	0	49	14	9	3
Idaho	370	173	10	38	8	6	3
Wyoming	264	115	0	15	1	8	0
Colorado	815	411	6	151	38	21	12
New Mexico	426	216	6	64	19	8	3
Arizona	603	188	3	100	28	15	6
Utah	373	167	17	23	5	9	4
Nevada	179	76	0	16	3	5	1
Pacific	8,284	2,716	596	1,802	509	207	161
Washington	1,131	539	46	191	53	31	12
Oregon	946	333	5	120	33	20	20
California.	5,531	1,506	0	1,234	333	117	104
Alaska	516	287	537	197	76	30	21
Hawaii	160	51	8	60	14	9	4

Source: U.S. Department of Commerce, Bureau of the Census.   * Grades 1 through 6.   † Grades 7 through 12.   ‡ Institutions granting degrees, offering degree-credit courses, or offering nondegree occupational curriculums.   § 1973 data.

School Year	Enrollment, grades 9-12	Population 14-17 years of age	Total number enrolled per 100 persons 14-17 years of age
1889–1890	359,949	5,354,653	6.7
1899–1900	699,403	6,152,231	11.4
1909–1910	1,115,398	7,220,298	15.4
1919–1920	2,500,176	7,735,841	32.3
1929–1930	4,804,255	9,341,221	51.4
1939–1940	7,123,009	9,720,419	73.3
1945–1946	6,237,133	9,056,000	68.9
1949–1950	6,453,009	8,404,768	76.8
1955–1956	7,774,975	9,207,000	84.4
1959–1960	9,599,810	11,154,879	86.1
Oct. 1970	14,796,000	15,718,000	94.1
Oct. 1973	15,354,000	16,522,000	92.9
Oct. 1974	15,529,000	16,711,000	92.9
Oct. 1975	15,698,000	16,766,000	93.6

Expanding interest in education and increasing enrollments resulted in a teacher shortage and a school building shortage. The trend was toward greater disparity between the number of pupils on the one hand and facilities and teaching personnel on the other. Studies by the U.S. Office of Education showed that even apparent gains in some directions were offset by losses in others when all principal factors were considered. For example, when the number of graduates from teacher training institutions rose from 25,000 in 1948 to 35,000 in 1950, this seemed to be an encouraging development. Closer investigation revealed that the increase was no more than enough to fill the normal number of vacancies caused by death, retirement, marriage, and change of occupation. Later statistics, however, showed a more favorable picture. The graduating class of 1961 produced approximately 44,658 graduates eligible to teach; 173,846 in 1964; 195,640 in 1973. In 1955 the pupil-teacher ratio in elementary schools was 30.2, in secondary schools, 20.9; in 1974 the pupil-teacher ratio in elementary schools was 22.7, in secondary schools, 18.7.

School Plant Needs. The school building shortage was due, not only to the great increase in enrollments, but also to the postponement of new construction during the war years, when the lack of building material and manpower made it difficult to build or even to maintain school buildings

PER CENT OF POPULATION 5-34 YEARS OF AGE ENROLLED IN SCHOOL, BY SEX AND RACE

Year	Male	Female	White	Racial Minorities
1960	60.0	52.8	56.4	55.9
1965	63.5	56.0	59.6	60.0
1970	62.6	55.5	58.7	60.8
1975	57.7	52.6	54.5	59.0

Source: U.S. Department of Commerce, Bureau of the Census.

properly. During most of the 1930 decade, school plant maintenance and building upkeep were neglected because of lack of funds. Consequently, from about 1931 through 1945, there was not much new construction, maintenance was neglected, and depreciation continued at an increasing rate. Some buildings became so dilapidated and obsolete that remodeling was impracticable. Then, before the postwar programs got under way, the schools were overwhelmed with increased enrollments, and the Korean War resulted in shortages of building

ELEMENTARY, SECONDARY, AND COLLEGE ENROLLMENT*

	Number enrolled						
	Public			Private			
Year	Elementary	Secondary	College	Elementary	Secondary	College	Total
1965	30,563,000	11,610,000	3,970,000	4,900,000	1,400,000	1,951,000	54,394,000
1970	32,577,000	13,332,000	6,428,000	4,100,000	1,300,000	2,153,000	59,890,000
1974	30,919,000	14,137,000	7,988,000	3,500,000	1,200,000	2,235,000	59,979,000
1984†	28,500,000	12,100,000	9,503,000	3,000,000	1,200,000	2,107,000	56,410,000

Source: U.S. Department of Commerce, Bureau of the Census. * Elementary—kindergarten through grade 8; secondary—grades 9 through 12; college—degree-credit and nondegree-credit enrollment at junior or community colleges, 4-year colleges, and graduate or professional schools. † Projected data.

material. In 1950 there were 128.2 thousand public elementary schools for 18.7 million students; in 1960, 91.9 thousand schools, 25.8 million students; in 1974, 65.1 thousand schools, 28 million students. On the secondary level, there were 24.5 thousand public secondary schools for 6.1 million students in 1950; 25.8 thousand schools, 9.2 million students in 1960; 25.9 thousand schools, 14.3 million students in 1974.

The percentage of school revenue provided by the federal government and by state governments has increased, while the percentage provided by local school districts has decreased gradually. In 1960 the percentage provided by the federal government was 6.9; in 1973, 11.0. State governments provided 29.1 per cent in 1960; 33.0 per cent in 1973. The percentage from local school districts was 39.3 in 1960; 31.5 in 1973.

Total expenditures for education in the United States are increasing constantly. With the exception of the years (1930–1940) following the economic depression, this always has been true. Total expenditures for public and nonpublic schools was $24.7 billion in 1960. This figure climbed to $89.2 billion in 1973.

Growth of High Schools. Of persons who entered high school in 1870, the girls were, for the most part, preparing to become teachers, and the boys were expecting to enter one of the professions. Only the larger communities supported high schools in those days, and only about one per cent of the children of high school age attended this school.

Following 1890 both small and large communities began to establish high schools, and high school enrollment increased rapidly. Enrollment approximately doubled each decade from 1910 to 1930; the increase from 1930 to 1941 was slower and after 1941 enrollment decreased for several years. A steady increase in enrollment that began in 1947 rose to 14,092,000 (grades 9 to 12) in 1972. Since then enrollment in grades 9 to 12 has changed only slightly. The percentage of change from 1950 to 1960 was 54.0; from 1960 to 1970, 43.6; and from 1970 to 1975, 6.6.

In 1975 2,816,000 persons graduated from high school, or approximately 74 per cent of the 18-year-olds. About 94 per cent of youth of high school age attended high school. In 1880 fewer than 3 out of every 100 persons of high school age were in public high schools, with approximately 1 of these 3 graduating.

Whereas in 1870 the average person found it possible to enter upon his life work with a little knowledge of reading and writing, the modern child finds that it is quite impossible to secure any advantageous position in the commercial or industrial world without a knowledge that extends very far beyond the rudimentary subjects taught in the elementary schools. If a person is going to enter industry, he or she must know something of the source of the raw materials with which the industry deals and must understand something of the scientific principles on which the industry depends. As a result of this and other forces boys and girls are remaining in school longer. Increasing numbers are using the high school as preparatory to college.

Increasing Complexity of Civic Relations. Citizenship has also come to be a more complex matter than it was in former days. Formerly, where communities were small and everyone knew personally the person who was sent to the legislature, voting was a matter of choice among acquaintances. As communities expanded, however, the problem of government became more complex, and the selection of the individual who should serve as a representative in the legislative assembly became infinitely more complicated, because of the lack of direct contact between voter and legislator. As a result, public intelligence with regard to governmental policies must today be cultivated through a broader knowledge of history and civics.

PUPILS TRANSPORTED TO SCHOOLS

Year*	Number of Pupils Transported	Per Cent of Pupils Enrolled	Expenditure for Transportation
1930	1,902,826	7.4	$ 54,823,000
1932	2,419,173	9.2	58,078,000
1934	2,794,724	10.6	53,908,000
1936	3,250,658	12.3	62,653,000
1938	3,769,242	14.5	75,637,000
1940	4,144,161	16.3	83,283,000
1942	4,503,081	18.3	92,922,000
1944	4,512,412	19.4	107,754,000
1946	5,056,966	21.7	129,756,000
1948	5,854,041	24.4	176,265,000
1950	6,947,384	27.7	214,504,000
1952	7,697,130	29.0	268,827,000
1954	8,411,719	32.8	307,437,000
1956	9,695,819	35.0	353,972,000
1958	10,861,689	36.5	416,491,000
1960	12,225,142	37.6	486,338,000
1966	15,500,000	40.0	787,000,000
1968	17,100,000	42.0	981,000,000
1970	18,200,000	43.0	1,219,000,000
1972†	19,500,000	46.0	1,508,000,000
1974	21,300,000	52.0	1,858,000,000

Source: U.S. Department of Health, Education, and Welfare; U.S. Department of Commerce, Bureau of the Census. * Refers to school year ending that year. † April 1971, Supreme Court ruled that busing of students may be ordered to achieve racial desegregation.

To be sure, American schools have not always developed these broader forms of knowledge as fully as they might, but it has come to be believed that they must if the citizens are to be better informed. It is generally accepted that it is quite impossible for a modern state to be conducted if its citizens have only elementary school training. Ever-increasing numbers of pupils are graduating from high school. Economic and social disturbances are bound to affect school enrollments, course subject-matter, and even teaching methods.

It may be said, almost literally, that the high school sprang into existence after the Civil War. Later panics and depressions in the economic world drove people to seek a broader education. World War I made the importance of intellectual and technical training so obvious that, since 1918, the enrollments of higher institutions have been steadily increasing. The beginning of space exploration by satellite in the late 1950s caused Americans to re-evaluate their educational system and expectations.

ENROLLMENT IN VOCATIONAL CLASSES

Year*	Total†	Agriculture	Consumer and Homemaking‡	Trades and Industry
1938	1,810,082	460,876	627,394	685,804
1940	2,290,741	584,133	818,766	758,409
1942	2,624,786	605,099	954,041	850,597
1944	2,001,153	469,959	806,605	543,080
1946	2,227,663	510,331	911,816	630,844
1948	2,836,121	640,791	1,139,766	762,628
1950	3,364,613	764,975	1,430,366	804,602
1952	3,165,988	746,402	1,391,389	793,213
1954	3,164,851	737,502	1,380,147	826,583
1956	3,413,159	785,599	1,486,816	883,719
1958	3,629,339	775,892	1,559,822	983,644
1960	3,768,149	796,237	1,588,109	938,490
1962	4,072,677	822,664	1,725,660	1,005,383
1966	6,070,000	907,000	1,898,000	1,269,000
1968	7,534,000	851,000	2,283,000	1,629,000
1970	8,794,000	853,000	2,570,000	1,906,000
1972	11,711,000	896,000	3,446,000	2,398,000
1974	13,794,000	976,000	3,703,000	2,824,000

Source: U.S. Department of Health, Education, and Welfare; U.S. Department of Commerce, Bureau of the Census. * Refers to school year ending that year. † Includes classes not shown separately. ‡ Prior to 1972, represents home economics.

YEAR*	DEGREES CONFERRED				PER CENT OF ALL DEGREES		
	Total	Bachelor's or first professional	Master's except first professional	Doctor's	Bachelor's or first professional	Master's except first professional	Doctor's
1948	318,749	272,311	42,449	3,989	85.4	13.3	1.3
1949	422,511	366,698	50,763	5,050	86.8	12.0	1.2
1950	498,373	433,734	58,219	6,420	87.0	11.7	1.3
1951	456,822	384,352	65,132	7,338	84.1	14.3	1.6
1952	403,194	331,924	63,587	7,683	82.3	15.8	1.9
1953	374,189	304,857	61,023	8,309	81.5	16.3	2.2
1954	358,699	292,880	56,823	8,996	81.7	15.8	2.5
1955	354,445	287,401	58,204	8,840	81.1	16.4	2.5
1956	379,495	311,298	59,294	8,903	82.0	15.6	2.3
1957	411,058	340,347	61,955	8,756	82.8	15.1	2.1
1958	440,304	365,748	65,614	8,942	83.1	14.9	2.0
1959	464,095	385,151	69,584	9,360	83.0	15.0	2.0
1960	479,215	394,889	74,497	9,829	82.4	15.5	2.1
1961	490,628	401,784	78,269	10,575	81.9	16.0	2.1
1962	516,996	420,485	84,889	11,622	81.3	16.4	2.2
1965	667,500	539,000	112,000	16,500	80.7	16.8	2.5
1966	714,200	555,000	141,000	18,200	77.7	19.7	2.6
1967	773,375	594,862	157,892	20,621	78.2	20.3	2.5
1968	871,832	671,591	177,150	23,091	77.0	20.3	2.6
1969	991,200	770,000	195,000	26,200	77.7	19.6	2.6
1970	1,071,900	833,000	209,000	29,900	77.7	19.5	2.8
1971	1,148,100	884,000	232,000	32,100	77.0	20.2	2.8
1972	1,224,400	938,000	253,000	33,400	76.6	20.7	2.7

Source: U.S. Department of Health, Education, and Welfare, Office of Education; U.S. Department of Commerce, Bureau of the Census. * Refers to school year ending that year.

Expansion of Higher Education. What has been said with regard to the expansion of the secondary schools can be repeated with regard to the expansion of higher education. In 1965, 501,000 people received bachelor's degrees (approximately 20 per cent of those persons 23 years old, or 25 per cent of the number of 1961 high school graduates). In 1974, 946,000 received bachelor's degrees (approximately 27 per cent of those persons 23 years old, or 33 per cent of the number of 1971 high school graduates). In 1965, 39.1 per cent of the people 18 to 21 years of age were attending an institution of higher education; in 1973, 47.1 per cent were attending.

The total enrollment, including faculty, of universities, colleges, professional schools, junior and teachers colleges, and normal schools in 1974 was 10,224,000. The total for 4-year institutions was 6,825,000; 2-year institutions, 2,198,000.

Higher Education and Democracy. The final conclusion to be drawn is that the school system of the United States has been seeking to attain the general democratic ideal of a higher education for everyone who is willing to spend the time and effort in securing such an education. It required a long period of development in American national life to bring even the common schools to the level at which the average person could be trained in subjects other than the rudiments of "the three R's." Once the common school reached its development, however, the demand for a higher education has grown with phenomenal rapidity. The median school years completed by those persons 25 years and over in 1960 was 10.6. By 1975 this figure had increased to 12.3 years.

REORGANIZATION OF EDUCATION

There are certain natural consequences that issue from these expanding ideals of a democratic school system. In the first place, there is a growing impatience with any delay in the introduction of useful subjects, such as natural science and civics. Formerly, the elementary schools did not attempt to teach the common people very much science or very much about the principles of government. These subjects were first introduced in the higher institutions of the American educational system. It was assumed that only people of the higher degrees of intellectual maturity could understand them.

Now that even the common people are sharing in a higher education, however, there is a disposition to introduce science and civics and all of the other subjects at the earliest possible moment. The result is that a reorganization of the curriculum of the lower schools is being carried forward very rapidly.

The Elective System. The administration of this broader course of study requires some flexibility in the arrangement of the program of individual pupils. Not all pupils will want the same type of training. Some of them are preparing to enter professions, while others are attending the higher schools with the expectation of entering upon industrial or commercial careers. The enriched course of study includes material appropriate to all of these different expectations, but no single individual can take advantage of all the different opportunities offered. The common practice in all higher institutions is, therefore, to allow students to select those types of training most directly related to their individual needs. This is perhaps one of the most radical changes that has taken place in the relations of the student and the school administration.

HISTORICAL SUMMARY OF PUBLIC ELEMENTARY AND SECONDARY SCHOOL STATISTICS: UNITED STATES, 1900 TO 1974*

POPULATION, PUPILS, AND INSTRUCTION STAFF	1900	1920	1940	1950	1960	1970	1974
Total population (thousands)†	75,995	104,512	130,880	148,665	179,323	203,200	209,800
Per cent of total population ages 5–17†	28.4	26.4	23.0	20.3	24.5	25.8	24.5
Total enrollment in elementary and secondary schools (thousands)	15,503	21,578	25,434	25,111	36,087	45,600§	45,400§
Per cent of total population enrolled	20.4	20.6	19.4	16.9	20.1	22.4	21.6
Per cent of population 5–17 years enrolled . .	71.9	78.3	84.4	83.2	82.2	86.9	88.2
Classroom teachers (thousands)‡	423	657	875	914	1,387	2,131	2,287
Per cent male	29.9	14.1	22.2	21.3	29.0	32.4 ‖	33.5 ‖
Average daily attendance (thousands)	10,633	16,150	22,042	22,284	32,477	41,900	41,400
Per cent of enrolled pupils attending daily	68.6	74.8	86.7	88.7	90.0	91.9	89.2
Average length of school term (in days)	144.3	161.9	175.0	177.9	178.0	178.9	178.7
Average number of days attended by each pupil enrolled.	99.0	121.2	151.7	157.9	160.2	161.7	159.5
Total instructional staff (thousands)	na	678	912	962	1,464	2,253	2,425

Source: U.S. Department of Commerce, Bureau of the Census. * Refers to school year ending that year. † Excludes armed forces abroad. ‡ Includes nonsupervisory staff. § As of fall of preceding year. ‖ Estimated.

FALL ENROLLMENT IN HIGHER EDUCATIONAL INSTITUTIONS*

ITEM	1960	1970	1974
Degree credit	3,583	7,920	9,023
Male	2,257	4,637	4,969
Female	1,326	3,284	4,055
4-year institutions	3,131	6,290	6,825
2-year institutions	451	1,630	2,198
Full-time	2,466	5,489	5,817
Part-time	1,117	2,431	3,206
Public	2,116	5,800	6,838
Private	1,467	2,120	2,185
Undergraduate.	3,227	6,889	7,833
Male	2,004	4,005	4,306
Female	1,223	2,884	3,527
4-year institutions	2,776	5,259	5,635
Full-time	2,077	4,234	4,429
Part-time	699	1,025	1,206
2-year institutions	451	1,630	2,198
Public	1,929	5,076	5,986
Private	1,298	1,813	1,847
First time enrolled	923	1,780	1,854
Graduate	356†	1,031	1,190
Nondegree credit	206	661	1,201

Source: U.S. Department of Commerce, Bureau of the Census. * Includes universities, colleges, professional schools, junior and teachers colleges, and normal schools. Figures in thousands. † Includes resident only.

The Lengthening Period of School. Related to the reorganization of education and partially resulting from it has been an increased length to the period of school for greater numbers of children. Indeed, the goal for America now seems to be that all children will not only have an elementary school and high school education but also will go to college or an institute of higher education for at least a year. Evidences pointing in this direction can be found in the accompanying tables. These tables show that increasing numbers of children are attending schools and colleges and staying longer in an educational setting. In 1975 there were enrolled in schools 97.0 per cent of children aged 5 to 13 years and 93.6 per cent of children 14 to 17 years. This is in sharp contrast to the year 1910 when 73.7 per cent of children aged 5 to 13 years and only 58.9 per cent of children 14 to 17 were enrolled in schools.

In addition to keeping children in school until they are older, the school term has been lengthened from an average 144.3 days in 1900 to 178.7 days in 1974. Summer schools have been instituted and students, especially at the secondary school level, are encouraged to take certain subjects in summer and others during the regular academic year. Thus are being organized year-round schools. Also, within the framework of the period of schooling, devices are being created to make the learning program as flexible as possible. Students in elementary schools may enroll for high school subjects if they are capable of learning them. Also, high school students can enroll in special college classes, either in summer or during the academic year. This flexibility has served to encourage students to continue their studies.

At each of the normal ends of the period of schooling—the first grade and college graduation—there are programs that encourage children and students to be in school. Nursery school and kindergarten programs are becoming more important and enrolling greater numbers of children. Also, graduate schools of universities are appealing to larger numbers of scholars, and students who previously would have left school after college graduation now continue into professional programs of graduate school.

THE SCIENCE OF EDUCATION

THE beginnings of the scientific study of education are to be traced to the German philosopher and educator, Herbart (1776–1841), who did his work between 1800 and 1841. He pointed out the fact that educational operations must be guided by scientific principles derived from the study of human nature, or psychology, and from the study of that science which deals with the rules of proper conduct, namely, ethics.

EXPERIMENTAL PSYCHOLOGY

The movement which Herbart inaugurated was effective in Germany in stimulating a number of lines of scientific inquiry. In the first place, it gave rise to a more careful study, in laboratories designed for that purpose, of the mental processes of adults and children. The development of the science of psychology during the last century is in a very large measure to be traced directly to the influence of Herbart. The movement was accelerated and augmented by the contributions of the physiologists and of those who were interested in measuring the processes of sensation.

The Child Study Movement. In 1881 G. Stanley Hall, who had just returned to Johns Hopkins university from a period of training in the psychological laboratory in Leipzig, Germany, began to collect and publish material on child psychology. He attracted a great deal of attention among teachers and school administrators for the views which he developed in regard to the reorganization of schools.

The "child study movement," as it was called, was carried forward vigorously by Hall and his students for a period of twenty years, and was one of the important sources of the present scientific study of education.

This movement suffered, however, because its methods of investigation were somewhat unsystematic and likely to lead to erroneous conclusions. The chief method of this school was that which has been called the "questionnaire" method. Various series of questions in regard to different aspects of children's mental lives were formulated. These were sent to parents and teachers in different parts of the country, and their answers were tabulated. Conclusions were drawn from these answers without very serious regard to the validity of the answers themselves. The results of the use of this method were numerous collections of interesting material about the development of children; but it was found that educational practice could not rely upon the relatively loose information thus collected.

Culture Epochs Theory. Herbart's influence was effective along lines other than those briefly traced in the foregoing statements about psychology. Numerous practice schools were set up in Germany, and theories in regard to education were tried out in these schools. One important theory of this sort was known as the "culture epochs theory." It was held that the line of development followed by children parallels closely the line of development which has been followed by the race. Thus, the race began with no ability to write and gradually evolved this ability. The race began with very crude graphic art and gradually refined this art through the cultivation of taste in color and through studies of form and perspective. Children's drawings show the same crudities as do those of primitive peoples, and the same stages of gradual development appear as children refine their taste for color and their knowledge of form. Such analogies as these encouraged the followers of Herbart to reach the general conclusion that they could lay out a course of study appropriate for the schools, provided they could

find by a careful study of the history of the race the different stages or epochs through which civilization has passed. A vigorous effort was accordingly made in Germany and in this country to prepare natural courses of study on this pattern. The result was an interest in such matters as the habits and abilities of children and primitive peoples, and much new and stimulating study was undertaken both of human nature and of materials to be used in instruction.

The culture epochs theory, like the child study movement, spent itself because of its crude generalizations; but, before it was abandoned, it had stimulated so much skepticism about the older traditional methods of teaching and had aroused so much interest in the possibilities of a new course of study that later generations of teachers and supervisors have profited greatly by its impulse.

Studies of Teaching Methods. Furthermore, the experimental schools which were set up by the followers of Herbart gave a great deal of attention to methods of teaching and developed new formulas to guide teachers in their work. The Herbartian movement came to the United States in very vigorous form during the '80's and led to the organization of a society of educators who called themselves the Herbart Society. The members of this group produced numerous books on methods of teaching and aroused the teachers of the country to the realization of the possibilities of improving their work.

Encouragement of Scientific Studies. In addition to the suggestions looking toward a science of education which can be traced directly to Herbart, there were natural forces at work in American civilization tending in the same direction. In the first place, as has been pointed out in an earlier section, great expansion was going forward in the American school. The secondary school was developing rapidly, and teaching was becoming a more and more highly specialized type of activity. By the early '90's, therefore, everything was ready for the launching of a movement which gradually gained impetus during the decades between 1890 and 1910, and which has gone forward rapidly since that time.

The Tests of J. M. Rice. In the early '90's an editor, Mr. J. M. Rice, began to collect for the magazine called *The Forum* a series of descriptive accounts of the great school systems of the country. He found such wide differences in the methods of work and in the achievements of the school systems which he visited that he ultimately decided to undertake a measurement of results secured in some of the subjects of instruction. He went to the leading cities of the United States and asked for permission to test the pupils in spelling and arithmetic. This he did during the years 1894 and 1895. The results were very astonishing. He found in his tests in spelling that, while there were the greatest differences in the amounts of time devoted to this subject in the school systems of different cities, the results seemed to show uniformly that children of a certain age can spell correctly about the same percentage of words. That is, it makes no difference how much time is given to instruction in spelling, children of the sixth grade will always show about the same degree of efficiency. Mr. Rice concluded that spelling develops as the child matures, almost independently of the work in the school.

His tests in arithmetic were no less astonishing in their results. They showed that children are by no means so well trained in this subject as their teachers had been in the habit of assuming. Furthermore, he found that the personality of the teacher is much more significant than any other factor in determining the success of instruction.

School people thought that the methods of testing were inadequate. But the facts were so impressive that, from that time on, numerous other investigators were led to devise tests and to examine in detail the results of instruction, not only in arithmetic, but in other subjects as well. Mr. Rice's investigation constituted, therefore, in a very definite sense, the starting point in the measurement movement, which in recent years has included all the subjects of the curriculum of the elementary school, and is now rapidly spreading into the high school and even into the field of college education.

Superintendent Maxwell's Reports. Superintendent Maxwell of New York City was another of the pioneers in the scientific movement in education. In the early years of this century, he called attention to the fact that numerous assumptions with regard to the progress of children through the grades of the elementary school were entirely without support in fact. His most striking pronouncement in regard to this matter was a statement that in New York schools a very considerable percentage of the pupils, instead of being in the grade in which they should be, according to their ages, were very far behind. To be exact, he said that 39 per cent of the children in the schools of New York City were below the grade in which they might normally be expected to be found.

The statements made by Superintendent Maxwell, with the tests which had been made by Rice and others who immediately followed him, proved to school people and to students of psychology and related subjects that there must be a very much more definite knowledge with regard to the actual success or failure of schools than that which could be gathered from the assumptions of teachers about the effectiveness of their work. Studies began to be made with regard to all of these matters, and the modern scientific movement was launched.

Biological and Anthropological Measurements. The scientific movement in education was influenced very early in its course by a parallel type of scientific development which was going on in biology and anthropology. Students of biology and of anthropology, who in the early stages of their sciences had depended on mere observation of the facts of life, began, about two decades ago, to realize that they must be much more exact in their information regarding plants and animals and human beings, if their sciences were to develop. They therefore began to measure and to make comparisons which were based on these exact measurements. They soon reached certain generalizations which have proved to be of very great importance in the study of education, as well as in the study of phenomena of other types. An example will serve to illustrate the type of measurement to which reference is here made.

The Normal Distribution of a Group. If, in a given large group of people, measurements of the heights of the individuals are made, it will be found that there are in the group a few very tall and a few very short persons. Between these two extremes, there is a distribution of the people, such that a gradual increase in the number of each class appears as one passes from the extremes, made up of very tall and very short people, toward the middle group, which is made up of those who are of average height. That is, while there are a few exceptionally tall people, there are a somewhat larger number who are very tall; there are a still larger number who are tall enough to attract attention but are neither exceptionally tall nor very tall. When we come to the average group, we find that it includes the largest number of individuals. Facts of this sort appear in any field in which a biological characteristic is measured.

Mental characteristics, like physical characteristics, seem to follow the same law of distribution. There are a few geniuses in the world and a few idiots: between these two extremes, the average members of society group themselves around the average ability.

This general discovery that individuals of a group distribute themselves around a center, or average, according to a definite law, has served to guide in a very important way the measurements which have been made in education. In measuring the ability of children to read or spell, it is found that members of any large group exhibit a tendency to collect around the average ability.

Stimulated by the early studies of the workers in the sciences and by the criticisms of schools made by Maxwell and other school people, students of education began to gather all of the available facts about school situations. They began to collect and compile school statistics on various matters. It may be well to follow their work in some detail.

Studies of Retardation. The term "retardation" was devised, by those who measured the progress of children through the schools, to indicate the fact that certain children fail of promotion in their school work, and hence fall behind the grades in which they ought to be if they had progressed steadily and successfully each year of their school lives. Thus, a child who is six years of age and just entering school may be accepted as a normal individual. If he fails to complete the work in the first grade satisfactorily, he becomes what is known as a "repeater," and he will be, not seven years of age, but eight, when he enters the second grade.

Acceleration. Acceleration is the opposite of retardation. If a child who is ten years of age and is in the fourth grade is allowed to pass directly into the sixth grade, thus gaining a year over children of like age, he is said to be accelerated. Theoretically, if the course of study administered in the elementary school were of average difficulty, bright children ought to be able to complete it in less time than dull children, and there ought to be as many accelerants as there are retards. The school, however, is not so organized as to push forward those who can do the work rapidly, and in most systems retardations accumulate without any balancing accelerations.

Grouping. For many years the schools were concerned more with acceleration of pupils than with the retarded child. Recently, however, efforts have been made to group children so that they will progress most effectively through the school program and retardation will be minimized. As a result several types of grouping have been effected. In one type the children are grouped according to their intellectual ability as demonstrated on intelligence tests. Schools often have what are termed "track" programs and students proceed through the school program on a "track" along with other children of the same intellectual capacity. Generally the tracks are of three levels: one for the children with the highest I.Q.; another for the average child; and a third for the child with the below-average I.Q. The classroom activities are designed for the level of ability of the students. The achievement of the students, therefore, varies at the end of the program according to the track in which they have been placed. Studies made recently have shown the desirability of using several kinds of evidence to determine the grouping of students. Still further studies question the desirability of separating students into groups based on ability.

One of the outcomes of the "track" system o grouping has been the advanced placement program Children selected early in the elementary school program are allowed to progress as rapidly as they desire through the elementary and secondary school programs. Many students take college level work in secondary schools and on entering college are enabled to enroll in advanced college classes. Some educators are now advocating the teaching of subjects in the elementary schools which have been considered high school or even college level subjects.

ACTUAL AND ESTIMATED SCHOOL ENROLLMENTS ACCORDING TO GRADE GROUPS*

School Year	Total	Elementary	High School	College
	000 omitted	000 omitted	000 omitted	000 omitted
1950 .	30,276	21,406	6,656	2,214
1955 .	37,426	27,086	7,961	2,379
1960 .	46,259	32,441	10,249	3,570
1965 .	53,769	35,120	12,975	5,675
1970 .	58,228	36,419	14,762	7,047
1975 .	58,041	33,573	15,903	8,564
1980 .	57,050	32,233	15,099	9,718
1985 .	58,880	35,404	13,781	9,695

*Estimates based on conservative figures Department of Commerce Bureau of Census.

Elimination. When a child leaves school he is said to be eliminated, especially if he leaves before completing the eighth grade. Elimination is heaviest among retarded pupils. These retarded pupils often reach the legal limit of compulsory education while in the lower grades. Thus a child who has lost two or three years through non-promotion may be found in the fifth or sixth grade at the time when he is fourteen years of age. Under the laws of many of the states, he is now allowed to leave school and enter upon some industrial task. A very large proportion of the children who are retarded and allowed under the law to leave school at fourteen years of age do so.

The present average age of completion of the eighth grade is 14.7 years. This average would be much higher if all who are eliminated remained in school.

Some of the most productive scientific studies carried on in the field of education in the early part of this century were studies of retardation and elimination. Great practical interest is attached to these studies. E. L. Thorndike and L. P. Ayres were leaders in this movement. Ayres prepared in 1909 a book entitled *Laggards in Our Public Schools,* as a summary of the studies which had been made up to that time. The influence of this book has been very large indeed. Most school systems now publish in their annual reports tables known as "age-grade tables," setting forth the number of children of different ages in each of the grades. Such a table calls attention to the retardation in the schools and stimulates teachers and administrators to try to improve the situation. So great has been the influence of such tables and studies of this matter, that the number of children who now complete the eighth grade is double that which it was before these scientific studies began.

DEVELOPMENT OF STANDARDS

A second type of scientific study in education is that which issued in the creation of scales and standards of school work. One of the earliest standards prepared was that which was worked out by E. L. Thorndike in 1909 in the form of a handwriting scale. Thorndike collected a large number of specimens of children's handwriting. These he submitted to competent judges, asking them to arrange the specimens in order of excellence. By a mathematical calculation of the judgments which he thus secured, Thorndike arranged the specimens in a series of equal steps from the poorest handwriting to the best. He then reproduced the selected specimens, which were separated from each other by equal steps of excellence, and published them as samples with which teachers could compare the work of their pupils. Any specimen of handwriting which was to be rated by the teacher could be held near the scale which had been prepared by Thorndike, and its relative position in the scale could be readily determined. The scale was marked with certain figures which made it possible to describe any given specimen in numerical terms.

The Handwriting Scale in Use. The importance of the handwriting scale consists in the fact that teachers no longer need to make the assumption that children in the different grades can write perfectly. It has long been known, of course, that third-grade children cannot equal the copy of the writing books, but just how far third-grade children commonly depart from that copy was not easily decided before the handwriting scale was perfected. It is now possible to compare the work of the third-graders, or that of any other children, with the standard scale, and to determine quite definitely the level of excellence which in general can be expected from pupils of the grade in question.

It may be remarked in passing that some people think of standardization as the reduction of all school work to absolute uniformity. That is not the significance of the term. School work can never be made absolutely uniform. One child's handwriting will differ in many ways from the handwriting of other children, but school work can be standardized in the sense that the teacher can ascertain the degree of excellence which has been attained and can govern his or her methods of instruction with this knowledge clearly in mind.

After Thorndike prepared the handwriting scale, numerous other workers perfected this and other scales for the study of children's work. There are scales for the measuring of excellence in English composition, scales for the measurement of various kinds of drawings, scales for the study of reading, and so on.

Thorndike is also known for his work in educational statistics. When he took his doctorate at Columbia in 1898 statistical treatments of test results were entirely new. Believing that "everything that exists exists in quantity" and could be measured to provide keys to scientific progress in learning, Thorndike devised intelligence tests that distinguished between the ability to learn and already acquired knowledge. Dean J. E. Russell of Teachers College said of him: "His service to pedagogical procedure has revolutionized educational administration."

Courtis Arithmetic Tests. One of the early instruments of educational measurement was the series of Courtis tests for the measurement of ability in arithmetic. By an ingenious composition of various number groups, S. A. Courtis prepared a series of exercises in the fundamental arithmetical operations of addition, subtraction, multiplication, and division. These were presented in such form that the pupils were asked to carry out at as rapid a pace as possible the various operations. The ability of any given child was measured by the number and accuracy of the operations which he could complete in a given period of time. The achievement of the whole grade could be measured by ascertaining the ability of the average child.

Spelling. In the field of spelling, early practices of schools were to teach it by resorting to the dictionary and selecting words in alphabetical order, arranging them in groups of gradually increasing length and complexity and making the children learn them. There was no limit to the number of words that the schoolmaster attempted to use in his drill of children.

Ayres conceived the idea of attempting to determine what words are needed in ordinary life. To this end he brought together the results of various studies of words. He ascertained what words recur in business correspondence by going through numerous business letters and tabulating the words which he found. The same thing was done with the Sunday newspaper and with the Bible. When all of these different lists of commonly used words were brought together, the astonishing result appeared that about one-half of the ordinary usage of words is limited to 50 common words, and the first 1000 words encountered in such a list exhaust the ordinary probabilities of use.

Ayres established, therefore, a list of 1000 most commonly employed words. He then gave these words to children in 84 school systems and found how far children of different grades are likely to be in error in spelling these common words. Through these measurements of error, he was able to arrange the words in ascending order of difficulty and to prepare a scale which can be used by any teacher to determine whether a given child or a given class has ordinary ability to spell common words.

Development of Scales and Tests. The preparation of scales and standards has gone forward very rapidly in recent years. Scales and tests have been developed in a wide variety of subjects and for many purposes. In educational circles great interest has been developed in the use of tests as devices to place students in the school program, to determine achievement, and to indicate qualifications for or interest in areas of study. More than 800 different standardized types of tests have been introduced for use in the schools. Because of the large number available and the claims of their supporters, efforts have been made to give information about the uses and misuses of tests to identify the better tests, to eliminate poor ones, and to compel test makers to produce tests which are more valid.

Classification of Tests. One of the important types of tests is the Achievement Battery. This is a series of tests designed primarily to survey achievement in the basic academic skills of children in the elementary schools, secondary schools, and colleges. As shown in the following table, there are wide variations in Achievement Batteries. They are designed also for special vocational skills. In these types of Achievement Batteries, there are subtests of the skills related to the vocation. Achievement Batteries are being used with considerable effectiveness when they are used to improve the curriculum or to aid in the development of the students. They can be harmful when they are used to limit the curriculum or to hold students to standards set by the test.

REPRESENTATIVE ACHIEVEMENT TEST BATTERIES

1. American School Achievement Tests. Grades 1, 2-3, 4-6, 7-9.
2. California Achievement Tests. Grades 1-14.
3. California Basic Skills Tests. Grades 4-6, 7-9.
4. California Tests in Social and Related Sciences. Grades 4-8, 9-12.
5. Contemporary Affairs: Every Pupil Test. Grades 7-12.
6. Co-operative General Culture Test. College.
7. Co-operative General Achievement Tests. Grades 12 and College entrance.
8. Current Affairs: Every Pupil Scholarship Test. High School.
9. General Scholarship Test For High School Seniors. Grade 12.
10. Graduate Record Examination: Area Tests. Sophomore through Graduate School. College.
11. Gray-Votaw-Rogers General Achievement Tests. Grades 1-3, 4-6, 5-9, 7-9.
12. Group Achievement Test: Dominion Tests 1934 Edition. Grade 8.
13. Group Achievement Tests: Niagara Edition Dominion Tests. Grade 8.
14. High School Fundamentals Evaluation Test. Grades 9-12.
15. Iowa Tests Of Basic Skills. Grades 3-9.
16. High School Placement Test. Entering High School Freshmen.
17. Iowa Tests Of Educational Development. Grades 9-13.
18. Municipal Battery: National Achievement Tests. Grades 3-6, 6-8.
19. National Achievement Tests. Grades 4-6, 7-9.
20. National Merit Scholarship Qualifying Test. High School Junior and Senior.
21. S.R.A. Achievement Series. Grades 2-4, 4-6, 6-9.
22. S.R.A. High School Placement Tests. Grades 8.5-9.5.
23. Scholastic Achievement Series. Grades 1.5-2.5, 2.5-3, 4-6, 7-9.
24. Sequential Tests Of Educational Progress. Grades 4-6, 7-9, 10-12, 13-14.
25. Stanford Achievement Test. Grades 1.9-3.5, 3-4, 5-6, 7-9.
26. Test For High School Entrants: National Achievement Tests. High School Entrants.
27. Tests Of Educational Development. High School and College.

Another type of test is that which examines Character and Personality. In tests of this sort, attempts are made to identify and measure character traits such as honesty, generosity, persistence, endurance, frustrability, and other qualities which make a personality. Widespread use of tests in this area is questionable at the present time because evidence is inadequate to support any contention for or against their validity as measures of total personality.

Many tests have been made to measure achievement and aptitude in the various individual subject areas of the school curriculum. Tests which have had extensive use are in English language, grammar, vocabulary, composition, poetry, and English literature; Mathematics including algebra, arithmetic, general mathematics, geometry, and trigonometry; the sciences of astronomy, biology, botany, chemistry, general science, nature study, physics, and zoology; foreign languages including French, German, Latin, and Spanish; the social studies of civics, current events, history, geography, economics, and political science; the commercial subjects of accounting, bookkeeping, business education, clerical ability, commercial law, and typewriting; fine arts of music and art. In the vocations there are accepted tests in agriculture, auto mechanics, industrial arts, mechanical aptitude, mechanical drawing, home economics, and occupations. In addition to these tests of the various subjects, there are others which test such things as handwriting, etiquette, religious education, safety education, academic aptitude, athletic ability, health and hygiene, general interests, logic, social manners, moral knowledge, reading readiness and achievement, reflective thinking, and study habits and skills. Tests have been developed to measure achievement or aptitude in nearly all forms of human endeavor. However, great care must be given to the selection of the proper test, administering it properly, and interpreting the results. There has been much misuse of tests which has caused harm to the individuals tested.

Other types of tests which are widely used are intelligence tests and sensory tests of motor ability, hearing, and vision. Thus it can be seen that in almost every area where there is need to determine mental growth some sort of test has been devised.

A Silent Reading Test. An example of a standard test may be found in the scale for the measurement of silent reading published by the Russell Sage Foundation of New York City. The directions for the tests and three examples of the reading passages used are given herewith:

DIRECTIONS

Giving the Tests.—1. See that each child has a pencil and that the teacher has a watch. 2. Distribute scales, face down. 3. Have children write on backs of sheets their names, grade, and date. 4. Tell children they are to have a test in reading. Hold scale up and explain that each paragraph tells them to do something to the picture above it with their pencils. They must read carefully, to make sure just what they are to do. They are to read and mark the paragraphs in order, starting at the top and working down, through the first, second, and third. They must do as many as they can in five minutes. 5. Make sure that the pupils understand; then tell them to turn papers over and begin. Allow exactly five minutes. Collect papers.

Marking the Papers. Count every paragraph correct in which the marking, no matter how crude it may be, exactly follows instructions. Count every paragraph wrong in which the marking does not exactly follow instructions. Remember this is a test of reading, not of drawing. The pupil's score is the number of paragraphs correctly marked. Write this number at the top of the paper.

Giving Credit. The credit to be assigned in each grade for each number of paragraphs correctly marked is shown in the table given below. A third-grade child having ten paragraphs right should be marked 80, a fourth-grade child having seven right, 50, and so on. Credits in table are for February 1. To adjust for other periods add or subtract from each child's mark as follows:

Grade 3 Oct. 1, +6 Dec. 1, +3 April 1, −3 June 1, −6
Grades 4-8   +2   +1   −1 June 1, −2

Give no marks less than 0 or more than 100. Write the credit the child receives at the top of his paper.

Results Usually Found. In the diagram shown under the table, columns show per cent of children in the average grade receiving each mark from 0 to 100. Figures below columns show marks or credits, and figures above columns show per cents of children commonly receiving those credits. Thus 12 per cent usually receive a mark of 50, eight per cent one of 68, and so on. The lowest third in the average class receive marks of from 0 to 38; the middle third, from 44 to 56, and the best third, from 62 to 100.

SPECIMENS OF TEST PASSAGES

1. This naughty dog likes to steal bones. When he steals one he hides it where no other dog can find it. He has just stolen two bones, and you must take your pencil and make two short, straight lines, to show where they are lying on the ground near the dog. Draw them as quickly as you can, and then go on.

2. This man is an Eskimo who lives in the far north where it is cold. There has just been a big storm, and all the ground is white with snow. The man has been walking and has made many footprints in it. With your pencil quickly make four of these in the snow just behind him.

3. This book is lying on the desk, but it is hard to make it stay open. With your pencil draw a single straight line to represent a ruler lying across the book to hold the pages open. Be sure to make the line from one side to the other, across the book, instead of making it go up and down.

Methods of Employing Tests. Such tests as have been described are used in various ways by different school officers. Teachers very frequently succeed in discovering by their use those pupils who are in need of special attention. They can then direct instruction to the remedy of the defects thus found. Such a use for the diagnosis of school difficulties is perhaps the most productive to which tests can be put.

Sometimes the superintendent of schools uses tests to find out whether teachers are getting on well with their classes. Such measurement of results for administrative purposes has proved to be very helpful in standardizing the practices of large school systems where the superintendent cannot come into personal contact with all of the teachers. The results in such cases must however be interpreted with great caution if injustices are to be avoided; for a teacher may very often have a class of low ability or of especially difficult type, as when she attempts to teach English to a group of children from homes where the English language is not spoken.

Tests have also been used in general school surveys where experts from outside a school system have been called in by the board of education or by the citizens in order to make a study of the virtues and defects of the system.

Improvements Based on Measurements. Schools have been greatly stimulated by the results of these studies. Measurement has given, first, a better understanding of what ought to be expected at the different levels of education. No teacher, however isolated, needs to be in any doubt as to the success or unsuccess of his work, because it is now thoroughly known what may be expected of children of different ages. Secondly, the tests and experiments have served as a means of deciding between different methods of instruction. Some methods are good and produce excellent results rapidly; other

CREDIT CORRESPONDING TO EACH NUMBER OF PARAGRAPHS MARKED IN EACH GRADE

Grade	0	1	2	3	4	5	6	7	8	9	10	11	12	13	14	15	16	17	18	19	20	Grade
3	0	26	32	38	44	50	56	62	68	74	80	86	92	98	100	..	..	..	..	..	..	3
4	0	14	20	26	32	38	44	50	56	62	68	74	80	86	92	98	100	..	..	..	..	4
5	0	8	14	20	26	32	38	44	50	56	62	68	74	80	86	92	98	100	..	..	..	5
6	0	2	8	14	20	26	32	38	44	50	56	62	68	74	80	86	92	98	100	..	..	6
7	..	0	2	8	14	20	26	32	38	44	50	56	62	68	74	80	86	92	98	100	..	7
8	..	..	0	2	8	14	20	26	32	38	44	50	56	62	68	74	80	86	92	98	100	8

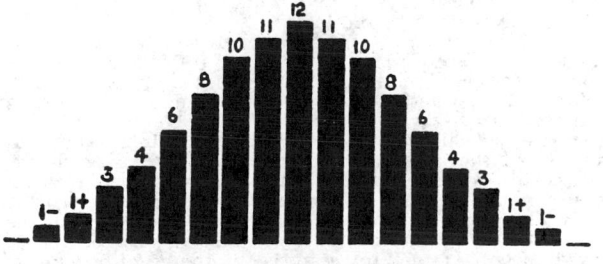

methods of teaching are less satisfactory, and students make slower progress when these less satisfactory methods are employed. With the scales and tests it is possible to determine accurately the rates of progress. It is, therefore, becoming increasingly difficult for a poor method of teaching to survive in a school. It is also becoming increasingly difficult for individual teachers to escape the necessity of cultivating at all times acquaintance with the best methods that have been devised for the treatment of the various topics in the course of study.

A type of test which has come into great prominence in recent years and has been very much discussed in connection with the work in the schools is the so-called general intelligence test. This has been applied in schools, and it has been employed also in industry in determining the efficiency of different sorts of workers. It has been used on a large scale by the United States armed forces since World War I, for the purposes of classifying recruits and officers.

This type of test originated many years ago in the experimental studies of the psychologist Ebbinghaus (1850–1909). Ebbinghaus devised a so-called completion test. He took a simple narrative and dropped out a word here and there. He then asked the person whose general intelligence he wanted to test to supply the omitted words. A comparison of different individuals showed that the persons of largest intelligence were those who could supply most rapidly and most correctly the missing words in the narrative. It is obvious that great service will be rendered to society if it is possible to devise some plan by which the general intelligence of a person can be rapidly measured, in the same way that his physical condition can be measured by his strength and endurance. Psychologists have, therefore, steadily pursued this matter in the effort to improve on the tests of Ebbinghaus and enlarge their application.

Cattell attempted to make use of the general intelligence test in the classification of college freshmen at Columbia university, during the late '90's, but his tests proved to be too crude for the purpose, and the results did not at that time seem very satisfactory. However, Cattell and his students pursued the matter until now numerous tests have been devised and are in use for measuring the general intelligence of all classes of students, as well as of persons who are to be selected for professional and business positions.

Binet and His Scale. In 1905 the Paris authorities asked the eminent psychologist Binet to devise some way of picking out the defective children in the elementary school. Binet devised, in response to this invitation, the now famous scale which bears his name.

The special character of Binet's scale lies in the fact that he brought together a number of questions and a number of tests of skill for each age. He thus set up a series of tests which ought to be passed by an ordinary child of three years of age and another set somewhat more difficult for children of four years of age, and so on up the scale. The way in which he determined the appropriateness of these tests for different ages was to try them out on a large number of pupils. He thus determined how far three-year-old children under ordinary circumstances can go in solving the various questions which he laid down in his series.

Various revisions of the Binet scales have been prepared, and a formula has been developed by means of which the relative intelligence of an individual can be expressed in a single numerical term. If the age of a person is compared with his achievements in the Binet series of tests, it can be determined whether the individual compares favorably with those of his own age or is above or below expectation. Thus, if a ten-year-old child passes the ten-year-old test and no higher, he has exactly fulfilled expectations. By dividing ten, the intellectual age of the child according to the expectations of the Binet scale, by his chronological age ten, we get the quotient one. This is known as the intelligence quotient and is commonly expressed by the letters I. Q. Another child of ten years of age might succeed in passing the test for twelve-year-old children; his I. Q. would then be 1.2. A third child of ten years of age might show a deficiency and be able to pass only the eight-year-old test. His I. Q. would be .8.

Stanford Revision of the Binet Scale. The following summary of the tests to be used with children of different ages constitutes the so-called Stanford revision of the Binet tests. The examples here given cover years three, four, five, and six. Similar lists have been prepared for the later years of the child's life.

THE STANFORD REVISION AND EXTENSION

"YEAR III. (6 tests, 2 months each.)
  1. Points to parts of body. (3 of 4.)
       Nose; eyes; mouth; hair.
  2. Names familiar objects. (3 of 5.)
       Key, penny, closed knife, watch, pencil.
  3. Pictures, enumeration or better. (At least 3 objects enumerated in one picture.)
       (a) Dutch Home; (b) River Scene; (c) Post-Office.
  4. Gives sex.
  5. Gives last name.
  6. Repeats 6 to 7 syllables. (1 of 3.)
  Al. Repeats 3 digits. (1 success in 3 trials. Order correct.)"

"YEAR IV. (6 tests, 2 months each.)
  1. Compare lines. (3 trials, no error.)
  2. Discrimination of forms. (Kuhlmann.) (Not over 3 errors.)
  3. Counts 4 pennies. (No error.)
  4. Copies square. (Pencil. 1 of 3.)
  5. Comprehension, 1st degree. (2 of 3.)
       (Stanford addition.) 'What must you do':
       'When you are sleepy?' 'Cold?' 'Hungry?'
  6. Repeats 4 digits. (1 of 3. Order correct.)
       (Stanford addition.)
  Al. Repeats 12 to 13 syllables. (1 of 3 absolutely correct or 2 with 1 error each.)"

"YEAR V. (6 tests, 2 months each.)
  1. Comparison of weights. (2 of 3.)
       3–15; 15–3; 3–15.
  2. Colors. (No error.)
       Red; yellow; blue; green.
  3. Æsthetic comparison. (No error.)
  4. Definitions, use or better. (4 of 6.)
       Chair; horse; fork; doll; pencil; table.
  5. Patience, or divided rectangle. (2 of 3 trials. 1 minute each.)
  6. Three commissions. (No error. Order correct.)
  A1. Age."

"YEAR VI. (6 tests, 2 months each.)
  1. Right and left. (No error.)
       Right hand; left ear; right eye.
  2. Mutilated pictures. (3 of 4 correct.)
  3. Counts 13 pennies. (1 of 2 trials, without error.)
  4. Comprehension, 2d degree. (2 of 3.) 'What's the thing for you to do':
       (a) 'If it is raining when you start to school?'
       (b) 'If you find that your house is on fire?'
       (c) 'If you are going some place and miss your car?'
  5. Coins. (3 of 4.)
       Nickel; penny; quarter; dime.
  6. Repeats 16 to 18 syllables. (1 of 3 absolutely correct, or 2 with 1 error each.)
  Al. Morning or afternoon."

Note.—Al. signifies alternative.

The following examples will serve to illustrate the way in which each of these lists of tests is elaborated in the instructions prepared for those who are to give the tests:

"III, 1. POINTING TO PARTS OF THE BODY

Procedure. After getting the child's attention, say: "Show me your nose.' 'Put your finger on your nose.'Same with the eyes, mouth, and hair.

"Tact is often necessary to overcome timidity. If two or three repetitions of the instruction fail to bring a response, point to the child's chin or ear and say: 'Is this your nose?' 'No?' 'Then where is your nose?' Sometimes, after one has tried two or three parts of the test without eliciting any response, the child may suddenly release his inhibitions and answer all the questions promptly. In case of persistent refusal to respond it is best not to harass the child for an answer, but to leave the test for a while and return to it later. This is a rule which applies generally throughout the scale. In the case of one exceptionally timid little girl, it was impossible to get any response by the usual procedure, but immediately when a doll was shown the child pointed willingly to its nose, eyes, mouth, and hair. The device was successful because it withdrew the child's attention from herself and centered it upon something objective.

"**Scoring.** Three responses out of four must be correct. Instead of pointing, the child sometimes responds by winking the eyes, opening the mouth, etc., which is counted as satisfactory.

"**Remarks.** Binet's purpose in this test is to ascertain whether the subject is capable of comprehending simple language. The ability to comprehend and use language is indeed one of the most reliable indications of the grade of mental development. The appreciation of gestures comes first, then the comprehension of language heard, next the ability to repeat words and sentences mechanically, and finally the ability to use language as a means of communication. The present test, however, is not more strictly a test of language comprehension than the others of the 3-year group, and in any case it could not be said to mark the *beginning* of the power to comprehend spoken language. That is fairly well advanced by the age of 2 years. The test closely resembles III, 2 (naming familiar objects), and III, 3 (enumeration of objects in a picture), except that it brings in a personal element and gives some clue to the development of the sense of self. All the data agree in locating the test at year III.

"**III, 2. NAMING FAMILIAR OBJECTS**

Procedure. Use a key, a penny, a closed knife, a watch, and an ordinary lead pencil. The key should be the usual large-sized doorkey, not one of the Yale type. The penny should not be too new, for the freshly made, untarnished penny resembles very little the penny usually seen. Any ordinary pocketknife may be used, and it is to be shown unopened. The formula is, 'What is this?' or, 'Tell me what this is.'

"**Scoring.** There must be at least three correct responses out of five. A response is not correct unless the object is named. It is not sufficient for the child merely to show that he knows its use. A child, for example, may take the pencil and begin to mark with it, or go to the door and insert the key in the lock, but this is not sufficient. At the same time we must not be too arbitrary about requiring a particular name. 'Cent' or 'pennies' for 'penny' is satisfactory, but 'money' is not. The watch is sometimes called 'a clock' or 'a tick-tock,' and we shall perhaps not be too liberal if we score these responses plus. 'Pen' for 'pencil,' however, is unsatisfactory. Substitute names for 'key' and 'knife' are rarely given. Mispronunciations due to baby-talk are of course ignored.

"**Remarks.** The purpose of this test is to find out whether the child has made the association between familiar objects and their names. The mental processes necessary to enable the child to pass this test are very elementary, and yet, as far as they go, they are fundamental. Learning the names of objects frequently seen is a form of mental activity in which the normally endowed child of 2 to 4 years finds great satisfaction. Any marked retardation in making such associations is a grave indication of the lack of that spontaneity which is so necessary for the development of the higher grades of intelligence. It would be entirely beside the point, therefore, to question the validity of the test on the ground that a given child may not have been taught the names of the objects used. Practically all children 3 years old, however poor their environment, have made the acquaintance of at least three of the five objects, and if intelligence is normal they have learned their names as a result of spontaneous inquiry.

"Always use the list of objects here given, because it has been standardized. Any improvised selection would be sure to contain some objects either less or more familiar than those in the standardized list. Note also that three correct responses out of five are sufficient. If we required five correct answers out of six (like Kuhlmann), or three out of three (like Binet, Goddard, and Huey), the test would probably belong at the 4-year level. Binet states that this test is materially harder than that of naming objects in a picture, since in the latter the child selects from a number of objects in the picture those he knows best, while in the former test he must name the objects we have arbitrarily chosen. This difference does not hold, however, if we require only three correct responses out of five for passing the test of naming objects, instead of Binet's three out of three. All else being equal, it is of course easier to recognize and name a real object shown than it is to recognize and name it from a picture.

"**III, 3. ENUMERATION OF OBJECTS IN PICTURES**

Procedure. Use the three pictures designated as 'Dutch Home,' 'River Scene,' and 'Post-Office.' Say, 'Now I am going to show you a pretty picture.' Then, holding first one before the child, close enough to permit distinct vision, say:

'Tell me what you see in this picture.' If there is no response, as sometimes happens, due to embarrassment or timidity, repeat the request in this form: 'Look at the picture and tell me everything you can see in it.' If there is still no response, say: 'Show me the . . . .' (naming some object in the picture). Only one question of this type, however, is permissible. If the child answers correctly, say, 'That is fine; now tell me everything you see in the picture.' From this point the responses nearly always follow without further coaxing. Indeed, if rapport has been properly cultivated before the test begins, the first question will ordinarily be sufficient. If the child names one or two things in a picture and then stops, urge him on by saying, 'And what else?' Proceed with pictures (b) and (c) in the same manner.

"**Scoring.** The test is passed if the child enumerates as many as three objects in one picture spontaneously; that is, without intervening questions or urging. Anything better than enumeration (as description or interpretation) is also acceptable, but description is rarely encountered before 5 years and interpretation rarely before 9 or 10.

"**Remarks.** The purpose of the test in this year is to find out whether the sight of a familiar object in a picture provokes recognition and calls up the appropriate name. The average child of 3 or 4 years is in what Binet calls 'the identification stage'; that is, familiar objects in a picture will be identified but not described, their relations to one another will not be grasped.

"In giving the test, always present the pictures in the same order, first Dutch Home, then River Scene, then Post-Office. The order of presentation will no doubt seem to the uninitiated too trivial a matter to insist upon, but a little experience teaches one that an apparently insignificant change in the procedure may exert a considerable influence upon the response. Some pictures tend more strongly than others to provoke a particular type of response. Some lend themselves especially to enumeration, others to description, others to interpretation. The pictures used in the Stanford revision have been selected from a number which have been tried, because they are more uniform in this respect than most others in use. However, they are not without their difference, picture (b), for example, tending more than the others to provoke description.

"There seems to be no disagreement as to the proper location of this test."

TESTS IN WORLD WARS I AND II

General Intelligence Tests. Since the improvement of the Binet scale, especially by Professor L. M. Terman of Leland Stanford Junior university significant programs for the measurement of intelligence have been conducted, principally by the schools and by the United States armed forces in World Wars I and II. World War I gave the intelligence-testing movement the greatest stimulus which it has ever had. The chief testing instrument used by the army during World War I was known as the Army Alpha Test reproduced below. During World War II, all branches of the armed forces used intelligence tests known as General Classification Tests. These were given to all enlisted personnel and to officers.

The chief purpose of these tests was to aid in eliminating all persons who were so incompetent that they could not understand and follow orders. Another purpose was to aid in the selection of those persons with the highest degree of intelligence for positions of command. The tests were also used to assist in making promotions from one rank to another rank. In brief, the tests were used in both wars to measure the degree of intelligence of the military personnel. Because of their success in the wars, their use in the schools of the nation received a tremendous impetus.

Occupational Tests. During World Wars I and II, the armed forces also needed a system of classification whereby they could place their personnel in the various occupations which were necessary for carrying on military operations. The locating of persons suited to the various occupations was effectively handled, in part, through a knowledge of the earlier occupations pursued by the persons. In many instances, however, it was necessary to place persons in occupations which were different from those pursued by them in civilian life, and tests were needed in order to avoid, so far as possible, misfit assignments.

Fortunately the methods for making such tests had been developed in much detail by psychologists and educationists even before World War I. With this beginning, many occupational tests were developed during World War I, and following that war and during World War II many other occupational tests were developed.

In 1940 war had become much more complex than in 1917. Many branches of the armed forces were confronted with the problem of selecting highly qualified men for difficult and specialized tasks. Candidates were given a battery of tests designed to provide a profile of aptitudes and abilities. The value of these tests as predictors was clearly reflected in lower "washout" rates.

After World War II the Army introduced the Aptitude Area System. This consisted originally of nine special aptitude tests called the Army Classification Battery and was given to all inductees. It included: A Verbal Test, Arithmetic Reasoning Test, Pattern Analysis Test, Mechanical Aptitude Test, Army Clerical Speed Test, Army Radio Code Aptitude Test, Shop Mechanics Test, Automotive Information Test, and Electronics Information Test.

One of the results of the impetus given to testing in World Wars I and II was the spread of the use of tests in the schools. Between 75% and 90% of all public elementary and secondary schools in the United States make use of standardized tests. A tremendous boost to testing was given in 1958 as a result of Title VA of the National Defense Education Act. This made funds available to states to establish and maintain a program for testing aptitudes and abilities of students in public secondary schools. Federal assistance was extended to private secondary schools under Section 504(B). By 1964 approximately 35% of all testing going on in secondary schools was being financed by the Federal Government and all 50 states were participating in the program.

REPRODUCTION OF ARMY ALPHA, FORM 5.

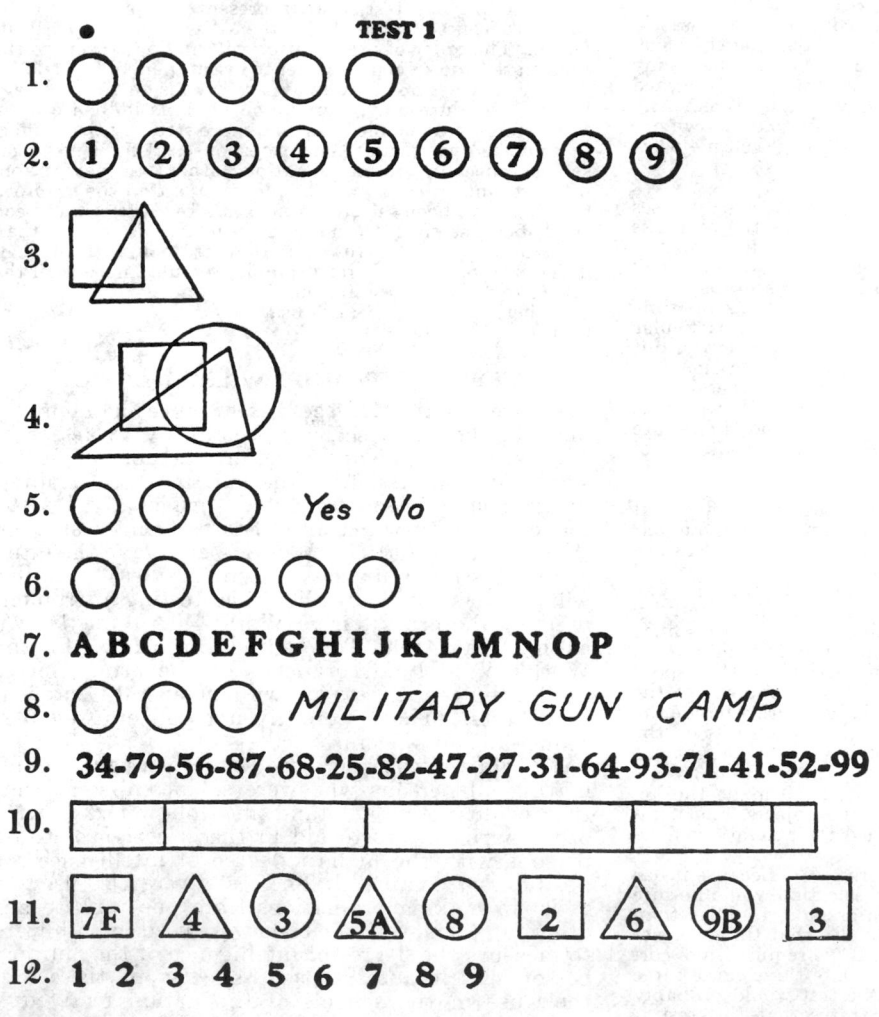

4. "Attention! Look at 4. When I say 'go,' make a figure 1 in the space which is in the circle, but not in the triangle or square, and also make a figure 2 in the space which is in the triangle and circle, but not in the square.—Go!" (Allow not over 10 seconds.)

(N.B. Examiner.—In reading 5, don't pause at the word CIRCLE as if ending a sentence.)

5. "Attention! Look at 5. If a machine gun can shoot more bullets a minute than a rifle, then (when I say 'go') put a cross in the second circle; if not, draw a line *under* the word No.—Go!" (Allow not over 10 seconds.)

6. "Attention! Look at 6. When I say 'go,' put in the second circle the right answer to the question: 'How many months has a year?' In the third circle do nothing, but in the fourth circle put any number that is a wrong answer to the question that you have just answered correctly.—Go!" (Allow not over 10 seconds.)

7. "Attention! Look at 7. When I say 'go,' *cross out* the letter just before C and also draw a line *under* the second letter before H.—Go!" (Allow not over 10 seconds.)

8. "Attention! Look at 8 Notice the three circles and the three words. When I say 'go,' make in the *first* circle the first letter of the *first* word; in the *second* circle the *first* letter of the *second* word; and in the *third* circle the last letter of the *third* word.—Go!" (Allow not over 10 seconds.)

This is an oral directions test. The directions given are as follows:

TEST I, FORM V

1. "Attention! 'Attention' always means 'Pencils up.' Look at the circles at 1. When I say 'go,' but not before, make a cross in the first circle and also a figure 1 in the third circle.—Go!" (Allow not over 5 seconds.)

2. "Attention! Look at 2, where the circles have numbers in them. When I say 'go,' draw a line from Circle 1 to Circle 4 that will pass *above* Circle 2 and *below* Circle 3.—Go!" (Allow not over 5 seconds.)

3. "Attention! Look at the square and triangle at 3. When I say 'go,' make a cross in the space which is in the triangle, but not in the square, and also make a figure 1 in the space which is in the triangle and in the square.—Go!" (Allow not over 10 seconds.)

9. "Attention! Look at 9. When I say 'go,' *cross out* each number that is more than 20, but less than 30.—Go!" (Allow not over 15 seconds.)

10. "Attention! Look at 10. Notice that the drawing is divided into five parts. When I say 'go,' put a 3 or a 2 in each of the two largest parts and any number between 4 and 7 in the part next in size to the smallest part.—Go!" (Allow not over 15 seconds.)

11. "Attention! Look at 11. When I say 'go,' draw a line through every even number that is not in a square and also through every odd number that is in a square with a letter.—Go!" (Allow not over 25 seconds.)

12. "Attention! Look at 12. If 7 is more than 5, then (when I say 'go') cross out the number 6 unless 6 is more than 8, in which case draw a line under the number 7.—Go!" (Allow not over 10 seconds.)

TEST 2

Get the answers to these examples as quickly as you can. Use the side of this page to figure on if you need to.

Samples
1. How many are 5 men and 10 men? Answer . . . . (15
2. If you walk 4 miles an hour for 3 hours, how far do you walk? Answer . . . (12

1. How many are 30 men and 7 men? Answer . . . (
2. If you save $7 a month for 4 months, how much will you save? Answer . . . . (
3. If 24 men are divided into squads of 8, how many squads will there be? Answer . . . . (
4. Mike had 12 cigars. He bought 3 more, and then smoked 6. How many cigars did he have left? Answer . . . . (
5. A company advanced 5 miles and retreated 3 miles. How far was it then from its first position? Answer (
6. How many hours will it take a truck to go 66 miles at the rate of 6 miles an hour? Answer . . . . (
7. How many cigars can you buy for 50 cents at the rate of 2 for 5 cents? Answer . . . . . . (
8. A regiment marched 40 miles in five days. The first day they marched 9 miles, the second day 6 miles, the third 10 miles, the fourth 8 miles. How many miles did they march the last day? Answer. (
9. If you buy two packages of tobacco at 7 cents each and a pipe for 65 cents, how much change should you get from a two-dollar bill? Answer . . . . (
10. If it takes 6 men 3 days to dig a 180-foot drain, how many men are needed to dig it in half a day? Answer . . . . (
11. A dealer bought some mules for $800. He sold them for $1,000, making $40 on each mule. How many mules were there? Answer . . . . (
12. A rectangular bin holds 400 cubic feet of lime. If the bin is 10 feet long and 5 feet wide, how deep is it? Answer . . . . (
13. A recruit spent one-eighth of his spare change for post cards and four times as much for a box of letter paper, and then had 90 cents left. How much money did he have at first? Answer . . . . . (
14. If 3½ tons of coal cost $21. what will 5½ tons cost? Answer . . . . (
15. A ship has provisions to last her crew of 500 men 6 months. How long would it last 1,200 men? Answer . . . . (
16. If a man runs a hundred yards in 10 seconds, how many feet does he run in a fifth of a second? Answer . . . . (
17. A U-boat makes 8 miles an hour under water and 15 miles on the surface. How long will it take to cross a 100-mile channel, if it has to go two-fifths of the way under water? Answer . . . . . . (
18. If 241 squads of men are to dig 4,097 yards of trench, how many yards must be dug by each squad? Answer . . . . (
19. A certain division contains 3,000 artillery, 15,000 infantry and 1,000 cavalry. If each branch is expanded proportionately until there are in all 20,900 men, how many will be added to the artillery? Answer . . . . (
20. A commission house which had already supplied 1,897 barrels of apples to a cantonment delivered the remainder of its stock to 29 mess halls. Of this remainder each mess hall received 54 barrels. What was the total number of barrels supplied? Answer. (

TEST 3

This is a test of common sense. Below are sixteen questions. Three answers are given to each question. You are to look at the answers carefully; then make a cross in the square before the best answer to each question, as in the sample:

Sample
Why do we use stoves? Because
☐ they look well
☒ they keep us warm
☐ they are black

Here the second answer is the best one and is marked with a cross. Begin with No. 1 and keep on until time is called.

1. Cats are useful animals, because
☐ they catch mice
☐ they are gentle
☐ they are afraid of dogs

2. Why are pencils more commonly carried than fountain pens? Because
☐ they are brightly colored
☐ they are cheaper
☐ they are not so heavy

3. Why is leather used for shoes? Because
☐ it is produced in all countries
☐ it wears well
☐ it is an animal product

4. Why judge a man by what he does rather than by what he says? Because
☐ what a man does shows what he really is
☐ it is wrong to tell a lie
☐ a deaf man cannot hear what is said

5. If you were asked what you thought of a person whom you didn't know. what should you say?
☐ I will go and get acquainted
☐ I think he is all right
☐ I don't know him and can't say

6. Streets are sprinkled in summer
☐ to make the air cooler
☐ to keep automobiles from skidding
☐ to keep down dust

7. Why is wheat better for food than corn? Because
☐ it is more nutritious
☐ it is more expensive
☐ it can be ground finer

8. If a man made a million dollars, he ought to
☐ pay off the national debt
☐ contribute to various worthy charities
☐ give it all to some poor man

9. Why do many persons prefer automobiles to street cars? Because
☐ an auto is made of higher grade materials
☐ an automobile is more convenient
☐ street cars are not as safe

10. The feathers on a bird's wings help him to fly because they
☐ make a wide, light surface
☐ keep the air off his body
☐ keep the wings from cooling off too fast

11. All traffic going one way keeps to the same side of the street because
☐ most people are right handed
☐ the traffic policeman insists on it
☐ it avoids confusion and collisions

12. Why do inventors patent their inventions? Because
☐ it gives them control of their inventions
☐ it creates a greater demand
☐ it is the custom to get patents

13. Freezing water bursts pipes because
☐ cold makes the pipes weaker
☐ water expands when it freezes
☐ the ice stops the flow of water

14. Why are high mountains covered with snow? Because
☐ they are near the clouds
☐ the sun seldom shines on them
☐ the air is cold there

15. If the earth were nearer the sun
☐ the stars would disappear
☐ our months would be longer
☐ the earth would be warmer

16. Why is it colder nearer the poles than near the equator? Because

☐ the poles are always farther from the sun

☐ the sunshine falls obliquely at the poles

☐ there is more ice at the poles

TEST 4

If the two words of a pair mean the same or nearly the same, draw a line under same. If they mean the opposite or nearly the opposite, draw a line under opposite. If you cannot be sure, guess. The two samples are already marked as they should be.

Samples { good—bad . . . . same—<u>opposite</u>
little—small . . . . . . <u>same</u>—opposite

1	wet—dry . . . . same—opposite	1
2	in—out . . . . same—opposite	2
3	hill—valley . . . . same—opposite	3
4	allow—permit . . . . . . same—opposite	4
5	expand—contract . . . . same—opposite	5
6	class—group . . . . same—opposite	6
7	former—latter . . . . . . same—opposite	7
8	confess—admit . . . . . . same—opposite	8
9	shy—timid . . . . same—opposite	9
10	delicate—tender . . . . . same—opposite	10
11	extinguish—quench . . . . same—opposite	11
12	cheerful—melancholy . . . same—opposite	12
13	accept—reject . . . . . . same—opposite	13
14	concave—convex . . . . . same—opposite	14
15	lax—strict . . . . same—opposite	15
16	assert—maintain . . . . . same—opposite	16
17	champion—advocate . . . . same—opposite	17
18	adapt—conform . . . . . . same—opposite	18
19	debase—exalt . . . . . . same—opposite	19
20	dissension—harmony . . . same—opposite	20
21	repress—restrain . . . . . same—opposite	21
22	bestow—confer . . . . . . same—opposite	22
23	amenable—tractable . . . same—opposite	23
24	avert—prevent . . . . . . same—opposite	24
25	reverence—veneration . . . same—opposite	25
26	fallacy—verity . . . . . . same—opposite	26
27	specific—general . . . . . same—opposite	27
28	pompous—ostentatious . . . same—opposite	28
29	accumulate—dissipate . . . same—opposite	29
30	apathy—indifference . . . . same—opposite	30
31	effeminate—virile . . . . . same—opposite	31
32	peculation—embezzlement . . same—opposite	32
33	benign—genial . . . . . . same—opposite	33
34	acme—climax . . . . . . same—opposite	34
35	largess—donation . . . . . same—opposite	35
36	innuendo—insinuation . . . same—opposite	36
37	vesper—matin . . . . . . same—opposite	37
38	aphorism—maxim . . . . . same—opposite	38
39	adjure—renounce . . . . . same—opposite	39
40	encomium—eulogy . . . . . same—opposite	40

TEST 5

The words A EATS COW GRASS in that order are mixed up and don't make a sentence; but they would make a sentence if put in the right order: A COW EATS GRASS, and this statement is true.

Again, the words HORSES FEATHERS HAVE ALL would make a sentence if put in the order ALL HORSES HAVE FEATHERS, but this statement is false.

Below are twenty-four mixed-up sentences. Some of them are true and some are false. When I say "go," take these sentences one at a time. Think what each **would** say if the words were straightened out, but don't write them yourself. Then, if what it **would** say is true, draw a line under the word "true"; if what it **would** say is false, draw a line under the word "false." If you can not be sure, guess. The two examples are already marked as they should be. Begin with No. 1 and work right down the page until time is called.

Samples { a eats cow grass . . . . . . true—false
horses feathers have all . . . . true—<u>false</u>

1	lions strong are . . . . true—false	1
2	houses people in live . . . . . . true—false	2
3	days there in are week eight a . . true—false	3
4	leg flies one have only . . . . . . true—false	4
5	months coldest are summer the . . true—false	5
6	gotten sea water sugar is from . . . true—false	6
7	honey bees flowers gather the from . true—false	7
8	and eat good gold silver to are . . true—false	8
9	president Columbus first the was America of . . . . true—false	9

10	making is bread valuable wheat for . . true—false	10
11	water and made are butter from cheese true—false	11
12	sides every has four triangle . . . . true—false	12
13	every times makes mistakes person at . true—false	13
14	many toes 'fingers as men as have . . true—false	14
15	not eat gunpowder to good is . . . . true—false	15
16	ninety canal ago built Panama years was the . . . . true—false	16
17	live dangerous is near a volcano to it . true—false	17
18	clothing worthless are for and wool cotton true—false	18
19	as sheets are napkins used never . . . true—false	19
20	people trusted intemperate be always can true—false	20
21	employ debaters irony never . . . . . true—false	21
22	certain some death of mean kinds sickness . . . . true—false	22
23	envy bad malice traits are and . . . . true—false	23
24	repeated call human for courtesies associations . . . . true—false	24

TEST 6

Samples {
2	4	6	8	10	12	*14*	*16*
9	8	7	6	5	4	*3*	*2*
2	2	3	3	4	4	*5*	*5*
1	7	2	7	3	7	*4*	*7*

Look at each row of numbers below, and on the two dotted lines write the two numbers that should come next.

3	4	5	6	7	8	. . . .	. . . .
10	15	20	25	30	35	. . . .	. . . .
8	7	6	5	4	3	. . . .	. . . .
3	6	9	12	15	18	. . . .	. . . .
5	9	13	17	21	25	. . . .	. . . .
8	1	6	1	4	1	. . . .	. . . .
27	27	23	23	19	19	. . . .	. . . .
1	2	4	8	16	32	. . . .	. . . .
8	9	12	13	16	17	. . . .	. . . .
9	9	7	7	5	5	. . . .	. . . .
19	16	14	11	9	6	. . . .	. . . .
2	3	5	8	12	17	. . . .	. . . .
11	13	12	14	13	15	. . . .	. . . .
29	28	26	23	19	14	. . . .	. . . .
18	14	17	13	16	12	. . . .	. . . .
81	27	9	3	1	⅓	. . . .	. . . .
20	17	15	14	11	9	. . . .	. . . .
16	17	15	18	14	19	. . . .	. . . .
1	4	9	16	25	36	. . . .	. . . .
3	6	8	16	18	36	. . . .	. . . .

TEST 7

Samples {
sky—blue : : grass—**table <u>green</u> warm big**
fish—swims : : man—**paper time <u>walks</u> girl**
day—night : : white—**red <u>black</u> clear pure**

In each of the lines below, the first two words are related to each other in some way. What you are to do in each line is to see what the relation is between the first two words, and underline the word in heavy type that is related in the same way to the third word. Begin with No. 1 and mark as many sets as you can before time is called.

1	gun—shoots : : knife—**run cuts hat bird**	1
2	ear—hear : : eye—**table hand see play**	2
3	dress—woman : : feathers—**bird neck feet bill** . .	3
4	handle—hammer : : knob—**key room shut door** .	4
5	shoe—foot : : hat—**coat nose head collar** . . .	5
6	water—drink : : bread—**cake coffee eat pie** . . .	6
7	food—man : : gasoline—**gas oil automobile spark**	7
8	eat—fat : : starve—**thin food bread thirsty** . . .	8
9	man—home : : bird—**fly insect worm nest** . . .	9
10	go—come : : sell—**leave buy money papers** . .	10
11	peninsula—land : : bay—**boats pay ocean Massachusetts**	11
12	hour—minute : : minute—**man week second short**	12
13	abide—depart : : stay—**over home play leave** . .	13
14	January—February : : June—**July May month year**	14
15	bold—timid : : advance—**proceed retreat campaign soldier**	15
16	above—below : : top—**spin bottom surface side**	16
17	lion—animal : : rose—**smell leaf plant thorn** . .	17
18	tiger—carnivorous : : horse—**cow pony buggy herbivorous**	18
19	sailor—navy : : soldier—**gun cap hill army** . . .	19
20	picture—see : : sound—**noise music hear bark** . .	20
21	success—joy : : failure—**sadness success fail work**	21
22	hope—despair : : happiness—**frolic fun joy sadness**	22
23	pretty—ugly : : attract—**fine repel nice draw** . . .	23
24	pupil—teacher : : child—**parent doll youngster obey**	24
25	city—mayor : : army—**navy soldier general private**	25

26 establish—begin : : abolish—**slavery wrong abolition end** 26
27 December—January : : last—**least worst month first** 27
28 giant—dwarf : : large—**big monster queer small** . 28
29 engine—caboose : : beginning—**commence cabin end train** 29
30 dismal—cheerful : : dark—**sad stars night bright** . 30
31 quarrel—enemy : : agree—**friend disagree agreeable foe** 31
32 razor—sharp : : hoe—**bury dull cuts tree** . . . 32
33 winter—summer : : cold—**freeze warm wet January** 33
34 rudder—ship : : tail—**sail bird dog cat** 34
35 granary—wheat : : library—**desk books paper librarian** 35
36 tolerate—pain : : welcome—**pleasure unwelcome friends give** 36
37 sand—glass : : clay—**stone hay bricks dirt** . . . 37
38 moon—earth : : earth—**ground Mars sun sky** . . 38
39 tears—sorrow : : laughter—**joy smile girls grin** . 39
40 cold—ice : : heat—**lightning warm steam coat** . 40

TEST 8

Notice the sample sentence:

People **hear** with the **eyes ears nose mouth**

The correct word is **ears**, because it makes the truest sentence.

In each of the sentences below you have four choices for the last word. Only one of them is correct. In each sentence draw a line under the one of these four words which makes the truest sentence. If you can not be sure, guess. The two samples are already marked as they should be.

Samples { People **hear** with the **eyes ears nose mouth**
         { France is in **Europe Asia Africa Australia**

1 **America** was discovered by **Drake Hudson Columbus Balboa** 1
2 **Pinochle** is played with **rackets cards pins dice** . . 2
3 The most prominent industry of **Detroit** is **automobiles brewing flour packing** 3
4 The **Wyandotte** is a kind of **horse fowl cattle granite** 4
5 The **U. S. School for Army Officers** is at **Annapolis West Point New Haven Ithaca** 5
6 **Food products** are made by **Smith & Wesson Swift & Co. W. L. Douglas B. T. Babbitt** 6
7 **Bud Fisher** was famous as an **actor author baseball player comic artist** 7
8 The **Guernsey** is a kind of **horse goat sheep cow** . 8
9 **Myrna Loy** is known as a **suffragist singer movie actress writer** 9
10 "**Hasn't scratched yet**" is used in advertising a **duster flour brush cleanser** 10
11 **Salsify** is a kind of **snake fish lizard vegetable** . . 11
12 **Coral** is obtained from **mines elephants oysters reefs** 12
13 **Rosa Bonheur** is famous as a **poet painter composer sculptor** 13
14 The **tuna** is a kind of **fish bird reptile insect** . . 14
15 **Emeralds** are usually **red blue green yellow** . 15
16 **Maize** is a kind of **corn hay oats rice** . . . 16
17 **Nabisco** is a **patent medicine disinfectant food product tooth paste** 17
18 **Velvet Joe** appears in advertisements of **tooth powder dry goods tobacco soap** 18
19 **Cypress** is a kind of **machine food tree fabric** . . 19
20 **Bombay** is a city in **China Egypt India Japan** . . 20
21 The **dictaphone** is a kind of **typewriter multigraph phonograph adding machine** 21
22 The **pancreas** is in the **abdomen head shoulder neck** 22
23 **Cheviot** is the name of a **fabric drink dance food** . 23
24 **Larceny** is a term used in **medicine theology law pedagogy** 24
25 The **Battle of Gettysburg** was fought in **1863 1813 1778 1812** 25
26 The **bassoon** is used in **music stenography bookbinding lithography** 26
27 **Turpentine** comes from **petroleum ore hides trees** 27
28 The number of a **Zulu's legs** is **two four six eight** 28
29 The **scimitar** is a kind of **musket cannon pistol sword** 29
30 **Nylon** is the name of a **metal vegetable textile bird** 30
31 The author of "**The Raven**" is **Stevenson Kipling Hawthorne Poe** 31
32 **Spare** is a term used in **bowling football tennis hockey** 32
33 A six-sided figure is called a **scholium parallelogram hexagon trapezium** 33

34 **Isaac Pitman** was most famous in **physics shorthand railroading electricity** 34
35 The **ampere** is used in measuring **wind power electricity water power rainfall** 35
36 The **Chrysler car** is made in **Buffalo Detroit Flint Toledo** 36
37 **Mauve** is the name of a **drink color fabric food** . 37
38 The **stanchion** is used in **fishing hunting farming motoring** 38
39 **Mica** is a **vegetable mineral gas liquid** . . . 39
40 **Scrooge** appears in **Vanity Fair The Christmas Carol Romola Henry IV** 40

Interpreting Results of the Alpha Test. The results of the army tests have been compiled by various writers in an effort to bring out the mental characteristics of the army recruits from different sections of the country and from different nationalities. One author has compiled the results of these tests in such a way as to show very definitely that the immigrants who come to the United States from the southeastern European countries are not able to pass the test with as high a grade as the immigrants who come from the northern European states. In view of the fact that recent immigration has been predominantly from the countries in the southeastern part of Europe, these findings raise grave social questions.

Another general fact brought out by these tests is that the average recruit was able to answer the tests only about as well as school children between 13 and 14 years of age. On the basis of this fact, the statement is sometimes made that the average American citizen is intellectually between 13 and 14 years of age. Against this statement it has been argued that the tests include only those types of intellectual effort which belong to a school training. Beyond 13 years of age the ordinary man does not continue to cultivate the same type of thinking which he cultivated in the school. Consequently, the test does not uncover the mental development which has been going on, for example, in business or in practical mechanics. There is nothing in the test to show what a man who works in a foundry has been learning since he left school.

Controversy as to the meaning of the test has arisen at another point also. There are some who regard the test as a measure of native ability, while others regard it as a measure of acquired information. If the test measures native ability, then it is not to be expected that anyone who passes the test well at any given time will be of low mental ability at any other time in his life. Conversely, anyone who is not able to pass the test at a level that comports with his age cannot be expected to show intellectual ability of a higher order later. Those who believe that the test measures acquired information, on the other hand, interpret the results to mean that a man has had certain intellectual opportunities if he passes the test well, and that he has been deprived of these opportunities if he does not pass well.

It has been shown very clearly that the ability of recruits from different states parallels closely the efficiency of the school systems of these states. This fact would seem to indicate that the test measures school training quite as much as it does native intelligence. In general, this latter conclusion is probably more nearly the exact truth than the statement that the test measures only native ability.

Applications of Intelligence Tests. There can be no doubt that the experience of the army demonstrated the value of the various tests which were used. Some people were so much impressed by the success of the army tests that they believed a method had been found of classifying all human beings for all sorts of purposes, and the most extreme positions have been taken with regard to the use of these tests.

For example, it has been asserted by some that anyone who passes with a low grade should not be educated in a high school, and certainly not in college, on the theory that it is uneconomical for society to bestow its training on those who are endowed with only moderate degrees of intelligence.

Furthermore, extremists have appeared in some school systems who would rearrange the classification of pupils, sometimes even to the extent of ignoring the judgment of teachers, putting into a given grade only those children who stand at the same level in a general intelligence test.

These extremists have been met by vigorous objectors who hold that it is quite impossible on the basis of a single test to determine a person's intelligence and his probable achievements in the intellectual world. The objectors have marshaled a large body of evidence to show that the tests are in need of elaboration if they are to be relied upon at all, and that it is necessary to administer more than one test before any reliance can be placed upon the classifications which they suggest.

As a matter of actual practice, these tests are now extensively used to supplement the judgments of teachers in classifying students in all grades of schools. This is undoubtedly the legitimate use to which they can be put. They cannot be used to the exclusion of the other evidences in regard to students' achievements, but they are proving in their refined forms to be very much more reliable than any other single type of evidence, and because of their extended use they certainly supply a basis for the comparison of educational institutions and of teachers.

Furthermore their extensive use has led to a careful scrutiny of all the other devices for measuring human ability, such as examinations and teachers' judgments. The net result has been a refinement of the methods of placing pupils in the school and of graduating them at the completion of their courses. The indirect advantages have therefore often equaled the direct.

Types of Intelligence Tests. Intelligence tests usually consist of a series of sub-tests which endeavor to measure the mental age of an individual as determined by his behavior in representative tasks. A device known as the Intelligence Quotient (IQ) is a means for summarizing the performance in this series of sub-tests.

A criticism of intelligence tests has been that the success one has with them depends on reading ability and a knowledge of a particular type of culture. To offset this criticism, a kind of intelligence test has been devised to overcome the limitation caused by the emphasis on verbalism. This is called the non-verbal test. The most widely used test of this type is the Army Beta Test. It is used to test those who are linguistically handicapped or are non-academic. Recently this test is being used in conjunction with or as a part of other verbal intelligence tests.

Types of Tests in Use. Numerous tests have been developed to determine the development of a child before the age of six years, and to predict his later status. The most effective of these endeavor to construct a scale by identifying what is considered to be normal behavior at the age in which the development is found. The resulting scales permit the identification of the child who is making more or less progress than others at a given age. However, the use of these tests as predictors is very dangerous. Also, expert interpretation of the scales is desirable in identifying what is considered to be normal behavior.

Performance tests are a type which provides essential information about the person being tested when he is handicapped on verbal tests. They are useful as a means of indicating how persons of borderline mental defects can be fitted into society. They are useful also as devices to supplement other forms of testing. Such tests are usually administered individually and great importance must be given to the expert who rates the performance of the person being tested.

A large number of tests have been constructed to measure special abilities in an individual. These have been useful in vocational guidance and vocational selection. Spatial and perceptual tests are of this type. They are of importance in determining suitability for work in the fields of engineering or architecture. Other tests have endeavored to group the elements of a performance to the task to be done and to set standards. Thus, such things as speed and reaction time, manual dexterity, aiming, steadiness, strength, and co-ordination have been tested in different types of activities related to a skill to determine the extent of abilities called for by a job. In addition, trade tests have been developed for use where knowledge of one job is important. The United States Employment Service has made wide use of this type of test. They are used as a screening device during short interviews. There are three groups usually tested: expert workers, beginners in the trade, and workers in closely related trades.

In the field of the arts, several tests have been designed to identify aptitude or ability in art. These tests attempt to determine judgment in art, measure the likelihood of success in drawing and painting, or test native capacities to see or hear.

Choosing the Proper Test. Because of the large number of tests being distributed and the possible dangers of the misuse of tests or the use of poor tests, it is important that careful selection of the proper test be made. There are several sources of information which the client can use to find out about the value of a test for his situation. The publishers of tests usually give in their catalogs brief descriptions of the tests and their costs. From a reading of these descriptions, the client may reach a decision about the worth of the test for his situation. *The Mental Measurements Yearbook* edited by O. K. Buros provides reviews of a wide variety of tests. This yearbook is published periodically and gives several reviews for each test included by outstanding experts in the field of testing. There are several other sources which review tests. *The National Education Association* and the *Encyclopedia of Vocational Guidance* are among these.

Selection of a test on the basis of the particular purpose for which it is to be used is important. Not all published tests are good tests. It has been found that often even in similar situations the same test may not be used appropriately. Tests tend to become outdated and a test which is excellent for a given situation may be entirely inappropriate to be used again. Some tests are designed for children and others for adults. In selection they must be examined to find what group they most readily fit. Some tests give specific measures and others provide a general picture. Here again the needs of the situation determine which test to choose. One of the practical considerations is the cost of the test. Costs involve more than the initial price. Scoring and interpreting the results of the test must be included in the cost. These may make wide variations in the total cost of a testing program. The time required for a test is also a consideration. Some tests are too long. The time required has an effect on the co-operation of the subject. On the other hand, a test which is too short may not do as thorough a job as a longer test. Experts in test construction are constantly at work trying to design tests of appropriate length.

The ease with which a test can be administered and scored must be considered because the proper administration of a test often provides serious problems. Administering a test usually requires proper space, atmosphere, timing, and expert guidance as the test is given. It may be difficult to supply these. Where classroom teachers can give tests in schools, they tend to take greater interest in the results. However, this may become a burden when teachers have to score large numbers of papers. Many of the published tests provide for machine scoring of the papers. A central agency gives this service for a fee or, as in the case of many school systems, a scoring machine is available. Since tests are used very often to compare results against others, it is desirable that results of proper equivalent tests shall be available. Often in testing programs, several tests of the same type are given so as to enable comparisons to be made. Also, the results of a test are compared with scores made by others on the same or like tests. Any test should be related to the interest of the person taking the test. He will then see the necessity for taking the test and will do as thorough a job as possible to get accurate results.

Usability becomes another important consideration in the selection of a test. Results often bring out strong prejudices in those who use them. Therefore, it is wise to have the test acceptable to those who will interpret the results. The usability of a test is related to the extent of information available about the test, the period of time of its usefulness, and the means for interpreting the results.

Interpreting the Scores of Tests. When a test is taken, a score is generally given as a report of the performance. The value thus placed on the results of the test is called the "raw score." Commonly this score is indicated by a numerical percentage grade or a letter indicating a rating of excellent, good, fair, poor, or unsatisfactory. It has been traditional practice to compare such grades with others and, although there may be little or no relationship between the scores thus given on tests, to interpret them alike. The standard practice over the years of scoring tests and comparing the results in this manner has raised many questions about the meaning of the scores. Many unfair judgments have been made about test results. Comparisons of scores have been made where such comparisons have not been warranted.

Raw scores have limited meaning unless they are related to some common standard. When a standard of reference is established, there is a proper measure to which the scores of tests can be referred for comparison. Then a more accurate picture is presented in the interpretation of a score and raw scores take on more meaning. In recent years, the makers of tests have attempted to make the meaning and accuracy of the raw scores greater by developing tests having standards which are usable for larger numbers of people.

In order to compare one score with a group of scores from the same test, a common procedure is to distribute all of the scores resulting from the test according to the frequency of each score. It is found usually that the scores distribute themselves so that "norms" or normal results can be seen showing the usual performance on the test. A score then can be compared with the "norm." A score above the norm indicates superior work and a score below the norm shows inferior quality. Another means for making comparison is to distribute the scores according to frequency and to express the score as a percentage of the group. This is called the percentile rank. Percentiles are counted upward. Therefore, a score at the 75 percentile means that there are 75 per cent of the scores below it. Scores at a given percentile rank may be compared easily with others. A third method for comparison is to find the average score on the test by adding all of the test scores and dividing this sum by the number of scores involved. The figure resulting is called the "mean" or average. Test experts endeavor to standardize scores by applying them to formulas which are designed to consider possible inaccuracies caused by the conditions of the testing procedure. As a result greater accuracy in determining the value of test scores has been achieved.

Testing Agencies. In the United States there are several agencies which have testing as a function. One of these is the Educational Testing Service. In 1947 three major educational groups involved in testing programs combined their testing functions to form the Educational Testing Service. These three were the American Council on Education, the Carnegie Foundation for the Advancement of Teaching, and the College Entrance Examination Board. On January 1, 1948 the new organization began its formal operations dedicated to the purposes of aiding in the discovery and development of human talents by providing tests and testing services for special needs of schools and colleges, governmental agencies, and the professions; to assist test users; to conduct educational and measurement research; and to explore undeveloped areas in testing.

Over the years the Educational Testing Service has expanded its programs and has become a major institution for the promotion of testing programs. Its services have been used widely by the government, schools and colleges, and industry. Four major areas of endeavor have characterized the work of this organization. It has developed a number of qualifying examinations to aid authorities in the placement of candidates in institutions of learning. A widely used examination of this type has been the College Entrance Examination which is designed to measure the scholastic ability of students applying for admission to college. Many colleges now include this examination as a regular part of the requirements for admission. It is given twice yearly in centers throughout the United States and other parts of the world. Each year approximately 500,000 candidates take this examination. Other qualifying examinations are the Graduate Record Examinations which aid colleges in evaluating achievement of students at various levels, or determine their fitness for graduate study; The National College Testing Programs for Freshmen and Sophomores in College; The National College Preparatory Testing Program; and the Secondary School Admissions Test which is designed to measure scholastic ability of students applying for admissions to secondary schools.

Another activity of the Educational Testing Service is to provide Scholarship services. It gives consultative services to non-collegiate sponsors of scholarship programs. Approximately 300,000 applicants for scholarships take scholarship tests offered by sponsors using these services. Also the Testing Service has a program entitled The Financial Statement Services. This is designed to provide colleges with a central financial transcript and computation service that collects and evaluates financial information relating to scholarship applicants.

A third activity of the Educational Testing Service which has broadened rapidly in its scope has been its aptitude testing program. The Selective Service College Qualifying Test was used to justify deferment of college students from military service. Other aptitude tests have been widely used in the selection of candidates for such professional schools, or professions as: Graduate School of Business Law School, Medical College, Actuary, Engineering, Foreign Science, Home Economics, Teaching and School Administration. In addition to tests of this sort, other aptitude tests have been developed to aid individual organizations or groups in determining special abilities or interests.

The fourth major area of concern of the Educational Testing Service has been research in the field of testing. Here the organization has centered its activities around the development of better tests, studies of the use of tests in areas heretofore untested, factors influencing test scores, norms and scales for tests, test theories, and personality measures.

Other organizations with major concerns in testing are the Psychological Corporation, Science Research Associates Incorporated, The California Test Bureau, and the World Book Company. The Psychological Corporation among its other activities prepared and conducts nationwide group testing programs for the evaluation of candidates for professional training. It also develops and sells a wide variety of aptitude, intelligence, personality, and achievement tests. Science Research Associates Incorporated is a private organization which provides a wide variety of testing services to schools. The National Merit Scholarship Qualifying Test designed by this organization has been used extensively to help select candidates for college scholarships. The California Test Bureau and the World Book Company both are private organizations which publish many types of tests usable by schools and industry.

LABORATORY STUDIES

Another and somewhat more elaborate form of scientific study which has contributed to the better organization of schools and to improved methods of teaching may be described under the name "laboratory studies." There are certain types of investigation which teachers cannot readily carry on in the classroom, the results of which are yet very useful in directing educational work. An illustration of this type is to be found in the studies which have been made on the maturing of the child's physical organism. A little child is immature in his physical structures in the same degree as he is immature in his intellectual development. The physical changes through which he passes are in some respects easier to observe and record than are the intellectual changes. A good deal of energy has therefore been devoted to taking physical measurements of children.

Reaction Measurements. Direct laboratory measurements of children's special abilities are also made. One of the earliest of these, which has been influential in affecting school practice, is the measurement of so-called "reaction times." The amount of effort necessary to carry out a certain intellectual process is indicated by the length of time which it requires. Thus it requires more time to work out an elaborate problem in multiplication than to solve a simple problem in addition. The exact measurement of time required for various mental processes can be made by means of elaborate time measuring devices used in the laboratory. By the use of such apparatus, it is found that a child can recognize a word in the same length of time that is required for him to recognize a single letter. This being the case, it is evidently much more economical, in the early stages of reading, to train him to recognize word-wholes rather than to require him to recognize the letters which make up words. Guided by these laboratory experiments and by practical experience, teachers have found it advantageous to abandon the A-B-C method of teaching reading in favor of the word-whole method.

Methods of Reading. In addition to the A-B-C method mentioned above, the *Phonetic Method* and the *Word Recognition* methods of reading have figured prominently in teaching children. In the Phonetic Method the syllables of a word are ' sounded out" and the child learns to identify words by assembling the component syllable sounds.* The syllable sounds are grouped into "families" and children learn these families. Once the sounds are learned, a child finds it easy to construct the total sound of a word through its parts. In this method it is necessary to give ear training to be sure that the child hears properly. A criticism of this method is that time is wasted on the process of learning the 'families" of sounds and breaking up of words into parts when the eye naturally sees the word as a whole. Critics believe that it would be better to train children to see the word as a whole and learn it that way.

The Word Recognition method is one which endeavors to train children to learn words as a whole. The child is taught simple words at first and then as he progresses the words become more difficult. Words used in the learning process are generally those which laboratory tests have proven children

---

*Evidence of current interest in this approach to the teaching of reading is seen in the publication of textbooks on *Phonics* and the holding of "Phonics Workshops" for teachers.

should know at different stages of intellectual and chronological age development. In the process of learning the words, their meaning is as important as recognition of the word. As words are learned, the child also learns to construct the words into meaningful sentences.

It is now generally agreed among experts in the teaching of reading that no one reading method is appropriate for all children. It has been found that the letter-by-letter spelling or sounding out of syllables is a slow and unnecessary process in most cases. The use of this method usually depends upon some special condition which would keep children from learning to read in the more natural way of word recognition. The A-B-C method depends on the previous learning of the alphabet. Today, educators believe that, because of the great variety of visual material available to most children, it is unnecessary to teach the alphabet before a child learns to read. It is agreed however that, although the Word Recognition method is the most natural way to read, the A-B-C method and the Phonetic method have places in the process of learning to read.

Reading and Eye Movements. The most productive laboratory studies that have been made of school subjects are the studies of the reading of pupils. The mental processes through which a child passes in looking at a series of words have been measured by photographing the movements of his eyes. If the eyes move rapidly across a page, the indication is that the child has been able to recognize the successive words fluently. If, on the other hand, the eyes move very slowly across a line of printed matter, it is evident that the child has not been able to recognize the successive words fluently.

Photographs of eye movements have brought out the fact that no one looks at each individual letter of a line of printed matter; the eye moves forward in steps of greater or less length. The reader takes in at each step a number of letters or words, and then moves forward to the next position, from which a new group of letters or words may be taken in. The length of the steps made by the reader is a fair measure of his range of recognition. It has been found that little children move their eyes in short steps along a line of printed matter. The trained adult, on the other hand, is able to take in whole phrases at a time, and his eye movements are rapid and long.

By means of similar photographs it has been possible to discover the various types of difficulty which arise in training children to read. It has also been possible to study minutely the effects of various methods of teaching, and in this way to devise ways to remedy defects in children who show incompetency in school work.

SCHOOL SURVEYS

During the same period in which scientific methods were used to improve the school program, steps were taken to measure the efficiency of an educational institution or school system. Communities began to conduct what are now known as school surveys. A number of earlier social surveys were organized to investigate such matters as the housing conditions in cities or the situation regarding employment. Following the examples of these social surveys, educators organized a number of general school surveys.

The first great school survey was that of New York City in 1912. The results of this survey were published in three large volumes and excited a tremendous amount of controversial discussion among school officers of the city. The question was pointedly raised whether the methods employed by the surveyors were adequate to the task of evaluating the work of a great school system. Since the New York City survey, there appeared in rapid succession reports of surveys of individual schools, city school systems, state school programs, and even surveys of school programs of national scope.

An important development in school surveys was the financial support of them by a wide variety of agencies. In some instances the individual school or school system financed the survey using local resources. In other instances, public agencies from the outside or private groups gave financial assistance. Many of the states now provide professional help to schools for the purpose of conducting school surveys and it is considered desirable for such surveys to be conducted periodically.

Types of Surveys. School surveys can be generally divided into Comprehensive or Special studies. Comprehensive surveys include studies of the school curriculum, school population trends, the educational status and growth of the pupils, the financial structure, the administrative organization, the faculty, and the nature of the facilities provided for the school program. A Special survey may include studies of any one or even a part of one of the above listed areas of the school program.

Survey Agencies. There are several kinds of agencies which conduct school surveys. Private companies have been established to give this service to schools. However, most school surveys have been made by university agencies or university professors. Certain state departments of education and the United States Office of Education have also made surveys.

BUREAUS OF RESEARCH

Finally, it is becoming common for school systems to provide themselves with agencies that can make continuous studies of their school operations. Many of the leading school systems of the country now have such bureaus of investigation.

All these indications of the mature application of the science of education make it certain that the preliminary stages of this movement have passed, and that the schools of the country will from this time on depend increasingly on scientific methods for the determination of their efficiency. A striking example of the use of scientific methods in administering a school system can be found in the city of Detroit, where the whole supervisory scheme is based on systematic tests, and where the organization of the classes in the schools is controlled by the measurements made by a department of research.

STUDIES OF THE CURRICULUM

A review of the development of the science of education would not be complete without indicating some of the newer lines of inquiry which in recent years have been pushed forward. The most productive of these relate to the curriculum of the schools. For a long time the courses administered in schools of all grades have simply followed traditions. Additions have, indeed, been made to the older curriculum, but these additions have come very slowly and they have not changed the essential character of the fundamental courses. There have been changes also in the fundamental courses, but these have been in the nature of slight revisions here and there, rather than radical reconstructions of the whole course.

In recent years, it has become apparent that a very large body of new instructional material must be put into the schools. The changes in social and industrial life, which have come with expanding civilization, require training of the young people of the country in lines which were never thought of when the school course was first laid down. The question immediately arises, under these conditions, as to what new subjects are most urgently demanded and how the time can be found for inserting them into the school program. Obviously, revision of the older courses must involve an elimination of any material which is not essential to a complete education. Additional material of value must be found. Studies of the curriculum have aimed, therefore, to discover what parts of existing courses may be dispensed with and what new material must be added

in order to make the school serviceable to the modern community.

Also it is becoming apparent that changes must be made in the organization of the curriculum as well as its subject matter. Ways of allowing and encouraging independent study on the part of the student, means for having students get special help from the teacher, ways of using the many new teaching devices which have been developed, and ways for allowing students to develop intellectually at their optimum rate are all to be considered as the curriculum is studied.

As a result of the curriculum studies now being made, more resources are being placed at the disposal of the teacher. Also, school buildings and equipment are being made available for longer periods of time for students, and facilities have been redesigned to meet modern needs. Students are encouraged to enroll in more subjects during their period of schooling.

Instructional Materials Centers. In order to help teachers and students take advantage of the many educational resources now becoming available, schools are beginning to establish instructional materials centers. In these are kept lists of available educational and curriculum materials. Also, there may be kept in them textbooks, resource units, films, slides, science equipment, and other kinds of instructional facilities. Teachers use the materials and return them to the center. Also, students may be assigned to the center for the purpose of independent study.

In some instances one center serves an entire school system and various schools draw on the materials of the center. In other cases each school is provided with its own center.

JOB ANALYSIS

Another type of study which is common is described by the term "job analysis." The children who go out of the schools must be prepared, as far as the school can prepare them, for the activities of life. If a boy is to become a salesman or a printer, the training which is given him during the last few years of his schooling ought to be intelligently directed toward these activities. This will be possible only if the actual demands of these activities are fully understood. Various educational agencies, therefore, have attempted to analyze the demands made upon the printer and the salesman. Careful tabulations of the daily routine of these and other occupations are undertaken, and in the light of these tabulations an effort is made to determine exactly what knowledge of a literary and scientific sort will best prepare one to deal with these demands.

This method of job analysis has suggested that schools include in their training much material which has been overlooked or ignored. For example, it is perfectly clear that the salesman must know how to meet people in such a way as to get their attention. The school has not ordinarily attempted to deal with such social matters and has nowhere in its curriculum provided for training in social leadership. The modern school is beginning to realize that success in life may depend upon direct emphasis on personal and social qualities quite as much as on spelling, arithmetic, and literature.

THE SCIENCE OF EDUCATION AND EDUCATIONAL REORGANIZATION

Enough of the scientific movement in education has been described to justify the assertion that schools in the United States are in process of constructive reorganization under the guidance of scientific investigators. The defects and virtues of the American educational system are being demonstrated by exact methods, and significant improvements are being introduced at a rate never before equaled in the history of schools.

MODERN SCHOOL SYSTEMS OF WORLD COUNTRIES.

EDUCATION IN GERMANY

THE school system of Germany has had four periods of development. The first period extends from the Napoleonic wars (1800–15) to the close of World War I in 1918. During this time the *Volksschule*, the *Gymnasium*, and the university were the major developments. The *Volksschule* was an eight year school for the laboring classes. This school was for children 6 to 14 years of age and was free to all. It was followed by a three year continuation school. The *Gymnasium* was a nine year classical school for pupils 9 to 18 years of age, largely of the upper classes. Similar to the *Gymnasium* in organization were the *Realgymnasium* and the *Oberrealschule* which were developed during the latter part of the period in response to a demand for more emphasis on modern languages and science. The first three years preparatory to entering these upper class schools were done in a separate elementary school known as the *Vorschule*. During this period the universities of Germany became world famous, and many graduate students from the United States and other countries attended them.

Period of the Republic. This, the second period, extends from the close of World War I to the coming to power of Adolph Hitler in 1933. During this period the most important school changes were (1) the establishment of an elementary school (*Grundschule*) for all children between the ages of 6 and 10; (2) the reforming of instruction in the upper years (10-14) of the *Volksschule*; and (3) the reform in the training of teachers.

Period of Hitler. The third period is that under Hitler from 1933 to the defeat of Germany in World War II in 1945. Although the structure of the school system did not change much during this period, the curriculum and teaching methods were radically changed. Hitler's *Mein Kampf* was widely used as a text, and the school system became a blatant instrument of propaganda for the Nazi party.

Period After Hitler. The fourth period began with the allied occupation of Germany after her military debacle. During their occupation the allied powers took steps to eliminate all Nazi materials and employees from the schools. All Nazi textbooks were ordered destroyed and more democratic ones procured.

Grundschule. As was stated above, this is a four year school for beginners, and all children attend it. It takes the place of the first four years of the old *Volksschule* and also of the preparatory work of the secondary schools. This school, provided by the Weimar Constitution of 1919, was an attempt to lessen the gap between the classes. It has practically eliminated illiteracy.

Secondary Schools. These schools admit pupils after they have had the four years of preparation provided by the *Grundschule*. They are tuition schools, and less than 15 per cent of the German youth attend them. The great majority of pupils continue their education from four to six years in the old *Volksschule* or in some type of *Mittleschule*, in which, in turn, they prepare for the vocational schools. In these vocational schools the pupils complete the thirteenth year of education at about the age of nineteen.

For those select pupils who are preparing for the universities and the professions, there is ample provision through the *Gymnasium*, which is the traditional school with emphasis on the languages; the *Realgymnasium*, with emphasis on Latin and the modern languages; the *Oberrealschule*, dedicated largely to mathematics and science with some emphasis on modern languages; and the *Deutsche Oberschule*, with a curriculum devoted largely to German culture and the arts. In recent years, all schools give some emphasis to German culture. During the 19th century the *Gymnasium* was by far the most important of these schools. In recent decades, however, these traditional classical schools have been giving away more and more to the modern schools with emphasis on science and social studies. These secondary schools are nine year institutions, beginning with the fifth grade. Their work is thus more advanced than that of the secondary school in the United States. While there are some provisions for pupils to pass from the *Volksschule* to these other secondary schools, only a small per cent of the pupils in these higher schools are from the working classes.

It may be noted that in the *Gymnasium* the study of Latin begins in the first year and continues throughout the curriculum of the *Gymnasium*, so that in the aggregate a pupil spends 68 year-hours in the study of this language. The result of this intensive study of Latin is that the average graduate of the *Gymnasium* is able to read any Latin text with ease. As compared with American institutions, these higher schools in Germany secure much more efficient results of the type just described than are secured in American colleges or universities, even among most students who specialize in the classical languages. The advantages of early specialization and continued study of a given subject are thus secured in full measure.

It is the universal attitude of the teachers in the higher institutions in Germany that the training which they give is much superior to that which is given in the American high school. On the other hand, it is to be pointed out that the breadth of training which is given in the *Gymnasium* is relatively less than the breadth of training given in an American school. For example, the opportunities for the study of general history are very slight. So also are the opportunities for the study of natural science. The curriculum of the *Gymnasium* is heavily loaded on the literary side, and, while it is intensive, it is lacking in the possibilities of general training.

The American high school, by contrast, aims at the cultivation of many different kinds of interests on the part of students.

Higher Education. In the 1930s there were 25 German universities. The enrollment of students in 1933 was about 88,000. By 1935 it had dropped to some 68,000, of whom 16 per cent were women. Of the total, no more than four per cent were from the working classes. In 1934 only 4700 new students were admitted to the universities; of them 700 were women. No Jews were admitted. University admission was based on examinations given for graduates of the *Gymnasium* or other schools of the same level. At that time, German universities were primarily research and professional institutions, not groups of colleges as in England.

By the mid-1970s, higher education in West Germany was less formalized—including universities, teacher-training colleges, and intermediate schools providing vocational education. There were also colleges of the humanities, as well as a college in Cologne for physical education. Higher technical colleges also offered vocational education.

By 1976 there were 264 higher academic institutions with slightly more than 840,000 students. Of these, some 283,000 were women and about 48,000 were foreign students. There were 49 universities with more than 555,000 students—of whom 178,000 were women. There were seven Catholic colleges of theology and four Protestant colleges of theology, with a combined enrollment of 1700 students. Thirty-three teacher-training colleges were attended by 78,000 students—51,000 of them were women. Twenty-five colleges of the humanities had an enrollment of 15,000 students, of whom 6500 were women.

The German student life is relatively free from restrictions. The university has complete jurisdiction over its students. A regular university court adjusts all matters of student discipline, and the student is answerable not to the city police but to the university court, it being assumed that as a non-resident of the city he is under the jurisdiction of the university rather than of the municipality.

The universities are maintained by grants, by student fees, and by appropriation from the state. An instructor receives a certain fee for each student who registers in his courses.

The University Professor.

The German university professor is socially of the highest rank. In many instances the rulers of Germany have decorated professors with civic honors. Their salaries are superior to those of any except the governmental officials of highest rank. There is a long period of apprenticeship before the professor can secure his appointment. He is first allowed to give lectures in the university in a capacity which is almost purely private. The title which attaches to his position at that stage is *Privatdocent*. If the young instructor is successful in his lectures at this level, he may be appointed to an assistant professorship, as it would be called in America. Ultimately, from this level he may be advanced to a full professorship.

The universities of Germany have no officer corresponding to the president of an American college. The academic professors meet from year to year and recommend three of their number from whom the Ministry of Education appoints a *rector*. The duties of this *rector*, however, are not at all those of the American college president; he is merely a temporary representative of the academic group, without authority over them.

Landjahr.

One of the first acts of the Nazi party was to create in 1934 an organization known as the *Landjahr*. The organization was an outgrowth of the Youth Movement founded in 1898, and under Hitler and his Nazi régime it became an effective instrument for molding in the Nazi pattern the attitude of German youth. The 1934 regulation creating the organization provided that all youth in the industrial cities who had completed eight years of elementary schooling must spend the next nine months in the rural districts. The youth were required to make contacts with the land, to learn to work, to see how people live in the country, to obtain physical training, and above all to become enthusiastic Nazis. Persons who spent this period in the organization were given preference when applying for admission to the universities. Most of them, however, found positions or were drafted into the armed services, and did not enter a university. Soon after the beginning of World War II in 1939, the organization was abandoned. It had, however, served a Nazi purpose.

Coeducation.

The sexes in Germany attend kindergarten together, and, to a degree, the university. In other schools, as a rule, the sexes are separated. By far the majority of the students in the secondary schools and the universities are men, but the percentage of women students is slowly increasing.

The Training of Teachers.

Germany was one of the first countries to require professional training for teachers. In amount of training, its secondary school teachers have for several decades led the world. Most secondary school teachers possess the Ph.D. degree or the equivalent. The elementary school teachers have had between two and three years of training, which is similar in amount to that of the typical teacher in the elementary schools of the United States. The secondary school teachers receive larger pay and have higher social standing than the elementary school teachers. As in the schools of the United States, the elementary school teachers have been struggling for professional and financial equality in comparison with the secondary school teachers. Their efforts have been rewarded but not to the extent that similar efforts in the United States have been rewarded.

Administration.

The German system of schools is decentralized; that is, administered and supported largely by the provinces or local states. Local autonomy was almost complete till the coming of the Nazis into power in 1933. Although this status continued to some degree during the Nazi régime, extensive supervisory power was given to the Central government. In control of this supervisory power, Hitler was enabled to change the entire philosophy of German education, to modify the curriculum, and to control the training, the appointment, the promotion, and even the thinking of the teachers. He brought the universities under his supervision, and practically extinguished academic freedom, which has been the historic pride of great universities everywhere.

The Curriculum.

In his *Mein Kampf*, Hitler gave specific suggestions for the new curriculum for the schools. In his totalitarian state, which was Germany during this régime, the schools were to be used to indoctrinate the youth concerning the Nazi policies. The following statement summarizes his views on how history was to be taught:

History in the German schools need not be greatly concerned about world attitudes and other nations. More attention must be given to German history. Tacitus was misinformed about the low cultural level of the early Germans. The Nordics have been most important in history. The Germans are pure Nordics. Propaganda and education go hand in hand. History is to be taught to discredit the Republic and to extol the Nazis. It is to be taught not impartially as a part of world history, but as German history.

EDUCATION IN FRANCE

The French school system consists of two distinct branches. The *école primaire* is the common school, and in it attendance is compulsory for all pupils to the thirteenth or fourteenth year. The subjects taught are history, geography, grammar, arithmetic, literature, drawing, manual training, and physical education.

The *école primaire* may be followed in the case of the brighter children by the *école supérieur*. At present, about 5 per cent of the children continue their studies in these superior schools. The number of, and the attendance at, these schools has grown rapidly during recent years.

Secularization of Schools.

There is one striking characteristic in which the French public schools differ from those of Germany. The French schools do not teach religion. Formerly the Church was dominant in the public schools of France as it was throughout Europe. After many struggles a law was passed in 1881, secularizing the French schools and substituting training in civics and morals for the earlier courses in religion. In 1886 a law was passed providing that no clerical teachers shall give instructions in the common schools. In 1904, teaching by the clerical congregations was suppressed, and public schools were substituted for those which had been controlled by the Church. The laws thus successively enacted provide that no teacher shall deal with religious matters.

Lycées, Collèges, and Universities.

The higher schools of France include the *lycées*, the *collèges* scattered throughout the country, and the universities, chief among which is the University of Paris.

The curriculum of the *lycée* is the traditional classical curriculum, and leads to the baccalaureate degree, which corresponds roughly to the American bachelor's degree. Lately a scientific course, corresponding to that of the *Realschule* of Germany, has been organized in some of the *lycées*. About

5 per cent of the population 11 to 18 years in age attend secondary schools. Approximately 150,000 attend the Catholic schools. The *Lycées for Girls* had an enrollment of 48,046 in 1935.

At the colleges, and more especially at the universities, instruction is made easily accessible to all comers. The method is that of the lecture. A great many students attend these lectures without attempting to secure any degree. The degree of doctor of philosophy conferred by the French universities is a higher degree than the degree of the same name conferred by the German universities. Indeed, before World War I, it was so difficult for a foreign student to qualify for this degree that very few such students were to be found in the French universities. Since that War, however, an effort has been made on the part of the French universities to interest foreign students in attendance at French institutions, and certain degrees have been provided with a view to accommodating foreign students to the French system of higher education. There are 17 of these universities in France, of which 5 are Catholic.

Control. The control of the French educational system is vested in a ministry of the central government. This minister of education prescribes in great detail the courses of study and the form of organization of all the institutions. Support of the lower schools is secured from taxation, while the support of the higher schools is derived very largely from student fees.

The Training of Teachers. In each so-called department or subdivision of the French state, there is a normal school for the training of boys and another for the training of girls who are to enter the teaching profession in the lower schools. Progress through one of these schools is dependent upon the success of the candidate in passing competitive examinations. Positions in the teaching profession are eagerly sought after, as they are permanent when once secured, and at the end of his professional career the teacher receives a pension for life.

The Training of Teachers for Higher Institutions. The normal school method of training teachers has been carried by France into its higher educational system. There is a special advanced school for those who are to teach in the *lycées* and in the *collèges*. Here the higher subjects of instruction are taught. This advanced normal school now has connection with the University of Paris.

Vocational Education. Attendance at vocational schools is nominally compulsory for part time. Since World War I, attendance has increased very rapidly.

Private Resources of the Universities. The law of 1896 gave the universities the rights of civil persons, that is, the right of accepting gifts and legacies, of holding private property, and of administering it without restrictions. Each university has a budget in which are included the receipts from fees for courses, from registration, and from library and laboratory fees paid by the students in accordance with the regulations. The income from this source may be spent on the following objects: expenses for laboratories, libraries, and collections; erection and maintenance of buildings; establishment of new courses; grants in the interest of students, as, for example, subsidies to student associations. The French universities have not, up to the present time, met with such generous donors as those of the American universities. A good beginning, however, has been made, and at the University of Paris the names of benefactors are inscribed on a marble tablet; while Lyon, Montpellier, Bordeaux, and others have also received important gifts.

ENGLISH EDUCATIONAL SYSTEM

Education in England is much less compactly organized than in France and Germany. England has followed the theory of individual freedom expressed by John Stuart Mill in 1859, which has resulted in a system of education that has three marked characteristics: (a) decentralization of responsibility and control, (b) the use of voluntary agencies in making provision for educational opportunities, and (c) marked freedom of the school administrators and teachers in matters relating to curricula, courses of study, and methods of teaching.

Ministry of Education. Historically, the United Kingdom consists of four distinct national units, England, Wales, Scotland, and Northern Ireland. Administratively, England and Wales comprise one unit and there are accordingly three distinct educational administrative systems in the United Kingdom. The Ministry of Education in London has no authority in Scotland, where the Scottish Educational Department is the appropriate department, and Northern Ireland has its own Ministry of Education.

The Ministry of Education in England, which displaced the old Board of Education, operates through its inspectors, whose headquarters are located in the areas wherein their work lies. The central authority is concerned chiefly with external features of the school rather than with internal matters, and, although their authority is final in some cases, there is a marked degree of local autonomy.

In the absence of a strongly centralized educational system, numerous voluntary agencies, including philanthropic societies, church organizations, and private enterprises of various kinds, supply educational facilities for the youth of England. This has given rise to "vested interests," whose contributions to the educational traditions of England must be reckoned with in any study of the educational system.

The administrators and teachers generally enjoy an unusual degree of freedom within their institutions. Teachers are not civil servants, that is, they are not servants of the state. They are employed and paid by the local authorities, and are subject to them rather than to the Ministry of Education. The latter serves only in an inspecting and advisory capacity. This practice is gradually producing greater homogeneity among the schools of England.

Types of Schools. School attendance is compulsory in England from the ages of 5 to 15 years. Two types of schools provide the necessary educational facilities for the children who come within these age limits. The first of these types is that provided by the local educational authorities. These schools are called *Provided Schools* or *Council Schools*, since they are provided by the local councils. In England and Wales, more than 6,850,000 children attend these publicly-maintained schools. The second type of school is provided by voluntary groups such as the Church of England or the Roman Catholic Church. Such schools are called *Voluntary Schools*. These schools may be aided financially by the government or they may be entirely independent. Of the approximately 9 million students in full-time attendance at schools, over 90 per cent attend publicly-provided or aided schools.

Both of these types of schools, or such of them as are recognized by the Ministry of Education, are maintained by the local educational authorities. Maintenance includes salaries for teachers, books, supplies, and equipment whether the school be Provided or Voluntary. Voluntary bodies must supply their own buildings and keep them in repair, but if they accept public grants they must submit to inspection by the Board of Education.

Teachers for the Provided schools are appointed by the local educational authorities. Those for the Voluntary schools are appointed by the voluntary bodies, subject to the approval of the local authorities. The latter may disapprove of a teacher only on educational grounds, however.

Religious instruction is given in all public elementary schools. In the provided schools this instruction must be non-sectarian. In the voluntary schools it conforms to the religious beliefs of the body providing the school.

Elementary Schools. Public elementary education in England has long been divided into three stages: the infant stage (from 5 to about 7 or 8 years of age), the junior stage (from 7 or 8 to about 11 years of age), and the senior stage (from about 11 to 14 years of age). Sometimes these three groups have separate schools, especially those in the junior and senior groups, but occasionally they are all grouped together in one school. The latter is likely to occur where the population is sparse.

Since 1926 the organization of public elementary education in England has been undergoing reorganization into primary (from 5 to about 11 years of age), and post-primary (11 to 14 years of age). The object of this reorganization is to make the post-primary schools meet the needs of the older children more adequately than those needs have been met in the past. This has given rise to new types of advanced public elementary schools. The reorganization is not yet complete throughout England.

Nursery school facilities are provided extensively by both public educational authorities and private or voluntary bodies. Such schools care for children between 2 and 5 years of age. Sometimes these provisions for nursery school education are attached to regular elementary schools; sometimes they consist of separate schools.

Secondary Schools. There are two general types of secondary schools—those which give a general education and the technical schools. In the main, the secondary schools provide general education and the most popular of this type of school is the *Secondary Modern School* which gives general education with a practical bias. A secondary school which has come into prominence is the Comprehensive School, which offers all types of secondary education desired by the students. About one-fourth of all secondary school students attend *Grammar Schools*, which are for students who hope to go to a university. Secondary Technical Schools offer education related to industry, commerce, and agriculture. The Public Schools are characteristic English schools. Most of these are Independent Schools. Some Public Schools, such as Eton, Harrow, Winchester, and Rugby, are famous in the history of English education.

Many secondary schools are not open to girls, the latter having secondary schools of their own. In the case of provided schools, local educational authorities decide how selection will be made to its secondary schools. More and more secondary schools are now being opened to girls.

Vocational Education. England provides a wide variety of opportunity for students wishing to specialize in particular vocational or technical school. Hence there are numerous technical, commercial, and art schools and colleges especially designed to meet this need. These schools enroll approximately one million students annually.

Adult Education. The movement for adult education began with university extension lectures at Cambridge in 1873. Since that time the movement has swept throughout England and is today furnishing thousands of classes for adults by means of universities and university colleges, voluntary organizations, local educational authorities, collegiate and other institutions, and charitable trusts.

The Examination System. The higher educational system of England is not as exclusive as the systems on the continent. England is unique in the fact that it has a system of examinations by which children who are especially competent and who have taken their lower training in the common, or board, schools may transfer, when ten years of age or older, to the secondary schools.

In this way England has succeeded in recruiting its upper classes from the lower levels of society much more liberally than have any of the other European nations. It is the pride of England that its civil service officers are drawn from all levels of society, and this fact is to be explained by the examination system just described. Matthew Arnold (1822–88), who was a school inspector, gave a name to this examination system which is commonly used everywhere in England. He called it the "educational ladder."

Municipal Secondary Schools and Universities. In recent years there has developed very rapidly in the great industrial cities of England a series of schools known as "municipal secondary schools" and "municipal universities." These institutions differ from the older secondary schools and universities in the fact that they lay much greater stress on the physical sciences and the practical engineering subjects. There has come up accordingly a sharp cleavage between the older classical type of training and the newer scientific type represented by these newer institutions.

Oxford (1110 or 1120?) and Cambridge (1229). At the head of the conservative type of higher education are the two great universities, Oxford and Cambridge. Both these universities were established in the medieval period, and are made up of separate colleges. These separate colleges can be traced back to religious orders. The whole organization can be understood by observing that the English university is an assemblage of living quarters or fraternity houses that have descended from the religious communities which originally established many of the colleges. As time went on, new colleges were established and endowed by wealthy patrons, some of them royal personages. The English university system thus provides for an intimate social life on the part of its students. The lectures which are conducted in these institutions are not regarded as the major contribution to the student's training. A tutorial system has gradually been evolved, which provides for each undergraduate the opportunity to associate intimately with a tutor who guides the student's readings and who engages him in discussions of what he has read. The student attends such lectures as interest him, but in the main his business is to read and to work independently in the field of his choice under the supervision and partial guidance of his tutor.

The result of this system is that a great many boys attend Oxford and Cambridge with no intention of studious effort. They go to the college merely for the purpose of spending a few years of their youth in pleasant intellectual surroundings. For these young men the college has a so-called "pass" course. On the other hand, those students who devote themselves to strenuous intellectual effort take what is known as the "honors" course. The examinations in these courses are very rigid, and the standards are so high that only a well trained specialist can complete the course.

The Rhodes Trust was founded in 1902 by Cecil Rhodes to provide scholarships to Oxford for 66 men annually. Thirty-two of these are selected from the United States. The Yearbook of Education, 1937, lists seventeen other large educational trusts in England and Scotland.

Examining Universities. There are also in England certain examining institutions. Thus the University of London is not altogether a teaching institution; it awards degrees to candidates who present themselves for examination after independent study in some particular field.

The Fisher Act. During World War I, English enthusiasm for a more liberal type of education ran very high, and there was enacted into the law by the British Parliament an educational code known as the Fisher act. This code provided that every child in Great Britain should be under the supervision of the Ministry of Education until the age of 18 years. The ministry was empowered to develop certain forms of industrial education for many of the pupils and to supervise the employment of all those children less than 18 years of age who were taken into the industries of Great Britain.

The plan laid down in the Fisher act has never been put into actual operation. The costs were found to be too great, and a commission which canvassed the matter reported that it would not be possible under economic conditions then prevailing to begin operating under the act. In 1929 Parliament took action increasing the age of compulsory education to 15 years, thus proceeding with the Fisher program.

Training of Teachers in England. England has numerous institutions for the training of teachers for the lower schools. These institutions are known as teacher training colleges. They are maintained in part by the localities in which they are situated, and in part by grants made by the central board of education for the maintenance of the individual students who are taking the courses.

New Education Bill. In 1944, Parliament enacted a new Education bill which reconstructed the whole system of public education in England and Wales. By this bill the school-leaving age was raised to 16 in 1947. The previous distinction between elementary education, which was compulsory for all, and secondary education, which was limited to pupils who could pass an entrance examination, was abolished. The school system was reorganized into three continuous parts—Primary, Secondary, and Further. In addition to these three parts, nursery schools were to be established by all local education authorities where there is sufficient demand. Attendance at these nursery schools, however, is not made compulsory.

The primary stage remains much as formerly, and includes children between the ages of 5 and 11. Secondary education is available to a much larger number of children and in a larger number of forms for children of various aptitudes.

The term "further education" includes university courses of all types, adult education, and compulsory part-time schooling for boys and girls under 18 who are no longer obtaining full-time instruction. The part-time instruction is given in new "Young People's Colleges," which are organized by local school authorities, and at which instruction is compulsory for at least 44 days in every year. In these colleges, the facilities for technical education are greatly increased.

Although England was already a leader in its provisions for pupil welfare, the new Education bill greatly extends such provisions. The provision for special education for the physically and mentally handicapped is enlarged. And provisions for religious instruction—denominational or undenominational—are made in all schools. In all primary and secondary schools the school day begins with worship. Schools containing pupils with various denominations follow an "Agreed Syllabus" in their religious instruction.

It is worthy of note that England enacted this legislation in 1944, during the dark days of World War II. By so doing she indicated to the whole world the importance of education. And she taxed herself more severely to meet the added cost entailed by the legislation.

RUSSIAN EDUCATIONAL SYSTEM

Education in Russia is a state monopoly. There are no church or private schools. Each of the sixteen republics which make up the U.S.S.R. has its own ministries of education, but these are subordinate to the central ministries which control education throughout the country.

The ministry of culture organized in 1953 is responsible for the organization of and teaching in all specialized secondary schools and the agricultural institutes.

A second central authority, the Ministry of Labor Reserves, controls all lower vocational education, including factory schools, but does not maintain them.

The local authorities are charged with the maintenance of pre-school institutions, primary and general secondary schools, and with adult education. The latest available statistics show that 60 per cent of educational expenditures are paid for by the local authorities, 19 per cent by the republics, and 23 per cent by the central government.

The educational system of Russia comprises the following types of schools: elementary schools, secondary schools, colleges, technical schools, workers' schools, and apprentice schools. Compulsory education extends from the age of 7 to 15, but is universally enforced only for ages 7 or 8 to 12. Kindergartens are provided for children of 3 to 7 but attendance is not compulsory, and only about 6 per cent of children attend.

Organization. Generally, the schools of Russia are organized on a 4-3-3- plan with completion of the program leading to the University or Institute. Children may enter Kindergarten from age three to seven years. Primary schools usually are four years in length although in some areas the schools have seven grades including both primary and secondary education.

The school system is uniform throughout the country in that all education is directed towards service to the state. All nationalities are permitted to use their mother tongue as a medium of instruction in their schools, but the Russian language is compulsory as a second language, beginning in the second grade, in all non-Russian schools. Public instruction everywhere is secular. Effort is made to establish separate schools for boys and girls.

A few pre-school institutions and those for adult education are maintained by trade unions, cooperatives, and collective farms, but they are under the strict control and supervision of public authorities. Primary schools are provided for all, and attendance is compulsory. Schools for the Liquidation of Illiteracy are provided for adults. Great numbers of advanced students assist in the work of these schools as a part of their service to the state.

On the secondary level, in addition to a wide system of secondary schools, are technical schools and "Workers' Faculties." The Workers' Faculties, called Rabfacs, were organized to give systematic preparation to experienced workers who were not ready for regular college work. On the higher levels, not only are there no tuition fees, but the students are supported, and, after graduation, employment is assured. Schools are open to all classes, and 75 per cent of students in the higher schools belong to the working classes.

In higher education there are two basic establishments—the University and the Institute. The university aims to train scientific workers with a view to research or to teaching in the secondary schools. Universities are divided into faculties, the most numerous of which are the faculties of physics, mathematics, philology, history, geography, biology, and chemistry. The course of study in the University usually lasts five years. Each of the republics has at least one university.

The Institutes teach special subjects such as medicine, pharmacy, mechanics, and mining. At the end of a course the student takes a State examination.

COMPARATIVE EDUCATION

The United Nations Educational, Scientific, and Cultural Organization (Unesco) is entrusted with the task of promoting the advancement of education throughout the world. In its efforts to fulfill this mission, Unesco has included in its program various provisions for the exchange of information about educational methods, activities, and achievements in different countries.

Comparative education, it points out, is a relatively new branch of the science of education which attempts to study educational conditions in different countries, so that increased understanding of those conditions and developments may stimulate and contribute to the general improvement of education in all countries.

"Educational concepts and movements," it goes on to say in its publication *World Handbook of Educational Organization and Statistics*, "though often characteristically national, have a way of traveling across frontiers. This process is as old as the history of education. Plato's ideas on education, originating in ancient Athens, are today a part of the universal heritage of mankind. So are also, in proportion to their recent origin, the educational theories of John Dewey growing out of the contemporary needs of American life. In the intervening 2400 years the amount of mutual borrowing has been so extensive that no treatise on the history of education has yet done full justice to it."

In some cases this educational exchange has taken the form of wholesale copying of methods of organization, of courses of study, of school programs, and even of textbooks. Unesco notes that students of comparative education rightly look with suspicion at wholesale borrowing and adoption by one country of the ideas and methods developed in another, because educational theories and practices develop as the result of the needs of the country where they originate, and there is danger that they may, to a greater or lesser degree, be unsuited to the country which adopts them.

In view of the prevalence of the practice, however, Unesco saw the needs for international statistics relating to the study of comparative education, but encountered difficulties in collecting up-to-date and reliable data for the intelligent appraisal of the educational conditions and achievements of different countries. While such statistics have become increasingly available through the efforts of national and international agencies, they are still unsatisfactory.

International Statistics. "The development of educational statistics," Unesco states, "has lagged far behind the statistics in other fields. The reasons for this are not hard to find. In the first place the regular collection and publication of statistics on a national scale has been a matter of slow and uneven growth in most countries. Subjects of more immediate need and tangible value, such as figures relating to territory and population, births and deaths, agricultural and industrial production, domestic and foreign trade, prices, wages and the cost of living are usually dealt with first. Statistics on education, public health, and other social services are either left out altogether, or prepared in a very rudimentary and summary form."

In the next place, Unesco proceeds to point out, education in many countries is still in the hands of local authorities or is a matter of private enterprise. Accordingly, except in those countries in which there is a high degree of centralized control over education, the national government often finds itself unable to collect complete statistical information from all local or private schools. For this reason, even the most diligent efforts of the central administrations frequently fail to meet the most elementary requirements of completeness, recency, and comparability.

"Finally," Unesco concludes, "educational ideas and methods, though susceptible of international exchange, cannot always be reduced to quantitative expression. On the other hand, such quantitative data as numbers of schools, teachers, and pupils are not suitable for direct international exchange. International requirements for the exchange of currency or commodities, for example, create a direct demand for such statistics on the international level. They even impose a certain degree of uniformity or comparability on the nationally collected statistics. But the need for international exchange of educational ideas and methods is only partially and indirectly met by the collection of statistics. Hence there is not the same sense of urgency regarding their international collection or standardization.

"Thus far, the attempts of international organizations to obtain the desirable statistics on education for international collections have often run far ahead of the actual availability of such statistics."

Illiteracy in Certain Countries. Some notion of the extent of education in a country is gained by examining the percentage of illiteracy of the country. The elimination of illiteracy is dependent on the establishment of schools and the enforcement of compulsory attendance laws. Countries that have longest made those provisions have the smallest amount of illiteracy. During recent years, every nation has been making an intensive effort to eliminate or decrease illiteracy.

ILLITERACY IN VARIOUS COUNTRIES OF THE WORLD*

Year	Country	Per cent†
1971	Algeria	73.6
1970	Argentina	7.4
1970	Brazil	33.8
1970	Chile	11.9
1964	Colombia	27.1
1963	Costa Rica	15.7
1960	Cyprus	24.1
1970	Dominican Republic	31.5
1962	Ecuador	32.5
1960	Egypt	80.5
1971	El Salvador	43.1
1971	Greece	15.6
1964	Guatemala	62.1
1971	Hong Kong	22:7‡
1970	Hungary	2.0
1961	India	72.2
1971	Indonesia	40.4§
1966	Iran	77.0
1961	Israel	15.8‖
1960	Jamaica	18.1
1960	Japan	2.2‡
1961	Jordan	67.6#
1970	Korea, Rep. of	12.4
1962	Liberia	91.1
1964	Libya	78.3
1966	Malawi	77.9**
1960	Mali	97.8††
1962	Mauritius	38.4‡‡
1970	Mexico	25.8
1971	Morocco	78.6
1963	Nicaragua	50.4
1960	Niger	99.1
1961	Pakistan	81.2§§
1970	Panama	21.7
1962	Paraguay	25.4
1961	Peru	39.4‖‖
1970	Philippines	16.7§
1970	Poland	2.2
1960	Portugal	38.1
1960	South Africa, Rep. of	43.0
1970	Spain	9.9
1969	Sri Lanka	19.1
1970	Syria	60.0
1970	Thailand	21.4
1970	Turkey	48.6
1969	United States	1.0‖
1970	U.S.S.R.	0.3##
1963	Uruguay	9.6
1971	Venezuela	17.6
1971	Yugoslavia	16.5
1969	Zambia	52.7

Source: U.S. Department of Commerce, Bureau of the Census. * Illiteracy: inability both to read or write in any, or a specified, language. Most European countries, Canada, U.S., Japan, Australia, and New Zealand have ceased to ask for information on illiteracy as the percentages are negligible. † Percentage of population age 15 and over. ‡ Illiteracy defined as never attended school. § Population age 10 and over. ‖ Population age 14 and over. # Includes persons with unknown literacy status. ** African population. †† Excludes nomad population; illiterate population excludes persons who can only read. ‡‡ Population age 13 and over. §§ Pakistani nationals only. ‖‖ Population age 17 and over; excludes Indian jungle population. ## Population ages 9 through 49.

EDUCATION IN THE UNITED STATES

THE PUBLIC SCHOOL SYSTEM

Wide Diversity of Schools. The present public school system in the United States is the result of the extension of the concept of the common school of colonial times. It now includes the vast majority of elementary and secondary schools of the country and in some instances has extended even to the university level.

Education is considered to be a state function and all institutions included within the public school system of the United States are under the control of the various states. As a result there is a great diversity of practices and standards. To safeguard education and to achieve the objectives set for it, people have insisted on provisions in State Constitutions and statutes quite different from those for other governmental services. States have followed a practice of treating the educational organization as a separate domain governed by laws peculiar to it and designed to keep control of education by the people themselves. Some similarity of organization has resulted from the national tendency to imitation, which leads a given institution to follow the example of similar institutions about it. Too, the decisions of the courts have established a body of common school law which has tended in some measure to render uniform the practices of different communities. Furthermore, private organizations have developed standards which have helped to influence the uniformity. In the main, however, despite the elements of commonality which exist, variety rather than uniformity is characteristic of American schools.

Absence of Federal Control. As has been pointed out in earlier sections, there is no central Federal control of schools in the United States. The Constitution makes no provision for participation by our Federal government in school activities. The result is that each of the states has gone its way without interference or supervision from the central government. The only way in which Federal authority has entered into educational matters is through subsidies of various forms, given either to the states or to particular types of institutions within a state.

The United States Office of Education. In April 1953 a new department of the Federal government, the Department of Health, Education, and Public Welfare took over the old Office of Education, which was a special bureau in the Department of the Interior. This office prepared and still prepares elaborate statistical reports, which have been so frequently drawn upon in the course of the earlier discussions of this section that it is hardly necessary to do more than refer to its statistical activities. It has absolutely no authority over public schools. It does not have authority even to demand statistical reports. In spite of this handicap, however, it has succeeded in developing the most valuable educational reports published by any government in the world. The United States Office of Education has been given the responsibility for the administration and supervision of various Federal laws related to education. This function has become increasingly important in recent years as these laws provide considerable Federal funds for public schools. In addition, the Office of Education often takes leadership in the promotion of national interest in education or co-operates with private, state, and local groups in studies of educational needs.

THE STATE AND THE LOCAL DISTRICT

Within the states very large authority has been left to the local district. Originally the entire control of the school was in the hands of the local district. Even the definition of the boundary of the district was a matter of relatively little concern to the state as a whole, because in the early days communities were so distinct from one another that their boundaries were obvious and natural. It was only after the states came to be somewhat thickly populated that problems of school support and school efficiency which concerned the larger community began to arise and the states assumed the authority which belongs to them. We find, accordingly, that schools were at first controlled by local officers rather than by the sovereign state. The result is that the states seem of late to have taken away from the local districts rights which the latter had long exercised.

Authority of the State. The movement toward centralization of authority in state departments of education has in some cases created friction with communities which regard this modern policy as a usurpation of their rights. Constitutionally, there can be no doubt that the state has a right to prescribe to the local districts in any degree which it will. Legislatures have been given power by State Constitutions which makes them the most important policy-making agent for education in a state. Legislatures establish the framework for education; they determine the scope of the system; they determine how public education is to be supported; they make direct appropriations for education; they create educational institutions; and they determine whether or not certain educational programs are to be authorized, expanded, decreased, or eliminated.

The Legislature usually authorizes a State education department to administer its policies. It may, however, provide for a State board of education to advise it regarding policy and to administer the educational program. The central agency may define the extent of the local district and may determine in all detail what shall be done within this district. While this is the constitutional right of the state, the practical fact is that the local district conducts its schools in very large measure according to its own desires, and local officers often look upon state supervision as indefensible interference.

Certification of Teachers. A conspicuous illustration of increasing state control is to be seen in the matter of the certification of teachers. In the colonies and in the older states the community selected the teacher. The trustee or the committee of the district not only employed the teacher but determined whether the qualifications of a given candidate were satisfactory; in other words, the local officers licensed the teacher. When the states began to organize more compact school systems, it immediately became apparent that local districts are not competent to license teachers. The judgment of the trustee is frequently biased by purely personal considerations. The various states, therefore, gradually assumed more or less control in this matter.

Since the assumption of control has been gradual and partial, there are a great many different practices in different parts of the country. There are still local districts which virtually select their own teachers without any large degree of state supervision. In many other cases a unit smaller than the state but larger than the local district has the power of certification. Especially common is certification by the county superintendent. The general tendency, however, is to prescribe by state law the qualifications necessary for a license to teach, and to enforce the requirement through the state department of education.

The results of the older and looser system are present, however, on every hand. A major reason for this has been the continued shortage of qualified teachers. The N.E.A. estimated that in 1960 the supply of beginning qualified teachers was less than one half of the demand. This, coupled with the fact that only about 73 per cent of graduating students, qualified to teach, enter teaching, provides a dismal picture of teacher supply. At the present time one

LIBRARIES IN THE UNITED STATES

Harvard's modern Lamont Library reflects the spirit of an institution that readily combines current business research with traditional scholarship.

The Library of Congress, on Capitol Hill, is the world's largest library building. Its book shelves are 250 miles long. The library houses important documents.

The "Library on Wheels" that seeks out its patrons is illustrated by this Bookmobile operating in Buffalo and Erie County, New York.

The new Public Library at Phoenix, Arizona is the key structure in a group of buildings dedicated to various cultural pursuits.

The new Pius XII Memorial Library at St. Louis University facilitates study and research through the latest improvements in lighting and equipment.

Extending public library service to surrounding areas has resulted in city-county mergers. The Charlotte-Mecklenburg County (N.C.) Library, above, illustrates this development.

Distinctive in its modern design and attractive in its setting, the Louisiana State Library at Baton Rouge invites visitors and patrons.

MODERN SCHOOL BUILDINGS

Welsh Valley Jr. H.S., Ardmore, Pa. (A Junior High)

Hoyt School, Madison, Wis. (An Elementary School)

Children's Retreat & Training School, Grand Rapids, Mich. (A Special Services School)

Shawnee-Mission East H.S., Prairie Village, Kansas (A Senior High)

Byrd Elementary, Chicago, Ill. (A large city Elementary)

North Shore H.S., Glen Head, L.I., N.Y. (A Jr-Sr. High)

Vincent G. Kling, Architect

El Camino (Calif.) College, Music & Commerce Complex (A Junior College)

Smith, Powell & Morgridge, Architects

State	1932	1940	1950	1961	1968	1972
Alabama	112	111	108	114	118	126
Alaska			27	29	27	29
Arizona	500	405	274	297	297	241
Arkansas	3,193	2,907	421	419	395	388
California	3,589	2,993	2,381	1,656	1,105	1,133
Colorado	2,041	1,868	1,533	340	181	187
Connecticut	161	169	172	177	179	169
Delaware	17	16	17	93	51	26
Dist. of Col.	1	1	1	1	1	3
Florida	67	67	67	67	67	94
Georgia	272	1,203	186	198	195	189
Hawaii			1	1	1	1
Idaho	1,418	1,195	810	137	117	117
Illinois	12,070	11,996	4,880	1,607	1,315	1,177
Indiana	1,292	1,156	1,056	900	395	316
Iowa	4,870	4,869	4,652	1,575	474	463
Kansas	8,748	7,394	5,257	2,414	336	331
Kentucky	384	262	237	211	199	191
Louisiana	66	67	67	67	66	66
Maine	518	510	492	460	323	291
Maryland	24	24	24	24	24	33
Massachusetts	355	351	351	378	406	373
Michigan	6,965	6,466	4,918	1,977	718	647
Minnesota	7,773	7,685	7,116	2,410	1,150	447
Mississippi	5,560	4,954	3,673	150	149	162
Missouri	8,764	8,661	6,273	1,732	815	636
Montana	2,439	2,066	1,381	1,050	840	552
Nebraska	7,244	7,063	6,769	3,560	2,172	1,374
Nevada	266	255	196	17	17	17
New Hampshire	244	241	240	230	183	167
New Jersey	552	559	559	588	593	609
New Mexico	98	1,730	107	91	90	89
New York	9,467	6,433	3,929	1,292	853	780
North Carolina	200	171	172	173	160	206
North Dakota	2,228	2,274	2,250	1,070	498	387
Ohio	2,043	1,668	1,509	862	691	641
Oklahoma	4,933	4,174	2,176	1,274	949	657
Oregon	2,234	2,015	1,179	510	376	353
Pennsylvania	2,587	2,535	2,524	958	597	531
Rhode Island	39	39	39	41	40	40
South Carolina	1,792	1,738	1,559	109	105	93
South Dakota	3,433	3,429	3,401	3,012	1,804	228
Tennessee	194	162	148	154	151	147
Texas	7,932	5,664	3,324	1,531	1,273	1,176
Utah	40	40	40	40	40	40
Vermont	268	60	265	267	253	272
Virginia	125	124	127	130	132	134
Washington	1,792	1,411	591	415	341	317
West Virginia	450	55	55	55	55	55
Wisconsin	7,662	7,392	5,792	2,400	493	467
Wyoming	400	375	316	212	180	70
Total U.S.	127,422	116,999	83,642	37,475	21,990	17.238

Source: N.E.A. Research Bulletin; U.S. Department of Commerce, Bureau of the Census.   * Refers to school year ending that year.

teacher in fourteen is an "emergency" or unqualified teacher.

Compulsory Attendance. In other respects, as well as in the employment of teachers, the state has found it necessary to assume control over the local districts. For example, the state has enacted compulsory attendance laws. This has been necessary because some districts are negligent and allow their children to grow up without proper schooling. When these children become adults, it is not the local district alone that suffers, but the whole commonwealth. The state can be economically and socially efficient only if its citizens are trained. The state, therefore, takes the local district and the family in hand and compels the education of all children.

State Departments of Education. Every state now has for its educational activity a chief executive officer, usually designated state superintendent or commissioner of education. In little more than one half of the states this officer is elected by popular vote. In a large number of states this officer is appointed by a state board of education and in a few others he or she is appointed by the governor. The majority of states provide in the state constitution the method of selection of the chief school officers. Consequently, only by revision of the state constitution, in these states, can a change be made in the method of selection. Despite this, 18 states made such a change between 1945 and 1954.

The state superintendent is frequently associated in the execution of the duties of his office, with a state board of education. Although all of the states have state education boards, the functions of these boards vary widely and so does the relationship of the state superintendent to them.

In every state the state superintendent has organized a department of subordinate officers to help supervise the educational program. There are wide differences in the functioning of these officers. In some states the central department is very active and powerful, in other states the central control is very slight.

State Participation in School Finance. The state always takes some share in the financial support of schools. Usually there is a state fund, derived from the sale of school lands or from certain forms of taxation, which is distributed to the local districts in proportion to the school population or as an incentive to the organization of some particular form of education, such as classes in agriculture or in physical culture. The state's share gradually has been increasing. In the United States in 1960 state governments paid 29.1 per cent of the expenses of public and nonpublic schools. In 1973 they paid 33 per cent. During the same period the federal government's financial responsibility increased from 6.9 per cent to 11 per cent.

CLASSROOM TEACHERS*

State	Total (1,000)	Average Salary ($1,000)
Alabama	36.7	10.6
Alaska	4.3	19.9†
Arizona	22.9	12.4
Arkansas	21.3	9.7
California	187.3	15.2
Colorado	26.8	12.0
Connecticut	35.0	12.6
Delaware	6.3	12.5
District of Columbia	6.7	na
Florida	72.9	10.5
Georgia	52.4	10.6
Hawaii	7.9	15.2‡
Idaho	9.0	10.2
Illinois	110.7	14.0
Indiana	52.3	12.0
Iowa	33.0	11.9
Kansas	25.6	10.7
Kentucky	31.8	9.8
Louisiana	42.1	10.1
Maine	11.8	10.3
Maryland	43.7	13.7
Massachusetts	64.1	11.9
Michigan	88.8	15.5
Minnesota	43.8	13.9
Mississippi	23.6	9.3
Missouri	48.3	10.5
Montana	9.4	11.2
Nebraska	18.2	10.0
Nevada	5.6	13.4
New Hampshire	8.8	10.5
New Jersey	80.1	13.4
New Mexico	12.9	11.0
New York	189.1	16.0§
North Carolina	54.3	11.0
North Dakota	7.6	10.1
Ohio	104.3	11.4
Oklahoma	29.8	9.6
Oregon	22.2	12.1
Pennsylvania	115.6	12.4
Rhode Island	9.2	13.4
South Carolina	27.9	9.9
South Dakota	8.1	9.3
Tennessee	39.9	10.3
Texas	143.4	11.4
Utah	12.7	11.4
Vermont	6.1	10.0
Virginia	58.4	11.3
Washington	33.6	13.6
West Virginia	20.1	10.5
Wisconsin	50.3	12.3
Wyoming	5.2	11.1

Source: U.S. Department of Commerce, Bureau of the Census. * For the school year ending June 1976. † Reduce by about 25 per cent to make purchasing power comparable to figures reported for other states. ‡ Reduce by about 19 per cent to make purchasing power comparable to figures reported for other states. § Median salary.

Intermediate School Districts. Because most states operate their schools through many small school districts it has been found desirable to organize some sort of intermediate unit for school administration. The intermediate units, operating between the state and local level, include counties, parts of counties and supervisory unions. The main responsibility of the units has not been the operation of schools, but rather the rendering of consultative services, inspectorial functions, and some additional services that a small school district would be unable to provide alone.

The Local School District. School districts vary in size and kind throughout the United States. They are organized for the purpose of promoting education within a given area of a state. In some instances the districts are concerned only with the educational program of some special area of education such as vocational education; special services such as health supervision, attendance services, or pupil transportation; or some level of education such as the elementary school or the secondary school. In other cases the officers of the district are empowered to promote all aspects of education. The school district usually has a trustee or a board of education selected from among the citizens of the district to operate the schools. These officers, in turn, usually employ professional educators to help in the running of the schools.

Organization of the Board of Education. In the history of American schools, boards of education have differed greatly in their size and in their mode of conducting business. As cities grew up during the last decades of the 19th century, many school boards became unwieldy bodies. Membership had formerly been on the basis of representation of city wards or on some other basis that led, during the rapid growth of the city, to a point at which the large size of the assembly made it almost impossible to do business. There has been a marked tendency, therefore, to reduce the size of the board to seven in the larger cities and to five or three in the smaller cities.

Another major item in this connection is the internal organization of the board. In some cases, boards of education have divided themselves into standing committees, each committee being in charge of some aspect of school work. Thus, a committee on finance and a committee on school buildings have been very common in such cases. Practical experience has shown that such a division of the board very frequently results in the assignment to these standing committees of all the business of the board in respect to the matter over which a committee has charge. The board as a whole then loses something of its effectiveness. Students of school organization recommend that boards be not divided into standing committees, and that committees be created only when it is necessary to make a study of some particular problem.

Powers of the Board of Education. Where there is a board of education, it is usually elected by vote. Sometimes it is appointed by some civil officer, such as the mayor or the judges. The board of education in many cities is historically descended from a committee of the common council. It is still very common for the board of education to be dependent on the city government in matters of finance. In other cases the board of education is constituted by state charter into an independent taxing body.

Among the important powers and responsibilities usually assigned to boards of education are the following: to provide facilities for the education of children; to determine who shall attend the schools and the discipline in the schools; to employ and discharge professional personnel to teach or administer in the schools; to develop rules and regulations for the running of the schools; to determine courses of study and instructional materials within the framework of state regulations; and to determine, within some limitations, the financing of the educational program.

The Superintendent of Schools. The relation of the board of education to the officers which it appoints has never been worked out with satisfactory clearness. The superintendent of schools is sometimes the executive officer of the board; that is, he carries out the resolutions of the board and is very definitely restricted in his activities by the votes of the board. In other cases the superintendent has powers assigned to him by law and is, in certain functions, independent of the board. For example, in the city of Saint Louis, Missouri, the superintendent of schools is empowered to nominate all teachers. The board of education can act in the appointment of teachers only on the nomination of the superintendent. In some other cities it is possible for the board of education to make appointments without even consulting the superintendent.

The relation of the board of education to the building principal and to the teacher who has charge of the individual classroom is ordinarily indirect. In most cases the superintendent is authorized by the board to direct the activities of these persons. On the other hand, there are cases where the board of education exercises direct supervision over the details of school organization. In general, this is regarded by students of school problems as a bad form of organization. It survives from the time when the lay officials of the school were in full charge of the employment of teachers and the equipment of the classroom.

In larger and more populous school districts, the superintendent often is assisted in his work by staff specialists. These may include persons given special responsibility for directing staff personnel and pupils activities, co-ordination of curriculums, or handling of any other of the many details of administration of the school program, which, in smaller districts, are assigned as a part of the superintendent's work.

The Business Manager. Boards of education have frequently found it advantageous, especially in the larger cities, to appoint an officer whose duty it is to carry on all of the business operations of the schools, such as purchasing supplies and keeping accounts. In many instances, this business manager has been made independent of the superintendent, on the theory that the superintendent is in charge of instruction, while the business manager is in charge of material equipment. Such a separation of business management from the instructional activities of the school is unfortunate, since the material equipment is always provided with a view to meeting educational needs. The best practice is that in which a special business officer is made responsible to the superintendent and through him to the board. In the smaller towns, it has been found advantageous to give the superintendent direct charge over the business organization of the schools.

Transportation of Pupils. A recent phenomenon of public education has been the consolidation of schools and school districts in rural areas. In a little more than twenty years, more than two-thirds of the one-room schools have been abandoned. In the same period of time the number of school districts has been reduced by more than one half. As consolidation has gone forward, the communities receive compensation for additional expenditures in the form of enlarged opportunities for rural children. It is perfectly clear that rural communities are increasingly demanding a share in the social facilities which were formerly restricted to the towns and cities. The development of consolidated school districts with schools having superior facilities has in some states followed the adoption of laws which provided at first only for transportation from rural districts to the centers where high schools existed.

With the advent of consolidation of small school districts the transportation of pupils has become increasingly important. Approximately thirty-five per cent of all children attending school are transported from their homes to the school. Both private and public carriers are used to transport children to school. Many school boards have provided district-owned school buses for school children. Elaborate

organizations are now provided for training of bus drivers and maintenance crews, routing of buses, and directing the program for efficiency and for the maximum safety of the children.

The School Lunch Program. As increasingly larger numbers of children have been transported long distances from their homes to attend school, it has become desirable to provide lunchrooms for them. Schools have therefore organized cafeterias to supply an adequate place for children to eat and also give opportunity for the children to get a "warm" meal. Since 1935 the Federal government has encouraged school-lunch programs in public schools by giving cash grants and allotting surplus commodities for school-lunch purposes. At the present time, an average of about one-third of the pupils attending public school are served by school-lunch programs.

School Advisory Committees. Recently changes have taken place in school districts, the number of members of school boards has decreased, and the problems associated with meeting the needs of the schools have become more complex. Because of these things, school boards and their administrative officers have often felt the need for help as school problems are studied. Therefore, informal committees have been formed to advise boards of education about methods desirable to solve particular problems. Particularly useful have been advisory committees which have helped boards to decide the proper types of school buildings desirable for a school district. These committees often give good advice about the selection of sites, sizes of schools, how to encourage approval by school patrons, and means for financing the schools. Other school affairs about which advisory committees have helped boards of education, are salary schedules for teachers, curriculums, grading systems, and personnel policies.

THE ELEMENTARY SCHOOL

Enough has been said of state educational organizations to make it clear that the schools of the United States are characterized by local differences. With this general qualification in mind, the following statement may be made with regard to the typical form of school organization in this country. In the main, the system is a *unit system*, that is, there are no parallel lines in the lower grades, as there are in Europe, designed to keep apart different classes of the population. All pupils begin in the same elementary school and progress into the high school.

Curriculum of Elementary Schools. The elementary school is usually divided into what is called lower primary and upper primary divisions. The lower primary division commonly consists of three grades. These three grades introduce the pupil to the work of the school and teach "the three R's." They also give the children some opportunity to cultivate observation of nature and to learn something of the fundamental laws of health. Following the primary training, the elementary-school program becomes very different in different parts of the country. The course of study varies and includes subjects which have gradually been added in the course of the development of American schools.

The following table shows the development of the elementary school subjects from the time of the first schools to the present. It will be observed that, when new subjects are added, the old ones are nearly always retained. Of course, innumerable changes of a practical nature have been made in the content of the various subjects. Likewise, many improvements have been made in the content of the various subjects and in teaching methods. During recent years there has been a marked tendency for teachers "to teach the child as well as the subject." In part as a result of the Progressive education movement, pupil interests and abilities are being considered by teachers more than ever before. Also, more services, such as health, free textbooks, libraries, guidance, extracurricular activities, lunch

DEVELOPMENT OF THE ELEMENTARY SCHOOL SUBJECTS FROM 1642 TO THE PRESENT

Subjects in 1642	Subjects in 1775
Reading	Reading
Writing	Writing
Bible	Arithmetic

Subjects in 1875	Subjects at Present
Reading	Reading
	Writing
Writing	Arithmetic
	Spelling
Arithmetic	Character Education
Spelling	Language and Grammar
	Geography
Conduct	History, Civics, and Current Events
Language and Grammar	Art
	Music
Geography	Science
History and Civics	Health Education and Supervised Play
Drawing	Safety Education
	Industrial Arts
Music	Home Economics
Nature Study	Agriculture
	Commercial subjects
Physical Exercises	Consumer Education
	Foreign Language

programs, and transportation, are now being provided than ever before.

Forms and Duration of Elementary Schools. The elementary school in many rural districts is organized in the form commonly known as the one-room school. A single teacher is in charge of the whole curriculum, and promotes the individual children as in his or her judgment they are ready to go forward with their work. In the larger communities the elementary school is graded; that is, the children of different states of maturity and school attainments are assembled in separate rooms, and each room has a teacher in charge of the work in that particular grade. The more highly organized elementary schools usually have, as stated previously, eight separate grades. In the larger cities and in some of the better organized rural areas a single school building often houses duplicate grades. In some of the less thoroughly organized schools, two or three grades are assembled in a single room in charge of a single teacher. With the development of school transportation, many one-room schools or schools with small enrollments have been abandoned and large elementary schools have taken their place. The number of one-room elementary schools in the United States is approximately one-third of that in 1930 and now children in rural areas often ride many miles to attend elementary school.

The elementary school is conducted in different communities for different numbers of days during the year. In the more highly organized states, 200 days a year constitute the regular program. In some rural districts this number is often reduced to 120 days or even less. In the United States there has been a steady trend in the direction of longer school terms.

Control of Elementary Schools. The method of control of the elementary school differs according to the size of the community. In smaller communities school trustees are usually in charge of the school. They have the power to employ the teacher and to provide for the material equipment of the school. The local lay school authorities are elected by the community, either at a town meeting or at a regular election. In the larger communities and populous school districts a board of education usually operates under a special charter from the state and has full administrative authority over the schools. It usually appoints, in addition to the teachers, a principal of each school building and a superintendent.

In most cases the teachers and principals are appointed upon the recommendation of the superintendents. In fact, the trend is distinctly toward accepting the recommendations of the superintendent in all professional matters.

In some instances the smaller districts are provided by the state with a supervisory officer. In many of the states the counties are organized having a county superintendent of schools who, like the state superintendent, is usually elected by popular vote.

THE JUNIOR HIGH SCHOOL

In recent years, a radical reform has taken place in the course of study and in the administration of the educational program for children of adolescent years. A new institution, commonly known as the junior high school, has been organized to include what normally would be the lower years of the adolescent period. Most frequently the junior high school includes the seventh and eighth grades of schooling. Often however the 9th grade is included. There were several reasons for this new organization. Formerly the elementary school did not include in its program the advanced studies, such as higher mathematics and foreign language, nor any of the subjects which lead directly into professional training.

The reason why these subjects were originally excluded is that, at the time the elementary program was first formulated, the average pupil usually went to school for only a very short period, and American parents were satisfied if their children enjoyed a relatively meager training in "the three R's" and other rudimentary subjects. Furthermore the example of the common school of Europe was at first strong in determining the practices of American elementary schools, and the common school of Europe, unlike the schools for the better classes, was very limited in its course of study. The American elementary school was originally organized, in respect to its subjects of instruction, with a very meager program, as though it were intended to serve only the common people, although as a matter of fact it has served to train all classes of pupils, including those who are to go forward to higher institutions.

The limitations under which the American elementary school operated in the past have, in recent years, been overcome in some measure through the sheer expansion of the educational system. Children who attended school so much more regularly and for so long a period that they have mastered the rudimentary or common branch subjects and, by the time they have entered the seventh grade, are ready to take more advanced work than they could have taken in earlier years. The demand has come to be very insistent, therefore, that the seventh and eighth grades include the beginnings of work which formerly belonged to the high school.

A second reason for the separate organization of the junior high school resulted from the gradual change in compulsory education laws in America. By these laws children were encouraged to stay in school longer, in most of the states, until the age of sixteen. The organization of a separate middle school above the elementary school grades provided opportunity to allow students to complete schooling close to the sixteen-year age and made a more natural termination point at the end of the ninth grade rather than the eighth.

A third reason was that the junior high school helped to orient the student into the high school program. It has been found that pupils in the seventh and eighth grades are mature enough to be dealt with in matters of discipline and social organization in a fashion wholly different from the way in which primary children and children in the fourth, fifth, and sixth grades ought to be handled. Junior high schools have been organized more closely along the lines of the high school. The external organization of the grades has undergone a modification in the direction of greater liberalizing of discipline. Pupils have been allowed to move about the building more freely than the younger children, and have been brought into contact with what is known as the departmental organization of their studies; that is, they have a number of teachers who are specialists in the different fields. The departmental form of organization has removed pupils to some extent from the close supervision of a single teacher which is common in the lower grades. Also, it has provided opportunity for more and better instruction in a wider range of subjects more closely related to the upper high school grades.

Curriculum of the Junior High School. In recent years the organization of junior high schools has been advocated on the basis of the unique contributions they can make to the education of children. It has been stressed that children of early adolescent age have certain peculiar characteristics and needs which can be provided for more effectively if the children are grouped separately in a junior high school. The program of studies has emphasized exploration of subjects which in the upper high school grades would be studied more seriously. Guidance of children into fields of interest has become an important aspect of the program. The junior high school enables the pupil to explore many potential fields of interest before he reaches the upper high school grades. At the same time he obtains a background for the subjects he will study in these grades. One of the significant aspects of the junior high school program has been the development of the *core curriculum*. In the core the teacher has a class for a daily block of time longer than one period, problems are studied which involve more than one subject and there is pupil-teacher planning in the development of projects for the course.

Advantages of Junior High Schools. Some advantages of the junior high school can be listed. These are:

1. Children of early adolescent period can be grouped together in facilities especially designed for their education.

2. The curriculum can be broader, and richer learning experiences are provided than in the 8-4 system.

3. Teachers with better preparation teach as subject specialists in the junior high school.

4. Better opportunities are provided for pupils to explore their interests, abilities, and talents in curricular and extra class programs, and to be guided into desired fields for advanced study.

5. Articulation between the elementary school and high school improves with organization of the junior high school.

6. Better building facilities, equipment, and athletic fields can be provided for children of this age group at less cost.

PUBLIC HIGH SCHOOLS

Turning from the elementary school and the junior high school to the high school, which is the highest unit of the public school system, we find diversity of practice and of organization even more pronounced than it was in the lower school.

The high school is typically four years in length and includes grades 9 through 12. However, there are high schools which have from two to six grades. The high school conducts its course with a view to preparing pupils either to enter directly upon the duties of adult life or to enter a college or other high institution. In the past, cities and large villages have been the centers which most commonly maintained high schools. Usually, in order to gain an enrollment large enough to maintain a high school the district has had to be somewhat larger than that which supplies pupils to the elementary school. In recent years rural communities have become very enthusiastic about organizing high schools. There has been considerable consolidation of small districts which maintain only elementary schools so that a high school program could be offered. Also, many school districts with both elementary and high schools have felt themselves to be too small to maintain an adequate high school program and so have consolidated. There are now striking examples to be found of rural high schools which serve districts lying entirely outside of any large centers of population.

Curriculum of High Schools. The courses of study in the high school cover a great variety of subjects. This condition is traceable to the fact that, at this higher level of education, there are few subjects which are regarded as essential to the training of every pupil, and there are evident differences in the individual needs of the pupils. Similarities which appear among high schools in the matter of curriculum arise very largely out of the fact that the tradition of higher education, as borrowed from Europe, is that of a classical training. Foreign languages, especially the ancient, and higher mathematics have therefore long been accepted items in the curriculum of American high schools. Even where the high school is organized by a community which is not preparing its pupils to go into the learned professions, there has been a disposition to continue the classical tradition.

In addition to the classical tradition or in some instances in direct opposition to it, there has been a growing tendency in American communities to provide courses which shall acquaint students with modern civilization. Since the high schools of the country have not been centrally controlled, this desire to enlarge the course of study has expressed itself in the greatest variety of experiments. Courses in science and in literature and in history and civics have been rapidly incorporated into the curriculum.

Commercial and industrial interests of late have demanded better training for those who are to enter these callings and the high school in its effort to meet this new social demand has introduced technical courses. In response to the commercial demand, typewriting, stenography, and bookkeeping have been organized and, in response to the industrial demand, home economics, agriculture, and technical courses have been opened upon an astonishingly large scale. Increasing attention is being given to health, physical education, and aesthetics in the high school program.

The common practice in high school is for a student to graduate when he has completed sixteen units of credit in an approved course of study beginning at grade nine. In small high schools only one or two courses of study may be offered. In the larger high schools the college preparatory course, the commercial course, the vocational or industrial course, and the general course are offered

Internal Organization of the High School. Ever since the beginning of the high school, there have been movements for revision of its internal organization. Recently Dr. James B. Conant, former president of Harvard University, examined the High School of the United States. He suggested that the high school should provide a general education for all future citizens, give opportunity for adequate training to those who were using the high school for terminal education, and a background for the college-bound youth. He suggested a series of standards in order to make these goals possible. These included having a school of adequate size, having adequate facilities, and having well-trained teachers. His study has led to examinations of these things in high schools throughout the United States.

Another study of the High School sponsored by the N.A.S.S.P. has encouraged sweeping changes in the internal organization of the High School. For some time it has been traditional for classes of the

High School to be organized into periods of 45 to 60 minutes in length with 6 or 7 of such periods constituting a school day. It is now suggested that there need be no uniformity about the length of periods, that some subjects of the high school should have longer periods of recitation than others. Furthermore, it is suggested that students be arranged into large groups of 75 to 150 for lectures in some subjects and that these be co-ordinated with small seminar groups of 15 to 20 students. Large blocks of time for independent study are being advocated in this type of grouping. The exponents of this plan for internal reorganization suggest that approximately 30 per cent of the student's weekly time be spent in large group instruction, 40 per cent in small group instruction, and 30 per cent in independent study. This plan has encouraged "team teaching" in which several teachers plan together the learning activities of the students and teach together, each teacher contributing his special skills.

Another recent innovation in the internal organization of the High School is the "school within a school." In this, a large school is divided into small units. Each unit may have a complete high school program or may have one phase of the total program. The unique features are that each unit has a complete faculty, student body, and administrative organization. The unit functions as a complete school, but shares facilities common with other units. Thus, it is believed that the advantages of the small school and the economies of the large school are welded together.

A third type of grouping of students is the "track" system. In this plan students are grouped homogeniously on the basis of their natural capacity to learn when they enter high school. Then they proceed throughout the high school program with the same group. A high school may have several of such "tracks" each with different content material in the same subjects. The purpose of the track system is to enable students to learn to their capacity. Thus, a group of students in one track may learn much more subject material than another during the same period of time in high school.

The significance of independent study has been emphasized by the development of machines for teaching. Educational psychologists are providing data which prove the value of various types of machines in the learning process. These enable the student to learn many different subject skills while studying independently and using a machine properly programmed for learning.

High School Districts. Some high schools are organized in special high school districts and are controlled by special high school boards. Approximately 7.5 per cent of all school districts maintaining high schools are organized in this way. In this type of school district high school pupils are drawn from several elementary schools. This special high school district may be organized to provide a comprehensive educational program or it may give only a technical or vocational education.

Break between Elementary and High Schools. Where the high school is part of the same system as the elementary schools, it is common for the pupils who complete the work of the eighth grade to pass without examination into the high school. At this point, however, in spite of the unit type of organization, there is a distinct educational break. The methods of instruction and the social atmosphere of the high school are much freer than were those of the elementary school.

The break encountered by students in passing from the lower to the high schools is due in part to the fact that the teachers in the two institutions are entirely different in preparation and outlook. Elementary school teachers have usually prepared for their professional careers in normal schools or teachers' colleges, while, especially in the better

grade of high schools, the teachers are college or university graduates. Even though a single board of education controls both schools, and even though there is a single superintendent in charge of the whole system, the elementary school and the high school represent two different types of education. Efforts in recent years have been toward minimizing the effects of the break between the elementary and secondary schools. Organization of the junior high school to retain many characteristics of the elementary school, orientation program which enables the elementary school child to learn about and even participate in the secondary school program before he enters high school, and standardization of admission procedures are ways used to bridge the gap between the elementary and secondary schools.

Types of High Schools. Whenever a community is able to give an enlarged curriculum for its high school, the question arises as to how to provide for the types of courses to be included. The solution to this problem is very different in various places. In certain cities the older high schools were those which devoted themselves to the academic curriculum and prepared students for college. As the curriculum expanded, separate schools were erected for technical and vocational education. Thus there came into being the technical high school, the vocational high school, the trade school, the commercial high school, and other types of special high schools. In other places, high schools such as the Manhattan High School of Women's Garment Trades in New York City or the Textile High School of Wooster, Massachussetts offer specialized curriculums in one or two subjects.

In recent years, the comprehensive high school, which offers both academic and technical programs has come into favor. The great majority of high schools endeavor to include a wide variety of subjects so that all students will find something of value to meet their interests and needs. In some high schools where enrollments are too small to support certain subjects students are permitted to take them by correspondence and, when the courses are completed to the satisfaction of the school authorities credits for them may be applied towards high school graduation. In other high schools where the school board cannot financially support equipment for vocational classes, pupils may enroll for vocational subjects and work in nearby factories under the instruction of trade journeymen and the supervision of school authorities.

The High School Unit. The process of standardizing high schools, which began with the report of the Committee of Ten referred to in the historical section, has gone so far as to develop a definite uniformity in the credits administered by these schools. Formerly it was the practice of high schools to give a number of different kinds of courses. Some of these consisted of two class exercises a week throughout the year; others were made up of four or five class exercises. Much confusion arose because of the variable programs of different schools. The colleges and secondary schools of the country were led by the Committee of Ten to approve a plan whereby each course should be of standard length.

In recent years a number of agencies have powerfully re-enforced the movement toward standardization. The result is that a so-called high school unit is now defined as 120 hours of classroom work in the course of a year, and all secondary schools are expected to report their work in these terms. The Carnegie Foundation engaged in a study which defined a unit as representing a year's study in any subject in a secondary school. The Unit constitutes approximately a quarter of a full year's work and the assumption is that the school has grades nine through twelve, is in session from 36 to 40 weeks, and a period is from 40 to 60 minutes in length. The Unit was to consist of at least 126 minute hours. This Unit so defined has grown to be commonly called "The Carnegie Unit." This study has been very helpful to state departments of education and accrediting agencies which have prepared approved lists of secondary schools and colleges.

Originally, the Carnegie study was made in connection with a plan for granting pensions to college teachers. The administration of pensions required that the foundation should determine when a given institution is an acceptable college. This in turn led back to the entrance requirements of the college, and so to a determination of the type of high school from which the college received its students. The Carnegie Foundation insisted, in its dealings with the colleges, that the entrance requirements should be definitely and clearly standardized.

This was the same demand which was made by accrediting associations and state departments of education. Now, in addition to the activities of these associations which select the higher grades of secondary schools for their approved lists, the state education departments and the state universities are active in preparing lists of lesser high schools which organize their courses in standard units even though they are not able to meet the complete standards of the major associations. The results secured by the preparation of these approved lists is a relatively high degree of uniformity, at least on the quantitative side of the administration of high school courses.

It has become almost universally standard for high schools to graduate students who have successfully completed an approved program of studies comprising 16 units of work beginning in the ninth grade of school. A few high school programs in special subject areas may require more than 16 units.

Methods of College Admissions. Prior to the organization of the standardizing associations, the common practice of American colleges was to administer entrance examinations to all students passing from the secondary school into college. The entrance examination system came to this country from England, where it is the chief means of regulating the work of all educational institutions. It is still the dominant method of college admission in the states east of the Allegheny mountains. The University of Michigan, established in 1837, devised the method of admission by certificate and thus broke away from the examination system of the older American institutions.

The theory on which the University of Michigan proceeded was that, as the highest institution of learning in the state, it had responsibilities which obligated it to provide through inspection and advice for the development, not only of its own courses, but also of the courses of the other institutions in the state. The University of Michigan, therefore, began to send members of its faculty to visit the high schools and encourage them in perfecting their methods of organization. When a student came from one of these inspected high schools he was received into the college as a satisfactory student, because the institution from which he came was known to conform to the requirements of the university. The certificate system has spread rapidly, especially in the Middle West and the West, and is today the accepted mode of college admission west of the Allegheny mountains.

In recent years the use of general intelligence tests has been advocated as a much better device than examination or certification to determine who shall pass from the high school into college. Elaborate studies have been made of the success with which the work of college students can be prognosticated on the basis of their school records, by entrance examinations in the particular subjects, or through general intelligence tests. It has been found that the school record and general intelligence tests are distinctly superior to examinations in particular subjects. General intelligence tests serve also to correct the estimate of the student based on his school record. The school record is determined in many instances by other considerations than native intelligence. Thus, an industrious student who is dull may sometimes make a better record than a bright student who is not attentive to his work. College officials have found it advantageous, therefore, in dealing with students, to collect the information supplementary to the school record, as a basis for the classification and administration of the school body.

Educational Guidance. With the growing complexity of the high school curriculum and with the influx into the high school of a student population that includes a great many different kinds of young people who are looking forward to all sorts of careers, it has become necessary to add to the administrative machinery of these schools agencies which shall be able to give students more advice than was formerly necessary in the choice of studies. As was pointed out in an earlier section, the high schools of 1870 had a very meager course of study, and students were very much of the same type. The very fact that they came to the schools showed that they had selected their careers and were prepared to fit into the very definite régime of the school.

The point has now been reached where nine of every ten children of the country who are of high school age are attending high school. Data from the U.S. Office of Education and the U.S. Census Bureau show that the proportion of youth of high school age staying in school has been steadily increasing and that the level of schooling among the total population has risen significantly in recent years. It is evident that there is no such definiteness in the expectations of students or of their teachers as was common at an earlier date. It is evident, too, that the youth who attend high schools now have wider dissimilarities in abilities, in intelligence, in interests, and needs. High school administrators are finding it necessary, therefore, to study the problems of course elections very carefully and to offer advice to students about the best ways of preparing themselves for those activities to which their capacities and desires lead them.

Most of the larger high schools of the country have recently added to their staff, for the purpose of giving such advice to students, special officers not formerly found in the schools. In some instances this officer may be an assistant principal in charge of student affairs; or there may be two assistants, one in charge of affairs of girls and one for boys. It is the business of this officer to supervise in an intimate way the social and personal activities of the students under his charge.

It is becoming more and more common for high schools to provide guidance counselors who give tests to youth to ascertain their interests and abilities, gather necessary information about the students to help them pursue their programs of study wisely, and advise them about courses of action in the progress of their programs. High schools now maintain extensive records for each student to aid the guidance counselor in his work.

One of the urgent problems of guidance is the choice of technical courses and the selection of suitable industrial opportunities for a given pupil. As a special phase of educational guidance, so-called vocational guidance has been provided in many schools. Vocational guidance in some cases has gone to the extent of providing courses in the industries of the city, so that pupils may become aware of the opportunities which are open to them in later life. Whether such special cases are given or not, it has been found desirable to give personal advice to students and to help them choose their courses and prepare themselves definitely for callings which are open to them. Another important work of guidance has been to learn as much as possible about each student to help place him in situations where learning is most effective for him, and to provide teachers with data so that they can help him learn efficiently. Guidance counselors, through testing programs, anecdotal records, case studies and devices help students to recognize their own abilities, needs, and personal goals.

Extracurricular Activities. The high school recognizes its obligation to the community in social as well as intellectual lines, and has accordingly provided, under the supervision of the school, intellectual, social, and athletic opportunities which were uncommon in the secondary schools of two decades ago. High school clubs have long been a part of the extracurricular activity of the school. However, in recent years many different types of clubs have been set up, with the view to drawing out the student's powers and encouraging him to take part in social activities which would not be aroused by the regular classroom exercises. In some high schools a regular period of the school day is set aside for club activity and thus clubs become closely aligned to classroom work. Intermural and interscholastic athletic programs are common in the high schools; the programs, assuming a personal character, aid the sports associated with the seasons of the year.

Various forms of student self-government have in some cases arisen out of these social activities. Not infrequently the high school has come to be a center of organization, not only for the young people of the community, but also for adults. Reference to this general matter will be made again in a later section dealing with the development of the community center movement.

Federal Encouragement of Technical Courses. In recent years the Federal government has encouraged the organization within high schools of special courses in agriculture and technical subjects. This encouragement has been given through certain supervisory agencies which have been provided from Washington, and through appropriations to the different states by the Federal government for the support of these special courses. The Federal government has no direct control over the secondary schools of the country, but it has set up elaborate machinery for approving plans made in various communities for the introduction of technical courses, and thus indirectly has exercised a great influence in the enlargement of the high school curriculum. Special reference will be made to this matter in a later section dealing with vocational education.

COLLEGES AND UNIVERSITIES

The lack of uniformity in American standards and practices, which has been a subject of frequent comment in earlier paragraphs, is nowhere more strikingly exhibited than in the organization of higher institutions of learning. Even the terms college and university are frequently interchanged, and in many cases the institutions which call themselves by these names are in reality devoting all of their energy to work of a grade which should be classified as belonging to the secondary school.

College. The college is typically a four-year institution, and is devoted to nonprofessional instruction or, as it is called, instruction in the liberal arts. Formerly the colleges, like the secondary schools, were dominated by the tradition of a classical education, but, as the various sciences have expanded and as modern languages have come to be recognized as equally important with classical languages, the range of college subjects has been enormously expanded. Furthermore, the adoption of the elective system has brought about a condition in American colleges, especially since 1880, which has encouraged the expansion of the curriculum into every possible field of human experience.

The differentiation of the college course has taken place most conspicuously in the junior and senior years. Many institutions have found it necessary, in order to meet the needs of their students, to introduce into these years professional courses leading into law, medicine, or other professions. Recently the practice has become more common to have a sharp division between the first two and the last two years of college, with a selection process for students wishing to enter the last two. The college generally consists of several departments. It is the usual practice for a student to specialize his study in one of these departments. The term "college" is now often identified with professional schools and there are such schools as Engineering College, Law College, Medical College, and so forth.

University. The term "university," when strictly used, designates an institution which differs from the college in that it is a composite institution including a number of professional schools or colleges. In almost every case, the universities of the country include a college of liberal arts and a graduate school as sub-divisions of their organization. Professional schools may be organized for any of the accepted professions. Thus we have schools for Medicine, Fine Arts, Law, Pharmacy, Dentistry, Engineering, Theology, Education, Music, Agriculture, and many others.

Degrees. With the multiplication of divisions in American universities, there has come a very great expansion of the list of degrees granted. A number of bachelor's degrees have been established for different types of courses. The most common of these, other than the Bachelor of Arts, is the Bachelor of Science. There are also degrees of Bachelor of Philosophy and Bachelor of Letters. Most of the professional schools, which offer degrees at the bachelor's level, have their own degree designation. There are, therefore, Bachelor of Education, Bachelor of Fine Arts, Bachelor of Engineering, and other such professional degrees.

The universities which give courses beyond the regular four years of the college confer numerous advanced degrees. The first of these, following the bachelor's degree, is the Master's degree. This is usually conferred on the basis of one year of graduate study, although some institutions have a set of scholarly achievements and use a minimum resident study as requirements for the degree. The study required for the Master's degree is very commonly spent in a single department or in a narrow range of closely related departments. The usual degree granted by a graduate school is the Master of Arts or a Master of Science degree. It is very uncommon for American institutions to grant the Master's degree on any basis other than the actual taking of courses in the institution itself.

Above the Master's degree is the Doctor's degree. The Doctor's degree of the graduate school is the Doctor of Philosophy. The character of this degree is determined very largely by the example of the German universities to which many American students went during the decades between 1880 and 1910. The Doctor of Philosophy degree is usually conferred after three years of resident study beyond the bachelor's degree. One of the essential requirements for this degree is the preparation of a thesis which shall demonstrate the ability of the candidate to produce an original piece of work in the field in which he is specializing. The Doctor's degree is also awarded for graduate study in many of the professional schools. Common professional school degrees are the Doctor of Education and Doctor of Medicine.

American universities confer a number of honorary degrees, chief among which is the degree of Doctor of Laws. This is conferred by an institution upon anyone who has contributed, especially in an administrative or civic way, to the betterment of the community. Other degrees on this same level are Doctor of Science and Doctor of Letters.

TOTAL AND FIRST-TIME DEGREE-CREDIT ENROLLMENT IN INSTITUTIONS OF HIGHER EDUCATION—1968

Region and State	Total Enrol. Fall 1968	First time Enrol. Fall 1968	Number of Institutions
Alabama	94,850	25,585	45
Alaska	7,193	2,638	3
Arizona	90,944	28,079	15
Arkansas	50,615	14,500	21
California	1,103,594	272,528	193
Colorado	102,822	24,979	29
Connecticut	106,234	24,896	47
Delaware	18,517	6,212	6
District of Col.	69,532	9,573	23
Florida	201,914	55,597	60
Georgia	108,816	24,811	58
Hawaii	25,614	9,118	5
Idaho	27,789	9,184	11
Illinois	390,831	106,547	133
Indiana	175,904	40,816	42
Iowa	103,516	29,990	51
Kansas	92,486	25,767	51
Kentucky	94,020	22,912	36
Louisiana	115,332	25,302	24
Maine	27,336	6,600	15
Maryland	124,093	27,824	48
Massachusetts	269,785	68,229	108
Michigan	342,995	85,038	86
Minnesota	148,621	35,046	56
Mississippi	68,667	22,761	42
Missouri	165,178	40,921	66
Montana	25,560	7,026	12
Nebraska	60,950	14,789	27
Nevada	10,109	2,537	2
New Hampshire	27,061	6,908	21
New Jersey	170,072	41,339	55
New Mexico	38,326	8,294	12
New York	704,009	143,026	214
North Carolina	148,370	44,486	89
North Dakota	27,676	8,358	14
Ohio	336,921	89,621	87
Oklahoma	106,130	26,720	35
Oregon	96,333	28,405	39
Pennsylvania	372,259	83,197	143
Rhode Island	44,740	10,550	14
S. Carolina	56,139	12,636	42
S. Dakota	28,909	7,388	17
Tennessee	122,373	28,512	52
Texas	379,379	97,967	114
Utah	69,916	14,707	10
Vermont	17,787	5,652	18
Virginia	127,526	37,293	57
Washington	153,902	52,984	39
W. Virginia	59,264	15,241	22
Wisconsin	172,239	43,133	60
Wyoming	13,816	4,493	7
U.S. Service Sc.	15,227	4,100	7
Canal Zone	1,190	359	1
Puerto Rico	54,138	13,702	5

Source: *Office of Education, U. S. Department of Health, Education and Welfare.*

Types of Higher Institutions. Three classes of universities and colleges may be distinguished from the point of view of their support and government. These are: privately-endowed institutions; state institutions; and municipal institutions. The most common form of American college is that which is dependent for its support upon private endowments. Two-thirds of the colleges of this country derived their initial support from religious bodies. Endowments come from many different sources to colleges. The funds given are usually committed to a board of trustees. Frequently the trustees are representatives of the religious bodies which organized the institution. In many instances, on the other hand, they constitute a self-perpetuating body. In all cases the board of trustees appoints an administrative head of the institution. There are more than twice as many private universities and colleges in the United States as there are public, although the public universities and colleges enroll many more students.

State Universities. Beginning with the state of Virginia and extending rapidly through the area which was at one time the Northwest Territory was a movement giving rise to institutions which have grown to be great state universities. The funds for their buildings and current expenses are supplied by the legislatures of their states. These institutions are universities in organization and are usually equipped with a full quota of professional work, especially in agriculture and engineering from subsidies granted by the Federal government. Many of the larger state universities are organized to operate in several locations in the state, thus serving all areas of the state. In this regard, one state university, that of New York, has no central campus but operates through a system of institutions both public and private throughout the state. All of the states of the United States now have state universities.

Municipal Universities and Colleges. The third type of organization which has become increasingly common is the municipal college or university. The first municipal university in this country was organized in Charleston, South Carolina in 1837. Others were at Louisville, Kentucky in 1846, City College in New York City in 1849; and one in Cincinnati, Ohio in 1873. From these early institutions many large cities of the United States modeled municipal universities to serve their citizens. Some cities, unwilling to support universities, have established municipal colleges, many of which have two-year programs.

The College Year. The college year, or university year, has ordinarily consisted of 36 to 40 weeks, the sessions beginning in the middle of September and ending with graduation exercises late in June. President Harper, at the time of organization of the University of Chicago, pointed out vigorously the lack of economy in an arrangement which left the

SCHOOL ENROLLMENTS BY TYPE OF SCHOOL—1930 TO 1967

Year	Total Fall Enrollment	Type of School			
		Kindergarten	Elementary School	High School	College or Professional
1967	50,800,553	2,432,373	29,209,742	12,246,690	6,911,748
1960	49,915,104		24,457,321	11,847,783	3,610,000
1958	42,279,493	2,135,917	27,991,073	8,868,586	3,283,917
1956	39,103,059	1,838,202	26,493,882	7,774,975	2,996,000
1950	31,319,271	1,175,312	21,031,929	6,453,009	2,659,021
1940	29,751,203	660,909	20,466,112	7,129,979	1,494,203
1930	29,652,377	786,463	22,953,377	4,811,800	1,100,737

Source: *U.S. Bureau of the Census.*

college buildings and equipment unused from the end of June until the middle of September. His original proposal was for four quarters of twelve weeks each, with a week of vacation after each quarter.

It has not been feasible to carry out this program. Generally colleges have operated on what is known as the semester plan. The college has two semesters during the academic year. The first semester begins in September shortly after Labor Day and ends during January or February of the following year. The second semester follows this and ends in May or June. Many colleges and universities operate a summer session during the period between June and September. The summer session varies in length at different institutions. A few universities are now operating on what is called a tri-semester plan. Here the attempt is made to eliminate waste in the use of buildings and to provide a program to accelerate the studies of students.

During the summer months teachers of high and elementary schools attend these summer sessions in such large numbers that the universities become, during this period, training places for the teachers in the lower schools. So vigorous has this movement become that boards of education are cognizant of it, and they offer inducements for their teachers to continue study by giving them additional compensation for it or by basing promotion within the school system on such study.

THE JUNIOR COLLEGE

The junior college is an institution offering training on the level of the first two college years, that is, the two years immediately following the close of the typical high school period. Although the beginnings of the movement reach back into the 19th century, the actual development of junior college units unassociated with universities covers a period of little more than three decades.

While the junior college first took hold in California and the Middle West, the South has proved a fertile field for the development of this type of institution. The movement has perhaps made the least progress in the New England and Middle Atlantic states. In these two groups the independent type is in the ascendent, in the South the church, and in the Middle and Western states the public.

The junior college is fast becoming a community college. Trends indicate that in time it will become a terminal college rather than merely the first two years of the four-year college. The Educational Directory of the United States Office of Education lists a total of 644 junior colleges of all types existing in the United States in 1963. By 1974 the number had increased to 973.

The History of the Movement. The beginnings of the junior college movement reach far back into the 19th century. As early as 1851, the year before he assumed the presidency of the University of Michigan, Henry Phillips Tappan recommended a differentiation between what he designated the "collegial" and the "executive" parts of education, terms which may be taken to have meant with him what we regard as, respectively, preparatory and professional education. He saw the organization for which he was contending exemplified in the relationship between the *Gymnasien* and the universities of Germany.

Perhaps the most influential of those who have fostered the junior college movement was William Rainey Harper, first president of the University of Chicago. President Harper was largely influential in the establishment, during the early years of the present century, of the first public junior colleges, —those maintained in connection with the high schools at Goshen, Indiana, and Joliet, Illinois (a township high school), the latter having maintained an uninterrupted existence to the present day. He encouraged also the establishment of junior colleges on private foundations, and contended that by becoming junior colleges many of the smaller colleges could find a logical place and function in the school system.

Among others who gave significant encouragement to the junior college, previously to and during the earliest stages of its actual development, are Edmund J. James, Alexis Lange, and David Starr Jordan.

The Place of the Junior College. The claims made for the junior college by its friends are many, among them the following: (1) that it will be able to give satisfactorily the first two years of college or university work; (2) that it will do much to popularize education on this level; (3) that it will hasten the provision of general and occupational training on this level for those who cannot or should not aspire to higher levels of training; (4) that it will accelerate the impending and desirable reorganization of higher education; and (5) that it will help in obviating the large amount of overlapping of high school and college courses which is known to exist at the present time.

That junior colleges are doing satisfactorily the first two years of college work is attested by the fact that most colleges and universities are admitting graduates of properly accredited junior units to third year standing. Comparison of the teaching staffs of junior colleges with those of other higher institutions shows the former to be somewhat less well prepared for the work, when consideration is given to periods of graduate study. At the same time, even in the present early stage of development, teachers in junior colleges are, on the average, much better prepared than are typical high school teachers, and they compensate to some extent for their present lack of graduate training by having had more experience than college and university teachers and by manifesting in class some superiority in teaching procedure. Salaries of teachers in public junior colleges are not so low as to lead to a misgiving that these institutions will not be able soon to compete with other higher institutions in order to secure a satisfactory teaching personnel.

There is evidence to indicate that, because of lowered costs and proximity to the prospective student, the public junior college is in a position to provide education on this level for a much larger proportion of the total population of the country than now receive it.

Reorganization. The tendencies of reorganization in secondary and higher education during a century have been in the direction of making a place for the junior college. The age of freshmen at Harvard experienced an advance of more than two years in the five decades from 1830 to 1880, and in other older Eastern colleges between the same dates large proportions of students entered at 12 to 17 years of age. During the same period and subsequently (by 1900), the extent of subjects required for admission increased from what was the equivalent of seven to nine units of work to fifteen or sixteen units. This is another way of saying that at least two more years of liberal education were being required for admission to college at the close of the last century than near its opening. While these changes were taking place, collegiate subjects were shifting downward, so that courses formerly open to upperclassmen only, like chemistry, physics, and history of English literature, were available for lowerclassmen, and had even been included in enriched rather than in diluted form in the upper high school years.

The operation of similar forces is seen in the gradually decreasing proportion of students enrolled in the upper years of separate colleges of liberal arts.

The tendency of students of such institutions when transferring to other schools is to enroll predominantly in professional curricula. In consequence, there is a decreasing proportion of men in the upper years of colleges of liberal arts, while in universities the number of men in the upper years increases out of proportion to the lower classes.

There can no longer be doubt that high school and freshmen and sophomore college courses have much in common. This means two things: first, that, being much alike, the line that divides secondary from college work as at present administered is artificial, for, if the work in the lower unit is "secondary" in character, that in the first two years of the upper unit is also largely secondary; second, that this identity involves much actual repetition for the individual student. The repetition results from giving similar work in two institutions, the upper of which knows little of what is going forward in the lower one.

Other types of claims which appear acceptable on behalf of the junior college are: (1) that, owing to smaller enrollments, there will appear in it less of the "depersonalization" of instruction which now tends to characterize the larger colleges and universities; (2) that in the new unit there will be better opportunities for laboratory training in leadership than in institutions in which leaders are largely selected from upperclassmen.

The Junior College and the Public School. From what has been said in description of the public junior college, it may be judged that, for the most part, it is an upward extension of the secondary school, with some measure of separation from the unit below. In communities with four-year high schools this means a 6–4–2 organization of public education. The junior-senior high school organization beginning with the seventh grade is, however, gaining such headway that in most cities, unless there is to be a regrouping of grades, we shall have a 6–3–3–2 organization, including in effect three secondary school units, two of them three years in length and the third two years in length.

It does not require much consideration of this plan or long experience with it to make one aware of its unwieldiness. In consequence, there has appeared an advocacy of a redistribution of the eight years of the new secondary school into two units of equal length,—a lower one to include the grades from the seventh through the tenth, and an upper to include the last two high school and the first two college years. Such a plan may be seen to be in harmony with the considerations supporting junior college reorganization already discussed. Small school systems will not, of course, even with generous provisions for state aid, be able to justify the support of the full eight-year period of secondary education. In this respect, however, the situation will in no wise differ from that now obtaining, in which communities maintain differing amounts of training beyond the elementary school, according to their resources and the number of children of secondary school age.

Junior Divisions in Universities. Another form of reorganization, which has something in common with the three main types of junior college referred to, is the horizontal separation of the first two from the last two years in certain universities, the lower unit being designated as the "junior college," "junior division," or "lower division," and the upper by corresponding names. By 1922 six universities had introduced this line of cleavage. By 1934 this number had increased to 136.

Recently, with the emphasis being made on the development of community colleges, universities have accelerated the organization of "junior divisions." Many state universities now offer the work of the first two years of college in "centers" located in the various areas of the state.

Public Junior Colleges. These are institutions which have developed in association with the public school system and which, with few exceptions, are maintained in connection with public high schools, usually with some attempt at separation. They are for the most part under the direction and control of local school authorities, and constitute an upward extension of the public school system, a natural step in evolution in communities which, in something like a satisfactory manner, have taken care of education on the lower levels.

The accompanying table shows that the publicly-controlled junior colleges are increasing in number, while privately-controlled ones are decreasing. As enrollments have gone up, one answer to the need for increasing facilities has been the junior college. Many experts believe that the needs of the citizenry can be met by this type of college rather than the regular four-year college. Following World War II junior colleges, particularly the public ones, have been showing a remarkable increase in enrollments.

Church Junior Colleges. Of the privately controlled junior colleges, approximately two-thirds are church operated. More than one-half of these are in the South. Practically all of the larger denominations are represented by at least one junior college, with the Baptists, Methodists, and Roman Catholics having the largest representation both in number of schools and in enrollments. Like other types of denominational schools, the church junior colleges give large emphasis to the creeds of the churches which sponsors them.

Independent Junior Colleges. The privately controlled independent junior college is often incorporated or it may be owned and operated by one or more persons, unincorporated. There are only 98 schools of this type, of which 38 are coeducational. Sixteen are for men, and 44 are for women. This is the least important of the three types both in the number of schools and in the total enrollment.

The table below gives the enrollment by subjects in 32 public junior colleges in California. Social sciences, English, and commerce and law lead the list. Ancient languages rank below aviation; home economics below art; mathematics below music. These enrollments indicate an important change in interests from a generation ago.

COURSES IN 32 CALIFORNIA PUBLIC JUNIOR COLLEGES

Subjects	Per cent of students enrolled	Subjects	Per cent of students enrolled
Social sciences	18.7	Art	3.8
English	18.0	Orientation	3.0
Commerce and law	11.1	Philosophy	2.7
Modern languages	9.5	Home economics	1.0
Physical sciences	9.1	Aviation	.5
Biological sciences	6.4	Civic health	.5
Music	6.2	Ancient languages	.3
Mathematics	5.0	Agriculture	.2
Engineering, etc.	3.9		

UNIVERSITY EXTENSION

The university extension movement began in England more than a century ago. Its motive was described by one of its early advocates in the question: "Though it may be impossible to bring the masses requiring education to the university, may it not be possible to carry the university to them?" After the movement had made much progress in England, it was brought to this country in 1887 through a discussion at a library conference in Albany, N. Y. Very shortly, centers were established in several cities, and in 1890 a society known as the American Society for the Extension of University Teaching was established and maintained by subscriptions in Philadelphia. In 1891 a number of important steps were taken: the state of

Education

Year	ALL JUNIOR COLLEGES		PUBLICLY CONTROLLED		PRIVATELY CONTROLLED	
	Number	Enrollment	Number	Enrollment	Number	Enrollment
1920	52	8,102	10	2,940	42	5,162
1924	132	20,559	39	9,240	93	11,319
1930	277	55,616	129	36,501	148	19,115
1934	322	78,480	152	55,869	170	22,611
1940	456	149,854	217	107,553	239	42,301
1944	413	84,616	210	56,439	203	28,177
1950	483	242,740	256	187,695	227	55,045
1954	518	325,804	293	272,036	225	53,768
1960	509	403,524	310	348,538	199	54,986
1965	633	841,437	399	737,890	234	103,547
1968	804	1,289,993	549	1,169,635	255	120,358
1969	813	1,528,000	577	1,413,000	236	116,000
1970	827	1,630,000	603	1,520,000	224	110,000
1971	854	1,725,000	637	1,623,000	217	103,000
1972	883	1,792,000	671	1,695,000	212	97,000
1973	929	1,922,000	709	1,829,000	220	93,000
1974	973	2,198,000	763	2,104,000	210	94,000

Source: U.S. Department of Health, Education, and Welfare, Office of Education; U.S. Department of Commerce, Bureau of the Census.

New York appropriated $10,000; the newly established University of Chicago took over a local society and began extension work on a large scale; and in December a national congress on university extension was held in Philadelphia.

Scope of the Movement. Following these early steps, the movement has spread over the whole country. The state universities especially have taken it up and are now engaged in a great variety of enterprises that are intended to carry opportunities of intellectual improvement to the people of their states. The work of the state universities is in many cases generously supported by appropriations made by the legislature. Local centers also contribute through payment of fees to the maintenance of classes or lecture courses, and many endowed colleges and universities cooperate with the state universities by sending out lecturers or conducting correspondence courses.

Variety of Extension Service. A brief summary of the types of service rendered may be attempted. First, there are bureaus of information. These prepare bibliographies and outlines for schools, clubs, and civic associations that are pursuing systematic studies, supply information on public health, child welfare, municipal problems, and like matters. Second, aid is given in organizing various forms of community activities, such as pageants, community exhibits, farm demonstrations, and other general occasions. Third, bulletins are published on legislation, on civic and state problems, and on recent scientific advances. Fourth, educational and entertainment films are supplied to clubs, churches, and schools. Fifth, packages of books are made up and lent to persons or organized groups who do not have access in their own towns to public libraries. Sixth, debates in schools or in clubs are organized and directed. In many cases selected reading material is supplied with the plans.

Seventh, classes are conducted in all kinds of subjects. Teachers' classes are conducted in educational subjects; farmers' classes in the mechanics of farm machinery; mothers' classes in the care of infants; general classes in literature, history, and science. These classes are conducted either wholly or in part by lecturers who come from the university, and often are made the basis of regular credit toward the degrees of the university. Eighth, correspondence courses are conducted. These also are often made the basis of credit toward graduation.

It may be remarked that the correspondence study phase of extension education has been developed by several large private institutions that devote their entire energy to this line of activity. These private correspondence schools usually specialize in commercial and mechanical courses with a view to giving practical education to students who have terminated their schooling early.

PROFESSIONAL SCHOOLS

The colleges and universities of the country lead into the professional schools. There was a time when training in law and medicine depended upon a general plan of apprenticeship training, whereby the candidate for admission to the profession associated himself with some experienced member of that profession and studied with him in private. Young men "read law," as the phrase put it, in the office of some law firm, or the prospective doctor acted as an assistant to some practitioner. Later the professional men organized institutions at which a number of candidates came together and paid fees for training. Professional schools thus grew up on a quasi-private basis and in many instances were very profitable because the instruction was given by men who secured their main salaries from the regular professions and took the student fees as additions to their incomes.

As the demands for professional training became more rigid, and especially after legal enactments began to prescribe more in detail the requirements for admission into the professions of law and medicine, the private professional schools found that they had to reconstruct their organization. It was no longer possible to give adequate instruction under conditions that were attractive to the instructors who devoted most of their time to other professional duties. Gradually professional schools began to be assimilated by universities, until finally the private professional training school has very largely disappeared.

Standardization in Medicine. The standardization of professional education is being pushed forward rapidly at the present time. The most vigorous movement of this type is exhibited in the schools devoted to the training of physicians. Under the guidance of the American Medical Council, a survey of the medical schools of the country was made in 1910 and it was found that most of the private institutions were very meager in their equipment and inadequate in their instruction. The Medical Council set up a system of grading medical schools, and, while it had no authority to enforce its grading and classification, the significance of its pronouncements was so great that most of the private medical schools were forced to close their doors. In this way a professional group acting without authority enforced a high standard upon institutions for professional training.

In the professions other than medicine the movement has taken the same general direction, but somewhat more slowly and without any concentrated effort on the part of any single powerful board.

Economy in Professional Training. One of the important problems with which these standardizing bodies for the professional schools have had to deal is that of the relation of professional education to the general training given in the college of liberal arts. In the United States the training of a candidate is so far behind that of European candidates in point of time that the professional person in the United States usually enters upon productive activities two years later than the European candidate. The reasons for this delay in American professional education have already been given in the preceding discussions of the organization of elementary and of secondary schools. Elementary education in the United States has never been so related to higher education as to introduce those who are going on into higher schools to the advanced subjects as early as do the European institutions.

The professional schools of the United States, however, have not in general gone back in their consideration to the high or the elementary schools, but have attempted to adjust their own relations with the college in such a way as to enable young people to get into the professional courses at a somewhat earlier date. There has been from time to time very vigorous discussion of the possibility of reducing the college course to two or three years. In many cases professional schools have been advised to accept students directly from the high school. At the present time there is no definite solution of this difficulty, and the probabilities are that a solution will not be reached until the professional schools and the higher institutions of learning canvass the whole problem of the organization of American education, from its elementary stages through the professional schools.

Technical Schools. Technical education of a higher grade has developed very rapidly in the United States. There are a number of engineering schools that are of university grade. These have been especially fostered by the land-grant colleges, and in some instances have come to be such important parts of the educational system that their courses have eclipsed in large measure the liberal arts training that formerly was characteristic of all higher institutions.

Many technical schools have developed co-operative programs with liberal arts colleges. In doing this, they have coordinated their curriculums so that a student may attend a four-year liberal arts college for three years, then transfer to a co-operating technical school for one year and obtain a professional degree.

Inequality of Educational Opportunity. The difference in the amount of money spent per pupil for education clearly indicates that the education supplied varies from state to state.

What is true of states is equally true of districts within the state. Neighboring districts having equal school registrations often differ in wealth in the most extreme degree. Rural children, in general, have much more meager educational opportunities than urban children. Often, inequalities occur in education because the school authorities are not willing to spend proper amounts of money for education. Some communities make greater effort than others for the support of their schools.

Bonded Indebtedness. In addition to the revenues for current expenses that are derived from taxes, the public schools of the United States have developed a method of securing funds for making payments on buildings and permanent improvements through the sale of bonds that must in the long run be paid for out of public funds. The amount of bonded indebtedness incurred for schools is very difficult to ascertain, but it is altogether certain that in many communities obligations have been assumed that constitute a very heavy burden for the future to carry.

SCHOOL FINANCE

The funds for the maintenance of the educational system described in the foregoing pages are derived from public taxes, Federal grants of land, student fees, and donations. In general, it may be said that the revenues for the support of elementary schools and high schools are all derived from taxes and grants of land. Revenues for higher education come from a variety of sources.

The greatest sources of income for public education are state and local governments. However, the Federal government is being urged to take an increasing interest in education, and programs in special areas of education are receiving federal support.

PUBLIC SCHOOL EXPENDITURES*

State	Total (millions)†	Average per Pupil‡
Alabama	863	1,090
Alaska	231	2,096
Arizona	801	1,415
Arkansas	433	881
California	6,596	1,320
Colorado	935	1,422
Connecticut	1,055	1,659
Delaware	213	1,606
District of Columbia	269	1,954
Florida	2,587	1,381
Georgia	1,237	1,114
Hawaii	286	1,545
Idaho	274	1,112
Illinois	3,458	1,452
Indiana	1,609	1,160
Iowa	947	1,455
Kansas	667	1,475
Kentucky	705	986
Louisiana	919	1,082
Maine	304	1,197
Maryland	1,457	1,516
Massachusetts	1,988	na
Michigan	3,108	1,366
Minnesota	1,653	1,513
Mississippi	511	997
Missouri	1,176	1,186
Montana	268	1,554
Nebraska	397	1,302
Nevada	187	1,261
New Hampshire	225	1,175
New Jersey	2,742	1,892
New Mexico	418	1,261
New York	7,385	2,179
North Carolina	1,538	1,099
North Dakota	174	1,207
Ohio	3,023	1,264
Oklahoma	709	1,130
Oregon	735	1,501
Pennsylvania	4,095	1,660
Rhode Island	274	1,481
South Carolina	701	1,030
South Dakota	185	1,094
Tennessee	995	969
Texas	3,294	1,094
Utah	412	1,084
Vermont	163	1,398
Virginia	1,445	1,197
Washington	1,271	1,443
West Virginia	485	1,071
Wisconsin	1,568	1,618
Wyoming	133	1,489

Source: U.S. Department of Commerce, Bureau of the Census. * In dollars; estimated; for school year ending June 30, 1976. † Includes interest on school debt. ‡ In average daily attendance.

Rapidly Increasing Costs. The increase in school expenditures in recent years has been a source of great anxiety to those who are in charge of public revenues. In all areas of school expenditures, costs have risen since World War II, and the number of pupils to be educated has increased. The question has been seriously raised in many quarters whether the public schools of this country can be carried forward on the scale which has been set by earlier practices of American communities. One of the chief problems which have led to this discussion in recent years is the problem of financing high schools. High school education is more costly than elementary education. A few years ago the attendance in high schools was relatively small, and, though the per capita expenditures were high, the aggregate expenditure for these schools was within easy possibility of support by the public. Since the high schools have increased in population so rapidly in recent years, they have made a very heavy demand on public resources. The estimates of future increases in high school enrollments make the problem very troublesome.

American communities do not usually understand why the cost of education in this country is so much higher than it is in other countries. No other nation has brought into its high schools anything like the proportion of the youth of the country represented in the high schools of the United States. Those who are disposed to advocate a curtailment of expenditures for public education in this country should recognize clearly the fact that they are asking the country to give up an experiment in popular education which is one of the unique characteristics of this democracy.

On the other hand, communities will have to recognize the fact that it is quite impossible to maintain public schools of the kind which exist in the United States without making very heavy demands on public funds. It is estimated that from one third to one half of the public revenues of the municipalities are expended in the maintenance of public schools.

State Appropriations for Education. In every state appropriations are made for education. Usually there are separate allotments made for the public elementary and secondary schools and for higher institutions of learning. The state usually distributes monies to the public elementary and secondary schools on the basis of the number of pupils in average attendance. Appropriations to universities take the form of direct grants or are given to the students of the institutions in the form of scholarships.

Individual Responsibility and Costs. These figures raise an interesting and important question regarding the individual's responsibility for the cost of his education. The student undoubtedly gains great personal advantage from his schooling. He is prepared to earn a higher wage than he would receive if he were uneducated. It is a perfectly legitimate question, therefore, to ask how far he should pay for this improvement in his earning capacity by paying tuition for his education. Especially in the higher institutions does this question become an immediate one in view of the fact that the resources of the higher schools are limited and the population of these institutions is rapidly increasing.

While it may be argued that the lower schools are necessary for the maintenance of the state and may legitimately be paid for by public moneys, it becomes very much more controversial to defend public support for higher education.

FEDERAL PARTICIPATION IN PUBLIC EDUCATION

In foregoing discussions it has been stated that the Federal government does not have any direct control over the school systems of the various states. It exerts some indirect control, however, through the standards which it establishes for school participation in the various educational funds which it appropriates.

The Federal government has shown its interest in education in three ways: first, through making land and money grants for education; second, through free distribution of surplus commodities; and, third, through establishing various educational agencies such as the United States Office of Education. Its land and money grants from the beginning to the present time would total several billion dollars, and during recent years its annual appropriations have amounted to several hundred million dollars. There has been a definite trend toward larger grants of money from the Federal government and a greater percentage of the total costs of education being borne by the Federal government.

The major appropriations at present being made by the Federal government for education are for the following purposes: education of active participants in World War II, vocational education in public secondary schools, higher education in land grant colleges, vocational rehabilitation, public schools in the District of Columbia, schools for Indians, education for military service, local school systems affected by Federal government programs, agricultural extension service, agricultural experiment stations, the school lunch program, and the United States Office of Education.

As a matter of historical development, the Federal government first became involved in education because of its relation to scientific and educational problems. The various departments of the Federal government find it necessary to employ experts as it participates in the scientific work of the nation. Many believe that the resources of the Federal government are necessary in some cases if scientific work is to go forward on a scale to insure adequate general information for the conduct of modern enterprises.

It becomes a matter of vital importance to the nation that experts be trained for the various lines of public service. Furthermore, when they undertake their work they must be supplied with suitable scientific equipment. The government has been forced, therefore, into the most intimate and vital contact with educational institutions of the country.

Land Grants. For reasons entirely foreign to those which were cited in the last paragraph, however, the Federal government was drawn into the support of public education. A publication of the office of education written by Professor F. H. Swift states the case as follows:

"On May 20, 1923, will occur the one hundred and thirty-eighth anniversary of the passage of one of the most famous and most significant ordinances ever enacted by the Congress of the United States. Out of this Ordinance of 1785 arose a national policy which has resulted in providing the states with vast grants for public education. This policy was not, however, positively assured until two years later, when Manasseh Cutler, one of the directors of the Ohio Company, held up the Congress of 1787 with the threat to buy land from some individual state unless his demands for school, university, and church lands should be granted.

"Congress, badly in need of money and fearful lest Cutler should carry out his threat, passed, on July 23, 1787, an ordinance authorizing the board of treasury to contract for the sale of lands to the Ohio Company on the terms demanded by Cutler, which included the following grants of land: Two townships for an institution of higher learning, and, within each township, one section of land for the ministry and one for schools. Thus began a national policy which resulted in granting to the states, Federal lands and moneys for public schools. Every one of the 30 public land states, i. e., states carved out of Federal domain, received extensive grants of Federal lands for endowing schools, which have been largely devoted to establishing permanent state endowments for public schools.

Extent of Grants. "Some Federal lands granted to the states have been given specifically for public schools; others, such as swamp lands, salt lands, and internal improvement lands, although not given specifically for schools, were devoted to schools by many states. Every public land state admitted prior to California, in 1850, received from the national government for the support of public schools the section numbered 16 in each congressional township. California and every subsequently admitted state, except Utah, Arizona, New Mexico, and Oklahoma, received sections 16 and 36. The first three of these states received sections 2 and 32 as well as 16 and 36. Oklahoma offers a special case also.

"In addition to township school sections aggregating approximately 73 millions of acres (73,155,075) (a), Congress, under separate acts, has granted to public land states approximately 11,000,000 acres of public domain for purposes of internal improvement; salt lands aggregating over 606,000 acres, and swamp lands aggregating more than 64,000,000 acres. It should be noted that lands granted as swamp lands, as in the case of Minnesota, sometimes proved to contain rich mineral deposits which made them among the most valuable lands granted to a state. From these various grants there have been given in all to the 30 public land states approximately 147,000 square miles of school lands, 101,000 square miles of swamp lands, 17,000 square miles of internal improvement lands, and 900 square miles of salt lands.

Colonial School Lands. "The policy of reserving for schools one or more sections of land in newly surveyed townships had become fairly well established in colonial days. As early as 1659, the general court of Massachusetts

---

"(a) Exclusive of approximately 21,000,000 acres of school lands reserved in Alaska; approximately 94,000,000 acres, if Alaskan reservations be included."

FEDERAL FUNDS FOR EDUCATION, 1974*

ITEM	AMOUNT
TOTAL	$13,079,000,000
Grants	12,727,000,000
Elementary-secondary education	4,207,000,000
Higher education	6,064,000,000
Vocational-technical and continuing education	2,456,000,000
Loans, higher education	352,000,000
Other educational funds	4,859,000,000

Source: U.S. Department of Commerce, Bureau of the Census. * For school year ending June 30, 1974.

granted the towns of Charlestown and Cambridge 1000 acres of land each on condition that they be forever appropriated to maintain a grammar school. In 1672, Connecticut granted 600 acres each to the four county towns of Fairfield, New London, New Haven, and Hartford for the support of a grammar school. In 1687, the Connecticut colony granted more than one-half of what is now Litchfield county to the towns of Hartford and Windsor to save this land from the cupidity of the royal governor Andros. Hartford and Windsor refused to restore this land to the colony when the troublesome times ceased. A controversy arose which resulted in a compromise. In 1726, the territory was divided in half. The eastern half was given to Hartford and Windsor. The colony took the western half, which it laid out in seven townships. Five of these townships were divided into 53 parts each. One of these 53 parts

EXPENDITURES FOR EDUCATION, 1973*

	PUBLIC AND PRIVATE	PUBLIC	PRIVATE
TOTAL	89,200,000,000	72,800,000,000	16,400,000,000
Elementary and secondary schools	57,800,000,000	52,100,000,000	5,700,000,000
Higher education	31,400,000,000	20,700,000,000	10,700,000,000

Source: U.S. Department of Commerce, Bureau of the Census. * For school year ending June 30, 1973.

SUMMARY OF PUBLIC SCHOOL STATISTICS, 1974*

School systems	16,730
Pupil enrollment†	
Total	45,400,000‡
Per cent of total population	21.6
Average daily attendance	41,400,000
Average length of term in days	178.7
Average number of days attended per pupil	159.5
Number of high school graduates	3,069,000
Instructional staff†	
Total	2,425,000
Classroom teachers§	2,287,000
Male ‖	766,000
Female ‖	1,521,000
Principals	100,000
Expenditures#	
Total	$56,970,000,000
Average annual salary per member of total instructional staff	$11,185
Expenditure per pupil in average daily attendance in day schools	$1,364
Revenue	
Total	$58,231,000,000
Federal	$4,930,000,000
State	$24,113,000,000
Local	$29,187,000,000

Source: U.S. Department of Commerce, Bureau of the Census. * Public elementary and secondary schools; for school year ending June 30, 1974. † Day schools only. ‡ As of fall 1973. § Includes nonsupervisory staff. ‖ Estimated. # In 1974 dollars.

in each town was reserved for the support of a town school, and two for the support of the ministry. In 1733, the assembly of the colony of Connecticut enacted that seven towns belonging to the colony be sold and the proceeds divided among the towns already settled, in proportion to their list of polls and ratable estate, the proceeds to be set apart by each town as a permanent school fund.

"From the proceeds of this policy of Connecticut two classes of permanent funds arose: (1) The fund belonging to the colony which was distributed among the towns of the colony; (2) funds belonging to new towns, arising from reservations of school lands within the towns.

"The colonial policy of reserving lands in each town was adopted soon after the formation of the Union by several states. Georgia, in 1783, provided for the reservation of 1000 acres of land in each county for the support of free schools. New York, in 1786, and Massachusetts, in 1788, provided for the reservation, in state-owned lands, of lots for schools and for the ministry."

Land-Grant Colleges. The interest of the Federal government in science, together with its method of appropriating land as a device for aiding the states in promoting education, led during the Civil War to the adoption of the so-called Morrill act of July 2, 1862. This act gave to each state 30,000 acres of public land for each senator and representative to which it was entitled in Congress, the states not having enough public lands within their borders receiving land scrip for the deficit. The money derived from the sale of these lands was to constitute an endowment fund, the interest of which was to be used for the support of "at least, one college, where the leading object shall be, without excluding other scientific and classical studies, and including military tactics, to teach such branches of learning as are related to agriculture and the mechanic arts, in such manner as the legislatures of the states may respectively prescribe, in order to promote the liberal and practical education of the industrial classes in the several pursuits and professions in life." The legislative assent of a state to the provisions of the act was made necessary before the state could participate in the benefits of the act.

On March 2, 1887, Congress appropriated $15,000 annually to each state, to be used by the state in conducting researches and in verifying experiments in the agricultural experiment stations under the direction of the land-grant colleges. The appropriations were made from money arising from the sale of public lands.

The second Morrill act, of August 30, 1890, appropriated annually, out of money derived from the sale of public lands, $15,000 to each state and territory for the further endowment and maintenance of the land-grant colleges, this to be increased annually by $1000 for ten years, after which time the amount for each state and territory was to be $25,000 annually. This money was to be applied only to instruction, and none of it could be used for buildings.

Subsequent acts have increased from time to time the appropriations to the institutions established under the acts mentioned in the foregoing paragraphs.

Many of the land-grant colleges were started in states which did not have state universities and in due time were expanded into state universities. Every state now has at least one land-grant college. Each of the Southern states has two such colleges, one for whites and the other for Negroes.

On the curriculum of higher education the land-grant colleges have exerted a large influence by popularizing the advantages of vocational education, especially in agriculture and engineering. Through their teaching, their research, and their extension work and other services they have promoted the rapid development of agriculture and engineering. Over the years they have had generous financial support from the Federal government and from the states.

After a period of somewhat slow growth in the later part of the 19th century, the new institutions began to develop rapidly about 1900. Their growth came partly through direct federal aid and partly through the increasing acceptance by the states of their obligations for the support of such institutions.

Often designated as the single most important contribution of the U.S. to higher education, the land-grant institutions, with the state universities, pioneered important innovations in higher education. These include the raising of the so-called "useful" arts, sciences, and professions to academic respectability; applied research as a valid function of higher education; the promotion of public service and continuing education; and the popularization of higher education at low cost.

Since World War II these institutions have taken an active lead in international cooperative programs, notably in agricultural and educational development in emerging nations. They have also been significantly responsible for the development in the U.S. of the world's leading agricultural productivity. The National Manpower Council in 1953 stated that "the most important single governmental step in connection with the training of scientific and professional personnel was the Morrill Act of 1862, which laid the basis for the country's extensive state college and university system."

In 1887 the Association of American Agricultural Colleges was formed. With the National Association of State Universities (founded in 1895), it has played a prime role in higher education and was among the founders of the American Council on Education (1918). The two associations merged in 1963 into the National Association of State Universities and Land-Grant Colleges, which now represents more than 100 institutions.

Other Federal Subsidies for Education. For many years the Federal government has made annual appropriations for various educational enterprises. The annual appropriations made by the Federal government to education are as follows:

United States Office of Education for Land-Grant Colleges, Vocational Education below college level. Smith-Hughes Act, George Barden Act, assistance to federally-affected areas for operation of schools and schoolhouse construction; *Public Health Service* for further research in health and for education of health personnel; surplus property distribution; vocational rehabilitation; Gallaudet College; American Printing House for the Blind; Howard University; *Department of Agriculture* for research in agriculture and agriculture stations, school lunch program; *Department of Commerce* for state marine academies, Federal marine schools for training and upgrading of marine personnel; *Department of Defense* for academic training of military personnel, education of children of military and civilian personnel overseas and military personnel while off duty; *Department of Interior* for education programs for Indians, Virgin Islands, and Pribilof Islands and children of Federal park employees; *Department of Justice* for vocational and general education in Federal penal institutions; *Department of State* for educational exchange programs; *Department of the Treasury* for the coast guard academy and tuition of coast guard personnel; *Atomic Energy Commission* for research and development of scientists, construction and operation of schools in centers operated by the Commission; *Canal Zone* for operation of schools; *District of Columbia* for public education; *International Cooperation Administration* for educational activities in undeveloped countries; *Veterans Administration* for administration of public laws 16,894, 346, and 550; *National Science Foundation* for research in mathematics, engineering, physical, biological, and medical sciences, and, in 1958, for the civilian space commission.

Congress in 1958 passed the National Defense Education Act which called for a total appropriation of $877 million to strengthen the American system of education. By this act, due to run four years, the states would appropriate a matching sum of $405 million. The allotments were scheduled for loans and fellowships to students in higher education; financial assistance for strengthening science, mathematics, and modern language instruction; guidance, counseling and testing; research and experimentation in effective use of television, radio, motion pictures and other audio-visual media for education and vocational education. Almost $71 million was borrowed by 15,115 college students under the National Defense Student Loan program in the 1960–61 academic year. The average loan was $470. The college put up $1.00 for every $9.00 received from the Federal government.

In the spring of 1962, Congress passed the Manpower Development Training Act to encourage vocational training and enable those untrained to get needed skill in vocations. And, in 1965, the Elementary and Secondary Education Act greatly increased the Federal funds appropriated for education.

Federal Land Grants. By its system of land grants to schools, the Federal government has given public education a mighty stimulus. This stimulus was much needed, especially in the early days when the financial resources of the people were limited and when a general interest in education had not yet risen among the people. The income from these land grants today provides less than one per cent of the support of public schools and colleges, but in the early days the income provided a much larger percentage.

Taking the place of Federal Land Grants have been grants of money by the Federal government for education. For the most part these have taken the form of grants to schools to aid in the development of new programs in special areas of education and scholarships for research within these programs.

The Federal Government uses different bases for determining apportionments. Following the Louisiana Purchase, assistance was given in proportion to land areas. The 16th section of each township from the public domain was given to help with the establishment and operation of a system of education. About ¾ of the states have received this type of Federal assistance.

A provision of the Morrill Act of 1862 authorized grants of 30,000 acres of the public lands to the states for each Senator and each Representative in Congress. The resulting grants were generally for the most populous states.

In some programs of assistance the Federal Government requires that State and local communities match any Federal funds allocated to them. The allotment procedure for vocational education which specifies that state and local funds must be provided in specific proportions is an example of the use of this base.

"G.I. Bill of Rights." According to the Serviceman's Adjustment Act of 1944 and as amended in 1945, any veteran of World War II who had at least 90 days of active service is entitled to at least 12 months of education at government expense, provided it is started not later than 4 years after separation from active service or 4 years after the end of the war, whichever date is the later. After that 12 months, he is entitled to an additional period equal to the time spent in active service after September 15, 1940, and before the end of the war. The total period was not to exceed 48 months, nor extend beyond 9 years after the end of the war.

The student could select his course and his school, provided it was on the list of the Veterans' Administration. For his fees and textbooks the government paid up to $500 per school year. It also paid a certain amount each month for his subsistence.

This act expired in July 1951 for all who were not already in continuous training. Another Federal act known as the "Korean G.I. Bill" was enacted. For the veteran with at least 90 days of service, the new act provided one and one half days of education for each day in service after June 27, 1950. The veteran must pursue an approved course of study not later than 3 years from the date of discharge from active duty and no training is allowable beyond eight years from that date.

As in the original G.I. Bill, the student could select his course and his school. The government gave monthly payments designated as "training allowance" instead of "subsistence." This included the costs of schooling and some aid toward living expenses. The size of the training allowance was based upon the dependency status of the veteran and the rate of the veteran's training time.

VOCATIONAL EDUCATION

The term "vocational education" has been used in recent times to cover those school courses which prepare for commercial and industrial pursuits. This is a very limited meaning of the words, because preparation for the professions is also in a very proper sense vocational education. If the broader meaning be attached to the term, all education is vocational. Harvard college, the first American institution of higher education, was a vocational school organized to train the clergy. Every college or technical school has in like manner been a school for the training of young men and women to enter upon the duties of adult life.

Considered in a narrower sense, vocational education, or preparation for commercial and industrial positions, is of comparatively recent origin in the United States. Formerly boys and girls were trained for such positions by being apprenticed to individual employers from whom they learned by imitation and without systematic instruction. The apprenticeship system began to break down, however, as soon as modern economic conditions became complex and especially when machine industry replaced the older and simpler handcrafts.

The first type of special training for practical business pursuits in this country was commercial education. The manufacturing processes by which raw materials are worked over were developed on an extensive scale in Europe rather than in this country.

Estimated "Life-Time" Income
For Men by Amount of Education

$174,000	Completion of less than 8 years of school
216,000	Completion of 8 years of school
320,000	Completion of 4 years of High School
520,000	Completion of 4 years of College

Source: *Statistical Abstract of the United States*, 1968.

Commercial Schools. As early as 1843, a man named Bartlett established in Philadelphia a school for the training of bookkeepers. Bartlett was followed by others, and soon every large city was supplied with a private business school or college which taught the elements of accounting and gave training in penmanship. These schools flourished because they supplied an urgent practical demand of the business world. Their courses were of short duration and highly intensive. The students were eager and there was a ready market for their services.

As business methods evolved, the courses of study in the private business schools also developed. When the typewriter came into common use, the schools transformed themselves in many cases into schools of typewriting and stenography.

In the early 1890's, the interest in commercial education had become so widespread that the attention of the public and of educators was drawn to it, and commercial courses for the public began to be advocated. In 1894 a group of commercial teachers met in Asbury Park and launched the movement. Since that date, high schools have rapidly developed courses in typewriting, stenography, and business methods, until now commercial education is one of the leading lines of instruction.

Manual Training. The first types of technical training to be adopted in this country were drawing and manual training. The exhibits of skilled workmanship brought from Europe to the Centennial exposition in Philadelphia in 1876 attracted the attention of Americans and convinced them that this country was far behind in the training of artisans. There was at that time no provision in the public schools for training pupils in manual skill. The European systems of woodworking were therefore borrowed and put into the school programs. This was especially true for the Swedish *Sloyd* system which emphasized the making of useful articles. Special schools were organized for the purpose of giving manual training courses. The first of these was the manual training school connected with Washington university at Saint Louis.

Manual training was advocated by its early promoters as a useful form of general training appropriate for all pupils, whether they were going into industry or the professions. Skill of hand, these promoters said, is just as important as reading and the sciences for a full development of personality.

The manual training movement has resulted in the introduction of handwork of some type into all schools. As a device for satisfying the demands of the business world for the training of workers, however, it has been superseded by a later and more distinctly technical type of education. Most schools now use the term "industrial arts" instead of manual training. An effort is made, also, to use the knowledge and skills of manual training as general education. Because of this, many new activities have been added to the manual training classes.

Technical Industrial Schools. In 1906 the state of Massachusetts appointed a commission on industrial and technical education. This commission pointed out that boys and girls were urgently needed in the machine industries, and that they were utterly unprepared by the ordinary schools for their places in factories. Indeed, it was clearly the belief of this commission that the ordinary forms of education are in many cases detrimental to industry. With the report of the Massachusetts commission there began a controversy which has been waged continuously from that time. On the one side have been arrayed the industrial leaders of the country, who have advocated two systems of schools, one for industrial workers, and one for the children of the upper classes of society who are to enter the professions. On the other side are the educators and other citizens, who hold that American public education must be a unit system unlike the dual system of Europe. This latter group advocates a reconstruction and liberalizing of common education, but insists that all the children of the United States shall be educated in the same school.

The National Society for the Promotion of Industrial Education, organized shortly after the Massachusetts commission had made its report, was the chief agency in inducing Congress to pass in 1917 the law creating the Federal board for vocational education. This board at first devoted its energy to the promotion of a dual system of education, but has since receded somewhat from that position and is at present co-operating with the high schools of the country in the establishment of industrial courses.

Agricultural Education. Parallel with the growth of technical education in industry, the schools have developed courses in agriculture. The department of agriculture has been influential in promoting such courses, and since 1914 has used a large Federal fund provided under the Smith-Lever act for this purpose.

Home Economics. Special training for girls in the arts of home making, cooking, and dressmaking has developed rapidly in recent years in the upper grades of elementary schools and in the high school.

Part-time and Co-operative Courses. Schools and industrial concerns have arranged to employ students on part-time programs so that there may be opportunities for these students to study and at the same time come into contact with practical processes. This type of work-study instruction has been widely adopted, both in colleges and in secondary schools since it was introduced by Herman Schneider in 1906 in the College of Engineering of the University of Cincinnati.

Smith-Lever Subventions. The Smith-Lever act, which became Federal law in 1914, is commonly known as the agricultural extension act. It provides Federal subventions to aid the states in promoting extension work in agriculture and home economics. The act made an appropriation for extension purposes but required each state or local community, or both, that might desire to participate in the funds, to match the Federal appropriation. This was the beginning of the use of the matching principle by the Federal government and, with few exceptions, such as in the case of grants made to the schools for defense training during World War II, the principle has been subsequently followed.

The extension work is carried on chiefly among adults but partly among youth of school age. Under the provisions of this act and its later amendments, approximately 90 per cent of the counties of the United States now employ agricultural agents and approximately 50 per cent of the counties employ demonstration agents of home economics. Approximately 15 per cent of the counties employ club-work agents who work exclusively with boys and girls in 4-H Club work and similar activities.

In each state the extension activities are supervised by the extension division of the land-grant college of the state. Each of these divisions publishes annually many bulletins and these have wide circulation, especially among the farm-

ing districts of the state. In addition to the day-to-day work of the county agents and of the club leaders, many institutes and other meetings are held every year.

All in all, these extension activities have constituted the largest experiment in adult education which the world has ever seen. They have not only improved agriculture but they have also improved the homes and the general environment of the rural areas.

Smith-Hughes Subventions. The approval of the Smith-Hughes law in 1917 marked the beginning of a new policy of the Federal government toward the financing of education; in brief, it started the policy of providing subventions for education lower than the college level. This act, which is often called the Federal Vocational Education act, provided for subventions to the secondary schools for instruction in agriculture, home economics, and industrial education. It also provided funds for the preparation of teachers of those subjects. According to the provisions of the act, the subvention was to amount to $1,860,-000 in 1917–18, and was to increase annually until a maximum of $7,367,000 was reached in 1925–26. The appropriations have been increased several times since 1925–26, and they now amount to more than $30,000,000 annually. The money is apportioned to the several states on the basis of total population, and in order to be eligible to receive it, the state or local community, or both, shall spend an equal amount for this work; each state and local community must also meet certain other standards prescribed by the act.

These vocational departments of agriculture, home economics, and industrial education are now found in thousands of schools, especially secondary schools, and thousands of new teachers are required annually by the departments. Salaries paid these teachers are somewhat higher than the average salary for teachers of the nation. They must serve 11 months, however, whereas the typical teacher serves only 8 or 9 months; and they must do much more community work than the typical teacher.

General supervision of the Smith-Hughes program is given by the United States office of education. More intensive supervision of the program is provided in each of the states by the division of vocational education of the state department of education. Such a division is required by the Smith-Hughes act. Any school desiring to organize a Smith-Hughes department, or a George-Deen department, should contact its state department of education.

George-Deen Subventions. The George-Deen legislation, enacted in 1937, provides an annual Federal subsidy for training workers for retail selling and other distributive occupation. Departments for the training of these distributive occupations are already found in hundreds of high schools, especially the large schools. The preparation given for such occupations is commonly called "distributive education."

As is the case with the Smith-Hughes subvention, the George-Deen funds are distributed to the states on the basis of total population, and in order to be eligible to receive them, the state or local community, or both, shall spend an equal amount for the program. Certain other standards must also be met.

George-Barden Act (Vocational Education Act of 1946). This Federal law passed in 1946 provided that funds allocated to the George-Deen subvention be replaced and additional funds were granted for vocational education. Under the act vocational education was developed further and funds were allowed to be used in connection with vocational guidance as well as vocational education.

Corporation Schools. Many industrial concerns have found it necessary to supplement the training given in the public schools by special courses for their own employees. Thus, department stores have found that they must train their salesmen, first, by giving them general information with regard to the duties of salespeople and, second, by giving them special instruction in regard to the particular commodities handled in that special establishment.

Another type of corporation school has been organized by industrial concerns. For example, there are schools for the training of printers. Young boys are taken into these schools and brought up in the trade. Instruction in such schools is much more systematic than was the training formerly given to an apprentice in the trade, and it is also more elaborate in that the boy who is attending the school is given some instruction, not only in the particular activi-

AMERICAN GENERALS AND ADMIRALS

General John J. Pershing
(1860–1948)
World War I Commander in Chief
American Expeditionary Force

General Ulysses S. Grant
(1822–1885)
Civil War Commander in Chief
of the Union Army
Eighteenth President of the U.S.

General Robert E. Lee
(1807–1870)
Civil War Commander
Armies of the Confederacy

General George C. Marshall
(1880–1959)
Army Chief of Staff (1939–45)
Secretary of State (1947–49)

General Dwight D. Eisenhower
(1890–1969)
World War II Supreme Commander
Allied Forces in Europe
Thirty-fourth President of the U.S.

General Douglas MacArthur
(1880–1964)
U. S. Armed Forces Commander
in the Far East, World War II
UN Forces Commander in Korea

General William C. Westmoreland
(1914–   )
Commander of U.S. Forces in Vietnam
Army Chief of Staff (1968–   )

Admiral Chester W. Nimitz
(1885–1966)
World War II Commander
of the Pacific Fleet
Chief of Naval Operations (1945–47)

General Maxwell D. Taylor
(1901–   )
UN Forces Commander in Korea
Army Chief of Staff (1955–59)

ARMED SERVICES SCHOOLS

The National War College situated at Fort McNair, D. C., is the top educational institution of our armed forces. Operated under the Joint Chiefs of Staff, it trains selected personnel of the armed forces and State Department in strategic planning and high level policy. There are about 114 students who study intensively for ten months.

This group of buildings at Colorado Springs, Colo., houses the United States Air Force Academy, newest of the Armed Forces schools.

The United States Military Academy at West Point has an authorized strength of 2496 cadets, who are under strict military control during the four year course. Graduates become 2nd lieutenants in the Army or Air Force.

The United States Naval Academy at Annapolis trains the officers for our Navy and Marine Corps. Properly qualified graduates receive commissions as Navy ensigns or Marine Corp 2nd lieutenants. Many foreign naval students are also trained.

The United States Coast Guard Academy at New London, Connecticut, was founded in 1876. Its cadets receive a four year course in engineering, military science and cultural subjects and become Coast Guard ensigns when they graduate. The U. S. Coast Guard is under the jurisdiction of the Secretary of the Treasury.

ties of the trade itself, but in the use of language and in the simpler elements of the sciences which contribute to the trade.

Continuation Schools. The general term "continuation school" has been used to refer to numerous types of organized education, sometimes conducted by the public school system itself, and very frequently conducted by institutions like the Young Men's Christian Association and the Young Women's Christian Association. A continuation school is a school in which students who have completed the ordinary course are carried further and are given training especially suited to the industrial and commercial activities which they are to take up in adult life.

In some states the laws require employers to release their minor workers for attendance on continuation schools during regular working hours in the week. Continuation classes are therefore to be distinguished from the evening courses often organized in public schools for the training of adults who are engaged in industry. Continuation classes are one phase of the general movement, which has been going on in recent years in this country, for the education of industrial workers.

Vocational Guidance. The recorded history of vocational guidance in connection with education and philanthropy begins about the year 1908, and is associated with the names of Frank Parsons in Boston and E. W. Weaver in New York. Parsons' initial efforts were sponsored by philanthropy, and placed major emphasis on two units of the guidance program,—occupational choice and the selection of training programs. The High School Teachers' Association, under the leadership of Mr. Weaver, sponsored the New York movement. The dissemination of occupational information and placement received equal emphasis with occupational choice and selection of training programs. Case study was employed in both cities. Neither effort received financial support from, or administrative recognition by, the public educational system.

From this informal beginning, vocational guidance has developed into a regular part of the program of many school systems. There are three distinct types of school activity which can properly be classed under the head of vocational guidance. First, numerous courses are now provided in high schools and colleges in which information regarding vocational opportunities is given. Second, pupils are offered, especially at the junior high school level, courses known as exploratory courses in which they are given an opportunity through short periods of contact with various lines of activity to discover whether they are interested in mechanical, artistic, literary, or commercial vocations and whether they have aptitude in any of these lines. Third, many schools have official advisers who make careful studies of pupils, testing their intelligence and abilities and consulting with them regarding their tastes and economic needs. Such advisers sometimes come in contact with pupils when they apply for work certificates. At other times they advise pupils throughout their whole school careers. The program of vocational guidance merges into the general program of educational guidance or, as it is sometimes called, the program of personnel guidance.

In its broadest sense, guidance is concerned with every phase of the life of the individual. Many educators, therefore, hold the view that it is the same as education. Other educators, on the contrary, believe that it is concerned only with crises in the life of the individual. The more important of these crises and types of guidance are the following:

1. School guidance
2. Vocational guidance
3. Leisure-time guidance
4. Health guidance

5. Character guidance
6. Home-membership guidance
7. Civic guidance

The Personnel Problem. Between 1908 and 1918 many educational systems and a large number of industrial plants instituted and operated a considerable variety of personnel units, or "special features," more or less independent of one another, but each intended to assist in the solution of some phase, or some phases, of the personnel problem. During the same period three or four national organizations came into being with the solution of personnel problems as their major objective. National vocational guidance conferences met in 1910 and 1912, and a permanent organization was perfected in 1913.

Organization on a national basis was a war-time accomplishment, and at the close of the war the association paid the penalty of overdevelopment on a nonprofessional basis and disbanded. The American Association of Public Employment Offices was launched in 1913 under the auspices of practical students of employment problems. Each of these organizations has been reorganized, and two have changed their names, but none has made any outstanding contribution to the solution of personnel problems. In addition to the above organizations a considerable number of national associations, with major objectives in other or allied fields, have been interested in and have made minor or local or national contribution within the personnel field. The Young Men's Christian Association, The Young Women's Christian Association, the Knights of Columbus, chambers of commerce, the American Association for Labor Legislation, and the Federated American Engineering Societies are illustrations.

World War and Personnel Programs. The war brought into prominence all the operating units of personnel programs and broadened the vision of both employer and educator relative to the interrelation of such units and the desirability of unification. The study of individual differences, which had long commanded the attention of educators, was applied to army personnel service under the direction of nationally known experts. Rating scales were developed, and the beginnings of job analysis, job classification, and job specification were borrowed from industry and were adapted to war emergencies. Rehabilitation programs tended to renew guidance activities in connection with vocational education; and training programs for counselors and personnel directors were offered by a number of colleges and universities. The United States Employment Service, the Training and Dilution Service, the War Labor Policies Board, the War Industries Board, and the Women in Industry Service are examples of war-time governmental services which were instituted to deal with personnel problems.

Overvaluation of war-time experimentation and results has tended to discredit the entire personnel movement, and the re-establishment of public confidence now confronts professional students of personnel problems. The standardization of personnel terminology and a fundamental philosophy of personnel service in its relation to all of the varied experiences which an individual meets in the process of occupational preparation and adjustment demand scientific determination. In the meantime, vocational guidance is still quite generally applied to educational and philanthropic efforts, while employm nt management, industrial relations, and personnel service are correspondingly common terms in industry. The Second International Conference, Barcelona, 1921, unanimously adopted the terms "vocational guidance" and "vocational selection." Vocational guidance was defined as the choice of an occupation for an individual; vocational selection, as the choice of an individual for a given occupation.

No agency has, as yet, instituted a unit program covering the entire personnel field. It is, however, generally conceded that when such a program is formulated it should co-ordinate all personnel functions and should include the study and interpretation of individual differences, methods of personality culture, and a number of other units. The problem is one of general estimation of all personal traits and of general education. The term "vocational guidance" seems too narrow to cover the whole series of broad considerations that thus appear to be important. The term "personnel guidance" has accordingly been suggested.

Personnel Guidance. The increasing complexity of the industrial activities and of the educational opportunities of the country have tended to confuse the individual in making a choice of his life work. Industrial concerns have found, also, that the securing and placement of workers is a complex and difficult task. This is the justification for emphasizing in schools and in industry personnel guidance.

Evening Schools. In the large cities evening classes are very commonly conducted by the public school system. These are attended either by those who seek a continuation of the regular school training or by adults who have had only a limited opportunity of education. In many cases the evening classes are especially organized for immigrants, to whom instruction is given in the use of the English language and in the facts about American institutions. In some cases these classes are organized into systematic curricula, especially by the Y. M. C. A. and similar organizations, and a student may pursue a systematic course leading to high school graduation or to very definite diplomas of a similar type.

Americanization Classes. The Americanization movement is the name given to a group of educational efforts which were greatly stimulated by World War I, and are aimed at the training of immigrants in a knowledge of American institutions. It became a matter of very keen social consciousness during the war that a great many communities made up of foreign-born persons are not acquainted with the institutions of government and social life in the United States. It was found in some of these communities, which have in a measure segregated themselves, that the cultivation of foreign languages has prevented even the children from becoming acquainted with American ways.

In the army, it became apparent that a great many foreigners did not use the English language with sufficient freedom to carry on intercourse with their American neighbors or to make use of the American newspaper. All of these discoveries with regard to the ineffectiveness of ordinary methods of instruction led the public schools and the Federal government, through its department of the interior, to undertake vigorous efforts for the training of all foreigners in the knowledge of American institutions and in the use of the English language. Many industrial concerns allowed their workers a certain amount of time each day to attend classes. These industrial concerns in many instances also provided space in which classes could be held. Sometimes the public school system supplied teachers; again volunteer workers gave instruction. Subsequent curtailment of immigration reduced somewhat the urgent necessity for this type of training, but in all parts of the country the Americanization movement stimulated attention to the need of training for citizenship.

Adult Education. This term was used in England for a long time before it became common in the United States. It referred originally to courses in which men and women who had had only limited educational opportunity were offered instruction in such subjects as religion, literature, and the lines of scientific knowledge which would be helpful to them in their practical lives.

In the United States the movement to provide similar opportunities for persons beyond the age when they could attend public schools began in a variety of different forms.

States have given impetus to the movement by providing funds to be used in public schools and colleges for adult education. In 1957 it was estimated by the *Bureau of the Census* that more than 8 million persons 14 years of age or over were enrolled in Adult Education classes.

In recent years the effort has been made to co-ordinate the various agencies which contribute to adult education. The American Association for Adult Education which was organized in 1926 is an organization which includes representatives of school systems and of philanthropic, social, and religious organizations, librarians, industrial leaders, and representatives of labor colleges and of such independent institutions as Cooper Union of New York, the Mechanics Institute of Rochester, N. Y., and Lewis Institute of Chicago.

Some of the early manifestations of the American movement for adult education are as follows:

Lyceums. An organized plan of instruction of adults was inaugurated under the name lyceum in Millbury, Mass., in 1826. This was a voluntary association of farmers and mechanics formed for "self-culture, community instruction, and mutual discussion of common public interests." By 1839 more than 3000 town lyceums were in existence. They usually met weekly and the members presented essays, gave lectures, or engaged in debates and discussions. Later the practice grew up of inviting paid lecturers to address the lyceums. A national organization was formed in 1831 and held conventions until 1839. The local lyceums continued to flourish until the time of the Civil War.

Chautauquas. The chautauqua institution grew out of an annually conducted camp meeting held by the Methodist Episcopal Church at Fair Point (later named Chautauqua), N. Y. In 1874 its character was changed, largely through the efforts of Bishop Vincent and Lewis Miller, from that of camp meeting to an assembly for studying Sunday school methods. Other subjects of instruction were offered until the whole field of education was covered. Popular entertainment and, later, drama were added. The institution was imitated by many other municipalities, and in 1904 a circuit plan was inaugurated by which the same speakers and entertainers appeared successively at different chautauquas. In the third decade of the 20th century, however, the popularity of the chautauqua circuits declined, in part at least, because of the advent of radio with its easily available program of entertainment and instruction.

Recent Extensions. One of the most widespread forms of adult education is that carried on by commercial correspondence schools. The work is almost wholly vocational and technical. Enrollment is estimated to exceed 2,000,000. See *Correspondence Schools.* Many of the larger universities, following the example of the University of Chicago, provide work by correspondence. Public evening schools and so-called continuation schools, supported by taxes, are numerous in urban centers. In addition there are thousands of business schools operated for a profit. The Y. M. C. A. and kindred organizations are active in supplying education, both vocational and general.

Education for workers is of two types—that offered by employers for immediate practical use in industry, and that provided by agencies for the workers. The Workers' Education bureau of America, organized in 1921, was made the agency for the educational program sponsored by the Ameri-

Science Demonstration at COSI. The Center of Science and Industry in Columbus, Ohio, provides a variety of activities for those who wish to gain a better understanding of past accomplishments and future possibilities in science and industry. Largely financed by donations from the community, the center is visited by over a quarter of a million people annually. (*Photo Courtesy COSI*)

Attentive observers at a **planetarium**—a projection showing an artificial sky in which moving planets of the solar system are seen in their relationship to the sun and to other planets. *(Photo courtesy Center of Science and Industry, Columbus, Ohio)*

An exhibit of the interior of a **coal mine** showing the basic structure of a mine, some of the tools used, and a bird in a cage, used to indicate to the miners the oxygen level in the mine. Coal has been mined for more than 1,000 years—the first coal mine in the U.S. was opened in Virginia during the 1740s. *(Photo courtesy Center of Science and Industry, Columbus, Ohio)*

can Federation of Labor, publishing textbooks and study outlines. Alumni schools have been organized by several colleges and universities and in some cases colleges have opened in the summer courses for persons who are not eligible for regular admission during the year.

The American Library Association, acting through the public libraries, has taken the initiative in bringing informing books to its readers through reading courses and the establishment of county libraries for rural districts. Public museums are usually centers of instruction on scientific topics, and many of the state and national parks provide education in nature lore. No small factor in the growth of adult education is the increasingly popular use of reference works in the home.

Illiteracy. A frequently used measure of the extent of education of a people is the percentage of illiteracy. In the United States, illiteracy is so small that the Census Bureau no longer asks questions regarding it on its census forms. A person unable to read and write in any language is categorized as an illiterate. Illiterates in the United States, generally, are those people who have migrated to the United States and do not use the English language or the few people who do not take advantage of the school system. In November 1969 1.0 per cent of the people 14 years of age and over in the United States were classified as illiterate. The percentage of illiterate whites was 0.7 per cent; the percentage of illiterate blacks was 3.6.

MEDIAN SCHOOL YEARS COMPLETED*

1940	1950	1960	1970	1973	1975
8.6	9.3	10.6	12.2	12.3	12.3

Source: U.S. Department of Commerce, Bureau of the Census. * Median school years completed by those persons 25 years old and over as of April in 1940 to 1960 and as of March in 1970 to 1975 in the United States.

MEDIAN SCHOOL YEARS COMPLETED, BY RACE AND SEX*

Race and Sex	1960	1970	1975
All Races	10.6	12.2	12.3
White	10.9	12.2	12.4
Female	11.2	12.2	12.3
Male	10.7	12.2	12.5
Black	8.0	9.9	10.9
Female	8.6	10.2	11.1
Male	7.7	9.6	10.7

Source: U.S. Department of Commerce, Bureau of the Census. * Median school years completed by those persons 25 years old and over as of March of year shown in the United States.

SCHOOL BUILDINGS

When American educational organization was relatively simple, the school buildings reflected the simplicity of the course of study and of the organization of the classes. The colleges and universities had the most elaborate structures. The design of buildings followed that of European universities or the prevailing style of buildings in America. More recently the function of the building has determined the type of architecture.

In the elementary and secondary schools, buildings range from one or two rooms to very large and elaborate structures. Generally the attempt has been made to eliminate the one-room buildings with their

simple desks and meager equipment. This type of building is gradually being replaced by a much more elaborate structure with fuller equipment. Some of the typical enlargements are as follows:

Playgrounds have been enlarged and equipped with apparatus; the heating and ventilating apparatus and the sanitary equipment of the school have been improved; desks have been provided which fit the pupils and furnish better conditions for schoolwork; greater attention has been paid to classroom lighting; rooms have been provided for special activities of the school such as laboratory and shop activities, dramatics, physical education and health, music, art, the lunch program, and the assembly program.

In many of the enlarged buildings the schools have been given responsibilities in addition to the education of elementary or secondary school children. They have become community educational centers. As such they are used for adult education programs and as public gathering places for educational meetings.

A number of problems have arisen as people decided to enlarge their school buildings. The costs of the larger buildings are greater. School authorities and citizens have had to make major decisions about educational programs, design, and size of facilities. In cities with high land values, it is sometimes necessary to erect a school building of several stories in order to provide outdoor space for school playgrounds. The larger buildings must of necessity be equipped with fire protection devices. The evolution of the modern school building has thus been in the direction of increasingly commodious housing for complex educational activities. As a result, many new ideas have developed in the design of school buildings. Some of the recent innovations in school design have been: the campus type of school at which several buildings, each housing special facilities, are located on a large compound; odd-shaped classrooms that deviate from a rectangular shape; and buildings shaped to eliminate corridors.

Standard Buildings. Standards have been set for school buildings. A number of devices have been developed for scoring buildings, so that communities may have a basis for judging the efficiency of any particular building.

In general the standards have been concerned with several major divisions of the building; its site, the structure of the building, the classroom, the special rooms, and the service systems. Scorecards have been designed to evaluate a school building and give numerical scores to the divisions. The building is rated on the basis of its score. The various points on the cards are scored with numbers that indicate the relative importance of each item in making up an estimate of the building as a whole.

Community Centers. There is a widespread movement in the United States in the direction of the use of school buildings for purposes other than the instruction of children. Some years ago attention was drawn to the fact that there is a great waste in public resources when school buildings are left empty during the late afternoon and evening after the children have gone home. Proper use of the buildings, it was pointed out, will make it possible for a community to carry on various lines of useful social activities at hours when the school building would otherwise be unused.

As a result of the agitation for the wider use of school plants, many school buildings have been equipped with auditoriums and other accommodations for social purposes. These auditoriums serve the regular school for assemblies and the community for all kinds of gatherings. For example, in the city of Rochester, New York, the school buildings have been extensively used for political meetings, social meetings, lectures, moving picture exhibitions, and other similar purposes. In the schools of the city of New York a regular system of free public lectures has been carried on for years, through which people in various parts of the city have been given access to types of information which can be contributed only by specialists in various fields of science and literature.

In the consolidated schools of Colorado, extensive programs of community betterment have been centered. These large consolidated schools are in some cases used for community church services; they have equipment for motion picture exhibitions; and they are used in many cases for meetings leading to the improvement of roads and to other civic undertakings. In one of the rural districts of Wisconsin a school became the center for a dairying business which was carried on co-operatively by all of the patrons of the school. In North Dakota, the consolidated schools have been used for dramatic exhibitions, and the people have found that various forms of public entertainment can be provided economically through these institutions. School buildings have been used also as demonstration centers for the extension courses given by state universities and by the Federal department of agriculture. Physical education has been stimulated through these community meetings, and in many cases the community has been led through these social gatherings to increase the school equipment.

EDUCATIONAL FOUNDATIONS

Gifts for the endowment of educational institutions have been common in America since the earliest colonial times. Recently several large donors have preferred to give, not to particular institutions, but to a general foundation empowered to distribute the funds to various institutions as may seem wise.

Peabody Education Fund. The first of the educational foundations was established in 1867 when George Peabody, of Massachusetts, gave to a board of trustees composed of fifteen men the sum of $3,000,000 to be used in the development of education in the more destitute portions of the Southern and the Southwestern states.

John F. Slater Fund. In 1882 John Slater set up a foundation which was to help in uplifting the "lately emancipated population of the Southern states."

The Carnegie Foundation. In 1905 Andrew Carnegie gave to a board of trustees $10,000,000 to be utilized for the purpose of pensioning college professors. The original plan adopted by this foundation, known as the Carnegie Foundation for the Advancement of Teaching, contemplated the retirement of college professors after 25 years of active service. It was assumed that after such a period of service it would be better for institutions to recruit their faculties by appointing younger men. At the same time the retired men would be able to carry on productive literary work which would increase the materials of instruction and promote the intellectual life of the nation.

Closely related to the Carnegie Foundation were certain scientific organizations set up by the same donor. The Carnegie Institute was established in 1902 for the purpose of promoting scientific research and publishing the results. It was assumed that many scientific and literary workers could greatly increase their output if they were supplied with research assistance. Carnegie also established a technical school in Pittsburgh, and ultimately created what is known as the Carnegie Corporation, holding large funds to be dispensed for any educational or charitable purpose.

The Carnegie Foundation has been a highly influential body in determining educational practice in this country. It was obliged to abandon its original plan for the pensioning of college professors. In lieu of this program, it has adopted a system of insurance which is much less expensive than the pension scheme originally projected.

In the course of its operations, the Carnegie Foundation has made numerous studies which have been used in defining the character of higher institutions. Reports have been prepared on schools of medicine, schools of law, and schools of engineering. Their regular reports have contained much information in regard to the organization of colleges and universities.

Other reports related to the studies made of higher education have been those dealing with the quality of teaching in the high school, the role of physical instruction in schools, and the development of a definition of a unit of instruction. The latter, commonly called the *Carnegie Unit*, has been used widely as a standard.

Another major project of the Carnegie Foundation was the establishment of and aid to libraries. Many libraries throughout America bear the name Carnegie because of the contributions made by the foundation to their support.

Rockefeller Boards. A great educational foundation was endowed by John D. Rockefeller in 1902, under the name of the General Education Board. This organization is closely related to the Rockefeller Institution of Medical Research and the Rockefeller Foundation, the latter being a general corporation supplied with large funds. It was created in 1913 by a special act of the legislature of the State of New York as a corporate body "to promote the well-being of mankind throughout the world."

The General Education Board has used its funds in large measure for the encouragement of colleges and universities. This encouragement has been rendered through direct donation to the endowments and through gifts to maintain higher salary schedules, the latter being a special type of appropriation which was undertaken in order to meet emergencies which arose in most institutions of higher learning after World War I.

The Russell Sage Foundation. The Russell Sage Foundation, established in 1907 by Mrs. Russell Sage after the death of her husband, has co-operated with numerous social agencies for the improvement of the administration of charities and other social enterprises. For a period during its history, the Russell Sage Foundation conducted a division of educational investigations. This division issued numerous reports, notably certain reports comparing the activities of different states in educational matters and showing the rank of these states in educational achievements. It also published elaborate studies and scales for measuring various types of school work such as scales for the measurement of handwriting, for spelling, and for reading.

The Cleveland Foundation. The Cleveland Foundation is a community organization established in 1914 by Mr. F. H. Goff in the city of Cleveland. At the time of the establishment of this foundation Mr. Goff was president of the Cleveland Trust Company. His experience with many of the large estates in Cleveland showed him that there are many persons of wealth who do not know how to dispose advantageously of such funds as they are willing to give to worthy enterprises. He induced a number of these persons to turn over their estates to a corporation made up of a board of trustees, appointed in part through public officials and in part by representative bodies of citizens. This board of trustees was constituted into a community trust, and was authorized by its charter to utilize such funds as came into its possession for any worthy social undertaking, especially in the city of Cleveland.

Acting under this charter, the Cleveland Foundation carried on an extensive survey of the public school system of the city. Reference has been made in an earlier paragraph to this survey, which is one of the most complete scientific studies of a school system that have been made in the United States. Following the school survey, came a survey of the recreational opportunities of the city, and then a survey of the administration of criminal law through the courts.

The activity of the Cleveland Foundation has been extensively imitated. The New York City Community Trust is organized on the same general plan as the Cleveland Foundation. In other parts of the country, also, bankers have seen in the example of the Cleveland Foundation the possibilities of such a proper and permanent organization of the estates of the country as will benefit the communities in which they have been accumulated. It seems probable that this type of foundation will be set up in a great many communities.

The Commonwealth Fund. The Commonwealth Fund is a relatively new foundation established in 1917 by the Harkness estate and chartered in New York. This foundation devotes itself to various philanthropic and educational enterprises. It has organized a special committee to deal with juvenile delinquency, is carrying on demonstration clinics in a number of cities, and is co-operating with juvenile courts. It has also organized a special committee to deal with the problems of educational research. This committee receives and acts upon various proposals made by students of education in different parts of the country, and subsidizes investigations which seem to be promising for the promotion of educational organization and research.

The Ford Foundation. The Ford Foundation was established in 1936 by Henry Ford and his son Edsel Ford for the administration of funds "for scientific, educational, and charitable purposes, all for the public welfare." The avowed purpose of its educational program is "to strengthen, expand, and improve educational facilities and to promote greater equality of educational opportunity." In 1951 the foundation began a program of assistance in five fields: the establishment of peace; strengthening of democracy; strengthening of the economy; education for a democratic society; and individual behavior and human relations. Both American and foreign institutions were involved. Economic, educational, and social assistance has been given to south and southeast Asia and the Near East. In December 1955 the Ford Foundation announced the allocation of $500,000,000 to 4157 privately-supported colleges, universities, and hospitals in the United States—the largest philanthropic donation ever made. The income for the Foundation is approximately $100,000,000 yearly.

The W. K. Kellogg Foundation. Established in 1930, this foundation had as its original purpose: "the promotion of the welfare, comfort, health, care, education, feeding, clothing, sheltering and safe guarding of children and youth." Later the purpose of the foundation was broadened to "receive and administer funds for educational or charitable purposes." The major activities of the foundation have been in education, medicine and public health, agriculture, dentistry, and nursing. One aspect of these activities

which has received special attention has been administration. The Cooperative Program in Educational Administration financed by a grant from this foundation has done much to stimulate interest in the administration of public schools. Eight centers were established for the program and approximately 140 institutions participated in a series of studies designated to analyze the problems of the school system and evaluate the school administrator's educational needs.

EDUCATIONAL SOCIETIES

Professional workers, engaged in the cultivation of literary and scientific subjects, are organized into numerous national societies. The American Historical Association, for example, includes those who are professionally connected with departments of history in colleges and universities and also many of those who give instruction in secondary schools. This association meets once a year in sessions at which papers are presented by its members, reporting the lines of research in which they are engaged. It also publishes a journal, the *Historical Review*, which includes original articles and reviews of all the publications in the field of history. The association appoints from time to time committees which make reports on various professional topics connected with the development of history as a subject of instruction. Especially significant have been the reports of committees outlining programs for history courses in secondary schools.

The statements which have been made about the American Historical Association can be repeated for a long list of learned societies both in the fields of the humanities and in the domains of the natural sciences.

American Association for the Advancement of Science. The associations which bring together representatives of the natural sciences are affiliated in one general organization known as the American Association for the Advancement of Science. This larger and more comprehensive organization is patterned after the older British association and is made up of a number of sections, such as the sections for chemistry, physics, mathematics, anthropology, and so on. The American association meets once a year for a winter session, at which time there are general sessions and sessions of each of the sections. In addition, there are occasional summer meetings which bring together certain divisions of the association.

National Education Association. Besides the special professional societies, there is an organization which includes teachers in all grades of schools. This is known as the National Education Association. This association, under various names, has been in existence since 1857. It is organized under a Federal charter, and has recently reconstructed its internal government so that the national meeting is now a representative body made up of delegates from the various state and local associations of teachers. The general association is subdivided for professional purposes into certain groups, such as the American Association of School Administrators, the classroom teachers, the department of higher education, and so on. These various divisions and departments organize programs at which papers are read, dealing with the special interest represented by the department. The general association, or representative assembly, deals with legislative matters and appoints committees and listens to their reports.

State Teachers' Associations. Affiliated with the national education organization are state associations. These in turn are made up in some states of sectional associations. Annual meetings are held by these associations, at which speakers present professional topics and committees report on various interests of the teaching body.

The National Catholic Educational Association. This is an organization of individuals and institutions interested in Catholic education. The origin of the association was in St. Louis, Missouri in 1904 where it grew out of a joint meeting of several other Catholic educational groups. Now there are seven departments of the association; Major Seminary, Minor Seminary, College and University, Secondary School, Elementary School, Special Education, and School Superintendent. At the present time the total membership is over 10,000. The association holds national and regional meetings. Important in its program is the publication of its *Newsletter, Catholic Education News Digest, Catholic High School Quarterly*, and other bulletins.

National Research Council. During World War I the National research council came into existence as a group of scientists contributing to the activities of the departments of war and navy and to the scientific inquiries which were necessary to provide the material resources of the country for the war. So significant were the contributions of the research council to the national war policies, that it was continued and has received generous endowments for its work. It now administers a series of fellowships and funds for the development of scientific research. It has its seat in Washington, and is directed by a staff of central officers, who not only administer the various divisions of the council but promote in general ways the development of science throughout the country.

The American Council and Other Bodies. Numerous other educational organizations have their seats in Washington. Notable among these are the American Academy of Science which is made up of 100 selected scientists; the American Geographical Society, which publishes a journal of geography but is otherwise only a loosely organized society; and, finally, the American Council on Education, which is one of the newest national educational organizations. The American Council is made up of representatives from various educational associations. It has a director and meets in annual session for the transaction of business. Among the constituent organizations which send delegates to the meetings of the American Council are the Association of American Universities, the Association of Land-Grant Colleges, the Association of State Universities, and other similar organizations.

Standardizing Associations. Mention has been made in an earlier paragraph of certain standardizing associations, such as the North Central Association of Colleges and Secondary Schools. These standardizing associations, while having no authority, prepare approved lists which designate selected colleges and secondary schools in various sections of the country as of high grade. The desire of institutions to appear on such lists is so keen that the associations have acquired very wide influence, even though they have no official public standing.

Mention may be made in this connection of certain professional organizations such as the American Medical Association. This is an organization, including all the physicians in the country, which publishes both a technical journal and a journal of a popular type intended to promote the interests of public sanitation and health. It has, through its central council, standardized medical schools. Similar professional associations exist among the lawyers, dentists, and other professional groups.

Parent-Teacher Associations. Numerous associations have been organized with a view to making the community better informed on school problems. Sometimes these organizations are initiated by school officers who find it desirable to get into closer communication with their patrons; sometimes they originate in the spontaneous desire of parents to improve the conditions which surround their children in the schools. They represent in a sense a revival of the town meeting, which was the original civic organization in control of the school district. While the town meeting has been replaced by representative assemblies for the enactment of ordinances and statutes, these newer forms of organization are felt by the community to be too remote from so vital an interest as the protection and schooling of children. While people are willing to leave property and public interests such as roadmaking and policing to their representatives, they want to be fully informed about the teachers who have charge of their children and about the organization of the school. The following statements are quoted from or based on bulletins published by the Office of Education, which describe the rise and development of these organizations:

Mothers' meetings inaugurated in 1855, in connection with the kindergarten movement in the United States, seem to have been the precursors of the parent-teacher associations. A mothers' conference was called by a kindergarten training teacher in Chicago in 1894. Three years later a national congress of mothers was called in Washington, D. C., by Alice McLellan Birney and others, in which the interests of all little children in the home and the community were discussed. A permanent organization of mothers was formed, and plans for the study of problems relating to child welfare were developed. In 1900, a formal charter was granted this organization in the District of Columbia.

National Organizations. Mothers and teachers discovered that they could accomplish more if united into a co-operative organization than was possible when each worked separately. Parent-teacher associations came into existence in response to the expressed need. Other organizations with various names but similar purposes came into existence also and united in this national organization. Among them were the parents' leagues, home and school associations, mothers' leagues, mothers' unions, preschool groups, reading circles, etc. In 1908, the National Congress of Mothers changed its name to include parent-teacher associations, and in 1915 a new charter was secured.

The movement has developed until the parent-teacher association has become the dominant national activity of parents and teachers. Membership grew from about 200,000 in 1920 to more than 1,500,000 in 1931. In 1958, the membership was 11,018,156. Summer courses for training leaders were given in colleges for the first time in 1922 at Columbia university.

The conditions under which the national organization operates may be briefly summarized as follows:

(1) The *annual convention* has all power over the conduct of the organization and is a delegate-voting body representing the state branches.

(2) The *board of managers* (composed of officers, state presidents, and the committee chairmen whom they elect) is authorized by the convention to carry on its work between the annual meetings, and must report annually to the convention.

(3) The *executive committee* is the servant of the board of managers and performs for it such duties as the board may assign to it, reporting to the board and the convention and having no independent authority.

(4) The *state branch* is the representative of the congress in the state and is pledged to carry out the objects and policies of the national organization.

(5) The *district organization* is the representative of the state branch in the district and is therefore pledged to carry out the state and national objects and policies in its territory.

(6) The *county council* represents the state branch in the county and carries the congress work to the individual members in every locality.

(7) The *local association* unites the members for carrying out the plans of the congress and for the promotion of the welfare of the children in the community.

(8) The *individual member* belongs directly to both the state and the national congress and is responsible for the attainment of its objects.

ACTIVITIES OF ORGANIZATIONS

A study of the reports of activities in parent-teacher associations in many states reveals a diversity of activities, but one general aim,—to surround children with conditions favorable to their growth. Among other things, this involves the education of parents in caring for the physical and mental health of preschool children. As one means of pursuing this object, the national organization, or congress, sponsors a so-called summer round-up of children, the purpose of which is to send to school in the first grade a class of children 100 per cent free from remediable defects. The method employed is to induce parents to secure in May a physical examination of their children who will begin school the following September, a second examination in September being held to determine the extent of corrections made.

Other objects, sponsored by special committees of the national congress, include safeguarding the health of school age children and the guidance of high school children by means of a study of social hygiene. For the latter purpose there is a committee on mental hygiene, headed by a competent psychologist.

The following list sets forth some of the concrete results of parent-teacher activities as reported by county superintendents:

1. Terms of schools lengthened.
2. School attendance improved.
3. System of uniform textbooks established.
4. Improvement in schoolhouses in sanitation and apparatus.
5. New school buildings erected.
6. Schools standardized.
7. Playground equipment purchased.
8. Instruments purchased for the schools.
9. Library books and pictures purchased for the schools.
10. School grounds beautified.
11. Warm noon lunch served.
12. Milk provided for underweight children.
13. Dental clinics established.
14. Physical examination of school children and remediable defects corrected.
15. Cases of tardiness lessened.
16. Junior banks organized.
17. Picture shows supervised.
18. Reading rooms sponsored.
19. Health crusades sponsored.
20. Scholarships created.
21. Standard of home life raised through child study.
22. Friction in community eliminated.
23. A friendly relationship between parents and teachers established, thus making discipline easier for teachers and creating a stimulus for better work among students.
24. The moral standard of the community improved.
25. Parents visit school, becoming acquainted with modern methods of education and curriculum.
26. Phases of child amusement and recreation in community improved.
27. Night schools established.
28. Work accomplished in the removal of illiteracy.
29. Community halls built.
30. More students finish eighth grades and high schools.
31. Kindergartens established.
32. Equipment for school lunches purchased.
33. As a whole, the parent-teacher association acts as a socializing and educating project in any community.

Preschool Groups. Two important activities which are the outgrowth of parent-teacher associations are the preschool study groups and reading groups. These consist of parents of little children under school age. Programs for these groups include the subjects of child care and training, proper diet for the young child, proper clothing, advice to expectant mothers.

The activities of the Co-operative Education Association of Virginia are, as indicated by the name, largely concerned with raising money in order to improve the school plant. They finance school lunches, improve the social and recreational life of the community, and co-operate with the school board in its efforts. Many libraries have been installed as a result of the efforts of these organizations.

SPECIAL TYPES OF AMERICAN SCHOOLS

Special Schools for Men and for Women. Higher schools exclusively for boys were organized in the early colonies and most of the older institutions, such as Harvard, Yale, and Princeton, are institutions exclusively for the training of boys.

The practice of excluding girls from schools led to the establishment of a group of secondary schools and colleges designed to give higher education to women. In 1820 Mrs. Emma Willard secured $4000 for the establishment of a female seminary in Troy, New York. Since then a number of great endowments have been devoted to the education of women at Vassar, Wellesley, Smith, and other centers.

Coeducation. The common schools generally are open to girls as well as to boys, but in some cases private secondary schools have opened their doors to boys only. Likewise, many private colleges enrolled only boys or only girls. As the Western states organized higher institutions supported by public taxation, and as the concept of the "common school" extended into secondary education, it became politically impossible to exclude women from the privileges of public institutions. Likewise, after World War II, as pressures for college education among young men and women increased, many higher institutions which formerly enrolled only one sex found it necessary to become coeducational. Many of the traditionally all-male or all-female colleges and universities have made arrangements to enroll both sexes. Thus Harvard University has Radcliffe College, and Vassar College has enrolled male students. At the present time many other institutions at the secondary school and college level are taking similar steps.

Correspondence Schools. The enthusiasm of President Harper of the University of Chicago, and others interested in wider education of all classes of people, led to the organization of correspondence courses under the supervision of universities and of special schools organized to administer such courses.

Education by correspondence had a wide appeal and many correspondence-study schools arose. Many have been very successful. One of the great limitations in their work is that many students start courses but do not have the persistence to carry them on.

The recent development of extensive programs of Adult Education carried on by institutions of higher education and public and private schools has almost entirely eliminated the need for correspondence schools except in the areas of certain technical skills. And the programs of adult education are being encouraged to spread their activities into these areas.

Experimental Schools. Many schools have been organized in different parts of the United States for the purpose of demonstrating the feasibility of some educational reform. These experimental schools often have been organized in connection with teacher-training institutions. One of the famous schools of this sort was the Dewey school, organized by John Dewey in Chicago for the purpose of correcting the formal practices of schools.

The University of Missouri developed an experimental school which attempted to have a course of study without the use of textbooks. Mrs. Johnson's school at Fairhope, Alabama was organized on the general principle that children should be allowed great freedom. Other schools have been established around such ideas as 1) a curriculum based on the study of great books; 2) a curriculum when a student concentrates on only one or two subjects at a time until they are mastered; and 3) curricula which enable a student to study independently and at his own pace for learning.

EDUCATION OF DEFECTIVES

There are certain types of physical and mental deficiencies which debar a student from participation in the ordinary activities of school life. Thus, a child who is blind is of necessity excluded by that defect from many of the ordinary school opportunities. The larger cities and most of the states have accordingly provided special institutions for the training of the blind. It is even more necessary to provide for children who are deaf.

Schools for the Blind. Various systems of training have been provided for the blind. It has been necessary to prepare a special type of book which can be read by touch. The earlier forms of letters used in books for the blind were reproductions of the ordinary alphabet, but it was soon found that this form of letters is not especially adapted to recognition through touch, and a point system, known as Braille, was substituted. In 1958 an audio machine was developed for reading by the blind.

Schools for the Deaf. In the training of the deaf there are two systems: one attempts to make the deaf person as nearly like a normal individual as possible by teaching him to understand what other people are saying through a careful observation of lip movements; the other system resorts to communication through hand movements, where various positions of the hand and fingers reproduce either the alphabet or word-wholes. Deafness is very frequently accompanied by inability to speak, and many of the schools for the deaf attempt to train their pupils, not only to recognize language when it is used by normal individuals, but also to participate in conversation through articulation which is acquired without the advantage of the sense of hearing. A deaf person has to learn to control his vocal cords by watching his own mouth and the vocal organs of others and then imitating the positions which produce sounds that he never hears.

Deficiencies in General Intelligence. Another group of defects which appear in abnormal individuals are very much more difficult to deal with. These are imbecility and feeble-mindedness. The most extreme cases in this group are of the custodial type and cannot be dealt with in the schools at all. For pupils who have some intelligence, but not a normal degree, special classes or special schools have been organized in many centers, and industrial training has been given as a substitute for ordinary school training, in the hope that the abnormal individuals may be made independent of charity. Formerly it was assumed that children of inferior intelligence should be associated with normal children in order that they might get the advantage of such association. It was also argued that normal children benefit by contact with slower children. It has become entirely evident, however, on the basis of accumulating experience, that the mixing of children of different degrees of intelligence is not an advantage, and methods have been developed of segregating children of inferior ability so that they may receive the special instruction necessary for their training.

The Emotionally Disturbed Child. Recently, great concern has been shown to the child who is emotionally disturbed. Special schools and classes are being organized for children with this defect. Increasing numbers of children have injuries to their personalities because of family situations or unfavorable social conditions. When a child is so afflicted often he cannot profit from instructions in the regular school or class. Teachers with special training and understanding of the problems of the emotionally disturbed person conduct educational programs which lead to the rehabilitation of children and enable them to take their places in society. Some states now have laws recognizing this condition in children and require that special classes or schools be organized when there are enough children classified as emotionally disturbed to form a class.

RELIGIOUS EDUCATION

The secular character of American schools has led to an elimination of religious instruction from the public schools. It is contended by many citizens that this is a misfortune, not merely because religion is thus in a measure eliminated from the common body of knowledge dispensed through the schools, but also because there is withdrawn from the schools the opportunity for the teaching of moral maxims and principles which would be advantageous in the training of the children. There has been a constant effort on the part of certain groups to re-introduce into the system of public instruction the teaching of the Bible and other forms of moral and religious subject matter. The result is that much legislation has been proposed and enacted, and numerous court decisions have been rendered on the general matter of the use of the Bible in the public schools. In some cases this legislation restricts the use of the Bible to a reading from the text without comment of any kind whatsoever. In other cases the decisions of the courts, based on legislation, have eliminated the Bible altogether from the school, making it illegal to read from the Bible even for opening exercises.

Various experiments are being tried to provide instruction in religion without attempting to modify the secular character of the schools. Experiments of this type have arranged some form of religious teaching outside of the regular school hours. In some cases children have been excused from the school for a period in the day and have gone to some neighboring church where religious instruction of suitable type has been given.

Other plans have arranged for instruction in Sunday schools to be supervised and credited by the public schools. The so-called Colorado plan is of this type. High schools approve the work of Sunday classes and treat such work as regular courses to be counted toward high school graduation.

Religious instruction has in recent years been greatly improved in Sunday schools as well as in classes of the type mentioned above. Many Protestant churches now provide normal classes for the training of teachers and a number of commissions have been active in reorganizing and enriching the courses of study used in Sunday schools.

Parochial Schools. Throughout its history, the Roman Catholic Church has been a patron of education. During the medieval period the clergy of this Church were the only teachers of the people. This special regard for education was retained by the Lutheran and various other Protestant bodies. At the present time, not satisfied with the instruction given in secular schools, these churches conduct numerous parochial schools and colleges. In these institutions, instruction in the conventional subjects is supplemented by instruction in religion and in Church history. In the case of the Roman Catholic Church, members of the religious orders are sometimes in charge of these schools. Since 1900 enrollments in elementary and secondary non-public schools have steadily increased both in numbers and percentage of the total students of full-time day schools. They now account for approximately 13 per cent of all full-time elementary and secondary school enrollments. The schools of the Roman Catholic Church enroll almost 90 per cent of these non-public school students. Protestant and other denominational schools account for about 6 per cent.

Of great concern to the Roman Catholic Church is its inability to support its extensive system of schools. Among plans suggested by leaders in the Church to do this are: that federal, state, and local tax funds be given for Church schools; that tax rebates be given to parents who send their children to parochial schools; and that the Church school system be reorganized.

Among the protestant churches the Lutheran Church has the largest number of students attending parochial schools. Other protestant churches having well-organized parochial schools are the Protestant Episcopal, Seventh-Day Adventist, Friends, Presbyterian, Methodist, Baptist, and Congregational churches.

The greatest concentration of parochial school enrollments is in ten states: New York, Pennsylvania, Illinois, Ohio, Michigan, New Jersey, California, Massachusetts, Wisconsin, and Missouri.

Control over the parochial schools is exercised by the various states in different ways. It was clearly determined in 1816 by the *Dartmouth Case* that private educational institutions had the right to exist. The *Oregon Case* in 1925 established that it was a violation of the 14th amendment to the U.S. Constitution for a state to require parents to send to public schools their children who were subject to the compulsory education laws.

Generally, the state laws regulating the parochial school are the same as those which apply to all individuals or organizations conducting businesses, charitable undertakings, or educational institutions. Legislation regarding the parochial schools is usually concerned with 1) incorporation, 2) state approval, 3) compulsory education, 4) public support, 5) tax exemptions, and 6) occupational licensing.

TEXTBOOKS

From the beginning, American common schools have been reading schools. In this respect they differ from the common schools of Europe, where instruction is given largely in oral form by the teacher. American schools have therefore needed from the outset a supply of reading books. As the curriculum was extended, reading material in each subject was put into the hands of the pupils, and they were required to prepare their lessons from this reading material.

The publication of textbooks, throughout American school history, has been left very largely to private initiative, and as a result there have grown up in connection with the schools of the country numerous large publishing houses which specialize in the preparation and publication of textbooks. The number of textbook publishers has increased in past years and the stiff competition has resulted in great improvement in appearance and content of textbooks. A large percentage of the salesmen for these companies are former teachers or school administrators and their work is done on a high plane of professional service to schools and teachers. Professional Bookmans Association of America (P.B.A.) was formed in 1947 and now has chapters from coast to coast. This organization emphasizes the professional aspect of selling and distributing textbooks, supplementary books, and reference books. There is also the American Textbook Publishers Institute (A.T.P.I.), an organization of publishers representing a high percentage of all publishers, which has the aim of improving all procedures which go into the making of modern textbooks.

State Regulation. Legislation has been passed providing for the official adoption by some authorized public body of a list of books which may be used in different grades of school. State textbook commissions are defended because they secure uniformity throughout the state, and this is regarded by some as an advantage, in that it permits children to move from center to center without being compelled to supply themselves with an entirely new equipment of school textbooks. On the other hand, state adoption is criticized because, at the time of adoptions, competition between various publishing houses frequently runs very high.

RADIO AND TELEVISION IN EDUCATION

In the early 1920's experimentation began with the use of radio in the classrooms. A notable experiment was made in Cleveland, Ohio schools, where radio lessons became a part of the curriculum. State-wide "School-Of-the-Air" programs have been developed and schools equipped with radios have had available to them a wide variety of educational subjects. In these programs a yearly schedule of educational topics is developed and schools are supplied with work books and teachers' manuals to supplement the broadcast. The movement for radio reception in the schools has been so widespread that now most of the schools of the United States are equipped with radio receiving sets and the Federal government has been encouraged to allow time on the air for educational programs. Schools use different means to take advantage of the many radio programs designed for educational use. A school may be equipped with a central radio receiving set and the desired program monitored to the classroom. In other schools each room is equipped with a receiving set. Another procedure used is to record a program on a tape recorder, edit it, and then present it to the students whenever the program fits the lesson.

A more recent teaching device is television. Experiments are now under way to determine its most effective use as an educational medium. Experimentation is taking place in two major areas: (1) the operation of equipment and the mechanics of using television as a teaching device; and (2) the development of proper programs for school use. A study in 1958 found that 50 institutions of higher education were experimenting with the use of closed circuit television in the classroom. Numerous secondary schools throughout the nation are beginning to use closed circuit television as a means to improve the quality of education. The *Ford Foundation* has given a large grant of money for the purpose of experimentation in the area of programming for educational television. One phase of the National Defense Education Act, passed by Congress in 1958, is concerned with research and experimentation in the use of the radio and television for educational purposes.

The first commercial television station owned by an educational institution was Iowa State College's commercial outlet, WOI-TV. Kansas State College of Manhattan, Kansas, was the first educational institution to apply for and be granted a non-commercial channel for television.

According to the United States Office of Education, there are presently 257 non-commercial educational television stations reserved. Of these over 60 are actually in operation. A total of 12 states have 65 state-wide networks of television devoted solely to education, either in operation or proposed. To show the interest developing in educational circles, 46 of the states have 199 colleges and universities which offer courses in Television. In addition, 268 colleges in 46 states and the District of Columbia offer college credit for network television courses. Television in the schools is not limited to colleges only. In 30 of the states, school districts report the regular use of television in the school programs.

A type of television of particular use to the schools is "Closed Circuit" television. This is a system which transmits a video signal from a sending camera to television receivers directly connected by a cable. In the use of this type of television, the installation can include a single room where one camera focuses on a speaker or demonstration and receiving sets are located in various areas of the room. By the use of this procedure, large rooms with large groups of students can have the closeness of small group procedures. Another use of "Closed Circuit" television provides for complex installations connecting numerous school buildings.

One experiment in educational television was the Mid-west Program on Airborne Television Instruction. At an altitude of 23,000 feet over Indiana UHF Channels number 72 and 76 were used to telecast to a six-state area of Illinois, Indiana, Kentucky, Michigan, Ohio, and Wisconsin. The potential audience was 5 million students in 13,000 schools. The program hoped to prove that television could be a means for economy in education while enriching the teaching of children.

A recent invention enables television pictures to be recorded on tape, called "Video Tape." This tape is usable for delayed re-broadcasting. Like radio tape recording, it can be edited and used by schools when the recording fits into the curriculum. At the present time, this invention is considered too costly to be practical for extensive school use.

EARLY CHILDHOOD EDUCATION

EARLY Childhood Education normally consists of a period previous to formal schooling (pre-school), kindergarten, and the primary grades (one through three) with a program adapted to the developmental needs of children 3 to 9 years of age.

During the first three or four years of life, a tremendous amount of learning takes place. These early years should be supplemented with an enriched program by providing the opportunity for each child to develop to his full potential.

Greater strides in research during the decade of 1960 will probably result in curriculum changes which will attain a better balance in basic education and surpass the progress of the past era.

DEVELOPMENT OF THE PRESCHOOL MOVEMENT

The preschool movement can be traced back as far as the 4th century B.C. when Plato stressed the importance of early childhood, and the necessity for family co-operation. A study of ancient history reveals that some of the early philosophers, preachers, and educational reformers considered the significance of parent-child relationships, and made plans for improved education for infants and young children. However, it is in the 17th century that early childhood education as we know it received its impetus.

As noted in the History of Education (pp. 1629–1634) several educational leaders have made valuable early contributions to the preschool movement. The pioneer work of Comenius, Rousseau, Basedow, Pestalozzi, and Froebel in this field is particularly noteworthy. More recently, important additions were made by Montessori, Dewey, and others. Early in the 20th century, organized planning for preschool training led to the introduction of institutions designed specifically for this purpose. In England (1908), for example, the consultation Committee of the Board of Education recommended good nursery schools to take care of children too young to attend regular schools.

The first preschools in America were adaptations of the English idea, differing however in aims, motives, and organization. The American preschool was promoted in the interest of psychological and educational research and was concerned with what could be learned from children rather than taught them. Social forces that prevailed in the country after 1890 further influenced their development. The number of schools increased rapidly following the close of World War I.

Nursery schools served chiefly the children of the middle classes prior to 1933 when the *Federal Emergency Relief Administration* aided in establishing federally-supported *Emergency Nursery Schools* principally for underprivileged children of the depression years. Their purpose was to provide employment for unemployed teachers and to promote physical, mental, social, and emotional well being for young children. The *Works Progress Administration* took over the supervision of the Emergency Schools in 1935. During World War II many of these schools revised their programs to meet the needs of children in defense areas.

The *National Association for Nursery Education* founded in 1931 has assumed leadership and guidance in the field. Other private and government organizations have promoted the popularity and public acceptance of nursery education by emphasizing the importance of the early formative years. The 20th-century school was planned not to give custodial care nor to impart specific moral or intellectual information, but to enrich experiences and to supplement rather than to supplant the activities of the home.

THE NURSERY SCHOOL PROGRAM

A Nursery School offers a valuable supervised educational program for children beginning at the approximate age of three years by making possible experiences which promote social, physical, mental, and emotional development. It aims to meet the developmental needs of the age levels before Kindergarten and to provide children with a variety of educational experiences. The term nursery school is often misused and should be differentiated from that of "day school" or "child care center."

Lack of legislation concerning facilities for nursery school age children in many states is responsible for the variety of institutions labeled "Nursery Schools." The diversity of organization and sponsorship makes it almost impossible to obtain accurate information and statistics concerning this area of preschool education. Existing programs range from mere baby sitting to well-run nursery schools which meet high educational standards. The type of organization, the methods of sponsorship, or the age of the children in attendance in no way determine the quality of the school. However, there is among preschool specialists some general agreement as to the essentials and objectives of a good nursery school. These are listed in a pamphlet by the National Association for Nursery School Education, written in 1942, entitled "Some Ways of Distinguishing a Good Nursery School."

The Nursery School program includes play periods and routine activities usually designated as free play time, juice time, story time, music time, rest time, and bathroom time. The schedule must be balanced and arranged to alternate listening with talking, active with quiet play and regulation with freedom. No element of the daily schedule should be rigid and as much leeway as the group needs and the school can manage should be given.

The programs of the three and four year olds differ in the allotment of time and kinds of experiences appropriate to the interests and needs of the age level. Because of the development of interest and greater physical ability, four year olds are capable of participating in more active group experiences, and performing some of the routine activities independently.

The free play period provides time to move about freely and a free choice of play materials to challenge the child's adaptability. Two free play periods are commonly found in the daily nursery school schedule, one of 45–60 minutes, and another of 30–40 minutes.

Periods devoted to music, group discussions, and stories are small group experiences. They should never exceed 20 minutes. The program should be flexible and often these activities can be incorporated in the free play period.

The number of days as well as the length of the nursery school day varies in different schools. Some meet for as little as one half day a week, others have a full day program including a morning and an afternoon session. At present there is no evidence or agreement that the preschool child benefits most from a program with a stated number of hours per day per week.

Nursery school groups should be small in order to give children individual attention and promote satisfactory group living. The younger the child is the smaller the group should be. For example, 20 4-year olds and 18 or fewer 3- or 2-year olds in one group is recommended.

The teacher-child ratio recommended by most authorities is one teacher for every ten 5-year olds, one teacher for every eight 4- and 3-year olds, and one teacher for every six 2-year olds. For health and safety reasons, it is desirable to have two adults supervising a group of nursery school children at all times.

A preschool group works best when children of like ages are grouped together. When the children are within a comparatively short age range, there are many opportunities for social adjustments, opportunities are present to give and take; to learn

"Childhood shows the man, as morning shows the day."—Milton

Shown here is a professor from Ohio Wesleyan University working with kindergarten students. The first kindergarten in the U.S. was established in Watertown, Wisconsin, in 1856 by Mrs. Carl S. Schurz. Games are a fundamental part of early education for children helping to develop their coordination and ability to follow instructions. The children here are playing "leap frog" and "crab walk." *(Photo courtesy M. Welch, Director of Public Relations, Ohio Wesleyan University)*

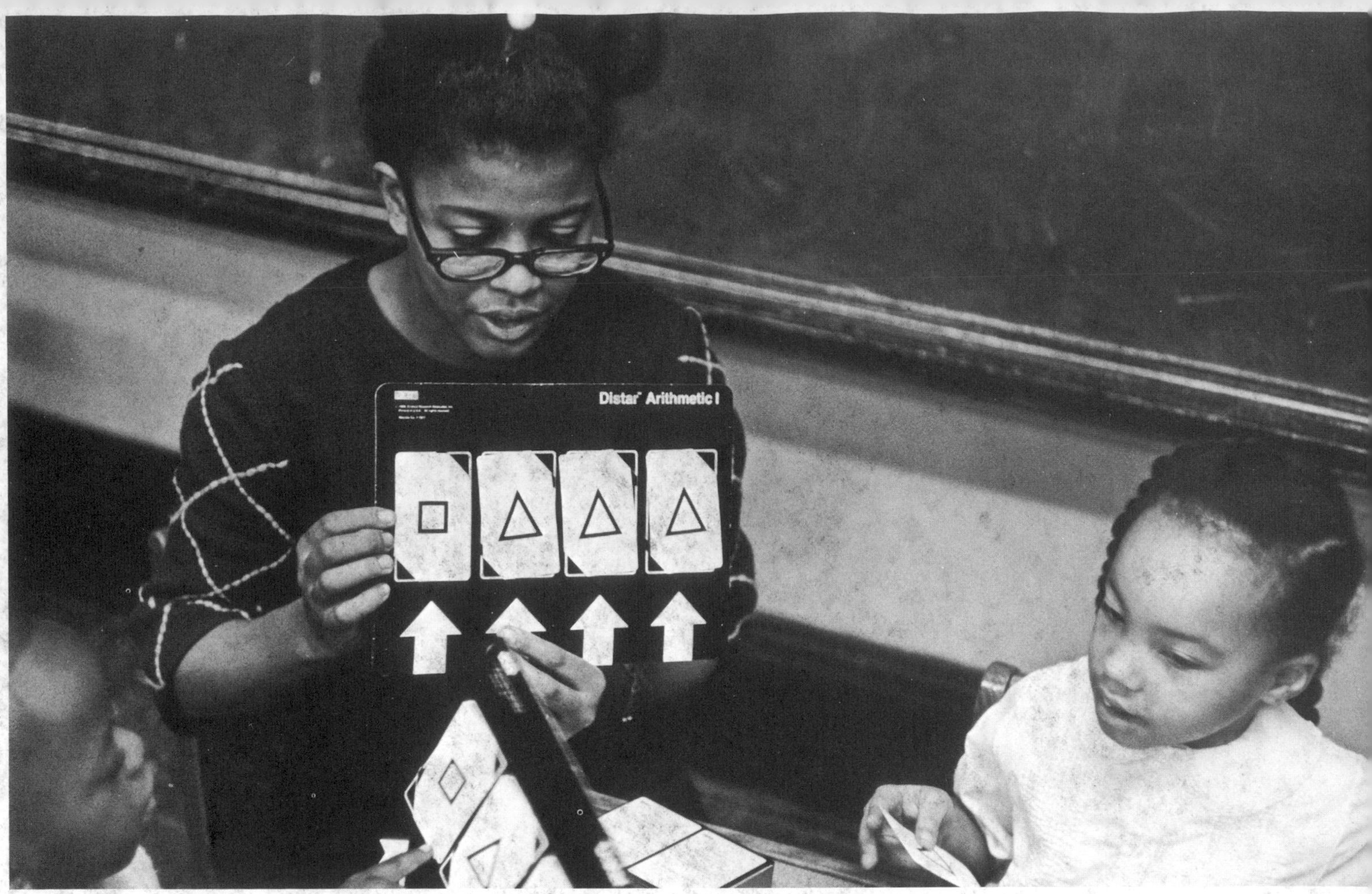

"Education alone can conduct us to that enjoyment which is at once best in quality and infinite in quantity."—Horace Mann (*Photos courtesy Distar Corporation*)

how to get along with peers; to lead and to follow; to consider the rights of others; to stand up for one's own rights; and to defend one's self. In some states an age of three years is suggested as the minimum entrance age.

The underlying principle of preschool education in the United States today is that the first six years of the child's life are the most important ones in the physical, mental, social, and emotional adjustment and many ills of adult life could be avoided through proper training in early childhood.

Preschool children need a wide variety of play material, sturdily built and washable. The following list is provided as a frame of reference for parents: Unit blocks made of hardwood, grouped with wooden or rubber animals, figures, small trucks, trains, airplanes, and boats. The housekeeping corner should contain a child size table, chairs, stove, refrigerators, beds, carriages, bedding, dishes and cooking utensils, ironing board, iron, broom, mop, dustpan, shelves or chest for storing, and a good supply of dressup clothes including purses, hats, belts, dresses, and suitcases. Art supplies should include easels, easel and finger paint, large brushes, a variety of size and kinds of paper, large crayons, blunt scissors, a clay and a storage crock. Water play utensils are such things as a galvanized tub, measuring cups, plastic and aluminum containers. Simple musical instruments such as drums, triangles, bells and percussion instruments; a good variety of apparatus for climbing, sliding and building; table and educational toys including wooden puzzles, beads, pegs and books; carpentry bench with sturdy hammers, saws, nails and soft wood; a sand box, piano and record player, round out the equipment. Basic furniture of appropriate size includes tables, chairs, storage shelves, lockers and low screens to provide partitions for some centers of interest.

TYPES OF NURSERY SCHOOLS

Nursery schools are of several types. A *Cooperative Nursery School* is one organized and administered by parents. Parents who form the group equip the school, administer policy, are responsible for financial support, employ teachers, and serve as assistants to the teaching staff.

The Private Nursery School typically is a proprietary school owned by the Director. Since it is a business venture, it must operate at a profit. Private Schools differ greatly in terms of fees charged, program and facilities, qualifications of teachers, and the socio-economic status of the families served. These private schools comprise about one-half of the existing Nursery Schools in the United States.

Religious Institutions have established educational centers for young children. The greatest numbers of these centers provide the regular nursery school educational program with the addition of the religious aspect.

The Laboratory Nursery School attempts to provide a rich creative experience for young children and in most instances is a center for Child Research and Parent Education. They have made a significant contribution to knowledge about the child and family living.

Nursery Schools for Exceptional Children are a recent contribution of education. They are for children who are handicapped in vision, hearing, movement, or have mental retardation. Such schools provide the special education needed for these children at an early age. Counseling help for parents is also one of their services.

Community Nursery Schools are organized, sponsored, and operated under some community auspice.

Settlement Nursery Schools place special focus on intercultural and interracial experiences whereby the special interests of various ethnic and racial groups contribute to the program to make understanding and acceptance of differences a primary goal.

Day Nurseries or *Child Care Centers* offer super-

vised group experiences to young children who cannot have adequate supervision in their own homes. They usually operate on an all-day, every-day basis.

Nursery Schools in the Public School System. The Nursery school is slowly finding a place in public education although relatively few are so organized and placed. California is the only state in which nursery schools are free and financed by State Education Department funds. In all other states, it is illegal to use public funds to operate a nursery school. The program in California is accomplished by means of the adult education program of the state.

Laws Governing Nursery Schools and Child Care Centers. Twenty-seven states have laws to protect children in Nursery Schools and Child Care Centers. However, the laws are often vague and unspecific, and enforcement is weak. Only twelve states regulate licensing of both nursery schools and child care centers and three states license nursery schools but not child care centers. Seven states have laws pertaining to professional qualifications for teachers of Nursery Schools but these do not apply to the staffs of Child Care Centers.

Only ten states specify penalties for violations of their laws regarding nursery school regulations. They have penalties which range from fines of $50 to $500 and six month to one year imprisonment.

THE KINDERGARTEN PROGRAM

The first kindergarten in the United States was established for German-speaking children in Watertown, Wisconsin in 1856 by Mrs. Carl S. Schurz. In 1860 Elizabeth Palmer Peabody opened the first kindergarten for English-speaking children in Boston, Massachusetts.

A study of kindergarten programs in various sections of the United States would seem to indicate that there has been little attempt to standardize them. The program may vary from school to school, and probably, even within a school system. However, with their diversities they all have some common elements. Children's learning in the kindergarten is foundational and basic to later learnings in the elementary school. Their learning is not acquired or recognized by the children as separate subjects. It is not achieved through drill, through subject teaching as may be appropriate later, or by the use of workbooks or textbooks. What and how much is learned differs with each child, depending upon his past experience, home environment, emotional stability, drive and native intelligence.

For purposes of identification to teachers and parents, the learnings in the kindergarten, basic to the later acquisition of more advanced knowledge and skills, may be grouped into Language Arts, Science, Health, Safety and Physical Education, Mathematics, Art and Music, Citizenship Education or Social Studies These are the same areas followed for the entire elementary school program.

The Language Arts Program is given 15% to 25% of the time of the average school week and includes: Story Time, Poetry, Exploring Books, Dramatizations, Corrective Speech Work, and Listening to the Teacher.

Citizenship Education occupies about 15% of the school week. Children are encouraged to become dependable members of the group. They share in the making and carrying out of plans and assume responsibility for care of equipment and materials. They learn of the interdependence of people and begin to understand celebrations of national holidays. Health, Safety, and Physical Education occupies 15% to 25% of the time. It includes dances and rhythm activities which use large muscles. Habits of safety in home, school, and community are stressed.

Mathematics is given approximately 10% of time. Here, making comparisons and counting as related to meaningful activities is done.

Science uses 10% of the time. The weather, stars,

seeds, pets and other animals are tools for discussions and learning activities.

Enrichment of Life Activities such as singing and other music experiences, art activities of painting, modeling, and construction are used for about 10% of the time.

Routines such as care of clothing, housekeeping, and classroom duties fill from 5% to 10% of the time.

Most kindergartens operate on a two and one-half or three hour session, one in the morning and one in the afternoon. Other programs are two-hour or all day sessions. The full day program is not widely used and, under present conditions, with the influx of small children in the elementary school, many schools cannot accommodate such a program.

THE PRIMARY PROGRAM

The primary school is generally interpreted as the place for providing the educational program for children of ages 6 through 9 years. The organization of the program may vary in different schools. In some, children are placed in grades 1, 2, and 3 according to maturity and accomplishment. In other schools the children are enrolled in an "ungraded school" program. Here the children stay in one group for a three-year period and learn at their own rate during their stay.

LANGUAGE ARTS WHICH INCLUDE
READING, WRITING, SPEECH
AND SPELLING

Reading. Learning to read and reading to learn prevails throughout the school program and appears to permeate the entire curriculum. Formal reading instruction in the first grade is preceded by a preparatory period, generally known as reading readiness. In this the child becomes acquainted with the procedures of learning to read from left to right and front to back. He also learns to distinguish likenesses and differences in objects, pictures, and forms.

Initial instruction in reading is usually informal and built around first hand experiences of the children. Reading readiness tests are often administered to determine the child's readiness in terms of vision, experience, and social maturity. Modern reading programs provide a variety of reading levels and reading materials of each grade level. A balance of oral and silent reading is used. Remedial reading programs either by the classroom teacher or reading specialist are used in some schools.

Alphabet. The *Initial Teaching Alphabet* made up of 44 characters by England's Sir James Pitman, with each symbol representing only one sound instead of the ABC alphabet of 26 letters, offers an interesting introduction to reading and writing.

Writing. Instruction in writing is begun some time during the first year of school. For the first two years the teacher and children use manuscript writing (letters more or less resembling those he reads). The reason for this is that the child learns and becomes familiar with the printed letters on his reading material. The transition from manuscript to cursive style is usually made in the third year of school.

Regular, brief supervised practice in writing is an essential part of the program. A less direct method is the attention given to penmanship in all written work in the various subject areas.

Speech and Spelling. During the early years of life children develop speech patterns. The school gives opportunity for conversations which under guidance enable them to acquire a wide vocabulary of meaningful words, to speak correctly, and to give facility in the use of language. The teacher sets a good example of speech.

Ability to spell correctly is not needed by the child until he has learned to write. Spelling instruction is centered around the words most frequently used in children's writings. Some children

have learned to spell about 140–150 words by the end of the second grade. Approximately 20 new words are introduced each week in the third year of school. At the end of this year the child usually has a writing vocabulary of about 750 words. Spelling should not be just a "subject" in the curriculum. It should be given attention in all written work throughout the school day.

Mathematics. In the first year of school attention is given to the development of a number concept. Teachers stress the learning of mathematics by doing measuring, manipulating, constructing rather than activities that depend upon listening and writing. Mathematics is made meaningful to children by using concrete experiences of number concepts as they appear in the normal classroom procedures.

Generally, during the second school year, single column addition to sums not exceeding 18, two-column addition, and subtraction without carrying or borrowing are introduced. In the third year addition and subtraction are extended to three columns of figures. Basic multiplication and division are taught and children begin to use simple fractions.

Citizenship Education, including History, Geography, Civics and Social Studies. Citizenship education is given through a series of guided learning experiences for children in which materials of history and geography are blended with events of the day. In the first and second years of school, direct first-hand experiences are the background of the curriculum. Field trips are taken around the school or the neighborhood, and gradually understanding of the environment is expanded to include a wider community. In the third year children begin to study their local community in a setting of the past as well as the present. Also they visit a few more remote communities. At this level social studies texts are introduced. Reading is supplemented with the use of globes, maps, and other teaching aids.

SCIENCE AND HEALTH

Science. Science information is firmly rooted through watching, touching, examining, and experimenting. Children become aware of changes and characteristics of things rather than the reason for these. Care of pets, collecting and examining nature objects, observing weather and seasonal changes are some of the common learning experiences. In the second year of school, the scientific method of problem solving is introduced with simple experiments.

Health. This program focuses attention on growth of good habits, attitudes and knowledge in the areas of food and eating habits, sleep and rest, care of teeth, eyes, ears, and cleanliness and mental health. Stress is also placed on safe practices at home, at school, and in the community. Health education is considered a basic requirement in the primary school curriculum, and is required by law in all states of the United States.

THE ARTS

In the first two years of school, children learn to sing many new songs and to play rhythm instruments. They are given opportunity to listen and respond to music. Awareness of rhythm, tempo, and pitch change are introduced with the reading of simple music in the third year of school.

A great variety of painting, modeling, and drawing experiences enables the child to develop concepts of form and design. The use of the materials is guided so that he becomes familiar with the use of color along with these concepts.

Dramatization on the nursery school and kindergarten levels is best on an informal and spontaneous basis. The use of puppets can be an effective way to use dramatization by observation.

LITERATURE

Many factors and experiences shape children's attitudes and abilities in reading and the appreciation of literature. The presence of books in the home and the kinds of use made of them by other members of the family may be among a child's first impressions. Encouragement of literary taste may be affected as much by a parent's obvious enjoyment of his own reading as by his conscious introduction of his child to the pleasures of reading.

Lullabies, chanting of nursery rhymes, and play with nonsense words or phrases train the infant's ear to the pleasures of listening and, most often in a natural way, in the imitation of the sounds he hears. The simplicity of Mother Goose rhymes has made them a favorite with children, and no age is too early for the parent to introduce them. The child's first experience may be to hear the verses recited at bedtime or at other times during the day, but when the parent opens the book of verses and reads them, the child makes another natural connection between the pleasures of the sounds and the pleasures that the book offers to those who read.

In many families, a set time for reading aloud or for telling stories may be a part of the day's schedule, but, in developing the child's interest, it is desirable for him to understand that reading is an effective means of enjoyment and information, whether or not it is programmed especially for his benefit.

Reading aloud to the young child should include time for the child to see illustrations that may accompany the text, and to ask questions or talk about what has been read or told. However, the time should not be a period of quizzing or of too-artificial teaching. Enjoyment and pleasure should be the keynotes, although the time should not be one of rare reward, but rather a customary time for sharing enjoyment in books. In this way, the child also develops other skills and attitudes that will be related throughout his life to the appreciation of literature. These include the ability to listen, an increasingly important skill in an era when much information is related to what one learns from various media; an appreciation of how to care for books; and a development of taste and knowledge of color, design, and other elements of good illustration in books.

Selection of books to read to children should allow, from as early an age as possible, for the child to participate in the activity of selection. This may apply to his choosing between several books available for reading at one time, or to choosing from a much wider selection in a bookstore or library. The relatively inexpensive books now available in neighborhood stores will undoubtedly find their way into a child's own library through purchase, or birthday or holiday gifts from relatives and friends, or through exchange with others.

Some general guides to the appeal that some themes or formats have for children may be set, but there are, throughout childhood, many differences among children and they should be encouraged to choose their own favorites. The first books chosen should be sturdy and easy to clean, so that children may be allowed to handle them with care without feeling unduly inhibited. One problem is the contrast between the child's small size and the relatively slow development of more precise muscular control. Pages should be large enough to turn easily, but not so large as to overwhelm the child. Large splashes of color and clear, clean lines in illustrations remain appealing throughout childhood, but may be necessities at first when children cannot focus on or appreciate detail. Simplicity in story line is an essential for the child whose attention span is short. Stories featuring children, families, pets, and other parts of their familiar environment are likely to be favorites. As experience widens, children may respond to more fanciful tales, as well as to books that give them information.

As children's books continue to represent approximately ten per cent of the titles published in the United States each year, and since the proportion that remain in print is higher than for adult titles, the task of selecting the best books for children becomes more difficult. Traditional nursery tales, such as "The Three Billy Goats Gruff," should form a part of each child's folk heritage, but he should also have the opportunity to know and enjoy what is new. Just as his interest is caught by an airplane or automobile as well as by a story of Indian or colonial days, the child should be able to find stories of other times as well as his own. His taste will be affected by many of the same events and environmental features that affect adults: references in the news or in conversation, recommendations from media, such as favorite television programs, or suggestions made by other children or adults. A familiar pitfall is for adults to assume that books that were their own favorites will naturally be as much loved by children of another generation. This is not always true, and even classics that survive two or three generations may eventually fail to hold interest. The parent who tries to force development of taste to follow a set pattern or his own preferences may set up barriers, rather than stepping-stones.

The sense of sharing also needs to be continued when children reach school age. Their pride in reading will be increased if they are encouraged to share in the reading at home, and parental interest and respect for the child's achievement should be sufficient reason for the parent to listen to his reading. At the same time, the child's mastery of reading should not be a reason for the parent or others to stop reading aloud. His level of appreciation exceeds his level of reading ability, and means that his acquaintance with good literature must be increased through reading or storytelling by others, as well as through his own efforts in reading.

Reviewing of current publications for children is difficult to find in depth and volume, but the parent should be alert to articles about children's books and reading in general periodicals, as well as in such special publications as *The Horn Book*, a periodical devoted to children's books and reading, and *The Bulletin of the Center for Children's Books*, a publication of reviews sponsored by the University of Chicago. However, since children's reading should include much that is already available, retrospective listings of recommended titles are also important for suggestions of reading within the family. Public or school libraries may provide original lists of good books, or may distribute those prepared by such groups as the Children's Services Division of the American Library Association. The purpose and scope of these lists are often indicated, and the lists should be used with these in mind.

For the parent who has not kept abreast of trends and changes in the reading materials published for children since his own childhood, the complexity, sophistication, and frankness of many titles written for children may be a shock. Taboos that were observed in publishing for many years (for example, depiction of a parent who smokes or drinks to excess, or descriptions of death or crimes) are no longer honored. The parent who wishes to oversee his child's reading must assume more responsibilities. At the same time, he should recognize that the changing social attitudes that have broken the taboos may be a reason for corresponding changes in parental attitudes about the selection of reading.

Although the child's reading interests and abilities expand and increase, he may choose to read some favorite books over and over. He may also wish to have the same stories told or read to him repeatedly. As long as he has access to more books from which to choose, this kind of repetition simply indicates continued pleasure in a story, and should not be discouraged. The elements that make the story a favorite may be discovered in other books that may become equally beloved.

REVIEW QUESTIONS

List the changes in the purposes of Education from Primitive Peoples to Modern Society 841

Characterize the schools organized in Europe in the 12th century. What was the first of these institutions? 841

Describe the origin of the common schools and indicate the part taken by the Church in their development 841, 846-847

Compare the early common and higher schools of Massachusetts as to purpose and curriculum 842

EDUCATIONAL INSTITUTIONS

What two classes of students were taught in the priestly schools of Egypt? 843

Name three important teachers of ancient Greece 843

Who was the great mathematician who worked at the University of Alexandria and what was his contribution to education? . . . 843-844

Whose writings have long formed the basis of Chinese education? 844

Indicate the present status of Chinese school systems 844

The educational system of what nation has served as a model for the schools of modern India? 844

Show how the Greeks came to be the teachers of Rome 844

Illustrate the work of Alcuin in the Palace School of Charlemagne 844-845

State evidences of Arab influence upon the intellectual life of Europe 845

Describe the organization and the purpose of the Jesuit schools 845

Trace the origin of the term "secondary school" and describe its development in Europe 845

Who were the leaders of the "neo humanism" movement in Germany? 845

Point out the reasons for the introduction of many new subjects into the secondary school curriculum 845-846

Describe the "public school" of England and tell the nature of its curriculum 846

Outline the general character of the European university 846

What is meant by "Academic Freedom?" . 846-847

What are the terms used for two types of students in the English University? 847

What was the one great advantage of the so-called Lancastrian movement? 847

Outline the provisions of the "General School Regulation" issued in Prussia by Frederick the Great 847

Why was the age of 14 adopted as the upper limit for compulsory school attendance in Prussia? 847

Enumerate the three grades of schools which existed in the American Colonies 847

Describe briefly the development of normal schools in the United States until 1860 . . 851

For what purpose were the first American colleges established? How did the University of Pennsylvania differ from others in origin and curriculum? 852

Indicate the importance of denominational colleges in the history of American higher education 852

Review the changes made in choice of professions by college graduates 852

Summarize the work of reformers in the history of education 854

Indicate the relation of the kindergarten to the teachings of Froebel 858

Point out some of the effects of Socrates' method of teaching 854

Into what four branches did Plato divide higher education? 854

Outline the ways in which Aristotle influenced medieval and modern education in Europe 854

Cite some methods of literary training advocated by Quintilian 855

What were the effects of the teaching of Alcuin? of Anselm? of Peter Abelard? . . 855

Describe the method of teaching employed by Saint Thomas Aquinas 855

Upon what subjects did Erasmus write? . . 855

What type of schools did Martin Luther advocate? 855

Discuss the objective of the order established by Loyola 855-856

To what educator can the modern organization of the German Gymnasium be attributed? . 856

Describe the contributions of two English educators of the 16th century 856

How is the influence of Comenius on modern education best stated? 856

What is the position of John Locke in respect to classical education? 856

Outline the plan of education for the individual as given by Rousseau 856

Describe some of the methods Basedow employed in his school 857

Estimate the rank of Pestalozzi among educational reformers 857-858

Outline the chief psychological teachings of Herbart 858

Summarize Froebel's leading educational principles 858-859

State the character of the contributions of Horace Mann and Henry Barnard to American education 859

Outline the contents of Herbert Spencer's four famous essays on education 859

What were the contributions of W. T. Harris to American education? 859-860

Describe the special educational contributions of Alfred Binet and Granville Stanley Hall . 860

Summarize Charles W. Eliot's notable reforms at Harvard University 860

On what was emphasis placed in the educational philosophy of John Dewey? 860

What were the contributions to American education by Charles Hubbard Judd? . . . 860

RECENT EXPANSION IN AMERICAN EDUCATION

Give evidences of increased schooling of Americans in recent years 861

List some reasons for development in periodical publication and circulation in the United States 862

Prove from postal statistics, that writing ability has been greatly extended since 1840 862

Explain the reasons for the school building shortage and the teachers shortage and the rising demand for school facilities . . . 863

Indicate some industrial changes which have occasioned the rapid growth of high schools . 866

THE SCIENCE OF EDUCATION

Outline the general method and the results of the child study movement 869

Describe briefly the place of the cultural Epochs Theory in American education . . 869

Describe the tests conducted by J. M. Rice . 869

Explain the meaning of the phrase "normal distribution" in a group 870

Point out the meaning of "retardation" and "acceleration." 870

Describe some methods used to group pupils in schools 870

What two educators led in studies of retardation and elimination of pupils? 871

How is the ability of a child measured by arithmetic tests? 872

Describe the possible uses and values of Achievement Battery Tests 872

Point out some improvements arising from the use of educational tests 874

What is the "Intelligence Quotient" or I.Q. and how is it determined? 874

For what purposes were the United States army tests devised? 875–876

Discuss the interpretation of the so-called Army Alpha Test 879

What is the major purpose of the Army Beta Test? 879

List some agencies which are promoting the use of tests and describe one of the major tests each has developed 881

Discuss the pros and cons of the ABC method, the Phonetic and Word recognition methods action and eye movements? 882

What important findings with respect to reading have followed laboratory studies of reaction and eye movements 882

Describe the methods used for studies of the school curriculum 883

Outline the methods employed in job analysis. 883

SCHOOLS IN FOREIGN COUNTRIES

Outline the general composition of the German school system in its four periods of recent development 884

Trace the history of secularization of French schools 885

Discuss the English examination system . . 887

Describe the organization of the universities of Oxford and Cambridge 887

What are some of the major features in the organization of Russian Education? . . . 888

In what countries of the world is illiteracy practically eliminated? In what countries is there more than 80% illiteracy? 889

EDUCATION IN THE UNITED STATES

Why is diversity rather than commonality a characteristic of the American schools? . . 890

Describe the functions of the United States Office of Education 890

Discuss the authority of the state in education 890

In what ways does the state directly contribute to the financial support of schools? 892

Discuss the role of the Board of Education in American education 892–893

What are the reasons for the development of the school lunch program? 893

Outline the growth of the elementary school curriculum 893

What have been some trends in the organization of the elementary school? 894

Describe three major reasons for the organization of the junior high school 894

What is meant by the core curriculum? . . . 895

Characterize the typical high school as to length of course and purpose 895

Describe the contributions of two recent studies made by the American high school . 896

What is meant by "The Carnegie Unit?" . . 897

Discuss the methods of college admission . 897–898

State one of the chief problems of educational guidance 897

Discuss extra curricular activities 898

Define the terms "College" and "University" and point out the difference between the two 899–900

What three types of universities and colleges are recognized? 899

What has been the development of the junior college? 900–901

Where and when did the university extension movement begin? 901

Indicate the variety of extension services in communities 902

What were the results of the standardizing work of the American Medical Council? . . 902

Discuss the problem of economy in professional training 903

Point out a fundamental cause of inequality of educational opportunity in America . . 903

Discuss the problems raised by the increasing costs of schools 904

Show how the Federal Government becomes involved in educational problems . . .904–905

Outline the history of Federal and colonial land grants for school purposes. Summarize the history of the policy of Federal land grants for colleges 906

What Federal subsidies for special education have recently been granted? 906

Describe the "G.I. Bill of Rights." 907

Define vocational education 907

Trace the histories of Commercial, Manual Training, and Technical Industrial Schools . 907

Summarize the extent of agricultural and industrial education under the Smith-Lever and the Smith-Hughes subventions . . . 908

List some of the common functions of guidance counselors 909

Outline the course of the Americanization movement 910

Describe briefly the different types of manifestations of the movement in Adult education 910

Discuss some of the innovations to schoolhouse design and explain why these have come about 911

List nine important educational foundations and cite the special work of each . . .912–913

Describe the organization of the National Education Association 913

List the activities of the P.T.A. 914–915

Summarize the growth of correspondence schools 915

Cite some examples of experimental schools 915

Trace the development of Parochial schools in the United States 916

Describe three procedures for using television in the schools 917

Of what does early childhood education normally consist? 918

How far back can the preschool movement be traced? 918

Describe the Nursery School program. How is the name misused? 918

When was the first Kindergarten in the United States established? 919

How are the learnings in Kindergarten grouped and what percentage of the school week is given to each program? 919

Describe the Primary Program 920

Who made up the *Initial Teaching* alphabet and of how many characters does it consist? . 920

When is instruction in writing begun? . . . 920

What methods are used to teach children to speak and spell correctly? 920

How do teachers stress the learning of mathematics? 920

What part do history and geography play in teaching Citizenship to children? 920

Do pets and nature objects help children in the study of science? Explain 920

What mediums are used to increase children's knowledge of objects, events, and the world in general? 920

How can parents be certain they are choosing the proper books for their children? . . . 921

What effects have changing social attitudes exerted on the writing and publishing of books for children and young people? . . 921

BIBLIOGRAPHY

EDUCATIONAL INSTITUTIONS

Brown, Elmer E.—The Making of Our Middle Schools. *Longmans*
Cubberly, E. P.—A Brief History of Education. *Houghton Mifflin*
Eby, F. and Arrowood, C. F.—The Development of Modern Education. *Prentice-Hall*
Good, H. G.—A History of Western Education. *Macmillan*
Graves, F. P.—A Students' History of Education. *Macmillan*
Monroe, Paul (Ed.)—A Cyclopedia of Education. *Macmillan*
Mulhern, J.—A History of Education. *Ronald Press*

EDUCATIONAL REFORMERS

Comenius, Johann A.—(Ed. Classics Series) *McGraw-Hill*
Compayre, G.—Pestalozzi and Elementary Education. *Crowell*
Davidson, Thomas—Aristotle and the Ancient Educational Ideals. *Scribner*
Dewey, John—Democracy and Education. *Macmillan*
—The School and Society. *Univ. of Chicago Press*
Graves, F. P.—Great Educators of Three Centuries. *Macmillan*
Hinsdale, B. A.—Horace Mann and the Common School Revival in the United States. *Scribner*
Hughes, Thomas—Loyola and the Educational System of the Jesuits. *Scribner*
Reisner, E. H. (Ed.)—Education Classics. *McGraw-Hill*
—Historical Foundation of Modern Education. *Macmillan*
Rousseau, Jean Jacques—Emile. *Dutton*
Ulich, R.—A History of Educational Thought. *Am. Book Co.*

EXPANSION OF AMERICAN EDUCATION

Reports of the United States Commissioner of Education, especially the Biennial Survey of Education, 1918 to date.
Proceedings of the National Education Association of the United States, 1857 to date.
Reports of the Chief State School Official of each state.
Yearbooks of the American Association for School Administrators, 1922 to date.
Yearbooks of the National Society for the Study of Education, 1902 to date.
Research Bulletins of the National Education Association, 1923 to date.

THE SCIENCE OF EDUCATION

Bingham, Walter V.—Aptitudes and Aptitude Testing. *Harper*
Buros, Oscar K.—The Fifth Mental Measurements Year Book *Gryphon Press*
English, H. B.—A Student's Dictionary of Psychological Terms. *Harper*
Freeman, F. N.—Mental Tests, Their History, Principles, and Applications. *Houghton Mifflin*
Good, Carter V. (Ed.)—Dictionary of Education. *McGraw-Hill*
Good, Carter V. (and others)—The Methodology of Educational Research. *Appleton-Century*
Greene, H. A. (and others)—Measurement and Evaluation in the Elementary School. *Longmans*
Monroe, W. S. (Ed.)—Encyclopedia of Educational Research. *Macmillan*
Peters, C. C. and Van Vorhis, W. R.—Statistical Procedures and Their Mathematical Bases. *McGraw-Hill*
Pressey, S. L.—Psychology and the New Education. *Harper*
Terman, L. M. and Merrill, Maude—Measuring Intelligence. *Houghton Mifflin*

Yearbooks of the National Society for the Study of Education:
—Intelligence. . . . Thirty-ninth Yearbook
—The Scientific Movement. Thirty-seventh Yearbook

MODERN SCHOOL SYSTEMS IN COUNTRIES OTHER THAN THE UNITED STATES

Kandel, I. L.—Comparative Education. *Houghton Mifflin*
Educational Yearbook of the International Institute of Teachers College, Columbia University, 1924 to date.
International Directory of Adult Education. *UNESCO*
International Yearbook of Education. *International Bureau of Education, Geneva*
Statesman's Yearbook, 1864 to date.

EDUCATION IN THE UNITED STATES

Barzun, Jacques—Teacher in America. *Little Brown*
—The House of Intellect *Harper*
Caswell, H. L. and Campbell, D. S.—Readings in Curriculum Development. *Am. Book Co.*
De Young, Chris A.—American Education. *McGraw-Hill*
Elsbree, W. S.—The American Teacher. *Am. Book Co.*
Jones, Howard Mumford—Reflections on Learning. *Rutgers Univ. Press*
Knight, E. W.—Education in the United States. *Ginn & Co.*
McGrath, Earl J.—Toward General Education. *Macmillan*
Reeder, W. G.—The Fundamentals of Public School Administration. *Macmillan*
Rickover, Hyman G.—Education and Freedom. *Dutton*
Rivlin, H. N. (Ed.)—Encyclopedia of Modern Education. *Philosophical Library*
Tead, Ordway—The Climate of Learning. *Harper*

The Elementary School

Adams, Fay—Educating American Children. *Ronald Press*
DeLima, A.—The Little Red Schoolhouse. *Macmillan*
Gesell, A. and Ilg, F.—The Child from Five to Ten. *Harper*
Porter, Martha P.—The Teacher in the New School. *World Book Co.*
Saucier, W. A.—Theory and Practice in the Elementary School. *Macmillan*
The Activity Movement, Thirty-third Yearbook of the National Society for the Study of Education.
Yearbooks of the Department of Elementary School Principals, 1921 to date.

The High School

Aikin, W. M.—The Story of the Eight-year Study *Harper*
Conant, James Bryant—The American High School Today *McGraw-Hill*
Crow, L. D. and Crow, Alice—Our Teen-age Boys and Girls. *McGraw-Hill*
Inglis, A. J.—Principles of Secondary Education. *Houghton Mifflin*
Koos, L. V.—Integrating High School and College. *Harper*
Education for All American Youth—A Report of the Educational Policies Commission.
The High School in a Changing World. 36th Year Book of the American Association of School Administrators.

Higher Education

Eels, Walter C. (Ed.)—American Junior Colleges. *Am. Council on Education*
Lindsay, E. E. and Holland, E. O.—College and University Administration. *Macmillan*
General Education in a Free Society; Report of the Harvard Committee. *Harvard Univ. Press*

English Language

CONTENTS GUIDE

	Page		Page
Abbreviations	1091	Language and Linguistics	987
Antonyms	1037	Latin Stems	951
Bibliography	1100	Letter Writing	1020
Book Lists	1033	Linguistic Theory	992
Business Letter Forms	1023	Literary Composition, Forms of	1015
Capital Letters	982	Oral Interpretation	1004
Children's Library	1035	Prefixes	948
Conjunctions	980	Prepositions	976
English Words from the Latin	953	Pronunciation, Correct	1008
Family Library	1032	Public Speaking	997
Famous First Lines	1089	Punctuation	983
Figures of Speech	1018	Questions, Review	1096
Foreign Phrases:		Radio and Television Speaking	1002
Latin	1078	Speech, Parts of	968
Modern Languages	1082	Spelling, Correct	961
Tourist Talk	1088	Suffixes	949
Good Usage	927	Synonyms and Antonyms	1037
Hawaiian Phrases	1088	Tourist Talk	1088
Heteronyms	967	Verb Forms	975
Homonyms	965	Word Building	947
		Writing and Speaking	992

Picture Guide: In the Shakespeare Country—Shakespeare's Church—Historic England.

IN THE SHAKESPEARE COUNTRY

a
Anne Hathaway's cottage at Shottery, Warwickshire, where young Shakespeare and his wife Anne, lived from 1582 to about 1584.

Photos a, b, and c courtesy of British Travel Association

b. Shakespeare's birthplace in Stratford-on-Avon, Warwickshire, is located on Henley Street and annually attracts thousands of visitors.

William Shakespeare. This portrait, supplied by the British Museum, is reproduced from a print in the first folio edition of his plays.

c. In this magnificent setting, the Royal Shakespeare Theatre at Stratford is a mecca for drama lovers of the world.

Shakespeare's church, Holy Trinity in Stratford-on-Avon, Warwickshire, England, was built during the 13th century. The spire was not added until 1763.

Historic England. *Above:* Stonehenge, on Salisbury Plain in Wiltshire, may date from as early as 1800 B.C. The monument's purpose is unknown, but one theory is that it was a temple or burial ground for ancient Britons. Excavations have yielded Stone Age relics and burial mounds of the Bronze Age. *Lower left:* **Big Ben,** the great clock-tower bell in the London Parliament, weighs 13 tons and was cast in 1856. It was named for Sir Benjamin Hall, London Commissioner of Works at the time. *Lower right:* **Windsor Castle,** residence of British monarchs, stands in Berkshire, 21 miles west of London. William the Conqueror first built a castle on the site. Rebuilt by later sovereigns, Windsor now covers some 24 acres. Queen Victoria and several English kings are buried here. (*Courtesy D. L. Sudduth*)

The English Language

INTRODUCTION

LANGUAGE, spoken and written, is mankind's most valuable asset. How language first arose has long been a matter of debate, but it is certain that it was originally much simpler than at present and that it developed from a group of bodily movements and from sounds with which certain meanings were arbitrarily associated. As men's experience became more varied and complex, such gestures and sounds were elaborated and multiplied until there arose what might be called spoken language. Written language followed, when an ingenious man thought of making marks to represent spoken words. By writing a symbol for each sound, an alphabet was devised and written speech was simplified. Thus communications could be sent long distances and thoughts could be recorded and preserved for the use of later times. Each generation was thereby enabled to instruct the next, and rapid progress in knowledge and in skill became possible.

Our English Tongue. To no people has there fallen a richer inheritance of language or a more splendid opportunity to further enrich and perfect that heritage than belongs to the English-speaking nations. The English language has grown to its present excellence through the development of one of the world's great literatures. This fact means that the work of scholars, poets, story-tellers, orators, and scientists has been contributing, through a thousand years, to enlarge, strengthen, and refine the English vocabulary and grammar. Moreover, the nations that speak this tongue have been modern pioneers in free, democratic government, with all that this implies in popular education, in free discussion of political questions, and in wide circulation of books, magazines, and newspapers.

The English and the Americans have been adventurous, trading, and colonizing people, sailing all the seas, exploring every continent, trading with, civilizing, and governing, peoples of every race. Whenever, for unaccustomed things, strange ways, or novel ideas, new words have been needed, these men of English speech have unhesitatingly adopted foreign words that met the need, and have assimilated them to the forms of the English language. Thus English has gained an unparalleled variety of synonyms and turns of speech, and it is better fitted than any other to be the language of a nation derived, as are the Americans, from people of many races.

In the European theater of World War II, men from America, England, Canada, Australia, and South Africa met upon the ground of a common language. Allowing for minor differences of dialect, colloquialisms, and slang, they understood and misunderstood one another in the English tongue, and they read the same newspapers and books, whether published in London, New York, Melbourne, Montreal, or Cape Town. In the post-war period, through its use in international trade and in the Proceedings of the United Nations, English has become universally recognized as a world language.

The Study of English. Language grows by adding new words, by giving new meanings to old words, and by developing the figurative or poetic senses of many words. All these processes depend upon increase of knowledge, upon invention and discovery, and upon the cultivation of art and poetry.

Words are, after all, only means to right understanding and true feeling; but many accurate, fine words are necessary to much good thinking. There is always a *best* word to express thought accurately and clearly. The student who would better his command of language will first direct his attention to those things which can be felt and seen, so that he may have something definite and concrete about which to talk or to write. He will next consult the dictionary for the meanings and the history of words; he will examine closely synonyms and antonyms for their accurate distinctions in meaning; nor will he fail to attend to the poetic suggestiveness of those words which give especial beauty both to the spoken and to the written phrase. He will, in a word, be always on his guard to avoid and to correct the errors and improprieties of usage which are likely to creep into his conversation.

Order of Study. English is treated in the following pages in a form to be referred to readily, to be used easily for help in speaking or writing, and to serve as a guide for systematic study. The various parts of the subject are arranged in the general order in which the boy or girl meets them in studying this most important of all school subjects. This arrangement would appear to be also the most convenient for older people.

Usage.—The correct and appropriate uses of words are given first place. During the early years of the child's life, before he knows much about sentences, he learns many words. Afterward, the value of his ability to use the correct and appropriate word, "to say the right thing in the right way," can never be overestimated. Therefore Usage, or approved uses of common words, is treated first.

Word Building and Spelling.—Again, the child's first words are naturally simple; most of them have but one syllable. In the beginning these are all nouns, for he does not yet know the use of the pronoun. By degrees, as the infant mind develops, the child finds the need of other words to express his thoughts and ideas. Soon he discovers that, by adding little syllables to the words with which he is already familiar, he can make himself understood. Thus unknowingly does the child arrive at the art of word building.

It will at once be seen that a knowledge of word building is of great value to the student of English as an aid in enlarging his vocabulary. For this reason, the section on Word Building follows Usage. It precedes the important subject of Spelling, because a knowledge of the structure of many English words helps equally both in grasping their meanings and in learning their component parts.

Pronunciation.—The guide of everyday usefulness has directed the making of the spelling and pronunciation lists. These are arranged to help the child with troublesome school words and also to give ready aid in the use of common words in business, in the household, and in social life. Correct spelling and correct pronunciation are essential to a perfect command of the English language.

Sentence Building, Capitals, Punctuation and *Linguistics.*—Following Word Building or etymology comes syntax or Sentence Building, which is the next important stage in the study of language. The essential rules and principles of grammar are given in this section, including the use of capital letters and punctuation marks, and Linguistics, or the science of language.

Speaking and Writing.—The section which presents helps in writing papers and essays and in making talks and speeches appropriately follows the study of words and sentences. To the student who desires advanced work in oral and in written language, this section is invaluable.

Forms of Literary Composition.—Having made an exhaustive study of words, sentences, and practical composition, the student is next introduced to the various forms of literature. In this section the principal divisions and subdivisions of prose and poetry are described and illustrated.

Letter Writing.—Because of its importance, Letter Writing follows Speaking and Writing in a separate section. The writing of an interesting letter may be counted as one of the finest accomplishments. In writing letters, we must apply the principles given in all the preceding sections on words, sentences, and composition.

Reading.—The language a person uses is influenced largely by the kind of books and papers he reads. Therefore a condensed guide to the best

types and examples of English reading is here given. The lists of books direct the reader to the masterpieces of English literature. They are arranged in groups suited to the various school grades. In each group are the books that teachers, librarians, and parents have found to interest most readily boys and girls of the corresponding grade or age. A lifetime might be spent in becoming acquainted with the books in these lists. Reading will reenforce all that can be learned from the preceding sections.

Synonyms and Antonyms.—The value of knowing the correct and appropriate word is pointed out above. We should now add to this the knowledge of how to choose with a nicety from among several appropriate words. It is this interest which leads to the study of the rich store of English Synonyms and Antonyms.

Foreign Words and Phrases and *Abbreviations.* Closing this department are two dictionaries— 1) Latin phrases frequently found in English books, and 2) phrases from Modern Languages, added to which are some examples of "tourist talk," consisting of current phrases useful to travelers; also a list of Abbreviations.

SELECTED GENERAL REFERENCES ON LANGUAGE

Abrams, Meyer H.—A Glossary of Literary Terms.
Holt '57
Barnouw, Erik—Mass Communication: Television, Radio, Film, Press . . . . *Holt '56*
Barzun, Jacques—The Modern Researcher.
Harcourt '63
Baugh, Albert C.—A History of the English Language . . . . *Meredith (Appleton) '57*
Bernstein, Theodore—Watch Your Language.
Atheneum '65
—More Language That Needs Watching.
Atheneum '64
—The Careful Writer . . . . . *Atheneum '65*
Bodmer, Frederick—The Loom of Language.
Norton '44
Bradley, Henry—The Making of English.
Walker '67
Cattell, N. R.—The New English Grammar.
MIT Press '69
Chisholm, William S.—The New English.
Funk & Wagnalls '69
Ferguson, Charles—Say It With Words.
Random House '59
Follett, Wilson—Modern American Usage.
Hill and Wang '66
Gates, Jean K.—Guide to the Use of Books and Libraries . . . . *McGraw-Hill '69*
Harbrace Guide to Dictionaries . . *Harcourt '63*
Hayakawa, S. I.—Language in Thought and Action.
Harcourt '65
Henle, Paul—Language, Thought, and Culture.
University of Michigan Press '58
Hilliard, Robert L.—Writing for Television and Radio . . . . *Hastings House '67*

Johnson, Elmer D.—Communication.
Scarecrow Press '66
Jordan, Archibald C.—The Writer's Manual.
World '66
Kierzek, John M. and Gibson, Walter—The Macmillan Handbook of English . . *Macmillan '60*
McCormick, Mona—Who-What-When-Where-How-Why Made Easy . *Quadrangle Books '71*
Menzel, D. H.; Jones, H. M.; Boyd, L. G.—Writing a Technical Paper . . . . *McGraw-Hill '66*
Morris, William and others—The American Heritage Dictionary of the English Language.
American Heritage/Houghton Mifflin '69
Neal, Harry E.—Nonfiction: From Idea to Published Book . . . . *Funk '64*
Nicolson, Margaret A.—A Practical Guide for Authors and Editors . . . . *Holt '67*
Perrin, Porter G. and others—Writer's Guide and Index to English . . . . . . *Scott, Foresman '66*
Schwartz, Robert J.—The Complete Dictionary of Abbreviations . . . . *Crowell '55*
Skillin, Marjorie E. and others—Words into Type.
Appleton-Century '64
Sledd, James and Ebbitt, Wilma R.—Dictionaries and That Dictionary . . . *Scott, Foresman '62*
Strunk, William and White, E. B.—The Elements of Style . . . . *Macmillan '62*
Turabian, Kate L.—A Manual for Writers of Term Papers, Theses, and Dissertations.
University of Chicago '67
University of Chicago Press—A Manual of Style '69
U. S. Government Printing Office Style Manual . '67
Webster's Third New International Dictionary of the English Language . . . . . . *Merriam '64*

GOOD USAGE

A PERSON's language reflects his social background, his geographic origin, and, especially, the extent of his education. By its form, it makes a good impression or an unfavorable one. That is why the question of correctness arises even before one's language is tested for the important qualities of clearness and accuracy. Mispronounced words, colloquialisms, malapropisms, incorrect idioms, and grammatical errors are noticed at once and can place a speaker or writer at a serious disadvantage. *How* he says a thing will attract more attention than *what* he says. On the other hand, if one's language is easy, confident, and fluent because correct, his listener or reader will accept the form without question and will think only about the subject matter.

Whether it is gained through formal instruction or through self-education, the ability to use language well comes only by observation, study, and practice. Because English is a living language and is therefore subject to change, the question of good usage is one that calls for constant attention. Whether certain words or forms of expression are acceptable or not is determined, not by an edict of some individual or group in authority, but by the consensus of the best writers and speakers who are using the language at any particular time.

The average person's first problem is to rid his speech of certain forms of expression that attract undue or unfavorable attention. Many expressions condemned by standard usage have resulted from someone's lazy habit of taking over ready-made phrases without regard to their repute or their real meaning. An effort to vary the phrasing is likely to uncover a fresh, interesting expression that will say the thing more effectively as well as more correctly.

Slang is an inclusive term for words and phrases that come into the language on trial, sometimes with very questionable associations, sometimes on a more respectable basis. At the outset it should be noted that not all new words should be classed as "slang". As the language grows, new meanings call for special words, which may be either coined or imported. The word "camouflage," for example, is a French importation that was accepted readily as a part of everyday English speech.

Certain words which began as slang abbreviations for longer expressions were challenged at first, but later gained a place for themselves. Examples are "cab," short for "cabriolet," "mob," for *mobile vulgus*, and "hoax," for "hocus pocus," itself a slang contraction for a Latin phrase used by impostors. Current abbreviations such as "gym" for "gymnasium," "exam," for "examination," and "mike," for "microphone," will readily suggest themselves. Whether any of these newer contractions will be accepted as standard usage is still open to question.

Slang from various questionable sources may be made almost respectable by the fashion of the moment. From the all-too-numerous examples, a few typical cases may be cited. Who hasn't heard, and perhaps used, such expressions as "so what?," "screwball," "sourpuss," "behind the eight ball," "cock-eyed," and "ritzy"? It may be argued that many such phrases are expressive. So is profanity, for that matter, but that doesn't qualify it as an example of good usage. But in addition to being undignified, slang is short-lived. Expressions like "twenty-three" and "skiddoo" are as outmoded today as the bathing suits of a generation ago. So a language that was artificial and synthetic to begin with has the added disadvantage of rapid obsolescence. If the habit of depending upon slang has not dulled his perception, the average person will turn with satisfaction to the dignity, accuracy, and perennial timeliness of standard English.

CORRECT USE OF SOME COMMON WORDS AND PHRASES

A. General usage in America approves the use of the article *a* before consonants, before initial *h* when sounded, and before the words *one* and *once: a house, a hospital, a historical society; a university; such a one.*

Colloquially, when two objects are thought of as belonging together or as used together, *a* need not be repeated: *a coat and hat; a cup and saucer; a sword and belt.* But, "She bought *a coat and a hat*," meaning two purchases, is correct.

The expression "*a black and white dress*" means but one, while "*a black and a white dress*" means two dresses—one black and one white. This second expression is awkward, and the form "*a black dress and a white one*" or "*a black dress and a white*" may be substituted. "They elected *a secretary and a treasurer*" implies two persons; but "*a secretary and treasurer*" implies one person.

Absolutely. This word, so frequently used instead of *indeed, assuredly, of course,* or *certainly,* should be discarded in favor of the accurate and appropriate word: "*Certainly* (not *absolutely*), I shall go." However, "It is *absolutely* certain that he will come" is correct when one intends to express positive assurance.

Accept, Except. *Accept* means "take when offered"; *except* means "leave out," "exclude": "I *accept* the gift." "We will *except* him from our requirements." Do not say "*accept of.*"

Acquire. This word should be distinguished from *obtain* and *procure.* We *acquire* that which we retain more or less permanently, but we *obtain* or *procure* anything which we enjoy temporarily. Thus, we *acquire* wealth, *obtain* a loan, *procure* supplies.

Across. "To get something *across,*" "to put a thing *across,*" "to come *across,*" are slang phrases. The first means usually "to make something understood," as an actor is said "to get it *across* (or *over*) to the audience." The second phrase implies *succeeding*; the third, *acceding,* as to a request or demand.

Adage. As this word describes a proverb, or old saying, one should never speak of an *old* adage.

Addict. This word, formed from the adjective *addicted,* has come into wide newspaper use. It means "one who has the habit of using" something generally harmful; as, "a drug *addict.*" It is widely used in medical works but has not yet come into general use. The term is a useful addition to our vocabulary. *Addicted* usually implies evil.

Addition. Number of verb. We say correctly, "Two and three *are* five," not "Two and three *is* five."

Administer. Do not say, "The man died from blows *administered* by the policeman." Oaths, medicine, affairs of state, are *administered.* Blows are *dealt.*

Admittance, Admission. In some uses these words are likely to be confused. *Admittance* refers to entrance to a place. "No *admittance*" means "entrance forbidden": "No *admittance* before 8 o'clock." *Admission* refers to entrance into a society or an audience, or into certain privileges: "*Admission* to the club depended upon scholarship." *Admission* may mean also the price or fee of entertainment: "*Admission* One Dollar."

Adore. This word means "worship," "venerate," or "hold in high respect or admiration." It is not appropriate to express a liking for chocolates.

Advert, Allude, Refer. The meanings of these words may be confused. We *advert* to that to which we turn the attention; we *allude* to a matter that we touch upon incidentally; we *refer* to a subject that we wish to bring back to notice.

Advise. In the jargon of business correspondence, "advise" is frequently misused to express some shading of "inform." Note the difference in the following example: "Our representative has informed (not 'advised') us of your application for additional credit. He advises us to grant the extension."

Advocate. Unlike propose, recommend, or urge, *advocate*, when used as a verb, is followed by a noun instead of a that-clause. We *recommend* that a measure be adopted; we *advocate* its adoption.

Aesthetic. This adjective preferably refers to abstract ideas, not to persons or objects. Do not speak of "an *aesthetic* person" or "an *aesthetic* decoration," but of "*aesthetic* standards" or "*aesthetic* considerations."

Affect. See *Effect.*

Affectation. Whether intentional or not, the use of "stylish" language arouses resentment in many people, who regard it as an assumption of superiority. The so-called "uppity" words may be clear and logically appropriate, but, because they are more bookish than conversational, they may produce an unfavorable reaction. Below are some typical pairs of what H. W. Fowler calls "working words" and "stylish words." Everyone can make up a similar list from his own experience.

WORKING WORDS	STYLISH WORDS
buy	purchase
class	category
drink	beverage
think	deem
wish	desire

Agendum, Agenda. The first (singular) indicates an item, as of business, to be considered; the second (plural), the list of all items for consideration or a program of business to be done.

Aggravate. Often inaccurately used when the speaker means *provoke, irritate,* or *anger.* The word means "increase" or "intensify." The following are correct uses: "His misery was *aggravated.*" "He is *irritated* by continually dealing with small matters." "She is easily *provoked* to jealousy."

Ago, Since. We say correctly, "a long time *ago*" and "some time *since*," or "many years *ago*" and "a few days *since*." *Ago* means before a certain time. If no point of time is specified, the word means before the present: "a year *ago* last Tuesday"; or, if we count back from the present, "a year *ago.*" *Since* means after a certain time and up to the present: "We have not met *since* 1910."

Agree. Do not use *agree* for *admit.* We *admit* a fact but *agree* in doing or thinking something. We may *admit* that a wall is not attractive but we *agree* in refusing to spend any more money to improve its appearance.

Agriculturist. Prefer this form to *agriculturalist.*

Aim. The not infrequent colloquial use of this word as a verb instead of *intend* or *plan,* as, "I *aim* to treat all customers fairly," is not approved by careful speakers, though formerly it was good English. As a noun, meaning "purpose," it is an excellent figurative word: "Young man, have an *aim* in life."

Ain't. Formerly classed by high authority as belonging to "illiterate speech," the contraction "*ain't*" for "*am not*" is not in good standing, despite recent efforts by publicists to make it respectable. Use it at your own risk, if at all, and hope your listeners will credit you with knowing better.

Alibi (Latin *elsewhere*). This standard legal term signifying absence from the scene of a crime, is also a familiar sports slang expression used loosely as an equivalent for "*excuse,*" "*explanation,*" or even "*apology.*"

Alike. This word should not be preceded by *both,* nor by *both just,* as in "These hats are *both alike*" or "*both just alike.*" Say, "These hats are *alike* (or *just alike*)." *Both* is superfluous in these phrases. See *Both* and *Just.*

All, All of. In spite of critics, popular usage has sanctioned the employment of *all of it, all of them,* like *some of them.* The idioms may be regarded as established. One may say either, "I have *all of it*" or "I have *it all.*" From the viewpoint of economy, *it all* is preferable.

Similarly, the phrase *all over* has established itself, as in the sentence, "We have searched *all over* the place."

Do not say, "This is *all* the *farther* I have read." The use is vulgar. Say, "This is as far as I have read" or "I have read no farther." See *Farther, Further.*

Allege. Do not use this word as a synonym for *say* or *tell,* as in "He *alleges* that the engine ran sixty miles an hour." Instead, "He *says* or *tells* us that, etc." The word has a legal sense, and with this meaning it is used in news writing. To say "The reasons *alleged* for the nomination are, etc." is to imply doubt as to the truth of what is *alleged* or to disclaim responsibility for the statement. See *Assert.*

All—not, Not—all. A common mistake among usually careful speakers is the failure to distinguish between these two logically different negatives. To say, "All people are not allergic to dust" is really equivalent to saying that none are allergic. On the other hand, by saying, "Not all people are allergic to dust," we convey the intended meaning that some are and some are not.

All right. The phrase should never be written *alright,* though formerly this usage was correct.

All together, Altogether. *All together* means "all in the same place at the same time" or "all acting at once": "We are *all together* in the business" or "Let us pull *all together*" or "Now, *all together,* boys." *Altogether* means "entirely"; as, "The time was *altogether* too short."

Almost, Nearly. These two adverbs should not be used indiscriminately. *Almost* suggests the ending of an act; *nearly,* its beginning. A man who receives an injury so severe that he barely comes off with his life *almost* loses it; a man who just escapes what would have killed him is *nearly* killed, or, as we say, "comes *very near* to being killed." These words are correctly used in "I have *almost* finished my work" and "I *nearly* ran over the child."

Alone, Only. To avoid ambiguity, observe the following distinction between these words: That is *alone* which is unaccompanied; that is *only* of which there is no other. "*Only* virtue makes us happy" means that nothing else can do it. "Virtue *alone* makes us happy" means that virtue unaided makes us happy. "This means of locomotion is used by man *only.*" See *Only.*

Already, All ready. Discriminate carefully between these terms. *Already* means "beforehand" or "so soon"; *all ready,* "everything prepared" or "prepared in every way."

Also. Like *only,* this particle is often misplaced, as in "If he is satisfied, I am satisfied *also.*" Write instead, "If he is satisfied, I *also* am satisfied." Place the word as close as possible to and usually following the word to which it applies.

Alternative. Do not use this word when more than two things are referred to. You may have the choice of three courses, not of three *alternatives.*

Alumni, Alumnæ. An *alumnus* is a graduate of a college, a university, or a school. *Alumni* (pronounced *ȧ-lŭm'nī*) is the masculine plural, but is used of men or women graduates. The feminine is *alumna*; plural, *alumnæ*, correctly pronounced *à-lŭm'nē*: "Association of Collegiate *Alumnæ*."

Amateur, Novice. *Amateur* means properly "one who pursues an art or plays a game *for the love of it*." The *amateur* may be highly skilled. The *novice* is a beginner; therefore, presumably unskilled.

Ambiguous. This word indicates uncertainty of meaning arising usually from lack of skill in the use of language. It is sometimes confused with "equivocal," which refers to intentional "double talk," in which more than one interpretation may best serve the speaker's purpose.

Ameliorated. This word means "bettered," "improved." "Her troubles are greatly *lessened* (not *ameliorated*)." We say correctly, "Conditions in the famine district have been *ameliorated*."

Amiable, Amicable. These two words of common origin appear so similar that important differences between them are sometimes overlooked. "Amiable" is a personal word, indicating a likeable or loveable disposition. "Amicable" is a more abstract term meaning friendly or agreeable, as in "an amicable settlement of a dispute."

Among. "He was there *among* the rest" should read "with the rest," because *rest* contradicts the idea of "mingling or including in a group" which is implied in *among*. "He was there *among* the first" is correct. *With* denotes simply accompaniment. Similarly, avoid such expressions as "*among one another, each other*." "*One another*" and "*each other*" imply individuals by themselves so that when they are used with *among* the resulting expression is self-contradictory. Say, "*among themselves*," "*with each other*," "*with one another*"; as "They exchanged hats *with each other*."

Amount. Used only of substances or material: "Only a small *amount* of grain could be purchased." Do not say, "a large *amount* of perfection" or "a large *amount* of people." *Degree of perfection* and *number of people* are correct.

Ample. This word should not be used, as it frequently is, to mean simply "sufficient." *Sufficient* means "enough to supply a need." *Ample* is a larger word and carries the sense of enough, as of space, time, supplies, with a wide margin for comfort or unforeseen demands.

An. Use this form of the article before words beginning with a vowel or a silent *h*; as, *an* inkpot, *an* oil well, *an* heir, *an* honor, *an* hour, *an* honest man.

And. See *Conjunctions*.

Answer, Reply. We *answer* a question, but we *reply* to a statement. *Reply* implies a more definitely planned expression than *answer*.

Ante-, Anti-. These prefixes are frequently confused. *Ante-* means "before"; *anti-* means "against" or "contrary to": "In *ante*-suffrage days the *anti*-suffragists were active." Pronounce the latter *ăn'tĭ*, not *ăn'tī*.

Antecedents. The use of this word to mean the ancestry and the past life of a person has good authority, though the use is of recent origin and the need for it infrequent. We may say of a person whose life history we wish to know, "What can you tell me of his *antecedents*?"

Anticipate. A stronger word than *expect* or *foresee*, and in some senses not synonymous with either. It means "take beforehand" (from Latin *ante*, "before," and *capere*, "to take"), "forestall," "get ahead of": "The committee was *anticipated* by the senator in introducing the water power bill."

The second meaning of the word is "look forward to," usually implying approval or enjoyment: "Only a few politicians *anticipated* his election" or "We *anticipated* a delightful vacation." One should say, "His death is daily *expected* (not *anticipated*)."

Antiquated, Ancient, Antique, Old. These words are frequently confused. *Old* is the opposite of *new, young, fresh; ancient* applies to what existed long ago, as *ancient states; antiquated* is a disparaging term for that which is old and in disuse or out of date, as "*antiquated* methods of business"; *antique* may be applied to something that has come down from olden times, as a vase or a piece of furniture, or to an imitation of the "real *antique*." See *Synonyms*.

Anxious. This word is often used loosely as a substitute for "eager" or some equally carefree expression. Note that in its original and correct sense, "anxious" conveys a suggestion of worry or concern.

Any. Sometimes used erroneously as an adverb to modify a verb; as, "Did you fish *any*?" Say rather, "Did you do *any* fishing?" *Any* should not be used for *all* in comparisons. Not, "That is the most beautiful car of *any* in the show," but "most beautiful car in the show." *Any* may modify adjectives; as, "*any* longer."

Anyhow, Anyway. Although sometimes disapproved as unscholarly, these are idiomatic expressions, meaning "in any event," "At any rate," or "be that as it may." Avoid *anyways* as vulgar.

Any place, Some place. These phrases should not be used for *anywhere* and *somewhere*. One should say, "I cannot find my umbrella *anywhere*," not "*any place*." One says properly, "I want to go *somewhere*"; but the expression "I want to go *some place*" is vulgar. The fault lies in needlessly using a noun in place of an adverb which accurately expresses the idea.

Anywheres. A vulgarism for *anywhere*. Similar vulgarisms are *somewheres* and *nowheres*.

A one. In such a sentence as "All who promised to come arrived, but not *a one* was on time," *a* is superfluous.

Apparently. This word stands midway between "seemingly," with its suggestion of deceptive outward appearances, and "evidently," with its convincing positiveness. "Apparently" can be inflected in such a way as to indicate various shades of meaning, but its rightful use is to describe what is clear to the eye or the understanding, but is not necessarily untrue.

Appear, Seem. *Appear* refers usually to what is evident to the senses: "The fruit *appears* to be well ripened." Every object may *appear*, but nothing *seems* except that which the mind admits to *appear* in a given form. Thus, *seems* is used to imply a result of thought or reflection: "He *seems* to be an honorable man."

Appreciate. Along with its suggestion of enjoyment, as in reference to works of art, "appreciate" is a serviceable word in some other common meanings. To say "We appreciate the difficulty of your situation" means that we understand sympathetically, not that we relish or enjoy the other person's difficulty. In a very different sort of context, "appreciate" means to grow in value, as in the case of property or investments.

Apt. Often misused for *likely*, and sometimes for *liable*. The following are examples of correct usage: "What is he *likely* to be doing?" "Where shall I be *likely* to find him?" *Liable* properly introduces some unhappy or disagreeable possibility: "If you go there, you are *liable* to incur his displeasure." *Apt* implies natural *fitness* or *tendency*: "Experienced men are *apt* to give good advice."

Arise, Arouse. The first form belongs to archaic, literary contexts: "I will *arise* and go to my father." In everyday use, *rise* is preferred: "We *rise* at six o'clock." *Arouse* refers to feelings: "This act *aroused* our anger." *Rouse* is used, transitively, in a literal sense: "We *roused* him from his slumbers."

As—as, So—as. Either combination may be used in negative statements involving comparison, but care should be taken to apply them appropriately. "James is not *as* tall *as* Tom" is a direct statement concerning the height of the two *without* implication that the speaker considers either of the persons spoken of as *tall*. But, if *so* be used instead of the first *as*, then it is understood that the second person referred to is notably tall in comparison with the first. Likewise, when age is spoken of, if one says, "My daughter is not *as* young *as* yours," the idea conveyed is that they may be nearly of the same age; but, by substituting *so* for the first *as*, one changes the sense and emphasizes the youth of the younger child and a marked difference between the two ages: "My daughter is not *so* young *as* yours."

As—as, only, may be used in affirmative declarative statements; as, "He is *as* good a man *as* anyone can find." *So—as*, however, is appropriate in some affirmative interrogative sentences when comparison is involved: "Is his estate *so* large *as* that?" Here an estate of great size is implied.

As for that is a vulgarism in such a sentence as "I do not know *as* I like him." Say, "*that* I like him." In such an erroneous expression as "Not *as* I am aware of," substitute *that* for *as*.

As a matter of fact. Trite phrase, overused by many speakers and writers. If emphasis is wanted, use a phrase specifically suited, such as: "Scientists agree that . ." or "It is universally understood that . .".

Aspiration, Ambition. *Aspiration* is exalted desire and properly implies striving for something high and ennobling; as, "To the *aspiration* of the poet we owe Milton's *Paradise Regained*." *Ambition* may imply worthy eagerness to achieve some great purpose, but it also connotes persistent, often overweening or inordinate, desire for personal advancement: "An *ambitious* man may *aspire* to greatness"; but it is used in the bad sense by Shakespeare in "*Ambition* should be made of sterner stuff." It is not properly used for *energy* or *fitness* for work, as in "He shows no *ambition* since his illness"; but it is correctly employed in "Repeated reverses curbed his *ambition*."

Assert, Allege. Two words often erroneously applied. Properly, one *asserts* that which one is ready to prove if called upon to do so, as a claim to property; one *alleges* that which is open to doubt or to question, as the existence of a will or the commission of a crime. See *Allege*.

As though. Often used for *as if*. This use has been condemned; but it is accepted as idiomatic English, notwithstanding the claim that it expresses a condition of remoteness approaching to impossibility; "We were received *as though* (or *as if*) there had been no war between our countries." *As if* is generally followed by a clause containing (1) a past subjunctive or (2) an infinitive expressing purpose or destination: (1) "Treating history *as if* it were a panorama intended to please the eye." "*As if* the dead the living should exceed." (2) "Buying agate and aluminum ware *as if* to set up housekeeping."

At. Redundant in the expressions "Where are we *at*?" "Where does he live *at*?"

At, In. *At* is a less definite word than *in*. Distinctions between them are not clearly drawn. The following examples, however, represent authoritative usage. We may say, "*in* the South," "*in* Chicago," also "The meeting was held *at* (or *in*) Baltimore." Of small towns or villages we say correctly, "They live *at* Walden"; but of larger cities, "His home is *in* Boston." To distinguish between points in a journey and the final destination, it is correct to say, "The ship calls *at* Halifax but docks *in* New York." A similar distinction is appropriate with the verb *arrive*. Either "We arrived *at* Denver," in which case the city is considered as one of the points to be reached in the journey, or "We arrived *in* Denver," which then is considered as the final stopping place. But, if the final destination is a small place, *at* is the correct word.

At all. An intensive colloquial phrase condemned by some critics, but entitled to standing as emphatic idiomatic English. There is a difference of emphasis between "I do not know him" and "I do not know him *at all*"; for, while the former denies acquaintance, it does not dispose of the possibility of acquaintance as emphatically as does the latter and more decided statement.

At best, At worst, At last. These are well-established idioms and are preferable to *at the best*, etc. They arose from an early joining of the preposition and the article into the form *atte*, whence *at*. See *Prepositions*.

At fault, In fault. Both phrases are correctly used for *in the wrong, in error, blameworthy*. *At fault* is the more common American usage.

Athletics. The word, when restricted to mean a system of physical exercises and training, should take a verb in the singular. But, when it is understood to mean the games and sports of a school, a verb in the plural is frequently used and is not incorrect. Similar use is current for *gymnastics* and *tactics*. Avoid the common error of saying *atheletics*, for the word is one of three syllables, *ath-let'ics*.

At one fell swoop. A trite expression, unpleasant to those hearers who appreciate its literary power in Shakespeare's *Macbeth*.

At that. This colloquialism used as an intensified ending is usually redundant and as such is better omitted: "The new car has arrived, and is a beauty *at that*." This construction has been traced to the use of the phrase in matters in which the cost of an article is considered; as, "Here is a good umbrella for $8.00 and cheap *at that* (price, understood)."

Audience. Often inaccurately used in place of spectators: The *audience* hears; the *spectators* see. Say: "the *spectators* at the ball game," not "the *audience*"; "the *audience* at the concert," not "the *spectators*."

Aught, Naught, Ought. *Aught* means "anything"; *naught* means "not anything," "nothing," or "cipher, 0." *Ought* is a verb, implying duty: "I *ought* to go." *Aught* or *ought* should never be used in the sense of *nothing* or a *cipher*.

Auspicious, Propitious. The word *auspicious* is applied to an occasion, the beginning of an important undertaking, or the like, and indicates that such occasions are favored by the conditions and by the circumstances. *Propitious* is applied to the conditions themselves and indicates that they are favorable. The word was originally applicable to a person or to a god and was later transferred to the signs which showed favor. A picnic has an *auspicious* beginning when the weather is *propitious*.

Avenge, Revenge. To *avenge* is to punish on behalf of another; to *revenge* is to punish on one's own behalf. We *avenge* a wrong to satisfy justice; but we may take *revenge* merely to satisfy our own angry resentment.

Averse, Aversion. *Averse to* is the accepted usage instead of *averse from*: "He was not *averse to* discussing his failure." Also *aversion to*: "His *aversion to* hard work is well known."

Avoid. This word means "to free oneself from" or "keep away from," but is often inaccurately used for *prevent* or *hinder*; as, "Nothing shall be lost if I can *avoid* it." Here *prevent* is the correct word to use: "if I can *prevent* it." But, "I shall not go if I can *avoid* it" is correct, for *avoid* here means "to free oneself from."

Awful, Awfully. Too frequently used as intensives. Avoid such phrases as "an *awful* shame," "*awfully* glad to see you." *Awful* is correctly used of that which fills with dread or inspires fear: "an *awful* catastrophe." Both of these words are colloquialisms that border on vulgarity when they are used in the sense of *extraordinary, highly remarkable,* or *excessively.*

Bad. Such phrases as *bad* cold, *bad* break, *bad* case are in wide colloquial use. Careful speakers try to use a more accurate and appropriate word, such as *serious, severe, troublesome.*

Badly, Bad. Discriminating people will try to avoid too general use of these words. When *feel* is used intransitively, like *seem,* the adjective *bad* (a predicate adjective) is grammatically correct: "She feels *bad* about the failure." In such a sentence as "I shall miss you *badly*," *very much* is to be preferred.

Balance. In bookkeeping, the sum to be added to the less or to be deducted from the greater of two amounts, as receipts and expenditures, so that the two "balance." It is incorrect to speak of the *balance* of a meal, the *balance* of an edition, etc. Here *rest* or *remainder* is correct. One may speak of the *balance* of an account.

Be back, Been to. Such expressions as "I will *be back* soon" and "I have *been to* town" are widely current. The first is approved, if *be back* signifies state or condition, not movement. For "I have *been to* town," one would better substitute "I have *been in* town." *In,* not *to,* is appropriate to the state or condition implied in *have been.*

Because. The word is a contraction of *by cause* and means "for the reason that." Therefore it is redundant in such constructions as "The reason we go is *because* we have been summoned." The correct form is "The *reason* we go is that we have been summoned" or, preferably, "We go *because* we have been summoned." The use of *why* after *because,* in "*because why,*" is a vulgarism in which *why* is redundant.

Begin, Commence. Although, historically, these words are precisely alike in meaning, *begin,* the Anglo-Saxon word, is preferred by careful speakers for general use. *Commence* has more formal associations and implies a beginning which involves a certain procedure and completion: One *begins* the practice of law, but one *commences* a lawsuit. We *begin* a day's work, but we *commence* a ceremony.

Behalf (on, in). A distinction worth noting is that *on behalf of* means "in the name of," while *in behalf of* means "in the interest of": "*On behalf of* the school, we thank you." "I make this appeal *in behalf of* the prisoner."

Beside, Besides. *Beside,* in present day usage, is a preposition and means "by the side of," as in "She stood *beside* the chair." *Besides* is either adverb or preposition and means "moreover," "beyond what has been said," or "in addition to": "*Besides,* they knew the road better"; "*Besides* wealth, he desired culture."

Better. This word is correctly used in the idiomatic form, *had better,* as in "We *had better* go."

Between. In its literal sense, this word applies to only two objects: "The candy was to be divided *between* the two boys, or *among* the four children."

When used of more than two objects, it brings them severally and individually into the relation expressed: "a treaty *between* three powers." One may say, "The steamers ply *between* San Francisco, Honolulu, and Yokohama."

"*Between* each desk there is a wide space." This is a frequent error. Say, "There is a wide space *between* each two desks" or "Wide spaces are left *between* desks."

Between may express contrast: "The two boys are brothers, but there is a great difference *between* them."

Biscuit. *Biscuits* is the correct plural. Although "Please pass the *biscuit*" is frequently heard, no one says, "Please pass the *cracker.*" There is a tendency to use *biscuit* as a collective singular by analogy with *bread,* but no one would say "Please pass the *roll*" of a number of rolls served at table.

Blame it on. A vulgarism used in place of *accuse* or *suspect:* "He *blames it on* his brother" should be "He *suspects* or *accuses* his brother" or "He *blames* his brother for it." In such an idiomatic phrase as "She is to *blame*" the passive meaning, "She is to be *blamed,*" is intended.

Both. Regarded as superfluous in the sentence "They are *both* alike." In "They *both* ran away from school," *both* has an intensive force. *Both,* as adjective or pronoun, may be applied to two objects or persons only. In "*Both* women spoke," *both* is an adjective; in "The general invited the colonel and the major and *both* went," *both* is a pronoun.

In the sentence, "They *both* met at the station," *both* is superfluous. "*Both* were alike good," meaning "*Both* were equally good," while approved usage, is not to be preferred to the latter sentence which is rhythmically perfect and linguistically sound.

As a conjunction, *both* may be used in connection with more than two things: "They lost all their property, *both* houses, barns, and crops."

Both of. Frequently condemned as colloquial; but the phrase has the support of literary usage, as in "*Both of* these arguments are sound."

Bother. Critics condemn this word when used as an imprecation or expression of impatience; as, "Oh, *bother* it all!" It is excellent English if used in the sense of *take trouble,* as in the sentence "You need not *bother* to return the paper."

Bound. In colloquial use to mean "determined" or "resolved," but challenged by the critics. *Bound* implies *compulsion* or *legal obligation*; as, "He is *bound* to pay it." "He is *bound* to do it" is correct if the person referred to is under obligation or promise, but not when the act depends on the resolution of the individual. Then say, "He is *certain, resolved,* or *determined* to do it." "He is *bound* to fail" should be "He is *sure* to fail." But we may say, "He is *bound* for destruction," meaning "He is *on the way* to destruction."

Brainy. A colloquialism meaning "mentally alert," "of quick understanding," or "of vigorous intellect"; as, a *brainy* man.

Broadcast. The past tense of this word is usually given as *broadcast.* In its new sense, however, of transmitting speech or programs by radio, the form *broadcasted* is so widely employed as to be regarded by many as standard usage.

Bunch. A word useful in describing bananas or grapes, but very objectionable slang when applied to people.

Bursted. A vulgarism sometimes rendered *busted.* Both are forms that cannot be too severely condemned, for the past participle and the past tense of the verb are the same as the infinitive, *burst.*

But. Frequently redundant before *that,* although sometimes required to make sense. When *but* is a preposition and *that* is a pronoun, there is no danger of error, for the meaning is "except that," as in "Nothing would please him *but that*." It is when both words are used as conjunctions that care must be exercised. In such a construction as "You need have no fear *that* she will go," the sense is clear that "she *will not* go"; but, in "You need have no fear *but that* she will go," the intention is clearly to express the feeling that "she is *sure* to go."

Best usage would eliminate *but* from "I have no doubt *but that* he will go," when the intention is to convey the feeling of certainty of his going. The form *but that* preceded by a negative becomes a positive—but it is more emphatic and less involved to say "I have no doubt *that* he will go."

"I cannot think (believe) *that* they will come" means that I believe strongly that they *will not* come; "I cannot think (believe) *but that* they will come" means that I must believe that they *will come*. "I can *but* believe him" means that, notwithstanding my own doubts, there is no other course open to me than to believe him; "I cannot *but* believe him" means that I am compelled to believe him—even against my will I am convinced. *But what* when used for *but that* is regarded as a vulgarism. These examples of the use of *but* illustrate what is meant by "English idiom."

By, With. *By* generally introduces the agent or doer; *with*, the instrument or means: "The window was broken *by* a boy *with* a ball." "The electricity is generated *by* water power." "The manager filled the theater *with* children." But, "The theater was crowded *by* the patrons of the opera."

By the name of. This phrase should not be confused with *of the name of*: "The business is owned by a man *of the name of* Brown." *Of the name* implies the real name; *by the name* suggests an assumed name; as, "Charles Farrar Browne was better known *by the name of* Artemus Ward than by his own name." It is well to substitute "a man *named* Brown" for "a man *of the name of* Brown."

By way of. We say correctly, "*by way of* illustration," meaning "*as* an illustration," or "*by way of* Cleveland" for "*through* Cleveland." In "He was *by way of* learning the country," *by way of* is an English colloquialism meaning "making progress in" or "occupied in."

Calamity. The word means, in an abstract sense, "source of misery or of loss," rather than the "loss" itself, for which it is often misused. *Calamities* are causes, of which *losses* may be the results. Any disaster produced by natural causes, as a hurricane, a cyclone, or a volcanic eruption, and attended by widespread destruction, is a *calamity* whether or not it be attended by loss of life.

Calculate. In the sense of *surmise, think, guess,* or *judge at random*, this word is a provincialism and is to be avoided: "I *think* (not *calculate*) tomorrow will be a fine day" but "His next move was *calculated* (that is, *designed*) to discourage his opponents."

Caliber. Often misused for *order*, as in "His work is of a higher *caliber* than hers." *Caliber* in its figurative sense applies to mental endowments. Thus, we may speak of a woman possessing great intellectual ability as being a person of *high caliber*, and of her work as being of high order, or excellent.

Can but, Cannot but. See *But*.

Can, May. Frequently confused. *Can* expresses power or ability; in most cases *may* expresses permission. Avoid "*Can* I speak to you a moment?" When you know that you *can speak* but wish merely for permission to do so, then substitute *may* for *can*. But, "*Can* you go?" is correct when the inquirer senses the possibility of obstacles that might prevent going; "*May* you go?" is also correct if permission to do so is involved.

Can not. Commonly and correctly written *cannot*. The origin of this form is in the shortened colloquial pronunciation of the two words.

Can't hardly. As *hardly* means "*not* easily" or "*not* quite," it must never be used with another negative as in this phrase. Substitute *can hardly*: "I *can hardly* believe the story."

Can't seem. Such an expression as "I *can't seem* to understand this problem" is to be avoided. Say, "I *seem unable* to understand." The inability is not in the *seeming* but in the *understanding*.

Capable, Susceptible. *Capable* is said of one's ability to do things, and in general it applies to the individual as having the capacity or intelligence to do; *susceptible* connotes action upon or sensitiveness to. Plans are *susceptible* of alteration; we are all *susceptible* to pain, that is, *capable* of being acted upon by it. One man may be *capable* of judging the fitness of another to fill a vacancy, yet he may not be *susceptible* to the blandishments of the applicant.

Capacity, Ability. These words are frequently confused. *Capacity* is the power of receiving or containing, and is used of the ability of the mind to accept ideas; it is the receptive mental faculty. *Ability* is power, either bodily or mental, and the word is sometimes used to describe mental endowments, or talents, of a superior kind. Some men possess the *ability* to help others although they have not the *capacity* to better their own conditions.

Carry. Provincial in the sense of *take, bring*, as in a carriage; as, "Father *carried* us all home with him." The word is archaic in the sense of *escort*: "He *carried* us to the party." Prefer "He *escorted* (*accompanied*) us."

Carry on. The phrase is in rather common colloquial use to mean "playing or behaving boisterously or indiscreetly." World War I gave us an intensified form of an old colloquial meaning, "maintain spirit and courage" or "keep work going in spite of difficulties."

Category. This formal word, preferably restricted to logical classification, should not be substituted indiscriminately for "class," "group," "rank," "species," and other more or less remotely associated synonyms.

Chairman. Correct usage sanctions *Mr. Chairman* and *Madam Chairman* as forms in which to address a presiding officer.

Cite, Quote. "Cite" means to refer definitely, as in footnotes listing sources and authorities. "Quote" is used only when the exact language of the source is given.

Claim. This word, as a verb, means "ask for" or "demand" by virtue of some authority or right, as in "We *claim* our share of the estate." It should not be used loosely for *say, assert, declare,* or *maintain*, as in "They *claim* that the water of the lake is warm."

Clever. As used in the sense of *good-natured* or *kindly*, this word is dialectal: "She is a *clever* woman." The commonly accepted sense today is *skillful, dexterous,* or *quick*. The word is used of mental alertness or mechanical ability. See *Synonyms*.

Clichés. The language is so full of ready-made phrases that it is easier to use them than to avoid them. Considered effective at first, these expressions have been worn threadbare by constant repetition. In the interest of freshness and originality, a different way of saying the thing should be attempted, at whatever cost in effort and initiative. It is really unnecessary to depend upon such stock phrases as "all nature seemed," "a bolt from the blue," "his better half," "the grim reaper," "the irony of fate," "wended our way," and "last but not least."

Clipped Endings. The practice of *"clipping"* the ending *-ing* is a vulgar error, as in *talkin'*, *walkin'*, *comin'*.

Coke Fiend. This is a vulgarism for an unfortunate individual addicted to cocaine or morphine. The term *addict* is the correct word to use. *Coke fiend* is in the same class as *rum hound* or *booze fighter*.

Commandeer. This word originated in South Africa during the Boer war. Its military meaning is "to compel to perform military service or to take for military purposes." As meaning "to take arbitrarily" it is in colloquial use only, the word *levy* or *requisition* being preferred by some as the literary term.

Company. The word is disapproved when used to mean "guests." Some writers look upon it as less formal, and therefore preferable, but no better word than *friends* need be used to express the intimacy of informal occasions. "The *company* has come" is decidedly provincial. "Our *friends* are here" and "The *guests* have arrived" serve to mark different degrees of formality.

Company, Corporation, Firm. With *company* or *firm*, either a singular or a plural verb is permissible; the word *corporation* takes a singular verb. A *corporation* is considered only as a unity, while one may think of a *company* or a *firm* either as a unit or as a number of partners.

Compared to, with. We may *compare* one thing *with* another in discussing the relative merits of both, but we *compare* one thing *to* another to point out some likeness: "*Compare* dead happiness *with* living woe." "*Compare* my life *with* his." "Life is *compared to* a voyage."

Comparison. In the *superlative degree*, comparison implies the inclusion of the things compared in a single group; in the *comparative degree* the things compared are thought of as in separate groups: *best of all; better than others*. See *Any, As, Else, Of*.

Complected. This is a dialectal word to be avoided. Say, "She is *dark-* (or *fair-*) *complexioned* (not *complected*)." Better still is the form, "She is of a dark (or fair) complexion." Frequently the simple "She is fair (or dark)" will serve.

Compliment, Complement. These words, so nearly alike and of the same origin, should not be confused. We say correctly, "They paid me the *compliment* of close attention" and "The ship had her *complement* (full number) of officers."

Comprised, Composed. These words are frequently confused. *Comprised* means "included"; *composed* means "made up" or "put together." We say correctly, "The ship's company *comprised* men of many nationalities," but "The bricks are *composed* of sand and clay."

Conclude, Decide. "Conclude" refers to the result of a reasoning process by which one reaches a point of mental certainty. "Decide" has to do with will and purpose. To decide is to resolve an issue or perhaps to settle upon a course of action.

Condone. The word should not be used for *compensate* or *atone*: "The abolition of the income tax would more than *compensate* (not *condone*) for the turmoil of an election." *Condone* means "forgive tacitly" or "overlook": "For the sake of tranquillity we *condone* many public faults."

Consequence. Etymologically, "a following together" and, from its original sense, "that which follows as a result of something that has preceded it." By an inversion, it has come to be used to signify importance or prominence acquired, as through the exercise of an office or through the ownership of land. Though some critics condemn this use of the word, it is authoritatively recognized and is logically sound: "He was a man of some *consequence* in his district."

Consider. The correct meaning of this word is "meditate," "deliberate," "reflect," "revolve in the mind." It should not be made to do service for *think, suppose*, and *believe*; as, "I *consider* that I have a bargain." This use, though frequent, is inappropriate.

Considerable. Frequently misused. Its association is with abstract rather than with concrete terms. A rich man may be one of *considerable* wealth, but we should not describe him as having *considerable* money. "We have had *considerable* rain" should be avoided. Prefer "an *abundance* of rain" or, more succinctly, "*plentiful* rain."

Contemptible, Contemptuous. Note the difference in point of view. A person who has done a wrong thing may be *contemptible*; that is, deserving of contempt. His attitude toward other people might be *contemptuous*; that is, he would show no regard for their judgments and opinions.

Continual, Continuous. The first of these words suggests recurring action, with intervals between; the second, unbroken occurrence, either in time or space: "Her *continual* nagging," "the *continuous* roar of the machinery."

Convince. This word, frequently misused in the sense of "persuade," means to gain mental assent, not to induce one to enter upon a course of action. "We persuaded (not convinced) him to go with us."

Correspond to, Correspond with. Things or people *correspond to* one another by agreeing or being parallel in certain respects; people *correspond with* one another by means of written communication.

Couple. The use of *couple* to mean merely "two" or "several" is vulgar or dialectal. The word correctly means "two like things or two persons acting in concert or so joined as to act together or to be considered together," as two mechanical parts or two partners in a dance.

Credible, Creditable. The latter word should not be used instead of *credible*, "believable." Say, "two *credible* (not *creditable*) witnesses." Say, "I am *credibly* (not *creditably*) informed." Formerly, *creditable* meant "credible," but this use is obsolete. It now means "commendable."

Curious. This word does not always mean "inquisitive," but frequently signifies "wrought with such care as to excite surprise" or "fashioned in such a way as to evoke surprise." The use of *curious* to mean "interesting," "unusual," or "novel" is sometimes condemned, but it is in good taste: "The museum possesses a collection of *curious* ornaments."

Data, Memoranda, Strata. These words are the plural forms of *datum, memorandum*, and *stratum*, but are sometimes construed erroneously as singulars: "The *datum* (singular) is here"; "The *data* (plural) are all here"; "This *memorandum* is clear"; "These *memoranda* are correct." To form the plural, an *s* has sometimes been added to the words *stratum, memorandum*, but never to *datum*. *Stratum*, being a technical word, should be more carefully used and its plural be written *strata*.

Deceiving. This should not be used in place of *trying to deceive*. When we suspect deception but are not *deceived*, we should say, not "He is *deceiving* me," but "He is *trying to deceive* me."

Defective, Deficient. "Defective" is used correctly to describe faultiness. "Deficient" refers to incompleteness in numbers or amount.

Delusion, Illusion. A "delusion" is an unsound idea arising within one's mind; an "illusion" is a false image from outside which deceives the senses, or sometimes an unreal concept that is more or less willingly accepted.

Demand. A transitive verb which always requires an object. We *demand* the payment of a debt. Do not say, "He *demanded* me to do it." Say, "He *demanded* that I should do it." "It" stands for the thing or act required. "They *demanded* their pay" is correct. The direct object of *demand* must be other than the person *of*, or *upon*, whom the demand is made.

Depot. See *Station*.

Deprecate, Depreciate. These words should not be confused. *Deprecate* means "regret," "express disapproval of": "His friends *deprecated* his hasty action." *Depreciate* means to "undervalue" or "decrease in value": "They *depreciated* the value of freedom"; "That stock has *depreciated* very greatly."

Desperately. The word should not be used to mean merely "seriously." It means "violently," "recklessly," "in a desperate manner." "He was *desperately* wounded" means wounded so seriously that he was beyond apparent hope of recovery.

Despite. This word may be preceded by *in* and followed by *of*, although *despite* has good standing as a preposition. Say, "*despite* all our efforts" or "*in spite of* all our efforts." *Notwithstanding* is a more dignified expression and has the same meaning.

Differ, Different. Persons or things *differ from* each other in appearance, size, etc. Persons may *differ with* each other in opinion. *Different from* is approved American usage, not *different to* or *different than*, both of which are accepted idioms in England, having substantial literary support, as of Goldsmith, John Henry Newman, and Thackeray. Shakespeare used *different from*.

Direct, Call. *To direct* some one's attention to a thing is more accurate and specific than *to call* his attention to a thing. Direct is the more formal.

Directly, Immediately. The use of *directly* as a synonym for *immediately* is sanctioned by good usage, though some critics pronounce it colloquial. One may say, "We will proceed *immediately* the train arrives" or "*immediately* after the train arrives." American usage prefers *immediately*. English usage favors *directly*.

Disapproval. Say, "He expressed *disapproval of* (not *with*) the dance."

Disinterested. Not lack of interest, but absence of partiality is indicated by this word. In the case of a controversy, for example, a disinterested third party is an unprejudiced observer.

Dissent. This word should be followed by *from*: "They *dissent from* our judgment." "They *dissent from* us." Compare *Differ*.

Do. Like other Anglo-Saxon verbs such as *make* or *put*, *do* has an almost unlimited variety of idiomatic uses. Examples are: "I *did* all the problems;" She *did* up the package;" "We could see that he was *done* for." Although many expressions containing *do* are informal, most of them are in good colloquial use and are popular because of their forcefulness. The various uses of *do* should be studied with the aid of a dictionary. Careful speakers will note the difference between acceptable and unauthorized forms. Thus they will say "I have *done* with the book," not "I am *done* (that is, *finished*,) with it."

Dock, Wharf. A *wharf* is a landing stage or pier; a *dock* is a body of water beside a *wharf* or between *wharves*. In American practice, *dock* is misused for *wharf*. Originally, *wharf* meant "bank" or "shore," and *dock* meant "ditch," "pit," or "pool." The distinction is more clearly apparent when one refers to the different forms of *dock* as *dry* or *graving dock*, *floating* and *wet dock*.

Don't, Doesn't. The first is a colloquial contraction for *do not*; the second, for *does not*. They should be used with care. Avoid "He *don't* want it." Say: "They *don't*," or "He *doesn't* want it."

Don't think. "I *don't think* it will rain" is an established idiom, as are other similar expressions in use.

Double Possessive. This construction is accepted as idiomatic English. Such phrases as "that house *of Brown's*" and "that car *of mine*" show the double possessive and may be used if required, but "*Brown's* house" and "*my* car" will usually express the thought more economically.

Doubtless. Because this word has become weakened through long use, it has given way in some cases to the stronger word "undoubtedly," or even to the intensive phrase, "beyond the shadow of a doubt." Other words denoting emphasis have fared similarly. Compare "soon" and "presently," which once meant "immediately."

Dozen, Dozens. After indications of price, *a dozen* or *the dozen* is correct. In American usage *a dozen* is preferred: "fifty cents *a dozen*." The phrases, "a pair," "a gross," "a tale," are used in like manner. Correctly we say, "several (or many) *dozens*"; but, when linked with definite numbers or used with *pairs*, *dozen* is the approved form, as, "four *dozen* pairs." See *Pair*.

Due to. That which may be attributed to a cause is *due to* it, but, to express cause or reason, *due to* is preferably used as a predicate complement: "His failure was *due to* unusual conditions." A sentence may begin with *because of* or *owing to*, but should not begin with *due to*. Example: *Because of* unusual conditions, he was unable to complete the work."

Each other. Properly applied to two only; *one another* must be used when the number referred to exceeds two. We say, "Great authors address themselves to *one another*," unless we refer to only two authors.

Eat, Ate, Eaten. These are the correct parts of the verb. Say, "He *ate* rapidly"; "I have *eaten* my dinner."

Effect, Affect. *Effect* means "bring about"; *affect* means "influence": "A man may *effect* a reform." "His ideas will *affect* the character of the reform." *Affect* may mean "pretend": "They *affect* an interest in the matter." *Effect* is sometimes used as a noun; *affect* is always a verb.

Effective. Associated with this word and related to it etymologically are several words that are usually differentiated from it in practice. Where "effective" means result-getting in a broad general sense, we speak of an "effectual" plea or prayer, an "efficacious" remedy, and an "efficient" machine or person.

Egoism, Egotism. One may be an *egoist*, that is, may habitually advocate the doctrine of *egoism*, or the pursuit of self-interest, as the supreme aim of human effort, and yet he may not be an *egotist*. *Egotism* is offensive conceit.

Either, Each, Both. Note the following correct expressions: "You may enter by *either* door (meaning *one* or the *other*)." "A bench is placed at *each* side of the doorway (that is, one on *one* side, one on the *other*)." "There were windows on *both* sides (or *each* side) of the doorway." Formerly, *either* was widely used in the sense of *each*, but this use is rare today.

Elemental, Elementary. "Elemental" refers to the basic forces or units of nature; "elementary" reduces anything to its simplest component parts for clear understanding.

Else, Else's. Such an expression as "Do not take *anyone else's* place" is good form and to be preferred to "Do not take *anyone's else* place," which has some defenders but is not accepted as sterling.

Else but. Avoid the use of *else* before *but* in the expression "I have no one *else but* you."

Emigrant, Immigrant. *Emigrants* are persons *going out* of a country, and *immigrants* are persons *coming into* it. *Emigrate* is derived from the Latin *e*, "out," and *migrare*, "to go from the land"; *immigrate*, from the Latin *im* for *in*, "into," and *migrare*.

Eminent, Imminent. Two words of similar sound but of widely different meanings. *Eminent* signifies "distinguished" or "well known": "He has become *eminent* in his profession." *Imminent* means "about to happen" or "threatening": "The defeat of the army was *imminent*."

Empty, Vacant. Anything that is "empty" is simply without contents or occupants. "Vacant" conveys the idea that it may have been occupied, or may be filled in the future.

Enclose, Inclose. The history of these words as well as general English usage favors *enclose* rather than *inclose*. But most recent dictionaries give *inclose* the preference. Either is correct.

Endorse, Indorse. Either form is correct, but, while *endorse* is used in literature, *indorse* finds favor in law and commerce. Do not say, "I *endorse* the movement." Say, "I *approve* it." Do not say, "*Indorse* the check *on the back*." Omit the last three words. *Indorse* means to write one's name *on the back* of commercial paper or documents.

Enjoyed the advantage. Trite phrase, elaborate and cumbersome substitute for "had."

Enthuse. It is better to speak of *being enthusiastic*. Typical of a large group of barbarisms known as "back-formations," *enthuse* is a coined verb suggested by the noun *enthusiasm*, but not derived from it by any proper linguistic procedure. Compare *burgle* (burglary), *laze* (lazy), and *orate* (oration). Although an occasional "back-formation" gains acceptance—for example, *diagnose, sidle, drowse,*—it is better as a rule to avoid such eccentric forms and to look for established synonyms.

Equally as well. An incorrect phrase. *As well* and *equally well* are correct forms.

Euphemisms. From an understandable wish to avoid offending sensitive ears, people tend to substitute long or abstract words for short plain ones. Thus, "imbibe" for "drink," "perspire" for "sweat," and "prevaricate" for "lie" stand for a long list of consciously watered-down synonyms. Not all of these substitute expressions are as ridiculous as "lady dog" and "gentleman cow," but euphemisms at best give an impression of linguistic timidity that is out of harmony with the times. People, especially moderns, are not so squeamish as these polite evasions would indicate. Within the bounds of decency, plain words are best.

Event, Eventuality. The first of these words indicates a definite happening; the second, an occurance considered as a possibility.

Ever so, Never so. *Ever so* is correctly used to mean "exceedingly." Both phrases are used to mean "however" or "no matter how," as in "were he *ever so* (or *never so*) rich." Modern usage prefers *ever so* in all such cases.

Excuse, Pardon. While *pardon* is the more formal official word in respect to offenses, and *excuse* the more familiar in respect to minor matters, a further distinction is to be noted. For instance, when interrupting a conversation, one says, "*Pardon* the interruption," and, when leaving a guest, "*Excuse* me."

Exemption, Immunity. One claims *exemption* from taxes or from duty; one acquires *immunity* from disease, as by inoculation, or is granted *immunity* from punishment.

Expect. As this word means "look forward to as a contingency," it should never be used of any retrogression, for one cannot *expect* backwards. Not, "I *expect* you thought I would come yesterday," but "I *suppose*, etc." "I *expect* you know all about it" should be "*imagine*," "*think*," or "*suspect* you know." But "We *expect* that they will come" or "We *expect* them" is correct. Compare *Anticipate*.

Extempore, Impromptu. An *extempore* address is one delivered without manuscript and without memorization, though previous preparation may have been made by thought upon the subject treated. An *impromptu* speech is given on the moment, without previous preparation.

Farther, Further. Careful speakers and writers use *farther* for distances in space and *further* for continuity of other kinds: "We walked *farther* today than yesterday"; "The chairman said *further* (that is, *in addition*) that all dues must be paid promptly." *Further*, then, is used for expressions of continuity, as of thought or action: "I had no *further* dealings with him"; "a *further* rise in temperature."

Fascinating. As that which *fascinates* operates on its object as by some irresistible power, *fascinating* should not be used when *charming* or *attractive* is meant. Properly, that is *fascinating* or *bewitching* which possesses the art to please beyond the power of resistance; as, "Her *fascinating* manner and words disarmed suspicion."

Faulty Comparisons. Avoid double comparatives and superlatives. Say, "*worse*," not "*worser*"; "*abler*," not "*more abler*." Avoid impossible comparisons. Say, "*more nearly perpendicular, more nearly universal*," not "*more perpendicular, more universal*." Use the comparative degree for two objects, the superlative for more than two.

Fearful. A much overworked word. The meanings of the nouns from which such words as *dreadful*, *terrible*, and *fearful* are derived should always be borne in mind when the adjectives are used. The colloquial use of these words to express intense feeling or annoyance easily passes into extravagant hyperbole. Do not describe the falling off a horse as a *terrible* but rather as a *serious* accident. "He was *fearful* for our safety," that is, "He *feared* that we were in danger" is correct.

Female. In polite speech this word is restricted to sex or to animals. When applied to women, it is derogatory, and it should not be used in such expressions as "What is more delightful than the blush of a beautiful young *female*!"

Feminine words. Although the suffix "ess" is available for converting masculine nouns to feminine ones, usage rejects or questions some words formed in this way, while accepting others. Examples of well-established feminine words are "actress," "governess," "hostess," and "stewardess." Doubtful ones include "authoress," "doctress," "editress," "manageress," and "poetess." In such cases, the masculine word may be preferable for both men and women. It is the only one possible for words like "clerk," "lecturer," "singer," "teacher," and "typist."

Fewer, Less. *Fewer* refers to number; *less*, to quantity. Instead of "There were not *less* than ten chapters in the book," we should say, "There were not *fewer* than ten chapters in the book." But say, "The box weighed not *less* than ten pounds."

Fine. An adjective which should not be used as an adverb. Do not say, "She sang that *fine*," when you mean "well." "I like that *fine*" and "He is doing *fine*" are incorrect. Say, "I like that *very much*" and "He is doing *well* or *very well*."

First-rate. Do not use this adjective as an adverb. "She plays *first-rate*" is a vulgarism. *First-*

rate means "of the highest excellence or quality." "He is a man of *first-rate* ability" is correct.

Fix. Often misused colloquially for *arrange* or *repair*: "I must *fix* the books." "Who *fixed* the dishes on the shelves?" "He had the clock *fixed*." It is vulgarly used thus: "I will *fix* him"; "The jury was *fixed*"; "You must *fix* up, if you go"; "Your affairs are in a bad *fix*." *Fix* means "fasten," "make firm," or "settle": "The hooks are *fixed* in the wall." "Their income is a *fixed* amount."

Folk, Folks. Often incorrectly used interchangeably. Both words are construed as plurals, but the first refers to *people* or *peoples* generally, as "folk tales" or "fairy folk." In colloquial usage, *folks* has displaced *folk*. In "My *folks* have gone South," *folks* signifies "relatives." In "the *folks* next door," the word means "neighbors."

Forceful, Forcible. We speak of a "*forceful* style" or a "*forceful* personality," but of *forcible* ejection or *forcible* action of any kind. In usage, *forcible* is the more common word, and *forceful* the more special one.

Former—Latter. These words should be used only when they really economize space and save the reader's time. By repeating the antecedents (nouns or phrases), one avoids sending the reader back to see which is *former* and which is *latter*. Sometimes, however, a disagreeable repetition is avoided by using "the *former*—the *latter*."

Fortuitous, Fortunate. "Fortuitous" refers to a chance happening that may be either favorable or unfavorable. "Fortunate" is restricted to favorable chance.

Funny. A word too frequently used when humor or amusement is not meant. Of something unusual, use *strange, odd, peculiar*, or a similar accurate word instead of *funny*: "It was a *peculiar* situation," not "*funny*" unless it is laughable.

Get, Got, Have. *Get*, like *do*, has many different meanings and is carelessly used. Avoid *get* for *be* and especially such expressions as "She will *get* laughed at for her pains." Say rather, "She will *be* laughed at, etc." If a man has inherited a fortune and has not dissipated it, we say correctly, "He *has* money"; if he obtains money through his own effort, we say correctly, "He *has gotten* money."

"*Get* a move on" is a forceful but inelegant Americanism for "Be quick about it."

Do not say, "*Get* up a show" when you mean plan or prepare. Colloquially, a *get-up* is an equipment consisting of dress and accessories and is very frequently correctly used, as in "a clever *get-up*" or "a stylish *get-up*." Avoid "Do you *get* me?" as the height of vulgarity.

"He *has got* to do it" is a common colloquialism. "He *has got* it to do" shows the wasteful character of the phrase. "He *has* it to do," "He *must* do it," or "He *has* to do it" is correct. We may, however, say correctly, "The cat *has got* the mouse," but "*caught* the mouse" is preferable.

Both *got* and *gotten* are correct forms of *get*, but careful writers tend to avoid *gotten*. As William Lyon Phelps said, "*Gotten* has *got* to go."

Get, meaning "become," is colloquial: "He will *get* well"; "as we *get* older."

Goes. In the phrase "anything *goes*" we have slang; in "the machine *goes*" we have idiomatic English. "That *goes* without saying" is a literal translation of a French idiom, in colloquial use.

Good. The use of the adjective *good* for the adverb *well* is vulgar. Avoid "I feel *good*" and "He is working *good*." Say rather: "I feel *well*"; "He is working *well*."

Grand. That which is *grand* is "magnificent," "noble," or "splendid," yet there is strong tendency to misapply the word. Today anything from a bit of chewing gum to Mt. Shasta is described as *grand*. The word should be used only of that which possesses grandeur.

Great. The indiscriminate use of this word is evidence of a poverty-stricken vocabulary: "We had a *great* time" is a colloquialism; "I like it *great*" is a vulgarism.

Had. "*Had* I thought of that, I should have come." This sentence is correct; but the common practice of inserting *have* after the pronoun is reprehensible. Shun "*Had* I have known," "*Had* I've known," "If I *had've*," "If I *had of* (uv)," if you wish to avoid being classed as illiterate.

Had better, as in "He *had better* look out," is excellent English idiom.

Had ought is a solecism for *should have*. *Ought* is not a participle. Say, "We *should have* or we *ought*," not "We *had ought*."

Hanged, Hung. Criminals are *hanged*, clothes are *hung*. This is an old distinction, still in force.

Hard, Hardly. The idiomatic adverb *hard* is in good use in such expressions as "He worked *hard*;" "Hit the line *hard*." *Hardly* cannot be used interchangeably with *hard*, because the two words differ in meaning. To say, "The battle was *hardly* won" may convey an idea opposite to the one intended. At best, the sentence is ambiguous. When a synonym for *scarcely* is needed, *hardly* is correctly used, as in the sentence "They will *hardly* succeed." In such cases the word is a useful negative of understatement. The adverb *hardly* is correctly followed by *when*, not *than*, as in "We had *hardly* taken our seats *when* the boat began to leak." The use of *hardly* with a negative added is a solecism, as in "I *can't hardly* tell." The correct form is "I *can hardly* tell."

Hate. A word that signifies "having a great aversion for," but used colloquially for *dislike* "I *hate* to do that kind of work." *Hate* is too strong a word for such use. Say, "I *dislike* to do that kind of work" or "I *detest* that kind of work."

Have to have. Avoid this useless repetition. Not, "I *have to have* my work done by three o'clock," but "I *must have* my work, etc." Do not say, "I *have got to get*" when "I *have to get*" is what you should say.

Healthful, Healthy. Note the distinction in meaning between these words. *Healthful* is applied to conditions or environments: "Children should be reared in *healthful* surroundings." *Healthy* describes a good physical condition, without disease. "A *healthy* mind in a *healthy* body is desirable."

Hear to it. We "*hear of*" an incident or "will not *hear of*" a course being pursued, but *hear to it* is archaic. *Hear* signifies "listen to"; formerly, "He will not *hear to* reason" was accepted as idiomatic, but it is now rendered "He will not *listen to* reason."

Hearty. "He ate a *hearty* breakfast" is good English idiom. *Hearty* means "strengthening" and "satisfying."

Hectic. A word which specifically means "habitual," "constitutional," being derived from the Greek *hexis*, "habit of body"; but it has come to mean "flushed" as with fever, or affected with such fever as accompanies tuberculosis. It is often misapplied, as in "*hectic* haste," in the sense of *feverish* or *excited*.

Hence, Thence, Whence. These words connote *removal from*; therefore, they should not be used with *from*. *Hence* is superfluous in such a sentence as "It will be many years *hence*, we apprehend, before he returns."

Historic, Historical. "Historic," a specialized word, means memorable; "historical," a more general term, means pertaining to history.

How. "I have heard *how*, in Italy, one is beset on all sides by beggars" should read "I have heard *that*, in Italy, etc." But "He told me *how* he worked his passage" is correct, since the reference is not to the fact, as in the first sentence, but to the manner of action.

How that and *as how*, as in "He told *how that* he would never return" or "He said *as how* he would go," are most objectionable colloquialisms.

However. Frequently misused for *how*, in such a sentence as "*However* could you tell such a story!" One should say, "*How* could you *ever* tell such a story!" *However* means "no matter what the extent of." "*However* careful you may be, you will make mistakes" is correct.

Hustle. Properly this word means "shove," "push," or "jostle roughly." Although frequently used colloquially for *hurry*, as in "*Hustle* that order along," it is not properly a synonym for *hurry*.

I, Me. These forms of the personal pronoun of the first person are frequently confused. *Me* is the form to use with a preposition. Say "between you and *me*," not "between you and *I*." Similarly, "with her (him) and *me*," not "with she (he) and *I*."

Idioms. Like every other living language, English is constantly forming idioms, that is, special combinations of words that do not follow the rules of either grammer or logic. Baffling to outsiders, these expressions are clear to the initiated and, despite their irregularity, are in good standing as language. Phrases like "by and large," "hold out," "make good," "pull through" and innumerable others illustrate this phase of English expression.

If. *Whether* in place of *if* is preferred by most authorities in sentences like these: "I do not know *if* (*whether*) the book will suit you"; "I wonder *if* (*whether*) he has come." The use of *if* for *whether* is colloquial or poetic. *Whether* is preferable to *if* especially where the additional idea of *or not* is implied. Compare "Let me know *if* you can go," and "Let me know *whether* you can go."

Ill, Sick. English usage confines the word *sick* chiefly to the meaning "nausea," as, *a sick headache;* but in America *ill* and *sick* are generally synonymous. However, we say: "He is a *sick* man," never "He is an *ill* man"; but, either "He is *ill*" or "He is *sick*."

In, Into. *In* is sometimes an adverb and sometimes a preposition, but its employment as an adverb is really an elliptical use of the preposition. As an adverb, *in* is correctly used in these sentences: "Come *in*," for here *in* means "into the house, room, etc."; and likewise, "Go *in*," meaning "Go into the room, house, etc." As a preposition, *in* may be used with verbs of rest or of motion and *into* with verbs of motion only: "He sat *in* his chair"; "The child runs *in* the yard"; "He walked *into* the house."

In back of. The expression "They sat *in back of* us," meaning "behind," though analogous to "They sat *in front of* us," is disapproved. *Behind* accurately expresses the thought. As to *in front of*, we have no corresponding preposition, since *before* may convey the idea of *facing* and thus may produce ambiguity.

Individual. The word is jocosely or contemptuously used for *person*. It is used correctly in "Changes both in *individuals* and in communities are often produced by trifles"; contemptuously in "That *individual* left here several hours ago."

Indulge. This word means "give oneself up to (something)"; "yield to one's longings or passions unrestrainedly"; "give free course to one's habits"; "humor to excess, as children." Thus, one *indulges* in idleness, or one *indulges* children's whims or wishes. While one may *indulge* a thirst for fame, one should avoid "I never *indulge*" as objectionable in declining an offer of refreshment.

Infer, Imply. These words are frequently confused. One *infers* or *reasons* or *draws a conclusion* from something heard or read. One may *imply* (*suggest*) in what one writes or says, for example "One *infers* from what Jefferson wrote that the Declaration of Independence *implies* belief in democracy."

Inferior to. Note that the correct form is *inferior to*, not *inferior than*. Example: "The substitute is nearly always *inferior to* the original product. *Superior to* is of course the corresponding idiom.

-ing. See *Clipped Endings*.

Ingenious, Ingenuous. *Ingenious* means "skillful," "inventive": "The boy is *ingenious* and loves machinery." *Ingenuous* means "candid," "frank," "open," "innocent," "guileless": "He made an *ingenuous* reply."

In our midst. Condemned by most critics as a substitute for *in the midst of* (*us*). The purist prefers *among us*.

In so far as. A phrase formed on the analogy of *in as much as*, but *so far as* expresses the thought and *far* is itself an adverb; therefore *in* is superfluous. "*In so far as* I know" should be "*so far as* I know." In "in as much as." *much* is a noun and requires a preposition to give the phrase adverbial force.

Intend. See *Mean*.

In or Under the circumstances. Both phrases are in good use. *Circumstances* may imply merely attendant conditions not thought of as seriously modifying action. *In* is then the proper preposition; as, "*In the circumstances* he hesitated." But when *action* is thought of as determined by the circumstances, as, "*Under the circumstances* prosecution of the case could not be avoided," *under* is the approved word.

Irrelevant. The word means "unconnected with" or "not related to": "His remarks were *irrelevant* to the discussion." Do not pronounce it *irrevelant*.

Is that so? Courtesy will prompt a thoughtful person to be careful *how* and *when* he uses this and the similar phrase, "You don't say so," for they imply doubt or disbelief as well as express surprise. As subject to equivocal interpretation they should be avoided. "I want to know," used in a similar sense, is vulgar.

Its, It's. Sheer carelessness causes many people to confuse the spelling of the possessive pronoun "its" ("A tree is known by its fruit") with the contraction of "it is" ("It's going to rain").

Junk. Colloquial or slang when used as a verb for *discard*, or "throw away as useless."

Just. This adverb is correctly used for *precisely*, *only, merely*, or *by a slight margin;* it is colloquial when the meaning is "quite," "very," "altogether," or "simply." Say, "I *just* missed the car," but not "The hostess was *just* lovely, but the food was *just* awful." Such a statement is ambiguous.

Kind. The word is singular. One should say, "this *kind*," not "these *kind*." But "those *kinds*," not "those *kind*," is correct.

Kind of. Avoid the use of *a* as a modifier before a noun when preceded by *kind of*. "What *kind of* man is he?" is correct. "What *kind of a* man is he?" is incorrect.

Kind of tired, amusing, etc., are slovenly speech. *Somewhat tired, rather amusing*, are preferred.

Lady. Address a woman who is a stranger to you as *Madam*, and not as *Lady*. Persons of culture do not say, "She is a fine *lady*," "a clever *lady*"; they use *woman* instead. Ladies say, "The *women* of America," "*women's* interests." In like manner use *man* or *men* instead of *gentleman* or *gentlemen*.

Last, Latest. We speak of an author's *latest* book, but hardly of his *last* book until he is dead. But we say properly, "Have you read the *last* number of this magazine?" Here *last* means "latest in a series."

Last two. This phrase is preferred by most authorities to *two last*: "They bought the *last two* copies."

Laundered. The clothes were *laundered*, not *laundried*.

Lay, Lie (verbs). *Lay* is transitive and denotes an *action* on an object; *lie* is intransitive and designates a *state* or a *condition*: "I *lay* the rug on the floor, and it *lies* there." "They *laid* him with his fathers." "He *lies* with his fathers." The following expressions are idiomatic: "A thing *lies* by us until we bring it into use"; "We *lay* it by for some future purpose."

The confusion arises probably from the fact that *lay* appears in both verbs. The words are correctly used in the following sentences:

I *lay* the book on the table today.
I *laid* it there yesterday.
I have *laid* it there every day.
I am *laying* it there now.
I *lie* on my bed today.
I *lay* there yesterday.
I have *lain* there every day.
I am *lying* there now.

Lay, Lie (nouns). Both of these words are in good use to signify the manner in which land *lies* in its relation to the surrounding country. "The *lay* of the land" is in popular favor; "the *lie* of the land" has the support of the scientists. The latter is the older English usage.

Learn, Teach. Formerly, *learn* and *teach* were used interchangeably, but now to confuse them is a mark of illiteracy. We *learn* things for ourselves; we try to *teach* others.

Leave, Let. One takes one's *leave*, after a call or visit. We ask *leave* or *permission*. One is *on leave*, that is, enjoying a permitted absence from his usual place of duty. Do not say "*Leave* him do it," but "*Let* him do it." Properly, one *leaves* (goes away from) a place, but he *lets* a person or thing alone, that is, does not meddle or interfere. Still, one correctly asks to be "*left* to himself," that is, asks others to "*leave*" or "go away from" him.

Legible, Readable. A "legible" piece of writing is clear to the eye, that is, easily deciphered. A "readable" book is one that invites reading because of its interesting style and content.

Lend, Loan. The verb *lend* is the general word to use when we supply something to another with the understanding that it is to be returned. Say, "*Lend* (not *loan*) me the books or money." The use of *loan* as a synonym for *lend*, although of English origin, has been condemned as an Americanism; but it has fallen into disuse except in financial circles. One says correctly, "He tried to get a *loan* from the bank," where *loan* is used as a noun. "The company *loans* money on good security"; here the word is used as a verb.

Less. See *Fewer*.

Let alone. A vulgarism when used to mean "excluding," "not to mention." Avoid such expressions as "The inconvenience was bad enough, *let alone* the expense."

Like, As. *Like* is not used for *as* in the New England States; the use is common in the South and the West. The phrase *like of that* should be avoided in "We spend our days fishing, canoeing, and the *like of that* (or *like that*)," for it is a vulgarism. Do not say: "Do *like* I do"; "I felt *like* I would faint"; "My feet were heavy *like*"; or "He had *liked* to have been killed," meaning "came near to being killed." Say: "Do *as* I do"; "I felt *as if*"; "My feet *seemed* heavy." But one may say, "She walks *like* a queen," meaning "in the manner of." To use the tautological phrase *like as if* is to display one's ignorance.

Like, Likely. The first is frequently erroneously used in conversation instead of the second. *Like* means "similar," "corresponding," "equal," and "resembling." *Likely*, as an adjective, means "probable," "suitable," "adaptable," or, adverbially, "to be reasonably expected." Avoid "He is *like* to call today" as illiterate. The following is correct: "In *like* circumstances, a repetition of the occurrence is *likely*."

Like, Love. See *Love*.

Literally. This word is often used for emphasis as a synonym for "actually," "positively" or some other intensive adverb. Its real meaning, "according to the letter," places it in direct opposition to "figuratively."

Loan. See *Lend*.

Locate. Colloquial for *settle* or *establish*. Prefer "He *settled* in Colorado"; "They *established* their business in Birmingham."

Lot, Lots. These words are in colloquial use for *much, many*; as, "a *lot* of money," "*lots* of people." Prefer "a *great deal* of money," "*much* money," "*many* people."

Love, Like. *Love* is a much abused English word. In modern practice *like* is used where taste is concerned and where no strong emotion is involved. One who delights in sweets is appropriately said to *like* candy. Of course one may *like* a person without *loving* him—that is, enjoy his companionship. We *love* wives, husbands, sweethearts, children, friends, truth, country.

Lunch, Luncheon. The second of these words is the more formal, or perhaps we should say, the more pretentious. Its use borders on verbal elegance. In general it will be avoided, except by people who *purchase* things instead of buying them, and who *reside*, not *live*, at a certain address.

Luxurious, Luxuriant. Do not confuse these words. The first describes that which is "gratifying to the senses"; the second means "growing in abundance." Correctly we speak of *luxurious* furnishings and of *luxuriant* foliage or vegetation.

-ly, adverbial suffix. Although "ly" is usually added to adjectives to form adverbs, only a misinformed purist would insist on using it in all cases. "Slow," for example, is a good adverb, with or without the "ly," and "fast" cannot use it. "Illy" and "thusly" are conspicuous examples of its mistaken application. Persons familiar with historical grammar will recall that adjectives ending in "ly" were once common. A few of them still persist, as "a comely lass," "a goodly number."

Mad. When used to signify "very angry," this word is a careless colloquialism. *Mad* properly means "crazy."

Manner, Manor. The correct phrase is *to the manner born*, not *to the manor born*. The phrase means "familiar with from birth."

Materialize. When used to mean "take shape" or "happen," the word is colloquial. Improperly used in the general sense of *appear*.

Mathematics. When considered as embracing the science of mathematics in its entirety as a concrete term, this word is construed with a verb in the singular; as, "*Mathematics is* the science that treats of quantities, their properties and relations, especially by the use of symbols"; "*Mathematics is* a subject in the course of study." But, when used distributively, to convey the idea of its different branches or divisions, the word is construed with a verb in the plural; as, "*Mathematics are* mere evolutions of necessary ideas." It should be borne in mind that mathematics are classified as *pure* or *abstract, applied* or *mixed,* and *qualitative,* as projective geometry.

Mean. Do not use *mean* as an adjective for *sick, unpleasant,* or *ashamed.* Say, "He felt *ashamed* of it," not "He felt *mean* about it."

Mean, Intend, Purpose. Best usage may be illustrated as follows: "By this statement I *mean,* etc."; "We *intend* to go"; "He *purposes* a thorough test of the machine." *Purpose* is a stronger word than *intend* and implies more careful thought.

Meanwhile. "Meanwhile" is an adverb of time equivalent to the phrase, "in the meantime." It is grammatically wrong, therefore, to say "in the meanwhile."

Meet. To say, "*Meet* Mr. A.," when introducing a friend, is bad form. But we say correctly, "Have you ever *met* Mrs. B.?" meaning "been introduced to." Prefer "I want you to *meet* Mrs. A." or "May I introduce Mr. A.?"

Middling. This word is an adjective, meaning "moderate," and should not be used as an adverb; therefore, we should not say that a thing is *middling* good, or that a thing is *middling* well done. "He resided in a town of *middling* size" is correct, but "of *moderate* size" is preferable.

Mighty. When used instead of *exceedingly very,* or *extremely,* this word is a colloquial intensive. Correctly used, *mighty* is a strong word indicating power of unusual force or quality; as, a *mighty* flood, a *mighty* monarch. It may connote uncommon size; as, *mighty* mountains.

Mistaken. The expression "If I am not *mistaken,*" though sometimes condemned as incorrect, is idiomatic and has been in use for several centuries with the sense "If I am not making a *mistake.*" "If I *mistake* not" is more formal, but it is thought by some to be stilted.

More than. Although its form implies plurality, this phrase is correctly construed as a singular: "*More than* one *is* there" or "There *is more than* one there."

Most. As a contraction of *almost,* this word is a provincialism: "The dress is *almost* (not *most*) finished." The use of *most* in the phrases *most perfect, most complete,* is sanctioned by good usage, on the ground that things are at best but relatively perfect or complete. Avoid the misuse of *most* in such colloquial forms as *most anybody* or *most anything.*

Muskrat. Do not say *mushrat.*

Mutual, Common. Recent writers do not insist so strongly upon the distinction between these two words. "We have *common* friends" or "We have *mutual* friends." *Mutual,* strictly, means "reciprocal," "existing between two parties"; but, because the meaning "ordinary" may be implied by the word *common,* many people prefer to say, "*mutual* friends," in spite of critics. There is, however, a clear and worth while distinction between the two words. *Common* means "belonging to all" as well as "ordinary." When we speak of a *mutual* friend we mean "one who reciprocates our friendship," and, when we refer to a *common* friend, we mean "one whose friendship we share in common

with other friends of his." The sentence "We have many friends in *common*" illustrates the point clearly, and is a good substitute for "We have many *common* friends." Persons interested in the same things have *common* interests. When they are interested in each other, their interest is *mutual.*

Myself. This pronoun is an emphatic or reflexive form for the first person and should be used only where emphasis is required, as in "Who did it? I *myself,*" that is, "I alone did it." It is incorrect to say, "Mary and *myself* were satisfied" or "Two friends and *myself* went." Say, "Two friends and I went" or "I went with two friends." Do not say, "*Myself,* I do not like it."

Named. See *By the name of.*

Neither, Neither nor. Because *neither,* like *either,* properly refers to one of two, it calls for a singular verb. Example: "Of the two leading candidates, *neither was* considered capable of filling the office." The singular is also used with *neither nor,* since the two persons or things mentioned are taken separately, and not together, as in "*Neither* John *nor* William is qualified."

New. Distinguish between *new* and *novel.* That which is *new* may be *novel,* but that which is *novel* need not be *new.* Anything striking or *different* from things with which we are familiar may be called *novel.* To say "*new* beginner" seems to argue utter indifference to the sense of words. To be a beginner is quite sufficient.

News. Notwithstanding its plural appearance, "news" is singular. Thus, we say "The news is good." Compare "acoustics," "politics" and other singular nouns ending in "s."

Nice. This word means "exact" or "discriminating," not "pleasant" or "good." A *nice* distinction is one resulting from discriminating reasoning; one who is *nice* in regard to matters of food is fastidious and hard to please; *nice* food is inviting, dainty food. Anything that is done or made with scrupulous exactness, precision, or accuracy is termed *nice;* as, a *nice* balance, that is, an exact balance; *nice* workmanship, that is, the result of skilled labor.

Nicely. This word is frequently misused in the attempt to make it do service for *well,* in this wise: "How will this pen do?" "*Nicely.*" "How are you?" "*Nicely.*" Use *well* or *very well,* for *nicely* means "accurately," "becomingly," "exactly."

None. A word that may be used with a verb in either the singular or the plural, depending on the intention of the person who uses it; as, "*None* of *these* things *move* me"; "*None* but the brave *deserves* the fair."

Nor, Not. Use *nor* and not *or* after *no* when the definite exclusion of two distinct persons or things is intended; as, "He has *no* father *nor* mother." But we use *or* when the following word merely explains the preceding: "The boy has *no* father *or* guardian." After *not,* when the single negation applies to both objects, use *or:* "They do *not* see *or* hear." But say, "They do *not* come, *nor* do they intend to come," where two separate negations are implied. Here *nor* is, logically, the equivalent of *and not.* For logic, watch the position of *not.* Do not say, for example, "All Democrats are *not* Free Traders," but "*Not* all Democrats are Free Traders."

No use. "It is *no use* to do that" should be "It is *of no use* to do that" or, preferably, "It is *useless* to do that."

Novice. See *Amateur.*

Nowhere. Do not say, "*nowhere* (or *nowheres*) near so much," because *nowhere* means "not in any place or anywhere" or, by extension, "at no time." "Not nearly so much" is correct.

Number. A word that can be correctly construed with a verb in the singular or the plural, depending on the idea to be expressed or the word on which emphasis is placed. We say correctly, when thinking of the individuals of a group, "A large *number were* (not *was*) there." Similarly, "There *are* a large *number* of people" or "There *are* many." But, if we intend to convey the idea of a unit, we say "The *number* of women present *was* small." When any phrase that has qualifying force seems to contradict in number the noun or verb with which it is used, an adjective should be substituted, so that the sentence shall correspond in form with the idea it is intended to convey. For example, "A *number* of changes *was* made," or "A *number* of changes *were* made." Better,—"*Numerous changes were* made."

Observance, Observation. *Observe* the following distinction: "Close *observation* of our customs shows too little *observance* of Sunday and of patriotic anniversaries." *Observation* means "the act of looking at or examining," or the result of such action. *Observance* implies recognition, as with service or ceremony.

Of, Off. See *Prepositions*. The two words are from the same source and are subject to confusion in common speech.

When *of* follows a superlative, the thing referred to as best, largest, etc., is to be thought of as included in a whole group; hence the rule requiring *of all* in the following: "She was the loveliest *of all* (not *any*)." "He was the least observed *of all* (not *all others*)." *Any* and *others* imply separation of groups for comparison, and are used appropriately only with the comparative degree: "He was less observed than *any* of the others (who were observed—understood)." *Any* requires *other(s)* or *one else* or a similar expression to follow it.

Off of, Off from. *Of* or *from*, in these phrases, should be omitted from such a sentence as the following: "The pears fell *off* (*of*) (*from*) the tree." *Off* expresses the idea of separation. *Of* and *from* are superfluous.

O. K. This commercial expression is used as noun, adjective, and verb: "Give this your *O. K.* (approval)"; "His work is *O. K.* (all right, correct)"; "He refused to *O. K.* (approve) the order." Since *O. K.* as an adjective means "all right," do not say "all *O. K.*": "The requisition is *O. K.* (not *all O. K.*)."

Old Adage. See *Adage*.

One—One's. While purists insist that *one*, as in the sentence "*One* meets *one's* friends in the city," should be followed by *one's* and never by *her* or *his*, usage sanctions either form where no ambiguity would result. But after *anyone, every one, no one*, etc., use *he* (*his*) or *she* (*hers*): "*No one* knows where *he* will meet an acquaintance." Never use *they* (*their*) with *one* in such a sentence as "*Every one* makes *his* own choice," for *one* is singular. Do not say, "When *one* travels, *you* want pleasant companions," for *one* is a pronoun of the third person, and any following pronoun used in its place should be of the same person. Generally, avoid the use of *one* when a repetition of the word would be required.

Ones. Instead of saying, "I do not like the other *ones*," say, "I do not like the *others*." *Ones* is in good use only in such phrases as "big *ones*" and "little *ones*": "Here are big stones and little *ones*."

One time, Then. Such expressions as her *one time* guardian and the *then* bishop of New York are convenient, clear, and economical, and they are approved by good authority.

Only. This word is probably more often misplaced than any other word in the language. "He *only* sang for us." "He sang *only* for us." The first sentence means that he *sang*, but did not *play* for us; the second means that he sang for *us* and not for anyone else. *Only* is regularly placed before the word it modifies: "*Only* he (or *only* John) sang for us. That is, no one else sang.

Onto, On to. The use of *onto* in such expressions as "He got *onto* the platform with difficulty" is justified by good authority. This use follows the analogy of *upon, into*, and others implying motion. Some authorities do not yet allow *onto*, although they approve *on to*, but the two forms have quite distinct uses. One should not say, "He walked *onto* the next town," but "He walked *on to* the next town."

Oral, Verbal. *Verbal* means "in words," either *spoken* or *written*; *oral* means "uttered by the mouth," "spoken."

Other. This word should not be omitted from sentences like the following: "He said that his wife was dressed better than any *other* woman there." The omission of *other* makes the statement include the person spoken of in the group with which she is compared. In stating a comparison avoid comparing a thing with itself.

Ought, Should. *Ought* is the stronger term. What we *ought* to do, we are morally bound to do: We *ought* to be truthful and honest, and we *should* be respectful to our elders.

Over, Across. There is a nice distinction between these words: A dog walks *across* the street, but he leaps *over* an obstruction. *Across* suggests merely passage from one limit to another; *over* also implies elevation. See *Prepositions*.

Overlook, Oversee. *Overlook* means, usually, "miss seeing," "not notice": "He *overlooked* the important point." *Oversee* means "supervise." *Look over* may mean "examine."

Own. The use of *own* to mean "admit to be true" or "concede" is supported by good usage; as, "He *owned* to his fault." Colloquially, *own* has come to mean "confess" or "clear one's mind of a matter," as in the sentence "He was accused and finally *owned* up."

Pair. With numbers, as "three *pairs*," best usage favors the plural, the use of the singular, as "three *pair*," being confined to trade cant. See *Dozen*.

Parcel post. This form is correct, not *parcels post*.

Partake. The word means, literally, "take part," "share." In this sense, several persons may *partake*, or one may *partake* with others. But the word is also in good use to mean "take" or "appropriate," without reference to sharing; as, "He *partook* of the food."

Party. The word should not be used generally for *person*. Not "the *party* that I saw," but "the *person* that I saw." We speak correctly, however, of the *parties* to a contract or an agreement.

Passive Progressive. Modern practice prefers "The church *is being built*" or "Cattle *are being sold* at fifty dollars a head" to the former usage "The church *is building*" or "Cattle *are selling*," etc." Say, "The boy *is being taught*," not "The boy *is teaching*," when the intention is to express the idea that the lad is receiving instruction.

Pep. Expressive slang for *energy, vigor*, but as yet it seems usually to need an apology.

Per. This preposition, originally taken from Latin phrases like *per diem* (by the day) and *per annum* (by the year), is often found in hybrid expressions such as "Ten dollars *per* day" or, worse still, in the clipped form, "Ten dollars *per*." It is much better to use consistent English, as in "Ten dollars *a* day."

Perform. Say, "She *plays* the piano beautifully," not "She *performs* beautifully on the piano." This sentence would be improved by using *well* or *admirably* in place of *beautifully*.

Place (verb). *Place* means "lay in position." Some authorities think one should say, "*place* a thing *into* a box"; but there is hardly enough of the idea of motion in the word *place* to justify *into*. *Place in* is more appropriate.

Plan on. "Do you *plan on* going?" A provincialism better expressed by "Do you *plan* going?"

Plebiscite. A word introduced into English from the French many years ago. Its recent revival is one of the results of World War I. The word means "a referendum, or vote of the people, in a district or state."

Plenty, Plentiful. One may say, "There will be *plenty* of fruit this fall"; but good usage calls for "Fruit will be *plentiful* (not *plenty*)." Used as an adverb, "plenty" has a colloquial crudity that is especially objectionable; for example, "plenty good" instead of "very good."

Plurality, Majority. "The president received a *plurality* of the votes cast for all candidates throughout the country" means that he received more than any other candidate. "The election of an officer requires a *majority*" means that election requires one vote or more in excess of half the total number of votes.

Point of view. Frequently expressed by *standpoint* or *viewpoint* in common usage. Most authorities frown upon *viewpoint* and prefer *point of view*. *Standpoint* is well established. Some would even use *angle* as a synonym. This last word is still colloquial, but there is a tendency to accept it.

Politics. American usage approves *politics is*; English usage approves *politics are*.

Ponderous phraseology. Either through deliberate affectation or through unconscious imitation of "fine" writing, people may fall into the habit of using showy or pedantic phraseology. For example, instead of being "thanked," a person may be "made the recipient of grateful acknowledgments." Charles Dickens depicted several characters whose linguistic finery emphasized the shabbiness of their personalities. Thus, instead of quoting the simple Anglo-Saxon saying that "a cat can look at a king," Mr. George, in *Martin Chuzzlewit*, translates: "I have heard it said that a cat is free to contemplate a monarch." On this subject, a word to the wise should be sufficient.

Possessive with Verbal Noun. "We did not know of *his* going." "The idea of *our* doing such a thing." "The fact of the *team's* playing at home interested him." These sentences represent approved usage. Occasionally, in the use of nouns, the possessive seems awkward or sounds harsh, and is omitted as unnecessary.

Post, Mail. The distinction in the use of these words is merely national. We *mail* letters in the United States and *post* them in Great Britain.

Posted. The use of this word for *informed*, in such expressions as "The man *posted* me" and "If I had been better *posted*," should be discouraged in favor of *informed*.

Practical, Practicable. *Practical* means "not theoretical" or "concerned with doing rather than with reasoning." *Practicable* means "capable of being done under given conditions": "A *practical* man will suggest *practicable* plans."

Practically, Virtually. These words are both used to mean "essentially" or "in reality": "The battle was *practically* over"; "He is *virtually* bankrupt." *Virtually* is preferred as expressing actuality in referring to conditions that exist but are not self-evident; for example, "Fighting continued *practically* all night, but the issue of the battle had already been *virtually* decided."

Prefer. "For making bread, do you *prefer* wheaten flour or corn flour?" "I *prefer* wheat *to* corn." Do not say, "I *prefer* wheat *rather than* corn." The *pre-* in *prefer* supplies the sense of *rather* or *before*.

Prejudice. This word connotes a bias or unfavorable attitude toward a person or thing and should not be used to indicate approbation, as in "The man is *prejudiced* in his favor." We should say, "He is *predisposed* (or *prepossessed*) in his favor."

Prepositions at Ends of Sentences. Sentences that end with prepositions are frequently more terse, always quite as idiomatic, and invariably simpler than they might be if differently constructed: "the man I gave it *to*" or "the man *to* whom I gave it"; "the verb it belongs *to*" or "the verb *to* which it belongs."

Pressure. This word in the sense of *influence* frequently carries a sinister meaning, but when it signifies *urgency* it is in good use; as, "the *pressure* of affairs or of business."

Pretty. Correctly used as an adverb, in such expressions as *pretty soon* or *pretty well*, meaning "rather," "somewhat." However, its repeated use tends to restrict one's vocabulary, to the exclusion of more appropriate words.

Preventive. Among careful speakers this word has never had any competition from the awkward and undesirable form *preventative*. Unless the long and the short form represent two different meanings, as in *visit* and *visitation*, the shorter one is always preferable. Compare the verbs *experiment* and *experimentalize*.

Previous to, Previously to. Both are in good use, but *previously* is necessary when the idea is adverbial: "*Previously to* our coming the affair had been settled." But we say correctly, "That event was *previous to* our coming." The same principle applies to *subsequent*, *relative*, etc.

Principal, Principle. *Principal*, usually an adjective ("The *principal* advantage"), is also used as a noun: "The *principal* of a school," "*principal* and interest." *Principle* is always a noun: "Both machines operate on this *principle*."

Proceeds. Use the plural verb with this word: "The *proceeds were* (not *was*) applied."

Procure. Usually, Anglo-Saxon *get* is preferable to Latin *procure*; e.g., "Where did you *get* it?", not "Where did you *procure* it?" *Procure* suggests provision for the future, as in the *procurement* of military supplies.

Promise. Often misused for *assure*, as in "I *promise* you I was agreeably surprised," which should be "I *assure* you, etc." The word *promise* refers to the future: "We *promise* to do our best."

Propose, Purpose. These words are not exact synonyms, as the following sentence shows: "I *propose* to build a house and *purpose* to live in it when it is ready." *Propose* implies a definite, specific plan; *purpose*, a more general intention.

Proposition. Commercial cant for *proposal*, *task*, or *undertaking*, all of which are preferable.

"Proud" words. At some time or other nearly everyone increases his working vocabulary by the addition of words that seem to lend distinction to his style. Through succeeding decades various words have served in this capacity. Once the favorite was "intriguing," then "devastating," then "priceless." As one man said when his attention was called to this matter, "Now that you have made me self-

conscious, I believe that 'currently' is currently my favorite." Caution regarding these "vogue" words is advisable for two reasons. First, they are likely to be overused; secondly, they soon become vague and general in meaning.

Prove. In the past tense and the past participle, *proved*, not *proven*, is correct, except in legal papers.

Providing. This should not be used for *provided*: "He offered to furnish a car, *provided* (not *providing*) the company would pay for gasoline and repairs."

Punch. Slang for *energy, effectiveness.*

Put. Like *do*, *put* has many meanings that are not in good literary use: *put*, meaning "go" or "get out"; *put up with* (endure); *put out* (displease); *put past*, as in "I should not *put it past* him," meaning "I suspect him to be capable of it"; *put up*, as in "He *put up* at the hotel (*stayed at*)." A forceful idiomatic phrase is *stay put.*

Quite. The word means "entirely," "completely," "altogether": "The building is *quite* complete." It means, in addition, "to a considerable extent or degree," "noticeably"; as, "The water is *quite* cold"; "The day was *quite* warm." The word is not properly used to mean "very" or "rather," as in "The book is *quite* interesting" or "She is *quite* ill." Such a colloquial phrase as *quite a bit* is questionable. *Quite some* is vulgar.

Raise. This word is applied in America to the bringing up of children, although formerly its use was common in this sense in England also. Modern usage applies the word to the breeding and rearing of animals and to the propagation and nurture of plants. Thus one may raise children, animals, and plants. Children and animals may be reared.

Re, In re. A piece of old law Latin transferred to business letters and not an abbreviation of *regarding*, as it is frequently taken to be. It means "matter," "in the matter of," or "on the subject of." The English phrase *referring to* is preferable and is, in fact, very generally used.

Real. Avoid the misuse of this word as an adverb in the sense of *very.* Say, "The house is *very* (not *real*) pleasant." The adverb *really* means "actually," as in "The story is *really* true."

Recipe, Receipt. The confusion of these two words is very old. Both words formerly meant a "medical formula," for which today we use the word prescription. While both are still applied to *cookery directions* there is a strong tendency in the best modern usage to reserve this sense for the word *recipe, receipt* being employed for commercial and other use in the sense of *receiving* or in *acknowledgment of receiving.* Say, "He paid the bill and was given a *receipt*"; "She has an excellent *recipe* for making clam chowder."

Recollect, Remember. *Recollect* refers to the recalling of events or facts, while *remember* refers to what may be in the mind continually: "He *remembers* very well his early youth." "I *recollect* now my first visit to the circus."

Regard. The plural of this word is sometimes erroneously used in the phrase *in regards to*, meaning "relating to," "concerning," or "about." It is correctly used in "He spoke *in regard to* bonuses."

Regrettable, Regretful. Strange to say, these words are often confused, even by otherwise careful speakers. An act may be "regrettable," that is, something to be regretted. A person's attitude may be "regretful" as he contemplates the act and its consequences.

Relations, Relatives. The following sentence illustrates the preferred use of these words: "One's *relations* with one's *relatives* may be pleasant or unpleasant." *Kin* or *kinsfolk* implies blood relationship.

Respectively, Respectfully. Do not confuse these words: "They were called *respectively* (that is, *in the order named*) Jim, Sam, and Al"; but "They were *respectfully* called (that is, *in a respectful manner*) James, Samuel, and Albert."

Risqué. Sometimes written *risky.* The words are not properly used as synonyms. That which is *risqué* is broadly suggestive to the point of obscenity; it borders on the obscene or questionable in art or writing: "a *risqué* story." In English usage, *risky* means "bold," "audacious," "daring," but lacks the equivocal force of the French word.

Same. Disapproved as a substitute for *it, they,* etc.: "We have sent the goods by express, and we hope you will receive *them* (not *same*) promptly." Legal usage allows *the same* for *it*: "If said tenant defaces *the same*, etc."

"Says I." A vulgarism.

Scared. Do not use *scared of* when you mean *scared by.* Many people use this phrase carelessly. Prefer *afraid of* or *fearful of.*

Scrap. This is commercial cant, meaning, as a verb, "discard" as out-of-date or unprofitable: "The ships and the plant will be *scrapped.*"

Secondhand. Say, "We bought the car *secondhand*, not *secondhanded.*"

See. The frequent interrogatory "*See?*," with which some persons sprinkle their conversation in their anxiety to secure attention, is most objectionable from the point of view either of manners or of language.

Seen. Not to be used for *saw*, which is the correct past tense of *see.* Avoid "I *seen* him last week" or "He *seen* that," as the height of vulgarity.

Sell. Formerly, "to *sell* a person" meant "to play a joke upon him." Now the same phrase is commercial cant, meaning "to *sell* something to him." Colloquially, *sell* may mean to convince.

Sequel. *Sequel* means "something that follows," as a continuation or consequence. It is used frequently of events or stories related in books: "The *Gay-Dombeys* may be called a *sequel* to *Dombey and Son*"; "The *sequel* of their marriage was a divorce."

Set, Sit. These verbs, like *lay* and *lie*, have long been subject to confusion. In modern usage, *set* is transitive; *sit* is intransitive. I *set* the hen, but she *sits* on her eggs. Incorrectly we speak of a *setting* hen, instead of a *sitting* hen. In Matthew, it was prophesied that Christ should come "*sitting* upon an ass," and his disciples took a colt and "*set* him thereon." The verbs are correctly used in these sentences: "My coat *sits* well"; "We will *sit* up," that is, "will not go to bed"; "Congress *sits.*" "We *set* down figures"; but "We *sit* down on the ground." But a very old intransitive use of *set* persists in the expressions, "the sun *sets*," "*sunset*," "*setting* sun," which are accepted as correct.

Sat.—This is both past tense and past participle of *sit.* I have *sat* is correct.

Sewage, Sewerage. *Sewerage* is the system of pipes and tunnels for carrying away the *sewage*, or waste matter, from buildings.

Shall, Will. These are auxiliary (helping) verbs, used to determine various modes and tenses of the action involved in a principal verb. In respect to these words, there are four important groups of idiomatic uses: (1) in declarative statements; (2) in questions; (3) in subordinate clauses; (4) in expressions of future requirement (veiled command).

1. *Declarative Statements.*—The following are the correct uses of *shall* and *will* with the personal pronouns, to express simple future action, declaratively and interrogatively:

DECLARATIVE	INTERROGATIVE
I shall	Shall I?
You will	Shall you?
He will	Will he?
We shall	Shall we?
You will	Shall you?
They will	Will they?

For the expression of the speaker's determination or command, *shall* and *will* exchange places in the foregoing table. For example: "I *shall*" becomes "I *will*"; "He *will*" becomes "He *shall*."

In the sense of *willing, determining, commanding,* or *requiring,* neither *shall* nor *will* has anything to do with "time," except as any command must be executed "after" it is given. This is clear in certain cases, where expression and action may well come together: "*Will* you sit here?" "Yes; I *will*," where the action is suited to the word, or, "*Wilt* thou have this woman to be thy wedded wife?" "I *will*."

2. *Questions.*—In questions, one uses the word expected in the answer: "*Shall* you speak?" expecting "I *shall* speak"; but "*Will* you speak?" expecting "I *will* speak."

But notice that "*Shall* you be glad to go?" is appropriate, while "*Will* you be glad to go?" is not, since gladness is not a matter of will. Only rarely may *will* be used interrogatively in the first person, because, as long as there is question in the mind, there is no will. Such a formal sentence as "We *will* ratify this treaty, *will* we not?" is approved; and we not infrequently exclaim, somewhat ironically, "Will I?" as if to say, "I *will* not" or "I certainly *will*."

3. *Subordinate Clauses.*—In subordinate clauses introduced by *that,* after such expressions as "It is said" or "Some one has said" or "It has been commanded," use the auxiliary that would be used in the original principal statement. For example: when the original statement or command was "He (or You) *shall* do the work," the clause of indirect quotation becomes "He has said that he (or you or I) *shall* do the work"; similarly, "He (or You) *will* do the work" becomes "He has said that he (or you or I) *will* do the work." In the former case *shall* retains its ancient force of obligation; in the latter, *will* retains its essential meaning of willingness or readiness. The following sentence further illustrates the use of *shall* to express determination: "We have decided that the contract *shall* be let to you, and that you *shall* follow specifications." If the subordinate clause follows such a verb as *suppose, think, believe,* or *know,* then the usage for *shall* and *will* in the subordinate clause is the same as for an independent declarative statement. Example: "I think that I *shall* never see a poem lovely as a tree."

In subordinate clauses introduced by such conjunctions as *if, when, whether,* or *although, shall* expresses simple future action in every person, while *will,* in every person, expresses willingness or determination. Examples: "If you *will* remember the rule, I *shall* be greatly obliged." "Although I *shall* see him, I *will* not speak." "If he *will* not meet me, I *will* not seek him."

Such use of *shall* is usually avoided by some other expression. Examples: "If I *see* him, I *will* speak"; "If he *does not meet* me, I *shall* not need to speak."

4. *Requirements and Commands.*—*Will* has a peculiar use to express a verbal command or a courteous request: "You *will* report back to headquarters on Sunday morning," that is, "You are required to report"; "You *will* please say no more about the matter" means that it is my wish, entreaty, or pleasure that you say no more about it.

Shape, Condition. A crude but common use of "shape" is to say that a person is "in bad shape" (ill), or that his affairs are "in good shape" (financially). The word "condition" is waiting to be used in such cases.

Should, Would. Although, in origin, these are past tenses of *shall* and *will,* they are now properly to be thought of as independent of the latter verbs. Their uses are highly idiomatic.

In affirmative principal clauses, *should* may express obligation in all persons: "I (You or He) *should* (ought to) attend the lecture." *Would,* in affirmative principal clauses and in all persons, may express willingness or determination dependent upon circumstances: "We (You, They) *would* come, if an invitation were given."

1. In the first person, *should,* and, in other persons, *would,* may express simply action dependent upon circumstances: "I *should* (They *would*) come, were it convenient."

2. In simple questions, the word expected in the answer is used: "*Should* he go?" "He *should*"; "*Would* you consider it?" "I *would*."

3. In *if* clauses, *should* expresses a condition involving action merely, *would* expresses a condition involving will: "If I *should* correct the error, the work would be approved"; "If you *would* permit me, I would correct the error."

4. *Would* may express intense desire: "I *would* that we might see them again." It expresses also, in reference to past time, habitual action: "He *would* walk up and down."

5. It should be observed that *would* is rarely used interrogatively in the first person except in such a half-ironical expression as "*Would* I?" implying "I certainly *would*" or "I certainly *would* not."

6. Many of the shades of meaning attached to *should* and *would* can be expressed only by changes in the tone of the voice. A fair-sized volume might be written about them.

Should seem, Would seem. These are useless locutions when plain *seem* or *seems* would express the meaning. They are appropriate, however, to suggest doubt, hesitation, or modesty in expressing a judgment.

Show me. Slang for *prove to me.*

Sick, Ill. See *Ill.*

Since when. This phrase, in which *when* is employed as a substantive, is used correctly in a relative clause: "We moved out West, *since when* (or *since which time*) we have not moved again." However, it is not approved in interrogative constructions; as, "*Since when* have you known that?" "How long have you known that?" is correct.

Sit up. We say to a child, "*Sit up,*" meaning "sit erectly." We *sit up,* that is, *remain out of bed* until a late hour. Compare the expressive slang, "Make one *sit up* and take notice." These phrases are not in good literary use.

Size up. Slang for *estimate, judge, classify. Up* is very frequent in careless colloquial speech and slang; as, *eat up, all up* (with), *stay up,* etc.

Slow, Slowly. Many adjectives in English need no change of form for adverbial use. *Fast* and *slow* are examples of these. Space economy on signs probably helps to maintain this form *slow* in such expressions as "Go *slow,*" though it has a long history in the language.

Smart. One should carefully observe the various meanings of this word. It is in good use for *bright, intelligent, brisk,* and *lively.* But in "He is a *smart* boy," the word may have the sense commonly attributed to it formerly, "sharp and impertinent," or that implied by bright and intelligent. After the English manner, one hears of *smart* clothes. The phrase *right smart*, meaning "much," "a good deal of," is provincial.

Smell of. We *smell* the rose, not *smell of* it. But we say properly, "The jar *smells of* rose leaves." The verb is transitive and intransitive.

So. Avoid using *so* as a bridge between the parts of a loose sentence. Example: "We couldn't find the house, *so* we started to go home, but it began to rain, *so* we waited," et cetera. Colloquial use of the adverb *so* without a that-clause is undesirable. Example: "The game was *so* exciting." But it is proper to say, "The book is *so* interesting that you will want to finish it at one sitting."

Some, Somewhat. *Some*, properly an indefinite adjective denoting number or quantity, is often used erroneously for *somewhat*, an adverb of degree, even by educated men and women. Such use appears frequently in the newspapers; but it is condemned as dialectal or provincial by all authorities, and it has no support in literary usage. Say, "I am *somewhat* tired," never "I am *some* tired"; "His estimate is *somewhat* greater," not "*some* greater." The colloquial use of *some*, to suggest exceptional quality or importance, as in "He is *some* manager," is equally to be disapproved.

Somewhere. "I have seen him some place" is not an acceptable substitute for the correct form, "I have seen him somewhere." The same distinction should be observed in "any place" and "anywhere."

Sort of. See *Kind*.

Split infinitive. Since an infinitive consists of a verb plus the particle "to," the insertion of an adverbial modifier between them creates a "split infinitive," for example: "Be careful to thoroughly mix the ingredients." Unsplitting the infinitive may be done either (1) by placing the adverb after the verb ("Be careful to mix the ingredients thoroughly") or (2) by placing it just before the verb ("Be careful thoroughly to mix the ingredients"). The first of these two constructions is simple and natural, and is usually preferable. Although the second arrangement is technically correct, it is formal and rather consciously precise. Sometimes it is also obscure. In the example cited above, there is a suggestion that "thoroughly" applies to "be careful" instead of to "mix." Anyway, the normal order is for the adverb to follow the verb.

Stand. Colloquial for *endure* in such an expression as "They can't *stand* it."

Stand a chance. Colloquial for *be likely*. "Does he *stand a chance* of election?" means "*Is he likely* to be elected?"

Stand for. Colloquial for *endure* or *allow*; as, "We will not *stand for* such conduct."

Standpoint. See *Point of view*.

State. We may say, "He *stated* his reasons in writing." *State* is a formal word and should not be used, as it frequently is in newspapers, to mean simply "say" or "tell."

Station, Depot. A *depot* is properly a place where goods or stores of any kind are kept; the places at which the trains of a railroad stop for passengers and the points they start from or arrive at are properly the *stations*. But, as a *depot* is a place of storage, so a *terminal* of a railroad line, where the rolling stock is kept to make up trains, may be spoken of correctly as a *depot*.

Stimulant, Stimulus. A stimulant is an agent that produces a temporary increase of energy. More abstractly, a stimulus is an exciting motive or impulse.

Stop, Stay. The colloquial phrases, *stop off*, *stop in*, *stop over*, are frowned on by critics. The first means to "step off" or "alight and stay at" some place; the second means "step in and call" or merely "call"; the last has gained position in railway cant, as in "*stop-over* privileges."

To stop is to arrest motion; *to stay* is to remain where motion is arrested. We may *stop* at a hotel; but how long we *stay* depends upon circumstances.

Storm. A violent commotion of the atmosphere is a *storm*. Avoid the word when referring to *rains* or *snows*, unless *rainstorms* or *snowstorms* are involved.

Street. Many careful speakers regard the expression "They live *in* John *street*" as better and more accurate than "They live *on* John *street*." General American usage seems to approve *on the street*. Colloquially, we say, "play *in the street*," one's house being thought of as bordering *on* the real *street*. "He has offices *in* Wall *street*" is a form of speech frequently heard. This implies the idea of the *street* as a financial center, including the buildings on it. The whole question turns upon our idea of what the word *street* includes.

Stricken. This form of the past participle of *strike* is used when misfortune or disability is implied: "He was *stricken* with fever"; "They were panic-*stricken*." *Struck* is the usual form for other meanings: "He was *struck* by a stone."

Stylish words. See *Affectation*.

Such. "I have never seen *such a small* man" should be "I have never seen *so small a* man," as may be seen by transposing the words of the first sentence, which then becomes "I have never seen a man *such small*." Similarly, *such a pretty*, *lovely*, etc., should be *so pretty a*, *lovely a*. However, in the sentence "It was *such a large* package as could not be carried in the car," *such a* is regarded as correct, meaning "a *large package* like this one."

Suffixes. See *Word Building*. Several suffixes are sources of common error, because of indiscriminate use:

-ette. This syllable is a French feminine diminutive, the masculine being *-et*. A *kitchenette*, then, is a little kitchen, feminine because of associations, probably. But *leatherette* is imitation leather. So we pass to the half-humorous, half-contemptuous *farmerette* and *suffragette*.

-let. This is another French ending, meaning "little." One should not say, "little *booklet*," the *little* being superfluous.

Sure. "He will *surely* be here," not "He will be here *sure*." "*Sure*, I'll do it" is slang. *Surely* is the adverb; *sure*, the adjective.

Suspicion. *Suspicion* is not in good use as a verb; prefer *suspect*.

Take. A verb, either transitive or intransitive. Combined with various prepositions and adverbs, it forms many idiomatic phrases and also many colloquial and slang phrases: "One *takes* leave," that is, assumes or receives permission to leave a place or a company; "One *takes to* a person," that is, *likes him*. Some uses, however, are to be avoided as vulgarisms: "She *took on* (scolded, raged, cried) dreadfully"; "School *takes up* at 8:30." Compare "*lets out* at 4:00," which is school cant.

Tasty. This word is an objectionable colloquialism for *tasteful*, when applied to persons, dress, furniture, etc. It is allowable in application to food. The following distinction is correct: Pie may be *tasty*, but the decorations of a room should be *tasteful*.

Tautology. Through carelessness, repetitive or overlapping expressions find their way into the speech of many people. Note such common examples as "*old* veteran," "*ancient* adage," "widow *woman*," and, somewhat more subtly, "consensus *of opinion*." A different case is provided by intentional repetition for emphasis, as in "the same identical person," and the purposeful repetition in legal phrasing, as in "I hereby give, devise and bequeath," etc.

Teach. See *Learn.*

Tenses, Sequence of. The general rule to be observed regarding tenses is that the verb in a dependent clause takes its tense from the verb in the main clause. Thus: "I think (present) that he is (present) honest" becomes "I thought (past) that he was (past) honest" when the tense of the main verb is changed. Usually, we can depend upon our "feeling for language" to save us from such mixed forms as "Give that others *might* live" instead of the correct sequence "Give that others *may* live."

Terminal prepositions. Puristic people insist on following a rigid rule that a sentence should never end with a preposition. For a vigorous, if slightly colloquial, statement like, "This is something worth thinking about," they would substitute the formal and rather prissy phrasing, "This is something about which it is worth while to think." What they overlook is the close relationship that often exists between verb and preposition, making the two practically one word. "He is a man you can count on" is good idiomatic English. It is natural and conversational as contrasted with the bookish style that results from transposing the preposition. Of course, terminal prepositions that are used unnecessarily and carelessly are properly condemned. For example, to say, "what we end up with" instead of "what we have left" is inexcusable. At the same time, no one should hesitate to use a prepositional ending that is natural and forceful.

Terrible, Frightful. These belong to the class of extravagant adjectives. *Terribly* and *frightfully* are similarly misused for *very* or *very much* or *extraordinarily*, when "terror" and "fright" are not involved. Save strong words for occasions that demand them.

Than. See *Any, Else, Of.*

That, So. *That* is not in good use as an adverb in such phrases as the following: "*that* good," "*that* worthy." "She was *so* worthy that they could not turn her away" is correct. Do not say, "She was *that* worthy, etc." *That*, however, is approved as a demonstrative adverb with expressions of measure or degree: "We could not stay *that* long"; "You will be *that* much farther on your way."

The. As in the case of the indefinite article, the repetition of the definite article *the* in such a series as "*the* bear, *the* deer, and *the* panther" serves to emphasize the individual separateness of the things named. Such repetition is necessary in expressions like the following, to avoid ambiguity: "*the* secretary and *the* treasurer (two persons)," "*the* finished and *the* unfinished manuscript (two manuscripts)." "*The* secretary and treasurer" means one person only.

If used before the first adjective, *the* should be used before each of a series of adjectives applied to one substantive, but distinguishing different objects; as, "*the* expensive, *the* cheap, and *the* medium-priced goods." See *A, An.*

Them, Those. Do not confuse these words. *Them* is the objective case of the plural third personal pronoun; *those* is a plural demonstrative adjective. Say "*those* facts," never "*them* facts."

Then. Used in such a phrase as "the *then* Chief Justice," this word is approved. The use has a long and honorable history. The phrase *then some* for *some more* is slang.

Thence. The preposition *from* with *thence* is superfluous. "He came *thence*" is correct.

Therefor, Therefore. These two look-alike words may seem to be alternative spellings for the same word, but they have quite different meanings. "Therefor," accented on the second syllable, is equivalent to the phrase, "for that." "Therefore," an adverb, introduces a conclusion based on a reasoning process that has already been indicated. It is accented on the first syllable.

Think for. Such a word as *suppose* or *suspect* should be substituted for the phrase *think for* in a barbarous sentence like "He hears more than you *think for*."

Those kind. "*That kind* of shoe is good," not "*those kind*." *Those* is plural; *kind* is singular. Care should be taken to preserve the number in the sentence. See *Kind.*

Through. *To be through* is an American colloquialism, meaning "to have finished," "to have done": "How soon will you *be through* with the work?" The phrase is frequently used and may be classed among our idioms.

To. Never say, "She was *to* my house yesterday." Use *at* in place of *to*. We say, colloquially, "I have been *to* town," and some critics allow the phrase as idiomatic. See *Be back.*

Together. In *meet together* or *converse together*, *together* is superfluous.

Tomorrow. One may say, "*Tomorrow is* or *will be* Monday." But one should say, "*Tomorrow will be* a memorable day."

Transparent, Translucent. *Transparent* means "clear," allowing light to pass so that objects may be seen through the substance. *Translucent* means "partially transparent," allowing light to pass but not permitting vision.

Transpire. Do not use this word to mean *happen*. We may say, "No information or news has *transpired*," meaning "None has become public."

Treat. A book *treats of* (not *treats on*) the subject of its contents.

Try. We *make* experiments, not *try* them, say some critics. Others point out that *try* experiments is laboratory usage; but *perform* is the more generally approved verb in this sense. "*Do* experiments" is school cant.

Try and. It is better to avoid the use of the phrase *try and do*. Use *try to do* instead. The use of this phrase is not quite like that of the phrase *come and see*, which is in good use.

Under the circumstances. See *In the circumstances.*

Unique. Since this word denotes one of a kind, it should not be used in the watered-down sense of unusual. Neither should it be accompanied by an adverb of degree, as in "very unique."

United States. Whether to use *is* or *are* after these words may be a political as well as a linguistic question. General usage approves *is*, though in government official usage there is warrant for *are*.

Universally, All. Do not say, "He was *universally* praised by *all* who heard him." The two words are so similar in meaning that the use of both is redundant. Say, "He was *universally* praised" or "He was praised by *all* who heard him."

Unkempt. Literally, the word means "uncombed," or, figuratively, "rough," "unpolished."

It is not to be used generally to mean "disordered," as in *unkempt* rooms. A person may be *unkempt*, a room never.

Up. Superfluously added to many verbs, as in *add up*, *open up*, etc. *Up* should be used with verbs only when it contributes definitely to the meaning or is in good colloquial use.

Use of Infinitive. The present infinitive is used after all tenses unless it refers to action occurring before the time implied in the assertion of the principal verb. Say, "He intended *to do* it," never "He intended *to have done* it." But "He is said *to have been* present" is correct, since his "being present" preceded the saying. *Ought*, being a defective verb, is followed by the present infinitive to express present or future duty, and by the perfect infinitive to express duty in past time: "They ought *to speak*"; "They ought *to have spoken*."

Verbs, Agreement of. The verb in a sentence must agree with the substantive of the subject in person and number. But there are several puzzling cases which give rise to frequent error.

(1) The subject includes substantives of different numbers: Either the master or his servants *are* at fault. Usage approves a verb agreeing with the nearest substantive. Usually it is better to recast such a sentence and avoid this construction: "The fault lies either with the master or his servants."

(2) Subject collective or distributive: "There *are* (*is*) six dollars in the drawer." If the thought is of the total amount of money, use the singular verb; if the idea of several pieces of money is uppermost, use the plural verb.

Verdict. A word loosely used for *opinion*. *Verdict* should be reserved for official decisions, as of a jury, or for opinion publicly and formally expressed: "That he is unreliable is the *opinion* (not the *verdict*) of all who know him."

Very. Most critics insist that *very* should not immediately precede a past participle used as an adjective. Not, "He was *very* pleased," but "He was *very much* pleased." *Very* may directly precede an adjective: "That is a *very* good article." Where the participle has chiefly an adjective sense, *very* is authoritatively used: "She is a *very* charming person."

View of, to. "He worked with a *view to* the establishment of a business." "We talked with a *view of* discovering each other's opinions." These sentences represent approved usage.

Viewpoint. *Point of view* is preferable. It has more character when used in a sentence in written English and in spoken English.

Vocation, Avocation. A person's *vocation* is his profession, his calling, his business; his *avocations* are the things that occupy him incidentally; "Mr. Wharton's *vocation* is banking; his *avocation* is photography."

Want, Need. *Need* refers to the actual fact of lack; *want* implies a personal sense or view of the situation. A man may *want* an automobile, when he does not *need* it for his business. Avoid using *want* and *need* loosely in the sense of *lack*.

Was, Is. When, in a subordinate clause, an unchanging truth or a present fact is to be stated, use *is*, not *was*, no matter what the tense of the principal verb: "He knew that ice *is* formed at 32°." The same rule applies to the use of the present tense of any verb: "They should have realized that war *settles* no disputes."

Ways. Wrongly used for *way*. "The house is a long *ways* off" should be "The house is a long *way* off."

Well, Why. The use of these words as exclamations of surprise or dismay may be defended, but too frequently they are simply drawling noises at the beginning of a sentence.

Went, Gone. These forms of the verb *go* are frequently confused. *Went* is the past tense; *gone* is the past participle. Say, "They *have gone* (not *have went*)."

What. "He would not believe *but what* I said it" should be "He would not believe *but that* I said it." See *But*.

Whence. "*Whence* came ye?" not "*From whence* came ye?" *Whence* means "from what place, source, or cause."

Whereabouts. In "His *whereabouts* is unknown," observe the correct singular verb.

Who, Whom. Avoid the common error of misusing *who* for *whom*. Say, "*Whom* are you thinking of?" not "*Who* are you thinking of?" "*Whom* did they mention?" not "*Who* did they mention?" *Whom* is the form to use as the object of a verb or preposition.

Whoever. One should write, "I will give it to *whoever* can use it," but, "I will give it to *whomever* you designate." The syntax of the pronoun in the subordinate clause determines the case.

Whole lot. As a substitute for *much* or *a great deal*, *whole lot* is only in vulgar use; as, "I don't care a *whole lot* for the theater."

Whose, Of which. Some critics object to the use of *whose* in referring to things, but there is precedent for the usage. Sometimes *of which* would bring in an awkward manner of speech. In such cases *whose* should be used: "This is the latest of those political changes *whose* causes we can easily find."

Widow woman. The word *woman* is superfluous here.

Without. This word is a preposition and should not take the place of the conjunction *unless*: "I shall not go *without* my father consents" should read "*unless* my father consents," or the expression might be changed to "*without* my father's consent," where *without* is a preposition.

Worst kind. A vulgarism frequently used in the sense of *very much*; as, "I want to go the *worst kind*."

Would have. Avoid the incorrect use of *would have* in conditional sentences. Not "If he *would have* come," but "If he *had* come." "*Would of*" is completely illiterate.

Yes. Avoid the various vulgar and provincial varieties of this important little word: *yeh, ya, yep, eh-uh*.

You-all. When used to mean simply "you," and applied to more than one person, this is a provincialism of the southern United States. It is not properly used to mean one person only.

Yours truly. This phrase used as a substitute for "I" or "me" is awkward and self-conscious. It arises from the same exaggerated modesty that prevents people from beginning a business letter with "I" and that causes essayists to introduce such circumlocutions as "from the standpoint of the present writer the conclusion seems evident" instead of saying "I think" or something equally natural and direct.

Z. The letter is *zee* or *zed*, the former being the common American name, the latter the British.

WORD BUILDING

To be skilled in language, one must know words and their right uses. The elements of spoken language are articulate sounds; those of written language are characters or letters which *represent* those sounds. From these elements, which are known as roots or stems, prefixes and suffixes, words are formed.

Roots. The *root* is the primitive form of any word and existed before the addition of prefix, suffix, or inflectional ending. The syllable preceding it is called the *prefix*; that which comes after it is named the *suffix*. For instance, the root of the word *prefix* is *fig* or *fix* from the Latin *figere*, "to attach"; the syllable *pre* signifies "before." Thus we get the meaning "to attach before." Similarly, the word *suffix*, from *sub* or *suf* meaning "under" or "after" and *figere* "to attach," means "to attach after." Since prefixes are attached before words or roots and suffixes are added at the end, prefixes or suffixes are called *affixes*, from *ad* or *af* meaning "to" and *figere* "to attach." Therefore, an *affix* is one or more letters or syllables added at the beginning or at the end of a word.

Stems. The *stem* is that part of a word to which the case endings or personal endings and tense signs are affixed; sometimes the *stem* is identical with the *root*, though generally it is derived from it with some formative suffix. Stems are so called because inflections were added to parts of words found in other languages, as branches are grafted to the stem or trunk of a tree. They have gradually been transplanted into the English language and may now be studied as constituent parts of our everyday speech. For example, in the Latin word *crucifigere*, "to crucify," we have the root *crux*, "a cross," changed into *cruci*, "to a cross," by the stem ending, *ci*; combining *cruci* and *figere*, which signifies "to attach," we get a word meaning "to attach to a cross."

By learning words from their etymology, we not only remember the meaning of the particular words thus studied, but we also immediately recognize all other words that are similarly formed.

Structure and Relations of Words. We know things best when we can relate them to other things and make comparisons. Besides, to understand a thing thoroughly we must know its parts; for instance, we know a house when we are familiar with its different rooms and the parts of its construction. Many words are built very much as houses are built; they have foundations, and to these are added various parts which are distinguished one from the other, thus making each word useful for definite purposes. We shall, therefore, learn words more intelligently if we are able to recognize the elements out of which they are built.

English has borrowed from Latin and Greek not only entire words, but also the elements of words; that is, stems, suffixes, and prefixes, out of which to make new combinations. By combining these elements, large groups of words have been built up, the words of each group being related through having the same stem.

An Aid to Memory. The meanings of words seldom used are easily forgotten. Recalling them is like groping in the dark. If, however, we know the elements of which these words are made, the difficulty largely disappears. Few people have time to learn Latin or Greek to get the meanings of these word elements; but the essential matters can be selected and grouped for ready reference and study. A little *grouping* of syllables will do away with much *groping* for word meanings. Learn the common meanings of the stems, prefixes, and suffixes given in this section. Master them, a few at a time. This study will largely increase your ability to remember and understand thousands of unfamiliar words.

It will also enable you to make much better use of the English dictionary.

Native and Foreign Words. The English language may be regarded as made up, for the most part, of the following groups of words:

1. Simple words retaining exactly or nearly their original Anglo-Saxon form and meaning; as, *man, will, and.*

2. Simple words borrowed from other languages, which words retain their original sense or become somewhat modified in meaning; as, *grand* (French), *pedal* (Latin).

3. Compound words made up of Anglo-Saxon, Latin, Greek, or other elements; as, *roadway* (Anglo-Saxon), *camshaft* (Dutch or French and Anglo-Saxon), *phonograph* (Greek).

4. Anglo-Saxon words formed of a stem and a prefix or suffix; as, *willful, undo, lengthen.*

5. Words made up of stems and prefixes or suffixes from other languages; as, *excise* (Latin), *engage* (French).

Short and Long Words. The English language, like every other cultivated tongue, comprises both short and long words, or, to express it better, "popular" and "learned" words. The former belong to the people in common—are limited to no particular class; the latter are words which may be used by educated speakers in ordinary conversation and are to be met with in general literature.

The short or popular words are those we have known from childhood—they are sufficient to express our immature thoughts and ideas. Later, the mind develops, and, through reading good literature, we become acquainted with a more formal and distinctive style of phraseology. It is thus unconsciously, yet naturally, that we pass from the use of simple words of Anglo-Saxon origin to those so-called learned words derived from the French, the Latin, or the Greek.

The following examples will illustrate methods of building up words to express more or less complicated ideas:

Cablegram, cable-gram (writing) means a writing or message sent by cable or wire.

Comprehensive, com (together) -prehens (grasping) -ive (adj.) means having the quality of seizing or grasping (much) together.

Cosmopolitan, cosmo (world) -polit (citizen) -an (adj.) means having the character or quality of a world citizen.

Impervious, im (not) -per (through) -vi (way) -ous (adj.) means having no way or passage through.

Periscope, peri (around) -scope (looker) means literally a looker around, or an instrument to look around with.

Prefixes and Suffixes. In the following lists are grouped the principal prefixes and suffixes and the most commonly used Latin stems of the English language. Their uses are illustrated by the analysis of about 350 common words. The principles illustrated in these lists may be applied generally, and the student will find his grasp of English meanings and spelling greatly improved by careful study of the significations, forms, and uses of the various word elements.

Prefixes commonly alter the meaning of the stem in some manner. Thus *hyper*tension adds the idea of excess; *un*wise contradicts the basic word. *Suffixes* may change only the meaning of a word, as in book*let*, but they frequently change its grammatical form also. For example, *ize* makes a verb out of an adjective (natural*ize*), and *ness* converts an adjective into an abstract noun (kind*ness*). It should be noted, however, that English often uses the same word for different parts of speech. Thus, without adding suffixes or otherwise changing its form, *iron* may be used as a noun ("The bridge is made of *iron*."), as a verb ("to *iron* a shirt"), or as an adjective ("He has an *iron* constitution.").

WORD FORMATIONS

Throughout the following lists of words compounded under *Prefixes*, the prefixes are printed in **boldface**, the rest of each word is printed in *italics*; thus, **ob**-*stinate*. Similarly, under *Suffixes*, the suffixes are in **boldface**, other syllables in *italics*; as, *verd*-**ant**. In the list of *Stems*, the stems are in **boldface**, other syllables in *italics*; as, *in*-**clus**-*ive*. Meanings of foreign language syllables not defined at the head of each group are given in parentheses; as, *pro* (forth) -**duce**. The word (noun), (adj.), (verb), (adv.), following a suffix, indicates that the suffix gives to the word of which it is a part the force of a noun, a verb, an adjective, or an adverb.

ANGLO-SAXON PREFIXES

A-, meaning *on* or *in*.
  A- *live* means *on* or *in* life.
  A- *board* means *on* board.
  A- *sleep* means *in* sleep.
Be-, meaning *affecting with* or *by*, or merely emphatic.
  Be- *witched* means *affected by* witchcraft.
  Be- *dewed* means wet as *with* dew.
  Be- *spattered* means spattered or spotted *all over*, as with mud.
For-, meaning *away* or *not*.
  For- *bid* means bid or command *not*, or refuse.
  For- *get* means *not* to hold, lose hold of.
  For- *give* means give or let go *away*.
  For- *bear* means keep *away* or *from*.
Fore-, meaning *in front*, *beforehand*, or *ahead of*.
  Fore- *arm* means the arm from elbow to hand.
  Fore- *tell* means tell *ahead of* time.
  Fore- *stall* means stop *beforehand*.
  Fore- *shadow* means to shadow or typify *beforehand*.
Half- and **No-,** as in half-done. nowhere.
Out-, meaning *excelling*.
  Out- *shine* means surpass (another) in brightness.
  Out- *play* means defeat at play.
To-, meaning *this* or *the*.
  To- *morrow* means *the* morrow or morning.
  To- *day* means *this* day.
Un-, a negative prefix.
  Un- *aware* means *not* heeding or noticing.
  Un- *kind* means *not* kind.
  Un- *fasten* means loosen bonds or fastenings.
  Un- *fair* means *not* fair.

LATIN PREFIXES

Ab-, meaning *from*, *not*.
  Ab- *duct* (lead) means lead *away*.
  Ab- *norm* (rule) -*al* (adj.) means *away* from the rule (norm).
  Ab- *sent* (being) means being *away* from, not present.
  Ab- *sorb* (suck in) means suck in *from*, as a blotter.
A-, Ad-, Ac-, Ag-, meaning *to*.
  A- *scribe* (write) means write *to* or give *to*, grant.
  Ad- *here* (stick) means stick *to*.
  Ac- *cede* (yield) means yield *to*.
  Ag- *gression* (stepping) means a stepping *to* or *forward*, crowding.
  Ag- *grav* (weight) -*ate* (verb) means add weight *to*, increase.
Ante-, meaning *before*.
  Ante- *cedent* (going) means going *before*.
  Ante- *date* means date *before* or *ahead of* time.
Bi-, Bis-, meaning *two*.
  Bi- *weekly* means every *two* weeks.
  Bis- *cuit* (cooked) means *twice* cooked (dry and hard).
  Bi- *sect* (cut) means cut in *two*.

Circum-, meaning *around*.
  Circum- *stance* (standing) means that which stands *around*, or accompanies.
  Circum- *scribe* (write) means write or draw *around*.
  Circum- *spect* (looking) means looking *around*, hence careful.
Com-, Con-, Co-, meaning *with*, *together*, or *completely*.
  Com- *pose* (place) means place *together*, to make.
  Con- *ceive* (take) means take to one's self *completely*, understand.
  Con- *dole* (sorrow) means sorrow *with*.
  Co- *oper* (work) -*ate* (verb) means work *together*.
Contra-, Contro-, meaning *against*.
  Contra- *dict* (speak) means speak *against*.
  Contro- *versy* (turning) means a turning *against*.
De-, meaning *down*, *out of*, *from*, *completely*.
  De- *scend* (climb) means climb *down*.
  De- *pend* (hang) means hang *down from*.
  De- *ment* (mind) -*ed* (adj.) means *out of* one's mind, insane.
  De- *port* (carry) means carry *from* or *away*.
  De- *nude* (bare) means make *completely* bare.
Dis-, Dif-, meaning *apart from*, *from*.
  Dis- *sect* (cut) means cut *apart*.
  Dis- *perse* (strew) means strew *apart*, scatter.
  Dis- *tend* (stretch) means stretch *apart*.
  Dis- *sent* (think) means think *apart* or *differently from*.
  Dif- *ferent* (bearing) means bearing *away from*, not like.
E-, Ef-, Ex-, meaning *from*, *out of*.
  E- *vade* (walk, go) means walk *away from*.
  Ef- *fect* (doing) means a doing *from*, something made *from* another.
  Ex- *claim* (cry) means cry *out*.
  Ex- *tort* (wrench) means wrench or force *from* or *out of*.
  Ex- *tradition* (giving over) means surrender *from*, as a prisoner is given over *from* one authority to another.
Extra-, meaning *outside*.
  Extra- *ordinary* (common) means *out of* the common.
  Extra- *territorial* means *out of* the territory.
In-, Il-, meaning *not* or *contrary*.
  In- *ept* (apt) means *not* apt or fit.
  In- *sensible* (feeling) means *not* feeling.
  In- *nocuous* (harmful) means *not* harmful.
  Il- *legal* (lawful) means *not* lawful.
In-, Im-, Il-, meaning *in*, *on*, or *upon*.
  In- *hale* (breathe) means breathe *in*.
  In- *voke* (call) means call *on* or *upon*.
  Im- *press* means press *upon*.
  Il- *lustr* (light) -*ate* (verb) means throw light *upon*.
Inter-, meaning *between*.
  Inter- *urban* (city) means *between* cities.
  Inter- *national* means *between* nations.
Intra-, Intro-, meaning *between*, *among*, or *within*.
  Intra- *mural* (wall) means *between* or *within* the walls.
  Intro- *duce* (lead) means lead *within* or *into* (knowledge).
Non-, meaning *not*.
  Non- *partisan* means *not* related to a party.
  Non- *entity* (something) means *not* anything.
Ob-, Op-, meaning *against*, *to*, *upon*.
  Ob- *stinate* (standing) means standing *against*.
  Ob- *ligate* (bind) means bind *to*, as *to* a promise.
  Op- *posite* (placed) means placed *against*.
  Op- *press* means press *upon*, crush; hence burden, tyrannize over.

Per-, meaning *through, completely, very.*
Per- *ceive* (take) means take *through* (thoroughly) therefore, learn.
Per- *manent* (staying) means staying *through,* continuing.
Per- *forate* (bore) means bore *through.*
Per- *verse* (turned) means turned *around.*

Post-, meaning *after.*
Post- *pone* (place) means place *after,* put off, or defer.
Post- *mortem* (death) means *after* death.
Post- *lude* (play) means (music) played *after.*

Pre-, meaning *before* (in time, place, rank, or degree).
Pre- *lude* (play) means play *before,* hence, music played *before.* Compare *Postlude.*
Pre- *face* (say or speak) means something said or spoken *before.*
Pre- *eminence* (elevation) means an elevation *before,* i.e., *above* others.
Pre- *vail* (strength) means be strong *before* or *in excess of,* hence to be master of.

Pro-, meaning *forth, forward.*
Pro- *pel* (drive) means drive *forward.*
Pro- *ceed* (go) means go *forward* or *forth.*
Pro- *ject* (throw) means throw or extend *forward.*
Pro- *mote* (move) means move *forward.*

Re-, meaning *again* or *back.*
Re- *form* (shape) means change *back,* or into a new shape or form.
Re- *pel* (drive) means drive *back.*
Re- *claim* (call) means call (for) *again,* hence get *back.*
Re- *view* (look at) means look at *again.*

Retro-, meaning *backward.*
Retro- *spect* (looking) means a looking *backward.*
Retro- *gression* (going) means a going *backward.*

Se-, meaning *from, away.*
Se- *cede* (go) means go *away* or *from,* withdraw,
Se- *duce* (lead) means lead *away.*
Se- *cure* (care) means *free from* care or anxiety.

Semi-, meaning *half.*
Semi- *annual* (yearly) means every six months or *half*-yearly.

Sub-, Sup-, Sus-, meaning *under.*
Sub- *marine* (sea) means *under* the sea.
Sub- *soil* means the layer of material *under* or *below* the surface soil.
Sup- *port* (carry) means carry *under,* that is, carry by being *under.*
Sus- *pend* (hang) means hang *under.*

Super-, Sur-, meaning *above, upon.*
Super- *structure* (building) means the building *above* the foundation.
Sur- *pass* means pass *over* or *above,* hence excel.
Sur- *tax* means a tax *above* another.

Trans-, Tra-, meaning *across.*
Trans- *fer* (carry) means carry *across.*
Tra- *verse* (turn, go) means turn or go *across.*

GREEK PREFIXES

A-, An-, meaning *without, not.*
A- *byss* (bottom) means *without* bottom.
A- *chromat* (color) *-ic* (adj.) means *not* colored.
An- *archy* (government) means *no* government.

Amphi-, meaning *around.*
Amphi- *theater,* means a theater *around* an open space.

Ana-, An-, meaning *up, according to, backward.*
Ana- *tom* (cut) *-y* (noun) means cutting *up.*
Ana- *gram* (writing) means a writing *backwards,* opposed to the usual order.
Ana- *logy* (ratio or proportion) means *up* to the proportion; hence, a resemblance, a likeness.

Anti-, meaning *against.*
Anti- *christian* means *opposed* to Christianity.
Anti- *pathy* (suffering) means a suffering *against,* hence opposition of feeling.

Cata-, Cath-, meaning *down, according to, in respect to.*
Cata- *lepsy* (falling) means a falling *down.*
Cata- *log* (name) means *according to* the name, a list so arranged.
Cath- *olic* (whole) means *in respect to* or *having to do with* the whole; hence, universal.

Dia-, meaning *through, across.*
Dia- *meter* (measure) means a measure or distance *through.*
Dia- *gonal* (angle) means *through* the angle or corner.
Dia- *gram* (writing) means a writing *through,* a plan or drawing.
Dia- *dem* (bind) means something that binds *across,* as a band or fillet across the head.

Hyper-, meaning *over, above.*
Hyper- *critical* means *over*-critical.

Hypo-, meaning *below* or *under.*
Hypo- *dermic* (skin) means *under* the skin.
Hypo- *thesis* (placed) means something placed *under,* as a foundation for reasoning.

Meta-, most often denoting change.
Meta- *phor* (carrying) means a carrying *over* (to another meaning).
Meta- *morphosis* (form) means a *change of* form.

Syl-, Sym-, Syn-, meaning *with, together.*
Syl- *lable* (taken) means taken *together.*
Sym- *pathy* (suffering) means suffering *with.* Compare *Condole.*
Syn- *opsis* (view) means a view *together,* hence a general view or exhibit.
Syn- *thetic* (put) means put *together.*

ANGLO-SAXON SUFFIXES

The following are the principal Anglo-Saxon sufr fixes. Like the prefixes, these are used with either Anglo-Saxon or foreign stems in their appropriate meanings.

-dom, noun suffix, meaning state or authority of, as in *kingdom.*

-ed, or **-d,** suffix for the past tense and the past participle of verb, as in *load, loaded; hear, heard.*

-en, a verb suffix, meaning to make or cause, as in *deepen, lengthen.*

-er, noun suffix, meaning the agent, as in *leade-* or *doer.*

-ful, noun or adjective suffix, meaning full or, sometimes, inclined to, as in *armful, handful, playful.*

-hood, noun suffix of state or quality, as in *manhood* or *hardihood.*

-ing, verbal noun or participial ending, conveying the idea of process, continuance, art, etc., as in *homing, speaking, painting.*

-ish, an adjective ending, with the meaning of resembling, somewhat like or inclined toward, as *bookish, childish.*

-le, a verb suffix often with frequentative and diminutive force, as in *handle, kindle, joggle, nestle, sprinkle.*

-less, adjective suffix, meaning lacking, deprived of, as in *armless, godless, homeless.*

-let, noun suffix, meaning little, as in *booklet, streamlet.*

-like, an adjective suffix, meaning resembling, as in *godlike.*

-ly, an adjective suffix, meaning resembling or having the quality of, as in *godly, homely;* also an adverbial suffix, as in *deeply, warmly.*

-ness, noun suffix, signifying quality, as in *lightness.*

-ship, noun suffix, signifying state, condition, office, or quality, as in *lordship, marksmanship.*

-some, an adjective suffix denoting considerable degree or quality, as in *handsome, wholesome, gladsome, winsome.*

-ty, meaning "ten times," as in *fifty.*

-wise, an adjective or adverbial suffix, signifying manner, as in *lengthwise, otherwise.*

-y, an adjective suffix, meaning like or pertaining to, as in *handy, windy;* or noun suffix, often equal to Latin *-ia* or French *-ie,* as in *history, villainy.*

SUFFIXES FROM THE LATIN, GREEK, AND FRENCH

-able, -ible, adjective suffix.
Vis (see) **-ible** means *possible to see.*
Sal (sell) **-able** means *possible to sell.*
Peace (peace) **-able** means *tending to peace.*
Terr (fright) **-ible** means *tending to create terror.*

-acious, -icious, adjective suffix.
Avar (greed) **-icious** means *given to greed, greedy.*
Aud (dare) **-acious** means *abounding in daring.*
Ten (hold) **-acious** means *given to holding.*

-acity, -icity, noun suffix, often equals *-ness.*
Cap (take) **-acity** means *power of holding* or *taking in.*
Authent (original) **-icity** means the *quality of genuineness.*
Loqu (talk) **-acity** means the *habit of excessive talking, talkativeness.*
Pugn (fight) **-acity** means *fighting quality.*

-acy, noun suffix.
Liter (letter) **-acy** means the *quality of knowing letters.*
Candid (white) **-acy** means *condition of whiteness* (Roman candidates for office were so called because clothed in white.).
Prim (first) **-acy** means the *state of being first or chief.*

-al, adjective or noun suffix.
Leg (law) **-al** means *according,* or *pertaining, to law.*
Plur (many) **-al** means *pertaining to more than one.*
Fin (end) **-al** means *pertaining to the end.*
Gener (class) **-al** means *pertaining to a whole class or body.*

-an, adjective suffix.
Hum (man) **-an** means *pertaining to mankind.*
Urb (city) **-an** means *pertaining to the city.*

-ant, -ent, adjective (-ing) or noun suffix.
Expect (await) **-ant** means *awaiting.*
Verd (green) **-ant** means *of green* or *like green.*
Ard (burn) **-ent** means *burning.*
Pot (power) **-ent** means *powerful.*
Visit **-ant** means *one who visits.*

-ary, adjective or noun suffix, signifying *like* or *connected with.*
Exempl (pattern) **-ary** means *fitted to be a model.*
Liter (letter) **-ary** means *having to do with letters.*
Plen (full) **-ary** means *having fullness* (as of power).

-ate, verb or adjective suffix.
Ex- (out) *cav* (hollow) **-ate** means *to make hollow, hollow out.*
Hibern (winter) **-ate** means *to winter, sleep through winter.*
Dis (out of) *-loc* (place) **-ate** means *to put out of place.*
Plac (please) **-ate** means *to please.*
Aspir (breath) **-ate** means *like breath, breathy.*
De (lacking) *-sper* (hope) **-ate** means *without hope.*

-ation, noun suffix.
Cre (make) **-ation** means *that which is made,* or *making.*
Ex (out of) *-clam* (cry) **-ation** means *that which is cried out,* or *a crying out.*
E (out of) *-limin* (bound) **-ation** means *putting out of bounds, getting rid of.*
Found (basis) **-ation** means *that on which anything stands* or *is founded.*

-ative, adjective suffix.
Authorit **-ative** means *serving for authority.*
Talk **-ative** means *inclined to talk.*
Tent (try) **-ative** means *serving for a trial* or *test.*

-fy, verb suffix.
Ampli (large) **-fy** means *make large.*
Veri (true) **-fy** means *make* or *establish as true.*
Testi (witness) **-fy** means *bear witness.*

-ic, adjective suffix.
Hero **-ic** means *like a hero.*
Poet **-ic** means *like poetry.*
Ascet (exercise, discipline) **-ic** means *pertaining to* or *characterized by self-denial.*

-ile, adjective suffix.
Ag (do, act) **-ile** means *capable of (easy) action.*
Fac (do) **-ile** means *fit for doing, easy.*
Duct (draw) **-ile** means *capable of being drawn,* as *metal into wire.*
Puer (child) **-ile** means *suited to,* or *like, a child.*

-ine (-in), adjective suffix.
Alkal (lye) **-ine** means *like an alkali* or *lye.*
Femin (woman) **-ine** means *pertaining to a woman.*
Sal (salt) **-ine** means *like salt.*

-ion, noun suffix, equals *-ing.*
Act (do) **-ion** means *the process of doing.*
Re (back) *-tent* (hold) **-ion** means *the act of holding back.*
Solut (loosen) **-ion** means *the process of loosening* or *clearing up.*

-ism, noun suffix.
American **-ism** means *a characteristic of,* or *the spirit of, America.*
Despot **-ism** means *the power of a despot.*
Buddh **-ism** means *the system of religion founded by Buddha.*

-ist, noun suffix.
Flor **-ist** means *seller of flowers.*
Pian **-ist** means *one who plays the piano.*

-ive, adjective suffix.
Primit (first) **-ive** means *like first things* or *beginnings.*
Ef (out) *-fus* (pour) **-ive** means *pouring out* or *like a pouring out.*

-ize, verb suffix.
Real **-ize** means *make real* or *think of as real.*
Civil **-ize** means *make civil* or *refined.*
Agon (struggle) **-ize** means *make,* or *go through, a struggle.*
Critic (judge) **-ize** means *judge* or *cause to pass under judgment.*

-or, noun suffix, equals *-er.*
Fact (do) **-or** means *a doer,* hence *something that affects a result.*
Con-duct (lead) **-or** means *one who leads (with).*
In-struct (build) **-or** means *one who builds* or *prepares (teaches).*

-ous, adjective suffix, often equals Anglo-Saxon *-y.*
Aque (water) **-ous** means *watery.*
Courage (boldness) **-ous** means *possessed of boldness.*
Lumin (light) **-ous** means *having* or *giving light.*
Por (hole) **-ous** means *full of minute holes* or *pores.*

-tude, noun suffix, often equals *-ness.*
Ampli (full) **-tude** means *fullness* or *large size.*
Soli (alone) **-tude** means *condition of being alone.*

-ure, noun suffix, often equals *-ing.*
Press **-ure** means a *pressing upon.*
En-clos (shut) **-ure** means a *shutting in.*

Latin Stems

Ag, Act, meaning *do.*
Act *-or* (noun) means *doer.*
Ag *-ent* (noun) means *doer,* especially for another, (derived through the French).
In (not) **-act** *-ive* (adj.) means not *doing* or *acting.*
Re (back) **-act** *-ion -ary* (adj.) means given to *acting back,* or acting according to former habits.

Anim, meaning *life.*
Anim *-al* (adj.) (having quality of) *-cule* (little) means a little thing *having life.*
Anim *-ated* (adj.) (having) means *lively.*
In (not) **-anim** *-ate* (adj.) means not *having life.*

Cap, Capt, Cept, Cip, meaning *take, get.*
Ac (to) **-cept** *-ance* (noun) (the act of) means the act of *taking* to one's self.
Cap *-able* (adj.) means able to *take.*
Cap *-acity* (noun) means power of *taking in* or *holding.*
Capt *-iv* (like) *-ate* (verb) means cause to be like one *taken.*
Con (together) **-cept** *-ion* (noun) (result) means the result of *taking* together or completely, e.g., an idea.
Per (through) **-cept** *-ion* (noun) means a *taking* thoroughly, seeing clearly.
Re (back) **-cept** *-ive* (adj.) (inclined to) means inclined to *take,* or *receive.*

Ced, Cess, meaning *move, go, yield.*
Ac (to) **-cede** means *yield* to.
Ac (to) **-cess** *-ible* (adj.) (possible) means possible to *go* to, or get at.
De (away) **-ced** *-ent* (noun) (one who) means one who *has gone* away, died.
Ex (from, beyond) **-ceed** means *go* beyond.
Pro (forward) **-ceed** means *go* forward.
Pro (forth) **-cess** *-ion -al* (noun) means something related to a *going* forth.
Re (back) **-cess** *-ion -al* (noun) means something related to a *going* back.
(These last two words are used of the music accompanying the entrance and the exit of a choir.)
Se (apart) **-cede** means *go* apart from.
Un (not) *-suc* (under) **-cess** *-ful -ly* (adverb) means not *going* or *following* under, that is, not attaining or succeeding.

Clud, Clus, meaning *close, shut.*
Con (completely) **-clude** means *shut* finally.
In (not) *-con* **-clus** *-ive* (adj.) *-ly* (adv.) means not *closing* completely.
In (in) **-clus** *-ive* (adj.) means *shutting* in or including.
Pre (before) **-clude** means *shut before,* hence put up a barrier against.
Se (away) **-clude** means *shut* away, withdraw.
Re (away) **-cluse** means one who is *shut away,* one who lives apart from society.

Dic, Dict, meaning *speak, tell, declare.*
Ab (away) **-dic** *-ate* (verb) means *speak* or *declare* away, as a position, a throne, give up.
De (apart) **-dic** *-ation* (noun) (an act) means an act of *speaking,* or *declaring* (a thing) apart; hence, setting apart, as a church.
Dict *-at* (the act) *-or* (noun) (agent) *-ial* (adj.) means characterized by the act or manner of a *speaker* or commander—like a dictator.
In (against) **-dict** *-ment* (noun) means a *declaration* against (a person), an accusation.

Domin, meaning *power* or *rule.*
Domin *-ant* (adj.) means *ruling, controlling,* or *principal.*
Domin *-ation* (noun) (state of) means the state or act of *ruling.*
Pre (above) **-domin** *-ate* (verb) means *rule* above or as superior to.

Duc, Duct, meaning *lead, draw, bring.*
Ad (to) **-duce** means *lead* or bring to, as proof to a statement.
Con (with) **-duc** *-ive* (adj.) (tending to) means tending to *lead,* or suitable to be led with, that is, helpful.
De (from) **-duce** means *draw* from, as a conclusion from a statement.
De (from) **-duct** *-ion* (noun) (act of) means a *taking* away from.
In (into) **-duct** *-ion* (noun) (act of) means a *leading* into, as an electric current is led into one coil from another.
Pro (forth) **-duce** means *bring* forth.
Pro (forth) **-duct** *-iv* (having power of) *-ity* (state of) means the state of having power of *bringing* forth.

Fac, Fact, Fect, Fict, meaning *make* or *do.*
Af (to) **-fect** means *do* to, as one thing does something to another.
Af (to) **-fect** *-ion* (noun) (-ing) means *making* toward, aspiring to, hence love.
Fac *-simile* (likeness) means a *made* likeness.
Fact *-ory* (noun) (place for) means a place for *making.*
Per (thoroughly) **-fect** means *made* completely.

Fer, Lat, meaning *bear, carry, move.*
Dif (apart) **-fer** *-ent* (adj.) means *bearing* apart.
E (from) **-lated** means *carried* from or out of, as out of one's usual self.
Ob (to) **-lat** *-ion* (noun) means something *borne* to or offered.
Re (back) **-late** means *bear* or *carry* back, that is, to some one or to something else, connect.
Super (above) **-lat** *-ive* (adj.) means *borne* over or above, the highest.
Un (not) *-trans* (across) **-lat** *-able* means not possible to *carry* across, as from one language to another.

Fid, meaning *belief, trust, faith.*
Con (with) **-fide** means share *trust* with.
Dif (apart) **-fid** *-ent* (adj.) means lacking *trust* or *faith,* especially in oneself.
In (not) **-fid** *-el* (noun) (one who) means one who lacks *faith,* unbeliever.

Fin, meaning *end* or *limit.*
De (from) **-fin** *-ition* (noun) (that which) means something that marks off or *limits* one thing from another.
In (not) **-fin** *-ite* (adj.) means not *limited.*
Un (not) *-con* (together) **-fin** *-ed* (Anglo-Saxon participle ending) means not *bounded* or shut in.
Fin *-ish* (verb) means make an *end.*

Flect, meaning *bend.*
De (from) **-flect** means *bend* from or aside.
Re (back) **-flect** *-ion* (-ing) means a *bending* back.

Flict, meaning *strike.*
Af (to, at) **-flict** means *strike* at.
In (on) **-flict** means *strike* on.

Frang, Frag, Fract, meaning *break.*
Frang *-ible* (adj.) means possible to *break.*
Frag *-ile* (adj.) means fitted, or likely, to *break.*
Frag *-ment* (noun) means that which is *broken.*
Fract *-ure* (noun) means a break or a result of *breaking.*

Grad, Gred, Gress, meaning *step, go.*
Con (together) **-gress** means that which *goes* together, hence, an official gathering or body.
De (down) **-grade** means cause to *step* down.

In (in) **-gred** *-i* *-ent* (noun) means that which *goes* into, as a part of a mixture.

Retro (backward) **-grade** (adj.) means *going* backward.

Un (not) *-pro* (forward) **-gress** *-ive* (adj.) means not *going* forward.

Leg, Lig, Lect, meaning *choose, pick, read.*

E (from) **-lect** *-or* (noun) means one who *chooses* from, as from a number of candidates.

In (not) *-e* (out) **-lig** *-ible* (adj.) means not possible to be *chosen.*

Intel (between) **-lig** *-ent* (adj.) means fitted to *select* between, or choose.

Leg *-ibil* *-ity* (noun) means *readableness.*

Se (from) **-lect** *-ive* (adj.) means fitted to *choose* from, or concerned with choosing.

Mand, Mend, probably from *manus* (hand) and *dare* (to give).

The stems imply authority.

Com (emphatic) **-mand** (verb) means exercise *authority.*

Com (emphatic) **-mend** *-at* *-ion* (noun) means an *authoritative* approval.

De (from) **-mand** (verb) means ask from with *authority.*

Mitt, Miss, meaning *send, let go.*

Ad (to) **-miss** *-ion* (noun) means a *sending* or letting in.

Com (with) **-mit** means *send* with.

Re (back) **-mit** means *send back,* hence *restore* or *forgive.*

Miss *-ive* (noun) means that which is *sent.*

Inter (between) **-miss** *-ion* (noun) means a *sending between,* hence an interruption or recess.

Per (through) **-miss** *-ion* (noun) means *letting go* altogether, allowing.

Mov, Mot, Mob, meaning *move.*

Auto (self) **-mob** *-ile* (adj.) means able to *move* itself. Used as noun.

Com (emphatic) **-mot** *-ion* (noun) means a disturbed, violent *moving.*

Mot *-or* (noun) means that which *moves.*

Pro (forward) **-mot** *-er* (noun) means one who *moves* (things) forward.

Re (back) **-move** means *move* back or away.

Pend, Pens, meaning *hang.*

Ap (to) **-pend** means *hang* to.

De (from) **-pend** *-ent* (noun) means one who *hangs* from.

Sus (under) **-pense** means a *hanging* under.

Pon, Pos, meaning *place, put.*

Com (together) **-pos** *-ite* (adj.) means *put* together.

Im (on) **-pos** *-it* *-ion* (noun) means something *put* upon, a burden.

Ex (forth, out) **-pon** *-ent* (noun) means *that which puts forth, sets out,* or *explains.*

Op (against) **-pon** *-ent* (noun) means one *placed* against.

Pro (forth) **-pose** means *put* forth or forward.

Port, meaning *carry.*

Ex (out) **-port** means *carry* out.

Im (in) **-port** means *carry* in.

Im (in) **-port** *-ant* (adj.) means *carrying* in, as if something weighty or of worth.

Re (back) **-port** means *carry* back.

Prob, meaning *proof, esteem.*

Prob *-at* *-ion* (noun) means a state or process of *proving.*

Re (back) **-prov** *-ing* *-ly* (adv.) means in a manner indicating withdrawal of *esteem.*

Reg, Rect, meaning *rule, lead, straight.*

Cor (with) **-rect** means *straight* with, as with some standard.

Di (apart, asunder, i.e., distinctly) **-rect** means distinctly *straight.*

E (out) **-rect** means *straight* out, or up, from.

Reg *-ul* *-ar* (adj.) means according to *rule.*

Reg *-ul* *-ate* (verb) means bring under *rule.*

Rupt, meaning *break, burst.*

Ab (off) **-rupt** means *broken off,* hence sudden or hasty.

Cor (together, altogether) **-rupt** means *break,* destroy completely.

Inter (between) **-rupt** means *break* in between.

Scrib, Script, meaning *write.*

De (down) **-scribe** means *write* down.

In (in or on) **-scribe** means *write* in or on.

Pre (before) **-script** *-ion* (noun) means something *written* before to be followed.

Sub (under) **-scribe** means *write* under, as one's name.

Sent, Sens, meaning *feel, think.*

Sense *-less* (adj.) means lacking *thought* or *feeling.*

Sent *-i* *-ment* (noun) means that which is *felt.*

Con (with) **-sent** means *feeling with,* hence agreement.

Sequ, Secut, meaning *follow.*

Con (with) **-sequ** *-ence* (noun) means that which *follows* with.

Per (through, thoroughly) **-secut** *-ion* (noun) means a *following* through to the end.

Sta, Sist, Stin, meaning *stand.*

As (to) **-sist** *-ance* (noun) means that which *stands* to or by.

Con (with) **-sist** *-ent* (adj.) means *standing,* or agreeing, with.

Per (through) **-sist** means *stand* through, hence remain unmoved, continue steadfastly.

De (apart) **-stine** means cause to *stand* apart, or to make fast for a particular end.

Un (not) **-sta** *-ble* (adj.) means not able to *stand.*

Tend, Tent, Tens, meaning *stretch.*

At (to) **-tend** means *stretch* to or toward.

Ex (out) **-tend** means *stretch* out.

Ex (out) **-tens** *-ive* (adj.) means *stretched* out.

In (to) **-tent** *-ion* (noun) means a *stretching* to or toward, as of the mind toward an object.

Tent, Tin, meaning *hold.*

Dis (apart) *-con* (together) **-tin** *-u* *-ous* (adj.) means not *holding* together, but apart.

Re (back) **-tent** *-ive* (adj.) means fitted with or able to *hold* back, or keep.

Tract, meaning *draw, lead.*

Con (together) **-tract** *-ion* (noun) means *drawing* together.

Re (back) **-tract** means *take* back.

Tract *-able* (adj.) means possible to be *led.*

Ven, meaning *come.*

Ad (to) **-vent** *-ure* (noun) means something that is *come* to or met, a happening.

Con (together) **-vent** *-ion* (noun) means a *coming* together.

Inter (between) **-vene** means *come* between.

Pre (before) **-vent** means *come* before.

Vert, Vers, meaning *turn.*

A (from) **-vert** means *turn* from.

Ir (not) *-re* (back) **-vers** *-ible* (adj.) means not possible to be *turned* back.

Sub (under) **-vert** means *turn* under or destroy.

Vid, Vis, meaning *see, look.*

In (not) **-vis** *-ible* (adj.) means not possible to be *seen.*

Pro (forward) **-vis** *-ion* (noun) means a *looking* forward, getting ready.

Re (again) **-vise** means *look at again,* hence examine again and alter.

Viv, Vit, meaning *live, life.*

Re (again) **-vive** means *live,* or cause to *live,* again

Vit *-al* (adj.) means like or connected with *life*

Viv *-ac* *-ious* (adj.), characterized by *life, lively.*

Voc, meaning *call.*

E (out) **-voke** means *call* out.

In (on) **-voc** *-ation* (noun) means a *calling* on.

Ir (not) *-re* (back) **-voc** *-able* (adj.) means not possible to be *called* back.

DERIVATION OF ENGLISH WORDS FROM THE LATIN

The foregoing list of prefixes, suffixes, and stems will aid in the study of the derivation of words. Moreover, it serves as a key to the means by which words are deduced from others known as primitives. Since more than half the words in the English language come directly or indirectly from the Latin, a study of the derivation of these words will be found of inestimable value.

While it is true that the study of one language may help one to learn another language, and that the study of Latin in particular makes one know English better, it does not follow that it is necessary to have studied Latin in order to understand words of Latin origin.

In the following groups of derivatives will be found first the Latin word with its English equivalent. That the structure of the English words built on the Latin may stand out as clearly as possible, the nominative and genitive (possessive) cases of the nouns have been given, while each verb is shown in the first person singular present indicative, together with the perfect participle.

No attempt has been made to give a list of all words derived from each root. With the aid of the dictionary, it will be found both interesting and instructive to see how many more words from the same root or stem may be added to the different groups. Always compare carefully each English word with the Latin word placed at the head of each group. Note how much or how little of the Latin word enters into the formation of the English word derived from it. The analysis of a few words taken from the list will serve as an excellent guide:

Capio is a Latin word meaning *I take*. It is formed from the verb stem *cap*. By attaching to the verb stem *cap* the Latin adjective suffix *a-ble* (able), meaning *tending* or *possible to*, we get the word *capable*, meaning *possible to take*, hence *having ability*.

The Latin word *duco*, *I lead*, is formed from the verb stem *duc*. The perfect participle of *duco* is *ductus*. The Latin stem, known as the supine stem, is *duct*. By affixing *intro*, a Latin prefix meaning *within* or *into*, and affixing the Latin noun suffix *ion*, meaning *the act of*, we get the word *introduction*, meaning the *act of leading into*.

Labor is a Latin word meaning *work*. The genitive singular, corresponding to the English possessive, is *laboris*. The stem is *labor*. By adding to the stem the Anglo-Saxon noun suffix *er*, meaning *one who does*, we get the word *laborer*, a workman.

Dens is a Latin word meaning *tooth*. The genitive singular is *dentis*. The stem is *dent*. By affixing to the stem the Greek noun suffix *ist*, meaning *one who is skilled in*, we get the word *dentist*, a tooth doctor. By adding to the stem *dent* the Latin prefix *tri*, meaning *three*, we get the word *trident*, meaning three toothed, hence a three-pronged fork or spear.

AL'TUS, high.

al'tar, a raised place for sacrifice.
al-tis'o-nant, high-sounding, lofty.
al'ti-tude, height, extent upward.

al'to, high, a term in music.
ex-alt', to raise, to extol, to elevate.
ex-al-ta'tion, a lifting up.

AN'GU-LUS, a corner. AN'GU-LI, of a corner.

an'gle, a corner.
an'gu-lar, having angles or corners.
e'qui-an-gu-lar, having equal angles.

quad'ran-gle, a figure having four angles, a square.
rec'tan-gle, a figure having right angles.
tri'an-gle, a three-angled figure.

AN'I-MA, life, breath. AN'I-MÆ, of life, breath.

an'i-mal, a living creature
an-i-mal'cule, a small animal.
an'i-mate, to impart life to.

an-i-ma'tion, state of possessing life.
in-an'i-mate, without life.
re-an'i-mate, to bring back to life.

AN'NUS, a year. AN'NI, of a year.

an-ni-ver'sa-ry, a yearly festival.
an'nu-al, yearly.
an-nu'i-tant, one who receives a yearly allowance.
an-nu'i-ty, an amount payable yearly.
bi-en'ni-al, occurring every two years.

cen-ten'ni-al, once in a hundred years.
per-en'ni-al, lasting for years.
su-per-an'nu-at-ed, disqualified by age.
su-per-an-nu-a'tion, a retiring allowance.
tri-en'ni-al, occurring every three years.

A'QUA, water A'QUÆ, of water.

a-qua-for'tis, (literally, powerful water) nitric acid.
a-qua'ri-um, an artificial pond for aquatic plants or animals.
a-qua'ri-us, the water bearer, a constellation.
a-quat'ic, adapted to water.

aq'ue-duct, a conduit for water.
a'que-ous, watery.
a'qui-form, in the form of water.
sub-a'que-ous, being under water.
ter-ra'que-ous, consisting of land and water.

AR'MA, arms, weapons AR-MO'RUM, of arms, weapons.

arm, a weapon, a limb.
ar'ma-ment, an armed force.
ar'mor-er, a maker of arms.
ar'mor-y, a place for arms, an arsenal.

ar'my, a body of soldiers.
dis-arm', to deprive of arms.
un-armed', without arms or weapons.

BE'NE, well, kindly.

ben-e-fac'tion, a doing good, a gift.
ben-e-fac'tor, one who benefits others.
ben-e-fi'cial, useful, advantageous.
ben'e-fit, aid, an act of kindness.

be-nev'o-lence, good will.
be-nev'o-lent, kind, charitable.
be-nign', gentle, mild.
be-nig'ni-ty, mildness, kindness.

CA'DO, I fall. CA'SUS, fallen.

ac'ci-dent, that which comes or falls by chance.
ca'dence, a fall of the voice.
case, condition, state.
cas'u-al, accidental, unexpected.

cas'u-al-ty, that which occurs by chance.
cas'u-ist, one who settles cases of conscience.
de-ca'dence, a falling away, a deterioration.
de-cay', to fall away, to decline.

CAL'CU-LUS, a pebble. **CAL'CU-LI**, of a pebble.

cal'cu-la-ble, that may be reckoned or depended on.
cal'cu-la-ry, pertaining to counting.
cal'cu-late, to count, to estimate, to plan.
cal-cu-la'tion, the process of counting.

cal'cu-la-tor, a ready reckoner, one who calculates.
cal'cu-li-form, shaped like a pebble.
cal'cu-lus, a stony concretion in the body, a disease; also a branch of mathematics.

CAP'I-O, I take. **CAP'TUS,** taken.

ac-cept', to take when offered.
ca'pa-ble, having ability, mental or physical.
ca-pa'cious, able to take on a large scale, spacious.
cap'tious, peevish, faultfinding.
cap'ti-vate, to capture, to take by charm.

cap'tive, one who is taken prisoner.
cap-tiv'i-ty, imprisonment, bondage.
cap'tor, one who takes or holds captive.
cap'ture, a seizure, a prize.

CA'PUT, the head. **CAP'I-TIS,** of the head.

cape, a headland.
cap'i-tal, standing at the head, chief.
cap-i-ta'tion, counting by heads.

pre-cip-i-ta'tion, headlong or rash haste.
re-ca-pit'u-late, to sum up or enumerate by heads.

CA'RO, flesh. **CAR'NIS,** of flesh.

car'nage, slain flesh, slaughter.
car'nal, fleshy, not spiritual.
car-na'tion, flesh color; a flower.

car-niv'o-rous, devouring flesh.
in-car'nate, clothed with flesh.
in-car-na'tion, state of being clothed with flesh.

CA'VE-O, I take care. **CAU'TUS,** avoided.

cau'tion, care, prudence.
cau'tion-a-ry, warning or caution.
cau'tious, careful, prudent.

ca've-at, a warning, a legal caution.
in-cau'tious, heedless, careless, rash.
pre-cau'tion, care beforehand.

CE'DO, I go, I yield, I give up. **CES'SUS,** given up.

cede, to give up, to grant, to surrender.
ces'sion, a yielding or a giving up.
con-cede', to yield, to grant, to admit to be true.
con-ces'sion, a conceding or yielding.
ex-ceed', to go beyond.
ex-cess', more than is necessary.

pre-cede', to go before.
pre-ced'ence, priority of place or rank.
pre-ced'ent, going before, previous.
prec'e-dent, an authoritative example.
pred-e-ces'sor, one who goes before.
pro-ceed', to go forward, to advance.

CEN'TRUM, the middle. **CEN'TRI,** of the middle.

cen'ter, the middle.
cen'tral, relating to the center.
cen-trif'u-gal, proceeding or flying away from the center.
cen-trip'e-tal, tending toward the center.

con'cen-trate, to bring to a common center.
con-cen'tric, having a common center.
ec-cen'tric, out of the center.
ec-cen-tric'i-ty, oddity.

CEN'TUM, a hundred.

cent, the hundredth part of a dollar.
cen'te-na-ry, a period of one hundred years.
cen-ten'ni-al, completing a hundred years.
cen'ti-pede, an insect with a hundred feet.

cen-tu'ri-on, the captain of a hundred soldiers.
cen'tu-ple, a hundredfold.
cen'tu-ry, one hundred consecutive years.

CIR'CU-LUS, dim. of **CIR'CUS,** a circle. **CIR'CU-LI,** of a circle.

cir'cle, a ring, a circumference.
cir'cled, surrounded.
cir'clet, a little circle.
cir'cuit, distance round any space or area.
cir-cu'i-tous, roundabout, indirect.

cir'cu-lar, in the form of a circle.
cir'cu-late, to move round.
cir'cus, an open space for sports.
en-cir'cle, to enclose in a circle, to surround.
sem-i-cir'cle, half of a circle.

CI'VIS, a citizen. **CI'VIS,** of a citizen.

civ'ic, pertaining to a city or a citizen.
civ'il, polite; pertaining to the rights of a citizen.
ci-vil'ian, a citizen, not a soldier.

ci-vil'i-ty, politeness; a state of civilization.
civ'i-lize, reclaim from savagery.
in-ci-vil'i-ty, neglect of courtesy.

CRE'DO, I believe. **CRED'I-TUS,** believed.

cre'dence, belief, credit.
cre-den'da, things to be believed.
cre-den'tial, that which gives a title to belief.
cred'i-ble, worthy of belief.
cred'it, belief, trust.
cred'i-ta-ble, worthy of belief.

cred'i-tor, one who believes, trusts, or credits.
cre-du'li-ty, belief, or readiness of belief.
cred'u-lous, believing too readily.
creed, that which is believed, doctrine.
dis-cred'it, to disbelieve.
in-cre-du'li-ty, unbelief.

CRE'O, I create. **CRE-A'TUS,** created.

cre-ate', to make, to form.
cre-a'tion, the act of creating.
cre-a'tive, having the power to create.
cre-a'tor, one who creates.

crea'ture, that which has been created.
re-cre-a'tion, making or forming anew.
rec-re-a'tion, refreshment after toil.

DENS, a tooth. **DEN'TIS,** of a tooth.

dent, a slight depression.
den'tal, pertaining to the teeth.
den'ti-frice, tooth powder, paste, or wash.

den'tist, a tooth doctor.
in-dent', to make a toothlike cut into.
tri'dent, a three-pronged fork or spear.

am‑bi‑dex'trous, using both hands equally.
dex'ter, pertaining to the right hand (heraldry).
dex‑ter'i‑ty, skill in using the hands.

dex'ter‑ous, clever, handy.
dex'ter‑ous‑ly, skillfully.
dex‑tral'i‑ty, state of being more efficient with the right hand.

DE'US, God. DE'I, of God. DI‑VI'NUS, from DI'VUS, pertaining to God.

de'i‑fy, to make a god of.
de'ist, one who believes in God, but denies supernatural revelation.
de'i‑ty, divinity, godhead.

di‑vine', holy, sacred.
div‑i‑na'tion, a foretelling of future events, the act of divining.
di‑vin'i‑ty, theology, the Deity.

DI'CO, I appoint, DI‑CA'TUS, appointed.

ab'di‑cate, to give up or relinquish.
ded'i‑cate, to devote to a special use.
in'di‑cate, to point out, to show.

in‑di‑ca'tion, a pointing out, a hint or suggestion.
in‑dic'a‑tive, pointing out.
pred'i‑cate, to proclaim, declare, affirm.

DI'CO, I say. DIC'TUS, said.

ben‑e‑dic'tion, a blessing.
con‑tra‑dict', to say against.
dic'tate, to say to, to declare with authority.
dic‑ta'tor, one who has power to command.
dic'tion, a mode of speech.
dic'tion‑a‑ry, a wordbook.

dic'tum, an authoritative statement.
in'ter‑dict, to forbid, to prohibit.
mal‑e‑dic'tion, evil speaking.
pre‑dict', to say beforehand.
val‑e‑dic'tion, a farewell.
ver'dict, opinion pronounced.

DI'ES, a day. DI‑E'I, of a day.

an‑te‑me‑rid'i‑an, before noon.
di'al, a plate marked with the hours of the day.
di'a‑ry, a daily record.
di‑ur'nal, daily.

me‑rid'i‑an, mid‑day, or noon.
post‑me‑rid'i‑an, after noon.
quo‑tid'i‑an, recurring daily.
si'ne di'e, without day.

DI'GE‑RO, I dissolve, separate. DI‑GES'TUS, dissolved, separated.

di‑gest' (verb), to dissolve (as of food).
di'gest (noun), a compilation, a compendium.
di‑gest'i‑ble, capable of being dissolved.
di‑ges'tion, the process of dissolving food.

di‑ges'tive, that which aids digestion.
in‑di‑gest'ed, not digested, without order.
in‑di‑gest'i‑ble, not easily dissolved.
in‑di‑ges'tion, lack of digestion, dyspepsia.

DI'VI‑DO, I divide. DI‑VI'SUS, divided.

di‑vide', to sever, to separate.
div'i‑dend, the number to be divided.
di‑vis'i‑ble, capable of being divided.

di‑vi'sion, the process of dividing.
di‑vi'sor, the number that divides.
in‑di‑vis'i‑ble, not separable into parts.

DOM'I‑NUS, a lord or master. DOM'I‑NI, of a lord or master.

dom'i‑nant, ruling, governing, prevailing.
dom'i‑nate, to exercise control over.
dom‑in‑eer', to rule with insolence.
do‑min'i‑cal, belonging to the Lord's day.

do‑min'ion, supreme authority, the power of ruling.
don, a Spanish title.
pre‑dom'i‑nance, superiority, ascendancy
pre‑dom'i‑nate, to prevail, to rule.

DU'CO, I lead. DUC'TUS, led.

don‑duct', to lead, to guide.
de‑duc'tion, a withdrawing, an inference.
duc'at, a ducal coin.
duc'tile, capable of being drawn out.
duke, a leader, a chief.
ed'u‑cate, to lead forth, to instruct.

in‑duct', to lead in, to install.
in‑tro‑duc'tion, a leading into.
pro‑duce', to bring forward, to lead forth.
pro‑duc'tive, having the power to produce, fertile.
re‑duc'tion, act of reducing, bringing down.
tra‑duce', to slander, to defame.

DU'RUS, hard, solid, lasting.

du'ra‑ble, able to endure, lasting.
dur'ance, personal restraint, imprisonment.
du‑ra'tion, continuance in time.

dur'ing, throughout.
en‑dur'ance, ability to bear, sufferance, patience.
en‑dure', to last, to withstand, to suffer.

ER'RO, I wander. ER‑RA'TUS, wandered.

err, to mistake, to wander from truth.
er'rant, roving, wandering.
er‑rat'ic, wandering, moving.

er‑ra'tum, an error or mistake in writing or printing.
er'ror, a wandering from the truth.

E‑RUM'PO, I burst forth, break out. E‑RUP'TUS, burst, broken out.

dis‑rupt', to break asunder forcibly.
dis‑rup'tion, bursting of rocks (in an earthquake).
e‑rum'pent, bursting out (as of buds).
e‑rupt', to burst forth (as a volcano).

e‑rup'tion, a breaking out.
e‑rup'tive, inclined to break out.
rup'ture, a breaking of tissues, or of a blood vessel.
rup'tured, having a hernia.

FAL'LO, I deceive FAL'SUS, deceived.

fal‑la'cious, misleading, deceptive.
fal'la‑cy, a deception.
fal'li‑ble, liable to err.
false, not true.

fal‑set'to, a feigned voice.
fal'si‑fy, to make false.
fal'si‑ty, an untruth.
in‑fal'li‑ble, not liable to err.

FE′RO, I carry, bring. LA′TUS, carried, brought.

con-fer′, to consult together.
de-fer′, to put off, to delay, to withhold.
fer′tile, capable of bearing, carrying.
pre-fer′, to carry before or regard as better.
re-late′, to bring into relation, to connect (as of facts).

rel′a-tive, that which can be brought close together, compared, connected.
trans-fer′, to carry over.
trans-late′, to carry across, to render into another language.

FI′DES, faith, trust. FI-DE′I, of faith, trust.

af-fi-da′vit, pledging one's faith, a declaration made on oath.
bo′na fi′de, in good faith.
con-fide′, to trust in.
con′fi-dence, a firm trust.

dif′fi-dence, want of faith.
fi-del′i-ty, faithfulness.
fi-du′ci-a-ry, one who holds in trust.
in-fi-del′i-ty, unfaithfulness, unbelief.
per′fi-dy, a breach of faith.

FI-GU′RA, a shape. FI-GU′RÆ, of a shape.

con-fig′ure, to give form or shape to.
dis-fig′ure, to deform, to deface.
ef′fi-gy, an image, a likeness.

fig′ur-a-tive, not literal.
fig′ure, a shape, a digit.
pre-fig′ure, to shape beforehand, to foreshadow.

FI′NIS, the end or limit. FI′NIS, of the end or limit.

con-fine′, to keep within limits.
con′fines, boundaries, limits.
de-fine′, to mark limits.
def′i-nite, clearly defined.

fi′nal, at an end.
fin′ish, to bring to an end.
fi′nite, having an end.
in′fi-nite, without end.

FIR′MUS, strong, durable.

af-firm′, to declare or assert positively.
con-firm′, to make strong, to corroborate.
firm, fixed, strong, durable.

in-firm′, weak, not strong.
in-fir′ma-ry, a place for the sick.
in-fir′mi-ty, weakness, feebleness.

FLAM′MA, a flame. FLAM′MÆ, of a flame.

flam′beau (*through Fr.*), a flaming torch.
flame, a stream of fire.
in-flame′, to kindle, to excite.

in-flam′ma-ble, capable of being easily set on fire.
in-flam-ma′tion, a heated swelling, an excitement.
in-flam′ma-to-ry, tending to inflame, kindle.

FO′LI-UM, a leaf. FO′LI-I, of a leaf.

cinque′foil (*through Fr.*), a five-leaved clover.
foil, a leaf or thin sheet of metal.
fo-li-a′ceous, having the texture of leaves.
fo′li-age, a cluster of leaves, flowers, and branches.

fo′li-ate, to beat into leaves.
fo′li-o, a four-paged sheet.
port-fo′li-o, case for loose leaves.
tre′foil (*through Fr.*), a three-leaved clover.

FOR′MA, form, appearance. FOR′MÆ, of form, of appearance.

form, shape, figure.
for′mal, according to form.
for-mal′i-ty, state of being formal, ceremony.
for-ma′tion, the act of forming.
in-for′mal, without ceremony.

mul′ti-form, having many shapes.
ref-or-ma′tion, a reforming or changing for the better.
re-for-ma′tion, forming anew.
trans-form′, to change form.
u′ni-form, alike in form.

FOR′TIS, strong, valiant.

com′fort, to give strength, to cheer.
ef′fort, to put forth strength.
en-force′, to put in force.
fort, a stronghold.
for-ti-fi-ca′tion, a strong place.
for′ti-fy, to make strong.

for-tis′si-mo (*It.*), in music, a direction to sing with the utmost strength.
for′ti-tude, strength or firmness of mind.
for′tress, a fortified place.
re-en-force′, to strengthen

FRA′TER, a brother. FRA′TRIS, of a brother.

con-fra-ter′ni-ty, a society, a brotherhood.
fra-ter′nal, brotherly.
fra-ter′ni-ty, brotherhood.

frat′er-nize, to join as brothers.
frat′ri-cide, killing a brother.
fri′ar (*through Fr.*), a monk.

FU′GI-O, I flee. FU′GI-TUS, fled.

cen-trif′u-gal, flying away from the center.
fu-ga′cious, fleeing away.
fu′gi-tive, a runaway.

ref′uge, a place of shelter.
ref-u-gee′, one who flees for refuge.
sub′ter-fuge, a fleeing under, or an artful evasion.

GRA′DI-OR, I step. GRES′SUS, stepped.

deg-ra-da′tion, a lowering in degree.
di-gress′, to step aside, to diverge.
e′gress, a stepping out of.
gra-da′tion, an advance step by step.
grade, step, rank, or degree.

grad′u-al, step by step.
grad′u-ate, to grade.
in′gress, a stepping into.
prog′ress, a stepping forward.
ret′ro-grade, stepping backward.

GRA′TUS, thankful, acceptable.

grate′ful, thankful, agreeable.
grat′i-fy, to delight, to please.
gra′tis, free, without recompense.

grat′i-tude, thankfulness.
gra-tu′i-tous, free, uncalled for.
gra-tu′i-ty, a free gift.

GREX, a flock. GRE'GIS, of a flock.

ag'gre-gate, to collect or unite into a mass.
con'gre-gate, to collect or assemble as a flock.
con-gre-ga'tion, a gathering, an assembly.

e-gre'gious, away from the flock, hence remarkably bad.
gre-ga'ri-ous, moving in flocks.
seg're-gate, to set apart, to separate.

HA'BE-O, I have. HAB'I-TUS, had, or held.

ex-hib'it, to hold forth to view.
hab'it, custom, use.
hab-i-ta'tion, a place held as an abode.

ha-bit'u-al, customary, commonly done.
in-hab'it, to dwell or live in.
pro-hib'it, to hold away, to prevent, to forbid.

HÆ'RE-O, I stick, or adhere. HÆ'SUS, adhered.

ad-here', to stick to.
ad-he'sion, a sticking to.
ad-he'sive, sticky.

co-her'ent, sticking together, cleaving.
in-co-her'ent, loose, unconnected.
in-her'ent, inseparable by nature.

HOS'PES, a host. HOS'PIT-IS, of a host (*through hostis*, a stranger, an enemy).

hos'pi-ta-ble, kind to guests.
hos'pi-tal, a place for the sick.
hos-pi-tal'i-ty, generosity, liberality toward guests.

host'ess, a female host, a landlady.
hos'tler, originally master of an inn, one who takes care of horses.

HU'MUS, the ground. HU'MI, of the ground.

ex-hu-ma'tion, the act of taking up from a grave.
ex-hume', to take up from the ground, to disinter.
hu-mil'i-ate, to reduce to a low condition.

hu-mil'i-ty, lowness of spirit (as on the ground).
in-hu-ma'tion, putting into the grave.
in-hume', to bury.

JU'DEX, a judge. JU'DI-CIS, of a judge.

ad-judge', to order or decree.
ad-ju'di-cate, to give sentence.
judge, one who decides.
judg'ment, decision, sentence.
ju-di'cial, pertaining to justice.

ju-di'cious, prudent, wise.
pre-judge', to decide before hearing.
prej'u-dice, judgment beforehand.
prej-u-di'cial, hurtful, injurious.
un-prej'u-diced, free from bias.

JUN'GO, I join. JUNC'TUS, joined.

ad'junct, something joined, but not essential.
con-join', to unite, to combine.
con-junc'tion, a connecting word.
en-join', to command, to order.

join, to unite.
junc'tion, a joining, a union.
junc'ture, a joint, or union.
sub-junc'tive, binding together, connecting.

JU'RO, I swear an oath. JU-RA'TUS, sworn on oath.

ab-ju-ra'tion, the act of forswearing.
ab-jure', to deny or renounce upon oath.
con-ju-ra'tion, solemn entreaty.
con-jure', to put under oath.

con'jure, to practice magic, to conspire.
con'jur-er, a juggler.
ju'ror, one of a jury.
ju'ry, a body of sworn men.

LA'BOR, work. LA-BO'RIS, of work.

e-lab'o-rate, to work out with care.
la'bor, hard work, toil.
lab'o-ra-to-ry, a scientist's workroom.

la'bor-er, a workman.
la-bo'ri-ous, toilsome, involving much labor.

LEV'O, I lift up. LE-VA'TUS, lifted up.

al-le'vi-ate, to lighten sorrow.
el'e-vate, to raise, to lift up.
el-e-va'tion, a lifting up.

le'ver, a bar for lifting.
lev'i-ty, lightness of manner.
lev'y, to raise money or soldiers.

LEX, a law. LE'GIS, of a law.

al-le'giance, loyalty
il-le'gal, unlawful.
le'gal, according to law.
le'gal-ize, to make lawful.

leg'is-late, to make laws.
leg'is-la-ture, the parliament or power that makes laws.
le-git'i-mate, lawful.

LO'CO, I place. LO-CA'TUS, placed.

a-lo-ca'tion, a placing for a set purpose.
dis'lo-cate, to displace, to disjoint.
lo'cal, belonging to a place.

lo-cal'i-ty, a place or situation.
lo'cate, to place.
lo-co-mo'tion, the act or power of changing place.

MAG'NUS, great. MA'JOR, greater.

mag-nif'i-cence, grandeur, spectacular beauty.
mag'ni-fy, to make great.
mag-nil'o-quence, pompous discourse.
mag'ni-tude, size, greatness.

ma'jor, greater, a military officer above a captain.
ma-jor'i-ty, the number greater than half; the age of 21 years.

MAN'DO, I command, MAN-DA'TUS, commanded.

com-mand', to give orders to.
com-mand'er, one who commands.
com-mand'ment, a precept.
coun-ter-mand', to revoke a command.

de-mand', to claim as a right.
man-da'mus, a legal order.
man'date, a command.
re-mand', to order or send back.

MA'NUS, a hand.   MA'NUS, of a hand.

a-man-u-en'sis, one who writes what another dictates, a copyist.

e-man'ci-pate, to set free, to liberate.

man'a-cles, handcuffs

ma-nip'u-late, to handle.

man'u-al, done by hand, a handbook.

man-u-fac'ture, made by hand or by machinery.

man-u-mit', to release from slavery, to set free.

man'u-script, literally, written by hand.

quad-ru'ma-nous, having four hands.

MAR'E, the sea.   MAR'IS, of the sea.

ma-rine', pertaining to the sea.

mar'i-ner, a seaman, a sailor.

mar'i-time, near the sea.

mer'maid (*through Fr.*), a sea monster.

sub-ma-rine', under the sea.

trans-ma-rine', across the sea.

ul-tra-ma-rine', a beautiful blue color (beyond the sea in color).

MI'GRO, I go from the land.   MI-GRA'TUS, gone from the land.

em'i-grant, one who leaves his own country.

em'i-grate, to leave one's country.

im'mi-grate, to settle in another country.

mi'grate, to remove to another country.

mi'gra-to-ry, roving, wandering.

trans-mi-gra'tion, removal from one place to another.

MI'NOR, MI'NUS, less (comparative of PAR'VUS, small, little).

di-min'ish, to lessen.

dim-i-nu'tion, a reduction in size, a lessening.

di-min'u-tive, small in size.

min'i-a-ture, a small likeness.

min'i-mum, smallest amount.

mi'nor, less, inferior.

mi-nor'i-ty, the smaller of two numbers (or parties) making up a whole; the state of being under age.

min'ute, a brief time, a moment.

mi-nute', very small, little.

MORS, death.   MOR'TIS, of death.

im-mor'tal, not subject to death.

im-mor'tal-ize, to cause to live forever.

mor'tal, subject to death.

mor-tal'i-ty, death.

mor-ti-fi-ca'tion, the death of a part of the body; vexation.

mor'ti-fy, to cause death; to humiliate.

MO'VE-O, I move.   MO'TUS, moved.

com-mo'tion, excited movement.

e-mo'tion, a movement of the mind.

mo'tion, a movement.

mo'tive, the moving power.

move, to put in motion.

move'ment, change of place or position.

pro-mote', to advance, to forward.

pro-mo'tion, a moving forward.

re-mov'al, a change of place.

re-move', to move from its place.

MUL'TUS, much, or many.

mul-ti-fa'ri-ous, having much diversity.

mul'ti-form, of many forms

mul-ti-lat'er-al, having many sides.

mul'ti-plex, manifold.

mul'ti-ply, to increase in number.

mul'ti-tude, a great number.

NA'VIS, a ship.   NA'VIS, of a ship.   NAU'TA, a sailor.   NAU'TÆ, of a sailor.

cir-cum-nav-i-ga'tion, sailing round the globe.

nau'ti-cal, seafaring.

nau'ti-lus, a shellfish that sails.

na'val, pertaining to ships.

nav-i-ga'tion, the art of sailing.

nav'i-ga-tor, a sailor.

na'vy, a fleet of ships.

NO'MEN, a name.   NO'MIN-IS, of a name.

de-nom-i-na'tion, a distinguishing name.

mis-no'mer (*through Fr.*), a wrong name.

no'men-cla-ture, a list of names in any art or science.

nom'i-nal, in name only.

nom'i-nate, to name.

nom'i-na-tive, the case denoting the subject of a finite verb.

nom-i-nee', a person named.

NO'VUS, new.

in-no-va'tion, introduction of something new.

nov'el, new.

nov'el-ty, newness.

nov'ice, a beginner.

no-vi'ti-ate, state of being a novice.

ren'o-vate, to make new, to renew.

NU'TRI-O, I nourish.   NU-TRI'TUS, nourished.

nour'ish (*through Fr.*), to cherish, to feed.

nour'ish-ing (*through Fr.*), promoting growth.

nour'ish-ment (*through Fr.*), act of nourishing.

nurse (*through Fr.*), one who nourishes.

nurs'er-y (*through Fr.*), apartment, in a house, appropriated to the care of children.

nur'ture (*through Fr.*), to feed, to foster.

nu'tri-ent, a nourishing substance.

nu'tri-ment, sustaining food.

nu-tri'tious, health giving.

OP'ER-A, work, labor.   OP'ER-Æ, of work, labor.

co-op'er-ate, to work together.

in-op'er-a-tive, not at work.

op'er-a, a musical play.

op'er-ate, to work, to act.

op-er-a'tion, action.

op'er-a-tor, one who performs.

OS, a bone.   OS'SIS, of a bone.

os'se-ous, bony.

os-sif'er-ous, containing or yielding bones.

os-si-fi-ca'tion, the process of changing into bone.

os'si-frage, the sea-eagle, or bone-breaker.

os'si-fy, to change into bone.

os-siv'o-rous, feeding on bones.

PA'TER, a father.   PA'TRIS, of a father.   PA'TRI-A, fatherland.   PA'TRI-Æ, of the fatherland.

com-pa'tri-ot, a fellow countryman.

pa-ter'nal, fatherly.

pa-ter'ni-ty, fatherhood.

pa'tri-arch, a father and ruler.

pa'tri-ot, a lover of his country.

pa'tri-ot-ism, a love of country.

PEN'DE-O, I hang. PEN'SUS, hung. PEN'DO, I weigh, or value. PEN'SUS, weighed or valued.

de-pend', to hang from, to rely upon.
ex-pend', to lay out, to use up.
ex-pense', money, time, etc. laid out.
im-pend'ing, hanging over, threatening.

pend'ant, (n.) something hanging.
pend'ent, (a.) something hanging, awaiting decision.
sus-pend', to hang, to delay.
sus-pen'sion, a temporary withholding, a hanging up.

PES, a foot. PE'DIS, of a foot.

bi'ped, a two-footed animal.
cen'ti-pede, having a hundred feet.
ex-pe'di-ent, apt or suitable.
ex'pe-dite, to hasten, to facilitate.
ex-pe-di'tion, haste, speed.
im-ped'i-ment, something which impedes or hinders.

ped'al, pertaining to the foot.
ped'es-tal, the base or foot of a pillar, vase, or lamp, etc.
pe-des'tri-an, one who goes on foot.
ped'i-cle, a little foot, hence the stalk, or stem of a flower.
quad'ru-ped, having four feet.

PE'TO, I seek. PE-TI'TUS, sought.

ap'pe-tite, desire, longing.
cen-trip'e-tal, directed toward the center.
com-pete', to strive with another.
com-pe-ti'tion, common strife for the same object.

im'pe-tus, the force with which a body is driven forward.
pe-ti'tion, a request, a seeking after something.
re-peat', to say again, to recite.

PO'NO, I put, or place. POS'I-TUS, put, or placed.

com-pose', to put together.
com-pos'i-tor, one who sets up printing type.
dis-pose', to put in place, to arrange.
ex-pose', to place out, to lay open.
ex-pos'i-tor, one who explains.
op-pose', to set against.

op'po-site, placed against.
po-si'tion, place, situation.
post, a place or station.
pos'ture, the mode in which anything is placed, an attitude.
sup-pose', to put under, or imagine.

POR'TO, I carry. POR-TA'TUS, carried.

ex-port', to carry out.
im-port', to carry in.
port, carriage, bearing, demeanor.
port'a-ble, capable of being carried.

por'ter, a carrier.
port'ly, of noble carriage, stately.
re-port', to carry back or give an account of.
sup-port', to sustain, to carry, to hold up.

PRI'MUS, first.

pri'ma fa'ci-e, at first view.
pri'ma-ry, first in order of time.
pri'mate, an archbishop, ranking first among others.
prime, of the first rank.
prim'er, a first book.

pri-me'val, belonging to the first ages.
prim'i-tive, original, pertaining to early times.
pri-mo-gen'i-ture, the right which belongs to the first-born.
pri-mor'di-al, first in order.

QUÆ'RO, I seek, I inquire. QUÆ-SI'TUS, sought.

ex'qui-site, sought out with care, hence, matchless, perfect.
in'quest, an inquiry into the cause of death.
in-quire', to seek into.
in-qui-si'tion, a searching into.
in-quis'i-tive, prying, curious.

que'ry, a question.
quest, search, inquiry.
re-quest', to ask, to solicit.
re-quire', to demand, to ask.

RA'DO, I scrape, I shave. RA'SUS, scraped.

a-brade', to scrape off.
ab-ra'sion, a rubbing off.
e-rase', to scratch or rub out.

e-ra'sure, a scratching out.
raze, to level with the ground.
ra'zor, a shaving knife.

RID'E-O, I laugh at. RI'SUS, laughed at.

de-ride', to laugh at.
de-ri'sion, scorn, mockery.
rid'i-cule, to expose to laughter.

ri-dic'u-lous, laughable, silly.
ris-i-bil'i-ty, proneness to laugh.
ris'i-ble, exciting laughter.

RO'GO, I ask, I demand. RO-GA'TUS, asked, demanded.

ar'ro-gance, pride, making undue claims to self-importance.
in-ter'ro-gate, to ask questions
in-ter-ro-ga'tion, inquiry.

in-ter-rog'a-tive, a word used in asking questions; as, *Who? What?*
su-per-er-o-ga'tion, doing more than is asked

SANC'TUS, holy, sacred.

sanc'ti-fy, to make holy.
sanc-ti-mo'ni-ous, having the appearance of holiness.
sanc'ti-ty, holiness.

sanc'tu-a-ry, a consecrated place.
sanc'tum sanc-to'rum, the most holy place.

SA'NUS, sound, healthful.

in-sane', of unsound mind.
in-san'i-ty, madness, lunacy.
san'a-tive, curative, tending to heal.

sane, sound, healthy.
san'i-ta-ry, pertaining to health.
san'i-ty, soundness of mind.

SCI'O, I know. SCI'ENS (pres. part.), knowing.

con'science, inward conviction or acknowledgment.
con'scious, aware of, knowing.
om-nis'cience, knowing all things.
pre'sci-ence, foreknowledge.

sci'ence, precise knowledge.
sci-en-tif'ic, according to science.
sci'o-list, a pretender to science, one who knows little.

SE'CO, I cut. SEC'TUS, cut.

bi-sect', to cut in two.
dis-sect', to cut in pieces.
dis-sec'tion, the art of cutting up, anatomy.
in'sect, a small animal that appears to be cut into or divided.

in'ter-sect, to cut between.
sec-ta'ri-an, belonging to a sect.
sec'tion, a cutting, a division.
seg'ment. a piece cut off.
tri-sect', to cut in three.

SER'VO, I preserve, I keep. SER-VA'TUS, preserved.

con-serv'a-tive, wishing to preserve.
con-serv'a-to-ry, a place where choice plants are preserved.
con-serve', to preserve from loss.

ob-serve', to notice, to keep in view.
res-er-va'tion, a keeping back.
re-serve', to keep back.
un-re-served', not kept back.

STRIN'GO, I bind, I hold fast. STRIC'TUS, bound or held.

as-trin'gent, binding, contracting.
con-strict', to draw together, to bind.
con-stric'tor, that which draws together; a class of serpents that crush their prey.

re-stric'tion, a holding back.
strict, held close, bound.
stric'ture, a contraction; a critical remark.
strin'gent, binding strongly.

TEN'DO, I stretch out. TEN'TUS or TEN'SUS, stretched out.

dis-ten'sion, a stretching asunder.
ex-tend', to spread out.
ex-ten'sion, a stretching out.
in-tense', strained, excessive.
pre-tend', to allege falsely.
pre-ten'sion, a claim, true or false.
su-per-in-tend', to overlook, to direct.

tend, to stretch towards.
tend'en-cy, direction, course.
ten'der, to offer, to stretch out the arm.
ten'don, a hard cord by which a muscle is attached to a bone.
tense, stretched to stiffness, rigid.
ten'sion, the state of being stretched.

TEN'E-O, I hold. TEN'TUS, held.

ab-stain', to hold back from.
ab'sti-nence, forbearance.
con-tain', to hold within limits.
con-tin'ue, to hold on.
de-tain', to hold from, to keep back.
de-ten'tion, a withholding.
main-tain', to uphold.

re-tain', to hold back, to keep.
ten'a-ble, capable of being held.
ten'ant, one who holds property of another.
ten'e-ment, that which is held by a tenant.
ten'et, a doctrine held.
ten'or, a state of holding on in a continuous course.
ten'ure, the manner of holding an estate.

TER'RA, the earth. TER'RÆ, of the earth.

dis-in-ter', to take out of the grave.
in-ter', to cover with earth, to bury.
in-ter'ment, burial, funeral.
sub-ter-ra'ne-an, underground.
ter'race, a raised level walk or platform of earth.

ter'ra cot'ta (*through It.*), cooked clay, potter's clay, of which statues and vases are made.
ter-ra'que-ous, consisting of land and water.
ter-res'tri-al, pertaining to the earth.

TEST'IS, a witness. TEST'IS, of a witness.

at-test', to bear witness.
pro-test', to declare, to witness against.
prot'es-tant, a Christian who rejects the tenets of the Roman Church.
test, a trial, a proof.

tes'ta-ment, a last will, a covenant.
tes'ti-fy, to bear witness to.
tes-ti-mo'ni-al, a writing which bears witness to one's character.

U'NUS, one. U-NI'US, of one.

u'ni-corn, a one-horned beast.
u'ni-form, of one appearance.
un'ion, concord, agreement.
u'ni-son, of one sound.

u'nit, a single thing.
u-nit'ed, joined, made one.
u'ni-ty, oneness, agreement.
u-niv'o-cal, of one meaning.

VE'RUS, true.

ve-ra'cious, observant of truth.
ve-rac'i-ty, truthfulness.
ver-i-fi-ca'tion, a proof of truth.

ver'i-fy, to prove true.
ver'i-ly, truly, indeed.
ver'i-ty, truth.

VI'A, a way, a road. VI'Æ, of a way, a road.

de'vi-ate, to go out of the way.
de-vi-a'tion, a wandering.
ob'vi-ate, to clear the way of
ob'vi-ous, easily discovered, plain, clear.

per'vi-ous, capable of being penetrated.
pre'vi-ous, going before.
vi'a, by the way of.
vi'a-duct, a large bridge built to carry a road.

VI'VO, I live. VIC'TUS, lived. VI'TA, life. VI'TÆ, of life.

re-vive', to live again, to arouse.
sur-vive', to live longer than, to outlive.
vi'tal, necessary to life.

vi-va'cious, full of life.
viv'id, lively, bright.
viv-i-sec'tion, anatomy practiced on living animals.

VO'LO, I wish, I am willing.

be-nev'o-lent, well-wishing, desirous of doing good.
in-vol'un-ta-ry, not having will or the power of choice.
ma-lev'o-lent, wishing evil.

vo-li'tion, the act of willing; the act of forming a purpose.
vol'un-ta-ry, of free will.
vol-un-teer', one who serves of free will.

CORRECT SPELLING

To be able to spell correctly is an accomplishment greatly to be desired. Two important elements enter into the habit of correct spelling: (1) to *observe* words correctly; (2) to *hear* words correctly. Errors often arise from a lack of *thoughtful attention* when studying spelling. In this way the impression made upon the mind by the word as a whole is *incorrect*, or the impression of the correct word has been so dimly made as to be easily forgotten. Difficult words are often more easily spelled because of the added attention they receive and, conversely, the short simple words are misspelled because attention is not directed to them.

It is well to be able to spell all words correctly, but especially should one be able to spell words in common use. Your stock of everyday words may number 2000 or 2500. These are the words of first importance in learning to spell.

The habit of consulting the dictionary is invaluable. The use of diacritical marks and the division of words into syllables are an aid to correct pronunciation; but it is only by practice and by a conscientious and frequent reference to the dictionary that proficiency in correct spelling can be acquired.

The meaning of words should be learned along with their spelling. This is particularly important in the case of homonyms, like *there* and *their*, which are pronounced the same but spelled differently. If the spelling and the meaning are learned together, no confusion arises in the use of these words.

How to Improve Your Spelling. With the hope of helping to overcome the poor spelling of the present day, the following suggestions are offered:

Pronounce words correctly and distinctly; clear enunciation is of great value.

Learn the analysis of words, that is, learn to recognize the syllables, prefixes, suffixes, and their values; for the analysis of words makes one's spelling more reliable.

With the analysis and meanings of words, associate their uses. This will lead to a mastery of words and tends to better power in spelling.

Make a special study of those words which by reason of a peculiar combination of letters present some difficulty; for example, *believe, receive, precede, proceed.*

Observe particularly silent letters, obscure vowels, or variations in vowel sounds which appear in certain words, as in *homage, heir, subtle, benefit, separate.*

A most troublesome factor in the spelling problem is the repetition of common errors. The habit of repeatedly misspelling the same words may be overcome by any method of study which directs special attention to them.

There is no better way to master the art of spelling than by repeated oral and written practice; for it is the *repetition* which forms the habit.

Because they lack special aptitude for spelling, or because of some difficulty not easily overcome, some persons believe they can never learn to spell. This is an error. Any person of average intelligence can learn to spell if he fully determines to do so, and then diligently strives toward the accomplishment of that end.

Spelling Lists. The following lists are prepared to give ever present help in spelling. They will be found useful for reference, for study, and for review. The first list contains one hundred "spelling demons" first published in *A Concrete Investigation of the Materials of English Spelling,* issued from the University of South Dakota. A comparison of these words with the spelling scale prepared by L. P. Ayres for the Russell Sage Foundation indicates that eighth grade pupils should earn marks of 90 to 100 on groups of 20 words each, selected from the list. However, a large number of these words are among those found to be most frequently misspelled in the

College Entrance Board examinations. The other lists have been prepared after a careful study of frequent spelling errors and everyday vocabularies, such as *The Child and His Spelling* by W. A. Cook and M. V. O'Shea and *The Spelling Vocabularies of Personal and Business Letters* by L. P. Ayres.

RULES FOR SPELLING

1. If a termination beginning with *e*, *i*, or *y* is added to a word ending in *c*, when *c* is not to be pronounced as *s*, *k* is inserted after *c*: *picnic, picnicking; traffic, trafficker.*

2. If a word of one syllable or a word accented on the last syllable ends in a single consonant preceded by a single vowel, the final consonant is doubled before a termination beginning with a vowel: *fit, fitting; clan, clannish; prefer, preferring; permit, permitted.*

3. When a digraph, that is, two coupled vowels, precedes the final consonant, or when the accent is not on the last syllable, or when it goes to a preceding syllable in the new word, the final consonant is not doubled before a termination beginning with a vowel: *sail, sailing; travel, traveler; benefit, benefited; prefer, preferable.* Exceptions are: *handicapped, humbugged.*

4. When a word ends in silent *e*, unless *e* is preceded by another vowel, the *e* is usually retained before a termination beginning with a consonant and omitted before a termination beginning with a vowel: *hide, hiding; come, coming; late, lateness; race, racial; provoke, provoking; fine, fineness; spite, spiteful, spiting; use, usable.* Exceptions: *judgment, acknowledgment, abridgment, duly, truly,* and *awful.*

5. Words ending in *ce* or *ge* do not drop the *e* before *able* or *ous*. Retaining *e* in this case preserves the soft sound of *g* and the *s* sound of *c*: *notice, noticeable; change, changeable.*

6. Words ending in *y* preceded by a consonant usually change *y* into *i* before an additional letter or syllable: *spy, spies; cry, crier; gratify, gratifies.* But *y* is not changed before *-ing*: *deny, denying; reply, replying.*

Words ending in *y* preceded by a vowel usually retain the *y* unchanged, as in *boy, boys, boyish, boyhood. Laid, paid, said,* are exceptions.

7. The spelling of many words in *ie* and *ei* may be determined by the following rule: If the coupled vowels follow *c*, the *e* comes first; if they follow *l* or *r*, the *i* comes first: *receive, believe, grief.* Some exceptions are: *financier, leisure, sleigh.*

8. In the singular number, the possessive of nouns is formed by adding to the noun an apostrophe and *s*: *Burns's, Jones's, St. James's, St. Giles's, Dickens's, Douglas's.*

The *s* is omitted in the singular when too many hissing sounds would come together: for *Jesus'* sake; for *conscience'* sake; for *goodness'* sake; *Damocles'* sword. When the word consists of more than two syllables, the apostrophe only is added: *Achilles'* sword; *Socrates'* wife; *Euripides'* dramas; *Demosthenes'* orations.

9. Derivatives formed from the Latin stem *ced* are usually spelled *cede*; the exceptions are *exceed, proceed, succeed.*

10. Generally spell in full rather than use abbreviations or numerals for the following: Titles of business, honor, or respect, preceding proper names; Christian names; numbers of fewer than three digits, unless the number is followed by a word of measure; all numbers beginning a sentence; the time of day, except when the number is used with A. M. or P. M.; numbers of centuries, sessions of congress, and the words "United States."

11. *Plurals.* Most nouns form the plural number by adding *s* or *es* to the singular: *state, states; inch, inches.*

The plural of numerals and of unusual or artificial word formations is formed by adding an apostrophe and *s*: *7's, 9's,* the *1900's, t's, y's.*

Plurals of proper names are generally formed by adding *s* or *es*: *Brown, Browns; James, Jameses.*

COMMON WORDS FREQUENTLY MISSPELLED

ONE HUNDRED SPELLING DEMONS

ache
again
always
among
answer
any
been
beginning
believe
blue
break
built
business
busy
buy
can't
choose
color
coming
cough
could
country
dear
doctor
does
done
don't
early
easy
enough
every
February
forty
friend

grammar
guess
half
having
hear
heard
here
hoarse
hour
instead
just
knew
laid
loose
lose
making
many
meant
minute
much
none
often
once
piece
quiet
raise
read
ready
said
says
seems
separate
shoes
since

some
straight
sugar
sure
tear
their
there
they
though
through
tired
tonight
too
trouble
truly
Tuesday
two
used
very
wear
Wednesday
week
where
whether
which
whole
women
won't
would
write
writing
wrote

SCHOOL WORDS

abbreviate
absence
absolutely
academy
accessory
accident
accidentally
accomplice
accomplish
accurate
accustom
acid
across
addition
adjoin
adjourn
affairs
affect
aggravate
algebraic
all right
almost
alphabet
already
ambition
ammonia
analogous
analysis
ancient
anecdote
angle
aniline (-in)
antarctic
antecedent
anthracite
Apollo
apostrophe
apparatus
apparent
appearance
appliance
appositive
architecture
arctic
argument
arithmetic
artificially
arouse
assembly
assignment
athletic
atmosphere
attempt

attendance
autobiography
auxiliary
avalanche
average
avoidance
awkward
barrier
battalion
benefit
biography
biology
blizzard
buoyant
cafeteria
candidate
canyon
caterpillar
chalk
changeable
chautauqua
chemistry
chosen
circuit
circumference
circumstance
citizenship
civilization
clever
climate
coherence
college
colloquial
combination
comedy
commencement
commission
communication
comparison
compulsory
concede
conceivable
conceive
conception
conscientious
consequence
conspicuous
contemplate
continent
continually
control
courageous
crater

criminally
criticism
crucifixion
crucify
curriculum
customary
cyclone
cylinder
daily
decide
decimal
declension
definitely
demonstrable
demonstrative
demonstrator
denominator
descend
description
descriptive
desirable
despair
desperately
develop
diagonal
dialogue (-log)
diameter
dictionary
difference
diligence
diphthong
disappear
discipline
disinfect
dismissal
dissatisfied
dissipated
distribute
division
dynasty
eclipse
e'er
effect
eighth
elegy
embarrass
emphasis
encouragement
encyclopedia
enemy
enmity
enthusiasm
envious

equation
equator
equipped
eraser
ere
erroneous
essential
exaggerate
examination
exceed
excel
excellent
exemption
exercise
exhibition
existence
expensive
explain
explanation
exposition
expression
extension
extremely
factoring
fascinate
felonious
figure
foreign
foresee
formally
formerly
frigid
gasoline
gauge (gage)
generally
genius
genuine
geology
geometry
glacier
granite
guard
gymnastics
happiness
height
hemisphere
hexagon
history
horizontal
humorous
hygiene
hypocrisy
hysterics
iambic
idiom
ignominious
ignominy
ignorance
illustrate
imagination
imperative
improvable
inborn
incident
incitement
incriminate
indefinitely
independence
independent
indictment
indispensable
infinite
infinitesimal
infinitive
influential
influentially
instigation
instigator
institute
intelligence
intelligible
intention
interrogative
intransitive
irregular
irresistible
island
isosceles
isthmus
its
it's
kindergarten
laboratory
later
latitude
latter

lead
lead pencil
learn
lecture
led
legend
lightning
literary
literature
livelihood
longitude
loyalty
Macaulay
machinist
malefactor
malign
malignant
malignity
maneuver
manual
marriage
martyr
martyrdom
mathematics
mechanic
mechanical
mechanism
mediocre
mediocrity
mercury
meridian
metaphor
metonymy
microscope
mirage
misspell
modifies
modifying
monosyllable
mountain
multiplication
municipal
muscular
naphtha
narration
nativity
neuter
nineteen
ninety
nominative
noticeable
numerator
obedience
occasion
occur
occurred
occurrence
o'clock
offense
omitted
opportunity
ostensible
ostentatious
oxygen
pageant
paragraph
parallel
paraphernalia
parliament
participial
participle
particularly
passed
passion
passionate
past
peaceful
peninsula
perfect
perfectly
perform
permanent
permission
perpendicular
perpetration
perpetrator
phenomenon
Philip
phrase
physics
physiology
picturesque
planet
plateau
poetry
polygon

polysyllable
positively
possess
possessive
possibility
practicable
practically
practice
prairie
precede
precinct
predicate
prejudice
preparation
principal
principle
prism
privilege
proceed
professor
progressive
pronounce
pronunciation
prophecy
prophesy
propitious
proportion
prove
psychology
punctuation
pyramid
quiet
quite
rabbit
rarefaction
rarefy
rareness
rarity
ravine
readiness
realize
reasonable
recess
recital
recognize
recollect
recommend
remember
remembrance
repellent
repetition
representative
review
rhetoric
rhythm
rhythmic
ridicule
rime (rhyme
sacrifice
sacrificial
sacrilege
sacrilegious
satire
satyr
saucy
scholarship
seize
semicircle
seminary
senate
sentence
separately
session
severely
shepherd
siege
signature
simile
socialist
soliloquies
soliloquy
solution
sometimes
sophomore
specific
specimen
speech
squirrel
statement
strait
strengthen
strenuous
studying
subordinate
subtraction
succeed

sufficiently
suit
suite
summary
superintendent
surely
susceptibility
susceptible
syllable
sympathize
synonym
syntax
synthesis
systematic
talented
tariff

technical
temperature
temptation
tendency
therefore
thermometer
tournament
tragedy
traveler
tropical
turpentine
twelfth
typical
unanimous
uncomfortable
undoubtedly

university
until
usually
vacation
valuable
vertical
villain
vocabulary
volume
wealthily
weird
whimper
wholly
zoology

Social and Personal Words

accept
accompany
acquaintance
aeronaut
aeroplane
affectionately
afford
agreeable
airplane
aisle
almanac
altar
amateur
angel
angry
animal
anniversary
announcement
annual
anxiety
apartment
apologize
appetite
appreciate
appreciative
arrangement
arrival
assistance
association
asylum
audience
automobile
bachelor
baggage
banquet
baptize
baseball
bazaar
bicycle
billiards
borrow
breakfast
burglar
campaign
candidate
canoe
captain
career
carriage
catechism
cathedral
celebration
cemetery
ceremony
chapel
chaperon
character
chauffeur
chivalry
circus
citizen
cologne
colonel
committee
complement
complexion
compliment

conductor
congregation
contribution
convenient
coquette
cordially
cousin
croquet
crowd
daughter
delegate
delicate
dentist
dependent
dietitian
din
diner
dining
dinner
disappoint
economical
elaborate
embarrassment
emergency
engagement
environment
etiquette
euchre
excursion
fashionable
fatigue
fellowship
fiancé
fiancée
funeral
garage
golf
grief
guest
hammock
harassment
heathen
heavy
heresy
hospitable
hungry
icicle
idol
innuendo
invitation
kodak
laugh
league
liquor
luncheon
magazine
majority
matron
mischief
missionary
mosquitoes
motor
mucilage
neighbor
niece
nuisance
occupy

oculist
optician
orchestra
organization
pamphlet
parade
parasol
passenger
pennant
phonograph
photographer
pianist
picnic
picnicking
plaguy
playwright
pleasure
priest
prodigal
prohibition
promenade
protégé
providence
psalm
quarrel
quoits
rehearse
relative
religious
rendezvous
repentance
restaurant
revival
scene
sight-seeing
sincerely
sleigh
souvenir
spectacles
suffrage
surprise
synagogue
tabernacle
taxicab
temperance
tenant
tenement
testament
theater
thief
tobacco
tournament
umbrella
umpire
unfortunate
valise
vaudeville
vilify
village
waltz
wasteful
wealth
whistle
wholesome
yacht

Business Words

acceptance
accommodate
accountant
accrued
acknowledge
acquire
acre

address
administration
advertise
affidavit
agency
agreement
allege

annuity
application
approximately
arbitration
article
assets
assignment

assure
attorney
auction
auditor
balance
bankrupt
bankruptcy
bargain
bookkeeper
brief
calculation
calendar
capacity
capital
cashier
catalogue (-log)
certificate
check
clerical
collateral
collectable (-ible)
commercial
commodity
competent
competition
compromise
comptroller
confidential
consideration
consignment
convenient
conveyance
corporation
correspondent
counterfeit
credentials
credit
creditor
criminal
customer
debt
debtor
decision
defer
deficit
delivery
depositor
diary
difficulty
discount
discussion
dividends
draft
due
economical
efficient
elevator
embezzle
employee
enterprise
especially

estimate
evidence
expenditure
expense
experience
factory
finally
finance
financial
financier
fiscal
foreclosure
foreign
forfeit
forgery
franchise
fraudulent
freight
government
guarantee
heir
hundred
immediate
indorsement
information
insolvency
installment
insurance
interest
inventory
investment
invoice
issue
itemized
items
janitor
journal
judgment
judicial
lease
ledger
legacy
legislature
liability
license
lucrative
machinery
manager
manufacture
material
maturity
mercantile
merchandise
millionaire
mortgage
mortgagee
mortgagor
municipal
necessary
notary
oblige

operator
parcel
particular
position
preferred
preliminary
president
probably
proceeds
profitable
profits
promissory
proprietor
purchase
receipt
recommend
reference
referring
register
regular
remittance
renewal
request
requisite
resources
respectfully
responsible
résumé
retail
revenue
salary
salesman
schedule
secretary
securities
sincerely
situation
speculate
stationery
statistics
stenographer
stockholder
storage
substantial
success
suggest
surplus
syndicate
taxes
telegraph
telephone
testimony
treasurer
typewriter
unique
usury
value
warehouse
warrant
weight
wholesale

Household Words

abscess
ague
alcohol
almond
ambulance
anesthetic
anoint
antitoxine
appendix
apron
artery
asbestos
asparagus
asthma
automatic
banana
bandage
baste
bilious
biscuit
blouse
bread
breathe
bronchitis
bruise
buffet
bungalow
bureau
butcher
button
cabbage
calico

cambric
camphor
cancer
cantaloupe
capsule
caramel
carpenter
cashmere
casserole
cataract
catarrh
ceiling
celery
cellar
cereal
chamois
chandelier
chiffonier
chloroform
chocolate
cholera
cinder
cinnamon
cloth
clothes
coat
cocoa
coffee
collar
contagious
convalescent
corduroy

cough
cretonne
crochet
croquette
crystal
cucumber
culinary
currant
curtain
dairy
desiccate
dessert
diamond
diarrhea
diary
digestion
diphtheria
disease
doily
dye
electricity
embroidery
enamel
epidemic
ether
faucet
feather
flannel
flour
forehead
fragile
frieze

furnace
furniture
gasoline (-ene)
gelatine
gingham
glycerine
grease
grippe (grip)
groceries
handkerchief
hearth
hemorrhage
herbs
hoarse
homeopathic
hosiery
hospital
inoculate
invalid
iodine (-in)
ironing
jewelry
kernel
kerosene
khaki
kimono
knead
knee
knife
knob
knot
knuckle
larynx
lattice
lemon
lemonade
lettuce
library
licorice
ligament
liniment
macaroni
mackerel
mackintosh
mahogany
mantelpiece
mattress
measles
measure
medicine
melon
meringue
milliner

mirror
molasses
muscle
mustard
nainsook
nausea
nervous
neuralgia
odor
omelet
organdie (-y)
ostrich
oyster
palate
paneling
paraffine
paralysis
pattern
peach
pear
peritonitis
perspiration
physically
physician
picture
pillow
pitcher
plaid
plaited
plumber
pneumonia
poached
porcelain
porch
portière
portrait
potatoes
poultice
poultry
prescription
ptomaine (-in)
pumpkin
quinine
radiator
raisin
raspberry
recipe
refrigerator
relief
remedy
reservoir
rheumatism
rhubarb

roast
salad
sandwich
sanitary
sateen
satin
saucer
sausage
scissors
settee
sieve
sirloin
skein
sleeve
specialist
spigot
spinach
steak
stomach
sugar
sulphur (-fur)
surgeon
syringe
taffeta
tailor
threshold
tissue
tomato
tongue
trousers
trousseau
tuberculosis
turkeys
turnip
typhoid
unbleached
utensil
vaccinate
vacuum
vanilla
vaseline (-in)
vegetable
veil
ventilate
ventilation
veranda
vinegar
waist
woolen
worsted
yolk
zephyr

Irregular Plurals

Singular	Plural
beef	beeves
calf	calves
elf	elves
half	halves
knife	knives
leaf	leaves
life	lives
loaf	loaves
self	selves
sheaf	sheaves
shelf	shelves
thief	thieves
wife	wives
wolf	wolves
ally	allies
city	cities
daisy	daisies
fairy	fairies
fancy	fancies
lady	ladies
lily	lilies
mystery	mysteries
gentleman	gentlemen
goose	geese
man	men
mouse	mice
tooth	teeth
woman	women
deer	deer
gross	gross
grouse	grouse
hose	hose
mackerel	mackerel
salmon	salmon
series	series
sheep	sheep
species	species

Singular	Plural
trout	trout
swine	swine
attorney at law	attorneys at law
commander in chief	commanders in chief
court-martial	courts-martial
editor in chief	editors in chief
father-in-law	fathers-in-law
governor-general	governors-general
maid of honor	maids of honor
man-of-war	men-of-war
son-in-law	sons-in-law
knight templar	knights templars
man-child	men-children
manservant	menservants
woman servant	women servants
alumna (feminine)	alumnæ
alumnus (masculine)	alumni
analysis	analyses
animalcule	animalcules
antithesis	antitheses
apparatus	apparatuses / apparatus
appendix	appendices / appendixes
axis	axes
bacillus	bacilli
bacterium	bacteria
bandit	banditti / bandits
basis	bases
beau	beaux / beaus
brother	brothers (relatives) / brethren (of the same society)
candelabrum	candelabra
cannon	cannons (individuals) / cannon (collectively)
cherub	cherubim (collectively) / cherubs
crisis	crises
cumulus	cumuli
curriculum	curricula / curriculums
datum	data
die	dies (for stamping) / dice (for gaming)
ellipsis	ellipses
erratum	errata
fish	fishes (individually) / fish (collectively)
foot	feet (parts of the body) / foot (infantry)
formula	formulæ / formulas
genius	geniuses (men of genius) / genii (spirits)
genus	genera
gymnasium	gymnasia / gymnasiums
head	heads (parts of bodies) / head (of cattle)
heathen	heathens (individuals) / heathen (collectively)
hippopotamus	hippopotami / hippopotamuses
horse	horses (animals) / horse (cavalry)
hypothesis	hypotheses
index	indexes (tables of reference) / indices (signs in algebra)
larva	larvæ
memorandum	memoranda / memorandums
nebula	nebulæ
oasis	oases
parenthesis	parentheses
penny	pennies (single coins) / pence (quantity in value)
phenomenon	phenomena
radius	radii
sail	sails (pieces of canvas) / sail (vessels)
seraph	seraphim (collectively) / seraphs
shot	shots (number of times fired) / shot (number of balls)
stratum	strata
synopsis	synopses
tableau	tableaux
terminus	termini
thesis	theses
trousseau	trousseaux
vertebra	vertebræ

HOMONYMS

Words pronounced the same but differing in spelling and in meaning.

air, that which we breathe.
ere, before.
e'er, ever.
heir, one that is to inherit.

aloud, audibly.
allowed, permitted.

altar, a place for worship.
alter, to change.

arc, part of a circle.
ark, as Noah's ark; a chest.

ascent, going up; an upward slope.
assent, to agree to.

ate, past tense of eat.
eight, twice four.

aught, anything.
ought, is (are) bound in duty.

bad, ill or wicked.
bade, past tense of bid.

bale, a bundle.
bail, surety for someone; a handle.

ball, a sphere; a dance.
bawl, to shout; to cry out.

band, that which binds; a narrow strip.
banned, forbidden.

bard, a poet.
barred, hindered; shut out.

bare, naked.
bear, to carry; a wild beast.

base, the lowest part; mean.
bass, the lowest part in harmonized music.

beech, a kind of tree.
beach, shore.

beer, a drink.
bier, anything on which the dead are carried to burial.

beet, a vegetable.
beat, to strike.

bell, a hollow metal body that rings or tolls.
belle, a beautiful or admired young woman.

berry, a small fruit.
bury, to inter; to conceal.

birth, being born; descent.
berth, a sleeping place.

bold, daring; courageous.
bowled, rolled, as in a game of bowling.

bole, the trunk of a tree.
boll, seed vessel of cotton plant.
bowl, a circular vessel.

bow, a weapon for shooting arrows; a kind of knot.
beau, a man of dress; a lover.

brake, a thicket.
break, to split.

bred, reared.
bread, baked flour.

breech, the lower or hinder part of a thing.
breach, a gap or opening.

brews, ferments; plots.
bruise, to crush; a contusion.

broach, a spit; to pierce.
brooch, an ornament for the breast.

brows, plur., the forehead.
browse, to eat the tender leaves of shrubs, as "sheep browse."

burrow, hole in ground made by an animal.
borough, a corporate town.
burro, a donkey.

by, a preposition and a prefix.
buy, to purchase.
bye, as in good-bye; a goal.
bi-, two, as in biweekly.

call, cry out; a visit.
caul, a membrane.

canon, a law; a rule.
cannon, a large gun.

canvas, a coarse cloth.
canvass, to solicit.

cast, to throw; a form.
caste, a tribe; a class.

cede, to give up.
seed, the embryo of a future plant.

ceiling, top, or covering, of a room.
sealing, tight closing, as with wax.

cell, a small cavity; a room.
sell, to exchange for a price.

cellar, an excavation in the ground.
seller, one who sells.

cent, a hundred; a coin.
sent, past tense of send.
scent, perfume; to smell.

cereal, pertaining to grain; food made of grain.
serial, pertaining to successive parts, as in a series.

cession, a giving up.
session, a sitting; a meeting.

chews, grinds with the teeth.
choose, to select.

choir, a company of singers.
quire, a set of sheets of paper.

cite, to summon; to quote.
site, place; position.
sight, the power of seeing; a look.

clause, part of a sentence.
claws, sharp nails or toes of animal or bird.

clime, a region; a country.
climb, to mount; to ascend.

core, an innermost part; a center.
corps, an organized company, as of soldiers.

course, a place for running; career.
coarse, not fine.

coward, one lacking in courage.
cowered, crouched through fear.

creek, a small stream.
creak, to make a harsh, grating noise.

crews, bodies of seamen for ships.
cruise, to sail from place to place on the ocean.
cruse, a small cup; a small bottle.

currents, streams.
currants, small fruit.

dew, moisture condensed and deposited from the air.
due, owing.

discreet, prudent; cautious.
discrete, distinct; disjoined.

doe, female of deer.
do, a musical sound name.
dough, unbaked bread.

done, performed.
dun, a color; to demand payment of debt.

dying, ceasing to live.
dyeing, shading or coloring.

faint, very fatigued; to swoon.
feint, a pretense.

fane, a temple.
fain, anxious; desirous.
feign, to pretend.

fare, money paid for a journey; food.
fair, beautiful; right; a market.

faun, a sylvan deity.
fawn, a young deer; to flatter meanly.

find, to discover.
fined, subject to a money penalty.

flour, fine part of meal.
flower, blossom of a plant.

fore, in front.
four, a number.

forth, forward; out.
fourth, the ordinal of four.

freeze, to congeal.
frieze, a coarse woolen fabric; an ornamented band on a wall.

gate, entrance; a door.
gait, way of walking.

gild, to overlay and adorn with gold.
guild, a society or corporation.

gilt, overlaid with gold.
guilt, responsibility for crime.

great, large.
grate, a fireplace; to rub against.

groan, deep sound of pain or sorrow.
grown, mature, fully developed.

guessed, estimated at random.
guest, one who is entertained.

hair, as of the head.
hare, an animal.

HOMONYMS (cont'd)

hall, a large room.
haul, to drag; to pull.

heel, the hind part of the foot.
heal, to cure; to grow sound.
he'll, contraction for "he will."

herd, a collection of cattle.
heard, past tense of hear.

hoard, to lay up in secret.
horde, a wandering tribe; a savage band.

hoes, uses a hoe.
hose, stockings; socks.
hose, rubber pipe.

I, a pronoun.
aye or **ay,** yes.
eye, organ of sight.

indite, to compose and write.
indict, to charge or accuse formally.

isle, a contraction for island.
aisle, passage in an auditorium.
I'll, contraction for "I will."

kernel, the central part.
colonel, chief officer of a regiment.

lane, a narrow passage.
lain, past participle of lie, to rest lengthwise on or against.

leaf, as of a book, a tree, etc.
lief, willingly.

least, little; beyond all others.
leased, held on lease.

led, past tense and participle of lead.
lead, a metal.

liar, one who tells lies.
lyre, a musical instrument.

lone, solitary; alone.
loan, a temporary grant.

male, opposite of female.
mail, armor; letters.

mane, the long hair on the neck of an animal.
main, the sea; principal; chief.

manner, method or way.
manor, an estate; a domain.

mantle, a cloak; a cover.
mantel, the slab or shelf above a fireplace.

marshal, a military or police officer.
martial, warlike.

maze, an intricate place.
maize, Indian corn.

mean, shabby; low; to intend.
mien, manner of look or appearance.

meet, fit; to assemble.
mete, to measure.
meat, food; flesh.

mind, the understanding.
mined, excavated.

miner, a worker in mines.
minor, one under age.

mite, something very small.
might, power; strength.

moan, to lament.
mown, cut down.

mussel, a shellfish.
muscle, the fleshy parts of an animal body.

mustard, a kind of plant.
mustered, assembled.

nave, hub of a wheel; main portion of a cathedral.
knave, a rogue.

nay, no.
neigh, cry of a horse.

need, want; poverty.
knead, to work the materials into dough.

new, not old.
knew, past tense of know.
gnu, a wild ox.

night, opposite of day.
knight, a title of honor.

no, opposite of yes.
know, to understand.

nose, the organ of smell.
noes, plural of no.
knows, has knowledge; understands

oar, implement for rowing a boat.
ore, metal as it comes from the earth.
o'er, contraction for over.

ode, a short poem.
owed, indebted to; past tense of owe.

our, a pronoun.
hour, sixty minutes.

pain, soreness.
pane, a piece of glass.

pair, two; a couple.
pare, to slice thinly.
pear, a kind of fruit.

passed, gone through; gone.
past, not present or future.

pause, a stop.
paws, feet of a beast.

peace, a state of quiet.
piece, a part.

pedal, a foot lever; to operate such a lever.
peddle, to sell from house to house.

peel, skin; outside.
peal, sound of bells.

peer, to look intently; an equal.
pier, a wharf.

plane, a perfectly flat or level surface; a kind of tree.
plain, level, flat country.

plate, a flat piece of metal; a shallow dish.
plait, to fold; to braid.

please, to delight or gratify.
pleas, pleadings in law; excuses.

plum, a fruit.
plumb, perpendicular; an instrument to determine whether a wall is perpendicular.

pray, to entreat.
prey, plunder.

prays, supplicates.
praise, approbation; to approve.
preys, attacks, as a wild beast.

principal, invested funds; chief.
principle, a fundamental rule or law.

quarts, measures of two pints each.
quartz, a variety of rock crystal.

rain, water from clouds.
rein, part of a harness; to check.
reign, to rule as a king.

rap, to strike sharply.
wrap, to wind or roll together; to fold.

rapped, struck.
rapt, transported; ravished.
wrapped, folded; enclosed.

rays, beams of light.
raise, to exalt; to lift up.
raze, to destroy utterly.

read, as a book; to study.
reed, a hollow cane.

red, a color.
read, past tense of read.

rest, peace; quiet.
wrest, to twist; to wrench.

right, just; correct.
rite, a ceremony.
write, to trace letters or characters.
wright, a workman.

road, a path; a way.
rode, past tense of ride.
rowed, propelled with oars.

rôle, a part in acting a play.
roll, a round thing; a register.

rood, fourth part of an acre.
rude, uncultivated; rough.
rued, grieved for.

root, as of a plant; origin.
route, direction; road.

ruff, an article of dress.
rough, unpolished; rugged.

rung, sounded, as a bell.
wrung, twisted.

rye, a sort of grain.
wry, crooked.

sac, a membranous receptacle.
sack, a large, strong bag.

sail, to navigate.
sale, act of selling.

sea, a wide expanse of water.
see, to perceive.

seam, a line of junction between pieces of cloth.
seem, to appear; to have a semblance.

sees, looks at.
seize, to take hold of.

skull, the whole bone of the head.
scull, a small boat; a light, short oar.

soared, mounted on the wing.
sword, a weapon of war.

sold, given for a price.
soled, furnished with a sole.

sore, painful.
soar, to mount by flight.

soul, the spirit.
sole, only; bottom of the foot; a fish

sow, to scatter seed.
sew, to fasten, as with a needle.
so, in this manner.

staid, steady; grave.
stayed, supported with ropes, as a mast.

stair, flight of steps.
stare, to look at.

stake, a pointed piece of wood.
steak, a slice of meat.

straight, direct; not curved.
strait, narrow; confined.

style, manner of dress or action.
stile, steps over a wall.

sucker, a young shoot of a tree.
succor, help; to relieve.

sum, the amount of anything; to add up.
some, more or less of a quantity.

sutler, one who follows a camp to sell provisions, etc.
subtler, more cunning; more acute.

sweet, pleasant; delightful.
suite, attendants; a set of rooms.

tale, a story.
tail, an appendage; hinder part.

taught, past tense and perfect participle of teach.
taut, stretched tight.

tear, water from the eye.
tier, a row; a series.

teem, to produce in abundance.
team, a pair of horses or oxen, working together.

their, possessive of they.
there, adv., in that place.

threw, past tense of throw.
through, from side to side, or from end to end.

throw, to cast; to fling.
throe, extreme pain.

time, fit season.
thyme, a garden plant.

told, expressed in words.
tolled, rung, as a bell.

tract, a quantity of land.
tracked, followed by the marks left.

two, a pair; twice one.
too, adv., also; excess, as too much.
to, preposition.

use, to apply or handle for some purpose.
ewes, female sheep.
yews, evergreen trees.

vale, a valley.
veil, a curtain, a covering.

vice, a fault.
vise, a tool.

wade, to walk through water.
weighed, past tense of weigh.

wait, to remain; to stay.
weight, heaviness; importance.

ware, sing. of wares; goods.
wear, to last; to endure.

waste, to squander.
waist, the middle part, as of the body.

wave, a moving ridge; to undulate.
waive, to defer; to abandon.

way, a road; manner.
weigh, to determine heaviness; to ponder.

wood, a forest; timber.
would, verb of wish or determination.

Words spelled the same but differing in sound and in meaning. Strictly, heteronyms, from the very etymology of the word, have no alliance between them except the accidental one of the same orthography. They are derived from different roots and their meanings are so distinct that their separate origin is at once indicated by such meanings. Mere change of accent, moreover, does not constitute a heteronym.

bass (bās), a term in music.
bass (băs), a fish.

bow (bou), the forward part of a vessel.
bow (bō), an archer's weapon; an implement for playing the violin; a knot.

chap (chăp), a fellow.
chap (chŏp), fleshy covering of a jaw.

dives (dīvz), goes under water.
Dives (dī'vēz), the rich man.

does (dōz), female deer.
does (dŭz), from the verb do.

gill (jĭl), quarter of a pint.
gill (gĭl), the organ of respiration of a fish.

glower (glou'ẽr), to stare.
glower (glō'ẽr), something that glows.

hinder (hĭn'dẽr), to prevent.
hinder (hĭn'dẽr), back part.

job (jŏb), petty work.
Job (jōb), a man's name.

lead (lĕd), a metal.
lead (lēd), to conduct.

lower (lō'ẽr), to descend.
lower (lou'ẽr), to frown.

manes (mānz), the hair on the neck of animals.
manes (mā'nēz), departed spirits.

mate (māt), a companion.
mate (mä'tā), a beverage.

mow (mō), to cut down.
mow (mou), a heap of grain; a compartment for storing grain.

mowing (mō'ĭng), the act of cutting.
mowing (mou'ĭng), to store away.

polish (pŏl'ĭsh), to shine.
Polish (pōl'ĭsh), adjective derived from Pole—pertaining to Poland.

poll (pŏl), a degree without honors.
poll (pōl), the head; a tax.

put (poŏt), to move; to push.
put (pŭt), a rustic; a clown.

repent (rē'pĕnt), creeping; prostrate; reptant.
repent (rê-pĕnt'), to feel penitence, contrition, or regret, for what one has done or has omitted to do.

row (rō), a rank or file; to propel with oars.
row (rou), a tumult.

sake (sāk), purpose, end, cause.
sake (sä'kĕ), liquor made from rice.

sewer (sū'ẽr), a ditch or a drain.
sewer (sō'ẽr), one who sews.

shower (shō'ẽr), one that exhibits.
shower (shou'ẽr), a light rain.

singer (sĭn'jẽr), one that singes.
singer (sĭng'ĕr), one that sings.

slough (slou, sloō), a hole full of mire; a marshy place.
slough (slŭf), cast-off skin of a serpent.

sow (sō), to scatter seeds.
sow (sou), female pig.

stingy (stĭn'jĭ), penurious.
stingy (stĭng'ĭ), piercing.

swinger (swĭng'ẽr), one that swings.
swinger (swĭn'jẽr), one that beats or chastises.

tarry (tär'ĭ), covered with, or like, tar.
tarry (tăr'ĭ), to abide at or in a place; to stay; to loiter; to delay.

tear (târ), to divide or separate on being pulled.
tear (tēr), a drop of limpid saline fluid secreted by the lachrymal gland.

tower (tou'ẽr), a high edifice; a citadel.
tower (tō'ẽr), that which tows.

wind (wĭnd), air in motion.
wind (wīnd), to twist.

wound (woōnd), an injury.
wound (wound), twisted.

SENTENCE BUILDING

ENGLISH GRAMMAR is both a science and an art. As a science, it investigates the principles in general on which the English language is based; as an art, it teaches the method of applying these principles in speaking and in writing the English language correctly.

In the whole range of school subjects there is none of greater importance than that of language. To facilitate the study of the English language, therefore, the true principles of grammar have been outlined in the following pages in a convenient form, expressed in a simple manner, and illustrated by appropriate examples.

THE ENGLISH SENTENCE

Word Groups. We express our thoughts in groups of words,—sentences, clauses, phrases.

A *sentence* is a group of words used to express a complete thought.

The complete sentence must always contain a subject and a predicate. The subject is the thing named; the predicate is the assertion about the thing named: "*Autumn* (subj.) *lingers* (pred.)."

In an imperative sentence, like "Go to him," the subject "you" is not usually expressed. This is an instance of *ellipsis*, or the omission of words otherwise necessary to grammatical completeness, when their meaning is well understood by the reader or hearer: "The knife belongs to Tom; the pencil (belongs) to William."

A *clause* is a group of words containing, like the sentence, a subject and a predicate, but used only as part of a complete sentence: "The motor, | which was new, | suddenly failed to work."

A clause may be either *independent* (principal) or *dependent* (subordinate): "He commanded, | who had never commanded before." The first words, *he commanded*, form an independent clause. The other words form a dependent clause; for, as they stand, they do not make a sentence. See *Complex Sentence.*

A *phrase* is a group of words so closely related as to express a single idea. The phrase is used as a part of speech: "*To become rich* (noun) was his ambition." "It was a matter *of importance* (adjective)." "Come *at your convenience* (adverb)."

Parts of Speech. In building sentences, we use name-words, action-words, modifiers, and connectives of various kinds. According to their use in sentences, these words are classified as *parts of speech*, of which there are eight:

1. A *noun* is a word used to name a person, a place, or a thing: *boy, city, foot, air, size.*

2. A *pronoun* is a word used in place of a noun: *it, her, none, who.*

Note.—Nouns, pronouns, and phrases or clauses used as nouns are called *substantives.*

3. A *verb* is a word used to say, or assert, something about a person, a place, or a thing: *walk, soften, drive, is.*

4. An *adjective* is a word used to modify, that is, describe or limit, a noun or pronoun: "*bright* sunshine," "*few* people," "I *alone.*"

5. An *adverb* is a word used to modify the meaning of a verb, an adjective, or another adverb: "speak *well*," "walk *swiftly*," "run *homeward*," "*very* pretty," "*so* quickly."

6. A *conjunction* is a word used to connect words, phrases, clauses, or sentences: *and, but, if, unless.*

7. A *preposition* is a word used to show the relation of some particular word, called its object, to another word: "flocks *of* birds (obj.)"; "strength *through* exercise (obj.)"; "peace *with* honor (obj.)."

8. An *interjection* is a word of exclamation used to express any emotion or feeling, as surprise, joy, grief, etc.: *ah! alas!*

Note.—Some words may be used as *several different parts of speech:*

Noun: "The *storm* was soon over."
Adjective: "The station displayed *storm* signals."
Verb: "The troops will *storm* the outworks."

Noun: "The *inside* of the house is pleasing."
Adjective: "He has *inside* information."
Adverb: "Will you step *inside?*"
Preposition: "*Inside* the door stood a clock."

Preposition: "I have been waiting *since* noon."
Conjunction: "*Since* I saw you, much has happened."

Adjective: "*Which* hat have you?"
Pronoun: "The hat *which* you see is mine."

Adjective: "*That* hat is mine."
Pronoun: "I want *that.*"
Conjunction: "He said *that* he would go."

PARTS OF THE SENTENCE

The Subject. The subject of a sentence is that about which the predicate asserts something: "*The weather* is cold." "*Health* counts for more than wealth."

Simple Subject.—The essential part of the *subject* is a substantive, that is, a noun, a pronoun, or a phrase or clause used as a noun. Noun means "name." The substantive is called the *essential*, or *simple*, *subject*, or the *subject substantive*: "A great *city* (noun substantive) is interesting"; "*She* (pro. substantive) is my friend"; "*To read well* (subst. phrase) requires much practice"; "*What he saw* (subst. clause) startled him."

Complete Subject.—The substantive with its modifiers is called the *complete subject*: "*His deposit* (subst.) *in the bank* (adj. phrase) | was large." The modifiers of the substantive may be adjectives, possessive nouns or pronouns, nouns in apposition, clauses or phrases used as adjectives or nouns.

The Predicate. The word *predicate* means "something said." The predicate of a sentence is that which is asserted about the subject: "Roses *were blooming.*"

The essential part of a predicate is a *verb*. We call the verb in the predicate the *essential*, or *simple*, *predicate*, or the *predicate verb*. "The car *ran* (pred. verb) *against the curb*." *Ran* is the simple predicate; *ran against the curb* is the complete predicate.

The relation between subject and predicate may be shown graphically, as in the following diagram. Note that the simple elements appear on the main line and the complex or subordinate ones below this line. The practice of sentence diagramming is strongly recommended.

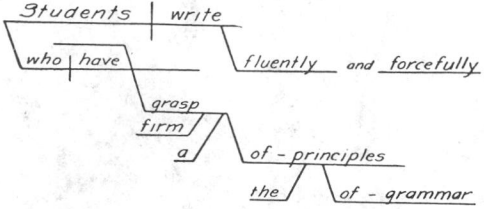

CLASSIFICATION OF SENTENCES

Kinds of Sentences. In respect to their *meaning*, sentences may be classified as declarative, interrogative, imperative, and exclamatory.

The *declarative sentence* makes a statement: "*John is not here.*"

The *interrogative sentence* asks a question: "*Where is my hat?*"

The *imperative sentence* gives a command; "*Answer his question.*"

The *exclamatory sentence* expresses a strong feeling, as of surprise, joy, etc.: "*How free are the pleasures of youth!*"

Note.—The foregoing is the common grouping of sentences. A more logical classification is the following: (1) *affirmative* and *negative*; (2) *declarative* and *interrogative*; (3) *exclamatory* and *nonexclamatory*.

Forms of Sentences. In respect to their *grammatical form*, sentences are simple, compound, or complex.

The *simple sentence* is a sentence of one clause, that is, a sentence having but one subject and one predicate. The simple sentence may be very short: "*Birds | sing.*" It may be longer, when the subject and the predicate are modified by several words and phrases: "*Those furs in the window | have been gathered from many different countries and climates.*"

A simple sentence may have a *compound subject*; as, "*The house and the grounds | are beautiful.*" It may have a *compound predicate*; as, "*They | sat and listened* to the music." Both subject and predicate may be compound; as, "*Mary and Elizabeth | lived and reigned* in England." These are important distinctions. Do not confuse the *long* sentence with the *complex* sentence.

The *compound sentence* is formed by two or more clauses of equal rank. These independent, or "coordinate," clauses may or may not be joined by coordinating conjunctions such as *and, but, for*: "A man approaches. | *and* | we recognize him;" "Some men are born great; | others achieve greatness."

The *complex sentence* is formed of a principal, or independent, clause and of one or more subordinate, or dependent, clauses. These subordinate clauses are introduced by subordinate conjunctions, such as *if, unless, because*, by relative pronouns, *who, which, what, that*, and by conjunctive adverbs, such as *when, where, while*: "I shall go *if it stops raining*"; "The child *that is happy* makes friends"; "Make hay *while the sun shines.*"

The Parts of Speech

Grammatical Relations. The relations of a word, a phrase, or a clause to other words in a sentence are called its *syntax* or *construction*. Either of these words means "placing or bringing together."

Inflection, in grammar, is the changing of the forms of words to indicate grammatical relation and change of meaning. Inflection of verbs is called *conjugation*. Inflection of nouns and pronouns is called *declension*. Inflection of adjectives and adverbs is called *comparison*.

In the English sentence, the grammatical relations of words are indicated by their position and by the use of connectives. The English language has dropped so many of the endings formerly attached to nouns and verbs that inflection in English grammar is of slight importance. So-called declension becomes in English the systematic arrangement in tables of the various forms of nouns and pronouns used for different cases and numbers. Conjugation consists in arranging in tables the various verb forms and verb phrases used for different modes and tenses.

Kinds of Substantives: Nouns and Pronouns

A *substantive* is a word, phrase, or clause used as a noun.

KINDS OF NOUNS

Proper Nouns. A *proper noun* is the name of a particular person, place, or thing. It is always written with a capital letter; as, *John, Paris, England, Europe.*

Common Nouns. A *common noun* is the name of any one of a class of persons, places, or things; as, *table, book, rabbit, boy, weather.*

Abstract Nouns. An *abstract noun* is the name of an idea: as, *honesty, hope, truth, system.*

Collective Nouns. A *collective noun* is the name of a group or collection of single things, considered as one; as, *crowd, army, jury, family, committee.*

Verbal Nouns. A *verbal noun*, or *gerund*, is the name of an action; as, *walking, skating, working.*

An *appositive* is a noun used after another noun or pronoun to describe or explain the meaning of that noun or pronoun. An appositive is said to be *in apposition to* the noun or pronoun it defines or explains: "Milton, the *poet*, became blind."

A *predicate noun* or *pronoun* is a noun or a pronoun that completes the predicate verb and refers to the subject: "Lincoln was *president*." "It is *I*."

KINDS OF PRONOUNS

Pronouns are classified as *personal, interrogative, demonstrative, relative* or *conjunctive*, and *indefinite*.

Personal Pronouns. The following are the forms of personal pronouns:

SINGULAR

	First Person	Second Person	Third Person Mas. Fem. Neut.
Nominative	I	you	he she it
Possessive	{ my, mine	{ your, yours	his { her, hers its
Objective	me	you	him her it

PLURAL

	First Person	Second Person	Third Person
Nominative	we	you	they
Possessive	{ our, ours	{ your, yours	{ their, theirs
Objective	us	you	them

The possessive forms given in the table are sometimes called *possessive pronouns*. They are pronouns in origin, but in use they are *possessive adjectives*.

Special Uses. *Ye* and *thou, thy, thine, thee*, are old forms, now seldom used except in poetry or in the language of religion.

The masculine pronouns, *he, his*, and *him*, are used also as of common gender: "Let every child use *his* own book."

You, whether referring to one person or more, always takes the plural verb.

It often stands as the *impersonal subject* of a verb: "*It* rains"; "*It* is cold"; "*It* grew dark."

It may be used as the *impersonal object* of a verb: "He footed *it* all the way"; "They are roughing *it* in the woods."

It is sometimes used as an introductory word, the real subject following the verb: "*It* is well to think before you speak." See *There*.

Compound Personal Pronouns. The word *self* added to *my, thy, your, him, her, it*, and the plural *selves* to *our, your, them*, form *compound personal pronouns*, often called *reflexive pronouns*. They are used chiefly (1) to express emphasis, with or without the simple pronoun: "I *myself* am positive"; "She talks of no one but *herself*." (2) as reflexive object of a verb, the object and the subject of the verb being the same person or thing: "He dressed *himself*"; "You will hurt *yourself*."

These pronouns have the same form for *nominative* and *objective* cases. They are not used in the *possessive*.

The simple personal pronoun is sometimes used reflexively in poetry: "I lay *me* down."

Interrogative Pronouns. Pronouns used in asking questions are *interrogative pronouns: who, which, what*. "*Who* is here?" "*Which* do you like?" "*What* did you say?"

Singular and Plural
Nominative who
Possessive whose
Objective whom

The interrogatives *which* and *what* have no declension or change of form, however used. *Who* and *whom* refer to persons only; the other forms, to persons or things.

Which, what, and *whose* are used also as *interrogative adjectives*: "*Which* train did he take?" "*What* number is that?" "*Whose* book is this?"

Demonstrative Pronouns. *This, that,* and the plurals, *these* and *those,* are called *demonstratives,* because they point out definitely the persons or things to which they refer. Latin *demonstrare* means "to point out": "*That* is the question"; "*Those* are the bills"; "The reasons are *these.*"

When used with nouns, like adjectives, the demonstratives are often called *demonstrative adjectives*: "*this* farm"; "*those* cattle."

Relative Pronouns. A relative pronoun is both pronoun and conjunction. As a *pronoun,* the word is used like a noun; as a *conjunction,* it joins clauses. Hence relative pronouns are sometimes called *conjunctive pronouns.* The relative pronouns are *who, which, what, that. As* and *but* may be used as relative pronouns.

Singular and Plural

Nominative	who	which
Possessive	whose	whose
Objective	whom	which

What and *that* have no change of form for the *nominative* and the *objective* and are not used in the *possessive.*

Who and *whom* refer to persons only.

Whose is used of both persons and things.

Which, as a relative, refers to things only.

That refers to both persons and things.

What may be called a *double relative,* being equivalent to *that which,* the demonstrative pronoun *that* and the relative pronoun *which*: "We know *what (that which)* he wants."

As is used as *relative pronoun*: "I want such *as (those which)* are desirable."

But is used as *relative pronoun*: "There is no fireside *but (that not)* has one vacant chair."

Which and *what* are used also as *relative adjectives*: "I know *which (that which)* book you mean"; "I see *what (that which)* reward she will receive."

Compound Relative Pronouns. *Who, which,* and *what* are combined with *ever* and *soever* to form *compound relative pronouns*: *whoever, whosoever, whichever, whichsoever, whatever, whatsoever.* The forms with *so* are rarely used.

Indefinite Pronouns. Indefinite pronouns do not point out definitely, but they refer in a general manner to persons or objects. Those commonly used are *each, every, either, neither, some, all, any, few, many, one, none, other, another, both.* Many of these words are used as indefinite adjectives:

(pro.) "*Some* dislike animals."

(adj.) "*Some* people dislike animals."

The only indefinite pronouns which have plural forms are *one* and *other*: "Give me a small *one* (sing.)"; "Give me small *ones* (plur.)"; "I want the *other* (sing.)"; "I want the *others* (plur.)."

Adjective Pronouns. The *demonstrative* and *indefinite pronouns* are also called *adjective pronouns,* because they are used both as adjectives and as nouns.

GRAMMATICAL RELATIONS OF NOUNS AND PRONOUNS

For nouns and pronouns, grammatical relations are said to be relations of *case, number, person,* and *gender.*

CASE

Nominative Case. The following are said to be in the *nominative* (naming) *case*:

1. A noun or pronoun used as subject: "The *boy* plays." "*He* came home."

2. A noun in apposition to a noun or pronoun in the nominative case: "John, my *brother,* is here." "She, the *woman* in black, wept bitterly."

3. A predicate noun or pronoun: "The man was *master.*" "It is *he* whom you want."

4. A noun or pronoun used in direct address: "*Citizens,* remember your duties"; "O *thou* that rollest above! whence are thy beams?"

5. A noun or pronoun used absolutely with a participle: "The *storm* abating, the air grew colder."

6. A noun or pronoun used in exclamation: "A *horse*! A *horse*! My kingdom for a horse." "*He,* lost!"

Objective Case. The following are said to be in the *objective case* (*objective* meaning "thrown, or directed, toward," as the action of a verb is directed toward a noun):

1. A noun, a pronoun, a phrase or a clause used as the object of a transitive verb (*transitive* meaning "going across," as the action of a verb goes across to the object): "James studies *spelling.*" "I like *her.*" "I tried *to learn a foreign language.*" "He said, '*I shall go.*'" "She knew *that all was well.*"

2. Indirect object: "He wrote (to) his *brother* (indirect object) a *letter* (direct object)."

One may recognize the indirect object by the possibility of using *to* before it without changing the meaning of the sentence.

3. The object of a preposition: "He went into the *store.*"

4. A word in apposition to a noun or pronoun in the objective case: "He found the house, a large stone *building.*"

5. Objective of exclamation: "Oh, happy *me*!"

6. A noun of time, distance, or quantity used adverbially. This is called an *adverbial objective*: "I slept four *hours*"; "He walked three *miles.*"

7. An objective complement (called also *predicate objective* and *adjunct accusative*): "They made him *chairman*"; "She called Mary *queen.*"

8. The secondary object: "They allowed each speaker an *hour.*" When such sentences are changed to the passive construction, the *secondary object* is retained as an object: "Each speaker was allowed an *hour.*"

9. A subject of an infinitive: "I know *him* to be truthful."

10. A predicate of an infinitive: "I know it to be *her.*"

Note.—Many recent authorities prefer the term *accusative case* for the foregoing constructions, except that of indirect object, for which they use the term *dative.*

Possessive Case. 1. A word expressing ownership or possession is in the *possessive case*: "*John's* books"; "*their* work."

2. When two nouns in the possessive case are in apposition, the second alone takes the possessive sign: "Webster the *statesman's* speeches"; "Jack the *giant-killer's* exploits."

3. The possessive form is used also to limit or define and does not necessarily indicate ownership: "six *days'* journey"; "*man's* duty"; "the *river's* brink."

Note.—Many authorities prefer the name *genitive* for the so-called possessive case.

Inflection.—English nouns have no inflection, or change of form, to denote cases, except the adding of the apostrophe and *s* for the possessive. See *Spelling.* Certain pronouns are inflected to denote cases. See *Kinds of Pronouns.*

Note.—Recent works on English grammar recommend the following classification of case forms and uses:

Forms,—*common* and *genitive.*

Uses,—*nominative, genitive, dative, accusative.*

SPECIAL USES

Compound names and groups of words add the possessive sign to the last word: "*William the Conqueror's* throne"; "the *king of England's* palace"; "my *father-in-law's* house."

Joint Possession. If two or more possessive nouns imply joint possession of the same thing, and are connected by *and*, the possessive sign is used with the last noun only:

"*Mary* and *John's* mother" implies common possession —one mother.

"*Mason* and *Hamlin's* organs."

"*Wheeler* and *Wilson's* store."

Separate Possession. If separate possession is implied, or if the nouns are connected by *or* or *nor*, each one takes the possessive sign:

"*Mary's* and *John's* mother" implies separate possession —two mothers.

"*Taft's* and *Wilson's* administration."

"Is that a *girl's* or a *boy's* voice?"

"He accepted neither the *skeptic's* nor the *clergyman's* view."

The possessive (genitive) case may be denoted by the objective case following the preposition *of*; "*Job's* patience," or "the patience *of Job*"; "*Somebody else's* work," or "the work *of somebody else*."

NUMBER

Nouns and pronouns denoting one person or thing are *singular*: *farm, wife*. Nouns and pronouns denoting more than one are *plural*: *farms, wives*. See *Spelling*.

Inflection.—English nouns regularly add *s* or *es* to form the plural. See *Spelling*. For pronoun plurals, see *Kinds of Pronouns*.

PERSON

The speaker or writer is the first person, *I, we*; the one addressed is the second person, *thou, you*; the person or thing spoken of is the third person, *he, it, they*.

Inflection.—English nouns are not inflected to distinguish person. See *Personal Pronouns*.

GENDER

In English, a noun or pronoun naming a male is *masculine*: *stag*. One naming a female, *feminine*: *girl*. One naming an object without sex, *neuter* (a Latin word, meaning "neither"): *tree*. Words which may be applied to either males or females are said to be of *common* gender: *animal*.

Inflection.—Nouns and pronouns are not inflected to distinguish gender. Personal pronouns have different forms to distinguish gender.

Antecedent. The substantive—word, phrase, or clause—for which a pronoun stands, and to which it refers, is called its *antecedent*, a Latin word, meaning "something going before":

"The man who planned the building made it his masterpiece." *Man* is the antecedent of *who* and of *his*.

"To sleep well, which is a blessing, is to repair and renew the body." *To sleep well* is a phrase, the antecedent of *which*.

Agreement. The pronoun is said to agree with its antecedent in *gender, person*, and *number*, but its *case* depends upon its use in the sentence:

"The book which you found is mine." The antecedent of *which* is *book*. *Book* is in the *nominative case*, the subject of *is*: *which* is in the *objective case*, the object of *found*.

"He is one of those who prefer winter." The antecedent of *who* is *those*, not *one*. Hence *who* is plural and requires a plural verb.

VERBS

KINDS OF VERBS

According to use, verbs are either *transitive* or *intransitive*.

Transitive Verbs. A transitive verb is one which requires an object to complete its meaning. The object, sometimes called *object complement*, names the receiver of the action of the verb: "The man *built* (verb) the *house* (object)."

Intransitive Verbs. An intransitive verb is one which does not require an object to complete its meaning. Some intransitives, however, need to be completed by a predicate noun or adjective, often called *attribute complement*, which refers to or modifies the subject: "That village *is* (verb) *Millville* (attribute complement)"; "The action *seems* (verb) *right* (attribute complement)."

GRAMMATICAL RELATIONS OF VERBS

The syntax of verbs involves relations of *voice, mode, tense, person*, and *number*. For the forms to express these, see *Table of Specimen Verb Forms*.

VOICE

Meaning of the Voices. *Voice* is often defined as that property of verbs which indicates whether the subject acts or is acted upon.

Active Voice.—If the subject is acting, the verb is in the *active*, or "doing," *voice*: "The man *broke* his cane."

Passive Voice.—If the subject is being acted upon, or receiving an action, the verb is in the *passive*, or "suffering," *voice*: "The cane *was broken*."

Forms to Denote Voice. The terms "active voice" and "passive voice" are applied also to the forms of the verb.

That form of the verb which shows that the subject is acting is called *active voice*: "Mary *broke* the dish."

That form of the verb which shows that the subject is acted upon is called *passive voice*: "The dish *was broken* by Mary." Some part of the verb *be* is joined to the past participle of a transitive verb to make the *passive voice*: *is sold, were made*.

Any transitive verb may be used in the passive voice, its object in the active becoming its subject in the passive: "The boy *lights* (active) the lamps"; "The lamps *are lighted* (passive) by the boy."

Intransitive verbs ordinarily are active, but some verbs are used either as intransitive or transitive: "He *spoke* (intrans.) truthfully"; "He *spoke* (trans.) the truth." When used transitively, such verbs may become passive: "The truth *was spoken* by him."

Some intransitive verbs, used with a following preposition, have a transitive meaning; as, *laugh at, look over, wonder at*: "He *laughed at* me"; "She *looked over* the work"; "They *wondered at* his skill." Such phrases are transitive in the fullest sense as tested by the passive construction: "I *was laughed at* by him"; "The work *was looked over* by her"; "His skill *was wondered at* by them."

MODE

Meaning of the Modes. *Mode* (or *mood*) may be defined as that property of verbs which shows the manner in which the action or state is conceived.

If the action or state expressed is thought of simply as a fact, the mode is *indicative*; if it is regarded as doubtful or merely as desired, the mode is *subjunctive*; if it is viewed as a command, the mode is *imperative*.

Forms to Denote Modes. The term "modes" is applied also to the several series of verb forms. In this use, *mode* is the form of the verb which shows the manner of expressing an action or a state.

The indicative mode states a fact or asks a simple question; as, "The sun shines"; "Has the rain been heavy?"

The indicative forms, however, are commonly used to express subjunctive and imperative ideas: "The dam will break if the river *rises* (condition)"; "You *will report* at seven (command)."

The imperative mode expresses a command or an entreaty; as, "*Come* here"; "*Have* mercy upon me."

The subjunctive mode makes a doubtful or conditional assertion; as, "Though he *slay* me, yet will I trust him."

For the so-called *potential mode*, see *Modal Auxiliaries*.

Meaning of Tenses. The *tense* of a verb indicates the time of the action or state.

As applied to verb forms, *tense* is the form the verb takes to indicate time.

According to the time expressed and the completeness or incompleteness of the action, state, or condition, the verb varies in tense.

Simple Tenses.—The simple (or incomplete) tenses, *present*, *past*, *future*, signify action or condition as continuing in present, past, or future time: "I *go*"; "I *went*"; "I *shall go*."

Perfect Tenses.—The perfect (or complete) tenses imply the completion of an act in present time (*present perfect*), in past time (*past perfect*), or in future time (*future perfect*): "I *hav gone*"; "I *had gone*"; "I *shall have gone.*" See *Table of Specimen Verb Forms.*

Other Tenses.—Some authorities distinguish a *past future* tense, as, "We thought he *would go,*" and a *past future perfect* tense, as, "We thought he *would have gone.*"

PERSON AND NUMBER

A verb must agree with its subject in person and in number: "I *do* not"; "He *does* not"; "You *do* not"; "They *do* not."

VERB FORMS

Inflection of Verbs, or Conjugation. In conjugation, English verbs change form to show voice, mode, tense, person, and number. The usually inflected forms are the third person singular of the present active indicative; the past active indicative; the present and past participles: *has, had, having, had.* For exceptions, see *Table of Specimen Verb Forms*: the verb *be*; *Subjunctive Mode.* See also *Thou Forms.*

Verb Phrases. All other mode, tense, and voice meanings are expressed by the simple verb or by verb phrases. A *verb phrase* is a group of verbs used as a single verb. A verb phrase is formed by prefixing an auxiliary (helping) verb to some infinitive or participle form of a principal verb: "Wars *shall cease*"; "It *may rain*"; "Fashions *have been changing.*"

Principal Parts. In order to conjugate any verb throughout its various modes and tenses, it is necessary to know only the *infinitive*, the *past tense*, and the *past participle*. These three, therefore, are called the *principal parts*: *find, found, found*; *go, went, gone.*

Regular Verbs. A regular (or weak) verb, in English, forms its past tense and past participle by adding *d* or *ed* to the present: *load, loaded*; *love, loved*; *wash, washed*; *persuade, persuaded.*

Irregular Verbs. An irregular (or strong) verb forms its past tense and past participle by a vowel change, frequently adding a change of ending: *hide, hid, hidden*; *drink, drank, drunk*; *eat, ate, eaten.*

A Defective Verb is one that lacks some of its principal parts; as, *ought, may, can.*

A Redundant Verb is one that has both a regular and an irregular form; as, *bereave, bereaved* or *bereft, bereaved* or *bereft.*

A Copulative Verb is an intransitive verb which connects the subject with a predicate noun or pronoun or with a predicate adjective. Such a verb is called a *linking* verb. Among intransitive verbs thus used are *be, become, seem, appear, feel, grow, remain, sit, stand*: "Mary *became* queen"; "He *grows* tall"; "She *feels* better."

A Reflexive Verb is a transitive verb, the subject and the object of which are the same individual: "I *wash* myself"; "He *contradicted* himself."

An Impersonal Verb is one used only in the third person singular with no definite personal subject: "It *rains*"; "It *snows.*"

Auxiliary Verbs. Auxiliary comes from the Latin *auxilium*, meaning "help"; hence, auxiliary verbs are verbs that help in the conjugation of other verbs. They are of two classes:

1. *Auxiliaries of tense and voice: will, shall, have, be, do, did.*

The forms of the auxiliary *be* used with a past participle make the passive voice; as, *are told, was told, shall have been told.*

Have and *had* are auxiliaries used with the past participle to form the present perfect and the past perfect tense, hence *have* and *had* are called "signs" of the perfect and past perfect tenses respectively:

Present Perfect.—I *have* told
Past Perfect.—I *had* told

Do and *did* are either emphatic or interrogative auxiliaries used with the present infinitive of another verb to form the present and past tenses respectively.

Present.—I *do* tell; *do* I tell?
Past.—I *did* tell; *did* I tell?

2. *Modal auxiliaries: may, might, can, could, would, should, must,* (in some cases *shall, will,* and *have*). For the uses of *shall, will, should, would,* see *Good Usage.*

The modal auxiliaries may be prefixed to the present infinitive or to the perfect infinitive of any verb in order to express various modes. They suggest doubt, permission, wish, ability, or duty: "I *may* tell, *may* have told"; "He *can* go"; "You *should* read."

May and *might* express permission, possibility, or doubt. *Might* was formerly used in the past tense, and it now expresses more doubt or dependence upon conditions than *may.* The time of the verb phrase formed with these auxiliaries is determined by the verb form following the auxiliary: "It *may* (*might*) have happened (past)."

Can and *could* express ability. *Can* signifies either present or future time: "We *can* go." *Could* may express past time: "Yesterday, I *could* do nothing." *Could* usually implies an uncertain condition: "They *could* have gone (if something had not interfered)."

Participles. Formed from a verb, usually by the addition of *ing* or *ed*, a participle retains the original verb meaning but is used in a subordinate or incidental way. Like the infinitive, the participle conveys in condensed form a verbal idea that might otherwise be expressed in a clause. Thus, instead of the sentence, "Because he walked rapidly, he soon reached the station," a parallel statement using a participle could be, "Walking rapidly, he soon reached the station." In the latter case, the word *walking* is a participle, which refers to "he." To avoid "dangling participles," every participial modifier should be placed next to its intended base.

In sentences like "Let *sleeping* dogs lie" and "A *burnt* child dreads the fire," the participle is used as an adjective. If it is not used in this way to modify a noun, it may be treated as a predicate adjective, as in the sentence "The visitor was *puzzled.*" In the opening sentence of a whimsical essay, Gilbert K. Chesterton illustrates the distinction between a true participle (action) and a participial adjective (condition): "Just now everybody is *revolting* in one sense of the word, except a few who are *revolting* in the other sense." The second *revolting* is really an adjective like "contemptible."

A verb has three participles:
Present participle—*speaking* (action is in progress): "He stood *speaking.*"
Past participle—*spoken* (action is completed): "A little word in kindness *spoken.*"
Perfect participle—*having spoken* (action is completed before the time implied in the principal verb): "*Having spoken* the word, he departed." See *Table of Specimen Verb Forms.*

Gerund or **Verbal Noun.** Verb forms ending in *-ing* are used also as nouns. They may be modified by adverbs, since they are verbal, or by adjectives, since they are used as nouns: "*Fishing constantly* (adv.) makes one taciturn"; "He found *good* (adj.) *fishing.*" A gerund may also take an object: "*Writing* the *letter* (obj.) was difficult."

When the gerund is preceded by an article, *a, an,* or *the,* or by an adjective, it requires a following phrase with *of,* signifying the *object* of its action: "The *building of* the ship took many days"; "Success depends upon careful *planning of* work."

The Subjunctive. With the exception of the forms given under the conjugation of *be,* English has no regularly inflected subjunctive forms. *Have* is used occasionally for *has* in the third person singular, and in other verbs the indicative singular third personal ending *s* is dropped, to make a subjunctive form: "If he *tell.*"

The ideas of *doubt, uncertainty, condition,* and *desire,* usually called *subjunctive,* are commonly expressed by the indicative or by various verb phrases. See *Good Usage: Should, Would.*

The past subjunctive *were* or *had* is often used in past conditional sentences when *if* is omitted. In such cases the verb precedes the subject: "*Were* I *going,* I should take supplies"; "*Had* we *thought* of it, we would have called on him."

The Infinitive. The *infinitive,* meaning "unlimited," is a form of the verb which partakes of the nature of a noun. It expresses action without person or number. The *present infinitive* represents incomplete action, *to go;* the *perfect infinitive* represents completed action. *to have gone.* Verb phrases are formed with the auxiliaries *be* and *have* to serve as present and perfect passive infinitives: *to be seen, to have been seen.* See *Table of Verb Forms.*

The English infinitive is usually preceded by the word *to,* which is a relic of an early stage of the language and no essential part of the infinitive. Most verbs, when they take a following infinitive, require the form with *to:* "I *want* him *to go.*" The following verbs generally take the infinitive without *to: bid, dare, feel, hear, let, make, need, see,* and all auxiliaries; as. "*See* him *go,*" "They *may return.*"

The infinitive may be used as a *noun,* as an *adjective,* or as an *adverb;* but it takes only an adverbial modifier, and, if transitive, may take an object: "*To tell* the *facts* (obj.) *accurately* (adv.) is difficult."

In the sentence "I want you to buy some oranges," some authorities regard *you to buy some oranges* as an *infinitive clause,* the object of the verb *want; you* is the subject and *oranges* is the object of *to buy.* Others call the *infinitive phrase, to buy some oranges,* the objective complement, and *you* the object complement, of the verb *want.*

Thou Forms. An old form of the second person singular in present and past tenses, now found only in poetical or religious use, is made by adding *st* or *est* to the first person singular: "*Thou tellest*"; "*Thou toldst*"; "*Thou hast*"; "*Thou hadst*"; "*Thou lovest*"; "*Thou lovedst.*" The verb *be* has the following forms: "*Thou art*"; "*Thou wast.*"

ADJECTIVES

Kinds of Adjectives according to Meaning. Adjectives are classified, according to meaning, as *limiting* and *descriptive.* An adjective modifies a noun or pronoun either by *limiting,* that is, setting it apart definitely from others, or by *describing,* that is, naming a quality of the thing for which the noun or pronoun stands. To say "a *third* report" is merely to set apart, or limit, the report as belonging to one class; to say "a *complete* report" is to describe it by a certain quality.

Such words as *three, five, eleven, second,* are limiting adjectives. They are called *numerals.* Those which merely give a number, as *two, four,* are called *cardinals;* those which designate an order in a series, as *seventh,* are called *ordinals.*

The, a, an, are limiting adjectives. *The* is called the *definite article; a* and *an* are called *indefinite articles. A* is used before consonant sounds, *an* before vowels. See *Good Usage.*

Kinds of Adjectives according to Use. Adjectives are commonly classified, according to their use in the sentence, as *attributive* and *predicate.*

Attributive Adjectives.—An adjective used in close connection with a noun is called an *attributive adjective,* although some prefer the term *adherent adjective.* Regularly the attributive adjective precedes its noun: "*pretty* flowers." For emphasis, it may sometimes be placed after the noun: "the city *beautiful.*"

Predicate Adjectives.—An adjective which modifies the noun of the subject but is placed in the predicate, usually following the verb, is called a *predicate adjective:* "The book is *large.*" For demonstrative, interrogative, relative, and indefinite adjectives, see *Kinds of Pronouns.*

Appositive Adjectives.—Some authorities distinguish a third type of adjective, the *appositive;* as, "The boy, *careless* and *indifferent,* paid no attention." Such adjectives do not limit their nouns but describe them. They usually follow the nouns.

Other adjectives regularly follow their nouns, some of them only as predicate adjectives,—*alone, awake, aware, asleep, alive:* "Man *alive!*" "The child is *asleep*"; "One star *alone.*"

Grammatical Relations. The use of English adjectives is very simple, because, except *this* and *that,* they are not inflected to distinguish gender, person, number, or case. The only inflection used is that employed to distinguish the degrees of comparison.

Comparison.—Most English adjectives are compared by adding to the simple form, or positive degree, of the adjective, *r* or *er,* to form the comparative degree, and *st* or *est,* to form the superlative: *high, higher, highest; fine, finer, finest.* The comparative degree expresses a greater or lesser degree of the quality named by the adjective; the superlative expresses the greatest or least degree of that quality.

For spelling changes with added syllables, see *Spelling.*

Many adjectives, especially those of more than two syllables, are compared by prefixing *more* or *less* for the comparative, *most* or *least* for the superlative: "*more* merciful"; "*least* troublesome." Some adjectives admit of both forms of comparison: *able, abler* (*more able*), *ablest* (*most able*). A few adjectives are compared irregularly: *bad, worse, worst; good, better, best.*

ADVERBS

Meaning of Adverbs. Adverbs modify the meaning of verbs, adjectives, and other adverbs, in respect to some one of the following ideas:

1. Place,—there, nowhere, yonder.
2. Time,—now, afterwards, soon.
3. Manner,—well, badly, thoroughly.
4. Cause,—therefore, consequently.
5. Number,—first, secondly, rarely.
6. Degree,—somewhat, more, highly.

They are classified, therefore, as adverbs of *place, time, manner, cause, number,* and *degree.*

Interrogative Adverbs. The adverbs *how, whence, wherefore, why,* and a few others are used to introduce questions, either direct or indirect: "*How* shall you go?" "They wanted to know *why* he did that."

Relative Adverbs. *As, how, now, since, so, thence, when, whence, whenever, where, wherever, whither, why,* and a few others are used to introduce *subordinate clauses.*

Forms. Most English adverbs end in *-ly.* Many of these are formed from adjectives: *quick* (adj.), *quickly* (adv.); *easy* (adj.), *easily* (adv.). Some adverbs have the same form as the corresponding adjectives: *early, hard, long, loud, deep.*

Caution.—*Goodly, lovely, manly, lonely,* and *homely* are adjectives.

Comparison.—Most adverbs are compared by prefixing to the simple form or positive degree *more* or *less* to form the comparative and *most* or *least* to form the superlative: easily, *more* easily, *most* easily; truly, *more* truly, *most* truly, *less* truly, *least* truly.

Some adverbs having the same form as the corresponding adjectives are compared by adding *er* and *est* to the simple form: *early, earlier, earliest; deep, deeper, deepest.*

A few adverbs are compared irregularly: *well, better, best; badly, worse, worst; much, more, most.*

There.—The adverb *there* is sometimes used to introduce a sentence, with no idea of place. When so used, *there* is called an *expletive,* because it "fills up" and is unnecessary to the sense: "*There* are many ways of doing good." See *It* under *Pronouns: Special Uses.*

The.—The definite article *the* is sometimes used as an adverb before comparatives: "*the* more, *the* merrier; *the* sooner, *the* better."

First.—The word *first* may be an adjective or an adverb: "The *first* (adj.) boy is my brother"; "He came *first* (adv.)." See *Good Usage.*

Position of Adverbs. Because great liberty is allowed as to the position of English adverbs, care should be taken so to place an adverb that its grammatical relation shall be clear.

PREPOSITIONS

Position of Prepositions. The word preposition comes from the Latin *pre,* before, and *ponere,* to place. Hence prepositions commonly stand before the words they govern ("Give the pencil *to him.*"); but they may come after them. In English this inversion occurs most frequently when the preposition governs a *relative* or an *interrogative word*: "They are people *whom* we know nothing *about*"; "*What* are you looking *for*?" See *Good Usage.*

Prepositional Phrases. The preposition and its object, with the modifiers of the object, form a phrase, which may be used as an adjective or an adverb: "The picture *on the screen* (adj.)"; "He ran *at top speed* (adv.)"; "Home *at last* (adv.)." Some prepositions form such close combinations with certain verbs that these expressions have the force of single words: *look over, laugh at, carry off.* See *Verbs, Prepositions.*

SUBORDINATE CLAUSES

According to use, subordinate clauses are *substantive, adjective,* and *adverbial.*

A *substantive clause* is a clause that performs the function of a noun: "*That he came* (subj. of verb) is true"; "I know *that he came* (obj. of verb)"; "He was anxious for *what had been promised him* (obj. of prep.)"; "He is *what he seems* (attribute complement)"; "The fact *that he did it* (appositive) is wonderful."

An *adjective clause* is a clause that modifies a noun or a pronoun. It may be introduced by a relative pronoun: "He *whom thou lovest* is sick"; "This is the tree *that we planted.*" It may be introduced by a conjunctive adverb: "The town *where* (in which) *she lived*"; "The time *when* (at which) *Rome was built.*"

An adjective clause may be *restrictive*: "I took the peach *that was ripe.*" It was a particular peach. *That was ripe* restricts or limits *peach,* telling which one was taken.

An adjective clause may be *non-restrictive*: "I read 'Marmion,' *which was written by Scott.*" *Marmion* defines what book was read. *Which was written by Scott* is a *non-restrictive* clause, merely adding another thought to the one already expressed. A comma is used after *Marmion* to separate the non-restrictive clause from the rest of the sentence.

Relative Clause.—A clause introduced by a relative pronoun is sometimes called a *relative clause*: "This tree, *which has stood for years,* bears no fruit."

An *adverbial clause* is a clause that modifies the meaning of a verb, an adjective, or another adverb.

Adverbial clauses are introduced by subordinate conjunctions or by conjunctive adverbs:

Time—"*When duty calls,* I obey."
Place—"*Where I go,* ye cannot come."
Degree—"It is better *than I expected.*"
Manner—"The child does *as he pleases.*"
Purpose—"He came *that he might learn.*"
Result—"She was so weak *that she fainted.*"
Cause—"The snow melted *because it rained.*"
Condition—"*If you do right,* you will win."
Concession—"*Though I failed,* I shall try again."

Conjunctions. See special section devoted to this subject.

PARSING

To parse a word is to classify it as a part of speech, explain its form, and show its relation to other words in the sentence.

In the sentence "He bought a car," *car* is a common noun, of neuter gender, in the third person, singular number, and in the objective case because it is the object of the verb *bought.*

Bought is an irregular, transitive verb. The principal parts are *buy, bought, bought.* It is active voice, indicative mode, past tense; third person, singular number, to agree with its subject *he.*

He is a personal pronoun. Its declension is singular, nom. *he,* poss. *his,* obj. *him*; plural, nom. *they,* poss. *their* or *theirs,* obj. *them.* Third person, singular number; nominative case, the subject of the verb *bought.*

SENTENCE ANALYSIS

To analyze a sentence, first classify the sentence according to *form* and *use.* Then point out the simple subject; the complete subject. Classify the modifiers of the simple subject, analyzing phrases and clauses. Point out the simple predicate; the complete predicate. Classify the modifiers of the simple predicate, analyzing phrases and clauses. If the sentence is complex or compound, also name and classify the clauses and the connectives which join them.

Simple Sentence. "Truth, crushed to earth, shall rise again" is a *simple, declarative* sentence. *Truth* is the *simple* subject; *truth, crushed to earth* is the *complete* subject; *crushed* is a participle formed from the verb *crush* and modifies the noun *truth; to earth* is an adverbial phrase, modifying *crushed; shall rise* is the *simple* predicate; *shall rise again* is the *complete* predicate; *shall rise* is the predicate verb, which is modified by the adverb *again.*

Complex Sentence. "Blessed is he who has found his work" is a *complex, declarative* sentence, composed of one independent clause, *blessed is he,* and one dependent clause, *who has found his work.* The subject of the independent clause is *he*; the predicate is *is blessed.* The predicate consists of the copulative verb *is* and the predicate adjective *blessed,* which modifies the subject *he.* The dependent clause, *who has found his work,* is an adjective clause modifying the pronoun *he.* The subject of the clause is the relative pronoun *who*; the complete predicate is *has found his work; has found* is the predicate verb, the direct object of which is *work; his* is a possessive pronoun modifying *work.* The relative pronoun *who* joins the two clauses; its antecedent is *he.*

TABLE OF SPECIMEN VERB FORMS
The Verb, **tell**. Principal Parts: *tell, told, told*
INDICATIVE MODE

ACTIVE VOICE   PASSIVE VOICE

Present Tense
Ordinary Form

SINGULAR	PLURAL	SINGULAR	PLURAL
I tell	We tell	I am told	We are told
You tell	You tell	You are told	You are told
He tells	They tell	He is told	They are told

Progressive Form

I am telling	We are telling	I am being told	We are being told
You are telling	You are telling	You are being told	You are being told
He is telling	They are telling	He is being told	They are being told

Emphatic Form

I do tell	We do tell	No corresponding forms in the passive voice.	
You do tell	You do tell		
He does tell	They do tell		

Negative Form

I do not tell	We do not tell	I am not told	We are not told
You do not tell	You do not tell	You are not told	You are not told
He does not tell	They do not tell	He is not told	They are not told

Negative Progressive Form

I am not telling	We are not telling	I am not being told	We are not being told
You are not telling	You are not telling	You are not being told	You are not being told
He is not telling	They are not telling	He is not being told	They are not being told

Present Perfect Tense

I have told	We have told	I have been told	We have been told
You have told	You have told	You have been told	You have been told
He has told	They have told	He has been told	They have been told

Past Tense
Ordinary Form

I told	We told	I was told	We were told
You told	You told	You were told	You were told
He told	They told	He was told	They were told

Progressive Form

I was telling	We were telling	I was being told	We were being told
You were telling	You were telling	You were being told	You were being told
He was telling	They were telling	He was being told	They were being told

Emphatic Form

I did tell	We did tell	No corresponding forms in the passive voice.	
You did tell	You did tell		
He did tell	They did tell		

Negative Form

I did not tell	We did not tell	I was not told	We were not told
You did not tell	You did not tell	You were not told	You were not told
He did not tell	They did not tell	He was not told	They were not told

Negative Progressive Form

I was not telling	We were not telling	I was not being told	We were not being told
You were not telling	You were not telling	You were not being told	You were not being told
He was not telling	They were not telling	He was not being told	They were not being told

Past Perfect, or Pluperfect, Tense

I had told	We had told	I had been told	We had been told
You had told	You had told	You had been told	You had been told
He had told	They had told	He had been told	They had been told

Future Tense

I shall tell	We shall tell	I shall be told	We shall be told
You will tell	You will tell	You will be told	You will be told
He will tell	They will tell	He will be told	They will be told

Future Perfect Tense

I shall have told	We shall have told	I shall have been told	We shall have been told
You will have told	You will have told	You will have been told	You will have been told
He will have told	They will have told	He will have been told	They will have been told

Infinitive Forms

Present.—(to) tell   Present.—(to) be told
Perfect.—(to) have told   Perfect.—(to) have been told

Participle Forms

Present.—telling   Present.—being told
Perfect.—having told   Past.—told
     Perfect.—having been told

Imperative Forms

Tell (Negative) Do not tell *or* Tell not   Be told (Negative) Do not be told *or* Be not told

The Verb **be**. Principal Parts: *am, was, been*

Present Tense		Past Tense	
SINGULAR	PLURAL	SINGULAR	PLURAL
I am	We are	I was	We were
You are	You are	You were	You were
He is	They are	He was	They were

The Verb **have**. Principal Parts: *have, had, had*

I have	We have	I had	We had
You have	You have	You had	You had
He has	They have	He had	They had

PREPOSITIONS

Through the study of prepositions, one gains a command of many idiomatic phrases found in every civilized language. Especially is this true of English, because English prepositions united with other words often take the place of corresponding inflected word forms in other languages.

From the following list of the more important English prepositions, the reader will learn the distinctive meanings attached to each according to the varied purposes for which it is used.

About. In its usual meanings of *around, close to, because of, concerning, not far from, over,* etc., this preposition is employed to express: (1) indefinite position, "The idlers hung *about* the saloon"; (2) in attendance on, "The king had his bodyguard *about* him"; (3) close at hand, on one's person, "He had no money *about* him"; (4) attention to, "We sent him *about (to attend to)* his business"; (5) abstract connection in the sense of concerning, "to see, ask, hear, write, think, dream *about* a thing." In expressing approximation, *about* has the force of an adverb of degree: "He is *about* my size."

Above. Commonly this word means *over, higher than, superior to*: "The colonel ranks *above* the major." "The airplane rose rapidly *above* the city." "Clouds seem to float just *above* the trees." "The man's record is *above* suspicion." "The president does not stand *above* the law." "Mr. Utterson could hear the footsteps *above* the hum of the city." "*Above* all, avoid the appearance of suspicion."

After. This word usually means *behind, following, as a result of, in spite of, for,* and *according to.* It may be used with the verb *be* and with any verb of motion, also after *seek, ask, hunt,* although, with these, modern usage generally prefers *for.* The following are examples of common usage: "The troops passed first and the supply train came *after (behind)* them." "It was *after (later than)* twelve when our friends left." "*After (as a result of)* careful examination the board approved the plans." "The picture is fashioned *after (according to)* an antique model." "Book *after* book was read." "Time *after* time Mr. Blank inquired *after (for)* you." "*After (in spite of)* all, they have failed." "*After* a while they grew tired."

Against. Common meanings: *opposite to* (in this sense expressed by *over against*), *opposed to, pressing upon, contrary, from.* Examples: "The mast stood out clearly *against (contrasting with)* the sky." "The governor had long held his ground *against* suffrage." "The machine was leaning *against (pressing upon)* the wall." "Such action seems *against (contrary to)* nature." "Defend us *against (from)* our enemies."

Along. Implies *motion* or *extension upon, at* or *near the side of.* In such connections it may mean *near, beside, following the line of*: "We wandered *along (beside)* the river bank." "Rare plants grow *along (by the side of)* that embankment." "Trees are planted *along (the whole length of)* the roadway." "The car proceeded *along (following the line of)* the Boston road."

Amid, Amidst. The two words do not differ essentially in meaning. Their first sense is that of *among, surrounded by,* used generally with plural *substantives*: "She dwelt *amid (surrounded by)* the ruins of her former glory." In an extended sense, the words apply to circumstances and conditions: "He was bewildered *amid (among)* the perplexities and temptations of his position." In poetry, *amid* is used with a singular noun to indicate *in the middle of,* or *surrounded by* some extended object: "She strayed *amid* the corn."

Among, Amongst. Like *amid* and *amidst,* these two words are interchangeable so far as meaning is concerned. Both words refer to several persons or things and convey the idea of dispersion or distribution. *Among* is the more common form: "We divided the profits *among* ourselves" (not *between,* unless only two persons are concerned). *Amongst* is the rarer, and perhaps more poetic, form.

Around, Round. Used interchangeably to signify motion or position *about, encircling, on all sides of, in all directions from, at random through*: "They made a journey *around (encircling)* the world." "*Around (on all sides of)* the mansion were gardens." "The beams of light radiate *around (in all directions from)* the central mass." "We spent the day riding *around (at random through)* the city." "They gathered *round (about)* the hearth."

At. This word primarily expresses the relation of *presence,* of *contact in place or time,* or of *direction towards.* (1) It designates more or less indefinitely the point or place where a thing is: "*at* the center," "*at* home," "*at* hand." (2) Sometimes it emphasizes contact with a place better than *in* or *by*: "*at* school," "*at* the helm." (3) It denotes presence at an event: "*at* the wedding," "*at* the ball"; also location of a feeling or quality: "sick *at* heart," "out *at* elbow." (4) It is likewise used to signify the end or object of directed effort: "look *at* it," "aim *at* the bull's eye"; similarly, with the verbs *strike, shout, wink, mock, laugh, be angry,* etc. (5) It implies action, occupation with, or employment: "*at* work," "*at* meals," "to pull *at* an oar."

Before. Usual meanings: *ahead of, preceding, face to face with, rather than, higher than.* Examples: "The visitors came *before (ahead of)* the appointed time." "The customer just *before (preceding)* you bought the last pound." "The culprit was brought *before (face to face with)* the judge." "The question is now *before (claiming the attention of) (subject to disposition by)* the house." "The ship drove *before* the wind." "Shakespeare comes *before (higher than)* Chaucer in rank though not in time."

Behind. Common meanings: *in the rear, at the back, toward the rear, not up with, supporting, backing.* Examples: "The garden was planted *behind* the house." "*Behind (in the rear of)* the army came the stragglers." "His shadow betrayed his presence *behind (at the back of)* the screen." "Many, worn out by the march, fell *behind (to the rear of)* their comrades." "His ideas are *behind (not up with)* the times." "The contractor did not have sufficient capital *behind (supporting)* him." "The train was *behind* time."

Below. Used literally of position or direction, signifying *lower than, under*: "The shot struck *below (lower than)* the water line." "The signature is placed on the line *below (under)* the complimentary close." "Three miles *below (farther down than)* the town, on the bank of the stream, stands the fort." Figuratively, *below* is used to express an inferior degree of rank, dignity, and excellence: "The corporal ranks *below* the sergeant." "They are as inferior as the fields are *below* the stars."

Beneath. This preposition is used generally of lower position. It suggests also influence or control and unworthiness. The following examples illustrate accurate uses of the word: "The plank roadway echoed *beneath* their tread." "Loch Katrine lay *beneath* him." "The trees were bent *beneath* their burden of fruit." "His knees shook *beneath* him." "The people were held *beneath* the yoke of the conqueror." "She thought her neighbors *beneath* her notice."

Beside. In its literal sense, used to mean *by the side of, near*: "The guard rode *beside* the carriage." Figuratively, *beside* is used to suggest comparison: "*Beside (in comparison with)* his son's achievement, his own seemed petty." *Beside* has the force of *outside of* in "*beside* himself" and "*beside* the question."

Besides. Formerly used interchangeably with *beside,* this word now signifies *over and above, in addition to, as well as,* and also *apart from*: "The house had many rooms *besides (in addition to)* those." "*Besides* (*as well as*) his income, he had other resources." "They are interested in nothing *besides* (*apart from*) their art."

Between. Used of position or movement in space separating two objects: "The courthouse was built *between* the rival towns." "He walks *between* his house and his office." *Between* is used also of intermediate qualities and conditions: "something intermediate *between* vice and virtue"; "a shade *between* orange and red." It may denote joint or reciprocal action either in agreement or opposition: "A struggle ensued *between* (*opposition*) the champions." "A compact was made *between* (*agreement*) the families." "*Between* them (*together*) they brought the game into camp." *Between* is likewise used to express confinement or restriction: "He took the bit *between* his teeth." It is employed particularly to signify privacy in conversation: "*between* ourselves," "*between* you and me."

Beyond. Used of an object in regard to both space and time, and signifying *farther on than, past, later than*: "They traveled *beyond* (*farther on than*) the mountains." "*Beyond* (*past*) the Alps lies Rome." "We were detained *beyond* (*past*) the usual hour of closing." Figuratively, the word is used in various senses of *exceeding* or *surpassing*: "The thing is *beyond* (*exceeds*) his power." "A scene lovely *beyond* (*surpassing*) expression was disclosed to view."

But. With the force of a preposition, *but* signifies *except, leaving out*: "The collector took all *but* (*except*) three." "There was no course open *but* (*except*) to submit." Some authorities treat these uses as conjunctive.

By. This word usually means *near, next to, in the course of, through the agency of, through the use of, according to* (*a specified unit of measure*). Examples: "The factory stands *by* (*near to*) the river." "Flight *by* (*in the course of the*) night was very dangerous." "No honest official is injured *by* (*through the agency of*) publicity." "*By* (*according to*) all physicians' rules he should have died." "More freight should be shipped *by* (*by way of*) water." "*By* whatever name it may be called, the tree is known *by* (*through the use of*) its fruit." "He works only *by* the day (work reckoned *according to* a day as a unit)." It may indicate a succession of units: "two *by* two"; "piece *by* piece"; "The timbers were dragged up the mountain one *by* one." The following are idiomatic expressions: "to take *by* and large" (to consider generally), "*by* seven o'clock," "to take *by* the hand," "two *by* the clock," "come *by*" (get), "do well *by* a person," "judge *by* appearance," "learn *by* experience," "take *by* surprise," "*by* the way," "*by* the pound," "*by* the book," "*by* hook and *by* crook," "*by* means of," "*by* dint of," "near *by*," "stand *by*" (help or support).

Down. Used literally of place and time and figuratively in various phrases, in the general sense of *descending direction*: "The machine sped easily *down* the incline." "A strange tradition comes *down* the years." The expression "*down* town" has the meaning of *into*, as denoting motion from a more elevated locality *down into* a lower one.

During. This word is used exclusively with reference to time, meaning *in the course of* or *throughout*: "We were repeatedly interrupted *during* (*in the course of*) the discussion." "*During* (*throughout*) this period a high temperature prevailed."

Except, Excepting. The two words are used interchangeably, in the sense of *exclusion* or *omission*: "Everybody was gay *except* the Major." "*Excepting* the last two articles, they adopted the agreement."

For. This preposition is a word of widely varied uses in reference to extent of space or of time, amounts of money, cause or occasion, purpose, seeking or reaching. It may mean *during, toward,*

in the interest of, in proportion to, in place of, in return, seeming, in relation to, in spite of. Examples: "The road was torn up *for* (*throughout*) a distance of half a mile." "The firm's note is good *for* (*to the extent of*) that amount." "The mayor was censured *for* (*because of his*) permitting the meeting." "The farmers gave them ball *for* (*in return for*) ball." "*For* (*in proportion to*) one who sees anything, ten people look." "*For* (*in spite of*) all his bluster, the man was a coward." The following phrases are idiomatic: "leave *for* a destination," "atone *for*," "argue *for*," "account *for*," "allow *for*," "apologize *for*," "pay *for*," "call *for*," "care *for*," "go *for*," "write *for*," "look *for*," "name *for*" (*after*), "to be well *for*," "*for* thirty dollars," "*for* once," "*for* a while," "indebted *for*," "a time *for* anything," "a taste *for* luxuries," "a longing *for* home," "*for* the asking," "the train *for* (*going to*) Philadelphia."

From. This word denotes primarily separation in space; but it is used also of a starting point in time, and it may express distinction of ideas and the relation of cause or source. Examples: "The house was placed about three hundred feet *from* the barn." "*From* boyhood he was interested in flowers and trees." "Men pass quickly *from* youth to age." "Skill arises *from* constant practice." "Deliver us *from* (*out of the power of*) evil."

In. This word may mean "*within* a place, a group of people or a society, or a period of time." It may denote also the end of a period of time or the object of a motion or a feeling. It may further be used in respect to manner, method, material, cause or occasion, and of duty or measure. *In* should be carefully distinguished from *into*, which implies motion or change only. Examples: "The family lives *in* Jamestown." "*In* the 19th century there were many wars." "The note is due *in* three months." "*In* whom can one put confidence?" "He took great delight *in* his friends." "*In* my judgment, the man is guilty." "The picture was done *in* oils." "Undoubtedly you spoke *in* haste."

We may say, "Come *in*"; but we must say, "Come *into* the house." The following are idiomatic expressions: "*in* the name of the law," "*in* time," "*in* wrath," "*in* health," "*in* doubt," "*in* error," "*in* scorn," "*in* fact," "*in* truth," "*in* love," "one *in* a thousand," "call *in* question," "hope *in*," "believe *in*," "trustworthy *in* word and deed," "originate *in*," "steeped *in*," "persist *in*."

Into. A preposition implying direction or motion, used regularly after the verbs *go, come, bring, put, send*, etc., also in referring to state or condition: "They went *into* the house." "He thrust the money *into* his purse." "The work extended well *into* the next month." "Their fathers had gone *into* business together." "The child burst *into* tears."

Notwithstanding. This word belongs to the class of participial prepositions. It means *in spite of* or *in the face of*: "The plan succeeded, *notwithstanding* strong opposition."

Of. This is the most commonly used English preposition. It may refer to position or location, distance, possession, extent of time, separation, source, material or character, relief. The following expressions will illustrate these meanings: "North *of* Boston," "the mountains *of* California," "a shore line *of* forty miles," "a creature *of* (*living only*) a day," "deprived *of* liberty," "the shadow *of* the glen," "a man *of* honor," "a form *of* great beauty," "cured *of* a cold," "a bridge *of* stone and iron." The following are idiomatic expressions: "fond *of*," "tired *of*," "best *of* all," "warned *of* danger," "hear *of*," "talk *of*," "beware *of*," "conscious *of*," "convicted *of*," "accounted *of*," "think well *of*," "afraid *of*," "big *of* heart," "*of* a cruel temper," "built *of*," "born *of*."

Off. This word means *from*, and is used chiefly to denote separation. It is employed idiomatically in various ways implying former dependence: "*off* one's hands," "*off* one's head." It sometimes indicates source or material with such verbs as *dine*, *eat*; as, "He dined *off* roast beef." It also signifies deduction or rebate; as, "They took it *off* the bill."

On, Upon. *On* and *upon* are nearly identical in meaning. *On* is used to indicate: (1) support or contact from elsewhere than beneath: "a fly *on* the wall"; (2) nearness: "a house situated *on* the river"; (3) employment or activity with or in respect to: "*on* the committee," "*on* duty," "*on* the run." It indicates the ground or basis of action: "stated *on* authority," "He bet *on* the red"; also position and boundary: "The town lay *on* the east." It likewise denotes state or condition: "*on* fire," "*on* sale," "*on* tap." Where simple contact or proximity to the surface is implied, *upon* is used interchangeably with *on*. The following are idiomatic uses: "The gifts arrived *on* time (*at the time set*)." "They bought the goods *on* time (*payment being deferred*)." "They lived *on* vegetables." To talk *on* or *upon* a subject implies more careful treatment of the theme than to talk *about* it.

Out. As a preposition, *out* is now obsolete or colloquial. *Out of* is used in its place. Examples: "He came *out of* (*from*) his retirement." "We frequently see things *out of* (*not according to*) their true proportion." "The bells were *out of* tune and harsh." The following are idiomatic phrases: "made *out of*," "*out of* order," "*out of* doors," "*out of* supplies," "*out of* season," "*out of* sight, *out of* mind."

Over. In the sense of *above*, this preposition is used to imply superiority, power, dignity, value, and preference; as, "to triumph *over* difficulties." It signifies *beyond*, in degree: "It cost *over* four dollars"; a whole surface: "to wander *over* the earth"; duration of time: "He let it soak *over* night." It has also the meanings of *across*, *from side to side*; as, "The dog leaped *over* the stream." *Over* is used idiomatically in such expressions as "*over* one's signature," "*over* head and ears in debt," etc.

Past: Used literally of space, time, and age signifying *beyond*, *farther on than*, *later than*: "He walked *past* (*farther on than*) the house." "They were just *past* (*beyond*) the boundary." "It is now ten minutes *past* (*later than*) twelve." "The old lady was *past* (*beyond the age of*) seventy." *Past* denotes also *beyond the power of*: "The man was troubled *past* endurance."

Round. See *Around*.

Save. Used in the sense of *except* or *excepting*: "There was no sign of human life *save* the chimney smoke."

Since. With the force of a preposition, this word is used altogether of time, signifying *from a time*, *within a following time*, and *duration*: "*Since* (*from*) that day we have not heard from him." "Where have you been *since* (*within the time after*) yesterday?" "It is a fortnight *since* he embarked."

Through. Used of space and time and in various other connections. It signifies *from one limit to another of*, *into every part of*, *passing within* in the sense of penetrating or transmitting, *during the period of*, *by means of*, *on account of*: "The hall runs *through* (*from end to end of*) the house." "The visitors were shown *through* (*into every part of*) the town." "A light shone *through* (*penetrating*) the woods." "The noise continued *through* (*during*) the night." "*Through* (*by means of*) his own perseverance, he held the position." "We were detained *through* (*on account of*) his blundering."

Throughout. The preposition *through*, reenforced by *out*, signifying *the whole of*, *every part of*, *space*, *region*, *period of time*, or *course of action*: "*throughout* the length and breadth of the land"; "*throughout* the night."

Till, Until. These words are used interchangeably in reference to time, signifying *to*, *up to*:

"They can wait *till* (*up to*) next week." "He will not reply to the letter *until* (*up to*) the end of the month."

To. Used primarily to denote relation of approach and arrival. It indicates that toward which there is movement—a terminal point: "He went *to* law about it." "She stretched her arms *to* heaven." Idiomatic uses: "The remarks were addressed *to* the audience." "Let us keep this *to* ourselves." "It was sweet *to* the taste." "We were bored *to* death." "The hall rang *to* the tramp of armed men." "The drawing was made *to* scale." "It was John *to* the very life."

Touching. Used with the force of a preposition in the sense of *concerning*, *with regard to*: "*Touching* the life of the interior villages, we have no authentic information."

Toward, Towards. Used interchangeably in the sense of *facing* or *looking in the direction of*, *approaching*, *aiming at*, *in respect to*: "The door was open *toward* (*facing*) the east." "A procession came *toward* (*approaching*) the village." "*Toward* (*approaching*) night the sky became overcast." "A strong trend *toward* (*aiming at*) independence was evident." "She maintained a critical attitude *towards* (*in respect to*) her family."

Under. The primary meaning of this word is *below*, *lower than*; as, "*under* a tree," "a cellar *under* the house." Hence, analogously it may have the meaning of *being weighed upon*, *oppressed*, or *controlled by* affliction, subjection, government, authority, and the like: "to travel *under* a heavy burden"; "to be brave *under* trials"; "*Under* (*during the government of*) the Tudors, England made great political progress."

Underneath. Used in the sense of *directly below*: "*Underneath* the desk, papers were piled."

Up. With respect to motion or position, this word signifies *from a lower to a higher place on or along*, *at a higher place upon*, *toward*, *near*, *at the top of*: "The party tramped *up* (*from a lower place*) the slope." "His farm lies *up* (*at a higher point upon*) the river." It may also denote movement from the coast to the interior; as, "to journey *up* the country." It may indicate direction from the mouth to the source of the river; as, "He sailed *up* the Hudson."

With. Denotes relation of contact or association. After the verbs *fight*, *contend*, *vie*, and the like, it has the meaning of *against*; as, "The Greeks fought *with* the Persians." "They are *with* (*in the employ of*) the telephone company." It may signify association in the sense of attribute; as, "a man *with* (*characterized by*) a clean record"; also the instrument or means; as, "He slew him *with* a sword" It may denote an accessory, as of contents, material, etc.; as, "to fill the stable *with* straw," "to line the hat *with* silk." *With* is used idiomatically in such phrases as "*with* all one's heart," "*with* tooth and nail," "to bear *with*," "to put up *with*," and the like.

Within. Used of place, signifying *inside of*: "*Within* the building were many curious objects." Used of time, signifying *inside the limits of*: "The train will arrive *within* an hour." The word is used of various other relations: "It is not *within* (*in the limits of*) his power to forbid the transfer." "Such an act does not come *within* (*in the scope of*) the court's jurisdiction." *Within* also implies limitation as to quantity: "He lived *within* his income."

Without. This word in the sense of *outside of* or *excluded from* is now seldom used and may be regarded as almost obsolete: "The poor folk dwelt *without* the walls." "She was *without* the pale of society." Its present meaning denotes *lack of*, *absence of*, *deprivation*: "The association was *without* (*lacked*) funds." "He was buried *without* (*deprived of*) the usual rites."

The following is a list of certain nouns, adjectives, and verbs, which require *special prepositions*:

Abhorrence *of* evil.

Abhorrent *to* his strict principles.

Abide *in* a place, *for* a while, *with* a company, *by* a promise.

Abound *in* vigor and courage, *with* theaters and churches.

Absolve *from* debt or allegiance or a charge of guilt.

A plant **absorbs** moisture *from* the air; one becomes absorbed *in* thought; nutriment may be absorbed *into* the system *through* the skin.

An **accessory** *to* the crime, *before* or *after* the fact; the accessories *of* an automobile.

The **accident** *of* family; an accident *to* the car.

Accommodate *to* circumstances, *with* money, material, etc.

Accompanied *by* several friends, *with* a suggestion.

Accord *with* (agree) looks or profession.

Accuse *of* a crime or fault.

Acquaint *with* the facts.

Acquaintance *with* a subject, *of* one person *with* another, *between* persons.

Acquit a person *of* a charge.

Active *in* temperament, *in* business, *for* an object or purpose, *with* instruments, *about* something.

Adapted *to* a use or situation, *for* a purpose, *from* a source, as *from* Shakespeare.

Adequate *to* a demand, *for* a purpose.

Admit *to* membership, *into* a house, *of* exceptions.

Admonish *of* error or duty, *against* a proposed act.

Advantage *of* education, *of* some one as "to get the advantage *of* us," *over* an opponent.

Advocate *of* free speech, *for* another person.

Affinity *between* colors and sounds, *of* one chemical element *for* another.

We **agree** *in* opinion *with* the speaker, *to* a proposition; persons agree *on* or *upon* a statement of principles, a contract, etc.; men should agree *among* themselves.

Alarm was felt *in* the village, *among* the women, *at* the sound.

Aliens *to* our national customs and thought; aliens *in* a country, *among* a people.

Alive *in* every fiber; alive *to* every good suggestion; alive *with* fervor, hope, resolve.

Allegiance *of* the citizen *to* the government; the government has a right to allegiance *from* the citizen.

Alliance *with* a state or people, *against* the common enemy, *for* offense and defense; alliance *of*, *between*, or *among* nations.

Allied. Wit allied *to* madness, a state allied *with* another.

Alter *from* one form *to* another.

Amazement *at* such reckless driving.

Ambitious *of* power.

Amused *with* toys, *at* a remark or a situation.

The **analogy** *between* a society and the plant body; the analogy *of* sound *to* light.

Anger *at* the insult prompted a retort in kind; anger *toward* an offender exaggerates the offense; angry *with* a person.

An **answer** *to* the question, *in* writing, *by* post, or *by* word of mouth.

Antipathy *to* (sometimes *for* or *against*) a person or thing; antipathy *between* two persons.

Anxious *for* a decision, *about* or *concerning* a person's safety.

An **apology** *to* a person *for* an error is fitting.

Appeal *to* an authority, *from* a decision, *for* help.

Appear *at* the theater, *among* the first, *on* or *upon* the surface, *to* the eye, *in* evidence, *in* print, *from* reports, *near* the place, *before* the audience, *through* the mist; appear *for* in behalf of, or *against* one in court.

Apportion *to* each a fair share; apportion the property *among* the creditors, *between* two claimants; apportion *according to* rank, etc.

Apprehensive *of* danger, *for* one's safety.

Approximation *to* the correct solution.

Arraign *at* the bar, *before* the court, *of* or *for* a crime, *on* or *upon* an indictment.

Arrested *for* crime, *on* suspicion, *by* the officer, *on*, *upon*, or *by virtue of* a warrant.

Ask *for* a thing; ask a thing *of* or *from* a person; ask *after* or *about* one's health, welfare, friends, etc.

Astonished *at* a situation or a person's attitude, *by* an event.

Attend *to* (listen) instructions, *on* or *upon* (wait) an official or dignitary.

Attended *by* a train of servants, *with* difficulties, advantages, etc.

Behavior *of* a person *to* or *toward* people, *on* or *upon* the streets, *before* the multitude, or *in* a place, *with* companions.

Benevolence *of* or *from* a person, *to* or *toward* others.

Break *to* pieces or *in* pieces, *into* several pieces (when the object is thought of as divided rather than shattered), *with* a friend, *away from* a habit; break *into* a house, *out of* prison; break *across* one's knee; break *through* a barrier.

Burn *in* fire; burn *with* fire; burn *to* the ground; burn *to* ashes; burn *through* the skin or the roof; burn *into* the conscience, etc.

Call *on* or *upon* a person (to visit him), *after* (by the name of), *in* question, *at* a house.

Care *of* a property, *for* the future, *about* a matter.

Carry *to* a place; carry *from* or *out of* a place; carry qualities *into* conduct; carry *across* the street, *over* the bridge; carry a cable *under* the sea.

Catch *at* a straw; catch a person *by* the collar; catch a ball *with* the hand; catch a disease *from* a patient; catch one *in* the act, a bird *in* a snare.

Cause *of* disaster; cause *for* interference.

Change a house gown *for* a street dress; change *from* a caterpillar *to* or *into* a butterfly.

Cheat one *of* his desires, *out of* a right.

Choose *from* or *from among* a number; choose *out of* the army; choose *between* two, *among* many; choose *for* a purpose.

Commit *to* a person *for* safe-keeping; commit *to* prison *for* trial.

Complain *of* a thing *to* a person, *of* one person *to* another, *of* or *against* a person *for* an act, *to* an officer, *before* the court, *about* a thing.

Concerned *with* a person, *in* a result, *in* a proceeding, *about* a matter, *for* a person's health, etc.

Concur *with* a person, *in* an opinion.

Confirm *by* testimony; confirm *in* a belief.

Conformity *with* an opinion, *to* an order, custom, etc.

Considerate *of* a person's feelings.

Contend *with* a person, difficulties, trials, temptations, etc., *for* a principle, a truth, *against* an obstacle, *for* an object.

Contrast two things, one *with* another.

Controversy *with* a person, *between* two or more, *about* or *over* a subject.

Conversant *with* a subject or the facts in a case.

Conversation *with* people, *between* or *among* persons, *about* a matter.

Convey *to* a friend, a purchaser, etc.; convey *from* one place *to* another; convey *by* express, *by* hand, etc.

Copy *after* a person, a model, an example, *from* life, nature, *from* or *out of* a work.

Correspond *with* a person, *to* ideas, models, etc.

Deliver *from* temptation, *out of* difficulty, trouble, etc., *of* an opinion.

Die *of* fever, *by* violence; die *for* one's country; die *at* sea, *in* one's bed, *in* agony; die *to* the world.

Differ *among* themselves, *from* one another, *from* or *with* another in judgment, opinion, etc., *about*, *concerning* a question, subject, etc.

Discriminate *between* two or more things, one thing *from* another, *against* a person.

Disgusted *with* a person, *at*, *by*, *with* a thing.

Divide *between* two, *among* two or more, *in* or *into* parts, something *with* another person, a thing *from* another, *upon* a question.

Draw water *from* or *out of* a well; draw one *into* an argument; draw *with* cords or ropes; the truck is drawn *by* a tractor *along* the road, *across* the lots, *over* the bridge, *through* the streets, *to* the station.

Employ *in*, *on*, *upon*, or *about* a work, business, etc., *for* a purpose, *at* a certain rate of salary or wage.

Entrance *into* a place, *on* or *upon* a work or course of action, *into* or *upon* office, *into* a contest, *by* or *through* a door, *within* the gates, *into* or *among* the company.

Envious *of* (formerly *at* or *against*) a person; envious *of* another's wealth or power.

Faint *with* hunger; faint *in* color.

Fall *under* censure, observation, etc., *from* a high place, *into* water, a hole, bad habits, etc., *on* or *upon* a foe, *among* thieves, *to* or *on* the ground.

Friendship *of* one person *for* or *toward* another, or friendship *between* persons.

Good *at* a business or task, *for* some purpose, *to* another person.

Gratified *at* an action or course of conduct.

Grief *at* a loss, *for* a friend.

Hanker *after* or *for* amusement, dainties, luxury, etc.

A result **happy** *for* a person; happy *at* a reply; happy *in* his home, *with* his friends, *among* his children; happy *at* a discovery, *over* a success.

Help *in* business or emergency, *with* money; help *to* success, *against* opposition.

Impatient *with* a person, *at* conduct, delay, etc., *for* something expected, *under* grief, misfortune, etc.

Injury *of* a cause; injury *to* a structure; injury *by* fire, *by* or *from* collision, interference, etc.

Inquisitive *about*, *concerning*, *in regard to*, *regarding* matters.

Join *to* something more numerous or greater, *with* something equal.

A **journey** *from* Naples *to* Rome, *through* Mexico, *across* the continent, *over* the sea; a journey *into* Asia, *among* savages, *by* land, *by* rail, *for* health, *on* foot, *on* the cars, etc.

We **listen** *for* what we expect or desire to hear; we listen *to* what we actually do hear.

Love *of* country, *for* humanity; love *to* or *toward* God and man.

Made *of*, *out of* or *from* certain materials, *into* a certain form, *for* a certain purpose or person; made *with* hands, *by* hand.

Martyr *for* or *to* a cause, *to* disease, disappointment, sorrow, etc.

Mastery *of* a subject or a task, *over* an enemy or opponent.

Mourn *for* a loss, *over* misfortune or trouble.

Necessary *to* a purpose, *for* or *to* a result or a person. unity is necessary *to* completeness; decision is necessary *for* command, *for* or *in* a commander.

Offended *at* a remark or course of action, *by* a word or act, *with* a person.

Opinion *on* a question, *about* a subject or a person.

Opportunity *of* doing something, *for* service, thought, etc.

Pardon *for* the offenders, *for* all offenses; pardon *of* offenders or offenses.

Patient *of* toil, *with* a person, *toward* learners, *under* difficulty.

Plead *with* the tyrant, *for* the captive; plead *against* injustice; plead *to* the indictment, *at* the bar, *before* the court.

Pleasant *to*, *with* or *toward* persons, *about* a matter.

Present *to* a person, a person *with* something.

Prevail *on*, *upon*, or *with* (to persuade), *over* or *against* (to overcome).

Profit *of* labor, *on* capital, *in* business.

Provide *with* supplies, *for* the future, *against* misfortune.

Purchase *at* a price, *at* a public sale, *of* or *from* a person; *for* cash, *with* money, *on* time.

Rejoice *at* an occurrence or an event, *in* personal qualities or possessions.

Relieve *from* pain, trouble, *of* duty or responsibility.

Reproach a person *for* acts.

Rise *from* slumber; rise *to* an occasion or responsibility, *at* a summons; rise *with* the dawn.

Security *for* the payment *of* a debt; security *to* the state, *for* the prisoner, *in* a specified sum; security *from* attack, *against* loss.

Send *from* the hand *to* or *toward* a mark; send *to* a friend *by* a messenger or *by* mail; send a person *into* danger.

Shelter *under* a roof *from* a storm, *in* a stronghold, *behind* or *within* walls.

Skillful *at* or *in* a task, *with* tools.

Strive *with* or *against* a person opposed or a thing in opposition, *for* something to be obtained.

Suffer *from* a disease, *by* some one's act or conduct, *with* another (sympathy).

Taste *of* food, etc., *for* painting, music.

Versed *in* a subject.

CONJUNCTIONS

The correct use of conjunctions is necessary to well constructed, intelligible sentences. No matter how accurate a writer's use of other words may be, if he does not indicate appropriately the relations between words or clauses, his sentences cannot be clear.

Conjunctions are divided into two general classes, *co-ordinate* and *subordinate*.

A *co-ordinate* conjunction connects words, phrases, or clauses of the same rank; as, *and*, *but*, *or*, *nor*, *either*, *neither*: "Sun *and* moon are heavenly bodies." "To be *or* not to be, that is the question." "Be not overcome of evil, *but* overcome evil with good."

A *subordinate* conjunction connects clauses of different rank; as, *since*, *unless*, *because*, *for*, *if*, *though*, *although*: "*Unless* it rains, the crops will fail."

Conjunctions include adverbs used as conjunctions and known as *conjunctive adverbs*, such as *when*, *where*, *whence*, *whereby*, *while*, *why*: "*While* we sleep, the body is rebuilt."

Correlative conjunctions are those which are used in pairs; as, *both—and*, *either—or*, *neither—nor*, *whether—or*, *though—yet*: "He *neither* ate *nor* slept." "*Though* all men deny Thee, *yet* will I not."

The following list of the more important English conjunctions shows varied shades of meaning that these parts of speech may assume, according to the demands of the different sentences in which they are used.

Although and **Though.** These words do not differ in meaning. They introduce concessive ideas: "We must be content with this, *though* we had hoped for more." "*Although* clear writing is difficult to produce, it is worth earnest endeavor." Equivalent phrases are: *in spite of the fact that*; *granted that*; *albeit*. *Even though* is more emphatic, as *although* was formerly more emphatic than *though*.

And. The most nearly universal connective. It is the original Saxon word used to join sentence elements that are grammatically alike and is the typical copulative of narration. It has, besides, a variety of effective uses as follows: (1) to intensify a statement,—"He talked on for hours *and* hours"; "They worked, *and* worked hard, to get results"; (2) as almost equivalent to *but*,—"It is one thing to plan *and* quite another to carry out plans"; (3) in such expressions as "There are boys *and* boys," indicating differences of condition, class, or character; (4) to express result,—"After long search he found the lode *and* became very wealthy." *And* may be used to begin a sentence, especially where some feeling or thought of surprise or reproach is implied: "*And* did you once see Shelley plain?" "*And* do you mean to tell me such a story?"

As. Used where comparisons of quality, close likeness, or proportion are implied: "He was as happy *as* only a man with a clear conscience can be"; "*As* we approached the rapids, the roar became deafening." *As* may denote cause or reason: "*As* the ship was unseaworthy, it was abandoned."

Because. Originally a phrase consisting of preposition and substantive, *by cause*. The word signifies *for the reason that* or *in consequence of*. See *For*.

Both. This conjunction is used regularly to precede the first of two co-ordinate words or phrases, and is followed by *and* before the second. It signifies *alike*, *as well as*, *too*, *also*; "a masterpiece for *both* argument and style." It may follow the co-ordinate words; as, "Malice mars logic and charity *both* (*alike*, *too*, *also*)."

But. Used in a great variety of ways, the primary sense being that of contrast or opposition: "His progress was slow *but* sure"; "We cannot *but* believe." Sometimes *but* implies a concession:

"Lincoln is dead, *but* the government at Washington still lives." *But* may mean "that—not": "There is no rose *but* bears its thorn."

Either. A disjunctive connective used before two co-ordinated alternatives and followed by the correlative *or*: "*Either* the light is distant *or* it is dim." "We must *either* stay where we are *or* risk being carried away by the flood."

Ere. A conjunction used mostly in poetry, thus differing from its synonym, *before*: "We shall meet *ere* set of sun." *Ere* must be distinguished carefully from *e'er*, which is a poetic contraction of *ever*.

Except. The use of *unless* instead of *except* is preferred by modern writers: "I will not be satisfied *unless* (*except*) you come." After *except* or *unless*, the phrases *it be*, *it were*, etc. are frequently used instead of repeating the principal verb: "He never goes to church *except it be* (he goes) to hear the music." "He seldom laughed *except it were* (he laughed) at his own jokes."

For. As a conjunction, *for* introduces only clauses or sentences of cause or reason. It should be distinguished carefully from *as*, *since*, *because*. *Because* is now used to introduce a real cause; as, "The water boils *because* it is heated." But one may say, "The water must be hot, *for* I saw John light the gas." In the latter case, *for* introduces a reason for a belief. *As* and *since* introduce causes or reasons that may be taken for granted: "*Since* (*as*) the hat was mine, I took it."

If. Used to introduce a clause of condition with the *subjunctive* signifying *doubt*, and with the *indicative* implying *suspended opinion* in regard to a statement: "*If* that be true, this is false." "He shall not secure the property *if* we can prevent it." *If* also introduces a concession, as equivalent to *although*: "*If* (*although*) he is competent, he sometimes makes mistakes."

Lest. Used to introduce a negative intention or purpose, equivalent to *that—not* or *for fear that*: "We hastened to return *lest* our friends should be alarmed."

Neither. The negative of *either*, used to introduce the first of two or more co-ordinate words or clauses, and followed by *nor*: "They had *neither* food *nor* clothing." "Quarter was *neither* given *nor* asked."

Nevertheless. In meaning, this compound is equivalent to *yet*, *notwithstanding*, or *in spite of that*: "Although entrance is forbidden, *nevertheless* they will use the house."

Nor. See *Neither*.

Notwithstanding. Equivalent in meaning to *although* or *in spite of the fact that*: "John was a stranger to most of the villagers, *notwithstanding* he had lived in Oakfield for thirty years."

Or. See *Either*.

Save. Used with the force of a conjunction, this word is equivalent to *except* or *unless*: "The night was still, *save* that the distant cataract rumbled steadily." "'Tis said there were no thought of hell, *save* (*unless*) hell were taught."

Since. This word denotes either sequence or duration in time or a logical relation. As applied to time, it signifies *from* a time or *subsequent to* or *during* a time: "Many years have passed *since* they met." "It is a fortnight *since* he embarked." Logically, *since* means *because* or *inasmuch as*: "*Since* she has inquired, you may give her the facts."

So. In its conjunctive use, this particle has the sense of *provided that*, *on condition that*; as, "They will be satisfied, *so* their children receive an education." It is used also to introduce a clause of result; as, "The car had disappeared, *so* the entire party walked home."

Than. Formerly this word was thought of both as conjunction and as preposition, and such expressions as "older *than* me," "taller *than* him" were allowable. Now, however, *than* is recognized only as a conjunction; hence one must say "older *than* I," "taller *than* he." The expression *than whom* is an exception to the rule given; as, "Roosevelt, *than whom* no American has been better loved or more sincerely hated." This construction is now universally approved.

That. A few common uses of *that* should be noticed. Besides being generally used to introduce an objective or adjective clause, *that* is likewise employed to denote time, definitely or indefinitely: "It is time *that* we should be going home." "We left the day *that* he arrived." It may also denote the relation of purpose or result: "He was given leave *that* he might go to Paris." Both in speaking and in writing we often omit *that* when the connection may readily be supplied: "We believe (*that*) the work can be done in a week."

Therefore. A conjunction of formal sense, used to introduce a conclusion or consequence. Its meanings may be expressed by *in consequence*, *for this reason*, *on that ground*, *consequently*: "We have completed our examination of the case; *therefore* we should make our report."

Till, Until. These two words are used as conjunctions without any difference in meaning. Their general sense is that of expectancy or continuance, expressed by (*up*) *to the time when*: "They could not vote *until* the polls were opened." "It was his custom to remain in the house *till* darkness had fallen."

Unless. A word compounded of *on* and *less*, and meaning literally *in less* or *on less*, that is, *on any less grounds or condition than*, the conditions being stated in a following clause. Other equivalent phrases are *if—not*, *in the event that—not*, *supposing that—not*. The following are typical uses of the word: "How shall they learn *unless* they are willing to hear?" "*Unless* the government's plans miscarry, the ships will be built." "I cannot explain his conduct, *unless* he has not been warned."

Whereas. A conjunction of two principal uses: (1) In formal documents and arguments, expressing the idea of *since*, *considering*, it introduces a preamble or a reason upon which a conclusion or a resolution is based: "*Whereas*, The society has accepted the plan of the committee, therefore, be it Resolved, etc." (2) Like *although*, it may imply a contradiction between the clause it introduces and a preceding statement: "They claimed a victory, *whereas* they had really lost the contest."

Whether. As a conjunction, this word introduces an implied question. (1) It may introduce alternatives, followed by *or* before the second alternative: "He was uncertain *whether* he should reply *or* be silent." When the second alternative is a negative of the first, it is frequently expressed by *not* or *no* following *or*: "They will move, *whether* the order arrives *or not*." (2) It may introduce a single indirect question, with an alternative omitted but implied: "We do not know *whether* he has read that book (*or not*) (*or some other*)."

While. Used of time, in the sense of *as long as* or *during the time that*: "*While* I was musing, the fire burned." It may also have the sense of *although*, implying some contradiction: "*While* the cloth is very heavy, it is not firm in texture."

Yet. As a conjunction, meaning *however*, *nevertheless*, *yet* implies usually some opposition, or unlikeness: "The board approved the plan, *yet* was not ready to act." "The tools are similar in form, *yet* very different in use." It may be used in the sense of *although*, signifying a concession: "They were determined, *yet* courteous."

CAPITAL LETTERS

In early forms of writing, capital letters were exclusively employed. Gradually small letters appeared and initial letters were used at the beginnings of sections and paragraphs only. Later the first word of a sentence was capitalized to call attention to its importance. Finally words within the sentence were treated in the same manner. It became the custom to begin every noun with a capital. This custom however, conducing to no useful end, has long since been laid aside.

Modern capitalization is determined somewhat by the thought to be conveyed. The chief uses of capitals are (1) to show the beginning of a unit of thought; (2) to give particular prominence to certain words, as names of countries, cities, persons, etc.; (3) to relieve the uniformity of the page.

Certain rules for capitalization are fixed. However, a slight variation in some instances may result from the individual usage of competent writers.

In the sciences, such as botany and geology, as well as in other departments of knowledge, certain customs of capitalization have become well established. Many of these special rules are to be found in the "stylebooks" issued by various publishers.

The following list contains the most generally approved rules and customs of capitalization in present day writing:

RULES FOR CAPITALS

1. The first word of every sentence should begin with a capital.

We receive good by doing good.
Always speak the truth.

2. The first word of every line of poetry should begin with a capital.

Like to a coin, passing from hand to hand,
Are common memories, and day by day
The sharpness of their impress wears away.

3. The first word of every direct quotation should begin with a capital.

Coleridge said, "Friendship is a sheltering tree."

4. The first word of every direct question should begin with a capital.

Ask yourself this question: Are you making the best use of your time?

5. The pronoun I and the interjection O should be capitalized.

Guide me, O thou great Jehovah.

6. Every proper noun should begin with a capital letter.

Europe, America, Chicago, James.

7. Words derived from proper nouns should begin with capitals unless, by long usage, they have lost all association with the nouns from which they are derived.

American, Americanize, Christian, Christianize, Roman, Hebrew, Elizabethan, etc.

But china dishes, india ink, prussian blue, turkey red, majolica ware, delft, castile soap, oriental rugs, galvanize, pasteurize, romance.

Capitalize all abbreviations of proper names.

Eng. (England), Sun. (Sunday), N. J. (New Jersey)

8. Names of geographical sections of the world, when used as proper nouns, should be capitalized.

The Far North, the Orient, the Near East, the Riviera, in the West.

9. The words North, South, East, and West and their compounds should begin with capitals whenever they refer to parts of the country, and not simply to points of the compass.

I have a friend in the South.
The river flows southwest.
Gold is found in the great Northwest.

10. The names of the days of the week, of the months of the year, and of feasts, fasts, festivals, and holidays, both religious and civic, should begin with capitals.

Tuesday, June, Arbor Day, Easter.

The names of the seasons are not capitalized except when personified.

The New England autumn is a delightful season.
Thou breath of Autumn's being.

11. Names of personified objects should be capitalized.

O Death! where is thy sting?
Then Memory disclosed her face divine.

12. All names and expressions which may be regarded as titles of the Deity should be capitalized.

Lord, God, Father, Son, Son of Man, Heavenly Father. But write King of kings, Father of mercies, Prince of peace, where the phrase is merely descriptive and not an essential part of the name.

As a rule, a personal pronoun referring to Deity should be capitalized when the meaning might otherwise be mistaken.

Be true thyself, and follow Me!

In general, do not capitalize a relative pronoun referring to Deity, because its antecedent is usually given.

Follow Him, whose truth shall deliver you.

13. The names of versions and of books and divisions of the Bible, names of sacred books of all religions, and titles of psalms and of parables should be capitalized.

Exodus, Psalms, New Testament, Epistle to the Romans, Sermon on the Mount, the Pentateuch, the Koran, Parable of the Vineyard.

14. The words street, river, gulf, sea, canal, coast, etc., may begin with capital letters when they are used in connection with proper names.

Bryant Street, Hudson River, Persian Gulf, North Sea, Erie Canal, Pacific Coast.

15. Names of political parties and of religious organizations, and generally the first word and all other important words in the names of societies and corporations, should be capitalized.

Conservative, Liberal, Republican, Democrat, Presbyterians, The Society for the Prevention of Cruelty to Animals.

16. Capitalize the first word and all other words, except articles, prepositions, and conjunctions, in titles of books, poems, essays, periodicals, plays, and pictures.

Gray's Elegy in a Country Churchyard.
Hawthorne's The Great Stone Face.
The Inside of the Cup.

Some publishers and the American Library Association capitalize only the first word and proper nouns and proper adjectives in titles.

A history of English local government.

17. Titles of honor, of respect, and of relationship, when used before the names of persons, should be capitalized; but, when used after the name, such titles are not capitalized.

King George, President Truman, Sir James, Uncle John, Aunt Edith.
Harry S. Truman, president of the United States; Honorable Joseph W. Martin, Jr., representative from Massachusetts. George VI, king of Great Britain.

Abbreviated titles of honor or respect should be capitalized.

James Bryce, D.C.L.; Dr. S. Weir Mitchell; Henry Brown, D.D., LL.D.

18. Names of important historical events and movements are capitalized.

The Revolution, the Reformation, the Colonial Period, the Renaissance, the Space Age.

19. In formal resolutions, capitalize the words Whereas and Resolved and the word immediately following each.

Whereas, This society, etc.; therefore, be it Resolved, That the office of secretary, etc.

PUNCTUATION

Punctuation is the art of separating composition or discourse into sentences, and members of a sentence, by means of certain marks or points (1) to make clear the author's meaning and (2) to show grammatical relations between words.

In spoken language, these relations are indicated by the pauses and by the inflections of the voice; but in written language there are no such aids, and it is necessary to supply the deficiency with definite marks.

As a means of conveying thought, punctuation does not generally receive the attention its importance demands. An omission, an insertion, or a transposition of points may completely alter the meaning of a sentence. To illustrate: An English statesman, having charged a government officer with dishonesty, was required publicly to retract the accusation in the House of Commons. The statesman read the following recantation: "I said he was dishonest, it is true; and I am sorry for it." The following day the papers printed the retraction thus: "I said he was dishonest; it is true, and I am sorry for it." By a simple transposition of the comma and the semicolon, the printed statement not only failed to carry an apology, but it also reiterated the original charge of dishonesty.

To a limited extent it is true that usage varies. But it is equally true that, as an art, punctuation is founded upon certain definite principles; and, while some latitude is allowed in their application, whatever directly violates these principles is incorrect and inadmissible.

Punctuation is, therefore, an essential part of good writing. A clear idea of what one wishes to say, a knowledge of the structure of sentences, and intelligent care in the application of definite rules will do much to perfect one in the use of this important art.

The generally accepted rules for punctuation are as follows:

Rules for Punctuation

The Period

1. A period should be placed at the close of every declarative or imperative sentence.

Washington is a beautiful city.
Think before you speak.

2. Place a period after all abbreviations, but not after chemical symbols, Roman numerals, per cent, or 8vo, 4to, 2d, 9th, etc. When an abbreviation ends a sentence, use only one period.

I know John Jones, M.D., LL.D.

When omission of letters is indicated by an apostrophe, a period is not used after the contraction: m'f'g for manufacturing; ass'n for association.

3. A period is not necessary after titles, headings, etc., on a page; but subheads and paragraph topics, not in separate lines, should be followed by a period.

The Exclamation Point

1. Place an exclamation point after every exclamatory sentence and after interjections and other expressions of emotion.

How welcome is the rain!
Alas! He died on the battlefield.
God forbid! May I never see it again!

In some cases, when an interjection is very closely connected with other words, the exclamation point is not placed between them, but is reserved for the close of the expression.

Oh, never may sun that morrow see!

2. The exclamation point is often used to express contempt or sarcasm.

And he is a writer!

The Interrogation Point

1. Place an interrogation point at the end of every direct question.

Is he telling the truth?
She asked, "When does school begin?"

The Colon

1. Place a colon between the great divisions of sentences, when minor subdivisions occur that are separated by semicolons.

We perceive the shadow to have moved along the dial, but did not see it moving; we observe that the grass has grown, though it was impossible to see it grow: so the advances we make in knowledge, consisting of minute and gradual steps, are perceivable only after intervals of time.

2. The colon separates a clause from the following clause or group of clauses illustrating or amplifying its meaning.

There is a singular and perpetual charm in a letter of yours: it never grows old; it never loses its novelty.

3. A colon precedes a formal enumeration of particulars.

Man consists of three parts: first, the body, with its sensual appetites; second, the mind, with its thirst for knowledge and other noble aspirations; third, the soul, with its undying principle.

4. A colon should be used before a long direct quotation.

Lord Bacon said: "Reading maketh a full man; conference, a ready man; writing, an exact man."

5. A colon follows *thus*, *as follows*, *this*, *these*, and similar expressions, introducing a statement or a series of clauses.

His credentials are as follows: he has studied economics; he has employed men; he has succeeded in business.

6. A colon usually follows the salutation in a letter.

My dear Mary: Sirs:

In short, informal letters, a comma may be used.

My dear Friend,

The Semicolon

1. A semicolon should be used to separate the parts of a compound sentence, when one or both members contain commas.

Mirth should be the embroidery of conversation, not the web; and wit the ornament of the mind, not the furniture.

2. When two clauses are joined by *for*, *but*, *and*, or an equivalent word, the one clause perfect in itself, and the other added as a matter of inference, contrast, or explanation, they are separated by a semicolon.

Economy is no disgrace; for it is better to live on a little than to outlive a great deal.

3. When the parts of a compound sentence, even though they are short, are not closely connected in thought, they should be separated by a semicolon.

Man proposes; God disposes.

4. If a series of expressions depends on a commencing or concluding portion of the sentence, the expressions should be separated by semicolons.

If we think of glory in the field; of wisdom in the cabinet; of the purest patriotism; of the highest integrity, public and private; of morals * * *,—the august figure of Washington presents itself as the personification of all these ideas.

5. A semicolon is commonly used before and a comma after *as*, *viz.*, *to wit*, *namely*, *for example*, *i.e.*, or *that is*, when they precede examples or illustrations.

We have three great bulwarks of liberty; viz., schools, colleges, and universities.

The Comma

1. All nouns of direct address should be set off by commas.

Mary, shut the door.
I say, John, it is not true.

2. Parenthetical expressions or additional expressions that break the directness of the statement should be set off by commas.

Industry, as well as genius, is essential to the production of great works.
It is mind, after all, that does the work of the world.

3. Words or expressions used in apposition should be set off from the rest of the sentence by commas.

Milton, the blind poet, wrote *Paradise Lost*.
We, the people of the United States, do ordain and establish this constitution.

4. A comma is used to mark the omission of words grammatically essential.

To err is human; to forgive, divine.
Go today if you can; if not, tomorrow.

5. A comma is used before a short direct quotation or question.

He said, "Time will tell."
Jane shouted, "Are you going?"

6. A nominative absolute construction or an expression used independently should be separated from the rest of the sentence by a comma.

To tell the truth, I do not know.
Rome having fallen, the world relapsed into barbarism.

7. A series of words in the same construction should be separated by commas.

Ulysses was wise, eloquent, cautious, and intrepid.
Men, women, and children filled the building.

8. When the subject consists of a series of words not joined by a conjunction, use a comma before the predicate.

Men, women, children, filled the building.

9. As a rule, when a clause is used as the subject of a verb, it should not, even though long, be followed by a comma, unless it ends with a verb.

That he is a man well qualified to fill the position must be admitted.
Whatever is, is right.

A comma is sometimes needed to prevent ambiguity.

He who teaches, often learns himself.

10. Use a comma between words in the same construction when they are modified in different ways.

They saw fields, and hills covered with trees.

11. When the separation of sentence elements is desirable and is slightly marked, a comma is used between co-ordinate clauses.

I heard him speak, but I made no reply.
Jane frowned, and her friend turned away.

12. Words used in pairs take a comma after each pair.

The dying man cares not for pomp or luxury, palace or estate, silver or gold.

13. A phrase or a clause out of its natural order should be separated from the rest of the sentence by a comma. If the sentence is short, the comma may be omitted.

Of the five races, the Caucasian is the most enlightened.
To those who labor, sleep is doubly pleasant.
With this I am satisfied.

14. In a complex sentence, if the dependent clause comes first, it should be followed by a comma.

Where I go, ye cannot come.

15. When two or more antecedent portions of a sentence have a common connection with some succeeding clause or word, a comma should be placed after each.

She is as tall, though not as handsome, as her sister.

16. A comma should be placed before a relative clause, when it is explanatory of the antecedent, or presents an additional thought.

Why ask John, who knows nothing about it?

A comma should not be placed between a restrictive adjunct or clause and that which it restricts.

Bring me the book that lies on the table.
Who can respect a man that is not governed by good principles?

Quotation Marks

1. Every direct quotation should be enclosed in double quotation marks.

Franklin said, "One today is worth two tomorrows."

2. A quotation within a quotation should be enclosed in single quotation marks.

Said he, "I quoted Burns's line, 'A man's a man for a' that.'"

3. Words or phrases of unusual, technical, or ironical meaning, or to which particular attention is directed, may be enclosed in single or double quotation marks.

Ann was made "master of ceremonies."
The phrase "producer to consumer" is popular.
He always talks about 'contacts and aerials.'

4. When a quotation consists of more than one paragraph, quotation marks should be placed at the *beginning* of *each* paragraph, but at the *end* of the *last* paragraph only.

The period and the comma are always placed inside the quotation marks. If at the close of a quotation any grammatical point other than the period or comma is required, it should be placed before the quotation marks if it is applicable to the quotation alone, but after them if it belongs to the sentence or member as a whole.

I read Tennyson's "In Memoriam."
He answered briefly, "Am I a knave that you should suspect me of this?"
Are our lots indeed cast "in the brazen age"?

The Parenthesis

1. Marks of parenthesis are used to enclose words loosely connected with the rest of the sentence in thought and structure.

Every star (and this great truth is inferred from indisputable facts) is the center of a planetary system.

Words within parenthesis should be punctuated as they would be in any other position, except before the last parenthetical mark. There, if the subject matter is complete in itself as regards both construction and sense, a period, an interrogation point, or an exclamation point should be used, according to the character of the sentence. If the parenthesis is incomplete in sense, there should be no point before the last mark.

Men are born equal (can you doubt it?); it is circumstances only that cast their lot in different stations.
Jane (such was her name) smiled sweetly.

The Dash

1. The dash is used to denote a sudden change in thought or in construction.

Closely following came—What do you suppose?

2. A dash is used after other points when a greater pause than they usually denote is required.

A traitor!—Yes.

3. A dash is used to set off parenthetical expressions which have a closer connection with the rest of the sentence than parenthesis marks would show.

You have a whole day—two days, if needful—to finish your work.

4. A dash is frequently used to set off an appositive or a supplementary word or phrase added for emphasis or for explanation.

He wrote an excellent article on chemistry—a subject to which he has devoted the greater part of his life.
Her features were plain but not repulsive—at least not so when you heard her speak.

The Hyphen

1. A hyphen should be used between syllables at the end of a line when a part of a word must be continued on the next line.

2. The hyphen is used in forming compound words which are not permanent compounds. Such words rightly united by a hyphen are of two kinds:

(1) Those used conventionally or for a certain occasion only.

A well-known man; fresh-water fish; open-hearth furnace.
After-deliberation showed they were wrong.

(2) Those which are attributively used as a phrase to transfer to an object a certain meaning that the literal sense of the words would not otherwise indicate.

A forget-me-not; Jack-in-the-pulpit; love-lies-bleeding.

An Early English Manuscript

Sumer is icumen in, loud sing cuckoo !
Groweth seed and bloweth mead and springeth the wood nu !
Ewe bleateth after lamb, loweth after calve cu,
Bullock sterteth, buck verteth, merry sing cuckoo !
        Cuckoo ! cuckoo !
Wel singes thu cuckoo : ne swick thu naver nu.

Along with Latin inscriptions, the words of the well-known "Cuckoo Song" are here reproduced from an old manuscript. Note the Anglo-Saxon characteristics which resemble modern German, as in "icumen" (gekommen) and "cu" (Kuh) for "cow." The now obsolete letter for "th" is seen in "springeth" and "the" in the third line. The long "s," which looks like an "f," appears here in both the English and the Latin script.

Geoffrey Chaucer (1328?–1400), the ''Father of English Poetry.'' Chaucer's storytelling ability was perhaps the greatest of all his talents. The *Canterbury Tales*, his most popular work, is one of the world's supreme masterpieces, but was left uncompleted at his death. Chaucer is credited, to a large degree, with the evolution of modern English, although the London dialect he used included many French words and spellings strange to later eyes. Among his works are: *The Flower and the Leaf, The Romaunt of the Rose, The Book of the Duchess, The House of Fame,* and *The Legend of Good Women.*

LANGUAGE AND LINGUISTICS

A person of native English speech who begins the study of any western European language, such as French or German, finds at once certain striking resemblances to English in forms of words and in grammar. The student of Latin and Greek observes similar likenesses among their evident dissimilarities. If he pursues his studies into the Slavic languages of Eastern Europe, such as Russian and Polish, he finds that they also resemble English in notable particulars. Further, similar phenomena appear to the student of certain ancient Asiatic languages, notably Zend and Sanskrit, the former spoken by the ancient Iranians or Persians, and deciphered only in the 19th century through its resemblance to Sanskrit, once the language of the Hindus.

Careful study of such facts has led scholars to the conclusion that all these languages are to be regarded as belonging to a great family of languages, sprung from a single tongue spoken by an ancient people of central Asia, to whom the term Aryan is sometimes applied. Properly, Aryan designates this ancient language, but it is used also to include all the ancient and modern languages which developed from it. This family is also called Indo-European, because its members are the great languages of India and Europe.

The outstanding characteristics of these Indo-European languages, which mark their relationship to each other and distinguish them from all others, are three: (1) They possess in common a number of words not found in other languages. (2) They indicate grammatical relations by means of endings added to words. (3) They are similar in the sounds they employ and in the general laws of their syntax. Other characteristics, also, such as uniform consonant changes, serve to distinguish groups and branches of languages within the general family. In the course of centuries, among different groups of people, the original consonant sounds in words have passed into other closely related sounds.

The close resemblance between the languages of Europe and those of India and Persia is shown clearly in the following table:

English	German	Latin	Greek	Zend	Tokhar	Sanskrit
mother	mutter	mater	mētēr	matar	macar	mātā
father	vater	pater	patēr	pitar	pacar	pitā
brother	bruder	frater	phratēr	brata	pracar	bhrātā

The Story of Old English. The beginnings of the English language, spoken today by more people than speak any one other tongue, are to be found in the dialects of the Saxons, Angles, and Jutes. At the invitation of British chieftains, these tribes came to Britain in the early part of the 5th century from the low-lying shores and islands of what are now the Dutch, German, and Danish North Sea coasts, bringing with them other adventurers from the Scandinavian countries. Having aided the Britons to drive back their foes, the Picts, these settlers turned upon the Britons themselves, forcing them back to the west and to the north. The Jutes settled in Kent, in the Southeast of England; the Angles, in the North, the East, and the Midlands; and the Saxons, in the South and the Southwest. The language of these tribes belonged to the West Germanic group of the Teutonic languages, and was more closely related to the Dutch than to the modern German.

From the old tongue of the conquered Britons a few words, such as *druid, bannock, down* (hill), *dun* (color), and perhaps *lawn* (land), with a few place names, entered the new language. The mingling of the dialects of the conquerors produced Anglo-Saxon or English Saxon, virtually a new language, the speech of the English Kin. This language had in it very little foreign element; it was highly inflected, and it formed new words from its own resources. Our words of common life, such as *while, nevertheless, man, god, loaf,* and *town,* indicate that Anglo-Saxon is still the bone and sinew of the English language.

Probably the tribes brought a few words of Latin origin, such as *mint* (money), *pound, mile, street,* and *church* (of Greek derivation), from the continent; for Roman and Greek merchants as well as Roman armies had penetrated to the lands along the North Sea. However, though the Romans had ruled Britain for 400 years and Latin had been spoken in the towns, the new conquerors seem to have found but few words they wished to adopt. The Latin *castra* (camp) survives in the name *Chester* and in other place names ending in *caster* and *cester*. The name *London,* of British origin, remains from this early time. But, with the coming of Christianity in the 6th century, numerous Latin words, such as *creed, verse, clerk, rose, lily,* and *turtle* (dove), were introduced. This number increased to perhaps 300 by the end of the 10th century.

In the 9th century the Danish or Scandinavian pirates overran the northeast districts of England,—Northumbria and Anglia; in the 10th century there were in this territory probably as many Danes as there were English; a Danish king ruled England in the early part of the 11th century. The conquest by the Danes was marked by pillage and cruelty, so that culture and literature were practically destroyed in the territory they ruled. For this reason, they left little trace of their language in the Anglo-Saxon of the time, though many words were preserved in local dialects and appeared in written English 200 years later. Curiously enough, these people gave to the English the word *law,* perhaps by way of the Dane law, as the district was called to which the West Saxon king Alfred at one time confined them. We owe to the Danes also such words as *call, care, fellow, husband, sister, die, same, thrive, take,* such place name endings as *-by, -thorpe, -thwaite,* and many surnames ending in *-son.*

While the Danes were harrying England, another body of Scandinavian rovers had settled in northern France. Normandy perpetuates the memory of these Northmen. Like their fellows in England, they adopted the tongue of their subjects, so producing the Norman French. Between these Normans and the Englishmen, intercourse grew in the 11th century. Edward the Confessor was educated in Normandy and to his court brought Normans, who made Norman French the language of the court society.

The Middle English Period. When William the Norman won the battle of Hastings in 1066, Anglo-Saxon fell to the position of the tongue of a conquered race, a people excluded from the court and from public office by decrees of the conqueror as well as by their own pride. Yet, though shut out from literary, courtly, and school use, the vitality of the language remained unimpaired. Not only did it maintain itself, but, when the struggle against royal tyranny in the 12th and the 13th century had wrung from King John a great charter written in Latin, and had brought Norman nobles and Saxon commons together in a common cause, English emerged as the language of the English Kin and their conquerors. We are told that about 1350 John Cornwall, a "master of grammar," changed instruction in his grammar school from French into English. In 1368 English was declared the language of the law courts. The poetry of Chaucer and the prose of the Wiclif-Purvey Bible raised the Midland dialect to the level of a literary language.

The language of this period, now called by scholars Middle English, was, however, very different from the Anglo-Saxon of 300 years earlier. It had dropped inflectional endings and had changed many spellings; it had lost some words and had borrowed from the French and the Latin many more. The arrangement of the words in a sentence was uncertain, since endings had been dropped and writers had set the words in what seemed to them, at the time, the best order. It was not until the 16th century that rules for word order were again reasonably well settled. A most important fact, however, is that in the 13th and the 14th century, through borrowing and Anglicizing, there began that generous enrichment of the language which has ever since characterized English speech.

The Anglo-Saxon Chronicle, which closed in 1154, contained a very few French words, such as *rent, treasure, countess,* and *castle;* but the immediate predecessors of Chaucer in the 14th century drew lavishly upon the French for synonyms and for words having no equivalent in the English. Already many Latin words had come in through the language of religion and the law. The new learning brought more, and, since most of the borrowed French words were of Latin origin, the total Latin element in English became very large. In everyday speech, however, the French is now the most striking part of our borrowed vocabulary.

From the 14th century to the 16th, with the Midland dialect, or London English, as a nucleus, the processes of forming the language on its new scale of greatness went on. Inflections were dropped, word order was fixed, spellings were changed, and new words were borrowed—some to be retained and others to be finally rejected. Thus the beginnings of modern English were prepared in the 16th century.

Making the Modern English. The 16th century translations of the Bible and the writings of Shakespeare and of other great Elizabethans contain many old forms of words and of grammar unfamiliar to us. But these works mark the beginning of modern English. Their wide circulation by means of the printing press has helped to stabilize the language, and, during the last three centuries, to make slower its rate of change in respect to spelling and grammar. However, as long as the language is living, changes will occur; some words will be dropped, new ones will be made or borrowed, and new meanings will be given to old words. In this modern period, the extension of commerce and the development of science have brought about the introduction of thousands of new words, science especially drawing very largely from the Greek.

A comparison of English synonyms tells vividly the story of this borrowing. For example, the word *royal* is from the French, *regal* is directly from the Latin, while *kingly* is the Anglo-Saxon word. These words, side by side, have taken on important distinctions of meaning. *Acute* is Latin, *keen* is Anglo-Saxon, *shrewd* appears in Middle English and probably is Anglo-Saxon. Similarly, *admit* is Latin; *receive* comes from the Latin through the French.

Another group of words, applying to manners and conduct, is illustrated by *brave,* which comes from either French or Italian. *Gallant* is directly from the French or Italian, though perhaps it was originally a German word. *Business* is of Anglo-Saxon or Danish origin, *trade* is Anglo-Saxon, while *profession* and *art* come from the Latin through the French. *Copy* comes from the French, *model* from the French or Italian, *pattern* from the French, *specimen* from the Latin. The business terms, *cost, expense, price, charge,* were very early taken into the language from the Old French.

The sources of the following synonyms, relating either to law or to religion, are interesting: *crime* comes from the Latin through the French, *vice* is from the same source, and *sin* is from the Anglo-Saxon; *holiness* is Anglo-Saxon, while *sanctity* comes directly from the Latin. The common word *draw* is Anglo-Saxon; its synonym, *haul,* is of French origin, perhaps originally from the German or

Scandinavian; while *pull* is Anglo-Saxon and *tug* is probably Scandinavian.

The following list of words of French origin will show to what degree the French element has been worked into our language of daily use: *age, air, aunt, beauty, boil, boot, broil, cape, card, chair, cloak, coat, cousin, cry, dainty, debt, dine, ease, engine, face, fame, fork, grace, hasty, jolly, justice, napkin, nephew, niece, peace, plate, river, roast, soil, supper, table, uncle, virtue.*

Another group will illustrate well the picturesque interest that may be found in English synonyms: *breeze* is French or Spanish; *gale* may be Danish; *blast* and *storm* are certainly Anglo-Saxon; *gust* finds a likely source in Icelandic; *tempest,* so common a colloquial word in New England, is from the Old French; while *hurricane* is a Carib word which has entered the English through the Spanish.

The Dutch were the sailors and traders of the 17th century, and they gave us such terms as *boom, skipper, sloop,* besides some common words like *spool* and *wagon.* From the Portuguese come the words *binnacle, caste,* and *junta.* From the Arabic, we get the words *alkali, algebra,* and *tariff.* Hebrew contributions to English are chiefly religious words: *cherub, seraph, hallelujah, Messiah, Satan, Jehovah. Cabal* is of this origin as is also *cinnamon,* itself borrowed by the Hebrew from some other source. *Pilgrim,* the earliest Italian word in English, is recorded in the 12th century. This was in the time of the Crusades. Since the 14th century, we have taken from the Italian many musical and art terms, such as *opera, fresco, prima donna, sonnet, cartoon, cameo.* Other words of Italian origin, some borrowed through the French, are *fiasco, alarm, piazza, balcony, caprice.*

American Words. America has added to our stock of words in several interesting ways. Exploration in the 16th and the 17th century brought us, through the Spanish, such words as *potato, tobacco, cargo,* and *banana.* The contact of Americans and Spaniards in the West has given us such words as *pueblo, burro, broncho, coyote, loco, adobe, mesa, cinch, tornado, ranch, canyon, arroyo,* and *stampede,* besides some slang words like *vamoose,* and, in the Southwest, hundreds of plant and place names, such as *chaparral, mesquite, madroña, manzanita,* and *tule, Sierra, Santa Fe,* and *Colorado.* At the present time, because of increasingly close relations with the South American countries, we are constantly getting words of Spanish origin, such as *peon* and *hacienda.* From the French in America we have taken over *depot, levee* (dike), *bayou,* and *crevasse,* also place names like *Butte, Boise, Saint Louis,* and *Terre Haute.* The Dutch in New York are responsible for the words *patroon* and *stoop* (porch or steps).

Out of our political life in America have come the words *congressional, presidential, federalist, nullification, gerrymander.* We have coined the word *mileage,* the word *eagle* means a coin, *corduroy* is American English for a kind of road, and we speak of *locating* land. *Outsider* and *creek* (stream) are Americanisms, while several old or dialect English words, such as *fall* (autumn), *rare* (underdone), *slump, spry, lam,* have been preserved in America. At Baltimore the word *clipper* was first applied to sharp-prowed, fast-sailing ships; and at Gloucester the first *schooner* was christened.

No less interesting are the words taken from the American Indians: *squaw, wigwam, pemmican, tepee, papoose, cayuse, hominy, moccasin, chinquapin, opossum, skunk, succotash, toboggan,* and very many place names like *Canandaigua, Spokane, Chautauqua, Chattahoochee,* and *Willamette.* Some of these Indian words, such as *tepee,* and place names, like *Willamette,* have been affected in form by the analogy of French, others by the Spanish, as *potato, tobacco.*

These illustrations will suggest that, in addition to the practical value to be realized from the study of words and the acquisition of skill in the use of

Mark Twain, whose boyhood experiences are reflected in his novel *Tom Sawyer*, was a great American humorist. His works—ranging from rustic comedy to philosophical discussions of mankind—have proved a rich vein of inspiration for dramatization.

A scene from Huckleberry Finn, Mark Twain's classic novel of life on the Mississippi River, is part of a mural the American artist Thomas Hart Benton painted for the Missouri State Capitol.

"When I was a boy, there was but one permanent ambition among my comrades in our village on the west bank of the Mississippi River. That was, to be a steamboatman."—Mark Twain

Life on the Mississippi

them, there is the further worth of such study as an approach to the history of the race. Words are the symbols of ideas, and ideas have made history.

Word Building. Many words, as they were needed to express ideas, have been built from simple forms by the process called "composition." The simplest sounds or groups of sounds that had, in the beginnings of language, a separate existence and meaning are called roots. Examples are *duc*, meaning "lead," *ag*, meaning "drive," *ed*, meaning "eat," *cad*, meaning "fall." By the addition of other so-called nominal roots, as *i* which appears now in the pronoun "it," we reach the stage of stems. So from *agri*, meaning "of a field," and *colere*, meaning "to cultivate," the Latin formed the word *agricola*, meaning "a cultivator of a field," or "a farmer."

Some simple words have had very little change from the earliest stems, except alteration of the vowel sound. Frequently this change has resulted from altering the position of the accent. The following will illustrate this development:

The word *arm* is from a root *ar*, meaning a "joint." This word is to be distinguished from the word *arms* or *arm*, meaning "weapons," which comes from the Latin, although the Latin word may be from the same source. The word *book* comes from the stem *boc*, meaning "beech," probably because in early times, in northern Europe, letters were carved upon blocks of beechwood or upon beech trees themselves.

Birth was not used in Old English but probably was taken later from the Old Norse. It is derived from an ancient Aryan stem allied to the Sanskrit *bhrti*, which meant "bearing." Bread was in Anglo-Saxon *bréad* and in Old Saxon *bröd*, having the meaning originally of "piece" or "fragment." The Anglo-Saxon rarely used this word to mean *bread*, employing instead the word *hláf* in the sense both of "bread" and of "loaf." However, before the beginning of the 13th century, *bread* came to mean the substance, and *hláf* assumed the limited meaning it still retains in loaf. *Comb* is from an ancient Teutonic root, related apparently to the Sanskrit *gambha*, meaning "jaw" or "teeth." *Deep* is from a very ancient root *dhup*, meaning originally "hollow." *God* seems to come from a root *g'heu*, meaning "to invoke." *Hand*, a common Teutonic word, is thought by some to be derived from a Gothic word *hinthan*, meaning "catch" or "take."

Language and History. In the vocabulary of the English tongue we find embodied the power men possess of readily and happily imaging or ideally representing the mysterious world in which we live. In our words are recorded their inventions as well as their ideals and schemes for the establishment of religion, society, and education. Here are mirrored the growth and the decay of ideas and ideals, the rise of the new and the displacement of the old. The lofty and the low in human thought and imagination are reflected in our language.

Our word *guest*, for example, is from the same root as is the Latin word *hostis* meaning "enemy," the original meaning of the root being "stranger." *Cheat* is from the old word *escheator*, the name of an officer whose duty it was to look after estates which, on the death of the owner, reverted to the state, a sense still retained in the legal term *escheat*. The real or suspected corruption of the *escheators* in the 15th or 16th century probably brought about the degradation of the word.

History finds still further illustration in such words as *cabal*, which comes from the Hebrew through the Latin and the French and meant originally "tradition." In the middle ages it came to mean "secret scheming," and in English this meaning was re-enforced by the fact that the initials of the names of five members of the Foreign Affairs Council of Charles II spelled this word *cabal*. In similar fashion, the words *earl* and *alderman* in their changing meanings represent much of English and American local government history.

The word *cross* suggests Christianity; but we should see in it also the early faith and learning of the great Irish schools of the 5th and the 6th century, from which the Norsemen of Northumbria took the word and passed it on to the Anglo-Saxons. Our word *world* also carries in its form the thinking of our pagan ancestors, who made it from *wer* meaning "man" and *old* meaning "age." It thus carries the sense of the "age of man or mankind," hence the "dwelling place of man."

In the early 13th century the foreign words in common use in English made up probably 12 per cent of the entire vocabulary. In Shakespeare's works the foreign element is estimated at 40 per cent. Today in our writing it is probably 60 per cent. It is estimated that in the dictionaries of today about 20 per cent of the words are of Anglo-Saxon origin, about 35 per cent are from the French, about 15 per cent from the Latin directly, about 12 per cent from the Greek. But the proportion of Anglo-Saxon words in our everyday speech is much greater than these figures show, because our grammar is English and our connective words, such as *or*, *and*, *but*, are Anglo-Saxon. The English language has borrowed vocabulary, but not syntax, and it has Anglicized foreign words. Therefore, in spite of great differences of spelling, pronunciation, and accent, we may include in the term *English* the Anglo-Saxon of the 7th century, the Middle English of the 14th century, and the tongue of today.

The making of dictionaries has maintained a record of words and usage which presents a vivid picture of the growth of the language in the last 300 years. Samuel Johnson's dictionary of 1755 contained about 15,000 words. The latest dictionaries record more than 400,000. It is estimated that the average person without special education may know and use from 5000 to 10,000 words, while the educated man may use and be familiar with the meanings of from 20,000 to 50,000.

SELECTED READINGS

ELEMENTARY

Alexander, Arthur—The Magic of Words.
Prentice Hall '61
Cahn, William and Rhoda—The Story of Writing: From Cave Art to Computer. *Harvey House '63*
Epstein, Sam and Beryl—The First Book of Words: Their Family Histories . . . . *Watts '54*
Ogg, Oscar—The 26 Letters . . . . . *Crowell '61*
Pei, Mario—All about Language . . *Lippincott '54*
Sparke, William—Story of the English Language . . . . *Abelard-Schuman '66*

ADVANCED

Barnett, Lincoln—The Treasure of Our Tongue.
New American Library '67
Bradley, Henry—*The Making of English.*
Walker '67
Carroll, John B.—The Study of Language.
Harvard University Press '53
Hogben, Lancelot—The Mother Tongue.
Norton '65
Hughes, John P.—The Science of Language.
Random House '62
Jespersen, Otto—Growth and Structure of the English Language . . . . *Norton '55*
—Language: Its Nature, Development and Origin . . . . *Norton '64*
Laird, Charlton—The Miracle of Language.
World '60
Marckwardt, Albert—American English.
. . . . *Oxford '58*
Mencken, H. L.—The American Language. Abridged edition . . . . *Knopf '63*
Pei, Mario—Voices of Man . *Humanities Press '64*

LINGUISTIC THEORY

In the section *Sentence Building*, English grammar is defined as a science that investigates the principles in general on which the English language is based. This section will discuss some attempts to formulate these general principles more precisely. We must also note the relevance of these formulations to the study of the language and to what in language study is not reached through linguistics.

FORMAL GRAMMAR

Linguistics Theories. The material in *Sentence Building* represents a distillation of grammatical knowledge that has accumulated for well over 2000 years. It is only because of certain developments in techniques of processing data and in modern mathematics that alternative ways of handling the "stuff" of language have become possible. We can now usefully distinguish between two general kinds of linguistic theories. One, a descriptive linguistic theory, has in general rejected the insights and conclusions of the ancients. The descriptivists ignore all but a narrowly defined set of data. Thus a descriptive grammar emerges as a statement of the patterns into which the sentences naturally fall.

The other theory, transformational grammar, has attempted to formulate the insights of traditional, classical grammar and thus to deepen our understanding of the insights, rejecting some and going beyond in others. For the *transformational* grammarian the data to be accounted for includes, not only the sentences of the language, but also the intuitions that speakers of a language have into their language about the relatedness of sounds in related words (*divine*, *divinity*, etc.), the relatedness of structures in related sentences (John hit the ball, the ball was hit by John, etc.). The descriptivist considers nothing but the sentences themselves fair game for analysis and rejects mentalistic data.

THE GOALS OF LINGUISTIC THEORY

The goals of linguistic theory are importantly: (**a**) to establish a set of generalizations or rules (a grammar) that explains consistently and adequately the sentences of English. This set of rules will then amount to a theory about the nature of the knowledge, subconscious to be sure, that speakers have of their language; (**b**) to learn how children internalize and acquire such a grammar, quickly and without much overt attention to learning the language of their environment; (**c**) to understand how speakers of a language bring their internalized grammar to bear in producing and receiving utterances; (**d**) to discover the universal properties of grammar and of language.

At present we know very little about (**b**) and (**c**), but we are beginning to understand (**a**) somewhat. Our understanding of it is a necessary prerequisite to the study of (**b**) and (**c**). Let us summarize what we have said of (**a**) so far. We understand a grammar of a language to be a set of rules in explanation of the sentences of the language. This set of rules must be finite in number, for the human mind in which the rules are neurally represented is of course of finite capacity. Language has, however, this peculiar property—the range of data, the possible data, is infinite, theoretically unlimited. Although all sentences are of a definite length, there is no sentence that can be said to be the longest. Thus the set of possible sentences in a language cannot itself be finite. A grammar must then explain infinity in a finite way. The ideas of deep and surface structures, of transformations, that allow certain structures such as a sentence to be embedded in other structures, are theoretically capable of handling this problem in a natural and adequate way. Furthermore, these notions are candidates for elaborating somewhat on (**d**) above, for universal properties of language.

PHONOLOGY: THE SOUND STRUCTURE OF LANGUAGE

Traditionally, grammars, have had little to say about phonology—at least school grammars. It is certainly of less interest, perhaps only less immediate interest, than the level of syntax, or sentence structure. This may be only because we attend to it less closely in using the language. As speakers and hearers, our purpose is to get quickly to meaning and to attend as little as possible to the actual sounds in the air.

However, the descriptive linguists made their most important contributions in the area of phonology. At this level of language structure they tried to establish the set of minimally distinct sounds for each language with which they worked. For example, since speakers could readily and consistently distinguish such pairs as *bat* and *pat*, it was clear that /b/ and /p/ were distinctive sound classes in English. (We shall follow the conventional practice of enclosing in virgules the symbol representing a distinctive sound class.) The differing /p/'s of *spat* (not followed by a puff of air—unaspirated), *pat* (aspirated), *tap* (often unexploded) do not constitute distinctive sound classes themselves—they are in fact members of the sound class /p/. Their differences are predictable on the basis of their positions with respect to the other sounds of the words.

The descriptive linguist thus worked to establish the set of distinctive sounds for each language and for each language to state the distribution of these classes and their members one to another. He also tried to describe the difference of stress or prominence of syllables in words and word groups. For example, in such pairs as *black bird* and *blackbird*, in the first case the vowel of *bird* is more prominent than *black*; in the second case the opposite is true.

But because these linguists operated without a sense of complicated rules that lead from abstract representations to concrete, their discussions of phonology lacked insight and generality. Again, neglecting notions of relatedness and concentrating too much on superficial identity, they missed the obvious. They recognized, for example, that the antepenultimate sound of *rejection* (re-jek'**sh**un) was the same as the first sound of *ship* (**sh**ip). But they failed to relate the /sh/ of *rejection* to the *t* of *reject*, to free this /sh/ from any but a superficial relationship to the /sh/ of *ship*.

The descriptivists noted that there was a difference between *black bird* and *blackbird* without accounting for the general properties of that difference. Consider that, if we say *black* and *bird* separately, they will have equal prominence.

In the discussion of phonology, generalizations of the power mentioned above are a goal, both in dealing with stress and with the relationships among individual sounds.

THE GENERAL STRUCTURE OF GRAMMARS

In a very informal way we have seen that generalizations about syntax and phonology, about sentence structure and sound structure, have much in common. There are abstract representations and rules that mediate from these to concrete representations—the structures and sounds of real-life sentences. About another aspect of language, *meaning*, very little in the way of formal analysis can be given. We know that the relationship between sound and meaning is an arbitrary one. There is no way, for instance, in a language one knows nothing about, to get the meaning of a word or a sentence from its sound alone, though one may well get the emotional intention from the quality of the voice alone. From this, one can suggest that it is the syntactic component of a grammar that forms a bridge between sound and meaning. The following diagram captures the relationships among the parts of a grammar:

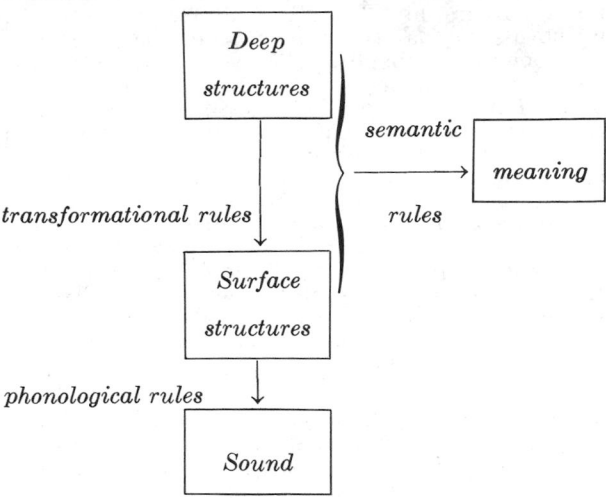

In receiving a sentence, one has somehow to construct from the sounds he hears a deep structure and its transformational relationship to a surface structure related to the sounds. From the deep structure and the transformations, meaning is somehow abstracted. Even more mysteriously, in uttering a sentence, a speaker must convert some intended meaning into sounds. Syntax in both these processes is the central component. This much seems certain. Exactly how it is that the mind attends to the finer details of the business of language, we have no idea. We are beginning to understand the nature of syntax and phonology and in that understanding lie the clues for understanding the nature of human intelligence itself.

THE USES OF LINGUISTICS

The uses of linguistics, real and imagined, are many. Here we shall deal only with the aims of formal grammar study. That is, why study the formal grammar of a language (English) of which you are a native speaker? And if it is studied, how should it be studied?

Goals of Grammar Study. Traditionally, the pedagogical aims of grammar study have been (a) to teach mental discipline, and (b) to improve verbal expression, both oral and written. What exactly *mental discipline* is to mean is not very clear, but we shall spend the greater part of this section trying to clarify what it *can* mean and *how* to accomplish it.

Mental Discipline. Some interesting substance can be given to the notion "mental discipline". It is clearly a goal of education to develop the intellect, to develop the rational powers of man so that he can introduce a sense of order into the chaos that surrounds him. In part, at least, this is what rational science is about—discovering the order underlying a seemingly confused and mad array of data. Insofar as grammar is a science, the goal of grammar is thus to discover a convincing order in the data of English. This point of view is exactly what we have presented in some detail above. If in the limited area of language that one is able to introduce to capture the order underlying chaos, it is possible that he may bring these analytic powers so developed to bear on other areas, discovering the order there or indeed that there is no order there.

From language study we can learn the ways of constructing theory. We can then hope that these ways will be transferred into other areas of study and life. This is what *mental discipline* can mean. Whether any of this is possible depends in part on how the formal properties of language are taught or learned. Traditionally, grammar teaching has simply consisted of a teacher or book presenting to the learner the formal rules of grammar. Rote learning is the rule. And this tradition has been maintained regardless of the theory of language from which the rules derive—presentation of rules and rote learning characterize the books and the teaching of traditional grammar, descriptive grammar, and transformational grammar.

If it is a goal of grammar study simply to learn a set of rules, then these books and the usual way of teaching from them will presumably reach that end. But, if the goal is for the individual or the class to reach towards an adequate and consistent theory of English sentences, then these materials and these ways of teaching are totally inadequate.

Learning Grammar. Granted that our goals are correct, we must consider other means of achieving them, for they will not be reached by rule-presentation and rote learning. Consider these alternatives:

(a) let the rules of a grammar book be taken as hypotheses, as terms in a theory of grammar, to be tested for their adequacy; (b) let the individual or class try to construct on the basis of their own sentences a set of rules, an hypothesis, about English sentences; then test the hypothesis against additional data and intuitions about English sentences.

Of course the notion of validating a grammar is quite far from what usually transpires in a grammar classroom, for grammar has come to be the Procrustean bed into which sentences must be crammed rather than a genuine scientific theory that must change, and be reformulated to accommodate the data. Grammar is truly a scientific endeavor only if it answers objections; if it ignores them, it is not.

Classroom grammar study can then be an attempt to construct a theory of what, as a speaker of the language, one already knows. Language, unlike history for example, is peculiarly adapted to this kind of study. For language is part of us all—it is ours by virtue of our humanness.

Working in ways sketched here, one can learn and teach grammar, seeking always better and more consistent generalizations that cover the data. Theories are constructed, destroyed, and modified as our preception of the data requires.

There are always questions of formal grammar left unanswered. It makes constructing a theory of a language all the more exciting and all the more engaging as a classroom activity.

The formal study of grammar should be approached with a desire to seek the best answers, to seek truth, not fiction. This search can best go forward in the framework of theory and pedagogy.

BEYOND GRAMMAR

There is, of course, much more than grammar to the study of language. Grammar is central, but there are other things of interest to deal with even though this must be done in quite informal ways. For example, what are we to say of meaning? of the structure of language units that go beyond the individual sentences? of the social and cultural connections of language, etc.? The present section concludes with some discussion of this last question.

In the formal structure of grammar, there are many slight differences among speakers of the same language. These *dialect* distinctions are attributable to nothing more than the natural separation of groups and individuals. Value judgments must be made carefully, since the differences are as natural as the geographical differences in similar plants and birds. It is often the case that the poor and the dispossessed speak a regional dialect different from that of the leaders of a community, and these differences are sometimes used to maintain the *status quo*. If society offers each person the same chances, then he will, up to his individual ability, develop ways of dealing with those chances in words and in actions.

WRITING AND SPEAKING

THE power to use effective language brings to its possessor ability to lead in social and civic affairs. Besides, more often than we commonly realize, personal success depends upon a command of good English.

Putting your thoughts together well in the sentences you speak or write is, therefore, always important. The social, professional, or business world measures you by the fitness of your language for the work you intend it to do. On the other hand, through persistent effort to adapt your language to your purposes, you gain a sense of self-command, an ease of manner, and a satisfying confidence in meeting people socially and in business.

Effective Language. Four requirements measure this fitness of language: *correctness, clearness, force, beauty.* Language is *correct* when it expresses thought in approved form. It is *clear* when those who hear or read it understand readily the thought of the speaker or writer. It is *forceful* when it interests those who hear or read it and impels them to respond according to the purposes of the speaker or writer. It is *beautiful* if it is correct, clear, and forceful, and also pleasing in sound or suggestion.

The art of expressing thought or feeling in effective language is called Rhetoric. The principles that govern the use of this effective language are rhetorical principles. One great principle underlies all others; namely, that true effectiveness of language depends upon the sincerity of the speaker or writer.

Semantics: Choosing and Arranging Words. Semantics is that branch of linguistics concerned with the meaning of words. Over and beyond the sincerity and enthusiasm of the speaker or writer is the choice of words to convey precise meaning, subtleties of connotation, avoidance of ambiguities, and to provide a climate of meaning by the use of well chosen words or signs. Language has no meaning apart from the thought it expresses.

You want to find pleasure in carrying on conversation with a friend or a stranger. You may have to make a report upon some work. You may want to sell a house or secure the interest and the support of voters in an election. You may want to persuade a friend to give up a harmful habit. You may have to convince a hostile audience of the truth of your opinions. In conversation you will be alert, interested, and responsive; in reporting, cool and accurate; in persuasion, positive, earnest, and impassioned. These are your personal problems. They will make you prize every help toward mastery of language.

Ordering of Thought. Both in speaking and in writing it is of the utmost importance to marshal the parts of a discourse into an effective order. This careful observance of arrangement should be followed both in regard to the discourse as a whole and in regard to each portion of it which deals with a single thought. The divisions into which a discourse falls when thus logically ordered are usually indicated by some more or less mechanical means. In speech, a judicious use of pauses and of vocal inflections serves the purpose, and in written compositions we employ the device of paragraphing.

The Paragraph. This term means a group of sentences in which a single subject is discussed, its beginning being marked usually by indention, or setting the first word a little to the right of the usual margin. This group of sentences may make a separate unit, as in the editorial columns of a newspaper, or it may serve as a division of a longer article. The structure and the length of the paragraph are matters of logic and convenience. Too long a paragraph, as well as a succession of very short ones, is to be avoided.

There are three important rhetorical requirements for a paragraph. The first requirement is *unity,* which means that there must be in the paragraph only one main thought. The second requirement is *coherence,* which implies that the sentences in the paragraph must be well connected and arranged so that each added thought helps to make the main idea clearer and more forceful. The third requirement is *emphasis,* which demands that the more important sentences shall be so placed in relation to the others as to draw immediate attention. Arranging sentences in contrasting pairs, or in order of climax, and alternating long and short sentences—these are means of securing emphasis. The beginning and the end of a paragraph are usually the most emphatic positions for sentences.

The purpose of the paragraph is to develop an idea, or, as often in stories, a single situation. Development means, literally, unfolding the subject so that the reader may understand the topic better or see the situation more clearly. To this end, give details, comparisons, and examples, or repeat ideas in slightly different words. Clearness is frequently effected by using vivid contrasts. The main idea should be stated in a single sentence, preferably either near the beginning or near the close of the paragraph. The following paragraph from *Ancient Times* by James H. Breasted illustrates well these methods of development:

"The Phœnicians learned the methods of manufacturing their goods, in almost all cases, from Egypt. There they learned to make glass and porcelain, to weave linen and dye it, to cast and hammer and engrave metal. On the other hand, we find that the *designs* employed in their art were international. Their metal platters they engraved with designs which they found in both Egypt and Asia. The art of Phœnicia was thus a kind of oriental composite or combination, drawn chiefly from the Nile and the Two Rivers. We remember that it was Phœnician workmen whom the Assyrian kings employed to make furniture and metal work for the royal palace. King Solomon likewise employed Phœnician workmen to build for him the Hebrew temple at Jerusalem (I Kings, V). After 1000 B. C. the Phœnicians were thus the artistic manufacturers of a great world extending from Nineveh on the east to Greece on the west."

GENERAL FORM OF DISCOURSE

Expression in language assumes, in relation to the purposes for which it is used, several well-recognized forms or types of discourse. We give talks or addresses, or we write papers or articles; we argue, explain, describe, or tell a story. Practical methods for everyday use of these various forms are given in the following paragraphs:

EXPLANATION

A pencil seems to be a simple, everyday thing, but you may sometime ask yourself: *How is this pencil made? What is it made of? Could it be made better?* You discover a problem that needs explanation or clearing up. This problem concerns the parts of the pencil and the relations between them. Other questions arise: *Why are these particular materials used in the pencil? What is the history of pencil making? Why is this thing called "pencil"?* Similarly, such subjects as *How is a gas engine made?* or *What is a bank?* call for explanation. *The clear, orderly answering of these questions is explanation.*

The first step in explanation is to divide the subject into topics to be discussed. The purpose of division is to give logical orderliness and simplicity, and consequently clearness, to your composition. The method to be followed is that of the outline, as illustrated in the following examples.

The headings in these specimen outlines are numbered in several different ways, any one of which may properly be used. In any outline, however, the numbering must be consistent throughout.

Subject. The Pencil.
Introduction.
1. The pencil is a thing of common use, but its nature, history, and manufacture are little understood.
2. The study of the pencil under these heads may be both interesting and suggestive.

Body.
1. Taking a common pencil apart.
   a. The case of wood, paper, or metal.
   b. The "lead."
2. The history of the pencil.
   a. Early forms.
   b. The word "pencil."
3. Process of manufacture.
   a. Preparation of materials.
   b. Construction.

Conclusion.
1. Skill with the pencil.
2. A stock of pencils in a store and the occupations it may suggest.

Such an outline may serve for a single treatment of the subject, or any one of the headings may be used as a separate topic. It should then be outlined in this same form. For example:

Subject.—A Stock of Pencils.
1. Pencils for drawing.
2. Pencils for various kinds of writing.
3. Pencils of different shapes and sizes.

The following is another common form of outline:

HOW TO USE CONCRETE

I. What is concrete?
   A. Elements.
   B. Mixtures.

II. Uses of concrete.
   A. Substitute for stone and wood.
   B. Unique uses.

III. Mixing concrete.
   A. Proportions.
   B. Method.

IV. Forms.
   A. Construction.
   B. Method of use.

The second step is to look up information. A common and practical method for preserving facts is to copy information on cards about 3 by 5 inches in size, one fact or topic to a card, with a reference to book and page where the facts were secured. The habit of thus looking up and noting facts will help to develop careful and trustworthy thinking

The third step in planning explanation is the finding of apt comparisons; for we learn by observing likenesses and differences between things. The unknown or unfamiliar thing should be compared with something known or familiar. For example, to make dimensions clear, use comparisons in addition to figures. Compare a length of 15 or 20 feet to the length of a room, the extent of a small surface to a table top. Such expressions as *T-shape, S-shape, U-shape* are useful. More imaginative comparisons are suggested by figures of speech.

DESCRIPTION

Generally speaking, the purpose of description is to appeal so vividly to the senses through language that the reader or hearer feels as if he were actually in the presence of the object described. To produce good description: (1) Indicate clearly your point of view, that is, your position with reference to the thing described. A railroad wreck may be described by one who was a passenger on the wrecked train or by a reporter who was sent to the wreck. Their mental points of view will be different. A building or a mountain may be described as seen from a near-by or from a distant point. These different physical points of view determine the nature of the description. (2) Choose words to convey sense impressions, as of *sight, sound, smell, taste, touch.* (3) Select and use only such details as help to make the total impression clear and vivid. Notice the indications of the point of view and the appeals to the senses of sight, touch, and hearing in the italicized words of the following paragraphs:

"It was *close on noon*: there was no *breath* of wind, and the heat was scarce *bearable* when the two men came on deck, had the boat manned, and *passed down*, one after another, into the stern sheets. A *white* shirt at the end of an oar served as a flag of truce; and the men, by direction, and to give it the better chance to be observed, *pulled* with extreme slowness. The isle *shook* before them like a place *incandescent* on the face of the lagoon *blinding copper* suns, no bigger than *sixpences*, danced and *stabbed* them in the eyeball. There went up from sand and sea, and even from the boat, a *glare* of *scathing* brightness; and as they could only peer abroad from between closed lashes, the excess of light seemed to be changed into a *sinister* darkness, comparable to that of a *thundercloud* before it bursts."—Stevenson: *The Ebb Tide.*

"There could not be a more *somber* aspect of external nature than as then seen *from the windows of my study.* The great *willow tree* had caught and retained among its leaves a whole cataract of water, to be shaken down at intervals by the frequent *gusts* of wind. All day long, and for a week together, the rain was *drip-drip-dripping* and *splash-splash-splashing* from the eaves and *bubbling* and *foaming* into the tubs beneath the spouts. The old, *unpainted* shingles of the house and outbuildings were *black* with moisture, and the mosses of ancient growth upon the walls looked *green* and *fresh*, as if they were the newest things and afterthought of Time. The usually *mirrored* surface of the *river* was *blurred* by an infinity of raindrops. The whole landscape had a completely *water-soaked* appearance, conveying the impression that the earth was wet through *like a sponge*; while the summit of a *wooded hill*, about a *mile distant*, was enveloped in a dense mist, where the demon of the tempest seemed to have his abiding-place, and to be plotting still direr inclemencies."—Hawthorne: *Mosses from an Old Manse.*

NARRATION

This most interesting form of composition is simply the telling of stories.

Narration without Plot. This is telling about a series of actual events,—a day's travel, the course of an investigation, or a report of some piece of work. For telling such a story the most important directions are these: Select carefully the details to be told. Make a connected account that moves straight forward in the time order of events and is not lost in little, unimportant matters.

The carefully written news story furnishes a good example. It usually begins with a *lead*, that is, a first sentence that summarizes the most important features of the account. Then the connected story, consisting of several sentences or paragraphs, follows. See *The Book or Article Review.*

Description finds its chief use in helping to make narration or explanation vivid and interesting.

Narration with Plot. The telling of a story in such a way as to arouse interest and hold the hearer or reader in suspense and uncertainty as to the outcome of events. You can spoil an *anecdote* or a *story* by giving the "point" too soon. Even anecdotes have miniature plots. Give the setting or background and introduce the characters first, then bring in their action or conversation, and finally "come to the point or climax." This method secures suspense while your audience waits for the climax. A master of English fiction is credited with the following recipe for story-telling: "Make them laugh; make them cry; but make them wait."

For the composition of other story forms, see *Forms of Literary Composition; The Book or Article Review,—Plot; The Scenario.*

SPECIAL FORMS OF DISCOURSE

We find the General Forms of Composition most frequently useful in the immediate telling of a story or in the preparation of a talk, a paper, or an essay. These occasions usually call for combinations of argument, explanation, description, and narration. The following suggestions are helps in real problems. They serve to answer the questions: What shall I put into the toast, the talk, or the club paper? What shall I leave out? How shall I begin? Getting started is often the hardest problem. See *Public Speaking.*

THE CLUB PAPER

As a member of some organization, a club or society, you are often expected to read papers upon various subjects. The theme or subject is usually given in the program or course of reading. Frequently, however, your topic is too big or too general. When you come to the task of preparing the paper, you must narrow the theme to something that you can treat interestingly in fifteen to thirty minutes. Here are four important principles:

a. Two or three important points, not more, can be treated well in a brief time. The attention of an audience is easily exhausted by too many details.

b. Perfection in speaking and writing is achieved by leaving out superfluous matter.

c. Statements of principles, conditions, or definitions must be made plain by clear illustrations or examples.

d. A brief anecdote or story is often worth pages of laborious explanation.

Suggestion.—Suppose, then, that you have your subject. Whatever it may be, remember that many of the most interesting facts and illustrations for most subjects are things right around you, things that you can see and hear. Any given topic is related to many other themes and to many other fields of knowledge. To point out some of these relations is to enhance the clearness as well as the interest of your paper.

A topic in art, for example, as you begin to look it up, will suggest related topics in literature, in history, in geography, in biography. As you follow these suggestions you will find your paper growing, not as a task, but as a pleasant interest. Make notes of what you find in your reading. Follow each hint of a related topic. Make more notes.

The Working Plan

Always prepare an *outline*, or *working plan*. An outline shows a general sketch or an indication of a plan, a system, or a course of thought. See *Explanation for suggestions about reading and cards. For suggestions as to interesting order of topics*, see *The Advertisement. For suggestions as to presenting the paper*, see *Public Speaking*.

The following plans represent typical ways of dealing with various kinds of subjects:

Subjects which fall under the general theme, *Community Plans*, are very frequently used in club programs. They may be concerned with material improvements in streets or buildings, or with political or social plans and organizations. The following well-tested general order of discussion is appropriate and effective. Either a single paper or a whole program may be built upon this plan. In the latter case, the subordinate topics become the titles of separate papers.

a. The situation outlined,
1. By a summary of facts, or
2. By a story or description.

b. Analogies, or comparisons with
1. Other communities, or
2. Other local projects or plans.

c. Proposals for action,
1. Clearly stated, and
2. Urged persuasively by appeal to such motives as the following: (1) community pride; (2) rivalry; (3) self interest; (4) duty; (5) moral ideals involved in religion and education.

An interesting type of paper is one which discusses *new discoveries* or *inventions* or *new ideas* put into action in society. In such a paper, do at least these four things:

a. Give a clear, brief statement of the discovery or idea or plan.

b. Illustrate with examples the meaning of a discovery or an idea, to make the matter clear and interesting.

c. Give the circumstances of the discovery or statement of the idea as nearly as possible in story form.

d. Show plainly how the thing affects the everyday interests of your audience. See *Suggestions* in the following outlines. This last point should never be neglected. Anything worth writing or talking about has a bearing on everyday life.

Specimen Outlines

The following outlines illustrate the application of the general plan to the discussion of special themes:

I. Subject. Advertising.

Suggestion: This topic needs to be narrowed or divided as follows:

1. What Use Do I Make of Advertisements?

Suggestion.—An intimate chat with two or three friends on the subject of advertising and its uses will help you. You will get their points of view, which will suggest to you a greater variety of topics and a better balanced treatment of your theme.

2. Some Interesting Advertising Pages.

Suggestion.—You need not depend merely upon description. Have the actual pages to show to your audience. Then you can better explain why they are interesting.

3. Art in Advertising.
a. The Printer's Work.
b. Opportunities for Artists.

4. The Store Window.
Window Dressing.

Suggestion.—An interesting way to begin such a topic is to describe an actual window, especially if your audience may have seen it. If you have studied it carefully, you can surprise your audience and arouse interest by showing what they have failed to notice.

5. Advertising Associations and Ad Clubs.

Suggestion.—Any topic about organizations raises at least four questions: (1) How did they come to be formed? (2) What are their purposes? (3) What do they do? (4) Of what use are they to us?

6. The Responsible Advertiser.

Suggestion.—This kind of topic raises such questions as the following: (1) What gives the advertiser power? (2) For what is he responsible? (3) Do advertisers acknowledge this responsibility? (4) What are the reasons for your answer to (3)? (5) What personal experiences have you had with advertisers?

II. Subject. The Health of a Community.

The field of this theme is so large that a single paper should, as a rule, be restricted to one of the subordinate topics:

1. The Food Supply.
a. Sources.

Suggestion.—To make a paper on this topic interesting, you should get some first-hand facts from your local market. Such investigation will enable you to use more intelligently the material from magazines and books.

b. Markets.
(1) Prices.
(2) Handling the Food Supply.

2. Sanitation.
a. Housebuilding.
b. Water Supply.
c. Sewerage.
d. Waste and Garbage Removal.
e. Flies, Microbes, and Vermin.

3. Control of Diseases.
Public Health Service.
(1) School Inspection.
(2) Hospital Service.
(3) Quarantine Regulations.

4. Public Parks and Playgrounds.

THE BOOK OR ARTICLE REVIEW

Treatments of historical, scientific, or literary themes frequently involve the reviewing of books or articles from magazines. In writing a book or article review, try (1) to convey a truthful, distinct impression of the outline—the plot, if the original is a story, or the logical plan, if it is a discussion—(2) to give a more specific idea of some notable feature of the work, and (3) to interest and instruct your audience so thoroughly that they will know whether they want to read the book or article.

By way of preparation, *read the material you are to review.* Then make sure that you have some general *reaction,* that is, some opinion or feeling about the book. Stating your own opinion or feeling furnishes a personal element which adds much to the worth and to the interest of your work.

Plot Outline. Remember that the outline or plot of a short story or of a novel concerns itself with the answers to six questions: *Who? What? When? Where? Why? How?* Usually the answers to the first four may be found very readily in a first reading of a story; they form the obvious framework for any tale. The writer of stories exercises his skill in cleverly managing the "How" and the "Why" of events and actions. Sometimes the answers to these two questions are reserved to the very end of the story and there made clear; in other cases one must draw one's own conclusions from the course of the narrative.

In planning a story review, especially for a rather brief paper, take a lesson from the *lead* of the newspaper reporter. The *lead* is an opening sentence in a news story, which summarizes accurately and concisely the substance of the article. It answers the six questions mentioned above. Such an opening sentence places the whole story briefly and concisely before the audience. Practice in writing such *leads* is a most valuable means of improving one's style of speaking or writing. Follow the lead with a brief outline of the plot. Then comment upon some especially interesting or important part of the book.

SUGGESTIVE OUTLINES

St. Ives, a novel by Robert Louis Stevenson.

Lead.—Viscount Anne de St. Ives, a poor private soldier of Napoleon, escapes from the military prison in Edinburgh, becomes heir, through his uncle's will, to a great English estate which had been settled on the older line of his family, marries a Scotch girl who had visited the prison, and becomes an English country gentleman.

I. Beginning.
 1. *Setting.*—
  a. The French prisoners in Edinburgh Castle beguile their time by making souvenirs and toys to sell to the visitors from the city.
  b. One of the prisoners, St. Ives, is a gentleman of attractive manners, but a bungling craftsman.
 2. *Inciting moments.*—
  a. St. Ives, by his handiwork and his courtesy, attracts the attention of a girl, Flora, who, with certain relatives, visits the prison.
  b. A London lawyer appears, gives St. Ives news, leaves him money and the address of his wealthy uncle.
 3. *Complications.*—
  a. St. Ives fights a duel, killing his opponent, who had used vile language about Flora.
  b. The English lieutenant, in command of the prison, suspects St. Ives's part in the duel and threatens to become a rival for Flora.
  c. On the eve of escape through a tunnel, St. Ives incurs the hatred of a soldier who knows of the duel. A threat of trial for murder hangs over St. Ives.

II. The Story of a Fugitive.
 1. By the aid of Flora's aunt, St. Ives escapes to England in the company of two drovers.
  Complication.—In a fight he kills or severely injures a third, a rival drover.
 2. In England he is invested with his uncle's estate.
  Complication.—This brings on him the deadly hatred of his disinherited cousin.
 3. With a carriage and a valet he goes back to Scotland to find Flora and to save his drover friends from prosecution.
  Complication.—His cousin follows and they meet at a ball. But St. Ives escapes in a balloon.

III. The End.
 1. After sundry adventures St. Ives gets to Paris.
  Complication.—His cousin tries to trap him.
 2. The London lawyer, his uncle's solicitor, appears just in time to discomfit the spy and save the hero.
 3. Back to Scotland and Flora.

Any story may be reviewed in this manner, by answering the six questions in an outline of about three main divisions.

Abstract. Many books and articles upon scientific, historical, or social themes call for the writing of abstracts. These are connected condensed statements of the theme and contents of the book or essay. Four qualities must be aimed at: (1) *accuracy,* that is, truth to the ideas presented in the original work; (2) *completeness,* that is, treatment of all essential parts of the original; (3) *clearness,* which is a matter of especial difficulty, because, in the effort merely to condense the matter, one is tempted to leave out words essential to the meaning; (4) *brevity,* which is to be desired and yet may be sacrificed to the other three qualities.

Remember that people who have not seen the original writing must be able to understand your abstract. Observe the following directions for planning your work:

(1) Following the idea suggested in connection with the *lead,* select a title or a topic sentence which will summarize the entire article.
(2) Choose similar titles or topic sentences for each section of the article.
(3) Separate the essential points and necessary illustrations from the unessential and unnecessary. The abstract must omit most of the merely illustrative content of the original article.
(4) Write the new condensed version of the article.
(5) Review the new version in order to condense it further.
(6) Be careful to give the last part of the article as full treatment as you give the first part.

Paraphrase. This is a method of interpreting a writing by turning it into simpler or more common language. It is a much more widely used kind of writing than many people suppose. The preacher and the teacher use paraphrase constantly. Commentaries on the Scriptures and upon the writings of many great authors, Dante or Shakespeare for example, consist very largely of paraphrase.

Four kinds of writings usually call for paraphrase: the work of (1) old authors, such as Spenser or Chaucer, whose language has become unfamiliar; (2) such learned authors as Darwin or Emerson, whose expressions need simplifying; (3) writers like Francis Bacon, whose style is very condensed and therefore needs enlargement and illustration; (4) poets like Browning, whose language is obscure or figurative and therefore needs to be rendered into plain and literal expression.

The writer of paraphrase should first determine to which of these classes his author belongs; then he can suit his manner to the need. The preacher and the Sunday school teacher may find it necessary to render the language of the Bible in more familiar forms. They may wish to enlarge a parable or a proverb by some simple illustration or to turn the figurative language of a psalm into plain, everyday speech. Again, the teacher of science may be obliged to simplify certain paragraphs found in a very condensed textbook. He will develop single sentences into paragraphs and add illustrations. The general method of planning the *abstract* applies also to making the paraphrase.

THE ADVERTISEMENT

The purpose of an advertisement is persuasion. In general, the successful writer of advertising "copy" uses simple, direct language and keeps the reader and his interests most prominent in the advertisement. As a phase of selling, advertising gives the reader fresh information, or rather news, concerning products and services that will meet his needs.

RADIO WRITING

A demand for this form of writing appeared for the first time in the decade 1920-30, when the radio audience came into being. Radio writing differs from other forms of composition by reason of the following facts. The words are written not to be read but to be spoken. The listener hears the speaker but does not see him. The potential audience comprises people of all ages, conditions, beliefs, prejudices, and levels of intelligence.

Simplicity of Language. The mixed character and educational attainments of the radio audience necessitate the use of the simplest possible language. Long and unusual words should be avoided. Sentences should be short and contain vivid word pictures. Words of varied meanings are undesirable. In short, one who prepares script for radio broadcasting should write not merely so that he may be understood but so that he cannot be misunderstood.

Sentences which look well on paper may not be effective when spoken. Hence one who writes for the radio should be "ear minded." Sentences should have a pleasing rhythm. Moreover, certain sounds are apt to be distorted by the microphone and should be avoided as far as possible. Thus a succession of sibilants, "explosive" consonants, and words like "herd" with its obscure "r" sound are difficult to enunciate intelligibly over the radio. Other words which are often heard unsatisfactorily include apathetic, incessantly, statistics, inimitable, egregious, indubitably, perpendicular, and population.

THE EDITORIAL

This is a special form of writing used in newspapers and magazines to interpret items of news or to give opinion about subjects of current interest. The editorial may be a mere summary of information gathered from any source for the convenience of the reader. It may be an argument in support of some policy, or an informing essay on a political, social, moral, historical, literary, or scientific theme. The editorial should be timely. The judgments expressed should be based upon accurate knowledge of facts and upon sincere belief, and the style should be at once popular and dignified. The methods of writing given under *Argument*, *Exposition*, and *The Paragraph* apply to the composition of the editorial.

THE SCENARIO

This is a succinctly written sketch or outline of the scenes, situations, characters, and action of a story or play. Writers of fiction generally use it in planning their work. Producers of moving pictures, however, have developed a special form and technique of the scenario. Scenario making has come to be the business of specially trained writers employed by the producers.

Parts of the Scenario. An approved form of the scenario includes the following parts:

1. A summary or synopsis of the story.—This is the form in which producers require that stories be submitted. The synopsis should be written in ordinary direct narrative style. Each paragraph should present the essential characters of a scene in clear, vivid, descriptive language and tell the action in words that mean action. Thoughts and feelings should be conveyed through the suggested acts and movements of the characters. Each succeeding paragraph must carry the story straight toward its culmination. Action should, as far as possible, be written in the present tense. Titles and subtitles may be put in, preferably in capital letters, but all other technical directions should be omitted.

2. A list of characters, with the scenes in which each appears, thus: *Old Man, 3, 8, 15.*

3. A "scene plot," or schedule of the various stage settings, with the numbers of the scenes in which each setting is used, thus: *Hotel Entrance, 4, 10, 11, 18.*

A "scene," in moving picture studio language, is a part of the action that can be taken from one position of the camera. A move of the camera ushers in a new scene, except where the camera moves along with the actors or follows them, as in a race or some street scene.

4. A list of properties, or "props."

5. An outline of the scenes, numbered in order.—This is called the "continuity." The paragraph devoted to each scene gives (a) place or setting, (b) the characters, (c) the attitudes and actions of the characters (pantomime), (d) the thought or feeling these are intended to convey. The following is an approved short form of such a paragraph:

SCENE 5

Railroad Station. College boys and girls leaving after graduation. A send-off. Margaret and Winston meet. Realization of parting, long to speak; both too proud, part stiffly. Train pulls in. Boys and girls enter cars, waving good-byes. Margaret, assisted by Jim, enters end coach, her eyes following Winston, who enters adjoining car. Train pulls out. *Dissolve* into:

SCENE 6

Winston Library. Winston gazing at picture.—

Producers now employ professional continuity writers to work up synopses into the finished action plot, or continuity. The best authorities, however, advise writers to prepare their own continuities before writing synopses to submit to producers. This method gives clearer and firmer structure to the story, because the writer has followed his characters through all the details of the action that makes the story for the screen.

VERSE

For many people the writing of verse is an interesting and amusing pastime. It is also one of the best means of improving one's command of language: (1) It calls for condensed and vivid expression and for a selection of words to produce good measure and rime; (2) it gives one occasion for searching out figurative language that will give variety, point, and concreteness to expression; (3) it improves one's appreciation of verse, which today forms so large a part of our current literature.

There is a wide and pleasant field for agreeable, witty, humorous, and fanciful verse. You may use it for a short, pointed speech. Often an unexpected "hit" is made in this way. Many epigrams, proverbs, mottoes, and sentiments are more vivid and more easily memorized, if expressed in couplets or quatrains.

Observe the following suggestions: (1) Verse must have a rhythm more striking and regular than that of prose or spoken conversation. (2) In English verse this rhythm is marked by the succession of beats or strong accents. Each *line* in English verse is made up of a number of feet. A *foot* consists of an accented syllable with one or more unaccented syllables closely connected with it. Several kinds of verse are named from the kinds of feet used and the number of accents to the line. (3) Select a model that you wish to imitate; read it over, beating out the accents with a pencil, until you get the swing of the lines. Such attention to a model will cure many a set of limping feet.

Rhythms. Recent writers of verse employ a wide variety of rhythms. They also use great freedom in choosing different lengths of line within the same poems. The best popular verse, however, keeps close to the well-established rules. The most common feet in English verse are the following:

a. Iambic (ĭ-ăm′bĭk), composed of two syllables, an accented preceded by an unaccented syllable;

b. Trochaic (trô-kā′ĭk), which is an accented syllable followed by an unaccented.

Two other types of feet, sometimes used, are:

a. Dactylic (dăk-tĭl′ĭk), which is an accented syllable followed by two unaccented;

b. Anapœstic (ăn′á-pĕs′tĭk), which is an accented syllable preceded by two unaccented.

A line of two accents is called a *dimeter* (dĭm′ê-tẽr); a line of three accents is called *trimeter* (trĭm′ê-tẽr); one of four accents, *tetrameter* (tĕt-răm′ê-tẽr); one of five accents, *pentameter* (pĕn-tăm′ê-tẽr).

SPECIMENS OF FEET AND METER

(Accented syllables are marked with ⎺; unaccented, with ⌣.)

Iambic.—
As flowers that bloom at morn, at eve decay.

Trochaic.—
Curls and ringlets of her tresses.

Dactylic.—
This is the story the sailorman told.

Anapæstic.—
Not a word, not a whisper, to soothe the sharp pain.

Mixed meter.—
Though it lashed the shallows that lined the beach.
Afar from the great sea deeps.

Dimeter.—
O'er folded blooms
On swirls of musk.

Trimeter.—
The lustrous blue of morn.
The night has a thousand eyes.

Tetrameter.—
They tempt the taste and charm the sight.
The crest and crowning of all good,
Life's final star, is Brotherhood.

Pentameter.—
Much have I traveled in the realms of gold,
And many goodly states and kingdoms seen.
Bowed by the weight of centuries he leans
Upon his hoe and gazes on the ground.

Rime. The agreement of syllables in sound. A syllable in the middle of a line may be rimed with one at the end: this is called *internal rime.* Usually, syllables are rimed at the ends of lines: this is called *end rime.* Lines of poetry are commonly written in groups of two or more, forming stanzas. The lines may rime in couplet or alternately or in some other of the patterns illustrated below. *Blank verse* is unrimed, usually iambic pentameter. *Free verse* is unrimed; and its rhythm is said to be a rhythm of thought rather than of accent. It is difficult to distinguish from rhythmical prose. At best, it is not a form for the amateur.

Specimens of Rime

Couplet.—
Why has not man a microscopic eye?
For this plain reason,—man is not a fly.

Bubble, Bubble, flows the stream,
Like an old tune through a dream.

Alternate rime.—
We, in some unknown power's employ,
Move on a rigorous line;
Can neither, when we will, enjoy
Nor, when we will, resign.

Quatrain with two rimed lines.—
I think that saving a child
And bringing him to his own
Is a derned sight better business
Than loafing round the throne.

Quatrain with two rimes.—
Why should I stay? Nor seed nor fruit have I
But, sprung at once to beauty's perfect round,
Nor loss nor gain nor change in me is found,—
A life—complete in death—complete to die.

Six-line stanza with two rimes.—
The hollow sea-shell, which for years hath stood
On dusty shelves, when held against the ear
Proclaims its stormy parent, and we hear
The faint, far murmur of the breaking flood.
We hear the sea. The Sea? It is the blood
In our own veins, impetuous and near.

Four lines with one rime.—
A little peach in an orchard grew,—
A little peach of emerald hue;
Warmed by the sun and wet by the dew
It grew.

Sonnet.—
What is a sonnet? 'Tis a pearly shell
That murmurs of the far-off murmuring sea,
A precious jewel carved most curiously;
It is a little picture painted well.
What is a sonnet? 'Tis the tear that fell
From the great poet's hidden ecstasy;
A two-edged sword, a star, a song—ah me!
Sometimes a heavy-tolling funeral bell.

This was the flame that shook with Dante's breath,
The solemn organ whereon Milton played,
And the clear glass where Shakespeare's shadow falls;
A sea this is—beware who ventureth!
For like a fiord the narrow floor is laid
Deep as mid-ocean to sheer mountain walls.
     Richard Watson Gilder.

The *Limerick* is a form of nonsense stanza, made up of five lines with two rimes. The first, second, and fifth lines rime, and the third and fourth lines. The following specimen well represents the limerick:

Said the Snail to the Tortoise: "You may
Find it hard to believe what I say;
  You will think it absurd,
  But I give you my word,
They fined me for speeding today."
     Oliver Herford.

The following school songs illustrate a method of adapting sentiment and words to a popular tune:

Tune: Come Back to Erin.
 Come back to Normal, Good English, Good English
  Back to the ones who have missed you so long.
 Come back to Normal, Good English, Good English!
  And all the building will ring with our song.

Tune: Row Your Boat.
 Watch, watch, watch your speech,
  Every word you say.
 Carefully, carefully, carefully, carefully
  Watch it every day.

PUBLIC SPEAKING

Public speaking, as commonly understood, though it does not lay claim to the more formal title of oratory, is nevertheless a term which includes that art. As oratory is the appeal of a high order of eloquence to the understanding and to the emotions, so, too, the province of public speaking is not only to entertain and inform, but also to convince and persuade.

Possibilities and Probabilities. Although it is not given to every one to become an orator, nevertheless, it is well within the scope and the power of the average intelligent person to become a good public speaker. Moreover, there never was a time when public speaking formed a more important factor in American life than it does today, nor was there ever a time when this talent brought to the individual more social and political influence.

Every citizen is likely at any time to be called upon to express his views on any topic which may be exercising the minds of the public. As an efficient member of the community, he should be ready to respond to the claim thus made upon him and be able to lay before his fellow-citizens or townsmen, in language at once clear and forceful, his opinions and his judgment on the question put before him for discussion.

Fundamentals. "What then," it will be asked, "is necessary in order to prepare one's self to become a successful public speaker?"

1. The first essential is a knowledge of one's fellow-men. By this is not meant that one must necessarily be a psychologist. He must, however, have an all-round knowledge of people in general, especially of the man in the street, with his prejudices to be overcome, his rights to be defended, and his wrongs to be rectified. Only in this way can a speaker get in touch with an audience. He must understand his audience before they will understand him.

2. In the second place, the speaker should have a knowledge of books. He should become acquainted with good literature. Not every intending speaker has had the advantages of a college training. He may not have enjoyed the privilege of extensive travel, and he may be wanting in that broader knowledge that comes only to those of wide and practical experience. But books are always open to him; they will furnish him with facts, ideas, and all that is needed for the illustration of his

subject. It was Bacon who said, "Reading maketh a full man." It is the man full of his subject, and thereby confident, who will interest and impress his audience.

3. As language is the chief means of conveying thought, it is a matter of the greatest importance to possess a ready command of words. To enlarge his vocabulary, the student of public speaking should make notes of all the new or strange words he meets in his general reading, or that he may hear in listening to lectures given by others. He should then make a point of using such words whenever opportunity offers; for it is by continuous use that they become his own.

The above three points sum up what may be regarded as the *remote preparation* for public speaking, in which lies in great measure the secret of success in this practical art. We now come to the *immediate preparation*, or the method to be followed in the actual planning and in the making of a speech.

Choice of Subject. Let the subject you choose be one of interest to yourself and one that is likely to be of interest to your audience. Remember you are to deliver a message. Unless you win the interest of your audience, your efforts to deliver a message will be in vain. Know beforehand the manner of audience you are about to address and adapt your subject to their capacity. In this way you will not be speaking "over their heads," and your purpose of convincing and persuading will be achieved.

The Plan. No matter how confident you may feel after you have gathered your material, always make in advance a plan or an outline of your intended talk or address. No builder undertakes the erection of a building until he has made a working plan of its different divisions, stories, and apartments. The same principle applies to an address. By making a plan you will put into your speech what you want to say, and will save time in saying it. Moreover, this much is due your audience. The habit of planning, if conscientiously cultivated, will enable you eventually to make a *mental* plan when opportunity will not allow of a penciled outline.

A speech to be convincing must be logical,— that is, it must be made up of an *introduction*, a *body*, and a *conclusion*. This rule is applicable to the formal address, to the simple talk at a club meeting, to an after-dinner speech, or to the toast at a wedding breakfast.

Introduction or Beginning. This should be a brief and clear forecasting of what the speaker proposes to discuss before or prove to his audience, and it should contain the logical scheme of his entire address. In plain words, he should let his hearers know how he intends to deal with his subject. In opening his speech his manner should be easy and natural. This end may be achieved in several ways; for instance, (1) by some happy compliment paid to the audience; (2) by reference to some interesting topic of the moment; (3) by an anecdote relating to some well-known character, or by a brief and apt quotation. In this simple manner a speaker may get in touch with his audience and at the same time may lead up to his subject.

Body of the Speech. This consists in the gradual and logical development of the proposition already set forth in your introduction. As you proceed in the unfolding of your main statements, make free use of illustration and comparison from other themes and topics familiar to your audience. This tends to greater clearness and insures interest. It is thus that you imperceptibly paint a background from which your word-picture will stand out in more sharply defined and vivid lines. As you pass from one point to another, revert occasionally to the argument already put forward, so that your audience may hold in mind the main divisions of your talk.

The Conclusion. The conclusion should be a careful summing up and welding together of the chief arguments developed in the body of the speech. They must be made to stand out lucidly and forcefully, and in such order that, by the presentation of their combined strength, conviction is driven home to the minds of those listening.

As has already been pointed out, public speaking may serve either to entertain, inform, convince, or persuade. The formal speech will always have dignity of form and of diction. So much will not be expected of the informal, short address, though the structure of each is essentially the same, both being built on the basis of logical thought. This being true, the informal speech is here dealt with, for practical purposes.

Informal Speeches. You may be called upon suddenly to say "a few words" in public, to propose a toast or to make an after-dinner speech, to take part in a discussion, or to talk as an executive to employees. A hundred different occasions may arise and demand from you some kind of address. You have to win the attention of your audience on the spur of the moment, and make your points as quickly. If you know the essentials that go to the making of a speech, as already stated above, a few hurried notes will be sufficient for the skeleton outline of what you intend to say.

A useful suggestive outline for the short talk or informal address is furnished by the following questions: 1—What is the fact or situation under discussion? 2—How has it come to be as it is? 3—How does it affect you? 4—What are you going to do about it?

Nucleus of an Informal Address. The nucleus, or concentrated matter, of a short talk may often be found (1) in the statement of some striking fact or incident, (2) in the presentation of clear and up-to-date statistics concerning a topic of real interest, (3) in the clever recital of a new story, or of an old one dressed in a new garb, and calculated to raise a laugh or a smile. The last method of beginning an address is perhaps the happiest of all, as by it the audience is warmed to sympathy with the speaker, the knowledge of which fact is no small aid to eloquence.

SOME STYLES OF SHORT TALKS

The occasions for the short talk are many, and there are almost as many styles as there are occasions. On the other hand, there are certain similarities to be noted in each, as the following examples will illustrate:

After-Dinner Speech. Usually, you have first to express some pointed sentiment in reference to the occasion, the host, or the guest of honor. A happy quotation or an adage which contains the gist of what you are about to say, will often serve as an appropriate *beginning*. Again, a half serious, half humorous comment will help in the development of the sentiment itself. Also, the flash light of a good crisp story will illumine your remarks so that your audience will see the point, and be won at once to your favor. As brevity is the soul of wit, so is it the essence of a good after-dinner speech.

Speech of Presentation or Award. Situations are constantly arising in which a gift or award is presented in token of friendship or in recognition of achievement. For example, a retiring employee receives a gift in recognition of his long service or an athlete is given a medal for outstanding proficiency. Whatever the occasion, the spokesman for the group making the award has an opportunity to show his best skill in paying tribute to the recipient. The theme of compliment and congratulation may be developed in various ways. It should always be handled with a light touch, but the degree and kind of humor depends, of course, on the persons present and the circumstances. How far whimsical humor may go, with entire appropriateness, is illustrated by

Sir James Barrie's famous compliment to Ellen Terry. He said, "The young men of my generation were madly, hopelessly in love with her. In fact, the standard formula for proposing marriage was for a young man to say to the woman of his second choice 'Since I can't have Miss Terry, may I please have you?'"

Impromptu Discussion. It may be that you are asked to take part in a running debate or discussion at which you happen to be present. In such a case you will have time to make a mental plan only. Nevertheless, you may adroitly begin your talk by referring to some salient fact or idea already mentioned in the debate, and thus gain time to put your thoughts in order. This is called a "point of contact" to which you may gradually attach your own trend of argument. Thus, often by an *impromptu* speech you can add to the interest of a debate by the orderly and well balanced presentment of your personal views. This happy facility comes from the persistent habit of making plans. To illustrate:

The debate is on the question of *safety*—an important topic to be discussed. Your opinion as an employer of labor, or as an employee, is sought on this subject. Possibly you will find a starting point for your talk by relating some accident which has taken place at the works or store in which you are employed. From this proceed to expand and make interesting your informal speech by putting forward your personal ideas on the best methods for preventing similar accidents in the future.

Again, the discussion may be on the question of *co-operation*. Once more you are asked to join in the debate. In such a case, a possible improvement in an industrial process, or a suggestion as to the better management of your business, may well supply you with a good opening and with excellent matter for an effective talk.

The examples given above illustrate some of the forms that a short address may take. It will be seen how some concrete and definite incidents, or accidents, may become the nucleus of your whole talk, and how, in time, you may find all the points you need to make a telling and striking address.

FORMS OF PUBLIC SPEAKING

The Expository Speech or Lecture. The aim of the expository speaker is to make something clear to his audience. It is usually the aim of the teacher. But there are many occasions outside of the school where a speaker has as his basic purpose the presentation of clarifying ideas. A new system of handling personnel may be set forth by a personnel director or a new plan for organized recreation may be presented by the chairman of the program committee. It is important for the speaker who is called upon to give clarifying information to keep his talk on an expository basis; that is, he must see to it that he does not bring in his own ax to grind and thus try to straddle exposition with persuasion. There are some six methods of exposition, any or all of which may be employed in a speech for clearness:

(1) *Comparison.* This is, perhaps, the most useful expository device. The audience is made to understand something new by having it compared with that which they already know. Analogy, which is a comparison of ratios, is a most useful form of comparison. When analogy is used the audience is enabled to understand a new relationship or process by seeing it compared to one with which they are familiar.

(2) *Analysis.* Through this device we come to understand something by having it taken apart for us. Thus we come to see the whole in terms of its parts. It is a good idea to remember that talks making use of analysis should end up with synthesis, so that the hearers see the relationship of the parts to the whole.

(3) *Definition.* Many effective speeches with clear-

ness as the end are based on the elaboration of a definition. We might, for instance, make an expository talk on Public Speaking by elaborating on the terms, and the relationship of the terms, in this definition: Public Speaking is the useful art of influencing human behavior through the medium of purposive speech.

(4) *Cause and Effect Relationship.* This method is often used where the material is of a historical character. A speaker might, for instance, explain Fascism by tracing its development in Germany.

(5) *Restatement.* When a speaker uses the expression, "in other words," and then goes on to give his audience another view of the same thing, he is using Restatement. It is different from *repetition* in that the same words are said over again in the latter.

(6) *Example.* The expository speaker uses *example* when he gives a demonstration, actually showing the thing he is explaining. The use of movies in teaching is an application of this method. It can also be said that illustrations by means of pictures or drawings on a blackboard are applications of the method. In the last few years, with the development of various techniques of visual education, expository presentations have been given added effectiveness by use of the example method.

Occasional and Commemorative Speeches. The purpose of the speaker in giving speeches at special occasions or in commemoration of some event or person is *Impressiveness*. The term Impressiveness is used to describe the purpose of those speeches in which the audience, already in agreement as to the concepts presented, is made to feel more deeply about them. Speeches of welcome, farewell speeches, speeches given when a gift is presented, and when one is accepted, have impressiveness as the purpose. Also those speeches given at dedication ceremonies and at anniversary gatherings have that purpose. Usually these speeches are eulogistic in character, that is, they are dominated by the mood of praise. Some of our finest oratory has been delivered at such occasions. The speakers have endeavored to catch the spirit of the hour, to voice the feelings of the listeners, to make the audience feel that their best thoughts and sentiments have been beautifully and effectively expressed.

It is in speeches of this kind that the expression comes close to the art of the poet. Metaphor, which is said to be the essence of poetry, is well employed in this form of speech composition. There also may be something of the rhythmic cadence of poetry. When the poetic element in such speech compositions springs from a genuine feeling of admiration of the subject being spoken of, there need be no fear of indulging in old-fashioned oratorical language. Love, affection, admiration, veneration, *when sincerely expressed*, is never out of date.

The Speech of Introduction. The function of the *speech of introduction* is to bring the speaker and the audience together in a proper spirit of acquaintanceship. It should meet this need and go no further. The listeners should be given that information about the speaker and his topic which will help them and the speaker. The introduction should be warm and friendly in spirit but should not embarrass the speaker by being eulogistic. It should be as short as possible and certainly should not encroach upon the speaker's topic. All too frequently the introducer is inclined to bask in the limelight of the main speaker, giving a speech of his own, indulging in oratorical flourishes, and generally stealing the main speaker's thunder.

DISCUSSION AND DEBATE

These two kinds of speaking are closely related in that they are a part of a general process, the process of arriving at a new point of view in regard to some public question. It can be said that *debate* picks up where discussion leaves off. Through the group discussion of a question or problem, a gathering of people may arrive at a point where it must decide whether or not to adopt a new policy in conducting its affairs. At this point debate begins: Should the new policy be adopted or not? For example, in group discussion the general question of obtaining proper medical care for the American people might be given consideration. At a certain point in the discussion the members of the group decide that the matter has reduced itself to the question: Should we or should we not adopt some form of nationalized health insurance? From that point on the gathering is on a debate basis. Following this line of thought, we shall give consideration first to the topic, group discussion.

Group Discussion. For hundreds of years the rhetoric of debating has been clearly set forth by textbook writers and followed by students in school debates and by lawyers and legislators. It is only in the last decade or so that the art of public discussion has been treated effectively in speech textbooks. However, public discussion of community and state problems has been effectively carried on in this country since the country's beginnings. The democratic method of open discussion of public questions was followed in New England Town Meetings in the 17th century. In the 18th century the same process of group thinking was to be observed in the Constitutional Convention. The delegates to the convention did not come to Philadelphia in 1787 to debate clearly defined issues nor to impress the gallery with persuasive oratory; they came to find a solution to a problem and to reach that solution by "negotiation and accommodation." We find the group discussion method manifested in the 19th century in the Lyceum and Chautauqua movements, the former being at its height in the middle of the century and the latter by the end of the century. The modern *open forum* movement had its beginnings in 1897 as a part of the adult education activities of Cooper Union in New York City. The movement was given fresh impetus in 1933 under the leadership of J. W. Studebaker, then superintendent of the Des Moines Public Schools. The Des Moines public Forums set the pattern for the discussion of public problems by citizens of a community. With the development of nationwide interest in this form of group thinking has come a substantial literature on the technique of discussion.

Today it is more important than ever that people be able to think through their problems in some cooperative fashion. We are no longer a world of isolated communities; the world itself is a community. This world community is endeavoring to find solutions to its problems in group discussions at the United Nations, in peace conferences, in industrial management-labor conferences, in organizations seeking racial harmony, and in international forums conducted by public spirited citizens.

The Process of Group Thinking. There are basically five steps in the process of thinking through to the solution of a problem. While it hardly can be said that any particular group discussion clearly follows the sequence, upon analysis it will be seen that the steps are involved. The steps are:

(1) Defining the problem.

(2) Analysis of the problem with the purpose of finding what values will be sought for in a solution.

(3) Suggestion of possible solutions or hypotheses.

(4) Consideration of relative merits of suggested solutions in the light of the values or criteria established in step two. Arrival at a tentative solution.

(5) Testing out the solution by visualizing it in operation.

A forum or discussion leader should keep these steps in mind in guiding a group in its problem solving efforts. He should have thought about the problem sufficiently beforehand and be sufficiently informed as to the basic aspects of the question so that he can detect tendencies to jump to conclusions, to reason in a circle, to generalize from insufficient evidence, to ignore minority interests, to fasten on trivial points, to indulge in personalities, and the many other all too human weaknesses to be found in our endeavors to be rational. When the leader sees that a member or members of the group are suggesting a solution before the problem has been adequately analyzed (step two) he should tactfully raise the question whether there are not values to be looked for in a solution which have not been considered and lead the members back to the second phase of the thought process. It will be found that this phase, the analysis step, is the one that is most difficult and which groups are prone to pass over too quickly. On the other hand, the leader must be on guard against having a preconceived solution to the problem and toward which he inflexibly directs the assembly. When that happens the discussion is no longer a co-operative, democratic process. The leader has become something of a dictator.

Types of Group Discussion. The type of group discussion taken up in the foregoing paragraphs is the type most commonly used. It is simple in its organization, there being only the chairman, or leader, and the gathering of people who sit before the leader, or with him around a table. This kind of discussion might be called the *conference* type. The unqualified word, *forum*, is also used as a term to describe this form of discussion.

Planning the Conference. The chairman or leader of the *conference* type of discussion must be imbued with the democratic principle of agreement in a group arrived at through full, free, and informed discussion. Collaboration for a common end should be the controlling objective. There are some things the leader can do to facilitate the attainment of that objective. He, himself, should command the respect of the group by being fair, tolerant, gracious, and firm, withal. He should be informed as regards the subject matter of the conference and as regards the process of democratic discussion. He should oversee the arrangements for the meeting, making sure that the room is a pleasant one, that the scheduled time for the meeting is a convenient one for the participants, that enough time is allotted for the meeting or meetings so that the group can arrive at a deliberative decision. When the discussion is going on he should carefully gauge the progress of the group, and if he sees that opposing interests are bringing about an impasse, he may well suggest a recess, in which heated tempers may cool off. Frequently important concessions are made during recesses, especially if during the recess the members can get together on a good-fellowship basis.

Besides the conference type of discussion there are six others, each type having a distinguishing characteristic. They are similar to each other in one respect, all being more formal than the conference type of discussion. The six types are: the *Panel-Forum*, the *Symposium-Forum*, the *Lecture-Forum*, the *Colloquy* or *Dialogue*, the *Public Hearing*, and the *Debate-Forum*.

The Panel-Forum. In this type of discussion a panel of two to six speakers sit on the platform along with the chairman and converse on some chosen topic for the benefit of the audience facing the platform. This is a popular form of discussion especially in educational circles. Usually the group, the panel and chairman, have a meeting beforehand at which an outline covering the material for discussion is worked out and each member of the panel is assigned some part of the outline on which to talk. The chairman should keep these points in mind in directing the discussion: No member of the panel should talk for more than one minute at a time. All discussion should be directed toward the audience. The chairman and panel members should remain seated, for the sake of informality. Spontaneity should be encouraged in the panel members. If two speak up at the same time, the chairman designates who shall talk first.

After the panel members have finished their conversation and the chairman has made a summary of the discourse, the audience should be called upon to participate in an open-forum discussion. They may contribute ideas or ask questions of the panel members. It is a good idea to allow as much as half of the meeting time for audience participation and to inform the audience beforehand that they will have that time for discussion.

The panel-forum, as are the remaining types to be presented here, is better suited to the conveying of information than to problem solving. When a problem is to be solved, it is best to use the *conference* type of discussion.

The Symposium-Forum. This type is similar to the panel-forum in that it is made up of a panel of speakers, from two to four, and who have designated points upon which to speak. It differs from it in that each member of the panel gives a set speech, running from five to ten minutes in length. After the panel members have spoken and the chairman has summarized, the chairman invites the audience to participate as in the panel-forum.

The Lecture-Forum. Here one speaker takes the place of a panel of speakers. There may be a chairman, who opens the meeting, introduces the speaker, and conducts the open forum when the speaker finishes. However, the lecturer himself may act as chairman. This type is better suited to the conveying of information than to problem solving.

The Colloquy or Dialogue. Three units are found on the platform in this type of discussion, a panel of experts, an audience panel, and the chairman. The audience panel is usually chosen from the audience at the time of the meeting. The chairman and the panel representing the audience begin the discussion, after the manner of the ordinary panel-forum. The members of the expert panel are called upon to supply evidence when the need for it becomes apparent and to give opinions when they are desired. The *colloquy* is well suited for conventions where experts in a particular field are available and where the audience-members have a specialized interest in the subject-matter.

The Public Hearing. There are two types of public hearings, that which is held by legislative committees and that held by representatives of governmental agencies. In both types a legislative committee or government representatives seek information, evidence, and existing opinion from members of organizations, pressure groups, or individual citizens. At hearings the committee members and the audience face each other and the space between them is allotted to the particular speaker who happens to be speaking. He addresses the committee with his back to the audience. In the legislative hearing, members of the committee ask questions of the speaker. In the second type, audience and speakers usually ask questions of the governmental representatives. The chief problem for the speaker in hearings is to make himself heard by the audience at his back without shouting to the committee.

The Debate-Forum. This type is similar to the Symposium-Forum except for the fact that in the former the panel of speakers is broken up into two units each taking the affirmative or negative on some debatable question. When the two sides have presented their arguments, the chairman invites the audience to participate. After perhaps twenty minutes of open-forum discussion a final summary is made by the opponent of the proposed solution and by the advocate of the proposed solution. The debate-forum is best used when the audience is familar with the problem and almost ready to decide what to do about it.

An *argument* is a reason given in support of a proposition. As a form of composition, argument is also the logical arrangement of a proposition and the reasons urged in support of it. Sometimes we merely defend an opinion; sometimes we try to convince others that certain opinions are true or false. When we use arguments to make people believe or act as we want them to, we use *persuasion*. Persuasion is the means by which a speaker or writer tries to move his audience to belief or action.

We succeed in persuasion partly through logical argument and partly through personal appeal to the sympathies and interests of an audience. Both these elements are necessary. Sometimes one plays the larger part, sometimes the other. Sincere human interest, added to a logical argument, is as necessary to a salesman as to a lawyer before a jury or to a preacher in his pulpit.

Debate. The best way to learn to argue well is to practice in formal discussions or debates. Free discussion of public questions is necessary to the welfare of people in a democracy. Therefore, schools, clubs, and societies should encourage such discussion and give opportunity for debate. Any debate centers in a question about which two opposing propositions can be made and supported by arguments. We cannot debate words or phrases. We may speak of discussing "taxes" or "freedom of speech"; but the discussion cannot proceed until we have put together a sentence or proposition about the subject. Preparation for debate calls first for selecting a debatable question. This is a question (1) on which opinions may reasonably differ, (2) on which material for evidence and proof s available, (3) which is of real interest.

The steps in planning an argument or a debate are the following:

1. State the question clearly and definitely. Propositions should be stated affirmatively, and should be so worded as to throw the burden of proof upon the affirmative. For example:

"Should the City of X purchase the local electric lighting plant?" or *"Should James W. go to college?"* Sometimes the question is stated in the form of a resolution: *"Resolved, That the City of X should purchase the local electric lighting plant."* The following form also is recommended by some teachers as a title for a debate: *"For and against the election of B. as mayor"; "For and against James W. going to college."*

2. Define concisely the terms used in the question. For instance, the terms "purchase" and "plant," in the first question, and the term "college," in the second, need definition.

3. Find the main *issues*, or special subordinate questions, on which the decision may turn. This discovery of issues is really a most vital part of argument; for clear statement of main issues eliminates useless talk about unimportant details. The following is the best method of finding the issues: (1) set down a number of opposing statements upon the question; (2) analyze these to find what are the exact points on which they conflict; (3) state these points as questions. These questions are the issues. Such an analysis of arguments on the question as to the electric lighting plant would probably reveal the following issues:

Is the present electric service unsatisfactory? Is owning and operating public utilities a wise policy for this city? Is some other management to be preferred?

These issues appear in the form of questions, to which the affirmative answers *yes* and the negative, *no*. The skillful debater takes account of these questions and sifts them until he has found those which seem really essential. Then, by answering these essential questions, he answers the main question. Such an argument may be outlined as follows:

The body, or *brief*, for the affirmative or negative side of the argument should thus take up the issues in order and answer each question, with reasons and evidence. Then, on the basis of the reasoning given, the *conclusion*, or final answer to the main question should be stated.

In a debate on any question, certain of the apparent issues may be set aside, by mutual agreement, before opening the discussion. They are then called "admitted matter," and the discussion, for the sake of brevity and clearness, takes up only the issues on which there is clear difference of opinion.

Logic. "*Why?*" is the student's most troublesome question but no progress in argumentative thinking can be made without clear answers to questions beginning with *Why*. The corresponding word in answers is *because*. One thing is true because another thing is true.

All reasoning must be based on long and careful observation of facts. *Logic*, which is the science or art of exact reasoning, teaches us how to arrange and test our propositions so that our conclusions shall be warranted.

The *syllogism* is a common form of logical reasoning. It may be represented as follows:

Major premise (general statement): Wooden houses can be burned.

Minor premise (particular statement): Mr. A's house is wooden.

Conclusion: Therefore, Mr. A's house can be burned.

To make this reasoning true, a sufficient number of cases must have been observed to justify the general statement. It must be certain also that Mr. A's house belongs to the general class of wooden houses.

If we said, "*Plants are good for food; geraniums are plants; therefore, geraniums are good for food,*" our reasoning would be faulty, because not all plants are good for food. Our general statement is untrue though our particular statement is true. If we said, "*Lumber is expensive; houses are made of lumber; therefore, houses are expensive,*" our reasoning would be faulty because not all houses are made entirely or mainly of lumber. The particular statement is untrue though the general statement and the fact stated in the conclusion are true. Therefore, in the first example, we would *distinguish* or *question* the *major* premise, *grant* the *minor*, and *deny* the *conclusion*; in the second, we would *grant* the *major*, *distinguish* the *minor*, and *deny* the *conclusion*.

Evidence and Proof. Answering these *why* questions involves evidence and proof. *Evidence* is any fact, testimony, or accepted principle, which tends to bring about a belief in the proposition which is being urged. Evidence may be direct or circumstantial. Direct evidence is such as immediately supports the proposition. For instance, a theft may have been committed, the thief pursued and caught; his possession of the stolen property and the testimony of the person who saw him steal would be *direct evidence*. If, however, no such evidence as this were available, *circumstantial evidence* might be used. This would be made up of facts about the suspected person and his movements, which would tend to show that he probably committed the deed. *Proof* is convincing evidence.

Formal Debate: Rules. In a formal debate each side must know which are the most important of the issues raised, and the debaters must remember that the decision depends upon the balance of argument. Every argument advanced by one side must be answered by the other. Unanswered argument stands, no matter how weak the evidence presented by the side using it. *Refutation*, or the answering of opponents' arguments, is very important.

The debating leagues of colleges and high schools have developed certain customs and rules for the conducting of debates. The most important of these follow:

1. *Selection of the Question.*—Usually one team proposes a question and the other team is allowed to choose to support either the affirmative or the negative side.

2. *Teams.*—Each side of the argument is maintained by a team of two (or three) members. An additional member, or alternate, is sometimes chosen. He may take one of the regular places in an emergency. Otherwise, he helps in the preparation of the debate.

3. *Teamwork.*—All members of the team should work together in preparing the debate. They should confer upon the selection of the important issues and the arrangement of material. Before the debate, each member of the team should be familiar with the entire argument, but the actual presentation should be divided among the three debaters. Each one should have a definite part of the case to present.

4. *Division of Work.*—The first speaker on each side has to state the position of his side, make one strong point, and win the attention and the interest of his audience. The second speaker has to maintain interest, make at least one striking argument, and refute some of his opponents' arguments. The last speaker has to drive home the strongest argument of his side, answer some of his opponents' arguments, and sum up the case.

5. *Organization of a Debate.*—A formal debate is organized with a chairman, a timekeeper, and usually three judges. The chairman calls the meeting to order, announces the question and any special rules for the discussion, and introduces the speakers. The timekeeper gives each speaker a signal one minute or two before his speech is to close and another, if necessary, when his time has expired.

6. *Order of Speaking.*—The speakers on the two sides alternate, first an affirmative and then a negative speaker. Usually the debaters give two series of speeches. The first consists of direct argument; the second, entirely of refutation. This second series of speeches is called rebuttal. The order of speakers in rebuttal may be changed from that followed in the direct argument. The affirmative may elect either to open or to close the rebuttal.

7. *Time.*—Each speaker in direct argument is allowed a definite time—six, eight, or ten minutes—for his direct speech and a shorter time for rebuttal. The first direct speakers and the last rebuttal speakers are sometimes allowed two or three minutes more than the others.

8. *Intermission.*—At the close of the direct speeches the debaters are allowed a brief intermission for conference before beginning the rebuttal.

9. *Limitations of Rebuttal.*—In rebuttal a speaker must confine himself to refuting his opponents' arguments. He is not allowed to bring in new material.

10. *Decision of the Judges.*—At the close of the debate the judges render their decision, usually without conferring. The chairman announces the decision, which is accepted as final.

RADIO AND TELEVISION SPEAKING

Reversing the development from silent to spoken movies, radio broadcasting was soon followed by the combination of visual with sound communication that is universally familiar as television. Unlike the change in motion pictures, however, it was not a case of the earlier form being eclipsed by the later one, but of the survival of both kinds, each with its own special function and appeal. Because radio broadcasting continued undiminished in importance following the advent of television, the problems of speaking common to both remained. In some respects, of course, the radio announcer or actor standing before a microphone had the advantage of simpler requirements and an informal atmosphere. Relaxed in shirt-sleeve comfort, he could read from a typed script held in his hand. If his delivery was *natural and spontaneous enough to indicate speaking instead of reading*, his audience would be unaware of the manuscript unless the sheets were rustled, in which case the noise would be picked up and magnified into a loud crackling sound. By contrast, the speaker facing a television audience would have to rely on his memory or be content with quick side glances at a teleprompter to keep his lines straight. In using the air waves for either medium, radio or television, the speaker would have to recognize certain obligations owed to the public.

Requirements for Speaking. For his audience, whether only listening or both seeing and listening, the speaker must meet certain minimum requirements. These include particularly distinct utterance, correct pronunciation, and a manner and tone of voice suited to the situation. His speech is not formal oratory but person-to-person communication on the intimate level of the living room or the conference table. When Queen Victoria, exasperated by a prime minister's loud conversation, said: "He talks to me as if I were a public meeting!" she was making a criticism that might well apply to radio speakers who disregard the amplifying possibilities of their medium.

Distinct utterance, always an asset to any speaker, is vitally important in radio and television. To the millions of listeners, the experience of hearing words spoken clearly by someone who is both intelligent and intelligible is almost like taking a course of study in the art of speaking. Perhaps without suspecting the extent of his influence, the speaker is actually teaching by example, and his pupils, of all ages, are legion. Obviously, the educational opportunities involved impose a great responsibility, not only on the person before the microphone but also on the broadcasting industry as a whole and on the regulating authorities. It is not that a renewal of a license would necessarily depend upon anything so specific as the enunciation of particular words. It is rather that a general standard of excellence needs to be maintained in a medium of communication whose existence is justified only by its contribution to public service.

No Room for Errors. The microphone and the volume control dial are potent instruments for exposing carelessness or unsuspected mannerisms in speech. Anyone who says "watt" instead of "what" or pronounces "winter" like "winner" will be enlightened, and probably shocked, when listening to a play-back of his own words. If these sounds have occurred in an audition, his failure is likely, and the reason for it should be evident. To forestall such an unhappy outcome, he will do well to give special attention to stressed and unstressed syllables, to "speech phrases" as units, and to word endings like *ing*, *ed*, and the plural *s*, along with inflections that are needed to bring out a particular shade of meaning. At the same time, however, he must see to it that his painstaking care is not noticeable to his audience. Art that conceals art, so important in many fields of endeavor, is nowhere more desirable than in speaking before a microphone. Deliberate striving for effect will get over to the listener and will cause amusement, annoyance, or possibly, that worst of all calamities, a twisting of the dial.

Your Pronunciation Is Showing. "What good," someone may ask, "is all this attention to distinct speaking if the wrong pronunciation is used in the first place?" A facetious answer might be that if a wrong sound is used it had better be slurred over rapidly in the hope that the speaker's mistake or uncertainty will not be too noticeable. An observation to be made here is that the speaker may not realize that he is wrong and may give the incorrect pronunciation with bold and positive distinctness. The member of a state legislature who accused his opponents of "chickenry" when he meant "chicanery" was doubtless an extreme case, but he could be a useful illustration of the principle involved. His speech would be remembered, but for the wrong reason.

Indeed, one of the great educational services of radio and television is that they have encouraged the study of pronunciation. A large section of the public that was formerly "eye-minded," recognizing words by sight without being sure how they were pronounced, has lately become "sound-conscious." They have discovered a fact sometimes forgotten, that language is fundamentally a matter of sounds and pauses, and only secondarily a collection of written or printed characters on a page.

Questions of preferred usage in regard to disputed pronunciations call for careful study or perhaps, as in the case of the British Broadcasting Corporation (BBC), a committee of experts to rule upon difficult choices. Whether he is guided by the recommendations of a committee or by the authority of leading dictionaries, the radio or television speaker is expected to ascertain and follow the best current usage in his pronunciation. As a beginning he might profitably turn to the pages on Correct Pronunciation in this department, and pronounce aloud the words that are given there, with diacritical markings. Continuation of this study would of course include similar exercises in the pronunciation of proper names, biographical, geographical, historical, and otherwise. Names of musical composers form an interesting special group. Many lists of such words are available which can be helpful in clearing up doubts in the speaker's mind and giving trustworthy guidance to his listeners.

The Manuscript. Not only problems in pronunciation but also many difficulties of utterance may be avoided in the preparation of the script. Whether the words are written by the person who is to speak them or by someone preparing a manuscript for him, the question of delivery should always be uppermost in the writer's mind or, so to speak, in his inner ear. Long sentences, with clauses that leave the reader gasping for breath, are bad in any kind of writing, but they are especially objectionable in spoken discourse. Medium-long sentences alternating with shorter ones can provide a rhythm that will be comfortable for both speaker and listener. Short, Anglo-Saxon words, because of their familiar sound and meaning, are usually preferable to learned, bookish terms. The latter sometimes turn out to be rumbling polysyllables requiring vocal gymnastics of the speaker. Words like "concatenation," "supererogation," or "sesquipedalian" are not likely to be spoken naturally by the average person or understood readily by his listeners. Even if the individual words offer no difficulty they may be found in awkward combinations like the phrase "river improvement movement" that was edited out of one manuscript. Removal or avoidance of "built-in" difficulties for speakers is a matter that requires constant attention. A famous case of revision for this purpose was the first radio broadcasting of bridge games. Immediate difficulty was experienced by listeners in differentiating between "the eight of clubs" and "the ace of clubs" and similar expressions, no matter how carefully the words were spoken. A small change in editing substituted the words "eight spot" to designate the card of lower value, and the speaker's problem was solved.

The Speaker's Qualification. Anyone who wishes to engage in radio or television work can look forward to a period of training and experience. His chances for success will of course be better if he can build on a foundation of natural aptitude plus general education. The National Broadcasting Company, in a pamphlet entitled *The Selection and Training of Radio Announcers*, listed the principal attributes desirable in a candidate as follows:

A good voice, clear enunciation, and pronunciation free of dialect or local peculiarities; ability to read well; sufficient knowledge of foreign languages for the correct pronunciation of names, places, titles, etc.; some knowledge of musical history, composition and composers; ability to read and interpret poetry; facility in extempore speech; selling ability in the reading of commercial continuity; ability to master the technical details in operating the switchboard; a college education.

The foregoing list, although referring specifically to radio, will apply equally, and with very few changes, to persons planning to work in television. In addition, the announcer who faces a visible audience should have a good "stage presence." The qualities of poise, animation, and naturalness that are reflected in the voice of the radio speaker should extend to the manner and appearance, to the entire personality, of the announcer or performer on television. Even so comparatively simple an assignment as delivering a commercial message is a test of the television announcer's all-round adequacy.

Range of Communication. The potential reach of radio and television communication and, correspondingly, the opportunity and responsibility of speakers, actors, and producers, may be glimpsed in a few statistics for 1967. Data compiled by the Federal Communications Commission and published in *Statistical Abstract* give the number of broadcasting stations in the United States, including Puerto Rico and the Virgin Islands as follows:

	Authorized	*On the Air*
AM Radio	4185	4085
FM Radio	1854	1560
Television	758	608

Even more impressive are the totals in terms of radio and television households in the United States, published by Billboard Publishing Co. as of January 1, 1967:

Radio Households*, U.S. Total	58,600,000
Television Households, U.S. Total	57,600,000

* *A radio household is defined as an occupied dwelling unit having one or more radio sets.*

FORMS OF ORAL INTERPRETATION

In schools, in clubs, in social gatherings, and in the home, there are occasions when we desire to read, recite, act out, or tell about something from the printed page. Many of us hesitate to do so for fear of being elocutionary. It is true that the exhibitionary kind of recitation that flourished in the nineties and in the first decade of this century has gone out of style and is heard today only when it is being satirized. But there is no reason why one should be fearful of communicating to others what he has found worth-while in our literature. The sincere expression of fine literature is never out of date.

There are four forms of oral interpretation which are frequently used, the characteristics of which will be presented here. They are: *Interpretative Reading, Recitation, Impersonation,* and *Story Telling.* These forms might be called patterns of delivery. Each form is made up of certain factors of delivery which are so integrated that they make a characteristic pattern. It is well for the speech student to know these patterns. When he does he will be able to be judicious in his oral interpretations. He will know when to act out and when to recite. He will avoid the mistake frequently made of acting out in a literal fashion that which should be suggested. In other words, he can avoid being told he is "elocutionary."

Principles of Oral Reading. There are certain techniques in oral interpretation which are applicable to all the forms mentioned in the foregoing paragraph and which we take up here preliminary to our discussion of the four specific forms.

Phrasing. A speech phrase is different from a grammatical phrase. In the sentence, "While John was walking up the hill, he stopped and looked back at the sunset," there are two grammatical phrases, "up the hill" and "at the sunset." These grammatical phrases are only a part of the two speech phrases which go to make up the sentence. A speech phrase is a unit of speech expression which presents some element of experience for the audience to grasp. That element may be an idea, an image, an action, an emotion, an attitude. Thus, in the sentence about John we have two elements of experience, that of John walking up the hill, and John's turning to look at the sunset.

Characteristics of a Speech Phrase. The speech phrase is a *unit* in several respects. It is a unit in its separateness. Usually it is separated from other phrases by a pause. Sometimes, however, a change in pitch or volume or rate may indicate the end of one phrase and the beginning of another. It is a unit in its presenting one pattern of experience, something which can be grasped and reacted to by the listeners. It is a unit in its cohesiveness. The words in the phrase, "while John was walking up the hill," tie up with each other much in the same way as the syllables of a polysyllabic word are related. In fact, we can say one speaks a speech phrase just as he would pronounce a many-syllabled word, such as *unconstitutional.* Finally, it is a unit in that it has a beginning, a middle, and an end. Almost always it has a key word or combination of words which form the backbone of the phrase. The reader, both in voice and bodily movement, leads up to this key word, emphasizes it, and returns from it.

Phrasing in Oral Reading. Once a reader gets a command of phrasing, most of the battle for good reading is won. He will be reading ideas and images rather than words. His voice will have the spontaneous character of conversation, because he is really thinking and responding to the content of his phrase units. He must always remember to look ahead, grasp the meaning of the phrase he is to read, and speak that phrase, with the aim of stirring up the same meaning in his audience.

Emphasis. It would seem that if one had caught the meaning of a phrase he would give the proper emphasis to the words. But this does not always follow, since we are inclined, at least in reading aloud, unconsciously to give less emphasis to important words when we, the readers, are no longer reading the material for the first time. In other words, because the content is no longer fresh to us, the kind of emphasis which comes with the spontaneous realization of ideas and feelings is lost.

Three Kinds of Emphasis. The voice should give prominence, usually through raising the pitch of the voice, to that which is new or which advances the thought of the material; to that which involves contrast or comparison; and to that which is given emotional intensification because of its importance. The first two in the above have to do with new ideas; the third, intensifying emphasis, has to do with old ideas. Terms used to designate these three kinds of emphasis are (in the order given above): *Assertive, Antithetic,* and *Intensive.* In the sentence which follows, those words which require *assertive* emphasis will be italicized; those requiring ANTITHETIC will appear in lightface caps; and those requiring **intensive** will be in boldface:

There abides *faith, hope,* and *charity,* **these three;** but the *greatest* of these is CHARITY.

"Faith, hope, and charity" are *new* ideas; that is, it is the first time they have been spoken of by the reader, and consequently they get the downward stroke in the pitch of the voice that goes with *Assertive* emphasis. "These three" involves the giving of emotional significance to something already taken up and is consequently given *Intensive* emphasis. In the word "greatest" the thought is advanced with a new *assertion* and that kind of emphasis is given the word. When "charity" is repeated at the end of the sentence it is used in a comparative sense and consequently receives *Antithetic* emphasis. We have already pointed out that the voice takes a downward stroke in pitch for assertive emphasis. For antithetic emphasis it does likewise, but before starting down it takes a slight upward turn giving the voice what is called a *circumflex* inflection. For intensive emphasis the voice remains on a high level of pitch until the whole idea has been intensified. Thus, in "these three" the voice remains on the same high pitch for both words.

In applying these principles of emphasis the important thing to remember is that the reader must be constantly on the alert so that he distinguishes between that which is *new* or *important* and that which is *old*. On the new and important ideas his voice jumps to a high level and descends with a quick stroke; on that which is old, his voice remains on the neutral, "taken-for-granted" level. We mention again here that "new" and "old" are always used in terms of the audience. Good oral reading involves the constant fluctuation of the voice between the level of stress and the level of words which have been referred to before. If the reader effectively applies the two techniques taken up in the foregoing paragraphs, namely, *phrasing* and *emphasis*, he will have the necessary oral reading fundamentals for performing in the specialized forms to be taken up below.

Interpretative Reading. In the reading of literature from the printed page for the benefit of a listening audience, the reader acts as a mediator between his material and his audience. His aim is to recreate the material in the minds and imaginations of his listeners. Therefore, it is important that he subordinate himself as a personality and a performer to that end. If he calls too much attention to himself by displaying his elocutionary facility or by literally acting out the happenings of his material, his listeners will be distracted from their imaginative activity and pay attention to what is happening on the platform. If he concentrates on stirring up the imaginations of his listeners through the use of *suggestion* (as opposed to the literal portrayal of acting) he will be properly carrying out his function as an Interpretative Reader.

The following points should be kept in mind as important in the technique of Interpretative Reading:

1. The reader's relationship to the audience is a *mediate* one.

2. The reader's activities are on a *suggestive* basis, as opposed to the *literal*.

3. Because it is the literature being read which is the audience's chief concern, the manuscript or book *must* be used. It is best to have the book on a reading-stand, thus freeing the reader for suggestive activity.

4. What the reader does with his voice and body must always be *spontaneous* or *extemporaneous* in character. Conscious control of the voice and body to the extent that we in the audience listen to the reader's interesting inflections and notice his graceful gestures interferes with imaginative activity in the audience.

Interpretative Reading Today. This form of oral reading was developed at the end of the last century as a reaction to the elocutionary display of the *recitation* vogue, which had swept the country. It is a form of speech activity, which when understood and not confused with recitation or acting, has a real place in our everyday life. We can use it in our clubs and in church meetings and in library reading-hours. It is particularly adaptable to the reading of plays and novels.

Recitation. While it is true that Recitation easily turns into a display of the performer's elocutionary virtuosity, it need not be so, if the reciter appreciates the true character of the form. When one recites he is doing much the same thing as when one sings a song. The beauty and story of a poem is being conveyed to an audience through the reciter's body and personality. The more interesting the personality of the reciter, the more interesting will be the performance as a whole. As William Butler Yeats has said, the reciter is "an interesting and exciting messenger." It can be seen that the reciter's rôle is somewhat different from that of the interpretative reader's. Whatever the reciter can do to make more interesting what he has to report, he is at liberty to do. But he must make sure that what he does always pertains to what he is reporting. It was when the old "elocutionists" indulged in exaggerated graceful movements and poses and when they overused their vocal variations that the message was lost in the process.

Characteristics of Recitation.

1. The material is *memorized*.

2. Poetry of a musical nature and ballads are especially suited to recitation.

3. *Literal elements* are not out of place. What the performer does is not subordinated to the material as it is in Interpretative Reading.

4. *Formalized elements* in delivery are permissible. The reciter may consciously attend to the musical patterns of his material. He may also take on the formal movements of stylized behavior, when the material permits of it.

5. The reciter's relationship to his audience is *direct*. There may be an element of *display* in the relationship.

Choral Speaking as a Kind of Recitation. The speaking of a piece of literature by a group is a popular activity in our schools today. Usually the material used is strongly musical in character. The director of the choral speaking choir strives for a clear-cut unison in the voices and for interesting variations in the use of the bass and alto voices in the group. There are several good books to be found now which explain the technique of speech choir directing and which give suggested methods for handling poetry on a choir basis.

Impersonation. This form of speaking is closely related to *acting*. When a performer takes a dramatic monologue, such as Browning's *My Last Dutchess*, memorizes it, and acts out the character of the duke in that famous piece of literature, he is *impersonating*. Monologues, long speeches from plays, and short scenes from plays having few characters are best suited to impersonation.

Characteristics of Impersonation.

1. The material is *memorized*.

2. *Literal elements* predominate over *suggested elements*. What the audience sees before them is of primary importance; their own imaginative activity is subordinated.

3. The performer's personality is *submerged* in the character he is portraying. In Recitation the performer's personality is very much in evidence.

4. Impersonation differs from *acting* in that costumes, scenery, and make-up are seldom used and the activity on the platform is usually limited to an area about four feet in diameter.

5. The impersonator tries to create an *illusion*. Through literal activity and through suggestion he tries to give the audience a picture of life, sometimes realistic, sometimes idealized.

Story Telling. This form of oral interpretation is closest to public speaking in its character. In preparing to tell a story the performer should go about it much in the same way as he would prepare an extemporaneous speech. He should read the story carefully and set the gist of it down in outline form. Then he should rehearse the telling of the story just as he would rehearse an extemporaneous speech. In telling the story to his audience he should have the same spontaneous quality which is so desirable in speech-making.

Characteristics of Story Telling.

1. The story is *not memorized*. Only those parts of the story which the public have come to know and expect to hear should be spoken from memory. The dialogue in the story of *The Three Bears* would be well given as it is found on the printed page.

2. Story telling is *not reciting*. The story teller is conversing *with* an audience rather than performing *for* it. His relationship to his audience is that of social intercourse.

3. The *literal* and the *suggested* go hand in hand in this form. At times the speaker may appeal to the imaginations of his listeners and at times he may act out his characters quite completely.

4. The story teller's personality should play the same part it does in public speaking. It should enhance what he has to say.

DELIVERY

The following words of Quintilian, the famous Roman orator and teacher of rhetoric, contain advice for the speaker which is as appropriate now as when they were written:

"In all kinds of public speaking, but especially in popular assemblies, it is a capital rule to attend to all the decorum of time, place, and character. No warmth of eloquence can atone for the neglect of this. That vehemence which is becoming in a person of character and authority may be unsuitable to the modesty expected from a young speaker. That sportive and witty manner which may suit one assembly is altogether out of place in a grave cause and solemn meeting. No one should ever rise to speak in public without forming to himself a just and strict idea of what suits his own age and character; what suits the subject, the hearers, the place, the occasion; and adjusting the whole train and manner of his speaking to this idea."

There are, in general, four methods of delivering speeches. Each has its especial strength and its peculiar weakness. It is important that a speaker should adopt for his main dependence the method to which his abilities are best suited.

Speaking from Manuscript. The use of a carefully prepared manuscript is the most certain method of delivering a speaker's thought completely, logically, and economically. It is especially appropriate for formal occasions, such as lectures, when the speaker's chief purpose is to convey information to his hearers. The weakness of this method lies in the tendency of the speaker to keep his eyes too closely riveted to his manuscript and thus lose the attention of his audience. The speaker who uses manuscript usually sacrifices some of the directness of address which is so important a quality of oratory. For the speaker of small experience, however, the use of manuscript during delivery is to be recommended.

Speaking from Notes. The speaker who uses notes, that is, an outline of the previously prepared manuscript, has the advantage of possessing a ready guide through his argument, while at the same time he is freer to meet unexpected situations than is the man who must follow a complete manuscript. This is a weighty consideration in discussion or debate. All notes, however, should be clearly written so that the speaker's eyes will not be taken from his audience for too long a time, while he attempts to decipher his outline.

Speaking from Memory. The memorized speech has the distinct advantage of permitting the speaker to look constantly at his audience. It does not, however, allow him to adapt himself readily to unforeseen circumstances, such as disturbances in an assembly or the necessity of answering unexpected arguments in debate. It is appropriate to formal occasions; for it permits the attainment of highly finished style both in composition and in delivery. The chief weakness of the method is that his effort to recall the memorized words may rob the speaker of directness and spontaneity. The ideal in the use of the memorized speech is to combine finished perfection of form with the appearance of that naturalness which marks the extemporaneous address.

Speaking Extemporaneously. Undoubtedly, the most effective form of public speaking is the extemporaneous address. This is to be defined as the presentation of thoroughly prepared thought in language which is the product of the occasion. As extemporaneous speaking is the most effective type of oratory, so it demands the most exacting and long-continued preparation and practice. However, the reward of the master of extemporaneous oratory is the consciousness of the most thorough command over his audiences. Extemporaneous speaking does not preclude the use of notes, and, for the short, informal address, the preparation of notes, outlining the thought to be clothed in extemporaneous language, is usually advisable.

Whichever of these general methods of speaking you choose to employ, you must observe certain well established principles pertaining to manner and to voice. The total effect of a speech is compounded of the words, the bodily attitudes, and the voice of the speaker. He must know how to adapt these elements to each other and to the spirit of his audience. It has well been said that the best oratorical style for a given individual is that of his best conversation.

The attainment of an effective manner before an audience is worthy of long and careful effort. Each speaker must study his own problems. However, there are two means which you will find to be fundamental:

1. Know your subject and your plan so well that you show *confidence* (a) by looking at your audience—letting them see your eyes, (b) by speaking directly to your audience—letting them see your lips move. The audience is entitled to this directness of address.

2. Be so thoroughly interested in your talk that you show ease (a) by standing so firmly *on both feet* that you can change your position without "teetering," (b) by such gestures with arms or body as are prompted by your thought and feeling *at the time*, (c) by directing your eyes and your voice at some time to every one in your audience, (d) by deep, steady breathing.

Gesture. The name for the bodily attitudes and movements and facial expressions by which a speaker supplements and emphasizes his words. Every speaker will use gesture in some way, because bodily movements are a fundamental mode of expressing ideas and feelings; and the more earnest and emphatic the speaker is, the more frequent and vigorous will be his gestures. Two rules you may well observe: (1) Do not try to repress all gesture. (2) Strive to make every gesture mean something definite. Superfluous gestures take the attention of your audience from what you are saying. Notice the gestures that you make spontaneously in conversation. Try to employ these and adapt them to the "enlarged conversation" of your public speech. We usually think of gestures as movements of the arms and hands. But remember that you can make many of your most effective gestures with your facial muscles, your head, or your whole body. This caution will help you to avoid the windmill method of gesture, or merely throwing your arms about. In gesture, as in every other phase of speaking, sincerity of thought and purpose is the best guard against meaningless expression.

Enunciation. For *good speech*, in uttering your own thoughts or reading orally the words of another, the first essential is this: *Carefully think your words and phrases.* Your voice will respond with wonderful accuracy to your understanding of the words you use. The second essential is this: Pronounce your words *distinctly and correctly*. This includes the true forming and arrangement of the sounds, faultless accent, and clear quality of voice. The list of words in the section entitled Correct Pronunciation will give you the precise sounds and accents for many words commonly used. For other words, consult unabridged dictionaries. Further, learn how to form these sounds exactly.

Voice Qualities. Pleasing and effective speech is very largely a result of the speaker's mastery of good voice qualities, the fundamental principle of which is proper breathing. Individual voices differ in quality because of the varied forms and conditions of the vocal cords and the resonance chambers of the mouth and nose. Each person has a normal quality of voice, which he uses in conversation, and by which it is possible to recognize him even when his features cannot be seen. But, by altering the shape of the mouth cavity or by opening or restricting the nasal and throat passages, each individual can produce several other qualities besides this normal one.

Eight qualities of the speaking voice are usually distinguished. Three of these the public speaker should cultivate: (1) *Normal*, which is a clear, resonant quality produced by the natural position of the vocal organs and the simple enunciation of vowels and consonants, the ordinary conversational voice. (2) *Orotund*, a fuller, clearer, and more resonant quality. It is appropriately used to express grandeur, sublimity, and similar thoughts and ideas of a lofty and impressive nature. The speaker should be careful not to use this quality too frequently, as it may easily pass into bombast and become unconvincing. (3) *Aspirate*, which is a breathy utterance either devoid of vocalization, as in a whisper, or partially vocalized, as in the so-called "stage whisper." The quality may suggest weakness or excessive emotion. It is sometimes used effectively in public speaking to give striking emphasis to an expression.

The remaining five qualities are generally undesirable and to be avoided in public speaking. They are confined to the art of the actor in portraying characters or in suggesting emotions with which they are associated. (4) *Guttural*, a throaty sound. (5) *Pectoral*, a hollow, breathy quality. (6) *Oral*, the result of a rather thin, mouth resonance. (7) *Nasal*, a quality characterized by a harsh twang. (8) *Falsetto*, a quality of tone above the speaker's natural range.

Cautions.—Three very common faults of American speech are *high pitch*, *nasality*, and *throatiness*. Too high a pitch of voice is due to nervousness and to lack of self-control. Nasality is not talking through the nose but failure to use the nasal cavity properly in speaking. It is frequently due to some obstruction of the nasal passages. Throatiness, or making sounds too low down in the throat, is usually caused by contraction of throat muscles.

Inflection. What punctuation is to written language, *inflection*, *change of pitch*, and *pauses* are to spoken language. The importance of changes of pitch in indicating emphasis was discussed under *emphasis* in the section on Oral Reading.

Change of Pitch. By pronouncing one of the words in a sentence with a decidedly high or low pitch as compared with the pitch of the others, you can give several additional meanings to the sentence. For instance: If *you* is given a higher pitch than *are going*, the sentence means that you are going and not some one else; pronouncing *are* with a higher pitch than *you* and *going* may indicate either surprise or decided determination. This abrupt shifting of the key, or tone, of speech *between* words, phrases, clauses, or sentences is called *change of pitch*.

Practice will show you the importance of this means of emphasis. It is, in fact, the natural method of marking off one idea from another in speech. If you think clearly, you can hardly keep such changes out of your voice.

Pauses. Plan your pauses as carefully as you arrange your words. Silences are the wells of thought. Definite pauses serve at least four main purposes: (1) They give your audience time to grasp important ideas. (2) They enable your audience to make the necessary transition from one thought to another and so to "follow" you. (3) They convey the impression that you are choosing your words carefully. (4) They impress your audience with a sense of your consideration for them. Thus, directly and indirectly, pauses serve to give emphasis to your speech.

Rate of Speaking. Just as the natural qualities of voice vary among individuals, so too their natural rates of speaking differ. Some people are naturally quick and nervous; others are slow and phlegmatic. It should be remembered, however, that the brain of the listener is capable of receiving and registering only a limited number of words in any given unit of time, and that a speaker should adjust his rate to the ability of the audience to take in what he says. Generally, it is unwise to exceed 125 words a minute in ordinary speaking. On the other hand, it is tiresome to listen to slow, drawling delivery. Hence, rate should be adapted (1) to the capability of the audience to grasp the speaker's meaning, as well as (2) to the nature of what is spoken.

It is important that, in the course of any speech or address, one should, from time to time, alter his rate of speaking. Change of rate (1) relieves monotony, (2) helps in emphasis, (3) suggests certain emotions or movements.

That which will quicken or retard a man's footsteps will also quicken or retard his rate of speaking. Narration, for example, is flowing, easy, and graceful; vehemence is firm and accelerated; anger and joy are sudden, sometimes hysterical. Again, dignity, authority, sublimity, and awe assume deeper tones and a slower movement. One may often hear a good speaker, at some sudden turn of thought or feeling, check himself in the full tide of utterance and give indescribable power to a passage by slackening his rate and by adopting a slow, deliberate enunciation.

Breathing. Breathe deeply and steadily, using the diaphragm and chest walls. Learn to feel your diaphragm, which is the flexible floor of your chest, expanding and moving downward as you "take in" breath. You can then control and steady its movement, keeping it expanded, and give *carrying power* to your voice. Practice this breathing. It will help you to avoid "stage fright." Take a "deep breath" before you begin to speak.

Correct Speech Sounds. These are secured by right breathing, proper shaping of the mouth, and correct placing of the various sounds. The voice is produced by vibrations, or waves, set up by the vocal cords in the column of air reaching from the lungs up into the mouth and the nose. The different shapes that the mouth cavity may take give special forms to these waves. The forms, thus produced, give rise to the *vowels*, or open voice sounds. Each vowel sound is made with the jaws and the flexible palate, lips, tongue, and cheeks in a definite position.

The cavities of the throat, nose, and mouth act as a *resonance chamber*, like an organ pipe or the body of a violin, to give volume and tone to the voice. Any obstruction, such as the mucus from a "cold," enlarged tonsils, or adenoids, interferes with the volume of the voice as well as with the purity and the clearness of its tone.

The *consonant sounds* we form by partially or entirely closing the mouth cavity with the teeth or tongue or lips. We thus, to some extent, shut off the vowel sound; at the same time, the friction or explosive force of the moving breath makes sounds which join or articulate with the vowels to form syllables.

A foreigner learning English pronounces a word like "concentrate" with the accent placed logically on the second, or "root" syllable. Then he learns that this word, like many others, has been affected by a recessive tendency which moved the accent to or toward the beginning, so that the correct pronunciation is *kŏn'sĕn-trāt*. However, as in spelling and other matters, the English language refuses to be consistent. The word *rê-mŏn'strāt* keeps the accent on the second syllable, while the comparable word *dĕm'ŏn-strāt* moves the accent back and changes both the syllabication and the vowel sounds. These are merely examples to indicate the need for careful examination of words in order to learn their present accepted pronunciation. At a time when many people are "eye-minded" and when reading aloud is almost a lost art, a study of diacritical marking for individual words is highly desirable. In this connection, a useful exercise for anyone would be the review and pronouncing aloud of the following list of more than 1600 words which have sometimes caused difficulty.

abbé, *a'bā'*
abdomen, *ăb-dō'mĕn*
abhor, *ăb-hôr'*
abhorrent, *ăb-hôr'ĕnt*
abject, *ăb-jĕkt'*
absent (adj.), *ăb'sĕnt*
absent (v.), *ăb-sĕnt'*
abstemious, *ăb-stē'mĭ-ŭs*
accent (n.), *ăk'sĕnt*
accent (v.), *ăk-sĕnt'*
accessory, *ăk-sĕs'ô-rĭ*
acclimate, *ă-klī'mĭt*
accompaniment, *ă-kŭm'pà-nĭ-mĕnt*
accuracy, *ăk'û-rà-sĭ*
acetylene, *ă-sĕt'ĭ-lēn*
acorn, *ā'kôrn*
acoustic, *ă-kōōs'tĭk*
acronym, *ăc'rō-nĭm*
actor, *ăk'tĕr*
acts, *ăkts*
acumen, *ă-kū'mĕn*
adagio, *à-dä'jō*
address, *ă-drĕs'*
adieu, *à-dū'*
adios, *ä'dyōs'*
adjourn, *ă-jûrn'*
adobe, *à-dō'bĭ*
adult, *à-dŭlt'*
adventure, *ăd-vĕn'chûr*
adverse, *ăd-vûrs'*
advertisement, *ăd-vûr'tĭz-mĕnt*
advertiser, *ăd'vĕr-tīz'ĕr*
aerial, *ēr'ĭ-ăl*
a fortiori, *ā fôr'shĭ-ō'rĭ*
aft, *àft*
after, *àf'tĕr*
again, *à-gĕn'*
agile, *ăj'ĭl*
alas, *à-làs'*
albino, *ăl-bī'nō*
alder, *ôl'dĕr*
algebra, *ăl'jê-brà*
alias, *ā'lĭ-ăs*
alien, *āl'yĕn*
allegro, *ä-lā'grō*
allies, *ă-līz'*
alloy, *ă-loi'*
alma mater, *ăl'mà mā'tĕr*
almond, *ä'mŭnd*
alpaca, *ăl-păk'à*
alpine, *ăl'pīn*
alternate (v.), *ôl'tĕr-nāt*
alternate (adj.) (n.), *ăl'tĕr-nĭt*
alternately, *ôl-tĕr'nĭt-lĭ*
alternative, *ôl-tûr'nà-tĭv*
aluminum, *à-lū'mĭ-nŭm*
alumnæ, *à-lŭm'nē*
alumni, *à-lŭm'nī*
amateur, *ăm'à-tûr'*
ambivalent, *ăm-bĭv'à-lĕnt*
ambrosia, *ăm-brō'zhĭ-à*
ameliorate, *à-mēl'yô-rāt*
amenable, *à-mē'nà-b'l*
amenity, *à-mĕn'ĭ-tĭ*
ammonia, *ă-mō'nĭ-à*
amortization, *ăm-ôr'tĭ-zā'shŭn*
amortize, *à-môr'tīz*
ampere, *ăm'pēr*
ancestor, *ăn'sĕs-tĕr*

ancestral, *ăn-sĕs'trăl*
anchor, *ăng'kĕr*
anchovy, *ăn-chō'vĭ*
ancient, *ān'shĕnt*
and, *ănd*
anemone, *à-nĕm'ô-nê*
angina pectoris, *ăn-jī'nà pĕk'tô-rĭs*
aniline, *ăn'ĭ-lĭn*
annihilate, *ă-nī'ĭ-lāt*
answer, *àn'sĕr*
antarctic, *ănt-ärk'tĭk*
anxiety, *ăng-zī'ĕ-tĭ*
anxious, *ăngk'shŭs*
aperient, *à-pēr'ĭ-ĕnt*
aperture, *ăp'ĕr-chûr*
aphelion, *ă-fē'lĭ-ŏn*
apostle, *à-pŏs''l*
apotheosis, *à-pŏth'ê-ō'sĭs*
apparatus, *ăp'à-rā'tŭs*
appellate, *ă-pĕl'āt*
appendicitis, *ă-pĕn'dĭ-sī'tĭs*
applicable, *ăp'lĭ-kà-b'l*
appreciation, *ă-prē'shĭ-ā'shŭn*
apricot, *ā'prĭ-kŏt*
apron, *ā'prŭn*
apropos, *ăp'rô-pō'*
aqua, *ăk' wà*
aquarium, *à-kwâr'ĭ-ŭm*
aqueduct, *ăk'wê-dŭkt*
arbutus, *är-bū'tŭs*
archangel, *ärk'ān'jĕl*
archbishop, *ärch'bĭsh'ŭp*
archetype, *är'kê-tīp*
archipelago, *är'kĭ-pĕl'à-gō*
architect, *är'kĭ-tĕkt*
archives, *är'kīvz*
archivist, *är'kê-vĭst*
arctic, *ärk'tĭk*
area, *ā'rê-à*
aria, *ä'rĭ-à*
arid, *ăr'ĭd*
armada, *är-mä'dà*
armistice, *är'mĭ-stĭs*
aroma, *à-rō'mä*
arras, *ăr'ăs*
arroyo, *ă-roi'ō*
artisan, *är'tĭ-zăn*
asafetida, *ăs'à-fĕt'ĭ-dà*
ascetic, *à-sĕt'ĭk*
ask, *àsk*
askance, *à-skăns'*
asparagus, *ăs-păr'à-gŭs*
asphalt, *ăs'fôlt*
aspirant, *ăs-pīr'ănt*
assay, *ă-sā'*
associate (v.), *ă-sō'shĭ-āt*
associate (n.), *-àt*
associate (adj.), *-àt*
association, *ă-sō'sĭ-ā'shŭn*
assume, *ă-sūm'*
asthma, *ăz'mà*
atheneum, *ăth'ê-nē'ŭm*
athletics, *ăth-lĕt'ĭks*
attaché, *ăt'à-shā'*
attorney, *ă-tûr'nĭ*
audacious, *ô-dā'shŭs*
audience, *ô'dĭ-ĕns*
au gratin, *ō'grà'tăN'*

aunt, *änt*
au revoir, *ō'rĕ-vwär'*
aurora borealis, *ô-rō'rà bō'rĕ-ā'lĭs*
authority, *ô-thŏr'ĭ-tĭ*
automobile, *ô'tô-mô-bēl'*
auxiliary, *ôg-zĭl'yà-rĭ*
avenue, *ăv'ê-nū*
aviator, *ā'vĭ-ā'tĕr*
avocado, *ăv'ô-kä'dō*
avoirdupois, *ăv'ĕr-dŭ-poiz'*
awry, *à-rī'*
axiom, *ăk'sĭ-ŭm*
aye, (yes) *ī*

bacilli, *bà-sĭl'ī*
bacillus, *bà-sĭl'ŭs*
bade, *băd*
badinage, *băd'ĭ-näzh'*
balcony, *băl'kô-nĭ*
ballad, *băl'ăd*
ballade, *bà-läd'*
ballet, *băl'à*
balm, *bäm*
banquet, *băng'kwĕt*
baptism, *băp'tĭz'm*
baptize, *băp-tīz'*
barbiturate, *bär-bĭt'û-rāt*
bargain, *bär'gĭn*
barrage, *bà-räzh'*
barrel, *băr'ĕl*
basin, *bā's'n*
basket, *bàs'kĕt*
bath, *bàth*
baton, *bà'tŏN'*
bayou, *bī'ōō*
because, *bê-kôz'*
bedstead, *bĕd'stĕd*
been, *bĭn*
begonia, *bê-gō'nĭ-à*
beige, *bāzh*
believe, *bê-lēv'*
belles-lettres, *bĕl'lĕt'r'*
belligerent, *bê-lĭj'ĕr-ĕnt*
bellows, *bĕl'ōz*
beloved (adj.), *bê-lŭv'ĕd*
beloved (part.), *bê-lŭvd'*
beneficent, *bê-nĕf'ĭ-sĕnt*
bequeath, *bê-kwēTH'*
bestial, *bĕst'yăl*
betrothal, *bê-trŏth'ăl*
bicycle, *bī'sĭk-'l*
biennial, *bī-ĕn'ĭ-ăl*
bijou, *bē'zhōō*
billet-doux, *bĭl'à-dōō*
bindery, *bīn'dĕr-ĭ*
biography, *bī-ŏg'rà-fĭ*
biology, *bī-ŏl'ô-jĭ*
bipartite, *bī-pär'tīt*
bismuth, *bĭz'mŭth*
blackguard, *blăg'ärd*
blanch, *blànch*
blanc mange, *blà-mänzh'*
blasé, *blä'zā'*
blaspheme, *blăs-fēm'*
blasphemous, *blăs'fê-mŭs*
blast, *blàst*
blatant, *blā'tănt*
blessed (adj.), *blĕs'ĕd*
blessed (part.), *blĕst*

blouse, *blouz*
blue, *blōō*
boisterous, *bois'tēr-ŭs*
bolero, *bô-lâr'ō*
boll weevil, *bōl wē'v'l*
bomb, *bŏm*
bona fide, *bō'nȧ fī'dĕ*
bon marché, *bôN'mȧr'shā'*
bonnet, *bŏn'ĕt*
borax, *bō'răks*
borrow, *bŏr'ō*
bosom, *bŏŏz'ŭm*
boudoir, *bōō' dwär*
bouquet, *bcō-kā'*
bourgeois, *bŏŏr' zhwä*
bourn (bound), *bōrn*
bourse, *bŏŏrs*
bovine, *bō'vīn*
bowlegged, *bō'lĕg'ĕd*
brand-new, *brănd'nū'*
brassière, *brȧ-zēr'*
breviary, *brē'vĭ-ĕr'ĭ*
brigand, *brĭg'ȧnd*
bristle, *brĭs''l*
brochure, *brô-shōōr'*
brogan, *brō'gȧn*
bromide, *brō'mīd*
bromine, *brō'mēn*
bronchitis, *brŏn-kī'tĭs*
brusque (brusk), *brŭsk*
buffet (sideboard), *bŏŏ-fā'*
bungalow, *bŭng'gȧ-lō*
buoy, *boi*
buoyant, *bōō'yȧnt*
bureaucracy, *bû-rŏk'rȧ-sĭ*
burlesque, *bûr-lĕsk'*
bursar, *bûr'sẽr*
business, *bĭz'nĕs*
butcher, *bŏŏch'ẽr*
butte, *būt*

cabal, *kȧ-băl'*
caballero, *kä'bäl-yā'rō*
cabaret, *kăb'ȧ-rā'*
cache, *kăsh*
cadaver, *kȧ-dăv'ẽr*
café, *kȧ'fā'*
cafeteria, *kăf'ĕ-tēr'ĭ-ȧ*
caisson, *kā'sŭn*
calf, *käf*
caliph, *kā'lĭf*
caliphate, *kăl'ĭ-fāt*
calk, *kôk*
calliope, *kȧ-lī'ô-pĕ*
calm, *käm*
caloric, *kȧ-lŏr'ĭk*
calorie, *kăl'ô-rĭ*
calve, *käv*
calyx, *kā'lĭks*
camembert, *kăm'ĕm-bâr'*
campanile, *kăm'pȧ-nē'lĕ*
cancel, *kăn'sĕl*
candelabra, *kăn'dĕ-lä'brȧ*
canine, *kā'nīn*
cañon, *kăn'yŭn*
cant, *kănt*
can't, *känt*
cantilever, *kăn'tĭ-lē'vẽr*
cantonment, *kăn-tŏn'mĕnt*
capitulate, *kȧ-pĭch'û-lāt*
capon, *kā'pŏn*
caprice, *kȧ-prēs'*
carafe, *kȧ-răf'*
carburetor, *kär'bû-rā'tẽr*
caricature, *kăr'ĭ-kȧ-chûr*
carillon, *kăr'ĭ-lŏn*
carrousel, *kăr' ŏŏ-sĕl*
cartridge, *kär'trĭj*
cashmere, *kăsh'mēr*
casino, *kȧ-sē'nō*

caste, *kȧst*
catalogue, *kăt'ȧ-lŏg*
catalpa, *kȧ-tăl'pȧ*
catch, *kăch*
catchup, *kăch'ŭp*
catechize, *kăt'ē-kīz*
catsup, *kăt'sŭp*
caveat, *kā'vē-ăt*
celestial, *sē-lĕs'chȧl*
celibacy, *sĕl'ĭ-bȧ-sĭ*
cello, *chĕl'ō*
celluloid, *sĕl'ū-loid*
cemetery, *sĕm'ē-tẽr-ĭ*
centenary, *sĕn'tē-nẽr'ĭ*
centennial, *sĕn-tĕn'ĭ-ăl*
centime, *sän'tēm*
century, *sĕn'chû-rĭ*
ceramic, *sē-răm'ĭk*
cerebrum, *sẽr'ē-brŭm*
chagrin, *shȧ-grĭn'*
challis, *shăl'ĭ*
chamois, *shăm'ĭ*
champagne, *shăm-pān*
chaos, *kā'ŏs*
chaperon, *shăp'ẽr-ōn*
character, *kăr'ăk-tẽr*
chargé d'affaires, *shär'zhā' dȧ'fâr'*
chartreuse, *shär-trûz'*
chassis, *shă'sĭ*
chasten, *chās''n*
chastise, *chăs-tīz'*
chastisement, *chăs'tĭz-mĕnt*
chatelaine, *shăt'ē-lān*
chauffeur, *shō'fûr*
chef, *shĕf*
chemise, *shē-mēz'*
chemisette, *shĕm'ĭ-zĕt*
chenille, *shē-nēl'*
chestnut, *chĕs'nŭt*
cheviot, *shĕv'ĭ-ŭt*
chew, *chōō*
chic, *shĕk*
chicane, *shĭ-kān'*
chicken, *chĭk'ĕn; -ĭn*
chiffon, *shĭ-fŏn'*
chiffonier, *shĭf'ô-nẽr'*
children, *chĭl'drĕn*
chimera, *kĭ-mē'rȧ*
chirography, *kī-rŏg'rȧ-fĭ*
chiropodist, *kī-rŏp'ô-dĭst*
chisel, *chĭz''l*
chocolate, *chŏk'ô-lĭt*
choleric, *kŏl'ẽr-ĭk*
chorister, *kŏr'ĭs-tẽr*
chorus, *kō'rŭs*
christen, *krĭs''n*
chyle, *kīl*
chyme, *kīm*
cinchona, *sĭn-kō'na*
cinematograph, *sĭn'ē-măt'ô-grȧf*
circuit, *sûr'kĭt*
circuitous, *sẽr-kū'ĭ-tŭs*
citadel, *sĭt'ȧ-dĕl*
civil, *sĭv'ĭl*
civilization, *sĭv'ĭ-lĭ-zā'shŭn*
clairvoyant, *klâr-voi'ȧnt*
clandestine, *klăn-dĕs'tĭn*
clapboard, *klăb'ẽrd*
clasp, *klȧsp*
class, *klȧs*
cleanly (adj.), *klĕn'lĭ*
cleanly (adv.), *klēn'lĭ*
clematis, *klĕm'ȧ-tĭs*
clew, *klōō*
clientele, *klī'ĕn-tĕl'*
clique, *klēk*
clothes, *klōTHz*
coadjutor, *kō-ăd-jōō'tẽr*
coagulate, *kô-ăg'û-lāt*
cocaine, *kô-kān'*
coccyx, *kŏk'sĭks*
codeine, *kō'dē-ēn*

coffee, *kŏf'ĭ*
cognac, *kō'nyȧk*
cognizance, *kŏg'nĭ-zȧns*
cognomen, *kŏg-nō'mĕn*
coiffure, *kwä-fūr'*
colander, *kŭl'ȧn-dẽr*
collation, *kŏ-lā'shŭn*
collect (n.), *kŏl'ĕkt*
collect (v.), *kŏ-lĕkt'*
colloquial, *kŏ-lō'kwĭ-ăl*
colosseum, *kŏl'ŏ-sē'ŭm*
colporteur, *kŏl'pōr'tẽr*
column, *kŏl'ŭm*
columnist, *kŏl'ŭm-nĭst*
combatant, *kŏm'bȧ-tănt*
combine (v.), *kŏm-bīn'*
combine (n.), *kŏm'bīn*
comeliness, *kŭm'lĭ-nĕs*
comely, *kŭm'lĭ*
comity, *kŏm'ĭ-tĭ*
commiserate, *kŏ-mĭz'ẽr-āt*
communal, *kŏm'û-năl*
commune (v.), *kŏ-mūn'*
commune (n.), *kŏm'ūn*
comparable, *kŏm'pȧ-rȧ-b'l*
complex (n.), *kŏm'plĕks*
complex (adj.), *kŏm-plĕks'*
comport, *kŏm-pōrt'*
compromise, *kŏm'prô-mīz*
comptroller, *kŏn-trōl'ẽr*
concave, *kŏn'kāv*
concerto, *kŏn-chẽr'tō*
conclude, *kŏn-klōōd'*
conclusive, *kŏn-klōō'sĭv*
concourse, *kŏn'kōrs*
concrete (n. and adj.), *kŏn'krēt*
condolence, *kŏn-dō'lĕns*
conduit, *kŏn'dĭt*
confidant, *kŏn'fĭ-dănt'*
confiscate, *kŏn'fĭs-kāt*
congé, *kôN'zhā'*
congenial, *kŏn-jēn'yȧl*
congregate, *kŏng'grē-gȧt*
congress, *kŏng'grĕs*
congruous, *kŏng'grōō-ŭs*
conjure, *kŏn-jōōr'*
connoisseur, *kŏn'ĭ-sûr'*
conquest, *kŏng'kwĕst*
conscientious, *kŏn'shĭ-ĕn'shŭs*
considerable, *kŏn-sĭd'ẽr-ȧ-b'l*
consignee, *kŏn'sĭ-nē'*
conspiracy, *kŏn-spĭr'ȧ-sĭ*
constable, *kŭn'stȧ-b'l*
consul, *kŏn'sŭl*
consummate, (v.) *kŏn'sŭ-māt*
contemplate, *kŏn'tĕm-plāt*
contemplative, *kŏn-tĕm'plȧ-tĭv*
continuity, *kŏn'tĭ-nū'ĭ-tĭ*
contractor, *kŏn'trăk-tẽr*
contrary, *kŏn'trẽr-ĭ*
contumely, *kŏn'tû-mē-lĭ*
conversant, *kŏn'vẽr-sȧnt*
coquetry, *kō'kĕ-trĭ*
coral, *kŏr'ăl*
cordial, *kôr'jăl*
cornet, *kôr'nĕt*
corolla, *kô-rŏl'ȧ*
corps, *kōr*
corral, *kŏ-răl'*
corridor, *kŏr'ĭ-dôr*
corrugate, *kŏr'ŏŏ-gȧt*
cortege, *kôr-tĕzh'*
cosmetic, *kŏz-mĕt'ĭk*
costume (n.), *kŏs'tūm*
costumer, *kŏs-tūm'ẽr*
cotillion, *kô-tĭl'yŭn*
coup, *kōō*
coupé, *kōō'pā'*
coupon, *kōō'pŏn*
courier, *kŏŏr'ĭ-ẽr*
courteous, *kûr'tē-ŭs*
courtier, *kōr'tĭ-ẽr*

cousin, *kŭz''n*
couturier, *kōō'tü'ryā'*
covetous, *kŭv'ĕ-tŭs*
crabbed, *krăb'ĕd*
cranberry, *krăn'bĕr-ĭ*
crèche, *krāsh*
credence, *krē'dĕns*
credulous, *krĕd'ŭ-lŭs*
creek, *krēk*
crêpe de Chine, *krāp'dĕ-shēn'*
crescendo, *krĕ-shĕn'dō*
crew, *krōō*
crucial, *krōō'shăl*
cruel, *krōō'ĕl*
crux, *krŭks*
cuisine, *kwē-zēn'*
culinary, *kū'lĭ-nĕr'ĭ*
culture, *kŭl'chŭr*
cuneiform, *kū-nē'ĭ-fôrm*
cupboard, *kŭb'ĕrd*
cupola, *kū'pô-là*
curator, *kû-rā'tĕr*
cycle, *sī'k'l*
cynosure, *sī'nô-shōōr*

dachshund, *däks'hōōnt'*
daguerreotype, *dȧ-gĕr'ô-tīp*
dahlia, *dăl'yȧ*
damage, *dăm'ĭj*
dance, *dȧns*
data, *dā'tȧ*
daub, *dôb*
deaf, *dĕf*
debacle, *dĕ-bä'k'l*
debauch, *dĕ-bôch'*
debenture, *dĕ-bĕn'chŭr*
débris, *dĕ-brē'*
début, *dā'bū*
debutante, *dĕb'ŭ-tänt'*
decade, *dĕk'ād*
decadence, *dĕ-kā'dĕns*
decent, *dē'sĕnt*
décolleté, *dā-kŏl'ĕ-tā; F. dȧ'kôl'tā'*
decorous, *dĕk'ô-rŭs*
dedicatory, *dĕd'ĭ-kȧ-tô'rĭ*
defalcate, *dĕ-făl'kāt*
defamation, *dĕf'ȧ-mā'shŭn*
deficit, *dĕf'ĭ-sĭt*
deign, *dān*
delicatessen, *dĕl'ĭ-kȧ-tĕs'ĕn*
delirious, *dĕ-lĭr'ĭ-ŭs*
de luxe, *dĕ lōōks'*
demagogic, *dĕm'ȧ-gŏj'ĭk*
demi-tasse, *dĕm'ĭ-tȧs'*
democratize, *dĕ-mŏk'rȧ-tīz*
demon, *dē'mŭn*
demonetization,
   dĕ-mŏn'ĕ-tĭ-zā'shŭn
demurrage, *dĕ-mûr'ĭj*
dénouement, *dā-nōō-mäN'*
depths, *dĕpths*
derisive, *dĕ-rī'sĭv*
deshabille, *dĕz'ȧ-bēl'*
desist, *dĕ-zĭst'*
despicable, *dĕs'pĭ-kȧ-b'l*
dessert, *dĭ-zûrt'*
destine, *dĕs'tĭn*
detail, *dĕ-tāl'*
detonation, *dĕt'ô-nā'shŭn*
detour, *dĕ'tōōr*
devoir, *dĕ-vwär'*
devotee, *dĕv'ô-tē'*
dew, *dū*
dexterous, *dĕk'stĕr-ŭs*
diagnostician, *dī'ăg-nŏs-tĭsh'ăn*
diastole, *dī-ăs'tô-lē*
dictator, *dĭk-tā'tĕr*
dictionary, *dĭk'shŭn-ĕr'ĭ*
diesel, *dē'zĕl*
dietetics, *dī'ĕ-tĕt'ĭks*
dietitian, *dī'ĕ-tĭsh'ăn*

different, *dĭf'ĕr-ĕnt*
diffuse (adj.), *dĭ-fūs'*
diffuse (v.), *dĭ-fūz'*
digest (v.), *dĭ-jĕst'*
digest (n.), *dī'jĕst*
digestion, *dĭ-jĕs'chŭn*
digitalis, *dĭj'ĭ-tăl'ĭs*
digraph, *dī'grȧf*
dilettante, *dĭl'ĕ-tăn'tĭ*
diocese, *dī'ô-sēs*
diphtheria, *dĭf-thēr'ĭ-ȧ*
diphthong, *dĭf'thŏng*
diploma, *dĭ-plō'mȧ*
direct, *dĭ-rĕkt'*
disaster, *dĭ-zȧs'tĕr*
disburse, *dĭs-bûrs'*
discern, *dĭ-zûrn'*
discipline, *dĭs'ĭ-plĭn*
discourse, *dĭs-kōrs'*
discretion, *dĭs-krĕsh'ŭn*
disdain, *dĭs-dān'*
disease, *dĭ-zēz'*
dishabille, *dĭs'ȧ-bēl'*
dishevel, *dĭ-shĕv'ĕl*
dispersion, *dĭs-pûr'shŭn*
disputant, *dĭs'pŭ-tănt*
district, *dĭs'trĭkt*
divan, *dī'văn*
diverge, *dī-vûrj'*
divulge, *dĭ-vŭlj'*
docile, *dŏs'ĭl*
domain, *dô-mān'*
domicile, *dŏm'ĭ-sĭl*
donkey, *dŏng'kĭ*
douche, *dōōsh*
drama, *drä'mȧ*
drawer, *drô'ĕr*
dromedary, *drŏm'ĕ-dĕr'ĭ*
drought, *drout*
drowned, *dround*
dubious, *dū'bĭ-ŭs*
due, *dū*
duty, *dū'tĭ*
dyspepsia, *dĭs-pĕp'shȧ*

eau de cologne, *ō dĕ kô-lōn'*
ebullition, *ĕb'ŭ-lĭsh'ŭn*
éclat, *ā'klä'*
economic, *ē-kō-nŏm'ĭk*
eczema, *ĕk'zĕ-mȧ*
edible, *ĕd'ĭ-b'l*
education, *ĕd'ŭ-kā'shŭn*
effigy, *ĕf'ĭ-jĭ*
effort, *ĕf'ĕrt*
ego, *ē'gō*
egret, *ē'grĕt*
electoral, *ē-lĕk'tĕr-ăl*
electrometer, *ē-lĕk'trŏm'ĕ-tĕr*
elegiac, *ĕ-lē'jĭ-ăc*
eleven, *ĕ-lĕv'ĕn*
élite, *ȧ'lēt'*
elm, *ĕlm;* not *ĕl'ŭm*
elongate, *ĕ-lŏng'găt*
embrasure, *ĕm-brā'zhĕr*
emeritus, *ĕ-mĕr'ĭ-tŭs*
emolument, *ĕ-mŏl'ŭ-mĕnt*
employee, *ĕm-ploi'ē*
enchant, *ĕn-chȧnt'*
encore, *äng-kōr', äng'kôr*
encyclical, *ĕn-sī'klĭ-kăl;*
   ĕn-sĭk'lĭ-kăl
endive, *ĕn'dīv*
enema, *ĕn'ĕ-mȧ*
enfranchise, *ĕn-frăn'chīz*
engine, *ĕn'jĭn*
ennui, *än'wē*
en route, *än rōōt'*
ensemble, *än-sŏm'b'l*
ensign (n.), *ĕn'sĭn*
entente, *äN'tänt'*
entree, *än'trā*
enunciate, *ĕ-nŭn'shĭ-āt*

envelope (n.), *ĕn'vĕ-lōp*
epaulet, *ĕp'ô-lĕt*
epistle, *ĕ-pĭs''l*
epitome, *ĕ-pĭt'ô-mĕ*
equine, *ē'kwīn*
equitable, *ĕk'wĭ-tȧ-b'l*
era, *ē'rȧ*
erasure, *ĕ-rā'zhŭr*
erratum, *ĕ-rā'tŭm*
erudite, *ĕr'ōō-dīt*
erysipelas, *ĕr'ĭ-sĭp'ĕ-lăs*
esquire, *ĕs-kwīr'*
etiquette, *ĕt'ĭ-kĕt*
etude, *ā'tūd*
euphemism, *ū'fĕ-mĭz'm*
euphonic, *ů-fŏn'ĭk*
evasive, *ĕ-vā'sĭv*
exaggeration, *ĕg-zăj'ĕr-ā'shŭn*
examine, *ĕg-zăm'ĭn*
example, *ĕg-zăm'p'l*
excise, *ĕk-sīz'*
exemplary, *ĕg-zĕm'plȧ-rĭ*
exhalation, *ĕks'hȧ-lā'shŭn*
exist, *ĕg-zĭst'*
exit, *ĕk'sĭt*
exogenous, *ĕks-ŏj'ĕ-nŭs*
exorbitant, *ĕg-zôr'bĭ-tănt*
expedient, *ĕks-pē'dĭ-ĕnt*
exponent, *ĕks-pō'nĕnt*
exquisite, *ĕks'kwĭ-zĭt*
extant, *ĕks'tănt*
extempore, *ĕks-tĕm'pô-rĕ*
extraordinary, *ĕks-trôr'dĭ-nĕr'ĭ*

facet, *făs'ĕt*
facile, *făs'ĭl*
facsimile, *făk-sĭm'ĭ-lē*
factory, *făk'tô-rĭ*
falcon, *fôl'kŭn*
fallen, *fôl'ĕn*
falsetto, *fôl-sĕt'ō*
family, *făm'ĭ-lĭ*
fancy, *făn'sĭ*
far, *fär*
fast, *făst*
faucet, *fô'sĕt*
favorite, *fā'vĕr-ĭt*
fecund, *fĕk'ŭnd*
fellow, *fĕl'ō*
feminine, *fĕm'ĭ-nĭn*
fête, *fāt*
fiancé, *fē'än-sā'*
fiancée, *fē'än-sā'*
fiasco, *fĕ-ăs'kō*
fichu, *fĭsh'ōō*
fidelity, *fĭ-dĕl'ĭ-tĭ*
figure, *fĭg'ŭr*
fillet, *fĭl'ĕt*
film, *fĭlm*
finale, *fĕ-nä'lā*
finance, *fĭ-năns'*
financier, *fĭn'ăn-sēr'*
finis, *fī'nĭs*
fleur-de-lis, *flûr'dĕ-lē'*
flew, *flōō*
floral, *flō'răl*
florid, *flŏr'ĭd*
florin, *flŏr'ĭn*
flute, *flōōt*
food, *fōōd*
forbade, *fŏr-băd'*
forehead, *fŏr'ĕd*
forest, *fŏr'ĕst*
formidable, *fôr'mĭ-dȧ-b'l*
forum, *fō'rŭm*
fountain, *foun'tĭn*
foyer, *foi'ā*
fragile, *frăj'ĭl*
frappé, *frȧ'pā'*
fraternize, *frăt'ĕr-nīz*
fricassee, *frĭk'ȧ-sē'*
friendship, *frĕnd'shĭp*

frontier, *frŭn-tēr'*
fuel, *fū'ĕl*
fulminate, *fŭl'mĭ-nāt*
funereal, *fû-nēr'ê-ăl*
fungi, *fŭn'jĭ*
furniture, *fûr'nĭ-chûr*
fusillade, *fū'zĭ-lād'*

gala, *gā'là*
gallery, *găl'ĕr-ĭ*
gangrene. *găng'grēn*
gape (v.), *gāp*
garage, *gà-räzh'*
garrulous, *găr'ū-lŭs*
gaseous, *găs'ê-ŭs*
gastritis, *găs-trī'tĭs*
gather, *găTH'ĕr*
gazetteer, *găz'ĕ-tēr'*
geisha, *gā'shà*
genealogy, *jĕn'ê-ăl'ô-jĭ*
generally, *jĕn'ĕr-ăl-ĭ*
genii, *jē'nĭ-ī*
genre, *zhäN'r'*
gentleman, *jĕn't'l-măn*
genuine, *jĕn' û-ĭn*
geography, *jê-ŏg'rà-fĭ*
geranium, *jê-rā'nĭ-ŭm*
gerrymander, *gĕr'ĭ-măn'dĕr*
gerund, *jĕr'ŭnd*
gesture, *jĕs'chûr*
get, *gĕt*
ghastly, *gàst'lĭ*
ghoul, *gōol*
gibber, *jĭb'ĕr*
gibbet, *jĭb'ĕt*
gin, *jĭn*
giraffe, *jĭ-ràf'*
girl, *gûrl*
gist, *jĭst*
gladiolus, *glăd'ĭ-ō'lŭs*
glycerin, *glĭs'ĕr-ĭn*
gneiss, *nīs*
golf, *gŏlf*
gondola, *gŏn'dô-là*
gone, *gŏn*
gospel, *gŏs'pĕl*
gourmet, *gōor'mā*
government, *gŭv'ĕrn-mĕnt*
granary, *grăn'à-rĭ*
granddaughter, *grănd'dô'tĕr*
grandeur, *grăn'dūr*
grasp, *gràsp*
grass, *gràs*
gratis, *grā'tĭs*
grimace, *grĭ-mās'*
grimy, *grīm'ĭ*
gripe, *grīp*
grisly, *grĭz'lĭ*
grotesque, *grô-tĕsk'*
grovel, *grŏv''l*
guardian, *gär'dĭ-ăn*
guillotine (n.), *gĭl'ô-tēn*
gymnasium, *jĭm-nā'zĭ-ŭm*
gyroscope, *jī'rô-skōp*

habitant, *hăb'ĭ-tănt*
habitué, *hà-bĭch' û-ā'*
hacienda, *ä-syĕn'dä*
handbook, *hănd'bŏŏk'*
handkerchief, *hăng'kĕr-chĭf*
hangar, *hăng'ĕr*
harass, *hăr'ăs*
harbinger, *här'bĭn-jĕr*
harem, *hā'rĕm*
hasten, *hās''n*
haunt, *hônt*
hearth, *härth*
heaven, *hĕv'ĕn*
hedonism, *hē'dŏn-ĭz'm*
hegemony, *hê-jĕm'ô-nĭ*
height, *hīt*
heinous, *hā'nŭs*

helm, *hĕlm*
hemoglobin, *hē'mô-glō'bĭn*
heroine, *hĕr'ô-ĭn*
hesitate, *hĕz'ĭ-tāt*
heteronym, *hĕt'ĕr-ô-nĭm'*
hieroglyphic, *hī'ĕr-ô-glĭf'ĭk*
highwayman, *hī'wā'măn*
hilarious, *hĭ-lâr'ĭ-ŭs*
hirsute, *hûr'sūt*
history, *hĭs'tô-rĭ*
hoist, *hoist*
holocaust, *hŏl'ô-kôst*
holograph, *hŏl'ô-gràf*
homage, *hŏm'ĭj*
homeopathic, *hō'mê-ô-păth'ĭk*
homestead, *hōm'stĕd*
homogeneous, *hō'mô-jē'nê-ŭs*
homonym, *hŏm'ô-nĭm*
honest, *ŏn'ĕst*
honorable, *ŏn'ĕr-à-b'l*
honorarium, *ŏn'ô-râr'ĭ-ŭm*
hoof, *hōof*
horrid, *hŏr'ĭd*
horse-radish, *hôrs'răd'ĭsh*
hospitable, *hŏs'pĭ-tà-b'l*
hovel, *hŭv'ĕl*
humble, *hŭm'b'l*
humor, *hū'mĕr*
hundred, *hŭn'drĕd*
hydraulics, *hī-drô'lĭks*
hydrometer, *hī-drŏm'ê-tĕr*
hygiene, *hī'jēn*
hygienic, *hī'jĭ-ĕn'ĭk*
hypocrisy, *hĭ-pŏk'rĭ-sĭ*
hypodermic, *hī-pô-dûr'mĭk*
hysteria, *hĭs-tēr'ĭ-à*
hysterical, *hĭs-tĕr'ĭ-kăl*

idea, *ī-dē'à*
ideal, *ī-dē'ăl*
ideology, *ĭd'ê-ŏl'ô-jĭ*
idiosyncrasy, *ĭd'ĭ-ô-sĭng'krà-sĭ*
ignoramus, *ĭg'nô-rā'mŭs*
illusory, *ĭ-lū'sô-rĭ*
illustrate, *ĭl'ŭs-trāt*
imbroglio, *ĭm-brōl'yō*
impious, *ĭm'pĭ-ŭs*
implacable, *ĭm-plā'kà-b'l*
importune, *ĭm'pŏr-tūn'*
impotent, *ĭm'pô-tĕnt*
improvise, *ĭm'prō-vīz*
inaugurate, *ĭn-ô'gû-rāt*
incise, *ĭn-sīz'*
incisive, *ĭn-sī'sĭv*
incognito, *ĭn-kŏg'nĭ-tō*
incomparable, *ĭn-kŏm'pà-rà-b'l*
incredulous, *ĭn-krĕj'û-lŭs*
incursion, *ĭn-kûr'zhŭn*
indisputable, *ĭn-dĭs'pû-tà-b'l*
industry, *ĭn'dŭs-trĭ*
inertia, *ĭn-ûr'shà*
inexplicable, *ĭn-ĕks'plĭ-kà-b'l*
inextricably, *ĭn-ĕks'trĭ-kà-blĭ*
infamous, *ĭn'fà-mŭs*
infantile, *ĭn'făn-tīl*
influence, *ĭn'flōo-ĕns*
ingénue, *ăN'zhā'nü'*
initiative, *ĭ-nĭsh'ĭ-ā'tĭv*
innocent, *ĭn'ô-sĕnt*
inopportune, *ĭn-ŏp'ŏr-tūn'*
inquiry, *ĭn-kwīr'ĭ*
insatiable, *ĭn-sā'shĭ-à-b'l*
insect, *ĭn'sĕkt*
insignia, *ĭn-sĭg'nĭ-à*
instead, *ĭn-stĕd'*
insulate, *ĭn'sû-lāt*
integer, *ĭn'tê-jĕr*
interesting, *ĭn'tĕr-ĕst-ĭng*
intermezzo, *ĭn'-tĕr-mĕd'zō*
international, *ĭn'tĕr-năsh'ŭn-ăl*
interpellate, *ĭn'tĕr-pĕl'āt*
interpellation, *ĭn'tĕr-pĕ-lā'shŭn*

interpolate, *ĭn-tûr'pô-lāt*
intricacy, *ĭn'trĭ-kà-sĭ*
intrigue, *ĭn-trēg'*
inundate, *ĭn'ŭn-dāt*
inveigle, *ĭn-vē'g'l*
iodine, *ī'ô-dīn*
irony, *ī'rô-nĭ*
irrefragable, *ĭ-rĕf'rà-gà-b'l*
irrefutable, *ĭ-rĕf'û-tà-b'l*
irremediable, *ĭr'rê-mē'dĭ-à-b'l*
irrevocable, *ĭ-rĕv'ô-kà-b'l*
isinglass, *ī'zĭng-glàs'*
isolate, *ī'sô-lāt*
italic, *ĭ-tăl'ĭk*
ivory, *ī'vô-rĭ*

jardiniére, *jär'dĭ-nēr'*
jocose, *jô-kōs'*
jostling, *jŏs'lĭng*
judgment, *jŭj'mĕnt*
jugular, *jŭg'û-lĕr*
jujitsu, *jōo-jĭt'sōo*
junta, *jŭn'tà*, pop. *hŭn'tà*
just, *jŭst*
jute, *jōot*
juvenile, *jōo'vê-nĭl*

kaleidoscope. *kà-lī'dô-skōp*
kept, *kĕpt*
kettle, *kĕt''l*
khaki, *kăk'ĭ*
khedive, *kĕ-dēv'*
kiln, *kĭl*
kimono, *kĭ-mō'nō*
kindergarten, *kĭn'dĕr-gär't'n*
kinetoscope, *kĭ-nē'tô-skōp*
kiosk, *kê-ŏsk'*
kismet, *kĭz'mĕt*
kitchen, *kĭch'ĕn*
knout, *nout*

laboratory, *lăb'ô-rà-tō'-rĭ*
laborer, *lā'bĕr-ĕr*
lamentable, *lăm'ĕn-tà-b'l*
language, *lăng'gwĭj*
largess, *lär'jĕs*
laryngitis, *lăr'ĭn-jī'tĭs*
larynx, *lăr'ĭngks*
laths, *làTHz*
lattice, *lăt'ĭs*
laudanum, *lô'dà-nŭm*
laugh, *làf*
lava, *lä'vä*
lavaliere, *lăv'à-lēr'*
layette, *lā-ĕt'*
leaped, *lēpt*
leapt, *lĕpt*
learned (adj.), *lûr'nĕd*
learned (v.), *lûrnd*
legate, *lĕg'ĭt*
legend, *lĕj'ĕnd*
legislature, *lĕj'ĭs-lā'chûr*
leisure, *lē'zhĕr*
length, *lĕngth*
lenient, *lē'nĭ-ĕnt*
leper, *lĕp'ĕr*
lese majesty, *lēz măj'ĕs-tĭ*
lethal, *lē'thăl*
lettuce, *lĕt'ĭs*
leverage, *lē'vĕr-àj*
liaison, *lē'ā-zŏn'*
libel, *lī'bĕl*
libertine. *lĭb'ĕr-tēn*
libido, *lĭ-bī'dō, lĭ-bē'dō*
librarian, *lī-brâr'ĭ-ăn*
library, *lī'brĕr'ĭ*
lichen, *lī'kĕn*
licorice, *lĭk'ô-rĭs*
lief, *lēf*
lilac, *lī'lăk*
limn, *lĭm*
lineament, *lĭn'ê-à-mĕnt*
lingerie, *lăN'zh'-rē'*

linoleum, *lĭ-nō'lē-ŭm*
linotype, *lĭn'ō-tīp'*
liqueur, *lē'kûr'*
liquor, *lĭk'ēr*
literati, *lĭt'ē-rā'tĭ*
literature, *lĭt'ēr-à-chûr*
lithographer, *lĭ-thŏg'rà-fēr*
livelong, *lĭv'lŏng'*
loath, *lōth*
loathe, *lōтн*
loggia, *lŏj'à*
longevity, *lŏn-jĕv'ĭ-tĭ*
long-lived, *lŏng'lĭvd'*
lower (threaten), *lou'ēr*
lure, *lūr*
lurid, *lū'rĭd*
lyceum, *lĭ-sē'ŭm*

machination, *măk'ĭ-nā'shŭn*
mackerel, *măk'ēr-ĕl*
madras, *mà-drăs'*
madre, *mä'drà*
maestro, *mä-ĕ'strô*
magazine, *măg'à-zēn'*
magna charta, *măg'nà kär'tà*
magnolia, *măg-nō'lĭ-à*
malaria, *mà-lâr'ĭ-à*
malefactor, *măl'ē-făk'tēr*
malign, *mà-līn'*
mallow, *măl'ō*
mama, *mä'mà*
mañana, *mä-nyä'nà*
mandamus, *măn-dā'mŭs*
mandatory, *măn'dà-tō'-rĭ*
mange, *mānj*
mania, *mā'nĭ-à*
maniacal, *mà-nī'à-kăl*
manor, *măn'ēr*
manufactory, *măn'ú-făk'tō-rĭ*
maraschino, *măr'à-skē'nō*
margarine, *mär'jà-rēn*
maritime, *măr'ĭ-tīm*
marquis, *mär'kwĭs*
marshmallow, *märsh'măl'ō*
masculine, *măs'kú-lĭn*
mask, *màsk*
massacred, *măs'à-kĕrd*
massage, *mà-säzh'*
masseur, *mă-sûr'*
masseuse, *mă-sûz'*
maté (drink), *mä'tā*
matinée, *măt'ĭ-nā'*
matron, *mā'trŭn*
mattress, *măt'rĕs*
mausoleum, *mô'sô-lē'ŭm*
mauve, *mōv*
mavournin, *mà-vōōr'nēn*
mayonnaise, *mä'ŏ-nāz'*
mayoralty, *mā'ēr-ăl-tĭ*
measure, *mĕzh'ēr*
mechanician, *mĕk'à-nĭsh'ăn*
medicament, *mē-dĭk'à-mĕnt*
medicinal, *mē-dĭs'ĭ-năl*
medieval, *mē'dĭ-ē'văl*
mediocre, *mē'dĭ-ō'kēr*
megrim, *mē'grĭm*
melee, *mā'lā*
memoir, *mĕm'wär*
memory, *mĕm'ô-rĭ*
ménage, *mà-näzh'*
meningitis, *mĕn'ĭn-jī'tĭs*
menu, *mĕn'ú*
mercantile, *mûr'kăn-tĭl*
mere (lake), *mēr*
meringue, *mē-răng'*
mesa, *mā'sä*
mésalliance, *mā'zăl'yăns'*
mesdames, *mā'dăm'*
mesmerism, *mĕz'mēr-ĭz'm*
messieurs, *mĕs'yĕrz*
metallurgy, *mĕt''l-ûr-jĭ*

metric, *mĕt'rĭk*
mezzo, *mĕd'zō*
microscopic, *mī'krô-skŏp'ĭk*
microscopy, *mī-krŏs'kô-pĭ*
migraine, *mī'grān*
militia, *mĭ-lĭsh'à*
mime, *mīm*
mineralogy, *mĭn'ēr-ăl'ô-jĭ*
mirage, *mĭ-räzh'*
misanthrope, *ĭs'ăn-thrōp*
miscellany, *mĭs'ē-lā-nĭ*
mischievous, *mĭs'chĭ-vŭs*
misconstrue, *mĭs'kŏn-strōō'*
miserable, *mĭz'ēr-à-b'l*
misogynist, *mĭ-sŏj'ĭ-nĭst*
mitten, *mĭt''n*
mnemonics, *nē-mŏn'ĭks*
mock, *mŏk*
moderate (adj.), *mŏd'ēr-ĭt*
modiste, *mô'dēst'*
modus vivendi, *mō'dŭs vĭ-vĕn'dī*
moiré, *mwä'rā'*
monetary, *mŏn'ē-tĕr'ĭ*
monogram, *mŏn'ô-grăm*
monologue, *mŏn'ô-lŏg*
monomania, *mŏn'ô-mā'nĭ-à*
monsieur, *mē-syû'*
monsignor, *mŏn-sē'nyôr*
morale, *mô-răl'*
mountain, *moun'tĭn*
mountainous, *moun'tĭ-nŭs*
municipal, *mu-nĭs'ĭ-păl*
museum, *mu-zē'ŭm*
mushroom, *mŭsh'rōōm*
musicale, *mū'zĭ-kàl'*
muskellunge, *mŭs'kē-lŭnj*
muskmelon, *mŭsk'mĕl'ŭn*
mustache, *mŭs-tàsh'*
mystery, *mĭs'tēr-ĭ*
mythology, *mĭ-thŏl'ô-jĭ*

naïve, *nä-ēv'*
nape, *nāp*
napery, *nā'pēr-ĭ*
naphtha, *năf'thà*
nasal, *nā'zăl*
nascent, *năs'ĕnt*
natatorium, *nā'tà-tō'rĭ-ŭm*
natural, *năch'ú-răl*
nature, *nā'chûr*
nausea, *nô'sē-à*
necessarily, *nĕs'ē-sēr'ĭ-lĭ*
necrology, *nē-krŏl'ô-jĭ*
nee, *nā*
negligee, *nĕg'lĭ-zhā'*
nephritis, *nē-frī'tĭs*
nepotism, *nĕp'ô-tĭz'm*
nervine, *nûr'vēn*
neuralgia, *nu-răl'jĭ-à*
neuritis, *nu-rī'tĭs*
neurosis, *nu-rō'sĭs*
nicety, *nī'sē-tĭ*
niche, *nĭch*
nirvana, *nĭr-vä'nà*
nomad, *nō'măd*
nom de plume, *nŏm'dĕ plōōm'*
nominative, *nŏm'ĭ-nà-tĭv*
nonchalant, *nŏn'shà-lănt*
nonpareil, *nŏn'pà-rĕl'*
nostalgia, *nŏs-tăl'jĭ-à*
notice, *nō'tĭs*
novice, *nŏv'ĭs*
noxious, *nŏk'shŭs*
nuance, *nü'äns'*
nuisance, *nū'săns*
nuncio, *nŭn'shĭ-ō*
nuptial, *nŭp'shăl*
nymph, *nĭmf*

oasis, *ô-ā'sĭs*
oaths, *ōтнz*
oatmeal, *ōt'mēl'*

obdurate, *ŏb'dû-rât*
obedient, *ô-bē'dĭ-ĕnt*
obeisance, *ô-bā'săns*
obelisk, *ŏb'ē-lĭsk*
obesity, *ô-bēs'ĭ-tĭ*
obiter dicta, *ŏb'ĭ-tēr dĭk'tà*
oblique, *ŏb-lēk'*; military, *lĭk'*
obscenity, *ŏb-sĕn'ĭ-tĭ*
occult, *ŏ-kŭlt'*
octave, *ŏk'tāv*
office, *ŏf'ĭs*
often, *ŏf'ĕn*
olden, *ōl'dĕn*
oleander, *ō'lē-ăn'dēr*
oleomargarine, *ō'lē-ô-mär'jà-rēn*
olfactory, *ŏl-făk'tô-rĭ*
on, *ŏn*
onerous, *ŏn'ēr-ŭs*
opponent, *ŏ-pō'nĕnt*
oral, *ō'răl*
orange, *ŏr'ĕnj*
orchestra, *ôr'kĕs-trà*
orchestral, *ôr-kĕs'trăl*
orchid, *ôr'kĭd*
ordeal, *ôr-dēl'*
ordinance, *ôr'dĭ-năns*
ordinarily, *ôr'dĭ-nĕr'ĭ-lĭ*
ordnance, *ôrd'năns*
orgy, *ôr'jĭ*
oriental, *ō'rĭ-ĕn'tăl*
orifice, *ŏr'ĭ-fĭs*
oriole, *ō'rĭ-ōl*
orthoepist, *ôr'thô-ĕp'ĭst*
orthopedic, *ôr'thô-pē'dĭk*
ostler, *ŏs'lēr*
overalls, *ō'vēr-ôlz'*

pacifist, *păs'ĭ-fĭst*
padre, *pä'drĭ*
padrone, *pä-drō'nà*
pageant, *păj'ĕnt*
pagination, *păj'ĭ-nā'shŭn*
pajama, *pà-jä'mà*
palatial, *pà-lā'shăl*
palette, *păl'ĕt*
palladium, *pă-lā'dĭ-ŭm*
palm, *päm*
palmistry, *päm'ĭs-trĭ*
paltry, *pôl'trĭ*
panacea, *păn'à-sē'à*
panegyric, *păn'ē-jĭr'ĭk*
panorama, *păn'ô-rä'mà*
papa, *pä'pà*
papier-mâché, *pä'pēr-mà-shā'*
papyrus, *pà-pī'rŭs*
paraffin, *păr'à-fĭn*
paramour, *păr'à-mōōr*
parasitic, *păr'à-sĭt'ĭk*
parasol, *păr'à-sŏl*
paresis, *pà-rē'sĭs*
parliament, *pär'lĭ-mĕnt*
parotid, *pà-rŏt'ĭd*
participle, *pär'tĭ-sĭ-p'l*
particularly, *pēr-tĭk'ú-làr-lĭ*
partner, *pärt'nēr*
partridge, *pär'trĭj*
passé, *pă-sā'*
pasteurize, *pàs'tēr-īz*
path, *pàth*
pathos, *pā'thŏs*
patience, *pā'shĕns*
patio, *pä'tĭ-ō*
patois, *păt'wä*
patriot, *pā'trĭ-ŭt*
patrol, *pà-trōl'*
patron, *pā'trŭn*
pecan, *pē-kăn'*
peculiar, *pē-kūl'yēr*
peculiarity, *pē-kū'lĭ-ăr'ĭ-tĭ*
pedagogue, *pĕd'à-gŏg*
pedagogy, *pĕd'à-gō'jĭ*
pedal, *pĕd'ăl*

pedometer, *pê-dŏm'ê-tẽr*
penal, *pē'nȧl*
penchant, *pän'shäN'; pĕn'chȧnt*
penitentiary, *pĕn'ĭ-tĕn'shȧ-rĭ*
peon, *pē'ŏn*
peony, *pē'ō-nĭ*
peremptory, *pẽr-ĕmp'tô-rĭ*
pergola, *pûr'gô-là*
perhaps, *pẽr-hăps'*
peril, *pĕr'ĭl*
period, *pēr'ĭ-ŭd*
periodic, *pēr'ĭ-ŏd'ĭk*
peritoneum, *pĕr'ĭ-tô-nē'ŭm*
peritonitis, *pĕr'ĭ-tô-nī'tĭs*
perpetuity, *pûr'pê-tū'ĭ-tĭ*
persist, *pẽr-sĭst'*
perspicuity, *pûr'spĭ-kū'ĭ-tĭ*
perspiration, *pûr'spĭ-rā'shŭn*
peso, *pā'sō*
petard, *pê-tärd'*
petite, *pê-tēt'*
petrel, *pĕt'rĕl*
pharmaceutic, *fär'mȧ-sū'tĭk*
pharyngitis, *făr'ĭn-jī'tĭs*
phial, *fī'ȧl*
philately, *fĭ-lăt'ĕ-lĭ*
philology, *fĭ-lŏl'ô-jĭ*
phlegmatic, *flĕg-măt'ĭk*
photogravure, *fō'tô-grȧ-vūr'*
phraseology, *frā'zê-ŏl'ô-jĭ*
physicist, *fĭz'ĭ-sĭst*
pianist, *pĭ-ăn'ĭst*
piano, *pĭ-än'ō*
picture, *pĭk'chûr*
pillow, *pĭl'ō*
pincers, *pĭn'sẽrz*
piquant, *pē'kȧnt*
pique, *pēk*
piqué, *pê-kā'*
pistachio, *pĭs-tăsh'ĭ-ō*
pith, *pĭth*
placard, *plăk'ärd*
placer, *plăs'ẽr*
plagiarist, *plā'jĭ-à-rĭst*
plague, *plāg*
plait, *plăt*
plant, *plȧnt*
plebiscite, *plĕb'ĭ-sĭt*
plenary, *plē'nȧ-rĭ*
plethora, *plĕth'ô-rȧ*
plural, *plōōr'ȧl*
pneumonia, *nŭ-mō'nĭ-ȧ*
poem, *pō'ĕm*
poignant, *poin'yȧnt*
poilu, *pwȧ'lü'*
poinsettia, *poin-sĕt'ĭ-ȧ*
poll, *pōl*
polonaise, *pō'lô-nāz'*
pomegranate, *pŏm'grăn'ĭt*
poniard, *pŏn'yẽrd*
poor, *pōōr*
porcine, *pôr'sīn*
portiere, *pôr'tyâr'*
posse, *pŏs'ê*
posterior, *pŏs-tēr'ĭ-ẽr*
postern, *pōs'tẽrn*
posthumous, *pŏs'chŭ-mŭs*
potato, *pô-tā'tō*
potpourri, *pō-pōō-rē'*
precedence, *prê-sēd'ĕns*
precedent (adj.), *prê-sēd'ĕnt*
precedent (n.), *prĕs'ê-dĕnt*
precise, *prê-sīs'*
predicament, *prê-dĭk'à-mĕnt*
preface, *prĕf'ĭs*
preferable, *prĕf'ẽr-à-b'l*
prelate, *prĕl'ĭt*
prelude (n.), *prĕl'ūd*
premature, *prē'mȧ-tūr'*
premier, *prē'mĭ-ẽr*
premise (n.), *prĕm'ĭs*
preparatory, *prê-păr'à-tō-rĭ*

presentation, *prĕz'ĕn-tā'shŭn*
president, *prĕz'ĭ-dĕnt*
presidio, *prê-sĭd'ĭ-ō*
presumptuous, *prê-zŭmp'chû-ŭs*
pretense, *prê-tĕns'*
pretext, *prē'tĕkst*
pretty, *prĭt'ĭ*
prima donna, *prē'mȧ dŏn'à*
prima facie, *prī'mȧ fā'shĭ-ē*
primates, *prī-mā'tēz*
pristine, *prĭs'tĭn*
prodigious, *prô-dĭj'ŭs*
produce (n.), *prŏd'ūs*
produce (v.), *prô-dūs'*
profile, *prō'fīl*
profuse, *prô-fūs'*
program, *prō'grăm*
progress (n.), *prŏg'rĕs*
projectile, *prô-jĕk'tĭl*
proletarian, *prō'lê-târ'ĭ-ȧn*
promenade, *prŏm'ê-näd'*
pronunciation, *prô-nŭn'sĭ-ā'shŭn*
propinquity, *prô-pĭng'kwĭ-tĭ*
propitious, *prô-pĭsh'ŭs*
pro rata, *prō rā'tȧ*
prosperous, *prŏs'pẽr-ŭs*
protean, *prō'tê-ȧn*
protégé, *prō'tê-zhā*
protein, *prō'tê-ĭn*
protestant, *prŏt'ĕs-tȧnt*
protrude, *prô-trōōd'*
prussic, *prŭs'ĭk*
psalm, *säm*
pseudonym, *sū'dô-nĭm*
psychiatry, *sī-kī'ȧ-trĭ*
psychic, *sī'kĭk*
psychosis, *sī-kō'sĭs*
ptomaine, *tō'mān*
publicist, *pŭb'lĭ-sĭst*
puerile, *pū'ẽr-ĭl*
pumpkin, *pŭmp'kĭn*
punitive, *pū'nĭ-tĭv*
purée, *pŭ-rā'*
pursue, *pẽr-sū'*
pyrites, *pĭ-rī'tēz*
pyrometer, *pī-rŏm'ê-tẽr*

quaff, *kwȧf*
quarrel, *kwŏr'ĕl*
quarter, *kwôr'tẽr*
quatrain, *kwŏt'rān*
quay, *kē*
queue, *kū*
quietus, *kwĭ-ē'tŭs*
quinine, *kwī'nīn; kwĭ-nēn'*
qui vive, *kê vēv'*
quixotic, *kwĭks'ŏt'ĭk*
quoit, *kwoit*
quorum, *kwō'rŭm*

rabies, *rā'bēz*
raceme, *rȧ-sēm'*
radish, *răd'ĭsh*
ragout, *rȧ-gōō'*
raillery, *rāl'ẽr-ĭ*
raja, *rä'jà*
rancor, *răng'kẽr*
ransack, *răn'săk*
rapier, *rā'pĭ-ẽr*
raspberry, *răz'bĕr-ĭ*
rather, *rȧTH'ẽr*
ratio, *rā'shĭ-ō*
ration, *rā'shŭn*
rational, *răsh'ŭn-ȧl*
rationale, *răsh'ŭn-ȧl*
recipe, *rĕs'ĭ-pē*
recitative (n.), *rĕs'ĭ-tȧ-tēv'*
reclamation, *rĕk'lȧ-mā'shŭn*
recluse, *rê-klōōs'*
recognizance, *rê-kŏg'nĭ-zȧns*
recognize, *rĕk'ŏg-nīz*
reconnaissance, *rê-kŏn'ȧ-sȧns*

reconnoiter, *rĕk'ô-noi'tẽr*
referable, *rĕf'ẽr-à-b'l*
referee, *rĕf'ẽr-ē'*
regalia, *rê-gā'lĭ-à*
régime, *rā'zhēm'*
regular, *rĕg'û-lẽr*
reiterate, *rê-ĭt'ẽr-āt*
renaissance, *rĕn'ĕ-zäns'*
rendezvous, *rän'dĕ-vōō*
reparable, *rĕp'à-rà-b'l*
repertoire, *rĕp'ẽr-twär*
replica, *rĕp'lĭ-kà*
reputable, *rĕp'û-tà-b'l*
requiem, *rē'kwĭ-ĕm (or rĕ')*
requital, *rê-kwīt'ȧl*
research, *rê-sûrch'*
reservoir, *rĕz'ẽr-vwôr*
residue, *rĕz'ĭ-dū*
resin, *rĕz'ĭn*
resolute, *rĕz'ô-lūt*
resonance, *rĕz'ô-nȧns*
resource, *rê-sōrs'*
respite, *rĕs'pĭt*
restaurant, *rĕs'tô-rȧnt*
restaurateur, *rĕs'tō'rȧ'tûr'*
résumé, *rā'zû-mā'*
reveille, *rĕv'ĕ-lĭ*
revenue, *rĕv'ê-nū*
reversion, *rê-vûr'shŭn*
revocable, *rĕv'ô-kà-b'l*
rheumatism, *rōō'mȧ-tĭz'm*
rhythm, *rĭTH'm*
ribald, *rĭb'ȧld*
ricochet, *rĭk'ô-shā'*
ridiculous, *rĭ-dĭk'û-lŭs*
rind, *rīnd*
rinse, *rĭns*
ripeness, *rīp'nĕs*
rise (n.), *rīz*
risk, *rĭsk*
robust, *rô-bŭst'*
roil, *roil*
romance, *rô-măns'*
roof, *rōōf*
room, *rōōm*
root, *rōōt*
roquefort, *rōk'fẽrt*
roseate, *rō'zê-ȧt*
rostrum, *rŏs'trŭm*
route, *rōōt*
routine, *rōō-tēn'*
rude, *rōōd*
rutabaga, *rōō'tȧ-bā'gà*

sabot, *sȧ'bō'*
sabotage, *săb'ô-täzh'*
saccharin, *săk'à-rĭn*
sachem, *sā'chĕm*
sachet, *sȧ-shā'*
sacrament, *săk'rȧ-mĕnt*
sacrifice, *săk'rĭ-fīs*
sacrilegious, *săk'rĭ-lē'jŭs*
safari, *sȧ-fä'rĭ*
sagacious, *sȧ-gā'shŭs*
said, *sĕd*
salary, *săl'à-rĭ*
saline, *sā'līn*
salmon, *săm'ŭn*
salon, *sȧ-lôn'*
salve, *säv*
sanatorium, *săn'à-tō'rĭ-ŭm*
sanguine, *săng'gwĭn*
sarcasm, *sär'kăz'm*
sarcophagus, *sär-kŏf'à-gŭs*
sarsaparilla, *sär'sȧ-pȧ-rĭl'à*
satin, *săt'ĭn*
satire, *săt'īr*
satyr, *săt'ẽr, sā'tẽr*
savage, *săv'ĭj*
savant, *sȧ'väN'*
says, *sĕz*
scallop, *skŏl'ŭp*

scared, *skârd*
scenario, *sĕ-nä′rĭ-ō*
scenic, *sē′nĭk*
schism, *sĭz′m*
schizophrenia, *skĭz′ō-frē′nĭ-à*
scion, *sī′ŭn*
scrofula, *skrŏf′ū-là*
séance, *sā′äns*
seckel, *sĕk″l*
secretary, *sĕk′rĕ-tĕr′ĭ*
sedative, *sĕd′à-tĭv*
seidlitz, *sĕd′lĭts*
seismic, *sīz′mĭk*
semiannual, *sĕm′ĭ-ăn′ū-ăl*
senile, *sē′nīl*
señora, *sā-nyō′rä*
separable, *sĕp′à-rà-b′l*
separate (v.), *sĕp′à-rāt*
separate (adj.), *sĕp′à-rĭt*
sesame, *sĕs′à-mĕ*
several, *sĕv′ẽr-ăl*
shampoo, *shăm-pōō′*
shan't, *shänt*
sheik, *shēk, shāk*
shillelagh, *shĭ-lā′là*
shrill, *shrĭl*
shrine, *shrīn*
sibilant, *sĭb′ĭ-lănt*
sidereal, *sī-dēr′ĕ-ăl*
signora, *sĕ-nyō′rä*
silhouette, *sĭl′ōō-ĕt′*
simultaneous, *sī′mŭl-tā′nĕ-ŭs*
since, *sĭns*
sinecure, *sī′nĕ-kūr*
sirup; syrup, *sĭr′ŭp*
ski, *skē*
skiing, *skē′ĭng*
slake, *slāk*
sleek, *slēk*
slept, *slĕpt*
smorgasbord, *smûr′găs-bôrd′*
snout, *snout*
sofa, *sō′fà*
soften, *sôf′ĕn*
soirée, *swä-rā′*
solace, *sŏl′ĭs*
solarium, *sō-lâr′ĭ-ŭm*
solemn, *sŏl′ĕm*
sombrero, *sŏm-brâr′ō*
sonata, *sō-nä′tà*
soprano, *sō-prä′nō*
sotto voce, *sōt′tô vō′chà*
souvenir, *sōō′vĕ-nēr′*
specie (coin), *spē′shĭ*
species, *spē′shĭz*
spinach, *spĭn′ĭch*
spirit, *spĭr′ĭt*
splenetic, *splĕ-nĕt′ĭk*
spouse, *spouz*
stalactite, *stà-lăk′tīt*
stalagmite, *stà-lăg′mīt*
static, *stăt′ĭk*
status, *stā′tŭs*
steady, *stĕd′ĭ*
stipend, *stī′pĕnd*
stirrup, *stĭr′ŭp*
stoicism, *stō′ĭ-sĭz′m*
stomach, *stŭm′ăk*
strata, *strā′tà*
strategic, *strà-tē′jĭk*
stratosphere, *străt′ô-sfēr*
strew, *strōō*
strychnine, *strĭk′nĭn*
student, *stū′dĕnt*
suave, *swäv*
subdue, *sŭb-dū′*
submarine(n), *sŭb′mà-rēn′*
subpoena, *sŭb-pē′nà*
subtle, *sŭt″l*
suburb, *sŭb′ûrb*
succinct, *sŭk-sĭngkt′*
suède, *swād*

suggest, *sŭg-jĕst′*
suit, *sūt*
suite, *swēt*
sumac, *shōō′măk*
sumptuous, *sŭmp′chû-ŭs*
superfluous, *sū-pûr′flōō-ŭs*
supple, *sŭp″l*
suppose, *sŭ-pōz′*
surcease, *sûr-sēs′*
surprise, *sĕr-prīz′*
surveillance, *sûr-vāl′ăns*
swan, *swŏn*
swept, *swĕpt*
syndicate, *sĭn′dĭ-kăt*
synod, *sĭn′ŭd*
syringe, *sĭ-rĭnj′*

table d'hote, *tà′blĕ dōt′*
taciturn, *tăs′ĭ-tûrn*
tallyho, *tăl′ĭ-hō′*
tapestry, *tăp′ĕs-trĭ*
task, *tàsk*
technique, *tĕk′nēk′*
tedious, *tē′dĭ-ŭs*
teething, *tēTH′ĭng*
telephonic, *tĕl′ĕ-fŏn′ĭk*
temperament, *tĕm′pẽr-à-mĕnt*
temperature, *tĕm′pẽr-à-chûr*
temporarily, *tĕm′pô-rẽr′ĭ-lĭ*
tenet, *tĕn′ĕt*
tepid, *tĕp′ĭd*
terrain, *tĕ-rān′*
tête-à-tête, *tāt′-à-tāt′*
textile, *tĕks′tĭl*
theater, *thē′à-tẽr*
thermostat, *thûr′mô-stăt*
thresh, *thrĕsh*
tiara, *tī-âr′à*
tincture, *tĭngk′chûr*
tolerable, *tŏl′ẽr-à-b′l*
tomato, *tô-mā′tō*
tongs, *tŏngz*
tonsorial, *tŏn-sō′rĭ-ăl*
tortoise, *tôr′tŭs*
toupee, *tōō-pā′*
tournament, *tōōr′nà-mĕnt*
tourniquet, *tōōr′nĭ-kĕt*
toward, *tō′ẽrd*
transmigrate, *trăns-mī′grāt*
transparent, *trăns-pâr′ĕnt*
travail, *trăv′āl*
travel, *trăv′ĕl*
traveler, *trăv′ĕl-ẽr*
traverse (n. v. adj.), *trăv′ẽrs*
treacle, *trē′k′l*
tribune, *trĭb′ūn*
trichina, *trĭ-kī′nà*
triumph, *trī′ŭmf*
trough, *trŏf*
trousseau, *trōō′sō′*
truculent, *trŭk′ū-lĕnt*
trustworthy, *trŭst′wûr′THĭ*
tube, *tūb*
tulip, *tū′lĭp*
tune, *tūn*
turnip, *tûr′nĭp*
turquoise, *tûr′koiz*

ukulele, *ū′kŭ-lā′lĕ*
ultimatum, *ŭl′tĭ-mā′tŭm*
umbrella, *ŭm-brĕl′à*
unaccented, *ŭn′ăk-sĕn′tĕd*
undersigned, *ŭn′dẽr-sīnd′*
unfrequented, *ŭn′frē-kwĕn′tĕd*
uninterested, *ŭn-ĭn′tẽr-ĕs-tĕd*
unprecedented, *ŭn-prĕs′ĕ-dĕn-tĕd*
untoward, *ŭn-tō′ẽrd*
usage, *ūs′ĭj*
used, *ūzd*
usually, *ū′zhōō-ăl-lĭ*
usurp, *ŭ-zûrp′*
usury, *ū′zhōō-rĭ*

vagary, *và-gâr′ĭ*
vagrant, *vā′grănt*
valance, *văl′ăns*
valet, *văl′ĕt*
valuable, *văl′ū-à-b′l*
vanquish, *văng′kwĭsh*
vase, *vās*
vast, *vàst*
vaudeville, *vōd′vĭl*
vehement, *vē′ĕ-mĕnt*
velvet, *vĕl′vĕt*
venal, *vē′năl*
venison, *vĕn′ĭ-z′n*
venous, *vē′nŭs*
ventriloquist, *vĕn-trĭl′ō-kwĭst*
veracious, *vĕ-rā′shŭs*
verbatim, *vûr-bā′tĭm*
verdigris, *vûr′dĭ-grēs*
version, *vûr′shŭn*
veterinary, *vĕt′ẽr-ĭ-nẽr′ĭ*
via, *vī′à*
vicar, *vĭk′ẽr*
vice versa, *vī′sĕ vûr′sà*
victim, *vĭk′tĭm*
victual, *vĭt″l*
vicuña, *vĭ-kōōn′yà*
vignette, *vĭn-yĕt′*
villain, *vĭl′ĭn*
vindictive, *vĭn-dĭk′tĭv*
vinous, *vī′nŭs*
virulent, *vĭr′ū-lĕnt*
virus, *vī′rŭs*
vis-à-vis, *vē′zà-vē′*
viscid, *vĭs′ĭd*
viscount, *vī′kount′*
visé, *vē′zā*
vitriol, *vĭt′rĭ-ŭl*
vituperation, *vĭ-tū′pẽr-ā′shŭn*
viva voce, *vī′và vō′sĕ*
viviparous, *vĭ-vĭp′à-rŭs*
volatile, *vŏl′à-tĭl*
volume, *vŏl′yŭm*
voluntarily, *vŏl′ŭn-tẽr′ĭ-lĭ*

waft, *wàft*
wainscot, *wān′skŭt*
warily, *wâr′ĭ-lĭ*
was, *wŏz*
wash, *wŏsh*
wasp, *wŏsp*
weird, *wērd*
well-bred, *wĕl′brĕd′*
when, *hwĕn*
where, *hwâr*
whisk, *hwĭsk*
whistler, *hwĭs′lẽr*
whole, *hōl*
whooping (cough), *hōōp′ĭng*
whortleberry, *hwûr′t′l-bĕr′ĭ*
widow, *wĭd′ō*
window, *wĭn′dō*
wiseacre, *wīz′ā′kẽr*
wistaria, *wĭs-tā′rĭ-à*
withes, *wĭths*
women, *wĭm′ĕn*
wondering, *wŭn′dẽr-ĭng*
wont (custom), *wŭnt*
wrath, *ràth*
wrestler, *rĕs′lẽr*

xenia, *zē′nĭ-à*
xylophone, *zī′lô-fōn*

yacht, *yŏt*
yolk, *yōk*

zealot, *zĕl′ŭt*
zenith, *zē′nĭth*
zodiacal, *zō-dī′à-kăl*
zoo, *zōō*
zoology, *zō-ŏl′ô-jĭ*

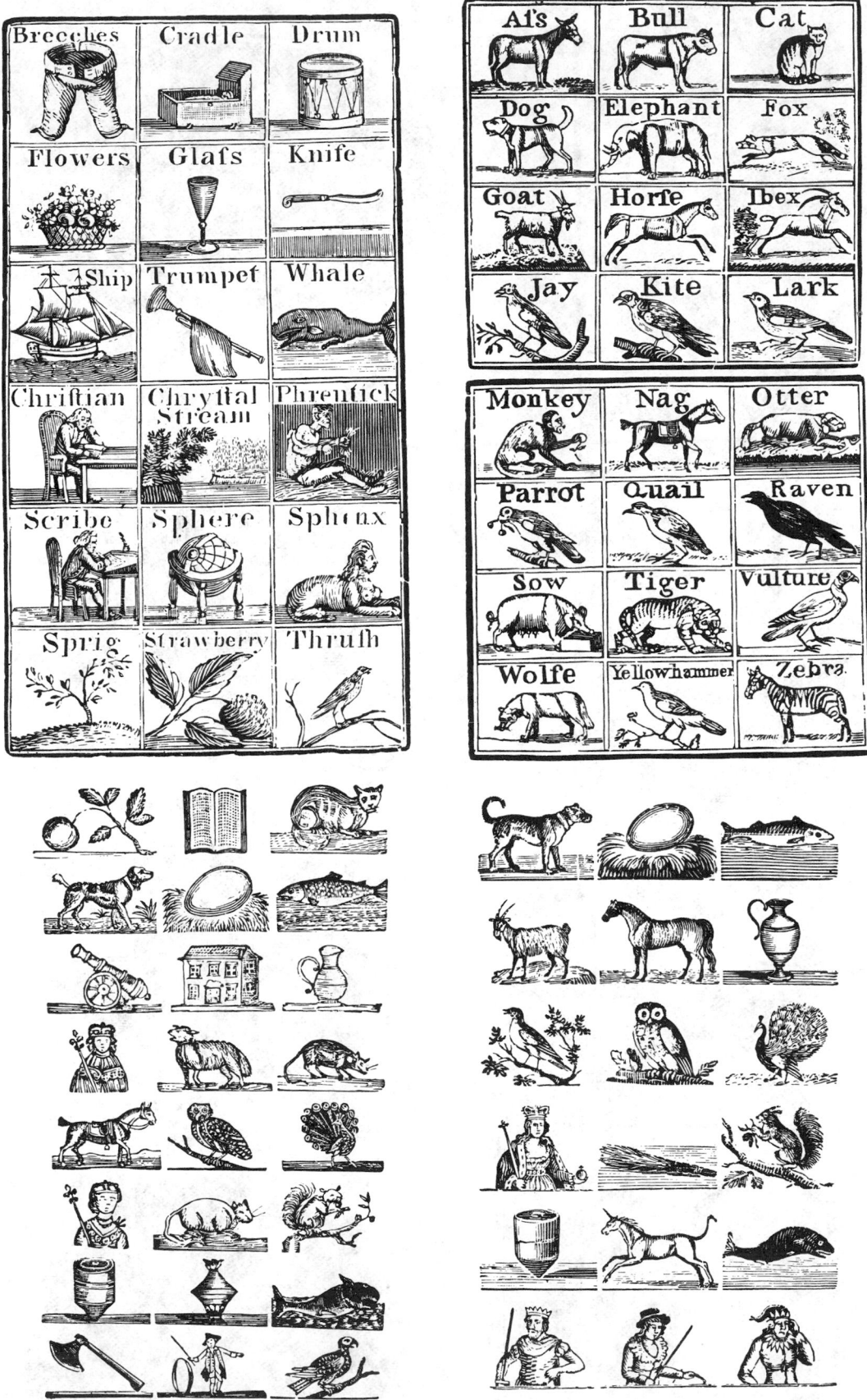

Wood engravings by Thomas Bewick (1753–1828) from *The English Spelling Book* compiled by William Mavor and published in 1801. The idea of using illustrations to help children learn has been utilized for many centuries. The *New England Primer,* which sold an estimated 2,000,000 copies in the 18th century, had an illustrated alphabet. *(1800 Woodcuts by Thomas Bewick and His School; edited by Blanche Cirker; Dover Publications, Inc., N.Y.)*

These wood engravings of libraries and reading were done by Thomas Bewick (1753–1828). The invention of the printing press (c.1450) marks the real beginning of modern libraries in Europe although the Bibliothèque Nationale of France was founded in 1367. The first library in the United States was founded in 1638 at Harvard College. (*1800 Woodcuts by Thomas Bewick and His School; edited by Blanche Cirker; Dover Publications, Inc., N.Y.*)

FORMS OF LITERARY COMPOSITION

Enjoyment in Reading. A good book is like an excellent dinner in good company, to which you bring a good digestion, a keen appetite, alert attention, and as ready a wit as you can muster. It is easy to indulge oneself in drifting idly through a maze of moving pictures. But some effort is necessary to keep the mind alert to the procession of thoughts on the printed page. If the author has written something worth while, he has taken much time to select the right words and set them in order. There is no higher pleasure than that of the reader who follows such an author through his pages and re-creates from the printed symbols his thought, his pictures, and his fancies. The book that you enjoy in this way becomes a part of your life.

Journals and Magazines. Business and professional people read the journals of their special interests. Members of churches, societies, and orders should read at least some of the papers and magazines published in their interest. Such reading is necessary to intelligent membership, as the reading of daily newspapers and weekly journals is necessary to efficient citizenship. But no one need read all of any paper or review. Let your special interest select and direct your attention. Reading the news that prompts to reflection upon the issues of the day is worth while; but trying to read the entire newspaper only produces a confused impression of many things, which serves to weaken the judgment. One should not, however, confine his reading to newspapers and magazines.

Books and Taste. The magazines offer, at small expense, acquaintance with the best literary work of the day. The novels of Charles Dickens were originally published in magazines. But the wise man will spend something for the sake of possessing at least a few good books. Even the public library cannot take the place of books on a shelf at home, whether home be a single room or a mansion. You may select your books according to your taste, but you should take pains to cultivate your taste.

A useful distinction has been drawn between the *literature of knowledge* and the *literature of power*. Keep this in mind in filling your bookshelf. Reliable volumes that contain the things one needs to know, or should be able to refer to on occasion, are of great importance; for exact information is indispensable. These make up the literature of knowledge. This class includes dictionaries, encyclopedias, histories, and books upon special sciences. Of even greater value are the books of power. These feed the imagination and inspire ideals. Such are the great biographies, classic stories, essays, and poetry. The wise man will value these, not for all they contain, but for what they actually bring to *him*. A single article in a work of reference, a single idea or fact in a history, one little poem out of a large volume, may be worth to you many times the cost of the book.

STORY OR NARRATIVE

Both of these words are derived from roots which mean simply *see* or *know*, but they have come to be applied to all accounts of events. The order of telling a story is either: (1) the time order in which things happen, as in history; or (2) an "arrangement" different from the time order. This "arrangement" may be made for the sake of (a) holding attention or (b) making clearer the relations of cause and effect among the events. Such an "arrangement" is called a plot, and stories so planned are fiction.

For plot outlines, refer to *The Book or Article Review* and *The Scenario* in the section Writing and Speaking.

Ancient Stories. Everybody likes a good story, and story-telling is very nearly, if not quite, the most ancient of the arts. The oldest discoverable collections of writing contain well-developed narratives in the form of myths and legends. A *myth* is an ancient tale which usually conveys some imaginative account of the origin of gods, various human arts, or natural phenomena. The *legend* is similar to the myth, but it is more directly concerned with the deeds of men. In the course of centuries, many of these tales were combined by master story-tellers into *epics*, which are stories of the lives and deeds of heroes, such as the *Iliad* and the *Odyssey*. The word epic comes from the Greek *epos*, meaning "speech" or "song," because these great stories were told or chanted for generations before the poems were actually written.

Medieval Romance. During the Middle Ages, long *romances* about the careers and conquests of Alexander and Charlemagne and their followers took shape from the tales and songs of minstrels who wandered from court to court and were welcomed in the castles for the entertainment they brought. The name *romance* was given to these stories because they were composed in the common Romance, or French, tongue rather than in the Latin of scholars. In similar manner, the romances of King Arthur and of the Holy Grail were built. Upon this fund of romance many modern writers have drawn. Tennyson embodied the Arthurian legends in the *Idylls of the King*.

In their early form, these stories were told in verse. Later they were recast in prose form by various writers. With these poems in prose there grew side by side the *prose tale*, which was a story of adventure, in which the events were strung together loosely and the interest depended on the strangeness of the events or the unforeseen outcome of the adventures. Several romantic prose tales were produced by Greek writers in the early Christian centuries. One of the most famous was *Apollonius of Tyre*. From this tale came Shakespeare's plot for *Pericles, Prince of Tyre*. To this general type of story belongs the series of tales known as the *Arabian Nights*. Washington Irving's *Tales of the Alhambra* furnish a more modern instance. Out of these loosely constructed legends there have developed in modern times the novel and the short story.

The Novel. Of the *novel* there are two general types. In the *romantic novel*, of which the stories of Sir Walter Scott are examples, the story is placed at a distance from the reader, in either time or space, and the strangeness of events and places contributes much to its interest. In romance our dreams come true. The *realistic novel* takes its subject matter from everyday affairs. The usual motives of people form the story, and the outcome must be made to seem reasonable and likely. William Dean Howells's work is among the best in the realistic style. The love motive is almost universal in the novel. The *psychological novel*, exemplified in Joyce's *Ulysses*, is primarily interested in recording the thoughts and feelings of the characters. The novel may vary in length from several thousand words to several hundred thousand.

The Short Story. The modern *short story* has been developed within the last hundred years. Its ancestors were many,—the Greek romances, the *fabliaux* in France, such tales as Boccaccio told in prose in Italy and Chaucer retold in verse in England; but it is a form clearly distinguished from all these. Edgar Allan Poe may be credited with the first characteristic work in the new form in America, and his stories are still reckoned among the best. The short story takes a small group of characters, carries them through a brief time, and, in rapid action, with a minimum of description, works out their fortunes and interactions. The story may vary in length from a few hundred to six or seven thousand words. The explanation of the plot must usually be cleverly concealed until the end of the story is reached, but it must then be made to seem reasonable and convincing. The works of Bret Harte, Francis R. Stockton, R. L. Stevenson, and Rudyard Kipling furnish examples of various types of the short story.

Special Forms of Prose Fiction. Both the novel and the short story appear in various special forms. The *mystery story*, for example, may be either long or short, but its plot turns upon some skillfully concealed relation between the events narrated. When this relation is revealed, in the end, as something very simple and commonplace, we have what is sometimes called a *surprise plot*. Or the mystery may be left as an unexplained something in the borderland of fancy or superstition, which human science has not yet mapped out. The mystery story is really a very primitive sort of tale, and many examples of it are to be found in early folklore. It carries all the thrills of unexpected and unexplained fortunes. Poe's *Gold Bug* and *Fall of the House of Usher* are classic examples of the modern mystery story.

The extraordinarily popular *detective story* is one sort of mystery tale, in which such a fascinatingly keen, questioning mind as that of Sir Arthur Conan Doyle's creation, Mr. Sherlock Holmes, is seen at work unraveling the tangled threads of the mystery. It is really a story built backward; for the real story is assumed to be already finished, and the detective is set to going over the obscure trail to discover the origin of the train of events. What we get is really two stories in one, the first being that of the original characters and events, the second, that of the detective and his discoveries. Such a story is *The Leavenworth Case*. The *adventure story* is more nearly like the old-fashioned tale. Its interest depends mostly upon the succession of unexpected and more or less complicated incidents calling for courage and address in the characters. *Robinson Crusoe*, *Treasure Island*, and *Kidnapped* are favorite examples of this kind.

Both the novel and the short story may be so written as to carry a special interest derived from the *location of the events*, from the *type of industry* in which the characters are engaged, or from the *class of society* in which they move. This last kind may involve only the people of one class of society. But more commonly it follows the ancient instinct of story-tellers for the effect of contrast. Then the clash of high and low, of rich and poor, which has interested mankind from the time of Aladdin and King Cophetua, furnishes the moving impulse.

The *historical novel* involves historical events as a necessary part of the story, and pictures some historical period. When it is based upon real scholarship and gives a trustworthy picture of the time in which its action is placed, it is not only interesting in itself but valuable as an aid to the study of history. *Hugh Wynne*, *The Crisis*, *The Cloister and the Hearth*, *Ivanhoe*, *Quentin Durward*, *The Last Days of Pompeii*, *The Conqueror*, *Quo Vadis*, and *Ben Hur* are excellent examples.

History. The almost universal desire for the true story finds satisfaction in *history*, the story of man's life from the beginning to the present time. Indeed, it is out of this material that most fiction and poetry are made. A knowledge of history is essential to a true education. An impartial and readable history, therefore, entitles its author to very high regard. The following works are masterpieces in this field: James F. Rhodes's *History of the United States*; Theodore Roosevelt's *Winning of the West*; Green's *History of England*; Ferrero's *Greatness and Decline of Rome*; Prescott's *Conquest of Mexico* and *Conquest of Peru*; Parkman's *France and England in the New World*; J. L. Motley's *Rise of the Dutch Republic*.

Biography. Second only to history in importance as a part of education, and in its masterpieces equally fascinating, is *biography*, or the life histories of important personages. To know the great thinkers and workers of the world through their biographies is not only interesting but of incalculable worth as an influence in developing character. The list of true and readable biographies is long. Many short lives have been written and published in such series as *American Statesmen* and *English Men of Letters*. The following are of high rank: Boswell's *Life of Johnson*, unique among biographies; Plutarch's *Parallel Lives of Illustrious Greeks and Romans*, an ancient work still full of interest; Morley's *Life of Gladstone*; Thayer's *Life of Cavour*; Carlyle's *Oliver Cromwell*; Palmer's *Life of Alice Freeman Palmer*; Booker Washington's *Up from Slavery*; Jacob Riis's *Making of an American*; Beveridge's *Life of John Marshall*. Letters and *journals* supplement biography.

Travel. Always and everywhere people are interested in *travelers' stories*, and many most entertaining books have been written to satisfy this appetite. A very large part of the *Odyssey* is made up of the wanderings of Odysseus, the Greek hero; the adventures of Sindbad the Sailor are proverbial; the book of the travels of Marco Polo through Asia is a classic. Among recent books, those of Harry Franck about his walking trips in various parts of the world are unique and interesting. The *Reminiscences of Rafael Pumpelly* contain some charming stories of travel in the 19th century. The stories of Arctic exploration by Peary and Stefansson, Roosevelt's travel and hunting narratives, the lives of Stanley and Livingstone, and Stevenson's chronicles of the South seas furnish mines of fascinating reading.

Folk Stories. The *folk tale*, or *folk story*, is what its name implies, a tale which has been told over and over again among the common people. This type of story is common to all peoples, and it is worthy of note that such stories circulated among widely separated peoples tell of similar adventures and teach similar truths. Many of these legends may be found in the collections made by Andrew Lang.

The *fairy tale* may be thought of as a type of folk story. Most fairy stories are of very ancient origin; some are modern. They are always concerned with a fanciful explanation of events and with the fate of people. The fairies are the little people of the air and the trees and the caves, who are either friendly or unfriendly to human folk. Some of these stories are very beautiful, while others are marred by the savage cruelty of barbarous times. Andersen's original tales and the *Märchen* gathered by the brothers Grimm offer excellent specimens of the fairy tale.

Stories That Teach. A very engaging type of story, of ancient origin, widely current in medieval times in Europe, and still to be found among remote and untutored peoples, is the *animal story*, in which the animals are personified, or endowed with human faculties. Frequently each sort of animal is supposed to embody a particular human trait, and the stories take on a moral flavor. In America, the finest examples of these tales are the Uncle Remus and Br'er Rabbit stories, retold in the negro dialect by Joel Chandler Harris.

Closely related to these animal stories are *fables*, pointed anecdotes in which animals are endowed with human qualities and are made to illustrate moral lessons. The fables of Æsop and of La Fontaine are universally popular.

The *parable* is a story of common events or happenings of every day, used to illustrate moral or religious truths. As the typical beginning of the old-fashioned story is "Once upon a time," so the typical beginning of the parable is "It is like." The New Testament affords us the best examples of the parable, though in one form or another a parable appears wherever any teaching of moral or social truth is to be done.

The *allegory* is a development of the story of common things which conveys moral and spiritual meanings. The allegory extends metaphor and personification into a story, in which the characters represent qualities, motives, or types of character. The morality plays of early English literature,

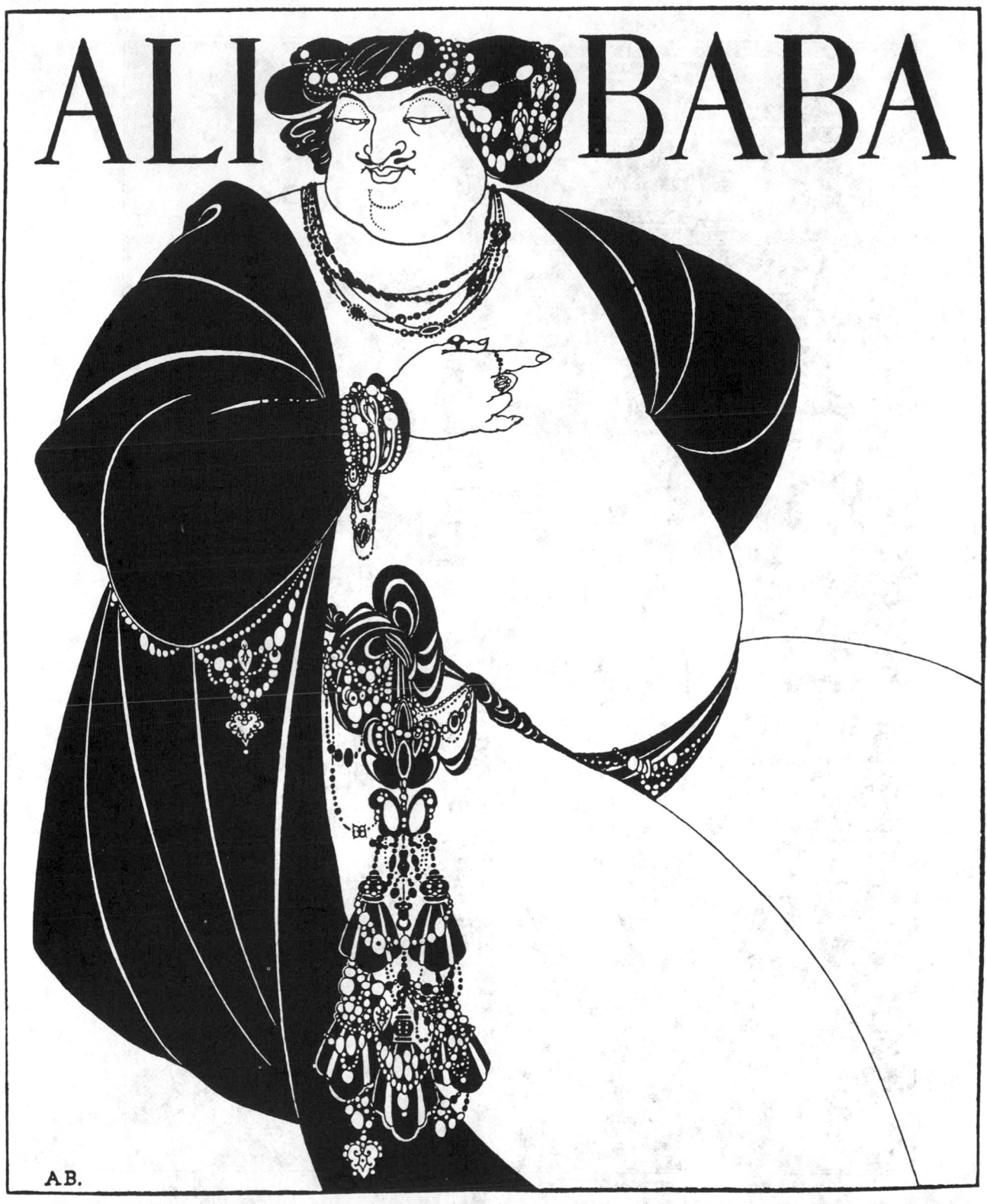

ALI BABA

Cover Design for "The Forty Thieves." This illustration by Aubrey Beardsley (1872–1898) was drawn in 1898 for his publisher Leonard Smithers, who had proposed an edition of Sir Richard Burton's translation of *Ali Baba and the Forty Thieves*. The popular folk tale occurs in some translations of *The Arabian Nights* or *The Thousand and One Nights*. The stories probably originated in ancient Persia and India. In the "frame-story" that ties all the others together, a king begins to kill each of his brides on the morning after his marriage. But one wife, Sharazad, beguiles him with a story every night until he finally relents and spares her life. Other popular tales from the collection include *Sinbad the Sailor* and *Aladdin's Lamp*. They were first introduced to the western world in Antoine Gallard's French translation published from 1704 to 1717. Notable English translations include those of Edward William Lane (1838), John Payne (1882–84), and Burton (1886–88). *(The Later Work of Aubrey Beardsley; Dover Publications, Inc., N.Y.)*

Frontispiece from "Volpone." One of the last illustrations Aubrey Beardsley did was for Ben Jonson's (c.1573–1637) 17th-century masterpiece *Volpone, or the Fox* (1606). Beardsley saw in Jonson's characterizations of Volpone and the servant Mosca qualities expressed in his own artwork. Beardsley even wrote a critical introduction to the play. He intended his illustrations for *Volpone* to be the climax to his artistic achievement. Before finishing the project, Beardsley died at Menton, France, in March 1898. Later that year, Leonard Smithers published the new edition using all that Beardsley had completed—the cover design, the frontispiece, and five initial letters. (*The Later Work of Aubrey Beardsley; Dover Publications, Inc., N.Y.*)

such as *Everyman*, and many modern short, poetic plays are really allegories. Indeed, the short allegory may be found frequently in fiction.

In English, the great prose allegory is Bunyan's *Pilgrim's Progress*. Dante's *Divine Comedy* is perhaps the greatest of the world's allegories. There is also much allegory in Tennyson's *Idylls of the King*.

DESCRIPTIVE PROSE

This type of composition appears as an important part of books on travel, art, architecture, cities, and natural scenery. The books of travel referred to under *Travel* contain many fine examples of this graphic style of writing.

EXPOSITION AND ARGUMENT

The logical development of themes is to be found in the form of *essays* on literary, historical, and scientific subjects, and in *speeches* and *orations*. The *essay* presents, either in serious or in light style, a writer's thoughts upon a subject, to inform, convince, explain, or entertain. The essays of Bacon, Addison, and Macaulay are English classics. Huxley was the great scientific essayist of the 19th century. Lord Bryce's *American Commonwealth* is a long essay, combining exposition and argument. Current magazines contain many essays upon a wide variety of subjects, in the form of editorials, special articles, and studies. The *speech* or *oration* is usually a discussion of a theme of public human interest, argumentative and persuasive in character, and prepared for a particular public occasion. The works of Edmund Burke, William Pitt, Patrick Henry, Daniel Webster, Abraham Lincoln, Stephen A. Douglas, Henry W. Grady, and Rufus Choate furnish examples of English and American oratory.

POETRY

When emotion and the creative imagination rule expression in language, we have poetry. The province of poetry is to kindle the imagination and inspire fine sentiments and high enthusiasms through beautiful language. English literature is rich in poetry that does just these things.

The Lyric. This is the simplest and most familiar form of poetry. The word *lyric* implies singing, but the lyric poem need not be set to music. It is simply the poet's personal expression of feeling, and it may be written upon any theme that arouses in him an emotional response. This theme is usually suggested by some person, place, or natural object. Usually the lyric is short, not more than a few stanzas, so that it can be read easily in a short time and grasped as a whole.

The songs of Robert Burns are among the purest lyrics in the English language. Tennyson's work includes many separate lyrics of very great beauty as well as numerous short songs inset in some of his longer poems. Rudyard Kipling's poetry should be read for a more rugged and vigorous type. Sidney Lanier produced several very beautiful lyrics, among which are *The Woods and the Master* and *The Marshes of Glynn*. James Whitcomb Riley's verses, even when he is telling a story, often seem to sing themselves. Riley is the great American master of the lyric in popular language. Joaquin Miller, among American poets, is to be read for his *Songs of the Sierras*. Among present day poets, also, the works of Alfred Noyes and John Masefield, in England, and of Richard Le Gallienne and Bliss Carman, in America, should be read.

The Sonnet. A lyric poem of the fixed length of fourteen iambic pentameter lines. Usually it has a first section of eight lines and a second section of six, though the sonnets of Shakespeare do not conform to this rule. The sonnet was adopted into English from the Italian. It is a form that requires the finest mastery both of language and of thought. Every reader of literature should be acquainted with some of the greater sonnets of Shakespeare and Milton and also with sonnets by poets of the present

day. As fine examples of the English sonnet, one may read Wordsworth's *To Milton*, Keats's *On Chapman's Homer*, and Rupert Brooke's series of sonnets under the title "*1914.*"

The Ode. A lyric adopted from the Greek, but altered greatly in form by various English poets. Today it is simply a poem written in dignified and elevated style, often for some set occasion. It varies, in length and metrical form, from such poems as Wordsworth's *Ode to Duty* and Shelley's *Ode to a Skylark* to a poem of the length of Lowell's *Commemoration Ode* or Tennyson's *Ode on the Death of the Duke of Wellington*.

Hymns and Songs. Hymns are written in stanzas usually of four or six lines with three or four accents to the line, though there is no special rule for these. *Popular songs* have most frequently the trochaic meter because of its lightness and rapidity of movement.

Elegies. These are funeral laments, often of a reflective character. Gray's *Elegy Written in a Country Churchyard* is an English classic.

Narrative Poetry. Aside from the great epics— the *Iliad*, the *Odyssey*, the *Æneid*, and *Paradise Lost*—and the metrical romances, such as those about Charlemagne and King Arthur, the most interesting form of narrative poetry is the *ballad*. This is really a folk story in lyric verse, though in modern use "ballad" means any short simple lyric. The manner of telling the story is frequently dramatic, that is, the characters are allowed to speak for themselves. The ballads of Robin Hood are perhaps the most familiar in English. These and many others may be found in such a collection as *English and Scottish Popular Ballads*, made by Francis J. Child.

Geoffrey Chaucer's *Canterbury Tales* mark the beginning of modern English narrative poetry. The stories of *Miles Standish* and *Evangeline*, as told by Longfellow, are familiar examples of the narrative poem of modern times. For many years the prose novel and the short story have crowded out the narrative poem, but it seems to be returning to favor in the work of several English and American poets. In America, Robert Frost was master of a type of short dramatic narrative, several examples of which are to be found in his volume *North of Boston*. John Masefield's *Dauber* and *Everlasting Mercy* and Alfred Noyes's *Drake* are excellent examples of poetic narratives.

Anthologies. The word means collections of flowers and was anciently used for compilations of short Greek poems and epigrams. Now it applies mostly to collections which represent the finest poetry of a given country, as an "American anthology," or poems about a certain class of subjects, as an "anthology of war poetry," or poems representing a certain type, as an "anthology of lyrics" or of hymns.

Vers libre, "Free Verse." This name is applied to a type of modern poetry in which the strict meters of the older verse do not appear and in which rime is rather deliberately rejected. Apart, therefore, from its arrangement in lines of irregular length, it is often difficult to distinguish this form of poetry from rhythmical prose. The writers of "free verse" attempt to make the rhythm of their poetry reflect truthfully the emotions that prompt them to write. Obviously, a poet must possess great skill to do this successfully. Hence very few pieces of good "free verse" have been written, the more successful being found in the works of Carl Sandburg, Amy Lowell, and Edgar Lee Masters.

DRAMA

A drama, or play, is essentially a story arranged to be told in action on the stage. This method of telling a story is very ancient, dating back to early festivals, when legends connected with the god or patron of a feast were represented with music, dancing, and recitation. The history of the stage and the drama in all countries shows more or less intimate connection with the service of religion as well as with the human love of entertainment.

English dramas are written either in verse or in prose. Sometimes the dramatists may use both forms in the same play, as Shakespeare did. At the present day, however, most plays that are to be both staged and printed are written in prose, for the modern public calls for a more "natural" mode of speech. The subject of the drama may be drawn from almost any source, according to the genius of the playwright, and, like the novel or short story, its manner may be romantic or realistic.

Tragedy and Comedy. Tragedy signifies a play of serious action and motive usually representing some human struggle having an adverse outcome. This struggle may be against the gods or fate, as in the ancient drama, against their own passions, as in the Shakespearean tragedies, or against their passions and social conditions, as in more modern plays. Comedy implies a lighter, more pleasant story, with a happy ending in place of the sad or disastrous close of tragedy. Few plays of the present day answer strictly to this classification, most of them exhibiting both tragedy and comedy.

Various Forms. We may have a *play of incident*, in which we are interested chiefly in what happens, or a *play of character*, in which we are interested chiefly in the people to whom things happen. The play may be said to belong either to *serious drama*, in the course of which some essential change or development in one or more characters is required, or to the *lighter drama*, in which there is frequently only change of situation or of relations among the characters. The *farce* is a light play of incident, carried to the extreme of artificial or ridiculous situations. The modern *melodrama* is characterized by exaggerated sensational features.

Goldsmith in the 18th century produced what is known as *comedy of manners*. He was followed by several playwrights in the same fashion. Plays in this class to be read are *The Good-Natured Man*, *She Stoops to Conquer*, *The Rivals*, and *The School for Scandal*.

A large number of English and American plays of recent years are to be classed as *social drama*. In these the method of the playwright is realistic, and his object is to portray the working of everyday human motives. Sometimes he rises to a discussion or criticism of modern social life and customs.

In America, William Vaughn Moody, Clyde Fitch, William Gillette, and Augustus Thomas produced plays suitable for reading and, among English playwrights, Sir Arthur W. Pinero, Henry Arthur Jones, and John Galsworthy did notable work.

There are in English several dramas which, while not successful on the stage, should be read by the student. Among these may be mentioned Tennyson's *Becket* and *Queen Mary*, and Browning's *The Falcon* and *Pippa Passes*.

During the 1920's there was marked interest in short plays of one or two acts, especially those of Lady Gregory, Lord Dunsany, and Sir James M. Barrie, but at the present time nothing important is being done in this field, and there is little interest in them. Dramas for television, however, have lately been receiving much attention. Some of the best writers for this medium are Norman Corwin, Paddy Chayefsky, and Horton Foote.

There is interest also in the *pageant*, which is simply an outdoor play with much action but with very little text. Its most frequent use is for portraying poetically the life and customs of past times, in celebrations of historical events.

For further references, see *Family Library*, *articles and tables on the various national literatures*, and the *Table of Modern World Literature*.

FIGURES OF SPEECH

Apt figures of speech are pictures of one's thoughts. A good comparison throws light on an idea, thereby helping people to understand it. For this reason, the language of the plain, matter-of-fact man is full of comparisons and figures, which he has inherited or unconsciously learned from those around him. He says, "plain as day," "heavy as lead," "level headed," as naturally as he says "see," "lift," or "think."

A *figure of speech* is a deviation from the usual application of words in order to impart clearness, force, and beauty to the composition. By saying "an army of ants" we give a vivid impression both of orderliness and of vastness in number. When David says "they were swifter than eagles" and "stronger than lions," we at once get a graphic description of the physical qualities of Saul and of Jonathan. Figures may be grouped in the four following classes:

I. Figures that picture a hidden resemblance or make use of a close association.

Simile (*sĭm'ĭ-lē*). In this figure, a likeness between things is expressed, usually by *like* or *as*, in the form of a comparison: "Sweet *as the morning air*." One may recount the kind words and acts and cheerfulness of a visitor and thus describe her prosaically very well, but if one says, "Her presence was *like a ray of sunshine* in a darkened room," the whole story is pictured in a single phrase. Other examples: "Quick *as lightning*"; "Abundant *as the light of the sun*"; "Deaf *as any tradesman's dummy*"; "A baby's feet, *like sea-shells pink*"; "Jolted *like a solitary penny* in an iron bank"; "White *as chalk*."

Metaphor (*mĕt'à-fôr*). The word means "carrying over," "transfer." In this figure, the word *like* or *as*, used in *simile*, is omitted, and, by an implied comparison, a new meaning or picture is transferred directly to the word: "He was a *tower* of strength"; "*Seeds* of truth"; "Lowliness is young ambition's *ladder*"; "Sail on, O *Ship* of State"; "Hours and minutes are *dollars* and *cents*."

The next two figures, *synecdoche* and *metonymy*, are similar in that the things suggested for comparison are more closely associated than those used in *simile* or *metaphor*. They are not uncommon in everyday speech, and their skillful use is a secret of much that is fascinating in literature. It is often difficult to classify an expression definitely as one or other of these figures. The name "metonymy" is often used for both.

Synecdoche (*sĭ-nĕk'dô-kē*). A figure in which a striking part of the object is used to signify the whole, or sometimes the whole to signify the part: "A thousand *hands* waved farewell"; "This *roof* (house) protects you"; "Now the *year* (the summer) is beautiful"; "*Ten thousand swords* would have leaped from their scabbards"; "The *hearths* (homes) of the nation"; "The *city* welcomed him."

Metonymy (*mē-tŏn'ĭ-mĭ*). A figure by which we put the cause for the effect, or the effect for the cause, as when we say, "He reads Milton," i. e., Milton's works; "Gray hairs should be respected," meaning old age; "My son, give me thy *heart*" (affection); "He was the *sigh* of his mother's soul" (the boy she loved).

Personification. The figure by which inanimate things or ideas are endowed with the qualities of human beings: "*Wisdom crieth* in the streets"; "*Hope hath* never lost *her* youth"; "The little *Road says*, Go";

> "The *Worm* aware of his intent
> *Harangued* him thus, right eloquent";

"Hark! *Truth proclaims*, thy triumphs cease"; "The *Sea saw* it and *fled*."

Allusion. A figure in which reference, direct or indirect, is made to some personage, incident, expression, or custom, with which the reader is familiar, to convey a vivid picture of the subject in hand: "A *Daniel* come to judgment"; "A *Napoleon* of finance"; "*They shall not pass.*"

II. Figures that depend for their force partly upon the arrangement of words in the sentence and partly upon the mental attitude of the speaker or writer.

Interrogation. This figure consists in asking a question with an implied contrary answer. Its force amounts to a vigorous denial: "*Am I a dog?*" "Hath the Lord said it, *and shall He not do it?*" "Hath He spoken it, *and shall He not make it good?*" "He that planted the ear, *shall He not hear?*" "He that formed the eye, *shall He not see?*" The figure is appropriate in intense expression, especially in oratory.

Apostrophe (*a-pŏs'trô-fê*). Another figure which is appropriate in oratory or in exalted poetry. It consists in turning aside from the usual order of words and addressing an object, an absent person, or a personified idea, thus bringing the object or idea vividly to the reader or audience: "O *Duty*, if that name thou love!" "O *Death!* where is thy sting?" "O *Grave!* where is thy victory?"

Vision. A figure closely akin to apostrophe but less forceful. This figure consists in describing a scene, an object, or an event as if it were immediately in view: "*I see before me the gladiator lie.*" The value of the figure consists in its vividness. The use of the historical present is a form of vision: "*I remember well the day I entered the room, the familiar objects are all before me, but my mother is not there.*"

Irony (*ī'rô-nĭ*). This consists in saying the opposite of what is meant. A classical illustration of irony is to be found in the repeated phrase of Mark Antony in *Julius Cæsar:* "They are *honorable* men"; "We have, to be sure, great reason to believe the *modest* man would not ask him for a debt, when he pursues his life." Modern writing is characterized rather by touches of irony than by a full development of the figure. It is a dangerous tool to use even occasionally and not at all fit for habitual employment.

Litotes (*lĭ'tô-tēz*). A figure of speech by which a strong affirmative is expressed simply by the negative of the contrary: "a citizen of *no mean city*," i. e., "of an important city"; "A storm of *no small force* drove our vessel before it"; "To be polite in word and in deed is a matter of *no slight significance.*"

Hyperbole (*hī-pĕr'bô-lē*). An exaggeration for the purpose of compelling attention: "*Every word that Webster used weighed a pound*";

"The sky *shrunk upward with unusual dread*
And trembling Tiber *div'd beneath his bed*";

"My song *shall blossom at your feet*
My heart *your throne shall be.*"

Euphemism (*ū'fê-mĭz'm*). A mild or inoffensive expression used in place of what is regarded as an unpleasant statement. "*He was in the habit of removing people's goods out of their houses without previous arrangement with the owners*"; "*He passed away.*" These are euphemisms for stealing and for death. In everyday conversation this figure often takes the form of understatement: "His experiment was not too successful."

III. Figures that are simply arrangements of well-chosen words to produce packed and pointed expression.

Antithesis (*ăn-tĭth'ê-sĭs*). This figure depends for its force upon vivid contrast of opposite terms or ideas. It gains power through the balanced construction involved in the sentence: "If one would be rich, *should he labor to increase his possessions, or to diminish his desires?*" "The Puritans hated bear baiting, *not because it gave pain to the bear, but because*

it gave pleasure to the spectators." Many catch phrases are antitheses: "*rich and poor*"; "*capital and labor.*"

Climax. An arrangement of words or groups of words in ascending order of force or importance: "*I know it, I concede it, I confess it, I proclaim it.*" "*Force, force to the utmost; force without stint or limit; the righteous, triumphant force which shall make right the law of the world and cast every selfish dominion down in the dust.*" The strongest expression must be placed last in order.

Epigram. A short, forceful expression which depends for its value upon its brevity and upon some surprise involved in it. The best epigrams imply some antithesis: "*The silence was audible*"; "*So good that he is good for nothing*"; "*Some laborious orators mistake perspiration for inspiration.*"

Epithet (*ĕp'ĭ-thĕt*). A descriptive word or phrase into which has been packed an important meaning or a vivid picture. The epithet is an important element in poetry, and many epithets have become common words. There are two kinds of epithets:

1. *Essential Epithets*, or names of qualities always associated with the thing described: "*green* grass"; "*bright* sword."

2. *Conventional Epithets*, such as adjectives which become commonly associated with certain names: "*honest* Abe"; "*doubting* Thomas"; "*bright-eyed* Athena." The Greek poems, the *Iliad* and the *Odyssey*, are particularly rich in epithets: "the *wine-dark* sea"; "*hollow* ships"; "*rosy-fingered* dawn." Other examples: "our *honored* dead"; "*daisied* fields."

IV. The following names are given to certain uses of words for their sound values:

Euphony (*ū'fô-nĭ*). A name applied to the pleasing effects of sounds produced by the combination of words in sentences or of phonetic elements in spoken words. Euphony is a fundamental requirement of poetry: "The most sounding and euphonic surname that English history or topography affords";

"The bells of Shandon that sound so grand on
The pleasant waters of the river Lee."

Onomatopœia (*ŏn'ô-măt'ô-pē'yà*). The word means name-making. Onomatopœia is the use of a word or phrase formed to imitate the sound of the thing signified. Many words in common use furnish examples: We say *rat tat tat* to denote a knocking at the door, *bow wow* to express the barking of a dog, or *buzz, buzz* to indicate the sound made by bees. Onomatopœia is frequently used in poetry where the sound of certain words is used to convey the sense; thus,

"When Ajax strives some rock's vast weight to throw
The line too labors, and the words move slow";

"And the *light Latin tripped* along her tongue
Amid the *roar of Irish gutturals.*"

Alliteration (*ă-lĭt'ĕr-ā'shŭn*). The use of a succession of words having the same initial letter or sound. The chief value of alliteration is in challenging attention. Alliterative phrases, also, are easily memorized: "*babbling babes*"; "*feathered fowl.*" Early English poetry used alliteration in place of rime and meter. The device is frequently used in modern poetry; as, for example, "*Still stands the forest primeval*"; "*Lisp of leaves and ripple of rain.*"

Assonance (*ăs'ô-năns*). A name applied to the recurrence of the same vowel sound in a group of words. Assonance is likely to become monotonous and disagreeable in prose or even in poetry, though sometimes it is used with good effect: "*So all day long the noise of battle rolled*"; "*Hark! Hark! the lark.*"

Among the arts of everyday life there is none more important than that of letter writing. Our business and social relations are so dependent upon our written communications that the ability to write a clear letter in correct form is regarded as an essential mark of an ordinary English education. No accomplishment is more highly prized than skill in writing tactful, effective business letters, unless it be the ability to write a graceful personal letter of friendship. The general principles that govern the writing of letters and many suggestions that will help the student of the art to perfect his work are given in the following pages. The very fact that a letter is taken as an index of the personal character of the writer should prompt us all to most careful study of this art which is at once so practical and so easy to master.

We all know the kind of letters we like to receive—social letters that are really sincere and hearty, like the personal talk of friends, business letters that are frank and clear and that bring the writers, as we say, face to face with us. The telephone conversation, instead of taking the place of the letter, has served to emphasize the importance of the personal, direct, well-planned letter, and to increase the demand for it. Telegrams often require "letters to follow," which state more completely the contents of the messages. Good business records demand letters to "confirm" important telephone conversations.

THE BUSINESS LETTER: PRINCIPLES

We judge people and business houses by the letters they write. First, the appearance of the letterhead, the quality of the paper, and the outward form or display of the letter attract or repel us; then the substance of the message and its style and its tone make their impression. All these elements contribute to the general effect of any letter and determine what the response to it shall be.

As we judge others, so we are judged. If our letters are to be worthy representatives of us and fulfill the missions on which they are sent, we must plan and construct them carefully and intelligently. No detail either of material or of dress can safely be neglected.

How do you plan your letters? Do you organize the ideas so that they can be quickly and easily understood? Do you present them with the ease of manner and with the touch of individuality that you would put into a personal interview? Do the sentences you write and the order in which you write them so clearly express what you wish to say that the reader will naturally make the response you want? Do you use the tone of courtesy and of respect that will leave in the reader's mind a pleasant impression and build his good will for you?

BUILDING YOUR LETTER

The object of practically every business letter is to secure action, either immediate or remote. But the reader is not likely to act as the writer wishes, unless it appears to his own advantage to do so. Hence, it is wise to study the merits of the proposed action from the reader's viewpoint, and to present them in such a light that he can see them plainly. In every legitimate transaction both sides profit, but it is necessary to lay greatest stress upon the reader's profit, since his self-interest is his most powerful incentive to action.

It is true that we all act upon suggestions, either in the form of commands or in the gentler forms of persuasion. First, however, our attention must be secured, our interest must be aroused, and we must have inducements to action. Hence, the following steps in the building of a business letter are well established and are of almost universal application: (1) Get the attention of the reader; (2) Give him definite information; (3) Arouse his interest; (4) Offer him an inducement to act or to respond to you; (5) Give him a positive suggestion or direction; (6) Close your letter with a courteous expression that leaves a good feeling behind it.

The following example illustrates one way of building the letter. The headings in the left margin are, of course, not a part of the letter.

(LETTERHEAD)

FOREST PRODUCTS ASSOCIATION

LUMBERMAN'S EXCHANGE
LASALLE AND MADISON STS., CHICAGO, ILLINOIS 60602

HOMES BUILDING DEPARTMENT
WALTER C. HINES, *Manager*

June 17, 19—

Mr. Thomas C. Parsons   Subject: *Expert Service*
22 Elm Street
Utica, New York 13501

Dear Sir:

ATTENTION
AND
INTEREST
(the
receiver's
point of
view)

As you say in your interesting reply to our advertisement, the time was, not so long ago, when a man built his house just as his neighbors built theirs. He used wood or brick or stone, because these were the only materials to be had. For the same reason, his roof was either shingle or slate.

Nowadays, however, as you suggest, a man tries to express his taste in a home. He wants also to fit his house artistically to its location. In response to these demands, the variety of available materials and of plans for their combination has been increased beyond the range of any one man's knowledge.

INFORMA-
TION

Right here is where we can help you. Our business is to bring to the solution of your problem the best possible expert knowledge of materials and construction. This service we are able to supply economically through our large co-operative organization.

INTEREST
AND
INDUCEMENT

We enable you to save money on the cost of building and to realize with greater satisfaction your ideals of convenience, quality, and beauty.

Two booklets, "Some How's of Houses" and "Forest to Finish," which we are mailing to you today, will give you a suggestion as to our method of service. You will notice that we propose to furnish unbiased advice about ALL kinds of building materials.

POSITIVE
SUGGESTION
AND
COURTESY

When you have examined these booklets, just fill out and sign the enclosed card. It will bring our nearest expert representative for a personal conference at any time you suggest.

Very truly yours,

Enclosure   *Walter C. Hines*

This letter, to be sure, is a sales letter and therefore exemplifies more clearly the steps mentioned above than does a collection letter or letter of adjustment. All business letters, however, are in a sense sales letters, since all attempt at least to "sell" the writer's viewpoint and to secure the reader's favorable response.

Of course you can make these several steps in ways as varied as the kinds of people concerned and as the nature of the services involved. So, the particular contents of letters will vary with circumstances. Many very short notes, such as orders or brief acknowledgments, will not show all the steps. In general, however, the opening of the letter should recognize the reader's viewpoint. Beyond this very important approach to the recipient, the contents of the letter should further prepare him for the letter's real message by impressing upon him a sense of the writer's reliability, thus arousing his confidence. The next step is either direct statement or tactful suggestion of the writer's viewpoint. Persuasion of the reader to accept and to act according to that viewpoint is the final step.

The Letter as a Talk. You may think of the letter as a substitute for face to face talk. Hence, imagine as clearly as you can the characteristics of your reader, his immediate problems, and those features of his surroundings which you might see clearly in a personal interview. You will thus be able to put into your letter the welcome personal element. For instance, a letter planned to sell an article to a lawyer or to a doctor will be different in its appeal from letters designed to reach a farmer or a merchant. *Plan your letter for your reader.*

It should be noted that the letters quoted here are only illustrations of principles and methods and are not offered as models or guides. Since conditions vary greatly and every letter should be written with its particular reader definitely in mind, no set of letters, however extensive, could safely be copied or closely imitated. Imitation of models, moreover, destroys the element of personal character that is so important a part of the good business letter.

The Letter as a Record. The letter is a more permanent thing than the conversation. (1) It serves as a ready means of confirmation and of record. (2) In it matters may be elaborated, or treated more definitely and more connectedly than in a conversation. (3) Most people find it easier to understand an object or a statement if they can see it. They have more confidence in their eyes than in their ears. Besides, they can take more time to study the thing or the word that is before their eyes. Hence the letter frequently offers an occasion for clear, detailed explanation, which the reader may have before him for continuous study or for repeated examination.

In modern practice, clear explanation is recognized as the best means of persuasion through letters. Argument is generally regarded as out of place in a business letter, except as it appears in the form of a conclusion based upon clear explanation. This is a principle also of the best modern advertising; for an advertisement is really an "open letter" of business.

STYLE: QUALITIES

The preceding paragraph will suggest that the business letter is not necessarily brief. In practice, however, it is usually, if possible, limited to one page. But it must always be *clear, concise, positive,* and *courteous.*

I. Clearness. This is a quality to be secured through right order, simple, direct statements, and pleasing mechanical form. If you first arouse attention and interest, the way to understanding is open; clearness means ease of understanding for the reader, but nothing is clear to an inattentive mind. Clearness through style involves: (1) the use of accurate, definite, familiar words and phrases; (2) the use of well-made and well-punctuated sentences; (3) good paragraphing.

1. Words and Phrases. The words in your letter should be "loaded"—each one should carry a definite meaning. The habit of using a limited stock of words is easy to fall into, but it is fatal to clearness, except in the narrow circle of persons familiar with them. Every business has its peculiar set of *stock phrases,* its *cant* or *jargon,* which is unfamiliar to many people. For them, it must be translated into expressions they can understand readily. The letter writer should study *Usage* and *Synonyms.* If he rejects a stock phrase like *in re,* he will be obliged to choose a fresh one. Here are some outworn phrases that good writers are careful to avoid:

Advise, in the sense of *inform* or *tell.* The word is used too often. *Inform* or *notify,* except in formal writing, would be better.

Along these lines. A good phrase, but, when used too often, *lines* becomes indefinite. *In this way* or *following these plans* may be more definite.

And oblige, as in the phrase, "*and oblige* Yours truly." An obvious short-cut in courtesy, and therefore lacking in courtesy. Write "We (or I) shall be greatly obliged."

As per. Use *according to,* or some other phrase. See *Good Usage.*

At all times, At this time. The false formality in these phrases often repeated robs them of force. Prefer *always* and *now.*

At hand or **Has come to hand.** An obsolete phrase. Write "We have your letter—," or leave the fact to be understood.

Attached hereto. Appropriate only in the briefest, routine forms.

At the present writing. Prefer *now* or *at present.*

Beg, as in "We *beg* to state." An expression to be used only in the most formal correspondence. Otherwise it suggests a false humility.

Complaint. The word has been displaced in favor of *claim* and *adjustment.* The business advantage is obvious.

Contents carefully noted. A dead phrase. Use some words that will really convey the personal interest intended: "We have read with particular care, etc."

Enclosed herewith or **We enclose herewith.** *Herewith* is unnecessary.

Enclosed please find. *Please* is superfluous. Write "You will find enclosed" or "We enclose."

Earliest convenience. A faulty choice of words assumed to be courteous because of their indefiniteness. "As soon as possible" or "as soon as convenient for you" is the meaning usually intended.

Esteemed, as in "your *esteemed* favor." This and the following word are old forms of courtesy worn out by too frequent use. Say simply "your letter."

Favor, as in "*favor* us with a reply." Save the word for times when a reply is a real favor or courtesy.

Hand you herewith. Originally supposed to suggest personal presence in a letter, this phrase has lost its meaning through too frequent repetition. To say simply "inclose," or "enclose," is usually sufficient.

Inst., Ult., Prox. These are not now in good use to indicate present, last, or next month.

Kindly, as in "thanking you *kindly.*" Superfluous. Kindness is implied in thanks.

Our Mr......... No longer good form. Omit *our,* or say "our representative," or use his official title; as, "our manager."

Participial Construction, as in "*Hoping* for an early reply." In English, the present participle frequently gives a weak form of expression. Its use in the conclusion of letters is to be avoided. Write, "We hope for."

Party, meaning *person.* See *Good Usage.*

Passive Construction, as in "goods *were not able to be shipped.*" Use active form of expression: "It was not possible to ship" or "We could not ship."

Permit me to say. This phrase is too formal for ordinary use. It seems to imply some straining of relations.

Pronouns or Articles Omitted, as in "*Received yours and contents noted.*" The pronoun *I* or *we* is good form and should be used.

Proposition, meaning *affair.* See *Good Usage.*

Recent date, as in "yours of *recent date.*" Exactness is preferable. Give precise date.

Same, as in "the *same* shall receive prompt attention." The word is overworked. Use regular pronouns, except in formal papers.

State, meaning *say.* See *Good Usage.*

The writer. People are not so much afraid of the first personal pronoun as they used to be. Use *I* or *we,* instead of *the writer* or *the undersigned,* except in official letters, reports, and other formal documents.

Valued, as in "your *valued* communication." False formality, except on special occasions.

Would say or **Wish to say.** Too frequently these are mere wasteful, roundabout phrases. Omit them.

Your obedient servant. Another worn-out form. Many of these business forms are relics of the old servant attitude of the shopkeeper toward a patron. Let your phrases of courtesy express self-respect.

2. Sentences. The sentence is the common unit of thought expression. In some special types of letters the separate phrase may be used to challenge attention, but good sentence structure is necessary to the good letter. See *Sentence Building.*

Three rhetorical types of sentences are recognized.

(1) *The loose sentence* simply adds idea to idea; it can be closed at any one of several different points and still be a complete sentence. Example: "Students from Central and South America are already coming to our colleges and universities in considerable numbers—and nothing has done so much to make Latin America acquainted with the United States."

(2) *The periodic sentence* is more rarely used and must be definitely planned in advance. It piles up one subordinate idea after another, preparatory to the main statement. Its advantage is in its effect of climax. Example: "That there is a serious housing shortage today, not only in the United States but throughout the civilized world, is a generally known fact."

(3) *The balanced sentence* is so called because it is built of contrasting clauses of similar form, which seem to balance each other like a pair of scales. This sentence is much used in advertising and in business letters. Its value lies in the emphasis and clearness which come from the contrasts in the sentence. Example: "Not only is order Heaven's first law, but it is the first and last law of Earth."

The skillful writer will adapt his sentence form to the subject in hand and to the purpose in view. He will vary the forms of his sentences to avoid monotony, for monotony is the foe of attention and, therefore, of clearness.

See *Punctuation.*

3. Paragraphs. The paragraph is the common form for the relating and the developing of ideas. In its construction, we must consider logic, style, and form. For *Paragraph Development*, refer to *Speaking and Writing* and see below under *Form.* The skillful letter writer will study the psychology of the paragraph. Good paragraph arrangement enables the reader to see the relationship of sentences that belong together as parts of the treatment of a single topic. It enables him also to get the intended emphasis by observing the position of the various sentences in the paragraph. The beginning and the end of a paragraph, as of a sentence, are the emphatic points.

The following is an excellent example of a business paragraph:

"Saving should be more than the accumulation of money. It should include the use of money to add to the total; in other words, investment. Reckless investment is speculation, but careful investment is the best form of saving."

The first sentence states a topic clearly; the second enlarges on the topic; the third, a balanced sentence, develops the "investment" idea and repeats, for emphasis, the word "saving," which thus is kept the most emphatic word in the paragraph.

II. Conciseness. One attains conciseness through using the exact word, and by using no more words than necessary. The quality is the result of precision and of economy in diction. Skill in this matter is to be attained through study of *Synonyms* and of *Usage.* Conciseness is not improved by omitting the pronoun subject from a sentence; as, "Received yours of the 24th." Always put the subject into the sentence. (The imperative sentence is an exception.)

III. Positiveness. This is a matter of *contents* and of *style.* It means direct, definite, unmistakable meaning in directions and suggestions.

Strive for positiveness in the *contents* of a business letter. The reason for this rule is psychological. We know how the mind works. Desired action is best secured by positive suggestion; undesired action is best prevented, not by negative suggestion, but by positive suggestion of the opposite action. For example: instead of saying, "Do not delay writing us," say, "Write to us at once."

IV. Courtesy. The true quality of courtesy arises from the writer's consideration for the interests and feelings of his reader. It is usually manifested, however, in the choice and in the use of expressions of politeness that have been well established by convention. It is often made even more evident by what the letter leaves unsaid. Words and phrases that might wound or irritate or might suggest lack of respect for the reader should be scrupulously avoided. The quality of courtesy should pervade the whole letter, but it is especially vital at the beginning and at the end. Most of the specimen letters quoted here illustrate the value of courtesy.

FORM

Good psychology prompts attention to the *mechanical form* of the letter as a means of securing attention and favorable consideration. Not only must the letter be easy to read, but it must invite reading. No matter how important or interesting the contents of a letter may be, if its form is not attractive, it may be a failure.

Legibility and Neatness. If a manuscript has a clean-cut, finished look, anyone who sees it will be predisposed in favor of the writer and his work. Conversely, an illegible or untidy manuscript creates an unfavorable impression that can hardly be overcome by good style and content. Letters written by hand need not display artistic shading or Spencerian flourishes, but they should meet the minimum requirements for legibility. That is, they should identify the written characters by giving them proper slant, looping, and spacing—by rounding the "m's" and "n's" and by sharpening the "u's." Even more important is the distinct separation of words. A little practice in observing these simple requirements for legibility will make anyone's writing acceptable.

Quality and Form of Stationery. This is the first consideration. Select good stationery; then write letters of corresponding quality. Generally, commercial letter paper is about 8½ by 11 inches in size. A half sized sheet, 6 by 10 or 5½ by 8, is sometimes used, although the best form is the full sized sheet for all letters. For mailing, this full sized sheet should be folded from the bottom so as to bring the bottom edge within about a half inch of the top. This folding makes the opening of the letter easy. If a letterhead is used, this folding may be made so as to leave a part of the letterhead visible. The folded sheet is then again folded twice, the first fold beginning about one-third of the distance from the right, bringing the sheet to a convenient size for the ordinary business envelope.

For the long or legal envelope, fold the bottom third of the page upward, then the top third down. This folding allows the reader, on opening the letter, to see the heading at once. Folding the top third down first and the bottom third upward makes insertion in the envelope easier. Formal official letters are frequently written on stationery of the social form, that is, on a four-page, folded sheet adapted for folding once to fit either an envelope of commercial size or the square type of envelope. It may carry a short form of letterhead either printed or engraved.

The envelope should, of course, match the paper in color and in quality. A short form of letterhead or return address is printed in the upper left-hand corner of the envelope, or sometimes on the flap of the envelope, as on social stationery.

In general, white paper of the "bond" type is always good form. If tinted papers are used, the color should be such as will not interfere with ease of reading.

Placing the Letter Upon the Page. This is very important. For the positions of the various parts there are set rules. The reader habitually looks for the address of the writer in the upper right-hand part of the page, for his own address and the salutation at the upper left-hand part, on lines slightly below the writer's address, and for a formal conclusion at the bottom. Examples of these rules and of permissible variations are shown in the following specimens.

CORRECT BUSINESS LETTER FORMS

I. The Heading. This contains the address of the sender and the date of writing. It is the first item in the business letter. A printed or engraved letterhead should contain the address of the individual or firm. The address so given need not be repeated. The following forms are approved to be placed in the upper right-hand part of the page. Care should be taken that this heading is not too near the right-hand side. When the heading takes two lines or three, the second and third lines may be indented; as,—

810 Jefferson Avenue,
Cleveland, Ohio 44113
June 28, 19—.

or, in block,

810 Jefferson Avenue,
Cleveland, Ohio 44113
June 28, 19—.

or,

725 Tremont St., Boston 02118
June 28, 19—.

To give a personal or social *tone* to the letter, numbers and dates may be written out. The following form for dates, in both heading and body of the letter, finds favor with some writers:

15 May, 19—.

II. The Introduction, or Address. This is the second item in the letter. It should be placed one or two lines below the heading and at the left of the page. The following forms are in good use:

1. Addressing a firm,—

> Messrs. Jones & Black
> 480 Main Street
> Buffalo, New York 14203

or, The Aetna Company
> 7 Archer Avenue
> Omaha, Nebraska 68107

or, Smith, Marks & Co.,
> P.O. Box 250
> Boston, Mass. 02101

2. Addressing an individual, as a member of a firm,—

> Mr. James T. Girard'
> President Girard Steel Company
> Box 1768, Plaza Sta.,
> St. Louis, Missouri 63199

3. Addressing an individual,—

> Mr. Thomas Brown
> 513 Sacramento Street
> San Francisco, California 94111

Note.—These addresses may be written in block. Some writers prefer not to use commas at the ends of lines in the heading or address. This practice is permissible. Periods also, except after abbreviations, may be omitted from the ends of these lines. Omission of marks must, however, be consistent:

16 Park Ave., Denver 80218
December 14, 19—

> Miss Jean Phillips
> 1014 Chamber of Commerce
> Columbus, Ohio 43215

The method of open punctuation, used in the above example, may be seen illustrated in the first sample letter under Letter Writing, by Walter C. Hines.

When the firm is addressed, but it is intended that the letter should go to some particular person, *Attention Mr. . . . . .* may be written at the right below the heading, or on a line with the salutation. Frequently, the *subject* of the letter is written at the right in line with the name of the firm or person addressed:

The Aetna Company   Subject: *Flour Shipment*
7 Archer Avenue
On aha, Nebraska 68107

Gentlemen: Attention Mr. Brown

4. Military Form,—

The following form is prescribed for U. S. Army correspondence:

U. S. ARMY RECRUITING STATION,
5 EAST SWAN STREET, BUFFALO, N. Y. 14203

825   22 November, 19—.
From: *Recruiting Officer.*
To: *The Adjutant General of the Army, Washington, D. C. 20301*
Subject: *Enlistments.*

This is called the "brief." It occupies the upper third of the ordinary sheet and is folded back so as to be immediately visible in files or on opening the envelope. The usual *salutation* and the usual *complimentary close* are omitted. The number (825) refers to the office files.

Many business houses use a similar form, especially for routine letters between departments.

5. Addressing a firm of women,—

> Mesdames Trigg & New
> 5314 Michigan Avenue
> Chicago, Illinois 60615

Note.—Some authorities permit omission of the period after *Mr.* and *Messrs.*

III. The Salutation. This is the third item.

1. In addressing a firm, *Gentlemen* is preferred to *Dear Sirs* by most writers. This form is used also in addressing firms made up of men and women.

2. In addressing a firm made up of women, *Ladies* is the usual salutation.

3. For individuals, *Dear Sir* is the usual form. *My dear Sir* is regarded as rather more formal. A little more informal, according to occasion, is *Dear Mr. Girard* or *My dear Mr. Girard.*

4. *Dear Madam* or, more formal, *My dear Madam* is appropriate in addressing either a married or an unmarried woman. *Dear Mrs. Smith* or, more formal, *My dear Mrs. Smith* may be used if the degree of acquaintanceship permits.

5. In addressing an unmarried woman, use such a form as *Dear Miss Walker* or, more formal, *My dear Miss Walker.*

6. In addressing a letter to a man *and* a woman, use the form *Dear Sir and Madam.*

Note.—The husband's title, as, *Doctor, Professor,* or *Reverend,* should never be prefixed to the wife's name.

In a letter to a doctor or a professor, the address may be *Dr. James Martin* or *James Martin, M. D.* (or *D. D., Ph. D., D. O., D. D. S.*), or *Professor Wm. James.* If *Dr.* precedes the name, the abbreviation for the degree should not follow. In such cases, the salutation may be *Dear Sir* or, less formal, *Dear Doctor Martin* or *Dear Professor James.*

Note.—In general, good taste seems to approve, even in business letters, the spelling out of a title in the salutation, although the abbreviation may be used.

Note.—In the punctuation of the salutation, usage varies. The colon is always correct. In short, informal letters, the comma may be used. The dash is superfluous. However, if the address takes more than three lines, the salutation may be made part of the first line of the letter and may be followed by colon and dash or by comma and dash:

Gentlemen:—In your letter of June 26, etc.

IV. The Body of the Letter. This should be well centered on the page. The margins at top and bottom should be approximately equal, and the margins at the sides should be kept, as nearly as possible, equal. It is easy to keep the left-hand margin regular, but some care is necessary to get an even right-hand margin. Wide margins at right and left are advisable for two reasons: (1) Short lines are easier to read than long ones; (2) the contrast of blank and filled spaces makes reading easier.

The Paragraphing of a Business Letter. This is perhaps the most important feature of its form. First of all, the paragraphs should be reasonably short, for a well broken page is more inviting to the eye and easier to read than solid masses of type. Secondly, the paragraphs should not have too great a contrast in length. Absolute uniformity is, of course, impossible and undesirable as well. Variety in the matter of length, however, should be only great enough to avoid monotony. Generally speaking, the paragraphs a the beginning and at the end of the letter should be somewhat shorter than those in the middle.

The following paragraph forms are in use:

The indented paragraph, like this one. The first line is set in from the margin a number of spaces approximately equal to the margin allowed.

The hanging paragraph, like this. The first line begins at the margin, and all other lines are indented a number of spaces equal to the margin allowed for the first line.

The blocked paragraph, like this. No line is given extra indention. This last type of paragraph calls for very wide margins and for extra space between paragraphs. Examples of these various forms of paragraphing are given in the specimen letters on the following pages. Margins should be at least one inch wide, and two blank lines should be left between paragraphs.

V. The Complimentary Close. In business letters this should be *Yours truly,* or *Yours very truly,* or *Respectfully yours, Very respectfully yours,* except in cases where the writer, because of close acquaintance, may prefer a more informal phrase, such as *Sincerely yours, Faithfully yours.* Never write *respectively* for *respectfully.*

Such an expression as *With sincerest regards, I am* should begin a new, indented line, just above the complimentary close.

Envelope. *The address on the envelope* and that in the letter should correspond accurately, although some authorities permit the omission of the street address in the letter. On the envelope, the first line of the address should be placed approximately halfway between the top and the bottom of the envelope, beginning about one-fourth of the length of the envelope from the left-hand end.

Additional directions, such as *in care of, c/o,* or *introducing,* may be placed at the lower left-hand corner. A post-office box number is usually placed in this position, to avoid having more than three, or at most four, lines in the address. Neither the abbreviation *No.* nor the sign # should be placed before the street address, but the postal zone number should be included. The address may be punctuated with commas at the ends of lines, except the last line, where a period should be used; or punctuation may be omitted entirely, except after abbreviations.

In *street numbers* involving *second* or *third,* it is sufficient to write *d* after the figures instead of *nd* or *rd;* as 32d, 23d. Many writers do not use *d* or *th.* To insure the return of a letter in case of failure of delivery, the writer's address should be placed on the outside of the envelope, either in the upper left-hand corner on the front of the envelope or on the flap at the back of the envelope.

Cautions. Certain things the careful writer will always do: (1) He will use the *correct* address of the person to whom he is writing and will make the salutation *appropriate;* (2) he will have the complimentary close *appropriate* and his own signature *legible.* If the writer of the letter is a woman, she will add to her signature whatever may be necessary to indicate whether or not she is married, as in the following:

(Mrs.) or (Miss) *Anna M. Worden.*

or,

(Mrs. J. C. Truman)   *Mary V. Truman.*

If there are "enclosures" in the letter, such as stamps, money, or papers, these should always be mentioned; and it is customary to write in the lower left-hand corner either the word *Enclosure* or the abbreviation *Enc.;* similarly, *Inclosure* or *Inc.*

Letters sent in the name of a firm by an official or employee may be signed as follows:

Knight, Lymmes, and Co.
By (or Per) L. R. Parsons.

APPROPRIATE FORMS IN ADDRESSING OFFICIALS AND DIGNITARIES

The President of the United States.
Name and address,—The President, White House (or Executive Mansion), Washington, D. C.
Salutation,—*Mr. President:* or *Sir:*
Close,—*Respectfully yours,* or *Very truly yours,*

The Vice President of the United States.
Name and address,—The Honorable..........,Vice President of the United States, Washington, D. C. or, To the Vice President of the United States, Washington, D. C.
Salutation,—*Sir:* or *Dear Sir:*
Close,—*Very truly yours,* or *Respectfully yours,*

Member of Cabinet.
Name and address,—The Secretary of State, Washington, D. C.
Salutation,—*Dear Mr. Secretary:*
Close,—*Yours very truly,*
or,
Name and address,—The Honorable the Secretary of the Treasury, Washington, D. C. or, The Honorable A............ B............, Secretary of the Treasury, Washington, D. C.
Salutation,—*Sir:* or *Dear Sir:*
Close,—*Very respectfully yours,*

Members of Congress.
Name and address,—The Hon. Martin Warren, United States Senate Washington, D. C.
or, The Hon. Martin Warren, House of Representatives, Washington, D. C.
Salutation,—*Sir:* or *Dear Sir:*
Close,—*Very truly yours,*

Foreign Ministers.
Name and address,—His Excellency,........,Ambassador to the Court of St. James, London. England.
Salutation,—*Your Excellency:* or *Sir:*
Close,—*Very truly yours,*

Governors.
Name and address,—His Excellency, the Governor of New York, Albany, N. Y.
or, His Excellency, the Governor, Albany, N. Y.
or, His Excellency, Governor S. M. Smith, Albany, N. Y.
Salutation,—*Your Excellency:* or *Sir:*
Close,—*Very truly yours,*

Mayors.
Name and address,—The Honorable ...., Mayor of New York City, New York City, N. Y.
Salutation,—*Sir:* or *Dear Sir:*
Close,—*Very truly yours,*

State Officers.
Name and address,—The Honorable Attorney-General of New York, Albany, N. Y.
or, The Honorable ...., Attorney-General of New York, Albany, N. Y.
Salutation,—*Sir:* or *Dear Sir:*
Close,—*Very truly yours,*

Judge of Supreme Court (or highest court of a State).
Name and address,—The Hon. William V. Hinton, State Capitol, Columbus, Ohio
Salutation,—*Dear Mr. Justice:*
Close,—*Yours very truly,*

Judge (other than Supreme Court).
Name and address,—The Hon. Henry A. Freeman State Circuit Court Building, Chicago, Ill.
Salutation,—*Dear Sir:* or (less formal) *Dear Judge Freeman:*
Close,—*Yours very truly,*

Minor Officials (City or County).
Name and address,—Mr. James Wingate, City Treasurer, City Hall, Des Moines, Iowa.
Salutation,—*Dear Sir:*
Close,—*Yours very truly,*

President of a University.
Name and address,—President Nathan M. Pusey, Harvard University, Cambridge, Mass.
Salutation,—*Dear Sir:* or (more formal) *My dear Sir:*
Close,—*Yours very truly,*

College or University Professor.
Name and address,—Professor Arthur K. Rimer, University of Denver, Denver, Colo. 80202 (Degree is usually omitted.)
Salutation,—*Sir:* or *Dear Sir:*
Close,—*Yours very truly,* or *Yours sincerely,*

Superintendent of Schools.
Name and address,—Superintendent Edward Jones, Department of Education, City Hall, Cleveland, Ohio 44114
Salutation,—*Sir:* or *Dear Sir:* or *My dear Sir:* or (very informally) *Dear Mr. Jones:*
Close,—*Yours very truly,* or *Yours sincerely,*

Protestant Clergyman.
Name and address,—The Reverend Thomas L. Warner, 1645 Earl Avenue, Harrisburg, Pa. 17109
Salutation,—*Sir:* or *Dear Sir:* or *My dear Sir:* or (very informally) *Dear Mr. Warner:*
Close,—*Yours very truly,* or *Yours sincerely,*

Parish Priest.
Name and address,—The Reverend Frederick E, Kane, 276 Francis Street, Detroit, Mich. 48217
Salutation,—*Reverend and dear Father:* or *Dear Reverend Father:*
Close,—*Yours sincerely,*

Jewish Rabbi.
Name and address,—Rabbi Stephen S. Wise, 340 W. 57th St., New York, N. Y. 10019
Salutation,—*Dear Sir:*
Close,—*Yours very truly,* or *Yours sincerely,*

Protestant Doctor of Divinity (or of Laws).
Name and address,—The Reverend Charles A. McArthur, D. D. (or LL. D.), 5927 Dorchester Avenue, Boston, Mass. 02224
Salutation,—*Sir:* or *Dear Sir:* or *My dear Sir:* or (very informally) *Dear Dr. McArthur:*
Close,—*Yours very truly,* or *Yours sincerely,*

The Pope.
Name and address,—His Holiness, Pope John XXIII The Vatican, Rome.
Salutation,—*Your Holiness:*
Close,—*Sincerely yours in Christ,*

Cardinal.
Name and address,—His Eminence, William Cardinal O'Connell, Archbishop of Boston, 25 Granby Street, Boston, Mass. 02215
Salutation,—*Your Eminence:*
Close,—*Faithfully your Eminence's servant,* or *Sincerely yours;* if the writer is a Catholic, the words "in Christ" are usually added.

Bishop.
Name and address,—The Most Reverend Moses E. Kiley, D. D., Bishop of Trenton, Trenton, N. J.
Salutation,—*Right Reverend and dear Bishop:* or *Right Reverend Bishop:* or, simply, and perhaps more commonly, *Sir:*
Close,—any of the ordinary forms, such as *Very truly yours,* or *Yours sincerely;* if the writer is a Catholic, the words "Sincerely yours in Christ" should be used.

Women in Religious Orders.
Name and address,—(1) The Reverend Mother Angela (in the case of the Mother Superior); (2) Sister Constance (in the case of a Sister); followed in each case by the address.
Salutation,—(1) *Reverend Mother:* (2) *Reverend Madam:* or *Dear Madam:*
Close,—*Yours sincerely,* or any of the more formal phrases.

Military Officer.
Name and address,—General Lyman L. Lemnitzer, Defense Department, Washington, D. C. 20301 or, The Commanding Officer, Niagara Falls Air Base, Niagara Falls, N. Y. 14306
Salutation,—*Sir:* or *Dear Sir:*
Close,—any of the ordinary forms.

Naval Officer.
Name and address,—Admiral Arleigh A. Burke, Naval Observatory, Washington, D. C. or, if at sea, U. S. S. *Pennsylvania,* c/o Postmaster, New York, N. Y. 10551
Salutation,—*Sir:* or *Dear Sir:*
Close,—any of the ordinary forms.

Note.—The salutation *Sir,* in nearly all cases, is used in formal official letters. This is also an approved salutation to use in addressing a letter to the editor of a newspaper or other journal. See *Official Letters.*

TYPES OF BUSINESS LETTERS

The following are the common types of letters. Each type has its own peculiar problems.

I. The Simple Order and **Reply.** This type, supplemented by the letter of inquiry and explanation, is the kind that most people have frequent occasion to use. Out of this simple exchange, however, may develop the elaborate system of *claim, adjustment,* and *follow-up* letters. Claim and adjustment letters, in particular, should be tactfully written. The wording should make plain the writer's intention to be accurate and fair.

1. Order for Goods.

> 572 East Avenue,
> Rochester, New York 14607
>
> April 3, 19—

Messrs. Rowen, Winstead, & Company
437 State Street
Chicago, Illinois 60605
Gentlemen:

Will you please send me by freight, addressed to James Wilson, Alton, N.Y., the following:

> 1 French row-motor;
> 1 set Franklin garage door tracks and hangers.

I enclose check for $96.25, net price as listed in your special March bulletin.

The building materials purchased from you last summer have proved so satisfactory that I am very glad to send you this further order. I hope that it can be shipped very promptly.

> Yours very truly,
Enc.   Robert T. Vane.

2. Request for Adjustment.

> 572 East Avenue,
> Rochester, N. Y. 14607
>
> July 6, 19—

Messrs. Rowen, Winstead, & Company
437 State Street
Chicago, Illinois 60605
Gentlemen:

I have had shipped to you today from Cayuga, N. Y., by insured parcel post, the propeller and housing from the row-motor which I recently purchased from you.

We have used this motor a very few times only. Yesterday, while we were on the river, the housing broke, and it was only by the merest accident that I was able to recover it at all. I do not know that the machine was subjected to any extraordinary strain, though, of course, it may have been. However, the metal looks to me as if it had been defective at the break. Will you please examine the housing and make such adjustment as you think is right.

I shall be glad to have this matter attended to promptly in order that we may have the engine to use as soon as possible.

> Yours very truly,
> Robert T. Vane.

3. Reply to Adjustment Request.

> (LETTERHEAD)
>
> July 8, 19—

Mr. Robert T. Vane
572 East Avenue
Rochester, New York 14607
Dear Sir:

We are very sorry to learn from your letter of July 6 that you have had trouble with the row-motor. We have not yet received the broken parts, but we appreciate the fact that during vacation time you will want a motor to use. Accordingly, we will ship by today's parcel post a propeller and housing to replace the broken parts.

When your shipment arrives, we will have an examination made and will make adjustment such as we think will thoroughly satisfy you. We appreciate your patronage and your good offices in our favor.

> Yours very truly,
> Rowen, Winstead, & Company
> By J. C. Marcus

4. Order for Magazine.

24 Winfield Street
Oswego, Illinois 60543
October 15, 19—

Time, the Weekly Newsmagazine
350 East 22nd Street
Chicago, Illinois 60616

Gentlemen:

I enclose money for $12.00 in payment for renewal of my subscription to Time, the Weekly Newsmagazine, for the year 196–.

Please note the change of address indicated at the head of this letter.

Former address: 371 Otis Ave., Kenmore, Ohio 44314

Yours very truly,

Enc.   *(Miss) Myra V. Killian.*

5. Letter to College Officer.

622 Plymouth Avenue
Harrisburg, Pa. 17109
July 13, 19—

Mr. James Harvey, Registrar
University of Illinois
Urbana, Ill. 61801

Dear Sir:

Will you please send me a copy of your application blank for entrance to the engineering school in Fairmount. I completed my high school course in June, and I am planning to enter college next fall. I should be glad to receive also a copy of your catalogue and other information that would be useful.

Very respectfully yours,

William D. Brown.

II. Letters of Agreement. These usually supplement contracts of various sorts, and should be worded as nearly as possible in the terms of the accompanying contract

III. The Sales or Advertising Letter. This has been very highly developed within the last few years. It is really the standard or type of all business letters. The psychological principles of the business letter, as stated before, apply with special force to this type, which has for its immediate purpose the securing of business. In present day practice, sales letters are frequently prepared in series, the whole series being planned to cover the steps already given for the typical business letter. The first letter is designed, for instance, to get attention; the last in the series is written as the "clincher," or final persuasive letter.

A short series of four or five letters may be used, each one distinctly different in contents and purpose. Again, a long series, sometimes called "continuous," may be employed, each letter differing only slightly from the others in point of view, all aimed at persuading the "prospect."

These series are the common form of the *follow-up systems.* The writer has a definite object in view, usually to secure a new field of business or to maintain interest and good will among his present clients. If his first letter fails to fulfil its purpose, he follows it up with others in which the methods of approach or inducements offered differ somewhat from those of the first. For example, the letter of the Forest Products Association (first sample under Letter Writing), might be followed by one giving some more definite, *interesting* details about the special uses of woods to arouse the attention and the interest of Mr. Parsons, should he fail to return the card. If he returns the card promptly, a second letter should precede the representative's call, introducing him and encouraging the fullest use of his services.

Such letters as the following (**6, 7**), when prepared as circular or form letters, should be so printed that the type style used in filling in the individual addresses shall be like that in the body of the letter. The whole then will have the appearance of a personal letter and will command attention.

6. Sales Letter.

(LETTERHEAD)

April 6, 19—

Mrs. Marion T. Archer
1432 Delavan Avenue
Albion, Indiana 46701

Dear Madam:

ATTENTION — *On that auto trip last summer, you enjoyed tremendously the road and the ride through beautiful scenery. But when you came to the inn at the end of the day, did you find your gowns in the smooth, dainty condition you could have wished for? Isn't it annoying to find the only things you have to "change to" all rumpled and creased?*

INTEREST — *The answer, of course, is a wardrobe trunk. It is a compact, dust-proof trunk in your car, and a handy, complete wardrobe in your hotel room.*

INFORMATION

INDUCEMENT — *Through an unusually large purchase of the widely known Plico trunks, we are able to offer, during the next week, a full stock at prices that mean to you a saving of more than one-third the usual cost of these high-grade trunks.*

POSITIVE SUGGESTION — *One look at the sturdy build of these trunks and their complete and dainty arrangement of trays and hangers for every sort of hat and garment will convince you that certainly, at these prices, you cannot afford another trip without such a convenience.*

Members of our sales staff are enthusiastic about these new Plico trunks, especially as regards the wide variety of types, conveniences, and styles offered. They will do their best to show you a wardrobe trunk which will best meet your individual traveling needs and your requirements in color and decorative treatment.

Come in early and make your selection before the present full stock is picked over by other buyers.

Very truly yours,

Eldridge, Warren and Company,
Per B. F. Warren,
Manager.

7. Sales Letter.

(LETTERHEAD)

THE SECRETARY OF THE TREASURY

Washington

October 1946

To Newspaper Publishers,
Editors and Ad Managers:

The first lesson in a democracy is that the Government belongs to its millions of citizens. It belongs to you—all of us. The Nation can be only as prosperous as are its cities, farms and communities of the individual families which inhabit them.

When you help to promote the sale of U. S. Savings Bonds, you help check inflation and subsequent depression. You help to maintain stable economy.

Stability alone is not enough. The ownership of Savings Bonds does more. It gives people an actual share in America. It presents the possibility of providing the funds for homes and higher education of your children, for old age security, and for emergencies. In other words, your effort in securing bond advertising provides for the security and prosperity of the individual and his family. Prosperous families mean prosperous communities. Prosperous communities mean a prosperous Nation.

That is how you help your Government—that is how you help yourself—when you assist in the U. S. Savings Bond Program.

I urge you to be of all the help you can.

Sincerely,

John W. Snyder
Secretary of the Treasury.

IV. The Collection Letter. Collection letters are of two main types,—routine notifications of indebtedness and personal requests for payment. The first of these are standard, impersonal notices, and are therefore inoffensive. Usually, such reminders are all that is necessary. If personal requests are needed, they should be courteous and should avoid the use of threats or other offensive measures except as a last resort. In order to be courteous, however, a collection letter need not be apologetic. Firmness not only enhances the prestige of the creditor but also gains the debtor's respect. Collection letters are usually prepared as a series which begins with a mild suggestion that payment would be appreciated and ends with an insistent demand. The orderly and systematic mailing of such a series is often more important in making the work of collection letters effective than is the construction of any individual letter. Every letter, however, should have the double purpose of securing the money due and also of retaining the debtor's good will.

8. Collection Letter.

(LETTERHEAD)

June 20, 19—

Mr. M. C. Harris
12 Arthur Street
Conneaut, Ohio 44030
Dear Sir:

We find on our books a charge against you of $15.87, under date of May 14. We wish to call your attention to the fact that this is past due.

Your prompt remittance will be appreciated.
Very truly yours,
Owen, James, and Co.

9. Collection Letter (*a little more insistent*).

(LETTERHEAD)

June 1, 19—

Mr. L. R. Converse
356 Oliver Street
Baltimore, Maryland 21202
Dear Sir:

According to our books, your account for invoice of April 7 amounting to $47.60 is unpaid and past due. We wrote you about this account on May 20, but we have had no reply. We wish again to call your attention to the need for payment.

Please give this matter your immediate attention.
Very truly yours,
Owen, James, and Co.

V. The Letter of Application. The letter of application is in most respects similar to the sales letter. The writer is attempting to sell his own services. To be sure, he must be somewhat more modest and restrained in talking about himself than he is in talking about commodities and the services of others. He should not, however, run the risk of making his letter awkward as well as hypocritical by avoiding the use of the first personal pronoun *I* or by any other device that has its basis in false modesty. If the reader is to desire the writer's services, he must know enough about them to be able to judge their value to him in his business.

10. Direct Application for Commercial Position.

419 Marshall Street,
Syracuse, New York 13210
February 3, 19—

Messrs. G. A. Case & Son
193 Broad Street
Syracuse, New York 13210
Gentlemen:

I wish to apply for the position in your engineering office which you mention in your advertisement in this morning's "Standard."

I am nineteen years old, a graduate of the Technical High School in the class of 19—. I have also completed a course in drafting in the Mechanics' Institute of Rochester. At present I am employed in the shops of the J. W. Atkins Company, Machinists.

I should be glad to be granted a personal interview at your convenience.

Yours very truly,
James Manson.

311 East Welker Street,
Buffalo, New York 14208
October 1, 19—

Box 176,
Buffalo Evening News.

Gentlemen:
Will you please consider me an applicant for the position mentioned in your advertisement in the Buffalo Evening News of October 1. My qualifications are as follows:

Education. I am a graduate of the Bennett High School of this city, in the class of 19—. My course included commercial work in bookkeeping, typewriting, and stenography. In all these subjects my standing was high.

Experience. During the last two years, I have been employed in the office of R. D. Ward & Son, Ellicott Square Building. My work has included stenography and general office assistance.

References. I can refer you, for information as to my ability and my character, to R. D. Ward & Son, and also to the following: Mr. J. W. Archer, head of Commercial Department, Bennett High School; Mr. Martin B. Allen, Supreme Court Judge.

Very truly yours,
Thomas R. Stafford.

VI. Letter of Resignation. The conclusion of an employee's services should be brought about in a courteous, businesslike manner, and this should be reflected in the correspondence. Although formal, in that it is a record of proceedings, the letter of resignation is usually somewhat personal in tone. Whereas the letter of application is nearly always directed to strangers, the letter terminating one's employment is addressed to persons with whom one has become acquainted. Also *consideration*, which is an important characteristic of "separation correspondence," can best be expressed in language that is more or less informal.

12.

Columbus, Ohio,
November 20, 19—

Mr. James B. Wilson, President
The Midwest Supply Company
Columbus, Ohio 43215

Dear Mr. Wilson:

Circumstances have arisen which make it necessary for me to be at home with my family in Cleveland. I am therefore submitting my resignation, effective January first, 196–. This will give you a month in which to find a successor for my position. Meanwhile, I will do everything I can to train the new person and otherwise insure the continuation of the work without loss of efficiency.

My stay with your firm has been very pleasant, and I regret the necessity of making a change. I am grateful to you and your associates for many courtesies that have been shown me. It is a privilege to have been a member of your organization.

Yours sincerely,
Susan T. Woodruff.

VII. Notes of Introduction. The writer should aim to make it easy for two of his friends to become acquainted with each other. The note may either be sent directly to the person whose good offices it bespeaks, or be given to the person introduced. In the latter case, the envelope is usually left unsealed. The wording should be frank and sincere and should suggest the opening for conversation.

13.

Tipton, Oklahoma 73570
May 7, 19—

Mr. Chas. R. Andrews, Trustee
School District No. 9
Tipton, Oklahoma 73570

My dear Mr. Andrews:

Miss Emily Smith desires to secure a position as assistant in your school. She holds a first grade certificate and has had three years of successful experience in our school. We regret to lose her, but she prefers your district because it is nearer to her home. I can recommend Miss Smith as a skillful teacher. She will exert an excellent influence in any school.

Very truly yours,
Charles J. Major,
Trustee of School District No. 4.

14.

North Concord, Vermont 05858
July 6, 19—

Mr. Walter C. Strong
84 Arlington Avenue
Pittsburgh, Pa. 15203

My dear Mr. Strong:

It gives me great pleasure to introduce to you my friend, Mr. Weston Beach, who is to become a resident in your city. You will find him an affable person. I shall greatly appreciate whatever courtesy you may show him in helping him to become acquainted.

Cordially yours,
Henry B. Johnson

VIII. Letters of Recommendation. Recommendations are sometimes included in notes of introduction, but often they are written as separate letters. They may be written as general letters addressed "To whom it may concern," or as special letters to some definite person.

15. General Recommendation.

Wicomico, Virginia 23184
May 10, 19—

To Whom It May Concern:

This is to certify that the bearer of this note, Miss Lillian Glades, was graduated from The Teachers' College, Cumberland University, and has since taught in the schools of this city. For the past three years she has taught in the Straymore School, and I have had opportunity to observe her work closely. I can recommend her as capable of filling any position in a city graded school.

John W. Grove,
Principal of Straymore School.

16. General Recommendation.

To Whom It May Concern:

Mr. Henry Laird has been in our employ as bookkeeper the past six years. He is a skilled accountant and a loyal man; in every way he has served us well. We regret to part with him. He goes at his own request because he feels that he should receive a higher salary than we can afford to pay.

We wish Mr. Laird every success.

Jones, Martin and Co.
Birmingham, Alabama,
June 26, 19—

17. Special Recommendation.

Lehigh University,
Bethlehem, Pa. 18015
January 1, 19—

Mr. Harvey W. Jonson
Superintendent of Public Works
Topeka, Kansas 66603
My dear Mr. Jonson:

We have in our junior class a young man, Mr. Thomas Redding, who has done excellent work in the engineering department. He is a fine, clean young man and has commanded the respect of instructors and students, alike. His home is in Nebraska, and he is anxious, on account of the illness of his father, to get employment for the next year or two near home.

I shall greatly appreciate it if you will interest yourself in him and help him to get work.

Very truly yours,
Thomas Benedict.

IX. The Formal or Official Letter. In formal or official letters, the heading is placed as in the business letter, but the best usage approves the spelling out of the date instead of the use of numerals.

In such letters, also, the address of the person to whom the letter is sent may be placed at the close of the letter, in the lower left-hand part of the sheet. The title of the person addressed, as Reverend or Honorable, should be spelled out and the initials or given name used. "The" is not necessary before these titles, although good formal usage approves such expressions as The Reverend Mr. Thomas in the body of the letter, and many good writers prefer this form for the address. The salutation in such a letter may be Dear Sir or simply Sir.

18. Note of Appreciation.

October eleventh,
Nineteen-sixty——

Dear Sir:

By formal vote the Rivoli Club last night instructed me, as secretary of the club, to convey to you their very sincere appreciation of your courtesy and genuine service in the address which you delivered before the club members and their guests on Friday evening, October 10.

I desire the privilege of adding also my own word of grateful acknowledgment.

Very sincerely yours,
James Wakefield.

The Honorable Thomas Downing,
7 Harris Street,
Denver, Colorado 80229

X. Excuse for Absence from School.

19.

Will Miss Stringer please excuse Frances Prescott's absence from school, March 4 and 5, on account of illness in the family.

Sarah C. Prescott.

(Mrs. J. W. Prescott),
March 6, 19—

20.

Dear Miss Townsend,

Please excuse James's absence from school, October tenth to fourteenth, on account of illness.

Very truly yours,
(Mrs.) James T. Orcutt.

Post Cards or **Postal Cards.** These are appropriate only for brief notices sent out by individuals or organizations, or for impersonal notes. They are not suitable for personal messages. Even the shortest note of any degree of intimacy should always be written as a letter and enclosed in an envelope. The Picture Post Card is no exception to this rule.

Telegrams. The rates for sending telegrams are based upon a message of twelve words, without punctuation. If punctuation is essential for clearness, the words comma, period, etc. may be inserted and paid for at regular word rates. No charge is made for the date, address, or signature. A message may be repeated back from the receiving office to the sender, for the sake of accuracy, at established rates.

Other classes of telegraphic service, known as night telegrams, night letters, and day letters, are also available. They offer the advantage either of lower rates or of greater length, but delivery is less prompt.

Cablegrams. Cablegrams, on account of higher cost, are more highly abbreviated than telegrams. The use of code words, that is, either ordinary words given unusual meanings by agreement of the sender and of the receiver, or artificial words whose meanings have been agreed upon, is common. Since the use of codes is governed by certain restrictions, however, the regulations of the cable companies should be consulted before writing a code message for transmission over their wires.

TAKING CARE OF THE DAILY MAIL

1. Read carefully letters received. Where the daily mail is heavy, have letters sorted into groups according to subject, as orders, inquiries, adjustment, etc. You can then deal with them more economically.

2. Keep incoming letters and envelopes together until you are certain that the writer's proper local address is in the letter. The omission of this item is a frequent offense.

3. Have your own local address on your letterhead. Omission of this often arouses in your correspondents the feeling that you are not a responsible business man.

4. *Reply promptly* to letters, usually within a day. If delay for full reply is necessary, acknowledge briefly the letter received, giving reasons for delay. Then, keep a reminder or "tickler file" to bring the matter again to your attention at the proper time.

5. *Plan your replies* to cover all points called for. Keep before you, while writing or dictating, the letter you are answering or a memorandum of its contents. An incomplete reply is annoying and unfair to your correspondent and to yourself.

6. *File together* in some orderly system the letters received and duplicates of your replies.

7. When replies are made by telegraph, *supplement and confirm* them by brief letters. These letters make useful records.

8. *Form letters*, printed on your regular stationery, to imitate typewriting, are convenient and economical when the same message is to go to a large number of people.

9. *Guide Forms.*—If your business does not call for much dictation of letters, you will find it worth while to prepare a few guide forms. These are letters prepared at leisure as carefully as possible, applying to various cases that arise frequently in your correspondence. Then, in the hurry of dictation, by making in the form letter only such changes as the particular case calls for, you can be certain of getting out a good letter.

10. *Filing.*—The purpose of filing correspondence is to keep an accurate, convenient record of past business and a guide for future correspondence. Any system used should be accurate, compact, readily accessible. There are in common use three systems:

a. *The Alphabetical System*, which is the simplest. In this system, letters are filed according to the names of the writers or the addressees; for example, letters received from and sent to *Williams* would be filed in a paper folder under *W*.

b. *The Subject System.*—The divisions of the file are made to correspond to the important items of the business: furnishings, clothing, etc. Usually an alphabetical order is kept within each subject.

c. *The Numerical System.*—In this system various subjects or correspondents are given numbers, and all papers connected with them are filed under the proper numbers in the file. The advantage of this is that it will take care of a file of any size and of any number of subjects. But a separate card index of names must be kept as a key. Each card carries the name of a subject or of a person and also the corresponding file number. The cards are arranged alphabetically.

Combination Systems are used also. Adapt your system to the requirements of your business, not your business to a system.

SOCIAL CORRESPONDENCE: FORMS

Stationery. Good usage approves a wide variety of forms and the indulgence of personal taste in the choice of stationery and in the writing of social letters and notes. The principles governing the form and appearance of business correspondence apply generally to social letters, but many informal variations from these rules are permitted.

White, unruled paper and envelopes to match are always in good taste, although pale-tinted papers which do not interfere with the clearness of the writing are permissible. Social note paper is usually a folded four-page sheet adapted to fold again once for the envelope. This paper, as well as the correspondence card, is prepared in various sizes and styles.

The Written Page. *The various parts of the letter*, as shown in the specimens, should be placed properly on the page, with due allowance for margins; no writing should be done in the margins. The heading should be placed as in the business

letter, or, informally, the street address of the writer may be omitted, the date alone being written at the top of the sheet. An approved custom is to write out the date fully instead of using figures. The address of the recipient may be omitted in very familiar notes; that of the writer may be placed at the top of the paper or at the end of the letter in the lower left-hand part of the page.

Beginning and **End.** In the *salutation*, whatever form seems appropriate to the writer is permissible. except that certain abrupt and uncouth forms, such as *James* or *Friend John*, are ruled out, and the name of the person is preferred by many to the old form *Dear Friend. My dear Friend*, in this case, seems to be regarded as informal. *The complimentary close* may take any one of several forms, according to the degree of formality or familiarity in the letter. In such expressions as *Sincerely yours, Truly yours, Affectionately yours*, the first word only is capitalized.

TYPES OF SOCIAL NOTES AND LETTERS

The social note, written either upon the usual note-size paper or upon the commonly used correspondence card, is an important form of social writing. Such notes are brief, and the best taste dictates that the language should be as cordial and courteous as it can be made. The following specimens will suggest forms of expression appropriate for these notes. The heading is placed as in business or social letters, generally as follows:

> *439 East 23d Street,*
> *June 7, 19—.*

or,

> *Lyons Place,*
> *November the Thirteenth.*

The salutation may be as follows: *My dear Mr. Martin, My dear Mrs. Smith*, or *My dear Mary.* Best usage requires the addressing of a married woman by her husband's given name: *Mrs. Henry T. Myers*, not *Mrs. Laura Myers*. A widow may use her own given name or her husband's, as she pleases. The address of the recipient is placed at the lower left-hand corner of the sheet or card, or the date and the address of the writer may occupy this position. The complimentary close may be as for the social letter.

INFORMAL NOTES

1. Invitation.

> *515 Martin Place,*
> *Thursday Evening.*

Dear Frank,
If you are free to accept an invitation for Saturday afternoon, Mrs. Archer and I shall be very glad to have you with us in a little auto party out at Fort Beach. We shall take luncheon with us, and I know you will enjoy the trip. We will call for you at two.
> *Very cordially yours,*
> *William S. Archer.*

2. Reply.

> *Friday Morning.*

My dear Archer:
I shall be more than glad to be one of your delightful party for tomorrow afternoon. and I shall be ready at two o'clock.
> *Sincerely yours,*
> *Frank Adams Bates.*

or,

3. Reply.

> *Friday Morning.*

Dear Will,
I am very sorry to miss the pleasant party I am sure you will have at the Fort, but, as I leave for Chicago at six this evening upon very important business, I shall not be able to be with you.
> *Very truly yours,*
> *Frank Adams Bates.*

4. Invitation.

Dear Mrs. Graham:

How about Thursday afternoon for a little theater party in honor of your guest, Miss Smith? If you and she are at liberty, I shall take pleasure in making the necessary arrangements for the play, and for tea at Huyler's later.

Sincerely yours,

Marie Langs.

909 Fountain Avenue
June the sixth

5. Reply.

Dear Miss Langs:

I thank you very much for your kind thoughtfulness for my guest. Miss Smith and I are delighted to set aside Thursday afternoon as you suggest.

Sincerely yours,

Julia Graham.

314 Kingsley Place
June the seventh

6. Note of Regret.

Dear Marie:

Such fascinating suggestions of "cake and tea and other things" you contrive to put into your note. I wonder if that same imagination of yours can help you to understand our disappointment at not being able to accept your invitation for Thursday afternoon. We have not words to express it. And all on account of an out-of-town appointment of such long standing that it must be kept on that particular afternoon.

Please try to imagine us just as "sorry as we can be."

Cordially yours,

Julia Graham.

7. Regrets.

Dear Miss Langs:

I regret that a previous engagement on the part of Miss Smith makes it impossible for us to accept your kind invitation for next Thursday afternoon.

Sincerely yours,

Julia Graham.

8. Invitation.

Sunnyslope Farm,
October 1, 19—

Dear Mrs. Walters,

My sister Margaret and I are inviting a few friends, quite informally, to meet our cousin, Mary Arthur, on Thursday afternoon. May we count on the pleasure of having you and your daughter, Miss Esther, with us?

Sincerely,

Sara Beeman.

9. Invitation.

The Poplars,
April 10, 19—

Dear Mrs. James:

Our Village Circle meets at our home on Monday evening next, April fifteenth. Mr. Williams and I shall be very glad to have you and Mr. James as our guests for the evening, that you may have an opportunity to meet some of your new neighbors.

Very cordially,
Harriet Williams.

10. Note with Birthday Gift.

Dear Miss Burns,

Please accept these flowers with my love and with the wish that you may enjoy many returns of this happy day.

Sincerely yours,
Helen Harvey.

73 Wellington Road
September tenth

11. Reply.

Thursday Morning.

Dear Miss Helen,

Your note and gift of beautiful flowers completed a day of perfect happiness. It is good to grow old when friends emphasize the years with increasing kindness. Thank you, dear friend, for the love which has never failed me.

Cordially yours,
Celia Burns.

The Bread-and-Butter Note. A short letter to some one whose informal hospitality one has enjoyed should never be neglected or postponed. Something like the following is appropriate, though the matter should vary according to the relations and hearts of people. The language of friendship and courtesy is none too familiar to our pens.

12.

Dear Mrs. Hartley,

Back at routine again, I catch myself fancying that I am yet in the little circle of your guests of last week.

That is the joy of such hospitality as yours,—that the memory of it lingers so long and happily.

Sincerely yours,

John W. Dare.

10 Martin Street
October 15, 19—

13.

Dear Alice:

I wish I could tell you how much I have benefited from the physical relaxation and mental stimulus of my week-end with you. I have come back to the good old grind with real enthusiasm, and it is all a result of your cleverly planned hospitality. Saturday's picnic alone put enough new life into me to last for some time. Thank you so much for all your thoughtfulness from beginning to end.

Cordially,
Marion.

35 Main Street, Overton
August 17, 19—

Letters of Condolence. Letters of condolence and sympathy are always difficult to write. Write only what is in your heart to say. In many instances the kindest thing is silence. The following letter of sympathy, now preserved in Oxford University, is a classic of this kind of expression, and appeals to us all.

14.

Executive Mansion,
Washington, November 21, 1864.

Dear Madam:

I have been shown in the files of the War Department a statement of the Adjutant General of Massachusetts, that you are the mother of five sons who have died gloriously on the field of battle. I feel how weak and fruitless must be any word of mine which should attempt to beguile you from the grief of a loss so overwhelming. But I cannot refrain from tendering to you the consolation that may be found in the thanks of the republic they died to save. I pray that our Heavenly Father may assuage the anguish of your bereavement, and leave you only the cherished memory of the loved and lost, and the solemn pride that must be yours to have laid so costly a sacrifice upon the altar of freedom.

Yours very sincerely and respectfully,

A. Lincoln.

To Mrs. Bixby,
Boston, Mass.

15.

December 7, 19—

Dear Margaret,

In the mail this morning came the sad news from Gertrude that your mother had passed away.

I wish I could be near you at this time to be of some comfort to you. But the greatest comfort you must have is the knowledge and feeling that your mother lived a full and happy life and left this world serene, largely because you and Emma and John did everything to make it so.

Affectionately,

Henry Jerome.

To Miss Margaret Jones.

16.

Dear Tom:

I am very sorry to hear that business affairs have been apparently "going into reverse" for you lately. Be sure that I believe your difficulties are only temporary. They can't be otherwise, with your ability and faithfulness. Here is my hand. If I can be of any help, call on me at once.

Sincerely yours,
Robert.

September 10, 19—

Letters of Congratulation. A letter of congratulation is easier to write.

17.

Dear Martin,

Heartiest congratulations on the good news. Of course I know you don't entirely deserve such good fortune as the promise of Frances to become your wife, but fortunately we are not always treated strictly according to our deserts. We shall all be happy in the happiness that is to be yours.

Sincerely your well-wisher,
Robert Howard.

April 8, 19—.

18.

384 Linden Avenue,
August 18, 19—.

Dear Louise,

We are all greatly delighted over the announcement in the newspaper that you have won a scholarship in the university. You have our heartiest congratulations on your success in this severe test, as well as our sincere good wishes for your enjoyment of college life and work.

Sincerely yours,
Arlene Benham.

FORMAL INVITATIONS AND REPLIES

Formal invitations are written in the third person and, for large affairs, are usually engraved or printed and mailed about two weeks in advance. An invitation sent out by a school, or a class in the school, a club, or any group of persons, is usually in the third person; and, if the invitation be to an entertainment, as at a church or a commencement program, no formal reply is needed. Formal replies, however, should always be sent where entertainment is to be provided for each individual, for the host or hostess will need to know how to provide.

The letters *R. S. V. P.* are sometimes put in the lower left-hand corner of an invitation. They stand for the French phrase, *Répondez s'il vous plaît*, meaning "Reply, if you please." The English words, *An answer will oblige* or *An answer is requested*, are now much used.

1. Invitation to Commencement Exercises.

The Senior Class of
Columbia Seminary
requests the pleasure of your presence at the
Commencement Exercises
June fifteenth to eighteenth

2. Invitation to Commencement Exercises.

The Faculty and Graduating Class
of the
Boston Teachers' Training School
invite you to attend the
Seventeenth Annual Commencement Exercises
Friday evening, April fifteenth, 19—
at half past eight o'clock
1124 Tremont Avenue

3. Formal Invitation to a Reception and Dance.

The Epsilon Mu Sorority
invites you to be present at a
reception and dance to be held at the

COLONIAL CLUB
Tuesday evening, April nineteenth
at half after eight o'clock

4. Wedding Invitation.

Mr. and Mrs. Joseph Suffolk
request the honor of your presence at the
marriage of their daughter
Mabel Grace
to
Mr. Andrew Jackman
Wednesday afternoon, June fifteenth
at three o'clock
Saint-Mary's-on-the-Hill Church

5. Acceptance of Wedding Invitation.

Mr. and Mrs. John T. Brown accept with pleasure the invitation of Mr. and Mrs. Joseph Suffolk to be present at the marriage of their daughter Mabel Grace on June fifteenth.

6. Announcement.

Mr. Andrew Jackman
Miss Mabel Grace Suffolk
Married
on Wednesday, June the fifteenth
Nineteen hundred and seventy—
Baltimore

Note.—At home cards are often inserted in the same envelope with the announcements.

7. For a Formal At Home.

Mrs. Jacques Randolph Stearns
At Home
on Wednesday, the seventh of December
from three until six o'clock
1106 Ballston Heights
to meet
Mrs. James Winchell Toynbee

8. Formal Note of Invitation.

Miss Belle Coe requests the pleasure of Miss Hinman's company on Thursday evening at eight o'clock.

128 Fremont St., January nine.

9. The Invitation Accepted.

Miss Hinman accepts with pleasure Miss Coe's invitation for Thursday evening at eight o'clock.

Wellington Place, January ten.

10. The Invitation Declined.

Miss Hinman sincerely regrets that she cannot accept Miss Coe's invitation for Thursday evening at eight o'clock.

Wellington Place, January ten.

11. A Less Formal Invitation. Calling cards are often used for small informal gatherings of friends.

At Home
Mrs. James Winchell Toynbee
Wednesday, January 14, 3 to 4.
40 College St.

12. Dinner Invitation.

1432 Lincoln Avenue
Mr. and Mrs. Thomas Dowd
request the pleasure of
Mr. James Morley's
company at dinner
On Wednesday evening, March the fifth
at eight o'clock

February the twenty-fifth

13. Acceptance.

415 Martin St.

Mr. James Morley accepts with pleasure the invitation of Mr. and Mrs. Thomas Dowd for Wednesday evening, March the fifth, at eight o'clock.

February the twenty-seventh.

14. Regrets.

Mr. James Morley sincerely regrets that a professional engagement made several months since prevents his acceptance of Mr. and Mrs. Thomas Dowd's kind invitation for Wednesday evening, March the fifth

February the twenty-seventh.

The collection of books that make up a family library represents the unity of the family's interests and needs, as well as the diversity of the approaches to reading and the use of books that individual members of the family make. When a portion of the collection is on view in the home, guests will often study it—not only to search for favorites of their own and to find new titles that may not be familiar to them, but also to get a sense of what the family enjoys. Thoughtfully selected and carefully maintained, the library may be an index to a family's characteristic personality, as well as a valuable aid to its pursuit of information and recreation.

Encyclopedias. Reference books of many kinds may be the cornerstone of the collection. There was a time when purchase of a single set of encyclopedias was considered the most important investment that a family could make in its book collection. Such a multivolume set is still a major investment and calls for care and consideration in selection. Examination of various sets in a library or other center where they may be available is an important part of the decision about purchase. Although reviews of encyclopedias are not frequent, the ones that appear should be read with care, and with special concern for the points they raise that are especially pertinent to family purchase.

When examining encyclopedias, a good technique is to select in advance several topics, including ones in several different subject areas and ones of varying timeliness, and to check several different encyclopedias, preferably ones of similar dates of publication, to see what differences there may be in treatment, accuracy, format, ease of locating information, and other important features of use.

Careful reading of the forewords of several sets is especially relevant in determining the audience to which the encyclopedia is primarily directed and in evaluating the internal aids, such as the index, maps, and the like, that will determine the set's usefulness.

Although the time and attention spent on the decision about purchase of an encyclopedia may be considerable, other additions to the family library should be made with the same concern. The tendency, even in today's mobile society, for families to retain their books and to move them frequently, should mean that the items finally selected are worth keeping. The aesthetic values of attractive bindings, clear print, illustrations that truly complement or enhance the text, and other characteristics should be considered as carefully as the titles themselves.

Nature of the Library. Since some of the books in a family library may come as gifts, and others selected by different members of the family at different times and for various purposes, there is likely to be variety in quality and appeal. Sentiment about the first book that prompted a child's interest in reading or the autographed copy presented by a new author may be responsible for a family's keeping some books long past the day when they are actively consulted or read. For other books, such as annuals or almanacs, there may be little reason to retain the books for any length of time. The library should be a constantly growing, changing collection, with some of the basic elements remaining, others changing as interests and attitudes change.

Many factors may determine what a family decides to keep in its library: the occupations of the parents, accessibility of materials in other libraries, the attitude of the children toward reading, the frequency of moves, and the size of the home.

Location. It is essential that there be at least one place where shelves in a convenient location allow for the collection and care of the family library. Ideally, there should be shelves or cupboards in several areas of the home where individual members of the family may keep their favorite books, or where ones currently being read can be kept within easy reach. Cookbooks in the kitchen, repair manuals in the workshop, nature guides in the car, are only a few examples.

Permanence of Appeal. The library should include books chosen for the permanence of their appeal, in addition to those that are useful or interesting only at a specific time in the family's life. Collections of prose and of poetry, for example, should be chosen with consideration for the range and quality of the selections. Their appeal to different members of the family may thus cause them to be kept in the library for many years.

Textbooks purchased during children's schooldays are too often kept as part of the library long after their value and accuracy have diminished. In such fields as science, it may be relatively easy to check for the current accuracy of materials. In the social sciences or in literature, such a check may be more difficult, but except in unusual instances, textbooks need not be kept beyond the period when the student consults them.

A family's shared interest in travel, hobbies, or other pastimes may be responsible for the development of an extensive segment of the library. Atlases, which are useful in the planning or the reminiscence of travels, may become outdated as new roads, buildings, or even new countries appear, and boundaries and natural features change. Atlases, however, provide an example of the exception that may warrant keeping material that is no longer currently accurate, but that is still desirable to have on hand to recall the experiences of a trip or to trace changes that have occurred in recent years. Travel guides tend to become dated quite rapidly, and the more specific and helpful they are at the time of purchase, the more rapid that dating may be. This is true in the case of prices quoted for fares, information about passports, prices for accommodations and meals, and even addresses for shops and other places to visit, which are subject to change. Again, the value of the book as an aid to planning may diminish, while an attachment to the places or events it helps to recall may be responsible for a family's choosing to keep the book on its shelves.

Such hobbies as stamp collecting, coin collecting, crafts, and various sports may cause the purchase of a large share of the family library. Especially when such titles are purchased as gifts for an individual of the family, his knowledge of the titles available in his field of interest should be considered, and the title chosen for him might best be selected with the understanding that he may exchange it.

A family's general reading for pleasure may span many subject areas and many kinds of books. The book that is to be read only once may be added to the library in paperback format, and kept only for a limited time. Readers of mysteries and science fiction frequently add books in these areas to their shelves, but except for those of a few favorite authors, they may not keep them as part of their permanent collection. Fiction of more lasting value may include literature and classics that have been tested by time, but the practice of purchasing sets of books by one author is less common than it once was. There are reprint editions of most major classics, and there are also special editions prepared for their aesthetic value. Both kinds may find a place in the library, and the choice may be chiefly a matter of taste. In some instances, however, where illustrations are an intrinsic part of the text, as in some of James Thurber's books, the careful selector of books will not be satisfied with editions in which the illustrations are omitted or are poorly reproduced.

Bookstores. The family engaged in developing its library may often have a problem in finding bookstores to serve its varied interests. Most of the all-purpose bookstores are in major metropolitan areas, and the problem of merchandising books of quality keeps their number low. Members of the family may thus find it helpful to keep lists of books

THE LINCOLN LIBRARY OF SPORTS CHAMPIONS

1

HENRY AARON, KAREEM ABDUL-JABBAR, HERB ADDERLEY, GROVER CLEVELAND ALEXANDER, MUHAMMAD ALI, DICK ALLEN, GEORGE ALLEN, PHOG ALLEN, TED ALLEN, BOBBY ALLISON, WALTER ALSTON, LANCE ALWORTH, GARY ANDERSON, PAUL ANDERSON, MARIO ANDRETTI, LUIS APARICIO, LUKE APPLING, EDDIE ARCARO, NATE ARCHIBALD, PAUL ARIZIN, ROONE ARLEDGE, TOMMY ARMOUR, HENRY ARMSTRONG, ARTHUR ASHE, RED AUERBACH, BRAULIO BAEZA, ERNIE BANKS, ROGER BANNISTER, RICK BARRY, SAMMY BAUGH, ELGIN BAYLOR, BOB BEAMON, CHUCK BEDNARIK.

The Lincoln Library of Sports Champions, covering more than 50 different sports, is for children and students of all ages. The 14-volume work contains stories of human interest, easy-to-read biographies of more than 500 sports personalities, and hundreds of photographs. *The Lincoln Library of Sports Champions* is not entirely reference. The set is also a much-needed reading motivator. The editors have selected outstanding personalities that account for the ever-growing popularity of sports. In choosing among the many sports stars, sheer ability was not the only reason for the inclusion of a particular person. The selection represents sports figures not only gifted with great skill, but looked upon by most as among the top in their profession.

Noted Americans in Language Arts: Top Left—**Edward P. Morgan** (1910–), **news commentator and broadcaster,** began his career as a reporter for the *Seattle Star*. He then became a correspondent for United Press, after that he worked for the *Chicago Daily News, Colliers Weekly,* and CBS, where he gained national recognition as a broadcaster.

Top Right—**William Morris** (1913–), **editor and newspaper columnist,** has played a large part in the compiling and publication of many dictionaries and encyclopedias. He was editor-in-chief for the *American Heritage Dictionary* and also served as an editor for *Funk and Wagnalls New Standard Dictionary.*

Bottom Left—**Milton Friedman** (1912–) was the recipient of the **1976 Nobel Prize in Economics.** A former economic advisor to Richard M. Nixon, Friedman resigned over a dispute concerning wage-and-price controls. He is a coauthor of the monumental *A Monetary History of the United States, 1867–1960.*

Bottom Right—**Daniel J. Boorstin** (1914–) was appointed **Librarian of Congress** in 1975. The former director of the National Museum of History and Technology of the Smithsonian Institution graduated from Harvard, Oxford, and Yale universities. A historian, Boorstin has written many books, including *The Lost World of Thomas Jefferson* and *The Americans: The Colonial Experience.*

they especially want when they have opportunities to shop. When it is possible to open an account or to order by mail, these sources may facilitate new purchases, and the catalogs or announcements that come to holders of accounts may help to keep them informed of what is new or available in bookstores. Shops that cater to special interests of readers, such as books on antiques, various periods of history, or children's literature, may offer more opportunities for the family to expand or compare its collection.

Personal and specialty bookshops have traditionally stressed their services in the selection of titles, and many are cooperative in suggesting titles and handling requests for books that are not currently in stock.

Care of Books. Caring for books is an important aspect of ownership of a home library. When dust jackets are available, they may help to enhance the appearance and prolong the life of the book if they are left in place. Transparent plastic jackets in adjustable sizes may be found in many book and stationery stores, and they may further preserve the jackets of the books themselves. When a book is added to the permanent collection, a bookplate showing family or individual ownership may be affixed to it. Just as the plastic jacket should be applied so that the endpapers, if decorated, are preserved as well as possible, the bookplate or some other simple statement of ownership should be placed near the front of the book on the endpapers or front pages before the text where it will be obvious to anyone examining the book, while it does not deface the book itself.

From the list given here it will be possible to form the nucleus of a private library which can serve for education and entertainment as well as for everyday use. A still wider range of selection may be had by consulting the bibliographies given in connection with different departments of these volumes.

REFERENCE WORKS

Title	Publisher
An Atlas: Readers Atlas	Rand McNally

English dictionaries: American Heritage or Webster's New International

Foreign Language dictionaries:
Cassell's New English-French French-English Dictionary
Pfeffer's Dictionary of Everyday Usage, German-English, English-German
Encyclopedias:
Junior emphasis A to Z: World Book, Compton's
Senior emphasis A to Z: Britannica, Americana, Colliers
Information departmentalized: The New Lincoln Library Encyclopedia
Webster's Biographical Dictionary

Other Sources:

Author	Title	Publisher
Bartlett, John—Familiar Quotations		Little Brown
Brewer, E. C.—Dictionary of Phrase and Fable		Lippincott
Cary, M. (Ed.)—The Oxford Classical Dictionary		Clarendon
Ellison, John W. (Ed.)—Complete Concordance of the Revised Standard Version of the Bible		Nelson
Dorland, W. A. and Miller, E. C. L.—American Illustrated Medical Dictionary		Saunders
Dyke, A. L.—Automobile and Gasoline Engine Encyclopedia (Latest Ed.)		Goodheart-Willcox
Keller, Helen R. (Ed.)—Reader's Digest of Books		Macmillan
Robert, Henry M.—Rules of Order (Rev. Ed.)		
Roget, Peter M.—Thesaurus (See *Synonyms*)		

GENERAL LITERATURE

Author	Title	Publisher
Æsop—Fables		
The Bible		
The Arabian Nights		
Bacon, Francis—Essays		
Botkin, Benj. A.—Treasury of American Folklore		Crown
Bunyan, John—Pilgrim's Progress		
Burke, Edmund—Reflections on the French Revolution		

Author	Title	Publisher
Cambridge History of American Literature		Macmillan
Cambridge History of English Literature		Macmillan
Cervantes, Miguel de—Don Quixote		
Chaucer, Goeffrey—The Canterbury Tales		
Chesterfield, Lord—Letters to his Son		Oxford
Cicero, Marcus Tullius—Essays		Dutton
Dante Alighieri—The Divine Comedy		Dutton
Demosthenes—Orations		Dutton
Emerson, R. W.—Essays (1st and 2d Series)		Macmillan
Galsworthy, John—Plays		Scribner
Garnett, R. and Gosse, E.—History of English Literature		
Homer—The Iliad and the Odyssey		Classics Club
Ibsen, Henrik—Selected Plays		Mod. Library
Lamb, Charles—Essays of Elia		Nelson
Legouis, Émile—History of English Literature		Macmillan
Machiavelli, Niccolo—The Prince		Oxford
Marcus Aurelius—Meditations		World Classics
Merejkowski, Dmitri—The Romance of Leonardo da Vinci		
Molière—Comedies		Mod. Library
Montaigne, Michel de—Essays		Dutton
Oates, W. J. and O'Neill, Eugene, Jr.—The Complete Greek Drama		Random House
Pepys, Samuel—Diary		Dutton
Plato—Dialogues and The Republic		Classics Club
Schuster, M. Lincoln—Treasury of the World's Great Letters		Simon & Schuster
Shakespeare—Plays (G. Lyman Kittredge, Ed.)		Ginn
Shaw, George Bernard—Nine Plays		Dodd Mead
Sheridan, Richard Brinsley—Plays		Oxford
Smith, Logan Pearsall—All Trivia		Harcourt Brace
Stevenson, R. L.—Virginibus Puerisque and Other Essays		
Thoreau, Henry D.—Walden		
Virgil—The Æneid		
Walton, Isaac—The Compleat Angler		

BIOGRAPHY

Adams, Henry—The Education of Henry Adams	
Adams, James T.—The Living Jefferson	Scribner
Boswell, James—Life of Johnson	Mod. Library
Bouyer, L. Newman: His Life and Spirituality	Kenedy
Canby, Henry S.—Thoreau	Peter Smith
Canning, John (Ed.)—100 Great Modern Lives	Hawthorn
Cellini, Benvenuto—Autobiography	Dutton
Eastman, Max—Einstein, Trotsky, Hemingway, Freud, and other great companions	Collier
Franklin, Benjamin—Autobiography	Macmillan
Freeman, Douglas Southall—Robert E. Lee	Scribner
Guedalla, Philip—Wellington	Harper
Holt, Rackham—George Washington Carver	Doubleday
Mersand, Jos. (Ed.)—Great American Short Biographies	
Phelps, William Lyon—Autobiography with Letters	Oxford
Plutarch—Lives	Mod. Library
Riis, Jacob—The Making of an American	Macmillan
Sandburg, Carl—Abraham Lincoln: The Prairie Years	
Sherwood, Robert—Roosevelt and Hopkins	Harper
Steffens, Lincoln—Autobiography	Harcourt Brace
Strachey, Lytton—Eminent Victorians	Harcourt Brace
Untermeyer, Louis—Makers of the Modern World	Sands
Van Doren, Carl—Benjamin Franklin	Viking
White, William A.—A Puritan in Babylon	Peter Smith

FICTION

Austen, Jane—Sense and Sensibility	Dutton
Balzac, Honore de—Old Goriot	Mod. Library
Bennett, Arnold—The Old Wives' Tale	Mod. Library
Bromfield, Louis—The Green Bay Tree	Stokes
Bronte, Emily—Wuthering Heights	Mod. Library
Buck, Pearl—The Good Earth	Grosset & Dunlap
Butler, Samuel—The Way of All Flesh	Dutton
Cather, Willa—Death Comes for the Archbishop	Knopf
Conrad, Joseph—Victory	Mod. Library
Cooper, James Fenimore—The Spy	Scribner
—The Last of the Mohicans	
Dickens, Charles—Pickwick Papers	Mod. Library
Dostoiévsky, F.—The Brothers Karamazov	Mod Library
—Crime and Punishment	Mod. Library
Drury, Allen—Advise and Consent	Doubleday
Dumas, Alexandre—The Count of Monte Cristo	Nelson
Flaubert, Gustave—Madame Bovary	Dutton
Forster, E. M.—Howard's End	Knopf
France, Anatole—The Crime of Sylvestre Bonnard	
Galsworthy, John—The Forsyte Saga	Scribner
Glasgow, Ellen—Barren Ground	Peter Smith
Hamsun, Knut—Growth of the Soil	Mod. Library
Hardy, Thomas—The Return of the Native	Macmillan
—Tess of the D'Urbervilles	Mod. Library
Harte, Bret—The Luck of Roaring Camp	Houghton Mifflin
Hawthorne, Nathaniel—The Scarlet Letter	Mod. Library
—The House of the Seven Gables	Dutton

Author	Title	Publisher

Hemingway, Ernest—For Whom the Bell Tolls   *Scribner*
Henry, O.—Great Short Novels (ed. by Rahv) *Peter Smith*
Hersey, John—A Bell for Adano   .   .   *Mod. Library*
Howells, William D.—The Rise of Silas Lapham
Houghton Mifflin
Hugo, Victor—The Hunchback of Notre Dame   .   *Dodd*
James, Henry—The American   .   .   *Houghton Mifflin*
Kafka, Franz—The Trial   .   .   .   .   *Knopf*
Kipling, Rudyard—Kim.   .   .   .   .   .   *Macmillan*
Lardner, Ring—Collected Short Stories   .   .   *Scribner*
Lewis, Sinclair—Babbitt   .   .   .   *Harcourt Brace*
—Arrowsmith   .   .   .   *Mod. Library*
Lytton, E. Bulwer—The Last Days of Pompeii   .   *Dutton*
Mann, Thomas—The Magic Mountain   .   .   .   *Knopf*
Marquand, John P.—The Late George Apley
Grosset & Dunlap
Maugham, Somerset—Of Human Bondage   *Mod. Library*
Maupassant, Guy de—Short Stories   .   .   .   .   *Dutton*
Meredith, George—The Egoist   .   .   .   .   .   *Oxford*
Michener, Thomas—Tales of the South Pacific *Macmillan*
Mitchell, Margaret—Gone With the Wind   .   *Macmillan*
Paton, Alan—Cry, the Beloved Country   .   .   *Scribner*
Poe, Edgar Allen—Tales   .   .   .   .   *Mod. Library*
Priestley, J. B.—The Good Companions   .   .   *Harper*
Reade, Charles—The Cloister and the Hearth   .   *Dutton*
Richardson, Samuel—Pamela   .   .   .   .   *Dutton*
Roberts, Kenneth—Northwest Passage   .   .   *Doubleday*
Rolland, Romain—Jean Christophe   .   *Mod. Library*
Scott, Sir Walter—The Heart of Midlothian   .   .   *Nelson*
—Waverly   .   .   .   .   .   .   *Nelson*
Sienkiewicz, H.—Quo Vadis?   .   .   .   .   .   *Dutton*
Steinbeck, John—Of Mice and Men   .   .   .   *Viking*
Stevenson, Robert Louis—The Strange Case of Dr. Jekyll
and Mr. Hyde   .   .   .   .   *Dutton*
Tarkington, Booth—Alice Adams   .   *Grosset & Dunlap*
Thackeray, William M.—Vanity Fair   .   .   *Mod. Library*
Thirkell, Angela—Love at All Ages   .   .   .   *Knopf*
Tolstóy, Leo—War and Peace   .   .   .   .   *Mod. Library*
—Anna Karenina   .   .   .   *Mod. Library*
Trollope, Anthony—Barchester Towers   .   .   .   *Dutton*
Twain, Mark—The Gilded Age   .   .   .   .   *Harper*
Wells, H. G.—Tono-Bungay   .   .   .   *Mod. Library*
Wescott, Edward—David Harum   .   .   .   *Peter Smith*
Wharton, Edith—Ethan Frome   .   .   .   .   *Scribner*
—The Age of Innocence   .   *Mod. Library*
Wilder, Thornton—The Bridge of San Luis Rey
Grosset & Dunlap
Wolfe, Thomas—Of Time and the River   .   .   *Scribner*
—You Can't Go Home Again   .   .   *Harper*

POETRY

Benét, Stephen Vincent—John Brown's Body   .   *Rinehart*
Browning, Robert—Selected Poems   .   .   .   .   *Oxford*
Burns, Robert—Poems   .   .   .   .   *Dutton*
Byron, George Gordon—Poems   .   .   .   .   .   *Oxford*
Dickinson, Emily—Bolts of Melody   .   .   .   .   *Harper*
Eliot, T. S.—Collected Poems   .   .   .   *Harcourt Brace*
Fitzgerald, Edward—Translation of the Rubaiyat of Omar
Khayyam   .   .   .   .   *Dutton*
Frost, Robert—Complete Poems   .   .   .   .   .   *Holt*
Housman, A. E.—A Shropshire Lad   .   .   .   .   *Holt*
Hubbell, J. B and Beaty, J. O.—An Introduction to Poetry
Macmillan
Keats, John—Poems   .   .   .   .   *Dutton*
Longfellow, Henry W.—Poems   .   .   .   *Mod. Library*
Masefield, John—Selected Poems   .   .   .   *Macmillan*
Millay, Edna St. Vincent—Collected Sonnets   .   *Harper*
Palgrave, Francis—Golden Treasury   .   .   .   .   *Dutton*
Rodman, Selden—100 Modern Poets   . *New Amer. Library*
Sandburg, Carl—Selected Poems   .   .   *Harcourt Brace*
Shelley, Percy Bysshe—Poems   .   .   .   .   .   *Oxford*
Tennyson, Alfred—Poems   .   .   .   .   .   .   *Oxford*
Whitman, Walt—Leaves of Grass   .   .   *Mod. Library*
Wordsworth, William—Poems   .   .   .   .   .   *Oxford*

HISTORY

Adams, Henry—Degredation of Democratic Dogma *Smith*
Adams, James T., ed.—Atlas of American History *Scribner*
Adams, James T.—The Epic of America   .   *Little Brown*
Beard, Charles A. and Mary—The Rise of American
Civilization   .   .   .   .   *Macmillan*
Carlyle, Thomas—The French Revolution   *Mod. Library*
Creasy, Edward S.—Fifteen Decisive Battles   .   .   *Dutton*
Creighton, Donald G.—Dominion of the North; A History
of Canada   .   .   .   .   .   .   *Houghton Mifflin*
Green, John Richard—A Short History of the English
People   .   .   .   .   *Dutton*
Hyma, A.—History of the Dutch in the Far East   .   *Wahr*
Johnson, Gerald W.—America is Born   .   .   .   *Morrow*
Langer, W. L.—An Encyclopedia of World History
Houghton Mifflin
Macaulay, T. B.—The History of England   .   .   *Dutton*
Motley, J. L.—The Rise of the Dutch Republic   *Dutton*
Parkman, Francis—The Oregon Trail   .   .   *Mod. Library*

Author	Title	Publisher

Seligman, E. R. H.—Economic Interpretation of History
Gordian
Toynbee, Arnold J.—A Study of History (Abridged ed.)
Oxford
Van Loon, H. W.—Story of Mankind   .   .   .   *Tudor*
Wells, H. G.—The Outline of History   .   .   *Garden City*
Whitehead, Alfred N.—Adventures in Ideas   *Macmillan*
Wilgus, A. Curtis—Argentina, Brazil, and Chili
since Independence   .   .   .   .   *Russell*

HOME AND COMMUNITY

Bromfield, Louis—Pleasant Valley   .   .   .   .   *Harper*
Crotty, William J. and Others—Political Parties and
Political Behavior   .   .   .   .   *Allyn & Bacon*
Doob, Leonard W.— Political Opinion and Propaganda
Shoe String
Goldstein, Philip—Triumph of Biology   .   .   *Doubleday*
Hoyt, E. P.—Condition Critical: Our Hospital Crisis   *Holt*
Inkeles, Alex—What is Sociology   .   .   *Prentice Hall*
Kent, Robert W.—How to Choose Your House and Live in
It Ever After   .   .   .   .   .   .   *Lee Inst.*
Lasswell, Harold D.—The Analysis of Political Behavior
Oxford
McDonald-Austin F.—American City Government and
Administration   .   .   .   .   *Crowell*
McLaughlin, Andrew C.—A Constitutional History of the
United States   .   .   .   .   *Appleton-Century*
Peach, W. N.—Principles of Economics, 3rd ed.   .   *Irwin*
Picton, Lionel J.—Nutrition and the Soil   .   *Devin-Adair*

HOME AND EDUCATION

Anshen, Melvin—An Introduction to Business *Macmillan*
Baebenroth, H. C. and Parkhurst, Charles C.—Modern
Business English   .   .   .   .   .   .   *Prentice-Hall*
Britten, Jessie D.—Practical Notes on Nursing Procedure
Williams & Wilkins
Carlson, P. A., Forkner, H. L., and Prickett, A. L.—
Twentieth Century Bookkeeping and Accounting
South-Western Pub. Co.
Craig, William—Care of Newly Born Infant, 3rd ed.
Williams & Wilkins
Crow, Lester D. and Alice—How to Study   .   .   *Collier*
Dacey, Norman F.—How to Avoid Probate   .   *Crown*
Davison, Eloise, Ed.—America's Housekeeping Book
Scribner
Durant, Will—The Story of Philosophy   .   .   *Garden City*
Farmer, Robert A.—How to Avoid Problems with your
Will   .   .   .   .   *Arco*
Greenbie, Marjorie—The Arts of Leisure   .   .   *Whittlesey*
Hunter, Beatrice—Consumer Beware!   .   .   *Devin-Adair*
Hurlock, Elizabeth B.—Child Growth and Development
McGraw
James, William—Psychology   .   .   .   .   .   *Harper*
Kling, Samuel G.—Legal Encyclopedia for the Home and
Business   .   .   .   .   *Pocket Books*
MacGibbon, Elizabeth G.—Fitting Yourself for Business
McGraw-Hill
Post, Emily—Etiquette   .   .   .   .   *Funk & Wagnalls*
Schifferes, Justus J.—How to Live Longer   .   .   *Collier*
Simpson, Jean I. and Taylor, Demetria—The Frozen Food
Cook Book   .   .   .   .   .   .   *Simon & Schuster*

POPULAR SCIENCE

Audubon, John J.—The Birds of America   .   .   *Macmillan*
Cox, Ian—Science Survey   .   .   .   *S. Low Marston*
Dampier, John B.—A History of Science   .   .   *Macmillan*
Ditmars, R. L.—Snakes of the World   .   .   .   *Macmillan*
Eddington, Sir Arthur—The Expanding Universe
Macmillan
Eiseley, Loren C.—Darwin's Century   .   .   .   *Doubleday*
Hecht, Selig—Explaining the Atom   .   .   .   .   *Viking*
Henney, Keith—Principles of Radio (5th ed.)   .   .   *Wiley*
Jaques, Harry E.—How to Know the Trees
Wm. C. Brown Co.
Jeans, Sir James—The Universe Around Us   .   *Macmillan*
Osborn, Fairfield—Our Plundered Planet   .   *Little Brown*
Peterson, Roger T.—A Field Guide to the Birds
Houghton Mifflin
Scheinfeld, Amram—Your Heredity and Environment
Stokes
Spencer, L. J.—A Key to Precious Stones   .   .   *Emerson*
Titiev, M.—Introduction to Cultural Anthropology   *Holt*
Whitehead, A. N.—Science and the Modern World
Macmillan

TRAVEL

Barretto, Larry—Bright Mexico   .   .   .   .   .   *Farrar*
—Hawaiian Holiday   .   .   .   *Dodd Mead*
Bertram, Kate and Richard—Caribbean Cruise   .   *Norton*
Fleming, Peter—Brazilian Adventure   .   .   .   *Scribner*
Franck, H. A., with Lanks, H. C.—Pan American Highway
Appleton-Century
Hammond, C. S. and Co. World Travelog   .   .   *Hammond*
Hatcher, Harlan—The Great Lakes   .   .   .   .   *Oxford*
Look at America Series   .   .   .   .   .   *Houghton Mifflin*

The title character from "The Scarecrow of Oz" written by L. Frank Baum and illustrated by John R. Neill. *The Scarecrow of Oz* was one of the many "Oz" books Baum dedicated his life to. These books created an Oz-mania with a large following among children. There was even a small newspaper called *The Osmopolitan* and Ozite clubs. *(Picture courtesy Rand McNally)*

The Wizard of Oz, from the book *The Scarecrow of Oz*, written by L. Frank Baum and illustrated by John R. Neill. Lyman Frank Baum began his career as a newspaperman before he turned to writing "American fairy tales," as he called them. He wrote a total of 14 Oz books, beginning with the *The Wonderful Wizard of Oz* (1900) and ending with *Glinda of Oz* (1920). He also wrote many other children's stories. *The Wizard of Oz* became a movie in 1939. The movie, one of the first to be filmed in color, starred Judy Garland as Dorothy, Ray Bolger as the Scarecrow, Jack Haley as the Tinman, Bert Lahr as the Lion, and Frank Morgan as the Wizard. Both the movie and the book have become classics. *(Picture courtesy Rand McNally)*

Author	Title	Publisher

Look magazine—Guide books prepared by the magazine and the following editors:
  Allen, Frederick—New York City
  Bromfield, Louis—The Midwest
  Chase, Mary Ellen—New England
  Cohn, David I.—The South
  Jackson, Joseph H.—The Far West
  Johnson, Gerald W.—The Central Northeast
  Stegner, Wallace—The Central Northwest
The Reader's Digest Family Reference Series: These
  United States . . . . *The Reader's Digest Ass'n*
Rivers of America Series . . . . *Rinehart*
  Banta, R. E.—The Ohio
  Beston, Henry—The St. Lawrence
  Canby, H. S.—The Brandywine
  Carmer, Carl—The Hudson
  Dana, Julia—The Sacramento
  Davis, Julia—The Shenandoah
  Gutheim, F.—The Potomac
  Vestal, Stanley—The Missouri
  Waters, Frank—The Colorado
  Way, F., Jr.—The Allegheny
Stein, Howard and Adeline—Budget Guide to Europe
  Van Nostrand
Ullman, James R.—Kingdom of Adventure: Everest *Sloane*
Vestal, Stanley—The Old Sante Fe Trail *Houghton Mifflin*

THE CHILDREN'S LIBRARY

Every child should own some books. Every child should have access to the books that develop his sympathy, broaden his understanding, deepen his appreciation—of people and of the world about him. To become familiar with books, the child needs constant contact with more and more books. And, if children are to love books and reading, the books provided must satisfy their needs and interests and always they must give joy and pleasure.

The following list is arranged for convenience by grades from third through tenth. Because children within the same grade frequently differ in reading ability, no child should be restricted to books classified under his own particular grade level.

Although this list has been chosen by competent authorities, it should not be regarded as a complete selection of "the best" books for children. With almost a thousand new titles for children published each year, persons assisting in selection should be alert to the new, as well as to the older books that have stood the acid test of childhood choice.

READING REFERENCES FOR ADULTS

Title	Author	Publisher
Bequest of Wings—Duff		*Viking*
Books, Children and Men—Hazard		*Horn Book*
Parent's Guide to Children's Reading—Larrick		*Doubleday*
Reading with Children—Eaton		*Viking*
Way of the Storyteller—Sawyer		*Viking*

I. READ-ALOUD AGE

STORY COLLECTIONS

Here and Now Story Book—Mitchell		*Dutton*
Little Bookroom—Farjeon		*Walck*
Once the Hodja—Kelsey		*McKay*
Once Upon a Time—Dobbs		*Random*
Told Under the Green Umbrella—		
Told Under the Christmas Tree—		
Association for Childhood Education		*Macmillan*

POETRY

Child's Garden of Verses—Stevenson		*Scribner*
Come Hither—de la Mare		*Knopf*
Favorite Poems, Old and New—Ferris		*Doubleday*
Gaily We Parade—Brewton		*Macmillan*
Inheritance of Poetry—Adshead and Duff		*Houghton*
Little Laughter—Love		*Crowell*
Rainbow in the Sky—Untermeyer		*Harcourt*
Rocket in My Pocket—Withers, comp.		*Holt*
Silver Pennies—Thompson, comp.		*Macmillan*
Sing-Song—Rossetti		*Macmillan*
Sung Under the Silver Umbrella—		
Association for Childhood Education International		
This Way, Delight—Read		*Pantheon*
Tirra Lirra—Richards		*Little*
World of Christopher Robin—Milne		*Dutton*

SONGS

American Folksongs for Children—Seeger		*Doubleday*
Book of Favorite Hymns—Bertail		*Garden City*
Cat Came Fiddling—Kapp		*Harcourt*
Sing for Christmas—Wheeler		*Dutton*
Singing Time—Coleman and Thorn		*Day*

Title	Author	Publisher

ABC AND MOTHER GOOSE BOOKS

ABC Book—Falls		*Doubleday*
ABC Bunny—Gag		*Coward*
Bible ABC—Hogarth		*Lippincott*
Lavender's Blue—Lines		*Watts*
Marguerite de Angeli's Book of Nursery and Mother Goose Rhymes		*Doubleday*
Real Mother Goose—Wright		*Rand*
Ring o' Roses—Brooke		*Warne*

PICTURE STORY BOOKS

Anatole and the Cat—Titus		*McGraw*
And to think that I saw it on Mulberry Street—Seuss		*Vanguard*
Angus and the Ducks—Flack		*Doubleday*
April's Kittens—Newberry		*Harper*
Big Snow—Hader		*Macmillan*
Blueberries for Sal—McCloskey		*Viking*
Boats on the River—Flack		*Viking*
Chanticleer and the Fox—Cooney		*Crowell*
Christ Child—Petersham		*Doubleday*
Country Bunny—Heyward		*Houghton*
Curious George—Rey		*Houghton*
Golden Goose Book—Brooke		*Warne*
Happy Lion—Fatio		*McGraw*
Hey Diddle, Diddle, Picture Book—Caldecott		*Warne*
In the Forest—Ets		*Viking*
Jeanne-Marie Counts her Sheep—Francoise		*Scribner*
Johnny Crow's Garden—Brooke		*Warne*
Little Auto—Lenski		*Oxford*
Little Bear—Minarik		*Harper*
Little House—Burton		*Houghton*
Make Way for Ducklings—McCloskey		*Viking*
Mike's House—Sauer		*Viking*
Millions of Cats—Gag		*Coward*
Over in the Meadow—Langstaff		*Harcourt*
Poppy Seed Cake—Clark		*Doubleday*
Prayer for a Child—Field		*Macmillan*
Rooster Crows—Petersham		*Macmillan*
Rosa-too-little—Felt		*Doubleday*
Snipp, Snapp, Snurr and the Red Shoes—Lindman		*Whitman*
Story of Baber—Brunhoff		*Random*
Story of Ferdinand—Leaf		*Viking*
Tale of Peter Rabbit—Potter		*Warne*
Timothy Turtle—Graham		*Viking*
A Tree is Nice—Udry		*Harper*
Umbrella—Yashima		*Viking*
White Snow, Bright Snow—Tresselt		*Lothrop*

II. GRADES THREE TO TEN

THIRD GRADE

Andy and the Lion—Daugherty		*Viking*
The Bears on Hemlock Mountain—Dalgliesh		*Scribner*
Billy and Blaze—Anderson		*Macmillan*
Cowboy Tommy—Tousey		*Hale*
Crow Boy—Yashima		*Viking*
Dash and Dart—Buff		*Viking*
Elf Owl—Buff		*Viking*
Five Chinese Brothers—Bishop		*Coward*
500 Hats of Bartholomew Cubbins—Seuss		*Vanguard*
In My Mother's House—Clark		*Viking*
Katy and the Big Snow—Burton		*Houghton*
Little Island—Macdonald		*Doubleday*
Little Pear—Lattimore		*Harcourt*
Little Toot—Gramatky		*Putnam*
Madeline—Bemelmans		*Viking*
My Father's Dragon—Gannett		*Random*
Ola—Aulaire		*Doubleday*
Painted Pig—Morrow		*Knopf*
Pedro, Angel of Olvera Street—Politi		*Scribner*
Pelle's New Suit—Beskow		*Harper*
Riding the Rails—Olds		*Houghton*
Roger and the Fox—Davis		*Doubleday*
Story about Ping—Flack		*Viking*
Swineherd—Andersen (tr. Blegvad)		*Harcourt*

FOURTH GRADE

Abraham Lincoln—Aulaire		*Doubleday*
Appleseed Farm—Douglas		*Abingdon*
Bed-knob and Broomstick—Norton		*Harcourt*
Betsy and Billy—Haywood		*Harcourt*
Birds in Their Homes—Webb		*Doubleday*
Blue Fairy Book—Lang		*Random*
Bright April—de Angeli		*Doubleday*
Charlotte's Web—White		*Harper*
Courage of Sarah Noble—Dalgliesh		*Scribner*
Dancing Cloud—Buff		*Viking*
Down, Down the Mountain—Credle		*Nelson*
Fast Sooner Hound—Bontemps		*Houghton*
First Bible, ill. by Sewell		*Oxford*
King of the Golden River—Ruskin		*World*
Little Boat Boy—Bothwell		*Harcourt*
Many Moons—Thurber		*Harcourt*
Melindy's Medal—Faulkner		*Messner*

Title	Author	Publisher
On Indian Trails with Daniel Boone—Meadowcroft		*Crowell*
Peachtree Island—Lawrence		*Harcourt*
Pierre Pidgeon—Kingman		*Houghton*
Pollywiggle's Progress—Bronson		*Macmillan*
Who Goes There?—Lathrop		*Macmillan*
World of Pooh—Milne		*Dutton*

FIFTH GRADE

Adventures of Pinocchio—Collodi		*Macmillan*
Æsop's Fables, ill. by Artzybasheff		*Viking*
Alice's Adventures in Wonderland—Carroll		*Macmillan*
At the Back of the North Wind—Macdonald		*Macmillan*
Away Goes Sally—Coatsworth		*Macmillan*
Bastable Children—		*Coward*
The Borrowers—Norton		*Harcourt*
Complete Nonsense Book—Lear		*Dodd*
Emil and the Detectives—Kastner		*Doubleday*
English Fairy Tales, ed. Jacobs		*Putnam*
Freddy, the Detective—Brooks		*Knopf*
Heidi—Spyri		*Lippincott*
Honk: The Moose—Stong		*Dodd*
Hundred Dresses—Estes		*Harcourt*
Just So Stories—Kipling		*Doubleday*
Little House in the Big Woods—Wilder		*Harper*
Little House on the Prairie—Wilder		*Harper*
Matchlock Gun—Edmonds		*Dodd*
Miss Hickory—Bailey		*Viking*
Misty of Chincoteague—Henry		*Rand*
The Moffats—Estes		*Harcourt*
Mr. Popper's Penguins—Atwater		*Little*
Paddle-to-the-Sea—Holling		*Houghton*
Peter and Wendy—Barrie		*Scribner*
Peterkin Papers—Hale		*Houghton*
Rabbit Hill—Lawson		*Viking*
The Rescuers—Sharp		*Little*
Ride on the Wind—Dalgliesh		*Scribner*
The Saturdays—Enright		*Rinehart*
Story of Dr. Dolittle—Lofting		*Lippincott*
Tales from Grimm—tr., Gag		*Coward*
Thee, Hannah!—de Angeli		*Doubleday*
This Boy Cody—Wilson		*Watts*
Wheel on the School—DeJong		*Harper*
Wind in the Willows—Grahame		*Scribner*
Wonder Clock—Pyle		*Harper*

SIXTH GRADE

Adventures of Odysseus and the Tale of Troy—Colum		*Macmillan*
Arabian Nights—ed. Lang		*Longmans*
Call It Courage—Sperry		*Macmillan*
Cartier Sails the St. Lawrence—Averill		*Harper*
Daughter of the Mountains—Rankin		*Viking*
Fairy Tales—Andersen		*Macmillan*
Gift of the Forest—Singh and Lownsbery		*McKay*
Golden Nature Guides—Zim		*Simon (Golden Press)*
Good Master—Seredy		*Viking*
Hans Brinker—Dodge		*Scribner*
Henry Reed—Robertson		*Viking*
Hitty: Her First 100 Years—Field		*Macmillan*
Homer Price—McCloskey		*Viking*
Jack Tales—Chase		*Houghton*
Judy's Journey—Lenski		*Lippincott*
Jungle Book—Kipling		*Doubleday*
Little Men—Alcott		*Grosset*
Little Vic—Gates		*Viking*
Little Women—Alcott		*Little*
Mary Poppins—Travers		*Harcourt*
Miracles on Maple Hill—Sorenson		*Harcourt*
Onion John—Krumgold		*Crowell*
Rebecca of Sunnybrook Farm—Wiggin		*Houghton*
Seabird—Holling		*Houghton*
Secret Garden—Burnett		*Lippincott*
Secret of the Andes—Clark		*Viking*
Shepherd's Nosegay—Fillmore		*Harcourt*
Strawberry Girl—Lenski		*Lippincott*
Swiss Family Robinson—Wyss		*Macmillan*
Thunder of the Gods—Hosford		*Holt*
Wonderful Adventures of Nils—Lagerlof		*Doubleday*

SEVENTH GRADE

Adventures of Tom Sawyer—Clemens		*Harper*
The Ark—Benary-Isbert		*Harcourt*
Blue Willow—Gates		*Viking*
Caddie Woodlawn—Brink		*Macmillan*
Children of the Sea—Bronson		*Harcourt*
Favorite Uncle Remus—Harris		*Houghton*
Golden Fleece—Colum		*Macmillan*
Junior Book of Insects—Teale		*Dutton*
Kidnapped—Stevenson		*Scribner*
King of the Wind—Henry		*Rand*
Lassie Come-home—Knight		*Winston*
Li Lun, Lad of Courage—Treffinger		*Abingdon*
Pecos Bill—Bowman		*Whitman*
Robinson Crusoe—Defoe		*Lippincott*
Roller Skates—Sawyer		*Viking*
Shuttered Windows—Means		*Houghton*

Title	Author	Publisher
Silver Chief, Dog of the North—O'Brien		*Winston*
Stars for Sam—Reed		*Harcourt*
Story of King Arthur and His Knights—Pyle		*Scribner*
Swallows and Amazons—Ransome		*Lippincott*
Treasure Island—Stevenson		*Scribner*
Vulpes, the Red Fox—George		*Dutton*
Yankee Doodle's Cousins—Malcolmson		*Houghton*

EIGHTH GRADE

Adventures of Huckleberry Finn—Clemens		*Harper*
Bambi—Salten		*Grosset*
Banner in the Sky—Ullman		*Lippincott*
Benjamin Franklin—Judson		*Follett*
Boys' Sherlock Holmes—Doyle		*Harper*
Boy with a Pack—Meader		*Harcourt*
Casting Away of Mrs. Lecks and Mrs. Aleshine—Stockton		*Meredith*
Chucklebait—Scoggins, ed.		*Knopf*
Daniel Boone—Daugherty		*Viking*
Fair Adventure—Gray		*Viking*
Harriet Tubman—Petry		*Crowell*
Lee of Virginia—Freeman		*Scribner*
Man Who Was Don Quixote—Busoni		*Prentice*
Mary McLeod Bethune—Sterne		*Knopf*
Men of Iron—Pyle		*Harper*
Merry Adventures of Robin Hood—Pyle		*Scribner*
Otto of the Silver Hand—Pyle		*Scribner*
Paul Bunyan—Shephard		*Harcourt*
Perilous Road—Steele		*Harcourt*
Peter the Great—Baker		*Vanguard*
Smoky—James		*Scribner*
Stories from Shakespeare—Chute		*World*
That Lively Man, Ben Franklin—Eaton		*Morrow*
These Happy Golden Years—Wilder		*Harper*
Trumpeter of Krakow—Kelly		*Macmillan*
Yankee Thunder—Shapiro		*Messner*
Young Fu—Lewis		*Winston*

NINTH GRADE

Abe Lincoln Grows Up—Sandburg		*Harcourt*
Adam of the Road—Gray		*Viking*
All-American—Tunis		*Harcourt*
Bewitching Betsy Bonaparte—Desmond		*Dodd*
Big Doc's Girl—Medearis		*Lippincott*
Big Red—Knelgaard		*Holiday*
Boy on Horseback—Steffens		*Harcourt*
David Copperfield—Dickens		*Macmillan*
David Livingstone, Foe of Darkness—Eaton		*Morrow*
Florence Nightingale—Nolan		*Messner*
George Washington's World—Foster		*Scribner*
Great Heritage—Shippen		*Viking*
Invincible Louisa—Meigs		*Little*
Jim Davis—Masefield		*Macmillan*
Johnny Tremain—Forbes		*Houghton*
Lone Journey—Eaton		*Harcourt*
Lost World—White		*Random*
Martha, Daughter of Virginia—Vance		*Dutton*
My Friend Flicka—O'Hara		*Lippincott*
Narcissa Whitman—Eaton		*Harcourt*
National Velvet—Bagnold		*Morrow*
On Safari—Waldeck		*Viking*
Vast Horizons—Lucas		*Viking*
Watch for a Tall White Sail—Bell		*Morrow*
Witch of Blackbird Pond—Speare		*Houghton*

TENTH GRADE

Book of Americans—Benét		*Rinehart*
Clouded Star—Parrish		*Harper*
Dark Frigate—Hawes		*Little*
Devil and Daniel Webster—Benét		*Rinehart*
Drums—Boyd		*Scribner*
Dune Boy—Teale		*Dodd*
Here I Stay—Coatsworth		*Coward*
Here is Alaska—Stefansson		*Scribner*
Ivanhoe—Scott		*Dodd*
Jane Eyre—Bronte		*Dodd*
Lad: A Dog—Terhune		*Dutton*
Lantern in Her Hand—Aldrich		*Meredith*
Les Miserables—Hugo		*Dodd*
Let the Hurricane Roar—Lane		*McKay*
Little Britches—Moody		*Norton*
Madame Curie—Sheean		*Garden City*
Moby Dick—Melville		*Winston*
Mrs. Mike—Freeman		*Coward*
My Antonia—Cather		*Houghton*
Old Man and the Sea—Hemingway		*Scribner*
Old Yeller—Gipson		*Harper*
Penn—Gray		*Viking*
Pride and Prejudice—Austen		*Dodd*
Red Chair Waits—Huggins		*Westminster*
The Sea Around Us—Carson		*Oxford*
Seventeenth Summer—Daly		*Dodd*
The Virginian—Wister		*Macmillan*
Wind, Sand and Stars—Saint Exupery		*Harcourt*
Winter Wheat—Walker		*Harcourt*
The Yearling—Rawlings		*Scribner*

Dr. Seuss—Theodor Seuss Geisel—cartoonist and author. The world of Dr. Seuss's books is alive with fantastic animals. Filled with humor, these children's stories have become popular with generation after generation—in books, on films, and on television. Here, partly revealed behind its creator, is the "Cat in the Hat," a favorite character. Other titles by Dr. Seuss include *And to Think That I Saw It on Mulberry Street, The 500 Hats of Bartholomew Cubbins, The Seven Lady Godivas, The King's Stilts, Horton Hatches the Egg, McElligot's Pool, If I Ran the Zoo, Scrambled Eggs Super!, On Beyond Zebra, If I Ran the Circus,* and *Green Eggs and Ham.* (*Courtesy Random House and Dr. Seuss*)

Abraham Lincoln—by Lynd Ward, author and illustrator of many books, including *The Biggest Bear,* a winner of the Caldecott Medal, and *God's Man,* a novel without words, the first woodcut story to appear in the U.S. This drawing appears in *Abraham Lincoln* by May McNeer, who also has written numerous books, including *Mark Twain, Armed With Courage,* and *My Friend Mac.* *(Photo courtesy Houghton Mifflin Company)*

SYNONYMS AND ANTONYMS

SYNONYMS are words that are grouped together because they express the same general idea, though they usually differ considerably from one another in shades of meaning. Examples are *custom, habit,* and *fashion.* Antonyms are words of opposite meaning, as *sharp, dull; long, short; weak, strong.*

The richness of a language in variety, flexibility, and precision may be measured by the number of synonyms it offers to writers and speakers. As English has grown from its Anglo-Saxon beginnings it has adopted and naturalized many words of foreign origin, which have become synonyms for native words. For example, the Latin word *transgression* is found side by side with the Anglo-Saxon word *sin.* Though seemingly equivalent in meaning, these words do not have the same effect upon the listener. Each word has its particular significance and its special overtones.

To cite a more elaborate example, a typical collection of synonyms can be gathered around the basic concept, *at the same time.* The group would include, among others, such words as *contemporary, synchronous, concurrent,* and *simultaneous.* From the standpoint of etymology, the first two words are exact equivalents. The Latin prefix *con* means with or together, the root form *temp* means time, and the word ends in a standard adjective suffix. A direct parallel for these word elements is seen in the Greek prefix *syn,* meaning with or together, the root form *chron,* meaning time, and the adjective suffix which ends the word. Having in mind only their literal meanings, one might suggest that either word would serve, and that two words for the same idea are superfluous. But these two words, although seemingly equivalent, are not interchangeable, and synonyms rarely are. We speak of contemporary writers, artists and other persons, but of synchronous motors. Taxes levied by the state and the nation may be concurrent, that is, running in parallel over the same period, and thus constituting double taxation. Explosions occurring at the same instant are said to be simultaneous. Each of the foregoing synonyms, though meaning essentially *at the same time,* has its own shade of meaning and its own set of associations.

Words with Overlapping Meanings. Occasionally situations arise in which a group of synonyms taken together can be more useful than any single example that might be chosen. To cite an illustration from everyday experience, take the phrasing of a statute requiring the purchase of a dog license, which begins with the words, "Any one who owns, keeps, or harbors . . . a dog," etc. Now here are three synonyms with related but different meanings. If you have a dog on your premises you may have acquired him by gift or purchase (owns), you may simply have him in your custody (keeps), or perhaps the dog has adopted you, as friendly mongrels have a way of doing, and you merely tolerate his presence as a permanent guest (harbors). The statute covers all three possibilities, and you must buy a license on the basis of whichever synonym applies to your particular case.

Choosing the Right Synonym. In contrast with the special case of legal phrasing, the usual problem is to choose just one word out of a group. A writer draws the various synonyms together and makes his selection, rejecting the unwanted words and keeping the one that fills the immediate need. For beginners, the process of selection may involve the consulting of reference sources and perhaps the compiling of written lists of words to be considered. More experienced writers and speakers can review the synonyms mentally, and of course very rapidly. Discrimination between words that goes on in this way is really an essential part of the thinking process. This fact is recognized in the popular short definition of thinking, "To think is to compare."

Precision is arrived at through a careful weighing of various possibilities.

In any given instance, the specific synonym chosen is valued, not only because it is precise in meaning, but also because it makes for economy of expression. The specific term is really the equivalent of a single base word plus a descriptive or explanatory phrase.

Antonyms. If an effect of clarification or emphasis can best be obtained by contrast, the choice will be among antonyms, or opposites, for the base word. To convey the positive idea of *able* by denying the contrary, it may be said of an applicant for a position that he is never *slipshod* or *slovenly* in his work. Such adjectives belong in a list of negative expressions contrasted with the base word, that is, in a list of antonyms. There are many cases in which the distinction between antonyms is more important than between the positive words from which they are derived or to which they correspond. For example, the positive forms *relevant* and *pertinent* are about as close to being interchangeable as any words that can be found. Their corresponding antonyms, *irrelevant* and *impertinent* show marked differences in shades of meaning.

Sometimes the antonyms are verbs, but more often they are adjectives or adverbs. In the latter case, a word of caution should be given. Laziness in word selection is encouraged by the fact that antonyms for adjectives and adverbs can be easily and cheaply formed. By prefixing *anti, dis, non, un,* or some other syllable of the kind, an antonym can be provided for almost any adjective or adverb. However, because the principle of variety is so important in every form of writing or speaking, only limited use should be made of the "prefix" type of antonym. To cite an extreme example, one would certainly not express the opposite of rich (wealthy) by coining a crude derivative word like *un-rich.* Instead, there could be a choice from a whole collection of words like *poor, indigent, penniless, poverty-stricken,* and other specific antonyms, ranging all the way to the possible but unlikely word *impecunious.*

How to Use. To get the greatest amount of value from the following dictionary of synonyms and antonyms, it is necessary that one should understand clearly the use of the index or key. Let us suppose, for example, that you are writing a letter in which you have used the word *trouble.* You may desire to repeat the idea of this word and yet you do not wish to employ the same word again. Perhaps you do not recall another word which will exactly express the thought you wish to convey.

Turn to the index or key beginning on page 1072 and find the word *trouble* with a reference to page 1070. You will also find *trouble* occurring twice followed by words in italics: once by *affliction* with a reference to page 1039 and once by *difficulty* with a reference to page 1051. First turn to page 1070 and there you will find *disturb* and *molest* as variant words. It may be that one of these will suit your purpose. But, if both words fail, next refer to page 1039 and look for *affliction.* Under it, in addition to *trouble,* are the words *distress, grief,* and *sorrow.* If up to this point you are not satisfied, you may turn to page 1051 and look for *difficulty.* Under it you find the additional synonyms *obstacle, impediment,* and *embarrassment,* with an explanation of how each word is used. Among all these synonyms, you are almost certain to find a word to suit the need. But, in the very rare case that you do not find the precise word, you will have received many suggestions which will enable you to convey the desired idea in a different manner; for, by glancing at the antonyms under the three paragraphs you have read, you will have seen *soothe, quiet, compose, caress, happiness, comfort, satisfaction, cheer, aid, help, assistance, relief,* and *encouragement.*

Abandon, desert, forsake, relinquish, surrender. The general idea which these words have in common is that of giving up or leaving something or someone. Specific applications are represented by the various synonyms used in the following phrases: abandon a ship or an infant or a project, or abandon oneself to despair; desert one's wife, regiment or husband; forsake one's companions or a cause to which one has been committed; relinquish a hold or a possession; surrender one's freedom, a fortress or an army (implying formal capitulation). In everyday language, one may surrender an insurance policy.
Antonyms.—Keep, maintain, protect, support.

Abbreviate, abridge, condense. The common purpose of reducing or shortening indicated by these words is accomplished in three ways. Abbreviate deals in fragments, as when it makes initials stand for words. Abridge selects and combines portions of a book or article, but the parts retained are essentially the same as in the original version. Condense keeps the main ideas of the original but rephrases them in more concise language, as in the writing of a summary or abstract.
Antonyms.—Amplify, expand, elaborate.

Abeyance, postponement, suspense. Actions proposed or undertaken are kept waiting, that is, held in abeyance, pending some future development. Postponement implies delay with a more definite intention to resume action. Suspense keeps the idea of interruption and adds to it an element of uncertainty, or perhaps anxiety.
Antonyms.—Continuation, resumption.

Abhor, detest, loathe. These terms all denote aversion. We may abhor an act that is shocking to our moral sense; we may detest a person who is guilty of such an act. Using a still stronger word, we may loathe something that offends our taste, whether it be unacceptable conduct or unappealing food. In the case of both physical and moral repugnance, loathe carries with it a strong sense of physical revulsion.
Antonyms.—Admire, esteem, approve, desire.

Ability, capacity, faculty, talent, genius. In general, ability means the power of doing, without specifying the quality or degree. It may be either physical or mental. Capacity, when applied to persons, is mental only. It looks to the future and estimates the possibility of knowledge that can be absorbed and the productive brain activity that can be expected. The analogy here is obviously with such physical and mechanical concepts as the cubic contents of a container and the productive output of a machine. Ability may be the result of health, strength, and training. Faculty is a gift of nature to the species; for example, a sense of sight or hearing. Talent is a special aptitude born in the individual; genius is a phenomenal endowment by nature which enables an individual to do the highest form of creative work.
Antonyms.—Inability, incompetence, stupidity.

Abject, servile, slavish, cringing. Different kinds and degrees of self-depreciation are indicated by these words. An abject apology shows extreme humility as well as regret. A servile attitude toward one's superiors and a slavish devotion to routine tasks might lead to a cringing acceptance of degradation which is the antithesis of dignity.
Antonyms.—Proud, independent, overbearing.

Abolish, abrogate, repeal, revoke, annul. The word abolish, usually suggesting an act of power or authority, conveys the idea of putting a total end to a thing and is applied particularly to those things which have been long in existence and are firmly established. Laws are either repealed, as by a vote of public assemblies, or abrogated, as by the enactment of new laws which supersede the old ones. Revoking is an act of individual authority—edicts are revoked—while annulling is an act of discretion following sober second thought or a change in conditions. For example, contracts are annulled.
Antonyms.—Establish, institute, confirm.

Absolute, despotic, arbitrary, tyrannical. Absolute power is independent of and superior to all other power: an absolute monarch is uncontrolled, either by men or by things. Despotic power is power exercised as by a master or lord. Despotic power is, therefore, as complete as absolute power but carries the added idea that the ruler has the right to treat his subjects according to his will or pleasure. With arbitrariness are associated the ideas of caprice and selfishness. With tyranny are associated the ideas of oppression and injustice. In modern use, both arbitrariness and tyranny are associated with despotism.
Antonyms.—Limited, constitutional, accountable, mild, lenient, just.

Accomplish, effect, execute, achieve. To accomplish an object signifies more than simply to effect a purpose, both as to the thing aimed at and the means employed in bringing it about. Extraordinary means are requisite for accomplishing and ordinary means, for effecting. To accomplish is properly said of that which a person sets before himself; but to effect, execute, and achieve do not relate to the views of a person acting, but to the thing brought about. What is executed is complicated in its nature, as to execute a design or project; what is achieved is of greater and worthier conception, as to achieve success in a profession.
Antonyms.—Fail, come short, default, give up.

Accuse, charge, impeach, arraign. The idea of asserting something to the prejudice of another is common to these terms. But accuse is said of acts; charge, of moral qualities constituting the character. We accuse a person of murder; we charge him with dishonesty. High officials are impeached; criminals are arraigned.
Antonyms.—Clear, discharge, exonerate, acquit.

Act, do, make. We always act when we do, but we do not always do when we act. Act is applied to either persons or things, as a spring or a lock acts; do applies in this sense to persons only. Act is generally used intransitively, as to act well or ill in this or that manner; do is usually transitive, as to do right or wrong, to do one's duty. To make is to bring a thing to being or form as to make a pen.

Act, work, operate. A machine works, but each of its parts is said to act; so beer works, and bread works. Sometimes act as well as work is taken in the sense of exerting a power upon other bodies and producing changes, as the sun acts on the plants. Operate is applied to matters of a general nature in science or morals, as a measure operates, or words may operate on the mind, or reasons may operate on the understanding.

Action, gesture, gesticulation, posture, attitude. All these terms are applied to the state of the body; the first three indicate a state of motion, the last two a state of rest. Action respects the movements of the body in general; gesture is an action indicative of some particular state of mind; gesticulation is the act of making gestures. Raising the arm is an action; bowing is a gesture. Posture and attitude both imply a mode of placing the body, but the posture is either natural or assumed; the attitude is always assumed or represented. We assume a sitting posture or an attitude of prayer.

Active, diligent, industrious, assiduous, laborious, busy, officious. We are active if we are only ready to exert our powers, whether to any end or not; we are diligent when we are active for some specific end; we are industrious when no time is left unemployed in some serious pursuit; we are assiduous if we do not leave a thing until it is finished; we are laborious when the bodily or mental powers are regularly employed in some hard labor. Busy implies continuous occupation. Officious implies being busy without discretion, especially about other people's affairs.
Antonyms.—Inert, indolent, lazy, trifling, idle, shiftless.

Actual, real, positive, true. What is actual has proof of its existence within itself, and may be exposed to the eye; what is real may be satisfactorily proved to exist; what is positive precludes the necessity of a proof. That is true which is genuine, in accord with evident facts or susceptible of proof.
Antonyms.—Supposititious, imaginary, doubtful, uncertain, false, artificial.

Actuate, impel, induce. One is actuated by motives, impelled by passions, and induced by reason or inclination. Whatever actuates is the result of reflection—it is a steady and fixed principle. Whatever impels is momentary and vehement, and often precludes reflection. Whatever induces is not vehement, though often momentary.
Antonyms.—Restrain, inhibit, impede, check.

Acute, keen, shrewd. An acute angle or a pointed instrument is sharp; the cutting edge of a knife is keen. In the mental sense, an argument may be acute, a reproach keen, and a judgment shrewd. Pain is sometimes acute, remorse keen, and suspicion shrewd.
Antonyms.—Dull, obtuse, stupid.

Adhere, stick, cohere. In the physical sense, an object attaches itself to another by adhering when their surfaces come in contact. If the objects are alike in composition they cohere, or unite on equal terms, and become unified. An object with a mucilaginous property or an animal with strong tentacles may stick to a surface. Figuratively, a man may adhere to a political party.
Antonyms.—Detach, disengage, separate.

Adjacent, abutting, juxtaposed. Two houses standing side by side are described as adjacent. If the lots which they occupy come together at a boundary line, the properties are said to be abutting. Objects or works of art placed side by side for comparison are said to be juxtaposed.
Antonyms.—Distant, separated, disjoined.

Admit, allow, permit, suffer, tolerate. Admit in this sense is used mostly of ideas and propositions, usually used with *of*. Allow is of more general application, frequently implying only a tacit refraining from refusal. We admit that which concerns ourselves; we allow that which is for the convenience of others. What is suffered may be burden-.some to the sufferer, if not morally wrong; what is tolerated is contrary to one's desires, and is suffered only because it cannot be prevented. Permit implies a positive grant of privilege.
Antonyms.—Forbid, refuse, withstand, prevent, deny.

Admit, receive. Persons are admitted to the tables, and into the familiarity or confidence of others; they are hospitably received by those who wish to be their entertainers. We admit willingly or reluctantly; we receive politely or rudely.
Antonyms.—Shut out, forbid, exclude.

Adoration, worship, reverence. Adoration is the service of the heart toward a superior being, in which we acknowledge our dependence and obedience by petition and thanksgiving; worship consists in the outward form of showing reverence to some supposed superior being. Reverence differs from adoration inasmuch as it has a mixture of awe, arising from consciousness of weakness and dependence, or of obligations for favors received.
Antonyms.—Contempt, dishonor, impiety, sacrilege.

Advance, proceed. Advance implies movement forward; proceed, movement from one point to another, also resumption of movement after a pause.
Antonyms.—Recede, retire, withdraw.

Advantage, benefit, utility. Advantage refers to external circumstances of profit, honor, and convenience; benefit, to the consequences of actions and events; utility respects the good which can be drawn from the use of any object. A large house or a particular situation may have its advantages; suitable exercise is attended with benefit; the utility of motor cars consists in their supplying means of rapid travel.
Antonyms.—Disadvantage, futility, worthlessness.

Adverse, antagonistic, hostile. Adverse criticism is definitely unfavorable; an antagonistic attitude combines opposition with personal dislike. Nations at odds or individuals who are parties to a public conflict are said to be hostile toward one another.
Antonyms.—Auspicious, favorable, friendly.

Advice, counsel. Advice is given by physicians and other professional persons who have special knowledge in some technical field. We receive counsel in matters of conduct from wiser, and usually older, persons who have a superior acquaintance with moral principles. It is assumed that both advice and counsel are sought, and not proffered gratuitously.

Affect, assume, pretend. To affect is to use forced efforts to appear to have that which one has not; to assume is to appropriate to oneself that which one has no right to have. One affects to have fine feelings, and assumes great importance. We pretend by making a false declaration. One affects indifference to praise and pretends to have wealth.

Affect, influence, sway, concern. Things affect our well being when they cause some change in our outward circumstances; they concern us when they come closer and touch our personal interests. We are influenced by the example of someone and swayed, that is, impelled to action, by his persuasive arguments.

Affectionate, kind, fond. We are affectionate toward relatives and close friends. Kindness includes a wider circle of recipients and is expressed in considerate action. Fondness implies a tender, indulgent, and often unreasoning liking. Originally, kind suggested natural affection, as in Hamlet's words, "A little more than kin, and less than kind."
Antonyms.—Indifferent, unfriendly, inconsiderate.

Affirm, assert. Affirm is said of facts; assert, of opinions. We affirm what we know; we assert what we believe.
Antonyms.—Deny, retract, repudiate.

Affliction, distress, trouble, grief, sorrow. Affliction is applied both to severe misfortune and to the deep sorrow of heart that may come from it. Grief is keen, poignant sorrow springing from a definite cause. Distress implies severe, painful trouble from physical or mental causes. Trouble may imply merely confusion of mind, or it may signify deep-seated disturbance.
Antonyms.—Happiness, comfort, satisfaction, cheer.

Affront, insult, outrage. To affront is to show reproach in the presence of others—it piques and mortifies; to insult is to attack with insolence—it irritates and provokes; to outrage is to combine all that is offensive, to add insult to injury.
Antonyms.—Honor, gratify, please, benefit.

Afraid, fearful, timorous, timid. Afraid is the most general of these words, implying either a slight or a high degree of fear. Fearful is a stronger word than afraid: one may be fearful of defeat and yet not afraid in a discreditable sense. Timid and timorous imply constitutional liability to fear, even of slight matters.
Antonyms.—Brave, bold, fearless, intrepid.

Agree, accede, consent, comply, acquiesce. Agree is the general term, meaning to fall in with. We accede by becoming a party to a thing; those who accede are on equal terms. We consent to a thing by authorizing it, we comply with a thing by allowing it; those who consent or comply are not on equal terms with those in whose favor the consent is given or compliance made. Consenting is an act of the will, complying an act of good nature or weakness. To acquiesce is quietly to accept; it is a passive act, dictated by prudence or duty.
Antonyms.—Disagree, dissent, refuse, decline, oppose.

Agreeable, pleasant, pleasing. Agreeable expresses a less vivid feeling than pleasant; pleasing marks a sentiment less vivid and distinct than either. A pleasing countenance denotes tranquillity and contentment; a pleasant countenance bespeaks happiness.
Antonyms.—Disagreeable, repulsive, irritating.

Aim, aspire. We aim at a certain proposed point by endeavoring to gain it; we aspire after that which we think ourselves entitled to, and which we flatter ourselves with gaining. Many men aim at riches and honor; it is the lot of but few to aspire to high office.

Aim, object, end. The aim is that which the person has in his own mind. The object lies in the thing. The end is that which follows or terminates any course or proceeding. It is the aim of the Christian to live peaceably; it is a mark of dullness or folly to act without an object; it is sophistry to suppose that the end will justify the means.

Air, manner, look, carriage, gait. Air lies in the whole person; manner refers to movement or action or expressive gesture. A man has the air of a common person; it discovers itself in all his manners. An air is noble or simple—it marks an elevation or simplicity of character; a manner is rude, rustic, or awkward, for want of culture, good society, and good example. We assume an air, and affect a manner. Look refers especially to the facial expression—an honest look. Carriage applies to the manner of holding or carrying the body. Gait is the manner of walking.

Alarm, terror, fright, consternation. Alarm is felt at the sudden approach of danger or signs of danger. Terror may arise from any appearance or event suggesting great harm or catastrophe; alarm prompts us to defense, and terror disarms us. Fright is a less vivid emotion than either, as it arises from the simple appearance or thought of danger. Consternation springs from the view of some very serious evil, and commonly affects many. Alarm affects the feelings, terror the understanding, and fright the senses; consternation seizes the whole mind and benumbs the faculties.
Antonyms.—Calmness, repose, confidence, self-command.

Alertness, alacrity. Alertness signifies an attitude and manner of keen readiness, promising prompt, spirited action. Alacrity implies a quick, willing response to impulse or demand from without.
Antonyms.—Inertness, sluggishness, languidness, apathy.

Allay, soothe, appease, mitigate, assuage. All these terms indicate a lessening of something painful. In a physical sense an irritating pain is allayed; a wounded part is soothed by affording ease and comfort. Extreme heat or thirst is allayed; extreme hunger is appeased; a punishment or suffering is mitigated. Temper or enthusiasm that is fervid and vehement is allayed; one soothes a mind that is distressed or irritated; one appeases what is tumultuous and boisterous; one mitigates the pains of others; one assuages grief or afflictions.
Antonyms.—Arouse, irritate, intensify, kindle, excite.

Alleviate, relieve. A pain is alleviated by making it less burdensome; a necessity is relieved by supplying what is wanted. Alleviate refers to internal feelings only; relieve, to either internal feelings or external circumstances. That alleviates which affords ease and comfort; that relieves which removes the pain.
Antonyms.—Aggravate, intensify.

Alliance, league, coalition, confederacy. An alliance, as of families or states, is a joining of resources for mutual benefit. A league is a more formal organization designed to serve the common interests of its members. A coalition is usually a temporary union, as of states or political parties, to meet a particular situation. A confederation is a union of hitherto separate political units in which their previously distinct powers are delegated to a central authority.

Allot, appoint, destine. Allot is used only for things; appoint and destine for persons or things. A space of ground is allotted for cultivation; a person is appointed as steward or governor; a youth is destined for a particular profession. Allot and appoint imply immediate purposes; destine implies remote purposes.

Allow, grant, bestow. That is allowed which may be expected, if not directly required; that is granted which is desired, or directly asked for; that is bestowed which is wanted as a matter of necessity. A grant comprehends in it something more important than an allowance, and passes between persons in a higher station; what is bestowed is of less value than either. A boy is allowed money for expenses; a king grants pensions to his officers; relief is bestowed on the indigent.
Antonyms.—Refuse, withhold, disallow.

Allowance, wages, fee, salary, stipend, pay, honorarium. An allowance is a gratuitous payment of money —it ceases at the pleasure of the donor. Compensation for labor, particularly common labor, is called wages. A fee is a specific sum paid for professional services. Salary (in ancient times "salt money") means fixed compensation paid regularly over a long interval. Stipend, less permanent than salary, is a fixed income for teachers, clergymen, and others over a stated period. Pay is a general word covering reward for services, but it is used specifically for compensation received by soldiers. A small fee, as for lectures, may be made to seem more impressive by being called an "honorarium."

Allude, refer, hint, suggest. To allude is not so direct as to refer, but it is more clear and positive than either hint or suggest. We allude to a circumstance by introducing something collaterally allied to it; we refer to an event by expressly introducing it into our discourse; we hint at a person's intentions by insinuating what may possibly happen; we suggest an idea by some expressions relative to it.

Alone, solitary, lonely, desolate. Alone states the fact of being by oneself. Solitary is a more subjective word which carries a suggestion of isolation. One can be lonely in a crowd, that is, without acquaintances or understanding friends. Desolate, when applied to a person, indicates grief resulting from irreparable loss. A desolate landscape shows ruin and destruction.
Antonyms.—Accompanied, attended.

Ambiguous, equivocal, cryptic. Ambiguous language is obscure, capable of being interpreted in more than one way. Equivocal speech, or "double-talk," is intentionally left open to different and perhaps opposite meanings. The Frenchman's equivocal compliment on a young woman, "Her beauty is equaled only by her intelligence," could be taken in either of two ways. A cryptic remark is vague or puzzling because of its brevity.
Antonyms.—Clear, definite, plain.

Amend, correct, mend, repair. Amend and correct are applied to works of the understanding. Amend signifies to remove faults or defects, generally by adding or taking away or altering, as in amending a law. To correct is to remove faults by revising or reshaping, as to correct copy. Mend, often used in reference to mechanical or textile objects, means to replace or restore a defective part. Repair indicates a more thorough restoration of the object to its former state. One mends a garment and repairs a bridge.
Antonyms.—Damage, impair, destroy.

Amicable, friendly. Amicable implies a negative sentiment, a freedom from discordance; friendly implies a positive feeling of regard, the absence of indifference. We make an amicable settlement and have a friendly understanding.
Antonyms.—Ill-tempered, unfriendly, hostile.

Amuse, divert, entertain. Amusement kills time pleasantly during idle moments. Anything diverting pleases by drawing our attention away from work or serious thinking. Entertainment is planned to give active enjoyment. It makes a calculated appeal to the senses, the understanding, or the critical faculties—sometimes to all three.
Antonyms.—Bore, annoy, tire.

Anger, resentment, wrath, ire, indignation, rage, fury. Anger is a sudden sentiment of displeasure; resentment is a continued anger; wrath is a heightened sentiment of anger, which is poetically expressed by the word ire. Indignation is a sentiment awakened by the unworthy and atrocious conduct of others; as it is exempt from personality it is not irreconcilable with the temper of a Christian. Rage is a vehement show of anger, and fury is an excess of rage.
Antonyms.—Patience, acquiescence, gentleness, self-control, serenity, calmness.

Animate, enliven, exhilarate. To be animated is to have, or seem to have, the faculties of a living creature, as in the alertness of a person or the movements of an animated cartoon. Enliven refers to a raising of one's spirits and a quickening of one's impulses. Exhilarate (note the related word "hilarity") carries the idea of merrymaking as a phase of extreme liveliness.
Antonyms.—Deaden, dull, depress.

Announce, proclaim, publish. We announce an event that is expected and just at hand; we proclaim an event that requires to be known by all the parties interested; we publish what is supposed likely to interest all who know it.
Antonyms.—Conceal, suppress, withhold.

Answer, reply, rejoinder, response. An answer is given to a question; a reply is made to an assertion or a letter; a rejoinder is made to a reply; a response is made in accordance with the words of another. We answer either for the purpose of affirmation, information, or contradiction; we always reply, or rejoin, in order to explain or confute; responses are made by way of assent or confirmation.
Antonyms.—Question, query, interrogation.

Answerable, responsible, accountable, amenable. Answerable and responsible convey the idea of a formal pledge or an implied obligation for the performance of some act or the fulfillment of some engagement. A person is accountable to his employer for the manner in which he has conducted business entrusted to him. Amenable refers more to one's disposition. A person is said to be amenable to reason, that is, open or susceptible.
Antonyms.—Independent, arbitrary, irresponsible.

Apologize, defend, justify, exculpate, excuse, plead. We apologize for an error by acknowledging ourselves guilty of it; we defend ourselves against a charge by proving its fallacy; we justify our conduct against any imputation by proving that it was blameless; we exculpate ourselves from all blame by proving that we took no part in the transaction. Excuse and plead are not grounded on any idea of innocence; a plea is frequently an idle or unfounded excuse, a frivolous attempt to lessen displeasure; we excuse ourselves for a neglect by alleging indisposition.

Apparent, visible, clear, plain, obvious, evident. That which is simply an object of sight is visible; that which presents itself to our view in any form, real or otherwise, is apparent. The stars themselves are visible to us; but their size is apparent. What is clear is to be seen in all its parts and in its proper colors; what is plain is seen by understanding; what is obvious presents itself readily to the mind of everyone; what is evident is unquestionably seen, and leaves no hesitation in the mind.
Antonyms.—Obscure, hidden, latent, doubtful.

Applause, acclamation, ovation. Applause is approval expressed by clapping of hands; acclamation calls for shouts and cries. Ovation represents still greater enthusiasm, in which an audience rises spontaneously and engages in prolonged cheering.
Antonyms.—Censure, hissing, booing.

Appoint, order, prescribe, ordain. To appoint is the act of either an equal or a superior; we appoint a meeting with any one at a given time and place; a king appoints his ministers. To order is the act of one invested with a partial authority; a master gives his orders to his servant. To prescribe is the act of one who is superior by virtue of his knowledge; a physician prescribes for his patient. To ordain is an act emanating from the highest authority; kings and councils ordain, but their ordinances must be conformable to what is ordained by the Divine Being.
Antonyms.—Forbid, prohibit, veto.

Apprehend, conceive, suppose, imagine. To apprehend is to become aware of something; to conceive is to create in the mind something that does not exist. One supposes, or conjectures, something that may be doubtful but seems probable and reasonable. One may imagine the most unreal creatures, objects or situations as well as realizable ones.

Approach, access, admittance. Approach signifies the coming near or toward an object, and consequently it is an unfinished act, but access and admittance are finished acts; access is coming to, or as close to, an object as is needful; admittance is coming into any place, or into the presence or society of any person.
Antonyms.—Recession, withdrawal, exclusion.

Approach, approximate. Approach means to draw or come nearer to, although the distance at any time may still be great. Approximate implies a very close approach—as close as conditions will permit.
Antonyms.—Avoid, miss, shun, evade.

Argue, evince, prove. To argue is to establish an indication amounting to probability; to evince denotes an indication so clear as to remove doubt; to prove marks an evidence so positive as to produce conviction.

Argument, reason, proof. An argument serves for defense; a reason, for justification; a proof, for conviction. Arguments are adduced in support of a hypothesis or a proposition; reasons are assigned in matters of belief and practice; proofs are collected to determine truth as to alleged facts.

Arise, rise, mount, ascend, climb, scale. Arise is used only in the sense of simply getting up, but rise is employed to express a continued motion upward. A person arises from his seat or his bed; a bird rises in the air; a person mounts a hill, and ascends a mountain. To climb is to rise step by step by clinging to a certain body; to scale is to rise as by an escalade, or species of ladder, employed in mounting the walls of fortified towns. Trees and mountains are climbed; walls are scaled.
Antonyms.—Settle, fall, descend, sink.

Arrogant, proud, presumptuous. The arrogant man seeks to impose his assumed superiority on others; he shows an aggressive self-assertion. A proud person is more quietly conscious of his own importance; he may stand aloof from people he considers inferior. A person is presumptuous who acts rashly in asserting claims for favors or attention; he lacks sufficient judgment for proper self-restraint.
Antonyms.—Modest, meek, humble, self-effacing.

Artist, artisan, mechanic, craftsman. The artist ranks higher than the artisan,—the former requires intellectual refinement, the latter nothing but to know the common, mechanical practice of an art or trade. The sculptor is an artist; the sign-painter is an artisan. Mechanic and artisan are used interchangeably. Craftsman implies technical skill and judgment; it is used of both artist and artisan. The mechanic is one whose work involves manual skill, or skill in the use of tools.

Ask, inquire, question, interrogate. We perform all these actions in order to get information; but we ask, for general purposes of convenience; we inquire from motives of curiosity; we question and interrogate from motives of discretion. Indifferent people ask of each other whatever they wish to know; learners inquire the reasons of things that are new to them; masters question their servants, or parents their children, when they wish to ascertain the real state of any case; magistrates interrogate criminals when they are brought before them.
Antonyms.—Answer, reply, respond.

Assemble, muster, collect. To assemble is to bring together by a call or invitation or, as machine parts, by mechanical process according to a plan; to muster is to bring together by an act of authority, or by a particular effort, into one point of view at one time, and from one quarter; to collect is to bring together at different times, and from different quarters.
Antonyms.—Adjourn, dismiss, scatter, disperse.

Assent, consent, approbation, concurrence. Assent concerns matters of judgment; consent, matters of conduct. We assent to what we admit to be true; we consent to what we allow to be done. Approbation is a species of assent, concurrence, of consent. To approve is not merely to assent to a thing as right, but to determine upon it positively; concurrence is properly the consent of many. Assent is given by equals or inferiors; consent, by superiors; approbation, by equals or superiors; concurrence, by equals.
Antonyms.—Dissent, refusal, disapproval, disagreement.

Association, society, company, partnership, corporation. Associations and societies are organizations for the promotion of literary, scientific, religious, or benevolent objects. Companies and partnerships are formed for business purposes. The partnership is the least stable of business organizations. A corporation is a more permanent organization, chartered by the state. It persists irrespective of the particular individuals owning or controlling its stock.

Asylum, refuge, shelter, retreat. Asylum is sought by a person who has no home; refuge by one who is apprehensive of danger; shelter by anyone who seeks protection from the elements. Retreat implies a wish for separation from the cares of life, an opportunity for meditation.

Attack, assail, assault. To attack is to make an approach in order to do some violence to the person; to assail or assault is to make a sudden and vehement attack. One assails by means of missiles, reproaches, or invective; one assaults by direct personal violence.
Antonyms.—Resist, withstand, sustain, defend.

Attempt, endeavor, effort, essay. An attempt is the act of setting about a thing with a view of effecting it; an endeavor is a continued attempt. An effort is to an attempt as a means is to an end; it is the act of calling forth those powers which are required in an attempt.

Attend, hear, listen. To attend is to have the mind intently engaged on what we hear; to listen is to strive to hear. People attend when they are addressed. Listen implies a lesser degree of heed than attend. To hear is merely to be conscious of sound.

Attentive, careful. We are attentive in order to understand and to improve; we are careful to avoid mistakes. Attentive refers to mental attitude; careful relates to mechanical action: we listen attentively; we read or write carefully.
Antonyms.—Inattentive, careless, heedless, indifferent.

Attract, allure, invite, engage. That is attractive which draws the attention toward itself; that is alluring which awakens desire; that is inviting which offers persuasion; that is engaging which takes possession of the mind.
Antonyms.—Repel, deter, estrange, disgust.

Austere, rigid, severe, rigorous, stern. The austere man is severe with himself; the rigid man binds himself to a rule. The manners of a man are austere when he refuses to take part in any social enjoyments. Severe is used with reference to conduct,—a man is severe in the restraints he imposes and the punishments he inflicts. Rigorous implies harshness. Sternness is a species of severity more in manner than in direct action; a commander may issue his commands sternly, or a despot may issue his stern decrees.
Antonyms.—Affable, gentle, indulgent, mild.

Avaricious, miserly, parsimonious, niggardly. An avaricious man shows his love of money in his ordinary dealings; but the miser lives for his money and suffers every privation rather than part with it. The avaricious man indulges his passion for money by parsimony, that is, by excessive personal saving, or by niggardly ways in his dealings with others.
Antonyms.—Unselfish, generous, lavish, free.

Awaken, excite, provoke, rouse, stir up. We awaken by a simple effort; we excite by repeated efforts or forcible means; we provoke by words, looks, or actions. The tender feelings are awakened; affections, or the passions in general, are excited; the angry passions are commonly provoked. We are roused from an extraordinary state by extraordinary means; we are stirred up from an ordinary to an extraordinary state.
Antonyms.—Calm, quiet, pacify, restrain.

Awe, reverence, dread. Awe and reverence both denote a strong sentiment of respect, mingled to some extent with fear. Of the two, awe is the stronger, being inspired, for example, by the great forces of nature and the contemplation of their Divine origin. Reverence, also a religious sentiment, is associated with quieter and less disturbed feelings. Dread is a haunting fear of what is to come.
Antonyms.—Irreverence, familiarity, assurance.

Awkward, clumsy, bungling. Awkward applies to outward deportment; clumsy, to the shape and make of the object. A person has an awkward gait; he is clumsy in his whole person. Bungling applies to the result of awkwardness and clumsiness in performing work.
Antonyms.—Adroit, dexterous, neat, skillful.

Axiom, maxim, aphorism, saying, adage, proverb, byword. The axiom is a truth of the first value, a self-evident proposition which is the basis of other truths. A maxim is a truth of the first moral importance for all practical purposes; an aphorism is a truth set apart for its pointedness and excellence. Adage and proverb are common sayings, the former among the ancients, the latter among the moderns. The byword is a casual saying, originating in some local circumstance, frequently used in contempt.

Babble, chatter, chat, prattle. Babbling denotes rapidity of speech, which renders it unintelligible; chatter is an imitation of the noise of speech properly applied to magpies or parrots, and figuratively to a corresponding mode of speech in human beings. The winter's fireside invites neighbors to assemble and chat away many an hour which might otherwise hang heavy on hand, or be spent less inoffensively. The prattling of babes has an interest for every feeling mind, but for parents it is one of the highest enjoyments.

Band, company, crew, gang. All these terms denote a small association for a particular object. A band is an association in which men are bound together by some strong obligation, whether taken in a good or a bad sense, as a band of soldiers, a band of robbers; a company marks an association for convenience, without any particular obligation, as a company of travelers, a company of strolling players. A crew marks an association collected by some external power, or by coincidence of plan and motive; in the former case it is used for a ship's crew, in the latter and bad sense of the word it is employed for any number of evil-minded persons met together from different quarters and co-operating for some bad purpose. Gang and crew are applied to companies of workmen under one leader or on one job, or to bands brought together for boisterous or disorderly purposes. Gang is applied to groups of boys who play together under a leader.

Banishment, exile, expulsion. Banishment follows from a decree of justice; exile, either by the necessity of circumstances or by an order of authority; banishment is a disgraceful punishment inflicted by tribunals upon delinquents; exile is a disgrace incurred without dishonor; exile removes us from our country; banishment or expulsion drives us from it ignominiously.
Antonyms.—Recall, reinstatement, repatriation.

Be, become, grow. Be is positive; become is relative: a person is what he is without regard to what he was; he becomes that which he was not before. To grow is to become by a gradual process. A man may become a good man from a vicious one, in consequence of a sudden action of his mind; but he grows in wisdom and virtue by means of an increase in knowledge and experience.
Antonyms.—Die, stagnate, diminish.

Be, exist, subsist. We say of qualities, of forms, of actions, of arrangement, of movement, and of every different relation, whether real, ideal, or qualificative, that they are; we say of matter, of spirit, of body, and of substances, that they exist. Man is man, and will be man under all circumstances and changes of life; he exists under every known climate and variety of heat or cold in the atmosphere. Subsist implies generally dependence upon outside aid for existence. Cities subsist on the productivity of the country.

Bear, yield. Both words mean to produce: bear respects animals and plants, which bear young or fruit; yield respects plants or inanimate objects, which yield increase.

Beat, defeat, overpower, rout, overthrow. An army is beaten in important engagements; it is defeated and may be routed in partial attacks; it is overpowered by numbers, and overthrown in set engagements. These words are similarly applied to the fortunes of persons.
Antonyms.—Aid, help, succor, befriend.

Beautiful, fine, fair, handsome, pretty. Beautiful implies a certain perfection of form, correctness of proportion, unity of impression, harmony of details. Applied to human beings it connotes some spiritual excellence. Fine implies perfection of finish and design, both interior and exterior. Fair conveys the idea of external smoothness and freedom from blemish. Handsome implies superficial excellence, of proportion in particular. Pretty is confined to objects of refinement, especially those small and dainty, as a pretty fancy, a pretty child.
Antonyms.—Plain, uncouth, coarse, deformed, ugly.

Becoming, comely, graceful. Becoming applies to the decorations of the person and to the deportment; comely refers to natural embellishments; graceful, to natural or artificial accomplishments. Manner is becoming; figure is comely; air, figure, or attitude is graceful.
Antonyms.—Unsuitable, awkward, homely, uncouth.

Beg, beseech, solicit, entreat, supplicate, implore, crave. To beg denotes a state of want; to beseech, entreat, and solicit, a state of urgent necessity; supplicate and implore, a state of abject distress; crave, the lowest state of physical want. One begs with importunity, beseeches with earnestness, entreats by the force of reasoning and strong representation; one solicits by virtue of one's interest, supplicates by a humble address, implores by every mark of dejection and humiliation.
Antonyms.—Command, demand, claim, extort, refuse.

Behavior, conduct. Behavior is more specific, and refers to acts, especially in the presence of or in reference to others. Conduct is more general and inclusive; it implies moral or ethical considerations governing behavior.

Belief, credit, trust, faith. Belief and credit are particular actions or sentiments; trust and faith are permanent dispositions of the mind. Things are entitled to our belief; persons are entitled to our credit; but people repose trust in others, or have faith in others. Belief is intellectual and may be quite impersonal. Faith and trust are personal and have immediate reference to conduct. Trust in God serves to dispel all anxious concern about the future.
Antonyms.—Doubt, denial, distrust, skepticism.

Benevolence, benignity, humanity, kindness, tenderness. Benevolence lies in the will; benignity, in the disposition or frame of mind. Humanity lies in the heart; kindness and tenderness, in the affections. Benevolence indicates a general good will to all mankind; benignity particular goodness or kindness of disposition. Humanity is a general tone of feeling; kindness and tenderness are particular modes of feeling.
Antonyms.—Malevolence, malignity, churlishness, harshness, brutality, ill will.

Bereave, deprive, strip. To bereave expresses more than deprive, but less than strip, which denotes a total and violent bereavement. One is bereaved of children, deprived of pleasures, and stripped of property. We are bereaved of that on which we set most value; the act of bereaving does violence to our inclination. We are deprived of the ordinary comforts and conveniences of life,—they cease to be ours. We are stripped of the things which we most want; we are thereby rendered, as it were, naked.
Antonyms.—Restore, supply, comfort, endow.

Blame, censure, condemn, reprove. To blame is simply to ascribe a fault to; to censure is to express disapprobation. The thing more than the person is blamed; the person more than the thing is censured. A person may be blamed for his good nature and censured for his negligence. That which is condemned is of a more serious nature, and it produces a stronger and more unfavorable expression of displeasure or disapprobation than that which is blamed; reprove is even more personal than censure. A reproof passes from one individual to another, or to a certain number of individuals.
Antonyms.—Praise, approve, applaud, countenance.

Blemish, stain, spot, speck, flaw, defect, fault. Whatever detracts from the seemliness of appearance is a blemish. In works of art the slightest dimness of color or want of proportion is a blemish. A stain or spot sufficiently characterizes itself as that which is superfluous and out of its place; a speck is a small spot; a flaw is a defect that prevents the substance from holding together properly, as a flaw in glazing on china, in a steel rail, in an argument. A blemish tarnishes; a stain spoils; a spot, speck, or flaw disfigures. Defect consists in the want of some specific essential in an object; fault conveys the idea not only of something wrong, but also of its relation to the author.

Blot out, expunge, erase, efface, cancel, obliterate. Letters are blotted out, so that they cannot be seen again; they are expunged, so as to signify that they cannot stand for anything; they are erased, so that the space may be used for other writing. Efface does not designate either the manner or the object; inscriptions on stone may be effaced, that is, rubbed off so as not to be visible. Cancel is principally confined to written or printed characters; they are canceled by striking through them with the pen. Letters are obliterated which are in any way made illegible.
Antonyms.—Write, record, confirm, perpetuate.

Bold, fearless, intrepid, undaunted. Boldness is a positive characteristic of the spirit; fearlessness is a negative state of the mind, that is, simply an absence of fear. A person may be bold through fearlessness, but he may be fearless without being bold; he may be fearless where there is no apprehension of danger or no cause for apprehension, but he is bold only when he is conscious or apprehensive of danger, and prepared to encounter it. A man is intrepid who has no fear where the most fearless might tremble; he is undaunted whose spirit is unabated by that which would make the stoutest heart yield.
Antonyms.—Afraid, fearful, cowardly, timid, fainthearted.

Booty, spoil, prey. Booty and spoil are used as military terms in attacks on any enemy; prey, in cases of particular violence. The soldier gets his booty; the combatant, his spoils; the carnivorous animal, his prey. Booty implies something of personal service to the captor; spoils, whatever serves to designate his triumph; prey includes whatever gratifies the appetite and is to be consumed.

Bound, limit, confine, circumscribe, restrict, enclose. Bound applies to the natural or political divisions of the earth: countries are bounded by mountains and seas. Limit applies to any artificial boundary,—landmarks in fields serve to show the limits of one man's ground. To confine is to shut within limits,—in this manner we confine cattle in a yard by means of walls. To circumscribe is literally to write or draw around, as a circle around a square or limits about our desires. To restrict is to exercise a strong degree of control: a person is restricted in his movements by the narrowness of a room; laws often restrict privileges. To enclose is to bound or limit on all sides, as a garden is enclosed.

Boundless, unbounded, unlimited, infinite. Space is boundless so long as no bounds to it have been discovered; desires are often unbounded which ought always to be bounded; power is sometimes unlimited which would be better limited. That is infinite which is without bound or end, as: the power of God; the series of figures in the decimal expression of the fraction ⅓.
Antonyms.—Confined, restricted, circumscribed, finite.

Bravery, courage, valor, gallantry. Bravery lies in the blood; courage lies in the mind. The latter depends on the reason, the former on the physical temperament. The first is a species of instinct; the second is a virtue. A man is brave in proportion as he is without thought of danger; he has courage in proportion as he reasons or reflects. Valor is a higher quality than either bravery or courage—it combines the fire of bravery with the determination and firmness of courage. Gallantry is extraordinary bravery combined with high-spirited manner.
Antonyms.—Fear, cowardice, dismay, effeminacy.

Breach, break, gap, chasm. A breach and a gap are the consequence of a violent removal which destroys the connection; a break and a chasm may arise from the absence of that which would form a connection. A breach in a wall is made by means of cannon; gaps in fences are commonly the effect of some violent effort to pass through; a break is made in a page of printing by leaving off in the middle of a line; a chasm is left when an earthquake causes a gaping fissure.

Break, bruise, squeeze, pound, crush. Break always implies the separation of the component parts of a body; bruise denotes simply to injure without separation of parts. Hard, brittle substances, as glass, are broken; soft, pulpy substances, as flesh or fruits, are bruised. Squeeze is used for soft substances or for gentle compression. To pound is properly to crush in a mortar, so as to produce a separation of parts. To crush is the most violent and destructive of all operations, which amounts to destroying the structure of a body.

Break, burst, crack, split. To break does not specify any particular manner or form of action,—what is broken may be broken in two or more pieces, broken short or lengthwise, and the like; to burst is to break suddenly and with violence, frequently also with noise. To crack and to split are modes of breaking lengthwise: the former in application to hard or brittle objects, as clay, or the things made of clay; the latter in application to wood or substances like coal or rock that have seams or lines of cleavage.
Antonyms.—Join, attach, mend, unite, weld.

Breeze, gale, blast, gust, storm, tempest, hurricane. A breeze is gentle; a gale is brisk, but steady: we have breezes on a calm summer's day; the mariner has favorable gales, which keep the sails on the stretch. A blast is impetuous. The blare of a trumpet, the breath of bellows, are blasts. A gust is sudden and vehement; storm, tempest, and hurricane include other particulars besides wind. A storm throws the whole atmosphere into commotion; it is a war of the elements, in which wind, rain, hail, and the like conspire to disturb the heavens. Tempest is a violent storm. Hurricane is a species of storm which exceeds all the rest in violence, duration, and area.
Antonyms.—Lull, calm, stillness, fair weather.

Brightness, luster, splendor, brilliancy. Brightness and luster are applied properly to natural lights; splendor and brilliancy have been more commonly applied to that which is artificial or unusual. There is always more or less brightness in the sun or moon; there is an occasional luster in all the heavenly bodies when they shine in their unclouded brightness; there is splendor in the eruptions of flame from a volcano or from an immense conflagration; there is brilliancy in a collection of diamonds.
Antonyms.—Dullness, dimness, shadow, obscurity, gloom.

Bring, take, fetch, carry. Bring commonly means to transport something from a point more or less distant to the place occupied by the speaker. Take implies removal of something from the speaker's position to another location. To fetch is to go and get something, then bring it to the speaker's position. Carry simply means to transport or take along something without regard to destination or point of origin.

Bulky, massive. Whatever is bulky is large, unwieldy, often awkward to handle, whether heavy or not; what is massive is compact in substance and combines solidity with large size.
Antonyms.—Compact, small, slight, slender.

Burial, interment. We bury in order to conceal. Interment is accompanied with religious ceremonies. Burial is confined to no object or place; interment refers properly to burial in the earth.

Business, occupation, employment, avocation, vocation. Business occupies all a person's thoughts as well as his time and powers. Occupation and employment occupy only his time and strength; the first is mostly regular, the object of our choice; the second is casual, depending on the will of another. Vocation is applied to one's regular work; avocation, to the occupation with which one occupies his time outside the regular routine of work.
Antonyms.—Recreation, amusement, relaxation, pastime.

Business, trade, profession, art. Buying or selling of merchandise is inseparable from trade; but the exercise of one's knowledge and experience for purposes of gain constitutes a business. A profession implies scholarship and skill in application of principles. An art involves skill in the practice of accepted rules and methods of work to produce practical results with definite materials. We speak of the profession of letters, but of the art of writing. Trade is used also of mechanical occupation, as the carpenter's trade.

Bustle, tumult, uproar. Bustle has most of hurry in it; tumult, most of disorder and confusion; uproar, most of noise: the hurried movements of one, or many, cause a bustle; the disorderly struggles of many constitute a tumult. The loud elevation of many opposing voices produces an uproar; uproar is the consequence either of general anger or of mirth.
Antonyms.—Calm, quietness, order, tranquillity.

Calamity, disaster, misfortune, mischance, mishap. A calamity is a great disaster or misfortune; a misfortune is a great mischance or mishap. Whatever is attended with destruction is a calamity; whatever occasions mischief to the person, or defeats or interrupts plans, is a disaster; whatever is accompanied with a loss of property or the deprivation of health is a misfortune; whatever diminishes the beauty or utility of objects is a mischance or a mishap.
Antonyms.—Success, blessing, boon, achievement.

Calculate, reckon, compute, count. To calculate denotes any numerical operation in general, but is particularly applicable to the abstract science of figures. The astronomer calculates motions of the heavenly bodies; the mathematician makes arithmetical calculations. To reckon is to enumerate and set down things in detail. Reckoning is applicable to the ordinary business of life: tradesmen keep their accounts by reckoning; children learn to reckon by various simple processes. Calculation is therefore the science; reckoning, the practical art of enumerating. To compute is to come at the result by calculation. We count one by one,—we count the minutes.

Calendar, almanac. A calendar is a system of marking the divisions of time or, specifically, a chart showing the days, weeks, and months of the year. To this information an almanac adds such data as the changes of the moon, the times of sunset and sunrise, the signs of the zodiac, and so on.

Call, cry, exclaim. Call is used on all ordinary occasions in order to draw a person to a spot, or for any other purpose, when one wishes to be heard. To cry is to call loudly on particular occasions. A call draws attention; a cry awakens alarm. To exclaim implies the expression of some particular feeling.
Antonyms.—Hush, listen, be silent.

Call, invite, summon. In the act of calling, any sounds may be used; we may call by simply raising the voice. Inviting may be a direct or indirect act; we may invite by looks or signs as well as by words, by writing as well as by speaking. To summon is an act of authority, as to summon witnesses.
Antonyms.—Dismiss, disperse, send away.

Calm, placid, serene, composed, collected. Physically, calm means free from violent action; mentally, free from disturbing emotion or passion. Placid implies ease and contentment of mind. We speak also of a calm sea and a placid lake. Serene implies clearness and composure of mind. A sky is serene when free from clouds and clear. The mind is composed when excitement has been allayed; it is collected when all its powers are at command.
Antonyms.—Agitated, stormy, violent, passionate.

Candor, openness, sincerity. Candor obliges us to acknowledge even that which may make against ourselves; it is disinterested. Openness impels us to utter whatever passes in the mind—it is unguarded. Sincerity assures that our words and actions are true to our thoughts and feelings —it is positive.
Antonyms.—Cunning, deceit, craft, duplicity.

Captious, cross, peevish, petulant, fretful. Captious marks a readiness to find fault; cross indicates a readiness to offend or go contrary to the wishes of others; peevish expresses a strong degree of crossness; fretful, a complaining impatience. Captiousness is the consequence of ill will or pique; crossness, of ill humor; peevishness and fretfulness, of a painful irritability. Petulance is the result either of a hasty temper or a sudden irritability.
Antonyms.—Considerate, good-natured, appreciative, thoughtful, patient.

Capture, seizure, prize. A capture is made by force of arms; a seizure is made by direct and personal force. Prize relates only to the thing taken and its value to the captor.

Care, charge, management. Care includes both charge and management; but, in the strict sense, it comprehends personal labor. Charge involves responsibility; management includes regulation and order. A gardener has the care of a garden; a nurse has charge of children; a steward has the management of a farm.

Care, solicitude, anxiety. Care is the most indefinite of the three; it may be accompanied with pain or not, according to the nature of the object or the intensity of the application. Care may be exercised with or without feeling; solicitude has desire, mixed with fear; anxiety has distress for the present, mixed with fear for the future.
Antonyms.—Satisfaction, indifference, unconcern, trust.

Careful, provident. Careful, or full of care, that is, having care, is the general term. To be provident is to be careful in preventing straits and difficulties. The term careful is applied for the most part to present matters, but provident only to that which is future. One is careful of his money, but provident toward a time of need.
Antonyms.—Careless, neglectful, reckless, heedless, spendthrift.

Carnage, slaughter, massacre, butchery. Carnage pictures heaped corpses; slaughter, the wholesale taking of lives as in battle. Butchery is the brutal word for killing men and women as cattle are killed. Massacre implies the killing or butchery of many defenseless men, women, and children.

Case, cause. The case is matter of fact; the cause is matter of question. A case involves circumstances and consequences; a cause involves reasons and arguments. A case is something to be learned; a cause is something to be decided.

Cause, occasion, create. What is caused seems to follow naturally. What is occasioned follows incidentally, or what occasions may be incidental, but necessary. What is created receives its existence arbitrarily. A wound causes pain; accidents occasion delay; busybodies create mischief.

Cause, reason, motive. A cause is that which brings about any event, act, or fact. "The Creator is the first cause of all things." A reason is an explanation devised by the mind for a fact, an event, or an action. We give reasons also for our beliefs, that is, the grounds for them. A motive is an influence that determines choice or action. Effects follow causes, conclusions follow reasons, and actions spring from motives.

Cautious, wary, circumspect. We must be cautious on all occasions where there is danger, but we must be wary where there is great danger. A tradesman must be cautious in his dealings with all men, but he must be wary when he has to deal with designing men. Circumspect implies attention to all the conditions and probable consequences of action. A man must be circumspect when he transacts business of particular importance and delicacy.
Antonyms.—Rash, impulsive, audacious, precipitate.

Cease, discontinue. Cease is used for either particular actions or general habits; discontinue, for general habits. A restless, spoiled child never ceases crying until it has obtained what it wants; it is a mark of impatience not to cease lamenting when one is in pain. A sensitive person discontinues his visits when they are found not to be agreeable.
Antonyms.—Continue, persist, persevere.

Celebrate, commemorate. Everything is celebrated which is distinguished by any marks of attention, without regard to the time of the event, whether present or past; nothing is commemorated but what has already passed in point of time.
Antonyms.—Forget, ignore, disregard.

Celestial, heavenly. Celestial is applied mostly in the natural sense of the heavens; heavenly is employed more commonly in a spiritual sense. Hence, we speak of the celestial globe as distinguished from the terrestrial, and of the celestial bodies. But we speak of the heavenly habitation, of heavenly joys or bliss, of heavenly spirits and the like.
Antonyms.—Terrestrial, earthly, mundane.

Censure, carp, cavil. To censure respects positive errors; to carp and cavil have regard to what is trivial or imaginary. The former is employed for errors in persons; the latter, for supposed defects in things. Carping and caviling are resorted to only to indulge ill nature or self-conceit; party politicians carp at the measures of administration; infidels cavil at the evidences of Christianity, because they are determined to disbelieve.
Antonyms.—Praise, approve, sanction, uphold.

Cessation, stop, rest, intermission. Cessation refers to the course of things; whatever does not go on has ceased; things cease of themselves. Stop implies an abrupt cessation, as if due to an outside force. Rest is cessation from labor or exertion—whatever does not move or exert itself is at rest. Intermission is cessation only for a time or at certain intervals. That which ceases or stops is supposed to be at an end; rest or intermission supposes a renewal.
Antonyms.—Stir, work, persistence, continuance.

Chance, fortune, fate. Chance applies to all things personal or otherwise; fortune and fate are applied most often to that which is personal. Chance neither forms, orders, nor designs; neither knowledge nor intention is attributed to it; its events are uncertain and variable. Fortune forms plans and designs, but without choice; we attribute to it an intention without discernment; it is said to be blind. Fate forms plans and chains of causes; intention, knowledge, and power are attributed to it—its views are fixed; its results are decisive.
Antonyms.—Choice, free will, purpose.

Change, exchange, barter, substitute. To change in respect to persons is to take one for another, without regard to whether they are alike or different,—as a king changes his ministers, or any person may change his servants. To exchange is to take one person in return for another who is in like condition, as prisoners are exchanged in time of war. In respect to things, to change is to take anything new or fresh, whether alike or different; clothes may be changed. To exchange is to take one thing for another, that is, either of the same kind or equivalent in value, as to exchange one commodity for another. To change may often be the result of caprice, but to exchange is always an act of either discretion or necessity. To barter is to give any commodity for other commodities. To substitute is to put one person or thing in the place of another for the purpose of doing any service or filling any office, as to substitute one for another in military service, or to substitute wood for steel in building.
Antonyms.—Keep, hold, retain.

Change, alteration, variation, vicissitude. Change refers to any difference in persons, things or circumstances. Alteration is a minor change purposely made in details without affecting the identity of the whole, as in the alteration of a garment. Vicissitudes are the unpredictable but inevitable ups and downs of life for which every one is supposed to be prepared.
Antonyms.—Uniformity, consistency, monotony.

Character, reputation. Character lies in the man; it is the mark of what he is. A person's reputation depends upon others; it is what they think of him.

Chasten, chastise. Chasten is used only of spiritual correction, as the chastening of men by God. Chastise implies physical pain or punishment with a corrective purpose.

Cheat, defraud, trick. One cheats by direct and gross falsehood or artifice; one defrauds by a settled plan or contrivance; one tricks by a sudden invention.

Check, chide, reprimand, reprove, rebuke. A person is checked that he may not continue to do what is offensive; he is chidden for what he has done, that he may not repeat it. People are checked by actions and looks, as well as by words; they are chidden by words only. A person may chide or reprimand in anger; he reproves and rebukes with coolness. Omissions or mistakes occasion or require a reprimand; irregularities of conduct give rise to reproof; and improprieties of behavior demand rebuke.
Antonyms.—Allow, indulge, abet, approve, laud.

Cheer, encourage, comfort. To encourage is to give heart or courage for action, to strengthen resolution. To cheer and to comfort apply to the spirits or feelings; but to cheer expresses more than to comfort, the former signifying to produce a lively sentiment, the latter to lessen or remove a painful one. We are cheered in the moments of despondence, whether from real or imaginary causes; we are comforted in the hour of distress; we are encouraged in times of timidity and fear.
Antonyms.—Sadden, grieve, hurt, dishearten.

Chief, principal, main. Chief respects order and rank; principal has regard to importance and respectability; main, to degree or quantity. We speak of a chief clerk, of a commander in chief, of the chief person in a city, but of the principal people in a city, of the principal circumstances in a narrative, and of the main object.
Antonyms.—Subordinate, minor, inferior, attendant.

Choose, select, pick. Choose implies an act of judgment in which a decision is made in favor of one or more out of a number of things. Select emphasizes the exercise of taste in reaching a similar decision. Picking is usually done more hastily and somewhat at random.
Antonyms.—Reject, cull.

Circumstance, situation. Circumstance is to situation as a part is to a whole: many circumstances constitute a situation; a situation is an aggregate of circumstances. A person is said to be in circumstances of affluence who has an abundance of everything essential to his comfort; he is in an easy situation when nothing exists to create uneasiness.

Circumstantial, particular, minute. A circumstantial account contains all the leading events; a particular account includes many smaller details; a minute treatment of the subject goes beyond this and includes every incident and movement, however trivial. Circumstantial evidence consists of ascertained facts objectively discovered as against personal testimony.
Antonyms.—General, cursory, indefinite.

Cite, quote. We quote exact words or the substance of a passage. We cite an author or a passage in his work by giving the exact location or reference, as line and page, so that the words may be found readily.

Civil, polite, obliging. Polite expresses more than civil; it is possible to be civil without being polite. Politeness seeks the opportunity to please: it prevents the necessity of asking by anticipating the wishes; it is full of delicate attentions, and is an active benevolence in the minor concerns of life. Civil applies to words or manner as well as to the action; obliging, to the action only. Civil and obliging both imply a desire to do a kindness.
Antonyms.—Rude, discourteous, ill-mannered, churlish.

Clandestine, secret. To do a thing clandestinely is to elude observation; to do a thing secretly is to do it without the knowledge of anyone. What is clandestine is forbidden, which is not necessarily the case with what is secret.
Antonyms.—Authorized, public, open.

Clasp, hug, embrace. To clasp is to enclose another in one's arms. To hug is to press tightly to the bosom, whether it is done by a person or a bear. The more refined term embrace means to enfold in the arms in token of friendship or affection. It implies mutuality of sentiment between the persons concerned.

Classify, arrange. The general qualities and attributes of things are to be considered in classifying; their fitness to stand by each other must be considered in arranging. Classification serves the purposes of either public policy or science; arranging is a matter of convenience to the individual himself.
Antonyms.—Mix, disorder, jumble, confuse, scatter.

Clean, cleanly, pure. Clean expresses a freedom from dirt or soil; cleanly, the disposition or habit of being clean. Pure is used in a moral sense, as a pure heart; it is used also to mean free from other substances, as a solution is chemically pure.
Antonyms.—Soiled, dirty, foul, filthy.

Clearly, distinctly. That is seen clearly of which one has an unobstructed view. Distinctly, a stronger word, conveys the idea of things seen so clearly that they are distinguished from other objects. The same use of these terms applies to hearing and the other senses.
Antonyms.—Dimly, faintly, vaguely.

Clearness, lucidity, brightness, vividness. A mere freedom from stain or dullness constitutes clearness; a shining clearness, as of crystal, constitutes lucidity; brightness supposes a certain strength of light; vividness, a freshness combined with strength, and with a degree of brilliancy.
Antonyms.—Dimness, dullness, cloudiness, darkness.

Clearness, perspicuity. Clearness springs from right distinguishing of the ideas discussed. Perspicuity is a quality of the style in which thought is expressed. The argument is clear; the language, perspicuous.
Antonyms.—Obscurity, indefiniteness, ambiguity, vagueness.

Clever, skillful, expert, dexterous. Cleverness is mental power employed in the ordinary concerns of life—a person is clever in business. Skill implies both mental and physical ability, especially in mechanical operations and in science: a physician, a lawyer, or an artist is skillful; one may have a skill in divination or a skill in painting. Expertness and dexterity require more physical than mental power exerted in minor arts and amusements—one is expert at throwing quoits, dexterous in the management of horses.
Antonyms.—Awkward, bungling, stupid, slow.

Close, conclude, finish. We may close anything, as a discourse or a meeting, at any point by simply ceasing to have any more to do with it; but we conclude in a definite and positive manner. To conclude is to bring to an end by determination; to finish is to bring to an end by completion. What is settled by arrangement and deliberation is properly concluded; what is begun and ended on a certain plan is said to be finished.
Antonyms.—Begin, open, start, commence, initiate.

Close, near. Close is more definite than near; houses which are almost joined stand close to each other; men stand close when they touch each other. Objects are near which are within sight; persons are near each other when they can converse together.
Antonyms.—Distant, far, remote, removed.

Coarse, rough, rude. In the physical sense, coarse refers to the composition and materials of bodies, as coarse bread, coarse meat, coarse cloth; rough applies to the surface of bodies, as rough wood and rough skin; rude respects the make or fashion of things,—as a rude bark, a rude utensil. The application of these words to manners and conduct follows their physical sense. A person's language may be coarse, his appearance rough, and his manner rude.
Antonyms.—Fine, refined, smooth, pleasant, suave, polished, civil, polite.

Cogent, forcible, strong. Cogency applies to reasons individually considered; force and strength, to modes of reasoning or expression. Cogent reasons impel to decisive conduct; strong conviction is produced by forcible reasoning conveyed in strong language.
Antonyms.—Feeble, ineffectual, unconvincing, weak.

Colleague, partner, associate. Colleague is used properly of people associated in high office, as in court or in legislature. It is used popularly by debaters associated on teams. Associate is a more general term. Used officially, it implies subordination, as an associate professor. Partner is used popularly of men associated for business and sharing common risks, especially in some hazardous undertaking.
Antonyms.—Opponent, rival, foe, adversary, competitor.

Combat, oppose. A person's views or attitudes are combated; his interests or his measures are opposed.
Antonyms.—Advocate, aid, promote, support.

Come, arrive. To come specifies neither time nor manner; to arrive is employed with regard to some particular period or circumstances. Guests arrive; trains arrive; what is to come is uncertain.
Antonyms.—Go, leave, depart, set out, take leave.

Comfort, pleasure, happiness. Comfort implies a freedom of the whole person from annoyance or pain, a positive feeling of contentment. Pleasure lies in a vivid and intense experience and is fleeting in its nature. Happiness is an abiding state of agreeable feeling.
Antonyms.—Uneasiness, pain, heartache, sorrow.

Command, direction, order, injunction, precept. A command is an exercise of power or authority; it is imperative and must be obeyed. Direction contains the idea of instruction; order, that of authority. Directions should be followed; orders, obeyed. A superior issues commands. Injunction imposes a duty by virtue of the authority which enjoins. A precept lays down or teaches such duties as already exist.

Antonyms.—Consent, leave, license, permission.

Commission, authorize, empower. We commission in matters where our own will and convenience are concerned; we authorize in matters where our personal authority is requisite; we empower in matters where the authority of the law is required.

Antonyms.—Refuse, prohibit, forbid, disallow, enjoin.

Commodious, convenient. Commodious is most often applied to that which contributes to the bodily ease and comfort; convenient, to whatever suits the purposes of men in their various transactions.

Antonyms.—Narrow, restraining, ill-contrived, awkward.

Commonly, generally, frequently, usually. What is commonly done is an action common to all; what is generally done is the action of the greatest part; what is frequently done is either the action of many, or an action many times repeated by the same person; what is usually done is done regularly by one or many.

Antonyms.—Rarely, occasionally, sometimes, seldom.

Communicate, impart. A thing may be communicated directly or indirectly, and to any number of persons, as to communicate intelligence by signal or otherwise. Impart is a direct action that passes between individuals, as to impart instruction.

Compatible, consistent. Compatibility has a reference principally to plans and measures; consistency, to character, conduct, and station. Everything which does not interrupt its prosecution is compatible with a plan; everything by which it is neither degraded nor elevated is consistent with a person's station.

Antonyms.—Discordant, incongruous, contradictory, inharmonious.

Compel, force, oblige, necessitate. To compel denotes moral rather than physical force; but to force is properly applied to the use of physical force or a violent degree of moral force. A man may be compelled to walk if he has no means of riding; he may be forced to go at the will of another. Oblige expresses only an indirect influence, which may be resisted or yielded to at discretion. We are compelled to do that which is repugnant to our will and our feelings. That which one is obliged to do may have the assent of the judgment, if not of the will. We are necessitated by circumstances, or by anything which puts it out of our power to do otherwise.

Antonyms.—Induce, persuade, invite, tempt, lead.

Compensation, amends, satisfaction, recompense, remuneration, reward. Compensation, whether in money or otherwise, means a return for service given. Amends attempts to repair damage done to someone's interests or feelings. It is voluntarily offered. A person who has a grievance may expect or demand, and possibly receive, satisfaction. Recompense, literally a paying back, carries the idea of reciprocal return, evening the score of favors done. Remuneration means the discharge of an obligation by payment of money. Reward is a token of appreciation, usually a generous one, that is given voluntarily.

Competent, fitted, qualified. Competent especially regards the mental endowments and attainments; fitted, the disposition and character; qualified, the artificial acquirements or natural qualities.

Antonyms.—Unprepared, unsuitable, ill-adapted.

Complain, lament. Complaint implies dissatisfaction; lamentation, grief. Complaint is expressed verbally; lamentation, either by words or signs. Complaint is made of personal grievances; lamentation may be made on account of others as well as of ourselves. We complain of our ill health, of our inconveniences, or of troublesome circumstances; we lament our inability to serve another.

Antonyms.—Rejoice, welcome, hail, approve.

Complaint, accusation. A complaint is usually made in matters that personally affect the complainant; an accusation is made of matters in general, but especially those of a moral nature. A complaint is made for the sake of obtaining redress; an accusation is made for the sake of ascertaining a fact or for the sake of bringing to punishment.

Antonyms.—Defense, justification, exoneration, acquittal.

Complete, finish, terminate. The characteristic idea of completing is that of making a thing altogether what it ought to be; that of finishing, the doing all that is intended to be done toward a thing; and that of terminating, simply putting an end to a thing.

Antonyms.—Begin, commence, initiate.

Complete, perfect, finished. That is complete which has no deficiency; that is perfect which has positive excellence; and that is finished which is at an end.

Antonyms.—Deficient, faulty, marred, unaccomplished.

Comply, conform, yield, submit. These words represent various kinds and degrees of acquiescence. One complies with requests or requirements, one conforms to customs or standards of behavior, one yields to temptation or to pressure of any sort, and one submits, usually with reluctance, to the will of another.

Antonyms.—Rebel, disobey, resist.

Compose, settle. We compose that which has been disjointed and separated, by bringing it together again; we settle that which has been disturbed and put in motion, by setting it at rest.

Antonyms.—Disturb, disarrange, confuse.

Composed, sedate. Composed implies a temporary state of mental quiet and calm, arising from mastery of the emotions. Sedate signifies a permanent habit of calm steadiness of temper.

Antonyms.—Agitated, disturbed, flighty, frolicsome.

Compound, compose. Compound applies in a physical sense only and refers especially to the mixing of substances in fixed proportions. Compose, in a physical, social, or moral sense, refers to the fact of a mixture of elements. The chemist compounds medicines carefully; society is composed of various classes. One composes music.

Antonyms.—Resolve, analyze, dissect, break up.

Comprise, comprehend, embrace, contain, include. A library comprises a variety of books; the whole is comprised within a small compass. Laws comprehend a number of cases. A discourse embraces a variety of topics. A society contains very many individuals; it includes none but those of a certain class, or it includes some of every class.

Antonyms.—Exclude, debar, except, omit.

Conceal, dissemble, disguise. To conceal is simply to abstain from making known what we wish to keep secret; to dissemble and disguise signify to conceal by assuming some false appearance. We conceal facts; we dissemble feelings; we disguise sentiments.

Antonyms.—Reveal, discover, divulge, show, unveil.

Conceal, hide, secrete. To conceal is to keep from observation; to hide is to put under cover; to secrete is to set at a distance or in unfrequented places.

Antonyms.—Show, expose, exhibit, disclose.

Conceit, fancy. Conceit applies only to internal objects; it is mental in the operation and the result; it is a species of invention. Fancy is applied to external objects, or whatever acts on the senses. Nervous people are subject to strange conceits; timid people fancy they hear sounds or see objects in the dark which awaken terror.

Antonyms.—Actuality, reality, fact.

Conceive, understand, comprehend. Conception is the simplest operation of the three: when we conceive we may have but one idea; when we understand or comprehend we have all the ideas which the subject is capable of presenting. The builder conceives plans; the scholar understands languages; the metaphysician attempts to explain many things which are not to be comprehended.

Conception, notion, idea, image. Conception is the general, scientific word for idea, the product of the mind's relating and constructive work. Notion implies more direct reference to the thing known. Idea is used popularly and vaguely for conception, fancy, and image. An image is the product of the picturing activity of the mind. We speak of the conception of immortality, of the idea of God, of a notion of proper conduct, of an image of a face.

Conciliate, reconcile. To conciliate is to get good will and affection for oneself; to reconcile is to unite the affections of two persons to each other.

Antonyms.—Disaffect, estrange, alienate.

Conclusion, inference, deduction, induction. A conclusion is a necessary consequence of certain admitted facts or statements. An inference is a probable conclusion; it may be hastily drawn from incomplete data. Induction is a process of reasoning from particular facts toward a general principle. Deduction is reasoning from a general principle, from which conclusions are drawn regarding particular facts to which the principle applies. Scientific conclusions are reached through the alternate use of induction and deduction.

Conclusive, convincing. Conclusive applies either to practical or theoretical matters; convincing, to what is theoretical only. An argument is convincing, a chain of reasoning conclusive.
Antonyms.—Uncertain, dubious, questionable, hypothetical.

Condition, station. Condition commonly refers to circumstances, education, birth, and the like; station refers rather to rank, occupation, or fixed mode of life.

Conduce, contribute. To conduce signifies to serve the full purpose; to contribute signifies only to serve a secondary purpose. Exercise conduces to health; it contributes to give vigor to the frame.
Antonyms.—Counteract, contravene, hinder, defeat.

Conduct, manage, direct. Conducting requires most wisdom and knowledge; managing, most action; direction, most authority. A lawyer conducts the cause intrusted to him; an agent manages the mercantile concerns for his employer; a superintendent directs the movements of all the subordinate agents.

Confederate, accomplice. A confederate is a partner in a plot or a secret association; an accomplice is a partner in some active violation of the laws.
Antonyms.—Rival, adversary, betrayer.

Confidence, trust. Confidence is an extraordinary trust, but trust is always ordinary unless the term be otherwise qualified. Confidence involves communication of a man's mind to another, but trust is confined to matters of action.
Antonyms.—Doubt, mistrust, suspicion, misgiving.

Confident, assured, positive, sanguine. A person is confident who has faith in his ability or in the soundness of his position. Any one who has an assured manner is, or seems to be, certain of success. One who is positive has no doubt concerning the accuracy of his information or the rightness of his position. A calm form of optimism is indicated by sanguine, which connotes good health and normal cheerfulness.
Antonyms.—Apprehensive, diffident, doubtful, vacillating.

Confirm, corroborate. Confirm is the stronger word, implying support by established facts or assured knowledge. Corroborate implies support of a statement or belief by added statements or attendant circumstances.
Antonyms.—Refute, confute, invalidate, annul, weaken.

Conformable, agreeable, suitable. Conformable is employed for matters of obligation; agreeable, for matters of choice; suitable, for matters of propriety and discretion. What is conformable accords with some prescribed form or given rule of others; what is agreeable accords with the feelings, tempers, or judgments of ourselves or others; what is suitable accords with outward circumstances.
Antonyms.—Inconsistent, ill-adapted, unwelcome, unfitted.

Confound, confuse. A person confounds one thing with another; objects become confused, or a person confuses himself. It is a common error among ignorant people to confound names, and among children to have their ideas confused on commencing a new study.
Antonyms.—Distinguish, separate, discriminate.

Confront, face. Confront implies to set face to face; face signifies to set the face toward any object. Witnesses are confronted; a person faces danger.
Antonyms.—Avoid, evade, shun, dodge.

Confusion, disorder. Confusion supposes the absence of all order; disorder, the derangement of order where it exists or is supposed to exist.
Antonyms.—Method, regularity, orderliness.

Confute, refute, disprove. Confute applies to what is argumentative; refute, to what is practical and personal; disprove, to whatever is represented or related. An argument is confuted by proving its fallacy; a charge is refuted by proving the innocence of the party charged; an assertion is disproved by proving that it is incorrect.
Antonyms.—Prove, substantiate, support, uphold, defend.

Connect, combine, unite. Things connected and combined remain distinct, but things united lose all individuality. Things the most dissimilar may be connected or

combined; things of the same kind only can be united. Houses are connected by means of a common passage; the armies of two nations are combined; two armies of the same nation are united.
Antonyms.—Separate, sever, disjoin, part.

Conqueror, victor. A conqueror is always supposed to add something to his possessions; a victor gains nothing but the superiority. Those who take possession of other men's lands by force of arms make a conquest; those who excel in any trial of skill are the victors.

Consent, permit, allow. As the act of an equal, we consent to that in which we have a common interest with others. We permit or allow what is for the accommodation of others: we allow by not opposing; we permit by a direct expression of our will. Contracts are formed by the consent of the parties who are interested. The proprietor of an estate permits his friends to sport on his grounds; he allows a passage through his premises.
Antonyms.—Refuse, forbid, prohibit, interdict.

Consequence, effect, result. A consequence follows of itself; an effect is brought about, or in other words, is produced directly by a cause. A result is the final outcome of a series of contributing causes.

Consider, reflect. To consider is employed for practical purposes; to reflect, for matters of speculation or moral improvement. Common objects call for consideration; the workings of the mind itself or objects purely spiritual occupy reflection.

Consonant, accordant, consistent. Consonant (with, to) implies such agreement as would avoid discord. Consistent (with) applies to agreement that avoids contradiction. Consonant and accordant are applied to matters of belief and sentiment; consistent, also to matters of conduct.
Antonyms.—Dissonant, discordant, incongruous, incompatible.

Constancy, stability, steadiness, firmness. Constancy involves the affections; stability, the opinions; steadiness, the action or the motives of action; firmness, the purpose or resolution.
Antonyms.—Variableness, fickleness, capriciousness.

Constitute, appoint, depute. To constitute is the act of a body or organization; to appoint and depute may be the act of either a body or an individual. The person who is deputed becomes the agent of the authority that appoints him; that is, he is a deputy.

Consult, deliberate. Consultations always require two persons at least; deliberations may be carried on either with a man's self or with others. An individual may consult with one or many; assemblies commonly deliberate.

Consummate, complete. Consummate refers to desires or plans or movements brought to fulfillment. Complete is applied in the sense of finishing according to design.
Antonyms.—Fail, fall short.

Contagious, infectious, epidemic. The first two words, very closely related in meaning, differ chiefly in their reference to the manner in which disease may be transmitted. One may contract a contagious disease by receiving germs directly from a sick person or through contact with something he has touched. In current usage infectious refers especially to communicable disease that is transmitted through agents, such as rats and mosquitoes. Contagion may pervade the atmosphere. Epidemic indicates a wide and usually rapid spread of some specific form of communicable disease.
Antonyms.—Antiseptic, hygienic, sanitary.

Contaminate, defile, pollute, taint, corrupt. Whatever is impure contaminates; what is gross and vile, in the natural sense, defiles and, in the moral sense, pollutes; what is contagious or infectious corrupts; what is corrupted may taint other things.
Antonyms.—Wash, purify, cleanse, disinfect.

Contemplate, meditate, muse. Different species of reflection are marked by these terms. We contemplate what is present or before our eyes; we meditate on what is past or absent. The heavens and all the works of the Creator are objects of contemplation; the ways of Providence are fit subjects for meditation. One muses on events or circumstances which have recently passed.

Contend, contest, dispute. To contend is simply to exert a force against a force; to contest is to struggle with an opponent for an object; to dispute, according to its original meaning, applies to opinions only and is distinguished from contend in this,—that the latter signifies to maintain one's own opinion, the former to call in question the opinion of another.
Antonyms.—Yield, give up, surrender, acknowledge.

Contentment, satisfaction. Contentment lies in ourselves; satisfaction is derived from external objects. One is contented when one wishes for no more; one is satisfied when one has obtained all one wishes. Contentment is within the reach of the poor man, to whom it is a continual feast; but satisfaction has never been procured by wealth, however enormous, or by ambition, however boundless.
Antonyms.—Desire, distress, trouble, regret, mourning.

Continual, continuous, perpetual, constant, continued. Continual implies possible intermission but also regular beginning again. Continuous admits of no pause or interruption. What is perpetual admits of no termination. There may be an end to that which is continual, and there may be intervals in that which is perpetual. Constant, like continuous, admits of no interruption, and it also admits of no change. What is continual may not always continue in the same state; but what is constant remains in the same state; what is continued ceases for a time, only to be taken up again.
Antonyms.—Changing, intermittent, desultory, broken, concluded.

Continuance, continuation, continuity, duration. Continuance describes an action that is prolonged without interruption. Continuation suggests resumption after an interval, as in the parts of a serial story. Continuity, a term frequently used with reference to radio programs, means the linking of different parts to form an unbroken sequence. Duration refers only to the extent of time through which an action is continued.
Antonyms.—Cessation, interruption, termination.

Continue, persevere, persist. We continue from habit or circumstances; we persevere from reflection and the exercise of our judgment; we persist from attachment to a desire or purpose. A child perseveres in a new study until he has mastered it; he persists in making a request until he has obtained the object of his desire.
Antonyms.—Pause, stop, give up, desist, forbear.

Continue, remain. Continue is associated with a state of action; remain, with a state of rest. We are said to continue to speak or to do anything, to remain stationary or in a position.
Antonyms.—Cease, leave off, depart, remove.

Contradict, deny. One contradicts terms by asserting something directly opposite; one denies by advancing arguments or by suggesting doubts or difficulties. Both these terms may therefore be used in reference to disputations. We may deny the truth of a position by contradicting the assertions that are advanced in its support.
Antonyms.—Admit, assert, corroborate, support, maintain.

Controvert, dispute. To controvert has regard to speculative points; to dispute respects matters of fact: there is more of opposition in controversy, more of doubt in disputing. A sophist controverts; a skeptic disputes.
Antonyms.—Agree, accord, harmonize, concur, unite.

Contumacious, rebellious. The contumacious resist only occasionally; the rebellious resist systematically. The contumacious stand only on certain points and oppose the individual; the rebellious set themselves up against the authority itself. Contumacious implies a proud contemptuous air.
Antonyms.—Compliant, deferential, obedient.

Convenient, suitable, proper. Convenient circumstances or arrangements contribute to the ease or comfort of an individual. Anything that is suitable fits the ends or purposes one has in view. Proper relates to etiquette or to moral fitness, as judged by generally received opinion.
Antonyms.—Unsuitable, inconvenient, unseemly.

Conversant, familiar, versed. Conversant implies close acquaintance, the result of study or of frequent contact. Familiar refers to knowledge obtained in a more routine fashion, incidental perhaps to everyday experience. Versed carries with it the idea of proficiency or skill, as in an art or a profession. A person is familiar with his surroundings, conversant with a language, and versed in the law or in some other profession.
Antonyms.—Ignorant, unacquainted.

Conversation, dialogue, conference, colloquy. A conversation is actually held between two or more persons: a dialogue is usually fictitious and written as if spoken: any number of persons may take part in a conversation, but a dialogue always refers to the two persons who are expressly engaged. A conference is specifically appointed and is usually on public concerns. The colloquy has the same character as the dialogue but is not confined to two people.

Convert, proselyte. Convert is more extensive in its sense and application than proselyte,—in its full sense it includes every change of opinion, without respect to the subject. Proselyte, in its original application, denoted changes only from one religious belief to another; it now means a new convert to a religion, a religious sect, or to some particular system or party.

Convince, persuade. A person is convinced who is brought, intellectually, to accept the truth of a proposition or the accuracy of a statement of fact. He is persuaded by something that appeals to his judgment or inclinations and thus influences his will. Convince leads to mental assent; persuade leads to action. An unfortunately common error of usage is to interchange these two words, as in the sentence, "I convinced him to go," which should be, "I persuaded him to go."

Convivial, social. The prominent idea in convivial is that of sensual indulgence, which usually includes drinking; the prominent idea in social is that of enjoyment through intercourse with society. We speak of convivial meetings, convivial enjoyments, or the convivial board; but we say social intercourse, social pleasure, social amusements, and the like.
Antonyms.—Temperate, retiring, cold, solitary.

Copy, imitate, mimic, parody, burlesque. To copy is to duplicate an original. Imitate follows the plan or pattern of the original but allows some freedom in the handling of details. Mimic suggests the adoption of mannerisms closely resembling those of another person in order to produce a comic effect. Like mimic, burlesque and parody are imitations with humorous intent. To parody is to create a parallel closely resembling a poem or some other work but introducing clever and witty departures from it. To burlesque a piece of writing is to give an exaggerated imitation of it that is a travesty on the original.

Coquette, jilt. The coquette makes a traffic of her own charms by seeking a multitude of admirers; the jilt sports with the sacred passion of love, and lightly casts off those previously accepted as lovers.

Correct, accurate, exact, nice. Correctness meets a given standard, whether of information, taste, or something else. Accurate indicates care in the observation and reporting of details. Exact emphasizes complete agreement with requirements and suggests a rigorous application of standards. Nice, as in the expression "a nice distinction," indicates refined taste and acute perception.
Antonyms.—Faulty, careless, erroneous.

Correction, discipline, punishment. As correction and discipline have commonly required punishment to render them efficacious, custom has affixed to them a strong resemblance in their application, although they are distinguished from each other by obvious marks of difference. The prominent idea in correction is that of making right what has been wrong. In discipline, the leading idea is that of instructing or regulating. In punishment, the leading idea is that of inflicting pain. We remove an evil by correction; we prevent it by discipline.

Correspond, accord. To correspond is to answer or conform to the description of something else. Things that correspond must be alike in size, shape, color, and every minute particular. To accord is to agree or to be in harmony and without conflict. Things that accord must be suited to each other. His disposition accords with his looks.

Cost, price, charge, expense. The cost of an article is the amount of money that was paid for it. We may say also that the cost of producing the article (labor, materials, etc.) determines the price asked for it. In other words, the price is fixed by the seller and the cost is met by the buyer. A charge is an amount demanded for services. In a more general sense, charges (for example, fixed charges) are the items taken together which represent the cost of doing business. Expenses are miscellaneous disbursements incidental to the carrying on of business or the conducting of private affairs.

Courage, fortitude, resolution. Courage respects action; fortitude respects passion: a man has courage to meet danger, fortitude to endure pain. Resolution simply marks the will not to recede; we require resolution not to yield to the first difficulties that offer.
Antonyms.—Fear, timidity, pusillanimity.

Cover, hide. The ruling idea in the word cover is that of throwing or putting something over a body; in the word hide is that of keeping carefully to one's self, from the observation of others.
Antonyms.—Show, reveal, expose.

Covey, flock, bevy. Covey, usually applied to quail, is one of many special collective nouns referring to animals. Compare *school* of fish and *pride* of lions. Flock, a more general term, suggests birds but may also apply to sheep, while the verb *to flock* may describe the coming together of a crowd of people, drawn to some point by a common impulse. Bevy, though properly associated with quail, is sometimes used in a mildly complimentary way to identify a group of women.

Cozy(sy), comfortable, snug. Cozy contains essentially the same ideas as its less colorful synonyms, in that it describes a place or situation conducive to relaxation—perhaps an armchair before the fire on a cold, stormy night. Comfortable, in addition to denoting physical ease, may suggest freedom from worry, financial or otherwise. Snug, which also describes an agreeable situation, emphasizes small but well-arranged quarters.

Credit, favor, influence. These terms mark the state we stand in with regard to others as flowing out of their sentiments toward ourselves. Credit arises from esteem; favor from good will or affection; influence from credit or favor or external circumstances. Influence is employed in directing others; weak people easily give their credit or bestow their favor, by which an influence is gained over them to bend them to the will of others.

Crime, vice, sin. A crime is a social offense; a vice is a personal offense. Every action which does injury to others, either individually or collectively, is a crime; that which does injury to ourselves is a vice. Crime consists in a violation of human laws; vice, in a violation of moral law; sin, in a violation of the Divine law.

Criminal, culprit, malefactor, felon, convict. When we wish to speak in general of those who by offenses against the laws or regulations of society have exposed themselves to punishment, we denominate them criminals; when we consider them as already brought before a tribunal, we call them culprits; when we consider them in regard to the moral turpitude of their character, as the promoters of evil rather than of good, we entitle them malefactors; when we consider them as offending by the grosser violations of the law, they are termed felons; when we consider them as already under the sentence of the law, we call them convicts.

Criterion, standard. The criterion is employed only in matters of judgment; the standard is used in the ordinary concerns of life. The former serves for determining the characters and qualities of things; the latter, for defining quantity and measure.

Cruel, barbarous, sadistic, brutal, savage. A cruel person has no regard for the sufferings of others. One who is barbarous shows a primitive ferocity not controlled by the restraints of civilized society. Sadistic people, if they are true followers of the Marquis de Sade, delight in inflicting tortures ingeniously contrived for their victims. Brutal people use coarser methods in causing pain to others. A savage person gives full play to animal instincts of ferocity.
Antonyms.—Kind, humane, gentle, refined, civilized.

Crying, weeping. Crying arises from an impatience in suffering bodily pains; weeping is occasioned by mental grief.

Cultivation, culture, civilization, refinement. Civilization implies for a people a high state of economic and social life. Cultivation primarily applies to the treatment of soil and plants to encourage growth. Applied to the human mind and character, it denotes the possession of training and refinement of which culture is the outcome. Culture comprehends the intellectual phases of civilization; in persons it implies a high mental, moral, and aesthetic development, with possession of graces and niceties of word and manner. Refinement connotes especially fineness and delicacy of feeling.
Antonyms.—Rusticity, rudeness, coarseness, crudity, savagery.

Cure, heal, remedy. Diseases are cured, wounds are healed; the former is a complex process, the latter is simple. Whatever requires to be cured is wrong in the system; whatever requires to be healed is occasioned externally by violence, and requires external applications. To remedy has a moral application; an omission, a deficiency, or a mischief, requires to be remedied.
Antonyms.—Injure, irritate, inflame, aggravate.

Curious, inquisitive, prying. Curious implies an interest in learning about things generally, especially matters not of immediate concern to the person. Inquisitive connotes a rather persistent and impertinent curiosity. Prying applies to an officious, unwelcome, disagreeable inquisitiveness.
Antonyms.—Uninterested, indifferent, apathetic, nonchalant.

Cursory, hasty, slight, desultory. An author will take a cursory view of those points which are not necessarily connected with his subject; an author who takes a hasty view of a subject will mislead by his errors; he who takes a slight view will disappoint by the shallowness of his information. Between cursory and desultory there is the same difference as between running and leaping: we run in a line, but we leap from one part to another; so remarks that are cursory have more or less connection, but remarks that are desultory are without any coherence.
Antonyms.—Detailed, careful, thorough, methodical, coherent.

Custom, habit, fashion, practice. Custom is the practice of doing a thing in like circumstances and in a uniform manner for definite reasons. Social customs regulate many important concerns of men. Habit is the series of acts, which, through practice, has become involuntary or reflex. Fashion is arbitrary and capricious, and is applied to matters of minor importance. Practice signifies actual doing or the thing done: it may be the practice of a person to do acts of charity, as the occasion requires; but, when he uniformly does a particular act of charity at any given period of the year, it is properly said to be his custom.

Danger, peril, hazard, risk. Danger is a general term for impending evil; peril suggests nearer and greater threat of harm, with the odds against the person threatened. Hazards are possibilities of danger that are latent in circumstances, as in road hazards for motorists. A risk is a chance of danger that is assumed voluntarily and with knowledge of a possible adverse outcome.

Daring, bold. He who is daring provokes resistance and courts danger; but the bold man is contented to overcome the resistance that is offered to him. A man may be bold in the use of words only; he must be daring in actions; he is bold in the defense of truth; he is daring in military enterprise.
Antonyms.—Fearful, hesitating, timorous, faint-hearted.

Dark, obscure, dim, mysterious, abstruse. Dark is opposed to light; obscure, to bright. What is dark is altogether hidden; what is obscure is not to be seen distinctly, or without an effort. Dim expresses a degree of darkness, but is employed more in relation to the person seeing than to the object seen. Any intricate affair, which involves the characters and conduct of men, may be mysterious. Obscure may be applied to things or ideas; abstruse to ideas only.
Antonyms.—Light, bright, clear, distinct, plain.

Deadly, mortal, fatal, lethal. Deadly implies strong probability of death. Mortal, a more poetic word, indicates that death has already occurred or is in process of occurring. Thus we speak of deadly peril and of a mortal wound. Fatal suggests a chain of circumstances that inevitably cause death. Lethal describes an agency or a physical substance that produces death, as a lethal dose of poison.
Antonyms.—Vital, life-giving, wholesome.

Debt, due. Debt, in its literal meaning, refers to an amount owed by some one in return for goods or services. The word may also express a moral obligation, as a debt of gratitude. Due is what is coming to someone, whether payable in money or in some other form of requital. According to the proverbial saying, we should even "give the Devil his due."

Deceit, deception, guile. Deceit is the habit of intentional falsehood. Deception, the act of misleading through false appearances, is not always blameworthy: a magician may practice deception. Guile implies crafty, insidious deceit.
Antonyms.—Honesty, truth, candor, sincerity.

Deceiver, impostor. Deceiver is the general term for a person who practices deception, fraud, trickery or chicanery. An impostor is a person who passes himself off as someone else.

Decency, decorum. Decency respects a man's conduct; decorum, his behavior.
Antonyms.—Unseemliness, impropriety, unfitness.

Decided, decisive. Decided marks that which is actually fixed and settled; decisive, that which appertains to decision. A person's aversion or attachment is decided; a sentence, a judgment, or a victory, is decisive.
Antonyms.—Indecisive, unsettled, doubtful.

Decided, determined, resolute. A man who is decided remains in no doubt; he who is determined is un-

influenced by the doubts or questions of others; he who is resolute is uninfluenced by the consequences of his actions.
Antonyms.—Irresolute, doubting, wavering, uncertain.

Decision, judgment, sentence. A decision has no respect to the agent; it may be said of one or many; it may be the decision of the court, of the nation, of the public, of a particular body of men, or of a private individual. But a judgment is given in a public court or among private individuals. A sentence is passed in a court of law or at the bar of a public assembly.

Decree, edict. A decree is a more solemn and deliberative act than an edict; on the other hand, an edict is more authoritative than a decree. A decree is the decision of one or many; an edict speaks the will of an individual. Councils and courts, as well as princes, make decrees. An edict is peculiar to a despotic government.

Dedicate, devote, consecrate, hallow. There is something more solemn in the act of dedicating than in that of devoting, but less than in that of consecrating. To dedicate and devote may be employed in both temporal and spiritual matters; to consecrate and hallow, only in the spiritual sense. An author dedicates a book to a friend or patron by prefacing it with the name and the complimentary inscription. We dedicate a house to the service of God; we devote our time to the benefit of our friends or to the relief of the poor. To consecrate is to declare sacred by means of religious ceremony. The church is consecrated; particular days are hallowed.
Antonyms.—Desecrate, profane.

Deduction, abatement. Both these words imply a taking from something. A person may make a deduction in an account for various reasons, but he makes an abatement in a demand when it is objected to as excessive.
Antonyms.—Increase, addition, augmentation.

Deface, disfigure, deform. Deface implies marring of the surface, frequently by destroying some of it, as letters or inscriptions. Disfigure applies to the deeper injury which mars beauty of form or shape. Deform means so to alter the structure as to produce a misshapen thing.
Antonyms.—Amend, better, improve, rectify.

Defective, deficient. Defective implies the quality or characteristic of lacking something or of being incomplete. Deficient is used with regard to the measure or character of the defect. A book may be defective in consequence of lacking some leaves. A man may be deficient in courage.
Antonyms.—Perfect, complete, unimpaired, whole.

Defend, protect, vindicate. A person may be defended in any particular case of actual danger or difficulty; he is protected from what may happen as well as what does happen. Defense respects the evil that threatens; protection involves the supply of necessities and the affording of comforts. Vindicate implies successful defense against a charge or accusation.
Antonyms.—Endanger, imperil, expose, betray.

Defendant, defender. Technically, a defendant is an accused person against whom a case is brought in court. A defender is one who actively repels attacks upon a person or a cause. A king may be designated as a Defender of the Faith.
Antonyms.—Prosecutor, plaintiff, accuser, assailant.

Definite, definitive. Anything that is definite has its limits or boundaries clearly fixed. Definitive, especially in reference to biographies or histories, means final and decisive. A definitive statement settles an argument once and for all.
Antonyms.—Vague, ambiguous, doubtful.

Deity, divinity. Deity signifies a divine person; divinity signifies the divine essence or power.

Dejection, depression, melancholy. Depression is but a degree of dejection. Slight circumstances may occasion a depression; distressing events occasion dejection: the death of a near and dear relative may be expected to produce dejection in persons of the greatest self-possession. Melancholy is a severe form of depression which amounts to a mental disease.
Antonyms.—Rapture, happiness, elation, felicity, cheerfulness.

Delegate, deputy. A delegate is an authorized representative sent by an organization to a convention or some other gathering. A deputy is usually a person designated, or "deputized," to act in the place of another, for example, as assistant to a sheriff or to some other executive officer. In the expression Chamber of Deputies a representative has a status more permanent than that of delegate; he is the legislative equivalent of the executive deputy.

Deliver, rescue, save. One may be delivered from any evil, whether great or small, and in any manner. To rescue is to deliver from a great impending danger or immediate evil, as to rescue from the hands of robbers or from the jaws of a wild beast. To save signifies to keep from evil.
Antonyms.—Abandon, destroy, surrender, lose.

Demand, require. We demand that which is owing and ought to be given; we require that which we wish and expect to have done. The creditor makes a demand on the debtor; the master requires a certain portion of duty from his servant.
Antonyms.—Appeal (for), entreat, request, beg.

Demur, doubt, hesitation, objection. Demurs often occur in matters of deliberation; doubt, in regard to matters of fact; hesitation, in matters of ordinary conduct; and objections, in matters of common consideration. Artabanes made many demurs to the proposed invasion of Greece by Xerxes. Doubts have been suggested respecting the veracity of Herodotus as a historian. It is not proper to ask that which cannot be granted without hesitation. There are but few things which we either attempt to do or recommend to others that are not liable to some kind of an objection.
Antonyms.—Certainty, approval, promptness, consent.

Demur, hesitate. We demur from doubt or difficulty; we hesitate from an undecided state of mind. Demurring is a matter of prudence, it is always grounded on some reason—a lawyer for the defense demurs to evidence presented by the prosecution, in the hope of throwing doubt upon its contents. Hesitating is rather a matter of feeling. When a request of a dubious nature is made of us, we hesitate in complying with it; one hesitates to voice objection to a plan about the wisdom of which his friends have no doubts.
Antonyms.—Assent, acquiesce, decide, proceed.

Denote, signify. Denote is employed with regard to things and their characters; signify, with regard to the thoughts or movements. A letter or character may be made to denote any number, as words are made to signify the intentions and wishes of the person.

Deny, refuse. Deny applies both to matters of fact and to matters of wish or request; refuse, only to the latter. We deny a report or we deny or refuse a request.
Antonyms.—Grant, accede (to), allow.

Deplore, lament. Deplore indicates keen regret over something already done that is regarded as serious and irreparable. We deplore the action or the conduct of some one who has acted in a regrettable way. Lament conveys the idea of personal grief over something that has happened. Whereas deplore proceeds mainly from one's judgment, lament involves chiefly the emotions.
Antonyms.—Rejoice (at), exult or glory (in).

Deposit, pledge, security. Pledge is the general term applying to anything given as assurance of fulfillment of an agreement. It may be a deposit, a term now generally used of money as commonly paid "to bind a bargain," or security, now usually some form of commercial paper, such as bonds, notes, etc.

Depravity, contamination, corruption. Depravity implies a state of moral degradation, whether innate or acquired. Contamination refers to the process of bringing about a low state of morals through the introduction of external impurities, just as the word is used literally to describe the introduction of disease germs into drinking water. Corruption suggests a more thoroughgoing impairment of any one's moral nature through evil influences that work from within.
Antonyms.—Virtue, goodness, correction, purification.

Depth, profundity. Depth is indefinite in its signification; profundity is a positive and considerable degree of depth. Moreover, the word depth is applied to objects in general; profundity is confined in its application to matters of thought or feeling.
Antonyms.—Shallowness, superficiality.

Derive, trace, deduce. The act of deriving is immediate and direct; that of tracing, a gradual process; that of deducing, a reasoning process. We discover causes and sources by derivation; we discover the course, progress, and commencement of things by tracing; we discover the grounds and reasons of things by deduction.

Desert, merit, worth. Desert is taken for that which is good or bad; merit, for that which is good only. We deserve praise or blame; we merit a reward. Worth is that which is absolutely valuable—it must be sought for on its own account.
Antonyms.—Demerit, worthlessness.

Design, purpose, intend, mean. To design is to plan in a steady, methodical manner; to purpose is to propose to oneself, with some degree of determination; to intend is to have in mind to do something—a less definite expression than the others. Mean still has a colloquial flavor, signifying a vague intention.

Desire, wish, covet. To desire is imperious—it demands gratification; to wish is less vehement—it consists of a strong inclination. To covet is to desire that which belongs to another.
Antonyms.—Dislike, detest, be averse to, spurn.

Desist, leave off. To desist is voluntary or involuntary; to leave off is voluntary. We are frequently obliged to desist, but we leave off at our option. He who annoys another must be made to desist; he who does not wish to offend will leave off when requested.
Antonyms.—Persist, continue, keep on.

Despair, desperation, despondency. Despair is a state of mind produced by the view of external circumstances; desperation and despondency may be the fruit of the imagination. The former therefore always rests on some ground; the latter are sometimes ideal. Desperation marks a state of vehement and impatient feeling; despondency is hopelessness, and is often a disease of the mind.
Antonyms.—Assurance, hopefulness, confidence, courage.

Destiny, destination. Destiny is the point or line marked out in the walk of life; destination is the place fixed upon in particular: as every man has his peculiar destiny, so every traveler has his particular destination. Destiny is altogether set above human control; destination is, however, under the specific control of an individual, either for himself or for another.

Destiny, fate, lot, doom. Destiny is used in regard to one's station and walk in life; fate, in regard to what one suffers; lot, in regard to what one gets or possesses; doom is the final destiny which terminates unhappily and depends mostly upon the will of another. Destiny is marked out; fate is fixed; a lot is assigned; a doom is decreed.

Destroy, consume, waste. To destroy is to break or shatter or by other means put anything beyond hope of restoration. A house may be destroyed by fire or it may fall to ruin. To consume is to use up, as to consume food or merchandise; to waste is to expend unnecessarily, extravagantly, to spend to no purpose, as to waste time or property.
Antonyms.—Build, repair, restore, supply, preserve.

Destruction, ruin. Destruction is an act of immediate violence; ruin is a gradual process. A thing is destroyed by some external action upon it; a thing falls to ruin of itself. A reputation is destroyed; a character is ruined.
Antonyms.—Construction, upbuilding, preservation.

Determine, resolve. We determine how or what we shall do—this requires examination and choice. We resolve that we will do what we have determined upon—this requires a firm spirit.
Antonyms.—Hesitate, waver, question, vacillate.

Deviate, wander, swerve, stray. Deviate always supposes a direct path which is departed from; wander includes no such idea. The act of deviating is commonly faulty; that of wandering is indifferent. To swerve is to deviate from that which one holds right; to stray is to wander in the same bad sense. Men swerve from their duty to consult their interest; the young stray from the path of rectitude to seek that of pleasure.
Antonyms.—Continue, advance, progress.

Devise, bequeath. In the technical sense, to devise is to give lands by a will duly attested according to law; to bequeath is to give personalty for possession after one's death by a less formal instrument.

Dictate, suggestion. Dictate signifies the thing uttered, and has an imperative sense; the suggestion signifies the thing intimated, and conveys the idea of its being proposed secretly or in a gentle manner. These terms are both applied, with this distinction, to acts of the mind. When conscience, reason, or passion present anything forcibly to the mind, it is called a dictate; when anything enters the mind in a casual manner, it is called a suggestion.

Dictionary, encyclopedia. The definition of words, with their various changes, modifications, uses, acceptations, and applications, are the proper subjects of a dictionary; the nature and properties of things, with their construction, uses, powers, etc., are the proper subjects of an encyclopedia.

Dictionary, lexicon, vocabulary, glossary. We speak of a lexicon of Greek or Latin, of a dictionary of a modern language. A vocabulary is a partial kind of dictionary, which may comprehend a simple list of words, with or without explanation, arranged in order or otherwise. A glossary is an explanatory vocabulary, which commonly serves to explain obsolete or technical terms.

Die, expire, perish. Die is the general word for cessation of life or extinction of being. Expire is a softened expression for die. Trees die and a flame expires; figuratively, a lease expires. Perish signifies utter decay and disappearance.
Antonyms.—Live, survive, persist, exist.

Difference, dispute, altercation, quarrel. A difference, as distinguished from the others, is generally of a less serious and personal kind; a dispute consists not only of angry words, but of much ill blood and unkind action; an altercation is a wordy dispute, in which difference of opinion is drawn out into a multitude of words; a quarrel is the most serious of all differences, which leads to every manner of violence.

Difference, distinction. Difference lies in the thing; distinction is the act of a person who recognizes differences. Those are equally bad logicians who make a distinction without a difference, or who make no distinction where there is a difference. A careful writer will make a distinction between synonyms.
Antonyms.—Similarity, likeness, agreement, identity.

Difference, variety, diversity, medley. Difference and variety seem to lie in the things themselves; diversity and medley are created either by accident or by design. A difference may lie in two objects only; a variety cannot exist without an assemblage. A difference is discovered by means of a comparison which the mind forms of objects to prevent confusion; variety strikes on the mind, and pleases the imagination with many agreeable images. Diversity arises from an assemblage of objects naturally contrasted; a medley is produced by a casual assemblage of objects often so illy suited as to produce a ludicrous effect.
Antonyms.—Likeness, sameness, correspondence.

Difficulty, obstacle, impediment, embarrassment, trouble. A difficulty is something or a circumstance that interferes with ease of action. Obstacle means anything directly opposed to one's effort toward an end. Impediment is like a clog or brake in hindering movement or progress. An embarrassment is any condition or circumstance that gives rise to confusion or perplexity, and so proves an obstacle or difficulty. Trouble is a general word applied to the circumstances or to feelings aroused by them.
Antonyms.—Aid, help, assistance, relief, encouragement.

Diffuse, prolix. Both words mark defects of style opposed to brevity. A diffuse writer is fond of amplification, the prolix writer is fond of circumlocution, minute details, and trifling particulars.
Antonyms.—Brief, concise, succinct, condensed.

Digress, deviate. Both in the original and the accepted sense, these words express going out of the ordinary course. We digress only in a narrative, whether written or spoken; we deviate in actions as well as in words, in our conduct as well as in writings.

Dilate, expand. Dilate implies enlargement, as a circular ripple on water widens; expand suggests enlargement in every direction, as a flower expands. A speaker dilates upon a theme, dwells upon it with many words; he expands his argument by discussing points in greater detail.
Antonyms.—Contract, condense, narrow, compress.

Diligent, expeditious, prompt. Diligent marks the interest one takes in doing something; he is diligent who loses no time, who keeps close to the work from inclination. Expeditious marks the desire one has to complete the thing begun. Prompt marks one's desire to get ready; he is prompt who sets about a thing without delay.
Antonyms.—Inattentive, neglectful, slow, hesitant, dilatory.

Disappear, vanish. A thing disappears either gradually or suddenly; it vanishes of a sudden: it disappears in the ordinary course of things; it vanishes by an unusual effort or as if by supernatural or magic power.
Antonyms.—Appear, arise, emerge.

Disapproval, dislike, disinclination. Disapproval is an act of the judgment; dislike, a matter of feeling and sentiments. Disinclination implies a mild or careless dislike, usually of something to be done.

Disapprove, dislike. Disapprove is an act of the judgment; dislike is an act of the will or of the affection. To approve or disapprove is peculiarly the part of a superior, or of one who determines the conduct of others; to dislike is altogether a personal act, in which the feelings of the individual are consulted.
Antonyms.—Approve, like, enjoy, delight in.

Disbelief, unbelief. Disbelief properly implies the believing that a thing is not, or refusing to believe that it is. Unbelief properly implies skepticism or a withholding of belief. As generally applied to religion, unbelief signifies disbelief of dogmas or doctrines, usually with the indication of willfulness. Disbelief is most properly applicable to the ordinary events of life; unbelief, to serious matters of opinion.

Disclaim, disown. One may disclaim responsibility for an act; he may disown his children.
Antonyms.—Claim, acknowledge, own, recognize.

Discord, strife, dissension, contention. Discord consists mostly in the feeling; strife consists mostly in the outward action. Discord evinces itself in various ways—by looks, words, or actions; strife displays itself in words or acts of violence. A collision of opinions produces dissension; a collision of interests produces contention; a collision of humors produces discord.
Antonyms.—Concord, peace, agreement.

Discover, reveal, betray, divulge. Discover suggests exposing to view something that has been hidden, or perhaps unknown. Reveal carries the idea of lifting a curtain or imparting information that has hitherto been kept secret. Betray indicates the violation of a confidence, or it might refer to evidence given involuntarily, as in the speech or action of an accused person. Divulge means giving up information with which one has been entrusted. There may be more reluctance than is associated with betray as a voluntary act, but in effect, divulge also suggests violation of a confidence.
Antonyms.—Conceal, hide, suppress.

Discredit, disgrace, reproach, scandal, dishonor, shame. Discredit interferes with a man's respectability; disgrace marks him out as an object of unfavorable distinction; reproach makes him a subject of adverse criticism; scandal makes him an object of offense or even of abhorrence. Dishonor connotes loss of dignity and favor; disgrace expresses positive reproach and fall from honorable regard; a consciousness of guilt and of the resulting disgrace will bring shame to a person. Shame, the consequence of open moral guilt, is the strongest of these words.
Antonyms.—Honor, favor, regard, respect, dignity.

Discuss, argue, debate. In discussing a question, one discourses upon it calmly and impartially, giving equal attention to pros and cons. Argue is a more personal word meaning to cite reasons and evidence, sometimes a bit heatedly, in support of one side. To debate is to present a formal, organized statement of the case for or against a proposition.

Disgust, loathing, nausea. Disgust is less than loathing, and loathing than nausea. When applied to sensible objects, we are disgusted with dirt; we loathe the smell of food if we have a sickly appetite; we nauseate medicine. When applied metaphorically, we are disgusted with affectation; we loathe the endearments of those who are offensive; we are nauseated by all the enjoyments of life, after having made an intemperate use of them and discovered their inanity.
Antonyms.—Desire, relish, craving.

Dishonest, knavish. What is dishonest violates the established laws of man; what is knavish supposes peculiar art and design in the accomplishment.
Antonyms.—Honorable, straightforward, upright.

Disjoint, dismember. Disjoint means to put out of joint, to dislocate, as a dislocated ankle, or to separate as the joints, as a tool or mechanism. Speech, when not well connected or when hesitating, may be called disjointed. Dismember implies mutilating or tearing apart of the animal or human body.
Antonyms.—Join, unite, assemble.

Dismay, daunt, appall. We are dismayed by alarming circumstances; we are daunted by terrifying circumstances; we are appalled by horrid circumstances.
Antonyms.—Hearten, encourage, incite, rouse.

Disorder, disease, distemper, malady. Disease connotes any deviation from health, whether in plants or animals. Disorder implies usually a slight, temporary sickness. Distemper is now used only of animal diseases. Malady carries the sense of lingering, deep-seated diseases, often with the idea of a morbid state of mind or spirits.

Disparity, inequality. Disparity applies to two objects which should meet or stand in coalition with each other; inequality is applicable to those that are compared with each other. The disparity of age, situation, and circumstances is to be considered with regard to persons entering into a matrimonial connection; the inequality in the portion of labor which is to be performed by two persons is a ground for the inequality of their recompense.
Antonyms.—Parity, equality, equivalence.

Dispassionate, cool. A person who is dispassionate is characteristically temperate in his opinions and judgments. Coolness implies self-control in situations likely to cause excitement. We speak of considering a quarrel dispassionately and of being cool in moments of danger.
Antonyms.—Excitable, hasty, hot.

Dispel, disperse. Dispel means to drive away, as doubt or gloom. It applies only to intangible things. Disperse means to drive apart, to scatter, as a crowd.
Antonyms.—Collect, gather, accumulate.

Dispense, distribute. Dispense is an indiscriminate action; distribute is a particularizing action: we dispense to all; we distribute to each individually. One dispenses charity, but he distributes gifts.
Antonyms.—Hold, keep, retain, withhold.

Displeasure, anger, disapprobation. Displeasure is a softened and gentle feeling. Anger is the intense feeling of dissatisfaction and resentment, rising often to vehement expression. Displeasure may be slight or intense, but it lacks the element of resentment and may not reveal its true intensity in words. Disapprobation is a definite sentiment of censure or of disapproval.
Antonyms.—Satisfaction, pleasure, approval.

Disposal, disposition. Disposal implies merely the removal of things; disposition implies their orderly or appropriate placing or arrangement.

Disposition, inclination. We may always expect a man to do that which he is disposed to do; but we cannot always calculate upon his executing that to which he is merely inclined. We indulge a disposition; we yield to an inclination. Disposition comprehends the whole state of the mind; inclination refers always to a particular object.

Disposition, temper. Disposition is permanent and settled; temper may be transitory and fluctuating. The disposition comprehends the springs and motives of actions; the temper influences the action of the moment. It is possible and not unusual to have a good disposition with a bad temper, and vice versa.

Disregard, neglect, slight. We disregard the warnings, the words, or opinions of others; we neglect their injunctions or their precepts. To disregard results from the settled purpose of the mind; to neglect, from a temporary forgetfulness or oversight. Slight is altogether an intentional act toward an individual.
Antonyms.—Attend to, regard, observe, respect.

Distant, far, remote. Distant is used to designate great space; far, only that which is ordinary. Astronomers estimate that the sun is nearly 93 million miles distant from the earth; a person lives not very far off, or a person is far from the spot. Remote expresses the relative idea of having disappeared from sight.
Antonyms.—Near, close, neighboring, contiguous.

Distinguish, discriminate. To distinguish, whether by the senses or the understanding, is to recognize differences between objects and ideas. Discriminate (literally, to divide) means to separate and select according to certain standards of judgment or taste. We may speak of a distinction as true, but of discrimination as nice, that is, exact.
Antonyms.—Confuse, overlook, confound.

Distinguished, conspicuous, noted, eminent, illustrious. A thing is distinguished in proportion as it is distinct or separate from others; it is conspicuous in proportion as it is easily seen; it is noted in proportion as it is widely known. Eminent applies to those things which set a man high in the circle of his acquaintances; illustrious applies to that which makes him shine before the world.
Antonyms.—Ordinary, common, unknown, humble.

Distress, anxiety, anguish, agony. Distress is the pain felt when in a strait from which we see no means of extricating ourselves; anxiety is that pain which one feels on the prospect of an evil. Distress always depends upon some outward cause; anxiety often lies in the imagination; anguish arises from the reflection on the evil that is past; agony springs from witnessing or suffering intense mental or bodily pain.
Antonyms.—Comfort, calm, apathy, tranquillity.

Distress, harass, perplex. A person is distressed either in his outward circumstances or in his feelings; he is harassed in mind or body; he is perplexed in his understanding more than in his feelings. A deprivation distresses; provocations and hostile measures harass; stratagems and ambiguous measures perplex.
Antonyms.—Soothe, console, comfort, compose.

Distrust, suspicion, diffidence. Distrust is said either of ourselves or of others; suspicion is said only of others; diffidence, only of ourselves. To be distrustful of a person is to impute no good of him; to be suspicious of a person is to impute positive evil to him. As regards oneself, a person may distrust his own powers for the execution of a particular office, or have a distrust of himself in company; he has a general diffidence, or he is naturally diffident.
Antonyms.—Trust, confidence, faith, self-confidence.

Disturb, interrupt. Disturb implies more or less constant breaking up or unsettling as regards one's attitude, activities or affairs. Interrupt connotes a sharp, sudden break in continuity. One's mind may be disturbed from within, but one's thinking is interrupted from without.
Antonyms.—Quiet, tranquilize, pacify.

Divide, distribute, share. We divide the thing; we distribute to the person. To share is to make into parts, the same as divide, and it is to give those parts to some persons, the same as distribute. The person who shares takes a part himself; he who distributes gives it all to others.
Antonyms.—Keep, reserve, withhold, retain.

Divide, separate. That is divided which has been or has been conceived to be a whole; that is separated which might be joined. An army may be divided into two or three divisions or portions; the divisions are frequently separated in their march.
Antonyms.—Join, connect, unite, unify, coalesce, fuse.

Doctrine, dogma, tenet. Although doctrine is historically understood to mean a body of principles taught by theologians and philosophers, the word is now used more generally to identify any formulated statement of theory or of principles governing action. Thus, we speak of the Monroe Doctrine or of Einstein's doctrine (theory) of relativity. Dogma refers to principles positively asserted and definitely laid down by some authority, for example, the leader or governing body of a church. A tenet is a belief that is commonly held, even though not formally taught or officially promulgated.

Doubt, question. Doubt lies altogether in the mind; it is a less active feeling than question: by the former we merely suspend decision; by the latter we actually demand proofs in order to assist us in deciding. We may doubt in silence; we cannot question without expressing doubt, directly or indirectly. We doubt the truth of a position; we question the veracity of an author.
Antonyms.—Accept, believe, assume.

Doubt, suspense. Doubt respects that which we should believe; suspense, that which we wish to know or ascertain. We are in doubt for lack of decisive, positive evidence; in suspense for lack of certainty about the future. Doubt interrupts our progress in the attainment of truth; suspense impedes us in the attainment of our objects.
Antonyms.—Confidence, certainty, assurance.

Draw, drag, haul, pull. Draw expresses here the idea common to the first three terms, namely, that of putting a body in motion from behind oneself or toward oneself. To drag is to draw a thing with violence, or to draw that which makes resistance; to haul is to drag it with still greater violence. To pull signifies only an effort to draw without the idea of motion; horses pull very long sometimes before they can draw a heavily laden cart uphill.

Dream, vision, reverie (revery). Primarily, dreams are visions, thoughts, or images passing in the mind during sleep. One's imagined ideals in life when far from realization are called dreams. A vision may come to one during waking hours. A reverie is a loose train of thought or imagery, running through the mind when one is awake but given over to musing—a waking dream or daydream.

Dull, gloomy, sad, dismal. When applied to natural objects, dull and gloomy denote the want of necessary light or life; in this sense metals are more or less dull according as they are stained with dirt. The weather is dull when the sun is obscured by clouds, and gloomy when the atmosphere is darkened by fogs or thick clouds. Dismal denotes not merely the want of that which is necessary, but also the presence of that which is repugnant to the senses. Dismal carries the sense of evil omen or unlucky foreboding. Sad implies a gloomy or downcast countenance and suggests grief.
Antonyms.—Bright, happy, joyous, merry, cheerful.

Durable, lasting, permanent. Durable is naturally said of material substances; lasting, of those which are spiritual, although in ordinary discourse sometimes they exchange offices. Permanent connotes fitness to endure or remain. We make permanent improvements of lasting or durable materials. That which perishes quickly is not durable; that which ceases quickly is not lasting; that which is only for a time is not permanent.
Antonyms.—Perishable, flimsy, unstable, temporary.

Duty, obligation. Duty has to do with the conscience, and arises from the natural relations of society; an obligation arises from circumstances and is a species of duty. He who guarantees to pay a sum of money contracts an obligation. He who marries contracts new duties.

Ease, quiet, rest. Ease implies absence of anything causing strain on mind or body. Quiet is freedom from external disturbance, such as noise or violence. Repose carries with it the idea of refreshing rest, especially sound sleep.
Antonyms.—Disturbance, toil, strain.

Ease, dexterity, facility. In reference to action, ease denotes such positive qualities as gracefulness and directness. Dexterity connotes a high degree of proficiency or skill. Facility adds the idea of lightness and speed in the performance of tasks.
Antonyms.—Difficulty, awkwardness, constraint.

Eclipse, obscure. Heavenly bodies are eclipsed by the passing of other bodies between them and the beholder; things are in general obscured which are in any way rendered less striking or visible. So, figuratively, real merit is eclipsed by the intervention of superior merit; it is often obscured by an ungracious exterior in the possessor or by his unfortunate circumstances.
Antonyms.—Reveal, show, illuminate.

Education, instruction, breeding. Instruction and breeding are to education as parts to a whole. Instruction implies the communication of knowledge, and breeding connotes the manners or outward conduct. Education comprehends the formation of the mind, the regulation of the heart, and the establishment of the principles. Good instruction makes one wiser; good breeding makes one more polished and agreeable.

Effect, produce, perform. To produce signifies to bring something forth or into existence; to perform, to do something completely. To effect is to produce a result by performing. Whatever is effected is the consequence of a specific design; it always requires, therefore, a rational agent. What is produced may follow incidentally, or arise from the action of an irrational agent or an inanimate object; what is performed is done by specific efforts.

Elderly, aged, old, senile. An elderly person has passed the meridian of life; an old man is approaching the normal maximum allotment of years; an aged person has reached this maximum or exceeded it. A senile person, whether old by the calendar or not, exhibits the characteristics commonly associated with older people, such as forgetfulness and childishness.
Antonyms.—Young, youthful.

Embarrassed, abashed, perplexed. A person is embarrassed by actions or circumstances that impede his freedom of movement or his ease in social contacts. He is abashed by something that shakes his self-confidence. Extensive dealings with others often cause him to be perplexed and thus to be both puzzled and confused.
Antonyms.—Self-possessed, confident, composed.

Emissary, spy. Both these words designate a person sent out by a body on some public concern among their enemies; but they differ in their office according to the etymology of the words. The emissary is sent so as to mix with the people to whom he goes, to be in all places, and to associate with every one individually, as may serve his purpose. The spy takes his station wherever he can best perceive what is passing; he keeps himself at a distance from all but such as may particularly aid him in the object of his search. The emissary is generally employed by those who have some illegitimate object to pursue; spies, on the other hand, are employed by all regular governments in a time of warfare.

Employ, use. We employ either persons or things; we use only things, unless, in an evil sense, we use persons. One may be employed in his own or another's affairs.
Antonyms.—Reject, discharge, overlook.

Encouraged, emboldened. One is encouraged (literally, heartened) toward a course of action by cheering words from others or by circumstances that seem favorable. Emboldened refers chiefly to the strengthening of resolution within oneself, preparatory to doing something audacious.

Antonyms.—Discouraged, frightened, intimidated.

End, terminate, close. End is a general term; an end may come by chance or intention. A discussion may end without being finished, closed, or properly terminated. Close implies a preceding opening in the sense of beginning, as we open and close meetings. Terminate implies usually a purposed end or definite means of ending. His visit was terminated by an abrupt departure. The lane terminated in a high wall.

Antonyms.—Begin, open, commence, initiate.

Endeavor, aim, strive, struggle. An endeavor springs from a sense of duty; we endeavor to do that which is right and avoid that which is wrong. Aiming is the fruit of an aspiring temper—the object aimed at is always something superior either in reality or imagination. Striving is the consequence of an ardent desire—the thing striven for is always conceived to be of importance. Struggling is the effect of necessity—it is proportioned to the difficulty of attainment; the thing struggled for is indispensably necessary.

Endeavor, attempt, effort. Endeavor indicates sustained exertion in the pursuit of an important objective; attempt carries the idea of an experimental undertaking in which one is prepared for failure. Effort is a more general word denoting the exertion of one's will and ability toward the accomplishing of some purpose.

Antonyms.—Rest, slackness, negligence.

Energy, force, vigor, power. Energy is power, thought of or expressed in terms of actual or possible work,—as electrical energy, the energy of his words. Force implies resistance to be overcome. Vigor connotes physical or mental power in daily use, as vigorous growth of a plant. Power is the most general term for ability to do,—as a powerful engine, a speaker of great power.

Antonyms.—Weakness, inefficiency, impotence, incapacity.

Enlarge, increase, extend. Enlarge is applied to dimension and extent; increase is applicable to quantity, signifying to become greater in size by the junction of other matter; extend signifies to make greater in space. We speak of enlarging a house, a room, premises, or boundaries; of increasing an army, or property, capital, expense; of extending the boundaries of an empire.

Antonyms.—Lessen, decrease, contract.

Enmity, animosity, hostility. Enmity lies in the heart; it is deep and malignant. Animosity, from *animus*, a spirit, lies in the passions—it is fierce and vindictive. Hostility, from *hostis*, a political enemy, lies in the action—it is mischievous and destructive. Enmity is altogether personal; hostility respects public or private measures; enmity often lies concealed in the heart and does not betray itself by any open act of hostility.

Antonyms.—Friendliness, love, affection, amity.

Enormous, prodigious, monstrous. The enormous goes beyond our rules of estimating and calculating; the prodigious raises our minds beyond their ordinary standard of thinking; the monstrous contradicts nature and the course of things, frequently with implications of evil.

Antonyms.—Small, minute, usual, natural, reasonable.

Enough, sufficient. Sufficient sometimes implies, more distinctly than enough, the idea of an end or purpose, but in general the words are used without distinction of meanings. Sufficient may be thought more genteel than enough.

Antonyms.—Scanty, sparing, meager.

Enterprising, adventurous. The enterprising character conceives great projects and pursues objects that are difficult to obtain. The adventurous character is contented with seeking that which is new and with placing himself in dangerous and unusual situations.

Antonyms.—Shrinking, contented.

Epithet, adjective. Epithet is the technical term of the rhetorician; adjective, that of the grammarian. The same word is an epithet as it qualifies the sense; it is an adjective as it is a part of speech. Thus, in the phrase, "Alexander the Great," great is an epithet, inasmuch as it designates Alexander in distinction from all other persons; it is an adjective as it expresses a quality in distinction from the noun, Alexander, which denotes a thing. In current usage, epithet may signify abuse or, at least, an unfavorable opinion.

Equal, even, equable, like, alike, uniform. Equal is said of degree, quantity, number, and dimensions, as equal in years; even is said of the surface and position of bodies—a board is made even with another board. Like is said of accidental qualities in things, as alike in color or in feature; uniform is said of things only as to their fitness to correspond; those which are unlike in color, shape, or make, are not uniform, and cannot be made to match as pairs. Equable signifies free from sudden or violent changes,—as an equable climate, equable temper.

Antonyms.—Variable, irregular, unlike, different.

Error, mistake, blunder, fault. Error is the general term, applied to the judgment or to conduct. Mistake is an error of choice; blunder, an awkward error of action. Fault is more serious error, implying frequently a flaw in character or habits.

Eruption, explosion. Eruption is the sudden, and perhaps later continuous, coming into view of something that has been confined, as the eruption of a volcano. Explosion signifies bursting with a noise, with violence, and, characteristically, with the disintegration of a substance.

Estimate, compute, rate. To estimate is to obtain the aggregate sum in one's mind either by an immediate or a progressive act; estimate allows for some inaccuracy in results. To compute is to obtain the sum by the gradual process of putting together items; to rate is to fix the relative value in one's mind by deduction and comparison. A builder estimates the expense of building a house on a given plan; a proprietor of houses computes the probable diminution in the value of his property in consequence of wear and tear; the surveyor rates the present value of lands or houses.

Eternal, endless, everlasting. The eternal is set above time; the endless lies within time. That is properly eternal which has neither beginning nor end; that is endless which has a beginning but no end; that which is everlasting has neither interruption nor cessation.

Antonyms.—Finite, temporary, transitory, passing.

Evade, equivocate. Evade means to turn away from a subject by calling attention to something else. To equivocate is to avoid a positive commitment by using ambiguous language.

Antonyms.—Confront, face.

Event, incident, episode. Event denotes an occurrence of major importance. An incident is a subordinate happening, usually attendant upon an event. An episode is an occurrence somewhat apart from the usual chain of happenings. Although of relatively minor importance, the episode is a self-contained narrative unit and deserves attention for its own sake.

Exact, extort. To exact is to demand peremptorily—it is commonly an act of injustice. To extort is to get with violence—it is an act of tyranny.

Exact, nice, particular. Exact indicates precision that meets objective standards of measurement. Nice refers to refined differentiation with regard to matters of taste; it represents a subjective form of precision. Particular suggests a conscientious attitude and close attention to minute details.

Antonyms.—Careless, crude, slipshod.

Example, instance, illustration. An example is a typical case used to explain a general principle or a classification. An instance is a concrete "case in point" offered in support of an assertion. Whereas instance is associated chiefly with evidence used in an argument, example and illustration are concerned primarily with instruction. Illustration, whether in words or pictures, gives a more complete, and usually a more interesting, view of the subject under consideration.

Example, pattern. The example must be followed generally; the pattern must be followed particularly, not only as to what but how a thing is to be done. The former serves as a guide to the judgment; the latter, to the actions.

Excite, incite, provoke. To excite is said more particularly of the inward feelings; incite is said of the external actions; provoke is said of both. A person's passions are excited; he is incited by any particular passion to a course of conduct; he is provoked to a particular step by some feeling.

Antonyms.—Calm, inhibit, deter, restrain.

Excursion, ramble, tour, trip, jaunt. Excursion is properly a journey out of one's usual range of travel. It may be long or short. A tour is usually a more carefully planned "round trip" of some length, as a tour of the lakes. Trip, formerly a short journey on foot, is now applied generally. Ramble is a purposeless, pleasant walk. Jaunt is a short ramble or journey.

Excuse, pardon. We excuse a person by exempting him from blame; we pardon by giving up the punishment of the offense one has committed. We excuse a small fault; we pardon a great fault; we excuse that which personally affects ourselves; we pardon that which offends against morals. Pardon is also conventionally used as a courteous term in place of excuse, as in "pardon the suggestion."
Antonyms.—Blame, condemn, convict, punish.

Execute, fulfill, perform. To execute is to bring about an end; it involves active measures and is peculiarly applicable to that which is extraordinary, or to that which requires particular spirit and talents. Schemes of ambition are executed. To fulfill is to satisfy a moral obligation. We fulfill the duties of citizens. To perform is to carry through by simple action or labor; it is more particularly applicable to the ordinary and regular business of life. We perform a work or a task.

Exercise, practice. Exercise is action for the purpose of stimulating or developing power; practice is regular exercise for the purpose of acquiring or increasing skill and ease of action.

Exigency, emergency. The exigency is more common but less pressing; the emergency is imperious when it comes, but it comes less frequently. A prudent traveler will never carry more money with him than will supply the exigencies of his journey; in case of an emergency he will borrow of his friends rather than risk his property.

Exonerate, exculpate, acquit. To exonerate is to relieve some one from suspicion or charge of moral guilt. Exculpate commonly refers to removal of blame in small matters, as when we exculpate (excuse) ourselves. Acquit carries the idea of a decision which frees one officially from a charge of misdoing.
Antonyms.—Accuse, blame, indict, convict.

Expediency, fitness. The expediency of a thing depends altogether upon the outward circumstances; the fitness is determined by a moral rule.

Expedient, resource. The expedient is an artificial means; the resource is a natural means. A cunning man is fruitful in expedients; a fortunate man abounds in resources.

Explain, expound, interpret. Single words or sentences are explained; a whole work, or a considerable part of it, is expounded; the sense of any writing or symbolical sign is interpreted.

Explain, illustrate, elucidate. To explain is simply to render intelligible; to illustrate and elucidate are to give additional clearness. Everything requires to be explained to one who is ignorant of it; but the best informed will require to have abstruse subjects illustrated and obscure subjects elucidated; that is, made light.

Expostulate, remonstrate. We expostulate in a tone of authority; we remonstrate in a tone of complaint. He who expostulates passes a censure and claims to be heard; he who remonstrates presents his case and requests to be heard.
Antonyms.—Abet, countenance, urge (on).

Extraneous, extrinsic, foreign. The extraneous is that which forms no necessary or natural part of anything. The extrinsic is that which forms a part or has a connection with a thing, but only in an indirect form; it is not an inherent or component part. The foreign is that which forms no part whatever, and has no kind of connection with an object or an incident.
Antonyms.—Essential, intrinsic, native.

Extraordinary, remarkable, phenomenal. All of these words represent a departure in some degree from common experience. Extraordinary (literally, beyond the ordinary) describes something so unusual as to attract attention. Remarkable, a word often applied to persons as well as to incidents and achievements, means deserving of special notice. Phenomenal describes unique occurrences or unexplainable facts observed by the senses.
Antonyms.—Common, ordinary, usual.

Extravagant, prodigal, lavish, profuse. The extravagant man spends his money without reason; the prodigal man spends it in excesses. One may be extravagant with a small sum where it exceeds one's means; one can be prodigal only with large sums. Lavish and profuse are properly applied to particular actions,—the former to denote an expenditure more or less wasteful or superfluous, the latter to denote a full supply without any sort of scant.
Antonyms.—Careful, thrifty, provident, sparing.

Exuberant, luxuriant. These terms are both applied to any flourishing growth or abundance: exuberance expresses the excess; luxuriance, the profusion. Luxuriant is the more usual and of wider application,—as luxuriant foliage, hair, fancy. Exuberant is applied specifically to the feelings,—as exuberant spirits, fancy, joy.
Antonyms.—Impoverished, scanty, poor, deficient, short.

Facetious, jocular, jocose. Facetious refers to comments that are intended to be taken lightly and to be appreciated for their wit. Jocular describes a jesting manner in action or conversation. A jocose person is one who is naturally inclined to be merry or sportively humorous.
Antonyms.—Serious, solemn, crabbed, lugubrious.

Factious, seditious. Factious is an epithet to characterize the tempers of men; seditious characterizes their conduct. The factious man attempts to raise himself into importance; he aims at authority, and seeks to interfere in the measures of government. The seditious man attempts to excite others and to provoke their resistance to established authority. The first wants to be a lawgiver; the second does not hesitate to be a lawbreaker.
Antonyms.—Loyal, complaisant, governable.

Fair, clear. Fair is used in a positive sense; clear, in a negative sense. There must be some brightness in what is fair; there must be no spots in what is clear. The weather is said to be fair, which is not only free from what is disagreeable, but somewhat enlivened by the sun; it is clear when it is free from clouds or mists.
Antonyms.—Dark, cloudy, murky, dull, stormy.

Faith, creed. These words are synonymous when taken for the thing trusted in or believed; but they differ in this; faith has always a reference to the principle in the mind; creed respects a formulated doctrine which is the object of belief.

Faith, fidelity. Faith here denotes a mode of action, namely, in acting true to the faith which others repose in us; fidelity, a disposition of the mind to adhere to that faith which others repose in us. We keep our faith; we show our fidelity.
Antonyms.—Untruth, faithlessness, treachery.

Faithless, perfidious, treacherous. A faithless man is faithless only for his own interest; a perfidious man is expressly so to the injury of another. Perfidy may lie in the will to do; treachery lies altogether in the thing done.
Antonyms.—Faithful, true, trustworthy, dependable.

Fall, downfall, ruin. Fall applies generally to decline from erectness or to descent from high position or state—it applies to things, institutions, and persons. Downfall now generally applies to descent from rank, place, or position—it implies destruction and ruin. The fall of Sedan brought the downfall of Napoleon and the ruin of French hopes.
Antonyms.—Elevation, ascent, rise.

Fallacious, deceitful, fraudulent. Fallacious applies to falsehood in opinion; deceitful, to that which is externally false: our logic is often fallacious; the appearances of things are often deceitful. Fallacious, as characteristic of the mind, excludes the idea of design; deceitful excludes the idea of mistake; fraudulent describes a gross species of the deceitful.
Antonyms.—Logical, true, real, genuine.

Fame, report, rumor, hearsay. Fame serves to form or establish a reputation either of a person or of a thing; it will be good or bad, according to circumstances,—the fame of our Savior's miracles went abroad through the land. A report serves to communicate information of events; it may be more or less correct according to the veracity or authenticity of the reporter. A rumor serves the purposes of fiction; it is more or less vague according to the temper of the times and the nature of the events. The hearsay is an indefinite report, passed from mouth to mouth, its origin quickly lost.

Famous, celebrated, renowned, illustrious. Famous signifies being of conspicuous note. It is applicable to that which causes a noise or sensation, to that which is talked of, written upon, discussed, and thought of, or to that which is circulated among all ranks and orders of men. Celebrated signifies kept in the memory by a celebration or memorial and is applicable to that which is praised and honored with solemnity. Renown means named about or repeatedly and signifies wide and exalted fame. Illustrious implies conspicuous nobility or worth.
Antonyms.—Unknown, obscure, commonplace, humble.

Fanciful, whimsical, capricious, fantastic. A fanciful tale, although a product of the imagination, may have consistency and may give a momentary impression of plausibility. A fantastic account of something is so exaggerated or so far from reality as to be beyond belief. Whimsical implies quaint turns of fancy or imagination indulged in by a person who is recognized as eccentric. A capricious person displays sudden, unreasonable changes of mind or temper.

Antonyms.—Logical, realistic, serious, regular.

Fancy, imagination. The fancy forms combinations, either real or unreal, as chance may direct; but the imagination is less often led astray. The fancy is busy in dreams, or when the mind is in a disordered state; but the imagination is supposed to act when the intellectual powers are in full play.

Fatigue, weariness, lassitude. Fatigue is an exhaustion of the animal or mental powers; weariness is a wearing out of the strength, or a breaking of the spirits; lassitude is a general relaxation of the animal frame.

Antonyms.—Freshness, strength, endurance, elasticity.

Fearful, dreadful, frightful, tremendous, terrible, terrific, horrible, horrid. A contest is fearful when the issue is important, the event doubtful; the thought of death is dreadful to one who feels himself unprepared. The frightful is less than the tremendous; the tremendous, less than the terrible; the terrible, less than the horrible. Shrieks may be frightful; thunder and lightning may be tremendous; the roaring of a lion is terrible; the glare of his eye terrific; the actual spectacle of killing is horrible or horrid. We may speak of a frightful, dreadful, terrible, or horrid dream, or of dreadful or terrible consequences.

Antonyms.—Pleasant, agreeable, inspiriting, encouraging.

Feel, be sensible, conscious. Feel is generally an indefinite word for a function of the senses and the emotions. Sensible has a more definite use in both cases, always with reference to some object, as to be sensible of light or of error, or of a friend's sympathy. One is aware of external things; conscious refers to the working of the mind in respect to either inner or outer purposes. The expression "conscious of a fault" may refer to the intellectual grasp of it; "sensible of a fault," to the emotion aroused by it.

Antonyms.—(Be) apathetic, indifferent, insensible.

Feign, pretend, simulate. Pretend, or pretend to, is the general word for assuming a false appearance or character. Feign implies more careful invention; simulate, more specific representation of resemblance. One pretends to be occupied; he feigns illness; but he simulates the action of a lunatic. Feign and simulate are very close synonyms.

Antonyms.—(Be) frank, sincere, open, ingenuous.

Felicitate, congratulate. Felicitate is the more formal term; congratulate, the more hearty word. Properly, we congratulate others only; we may felicitate others or ourselves.

Female, feminine, effeminate. Female applies to animal and human species. Feminine connotes the qualities and characteristics peculiar to woman. Effeminate implies reproach for men marked by weak or womanish qualities.

Antonyms.—Male, masculine, mannish, manly.

Ferocious, fierce, savage. All these imply predominance of brute passion. Ferocious signifies a settled, bloodthirsty cruelty or the appearance of it. Fierce connotes blazing, angry temper or sometimes simply an intense purpose or determination. Savage, whether applied to nature, animals, or men, signifies a disposition or character untamed, heartless, of a natural cruelty.

Antonyms.—Gentle, mild, tame, civilized.

Fervent, ardent. Fervent implies warmth of feeling, earnestness. Ardent connotes keen passion, burning enthusiasm in a cause or in pursuit of a purpose. We may speak of fervent prayers and ardent lovers.

Antonyms.—Cold, dispassionate, sluggish, phlegmatic.

Final, conclusive. Final designates simply the circumstance of being the last. Conclusive implies fitness to be final because of being convincing. Final proof may be the last introduced in a discussion; conclusive proof shuts off further argument. If the reasoning is conclusive the conclusion will be final.

Antonyms.—Temporary, tentative, partial, inconclusive.

Find, discover, invent. Find is the general word for coming to know or bringing to knowledge what was not known before. We discover the things not before known to exist; we invent combinations or processes. Iron was discovered; processes for making steel were invented. The principles of flying were discovered; the airplane was invented.

Antonyms.—Imitate, copy, reproduce.

Fine, delicate, nice. Fine, in the natural sense, denotes smallness in general. Delicate denotes a degree of fineness that is agreeable to the taste. Thread is said to be fine; silk is said to be delicate, when to fineness of texture it adds softness. Nice is said of what is agreeable to a discriminating taste and judgment.

Antonyms.—Coarse, crude, uncouth, unrefined.

Finite, limited. Finite is the natural property of things; limited is the artificial property. The former is opposite only to the infinite; but the latter, which lies within the finite, is opposed to the unlimited or the infinite. This world is finite and space infinite; one's powers or resources are limited.

Antonyms.—Infinite, illimitable, boundless.

Firm, fixed, solid, stable. Firm implies steadiness. Fixed denotes the state of being secure; solid implies power of resisting deforming forces; stable implies ability to maintain a constant position. That is firm which is not easily shaken; that is fixed which is fastened to something else, and not easily torn away; that is solid which is able to bear and does not easily give way; that is stable which is able to make a stand against resistance or the effects of time.

Antonyms.—Insecure, unstable, shaky, loose.

Fit, apt. A house is fit for the accommodation of the family, according to the plan of the builder; the young mind is apt to receive either good or bad impressions.

Antonyms.—Ill-adapted, inappropriate, unsuitable.

Flattery, compliment, praise. Flattery refers to insincere praise which plays upon a person's vanity, usually with an ulterior motive on the part of the flatterer. Compliment may be either sincere or insincere praise, but in any case it arises from some specific occasion and does not suggest deliberate, far-reaching design. Praise is a natural and usually disinterested expression of appreciation. It rests on proven merit.

Antonyms.—Detraction, censure, disparagement.

Flexible, pliable, pliant, supple, limber. Flexible implies ease of bending or of being changed in shape—figuratively, susceptible to external impression. Pliable suggests ease of bending, folding, or working (as with the hands). Pliant implies more distinctly an inherent quality of easy bending to meet resistance. Figuratively, pliable suggests readiness for control (especially by evil influence); pliant suggests a temper of easy complaisance or accommodation. Supple implies freedom of easy movement. Limber applies to flexible material objects.

Antonyms.—Rigid, stiff, cross-grained, unyielding, stubborn, unbending, intractable.

Fluctuate, waver. To fluctuate conveys the idea of alternate movement; to waver, that of constant motion backward and forward. When applied in the moral sense, to fluctuate designates the action of the spirits or the opinions; to waver is said of the will or purpose.

Antonyms.—Stand, (be) firm, determined, resolute.

Follow, pursue. The idea of going after any object in order to reach or obtain it is common to these terms, but under different circumstances: to follow a person implies usually a friendly intention; to pursue, a hostile intention.

Antonyms.—Lead, go ahead of, flee from.

Follow, succeed, ensue. Follow and succeed are used of persons and things; ensue, of things only. Follow, in respect of persons, denotes going in order; succeed denotes going or being in the same place immediately after another. Many persons may follow one another at the same time, but only one individual properly succeeds another. Ensue is used in specific cases,—quarrels too often ensue from the conversations of violent men who differ either in religion or politics.

Antonyms.—Lead, precede, occasion.

Folly, foolery. Folly is the general word for inconsiderate, foolish conduct, especially when leading to easily foreseen disaster. Foolery implies absurd, nonsensical, though frequently amusing, performances.

Antonyms.—Sense, sobriety, prudence, judgment.

Fool, idiot, buffoon. Fool, as commonly used, signifies one who acts or talks senselessly, or one who uses no judgment. Buffoon—a word, like fool, connected in origin with wind, windbag—signifies a state fool or clown. Idiot implies lack of reasoning powers; imbecile, meaning weak-minded, is the proper synonym for this word.

Foolhardy, adventurous, rash. The foolhardy man ventures in defiance of consequences; the adventurous man ventures from a love of the arduous and the bold; the rash man ventures for want of thought.

Antonyms.—Calculating, hesitating, cautious, careful.

Force, violence. The arm of justice must exercise force in order to bring offenders to a proper account; one nation exercises violence against another in the act of carrying on war. Force is mostly conformable to reason and equity; violence is always resorted to for the attainment of that which is unattainable by law. Force is often something desirable; violence is always something hurtful. We ought to listen to arguments which have force in them; we endeavor to correct the violence of all angry passions.
Antonyms.—Indulgence, clemency, gentleness, kindness.

Foretell, predict, prophesy, prognosticate. Foretell frequently implies some occult powers; predict generally implies reasonable inference from facts, though the words are used loosely to mean merely "tell before." Prophesy implies inspiration or great assurance on the part of the speaker that his predictions are true. Prognosticate means to predict from observation of symptoms, as a physician prognosticates. The word is sometimes used humorously for predict.

Forgetfulness, oblivion. Forgetfulness characterizes the person or that which is personal; oblivion, the state of the thing. The former refers to him who forgets; the latter to that which is forgotten.
Antonyms.—Remembrance, memory, recollection.

Forgive, pardon, absolve, remit. Individuals forgive each other personal offenses; they pardon offenses against law and morals. The former is an act of Christian charity; the latter, an act of clemency. To remit is to refrain from inflicting—it has more particular regard to the punishment. Remission is granted by an authority—it arrests the execution of justice. To absolve is to free from penalty either by the civil judge or the ecclesiastical minister—it re-establishes the accused in the rights of innocence.
Antonyms.—Condemn, convict, punish, inflict.

Form, ceremony, rite, observance. Form respects all determinate modes of acting and speaking, adopted by society at large, in every transaction of life; ceremony respects those forms of outward behavior which are made the expressions of respect and deference; rite and observance are applied to ceremonies, especially those of religion.

Form, fashion, mold, shape. Form conveys the idea of producing. When we wish to represent a thing as formed in any distinct or remarkable way, we may speak of it as fashioned. God formed man out of the dust of the ground; he fashioned him after his own image. When we wish to represent a thing as formed according to a precise rule, we should say it is molded. Thus the habits of a man are molded at the will of a superior. When we wish to represent a thing as receiving the qualities which distinguish it from others, we talk of shaping it.
Antonyms.—Break, destroy, demolish, mutilate.

Formidable, dreadful, terrible, shocking. The formidable acts neither suddenly nor violently; the dreadful may act violently but not suddenly. Thus the appearance of an army may be formidable, but that of a field of battle is dreadful. The terrible and the shocking act both suddenly and violently, but the former acts both on the senses and the imagination, the latter on the moral feelings. Thus the glare of the tiger's eye is terrible; the unexpected news of a friend's death is shocking.
Antonyms.—Weak, trivial, commonplace, insignificant.

Forsaken, forlorn, destitute. To be forsaken is to be deprived of the company and the assistance of those we have looked to; to be forlorn is to be lost—to be without a guide in an unknown road; to be destitute is to be deprived of the first necessaries of life.
Antonyms.—Protected, cherished, cared for, supported, supplied.

Forswear, perjure, suborn. To forswear is applied to all kinds of oaths; to perjure is employed only for such oaths as have been administered by the civil magistrate. A soldier forswears himself who breaks his oath of allegiance by desertion; a man perjures himself in a court of law who swears to the truth of that which he knows to be false. Suborn signifies to make to forswear. A perjured man has all the guilt upon himself; but he who is suborned shares his guilt with the suborner.

Foster, cherish, harbor, indulge. These terms are all employed here in the moral acceptation, to express the idea of giving nourishment to an object. To foster in the mind is to keep with care and positive endeavors, as when one fosters prejudices by encouraging everything which favors them; to cherish in the mind is to hold dear or set a value upon, as when one cherishes good sentiments by dwelling upon them with inward satisfaction. To harbor is to allow room in the mind, and it is generally taken in the worst sense of giving admission to that which ought to be excluded, as when one harbors resentment by permitting it to have a resting place in the heart. To indulge in the mind is to give the whole mind to it, to make it the chief source of pleasure, as when one indulges an affection by making the will and the outward conduct bend to its gratifications.
Antonyms.—Cast off, reject, refrain from, abjure, forswear.

Foundation, ground, basis. A report is said to be without any foundation when it has taken its rise in mere conjecture or in some arbitrary cause independent of all fact. A man's suspicion is said to be without ground when not supported by external evidence. Foundation and base are the lowest parts of a structure; but the former lies underground, the latter stands above. Basis is used now only in the figurative sense. Rumor which has no basis in fact may be called baseless fabrication.

Fragile, frail, brittle. That is fragile which, like a flower or a vase, is easily broken or destroyed; brittle implies liability to crack or shatter, as an eggshell. Frail is close to fragile in meaning, but it is applied to weak physical or mental natures. The human body is frail or a person's virtue shows frailty.
Antonyms.—Tough, strong, firm, unbreakable.

Frank, candid, ingenuous, free, open, plain. The frank man is under no constraint; his thoughts and feelings are both set at ease, and his lips are ever ready to give utterance to the dictates of his heart. The candid man has nothing to conceal; he speaks without regard to self-interest or to any like consideration—he speaks only the truth. The ingenuous man throws off all disguise; he scorns all artifice and brings everything to light—he speaks the whole truth. Free, open, and plain have not so high an office as the first three. Frank, free, and open men all speak without constraint, but the frank man is not impertinent nor indiscreet. The plain man speaks plainly but truly—he gives no false coloring to his speech.
Antonyms.—Insincere, disingenuous, close, reserved, shuffling.

Free, exempt, immune. Free describes the negative condition of absence from restraint or obligation. One who is exempt is relieved from the necessity of meeting common legal requirements, such as taxes or jury duty or military service. Immunity indicates a privileged situation with regard to small obligations, or it may mean a condition in which one is no longer susceptible to disease.
Antonyms.—Bound, restricted, liable.

Free, familiar. To be free is to be disengaged from the constraints which the ceremonies of social intercourse impose; to be familiar is to be upon the footing of a friend or a relative or of one of the same family.
Antonyms.—Restrained, reserved, distant.

Free, liberal. To be free signifies to act or think at will; to be liberal is to act according to the dictates of a large heart and an enlightened mind.
Antonyms.—Narrow, constrained, conservative.

Frequent, resort to, haunt. Frequent is generally used only of resorting often or repeatedly to a place and applies either to one person or to several together. Resort implies the gathering of a number of people in a place. Haunt implies frequenting continually or pertinaciously when unwelcome. He haunted the neighborhood or the memory haunts him.

Frighten, intimidate. Danger immediately present or evident to the senses frightens; danger distant but apprehended intimidates.
Antonyms.—Attract, encourage, stimulate.

Gape, stare, gaze. Gape and stare are taken in an ill sense. The former indicates the astonishment of gross ignorance; the latter, not only ignorance but impertinence. Gaze is taken in a good sense, as indicating a feeling of astonishment, pleasure, or curiosity.

Gather, collect. To gather signifies to bring things of a kind together; to collect annexes also the idea of binding or forming into a whole. We gather that which is scattered in different parts, as stones are gathered into a heap; vessels are collected so as to form a fleet.
Antonyms.—Scatter, disperse, separate.

General, universal, common. General refers to characteristics, actions or practices associated with all members of a group. Universal goes farther and admits of no exceptions. Common is a milder word describing shared characteristics or usual actions.
Antonyms.—Particular, specific, individual.

Genteel, polite. Gentility respects rank in life; politeness, the refinement of the mind and outward behavior. Genteel indicates now a pretension of superiority. All decent, intelligent people are polite; a decayed gentleman may be genteel.

Antonyms.—Common, uncouth, unpolished.

Gentle, tame. Gentle implies quietness, kindness; tame implies obedience and willingness, often with some lack of spirit.

Antonyms.—Fierce, wild, spirited.

Gift, present, donation. The gift is an act of generosity or condescension—it contributes to the benefit of the receiver. The present is an act of kindness, courtesy, or respect—it contributes to the pleasure of the receiver. The gift is private and benefits the individual; the donation is public and serves some general purpose. What is given to relieve the necessities of any poor person is a gift; what is given to support an institution is a donation.

Give, grant, bestow, present, award. To give is to transmit something one has to someone else. The gift, or thing transmitted, is for the benefit or use of the recipient. One grants a favor or a pardon or a sum of money intended for a specific use. A grant may be made by a person to a subordinate or by an organization to an individual. Bestow suggests the settling of something having considerable value upon a designated recipient. To present something is to transmit it usually as a token of esteem or good wishes. Presents pass between individuals. An award is made to a person or group by judges or some other authority in recognition of merit.

Antonyms.—Withhold, refuse, deny.

Give up, abandon, resign, forego. To give up is applied to familiar cases; abandon, to matters of importance. One gives up an idea, an intention, a plan, and the like; one abandons a project, a scheme, a measure of government. A man gives up his situation by a positive act of his choice; he resigns his office when he feels it inconvenient to hold it. So, likewise, we give up expectations and resign hopes; we resign that which we have, and we forego that which we might have.

Antonyms.—Hold fast, guard, retain, enjoy, seize.

Glaring, barefaced. Glaring designates the thing; barefaced characterizes the person. A glaring falsehood is that which strikes the observer in an instant as a falsehood; a barefaced lie or falsehood betrays the effrontery of him who utters it.

Glimpse, glance. Glimpse is a casual or fleeting view determined by the position or movement of the object or the observer; a glance is a hasty look, determined by the eye alone. From a moving car one, glancing at the landscape, catches glimpses of trees.

Glory, boast, vaunt. To glory is to exult or to rejoice; to boast is to set forth to one's advantage; to vaunt is to set oneself up before others. To glory is more particularly the act of the mind, the indulgence of the internal sentiment; to boast denotes rather the expression of the sentiment; to vaunt is properly to proclaim praises aloud and is taken either in an indifferent or in a bad sense.

Glory, honor. Glory is something dazzling and widely diffused; honor is something less splendid but more solid. Glory impels to extraordinary efforts and to great undertakings; honor induces to a discharge of one's duty.

Antonyms.—Shame, discredit, disgrace.

Godlike, divine, heavenly. Godlike is a more expressive but less common term than divine. The former is used only as an epithet of peculiar praise for an individual; divine is generally employed for that which appertains to a superior being, in distinction from that which is human. A heavenly being denotes an angel or inhabitant of heaven, in distinction from earthly beings.

Antonyms.—Human, earthly.

Good nature, good humor. Good nature and good humor both imply the disposition to please and be pleased, but the former is habitual and permanent while the latter is temporary and partial. The former lies in the nature and frame of the mind, the latter in the state of the spirits.

Antonyms.—Ill nature, ill humor, sullenness, petulance.

Govern, rule, regulate. The exercise of authority enters more or less into the signification of these terms, but to govern implies the exercise likewise of judgment and knowledge. To rule implies rather the unqualified exercise of power, the making the will the rule. A king governs his people by means of wise laws and an upright administration; a despot rules over a nation according to his arbitrary decision. To regulate is to govern or control simply by judgment; the word is applicable to things of minor moment, where the force of authority is not so requisite. One governs the affairs of a nation or a large body where great interests are involved; one regulates the concerns of an individual.

Government, administration. Both these terms may be employed to designate either the act of governing and administering or the persons governing and administering. In both cases government has a more extensive meaning than administration. The former includes every exercise of authority; administration implies only that exercise of authority which consists in putting the laws or the will of another in force. When we speak of the government, as it respects the persons, it implies the whole body of constituted authorities; but the administration implies only that part which puts in execution the intentions of the whole.

Grace, charm, elegance. Grace is altogether physical; charm is either physical or mental. Grace qualifies the action of the body; charm is an inherent quality in the person. A lady moves, dances, and walks with grace; the charms of her person are equal to those of her mind. A graceful figure is rendered so by the deportment of the body. A comely figure has that in itself which pleases the eye. Grace is a quality pleasing to the eye, but elegance is a quality of a higher nature and inspires admiration. Elegance implies niceties and polish of manner. All these words are extended in meaning, figuratively, to language and dress.

Gratify, indulge, humor. To gratify is a positive act of the choice; to indulge is a negative act of the will, a yielding of the mind to circumstances. One gratifies his desires or appetites; he indulges his humors or indulges in pleasures. We gratify and indulge others as well as ourselves, and mostly in the good sense. To gratify, when directed toward others, is an act of generosity. To indulge is to yield to the wishes or to be lenient to the infirmities of others—it is an act of kindness or good nature. To humor is taken mostly in an unfavorable sense, bordering on placate or appease.

Antonyms.—Restrict, mortify, discipline, restrain.

Gratuitous, voluntary. Gratuitous implies a giving or conferring beyond what is required; voluntary connotes free, willing, uncompelled action.

Antonyms.—Obligatory, compulsory, necessary, demanded.

Grave, serious, solemn. Grave expresses more than serious. It bespeaks not merely the absence of mirth, but that heaviness of mind which is displayed in all the movements of the body. Serious, on the other hand, bespeaks no depression but simply steadiness of action and a refraining from all that is jocular. A judge pronounces the solemn sentence of condemnation in a solemn manner; a preacher delivers many solemn warnings to his hearers.

Antonyms.—Light, cheery, frivolous, gay.

Great, grand, sublime. These terms are synonymous only in their moral application. Great simply designates extent; grand includes likewise the idea of excellence and superiority. A great undertaking characterizes only the extent of the undertaking; a grand undertaking bespeaks its superior excellence. A scene may be either grand or sublime. It is grand as it fills the imagination with its immensity; it is sublime as it elevates the imagination beyond the surrounding and less important objects.

Antonyms.—Mean, petty, unimpressive, ordinary.

Great, large, big. Great applies to all sorts of dimensions by which things are measured; large usually refers to magnitude, bulk, or scope. Big denotes great as to expansion or capacity. Great suggests the impression on the speaker, and is used more often of abstract ideas. Large suggests absolute size, and is used mostly of things. Big is in loose colloquial use for all these meanings of great and large.

Antonyms.—Little, small, diminutive, inconsiderable.

Groan, moan. Groan is a deep sound produced by hard breathing; moan is a plaintive, long-drawn sound produced by the organs of utterance. The groan proceeds involuntarily as an expression of severe pain, either of body or mind; the moan proceeds often from the desire of awakening attention or exciting compassion.

Gross, coarse. These terms are synonymous in their moral application. A person becomes gross by an unrestrained indulgence of his sensual appetites, particularly in eating and drinking; he is coarse from the want of polish either as to his mind or manners.

Antonyms.—Refined, polished, delicate, elegant.

Guard, defend, watch. To guard, in its largest sense, comprehends both watching and defending, that is, both preventing the attack and resisting it when it is made. In the restricted sense, to guard is properly to keep off an enemy; to defend is to drive him away when he makes the attack. Watch, like guard, consists in looking to the danger, but it does not necessarily imply the use of any means to prevent the danger—he who watches gives an alarm.

Guess, conjecture, surmise. We guess when we have no means or facts from which to reason. Conjecture is to conclude upon incomplete evidence. Surmise implies still slighter foundation for opinion.
Antonyms.—Reason, calculate, compute, conclude.

Guest, visitor, or visitant. Guest signifies one who is entertained; visitor or visitant is the one who pays the visit. The visitor simply comes to see the person, but the guest partakes also of hospitality. Visitant implies a visitor from outside one's sphere or usual environment, as a supernatural visitant.

Guise, habit. The guise is that which is unusual and often only occasional; the habit is that which is usual among particular classes. A person sometimes assumes the guise of a peasant, in order the better to conceal himself; he who devotes himself to the clerical profession puts on the habit of a clergyman.

Habitation, home, house, residence. Habitation implies merely a dwelling place; house refers to a building constructed purposely for dwelling. Home is usually restricted to mean a dwelling endeared as the scene of domestic ties and family life. Residence is a more formal term than house, though less exact.

Happen, chance. Happen applies to all events, without including any collateral idea; chance comprehends likewise the idea of lack of causation in events. Whatever comes to pass happens, whether regularly in the course of things or particularly and out of the order; whatever chances happens altogether without concert or intention and often without apparent relation to any other thing.

Happy, fortunate. Both words are applied to the external circumstances of a man. The former conveys the idea of that which is abstractly good; the latter implies rather what is agreeable to one's wishes. A man is happy in his marriage; he is fortunate in his trading concerns. Happy excludes the idea of chance; fortunate excludes the idea of personal effort.
Antonyms.—Unlucky, unsuccessful, infelicitous.

Harbor, haven, port. The idea of a resting place for vessels is common to these terms. Harbor carries with it little more than the common idea of affording a resting or anchoring place; haven conveys the idea of security; port conveys the idea of an enclosure. A haven is a natural harbor; a port is an artificial harbor.

Hard, firm, solid. That is hard which will not yield to a closer compression; that is firm which will not yield so as to produce a separation. Ice is hard, so far as respects itself, when it resists every pressure; it is firm, with regard to the water which it covers, when it is so closely bound as to resist every weight without breaking. Hard and solid respect the internal constitution of bodies and the adherence of the component parts, but hard denotes a much closer degree of adherence than solid.
Antonyms.—Soft, yielding, fluid.

Hasten, hurry, speed, expedite, dispatch. To hasten expresses little more than the general idea of quickness in moving toward a point; he hastens who runs to get to the end of his journey. Hurry implies planless and restless or perturbed haste. The word speed includes not only quick but forward movement. He who speeds goes effectually forward and comes to his journey's end the soonest. This idea is excluded from the term haste, which may often be a planless, unsuitable quickness. Hence the proverb, "The more haste, the worse speed." Expedite and dispatch are terms of higher import, in application to the most serious concerns in life. Expedite expresses a process, a bringing forward toward an end; dispatch implies a putting an end to, making a clearance. We do everything in our power to expedite a business; we dispatch a great deal of business within a given time.
Antonyms.—Impede, retard, clog, check.

Hateful, odious. Hateful is properly applied to whatever violates general principles of morality: lying and swearing are hateful vices. Odious is more commonly applied to such things or persons as excite especial repugnance by their nature or conduct.
Antonyms.—Pleasing, attractive, desirable.

Hatred, enmity, antipathy. Hatred refers to intense personal dislike; it is therefore stronger than the abstract term hate. Enmity is a strong feeling of ill will. Antipathy is aversion on a temperamental basis; it is felt, rather than explained.
Antonyms.—Love, amity, friendship, attraction.

Haughtiness, disdain, arrogance. Haughtiness is founded on the high opinion we entertain of ourselves; disdain, on the low opinion we have of others; arrogance is the result of both, but, if anything, more of the former than of the latter. Haughtiness and disdain are properly sentiments of the mind; arrogance, a mode of acting resulting from a state of mind.
Antonyms.—Modesty, respectfulness, consideration, courtesy.

Have, possess. One may be said to have what is in one's hand or within one's reach, but to possess is to have as one's own. A clerk has the money which he has fetched for his employer; the latter possesses the money which he has the power of turning to his use.

Healthful, wholesome, salubrious, salutary. Healthful is applied to exercise, to air, situation, climate, and most other things except food, to which wholesome is commonly applied. The life of a farmer is reckoned the most healthful; the simplest diet is the most wholesome. Healthful and wholesome are rather negative in their sense; salubrious and salutary are positive. That is healthful and wholesome which does no injury to the health; that is salubrious which serves to improve the health; that is salutary which serves to remove a disorder.
Antonyms.—Hurtful, deleterious, unwholesome.

Heap, pile, accumulate. To heap is to bring together numerous objects, placing them loosely in a moundlike mass. Pile suggests a more careful placing of the objects gathered, with one unit laid on top of another. Accumulate is a more general word used to describe the collecting of things and the gradual growth of their number.

Hearty, warm, sincere, cordial. There are cases in which it may be peculiarly proper to be hearty, as when we are supporting the cause of religion and of virtue; there are other cases in which it is peculiarly proper to be warm, as when our affections ought to be roused in favor of our friends. In all cases we ought to be sincere when we express either a sentiment or a feeling; it is peculiarly happy to be on terms of cordial regard with those who stand in any close relation to us. The man himself should be hearty; his heart should be warm; professions should be sincere; a reception, cordial.
Antonyms.—Formal, cold, insincere, indifferent.

Heed, care, attention. Heed applies to matters of importance to one's moral conduct; care, to matters of minor import. A man is required to take heed; a child is required to take care. The former exercises his understanding in taking heed; the latter exercises his thoughts and his senses in taking care. We speak of giving heed and paying attention. Heed is applied only to that which is conveyed to us by another, in the shape of a direction, a caution, or an instruction; the latter is said of everything which we keep within our notice.
Antonyms.—Heedlessness, carelessness, oversight, neglect, rashness.

Help, aid, assist. In everyday usage, help is the common word and assist is a genteelism which says the same thing. In natural, informal style we ask, "May I help you?" instead of using the more formal expression, "May I assist you?" However, in its more legitimate use, assist adds the idea of standing by, recalling something of its original French meaning of being present. Aid suggests response to a need; in this way it is specialized within the general meaning of the inclusive word help.
Antonyms.—Oppose, hinder, obstruct.

Hesitate, falter, stammer, stutter. A person who is not in the habit of public speaking or of collecting his thoughts into a set form will be apt to hesitate even in familiar conversation; he who first addresses a public assembly will be apt to falter. Children who first begin to read will stammer at hard words; one who has an impediment in his speech will stutter when he attempts to speak in a hurry.

Heterodoxy, heresy. Heterodoxy means a belief different from an accepted doctrine; heresy usually implies pernicious erroneous doctrine. But one who has heterodox opinions is a heretic.
Antonyms.—Orthodoxy, conformity.

High, tall, lofty. High is the general word meaning elevated above some point of reference; for example, a high mountain towers above a plain. Tall, the opposite of short, suggests the unusual height of something as compared with others of its class; for example, a tall tree or a tall man. Lofty is a more poetic term implying elevated in sentiment or in a moral sense.

Antonyms.—Low, short, base.

Hinder, stop. To hinder is to interfere with the progress of a person or a thing; to stop implies entire, and usually sudden, cessation of motion.

Antonyms.—Further, promote, advance.

Hold, keep, detain, retain. To hold is a physical act and requires a degree of bodily strength, or at least the use of the limbs; to keep is simply to have by one at one's pleasure. Detain and retain are modes of keeping. The former signifies keeping back what belongs to another; the latter signifies keeping a long time for one's own purpose.

Antonyms.—Give up, surrender, return, restore.

Hold, occupy, possess. We hold a thing for a long or a short time; we occupy it permanently; we hold it for ourselves or others; we occupy it only for ourselves. We hold it for various purposes; we occupy only for the purpose of converting it to our private use. To occupy is to hold only under a certain compact; to possess is to hold as one's own.

Holiness, sanctity. Holiness implies inherent qualities of piety and godliness; sanctity is a character given or conferred upon persons or places because of relation to holy men or things. A priest should be holy; there is an air of sanctity about a church.

Antonyms.—Profaneness, impiety.

Hollow, empty. That is hollow which has an empty space, or cavity, as a hollow tree. That which has nothing in it is empty, as an empty chair.

Antonyms.—Solid, full.

Holy, sacred, divine. Whatever is most intimately connected with religion and with religious worship, in its purest state, is holy, uncontaminated by any worldly thought, and elevated in the greatest possible degree, so as to suit the nature of an infinitely perfect and exalted Being. The sacred derives its sanction from human institutions, and is connected rather with our moral than our religious duties. What is holy is altogether spiritual and abstracted from the earthly. The divine is often contrasted with the human, but there are many human things that are denominated divine. What is divine, therefore, may be so superlatively excellent as to be conceived of as having the stamp of inspiration from the Deity.

Antonyms.—Human, profane, secular.

Honor, reverence, respect. To honor is only an outward act; to reverence either is an act of the mind or is the outward expression of a sentiment; to respect is mostly an act of the mind, though it may admit of being expressed by some outward act. We honor God by adoration and worship; we honor our parents by obeying them and giving them our personal service; we reverence our Maker by cherishing in our minds a dread of offending him; we respect a person or a thing that is lofty, worthy, or honorable.

Antonyms.—Scorn, contemn, despise, disdain.

Hot, fiery, burning, ardent. In the figurative application, a temper is said to be hot or fiery; rage is burning; the mind is ardent in pursuit of an object. Zeal may be hot, fiery, burning, or ardent; but in the first three cases it denotes the intemperance of the mind when heated by religion or politics. Ardent is admissible so long as it is confined to a good object.

Antonyms.—Cool, calm, stolid, dispassionate.

Human, humane. The human race or human beings are opposed to the irrational part of the creation; a humane race or a humane individual is opposed to one that is cruel and fond of inflicting pain.

Antonyms.—Animal, divine, beastly, inhuman, cruel.

Humble, modest, submissive. A man is humble from a sense of his comparative inferiority to others in point of station and outward circumstances; he is humble from a sense of his imperfections, and a consciousness of not being what he ought to be. He is modest, inasmuch as he sets but little value on his qualifications, acquirements, and endowments. Between humble and submissive there is this prominent feature of distinction,—that the former marks a temper of mind, the latter a mode of action. We may be submissive because we are humble; but we may likewise be submissive from fear, from interested motives.

Antonyms.—Haughty, arrogant, vain, conceited, obstinate.

Humor, temper, mood. Humor is fluctuating, so that it varies continually in the same mind; temper is a more permanent quality, showing itself to be the same whenever it appears at all. Humor makes a man appear different at different times; temper makes him different from others.

Hence we speak of the humor of the moment, the temper of youth or old age. Humor and mood denote temporary states of feeling, but mood is of a rather more pervasive, controlling nature than humor, which seems more capricious. There is no calculating on the humor of the man; it depends upon his mood whether he does work ill or well.

Hurtful, pernicious, noxious, noisome. Between hurtful and pernicious there is the same distinction as between hurting and destroying: that which is hurtful may hurt in various ways; but that which is pernicious necessarily tends to destruction. Confinement is hurtful to the health; bad company is pernicious to the morals. Noxious and noisome are forms of the hurtful. That which is noxious inflicts a direct injury; that which is noisome inflicts it indirectly. Noxious insects are such as wound; noisome vapors are such as tend to create disorders.

Antonyms.—Healthful, wholesome, salutary, salubrious.

Ideal, imaginary. The ideal improves upon the real by selecting merits and eliminating defects; hence, the definition, "Art is idealized imitation of nature." The imaginary departs freely from reality. An ideal commonwealth, or Utopia, is developed from known principles of government and thus bears a certain relationship to actual states, however much it may improve upon them. The fanciful description of a country governed wisely by horses, in *Gulliver's Travels,* is created by the imagination working with complete abandon. Invention, whether mechanical or literary, can utilize imaginary concepts to excellent advantage.

Antonyms.—Real, actual, practical.

Idle, lazy, indolent. One is termed idle who will do nothing useful; one is lazy who will do nothing at all without great reluctance; one is indolent who does not care to do anything or undertake anything.

Antonyms.—Busy, industrious, energetic, active.

Illuminate, illumine, enlighten. We illuminate by means of artificial lights; the sun illuminates the world by its own light. Preaching and instruction enlighten the minds of men. Illumine is but a poetic variation of illuminate. Figuratively, we speak of an illuminating remark. Illuminating examples are an aid to understanding principles.

Antonyms.—Darken, shadow, obscure, cloud.

Imminent, impending. Both terms are used in regard to some evil that is exceedingly near. Imminent conveys no idea of duration; impending excludes the idea of what is momentary. A person may be in imminent danger of losing his life in one instant, and the danger may be over the next instant; but an impending danger is that which has been long in existence and gradually approaching.

Antonyms.—Doubtful, unexpected, improbable, unheralded, unlikely.

Impair, injure. To impair is a progressive mode of injuring; to injure is to do harm either by degrees or by an instantaneous act. Straining of the eyes impairs the sight, but a blow injures rather than impairs the eye.

Antonyms.—Benefit, help, remedy, repair.

Imperious, lordly, domineering, overbearing. A person's temper or his tone is said to be imperious; his air or deportment is lordly; his tone is domineering. Overbearing is employed for men in the general relations of society, whether superiors or equals. A man of an imperious temper and some talent will frequently be so overbearing in the assemblies of his equals as to awe the rest into silence.

Antonyms.—Servile, submissive, humble, pliant.

Implicate, involve. Implicate denotes folding into a thing; involve, rolling into a thing. To implicate therefore marks something less entangled than to involve; for that which is folded may be folded only once, but that which is rolled is turned many times. In application to human affairs, therefore, people are said to be implicated who have taken ever so small a share in a transaction; they are involved only when they are deeply concerned. Implicate is now always used in an unfavorable sense. Involve may have this sense also, but is of more general use.

Antonyms.—Extricate, disentangle.

Impugn, attack. He who impugns may sometimes proceed insidiously to undermine the faith of others; he who attacks always proceeds directly with more or less violence.

Antonyms.—Defend, uphold, vindicate.

Inability, disability. Inability refers to weakness or powerlessness that is inherent and always has been present. Disability indicates that power formerly possessed has been lost, either temporarily or permanently.

Antonyms.—Ability, competence.

Inadvertency, inattention, oversight. Anyone may be guilty of inadvertency, since the mind that is occupied by several subjects may be concentrated so closely on one that another may escape notice. Inattention denotes a willful lack of attention. It is always a fault, or at least a discourtesy. Oversight, a species of inadvertency, is perhaps a more pardonable fault, since it suggests passing by something in haste, and usually in spite of good intentions.
Antonyms.—Attention, care, scrutiny.

Inclination, tendency, propensity, proneness. Inclination denotes a leaning in the direction of something or a first movement toward it. Tendency is a more settled and persistent form of inclination. It provides a more reliable basis for the prediction of someone's conduct. Propensity, which in its milder form may be no more than a flair or a predilection, is often an inherent tendency such as an appetite for drink or some other kind of craving. Proneness is something outside the will and is the result of circumstances difficult to explain, as when we say that a particular individual is "accident-prone."
Antonyms.—Aversion, repugnance.

Inconvenience, annoy, molest. To inconvenience anyone is to interfere with his plans, his movements, or his comfort. To annoy him is to impose a strain on his patience or equanimity. Molest indicates a serious and often malicious invasion of a person's rights or security.
Antonyms.—Accommodate, appease, gratify.

Increase, grow. Things that increase become larger or more numerous, either gradually or quickly. Grow implies a gradual increase brought about by an organic cause. A tree grows; the profit from a business increases.
Antonyms.—Decrease, diminish, shrink.

Indebted, obliged. Indebted is more binding and positive than obliged. We are indebted to whoever confers an essential service; we are obliged to him who does us any service. A man is indebted to another for the preservation of his life; he is obliged to him for an ordinary act of civility.

Indifferent, unconcerned, regardless. Indifferent applies only to the will; unconcerned, to either the will or the understanding; regardless, to the understanding only. We are indifferent about matters of minor consideration; we are unconcerned about, or regardless of, serious matters that have remote consequences. An author will seldom be indifferent about the success of his work; he ought not to be unconcerned about the influence which his writings may have on the public, or regardless of the estimation in which his own character as a man may be held.
Antonyms.—Heedful, anxious, careful, mindful, observant.

Indubitable, unquestionable, indisputable, undeniable, incontrovertible, irrefragable. When a fact is supported by such evidence as admits of no kind of doubt, it is termed indubitable; the authority of a man whose character for integrity stands unimpeached, is termed unquestionable authority; when a thing is believed to exist on the evidence of every man's senses, it is termed undeniable; when a sentiment has always been held as either true or false, without dispute, it is termed indisputable; when arguments have never been refuted in any degree, they are termed incontrovertible; when arguments have never been satisfactorily answered, they are termed irrefragable.
Antonyms.—Doubtful, questionable, uncertain, dubious.

Indulgent, fond. Indulgence lies more in forbearing from the exercise of authority; fondness, in the outward behavior and endearments. They may both arise from an excess of kindness or love. An indulgent parent is seldom a prudent parent; a fond parent is foolishly tender and loving.
Antonyms.—Strict, stern, exacting.

Infamous, scandalous. Infamous and scandalous are both said of that which is liable to excite great displeasure in the minds of all who hear it, and to degrade the offenders in the general estimation. But the infamous seems to be that which produces greater publicity and more general reprehension than the scandalous, consequently it is more serious in its nature and a greater violation of good morals.
Antonyms.—Honorable, respectable, creditable.

Inform, instruct, teach. To inform is the act of persons in all conditions; to instruct and teach are the acts of superiors, either on one ground or another. One informs by virtue of an accidental superiority or priority of knowledge; one instructs by virtue of superior knowledge or superior station; one teaches by virtue of superior knowledge rather than of station.
Antonyms.—Misinform, delude, mislead.

Ingenuity, wit. Ingenuity comprehends invention; wit in this sense implies only quickness of apprehension. He had the ingenuity to make good use of the opportunity if he had had the wit to see it.
Antonyms.—Dullness, slowness, stupidity.

Injustice, injury, wrong. Injustice is unfairness toward someone, as in an action or a judgment which violates his rights. Injury refers to more tangible damage, causing loss or pain to the victim. The word wrong reflects upon the doer and denotes a flagrant kind of injustice.
Antonyms.—Justice, right, benefit.

Inside, interior. The term inside may be applied to bodies of any magnitude, small or large; interior is peculiarly appropriate to bodies of great magnitude. We may speak of the inside of a nutshell but not of its interior. The interior of the church was beautifully decorated.
Antonyms.—Outside, exterior.

Insinuation, reflection. An insinuation always deals in half words; a reflection is commonly open. They are both leveled at the individual with no good intent. The insinuation is general and may be employed to convey any unfavorable sentiment; the reflection is particular and commonly passes between persons in close connection.

Insist, persist. Both these terms express the idea of resting or keeping to a thing; but insist signifies to rest on a point, and persist signifies to keep on with a thing, to carry it through. We insist on a matter by maintaining it; we persist in a thing by continuing to do it.
Antonyms.—Desist, yield, abandon, forego, cease.

Insolvency, failure, bankruptcy. Insolvency is a state; failure, an act flowing out of that state; bankruptcy, an effect of that act. Insolvency is a condition of not being able to pay one's debts; failure is a cessation of business, from the want of means to carry it on; bankruptcy is a legal surrender of all one's remaining goods into the hands of one's creditors, in consequence of a real or supposed insolvency.
Antonyms.—Solvency, soundness.

Instant, moment. A dutiful child comes the instant he is called; a prudent person embraces the favorable moment. When both words have respect to the present time, instant expresses a much shorter space than moment.

Insurrection, sedition, rebellion, revolt. There may be an insurrection against usurped power, which is always justifiable; but sedition and rebellion are leveled against power universally acknowledged to be legitimate. Insurrection is always open,—it is a rising up of many in a mass, but it does not imply any concerted, or any specifically active, measure. Rebellion is the consummation of sedition; the scheme of opposition which has been digested in secrecy breaks out into open hostilities and becomes rebellion. Revolt is mostly taken either in an indifferent or a good sense for resisting a foreign dominion which has been imposed by force of arms.
Antonyms.—Subjection, obedience, submission, acquiescence, allegiance.

Intellect, genius, talent. Intellect is the power or faculty of knowing, improved by cultivation and exercise,—in this sense we speak of a man of intellect, or of a work that displays great intellect. Genius is the particular bent of the intellect which is born with a man, as a genius for poetry, painting, or music. Talent is a particular mode of intellect which qualifies its possessor to do some things better than others, as a talent for learning languages, a talent for the stage, etc.

Interchange, reciprocity. Interchange is an act; reciprocity is an attitude as well as an act. By an interchange of sentiment, friendships are engendered; the reciprocity of good services is what renders them doubly acceptable to those who do them and to those who receive them.

Interest, concern. We have an interest in whatever touches or comes near to our feelings or our external circumstances; we have a concern in that which demands our attention. Interest may be slight or intense; concern implies a serious care about something.
Antonyms.—Indifference, apathy, unconcern, insensibility.

Interval, respite. The term interval respects time only; respite includes the idea of ceasing from action for a time. Intervals of ease are a respite to one who is oppressed with labor.

Intervention, interposition. The light of the moon is obstructed by the intervention of the clouds; the life of an individual is preserved by the interposition of a superior.

Intrude, obtrude. To intrude is to go into any society unasked and undesired; to obtrude is to put oneself in the way of another by joining the company and taking a part in the conversation without invitation or consent.
Antonyms.—Recede, withdraw, remove.

Invalid, patient. An invalid is so called because he lacks his ordinary share of health and strength; the patient is one who is laboring under some bodily suffering for which he is receiving care and treatment.

Invest, endue, or **endow.** One is invested with that which is external; one is endued with that which is internal. We invest a person with an office or a dignity; a person is endued with good qualities. Endow carries the sense of bestowing upon, supplying, or equipping. One may endow a college; a man is richly endowed with intellect or ability; but he is endued with piety or virtue.
Antonyms.—Divest, deprive, strip, dispossess.

Irrational, foolish, absurd, preposterous. Irrational is applicable more frequently to the thing than to the person, to the principle than to the practice. Foolish, on the contrary, is commonly applicable to the person as well as to the thing, to the practice rather than to the principle; absurd is applied to anything, however trivial, which in the smallest degree offends our understanding. The conduct of children is therefore often foolish, but not absurd and preposterous. It is absurd for a man to persuade another to do that which he in like circumstances would object to do himself; it is preposterous for a man to expose himself to the ridicule of others, and then be angry with those who will not treat him respectfully.
Antonyms.—Reasonable, rational, sensible, consistent.

Irreligious, profane, impious. All men who are not positively actuated by principles of religion are irreligious. Profanity and impiety are, however, of a heinous nature; they consist not in the mere absence of regard for religion, but in a positive contempt for it and open outrage against its laws. The profane man treats what is sacred as if it were profane. The impious man is directly opposed to the pious man. The former is filled with defiance and rebellion against his Maker; the latter is filled with love and fear.
Antonyms.—Religious, pious, God-fearing, reverent.

Jealousy, envy. We are jealous of what is our own; we are envious of what is another's. Jealousy fears to lose what it has; envy is pained at seeing others have that which it wants for itself.
Antonyms.—Friendliness, magnanimity, generosity, trust.

Journey, travel, voyage. Journey signifies the course that is taken in the space of a day or, in general, any comparatively short passage from one place to another. Travel signifies such a course or passage as requires labor and causes fatigue; in general, any long course. Voyage is now confined to passages by sea.

Joy, gladness, mirth. What creates joy and gladness is of a permanent nature; that which creates mirth is temporary. Joy is the most vivid sensation in the soul; gladness is the same in quality but inferior in degree. Joy is awakened in the mind by the most important events in life.
Antonyms.—Sorrow, sadness, distress, mourning.

Judgment, discretion, prudence. Judgment is conclusive,—it decides by positive inference, and it enables a person to discover the truth. Discretion is intuitive,—it discerns or perceives what is in all probability right. A person who exercises prudence does not inconsiderately expose himself to danger; a measure is prudent that guards against the chances of evil; the impetuosity of youth naturally impels to imprudence.
Antonyms.—Foolishness, recklessness, injudiciousness.

Justness, correctness. We estimate the value of remarks by their justness, that is, by their accordance with certain admitted principles. Correctness of outline is of the first importance in drawing; correctness of dates enhances the value of a history.
Antonyms.—Looseness, inexactness, inaccuracy, partiality.

Keep, preserve, save. The idea of having in one's possession is common to all these terms, which is, however, the simple meaning of keep. To preserve signifies to keep with care and free from all injury; to save is to keep laid up in a safe place and free from destruction.
Antonyms.—Lose, neglect, waste.

Keeping, custody. Keeping amounts to little more than having purposely in one's possession; but custody is a particular kind of keeping, for the purpose of preventing an escape. Inanimate objects may be in one's keeping; but a prisoner or that which is in danger of getting away is placed in custody.

Know, be acquainted with. We may know things or persons in various ways; we may know them by name only; or we may know their internal properties or characters. One is acquainted with either a person or a thing only in a direct manner, and by an immediate intercourse in one's own person.

Knowledge, science, learning, erudition. Knowledge is a general term which simply implies the thing known; science is the department of systematized knowledge; learning is that kind of knowledge which one derives from schools or through the medium of personal instruction; erudition is scholastic knowledge obtained by profound research.
Antonyms.—Illiteracy, ignorance, smattering.

Land, country. The term land, in its proper sense, excludes the idea of habitation; the term country excludes that of the earth or the parts of which it is composed. Hence we speak of the land as rich or poor according to what it yields; of a country as rich or poor according to what its inhabitants possess.

Large, big, great. Large refers to magnitude—to above-average size, capacity or number. Big implies particularly bulk. Great, formerly a close synonym and practically interchangeable with large, is now used more to signify importance and other abstract ideas.
Antonyms.—Small, diminutive, trivial.

Laudable, praiseworthy, commendable. Things are laudable in themselves; they are praiseworthy or commendable in this or that person. That which is laudable is entitled to encouragement and general approbation. An honest endeavor to be useful to one's family or oneself is at all times laudable. What is praiseworthy obtains the respect of all men.
Antonyms.—Censurable, reprehensible, blameworthy.

Lay or **take hold of, catch, seize, snatch.** To lay or take hold of is here the generic expression; it denotes simply getting into one's possession, which is the common idea in the signification of all these terms, which differ in regard to the motion in which the action is performed. To catch is to lay hold of with an effort; to seize is to lay hold of with violence; to snatch is to lay hold of by a sudden effort.
Antonyms.—Let go, let slip, miss, lose.

Lead, conduct, guide. One leads by helping a person onward in any manner, as to lead a child by the hand; conduct and guide are different modes of leading,—the former by virtue of one's office or authority, the latter by one's knowledge or power, as to conduct an army, to guide a traveler in an unknown country.

Lean, incline, bend. In the proper sense, lean and incline are both said of the position of bodies; bend is said of the shape of bodies. That which leans, rests on one side or in a sideward direction; that which inclines, turns only in a slight degree; that which bends, forms a curvature.
Antonyms.—Rise, be erect, straighten.

Leave, quit, relinquish. We leave that to which we may intend to return; we quit that to which we return no more; we relinquish something unwillingly. We leave persons or things; we quit and relinquish things only.
Antonyms.—Stay by, retain, keep, hold.

Lethargy, lassitude, languor, stupor. Lethargy, a general term for sluggishness, describes a state of inactivity that is usually temporary, the result of overeating or perhaps physical exertion. Lassitude, suggesting weariness caused by worry or strain, emphasizes listlessness, inertia of the mind or spirit. Languor indicates the sort of faintness that is associated with a delicate constitution or with soft living. Stupor suggests a condition approaching insensibility, the result of fatigue or possibly of narcotic poisoning. None of the foregoing synonyms would apply to a phlegmatic person, whose slowness of reaction is constitutional, characteristic, and entirely comfortable.
Antonyms.—Alertness, vigor, energy, sprightliness.

Liberal, generous, bountiful, munificent. A liberal person is open-handed in spending his money; a liberal offer goes beyond what might be expected. Anyone who is generous is warm-hearted and unselfish; he gives cheerfully to needy people and worthy causes. Bountiful implies lavish giving by a wealthy person. Munificent goes beyond bountiful and indicates a truly princely largess.
Antonyms.—Stingy, close-fisted, niggardly.

Liberal, progressive, radical. Like many other words that express shades of political opinion, liberal is a term of either praise or reproach, according to one's point of view.

In the sense of a disposition to accept new ideas and put them into practice, liberal, referring to attitude, is closely related to progressive, which refers chiefly to policies and actions. Both liberal and progressive are words likely to be used by people who wish to speak well of themselves. These are almost fighting words to their conservative opponents, whose favorite term of denunciation is the still stronger word radical. Having a literal meaning connected with root, radical suggests an extreme departure from accepted ideas, leading to a "root-and-branch" destruction of the present system.
Antonyms.—Conservative, moderate, tory.

Lift, heave, hoist. We lift with or without an effort; we heave and hoist always with an effort. We lift a child up to let him see anything more distinctly; workmen heave the stones or beams which are used in a building; they hoist materials to the upper parts of the structure.
Antonyms.—Drop, lower, let fall.

Likeness, resemblance, similarity. Likeness refers to either external or internal properties; resemblance, only to the external properties; similarity applies to the circumstances or properties. We speak of a likeness between two persons, of a resemblance in the cast of the eye, of a similarity in age and disposition.
Antonyms.—Unlikeness, dissimilarity, contrast, difference.

Linger, tarry, loiter, lag, saunter. To linger is to stop altogether, or to move but slowly forward; to tarry is properly to suspend one's movements: the former proceeds from reluctance to leave the spot on which we stand; the latter, from motives of discretion. To loiter is to move slowly and reluctantly. To lag is to move more slowly than others. To saunter is altogether the act of an idler; those who have no object in moving either backward or forward will saunter if they move at all.
Antonyms.—Hasten, hurry, press forward, rush, march.

Literate, educated, learned. Although the word literate could formerly be applied to a learned or literary person, its present meaning is generally restricted to the mere ability to read and write, at the lowest level of schooling. In Fourteenth Century England, literate presupposed a knowledge of Latin, the universal language of scholarship, as is shown by the following quotation from official instructions for administering the Coronation oath: "If the King is illiterate, let him swear in French." Educated goes considerably beyond literate as a description of one's schooling, while learned goes still farther and indicates the accomplishments of a scholar.
Antonyms.—Illiterate, ignorant, unlettered.

Little, small, diminutive. What is little is so in the ordinary sense in respect to size; it is properly opposed to great. The small is that which is less than others in point of bulk; it is opposed to the large. The diminutive is that which is less than it ought to be, as a person who is below the ordinary stature is said to be diminutive in stature.
Antonyms.—Large, great, big, huge, immense.

Look, appearance. Look or looks refers to an impression a person or thing makes; appearance implies outward characteristics. He presented a travel-stained appearance, but he had the look of a gentleman.

Lose, miss. What is lost is supposed to be entirely and irrecoverably gone; what is missed may be only out of sight or not at hand at the time when it is wanted.
Antonyms.—Find, hold, have.

Madness, frenzy, rage, fury. Madness is a confirmed derangement in the organ of thought; frenzy is only a temporary derangement from the violence of any disease or from any other cause. Rage refers more immediately to the agitation that exists within the mind; fury refers to that which shows itself outwardly. A person contains or stifles his rage, but his fury breaks out into some external mark of violence.
Antonyms.—Sanity, calmness, patience, self-control.

Magnificence, splendor, pomp. Magnificence lies not only in the number and the extent of the objects presented, but in the degree of richness as to their coloring and quality. Splendor is but a characteristic of magnificence, attached to such objects as dazzle the eye by the quantity of light or by the beauty and strength of coloring. Pomp signifies, in general, formality and ceremony.
Antonyms.—Plainness, meanness, simplicity, somberness.

Make, form, produce, create. To make is the most general and unqualified term; to form signifies to make after a given shape or pattern; to produce is to bring forth into the light, to call into existence; to create is to bring into existence by an absolute exercise of power.

Malevolence, maliciousness, malignity. Malevolence has a deep root in the heart and is a settled part of the character; we denominate the person malevolent, to designate the ruling temper of his mind. Maliciousness may be applied as an epithet to particular parts of a man's character or conduct; one may have a malicious joy or pleasure in seeing the distresses of another. Malignity is not so often employed to characterize the person as to describe the thing; the malignity of a design is estimated by the degree of mischief which was intended.
Antonyms.—Good will, kindness, good nature, benevolence.

Manly, masculine, virile. Manly refers to behavior and indicates possession or manifestation of qualities considered most admirable in a man. Masculine denotes physical attributes such as size, strength, and vigor, or it may suggest courage and other characteristics associated with adult male human beings. Virility emphasizes vigor and robust physical health.
Antonyms.—Boyish, effeminate, weak.

Manners, morals. Manners applies to the minor forms of acting with others and toward others; morals includes the important duties of life. By an attention to good manners we render ourselves good companions; by an observance of good morals we become good members of society.

Mark, trace, vestige. Mark implies a fresh and uninterrupted line; trace a more or less temporary mark left by something or someone passing. Originally meaning footstep, vestige now means a faint remaining sign of something that has been lost or has disappeared. In physiology vestigial organs are parts of the body which are now imperfectly developed but were formerly more important, such as the vermiform appendix.

Martial, warlike, military. We speak of martial array, martial preparations, martial law, a court-martial, but of a warlike nation, meaning a nation which is fond of war, of a warlike spirit or temper, or a warlike appearance. We speak of military in distinction from naval, as military expeditions, military movements, and the like.
Antonyms.—Peaceful, unwarlike, civilian, unsoldierly.

Memory, remembrance, recollection, reminiscence. Memory is the power to recall experiences; remembrance is the act of recalling. Recollection, frequently used for both the power and the act, implies a conscious effort to bring back details from past experience. Reminiscence, a sort of autobiographical musing, seeks to recapture images and happenings stored long ago in the mind.
Antonyms.—Forgetfulness, oblivion.

Mercantile, commercial. Mercantile applies to the actual transaction of business or to a transfer of merchandise by sale or by purchase. Commercial comprehends the theory and practice of exchange; hence we speak in a peculiar manner of a mercantile house, a mercantile situation, and the like, but of a commercial education, a commercial people, and the like.

Mitigate, alleviate, assuage. Mitigate, meaning literally to soften, describes the process of lessening harshness, suffering, or anything else that is unpleasant. Alleviate, used mainly with reference to physical suffering, provides, not a cure, but a temporary remedy to relieve distress. Assuage deals with the emotions, particularly grief or sorrow, and seeks to make one's mental suffering more endurable.
Antonyms.—Aggravate, intensify.

Mix, mingle, blend. Mix is here a general and indefinite term, signifying simply to put together, but we may mix two or several things. We mingle several objects; things are mixed so as to lose all distinction, but they may be mingled and yet retain a distinction. To blend is only partially to mix, as colors blend which shade into each other.
Antonyms.—Distinguish, separate, segregate, sort.

Modesty, bashfulness, diffidence. Modesty refrains from boasting and preserves a wholesome awareness of its own limitations. Bashfulness is shy because of youth or inexperience and hence is the cause of hesitation and awkwardness in dealing with others. Diffidence is distrust of one's powers, though it need imply no more than hesitation about beginning an undertaking. Because diffidence is a useful corrective for overconfidence, the diffident person may do very well, once he has started.
Antonyms.—Boldness, forwardness, egotism.

Moisture, humidity, dampness. Moisture is used in general to express any small degree of infusion of a liquid into a body; humidity is employed scientifically to describe the state of holding any portion of such liquid. Hence we speak of moisture on a table, moisture on paper, but of the

humidity of the air. Dampness is the popular term for the condition resulting from a permeating of a substance by moisture, as a wall or the earth may be damp.
Antonyms.—Aridity, drought, dryness.

Money, cash. Money is applied to everything which serves as a circulating medium; cash is, in ordinary use, coin or paper, legal tender, actually in hand for use.

Motion, movement. We speak of a state of motion as opposed to a state of rest, of perpetual motion, the laws of motion, and the like. On the other hand, we use movement generally in speaking of change of position, as an upward movement, a person's movements. As applied to a person, motion implies gesture.
Antonyms.—Rest, quiet, pause.

Moving, affecting, pathetic The good or bad feelings may be moved; the tender feelings only are affected. A field of battle is a moving spectacle; the death of a friend is an affecting spectacle. The pathetic applies only to what is addressed to the heart; hence an address is pathetic.

Mutual, reciprocal, common. Mutual describes a shared feeling between two persons in which the sentiment of each toward the other is similar in kind and equal in intensity. The word could refer to hostility on this basis, but is more often associated with respect or affection. Reciprocal, indicating an exchange on equal terms, is not restricted to feelings, but could apply to favors or actions. It frequently suggests a response in kind by one party after the other has taken the initiative, or in other words, a return exchange. Common, a more general term, relates to shared experiences that do not involve an interchange between the persons concerned. Even people who have no direct relationship with one another may have ideas, friends, or property in common. Incidentally, the phrase "in common" provides a way of correcting without ambiguity such faulty expressions as "mutual friend," made popular by the title of a Dickens novel.
Antonyms.—Individual, separate.

Naïve, ingenuous, unsophisticated. A naïve person is free from artificiality or guile. Formerly used in a favorable sense, to denote naturalness with fresh and charming simplicity, the word more recently has come to suggest amusing gullibility. Ingenuous connotes a sort of childish innocence, or perhaps a disconcerting frankness in contrast with the evasiveness of designing people. Unsophisticated implies lack of experience and want of worldly wisdom.
Antonyms.—Urbane, artful, worldly-wise.

Name, nickname, pseudonym, acronym. Name is a general word used to identify persons, objects, and, in fact, almost anything. A nickname, which may be either an abbreviation of a person's real name or a substitute for it, is usually applied in affection or derision by the person's associates. A pseudonym is a fictitious name, for example, a pen name adopted by an author. Acronym, a word of comparatively recent origin, means a synthetic word formed by a series of initial letters, as CARE, WAVE, NATO. An extreme example of this popular word coinage is MOUSE, which stands for Medium Orbital Unmanned Satellite of the Earth.

Native, natural. Of a person we may say that his worth is native, to indicate that it is some valuable property which is born with him; we may say that it is natural, as opposed to that which is acquired.
Antonyms.—Acquired, adventitious, affected.

Neglect, omit. To neglect is to disregard, to treat with little or no attention or respect; to omit is to leave out, to leave unnoticed or undone. We neglect an opportunity, we neglect the means, the time, the use, and the like; we omit a word, a sentence, or a figure, and we may omit an item from the day's work. To omit does not always involve the censure that attends neglect.
Antonyms.—Attend to, notice, grasp, insert.

Neighborhood, locality, vicinity. Neighborhood refers to a community, with emphasis on the comparative nearness of the inhabitants to one another. Locality is more of a geographical and impersonal term fixing the area within which something is situated. Vicinity implies nearness to a point or place of reference, for example, the vicinity of Washington.

New, novel, modern, fresh, recent. All these epithets are applied to what has not long existed. New expresses this idea simply without any qualifications; novel is something strange or unexpected; the modern is the thing of today, as distinguished from that which existed in former times; the fresh is that which is so new as not to be the worse for use, or that which has not been before used or employed; the recent is that which is so new as to appear as if it were just made or done.
Antonyms.—Old, familiar, accustomed, ancient, stale.

News, tidings, information, intelligence, notice. News is the general term for communicated knowledge of happenings. Tidings is used poetically in the same sense. Information implies knowledge of some particular thing or event. Intelligence implies that the knowledge has been gained systematically or through organized agencies. Notice involves announcement, especially of a formal nature.

Notice, remark, observe. To notice is a more cursory action than to remark; we may notice a thing by a single glance, or on merely turning the head. To remark supposes a reaction of the mind on an object. We observe things in order to judge of, or draw conclusions from, them, as to observe the condition of the weather. We remark things as matters of fact, as to remark the manner of a speaker.
Antonyms.—Overlook, pass over, disregard, slight.

Noticeable, conspicuous, prominent, remarkable, striking. All of these synonyms describe persons or things that attract attention in varying degrees and with different effects on the observer. Noticeable, the most general term, is neutral and carries rather mild emphasis. In fact, hairsplitting critics have argued with some justification that the word noticeable is superfluous, since anything that was not perceptible would not be mentioned in the first place. Nevertheless, the word is useful in many contexts, and particularly where a certain degree of understatement is desirable. Conspicuous, often used with deprecatory overtones, may suggest that a person or thing commands more attention than is warranted. However, the word may also be used in a favorable sense, as in the phrase "conspicuous for bravery." Although neutral in a phrase like "prominent features of the landscape," the word prominent in reference to persons connotes favorable distinction. Remarkable suggests attributes or qualities, usually of a commendable sort, that are encountered unexpectedly and with some degree of pleasure. Striking applies to something that makes a strong bid for the observer's attention and creates a lasting impression.
Antonyms.—Obscure, hidden, inconspicuous.

Numeral, numerical. Numeral, or belonging to number, is applied to a class of words in grammar, as a numeral adjective or a numeral noun. Numerical, or containing number, is applied to whatever involves number or calculation of numbers, as a numerical difference, where there is a difference between any two numbers or a difference expressed by numbers.

Obedient, submissive, obsequious. One is obedient to command, submissive to power or the will, obsequious to persons. Obedient is always taken in a good sense; submissive, in a humble sense; obsequious, in a mean sense.
Antonyms.—Rebellious, stubborn, recalcitrant, self-respecting.

Object, oppose. To object to a thing is to propose or start something against it; but to oppose it is to set oneself up steadily against it.
Antonyms.—Support, maintain, promote, encourage.

Obnoxious, offensive. In the sense of giving offense, obnoxious implies as much as hateful, offensive little more than displeasing. A man is obnoxious to a party, whose interest or principles he is opposed to; he may be offensive to an individual merely on account of his manners or on account of any particular actions.
Antonyms.—Acceptable, agreeable, pleasing, attractive.

Occasion, opportunity. The occasion is that which offers us the possibility of doing an act or the chance of giving rise to a result. The opportunity is that which invites to action—it tempts us to embrace the moment for taking the step.

Occasional, casual. Occasional carries with it the idea of infrequency; casual, that of unfixedness or the absence of all design. Our acts of charity may be occasional, but they ought not to be casual.
Antonyms.—Regular, systematic, frequent, periodic.

Offender, delinquent. Those who do forbidden or prohibited acts are offenders; those who fail in required or prescribed conduct are delinquents.

Offspring, progeny, issue. Offspring is a familiar term applicable to one or many children; progeny is employed only as a collective noun for a number; issue is used in an indefinite manner without particular regard to number. When we speak of the children themselves we call them the offspring; when we speak of the parents we call the children their progeny. Issue is used only in regard to a man that is deceased.
Antonyms.—Parents, parentage, stock.

Ominous, fateful, portentous. These three words are closely related in their ancient origin and are fairly similar in their present use. Ominous, once associated superstitiously with evil omens, is now used more broadly to describe anything that bodes ill or seems threatening. Fateful, a stronger term, suggests a happening or turn of events pointing definitely toward a disastrous outcome. Portentous is a somewhat more poetic word hinting darkly of calamity in prospect.
Antonyms.—Favorable, auspicious.

Opinionated, conceited, egotistical. An opinionated man is not only fond of his own opinion but full of his own opinion; he has an opinion on everything, which is the best possible opinion. A conceited man has an inordinately high opinion of his own talent,—it is not only high in competition with others, but it is so high as to be set above others. The egotistical man makes himself the darling object of his own contemplation; he admires and loves himself to such a degree that he can talk and think of nothing else.
Antonyms.—Modest, generous, simple, unassuming.

Option, choice. The option or the power of choosing is given; the choice itself is made. Hence we say a thing is at a person's option, or it is his own option, or the option is left to him, in order to designate his freedom of choice more strongly than the word choice itself expresses it.
Antonyms.—Necessity, compulsion.

Outward, external, exterior. Outward signifies tending out from or appearing on the outside. Exterior applies to the outer side or face, as the exterior of a building. External adds to the idea of exterior the notion of whatever is outside and separate from a thing.
Antonyms.—Inward, internal, interior.

Paint, depict. To paint is employed either literally to represent figures on paper, or figuratively to represent circumstances and events by means of words; to depict is used mostly in this latter sense, but paint expresses a greater exercise of the imagination than the latter. It is the art of the poet to paint nature in lively colors; it is the art of the historian or the narrator to depict in strong colors a real scene of misery.

Palatable, appetizing, tasty. Palatable food is acceptable to the palate, but the word arouses little enthusiasm, even though it adds something to edible. Figuratively, we speak of advice or criticism as being palatable or the reverse, and in this connection the word seems a bit more expressive than when used in its literal sense. Appetizing has a kind of lip-smacking suggestion that makes the food it describes appealing. Tasty is a word for epicurean diners, or possibly gourmets. Many other synonyms can be assembled which awaken anticipation of savory puddings, piquant relishes and toothsome desserts. Writing in this vein offers unlimited opportunity for a display of verbal gusto that may or may not be justified by the actual foods recommended.
Antonyms.—Distasteful, insipid, offensive, nauseous.

Part, piece, patch. Things may be divided into parts without any express separation; but when divided into pieces they are actually cut asunder. Hence we may speak of a loaf as divided into twelve parts when it is only conceived to be so, and divided into twelve pieces when it is really so. The patch is that which is always broken and disjointed, a something imperfect; many things may be formed out of a piece, but the patch serves only to fill up a rent or break.

Particular, individual. Particular is much more specific than individual. The particular confines us to one object only of many; the individual may be any one object among many.
Antonyms.—General, collective, common.

Peace, quiet, calm, tranquillity. Peace implies an exemption from public or private broils; quiet implies a freedom from noise or interruption. Calm is a form of quiet which applies to objects in the natural or the moral world; it indicates the absence of violent motion as well as violent noise. Tranquillity expresses the situation as it exists in the present moment, independently of what goes before or after; it is sometimes applicable to society, sometimes to natural objects, and sometimes to the mind.
Antonyms.—War, disturbance, noise, commotion, storm, violence.

Pedantic, academic, bookish. An exhibition of learning which appears to be valued chiefly for learning's sake shows a person to be pedantic. This is particularly true when the exhibitionist displays the technical vocabulary of scholarly research. Academic refers not so much to personal characteristics of scholars as to dryness and abstractness of subject matter. The word also suggests a theoretical rather than a practical approach to subjects and issues. When we say, "That question is purely academic," we mean that it is too remote from present reality to be tested in practice. Bookish describes a person who has learned more from reading than from living.
Antonyms.—Natural, realistic, practical.

Penurious, economical, saving, sparing, thrifty, niggardly. To be economical is a virtue in those who have but narrow means. Saving implies care in the use of money. To be sparing is to use frugally or stintingly; thrifty suggests careful management; penurious means miserly or sparing in regard to the use of money; niggardly implies spending grudgingly or letting go in the smallest possible quantities.
Antonyms.—Generous, lavish, extravagant, unthrifty, wasteful.

Perpetrate, commit. One may commit offenses of various degrees and magnitude; but one perpetrates crimes only, and those of the more heinous kind.

Pillar, column. A pillar is an upright supporting part of a structure. Figuratively, a pillar of a church or of society is a person who plays an essential part in supporting the organization. Columns—for example, columns in the Grecian orders—are more for ornament than for support.

Piteous, doleful, woeful, rueful. Piteous is applicable to one's external expression of bodily or mental pain; a child makes piteous lamentations when it suffers from hunger or has lost its way. Doleful applies to those sounds which awaken a feeling of pain; there is something doleful in the tolling of a funeral bell or in the sound of a muffled drum. Woeful applies to the circumstances and situations of men; a scene is woeful in which we witness a large family of young children suffering under the complicated horrors of sickness and want. Rueful applies to the outward indications of inward sorrow depicted in looks or countenance.
Antonyms.—Happy, joyous, merry, cheerful.

Pity, compassion. Pity is excited principally by the weakness or degraded condition of the subject; compassion, by his uncontrollable and inevitable misfortunes.
Antonyms.—Pitilessness, hardness, antipathy.

Playful, gamesome, sportive. Playful is applicable to youth or childhood, when there is the greatest disposition to play. Gamesome and sportive are applied to persons of maturer years, the former in the bad sense, and the latter in the good sense. A person may be said to be gamesome who gives in to idle jests, or sportive who indulges in harmless sport.
Antonyms.—Sober, dull, serious, gloomy.

Poise, balance. To poise is properly to keep the weight from pressing on either side; to balance is to adjust or equalize two forces. The idea of bringing into an equilibrium is common to both terms. A thing is poised as respects itself; it is balanced as respects other things.
Antonyms.—Mispoise, unbalance, tilt, upset.

Poison, venom. Poison is the general word for substances deadly when introduced into the human system. Venom now means the particular poison of serpents, etc. It applies figuratively to hatred or malignity as blighting to life.

Politeness, polish, refinement. Politeness and polish do not extend to anything but externals; refinement applies as much to the mind as to the body. Rules of conduct and contact with good society will make a man polite; lessons in dancing will serve to give a polish; refined manners or principles will naturally arise out of refinement in mind.
Antonyms.—Impoliteness, rudeness, crudity, boorishness.

Pour, spill. We pour with design; we spill by accident. We pour water over a plant or a garden; we spill it on the ground.

Powerful, potent, mighty. Powerful is applicable to strength as well as to power: a powerful man is one who by size and make can easily overpower another; a powerful person is one who has much in his power. Potent is used only in this latter sense, in which it expresses a larger extent of power; a potent monarch is much more than a powerful prince. Mighty expresses a still higher degree of power; might is power unlimited by any consideration or circumstance. A giant is called mighty in the physical sense; genius which takes everything within its grasp is said to be mighty.
Antonyms.—Weak, impotent, powerless, feeble.

Predicament, dilemma, quandary, plight. A predicament is an uncomfortable situation from which one cannot easily be extricated, either by his own efforts or by the help of others. A dilemma, literally a two-horned situation, is a condition in which two ways of escape are offered, both of which are unacceptable. Historically, dilemma was generally understood to mean a trap set by an opponent in debate, but the word now has much wider application, as for example in describing a choice between two evils or, in fact, between equally undesirable alternatives of any kind. A quandary is a state of perplexity that paralyzes effort and leaves one helpless. Robert Benchley's book, *My Ten Years in a Quandary*, brings out the humorous implications of the word. Plight indicates a sorry situation in which the victim becomes an object of pity or, at least, of sympathy. Whereas one who is in a predicament may experience nothing worse than embarrassment or mild discomfort, the person who is in a plight suffers real distress.

Preliminary, preparatory, introductory. Preliminary indicates a kind of getting ready or warming up in advance of an undertaking. Preparatory refers to still earlier activity, as in collecting needed materials or obtaining instruction required for a task. Introductory leads directly into a job or a piece of writing and may thus be considered a part of the main action.
Antonyms.—Following, concluding, final.

Press, squeeze, pinch, grip. The forcible action of one body on another is included in all these terms. In the word press this is the only idea; the rest differ in the circumstances. We may press with the foot, the hand, or any particular limb. One squeezes commonly with the hand. One pinches either with the fingers or with an instrument constructed in a similar form; one grips with teeth, hands, or any instrument that can gain hold of the object.
Antonyms.—Ease, let go, relieve, relax.

Presumptive, presumptuous, presuming. A presumptive heir is one presumed or expected to be heir; presumptive evidence is evidence founded on some supposition; so likewise presumptive reasoning. But a presumptuous man, a presumptuous thought, a presumptuous behavior, all indicate an overconfidence in regard to one's own powers.

Privacy, retirement, seclusion. Privacy is opposed to publicity; he who lives in privacy is one who follows no public line, who lives so as to be little known. Retirement is opposed to openness or freedom of access: he who lives in retirement withdraws from the society of others. Seclusion is excess of retirement: he who lives in seclusion bars all access to himself and shuts himself from the world.
Antonyms.—Publicity, prominence, notoriety.

Proceeding, transaction. Proceeding signifies literally going forward; transaction, the thing carried through. We are witnesses to the whole proceeding; we inquire into the whole transaction.

Production, performance, work. The term production cannot be employed without specifying or referring to the source from which it is brought forth or the means by which it is brought forth, as the production of art, the production of the inventive faculty. A performance cannot be spoken of without referring to the individual by whom it has been executed; hence we speak of this or that person's performance. When we wish to specify anything that results from labor, it is termed a work; in this manner we speak either of the work of one's hands, or of a work of the imagination.

Profligate, abandoned, reprobate. A profligate man has lost all by his vices. An abandoned man gives way to his passions, which, having the entire sway over him, naturally impel him to every excess. The reprobate man is one who has been reproved until he becomes insensible to reproof, and becomes a prey to the malignity of his own vices.
Antonyms.—Virtuous, high-principled, self-controlled, conscientious.

Prominent, conspicuous, noticeable. Prominent carries the idea of extending or projecting beyond some point of reference: a prominent nose stands out from the face; a prominent man stands out from the crowd. Conspicuous persons or things attract attention so singularly that the eye cannot miss them. Noticeable is a milder and sometimes less offensive term for the idea in conspicuous.
Antonyms.—Obscure, retiring, inconspicuous.

Promise, engagement. In promises the faith of an individual is admitted upon his word, and built upon as if it were a deed; in engagements the intentions of an individual for the future are all that are either implied or understood.

Proportionate, commensurate, adequate. Proportionate implies an adaptation to some assumed standard, as a reward may be proportionate to an act. Commensurate connotes greater accuracy of measurement, as a man's powers may be commensurate with his task. Adequate signifies sufficient, without the implications of the other words.
Antonyms.—Disproportionate, incommensurate, unequal, inadequate.

Provide, procure, furnish, supply. Provide and procure are both actions that have a special reference to the future; furnish and supply are employed for that which is of immediate concern. One provides a dinner in the contemplation that some persons are coming to partake of it; one procures help in the contemplation that it may be wanted. We furnish materials for a building as they are needed. One supplies a family with any article of domestic use.
Antonyms.—Miss, fail of, withhold, deprive of.

Publish, promulgate, divulge, reveal, disclose. To publish is the most general of these terms, conveying in its extended sense the idea of making known; it is in many respects indefinite,—we may publish to many or few. To promulgate is always to make known to many. We may publish that which is a domestic or a national concern; we promulgate properly only that which is of general interest; we divulge things intended to be kept secret; we commonly divulge the secrets or the crimes of another; we reveal the secret or the mystery of a transaction; we disclose from beginning to end an affair which has never before been known or accounted for.
Antonyms.—Hide, conceal, suppress, hush up.

Put, place, lay, set. To put is a general term meaning to bring to a position,—we may put a thing into one's room, one's desk, one's pocket, and the like. To place is to put in a specific manner, and for a specific purpose, as one places a book on a shelf. To lay and to set are still more specific than place, the former being applied only to such things as can be made to lie, and set only to such as can be made to stand. A book may be said to be laid on the table when placed in a downward position, and set when placed on one end.
Antonyms.—Take up, move, remove, disturb.

Qualification, accomplishment. The qualification serves the purpose of utility; the accomplishment serves to adorn. By the first we are enabled to make ourselves useful; by the second we are enabled to make ourselves agreeable.

Quarrel, broil, feud. Quarrel is the general and ordinary term; broil and feud, including active hostility, are particular terms. The idea of a variance between two or more persons is common to these terms; but the first involves the complaints and charges which are reciprocally made. Broil implies the confusion and the entanglement which arise from a contention and a collision of interests; feud, the mutual hostilities which arise out of the variance.

Question, query, questionnaire, quiz. Questions and queries are both put for the sake of obtaining an answer. Question, the more general term, may apply to either reasonable or unreasonable inquiries. It may even be used at times to entrap the person asked, as in the case of so-called loaded or leading questions. A query is usually a rational inquiry and may be addressed to a scholar or some other authority. A questionnaire is an organized group of questions designed to aid someone in making an investigation. A quiz is a brief off-hand test of a person's information.
Antonyms.—Answer, reply, report.

Radiance, brilliancy. Radiance denotes the emission of rays and is therefore peculiarly applicable to bodies naturally luminous, like the heavenly bodies; brilliancy denotes the whole body of light emitted, and it may therefore be applied equally to natural and artificial light. Radiance implies the activity of the shining source of light; figuratively we speak of a radiant face or personality. Brilliancy applies specifically to the appearance; figuratively we speak of a brilliant wit.
Antonyms.—Dullness, murkiness, darkness, dimness.

Rapacious, ravenous, voracious. Rapacious is the quality peculiar to beasts of prey, or to what is like beasts of prey. A lion is rapacious when it seizes on its prey; it is ravenous in the act of consuming it. The word ravenous respects the haste with which one eats; the word voracious respects the quantity which one consumes. A ravenous person is loath to wait for the dressing of his food; he consumes it without any preparation. A voracious person not only eats in haste, but he consumes great quantities, and continues to do so for a long time.
Antonyms.—Frugal, fastidious, dainty.

Rashness, temerity, haste, precipitancy. Rashness is a general and indefinite term, in the signification of which an improper celerity is the leading idea; in temerity the leading idea is want of consideration, springing mostly from an overweening confidence, or from a presumption of character. Haste and precipitancy are but modes or characteristics of rashness and are consequently employed only in particular cases, as haste in regard to our movements and precipitancy in regard to our measures.
Antonyms.—Prudence, deliberation, caution, circumspection.

Ready, prompt, apt. Ready is in general applied to that which has been intentionally prepared for a given purpose; prompt is applied to that which is at hand so as to answer the immediate purpose; apt is applied to that which is fit, or from its nature has a tendency to produce effects.
Antonyms.—Unprepared, unfit, dilatory, unavailable.

Reclaim, reform. Reclaim signifies to call back to its right place that which has gone astray; reform signifies to form anew that which has changed its form; the words are allied only in their application to the moral character. A man is reclaimed from his vicious courses by the force of advice or exhortation; he may be reformed by various means, external or internal.
Antonyms.—Corrupt, degrade, impair, vitiate, confirm.

Recover, retrieve, repair, recruit, restore. We repair that which has been injured; we recruit that which has been diminished; we recover that which has been taken away; we retrieve our misfortunes or our lost reputation; we restore that which has been lost or misplaced, as health or money.
Antonyms.—Lose, lessen, wreck, diminish, injure.

Redundant, wordy, prolix, tautological. These synonyms all refer to the use of unnecessary words. A redundant style of expression substitutes phrases for single words and circumlocutions for direct statements. A person given to wordiness shows delight in using words for their own sake. He is inclined to pile up synonyms instead of choosing the particular one that fits. Prolix suggests a drawing out of subject matter, with resulting bulkiness of expression. Tautological describes the common fault of repetition, as in a phrase like "old veteran," where the idea of old is already present in veteran.
Antonyms.—Concise, succinct, terse, pithy.

Reform, reformation. Whatever undergoes such a change as to give a new form to an object occasions a reform; when such a change is produced in the moral character, it is termed a reformation. The concerns of a state require occasional reform; those of an individual require reformation.

Refuse, decline, reject, repel, rebuff. We refuse what is asked of us, for want of inclination to comply; we decline what is proposed, from motives of discretion; we reject what is offered to us, because it does not fall in with our views. To repel is to reject with violence; to rebuff is to refuse with contempt or with what may be considered as such.
Antonyms.—Accept, receive, acquiesce, comply, welcome.

Relevant, pertinent, apposite. In logic, an idea is considered to be relevant if it belongs clearly to a given subject and helps to explain it. Anything that is pertinent, for example, "a pertinent observation," goes to the heart of a discussion or presents an important phrase of a subject. Something apposite, as "an apposite remark," illuminates a discussion with striking effect. It may even be considered a flash of inspiration. Like wit, it combines appropriateness with unexpectedness.
Antonyms.—Irrelevant, foreign, extraneous.

Repeat, recite, rehearse, recapitulate. To repeat is to say or utter again; to recite is to repeat in a formal manner; to rehearse is to repeat or recite by way of preparation; to recapitulate is to repeat the chapters or principal heads of any discourse, or to summarize the main points.

Repress, restrain, restrict, suppress. Repress implies usually a temporary holding back of something from action; restrain is a stronger word, frequently implying physical force and more permanent holding back. Restrict adds to restrain the idea of bounds within which the restricted activity is free. Suppress implies permanent repression or stifling of activity.
Antonyms.—Release, loose, arouse, set free, incite.

Reproach, rebuke, reprimand. Reproach is a general term for an expression of disapproval with regard to someone's character or conduct. Rebuke implies an immediate reaction in criticism of someone's wrong conduct. Specifi-

cally, it suggests a form of justified scolding. A reprimand is a considered rebuke administered formally by a superior.
Antonyms.—Praise, commendation.

Reputation, fame, renown. Reputation is the estimate formed by others. It may be good or bad. Fame often means widespread reputation. Renown is both widespread and favorable.
Antonyms.—Ignominy, infamy.

Restore, return, repay. We restore upon a principle of equity; we return upon a principle of justice and honor; we repay upon a principle of undeniable right. We cannot always claim that which ought to be restored; we not only claim but enforce the claim in regard to what is to be returned or repaid.
Antonyms.—Withhold, retain, default.

Retard, hinder, thwart. We retard, or slow down, the progress of an action. We hinder people who are doing something by interfering with their freedom of action. We thwart unworthy plans and purposes, and in so doing frustrate the activities of their originators.
Antonyms.—Accelerate, further, help.

Right, claim, privilege. Right, in its full sense, is altogether an abstract thing which is independent of human laws and regulations; claims and privileges are altogether connected with the establishments of civil society. We have often a claim to a thing which is not in our power to substantiate; and, on the other hand, claims are set up in cases which are totally unfounded on any right. Privileges are rights granted to individuals, depending either on the will of the grantor, on the circumstances of the receiver, or on both; privileges are, therefore, partial rights transferable at the discretion of persons individually or collectively.
Antonyms.—Duty, obligation, responsibility.

Royal, regal, kingly. Royal signifies belonging to a king, in its most general sense; regal signifies appertaining to a king, in its particular application. A royal carriage, a royal residence, royal authority—all designate the general and ordinary appurtenances of a king. Regal government, regal state, regal power, denote the peculiar properties of a king; kingly always implies what is becoming a king, or after the manner of a king—a kingly crown is such as a king ought to wear.

Rural, rustic. Rural applies to all country objects except man; it is, therefore, often connected with the charms of nature. Rustic, as here compared, applies only to persons or to what is personal, with reference to the country—it is generally associated with the want of culture.
Antonyms.—Urban, refined, cultured, urbane.

Safe, secure. We may be safe without using any particular measures; but none can reckon on any degree of security without great precaution. A person may be safe on the top of a coach; but, if he wish to be secure from falling off, he must be fastened.
Antonyms.—Unsafe, insecure, endangered.

Salute, salutation. A salute may consist of either a word or an action; salutations pass from one friend to another. The salute may be either direct or indirect; the salutation is always direct and personal. Guns are fired by way of a salute. Bows are given in the way of a salutation.

Satisfy, please, gratify. What satisfies is not always adapted to please; nor is that which pleases that which will always satisfy: plain food satisfies a hungry person; it does not please him when he is not hungry. To gratify is to please in a high degree, to produce a vivid pleasure; we may be pleased with trifles; but we are commonly gratified with such things as act strongly either on the senses or the affections.
Antonyms.—Displease, offend, disgust, anger.

Seaman, sailor, mariner. All these words denote persons occupied in navigation. The seaman, as the word implies, follows his business on the sea. The sailor and the mariner are both specific terms to designate the seaman; every sailor and every mariner is a seaman, although not every seaman is a sailor or a mariner. The former is one who is employed about the work of the vessel; the latter is one who traverses the ocean to and fro, and passes his life upon it.

Secret, hidden, latent, occult, mysterious. What is secret is known to some one; what is hidden may be known to no one. It rests in the breast of an individual to keep a thing secret; it depends on the course of things if anything remains hidden. The latent is the secret or the concealed, especially concealed forces which give no hint of their presence by external appearances; a latent fury may exist in an apparently gentle tiger. An occult science is one that is hidden from the view of persons in general, and is attainable by but few; occult causes or qualities are those which lie too remote to be discovered by the inquirer. The operations of Providence are said to be mysterious, as they are altogether past our finding out.

Antonyms.—Open, revealed, evident, plain, understandable.

See, perceive, observe. The eye sees when the mind is absent; the mind and the eye or other senses perceive in conjunction. Hence, we may say that a person sees, but does not perceive. We observe not by a mere simple act of the mind, but by its positive and fixed exertion.

Seem, appear. Seem is said of that which is dubious, contingent, or future; appear, of that which is actual, positive, and past. A thing seems strange which we are led to conclude is strange from what we see of it; a thing appears clear when we have a clear conception of it.

Sensualist, voluptuary, epicure. The sensualist lives for the indulgence of his senses; the voluptuary is devoted to his pleasures, and, as far as these pleasures are the pleasures of sense, the voluptuary is a sensualist. The epicure as one who makes the pleasures of sense his god, and in this sense he is a sensualist and a voluptuary. In the application of these terms, however, the sensualist is one who is a slave to the grossest appetites; the voluptuary is one who studies his pleasures so as to make them the most valuable to himself; the epicure is a kind of voluptuary who practices more than ordinary refinement in the choice of his pleasures, especially of food.

Antonyms.—Stoic, ascetic, hermit.

Servant, domestic, menial, drudge. In the term servant is included the idea of service performed; in the term domestic, the idea of one belonging to the house or family; in the word menial is included the idea of servile labor; and in the term drudge, that of wearisome labor.

Antonyms.—Master, mistress, employer, boss.

Shade, shadow. Both these terms express that darkness which is occasioned by the sun's rays being intercepted by any body; shade simply expresses the absence of light; hadow signifies also the figure of the body which intercepts he light.

Antonyms.—Light, brightness, sunshine.

Sharp, acute, keen. The general property expressed by these epithets is that of ability to cut. The term sharp is generic and indefinite; the two others are modes of sharpness differing in circumstance or in degree. Acute is not only more than sharp in the common sense, but signifies also sharp-pointed; a knife may be sharp, but a needle is properly acute. Things are sharp that have either a long or a pointed edge; but keen is applicable only to the long edge, and that in the highest degree of sharpness. A common knife may be sharp; a razor or a lancet is properly said to be keen. All these words are applied figuratively to mental ability, their meanings corresponding to their literal senses.

Antonyms.—Dull, blunt, obtuse.

Short, concise, terse, succinct. To the general word short, in reference to brevity in writing or speaking, concise adds the idea of compactness. Terse combines brevity with wit and polish, as in a proverb or an epigram. Succinct compresses a great deal into a small space.

Antonyms.—Bulky, redundant, diffuse, wordy.

Show, exhibition, representation, sight, spectacle. A show consists of that which merely pleases the eye—it is not a matter either of taste or art, but merely of curiosity. An exhibition, on the contrary, presents some effort of talent or some work of genius; a representation sets forth the image or imitation of something by the power of art. Hence we speak of a show of wild beasts, an exhibition of paintings, and a theatrical representation; sights and spectacles present themselves to view. Whatever excites notice is a sight; a spectacle, on the contrary, is that kind of sight which has something in it to interest either the heart or the head of the observer. Processions are sights; battles or bullfights are spectacles.

Showy, pretentious, ostentatious, pompous. These words, all connoting fundamental insincerity, have in common the idea of vainglorious display. Showy refers chiefly to the spectacle itself, though the vanity of the person responsible for the exhibition is clearly implied. Pretentious seeks to make much out of little, while ostentatious presents a person's wealth, generosity or other possession or quality with elaborate flourishes. Pompous describes the self-important manner of the person concerned. All the synonyms listed picture the person or display in an unfavorable or perhaps a humorous light.

Antonyms.—Modest, reserved, sincere, self-effacing.

Sick, sickly, diseased, morbid. Sick denotes a partial state of illness; sickly, a permanent state of the body, a proneness to be sick. He who is sick may be made well; but he who is sickly is seldom really well. Sickly expresses a permanent state of indisposition unless otherwise qualified; but diseased expresses a violent state of derangement without specifying its duration. Sickly and morbid are applied to the habitual state of the feelings or character: a sickly sentimentality; a morbid sensibility.

Antonyms.—Well, healthy, whole, cheerful.

Sign, signal. The sign enables us to recognize an object; it is, therefore, sometimes natural. Signal serves to give warning; it is always arbitrary.

Simple, single, singular. We may speak of a simple matter as something easily grasped or understood. A single instance or circumstance is unaccompanied by any other; a singular instance is one that rarely has its like.

Antonyms.—Complex, complicated, accompanied, common

Simulation, dissimulation. Simulation is making oneself like what one is not; dissimulation is making oneself appear unlike what one really is. The hypocrite puts on the semblance of virtue to recommend himself to the virtuous; the dissembler conceals his vices when he wants to gain the simple or the ignorant to his side.

Antonyms.—Truth, frankness, sincerity, ingenuousness.

Slack, loose. Slack is said only of that which is tied, or of that with which anything is tied; loose is said of any substances, the parts of which do not adhere closely.

Antonyms.—Taut, tight, stretched, compact.

Slant, slope. Slant is said of small bodies only; slope is said indifferently of all bodies, large and small. A book may be made to slant by lying in part on another book on a desk or a table; but a piece of ground is said to slope.

Antonyms.—Be perpendicular, erect, level.

Slip, slide, glide. Slip is an involuntary, and slide a voluntary, motion. Those who go on the ice in fear will slip; boys slide on the ice by way of amusement. To slip and slide are lateral movements of the feet; but to glide is the movement of the whole body, and just that easy motion which is made by slipping, sliding, flying, or swimming. A person glides along the surface of the ice when he slides; a vessel glides along through the water.

Soak, drench, steep. A person's clothes are soaked in rain when the water has penetrated every thread; he himself is drenched in the rain when it has penetrated, as it were, his very body. Steep respects a manner of soaking employed as an artificial process. Soak is, however, a permanent action by which hard things are rendered soft; steep is a temporary action by which soft bodies become penetrated with a liquid. Dried fruits are prepared for eating by soaking; herbs are steeped to extract their essences or flavors.

Antonyms.—Dry, dehydrate, desiccate, evaporate.

Social, sociable. Social people seek others; sociable people are sought for by others.

Antonyms.—Solitary, retiring, uncompanionable.

Solicitation, importunity. Solicitation is general; importunity is particular. Solicitation itself may give trouble to a certain extent, but it is not always unreasonable; importunity is troublesome, insistent solicitation.

Solitary, desert, desolate. Solitary simply denotes the absence of all beings of the same kind—a place is solitary to a man where there is no human being but himself. Desert conveys the idea of a place made solitary by being shunned, because of its unfitness as a place of residence. Desolate conveys the idea of a place made solitary or bare of inhabitants and of all traces of habitation by violent means.

Antonyms.—Populous, peopled, cultivated, inhabited, fruitful.

Sound, sane, healthy. Sound is extended in its application to all things that are in the state in which they ought to be to preserve their vitality. A horse is said to be sound in mind and limb; a tree is sound when not decayed in any part. Healthy expresses more than either sound or sane; we are healthy in every part, but we are sound in that which is essential to life. He who is sound may live, but he who is healthy enjoys life. Sane is applicable to human beings, in the same sense, but with reference to the mind; a sane person is one of sound mind.

Antonyms.—Decayed, diseased, flawed, corrupt.

Speak, say, tell. To speak may simply consist in uttering an articulate sound; but to say is to communicate some idea by means of words. A child begins to speak the moment it opens its lips to utter any acknowledged sound; but it will be some time before it can say anything. To say is to communicate that which passes in our own minds, to express our ideas and feelings as they rise. To tell is to communicate events or circumstances respecting ourselves or others.

Specious, plausible, colorable. These words represent different kinds and degrees of acceptableness in a claim or an argument. A specious argument is fraudulent even though it may seem outwardly and momentarily convincing. Plausible explanations commend themselves to one's reason, though they are admittedly subject to further consideration, and perhaps revision or rejection. Colorable evidence is that which seems valid on the face of it. Circumstances point in its favor. Specious is the only word in the group that suggests intentional deception.
Antonyms.—Sound, valid, convincing.

Spread, expand, diffuse. To spread may be said of anything which comes to occupy more space than it has done, whether by a direct separation of its parts or by an accession to the substance; but to expand is to spread by means of extending or unfolding the parts. A mist spreads over the earth; a flower expands its leaves. To diffuse is to scatter, to cause to spread, as to diffuse information.
Antonyms.—Contract, condense, restrict, close, draw in.

Staff, stay, prop, support. Anything may be called a staff which holds up after the manner of a staff, particularly as it relates to persons, as bread is said to be the staff of life. The stay makes a thing secure for the time being—it keeps it in its place. A prop is usually of a temporary nature; a support is more permanent. Every pillar on which a building rests is a support; the timbers which keep a damaged structure from falling are props.

Stain, soil, sully, tarnish. All these terms imply the act of diminishing the brightness of an object, but the term stain denotes something grosser than the other terms, and is applied to inferior objects. Things which are not remarkable for purity or brightness may be stained, as hands when stained with blood. Nothing is sullied or tarnished but what has some intrinsic value. A fine picture or piece of writing may be easily soiled by a touch of the finger. The finest silver is the soonest tarnished; a man's life may be stained by the commission of some gross immorality; his honor may be sullied, or his glory tarnished.
Antonyms.—Cleanse, clean, brighten, polish, clear.

Stalwart, strong, brawny, sturdy. From its original Anglo-Saxon meaning of serviceable, stalwart has usually emphasized the idea of physical strength, by which one is fitted for service. Hence its association with strong and brawny in their reference to muscular development. A related meaning of stalwart which has partially displaced the notion of muscularity is that of fortitude, strength of purpose, dependability. Here the word comes closer to sturdy and shares with it a connotation of resoluteness.

Starry, stellar, astral. Although closely related in origin, these words, all pertaining to star, have rather widely different associations. Starry is the poetic, or at least non-technical, term for celestial bodies, or perhaps for a person's contemplation of them. Thus the current adjective *starry-eyed* indicates someone's preoccupation with things beyond the range of earthly practicalities. Starry is descriptive, suggesting brilliance and remoteness n the celestial object, while stellar is a working word used technically to convey an astronomical concept. We may speak of a stellar eclipse, but not of a starry one. Astral takes us out of astronomy into the field of occult influences, manifestations or ideas that are assumed to be associated with the stars.

Stately, majestic, grand, grandiose. These synonyms are representative of a large group of words, including magnificent, splendid, princely, august, noble, regal, and sumptuous. All of these related terms are used to describe a display, an official ceremony, or something else that is impressive for its size, richness, beauty, or other distinguished qualities. Stately connotes dignity, gracefulness, and restraint, as in the bearing of a person or the measured tread of a band marching to music. Majestic refers to something that is not only imposing because of its size and beauty but also inspiring by reason of its solemnity.

Grand, if not misapplied, conveys the ideas of size and beauty in the works of man and of sublimity in the works of nature. Grandiose suggests pretentiousness, a kind of sham grandeur that is too exaggerated to be taken seriously.

Steal, pilfer, purloin. Steal, whose everyday meaning is all-too familiar, has accumulated a large collection of synonyms, most of which are euphemisms for the plain word denoting a crime of property. If, instead of steal, the word for appropriating someone else's possessions is pilfer, there seems to be a partial scaling down of guilt, as in the removal of small sums from a petty cash drawer or the depredations of children with "sticky fingers." Purloin, being a literary word and therefore seldom used in common parlance, may be considered almost complimentary in its glossing over of guilt. Whether the act is denoted by steal, pilfer, purloin or some other expression, the illegal transfer of property remains the same so far as its rightful owner is concerned.

Steep, abrupt, precipitous, sheer. When the angle of ascent or descent approaches the perpendicular, an incline is said to be steep. If its departure from a given plane of reference is sudden, the slope may be described as abrupt. If a descent is not only sudden but also headlong, it is called precipitous. Sheer describes a drop straight down, or perhaps a cliff that towers directly above a point of observation. The words precipitous and sheer deal not only with the angle of the incline but also with the feelings of the person who is present at the scene.

Stereotyped, trite, hackneyed, bromidic, platitudinous. There is great need for words to describe lack of originality in people's writing or speaking. Stereotyped is particularly useful for this purpose because it indicates the mechanical following of a fixed pattern, as if the language it describes had been previously cast in a mold. A trite expression probably had merit when it was fresh and has been repeated for that reason. Having been handed down through decades or perhaps even centuries, it has become as flat as a wornout proverb. "Ignorance is bliss," "sadder but wiser," and countless other phrases bear witness to this observation. In hackneyed, the "wornout" suggestion is pictorially conveyed by the image of a horse that has been overworked beyond the point of response. Bromidic came into use after the appearance of a small volume, *Are You a Bromide?*, by Gelett Burgess. People whose conversation offered nothing more original than such comments as "Better late than never" were enabled to classify themselves, or others might do it for them. Platitudinous language is used by orators who utter commonplaces volubly and sonorously.

Sterile, aseptic, antiseptic. Sterile describes a condition of freedom from bacteria or any kind of living organisms. Surgical instruments, for example, are rendered sterile by heating. Aseptic refers to preventive measures which avoid contact between a person and any source of infection. Antiseptic indicates the destruction of microorganisms that are already present. Commonly used as a noun, the word means any substance capable of destroying germs.

Stigma, brand, blot. Originally meaning a mark burned or made by a pointed instrument, a stigma was the visible sign that a person was a criminal or a slave. In this sense the word was almost an exact equivalent for brand, which denotes a mark made by a hot iron on animals, and formerly on human beings. Gradually, stigma has come to mean not so much an actual mark as a reproach, an unfavorable association that has not resulted from the fault of the one who carries it but has been applied from the outside as a means of discrediting him. Name-calling and the attribution of guilt by association are well-known devices for detraction. Guedalla's famous pun on "Any stick to beat a dog" "Any stigma to beat a dogma," contains a wise observation on the modern stigma technique. In contrast with a reproach gratuitously offered by outsiders, a blot—for example, "a blot in the scutcheon"—arises from some fault within the person who bears it, or within his family. He may live it down eventually, but in the meantime he must assume responsibility for it.

Stir, move. We may move in any manner, but to stir is to move so as to disturb the rest and composure of either the body or the mind.

Story, tale. Story is either a narrative of fictitious happenings or an account of actual events, as in a news story. Tale implies a longer, more wandering narrative or sometimes a made-up report of events intended for deceptive purposes.

Stream, current, tide. All rivers are streams, more or less gentle according to the nature of the ground through which they pass. The force of the current is very much increased by the confinement of any water between rocks, or between artificial embankments. The tide is high or low, strong or weak, at different hours of the day; when the tide is high, the current is strongest. Stream is the general term implying flow; current implies a more or less definite direction and rate of flow; tide applies to a regular flow, alternating in direction. In these senses the words are applied figuratively to human affairs.

Successive, alternate. The successive may be accidental or intentional; the alternate is always intentional. It may rain for three successive days, or a fair may be held for three successive days. Trees are placed sometimes in alternate order, when every other tree is of the same size and kind.

Surround, encompass, environ, encircle. We may surround an object by stationing people at certain distances all round it; in this manner a person may be surrounded by other persons; a garden is surrounded by a wall. Encompass applies to objects of a great or indefinite extent, as the earth is encompassed by the air. To surround is to extend around an object of any form; but to environ and to encircle carry with them the idea of forming a circle round an object. Thus a town or a valley may be environed by hills, a basin of water may be encircled by trees, or the head may be encircled by a wreath of flowers.

Sympathy, compassion, commiseration, condolence. Sympathy has the literal meaning of fellow feeling, that is, a kindred or like feeling, or feeling in company with another. Compassion, commiseration, and condolence signify a like suffering, or a suffering in company. Sympathy preserves its original meaning in its application, for we laugh or cry because of sympathy. Compassion is altogether a moral feeling, which makes us enter into the distresses of others. We may sympathize with others without essentially serving them; but, if we feel compassion, we naturally turn our thoughts toward relieving them. Commiseration is awakened toward those who are in an abject state of misery. Condolence is expressed sympathy.
Antonyms.—Antipathy, harshness, mercilessness, unkindliness, inhumanity.

Tease, vex, taunt, tantalize, torment. To tease is applied to that which is most trifling; torment, to that which is most serious. We are teased by a fly that buzzes in our ears; we are vexed by the carelessness and stupidity of our servants; we are taunted by the sarcasms of others; we are tantalized by the fair prospects which present themselves only to disappear again; we are tormented by the importunities of troublesome beggars or by the pain of anxious fears.
Antonyms.—Calm, comfort, gratify, satisfy, console, relieve.

Thick, dense. We speak of thick in regard to hard or soft bodies, as a thick board or thick cotton; we speak of thick in regard to solid or liquid bodies, as a thick cheese or thick milk. Dense specifically adds the idea of great closeness of parts and consequent weight and solidity. Applied to mind, dense is a stronger term than thick.
Antonyms.—Thin, tenuous, rarefied, quick, clever.

Think, suppose, imagine, believe, deem. We think a thing right or wrong; we suppose it to be true or false; we imagine it to be real or unreal. In regard to moral points, in which case the word deem may be compared with the others, to think is to draw a conclusion from certain premises. I think that a man has acted wrongly. To suppose is to take up an idea arbitrarily or at pleasure; to imagine is to take up an idea by accident, or without any connection with the truth or reality. To deem is to form a conclusion; things are deemed hurtful or otherwise in consequence of observation. We think as the thing strikes us at the time; we believe as the result of a course of thought.
Antonyms.—Know, prove, demonstrate.

Threat, menace. We may be threatened with either small or great evils; but we are menaced only with great evils.
Antonyms.—Attraction, allurement, enticement.

Timely, seasonable, opportune. Anything that is timely comes just when it is of greatest interest or value. Seasonable refers to occurrences, or perhaps articles of merchandise, which come at appropriate periods of the year. Opportune suggests a sort of accidental fitness, as in the case of help which arrives "in the nick of time."
Antonyms.—Ill-timed, inopportune, unseasonable.

Torment, torture. Torture is an excess of torment. We may be tormented by a variety of indirect means; but we are mostly said to be tortured by the direct means that may be compared to the rack or a similar instrument.
Antonyms.—Comfort, ease, solace.

Trembling, tremor, trepidation. Trembling expresses any degree of involuntary shaking of the frame, from the affection of either the body or the mind; cold, nervous affections, fear, and the like are the ordinary causes of trembling. Tremor is a slight degree of trembling, which arises mostly from a mental affection; when the spirits are agitated, the mind is thrown into a tremor by any trifling incident. Trepidation is more violent and springs from fear or alarm; it shows itself in the action, or the different movements of the body, rather than in the body.
Antonyms.—Firmness, immobility, steadiness, self-command.

Trouble, disturb, molest. Trouble is the most general in its application; we may be troubled by the want of a thing, or troubled by what is unsuitable; we are disturbed and molested only by that which actively troubles. Trouble may be permanent; disturbance and molestation are temporary, and both refer to the peace which is destroyed. A disturbance ruffles or throws out of a tranquil state; a molestation burdens or bears hard on either the body or the mind.
Antonyms.—Soothe, quiet, compose, caress.

Truth, veracity. Truth belongs to the thing; veracity to the person. The truth of a story is admitted upon the veracity of the narrator.
Antonyms.—Deception, falsehood, falsity.

Turn, bend, twist, distort, wring, wrest, wrench. We turn a thing by moving it about a fixed point; thus we turn the earth over. To bend is simply to change direction; thus a stick is bent, or a body may bend its direction to a certain point. To twist is to bend many times, to make many turns. To distort is to turn or twist out of the right form; thus the face is distorted in convulsions. To wring is to twist with violence; thus linen that has been wetted is wrung. To wrest or wrench is to separate from a body by means of twisting; thus a stick may be wrested out of the hand, or a hinge wrenched off the door.

Turn, wind, whirl, twirl, writhe. To turn is to cause to rotate; wind is to turn a thing around in a regular manner; whirl, to turn it around in a violent manner; twirl, to turn it around in an irregular and unmeaning way. Writhe implies a twisting about within the thing itself, a contortion, as writhing in pain.

Unbelief, infidelity, incredulity. Unbelief implies a settled doubting state of mind; infidelity carries the idea of unfaithfulness to vows or responsibilities; incredulity is a doubting attitude toward tales more or less strange. In religion both unbelief and infidelity convey a sense of failure in duty, the latter being the stronger word.
Antonyms.—Belief, faith, faithfulness, credulity.

Understanding, intellect, intelligence. Understanding is employed to describe a familiar and easy power or operation of the mind in forming distinct ideas of things. Intellect is employed to mark the same operation in regard to higher and more abstruse objects. Understanding applies to the first exercise of the rational powers; it is therefore aptly said of children and savages that they employ their understandings on the simple objects of perception. Intellect, being a matured state of the understanding, is most properly applied to the efforts of those who have their powers in full vigor. Intelligence is less abstract, and is used of a particular person, often to denote large understanding or capacity for understanding.

Unspeakable, ineffable, unutterable, inexpressible. Unspeakable is sometimes used in religion to refer to those objects which are above human conception and surpass the power of language to describe, as the unspeakable goodness of God. Ineffable is said of such objects as cannot be painted in words with adequate force, as the ineffable sweetness of a person's look. Unspeakable is now applied especially to things too evil for utterance; ineffable is used of things too high or good for utterance. Unutterable and inexpressible are extended in their signification to that which is incommunicable by signs from one being to another. Grief is unutterable which it is not in the power of the sufferer by any sounds to bring home to the feelings of another; grief is inexpressible that is not to be expressed by looks, or words, or any sign.
Antonyms.—Common, commonplace, obvious, trivial.

Unworthy, worthless. Unworthy is a term of less reproach than worthless: the former signifies not to be worthy of praise or honor; the latter signifies to be without all worth, and consequently in the fullest sense bad. There are many unworthy members in every religious community; but every society that is conducted upon proper principles will take care to exclude worthless members.
Antonyms.—Worthy, estimable, admirable, noble.

Usage, custom. Usage is what one has been long accustomed to do; custom is what one generally does. The usage acquires force and sanction by dint of time; the custom acquires sanction by the frequency of its appearance or by the numbers following it.
Antonyms.—Innovation, novelty, fancy.

Utter, speak, articulate, pronounce. Utter signifies to put out; that is, to send forth a sound. This, therefore, is a more general term than speak, which is to utter an intelligible sound. We may utter a groan; we speak words only, or that which is intended to serve as words. Speak, therefore, is only a form of utterance—a dumb man has utterance, but not speech. Articulate and pronounce are modes of speaking. To articulate, from *articulum,* "a joint," is to pronounce distinctly the letters or syllables of words; this is the first effort of a child beginning to speak. To pronounce is to speak words intelligibly.
Antonyms.—Mutter, mumble.

Value, prize, esteem. To value is to estimate the worth, real or supposed, relative or absolute, of a thing; in this sense men value gold above silver, or an appraiser values goods. Prize and esteem are taken only as mental actions; the former is taken in reference to sensible or moral objects, the latter, only to moral objects. We may value books according to their market price, or we may value them according to their contents; we prize books only for their contents; in this sense prize is a much stronger term than value.
Antonyms.—Contemn, disregard, depreciate, disprize, despise.

Vex, annoy, bother, irk. Any of the various kinds of disturbance which these words imply is a sufficient tax on our endurance, though some are perhaps more serious than others. Vex, a rather strong word, suggests worry added to perplexity. Annoy refers to a comparatively mild attack upon our comfort, such as the buzzing of a fly, but its persistence makes it unwelcome. Bother is objectionable because it suggests a needless invasion of our quiet or comfort. Irk connotes a rather severe trial of our patience, with sometimes a violation of our sense of justice or fairness.
Antonyms.—Comfort, soothe, please, gratify.

View, survey, prospect. We take a view or survey; the prospect presents itself. The view is of an indefinite extent; the survey is always comprehensive in its nature. Ignorant people take but narrow views of things; the capacious mind of a genius takes a survey of all nature. Prospect, used literally, signifies an outlook as from a window; figuratively, it implies a person's outlook or view toward the future.

Violent, furious, boisterous, vehement, impetuous. A man is violent in his opinions, violent in his measures, violent in his resentments; he is furious in his anger, or has a furious temper; he is vehement in his affections or passions, vehement in love, vehement in zeal, vehement in pursuing an object. Violence transfers itself to some external object on which it acts with force; but vehemence respects that manner of violence which is confined to the person himself; we may dread violence, because it is always liable to do mischief. Impetuosity is rather the extreme of violence or vehemence. An impetuous attack is an excessively violent attack; an impetuous character is an excessively vehement character. Boisterous is said of the manner and of the behavior rather than of the mind.
Antonyms.—Mild, quiet, gentle, cool, collected, self-restrained.

Wakefulness, watchfulness, vigilance. Wakefulness is an affair of the body and depends upon the temperament; watchfulness is an affair of the will and depends upon the determination. Some persons are more wakeful than they wish to be; few are as watchful as they ought to be. Vigilance expresses a high degree of watchfulness. A sentinel is watchful who on ordinary occasions keeps good watch; but it is necessary for him, on extraordinary occasions, to be vigilant in order to detect whatever may pass.
Antonyms.—Drowsiness, heedlessness, inattention, negligence.

Want, need, lack. To want is to be without that which contributes to our comfort or is an object of our desires; to need is to be without that which is essential to our existence or our purposes. To lack expresses little more than the general idea of being without. It is usual to consider what we want as artificial, and what we need as natural and indispensable. What one man wants is a superfluity to another; but that which is needed by one is in like circumstances needed by all.
Antonyms.—Have, share, possess.

Wave, billow, surge, breaker. Waves which swell more than ordinarily are termed billows; waves which rise higher than usual are termed surges; waves which dash against the shore, or against vessels, with more than ordinary force, are termed breakers.

Weak, feeble, infirm. We may be weak in body or in mind; we are feeble and infirm only in the body; we may be weak from disease, or weak by nature—both words convey the gross idea of a defect. But the terms feeble and infirm are qualified expressions for weakness. An old man is feeble from age; he may likewise be infirm in consequence of sickness.
Antonyms.—Strong, sound, healthy, well.

Weight, burden, load. A person may sink under the weight that rests upon him; a platform may break down from the weight upon it; a person sinks under his burden or load; a cart breaks down from the load.

Whole, entire, complete, total, integral. Whole excludes subtraction; entire excludes division; complete excludes deficiency. A whole orange has had nothing taken from it; an entire orange is not yet cut; a complete orange is grown to its full size. Total is the opposite of partial. Integral is applied now to parts or to numbers not broken.

Will, wish. We can will nothing but what we can effect; we may wish for many things which lie above our reach.

Wisdom, prudence. Wisdom directs all matters present or to come; prudence, which acts by foresight, directs what is to come. Rules of conduct are framed by wisdom, and it is the part of prudence to apply these rules to the business life.
Antonyms.—Unwisdom, imprudence, indiscretion, folly.

Wonder, miracle, marvel, prodigy, monster. Wonders are natural; miracles are supernatural. The whole creation is full of wonders; the Bible contains accounts of miracles. Wonders are real; marvels are often fictitious; prodigies are extravagant and imaginary; monsters are violations of the laws of nature. The production of a tree from a grain of seed is a wonder; but a calf with two heads is a monster.

Wonder, surprise, astonishment, amazement. Wonder is the feeling induced by something strange or unusual. Surprise has the idea of sudden wonder. Astonishment is stronger, and includes failure to understand. Amazement adds the idea of bewilderment at something strange or unexpected.
Antonyms.—Comprehension, coolness, composure.

Work, labor, toil, drudgery, task. Every member of society must work for his support, if he is not in independent circumstances. The poor are obliged to labor for their daily subsistence; some are compelled to toil incessantly for the pittance which they earn. Drudgery falls to the lot of those who are the lowest in society. A man wishes to complete his work; he is desirous of resting from his labor; he seeks for a respite from his toil; he submits to drudgery. Task is a work imposed by others, and it is, consequently, more or less burdensome.
Antonyms.—Play, ease, relaxation, recreation, amusement.

Writer, author. Writer refers us to the act of writing; author, to the act of inventing. There are, therefore, many writers who are not authors; but there is no author of books who may not be termed a writer. Compilers and contributors to periodical works are properly writers, though not always entitled to the name of authors. Poets and historians are properly termed authors rather than writers.

Youthful, juvenile, puerile. Of these three words, youthful is the one most often used in a favorable sense, referring to a natural and usually admirable kind of youngness. Even an older person may be credited with youthful traits, or at least with a youthful spirit. Juvenile and puerile, the Latin words for youthful and boyish, respectively, are frequently used in a deprecatory way to describe immature conduct in adults. Of the two, puerile is the stronger term of disparagement.
Antonyms.—Mature, adult, grown-up.

KEY TO THE DICTIONARY OF SYNONYMS

The following is an index to the synonyms which occur in the preceding section. Combined in a single alphabetical list are the key words, in italics, and the other words, printed in Roman type, which appear as synonyms in connection with the various key words. In the index, each of these secondary words is followed by the italicized key word under which its meaning is discussed in the text. Sometimes the same key word, used in a different sense or having a different grammatical classification, heads more than one group of synonyms. This is shown in the index below by numerals in parentheses placed in line with the key word. Similarly, the same secondary words, having different shades of meaning, may be listed under more than one key word. In every instance, the page reference at the right of the column is to the key word concerned.

Abandon 1038
Abandon, *give up* . 1058
Abandoned, *profligate* 1066
Abashed, *embarrassed* 1053
Abatement, *deduction* 1050
Abbreviate 1038
Abeyance 1038
Abhor 1038
Ability 1038
Abject 1038
Abolish 1038
Abridge, *abbreviate* . 1038
Abrogate, *abolish* . 1038
Abrupt, *steep* . . 1069
Absolute 1038
Absolve, *forgive* . 1057
Abstruse, *dark* . . 1049
Absurd, *irrational* . 1062
Abutting, *adjacent* . 1039
Academic, *pedantic* . 1065
Accede, *agree* . . 1039
Access, *approach* . 1041
Acclamation, *applause* 1040
Accomplice, *confeder-
ate* 1047
Accomplish 1038
Accomplishment, *quali-
fication* 1066
Accord, *correspond* . 1048
Accordant, *consonant* . 1047
Accountable, *answer-
able* 1040
Accumulate, *heap* . 1059
Accurate, *correct* . . 1048
Accusation, *complaint* . 1046
Accuse 1038
Achieve, *accomplish* . 1038
Acquiesce, *agree* . . 1039
Acquit, *exonerate* . . 1055
Acronym, *name* . . 1064
Act (2) 1038
Action 1038
Active 1038
Actual 1038
Actuate 1038
Acute 1038
Acute, *sharp* . . . 1068
Adage, *axiom* . . 1041
Adequate, *proportion-
ate* 1066
Adhere 1038
Adjacent 1039
Adjective, *epithet* . 1054
Administration, *gov-
ernment* 1058
Admit (2) 1039
Admittance, *approach* 1041
Adoration 1039
Advance 1039
Advantage 1039
Adventurous, *enter-
prising* 1054
Adventurous, *foolhardy* 1056
Adverse 1039
Advice 1039
Affect (2) 1039
Affecting, *moving* . 1064
Affectionate . . . 1039
Affirm 1039
Affliction 1039

Affront 1039
Afraid 1039
Aged, *elderly* . . . 1053
Agony, *distress* . . 1052
Agree 1039
Agreeable 1039
Agreeable, *conformable* 1047
Aid, *help* 1059
Aim (2) 1039
Aim, *endeavor* . . 1054
Air 1039
Alacrity, *alertness* . 1039
Alarm 1039
Alertness 1039
Alike, *equal* . . . 1054
Allay 1039
Alleviate 1040
Alleviate, *mitigate* . 1063
Alliance 1040
Allot 1040
Allow 1040
Allow, *admit* . . . 1039
Allow, *consent* . . 1047
Allowance 1040
Allude 1040
Allure, *attract* . . 1041
Almanac, *calendar* . 1043
Alone 1040
Alteration, *change* . 1044
Altercation, *difference* . 1051
Alternate, *successive* . 1070
Amazement, *wonder* . 1071
Ambiguous 1040
Amenable, *answerable* . 1040
Amend 1040
Amends, *compensation* 1046
Amicable 1040
Amuse 1040
Anger 1040
Anger, *displeasure* . 1052
Anguish, *distress* . 1052
Animate 1040
Animosity, *enmity* . 1054
Announce 1040
Annoy, *inconvenience* . 1061
Annoy, *vex* 1071
Annul, *abolish* . . 1038
Answer 1040
Answerable 1040
Antagonistic, *adverse* . 1039
Antipathy, *hatred* . 1059
Antiseptic, *sterile* . 1069
Anxiety, *care* . . . 1044
Anxiety, *distress* . 1052
Aphorism, *axiom* . 1041
Apologize 1040
Appall, *dismay* . . 1052
Apparent 1040
Appear, *seem* . . . 1068
Appearance, *look* . 1063
Appease, *allay* . . 1039
Appetizing, *palatable* 1065
Applause 1040
Appoint 1040
Appoint, *allot* . . 1040
Appoint, *constitute* . 1049
Apposite, *relevant* . 1067
Apprehend 1041
Approach (2) . . . 1041
Approbation, *assent* . 1041
Approximate, *approach* 1041

Apt, *fit* 1056
Apt, *ready* 1067
Arbitrary, *absolute* . 1038
Ardent, *fervent* . . 1056
Ardent, *hot* . . . 1060
Argue 1041
Argue, *discuss* . . 1052
Argument 1041
Arise 1041
Arraign, *accuse* . . 1038
Arrange, *classify* . 1045
Arrive, *come* . . . 1045
Arrogance, *haughtiness* 1059
Arrogant 1041
Art, *business* . . . 1043
Articulate, *utter* . 1071
Artisan, *artist* . . 1041
Artist 1041
Ascend, *arise* . . . 1041
Aseptic, *sterile* . . 1069
Ask 1041
Aspire, *aim* . . . 1039
Assail, *attack* . . 1041
Assault, *attack* . . 1041
Assemble 1041
Assent 1041
Assert, *affirm* . . 1039
Assiduous, *active* . 1038
Assist, *help* . . . 1059
Associate, *colleague* . 1045
Association 1041
Assuage, *allay* . . 1039
Assuage, *mitigate* . 1063
Assume, *affect* . . 1039
Assured, *confident* . 1047
Astral, *starry* . . 1069
Astonishment, *wonder* . 1071
Asylum 1041
Attack 1041
Attack, *impugn* . . 1060
Attempt 1041
Attempt, *endeavor* . 1054
Attend 1041
Attention, *heed* . . 1059
Attentive 1041
Attitude, *action* . 1038
Attract 1041
Austere 1041
Author, *writer* . . 1071
Authorize, *commission* 1046
Avaricious 1041
Avocation, *business* . 1043
Awaken 1041
Award, *give* . . . 1058
Awe 1041
Awkward 1041
Axiom 1041

Babble 1042
Balance, *poise* . . 1065
Band 1042
Banishment 1042
Bankruptcy, *insolvency* 1061
Barbarous, *cruel* . . 1049
Barefaced, *glaring* . 1058
Barter, *change* . . 1044
Bashfulness, *modesty* . 1063
Basis, *foundation* . 1057
Be (2) 1042
Be acquainted with,
know 1062
Bear 1042
Beat 1042
Beautiful 1042
Become, *be* . . . 1042
Becoming 1042
Beg 1042
Behavior 1042
Belief 1042
Believe, *think* . . 1071
Bend, *lean* 1062
Bend, *turn* 1070
Benefit, *advantage* . 1039
Benevolence . . . 1042
Benignity, *benevolence* . 1042
Bequeath, *devise* . 1051
Bereave 1042
Beseech, *beg* . . . 1042
Bestow, *allow* . . 1040
Bestow, *give* . . . 1058
Betray, *discover* . 1052
Bevy, *covey* . . . 1049
Big, *great* 1058
Big, *large* 1062
Billow, *wave* . . . 1071
Blame 1042

Blast, *breeze* . . . 1043
Blemish 1042
Blend, *mix* 1063
Blot, *stigma* . . . 1069
Blot out 1042
Blunder, *error* . . 1054
Boast, *glory* . . . 1058
Boisterous, *violent* . 1071
Bold 1042
Bold, *daring* . . . 1049
Bookish, *pedantic* . 1065
Booty 1043
Bother, *vex* . . . 1071
Bound 1043
Boundless 1043
Bountiful, *liberal* . 1062
Brand, *stigma* . . 1069
Bravery 1043
Brawny, *stalwart* . 1069
Breach 1043
Break (2) 1043
Break, *breach* . . 1043
Breaker, *wave* . . 1071
Breeding, *education* . 1053
Breeze 1043
Brightness 1043
Brightness, *clearness* . 1045
Brilliancy, *brightness* . 1043
Brilliancy, *radiance* . 1066
Bring 1043
Brittle, *fragile* . . 1057
Broil, *quarrel* . . 1066
Bromidic, *stereotyped* . 1069
Bruise, *break* . . 1043
Brutal, *cruel* . . . 1049
Buffoon, *fool* . . . 1056
Bulky 1043
Bungling, *awkward* . 1041
Burden, *weight* . . 1071
Burial 1043
Burlesque, *copy* . . 1048
Burning, *hot* . . . 1060
Burst, *break* . . . 1043
Business (2) . . . 1043
Bustle 1043
Busy, *active* . . . 1038
Butchery, *carnage* . 1044
Byword, *axiom* . . 1041

Calamity 1043
Calculate 1043
Calendar 1043
Call (2) 1043
Calm 1044
Calm, *peace* . . . 1065
Cancel, *blot out* . . 1042
Candid, *frank* . . 1057
Candor 1044
Capacity, *ability* . 1038
Capricious, *fanciful* . 1055
Captious 1044
Capture 1044
Care (2) 1044
Care, *heed* 1059
Careful 1044
Careful, *attentive* . 1041
Carnage 1044
Carp, *censure* . . 1044
Carriage, *air* . . . 1039
Carry, *bring* . . . 1043
Case 1044
Cash, *money* . . . 1064
Casual, *occasional* . 1064
Catch, *lay hold of* . 1062
Cause (2) 1044
Cause, *case* . . . 1044
Cautious 1044
Cavil, *censure* . . 1044
Cease 1044
Celebrate 1044
Celebrated, *famous* . 1055
Celestial 1044
Censure 1044
Censure, *blame* . . 1042
Ceremony, *form* . . 1057
Cessation 1044
Chance 1044
Chance, *happen* . . 1059
Change (2) 1044
Character 1044
Charge, *accuse* . . 1038
Charge, *care* . . . 1044
Charge, *cost* . . . 1048
Charm, *grace* . . 1058
Chasm, *breach* . . 1043
Chasten 1044

Chastise, *chasten* . . . 1044
Chat, *babble* 1042
Chatter, *babble*. . . . 1042
Cheat 1044
Check 1045
Cheer 1045
Cherish, *foster* . . . 1057
Chide, *check* 1045
Chief 1045
Choice, *option* . . . 1065
Choose 1045
Circumscribe, *bound* . 1043
Circumspect, *cautious*. 1044
Circumstance 1045
Cite 1045
Civil 1045
Civilization, *culti-*
 vation 1049
Claim, *right* 1067
Clandestine 1045
Clasp 1045
Classify 1045
Clean 1045
Cleanly, *clean* . . . 1045
Clear, *apparent* . . . 1040
Clear, *fair*. 1055
Clearly 1045
Clearness 1045
Clever 1045
Climb, *arise* 1041
Close (2) 1045
Close, *end* 1054
Clumsy, *awkward* . . 1041
Coalition, *alliance* . . 1040
Coarse 1045
Coarse, *gross* 1058
Cogent 1045
Cohere, *adhere* . . . 1038
Colleague 1045
Collect, *assemble* . . 1041
Collect, *gather* . . . 1057
Collected, *calm* . . . 1044
Colloquy, *conversation* 1048
Colorable, *specious* . 1069
Column, *pillar* . . . 1065
Combat 1045
Combine, *connect*. . . 1047
Come 1045
Comely, *becoming* . . 1042
Comfort 1045
Comfort, *cheer* . . . 1045
Comfortable, *cozy* . . 1049
Command 1045
Commemorate, *cele-*
 brate 1044
Commendable, *laud-*
 able 1062
Commensurate, *propor-*
 tionate 1066
Commercial, *mercan-*
 tile 1063
Commiseration, *sym-*
 pathy 1070
Commission 1046
Commit, *perpetuate* . 1065
Commodious 1046
Common, *general*. . . 1057
Common, *mutual*. . . 1064
Commonly 1046
Communicate 1046
Company, *association* 1041
Company, *band* . . . 1042
Compassion, *pity*. . . 1065
Compassion, *sympathy* 1070
Compatible 1046
Compel 1046
Compensation 1046
Competent 1046
Complain 1046
Complete (2) 1046
Complete, *consummate* 1047
Complete, *whole* . . 1071
Compliment, *flattery* . 1056
Comply 1046
Comply, *agree* . . . 1039
Compose 1046
Compose, *compound* . 1046
Composed 1046
Composed, *calm* . . . 1044
Compound 1046
Comprehend, *conceive* 1046
Comprehend, *comprise* 1046
Comprise 1046
Compute, *calculate* . 1043
Compute, *estimate* . . 1054
Conceal (2) 1046

Conceit 1046
Conceited, *opinionated* 1065
Conceive 1046
Conceive, *apprehend* . 1041
Conception 1046
Concern, *affect* . . . 1039
Concern, *interest* . . 1061
Conciliate 1046
Concise, *short* . . . 1068
Conclude, *close* . . . 1045
Conclusion 1046
Conclusive 1047
Conclusive, *final* . . 1056
Concurrence, *assent* . 1041
Condemn, *blame* . . 1042
Condense, *abbreviate* 1038
Condition 1047
Condolence, *sympathy* 1070
Conduce 1047
Conduct 1047
Conduct, *lead* . . . 1062
Conduct, *behavior* . . 1042
Confederacy, *alliance* 1040
Confederate 1047
Conference, *conversa-*
 tion 1048
Confidence 1047
Confident 1047
Confine, *bound* . . . 1043
Confirm 1047
Conform, *comply* . . 1046
Conformable 1047
Confound 1047
Confront 1047
Confuse, *confound* . . 1047
Confusion 1047
Confute 1047
Congratulate, *felici-*
 tate 1056
Conjecture, *guess* . . 1059
Connect 1047
Conqueror 1047
Conscious (be), *feel* . 1056
Consecrate, *dedicate* . 1050
Consent 1047
Consent, *agree* . . . 1039
Consent, *assent* . . . 1041
Consequence 1047
Consider 1047
Consistent, *compatible*. 1046
Consistent, *consonant* 1047
Consonant 1047
Conspicuous, *distin-*
 guished 1052
Conspicuous, *noticeable* 1064
Conspicuous, *promi-*
 nent 1066
Constancy 1047
Constant, *continual*. . 1048
Consternation, *alarm* 1039
Constitute 1047
Consult 1047
Consume, *destroy*. . . 1051
Consummate 1047
Contagious 1047
Contain, *comprise* . . 1046
Contaminate 1047
Contamination, *deprav-*
 ity 1050
Contemplate 1047
Contend 1047
Contention, *discord* . 1052
Contentment 1048
Contest, *contend* . . 1047
Continual 1048
Continuance 1048
Continuation, *continu-*
 ance 1048
Continue (2) 1048
Continued, *continual* . 1048
Continuity, *continu-*
 ance 1048
Continuous, *continual*. 1048
Contradict 1048
Contribute, *conduce* . 1047
Controvert 1048
Contumacious 1048
Convenience 1048
Convenient, *commo-*
 dious 1046
Conversant 1048
Conversation 1048
Convert 1048
Convince 1048
Convincing, *conclusive* 1047
Convict, *criminal* . . 1049

Convivial 1048
Cool, *dispassionate* . . 1052
Copy 1048
Coquette 1048
Cordial, *hearty* . . . 1059
Corporation, *associa-*
 tion 1041
Correct 1048
Correct, *amend* . . . 1040
Correction 1048
Correctness, *justness* 1062
Correspond 1048
Corroborate, *confirm* . 1047
Corrupt, *contaminate* . 1047
Corruption, *depravity* . 1050
Cost 1048
Counsel, *advice* . . . 1039
Count, *calculate* . . 1043
Country, *land* . . . 1062
Courage 1048
Courage, *bravery* . . 1043
Cover 1048
Covet, *desire* 1051
Covey 1049
Cozy (sy) 1049
Crack, *break* 1043
Craftsman, *artist* . . 1041
Crave, *beg*. 1042
Create, *cause* 1044
Create, *make* 1063
Credit 1049
Credit, *belief* 1042
Creed, *faith* 1055
Crew, *band* 1042
Crime 1049
Criminal 1049
Cringing, *abject* . . 1038
Criterion 1049
Cross, *captious* . . . 1044
Cruel 1049
Crush, *break* 1043
Cry, *call* 1043
Crying 1049
Cryptic, *ambiguous* . 1040
Culprit, *criminal* . . 1049
Cultivation 1049
Culture, *cultivation* . 1049
Cure 1049
Curious 1049
Current, *stream* . . . 1070
Cursory 1049
Custody, *keeping* . . 1062
Custom 1049
Custom, *usage* . . . 1071

Dampness, *moisture* 1063
Danger 1049
Daring 1049
Dark 1049
Daunt, *dismay* . . . 1052
Deadly 1049
Debate, *discuss* . . . 1052
Debt 1049
Deceit 1049
Deceitful, *fallacious* . 1055
Deceiver 1049
Decency 1049
Deception, *deceit* . . 1049
Decided (2) 1049
Decision 1049
Decisive, *decided* . . 1049
Decline, *refuse* . . . 1067
Decorum, *decency* . . 1049
Decree 1050
Dedicate 1050
Deduce, *derive* . . . 1050
Deduction 1050
Deduction, *conclusion*. 1046
Deem, *think* 1070
Deface 1050
Defeat, *beat* 1042
Defect, *blemish* . . . 1042
Defective 1050
Defend 1050
Defend, *apologize* . . 1040
Defend, *guard* . . . 1058
Defendant 1050
Defender, *defendant* . 1050
Deficient, *defective* . 1050
Defile, *contaminate* . 1047
Definite 1050
Definitive, *definite* . 1050
Deform, *deface* . . . 1050
Defraud, *cheat* . . . 1044
Deity 1050
Dejection 1050

Delegate 1050
Deliberate, *consult* . . 1047
Delicate, *fine* . . . 1056
Delinquent, *offender* . 1064
Deliver 1050
Demand. 1050
Demur (2) 1050
Denote 1050
Dense, *thick* 1070
Deny 1050
Deny, *contradict* . . 1048
Depict, *pain* 1065
Deplore 1050
Deposit 1050
Depravity 1050
Depression, *dejection* . 1050
Deprive, *bereave* . . 1042
Depth 1050
Depute, *constitute* . . 1047
Deputy, *delegate* . . 1050
Derive 1050
Desert 1050
Desert, *abandon* . . . 1038
Desert, *solitary* . . . 1068
Design 1051
Desire 1051
Desist 1051
Desolate, *alone* . . . 1040
Desolate, *solitary* . . 1068
Despair 1051
Desperation, *despair* . 1051
Despondency, *despair*. 1051
Despotic, *absolute* . . 1038
Destination, *destiny* . 1051
Destine, *allot* . . . 1040
Destiny (2) 1051
Destitute, *forsaken* . 1057
Destroy 1051
Destruction 1051
Desultory, *cursory* . . 1049
Detain, *hold* 1060
Determine 1051
Determined, *decided* . 1049
Detest, *abhor* . . . 1038
Deviate 1051
Deviate, *digress* . . 1051
Devise 1051
Devote, *dedicate* . . 1050
Dexterity, *ease*. . . 1053
Dexterous, *clever* . . 1045
Dialogue, *conversation* 1048
Dictate 1051
Dictionary (2) 1051
Die 1051
Difference (3) 1051
Difficulty 1051
Diffidence, *distrust* . 1053
Diffidence, *modesty* . 1063
Diffuse 1051
Diffuse, *spread* . . . 1069
Digress 1051
Dilate 1051
Dilemma, *predicament* 1065
Diligent 1051
Diligent, *active* . . . 1038
Dim, *dark* 1049
Diminutive, *little* . . 1063
Direct, *conduct*. . . 1047
Direction, *command* . 1045
Disappear 1051
Disapprobation, *dis-*
 pleasure 1052
Disapproval 1051
Disapprove 1052
Disaster, *calamity* . . 1043
Disbelief 1052
Discipline, *correction* 1048
Disclaim 1052
Disclose, *publish* . . 1066
Discontinue, *cease* . . 1044
Discord 1052
Discover. 1052
Discover, *find* . . . 1056
Discredit 1052
Discretion, *judgment* 1062
Discriminate, *distin-*
 guish 1052
Discuss 1052
Disdain, *haughtiness* 1059
Disease, *disorder* . . 1052
Diseased, *sick* . . . 1068
Disfigure, *deface* . . 1050
Disgrace, *discredit* . 1052
Disguise, *conceal* . . 1046
Disgust 1052
Dishonest 1052

Dishonor, *discredit* . . 1052
Disinclination, *disapproval* 1051
Disjoint 1052
Dislike, *disapproval* . 1051
Dislike, *disapprove* . . 1052
Dismal, *dull* 1053
Dismay 1052
Dismember, *disjoint* . . 1052
Disorder 1052
Disorder, *confusion* . . 1047
Disown, *disclaim* . . 1052
Disparity 1052
Dispassionate . . . 1052
Dispatch, *hasten* . . . 1059
Dispel 1052
Dispense 1052
Disperse, *dispel* . . . 1052
Displeasure 1052
Disposal 1052
Disposition (2) . . . 1052
Disposition, *disposal* . 1052
Disprove, *confute* . . 1047
Dispute, *contend* . . 1047
Dispute, *controvert* . . 1048
Dispute, *difference* . . 1051
Disregard 1052
Dissemble, *conceal* . . 1046
Dissension, *discord* . . 1052
Dissimulation, *simulation* 1068
Distant 1052
Distemper, *disorder* . . 1052
Distinction, *difference* . 1051
Distinctly, *clearly* . . 1045
Distinguish 1052
Distinguished . . . 1052
Distort, *turn* 1070
Distress 1052
Distress, *affliction* . . 1039
Distribute, *dispense* . . 1052
Distribute, *divide* . . 1053
Distrust 1053
Disturb 1053
Disturb, *trouble* . . . 1070
Diversity, *difference* . 1051
Divert, *amuse* . . . 1040
Divide (2) 1053
Divine, *godlike* . . . 1058
Divine, *holy* 1060
Divinity, *deity* . . . 1050
Divulge, *discover* . . 1052
Divulge, *publish* . . 1066
Do, *act* 1038
Doctrine 1053
Dogma, *doctrine* . . 1053
Doleful, *piteous* . . . 1065
Domestic, *servant* . . 1068
Domineering, *imperious* 1060
Donation, *gift* . . . 1058
Doom, *destiny* . . . 1051
Doubt (2) 1053
Doubt, *demur* . . . 1050
Downfall, *fall* . . . 1055
Drag, *draw* 1053
Draw 1053
Dread, *awe* 1041
Dreadful, *fearful* . . 1056
Dreadful, *formidable* . 1057
Dream 1053
Drench, *soak* . . . 1068
Drudge, *servant* . . 1068
Drudgery, *work* . . 1071
Due, *debt* 1049
Dull 1053
Durable 1053
Duration, *continuance* 1048
Duty 1053

Ease 1053
Eclipse 1053
Economical, *penurious* 1065
Edict, *decree* . . . 1050
Educated, *literate* . . 1063
Education 1053
Efface, *blot out* . . 1042
Effect 1053
Effect, *accomplish* . . 1038
Effect, *consequence* . 1047
Effeminate, *female* . . 1056
Effort, *attempt* . . . 1041
Effort, *endeavor* . . 1054
Egotistical, *opionated* 1065
Elderly 1053

Elegance, *grace* . . . 1058
Elucidate, *explain* . . 1055
Embarrassed 1053
Embarrassment, *difficulty* 1051
Emboldened, encouraged 1053
Embrace, *clasp* . . . 1045
Embrace, *comprise* . . 1046
Emergency, *exigency* . 1055
Eminent, *distinguished* 1052
Emissary 1053
Employ 1053
Employment, *business* 1043
Empower, *commission* 1045
Empty, *hollow* . . . 1060
Encircle, *surround* . . 1070
Enclose, *bound* . . . 1043
Encompass, *surround* . 1070
Encourage, *cheer* . . 1045
Encouraged 1053
Encyclopedia, *dictionary* 1051
End 1054
End, *aim* 1039
Endeavor (2) 1054
Endeavor, *attempt* . . 1041
Endless, *eternal* . . 1054
Endow, *invest* . . . 1062
Endue, *invest* . . . 1062
Energy 1054
Engage, *attract* . . . 1041
Engagement, *promise* . 1066
Enlarge 1054
Enlighten, *illuminate* . 1060
Enliven, *animate* . . 1040
Enmity 1054
Enmity, *hatred* . . . 1059
Enormous 1054
Enough 1054
Ensue, *follow* . . . 1056
Enterprising 1054
Entertain, *amuse* . . 1040
Entire, *whole* . . . 1071
Entreat, *beg* 1042
Environ, *surround* . . 1070
Envy, *jealousy* . . . 1062
Epicure, *sensualist* . . 1068
Epidemic, *contagious* . 1047
Episode, *event* . . . 1054
Epithet 1054
Equable, *equal* . . . 1054
Equal 1054
Equivocal, *ambiguous* 1040
Equivocate, *evade* . . 1054
Erase, *blot out* . . 1042
Error 1054
Erudition, *knowledge* . 1062
Eruption 1054
Essay, *attempt* . . . 1041
Esteem, *value* . . . 1071
Estimate 1054
Eternal 1054
Evade 1054
Even, *equal* 1054
Event 1054
Everlasting, *eternal* . 1054
Evident, *apparent* . . 1040
Evince, *argue* . . . 1041
Exact (2) 1054
Exact, *correct* . . . 1048
Example 1054
Excite 1054
Excite, *awaken* . . . 1041
Exchange, *change* . . 1044
Exclaim, *call* . . . 1043
Exculpate, *apologize* . 1040
Exculpate, *exonerate* . 1055
Excursion 1054
Excuse 1055
Excuse, *apologize* . . 1040
Execute 1055
Execute, *accomplsh* . 1038
Exempt, *free* . . . 1057
Exercise 1055
Exhibition, *show* . . 1068
Exhilarate, *animate* . 1040
Exigency 1055
Exile, *banishment* . . 1042
Exist, *be* 1042
Exonerate 1055
Expand, *dilate* . . . 1051
Expand, *spread* . . . 1069
Expediency 1055
Expedient 1055
Expedite, *hasten* . . 1059

Expeditious, *diligent* . 1051
Expense, *cost* . . . 1048
Expert, *clever* . . . 1045
Explain (2) 1055
Explosion, *eruption* . 1054
Expostulate 1055
Expound, *explain* . . 1055
Expire, *die* 1051
Expulsion, *banishment* 1042
Expunge, *blot out* . . 1042
Extend, *enlarge* . . 1054
Exterior, *outward* . . 1065
External, *outward* . . 1065
Extort, *exact* . . . 1054
Extraneous 1055
Extraordinary . . . 1055
Extravagant 1055
Extrinsic, *extraneous* . 1055
Exuberant 1055

Face, *confront* . . . 1047
Facetious 1055
Facility, *ease* . . . 1053
Factious 1055
Faculty, *ability* . . . 1038
Failure, *insolvency* . 1061
Fair 1055
Fair, *beautiful* . . . 1042
Faith (2) 1055
Faith, *belief* . . . 1042
Faithless 1055
Fall 1055
Fallacious 1055
Falter, *hesitate* . . 1059
Fame 1055
Fame, *reputation* . . 1067
Familiar, *conversant* . 1048
Familiar, *free* . . . 1057
Famous 1055
Fanciful 1055
Fancy 1056
Fancy, *conceit* . . . 1046
Fantastic, *fanciful* . . 1055
Far, *distant* 1052
Fashion, *custom* . . 1049
Fashion, *form* . . . 1057
Fatal, *deadly* . . . 1049
Fate, *chance* . . . 1044
Fate, *destiny* . . . 1051
Fateful, *omnious* . . 1065
Fatigue 1056
Fault, *blemish* . . . 1042
Fault, *error* 1054
Favor, *credit* . . . 1049
Fearful 1056
Fearful, *afraid* . . . 1039
Fearless, *bold* . . . 1042
Fee, *allowance* . . . 1040
Feeble, *weak* . . . 1071
Feel 1056
Feign 1056
Felicitate 1056
Felon, *criminal* . . 1049
Female 1056
Feminine, *female* . . 1056
Ferocious 1056
Fervent 1056
Fetch, *bring* . . . 1043
Feud, *quarrel* . . . 1066
Fidelity, *faith* . . . 1055
Fierce, *ferocious* . . 1056
Fiery, *hot* 1060
Final 1056
Find 1056
Fine 1056
Fine, *beautiful* . . . 1042
Finish, *close* . . . 1045
Finish, *complete* . . 1046
Finished, *complete* . . 1046
Finite 1056
Firm 1056
Firm, *hard* 1059
Firmness, *constancy* . 1047
Fit 1056
Fitness, *expediency* . 1055
Fitted, *competent* . . 1046
Fixed, *firm* 1056
Flattery 1056
Flaw, *blemish* . . . 1042
Flexible 1056
Flock, *covey* . . . 1049
Fluctuate 1056
Follow 1056
Folly 1056
Fond, *affectionate* . . 1039
Fond, *indulgent* . . 1061

Fool 1056
Foolery, *folly* . . . 1056
Foolhardy 1056
Foolish, *irrational* . . 1062
Force 1057
Force, *compel* . . . 1046
Force, *energy* . . . 1054
Forcible, *cogent* . . 1045
Forgo, *give up* . . 1058
Foreign, *extraneous* . 1055
Foretell 1057
Forgetfulness . . . 1057
Forgive 1057
Forlorn, *forsaken* . . 1057
Form (2) 1057
Form, *make* . . . 1063
Formidable 1057
Forsake, *abandon* . . 1038
Forsaken 1057
Forswear 1057
Fortitude, *courage* . . 1048
Fortunate, *happy* . . 1059
Fortune, *chance* . . 1044
Foster 1057
Foundation 1057
Fragile 1057
Frail, *fragile* . . . 1057
Frank 1057
Fraudulent, *fallacious* . 1055
Free (3) 1057
Free, *frank* 1057
Frenzy, *madness* . . 1063
Frequent 1057
Frequently, *commonly* 1046
Fresh, *new* 1064
Fretful, *captious* . . 1044
Friendly, *amicable* . . 1040
Fright, *alarm* . . . 1039
Frighten 1057
Frightful, *fearful* . . 1056
Fulfill, *execute* . . 1055
Furious, *violent* . . 1071
Furnish, *provide* . . 1066
Fury, *anger* . . . 1040
Fury, *madness* . . . 1063

Gait, *air* 1039
Gale, *breeze* . . . 1043
Gallantry, *bravery* . . 1043
Gamesome, *playful* . 1065
Gang, *band* . . . 1042
Gap, *breach* . . . 1043
Gape 1057
Gather 1057
Gaze, *gape* 1057
General 1057
Generally, *commonly* . 1046
Generous, *liberal* . . 1062
Genius, *ability* . . . 1038
Genius, *intellect* . . 1061
Genteel 1058
Gentle 1058
Gesticulation, *action* . 1038
Gesture, *action* . . 1038
Gift 1058
Give 1058
Give up 1058
Gladness, *joy* . . . 1062
Glance, *glimpse* . . 1058
Glaring 1058
Glide, *slip* 1068
Glimpse 1058
Gloomy, *dull* . . . 1053
Glory (2) 1058
Glossary, *dictionary* . 1051
Godlike 1058
Good humor, *good nature* 1058
Good nature 1058
Govern 1058
Government 1058
Grace 1058
Graceful, *becoming* . 1042
Grand, *great* . . . 1058
Grand, *stately* . . . 1069
Grandiose, *stately* . . 1069
Grant, *allow* . . . 1040
Grant, *give* 1058
Gratify 1058
Gratify, *satisfy* . . 1067
Gratuitous 1058
Grave 1058
Grave 1058
Great 1058
Great, *large* 1062
Grief, *affliction* . . 1039

Grip, *press* 1066
Groan 1058
Gross 1058
Ground, *foundation* . . 1057
Grow, *be* 1042
Grow, *increase* . . . 1061
Guard 1058
Guess 1059
Guest 1059
Guide, *lead* 1062
Guile, *deceit* 1049
Guise 1059
Gust, *breeze* 1043

Habit, *custom* 1049
Habit, *guise* 1059
Habitation 1059
Hackneyed, *stereotyped* 1069
Hallow, *dedicate* . . . 1050
Handsome, *beautiful* . . 1042
Happen 1059
Happiness, *comfort* . . 1045
Happy 1059
Harass, *distress* . . . 1053
Harbor 1059
Harbor, *foster* 1057
Hard 1059
Haste, *rashness* . . . 1067
Hasten 1059
Hasty, *cursory* . . . 1049
Hateful 1059
Hatred 1059
Haughtiness 1059
Haul, *draw* 1053
Haunt, *frequent* . . . 1057
Have 1059
Haven, *harbor* . . . 1059
Hazard, *danger* . . . 1049
Heal, *cure* 1049
Healthful 1059
Healthy, *sound* . . . 1068
Heap 1059
Hear, *attend* 1041
Hearsay, *fame* . . . 1055
Hearty 1059
Heave, *lift* 1063
Heavenly, *celestial* . . 1044
Heavenly, *godlike* . . 1058
Heed 1059
Help 1059
Heresy, *heterodoxy* . . 1059
Hesitate 1059
Hesitate, *demur* . . . 1050
Hesitation, *demur* . . 1050
Heterodoxy 1059
Hidden, *secret* . . . 1067
Hide, *conceal* 1046
Hide, *cover* 1048
High 1059
Hinder 1060
Hinder, *retard* . . . 1067
Hint, *allude* 1040
Hoist, *lift* 1063
Hold (2) 1060
Holiness 1060
Hollow 1060
Holy 1060
Home, *habitation* . . 1059
Honor 1060
Honor, *glory* 1058
Honorarium, *allowance* 1040
Horrible, *fearful* . . . 1056
Horrid, *fearful* . . . 1056
Hostile, *adverse* . . . 1039
Hostility, *enmity* . . . 1054
Hot 1060
House, *habitation* . . . 1059
Hug, *clasp* 1045
Human 1060
Humane, *human* . . . 1060
Humanity, *benevolence* 1042
Humble 1060
Humidity, *moisture* . . 1063
Humor 1060
Humor, *gratify* . . . 1058
Hurricane, *breeze* . . 1043
Hurry, *hasten* . . . 1059
Hurtful 1060

Ideal 1060
Idiot, *fool* 1056
Idle 1060
Illume, *illuminate* . . 1060
Illuminate 1060
Illustrate, *explain* . . 1055
Illustration, *example* . 1054

Illustrious, *distin-*
guished 1052
Illustrious, *famous* . . 1055
Image, *conception* . . 1046
Imaginary, *ideal* . . . 1060
Imagination, *fancy* . . 1056
Imagine, *apprehend* . . 1041
Imagine, *think* . . . 1070
Imitate, *copy* 1048
Imminent 1060
Immune, *free* 1057
Impair 1060
Impart, *communicate* . 1046
Impeach, *accuse* . . . 1038
Impediment, *difficulty* . 1051
Impel, *actuate* . . . 1038
Impending, *imminent* . 1060
Imperious 1060
Impetuous, *violent* . . 1071
Impious, *irreligious* . . 1062
Implicate 1060
Implore, *beg* 1042
Importunity, *solici-*
tation 1068
Impostor, *deceiver* . . 1049
Impugn 1060
Inability 1060
Inadvertency 1061
Inattention, *inad-*
vertency 1061
Incident, *event* . . . 1054
Incite, *excite* 1054
Inclination 1061
Inclination, *disposi-*
tion 1052
Incline, *lean* 1062
Include, *comprise* . . 1046
Incontrovertible, *in-*
dubitable 1061
Inconvenience 1061
Increase 1061
Increase, *enlarge* . . . 1054
Incredulity, *unbelief* . 1070
Indebted 1061
Indifferent 1061
Indignation, *anger* . . 1040
Indisputable, *indu-*
bitable 1061
Individual, *particular* . 1065
Indolent, *idle* 1060
Indubitable 1061
Induce, *actuate* . . . 1038
Induction, *conclusion* . 1046
Indulge, *foster* . . . 1057
Indulge, *gratify* . . . 1058
Indulgent 1061
Industrious, *active* . . 1038
Ineffable, *unspeakable* . 1070
Inequality, *disparity* . 1052
Inexpressible, *un-*
speakable 1070
Infamous 1061
Infectious, *contagious* . 1047
Inference, *conclusion* . 1041
Infidelity, *unbelief* . . 1070
Infinite, *boundless* . . 1043
Infirm, *weak* 1071
Influence, *affect* . . . 1039
Influence, *credit* . . . 1049
Inform 1061
Information, *news* . . 1064
Ingenuity 1061
Ingenuous, *frank* . . 1057
Ingenuous, *naive* . . 1064
Injunction, *command* . 1045
Injure, *impair* . . . 1060
Injury, *injustice* . . . 1061
Injustice 1061
Inquire, *ask* 1041
Inquisitive, *curious* . . 1049
Inside 1061
Insinuation 1061
Insist 1061
Insolvency 1061
Instance, *example* . . 1054
Instant 1061
Instruct, *inform* . . . 1061
Instruction, *education* . 1053
Insult, *affront* . . . 1039
Insurrection 1061
Integral, *whole* . . . 1071
Intellect 1061
Intellect, *understand-*
ing 1070
Intelligence, *news* . . 1064

Intelligence, *under-*
standing 1070
Intend, *design* . . . 1051
Interchange 1061
Interest 1061
Interior, *inside* . . . 1061
Interment, *burial* . . 1043
Intermission, *cessation* 1044
Interposition, *inter-*
vention 1061
Interpret, *explain* . . 1055
Interrogate, *ask* . . . 1041
Interrupt, *disturb* . . 1053
Interval 1061
Intervention 1061
Intimidate, *frighten* . . 1057
Intrepid, *bold* . . . 1042
Introductory, *prelim-*
inary 1066
Intrude 1062
Invalid 1062
Invent, *find* 1056
Invest 1062
Invite, *attract* . . . 1041
Invite, *call* 1043
Involve, *implicate* . . 1060
Ire, *anger* 1040
Irk, *vex* 1071
Irrational 1062
Irrefragable, *indubi-*
table 1061
Irreligious 1062
Issue, *offspring* . . . 1064

Jealousy 1062
Jilt, *coquette* 1048
Jocose, *facetious* . . . 1055
Jocular, *facetious* . . 1055
Journey 1062
Joy 1062
Judgment 1062
Judgment, *decision* . . 1050
Justify, *apologize* . . 1040
Justness 1062
Juvenile, *youthful* . . 1071
Juxtaposed, *adjacent* . 1039

Keen, *acute* 1038
Keen, *sharp* 1068
Keep 1062
Keep, *hold* 1060
Keeping 1062
Kind, *affectionate* . . 1039
Kindness, *benevolence* . 1042
Kingly, *royal* 1067
Knavish, *dishonest* . . 1052
Know 1062
Knowledge 1062

Labor, *work* 1071
Laborious, *active* . . . 1038
Lack, *want* 1071
Lag, *linger* 1063
Lament, *complain* . . 1046
Lament, *deplore* . . . 1050
Land 1062
Languor, *lethargy* . . 1062
Large 1062
Large, *great* 1058
Lassitude, *fatigue* . . 1056
Lassitude, *lethargy* . . 1062
Lasting, *durable* . . . 1053
Latent, *secret* 1067
Laudable 1062
Lavish, *extravagant* . . 1055
Lay, *put* 1066
Lay hold of 1062
Lazy, *idle* 1060
Lead 1062
League, *alliance* . . . 1040
Lean 1062
Learned, *literate* . . . 1063
Learning, *knowledge* . 1062
Leave 1062
Leave off, *desist* . . . 1051
Lethal, *deadly* . . . 1049
Lethargy 1062
Lexicon, *dictionary* . . 1051
Liberal 1062
Liberal, *free* 1057
Lift 1063
Like, *equal* 1054
Likeness 1063
Limber, *flexible* . . . 1056
Limit, *bound* 1043
Limited, *finite* . . . 1056

Linger 1063
Listen, *attend* . . . 1041
Literate 1063
Little 1063
Load, *weight* 1071
Loathe, *abhor* . . . 1038
Loathing, *disgust* . . 1052
Locality, *neighbor-*
hood 1064
Lofty, *high* 1059
Loiter, *linger* 1063
Lonely, *alone* 1040
Look 1063
Look, *air* 1039
Lordly, *imperious* . . 1060
Loose, *slack* 1068
Lose 1063
Lot, *destiny* 1051
Lucidity, *clearness* . . 1045
Luster, *brightness* . . 1043
Luxuriant, *exuberant* . 1055

Madness 1063
Magnificence 1063
Main, *chief* 1045
Majestic, *stately* . . . 1069
Make 1063
Make, *act* 1038
Malady, *disorder* . . . 1052
Malefactor, *criminal* . 1049
Malevolence 1063
Maliciousness, *malev-*
olence 1063
Malignity, *malevolence* 1063
Manage, *conduct* . . . 1047
Management, *care* . . 1044
Manly 1063
Manner, *air* 1039
Manners 1063
Mariner, *seaman* . . . 1067
Mark 1063
Martial 1063
Marvel, *wonder* . . . 1071
Masculine, *manly* . . 1063
Massacre, *carnage* . . 1044
Massive, *bulky* . . . 1043
Maxim, *axiom* . . . 1041
Mean, *design* 1051
Mechanic, *artist* . . . 1041
Meditate, *contemplate* . 1047
Medley, *difference* . . 1051
Melancholy, *dejection* . 1050
Memory 1063
Menace, *threat* . . . 1070
Mend, *amend* 1040
Menial, *servant* . . . 1068
Mercantile 1063
Merit, *desert* 1050
Mighty, *powerful* . . 1065
Military, *martial* . . . 1063
Mimic, *copy* 1048
Mingle, *mix* 1063
Minute, *circumstan-*
tial 1045
Miracle, *wonder* . . . 1071
Mirth, *joy* 1062
Mischance, *calamity* . 1043
Misfortune, *calamity* . 1043
Miserly, *avaricious* . . 1041
Mishap, *calamity* . . 1043
Miss, *lose* 1063
Mistake, *error* . . . 1054
Mitigate 1063
Mitigate, *allay* . . . 1039
Mix 1063
Moan, *groan* 1058
Modern, *new* 1064
Modest, *humble* . . . 1060
Modesty 1063
Moisture 1063
Mold, *form* 1057
Molest, *inconvenience* . 1061
Molest, *trouble* . . . 1070
Moment, *instant* . . . 1061
Money 1064
Monster, *wonder* . . 1071
Monstrous, *enormous* . 1054
Mood, *humor* 1060
Morals, *manners* . . . 1063
Morbid, *sick* 1068
Mortal, *deadly* . . . 1049
Motion 1064
Motive, *cause* 1044
Mount, *arise* 1041
Move, *stir* 1069
Movement, *motion* . . 1064

Moving 1064
Munificent, *liberal* . . 1062
Muse, *contemplate* . . 1047
Muster, *assemble* . . 1041
Mutual 1064
Mysterious, *dark* . . 1049
Mysterious, *secret* . . 1067

Naive 1064
Name. 1064
Native 1064
Natural, *native* . . . 1064
Nausea, *disgust* . . 1052
Near, *close* 1045
Necessitate, *compel* . 1046
Need, *want* 1071
Neglect 1064
Neglect, *disregard* . . 1052
Neighborhood . . . 1064
New 1064
News 1064
Nice, *exact* 1054
Nice, *fine* 1056
Nickname, *name* . . 1064
Niggardly, *avaricious* . 1041
Niggardly, *penurious* . 1065
Noisome, *hurtful* . . 1060
Noted, *distinguished* . 1052
Notice 1064
Notice, *news* 1064
Noticeable, *prominent* . 1066
Notion, *conception* . . 1046
Novel, *new* 1064
Noxious, *hurtful* . . 1060
Numeral 1064
Numerical, *numeral* . 1064

Obedient 1064
Object. 1064
Object, *aim* 1039
Objection, *demur* . . 1050
Obligation, *duty* . . 1053
Oblige, *compel* . . . 1046
Obliged, *indebted* . . 1061
Obliging, *civil* . . . 1045
Obliterate, *blot out* . 1042
Oblivion, *forgetfulness* . 1057
Obnoxious 1064
Obscure, *dark* . . . 1049
Obscure, *eclipse* . . 1053
Obsequious, *obedient* . 1064
Observance, *form* . . 1057
Observe, *notice* . . . 1064
Observe, *see* 1068
Obstacle, *difficulty* . . 1051
Obtrude, *intrude* . . 1062
Obvious, *apparent* . . 1040
Occasion 1064
Occasion, *cause* . . 1044
Occasional 1064
Occult, *secret* . . . 1067
Occupation, *business* . 1043
Occupy, *hold* . . . 1060
Odious, *hateful* . . 1059
Offender 1064
Offensive, *obnoxious* . 1064
Officious, *active* . . 1038
Offspring 1064
Old, *elderly* 1053
Ominous 1065
Omit, *neglect* . . . 1064
Open, *frank* 1057
Openness, *candor* . . 1044
Operate, *act* 1038
Opinionated 1065
Opportune, *timely* . . 1070
Opportunity, *occasion* . 1064
Oppose, *combat* . . 1045
Oppose, *object* . . . 1064
Option 1065
Ordain, *appoint* . . 1040
Order, *appoint* . . . 1040
Order, *command* . . 1045
Ostentatious, *showy* . 1068
Outrage, *affront* . . 1039
Outward 1065
Ovation, *applause* . . 1040
Overbearing, *imperious* 1060
Overpower, *beat* . . 1042
Oversight, *inadvertency* 1061
Overthrow, *beat* . . 1042

Paint 1065
Palatable 1065
Pardon, *excuse* . . . 1055

Pardon, *forgive.* . . 1057
Parody, *copy* 1048
Parsimonious, *avaricious* 1041
Part 1065
Particular 1065
Particular, *circumstantial* 1045
Particular, *exact* . . 1054
Partner, *colleague* . . 1045
Partnership, *association* 1041
Patch, *part* 1065
Pathetic, *moving* . . 1064
Patient, *invalid* . . 1062
Pattern, *example* . . 1054
Pay, *allowance* . . . 1040
Peace 1065
Pedantic 1065
Peevish, *captious* . . 1044
Penurious 1065
Perceive, *see* 1068
Perfect, *complete* . . 1046
Perfidious, *faithless* . 1055
Perform, *effect* . . . 1053
Perform, *execute* . . 1055
Performance, *production* 1066
Peril, *danger* 1049
Perish, *die* 1051
Perjure, *forswear* . . 1057
Permanent, *durable* . 1053
Permit, *admit* . . . 1039
Permit, *consent* . . 1047
Pernicious, *hurtful* . 1060
Perpetuate 1065
Perpetual, *continual* . 1048
Perplex, *distress* . . 1053
Perplexed, *embarrassed* 1053
Persevere, *continue* . 1048
Persist, *continue* . . 1048
Persist, *insist* . . . 1061
Perspicuity, *clearness* . 1045
Persuade, *convince* . 1048
Pertinent, *relevant* . 1067
Petulant, *captious* . . 1044
Phenomenal, *extraordinary* 1055
Pick, *choose* 1045
Piece, *part* 1065
Pile, *heap* 1059
Pilfer, *steal* 1069
Pillar 1065
Pinch, *press* 1066
Piteous 1065
Pity 1065
Place, *put* 1066
Placid, *calm* 1044
Plain, *apparent* . . 1040
Plain, *frank* 1057
Platitudinous, *stereotyped* 1069
Plausible, *specious* . 1069
Playful 1065
Plead, *apologize* . . 1040
Pleasant, *agreeable* . 1039
Please, *satisfy* . . . 1067
Pleasing, *agreeable* . 1039
Pleasure, *comfort* . . 1045
Pledge, *deposit* . . . 1050
Pliable, *flexible* . . 1056
Pliant, *flexible* . . . 1056
Plight, *predicament* . 1065
Poise 1065
Poison 1065
Polish, *politeness* . . 1065
Polite, *civil* 1045
Polite, *genteel* . . . 1058
Politeness 1065
Pollute, *contaminate* . 1047
Pomp, *magnificence* . 1063
Pompous, *showy* . . 1068
Portentous, *ominous* . 1065
Positive, *actual* . . . 1038
Port, *harbor* 1059
Positive, *confident* . 1047
Possess, *have* . . . 1059
Possess, *hold* . . . 1060
Postponement, *abeyance* 1038
Posture, *action* . . 1038
Potent, *powerful* . . 1065
Pound, *break* . . . 1043
Pour 1065
Power, *energy* . . . 1054
Powerful 1065

Practice, *custom* . . 1049
Practice, *exercise* . . 1055
Praise, *flattery* . . . 1056
Praiseworthy, *laudable* 1062
Prattle, *babble* . . . 1042
Precept, *command* . . 1045
Precipitancy, *rashness* 1067
Precipitous, *steep.* . . 1069
Predicament 1065
Predict, *foretell* . . 1057
Preliminary 1066
Preparatory, *preliminary* 1066
Preposterous, *irrational* 1062
Prescribe, *appoint* . . 1040
Present, *gift* 1058
Present, *give* 1058
Preserve, *keep* . . . 1062
Press 1066
Presuming, *presumptive* 1066
Presumptive 1066
Presumptuous, *arrogant* 1041
Presumptuous, *presumptive* 1066
Pretend, *affect* . . . 1039
Pretend, *feign* . . . 1056
Pretentious, *showy* . . 1068
Pretty, *beautiful* . . 1042
Prey, *booty* 1043
Price, *cost* 1048
Principal, *chief.* . . 1045
Privacy 1066
Privilege, *right* . . . 1067
Prize, *capture* . . . 1044
Prize, *value* 1071
Proceed, *advance* . . 1039
Proceedings 1066
Proclaim, *announce* . 1040
Procure, *provide* . . 1066
Prodigal, *extravagant* 1055
Prodigious, *enormous* 1054
Prodigy, *wonder* . . 1071
Produce, *effect* . . . 1053
Produce, *make* . . . 1063
Production 1066
Profane, *irreligious* . 1062
Profession, *business.* . 1043
Profligate 1066
Profundity, *depth* . . 1050
Profuse, *extravagant* . 1055
Progeny, *offspring* . . 1064
Prognosticate, *foretell* 1057
Progressive, *liberal* . 1062
Prolix, *diffuse* . . . 1051
Prolix, *redundant* . . 1067
Prominent 1066
Prominent, *noticeable* 1064
Promise 1066
Prompt, *diligent* . . 1051
Prompt, *ready* . . . 1067
Promulgate, *publish* . 1066
Pronounce, *utter* . . 1071
Proof, *argument* . . 1041
Prop, *staff* 1069
Propensity, *inclination* 1061
Proper, *convenient* . 1048
Prophesy, *foretell* . . 1057
Proportionate . . . 1066
Proselyte, *convert.* . . 1048
Prospect, *view* . . . 1071
Protect, *defend* . . . 1050
Proud, *arrogant* . . 1041
Prove, *argue* 1041
Proverb, *axiom* . . . 1041
Provide 1066
Provident, *careful* . . 1044
Provoke, *awaken* . . 1041
Provoke, *excite.* . . 1054
Prudence, *judgment.* . 1062
Prudence, *wisdom* . . 1071
Prying, *curious* . . . 1049
Pseudonym, *name* . . 1064
Publish 1066
Publish, *announce* . . 1040
Puerile, *youthful* . . 1071
Pull, *draw* 1053
Punishment, *correction* 1048
Pure, *clean* 1045
Purloin, *steal* . . . 1069
Purpose, *design* . . 1051
Pursue, *follow* . . . 1056

Put 1066

Qualification . . . 1066
Qualified, *competent* . 1046
Quandary, *predicament* 1065
Quarrel 1066
Quarrel, *difference* . . 1051
Query, *question* . . . 1066
Question 1066
Question, *ask* . . . 1041
Question, *doubt* . . 1053
Questionnaire, *question* 1066
Quiet, *ease* 1053
Quiet, *peace* 1065
Quit, *leave* 1062
Quiz, *question* . . . 1066

Radiance 1066
Radical, *liberal* . . . 1062
Rage, *anger* 1040
Rage, *madness* . . . 1063
Ramble, *excursion* . . 1054
Rapacious 1066
Rash, *foolhardy* . . 1056
Rashness 1067
Rate, *estimate* . . . 1054
Ravenous, *rapacious* . 1066
Ready 1067
Real, *actual* 1038
Reason, *argument* . . 1041
Reason, *cause* . . . 1044
Rebellion, *insurrection* 1061
Rebellious, *contumacious* 1048
Rebuff, *refuse* . . . 1067
Rebuke, *check* . . . 1045
Rebuke, *reproach.* . . 1067
Recapitulate, *repeat* . 1067
Receive, *admit* . . . 1039
Recent, *new* 1064
Reciprocal, *mutual* . 1064
Reciprocity, *interchange* 1061
Recite, *repeat* . . . 1067
Reckon, *calculate* . . 1043
Reclaim 1067
Recollection, *memory* . 1063
Recompense, *compensation* 1046
Reconcile, *conciliate* . 1046
Recover 1067
Recruit, *recover* . . 1067
Redundant 1067
Refer, *allude.* . . . 1040
Refinement, *cultivation* 1049
Refinement, *politeness* 1065
Reflect, *consider* . . 1047
Reflection, *insinuation* 1061
Reform 1067
Reform, *reclaim* . . 1067
Reformation, *reform* . 1067
Refuge, *asylum* . . . 1041
Refuse 1067
Refuse, *deny.* . . . 1050
Refute, *confute.* . . 1047
Regal *royal* 1067
Regardless, *indifferent* 1061
Regulate, *govern* . . 1058
Rehearse, *repeat* . . 1067
Reject, *refuse* . . . 1067
Relevant. 1067
Relieve, *alleviate* . . 1040
Rejoinder, *answer* . . 1040
Relinquish, *abandon* . 1038
Relinquish, *leave* . . 1062
Remain, *continue.* . . 1048
Remark, *notice* . . . 1064
Remarkable, *extraordinary* 1055
Remarkable, *noticeable* 1064
Remedy, *cure* . . . 1049
Remembrance, *memory* 1063
Reminiscence, *memory* 1063
Remit, *forgive* . . . 1057
Remonstrate, *expostulate* 1055
Remote, *distant* . . 1052
Remuneration, *compensation* 1046
Renown, *reputation* . 1067
Renowned, *famous* . . 1055
Repair, *amend* . . . 1040
Repair, *recover* . . . 1067
Repay, *restore* . . . 1067

Repeal, abolish 1038
Repeat 1067
Repel, refuse 1067
Reply, answer 1040
Report, fame 1055
Representation, show . . 1068
Repress 1067
Reprimand, check . . . 1045
Reprimand, reproach . . 1067
Reproach 1067
Reproach, discredit . . 1052
Reprobate, profligate . . 1066
Reprove, blame . . . 1042
Reprove, check . . . 1045
Reputation 1067
Reputation, character . . 1044
Require, demand . . . 1050
Rescue, deliver 1050
Resemblance, likeness . 1063
Resentment, anger . . . 1040
Residence, habitation . 1059
Resign, give up . . . 1058
Resolute, decided . . . 1049
Resolution, courage . . 1048
Resolve, determine . . 1051
Resort to, frequent . . 1057
Resource, expedient . . 1055
Respect, honor . . . 1060
Respite, interval . . . 1061
Response, answer . . . 1040
Responsible, answer-
    able 1040
Rest, cessation . . . 1044
Rest, ease 1053
Restore 1067
Restore, recover . . . 1067
Restrain, repress . . . 1067
Restrict, bound . . . 1043
Restrict, repress . . . 1067
Result, consequence . . 1047
Retain, hold 1060
Retard 1067
Retirement, privacy . . 1066
Retreat, asylum . . . 1041
Retrieve, recover . . . 1067
Return, restore . . . 1067
Reveal, discover . . . 1052
Reveal, publish . . . 1066
Reverence, adoration . . 1039
Reverence, awe . . . 1041
Reverence, honor . . . 1060
Reverie, dream . . . 1053
Revoke, abolish . . . 1038
Revolt, insurrection . . 1061
Reward, compensation . 1046
Right 1067
Rigid, austere 1041
Rigorous, austere . . . 1041
Rise, arise 1041
Risk, danger 1049
Rite, form 1057
Rough, coarse 1045
Rouse, awaken . . . 1041
Rout, beat 1042
Royal 1067
Rude, coarse 1045
Rueful, piteous . . . 1065
Ruin, destruction . . . 1051
Ruin, fall 1055
Rule, govern 1058
Rumor, fame 1055
Rural 1067
Rustic, rural 1067

Sacred, holy 1060
Sad, dull 1053
Sadistic, cruel 1049
Safe 1067
Sailor, seaman . . . 1067
Salary, allowance . . . 1040
Salubrious, healthful . 1059
Salutary, healthful . . 1059
Salutation, salute . . 1067
Salute 1067
Sanctity, holiness . . 1060
Sane, sound 1068
Sanguine, confident . . 1047
Satisfaction, compen-
    sation 1046
Satisfaction, content-
    ment 1048
Satisfy 1067
Saunter, linger . . . 1063
Savage, cruel 1049
Savage, ferocious . . 1056
Save, deliver 1050

Save, keep 1062
Saving, penurious . . 1065
Say, speak 1069
Saying, axiom 1041
Scale, arise 1041
Scandal, discredit . . 1052
Scandalous, infamous . 1061
Science, knowledge . . 1062
Seaman 1067
Seasonable, timely . . 1070
Seclusion, privacy . . 1066
Secret 1067
Secret, clandestine . . 1045
Secrete, conceal . . . 1046
Secure, safe 1067
Security, deposit . . . 1050
Sedate, composed . . 1046
Sedition, insurrection . 1061
Seditious, factious . . 1055
See 1068
Seem 1068
Seize, lay hold of . . 1062
Seizure, capture . . . 1044
Select, choose 1045
Senile, elderly 1053
Sensible (be), feel . . 1056
Sensualist 1068
Sentence, decision . . 1050
Separate, divide . . . 1053
Serene, calm 1044
Serious, grave 1058
Servant 1068
Servile, object 1038
Set, put 1066
Settle, compose . . . 1046
Severe, austere . . . 1041
Shade 1068
Shadow, shade . . . 1068
Shame, discredit . . . 1052
Shape, form 1057
Share, divide 1053
Sharp 1068
Sheer, steep 1069
Shelter, asylum . . . 1041
Shocking, formidable . 1057
Short 1068
Show 1068
Showy 1068
Shrewd, acute 1038
Sick 1068
Sickly, sick 1068
Sight, show 1068
Sign 1068
Signal, sign 1068
Signify, denote . . . 1050
Similarity, likeness . . 1063
Simple 1068
Simulate, feign . . . 1056
Simulation 1068
Sin, crime 1049
Sincere, hearty . . . 1059
Sincerity, candor . . . 1044
Single, simple 1068
Singular, simple . . . 1068
Situation, circumstance 1045
Skillful, clever 1045
Slack 1068
Slant 1068
Slaughter, carnage . . 1044
Slavish, abject . . . 1038
Slide, slip 1068
Slight, cursory . . . 1049
Slight, disregard . . . 1052
Slip 1068
Slope, slant 1068
Small, little 1063
Snatch, lay hold of . . 1062
Snug, cozy 1049
Soak 1068
Sociable, social . . . 1068
Social 1068
Social, convivial . . . 1048
Society, association . . 1041
Soil, stain 1069
Solemn, grave 1058
Solicit, beg 1042
Solicitation 1068
Solicitude, care . . . 1044
Solid, firm 1056
Solid, hard 1059
Solitary 1068
Solitary, alone 1040
Soothe, allay 1039
Sorrow, affliction . . . 1039
Sound 1068
Sparing, penurious . . 1065

Speak 1069
Speak, utter 1071
Specious 1069
Speck, blemish . . . 1042
Spectacle, show . . . 1068
Speed, hasten 1059
Spill, pour 1065
Splendor, brightness . 1043
Splendor, magnificence 1063
Split, break 1043
Spoil, booty 1043
Sportive, playful . . . 1065
Spot, blemish 1042
Spread 1069
Spy, emissary 1053
Squeeze, break . . . 1043
Squeeze, press . . . 1066
Stability, constancy . . 1047
Stable, firm 1056
Staff 1069
Strain 1069
Strain, blemish . . . 1042
Stalwart 1069
Stammer, hesitate . . 1059
Standard, criterion . . 1049
Stare, gape 1057
Starry 1069
Stately 1069
Station, condition . . 1047
Stay, staff 1069
Steadiness, constancy . 1047
Steal 1069
Steep 1069
Steep, soak 1068
Stellar, starry 1069
Stereotyped 1069
Sterile 1069
Stern, austere 1041
Stick, adhere 1038
Stigma 1069
Stipend, allowance . . 1040
Stir 1069
Stir up, awaken . . . 1041
Stop, cessation . . . 1044
Stop, hinder 1060
Storm, breeze 1043
Story 1069
Stray, deviate 1051
Stream 1070
Strife, discord 1052
Striking, noticeable . . 1064
Strip, bereave 1042
Strive, endeavor . . . 1054
Strong, cogent 1045
Strong, stalwart . . . 1069
Struggle, endeavor . . 1054
Stupor, lethargy . . . 1062
Sturdy, stalwart . . . 1069
Stutter, hesitate . . . 1059
Sublime, grand . . . 1058
Submissive, humble . . 1060
Submissive, obedient . 1064
Submit, comply . . . 1046
Suborn, forswear . . . 1057
Subsist, be 1042
Substitute, change . . 1044
Succeed, follow . . . 1056
Successive 1070
Succinct, short . . . 1068
Suffer, admit 1039
Sufficient, enough . . 1054
Suggest, allude . . . 1040
Suggestion, dictate . . 1051
Suitable, conformable . 1047
Suitable, convenient . 1048
Sully, stain 1069
Summon, call 1043
Supple, flexible . . . 1056
Supplicate, beg . . . 1042
Supply, provide . . . 1066
Support, staff 1069
Suppose, apprehend . . 1041
Suppose, think . . . 1070
Suppress, repress . . 1067
Surge, wave 1071
Surmise, guess . . . 1059
Surprise, wonder . . . 1071
Surrender, abandon . . 1038
Surround 1070
Survey, view 1071
Suspense, abeyance . . 1038
Suspense, doubt . . . 1053
Suspicion, distrust . . 1053
Sway, affect 1039
Swerve, deviate . . . 1051
Sympathy 1070

Taint, contaminate . . 1047
Take, bring 1043
Tale, story 1069
Talent, ability 1038
Talent, intellect . . . 1061
Tall, high 1059
Tame, gentle 1058
Tantalize, tease . . . 1070
Tarnish, stain 1069
Tarry, linger 1063
Task, work 1071
Tasty, palatable . . . 1065
Taunt, tease 1070
Tautological, redun-
    dant 1067
Teach, inform 1061
Tease 1070
Tell, speak 1069
Temerity, rashness . . 1067
Temper, disposition . . 1052
Temper, humor . . . 1060
Tempest, breeze . . . 1043
Tendency, inclination . 1061
Tenderness, benevo-
    lence 1042
Tenet, doctrine . . . 1053
Terminate, complete . 1046
Terminate, end . . . 1054
Terrible, fearful . . . 1056
Terrible, formidable . . 1057
Terrific, fearful . . . 1056
Terror, alarm 1039
Terse, short 1068
Thick 1070
Think 1070
Threat 1070
Thrifty, penurious . . 1065
Thwart, retard . . . 1067
Tide, stream 1070
Tidings, news 1064
Timely 1070
Timid, afraid 1039
Timorous, afraid . . . 1039
Toil, work 1071
Tolerate, admit . . . 1039
Torment 1070
Torment, tease . . . 1070
Torture, torment . . . 1070
Total, whole 1071
Tour, excursion . . . 1054
Trace, derive 1050
Trace, mark 1063
Trade, business . . . 1043
Tranquillity, peace . . 1065
Transaction, proceed-
    ing 1066
Travel, journey . . . 1062
Treacherous, faithless . 1055
Trembling 1070
Tremendous, fearful . 1056
Tremor, trembling . . 1070
Trepidation, trembling 1070
Trick, cheat 1044
Trip, excursion . . . 1054
Trite, stereotyped . . 1069
Trouble 1070
Trouble, affliction . . 1039
Trouble, difficulty . . 1051
True, actual 1038
Trust, belief 1042
Trust, confidence . . . 1047
Truth 1070
Tumult, bustle . . . 1043
Turn (2) 1070
Twirl, turn 1070
Twist, turn 1070
Tyrannical, absolute . 1038

Unbelief 1070
Unbelief, disbelief . . 1052
Unbounded, boundless 1043
Unconcerned, indiffer-
    ent 1061
Undaunted, bold . . . 1042
Undeniable, indubitable 1061
Understand, conceive . 1046
Understanding 1070
Uniform, equal . . . 1054
Unite, connect . . . 1047
Universal, general . . 1057
Unlimited, boundless . 1043
Unquestionable, indu-
    bitable 1061
Unsophisticated, naive 1064
Unspeakable 1070

Unutterable, *unspeak-*	
able	1070
Unworthy	1071
Uproar, *bustle*	1043
Usage	1071
Use, *employ*	1053
Usually, *commonly*	1046
Utility, *advantage*	1039
Utter	1071
Valor, *bravery*	1043
Value	1071
Vanish, *disappear*	1051
Variation, *change*	1044
Variety, *difference*	1051
Vaunt, *glory*	1058
Vehement, *violent*	1071
Venom, *poison*	1065
Veracity, *truth*	1070
Versed, *conversant*	1048
Vestige, *mark*	1063
Vex	1071
Vex, *tease*	1070
Vice, *crime*	1049
Vicinity, *neighborhood*	1064
Vicissitude, *change*	1044
Victor, *conqueror*	1047
View	1071
Vigilance, *wakefulness*	1071
Vigor, *energy*	1054
Vindicate, *defend*	1050
Violence, *force*	1057
Violent	1071
Virile, *manly*	1063
Visible, *apparent*	1040
Vision, *dream*	1053
Visitant, *guest*	1059
Visitor, *guest*	1059
Vividness, *clearness*	1045
Vocabulary *dictionary*	1061
Vocation, *business*	1043
Voluntary, *gratuitous*	1058
Voluptuary, *sensualist*	1068
Voracious, *rapacious*	1066
Voyage, *journey*	1062
Wages, *allowance*	1040
Wakefulness	1071
Wander, *deviate*	1051
Want	1071
Warlike, *martial*	1063
Warm, *hearty*	1059
Wary, *cautious*	1044
Waste, *destroy*	1051
Watch, *guard*	1058
Watchfulness, *wakeful-*	
ness	1071
Wave	1071
Waver, *fluctuate*	1056
Weak	1071
Weariness, *fatigue*	1056
Weeping, *crying*	1049
Weight	1071
Whimsical, *fanciful*	1055
Whirl, *turn*	1070
Whole	1071
Wholesome, *healthful*	1059
Will	1071
Wind, *turn*	1070
Wisdom	1071
Wish, *desire*	1051
Wish, *will*	1071
Wit, *ingenuity*	1061
Woeful, *piteous*	1065
Wonder (2)	1071
Wordy, *redundant*	1067
Work	1071
Work, *act*	1038
Work, *production*	1066
Worship, *adoration*	1039
Worth, *desert*	1050
Worthless, *unworthy*	1071
Wrath, *anger*	1040
Wrench, *turn*	1070
Wrest, *turn*	1070
Wring, *turn*	1070
Writer	1071
Writhe, *turn*	1070
Wrong, *injustice*	1061
Yield, *bear*	1042
Yield, *comply*	1046
Youthful	1071

References for Further Study

No process of self-education is more rewarding than the cultivation of a good working vocabulary. The importance of such study is universally recognized. A popular magazine of large circulation has consistently devoted space to a department called "Increasing Your Word Power," and many newspapers regularly publish articles dealing with the same subject. Such instruction for the public, supplementing the work of schools and textbooks, clearly indicates both the need and the widespread demand for a better understanding of words and their uses.

It will be noted that in all such discussions the main emphasis is not merely on the expansion of one's vocabulary—for example, the learning of three new words a day. The measure of anyone's progress is qualitative, not quantitative. Each word has overtones derived from its origin, background and associations, and whenever ideas of importance are to be expressed, the search is for the one particular word that best conveys the intended meaning. Moreover, each word has a precise definition that sets it apart from other words, even from some that are closely associated with it. Additional suggestions will be found in the works cited below.

Evans, Bergen and Cornelia—A Dictionary of Contemporary American Usage. *Random House*

Fernald, James C.—Standard Handbook of Synonyms, Antonyms and Prepositions.
Funk & Wagnalls

Hogan, Homer—Dictionary of American Synonyms.
Philosophical Library

Laird, Charlton G.—Promptory. *Holt*

Nicholson, Margaret—A Dictionary of American English Usage. *Oxford University Press*

Reifer, Mary—Dictionary of New Words.
Philosophical Library

Roget, P. M.—Thesaurus. *Crowell*

Webster—Dictionary of Synonyms. *Merriam*

DICTIONARY OF LATIN WORDS AND PHRASES

A considerable number of Latin words and phrases have found their way into English. Some of these are familiar legal terms; some are church terms; some are quotations from poets; and some are merely convenient expressions without an exact English equivalent. Often they cannot be understood without some information in regard to the manner in which they were used in the past. It is frequently necessary to know the meaning which was attached to such phrases by those who spoke Latin and also to know the precise sense in which they have come to be employed in English. Such information is seldom given in the ordinary Latin dictionaries and yet it is necessary for an adequate understanding of the terms. The following is a list of Latin words and phrases which are frequently met with; it is particularly valuable in that it contains the pronunciation and the meaning of all terms used.

Roman Pronunciation. The Roman method of pronunciation is an approximation to the ancient pronunciation of the Latin language, or to that used by the Romans themselves in the days of Cicero and Augustus. It is the system now used almost exclusively in the public schools, and is the one employed in the preparation of the following list.

But many Latin words and phrases have become so thoroughly anglicized that it would be pedantic to disregard their customary English pronunciation. Therefore, the English pronunciation of an anglicized word or phrase is given in parentheses immediately after the Roman.

The key to the Roman method is as follows:

Vowels and Diphthongs

Long vowels (marked ‾) are supposed to take twice as long to utter as short vowels (marked ˘). All diphthongs are long. The following table shows the *approximate* sound of the Latin vowels and diphthongs:—

ā is pronounced like *a* in *father*
ă is pronounced like *a* in *what*
ē is pronounced like *e* in *prey*
ĕ is pronounced like *e* in *met*
ī is pronounced like *i* in *machine*
ĭ is pronounced like *i* in *pin*
ō is pronounced like *o* in *note* (close *o*)
ŏ is pronounced like *aw* in *law* (open *o*—uttered very rapidly)
ū is pronounced like *u* in *rude*
ŭ is pronounced like *u* in *pull*
ȳ is pronounced like *French u* or *German ü*
y̆ is pronounced like *French u* or *German ü* (but uttered very rapidly)
ae is pronounced like *ai* in *aisle*
au is pronounced like *ow* in *how*
eu is pronounced like *eh-oo* (run rapidly together)
oi is pronounced like *oi* in *boil*

Consonants

The consonants have *approximately* the same sounds as in English, with the following exceptions:—

c is pronounced like *k* (never like *s*)
g is pronounced like *g* in *get* (never like English *j*)
j is pronounced like *y* in *yet* (never like English *j*)
s is pronounced like *s* in *sin* (never like *z*)
t is pronounced like *t* in *tin* (never like *sh*)
v is pronounced like *w* in *win* (never like *v* in *very*)
ch* is pronounced like *k-h* (in *back home*)
ph* is pronounced like *p-h* (in *up hill*)
th* is pronounced like *t-h* (in *at home*)

* But these three aspirates are commonly, if improperly, pronounced as *k*, *f*, and *th* (in *thin*) respectively.

A, The first letter of the European alphabets, has, in the English language, three different sounds, which may be termed the broad, open, and slender.

The broad sound resembling that of the German *a* is found, in many of our monosyllables, as *all*, *wall*, *malt*, *salt*; in which *a* is pronounced as *au* in *cause*, or *aw* in *law*. Many of these words were anciently written with *au*, as *fault*, *waulk*; which happens to be still retained in *fault*. This was probably the ancient sound of the Saxons, since it is almost uniformly preserved in the rustic pronunciation, and the Northern dialects, as *maun* for *man*, *haund* for *hand*.

A open, not unlike the *a* of the Italians, is found in *father*, *rather*, and more obscurely in *fancy*, *fast*, &c.

A slender or close, is the peculiar *a* of the English language, resembling the sound of the French *e* masculine, or diphthong *ai* in *pais*, or perhaps a middle sound between them, or between the *a* and *e*; to this the Arabic *a* is said nearly to approach. Of this sound we have examples in the words, *place*, *face*, *waste*, and all those that terminate in *ation*; as, *relation*, *nation*, *generation*.

A is short, as, *glass*, *grass*; or long, as, *glaze*, *graze*: it is marked long, generally, by an *e* final, *plane*, or by an *i* added, as, *plain*.

A, an article set before nouns of the singular number; *a man, a tree*; denoting the number *one*, as, *a man is coming*, that is, *no more than one*; or an indefinite indication, as, *a man may come this way*; that is, *any man*. This article has no plural signification. Before a word beginning with a vowel, it is written *an*, as, *an ox*, *an egg*, of which *a* is the contraction.

A is sometimes a noun; as, a great *A*, a little *a*.

A is placed before a participle, or participial noun; and is considered by Wallis as a contraction of *at*, when it is put before a word denoting some action not yet finished; as, I am *a* walking. It also seems to be anciently contracted from *at*, when placed before local surnames; as, Thomas *a* Becket. In other cases, it seems to signify *to*, like the French *à*.

> *A* hunting Chloe went.   *Prior.*

> They go *a* begging to a bankrupt's door.   *Dryd.*

> May pure contents for ever pitch their tents
> Upon these downs, these meads, these rocks, these mountains,
> And peace still slumber by these purling fountains!
>   Which we may every year
> Find when we come *a* fishing here.   *Wotton.*

Now the men fell *a* rubbing of armour, which a great while had lain oiled; the magazines of munition are viewed; the officers of remains called to account.   *Wotton.*

Another falls *a* ringing a Pescennius Niger, and judiciously distinguishes the sound of it to be modern. *Addison on medals.*

A has a peculiar signification, denoting the proportion of one thing to another. Thus we say, The landlord hath a hundred *a* year; The ship's crew gained a thousand pounds *a* man.

The river Inn, that had been hitherto shut up among mountains, passes generally through a wide open country, during all its course through Bavaria; which is a voyage of two days, after the rate of twenty leagues *a* day.   *Addison on Italy.*

A is used in burlesque poetry, to lengthen out a syllable, without adding to the sense.

Vol. I.

B

> For cloves and nutmegs to the line-*a*,
> And even for oranges to China.   *Dryden.*

A is sometimes, in familiar writings, put by a barbarous corruption for *he*.

A, in composition, seems to have sometimes the power of the French *a* in these phrases, *a droit, a gauche*, &c. and sometimes to be contracted from *at*; as, *aside, aslope, afoot, asleep, athirst, aware*.

> If this, which he avouches, does appear,
> There is no flying hence, nor tarrying here.
> I gin to be *a weary* of the sun;
> And wish the state of the world were now undone.
>   *Shakespeare's Macbeth.*

> And now a breeze from shore began to blow,
> The sailors ship their oars, and cease to row;
> Then hoist their yards *a-trip*, and all their sails
> Let fall, to court the wind, and catch the gales.
>   *Dryden's Ceyx and Alcyone.*

A is sometimes redundant; as, *arise, arouse, awake*; the same with *rise, rouse, wake*.

A, in abbreviations, stands for *artium*, or arts; as, A. B. bachelor of arts, *artium baccalaureus*; A. M. master of arts, *artium magister*; or, *anno*; as, A. D. *anno domini*.

AB, at the beginning of the names of places, generally shews that they have some relation to an abbey.

ABA´CKE. *adv.* obsolete. Backwards.

> But when they came where thou thy skill didst show,
> They drew *abacke*, as half with shame confound,
> Shepherds to see them in their art outgo.   *Spens. Past.*

ABA´CTOR. *n. s.* [Lat. *abactor*, a driver away.] Those who drive away or steal cattle in herds, or great numbers at once, in distinction from those that steal only a sheep or two. *Blount.*

A´BACUS. *n. s.* [Lat. *abacus*.]

1. A counting-table, anciently used in calculations.

2. In architecture, it is the uppermost member of a column, which serves as a sort of crowning both to the capital and column.   *Dict.*

ABAFT. *adv.* [of *abaftan*, Sax. Behind.] From the fore-part of the ship, towards the stern.   *Dict.*

ABAI´SANCE. *n. s.* [from the French *abaiser*, to depress, to bring down.] An act of reverence, a bow. *Obeysance* is considered by Skinner as a corruption of *abaisance*, but is now universally used.

To ABA´LIENATE. *v. a.* [from *abalieno*, Lat.] To make that another's which was our own before.   *Calv. Lex. Jur.* A term of the civil law, not much used in common speech.

ABALIENA´TION. *n. s.* [Lat. *abalienatio*.] A giving up one's right to another person; or a making over an estate, goods, or chattels by sale, or due course of law.   *Dict.*

To ABA´ND. *v. a.* [A word contracted from abandon, but not now in use. See ABANDON.] To forsake.

> Those foreigners which came from far
> Grew great, and got large portions of land,
> That in the realm, ere long, they stronger are
> Than they which sought at first their helping hand,
> And Vortiger enforced the kingdom to *aband*.
>   *Spenser's Fairy Queen, b. ii. cant. 10.*

To ABA´NDON. *v. a.* [Fr. *abandonner*. Derived, according to *Menage*, from the Italian *abandonare*, which signifies to forsake his colours; *bandum* [*vexillum*] *deserere*. *Pasquier* thinks

it

Dr. Samuel Johnson, critic, essayist, and lexicographer of 18th-century England.

AB INITIO, *ăb ĭn-ĭ′tĭ-ō (ăb ĭn-ĭsh′ĭ-ô)*. From the beginning.

AB OVO AD MALA, *ăb ō′vō ăd mā′lă*. From the eggs to the apples; from beginning to end. The Roman dinner began with eggs and ended with apples.

ABSIT OMEN, *ăb′sĭt ō′mĕn*. May no harm come from it, that is, from a word just used.

AD ASTRA PER A PERA, *ăd ăs′tră pĕr ăs′pĕ-ră*. To the stars through difficulties. Motto of Kansas.

AD CAPTANDUM VULGUS, *ăd căp-tăn′dŭm vŭl′gŭs*. To attract the rabble, like "playing to the gallery."

AD INFINITUM, *ăd ĭn′fĭ-nĭ′tŭm (ăd ĭn′fĭn-ĭ′tŭm)*. To infinity without end.

AD LIBITUM, *ăd lĭb′ĭ-tŭm*. At one's pleasure.

AD NAUSEAM, *ăd nau′sĕ-ăm (ăd nô′sĕ-ăm)*. To the point of disgusting or nauseating.

AD REM, *ăd rĕm*. To the purpose; to the point.

AD VALOREM, *ăd vă-lō′rĕm (ăd văl-ō′rĕm)*. According to value.

ÆQUO ANIMO, *æ′quō ăn′ĭ-mô*. With a calm mind; with equanimity.

ÆTATIS SUÆ, *æ-tā′tĭs sŭ′æ*. Aged; in the year of his or her age.

ÆTERNUM VALE! *æ-tĕr′nŭm vă′lē*. Farewell forever!

A FORTIORI, *ā fŏr′tĭ-ō′rĭ (ā fŏr′shĭ-ō′rĭ)*. For the stronger reason; all the more.

ALIAS, *ā′lĭ-ās (ā′lĭ-ăs)*. Otherwise; generally indicating the variant of a name.

ALMA MATER, *ăl′mă mā′tĕr (ăl′mă mā′tĕr)*. Beloved or foster mother; one's college or university.

ALTER EGO, *ăl′tĕr ĕ′gô (ăl′tĕr ē′gô)*. Another or second self.

ANNO DOMINI, *ăn′nō dŏ′mĭ-nĭ (ăn′ô dŏm′ĭ-nĭ)*. In the year of our Lord. *A. D.*

ANNO URBIS CONDITÆ, *ăn′nō ŭr′bĭs cŏn′dĭ-tæ*. In the year of the founding of the city (Rome, 753 B. C.). A Roman method of dating. *A.U.C.*

ANTE BELLUM, *ăn′tĕ bĕl′lŭm (ăn′tĕ bĕl′ŭm)*. Before the war.

A POSSE AD ESSE, *ā pŏs′sĕ ăd ĕs′sĕ*. From possibility to actuality.

A POSTERIORI, *ā pŏs′tĕ-rĭ-ō′rĭ (ā pŏs′tĕ-rĭ-ō′rĭ)*. By induction; an *a posteriori* argument,—inferring causes from effects.

A PRIORI, *ā prĭ-ō′rĭ (ā prī-ō′rĭ)*. Deductively; an *a priori* argument,—one which infers effects from known causes.

ARS ARTIUM OMNIUM CONSERVATRIX, *ărs ăr′tĭ-ŭm ŏm′nĭ-ŭm cŏn′sĕr-vā′trĭx*. The art preservative of all arts,—printing.

ARS EST CELARE ARTEM, *ărs ĕst cē-lā′rĕ ăr′tĕm*. Art is to conceal art.

ARS LONGA, VITA BREVIS, *ărs lŏn′gă vĭ′tă brĕ′vĭs*. Art is long, life is short. A Latin translation from Hippocrates.

ARTIUM MAGISTER, *ăr′tĭ-ŭm mă-gĭs′tĕr (ăr′shĭ-ŭm mă-jĭs′tĕr)*. Master of arts.

ASINUS AD LYRAM, *ăs′ĭ-nŭs ăd lў′răm*. An ass at the harp; an awkward fellow.

AUDACES FORTUNA JUVAT, *au-dā′cēs fŏr-tū′nă jŭ′văt*. Fortune favors the bold. A paraphrase from Virgil.

AUT CÆSAR AUT NIHIL, *aut cæ′săr aut nĭ′hĭl*. Either Cæsar or nothing. A saying attributed to Cæsar Borgia and applicable to those unduly ambitious.

AUT VINCERE AUT MORI, *aut vĭn′cĕ-rĕ aut mŏ′rĭ*. To conquer or die.

AVE, IMPERATOR! MORITURI TE SALUTANT, *ă′vē ĭm′pĕ-rā′tŏr mŏ′rĭ-tū′rĭ tē să-lū′tănt*. Hail, Emperor! Those about to die salute thee.—Suetonius. Cry of the Roman gladiators on entering the arena.

BEATÆ MEMORIÆ, *bĕ-ā′tæ mĕ-mŏ′rĭ-æ*. Of blessed or happy memory.

BIS PUERI SENES, *bĭs pŭ′ĕ-rĭ sĕ′nēs*. Old men are in second childhood.

BONAFIDE, *bŏ′nă fĭ′dē (bō′nă fĭ′dê)*. In·good faith.

BONAFIDES, *bŏ′nă fĭ′dēs (bō′nă fĭ′dêz)*. Good faith; word of honor.

BONUM VINUM LÆTIFICAT COR HOMINIS, *bŏ′nŭm vĭ′nŭm æ-tĭ′flĭ-căt cŏr hŏm′ĭ-nĭs*. Good wine gladdens man's heart.

CACOETHES SCRIBENDI, *că′cŏ-ē′thĕs scrī-bĕn′dĭ*. The incurable passion for scribbling.—Juvenal.

CARCERE DURO, *căr′cĕ-rĕ dū′rō*. In durance vile; at hard labor.

CARPE DIEM, *căr′pĕ dĭ′ĕm*. Seize the day, enjoy life. —Horace.

CASUS BELLI, *că′sŭs bĕl′lĭ (kă′sŭs bĕl′ĭ)*. The cause that brings about war.

CAVEAT EMPTOR, *kă′vê-ăt ĕmp′tŏr*. Let the buyer beware. An old maxim of the common law, which still applies to titles of real estate transferred.

CEDANT ARMA TOGÆ, *cē′dănt ăr′mă tŏ′gæ*. Let arms give place to the toga.—Cicero. Let the statesman's glory outshine the soldier's.

CETERIS PARIBUS, *cē′tĕ-rĭs păr′ĭ-bŭs*. Other things being equal,—expressing a condition.

CIVIS ROMANUS SUM, *cĭ′vĭs rō-mā′nŭs sŭm*. I am a Roman citizen.

COGITO, ERGO SUM, *cŏ′gĭ-tō ĕr′gō sŭm*. I think, therefore I exist. The basis of Descartes's philosophy.

CONSENSUS OMNIUM, *cŏn-sĕn′sŭs ŏm′nĭ-ŭm*. Universal agreement

CONSUETUDO PRO LEGE SERVATUR, *cŏn′suĕ-tū′dō prō lē′gĕ sĕr-vā′tŭr*. Custom is held as law. The basis of English common law.

CORPUS DELICTI, *cŏr′pŭs dē-lĭc′tĭ*. The body of a crime; anything which serves to prove its commission; essential proof in a case.

CREDO QUIA ABSURDUM, *crē′dō quĭ′ă ăb-sŭr′dŭm*. I believe because it is absurd; the conquest of reason by faith.

CRUX, *crŭx*. A cross, a difficulty; as, the crux of the matter.

CUI BONO? *cŭ′ĭ bŏ′nō (kĭ bō′nō)*. To whose advantage? The criminal may possibly be traced by the answer to the question.

CUI FORTUNA IPSA CEDIT, *cŭ′ĭ fŏr-tū′nă ĭp′să cē′dĭt*. To whom Fortune herself yields; that is, a lucky person.

CUIQUE SUUM, *cŭ′ĭ quĕ sŭ′ŭm*. Let each one have his own.

CUM GRANO SALIS, *cŭm grā′nō să′lĭs*. With a pinch of salt; not to be taken seriously.

DA LOCUM MELIORIBUS, *dā lŏ cŭm mĕ′lĭ-ō′rĭ--bŭs*. Give place to your betters.

DE FACTO, *dē făc′tō*. Actually; as a matter of fact.

DE GUSTIBUS NON EST DISPUTANDUM, *dē gŭs′tĭ-bŭs nōn ĕst dĭs′pŭ-tăn′dŭm*. There's no use disputing about tastes,—an old scholastic proverb.

DEI GRATIA, *dē′ĭ grā′tĭ-ă (dē′ĭ grā′shĭ-ă)*. By the grace or favor of God. Part of the inscription on British coinage.

DE JURE, *dē jŭ′rĕ (dē jū′rê)*. Lawfully, by right.

DELENDA EST CARTHAGO, *dē-lĕn′dă ĕst căr-thā′gō*. Carthage must be destroyed. Applicable to the intention of overcoming a difficulty.

DE MORTUIS NIL NISI BONUM, *dē mŏr′tŭ-ĭs nĭl nĭ′sĭ bŏ′nŭm*. Say nothing but good of the dead.

DE NOVO *dē nō′-vō*. From the beginning; anew.

DEO GRATIAS, *dē′ō grā′tĭ-ās (dē′ô grā′shĭ-ăs)*. Thanks be to God. Used in the liturgy of the Mass.

DEO VOLENTE, *dē′ō vŏ-lĕn′tĕ*. God willing. *D. V.*

DE PROFUNDIS, *dē prŏ-fŭn′dĭs*. Out of the depths. An appeal made *de profundis*, that is, in dire distress.

DEUS EX MACHINA, *dē′ŭs ĕx măch′ĭn-ă*. A god from a machine; an artificial solution of a problem, from the practice in the Greek drama of introducing a god by stage machinery to bring an otherwise insoluble plot to a satisfactory end.

DIES IRÆ, *dī′ēs ĭ′ræ*. The day of wrath; the judgment day. The title of a celebrated Latin hymn.

DIVIDE ET IMPERA, *dī′vĭ-dĕ ĕt ĭm′pĕ-ră*. Divide and rule. A motto of Roman imperialism.

DOCTUS CUM LIBRO, *dŏc′tŭs cŭm lĭ′brō*. Learned with the aid of a book.

DOMINUS VOBISCUM, *dŏm′ĭ-nŭs vō-bĭs′cŭm*. The Lord be with you,—words used frequently in the Roman liturgy.

DONEC ERIS FELIX MULTOS NUMERABIS AMICOS, *dō′nĕc ĕ′rĭs fē′lĭx mŭl′tōs nŭ′mĕ-rā′bĭs ă-mī′cōs*. While you are happy, you will count many friends.—Ovid.

DULCE ET DECORUM EST PRO PATRIA MORI, *dŭl′cĕ ĕt dĕ-cō′rŭm ĕst prō pă′trĭ-ă mŏ′rĭ*. It is sweet and glorious to die for one's country.—Horace.

DUX FEMINA FACTI, *dŭx fē′mĭ-nă făc′tĭ*. A woman was the leader in the adventure.—Virgil.

ECCE HOMO! *ĕc′cĕ hŏ′mō (ĕk′sĕ hō′mô)*. Behold the man! Applied specifically to any picture of Christ wearing the crown of thorns.

EDITIO PRINCEPS, *ē-dĭ′tĭ-ō prin′cĕps (ê-dĭsh′ĭ-ô prĭn′sĕps)*. A first edition of a printed work.

EGO SUM QUI SUM, *ĕ′gō sŭm quĭ sŭm*. I am who I am.— Exodus III:14. The answer of the Supreme Being to Moses.

EHEU! FUGACES LABUNTUR ANNI, *ē′heu fŭ-gā′cēs lă-bŭn′tŭr ăn′nĭ*. Alas! how the years slip by.—Horace.

E PLURIBUS UNUM, *ē plŭ′rĭ-bŭs ū′nŭm* From many, one. Motto of the United States of America.

ERRARE EST HUMANUM, *ĕr-rā′rĕ ĕst hū-mā′nŭm*. To err is human.

ESSE QUAM VIDERI, *ĕs′sĕ quăm vĭ-dē′rĭ*. To be, rather than to seem.

ESTO QUOD ESSE VIDERIS, *ĕs′tō quŏd ĕs′sĕ vĭ-dē′rĭs*. Be what you seem to be.

ET CETERA, *ĕt cē′tĕ-ră (ĕt sĕt′ê-ră)*. And the rest; *etc.*, *&c.*

ET IN ARCADIA EGO! *ĕt ĭn ăr-cā′dĭ-ă ĕ′gô*. I, too, once lived in Arcadia! An exclamation of regret for happiness no longer possessed.

ET SEQUENTIA, *ĕt sĕ-quĕn′tĭ-ă*. And what follows; *et seq.*

ET TU, BRUTE! *ĕt tū brū′tĕ*. And thou also, Brutus! Usually given as the last words of Julius Cæsar, when he saw Brutus among his murderers.

EX CATHEDRA, *ĕx că′thĕ-dră (ĕks kă′thê-dră)*. "From the chair." A statement bearing unquestionable authority.

EX DONO, *ĕx dō′nō*. As a gift. Used preceding the name of a public benefactor on what he has presented.

EXEMPLI GRATIA, *ĕx-ĕm′plĭ grā′tĭ-ă (ĕg-zĕm′plĭ grā′shĭ-ă)*. By way of example,—written *e.g.*

EXEUNT OMNES; EXIT, *ĕx′ĕ-ŭnt ŏm′nēs ĕx′ĭt (ĕks′ê-ŭnt ŏm′nēz ĕk′sĭt)*. All go out; he or she goes out.

EX NIHILO NIHIL FIT, *ĕx nĭ′hĭ-lō nĭ′hĭl fĭt*. From nothing, nothing comes.

Ex parte, *ĕx pär'tĕ*. On one side only. An *ex parte* argument.

Experto crede, *ĕx-pĕr'tō crē'dĕ*. Believe one who has tried it.—Virgil.

Ex tempore, *ĕx tĕm'pŏ-rĕ (ĕks tĕm'pô-rê)*. Offhand; without preparation.

Facile princeps, *fă'cĭ-lĕ prin'cĕps (făs'ĭ-lê prin'sĕps)*. The acknowledged chief; one who stands indisputably first.—Cicero.

Facilis descensus Averni, *fă'cĭ-lĭs dē-scēn'sŭs ă-vĕr'nĭ*. The descent to hell is easy.—Virgil. It is easy enough to get into trouble.

Fama volat, *fā'mă vŏ'lăt*. Fame flies,—expressing the rapidity with which news is spread.

Felix culpa, *fē'lĭx cŭl'pă*. Happy fault.—St. Augustine. Applicable when a mistake turns out to be a benefit.

Feræ naturæ, *fĕ'ræ nā-tū'ræ*. Of a wild nature. Applied to wild beasts.

Festina lente, *fēs-tī'nă lĕn'tĕ*. Make haste slowly; don't rush serious work.

Fiat justitia ruat cælum, *fī'ăt jūs-tĭ'tĭ-ă rŭ'ăt cœ'lŭm*. Let justice be done though the heavens should fall.

Fiat lux, *fī'ăt lŭx*. Let there be light.

Fidei defensor, *fĭ'dĕ-ī dē-fĕn'sŏr*. Defender of the faith.

Fidus Achates, *fĭ'dŭs ă-chā'tēs (fĭ'dŭs â-kā'tēz)*. Faithful Achates.—Virgil. A trusty friend.

Flagrante delicto, *flă-grăn'tĕ dē-lĭc'tō*. The crime blazing; red-handed; in the very act.

Fortiter, fideliter, feliciter, *fŏr'tĭ-tĕr fĭ-dēl'ĭ-tĕr fē-lĭc'ĭ-tĕr*. Boldly, faithfully, successfully.

Fortiter in re, *fŏr'tĭ-tĕr ĭn rĕ*. With firmness in action.

Fugit irreparabile tempus, *fŭ'gĭt ĭr're-pă-rā'bĭ-lĕ tĕm'pŭs*. Time flies, never to be recalled.—Virgil.

Gaudeamus igitur, *gaud-ĕ-ā'mŭs ĭ'gĭ-tŭr*. Therefore, let us rejoice,—the burden of a macaronic song.

Gloria in excelsis Deo, *glō'rĭ-ă ĭn ĕx-cĕl'sĭs dĕ'ō (glō'rĭ-à ĭn ĕk-sĕl'sĭs dē'ô)*. Glory to God in the highest.

Gradus ad Parnassum, *grā'dŭs ăd pär-nās'sŭm*. A step to Parnassus; aid in writing Latin poetry; a work on Latin verse-making containing rules and examples.

Græcum est, non legitur, *græ'cŭm ĕst nōn lĕ'gĭ-tŭr*. It is Greek, so skip it; don't meddle with what you know nothing about.

Gratis pro Deo, *grā'tĭs prō dĕ'ō*. Freely for God,—the manner in which charity should be bestowed.

Habeas corpus, *hă'bĕ-ās cŏr'pŭs (hā'bê-ăs cŏr'pŭs)*. Have the body. A writ issued for the purpose of bringing a person before a court or a judge, usually to determine whether he should be retained in custody or given his freedom.

Hic et nunc, *hīc ĕt nŭnc*. Here and now.

Hic jacet, *hīc jă'cĕt (hĭk jā'sĕt)*. Here lies. Inscribed on tombstones.

Hinc illæ lacrimæ, *hĭnc ĭl'læ lă'crĭ-mæ*. Hence these tears.—Terence. This is the cause of the trouble.

Homo sum; humani nihil a me alienum puto, *hŏ'mō sŭm hū-mā'nĭ nĭ'hĭl ā mē ă'lĭ-ē'nŭm pŭ'tō*. I am a man; there is naught which touches man that is not my concern.—Terence.

Hortus siccus, *hŏr'tŭs sĭc'cŭs*. A dry garden; a collection of dried plants; a herbarium.

Imperium in imperio, *ĭm-pĕ'rĭ-ŭm ĭn ĭm-pĕ'rĭ-ō*. A government existing within another. Said of a power set up against constituted authority.

Imprimatur, *ĭm'prī-mā'tŭr*. It may be published. A censor's permission at the beginning of certain Catholic works.

In esse, *ĭn ĕs'sĕ*. In being.

In extenso, *ĭn ĕx-tēn'sō (ĭn ĕks-tĕn'sô)*. Entirely, at full length; as, to treat a subject *in extenso*.

In extremis, *ĭn ĕx-trē'mĭs (ĭn ĕks-trē'mĭs)*. In very bad circumstances; at the point of death.

Infra dignitatem, *ĭn'fră dĭg'nĭ-tā'tĕm*. Beneath one's dignity, *infra dig*.

In hoc signo vinces, *ĭn hōc sĭg'nō vĭn'cēs (ĭn hŏk sĭg'nô vĭn'sēz)*. In this sign thou shalt conquer. The motto is said to have been adopted by Constantine after his vision of a cross in the heavens just before his decisive battle with Maxentius, 312 A. D.

Initium sapientiæ timor Domini, *ĭ-nĭ'tĭ-ŭm să'pĭ-ĕn'tĭ-æ tĭm'ŏr dŏm'ĭ-nĭ*. The fear of the Lord is the beginning of wisdom.

In loco parentis, *ĭn lŏ'cō pă-rĕn'tĭs (ĭn lō'kŏ pâ-rĕn'tĭs)*. In the place of a parent.

In medias res, *ĭn mĕ'dĭ-ās rēs*. Into the middle of the subject; without wasting words.

In memoriam, *ĭn mĕ-mō'rĭ-ăm (ĭn mê-mō'rĭ-ăm)*. In memory of.

In perpetuam rei memoriam, *ĭn pĕr-pĕt'ŭ-ăm rĕ'ī mĕ-mō'rĭ-ăm*. In everlasting remembrance of the event.

In posse, *ĭn pŏs'sĕ*. In possible existence.

In propria persona, *ĭn prŏ'prĭ-ā pĕr-sō'nă*. In one's own person.

(In) re, *ĭn rē (ĭn rē)*. In the matter of, concerning; as, *(in) re* the election.

In situ, *ĭn sĭ'tū (ĭn sĭ'tú)*. In position; the actual spot. A phrase especially employed in mineralogy.

In statu quo, *ĭn stă'tū quō (ĭn stā'tú kwō)*. In its former state.

Integer vitæ scelerisque purus, *ĭn'tĕ-gĕr vī'tæ scĕ'lĕ-rĭs'quĕ pū'rŭs*. A man upright in life and free from blame.—Horace.

Intelligenti pauca, *ĭn-tĕl'lĭ-gĕn'tĭ pau'că*. But few words necessary for one who is intelligent (also *verbum sapienti*, *verb. sap.*).

Inter alia, *ĭn'tĕr ā'lĭ-ă (ĭn' tĕr ā'lĭ-à)*. Among other things.

Inter nos, *ĭn'tĕr nōs (ĭn'tĕr nōs)*. Between, among ourselves.

In toto, *ĭn tŏ'tō*. In the whole; entirely.

In vacuo, *ĭn vă'cū-ō (ĭn văk'ú-ô)*. In a vacuum.

In vino veritas, *ĭn vī'nō vĕr'ĭ-tās*. In wine there's truth; a man becomes more confidential when he drinks.

Ipse dixit, *ĭp'sĕ dĭx'ĭt (ĭp'sĕ dĭk'sĭt)*. He himself has said it; a mere assertion.

Ipsissima verba, *ĭp-sĭs'sĭ-mă vĕr'bă*. The identical words.

Ipso facto, *ĭp'sō făc'tō (ĭp'sô făk'tô)*. By the very fact; actually.

Ita est, *ĭ'tă ĕst*. It is so.

Jacta alea esto, *jăc'tă ā'lĕ-ă ĕs'tō*. Let the die be cast.—Julius Cæsar. It is probable that the exact words uttered by Julius Cæsar on crossing the Rubicon were from a Greek play of Menander, the Latin being a translation.

Jus civile, *jūs cĭ-vī'lĕ (jŭs sĭ-vī'lê)*. The law of citizens. The Roman law applied to citizens. See *Jus gentium*.

Jus est ars boni et justi, *jūs ĕst ärs bŏ'nĭ ĕt jūs'tĭ*. Right is the art of the good and of the just.

Jus gentium, *jūs gĕn'tĭ-ŭm (jŭs jĕn'shĭ-ŭm)*. The law of nations. The Roman law applied to foreigners, or between foreigners and citizens. See *Jus civile*.

Labor omnia vincit improbus, *lă'bŏr ŏm'nĭ-ă vĭn'cĭt ĭm'prŏ-bŭs*. Stubborn labor overcomes all things.—Virgil.

Lapsus calami, *lăp'sŭs că'lă-mĭ (lăp'sŭs kăl'â-mĭ)*. A slip of the pen.

Lapsus linguæ, *lăp'sŭs lĭn'guæ (lăp'sŭs lĭng'gwê)*. A slip of the tongue.

Lares et penates, *lă'rēs ĕt pĕ-nā'tēs (lā'rêz ĕt pê-nā'têz)*. Household gods.

Latet anguis in herba, *lă'tĕt ăn'guĭs ĭn hĕr'bă*. A snake lies hid in the grass.—Virgil. Said by way of warning.

Lato sensu, *lā'tō sĕn'sū*. In a broad sense; with a wide meaning.

Laudator temporis acti, *lau-dā'tŏr tĕm'pŏ-rĭs āc'tĭ*. One who praises the good old days,—generally to the disparagement of the present.—Horace.

Laus Deo, *laus dĕ'ō*. Praise to God.

Levius fit patientia quidquid corrigere est nefas, *lĕ'vĭ-ŭs fĭt pă'tĭ-ĕn'tĭ-ă quĭd'quĭd cŏr-rĭ'gĕ-rĕ ĕst nĕ'făs*. What cannot be cured may be lightened by patience.—Horace.

Lex talionis, *lĕx tăl'ĭ-ō'nĭs*. The law of retaliation.

Loco citato, *lŏ'cō cĭ-tā'tō (lō'kŏ sĭ-tā'tō)*. In the place quoted. (*loc. cit.*)

Magister dixit, *mă-gĭs'tĕr dĭx'ĭt (mă-jĭs'tĕr dĭks'ĭt)*. The master has said it,—hence no more argument.

Magna cum laude, *mīg'nă cŭm lau'dĕ*. With high honors.

Magnum opus, *măg'nŭm ŏ'pŭs (măg'nŭm ō'pŭs)*. A great undertaking; the great work of a man's life.

Mater familias, *mā'tĕr fă-mĭ'lĭ-ās (mā'tĕr fâ-mĭl'ĭ-ăs)*. The mother of the family.

Materiam superabat opus, *mā-tĕ'rĭ-ăm sŭ'pĕ-rā'băt ŏ'pŭs*. The workmanship surpassed the materials.—Ovid.

Mea culpa, *mĕ'ă cŭl'pă (mē'â kŭl'pă)*. Through my fault.

Medice cura teipsum, *mĕd'ĭ-cĕ cū'ră tē-ĭp'sŭm*. Doctor, cure yourself; practice what you preach.

Memento homo quia pulvis es, *mĕ-mĕn'tō hŏ'mō quĭ'ă pŭl'vĭs ĕs*. Remember, man, thou art but dust.

Mens sana in corpore sano, *mēns sā-'nă ĭn cŏr'pŏ-rĕ sā-nō*. A sound mind in a sound body.—Juvenal. Often wrongly interpreted to mean that the one depends on the other.

Minima de malis, *mĭn'ĭ-mă dē mă'lĭs*. Of evils, choose the least.

Mirabile dictu, *mĭ-rā'bĭ-lĕ dĭc'tū*. Wonderful to relate.

Mirabile visu, *mĭ-rā'bĭ-lĕ vĭ'sū*. A wonderful sight.

Modus operandi, *mŏ'dŭs ŏ'pĕ-răn'dĭ (mō'dŭs ŏp-ēr-ăn'dĭ)*. Mode, or manner, of working.

Modus vivendi, *mŏ'dŭs vĭ-vĕn'dĭ (mō'dŭs vĭ-vĕn'dĭ)*. Mode, or manner, of living.

Multi sunt vocati, pauci vero electi, *mŭl'tĭ sŭnt vŏ-cā'tĭ pau'cī vē'rō ē-lēc'tĭ*. Many are called, but few are chosen.

Multum in parvo, *mŭl'tŭm ĭn pär'vō*. Much in little.

Mutato nomine, *mū-tā'tō nōm'ĭ-nĕ*. The name being changed; the story fits you.

Necessitas non habet legem, *nĕ-cĕs'sĭ-tās nōn hă'bĕt lē'gĕm.* Necessity knows no law.

Ne plus ultra, *nē plŭs ŭl'trā (nē plŭs ŭl'trā).* Nothing beyond. The *ne plus ultra* of elegance; also *nec* or *non plus ultra.* Hercules engraved these words on the summits of Abyla and Calpe, the modern Iebel Musa and Gibraltar, the "Pillars of Hercules."

Ne quid nimis, *nē quĭd nĭ'mĭs.* Let there be nothing too much; excess is a fault.

Nescit vox missa reverti, *nĕ'scĭt vōx mĭs'să rĕ-vĕr'tĭ.* A word uttered cannot be recalled.

Nihil obstat, *nĭ'hĭl ŏb'stăt.* Nothing prevents; there is no objection. A phrase sometimes placed at the beginning of books. See *Imprimatur.*

Nil admirari, *nĭl ăd'mĭ-rā'rĭ.* To be astonished at nothing. —Horace. A *nil admirari* state of mind.

Nil novi sub sole, *nĭl nŏ'vĭ sŭb sō'lĕ.* Nothing new under the sun.

Nolens volens, *nō'lēns vŏ'lēns (nō'lĕnz vō'lĕnz).* Whether one will or not.

Noli me tangere, *nō'lĭ mē tăn-gĕ,ĕr.* Touch me not.

Nolle prosequi, *nŏl'lĕ prŏ'sĕ-qui (nŏl'ê prŏs'ê-kwi).* To be unwilling to proceed. A legal phrase to indicate the abandonment of a suit.

Non est, *nōn ĕst (nŏn ĕst).* It is not; wanting; minus.

Non multa, sed multum, *nōn mŭl'tă sĕd mŭl'tŭm.* Not many things, but much; quality, not quantity.

Non nova sed nove, *nōn nŏ'vă sĕd nŏ'vĕ.* Not new things, but old things in a new manner.

Non omnia possumus omnes, *nōn ŏm'nĭ-ă pŏs'sŭ-mŭs ŏm'nēs.* We cannot all of us do everything.—Virgil.

Non possumus, *nōn pŏs'sŭ-mŭs (nŏn pŏs'ŭ-mŭs).* We cannot,—an irrevocable refusal; as, to utter a *non possumus.*

Non sequitur, *nōn sĕ'quĭ-tŭr (nŏn sĕk'wĭ-tŭr).* It does not follow; an unwarranted conclusion.

Nosce teipsum, *nōs'cĕ tē-ĭp'sŭm.* Know thyself. From the Greek inscription written over the entrance to the Delphian temple.

Nota bene, *nŏ'tā bĕ'nĕ (nō'tà bē'nĕ).* Mark well; give good heed. *N. B.*

Nunc est bibendum, *nŭnc ĕst bĭ-bĕn'dŭm.* It is time for a drink.—Horace.

Obiit, *ŏb'ĭ-ĭt.* He (or she) died.

Obiter dicta, *ŏb'ĭ-tĕr dĭc'tă.* Things said incidentally; an unofficial expression or opinion.

Oculos habent et non videbunt, *ŏc'ŭ-lōs hă'bĕnt ĕt nōn vĭ-dē'bŭnt.* They have eyes but will not see. Said of those who are obstinate.

Odi profanum vulgus, *ō'dĭ prŏ-fā'nŭm vŭl'gŭs.* I hate the vulgar crowd.—Horace.

Odium theologicum, *ō'dĭ-ŭm thē'ō-lŏ'gĭ-cŭm (ō'dĭ-ŭm thē'ô-lŏ'jĭ-cŭm).* The hatred of theologians.

Omne ignotum pro magnifico est, *ŏm'nĕ ĭg-nō'tŭm prō măg-nĭ'fĭ-cō ĕst.* Everything unknown is magnified; distance lends enchantment.—Tacitus.

Omnia vincit amor, *ŏm'nĭ-ă vĭn'cĭt ă'mŏr.* Love conquers all things.—Virgil.

Ora pro nobis, *ō'rā prō nō'bĭs.* Pray for us.

O sancta simplicitas! *ō sānc'tă sĭm-plĭ'cĭ-tās.* O blessed simplicity!—said ironically.

O tempora! O mores! *ō tĕm'pŏ-ră ō mō'rēs.* Alas, for the age we live in and its manners!—Cicero.

O terque quaterque beati! *ō tĕr'quĕ quă-tĕr'quĕ bĕ-ā'tĭ.* O thrice and again happy!—Virgil. Meaning,—those who die for their country.

Otium cum dignitate, *ō'tĭ-ŭm cŭm dĭg'nĭ-tā'tĕ.* Ease with dignity.—Cicero. A phrase applied humorously to stout people.

Panem et circenses, *pā'nĕm ĕt cĭr-cĕn'sēs.* Bread and the games.—Juvenal. Words applied contemptuously to those who think only of pleasure.

Particeps criminis, *pär'tĭ-cĕps crĭ'mĭ-nĭs (pär'tĭ-sĕps crĭ'-mĭ-nĭs).* An accomplice.

Parturiunt montes, nascetur ridiculus mus, *pär-tŭ'rĭ-ŭnt mŏn'tēs nās-cē'tŭr rĭ-dĭ'cŭ-lŭs mŭs.* The mountains labor, a ridiculous mouse will be born; big boasting results in nothing.—Horace.

Pater familias, *pā'tĕr fă-mĭl'ĭ-ās (pā'tĕr fà-mĭl'ĭ-ăs).* The father of the family.

Pater noster, *pā'tĕr nŏs'tĕr (pā'tĕr nŏs'tĕr).* Our father.

Pater patriæ, *pā'tĕr pā'trĭ-æ.* The father of his country.

Patres conscripti, *pā'trēs cŏn-scrip'tĭ (pā'trēz kŏn-skrĭp'tĭ).* The conscript fathers; the Roman senate. The words are often jocularly applied to the members of a town council.

Pauca sed bona, *pau'că sĕd bŏ'nă.* A few things, but good things.

Pax vobiscum! *păx vō-bĭs cŭm.* Peace be with you!

Peccavi, *pĕc-cā'vĭ.* I have sinned. Used to acknowledge one's mistake.

Per jocum, *pĕr jŏ'cŭm.* For fun.

Per jovem! *pĕr jŏ'vĕm.* By Jove! By Jupiter!

Per saltum, *pĕr săl'tŭm.* By a jump.

Per se, *pĕr sē.* Of itself; without other support.

Persona grata, *pĕr-sō'nă grā'tă.* A favored person; one always welcome. In diplomacy, a *persona non grata* is an unacceptable ambassador or other official representative from a foreign country.

Poeta nascitur, orator fit, *pŏ-ē'tă nās'cĭ-tŭr ō-rā'tŏr fĭt.* The poet is born, the orator made. The French say: "You can learn to cook but not to grill."

Pons asinorum, *pŏns ă'sĭ-nō'rŭm (pŏnz ăs'ĭ-nō'rŭm).* The bridge of asses. Applied to first difficult proposition in Euclid's textbook of geometry.

Post hoc ergo propter hoc, *pŏst hōc ĕr'gō prŏp'tĕr hōc.* After that, therefore, on account of that; bad logic, taking an antecedent as a cause.

Potius mori quam fœdari, *pŏ'tĭ-ŭs mŏ'rĭ quăm fœ-dā'rĭ.* Death before dishonor.

Prima facie, *prĭ'mă fă'cĭ-ē (prĭ'mà fā'shĭ-ê).* At the first glance; as, *prima facie* evidence.

Primo mihi, *prĭ'mō mĭ'hĭ.* First of all myself. Motto of the egotist.

Primum vivere deinde philosophari, *prĭ'mŭm vĭv'ĕ-rĕ dĕ-ĭn'dĕ phĭ-lŏ'sŏ-phā'rĭ.* Earn your living first, then you may talk.

Primus inter pares, *prĭ'mŭs ĭn'tĕr pā'rēs.* First among equals; for example, the president of a republic.

Principia, non homines, *prĭn-cĭ'pĭ-ă nōn hŏ'mĭ-nēs.* Principles, not men.

Pro aris et focis, *prō ā'rĭs ĕt fŏ'cĭs.* For altars and hearths; for faith and fatherland.

Pro bono publico, *prō bŏ'nō pŭb'lĭ-cō (prō bō'nô pŭb'lĭ-kô).* For the public good.

Pro forma, *prō fŏr'mā.* As a matter of form.

Proh pudor! *prōh pŭ'dŏr.* For shame!

Propaganda fide, *prō'pā-găn'dā fĭ'dē (prō'pâ-găn'dà fĭ dê).* For extending the faith.

Pro tempore, *prō tĕm'pŏ-rĕ (prō tĕm'pô-rê).* For the time being. *Pro tem.*

Qualis pater talis filius, *quā'lĭs pă'tĕr tā'lĭs fĭ'lĭ-ŭs.* Like father, like son; a chip of the old block.

Quandoque bonus dormitat Homerus, *quăn-dō'quĕ bŏ'nŭs dŏr-mĭ'tăt hŏ-mē'rŭs.* Even the good Homer sometimes nods.—Horace. Not even the greatest always excel.

Quid nunc? *quĭd nŭnc (quĭd nŭnc).* What now? A newsmonger or gossip.

Quod erat demonstrandum, *quŏd ĕ'răt dē'mōn-străn'dŭm (kwŏd ĕr'ăt dē'mŏn-străn'dŭm).* Which was to be proved. *Q.E.D.*

Quod erat faciendum, *quŏd ĕ'răt fă'cĭ-ĕn'dŭm.* Which was to be done. *Q.E.F.*

Quod scripsi scripsi, *quŏd scrĭp'sĭ scrĭp'sĭ.* What I have written, I have written. To express an unalterable decision. Words attributed to Pontius Pilate.

Quomodo vales? *quŏ'mŏ-dō vă'lēs.* How are you?

Quot homines, tot sententiæ, *quŏt hŏ'mĭ-nēs tŏt sĕn-tĕn'tĭ-æ.* As many opinions as there are persons.—Terence. Too many cooks spoil the broth.

Rara avis in terris, *rā'ră ă'vĭs ĭn tĕr'rĭs.* A rare bird on earth.—Juvenal. Sometimes used of a sly or knowing person.

Reductio ad absurdum, *rĕ-dŭc'tĭ-ō ăd ăb-sŭr'dŭm (rê-dŭk-shĭ-ô ăd ăb-sŭr'dŭm).* A reducing to an absurdity.

Religio laici, *rĕ-lĭ'gĭ-ō lā'ĭ-cī (rĕ-lĭj'ĭ-ô lā'ĭ-sĭ).* The religion of a layman.

Religio medici, *rĕ-lĭ'gĭ-ō mĕ'dĭ-cī (rĕ-lĭj'ĭ-ô mĕd'ĭ-sĭ).* The religion of a physician.

Requiescat in pace, *rĕ'qui-ēs'căt ĭn pā'cĕ (rĕk'wĭ-ĕs'kăt ĭn pā'sê).* May he rest in peace. *R.I.P.*

Res judicata, *rēs jū'dĭ-cā'tă.* A matter decided; a case already settled. The French phrase is *chose jugée.*

Res, non verba, *rēs nōn vĕr'bă.* Deeds not words. The secret of success.

Rus in urbe, *rŭs ĭn ŭr'bĕ (rŭs ĭn ŭr'bê).* A residence in or near town, with many of the advantages of the country.

Salus populi suprema lex, *să'lūs pŏ'pŭ-lĭ sŭ-prē'mă lēx.* The welfare of the people is the first law.—From the Laws of the XII Tables.

Sanctum sanctorum, *sānc'tŭm sānc-tō'rŭm (sănk'tŭm sănk-tō'rŭm).* The holy of holies.

Sapiens nihil affirmat quod non probet, *să'pĭ-ēns nĭ'hĭl ăf-fĭr'măt quŏd nōn prŏ'bĕt.* A wise man says nothing he cannot prove.

Semper fidelis, *sĕm'pĕr fĭ-dē'lĭs.* Always faithful.

Servus servorum Dei, *sĕr-vŭs sĕr-vŏ'rŭm dē'ĭ.* Servant of the servants of God. A title used by the pope.

Sesquipedalia verba, *sēs'qui-pĕ-dā'lĭ-ă vĕr'bă.* Words a foot and a half long.—Horace. Pompous twaddle with little meaning.

Sic semper tyrannis, *sĭc sĕm'pĕr tў-răn'nĭs (sĭk sĕm'pĕr tĭ-răn'ĭs).* Thus ever to tyrants. The motto of Virginia.

Sic transit gloria mundi, *sĭc trăn'sĭt glō'rĭ-ă mŭn'dĭ.* Thus passes the glory of the world. Words addressed to the pope on his election,—accompanied by the burning of flax.

Silent leges inter arma, *sĭ'lĕnt lē'gēs ĭn'tĕr ăr'mă.* The laws are silent in the midst of arms.—Cicero.

SIMILIA SIMILIBUS CURANTUR, *sĭ-mĭl'ĭ-ă sĭ-mĭl'ĭ-bŭs cū-răn'tŭr.* Like things are cured by like. The principle of homeopathy.

SI MONUMENTUM REQUIRIS, CIRCUMSPICE, *sĭ mŏn'ŭ-měn'tŭm rĕ-qui'rĭs cĭr-cŭm'spĭ-cĕ.* If you seek my monument, look around. The epitaph of Sir Christopher Wren in St. Paul's Cathedral, of which he was the architect.

SINE DIE, *sĭ'nĕ dĭ'ē (sī'nê dī'ê).* Without a day; finally. E.g., an adjournment *sine die*.

SINE QUA NON, *sĭ'nĕ quā nŏn (sī'nê kwā nŏn).* Without which, not; essential; as, a *sine qua non* condition.

SI VIS PACEM PARA BELLUM, *sĭ vĭs pā'cĕm păr'ă bĕl'lŭm.* If you wish peace, prepare for war. A specious maxim.

SOLITUDINEM FACIUNT, PACEM APPELLANT, *sŏ'lĭ-tū'dĭ-nĕm fā'cĭ-ŭnt pā'cĕm ăp-pĕl'lănt.* They make a wilderness and call it peace.—Tacitus.

SOL LUCET OMNIBUS, *sŏl lū'cĕt ŏm'nĭ-bŭs.* The sun shines for all; even the poorest have certain natural rights.

SPIRITUS PROMPTUS EST, CARO AUTEM INFIRMA, *spĭr'ĭ-tŭs prŏmp'tŭs ĕst că'rō au'tĕm ĭn-fĭr'mă.* The spirit is willing, but the flesh is weak; good-natured but indolent.

STATU QUO ANTE BELLUM, *stā'tū quō ăn'tĕ bĕl'lŭm (stā'tû kwō ăn'tê bĕl'ŭm).* As things were before the war, or in *statu quo*. Used to express the unchanged state of things in general.

SUB LEGE LIBERTAS, *sŭb lē'gĕ lĭ-bĕr'tăs.* Liberty under the law; the only freedom compatible with order.

SUB PŒNA, *sŭb pœ'nā (sŭb pē'nà).* Under a penalty. A judicial writ requiring attendance at a certain time and place under penalty.

SUB ROSA, *sŭb rŏ'sā (sŭb rō'zà).* Under the rose; secretly.

SUB SPECIE, *sŭb spē'cĭ-ē.* Under the appearance of.

SUFFICIT DIEI MALITIA SUA, *sŭf'fĭ-cĭt dĭ-ē'ĭ mă-lĭ'tĭ-ă sū'ă.* Sufficient for the day is the evil thereof; don't meet trouble halfway.

SUI GENERIS, *sū'ī gĕ'nĕ-rĭs (sū'ī jĕn'ĕr-ĭs).* Of its own kind; unlike any other.

SUMMA CUM LAUDE, *sŭm'mā cŭm lau'dĕ.* With highest honors.

SUNT LACRIMÆ RERUM, *sŭnt lă'crĭ-mæ rē'rŭm.* There are tears for suffering.—Virgil.

SURSUM CORDA, *sŭr'sŭm cŏr'dă.* Lift up your hearts; take courage.

TÆDIUM VITÆ, *tœ'dĭ-ŭm vī'tœ (tē'dĭ-ŭm vī'tê).* The weariness of life, which comes from doing nothing.

TE DEUM LAUDAMUS, *tē dĕ'ŭm lau-dā'mŭs (tē dē'ŭm lô-dā'mŭs).* We praise thee, O God.

TEMPUS EDAX RERUM, *tĕm'pŭs ĕ'dāx rē'rŭm.* Time is the devourer of all things.—Ovid.

TEMPUS FUGIT, *tĕm'pŭs fŭ'gĭt (tĕm'pŭs fū'jĭt).* Time flies.

TEMPUS OMNIA REVELAT, *tĕm'pŭs ŏm'nĭ-ă rĕ-vē'lăt.* Time reveals all things.

TERMINUS AD QUEM, *tĕr'mĭ-nŭs ăd quĕm.* The limit to which; the goal.

TERMINUS A QUO, *tĕr'mĭ-nŭs ā quō.* The limit from which; the starting point.

TERRA FIRMA, *tĕr'ră fĭr'mă (tĕr'à fĕr'mà).* The firm land; the continent.

TERRA INCOGNITA, *tĕr'ră ĭn-cŏg'nĭ-tă (tĕr'à ĭn-kŏg'nĭ-tà).* An unknown land.

TERTIUM QUID, *tĕr'tĭ-ŭm quĭd (tĕr'shĭ-ŭm kwĭd).* A third something, produced by the union of two different things or the collision of two opposing forces.

TIBI GRATIAS, *tĭb'ĭ grā'tĭ-ăs.* Thank you.

TIMEO DANAOS ET DONA FERENTES, *tĭm'ĕ-ŏ dă'nă-ōs ĕt dō'nă fĕ-rĕn'tēs.* I fear the Greeks even when they bring gifts. The guileful should never be trusted.—Virgil.

TIMEO HOMINEM UNIUS LIBRI, *tĭm'ĕ-ō hŏm'ĭnĕm ū-nī'ŭs lĭ'brī.* I fear the man of one book; he who possesses thorough knowledge of a book is a redoubtable adversary.—St. Thomas Aquinas.

TU QUOQUE, *tū quŏ'quĕ (tū kwō'kwê).* Thou also; a *tu quoque* argument, that is, a weak and worthless one.

UBI BENE IBI PATRIA, *ŭ'bĭ bĕ'nĕ ĭ'bĭ pă'trĭ-ă.* Where one is well off, there is his country. A paraphrase of Pacuvius.

ULTIMA RATIO REGUM, *ŭl'tĭ-mă rā'tĭ-ō rē'gŭm.* The last argument of kings,—engraved on French cannon by order of Louis XIV.

ULTRA VIRES, *ŭl'tră vī'rēs (ŭl'trà vī'rēz).* Beyond power; transcending authority. A phrase used frequently in relation to acts by corporations in excess of their legal rights.

UT INFRA; UT SUPRA, *ŭt ĭn'frā ŭt sŭ'prā.* As below; as above (quoted). Direction notes in books.

VADE MECUM, *vā'dĕ mē'cŭm (vā'dĕ' mē'cŭm).* Go with me; a constant companion.

VÆ VICTIS, *vœ vĭc'tĭs.* Woe to the conquered. Said to have been the exclamation of Brennus, when he threatened to exterminate the Romans.

VARIORUM, *vā'rĭ-ō'rŭm.* Of various things. With the comments of various critics; as, a *variorum* edition of Shakespeare.

VENI, VIDI, VICI, *vē'nī vī'dī vī'cī (vē'nī vī'dī vī'sī).* I came, I saw, I conquered. The laconic dispatch in which Julius Cæsar announced to the Senate his victory in Asia Minor.

VERBUM SAPIENTI (see INTELLIGENTI PAUCA).

VIA MEDIA, *vī'ă mĕ'dĭ-ă (vī'à mē'dĭ-à).* A middle course.

VICE VERSA, *vī'cĕ vĕr'sā (vī'sê vĕr'sà).* The terms being interchanged.

VI ET ARMIS, *vī ĕt ăr'mĭs.* By main force.

VIR BONUS DICENDI PERITUS, *vĭr bŏ'nŭs dī-cĕn'dī pĕ-rī'tŭs.* A good man skilled in the art of speaking. The Roman definition of an orator.

VIS COMICA, *vĭs cŏm'ĭ-că.* The comic element or power; the gift of causing laughter.—Julius Cæsar.

VIS INERTIÆ, *vĭs ĭn-ĕr'tĭ-œ (vĭs ĭn-ĕr'shĭ-ê).* The power of inertia.

VIVA VOCE, *vī'vă vō'cĕ (vī'và vō'sê).* With the living voice; by word of mouth.

VIVE VALEQUE! *vī'vĕ văl-ē'quĕ.* Long life and prosperity!—Horace. Used at the end of letters.

VOX CLAMANTIS IN DESERTO, *vōx clā-măn'tĭs ĭn dē-sĕr'tō.* A voice crying in the wilderness. Said of one whose advice is not heeded.

VOX ET PRÆTEREA NIHIL, *vōx ĕt prœ-tĕ'rĕ-ā nĭ'hĭl.* A voice and nothing more; sound without sense.

VOX POPULI VOX DEI, *vōx pŏ'pŭ-lĭ vōx dē'ĭ (vŏks pŏp'ŭ-lĭ vŏks dē'ĭ).* The voice of the people, God's voice.

VULNERANT OMNES, ULTIMA NECAT, *vŭl'nĕ-rănt ŏm'nēs ŭl'tĭ-mă nĕ'căt.* They all wound, the last kills. An inscription found on old clocks referring to the hours.

WORDS AND PHRASES FROM MODERN LANGUAGES

All phrases from the Italian are marked (It.); those from the Spanish, (Sp.); and those from the German, (Ger.). The unmarked phrases are from the French.

The key to pronunciation of the following list of words and phrases will be found in the introductory pages of this volume.

ABANDON, *ä'băn'dôn'.* Unconstraint; an amiable negligence in speech or manner.

A BAS, *à bä'.* Down with (disapproving).

À BAS L'INJUSTICE, *à bä' lăn'zhüs'tēs'.* Down with injustice.

ABSENCE D'ESPRIT, *ȧp'säns' dĕs'prē'.* Absence of mind.

À CHEVAL, *à shĕ-väl'.* On horseback.

A CHICO PAJARILLO CHICO NIDILLO (Sp.), *ä chē'kō pä-Hȧrēl'yō chē'kō nē-THĒl'yō.* Little bird, little nest; adapt your manners to your company.

A COMPTE, *à kônt'.* On account.

À CORPS PERDU, *à kôr' pĕr'dü'.* Headlong; desperately.

À COUVERT, *à kōō'vĕr'.* Under cover; protected; sheltered.

A DEUX MAINS, *à dû' măn'.* With or for both hands; having a double office or employment.

À DISCRÉTION, *à dĕs'krā'syôn'.* At discretion; unrestrictedly.

A DONDE FUERES HAZ LO QUE VIERES (Sp.), *ä dôn'dä fwä'rĕs äth lō kä vyä'rĕs.* Where you are, do what you see; when in Rome, do as Rome does.

A DROI TE, *à drwät'.* To the right.

AFFAIRE D'AMOUR, *à'fâr' dȧ'mōōr'.* A love affair.

AFFAIRE D'HONNEUR, *à'fâr' dô'nûr'.* An affair of honor; a duel.

AFFAIRE DE CŒUR, *à'fâr' dĕ kûr'.* An affair of the heart; a love affair.

A FIN, *à făn'.* To the end or object.

A FOND, *à fôn'.* To the bottom; thoroughly.

À GAUCHE, *à gōsh'.* To the left.

À GENOUX, *à zhĕ-nōō'.* On one's knees; kneeling.

À GRANDS FRAIS, *à grän' frĕ'.* At great expense.

À HAUTE VOIX, *à ōt' vwä'.* Aloud.

À HUIS CLOS, *à üê' klō'.* With closed doors; secretly.

À L'ABANDON, *à lä'băn'dôn'.* In confusion; uncared for.

À LA BELLE ÉTOILE, *à lä bĕl' ā'twäl'.* Under the canopy of heaven; in the open air at night.

A LA BONNE HEURE, *à lä bô'nûr'.* Well done! That's something like!

A L'ABRI, *à lä'brē'.* Under shelter.

À LA CAMPAGNE, *à lä kän'pàn'y'.* In the country.

À LA CARTE, *à lä kärt'.* By the bill of fare; to dine *a la carte*.

À LA CRÉOLE, *à lä krā'ôl'.* With tomatoes.

À LA DÉROBÉE, *à lä dā'rô'bä'.* Stealthily.

À LA FRANÇAISE, *à lä frän'sàz'.* In the French fashion.

A LA GRECQUE, *à lä grĕk'.* After the Greek fashion.

A LA MODE, *à lä môd'.* In the fashion; according to the custom or fashion.

A LA TEMPESTAD SIGUE LA CALMA (Sp.), *ä lä tĕm-pĕs-täth' sē'gä lä käl'mä.* After the storm comes the calm.

AL BUON VINO NON BISOGNA FRASCA (It.), *äl bwôn vē'nō nōn bē-zōn'yä fräs'kä.* Good wine needs no bush.

AL CONTADO (Sp.), *äl kôn-tä'THō.* For cash; ready money.

A L'ENVI, *à län'vē'.* In emulation of one another.

AL FRESCO (It.), *äl fräs'kō.* In the open air.

A L'IMPROVISTE, *à län'prō'vēst'.* Unawares; on a sudden.

ALLA VOSTRA SALUTE (It.), *äl'lä vôs'trä sä-lōō'tĕ.* To your good health.

ALLEZ-VOUS-EN, *à'lä'vōō'zäN'.* Away with you; be off.

ALLONS, *à'lôN'.* Come; now then!

AL PIÙ (It.), *äl pyōō'.* At most.

A MAIN ARMÉE, *à mäN'när'mā'.* By force of arms.

AM ANFANG (Ger.), *äm än'fäng.* In the beginning.

AMAR Y SABER NO PUEDE SER (Sp.), *ä-mär' ē sä-bĕr' nō pwä'THä sĕr.* No one can love and be wise at the same time.

AMENDE HONORABLE, *à'mäN'dô'nô'rä'bl'.* Fit reparation; a satisfactory apology.

À MERVEILLE, *à mĕr'vā'y'.* Marvelously; to perfection.

AMI DE COUR, *à'mē' dĕ kōōr'.* A friend of the court; a false friend; one who is not to be depended on.

AMI DU PEUPLE, *à'mē' dü pû'pl'.* Friend of the people.

AMI EN VOIE, *à'mē' än vwä.* A friend at court; one who has influence.

AMOR CON AMOR SE PAGA (Sp.), *ä-môr' kôn ä-môr' sā pä'gä.* Love is paid with love; one good turn deserves another.

AMOUR PROPRE, *à'mōōr' prô'pr'.* Vanity; self-respect.

ANCIEN RÉGIME, *äN'syäN' rā'zhēm'.* The former condition of things; of French government before 1789.

À OUTRANCE, *à ōō'träNs'.* To the death; to the last extremity.

À PAS DE GÉANT, *à pä' dĕ zhā'äN'.* With a giant's stride.

À PAS DE LOUP, *à pä' dĕ lōō'.* With stealthy steps.

À PERTE DE VUE, *à pĕrt' dĕ vü'.* Till out of sight.

À PEU PRÈS, *à pû' prā'.* Nearly.

À PIED, *à pyä'.* On foot.

À POINT, *à pwäN'.* Just in time; to a turn; exactly right.

APRÈS NOUS LE DÉLUGE, *àp'rä' nōō' lĕ dā'lüzh'.* After us, the deluge.

À PRIMA VISTA (It.), *ä prē'mä vĭs'tä.* At the first glance.

À PROPOS, *à prô'pō'.* To the point; pertinently.

À PROPOS DE RIEN, *à prô'pō' dĕ ryäN'.* Apropos to nothing; motiveless; for nothing at all.

AQUÍ SE HABLA ESPAÑOL (Sp.), *ä-kē' sā ä'blä ĕs-pä-nyôl'.* Spanish is spoken here.

ARGENT COMPTANT, *är'zhäN' kôN'täN'.* Ready money.

ARMUTH IST KEINE SCHANDE (Ger.), *är'mōōt ĭst kī'nĕ shän'dĕ.* Poverty is no disgrace.

ARRIÈRE PENSÉE, *à'ryâr' päN'sā'.* Mental reservation; unavowed purpose.

À TORT ET À TRAVERS, *à tôr'tā à trä'vâr'.* At random.

AU BOUT DE SON LATIN, *ō bōō' dĕ sôN' lä'täN'.* At the end of his Latin; at one's wit's end; in a fix.

AU CONTRAIRE, *ō kôN'trâr'.* On the contrary.

AU COURANT, *ō kōō'räN'.* Well acquainted with; well informed.

AU DÉSESPOIR, *ō dā'zĕs'pwär'.* In despair.

AU FAIT, *ō fĕ'.* Expert; up-to-date.

AU FOND, *ō fôN'.* At bottom; at heart; really.

AU GRATIN, *ō grä'täN'.* With cheese or bread raspings to form a crust.

AU JUS, *ō zhü'.* With the natural juice.

AU PAS DE CHARGE, *ō pä dĕ shärzh'.* Double quick time.

AU PIS ALLER, *ō pē' zà'lā'.* At the very worst; let the worst come to the worst. *Un pis aller* means a last resource, a makeshift.

AU RESTE, *ō rĕst'.* As for the rest.

AU REVOIR, *ō rĕ-vwär'.* Till we meet again.

AUSSITÔT DIT, AUSSITÔT FAIT, *ō'sĕ'tō' dē' ō'sĕ'tō' fĕ'.* No sooner said than done.

AUTANT D'HOMMES, AUTANT D'AVIS, *ō'täN' dôm' ō'täN' dà'vē'.* Many men, many minds.

AUTRE FOIS, *ō'tr' fwä'.* Another time.

AUX ARMES, *ō zärm'.* To arms.

À VOLONTÉ, *à vô'lôN'tä'.* At pleasure.

À VOTRE SANTÉ, *à vô'tr' säN'tä'.* To your health.

À VUESTRA SALUD (Sp.), *à vwäs'trä sä-lōōTH'.* To your health; good health.

BALLON D'ESSAI, *bà'lôN' dĕs'sĕ'.* A balloon sent up to test the direction of air currents,—hence, anything said or done to gauge public feeling on any question.

BAS BLEU, *bä' blû'.* A bluestocking; a woman who seeks a reputation for learning.

BEAUX YEUX, *bō' zyû'.* Handsome eyes, a fair face.

BEL ESPRIT, *bĕl' ĕs'prē'.* A wit; a genius.

BEN TROVATO (It.), *bĕn trō-vä'tō.* Well invented.

BÊTE NOIRE, *bât' nwär'.* A black beast; a bore; a nuisance.

BILLET DOUX, or BILLET D'AMOUR, *bē'yĕ' dōō'* or *bē'yĕ' dä'mōōr'.* A love letter.

BIZARRE, *bē'zär'.* Odd; fantastic.

BLASÉ, *blä'zä'.* Surfeited; term applied to a pose of indifference.

BON AMI, *bôn'nà'mē'.* Good friend.

BON GRÉ, MAL GRÉ, *bôN' grä' mäl' grä'.* With good or bad grace; willing or unwilling.

BONHOMIE, *bôN'nô'mē'.* Good nature; simplicity.

BON JOUR, *bôN' zhōōr'.* Good day; good morning.

BON MOT, *bôN' mô'.* A witticism.

BONNE ET BELLE, *bôn' nä-bĕl'.* Good and handsome,— said of a woman.

BONNE FOI, *bôn' fwä'.* Good faith.

BON SOIR, *bôN' swär'.* Good evening.

BON TON, *bôN' tôN'.* Good breeding; the style and manner of gentlefolk.

BOUTE-EN-TRAIN, *bōō' täN trăN'.* Mirth inspirer, merry companion.

BREVETÉ, *brĕv'-tā'.* Patented.

BUENAS NOCHES (Sp.), *bwä'näs nō'chĕs.* Good evening.

BUENAS TARDES (Sp.), *bwä'näs tär'dĕs.* Good afternoon.

BUENO (Sp.), *bwä'nō.* Good; all right.

BUENOS DIAS (Sp.), *bwä'nōs dē'äs.* Good morning.

CADA ONEJA CON SU PAREJA (Sp.), *kä'THä ō-nā'Hä kôn sōō pä-rā'Hä.* Every sheep with its like; birds of a feather flock together.

CADA UNO SABE DONDE LE APRIETA EL ZAPATO (Sp.), *kä'THä ōō'nō sä'bĕ dôn'dä lä ä-pryä'tä ĕl thä-pä'tō.* Each one knows where his own shoe pinches.

CARTE BLANCHE, *kärt' blänsh'.* Full power; full permission.

CASTELLO CHE DÀ ORECCHIA SI VUOL RENDERE (It.), *käs-tĕl'lō kā dä ō-rāk'kyä sē vwôl rĕn'dĕ-rĕ.* The fortress that parleys soon surrenders.

CELA VA SANS DIRE, *sĕ-là' và' säN dēr'.* That goes without saying; that is understood.

CE N'EST QUE LE PREMIER PAS QUI COÛTE, *sĕ nĕ' kĕ lĕ prĕ-myā' pä' kĕ' kōōt'.* It is only the first step that is difficult.

C'EST À DIRE, *sĕ' tä' dēr'.* That is to say.

C'EST UNE AUTRE CHOSE, *sĕ'tün' ō'tr' shōz'.* That is quite another thing.

CHACUN À SON GOÛT, *shà'kûn' nà sôN' gōō'.* Every one to his taste.

CHACUN TIRE DE SON CÔTÉ, *shà'kûn' tēr' dĕ sôN' kō-tā'.* Every one inclines to his own side or party.

CHANSON DE GESTE, *shäN'sôN' dĕ zhĕst'.* A song of heroic deeds; medieval French epic poem.

CHAPEAU DE BRAS, *shà'pō' dĕ brä'.* A military cocked hat.

CHAPELLE ARDENTE, *shà'pĕl' är'däNt'.* The chamber where a dead body lies in state.

CHÂTEAU, *shà'tō'.* A castle.

CHAUVINISTE, *shō'vē'nĕst'.* Over-aggressive patriot; "jingo."

CHEF-D'ŒUVRE, *shĕ'dû'vr'.* A masterpiece; a crowning piece of work.

CHEMIN DE FER, *shĕ-mäN' dĕ fâr'.* Iron road; a railway.

CHERCHEZ LA FEMME *shĕr'shā' là fäm'.* Find the woman. Compare the Latin, Dux femina facti.

CHÈRE AMIE, *shâr' à'mē'.* A dear (female) friend.

CHE SARÀ, SARÀ (It.), *kā sä-rä' sä-rä'.* What will be, will be.

CHEVAL DE BATAILLE, *shĕ-väl' dĕ bà'tä'y'.* A war horse; chief dependence or support; one's strong point.

CHI LO SA? (It.), *kē lō sä.* Who knows?

CHI TACE CONFESSA (It.), *kē tä'chĕ kôn-fĕs'sä.* He who keeps silent admits his guilt

CHI VA PIANO VA SANO (It.), *kē vä pyä'nō vä sä'nō.* Who goes slowly goes surely.

CI GÎT, *sē zhē'.* Here lies. (A common inscription on tombstones)

COMME IL FAUT, *kô mēl fō'.* Proper; as it should be.

COMMENT VOUS PORTEZ VOUS? *kô'mäN' vōō' pôr'tä' vōō'.* How are you?

¿COMO SE DICE EN INGLES—? (Sp.), *kō'mō sä dē'thä ĕn ēn'glĕs.* How do you say in English—?

¿COMO SE ESCRIBE EN ESPAÑOL? (Sp.), *kō'mō sä ĕs-krē'bä ĕn ĕs'pä-nyôl'.* How is it written in Spanish?

¿COMO SE PRONUNCIA ESA PALABRA? (Sp.), *kō'mō sä prō-nōōn'thyä ā'sä pä-lä'brä.* How is this word pronounced?

¿COMO VA? (colloq. Sp.), *kō'mō vä.* How are you?

COMPAGNON DE VOYAGE, *kôN'pä'nyôN' dĕ vwä'yäzh'.* A traveling companion.

COMPTE RENDU, *kôNt' räN'dü'.* An account rendered; a report.

CONCIERGE, *kôN'syârzh.* A portress, hall porter, lodge keeper.

CONCOURS, *kôN'kōōr'.* Competition (as for a prize); contest.

CON DILIGENZA (It.), *kôn dē-lē-jēn'tsä.* With diligence.

CON DOLORE (It.), *kôn dō-lō'rĕ.* With grief; sadly.

CON MUCHO GUSTO (Sp.), *kôn mōō'chō gōō'stō.* With great pleasure.

CONSEIL D'ÉTAT, *kôN'sĕ'y' dä'tä'.* A council of state; a privy council.

CONSOMMÉ, *kôN'sô'mä'.* A clear soup.

CON TRABAJAR ADELANTAMOS (Sp.), *kôn trä-bä-Här' ä' THĕl-än-tä'mōs.* By working we progress.

CONTRETEMPS, *kôN'tr'-täN'.* An awkward mishap.

CORDON SANITAIRE, *kôr'dôN' sà'nē'târ'.* A line of sentries to prevent, as far as possible, the spread of contagion or pestilence. (Used also of other precautionary measures.)

COULEUR DE ROSE, *kōō'lûr' dĕ rōz'.* Rose color.

Coup, kōō. A stroke; a blow; a thrust; a dig.

Coup de grace, kōō' dĕ gräs'. A finishing-stroke. (Formerly applied to the fatal blow by which the executioner put an end to the torments of a culprit broken on the wheel.)

Coup de main, kōō' dĕ măn'. A sudden attack; an enterprise (military); an undertaking; a helping hand.

Coup de maître, kōō' dĕ mâ'tr'. A master stroke.

Coup d'essai, kōō' dā'sĕ'. A first attempt; an experiment.

Coup d'état, kōō' dā'tä'. A stroke of policy, bringing about a sudden change of government (usually by unconstitutional means).

Coup d'œil, kōō' dŭ'y'. A rapid glance; a view.

Coup de pied, kōō dĕ pyā'. A kick.

Coup de poing, kōō dĕ pwăn'. A blow of the fist; a punch.

Courage sans peur, kōō'räzh' sän pûr'. Fearless courage.

Courant d'air, kōō'rän' dâr'. A draft.

Course de chevaux, kōōrs' dĕ shĕ-vō'. A horse race.

Coûte que coûte, kōōt' kĕ' kōōt'. Cost what it may; at any price.

Cuisine, küē'zĕn'. A kitchen; cookery.

Dame d'honneur, dăm' dŏ'nûr'. A maid of honor.

Dar la mano a (Sp. and It.), där lä mä'nō ä. To give the hand to; to shake hands with.

Dar un paseo (Sp.), där ōōn pä-sā'ō. To take a walk.

Das geht Sie nichts an (Ger.), däs gät zē nĭкts än. That does not concern you.

De bonne grâce, dĕ bôn' gräs'. With good will; willingly.

Début, dā'bü'. First appearance.

Débutante, dā'bü'tänt'. A young lady just entering society.

De but en blanc, dĕ bü' län blän'. Bluntly; right off.

Décolleté, dā'kŏ'l'-tā'. Wearing a low-necked dress.

Dégagé, dā'gä'zhā'. Free; easy; without constraint.

De gaieté de cœur, dĕ gä'tā' dĕ kûr'. In sport; sportively.

De la fama el atajo se entra por el trabajo (Sp.), dä lä fä'mä ĕl ä-tä'Hō sä ĕn'trä pōr ĕl trä-bä'Hō. The path of fame begins by work.

De mal en pis, dĕ mäl' än pē'. From bad to worse.

Déme la mano (Sp.), dā'mä lä mä'nō. Give me your hand; shake hands.

De moda (Sp.), dä mō'THä. Fashionable.

Dénouement, dā'nōō'män'. An unraveling or disclosure, as of a plot in a play; a wind-up; a catastrophe.

Dernier ressort, dĕr'nyā' rĕ-sôr'. The last resource.

Désagrément, dā'zä'grā'män'. Something disagreeable or unpleasant.

De sol á sol (Sp.), dä sôl ä sôl. From morning till night.

Dieu est toujours pour les plus gros bataillons, dyû'ĕ' tōō'zhōōr' pōōr lä plü' grō' bä'tä'yŏn'. God is always on the side of the largest battalions; the largest army has the best chance.

Dieu et mon droit, dyû' ā môn' drwä'. God and my right. Motto on the British royal coat of arms.

Dieu vous garde, dyû' vōō' gärd'. God protect you.

Di grado in grado (It.), dē grä'dō ĭn grä'dō. Step by step; gradually.

Dios me libre de hombre de un libro (Sp.), dē'ôs mä lē'brä dä ôm'brä dä ōōn lē'brō. God deliver me from a man of one book.

Di salto (It.), dē säl'tō. By leaps.

Dispénseme usted (Sp.), dēs-pĕn'sä-mä ōōs-tĕтH'. I beg your pardon; allow me.

Di tutti novello par bello (It.), dē tōōt'tĕ nō-vĕl'lō pär bĕl'lō. Everything new seems beautiful.

Dolce far niente (It.), dōl'chĕ fär nyĕn'tĕ. The sweet do-nothing; sweet idleness.

Donnant donnant, dôn'nän' dôn'nän'. Give and take.

Dorer la pilule, dō'rā' lä pē'lül'. To gild the pill.

Double entente, dōōb'län'tänt'. Double meaning.

Durante vita (It.), dōō-rän'tä vē'tä. During life.

Eau de cologne, ō' dĕ kō-lôny''. Cologne water.

Eau de vie, ō' dĕ vē'. Water of life—applied usually to brandy.

Éclat, ā'klä'. Splendor, brilliancy.

Édition de luxe, ā'dē'syôn' dĕ lüks'. A costly edition of a book, handsomely bound, and usually well illustrated.

Ehrlich währt am längsten (Ger.), âr'lĭk vârt äm lĕngs'tĕn. Honesty is the best policy.

Eile mit Weile (Ger.), ī'lĕ mĭt vī'lĕ. Make haste slowly.

Eine Schwalbe macht keinen Sommer (Ger.), ī'nĕ shväl'bĕ mäkt kī'nĕn zô'mĕr. One swallow does not make a summer.

Ein gebranntes Kind scheut das Feuer (Ger.), ĭn gä-brän'tĕs kĭnt shoit däs foi'ĕr. A burnt child dreads the fire.

Élan, ā'län'. Military dash; quick, sudden movement.

El árbol se conoce por su fruto (Sp.), ĕl är'bôl sä kō-nō'thä pôr sōō frōō'tō. The tree is known by its fruit.

El ejercicio hace maestro (Sp.), ĕl ĕH-ĕr-thē'thyō ä'thä mä-ĕs'trō. Exercise makes the master; practice makes perfect.

Élite, ā'lēt'. A select body of persons; society.

El trabajo hace la vida agradable (Sp.), ĕl trä-bä'Hō ä'thä lä vē'THä ä-grä-THä'blä. Work makes life worth living. (cf. Ger. Arbeit macht das Leben susz.)

Embarras des richesses, än'bä'rä' dä rē'shĕs'. The plague of riches; difficulty of choice.

Embonpoint, än'bôn'pwän'. Roundness; corpulence; mostly used in humorous reference.

En ami, än nä'mē'. As a friend.

En arrière, än nä'ryâr'. In the rear; behind.

En attendant, än nä'tän'dän'. In the meantime.

En avant, än nä'vän'. Forward.

En badinant, än bä'dē'nän'. In sport; jestingly.

En casa (Sp.), ĕn kä'sä. At home.

En cueros, en cueros vivos (Sp.), ĕn kwä'rōs vē'vōs. Naked; without clothing.

Ende gut, Alles gut (Ger.), ĕn'dĕ gōōt ä'lĕs gōōt. All's well that ends well.

En déshabillé, än dā'zä'bē'yä'. Carelessly dressed as at early morning; unprepared.

En Dieu est tout, än dyû' ĕ tōō'. In God are all things.

En effet, än nĕ'fĕ'. Indeed; really; in effect.

En famille, än fä'mē'y'. With one's family; at home.

Enfant gâté, än'fän' gä'tä'. A spoiled child.

Enfants perdus, än'fän' pĕr'dü'. Lost children; a forlorn hope.

Enfant terrible, än'fän' tĕ'rē'bl'. A child or person whose acts or remarks are embarrassing.

Enfant trouvé, än'fän' trōō'vä'. A foundling.

Enfin, än'fän'. In short; finally; at last.

En grande tenue or toilette, än' gränd' tĕ-nü' or twä'lĕt'. In full official, or evening, dress.

En masse, än' mäs'. In a body or mass.

Ennui, än'nwē'. Weariness; boredom.

En passant, än' pä'sän'. In passing; by the way.

En plein jour, än' plän' zhōōr'. In broad daylight.

En queue, än' kû'. Immediately after; in the rear. Used especially of persons waiting in line, as at the door of a theater or at the ticket office of a railway station.

En rapport, än' rä'pôr'. In harmony, relation, or agreement.

En règle, än' rĕg'l'. Regular; in order.

En route, än' rōōt'. On the way.

Ensemble, än'sän'bl'. The whole; together.

En suite, än' süēt'. In company; in a set.

Entente cordiale, än'tänt' kôr'dyäl'. A good understanding, especially between two states.

Entêté, än'tĕ'tä'. Headstrong.

Entourage, än'tōō'räzh'. Surroundings; associates.

Entre deux feux, än'tr' dû' fû'. Between two fires.

Entre deux vins, än'tr' dû' vän'. Between two wines; half drunk.

Entrée, än'trā'. Entry; first course.

Entre nous, än'tr' nōō'. Between ourselves; in confidence.

En venir aux coups, än' vĕ-nēr' ō kōō'. To come to blows.

En verité, än' vä'rē'tä'. In truth; really.

En vez de oro es dorado (Sp.), ĕn väth dä ō'rō ĕs dō-rä'тHō. In place of gold 'tis only gilt; a false friend.

En voiture! än' vwä'tür'. All aboard!

E pur si muove! (It.), ā pōōr sē mwô'vĕ. Nevertheless it moves! (Supposed words of Galileo after his condemnation; referring to the motion of the earth.)

Es freut mich sehr (Ger.), ĕs froit mĭк zär. I am very glad.

Est ist nicht Alles Gold, was glänzt (Ger.), ĕs ĭst nĭkt ä'lĕs gôlt väs glĕntst. All is not gold that glitters.

Esprit de corps, ĕs'prē' dĕ kôr'. The animating spirit of a collective body of persons, as of a regiment, the bar, the clergy, a school.

Esprit des lois, ĕs'prē' dä lwä'. Spirit of the laws.

Es thut mir leid (Ger.), ĕs tōōt mēr līt. I am sorry.

Ewigkeit (Ger.), ā'vĭk-kīt. Eternity.

Façon de parler, fä'sôn' dĕ pär'lā'. Manner of speaking; phrase; locution.

Faire bonne mine, fâr' bôn' mēn'. To look pleasant.

Faire les cent coups, fâr' lä sän' kōō'. To play all sorts of tricks.

Faire sans dire, fâr' sän' dēr'. To act without ostentation.

Faire son devoir, fâr' sôn' dĕ-vwär'. To do one's duty.

Fait accompli, fĕ'tä'kôn'plē'. An accomplished fact.

Faux pas, fō' pä'. A false step; an act of indiscretion.

Femme de chambre, fäm' dĕ shän'br'. A chambermaid.

Femme de charge, fäm' dĕ shärzh'. A housekeeper.

Fête, fāt. A feast; festival; holiday.

Fête champêtre, fāt' shän'pâ'tr'. A rural out-of-door feast; a festival in the fields.

Feu de joie, fû' dĕ zhwä'. A bonfire or discharge of firearms as a sign of rejoicing.

Fille de chambre, fē'y' dĕ shän'br'. A chambermaid.

Fille d'honneur, fē'y' dŏ'nûr'. A maid of honor; a lady in waiting.

Fleur-de-lis, flûr'dĕ-lē'. The flower of the lily. The coat of arms of France (a heraldic iris).

FRISCH BEGONNEN, HALB GEWONNEN (Ger.), *frĭsh bĕ-gŏn'nĕn hälp gĕ-vŏn'nĕn.* Well begun is half done.

FROIDES MAINS, CHAUDE AMOUR, *frwäd' măn' shō'dä'mōōr'.* Cold hands, warm heart.

FRONT À FRONT, *frôn'tä frôn'.* Face to face.

FUYEZ LES DANGERS DU LOISIR, *füe'yā' lä dän'zhä' dü lwä'zēr'.* Fly from the dangers of leisure.

GAIETÉ DE CŒUR, *gâ'tā' dĕ kŭr'.* Gaiety of heart.

GARÇON, *gàr'sôn'.* A lad; a waiter.

GARDE À CHEVAL, *gàr'dä shĕ-vàl'.* A mounted guard.

GARDE DU CORPS, *gàrd' dü kôr'.* A bodyguard.

GARDEZ LA FOI, *gàr'dā' lä fwä'.* Keep the faith.

GARDEZ-VOUS-EN BIEN, *gàr'dā' vōō' zän byăn'.* Don't you do it; do nothing of the kind.

GENDARME, *zhän'därm'.* Policeman; a turbulent woman; a flaw (as in a diamond).

GENS DE CONDITION, *zhän' dĕ kôn'dē'syŏn'.* People of rank.

GENS DE MÊME FAMILLE, *zhän' dĕ mâm' fà'mē'y'.* People of the same family; birds of a feather.

GENTILHOMME, *zhän'tē'yŏm'.* A gentleman; a nobleman.

GIOVINE SANTO, DIAVOLO VECCHIO (It.), *jō'vē-nĕ sän'tō dyä'vō-lō vĕk'kyō.* A young saint, an old devil.

GLEICH UND GLEICH GESELLT SICH GERN (Ger.), *glīk ōōnt glīk gĕ-zĕlt' zĭk gärn.* Birds of a feather flock together.

GLI ASSENTI HANNO TORTO (It.), *lyē äs-sĕn'tē än'nō tôr'tō.* The absent are in the wrong.

GOUTTE À GOUTTE, *gōō'tä-gōōt'.* Drop by drop.

GOUVERNANTE, *gōō'vĕr'nänt'.* A governess; housekeeper.

GRÂCE À DIEU, *grä'sä dyŭ'.* Thanks be to God.

GRANDE CHÈRE ET BEAU FEU, *gränd' shăr' ā bō' fŭ'.* Good fare and a good fire; comfortable quarters.

GRAND MERCI, *grän' mĕr'sē'.* Many thanks.

GROSSE TÊTE ET PEU DE SENS, *grōs' tât' ā pŭ' dĕ sän'.* A big head and little sense.

GUERRA Á CUCHILLO (Sp.), *gär'rä ä kōō-chĕl'yō.* War to the knife.

GUERRE À MORT, *gâr à môr'.* War to the death.

GUTEN MORGEN (Ger.), *gōōt'ĕn môr'gĕn.* Good morning.

HACE BUEN TIEMPO (Sp.), *ä'thä bwän tyĕm'pō.* It is fine weather.

HASTA LUEGO (Sp.), *äs'tä lwä'gō.* Until by and by; I'll see you later.

HASTA OTRA VEZ (Sp.), *äs'tä ō'trä väth.* Until another time; till we meet again.

HASTA MAÑANA (Sp.), *äs'tä män-yä'nä.* Good-by; until tomorrow.

HAUT GOÛT, *ō' gōō'.* High flavor; elegant taste.

HAUT TON, *ō' tŏn'.* Highest fashion.

HOMME D'AFFAIRES, *ôm' dà'fâr'.* A man of business; an agent.

HOMME DE ROBE, *ôm' dĕ rŏb'.* A person in a civil office.

HOMME D'ESPRIT, *ôm' dĕs'prē'.* A wit; a genius.

HOMME D'ÉTAT, *ôm' dä'tä'.* A statesman.

HONI SOIT QUI MAL Y PENSE, *ô'nē' swä' kē' màl' ē päns'.* Evil to him who evil thinks. (The motto of the Order of the Garter.)

HORS DE COMBAT, *ôr' dĕ kôn'bä'.* Out of the fight; disabled; unfit to continue a contest.

HORS DE LA LOI, *ôr' dĕ là lwä'.* Outlawed.

HORS DE PROPOS, *ôr' dĕ prō'pō'.* Wide of the point; inapplicable.

HORS DE SAISON, *ôr' dĕ sĕ'zŏn'.* Out of season; unseasonable.

HORS D'ŒUVRE, *ôr' dŭv'r'.* Out of course; a side dish; a digression.

HÔTEL DE VILLE, *ô'tĕl' dĕ vēl'.* A town hall.

HÔTEL DIEU, *ô'tĕl' dyŭ'.* The chief hospital of a town.

HÔTEL GARNI, *ô'tĕl' gär'nē'.* Furnished lodgings.

ICH DIEN (Ger.), *ĭk dēn'.* I serve.

IDÉE FIXE, *ē'dā' fēks'.* A fixed idea; a mental conviction or attitude.

IGNORANCE CRASSE, *ēn'yô'räns' kräs'.* Gross ignorance.

I GRAN DOLORI SONO MUTI (It.), *ē grän dō-lō'rē sō'nō mōō'tē.* Great griefs are silent.

IL FAUT DE L'ARGENT, *ēl fō' dĕ làr'zhän'.* Money is needed.

IL N'A NI BOUCHE NI ÉPERON, *ēl nà' nē bōōsh' nē äp'-rôn'.* He has neither mouth nor spur; he has neither wit nor courage.

IL NE FAUT JAMAIS DÉFIER UN FOU, *ēl nĕ fō' zhà'mĕ' dä'fyä' ûn fōō'.* One should never provoke a fool.

IL NE FAUT POINT DISPUTER DES GOÛTS, *ēl nĕ fō' pwän' dĕs'pü'tä' dā gōō'.* There is no accounting for tastes.

IL N'EST SAUCE QUE D'APPÉTIT, *ēl nĕ' sōs' kĕ dà'pä'tē'.* Hunger is the best sauce.

IL SOUFFLE LE CHAUD ET LE FROID, *ēl sōōf'l' lĕ shō ā lĕ frwä'.* He blows hot and cold; he's a timeserver.

IMPOLI, *än'pō'lē'.* Unpolished; rude.

IN UN GIORNO NON SI FE' ROMA (It.), *ēn ōōn jôr'nō nōn sē fä rō'mä.* Rome was not built in a day.

JAMAIS BON COUREUR NE FUT PRIS, *zhà'mĕ' bŏn kōō'rŭr' nĕ fü' prē'.* A good runner is not to be taken; old birds are not to be caught with chaff.

JE NE SAIS QUOI, *zhĕ nĕ sà' kwä'.* I know not what; hard to describe; used humorously, as a "je ne sais quoi."

JE N'OUBLIERAI JAMAIS, *zhĕ nōō'blyä'rä' zhà'mĕ'.* I will never forget.

JE SUIS PRÊT, *zhĕ süĕ' prĕ'.* I am ready.

JET D'EAU, *zhĕ' dō'.* A fountain; a jet of water.

JEU DE MOTS, *zhû' dĕ mō'.* A play upon words; a pun.

JEU D'ESPRIT, *zhû' dĕs'prē'.* A witticism.

JEU DE THÉÂTRE, *zhû dĕ tä'ät'r'.* A stage trick; claptrap.

JEUNESSE DORÉE, *zhû'nĕs' dō'rā'.* Gilded youth.

JOUER DE BONHEUR, *zhwä' dĕ bô'nûr'.* To be in luck.

L'ADDITION, *là'dē'syŏn'.* The bill.

L'ADDITION S'IL VOUS PLAÎT, *là'dē'syŏn' sē vōō' plĕ'.* Give me my bill please.

LA CARIDAD BIEN ORDENADA EMPIEZA POR UNO MISMO (Sp.), *lä kä-rē-THäd' byän ôr-dā-nä'thä ĕm-pyä'thä pŏr ōō'nō mēs'mō.* Charity well directed begins with oneself; charity begins at home.

LA COSTUMBRE ES OTRA NATURALEZA (Sp.), *lä kôs-tōōm'brä ĕs ō'trä nä'tōō-rä-lā'thä.* Custom is second nature.

LA CRITIQUE EST AISÉE, L'ART EST DIFFICILE, *là krē'tēk' ĕ'tä'zā' làr'ĕ' dē'fē'sēl'.* Criticism is easy enough, but art is difficult.

LADE NICHT ALLES IN EIN SCHIFF (Ger.), *lä'dĕ nĭkt ä'lĕs ĭn īn shĭf.* Do not load all in one ship; do not put all your eggs into one basket.

L'ADVERSITÉ FAIT LES HOMMES, ET LE BONHEUR LES MONSTRES, *läd'vĕr'sē'tä' fĕ' lä'zôm' ā lĕ bô'nûr' lä mŏn'str'.* Adversity makes men, and prosperity, monsters.

LA FORTUNA AIUTA I PAZZI (It.), *lä fôr-tōō'nä ä-yōō'tä ē pät'sē.* Fortune helps fools.

LA FORTUNE PASSE PARTOUT, *là fôr'tün' päs' pàr'tōō'.* Fortune passes everywhere; all men are subject to the vicissitudes of fortune.

LAISSEZ FAIRE, *lĕ'sā' fâr'.* Let it alone.—A *laissez faire* (careless) attitude.

LOYAUTÉ M'OBLIGE, *lwä'yō'tā' mô'blēzh'.* Loyalty binds me

L'AMOUR ET LA FUMÉE NE PEUVENT SE CACHER, *là'mōōr' ā là fü'mä' nĕ pŭv' sĕ kà'shä'.* Love and smoke cannot be hidden.

LA PATIENCE EST AMÈRE, MAIS SON FRUIT EST DOUX, *là pà'syän' sĕ'tä'mâr' mĕ sôn' früĕ' tĕ' dōō'.* Patience is bitter, but its reward is sweet.

LA PLUMA ES LENGUA DEL ALMA (Sp.), *lä plōō'mä ĕs lĕn'gwä dĕl äl'mä.* The pen is the tongue of the mind.

LA POINTE DU JOUR, *là pwänt' dü zhōōr'.* Daybreak.

LA POVERTÀ È LA MADRE DI TUTTE LE ARTI (It.), *lä pō-vĕr-tä' ĕ lä mä'drĕ dē tōōt'tä lä är'tē.* Poverty is the mother of all the arts.

L'ARGENT, *làr'zhän'.* Silver; money.

L'ART POUR L'ART, *làr' pōōr làr'.* Art for art's sake.

LASCIATE OGNI SPERANZA, VOI CH'ENTRATE (It.), *lä-shä'tĕ ōn'yē spĕr-än'tsä vō'ē kän-trä'tĕ.* All hope abandon, ye who enter here. The inscription over the gates of hell in Dante's "Inferno" (III.9).

L'AVENIR, *làv'nēr'.* The future.

LA VERDAD ES AMARGA (Sp.), *lä vĕr-däth' ĕs ä-mär'gä.* Truth is bitter.

LA VERTU EST LA SEULE NOBLESSE, *là vĕr'tü' ĕ là sŭl' nô'blĕs'.* Virtue is the sole nobility.

LE BEAU MONDE, *lĕ bō' mŏnd'.* The world of fashion; society.

LE BON TEMPS VIENDRA, *lĕ bôn' tän' vyăn'drä'.* There's a good time coming.

LE COÛT EN ÔTE LE GOÛT, *lĕ kōō'tän' ōt' lĕ gōō'.* The expense takes away the pleasure.

LE DEMI-MONDE, *lĕ dĕ-mē'mŏnd'.* The half-world, that is, of women of equivocal reputation, demimondaines.

LE JEU N'EN VAUT PAS LA CHANDELLE, *lĕ zhû'nän' vō' pà' là shän'dĕl'.* The game is not worth the candle; the object is not worth the trouble.

LE MALHEUR NE VIENT JAMAIS SEUL, *lĕ màl'ûr' nĕ vyăn' zhä'mĕ' sûl'.* Misfortune never comes alone.

LE MONDE EST LE LIVRE DES FEMMES, *lĕ mŏn'dĕ' lĕ lēv'r' dä fàm'.* The world is woman's book.

L'EMPIRE DES LETTRES, *län'pēr' dā lĕt'r'.* The empire of letters.

LE PAROLE SON FEMMINE, E I FATTI SON MASCHI (It.), *lä pä-rō'lĕ sôn fäm'mē-nĕ ĕ ē fät'tĕ sôn mäs'kē.* Words are feminine, and deeds are masculine.

LES CONVENANCES, *lä kôn'v'-näns'.* The proprieties; the rules of politeness.

LÈSE MAJESTÉ, *lĕz' mä'zhĕs'tä'.* High treason.

LES MURAILLES ONT DES OREILLES, *lä mü'rä'y'-zŏn' dä' zô'rä'y'.* Walls have ears.

LES PLUS SAGES NE LE SONT PAS TOUJOURS, *lä plü' säzh' nĕ lĕ sôn' pàs tōō'zhōōr'.* The wisest are not always wise.

LE TOUT ENSEMBLE, *lĕ tōō'tän'sän'bl'.* The whole taken together.

LETTRE DE CACHET, *lĕt'r' dĕ kà'shä'.* A sealed letter containing orders; a royal warrant, usually authorizing the imprisonment, without trial, of a person named therein.

LE VRAI N'EST PAS TOUJOURS VRAISEMBLABLE, *lĕ vrĕ' nĕ' pàs' tōō'zhōōr' vrĕ'sän'blä'bl'* Truth is not always probable.

L'HOMME PROPOSE, ET DIEU DISPOSE, *lôm' prô'pōz' ā dyú' dĕs'pōz'.* Man proposes and God disposes.

L'INCONNU, *lăn'kô'nü'.* The unknown.

L'INCROYABLE, *lăn'krwä'yà'bl'.* The incredible; the marvelous. (The word incroyable was applied substantively to the fops of the Directory period in the great French Revolution.)

LINGERIE, *lăn'zh'-rē'.* Linen goods; also, collectively, all the linen, cotton, and lace articles of a woman's wardrobe.

LITTÉRATEUR, *lĕ'tā'rà'tûr'.* A literary man.

LO BARATO ES CARO (Sp.), *lō bä-rä'tō ĕs kä'rō.* A bargain is dear.

LO MÁS PRONTO POSIBLE (Sp.), *lō mäs prôn'tō pō-sē'blä.* As soon as possible.

LO QUE NO SE PUEDE REMEDIAR SE HA DE AGUANTAR (Sp.), *lō kä nō sä pwä'THä rä-mä'THē-är' sä ä' THä ä-gwän-tär'.* What cannot be cured must be endured.

LOYAUTE' M'OBLIGE, *lwä' yō' tä' mô' blēzh'.* Loyalty binds me.

MA CHÈRE, *mà' shâr'.* My dear (fem.).

MADEMOISELLE, *mȧd'mwȧ'zĕl'.* Miss.

MAESTRO DI COLOR CHE SANNO (It.), *mä-ĕs'trō dē kō-lōr' kä sän'nō.* Master of those that know. (Applied by Dante to Aristotle.)

MA FOI, *mà' fwä'.* Upon my faith; upon my word.

MAINTIENS LE DROIT, *măn'tyăn' lĕ drwä'.* Maintain the right.

MAISON DE CAMPAGNE, *mâ'zôn' dē kän'pàn'y'.* A country house.

MAISON DE SANTÉ, *mâ'zôn' dĕ sän'tä'.* A private asylum or hospital.

MAISON DE VILLE, *mâ'zôn' dē vēl'.* A town hall.

MAÎTRE D'HÔTEL, *mâ'tr' dô'tĕl'.* A house steward.

MALADIE DU PAYS, *mȧ'lä'dē' dü pĕ'ē'.* Homesickness.

MAL À PROPOS, *măl' à' prô'pō'.* Out of place; ill suited.

MAL DE MER, *măl' dē mâr'.* Seasickness.

MALENTENDU, *măl'än'tän'dü'.* A misunderstanding; a mistake.

MALGRÉ NOUS, *măl'grä' nōō'.* In spite of us.

MALHEUR NE VIENT JAMAIS SEUL, *mȧ'lûr' nĕ vyăn' zhä'mĕ' sŭl'.* Misfortunes never come singly.

MARDI GRAS, *märd'ē' grä'.* Shrove Tuesday.

MARIAGE DE CONSCIENCE, *mä'ryäzh' dĕ kôn'syäns'.* A private marriage.

MARIAGE DE CONVENANCE, *mä'ryäzh' dĕ kôn'v'-näns'.* A marriage of convenience, or from interested motives.

MARQUER LE PAS, *mär'kä' lĕ pä'.* To mark time.

MARZO VENTOSO Y ABRIL LLUVIOSO SACAN Á MAYO HERMOSO (Sp.), *mär'thō vĕn-tō'sō ē ä-brēl' lyōō'vyō'sō sä'kän ä mī'ō ĕr-mō'sō.* Windy March and showery April bring flowery May.

MÁS QUIERO ASNO QUE ME LLEVE QUE CABALLO QUE ME DERRUEQUE (Sp.), *mäs kyä'rō äs'nō kä mä lyä'vä kä kä-bäl'yō kä mä dĕr-rwä'kä.* I prefer the ass that carries me to the horse that throws me.

MÁS SABE UN NECIO PREGUNTAR QUE PUEDEN CIEN SABIOS CONTESTAR (Sp.), *mäs sä'bä ōōn nĕ'thyō prä-gōōn'tär kä pwä'THĕn thyĕn sä'byōs kōn-tĕs-tär'.* One fool can ask more questions than a hundred learned men can answer.

MÁS VALE PÁJARO EN MANO QUE CIENTO VOLANDO (Sp.), *mäs vä'lä pä'Hä-rō ĕn mä'nō kä thyĕn'tō vō-län'dō.* A bird in the hand is worth two in the bush (a hundred flying).

MÁS VALE TARDE QUE NUNCA (Sp.), *mäs vä'lä tär'dä kä nōōn'kä.* Better late than never.

MÁS VALE UN TOMA QUE DOS TE DARÉ (Sp.), *mäs vä'lä ōōn tō'mä kä dôs tĕ dä-rä'.* One "take" is better than two "I'll give."

MAUVAISE HONTE, *mō'vä' zônt'.* False modesty.

MAUVAIS GOÛT, *mō'vĕ' gōō'.* False taste.

MI CARO AMIGO (Sp.), *mē kä'rō ä-mē'gō.* My dear friend.

MIR IST ALLES EINERLEI (Ger.), *mēr ĭst ä'lĕs ī'nĕr-lī.* It's all the same to me.

MISE-EN-SCÈNE, *mē'zän'sân'.* The staging of a play.

MON AMI, *môn' nà'mē'.* My friend.

MON CHER, *môn' shâr'.* My dear (fellow).

MONSIEUR, *mė-syû'.* Sir; Mr.; gentleman.

MOT DU GUET, *mō' dü gĕ'.* A watchword.

MOTS D'USAGE, *mō' dü'zäzh'.* Words in common use.

MUCHOS POCOS HACEN UN MUCHO (Sp.), *mōō'chōs pō'kōs ä'thĕn ōōn mōō'chō.* Many littles make much; many a mickle makes a muckle.

MURAGLIA BIANCA, CARTA DI MATTO (It.), *mōō-räl'yä byän'kä, kär'tä dē mät'tō.* A white wall is the fool's paper.

NAÏVE, *nà'ēv'.* Having unaffected simplicity.

NAÏVETÉ, *nà'ēv''tä'.* Native simplicity.

NÉE, *nā.* Born; maiden name.

NÉGLIGÉ, *nā'glē'zhä'.* A morning dress.

NESSUN MAGGIOR DOLORE CHE RICORDARSI DEL TEMPO FELICE NELLA MISERIA (It.), *nĕs-sōōn' mä-jōr' dō-lō'rĕ kä rē-kôr-där'sē däl tĕm'pō fĕ-lē'chĕ näl'lä mē-zä'rē-ä.* No greater sorrow than to remember happy days when in misery.—Dante.

NEUE BESEN KEHREN GUT (Ger.), *noi'ĕ bā'zĕn kā'rĕn gōōt;* A new broom sweeps clean.

NI FIRMES CARTAS QUE NO LEAS, NI BEBAS AGUA QUE NO VEAS (Sp.), *nē fēr'mĕs kär'täs kä nō lä'äs nē bä'bäs ä'gwä kä nō vä'äs.* Sign no letter you have not read, nor drink water you cannot see; be very cautious.

NI L'UN NI L'AUTRE, *nē lûn' nē lō'tr'.* Neither the one nor the other.

N'IMPORTE, *năn'pôrt'.* It is of no consequence.

NOBLESSE OBLIGE, *nô'blĕs' ô'blēzh'.* Nobility imposes obligations; much is expected from persons of good position.

NO ES ORO TODO QUE RELUCE (Sp.), *nō ĕs ō'rō tō'THō kä rä-lōō'thä.* All is not gold that glitters.

NO HAY BIEN NI MAL QUE CIEN AÑOS DURE (Sp.), *nō ī byän nē mäl kä thyän än'yōs dōō'rä.* No good or evil lasts a hundred years.

NO HAY DE QUE (Sp.), *nō ī dā kä.* You are welcome; don't mention it.

NO IMPORTA (Sp.), *nō ēm-pōr'tä.* No matter; 'tis all the same.

NO LAS MERECE (Sp.), *nō läs mä-rä'thä.* It is not worth it (in answer to *Gracias*).

NOM DE GUERRE, *nôn' dĕ gâr'.* A war-name; an assumed name in controversy.

NOM DE PLUME, *nôn dĕ plüm'.* An assumed title; a pen name.

NON MI RICORDO (It.), *nôn mē rē-kôr'dō.* I do not remember.

NON OGNI FIORE FA BUON ODORE (It.), *nôn ōn'yē fyō'rĕ fä bwōn ō-dō'rĕ.* It is not every flower that smells sweet.

NON VENDER LA PELLE DELL' ORSO PRIMA DI PIGLIARLO (It.), *nôn vän'dĕr lä pĕl'lĕ däll ōr'sō prē'mä dē pēl-yär'lō.* Don't sell the bearskin before you have caught the bear.

NO SE GANÓ ZAMORA EN UNA HORA (Sp.), *nō sä gä-nō' thä-mō'rä ĕn ōō'nä ō'rä.* (Zamora was not won in an hour), Rome was not built in a day.

NO SE PERMITE HURTAR PARA DAR POR DIOS (Sp.), *nō sä pĕr-mē'tä ōōr-tär' pä'rä där pôr dē'ôs.* It is not lawful to steal in order to give to God.

NOT KENNT KEIN GEBOT (Ger.), *nōt kĕnt kīn gä-bōt'.* Necessity knows no law.

NOTRE DAME, *nô'tr' däm'.* Our Lady; the Virgin Mary; the great cathedral of Paris.

NOUS AVONS CHANGÉ TOUT CELA, *nōō'zà'vôn' shän'zhä' tōō' sē-lä'.* We have changed all that.

NOUS VERRONS, *nōō' vĕ'rôn'.* We shall see.

NOUVELLES, *nōō'vĕl'.* News.

NO VALE LA PENA (Sp.), *nō vä'lä lä pä'nä.* It is not worth the trouble.

NO VALE NADA (Sp.), *nō vä'lä nä'THä.* It is worthless; no use; no matter.

NUL BIEN SANS PEINE, *nül' byăn' sän pân'.* No pains, no gains

NULLA NUOVA, BUONA NUOVA (It.), *nōōl'lä nwô'vä, bwô'nä nwô'vä.* No news is good news.

OGNI BOTTEGA HA LA SUA MALIZIA (It.), *ōn'yē bŏt-tā'gä ä lä sōō'ä mä-lē'tsyä.* Every shop has its trick; there are tricks in all trades.

OJOS QUE NO VEN, CORAZÓN QUE NO SIENTE (Sp.), *ō'hōs kä nō vĕn' kō-rä-thôn' kä nō syĕn'tä.* Eyes that see not, heart that feels not; out of sight, out of mind.

OLLA PODRIDA (Sp.), *ôl'yä pō-THrĕ'THä.* A heterogeneous mixture; a stew of meat and vegetables.

ON CONNAÎT L'AMI AU BESOIN, *ôn kô'nä' là'mē' ō bĕ-zwăn'.* A friend is known in time of need; a friend in need is a friend indeed.

ON DIT, *ôn' dē'.* They say; a rumor.

ORO È CHE ORO VALE (It.), *ō'rō ĕ kä ō'rō vä'lĕ.* That is gold which is worth gold.

OUBLIER JE NE PUIS, *ōō'blyä' zhĕ nĕ püē'.* I can never forget.

OUÏ-DIRE, *ōō-ē' dēr'.* Hearsay.

OUVRAGE DE LONGUE HALEINE, *ōō'vräzh' dĕ lôn'gà'lăn'.* A work of time.

PARA TRABAJAR HACEN FALTA LOS BURROS (Sp.), *pä'rä trä-bä-Här' ä'thĕn fäl'tä lōs bōōr'rōs.* For work you must have the donkeys; let others do the work while you pocket the results.

PAR CI, PAR LÀ, *pär sē' pär lä'.* Here and there.

PAR EXCELLENCE, *pär ĕk'sĕ'läns'.* Pre-eminently.

PAR EXEMPLE, *pär ĕg'zän'pl'.* For instance.

PAROLE D'HONNEUR, *pà'rôl' dô'nûr'.* Word of honor.

PARTOUT, *pär'tōō'.* Everywhere.

PARVENU, *pär've-nü'.* An upstart.

PAS À PAS, *pä'zà'pä'.* Step by step.

PASSÉE, *pä'sä'.* Worn; faded, said of a woman no longer young.

PÂTÉ DE FOIE GRAS, *pä'tä' dĕ fwä' grä'.* A pie made from the livers of geese.

PEINE FORTE ET DURE, *pân' fôr'tä dür'.* Very severe punishment; a kind of judicial torture.

PENSÉE, *pän'sä'.* A thought expressed in terse, vigorous language.

PÈRE DE FAMILLE, *pâr dĕ fà'mē'y'.* The father of the family.

PERDU, *pĕr'dü'*. Lost.

PER PIÙ STRADE SI VA A ROMA (It.), *pär pyōō' strä'dĕ sē vä ä rō'mä*. There are many roads to Rome.

PERRO QUE LADRA NO MUERDE (Sp.), *pĕr'rō kä lä'THrä nō mwĕr'dä*. His bark is worse than his bite.

PETIT, *pē-tē'*. Small.

PETIT À PETIT L'OISEAU FAIT SON NID, *pē-tē' tä pē-tē' lwä'zō' fä sôN nē*. Little by little the bird builds its nest.

PETIT COUP, *pē-tē' kōō'*. A small mask; a domino.

PETIT-MAÎTRE, *pē-tē' mâ'tr'*. A little master; a fop.

PEU À PEU, *pû'ä pû'*. Little by little; by degrees.

PEU S'EN FAUT, *pû' säN fō'*. Nearly so; very near.

PIED À TERRE, *pyä' tä târ'*. A resting place; a temporary lodging.

PIGLIAR DUE COLOMBI A UNA FAVA (It.), *pēl-yär' dōō'ĕ kō-lōm'bē ä ōō'nä fä'vä*. To catch two pigeons with one bean; to kill two birds with one stone.

PIS ALLER, *pē' zä'lā'*. The worst or last shift.

POCO A POCO (It.), *pô'kō ä pô'kō*. Little by little; by degrees.

POINT D'APPUI, *pwäN' dä'püē'*. Prop; point of support.

POMMES DE TERRE, *pôm' dĕ târ'*. Potatoes (apples of the earth).

POR DONDE MENOS SE PIENSA SALTA EL LIEBRE, *pôr dôn'dä mä'nôs sä pyĕn'sä säl'tä ĕl lyä'brä*. The hare leaps whence you least expect; never be surprised.

PORTER UN COUP FUNESTE, *pôr'tä' ûn kōō' fü-nĕst'*. To deal a fatal blow.

POT-POURRI, *pô'pōō'rē'*. A medley.

POUR ACQUIT, *pōōr ä'kē'*. Paid; settled. (The usual form of receipt.)

POUR FAIRE RIRE, *pōōr fâr' rēr'*. For fun; for a joke.

POUR FAIRE VISITE, *pōōr fâr' vē'zēt'*. To pay a visit,—written in the corner of a visiting card to notify of a formal call.

POUR PASSER LE TEMPS, *pōōr pä'sä' lĕ täN'*. To while away the time.

POUR PRENDRE CONGÉ, *pōōr präN'dr' kôN'zhā'*. To take leave. Usually abbreviated to P.P.C. on a visiting card.

PRENDRE LA LUNE AVEC LES DENTS, *präN'dr' lä lün' ä'vĕk' lä däN'*. To seize the moon in one's teeth; to aim at impossibilities.

PRESTO MATURO, PRESTO MARCIO (It.), *prĕs'tō mä-tōō'rō prĕs'tō mär'chō*. Soon ripe, soon rotten.

PRÊT D'ACCOMPLIR, *prĕ' dä'kôN'plēr'*. Ready to accomplish.

PRÊT POUR MON PAYS, *prĕ' pōōr' môN' pĕ'ē'*. Ready for my country.

PREUX CHEVALIER, *prû' shĕ-vä'lyä'*. A brave knight.

PROTÉGÉ, *prô'tā'zhā'*. One protected by another; one to whom patronage is given.

PURÉE, *pü'rä'*. A thick soup, or mashed potatoes.

PURÉE AUX CROUTONS, *pü'rä' ō krōō'tôN'*. A thick soup with small cubes of toasted bread.

QUELQUE CHOSE, *kĕl'k' shōz'*. Something; a trifle.

¿QUE QUIERE DECIR ESO? (Sp.) *kä kyä'rä dä-thēr' ä'sō*. What does that mean?

QUERIDO AMIGO MIO (Sp.), *kä-rē'THō ä-mē'gō mē'ō*. My dear friend.

QUI A BU BOIRA, *kē' ä' bü' bwä'rä'*. The tippler will go on tippling; it is hard to break off bad habits.

QUIEN ABROJOS SIEMBRA, ESPINAS COGE (Sp.), *kyän ä-brō'Hôs syäm'brä ĕs-pē'näs kō'Hä*. He who sows brambles reaps thorns.

QUIEN CALLA OTORGA (Sp.), *kyän käl'yä ō-tôr'gä*. Silence gives consent.

QUIEN MÁS TIENE MÁS QUIERE (Sp.), *kyän mäs tyä'nä mäs kyä'rä*. The more one has, the more one wants.

QUIEN MUCHO DUERME, POCO APRENDE (Sp.), *kyän mōō'chō dwĕr'mä pô'kō ä-prĕn'dä*. He who sleeps much learns little; the indolent make little headway.

QUIEN POCO SABE, PRESTO LO REZA (Sp.), *kyän pô'kō sä'bä prĕs'tō lō rä'thä*. He who knows little soon tells it.

QUIEN QUITA LA OCASIÒN, QUITA EL PECADO (Sp.), *kyän kē'tä lä ō-kä-syôn' kē'tä ĕl pä-kä'THō*. He who avoids the occasion avoids sin.

¿QUIÉN SABE? (Sp.), *kyän sa-bä*. Who knows?

QUIEN TODO LO QUIERE TODO LO PIERDE (Sp.), *kyän tō'THō lō kyä'rä tō'THō lō pyĕr'dä*. Who wants all loses all.

QU'IL SOIT COMME IL EST DÉSIRÉ, *kēl' swä' kô'mē' lĕ' dä'zē'rä'*. Let it be as desired.

QUI AIME BERTRAND AIME SON CHIEN, *kē'âm' bĕr'träN' âm' sôN' shyäN'*. Love me, love my dog.

QUI N'A SANTÉ, N'A RIEN, *kē' nä' säN'tä' nä' ryäN'*. He who has not health has nothing.

QUI PRÊTE À L'AMI PERD AU DOUBLE, *kē' prät' ä lä'mē' pĕr' tō' dōō'bl'*. Loan oft bosses both itself and friend.

QUI VA LÀ? *kē' vä' lä'*. Who goes there?

QUI VIVE? *kē' vēv'*. Who goes there? On the "qui vive," adroit, watchful.

RAISON D'ÉTAT, *rĕ'zôN' dä'tä'*. Interest of the state.

RAISON D'ÊTRE, *rĕ'zôN' dâ'tr'*. The reason for a thing's existence.

RÉGIME, *rä'zhēm'*. Mode or style of rule or management.

RENDEZVOUS, *räN'dā'vōō'*. A place of meeting.

RENDEZ MES DEVOIRS, *räN'dā' mä' dĕ-vwär'*. Pay my respects.

RENTRER EN GRÂCE, *räN'trä' äN gräs'*. To be restored to favor.

RÉPONDEZ S'IL VOUS PLAÎT (R.S.V.P.), *rä'pôN'dä' sēl vōō' plĕ'*. Reply if you please, written on invitation cards.

RÉPONDRE EN NORMAND, *rä'pôN'dr' äN nôr'mäN'*. To answer in Norman; to speak evasively.

RÉSUMÉ, *rä'zü'mä'*. A summing up.

RETE NUOVA NON PIGLIA UCCELLO VECCHIO (It.), *rä'tĕ nwō'vä nôn pēl'yä ōōt-shĕl'lō vĕk'kyō*. A new net won't catch an old bird.

REVENONS À NOS MOUTONS, *rĕ-vnôN' à nô' mōō'tôN'*. Let us return to our sheep; let us come back to our subject.

RIEN N'EST BEAU QUE LE VRAI, *ryäN' nĕ' bô' kĕ lĕ vrä'*. There is nothing beautiful but truth.

RIRA BIEN QUI RIRA LE DERNIER, *rē'rä' byäN' kē' rē'rä' lĕ dĕr'nyä'*. He laughs best who laughs last.

RIRE ENTRE CUIR ET CHAIR; RIRE SOUS CAPE, *rēr' äN'tr-küēr' ā shâr'; rēr' sōō' käp'*. To laugh in one's sleeve.

ROBE DE CHAMBRE, *rôb' dĕ shäN'br'*. A dressing gown; a morning gown.

ROBE DE NUIT, *rôb' dĕ nüē'*. A nightdress.

RÔLE, *rōl*. A part in a performance.

RUSE DE GUERRE, *rüz' dĕ gâr'*. A military stratagem.

SALUD Y PESETAS! (Sp.), *sä-lōōTH' ē pä-sä'täs*. Health and money (a toast).

SANAN CUCHILLADAS, MÁS NO MALAS PALABRAS (Sp.), *sä'nän kōō'chĕl-yä'THäs mäs nō mä'läs pä-lä'bräs*. Wounds from a knife will heal, but not those from the tongue.

SANS CÉRÉMONIE, *säN sä'rä'mō'nē'*. Without ceremony.

SANS PEUR ET SANS REPROCHE, *säN pûr' ä säN rĕ-prôsh'*. Fearless and stainless.

SANS RIME ET SANS RAISON, *säN rēm'ä säN rĕ'zôN'*. Without rime or reason.

SANS SOUCI, *säN sōō'sē'*. Free from care.

SAUVE QUI PEUT, *sōv' kē' pû'*. Save yourselves; let each one look out for himself; headlong flight.

SAVOIR FAIRE, *sä'vwär' fâr'*. Tact.

SAVOIR VIVRE, *sä'vwär' vē'vr'*. Good breeding.

SDEGNO D'AMANTE POCO DURA (It.), *zdän'yō dä-män'tĕ pô'kō dōō'rä*. A lover's anger is short-lived.

SÉANCE, *sä'äNs'*. A sitting given for a painting; an assembly gathered for some set purpose.

SE FAIRE JOUR, *sĕ fâr' zhōōr'*. To force one's way.

SELON LES RÈGLES, *sĕ-lôN' lä rĕg'l'*. According to rule.

SEMPRE IL MAL NON VIEN PER NUOCERE (It.), *sĕm'prĕ ēl mäl nôn vyĕn pär nwôt'shä-rĕ*. Misfortune is not always an evil.

SE NON È VERO, È BEN TROVATO (It.), *sĕ nôn ĕ vä'rō ĕ bĕn trō-vä'tō*. If it is not true, it is cleverly invented.

SÍ GRACIAS (Sp.), *sē grä'thyäs*. Yes, thank you.

SI JEUNESSE SAVAIT, SI VIEILLESSE POUVAIT, *sĕ zhû'nĕs' sä'vä' sĕ vyä'yĕs' pōō'vä'*. If youth but knew, if age but had strength.

SI JUVENTUD SUPIERA Y SI VEJEZ PUDIERA (Sp.), *sē Hōō-vĕn-tōōTH' sōō-pyä'rä ē sē vä-Häth' pōō-THyä'rä*. If youth but knew, if age but had strength; lost chances.

SOIRÉE, *swä'rä'*. An evening party.

SOUFFLER LE CHAUD ET LE FROID, *sōō'flä' lĕ shō' ā lĕ frwä'*. To blow hot and cold.

SOUS UN FAUX JOUR, *sōō' zûn fō' zhōōr'*. In a bad light.

SO VIEL ICH WEISS (Ger.), *zō fēl ĭk vĭs*. As far as I know.

STURM UND DRANG (Ger.), *shtōōrm ōōnt dräng*. Storm and stress.

TABLE D'HÔTE, *tä'bl' dōt'*. Table of the host; a meal served entire, not from separate orders.

TÂCHE SANS TACHE, *täsh' säN täsh'*. A work without a stain.

TANT MIEUX, *täN' myû'*. So much the better.

TANT PIS, *täN' pē'*. So much the worse.

TEL MAÎTRE, TEL VALET, *tĕl mä'tr' tĕl vä'lä'*. Like master, like man.

TÊTE-À-TÊTE, *tâ'tä-tât'*. A conversation between two parties.

TOUJOURS PERDRIX, *tōō'zhōōr' pĕr'drē'*. Always partridges; the same thing over and over again; too much of a good thing.

TOUJOURS PRÊT, *tōō'zhōōr' prĕ'*. Always ready.

TOUR DE FORCE, *tōōr' dĕ fôrs'*. A feat of strength or skill.

TOUT À FAIT, *tōō'tä-fĕ'*. Wholly; entirely.

TOUT À L'HEURE, *tōō'tä-lûr'*. Presently; just now.

TOUT AU CONTRAIRE, *tōō'tō-kôN'trâr'*. Quite the contrary.

TOUT À VOUS, *tōō'tä-vōō'*. Entirely yours.

TOUT BIEN OU RIEN, *tōō' byäN'nōō ryäN'*. All well or nothing.

TOUT DE SUITE, *tōō'dĕ-süēt'*. Immediately.

TOUT ENSEMBLE, *tōō'täN'säN'bl'*. All together, entire effect (of a work of art).

TOUT LE MONDE EST SAGE APRÈS COUP, *tōō' lĕ môN'dĕ'sàzh' ä'prĕ' kōō'*. Everybody is wise after the event,—when it's too late.

TRADUTTORI, TRADITORI (It.), *trä-dōōt-tō'rē trä-dē-tō'rē*. Translators are traitors,—they often give a wrong meaning to an author.

TRAVAUX FORCÉS, *trä'vō' fôr'sä'*. Hard labor (legal sentence).

TUTTE LE STRADE CONDUCONO A ROMA (It.), tŏōt′tĕ lĕ strä′dĕ kŏn-dōō′kō-nō ä rō′mä. All roads lead to Rome.

UEBUNG MACHT DEN MEISTER (Ger.), ü′bōōng mäᴋt dĕn mĭs′tĕr. Practice makes perfect.

UN BIENFAIT N'EST JAMAIS PERDU, ûn byăn′fĕ′ nĕ′ zhä′mĕ′ pĕr′dü′. A kindness is never lost.

UN SOT À TRIPLE ÉTAGE, ûn sŏ′ä trĕ′pl′ ä′täzh′. A consummate fool.

UN "TIENS" VAUT MIEUX QUE DEUX "TU L'AURAS," ûn tyăn′ vō′ myŭ′ kĕ dû tü lō′rä′. One "take it" is worth two "you shall have it"; a bird in the hand is worth two in the bush.

VALET DE CHAMBRE, vä′lä′ dĕ shäɴ′br′. An attendant.

VAMOS (Sp.), vä′mōs. Let us go; now, then!

VAYA USTED CON DIOS (Sp.), vä′yä ōōs-tĕth′ kŏn dē′ōs. Go with God; good-by and good luck!

VEDI NAPOLI E POI MORI (It.), vä′dē nä′pō-lē ĕ pō′ē mō′rē. See Naples and then die.

VERDADES Y ROSAS TIENEN ESPINAS (Sp.), vĕr-dä′thĕs ē rō′säs tyä′nĕn ĕs-pē′näs. Truth and roses have their thorns.

VÉRITÉ SANS PEUR, vä′rē′tä′ säɴ pûr′. Truth without fear.

VIELE HÄND' MACHEN BALD EIN END' (Ger.), fē′lĕ hĕnt′ mäk′ĕn bält ĭn ĕnt′. Many hands make quick work.

VIGUEUR DE DESSUS, vē′gûr′ dĕ dĕ-sü′. Strength from on high.

VINO DENTRO, SENNO FUORI (It.), vē′nō dän′trō sän′nō fwô′rē. When the wine is in, the wit is out.

VIS-À-VIS, vē′zä vē′. Face to face.

VIVE LA BAGATELLE, vēv′ lä bä′gä′tĕl′. Success to trifles! Said on hearing something ridiculous related.

VIVE LE ROI, vēv′ lĕ rwä′. Long live the king.

VOILÀ, vwä′lä′. See there; there is; there!

VOILÀ TOUT, vwä′lä′ tōō′. That's all; there you are!

VOILÀ UNE AUTRE CHOSE, vwä′lä′ ü′nō′tr′ shōz′. That's quite another thing.

VOIR LE DESSOUS DES CARTES, vwär lĕ dĕ-sōō′ dä kärt′. To see the face of the cards; to be in the secret.

VOUS Y PERDREZ VOS PAS, vōō′zē pĕr′drä′ vō′ pä′. You will have your walk for nothing; you will lose your labor over it.

WAS FEHLT IHNEN? (Ger.), väs fält ē′nĕn. What ails you? What is the matter with you?

WIE DIE ARBEIT, SO DER LOHN (Ger.), vē dē är′bĭt zō där lōn. As the labor, so the reward.

ZEITGEIST (Ger.), tsĭt′gĭst. The spirit of the age.

HAWAIIAN PHRASES

Noted for its prominent vowel sounds, the language originally spoken by natives of Hawaii (ha wy′ee) has a musical quality and an exotic charm. Although English is the standard medium of communication, many visitors to the fiftieth state will pick up some phrases as linguistic souvenirs. Here are a few examples:

ALOHA AHIAHI (ä lō′hä ä hē ä′hē)—Good evening.

ALOHA AU IA OE (ä lō′hä ou ē′ä ō′ä)—I love you.

ALOHA KAKAHIAKA (ä lō′hä kä kä hē ä′kä)—Good morning.

ALOHA NUI LOA (ä lō′hä nōō′ē lō′ä)—Much love.

HAUOLI LA HANAU (hou ō′ lē lä hä nä′oo)—Happy birthday.

HAUOLI MAKAHIKI HOU (hou ō′lē mä kä hē′kē hō′oo)—Happy New Year.

MAHALO NUI LOA (mä hä′lō nōō′ē lō′ä)—Many thanks.

MAIKAI (mĭ′kĭ)—I am fine.

MELE KALIKIMAKA (mä′lä kä lē kē mä′kä)—Merry Christmas.

PEHEA OE? (pä hä ä ō ä)—How are you?

TOURIST TALK—EXCERPTS FROM A FOREIGN PHRASE BOOK

As George Bernard Shaw once pointed out, a traveler attempting to use the language of a foreign country will get all the more attention if his speech is halting and fractured, and is therefore barely understandable. The natives are suspicious of a stranger whose accent and idiom are faultless, but they find linguistic clumsiness amusing, and they are pleased at their own cleverness in grasping a foreigner's partly hidden meaning. Since pronunciation is usually the chief obstacle, the prospective tourist will do well to take instruction in this, supplemented perhaps by drill with phonograph records, in order to be sure of pronouncing approximately the sounds that will make his phrases intelligible.

The examples of tourist phrases given in the following collection are typical, but of course are merely illustrative. Because each traveler has his own individual needs based on particular situations, his phrase book collection will naturally be a highly personalized one. In case of emergencies he can probably fall back on English, but meanwhile a good part of his enjoyment will come from attempting, more or less successfully, to speak like a native.

ENGLISH	FRENCH	GERMAN	SPANISH	ITALIAN
Where does this train go to?	Où va ce train?	Wohin fährt dieser Zug?	¿Adónde va este tren?	Dove va questo treno?
When does the train for .... start?	À quelle heure le train pour .... part-il?	Wann geht der Zug nach .... fort?	¿A qué hora sale el tren para ....?	A che ora parte il treno par ....?
Is there a dining car on this train?	Ya-t-il un wagon-restaurant à ce train?	Hat der Zug einen Speisewagon?	¿Hay (Wagón) comedor (o restaurante) en este tren?	C'e un vagone ristorante in questo treno?
How long does the boat stop at ....?	Combien de temps le bateau s' arrête-il à ....?	Wie lange legt das Boot in .... an?	¿Cuanto tiempo para el buque en ....?	Che fermata fa il battello a ....?
Please take me to the .... airport.	Veuillez me conduire a l'aéroport de	Fahren Sie mich bitte zum Flugplatz in	Haga el favor de conducir me a la estación .... de aviación.	Per favore, portate mi all' aeroporto di ....
Is smoking allowed?	Peut-on fumer?	Ist Rauchen gestattet?	¿Se permite fumar?	Ē permess d fumare?
I have nothing to declare.	Je n'ai rien à déclarer.	Ich habe nichts zu verzollen.	No tengo nada que declarar.	Non ho nulla da dichiarare.
Please give me back my passport.	Veuillez me rendre mon passeport.	Kann ich meinen Pass zuruckhaben?	Haga el favor de devolver me mi passaporte.	Prego di restituir mi il passaporto.
Which is the way to the station?	Quel est le chemin qui conduit à la gare?	Welches ist der Weg nach dem Bahnhof?	¿Cuál es el camino de la estación?	Qual' è la strada per la stazione?

ENGLISH	FRENCH	GERMAN	SPANISH	ITALIAN
Where does this road lead to?	Où conduit cette route?	Wohin führt diese Strasse?	¿Adonde conduce este camino?	Dove porta questa estrada?
Cabby! Are you disengaged?	Cocher! Êtes-vous libre?	Kutscher! Sind Sie frei?	!Cochero! Está usted libre?	Cocchiere! Siete libero?
Where can I get a bus to . . . .?	Où puis-je prendre un omnibus pour . . . .?	Wo kann ich einen Bus nach . . . . Bekommen?	¿En dónde puedo tomar el ómnibus para . . . .?	Dove posso prendere un omnibus per . . . .?
Which is the best hotel at . . . .?	Quel est le meilleur hôtel de . . . .?	Welches ist das beste Hotel in . . . .?	¿Cuál es el mejor hotel en . . . .?	Qual' e il migliore albergo a . . . .?
Kindly post this letter.	Veuillez mettre cette lettre à la poste.	Würden Sie bitte diesen Brief einwerfen.	Haga el favor de echarme esta carta al correo.	Favorisca impostarmi questa lettera.
At what time is the set meal?	À quelle heure est la table d'hôte?	Um wieviel Uhr ist die Table d'hôte?	¿A qué hora sirven la comida?	A che ora è la tavola rotonda?
Give me the bill of fare, please.	Donnez-moi la carte, s'il vous plait.	Geben Sie mir bitte die Speisekarte.	Haga el favor de darme la lista de platos.	Datemi il menu, per favore.
I will take the set dinner.	Je dinerai à la table d'hôte.	Ich nehme das Menu.	Comeré a la table d'hôte.	Io mangerò alla tavola rotonda.
Some more bread, if you please.	Encore du pain, s'il vous plait.	Noch etwas Brot, bitte.	Haga el favor de darme más pan.	Un altro poco di pane, per placere.
Thank you, I have enough.	Merci, j'en ai assez.	Danke, ich habe genug.	Gracias, hasta ya o con eso basta.	Grazie, ne ho abbastanza.
Waiter! another cup of coffee.	Garçon! Encore une tasse de café.	Ober! Noch eine Tasse Kaffee, bitte.	!Camarero! Otra taza de cafe.	Cameriere! Un' altra tazzina di caffe.
Can I borrow a book?	Puis-je emprunter un livre?	Kann ich ein Buch asuborgen?	¿Puedo tomar un libro prestado?	Posso avere in prestito un libro?
Please make up this prescription.	Veuillez préparer cette ordonnance.	Können Sie mir bitte diesen Rezept herstellen.	Haga el favor de preparme esta receta.	Per favore, preparatemi questa ricetta.
I want a lounge suit.	Il me faut un complet veston.	Ich möchte einen Strassenanzug.	Necessito un traje de americana.	Io desidero un vestito completo da mattina.
I wish to cash this traveller's check.	Je désire encassier ce cheque de voyage.	Ich mochte diesen traveller's cheque einlösen.	Deseo cobrar este traveller's cheque.	Desidero incassare questo traveller's cheque.

From TRAVELLERS' FOREIGN PHRASE BOOK by J. O. Kettridge
Quoted by permission of the Publishers,
Routledge & Kegan Paul, Ltd.

SOME FAMOUS FIRST LINES

Many of the "poems every one should know" are recognized better by their opening lines than by their titles. In some cases, a poem worth remembering may not even have a title. For example, a great sonnet by Shakespeare may be designated only by the Roman numeral XXXIII, which is no more revealing than the label "Opus 33" for a piece of music. However, for those who know and appreciate Shakespeare's poem, its opening words, "Full many a glorious morning have I seen," will immediately identify it. In many cases, the first line contains the key to the thought and acquaints the reader at once with the concept of the poem as a whole. From another point of view, it may be said that, originally, the first line gave the poet a running start into the process of composition. Until he had a good first line to give him impetus, he was not ready to write the poem.

Those who recognize poems by their first lines may or may not remember the lines that come next. People differ greatly in their ability to memorize long passages of poetry, but they can usually remember the opening words from their favorites, in the same way that they recall the opening bars of a well-liked symphony or overture. The famous first lines quoted below may lead either to the renewing of old acquaintance or, in some cases, to the addition of hitherto unknown works of poetry.

Afoot and light-hearted, I take the open road
    WALT WHITMAN—*Song of the Open Road*
A garden is a lovesome thing, God wot!
    THOMAS EDWARD BROWN—*My Garden*
A gentle Knight was pricking on the plaine
    EDMUND SPENSER—*The Faerie Queene*
A late lark twitters from the quiet skies
    WILLIAM E. HENLEY—*Margaritae Sorori*
All I could see from where I stood
    EDNA ST. VINCENT MILLAY—*Renascence*

All thoughts, all passions, all delights
    SAMUEL TAYLOR COLERIDGE—*Love*
And did those feet in ancient time
    WILLIAM BLAKE—From *Milton*
April is the cruellest month, breeding
    T. S. ELIOT—*The Waste Land*
Ask me no more where Jove bestows
    THOMAS CAREW—*Ask Me no More*
A thing of beauty is a joy forever
    JOHN KEATS—*Endymion*

A sweet disorder in the dress
ROBERT HERRICK—*Delight in Disorder*

Ay, tear her tattered ensign down!
OLIVER WENDELL HOLMES—*Old Ironsides*

Bards of passion and of mirth
JOHN KEATS—*Bards of Passion*

Behind him lay the great Azores
JOAQUIN MILLER—*Columbus*

Bowed by the weight of centuries, he leans
EDWIN MARKHAM—*The Man with the Hoe*

Breathes there a man with soul so dead
SIR WALTER SCOTT—*Patriotism*

Bright Star! would I were steadfast as thou art
JOHN KEATS—*Sonnet*

By the rude bridge that arched the flood
RALPH WALDO EMERSON—*Concord Hymn*

Come live with me and be my love
CHRISTOPHER MARLOWE—*The Passionate Shepherd*

Come Sleep, O Sleep! the certain knot of peace
SIR PHILIP SIDNEY—*Sleep*

Crabbed Age and Youth
WILLIAM SHAKESPEARE—*The Passionate Pilgrim*

Death, be not proud, though some have called thee
JOHN DONNE—Sonnet, *Death*

Drink to me only with thine eyes
BEN JONSON—*To Celia*

Ethereal minstrel! pilgrim of the sky!
WILLIAM WORDSWORTH—*To the Skylark*

Fair stood the wind for France
MICHAEL DRAYTON—*Agincourt*

Fear death? To feel the fog in my throat
ROBERT BROWNING—*Prospice*

Gather ye rosebuds while ye may
ROBERT HERRICK—*To the Virgins*

Give a man a horse he can ride
JAMES THOMSON—*Gifts*

God of our fathers, known of old
RUDYARD KIPLING—*Recessional*

Had we but world enough, and time
ANDREW MARVEL—*To His Coy Mistress*

Hail to thee, blithe spirit!
PERCY BYSSHE SHELLEY—*To a Skylark*

Happy those early days when I
HENRY VAUGHAN—*The Retreat*

Harp of the North, farewell! the hills grow dark
SIR WALTER SCOTT—*Lay of the Last Minstrel*

Helen, thy beauty is to me
EDGAR ALLAN POE—*To Helen*

Hence, loathed Melancholy
JOHN MILTON—*L'Allegro*

Here's to the maiden of bashful fifteen
RICHARD BRINSLEY SHERIDAN—*Drinking Song*

How do I love thee? Let me count the ways
ELIZABETH BARRETT BROWNING—*Sonnet*

How happy is he born and taught
SIR H. WOTTON—*The Character of a Happy Life*

How sleep the brave who sink to rest
WILLIAM COLLINS—*How Sleep the Brave*

I bargained with Life for a penny
JESSIE B. RITTENHOUSE—*My Wage*

I come from nothing, but from where
ALICE MEYNELL—*A Song of Derivations*

If I should die, think only this of me
RUPERT BROOKE—*The Soldier*

If I were Lord of Tartary
WALTER DE LA MARE—*Tartary*

I fled him, down the nights and down the days
FRANCIS THOMPSON—*The Hound of Heaven*

I must go down to the seas again
JOHN MASEFIELD—*Sea-fever*

In after days when grasses high
AUSTIN DOBSON—*In After Days*

In the grey wastes of dread,
ROY CAMPBELL—*Horses on the Camargue*

In Xanadu did Kubla Khan
SAMUEL TAYLOR COLERIDGE—*Kubla Khan*

I saw Eternity the other night
HENRY VAUGHAN—*A Vision*

It is portentous, and a thing of state
V. LINDSAY—*Abraham Lincoln Walks at Midnight*

I wandered lonely as a cloud
WILLIAM WORDSWORTH—*Daffodils*

Jenny kiss'd me when we met
LEIGH HUNT—*Jenny Kiss'd Me*

Let me live out my years in heat of blood
J. G. NEIHARDT—*Let Me Live Out My Years*

Much have I traveled in the realms of gold
JOHN KEATS—Sonnet, *Chapman's Homer*

My days among the dead are past
ROBERT SOUTHEY—*The Scholar*

My hair is gray, but not with years
LORD BYRON—*The Prisoner of Chillon*

My heart aches, and a drowsy numbness pains
JOHN KEATS—*Ode to a Nightingale*

No coward soul is mine
EMILY BRONTE—*Last Lines*

Of Man's first disobedience and the first
JOHN MILTON—*Paradise Lost*

Others abide our question, thou art free
MATTHEW ARNOLD—Sonnet, *Shakespeare*

Out of the night that covers me
W. E. HENLEY—*Invictus*

Over his keys the musing organist
J. RUSSELL LOWELL—*The Vision of Sir Launfal*

O Wild West Wind, thou breath of Autumn's being
PERCY BYSSHE SHELLEY—*Ode to the West Wind*

Say not the struggle nought availeth
ARTHUR HUGH CLOUGH—*Say Not the Struggle*

Serene, I fold my hands and wait
JOHN BURROUGHS—*Waiting*

Shall I compare thee to a summer's day?
WILLIAM SHAKESPEARE—*Sonnet XVIII*

She walks in beauty like the night
LORD BYRON—*She Walks in Beauty*

Slowly, silently, now the moon
WALTER DE LA MARE—*Silver*

Speak! speak! thou fearful guest
H. W. LONGFELLOW—*The Skeleton in Armor*

Sweet Auburn! Loveliest village of the plain
OLIVER GOLDSMITH—*The Deserted Village*

Swiftly walk over the western wave,
PERCY BYSSHE SHELLEY—*To the Night*

Tears, idle tears, I know not what they mean
ALFRED LORD TENNYSON—*Tears*, from *The Princess*

Tell me not, sweet, I am unkind
RICHARD LOVELACE—*To Lucasta*

The Assyrian came down like a wolf on the fold
LORD BYRON—*The Destruction of Sennacherib*

The blessed Damozel lean'd out
DANTE GABRIEL ROSSETTI—*The Blessed Damozel*

The glories of our blood and state
JAMES SHIRLEY—*Dirge*

The red rose whispers of passion
JOHN BOYLE O'REILLEY—*A White Rose*

There was a time when meadow, grove, and stream
W. WORDSWORTH—Ode, *Intimations of Immortality*

The splendor falls on castle walls
ALFRED LORD TENNYSON—*Bugle Song*

The sun that brief December day
JOHN GREENLEAF WHITTIER—*Snowbound*

The time you won your town the race
A. E. HOUSMAN—*To an Athlete Dying Young*

The wind was a torrent of darkness
ALFRED NOYES—*The Highwayman*

The world is too much with us; late and soon
WILLIAM WORDSWORTH—*Sonnet*

The year's at the spring
ROBERT BROWNING—*Pippa Passes*

Thou still unravished bride of quietness
JOHN KEATS—*Ode On a Grecian Urn*

'Twas at the royal feast for Persia won
JOHN DRYDEN—*Alexander's Feast*

Two roads diverged in a yellow wood
ROBERT FROST—*The Road Not Taken*

Under the wide and starry sky
ROBERT LOUIS STEVENSON—*Requiem*

Wake! For the Sun, who scattered into flight
EDWARD FITZGERALD—Trans., *The Rubaiyat*

We are the music-makers
ARTHUR O'SHAUGHNESSY—*Ode*

What dire offence from amorous causes springs
ALEXANDER POPE—*The Rape of the Lock*

What is this life if, full of care,
W. H. DAVIES—*Leisure*

When all the world is young, lad
CHARLES KINGSLEY—*"The Old, Old Song"*

When I consider how my light is spent
JOHN MILTON—*Sonnet on his Blindness*

When I consider Life, and its few years,
LIZETTE WOODWORTH REESE—Sonnet, *Tears*

When the hounds of Spring are on Winter's traces
A. C. SWINBURNE—Chorus from *Atalanta*

When you are old and gray and full of sleep
WILLIAM BUTLER YEATS—*When You Are Old*

Whither, O splendid ship, thy white sails crowding
ROBERT BRIDGES—*A Passer-by*

Why so pale and wan, fond lover?
SIR J. SUCKLING—*Encouragements to a Lover*

Ye distant spires, ye antique towers
THOMAS GRAY—Ode, *Eton College*

Yet once more, O ye laurels, and once more
JOHN MILTON—*Lycidas*

CHARACTERS FROM FICTION

Illustration by E. W. Kemble from
HUCKLEBERRY FINN by Mark Twain

Illustration by John Tenniel from
ALICE'S ADVENTURES IN WONDERLAND
by Lewis Carroll

Illustration by R. Caldecott from
JOHN GILPIN'S RIDE by William Cowper

Illustration by Gustave Doré from
DON QUIXOTE by Cervantes

Illustration by
George Cruikshank
from
OLIVER TWIST
by Charles Dickens

Illustration by
A. B. Frost from
THE UNCLE REMUS STORIES
by Joel Chandler Harris

FAMOUS NAMES IN LITERATURE

Becky Sharp   By *Frederick Barnard*

Of the many names on this page, perhaps the greatest challenge to illustrators is the fascinating, unscrupulous heroine of Thackeray's novel, *Vanity Fair*. Becky Sharp was selfish, unprincipled, and very clever. She succeeded in marrying Colonel Crawley, who was disinherited because of his marriage to her. After several unsavory scandals, Becky reversed her character and became pious and charitable.

Jane Eyre   By *Sigismond de Ivanowski*
Used by permission of
Appleton-Century-Crofts, Inc.

Jane Eyre, the heroine of a novel by Charlotte Brontë, was governess in the family of Mr. Rochester, with whom she fell in love. Mr. Rochester's wife, who was mentally ill, committed suicide. Later Jane Eyre and Mr. Rochester were married.

Sigismond de Ivanowski's illustrations for the Century Series, *Heroines of Fiction*, included some of Tolstoy's principal characters as well as Jane Eyre.

Mr. Darcy and Sir William Lucas
from *Pride And Prejudice*   By *Hugh Thomson*

Thomson's problem was to catch the spirit of Jane Austen's depiction of character—perceptive, mildly satirical, yet sympathetic.

DICTIONARY OF ABBREVIATIONS

Note:—In some abbreviations, particularly those used for government agencies, the periods after the initials are customarily omitted. In fact, many such combinations of initials are treated as actual words. (See *Acronyms*.)

A. Alto.
A1. First class.
A., a., adj. Adjective.
A., ans. Answer.
a., @. (Lat. *ad*), To; At.
A. A. Alcoholics Anonymous.
AAA. Agricultural Adjustment Agency; American Automobile Association.
A. A. A. & L. American Academy of Arts and Letters.
A. A. A. S. American Association for the Advancement of Science.
AAF. Army Air Forces.
A. A. O. N. M. S. Ancient Arabic Order of the Nobles of the Mystic Shrine.
a. a. r. Against all risks.
A. & A. S. R. Ancient and Accepted Scottish Rite.
AASA. American Ass'n of School Administrators.
A. A. S. S. (Lat. *Academiæ Antiquarinæ Societatis Socius*), Member of the American Antiquarian Society.
A. A. U. P. American Association of University Professors.
A. A. U. W. American Association of University Women.
A. B. (Lat. *artium baccalaureus*), Bachelor of Arts.
Abbr., Abbrev. Abbreviated, abbreviation.
ABC. American Broadcasting Corp.
Abp. Archbishop.
A. B. S. American Bible Society.
A. C. (Lat. *ante Christum*), Before Christ; Analytical Chemist; Alternating Current; Air Corps; Athletic Club.
Acc., Acct. Account.
A. D. (Lat. *anno Domini*), In the year of our Lord.
Ad., advt. Advertisement. Plur. *ads.*
A. D. C. Aide-de-camp.
Ad. inf. To infinity.
Adjt. Adjutant.
Adjt. Gen. Adjutant General.
Ad lib., Ad libit. (Lat. *ad libitum*), At pleasure.
Adm. Admiral.
Admr. Administrator.
Admx. Administratrix.
Adv. Advertising; Advocate; Adverb.
Æ., Æt. (Lat. *ætatis*), Of age, aged.
AEC. Atomic Energy Commission.
A.E.F. American Expeditionary Force.
AFL-CIO. American Federation of Labor and Congress of Industrial Organizations.
Agr., Agric. Agriculture, agricultural.
Agt. Agent.
A. H. (Lat. *anno Hegiræ*), In the year of the Hegira, or flight of Mohammed.
A. H. C. American Hospital Corps.
A. H. M. S. American Home Missionary Society.
A. H. S. (Lat. *anno humanæ salutis*), In the year of human salvation.
A. I. D. American Institute of Decorators; Agency for International Development.
AKC. American Kennel Club.
A. L. American Legion.
ALA. American Library Ass'n.
Ala., Al. Alabama.
Alas., Ak. Alaska.
Ald. Alderman.
A. L. of H. American Legion of Honor.
Alta. Alberta.
A. M. (Lat. *anno mundi*), In the year of the world.
A. M. (Lat. *ante meridiem*), Before noon.
A. M. (Lat. *artium magister*), Master of Arts.
Am., Amer. America, American.
AMA. American Medical Association.
A. M. D. Army Medical Department.

Amp. Ampere; amperage.
Amt. Amount.
AMVETS. American Veterans (World War II).
A. N. Anglo-Norman.
an. (Lat. *anno*), In the year.
Anat. Anatomy, anatomical.
Anc. Ancient.
Anon. Anonymous.
A. N. S. Army Nursing Service.
Ant., Antiq. Antiquities, antiquarian.
ANZAC. Australian and New Zealand Army Corps.
A. O. H. Ancient Order of Hibernians.
A. O. U. American Ornithologists' Union.
A. O. U. W. Ancient Order of United Workmen.
AP. Associated Press.
Ap., App. Apostle, apostles; Appendix.
Apl., Apr. April.
APO. Army Post Office.
Apoc. Apocalypse; Apocrypha.
Apog. Apogee.
approx. Approximate, -ly.
A. P. S. Associate of the Pharmaceutical Society.
Aq. (Lat. *aqua*), Water.
Ar., Arab. Arabic, Arabian.
Ar., Arr. Arrives, arrived, arrival.
A. R. A. Associate of the Royal Academy.
Aram. Aramaic.
ARC. American Red Cross.
Arch. Architecture.
Archæol. Archæology.
Archd. Archdeacon; Archduke.
Ariz., Az. Arizona.
Ark., Ar. Arkansas.
Arm. Armorican; Armenian.
ARP. Air-raid precautions.
Art. Article; Artificial; Artillery.
A. S., A.-S. Anglo-Saxon.
ASCAP. American Society of Composers, Authors, and Publishers.
ASEE. American Society for Engineering Education.
ASPCA. American Society for Prevention of Cruelty to Animals.
Assoc., Assn. Association.
Asst. Assistant.
A. S. S. U. American Sunday School Union.
Astrol. Astrology.
Astron. Astronomy, astronomical.
ATC. Air Transport Command.
A. T. S. American Tract Society; Army Transport Service.
Atty. Attorney.
A. U. A. American Unitarian Ass'n.
Aug. Augustus; August.
A. V. Authorized Version.
Avoir. Avoirdupois.
Awol. Absent without leave.

B. Bass; Book.
b. Born.
B., Brit. British.
B. A. Bachelor of Arts.
Bal. Balance.
Balt., Balto. Baltimore.
Bap., Bapt. Baptist.
Bar. Barrel; Barometer.
Bart., Bt. Baronet.
Bat., Batt. Battalion, battery.
B. B. C. British Broadcasting Corp.
bbl. Barrel. Plur. *bbls.*
B. C. Before Christ; British Columbia.
B. Ch. (Lat. *baccalaureus chirurgiæ*), Bachelor of Surgery.
B. C. L. (Lat. *baccalaureus civilis legis*), Bachelor of Civil Law.
B. C. S. Bachelor of Commercial Science.
B. D. (Lat. *baccalaureus divinitatis*), Bachelor of Divinity.
Bd. Bound; Bond; Board; Band.
Bdls. Bundles.
Bds. Bound in boards.

B. E. Bachelor of Engineering; Bachelor of Elocution
b. e. Bill of exchange.
Belg. Belgic, Belgian.
Ben., Benj. Benjamin.
Berks. Berkshire (England).
Bib. Bible, biblical.
Biog. Biography, biographical.
Biol. Biology, biological.
B/L. Bill of lading.
B. L., B.LL. (Lat. *baccalaureus legum*), Bachelor of Laws.
bldg. Building.
B. M. (Lat. *baccalaureus medicinæ*), Bachelor of Medicine.
B. M., B. Mus. (Lat. *baccalaureus musicæ*), Bachelor of Music.
BMEWS. Ballistic Missile Early Warning System.
Bot. Botany, botanical.
Bp. Bishop.
B. P. O. E. Benevolent and Protective Order of Elks.
Br., Bro. Brother.
Brig. Brigade, brigadier.
Brig. Gen. Brigadier General.
B. S. Bachelor of Surgery; Bachelor of Science.
B. S. A. Boy Scouts of America.
B. Sc. (Lat. *baccalaureus scientiæ*), Bachelor of Science.
bu., bush. Bushel.
B. V. Blessed Virgin.
B. V. M. Blessed Virgin Mary.
B. W. I. British West Indies.

c. About (for approximate dates).
C. Cent, cents; Centigrade; Consul; Centime, centimes; Hundred.
C., Cap. (Lat. *caput*), Chapter.
C. A. Chartered Accountant.
CAA. Civil Aeronautics Administration.
CAB. Civil Aeronautics Board.
Cal. Calendar.
Cal., Calif. California.
Cam., Camb. Cambridge.
Cant. Canticle; Canterbury.
Cantab. (Lat. *Cantabrigiensis*), Of Cambridge.
CAP. Civil Air Patrol.
Caps. Capitals.
Capt. Captain.
car., k. Carat.
Card. Cardinal.
CARE. Co-operative for American Relief Everywhere.
Cath. Catharine; Catholic; Cathedral.
C. B. Companion of the Bath.
CBC. Canadian Broadcasting Corp.
CBS. Columbia Broadcasting System.
C. C. Catholic Clergyman, Catholic Curate.
CCC. Civilian Conservation Corps.
C. D. S. Companion of the Distinguished Service Order.
C. D. V. or *c. d. v.* Carte-de-Visite.
C. E. Civil Engineer.
Celt. Celtic.
Cent. (Lat. *centum*), Hundred; Centigrade.
Cert., Certif. Certify, certificate.
Cf. (Lat. *confer*), Compare.
c. f. i. Cost, freight, and insurance.
c. ft. Cubic feet.
C. G. Coast guard; Commissary General; Consul General.
C. G. S. Centimeter-Gram-Second.
Ch. Church; Chapter.
Chal., Chald. Chaldee.
Chanc. Chancellor, chancery.
Chap. Chapter; Chaplain.
Chas. Charles.
Chem. Chemistry, chemical.
Chin. Chinese.
Chr. Christ; Christian.
Chron. Chronology, chronological.
C. I. Order of the Crown of India.
CIA. Central Intelligence Agency.
C.I.F. Cost, Insurance, freight.

1091

Cit. Citation; Citizen.
Civ. Civil.
C. J. Chief Justice.
Cl. Clergyman.
Clk. Clerk.
cm. Centimeter.
C. M. Common meter.
C. M. (Lat. *chirurgiæ magister*), Master in Surgery.
CO. Commanding Officer.
Co. Company; County.
C. O. D. Cash on Delivery; Collect (payment) on delivery.
. *of C.* Chamber of Commerce.
Col. Colonel; Colossians: Column.
Coll. College; Collection.
Colloq. Colloquial, colloquialism.
Colo., Co. Colorado.
Com. Commander; Commerce; Commissioner; Committee; Commodore.
Comm. Commentary; Commerce.
Comp. Compare, comparative; Compound, compounded.
Compar. Comparative.
Com. Ver. Common Version.
Con. (Lat. *contra*), Against.
Conelrad. Control of Electronic Radiation.
Cong. Congregation, Congregational, Congregationalist; Congress.
Conj. Conjunction.
Conn., Ct. Connecticut.
Cont. Contents; Continued.
Co-op. Co-operative.
Cop., Copt. Coptic.
Cor. Corinthians.
Corrup. Corruption, corrupted.
Cor. Sec. Corresponding Secretary.
C. P. Clerk of the Peace; Common Pleas.
c. p. Chemically pure.
C. P. A. Certified Public Accountant; Civilian Production Administration.
C. Q. D. Come quick—danger.
Cr. Credit, creditor.
Cres. Crescendo.
Crim. con. Criminal conversation, or adultery.
cryst., crystal. Crystallography.
C. S. Christian Science.
C. S. A. Confederate States of America.
Csks. Casks.
Ct. (Lat. *centum*), A hundred.
Ct. Court.
C. T. A. U. Catholic Total Abstinence Union.
ctge. Cartage.
Cu., Cub. Cubic.
Cu. ft. Cubic foot.
Cur., Curt. Current—this month.
CVA. Columbia Valley Authority.
Cwt. Hundredweight(s).
C. Y. M. A. Catholic Young Men's Association.
C. Z. Canal Zone.

D. Deputy; Democrat; Dutch.
d. (Lat. *denarius, denarii*), Penny, pence.
d. Died; Daughter.
D. A. District Attorney.
Dan. Daniel; Danish.
D. A. R. Daughter(s) of the American Revolution.
Dat. Dative.
D. C. Doctor of Chiropractic.
D. C. (Ital. *da capo*), From the beginning; Direct Current.
D. C., Dist. Col. District of Columbia.
D. C. L. Doctor of Civil (or Canon) Law.
D. D. (Lat. *divinitatis doctor*), Doctor of Divinity.
D-Day. Day designated for military operation against enemy.
D. D. S. Doctor of Dental Surgery.
D E. Dynamic Engineer.
Dec. December.
decim. Decimeter.
Def. Definition; Defendant.
Deg. Degree, degrees.
Del., De. Delaware.
Del. (Lat. *delineavit*), He (or she) drew.
D. Eng. Doctor of Engineering.

Dep., Dept. Department; Deputy; Deposit.
Der. Derived, derivation.
Deut. Deuteronomy.
DEW. Distant Early Warning.
dft. Draft; Defendant.
D. G. (Lat. *Dei gratia*), By the grace of God.
Dict. Dictionary.
Dim., Dimin. Diminutive.
Dis., Disct. Discount.
Dist. District.
Div. Divide, dividend, division, divisor.
D. Lit., D. Litt. Doctor of Literature.
D. M., D. Mus. Doctor of Music.
D. M. D. Doctor of Dental Medicine.
DNA. Deoxyribonucleic Acid.
D. O. Doctor of Osteopathy; Doctor of Oratory.
Do. (Ital. *ditto*), The same.
Dols. Dollars.
Doz. Dozen.
D.P. Displaced Person.
Dpt. Deponent; Department.
Dr. Debtor; Doctor; Dram, drams.
D. S. (Ital. *dal segno*), From the sign.
D. S., D. Sc. Doctor of Science.
D. S. C. Distinguished Service Cross.
D. S. M. Distinguished Service Medal.
D. S. O. Distinguished Service Order.
DST. Daylight Saving Time.
D. T. (Lat. *doctor theologiæ*), Doctor of Theology.
Du. Dutch; Duke.
Duo., 12mo. Duodecimo (twelve folds).
D. V. (Lat. *Deo volente*), God willing.
D. V. M. Doctor of Veterinary Medicine.
D. V. S. Doctor of Veterinary Surgery.
dwt. (Lat. *denarius*, and English *weight*), Pennyweight, pennyweights.
Dyn., Dynam. Dynamics.

E. East, Eastern; English.
Ea. Each.
Eben. Ebenezer.
Eccl., Eccles. Ecclesiastical.
Econ. Economy, economics.
Ed. Editor; Edition; Edinburgh.
Ed., Edm. Edmund.
Ed.D. Doctor of Education.
Edin. Edinburgh.
Edw. Edward.
E. E. Errors excepted; Electrical Engineer.
EEC. European Economic Community (Common Market).
e. g. (Lat. *exempli gratia*), For example.
Elec., Elect. Electric, electricity.
Eliz. Elizabeth, Elizabethan.
e. m. f. Electromotive force.
Emp. Emperor, empress.
Enc., Encl. Enclosure.
Ency., Encyc. Encyclopedia.
E. N. E. East northeast.
Eng. England, English.
Eng., Engin. Engineer, engineering.
Ent., Entom. Entomology.
Eph. Ephesians; Ephraim.
Epiph. Epiphany.
Epis., Episc. Episcopal.
Epis., Epist. Epistle, epistolary.
ER. Endoplasmic Reticulum.
ERP. European Recovery Program.
E. S. E. East southeast.
ESP. Extra-sensory perception.
EST. Eastern Standard Time.
Esq., Esqr. Esquire.
et al. (Lat. *et alibi*), And elsewhere.
et al. (Lat. *et alii, aliæ,* or *alia*), And others.
etc., &c. (Lat. *et cetæri, cæteræ,* or *cætera*), And the others, and so forth.
Ethnol. Ethnology, ethnological.
Etym. Etymology.
Ex. Example; Examined; Exception; Exodus; Export; Executive.
Exch. Exchange; Exchequer.
Exd. Examined.
Exec., Exr. Executor.
Execx., Exrx. Executrix.
Ex. Gr. (Lat. *exempli gratia*), For example.
Exod. Exodus.
Exon. (Lat. *Exonia*), Exeter.
exp. Express; Export; Expense.

Ezek. Ezekiel.
F. Fellow; Fahrenheit; France.
f. Farthing, farthings; Folio; Feminine.
f. Franc, francs.
Fahr. Fahrenheit.
F. & A. M. Free and Accepted Masons.
f. a. s. Free alongside ship.
FBI. Federal Bureau of Investigation.
FCA. Farm Credit Association.
FCC. Federal Communications Commission.
Fcp. Foolscap.
F. D., Fid. Def. (Lat. *fidei defensor*), Defender of the Faith.
FDIC. Federal Deposit Insurance Corp.
Feb. February.
Fec. (Lat. *fecit*), He (or she) did it.
Fem. Feminine.
FEPC. Fair Employment Practice Committee.
F. F. V. First Families of Virginia.
F. G. S. Fellow of the Geological Society.
FHA. Federal Housing Administration.
F. I. A. Fellow of the Institute of Actuaries.
F. I. C. Fellow of the Chemical Institute.
Fig. Figure, figurative, figuratively.
Finn. Finnish.
Fl. Flemish; Florin, florins; Flourished.
Fla., Fl. Florida.
FLA. Federal Loan Administration.
F. M. Field Marshal; Frequency Modulation.
fo., fol. Folio.
f. o. b. Free on board.
fol. Folio; Following.
For. Foreign.
for'd., fwd. Forward, forwarded.
FPC. Federal Power Commission.
Fr. France, French; Francis; Francs.
F. R. A. S. Fellow of the Royal Astronomical Society.
Fred. Frederick.
F. R. G. S. Fellow of the Royal Geographical Society.
Fri. Friday.
FRS. Federal Reserve System.
F. R. S. Fellow of the Royal Society.
F. R. S. L. Fellow of the Royal Society of Literature.
frt. Freight.
FSA. Federal Security Administration.
ft. Foot, feet.
FTC. Federal Trade Commission.
Fth. Fathom.
Fur. Furlong.

G. Genitive; Guinea, guineas; Gulf.
Ga. Georgia.
Gael. Gaelic.
Gal. Galatians.
Gal., Gall. Gallon.
G. A. R. Grand Army of the Republic.
GATT. General Agreement on Tariffs and Trade.
G. B. Great Britain.
G. C. B. Grand Cross of the Bath.
G. C. L. H. Grand Cross of the Legion of Honor.
G. C. S. I. Grand Commander of the Star of India.
G. C. V. O. Grand Cross of the Royal Victorian Order.
G. D. Grand Duke, Grand Duchess.
Gen., Genl. General.
Gen. Genesis; Genitive.
Gend. Gender.
Geo. George.
Geog. Geography, geographical.
Geol. Geology, geological.
Geom. Geometry, geometrical.
Ger., Germ. German, Germany.
G. H. Q. General Headquarters.
Gi. Gill, gills.
G. I. Government Issue.
G. L. Grand Lodge.
G. M. Grand Master.
Gm. Gram.
GMT. Greenwich Mean Time.
Go., Goth. Gothic.
G. O. P. Grand Old Party (applied to Republican party).
Gov. Governor, government.

Gov.-Gen. Governor-General.
Govt. Government.
Gr. Grain(s); Great; Greek; Gross.
gr. gram(s).
Gram. Grammar, grammatical.
Gro. Gross.
G. T. Good Templars; Grand Tyler.
Gtt. (Lat. *guttæ*), Drops.
H., hr. Hour, hours.
Hag. Haggai.
Hamps. Hampshire.
Haw., Hi. Hawaii.
H. C. House of Commons.
h. e. (Lat. *hoc est*), That is or this is; (*hic est*), Here is.
Heb., Hebr. Hebrew, Hebrews.
HEW. Department of Health, Education and Welfare.
H. H. His (or Her) Highness; His Holiness (the Pope).
Hhd. Hogshead, hogsheads.
H.I.H. His (or Her) Imperial Highness.
Hind. Hindu, Hindustan, Hindustani.
Hist. History, historical.
H. J. (Lat. *hic jacet*), Here lies.
H. J. S. (Lat. *hic jacet sepultus*), Here lies buried.
H. M. His (or Her) Majesty.
H. M. S. His (or Her) Majesty's service, ship, or steamer.
Hon., Honble. Honorable.
Hor., Horol. Horology, horological.
Hort., Hortic. Horticulture, horticultural.
H. P. Half pay; High priest; Horse power.
H. R. House of Representatives.
H. R. H. His (or Her) Royal Highness.
Hun., Hung. Hungary, Hungarian.
Hyd., Hydros. Hydrostatics.
Hydraul. Hydraulics.
Hypoth. Hypothesis, hypothetical.
I., Isl. Island.
Ia. Iowa.
Ib., Ibid. (Lat. *ibidem*), In the same place.
ICBM. Intercontinental ballistic missile.
ICC. Interstate Commerce Com's'n; Indian Claims Com's'n.
Ice., Icel. Iceland, Icelandic.
Ich., Ichth. Ichthyology.
Ida., Id. Idaho.
IDA. International Development Ass'n.
i. e. (Lat. *id est*), That is.
I. H. S. Greek contraction for Jesus, —used as abbrev. for Lat. *Jesus Hominum Salvator*, "Jesus, the Savior of Men," and *In hoc signo*, "In this sign (cross)."
Ill. Illinois.
ILO. International Labor Organization.
Imp. (Lat. *imperator*), Emperor; Imperial; Impersonal.
In. Inch, inches.
Incog. (Ital. *incognito*), Unknown.
Ind. India, Indian; Indiana.
In lim. (Lat. *in limine*), At the outset.
In loc. (Lat. *in loco*), In its place.
in re. In regard to.
I. N. R. I. (Lat. *Jesus Nazarenus Rex Iudæorum*), Jesus of Nazareth, King of the Jews.
Ins. Insurance.
Inst. Instant; The present month; Institute, institution.
Int. Interest.
Int. Dept. Department of the Interior.
Intrans. Intransitive.
Int. Rev. Internal Revenue.
Intro., Introd. Introduction.
I. O. O. F. Independent Order of Odd Fellows.
I. O. R. M. Improved Order of Red Men.
I. O. U. I owe you.
I. Q. Intelligence Quotient.
i. q. (Lat. *idem quod*), The same as.
Ir. Ireland, Irish.

IRBM. Intermediate range ballistic missile.
IRS. Internal Revenue Service.
Is., Isa. Isaiah.
I. S. Irish Society.
I. S. M. (Lat. *Jesus Salvator Mundi*), Jesus, Savior of the World.
It., Ital. Italy, Italian; Italic.
Itin. Itinerary.
J. Judge; Justice.
Jac. Jacob, Jacobus (—James).
JAG. Judge Advocate General.
Jan. January.
Jav. Javanese.
J. C. Jesus Christ.
J. C. D. (Lat. *juris civilis doctor*), Doctor of Civil Law.
J. D. (Lat. *jurum doctor*), Doctor of Laws.
Jer. Jeremiah.
J. H. S. See *I. H. S.*
Jno. John.
Jon., Jona. Jonathan.
Jos. Joseph.
Josh. Joshua.
Jour. Journal; Journey.
J. P. Justice of the Peace.
Jr. Juror; Junior.
J. R. Joint Resolution.
J. U. D. (Lat. *Juris utriusque doctor*), Doctor of both laws (of civil and canon law).
Jud. Judith; Judicial.
Judg. Judges.
Jul. July; Julius, Julian.
Jun., Je. June.
K. King; Knight.
k. Karat.
Kans., Kan., Ks. Kansas.
K. B. Knight of the Bath; King's Bench.
K. C. King's Counsel; Knights of Columbus; Kansas City.
kg. Kilogram.
Ki. Kings.
Kingd. Kingdom.
K. L. H. Knight of the Legion of Honor.
K. M. Knight of Malta.
km. Kilometer.
K. P. Knight of St. Patrick.
K. of P. Knights of Pythias.
Kt. Knight.
K. T. Knight Templar.
Kw. Kilowatt.
Kwh. Kilowatt hour.
Ky. Kentucky.
L. Latin; Lake; Lord; Lady.
L., l., £. (Lat. *libra*), Pound, pounds (sterling).
L., lb., ℔. (Lat. *libra*), Pound, pounds (weight).
La., Lou. Louisiana.
Lat. Latin; Latitude.
LC. Landing Craft.
l. c. Lower case (in printing).
L. c., loc. cit. (Lat. *loco citato*), In the passage cited.
l/c. Letter of credit.
L. D. S. Licentiate of Dental Surgery; Latter Day Saints.
Leg., Legis. Legislature, legislative.
Lev., Levit. Leviticus.
Lex. Lexicon.
Lexicog. Lexicography, lexicographer, lexicographical.
L. H. D. (Lat. *Litterarum Humanarum Doctor*), Doctor of Humanities.
L. I. Light Infantry; Long Island.
Lib. (Lat. *liber*), Book; Library, librarian.
Lieut., Lt. Lieutenant.
Lieut. Col. Lieutenant Colonel.
Lieut. Gen. Lieutenant General.
Lieut. Gov. Lieutenant Governor.
Linn. Linnæus, Linnæan.
Liq. Liquor, liquid.
Lit. Literally, literature, literary.
Lit. D., Litt. D. (Lat. *literarum doctor*), Doctor of Literature.
LL. B. (Lat. *legum baccalaureus*), Bachelor of Laws.

LL. D. (Lat. *legum doctor*), Doctor of Laws.
LL. M. Master of Laws.
L. M. Long meter.
loc. cit. In the place quoted.
Lon., Lond. London.
Lon., Long. Longitude.
Loq. (Lat. *loquitur*), He (or she) speaks.
LP. Long play (phonograph record).
LSD. Lysergic acid diethylamide.
L. s. d. (Lat. *libræ, solidi, denarii*), Pounds, shillings, pence.
Lt. Lieutenant.
Ltd. Limited.
Lt. Inf. Light Infantry.
LTL. Less than truckload.
Luth. Lutheran.
m. Married; Masculine; Meter, meters; Mile, miles; Minute, minutes.
M. Marquis; Middle; Monday; Morning; Monsieur.
M. (Lat. *mille*), Thousand.
M. (Lat. *meridies*), Meridian; Noon.
MA. Master of Arts.
Mac., Macc. Maccabees.
MAD. Magnetic airborne detector.
Maj. Major.
Maj. Gen. Major General.
Mal. Malachi; Malay, Malayan.
Man. Manitoba.
Manuf. Manufactures, manufacturing.
Mar. March; Maritime.
Marq. Marquis.
Mas., Masc. Masculine.
Mass., Ma. Massachusetts.
M. Ast. S. Member of the Astronomical Society.
Math. Mathematics, mathematical.
Matt. Matthew.
M. B. (Lat. *medicinæ baccalaureus*), Bachelor of Medicine.
M. B. (Lat. *musicæ baccalaureus*), Bachelor of Music.
MC. Member of Congress; Master of Ceremonies.
MD. Muscular dystrophy.
M. D. (Lat. *medicinæ doctor*), Doctor of Medicine.
Md. Maryland.
Mdlle., Mlle. (Fr. *mademoiselle*), Miss.
Mdse. Merchandise.
M. E. Most Excellent; Military Engineer; Mining Engineer; Mechanical Engineer; Methodist Episcopal.
Me. Maine.
Meas. Measure.
Mech. Mechanics, mechanical.
Med. Medicine, medical; Medieval.
Med. Lat. Medieval Latin.
Mem. Memorandum, memoranda.
Messrs., MM. (Fr. *messieurs*), Gentlemen.
Met. Metaphysics, metaphysical.
Metal., Metall. Metallurgy.
Metaph. Metaphysics; Metaphorically.
Meteor. Meteorology, meteorological.
Meth. Methodist.
Mex. Mexico, Mexican.
MFH. Master of Fox Hounds.
Mfr. Manufacturer; manufacture.
mg. Milligram.
Mi. Michigan.
M. I. C. E. Member of the Institute of Civil Engineers.
Mich. Michaelmas; Michigan.
Mid. Middle; Midshipman.
Mil., Milit. Military.
M. I. M. E. Member of the Institute of Mining Engineers.
Min. Mineralogy, mineralogical; Minute, minutes.
Minn., Mn. Minnesota.
Min. Plen. Minister Plenipotentiary.
Miss., Ms. Mississippi.
ML. Master of Laws; Multiple listing (real estate).
mm. Millimeters.
Mme. Madame.
M. O. Money order.
Mo. Missouri; Month.
Mod. Modern.
Mon. Monday.

Mons. (Fr. *monsieur*), Sir; Mr.
Mont. Montana.
M. P. Member of Parliament; Military Police.
M. P. P. Member of Provincial Parliament.
Mr. Master, Mister.
M. R. G. S. Member of the Royal Geographical Society.
M. R. I. Member of the Royal Institute.
Mrs. Mistress.
M. S. Master of Surgery; Master of Science.
Ms. Manuscript; *Mss.* Manuscripts.
MS. Multiple sclerosis.
MSG. Monosodium glutamate.
MST. Mountain Standard Time.
Mt. Montana, Mount; *Mts.* mountains.
mth., mo. Month.
Mus. Museum; Music, musical.
Mus. B. (Lat. *musicæ baccalaureus*), Bachelor of Music.
Mus. D., Mus. Doc., Mus. Doct. (Lat. *musicæ doctor*), Doctor of Music.
MVA. Missouri Valley Authority.
M. V. O. Member of the Royal Victorian Order.
M. W. A. Modern Woodmen of America.
Myth. Mythology, mythological.
N. Noon; North; Noun; Number; New; Neuter.
N. A. North America, North American.
NAA. National Aeronautic Ass'n.
NAACP. National Association for the Advancement of Colored People.
Nah. Nahum.
NAM. Nat'l Ass'n of Manufacturers.
NAS. National Academy of Sciences.
NASA. National Aeronautics and Space Administration.
Nat. Natural; National.
Nat. Hist. Natural History.
NATO. North Atlantic Treaty Organization.
Naut. Nautical.
Nb. Nebraska.
N. B. New Brunswick.
N. B. (Lat. *nota bene*), Note well; Take notice.
NBC. National Broadcasting Company.
N. C. North Carolina.
N. Dak., N. D. North Dakota.
N. E. New England, Northeast.
N. E. A. National Education Ass'n.
Nebr., Neb. Nebraska.
Neg. Negative, negatively.
Neh. Nehemiah.
Nem. con. (Lat. *nemine contradicente*), No one contradicting, unanimously.
Nem. diss. (Lat. *nemine dissentiente*), No one dissenting, unanimously.
Neth. Netherlands.
Neut. Neuter.
Nev. Nevada.
New Test., N. T. New Testament.
N. F. Newfoundland.
N. H. New Hampshire.
N. J. New Jersey.
N. L., N. Lat. North Latitude.
NLRB. Nat'l Labor Relations Board.
NMB. National Mediation Board.
N. Mex., N. M. New Mexico.
NNE. North northeast.
No., Nos. Number, numbers.
nol. pros. (Lat. *nolle prosequi*), To be unwilling to prosecute.
Nom., Nomin. Nominative.
non-com. Non-commissioned officer.
Non con. Non-content, dissentient. (The formula in which Members of the House of Lords vote.)
Non obst. (Lat. *non obstante*), Notwithstanding.
Non pros. (Lat. *non prosequitur*), He does not prosecute.
Non seq. (Lat. *non sequitur*), It does not follow (as a consequence).
Nor., Norm. Norman.
Nor. Fr., Norm. Fr. Norman French.
Norw. Norway, Norwegian, Norse.
Nov. November.

N. P. Notary Public.
NROTC. Naval Reserve Officers' Training Corps.
N. S. New style; Nova Scotia.
NSF. Nat'l Science Foundation.
N. S. J. C. (Fr. *Notre Seigneur Jesus Christ*), Our Lord Jesus Christ.
N. S. W. New South Wales.
Num., Numb. Numbers.
N. V. M. Nativity of the Virgin Mary.
N. W. Northwest, northwestern.
N. Y. New York.
N. Z., N. Zeal. New Zealand.
O. (unofficial) Ohio; Old.
OAS. Organization of American States.
OAU. Organization of African Unity.
ob. (Lat. *obiit*), He (or she) died.
Obj. Objective.
Obs. Obsolete.
Oct. October.
Oct., 8vo. Octavo.
Oh. Ohio.
O. K. "All correct."
Okla. Oklahoma.
Old Test., O. T. Old Testament.
Olym. Olympiad.
O. M. Order of Merit.
O. M. I. Order of Mary Immaculate.
Ont. Ontario
Op. Opposite, opposition.
Opt. Optative; Optics, optical.
Ord., Ordn. Ordnance.
Oreg., Ore. Oregon.
Orig. Original, originally.
Ornith. Ornithology, ornithological.
O. S. Old Style; Old Saxon.
O. S. A. Order of St. Augustine.
O. S. B. Order of St. Benedict.
O. S. F. Order of St. Francis.
Oxf. Oxford.
Oxon. (Lat. *Oxonia, Oxoniensis*), Oxford, of Oxford.
Oz. Ounce. (The *z* in this contraction and in *viz.* represents an old symbol (ʒ), used to mark a terminal contraction.)
P. Page; Participle; Past; Pole; Port.
Pa. Pennsylvania.
Pal., Palæont. Palæontology, palæontological.
Par. Paragraph.
Parl. Parliament, parliamentary.
Part. Participle.
Payt. Payment.
Pd. Paid.
Pd. D. Doctor of Pedagogy.
P. E. Protestant Episcopal.
P. E. I. Prince Edward Island.
P. E. N. Poets, Playwrights, Editors, Essayists, and Novelists (International).
Pent. Pentecost.
Per., Pers. Persian; Person, personal.
Per. an. (Lat. *per annum*), Yearly.
Per cent., per ct. (Lat. *per centum*), By the hundred.
Peruv. Peruvian.
pfd. Preferred.
Phar., Pharm. Pharmacy.
Ph. B. (Lat. *philosophiæ baccalaureus*), Bachelor of Philosophy.
Ph. D. (Lat. *philosophiæ doctor*), Doctor of Philosophy.
Phil. Philip; Philippians; Philosophy, philosophical.
Phil., Phila. Philadelphia.
Philol. Philology.
Philos. Philosophy, philosophical.
Ph. M. Master of Philosophy.
PHS. Public Health Service.
Phys. Physics, physical.
Physiol. Physiology, physiological.
Pinx., Pxt. (Lat. *pinxit*), He (or she) painted it.
Pk. Peck.
Pl. Place; Plate; Plural.
Plf., Plff., Pltff. Plaintiff.
Plur. Plural.
P. M. (Lat. *post meridiem*), Afternoon.
P. M. Past Master; Peculiar meter; Postmaster.

P. O. Post Office.
Pol. Polish, Poland.
Polit. Econ. Political Economy.
Pop. Population.
Port. Portugal, Portuguese.
POW. Prisoner of War.
Pp. Pages.
P. P. Parish Priest.
P. P. C. (Fr. *pour prendre congé*), To take leave. See *T. T. L.*
Pph. Pamphlet.
Pr. Present; Priest; Prince.
Pr. par. Present participle.
P. R. (Lat. *Populus Romanus*), The Roman People; Puerto Rico.
P. R. C. (Lat. *post Roman conditam*), After the building of Rome.
Pref. Prefix; Preface.
Pres. President; Present.
Prim. Primary.
Prin. Principal.
Prob. Problem; Probable, probably.
Prof. Professor.
Pron. Pronoun; Pronounced, pronunciation.
Pro tem. (Lat. *pro tempore*), For the time being.
Prov. Proverbs, proverbial, proverbially; Provincial; Provost.
Prox. (Lat. *proximo*), Next; Of the next month.
Prus. Prussia, Prussian.
P. S. (Lat. *post scriptum*), Postscript.
Ps., Psa. Psalm, psalms.
pseud. Pseudonym.
pt. Part; Payment; Point; Port.
PTA. Parent-Teacher Association.
Pub. Public; Published, publisher.
Pvt., pte. Private.
Pwt. Pennyweight.
Q., Qu. Query; Question.
q. e. (Lat. *quod est*), Which is.
Q. E. D. (Lat. *quod erat demonstrandum*), Which was to be proved.
Q. M. Quartermaster.
Qr. Quarterly; Quire.
Qt. Quart.
Quar., quart. Quarterly.
Quar., 4to. Quarto.
Que. Quebec.
q. v. (Lat. *quod vide*), Which see.
R. Réaumur; River.
R. (Lat. *rex*), King; (Lat. *regina*), Queen.
R. A. Royal Academy, Royal Academician; Rear Admiral; Royal Arch; Royal Artillery; Royal Art.
Rad. (Lat. *radix*), Root.
RAF. Royal Air Force.
R. C. Roman Catholic; Red Cross.
R. E. Reformed Episcopal.
REA. Rural Electrification Administration.
Rec. Recipe; Receipt.
Recd. Received.
Recpt. Receipt.
Ref. Reference; Referee.
Ref. Ch. Reformed Church.
Reg. Regular; Registered.
Reg., Regr. Registrar.
Reg., Regt. Regiment.
Rel. Religion, religious.
Rel. Pron. Relative Pronoun.
Rem. Remark, remarks.
Rep. Report; Representative.
Rep., Repub. Republic; Republican.
Res. Reserve; Residence.
Rev. Revelation; Revenue; Reverend; Review; Revise.
Rev. Stat. Revised Statutes.
RFC. Reconstruction Finance Corp.
R. F. D. Rural Free Delivery.
Rhet. Rhetoric, rhetorical.
R. I. Rhode Island.
R. I. P. (Lat. *requiescat in pace*), May he (or she) rest in peace.
Riv. River.
R. N. Registered Nurse; Royal Navy.
RNA. Ribonucleic Acid.
Rom. Roman, Romans.
Rom. Cath. Roman Catholic.
ROTC. Reserve Officers' Training Corps.

R. R. Railroad.
R. S. V. P. (Fr. *Répondez s'il vous plaît*), Please reply.
Rt. Right.
Rt. Hon. Right Honorable.
Rt. Rev. Right Reverend.
Russ. Russia, Russian.
R. V. Revised Version.
Ry. Railway.

S. Saint; Saturday; Section; Shilling; Sign; Signor; Solo; Soprano; South; Sun; Sunday; Sabbath.
s. Second, seconds; See; Singular; Son; Succeeded.
S. A. South Africa; South America; Salvation Army.
Sab. Sabbath.
SAC. Strategic Air Command.
Sam. Samuel.
Sans., Sansc., Sansk., Skr. Sanscrit, Sanskrit.
Sask. Saskatchewan.
Sat. Saturday.
Sax. Saxon, Saxony.
SBA. Small Business Administration.
S. C. South Carolina.
S. caps., Sm. caps. Small capitals (in printing).
Sc. B. (Lat. *scientiæ baccalaureus*), Bachelor of Science.
Sc. D. (Lat. *scientiæ doctor*), Doctor of Science.
Sch. (Lat. *scholium*), A note.
Sci. Science.
Scot., Sc. Scotland, Scotch, Scottish.
Scrip., Script. Scripture, scriptural.
Sculp. Sculpture.
Sculp., Sculpt., Sc. (Lat. *sculpsit*), He (or she) engraved it.
S. D. Doctor of Science.
S. Dak., S. D. South Dakota.
SE. Southeast.
SEATO. Southeast Asia Treaty Organization.
SEC. Securities and Exchange Commission.
Sec. Second.
Sec., Sect. Section.
Sec., Secy. Secretary.
Sen. Senate, senator.
Sen. Doc. Senate Document.
Sep., Sept. September.
Seq. (Lat. *sequentes, sequentia*), The following, or the next.
Serg., Sergt. Sergeant.
Sess. Session.
SHAPE. Supreme Headquarters Allied Powers in Europe.
sic. As in the original (mistake uncorrected).
S. J. Society of Jesus.
Slav. Slavonic.
Snafu. Situation normal, all fouled up.
SNAP. Systems of Nuclear Auxiliary Power.
Soc., Socy. Society.
Sol. Gen. Solicitor-General.
S. O. S. Wireless distress signal at sea.
Sp. Spain, Spanish; Spirit.
s. p (Lat. *sine prole*), Without issue.
SPARS. (Lat. *Semper parati* [æ]), Always ready; Coast Guard motto and translation, initials being used as designation for Women's Coast Guard Reserves.
SPCA. Society for the Prevention of Cruelty to Animals.
SPCC. Society for the Prevention of Cruelty to Children.
Spec. Special, specially.
sp. gr , s. g. Specific gravity.
S. P. Q. R. (Lat. *Senatus Populusque Romanus*), The Senate and the People of Rome.
sq. Square; *sq. ft.* Square foot, feet; *sq. in.* Square inch(es); *sq. m.* Square mile(s); *sq. yd.* Square yard(s); *sq. rd.* Square rod(s).
Sr. Senior.
S. R. Senate Resolution.
SRO. Standing room only!
SS. Sunday School; Steamship.
SSA. Social Security Administration.

SSE. South-southeast.
SSW. South-southwest.
St. Saint; Stone; Street.
st. (Lat. *stet*), Let it stand (in printing).
Stat. Statute, statutes; Statuary.
STD. (Lat. *sacræ theologiæ doctor*), Doctor of Sacred Theology.
ster., stg. Sterling.
Str. Steamer; Strait.
Subst. Substantive; Substitute.
Sun., Sund. Sunday.
Sup. Superior; Superlative; Supplement; Supine.
Sup. Ct. Supreme Court.
Supt. Superintendent.
Surg. Surgeon, surgery.
Surg.-Gen. Surgeon-General.
Surv. Surveying, surveyor.
Surv.-Gen. Surveyor-General.
SW. Southwest.
Sw. Sweden, Swedish.
Swit., Switz. Switzerland.
Syn. Synonym, synonymous.
Syr. Syria, Syriac.

T. Tenor; Ton; Tun; Tuesday.
Tab. Table; Tabular statement.
Tass. The Soviet News Agency.
Tcs. Tierces.
Tech. Technical, technically.
Tenn., Tn. Tennessee.
Term. Termination.
Teut. Teutonic.
Tex., Tx. Texas.
Text. rec. (Lat. *textus receptus*), The received text.
Th. Thomas; Thursday.
Theo. Theodore.
Theol. Theology.
Tho., Thos. Thomas.
Thu., Thur., Thurs. Thursday.
Tim. Timothy.
Tit. Title; Titus.
TNT. Trinitrotoluene, an explosive.
Tob. Tobit.
Tom. Tome, volume.
Tonn. Tonnage.
Topog. Topography, topographical.
Tr. Translation, translator, translated; Transpose; Treasurer; Trustee.
Trans. Transaction; Translation, translator, translated.
Treas. Treasurer.
Trig., Trigon. Trigonometry, trigonometrical.
Trin. Trinity.
T. T. L. To take leave. See *P. P. C.*
Tu., Tues. Tuesday.
Turk. Turkey, Turkish.
TVA. Tennessee Valley Authority.
twp. Township.
Typ. Typographer.
Typog. Typography, typographical.

UAR. United Arab Republic.
u.c. Upper Case (Capital letters in printing).
UFO. Unidentified flying object.
U. J. D. See *J. U. D.*
UK. United Kingdom.
Ult. (Lat. *ultimo*), Last; Of the last month.
UN. United Nations.
UNESCO. United Nations Educational, Scientific, and Cultural Organization.
UNICEF. United Nations Internat'l Children's Emergency Funds.
Unit. Unitarian.
Univ. University.
UPI. United Press International.
U. S. United States.
USA. United States of America; United States Army.
USAF. United States Air Force.
USCG. United States Coast Guard.
USES. United States Employment Service.
USIA. United States Information Agency.
U. S. L. United States Legation.
U. S. M. United States mail; United States marine.
U. S. M. A. United States Military Academy.
U. S. N. United States Navy.

U. S. N. A. United States Naval Academy.
USO. United Service Organizations.
U. S. S. United States Senate; United States ship or steamer.
U. S. S. Ct. United States Supreme Court.
USSR. Union of Soviet Socialist Republics (Russia).

V. Verb; Verse; Victoria; Violin.
V. (Lat. *vide*), See.
V. A. Vicar Apostolic; Vice Admiral; Veterans Administration.
Va. Virginia.
Val. Valve; Value.
Vat. Vatican.
V. C. Victoria Cross.
V-E Day. Official date of Germany's surrender in World War II.
V. F. W. Veterans of Foreign Wars.
V. G. Vicar General.
V.I. Virgin Islands.
Vice pres. Vice President.
Vid. (Lat. *vide*), See.
VIP. Very important person.
Vis., Visc. Viscount.
VISTA. Volunteers in Service to America.
Viz. (Lat. *videlicet*), Namely; To wit. See *Oz.*
V-J Day. Official date of Japan's surrender in World War II.
Voc. Vocative.
Vol., Vols. Volume, Volumes.
V. P. Vice President.
V. Rev. Very Reverend.
V. S. Veterinary surgeon.
vs., v. (Lat. *versus*), Against.
Vt. Vermont.
Vul., Vulg. Vulgate.

W. Wednesday; Week; Welsh; West, western.
WAC. Women's Army Corps.
WAF. Women in the Air Force.
Wash., Wa. Washington.
WAVES. Women Appointed for Volunteer Emergency Service (Women's naval reserve).
W. C. A. Women's Christian Ass'n.
W. C. T. U. Women's Christian Temperance Union.
Wed. Wednesday.
Wel. Welsh.
w. f. Wrong font (in printing).
WHO. World Health Organization.
W. I. West Indies, West Indian.
Wis., Wisc., Wi. Wisconsin.
Wk. Week.
W. Long. West Longitude.
Wm. William.
WNW. West northwest.
W. R. C. Women's Relief Corps.
WSW. West southwest.
Wt. Weight.
W. Va., W.V. West Virginia.
Wyo., Wy. Wyoming.

X., Xt. Christ.
Xm., Xmas. Christmas.
Xn., Xtian. Christian.
Xnty. Christianity.
Xper., Xr. Christopher.

Y. Year.
Yd. Yard; *Yds.* Yards.
YMCA. Young Men's Christian Ass'n.
Y. M. Cath. A. Young Men's Catholic Association.
YMHA. Young Men's Hebrew Ass'n.
Y. P. S. C. E. Young People's Society of Christian Endeavor.
Yr. Year; Younger; Your.
Yrs. Years; Yours.
YWCA. Young Women's Christian Ass'n.

Zach. Zachary.
Zech. Zechariah.
Zeph. Zephaniah.
Z. G. Zoological Gardens.
ZIP. Zone Improvement Program.
Zool. Zoology, zoological.

REVIEW QUESTIONS

THE following list of *review* questions has been prepared to serve as a *review* of the preceding subject matter on the English language. As the questions have been arranged in logical order for the proper development of each subject, they should serve also to suggest a thorough and systematic *course of study* for those who desire to improve their everyday English.

Although the list contains several hundred questions, it includes but a small fraction of the thousands of questions which the English department will answer. A similar list will be found at the end of each of the other departments.

GOOD USAGE

In *a secretary and treasurer,* how many persons are implied? 927
Which is correct, "Two and three *are* five" or "Two and three *is* five"? 927
In what sense is the word *adore* correctly used? . 927
Distinguish between being *almost* killed and being *nearly* killed. Illustrate 928
In regard to usage, compare the following words: *alumni, alumna, alumnus, alumnæ* . . 928
Which word suggests the greater quantity, *ample* or *sufficient?* 929
Distinguish between *answer* and *reply* 929
Is there any difference between *antiquated, ancient, antique,* and *old?* 929
What is the difference between *appear* and *seem?* Show the correct use of these words . 929
Give accurately the use of each of the following words: *apt, likely, liable* 929
Distinguish between *aspiration* and *ambition* . 930
Contrast the meanings of the words *audience* and *spectators.* 930
When do we *avenge* wrong and when do we *revenge* wrong? 930
What is wrong with the sentence "I shall miss you badly"? 931
Is it correct to say "the *balance* of the dinner"? In what sense is this word correctly used? . 931
Is it more accurate to say "We began the day's work" or "We commenced the day's work"? 931
In speaking of how many objects is the word *between* correctly applied? 931
Illustrate the correct use of *had better* as an idiom 931
Explain the distinction in the use of the words *by* and *with* 932
What rule governs the use of *can* and *may?* . 932
What is wrong in this sentence: "I can't hardly believe the story"? 932
Distinguish between *capacity* and *ability* . . . 932
Compare the meanings of the words *cite* and *quote.* 932
When should we say *compared to* and when *compared with?* 933
When should we say *correspond to* and when *correspond with?* 933
In what sense is the word *couple* correctly used? 933
Distinguish between *credible* and *creditable.* . 933
Give sentences showing the correct use of the following: the singular of *data;* the plural of *memorandum* 933
Is it more accurate to *direct* or to *call* one's attention to a thing? 934
What preposition correctly follows the use of the word *dissent?* 934
What is meant by the *double possessive?* Illustrate two forms of the double possessive . . 934
How are the words *effect* and *affect* correctly used? Which may be a noun? 934

Distinguish between *emigrant* and *immigrant* . 935
Do we *endorse* or *indorse* a check? Explain . 935
When do we *excuse* and when do we *pardon?* . 935
What rule applies to the use of the words *farther* and *further?* 935
What rule distinguishes the use of the words *fewer* and *less?* Illustrate 935
Why should *fine* not be used as an adverb? . . 935
To what should the word *grand* be applied? . . 936
Give examples showing the correct use of *hard* . 936
Do we *hate* or do we *dislike* to do certain things? 936
Distinguish between the use of *historic* and *historical* 936
What is the rule for the use of the prepositions *in* and *into?* Which of the two is sometimes an adverb? 937
When do we use the phrase *in the circumstances* and when *under the circumstances?* . 937
Is your pronunciation of *irrelevant* correct? . . 937
Do we like *this* kind or *these* kind of apples? *that* kind or *those* kind of books? 937
What word should generally be used instead of *lady?* 938
Are clothes *laundered* or *laundried?* 938
Illustrate the correct use of the verbs *lay* and *lie.* 938
Give sentences in which the words *lay* and *lie* are used as nouns 938
How do *legible* and *readable* differ in meaning? . 938
Do we *lend* money or do we *loan* it? Give a sentence showing *loan* as a noun 938
Illustrate *mathematics* used correctly with a singular verb; with a plural verb 939
Explain clearly the use of the verb *meet* when introducing a friend 939
Is there any difference in meaning between a *mutual* friend and a *common* friend? 939
Illustrate *none* used correctly with both a singular and a plural verb. 939
Give a sentence showing *number* used correctly as subject of a singular verb; of a plural verb . 940
Distinguish between *oral* and *verbal* message . 940
Find the error in the sentence: "I am glad that ordeal is over with." 940
Is it preferable to say "three pairs of shoes" or "three pair of shoes"? 940
What is the meaning of *majority?* of *plurality?* . 941
Distinguish between *practical* and *practicable* . 941
What are "proud" words? Illustrate their use 941
Distinguish between *recipe* and *receipt* 942
Illustrate the proper use of the words *regrettable* and *regretful* 942
Explain and illustrate the correct use of *respectively* and *respectfully* 942
Explain clearly the use of the words *set* and *sit* . 942
Distinguish between *sewage* and *sewerage* . . . 942
Mention two adjectives which have the same form when used as adverbs. 943
What is meant by the *split infinitive?* When is it permissible? 944
Is there any difference between *station* and *depot?* 944
Point out the error in this sentence: "I have never seen such a pretty car." 944
Is it correct to say, "the finished and unfinished manuscript"? Give a reason for your answer 945
Is it ever permissible to use the word *whose* in referring to things? 946

WORD BUILDING

From what elements are words formed? . . . 947
What is meant by the *root* of a word? 947
What is meant by the *stem* of a word? 947
How does the *root* of a word differ from the *stem?* 947
Of what advantage is a knowledge of *roots* and *stems?* 947
What is a *prefix?* a *suffix?* 947
Explain the meaning of *affixes* 947
Show how the following words are built: *cable-gram, periscope* 947
Name three Anglo-Saxon prefixes 948
What is the meaning of each of the following prefixes: *dis, contra, circum, non?* 948
Show the formation of the following words: *descent, illegal, exclaim, unkind, forgive.* . . 948
Mention three Anglo-Saxon suffixes . . . 949
What is the meaning of each of the following prefixes: *semi, re, hypo, sub, trans, pre, per, pro?* 949
What is the meaning of each of the following suffixes: *like, er, ful, ly?* 949
Name a suffix which may be adjective or verbal 950
What Latin suffix corresponds to the Anglo-Saxon suffix *er?* Illustrate 950
Show how the following words are built: *factor, florist, legal, creation, peaceable, feminine* . . 950
Name two suffixes which may be adjective or noun and give words showing both uses . . 950
Name an adjective built upon each of the following stems: *cap, fin, clus, duc* 950
Give two words built upon the stem *dict*, each having a prefix and a suffix 951
Explain the meaning of the following words by showing how they are built: *dependent, unstable, senseless* 952
Show how the word *automobile* is built 952
Point out the stems, prefixes, and suffixes in the following words: *irrevocable, convention, vital*. 952
Show how adjectives are formed from verb stems 952

DERIVATION OF ENGLISH WORDS FROM THE LATIN

Explain in what way the study of English words from the Latin is of use to you 953
Mention three nouns from the Latin word *bene*. 953
What Latin word means "I believe"? From the stem of this word, build two English nouns. 954
Explain the derivation of the following: *dictionary, indigestible, division* 955
From the supine stem of *duco* form three English nouns 955
What Latin verb is the source of the word *relative?* 956
What is the meaning of *gratus?* Name three words derived from *gratus* 956
From what Latin word is each of the following words derived: *illegal, allegiance, legitimate?*. 957
By pointing out the stems, prefixes, and suffixes, explain how these words are built: *interrogative, competition, portable* 959
Explain the derivation of *reservation, bisect, tenant* 960
What Latin word means "I live"? Name a noun, an adjective, and a verb derived from it 960

SPELLING

Mention some aids in mastering the art of spelling 961
How is the possessive case of nouns formed? 961
Show the possessive of the following words: *Achilles, Dickens, conscience*. 961

What is the plural of each of the following words: *thief, goose, ally, mouse?* 964
Why are the following words called homonyms: *wait, weight; time, thyme?* 967
What are heteronyms? 967
Mention two words which are heteronyms . . 967

SENTENCE BUILDING

What is a sentence? What two parts are essential to the building of a sentence? Illustrate. 968
How does a clause differ from a sentence? . . 968
What is meant by a *part of speech?* 968
Name the different parts of speech and define and illustrate each 968
What is a substantive? 968
Illustrate a simple sentence having a compound subject and a compound predicate 969
How does a complex sentence differ from a compound sentence? 969
What is meant by *inflection* of words? . . . 969
What is an *appositive?* a *predicate noun?* . . 969
Name five kinds of pronouns 969
What are interrogative pronouns? 969
Show the difference between an interrogative pronoun and an interrogative adjective . . 970
Give a sentence containing a demonstrative pronoun; a demonstrative adjective 970
Give a sentence containing a relative pronoun; an adjective pronoun; an indefinite pronoun. 970
By means of a sentence, show the use of the *direct* and the *indirect* object 970
What change in English nouns is made to show the possessive case? 970
By what other name is the possessive case known? 970
Write a sentence which shows the possessive case of two nouns implying separate possession 971
Explain and illustrate the meaning of the singular and the plural number 971
Define antecedent 971
Explain and illustrate the meaning of a *transitive* verb; an *intransitive* verb 971
As applied to verbs, what does *mode* show? . . 971
Explain the mode of each verb in the following sentence: "If thine enemy hunger, feed him." 971
What do we call the form the verb takes to show *time?* 972
Explain what is meant by a *copulative* verb. . 972
Define and illustrate an *impersonal* verb. Why are such verbs called impersonal? 972
What is an *auxiliary* verb? Why is it so called? 972
What auxiliary verb is a "sign" of the present perfect tense? of the past perfect tense? . . 972
Give a sentence containing an irregular, transitive verb in the active voice, indicative mode, past perfect tense, first person, plural number 971–972
What is a *participle?* 972
What is a *gerund?* How does a *gerund* differ from a *participle?* 973
What word usually precedes the English infinitive? 973
Classify the following adjectives as *limiting* or *descriptive: large, those, green, five, troublesome* 973
Give a sentence containing an *appositive* adjective 973
Name the degrees in the comparison of adjectives and explain each 973
By the use of an indirect question, illustrate an interrogative adverb 973
Give a sentence containing *when* used as an *interrogative* adverb; as a *relative* adverb . . . 975
How are adverbs compared? Illustrate . . . 974
Illustrate the following: *the* as adjective; *the* as adverb; *first* as adverb; *first* as adjective 973, 974
Define and illustrate an *adjective* clause; an *adverbial* clause; a *substantive* clause 974
What determines whether a clause is substantive, adjective, or adverbial? 974

By means of sentences, explain the difference between a *restrictive* and a *non-restrictive* clause 974

Illustrate a *substantive* clause the object of a preposition; an *adverbial* clause of condition . 974

Use *where* to introduce an *adjective* clause; an *adverbial* clause; a *substantive* clause 974

PREPOSITIONS AND CONJUNCTIONS

By the use of sentences, show three meanings of the preposition *before* 976

Give sentences showing the following words used as prepositions: *within, without, toward, through* 978

Is one ambitious *of* or *for* power? 979

Illustrate the following prepositions used correctly with the verb *divide: into, with, between, among* 979

Is it correct to say angry *at* or *with* a person? . 979

When should one say offended *at* and when offended *with?* 980

Is a person relieved *of* or *from* pain? 980

Into what two general classes are conjunctions divided? 980

What are *correlative* conjunctions? Give sentences to illustrate 980

Give a sentence in which *for* is used as a preposition; as a conjunction 977, 981

CAPITAL LETTERS

What are the chief uses of capital letters? . . 982

In the following sentence, why is the word *grave* capitalized: "O Grave! where is thy victory?" 982

Should the names of the seasons be capitalized? 982

Give the rule for the capitalization of titles of office or of honor. When should such titles not begin with capitals? How should abbreviated titles be written? 982

Explain the capitalization of words derived from proper nouns 982

Illustrate the correct use of the word *president* written with a capital; with a small letter . 982

PUNCTUATION

What is the object of punctuation? Explain its importance 983

Show how the transposition of punctuation marks may alter the meaning of a sentence . 983

Give three illustrations of different rules for the use of the colon 984

When is the semicolon used between clauses joined by *for, but,* and? When is it used between the parts of a compound sentence? . 984

By giving two illustrations, show the uses of the dash as a mark of punctuation 984

State two uses of the hyphen 984

LANGUAGE AND LINGUISTICS

How did the English language come to be so generally spoken? 987

Explain the relationship of the English language to other tongues 987

What early tongue is called the basis of the English language? 987

What kind of words were brought into the English language by the introduction of Christianity? 987

What effect had the conquest of the Danes upon the culture and the language of the people of England? 987

What was the language of the Northmen? . . 987

After the Norman conquest, which classes spoke the Saxon language? Which spoke French? . 988

What influences made the Latin element in the English language so large? 988

What great literary works mark the beginning of the modern English period? 988

How did the printing press affect the growth of the English language? 988

WRITING AND SPEAKING

What is rhetoric? 992

Upon what does true effectiveness of language depend? 992

Name several well-defined forms of discourse . 992

What form of discourse is used in the telling of stories? 992

What is a paraphrase? Illustrate by example. 995

What is the purpose of the *editorial?* 996

Define the *scenario.* Explain its parts . . . 996

Of what does *verse* consist? 996

In English verse, what is a *foot?* 996

Name and define the most common *feet* in English verse 997

Distinguish between *rhythm* and *rime* . . 996–997

State what is meant by a *stanza* 997

PUBLIC SPEAKING

Mention three requisites of the successful public speaker 997

What is the first step in planning a speech? . 998

Of what three chief divisions must a well arranged speech consist? 998

Give two appropriate suggestions for the beginning of an after-dinner speech 998

What three points should be covered when proposing a toast at a wedding breakfast? . 998

Upon what combined forces does the total effect of a speech depend? 999

Name three speech occasions for which the *purpose* may be *Impressiveness* 999

List three common faults of speeches of introduction 999

Why may we say *debate* is one of the final steps in the discussion process? 999

In what New England gatherings were *open forum discussions* first held in America? . .1000

Give the *five steps* in the process of group thinking 1000

What is the essential duty of the leader in group discussion? 1000

List five points for the leader of a *conference* to keep in mind 1000

In the *panel-forum* how much time should be allowed for audience participation? 1000

When is it best to use the *debate-forum* type of discussion? 1001

What is the purpose of argumentative discourse? 1901

State the aim of *persuasion* 1001

What constitutes *debate?* 1001

RADIO-TELEVISION SPEAKING

How do the speaker's problems differ as between radio and television? 1002

What are the requirements for a radio or television speaker? 1003

How can the script writer help or hinder smooth delivery for the speaker? 1003

Cite examples of "built-in" difficulties in scripts prepared for speakers? 1003

What principal attributes are mentioned in the pamphlet *The Selection and Training of Announcers?* 1003

What constitutes a good "stage presence" for a speaker? 1004

FORMS OF ORAL INTERPRETATION

Why is phrasing so important in oral reading?.1004
What are the three forms of speech emphasis?.1004
Should one memorize in *interpretative reading?*.1005
What type of material is best suited to Impersonation?................1005
What is the best means of obtaining an effective manner in delivery?........1006
How can one acquire *good speech* in delivery?.1007
Mention eight qualities of the speaking voice.1007
In changing the pitch of the voice, what should one be careful to avoid?........1007
Show how the inflection of the voice may alter the meaning of a sentence.........1007
Name five means of securing emphasis in oratory................1007
Of what importance in public speaking is the habit of right breathing?........1007

PRONUNCIATION

Pronounce correctly the following: chauffeur, décolleté, entente, masseur, masseuse, menu, morale, passé, protégé, résumé, seidlitz, suite, ukulele.......1008–1009
What is the correct pronunciation of each of the following words: clique, clematis, forehead, khaki, jardinière, monetary?....1009–1012

FORMS OF LITERARY COMPOSITION

Mention several sources of good literature..1015
What are the distinguishing features of the *romance story*, the *novel*, and the *short story?*.1015
Distinguish between *history* and *biography.*..1016
What book furnishes the best examples of the parable?................1016
Mention three historical novels......1016
Name five forms of poetry.......1017
Distinguish the ode from other forms of poetry.1017
What is the nature of an elegy? Give a well-known example of elegy.........1017
Name four great epics.........1017
Of what form of poetry are *Miles Standish* and *Evangeline* examples?.........1017
What is a sonnet? Name two authors who have composed sonnets............1017
Explain the characteristics of the drama.1017–1018

FIGURES OF SPEECH

What is a *figure of speech?* Illustrate....1018
What is a *simile?* By what words is it usually introduced? Give two examples of *simile*.1018
How does a *metaphor* differ from a *simile?* Give sentences to show this difference....1018
Define and illustrate *synecdoche*....1018
In the following sentence, change the *simile* to a *metaphor* "He shall be like a tree planted by the rivers of water."........1018
Give three examples of *personification*....1018
Explain the following figures and illustrate each: *apostrophe, irony, alliteration*....1019

LETTER WRITING

Why is the study of letter writing of so great importance?..............1020
Name four requisites of a business letter...1020
Name the first three items in the building of a business letter.............1023
Show a correct form of *introduction* to a business letter................1023
In the punctuation of the salutation, is the colon or the comma to be preferred? Explain 1023
Where is the address properly placed on the envelope? the postal ZIP Code?....1024
Should the address on the envelope be punctuated? Explain and illustrate.......1024
In what person are formal invitations always written? In what person should the reply to a formal invitation be written?......1031

What is the meaning of *R.S.V.P.*, sometimes placed in the lower left-hand corner of an invitation?................1031

SYNONYMS AND ANTONYMS

What is the meaning of the word *synonym?* of the word *antonym?*.........1037
Explain the correct use of *abandon, desert, forsake, relinquish*............1038
How does *ability* differ from *talent?*......1038
In meaning, which is the stronger word, *afraid* or *fearful?*............1039
How does *carriage* differ from *gait?*......1039
When is pain *alleviated* and when is it *relieved?*.1040
Compare the meanings of *alone, solitary, lonely*.1040
Distinguish between *anger* and *rage*......1040
Do we *assent* or *consent* to matters of conduct?.1041
In meaning, which is the broader term— *conduct* or *behavior?* Explain........1042
Give an antonym of each of the following: *belief, credit, trust, faith*.........1042
Explain the words *bravery* and *courage*. How does *valor* compare with *bravery* or *courage?*.1043
What is a *calamity?* a *disaster?* Was the sinking of the Titanic a *calamity* or a *disaster?*.1043
How does *capture* differ from *seizure?*....1044
Distinguish between things *heavenly* and things *celestial*. Give an antonym of each word.1044
Explain the difference between one's *character* and one's *reputation*.........1044
Do we *cite* authors or do we *quote* them?...1045
Distinguish between *effect* and *result*....1047
When do we *cry* and when do we *weep?*...1049
Contrast the meanings of *crime, vice,* and *sin*.1049
What is the difference between a *remedy* and a *cure?*................1049
In what way is *habit* formed? How does *custom* differ from *habit?*............1049
What is the distinction between *cozy* and *comfortable?*................1049
Of what word is *plaintiff* an antonym? Of what word is it a synonym?.........1050
Is *deity* the same as *divinity?* Explain....1050
If a building were hit by a bomb, would it be *destroyed* or *ruined?*............1051
Give the difference between *intend* and *purpose*. Which is the stronger in meaning—*purpose* or *design?*.........1051
Mention a synonym of *difficulty;* an antonym of *determine*................1051
Is it possible to have a bad *temper* with a good *disposition?* Give a reason for your answer.1052
Upon what does the *expediency* of a thing depend? What determines its *fitness?*....1055
When do we *forgive* and when do we *pardon?*.1057
How do *free* and *liberal* differ in usage?....1057
Explain the difference between *habitation* and *home;* between *house* and *residence*....1059
Is a tree *high* or *tall?* Is the bird's nest in the top of the tree *high* or *lofty?*........1059
Distinguish between *human* race and *humane* race................1060
Are *inability* and *disability* the same? Explain.1060
Compare the meaning of *annoy* with that of *molest*................1061
A man saved a boy's life. Is the boy *indebted* or *obliged* to the man?.........1061
Is there any difference between *joy* and *gladness?* Explain............1062
Mention a synonym and an antonym of *large*.1062
Explain the difference between a person's *manners* and his *morals*.........1063
When is a thing *poised* and when is it *balanced?*.1065
Mention a word opposed in meaning to each of the following: *powerful, mighty, peace*.1065
State the difference between a *sign* and a *signal*.1068
In regard to usage, compare the following words: *speak, say, tell*.........1069
How does *understanding* differ from *intellect?* from *intelligence?*.........1070

BIBLIOGRAPHY

HISTORY OF THE ENGLISH LANGUAGE

Baugh, A. C.—A History of the English Language *Appleton*
Bloomfield, L.—Language . . . . *Holt*
Brin, Joseph G.—Applied Semantics . *Humphries*
Graff, W. L.—Language and Languages . *Russell*
Greenough, J. B. and Kittredge, G. L.—Words and Their Ways of Speech . . . . *Macmillan*
Nelson, Francis—History of English . *Macmillan*
Robertson, S.—The Development of Modern English . . . . *Prentice-Hall*

GOOD USAGE

Dean, Leonard F.—Essays on Language and Usage. *Oxford*
Evans, Bergen and Cornelia—A Dictionary of Contemporary American Usage . . . . *Random*
Fowler, H. W.—A Dictionary of Modern English Usage . . . . *Oxford*
Glover, D. M.—Daily Guide to Correct English. *Christopher*
Ives, Sumner—A New Handbook for Writers. *Knopf*
Partridge, Eric—The Concise Usage and Abusage. *Citadel*
Taintor, Sarah A.—The Secretary's Handbook. *Macmillan*

WORD BUILDING

Brown, Ivor J.—A Word in Your Ear . . *Dutton*
Ernst, Margaret S.—More About Words . *Knopf*
Garrison, Webb—What's In a Word . *Abingdon*
MacDonald, A. M., ed.—Chambers Etymological Dictionary . . . . *Littlefield*

SPELLING AND PRONUNCIATION

Allen, Robert L., and Others—English Sounds and Their Spelling . . . . *Crowell*
Colby, Frank—University Pronouncing Dictionary of Troublesome Words . . . . . *Apollo*
Crowell, Thomas L., Jr.—NBC Handbook of Pronunciation, 3rd Ed. . . . . *Crowell*
Gleeson, Ruth and Colvin, James—Words Most Often Misspelled and Mispronounced *Pocket Books*
Thomas, Charles K.—An Introduction to the Phonetics of American English . . . . . *Ronald*

DICTIONARIES

New Standard Dictionary . . *Funk and Wagnalls*
Webster's New International Dictionary . *Merriam*
Oxford English Dictionary . . . . . *Oxford*
Craigie, Sir Wm. A.—A Dictionary of American English . . . . . *Univ. of Chicago Press*
Desk Dictionaries for Ready Reference:
    American College Dictionary . . . *Harper*
    College Standard Dictionary *Funk and Wagnalls*
    Webster's Collegiate Dictionary . . . *Merriam*
    The Winston Dictionary . . . . . *Winston*

SENTENCE BUILDING

Bryant, M. M.—Functional English Grammar *Heath*
Curme, G. O.—Parts of Speech and Accidence *Heath*
Faulkner, Claude W.—Writing Good Sentences *Scribner*
Fernald, J. C.—English Grammar Simplified *Funk and Wagnalls*
Fries, Charles C.—The Structure of English *Harcourt*
Gleason, H. A., Jr.—Linguistics and English Grammar . . . . *Holt*
Romine, Jack S.—Sentence Mastery *Prentice-Hall*

PUNCTUATION AND CAPITALIZATION

Collins, F. W.—Authors' and Printers' Dictionary *Oxford*
Hutchinson, Lois D.—Standard Handbook for Secretaries, 7th ed. . . . . *McGraw-Hill*
Prentice-Hall Editorial Staff—Punctuation Made Easy . . . . *Prentice-Hall*
West, L.—300 Commas . . . . . . *McGraw-Hill*

LINGUISTICS

Chomsky, N.—Syntactic Structures . . . *Mouton*
Chomsky, N. and Halle, Morris—The Sound Pattern of English . . . . *Harper*
Gleason, H. A.—Linguistics and English Grammar. *Holt*
Hymes, D.—Language in Culture and Society. *Harper*

WRITING AND SPEAKING

Archer, Wm.—Playmaking . *Small, Maynard & Co.*
Cypreansen, Lucille—Speech Development, Improvement and Correction . . . . . . *Ronald*
Ferguson, Charles W.—Say It with Words . *Knopf*
Fields, Victor A.—Voice and Diction . *Macmillan*
Flesch, R.—The Art of Plain Talk . *Harper*
Ford, N. A. and Waters, Turpin—Basic Skills for Better Writing, Vols. A & B, paper . . *Putnam*
Guth, Hans P.—Words and Ideas . . . *Wadsworth*
Hodges, John C. and Laws, S. Y.—Harbrace Writing Counsel. . . . . *Harcourt*
Hook, Julius N.—Guide to Good Writing: Grammar, Style and Usage . . . . . . *Ronald*
Ives, Sumner—New Handbook for Writers . *Knopf*
Loren, B. B.—English Essentials . . . *Macmillan*
Nelson, Herbert B.—English Essentials. *Littlefield*
Quiller-Couch, Sir Arthur—On the Art of Writing. *Putnam*
Shaw, Harry—Errors in English and Ways to Correct Them . . . . *Barnes & Noble*
Wallace, Karl R.—A History of Speech Education in America . . . . *Appleton*

FORMS OF SPEAKING

Baird, Albert C.—American Public Addresses. *McGraw-Hill*
Culp, Ralph B.—Basic Types of Speech. *Brown Co., W. C.*
Machelin, E.—Speech for the Stage . *Theatre Arts*
Monroe, A. H.—Principles and Types of Speech. *Scott-Foresman*
Sanford, Wm. P. and Yeager, W. H.—Effective Business Speech . . . . *McGraw-Hill*
Sarett, Lew and Others—Basic Principles of Speech, 4th ed. . . . . *Houghton*
Simmons, Harry—How to Talk your Way to Success . . . . *Prentice-Hall*
Zemlin, W.—Speech and Hearing Science. *Prentice-Hall*

LETTER WRITING

Aurner, Robert R.—Effective Business English. *South-Western*
Prentice-Hall Editorial Staff—How to Write a Good Letter . . . . *Prentice-Hall*
Shidle, N. C.—Art of Successful Communication. *McGraw-Hill*

SYNONYMS AND ANTONYMS

Allen, F. S.—Synonyms and Antonyms . *Harper*
Basescu, Sophie—Know the Word . . . *Helios*
Fernald, J. C.—Standard Handbook of English Synonyms, Antonyms, and Prepositions. *Funk and Wagnalls*
Roget, Peter—Thesaurus of English Words and Phrases (3rd ed.) . . . . *Grossett and Dunlap*
Soule, R. and Howsam, G.—Dictionary of English Synonyms, Antonyms, and Parallel Exp. *Shalom*
Synonyms, Antonyms, and Homonyms *Hawthorne*
Trench, R. C.—On the Study of Words . *Dutton*